2017 Canadian
Key Business Directory
épertoire des principales
entreprises Canadiennes
2017

This directory is the property of Mergent Inc.
Ce répertoire est la propriété de Mergent Inc.
Mergent Inc.
444 Madison Ave, Suite 1710
New York, NY 10022

Copyright © 2017

ISBN 9781682004265
Printed in the U.S.A.

Disclaimer

Any purchaser, reader or user of this directory assumes all responsibility for actions taken as a result of information provided herein. Any purchaser, reader or user agrees that D&B, its employees, subsidiaries and partners hold no liability for the interpretations derived from this directory and any subsequent actions taken as a result of that interpretation including, but not limited to, advertising, direct mailing, telemarketing and business decisions.

Démenti

N'importe quel acheteur, lecteur ou utilisateur de ce répertoire assume toute la responsabilité des mesures prises en raison des informations fournies ci-inclus. N'importe quel acheteur, lecteur ou utilisateur sont en accord que D&B, ses employés, les subsidiaires et les associés ne tiennent aucune responsabilité pour les traductions dérives de ce répertoire et d'aucune mesure subséquent pris en raison de cette interprétation.

Notice concerning use for compilation or dissemination to third parties

Subscribers to D&B Canada publications are not authorized, even on occasion, to use any D&B publication to: compile mailing lists, marketing aids, and other types of data, for sales or otherwise to a third party. Any subscriber doing so will be in direct violation of the contractual agreement under which the Directory is provided to the subscriber. D&B Canada does not permit or acquiesce in such uses of its publications. Any subscriber or other person who does not understand any aspect of this policy, please contact: D&B's Corporate Marketing and Public Affairs office at 1.800.INFO.DNB (1.800.463.6362).

Avis concernant l'utilisation aux fins de dissémination à une tierce partie

Les souscripteurs aux publications de D&B ne sont pas autorisés à utiliser, même occasionnellement, ces publications pour compiler des listes d'adresses, des supports à la commercialisation et d'autres types d'informations, et à les vendre, sinon les offrir à une tierce partie. Tout souscripteur qui agit ainsi est en violation de l'entente contractuelle sous laquelle le répertoire est fourni au souscripteur. D&B ne permet pas et n'accepte pas que ses publications soient utilisées pour les fins précitées. Tout souscripteur ou autre personne qui s'engage dans des actions non autorisées ou qui les encourage doit s'attendre à subir des conséquences d'ordre juridique et financier. Aucun amendement ou renonciation à l'entente n'engage les parties, à moins d'être exprimés par écrit et signés par un fondé de pouvoir de D&B Canada et par le souscripteur. Au cas où un souscripteur, ou toute autre personne, aurait des doutes quant à l'une des dispositions de cette politique, veuillez communiquer avec le Service de commercialisation et des affaires publiques de D&B Canada au 1.800.INFO.DNB (1.800.463.6362).

What's Inside?
Le contenu

Volume 1
Sales, Employee Stats and County Information

Section I   Geographic Index

An alphabetical listing of businesses by geographic location.
Business information listed includes all details outlined above.

Inscriptions par région géographique

Une liste des entreprises dans l'ordre alphabétique par région géographique.
Chaque inscription comporte tous les éléments ci-dessus

Volume 2

Section I1   Line of Business Index SIC Codes

A numerical listing of businesses by SIC Code.
Business information listed includes all details outlined above.
An SIC Code table is available at the end of this section.

Inscriptions par domaine d'exploitation Codes C.I.S.

Une liste des entreprises dans l'ordre numérique par code C.I.S.
Chaque inscription comporte tous les éléments ci-dessus.
Un tableau des codes C.I.S. figure à la fin de cette section.

Section III   Alphabetic Listing

An alphabetical listing of businesses.
Business information listed includes:
Legal business name and address; reference to parent company; number of employees; sales
volume; space occupied; headquarters, branch, single location indicator; primary line of business
(SIC code) and description; D-U-N-S® Number; officers and management contact names on file.

Source d'information centrale inscriptions dans l'ordre alphabétique

Une liste des entreprises dans l'ordre alphabétique.
Chaque inscription comporte les renseignements suivants :
Raison sociale juridique de l'entreprise et son adresse, une référence à la compagnie mère, la taille
du personnel, le chiffre d'affaires, la surface occupée, un indicateur siège social, succursale,
emplacement unique, le domaine d'exploitation principal (code C.I.S.) et une description, le numéro
D-U-N-S®, les personnes-ressources au sein des membres du bureau de direction et de la direction
disponibles.

Key Business Terms Used by D&B

Branch: A secondary location of a company reporting to a headquarters or subsidiary. Branches carry the same primary name as their headquarters and can only report to a headquarters of subsidiary establishment.

Division: A separate operating unit of a corporation with a division name, performing a specific activity.

Headquarters: An establishment that has a branch or branches operating under the same legal name.

Parent: A business establishment that controls another company through ownership of all or a majority of its shares.

Single Location: A business establishment with no branches reporting to it. A single location may be a parent or subsidiary.

Subsidiary: A corporation which is more than 50% owned by another company. Subsidiary companies are formed for several purposes. The subsidiary may conduct business totally different from that of the parent company, or may be at a different location.

D-U-N-S® Number: The D-U-N-S® Number is proprietary to D&B and helps to distinguish a business and identify it as a unique establishment. Assigned and maintained by D&B, these computer generated numbers provide common identification standards for most business establishments.

Trade Name: A trade name is used by a business for advertising and buying purposes. This should not be confused with a branch or division name. A trade name does not have to be registered.

Glossaire des mots clés de D&B

Compagnie mère : Une compagnie qui contrôle une autre compagnie grâce à la possession de toutes ou d'une tranche majoritaire des actions de cette compagnie.

Division : Une unité particulière d'une compagnie avec sa dénomination et ses propres actvités. Une division peut comporter des membres du bureau de direction mais n'a pas de capital et n'est pas constituée en compagnie.

Emplacement unique : Un établissement commercial qui n'exploite pas de succursale. Un emplacement unique peut être une compagnie mère et, ou, un filiale.

Filiale : Une compagnie dont plus de 50 % des actions sont détenues par une autre compagnie. Une filiale peut être constituée pour diverses raisons. Les activités d'une filiale peuvent être totalement différentes de celles de la compagnie mère, et elle peut être exploitée d'un emplacement différent.

Numéros D-U-N-S® : Les numéros D-U-N-S® servent à l'identification de chaque établissement unique. Affectés et mis à jour par D&B, ces numéros d'identification informatisés s'avèrent la norme en matière d'identification des établissements commerciaux.

Profil commercial (appellation commerciale) : Une dénomination utilisée par une entreprise aux fins de publicité et, ou, d'achat. À ne pas confondre avec une dénomination de succursale ou de division. Un profil commercial peut être enregistré ou non.

Siège social : Une entreprise qui exploite une ou des succursales sous la même raison sociale reconnue.

Succursale : Un emplacement secondaire d'une compagnie relevant du siège social ou d'une filiale. Une succursale est exploitée sous la même raison sociale principale que le siège social et relève exclusivement du siège social ou d'une filiale.

How to Use a D&B Canadian Directory Listing

The D&B Canadian Directories together, contain more than 140,000 business listings and close to 500,000 contact names. The types of businesses reported on varies between directories.

The Canadian Key Business Directory

This directory contains listings of Canadian businesses with one or more of the following: $5 million in sales, 50 employees at a single or headquarters location, or 250 employees total. Public and private schools are excluded.

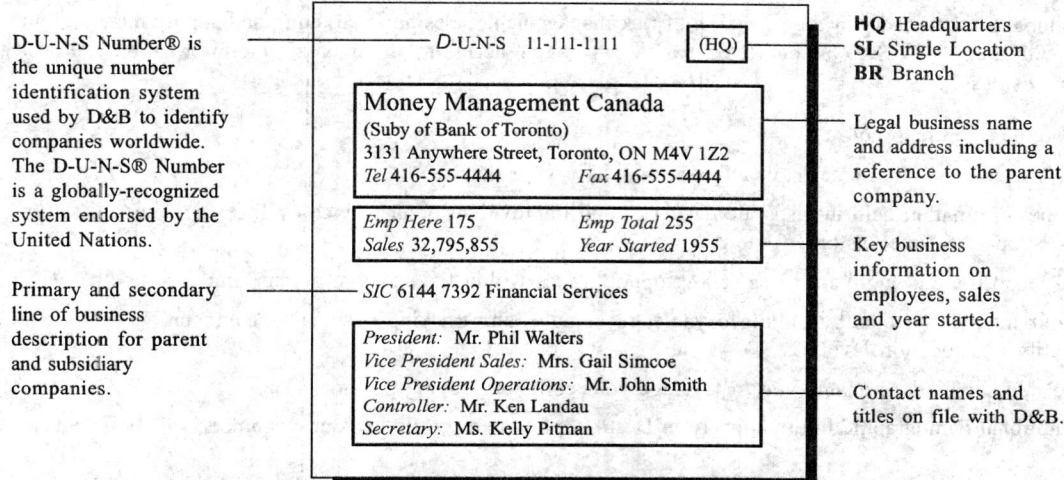

D-U-N-S Number® is the unique number identification system used by D&B to identify companies worldwide. The D-U-N-S® Number is a globally-recognized system endorsed by the United Nations.

Primary and secondary line of business description for parent and subsidiary companies.

HQ Headquarters
SL Single Location
BR Branch

Legal business name and address including a reference to the parent company.

Key business information on employees, sales and year started.

Contact names and titles on file with D&B.

Utilisation des inscriptions dans les répertoires canadiens de D&B

Au total, les répertoires commerciaux canadiens de D&B comportent plus de 140 000 inscriptions d'entreprises et près de 500 000 de personnes-ressources. Les types d'entreprises répertoriées varient d'un répertoire à l'autre.

Le Répertoire des principales entreprises canadiennes

Ce répertoire comporte les inscriptions des entreprises canadiennes qui répondent à un ou plus des critères suivants : chiffre d'affaires de 5 millions de dollars, personnel de 50 au siège social ou à un emplacement unique, ou de 250 au total. Les maisons d'enseignement publiques et privées ne sont pas répertoriées.

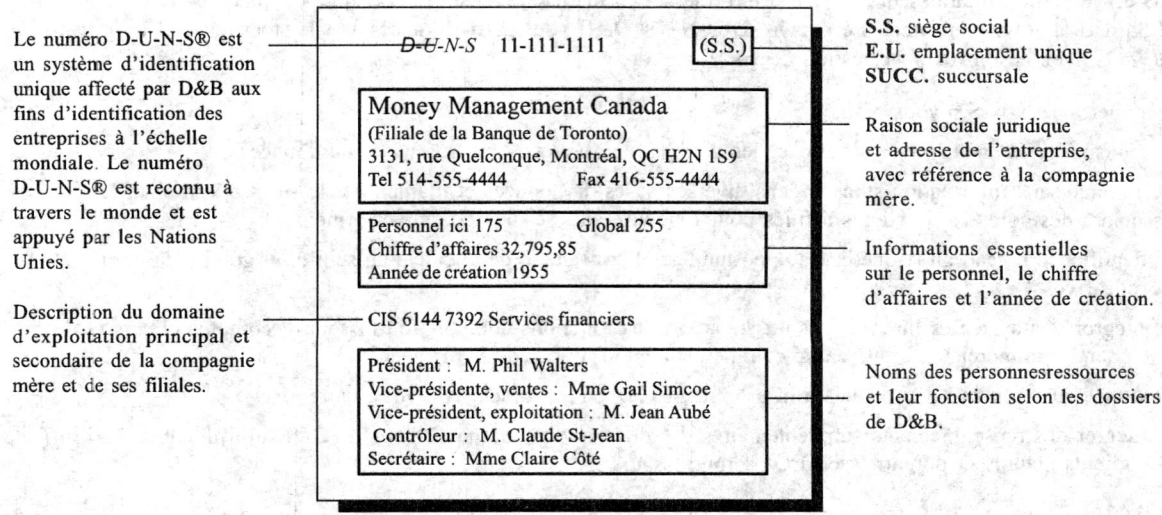

Le numéro D-U-N-S® est un système d'identification unique affecté par D&B aux fins d'identification des entreprises à l'échelle mondiale. Le numéro D-U-N-S® est reconnu à travers le monde et est appuyé par les Nations Unies.

Description du domaine d'exploitation principal et secondaire de la compagnie mère et de ses filiales.

S.S. siège social
E.U. emplacement unique
SUCC. succursale

Raison sociale juridique et adresse de l'entreprise, avec référence à la compagnie mère.

Informations essentielles sur le personnel, le chiffre d'affaires et l'année de création.

Noms des personnes-ressources et leur fonction selon les dossiers de D&B.

D&B D-U-N-S® Number

In today's global economy, D&B's Data Universal Numbering System, the D&B D-U-N-S® Number, has become the standard for keeping track of more than 97 million businesses and their corporate relationships worldwide. D-U-N-S® Numbers are unique nine-digit identification sequences that act as the nuts and bolts of D&B's database. They provide a secure identification for individual business entities while linking corporate family structures. Used by the world's most influential standards-setting organizations, the D-U-N-S® Number is recognized, recommended or required by more than 50 global associations including the United Nations, the U.S. Federal Government and the European Community.

D&B is the global market leader in the provision of risk management, sales and marketing and supply management information. With the D-U-N-S® Number, D&B can help you gain access to and maintain the information you need to manage your business.

D-U-N-S® Numbers can help you:

- Consolidate, cleanse and eliminate duplicate records within your databases
- Streamline the information held in disparate databases and improve customer service by linking related customer accounts to support a "one customer" view
- Identify risk exposure and highlight cross-selling opportunities within the same corporate family group
- Integrate your internal systems by linking payables/receivables and tracking business documentation to the business entity and location level
- Link interrelated suppliers to enable you to leverage your corporate buying power
- Integrate additional demographic information from D&B to provide a profile of your customers, suppliers and prospects

Le numéro D-U-N-S® D&B

Dans l'économie à l'échelle mondiale d'aujourd'hui, le Système de numérotage universel de données D&B, le numéro D-U-N-S® D&B, est devenu la norme d'identification de plus de 97 millions d'entreprises et de leurs affiliations corporatives à travers le monde. Les numéros D-U-N-S® D&B sont un numéro d'identification unique à neuf chiffres et ils constituent l'élément d'association primordial dans la base de données D&B. Ils permettent l'identification de chaque entreprise et l'association d'entreprises qui sont membres d'une même famille corporative. Utilisés par les organismes mondiaux les plus influents en matière d'établissement de normes, ils sont reconnus, recommandés ou requis par plus de 50 associations mondiales, y compris l'organisation des Nations Unies, le Gouvernement fédéral des É.-U. et la Communauté européenne.

D&B est le premier fournisseur mondial d'information en matière de gestion du risque, de vente, de marketing et de gestion de l'approvisionnement. Le numéro D-U-N-S® D&B vous permet l'accès à et le stockage de l'information dont vous avez besoin pour la gestion de votre entreprise.

Les numéros D-U-N-S® vous permettent :

- De consolider, de nettoyer et d'éliminer les doubles de dossiers dans vos bases de données
- De rationaliser l'information stockée dans diverses bases de données et d'améliorer le service à la clientèle en associant des comptes de clients affiliés pour répondre aux besoins du "client principal"
- D'identifier le niveau du risque et les opportunités de croisement de clientèle au sein d'un groupe de familles corporatives
- D'intégrer vos systèmes internes par l'association des fonctions comptes fournisseurs / comptes clients et de documents commerciaux, à une entité commerciale et au niveau de l'emplacement
- D'associer des fournisseurs affiliés afin d'optimiser le pouvoir d'achat de votre entreprise
- D'intégrer des renseignements supplémentaires d'ordre démographique obtenus de D&B afin d'établir un profil de vos clients actuels et potentiels et de vos fournisseurs

Put the D-U-N-S® Number at the Core of Your Sales and Marketing, Risk Management and Supply Management Operations

- Within enterprise wide solutions, the D-U-N-S® Number ensures accurate data—giving you confidence in the quality of the information you use to manage your business.

- In database marketing applications, D-U-N-S® Numbering allows customers to use D&B's demographic information to profile their best customers and create a model using their characteristics to identify which business are their warmest prospects.

- In risk management, the D-U-N-S® Number can link customer files to respective parent companies to provide a view of your total credit exposure within a single corporate family. This insight into customers' corporate structures means that credit limits can be managed intelligently and collections efforts prioritized.

- The D-U-N-S® Number helps ensure receivables management efforts are carefully managed and properly targeted by pinpointing customer locations and identifying important corporate relationships.

- In supply management, the D-U-N-S® Number enables a better understanding of your supplier base by helping identify duplicate records and providing linkage information on supplier family trees. This understanding allows you to leverage your purchasing power, cut costs out of the purchasing process and reduce the number of redundant suppliers worldwide.

- For companies with an e-commerce strategy, the D-U-N-S® Number can be used as a means of identifying suppliers, trading partners and customers. Companies wishing to be recognized as a credible supplier of online services can use their D-U-N-S® Number as a means of identification allowing potential customers to verify their business credentials before starting a trading relationship.

Intégrez le numéro D-U-N-S® au sein de vos activités de vente et de marketing, de gestion du risque et de gestion de l'approvisionnement

- Peu importe les solutions utilisées au sein de votre entreprise, le numéro D-U-N-S® assure l'exactitude des données - vous pouvez ainsi avoir confiance à la qualité de l'information que vous utilisez dans la gestion de votre entreprise.

- Pour les applications base de données de marketing, le numéro D-U-N-S® permet aux clients d'utiliser l'information d'ordre démographique de D&B afin d'établir un profil de leurs meilleurs clients, et de créer un modèle en se fondant sur leurs caractéristiques pour identifier les entreprises qui s'avèrent les meilleurs clients potentiels.

- En matière de gestion du risque, le numéro D-U-N-S® permet d'associer des dossiers de clients à leur compagnie mère respective afin d'obtenir une vue d'ensemble du risque relatif à toute une famille corporative. Cette vue d'ensemble d'une structure corporative permet une gestion intelligente des plafonds de crédit et l'établissement d'un ordre de priorité en ce qui a trait aux mesures de recouvrement.

- Le numéro D-U-N-S® aide à assurer que la gestion des comptes clients est bien planifiée et bien orientée, par l'identification des emplacements des clients et des liens corporatifs importants.

- En matière de gestion de l'approvisionnement, le numéro D-U-N-S® vous permet de bien connaître votre base de fournisseurs en vous permettant d'identifier les dossiers en double et les liens du réseau filiales de vos fournisseurs. Ainsi, vous êtes en mesure d'optimiser votre pouvoir d'achat, de diminuer vos coûts d'approvisionnement et de réduire le surnombre de fournisseurs à l'échelle internationale.

- En matière de commerce électronique, le numéro D-U-N-S® s'avère une façon d'identifier les fournisseurs, les partenaires d'affaires et les clients. Les entreprises qui souhaitent être reconnues comme un fournisseur fiable de services en ligne, peuvent utiliser leur numéro D-U-N-S® à titre d'élément d'identification ce qui permet aux clients potentiels de vérifier leur situation commerciale avant d'amorcer une relation d'affaires.

How is a D-U-N-S® Number Assigned?

The D-U-N-S® Number is solely maintained by D&B. When a business is first entered into the D&B business information database we assign each location that has its own unique, separate and distinct operation, its own D-U-N-S® Number. For more information call 1.800.INFO.DNB (1.800.463.6362) or visit www.dnb.ca.

Comment un numéro D-U-N-S® est-il affecté?

Seule D&B affecte un numéro D-U-N-S®. Lors de l'intégration d'une entreprise à la base de données commerciale D&B, nous affectons un numéro D-U-N-S® unique à chacun des emplacements avec des activités particulières, indépendantes et distinctes. Pour plus de renseignements, veuillez composer 1.800.INFO.DNB (1.800.463.6362) ou visiter www.dnb.ca/fr.

D&B Ensures Data Accuracy with our Trademarked DUNSRight™ Quality Process

The DUNSRight™Quality Process is D&B's quality assurance program to ensure data quality. Our five quality drivers:

- *Global Data Collection* brings together data from a variety of worldwide sources
- *Entity Matching* is a patented process that produces a single, accurate picture of each business and our next generation of matching technology will help you find more businesses in our database
- *D-U-N-S® Numbers,* unique to each business, are a means of identifying and tracking every activity of a business
- *Corporate Linkage* exposes risk by showing related businesses such as subsidiaries and parent companies
- *Predictive Indicators* use statistical analysis to indicate how companies may perform in the future

L'exactitude des données D&B est assurée par notre processus de qualité breveté DUNSRight™

Le processus de qualité DUNSRight™ est le programme d'assurance de la qualité des données D&B. Voici nos cinq moteurs de la qualité :

- *Collecte de données internationales* auprès de nombreuses sources à travers le monde
- *Assortiment d'entités*, un processus breveté qui donne une image précise de chaque entreprise, notre prochaine génération de technologies vous permettra d'avoir accès à davantage d'entreprises dans notre base de donnée
- *Numéros D-U-N-S®*, un numéro unique affecté à chaque entreprise aux fins d'identification et de suivi de toutes les activités d'une entreprise
- *Association de sociétés*, signale le risque en précisant les entreprises affiliées telles les filiales et les compagnies mères
- *Indicateurs de prévision*, fondés sur une analyste statistique, ils indiquent comment une entreprise est susceptible de se comporter ultérieurement

COMPANY	SALES ($)	RANK	EMPLOYEES HERE	PRIMARY SIC CODE
LOBLAW COMPANIES LIMITED 1 Presidents Choice Cir, Brampton, ON L6Y 5S5, Tel (905) 459-2500	34,308,433,325	1	80	5411
CANADIAN TEST CASE 167 5770 Hurontario St, Mississauga, ON L5R 3G5, Tel	28,788,247,200	2	6	7389
Toronto-Dominion Bank, The (*Suby of* **TORONTO-DOMINION BANK, THE**) 55 King St W, Toronto, ON M5K 1A2, Tel (416) 982-5722	27,356,640,075	3	5,000	6021
CANADIAN TEST CASE 177 CORP 6750 Century Ave Suite 305, Mississauga, ON L5N 2V8, Tel (905) 812-5920	26,557,153,480	4	120	5812
Canadian Test Case 185 (*Suby of* **CANADIAN TEST CASE 185**) 6750 Century Ave Suite 300, Mississauga, ON L5N 2V8, Tel (905) 999-2222	25,186,611,516	5	300	3714
WORKERS COMPENSATION BOARD OF PRINCE EDWARD ISLAND 14 Weymouth St, Charlottetown, PE C1A 4Y1, Tel (902) 368-5680	25,014,097,224	6	0	6331
▲ **CONOCOPHILLIPS WESTERN CANADA PARTNERSHIP** 401 9 Ave Sw Suite 1600, Calgary, AB T2P 3C5, Tel (403) 233-4000	23,259,407,800	7	2,500	1382
TD CAPITAL TRUST II 55 King St, Toronto, ON M5K 1A2, Tel (416) 308-6963	22,865,111,600	8	5	6541
Royal Bank Of Canada (*Suby of* **ROYAL BANK OF CANADA**) 200 Bay St, Toronto, ON M5J 2J5, Tel (416) 974-3940	20,724,267,953	9	500	6021
GREAT-WEST LIFE ASSURANCE COMPANY, THE 100 Osborne St N Suite 4c, Winnipeg, MB R3C 1V3, Tel (204) 946-1190	20,289,481,800	10	2,775	6324
SOBEYS INC 115 King St, Stellarton, NS B0K 0A2, Tel (902) 752-8371	19,163,076,970	11	500	5411
▲ **EOG RESOURCES CANADA INC** 700 9 Ave Sw Suite 1300, Calgary, AB T2P 3V4, Tel (403) 297-9100	13,806,455,248	12	100	1311
Agrium Canada Partnership (*Suby of* **AGRIUM CANADA PARTNERSHIP**) 13131 Lake Fraser Dr Se, Calgary, AB T2J 7E8, Tel (403) 225-7000	13,665,000,000	13	335	2873
SOBEYS CAPITAL INCORPORATED 115 King St, Stellarton, NS B0K 0A2, Tel (902) 752-8371	12,031,219,430	14	200	5141
HUDSON'S BAY COMPANY 401 Bay St Suite 500, Toronto, ON M5H 2Y4, Tel (800) 521-2364	11,016,690,335	15	600	5311
KOODO MOBILE-SCARBOROUGH 200 Consilium Pl Suite 1600, Scarborough, ON M1H 3J3, Tel (647) 837-6252	10,405,523,600	16	40,000	4899
KRAFT HEINZ CANADA ULC 95 Moatfield Dr Suite 316, North York, ON M3B 3L6, Tel (416) 441-5000	9,277,025,966	17	350	2043
EMPRO HOLDINGS LIMITED 115 King St, Stellarton, NS B0K 0A2, Tel (902) 755-4440	9,175,230,720	18	3	6712
PROVIGO DISTRIBUTION INC 400 Av Sainte-Croix, Saint-Laurent, QC H4N 3L4, Tel (514) 383-3000	7,763,254,837	19	800	5141
Federated Co-Operatives Limited (*Suby of* **FEDERATED CO-OPERATIVES LIMITED**) 401 22nd St E, Saskatoon, SK S7K 0H2, Tel (306) 244-3311	6,825,681,252	20	500	4225
Canada Post Corporation (*Suby of* **CANADA POST CORPORATION**) 2701 Riverside Dr, Ottawa, ON K1A 1L5, Tel (613) 734-8440	6,019,551,280	21	2,500	4311
▲ **LEIDOS, INC** 60 Queen St Suite 1516, Ottawa, ON K1P 5Y7, Tel (613) 563-7242	4,696,932,100	22	0	7371
▲ **CBRE LIMITED** 145 King St W Suite 1100, Toronto, ON M5H 1J8, Tel (416) 362-2244	4,459,066,141	23	1,800	8748
Compagnie d'Assurances Generales TD (*Suby of* **TORONTO-DOMINION BANK, THE**) 50 Boul Cremazie O Bureau 1200, Montreal, QC H2P 1B6, Tel (514) 382-6060	4,365,125,414	24	0	6311
EDWARD D. JONES & CO. CANADA HOLDING CO., INC 90 Burnhamthorpe Rd W Suite 902, Mississauga, ON L5B 3C3, Tel (905) 306-8600	4,331,255,000	25	1,600	6211
SOBEYS WEST INC 1020 64 Ave Ne, Calgary, AB T2E 7V8, Tel (403) 730-3500	4,182,909,892	26	600	5411
LIQUOR CONTROL BOARD OF ONTARIO, THE 55 Lake Shore Blvd E Suite 874, Toronto, ON M5E 1A4, Tel (416) 365-5900	4,174,116,090	27	100	5921
Finning International Inc (*Suby of* **FINNING INTERNATIONAL INC**) 666 Burrard St Suite 1000, Vancouver, BC V6C 2X8, Tel (604) 691-6444	4,162,722,060	28	897	5084
MAGNA SEATING INC 337 Magna Dr, Aurora, ON L4G 7K1, Tel (905) 726-2462	3,820,951,859	29	100	3714
INSURANCE CORPORATION OF BRITISH COLUMBIA 151 Esplanade W Suite 135, North Vancouver, BC V7M 3H9, Tel (604) 661-2800	3,797,134,051	30	1,500	6331
▲ Molson Coors Canada Inc (*Suby of* **MOLSON COORS BREWING COMPANY**) 33 Carlingview Dr, Etobicoke, ON M9W 5E4, Tel (416) 679-1786	3,567,500,000	31	3	2082
Lions Gate Entertainment Corp (*Suby of* **LIONS GATE ENTERTAINMENT CORP**) 250 Howe St Fl 20, Vancouver, BC V6C 3R8, Tel (877) 848-3866	3,201,500,000	32	0	7812
Purolator Holdings Ltd (*Suby of* **CANADA POST CORPORATION**) 5995 Avebury Rd Suite 100, Mississauga, ON L5R 3T8, Tel (905) 712-1251	3,158,177,896	33	1,300	4731
Martinrea International Inc (*Suby of* **MARTINREA INTERNATIONAL INC**) 3210 Langstaff Rd, Vaughan, ON L4K 5B2, Tel (289) 982-3000	3,152,834,061	34	100	3499
▲ **CIT FINANCIAL LTD** 207 Queens Quay W Suite 700, Toronto, ON M5J 1A7, Tel (416) 507-2400	3,102,824,457	35	300	6153
FGL ACQUISITIONCO LIMITED 2180 Yonge St, Toronto, ON M4S 2B9, Tel (416) 480-3000	3,091,066,240	36	1	6712
CAPITALE ASSUREUR DE L'ADMINISTRATION PUBLIQUE INC, LA 625 Rue Jacques-Parizeau, Quebec, QC G1R 2G5, Tel (418) 644-4106	2,920,397,939	37	400	6311

COMPANY	SALES ($)	RANK	EMPLOYEES HERE	PRIMARY SIC CODE
Just Energy Group Inc (*Suby of* **JUST ENERGY GROUP INC**) 6345 Dixie Rd Suite 200, Mississauga, ON L5T 2E6, *Tel* (905) 670-4440	2,859,903,318	38	0	4911
Ferus Inc (*Suby of* **THE ENERGY & MINERALS GROUP**) 401 9 Ave Sw Suite 916, Calgary, AB T2P 3C5, *Tel* (403) 517-8777	2,707,034,375	39	50	4925
▲ **PLAINS MIDSTREAM CANADA ULC** 607 8 Ave Sw Suite 1400, Calgary, AB T2P 0A7, *Tel* (403) 298-2100	2,666,056,939	40	570	4612
Purolator Inc. (*Suby of* **CANADA POST CORPORATION**) 5995 Avebury Rd, Mississauga, ON L5R 3P9, *Tel* (905) 712-1084	2,447,247,799	41	350	4731
Newport Partners Holdings LP (*Suby of* **NEWPORT PARTNERS HOLDINGS LP**) 469 King St W, Toronto, ON M5V 1K4, *Tel* (416) 867-7555	2,418,298,913	42	1	6722
SOCIETE DES ALCOOLS DU QUEBEC 905 Av De Lorimier, Montreal, QC H2K 3V9, *Tel* (514) 254-6000	2,405,791,207	43	100	5921
Gestion Laberge Inc (*Suby of* **GESTION LABERGE INC**) 6245 Boul Wilfrid-Hamel, L'Ancienne-Lorette, QC G2E 5W2, *Tel* (418) 667-1313	2,403,690,262	44	75	6712
FRASER HEALTH AUTHORITY 13450 102 Ave Suite 400, Surrey, BC V3T 0H1, *Tel* (604) 587-4600	2,365,677,737	45	12,000	8062
SCDA (2015) INC 1245 Rue Sherbrooke O Bureau 2100, Montreal, QC H3G 1G3, *Tel* (514) 499-8855	2,359,494,474	46	1,600	6311
LOBLAWS SUPERMARKETS LIMITED 1 Presidents Choice Cir, Brampton, ON L6Y 5S5, *Tel* (905) 459-2500	2,307,382,138	47	300	5411
Asig Canada Ltd (*Suby of* **ASIG CANADA LTD**) 8501 Mississauga Rd Suite 302, Brampton, ON L6Y 5G8, *Tel* (905) 497-4114	2,256,966,294	48	0	5172
▲ **GENERAL MOTORS OF CANADA COMPANY** 1908 Colonel Sam Dr, Oshawa, ON L1H 8P7, *Tel* (905) 644-5000	2,110,607,130	49	450	3711
▲ Lennox Industries (Canada) Ltd (*Suby of* **LENNOX INTERNATIONAL INC.**) 400 Norris Glen Rd, Etobicoke, ON M9C 1H5, *Tel* (416) 621-9302	2,037,062,744	50	350	3634
Canadian Test Case 168 Inc. (*Suby of* **CANADIAN TEST CASE 168 INC.**) 5770 Hurontario St, Mississauga, ON L5R 3G5, *Tel*	2,020,680,000	51	375	3714
▲ Masonite International Corporation (*Suby of* **MASONITE INTERNATIONAL CORPORATION**) 2771 Rutherford Rd, Concord, ON L4K 2N6, *Tel* (905) 482-2370	1,973,964,000	52	50	2431
ZEHRMART INC 1 Presidents Choice Cir, Brampton, ON L6Y 5S5, *Tel* (905) 459-2500	1,968,728,648	53	150	5411
NEXEN ENERGY ULC 801 7 Ave Sw Suite 2900, Calgary, AB T2P 3P7, *Tel* (403) 699-4000	1,937,370,362	54	300	1382
CU INC 909 11 Ave Sw Suite 700, Calgary, AB T2R 1N6, *Tel* (403) 292-7500	1,903,106,585	55	0	4931
HYDRO ONE NETWORKS INC 483 Bay St Suite 1000, Toronto, ON M5G 2P5, *Tel* (416) 345-5000	1,897,124,121	56	500	4911
LNA HOLDINGS ULC 334 Av Avro, Pointe-Claire, QC H9R 5W5, *Tel* (514) 428-7150	1,887,416,320	57	1	6712
Keyera Corp (*Suby of* **KEYERA CORP**) 144 4 Ave Sw Suite 600, Calgary, AB T2P 3N4, *Tel* (403) 205-8300	1,855,749,335	58	250	1389
▲ Home Depot of Canada Inc (*Suby of* **THE HOME DEPOT INC**) 1 Concorde Gate Suite 900, North York, ON M3C 4H9, *Tel* (416) 609-0852	1,729,168,590	59	110	5251
INTACT INSURANCE COMPANY 700 University Ave Suite 1500, Toronto, ON M5G 0A1, *Tel* (416) 341-1464	1,720,267,385	60	200	6331
ILLINOIS CENTRAL RAILROAD 935 Rue De La Gauchetiere O Bureau 11, Montreal, QC H3B 2M9, *Tel* (514) 399-4536	1,713,287,600	61	3,218	4011
Western Financial Group Inc (*Suby of* **WESTERN FINANCIAL GROUP INC**) 1010 24 St Se, High River, AB T1V 2A7, *Tel* (403) 652-2663	1,689,259,087	62	119	6311
TOYOTA MOTOR MANUFACTURING CANADA INC 1055 Fountain St N, Cambridge, ON N3H 4R7, *Tel* (519) 653-1111	1,688,456,519	63	0	3711
▲ **AECOM ENERGY SERVICES LTD** 6025 11 St Se Suite 240, Calgary, AB T2H 2Z2, *Tel* (403) 218-7100	1,668,465,288	64	40	1389
STANTEC CONSULTING LTD 10160 112 St Nw, Edmonton, AB T5K 2L6, *Tel* (780) 917-7000	1,665,546,860	65	1,400	8711
CHICAGO, CENTRAL & PACIFIC RAILROAD COMPANY (INC) 935 Rue De La Gauchetiere O, Montreal, QC H3B 2M9, *Tel* (514) 399-4536	1,657,726,080	66	3,218	4011
RBC Life Insurance Company (*Suby of* **ROYAL BANK OF CANADA**) 6880 Financial Dr Suite 1000, Mississauga, ON L5N 8E8, *Tel* (905) 816-2746	1,579,890,998	67	400	6311
MICHELIN AMERIQUE DU NORD (CANADA) INC 2500 Boul Daniel-Johnson Bureau 500, Cote Saint-Luc, QC H7T 2P6, *Tel* (450) 978-4700	1,559,251,800	68	150	5014
TRILOGY RETAIL ENTERPRISES L.P 161 Bay St Suite 4900, Toronto, ON M5J 2S1, *Tel* (416) 943-4110	1,540,112,450	69	6,000	6712
RBC Dominion Securities Inc (*Suby of* **ROYAL BANK OF CANADA**) 200 Bay St, Toronto, ON M5J 2W7, *Tel* (416) 842-2000	1,507,016,865	70	1,000	6282
ORICA CANADA INC 301 Rue De L'Hotel-De-Ville, Brownsburg-Chatham, QC J8G 3B5, *Tel* (450) 533-4201	1,505,544,045	71	550	2892
▲ Costco Wholesale Canada Ltd (*Suby of* **COSTCO WHOLESALE CORPORATION**) 415 West Hunt Club Rd, Nepean, ON K2E 1C5, *Tel* (613) 221-2010	1,498,539,817	72	190	5099
BANK OF NOVA SCOTIA TRUST COMPANY, THE 1 Queen St E Suite 1200, Toronto, ON M5C 2W5, *Tel* (416) 866-7829	1,483,001,280	73	0	6021
BP Canada Energy Company (*Suby of* **BP P.L.C.**) 240 4 Ave Sw, Calgary, AB T2P 4H4, *Tel* (403) 233-1313	1,473,295,415	74	2,100	1311

COMPANY	SALES ($)	RANK	EMPLOYEES HERE	PRIMARY SIC CODE
Pivot Technology Solutions, Inc (*Suby of* **PIVOT TECHNOLOGY SOLUTIONS, INC**) 161 Bay St Suite 1020, Toronto, ON M5J 2S1, *Tel* (647) 788-2034	1,470,841,000	75	0	8731
VALE CANADA LIMITED 200 Bay St Suite 1600, Toronto, ON M5J 2K2, *Tel* (416) 361-7511	1,441,411,589	76	200	1629
CI Financial Corp (*Suby of* **CI FINANCIAL CORP**) 2 Queen St E, Toronto, ON M5C 3G7, *Tel* (416) 364-1145	1,441,050,354	77	500	6282
Commission des Normes, de Lequite, de la Sante et de la Securite du Travail, La (*Suby of* **COMMISSION DES NORMES, DE LEQUITE, DE LA SANTE ET DE LA SECURITE DU TRAVAIL, LA**) 524 Rue Bourdages Bureau 370, Quebec, QC G1K 7E2, *Tel* (877) 639-0744	1,433,604,794	78	1,000	6331
J. D. Irving, Limited (*Suby of* **J. D. IRVING, LIMITED**) 300 Union St Suite 5, Saint John, NB E2L 4Z2, *Tel* (506) 632-7777	1,422,733,650	79	1,200	2421
Frontera Energy Corporation (*Suby of* **FRONTERA ENERGY CORPORATION**) 333 Bay St Suite 1100, Toronto, ON M5H 2R2, *Tel* (416) 362-7735	1,411,711,000	80	30	1381
IMPERIAL OIL LIMITED Po Box 3004 Stn Main, Sarnia, ON N7T 7M5, *Tel* (519) 339-4015	1,398,780,000	81	950	2911
ATCO GAS AND PIPELINES LTD 909 11 Ave Sw Suite 1200, Calgary, AB T2R 1L7, *Tel* (403) 245-7060	1,398,510,698	82	400	4923
GROUPE VOLVO CANADA INC 35 Boul Gagnon, Sainte-Claire, QC G0R 2V0, *Tel* (418) 883-3391	1,395,373,388	83	950	5012
MEG ENERGY CORP 3 Ave Sw Suite 600 25 Fl, Calgary, AB T2P 0G5, *Tel* (403) 770-0446	1,380,387,629	84	617	1311
Cenovus FCCL Ltd (*Suby of* **CENOVUS ENERGY INC**) 500 Centre St Se Suite 766, Calgary, AB T2G 1A6, *Tel* (403) 766-2000	1,339,339,570	85	0	1311
PETROKAZAKHSTAN INC 140 4 Ave Sw Suite 1460, Calgary, AB T2P 3N3, *Tel* (403) 221-8435	1,339,339,570	86	0	1311
HSBC BANK CANADA 885 Georgia St W, Vancouver, BC V6C 3G1, *Tel* (604) 685-1000	1,289,940,880	87	300	6021
ALGOMA STEEL INC 105 West St, Sault Ste. Marie, ON P6A 7B4, *Tel* (705) 945-2351	1,288,313,550	88	2,300	5051
FORTISBC PACIFIC HOLDINGS INC 1975 Springfield Rd Suite 100, Kelowna, BC V1Y 7V7, *Tel* (250) 469-8000	1,286,779,440	89	2,000	4911
WORKERS' COMPENSATION BOARD ALBERTA 9912 107 St Nw, Edmonton, AB T5K 1G5, *Tel* (780) 498-3999	1,277,955,398	90	500	6331
AMBATOVY JOINT VENTURE 2200 Lake Shore Blvd W, Etobicoke, ON M8V 1A4, *Tel* (416) 924-4551	1,277,421,192	91	8,000	1061
NEXEN HOLDINGS (USA) INC 801 7 Ave Sw Suite 200, Calgary, AB T2P 3P7, *Tel* (403) 234-6700	1,272,955,845	92	0	1311
AMEC FOSTER WHEELER INC 2020 Winston Park Dr Suite 700, Oakville, ON L6H 6X7, *Tel* (905) 829-5400	1,263,097,792	93	535	6719
MASTER CREDIT CARD TRUST 100 University Ave Suite 800, Toronto, ON M5J 2Y1, *Tel* (416) 867-6785	1,262,891,271	94	1	6726
BROOKFIELD RENEWABLE ENERGY PARTNERS L.P. 41 Rue Victoria, Gatineau, QC J8X 2A1, *Tel* (819) 561-2722	1,251,786,730	95	0	8731
SHAW CABLESYSTEMS G.P. 630 3 Ave Sw, Calgary, AB T2P 4L4, *Tel* (403) 750-4500	1,239,865,056	96	5,600	4841
ALBERTA TREASURY BRANCHES 10020 100 St Nw Suite 2100, Edmonton, AB T5J 0N3, *Tel* (780) 408-7000	1,227,656,561	97	200	6036
▲ **ADESA AUCTIONS CANADA CORPORATION** 55 Auction Lane 2nd Floor, Brampton, ON L6T 5P4, *Tel* (905) 790-7653	1,201,469,475	98	35	5012
EXPORT DEVELOPMENT CANADA 150 Slater St, Ottawa, ON K1A 1K3, *Tel* (613) 598-2500	1,163,910,240	99	1,000	6111
Spin Master Corp (*Suby of* **SPIN MASTER CORP**) 450 Front St W, Toronto, ON M5V 1B6, *Tel* (416) 364-6002	1,154,454,000	100	0	6712
▲ Imperial Oil Resources Limited (*Suby of* **EXXON MOBIL CORPORATION**) 237 4 Ave Sw Suite 4063, Calgary, AB T2P 4K3, *Tel* (800) 567-3776	1,154,019,392	101	1,500	1382
TECK COAL LIMITED 205 9 Ave Se Suite 1000, Calgary, AB T2G 0R3, *Tel* (403) 767-8500	1,151,100,964	102	150	1221
SODEXO QUEBEC LIMITEE 930 Rue Wellington Bureau 100, Montreal, QC H3C 1T8, *Tel* (514) 866-5561	1,149,422,868	103	30	8741
REDBERRY FRANCHISING CORP 401 The West Mall Suite 700, Etobicoke, ON M9C 5J4, *Tel* (416) 626-6464	1,143,269,520	104	55	6794
AMER SPORTS CANADA INC 2220 Dollarton Hwy Unit 110, North Vancouver, BC V7H 1A8, *Tel* (604) 960-3001	1,137,238,431	105	1,000	5091
▲ **UNION GAS LIMITED** 50 Keil Dr N Suite 2001, Chatham, ON N7L 3V9, *Tel* (519) 352-3100	1,130,917,205	106	900	4923
▲ ABC Group Inc (*Suby of* **CERBERUS CAPITAL MANAGEMENT, L.P.**) 2 Norelco Dr, North York, ON M9L 2X6, *Tel* (416) 246-1782	1,124,981,033	107	150	3089
SYNCREON HOLDINGS INC 999 Boundary Rd, Oshawa, ON L1J 8P8, *Tel* (905) 743-6277	1,104,300,000	108	5	4783
BRIDGESTONE CANADA INC 5770 Hurontario St Suite 400, Mississauga, ON L5R 3G5, *Tel* (877) 468-6270	1,094,410,500	109	2,100	5014
FCA CANADA INC 1 Riverside Dr W, Windsor, ON N9A 5K3, *Tel* (519) 973-2000	1,055,303,565	110	1	3711

▲ **ENERGIE VALERO INC**

COMPANY	SALES ($)	RANK	EMPLOYEES HERE	PRIMARY SIC CODE
1801 Av Mcgill College Bureau 1300, Montreal, QC H3A 2N4, *Tel* (514) 982-8200	1,053,260,665	111	425	5172
SASKATOON REGIONAL HEALTH AUTHORITY 410 22nd St E, Saskatoon, SK S7K 5T6, *Tel* (306) 655-3300	1,052,552,335	112	3,500	8062
SOBEYS QUEBEC INC 11281 Boul Albert-Hudon, Montreal-Nord, QC H1G 3J5, *Tel* (514) 324-1010	1,046,183,477	113	800	5141
▲ Chevron Canada Limited (*Suby of* **CHEVRON CORPORATION**) 1050 Pender St W Suite 1200, Vancouver, BC V6E 3T4, *Tel* (604) 668-5300	1,039,501,200	114	350	2911
▲ **CUSTOM HOUSE ULC** 3680 Uptown Blvd Suite 300, Victoria, BC V8Z 0B9, *Tel* (888) 987-7612	1,029,037,713	115	100	6099
WSP CANADA GROUP LIMITED 100 Commerce Valley Dr W, Thornhill, ON L3T 0A1, *Tel* (905) 882-1100	1,028,016,263	116	0	8711
▲ **UNITED PARCEL SERVICE CANADA LTD** 1022 Champlain Ave, Burlington, ON L7L 0C2, *Tel* (905) 676-1708	1,027,505,538	117	100	4212
ALLSTREAM BUSINESS INC 7550 Birchmount Rd, Markham, ON L3R 6C6, *Tel* (416) 345-2000	1,025,535,599	118	2,000	4899
3522997 CANADA INC 180 Montee De Liesse, Saint-Laurent, QC H4T 1N7, *Tel* (514) 341-6161	1,025,152,250	119	4,000	6712
SASKATCHEWAN GOVERNMENT INSURANCE 2260 11th Ave Suite 18, Regina, SK S4P 0J9, *Tel* (306) 751-1200	1,021,223,304	120	1,000	6331
FORTISBC ENERGY INC 1111 Georgia St W Suite 1000, Vancouver, BC V6E 4M3, *Tel* (604) 443-6525	1,017,293,640	121	300	4923
▲ **ENBRIDGE ENERGY DISTRIBUTION INC** 500 Consumers Rd, North York, ON M2J 1P8, *Tel* (416) 492-5000	1,012,061,346	122	400	4924
NOVA SCOTIA POWER INCORPORATED 1223 Lower Water St, Halifax, NS B3J 3S8, *Tel* (902) 428-6230	1,002,958,620	123	600	4911
UNIVERSITY OF MANITOBA THE 66 Chancellors Cir Rm 406, Winnipeg, MB R3T 2N2, *Tel* (204) 474-8167	998,394,219	124	300	8221
LONDON DRUGS LIMITED 12251 Horseshoe Way, Richmond, BC V7A 4X5, *Tel* (604) 272-7400	991,025,188	125	350	5912
Consumers' Co-operative Refineries Limited (*Suby of* **FEDERATED CO-OPERATIVES LIMITED**) 550 9th Ave E, Regina, SK S4P 3A1, *Tel* (306) 721-5353	974,532,375	126	0	2911
2206997 Ontario Inc (*Suby of* **2206997 ONTARIO INC**) 939 Eglinton Ave E Suite 201, Toronto, ON M4G 4H7, *Tel* (416) 696-7700	965,599,920	127	1	8748
ENSIGN DRILLING INC 400 5 Ave Sw Suite 1000, Calgary, AB T2P 0L6, *Tel* (403) 262-1361	948,861,850	128	75	1381
GREAT LAKES BASIN ENERGY L.P. 1055 Georgia St W Suite 1100, Vancouver, BC V6E 3R5, *Tel* (604) 488-8000	941,397,120	129	2,200	4924
MAN CANADA AHL ALPHA FUND 70 York St Suite 1202, Toronto, ON M5J 1S9, *Tel* (416) 775-3646	921,566,472	130	1	6726
University of Saskatchewan (*Suby of* **UNIVERSITY OF SASKATCHEWAN**) 105 Administration Pl Suite E, Saskatoon, SK S7N 5A2, *Tel* (306) 966-4343	918,800,689	131	1,100	8221
CWA ENGINEERS INC 2925 Virtual Way Suite 380, Vancouver, BC V5M 4X5, *Tel* (604) 526-2275	917,966,185	132	44	8711
▲ Amex Canada Inc (*Suby of* **AMERICAN EXPRESS COMPANY**) 2225 Sheppard Ave E, Toronto, ON M2J 5C2, *Tel* (905) 474-8000	912,008,750	133	2,000	6099
PEPSI BOTTLING GROUP (CANADA), ULC, THE 5205 Satellite Dr, Mississauga, ON L4W 5J7, *Tel* (905) 212-7377	909,563,550	134	257	2086
Wheaton Precious Metals Corp (*Suby of* **WHEATON PRECIOUS METALS CORP**) 1021 Hastings St W Suite 3500, Vancouver, BC V6E 0C3, *Tel* (604) 684-9648	891,557,000	135	0	1044
PCL CONSTRUCTORS CANADA INC 2085 Hurontario St Suite 400, Mississauga, ON L5A 4G1, *Tel* (905) 276-7600	881,237,142	136	500	1542
▲ **LOWE'S COMPANIES CANADA, ULC** 5150 Spectrum Way, Mississauga, ON L4W 5G2, *Tel* (905) 219-1000	880,489,728	137	150	5211
GROUPE RESTAURANTS IMVESCOR INC 8250 Boul Decarie Bureau 310, Montreal, QC H4P 2P5, *Tel* (514) 341-5544	878,062,162	138	30	6794
Royal Trust Corporation of Canada (*Suby of* **ROYAL BANK OF CANADA**) 77 King St W Suite 3800, Toronto, ON M5K 2A1, *Tel* (416) 974-1400	872,488,007	139	0	6021
FARM CREDIT CANADA 1800 Hamilton St, Regina, SK S4P 4L3, *Tel* (306) 780-8100	855,688,243	140	700	6159
Resolve Corporation (*Suby of* **2206997 ONTARIO INC**) 2 Robert Speck Pky Suite 1600, Mississauga, ON L4Z 1H8, *Tel* (905) 306-6200	852,131,109	141	300	8748
AECON CONSTRUCTION GROUP INC 20 Carlson Crt Suite 800, Etobicoke, ON M9W 7K6, *Tel* (416) 293-7004	846,635,963	142	250	1541
JAZZ AVIATION LP 3 Spectacle Lake Dr Suite 100, Dartmouth, NS B3B 1W8, *Tel* (902) 873-5000	837,296,993	143	650	4512
Enerflex Ltd (*Suby of* **ENERFLEX LTD**) 1331 Macleod Trail Se Suite 904, Calgary, AB T2G 0K3, *Tel* (403) 387-6377	836,245,596	144	50	3563
NOVA SCOTIA HEALTH AUTHORITY 1276 South Park St Suite 1278, Halifax, NS B3H 2Y9, *Tel* (902) 473-5117	834,962,251	145	200	8062
R.G.F.M. Bertucci Management Corp Inc (*Suby of* **R.G.F.M. BERTUCCI MANAGEMENT CORP INC**) 2040 Rue Peel, Montreal, QC H3A 1W5, *Tel* (514) 861-9971	832,641,904	146	1	6712
Canadian Blood Services (*Suby of* **CANADIAN BLOOD SERVICES**) 1800 Alta Vista Dr, Ottawa, ON K1G 4J5, *Tel* (613) 739-2300	830,976,351	147	400	8099

COMPANY	SALES ($)	RANK	EMPLOYEES HERE	PRIMARY SIC CODE
Diageo Canada Inc (*Suby of* **DIAGEO PLC**) 401 The West Mall Suite 800, Toronto, ON M9C 5P8, *Tel* (416) 626-2000	826,644,731	148	70	2085
REGIONAL HEALTH AUTHORITY NB 155 Pleasant St, Miramichi, NB E1V 1Y3, *Tel* (506) 623-5500	822,036,011	149	1,000	8062
Cenovus Energy Inc (*Suby of* **CENOVUS ENERGY INC**) 500 Centre St Se, Calgary, AB T2P 0M5, *Tel* (403) 766-2000	820,960,832	150	1,386	1382
EXTENDICARE (CANADA) INC 3000 Steeles Ave E Suite 700, Markham, ON L3R 9W2, *Tel* (905) 470-1400	820,005,307	151	120	8051
University of Waterloo (*Suby of* **UNIVERSITY OF WATERLOO**) 200 University Ave W, Waterloo, ON N2L 3G1, *Tel* (519) 888-4567	817,080,457	152	0	8221
CANFOR PULP PRODUCTS INC 1700 75th Ave W Unit 230, Vancouver, BC V6P 6G2, *Tel* (604) 661-5421	815,014,826	153	0	6712
Transport TFI 21, S.E.C. (*Suby of* **TRANSPORT TFI 21, S.E.C.**) 8801 Rte Transcanadienne Bureau 500, Saint-Laurent, QC H4S 1Z6, *Tel* (514) 856-7500	813,438,844	154	50	5021
RICHARDSON INTERNATIONAL LIMITED 1 Lombard Pl Suite 2800, Winnipeg, MB R3B 0X3, *Tel* (204) 934-5961	812,125,552	155	400	5153
Algonquin Power & Utilities Corp (*Suby of* **ALGONQUIN POWER & UTILITIES CORP**) 354 Davis Rd, Oakville, ON L6J 2X1, *Tel* (905) 465-4500	810,664,234	156	0	6712
CANADIAN NUCLEAR LABORATORIES LTD. 286 Plant Rd, Chalk River, ON K0J 1J0, *Tel* (613) 584-3311	809,424,934	157	0	2819
Wawanesa Mutual Insurance Company, The (*Suby of* **WAWANESA MUTUAL INSURANCE COMPANY, THE**) 191 Broadway Suite 100, Winnipeg, MB R3C 3P1, *Tel* (204) 985-3811	806,653,499	158	217	6331
Sunnybrook Health Sciences Centre Foundation (*Suby of* **SUNNYBROOK HEALTH SCIENCES CENTRE FOUNDATION**) 2075 Bayview Ave Suite 747, Toronto, ON M4N 3M5, *Tel* (416) 480-6100	803,787,987	159	7,000	8011
▲ **DEVON CANADA CORPORATION** 400 3 Ave Sw Suite 2000, Calgary, AB T2P 4H2, *Tel* (403) 232-7100	795,131,793	160	200	1311
AGRICULTURE FINANCIAL SERVICES CORPORATION 5718 56 Ave, Lacombe, AB T4L 1B1, *Tel* (403) 782-8200	792,475,111	161	300	6159
TRAVELEX CANADA LIMITED 100 Yonge St, Toronto, ON M5C 2W1, *Tel* (416) 359-3700	790,602,145	162	500	6099
Camso Inc (*Suby of* **CAMSO INC**) 2633 Rue Macpherson, Magog, QC J1X 0E6, *Tel* (819) 823-1777	785,057,132	163	75	3569
BANQUE DE DEVELOPPEMENT DU CANADA 5 Place Ville-Marie Bureau 400, Montreal, QC H3B 5E7, *Tel* (514) 283-5904	777,423,156	164	750	6141
HOLLISWEALTH ADVISORY SERVICES INC. 1 Adelaide St E Suite 2700, Toronto, ON M5C 2V9, *Tel* (416) 350-3250	773,275,177	165	200	6282
Rogers Communications Canada Inc (*Suby of* **ROGERS COMMUNICATIONS INC**) 333 Bloor St E 9th Fl, Toronto, ON M4W 1G9, *Tel* (416) 935-7777	773,129,018	166	5	4841
▲ General Electric Canada Company (*Suby of* **GENERAL ELECTRIC COMPANY**) 2300 Meadowvale Blvd Suite 100, Mississauga, ON L5N 5P9, *Tel* (905) 858-5100	770,173,149	167	500	3625
ATS Automation Tooling Systems Inc (*Suby of* **ATS AUTOMATION TOOLING SYSTEMS INC**) 730 Fountain St N Suite 2b, Cambridge, ON N3H 4R7, *Tel* (519) 653-6500	769,509,223	168	100	3569
BRICK LTD., THE 16930 114 Ave Nw, Edmonton, AB T5M 3S2, *Tel* (780) 930-6000	766,978,635	169	0	5712
North Atlantic Refining Limited (*Suby of* **PEAK STRATEGIC SILVER PARTNERS**) 1 Refining Rd, Come By Chance, NL A0B 1N0, *Tel* (709) 463-8811	766,087,350	170	600	2911
SUNCOR ENERGY PRODUCTS PARTNERSHIP 150 6 Ave Sw, Calgary, AB T2P 3Y7, *Tel* (403) 296-8000	766,087,350	171	200	2911
Indigo Books & Music Inc (*Suby of* **INDIGO BOOKS & MUSIC INC**) 468 King St W Suite 500, Toronto, ON M5V 1L8, *Tel* (416) 646-8945	765,706,765	172	200	5942
Centerra Gold Inc (*Suby of* **CENTERRA GOLD INC**) 1 University Ave Suite 1500, Toronto, ON M5J 2P1, *Tel* (416) 204-1241	760,758,000	173	50	1081
▲ Molson Coors Canada Holdco ULC (*Suby of* **MOLSON COORS BREWING COMPANY**) 33 Carlingview Dr, Etobicoke, ON M9W 5E4, *Tel* (416) 679-1786	760,432,640	174	1	6712
MAGNA POWERTRAIN INC 50 Casmir Crt, Concord, ON L4K 4J5, *Tel* (905) 532-2100	745,147,629	175	25	3714
MERCEDES-BENZ CANADA INC 98 Vanderhoof Ave, Toronto, ON M4G 4C9, *Tel* (416) 425-3550	744,199,140	176	289	5012
Crius Energy Trust (*Suby of* **CRIUS ENERGY TRUST**) 100 King St W Suite 3400, Toronto, ON M5X 1A4, *Tel* (416) 644-1753	743,795,000	177	0	4924
TORONTO HYDRO-ELECTRIC SYSTEM LIMITED 14 Carlton St, Toronto, ON M5B 1K5, *Tel* (416) 542-3100	741,280,712	178	170	4911
SQI HOLDINGS II INC 115 King St, Stellarton, NS B0K 0A2, *Tel* (902) 752-8371	737,267,874	179	1	6712
3077578 Nova Scotia Corp (*Suby of* **3077578 NOVA SCOTIA CORP**) 620 Richmond St, London, ON N6A 5J9, *Tel* (519) 453-9600	736,200,000	180	2	5074
PHILIPS ELECTRONICS LTD 281 Hillmount Rd, Markham, ON L6C 2S3, *Tel* (905) 201-4100	732,934,971	181	300	5064
▲ Winners Merchants International L.P. (*Suby of* **THE TJX COMPANIES INC**) 60 Standish Crt, Mississauga, ON L5R 0G1, *Tel* (905) 405-8000	729,607,000	182	600	5651
SIGNET DEVELOPMENT CORPORATION 150 Signet Dr, North York, ON M9L 1T9, *Tel* (416) 749-9300	728,150,880	183	1,700	6553

ATCO ELECTRIC LTD

COMPANY	SALES ($)	RANK	EMPLOYEES HERE	PRIMARY SIC CODE
10035 105 St Nw, Edmonton, AB T5J 2V6, *Tel* (800) 668-2248	717,349,602	184	400	4911
James Richardson & Sons, Limited (*Suby of* **JAMES RICHARDSON & SONS, LIMITED**) 1 Lombard Pl Suite 3000, Winnipeg, MB R3B 0Y1, *Tel* (204) 953-7970	716,619,995	185	20	5153
GENSTAR CAPITAL, ULC 1001 Corporate Dr, Burlington, ON L7L 5V5, *Tel* (905) 319-5645	716,237,000	186	2,800	6719
▲ Coca-Cola Refreshments Canada Company (*Suby of* **THE COCA-COLA COMPANY**) 335 King St E, Toronto, ON M5A 1L1, *Tel* (416) 424-6000	715,014,860	187	383	2086
McMaster University (*Suby of* **MCMASTER UNIVERSITY**) 1280 Main St W Gh209, Hamilton, ON L8S 4L8, *Tel* (905) 525-9140	714,324,553	188	0	8221
NORTON ROSE CANADA LLP 400 3 Ave Sw Suite 3700, Calgary, AB T2P 4H2, *Tel* (403) 267-8222	707,580,160	189	300	8111
Hamilton Health Sciences Corporation (*Suby of* **HAMILTON HEALTH SCIENCES CORPORATION**) 1200 Main St W, Hamilton, ON L8S 4J9, *Tel* (905) 521-2100	695,826,196	190	4,000	8062
COMBINED INSURANCE COMPANY OF AMERICA 7300 Warden Ave Suite 300, Markham, ON L3R 0X3, *Tel* (905) 305-1922	689,192,320	191	0	6321
CPPIB ZAMBEZI HOLDINGS INC 1 Queen St E Suite 2600, Toronto, ON M5C 2W5, *Tel* (416) 868-4075	688,033,900	192	2,000	4731
DESJARDINS HOLDING FINANCIER INC 1 Rue Complexe Desjardins S 40e Etage, Montreal, QC H5B 1J1, *Tel* (418) 838-7870	687,216,833	193	100	6411
TATA COMMUNICATIONS (CANADA) LTD 1555 Rue Carrie-Derick, Montreal, QC H3C 6W2, *Tel* (514) 868-7272	670,337,265	194	400	4899
▲ ExxonMobil Canada Ltd (*Suby of* **EXXON MOBIL CORPORATION**) 237 4 Ave Sw, Calgary, AB T2P 4K3, *Tel* (403) 232-5300	669,706,265	195	500	1311
Canaccord Genuity Group Inc (*Suby of* **CANACCORD GENUITY GROUP INC**) 609 Granville St Suite 2200, Vancouver, BC V6C 1X6, *Tel* (604) 643-7300	669,518,331	196	345	6211
DESJARDINS ASSURANCES GENERALES INC 6300 Boul De La Rive-Sud, Levis, QC G6V 6P9, *Tel* (418) 835-4850	668,976,658	197	625	6331
COMPASS GROUP CANADA LTD 1 Prologis Blvd Suite 400, Mississauga, ON L5W 0G2, *Tel* (905) 795-5100	663,431,645	198	150	5812
Detour Gold Corporation (*Suby of* **DETOUR GOLD CORPORATION**) 199 Bay St Suite 4100, Toronto, ON M5L 1E2, *Tel* (416) 304-0800	658,286,000	199	425	1081
▲ Molson Coors Callco ULC (*Suby of* **MOLSON COORS BREWING COMPANY**) 33 Carlingview Dr, Etobicoke, ON M9W 5E4, *Tel* (416) 679-1786	655,578,757	200	2	6712
▲ Emerson Electric Canada Limited (*Suby of* **EMERSON ELECTRIC CO.**) 66 Leek Crescent, Richmond Hill, ON L4B 1H1, *Tel* (905) 948-3401	653,727,872	201	3,000	5063
FUNDEX INVESTMENTS INC 400 Applewood Cres, Concord, ON L4K 0C3, *Tel* (905) 305-1651	642,054,160	202	0	6211
LILYDALE INC 7727 127 Ave Nw, Edmonton, AB T5C 1R9, *Tel* (780) 448-0990	640,230,143	203	300	5144
PCL INDUSTRIAL CONSTRUCTORS INC 9915 56 Ave Nw, Edmonton, AB T6E 5L7, *Tel* (780) 733-5500	635,135,233	204	100	1541
OCEANAGOLD CORPORATION 777 Hornby Street Suite 1910, Vancouver, BC V6Z 1S4, *Tel* (604) 235-3360	628,634,000	205	950	1081
▲ Altalink, L.P. (*Suby of* **BERKSHIRE HATHAWAY INC.**) 2611 3 Ave Se, Calgary, AB T2A 7W7, *Tel* (403) 267-3400	623,388,971	206	1	4911
LIQUOR STORES LIMITED PARTNERSHIP 10508 82 Ave Nw Suite 300, Edmonton, AB T6E 2A4, *Tel* (780) 944-9994	622,661,219	207	0	5921
▲ Marmon/Keystone Canada Inc (*Suby of* **BERKSHIRE HATHAWAY INC.**) 1220 Heritage Rd, Burlington, ON L7L 4X9, *Tel* (905) 319-4646	621,708,343	208	50	5051
▲ Genuine Parts Holdings ULC (*Suby of* **GENUINE PARTS COMPANY**) 7025 Rue Ontario E, Montreal, QC H1N 2B3, *Tel* (514) 256-5031	619,660,160	209	6	5013
CENTRE DE SANTE ET DE SERVICES SOCIAUX DE LAVAL 1755 Boul Rene-Laennec, Cote Saint-Luc, QC H7M 3L9, *Tel* (450) 668-1010	619,149,350	210	2,815	8062
Franco-Nevada Corporation (*Suby of* **FRANCO-NEVADA CORPORATION**) 199 Bay St Suite 2000, Toronto, ON M5L 1G9, *Tel* (416) 306-6300	610,200,000	211	0	6211
NALCOR ENERGY 500 Columbus Dr, St. John'S, NL A1B 4K7, *Tel* (709) 737-1440	609,541,445	212	0	4911
▲ **MDC PARTNERS INC** 45 Hazelton Ave, Toronto, ON M5R 2E3, *Tel* (416) 960-9000	607,981,513	213	0	7311
FINANCIERE BANQUE NATIONALE & CIE INC 1155 Rue Metcalfe Bureau 400, Montreal, QC H3B 4S9, *Tel* (514) 879-2222	598,757,900	214	0	6211
Royal Bank Holding Inc (*Suby of* **ROYAL BANK OF CANADA**) 200 Bay St, Toronto, ON M5J 2J5, *Tel* (416) 947-8393	597,037,408	215	0	6211
▲ **AECOM CANADA LTD** 3292 Production Way, Burnaby, BC V5A 4R4, *Tel* (604) 444-6400	595,894,063	216	100	8742
NATIONAL BANK GROUP INC 600 Rue De La Gauchetiere O Bureau 11e, Montreal, QC H3B 4L2, *Tel* (514) 394-6611	593,032,960	217	1	6211
Groupe Sante Sedna Inc (*Suby of* **GROUPE SANTE SEDNA INC**) 1010 Rue Sherbrooke O Bureau 2405, Montreal, QC H3A 2R7, *Tel* (514) 844-8760	592,028,160	218	10	8741
Ivari Canada ULC (*Suby of* **WILTON RE LTD**) 5000 Yonge St Suite 500, North York, ON M2N 7E9, *Tel* (416) 883-5000	589,916,931	219	500	6311
Kelsey's Restaurants Inc (*Suby of* **CARA HOLDINGS LIMITED**) 387 Gloucester Ave, Oakville, ON L6J 3X3, *Tel*	584,243,980	220	40	5812

COMPANY	SALES ($)	RANK	EMPLOYEES HERE	PRIMARY SIC CODE
REPSOL CANADA ENERGY PARTNERSHIP 888 3 St Sw Suite 2000, Calgary, AB T2P 5C5, *Tel* (403) 237-1234	582,591,190	221	200	1382
3072410 CANADA INC 1001 Rue Yamaska E, Farnham, QC J2N 1J7, *Tel* (450) 293-3173	581,879,680	222	1	6712
SEMTECH CANADA INC 4281 Harvester Rd, Burlington, ON L7L 5M4, *Tel* (905) 632-2996	578,827,000	223	350	3679
Baytex Energy Corp (*Suby of* **BAYTEX ENERGY CORP**) 520 3 Ave Sw Suite 2800, Calgary, AB T2P 0R3, *Tel* (587) 952-3000	576,993,366	224	147	1311
Tervita Corporation (*Suby of* **TERVITA CORPORATION**) 140 10 Ave Se Suite 1600, Calgary, AB T2G 0R1, *Tel* (403) 233-7565	573,835,906	225	800	8748
SF INSURANCE PLACEMENT CORPORATION OF CANADA 333 First Commerce Dr, Aurora, ON L4G 8A4, *Tel* (905) 750-4100	573,398,141	226	30	6331
▲ General Electric Capital Canada (*Suby of* **GENERAL ELECTRIC COMPANY**) 2300 Meadowvale Blvd, Mississauga, ON L5N 5P9, *Tel* (905) 858-5100	570,187,871	227	250	6153
▲ Weyerhaeuser Company Limited (*Suby of* **WEYERHAEUSER COMPANY**) 1140 Pender St W Suite 440, Vancouver, BC V6E 4G1, *Tel* (604) 661-8000	569,093,460	228	200	2421
MANITOBA AGRICULTURAL SERVICES CORPORATION 1525 1st St Unit 100, Brandon, MB R7A 7A1, *Tel* (204) 726-6850	559,196,817	229	35	6159
EVERTRUST DEVELOPMENT GROUP CANADA INC 3100 Steeles Ave E Suite 302, Markham, ON L3R 8T3, *Tel* (647) 501-2345	556,690,141	230	3,000	1542
▲ Federal Express Canada Corporation (*Suby of* **FEDEX CORPORATION**) 5985 Explorer Dr Suite 313, Mississauga, ON L4W 5K6, *Tel* (800) 463-3339	553,260,988	231	6,000	4212
Pratt & Whitney Canada Corp (*Suby of* **PRATT AERO LIMITED PARTNERSHIP**) 1000 Boul Marie-Victorin, Longueuil, QC J4G 1A1, *Tel* (450) 677-9411	552,677,303	232	5,000	3519
▲ General Dynamics Land Systems - Canada Corporation (*Suby of* **GENERAL DYNAMICS CORPORATION**) 1991 Oxford St E Bldg 15, London, ON N5V 2Z7, *Tel* (519) 964-5900	551,282,136	233	2,000	3711
Wolseley Holdings Canada Inc (*Suby of* **WOLSELEY PLC**) 880 Laurentian Dr Suite 1, Burlington, ON L7N 3V6, *Tel* (905) 335-7373	548,077,008	234	8	6712
Cara Holdings Limited (*Suby of* **CARA HOLDINGS LIMITED**) 21 Bedford Rd Suite 200, Toronto, ON M5R 2J9, *Tel* (416) 944-1101	546,739,286	235	4	5812
▲ JDS Uniphase Corporation (*Suby of* **VIAVI SOLUTIONS INC.**) 61 Bill Leathem Dr, Nepean ON K2J 0P7, *Tel* (613) 843-3000	541,406,875	236	0	3661
Simcoe County District School Board, The (*Suby of* **SIMCOE COUNTY DISTRICT SCHOOL BOARD, THE**) 1170 Hwy 26, Midhurst, ON L0L 1X0, *Tel* (705) 734-6363	540,750,049	237	180	8211
HUSKY INJECTION MOLDING SYSTEMS LTD 500 Queen St S, Bolton, ON L7E 5S5, *Tel* (905) 951-5000	540,273,984	238	500	6712
JOHNSON CONTROLS NOVA SCOTIA U.L.C. 56 Leek Cres, Richmond Hill, ON L4B 1H1, *Tel* (866) 468-1484	534,656,010	239	200	2531
Capstone Mining Corp (*Suby of* **CAPSTONE MINING CORP**) 510 Georgia St W Suite 2100, Vancouver, BC V6B 0M3, *Tel* (604) 684-8894	529,402,000	240	0	1081
MAC'S CONVENIENCE STORES INC 305 Milner Ave Suite 400, Toronto, ON M1B 0A5, *Tel* (416) 291-4441	526,776,254	241	110	5411
SINOPEC DAYLIGHT ENERGY LTD 112 4 Ave Sw Suite 2700, Calgary, AB T2P 0H3, *Tel* (403) 266-6900	525,564,120	242	0	2911
GERDAU AMERISTEEL CORPORATION 1801 Hopkins St, Whitby, ON L1N 5T1, *Tel* (905) 668-3535	525,317,040	243	500	3312
NATIONAL MONEY MART COMPANY 401 Garbally Rd, Victoria, BC V8T 5M3, *Tel* (250) 595-5211	524,081,855	244	300	6099
TAQA NORTH LTD 308 4 Ave Sw Suite 2100, Calgary, AB T2P 0H7, *Tel* (403) 724-5000	520,010,475	245	0	1311
▲ **WEETABIX OF CANADA LIMITED** 751 D'Arcy St, Cobourg, ON K9A 4B1, *Tel* (905) 372-5441	518,020,970	246	260	2043
SERVICES AEROPORTUAIRE HANDLEX INC 5959 Boul De La Cote-Vertu, Saint-Laurent, QC H4S 2E6, *Tel*	516,668,160	247	300	4581
DELTA FOODS INTERNATIONAL INC 5630 Montgomery Pl, Vancouver, BC V6T 2C7, *Tel* (778) 370-0576	508,771,750	248	1,003	5146
858317 Alberta Ltd (*Suby of* **858317 ALBERTA LTD**) 3825 34 St Ne Suite 113, Calgary, AB T1Y 6Z8, *Tel* (403) 301-0260	507,223,040	249	1	6712
Aritzia Inc (*Suby of* **ARITZIA INC**) 611 Alexander St Suite 118, Vancouver, BC V6A 1E1, *Tel* (604) 251-3132	506,938,135	250	15	6712
VERSACOLD GROUP LIMITED PARTNERSHIP 2115 Commissioner St Suite 1, Vancouver, BC V5L 1A6, *Tel* (604) 255-4656	503,465,081	251	100	4222
First Capital Realty Inc (*Suby of* **GAZIT AMERICA INC**) 85 Hanna Ave Suite 400, Toronto, ON M6K 3S3, *Tel* (416) 504-4114	500,210,079	252	17	6512
NEWFOUNDLAND POWER INC 55 Kenmount Rd, St. John'S, NL A1B 3P8, *Tel* (709) 737-5600	497,138,333	253	200	4911
BroadGrain Commodities Inc (*Suby of* **BROADGRAIN HOLDINGS INC**) 18 King St E Suite 900, Toronto, ON M5C 1C4, *Tel* (416) 504-0070	494,437,800	254	55	5153
MINAS BASIN HOLDINGS LIMITED 50 Main St, Hantsport, NS B0P 1P0, *Tel*	493,744,800	255	0	6712
Wolseley Canada Inc (*Suby of* **WOLSELEY PLC**) 880 Laurentian Dr Suite 1, Burlington, ON L7N 3V6, *Tel* (905) 335-7373	492,484,725	256	200	5074
CALDIC CANADA INC 6980 Creditview Rd, Mississauga, ON L5N 8E2, *Tel* (905) 812-7300	492,030,568	257	174	2043

COMPANY	SALES ($)	RANK	EMPLOYEES HERE	PRIMARY SIC CODE
SSR Mining Inc (*Suby of* **SSR MINING INC**) 1055 Dunsmuir St Suite 800, Vancouver, BC V7X 1G4, *Tel* (604) 689-3846	490,986,000	258	10	1044
Priszm Canadian Operating Trust (*Suby of* **PRISZM CANADIAN OPERATING TRUST**) 101 Exchange Ave, Concord, ON L4K 5R6, *Tel* (416) 739-2900	484,525,200	259	0	6712
CALIAN LTD 340 Legget Dr Suite 101, Kanata, ON K2K 1Y6, *Tel* (613) 599-8600	484,234,309	260	100	4899
EPCOR POWER (WILLIAMS LAKE) LTD 10065 Jasper Ave Nw, Edmonton, AB T5J 3B1, *Tel* (780) 412-3191	482,554,560	261	750	4911
PEYTO EXPLORATION & DEVELOPMENT CORP 600 3rd Ave Suite 300, Calgary, AB T2P 0G5, *Tel* (403) 261-6081	480,812,149	262	50	1382
▲ Dominicn Of Canada General Insurance Company, The (*Suby of* **THE TRAVELERS COMPANIES INC**) 165 University Ave Suite 101, Toronto, ON M5H 3B9, *Tel* (416) 362-7231	477,892,585	263	200	6331
▲ **ECOLAB CO.** 5105 Tomken Rd Suite 1, Mississauga, ON L4W 2X5, *Tel* (905) 238-0171	476,175,516	264	60	2842
▲ **FIRST CHOICE HAIRCUTTERS LTD** 6400 Millcreek Dr, Mississauga, ON L5N 3E7, *Tel* (905) 858-8100	475,922,646	265	20	6794
MAGNA EXTERIORS INC 50 Casmir Crt, Concord, ON L4K 4J5, *Tel* (905) 669-2888	475,630,803	266	1,000	3714
NABORS DRILLING CANADA ULC 500 4 Ave Sw Suite 2800, Calgary, AB T2P 2V6, *Tel* (403) 263-6777	473,991,487	267	0	6712
TELUS COMMUNICATIONS (QUEBEC) INC 6 Rue Jules-A.-Brillant Bureau 20602, Rimouski, QC G5L 1W8, *Tel* (418) 723-2271	473,991,487	268	100	6712
INLAND PACIFIC RESOURCES INC 1188 Georgia St W Suite 1160, Vancouver, BC V6E 4A2, *Tel* (604) 697-6700	471,168,000	269	2,000	1623
MANULIFE CANADA LTD 500 King St N, Kitchener, ON N2J 4Z6, *Tel* (519) 747-7000	467,928,720	270	255	6311
▲ Weight Watchers Canada, Ltd (*Suby of* **WEIGHT WATCHERS INTERNATIONAL, INC.**) 2295 Bristol Cir Unit 200, Oakville, ON L6H 6P8, *Tel* (905) 491-2100	466,547,088	271	120	8099
3958230 Canada Inc (*Suby of* **3958230 CANADA INC**) 600 Boul De Maisonneuve O Bureau 2200, Montreal, QC H3A 3J2, *Tel* (450) 646-9760	465,793,225	272	2	6712
Canerector Inc (*Suby of* **CANERECTOR INC**) 1 Sparks Ave, North York, ON M2H 2W1, *Tel* (416) 225-6240	465,124,463	273	6	3443
LA CAPITALE FINANCIAL SECURITY INSURANCE COMPANY 7150 Derrycrest Dr Suite 1150, Mississauga, ON L5W 0E5, *Tel* (905) 795-2300	463,930,850	274	180	6321
Compagnie Trust Royal, La (*Suby of* **ROYAL BANK OF CANADA**) 1 Place Ville-Marie Bureau 600, Montreal, QC H3B 1Z5, *Tel*	459,781,440	275	50	6021
MACKENZIE FINANCIAL CORPORATION 180 Queen St W Suite 1600, Toronto, ON M5V 3K1, *Tel* (416) 355-2537	459,459,530	276	1,100	6722
FIRST URANIUM CORPORATION 77 King St W Suite 400, Toronto, ON M5K 0A1, *Tel* (416) 306-3072	458,254,593	277	500	1094
OIL TECHNOLOGY OVERSEAS INC 336 Copperfield Blvd Se, Calgary, AB T2Z 4R6, *Tel*	457,585,920	278	2	1389
CINRO RESOURCES INC 100 King St W, Toronto, ON M5X 2A1, *Tel*	454,971,600	279	700	3341
OANDO ENERGY RESOURCES INC 112 4th Ave Sw Suite 1230, Calgary, AB T2P 0H3, *Tel* (403) 719-9152	454,965,000	280	1	1382
AVELIA GROUPE 951 Rue Reverchon, Saint-Laurent, QC H4T 4L2, *Tel*	453,204,720	281	1,700	1541
BPO PROPERTIES LTD 181 Bay St Suite 330, Toronto, ON M5J 2T3, *Tel* (416) 363-9491	453,127,712	282	1	6719
AXA PACIFIC INSURANCE COMPANY 999 Hastings St W Suite 200, Vancouver, BC V6C 2W2, *Tel* (604) 669-0595	452,506,386	283	4	6321
▲ Canada Imperial Oil Limited (*Suby of* **EXXON MOBIL CORPORATION**) 237 4 Ave Sw Suite 2480, Calgary, AB T2P 0H6, *Tel* (800) 567-3776	451,407,851	284	150	5172
BFL CANADA INSURANCE SERVICES 1167 Kensington Cres Nw Suite 200, Calgary, AB T2N 1X7, *Tel* (403) 451-4132	449,208,234	285	350	6311
ACIER GENDRON LTEE 2270 Rue Garneau, Longueuil, QC J4G 1E7, *Tel* (450) 442-9494	448,104,650	286	800	5051
Sun Country Health Region (*Suby of* **SUN COUNTRY HEALTH REGION**) 808 Souris Valley Rd, Weyburn, SK S4H 2Z9, *Tel* (306) 842-8399	444,733,263	287	100	8099
COMPAGNIE D'ASSURANCE BELAIR INC, LA 7101 Rue Jean-Talon E Bureau 300, Anjou, QC H1M 3T6, *Tel* (514) 270-1700	444,403,624	288	450	6331
EXPERTECH NETWORK INSTALLATION INC 240 Attwell Dr, Etobicoke, ON M9W 5B2, *Tel*	444,272,160	289	100	1623
International Group, Inc, The (*Suby of* **IGI HOLDINGS, INC**) 50 Salome Dr, Scarborough, ON M1S 2A8, *Tel* (416) 293-4151	443,787,000	290	0	2911
Prophecy Development Corp (*Suby of* **PROPHECY DEVELOPMENT CORP**) 409 Granville St Suite 1610, Vancouver, BC V6C 1T2, *Tel* (604) 569-3661	442,725,528	291	0	1221
Canadian Apartment Properties Real Estate Investment Trust (*Suby of* **CANADIAN APARTMENT PROPERTIES REAL ESTATE INVESTMENT TRUST**) 11 Church St Suite 401, Toronto, ON M5E 1W1, *Tel* (416) 861-5771	441,443,065	292	125	6722
Fido Solutions Inc (*Suby of* **ROGERS COMMUNICATIONS INC**) 800 Rue De La Gauchetiere O Bureau 4000, Montreal, QC H5A 1K3, *Tel* (514) 937-2121	439,795,633	293	300	4899

Saputo Produits Laitiers Canada S.E.N.C. (*Suby of* **SAPUTO PRODUITS LAITIERS CANADA S.E.N.C.**)

COMPANY	SALES ($)	RANK	EMPLOYEES HERE	PRIMARY SIC CODE
2365 Ch De La Cote-De-Liesse, Saint-Laurent, QC H4N 2M7, *Tel* (514) 328-6663	439,442,296	294	150	2022
NOVA SCOTIA LIQUOR CORPORATION 93 Chain Lake Dr, Halifax, NS B3S 1A3, *Tel* (902) 450-6752	438,879,911	295	150	5921
ALLEN & ASSOCIATES INC 60 Collier St Unit 217, Barrie, ON L4M 1G8, *Tel* (705) 443-4473	438,058,500	296	2	8748
Morneau Shepell Inc (*Suby of* **MORNEAU SHEPELL INC**) 895 Don Mills Rd Suite 700, North York, ON M3C 1W3, *Tel* (416) 445-2700	437,912,000	297	17	6722
CHILDREN'S & WOMEN'S HEALTH CENTRE OF BRITISH COLUMBIA BRANCH 4500 Oak St, Vancouver, BC V6H 3N1, *Tel* (604) 875-2424	437,553,850	298	2,000	8069
Prairie Mountain Health (*Suby of* **PRAIRIE MOUNTAIN HEALTH**) 192 1st Ave W, Souris, MB R0K 2C0, *Tel* (204) 483-5000	436,111,201	299	20	8011
CANADA FIRE EQUIPMENT INC 31 Bache Ave, Keswick, ON L4P 0C7, *Tel* (905) 535-2777	435,220,500	300	3,300	5999
CIBC WORLD MARKETS INC 161 Bay St Suite 700, Toronto, ON M5J 2S1, *Tel* (416) 594-7000	433,125,500	301	50	6211
▲ Veritiv Canada, Inc (*Suby of* **VERITIV CORPORATION**) 4300 Rue Hickmore, Saint-Laurent, QC H4T 1K2, *Tel* (514) 367-3111	432,875,833	302	69	5111
Eldorado Gold Corporation (*Suby of* **ELDORADO GOLD CORPORATION**) 550 Burrard St Suite 1188, Vancouver, BC V6C 2B5, *Tel* (604) 687-4018	432,727,000	303	35	1041
Intrawest ULC (*Suby of* **HAWK HOLDING COMPANY, LLC**) 375 Water St Suite 710, Vancouver, BC V6B 5C6, *Tel* (604) 695-8200	431,392,998	304	75	7011
▲ Xerox Canada Ltd (*Suby of* **XEROX CORPORATION**) 5650 Yonge St Suite 900, North York, ON M2M 4G7, *Tel* (416) 733-6501	426,820,095	305	350	5999
FORTISALBERTA INC 320 17 Ave Sw, Calgary, AB T2S 2V1, *Tel* (403) 514-4000	423,253,715	306	1,000	4911
INSTALOANS INC 17631 103 Ave Nw, Edmonton, AB T5S 1N8, *Tel* (780) 408-5110	420,916,050	307	50	6141
Great Canadian Gaming Corporation (*Suby of* **GREAT CANADIAN GAMING CORPORATION**) 95 Schooner St, Coquitlam, BC V3K 7A8, *Tel* (604) 303-1000	418,934,928	308	250	7999
Pengrowth Energy Corporation (*Suby of* **PENGROWTH ENERGY CORPORATION**) 222 3 Ave Sw Suite 2100, Calgary, AB T2P 0B4, *Tel* (403) 233-0224	418,786,999	309	1	1311
THOMAS & BETTS FABRICATION INC 700 Av Thomas, Saint-Jean-Sur-Richelieu, QC J2X 2M9, *Tel* (450) 347-5318	417,872,550	310	140	3644
▲ McDonald's Restaurants Of Canada Limited (*Suby of* **MCDONALD'S CORPORATION**) 1 Mcdonalds Pl, North York, ON M3C 3L4, *Tel* (416) 443-1000	417,043,361	311	300	5812
TRILON BANCORP INC 181 Bay St Suite 4420, Toronto, ON M5J 2T3, *Tel* (416) 363-0061	416,891,520	312	6	6141
POSTMEDIA NETWORK INC 365 Bloor St E Suite 1601, Toronto, ON M4W 3L4, *Tel* (416) 383-2300	414,562,697	313	200	2711
TOYOTA CANADA INC 1 Toyota Pl, Scarborough, ON M1H 1H9, *Tel* (416) 438-6320	414,154,603	314	425	5012
ATI Technologies ULC (*Suby of* **ATI TECHNOLOGIES ULC**) 1 Commerce Valley Dr E, Thornhill, ON L3T 7X6, *Tel* (905) 882-7589	413,833,090	315	1,200	3577
Lucky Star Holdings Inc (*Suby of* **LUCKY STAR HOLDINGS INC**) 233 Court St S, Thunder Bay, ON P7B 2X9, *Tel* (807) 345-0571	413,776,640	316	0	5031
▲ Tetra Tech Canada Inc (*Suby of* **TETRA TECH, INC.**) 14940 123 Ave Nw, Edmonton, AB T5V 1B4, *Tel* (780) 451-2121	413,030,523	317	500	8711
WORLEYPARSONS CANADA SERVICES LTD 8500 Macleod Tr Se, Calgary, AB T2H 2N1, *Tel* (403) 258-8000	413,030,523	318	3,000	8711
SAP CANADA INC 4120 Yonge St Suite 600, North York, ON M2P 2B8, *Tel* (416) 229-0574	409,253,485	319	304	7372
NISSAN CANADA INC 5290 Orbitor Dr, Mississauga, ON L4W 4Z5, *Tel* (905) 602-0792	404,507,600	320	250	5012
REXEL CANADA ELECTRICAL LTD 5600 Keaton Cres, Mississauga, ON L5R 3G3, *Tel* (905) 712-4004	401,648,654	321	181	5063
F&P MFG., INC 1 Nolan Rd, Tottenham, ON L0G 1W0, *Tel* (905) 936-3435	400,325,663	322	630	3714
Vision 7 International Inc (*Suby of* **VISION 7 INTERNATIONAL INC**) 300 Rue Saint-Paul Bureau 300, Quebec, QC G1K 7R1, *Tel* (418) 647-2727	399,167,990	323	1	6712
Vision 7 Communications Inc (*Suby of* **VISION 7 INTERNATIONAL INC**) 300 Rue Saint-Paul Bureau 300, Quebec, QC G1K 7R1, *Tel* (418) 647-2727	399,022,068	324	27	6712
Edmonton Catholic Separate School District No.7 (*Suby of* **EDMONTON CATHOLIC SEPARATE SCHOOL DISTRICT NO.7**) 9807 106 St Nw Suite 7, Edmonton, AB T5K 1C2, *Tel* (780) 441-6000	398,305,864	325	120	8211
D+H LIMITED PARTNERSHIP 120 Bremner Blvd 30th Fl, Toronto, ON M5J 0A8, *Tel* (416) 696-7700	393,987,780	326	500	6211
Northland Properties Corporation (*Suby of* **NORTHLAND PROPERTIES CORPORATION**) 1755 Broadway W Suite 310, Vancouver, BC V6J 4S5, *Tel* (604) 730-6610	393,987,780	327	60	7011
ASSOCIATION DES GESTIONNAIRES DE L'HOPITAL SAINTE-JUSTINE 3175 Ch De La Cote-Sainte-Catherine, Montreal, QC H3T 1C5, *Tel* (514) 345-4931	392,712,950	328	3,500	8069
SMTC NOVA SCOTIA COMPANY 635 Hood Rd, Markham, ON L3R 4N6, *Tel* (905) 479-1810	392,575,360	329	2	3672
EXCHANGE CORPORATION CANADA INC 4831 Miller Rd Suite 206, Richmond, BC V7B 1K7, *Tel* (604) 656-1700	392,163,763	330	4	6099

COMPANY	SALES ($)	RANK	EMPLOYEES HERE	PRIMARY SIC CODE
London Agricultural Commodities Inc (*Suby of* **MICHIGAN AGRICULTURAL COMMODITIES, INC.**) 1615 North Routledge Pk Unit 43, London, ON N6H 5L6, *Tel* (519) 473-9333	390,107,000	331	27	6799
FLIGHT CENTRE TRAVEL GROUP (CANADA) INC 1133 Melville St Suite 600s, Vancouver, BC V6E 4E5, *Tel* (604) 682-5202	389,756,059	332	300	4724
Sino-Forest Corporation (*Suby of* **SINO-FOREST CORPORATION**) 90 Burnhamthorpe Rd W Suite 1208, Mississauga, ON L5B 3C3, *Tel*	386,946,720	333	10	2421
ONTARIO LOTTERY AND GAMING CORPORATION 4120 Yonge St Suite 420, North York, ON M2P 2B8, *Tel* (416) 224-1772	380,344,129	334	300	7999
BELL EXPRESSVU INC 100 Wynford Dr Suite 300, North York, ON M3C 4B4, *Tel* (416) 383-6600	377,425,200	335	1,170	4841
SITA INFORMATION NETWORKING COMPUTING CANADA INC 777 Walker'S Line, Burlington, ON L7N 2G1, *Tel* (905) 681-6200	376,648,901	336	1	7371
▲ **DANA CANADA CORPORATION** 656 Kerr St, Oakville, ON L6K 3E4, *Tel* (905) 849-1200	376,472,685	337	60	3714
COAL VALLEY PARTNERSHIP 10235 101 St Nw Unit 1600, Edmonton, AB T5J 3G1, *Tel* (780) 420-5810	371,654,558	338	1	1221
Ottawa Catholic District School Board (*Suby of* **OTTAWA CATHOLIC DISTRICT SCHOOL BOARD**) 570 West Hunt Club Rd, Nepean, ON K2G 3R4, *Tel* (613) 224-2222	371,611,350	339	330	8211
SASKATCHEWAN CROP INSURANCE CORPORATION 484 Prince William Dr, Melville, SK S0A 2P0, *Tel* (306) 728-7200	370,727,912	340	121	6331
▲ ITW Canada Inc (*Suby of* **ILLINOIS TOOL WORKS INC.**) 120 Travail Rd, Markham, ON L3S 3J1, *Tel* (905) 201-8399	369,822,500	341	50	5084
Algonquin Power Income Fund (*Suby of* **ALGONQUIN POWER INCOME FUND**) 2845 Bristol Cir, Oakville, ON L6H 7H7, *Tel* (905) 465-4500	369,739,045	342	0	6722
SIEMENS CANADA LIMITED 1577 North Service Rd E, Oakville, ON L6H 0H6, *Tel* (905) 465-8000	369,691,867	343	300	3625
ROLLS-ROYCE HOLDINGS CANADA INC 9500 Ch De La Cote-De-Liesse, Lachine, QC H8T 1A2, *Tel* (514) 631-3541	369,376,080	344	1	6712
RODFAM HOLDINGS LIMITED 2575 Airport Rd, Windsor, ON N8W 1Z4, *Tel* (519) 969-3350	369,179,760	345	1	6712
SMS EQUIPMENT INC 53113 Range Road 263a, Acheson, AB T7X 5A5, *Tel* (780) 454-0101	368,156,675	346	200	5082
MPT UTILITIES EUROPE LTD 155 Wellington St W, Toronto, ON M5V 3H1, *Tel* (416) 649-1300	365,727,250	347	550	4911
Halifax Regional School Board (*Suby of* **HALIFAX REGIONAL SCHOOL BOARD**) 33 Spectacle Lake Dr, Dartmouth, NS B3B 1X7, *Tel* (902) 464-2000	365,409,362	348	200	8211
▲ Gap (Canada) Inc (*Suby of* **THE GAP INC**) 60 Bloor St W Suite 1501, Toronto, ON M4W 3B8, *Tel* (416) 921-2225	364,803,500	349	65	5651
TD Securities Inc (*Suby of* **TORONTO-DOMINION BANK, THE**) 66 Wellington St W, Toronto, ON M5K 1A2, *Tel* (416) 307-8500	364,803,500	350	1,600	6211
CENTRE DE SANTE ET DE SERVICES SOCIAUX PIERRE-BOUCHER 1333 Boul Jacques-Cartier E, Longueuil, QC J4M 2A5, *Tel* (450) 468-8410	364,139,520	351	0	8062
Chemco Electrical Contractors Ltd (*Suby of* **BALM MANAGEMENT ENTERPRISES LTD**) 3135 4 St, Nisku, AB T9E 8L1, *Tel* (780) 436-9570	359,893,194	352	120	1731
LANTIC INC 4026 Rue Notre-Dame E, Montreal, QC H1W 2K3, *Tel* (514) 527-8686	359,623,290	353	300	2062
DELTA HOTELS LIMITED 77 King St W Suite 2300, Toronto, ON M5K 2A1, *Tel* (416) 874-2000	357,945,194	354	750	8741
▲ ESIT Canada Enterprise Services Co (*Suby of* **DXC TECHNOLOGY COMPANY**) 1969 Upper Water St, Halifax, NS B3J 3R7, *Tel*	357,507,430	355	885	5734
EPCOR DISTRIBUTION & TRANSMISSION INC 10423 101 St Nw Suite 2000, Edmonton, AB T5H 0E8, *Tel* (780) 412-3414	356,267,098	356	45	4911
CONNORS BROS. CLOVER LEAF SEAFOODS COMPANY 80 Tiverton Crt Suite 600, Markham, ON L3R 0G4, *Tel* (905) 474-0608	355,683,413	357	5	5146
Thomson Tremblay Inc (*Suby of* **R.G.F.M. BERTUCCI MANAGEMENT CORP INC**) 2040 Rue Peel Bureau 200, Montreal, QC H3A 1W5, *Tel* (514) 861-9971	355,075,000	358	45	7361
UNILEVER CANADA INC 160 Bloor St E Suite 1400, Toronto, ON M4W 3R2, *Tel* (416) 964-1857	354,151,238	359	200	2099
Avigilon Corporation (*Suby of* **AVIGILON CORPORATION**) 555 Robson St 3rd Fl, Vancouver, BC V6B 3K9, *Tel* (604) 629-5182	353,622,000	360	90	3651
▲ Stream International Canada ULC (*Suby of* **CONVERGYS CORPORATION**) 540 Dundas St W, Belleville, ON K8P 1B8, *Tel* (613) 961-5400	353,373,375	361	0	7374
NEW BRUNSWICK LIQUOR CORPORATION 170 Wilsey Rd, Fredericton, NB E3B 5J1, *Tel* (506) 452-6826	348,026,700	362	100	5921
Borden Ladner Gervais LLP (*Suby of* **BORDEN LADNER GERVAIS LLP**) 22 Adelaide St W Suite 3400, Toronto, ON M5H 4E3, *Tel* (416) 367-6000	347,633,150	363	600	8111
CENTRE HOSPITALIER PIERRE LE GARDEUR 911 Montee Des Pionniers, Terrebonne, QC J6V 2H2, *Tel* (450) 654-7525	346,406,640	364	3,700	8062
▲ **AMERICREDIT FINANCIAL SERVICES OF CANADA LTD** 200 Jameson Dr, Peterborough, ON K9K 2N3, *Tel* (705) 876-3900	345,269,346	365	450	6141
Upper Grand District School Board, The (*Suby of* **UPPER GRAND DISTRICT SCHOOL BOARD, THE**) 500 Victoria Rd N, Guelph, ON N1E 6K2, *Tel* (519) 766-9140	344,843,254	366	80	8211
TARKETT INC 1001 Rue Yamaska E, Farnham, QC J2N 1J7, *Tel* (450) 293-3173	343,717,858	367	230	2851

COMPANY	SALES ($)	RANK	EMPLOYEES HERE	PRIMARY SIC CODE
MSN WIRELESS INC 1315 Derry Rd E Suite 6a, Mississauga, ON L5T 1B6, *Tel* (416) 745-9900	343,541,120	368	1,354	4899
Bantrel Co. (*Suby of* **BECHTEL GROUP, INC.**) 1201 Glenmore Trail Sw Suite 1061, Calgary, AB T2V 4Y8, *Tel* (403) 290-5000	342,039,762	369	2,525	8711
Upper Canada District School Board, The (*Suby of* **UPPER CANADA DISTRICT SCHOOL BOARD, THE**) 225 Central Ave W, Brockville, ON K6V 5X1, *Tel* (613) 342-0371	341,747,210	370	100	8211
CENTRE DE SANTE ET DE SERVICES SOCIAUX DU SUD-QUEST-VERDUN 6161 Rue Laurendeau, Montreal, QC H4E 3X6, *Tel* (514) 762-2777	341,500,030	371	20	8062
SONEPAR CANADA INC 250 Chrysler Dr Unit 4, Brampton, ON L6S 6B6, *Tel* (905) 696-2838	341,456,076	372	50	5063
Fondation du Centre de Sante et de Services Sociaux de Trois-Rivieres (*Suby of* **FONDATION DU CENTRE DE SANTE ET DE SERVICES SOCIAUX DE TROIS-RIVIERES**) 155 Rue Toupin, Trois-Rivieres, QC G8T 3Z8, *Tel* (819) 370-2100	339,654,600	373	0	8742
MANITOBA PUBLIC INSURANCE CORPORATION, THE 234 Donald St Suite 912, Winnipeg, MB R3C 4A4, *Tel* (204) 985-7000	337,727,050	374	700	8743
▲ **EECOL HOLDINGS LTD** 63 Sunpark Dr Se, Calgary, AB T2X 3V4, *Tel* (403) 571-8400	337,165,316	375	4	5063
DAY & ROSS INC 398 Main St, Hartland, NB E7P 1C6, *Tel* (506) 375-4401	334,889,613	376	100	4213
ALCOA CANADA CIE 1 Place Ville-Marie Bureau 2310, Montreal, QC H3B 3M5, *Tel* (514) 904-5030	334,087,045	377	100	3334
AVI-SPL CANADA LTD 35 East Beaver Creek Rd Suite 1, Richmond Hill, ON L4B 1B3, *Tel* (866) 797-5635	332,919,674	378	75	4813
JIFFY TELECOMMUNICATIONS INC 100 King St W Suite 5600, Toronto, ON M5X 2A1, *Tel*	332,857,450	379	1,300	4899
G4S SECURE SOLUTIONS (CANADA) LTD 703 Evans Ave Suite 103, Toronto, ON M9C 5E9, *Tel* (416) 620-0762	332,813,634	380	50	7381
ATCO POWER ALBERTA LTD 919 11 Ave Sw Suite 1400, Calgary, AB T2R 1P3, *Tel* (403) 209-6900	332,451,650	381	500	4911
▲ JBS Canada Inc (*Suby of* **TYSON FOODS, INC.**) 1 Transcanada Hwy, Brooks, AB T1R 1C6, *Tel* (403) 362-3326	331,860,758	382	7	2011
SODEXO CANADA LTD 1100 Burloak Dr Unit 401, Burlington, ON L7L 6B2, *Tel* (905) 632-8592	331,752,303	383	60	5812
400369 Alberta Ltd (*Suby of* **400369 ALBERTA LTD**) 13220 St Albert Trail Nw Suite 303, Edmonton, AB T5L 4W1, *Tel* (780) 477-2233	330,474,780	384	3	6712
MBNA Canada Bank (*Suby of* **TORONTO-DOMINION BANK, THE**) 1600 James Naismith Dr Suite 800, Gloucester, ON K1B 5N8, *Tel* (613) 907-4800	330,001,246	385	1,250	6021
PILOT INSURANCE COMPANY 90 Eglinton Ave W Suite 102, Toronto, ON M4R 2E4, *Tel* (416) 487-5141	329,088,755	386	150	6331
▲ **CELESTICA INTERNATIONAL INC** 844 Don Mills Rd, North York, ON M3C 1V7, *Tel* (416) 448-5800	328,906,836	387	0	3679
MARTINREA AUTOMOTIVE INC 3210 Langstaff Rd, Vaughan, ON L4K 5B2, *Tel* (289) 982-3000	328,323,150	388	400	3499
SMS CONSTRUCTION AND MINING SYSTEMS INC 53113 Range Road 263a, Acheson, AB T7X 5A5, *Tel* (780) 948-2200	328,323,150	389	106	5082
INVESTORS PREMIUM MONEY MARKET FUND 447 Portage Ave, Winnipeg, MB R3C 3B6, *Tel* (204) 957-7383	327,966,720	390	800	6722
SIFTON PROPERTIES LIMITED 195 Dufferin Ave Suite 800, London, ON N6A 1K7, *Tel* (519) 434-1000	327,885,386	391	40	6553
▲ State Street Trust Company Canada (*Suby of* **STATE STREET CORPORATION**) 30 Adelaide St E Suite 1100, Toronto, ON M5C 3G8, *Tel* (416) 362-1100	326,861,440	392	900	6719
Workplace Health, Safety & Compensation Commission of New Brunswick (*Suby of* **WORKPLACE HEALTH, SAFETY & COMPENSATION COMMISSION OF NEW BRUNSWICK**) 1 Portland St, Saint John, NB E2L 3X9, *Tel* (506) 632-2200	326,314,584	393	100	6331
FORD AUTO SECURITIZATION TRUST 100 University Ave Suite 800, Toronto, ON M5J 2Y1, *Tel* (905) 845-2511	326,158,290	394	1	6726
Commission Scolaire de la Riviere-du-Nord (*Suby of* **COMMISSION SCOLAIRE DE LA RIVIERE-DU-NORD**) 995 Rue Labelle Bureau 1, Saint-Jerome, QC J7Z 5N7, *Tel* (450) 438-3131	325,147,250	395	100	8211
FOSTER'S RED & WHITE LTD 4 Robinson Dr, Bruce Mines, ON P0R 1C0, *Tel* (705) 785-3728	322,408,100	396	1,614	5411
▲ Aviscar Inc (*Suby of* **AVIS BUDGET GROUP, INC.**) 1 Convair Dr, Etobicoke, ON M9W 6Z9, *Tel* (416) 213-8400	321,985,497	397	400	7514
CURTIS INTERNATIONAL LTD 315 Attwell Dr, Etobicoke, ON M9W 5C1, *Tel* (416) 674-2123	321,543,055	398	37	5065
Hema-Quebec (*Suby of* **HEMA-QUEBEC**) 4045 Boul De La Cote-Vertu, Saint-Laurent, QC H4R 2W7, *Tel* (514) 832-5000	321,428,422	399	915	8099
993106 Alberta Ltd (*Suby of* **993106 ALBERTA LTD**) 1444 78 Ave Nw, Edmonton, AB T6P 1L7, *Tel* (780) 438-5930	320,953,850	400	40	5172
2063412 Investment LP (*Suby of* **2063412 INVESTMENT LP**) 302 Town Centre Blvd Suite 200, Markham, ON L3R 0E8, *Tel* (905) 477-4006	319,155,287	401	100	8052
SYNCREON NOVA SCOTIA ULC 999 Boundary Rd, Oshawa, ON L1J 8P8, *Tel* (905) 743-6277	319,020,000	402	1	4783
▲ Ford Credit Canada Limited (*Suby of* **FORD MOTOR COMPANY**) The Canadian Rd, Oakville, ON L6J 5C7, *Tel* (905) 845-2511	318,984,180	403	27	6141

COMPANY	SALES ($)	RANK	EMPLOYEES HERE	PRIMARY SIC CODE
STATOIL CANADA LTD 308 4 Ave Sw Suite 3600, Calgary, AB T2P 0H7, *Tel* (403) 234-0123	318,000,742	404	350	1311
RECOCHEM INC 850 Montee De Liesse, Saint-Laurent, QC H4T 1P4, *Tel* (514) 341-3550	316,287,715	405	225	2899
URANIUM ONE INC 333 Bay St Suite 1200, Toronto, ON M5H 2R2, *Tel* (647) 788-8500	314,600,000	406	22	1094
Corporation de Developpement Cuirs Bentley Inc, La (*Suby of* **CORPORATION DE DEVELOPPEMENT CUIRS BENTLEY INC, LA**) 375 Boul Roland-Therrien Bureau 210, Longueuil, QC J4H 4A6, *Tel* (450) 651-5000	314,022,853	407	3	6712
CLYDESDALE RESOURCES INC 9239 95 St Nw, Edmonton, AB T6C 3W9, *Tel*	313,929,367	408	3	1081
Grand River Hospital Corporation (*Suby of* **GRAND RIVER HOSPITAL CORPORATION**) 835 King St W, Kitchener, ON N2G 1G3, *Tel* (519) 742-3611	312,910,166	409	1,900	8062
▲ **MONDELEZ CANADA INC** 2660 Matheson Blvd E Suite 100, Mississauga, ON L4W 5M2, *Tel* (289) 374-4000	310,155,936	410	3,200	2032
Cavendish Farms Corporation (*Suby of* **J. D. IRVING, LIMITED**) 100 Prom Midland, Dieppe, NB E1A 6X4, *Tel* (506) 858-7777	310,082,975	411	100	5142
Supermarches GP Inc, Les (*Suby of* **SUPERMARCHES GP INC, LES**) 1665 Boul Benoit-Gaboury, Mont-Joli, QC G5H 3J1, *Tel* (418) 775-2214	309,204,000	412	30	5411
Centre de Sante et de Services Sociaux Haut-Richelieu-Rouville (*Suby of* **CENTRE DE SANTE ET DE SERVICES SOCIAUX HAUT-RICHELIEU-ROUVILLE**) 978 Boul Du Seminaire N, Saint-Jean-Sur-Richelieu, QC J3A 1E5, *Tel* (450) 358-2572	308,909,520	413	250	8062
Grain Millers Canada Corp (*Suby of* **GRAIN MILLERS, INC.**) 1 Grain Millers Dr, Yorkton, SK S3N 3Z4, *Tel* (306) 783-2931	308,801,213	414	0	2043
HYDRO OTTAWA LIMITED 3025 Albion Rd N, Ottawa, ON K1V 9V9, *Tel* (613) 738-6400	308,801,213	415	0	4911
ELLISDON CORPORATION 2045 Oxford St E, London, ON N5V 2Z7, *Tel* (519) 455-6770	308,471,981	416	0	1542
Canada Goose Holdings Inc (*Suby of* **BAIN CAPITAL, LP**) 250 Bowie Ave, Toronto, ON M6E 4Y2, *Tel* (888) 668-0625	307,358,686	417	0	2331
DELOITTE MANAGEMENT SERVICES LP 121 King St W Suite 300, Toronto, ON M5H 3T9, *Tel* (416) 775-2364	306,434,940	418	400	8721
GROUPE PAGES JAUNES CORP 16 Place Du Commerce, Verdun, QC H3E 2A5, *Tel* (514) 934-2000	306,392,979	419	800	4899
ERICSSON CANADA INC 8400 Boul Decarie, Mont-Royal, QC H4P 2N2, *Tel* (514) 345-7900	305,126,130	420	200	5065
▲ Molson Inc (*Suby of* **MOLSON COORS BREWING COMPANY**) 1555 Rue Notre-Dame E, Montreal, QC H2L 2R5, *Tel* (514) 521-1786	304,350,000	421	0	5181
ST. JOSEPH'S HEALTHCARE FOUNDATION, HAMILTON 224 James St S, Hamilton, ON L8P 3A9, *Tel* (905) 521-6036	303,589,473	422	0	8699
ENBRIDGE INCOME FUND 425 1 St Sw Suite 3000, Calgary, AB T2P 3L8, *Tel* (403) 767-3642	303,297,630	423	269	4922
SCHENKER OF CANADA LIMITED 5935 Airport Rd Suite 9, Mississauga, ON L4V 1W5, *Tel* (905) 676-0676	303,187,850	424	120	4731
LAWTON'S DRUG STORES LIMITED 236 Brownlow Ave Suite 270, Dartmouth, NS B3B 1V5, *Tel* (902) 468-1000	302,581,474	425	100	5912
VENTILATION BELLE-RIVE INC 2001 Rue De La Metropole Bureau 712, Longueuil, QC J4G 1S9, *Tel* (450) 332-9832	301,686,000	426	20	1711
Financiere Micadco Inc (*Suby of* **GROUPE MICHEL CADRIN INC**) 600 Boul Charest E Bureau 3036, Quebec, QC G1K 3J4, *Tel* (418) 529-6121	301,440,000	427	50	6712
ROBINSON SOLUTIONS (CANADA) INC 1456 Centennial Dr, Kingston, ON K7P 0K4, *Tel* (613) 389-7611	301,440,000	428	3	6712
TECK-BULLMOOSE COAL INC 550 Burrard St Suite 3300, Vancouver, BC V6C 0B3, *Tel* (604) 699-4000	300,762,240	429	505	1221
ASSOCIATION GENERALE DES ETUDIANTS ET ETUDIANTES DU COLLEGE LIONEL-GROULX INC 100 Rue Duquet, Sainte-Therese, QC J7E 3G6, *Tel*	299,987,650	430	3,000	8641
Evraz Inc. NA Canada (*Suby of* **EVRAZ PLC**) 100 Armour Rd, Regina, SK S4P 3C7, *Tel* (306) 924-7700	298,856,595	431	1,000	3312
NORDION (CANADA) INC 447 March Rd, Kanata, ON K2K 1X8, *Tel* (613) 592-2790	298,856,595	432	0	2819
TRANSCONTINENTAL PRINTING INC 1 Place Ville-Marie Bureau 3240, Montreal, QC H3B 3N2, *Tel* (514) 954-4000	296,804,128	433	160	2752
NOVA CHEMICALS CORPORATION 1000 7 Ave Sw Suite 1000, Calgary, AB T2P 5L5, *Tel* (403) 750-3600	295,490,835	434	50	2821
HIRAM WALKER & SONS LIMITED 2072 Riverside Dr E, Windsor, ON N8Y 4S5, *Tel* (519) 254-5171	295,198,992	435	350	2085
AREVA RESOURCES CANADA INC 817 45th St W, Saskatoon, SK S7L 5X2, *Tel* (306) 343-4500	294,871,840	436	0	1094
Southern Alberta Institute of Technology (*Suby of* **SOUTHERN ALBERTA INSTITUTE OF TECHNOLOGY**) 1301 16 Ave Nw Suite 201, Calgary, AB T2M 0L4, *Tel* (403) 284-7248	294,757,446	437	17	8222
CAMPUS LIVING CENTRES INC 5405 Eglinton Ave W Suite 214, Etobicoke, ON M9C 5K6, *Tel* (416) 620-0635	294,480,000	438	7	1531
Vente d'Auto H Gregoire Ltee (*Suby of* **VENTE D'AUTO H GREGOIRE LTEE**) 625 Rue Dubois, Saint-Eustache, QC J7P 3W1, *Tel*	294,480,000	439	0	5511

COMPANY	SALES ($)	RANK	EMPLOYEES HERE	PRIMARY SIC CODE
VIDEOTRON SERVICE INFORMATIQUE LTEE 300 Av Viger E Bureau 6, Montreal, QC H2X 3W4, *Tel* (514) 281-1232	294,480,000	440	4,000	7374
Gestion Francois Roberge Inc (*Suby of* **GESTION FRANCOIS ROBERGE INC**) 4320 Av Pierre-De Coubertin, Montreal, QC H1V 1A6, *Tel* (514) 256-9446	293,158,552	441	1	6712
SONY OF CANADA LTD 115 Gordon Baker Rd, North York, ON M2H 3R6, *Tel* (416) 499-1414	293,139,338	442	200	5064
10663 NEWFOUNDLAND LTD Gd Happy Valley-Goose Bay Stn C, Happy Valley-Goose Bay, NL A0P 1C0, *Tel* (709) 896-2421	292,176,000	443	120	4424
▲ **SAFETY-KLEEN CANADA INC.** 300 Woolwich St S Rr 2, Breslau, ON N0B 1M0, *Tel* (519) 648-2291	291,926,587	444	100	2992
SOURCE (BELL) ELECTRONICS INC, THE 279 Bayview Dr, Barrie, ON L4M 4W5, *Tel* (705) 728-2262	291,842,800	445	372	5731
TD Waterhouse Canada Inc (*Suby of* **TORONTO-DOMINION BANK, THE**) 77 Bloor St W Suite 3, Toronto, ON M5S 1M2, *Tel* (416) 982-7686	291,842,800	446	1,200	6211
GCT Canada Limited Partnership (*Suby of* **GCT GLOBAL CONTAINER TERMINALS INC**) 1285 Franklin St, Vancouver, BC V6A 1J9, *Tel* (604) 267-5200	291,233,586	447	114	4491
SOCIETE DES CASINOS DU QUEBEC INC, LA 500 Rue Sherbrooke O Bureau 1500, Montreal, QC H3A 3C6, *Tel* (514) 282-8000	291,186,154	448	769	7999
Aecom Production Services Ltd (*Suby of* **AECOM PRODUCTION SERVICES LTD**) 18817 Stony Plain Rd, Edmonton, AB T5S 0C2, *Tel* (780) 486-7000	290,529,507	449	100	1389
William Osler Health System (*Suby of* **WILLIAM OSLER HEALTH SYSTEM**) 2100 Bovaird Dr E, Brampton, ON L6R 3J7, *Tel* (905) 494-2120	288,778,451	450	2,500	8062
Evertz Technologies Limited (*Suby of* **EVERTZ TECHNOLOGIES LIMITED**) 5292 John Lucas Dr, Burlington, ON L7L 5Z9, *Tel* (905) 335-3700	288,634,237	451	0	3669
HOLDING DESSAU INC. 1200 Boul Saint-Martin O Bureau 300, Montreal, QC H7S 2E4, *Tel* (514) 281-1010	288,001,440	452	2	8742
RICOH CANADA INC 5560 Explorer Dr Suite 100, Mississauga, ON L4W 5M3, *Tel* (905) 795-9659	287,319,237	453	200	5044
CENTRAL REGIONAL HEALTH AUTHORITY 50 Union St, Grand Falls-Windsor, NL A2A 2E1, *Tel* (709) 292-2500	286,390,985	454	500	8062
Commission Scolaire de la Seigneurie-Des-Mille-Iles (*Suby of* **COMMISSION SCOLAIRE DE LA SEIGNEURIE-DES-MILLE-ILES**) 430 Boul Arthur-Sauve Bureau 3050, Saint-Eustache, QC J7R 6V7, *Tel* (450) 974-7000	285,431,454	455	175	8211
LINDE CANADA LIMITED 5860 Chedworth Way, Mississauga, ON L5R 0A2, *Tel* (905) 501-1700	285,169,829	456	150	5169
▲ **WYNDHAM WORLDWIDE CANADA INC** 180 Crown St Suite 200, Saint John, NB E2L 2X7, *Tel* (506) 646-2700	284,960,290	457	0	4899
Osprey Media Publishing Inc (*Suby of* **PLACEMENTS PELADEAU INC, LES**) 100 Renfrew Dr Suite 110, Markham, ON L3R 9R6, *Tel* (905) 752-1132	283,735,262	458	50	2711
▲ Fluor Canada Ltd (*Suby of* **FLUOR CORPORATION**) 55 Sunpark Plaza Se, Calgary, AB T2X 3R4, *Tel* (403) 537-4000	282,941,595	459	1,900	8711
BELL TECHNICAL SOLUTIONS INC 75 Rue J.-A.-Bombardier Suite 200, Boucherville, QC J4B 8P1, *Tel* (450) 449-1120	282,698,700	460	90	1731
CORREIA ENTERPRISES LTD 375 Nairn Ave, Winnipeg, MB R2L 0W8, *Tel* (204) 668-4420	281,344,000	461	7,000	7349
TEMPLETON, FRANKLIN MUTUAL BEACON FUND 200 King St W Suite 1500, Toronto, ON M5H 3T4, *Tel* (416) 957-6000	280,344,960	462	700	6722
▲ **SANMINA-SCI SYSTEMS (CANADA) INC** 330 Progress Ave, Scarborough, ON M1P 2Z4, *Tel*	280,246,800	463	0	3672
▲ Tetra Tech QE Inc (*Suby of* **TETRA TECH, INC.**) 5100 Rue Sherbrooke E Bureau 900, Montreal, QC H1V 3R9, *Tel* (514) 257-0707	279,712,448	464	2,000	8711
Casino Niagara Limited (*Suby of* **CASINO NIAGARA LIMITED**) 4342 Queen St, Niagara Falls, ON L2E 7J7, *Tel* (905) 374-6928	279,494,750	465	0	7999
Colabor Limited Partnership (*Suby of* **GROUPE COLABOR INC**) 580 Industrial Rd, London, ON N5V 1V1, *Tel* (800) 265-9267	279,452,573	466	500	5141
177293 CANADA LTD 150 6 Ave Sw, Calgary, AB T2P 3Y7, *Tel* (403) 296-8000	279,393,300	467	15	1311
AVIVA CANADA INC 10 Aviva Way Suite 100, Markham, ON L6G 0G1, *Tel* (416) 288-1800	279,220,599	468	1,250	6411
HOME TRUST COMPANY 145 King St W Suite 2300, Toronto, ON M5H 1J8, *Tel* (416) 360-4663	279,220,599	469	300	6021
CARGOJET HOLDINGS LTD 350 Britannia Rd E Unit 5-6, Mississauga, ON L4Z 1X9, *Tel* (905) 501-7373	278,413,071	470	1	4581
SWISSPORT CANADA HANDLING INC 6500 Silver Dart Dr, Mississauga, ON L5P 1A2, *Tel* (905) 676-2888	278,413,071	471	267	4581
AXA INSURANCE (CANADA) 5700 Yonge St Suite 1400, North York, ON M2M 4K2, *Tel* (416) 218-4175	277,704,356	472	200	6331
DHL EXPRESS (CANADA) LTD 18 Parkshore Dr, Brampton, ON L6T 0G7, *Tel* (905) 861-3400	276,666,974	473	150	4212
GREATER VANCOUVER REGIONAL DISTRICT, THE 4330 Kingsway, Burnaby, BC V5H 4G7, *Tel* (604) 451-6575	276,479,329	474	1,500	8741
TELUS SOLUTIONS EN SANTE INC 22e Etage 630, Boul Rene-Levesque O, Montreal, QC H3B 1S6, *Tel* (514) 665-3050	276,420,694	475	50	7372
AECON LOCKERBIE INDUSTRIAL INC				

COMPANY	SALES ($)	RANK	EMPLOYEES HERE	PRIMARY SIC CODE
14940 121a Ave Nw, Edmonton, AB T5V 1A3, *Tel* (780) 452-1250	275,631,233	476	40	1542
▲ Startek Canada Services Ltd (*Suby of* **STARTEK, INC.**) 100 Innovation Dr, Kingston, ON K7K 7E7, *Tel* (613) 531-6350	275,013,760	477	560	8748
Comark Inc (*Suby of* **COMARK INC**) 6789 Millcreek Dr, Mississauga, ON L5N 5M4, *Tel* (905) 567-7375	273,967,429	478	150	5621
Integrated Distribution Systems Limited Partnership (*Suby of* **INTEGRATED DISTRIBUTION SYSTEMS LIMITED PARTNERSHIP**) 3280 Wharton Way, Mississauga, ON L4X 2C5, *Tel* (905) 212-3300	273,602,625	479	50	5084
CO-OPERATORS GENERAL INSURANCE COMPANY 130 Macdonell St, Guelph, ON N1H 2Z6, *Tel* (519) 824-4400	272,654,136	480	500	6411
BUHLER EZEE-ON, INC 5110 62 St, Vegreville, AB T9C 1N6, *Tel* (780) 632-2126	271,612,600	481	85	3523
GREENHILLS MINE JOINT VENTURE Gd, Elkford, BC V0B 1H0, *Tel* (250) 865-3097	271,061,920	482	460	1221
BROOKFIELD PROPERTIES LTD 181 Bay St Suite 330, Toronto, ON M5J 2T3, *Tel* (416) 369-2300	270,703,438	483	100	6512
CAPE BRETON DISTRICT HEALTH AUTHORITY 1482 George St, Sydney, NS B1P 1P3, *Tel* (902) 567-8000	269,487,797	484	1,000	8062
Parkland Regional Health Authority Inc (*Suby of* **PARKLAND REGIONAL HEALTH AUTHORITY INC**) 625 3rd St Sw, Dauphin, MB R7N 1R7, *Tel* (204) 638-2118	268,281,600	485	50	8062
CBI Limited (*Suby of* **CBI LIMITED**) 3300 Bloor St W Suite 900, Etobicoke, ON M8X 2X2, *Tel* (800) 463-2225	268,104,685	486	50	8049
FORTISBC INC 1975 Springfield Rd Suite 100, Kelowna, BC V1Y 7V7, *Tel* (604) 576-7000	266,642,023	487	80	4911
GROUPE TH INC 4655 Boul Wilfrid-Hamel, Quebec, QC G1P 2J7, *Tel* (418) 871-8151	266,113,710	488	7	8711
▲ **WALMART CANADA LOGISTICS ULC** 6800 Maritz Dr, Mississauga, ON L5W 1W2, *Tel* (905) 670-9966	265,576,948	489	800	4225
EGI Financial Holdings Inc (*Suby of* **EGI FINANCIAL HOLDINGS INC**) 2680 Matheson Blvd E Suite 300, Mississauga, ON L4W 0A5, *Tel* (905) 214-7880	264,908,869	490	0	6411
ENBRIDGE PIPELINES (SASKATCHEWAN) INC 402 Kensington Ave, Estevan, SK S4A 2K9, *Tel* (306) 634-2681	264,888,682	491	15	4612
Comcare (Canada) Limited (*Suby of* **COMCARE (CANADA) LIMITED**) 339 Wellington Rd Suite 200, London, ON N6C 5Z9, *Tel* (800) 663-5775	264,664,320	492	70	8049
RBC General Insurance Company (*Suby of* **ROYAL BANK OF CANADA**) 6880 Financial Dr Suite 200, Mississauga, ON L5N 7Y5, *Tel* (905) 816-5400	263,860,055	493	410	6331
CANADIAN NORTH INC 5109 48 St 202 Nunasi Bldg., Yellowknife, NT X1A 1N5, *Tel* (867) 669-4000	263,852,120	494	76	4729
LEDVANCE LTD 5450 Explorer Dr Suite 100, Mississauga, ON L4W 5N1, *Tel* (905) 361-9327	262,658,520	495	130	3641
SOVEREIGN GENERAL INSURANCE COMPANY, THE 6700 Macleod Trl Se Suite 140, Calgary, AB T2H 0L3, *Tel* (403) 298-4200	262,046,595	496	75	6411
CP ENERGY MARKETING INC 505 2 St Sw Suite 84, Calgary, AB T2P 1N8, *Tel* (403) 717-4600	261,842,450	497	1,600	8711
NATIONAL BANK TRUST INC 600 Rue De La Gauchetiere O Bureau 2800, Montreal, QC H3B 4L2, *Tel* (514) 871-7100	261,781,052	498	0	6021
WORKPLACE HEALTH SAFETY & COMPENSATION COMMISSION OF NEWFOUNDLAND AND LABRADOR 148 Forest Rd Unit 146, St. John'S, NL A1A 1E6, *Tel* (709) 778-1000	261,701,405	499	190	6331
CENTRE DE SANTE ET DE SERVICES SOCIAUX DE CHICOUTIMI 305 Rue Saint-Vallier, Chicoutimi, QC G7H 5H6, *Tel* (418) 541-1046	260,320,365	500	2,200	8011
AGROMEX INC 251 235 Rte, Ange-Gardien, QC J0E 1E0, *Tel* (450) 293-3694	259,875,300	501	150	2011
▲ Molson Breweries Of Canada Limited (*Suby of* **MOLSON COORS BREWING COMPANY**) 33 Carlingview Dr, Etobicoke, ON M9W 5E4, *Tel* (416) 679-1786	259,875,300	502	0	5181
▲ PPG Architectural Coatings Canada Inc (*Suby of* **PPG INDUSTRIES, INC.**) 2025 Rue De La Metropole, Longueuil, QC J4G 1S9, *Tel* (514) 527-5111	259,521,210	503	150	2851
Simcoe Muskoka Catholic District School Board (*Suby of* **SIMCOE MUSKOKA CATHOLIC DISTRICT SCHOOL BOARD**) 46 Alliance Blvd, Barrie, ON L4M 5K3, *Tel* (705) 722-3555	258,857,776	504	100	8211
3346625 Canada Inc (*Suby of* **3346625 CANADA INC**) 54 Rang De La Montagne, Rougemont, QC J0L 1M0, *Tel* (450) 469-2912	258,763,543	505	2	6712
BESSEMER & LAKE ERIE RAILROAD 935 Rue De La Gauchetiere O Bureau 11, Montreal, QC H3B 2M9, *Tel* (514) 399-4536	258,553,440	506	502	4011
BULUTH MISSABE & IRON RANGE RAILROAD 935 Rue De La Gauchetiere O Bureau 4eme, Montreal, QC H3B 2M9, *Tel* (514) 399-4536	258,553,440	507	502	4011
CIRQUE DU SOLEIL INC 8400 2e Av, Montreal, QC H1Z 4M6, *Tel* (514) 722-2324	258,056,173	508	2,560	7999
GREAT CANADIAN CASINOS INC 95 Schooner St, Coquitlam, BC V3K 7A8, *Tel* (604) 303-1000	258,056,173	509	10	7999
LifeMark Health Management Inc (*Suby of* **AUDAX GROUP, L.P.**) 20 Eglinton Ave W Suite 600, Toronto, ON M4R 1K8, *Tel* (416) 485-1344	257,259,428	510	13	8741
MARK'S WORK WEARHOUSE LTD 1035 64 Ave Se Suite 30, Calgary, AB T2H 2J7, *Tel* (403) 255-9220	257,186,468	511	382	5699

▲ Moore Canada Corporation (*Suby of* **R. R. DONNELLEY & SONS COMPANY**)

COMPANY	SALES ($)	RANK	EMPLOYEES HERE	PRIMARY SIC CODE
6100 Vipond Dr, Mississauga, ON L5T 2X1, Tel (905) 362-3100	255,873,175	512	400	6712
Willsonia Industries Limited (Suby of **WILLSONIA INDUSTRIES LIMITED**) 140 Bond St W, Oshawa, ON L1J 8M2, Tel (905) 723-3321	255,804,960	513	1	6712
ACCENTURE BUSINESS SERVICES FOR UTILITIES INC 510 Georgia St W Suite 2075, Vancouver, BC V6B 0M3, Tel (604) 646-5000	254,158,043	514	0	8741
STAR CHOICE TELEVISION NETWORK INCORPORATED 2924 11 St Ne, Calgary, AB T2E 7L7, Tel (403) 538-4672	252,305,280	515	200	4841
Insight Film Studios Ltd (Suby of **INSIGHT FILM STUDIOS LTD**) 112 6th Ave W, Vancouver, BC V5Y 1K6, Tel (604) 623-3369	252,073,008	516	100	7812
Fondation de L'Institut Universitaire en Sante Mentale de Montreal (Suby of **FONDATION DE L'INSTITUT UNIVERSITAIRE EN SANTE MENTALE DE MONTREAL**) 7401 Rue Hochelaga, Montreal, QC H1N 3M5, Tel (514) 251-4000	251,130,679	517	0	8063
HALIFAX HANGERS LIMITED Hangar No 1 St John'S International Airport, St. John'S, NL A1A 5B5, Tel (709) 576-1800	250,396,160	518	1	6719
▲ ICT Canada Marketing Inc (Suby of **SYKES ENTERPRISES INCORPORATED**) 400 Main St Suite 2004, Saint John, NB E2K 4N5, Tel (506) 653-9050	249,592,320	519	2	7389
CLEARWATER SEAFOODS LIMITED PARTNERSHIP 757 Bedford Hwy, Bedford, NS B4A 3Z7, Tel (902) 443-0550	249,233,751	520	0	2092
SECURITAS CANADA LIMITED 265 Yorkland Blvd Suite 500, North York, ON M2J 1S5, Tel (416) 774-2500	249,160,791	521	45	7381
GARDEWINE GROUP INC 60 Eagle Dr, Winnipeg, MB R2R 1V5, Tel (204) 633-5795	247,409,734	522	50	4731
9103-9834 Quebec Inc (Suby of **9103-9834 QUEBEC INC**) 400 Boul Saint-Joseph Bureau 2, Drummondville, QC J2C 2A8, Tel (819) 475-3928	246,283,440	523	0	5999
IBERIAN MINERALS CORP 181 Bay St Suite 2830, Toronto, ON M5J 2T3, Tel	245,321,000	524	10	1081
Entreprises Mirca Inc, Les (Suby of **ENTREPRISES MIRCA INC, LES**) 3901 Rue Jarry E Bureau 250, Montreal, QC H1Z 2G1, Tel (514) 253-3110	245,147,952	525	0	6712
Groupe Deschenes Inc (Suby of **ENTREPRISES MIRCA INC, LES**) 3901 Rue Jarry E Bureau 250, Montreal, QC H1Z 2G1, Tel (514) 253-3110	244,929,070	526	20	6712
Ascendant Resources Inc (Suby of **ASCENDANT RESOURCES INC**) 79 Wellington St W Suite 2100, Toronto, ON M5K 1H1, Tel (647) 796-0066	244,710,188	527	0	1382
▲ BPR Inc (Suby of **TETRA TECH, INC.**) 4655 Boul Wilfrid-Hamel, Quebec, QC G1P 2J7, Tel (418) 871-8151	244,629,282	528	300	8711
Martin, Ian Technology Staffing Limited (Suby of **MARTIN, IAN TECHNOLOGY STAFFING LIMITED**) 465 Morden Rd, Oakville, ON L6K 3W6, Tel (905) 815-1600	244,614,720	529	2	6712
SOCAN Foundation, The (Suby of **SOCAN FOUNDATION, THE**) 41 Valleybrook Dr, North York, ON M3B 2S6, Tel (416) 445-8700	244,113,915	530	3	7389
Value Village Stores, Inc (Suby of **SAVERS, INC.**) 7350 Edmonds St, Burnaby, BC V3N 1A8, Tel (604) 540-4916	243,070,031	531	5	5399
HOPITAL CHARLES LEMOYNE 3120 Boul Taschereau, Greenfield Park, QC J4V 2H1, Tel (450) 466-5000	241,856,800	532	2,500	8062
▲ Computer Sciences Canada Inc (Suby of **DXC TECHNOLOGY COMPANY**) 555 Legget Dr, Kanata, ON K2K 2X3, Tel (613) 591-1810	241,510,779	533	150	7373
Brookfield Capital Partners II L.P. (Suby of **BROOKFIELD CAPITAL PARTNERS II L.P.**) 181 Bay St Suite 300, Toronto, ON M5J 2T3, Tel (416) 363-9491	241,451,000	534	1	3088
Commission Scolaire Des Premieres-Seigneuries (Suby of **COMMISSION SCOLAIRE DES PREMIERES-SEIGNEURIES**) 643 Av Du Cenacle, Quebec, QC G1E 1B3, Tel (418) 666-4666	240,388,128	535	150	8211
120776 CANADA INC 700 Rue Canadel, Louiseville, QC J5V 3A4, Tel (819) 228-8471	239,929,250	536	950	6712
▲ **SERVICES DE CAFE VAN HOUTTE INC** 3700 Rue Jean-Rivard, Montreal, QC H1Z 4K3, Tel (514) 593-7711	239,314,080	537	1	5046
PERSONAL INSURANCE COMPANY, THE 3 Robert Speck Pky Suite 550, Mississauga, ON L4Z 3Z9, Tel (905) 306-5252	238,946,293	538	355	6331
RICHARDSON MILLING LIMITED 1 Can-Oat Dr, Portage La Prairie, MB R1N 3W1, Tel (204) 857-9700	238,873,332	539	500	5153
RICHARDSON PIONEER LIMITED 1 Lombard Pl Suite 2700, Winnipeg, MB R3B 0X8, Tel (204) 934-5961	238,873,332	540	100	5153
SEQUOIA RESOURCES CORP 605 5 Ave Sw Suite 3200, Calgary, AB T2P 3H5, Tel (403) 269-4400	238,565,525	541	0	1311
CHUBB INSURANCE COMPANY OF CANADA 1 Adelaide St E Suite 1500, Toronto, ON M5C 2V9, Tel (416) 863-0550	238,305,650	542	250	6331
WILLIAMS OPERATING CORPORATION 550 Burrard St Suite 3300, Vancouver, BC V6C 0B3, Tel (604) 699-4000	238,234,320	543	400	1221
CHALLENGER MOTOR FREIGHT INC 300 Maple Grove Rd, Cambridge, ON N3E 1B7, Tel (519) 653-6226	238,219,025	544	1,200	4213
ELLISDON CONSTRUCTION LTD 2045 Oxford St E, London, ON N5V 2Z7, Tel (519) 455-6770	237,778,921	545	80	1541
Societe Makivik (Suby of **SOCIETE MAKIVIK**) 1111 Boul Dr.-Frederik-Philips, Saint-Laurent, QC H4M 2X6, Tel (514) 745-8880	237,560,039	546	70	4512
Burnbrae Farms Limited (Suby of **BURNBRAE HOLDINGS LTD**) 3356 County Road 27, Lyn, ON K0E 1M0, Tel (613) 345-5651	237,122,275	547	800	5144

CANADIAN FOREST PRODUCTS LTD

COMPANY	SALES ($)	RANK	EMPLOYEES HERE	PRIMARY SIC CODE
1700 75th Ave W Unit 100, Vancouver, BC V6P 6G2, *Tel* (604) 661-5241	237,122,275	548	120	2421
WEINS CANADA INC				
3120 Steeles Ave E, Markham, ON L3R 1G9, *Tel* (905) 948-0977	237,122,275	549	190	5511
SEACLIFF CONSTRUCTION CORP				
1066 Hastings St W, Vancouver, BC V6E 3X2, *Tel* (604) 601-8206	237,092,899	550	100	8742
CARMACKS ENTERPRISES LTD				
701 25 Ave, Nisku, AB T9E 0C1, *Tel* (780) 955-5545	236,551,590	551	50	1611
NOVA FORGE CORP				
34 Power Plant Rd, Trenton, NS B0K 1X0, *Tel* (902) 752-0989	236,479,950	552	900	3743
MINCORP EXCHANGE INC				
20 Queen St W Unit 702, Toronto, ON M5H 3R3, *Tel*	236,369,280	553	112	6099
ENMAX POWER SERVICES CORP				
239 Mayland Pl Ne, Calgary, AB T2E 7Z8, *Tel* (403) 514-3000	235,736,022	554	493	4911
GO BEE INDUSTRIES INC				
300 York Blvd, Hamilton, ON L8R 3K6, *Tel*	235,582,250	555	1,000	7319
SYNDICAT DES INFIRMIERES, INHALOTHERAPEUTES ET INFIRMIERES AUXILIAIRES DE LAVAL (CSQ)				
2725 Ch Sainte-Foy Bureau 656, Quebec, QC G1V 4G5, *Tel* (418) 656-4710	235,566,900	556	2,100	8069
SOCIETE GENERALE (CANADA)				
1501 Av Mcgill College Bureau 1800, Montreal, QC H3A 3M8, *Tel* (514) 841-6000	235,298,258	557	115	6081
BML GROUP LIMITED				
5905 Campus Rd, Mississauga, ON L4V 1P9, *Tel* (905) 676-1293	234,828,387	558	1,000	6719
NOVA PETROCHEMICALS LTD				
1000 7 Ave Sw, Calgary, AB T2P 5L5, *Tel* (403) 750-3600	234,828,387	559	1,000	6712
▲ Tetra Tech Canada Holding Corporation (*Suby of* **TETRA TECH, INC.**)				
6835 Century Ave, Mississauga, ON L5N 7K2, *Tel* (905) 369-3000	234,828,387	560	5	6712
CANAC IMMOBILIER INC				
6245 Boul Wilfrid-Hamel Bureau 400, L'Ancienne-Lorette, QC G2E 5W2, *Tel* (418) 667-1313	234,787,533	561	75	5211
TRANSGAS LIMITED				
1777 Victoria Ave Suite 700, Regina, SK S4P 4K5, *Tel* (306) 777-9500	234,407,521	562	120	4923
Porter Airlines Inc (*Suby of* **PORTER AVIATION HOLDINGS INC**)				
4-1 Island Airport, Toronto, ON M5V 1A1, *Tel* (416) 203-8100	234,057,926	563	1,500	4581
Groupe Michel Cadrin Inc (*Suby of* **GROUPE MICHEL CADRIN INC**)				
600 Boul Charest E, Quebec, QC G1K 3J4, *Tel* (418) 529-6121	234,017,920	564	0	5912
Centre Hospitalier du Centre la Mauricie (*Suby of* **CENTRE HOSPITALIER DU CENTRE LA MAURICIE**)				
50 119e Rue, Shawinigan-Sud, QC G9P 5K1, *Tel* (819) 536-7500	234,013,440	565	0	8062
Groupe Master Inc, Le (*Suby of* **GESTION GROUPE MASTER INC**)				
1675 Boul De Montarville, Boucherville, QC J4B 7W4, *Tel* (514) 527-2301	233,839,044	566	150	5075
CENTRE DE SANTE ET DE SERVICES SOCIAUX DU PONTIAC				
160 Ch De La Chute, Fort-Coulonge, QC J0X 1V0, *Tel* (819) 683-3000	233,697,592	567	15	8062
BORALEX POWER INCOME FUND				
36 Rue Lajeunesse, Kingsey Falls, QC J0A 1B0, *Tel* (819) 363-5860	232,726,300	568	11	4911
Grand Erie District School Board (*Suby of* **GRAND ERIE DISTRICT SCHOOL BOARD**)				
349 Erie Ave, Brantford, ON N3S 2H7, *Tel* (519) 756-6301	232,284,099	569	600	8211
Fidelity Investments Canada ULC (*Suby of* **FMR LLC**)				
483 Bay St Suite 200, Toronto, ON M5G 2N7, *Tel* (416) 307-5200	231,577,262	570	600	6722
▲ Bell Helicopter Textron Canada Limitee (*Suby of* **TEXTRON INC.**)				
12800 Rue De L'Avenir, Mirabel, QC J7J 1R4, *Tel* (450) 971-6500	230,628,773	571	0	3721
PRINCESS AUTO LTD				
475 Panet Rd, Winnipeg, MB R2C 2Z1, *Tel* (204) 667-4630	230,555,812	572	300	5251
Commission Scolaire des Decouvreurs (*Suby of* **COMMISSION SCOLAIRE DES DECOUVREURS**)				
945 Av Wolfe Bureau 100, Quebec, QC G1V 4E2, *Tel* (418) 652-2121	230,099,200	573	100	8211
REVERA LONG TERM CARE INC				
600 Jamieson Pky, Cambridge, ON N3C 0A6, *Tel* (519) 622-1840	229,903,015	574	85	8051
NATIONAL TIRE DISTRIBUTORS INC				
5035 South Service Rd 4th Fl, Burlington, ON L7L 6M9, *Tel* (877) 676-0007	229,826,205	575	40	5014
British Columbia's Childrens Hospital (*Suby of* **BRITISH COLUMBIA'S CHILDRENS HOSPITAL**)				
4480 Oak St Suite B321, Vancouver, BC V6H 3V4, *Tel* (604) 875-2345	229,268,646	576	0	8069
Cona Resources Ltd (*Suby of* **CONA RESOURCES LTD**)				
421 7 Ave Sw Suite 1900, Calgary, AB T2P 4K9, *Tel* (403) 930-3000	228,368,352	577	0	1311
ROLLS-ROYCE CANADA LIMITEE				
9500 Ch De La Cote-De-Liesse, Lachine, QC H8T 1A2, *Tel* (514) 631-3541	228,002,188	578	1,400	4581
▲ Tetra Tech QC Inc (*Suby of* **TETRA TECH, INC.**)				
5100 Rue Sherbrooke E Bureau 900, Montreal, QC H1V 3R9, *Tel* (514) 257-0707	227,949,385	579	1,300	8711
VIDEON CABLESYSTEMS INC				
630 3 Ave Sw Suite 900, Calgary, AB T2P 4L4, *Tel* (403) 750-4500	227,587,200	580	900	4841
EASYFINANCIAL SERVICES INC				
33 City Centre Dr Suite 510, Mississauga, ON L5B 2N5, *Tel* (905) 272-2788	227,572,454	581	57	6141
Administration Lver Inc (*Suby of* **GESTION FRANCOIS ROBERGE INC**)				
4320 Av Pierre-De Coubertin, Montreal, QC H1V 1A6, *Tel* (514) 256-9446	226,834,816	582	4	6712
Syndicat des Professionnelles en Soins de Sante Lac St-Jean Est (*Suby of* **SYNDICAT DES PROFESSIONNELLES EN SOINS DE SANTE LAC ST-JEAN EST**)				
300 Boul Champlain, Alma, QC G8B 3N8, *Tel* (418) 662-1424	226,436,400	583	800	6371
All Seniors Care Holdings Inc (*Suby of* **ALL SENIORS CARE HOLDINGS INC**)				
175 Bloor St E Suite 601, Toronto, ON M4W 3R8, *Tel* (416) 323-3773	226,158,960	584	0	6513

COMPANY	SALES ($)	RANK	EMPLOYEES HERE	PRIMARY SIC CODE
Canaccord Genuity Corp (*Suby of* **CANACCORD GENUITY GROUP INC**) 609 Granville St Suite 2200, Vancouver, BC V7Y 1H2, *Tel* (604) 684-5992	226,158,960	585	500	6211
Major Drilling Group International Inc (*Suby of* **MAJOR DRILLING GROUP INTERNATIONAL INC**) 111 St George St Suite 100, Moncton, NB E1C 1T7, *Tel* (506) 857-8636	225,683,575	586	27	1481
CONESTOGA MEAT PACKERS LTD 313 Menno St, Breslau, ON N0B 1M0, *Tel* (519) 648-2506	225,242,100	587	807	5147
LUXOTTICA RETAIL CANADA INC 2000 Argentia Rd Suite 2, Mississauga, ON L5N 1V8, *Tel* (905) 858-0008	225,225,260	588	15	5995
Westport Fuel Systems Inc (*Suby of* **WESTPORT FUEL SYSTEMS INC**) 1750 75th Ave W Suite 101, Vancouver, BC V6P 6G2, *Tel* (604) 718-2000	224,895,000	589	150	3519
▲ Apache Canada Ltd (*Suby of* **APACHE CORPORATION**) 421 7 Ave Sw Suite 2800, Calgary, AB T2P 4K9, *Tel* (403) 261-1200	224,500,074	590	200	1382
TSX VENTURE EXCHANGE INC 300 5 Ave Sw, Calgary, AB T2P 3C4, *Tel* (403) 218-2800	224,445,634	591	100	6231
Algoma District School Board (*Suby of* **ALGOMA DISTRICT SCHOOL BOARD**) 644 Albert St E, Sault Ste. Marie, ON P6A 2K7, *Tel* (705) 945-7111	224,368,535	592	60	8211
SAMSUNG ELECTRONICS CANADA INC 2050 Derry Rd W Suite 1, Mississauga, ON L5N 0B9, *Tel* (905) 542-3535	223,925,884	593	182	5064
AON Inc (*Suby of* **AON GROUP INC**) 307 Aylmer St N, Peterborough, ON K9J 7M4, *Tel* (705) 742-5445	223,568,000	594	60	6553
▲ **WILLBROS CONSTRUCTION SERVICES (CANADA) LP** 1103 95 St Sw Suite 201, Edmonton, AB T6X 0P8, *Tel* (403) 817-2265	223,492,758	595	466	1623
IZAAK WALTON KILLAM HEALTH CENTRE, THE 585 0/5980 University Ave, Halifax, NS B3K 6R8, *Tel* (902) 470-8888	223,441,330	596	3,500	8069
Parrish & Heimbecker, Limited (*Suby of* **PARRISH & HEIMBECKER, LIMITED**) 201 Portage Ave Suite 1400, Winnipeg, MB R3B 3K6, *Tel* (204) 956-2030	223,259,742	597	25	6712
CANADA BREAD COMPANY, LIMITED 10 Four Seasons Pl Suite 1200, Etobicoke, ON M9B 6H7, *Tel* (416) 622-2040	221,362,764	598	200	2051
Placements Lauzon Inc (*Suby of* **PLACEMENTS LAUZON INC**) 2101 Cote Des Cascades, Papineauville, QC J0V 1R0, *Tel* (819) 427-5144	221,164,616	599	1	5031
GROUPE BELL NORDIQ INC 7151 Rue Jean-Talon E Bureau 700, Anjou, QC H1M 3N8, *Tel* (514) 493-5300	220,693,452	600	140	4899
Hewitt Associates Corp (*Suby of* **TEMPO ACQUISITION, LLC**) 2 Sheppard Ave E Suite 1500, North York, ON M2N 7A4, *Tel* (416) 225-5001	220,027,754	601	50	8748
NORTH WEST REDWATER PARTNERSHIP 140 4 Ave Sw Suite 2800, Calgary, AB T2P 3N3, *Tel* (403) 398-0900	219,976,511	602	201	2911
TRENCH LIMITED 71 Maybrook Dr, Scarborough, ON M1V 4B6, *Tel* (416) 298-8108	219,767,879	603	300	3699
2151177 ONTARIO INC 166 Norseman St, Etobicoke, ON M8Z 2R4, *Tel*	219,682,080	604	1	6712
Administration F.L.T. Ltee (*Suby of* **ADMINISTRATION F.L.T. LTEE**) 3075 Aut Transcanadienne, Pointe-Claire, QC H9R 1B4, *Tel* (514) 694-5855	219,682,080	605	3	6712
HAMILTON UTILITIES CORPORATION 55 John St N, Hamilton, ON L8R 3M8, *Tel* (905) 317-4781	219,347,840	606	5	4911
▲ Caleres Canada, Inc (*Suby of* **CALERES, INC.**) 1857 Rogers Rd, Perth, ON K7H 1P7, *Tel* (613) 267-0348	219,091,493	607	35	5139
GUESS? CANADA CORPORATION 8275 19e Av, Montreal, QC H1Z 4K2, *Tel* (514) 593-4107	218,882,100	608	58	5136
KPMG LLP (*Suby of* **KPMG LLP**) 333 Bay St Suite 4600, Toronto, ON M5H 2S5, *Tel* (416) 777-8500	218,882,100	609	150	8721
Les Placements Yellow Inc (*Suby of* **LES PLACEMENTS YELLOW INC**) 5665 Boul Saint-Laurent, Montreal, QC H2T 1S9, *Tel* (514) 273-0424	218,882,100	610	0	6712
NUTRECO CANADA INC 150 Research Lane Suite 200, Guelph, ON N1G 4T2, *Tel* (519) 823-7000	218,882,100	611	35	2048
Rio Tinto Fer et Titane Inc (*Suby of* **RIO TINTO PLC**) 1625 Rte Marie-Victorin, Sorel-Tracy, QC J3R 1M6, *Tel* (450) 746-3000	218,882,100	612	0	3399
VENTURE STEEL INC 60 Disco Rd, Etobicoke, ON M9W 1L8, *Tel* (416) 798-9396	218,882,100	613	0	5051
170592 Canada Inc (*Suby of* **170592 CANADA INC**) 11450 Ch Cote-De-Liesse, Dorval, QC H9P 1A9, *Tel* (514) 631-3341	218,544,000	614	1	6712
VUTEQ CANADA INC 920 Keyes Dr, Woodstock, ON N4V 1C2, *Tel* (519) 421-0011	218,045,200	615	750	3089
EXXONMOBIL BUSINESS SUPPORT CENTRE CANADA ULC 95 Boundary Dr, Moncton, NB E1G 5C6, *Tel* (800) 567-3776	217,610,250	616	1,100	8742
▲ G&K Services Canada Inc (*Suby of* **CINTAS CORPORATION**) 6299 Airport Rd Suite 101, Mississauga, ON L4V 1N3, *Tel* (905) 677-6161	217,082,501	617	35	7213
SASKATCHEWAN INSTITUTE OF APPLIED SCIENCE AND TECHNOLOGY 119 4th Ave S Suite 400, Saskatoon, SK S7K 5X2, *Tel* (866) 467-4278	216,521,886	618	65	8222
▲ Chevron Resources Ltd (*Suby of* **CHEVRON CORPORATION**) 500 5 Ave Sw Suite 700, Calgary, AB T2P 0L7, *Tel* (403) 234-5000	216,264,506	619	250	1311
▲ ABC Group Limited (*Suby of* **CERBERUS CAPITAL MANAGEMENT, L.P.**) 2 Norelco Dr, North York, ON M9L 2X6, *Tel* (416) 246-1782	215,869,749	620	1	6712
North Eastman Health Association Inc (*Suby of* **NORTH EASTMAN HEALTH ASSOCIATION INC**) 24 Aberdeen Ave, Pinawa, MB R0E 1L0, *Tel* (204) 753-2012	215,529,600	621	20	8741

COMPANY	SALES ($)	RANK	EMPLOYEES HERE	PRIMARY SIC CODE
FMC Technologies Canada Ltd (*Suby of* **RELIANCE OILFIELD SERVICES, LLC**) 333 11 Ave Sw Suite 1000, Calgary, AB T2R 1L9, *Tel* (403) 262-4000	215,379,986	622	75	1389
▲ Skyline (PHP) Canada ULC (*Suby of* **NUCOR CORPORATION**) 1400 Rue Marie-Victorin Bureau 216, Saint-Bruno, QC J3V 6B9, *Tel* (450) 461-6366	215,263,374	623	5	5051
LANXESS CANADA CO./CIE 25 Erb St, Elmira, ON N3B 3A3, *Tel* (519) 669-1671	215,088,144	624	218	2992
TRAVELBRANDS INC 5450 Explorer Dr Suite 300, Mississauga, ON L4W 5N1, *Tel* (416) 649-3939	214,577,419	625	400	4725
WEIR CANADA, INC 2360 Millrace Crt, Mississauga, ON L5N 1W2, *Tel* (905) 812-7100	214,285,800	626	110	5084
▲ Wendy's Restaurants Of Canada Inc (*Suby of* **THE WENDY'S COMPANY**) 240 Wyecroft Rd, Oakville, ON L6K 2G7, *Tel* (905) 337-8041	214,191,382	627	100	5812
9268-4935 QUEBEC INC 695 90e Av, Lasalle, QC H8R 3A4, *Tel* (514) 368-1505	214,160,950	628	3	6712
ARMOUR TRANSPORT INC 689 Edinburgh Dr, Moncton, NB E1E 2L4, *Tel* (506) 857-0205	214,066,694	629	800	4213
IPSOS LIMITED PARTNERSHIP 1285 Pender St W Suite 200, Vancouver, BC V6E 4B1, *Tel* (778) 373-5000	214,066,694	630	100	8732
ELLISDON CONSTRUCTION SERVICES INC 2045 Oxford St E, London, ON N5V 2Z7, *Tel* (519) 455-6770	213,704,122	631	0	1542
PRINCESS GROUP INC 475 Panet Rd, Winnipeg, MB R2C 2Z1, *Tel* (204) 667-4630	213,419,520	632	2	5251
BUHLER INDUSTRIES INC 1260 Clarence Ave, Winnipeg, MB R3T 1T2, *Tel* (204) 661-8711	212,685,858	633	0	3524
HARVEST OPERATIONS CORP 700 2nd St Sw Suite 1500, Calgary, AB T2P 2W1, *Tel* (403) 265-1178	212,500,009	634	250	1311
CUDDY INTERNATIONAL CORPORATION 1226 Trafalgar St, London, ON N5Z 1H5, *Tel* (800) 265-1061	211,534,800	635	180	2015
2063414 Ontario Limited (*Suby of* **2063414 ONTARIO LIMITED**) 302 Town Centre Blvd Suite 200, Markham, ON L3R 0E8, *Tel* (905) 477-4006	211,409,920	636	40	8051
EXXONMOBIL CANADA ENERGY 237 4 Ave Sw, Calgary, AB T2P 4K3, *Tel* (403) 260-7910	211,270,162	637	150	1382
▲ **ENBRIDGE COMMERCIAL SERVICES INC** 500 Consumers Rd, North York, ON M2J 1P8, *Tel* (416) 492-5000	210,553,200	638	1,000	8741
Fortuna Silver Mines Inc (*Suby of* **FORTUNA SILVER MINES INC**) 200 Burrard St Suite 650, Vancouver, BC V6C 3L6, *Tel* (604) 484-4085	210,255,000	639	0	1044
GDI SERVICES (CANADA) LP 60 Worcester Rd, Etobicoke, ON M9W 5X2, *Tel* (416) 736-1144	210,126,816	640	30	7349
TRANSELEC/COMMON INC 2075 Boul Fortin, Cote Saint-Luc, QC H7S 1P4, *Tel* (514) 382-1550	210,126,816	641	200	1623
Lakeridge Health (*Suby of* **LAKERIDGE HEALTH**) 850 1/4 Champlain Ave, Oshawa, ON L1J 8R2, *Tel* (905) 576-8711	208,740,563	642	200	8062
▲ Industries Mondiales Armstrong Canada Ltee, Les (*Suby of* **ARMSTRONG WORLD INDUSTRIES, INC.**) 1595 Boul Daniel-Johnson Bureau 300, Montreal-Ouest, QC H7V 4C2, *Tel* (450) 902-3900	207,900,240	643	0	3996
COMPUTERSHARE TRUST COMPANY OF CANADA 100 University Ave Suite 800, Toronto, ON M5J 2Y1, *Tel* (416) 263-9200	207,792,074	644	400	6733
HGS CANADA INC 82 Hillstrom Ave, Charlottetown, PE C1E 2C6, *Tel* (902) 370-3200	207,312,380	645	25	7379
CENTRE DE SANTE ET DE SERVICE SOCIAUX D'ARTHABASKA-ERABLE 61 Rue De L'Ermitage, Victoriaville, QC G6P 6X4, *Tel* (819) 758-7511	206,652,750	646	2,300	8062
9074-8898 QUEBEC INC 3195 Ch De Bedford, Montreal, QC H3S 1G3, *Tel* (514) 376-6240	205,984,000	647	500	2342
CENTRE DE SANTE ET DE SERVICES SOCIAUX DU SUROIT 150 Rue Saint-Thomas, Salaberry-De-Valleyfield, QC J6T 6C1, *Tel* (450) 371-9920	205,582,080	648	0	8069
SAIPEM CANADA INC 530 8 Ave Sw Suite 2700, Calgary, AB T2P 3S8, *Tel* (403) 441-2793	205,238,449	649	800	1629
AGF CANADIAN RESOURCES FUND LIMITED 66 Wellington St W, Toronto, ON M5K 1E9, *Tel* (800) 268-8583	204,979,200	650	500	6722
BOULANGERIE VACHON INC 8770 Boul Langelier Bureau 230, Saint-Leonard, QC H1P 3C6, *Tel* (514) 326-5084	204,695,111	651	50	5149
▲ **UPS SCS, INC** 4156 Mainway, Burlington, ON L7L 0A7, *Tel* (905) 315-5500	204,202,694	652	300	4212
ACME ENERGY MARKETING LTD 444 5 Ave Sw Suite 1010, Calgary, AB T2P 2T8, *Tel* (403) 517-5500	204,175,039	653	5	5172
1127770 B.C. LTD 777 Broadway W, Vancouver, BC V5Z 4J7, *Tel*	203,998,117	654	1,398	5047
ALECTRA UTILITIES CORPORATION 55 John St N, Hamilton, ON L8R 3M8, *Tel* (905) 522-6611	203,268,510	655	345	4911
Hammond Power Solutions Inc (*Suby of* **HAMMOND POWER SOLUTIONS INC**) 595 Southgate Dr, Guelph, ON N1G 3W6, *Tel* (519) 822-2441	203,249,268	656	800	3612
CARTONS ST-LAURENT INC 630 Boul Rene-Levesque O Bureau 3000, Montreal, QC H3B 1S6, *Tel* (514) 744-6461	202,111,440	657	1,000	2657
CASCADES GROUPE PAPIERS FINS INC 7280 West Credit Ave, Mississauga, ON L5N 5N1, *Tel* (905) 813-9400	202,028,178	658	0	2621

COMPANY	SALES ($)	RANK	EMPLOYEES HERE	PRIMARY SIC CODE
BUNGE CANADA HOLDINGS 1 ULC 2190 South Service Rd W, Oakville, ON L6L 5N1, *Tel* (905) 825-7900	201,581,150	659	1	6712
Upper Lakes Group Inc (*Suby of* **UPPER LAKES GROUP INC**) 250 Merton St Suite 403, Toronto, ON M4S 1B1, *Tel* (416) 920-7610	201,152,650	660	35	4432
GOLDEN CREDIT CARD TRUST 100 University Ave Suite 800, Toronto, ON M5J 2Y1, *Tel* (416) 955-2420	201,018,712	661	3	6021
Crocodile Labour Services Inc (*Suby of* **CROCODILE LABOUR SERVICES INC**) 343 Railway St, Vancouver, BC V6A 1A4, *Tel* (604) 681-1298	200,960,000	662	0	7361
▲ Baker Hughes Canada Company (*Suby of* **BAKER HUGHES, A GE COMPANY**) 401 9 Ave Sw Suite 1000, Calgary, AB T2P 3C5, *Tel* (403) 537-3400	200,641,925	663	200	5084
TST SOLUTIONS L.P. 5200 Maingate Dr, Mississauga, ON L4W 1G5, *Tel* (905) 625-7601	200,641,925	664	80	4213
AGF ALL WORLD TAX ADVANTAGE GROUP LIMITED Gd, Toronto, ON M5J 2W7, *Tel* (416) 367-1900	200,246,400	665	500	6722
South West Terminal Ltd (*Suby of* **SOUTH WEST TERMINAL LTD**) Gd, Gull Lake, SK S0N 1A0, *Tel* (306) 672-4112	200,130,807	666	0	4221
TD Life Insurance Company (*Suby of* **TORONTO-DOMINION BANK, THE**) 55 King St W, Toronto, ON M5K 1A2, *Tel*	198,744,947	667	200	6311
ENWIN UTILITIES LTD 787 Ouellette Ave Suite 517, Windsor, ON N9A 4J4, *Tel* (519) 255-2727	198,717,979	668	339	4911
▲ **ARAMARK ENTERTAINMENT SERVICES (CANADA) INC** 1000 Palladium Dr Suite 107, Kanata, ON K2V 1A4, *Tel* (613) 599-0230	198,631,354	669	0	8742
Board of Education of School District No. 57 (Prince George), The (*Suby of* **BOARD OF EDUCATION OF SCHOOL DISTRICT NO. 57 (PRINCE GEORGE), THE**) 2100 Ferry Ave, Prince George, BC V2L 4R5, *Tel* (250) 561-6800	198,454,487	670	120	8211
SINTRA INC 4984 Place De La Savane, Montreal, QC H4P 2M9, *Tel* (514) 341-5331	198,307,183	671	25	1611
Dundee Corporation (*Suby of* **DUNDEE CORPORATION**) 1 Adelaide St E Suite 2100, Toronto, ON M5C 2V9, *Tel* (416) 350-3388	198,176,043	672	0	6211
▲ **KBR INDUSTRIAL CANADA CO.** 3300 76 Ave Nw, Edmonton, AB T6P 1J4, *Tel* (780) 468-1341	198,161,261	673	998	1541
STACKPOLE INTERNATIONAL POWDER METAL, LTD. 1325 Cormorant Rd, Ancaster, ON L9G 4V5, *Tel* (905) 304-9455	198,161,261	674	42	3714
NEWFOUNDLAND LABRADOR LIQUOR CORPORATION 90 Kenmount Rd, St. John'S, NL A1B 3R1, *Tel* (709) 724-1100	197,691,048	675	105	5921
Altamart Investments (1993) Ltd (*Suby of* **ALTAMART INVESTMENTS (1993) LTD**) 9020 90 St, Peace River, AB T8S 1Z4, *Tel* (780) 624-4200	197,342,720	676	13	5411
Innvest Properties Corp (*Suby of* **INNVEST PROPERTIES CORP**) 200 Bay St Suite 2200, Toronto, ON M5J 2J2, *Tel* (416) 607-7100	196,993,890	677	70	7011
COASTAL SHIPPING LIMITED 128 Main St, Lewisporte, NL A0G 3A0, *Tel* (709) 535-6944	196,337,244	678	5	4424
Nasco Services Inc (*Suby of* **CROCODILE LABOUR SERVICES INC**) 343 Railway St, Vancouver, BC V6A 1A4, *Tel* (604) 681-1298	196,320,000	679	17	7361
RIDLEY INC 34 Terracon Pl, Winnipeg, MB R2J 4G7, *Tel* (204) 956-1717	196,205,852	680	6	2048
SOFTCHOICE CORPORATION 173 Dufferin St Suite 200, Toronto, ON M6K 3H7, *Tel* (416) 588-9002	196,118,362	681	600	7371
CANON CANADA INC 8000 Mississauga Rd, Brampton, ON L6Y 0C3, *Tel* (905) 795-1111	194,906,475	682	300	5044
▲ NCR Canada Corp (*Suby of* **NCR CORPORATION**) 50 Northland Rd, Waterloo, ON N2V 1N3, *Tel* (905) 826-9000	194,906,475	683	200	5044
Peterborough Victoria Northumberland and Clarington Catholic District School Board (*Suby of* **PETERBOROUGH VICTORIA NORTHUMBERLAND AND CLARINGTON CATHOLIC DISTRICT SCHOOL BOARD**) 1355 Lansdowne St W, Peterborough, ON K9J 7M3, *Tel* (705) 748-4861	194,779,404	684	70	8211
417289 B.C. Ltd (*Suby of* **417289 B.C. LTD**) 570 Granville St Suite 400, Vancouver, BC V6C 3P1, *Tel* (604) 689-4005	194,749,440	685	0	6712
O.C. Holdings '87 Inc (*Suby of* **O.C. HOLDINGS '87 INC**) 1345 Cliveden Ave, Delta, BC V3M 6C7, *Tel* (604) 515-4555	194,651,280	686	2	5142
FOUNTAIN TIRE LTD 1006 103a St Sw Suite 103, Edmonton, AB T6W 2P6, *Tel* (780) 464-3700	194,586,187	687	200	5531
MAXXAM ANALYTICS INTERNATIONAL CORPORATION 1919 Minnesota Crt Suite 500, Mississauga, ON L5N 0C9, *Tel* (905) 288-2150	194,559,975	688	90	8734
GDTM Inc (*Suby of* **GDTM INC**) 1970 Rue Des Toitures, Trois-Rivieres, QC G8V 1V9, *Tel* (819) 374-8784	194,025,541	689	0	5031
▲ **PRIMERICA LIFE INSURANCE COMPANY OF CANADA** 2000 Argentia Rd Suite 5, Mississauga, ON L5N 1P7, *Tel* (905) 812-3520	193,783,619	690	170	6311
LE CENTRE DE SANTE ET DE SERVICES SOCIAUX DE BORDEAUX-CARTIERVILLE-SAINT-LAURENT 555 Boul Gouin O, Montreal, QC H3L 1K5, *Tel* (514) 331-3020	193,769,500	691	2,003	8062
Hotel-Dieu Grace Healthcare (*Suby of* **HOTEL-DIEU GRACE HEALTHCARE**) 1030 Ouellette Ave, Windsor, ON N9A 1E1, *Tel* (519) 255-2260	193,465,150	692	0	8062
CUMIS LIFE INSURANCE COMPANY 151 North Service Rd, Burlington, ON L7R 4C2, *Tel* (905) 632-1221	192,517,815	693	100	6311
Groupe Cooperatif Dynaco (*Suby of* **GROUPE COOPERATIF DYNACO**) 205 Av Industrielle Bureau 200, La Pocatiere, QC G0R 1Z0, *Tel* (418) 856-3807	192,071,250	694	25	5251

COMPANY	SALES ($)	RANK	EMPLOYEES HERE	PRIMARY SIC CODE
NOVA SCOTIA COMMUNITY COLLEGE 5685 Leeds St, Halifax, NS B3K 2T3, *Tel* (902) 491-6722	191,896,779	695	75	8222
Decima Inc (*Suby of* **DECIMA INC**) 160 Elgin St Suite 1800, Ottawa, ON K2P 2P7, *Tel* (613) 230-2200	191,215,680	696	500	8732
Primmum Insurance Company (*Suby of* **TORONTO-DOMINION BANK, THE**) 50 Boul Cremazie O Bureau 1200, Montreal, QC H2P 1B6, *Tel* (514) 382-6060	191,157,034	697	260	6331
A.P. PLASMAN INC. 5245 Burke St Suite 1, Windsor, ON N9A 6J3, *Tel* (519) 737-6984	190,938,152	698	100	3089
▲ **ELECTRONICS BOUTIQUE CANADA INC** 8995 Airport Rd Suite 512, Brampton, ON L6T 5T2, *Tel* (905) 790-9262	189,697,820	699	100	5734
▲ State Street Bank & Trust Company (*Suby of* **STATE STREET CORPORATION**) 30 Adelaide St E Suite 1100, Toronto, ON M5C 3G8, *Tel* (416) 362-1100	189,535,719	700	0	6211
ALIMENTS SAPUTO LIMITEE 6869 Boul Metropolitain E, Saint-Leonard, QC H1P 1X8, *Tel* (514) 328-6662	189,333,017	701	70	5141
AIRPORT TERMINAL SERVICE INC CANADIAN 6500 Silver Dart Dr Unit 211, Mississauga, ON L5P 1B1, *Tel* (905) 405-9550	189,252,480	702	300	4581
Laliberte & Associes Inc (*Suby of* **LALIBERTE & ASSOCIES INC**) 8790 Rue Lajeunesse, Montreal, QC H2M 1R6, *Tel* (514) 381-8081	189,252,480	703	0	8741
COAST MOUNTAIN BUS COMPANY LTD 287 Nelson'S Crt Suite 700, New Westminster, BC V3L 0E7, *Tel* (778) 375-6400	187,436,038	704	300	4111
CNOOC CANADA ENERGY LTD. 801 7 Ave Sw, Calgary, AB T2P 3P7, *Tel* (403) 699-4000	187,370,091	705	350	1382
8504741 CANADA INC 1000 Rue De La Gauchetiere O Bureau 2500, Montreal, QC H3B 0A2, *Tel* (514) 392-1900	186,958,074	706	1	6712
TECHNOLOGIES METAFORE INC 9393 Boul Louis-H.-Lafontaine, Anjou, QC H1J 1Y8, *Tel* (514) 354-3810	186,863,841	707	1,000	7371
▲ **TICKETMASTER CANADA HOLDINGS ULC** 1 Blue Jays Way Suite 3900, Toronto, ON M5V 1J3, *Tel* (416) 345-9200	185,856,400	708	1	6712
▲ **RYERSON CANADA, INC** 1219 Corporate Dr Suite 2, Burlington, ON L7L 5V5, *Tel* (416) 622-3100	185,320,178	709	40	5051
Targray Technologie Internationale Inc (*Suby of* **THOMAS A.G. RICHARDSON INVESTISSEMENT INC**) 18105 Rte Transcanadienne, Kirkland, QC H9J 3Z4, *Tel* (514) 695-8095	184,911,250	710	0	5049
Societe d'Hypotheque de la Banque Royale (*Suby of* **ROYAL BANK OF CANADA**) 1 Place Vil e-Marie, Montreal, QC H3C 3A9, *Tel* (514) 874-7222	184,740,450	711	700	6162
▲ **ANIXTER POWER SOLUTIONS CANADA INC** 188 Purdy Rd, Colborne, ON K0K 1S0, *Tel* (905) 355-2474	184,251,588	712	100	5085
ENERCARE SOLUTIONS INC 4000 Victoria Park Ave, North York, ON M2H 3P4, *Tel* (905) 695-7788	184,169,389	713	0	6719
COMPLEXE DE L'AUTO PARK AVENUE INC 4505 Boul Metropolitain E Bureau 201, Saint-Leonard, QC H1R 1Z4, *Tel* (514) 899-9000	184,050,000	714	4	5511
BMW CANADA INC 50 Ultimate Dr, Richmond Hill, ON L4S 0C8, *Tel* (905) 770-1758	183,905,087	715	203	5012
CSSS DE CHICOUTIMI 305 Rue Saint-Vallier, Chicoutimi, QC G7H 5H6, *Tel* (418) 541-1000	183,827,400	716	1,900	8062
Medicine Hat Co-Op Limited (*Suby of* **MEDICINE HAT CO-OP LIMITED**) 3030 13 Ave Se Suite 100, Medicine Hat, AB T1B 1E3, *Tel* (403) 528-6604	183,738,893	717	100	5411
PANASONIC CANADA INC 5770 Ambler Dr Suite 70, Mississauga, ON L4W 2T3, *Tel* (905) 624-5010	183,642,082	718	300	5064
▲ **FOOT LOCKER CANADA CO** 230 Barmac Dr, North York, ON M9L 2Z3, *Tel* (416) 748-4210	183,277,278	719	40	5661
ONTARIO NORTHLAND TRANSPORTATION COMMISSION 555 Oak St E, North Bay, ON P1B 8E3, *Tel* (705) 472-4500	183,204,318	720	600	4899
THOMPSON HEALTH REGION 311 Columbia St, Kamloops, BC V2C 2T1, *Tel* (250) 314-2784	182,407,100	721	2,000	8093
▲ **WTH Canada, Inc** (*Suby of* **AVIS BUDGET GROUP, INC.**) 1 Convair Dr, Etobicoke, ON M9W 6Z9, *Tel* (416) 213-8400	182,036,947	722	1	6712
CANAC-MARQUIS GRENIER LTEE 6245 Boul Wilfrid-Hamel, L'Ancienne-Lorette, QC G2E 5W2, *Tel* (418) 667-1313	181,818,064	723	100	6719
KIK Holdco Company Inc (*Suby of* **KIK CUSTOM PRODUCTS INC**) 101 Macintosh Blvd, Concord, ON L4K 4R5, *Tel* (905) 660-0444	181,818,064	724	850	6719
SERVICES MATREC INC 4 Ch Du Tremblay Bureau 625, Boucherville, QC J4B 6Z5, *Tel* (450) 641-3070	181,818,064	725	80	6712
RBC Insurance Holdings Inc (*Suby of* **ROYAL BANK OF CANADA**) 6880 Financial Dr Suite 200, Mississauga, ON L5N 7Y5, *Tel* (905) 949-3663	181,792,320	726	0	6411
INDUSTRIELLE ALLIANCE, ASSURANCE AUTO ET HABITATION INC 925 Grande Allee O Bureau 230, Quebec, QC G1S 1C1, *Tel* (418) 650-4600	181,599,182	727	0	6331
STANTEC CONSULTING INTERNATIONAL LTD 10160 112 St Nw, Edmonton, AB T5K 2L6, *Tel* (780) 917-7000	180,577,733	728	250	8711
STANTEC GEOMATICS LTD 10160 112 St Nw, Edmonton, AB T5K 2L6, *Tel* (780) 917-7000	180,577,733	729	100	8713
Commission Scolaire des Phares (*Suby of* **COMMISSION SCOLAIRE DES PHARES**) 435 Av Rouleau, Rimouski, QC G5L 5W6, *Tel* (418) 723-5927	179,829,120	730	65	8211

Community Care Access Centre of London and Middlesex (*Suby of* **COMMUNITY CARE ACCESS CENTRE OF LON-DON AND MIDDLESEX**)

COMPANY	SALES ($)	RANK	EMPLOYEES HERE	PRIMARY SIC CODE
356 Oxford St W, London, ON N6H 1T3, *Tel* (519) 473-2222	179,795,737	731	100	8059
Pacific Link Communications Inc (*Suby of* **PACIFIC LINK COMMUNICATIONS INC**) 570 Alden Rd Suite 11, Markham, ON L3R 8N5, *Tel* (905) 305-8100	179,363,600	732	93	5999
TREO DRILLING SERVICES L.P. 285160 Kleysen Way, Rocky View County, AB T1X 0K1, *Tel* (403) 723-8600	178,274,456	733	430	1381
TD Financing Services Home Inc (*Suby of* **TORONTO-DOMINION BANK, THE**) 25 Booth Ave Suite 101, Toronto, ON M4M 2M3, *Tel* (416) 463-4422	178,242,990	734	200	6141
Yanke Holdings Ltd (*Suby of* **YANKE HOLDINGS LTD**) 1359 Fletcher Rd, Saskatoon, SK S7M 5H5, *Tel* (306) 955-4221	177,950,080	735	1	6712
▲ **BWXT CANADA LTD** 581 Coronation Blvd, Cambridge, ON N1R 3E9, *Tel* (519) 621-2130	177,367,462	736	900	3621
CANYON SERVICES GROUP INC 645 7 Ave Sw Suite 2900, Calgary, AB T2P 4G8, *Tel* (403) 266-0202	177,193,794	737	200	1389
Goderich Elevators Limited (*Suby of* **PARRISH & HEIMBECKER, LIMITED**) 230 Harbour St, Goderich, ON N7A 3Y5, *Tel* (519) 524-7367	177,148,580	738	17	4221
Nova Agri Inc (*Suby of* **DYKEVIEW FARMS LIMITED**) 1225 Middle Dyke Rd, Centreville, NS B0P 1J0, *Tel* (902) 582-1445	177,148,580	739	0	4221
Koch Fertilizer Canada, ULC (*Suby of* **KOCH INDUSTRIES, INC.**) 1400 17th St E, Brandon, MB R7A 7C4, *Tel* (204) 729-2900	176,888,454	740	220	2873
Toys 'R' Us (Canada) Ltd (*Suby of* **TOYS "R" US, INC.**) 2777 Langstaff Rd, Concord, ON L4K 4M5, *Tel* (905) 660-2000	176,628,579	741	250	5945
▲ **AMERICAN EAGLE OUTFITTERS CANADA CORPORATION** 450 Courtneypark Dr W, Mississauga, ON L5W 1Y6, *Tel* (289) 562-8000	176,346,012	742	10	5651
REGIONAL TIRE DISTRIBUTORS INC 16408 121a Ave Nw, Edmonton, AB T5V 1J9, *Tel* (780) 483-1391	176,015,750	743	347	5014
90401 Canada Ltee (*Suby of* **90401 CANADA LTEE**) 790 Rue Begin, Saint-Laurent, QC H4M 2N5, *Tel* (514) 334-5000	175,609,950	744	5	6712
LONE STAR GROUP OF COMPANIES HOLDINGS INC 32 Colonnade Rd Suite 900, Nepean, ON K2E 7J6, *Tel* (613) 727-1966	175,609,950	745	700	6712
▲ **PETRO-CANADA LUBRICANTS INC** 2310 Lakeshore Rd W, Mississauga, ON L5J 1K2, *Tel* (905) 804-3600	175,470,484	746	83	5172
ASSURANCE MARTIN & CYR INC 460 Rue Mcgill, Montreal, QC H2Y 2H2, *Tel* (514) 527-9546	175,438,080	747	706	6712
TRQSS, INC 255 Patillo Rd, Tecumseh, ON N8N 2L9, *Tel* (519) 973-7400	175,415,828	748	700	2399
Groupe Gaudreault Inc, Le (*Suby of* **LE GROUPE GAUDREAULT INC**) 1500 Rue Raymond-Gaudreault, Repentigny, QC J5Y 4E3, *Tel* (450) 585-1210	175,136,640	749	600	6712
All Seniors Care Living Centres Ltd (*Suby of* **ALL SENIORS CARE HOLDINGS INC**) 175 Bloor St E Suite 601, Toronto, ON M4W 3R8, *Tel* (416) 323-3773	175,105,680	750	30	6513
NOVA CENTRAL SCHOOL DISTRICT 203 Elizabeth Dr, Gander, NL A1V 1H6, *Tel* (709) 256-2547	175,084,728	751	1,000	8211
▲ **PRO CANADIAN HOLDINGS I, ULC** 1969 Upper Water St Suite 1300, Halifax, NS B3J 3R7, *Tel* (902) 425-6500	175,084,728	752	1	6712
CONNEXIM, SOCIETE EN COMMANDITE 505 Boul De Maisonneuve O, Montreal, QC H3A 3C2, *Tel*	174,935,680	753	700	4899
Board of Education of School District No. 35 (Langley) (*Suby of* **BOARD OF EDUCATION OF SCHOOL DISTRICT NO. 35 (LANGLEY)**) 4875 222 St, Langley, BC V3A 3Z7, *Tel* (604) 534-7891	174,549,577	754	0	8211
7577010 Canada Inc (*Suby of* **GESTION BMR INC**) 1501 Rue Ampere Bureau 200, Boucherville, QC J4B 5Z5, *Tel* (450) 655-2441	174,203,076	755	1	5211
Dillon Consulting Inc (*Suby of* **DILLON CONSULTING INC**) 235 Yorkland Blvd Unit 800, North York, ON M2J 4Y8, *Tel* (416) 229-4646	173,930,880	756	2	6712
MEDISYS HOLDING LP 500 Rue Sherbrooke O Bureau 1100, Montreal, QC H3A 3C6, *Tel* (514) 845-1211	173,930,880	757	700	6712
Spicers Canada ULC (*Suby of* **CNG CANADA HOLDING INC.**) 200 Galcat Dr, Woodbridge, ON L4L 0B9, *Tel* (905) 265-5000	173,281,663	758	200	5111
CANWEL BUILDING MATERIALS LTD 1055 West Georgia St Suite 1100, Vancouver, BC V6E 3P3, *Tel* (604) 432-1400	173,250,200	759	50	5039
RBC Dominion Securities Limited (*Suby of* **ROYAL BANK OF CANADA**) 200 Bay St, Toronto, ON M5J 2J5, *Tel* (888) 820-8006	173,250,200	760	0	6211
Scoular Canada Ltd (*Suby of* **THE SCOULAR COMPANY**) 10201 Southport Rd Sw Suite 1110, Calgary, AB T2W 4X9, *Tel* (403) 720-9050	173,250,200	761	20	6799
ALBIAN SANDS ENERGY INC Gd Lcd Main, Fort Mcmurray, AB T9H 3E2, *Tel* (780) 713-4400	173,062,780	762	420	1382
HYDRO ALUMINIUM CANADA INC 2000 Av Mcgill College Bureau 2310, Montreal, QC H3A 3H3, *Tel* (514) 840-9110	172,823,139	763	2	3334
Le Chateau Inc (*Suby of* **LE CHATEAU INC**) 105 Boul Marcel-Laurin, Saint-Laurent, QC H4N 2M3, *Tel* (514) 738-7000	172,690,336	764	300	5621
Commission Scolaire des Rives-du-Saguenay (*Suby of* **COMMISSION SCOLAIRE DES RIVES-DU-SAGUENAY**) 36 Rue Jacques-Cartier E, Chicoutimi, QC G7H 1W2, *Tel* (418) 698-5000	172,634,673	765	100	8211
AstraZeneca Canada Inc (*Suby of* **ASTRAZENECA PLC**) 1004 Middlegate Rd Suite 5000, Mississauga, ON L4Y 1M4, *Tel* (905) 277-7111	172,557,199	766	800	2834
Rainbow District School Board (*Suby of* **RAINBOW DISTRICT SCHOOL BOARD**) 69 Young St, Sudbury, ON P3E 3G5, *Tel* (705) 377-4615	172,438,480	767	50	8211

COMPANY	SALES ($)	RANK	EMPLOYEES HERE	PRIMARY SIC CODE
KINGSWAY LINKED RETURN OF CAPITAL TRUST 40 King St W 26 Flr, Toronto, ON M5H 3Y2, *Tel* (416) 945-4160	172,278,000	768	1	6726
SAFRAN LANDING SYSTEMS CANADA INC 574 Monarch Ave, Ajax, ON L1S 2G8, *Tel* (905) 683-3100	172,114,291	769	600	3728
PARKBRIDGE LIFESTYLE COMMUNITIES INC 500 4 Ave Sw Suite 1500, Calgary, AB T2P 2V6, *Tel* (403) 215-2100	171,864,198	770	25	6719
0429746 B.C. Ltd (*Suby of* **O.C. HOLDINGS '87 INC**) 1345 Cliveden Ave, Delta, BC V3M 6C7, *Tel* (604) 515-4555	171,777,573	771	280	5142
▲ Oracle Canada ULC (*Suby of* **ORACLE CORPORATION**) 100 Milverton Dr Suite 100, Mississauga, ON L5R 4H1, *Tel* (905) 890-8140	171,777,573	772	0	7371
VARSTEEL LTD 220 4 St S Suite 330, Lethbridge, AB T1J 4J7, *Tel* (403) 320-1953	171,165,802	773	35	5051
INTERTAPE POLYMER INC 9999 Boul Cavendish Bureau 200, Saint-Laurent, QC H4M 2X5, *Tel* (514) 731-7591	169,611,946	774	2,000	2295
TWC Enterprises Limited (*Suby of* **TWC ENTERPRISES LIMITED**) 15675 Dufferin St, King City, ON L7B 1K5, *Tel* (905) 841-5372	169,411,989	775	0	7999
▲ Lear Corporation Canada Ltd (*Suby of* **LEAR CORPORATION**) 530 Manitou Dr, Kitchener, ON N2C 1L3, *Tel* (519) 895-1600	169,265,445	776	250	2531
CAPE BRETON-VICTORIA REGIONAL SCHOOL BOARD 275 George St, Sydney, NS B1P 1J7, *Tel* (902) 564-8293	169,106,655	777	35	8211
CENTRE DE SANTE ET DE SERVICES SOCIAUX DE QUEBEC-NORD 4e Etage 2915, Av Du Bourg-Royal, Quebec, QC G1C 3S2, *Tel* (418) 661-5666	169,087,503	778	100	8011
VITALAIRE CANADA INC 6990 Creditview Rd Unit 6, Mississauga, ON L5N 8R9, *Tel* (905) 855-0411	169,049,942	779	70	5169
CAPITALE ASSURANCES ET GESTION DU PATRIMOINE INC, LA 625 Rue Saint-Amable, Quebec, QC G1R 2G5, *Tel* (418) 644-4200	168,904,021	780	1	6311
Canadian Linen and Uniform Service Co (*Suby of* **AMERIPRIDE SERVICES, INC.**) 20 Atomic Ave, Etobicoke, ON M8Z 5L1, *Tel* (416) 354-3100	168,758,099	781	2	7213
DEFENCE CONSTRUCTION (1951) LIMITED 350 Albert St Suite 1900, Ottawa, ON K1R 1A4, *Tel* (613) 998-9548	168,745,695	782	120	8741
GREYHOUND CANADA TRANSPORTATION ULC 877 Greyhound Way Sw, Calgary, AB T3C 3V8, *Tel* (403) 218-3000	167,792,819	783	350	4131
ENCOREFX INC 517 Fort St Fl 2, Victoria, BC V8W 1E7, *Tel* (250) 412-1290	167,619,569	784	5	6099
HENNIGES AUTOMOTIVE SEALING SYSTEMS CANADA INC 100 Kennedy St, Welland, ON L3B 0B4, *Tel*	167,600,640	785	800	3069
POLAR EXPLOSIVES LTD 349 Old Airport Rd Suite 104, Yellowknife, NT X1A 3X6, *Tel* (867) 880-4613	167,451,863	786	540	5169
▲ AIG Insurance Company of Canada (*Suby of* **AMERICAN INTERNATIONAL GROUP, INC.**) 145 Wellington St W Suite 1400, Toronto, ON M5J 1H8, *Tel* (416) 596-3000	167,225,924	787	0	6331
▲ **MICROSEMI STORAGE SOLUTIONS LTD** 8555 Baxter Pl Suite 105, Burnaby, BC V5A 4V7, *Tel* (604) 415-6000	167,152,964	788	300	3661
▲ Campbell Company of Canada (*Suby of* **CAMPBELL SOUP COMPANY**) 60 Birmingham St, Etobicoke, ON M8V 2B8, *Tel* (416) 251-1131	166,886,466	789	700	2032
Builders Energy Services Ltd (*Suby of* **BUILDERS ENERGY SERVICES LTD**) 250 2 St Sw Suite 1100, Calgary, AB T2P 0C1, *Tel* (403) 693-2378	166,184,880	790	40	1389
CANADIAN TEST CASE 29-B 5770 Hurontario St, Mississauga, ON L5R 3G5, *Tel* (905) 812-5922	166,073,650	791	50	6324
▲ **WESTERN INVENTORY SERVICE LTD** 3770 Nashua Dr Suite 5, Mississauga, ON L4V 1M5, *Tel* (905) 677-1947	165,870,750	792	50	7389
KENWORTH TORONTO LTD 500 Creditstone Rd, Concord, ON L4K 3Z3, *Tel* (905) 695-0740	165,713,816	793	75	5012
Granite REIT Inc (*Suby of* **GRANITE REIT INC**) 77 King St W Suite 4010, Toronto, ON M5K 2A1, *Tel* (647) 925-7500	165,237,433	794	0	6712
CENTRE DE SANTE ET DE SERVICES SOCIAUX DE GATINEAU 85 Rue Bellehumeur Bureau 301, Gatineau, QC J8T 8B7, *Tel* (819) 966-6016	165,194,066	795	0	8062
Greenwich Associates ULC (*Suby of* **GREENWICH ASSOCIATES LLC**) 1220 Sheppard Ave E Suite 201, North York, ON M2K 2S5, *Tel* (416) 493-6111	165,001,808	796	62	8732
SAINE MARKETING INC 1600 Boul Rene-Levesque O Bureau 1800, Montreal, QC H3H 1P9, *Tel* (514) 931-8236	165,001,808	797	900	8732
Societe en Commandite Avions C Series (*Suby of* **SOCIETE EN COMMANDITE AVIONS C SERIES**) 800 Boul Rene-Levesque W Bureau 2900, Montreal, QC H3B 1Y8, *Tel* (514) 855-5000	164,745,261	798	0	3721
BRITISH COLUMBIA MENTAL HEALTH SOCIETY 2601 Lougheed Hwy, Coquitlam, BC V3C 4J2, *Tel* (604) 524-7000	164,712,480	799	1,700	8063
HMZ METALS INC 2 Toronto St Suite 500, Toronto, ON M5C 2B6, *Tel*	164,686,720	800	400	3339
▲ **HENRY SCHEIN CANADA, INC** 345 Townline Rd Ss 4, Niagara On The Lake, ON L0S 1J0, *Tel* (905) 646-1711	164,587,690	801	260	5047
SHOPPERS DRUG MART CORPORATION 243 Consumers Rd, North York, ON M2J 4W8, *Tel* (416) 493-1220	164,234,536	802	100	5912
CDSL CANADA LIMITED 1900 Albert St Unit 700, Regina, SK S4P 4K8, *Tel* (306) 761-4000	164,161,575	803	250	7379
SYNCREON CANADA INC 999 Boundary Rd, Oshawa, ON L1J 8P8, *Tel* (905) 743-6277	164,161,575	804	44	4783

COMPANY	SALES ($)	RANK	EMPLOYEES HERE	PRIMARY SIC CODE
Le Centres Jeunesse de Montreal Institut Universitaire (*Suby of* **LE CENTRES JEUNESSE DE MONTREAL INSTITUT UNIVERSITAIRE**) 4675 Rue Belanger, Montreal, QC H1T 1C2, *Tel* (514) 593-3979	163,943,200	805	135	8322
▲ Chrysler Financial Services Canada Inc (*Suby of* **CERBERUS CAPITAL MANAGEMENT, L.P.**) 1 Riverside Dr W, Windsor, ON N9A 5K3, *Tel* (519) 973-2000	163,211,383	806	30	6153
Wawanesa Life Insurance Company, The (*Suby of* **WAWANESA MUTUAL INSURANCE COMPANY, THE**) 200 Main St Suite 400, Winnipeg, MB R3C 1A8, *Tel* (204) 985-3940	163,022,917	807	78	6311
INGRAM MICRO INC 55 Standish Crt Suite 1, Mississauga, ON L5R 4A1, *Tel* (905) 755-5000	162,422,063	808	800	5045
BOARD OF GOVERNOR'S OF RED RIVER COLLEGE, THE 2055 Notre Dame Ave, Winnipeg, MB R3H 0J9, *Tel* (204) 632-3960	161,988,937	809	750	8222
ALLIED DOMECQ CANADA LTD 2072 Riverside Dr E, Windsor, ON N8Y 4S5, *Tel* (519) 254-5171	161,964,000	810	3	5182
EDMONTON TRAILER MANUFACTURING LTD 16908 128a Ave Nw, Edmonton, AB T5V 1K7, *Tel* (403) 744-5120	161,316,108	811	706	3531
G. Cooper Equipment Rentals Limited (*Suby of* **G. COOPER EQUIPMENT RENTALS LIMITED**) 33 Racine Rd, Etobicoke, ON M9W 2Z4, *Tel* (416) 744-5000	161,170,186	812	12	7353
Ceger Inc (*Suby of* **CEGER INC**) 1180 Rue Bersimis, Chicoutimi, QC G7K 1A5, *Tel* (418) 543-4938	161,169,920	813	50	6712
TEVA CANADA LIMITED 30 Novopharm Crt, Scarborough, ON M1B 2K9, *Tel* (416) 291-8876	161,036,061	814	300	2834
Benapac Inc (*Suby of* **BENAPAC INC**) 700 Education Rd, Cornwall, ON K6H 6B8, *Tel* (613) 933-1700	160,595,350	815	150	5013
AON REED STENHOUSE INC 20 Bay St Suite 2400, Toronto, ON M5J 2N8, *Tel* (416) 868-5500	160,429,685	816	314	6411
Dynamic Mutual Funds (*Suby of* **DYNAMIC MUTUAL FUNDS**) 1 Adelaide St E Suite 2900, Toronto, ON M5C 2V9, *Tel* (416) 363-5621	160,197,120	817	0	6722
BRITISH COLUMBIA CANCER AGENCY BRANCH 600 10th Ave W, Vancouver, BC V5Z 4E6, *Tel* (604) 877-6000	159,117,360	818	1,010	8069
COLLEGE D'ENSEIGNEMENT GENERAL & PROFESSIONEL STE-FOY 2410 Ch Sainte-Foy, Quebec, QC G1V 1T3, *Tel* (418) 659-6600	159,073,600	819	1,100	8221
▲ Masco Canada Limited (*Suby of* **MASCO CORPORATION**) 350 South Edgeware Rd, St Thomas, ON N5P 4L1, *Tel* (519) 633-5050	159,065,135	820	410	3432
FORMULA POWELL L.P. Gd Stn Main, Grande Prairie, AB T8V 2Z7, *Tel* (780) 539-5910	158,523,933	821	0	4213
GLOVIS CANADA, INC 5770 Hurontario St Suite 700, Mississauga, ON L5R 3G5, *Tel* (905) 361-1342	158,334,665	822	0	4212
International Graphics ULC (*Suby of* **TAYLOR CORPORATION**) 505 Douro St, Stratford, ON N5A 3S9, *Tel* (519) 271-3010	157,086,244	823	0	2678
LUFF INDUSTRIES LTD 235010 Wrangler Rd, Rocky View County, AB T1X 0K3, *Tel* (403) 279-3555	156,961,193	824	86	3535
Chignecto Central Regional School Board (*Suby of* **CHIGNECTO CENTRAL REGIONAL SCHOOL BOARD**) 60 Lorne St, Truro, NS B2N 3K3, *Tel* (902) 897-8900	156,793,650	825	2,717	8211
Innovapost Inc (*Suby of* **CANADA POST CORPORATION**) 365 March Rd, Kanata, ON K2K 3N5, *Tel* (613) 270-6262	156,426,614	826	290	7372
AltaGas Utilities Inc (*Suby of* **ALTAGAS HOLDING LIMITED PARTNERSHIP NO. 1**) 5509 45 St, Leduc, AB T9E 6T6, *Tel* (780) 986-5215	156,143,915	827	70	4923
Abatement Technologies Limited (*Suby of* **ABATEMENT TECHNOLOGIES, INC.**) 7 High St, Fort Erie, ON L2A 3P6, *Tel* (905) 871-4720	155,187,409	828	40	3634
CARDINAL RIVER COALS LTD Gd, Hinton, AB T7V 1V5, *Tel* (780) 692-5100	154,968,527	829	350	1221
▲ **TOTAL E&P CANADA LTD** 240 4 Ave Sw Suite 2900, Calgary, AB T2P 4H4, *Tel* (403) 571-7599	154,676,684	830	170	1311
Groupe TNT Inc (*Suby of* **GROUPE TNT INC**) 20845 Ch De La Cote N Bureau 200, Boisbriand, QC J7E 4H5, *Tel* (450) 431-7887	154,541,956	831	0	1521
CPP INVESTMENT BOARD PRIVATE HOLDINGS (2) INC. One Queen St E Suite 2500, Toronto, ON M5C 2W5, *Tel* (416) 868-4075	154,305,450	832	886	6371
Corel Corporation (*Suby of* **VECTOR CAPITAL MANAGEMENT, L.P.**) 1600 Carling Ave Suite 100, Ottawa, ON K1Z 8R7, *Tel* (613) 728-8200	154,279,303	833	450	7371
Interlake Regional Health Authority Inc (*Suby of* **INTERLAKE REGIONAL HEALTH AUTHORITY INC**) 589 3rd Ave S, Stonewall, MB R0C 2Z0, *Tel* (204) 467-4742	154,165,024	834	0	8062
▲ Sonoco Plastics Canada ULC (*Suby of* **SONOCO PRODUCTS COMPANY**) 245 Britannia Rd E, Mississauga, ON L4Z 4J3, *Tel* (905) 624-2337	153,413,052	835	300	3089
Portefeuille Soucy Inc (*Suby of* **SOUCY HOLDING INC**) 5450 Rue Saint-Roch S, Drummondville, QC J2B 6V4, *Tel* (819) 474-6666	153,392,400	836	0	3795
Services Financiers NCO, Inc (*Suby of* **EGS SHELL COMPANY, INC.**) 75 Rue De Port-Royal E Bureau 240, Montreal, QC H3L 3T1, *Tel* (514) 385-4444	153,217,470	837	1,000	7322
Securite Nationale Compagnie d'Assurance (*Suby of* **TORONTO-DOMINION BANK, THE**) 50 Boul Cremazie O Bureau 1200, Montreal, QC H2P 1B6, *Tel* (514) 382-6060	153,144,509	838	1,500	6411
CAPITAL CARE GROUP INC 9925 109 St Nw Suite 500, Edmonton, AB T5K 2J8, *Tel* (780) 448-2400	152,939,997	839	0	8051
Leger Marketing Inc (*Suby of* **LEGER MARKETING INC**) 507 Place D'Armes Bureau 700, Montreal, QC H2Y 2W8, *Tel* (514) 845-5660	152,540,640	840	425	8732

Transport Thibodeau Saguelac Marcan Inc (*Suby of* **GROUPE THIBODEAU INC**)

COMPANY	SALES ($)	RANK	EMPLOYEES HERE	PRIMARY SIC CODE
128 2e Av, Portneuf, QC G0A 2Y0, *Tel*	152,344,320	841	750	4213
TransGlobe Property Management Services Ltd (*Suby of* **TRANSGLOBE PROPERTY MANAGEMENT SERVICES LTD**)				
5935 Airport Rd Suite 600, Mississauga, ON L4V 1W5, *Tel*	152,148,000	842	250	6531
CONTITECH CANADA, INC				
237 Brunel Rd, Mississauga, ON L4Z 1X3, *Tel* (905) 366-2010	152,123,060	843	30	3069
AIRPORT TERMINAL SERVICES CANADIAN COMPANY				
8075 22 St Ne, Calgary, AB T2E 7Z6, *Tel* (403) 291-0965	151,977,138	844	25	4581
Alliance Corporation (*Suby of* **ALLIANCE HOLDCO INC**)				
2395 Meadowpine Blvd, Mississauga, ON L5N 7W6, *Tel* (905) 821-4797	151,964,200	845	100	5065
ASSANTE CAPITAL MANAGEMENT LTD				
2 Queen St E Suite 1900, Toronto, ON M5C 3G7, *Tel* (416) 348-9994	151,903,435	846	2	6211
WIPRO SOLUTIONS CANADA LIMITED				
10040 104 St Nw Suite 100, Edmonton, AB T5J 0Z2, *Tel* (780) 420-7875	151,680,550	847	0	8742
FIDUCIE DESJARDINS INC				
1 Complexe Desjardins Tour S, Montreal, QC H5B 1E4, *Tel* (514) 286-9441	151,174,570	848	700	6733
928338 ONTARIO INC				
300 Supertest Rd, North York, ON M3J 2M2, *Tel*	150,920,960	849	1	5621
▲ **Starbucks Coffee Canada, Inc** (*Suby of* **STARBUCKS CORPORATION**)				
5140 Yonge St Suite 1205, North York, ON M2N 6L7, *Tel* (416) 228-7300	150,809,767	850	100	5812
CAM CLARK FORD SALES LTD				
925 Veterans Blvd Nw Bay 1, Airdrie, AB T4A 2G6, *Tel* (403) 948-6660	150,720,000	851	300	5511
Kluskus Holdings Ltd (*Suby of* **KLUSKUS HOLDINGS LTD**)				
9011 50 St Nw, Edmonton, AB T6B 2Y2, *Tel* (780) 468-4300	150,653,250	852	3	6712
▲ **Goodrich Aerospace Canada Ltd** (*Suby of* **UNITED TECHNOLOGIES CORPORATION**)				
1400 South Service Rd W, Oakville, ON L6L 5Y7, *Tel* (905) 827-7777	150,590,885	853	580	3728
TRANSPORT QUIK X INC				
6767 Davand Dr, Mississauga, ON L5T 2T2, *Tel* (905) 670-5770	150,554,424	854	200	4213
MAMMOET CANADA HOLDINGS INC				
7504 Mclean Rd E, Guelph, ON N1H 6H9, *Tel* (519) 740-0550	149,948,048	855	70	6712
132179 Canada Inc (*Suby of* **132179 CANADA INC**)				
11500 Boul Armand-Bombardier, Montreal, QC H1E 2W9, *Tel*	149,841,650	856	1	6712
TRAVAILLEURS CANADIEN DE L'AUTOMOBILE SECTION LOCALE 62				
9045 Ch Cote-De-Liesse Bureau 203, Dorval, QC H9P 2M9, *Tel* (514) 636-8080	148,614,240	857	1,044	8631
BIRD CONSTRUCTION COMPANY LIMITED				
5700 Explorer Dr Suite 400, Mississauga, ON L4W 0C6, *Tel* (905) 602-4122	148,475,025	858	50	1542
3858065 Canada Inc (*Suby of* **3858065 CANADA INC**)				
2525 Rue Canadien, Drummondville, QC J2C 7W2, *Tel*	148,408,960	859	5	6712
LAKOTA DRILLING INC				
1704 5 St, Nisku, AB T9E 8P8, *Tel* (780) 955-7535	148,408,960	860	600	6712
COGENT POWER INC				
845 Laurentian Dr, Burlington, ON L7N 3W7, *Tel* (905) 637-3033	148,256,142	861	310	4911
▲ **Neenah Paper Company of Canada** (*Suby of* **NEENAH PAPER, INC.**)				
260 Abercrombie Rd, New Glasgow, NS B2H 1K8, *Tel* (902) 752-8461	148,221,600	862	0	2621
COMPAGNIE D'ASSURANCE SONNET				
5 Place Ville-Marie Bureau 1400, Montreal, QC H3B 0A8, *Tel* (514) 875-5790	148,110,221	863	210	6331
ARSLANIAN CUTTING WORKS NWT LTD				
106 Archibald St, Yellowknife, NT X1A 2P4, *Tel* (867) 873-0138	148,025,280	864	48	3915
Canacol Energy Ltd (*Suby of* **CANACOL ENERGY LTD**)				
525 8 Ave Sw Suite 4500, Calgary, AB T2P 1G1, *Tel* (403) 561-1648	147,985,000	865	0	1311
MARCOUX BROS. TRUCKING LTD				
2815 Lorne Ave, Saskatoon, SK S7J 0S5, *Tel* (306) 955-4221	147,977,600	866	1	4783
PERSONNEL UNIQUE CANADA INC				
455 Boul Fenelon Bureau 210, Dorval, QC H9S 5T8, *Tel* (514) 633-6220	147,609,750	867	750	8741
▲ **ANIXTER CANADA INC**				
200 Foster Cres, Mississauga, ON L5R 3Y5, *Tel* (905) 568-8999	147,599,496	868	450	5063
VITA MILLS INC				
7453 Progress Way, Delta, BC V4G 1E7, *Tel*	147,436,320	869	0	2043
AMERICAN & EFIRD CANADA INCORPOREE				
8301 Boul Ray-Lawson, Anjou, QC H1J 1X9, *Tel* (514) 352-4800	147,262,670	870	0	2284
BELRON CANADA INCORPOREE				
8288 Boul Pie-Ix, Montreal, QC H1Z 3T6, *Tel* (514) 593-8000	147,262,670	871	250	7536
SASKATCHEWAN HOUSING CORPORATION				
1920 Broad St Suite 900, Regina, SK S4P 3V6, *Tel* (306) 787-4177	147,133,142	872	100	6531
FEDERATED INSURANCE COMPANY OF CANADA				
255 Commerce Drive, Winnipeg, MB R3C 3C9, *Tel* (204) 786-6431	146,916,170	873	130	6331
Groupe Thibodeau Inc (*Suby of* **GROUPE THIBODEAU INC**)				
128 2e Av, Portneuf, QC G0A 2Y0, *Tel*	146,901,760	874	1	4213
▲ **2011767 Ontario Inc** (*Suby of* **ANSYS, INC.**)				
554 Parkside Dr, Waterloo, ON N2L 5Z4, *Tel* (519) 886-8000	146,628,900	875	3	6712
CORNER BROOK PULP AND PAPER LIMITED				
1 Mills Rd, Corner Brook, NL A2H 6B9, *Tel* (709) 637-3104	146,532,160	876	264	2621
Dillon Projects Limited (*Suby of* **DILLON CONSULTING INC**)				
235 Yorkland Blvd Suite 800, North York, ON M2J 4Y8, *Tel* (416) 229-4646	146,198,400	877	0	8741

COMPANY	SALES ($)	RANK	EMPLOYEES HERE	PRIMARY SIC CODE
▲ 3M Canada Company (*Suby of* **3M COMPANY**) 300 Tartan Dr, London, ON N5V 4M9, *Tel* (519) 451-2500	145,921,400	878	1,200	2891
▲ INVESCO CANADA LTD 5140 Yonge St Suite 800, North York, ON M2N 6X7, *Tel* (800) 874-6275	145,921,400	879	800	6211
▲ Jacobs Industrial Services (*Suby of* **JACOBS ENGINEERING GROUP INC.**) 1104 70 Ave Nw, Edmonton, AB T6P 1P5, *Tel* (780) 468-2533	145,921,400	880	25	7349
▲ Jacobs Industrial Services Ltd (*Suby of* **JACOBS ENGINEERING GROUP INC.**) 205 Quarry Park Blvd Se Suite 200, Calgary, AB T2C 3E7, *Tel* (403) 258-6399	145,921,400	881	25	7349
PARMALAT CANADA INC 405 The West Mall 10th Fl, Etobicoke, ON M9C 5J1, *Tel* (416) 626-1973	145,921,400	882	100	2023
RBC Global Asset Management (U.S.) Inc. (*Suby of* **ROYAL BANK OF CANADA**) 155 Wellington St W 22 Flr, Toronto, ON M5V 3K7, *Tel* (416) 974-5008	145,921,400	883	1,000	6282
CFS International Inc (*Suby of* **CFS INTERNATIONAL INC**) 1951 Leslie St, North York, ON M3B 2M3, *Tel* (416) 385-2882	145,495,598	884	10	2321
CHEMTRADE LOGISTICS (US) INC 155 Gordon Baker Rd Suite 300, North York, ON M2H 3N5, *Tel* (416) 496-5856	145,374,960	885	450	5169
▲ Laboratoires Abbott Limitee (*Suby of* **ABBOTT LABORATORIES**) 8625 Rte Transcanadienne, Saint-Laurent, QC H4S 1Z6, *Tel* (514) 832-7000	145,337,714	886	300	2834
PHARMASCIENCE INC 6111 Av Royalmount Bureau 100, Montreal, QC H4P 2T4, *Tel* (514) 340-1114	145,337,714	887	650	2834
▲ Electronic Arts (Canada) Inc (*Suby of* **ELECTRONIC ARTS INC.**) 4330 Sanderson Way, Burnaby, BC V5G 4X1, *Tel* (604) 456-3600	144,681,068	888	20	7371
Cie Materiaux de Construction BP Canada, La (*Suby of* **3077578 NOVA SCOTIA CORP**) 9510 Rue Saint-Patrick, Lasalle, QC H8R 1R9, *Tel* (514) 364-0161	144,462,186	889	300	2493
Ernst & Young LLP (*Suby of* **ERNST & YOUNG LLP**) 222 Bay St 21 Fl, Toronto, ON M5K 1J7, *Tel* (416) 864-1234	144,462,186	890	3,000	8721
JOHN BUHLER INC 1260 Clarence Ave, Winnipeg, MB R3T 1T2, *Tel* (204) 661-8711	143,537,791	891	300	3523
Freson Market Ltd (*Suby of* **ALTAMART INVESTMENTS (1993) LTD**) 4401 48 St Unit 130, Stony Plain, AB T7Z 1N3, *Tel* (780) 968-6924	143,294,815	892	8	5411
Johnvince Foods (*Suby of* **JOHNVINCE FOODS**) 555 Steeprock Dr, North York, ON M3J 2Z6, *Tel* (416) 636-6146	143,148,893	893	400	5145
GT CANADA MEDICAL PROPERTIES REAL ESTATE INVESTMENT TRUST 161 Bay St, Toronto, ON M5J 2S1, *Tel* (416) 572-2170	143,057,232	894	3	6799
▲ Procor Limited (*Suby of* **BERKSHIRE HATHAWAY INC.**) 2001 Speers Rd, Oakville, ON L6L 2X9, *Tel* (905) 827-4111	142,857,051	895	0	4741
Acosta Canada Corporation (*Suby of* **ACOSTA INC.**) 250 Rowntree Dairy Rd, Woodbridge, ON L4L 9J7, *Tel* (905) 264-0466	142,844,790	896	150	5141
▲ Westrock Company of Canada Inc (*Suby of* **WESTROCK COMPANY**) 15400 Rue Sherbrooke E Bureau A-15, Pointe-Aux-Trembles, QC H1A 3S2, *Tel* (514) 642-9251	142,671,540	897	300	2657
FRANCHISE COMPANY INC, THE 5397 Eglinton Ave W Suite 108, Etobicoke, ON M9C 5K6, *Tel* (416) 620-4700	142,668,611	898	9	6794
▲ GE Water & Process Technologies Canada (*Suby of* **GENERAL ELECTRIC COMPANY**) 3239 Dundas St W, Oakville, ON L6M 4B2, *Tel* (905) 465-3030	142,584,915	899	1	5169
LUXOTTICA CANADA INC 2000 Argentia Rd Suite 2, Mississauga, ON L5N 1V8, *Tel* (905) 858-0008	142,273,365	900	15	5995
Superclub Videotron Ltee, Le (*Suby of* **PLACEMENTS PELADEAU INC, LES**) 4545 Rue Frontenac Bureau 101, Montreal, QC H2H 2R7, *Tel* (514) 372-5200	141,827,100	901	60	6794
Exova Canada Inc (*Suby of* **EXOVA, INC.**) 2395 Speakman Dr Suite 583, Mississauga, ON L5K 1B3, *Tel* (905) 822-4111	141,543,758	902	600	8734
▲ Rexall Pharmacy Group Ltd (*Suby of* **MCKESSON CORPORATION**) 5965 Coopers Ave, Mississauga, ON L4Z 1R9, *Tel* (905) 501-7800	141,543,758	903	20	5912
Commission de la Construction du Quebec (*Suby of* **COMMISSION DE LA CONSTRUCTION DU QUEBEC**) 3530 Rue Jean-Talon O, Montreal, QC H3R 2G3, *Tel* (514) 341-7740	141,475,840	904	400	8611
ELLIOTT & PAGE LIMITED 200 Bloor St E Suite 1, Toronto, ON M4W 1E5, *Tel* (416) 581-8300	141,475,840	905	345	6722
UNIQUE ASSURANCES GENERALES INC, L' 625 Rue Saint Amable, Quebec, QC G1K 0E1, *Tel* (418) 683-2711	141,285,538	906	105	6331
▲ GENERAL MOTORS FINANCIAL OF CANADA, LTD. 2001 Sheppard Ave E Suite 600, Toronto, ON M2J 4Z8, *Tel* (416) 753-4000	141,025,663	907	200	6159
2278988 Ontario Inc (*Suby of* **GROUPE COLABOR INC**) 1620 Boul De Montarville, Boucherville, QC J4B 8P4, *Tel* (450) 449-4911	140,761,440	908	400	5141
School District No. 44 (North Vancouver) (*Suby of* **SCHOOL DISTRICT NO. 44 (NORTH VANCOUVER)**) 2121 Lonsdale Ave, North Vancouver, BC V7M 2K6, *Tel* (604) 903-3444	140,539,433	909	800	8211
KILDAIR SERVICE ULC 1000 Montee Des Pionniers Bureau 110, Terrebonne, QC J6V 1S8, *Tel* (450) 756-8091	140,532,550	910	25	5172
COMPAGNIE MEXX CANADA 905 Rue Hodge, Saint-Laurent, QC H4N 2B3, *Tel* (514) 383-5555	140,312,788	911	750	5137
Steeplejack Services (Scaffolding) Ltd (*Suby of* **BROCK CANADA INC**) 8925 62 Ave Nw, Edmonton, AB T6E 5L2, *Tel* (780) 465-9016	140,178,720	912	5	1799
COMBINED INSURANCE CO OF AMERICA 733 Boul Frontenac O Bureau 200, Thetford Mines, QC G6G 7X9, *Tel* (450) 645-9030	140,030,089	913	0	6321
HOLT, RENFREW & CIE, LIMITEE 60 Bloor St W Suite 1100, Toronto, ON M4W 3B8, *Tel* (416) 922-2333	140,011,583	914	200	5621

COMPANY	SALES ($)	RANK	EMPLOYEES HERE	PRIMARY SIC CODE
NORTHWESTEL INC 301 Lambert St Suite 2727, Whitehorse, YT Y1A 1Z5, *Tel* (867) 668-5300	139,935,857	915	275	4899
CANEXUS CHEMICALS CANADA LTD 144 4 Ave Sw Unit 2100, Calgary, AB T2P 3N4, *Tel* (403) 571-7300	139,558,925	916	0	5169
Commission Scolaire des Chenes (*Suby of* **COMMISSION SCOLAIRE DES CHENES**) 457 Rue Des Ecoles Bureau 846, Drummondville, QC J2B 1J3, *Tel* (819) 478-6700	139,392,300	917	100	8211
CENTRE DE SANTE ET DE SERVICES SOCIAUX DU COEUR-DE-L'ILE 1385 Rue Jean-Talon E, Montreal, QC H2E 1S6, *Tel* (514) 495-6767	139,136,055	918	1,300	8062
▲ **SILGAN PLASTICS CANADA INC** 1575 Drew Rd, Mississauga, ON L5S 1S5, *Tel* (905) 677-2324	138,773,410	919	120	3089
TerraVest Capital Inc (*Suby of* **TERRAVEST CAPITAL INC**) 4901 Bruce Rd, Vegreville, AB T9C 1C3, *Tel* (403) 364-0064	138,532,514	920	0	3714
▲ Applied Industrial Technologies, LP (*Suby of* **APPLIED INDUSTRIAL TECHNOLOGIES, INC.**) 143 Wheeler St, Saskatoon, SK S7P 0A4, *Tel* (306) 931-0888	138,167,035	921	25	5085
HAGEMEYER CANADA INC 4810 92 Ave Nw, Edmonton, AB T6B 2X4, *Tel* (780) 468-3366	138,167,035	922	150	5085
Sir Wilfrid Laurier School Board (*Suby of* **SIR WILFRID LAURIER SCHOOL BOARD**) 235 Montee Lesage Bureau 1, Rosemere, QC J7A 4Y6, *Tel* (450) 621-5600	138,059,520	923	75	8211
TRANSPORT GUILBAULT CANADA INC 435 Rue Faraday, Quebec, QC G1N 4G6, *Tel* (514) 521-9023	137,768,500	924	200	4213
SASKATCHEWAN GAMING CORPORATION 1880 Saskatchewan Dr, Regina, SK S4P 0B2, *Tel* (306) 565-3000	137,588,354	925	600	7999
Graybar Canada Limited (*Suby of* **GRAYBAR ELECTRIC COMPANY, INC.**) 3600 Joseph Howe Dr, Halifax, NS B3L 4H7, *Tel* (902) 457-8787	137,127,533	926	80	5063
Marine Harvest North America Inc (*Suby of* **MARINE HARVEST NORTH AMERICA INC**) 1334 Island Hwy Suite 124, Campbell River, BC V9W 8C9, *Tel* (250) 850-3276	136,957,500	927	3	6712
NURUN INC 740 Rue Notre-Dame O Bureau 600, Montreal, QC H3C 3X6, *Tel* (514) 392-1900	136,867,658	928	120	7371
COGECO CONNEXION INC 5 Place Ville-Marie Bureau 1700, Montreal, QC H3B 0B3, *Tel* (514) 764-4700	136,436,509	929	0	4841
CN WORLDWIDE AMERIQUE DU NORD (CANADA) INC 935 Rue De La Gauchetiere O, Montreal, QC H3B 2M9, *Tel* (514) 399-5430	136,347,907	930	100	4011
Opinion Search Inc (*Suby of* **DECIMA INC**) 160 Elgin St Suite 1800, Ottawa, ON K2P 2P7, *Tel* (613) 230-9109	136,250,880	931	400	8732
ZCL Composites Inc (*Suby of* **ZCL COMPOSITES INC**) 1420 Parsons Rd Sw, Edmonton, AB T6X 1M5, *Tel* (780) 466-6648	136,185,656	932	80	3299
▲ RPM Canada Company (*Suby of* **RPM INTERNATIONAL INC.**) 95 Sunray St, Whitby, ON L1N 9C9, *Tel* (905) 430-3333	136,001,407	933	450	2851
LAUZON - PLANCHERS DE BOIS EXCLUSIFS INC 2101 Cote Des Cascades, Papineauville, QC J0V 1R0, *Tel* (819) 427-5144	135,789,609	934	250	5031
Filtex Inc (*Suby of* **FILTEX INC**) 5060 Rue Francois-Cusson, Lachine, QC H8T 1B3, *Tel*	135,695,376	935	9	2284
TSG ENERGY SERVICES LTD 311 253 Gregoire Dr, Fort Mcmurray, AB T9H 4G7, *Tel* (780) 799-2772	135,695,376	936	600	1623
GESTION JEAN & GUY HURTEAU INC 21 Rue Paul-Gauguin, Candiac, QC J5R 3X8, *Tel* (450) 638-2212	135,648,000	937	550	6712
CITIZENS BANK OF CANADA 815 Hastings St W Suite 401, Vancouver, BC V6C 1B4, *Tel* (604) 682-7171	135,506,910	938	350	6021
Viridian Inc (*Suby of* **AGRIUM CANADA PARTNERSHIP**) 13131 Lake Fraser Dr Se, Calgary, AB T2J 7E8, *Tel* (403) 225-7000	135,488,020	939	200	2873
Centre Hospitalier Et Centre De Readaptation Antoine-Labelle (*Suby of* **CENTRE HOSPITALIER ET CENTRE DE READAPTATION ANTOINE-LABELLE**) 757 Rue De La Madone, Mont-Laurier, QC J9L 1T3, *Tel* (819) 623-1234	135,435,750	940	100	8062
Commission Scolaire de la Jonquiere (*Suby of* **COMMISSION SCOLAIRE DE LA JONQUIERE**) 3644 Rue Saint-Jules, Jonquiere, QC G7X 2K9, *Tel* (418) 542-7551	134,871,840	941	0	8211
Centre De Sante Et Services Sociaux Du Pontiac (*Suby of* **CENTRE DE SANTE ET SERVICES SOCIAUX DU PONTIAC**) 200 Rue Argue, Shawville, QC J0X 2Y0, *Tel* (819) 647-2211	134,844,160	942	35	8099
Air Inuit Ltee (*Suby of* **SOCIETE MAKIVIK**) 6005 Boul De La Cote-Vertu, Saint-Laurent, QC H4S 0B1, *Tel* (514) 905-9445	134,658,814	943	600	4512
▲ Societe Conseil Groupe LGS (*Suby of* **INTERNATIONAL BUSINESS MACHINES CORPORATION**) 1360 Boul Rene-Levesque O Bureau 400, Montreal, QC H3G 2W6, *Tel* (514) 964-0939	134,615,405	944	300	8741
ANNAPOLIS VALLEY REGIONAL SCHOOL BOARD 121 Orchard St Rr 3, Berwick, NS B0P 1E0, *Tel* (902) 538-4600	134,361,474	945	60	8211
▲ **HAIN-CELESTIAL CANADA, ULC** 180 Attwell Dr Suite 410, Etobicoke, ON M9W 6A9, *Tel* (416) 849-6210	134,355,530	946	50	2075
College Of New Caledonia, The (*Suby of* **COLLEGE OF NEW CALEDONIA, THE**) 3330 22nd Ave, Prince George, BC V2N 1P8, *Tel* (250) 562-2131	134,281,883	947	800	8221
▲ **ELECTRO-MOTIVE DIESEL INC** 75 Diesel Dr, Concord, ON L4K 1B9, *Tel* (905) 761-4964	134,281,883	948	0	3743
EAST CENTRAL DISTRICT HEALTH BOARD Po Box 5027 Stn Main, Yorkton, SK S3N 3Z4, *Tel* (306) 786-0113	134,140,800	949	1,400	8062
CADILLAC FAIRVIEW CORPORATION LIMITED, THE 20 Queen St W Suite 500, Toronto, ON M5H 3R4, *Tel* (416) 598-8200	134,101,767	950	200	6512

COMPANY	SALES ($)	RANK	EMPLOYEES HERE	PRIMARY SIC CODE
PENN WEST PETROLEUM 111 5 Ave Sw Suite 800, Calgary, AB T2P 3Y6, *Tel* (403) 777-2500	133,955,845	951	200	1311
HONDA CANADA FINANCE INC 180 Honda Blvd Suite 200, Markham, ON L6C 0H9, *Tel* (905) 888-4188	133,664,002	952	132	6141
ACADIA STUDENTS' UNION INC 30 Highland Ave, Wolfville, NS B4P 2R5, *Tel* (902) 585-2110	133,445,120	953	80	6321
Coffrages C.C.C. Ltee, Les (*Suby of* **COFFRAGES C.C.C. LTEE, LES**) 435 Rue De Port-Royal O, Montreal, QC H3L 2C3, *Tel* (514) 382-2151	133,399,440	954	0	3271
CANCERCARE MANITOBA 675 Mcdermot Ave Suite 1160, Winnipeg, MB R3E 0V9, *Tel* (204) 787-4143	133,315,996	955	647	8069
SERVICES KAMTECH INC 5055 Rue Levy, Saint-Laurent, QC H4R 2N9, *Tel* (418) 808-4276	133,301,280	956	30	1541
GESTION CANADADIRECT INC 743 Av Renaud, Dorval, QC H9P 2N1, *Tel* (514) 422-8557	133,104,960	957	700	8732
Service a la Clientele Alorica Ltee (*Suby of* **ALORICA INC.**) 75 Rue De Port-Royal E Bureau 240, Montreal, QC H3L 3T1, *Tel* (514) 385-4444	132,715,513	958	1,400	4813
▲ **IRON MOUNTAIN CANADA OPERATIONS ULC** 195 Summerlea Rd, Brampton, ON L6T 4P6, *Tel* (905) 792-7099	132,679,923	959	15	4226
CANADIAN COAST GUARD AUXILIARY (CENTRAL AND ARCTIC) INC 577 Kingston Rd Suite 206, Toronto, ON M4E 1R3, *Tel* (416) 463-7283	132,516,000	960	811	8699
FLOWERS CANADA INC 99 Fifth Ave Suite 305, Ottawa, ON K1S 5K4, *Tel* (800) 447-5147	132,417,840	961	958	8611
▲ Moores The Suit People Inc (*Suby of* **TAILORED BRANDS, INC.**) 129 Carlingview Dr, Etobicoke, ON M9W 5E7, *Tel* (416) 675-1900	132,277,749	962	80	5611
CLUB SOCIAL DES EMPLOYES-ES DU CENTRE DE SANTE ET DE SERVICES SOCIAUX DE CHARLEVOIX, LE 74 Rue Ambroise-Fafard, Baie-Saint-Paul, QC G3Z 2J6, *Tel* (418) 435-5150	132,189,903	963	0	8062
CHC HELICOPTERS CANADA INC 4740 Agar Dr, Richmond, BC V7B 1A3, *Tel* (604) 276-7500	131,985,906	964	200	4522
▲ Cardinal Health Canada Inc (*Suby of* **CARDINAL HEALTH, INC.**) 1000 Tesma Way, Concord, ON L4K 5R8, *Tel* (905) 417-2900	131,926,060	965	50	5047
TORONTO COMMUNITY HOUSING CORPORATION 931 Yonge St Suite 400, Toronto, ON M4W 2H2, *Tel* (416) 981-5500	131,912,946	966	50	6531
Brock Canada Inc (*Suby of* **BROCK CANADA INC**) 8925 62 Ave Nw, Edmonton, AB T6E 5L2, *Tel* (780) 465-9016	131,839,985	967	40	1389
Strike Group Inc (*Suby of* **STRIKE GROUP INC**) 505 3 St Sw Suite 1300, Calgary, AB T2P 3E6, *Tel* (403) 232-8448	131,839,985	968	10	1389
MARINE ATLANTIC INC 10 Fort William Pl Suite 302, St. John'S, NL A1C 1K4, *Tel* (709) 772-8957	131,670,152	969	7	4482
Bulova Developments Inc (*Suby of* **BULOVA DEVELOPMENTS INC**) 128 2 Ave Se Suite 200, Calgary, AB T2G 5J5, *Tel* (403) 699-8830	131,528,320	970	16	6553
Former Restoration L.P. (*Suby of* **INTERSTATE RESTORATION LLC**) 60 Admiral Blvd, Mississauga, ON L5T 2W1, *Tel* (905) 696-2900	131,329,260	971	25	1771
INTRIA ITEMS INC 5705 Cancross Ct, Mississauga, ON L5R 3E9, *Tel* (905) 755-2400	131,329,260	972	100	7374
WINDSOR CASINO LIMITED 377 Riverside Dr E, Windsor, ON N9A 7H7, *Tel* (519) 258-7878	131,329,260	973	3,000	7011
▲ United Technologies Canada Ltd (*Suby of* **UNITED TECHNOLOGIES CORPORATION**) 1 Brunswick Pl Suite 1500, Saint John, NB E2K 1B5, *Tel* (506) 633-2715	131,237,027	974	1	6712
ONTARIO CLEAN WATER AGENCY 1 Yonge St Suite 1700, Toronto, ON M5E 1E5, *Tel* (416) 314-5600	131,200,052	975	100	4941
9269-2631 QUEBEC INC 191 Rue Delage, Riviere-Du-Loup, QC G5R 6E2, *Tel* (418) 862-6941	130,803,901	976	0	2621
Hood Packaging Corporation (*Suby of* **HOOD PACKAGING CORPORATION**) 2380 Mcdowell Rd, Burlington, ON L7R 4A1, *Tel* (905) 637-5611	130,803,901	977	25	2674
Groupe Colabor Inc (*Suby of* **GROUPE COLABOR INC**) 1620 Boul De Montarville, Boucherville, QC J4B 8P4, *Tel* (450) 449-4911	130,745,574	978	10	5141
SPOOKY LURKER NETWORKS Gd, Blumenort, MB R0A 0C0, *Tel* (204) 381-1230	130,723,520	979	546	4813
▲ **EECOL ELECTRIC ULC** 63 Sunpark Dr Se, Calgary, AB T2X 3V4, *Tel* (403) 253-1952	130,526,692	980	25	5063
GESTIONS MILLER CARMICHAEL INC 3822 Av De Courtrai, Montreal, QC H3S 1C1, *Tel* (514) 735-4361	130,062,000	981	540	6712
NEXANS CANADA INC 140 Allstate Pky Suite 300, Markham, ON L3R 0Z7, *Tel* (905) 944-4300	129,937,650	982	70	3312
ROBERT BOSCH INC 6955 Creditview Rd, Mississauga, ON L5N 1R1, *Tel* (905) 826-6060	129,937,650	983	0	5085
TROTTER AND MORTON BUILDING TECHNOLOGIES INC 5711 1 St Se, Calgary, AB T2H 1H9, *Tel* (403) 255-7535	129,937,650	984	345	1711
BENTLEYS OF LONDON SLACKS LTD 1309 Mountain Ave, Winnipeg, MB R2X 2Y1, *Tel* (204) 786-6081	129,247,300	985	1,500	2339
KILLAM PROPERTIES INC 3700 Kempt Rd Suite 100, Halifax, NS B3K 4X8, *Tel* (902) 453-9000	129,233,390	986	5	6513
GATES CANADA INC 225 Henry St Suite 8, Brantford, ON N3S 7R4, *Tel* (519) 759-4141	129,140,439	987	163	5085

COMPANY	SALES ($)	RANK	EMPLOYEES HERE	PRIMARY SIC CODE
KINDERSLEY TRANSPORT LTD 2411 Wentz Ave, Saskatoon, SK S7K 3V6, *Tel* (306) 934-1911	129,099,073	988	270	4213
Catholic District School Board of Eastern Ontario (*Suby of* **CATHOLIC DISTRICT SCHOOL BOARD OF EASTERN ONTARIO**) 2755 Highway 43, Kemptville, ON K0G 1J0, *Tel* (613) 258-7757	128,815,360	989	30	8211
Elk Island Public Schools Regional Division No. 14 (*Suby of* **ELK ISLAND PUBLIC SCHOOLS REGIONAL DIVISION NO. 14**) 683 Wye Rd, Sherwood Park, AB T8B 1N2, *Tel* (780) 464-3477	128,815,360	990	160	8211
PETON DISTRIBUTORS INC 225 Royal Crest Crt, Markham, ON L3R 9X6, *Tel* (905) 946-1200	128,722,141	991	0	5149
FACTORY MUTUAL INSURANCE CO 165 Commerce Valley Dr W Suite 500, Thornhill, ON L3T 7V8, *Tel* (905) 763-5555	128,589,600	992	0	6331
▲ **RGIS CANADA ULC** 2560 Matheson Blvd E Suite 224, Mississauga, ON L4W 4Y9, *Tel* (905) 206-1107	128,491,440	993	100	7389
CORUS MEDIA HOLDINGS INC 121 Bloor St E Suite 1500, Toronto, ON M4W 3M5, *Tel* (416) 967-1174	128,410,832	994	250	4833
BROOKFIELD FOODS LIMITED 4135 Scotsburn Rd, Scotsburn, NS B0K 1R0, *Tel*	128,156,744	995	6	5142
PAYLESS CORP 5965 Coopers Ave, Mississauga, ON L4Z 1R9, *Tel* (905) 502-5965	127,968,278	996	6	5912
Hogg Robinson Canada Inc (*Suby of* **HOGG ROBINSON GROUP PLC**) 370 King St W Suite 700, Toronto, ON M5V 1J9, *Tel* (416) 593-8866	127,779,812	997	70	8742
1732187 ONTARIO INC 1905 Blackacre Dr Rr 1, Oldcastle, ON N0R 1L0, *Tel* (519) 737-9948	127,685,580	998	1,200	3544
IKO INDUSTRIES LTD 80 Stafford Dr, Brampton, ON L6W 1L4, *Tel* (905) 457-2880	127,681,225	999	200	2952
Conseil de Vie Etudiante de l'Ecole Nationale Aerotechnique College Edouard-Montpetit Inc (*Suby of* **CONSEIL DE VIE ETUDIANTE DE L'ECOLE NATIONALE AEROTECHNIQUE COLLEGE EDOUARD-MONTPETIT INC**) 945 Ch De Chambly, Longueuil, QC J4H 3M6, *Tel* (450) 679-2631	127,591,347	1000	0	8221

COMPANY	EMPLOYEES HERE	RANK	SALES ($)	PRIMARY SIC CODE
QUINCAILLERIE RICHELIEU LTEE 800 Rue Beriault, Longueuil, QC J4G 1R8, *Tel* (450) 674-0888	60,514	1	0	5072
KOODO MOBILE-SCARBOROUGH 200 Consilium Pl Suite 1600, Scarborough, ON M1H 3J3, *Tel* (647) 837-6252	40,000	2	10,405,523,600	4899
Toronto-Dominion Bank, The (*Suby of* **TORONTO-DOMINION BANK, THE**) 66 Wellington St W, Toronto, ON M5K 1A2, *Tel* (416) 944-5746	40,000	3	0	6021
COMPAGNIE DES CHEMINS DE FER NATIONAUX DU CANADA 277 Front St W, Toronto, ON M5A 1E1, *Tel* (888) 888-5909	21,967	4	0	4111
▲ John Deere Landscapes Ltd (*Suby of* **SITEONE LANDSCAPE SUPPLY, INC.**) 9415 48 St Se, Calgary, AB T2C 2R1, *Tel* (403) 236-0102	20,000	5	0	1629
Centre Jeunesse de la Mauricie et du Centre-du-Quebec, Le (*Suby of* **CENTRE JEUNESSE DE LA MAURICIE ET DU CENTRE-DU-QUEBEC, LE**) 1455 Boul Du Carmel, Trois-Rivieres, QC G8Z 3R7, *Tel* (819) 378-5590	18,000	6	0	8322
Penske Truck Leasing Canada Inc (*Suby of* **PENSKE CORPORATION**) 2500 Boul Pitfield, Saint-Laurent, QC H4S 1Z7, *Tel* (514) 333-4080	15,000	7	0	7513
FRASER HEALTH AUTHORITY 13450 102 Ave Suite 400, Surrey, BC V3T 0H1, *Tel* (604) 587-4600	12,000	8	2,365,677,737	8062
OTTAWA HOSPITAL, THE 1053 Carling Ave Suite 119, Ottawa, ON K1Y 4E9, *Tel* (613) 722-7000	12,000	9	0	8062
CENTRE HOSPITALIER UNIVERSITAIRE DE QUEBEC 10 Rue De L'Espinay Bureau 520, Quebec, QC G1L 3L5, *Tel* (418) 525-4444	8,964	10	0	8062
AMBATOVY JOINT VENTURE 2200 Lake Shore Blvd W, Etobicoke, ON M8V 1A4, *Tel* (416) 924-4551	8,000	11	1,277,421,192	1061
▲ G&K Services Canada Inc (*Suby of* **CINTAS CORPORATION**) 2665 Av Dalton Bureau 10, Quebec, QC G1P 3S8, *Tel* (418) 658-0044	8,000	12	0	7218
Banque Toronto-Dominion, La (*Suby of* **TORONTO-DOMINION BANK, THE**) 55 King St W, Toronto, ON M5K 1A2, *Tel* (416) 982-2322	7,000	13	0	6021
CORREIA ENTERPRISES LTD 375 Nairn Ave, Winnipeg, MB R2L 0W8, *Tel* (204) 668-4420	7,000	14	281,344,000	7349
Sunnybrook Health Sciences Centre Foundation (*Suby of* **SUNNYBROOK HEALTH SCIENCES CENTRE FOUNDATION**) 2075 Bayview Ave Suite 747, Toronto, ON M4N 3M5, *Tel* (416) 480-5100	7,000	15	803,787,987	8011
ALBERTA HEALTH SERVICES 1403 29 St Nw Suite 1403, Calgary, AB T2N 2T9, *Tel* (403) 670-1110	6,000	16	0	8011
▲ Federal Express Canada Corporation (*Suby of* **FEDEX CORPORATION**) 5985 Explorer Dr Suite 313, Mississauga, ON L4W 5K6, *Tel* (800) 463-3339	6,000	17	553,260,988	4212
TRILOGY RETAIL ENTERPRISES L.P 161 Bay St Suite 4900, Toronto, ON M5J 2S1, *Tel* (416) 943-4110	6,000	18	1,540,112,450	6712
SHAW CABLESYSTEMS G.P. 630 3 Ave Sw, Calgary, AB T2P 4L4, *Tel* (403) 750-4500	5,600	19	1,239,865,056	4841
BOMBARDIER INC 123 Garratt Blvd, North York, ON M3K 1Y5, *Tel* (416) 633-7310	5,000	20	0	3721
EASTERN REGIONAL INTEGRATED HEALTH AUTHORITY 154 Lemarchant Rd, St. John'S, NL A1C 5B8, *Tel* (709) 777-6300	5,000	21	0	8062
Pratt & Whitney Canada Corp (*Suby of* **PRATT AERO LIMITED PARTNERSHIP**) 1000 Boul Marie-Victorin, Longueuil, QC J4G 1A1, *Tel* (450) 677-9411	5,000	22	552,677,303	3519
Rogers Communications Inc (*Suby of* **ROGERS COMMUNICATIONS INC**) 333 Bloor St E 10 Fl, Toronto, ON M4W 1G9, *Tel* (416) 935-2303	5,000	23	0	4899
Toronto-Dominion Bank, The (*Suby of* **TORONTO-DOMINION BANK, THE**) 55 King St W, Toronto, ON M5K 1A2, *Tel* (416) 982-5722	5,000	24	27,356,640,075	6021
Toronto-Dominion Bank, The (*Suby of* **TORONTO-DOMINION BANK, THE**) 2885 Bayview Ave, North York, ON M2K 0A3, *Tel* (416) 733-1015	5,000	25	0	6021
UNIVERSITE DU QUEBEC 1200 Rue Berri, Montreal, QC H2L 4S6, *Tel* (514) 987-3000	5,000	26	0	8221
CANADIAN NATURAL RESOURCES LIMITED Hwy 63, Fort Mcmurray, AB T9H 5N4, *Tel* (780) 828-2500	4,500	27	0	1311
ONTARIO LOTTERY AND GAMING CORPORATION 6380 Fallsview Blvd, Niagara Falls, ON L2G 7X5, *Tel* (905) 358-7654	4,500	28	0	7999
VANCOUVER ISLAND HEALTH AUTHORITY 3045 Gibbins Rd, Duncan, BC V9L 1E5, *Tel* (250) 709-3000	4,500	29	0	8011
CALGARY BOARD OF EDUCATION 47 Fyffe Rd Se, Calgary, AB T2H 1B9, *Tel* (403) 777-6420	4,030	30	0	8211
3522997 CANADA INC 180 Montee De Liesse, Saint-Laurent, QC H4T 1N7, *Tel* (514) 341-6161	4,000	31	1,025,152,250	6712
APOTEX INC 200 Barmac Dr, North York, ON M9L 2Z7, *Tel* (800) 268-4623	4,000	32	0	2834
City of Ottawa (*Suby of* **CITY OF OTTAWA**) 1500 St. Laurent Blvd, Ottawa, ON K1G 0Z8, *Tel* (613) 741-6440	4,000	33	0	4111
COMPAGNIE DE TELEPHONE BELL DU CANADA OU BELL CANADA, LA 1 Carref Alexander-Graham-Bell, Verdun, QC H3E 3B3, *Tel*	4,000	34	0	4899
HALTON DISTRICT SCHOOL BOARD 1474 Wallace Rd, Oakville, ON L6L 2Y2, *Tel*	4,000	35	0	8211
Hamilton Health Sciences Corporation (*Suby of* **HAMILTON HEALTH SCIENCES CORPORATION**) 1200 Main St W, Hamilton, ON L8S 4J9, *Tel* (905) 521-2100	4,000	36	695,826,196	8062

COMPANY	EMPLOYEES HERE	RANK	SALES ($)	PRIMARY SIC CODE
UNIVERSITE LAVAL 1030 Av Des Sciences Humaines, Quebec, QC G1V 0A6, *Tel* (418) 656-2131	4,000	37	0	8221
UNIVERSITE DU QUEBEC 405 Rue Sainte-Catherine E, Montreal, QC H2L 2C4, *Tel* (514) 987-3000	4,000	38	0	8221
VIDEOTRON SERVICE INFORMATIQUE LTEE 300 Av Viger E Bureau 6, Montreal, QC H2X 3W4, *Tel* (514) 281-1232	4,000	39	294,480,000	7374
BRUCE POWER L.P. 700 University Ave Suite 200, Toronto, ON M5G 1X6, *Tel* (519) 361-2673	3,700	40	0	4911
CENTRE HOSPITALIER PIERRE LE GARDEUR 911 Montee Des Pionniers, Terrebonne, QC J6V 2H2, *Tel* (450) 654-7525	3,700	41	346,406,640	8062
ONTARIO POWER GENERATION INC 1675 Montgomery Park Rd, Pickering, ON L1V 2R5, *Tel* (905) 839-1151	3,600	42	0	4911
ASSOCIATION DES GESTIONNAIRES DE L'HOPITAL SAINTE-JUSTINE 3175 Ch De La Cote-Sainte-Catherine, Montreal, QC H3T 1C5, *Tel* (514) 345-4931	3,500	43	392,712,950	8069
BOMBARDIER INC 400 Ch De La Cote-Vertu, Dorval, QC H4S 1Y9, *Tel* (514) 855-5000	3,500	44	0	3721
CANADA POST CORPORATION 555 Rue Mcarthur Bureau 1506, Saint-Laurent, QC H4T 1T4, *Tel* (514) 345-4571	3,500	45	0	4311
IZAAK WALTON KILLAM HEALTH CENTRE, THE 585 0/5980 University Ave, Halifax, NS B3K 6R8, *Tel* (902) 470-8888	3,500	46	223,441,330	8069
SASKATOON REGIONAL HEALTH AUTHORITY 410 22nd St E, Saskatoon, SK S7K 5T6, *Tel* (306) 655-3300	3,500	47	1,052,552,335	8062
SECURITE KOLOSSAL INC 325 Rue Du Marais Bureau 220, Quebec, QC G1M 3R3, *Tel* (418) 683-1713	3,500	48	0	7381
UNIVERSITE DU QUEBEC 1440 Rue Saint-Denis, Montreal, QC H3C 3P8, *Tel* (514) 987-3092	3,500	49	0	8221
CANADA FIRE EQUIPMENT INC 31 Bache Ave, Keswick, ON L4P 0C7, *Tel* (905) 535-2777	3,300	50	435,220,500	5999
CHICAGO, CENTRAL & PACIFIC RAILROAD COMPANY (INC) 935 Rue De La Gauchetiere O, Montreal, QC H3B 2M9, *Tel* (514) 399-4536	3,218	51	1,657,726,080	4011
ILLINOIS CENTRAL RAILROAD 935 Rue De La Gauchetiere O Bureau 11, Montreal, QC H3B 2M9, *Tel* (514) 399-4536	3,218	52	1,713,287,600	4011
GOVERNMENT OF THE PROVINCE OF BRITISH COLUMBIA 6951 Westminster Hwy, Richmond, BC V7C 1C6, *Tel* (604) 273-2266	3,200	53	0	6331
IZAAK WALTON KILLAM HEALTH CENTRE, THE Gd, Halifax, NS B3K 6R8, *Tel* (902) 470-6682	3,200	54	0	8731
▲ **MONDELEZ CANADA INC** 2660 Matheson Blvd E Suite 100, Mississauga, ON L4W 5M2, *Tel* (289) 374-4000	3,200	55	310,155,936	2032
BLACK GOLD REGIONAL DIVISION #18 105 Athabasca Ave, Devon, AB T9G 1A4, *Tel* (780) 987-3709	3,025	56	0	8211
Financiere Micadco Inc (*Suby of* **GROUPE MICHEL CADRIN INC**) 9550 Boul De L'Ormiere, Quebec, QC G2B 3Z6, *Tel* (418) 842-9221	3,020	57	0	5912
ALBERTA HEALTH SERVICES 3942 50a Ave, Red Deer, AB T4N 4E7, *Tel* (403) 343-4422	3,000	58	0	8062
ASSOCIATION GENERALE DES ETUDIANTS ET ETUDIANTES DU COLLEGE LIONEL-GROULX INC 100 Rue Duquet, Sainte-Therese, QC J7E 3G6, *Tel*	3,000	59	299,987,650	8641
BMO NESBITT BURNS INC 1 First Canadian Pl 21st Fl, Toronto, ON M5X 1H3, *Tel* (416) 359-4000	3,000	60	0	6211
BANK OF MONTREAL 4100 Gordon Baker Rd, Scarborough, ON M1W 3E8, *Tel* (416) 508-7618	3,000	61	0	8731
CANADA POST CORPORATION 2701 Riverside Dr, Ottawa, ON K1A 0B1, *Tel* (613) 734-8440	3,000	62	0	4311
CANADIAN BROADCASTING CORPORATION 250 Front St W, Toronto, ON M5V 3G5, *Tel* (416) 205-3311	3,000	63	0	4832
CANADIAN BROADCASTING CORPORATION 205 Wellington St W, Toronto, ON M5V 3G7, *Tel*	3,000	64	0	4833
CANADIAN BROADCASTING CORPORATION 1400 Boul Rene-Levesque E, Montreal, QC H2L 2M2, *Tel* (514) 597-6000	3,000	65	0	4833
Casino Niagara Limited (*Suby of* **CASINO NIAGARA LIMITED**) 5705 Falls Ave, Niagara Falls, ON L2G 3K6, *Tel* (905) 374-3598	3,000	66	0	7999
CENTRE HOSPITALIER UNIVERSITAIRE DE QUEBEC 775 Rue Saint-Viateur Unite 130a, Quebec, QC G2L 2Z3, *Tel* (418) 622-1008	3,000	67	0	8062
CENTRE DE SANTE ET DE SERVICES SOCIAUX DE QUEBEC-NORD 190 76e Rue E, Quebec, QC G1H 7K4, *Tel* (418) 628-6808	3,000	68	0	8011
▲ Emerson Electric Canada Limited (*Suby of* **EMERSON ELECTRIC CO.**) 66 Leek Crescent, Richmond Hill, ON L4B 1H1, *Tel* (905) 948-3401	3,000	69	653,727,872	5063
Ernst & Young LLP (*Suby of* **ERNST & YOUNG LLP**) 222 Bay St 21 Fl, Toronto, ON M5K 1J7, *Tel* (416) 864-1234	3,000	70	144,462,186	8721
EVERTRUST DEVELOPMENT GROUP CANADA INC 3100 Steeles Ave E Suite 302, Markham, ON L3R 8T3, *Tel* (647) 501-2345	3,000	71	556,690,141	1542
GREAT-WEST LIFE ASSURANCE COMPANY, THE 60 Osborne St N, Winnipeg, MB R3C 1V3, *Tel* (204) 926-5394	3,000	72	0	6311
MANUFACTURERS LIFE INSURANCE COMPANY, THE 500 King St N, Waterloo, ON N2J 4C6, *Tel* (519) 747-7000	3,000	73	0	6311

COMPANY	EMPLOYEES HERE	RANK	SALES ($)	PRIMARY SIC CODE
MCGILL UNIVERSITY HEALTH CENTRE 687 Av Des Pins O Bureau 1408, Montreal, QC H3A 1A1, *Tel* (514) 934-1934	3,000	74	0	8062
Rogers Communications Canada Inc (*Suby of* **ROGERS COMMUNICATIONS INC**) 1 Mount Pleasant Rd Suite 115, Toronto, ON M4Y 2Y5, *Tel* (416) 935-1100	3,000	75	0	6712
WINDSOR CASINO LIMITED 377 Riverside Dr E, Windsor, ON N9A 7H7, *Tel* (519) 258-7878	3,000	76	131,329,260	7011
WORLEYPARSONS CANADA SERVICES LTD 8500 Macleod Tr Se, Calgary, AB T2H 2N1, *Tel* (403) 258-8000	3,000	77	413,030,523	8711
CENTRE DE SANTE ET DE SERVICES SOCIAUX DE LAVAL 1755 Boul Rene-Laennec, Cote Saint-Luc, QC H7M 3L9, *Tel* (450) 668-1010	2,815	78	619,149,350	8062
GENSTAR CAPITAL, ULC 1001 Corporate Dr, Burlington, ON L7L 5V5, *Tel* (905) 319-5645	2,800	79	716,237,000	6719
GREAT-WEST LIFE ASSURANCE COMPANY, THE 100 Osborne St N Suite 4c, Winnipeg, MB R3C 1V3, *Tel* (204) 946-1190	2,775	80	20,289,481,800	6324
Chignecto Central Regional School Board (*Suby of* **CHIGNECTO CENTRAL REGIONAL SCHOOL BOARD**) 60 Lorne St, Truro, NS B2N 3K3, *Tel* (902) 897-8900	2,717	81	156,793,650	8211
QUINTERRA PROPERTY MAINTENANCE INC 1681 Chestnut St Suite 400, Vancouver, BC V6J 4M6, *Tel* (604) 689-1800	2,700	82	0	7349
GOUVERNEMENT DE LA PROVINCE DE QUEBEC 333 Boul Jean-Lesage, Quebec, QC G1K 8Z2, *Tel* (418) 528-4338	2,654	83	0	6411
CIRQUE DU SOLEIL INC 8400 2e Av, Montreal, QC H1Z 4M6, *Tel* (514) 722-2324	2,560	84	258,056,173	7999
Bantrel Co. (*Suby of* **BECHTEL GROUP, INC.**) 1201 Glenmore Trail Sw Suite 1061, Calgary, AB T2V 4Y8, *Tel* (403) 290-5000	2,525	85	342,039,762	8711
ALBERTA HEALTH SERVICES 7007 14 St Sw, Calgary, AB T2V 1P9, *Tel* (403) 943-3000	2,500	86	0	8011
BANK OF NOVA SCOTIA, THE 2201 Eglinton Ave E Suite 1, Scarborough, ON M1L 4S2, *Tel* (416) 701-7307	2,500	87	0	6021
Canada Post Corporation (*Suby of* **CANADA POST CORPORATION**) 2701 Riverside Dr, Ottawa, ON K1A 1L5, *Tel* (613) 734-8440	2,500	88	6,019,551,280	4311
CANADIAN FOREST PRODUCTS LTD 1000 Industrial Road 1, Cranbrook, BC V1C 4C6, *Tel* (250) 426-6241	2,500	89	0	2421
COMPAGNIE DES CHEMINS DE FER NATIONAUX DU CANADA 11703 127 Ave Nw, Edmonton, AB T5E 0C9, *Tel* (780) 472-3486	2,500	90	0	4011
▲ **CONOCOPHILLIPS WESTERN CANADA PARTNERSHIP** 401 9 Ave Sw Suite 1600, Calgary, AB T2P 3C5, *Tel* (403) 233-4000	2,500	91	23,259,407,800	1382
GOVERNING COUNCIL OF THE UNIVERSITY OF TORONTO 27 King'S College Cir, Toronto, ON M5S 1A1, *Tel* (416) 978-5850	2,500	92	0	8221
HOPITAL CHARLES LEMOYNE 3120 Boul Taschereau, Greenfield Park, QC J4V 2H1, *Tel* (450) 466-5000	2,500	93	241,856,800	8062
SUN LIFE ASSURANCE COMPANY OF CANADA 1155 Rue Metcalfe Bureau 20, Montreal, QC H3B 2V9, *Tel* (514) 866-6411	2,500	94	0	6311
William Osler Health System (*Suby of* **WILLIAM OSLER HEALTH SYSTEM**) 2100 Bovaird Dr E, Brampton, ON L6R 3J7, *Tel* (905) 494-2120	2,500	95	288,778,451	8062
▲ JBS Canada Inc (*Suby of* **TYSON FOODS, INC.**) Gd Stn Main, Brooks, AB T1R 1E4, *Tel* (403) 362-3457	2,400	96	0	2011
ALGOMA STEEL INC 105 West St, Sault Ste. Marie, ON P6A 7B4, *Tel* (705) 945-2351	2,300	97	1,288,313,550	5051
CENTRE DE SANTE ET DE SERVICE SOCIAUX D'ARTHABASKA-ERABLE 61 Rue De L'Ermitage, Victoriaville, QC G6P 6X4, *Tel* (819) 758-7511	2,300	98	206,652,750	8062
SUNCOR ENERGY INC Gd, Fort Mcmurray, AB T9H 3E3, *Tel* (780) 713-7163	2,300	99	0	1311
CENTRE DE SANTE ET DE SERVICES SOCIAUX DE CHICOUTIMI 305 Rue Saint-Vallier, Chicoutimi, QC G7H 5H6, *Tel* (418) 541-1046	2,200	100	260,320,365	8011
GREAT LAKES BASIN ENERGY L.P. 1055 Georgia St W Suite 1100, Vancouver, BC V6E 3R5, *Tel* (604) 488-8000	2,200	101	941,397,120	4924
HYDRO-QUEBEC 2625 Boul Lebourgneuf Bureau 14, Quebec, QC G2C 1P1, *Tel* (418) 845-6600	2,200	102	0	4911
SCANFIELD HOLDINGS LIMITED 2 Jane St Suite 211, Toronto, ON M6S 4W8, *Tel* (416) 763-4531	2,191	103	60,464,200	6553
MAPLE LEAF FOODS INC 6355 Richmond Ave E, Brandon, MB R7A 7M5, *Tel* (204) 571-2500	2,186	104	0	2011
McMaster University (*Suby of* **MCMASTER UNIVERSITY**) Po Box 2000 Stn Lcd 1, Hamilton, ON L8N 3Z5, *Tel* (905) 521-2100	2,182	105	0	8221
BP Canada Energy Company (*Suby of* **BP P.L.C.**) 240 4 Ave Sw, Calgary, AB T2P 4H4, *Tel* (403) 233-1313	2,100	106	1,473,295,415	1311
BRIDGESTONE CANADA INC 5770 Hurontario St Suite 400, Mississauga, ON L5R 3G5, *Tel* (877) 468-6270	2,100	107	1,094,410,500	5014
EDMONTON NORTHLANDS 7424 118 Ave Nw, Edmonton, AB T5B 4M9, *Tel* (780) 471-7210	2,100	108	0	7922
SYNDICAT DES INFIRMIERES, INHALOTHERAPEUTES ET INFIRMIERES AUXILIAIRES DE LAVAL (CSQ) 2725 Ch Sainte-Foy Bureau 656, Quebec, QC G1V 4G5, *Tel* (418) 656-4710	2,100	109	235,566,900	8069
ST. JOSEPH'S HEALTH CARE, LONDON 298 Grosvenor St, London, ON N6A 1Y8, *Tel* (519) 646-6000	2,030	110	0	6324

COMPANY	EMPLOYEES HERE	RANK	SALES ($)	PRIMARY SIC CODE
LE CENTRE DE SANTE ET DE SERVICES SOCIAUX DE BORDEAUX-CARTIERVILLE-SAINT-LAURENT 555 Boul Gouin O, Montreal, QC H3L 1K5, *Tel* (514) 331-3020	2,003	111	193,769,500	8062
NATIONAL FIBERS INC 1655 Sismet Rd Unit 8, Mississauga, ON L4W 1Z4, *Tel* (905) 238-6181	2,001	112	118,525,900	4213
ALLSTREAM BUSINESS INC 7550 Birchmount Rd, Markham, ON L3R 6C6, *Tel* (416) 345-2000	2,000	113	1,025,535,599	4899
▲ Amex Canada Inc (*Suby of* **AMERICAN EXPRESS COMPANY**) 2225 Sheppard Ave E, Toronto, ON M2J 5C2, *Tel* (905) 474-8000	2,000	114	912,008,750	6099
B. GINGRAS ENTERPRISES LTD 4505 101 St Nw, Edmonton, AB T6E 5C6, *Tel* (780) 435-3355	2,000	115	81,160,000	7349
Banque Toronto-Dominion, La (*Suby of* **TORONTO-DOMINION BANK, THE**) 79 Wellington St W, Toronto, ON M5K 1A2, *Tel* (416) 982-8990	2,000	116	0	6021
BELL MEDIA INC 9 Channel Nine Crt, Scarborough, ON M1S 4B5, *Tel* (416) 332-5000	2,000	117	0	4833
BELL MOBILITE INC 200 Boul Bouchard Bureau 500, Dorval, QC H9S 5X5, *Tel* (514) 420-7700	2,000	118	0	5999
CDSL CANADA LIMITED 2480 Meadowvale Blvd Suite 100, Mississauga, ON L5N 8M6, *Tel* (905) 858-7100	2,000	119	0	7379
CPPIB ZAMBEZI HOLDINGS INC 1 Queen St E Suite 2600, Toronto, ON M5C 2W5, *Tel* (416) 868-4075	2,000	120	688,033,900	4731
CANADIAN NATURAL RESOURCES LIMITED 324 8 Ave Sw Suite 1800, Calgary, AB T2P 2Z2, *Tel* (403) 517-6700	2,000	121	0	1311
CARGILL LIMITED 472 Avenue & Hwy Suite 2a, High River, AB T1V 1P4, *Tel* (403) 652-4688	2,000	122	0	2011
CENTRE HOSPITALIER DE L'UNIVERSITE DE MONTREAL 1560 Rue Sherbrooke E, Montreal, QC H2L 4M1, *Tel* (514) 890-8000	2,000	123	0	8062
CHILDREN'S & WOMEN'S HEALTH CENTRE OF BRITISH COLUMBIA BRANCH 4500 Oak St, Vancouver, BC V6H 3N1, *Tel* (604) 875-2424	2,000	124	437,553,850	8069
▲ **ENBRIDGE GAS DISTRIBUTION INC** Scarborough, Toronto, ON M1K 5E3, *Tel* (416) 492-5000	2,000	125	0	4612
FORTISBC PACIFIC HOLDINGS INC 1975 Springfield Rd Suite 100, Kelowna, BC V1Y 7V7, *Tel* (250) 469-8000	2,000	126	1,286,779,440	4911
▲ General Dynamics Land Systems - Canada Corporation (*Suby of* **GENERAL DYNAMICS CORPORATION**) 1991 Oxford St E Bldg 15, London, ON N5V 2Z7, *Tel* (519) 964-5900	2,000	127	551,282,136	3711
GOUVERNEMENT DE LA PROVINCE DE QUEBEC 116 Boul Lonel-Emond, Gatineau, QC J8Y 1W7, *Tel*	2,000	128	0	8062
GREAT-WEST LIFE ASSURANCE COMPANY, THE 190 Simcoe St, Toronto, ON M5T 3M3, *Tel* (416) 597-1440	2,000	129	0	6311
HOLDING BELL MOBILITE INC 5099 Creekbank Rd, Mississauga, ON L4W 5N2, *Tel* (416) 674-2220	2,000	130	0	5999
HONDA CANADA INC 4700 Tottenham Rd, Alliston, ON L9R 1A2, *Tel* (705) 435-5561	2,000	131	0	3711
INLAND PACIFIC RESOURCES INC 1188 Georgia St W Suite 1160, Vancouver, BC V6E 4A2, *Tel* (604) 697-6700	2,000	132	471,168,000	1623
INTERTAPE POLYMER INC 9999 Boul Cavendish Bureau 200, Saint-Laurent, QC H4M 2X5, *Tel* (514) 731-7591	2,000	133	169,611,946	2295
LAKEHEAD UNIVERSITY 955 Oliver Rd Suite 2008, Thunder Bay, ON P7B 5E1, *Tel* (807) 343-8110	2,000	134	0	8221
MCGILL UNIVERSITY HEALTH CENTRE 3801 Rue University Bureau 548, Montreal, QC H3A 2B4, *Tel* (514) 398-6644	2,000	135	0	8062
MCGILL UNIVERSITY HEALTH CENTRE 2300 Rue Tupper Bureau F372, Montreal, QC H3H 1P3, *Tel* (514) 412-4307	2,000	136	0	8069
NOVA SCOTIA COMMUNITY COLLEGE 5685 Leeds St, Halifax, NS B3K 2T3, *Tel* (902) 491-6774	2,000	137	0	8221
NOVA SCOTIA HEALTH AUTHORITY 1278 Tower Rd, Halifax, NS B3H 2Y9, *Tel* (902) 473-1787	2,000	138	0	8062
Prairie North Regional Health Authority (*Suby of* **PRAIRIE NORTH REGIONAL HEALTH AUTHORITY**) 1092 107th St, North Battleford, SK S9A 1Z1, *Tel* (306) 446-6600	2,000	139	3,766,859	8062
PROVINCE OF PEI 60 Riverside Dr, Charlottetown, PE C1A 8T5, *Tel* (902) 894-2111	2,000	140	0	8062
Rio Tinto Alcan Inc (*Suby of* **RIO TINTO PLC**) 1 Smelter Site Rd, Kitimat, BC V8C 2H2, *Tel* (250) 639-8000	2,000	141	0	3334
SEARS CANADA INC 1908 7th Ave, Regina, SK S4R 5E1, *Tel* (306) 569-1711	2,000	142	0	5399
SEARS CANADA INC 1655 Rue Beaulac, Saint-Laurent, QC H4R 1Z1, *Tel* (514) 335-5824	2,000	143	0	5311
Station Mort Tremblant Inc (*Suby of* **HAWK HOLDING COMPANY, LLC**) 1000 Ch Des Voyageurs, Mont-Tremblant, QC J8E 1T1, *Tel* (819) 681-3000	2,000	144	87,552,840	7011
Station Mort-Tremblant Societe en Commandite (*Suby of* **HAWK HOLDING COMPANY, LLC**) 1000 Ch Des Voyageurs, Mont-Tremblant, QC J8E 1T1, *Tel* (819) 681-2000	2,000	145	87,552,840	7011
▲ Tetra Tech QE Inc (*Suby of* **TETRA TECH, INC.**) 5100 Rue Sherbrooke E Bureau 900, Montreal, QC H1V 3R9, *Tel* (514) 257-0707	2,000	146	279,712,448	8711
THOMPSON HEALTH REGION 311 Columbia St, Kamloops, BC V2C 2T1, *Tel* (250) 314-2784	2,000	147	182,407,100	8093

COMPANY	EMPLOYEES HERE	RANK	SALES ($)	PRIMARY SIC CODE
UNIFOR 1111 Homer Watson Blvd, Kitchener, ON N2C 2P7, *Tel*	2,000	148	0	8631
CSSS DE CHICOUTIMI 305 Rue Saint-Vallier, Chicoutimi, QC G7H 5H6, *Tel* (418) 541-1000	1,900	149	183,827,400	8062
▲ Fluor Canada Ltd (*Suby of* **FLUOR CORPORATION**) 55 Sunpark Plaza Se, Calgary, AB T2X 3R4, *Tel* (403) 537-4000	1,900	150	282,941,595	8711
Grand River Hospital Corporation (*Suby of* **GRAND RIVER HOSPITAL CORPORATION**) 835 King St W, Kitchener, ON N2G 1G3, *Tel* (519) 742-3611	1,900	151	312,910,166	8062
BOMBARDIER INC 200 Ch De La Cote-Vertu Bureau 1110, Dorval, QC H4S 2A3, *Tel* (514) 420-4000	1,800	152	0	3721
▲ **CBRE LIMITED** 145 King St W Suite 1100, Toronto, ON M5H 1J8, *Tel* (416) 362-2244	1,800	153	4,459,066,141	8748
CANADIAN CORPS OF COMMISSIONAIRES (NORTHERN ALBERTA) 10633 124 St Nw Suite 101, Edmonton, AB T5N 1S5, *Tel* (780) 451-1974	1,800	154	72,370,867	7381
FRASER HEALTH AUTHORITY 3935 Kincaid St, Burnaby, BC V5G 2X6, *Tel* (604) 434-3992	1,800	155	0	8062
UNIVERSITE DU QUEBEC 3351 Boul Des Forges, Trois-Rivieres, QC G8Z 4M3. *Tel* (819) 376-5011	1,800	156	0	8221
AVELIA GROUPE 951 Rue Reverchon, Saint-Laurent, QC H4T 4L2, *Tel*	1,700	157	453,204,720	1541
BRITISH COLUMBIA MENTAL HEALTH SOCIETY 2601 Lougheed Hwy, Coquitlam, BC V3C 4J2, *Tel* (604) 524-7000	1,700	158	164,712,480	8063
▲ **CONOCOPHILLIPS WESTERN CANADA PARTNERSHIP** 401 9th Ave Sw, Calgary, AB T2P 2H7, *Tel* (403) 260-8000	1,700	159	0	1311
▲ Praxair Canada Inc (*Suby of* **PRAXAIR, INC.**) 834 51st St E Suite 5, Saskatoon, SK S7K 5C7, *Tel* (306) 242-3325	1,700	160	0	2813
SEARS CANADA INC 500 College St E, Belleville, ON K8N 5T2, *Tel* (613) 391-3106	1,700	161	0	4225
SIGNET DEVELOPMENT CORPORATION 150 Signet Dr, North York, ON M9L 1T9, *Tel* (416) 749-9300	1,700	162	728,150,880	6553
MOHAWK COLLEGE OF APPLIED ARTS AND TECHNOLOGY, THE 135 Fennell Ave W, Hamilton, ON L9C 1E9, *Tel* (905) 575-1212	1,650	163	0	8222
FOSTER'S RED & WHITE LTD 4 Robinson Dr, Bruce Mines, ON P0R 1C0, *Tel* (705) 785-3728	1,614	164	322,408,100	5411
CP ENERGY MARKETING INC 505 2 St Sw Suite 84, Calgary, AB T2P 1N8, *Tel* (403) 717-4600	1,600	165	261,842,450	8711
CENTRE DE SANTE ET DE SERVICES SOCIAUX DU SUD-QUEST-VERDUN 4000 Boul Lasalle, Verdun, QC H4G 2A3, *Tel* (514) 362-1000	1,600	166	0	8062
EDWARD D. JONES & CO. CANADA HOLDING CO., INC 90 Burnhamthorpe Rd W Suite 902, Mississauga, ON L5B 3C3, *Tel* (905) 306-8600	1,600	167	4,331,255,000	6211
SCDA (2015) INC 1245 Rue Sherbrooke O Bureau 2100, Montreal, QC H3G 1G3, *Tel* (514) 499-8855	1,600	168	2,359,494,474	6311
TD Securities Inc (*Suby of* **TORONTO-DOMINION BANK, THE**) 66 Wellington St W, Toronto, ON M5K 1A2, *Tel* (416) 307-8500	1,600	169	364,803,500	6211
ERICSSON CANADA INC 8400 Boul Decarie, Mont-Royal, QC H4P 2N2, *Tel* (514) 345-7900	1,550	170	0	5065
CARGILL LIMITED 781 York Rd, Guelph, ON N1E 6N1, *Tel* (519) 823-5200	1,540	171	0	2011
ATLATSA RESOURCES CORPORATION 666 Burrard St Suite 1700, Vancouver, BC V6C 2X8, *Tel* (604) 631-1300	1,500	172	120,339,846	1081
Bantrel Co. (*Suby of* **BECHTEL GROUP, INC.**) 700 6 Ave Sw Suite 1400, Calgary, AB T2P 0T8, *Tel* (403) 290-5000	1,500	173	0	8711
BENTLEYS OF LONDON SLACKS LTD 1309 Mountain Ave, Winnipeg, MB R2X 2Y1, *Tel* (204) 786-6081	1,500	174	129,247,300	2339
BUY-LOW FOODS LTD 19676 Telegraph Trail, Langley, BC V1M 3E5, *Tel* (604) 888-1121	1,500	175	0	5141
CANADIAN IMPERIAL BANK OF COMMERCE 5650 Yonge St Suite 1400, North York, ON M2M 4G3, *Tel* (416) 218-9922	1,500	176	0	4899
CANADIAN NATIONAL EXHIBITION ASSOCIATION 210 Princes Blvd, Toronto, ON M6K 3C3, *Tel* (416) 263-3600	1,500	177	57,055,267	7996
COMPAGNIE MINIERE IOC INC Gd, Labrador City, NL A2V 2L8, *Tel* (709) 944-8400	1,500	178	0	1011
▲ Corrpro Canada, Inc (*Suby of* **AEGION CORPORATION**) 8607 101 St, Fort St. John, BC V1J 5K4, *Tel* (250) 787-9100	1,500	179	0	8711
▲ Ford Motor Company of Canada, Limited (*Suby of* **FORD MOTOR COMPANY**) Gd, St Thomas, ON N5P 3W1, *Tel*	1,500	180	0	3711
▲ General Dynamics Land Systems - Canada Corporation (*Suby of* **GENERAL DYNAMICS CORPORATION**) 1941 Robertson Rd, Ottawa, ON K2H 5B7, *Tel* (613) 596-7222	1,500	181	0	3711
GOVERNING COUNCIL OF THE UNIVERSITY OF TORONTO 55 Harbord St Suite 1048, Toronto, ON M5S 2W6, *Tel* (416) 978-7375	1,500	182	0	8221
GREATER VANCOUVER REGIONAL DISTRICT, THE 4330 Kingsway, Burnaby, BC V5H 4G7, *Tel* (604) 451-6575	1,500	183	276,479,329	8741
HUDSON BAY MINING AND SMELTING CO., LIMITED Gd, Flin Flon, MB R8A 1N9, *Tel* (204) 687-2385	1,500	184	0	1021

COMPANY	EMPLOYEES HERE	RANK	SALES ($)	PRIMARY SIC CODE
▲ IBM Canada Limited (*Suby of* **INTERNATIONAL BUSINESS MACHINES CORPORATION**) 23 Boul De L'Aeroport, Bromont, QC J2L 1A3, *Tel* (450) 534-6000	1,500	185	0	3674
▲ IBM Canada Limited (*Suby of* **INTERNATIONAL BUSINESS MACHINES CORPORATION**) 105 Moatfield Dr Suite 100, North York, ON M3B 0A4, *Tel* (905) 316-5000	1,500	186	0	7299
INTRIA ITEMS INC 155 Britannia Rd E Suite 200, Mississauga, ON L4Z 4B7, *Tel* (905) 502-4592	1,500	187	0	7374
▲ Imperial Oil Resources Limited (*Suby of* **EXXON MOBIL CORPORATION**) 237 4 Ave Sw Suite 4063, Calgary, AB T2P 4K3, *Tel* (800) 567-3776	1,500	188	1,154,019,392	1382
INSURANCE CORPORATION OF BRITISH COLUMBIA 151 Esplanade W Suite 135, North Vancouver, BC V7M 3H9, *Tel* (604) 661-2800	1,500	189	3,797,134,051	6331
LOBLAWS SUPERMARKETS LIMITED 1460 Merivale Rd, Nepean, ON K2E 5P2, *Tel* (613) 226-6001	1,500	190	0	5411
MERA NETWORKS INC 15 Wertheim Crt Suite 306, Richmond Hill, ON L4B 3H7, *Tel* (905) 882-4443	1,500	191	24,778,416	7371
MUNICIPAL CONTRACTING LIMITED 927 Rocky Lake Dr, Waverley, NS B2R 1S1, *Tel* (902) 835-3381	1,500	192	0	1611
NIAGARA 21ST GROUP INC 6740 Fallsview Blvd, Niagara Falls, ON L2G 3W6, *Tel* (905) 357-7300	1,500	193	0	7011
Porter Airlines Inc (*Suby of* **PORTER AVIATION HOLDINGS INC**) 4-1 Island Airport, Toronto, ON M5V 1A1, *Tel* (416) 203-8100	1,500	194	234,057,926	4581
PUROLATOR INC. 62 Vulcan St, Etobicoke, ON M9W 1L2, *Tel* (416) 241-4496	1,500	195	0	4731
SECURITAS CANADA LIMITED 1980 Rue Sherbrooke O Bureau 300, Montreal, QC H3H 1E8, *Tel* (514) 935-2533	1,500	196	0	7381
Securite Nationale Compagnie d'Assurance (*Suby of* **TORONTO-DOMINION BANK, THE**) 50 Boul Cremazie O Bureau 1200, Montreal, QC H2P 1B6, *Tel* (514) 382-6060	1,500	197	153,144,509	6411
ST AMANT INC 440 River Rd, Winnipeg, MB R2M 3Z9, *Tel* (204) 256-4301	1,500	198	91,405,913	8059
ST. JOSEPH'S HEALTH CARE, LONDON 268 Grosvenor St, London, ON N6A 4V2, *Tel* (519) 646-6100	1,500	199	0	8093
TECK METALS LTD 25 Aldridge Ave, Trail, BC V1R 4L8, *Tel* (250) 364-4222	1,500	200	0	1081
TRICAN WELL SERVICE LTD 418 11979 40 St Se, Calgary, AB T2Z 4M3, *Tel* (403) 723-3688	1,500	201		1389
WINNIPEG REGIONAL HEALTH AUTHORITY, THE 820 Sherbrook St Suite 543, Winnipeg, MB R3A 1R9, *Tel* (204) 774-6511	1,500	202	0	8062
REGINA QU'APPELLE REGIONAL HEALTH AUTHORITY 4101 Dewdney Ave, Regina, SK S4T 1A5, *Tel* (306) 766-2222	1,440	203	0	8062
URGENCES-SANTE 6700 Rue Jarry E, Montreal, QC H1P 0A4, *Tel* (514) 723-5600	1,426	204	93,853,709	4119
EAST CENTRAL DISTRICT HEALTH BOARD Po Box 5027 Stn Main, Yorkton, SK S3N 3Z4, *Tel* (306) 786-0113	1,400	205	134,140,800	8062
ROLLS-ROYCE CANADA LIMITEE 9500 Ch De La Cote-De-Liesse, Lachine, QC H8T 1A2, *Tel* (514) 631-3541	1,400	206	228,002,188	4581
Service a la Clientele Alorica Ltee (*Suby of* **ALORICA INC.**) 75 Rue De Port-Royal E Bureau 240, Montreal, QC H3L 3T1, *Tel* (514) 385-4444	1,400	207	132,715,513	4813
STANTEC CONSULTING LTD 10160 112 St Nw, Edmonton, AB T5K 2L6, *Tel* (780) 917-7000	1,400	208	1,665,546,860	8711
1127770 B.C. LTD 777 Broadway W, Vancouver, BC V5Z 4J7, *Tel*	1,398	209	203,998,117	5047
Cenovus Energy Inc (*Suby of* **CENOVUS ENERGY INC**) 500 Centre St Se, Calgary, AB T2P 0M5, *Tel* (403) 766-2000	1,386	210	820,960,832	1382
MSN WIRELESS INC 1315 Derry Rd E Suite 6a, Mississauga, ON L5T 1B6, *Tel* (416) 745-9900	1,354	211	343,541,120	4899
Hamilton Health Sciences Corporation (*Suby of* **HAMILTON HEALTH SCIENCES CORPORATION**) 711 Concession St Suite 201, Hamilton, ON L8V 1C3, *Tel* (905) 521-2100	1,345	212	0	8062
BRIDGESTONE CANADA INC 1200 Boul Firestone, Joliette, QC J6E 2W5, *Tel* (450) 756-1061	1,300	213	0	3011
CENTRE DE SANTE ET DE SERVICES SOCIAUX DE LA VIEILLE-CAPITALE 50 Rue Saint-Joseph E, Quebec, QC G1K 3A5, *Tel* (418) 529-2572	1,300	214	0	8322
CENTRE DE SANTE ET DE SERVICES SOCIAUX DU COEUR-DE-L'ILE 1385 Rue Jean-Talon E, Montreal, QC H2E 1S6, *Tel* (514) 495-6767	1,300	215	139,136,055	8062
▲ General Electric Canada Company (*Suby of* **GENERAL ELECTRIC COMPANY**) 107 Park St N Suite 2, Peterborough, ON K9J 7B5, *Tel* (705) 748-8486	1,300	216	0	3625
GOUVERNEMENT DE LA PROVINCE DE QUEBEC 525 Boul Wilfrid-Hamel, Quebec, QC G1M 2S8, *Tel* (418) 529-9141	1,300	217	0	8011
GOUVERNEMENT DE LA PROVINCE DE QUEBEC 525 Boul Wilfrid-Hamel, Quebec, QC G1M 2S8, *Tel* (418) 649-3700	1,300	218	0	8093
GOVERNING COUNCIL OF THE SALVATION ARMY IN CANADA, THE 300 Booth Dr, Winnipeg, MB R3J 3M7, *Tel* (204) 837-8311	1,300	219	116,848,796	8062
HUDSON'S BAY COMPANY 674 Granville St Suite 9999, Vancouver, BC V6C 1Z6, *Tel* (604) 681-6211	1,300	220	0	5311
JIFFY TELECOMMUNICATIONS INC 100 King St W Suite 5600, Toronto, ON M5X 2A1, *Tel*	1,300	221	332,857,450	4899

COMPANY	EMPLOYEES HERE	RANK	SALES ($)	PRIMARY SIC CODE
OMNI HOLDINGS INC 1840 Lansdowne St W Unit 12, Peterborough, ON K9K 2M9, *Tel* (705) 748-6631	1,300	222	81,589,760	8051
OTTAWA HOSPITAL, THE 725 Parkdale Ave, Ottawa, ON K1Y 4E9, *Tel* (613) 761-4395	1,300	223	0	8733
Purolator Holdings Ltd (*Suby of* **CANADA POST CORPORATION**) 5995 Avebury Rd Suite 100, Mississauga, ON L5R 3T8, *Tel* (905) 712-1251	1,300	224	3,158,177,896	4731
▲ Tetra Tech QC Inc (*Suby of* **TETRA TECH, INC.**) 5100 Rue Sherbrooke E Bureau 900, Montreal, QC H1V 3R9, *Tel* (514) 257-0707	1,300	225	227,949,385	8711
Sault Area Hospital (*Suby of* **SAULT AREA HOSPITAL**) 750 Great Northern Rd Suite 1, Sault Ste. Marie, ON P6B 0A8, *Tel* (705) 759-3434	1,292	226	90,471,268	8062
AVIVA CANADA INC 10 Aviva Way Suite 100, Markham, ON L6G 0G1, *Tel* (416) 288-1800	1,250	227	279,220,599	6411
MBNA Canada Bank (*Suby of* **TORONTO-DOMINION BANK, THE**) 1600 James Naismith Dr Suite 800, Gloucester, ON K1B 5N8, *Tel* (613) 907-4800	1,250	228	330,001,246	6021
United Steelworkers Of America (*Suby of* **UNITED STEELWORKERS**) 1 Diamond St, Trenton, NS B0K 1X0, *Tel*	1,201	229	0	8631
1732187 ONTARIO INC 1905 Blackacre Dr Rr 1, Oldcastle, ON N0R 1L0, *Tel* (519) 737-9948	1,200	230	127,685,580	3544
▲ 3M Canada Company (*Suby of* **3M COMPANY**) 300 Tartan Dr, London, ON N5V 4M9, *Tel* (519) 451-2500	1,200	231	145,921,400	2891
ATI Technologies ULC (*Suby of* **ATI TECHNOLOGIES ULC**) 1 Commerce Valley Dr E, Thornhill, ON L3T 7X6, *Tel* (905) 882-7589	1,200	232	413,833,090	3577
BEAUWARD SHOPPING CENTRES LTD 3200 Boul Laframboise Bureau 1009, Saint-Hyacinthe, QC J2S 4Z5 *Tel* (450) 773-8282	1,200	233	0	6512
BOMBARDIER INC 9501 Av Ryan, Dorval, QC H9P 1A2, *Tel* (514) 855-5000	1,200	234	0	8711
Brewers' Distributor Ltd (*Suby of* **BREWERS' DISTRIBUTOR LTD**) 1711 Kingsway Ave, Port Coquitlam, BC V3C 0B6, *Tel* (604) 927-4055	1,200	235	0	5181
CRH CANADA GROUP INC 435 Rue Jean-Neveu, Longueuil, QC J4G 2P9, *Tel* (450) 651-1117	1,200	236	0	3241
CHALLENGER MOTOR FREIGHT INC 300 Maple Grove Rd, Cambridge, ON N3E 1B7, *Tel* (519) 653-6226	1,200	237	238,219,025	4213
City of Winnipeg, The (*Suby of* **CITY OF WINNIPEG, THE**) 65 Ellen St, Winnipeg, MB R3A 0Z8, *Tel* (204) 986-6308	1,200	238	0	4119
▲ Coca-Cola Refreshments Canada Company (*Suby of* **THE COCA-COLA COMPANY**) 15 Westcreek Blvd Suite 1, Brampton, ON L6T 5T4, *Tel* (905) 874-7200	1,200	239	0	2086
Commission Scolaire Eastern Townships (*Suby of* **COMMISSION SCOLAIRE EASTERN TOWNSHIPS**) 101 Rue Du Moulin Bureau 205, Magog, QC J1X 4A1, *Tel* (819) 868-3100	1,200	240	0	8331
CONSEILLERS EN GESTION ET INFORMATIQUE CGI INC 410 Boul Charest E Bureau 700, Quebec, QC G1K 8G3, *Tel* (418) 623-0101	1,200	241	0	7379
EC RESTAURANTS (CANADA) CORP 6001 1a St Sw Suite 200, Calgary, AB T2H 0G5, *Tel* (403) 263-4323	1,200	242	50,319,200	5812
GOUVERNEMENT DE LA PROVINCE DE QUEBEC 3510 Rue Cambronne, Quebec, QC G1E 7H2, *Tel* (418) 661-3700	1,200	243	0	8399
HUDSON'S BAY COMPANY 176 Yonge St, Toronto, ON M5C 2L7, *Tel* (416) 861-9111	1,200	244	0	5311
INTERIOR HEALTH AUTHORITY 2101 32 St, Vernon, BC V1T 5L2, *Tel* (250) 545-2211	1,200	245	0	8062
J. D. Irving, Limited (*Suby of* **J. D. IRVING, LIMITED**) 300 Union St Suite 5, Saint John, NB E2L 4Z2, *Tel* (506) 632-7777	1,200	246	1,422,733,650	2421
OLYMEL S.E.C. 568 Ch De L'Ecore S, Vallee-Jonction, QC G0S 3J0, *Tel* (418) 253-5437	1,200	247	0	2011
SNC-LAVALIN INC 605 5 Ave Sw Suite 1400, Calgary, AB T2P 3H5, *Tel* (403) 294-2100	1,200	248	0	8711
STANDARD AERO LIMITED 33 Allen Dyne Rd, Winnipeg, MB R3H 1A1, *Tel* (204) 775-9711	1,200	249	116,943,885	7538
SYNDICAT DES INSPECTEURS ET DES REPARTITEURS DU RESEAU DE TRANSPORT DE LA CAPITALE (FISA) 720 Rue Des Rocailles, Quebec, QC G2J 1A5, *Tel* (418) 627-2351	1,200	250	58,739,550	4111
TD Waterhouse Canada Inc (*Suby of* **TORONTO-DOMINION BANK, THE**) 77 Bloor St W Suite 3, Toronto, ON M5S 1M2, *Tel* (416) 982-7686	1,200	251	291,842,800	6211
University of Saskatchewan (*Suby of* **UNIVERSITY OF SASKATCHEWAN**) 107 Wiggins Rd Suite B103, Saskatoon, SK S7N 5E5, *Tel* (306) 966-1625	1,200	252	0	8221
VALEURS MOBILIERES DESJARDINS INC 2 Complexe Desjardins Tour E 15 +Tage, Montreal, QC H5B 1J2, *Tel* (514) 286-3180	1,200	253	0	6211
WORLEYPARSONS CANADA SERVICES LTD 5008 86 St Nw Suite 120, Edmonton, AB T6E 5S2, *Tel* (780) 440-5300	1,200	254	0	8711
BELL EXPRESSVU INC 100 Wynford Dr Suite 300, North York, ON M3C 4B4, *Tel* (416) 383-6600	1,170	255	377,425,200	4841
BOMBARDIER INC 1800 Boul Marcel-Laurin, Saint-Laurent, QC H4R 1K2, *Tel* (514) 855-5000	1,100	256	0	3812
CENTRE DE SANTE ET DE SERVICES SOCIAUX-INSTITUT UNIVERSITAIRE DE GERIATRIE DE SHERBROOKE 1036 Rue Belvedere S, Sherbrooke, QC J1H 4C4, *Tel*	1,100	257	69,889,920	8051
▲ **CITIGROUP GLOBAL MARKETS CANADA INC** 2920 Matheson Blvd E, Mississauga, ON L4W 5R6, *Tel* (905) 624-9889	1,100	258	0	6722

COMPANY	EMPLOYEES HERE	RANK	SALES ($)	PRIMARY SIC CODE
COLLEGE D'ENSEIGNEMENT GENERAL & PROFESSIONEL STE-FOY 2410 Ch Sainte-Foy, Quebec, QC G1V 1T3, *Tel* (418) 659-6600	1,100	259	159,073,600	8221
CONCORDIA HOSPITAL 1095 Concordia Ave, Winnipeg, MB R2K 3S8, *Tel* (204) 667-1560	1,100	260	98,850,312	8062
CREATIVE VISTAS ACQUISITION CORP 2100 Forbes St, Whitby, ON L1N 9T3, *Tel* (905) 666-8676	1,100	261	124,387,428	1731
EXXONMOBIL BUSINESS SUPPORT CENTRE CANADA ULC 95 Boundary Dr, Moncton, NB E1G 5C6, *Tel* (800) 567-3776	1,100	262	217,610,250	8742
MACKENZIE FINANCIAL CORPORATION 180 Queen St W Suite 1600, Toronto, ON M5V 3K1, *Tel* (416) 355-2537	1,100	263	459,459,530	6722
MATSQUI-SUMAS-ABBOTSFORD GENERAL HOSPITAL SOCIETY 32900 Marshall Rd, Abbotsford, BC V2S 0C2, *Tel* (604) 851-4700	1,100	264	102,969,840	8062
▲ Stream International Canada ULC (*Suby of* **CONVERGYS CORPORATION**) 7955 Evans Rd, Chilliwack, BC V2R 5R7, *Tel* (604) 702-5100	1,100	265	0	7389
University of Saskatchewan (*Suby of* **UNIVERSITY OF SASKATCHEWAN**) 105 Administration Pl Suite E, Saskatoon, SK S7N 5A2, *Tel* (306) 966-4343	1,100	266	918,800,689	8221
MAGNA INTERNATIONAL INC 345 University Ave Suite 1, Belleville, ON K8N 5T7, *Tel* (613) 969-1122	1,090	267	0	3647
▲ Schering-Plough Canada Inc (*Suby of* **MERCK & CO., INC.**) 16750 Rte Transcanadienne, Kirkland, QC H9H 4M7, *Tel* (514) 426-7300	1,078	268	106,595,583	2834
LABATT BREWING COMPANY LIMITED 50 Av Labatt Bureau 42, Lasalle, QC H8R 3E7, *Tel* (514) 366-5050	1,070	269	0	2082
TECK COAL LIMITED Gd, Sparwood, BC V0B 2G0, *Tel* (250) 425-8325	1,060	270	0	1221
HAWORTH, LTD 222 5 Ave Sw Suite 112, Calgary, AB T2P 0L1, *Tel* (403) 203-6000	1,050	271	119,802,513	2542
VANCOUVER COMMUNITY COLLEGE 250 Pender St W Suite 358, Vancouver, BC V6B 1S9, *Tel* (604) 443-8300	1,050	272	0	8221
TRAVAILLEURS CANADIEN DE L'AUTOMOBILE SECTION LOCALE 62 9045 Ch Cote-De-Liesse Bureau 203, Dorval, QC H9P 2M9, *Tel* (514) 636-8080	1,044	273	148,614,240	8631
HOTEL DIEU HEALTH SCIENCES HOSPITAL, NIAGARA 155 Ontario St, St Catharines, ON L2R 5K2, *Tel*	1,015	274	91,217,447	8062
BRITISH COLUMBIA CANCER AGENCY BRANCH 600 10th Ave W, Vancouver, BC V5Z 4E6, *Tel* (604) 877-6000	1,010	275	159,117,360	8069
FRONTIER SCHOOL DIVISION 1 Rossville Rd, Norway House, MB R0B 1B0, *Tel* (204) 359-4100	1,005	276	0	8211
DELTA FOODS INTERNATIONAL INC 5630 Montgomery Pl, Vancouver, BC V6T 2C7, *Tel* (778) 370-0576	1,003	277	508,771,750	5146
AMEC FOSTER WHEELER AMERICAS LIMITED 801 6 Ave Sw Suite 900, Calgary, AB T2P 3W3, *Tel* (403) 298-4170	1,000	278	0	8711
ALBERTA HEALTH SERVICES 10230 111 Ave Nw Suite 2e, Edmonton, AB T5G 0B7, *Tel* (780) 735-7999	1,000	279	0	8062
ALIMENTS OLYMPUS (CANADA), LES 3201 Boul Taschereau, Greenfield Park, QC J4V 2H4, *Tel*	1,000	280	38,918,188	5812
ALUMINERIE DE BECANCOUR INC 5555 Rue Pierre-Thibault Bureau 217, Becancour, QC G9H 2T7, *Tel* (819) 294-6101	1,000	281	0	3463
AMER SPORTS CANADA INC 2220 Dollarton Hwy Unit 110, North Vancouver, BC V7H 1A8, *Tel* (604) 960-3001	1,000	282	1,137,238,431	5091
Atlific Inc (*Suby of* **3376290 CANADA INC**) 4960 Clifton Hill, Niagara Falls, ON L2G 3N4, *Tel* (905) 358-3293	1,000	283	0	7011
Attraction Images Productions Inc (*Suby of* **ATTRACTION MEDIA INC**) 5455 Av De Gaspe Bureau 804, Montreal, QC H2T 3B3, *Tel* (514) 285-7001	1,000	284	114,548,299	7922
BML GROUP LIMITED 5905 Campus Rd, Mississauga, ON L4V 1P9, *Tel* (905) 676-1293	1,000	285	234,828,387	6719
BLACKBERRY LIMITED 2240 University Ave E, Waterloo, ON N2K 0A9, *Tel* (519) 888-7465	1,000	286	0	3663
CANAC-MARQUIS GRENIER LTEE 947 Av Royale, Quebec, QC G1E 1Z9, *Tel* (418) 667-1729	1,000	287	0	5039
▲ Canada Imperial Oil Limited (*Suby of* **EXXON MOBIL CORPORATION**) 602 Christina St S, Sarnia, ON N7T 7M5, *Tel* (519) 339-2000	1,000	288	0	5172
CANADIAN TIRE SERVICES LIMITED 1000 East Main St, Welland, ON L3B 3Z3, *Tel* (905) 735-3131	1,000	289	0	6153
CAPE BRETON DISTRICT HEALTH AUTHORITY 1482 George St, Sydney, NS B1P 1P3, *Tel* (902) 567-8000	1,000	290	269,487,797	8062
CARTONS ST-LAURENT INC 630 Boul Rene-Levesque O Bureau 3000, Montreal, QC H3B 1S6, *Tel* (514) 744-6461	1,000	291	202,111,440	2657
Cavendish Farms Corporation (*Suby of* **J. D. IRVING, LIMITED**) Gd, Kensington, PE C0B 1M0, *Tel* (902) 836-5555	1,000	292	0	5142
CENTRE HOSPITALIER DE L'UNIVERSITE DE MONTREAL 1058 Rue Saint-Denis, Montreal, QC H2X 3J4, *Tel* (514) 890-8000	1,000	293	0	8062
CENTRE DE SANTE ET SERVICES SOCIAUX DE MONTMAGNY - L'ISLET 10 Rue Alphonse, Saint-Fabien-De-Panet, QC G0R 2J0, *Tel* (418) 249-2572	1,000	294	0	8062
CENTRE FOR ADDICTION AND MENTAL HEALTH 175 Brentcliffe Rd, Toronto, ON M4G 0C5, *Tel* (416) 425-3930	1,000	295	0	8093

COMPANY	EMPLOYEES HERE	RANK	SALES ($)	PRIMARY SIC CODE
Commission des Normes, de Lequite, de la Sante et de la Securite du Travail, La (*Suby of* **COMMISSION DES NORMES, DE LEQUITE, DE LA SANTE ET DE LA SECURITE DU TRAVAIL, LA**) 524 Rue Bourdages Bureau 370, Quebec, QC G1K 7E2, *Tel* (877) 639-0744	1,000	296	1,433,604,794	6331
COMPAGNIE DES CHEMINS DE FER NATIONAUX DU CANADA 1 Administration Rd, Vaughan, ON L4K 1B9, *Tel* (905) 669-3128	1,000	297	0	4011
CONSEIL SCOLAIRE CATHOLIQUE DE DISTRICT DES GRANDES RIVIERES, LE 75 Queen St, Kapuskasing, ON P5N 1H5, *Tel* (705) 335-6091	1,000	298	0	8211
CORPORATION OF THE CITY OF TORONTO 4330 Dufferin St Suite 28, North York, ON M3H 5R9, *Tel* (416) 392-2000	1,000	299	0	4119
ELECTROLUX CANADA CORP 802 Boul De L'Ange-Gardien, L'Assomption, QC J5W 1T6, *Tel* (450) 589-5701	1,000	300	0	3634
▲ **ENBRIDGE COMMERCIAL SERVICES INC** 500 Consumers Rd, North York, ON M2J 1P8, *Tel* (416) 492-5000	1,000	301	210,553,200	8741
▲ **ENBRIDGE PIPELINES INC** 10201 Jasper Ave Nw, Edmonton, AB T5J 3N7, *Tel*	1,000	302	0	4612
Evraz Inc. NA Canada (*Suby of* **EVRAZ PLC**) 100 Armour Rd, Regina, SK S4P 3C7, *Tel* (306) 924-7700	1,000	303	298,856,595	3312
EXPORT DEVELOPMENT CANADA 150 Slater St, Ottawa, ON K1A 1K3, *Tel* (613) 598-2500	1,000	304	1,163,910,240	6111
FYI EYE CARE SERVICE AND PRODUCTS INC 1211 99 St, Grande Prairie, AB T8V 6X9, *Tel* (780) 532-2969	1,000	305	78,626,160	8042
▲ Ford Motor Company of Canada, Limited (*Suby of* **FORD MOTOR COMPANY**) 3223 Lauzon Pky, Windsor, ON N9A 6X3, *Tel* (519) 944-8784	1,000	306	0	5521
▲ Ford Motor Company of Canada, Limited (*Suby of* **FORD MOTOR COMPANY**) 1 Quality Way, Windsor, ON N9A 6X3, *Tel* (519) 944-8658	1,000	307	0	3714
▲ Ford Motor Company of Canada, Limited (*Suby of* **FORD MOTOR COMPANY**) 2900 Trenton St, Windsor, ON N9A 7B2, *Tel* (519) 257-2000	1,000	308	0	3322
FORTISALBERTA INC 320 17 Ave Sw, Calgary, AB T2S 2V1, *Tel* (403) 514-4000	1,000	309	423,253,715	4911
FRASER HEALTH AUTHORITY 11666 Laity St, Maple Ridge, BC V2X 5A3, *Tel* (604) 463-4111	1,000	310	0	8062
GAY LEA FOODS CO-OPERATIVE LIMITED 20 Morley St, Hamilton, ON L8H 3R7, *Tel* (905) 544-6281	1,000	311	0	2021
▲ General Electric Canada Company (*Suby of* **GENERAL ELECTRIC COMPANY**) 2 Boul De L'Aeroport, Bromont, QC J2L 1S6, *Tel* (450) 534-0917	1,000	312	0	3625
GO BEE INDUSTRIES INC 300 York Blvd, Hamilton, ON L8R 3K6, *Tel*	1,000	313	235,582,250	7319
GREATER TRAIL COMMUNITY HEALTH COUNCIL 1200 Hospital Bench, Trail, BC V1R 4M1, *Tel* (250) 368-3311	1,000	314	89,898,187	8062
GROUPE PAGES JAUNES CORP 2600 Boul Laurier Bureau 128, Quebec, QC G1V 4Y4, *Tel* (418) 656-1530	1,000	315	0	4899
HATCH LTD 4342 Queen St Suite 500, Niagara Falls, ON L2E 7J7, *Tel* (905) 374-5200	1,000	316	0	8711
▲ Hecla Quebec Inc (*Suby of* **HECLA MINING COMPANY**) 1010 3e Rue, Val-D'Or, QC J9P 4B1, *Tel* (819) 874-4511	1,000	317	0	1041
▲ IBM Canada Limited (*Suby of* **INTERNATIONAL BUSINESS MACHINES CORPORATION**) 10044 108 St Nw Suite 401, Edmonton, AB T5J 3S7, *Tel* (780) 642-4100	1,000	318	0	3571
MAGNA CLOSURES INC 521 Newpark Blvd, Newmarket, ON L3X 2S2, *Tel* (905) 853-1800	1,000	319	0	5013
MAGNA EXTERIORS INC 50 Casmir Crt, Concord, ON L4K 4J5, *Tel* (905) 669-2888	1,000	320	475,630,803	3714
MAGNA INTERNATIONAL INC 1 Cosma Crt, St Thomas, ON N5P 4J5, *Tel* (519) 633-8400	1,000	321	0	3714
MAINTENANCE SERVIKO INC 2670 Rue Duchesne Bureau 100, Saint-Laurent, QC H4R 1J3, *Tel* (514) 332-2600	1,000	322	98,160,000	7361
MASCAREN INTERNATIONAL INC 500a Danforth Ave Suite 304, Toronto, ON M4K 1P6, *Tel* (416) 465-6690	1,000	323	98,160,000	7363
MINES AGNICO EAGLE LIMITEE 20 Rte 395 Cadillac, Rouyn-Noranda, QC J0Y 1C0, *Tel* (819) 759-3644	1,000	324	0	1241
▲ Molson Canada 2005 (*Suby of* **MOLSON COORS BREWING COMPANY**) 1 Carlingview Dr, Etobicoke, ON M9W 5E5, *Tel* (416) 675-1786	1,000	325	0	2082
Morneau Shepell Ltd (*Suby of* **MORNEAU SHEPELL INC**) 800 Square Victoria Bureau 4000, Montreal, QC H4Z 0A4, *Tel* (514) 878-9090	1,000	326	0	8999
NOVA PETROCHEMICALS LTD 1000 7 Ave Sw, Calgary, AB T2P 5L5, *Tel* (403) 750-3600	1,000	327	234,828,387	6712
NEWLY WEDS FOODS CO. 1381 Rue Ampere, Boucherville, QC J4B 5Z5, *Tel* (450) 641-2200	1,000	328	0	2099
NORTEL NETWORKS LIMITED 250 Sidney St, Belleville, ON K8P 3Z3, *Tel*	1,000	329	0	4899
NOVA CENTRAL SCHOOL DISTRICT 203 Elizabeth Dr, Gander, NL A1V 1H6, *Tel* (709) 256-2547	1,000	330	175,084,728	8211
PF RESOLU CANADA INC 2001 Neebing Ave, Thunder Bay, ON P7E 6S3, *Tel* (807) 475-2400	1,000	331	0	2621
PROVIDENCE HEALTH CARE SOCIETY				

COMPANY	EMPLOYEES HERE	RANK	SALES ($)	PRIMARY SIC CODE
3080 Prince Edward St, Vancouver, BC V5T 3N4, *Tel* (604) 877-8302	1,000	332	0	8062
RBC Dominion Securities Inc (*Suby of* **ROYAL BANK OF CANADA**) 200 Bay St, Toronto, ON M5J 2W7, *Tel* (416) 842-2000	1,000	333	1,507,016,865	6282
RBC Global Asset Management (U.S.) Inc. (*Suby of* **ROYAL BANK OF CANADA**) 155 Wellington St W 22 Flr, Toronto, ON M5V 3K7, *Tel* (416) 974-5008	1,000	334	145,921,400	6282
REGINA EXHIBITION ASSOCIATION LIMITED 1700 Elphinstone St, Regina, SK S4P 2Z6, *Tel* (306) 781-9200	1,000	335	73,129,200	7999
REGIONAL HEALTH AUTHORITY NB 155 Pleasant St, Miramichi, NB E1V 1Y3, *Tel* (506) 623-5500	1,000	336	822,036,011	8062
Rio Tinto Alcan Inc (*Suby of* **RIO TINTO PLC**) 3000 Rue Des Pins O, Alma, QC G8B 5W2, *Tel* (418) 480-6000	1,000	337	0	3399
SASKATCHEWAN GOVERNMENT INSURANCE 2260 11th Ave Suite 18, Regina, SK S4P 0J9, *Tel* (306) 751-1200	1,000	338	1,021,223,304	6331
SASKATCHEWAN INSTITUTE OF APPLIED SCIENCE AND TECHNOLOGY 1130 Idylwyld Dr And 33rd St, Saskatoon, SK S7K 3R5, *Tel* (866) 467-4278	1,000	339	0	8222
Services Financiers NCO, Inc (*Suby of* **EGS SHELL COMPANY, INC.**) 75 Rue De Port-Royal E Bureau 240, Montreal, QC H3L 3T1, *Tel* (514) 385-4444	1,000	340	153,217,470	7322
Services Financiers NCO, Inc (*Suby of* **EGS SHELL COMPANY, INC.**) 11125 124 St, Surrey, BC V3V 4V2, *Tel* (604) 953-2801	1,000	341	0	7322
SLEEP COUNTRY CANADA INC 805 Boyd St Suite 100, New Westminster, BC V3M 5X2, *Tel* (604) 515-9711	1,000	342	0	5712
Specialty Care Inc (*Suby of* **SPECIALTY CARE INC**) 10260 Kennedy Rd, Brampton, ON L6Z 4N7, *Tel* (905) 495-4695	1,000	343	0	8059
TECHNOLOGIES METAFORE INC 9393 Boul Louis-H.-Lafontaine, Anjou, QC H1J 1Y8, *Tel* (514) 354-3810	1,000	344	186,863,841	7371
TEMBEC INC 1 Government Rd W, Kapuskasing, ON P5N 2X8, *Tel* (705) 337-9784	1,000	345	0	2621
Tervita Corporation (*Suby of* **TERVITA CORPORATION**) 27123 Hwy 597 Suite 13, Blackfalds, AB T0M 0J0, *Tel* (403) 885-0075	1,000	346	0	1389
UNIVERSITY OF OTTAWA 451 Smyth Rd Suite Rgn, Ottawa, ON K1H 8M5, *Tel* (613) 562-5800	1,000	347	0	8221
VEOLIA ES CANADA SERVICES INDUSTRIELS INC 7950 Av Pion, Saint-Hyacinthe, QC J2R 1R9, *Tel* (450) 796-6060	1,000	348	0	4953
VIGOUR LIMITED PARTNERSHIP 2121 Argentia Rd Suite 301, Mississauga, ON L5N 2X4, *Tel* (905) 821-1161	1,000	349	62,699,520	8051
William Osler Health System (*Suby of* **WILLIAM OSLER HEALTH SYSTEM**) 101 Humber College Blvd, Etobicoke, ON M9V 1R8, *Tel* (416) 494-2120	1,000	350	0	8062
Woodbine Entertainment Group (*Suby of* **WOODBINE ENTERTAINMENT GROUP**) 555 Rexdale Blvd, Toronto, ON M9W 5L2, *Tel* (416) 675-7223	1,000	351	325,565	7948
BLAKE, CASSELS & GRAYDON LLP 199 Bay St Suite 4000, Toronto, ON M5V 1V3, *Tel* (416) 863-2400	999	352	0	8111
▲ **KBR INDUSTRIAL CANADA CO.** 3300 76 Ave Nw, Edmonton, AB T6P 1J4, *Tel* (780) 468-1341	998	353	198,161,261	1541
Roman Catholic Archdiocese of Vancouver, The (*Suby of* **ROMAN CATHOLIC ARCHDIOCESE OF VANCOUVER, THE**) 4885 Saint John Paul Ii Way, Vancouver, BC V5Z 0G3, *Tel* (604) 683-0281	986	354	84,903,843	8661
ACCEO SOLUTIONS INC 7710 Boul Wilfrid-Hamel, Quebec, QC G2G 2J5, *Tel* (418) 877-0088	960	355	0	7372
FLOWERS CANADA INC 99 Fifth Ave Suite 305, Ottawa, ON K1S 5K4, *Tel* (800) 447-5147	958	356	132,417,840	8611
120776 CANADA INC 700 Rue Canadel, Louiseville, QC J5V 3A4, *Tel* (819) 228-8471	950	357	239,929,250	6712
CENTRE HOSPITALIER FLEURY 2180 Rue Fleury E, Montreal, QC H2B 1K3, *Tel* (514) 383-9311	950	358	88,932,960	8062
GROUPE VOLVO CANADA INC 35 Boul Gagnon, Sainte-Claire, QC G0R 2V0, *Tel* (418) 883-3391	950	359	1,395,373,388	5012
IMPERIAL OIL LIMITED Po Box 3004 Stn Main, Sarnia, ON N7T 7M5, *Tel* (519) 339-4015	950	360	1,398,780,000	2911
MAGNA INTERNATIONAL INC 333 Market Dr, Milton, ON L9T 4Z7, *Tel* (905) 878-5571	950	361	0	3714
NIAGARA HEALTH SYSTEM 5546 Portage Rd, Niagara Falls, ON L2G 5X8, *Tel* (905) 378-4647	950	362	0	8062
OCEANAGOLD CORPORATION 777 Hornby Street Suite 1910, Vancouver, BC V6Z 1S4, *Tel* (604) 235-3360	950	363	628,634,000	1081
SOEURS DE LA CHARITE D'OTTAWA, LES 43 Bruyere St, Ottawa, ON K1N 5C8, *Tel* (613) 562-0050	950	364	0	8661
9130-1168 QUEBEC INC 298 Boul Armand-Theriault Bureau 2, Riviere-Du-Loup, QC G5R 4C2, *Tel* (418) 862-7848	926	365	0	6512
Hema-Quebec (*Suby of* **HEMA-QUEBEC**) 4045 Boul De La Cote-Vertu, Saint-Laurent, QC H4R 2W7, *Tel* (514) 832-5000	915	366	321,428,422	8099
▲ Stream International Canada ULC (*Suby of* **CONVERGYS CORPORATION**) 95 Union St, Glace Bay, NS B1A 2P6, *Tel* (902) 842-3800	909	367	0	7389
2168587 ONTARIO LTD 50 Marmora St, North York, ON M9M 2X5, *Tel* (416) 661-7744	900	368	0	2053

COMPANY	EMPLOYEES HERE	RANK	SALES ($)	PRIMARY SIC CODE
4659555 MANITOBA LTD 330a King St, Winnipeg, MB R3B 3H4, *Tel* (204) 989-5820	900	369	84,809,610	7361
ALBERTA HEALTH SERVICES Gd Stn Main, Ponoka, AB T4J 1R9, *Tel* (403) 783-7600	900	370	0	8011
ALBERTA TREASURY BRANCHES 229 33 St Ne Suite 400, Calgary, AB T2A 4Y6, *Tel* (403) 974-6850	900	371	0	8742
APOTEX INC 50 Steinway Blvd Suite 3, Etobicoke, ON M9W 6Y3, *Tel* (416) 675-0338	900	372	0	2834
▲ **BWXT CANADA LTD** 581 Coronation Blvd, Cambridge, ON N1R 3E9, *Tel* (519) 621-2130	900	373	177,367,462	3621
BAYER INC 1265 Vidal St S, Sarnia, ON N7T 7M2, *Tel* (519) 337-8251	900	374	0	2822
CARGILL LIMITED 10 Cuddy Blvd, London, ON N5V 5E3, *Tel* (519) 453-4996	900	375	0	2015
Coutts, William E. Company, Limited (*Suby of* **HALLMARK CARDS, INCORPORATED**) 501 Consumers Rd, North York, ON M2J 5E2, *Tel* (416) 492-1300	900	376	0	2771
CROSS, DR G B MEMORIAL HOSPITAL 67 Manitoba Dr, Clarenville, NL A5A 1K3, *Tel* (709) 466-3411	900	377	86,211,840	8062
DESJARDINS GROUPE D'ASSURANCES GENERALES INC 5070 Dixie Rd, Mississauga, ON L4W 1C9, *Tel* (905) 366-4430	900	378	0	6411
GOUVERNEMENT DE LA PROVINCE DE QUEBEC 50 Rue Saint-Patrice E, Magog, QC J1X 3X3, *Tel* (819) 843-2572	900	379	0	8062
INTACT INSURANCE COMPANY 321 6 Ave Sw Suite 1200, Calgary, AB T2P 3H3, *Tel* (403) 269-7961	900	380	0	6331
KIK OPERATING PARTNERSHIP 2000 Kipling Ave, Etobicoke, ON M9W 4J6, *Tel* (416) 743-6255	900	381	0	2842
▲ **KNOLL NORTH AMERICA CORP** 1000 Arrow Rd, North York, ON M9M 2Y7, *Tel* (416) 741-5453	900	382	79,521,842	2521
NOVA FORGE CORP 34 Power Plant Rd, Trenton, NS B0K 1X0, *Tel* (902) 752-0989	900	383	236,479,950	3743
Peter Kiewit Infrastructure Co. (*Suby of* **PETER KIEWIT SONS', INC.**) 9500 100 St Se, Calgary, AB T3S 0A2, *Tel*	900	384	0	1611
Presse, Ltee, La (*Suby of* **GESCA LTEE**) 750 Boul Saint-Laurent, Montreal, QC H2Y 2Z4, *Tel* (514) 285-7000	900	385	74,638,796	2711
▲ Procter & Gamble Inc (*Suby of* **THE PROCTER & GAMBLE COMPANY**) 1475 California Ave, Brockville, ON K6V 6K4, *Tel* (613) 342-9592	900	386	0	2841
PWC MANAGEMENT SERVICES LP 10190 152a St 3 Fl, Surrey, BC V3R 1J7, *Tel* (604) 806-7000	900	387	0	8721
REGIONAL HEALTH AUTHORITY A 1750 Sunset Dr, Bathurst, NB E2A 4L7, *Tel* (506) 544-3000	900	388	0	8062
RELIGIOUS HOSPITALLERS OF SAINT JOSEPH OF THE HOTEL DIEU OF KINGSTON 166 Brock St, Kingston, ON K7L 5G2, *Tel* (613) 549-2680	900	389	0	8069
REVOLUTION ENVIRONMENTAL SOLUTIONS ACQUISITION GP INC 6110 27 St Nw, Edmonton, AB T6P 1Y5, *Tel* (780) 450-7664	900	390	63,230,276	8731
Royal Bank Of Canada (*Suby of* **ROYAL BANK OF CANADA**) 1260 Taylor Ave, Winnipeg, MB R3M 3Y8, *Tel* (204) 499-7000	900	391	0	7299
SAINE MARKETING INC 1600 Boul Rene-Levesque O Bureau 1800, Montreal, QC H3H 1P9, *Tel* (514) 931-8236	900	392	165,001,808	8732
SIEMENS CANADA LIMITED 30 Milton Ave, Hamilton, ON L8L 6E6, *Tel* (905) 528-8811	900	393	0	3511
SOBEYS CAPITAL INCORPORATED 12910 156 St Nw, Edmonton, AB T5V 1E9, *Tel* (780) 447-1440	900	394	0	5141
St Joseph's General Hospital (*Suby of* **ST JOSEPH'S GENERAL HOSPITAL**) 2137 Comox Ave, Comox, BC V9M 1P2, *Tel* (250) 339-1451	900	395	76,535,774	8062
▲ State Street Trust Company Canada (*Suby of* **STATE STREET CORPORATION**) 30 Adelaide St E Suite 1100, Toronto, ON M5C 3G8, *Tel* (416) 362-1100	900	396	326,861,440	6719
▲ **UNION GAS LIMITED** 50 Keil Dr N Suite 2001, Chatham, ON N7L 3V9, *Tel* (519) 352-3100	900	397	1,130,917,205	4923
UNIVERSITY OF BRITISH COLUMBIA, THE 2329 West Mall, Vancouver, BC V6T 1Z4, *Tel* (604) 822-2172	900	398	0	8221
VIDEON CABLESYSTEMS INC 630 3 Ave Sw Suite 900, Calgary, AB T2P 4L4, *Tel* (403) 750-4500	900	399	227,587,200	4841
▲ **WALMART CANADA LOGISTICS ULC** 3400 39 Ave Ne, Calgary, AB T1Y 7J4, *Tel* (403) 250-3648	900	400	0	4225
Finning International Inc (*Suby of* **FINNING INTERNATIONAL INC**) 666 Burrard St Suite 1000, Vancouver, BC V6C 2X8, *Tel* (604) 691-6444	897	401	4,162,722,060	5084
T.E.C.M. LIMITED 103 Kinkora Dr, Winnipeg, MB R3R 2P5, *Tel* (204) 227-8556	890	402	92,172,240	3625
CPP INVESTMENT BOARD PRIVATE HOLDINGS (2) INC. One Queen St E Suite 2500, Toronto, ON M5C 2W5, *Tel* (416) 868-4075	886	403	154,305,450	6371
▲ ESIT Canada Enterprise Services Co (*Suby of* **DXC TECHNOLOGY COMPANY**) 1969 Upper Water St, Halifax, NS B3J 3R7, *Tel*	885	404	357,507,430	5734
KIK Holdco Company Inc (*Suby of* **KIK CUSTOM PRODUCTS INC**) 101 Macintosh Blvd, Concord, ON L4K 4R5, *Tel* (905) 660-0444	850	405	181,818,064	6719

COMPANY	EMPLOYEES HERE	RANK	SALES ($)	PRIMARY SIC CODE
KUNTZ ELECTROPLATING INC 851 Wilson Ave, Kitchener, ON N2C 1J1, *Tel* (519) 893-7680	850	406	57,274,150	3471
RIVERVIEW HEALTH CENTRE INC 1 Morley Ave, Winnipeg, MB R3L 2P4, *Tel* (204) 478-6203	850	407	47,734,066	8051
ROCKY MOUNTAIN DEALERSHIPS INC 260180 Writing Creek Cres, Rocky View County, AB T4A 0M9, *Tel* (403) 513-7000	850	408	0	5082
TOROMONT INDUSTRIES LTD 65 Villiers St, Toronto, ON M5A 3S1, *Tel* (416) 465-7581	850	409	0	3585
GUNGNIR RESOURCES INC 1688 152 St Suite 404, Surrey, BC V4A 4N2, *Tel* (604) 683-0484	833	410	90,544,229	1041
Cambrian College of Applied Arts & Technology, The (*Suby of* **CAMBRIAN COLLEGE OF APPLIED ARTS & TECH-NOLOGY, THE**) 1400 Barrydowne Rd, Sudbury, ON P3A 3V8, *Tel* (705) 566-8101	830	411	123,870,450	8222
OMEGA DIRECT RESPONSE INC 30 Wertheim Crt Unit 12, Richmond Hill, ON L4B 1B9, *Tel* (416) 733-9911	825	412	54,884,450	7389
HYDRO-QUEBEC 140 Boul Cremazie O, Montreal, QC H2P 1C3, *Tel* (514) 858-8500	821	413	0	8731
CANADIAN COAST GUARD AUXILIARY (CENTRAL AND ARCTIC) INC 577 Kingston Rd Suite 206, Toronto, ON M4E 1R3, *Tel* (416) 463-7283	811	414	132,516,000	8699
CONESTOGA MEAT PACKERS LTD 313 Menno St, Breslau, ON N0B 1M0, *Tel* (519) 648-2506	807	415	225,242,100	5147
ACIER GENDRON LTEE 2270 Rue Garneau, Longueuil, QC J4G 1E7, *Tel* (450) 442-9494	800	416	448,104,650	5051
ARMOUR TRANSPORT INC 689 Edinburgh Dr, Moncton, NB E1E 2L4, *Tel* (506) 857-0205	800	417	214,066,694	4213
AstraZeneca Canada Inc (*Suby of* **ASTRAZENECA PLC**) 1004 Middlegate Rd Suite 5000, Mississauga, ON L4Y 1M4, *Tel* (905) 277-7111	800	418	172,557,199	2834
BELL ALIANT REGIONAL COMMUNICATIONS INC Gd, Saint John, NB E2L 4K2, *Tel* (506) 658-7169	800	419	0	4899
BELL MEDIA INC 444 Front St W, Toronto, ON M5V 2S9, *Tel* (416) 585-5000	800	420	0	5192
BOMBARDIER INC 1101 Rue Parent, Saint-Bruno, QC J3V 6E6, *Tel* (514) 861-9481	800	421	0	4111
Burnbrae Farms Limited (*Suby of* **BURNBRAE HOLDINGS LTD**) 3356 County Road 27, Lyn, ON K0E 1M0, *Tel* (613) 345-5651	800	422	237,122,275	5144
▲ CMC Electronique Inc (*Suby of* **ESTERLINE TECHNOLOGIES CORP**) 600 Boul Dr.-Frederik-Philips, Saint-Laurent, QC H4M 2S9, *Tel* (514) 748-3148	800	423	117,320,806	8711
CANADA LIFE ASSURANCE COMPANY, THE 1901 Scarth St Suite 414, Regina, SK S4P 4L4, *Tel* (306) 751-6000	800	424	0	6311
CANADA POST CORPORATION Gd Stn Terminal, Vancouver, BC V6B 3P7, *Tel*	800	425	0	4311
CANADIAN PACIFIC RAILWAY COMPANY 1 Old Lodge Rd, Jasper, AB T0E 1E0, *Tel* (780) 852-6406	800	426	0	7011
CARGILL LIMITED 71 Rexdale Blvd, Etobicoke, ON M9W 1P1, *Tel*	800	427	0	2011
CENTRE BUTTERS-SAVOY ET HORIZON 1255 Rue Beauregard Bureau 2201, Longueuil, QC J4K 2M3, *Tel* (450) 679-6511	800	428	40,192,000	8361
CENTRE HOSPITALIER UNIVERSITAIRE DE QUEBEC 2705 Boul Laurier Bureau 4, Quebec, QC G1V 4G2, *Tel* (418) 654-2244	800	429	0	8731
CENTRE DE SANTE ET DE SERVICE SOCIAUX LES ESKERS DE L'ABITIBI 632 1re Rue O, Amos, QC J9T 2N2, *Tel* (819) 732-3271	800	430	0	8062
Centre de Sante et de Services Sociaux de Becancour-Nicolet-Yamaska (*Suby of* **CENTRE DE SANTE ET DE SER-VICES SOCIAUX DE BECANCOUR-NICOLET-YAMASKA**) 675 Rue Saint-Jean-Baptiste, Nicolet, QC J3T 1S4, *Tel* (819) 293-2071	800	431	112,203,700	8069
CHOEUR DU CEGEP DE SHERBROOKE 475 Rue Du Cegep, Sherbrooke, QC J1E 4K1, *Tel* (819) 564-6350	800	432	107,425,506	8221
College Of New Caledonia, The (*Suby of* **COLLEGE OF NEW CALEDONIA, THE**) 3330 22nd Ave, Prince George, BC V2N 1P8, *Tel* (250) 562-2131	800	433	134,281,883	8221
COLLEGE D'ENSEIGNEMENT GENERAL ET PROFESSIONNEL JOHN ABBOTT 21275 Rue Lakeshore, Sainte-Anne-De-Bellevue, QC H9X 3L9, *Tel* (514) 457-6610	800	434	107,425,506	8221
DESSAU INC 1060 Boul Robert-Bourassa Unite 600, Montreal, QC H3B 4V3, *Tel* (514) 281-1033	800	435	0	8711
DICOM TRANSPORTATION GROUP CANADA, INC 10755 Ch Cote-De-Liesse, Dorval, QC H9P 1A7, *Tel* (514) 631-1242	800	436	0	4212
▲ Dow Chemical Canada ULC (*Suby of* **THE DOW CHEMICAL COMPANY**) Gd, Fort Saskatchewan, AB T8L 2P4, *Tel* (780) 998-8000	800	437	0	2899
Ernst & Young LLP (*Suby of* **ERNST & YOUNG LLP**) 800 Boul Rene-Levesque O Bureau 1900, Montreal, QC H3B 1X9, *Tel* (514) 875-6060	800	438	0	8721
FAIRMONT HOTELS & RESORTS INC 111 Lake Louise Dr, Lake Louise, AB T0L 1E0, *Tel* (403) 522-1818	800	439	0	7011
FAIRMONT HOTELS & RESORTS INC 405 Spray Ave, Banff, AB T1L 1J4, *Tel* (403) 762-6860	800	440	0	7011
FAIRMONT HOTELS INC 900 Boul Rene-Levesque O, Montreal, QC H3B 4A5, *Tel* (514) 861-3511	800	441	0	7011

COMPANY	EMPLOYEES HERE	RANK	SALES ($)	PRIMARY SIC CODE
FEDERATION DES CAISSES DESJARDINS DU QUEBEC				
3155 Boul De L'Assomption, Montreal, QC H1N 3S8, *Tel* (514) 253-7300	800	442	0	4899
FUJITSU				
2000 Boul Lebourgneuf Bureau 300, Quebec, QC G2K 0B8, *Tel* (418) 840-5100	800	443	80,384,000	7379
G4S SECURE SOLUTIONS (CANADA) LTD				
2 Lansing Sq Suite 204, North York, ON M2J 4P8, *Tel* (416) 490-8329	800	444	0	7381
GOVERNMENT OF THE PROVINCE OF ALBERTA				
10155 102 St Nw Suite 1109, Edmonton, AB T5J 4L4, *Tel* (780) 427-8392	800	445	0	8999
GROUPE PAGES JAUNES CORP				
16 Place Du Commerce, Verdun, QC H3E 2A5, *Tel* (514) 934-2000	800	446	306,392,979	4899
Hammond Power Solutions Inc (*Suby of* **HAMMOND POWER SOLUTIONS INC**)				
595 Southgate Dr, Guelph, ON N1G 3W6, *Tel* (519) 822-2441	800	447	203,249,268	3612
HENNIGES AUTOMOTIVE SEALING SYSTEMS CANADA INC				
100 Kennedy St, Welland, ON L3B 0B4, *Tel*	800	448	167,600,640	3069
HOPITAL L'HOTEL DIEU D'ARTHABASKA				
5 Rue Des Hospitalieres, Victoriaville, QC G6P 6N2, *Tel* (819) 357-1151	800	449	74,896,080	8062
HUMBER RIVER HOSPITAL				
2111 Finch Ave W, Toronto, ON M3N 1N1, *Tel* (416) 744-2500	800	450	0	8062
HUSKY OIL OPERATIONS LIMITED				
5650 52 St, Lloydminster, AB T9V 0R7, *Tel*	800	451	0	1311
INTRIA ITEMS INC				
8301 Rue Elmslie, Lasalle, QC H8N 3H9, *Tel* (514) 368-5222	800	452	0	7374
INGRAM MICRO INC				
55 Standish Crt Suite 1, Mississauga, ON L5R 4A1, *Tel* (905) 755-5000	800	453	162,422,063	5045
INTERIOR HEALTH AUTHORITY				
311 Columbia St, Kamloops, BC V2C 2T1, *Tel* (250) 374-5111	800	454	0	8062
▲ **INVESCO CANADA LTD**				
5140 Yonge St Suite 800, North York, ON M2N 6X7, *Tel* (800) 874-6275	800	455	145,921,400	6211
INVESTORS PREMIUM MONEY MARKET FUND				
447 Portage Ave, Winnipeg, MB R3C 3B6, *Tel* (204) 957-7383	800	456	327,966,720	6722
KPMG LLP (*Suby of* **KPMG LLP**)				
777 Dunsmuir St Suite 900, Vancouver, BC V7Y 1K3, *Tel* (604) 691-3000	800	457	0	8721
KIRKLAND LAKE GOLD LTD				
1350 Government Rd W, Kirkland Lake, ON P2N 3J1, *Tel* (705) 567-5208	800	458	0	1081
LEDCOR INDUSTRIES INC				
1067 Cordova St W Suite 1200, Vancouver, BC V6C 1C7, *Tel* (604) 681-7500	800	459	110,793,503	1611
London Health Sciences Centre Research Inc (*Suby of* **LONDON HEALTH SCIENCES CENTRE RESEARCH INC**)				
750 Base Line Rd E Suite 300, London, ON N6C 2R5, *Tel* (519) 667-6649	800	460	857,947	8733
MAIBEC INC				
24 6e Rang Bureau 6, Saint-Pamphile, QC G0R 3X0, *Tel* (418) 356-3331	800	461	0	2421
MANUFACTURERS LIFE INSURANCE COMPANY, THE				
2727 Joseph Howe Dr, Halifax, NS B3L 4G6, *Tel* (902) 453-4300	800	462	0	6311
MANUFACTURERS LIFE INSURANCE COMPANY, THE				
2000 Rue Mansfield Unite 300, Montreal, QC H3A 2Z4, *Tel* (514) 288-6268	800	463	0	6311
MATRIX LOGISTICS SERVICES LIMITED				
2675 Steeles Ave W, Brampton, ON L6Y 5X3, *Tel* (905) 451-6792	800	464	0	4225
Metropolitan Entertainment Group (*Suby of* **GREAT CANADIAN GAMING CORPORATION**)				
1983 Upper Water St, Halifax, NS B3J 3Y5, *Tel* (902) 425-7777	800	465	51,628,560	7999
▲ **METROPOLITAN LIFE HOLDINGS LIMITED**				
99 Bank St, Ottawa, ON K1P 6B9, *Tel* (613) 560-7446	800	466	103,795,840	6531
MULTI-MARQUES INC				
3455 Av Francis-Hughes, Sainte-Rose, QC H7L 5A5, *Tel* (450) 669-2222	800	467	126,920,880	2051
NIAGARA HEALTH SYSTEM				
142 Queenston St, St Catharines, ON L2R 2Z7, *Tel* (905) 684-7271	800	468	0	8062
NORDION INC				
3680 Gilmore Way, Burnaby, BC V5G 4V8, *Tel* (604) 431-5005	800	469	0	8071
▲ PACCAR of Canada Ltd (*Suby of* **PACCAR INC**)				
10 Rue Sicard, Sainte-Therese, QC J7E 4K9, *Tel* (450) 435-6171	800	470	0	3711
PROVIGO DISTRIBUTION INC				
400 Av Sainte-Croix, Saint-Laurent, QC H4N 3L4, *Tel* (514) 383-3000	800	471	7,763,254,837	5141
Restigouche Health Authority (*Suby of* **RESTIGOUCHE HEALTH AUTHORITY**)				
189 Lily Lake Rd, Campbellton, NB E3N 3H3, *Tel* (506) 789-5000	800	472	109,781,329	8062
Rio Tinto Alcan Inc (*Suby of* **RIO TINTO PLC**)				
5000 Rte Du Petit Parc, La Baie, QC G7B 4G9, *Tel* (418) 697-9600	800	473	0	3334
SAIPEM CANADA INC				
530 8 Ave Sw Suite 2700, Calgary, AB T2P 3S8, *Tel* (403) 441-2793	800	474	205,238,449	1629
School District No. 44 (North Vancouver) (*Suby of* **SCHOOL DISTRICT NO. 44 (NORTH VANCOUVER)**)				
2121 Lonsdale Ave, North Vancouver, BC V7M 2K6, *Tel* (604) 903-3444	800	475	140,539,433	8211
Services Financiers NCO, Inc (*Suby of* **EGS SHELL COMPANY, INC.**)				
345 Queen St E, Sault Ste. Marie, ON P6A 1Z2, *Tel*	800	476	0	7389
SOBEYS CAPITAL INCORPORATED				
11281 Boul Albert-Hudon, Montreal-Nord, QC H1G 3J5, *Tel* (514) 324-5700	800	477	0	5141
SOBEYS QUEBEC INC				
11281 Boul Albert-Hudon, Montreal-Nord, QC H1G 3J5, *Tel* (514) 324-1010	800	478	1,046,183,477	5141

COMPANY	EMPLOYEES HERE	RANK	SALES ($)	PRIMARY SIC CODE
SUN LIFE ASSURANCE COMPANY OF CANADA 2255 Sheppard Ave E Suite 135a, North York, ON M2J 4Y1, *Tel* (416) 496-4500	800	479	0	6311
SUPRALIMENT S.E.C. 25 125 Rte E, Saint-Esprit, QC J0K 2L0, *Tel* (450) 839-7258	800	480	0	2011
SYMCOR INC 8 Prince Andrew Pl, North York, ON M3C 2H4, *Tel* (905) 273-1000	800	481	0	8741
Syndicat des Professionnelles en Soins de Sante Lac St-Jean Est (*Suby of* **SYNDICAT DES PROFESSIONNELLES EN SOINS DE SANTE LAC ST-JEAN EST**) 300 Boul Champlain, Alma, QC G8B 3N8, *Tel* (418) 662-1424	800	482	226,436,400	6371
TEMBEC INC 10 Ch Gatineau, Temiscaming, QC J0Z 3R0, *Tel* (819) 627-4387	800	483	0	2611
Tervita Corporation (*Suby of* **TERVITA CORPORATION**) 140 10 Ave Se Suite 1600, Calgary, AB T2G 0R1, *Tel* (403) 233-7565	800	484	573,835,906	8748
Toronto-Dominion Bank, The (*Suby of* **TORONTO-DOMINION BANK, THE**) 12 Concord Pl, Toronto, ON M3C 2R8, *Tel* (416) 462-2054	800	485	0	6021
▲ **WALMART CANADA LOGISTICS ULC** 6800 Maritz Dr, Mississauga, ON L5W 1W2, *Tel* (905) 670-9966	800	486	265,576,948	4225
▲ Winners Merchants International L.P. (*Suby of* **THE TJX COMPANIES INC**) 3185 American Dr, Mississauga, ON L4V 1B8, *Tel* (905) 672-2228	800	487	0	5651
CAPILANO UNIVERSITY 2055 Purcell Way Suite 284, North Vancouver, BC V7J 3H5, *Tel* (604) 986-1911	797	488	31,559,191	8221
▲ General Dynamics Produits de Defense et Systemes Tactiques-Canada Inc (*Suby of* **GENERAL DYNAMICS CORPORATION**) 5 Montee Des Arsenaux, Repentigny, QC J5Z 2P4, *Tel* (450) 581-3080	790	489	0	3483
ST. JOSEPH'S HEALTH CARE, LONDON 850 Highbury Ave N, London, ON N5Y 1A4, *Tel* (519) 455-5110	786	490	0	8093
▲ **NAVISTAR CANADA, INC** 508 Richmond St, Chatham, ON N7M 1R3, *Tel*	777	491		3711
ALLIED INTERNATIONAL CREDIT CORP 16635 Yonge St Suite 26, Newmarket, ON L3X 1V6, *Tel* (905) 470-8181	775	492	28,846,155	4899
SOCIETE DES CASINOS DU QUEBEC INC, LA 500 Rue Sherbrooke O Bureau 1500, Montreal, QC H3A 3C6, *Tel* (514) 282-8000	769	493	291,186,154	7999
ARBEC, BOIS D'OEUVRE INC 1053 Boul Ducharme, La Tuque, QC G9X 3C3, *Tel* (514) 327-2733	750	494	71,136,683	2421
BANQUE DE DEVELOPPEMENT DU CANADA 5 Place Ville-Marie Bureau 400, Montreal, QC H3B 5E7, *Tel* (514) 283-5904	750	495	777,423,156	6141
BLUE TREE HOTELS INVESTMENT (CANADA), LTD Westin Harbour Castle, Toronto, ON M5J 1A6, *Tel* (416) 869-1600	750	496	0	7011
BOARD OF GOVERNOR'S OF RED RIVER COLLEGE, THE 2055 Notre Dame Ave, Winnipeg, MB R3H 0J9, *Tel* (204) 632-3960	750	497	161,988,937	8222
Cavendish Agri Services Limited (*Suby of* **J. D. IRVING, LIMITED**) 25532 Main Hwy Suite 2, Summerside, PE C1N 4J9, *Tel* (902) 836-5555	750	498	0	2037
CENTRE HOSPITALIER JACQUES VIGER 1051 Rue Saint-Hubert, Montreal, QC H2L 3Y5, *Tel* (514) 842-7181	750	499	36,810,000	8361
COMPAGNIE MEXX CANADA 905 Rue Hodge, Saint-Laurent, QC H4N 2B3, *Tel* (514) 383-5555	750	500	140,312,788	5137
COMPAGNIE DES CHEMINS DE FER NATIONAUX DU CANADA 1108 Industrial Way, Prince George, BC V2N 5S1, *Tel* (250) 561-4190	750	501	0	4111
DELTA HOTELS LIMITED 77 King St W Suite 2300, Toronto, ON M5K 2A1, *Tel* (416) 874-2000	750	502	357,945,194	8741
EPCOR POWER (WILLIAMS LAKE) LTD 10065 Jasper Ave Nw, Edmonton, AB T5J 3B1, *Tel* (780) 412-3191	750	503	482,554,560	4911
Grand Forest Holdings Incorporated (*Suby of* **J. D. IRVING, LIMITED**) Gd, Summerside, PE C1N 4J9, *Tel* (902) 836-5555	750	504	0	5142
HYDRO-QUEBEC 1800 Boul Lionel-Boulet, Varennes, QC J3X 1P7, *Tel* (450) 652-8011	750	505	0	8731
KPH TURCOT, UN PARTENARIAT S.E.N.C 4333 Boul De La Grande-Allee, Boisbriand, QC J7H 1M7, *Tel* (450) 435-5756	750	506	106,157,819	8742
KPMG LLP (*Suby of* **KPMG LLP**) 600 Boul De Maisonneuve O Unite 1500, Montreal, QC H3A 0A3, *Tel* (514) 840-2100	750	507	0	8721
MAGNA SEATING INC 201 Patillo Rd, Tecumseh, ON N8N 2L9, *Tel* (519) 727-6222	750	508	0	2531
MANULIFE CANADA LTD 2000 Rue Mansfield Unite 200, Montreal, QC H3A 2Z4, *Tel* (514) 845-1612	750	509	0	8742
NEW BRUNSWICK POWER CORPORATION 122 Countyline Rd, Maces Bay, NB E5J 1W1, *Tel*	750	510	0	4911
PERSONNEL UNIQUE CANADA INC 455 Boul Fenelon Bureau 210, Dorval, QC H9S 5T8, *Tel* (514) 633-6220	750	511	147,609,750	8741
POSTMEDIA NETWORK INC 215 16 St Se, Calgary, AB T2E 7P5, *Tel* (403) 235-7168	750	512	0	2711
PRICEWATERHOUSECOOPERS LLP 1250 Boul Rene-Levesque O Bureau 2800, Montreal, QC H3B 4W8, *Tel* (514) 205-5000	750	513	0	8721
SUN GRO HORTICULTURE CANADA LTD Gd, Elma, MB R0E 0Z0, *Tel* (204) 426-2121	750	514	61,292,800	1499

COMPANY	EMPLOYEES HERE	RANK	SALES ($)	PRIMARY SIC CODE
SWISSPORT CANADA INC Gd, Richmond, BC V7B 1Y4, *Tel* (604) 303-4550	750	515	0	4581
Transport Thibodeau Saguelac Marcan Inc (*Suby of* **GROUPE THIBODEAU INC**) 128 2e Av, Portneuf, QC G0A 2Y0, *Tel*	750	516	152,344,320	4213
VUTEQ CANADA INC 920 Keyes Dr, Woodstock, ON N4V 1C2, *Tel* (519) 421-0011	750	517	218,045,200	3089
GOUVERNEMENT DE LA PROVINCE DE QUEBEC 7843 Rue Des Santolines, Quebec, QC G1G 0G3, *Tel* (418) 683-2511	741	518	0	8361
WATERVILLE TG INC 10 Rue Du Depot, Waterville, QC J0B 3H0, *Tel* (819) 837-2421	728	519	106,860,109	2891
Royal Bank Of Canada (*Suby of* **ROYAL BANK OF CANADA**) 90 Sparks St Suite 300, Ottawa, ON K1P 5B4, *Tel* (613) 564-3100	725	520	0	6021
BELL ALIANT REGIONAL COMMUNICATIONS INC 1505 Barrington St Suite 1102, Halifax, NS B3J 3K5, *Tel* (902) 487-4609	711	521	0	4899
SOCIETE DE TRANSPORT DE LAVAL 2250 Av Francis-Hughes, Montreal, QC H7S 2C3, *Tel* (450) 662-5400	707	522	33,472,560	4111
ASSURANCE MARTIN & CYR INC 460 Rue Mcgill, Montreal, QC H2Y 2H2, *Tel* (514) 527-9546	706	523	175,438,080	6712
EDMONTON TRAILER MANUFACTURING LTD 16908 128a Ave Nw, Edmonton, AB T5V 1K7, *Tel* (403) 744-5120	706	524	161,316,108	3531
902316 ONTARIO LIMITED 200 Hanlan Rd Suite A, Woodbridge, ON L4L 3P6, *Tel* (905) 850-5544	700	525	32,981,515	2789
▲ ADP Canada Co (*Suby of* **AUTOMATIC DATA PROCESSING, INC.**) 3250 Bloor St W Suite 1600, Etobicoke, ON M8X 2X9, *Tel* (416) 207-2900	700	526	103,950,120	8721
ALBERTA HEALTH SERVICES 10030 107 St Nw Suite 700, Edmonton, AB T5J 3E4, *Tel* (780) 735-0986	700	527	0	8062
ALCOA CANADA CIE 100 Rte Maritime, Baie-Comeau, QC G4Z 2L6, *Tel* (418) 296-3311	700	528	0	3354
ARCELORMITTAL PRODUITS LONGS CANADA S.E.N.C. 3900 Rte Des Acieries, Contrecoeur, QC J0L 1C0, *Tel* (450) 392-3226	700	529	0	3312
BBA Inc (*Suby of* **GROUPE BBA INC**) 10 Carlson Crt Suite 420, Toronto, ON M9W 6L2, *Tel* (416) 585-2115	700	530	0	8711
BARRY GROUP INC 1 Masonic Terrace, Clarenville, NL A5A 1N2, *Tel* (709) 466-7186	700	531	0	2092
BELLEMARE ENVIRONNEMENT 11450 Boul Industriel, Trois-Rivieres, QC G9A 5E1, *Tel* (819) 697-2227	700	532	51,239,520	8731
▲ Best Buy Canada Ltd (*Suby of* **BEST BUY CO., INC.**) 9250 Airport Rd Suite 1, Brampton, ON L6S 6K5, *Tel* (905) 494-7272	700	533	0	5065
▲ Campbell Company of Canada (*Suby of* **CAMPBELL SOUP COMPANY**) 60 Birmingham St, Etobicoke, ON M8V 2B8, *Tel* (416) 251-1131	700	534	166,886,466	2032
CANADA BREAD COMPANY, LIMITED 3455 Av Francis-Hughes, Sainte-Rose, QC H7L 5A5, *Tel* (450) 669-2222	700	535	0	5461
CARGILL LIMITED 7901 Rue Samuel-Hatt, Chambly, QC J3L 6V7, *Tel* (450) 447-4600	700	536	0	5153
CENTRE HOSPITALIER ET CENTRE DE READAPTATION ANTOINE-LABELLE 1525 Rue L'Annonciation N, Riviere-Rouge, QC J0T 1T0, *Tel* (819) 275-2411	700	537	0	8062
CINRO RESOURCES INC 100 King St W, Toronto, ON M5X 2A1, *Tel*	700	538	454,971,600	3341
▲ Com Dev Ltd (*Suby of* **HONEYWELL INTERNATIONAL INC.**) 155 Sheldon Dr, Cambridge, ON N1R 7H6, *Tel* (519) 622-2300	700	539	104,479,722	3669
▲ Computer Sciences Canada Inc (*Suby of* **DXC TECHNOLOGY COMPANY**) 1360 Boul Rene-Levesque O Bureau 300, Montreal, QC H3G 2W7, *Tel*	700	540	0	7379
▲ **CONCENTRIX TECHNOLOGIES SERVICES (CANADA) LIMITED** 720 Coverdale Rd, Riverview, NB E1B 3L8, *Tel* (506) 860-5900	700	541	0	4899
CONNEXIM, SOCIETE EN COMMANDITE 505 Boul De Maisonneuve O, Montreal, QC H3A 3C2, *Tel*	700	542	174,935,680	4899
CONNORS BROS. CLOVER LEAF SEAFOODS COMPANY 180 Brunswick St, Blacks Harbour, NB E5H 1G6, *Tel* (506) 456-1610	700	543	0	5146
ERNST & YOUNG INC 800 Boul Rene-Levesque O Bureau 1900, Montreal, QC H3B 1X9, *Tel* (514) 875-6060	700	544	0	8721
Ernst & Young LLP (*Suby of* **ERNST & YOUNG LLP**) 1 Place Ville-Marie Bureau 2400, Montreal, QC H3B 3M9, *Tel* (514) 875-6060	700	545	0	8721
FAIRMONT HOTELS & RESORTS INC 900 Boul Rene-Levesque O, Montreal, QC H3B 4A5, *Tel* (514) 861-3511	700	546	0	7011
FARM CREDIT CANADA 1800 Hamilton St, Regina, SK S4P 4L3, *Tel* (306) 780-8100	700	547	855,688,243	6159
FIDUCIE DESJARDINS INC 1 Complexe Desjardins Tour S, Montreal, QC H5B 1E4, *Tel* (514) 286-9441	700	548	151,174,570	6733
▲ Ford Motor Company of Canada, Limited (*Suby of* **FORD MOTOR COMPANY**) 6500 Cantelon Dr, Windsor, ON N8T 0A6, *Tel* (519) 251-4401	700	549	0	3711
GEM HEALTH CARE GROUP LIMITED 15 Shoreham Ln Suite 101, Halifax, NS B3P 2R3, *Tel* (902) 429-6227	700	550	0	6712
GESTION CANADADIRECT INC 743 Av Renaud, Dorval, QC H9P 2N1, *Tel* (514) 422-8557	700	551	133,104,960	8732

COMPANY	EMPLOYEES HERE	RANK	SALES ($)	PRIMARY SIC CODE
GOVERNMENT OF THE PROVINCE OF ALBERTA 5718 56 Ave, Lacombe, AB T4L 1B1, *Tel* (403) 782-8309	700	552	0	6331
GOVERNORS OF THE UNIVERSITY OF ALBERTA, THE 45 University Campus Nw Rm 410, Edmonton, AB T6G 2P5, *Tel* (780) 492-2131	700	553	0	8731
GROUPE CANAM INC 115 Boul Canam N, Saint-Gedeon-De-Beauce, QC G0M 1T0, *Tel* (418) 582-3331	700	554	0	3441
▲ Hershey Canada Inc (*Suby of* **HERSHEY COMPANY**) 375 Pleasant St, Dartmouth, NS B2Y 4N4, *Tel*	700	555	0	2064
I.M.P. GROUP LIMITED 10225 Av Ryan, Dorval, QC H9P 1A2, *Tel* (514) 636-7070	700	556	0	4581
L'INDUSTRIELLE-ALLIANCE SERVICES IMMOBILIERS INC 3810 Rue De Marly, Quebec, QC G1X 4B1, *Tel* (418) 651-7308	700	557	85,218,000	6513
LONE STAR GROUP OF COMPANIES HOLDINGS INC 32 Colonnade Rd Suite 900, Nepean, ON K2E 7J6, *Tel* (613) 727-1966	700	558	175,609,950	6712
MAGELLAN AEROSPACE LIMITED 660 Berry St, Winnipeg, MB R3H 0S5, *Tel* (204) 775-8331	700	559	0	3728
MANITOBA PUBLIC INSURANCE CORPORATION, THE 234 Donald St Suite 912, Winnipeg, MB R3C 4A4, *Tel* (204) 985-7000	700	560	337,727,050	8743
MAPLE LEAF FOODS INC 100 Ethel Ave, Toronto, ON M6N 4Z7, *Tel* (416) 767-5151	700	561	0	2015
MAPLE TERRAZZO MARBLE & TILE INCORPORATED 200 Edgeley Blvd Unit 9, Concord, ON L4K 3Y8, *Tel* (905) 760-1776	700	562	0	8631
MCMASTER STUDENTS UNION INCORPORATED 1280 Main St W Rm 1, Hamilton, ON L8S 4K1, *Tel* (905) 525-9140	700	563	99,632,400	8631
MEDISYS HOLDING LP 500 Rue Sherbrooke O Bureau 1100, Montreal, QC H3A 3C6, *Tel* (514) 845-1211	700	564	173,930,880	6712
Meloche Monnex Inc (*Suby of* **TORONTO-DOMINION BANK, THE**) 50 Boul Cremazie O Bureau 1200, Montreal, QC H2P 1B6, *Tel* (514) 382-6060	700	565	126,076,090	6411
METROLINX 200 Steeprock Dr, North York, ON M3J 2T4, *Tel*	700	566	0	4011
MULTI-MARQUES INC 3443 Av Francis-Hughes Bureau 1, Laval, QC H7L 5A6, *Tel* (450) 629-9444	700	567	0	5149
NTT DATA CANADA, INC. 2000 Barrington St Suite 300, Halifax, NS B3J 3K1, *Tel* (902) 422-6036	700	568	94,232,900	7379
NEMO PRODUCTIONS - CAN, INC 8035 Glenwood Dr, Burnaby, BC V3N 5C8, *Tel*	700	569	119,755,200	7829
NORTHWOODCARE INCORPORATED 2615 Northwood Terr, Halifax, NS B3K 3S5, *Tel* (902) 454-8311	700	570	34,356,000	8361
OLYMEL S.E.C. 57 125 Rte, Saint-Esprit, QC J0K 2L0, *Tel* (450) 839-7258	700	571	0	2011
OLYMEL S.E.C. 125 Rue Saint-Isidore, Saint-Esprit, QC J0K 2L0, *Tel* (450) 839-7258	700	572	0	2011
ONTARIO POWER GENERATION INC 800 Kipling Ave Suite 1, Etobicoke, ON M8Z 5G5, *Tel* (416) 231-4111	700	573	0	4911
PEARSON CANADA INC 195 Harry Walker Pky N Suite A, Newmarket, ON L3Y 7B3, *Tel* (905) 853-7888	700	574	0	2731
▲ PepsiCo Canada ULC (*Suby of* **PEPSICO, INC.**) 14 Hunter St E, Peterborough, ON K9J 7B2, *Tel* (705) 743-6330	700	575	0	2043
PRICEWATERHOUSECOOPERS LLP 2640 Boul Laurier Bureau 1700, Quebec, QC G1V 5C2, *Tel* (418) 522-7001	700	576	0	8721
PRINCE ALBERT PARKLAND REGIONAL HEALTH AUTHORITY 1521 6th Ave W, Prince Albert, SK S6V 5K1, *Tel* (306) 765-6400	700	577	14,420,549	8062
▲ Procter & Gamble Inc (*Suby of* **THE PROCTER & GAMBLE COMPANY**) 4711 Yonge St, North York, ON M2N 6K8, *Tel* (416) 730-4711	700	578	38,158,446	2841
PROVIGO DISTRIBUTION INC 180 Ch Du Tremblay, Boucherville, QC J4B 7W3, *Tel* (450) 449-8000	700	579	0	5148
SASKATOON REGIONAL HEALTH AUTHORITY 701 Queen St Suite 1237, Saskatoon, SK S7K 0M7, *Tel* (306) 655-8000	700	580	0	8062
SEARS CANADA INC 9501 Highway 50, Woodbridge, ON L4H 2B9, *Tel* (905) 893-5284	700	581	0	4225
Services Financiers NCO, Inc (*Suby of* **EGS SHELL COMPANY, INC.**) 33 Sinclair Blvd Unit 4, Brantford, ON N3S 7X6, *Tel* (519) 750-6000	700	582	0	7322
SITEL CANADA CORPORATION 3250 Bloor St W, Etobicoke, ON M8X 2X9, *Tel*	700	583	98,671,360	7389
Societe d'Hypotheque de la Banque Royale (*Suby of* **ROYAL BANK OF CANADA**) 1 Place Ville-Marie, Montreal, QC H3C 3A9, *Tel* (514) 874-7222	700	584	184,740,450	6162
SOUTH SHORE DISTRICT HEALTH AUTHORITY 90 Glen Allan Dr, Bridgewater, NS B4V 3S6, *Tel* (902) 527-2266	700	585	95,621,669	8062
SUNCOR ENERGY INC 2489 North Sheridan Way, Mississauga, ON L5K 1A8, *Tel* (905) 804-4500	700	586	0	1389
TRQSS, INC 255 Patillo Rd, Tecumseh, ON N8N 2L9, *Tel* (519) 973-7400	700	587	175,415,828	2399
TELE-MOBILE COMPANY 8851 Rte Transcanadienne Bureau 1, Saint-Laurent, QC H4S 1Z6, *Tel* (514) 832-2000	700	588	0	4899

COMPANY	EMPLOYEES HERE	RANK	SALES ($)	PRIMARY SIC CODE
TEMPLETON, FRANKLIN MUTUAL BEACON FUND 200 King St W Suite 1500, Toronto, ON M5H 3T4, *Tel* (416) 957-6000	700	589	280,344,960	6722
UNIFOR 15 Westcreek Blvd Suite 1, Brampton, ON L6T 5T4, *Tel* (905) 874-4026	700	590	0	8631
VECIMA NETWORKS INC 150 Cardinal Pl, Saskatoon, SK S7L 6H7, *Tel* (306) 955-7075	700	591	0	8731
WELLINGTON CATHOLIC DISTRICT SCHOOL BOARD 200 Clair Rd W, Guelph, ON N1L 1G1, *Tel* (519) 822-8502	700	592	0	8211
WORLEYPARSONS CANADA SERVICES LTD 9405 50 St Nw Suite 101, Edmonton, AB T6B 2T4, *Tel*	700	593	0	8711
SUPERIOR TRUSS CO LTD 165 Industrial Rd, Oak Bluff, MB R4G 0A5, *Tel* (204) 888-7663	690	594	106,307,280	2439
CENTRE DE SANTE ET DE SERVICES SOCIAUX DE DORVAL-LACHINE-LASALLE 650 16e Av, Lasalle, QC H8P 2S3, *Tel* (514) 637-2351	685	595	0	8062
ST. JOSEPH'S HEALTH CARE, LONDON Gd, St Thomas, ON N5P 3V9, *Tel* (519) 631-8510	667	596	0	8093
KRUGER PRODUCTS L.P. 100 1e Av, Crabtree, QC J0K 1B0, *Tel* (450) 754-2855	662	597	0	2676
▲ Raytheon Canada Limited (*Suby of* **RAYTHEON COMPANY**) 450 Leitz Rd Suite 2, Midland, ON L4R 5B8, *Tel* (705) 526-5401	662	598	0	3827
HOLT, RENFREW & CIE, LIMITEE 737 Dunsmuir St, Vancouver, BC V6C 1N5, *Tel* (604) 681-3121	660	599	0	5621
AON REED STENHOUSE INC 700 De La Gauchetiere O Bureau 1800, Montreal, CC H3B 0A4, *Tel* (514) 842-5000	650	600	0	6411
AGNICO EAGLE MINES LIMITED 10200 Rte De Preissac, Rouyn-Noranda, QC J0Y 1C0, *Tel* (819) 759-3700	650	601	0	1041
AGROPUR COOPERATIVE 510 Rue Principale, Granby, QC J2G 2X2, *Tel* (450) 375-1991	650	602	0	2022
Aluma Systems Inc (*Suby of* **CLAYTON, DUBILIER & RICE, INC.**) Gd Lcd Main, Fort Mcmurray, AB T9H 3E2, *Tel* (780) 790-4852	650	603	0	1799
ATTRIDGE TRANSPORTATION INCORPORATED 27 Mill St S, Waterdown, ON L0R 2H0, *Tel* (905) 690-2632	650	604	0	4141
BOMBARDIER TRANSPORTATION CANADA INC 1001 Montreal St, Thunder Bay, ON P7C 4V6, *Tel* (807) 475-2810	650	605	0	3743
CANADIAN PACIFIC RAILWAY COMPANY 4599 Chateau Blvd, Whistler, BC V0N 1B4, *Tel* (604) 938-2086	650	606	0	7011
Cara Operations Limited (*Suby of* **CARA HOLDINGS LIMITED**) 1185 Rue Rodolphe-Page Bureau 1, Dorval, QC H4Y 1H3, *Tel* (514) 636-5824	650	607	0	5812
Cegep de Trois-Rivieres (*Suby of* **CEGEP DE TROIS-RIVIERES**) 3500 Rue De Courval, Trois-Rivieres, QC G8Z 1T2, *Tel* (819) 376-1721	650	608	94,704,065	8222
Centre de Protection et de Readaptation de la Cote-Nord (*Suby of* **CENTRE DE PROTECTION ET DE READAPTATION DE LA COTE-NORD**) 835 Boul Jolliet, Baie-Comeau, QC G5C 1P5, *Tel* (418) 589-9927	650	609	0	8361
Centres Jeunesse de Lanaudiere, Les (*Suby of* **CENTRES JEUNESSE DE LANAUDIERE, LES**) 1170 Rue Ladouceur, Joliette, QC J6E 3W7, *Tel* (450) 759-0755	650	610	0	8641
COLLEGE LIONEL-GROULX 100 Rue Duquet, Sainte-Therese, QC J7E 3G6, *Tel* (450) 430-3120	650	611	87,353,898	8221
Commission Scolaire Central Quebec (*Suby of* **COMMISSION SCOLAIRE CENTRAL QUEBEC**) 2046 Ch Saint-Louis, Quebec, QC G1T 1P4, *Tel* (418) 681-7705	650	612	64,407,680	8211
CORPORATION DE L'ECOLE DES HAUTES ETUDES COMMERCIALES DE MONTREAL, LA 3000 Ch De La Cote-Sainte-Catherine, Montreal, QC H3T 2A7, *Tel* (514) 340-6000	650	613	90,994,320	8221
JAZZ AVIATION LP 3 Spectacle Lake Dr Suite 100, Dartmouth, NS B3E 1W8, *Tel* (902) 873-5000	650	614	837,296,993	4512
▲ McCann WorldGroup Canada Inc (*Suby of* **THE INTERPUBLIC GROUP OF COMPANIES INC**) 200 Wellington St W Suite 1300, Toronto, ON M5V 0N6, *Tel* (416) 594-6000	650	615	84,050,726	7311
MORRISON HERSHFIELD LIMITED 9515 Montrose Rd, Port Robinson, ON L0S 1K0, *Tel* (905) 394-3900	650	616	0	4899
▲ NCR Canada Corp (*Suby of* **NCR CORPORATION**) 580 Weber St E, Kitchener, ON N2H 1G8, *Tel*	650	617	0	3578
PHARMASCIENCE INC 6111 Av Royalmount Bureau 100, Montreal, QC H4P 2T4, *Tel* (514) 340-1114	650	618	145,337,714	2834
RESIDENCE SAINT-CHARLES BARROMEE 66 Boul Rene-Levesque E, Montreal, QC H2X 1N3 *Tel* (514) 861-9331	650	619	70,577,040	8069
Rio Tinto Alcan Inc (*Suby of* **RIO TINTO PLC**) 1954 Rue Davis, Jonquiere, QC G7S 3B6, *Tel* (418) 699-2131	650	620	0	4911
▲ **ROCKWELL AUTOMATION CANADA CONTROL SYSTEMS** 135 Dundas St, Cambridge, ON N1R 5N9, *Tel* (519) 623-1810	650	621	124,368,720	3625
Safway Services Canada, ULC (*Suby of* **SAFWAY GROUP HOLDING LLC**) 1005 Memorial Dr Unit 3, Fort Mcmurray, AB T9K 0K4, *Tel* (780) 791-6473	650	622	0	1799
UNIVERSITE DU QUEBEC 300 Allee Des Ursulines, Rimouski, QC G5L 3A1, *Tel* (418) 723-1986	650	623	0	8221
▲ Weyerhaeuser Company Limited (*Suby of* **WEYERHAEUSER COMPANY**) Gd Stn Main, Grande Prairie, AB T8V 3A9, *Tel* (780) 539-8500	650	624	0	5031
POSTMEDIA NETWORK INC				

COMPANY	EMPLOYEES HERE	RANK	SALES ($)	PRIMARY SIC CODE
10006 101 St Nw, Edmonton, AB T5J 0S1, *Tel* (780) 429-5100	648	625	0	2711
CANCERCARE MANITOBA				
675 Mcdermot Ave Suite 1160, Winnipeg, MB R3E 0V9, *Tel* (204) 787-4143	647	626	133,315,996	8069
CENTENNIAL 2000 INC				
4412 Manilla Rd Se Suite 1, Calgary, AB T2G 4B7, *Tel* (403) 214-0044	645	627	103,494,400	2011
ALBERTA HEALTH SERVICES				
4405 South Park Dr, Stony Plain, AB T7Z 2M7, *Tel* (780) 968-3600	640	628	0	8062
▲ Autoliv Canada Inc (*Suby of* **AUTOLIV, INC.**)				
351 Queen St N, Tilbury, ON N0P 2L0, *Tel* (519) 682-9501	640	629	0	3089
SNC-LAVALIN INC				
195 The West Mall, Etobicoke, ON M9C 5K1, *Tel* (416) 252-5311	640	630	0	8711
▲ Sykes Assistance Services Corporation (*Suby of* **SYKES ENTERPRISES INCORPORATED**)				
248 Pall Mall St, London, ON N6A 5P6, *Tel* (519) 434-3221	640	631	109,404,397	7549
Association generale des Etudiants du C.E.G.E.P. de St-Jerome Inc, L (*Suby of* **ASSOCIATION GENERALE DES ETUDIANTS DU C.E.G.E.P. DE ST-JEROME INC, L**)				
455 Rue Fournier Bureau 450, Saint-Jerome, QC J7Z 4V2, *Tel* (450) 435-7147	638	632	94,044,150	8221
Universite de Moncton (*Suby of* **UNIVERSITE DE MONCTON**)				
18 Av Antonine-Maillet, Moncton, NB E1A 3E9, *Tel* (506) 858-4000	636	633	83,904,805	8221
F&P MFG., INC				
1 Nolan Rd, Tottenham, ON L0G 1W0, *Tel* (905) 936-3435	630	634	400,325,663	3714
▲ Campbell Company of Canada (*Suby of* **CAMPBELL SOUP COMPANY**)				
1400 Mitchell Rd S, Listowel, ON N4W 3G7, *Tel*	625	635	0	5142
DESJARDINS ASSURANCES GENERALES INC				
6300 Boul De La Rive-Sud, Levis, QC G6V 6P9, *Tel* (418) 835-4850	625	636	668,976,658	6331
Black Bond Books Ltd (*Suby of* **BLACK BOND BOOKS LTD**)				
32555 London Ave Suite 344, Mission, BC V2V 6M7, *Tel*	619	637	0	5942
MEG ENERGY CORP				
3 Ave Sw Suite 600 25 Fl, Calgary, AB T2P 0G5, *Tel* (403) 770-0446	617	638	1,380,387,629	1311
SUPRALIMENT S.E.C.				
183 Rte Du President-Kennedy, Saint-Henri-De-Levis, QC G0R 3E0, *Tel* (418) 882-2282	617	639	0	2011
ENERGY & CHEMICAL WORKERS UNION LOCAL 530				
10208 99 Ave, Fort Saskatchewan, AB T8L 1Y1, *Tel* (780) 998-2074	605	640	88,120,960	8631
AMEC FOSTER WHEELER AMERICAS LIMITED				
111 Dunsmuir St Suite 400, Vancouver, BC V6B 5W3, *Tel* (604) 664-4315	600	641	0	8711
AGENCE DE LA SANTE ET DES SERVICES SOCIAUX DE LA MONTEREGIE, L'				
1255 Rue Beauregard, Longueuil, QC J4K 2M3, *Tel* (450) 679-6772	600	642	27,610,240	8399
Agrium Inc (*Suby of* **AGRIUM CANADA PARTNERSHIP**)				
16 Agrium Rd, Vanscoy, SK S0L 3J0, *Tel* (306) 668-4343	600	643	0	1474
AIR CANADA				
355 Portage Ave Suite 3850, Winnipeg, MB R3B 0J6, *Tel* (204) 941-2684	600	644	0	4512
Air Inuit Ltee (*Suby of* **SOCIETE MAKIVIK**)				
6005 Boul De La Cote-Vertu, Saint-Laurent, QC H4S 0B1, *Tel* (514) 905-9445	600	645	134,658,814	4512
Akita Drilling Ltd (*Suby of* **AKITA DRILLING LTD**)				
2302 8 St, Nisku, AB T9E 7Z2, *Tel* (780) 955-6700	600	646	0	1381
ALBERTA HEALTH SERVICES				
10101 Southport Rd Sw, Calgary, AB T2W 3N2, *Tel* (403) 943-0755	600	647	0	8011
ASSOCIATION DE PARENTS DU CENTRE GABRIELLE MAJOR				
8150 Boul Metropolitain E, Anjou, QC H1K 1A1, *Tel*	600	648	31,705,680	8322
BAYER INC				
7600 Rte Transcanadienne, Pointe-Claire, QC H9R 1C8, *Tel* (514) 697-5550	600	649	0	2834
BELLEVUE PATHE HOLDINGS LTD				
2100 Rue Sainte-Catherine O Bureau 1000, Montreal, QC H3H 2T3, *Tel* (514) 939-5000	600	650	65,130,900	7812
Borden Ladner Gervais LLP (*Suby of* **BORDEN LADNER GERVAIS LLP**)				
22 Adelaide St W Suite 3400, Toronto, ON M5H 4E3, *Tel* (416) 367-6000	600	651	347,633,150	8111
BOULANGERIE VACHON INC				
380 Rue Notre-Dame N, Sainte-Marie, QC G6E 2K7, *Tel* (418) 387-5421	600	652	0	5149
CLSC -CHSLD DE ROSEMONT				
3311 Boul Saint-Joseph E, Montreal, QC H1X 1W3, *Tel* (514) 524-3541	600	653	28,760,880	8399
CANADA POST CORPORATION				
393 Millen Rd, Stoney Creek, ON L8E 5A8, *Tel* (905) 664-0009	600	654	0	4311
CANADIAN UNION OF POSTAL WORKERS				
3719 Walker Rd, Windsor, ON N8W 3S9, *Tel* (519) 944-4102	600	655	0	8631
Canpar Transport L.P. (*Suby of* **CANPAR TRANSPORT L.P.**)				
205 New Toronto St, Toronto, ON M8V 0A1, *Tel* (416) 869-1332	600	656	0	4213
Cara Operations Limited (*Suby of* **CARA HOLDINGS LIMITED**)				
6260 Miller Rd, Richmond, BC V7B 1B3, *Tel* (604) 278-9144	600	657	0	5812
CENTRE DE SANTE SERVICES SOCIAUX MARIA CHAPDELAINE				
2000 Boul Du Sacre-Coeur, Dolbeau-Mistassini, QC G8L 2R5, *Tel* (418) 276-1234	600	658	52,166,901	8062
CENTRE DE SANTE ET DE SERVICES SOCIAUX DE LAVAL				
800 Boul Chomedey Bureau 200, Montreal-Ouest, QC H7V 3Y4, *Tel* (450) 682-2952	600	659	0	8399
CENTRE DE SANTE ET DE SERVICES SOCIAUX DE LA VALLEE-DE-LA-BATISCAN				
90 Rang Riviere Veillette, Sainte-Genevieve-De-Batiscan, QC G0X 2R0, *Tel* (418) 362-2727	600	660	0	8399
CENTRE DE SOINS PROLONGES GRACE DART				
5155 Rue Sainte-Catherine E, Montreal, QC H1V 2A5, *Tel* (514) 255-2833	600	661	66,718,720	8069

COMPANY	EMPLOYEES HERE	RANK	SALES ($)	PRIMARY SIC CODE
COLLEGE ENSEIGNANT GENERAL ET PROFESSIONNEL MONTMORENCY 475 Boul De L'Avenir, Montreal, QC H7N 5H9, *Tel* (450) 975-6100	600	662	80,569,130	8221
COLLEGE D'ENSEIGNEMENT GENERAL ET PROFESSIONNEL LIMOILOU 1300 8e Av Bureau 1400, Quebec, QC G1J 5L5, *Tel* (418) 647-6600	600	663	86,739,750	8221
COMMUNITY LIVING ESSEX COUNTY 13158 Tecumseh Rd E, Windsor, ON N8N 3T6, *Tel* (519) 979-0057	600	664	0	8322
COMPAGNIE DES CHEMINS DE FER NATIONAUX DU CANADA Gd, Concord, ON L4K 1B9, *Tel* (905) 669-3302	600	665	0	4011
CONFEDERATION DES SYNDICATS NATIONAUX (C.S.N.) 1601 Av De Lorimier, Montreal, QC H2K 4M5, *Tel* (514) 529-4993	600	666	0	8631
CORPORATION OF THE CITY OF TORONTO 789 Yonge St, Toronto, ON M4W 2G8, *Tel* (416) 393-7131	600	667	0	8231
CORPS CANADIEN DES COMMISSIONNAIRES DIVISION DE QUEBEC 3405 Boul Wilfrid-Hamel Bureau 330, Quebec, QC G1P 2J3, *Tel* (418) 681-0609	600	668	25,128,960	7381
Exova Canada Inc (*Suby of* **EXOVA, INC.**) 2395 Speakman Dr Suite 583, Mississauga, ON L5K 1B3, *Tel* (905) 822-4111	600	669	141,543,758	8734
FP Canadian Newspapers Limited Partnership (*Suby of* **FP CANADIAN NEWSPAPERS LIMITED PARTNERSHIP**) 1355 Mountain Ave, Winnipeg, MB R2X 3B6, *Tel* (204) 697-7000	600	670		2711
FAIRMONT HOTELS & RESORTS INC 181 Rue Richelieu Bureau 200, La Malbaie, QC G5A 1X7, *Tel* (418) 665-3703	600	671	0	7011
FAIRMONT HOTELS & RESORTS INC 4599 Chateau Blvd, Whistler, BC V0N 1B4, *Tel* (604) 938-8000	600	672	0	7011
FAMILY AND CHILDREN SERVICES OF FRONTENAC AND CLINICS ADDINGTON 1479 John Counter Blvd, Kingston, ON K7M 7J3, *Tel* (613) 545-3227	600	673	29,440,640	8399
Fidelity Investments Canada ULC (*Suby of* **FMR LLC**) 483 Bay St Suite 200, Toronto, ON M5G 2N7, *Tel* (416) 307-5200	600	674	231,577,262	6722
FUJITSU CONSEIL (CANADA) INC 2960 Boul Laurier Bureau 400, Quebec, QC G1V 4S1, *Tel*	600	675		7379
GDI SERVICES (CANADA) LP 931 Leathorne St Unit E, London, ON N5Z 3M7, *Tel* (519) 681-3330	600	676	0	7349
GATEWAY CASINOS & ENTERTAINMENT INC 350 Gifford St Suite 1, New Westminster, BC V3M 7A3, *Tel* (604) 777-2946	600	677	0	7011
GIBRALTAR MINES LTD 1040 Georgia St W, Vancouver, BC V6E 4H1, *Tel* (778) 373-4533	600	678	7,296,070	1081
Gienow Windows & Doors Inc (*Suby of* **H.I.G. CAPITAL INC.**) 7140 40 St Se, Calgary, AB T2C 2B6, *Tel* (403) 203-8200	600	679	79,155,636	2431
GOUVERNEMENT DE LA PROVINCE DE QUEBEC 475 Boul De Maisonneuve E, Montreal, QC H2L 5C4, *Tel* (514) 873-1100	600	680	0	8231
GOUVERNEMENT DE LA PROVINCE DE QUEBEC 4255 Av Papineau, Montreal, QC H2H 2P6, *Tel* (514) 526-4981	600	681	0	7041
GOVERNMENT OF THE PROVINCE OF ALBERTA 9820 106 St Nw Suite 534, Edmonton, AB T5K 2J6, *Tel* (780) 427-3076	600	682	0	6289
GOVERNMENT OF THE PROVINCE OF ALBERTA 10726 106 Ave, Grande Prairie, AB T8V 4C4, *Tel* (780) 539-2057	600	683	0	8221
Grand Erie District School Board (*Suby of* **GRAND ERIE DISTRICT SCHOOL BOARD**) 349 Erie Ave, Brantford, ON N3S 2H7, *Tel* (519) 756-6301	600	684	232,284,099	8211
Groupe Gaudreault Inc, Le (*Suby of* **LE GROUPE GAUDREAULT INC**) 1500 Rue Raymond-Gaudreault, Repentigny, QC J5Y 4E3, *Tel* (450) 585-1210	600	685	175,136,640	6712
HATCH CORPORATION 5 Place Ville-Marie Bureau 1400, Montreal, QC H3B 2G2, *Tel* (514) 861-0583	600	686	0	8711
HATCH LTD 5 Place Ville-Marie Bureau 1400, Montreal, QC H3B 2G2, *Tel* (514) 861-0583	600	687	0	8711
HONDA CANADA INC 180 Honda Blvd Suite 200, Markham, ON L6C 0H9, *Tel* (905) 888-8110	600	688	106,569,260	3711
HUDSON'S BAY COMPANY 2 Bloor St E Suite 52, Toronto, ON M4W 3H7, *Tel* (416) 972-3313	600	689	0	5311
HUDSON'S BAY COMPANY 401 Bay St Suite 500, Toronto, ON M5H 2Y4, *Tel* (800) 521-2364	600	690	11,016,690,335	5311
HYDRO-QUEBEC 5050 Boul Des Gradins Bureau 200, Quebec, QC G2J 1P8, *Tel* (418) 624-2811	600	691	0	8631
▲ ICT Canada Marketing Inc (*Suby of* **SYKES ENTERPRISES INCORPORATED**) 720 Coverdale Rd Unit 9, Riverview, NB E1B 3L8, *Tel* (506) 387-9050	600	692	0	7389
IMPERIAL TOBACCO COMPAGNIE LIMITEE 107 Woodlawn Rd W, Guelph, ON N1H 1B4, *Tel*	600	693	0	2111
IMPRIMERIES TRANSCONTINENTAL 2005 S.E.N.C. 2049 20th St E, Owen Sound, ON N4K 5R2, *Tel* (519) 376-8330	600	694	0	2732
INSTITUT PHILIPPE PINEL DE MONTREAL 10905 Boul Henri-Bourassa E, Montreal, QC H1C 1H1, *Tel* (514) 648-8461	600	695	58,110,720	8063
Ironhorse Corporation (*Suby of* **IRONHORSE CORPORATION**) 9 Capella Crt Suite 200, Ottawa, ON K2E 8A7, *Tel* (613) 228-2813	600	696	51,534,000	7389
JOHNSON INC 95 Elizabeth Ave, St. John'S, NL A1B 1R6, *Tel* (709) 737-1500	600	697	0	6411
Kerry's Place Autism Services (*Suby of* **KERRY'S PLACE AUTISM SERVICES**) 34 Berczy St Unit 190, Aurora, ON L4G 1W9, *Tel* (905) 841-6611	600	698	30,278,691	8399

COMPANY	EMPLOYEES HERE	RANK	SALES ($)	PRIMARY SIC CODE
LAKOTA DRILLING INC 1704 5 St, Nisku, AB T9E 8P8, *Tel* (780) 955-7535	600	699	148,408,960	6712
LANGUAGES OF LIFE INC 99 Fifth Ave Suite 14, Ottawa, ON K1S 5K4, *Tel* (613) 232-9770	600	700	37,221,996	7389
▲ **LOCKHEED MARTIN CANADA INC** 45 O'Connor St Suite 870, Ottawa, ON K1P 1A4, *Tel* (613) 688-0698	600	701	77,046,499	3625
MAGNA SEATING INC 564 Newpark Blvd, Newmarket, ON L3X 2S2, *Tel* (905) 853-3604	600	702	0	2531
MAGNA SEATING INC 550 Newpark Blvd, Newmarket, ON L3X 2S2, *Tel* (905) 895-4701	600	703	0	2531
MAPLE LEAF FOODS INC 6985 Financial Dr, Mississauga, ON L5N 0A1, *Tel* (905) 285-5000	600	704	0	2011
MCELHANNEY ASSOCIATES LAND SURVEYING LTD 8808 72 St, Fort St. John, BC V1J 6M2, *Tel* (250) 787-0356	600	705	0	8713
MEMORIAL UNIVERSITY OF NEWFOUNDLAND 155 Ridge Road, St. John'S, NL A1C 5R3, *Tel* (709) 778-0483	600	706	0	8222
MONTCALM SERVICES TECHNIQUES INC 695 90e Av, Lasalle, QC H8R 3A4, *Tel*	600	707	23,558,400	7349
NAV CANADA 7421 135 St, Surrey, BC V3W 0M8, *Tel* (604) 598-4805	600	708	0	4899
NIAGARA COLLEGE OF APPLIED ARTS & TECHNOLOGY 5881 Dunn St, Niagara Falls, ON L2G 2N9, *Tel* (905) 374-7454	600	709	0	8221
North Atlantic Refining Limited (*Suby of* **PEAK STRATEGIC SILVER PARTNERS**) 1 Refining Rd, Come By Chance, NL A0B 1N0, *Tel* (709) 463-8811	600	710	766,087,350	2911
NORTHBRIDGE GENERAL INSURANCE CORPORATION 105 Adelaide St W Suit 700, Toronto, ON M5H 1P9, *Tel* (416) 350-4400	600	711	0	6331
NOVA SCOTIA POWER INCORPORATED 1223 Lower Water St, Halifax, NS B3J 3S8, *Tel* (902) 428-6230	600	712	1,002,958,620	4911
ONTARIO NORTHLAND TRANSPORTATION COMMISSION 555 Oak St E, North Bay, ON P1B 8E3, *Tel* (705) 472-4500	600	713	183,204,318	4899
ONTARIO POWER GENERATION INC 34 Regional Rd 55, Nanticoke, ON N0A 1L0, *Tel* (519) 587-2201	600	714	0	4911
PARKER HANNIFIN CANADA 1305 Clarence Ave, Winnipeg, MB R3T 1T4, *Tel* (204) 452-6776	600	715	0	3625
PARKLAND COMMUNITY LIVING AND SUPPORTS SOCIETY 6010 45 Ave, Red Deer, AB T4N 3M4, *Tel* (403) 347-3333	600	716	28,760,880	8322
Pioneer Village Special Care Corporation (*Suby of* **REGINA PIONEER VILLAGE LTD**) 430 Pioneer Dr, Regina, SK S4T 6L8, *Tel* (306) 757-5646	600	717	30,144,000	8361
POTASH CORPORATION OF SASKATCHEWAN INC Gd, Lanigan, SK S0K 2M0, *Tel* (306) 365-2030	600	718	0	1474
PRICEWATERHOUSECOOPERS LLP 250 Howe St Suite 700, Vancouver, BC V6C 3S7, *Tel* (604) 806-7000	600	719	0	8721
▲ Procter & Gamble Inc (*Suby of* **THE PROCTER & GAMBLE COMPANY**) 211 Bayview Fairways Dr, Thornhill, ON L3T 2Z1, *Tel* (416) 730-4872	600	720	0	5099
Resolve Corporation (*Suby of* **2206997 ONTARIO INC**) 197 Dufferin St Suite 100, Bridgewater, NS B4V 2G9, *Tel* (902) 541-3600	600	721	0	8742
Rio Tinto Alcan Inc (*Suby of* **RIO TINTO PLC**) 6000 6e Av, La Baie, QC G7B 4G9, *Tel* (418) 697-9540	600	722	0	3365
Rio Tinto Alcan Inc (*Suby of* **RIO TINTO PLC**) 1955 Boul Mellon, Jonquiere, QC G7S 0L4, *Tel* (418) 699-2002	600	723	0	3334
ROYAL & SUN ALLIANCE INSURANCE COMPANY OF CANADA 2225 Erin Mills Pky Suite 1000, Mississauga, ON L5K 2S9, *Tel* (905) 403-2333	600	724	0	6331
SMS EQUIPMENT INC 22k Highway 63 North, Fort Mcmurray, AB T9H 3G2, *Tel* (780) 743-2622	600	725	0	5082
SAFRAN LANDING SYSTEMS CANADA INC 574 Monarch Ave, Ajax, ON L1S 2G8, *Tel* (905) 683-3100	600	726	172,114,291	3728
SASKATCHEWAN GAMING CORPORATION 1880 Saskatchewan Dr, Regina, SK S4P 0B2, *Tel* (306) 565-3000	600	727	137,588,354	7999
SECURITY OFFICER CAREER COLLEGE 8055 Coronet Rd Nw, Edmonton, AB T6E 4N7, *Tel*	600	728	117,792,000	6211
SERVICES DE READAPTATION SUD OUEST ET DU RENFORT, LES 30 Rue Saint-Thomas Bureau 200, Salaberry-De-Valleyfield, QC J6T 4J2, *Tel* (450) 371-4816	600	729	0	8361
SHAW CABLESYSTEMS G.P. 10450 178 St Nw, Edmonton, AB T5S 1S2, *Tel* (780) 490-3555	600	730	0	4841
SHERRITT INTERNATIONAL CORPORATION 10101 114 St, Fort Saskatchewan, AB T8L 2T3, *Tel* (780) 992-7000	600	731	0	3339
SOBEYS CAPITAL INCORPORATED 100 Nordeagle Ave, Whitby, ON L1N 9S1, *Tel* (905) 665-9318	600	732	0	4225
SOBEYS CAPITAL INCORPORATED 6355 Viscount Rd, Mississauga, ON L4V 1W2, *Tel*	600	733	0	5141
SOBEYS WEST INC 1020 64 Ave Ne, Calgary, AB T2E 7V8, *Tel* (403) 730-3500	600	734	4,182,909,892	5411
SOCIETE DE TRANSPORT DE MONTREAL 7770 Rue Saint-Patrick, Lasalle, QC H8N 1V1, *Tel* (514) 280-6382	600	735	0	4111

COMPANY	EMPLOYEES HERE	RANK	SALES ($)	PRIMARY SIC CODE
SOCIETE EN COMMANDITE REVENUE NORANDA 860 Boul Gerard-Cadieux, Salaberry-De-Valleyfield, QC J6T 6L4, *Tel* (450) 373-9144	600	736	0	3339
SOFTCHOICE CORPORATION 173 Dufferin St Suite 200, Toronto, ON M6K 3H7, *Tel* (416) 588-9002	600	737	196,118,362	7371
SPEEDY CREEK (1997) LTD 17724 102 Ave Nw, Edmonton, AB T5S 1H5, *Tel*	600	738	0	5812
ST. LAWRENCE COLLEGE OF APPLIED ARTS AND TECHNOLOGY, THE 2 St Lawrence Dr, Cornwall, ON K6H 4Z1, *Tel* (613) 933-6080	600	739	0	8221
Structures Barrette Inc (*Suby of* **GDTM INC**) 555 Rang Saint-Malo, Trois-Rivieres, QC G8V 0A8, *Tel* (819) 374-6061	600	740	0	5031
SUNCOR ENERGY INC 11701 Rue Sherbrooke E, Pointe-Aux-Trembles, QC H1B 1C3, *Tel* (514) 640-8000	600	741	0	2911
TELUS COMMUNICATIONS INC 11 King St W Suite C115, Toronto, ON M5H 4C7, *Tel* (416) 507-7400	600	742	0	4899
TSG ENERGY SERVICES LTD 311 253 Gregoire Dr, Fort Mcmurray, AB T9H 4G7, *Tel* (780) 799-2772	600	743	135,695,376	1623
TECHART WOODWORKS LTD 11220 Voyageur Way Unit 10, Richmond, BC V6X 3E1, *Tel* (604) 276-2282	600	744	63,324,509	2431
TECHNICOLOR SERVICES CREATIFS CANADA INC 2101 Rue Sainte-Catherine O Bureau 300, Montreal, QC H3H 1M6, *Tel* (514) 939-5060	600	745	55,613,314	7812
THE LAKE LOUISE SKI AREA LTD 1333 8 St Sw Suite 908, Calgary, AB T2R 1M6, *Tel* (403) 244-4449	600	746	35,337,600	7011
TRANSCONTINENTAL PRINTING INC 275 Wellington St E, Aurora, ON L4G 6J9, *Tel* (905) 841-4400	600	747	0	2752
TRANSCONTINENTAL PRINTING INC 1590 20th St E, Owen Sound, ON N4K 5R2, *Tel* (519) 371-5171	600	748	0	2752
TYCO SAFETY PRODUCTS CANADA LTD 95 Bridgeland Ave, North York, ON M6A 1Y7, *Tel* (905) 760-3000	600	749	0	3699
▲ **UPS SCS, INC** 4156 Mainway, Burlington, ON L7L 0A7, *Tel* (905) 315-5500	600	750	0	7389
UNIFOR 20 Walnut St, St Catharines, ON L2T 1H5, *Tel* (905) 227-7717	600	751	0	8631
UNIVERSITY OF THE FRASER VALLEY 45190 Caen Ave, Chilliwack, BC V2R 0N3, *Tel* (604) 792-0025	600	752	0	8221
VIA RAIL CANADA INC 65 Front St W Suite 222, Toronto, ON M5J 1E6, *Tel* (888) 842-7245	600	753	0	4111
WE CARE HEALTH SERVICES INC 160 Traders Blvd E Suite 208, Mississauga, ON L4Z 3K7, *Tel* (905) 275-7250	600	754	0	8051
▲ Winners Merchants International L.P. (*Suby of* **THE TJX COMPANIES INC**) 60 Standish Crt, Mississauga, ON L5R 0G1, *Tel* (905) 405-8000	600	755	729,607,000	5651
Centre De Sante Des Etchemin (*Suby of* **CENTRE DE SANTE DES ETCHEMIN**) 331 Rue Du Sanatorium Rr 1, Lac-Etchemin, QC G0R 1S0, *Tel* (418) 625-3101	590	756	59,484,160	8063
GROUPE LUMENPULSE INC 1751 Rue Richardson Bureau 1505, Montreal, QC H3K 1G6, *Tel* (514) 937-3003	587	757	64,278,377	3646
DESJARDINS SECURITE FINANCIERE, COMPAGNIE D'ASSURANCE VIE 95 Rue Des Commandeurs, Levis, QC G6V 6P6, *Tel* (418) 838-7800	582	758	0	6311
947465 ONTARIO LTD 573 Admiral Crt, London, ON N5V 4L3, *Tel* (519) 455-1390	580	759	17,218,725	4151
▲ Goodrich Aerospace Canada Ltd (*Suby of* **UNITED TECHNOLOGIES CORPORATION**) 1400 South Service Rd W, Oakville, ON L6L 5Y7, *Tel* (905) 827-7777	580	760	150,590,885	3728
CATALYST PAPER CORPORATION 8541 Hay Road N, Crofton, BC V0R 1R0, *Tel* (250) 246-6100	578	761	0	2621
HALIFAX REGIONAL MUNICIPALITY 200 Ilsley Ave, Dartmouth, NS B3B 1V1, *Tel* (902) 490-6614	576	762	0	4111
NORTH EAST MENTAL HEALTH CENTRE (NORTH BAY CAMPUS) 4700 Highway 11 N, North Bay, ON P1B 8G3, *Tel* (705) 474-1200	575	763	57,072,640	8063
ALIMENTS PRINCE, S.E.C. 255 Rue Rocheleau, Drummondville, QC J2C 7G2, *Tel* (819) 475-3030	570	764	0	2013
▲ **PLAINS MIDSTREAM CANADA ULC** 607 8 Ave Sw Suite 1400, Calgary, AB T2P 0A7, *Tel* (403) 298-2100	570	765	2,666,056,939	4612
SOCIETE EN COMMANDITE MANOIR RICHELIEU 181 Rue Richelieu Bureau 200, La Malbaie, QC G5A 1X7, *Tel* (418) 665-3703	570	766	24,952,559	7011
VENTRA GROUP CO 530 Park St, Beaverton, ON L0K 1A0, *Tel* (705) 426-7311	570	767	0	3423
SOCIETE DE TRANSPORT DE MONTREAL 8150 Rue Larrey, Anjou, QC H1J 2J5, *Tel* (514) 280-5913	560	768	0	4111
▲ Startek Canada Services Ltd (*Suby of* **STARTEK, INC.**) 100 Innovation Dr, Kingston, ON K7K 7E7, *Tel* (613) 531-6350	560	769	275,013,760	8748
ALMA MATER SOCIETY OF QUEEN'S UNIVERSITY INCORPORATED 99 University Ave, Kingston, ON K7L 3N5, *Tel* (613) 533-2725	550	770	53,202,720	8641
CHSLD JUIFS DE MONTREAL 5725 Av Victoria Bureau 131, Montreal, QC H3W 3H6, *Tel* (514) 738-4500	550	771	59,681,280	8069
COLLEGE DE BOIS-DE-BOULOGNE 10555 Av Du Bois-De-Boulogne, Montreal, QC H4N 1L4, *Tel* (514) 332-3000	550	772	76,957,440	8221

COMPANY	EMPLOYEES HERE	RANK	SALES ($)	PRIMARY SIC CODE
COMPAGNIE DES CHEMINS DE FER NATIONAUX DU CANADA 150 Pandora Ave W, Winnipeg, MB R2C 4H5, *Tel* (204) 235-2626	550	773	0	4789
FAIRMONT HOTELS & RESORTS INC 1 Lodge Rd, Jasper, AB T0E 1E0, *Tel* (780) 852-3301	550	774	0	7011
Ganz (*Suby of* **GANZ**) 1 Pearce Rd, Woodbridge, ON L4L 3T2, *Tel* (905) 851-6661	550	775	90,033,504	5199
GESTION JEAN & GUY HURTEAU INC 21 Rue Paul-Gauguin, Candiac, QC J5R 3X8, *Tel* (450) 638-2212	550	776	135,648,000	6712
GLOBAL UPHOLSTERY CO. INC 565 Petrolia Rd, North York, ON M3J 2X8, *Tel* (416) 739-5000	550	777	0	2522
GOLDER ASSOCIATES LTD 2535 3 Ave Se Suite 102, Calgary, AB T2A 7W5, *Tel* (403) 299-5600	550	778	0	8748
MPT UTILITIES EUROPE LTD 155 Wellington St W, Toronto, ON M5V 3H1, *Tel* (416) 649-1300	550	779	365,727,250	4911
ORICA CANADA INC 301 Rue De L'Hotel-De-Ville, Brownsburg-Chatham, QC J8G 3B5, *Tel* (450) 533-4201	550	780	1,505,544,045	2892
OTTAWA HOSPITAL, THE 1967 Riverside Dr Suite 323, Ottawa, ON K1H 7W9, *Tel* (613) 738-7100	550	781	0	8062
Peel District School Board (*Suby of* **PEEL DISTRICT SCHOOL BOARD**) 5650 Hurontario St Suite 106, Mississauga, ON L5R 1C6, *Tel* (905) 890-1099	550	782	1,555,786	8211
SERVICES DES BENEVOLES DU CENTRE HOSPITALIER BAIE-DES-CHALEURS INC 419 Boul Perron, Maria, QC G0C 1Y0, *Tel* (418) 759-3443	550	783	53,261,250	8062
SOBEYS WEST INC 3440 56 Ave Se, Calgary, AB T2C 2C3, *Tel* (403) 279-2555	550	784	0	2011
SPORT MASKA INC 3400 Rue Raymond-Lasnier, Saint-Laurent, QC H4R 3L3, *Tel* (514) 461-8000	550	785	78,505,713	3949
TOLKO INDUSTRIES LTD 844 Otter Lake Cross Rd, Armstrong, BC V0E 1B6, *Tel* (250) 546-3171	550	786	0	2421
SPOOKY LURKER NETWORKS Gd, Blumenort, MB R0A 0C0, *Tel* (204) 381-1230	546	787	130,723,520	4813
CASCADES CANADA ULC 520 Rue Commerciale N, Temiscouata-Sur-Le-Lac, QC G0L 1E0, *Tel* (418) 854-2803	542	788	0	2631
C.P. LOEWEN ENTERPRISES LTD 77 Pth 52 W, Steinbach, MB R5G 1B2, *Tel* (204) 326-6446	540	789	58,212,067	2431
GESTIONS MILLER CARMICHAEL INC 3822 Av De Courtrai, Montreal, QC H3S 1C1, *Tel* (514) 735-4361	540	790	130,062,000	6712
LANDING TRAIL PETROLEUM CO 253 Gregoire Dr Unit 311, Fort Mcmurray, AB T9H 4G7, *Tel* (780) 799-2772	540	791	118,969,920	1389
MECANIQUE A VAPEUR MAURICE ENR 5445 Av De Gaspe Bureau 99, Montreal, QC H2T 3B2, *Tel*	540	792	53,006,400	3599
POLAR EXPLOSIVES LTD 349 Old Airport Rd Suite 104, Yellowknife, NT X1A 3X6, *Tel* (867) 880-4613	540	793	167,451,863	5169
VIANDES DU BRETON INC, LES 150 Ch Des Raymond, Riviere-Du-Loup, QC G5R 5X8, *Tel* (418) 863-6711	540	794	62,892,123	2011
AMEC FOSTER WHEELER INC 2020 Winston Park Dr Suite 700, Oakville, ON L6H 6X7, *Tel* (905) 829-5400	535	795	1,263,097,792	6719
Rogers Communications Inc (*Suby of* **ROGERS COMMUNICATIONS INC**) 40 Weber St E Suite 500, Kitchener, ON N2H 6R3, *Tel* (519) 585-2400	535	796	0	4899
College d'Enseignement General et Professionnel de Jonquiere (*Suby of* **COLLEGE D'ENSEIGNEMENT GENERAL ET PROFESSIONNEL DE JONQUIERE**) 2505 Rue Saint-Hubert, Jonquiere, QC G7X 7W2, *Tel* (418) 547-2191	532	797	79,536,800	8221
HUDSON'S BAY COMPANY 145 Carrier Dr, Etobicoke, ON M9W 5N5, *Tel* (416) 798-5755	530	798	0	5099
TECK COAL LIMITED Gd, Sparwood, BC V0B 2G0, *Tel* (250) 425-2555	530	799	0	1221
UNIFOR 1045 Gibsons Way, Gibsons, BC V0N 1V4, *Tel* (604) 886-2722	530	800	0	8631
PHX ENERGY SERVICES CORP 250 2 St Sw Suite 1400, Calgary, AB T2P 0C1, *Tel* (403) 543-4466	529	801	109,763,768	1381
2953-6778 QUEBEC INC 549 Rue De Verrazano Bureau 3000, Boucherville, QC J4B 7W2, *Tel* (450) 449-1516	525	802	61,840,800	1711
LAW SOCIETY OF UPPER CANADA, THE 130 Queen St W Suite 100, Toronto, ON M5H 2N6, *Tel* (416) 947-3315	525	803	0	8111
GOWLING WLG (CANADA) LLP 100 King St W Suite 1600, Toronto, ON M5X 1G5, *Tel* (416) 862-7525	524	804	0	8111
A.P. PLASMAN INC. 418 Silver Creek Industrial Dr Rr1, Tecumseh, ON N8N 4Y3, *Tel* (519) 727-4545	520	805	0	3089
APOTEX INC 380 Elgin Mills Rd E, Richmond Hill, ON L4C 5H2, *Tel* (905) 884-2050	520	806	0	2834
GOUVERNEMENT DE LA PROVINCE DE QUEBEC 800 Sq Victoria 22e Etage, Montreal, QC H4Z 1G3, *Tel* (514) 395-0337	520	807	0	8741
TECK COAL LIMITED Gd, Elkford, BC V0B 1H0, *Tel* (250) 865-2271	520	808	0	1221

▲ **WAL-MART CANADA CORP**

COMPANY	EMPLOYEES HERE	RANK	SALES ($)	PRIMARY SIC CODE
1051 Garner Rd W Suite 3127, Ancaster, ON L9G 3K9, *Tel* (905) 648-9980	520	809	0	5311
Joey Tomato's (*Suby of* **JOEY TOMATO'S**) 505 Burrard St Suite 950, Vancouver, BC V7X 1M4, *Tel* (604) 699-5639	513	810	21,301,760	5812
A.G. SIMPSON AUTOMOTIVE INC 901 Simcoe St S, Oshawa, ON L1H 4L1, *Tel* (905) 571-2121	510	811	0	3465
GOLDCORP CANADA LTD 4315 Goldmine Rd, South Porcupine, ON P0N 1H0, *Tel* (705) 235-3221	510	812	0	1041
GROUPE DE SECURITE GARDA INC, LE 8989 Macleod Trail Sw Suite 118, Calgary, AB T2H 0M2, *Tel* (403) 517-5899	510	813	0	7381
▲ **NESTLE CANADA INC** 72 Sterling Rd, Toronto, ON M6R 2B6, *Tel* (416) 535-2181	505	814	0	2064
PRT GROWING SERVICES LTD 355 Burrard St Suite 410, Vancouver, BC V6C 2G8, *Tel* (604) 687-1404	505	815	0	7389
TECK-BULLMOOSE COAL INC 550 Burrard St Suite 3300, Vancouver, BC V6C 0B3, *Tel* (604) 699-4000	505	816	300,762,240	1221
Dentons Canada LLP (*Suby of* **DENTONS CANADA LLP**) 77 King St W Suite 400, Toronto, ON M5K 2A1, *Tel* (416) 863-4511	504	817	118,123,373	8111
▲ General Dynamics Land Systems - Canada Corporation (*Suby of* **GENERAL DYNAMICS CORPORATION**) 1020 68 Ave Ne, Calgary, AB T2E 8P2, *Tel* (403) 295-6700	503	818	0	7371
BESSEMER & LAKE ERIE RAILROAD 935 Rue De La Gauchetiere O Bureau 11, Montreal, QC H3B 2M9, *Tel* (514) 399-4536	502	819	258,553,440	4011
BULUTH MISSABE & IRON RANGE RAILROAD 935 Rue De La Gauchetiere O Bureau 4eme, Montreal, QC H3B 2M9, *Tel* (514) 399-4536	502	820	258,553,440	4011
CANRIG DRILLING TECHNOLOGY LTD 5250 94 Ave Se Suite 5250, Calgary, AB T2C 3Z3, *Tel* (403) 279-3466	501	821	105,823,547	1389
STIKEMAN ELLIOTT LLP 1155 Boul Rene-Levesque O Unite B01, Montreal, QC H3B 4P9, *Tel* (514) 397-3000	501	822	0	8111
2936950 Canada Inc (*Suby of* **CORPORATION DEVELOPPEMENT KNOWLTON INC**) 315 Ch De Knowlton, Knowlton, QC J0E 1V0, *Tel* (450) 243-6161	500	823	46,724,160	2844
3104346 CANADA INC 576 Rue Sainte-Catherine E Bureau 111, Montreal, QC H2L 2E1, *Tel* (514) 845-3345	500	824	20,799,360	5812
9074-8898 QUEBEC INC 3195 Ch De Bedford, Montreal, QC H3S 1G3, *Tel* (514) 376-6240	500	825	205,984,000	2342
AGF ALL WORLD TAX ADVANTAGE GROUP LIMITED Gd, Toronto, ON M5J 2W7, *Tel* (416) 367-1900	500	826	200,246,400	6722
AIM Holding Trust (*Suby of* **ART IN MOTION INCOME FUND**) 2000 Brigantine Dr, Coquitlam, BC V3K 7B5, *Tel* (604) 525-3900	500	827	102,536,320	6712
AMEC FOSTER WHEELER INC 801 6 Ave Sw Suite 900, Calgary, AB T2P 3W3, *Tel* (403) 298-4170	500	828	0	6712
AON CONSULTING INC 700 Rue De La Gauchetiere O Bureau 1900, Montreal, QC H3B 0A7, *Tel* (514) 845-6231	500	829	0	8999
ARLANXEO CANADA INC 1265 Vidal St S, Sarnia, ON N7T 7M2, *Tel* (519) 337-8251	500	830	90,179,425	2822
ATCO POWER ALBERTA LTD 919 11 Ave Sw Suite 1400, Calgary, AB T2R 1P3, *Tel* (403) 209-6900	500	831	332,451,650	4911
ABILITY JANITORIAL SERVICES LIMITED 870 Campbell Ave Suite 2, Ottawa, ON K2A 2C5, *Tel*	500	832	19,632,000	7349
▲ Acklands - Grainger Inc (*Suby of* **W.W. GRAINGER, INC.**) 50 Minthorn Blvd, Thornhill, ON L3T 7X8, *Tel* (905) 763-3474	500	833	0	5084
ADVOCATE HEALTH CARE PARTNERSHIP (NO. 1) 429 Walmer Rd, Toronto, ON M5P 2X9, *Tel* (416) 967-6949	500	834	29,400,665	8051
AECON CONSTRUCTION AND MATERIALS LIMITED 20 Carlson Crt Suite 800, Etobicoke, ON M9W 7K6, *Tel* (905) 454-1078	500	835	68,437,137	1629
AEROPORTS DE MONTREAL 580 Boul Stuart-Graham S, Dorval, QC H4Y 1G4, *Tel* (514) 633-2811	500	836	0	4581
AGF CANADIAN RESOURCES FUND LIMITED 66 Wellington St W, Toronto, ON M5K 1E9, *Tel* (800) 268-8583	500	837	204,979,200	6722
ALAMOS GOLD INC 259 Matheson St, Matachewan, ON P0K 1M0, *Tel* (705) 565-9800	500	838	0	1041
ALBERTA HEALTH SERVICES 31 Sunpark Plaza Se Suite 113, Calgary, AB T2X 3W5, *Tel* (403) 943-9300	500	839	0	8093
ALBERTA HEALTH SERVICES 6910 47 St, Wetaskiwin, AB T9A 3N3, *Tel* (780) 361-7100	500	840	0	8062
ALBERTA HEALTH SERVICES 4210 48 St, Leduc, AB T9E 5Z3, *Tel* (780) 986-7711	500	841	0	8062
ALERIS ALUMINIUM CANADA S.E.C. 290 Rue Saint-Laurent, Trois-Rivieres, QC G8T 6G7, *Tel*	500	842	33,472,560	3463
APOTEX INC 285 Garyray Dr, North York, ON M9L 1P2, *Tel* (416) 749-9300	500	843	0	2834
ARMATURES BOIS-FRANCS INC 249 Boul De La Bonaventure, Victoriaville, QC G6T 1V5, *Tel* (819) 758-7501	500	844	77,484,263	3443
Assante Wealth Management Ltd (*Suby of* **CI FINANCIAL CORP**) 20 Queen St E, Toronto, ON M5C 3G7, *Tel* (416) 364-1145	500	845	94,429,920	8742

COMPANY	EMPLOYEES HERE	RANK	SALES ($)	PRIMARY SIC CODE
ASSOCIATION DES GENS D'AFFAIRES & PROFESSIONNELS ITALO-CANADIENS INC, L' 8370 Boul Lacordaire Bureau 310, Saint-Leonard, QC H1R 3Y6, *Tel* (514) 254-4929	500	846	73,620,000	8621
Asurion Canada, Inc (*Suby of* **NEW ASURION CORPORATION**) 11 Ocean Limited Way, Moncton, NB E1C 0H1, *Tel* (506) 386-9200	500	847	115,718,001	4899
ATLANTIC HOTELS PARTNERSHIP 510 Hastings St W, Vancouver, BC V6B 1L8, *Tel* (604) 687-8813	500	848	30,144,000	7011
BELL MOBILITE INC 2925 Virtual Way Suite 400, Vancouver, BC V5M 4X5, *Tel* (604) 678-4160	500	849	0	4899
BETHANY CARE SOCIETY 916 18a St Nw Suite 3085, Calgary, AB T2N 1C6, *Tel* (403) 284-0161	500	850	0	8051
BLACK & MCDONALD LIMITED 31 Pullman Crt, Scarborough, ON M1X 1E4, *Tel* (416) 298-9977	500	851	0	1711
BOMBARDIER INC 1500 Airport Rd, North Bay, ON P1B 8G2, *Tel*	500	852	0	8711
BOMBARDIER TRANSPORTATION CANADA INC 230 Rte O Bureau 130, La Pocatiere, QC G0R 1Z0, *Tel* (418) 856-1232	500	853	0	5088
CH-CHSLD DE PAPINEAU 500 Rue Belanger, Gatineau, QC J8L 2M4, *Tel* (819) 986-3341	500	854	25,816,080	8399
CI Financial Corp (*Suby of* **CI FINANCIAL CORP**) 2 Queen St E, Toronto, ON M5C 3G7, *Tel* (416) 364-1145	500	855	1,441,050,354	6282
CML INTERNATIONAL INC 414 16 Ave Nw Suite 414, Calgary, AB T2M 0J1, *Tel* (403) 203-8772	500	856	20,290,000	2396
CT Financial Assurance Company (*Suby of* **TORONTO-DOMINION BANK, THE**) 55 King St W, Toronto, ON M5K 1A2, *Tel*	500	857	45,016,752	6411
CALEDON SAND & GRAVEL INC 14442 Regional Road 50 Suite 50, Bolton, ON L7E 3E2, *Tel* (905) 951-2244	500	858	0	5032
Canaccord Genuity Corp (*Suby of* **CANACCORD GENUITY GROUP INC**) 609 Granville St Suite 2200, Vancouver, BC V7Y 1H2, *Tel* (604) 684-5992	500	859	226,158,960	6211
CANADA POST CORPORATION 280 Progress Ave, Scarborough, ON M1P 2Z4, *Tel* (416) 299-4577	500	860	0	4311
CANADA POST CORPORATION 2800 Keele St, Toronto, ON M3M 2G4, *Tel*	500	861	0	4311
CANADEL INC 700 Rue Canadel, Louiseville, QC J5V 3A4, *Tel* (819) 228-8471	500	862	0	2511
CANADIAN BROADCASTING CORPORATION 700 Hamilton St, Vancouver, BC V6B 2R5, *Tel* (604) 662-6000	500	863	0	4832
CANADIAN PACIFIC RAILWAY COMPANY 1100 Rue De La Gauchetiere, Montreal, QC H3C 3E4, *Tel* (514) 395-5151	500	864	0	4111
CANADIAN WESTERN BANK 666 Burrard St 22nd Fl, Vancouver, BC V6C 2X8, *Tel* (604) 669-0081	500	865	0	6021
CAPITAL CARE GROUP INC 8740 165 St Nw Suite 438, Edmonton, AB T5R 2R8, *Tel* (780) 341-2300	500	866	0	8051
CASCADES CANADA ULC 2755 Rue Viau, Montreal, QC H1V 3J4, *Tel* (514) 251-3800	500	867	0	2652
CATHOLIC SOCIAL SERVICES 5104 48 Ave, Red Deer, AB T4N 3T8, *Tel* (403) 347-8844	500	868	0	8361
CENTRAL REGIONAL HEALTH AUTHORITY 50 Union St, Grand Falls-Windsor, NL A2A 2E1, *Tel* (709) 292-2500	500	869	286,390,985	8062
CENTRE JEUNESSE DE L'ESTRIE 340 Rue Dufferin, Sherbrooke, QC J1H 4M7, *Tel*	500	870	0	8322
CENTRE DE SANTE ET DE SERVICES SOCIAUX JEANNE-MANCE 1440 Rue Dufresne, Montreal, QC H2K 3J3, *Tel* (514) 527-8921	500	871	0	8361
CENTRE DE SANTE ET DE SERVICES SOCIAUX DE KAMOURASKA 575 Av Martin, Saint-Pascal, QC G0L 3Y0, *Tel* (418) 856-7000	500	872	48,391,650	8062
Centre de Sante et de Services Sociaux de la Haute-Gaspesie (*Suby of* **CENTRE DE SANTE ET DE SERVICES SOCIAUX DE LA HAUTE-GASPESIE**) 50 Rue Du Belvedere, Sainte-Anne-Des-Monts, QC G4V 1X4, *Tel* (418) 797-2744	500	873	0	8621
CENTRE DE SANTE ET DE SERVICES SOCIAUX DES SOMMETS 234 Rue Saint-Vincent, Sainte-Agathe-Des-Monts, QC J8C 2B8, *Tel* (819) 324-4055	500	874	16,134,800	8051
CENTRE DE SANTE ET DE SERVICES SOCIAUX DU PONTIAC 2135 Rue De La Terrasse-Cadieux, Quebec, QC G1C 1Z2, *Tel* (418) 667-3910	500	875	0	8051
CENTRE DE SERVICE SANTE ET SOCIAUX DU GRAND LITTORAL 9330 Boul Du Centre-Hospitalier, Levis, QC G6X 1L6, *Tel* (418) 380-8993	500	876	76,666,240	8062
CHEVALIER DE COLOMB (CONSEIL NO 1093) 170 Rue Saint-Antoine N, Granby, QC J2G 5G8, *Tel* (450) 375-1093	500	877	48,392,880	8641
CHINMAYA MISSION (HALTON REGION) 206 Locke St S, Hamilton, ON L8P 4B4, *Tel* (905) 570-0159	500	878	73,620,000	8621
CINRAM CANADA OPERATIONS ULC 400 Nugget Ave, Scarborough, ON M1S 4A4, *Tel* (416) 332-9000	500	879	0	3652
CITY OF EDMONTON 3 Sir Winston Churchill Sq Nw Suite 5, Edmonton, AB T5J 2C3, *Tel* (780) 718-8941	500	880	0	4953
▲ **CLEAN HARBORS ENERGY AND INDUSTRIAL SERVICES CORP.** 3902 77 Ave, Leduc, AB T9E 0B6, *Tel* (780) 980-1868	500	881	0	7349

CO-OPERATORS GENERAL INSURANCE COMPANY

COMPANY	EMPLOYEES HERE	RANK	SALES ($)	PRIMARY SIC CODE
130 Macdonell St, Guelph, ON N1H 2Z6, Tel (519) 824-4400	500	882	272,654,136	6411
CO-OPERATORS GROUP LIMITED, THE				
1920 College Ave, Regina, SK S4P 1C4, Tel (306) 347-6200	500	883	0	6411
Colabor Limited Partnership (*Suby of* **GROUPE COLABOR INC**)				
580 Industrial Rd, London, ON N5V 1V1, Tel (800) 265-9267	500	884	279,452,573	5141
CONESTOGA COLLEGE COMMUNICATIONS CORPORATION				
299 Doon Valley Dr, Kitchener, ON N2G 4M4, Tel (519) 748-5220	500	885	62,892,123	8222
CONSEIL SCOLAIRE ACADIEN PROVINCIAL				
3435 Rte 206, Petit De Grat, NS B0E 2L0, Tel (902) 226-5232	500	886	0	8211
Consumers' Co-operative Refineries Limited (*Suby of* **FEDERATED CO-OPERATIVES LIMITED**)				
650 E 9th Ave N, Regina, SK S4P 3A1, Tel (306) 721-5353	500	887	0	2911
COOP FEDEREE, LA				
3250 Boul Laurier E, Saint-Hyacinthe, QC J2R 2B6, Tel (450) 773-6661	500	888	0	5144
CORPORATION DE CEGEP ANDRE-LAURENDEAU				
1111 Rue Lapierre Bureau 300, Lasalle, QC H8N 2J4, Tel (514) 364-3320	500	889	69,988,080	8221
CORUS ENTERTAINMENT INC				
800 Rue De La Gauchetiere O Bureau 1100, Montreal, QC H5A 1M1, Tel (514) 767-9250	500	890	0	7922
D+H LIMITED PARTNERSHIP				
120 Bremner Blvd 30th Fl, Toronto, ON M5J 0A8, Tel (416) 696-7700	500	891	393,987,780	6211
Decima Inc (*Suby of* **DECIMA INC**)				
160 Elgin St Suite 1800, Ottawa, ON K2P 2P7, Tel (613) 230-2200	500	892	191,215,680	8732
DELOITTE LLP				
850 2 St Sw Suite 700, Calgary, AB T2P 0R8, Tel (403) 267-1700	500	893	0	8721
DESJARDINS SECURITE FINANCIERE, COMPAGNIE D'ASSURANCE VIE				
1 Complex Desjardins, Montreal, QC H5B 1E2, Tel (514) 285-7700	500	894	0	6311
DESJARDINS SECURITE FINANCIERE, COMPAGNIE D'ASSURANCE VIE				
1 Complexe Desjardins, Montreal, QC H5B 1E2, Tel (514) 285-3000	500	895	0	6311
DESJARDINS SECURITE FINANCIERE, COMPAGNIE D'ASSURANCE VIE				
2 Complexe Desjardins Tour E, Montreal, QC H5B 1E2, Tel (514) 350-8700	500	896	0	6311
DUFFERIN-PEEL CATHOLIC DISTRICT SCHOOL BOARD				
950 North Park Dr, Brampton, ON L6S 3L5, Tel (905) 792-2282	500	897	0	8211
DUFFERIN-PEEL CATHOLIC DISTRICT SCHOOL BOARD				
4235 Golden Orchard Dr, Mississauga, ON L4W 3G1, Tel (905) 624-4529	500	898	0	8211
▲ ESIT Canada Enterprise Services Co (*Suby of* **DXC TECHNOLOGY COMPANY**)				
370 Welton St, Sydney, NS B1P 5S4, Tel (902) 563-4600	500	899	0	7371
▲ Electronic Arts (Canada) Inc (*Suby of* **ELECTRONIC ARTS INC.**)				
3 Place Ville-Marie Bureau 12350, Montreal, QC H3B 0E7, Tel (514) 448-8800	500	900	0	7371
▲ **ENERGIE VALERO INC**				
165 Ch Des Iles, Levis, QC G6V 7M5, Tel (418) 837-3641	500	901	0	2911
Evraz Inc. NA Canada (*Suby of* **EVRAZ PLC**)				
7201 Ogden Dale Rd Se, Calgary, AB T2C 2A4, Tel (403) 279-3351	500	902	0	3312
EXTENDICARE (CANADA) INC				
700 Dorval Sr Suite 111, Oakville, ON L6K 3V3, Tel (905) 847-1025	500	903	0	8051
EXTENDICARE (CANADA) INC				
509 Glendale Ave Suite 200, Niagara On The Lake, ON L0S 1J0, Tel (905) 682-6555	500	904	0	8051
▲ ExxonMobil Canada Ltd (*Suby of* **EXXON MOBIL CORPORATION**)				
237 4 Ave Sw, Calgary, AB T2P 4K3, Tel (403) 232-5300	500	905	669,706,265	1311
F&P MFG., INC				
275 Wright Blvd, Stratford, ON N5A 7Y1, Tel	500	906	0	3714
FEDSEC CORPORATION				
60 St Clair Ave E Suite 1000, Toronto, ON M4T 1N5, Tel (416) 323-9911	500	907	20,908,080	7381
FAIRMONT HOTELS & RESORTS INC				
900 Georgia St W, Vancouver, BC V6C 2W6, Tel (604) 684-3131	500	908	0	7011
FAIRMONT HOTELS & RESORTS INC				
1 Rideau St, Ottawa, ON K1N 8S7, Tel (613) 241-1414	500	909	0	7011
Federated Co-Operatives Limited (*Suby of* **FEDERATED CO-OPERATIVES LIMITED**)				
401 22nd St E, Saskatoon, SK S7K 0H2, Tel (306) 244-3311	500	910	6,825,681,252	4225
FEDERATION DES CAISSES DESJARDINS DU QUEBEC				
1 Complex Desjardins, Montreal, QC H5B 1B2, Tel (514) 281-7000	500	911	0	6062
FIRST URANIUM CORPORATION				
77 King St W Suite 400, Toronto, ON M5K 0A1, Tel (416) 306-3072	500	912	458,254,593	1094
FLEX-N-GATE CANADA COMPANY				
775 Technology Dr, Peterborough, ON K9J 6Z8, Tel (705) 742-3534	500	913	0	3714
▲ Ford Motor Company of Canada, Limited (*Suby of* **FORD MOTOR COMPANY**)				
1000 Henry Ford, Windsor, ON N9A 7E8, Tel (519) 257-2020	500	914	0	3519
GHD CONSULTANTS LTEE				
445 Av Saint-Jean-Baptiste Bureau 390, Quebec, QC G2E 5N7, Tel (418) 658-0112	500	915	0	8621
▲ General Electric Canada Company (*Suby of* **GENERAL ELECTRIC COMPANY**)				
2300 Meadowvale Blvd Suite 100, Mississauga, ON L5N 5P9, Tel (905) 858-5100	500	916	770,173,149	3625
▲ General Electric Canada Company (*Suby of* **GENERAL ELECTRIC COMPANY**)				
1290 S Service Rd W, Oakville, ON L6L 5T7, Tel (905) 849-5048	500	917	0	3625
GERDAU AMERISTEEL CORPORATION				
1801 Hopkins St, Whitby, ON L1N 5T1, Tel (905) 668-3535	500	918	525,317,040	3312

COMPANY	EMPLOYEES HERE	RANK	SALES ($)	PRIMARY SIC CODE
GLACE BAY HEALTH CARE FACILITY 300 South St, Glace Bay, NS B1A 1W5, *Tel* (902) 849-5511	500	919	46,822,320	8062
GOLDCORP INC 853 Boul Rideau, Rouyn-Noranda, QC J0Z 2X0, *Tel* (819) 764-6400	500	920	0	1041
GOLDFINGER JEWELRY INC Gd, Richmond, BC V7E 3E6, *Tel* (604) 275-0061	500	921	85,508,480	8733
▲ Goodyear Canada Inc (*Suby of* **THE GOODYEAR TIRE & RUBBER COMPANY**) 388 Goodyear Rd, Napanee, ON K7R 3L2, *Tel* (613) 354-7411	500	922	0	3011
GOUVERNEMENT DE LA PROVINCE DE QUEBEC 11000 Rue Des Montagnards Rr 1, Beaupre, QC G0A 1E0, *Tel* (418) 661-5666	500	923	0	8361
GOUVERNEMENT DE LA PROVINCE DE QUEBEC 375 Rue Argyll, Sherbrooke, QC J1J 3H5, *Tel* (819) 821-1170	500	924	0	8051
GOUVERNEMENT DE LA PROVINCE DE QUEBEC 100 Rue Laurier, Gatineau, QC K1A 0M8, *Tel* (819) 776-7000	500	925	0	8412
GOUVERNEMENT DE LA PROVINCE DE QUEBEC 475 Boul De Maisonneuve E, Montreal, QC H2L 5C4, *Tel* (514) 873-1100	500	926	0	8231
GOVERNING COUNCIL OF THE UNIVERSITY OF TORONTO 190 Elizabeth St, Toronto, ON M5G 2C4, *Tel* (416) 978-8383	500	927	0	8221
GOVERNING COUNCIL OF THE UNIVERSITY OF TORONTO 215 Huron St, Toronto, ON M5S 1A2, *Tel* (416) 978-2142	500	928	0	8221
GOVERNING COUNCIL OF THE UNIVERSITY OF TORONTO 1265 Military Trail Suite 303, Scarborough, ON M1C 1A4, *Tel* (416) 287-7033	500	929	0	8221
GOVERNMENT OF ONTARIO 400 University Ave 14th Flr, Toronto, ON M7A 1T7, *Tel* (416) 326-7600	500	930	0	8111
▲ Grand & Toy Limited (*Suby of* **OFFICE DEPOT, INC.**) 200 Aviva Park Dr, Woodbridge, ON L4L 9C7, *Tel* (416) 401-6300	500	931	0	5112
GROUPE BOUTIN INC 128 Ch Du Tremblay, Boucherville, QC J4B 6Z6, *Tel* (450) 449-7373	500	932	0	4213
GROUPE ROBERT INC 20 Boul Marie-Victorin, Boucherville, QC J4B 1V5, *Tel* (514) 521-1011	500	933	0	4212
GROUPE VOLVO CANADA INC 1000 Boul Industriel Bureau 1160, Saint-Eustache, QC J7R 5A5, *Tel* (450) 472-6410	500	934	0	3711
H.B. GROUP INSURANCE MANAGEMENT LTD 5600 Cancross Crt, Mississauga, ON L5R 3E9, *Tel* (905) 507-6156	500	935	0	6331
▲ Hershey Canada Inc (*Suby of* **HERSHEY COMPANY**) 1 Hershey Dr, Smiths Falls, ON K7A 4T8, *Tel*	500	936	0	2066
HUSKY INJECTION MOLDING SYSTEMS LTD 500 Queen St S, Bolton, ON L7E 5S5, *Tel* (905) 951-5000	500	937	540,273,984	6712
HYDRO ONE NETWORKS INC 483 Bay St Suite 1000, Toronto, ON M5G 2P5, *Tel* (416) 345-5000	500	938	1,897,124,121	4911
IMMEUBLES JACQUES ROBITAILLE INC, LES 7175 Boul Wilfrid-Hamel, Quebec, QC G2G 1B6, *Tel* (418) 872-9831	500	939	58,896,000	7011
Imperial Parking Canada Corporation (*Suby of* **GATES GROUP CAPITAL PARTNERS, LLC**) 515 Hastings St W Suite 600, Vancouver, BC V6B 0B2, *Tel* (604) 681-7311	500	940	46,621,887	7521
▲ InVentiv Health Clinique Inc (*Suby of* **INC RESEARCH HOLDINGS, INC.**) 2500 Rue Einstein, Quebec, QC G1P 0A2, *Tel* (418) 527-4000	500	941	51,715,185	8731
INDUSTRIELLE ALLIANCE, ASSURANCE ET SERVICES FINANCIERS INC 925 Grande Allee O Bureau 200, Quebec, QC G1S 4Z4, *Tel* (418) 686-7738	500	942	0	6411
INSTITUTE OF CIRCULATORY AND RESPIRATORY HEALTH 5000 Rue Belanger, Montreal, QC H1T 1C8, *Tel* (514) 593-7431	500	943	48,391,650	8062
Intrawest Resort Ownership Corporation (*Suby of* **HAWK HOLDING COMPANY, LLC**) 375 Water St Suite 326, Vancouver, BC V6B 5C6, *Tel* (604) 689-8816	500	944	89,483,728	6531
IVACO ROLLING MILLS 2004 L.P. 1040 Hwy 17, L'Orignal, ON K0B 1K0, *Tel* (613) 675-4671	500	945	54,720,525	3312
Ivari Canaca ULC (*Suby of* **WILTON RE LTD**) 5000 Yonge St Suite 500, North York, ON M2N 7E9, *Tel* (416) 883-5000	500	946	589,916,931	6311
JTI-MACDONALD CORP 2455 Rue Ontario E Bureau 4, Montreal, QC H2K 1W3, *Tel* (514) 598-2525	500	947	0	2111
Kelowna Flightcraft Air Charter Ltd (*Suby of* **RAINMAKER INDUSTRIES INC**) 5655 Airport Way Suite 1, Kelowna, BC V1V 1S1, *Tel* (250) 491-5500	500	948	104,831,760	4512
KUEHNE + NAGEL LTD 2300 Hogan Dr, Mississauga, ON L5N 0C8, *Tel* (905) 567-4168	500	949	0	4731
Langara Ccllege (*Suby of* **LANGARA COLLEGE**) 100 49th Ave W, Vancouver, BC V5Y 2Z6, *Tel* (604) 323-5511	500	950	96,211,755	8221
LARSEN PACKERS LIMITED 326 Main St Rr 3, Berwick, NS B0P 1E0, *Tel*	500	951	83,699,840	2011
LEE VALLEY TOOLS LTD 1090 Morrison Dr, Ottawa, ON K2H 1C2, *Tel* (613) 596-0350	500	952	101,524,617	5251
LENOVO (CANADA) INC 10 York Mills Rd Suite 400, North York, ON M2P 2G4, *Tel* (855) 253-6686	500	953	55,523,093	3571
LONDON HEALTH SCIENCES CENTRE 375 South St, London, ON N6A 4G5, *Tel* (519) 685-8500	500	954	0	8062
LONDON HEALTH SCIENCES CENTRE 339 Windermere Rd, London, ON N6A 5A5, *Tel* (519) 663-3197	500	955	0	8011

COMPANY	EMPLOYEES HERE	RANK	SALES ($)	PRIMARY SIC CODE
MMCC SOLUTIONS CANADA COMPANY 75 Eglinton Ave E, Toronto, ON M4P 3A4, *Tel* (416) 922-3519	500	956	71,647,407	7389
MAGELLAN AEROSPACE LIMITED 634 Magnesium Rd, Haley Station, ON K0J 1Y0, *Tel* (613) 432-8841	500	957	0	3365
MAGNA INTERNATIONAL INC 170 Edward St, St Thomas, ON N5P 4B4, *Tel* (519) 633-7080	500	958	0	3714
MAGNA SEATING INC 455 Magna Dr, Aurora, ON L4G 7A9, *Tel* (905) 713-6050	500	959	0	3465
MAGNA STRUCTURAL SYSTEMS INC 1 Conlon Dr, Perth, ON K7H 3N1, *Tel* (613) 267-7557	500	960	0	3365
▲ Marsh Canada Limited (*Suby of* **MARSH & MCLENNAN COMPANIES, INC.**) 120 Bremner Blvd Suite 800, Toronto, ON M5J 0A8, *Tel* (416) 868-2600	500	961	106,895,373	6411
▲ Mercer (Canada) Limited (*Suby of* **MARSH & MCLENNAN COMPANIES, INC.**) 1981 Av Mcgill College Bureau 800, Montreal, QC H3A 3T5, *Tel* (514) 285-1802	500	962	0	8999
METROLINX 20 Bay St Suite 901, Toronto, ON M5J 2N8, *Tel* (416) 874-5900	500	963	0	4011
Minto Apartments Limited (*Suby of* **MINTO APARTMENTS LIMITED**) 90 Sheppard Ave E Suite 500, North York, ON M2N 3A1, *Tel* (416) 977-0777	500	964	113,089,085	6531
NDG FINANCIAL CORP Gd Stn Terminal, Vancouver, BC V6B 3P7, *Tel*	500	965	96,661,760	8742
NAPOLEON HOME COMFORT BARRIE INC 24 Napoleon Rd, Barrie, ON L4M 0G8, *Tel* (705) 721-1214	500	966	49,849,204	5719
▲ **NESTLE CANADA INC** 980 Wilton Grove Rd, London, ON N6N 1C7, *Tel* (519) 686-0182	500	967	0	2023
Nordstrong Equipment Limited (*Suby of* **CANERECTOR INC**) 15475 Madrona Dr, Surrey, BC V4A 5N2, *Tel*	500	968	0	3535
NORTH YORK GENERAL HOSPITAL 555 Finch Ave W Suite 262, North York, ON M2R 1N5, *Tel* (416) 633-9420	500	969	0	8062
NORTHERN ALBERTA INSTITUTE OF TECHNOLOGY 10504 Princess Elizabeth Ave Nw, Edmonton, AB T5G 3K4, *Tel* (780) 378-5060	500	970	0	8222
NORTON ROSE CANADA S.E.N.C.R.L., S.R.L. 1 Place Ville-Marie Bureau 2500, Montreal, QC H3B 4S2, *Tel* (514) 847-4747	500	971	59,551,150	8111
O I EMPLOYEE LEASING INC 188 Mohawk St, Brantford, ON N3S 2X2, *Tel* (519) 752-2230	500	972	29,448,000	8721
OMNILOGIC SYSTEMS COMPANY 833 4 Ave Sw Suite 900, Calgary, AB T2P 3T5, *Tel* (403) 232-6664	500	973	50,240,000	7379
ONTARIO LOTTERY AND GAMING CORPORATION 70 Foster Dr Suite 800, Sault Ste. Marie, ON P6A 6V2, *Tel* (705) 946-6464	500	974	0	7999
ONTARIO LOTTERY AND GAMING CORPORATION 380 Second St, Gananoque, ON K7G 2J9, *Tel* (866) 266-8422	500	975	0	7999
ONTARIO PUBLIC SERVICE EMPLOYEES UNION 67 Beresford Cres, Brampton, ON L6P 2M1, *Tel* (416) 326-2591	500	976	0	8631
ONTARIO RIBS INC 56 The Esplanade Suite 201, Toronto, ON M5E 1A7, *Tel* (416) 864-9775	500	977	21,000,150	5812
PCL CONSTRUCTORS CANADA INC 2085 Hurontario St Suite 400, Mississauga, ON L5A 4G1, *Tel* (905) 276-7600	500	978	881,237,142	1542
PCS SALES (CANADA) INC Gd, Allan, SK S0K 0C0, *Tel* (306) 257-3312	500	979	0	1474
PF RESOLU CANADA INC 7 Mill Rd, Grand Falls-Windsor, NL A2A 1B8, *Tel* (709) 292-3000	500	980	0	2621
▲ **PVH CANADA, INC** 7445 Ch De La Cote-De-Liesse, Saint-Laurent, QC H4T 1G2, *Tel* (514) 278-6000	500	981	0	5136
PATHEON INC 111 Consumers Dr, Whitby, ON L1N 5Z5, *Tel* (905) 668-3368	500	982	0	2834
▲ PepsiCo Canada ULC (*Suby of* **PEPSICO, INC.**) 1001 Bishop St N, Cambridge, ON N3H 4V8, *Tel* (519) 653-5721	500	983	0	2096
▲ PepsiCo Canada ULC (*Suby of* **PEPSICO, INC.**) 12 Clipper Crt, Brampton, ON L6W 4T9, *Tel* (905) 460-2400	500	984	0	5145
▲ **PLAINS MIDSTREAM CANADA ULC** Gd Lcd Main, Swift Current, SK S9H 3V4, *Tel* (306) 773-9381	500	985	0	4612
Portage La Prairie School Division (*Suby of* **PORTAGE LA PRAIRIE SCHOOL DIVISION**) 535 3rd St Nw, Portage La Prairie, MB R1N 2C4, *Tel* (204) 857-8756	500	986	52,908,240	8211
POSTMEDIA NETWORK INC 200 Granville St Suite 1, Vancouver, BC V6C 3N3, *Tel* (604) 605-2000	500	987	0	2711
▲ Prairie Mines & Royalty ULC (*Suby of* **WESTMORELAND COAL COMPANY**) Gd, Edson, AB T7E 1W1, *Tel* (780) 794-8100	500	988	0	1221
PRINCE RUPERT SCHOOL DISTRICT 52 634 6th Ave E, Prince Rupert, BC V8J 1X1, *Tel* (250) 627-0772	500	989	0	8211
PROVIDENCE CARE CENTRE 752 King St W, Kingston, ON K7L 4X3, *Tel* (613) 548-5567	500	990	0	8063
PROVIGO DISTRIBUTION INC 8000 Rue Armand-Viau Bureau 500, Quebec, QC G2C 2E2, *Tel*	500	991	0	5141
Q & I COMPUTER SYSTEMS INC 115 Symons St, Etobicoke, ON M8V 1V1, *Tel* (416) 253-5555	500	992	95,706,000	7371

COMPANY	EMPLOYEES HERE	RANK	SALES ($)	PRIMARY SIC CODE
REGROUPEMENT DES C H S L D DES TROIS RIVES, LE 408 Av Saint-Charles, Vaudreuil-Dorion, QC J7V 7M9, *Tel* (450) 455-6177	500	993	31,705,680	8051
Reseau de Transport de Longueuil (*Suby of* **RESEAU DE TRANSPORT DE LONGUEUIL**) 1150 Boul Marie-Victorin, Longueuil, QC J4G 2M4, *Tel* (450) 442-8600	500	994	48,531,840	4111
RICHARDSON MILLING LIMITED 1 Can-Oat Dr, Portage La Prairie, MB R1N 3W1, *Tel* (204) 857-9700	500	995	238,873,332	5153
ROXUL INC 8024 Esquesing Line, Milton, ON L9T 6W3, *Tel* (905) 878-8474	500	996	29,184,280	3296
Royal Bank Of Canada (*Suby of* **ROYAL BANK OF CANADA**) 1307 Av Van Horne, Outremont, QC H2V 1K7, *Tel* (514) 495-5904	500	997	0	6021
Royal Bank Of Canada (*Suby of* **ROYAL BANK OF CANADA**) 200 Bay St, Toronto, ON M5J 2J5, *Tel* (416) 974-3940	500	998	20,724,267,953	6021
SMART TECHNOLOGIES ULC 501 Palladium Dr, Kanata, ON K2V 0A2, *Tel*	500	999	0	3674
SNC-LAVALIN INTERNATIONAL INC 605 5 Ave Sw Suite 1400, Calgary, AB T2P 3H5, *Tel* (403) 294-2100	500	1000	0	8711

SIC	DESCRIPTION	0-19	20-49	50-99	100-OVER	TOTAL	PRIMARY SIC ONLY
0115	Corn	0	2	0	0	2	0
0119	Cash grains, nec	3	2	1	0	6	0
0134	Irish potatoes	1	0	0	0	1	0
0139	Field crops, except cash grain	1	0	0	0	1	0
0161	Vegetables and melons	1	0	0	0	1	0
0175	Deciduous tree fruits	1	0	0	0	1	0
0181	Ornamental nursery products	1	0	0	0	1	0
0191	General farms, primarily crop	2	0	1	0	3	0
0213	Hogs	3	0	1	0	4	0
0214	Sheep and goats	0	0	1	0	1	0
0241	Dairy farms	1	0	0	0	1	0
0251	Broiler, fryer, and roaster chickens	1	1	2	0	4	0
0252	Chicken eggs	0	0	0	1	1	0
0253	Turkeys and turkey eggs	1	0	0	1	2	0
0254	Poultry hatcheries	0	1	0	0	1	0
0259	Poultry and eggs, nec	6	0	0	1	7	0
0273	Animal aquaculture	1	0	0	0	1	0
0291	General farms, primarily animals	0	0	1	0	1	0
0711	Soil preparation services	2	2	0	1	5	0
0721	Crop planting and protection	0	2	0	0	2	0
0722	Crop harvesting	1	1	0	0	2	0
0723	Crop preparation services for market	12	2	2	2	18	0
0742	Veterinary services, specialties	1	0	0	0	1	0
0751	Livestock services, except veterinary	0	0	0	1	1	0
0752	Animal specialty services	47	0	0	0	47	0
0762	Farm management services	1	1	0	0	2	0
0781	Landscape counseling and planning	0	0	4	4	8	0
0782	Lawn and garden services	1	0	1	1	3	0
0811	Timber tracts	1	0	0	0	1	0
0831	Forest products	2	1	0	0	3	0
0851	Forestry services	6	2	1	0	9	0
0912	Finfish	0	1	0	0	1	0
1011	Iron ores	6	1	1	3	11	10
1021	Copper ores	35	4	1	3	43	36
1031	Lead and zinc ores	13	0	0	0	13	3
1041	Gold ores	52	14	10	15	91	70
1044	Silver ores	12	2	0	1	15	7
1061	Ferroalloy ores, except vanadium	11	1	0	3	15	7
1081	Metal mining services	161	18	18	22	219	189
1094	Uranium-radium-vanadium ores	14	1	1	2	18	17
1099	Metal ores, nec	4	0	1	0	5	5
1221	Bituminous coal and lignite-surface mining	18	2	6	16	42	39
1222	Bituminous coal-underground mining	0	0	1	0	1	1
1231	Anthracite mining	2	0	0	0	2	2
1241	Coal mining services	15	4	1	5	25	19
1311	Crude petroleum and natural gas	354	55	19	41	469	412
1321	Natural gas liquids	19	7	5	2	33	14
1381	Drilling oil and gas wells	93	33	10	18	154	123
1382	Oil and gas exploration services	310	47	23	33	413	340
1389	Oil and gas field services, nec	592	153	63	52	860	744
1411	Dimension stone	15	3	3	2	23	22
1422	Crushed and broken limestone	16	9	4	7	36	24
1423	Crushed and broken granite	0	1	0	0	1	1
1429	Crushed and broken stone, nec	11	6	1	0	18	12
1442	Construction sand and gravel	21	7	3	2	33	22
1446	Industrial sand	4	2	0	0	6	5
1455	Kaolin and ball clay	0	0	1	0	1	1
1459	Clay and related minerals, nec	4	0	0	0	4	3
1474	Potash, soda, and borate minerals	10	3	1	9	23	19
1475	Phosphate rock	1	0	1	0	2	2
1479	Chemical and fertilizer mining	7	5	2	5	19	13
1481	NonMetallic mineral services	56	15	6	4	81	63
1499	Miscellaneous nonMetallic minerals, except fuels	29	16	10	7	62	52
1521	Single-family housing construction	267	57	24	18	366	307
1522	Residential construction, nec	120	41	13	19	193	128
1531	Operative builders	38	5	3	1	47	38
1541	Industrial buildings and warehouses	239	81	37	35	392	263
1542	Nonresidential construction, nec	297	93	44	34	468	303
1611	Highway and street construction	346	82	64	49	541	454
1622	Bridge, tunnel, and elevated highway construction	54	13	3	5	75	31
1623	Water, sewer, and utility lines	186	57	34	46	323	229
1629	Heavy construction, nec	157	44	30	23	254	176
1711	Plumbing, heating, air-conditioning	343	107	96	37	583	402
1721	Painting and paper hanging	17	7	14	3	41	27
1731	Electrical work	436	117	90	45	688	511
1741	Masonry and other stonework	16	4	20	3	43	33
1742	Plastering, drywall, and insulation	58	10	31	3	102	86
1743	Terrazzo, tile, marble and mossaic work	2	0	3	1	6	3
1751	Carpentry work	51	15	18	4	88	52

SIC	DESCRIPTION	0-19	20-49	50-99	100-OVER	TOTAL	PRIMARY SIC ONLY
1752	Floor laying and floor work, nec	27	13	4	2	46	20
1761	Roofing, siding, and sheetMetal work	58	25	29	10	122	100
1771	Concrete work	64	22	16	7	109	77
1781	Water well drilling	12	3	0	3	18	9
1791	Structural steel erection	45	19	17	10	91	42
1793	Glass and glazing work	56	5	3	2	66	27
1794	Excavation work	64	13	34	11	122	76
1795	Wrecking and demolition work	13	4	4	2	23	18
1796	Installing building equipment	75	25	13	8	121	68
1799	Special trade contractors, nec	247	80	63	18	408	271
2011	Meat packing plants	50	11	9	52	122	105
2013	Sausages and other prepared meats	21	5	13	13	52	36
2015	Poultry slaughtering and processing	15	6	4	28	53	40
2021	Creamery butter	3	1	2	4	10	6
2022	Cheese; natural and processed	20	5	8	18	51	36
2023	Dry, condensed and evaporated dairy products	9	5	5	9	28	18
2024	Ice cream and frozen deserts	13	6	5	5	29	15
2026	Fluid milk	17	7	6	14	44	32
2032	Canned specialties	14	4	5	8	31	23
2033	Canned fruits and specialties	17	7	11	9	44	35
2034	Dried and dehydrated fruits, vegetables and soup mixes	1	1	2	1	5	3
2035	Pickles, sauces, and salad dressings	5	0	6	6	17	5
2037	Frozen fruits and vegetables	9	2	5	5	21	18
2038	Frozen specialties, nec	12	4	6	6	28	20
2041	Flour and other grain mill products	33	11	10	5	59	37
2043	Cereal breakfast foods	5	2	2	5	14	11
2044	Rice milling	1	1	0	0	2	0
2045	Prepared flour mixes and doughs	3	0	3	3	9	5
2046	Wet corn milling	3	4	0	2	9	7
2047	Dog and cat food	9	1	2	5	17	11
2048	Prepared feeds, nec	72	36	8	4	120	106
2051	Bread, cake, and related products	106	16	45	38	205	173
2052	Cookies and crackers	6	1	7	4	18	8
2053	Frozen bakery products, except bread	6	2	4	2	14	7
2061	Raw cane sugar	1	0	1	0	2	2
2062	Cane sugar refining	5	1	0	2	8	8
2063	Beet sugar	0	1	0	0	1	1
2064	Candy and other confectionery products	21	6	11	19	57	34
2066	Chocolate and cocoa products	68	4	5	5	82	66
2067	Chewing gum	1	0	0	1	2	2
2068	Salted and roasted nuts and seeds	2	1	0	1	4	4
2075	Soybean oil mills	0	0	1	0	1	1
2076	Vegetable oil mills, nec	1	1	2	2	6	4
2077	Animal and marine fats and oils	4	0	0	1	5	3
2079	Edible fats and oils	20	4	7	5	36	26
2082	Malt beverages	72	11	9	13	105	88
2083	Malt	8	2	0	0	10	10
2084	Wines, brandy, and brandy spirits	123	5	9	7	144	139
2085	Distilled and blended liquors	13	2	5	4	24	21
2086	Bottled and canned soft drinks	23	3	12	17	55	51
2087	Flavoring extracts and syrups, nec	2	1	7	3	13	2
2091	Canned and cured fish and seafoods	10	1	4	8	23	19
2092	Fresh or frozen packaged fish	34	9	9	9	61	52
2095	Roasted coffee	5	0	1	4	10	8
2096	Potato chips and similar snacks	72	9	3	17	101	97
2097	Manufactured ice	13	3	1	0	17	17
2098	Macaroni and spaghetti	2	3	3	4	12	7
2099	Food preparations, nec	53	18	16	21	108	68
2111	Cigarettes	8	1	1	3	13	13
2121	Cigars	1	0	1	1	3	1
2131	Chewing and smoking tobacco	3	1	1	0	5	2
2141	Tobacco stemming and redrying	0	1	0	0	1	1
2211	Broadwoven fabric mills, cotton	6	3	1	4	14	11
2221	Broadwoven fabric mills, manmade	5	3	3	6	17	12
2231	Broadwoven fabric mills, wool	3	2	1	1	7	6
2241	Narrow fabric mills	5	1	4	2	12	11
2251	Women's hosiery, except socks	4	1	2	3	10	7
2252	Hosiery, nec	2	0	2	0	4	2
2253	Knit outerwear mills	2	0	0	0	2	1
2254	Knit underwear mills	1	0	0	0	1	0
2258	Lace and warp knit fabric mills	1	2	0	0	3	2
2259	Knitting mills, nec	0	0	1	0	1	0
2261	Finishing plants, cotton	0	0	1	0	1	1
2262	Finishing plants, manmade	0	0	0	1	1	0
2269	Finishing plants, nec	1	2	2	0	5	4
2273	Carpets and rugs	5	1	2	3	11	10
2281	Yarn spinning mills	1	0	1	1	3	1
2282	Throwing and winding mills	1	1	0	1	3	3
2284	Thread mills	3	1	0	1	5	3

SIC	DESCRIPTION	0-19	20-49	50-99	100-OVER	TOTAL	PRIMARY SIC ONLY
2295	Coated fabrics, not rubberized	8	2	4	2	16	11
2296	Tire cord and fabrics	2	1	0	1	4	3
2297	Nonwoven fabrics	3	1	1	3	8	7
2298	Cordage and twine	3	1	2	1	7	4
2299	Textile goods, nec	12	4	5	7	28	17
2311	Men's and boy's suits and coats	6	0	5	3	14	10
2321	Men's and boy's furnishings	4	2	3	2	11	7
2322	Men's and boy's underwear and nightwear	5	1	1	1	8	5
2325	Men's and boys' trousers and slacks	11	4	3	0	18	4
2326	Men's and boy's work clothing	6	5	3	4	18	14
2329	Men's and boy's clothing, nec	29	11	15	10	65	22
2331	Women's and misses' blouses and shirts	99	1	2	1	103	101
2335	Women's, junior's, and misses' dresses	8	3	2	2	15	7
2337	Women's and misses' suits and coats	13	3	3	3	22	9
2339	Women's and misses' outerwear, nec	160	19	15	8	202	95
2341	Women's and children's underwear	5	0	2	2	9	3
2342	Bras, girdles, and allied garments	1	0	1	1	3	1
2353	Hats, caps, and millinery	7	0	2	2	11	9
2361	Girl's and children's dresses, blouses	0	0	1	0	1	0
2369	Girl's and children's outerwear, nec	5	1	0	0	6	2
2371	Fur goods	1	0	0	0	1	1
2381	Fabric dress and work gloves	3	2	1	0	6	5
2384	Robes and dressing gowns	1	0	0	0	1	0
2386	Leather and sheep-lined clothing	13	0	3	0	16	15
2387	Apparel belts	0	1	0	2	3	2
2389	Apparel and accessories, nec	9	2	1	2	14	6
2391	Curtains and draperies	3	1	1	0	5	4
2392	Household furnishings, nec	21	4	4	2	31	12
2393	Textile bags	1	0	2	1	4	2
2394	Canvas and related products	13	4	5	4	26	20
2395	Pleating and stitching	7	1	0	2	10	3
2396	Automotive and apparel trimmings	4	2	3	1	10	5
2399	Fabricated textile products, nec	10	2	2	7	21	12
2411	Logging	38	17	6	4	65	49
2421	Sawmills and planing mills, general	99	29	41	87	256	212
2426	Hardwood dimension and flooring mills	16	3	5	10	34	20
2429	Special product sawmills, nec	5	4	4	3	16	14
2431	Millwork	85	24	41	30	180	135
2434	Wood kitchen cabinets	44	7	21	6	78	59
2435	Hardwood veneer and plywood	10	6	4	9	29	21
2436	Softwood veneer and plywood	2	0	2	6	10	6
2439	Structural wood members, nec	22	10	10	8	50	34
2441	Nailed wood boxes and shook	1	1	1	1	4	3
2448	Wood pallets and skids	12	3	11	4	30	22
2449	Wood containers, nec	4	1	0	0	5	3
2451	Mobile homes	0	2	0	0	2	2
2452	Prefabricated wood buildings	35	4	7	7	53	38
2491	Wood preserving	13	4	7	1	25	20
2493	Reconstituted wood products	8	0	2	10	20	13
2499	Wood products, nec	31	14	8	12	65	43
2511	Wood household furniture	16	3	11	11	41	30
2512	Upholstered household furniture	4	6	4	2	16	11
2514	Metal household furniture	10	0	5	2	17	11
2515	Mattresses and bedsprings	11	2	6	3	22	19
2517	Wood television and radio cabinets	1	0	3	1	5	4
2519	Household furniture, nec	3	0	5	2	10	6
2521	Wood office furniture	15	3	7	7	32	18
2522	Office furniture, except wood	21	1	6	11	39	35
2531	Public building and related furniture	20	4	5	14	43	21
2541	Wood partitions and fixtures	29	5	20	2	56	36
2542	Partitions and fixtures, except wood	23	4	9	8	44	32
2591	Drapery hardware and window blinds and shades	9	3	1	2	15	9
2599	Furniture and fixtures, nec	6	4	11	3	24	10
2611	Pulp mills	31	4	8	33	76	57
2621	Paper mills	56	8	9	33	106	86
2631	Paperboard mills	17	4	8	13	42	34
2652	Setup paperboard boxes	1	0	1	2	4	4
2653	Corrugated and solid fiber boxes	18	9	7	24	58	48
2655	Fiber cans, drums, and similar products	13	6	8	2	29	26
2656	Sanitary food containers	1	0	3	1	5	4
2657	Folding paperboard boxes	15	3	3	10	31	27
2671	Paper; coated and laminated packaging	12	6	2	4	24	18
2672	Paper; coated and laminated, nec	9	4	3	6	22	17
2673	Bags: plastic, laminated, and coated	7	5	10	6	28	24
2674	Bags: uncoated paper and multiwall	2	3	2	5	12	7
2675	Die-cut paper and board	2	1	3	1	7	1
2676	Sanitary paper products	7	2	3	12	24	18
2677	Envelopes	4	3	1	3	11	11
2678	Stationery products	3	3	1	0	7	6

SIC	DESCRIPTION	0-19	20-49	50-99	100-OVER	TOTAL	PRIMARY SIC ONLY
2679	Converted paper products, nec	23	5	10	20	58	39
2711	Newspapers	213	62	40	43	358	346
2721	Periodicals	54	32	6	14	106	80
2731	Book publishing	54	15	12	13	94	76
2732	Book printing	11	4	2	3	20	15
2741	Miscellaneous publishing	20	8	4	5	37	22
2752	Commercial printing, lithographic	164	26	26	37	253	221
2754	Commercial printing, gravure	5	0	1	2	8	4
2759	Commercial printing, nec	86	22	29	19	156	87
2761	Manifold business forms	25	2	6	7	40	35
2771	Greeting cards	13	1	0	2	16	13
2782	Blankbooks and looseleaf binders	6	3	4	3	16	14
2789	Bookbinding and related work	4	0	13	4	21	16
2791	Typesetting	1	0	0	0	1	1
2796	Platemaking services	1	0	1	1	4	3
2812	Alkalies and chlorine	5	0	0	2	7	4
2813	Industrial gases	117	18	8	4	147	134
2816	Inorganic pigments	5	2	2	2	11	10
2819	Industrial inorganic chemicals, nec	92	26	13	13	144	113
2821	Plastics materials and resins	32	13	20	14	79	64
2822	Synthetic rubber	4	1	2	4	11	8
2824	Organic fibers, noncellulosic	10	2	1	1	14	13
2833	Medicinals and botanicals	6	1	4	2	13	12
2834	Pharmaceutical preparations	75	20	14	50	159	134
2835	Diagnostic substances	5	0	1	1	7	6
2836	Biological products, except diagnostic	14	1	0	2	17	14
2841	Soap and other detergents	9	3	8	8	28	19
2842	Polishes and sanitation goods	16	10	9	6	41	29
2843	Surface active agents	1	0	0	0	1	0
2844	Toilet preparations	67	10	8	11	96	52
2851	Paints and allied products	119	19	11	14	163	137
2865	Cyclic crudes and intermediates	2	4	3	2	11	6
2869	Industrial organic chemicals, nec	31	16	4	8	59	40
2873	Nitrogenous fertilizers	23	2	3	6	34	31
2874	Phosphatic fertilizers	18	6	1	5	30	23
2875	Fertilizers, mixing only	18	6	4	0	28	20
2879	Agricultural chemicals, nec	27	6	2	6	41	32
2891	Adhesives and sealants	62	13	2	13	90	68
2892	Explosives	49	6	0	3	58	54
2893	Printing ink	18	3	1	0	22	19
2899	Chemical preparations, nec	62	25	16	12	115	79
2911	Petroleum refining	202	16	10	27	255	226
2951	Asphalt paving mixtures and blocks	33	12	2	4	51	29
2952	Asphalt felts and coatings	11	1	2	3	17	11
2992	Lubricating oils and greases	24	8	0	3	35	24
3011	Tires and inner tubes	15	3	0	6	24	19
3021	Rubber and plastics footwear	8	0	2	0	10	10
3052	Rubber and plastics hose and beltings	13	1	1	3	18	12
3053	Gaskets; packing and sealing devices	16	2	2	4	24	13
3061	Mechanical rubber goods	3	1	1	1	6	4
3069	Fabricated rubber products, nec	19	15	8	10	52	40
3081	Unsupported plastics film and sheet	21	6	12	11	50	43
3082	Unsupported plastics profile shapes	0	0	0	1	1	1
3083	Laminated plastics plate and sheet	6	2	0	2	10	8
3084	Plastics pipe	12	8	1	5	26	8
3085	Plastics bottles	1	1	0	1	3	1
3086	Plastics foam products	23	12	9	11	55	40
3087	Custom compound purchased resins	1	1	1	1	4	4
3088	Plastics plumbing fixtures	7	4	1	4	16	10
3089	Plastics products, nec	147	37	40	84	308	241
3111	Leather tanning and finishing	2	0	1	0	3	1
3142	House slippers	1	0	0	0	1	0
3143	Men's footwear, except athletic	11	0	2	1	14	11
3144	Women's footwear, except athletic	6	0	3	1	10	3
3149	Footwear, except rubber, nec	5	0	1	0	6	2
3151	Leather gloves and mittens	2	1	2	0	5	2
3161	Luggage	2	0	0	1	3	1
3171	Women's handbags and purses	8	1	1	0	10	0
3172	Personal leather goods, nec	6	1	1	1	9	2
3199	Leather goods, nec	2	0	1	1	4	3
3211	Flat glass	15	5	2	9	31	24
3221	Glass containers	5	1	0	1	7	7
3229	Pressed and blown glass, nec	13	2	0	1	16	11
3231	Products of purchased glass	18	5	5	6	34	21
3241	Cement, hydraulic	18	4	2	4	28	26
3251	Brick and structural clay tile	5	2	2	4	13	11
3253	Ceramic wall and floor tile	4	1	1	0	6	5
3255	Clay refractories	10	0	1	1	12	8
3259	Structural clay products, nec	5	0	1	1	8	7

SIC	DESCRIPTION	0-19	20-49	50-99	100-OVER	TOTAL	PRIMARY SIC ONLY
3261	Vitreous plumbing fixtures	2	0	0	0	2	2
3263	Semivitreous table and kitchenware	1	0	0	0	1	0
3264	Porcelain electrical supplies	1	0	0	0	1	0
3269	Pottery products, nec	1	0	0	1	2	2
3271	Concrete block and brick	23	7	4	2	36	24
3272	Concrete products, nec	51	27	15	15	108	76
3273	Ready-mixed concrete	115	26	10	14	165	130
3274	Lime	5	6	3	2	16	11
3275	Gypsum products	7	3	4	5	19	18
3281	Cut stone and stone products	15	3	6	1	25	19
3291	Abrasive products	5	4	2	4	15	11
3292	Asbestos products	2	0	0	0	2	1
3295	Minerals, ground or treated	10	2	3	3	18	11
3296	Mineral wool	10	2	3	4	19	14
3297	Nonclay refractories	9	3	2	1	15	14
3299	NonMetallic mineral products,	16	5	9	3	33	27
3312	Blast furnaces and steel mills	76	29	16	33	154	122
3313	ElectroMetallurgical products	3	0	1	0	4	3
3315	Steel wire and related products	11	4	1	0	16	12
3316	Cold finishing of steel shapes	7	3	0	1	11	5
3317	Steel pipe and tubes	3	2	3	4	12	9
3321	Gray and ductile iron foundries	5	0	4	9	18	15
3322	Malleable iron foundries	0	0	1	2	3	2
3324	Steel investment foundries	3	2	0	2	7	4
3325	Steel foundries, nec	14	0	1	6	21	18
3331	Primary copper	1	0	0	0	1	0
3334	Primary aluminum	8	1	1	8	18	17
3339	Primary nonferrous Metals, nec	16	3	3	4	26	18
3341	Secondary nonferrous Metals	12	3	2	3	20	14
3351	Copper rolling and drawing	2	1	0	1	4	3
3353	Aluminum sheet, plate, and foil	5	0	0	1	6	2
3354	Aluminum extruded products	4	1	3	5	13	10
3355	Aluminum rolling and drawing, nec	1	1	2	1	5	2
3356	Nonferrous rolling and drawing, nec	1	1	0	1	3	1
3357	Nonferrous wiredrawing and insulating	14	3	3	1	21	17
3364	Nonferrous die-castings except aluminum	1	2	0	2	5	3
3365	Aluminum foundries	8	4	5	6	23	18
3366	Copper foundries	0	1	2	0	3	2
3369	Nonferrous foundries, nec	6	1	2	4	13	7
3398	Metal heat treating	15	3	2	1	21	19
3399	Primary Metal products	16	3	3	2	24	22
3411	Metal cans	3	3	1	5	12	12
3412	Metal barrels, drums, and pails	6	2	3	0	11	8
3421	Cutlery	4	1	0	0	5	1
3423	Hand and edge tools, nec	8	2	1	4	15	9
3425	Saw blades and handsaws	5	2	0	0	7	5
3429	Hardware, nec	43	12	13	10	78	52
3431	Metal sanitary ware	13	2	3	5	23	17
3432	Plumbing fixture fittings and trim	3	1	0	2	6	5
3433	Heating equipment, except electric	18	7	8	6	39	34
3441	Fabricated structural Metal	50	27	13	15	105	72
3442	Metal doors, sash, and trim	59	13	9	22	103	65
3443	Fabricated plate work (boiler shop)	63	23	19	20	125	83
3444	Sheet Metalwork	71	24	21	9	125	69
3446	Architectural Metalwork	11	7	11	4	33	17
3448	Prefabricated Metal buildings and components	35	4	5	3	47	33
3449	Miscellaneous Metalwork	27	7	3	2	39	30
3451	Screw machine products	2	0	0	0	2	1
3452	Bolts, nuts, rivets, and washers	9	6	3	2	20	17
3462	Iron and steel forgings	18	6	2	3	29	21
3463	Nonferrous forgings	3	0	1	4	8	5
3465	Automotive stampings	21	7	9	26	63	43
3466	Crowns and closures	0	1	0	1	2	1
3469	Metal stampings, nec	60	12	14	14	100	56
3471	Plating and polishing	10	9	13	3	35	27
3479	Metal coating and allied services	35	20	26	5	86	65
3482	Small arms ammunition	1	0	0	0	1	1
3483	Ammunition, except for small arms, nec	4	0	0	1	5	3
3484	Small arms	2	0	0	1	3	2
3489	Ordnance and accessories, nec	1	0	0	0	1	0
3491	Industrial valves	17	3	2	1	23	15
3492	Fluid power valves and hose fittings	14	9	3	10	36	16
3493	Steel springs, except wire	3	1	1	3	8	6
3494	Valves and pipe fittings, nec	33	10	2	12	57	43
3495	Wire springs	2	0	1	0	3	1
3496	Miscellaneous fabricated wire products	38	10	10	3	61	45
3497	Metal foil and leaf	3	1	1	1	6	4
3498	Fabricated pipe and fittings	23	9	6	6	44	35
3499	Fabricated Metal products, nec	73	18	32	20	143	99

SIC	DESCRIPTION	0-19	20-49	50-99	100-OVER	TOTAL	PRIMARY SIC ONLY
3511	Turbines and turbine generator sets	15	0	0	3	18	16
3519	Internal combustion engines, nec	10	2	2	5	19	14
3523	Farm machinery and equipment	35	8	10	13	66	51
3524	Lawn and garden equipment	3	2	0	1	6	4
3531	Construction machinery	87	19	8	14	128	86
3532	Mining machinery	32	9	10	4	55	39
3533	Oil and gas field machinery	68	24	14	13	119	86
3534	Elevators and moving stairways	11	6	2	3	22	18
3535	Conveyors and conveying equipment	21	8	5	5	39	27
3536	Hoists, cranes, and monorails	13	2	3	0	18	9
3537	Industrial trucks and tractors	11	5	8	3	27	21
3541	Machine tools, Metal cutting type	15	8	10	0	33	24
3542	Machine tools, Metal forming type	3	6	4	0	13	7
3544	Special dies, tools, jigs, and fixtures	24	6	20	12	62	48
3545	Machine tool accessories	19	6	3	8	36	23
3546	Power-driven handtools	3	0	0	0	3	3
3547	Rolling mill machinery	3	0	1	0	4	3
3548	Welding apparatus	16	6	2	5	29	17
3549	Metalworking machinery, nec	3	3	0	3	9	6
3552	Textile machinery	6	0	0	0	6	3
3553	Woodworking machinery	11	2	5	3	21	14
3554	Paper industries machinery	7	1	1	2	11	6
3555	Printing trades machinery	6	1	2	1	10	5
3556	Food products machinery	12	6	3	4	25	21
3559	Special industry machinery, nec	30	8	6	2	46	28
3561	Pumps and pumping equipment	52	9	3	7	71	57
3562	Ball and roller bearings	8	0	1	3	12	9
3563	Air and gas compressors	25	7	3	1	36	29
3564	Blowers and fans	19	7	5	4	35	21
3565	Packaging machinery	7	6	2	1	16	13
3566	Speed changers, drives, and gears	2	2	0	2	6	4
3567	Industrial furnaces and ovens	16	5	5	5	31	18
3568	Power transmission equipment, nec	11	4	0	3	18	10
3569	General industrial machinery, nec	80	27	21	18	146	101
3571	Electronic computers	25	5	1	7	38	33
3572	Computer storage devices	1	0	0	0	1	1
3577	Computer peripheral equipment, nec	17	1	1	5	24	18
3578	Calculating and accounting equipment	16	2	2	2	22	17
3579	Office machines, nec	13	5	1	1	20	13
3581	Automatic vending machines	4	2	2	0	8	5
3585	Refrigeration and heating equipment	31	7	17	7	62	41
3586	Measuring and dispensing pumps	1	1	0	0	2	1
3589	Service industry machinery, nec	61	15	8	5	89	67
3592	Carburetors, pistons, piston rings and valves	4	0	0	2	7	5
3593	Fluid power cylinders and actuators	6	2	1	4	13	11
3594	Fluid power pumps and motors	1	0	0	0	1	0
3596	Scales and balances, except laboratory	8	2	2	0	12	8
3599	Industrial machinery, nec	105	36	42	12	195	116
3612	Transformers, except electric	15	4	4	11	34	21
3613	Switchgear and switchboard apparatus	12	4	3	5	24	14
3621	Motors and generators	30	6	5	11	52	32
3624	Carbon and graphite products	1	0	1	0	2	1
3625	Relays and industrial controls	69	26	17	18	130	113
3629	Electrical industrial apparatus, nec	4	1	0	0	5	3
3631	Household cooking equipment	3	1	1	1	6	5
3632	Household refrigerators and freezers	3	0	0	1	4	2
3633	Household laundry equipment	1	0	0	1	2	2
3634	Electric housewares and fans	17	3	1	3	24	20
3635	Household vacuum cleaners	0	1	0	0	1	0
3639	Household appliances, nec	8	0	0	1	9	8
3641	Electric lamps	4	0	0	3	7	6
3643	Current-carrying wiring devices	10	2	5	4	21	13
3644	Noncurrent-carrying wiring devices	10	8	1	2	21	19
3645	Residential lighting fixtures	8	2	1	5	16	8
3646	Commercial lighting fixtures	9	3	0	7	19	9
3647	Vehicular lighting equipment	1	0	3	2	6	4
3648	Lighting equipment, nec	14	8	1	1	24	15
3651	Household audio and video equipment	18	5	3	3	29	16
3652	Prerecorded records and tapes	4	1	1	1	7	5
3661	Telephone and telegraph apparatus	17	0	1	3	21	16
3663	Radio and t.v. communications equipment	33	7	3	11	54	45
3669	Communications equipment, nec	46	14	8	9	77	56
3671	Electron tubes	1	2	1	2	6	3
3672	Printed circuit boards	8	2	2	2	14	12
3674	Semiconductors and related devices	25	4	0	8	37	25
3675	Electronic capacitors	2	0	0	0	2	1
3677	Electronic coils and transformers	6	1	1	1	9	8
3678	Electronic connectors	5	0	1	2	8	5
3679	Electronic components, nec	33	11	9	22	75	48

SIC	DESCRIPTION	0-19	20-49	50-99	100-OVER	TOTAL	PRIMARY SIC ONLY
3691	Storage batteries	3	1	3	0	7	7
3692	Primary batteries, dry and wet	4	2	0	0	6	5
3694	Engine electrical equipment	8	5	3	1	17	12
3695	Magnetic and optical recording media	1	0	2	0	3	1
3699	Electrical equipment and supplies, nec	72	13	13	12	110	78
3711	Motor vehicles and car bodies	19	9	6	23	57	44
3713	Truck and bus bodies	24	10	7	0	41	32
3714	Motor vehicle parts and accessories	76	33	25	83	217	174
3715	Truck trailers	7	4	3	5	19	14
3716	Motor homes	2	0	3	1	6	6
3721	Aircraft	16	3	0	5	24	21
3724	Aircraft engines and engine parts	2	0	0	4	6	2
3728	Aircraft parts and equipment, nec	28	2	9	14	53	41
3731	Shipbuilding and repairing	12	7	9	4	32	23
3732	Boatbuilding and repairing	3	5	7	6	21	17
3743	Railroad equipment	16	1	1	5	23	16
3751	Motorcycles, bicycles and parts	2	0	1	2	5	2
3769	Space vehicle equipment, nec	1	0	0	1	2	2
3792	Travel trailers and campers	1	0	1	1	3	1
3795	Tanks and tank components	1	0	1	3	5	4
3799	Transportation equipment, nec	5	1	1	3	10	6
3812	Search and navigation equipment	21	11	4	7	43	27
3821	Laboratory apparatus and furniture	10	3	3	1	17	8
3822	Environmental controls	38	16	9	3	66	57
3823	Process control instruments	37	7	4	14	62	35
3824	Fluid meters and counting devices	12	1	1	1	15	10
3825	Instruments to measure electricity	27	7	4	3	41	24
3826	Analytical instruments	7	1	0	0	8	6
3827	Optical instruments and lenses	22	7	3	9	41	25
3829	Measuring and controlling devices, nec	21	8	4	3	36	20
3841	Surgical and medical instruments	31	6	5	5	47	32
3842	Surgical appliances and supplies	51	15	11	7	84	66
3843	Dental equipment and supplies	6	2	0	0	8	8
3844	X-ray apparatus and tubes	2	1	0	0	3	1
3845	Electromedical equipment	7	1	2	1	11	6
3851	Ophthalmic goods	37	1	0	5	43	34
3861	Photographic equipment and supplies	4	3	4	1	12	8
3873	Watches, clocks, watchcases, and parts	2	1	1	1	5	2
3911	Jewelry, precious Metal	11	0	5	1	17	14
3914	Silverware and plated ware	1	1	0	0	2	2
3915	Jewelers' materials and lapidary work	2	2	0	0	4	4
3931	Musical instruments	5	2	3	2	12	7
3942	Dolls and stuffed toys	0	1	0	1	2	1
3944	Games, toys, and children's vehicles	13	0	3	1	17	9
3949	Sporting and athletic goods, nec	25	2	12	7	46	38
3951	Pens and mechanical pencils	2	0	0	0	2	2
3952	Lead pencils and art goods	5	1	1	1	8	4
3953	Marking devices	4	3	1	1	9	7
3955	Carbon paper and inked ribbons	9	0	2	0	11	8
3961	Costume jewelry	5	2	1	0	8	6
3965	Fasteners, buttons, needles, and pins	9	0	3	0	12	10
3991	Brooms and brushes	9	0	2	0	11	11
3993	Signs and advertising specialties	45	12	28	4	89	65
3995	Burial caskets	1	0	1	2	4	4
3996	Hard surface floor coverings, nec	3	0	0	3	6	2
3999	Manufacturing industries, nec	76	10	13	5	104	78
4011	Railroads, line-haul operating	104	54	19	36	213	209
4013	Switching and terminal services	11	0	1	1	13	12
4111	Local and suburban transit	168	38	39	57	302	259
4119	Local passenger transportation, nec	183	40	12	16	251	220
4121	Taxicabs	16	5	25	6	52	44
4131	Intercity and rural bus transportation	126	12	13	11	162	143
4141	Local bus charter service	6	3	8	3	20	9
4142	Bus charter service, except local	71	18	33	26	148	90
4151	School buses	119	44	65	58	286	267
4173	Bus terminal and service facilities	43	5	5	1	54	46
4212	Local trucking, without storage	570	192	171	91	1,024	612
4213	Trucking, except local	944	266	170	115	1,495	1,167
4214	Local trucking with storage	108	35	32	12	187	132
4215	Courier services, except by air	20	4	2	3	29	18
4221	Farm product warehousing and storage	216	16	8	2	242	226
4222	Refrigerated warehousing and storage	36	12	11	4	63	51
4225	General warehousing and storage	680	105	70	56	911	620
4226	Special warehousing and storage, nec	86	36	11	7	140	93
4231	Trucking terminal facilities	29	4	1	7	41	34
4311	U.s. postal service	4,052	181	64	47	4,344	4,311
4412	Deep sea foreign transportation of freight	14	2	2	1	19	15
4424	Deep sea domestic transportation of freight	22	3	2	7	34	28
4432	Freight transportation on the great lakes	5	1	0	4	10	7

SIC	DESCRIPTION	0-19	20-49	50-99	100-OVER	TOTAL	PRIMARY SIC ONLY
4449	Water transportation of freight	15	1	1	3	20	15
4482	Ferries	64	6	4	4	78	76
4489	Water passenger transportation	3	0	4	0	7	4
4491	Marine cargo handling	46	16	6	5	73	62
4492	Towing and tugboat service	9	3	0	0	12	11
4493	Marinas	20	4	9	2	35	25
4499	Water transportation services,	10	7	3	2	22	14
4512	Air transportation, scheduled	198	27	14	30	269	243
4513	Air courier services	4	1	1	2	8	3
4522	Air transportation, nonscheduled	79	30	10	12	131	101
4581	Airports, flying fields, and services	159	32	19	34	244	209
4612	Crude petroleum pipelines	77	13	7	8	105	91
4613	Refined petroleum pipelines	12	2	0	1	15	15
4619	Pipelines, nec	42	8	5	1	56	49
4724	Travel agencies	681	50	21	8	760	710
4725	Tour operators	86	24	15	11	136	102
4729	Passenger transportation arrangement	49	5	3	1	58	39
4731	Freight transportation arrangement	770	175	70	76	1,091	952
4741	Rental of railroad cars	15	1	2	1	19	14
4783	Packing and crating	24	12	2	2	40	21
4785	Inspection and fixed facilities	35	4	1	2	42	37
4789	Transportation services, nec	42	13	8	9	72	51
4812	Radiotelephone communication	314	15	1	0	330	272
4813	Telephone communication, except radio	320	42	30	32	424	253
4822	Telegraph and other communications	6	0	0	0	6	2
4832	Radio broadcasting stations	165	85	51	26	327	285
4833	Television broadcasting stations	95	31	32	37	195	161
4841	Cable and other pay television services	124	16	11	12	163	131
4899	Communication services, nec	891	120	59	104	1,174	1,041
4911	Electric services	483	111	44	62	700	671
4922	Natural gas transmission	68	9	9	9	95	79
4923	Gas transmission and distribution	83	12	5	10	110	103
4924	Natural gas distribution	73	18	9	9	109	94
4925	Gas production and/or distribution	31	4	3	2	40	29
4931	Electric and other services combined	11	6	1	1	19	14
4932	Gas and other services combined	9	3	0	0	12	8
4941	Water supply	87	13	5	3	108	99
4952	Sewerage systems	5	1	0	0	6	5
4953	Refuse systems	510	114	52	39	715	630
4959	Sanitary services, nec	34	9	13	8	64	33
4961	Steam and air-conditioning supply	11	5	0	0	16	10
4971	Irrigation systems	19	4	2	2	27	25
5012	Automobiles and other motor vehicles	111	37	17	26	191	147
5013	Motor vehicle supplies and new parts	740	137	44	40	961	678
5014	Tires and tubes	110	26	2	4	142	98
5015	Motor vehicle parts, used	24	4	3	2	33	22
5021	Furniture	74	20	19	3	116	69
5023	Homefurnishings	145	37	10	12	204	130
5031	Lumber, plywood, and millwork	232	63	18	28	341	257
5032	Brick, stone, and related material	299	61	30	12	402	311
5033	Roofing, siding, and insulation	68	16	6	1	91	73
5039	Construction materials, nec	285	71	29	27	412	298
5043	Photographic equipment and supplies	19	3	2	3	27	19
5044	Office equipment	151	39	23	25	238	202
5045	Computers, peripherals, and software	210	39	28	27	304	218
5046	Commercial equipment, nec	85	21	13	5	124	77
5047	Medical and hospital equipment	191	53	30	19	293	219
5048	Ophthalmic goods	21	2	0	2	25	24
5049	Professional equipment, nec	111	31	11	8	161	113
5051	Metals service centers and offices	337	76	37	28	478	417
5052	Coal and other minerals and ores	7	0	0	0	7	3
5063	Electrical apparatus and equipment	498	91	32	38	659	491
5064	Electrical appliances, television and radio	113	13	5	8	139	109
5065	Electronic parts and equipment, nec	315	60	39	28	442	287
5072	Hardware	169	31	24	10	234	148
5074	Plumbing and heating equipment and supplies (hydronics)	483	71	26	20	600	490
5075	Warm air heating and air conditioning	328	57	14	6	405	241
5078	Refrigeration equipment and supplies	102	12	10	1	125	68
5082	Construction and mining machinery	307	70	31	23	431	347
5083	Farm and garden machinery	208	66	13	10	297	200
5084	Industrial machinery and equipment	1,143	279	92	62	1,576	1,146
5085	Industrial supplies	1,224	134	46	32	1,436	1,225
5087	Service establishment equipment	279	34	12	11	336	260
5088	Transportation equipment and supplies	61	17	1	4	83	54
5091	Sporting and recreation goods	115	26	10	11	162	125
5092	Toys and hobby goods and supplies	98	7	7	4	116	40
5093	Scrap and waste materials	71	17	8	2	98	74
5094	Jewelry and precious stones	23	8	1	2	34	23
5099	Durable goods, nec	233	53	31	76	393	241

SIC	DESCRIPTION	0-19	20-49	50-99	100-OVER	TOTAL	PRIMARY SIC ONLY
5111	Printing and writing paper	36	6	3	4	49	45
5112	Stationery and office supplies	87	27	15	7	136	109
5113	Industrial and personal service paper	55	16	10	6	87	56
5122	Drugs, proprietaries, and sundries	265	46	20	40	371	289
5131	Piece goods and notions	69	9	6	1	85	60
5136	Men's and boy's clothing	126	35	18	13	192	134
5137	Women's and children's clothing	234	47	23	22	326	162
5139	Footwear	76	7	3	4	90	59
5141	Groceries, general line	373	76	81	122	652	535
5142	Packaged frozen goods	61	13	17	22	113	58
5143	Dairy products, except dried or canned	85	19	13	18	135	82
5144	Poultry and poultry products	15	7	3	12	37	24
5145	Confectionery	107	17	13	18	155	78
5146	Fish and seafoods	58	17	10	9	94	72
5147	Meats and meat products	43	18	14	20	95	55
5148	Fresh fruits and vegetables	47	20	14	25	106	70
5149	Groceries and related products, nec	308	63	43	45	459	284
5153	Grain and field beans	249	35	11	6	301	269
5154	Livestock	18	14	1	0	33	30
5159	Farm-product raw materials, nec	7	6	4	1	18	16
5162	Plastics materials and basic shapes	50	10	4	4	68	49
5169	Chemicals and allied products, nec	497	71	36	25	629	512
5171	Petroleum bulk stations and terminals	87	15	7	3	112	80
5172	Petroleum products, nec	389	57	18	18	482	387
5181	Beer and ale	233	11	5	9	258	33
5182	Wine and distilled beverages	211	24	8	5	248	42
5191	Farm supplies	353	67	25	13	458	284
5192	Books, periodicals, and newspapers	63	9	6	6	84	69
5193	Flowers and florists supplies	20	6	5	0	31	27
5194	Tobacco and tobacco products	59	10	4	4	77	43
5198	Paints, varnishes, and supplies	279	11	3	4	297	207
5199	Nondurable goods, nec	224	25	19	44	312	150
5211	Lumber and other building materials	546	143	80	192	961	619
5231	Paint, glass, and wallpaper stores	283	8	6	13	310	213
5251	Hardware stores	346	117	72	165	700	472
5261	Retail nurseries and garden stores	197	42	20	105	364	162
5271	Mobile home dealers	8	0	0	0	8	4
5311	Department stores	601	94	82	418	1,195	1,151
5331	Variety stores	544	47	5	2	598	547
5399	Miscellaneous general merchandise	534	136	69	61	800	575
5411	Grocery stores	3,802	431	509	732	5,474	4,424
5421	Meat and fish markets	110	14	9	15	148	105
5431	Fruit and vegetable markets	30	21	20	23	94	57
5441	Candy, nut, and confectionery stores	184	7	2	5	198	153
5451	Dairy products stores	43	7	5	2	57	26
5461	Retail bakeries	177	45	79	35	336	231
5499	Miscellaneous food stores	497	27	7	10	541	481
5511	New and used car dealers	365	256	98	23	742	660
5521	Used car dealers	35	17	6	2	60	40
5531	Auto and home supply stores	1,249	226	77	27	1,579	1,048
5541	Gasoline service stations	1,898	86	39	15	2,038	1,614
5551	Boat dealers	20	13	3	1	37	17
5561	Recreational vehicle dealers	28	16	3	0	47	17
5571	Motorcycle dealers	24	19	3	1	47	30
5599	Automotive dealers, nec	18	16	1	1	36	15
5611	Men's and boys' clothing stores	796	59	12	10	877	629
5621	Women's clothing stores	2,490	125	28	19	2,662	2,465
5632	Women's accessory and specialty stores	899	45	12	14	970	483
5641	Children's and infants' wear stores	280	41	7	2	330	185
5651	Family clothing stores	1,300	366	98	33	1,797	1,460
5661	Shoe stores	1,527	78	12	2	1,619	1,442
5699	Miscellaneous apparel and accessory stores	670	61	18	8	757	461
5712	Furniture stores	849	243	100	26	1,218	988
5713	Floor covering stores	70	16	4	2	92	71
5714	Drapery and upholstery stores	21	5	2	0	28	12
5719	Miscellaneous homefurnishings	522	113	35	12	682	484
5722	Household appliance stores	179	41	34	10	264	147
5731	Radio, television, and electronic stores	222	36	92	30	380	283
5734	Computer and software stores	426	131	43	18	618	389
5735	Record and prerecorded tape stores	48	2	4	2	56	35
5736	Musical instrument stores	104	29	26	8	167	121
5812	Eating places	3,249	1,331	1,559	398	6,537	5,876
5813	Drinking places	62	36	182	51	331	83
5912	Drug stores and proprietary stores	1,012	234	89	127	1,462	1,285
5921	Liquor stores	1,968	118	47	34	2,167	1,923
5932	Used merchandise stores	271	20	6	5	302	238
5941	Sporting goods and bicycle shops	427	205	80	22	734	591
5942	Book stores	310	46	31	14	401	371
5943	Stationery stores	166	225	51	10	452	394

SIC	DESCRIPTION	0-19	20-49	50-99	100-OVER	TOTAL	PRIMARY SIC ONLY
5944	Jewelry stores	438	10	6	1	455	438
5945	Hobby, toy, and game shops	227	53	19	5	304	212
5946	Camera and photographic supply stores	65	5	2	4	76	62
5947	Gift, novelty, and souvenir shop	497	39	35	14	585	432
5948	Luggage and leather goods stores	35	3	2	2	42	29
5949	Sewing, needlework, and piece goods	124	20	1	3	148	145
5961	Catalog and mail-order houses	144	18	16	12	190	87
5962	Merchandising machine operators	27	9	8	1	45	22
5963	Direct selling establishments	98	19	10	7	134	82
5983	Fuel oil dealers	113	8	7	4	132	96
5984	Liquefied petroleum gas dealers	177	25	2	2	206	153
5989	Fuel dealers, nec	2	0	0	0	2	0
5992	Florists	30	5	10	8	53	37
5993	Tobacco stores and stands	61	4	14	13	92	12
5994	News dealers and newsstands	16	2	1	1	20	7
5995	Optical goods stores	434	9	3	5	451	424
5999	Miscellaneous retail stores, nec	2,459	358	139	169	3,125	2,280
6011	Federal reserve banks	12	4	1	0	17	17
6019	Central reserve depository, nec	1	0	0	0	1	1
6021	National commercial banks	5,218	1,262	71	51	6,602	6,570
6035	Federal savings institutions	5	0	0	0	5	4
6036	Savings institutions, except federal	131	44	1	3	179	176
6062	State credit unions	1,233	196	45	21	1,495	1,487
6081	Foreign bank and branches and agencies	10	1	0	1	12	12
6082	Foreign trade and international banks	1	1	0	0	2	2
6091	Nondeposit trust facilities	10	1	1	0	12	11
6099	Functions related to deposit banking	927	20	8	8	963	867
6111	Federal and federally sponsored credit agencies	46	4	2	3	55	49
6141	Personal credit institutions	643	37	6	7	693	640
6153	Short-term business credit institutions, except agricultural	52	12	3	10	77	64
6159	Miscellaneous business credit institutions	286	34	7	12	339	289
6162	Mortgage bankers and loan correspondents	193	19	5	11	228	162
6163	Loan brokers	162	5	2	1	170	125
6211	Security brokers and dealers	1,669	211	73	51	2,004	1,854
6221	Commodity contracts brokers, dealers	12	5	0	1	18	13
6231	Security and commodity exchanges	15	5	0	1	21	19
6282	Investment advice	513	67	35	19	634	500
6289	Security and commodity service	15	4	1	3	23	18
6311	Life insurance	728	131	45	44	948	728
6321	Accident and health insurance	190	43	12	18	263	122
6324	Hospital and medical service plans	21	6	4	8	39	28
6331	Fire, marine, and casualty insurance	496	76	32	84	688	594
6351	Surety insurance	81	20	7	12	120	59
6361	Title insurance	11	0	1	3	15	10
6371	Pension, health, and welfare funds	27	16	2	5	50	19
6399	Insurance carriers, nec	14	1	0	2	17	13
6411	Insurance agents, brokers, and service	2,075	225	96	94	2,490	2,183
6512	Nonresidential building operators	389	89	40	27	545	403
6513	Apartment building operators	857	58	52	24	991	858
6514	Dwelling operators, except apartments	31	2	4	2	39	24
6515	Mobile home site operators	10	0	0	0	10	3
6517	Railroad property lessors	2	0	0	0	2	2
6519	Real property lessors, nec	79	9	11	9	108	68
6531	Real estate agents and managers	1,209	174	114	69	1,566	1,418
6541	Title abstract offices	13	3	0	0	16	12
6552	Subdividers and developers, nec	41	17	4	3	65	46
6553	Cemetery subdividers and developers	175	41	13	9	238	171
6712	Bank holding companies	1,817	111	129	174	2,231	1,207
6719	Holding companies, nec	294	25	20	24	363	250
6722	Management investment, open-end	281	40	12	20	353	318
6726	Investment offices, nec	67	3	1	3	74	61
6732	Trusts: educational, religious, etc	23	1	1	1	26	24
6733	Trusts, nec	36	9	2	4	51	36
6792	Oil royalty traders	6	2	0	0	8	6
6794	Patent owners and lessors	260	32	37	24	353	112
6798	Real estate investment trusts	27	1	2	2	32	27
6799	Investors, nec	89	7	7	1	104	89
7011	Hotels and motels	374	199	413	222	1,208	1,113
7021	Rooming and boarding houses	14	2	4	2	22	10
7032	Sporting and recreational camps	66	22	21	6	115	81
7033	Trailer parks and campsites	61	8	5	0	74	54
7041	Membership-basis organization hotels	21	4	3	5	33	27
7211	Power laundries, family and commercial	21	2	5	1	29	26
7212	Garment pressing and cleaners' agents	14	0	0	1	15	12
7213	Linen supply	40	13	18	16	87	74
7215	Coin-operated laundries and cleaning	22	4	2	3	31	22
7216	Drycleaning plants, except rugs	47	4	6	1	58	47
7217	Carpet and upholstery cleaning	15	2	8	2	27	15
7218	Industrial launderers	31	14	12	17	74	55

SIC	DESCRIPTION	0-19	20-49	50-99	100-OVER	TOTAL	PRIMARY SIC ONLY
7219	Laundry and garment services, nec	108	5	6	5	124	95
7221	Photographic studios, portrait	63	2	1	2	68	61
7231	Beauty shops	532	19	12	7	570	542
7241	Barber shops	5	0	0	0	5	2
7251	Shoe repair and shoeshine parlors	1	1	0	0	2	0
7261	Funeral service and crematories	315	42	4	2	363	347
7291	Tax return preparation services	551	27	18	6	602	506
7299	Miscellaneous personal service	251	51	73	40	415	188
7311	Advertising agencies	111	37	25	23	196	158
7312	Outdoor advertising services	30	3	2	1	36	35
7313	Radio, television, publisher representatives	23	2	3	0	28	21
7319	Advertising, nec	47	17	7	12	83	63
7322	Adjustment and collection services	48	14	7	12	81	60
7323	Credit reporting services	28	4	4	3	39	34
7331	Direct mail advertising services	24	3	10	3	40	31
7334	Photocopying and duplicating services	76	19	7	2	104	53
7335	Commercial photography	17	2	3	2	24	17
7336	Commercial art and graphic design	34	14	12	8	68	43
7338	Secretarial and court reporting	13	2	2	1	18	15
7342	Disinfecting and pest control services	68	18	6	2	94	89
7349	Building maintenance services, nec	200	48	107	78	433	370
7352	Medical equipment rental	7	0	2	1	10	7
7353	Heavy construction equipment rental	291	77	30	10	408	317
7359	Equipment rental and leasing, nec	568	69	38	35	710	485
7361	Employment agencies	525	64	54	32	675	610
7363	Help supply services	153	21	23	11	208	163
7371	Custom computer programming services	337	97	82	82	598	487
7372	Prepackaged software	170	52	37	35	294	196
7373	Computer integrated systems design	53	13	6	12	84	45
7374	Data processing and preparation	85	21	24	34	164	111
7375	Information retrieval services	9	1	2	1	13	9
7376	Computer facilities management	11	6	5	5	27	23
7377	Computer rental and leasing	7	2	1	1	11	4
7378	Computer maintenance and repair	64	19	13	6	102	41
7379	Computer related services, nec	187	53	45	58	343	238
7381	Detective and armored car services	163	27	59	88	337	319
7382	Security systems services	50	6	15	9	80	39
7383	News syndicates	48	3	1	1	53	48
7384	Photofinish laboratories	42	18	11	10	81	23
7389	Business services, nec	1,466	328	285	212	2,291	1,786
7513	Truck rental and leasing, no drivers	612	61	16	8	697	452
7514	Passenger car rental	692	40	8	8	748	710
7515	Passenger car leasing	98	24	19	8	149	68
7519	Utility trailer rental	313	21	8	3	345	271
7521	Automobile parking	95	12	5	5	117	107
7532	Top and body repair and paint shops	139	34	38	8	219	115
7533	Auto exhaust system repair shops	27	0	1	1	29	20
7534	Tire retreading and repair shops	110	14	2	2	128	15
7536	Automotive glass replacement shops	201	5	2	1	209	192
7537	Automotive transmission repair shops	8	4	2	1	15	6
7538	General automotive repair shops	440	208	107	28	783	215
7539	Automotive repair shops, nec	101	25	8	8	142	43
7542	Carwashes	114	8	5	2	129	43
7549	Automotive services, nec	76	12	16	5	109	65
7622	Radio and television repair	9	3	3	2	17	4
7623	Refrigeration service and repair	36	10	6	0	52	35
7629	Electrical repair shops	137	39	21	11	208	93
7631	Watch, clock, and jewelry repair	27	0	1	0	28	6
7641	Reupholstery and furniture repair	3	2	4	0	9	3
7692	Welding repair	23	9	16	4	52	20
7694	Armature rewinding shops	8	5	4	1	18	14
7699	Repair services, nec	603	219	105	50	977	397
7812	Motion picture and video production	71	12	13	11	107	89
7819	Services allied to motion pictures	11	8	6	2	27	17
7822	Motion picture and tape distribution	20	7	4	1	32	25
7829	Motion picture distribution services	2	0	2	1	5	2
7832	Motion picture theaters, except drive-in	136	90	18	13	257	250
7833	Drive-in motion picture theaters	0	0	1	0	1	0
7841	Video tape rental	133	7	6	2	148	99
7911	Dance studios, schools, and halls	2	2	5	1	10	8
7922	Theatrical producers and services	62	26	15	14	117	87
7929	Entertainers and entertainment groups	21	5	8	2	36	28
7933	Bowling centers	12	6	3	0	21	16
7941	Sports clubs, managers, and promoters	55	16	3	5	79	64
7948	Racing, including track operation	4	1	6	13	24	19
7991	Physical fitness facilities	237	73	54	32	396	330
7992	Public golf courses	45	21	67	18	151	116
7993	Coin-operated amusement devices	20	0	7	8	35	13
7996	Amusement parks	27	3	7	6	43	40

SIC	DESCRIPTION	0-19	20-49	50-99	100-OVER	TOTAL	PRIMARY SIC ONLY
7997	Membership sports and recreation clubs	67	29	113	31	240	204
7999	Amusement and recreation, nec	993	211	157	89	1,450	862
8011	Offices and clinics of medical doctors	478	82	62	53	675	577
8021	Offices and clinics of dentists	52	8	13	0	73	66
8041	Offices and clinics of chiropractors	5	0	0	0	5	0
8042	Offices and clinics of optometrists	72	4	2	2	80	55
8043	Offices and clinics of podiatrists	5	0	0	0	5	4
8049	Offices of health practitioner	263	25	24	16	328	235
8051	Skilled nursing care facilities	148	71	260	266	745	677
8052	Intermediate care facilities	16	2	8	6	32	32
8059	Nursing and personal care, nec	144	42	67	66	319	245
8062	General medical and surgical hospitals	320	88	98	244	750	710
8063	Psychiatric hospitals	12	3	0	12	27	23
8069	Specialty hospitals, except psychiatric	99	20	20	37	176	146
8071	Medical laboratories	609	25	10	15	659	632
8072	Dental laboratories	13	5	7	0	25	22
8082	Home health care services	121	18	29	28	196	178
8092	Kidney dialysis centers	3	1	0	2	6	4
8093	Specialty outpatient clinics, nec	410	73	62	44	589	462
8099	Health and allied services, nec	149	22	14	13	198	162
8111	Legal services	598	83	94	76	851	804
8211	Elementary and secondary schools	3,920	6,178	2,768	543	13,409	13,296
8221	Colleges and universities	746	185	96	143	1,170	1,126
8222	Junior colleges	116	20	16	21	173	162
8231	Libraries	895	89	23	12	1,019	993
8243	Data processing schools	33	12	2	4	51	26
8244	Business and secretarial schools	17	2	6	3	28	21
8249	Vocational schools, nec	50	21	14	8	93	82
8299	Schools and educational services, nec	342	82	47	21	492	389
8322	Individual and family services	1,666	295	197	138	2,296	1,981
8331	Job training and related services	304	47	44	17	412	318
8351	Child day care services	764	231	89	18	1,102	771
8361	Residential care	693	191	208	189	1,281	1,182
8399	Social services, nec	1,286	160	61	65	1,572	1,317
8412	Museums and art galleries	107	19	7	9	142	133
8422	Botanical and zoological gardens	7	1	1	1	10	8
8611	Business associations	187	15	6	7	215	189
8621	Professional organizations	324	55	10	21	410	368
8631	Labor organizations	785	27	12	29	853	846
8641	Civic and social associations	1,125	31	42	19	1,217	1,176
8651	Political organizations	11	0	2	1	14	13
8661	Religious organizations	2,295	47	64	13	2,419	2,356
8699	Membership organizations, nec	601	82	18	23	724	621
8711	Engineering services	905	235	157	166	1,463	1,281
8712	Architectural services	108	16	19	15	158	122
8713	Surveying services	118	26	12	12	168	149
8721	Accounting, auditing, and bookkeeping	596	137	103	94	930	856
8731	Commercial physical research	283	68	54	62	467	363
8732	Commercial nonphysical research	132	33	20	41	226	168
8733	Noncommercial research organizations	82	16	13	26	137	105
8734	Testing laboratories	184	35	17	24	260	183
8741	Management services	1,271	205	130	137	1,743	1,306
8742	Management consulting services	1,295	170	98	110	1,673	1,148
8743	Public relations services	116	26	14	14	170	123
8744	Facilities support services	5	1	0	0	6	4
8748	Business consulting, nec	868	141	65	76	1,150	851
8811	Private households	3	0	0	0	3	2
8999	Services, nec	171	37	20	17	245	200
9111	Executive offices	1	0	0	0	1	0
9121	Legislative bodies	75	7	3	5	90	0
9199	General government, nec	2	0	1	0	3	0
9211	Courts	1	0	0	0	1	0
9221	Police protection	1	0	1	0	2	0
9223	Correctional institutions	4	1	0	1	6	0
9224	Fire protection	2	3	1	1	7	0
9229	Public order and safety, nec	2	2	0	1	5	0
9311	Finance, taxation, and monetary policy	7	4	2	0	13	0
9411	Administration of educational programs	16	4	2	2	24	0
9431	Administration of public health programs	25	3	3	5	36	0
9441	Administration of social and manpower programs	35	5	0	3	43	0
9511	Air, water, and solid waste management	3	0	0	0	3	0
9512	Land, mineral, and wildlife conservation	6	5	1	1	13	0
9531	Housing programs	3	0	2	0	5	0
9611	Administration of general economic programs	10	2	1	1	14	0
9621	Regulation, administration of transportation	5	1	0	0	6	0
9641	Regulation of agricultural marketing	11	2	0	1	14	0
9651	Regulation, miscellaneous commercial sectors	5	1	0	0	6	0
9721	International affairs	3	0	1	0	4	0
	TOTALS	134,891	29,579	18,043	13,767	196,280	158,639

NUMBER OF BUSINESSES BY COUNTY

BRITISH COLUMBIA

Alberni - Clayoquot 157

Bulkley - Nechako 254

Capital 1,769

Cariboo 335

Central Coast 22

Central Fraser-Val 551

Central Kootenay 326

Central Okanagan 943

Columbia - Shuswap 256

Comox - Strathcona 509

Cowichan Valley 334

East Kootenay 415

Fraser-Fort George 656

Greater Vancouver 10,698

Kitimat - Stikine 293

Kootenay Boundary 156

Mount Waddington 104

Nanaimo 756

North Okanagan 89

Okanagn-Similkameen 382

Peace River - Laird 571

Powell River 86

Skeena-Qn-Charlotte 140

Squamish - Lillooet 242

Stikine Region 13

Sunshine Coast 127

Thompson - Nicola 758

NEW BRUNSWICK

Albert 18

Charlotte 112

Gloucester 289

NOVA SCOTIA

ONTARIO

PRINCE EDWARD ISLAND

QUEBEC

2017 Canadian Key Business Directory

Répertoire des principales entreprises Canadiennes 2017

Section I

Geographic Index

Inscriptions par
région géographique

Acheson, AB T7X

D-U-N-S 24-802-3769   (SL)
ADLER FIRESTOPPING LTD
53016 Hwy 60 Unit 23, Acheson, AB, T7X 5A7
(780) 962-9495
Emp Here 55   *Sales* 2,845,467
SIC 7389 Business services, nec

D-U-N-S 24-396-7296   (HQ)
ADLER INSULATION 2005 LTD
(*Suby of* Adler Insulation 2005 Ltd)
53016 Hwy 60 Unit 23, Acheson, AB, T7X 5A7
(780) 962-9495
Emp Here 25   *Emp Total* 50
Sales 4,231,721
SIC 1742 Plastering, drywall, and insulation

D-U-N-S 25-268-4774   (BR)
ALLIED BLOWER & SHEET METAL LTD
53016 Hwy 60 Unit 36, Acheson, AB, T7X 5A7
(780) 962-6464
Emp Here 35
SIC 1796 Installing building equipment

D-U-N-S 20-212-7622   (BR)
ARMTEC LP
ARMTEC
26229 Township Road 531a Suite 205, Acheson, AB, T7X 5A4
(780) 444-1560
Emp Here 76
SIC 3272 Concrete products, nec

D-U-N-S 24-346-8225   (BR)
BMG HOLDINGS LTD
BARRETT EXPLORER
26229 Township Road 531a Suite 201, Acheson, AB, T7X 5A4
(780) 962-8200
Emp Here 30
SIC 5012 Automobiles and other motor vehicles

D-U-N-S 24-947-5984   (SL)
BEARCOM MANAGEMENT GROUP
BUS CENTRE
26230 Twp Rd 531a Suite 103, Acheson, AB, T7X 5A4
(780) 962-4645
Emp Here 20   *Sales* 9,338,970
SIC 5012 Automobiles and other motor vehicles
Owner Paul Gabbey

D-U-N-S 24-004-2622   (HQ)
CANADIAN LYNDEN TRANSPORT LTD
LYNDEN TRANSPORT
(*Suby of* Lynden Incorporated)
53016 Hwy 60 Suite 20, Acheson, AB, T7X 5A7
(780) 960-9444
Emp Here 57   *Emp Total* 2,500
Sales 7,369,031
SIC 4213 Trucking, except local
Pr Pr Walter Rakiewich
Treas Ken Loving
Ex Dir Jim Jansen

D-U-N-S 24-395-3200   (BR)
CLEAN HARBORS INDUSTRIAL SERVICES CANADA, INC
26220 Township Rd 531a, Acheson, AB, T7X 5A4
(780) 962-3442
Emp Here 60
SIC 1389 Oil and gas field services, nec

D-U-N-S 25-976-9503   (HQ)
CONTINENTAL CARTAGE INC
(*Suby of* Kluskus Holdings Ltd)
26215 Township Road 531a Uni 412, Acheson, AB, T7X 5A4
(780) 452-9414
Emp Here 58   *Emp Total* 603
Sales 9,988,687

SIC 4213 Trucking, except local
Pr Pr John Assman
VP VP Lawrence Cantera

D-U-N-S 24-784-3969   (SL)
DIAMONDGEAR INDUSTRIAL MANUFAC-TURING LTD
DIAMONDGEAR
26229 Twp Rd 531a Suite 206, Acheson, AB, T7X 5A4
(780) 451-3912
Emp Here 36   *Sales* 7,223,109
SIC 5063 Electrical apparatus and equipment
Pr Pr Jeffrey Sheckger

D-U-N-S 25-099-8978   (BR)
DRIVE PRODUCTS INC
26230 Township Road 531a Unit 111, Acheson, AB, T7X 5A4
(780) 960-6826
Emp Here 100
SIC 5084 Industrial machinery and equipment

D-U-N-S 24-786-1552   (BR)
DRIVE PRODUCTS INC
Bldg 531a, Acheson, AB, T7X 5A4

Emp Here 30
SIC 5013 Motor vehicle supplies and new parts

D-U-N-S 24-702-2494   (BR)
FLYNN CANADA LTD
26229 Township Rd 531a Suite 213, Acheson, AB, T7X 5A4
(780) 948-4200
Emp Here 60
SIC 1761 Roofing, siding, and sheetMetal work

D-U-N-S 25-128-1023   (BR)
FLYNN CANADA LTD
26229 Township Road 531a Suite 213, Acheson, AB, T7X 5A4
(780) 948-4200
Emp Here 20
SIC 7389 Business services, nec

D-U-N-S 24-583-5694   (BR)
FORBES BROS. LTD
53016 Hwy 60 Suite 605, Acheson, AB, T7X 5A7
(780) 960-1950
Emp Here 20
SIC 1623 Water, sewer, and utility lines

D-U-N-S 20-174-5515   (BR)
FORTISALBERTA INC
53030 Hwy 60 Suite 1, Acheson, AB, T7X 5A4
(780) 960-7200
Emp Here 38
SIC 4911 Electric services

D-U-N-S 20-182-1068   (SL)
GANOTEC WEST ULC
(*Suby of* Peter Kiewit Sons', Inc.)
26230 Township Road 531a Unit 131, Acheson, AB, T7X 5A4
(780) 960-7450
Emp Here 200   *Sales* 39,617,660
SIC 1541 Industrial buildings and warehouses
Pr Pr Creg Ratcliffe

D-U-N-S 25-386-7162   (SL)
GENICS INC
53016 Hwy 60 (561 Acheson Rd), Acheson, AB, T7X 5A7
(780) 962-1000
Emp Here 75   *Sales* 8,536,396
SIC 2491 Wood preserving
Pr Pr Calvin Wall
Wesley Wall

D-U-N-S 20-327-8551   (BR)
GREAT PACIFIC INDUSTRIES INC
OVERWAITEA FOOD GROUP
26308 Township Road 525a Unit 24, Acheson, AB, T7X 5A6

(780) 948-7400
Emp Here 20
SIC 4225 General warehousing and storage

D-U-N-S 24-397-1207   (SL)
HAYWORTH EQUIPMENT SALES INC
26229 Twp Rd 531a, Acheson, AB, T7X 5A4
(780) 962-9100
Emp Here 30   *Sales* 10,944,105
SIC 5511 New and used car dealers
Pr Pr Doreen Schmidek
Gary Schmidek

D-U-N-S 20-072-7001   (BR)
INTEGRATED DISTRIBUTION SYSTEMS LIMITED PARTNERSHIP
WAJAX EQUIPMENT
26313 Township Road 531a, Acheson, AB, T7X 5A3
(780) 487-6700
Emp Here 100
SIC 5084 Industrial machinery and equipment

D-U-N-S 24-991-2184   (SL)
JANDEL HOMES LTD
26230 Twp Rd 531a, Acheson, AB, T7X 5A4
(780) 960-4232
Emp Here 40   *Sales* 12,768,123
SIC 6552 Subdividers and developers, nec
Pr Mark Huchulak

D-U-N-S 20-845-4459   (BR)
KAL TIRE LTD
26308 Township Road 531a, Acheson, AB, T7X 5A3
(780) 960-3930
Emp Here 27
SIC 5531 Auto and home supply stores

D-U-N-S 20-082-8002   (SL)
KICHTON CONTRACTING LTD
26229 Township Road 531a Unit 204, Acheson, AB, T7X 5A4
(780) 447-1882
Emp Here 50   *Sales* 4,711,645
SIC 1794 Excavation work

D-U-N-S 20-203-9835   (BR)
LIEBHERR-CANADA LTD
53016 Hwy 60 Unit 208, Acheson, AB, T7X 5A7
(780) 962-6088
Emp Here 20
SIC 5082 Construction and mining machinery

D-U-N-S 24-255-2144   (HQ)
MYSHAK CRANE AND RIGGING LTD
(*Suby of* Myshak Equipment Ltd)
53016 Hwy 60 Suite 42b, Acheson, AB, T7X 5A7
(780) 960-9790
Emp Here 50   *Emp Total* 62
Sales 24,324,990
SIC 7389 Business services, nec
Pr Pr Corey Mitchell

D-U-N-S 20-302-0029   (HQ)
NCSG CRANE & HEAVY HAUL SERVICES LTD
53016 Hwy 60 Unit 817, Acheson, AB, T7X 5A7
(780) 960-6300
Emp Here 40   *Emp Total* 350
Sales 16,124,315
SIC 7353 Heavy construction equipment rental
Pr Pr Edward (Ted) J. Redmond
Darin Coutu
VP Fin Heather Maccallum

D-U-N-S 24-313-5287   (BR)
NELSON LUMBER COMPANY LTD
WINTERBURN TRUSS DIV OF
53027 Hwy 60, Acheson, AB, T7X 5A4
(800) 661-6526
Emp Here 20
SIC 5211 Lumber and other building materials

D-U-N-S 20-109-0243   (SL)

NORTH AMERICAN ROAD LTD
53016 Hwy 60 Suite 2, Acheson, AB, T7X 5A7
(780) 960-7171
Emp Here 50   *Sales* 7,538,632
SIC 1611 Highway and street construction
Pr Pr Martin Gouin
Ch Bd Yvon J Gouin

D-U-N-S 20-982-7158   (BR)
NOVA POLE INTERNATIONAL INC
26229 Township Road 531a Suite 203, Acheson, AB, T7X 5A4
(780) 962-0010
Emp Here 23
SIC 2499 Wood products, nec

D-U-N-S 24-417-5936   (HQ)
POWELL CANADA INC
(*Suby of* Powell Industries, Inc.)
53032 Range Road 263a, Acheson, AB, T7X 5A5
(780) 948-3300
Emp Here 325   *Emp Total* 2,323
Sales 35,021,136
SIC 1731 Electrical work
Michael Lucas
Pr Pr Peter Didaskalos
VP VP Milburn Honeycutt
Don Madison

D-U-N-S 20-734-1108   (HQ)
SMS CONSTRUCTION AND MINING SYS-TEMS INC
SMS RENTS
53113 Range Road 263a, Acheson, AB, T7X 5A5
(780) 948-2200
Emp Here 106   *Emp Total* 66,583
Sales 328,323,150
SIC 5082 Construction and mining machinery
Pr Hitoshi Kai
VP Susan Berggren
Shinji Matsumura

D-U-N-S 20-059-4302   (HQ)
SMS EQUIPMENT INC
53113 Range Road 263a, Acheson, AB, T7X 5A5
(780) 454-0101
Emp Here 200   *Emp Total* 66,583
Sales 368,156,675
SIC 5082 Construction and mining machinery
Pr Michael Granger
Robin Heard
Dir Fin Joe Noonan

D-U-N-S 24-397-3740   (HQ)
SPRUCELAND MILLWORKS INC
TIMU FOREST PRODUCTS DIV OF
(*Suby of* B.D.K. Properties Ltd)
53016 Hwy 60 Unit 803, Acheson, AB, T7X 5A7
(780) 962-6333
Emp Here 125   *Emp Total* 12
Sales 13,059,965
SIC 2431 Millwork
Pr Pr Ben Sawatzky
VP VP Willy Sawatzky
Greg Schellenberg

D-U-N-S 24-367-4343   (BR)
SYSCO CANADA, INC
SYSCO EDMONTON
(*Suby of* Sysco Corporation)
26210 Township Road 531a, Acheson, AB, T7X 5A4

Emp Here 50
SIC 5141 Groceries, general line

D-U-N-S 20-267-0399   (BR)
TERVITA CORPORATION
CONCORD WELL SERVICING
(*Suby of* Tervita Corporation)
53016 Hwy 60 Suite 11, Acheson, AB, T7X 5A7
(780) 962-4334
Emp Here 35

SIC 1389 Oil and gas field services, nec

D-U-N-S 24-377-6536   (SL)
TRIPLE RANDOM INC
53016 Hwy 60 Unit 46, Acheson, AB, T7X 5A7
(780) 979-0717
Emp Here 50   Sales 3,939,878
SIC 4212 Local trucking, without storage

D-U-N-S 24-716-7729   (HQ)
WESTERN STAR TRUCKS (NORTH) LTD
26124 Township Rd 531a, Acheson, AB, T7X 5A1
(780) 453-3452
Emp Here 75   Emp Total 90
Sales 35,750,743
SIC 5511 New and used car dealers
Pr Pr Barry Robinson
VP VP Scott Robinson
David Robinson
Jim Sand

D-U-N-S 24-395-4559   (HQ)
WESTQUIP DIESEL SALES (ALTA) LTD
26229 Twp Rd 531a Suite 208, Acheson, AB, T7X 5A4
(780) 960-5560
Emp Here 22   Emp Total 14
Sales 5,630,632
SIC 5084 Industrial machinery and equipment
Pr Pr Eugene W Dumont

Acme, AB T0M

D-U-N-S 25-360-3914   (BR)
GOLDEN HILLS SCHOOL DIVISION #75
ACME SCHOOL
610 Walsh Ave, Acme, AB, T0M 0A0
(403) 546-3845
Emp Here 20
SIC 8211 Elementary and secondary schools

Airdrie, AB T4A

D-U-N-S 20-515-6297   (HQ)
642354 ALBERTA LTD
TIM HORTONS
(Suby of 642354 Alberta Ltd)
185 East Lake Cres Ne, Airdrie, AB, T4A 2H7
(403) 912-1230
Emp Here 60   Emp Total 74
Sales 2,261,782
SIC 5812 Eating places

D-U-N-S 25-193-4923   (BR)
ADESA AUCTIONS CANADA CORPORATION
ADESA CALGARY
1621 Veterans Blvd Nw, Airdrie, AB, T4A 2G7
(403) 912-4400
Emp Here 200
SIC 5012 Automobiles and other motor vehicles

D-U-N-S 25-365-1061   (BR)
AIRDRIE, CITY OF
EASTLAKE RECREATION WELLNESS CENTER
800 East Lake Blvd Ne, Airdrie, AB, T4A 2K9
(403) 948-8804
Emp Here 65
SIC 7999 Amusement and recreation, nec

D-U-N-S 25-197-5970   (BR)
BURNCO ROCK PRODUCTS LTD
134 East Lake Blvd Ne, Airdrie, AB, T4A 2G2
(403) 948-1115
Emp Here 24
SIC 3273 Ready-mixed concrete

D-U-N-S 24-416-1444   (SL)
BOUNDARY TECHNICAL GROUP INC

421 East Lake Rd Ne Unit 8, Airdrie, AB, T4A 2J7
(403) 948-2198
Emp Here 30   Sales 2,626,585
SIC 8713 Surveying services

D-U-N-S 24-298-3476   (SL)
CAM CLARK FORD SALES LTD
925 Veterans Blvd Nw Bay 1, Airdrie, AB, T4A 2G6
(403) 948-6660
Emp Here 300   Sales 150,720,000
SIC 5511 New and used car dealers
Pr Pr Cameron Clark
Kevin Clark
Dir Chris Clark
Kim Robert Clark
Irving Veno
Wendy Dickman
Anita Cob

D-U-N-S 24-518-0864   (BR)
CHAMCO INDUSTRIES LTD
(Suby of Chamco Industries Ltd)
553 Kingsview Way Se Suite 110, Airdrie, AB, T4A 0C9
(403) 945-8134
Emp Here 75
SIC 5084 Industrial machinery and equipment

D-U-N-S 24-389-5021   (BR)
COSTCO WHOLESALE CANADA LTD
(Suby of Costco Wholesale Corporation)
1003 Hamilton Blvd Ne, Airdrie, AB, T4A 0G2
(403) 945-4250
Emp Here 100
SIC 4731 Freight transportation arrangement

D-U-N-S 24-807-2159   (BR)
EFCO CANADA CO
EFCO
527 East Lake Blvd Ne, Airdrie, AB, T4A 2G3
(403) 948-5426
Emp Here 30
SIC 5051 Metals service centers and offices

D-U-N-S 20-555-3501   (BR)
GLOVER INTERNATIONAL TRUCKS LTD
(Suby of Glover International Trucks Ltd)
78 East Lake Cres Ne, Airdrie, AB, T4A 2H4
(403) 948-2011
Emp Here 20
SIC 5531 Auto and home supply stores

D-U-N-S 24-533-3013   (BR)
IPAC SERVICES CORPORATION
(Suby of IPAC Services Corporation)
32 East Lake Cres Ne, Airdrie, AB, T4A 2H3
(403) 948-1155
Emp Here 60
SIC 1382 Oil and gas exploration services

D-U-N-S 25-187-7163   (BR)
LOBLAWS INC
EXTRA FOODS 9009
1050 Yankee Valley Blvd Se, Airdrie, AB, T4A 2E4
(403) 912-3800
Emp Here 116
SIC 5411 Grocery stores

D-U-N-S 20-366-3778   (SL)
MACK'S CUSTOM WELDING & FABRICATION INC
MACKSTEEL
143 East Lake Blvd Ne, Airdrie, AB, T4A 2G1

Emp Here 26   Sales 5,180,210
SIC 1541 Industrial buildings and warehouses
Ryan Hennessey
Pr Pr Sean Mackenzie

D-U-N-S 20-598-3729   (SL)
NORTH HILL MOTORS (1975) LTD
AIRDRIE CHRYSLER DODGE JEEP
139 East Lake Cres Ne, Airdrie, AB, T4A 2H7
(403) 948-2600
Emp Here 70   Sales 32,981,515

SIC 5511 New and used car dealers
Pr Pr Larry Mccook
Zia Khan
Bradley Styner
Jolayne Leger

D-U-N-S 24-076-4360   (BR)
RADIOLOGY CONSULTANTS ASSOCIATED
110 Mayfair Close Se, Airdrie, AB, T4A 1T6
(403) 777-3040
Emp Here 300
SIC 8748 Business consulting, nec

D-U-N-S 20-710-7074   (BR)
ROCKY VIEW SCHOOL DIVISION NO. 41, THE
BERT CHURCH HIGH SCHOOL
1010 East Lake Blvd Ne, Airdrie, AB, T4A 2A1
(403) 948-3800
Emp Here 50
SIC 8211 Elementary and secondary schools

D-U-N-S 20-710-7298   (BR)
ROCKY VIEW SCHOOL DIVISION NO. 41, THE
ROCKYVIEW VIRTUAL SCHOOL AND LEARNING CONNECTION
925 Irricana Rd Northeast Bay2, Airdrie, AB, T4A 2G6
(403) 948-4360
Emp Here 36
SIC 8211 Elementary and secondary schools

D-U-N-S 20-071-1583   (BR)
ROCKY VIEW SCHOOL DIVISION NO. 41, THE
R J HAWKEY ELEMENTARY SCHOOL
233 Big Springs Dr Se, Airdrie, AB, T4A 1C4
(403) 948-3939
Emp Here 43
SIC 8211 Elementary and secondary schools

D-U-N-S 20-591-8282   (BR)
ROCKY VIEW SCHOOL DIVISION NO. 41, THE
MEADOWBROOK MIDDLE SCHOOL
1791 Meadowbrook Dr Se, Airdrie, AB, T4A 1V1
(403) 948-5656
Emp Here 20
SIC 8211 Elementary and secondary schools

D-U-N-S 24-191-2273   (BR)
TRANSCANADA PIPELINES LIMITED
1401 Veterans Blvd Nw, Airdrie, AB, T4A 2G7
(403) 948-8111
Emp Here 50
SIC 1623 Water, sewer, and utility lines

D-U-N-S 25-385-3493   (SL)
UNIVERSAL WELD OVERLAYS INC
135 East Lake Blvd Ne, Airdrie, AB, T4A 2G1
(403) 948-1903
Emp Here 30   Sales 11,786,895
SIC 7692 Welding repair

D-U-N-S 20-199-6670   (BR)
WENDY'S RESTAURANTS OF CANADA INC
WENDY'S
(Suby of The Wendy's Company)
180 East Lake Cres Ne, Airdrie, AB, T4A 2H8
(403) 948-2108
Emp Here 30
SIC 5812 Eating places

Airdrie, AB T4B

D-U-N-S 20-769-5110   (SL)
1021416 ALBERTA LTD
OUR FLAMES RESTAURANT
216 Edmonton Trail Ne, Airdrie, AB, T4B 1R9
(403) 948-9335
Emp Here 50   Sales 1,819,127
SIC 5812 Eating places

D-U-N-S 20-638-2686   (BR)
ATCO GAS AND PIPELINES LTD
ATCO GAS, DIV OF
84 Gateway Dr Ne, Airdrie, AB, T4B 0J6
(403) 948-2973
Emp Here 50
SIC 4619 Pipelines, nec

D-U-N-S 24-128-3774   (BR)
ALBERTA HEALTH SERVICES
AIRDRIE REGIONAL HEALTH CENTRE
604 Main St S, Airdrie, AB, T4B 3K7
(403) 912-8400
Emp Here 50
SIC 8062 General medical and surgical hospitals

D-U-N-S 25-231-7284   (BR)
ALBERTA TREASURY BRANCHES
ATB FINANCIAL
404 Main St Se, Airdrie, AB, T4B 3C3
(403) 948-5828
Emp Here 23
SIC 6036 Savings institutions, except federal

D-U-N-S 20-552-3991   (HQ)
BARNSLEY INVESTMENTS LTD
MCDONALDS
(Suby of Barnsley Investments Ltd)
104 Edmonton Trail Ne Suite 1, Airdrie, AB, T4B 1S1
(403) 948-6000
Emp Here 30   Emp Total 60
Sales 1,824,018
SIC 5812 Eating places

D-U-N-S 25-616-4070   (BR)
BETHANY CARE SOCIETY
BETHANY AIRDRIE
1736 1 Ave Nw Suite 725, Airdrie, AB, T4B 2C4
(403) 948-6022
Emp Here 125
SIC 8051 Skilled nursing care facilities

D-U-N-S 20-713-0837   (BR)
CALGARY ROMAN CATHOLIC SEPARATE SCHOOL DISTRICT #1
ST. MARTIN DE PORRES HIGH SCHOOL
410 Yankee Valley Blvd Sw, Airdrie, AB, T4B 2M1
(403) 500-2041
Emp Here 30
SIC 8211 Elementary and secondary schools

D-U-N-S 25-269-6919   (BR)
CALGARY ROMAN CATHOLIC SEPARATE SCHOOL DISTRICT #1
OUR LADY QUEEN OF PEACE SCHOOL
1820 1 Ave Nw, Airdrie, AB, T4B 2E6
(403) 948-4661
Emp Here 60
SIC 8211 Elementary and secondary schools

D-U-N-S 24-337-2427   (BR)
FULMER DEVELOPMENT CORPORATION, THE
PIZZA HUT
(Suby of Fulmer Development Corporation, The)
108 Edmonton Trail Ne, Airdrie, AB, T4B 1R9
(403) 912-3440
Emp Here 20
SIC 5812 Eating places

D-U-N-S 24-361-7169   (BR)
HOME DEPOT OF CANADA INC
HOME DEPOT
(Suby of The Home Depot Inc)
2925 Main St Se, Airdrie, AB, T4B 3G5
(403) 945-3865
Emp Here 100
SIC 5251 Hardware stores

D-U-N-S 20-977-9318   (SL)
KITASKINAW EDUCATION AUTHORITY
90 Ashwood Rd Se, Airdrie, AB, T4B 1G8
(780) 470-5657
Emp Here 52   Sales 3,502,114

SIC 8211 Elementary and secondary schools

D-U-N-S 24-075-2589   (BR)
MARK'S WORK WEARHOUSE LTD
WORK WORLD
202 Veterans Blvd Ne Suite 100, Airdrie, AB, T4B 3P2
(403) 948-7768
Emp Here 20
SIC 5963 Direct selling establishments

D-U-N-S 20-027-3733   (BR)
ROCKY VIEW SCHOOL DIVISION NO. 41, THE
A E BOWERS ELEMENTARY SCHOOL
1721 Summerfield Blvd Se, Airdrie, AB, T4B 1T3
(403) 948-4511
Emp Here 35
SIC 8211 Elementary and secondary schools

D-U-N-S 20-025-4949   (BR)
ROCKY VIEW SCHOOL DIVISION NO. 41, THE
ECOLE EDWARDS ELEMENTARY
241 Jensen Dr Ne, Airdrie, AB, T4B 0G2
(403) 948-5922
Emp Here 62
SIC 8211 Elementary and secondary schools

D-U-N-S 20-591-8472   (BR)
ROCKY VIEW SCHOOL DIVISION NO. 41, THE
CLAYTON MIDDLE SCHOOL
305 Acacia Dr Se, Airdrie, AB, T4B 1G2
(403) 948-2445
Emp Here 60
SIC 8211 Elementary and secondary schools

D-U-N-S 20-591-7326   (BR)
ROCKY VIEW SCHOOL DIVISION NO. 41, THE
ECOLE AIRDRIE MIDDLE SCHOOL
332 1 Ave Ne Suite 9, Airdrie, AB, T4B 2K5
(403) 948-5969
Emp Here 40
SIC 8211 Elementary and secondary schools

D-U-N-S 20-591-9082   (BR)
ROCKY VIEW SCHOOL DIVISION NO. 41, THE
RALPH MCCALL ELEMENTARY SCHOOL
1505 1 Ave Nw, Airdrie, AB, T4B 2L9
(403) 948-7030
Emp Here 40
SIC 8211 Elementary and secondary schools

D-U-N-S 20-031-2192   (BR)
ROCKY VIEW SCHOOL DIVISION NO. 41, THE
GEORGE MCDOUGALL HIGH SCHOOL
412 3 Ave Ne, Airdrie, AB, T4B 1R7
(403) 948-5935
Emp Here 70
SIC 8211 Elementary and secondary schools

D-U-N-S 25-217-4065   (BR)
SHOPPERS DRUG MART CORPORATION
SHOPPERS DRUG MART
505 Main St S, Airdrie, AB, T4B 3K3
(403) 948-5858
Emp Here 20
SIC 5912 Drug stores and proprietary stores

D-U-N-S 24-363-3877   (BR)
SOBEYS WEST INC
AIRDRIE SAFEWAY
505 Main St, Airdrie, AB, T4B 2B8
(403) 948-4838
Emp Here 100
SIC 5411 Grocery stores

D-U-N-S 24-634-2310   (BR)
STARBUCKS COFFEE CANADA, INC
STARBUCKS
(*Suby of* Starbucks Corporation)
114 Sierra Springs Dr Se Unit 101, Airdrie, AB, T4B 3G6

(403) 945-8107
Emp Here 28
SIC 5812 Eating places

D-U-N-S 25-556-3454   (BR)
UNITED FARMERS OF ALBERTA CO-OPERATIVE LIMITED
UFA AIRDRIE FARM SUPPLY, DIV OF
613 Edmonton Trail Ne, Airdrie, AB, T4B 3J6
(403) 948-5913
Emp Here 32
SIC 5083 Farm and garden machinery

D-U-N-S 24-317-5317   (BR)
WAL-MART CANADA CORP
2881 Main St Se Suite 1050, Airdrie, AB, T4B 3G5
(403) 945-1295
Emp Here 200
SIC 5311 Department stores

Alberta Beach, AB T0E

D-U-N-S 20-029-7492   (BR)
NORTHERN GATEWAY REGIONAL DIVISION #10
GRASMERE SCHOOL
Gd, Alberta Beach, AB, T0E 0A0
(780) 924-3758
Emp Here 30
SIC 8211 Elementary and secondary schools

Alder Flats, AB T0C

D-U-N-S 20-023-9700   (BR)
WETASKIWIN REGIONAL PUBLIC SCHOOLS
ALDER FLATS ELEMENTARY SCHOOL
(*Suby of* Wetaskiwin Regional Public Schools)
Gd, Alder Flats, AB, T0C 0A0
(780) 388-3881
Emp Here 20
SIC 8211 Elementary and secondary schools

Aldersyde, AB T0L

D-U-N-S 20-651-5319   (BR)
DOUBLE R BUILDING PRODUCTS LTD
TRUSS & FLOOR DIVISION
1 Maple Leaf Rd, Aldersyde, AB, T0L 0A0
(403) 652-4011
Emp Here 25
SIC 5039 Construction materials, nec

D-U-N-S 20-952-4680   (SL)
MULLEN TRUCKING CORP
80079 Maple Leaf Rd E Unit 100, Aldersyde, AB, T0L 0A0
(403) 652-8888
Emp Here 150   *Sales* 19,407,546
SIC 4213 Trucking, except local
 Murray Mullen

Alix, AB T0C

D-U-N-S 24-880-7711   (SL)
RAHR MALTING CANADA LTD
Hwy 12 E, Alix, AB, T0C 0B0
(403) 747-2777
Emp Here 40
SIC 2083 Malt

D-U-N-S 20-029-3319   (BR)
WOLF CREEK SCHOOL DIVISION NO.72
ALIX M A C SCHOOL
4723 49th St, Alix, AB, T0C 0B0

(403) 747-2778
Emp Here 30
SIC 8211 Elementary and secondary schools

Alliance, AB T0B

D-U-N-S 24-949-8411   (SL)
HUTTERIAN BRETHREN OF SOUTH BEND
SOUTH BEND COLONY
1539 12 West Of 4th, Alliance, AB, T0B 0A0
(780) 879-2170
Emp Here 56   *Sales* 2,845,467
SIC 7389 Business services, nec

Altario, AB T0C

D-U-N-S 20-711-1639   (BR)
PRAIRIE LAND REGIONAL DIVISION 25
ALTARIO SCHOOL
Gd, Altario, AB, T0C 0E0
(403) 552-3828
Emp Here 32
SIC 8211 Elementary and secondary schools

Amisk, AB T0B

D-U-N-S 20-710-0871   (BR)
BUFFALO TRAIL PUBLIC SCHOOLS REGIONAL DIVISION NO. 28
AMISK ELEMENTARY SCHOOL
4911 53rd St, Amisk, AB, T0B 0B0
(780) 856-3771
Emp Here 50
SIC 8211 Elementary and secondary schools

Andrew, AB T0B

D-U-N-S 20-023-9775   (BR)
ELK ISLAND PUBLIC SCHOOLS REGIONAL DIVISION NO. 14
ANDREW SCHOOL
4922 50 Ave, Andrew, AB, T0B 0C0
(780) 365-3501
Emp Here 32
SIC 8211 Elementary and secondary schools

Ardmore, AB T0A

D-U-N-S 20-713-4862   (BR)
NORTHERN LIGHTS SCHOOL DIVISION NO. 69
ARDMORE SCHOOL
4801 48th St, Ardmore, AB, T0A 0B0
(780) 826-5144
Emp Here 50
SIC 8211 Elementary and secondary schools

D-U-N-S 20-280-2141   (BR)
ROCKWELL SERVICING INC
ENSIGN ROCKWELL SERVICING
440 Hwy 28, Ardmore, AB, T0A 0B0
(780) 826-6464
Emp Here 150
SIC 1389 Oil and gas field services, nec

Ardrossan, AB T8E

D-U-N-S 20-068-3170   (BR)
ELK ISLAND CATHOLIC SEPARATE REGIONAL DIVISION NO. 41

HOLLY REDEEMER CATHOLIC SCHOOL
53117 Range Road 222 Suite 222, Ardrossan, AB, T8E 2M8
(780) 922-4522
Emp Here 33
SIC 8211 Elementary and secondary schools

D-U-N-S 20-785-8015   (BR)
ELK ISLAND PUBLIC SCHOOLS REGIONAL DIVISION NO. 14
ARDROSSAN JUNIOR SENIOR HIGH
53129 Range Road 222, Ardrossan, AB, T8E 2M8
(780) 922-2228
Emp Here 75
SIC 8211 Elementary and secondary schools

D-U-N-S 20-023-9726   (BR)
ELK ISLAND PUBLIC SCHOOLS REGIONAL DIVISION NO. 14
ARDROSSAN ELEMENTARY SCHOOL
53131 Range Road 222, Ardrossan, AB, T8E 2M8
(780) 922-2066
Emp Here 45
SIC 8211 Elementary and secondary schools

D-U-N-S 24-862-6173   (BR)
PIONEER HI-BRED LIMITED
PIONEER HI-BRED PRODUCTION
(*Suby of* E. I. Du Pont De Nemours and Company)
22220 16 Hwy, Ardrossan, AB, T8E 2L4
(780) 922-4168
Emp Here 20
SIC 2824 Organic fibers, noncellulosic

Ashmont, AB T0A

D-U-N-S 20-023-9643   (BR)
ST. PAUL EDUCATION REGIONAL DIVISION NO 1
ASHMONT ELEMENTARY COMMUNITY SCHOOL
Gd, Ashmont, AB, T0A 0C0
(780) 726-3877
Emp Here 64
SIC 8211 Elementary and secondary schools

D-U-N-S 20-023-9650   (BR)
ST. PAUL EDUCATION REGIONAL DIVISION NO 1
ASHMONT SECONDARY SCHOOL
1 Main St, Ashmont, AB, T0A 0C0
(780) 726-3793
Emp Here 35
SIC 8211 Elementary and secondary schools

Athabasca, AB T9S

D-U-N-S 25-156-5040   (BR)
ALBERTA HEALTH SERVICES
ATHABASCA COMMUNITY HEALTH SERVICES
3401 48 Ave, Athabasca, AB, T9S 1M7
(780) 675-2231
Emp Here 50
SIC 8062 General medical and surgical hospitals

D-U-N-S 25-628-5545   (BR)
ALBERTA HEALTH SERVICES
ATHABASCA HEALTHCARE CENTRE
3100 48 Ave, Athabasca, AB, T9S 1M9
(780) 675-6000
Emp Here 147
SIC 8062 General medical and surgical hospitals

D-U-N-S 24-113-6139   (BR)
ASPEN VIEW PUBLIC SCHOOL DIVISION NO. 78

LANDING TRAIL INTERMEDIATE SCHOOLS
(Suby of Aspen View Public School Division No. 78)
5502 48 Ave, Athabasca, AB, T9S 1L3
(780) 675-2213
Emp Here 50
SIC 8211 Elementary and secondary schools

D-U-N-S 20-358-0258   (BR)
ASPEN VIEW PUBLIC SCHOOL DIVISION NO. 78
WHISPERING HILLS PRIMARY
(Suby of Aspen View Public School Division No. 78)
3001 Whispering Hills Dr, Athabasca, AB, T9S 1N3
(780) 675-4546
Emp Here 40
SIC 8211 Elementary and secondary schools

D-U-N-S 25-100-6151   (BR)
BUY-LOW FOODS LTD
4919 48 St, Athabasca, AB, T9S 1B9
(780) 675-2236
Emp Here 50
SIC 5411 Grocery stores

D-U-N-S 25-011-0954   (BR)
EXTENDICARE (CANADA) INC
EXTENDICARE ATHABASCA
4517 53 St, Athabasca, AB, T9S 1K4
(780) 675-2291
Emp Here 70
SIC 8051 Skilled nursing care facilities

D-U-N-S 20-880-3911   (BR)
FIRSTCANADA ULC
FIRST STUDENT CANADA
Po Box 327 Stn Main, Athabasca, AB, T9S 2A3
(780) 675-4220
Emp Here 40
SIC 4151 School buses

D-U-N-S 20-734-8603   (BR)
INDEPENDENT ELECTRIC AND CONTROLS LTD
3404 53 St, Athabasca, AB, T9S 1B2
(780) 675-9456
Emp Here 20
SIC 1389 Oil and gas field services, nec

D-U-N-S 20-793-7009   (BR)
PYRAMID CORPORATION
3706 53 St, Athabasca, AB, T9S 1B2
(780) 675-9234
Emp Here 25
SIC 1731 Electrical work

D-U-N-S 20-860-0838   (BR)
SOURCE (BELL) ELECTRONICS INC, THE
SOURCE, THE
4913a 49 St, Athabasca, AB, T9S 1C5
(780) 675-5557
Emp Here 25
SIC 5999 Miscellaneous retail stores, nec

Atikameg, AB T0G

D-U-N-S 20-711-6596   (BR)
WHITE FISH LAKE FIRST NATION #459
ATIKAMEG SCHOOL
Gd, Atikameg, AB, T0G 0C0
(780) 767-3797
Emp Here 35
SIC 8211 Elementary and secondary schools

Balzac, AB T0M

D-U-N-S 24-647-4019   (HQ)
ALTA GENETICS INC
263090 Range Road 11, Balzac, AB, T0M 0E0

(403) 226-0666
Emp Here 280   *Emp Total* 12,937
Sales 115,653,000
SIC 5159 Farm-product raw materials, nec
Pr Pr Cees Hartmans
Dir Wijnand Pon
   Hans Hannema
   Paul Hunt

D-U-N-S 24-827-8413   (BR)
PREMIER TECH HOME & GARDEN INC
291227 Westland Dr, Balzac, AB, T0M 0E0
(403) 516-3770
Emp Here 20
SIC 5191 Farm supplies

D-U-N-S 24-015-8584   (SL)
REDSON RESOURCE MANAGEMENT LTD
BUCARS R.V. CENTRE
262109 Rge Rd 10, Balzac, AB, T0M 0E0
(403) 207-1666
Emp Here 50   *Sales* 3,648,035
SIC 7538 General automotive repair shops

Banff, AB T0L

D-U-N-S 24-333-7347   (BR)
BANFF CARIBOU PROPERTIES LTD
KEG STEAKHOUSE & BAR
117 Banff Ave, Banff, AB, T0L 0C0
(403) 760-3030
Emp Here 35
SIC 5812 Eating places

Banff, AB T1L

D-U-N-S 20-048-3175   (SL)
567945 ALBERTA LTD
HENRY'S ELECTRIC
116 Eagle Cres, Banff, AB, T1L 1A3
(403) 762-3287
Emp Here 52   *Sales* 4,523,563
SIC 1731 Electrical work

D-U-N-S 20-720-2743   (BR)
ALBERTA HEALTH SERVICES
MINERAL SPRINGS HOSPITAL
305 Lynx St, Banff, AB, T1L 1H7
(403) 762-2222
Emp Here 200
SIC 8062 General medical and surgical hospitals

D-U-N-S 24-341-9954   (BR)
BANFF CARIBOU PROPERTIES LTD
BANFF PTARMIGAN
337 Banff Ave, Banff, AB, T1L 1B1
(403) 762-2207
Emp Here 50
SIC 7011 Hotels and motels

D-U-N-S 20-723-6428   (BR)
BANFF CARIBOU PROPERTIES LTD
BANFF LODGING COMPANY
901 Hidden Ridge Way, Banff, AB, T1L 1H8
(403) 762-3544
Emp Here 40
SIC 7011 Hotels and motels

D-U-N-S 24-345-4464   (BR)
BANFF CARIBOU PROPERTIES LTD
BANFF CARIBOU LODGE & SPA
521 Banff Ave, Banff, AB, T1L 1B7
(403) 762-5887
Emp Here 60
SIC 7011 Hotels and motels

D-U-N-S 20-300-7471   (BR)
BANFF CARIBOU PROPERTIES LTD
BANFF ROCKY MOUNTAIN RESORT
1029 Banff Ave, Banff, AB, T1L 1A2
(403) 762-5531
Emp Here 70

SIC 7011 Hotels and motels

D-U-N-S 25-389-4109   (HQ)
BREWSTER INC
PACKAGE TOURS, A DIV OF
100 Gopher St, Banff, AB, T1L 1J3
(403) 762-6700
Emp Here 175   *Emp Total* 225
Sales 53,626,115
SIC 4725 Tour operators
Pr David G Morrison
   James Fraser
VP Fin Terry Holt
VP Opers Andrew Whittick

D-U-N-S 24-440-1188   (HQ)
CANADIAN CO CO TOURS, INC
(Suby of Canadian Co Co Tours, Inc)
220 Bear St Suite 205, Banff, AB, T1L 1A2
(403) 762-5600
Emp Here 48   *Emp Total* 80
Sales 24,594,787
SIC 4725 Tour operators
Pr Pr Shintaro Wakatsuki

D-U-N-S 20-440-9049   (HQ)
CANADIAN MOUNTAIN HOLIDAYS LIMITED PARTNERSHIP
CMH HELI-SKIING & HIKING
(Suby of Hawk Holding Company, LLC)
217 Bear St, Banff, AB, T1L 1J6
(403) 762-7100
Emp Here 45   *Emp Total* 5,350
Sales 23,388,777
SIC 7011 Hotels and motels
Pr Pr Walter Bruns
Dir Lynda Murdock

D-U-N-S 20-107-7109   (BR)
CANADIAN ROCKIES REGIONAL DIVISION NO 12
BANFF ELEMENTARY SCHOOL
325 Squirrel S, Banff, AB, T1L 1H1
(403) 762-4465
Emp Here 35
SIC 8211 Elementary and secondary schools

D-U-N-S 20-003-5181   (BR)
CANADIAN ROCKIES REGIONAL DIVISION NO 12
BANFF COMMUNITY HIGH SCHOOL
330 Banff Ave, Banff, AB, T1L 1K1
(403) 762-4411
Emp Here 27
SIC 8211 Elementary and secondary schools

D-U-N-S 24-906-8420   (SL)
EARLS RESTAURANT (BANFF) LTD
229 Banff Ave, Banff, AB, T1L 1B9
(403) 762-4414
Emp Here 65   *Sales* 1,969,939
SIC 5812 Eating places

D-U-N-S 24-340-2695   (BR)
FGL SPORTS LTD
ATMOSPHERE
122 Banff Ave, Banff, AB, T1L 1C1
(403) 760-8249
Emp Here 20
SIC 5941 Sporting goods and bicycle shops

D-U-N-S 24-674-8230   (BR)
FAIRMONT HOTELS & RESORTS INC
FAIRMONT BANFF SPRINGS, THE
405 Spray Ave, Banff, AB, T1L 1J4
(403) 762-6860
Emp Here 800
SIC 7011 Hotels and motels

D-U-N-S 24-075-4817   (BR)
GAP (CANADA) INC
GAP
(Suby of The Gap Inc)
317 Banff Ave Suite 9m, Banff, AB, T1L 1B1
(403) 760-8630
Emp Here 20
SIC 5651 Family clothing stores

D-U-N-S 25-318-8940   (BR)
GREAT CANADIAN RAILTOUR COMPANY LTD
GRAY LINE WEST
(Suby of Armstrong Hospitality Group Ltd)
141 Eagle Cres, Banff, AB, T1L 1B4

Emp Here 63
SIC 4142 Bus charter service, except local

D-U-N-S 25-022-5588   (BR)
HUDSON'S BAY COMPANY
BAY, THE
125 Banff Ave, Banff, AB, T1L 1A1
(403) 762-5525
Emp Here 45
SIC 5399 Miscellaneous general merchandise

D-U-N-S 25-092-7287   (BR)
LULULEMON ATHLETICA CANADA INC
LULULEMON
121a Banff Ave, Banff, AB, T1L 1B4
(403) 760-3303
Emp Here 20
SIC 2339 Women's and misses' outerwear, nec

D-U-N-S 24-905-3695   (SL)
MELISSA'S MISSTEAK RESTAURANT LTD
MELISSA'S RESTAURANT AND BAR
218 Lynx St, Banff, AB, T1L 1A9
(403) 762-5511
Emp Here 60   *Sales* 1,824,018
SIC 5812 Eating places

D-U-N-S 25-366-0757   (SL)
OLD SPAGHETTI FACTORY, THE
317 Banff Ave 2nd Fl, Banff, AB, T1L 1A2
(403) 760-2779
Emp Here 50   *Sales* 1,532,175
SIC 5812 Eating places

D-U-N-S 24-322-2101   (SL)
PEACOCK CAPITAL LTD
229 Bear St 3 Fl, Banff, AB, T1L 1B1
(403) 762-2642
Emp Here 50   *Sales* 6,791,040
SIC 6712 Bank holding companies
Pr Pr Wilhelmus Pauw

D-U-N-S 20-798-6436   (BR)
REXALL PHARMACY GROUP LTD
REXALL
(Suby of McKesson Corporation)
317 Banff Ave, Banff, AB, T1L 1C3
(403) 762-2245
Emp Here 24
SIC 5912 Drug stores and proprietary stores

D-U-N-S 20-199-6068   (SL)
SALTLIK STEAKHOUSE
221 Bear St, Banff, AB, T1L 1B3
(403) 762-2467
Emp Here 60   *Sales* 1,824,018
SIC 5812 Eating places

D-U-N-S 24-342-4582   (SL)
SILVERTIP LODGE INC
(Suby of Intrawest Resorts Holdings, Inc.)
217 Bear St, Banff, AB, T1L 1J6
(403) 762-7100
Emp Here 50   *Sales* 2,598,753
SIC 7011 Hotels and motels

D-U-N-S 25-271-0587   (BR)
SOBEYS WEST INC
BANFF SAFEWAY
318 Main St, Banff, AB, T1L 1B4
(403) 762-5378
Emp Here 20
SIC 5411 Grocery stores

D-U-N-S 25-592-0399   (BR)
YOUNG WOMEN'S CHRISTIAN ASSOCIATION OF GREATER TORONTO
YWCA BANFF
Gd Stn Main, Banff, AB, T1L 1H1
(403) 762-3560
Emp Here 30

SIC 7011 Hotels and motels

Barnwell, AB T0K

D-U-N-S 20-028-3328   (BR)
BOARD OF TRUSTEES OF HORIZON SCHOOL DIVISION NO 67
BARNWELL SCHOOL
320 Heritage Rd, Barnwell, AB, T0K 0B0
(403) 223-2902
Emp Here 20
SIC 8211 Elementary and secondary schools

Barrhead, AB T7N

D-U-N-S 25-230-4837   (SL)
623878 ALBERTA LTD
BARRHEAD NEIGHBOURHOOD INN
6011 49 St, Barrhead, AB, T7N 1A5
(780) 674-3300
Emp Here 50   *Sales* 2,188,821
SIC 7011 Hotels and motels

D-U-N-S 20-719-0492   (BR)
A & W FOOD SERVICES OF CANADA INC
BARRHEAD A & W
4902 50 Ave, Barrhead, AB, T7N 1A6
(780) 674-7666
Emp Here 20
SIC 5812 Eating places

D-U-N-S 25-764-1555   (BR)
ALBERTA HEALTH SERVICES
BARRHEAD CONTINUING CARE CENTER
5336 59 Ave, Barrhead, AB, T7N 1L2
(780) 674-4506
Emp Here 200
SIC 8052 Intermediate care facilities

D-U-N-S 25-012-8592   (BR)
ALBERTA HEALTH SERVICES
BARRHEAD HEALTHCAPE CENTRE
4815 51 Ave, Barrhead, AB, T7N 1M1
(780) 674-2221
Emp Here 130
SIC 8062 General medical and surgical hospitals

D-U-N-S 20-920-4119   (BR)
ALBERTA HEALTH SERVICES
BARRHEAD COMMUNITY HEALTH SERVICES
6203 49 St, Barrhead, AB, T7N 1A1
(780) 674-3408
Emp Here 40
SIC 8011 Offices and clinics of medical doctors

D-U-N-S 20-578-2613   (BR)
ALBERTA TREASURY BRANCHES
ATB FINANCIAL
Gd Stn Main, Barrhead, AB, T7N 1B8
(780) 674-2241
Emp Here 20
SIC 6036 Savings institutions, except federal

D-U-N-S 24-113-5313   (BR)
BANQUE TORONTO-DOMINION, LA
TORONTO-DOMINION BANK, THE
(*Suby of* Toronto-Dominion Bank, The)
5037 50 St, Barrhead, AB, T7N 1A5
(780) 674-2216
Emp Here 25
SIC 6021 National commercial banks

D-U-N-S 24-346-0107   (SL)
BARRCANA HOMES INC
59504 Range Rd 32, Barrhead, AB, T7N 1A4
(780) 305-0505
Emp Here 206   *Sales* 27,068,420
SIC 2452 Prefabricated wood buildings
Pr Pr John Bennett

Dir Richard B. Hajduk
Dir Albert Vanleeuwen
Fin Ex Randy Fries

D-U-N-S 24-642-4659   (SL)
BARRHEAD & DISTRICT SOCIAL HOUSING ASSOCIATION
4321 52 Ave, Barrhead, AB, T7N 1M6
(780) 674-2787
Emp Here 44   *Sales* 5,535,840
SIC 6531 Real estate agents and managers
Dorothy Clarke
Cliff Tuininga
Ken Killeen
Darrell Troock
Bert Proft

D-U-N-S 24-328-2829   (SL)
BLUE HERON SUPPORT SERVICES ASSOCIATION
Gd Stn Main, Barrhead, AB, T7N 1B8
(780) 674-4944
Emp Here 170   *Sales* 6,201,660
SIC 8361 Residential care
Dir Ralph Helder

D-U-N-S 20-949-8117   (BR)
FRESON MARKET LTD
MEDICINE SHOPPE PHARMACY
(*Suby of* Altamart Investments (1993) Ltd)
5020 49 St, Barrhead, AB, T7N 1G4
(780) 674-3784
Emp Here 80
SIC 5912 Drug stores and proprietary stores

D-U-N-S 25-767-5462   (BR)
MMD SALES LTD
DEERLINE SALES LTD.
6111 49 St, Barrhead, AB, T7N 1A4
(780) 674-2213
Emp Here 22
SIC 5083 Farm and garden machinery

D-U-N-S 24-342-2289   (BR)
PEMBINA HILLS REGIONAL DIVISION 7
SUPPORT SERVICES COMPLEX
5310 49 St, Barrhead, AB, T7N 1P3
(780) 674-8510
Emp Here 20
SIC 4111 Local and suburban transit

D-U-N-S 20-713-2593   (BR)
PEMBINA HILLS REGIONAL DIVISION 7
BARRHEAD ELEMENTARY SCHOOL
5103 53 Ave, Barrhead, AB, T7N 1N9
(780) 674-8518
Emp Here 74
SIC 8211 Elementary and secondary schools

D-U-N-S 25-269-5945   (BR)
PEMBINA HILLS REGIONAL DIVISION 7
BARRHEAD COMPOSITE HIGH SCHOOL
5307 53 Ave, Barrhead, AB, T7N 1P2
(780) 674-8521
Emp Here 85
SIC 8211 Elementary and secondary schools

D-U-N-S 24-396-5279   (BR)
POLLARD BANKNOTE INCOME FUND
6203 46 St, Barrhead, AB, T7N 1A1
(780) 674-4750
Emp Here 80
SIC 7999 Amusement and recreation, nec

D-U-N-S 24-026-7096   (SL)
RICHARDSON MILLING LIMITED
Po Box 4615 Stn Main, Barrhead, AB, T7N 1A5
(780) 674-3960
Emp Here 30   *Sales* 59,754,813
SIC 2043 Cereal breakfast foods
Manager Anthony Hiscock

D-U-N-S 20-192-4565   (BR)
SERVUS CREDIT UNION LTD
BARRHEAD BRANCH
4929 50 Ave, Barrhead, AB, T7N 1A4
(780) 674-3348
Emp Here 20

SIC 6062 State credit unions

D-U-N-S 25-315-4835   (BR)
TORONTO-DOMINION BANK, THE
TD BANK
(*Suby of* Toronto-Dominion Bank, The)
5037 50th St, Barrhead, AB, T7N 1A5
(780) 674-2216
Emp Here 30
SIC 6021 National commercial banks

D-U-N-S 20-920-4242   (BR)
WESTLOCK MOTORS LTD
GRIZZLY TRAIL MOTORS
6201 49th St, Barrhead, AB, T7N 1A4
(780) 674-2236
Emp Here 30
SIC 5511 New and used car dealers

Bashaw, AB T0B

D-U-N-S 20-821-2188   (BR)
ARNETT & BURGESS OIL FIELD CONSTRUCTION LIMITED
5024 46 Ave, Bashaw, AB, T0B 0H0
(780) 372-3954
Emp Here 20
SIC 1629 Heavy construction, nec

Bassano, AB T0J

D-U-N-S 25-329-2668   (BR)
ALBERTA HEALTH SERVICES
BASSANO HOSPITAL
Gd, Bassano, AB, T0J 0B0
(403) 641-3183
Emp Here 50
SIC 8011 Offices and clinics of medical doctors

D-U-N-S 20-642-6749   (BR)
BASSANO FARMS LTD
415 10 St, Bassano, AB, T0J 0B0
(403) 641-3933
Emp Here 30
SIC 5431 Fruit and vegetable markets

D-U-N-S 20-655-0506   (BR)
GRASSLANDS REGIONAL DIVISION 6
NEWELL COLONY SCHOOL
Gd, Bassano, AB, T0J 0B0

Emp Here 40
SIC 8211 Elementary and secondary schools

D-U-N-S 20-712-0200   (BR)
GRASSLANDS REGIONAL DIVISION 6
CLEARVIEW COLONY SCHOOL
Gd, Bassano, AB, T0J 0B0

Emp Here 50
SIC 8211 Elementary and secondary schools

D-U-N-S 20-653-8204   (BR)
GRASSLANDS REGIONAL DIVISION 6
BASSANO SCHOOL
240 6th Ave, Bassano, AB, T0J 0B0
(403) 641-3577
Emp Here 30
SIC 8211 Elementary and secondary schools

Bawlf, AB T0B

D-U-N-S 20-025-4741   (BR)
BATTLE RIVER REGIONAL DIVISION 31
BAWLF SCHOOL
202 King St, Bawlf, AB, T0B 0J0
(780) 373-3784
Emp Here 25

SIC 8211 Elementary and secondary schools

Beaumont, AB T4X

D-U-N-S 20-915-5485   (SL)
751768 ALBERTA INC
T-REX
84 Bonin Cres, Beaumont, AB, T4X 1N7

Emp Here 25   *Sales* 5,653,974
SIC 1623 Water, sewer, and utility lines
Pr Troy Gendreau

D-U-N-S 20-028-8699   (BR)
BLACK GOLD REGIONAL DIVISION #18
ECOLE JE LAPOINTE SCHOOL
4801 55 Ave, Beaumont, AB, T4X 1K2
(780) 929-5988
Emp Here 27
SIC 8211 Elementary and secondary schools

D-U-N-S 20-709-8091   (BR)
BLACK GOLD REGIONAL DIVISION #18
ECOLE COLONIALE ESTATES SCHOOL
37 Coloniale Way, Beaumont, AB, T4X 1M7
(780) 929-5904
Emp Here 50
SIC 8211 Elementary and secondary schools

D-U-N-S 20-709-7861   (BR)
BLACK GOLD REGIONAL DIVISION #18
ECOLE SECONDAIRE BEAUMONT HIGH SCHOOL
5417 43 Ave, Beaumont, AB, T4X 1K1
(780) 929-6282
Emp Here 80
SIC 8211 Elementary and secondary schools

D-U-N-S 25-317-1169   (BR)
BLACK GOLD REGIONAL DIVISION #18
ECOLE BEAU MEADOW SCHOOL
4322 44 St, Beaumont, AB, T4X 1K3
(780) 929-2175
Emp Here 45
SIC 8211 Elementary and secondary schools

D-U-N-S 25-317-1128   (BR)
BLACK GOLD REGIONAL DIVISION #18
ECOLE BELLEVUE SCHOOL
5103 50 Ave, Beaumont, AB, T4X 1K4
(780) 929-8663
Emp Here 50
SIC 8211 Elementary and secondary schools

D-U-N-S 24-101-1423   (BR)
LOBLAWS INC
EXTRA FOODS
5201 30 Ave, Beaumont, AB, T4X 1T9
(780) 929-2043
Emp Here 50
SIC 5431 Fruit and vegetable markets

D-U-N-S 20-138-8761   (BR)
SOBEYS CAPITAL INCORPORATED
BEAUMONT SOBEYS
5700 50 St, Beaumont, AB, T4X 1M8
(780) 929-2749
Emp Here 150
SIC 5411 Grocery stores

Beaverlodge, AB T0H

D-U-N-S 20-959-8627   (BR)
ALBERTA HEALTH SERVICES
BEAVERLODGE PUBLIC HEALTH CENTRE
412 10a St, Beaverlodge, AB, T0H 0C0
(780) 354-2647
Emp Here 20
SIC 8062 General medical and surgical hospitals

D-U-N-S 24-346-5437   (BR)

GOVERNMENT OF THE PROVINCE OF AL-BERTA
BEAVERLODGE MUNICIPAL HOSPITAL
Gd, Beaverlodge, AB, T0H 0C0
(780) 354-2136
Emp Here 150
SIC 8062 General medical and surgical hospitals

D-U-N-S 20-027-4327   (BR)
PEACE WAPITI SCHOOL DIVISION NO.76
BEAVERLODGE REGIONAL HIGH SCHOOL
1034 2nd Ave, Beaverlodge, AB, T0H 0C0
(780) 354-2189
Emp Here 35
SIC 8211 Elementary and secondary schools

D-U-N-S 20-030-6426   (BR)
PEACE WAPITI SCHOOL DIVISION NO.76
BEAVERLODGE ELEMENTARY SCHOOL
1009 5th Ave, Beaverlodge, AB, T0H 0C0
(780) 354-2446
Emp Here 40
SIC 8211 Elementary and secondary schools

D-U-N-S 20-809-6909   (SL)
TARTAN SALES (1973) LTD
TARTAN FORD
202 10 St, Beaverlodge, AB, T0H 0C0

Emp Here 22   *Sales* 11,159,500
SIC 5511 New and used car dealers
  Allen E Gaudin
Pr Pr A Esdale Gaudin
  Merrilee Gaudin

D-U-N-S 20-064-4172   (BR)
TERVITA CORPORATION
(*Suby of* Tervita Corporation)
302 3rd Ave W, Beaverlodge, AB, T0H 0C0
(780) 354-3279
Emp Here 28
SIC 8748 Business consulting, nec

D-U-N-S 20-616-8593   (SL)
VI-AL HOLDINGS LTD
BEAVERLODGE MOTOR INN
116 6a St, Beaverlodge, AB, T0H 0C0
(780) 354-2291
Emp Here 60   *Sales* 2,626,585
SIC 7011 Hotels and motels

Beiseker, AB T0M

D-U-N-S 24-272-1561   (HQ)
CHS COUNTRY OPERATIONS CANADA, INC
CHS CANADA
714 1 Ave, Beiseker, AB, T0M 0G0
(403) 947-3767
Emp Here 27   *Emp Total* 12,167
Sales 4,377,642
SIC 5261 Retail nurseries and garden stores

D-U-N-S 20-592-1104   (BR)
ROCKY VIEW SCHOOL DIVISION NO. 41, THE
BEISEKER COMMUNITY SCHOOL
415 2 Ave, Beiseker, AB, T0M 0G0
(403) 947-3883
Emp Here 20
SIC 8211 Elementary and secondary schools

Bentley, AB T0C

D-U-N-S 25-849-8971   (BR)
ALBERTA HEALTH SERVICES
BENTLEY CARE CENTRE
52 Ave Unit 4834, Bentley, AB, T0C 0J0
(403) 748-4115
Emp Here 30

SIC 8051 Skilled nursing care facilities

D-U-N-S 20-023-9882   (BR)
WOLF CREEK SCHOOL DIVISION NO.72
BENTLEY SCHOOL
5314 49 St, Bentley, AB, T0C 0J0
(403) 748-3770
Emp Here 50
SIC 8211 Elementary and secondary schools

Black Diamond, AB T0L

D-U-N-S 20-260-1147   (BR)
ALBERTA HEALTH SERVICES
OILFIELDS GENERAL HOSPITAL
717 Government Rd, Black Diamond, AB, T0L 0H0
(403) 933-2222
Emp Here 60
SIC 8062 General medical and surgical hospitals

Blackfalds, AB T0C

D-U-N-S 25-115-2716   (SL)
CONTROL TECHNOLOGY INC
4305 South St, Blackfalds, AB, T0C 0B0
(403) 885-2677
Emp Here 42   *Sales* 5,326,131
SIC 1389 Oil and gas field services, nec
Pr Pr Sylvia Eastcott
  Linda Eastcott
Genl Mgr James Evans

Blackfalds, AB T0M

D-U-N-S 25-708-9792   (BR)
ACCEDE ENERGY SERVICES LTD
JET RENTALS AND SALES
27312 Twp Rd Unit 12, Blackfalds, AB, T0M 0J0

Emp Here 25
SIC 7353 Heavy construction equipment rental

D-U-N-S 24-174-2001   (BR)
COMPAGNIE DES CHEMINS DE FER NA-TIONAUX DU CANADA
COMPAGNIE DES CHEMINS DE FER NA-TIONAUX DU CANADA
27001 597 Hwy, Blackfalds, AB, T0M 0J0
(403) 350-1830
Emp Here 20
SIC 4011 Railroads, line-haul operating

D-U-N-S 24-862-9797   (BR)
FMC TECHNOLOGIES CANADA LTD
(*Suby of* Reliance Oilfield Services, LLC)
253 Township Rd 394 Suite 27312, Blackfalds, AB, T0M 0J0
(780) 926-2108
Emp Here 210
SIC 1389 Oil and gas field services, nec

D-U-N-S 24-387-5403   (SL)
FORCE PILE AND FOUNDATIONS INC
(*Suby of* Site Energy Services Ltd)
27312 - 213 Twp 394, Blackfalds, AB, T0M 0J0
(403) 341-0030
Emp Here 130   *Sales* 17,802,411
SIC 1629 Heavy construction, nec
Pr Pr Dallas T. Lenius
VP VP Dean Hall
  John S. Runge

D-U-N-S 24-364-2480   (BR)
FORMULA POWELL L.P.
4300 St Division 7 S, Blackfalds, AB, T0M 0J0

(403) 885-5151
Emp Here 30
SIC 4213 Trucking, except local

D-U-N-S 20-826-4663   (SL)
HECK TRANSWORLD INC
Gd, Blackfalds, AB, T0M 0J0
(403) 885-2402
Emp Here 80   *Sales* 16,130,550
SIC 1389 Oil and gas field services, nec
Pr Pr Lawrence Heck
  Vivian Heck

D-U-N-S 24-951-6696   (BR)
INTEGRATED DISTRIBUTION SYSTEMS LIMITED PARTNERSHIP
WAJAX EQUIPMENT
5424 Blackfalds Industrial Way, Blackfalds, AB, T0M 0J0
(403) 885-5604
Emp Here 25
SIC 5084 Industrial machinery and equipment

D-U-N-S 24-733-6183   (BR)
PROCRANE INC
STERLING CRANE DIV.
(*Suby of* Berkshire Hathaway Inc.)
Gd Hwy 2 And Sec 597 Joffre Rd, Blackfalds, AB, T0M 0J0
(403) 885-6000
Emp Here 20
SIC 7353 Heavy construction equipment rental

D-U-N-S 20-207-6084   (BR)
SHAWCOR LTD
GUARDIAN A ASHAWCOR CO
Henry St, Blackfalds, AB, T0M 0J0
(403) 346-2233
Emp Here 20
SIC 1389 Oil and gas field services, nec

D-U-N-S 20-892-1747   (BR)
TERVITA CORPORATION
(*Suby of* Tervita Corporation)
27312 Hwy 597 Suite 13, Blackfalds, AB, T0M 0J0
(403) 885-0075
Emp Here 1,000
SIC 1389 Oil and gas field services, nec

D-U-N-S 20-287-6744   (BR)
TOTAL OILFIELD RENTALS LIMITED PART-NERSHIP
27322-13 Twp Rd, Blackfalds, AB, T0M 0J0
(403) 885-4166
Emp Here 20
SIC 4213 Trucking, except local

D-U-N-S 20-653-8717   (BR)
WOLF CREEK SCHOOL DIVISION NO.72
IRONRIDGE ELEMENTARY CAMPUS
4710 Broadway Ave, Blackfalds, AB, T0M 0J0
(403) 885-4646
Emp Here 35
SIC 8211 Elementary and secondary schools

Blackfoot, AB T0B

D-U-N-S 24-835-6144   (BR)
GIBSON ENERGY ULC
CANWEST PROPANE
5503 63rd Ave, Blackfoot, AB, T0B 0L0
(780) 875-0070
Emp Here 25
SIC 5172 Petroleum products, nec

Blairmore, AB T0K

D-U-N-S 24-346-1910   (BR)
ALBERTA HEALTH SERVICES
CROWSNEST PASS HEALTH CENTRE

2001 107 St, Blairmore, AB, T0K 0E0
(403) 562-5011
Emp Here 160
SIC 8062 General medical and surgical hospitals

D-U-N-S 20-655-0043   (BR)
LIVINGSTONE RANGE SCHOOL DIVISION NO 68
ISABELLE SELLON SCHOOL
12602 18th Ave, Blairmore, AB, T0K 0E0
(403) 562-8815
Emp Here 21
SIC 8211 Elementary and secondary schools

D-U-N-S 20-771-5314   (BR)
LOBLAWS INC
EXTRA FOODS
12361 20th Ave, Blairmore, AB, T0K 0E0

Emp Here 40
SIC 5411 Grocery stores

Blue Ridge, AB T0E

D-U-N-S 25-533-7180   (BR)
WEST FRASER MILLS LTD
RANGER BOARD
Gd, Blue Ridge, AB, T0E 0B0
(780) 648-6333
Emp Here 120
SIC 2421 Sawmills and planing mills, general

Bon Accord, AB T0A

D-U-N-S 20-898-4823   (SL)
OAK HILL FOUNDATION
OAK HILL BOYS RANCH
Gd, Bon Accord, AB, T0A 0K0
(780) 921-2121
Emp Here 60   *Sales* 2,188,821
SIC 8361 Residential care

D-U-N-S 20-025-9450   (BR)
STURGEON SCHOOL DIVISION #24
BON ACCORD COMMUNITY SCHOOL
28 Range Rd 240 Hwy, Bon Accord, AB, T0A 0K0
(780) 921-3559
Emp Here 30
SIC 8211 Elementary and secondary schools

Bonnyville, AB T9N

D-U-N-S 24-345-5776   (BR)
ALBERTA HEALTH SERVICES
BONNYVILLE COMMUNITY HEALTH SER-VICES
4904 50th Ave, Bonnyville, AB, T9N 2G4
(780) 826-3381
Emp Here 40
SIC 8062 General medical and surgical hospitals

D-U-N-S 25-645-8225   (BR)
BAKER HUGHES CANADA COMPANY
BAKER ATLAS
(*Suby of* Baker Hughes, A GE Company)
5816 50 Ave, Bonnyville, AB, T9N 2N6
(780) 826-3409
Emp Here 20
SIC 1389 Oil and gas field services, nec

D-U-N-S 24-907-0012   (HQ)
BEAR SLASHING LTD
7402 50 Ave, Bonnyville, AB, T9N 0B7
(780) 826-8048
Emp Here 40   *Emp Total* 40
Sales 6,063,757

SIC 1389 Oil and gas field services, nec
Pr Pr Danny Dion

D-U-N-S 25-011-6860   (SL)
BONNYVILLE HEALTH CENTRE
5001 Lakeshore Dr, Bonnyville, AB, T9N 2J7
(780) 826-3311
Emp Here 280   Sales 26,828,160
SIC 8062 General medical and surgical hospitals
Alex Smyl

D-U-N-S 24-767-4708   (SL)
BONNYVILLE NEIGHBOURHOOD INN INC
BONNYVILLE NEIGHBORHOOD INN
5011 66 St, Bonnyville, AB, T9N 2L9
(780) 826-3300
Emp Here 50   Sales 1,532,175
SIC 5812 Eating places

D-U-N-S 25-195-3600   (BR)
CANADIAN NATURAL RESOURCES LIMITED
Gd Stn Main, Bonnyville, AB, T9N 2J6
(780) 826-8110
Emp Here 293
SIC 1311 Crude petroleum and natural gas

D-U-N-S 20-771-7229   (SL)
CANALTA
BOSTON PIZZA
4402 41 Ave, Bonnyville, AB, T9N 2E5
(403) 846-2343
Emp Here 60   Sales 1,824,018
SIC 5812 Eating places

D-U-N-S 20-794-6570   (BR)
CATHOLIC SOCIAL SERVICES
5201 44 St, Bonnyville, AB, T9N 2H1
(780) 826-3935
Emp Here 50
SIC 8399 Social services, nec

D-U-N-S 20-915-6624   (BR)
CLEAN HARBORS ENERGY AND INDUSTRIAL SERVICES CORP.
6215 52 Ave, Bonnyville, AB, T9N 2L7
(780) 812-3035
Emp Here 50
SIC 1389 Oil and gas field services, nec

D-U-N-S 20-322-0009   (BR)
ENTREC CORPORATION
4902 66 St, Bonnyville, AB, T9N 2R5
(780) 826-4565
Emp Here 100
SIC 4213 Trucking, except local

D-U-N-S 20-321-9993   (BR)
ENTREC CORPORATION
6708 50 Ave, Bonnyville, AB, T9N 0B7
(780) 808-9123
Emp Here 150
SIC 4213 Trucking, except local

D-U-N-S 25-011-0970   (BR)
EXTENDICARE (CANADA) INC
EXTENDICARE BONNYVILLE
4602 47 Ave, Bonnyville, AB, T9N 2E8
(780) 826-3341
Emp Here 65
SIC 8051 Skilled nursing care facilities

D-U-N-S 24-000-7174   (BR)
FLINT ENERGY SERVICES LTD.
6015 50 Ave, Bonnyville, AB, T9N 2L3
(780) 826-1988
Emp Here 50
SIC 1389 Oil and gas field services, nec

D-U-N-S 25-999-7203   (BR)
INDEPENDENT ELECTRIC AND CONTROLS LTD
6003 47 Ave Suite 5, Bonnyville, AB, T9N 0B3

Emp Here 50
SIC 1731 Electrical work

D-U-N-S 20-968-7610   (BR)
INTER PIPELINE LTD
COLD LAKE PIPELINE LP
Gd Stn Main, Bonnyville, AB, T9N 2J6
(780) 343-2000
Emp Here 25
SIC 1382 Oil and gas exploration services

D-U-N-S 25-266-3190   (BR)
KAEFER INTEGRATED SERVICES LTD
5002 55 Ave, Bonnyville, AB, T9N 2K6
(780) 826-4737
Emp Here 30
SIC 1742 Plastering, drywall, and insulation

D-U-N-S 20-029-0364   (BR)
LAKELAND LODGE AND HOUSING FOUNDATION
BONNYLODGE
4712 47 Ave Suite 214, Bonnyville, AB, T9N 2E7
(780) 826-3911
Emp Here 21
SIC 7389 Business services, nec

D-U-N-S 24-399-3631   (SL)
LAKELAND PETROLEUM SERVICES CO-OPERATIVE LTD
LAKELAND CO-OP
6020 54 Ave, Bonnyville, AB, T9N 2M8
(780) 826-3349
Emp Here 21   Sales 38,554,597
SIC 5171 Petroleum bulk stations and terminals
Terry Shenher
Pr Pr Jacques Ouellette
VP VP Dwayne Shultz
Louise Bellamy
Greg Sawchuk
Victor Koluk
Colin Balan
Denis Dery
John Irwin

D-U-N-S 25-174-6053   (BR)
LAKELAND ROMAN CATHOLIC SEPARATE SCHOOL DISTRICT NO. 150
NOTRE DAME ELEMENTARY SCHOOL
4711 48 St, Bonnyville, AB, T9N 2E6
(780) 826-3485
Emp Here 35
SIC 8211 Elementary and secondary schools

D-U-N-S 20-713-5802   (BR)
LAKELAND ROMAN CATHOLIC SEPARATE SCHOOL DISTRICT NO. 150
ECOLE NOTRE DAME SENIOR HIGH SCHOOL
49 Po Box 5006 Stn Main, Bonnyville, AB, T9N 2G3
(780) 826-3245
Emp Here 25
SIC 8211 Elementary and secondary schools

D-U-N-S 20-028-4409   (BR)
LAKELAND ROMAN CATHOLIC SEPARATE SCHOOL DISTRICT NO. 150
DR BERNARD BROSSEAU SCHOOL
4301 38 St, Bonnyville, AB, T9N 2P9
(780) 826-7005
Emp Here 37
SIC 8211 Elementary and secondary schools

D-U-N-S 24-364-7539   (BR)
NATIONAL-OILWELL CANADA LTD
NATIONAL OILWELL VARCO
(Suby of National Oilwell Varco, Inc.)
5402 55 Ave Unit 2, Bonnyville, AB, T9N 2K6
(780) 826-2263
Emp Here 21
SIC 1381 Drilling oil and gas wells

D-U-N-S 25-580-7604   (BR)
NELSON LUMBER COMPANY LTD
5201 43 St, Bonnyville, AB, T9N 0B2
(780) 826-3140
Emp Here 25

SIC 5211 Lumber and other building materials

D-U-N-S 20-023-9684   (BR)
NORTHERN LIGHTS SCHOOL DIVISION NO. 69
DUCLOS SCHOOL
4801 52 Ave, Bonnyville, AB, T9N 2R4
(780) 826-3992
Emp Here 35
SIC 8211 Elementary and secondary schools

D-U-N-S 20-713-5026   (BR)
NORTHERN LIGHTS SCHOOL DIVISION NO. 69
H E BOURGAIN SCHOOL
4313 39 St, Bonnyville, AB, T9N 2R1
(780) 826-3322
Emp Here 28
SIC 8211 Elementary and secondary schools

D-U-N-S 25-011-6837   (BR)
NORTHERN LIGHTS SCHOOL DIVISION NO. 69
BONNYVILLE CENTRALIZED HIGH SCHOOL
4908 49th Ave, Bonnyville, AB, T9N 2J7
(780) 826-3366
Emp Here 25
SIC 8211 Elementary and secondary schools

D-U-N-S 20-592-1054   (BR)
NORTHERN LIGHTS SCHOOL DIVISION NO. 69
H E BOURGOIN SCHOOL
4313 39 St, Bonnyville, AB, T9N 2R1
(780) 826-3323
Emp Here 20
SIC 8211 Elementary and secondary schools

D-U-N-S 24-059-3256   (BR)
PYRAMID CORPORATION
5718 54 Ave, Bonnyville, AB, T9N 0E4
(780) 826-4227
Emp Here 30
SIC 1731 Electrical work

D-U-N-S 24-236-1389   (SL)
S.S. PEVACH VENTURES LTD
SCORPION INDUSTRIES
Gd Stn Main, Bonnyville, AB, T9N 2J6
(780) 826-2161
Emp Here 50   Sales 3,939,878
SIC 4212 Local trucking, without storage

D-U-N-S 24-773-0422   (BR)
TARPON ENERGY SERVICES LTD
TARPON ENERGY SERVICES
5001 55 Ave, Bonnyville, AB, T9N 0A7
(780) 594-1204
Emp Here 80
SIC 1389 Oil and gas field services, nec

D-U-N-S 24-624-4524   (BR)
VARCO CANADA ULC
(Suby of National Oilwell Varco, Inc.)
5402 55 Ave Suite 2, Bonnyville, AB, T9N 2K6
(780) 826-2263
Emp Here 33
SIC 7353 Heavy construction equipment rental

Bow Island, AB T0K

D-U-N-S 24-097-9562   (BR)
ALBERTA HEALTH SERVICES
BOW ISLAND HEALTH CENTRE
938 Centre St, Bow Island, AB, T0K 0G0
(403) 545-3200
Emp Here 20
SIC 8062 General medical and surgical hospitals

D-U-N-S 20-029-3301   (BR)
PRAIRIE ROSE SCHOOL DIVISION NO 8
SENATOR GERSHAW SCHOOL

104 First Ave W, Bow Island, AB, T0K 0G0
(403) 545-6822
Emp Here 27
SIC 8211 Elementary and secondary schools

D-U-N-S 25-506-3497   (BR)
VITERRA INC
SASKATCHEWAN WHEAT POOL
801 1st Ave E, Bow Island, AB, T0K 0G0
(403) 545-2227
Emp Here 22
SIC 4221 Farm product warehousing and storage

Boyle, AB T0A

D-U-N-S 20-021-3192   (BR)
ALBERTA HEALTH SERVICES
BOYLE HEALTHCARE CENTRE
5004 Lakeview Rd, Boyle, AB, T0A 0M0
(780) 689-3732
Emp Here 50
SIC 8069 Specialty hospitals, except psychiatric

D-U-N-S 20-653-9467   (BR)
ASPEN VIEW PUBLIC SCHOOL DIVISION NO. 78
BOYLE SCHOOL
(Suby of Aspen View Public School Division No. 78)
5032 Taylor Rd, Boyle, AB, T0A 0M0
(780) 689-3647
Emp Here 36
SIC 8211 Elementary and secondary schools

D-U-N-S 20-073-9613   (SL)
BOYLE CO-OPERATIVE ASSOCIATION LIMITED
4802 Taylor Rd, Boyle, AB, T0A 0M0
(780) 689-3751
Emp Here 70   Sales 13,087,050
SIC 5541 Gasoline service stations
Genl Mgr Fran Hall
Pr Pr Roy Nilsen
VP VP Dan Walker
Irene Luchka
Bonnie Lega
Elmer Kennedy
Bill Goodwin
Curtis Gunderson

D-U-N-S 25-315-3753   (BR)
MILLAR WESTERN INDUSTRIES LTD
MILLAR WESTERN FOREST PRODUCTS
Gd, Boyle, AB, T0A 0M0

Emp Here 180
SIC 2421 Sawmills and planing mills, general

Bragg Creek, AB T0L

D-U-N-S 20-710-7181   (BR)
ROCKY VIEW SCHOOL DIVISION NO. 41, THE
BANDED PEEK SCHOOL
Gd, Bragg Creek, AB, T0L 0K0
(403) 949-2292
Emp Here 25
SIC 8211 Elementary and secondary schools

Breton, AB T0C

D-U-N-S 20-592-1260   (BR)
WILD ROSE SCHOOL DIVISION NO. 66
BRETON HIGH SCHOOL
(Suby of Wild Rose School Division No. 66)
Gd, Breton, AB, T0C 0P0

(780) 696-3633
Emp Here 20
SIC 8211 Elementary and secondary schools

D-U-N-S 20-592-1252   (BR)
WILD ROSE SCHOOL DIVISION NO. 66
BRETON ELEMENTARY SCHOOL
(*Suby of* Wild Rose School Division No. 66)
4715 51 St Breton, AB, T0C 0P0
(780) 696-3555
Emp Here 20
SIC 8211 Elementary and secondary schools

Brocket, AB T0K

D-U-N-S 20-509-6790   (BR)
PEIGAN (PIIKANI) NATION ADMINISTRATION
PEIGAN HEALTH SERVICE
(*Suby of* Peigan (Piikani) Nation Administration)
15th Ave, Brocket, AB, T0K 0H0
(403) 965-3809
Emp Here 20
SIC 8011 Offices and clinics of medical doctors

Brooks, AB T1R

D-U-N-S 25-135-7463   (BR)
ALBERTA HEALTH SERVICES
BROOKS HEALTH CENTRE
440 3 St E Suite 300, Brooks, AB, T1R 0X8
(403) 501-3232
Emp Here 300
SIC 8062 General medical and surgical hospitals

D-U-N-S 25-969-9486   (BR)
ALBERTA HEALTH SERVICES
BROOKS EMS
515 1st Ave Se, Brooks, AB, T1R 0H6
(403) 362-7575
Emp Here 32
SIC 8011 Offices and clinics of medical doctors

D-U-N-S 25-231-7201   (BR)
ALBERTA TREASURY BRANCHES
ATB FINANCIAL
219 2 St E, Brooks, AB, T1R 0G8
(403) 362-3351
Emp Here 20
SIC 6036 Savings institutions, except federal

D-U-N-S 25-105-1751   (BR)
BAKER HUGHES CANADA COMPANY
BAKER ATLAS
(*Suby of* Baker Hughes, A GE Company)
380 Well St, Brooks, AB, T1R 1C2
(403) 362-2736
Emp Here 30
SIC 1389 Oil and gas field services, nec

D-U-N-S 24-376-9945   (BR)
BIG COUNTRY ENERGY SERVICES LIMITED PARTNERSHIP
350 Aquaduct Dr, Brooks, AB, T1R 1B2
(403) 362-3222
Emp Here 100
SIC 1623 Water, sewer, and utility lines

D-U-N-S 24-159-5131   (SL)
BROOKS GOLF CLUB
1311 1 Ave E, Brooks, AB, T1R 1C3
(403) 362-2998
Emp Here 50   *Sales* 2,425,503
SIC 7997 Membership sports and recreation clubs

D-U-N-S 20-583-0966   (BR)
CHRIST THE REDEEMER CATHOLIC SEP-

ARATE REGIONAL DIVISION NO. 3
HOLY FAMILY ACADEMY
440 1 St W Suite 1, Brooks, AB, T1R 1L7
(403) 362-8001
Emp Here 50
SIC 8211 Elementary and secondary schools

D-U-N-S 20-574-6618   (BR)
CHRIST THE REDEEMER CATHOLIC SEPARATE REGIONAL DIVISION NO. 3
ST JOSEPH COLLEGIATE
408 1 St W, Brooks, AB, T1R 0V8
(403) 362-5989
Emp Here 35
SIC 8211 Elementary and secondary schools

D-U-N-S 20-133-9459   (BR)
CITY OF BROOKS
BROOKS RECREATION CENTRE
111 4 Ave W, Brooks, AB, T1R 1B7
(403) 362-3622
Emp Here 30
SIC 7999 Amusement and recreation, nec

D-U-N-S 25-269-5333   (BR)
CURTIN, AUSTIN SALES LTD
CANADIAN TIRE STORE # 212
(*Suby of* Curtin, Austin Sales Ltd)
404 Cassils Rd W Suite 212, Brooks, AB, T1R 0W3
(403) 362-4222
Emp Here 20
SIC 5531 Auto and home supply stores

D-U-N-S 24-786-7666   (HQ)
DERANWAY ENTERPRISES LTD
(*Suby of* Deranway Enterprises Ltd)
Gd Stn Main, Brooks, AB, T1R 1E4
(403) 362-5120
Emp Here 36   *Emp Total* 50
Sales 8,480,961
SIC 1389 Oil and gas field services, nec
Pr Pr Dennis Finkbeiner
   Don Finkbeiner
   Wayne Finkbeiner

D-U-N-S 20-829-6632   (BR)
ENCANA CORPORATION
2249 College Dr E, Brooks, AB, T1R 1G5
(403) 793-4400
Emp Here 180
SIC 1311 Crude petroleum and natural gas

D-U-N-S 20-703-0466   (BR)
FMC TECHNOLOGIES CANADA LTD
(*Suby of* Reliance Oilfield Services, LLC)
380 Well St, Brooks, AB, T1R 1C2
(403) 363-0028
Emp Here 100
SIC 1381 Drilling oil and gas wells

D-U-N-S 24-354-4264   (BR)
FLINT FLUID HAUL SERVICES LTD
10 Industrial Rd, Brooks, AB, T1R 1B5
(403) 793-8384
Emp Here 80
SIC 4212 Local trucking, without storage

D-U-N-S 25-105-6610   (BR)
FLINT INFRASTRUCTURE SERVICES LTD
FLINT FIELD SERVICES
1 Tree Rd, Brooks, AB, T1R 1C6

Emp Here 75
SIC 1623 Water, sewer, and utility lines

D-U-N-S 24-440-7110   (BR)
FRESON MARKET LTD
IGA
(*Suby of* Altamart Investments (1993) Ltd)
330 Fairview Ave W, Brooks, AB, T1R 1K7
(403) 362-4109
Emp Here 120
SIC 5411 Grocery stores

D-U-N-S 24-128-3790   (BR)
GRANT PRODUCTION TESTING SERVICES LTD

(*Suby of* Grant Corporation)
Aquaduct Po Box 440 Stn Main, Brooks, AB, T1R 1B4

Emp Here 150
SIC 1389 Oil and gas field services, nec

D-U-N-S 25-011-7140   (HQ)
GRASSLANDS REGIONAL DIVISION 6
GRASSLANDS PUBLIC SCHOOLS
(*Suby of* Grasslands Regional Division 6)
745 2 Ave E Suite 1, Brooks, AB, T1R 1L2
(403) 793-6700
Emp Here 35   *Emp Total* 500
Sales 43,158,668
SIC 8211 Elementary and secondary schools
Treas Lee Ann Woods
Ch Bd Karen Bartsch

D-U-N-S 20-711-9988   (BR)
GRASSLANDS REGIONAL DIVISION 6
UPLANDS ELEMENTARY SCHOOL
145 Upland Blvd, Brooks, AB, T1R 0R1
(403) 362-2660
Emp Here 70
SIC 8211 Elementary and secondary schools

D-U-N-S 25-325-3181   (BR)
GRASSLANDS REGIONAL DIVISION 6
BROOKS COMPOSITE HIGH SCHOOL
(*Suby of* Grasslands Regional Division 6)
650 4 Ave E Suite 849, Brooks, AB, T1R 0Z4
(403) 362-4814
Emp Here 50
SIC 8211 Elementary and secondary schools

D-U-N-S 20-712-0127   (BR)
GRASSLANDS REGIONAL DIVISION 6
GRIFFIN PARK SCHOOL
805 4 Ave W, Brooks, AB, T1R 0Z2
(403) 362-7555
Emp Here 45
SIC 8211 Elementary and secondary schools

D-U-N-S 20-712-0051   (BR)
GRASSLANDS REGIONAL DIVISION 6
EASTBROOK ELEMENTARY SCHOOL
417 7 St E, Brooks, AB, T1R 0B4
(403) 362-5464
Emp Here 35
SIC 8211 Elementary and secondary schools

D-U-N-S 20-711-9897   (BR)
GRASSLANDS REGIONAL DIVISION 6
BROOKS JUNIOR HIGH SCHOOL
124 4 Ave E, Brooks, AB, T1R 0Z3
(403) 362-3524
Emp Here 40
SIC 8211 Elementary and secondary schools

D-U-N-S 20-653-9384   (BR)
GRASSLANDS REGIONAL DIVISION 6
BOW CITY HUTTERIAN COLONY SCHOOL
Gd Stn Main, Brooks, AB, T1R 1E4
(403) 362-3378
Emp Here 40
SIC 8211 Elementary and secondary schools

D-U-N-S 20-827-2161   (SL)
GRID DEVELOPMENTS LTD
HERITAGE INN HOTEL AND CONVENTION CENTRE
1217 2 St W, Brooks, AB, T1R 1P7
(403) 362-6666
Emp Here 60   *Sales* 2,626,585
SIC 7011 Hotels and motels

D-U-N-S 20-002-8889   (BR)
JBS CANADA INC
LAKESIDE PACKERS
(*Suby of* Tyson Foods, Inc.)
Gd Stn Main, Brooks, AB, T1R 1E4
(403) 362-3457
Emp Here 2,400
SIC 2011 Meat packing plants

D-U-N-S 25-266-6110   (BR)
MNP LLP

247 1st St W, Brooks, AB, T1R 1C1
(403) 362-8909
Emp Here 20
SIC 8721 Accounting, auditing, and bookkeeping

D-U-N-S 20-004-6477   (BR)
MEDICINE HAT COLLEGE
BROOKS CAMPUS
200 Horticultural Station Rd E, Brooks, AB, T1R 1E5
(403) 362-1677
Emp Here 40
SIC 8222 Junior colleges

D-U-N-S 20-200-0688   (BR)
NABORS DRILLING CANADA LIMITED
NABORS PRODUCTION SERVICES, DIV OF
Gd Stn Main, Brooks, AB, T1R 1E4
(403) 362-6600
Emp Here 112
SIC 1389 Oil and gas field services, nec

D-U-N-S 24-961-6822   (BR)
NEWALTA CORPORATION
Gd Stn Main, Brooks, AB, T1R 1E4
(403) 362-4266
Emp Here 21
SIC 4953 Refuse systems

D-U-N-S 24-051-9392   (BR)
NINE ENERGY CANADA INC
IPS
349 Wells St, Brooks, AB, T1R 1B9

Emp Here 50
SIC 1389 Oil and gas field services, nec

D-U-N-S 20-711-1951   (BR)
PRAIRIE LAND REGIONAL DIVISION 25
BARRIE CREEK COMMUNITY SCHOOL
Rr 2 Stn Main, Brooks, AB, T1R 1E2

Emp Here 50
SIC 8211 Elementary and secondary schools

D-U-N-S 24-674-2423   (BR)
ROCKWELL SERVICING INC
ENSIGN ROCKWELL SERVICING
289 Aquaduct Dr E, Brooks, AB, T1R 1B6
(403) 362-3346
Emp Here 60
SIC 1389 Oil and gas field services, nec

D-U-N-S 20-439-5743   (SL)
SMITH TRUCKING SERVICE (1976) LTD
1 Tree Rd, Brooks, AB, T1R 1B6
(403) 362-4071
Emp Here 20   *Sales* 1,605,135
SIC 4212 Local trucking, without storage

D-U-N-S 25-271-0629   (BR)
SOBEYS WEST INC
SAFEWAY
550 Cassils Rd W Suite 100, Brooks, AB, T1R 0W3
(403) 362-6851
Emp Here 85
SIC 5411 Grocery stores

D-U-N-S 25-369-4186   (SL)
TAZ WELL SERVICING LTD
303 8 St E, Brooks, AB, T1R 1B8

Emp Here 25   *Sales* 9,536,300
SIC 1381 Drilling oil and gas wells

D-U-N-S 25-967-8316   (BR)
TRICAN WELL SERVICE LTD
390 Aquaduct Dr, Brooks, AB, T1R 1B9
(403) 362-5050
Emp Here 40
SIC 1389 Oil and gas field services, nec

D-U-N-S 20-916-2317   (BR)
WAL-MART CANADA CORP
WALMART
917 3 St W Suite 3658, Brooks, AB, T1R 1L5

(403) 793-2111
Emp Here 100
SIC 5199 Nondurable goods, nec

Bruderheim, AB T0B

D-U-N-S 20-281-5809   (BR)
BRUDERHEIM ENERGY TERMINAL LTD
(*Suby of* Cenovus Energy Inc)
555018 Range Road 202, Bruderheim, AB, T0B 0S0
(403) 604-6605
Emp Here 60
SIC 5169 Chemicals and allied products, nec

D-U-N-S 24-344-0307   (BR)
SUPERIOR PLUS LP
Gd, Bruderheim, AB, T0B 0S0
(780) 796-3900
Emp Here 26
SIC 2819 Industrial inorganic chemicals, nec

Buck Lake, AB T0C

D-U-N-S 20-070-2590   (BR)
PENN WEST PETROLEUM LTD
Gd, Buck Lake, AB, T0C 0T0
(780) 388-3740
Emp Here 30
SIC 1389 Oil and gas field services, nec

D-U-N-S 20-260-1142   (BR)
WETASKIWIN REGIONAL PUBLIC SCHOOLS
BUCK MOUNTAIN CENTRAL SCHOOL
(*Suby of* Wetaskiwin Regional Public Schools)
Gd, Buck Lake, AB, T0C 0T0
(780) 388-3900
Emp Here 26
SIC 8211 Elementary and secondary schools

Buffalo Head Prairie, AB T0H

D-U-N-S 20-655-3369   (BR)
FORT VERMILION SCHOOL DIVISON 52
BUFFALO HEAD PRAIRIE SCHOOL
(*Suby of* Fort Vermilion School Divison 52)
Gd, Buffalo Head Prairie, AB, T0H 4A0
(780) 928-2282
Emp Here 22
SIC 8211 Elementary and secondary schools

Burdett, AB T0K

D-U-N-S 20-654-1026   (BR)
PRAIRIE ROSE SCHOOL DIVISION NO 8
BURDETT SCHOOL
610 Main St, Burdett, AB, T0K 0J0
(403) 833-3841
Emp Here 25
SIC 8211 Elementary and secondary schools

Cadotte Lake, AB T0H

D-U-N-S 20-653-3106   (BR)
NORTHLAND SCHOOL DIVISION 61
LITTLE BUFFALO SCHOOL
Gd, Cadotte Lake, AB, T0H 0N0
(780) 629-3950
Emp Here 21
SIC 8211 Elementary and secondary schools

Calgary, AB T1X

D-U-N-S 24-126-0251   (BR)
ALBERTA CONFERENCE OF THE SEVENTH-DAY ADVENTISTS CHURCH
GARDEN ROAD CHURCH
155 100 St Ne, Calgary, AB, T1X 0L4
(403) 280-3500
Emp Here 30
SIC 8661 Religious organizations

D-U-N-S 20-831-6414   (BR)
MEMORIAL GARDENS CANADA LIMITED
MOUNTAIN VIEW MEMORIAL GARDENS
1515 100 St Se, Calgary, AB, T1X 0L4
(403) 272-9824
Emp Here 40
SIC 7261 Funeral service and crematories

Calgary, AB T1Y

D-U-N-S 25-519-8301   (BR)
1009833 ALBERTA LTD
PETLAND
3363 26 Ave Ne, Calgary, AB, T1Y 6L4
(403) 543-7711
Emp Here 40
SIC 5999 Miscellaneous retail stores, nec

D-U-N-S 24-325-0946   (BR)
1221295 ONTARIO INC
ALLIANCE GROUP
3424 26 St Ne Unit 3, Calgary, AB, T1Y 4T7
(403) 692-6283
Emp Here 60
SIC 7361 Employment agencies

D-U-N-S 20-305-5251   (BR)
668824 ALBERTA LTD
VISIONS THE BEST NAME IN ELECTRONICS
2930 32 Ave Ne, Calgary, AB, T1Y 5J4
(403) 250-9107
Emp Here 25
SIC 5065 Electronic parts and equipment, nec

D-U-N-S 25-922-4897   (SL)
689109 ALBERTA LTD
ARBY'S RESTAURANTS
(*Suby of* Hanson Restaurants Inc)
2791 32 Ave Ne, Calgary, AB, T1Y 2G1
(403) 291-2229
Emp Here 20   *Sales* 605,574
SIC 5812 Eating places

D-U-N-S 24-318-8682   (BR)
ALS CANADA LTD
ALS LABRATORY GROUP
2559 29 St Ne, Calgary, AB, T1Y 7B5
(403) 407-1800
Emp Here 30
SIC 8731 Commercial physical research

D-U-N-S 24-334-3238   (BR)
ATCO GAS AND PIPELINES LTD
3055 37 Ave Ne, Calgary, AB, T1Y 6A2
(403) 219-8600
Emp Here 20
SIC 4923 Gas transmission and distribution

D-U-N-S 25-272-0144   (SL)
ABM COLLEGE
3880 29 St Ne Suite 200, Calgary, AB, T1Y 6B6
(403) 719-4300
Emp Here 49   *Sales* 5,107,249
SIC 8221 Colleges and universities
Prin Mohammad Baten

D-U-N-S 20-966-6432   (BR)
ALBERTA MOTOR ASSOCIATION
A M A
3650 20 Ave Ne, Calgary, AB, T1Y 6E8

(403) 590-0001
Emp Here 50
SIC 8699 Membership organizations, nec

D-U-N-S 20-703-7610   (BR)
BAILEY METAL PRODUCTS LIMITED
(*Suby of* Bailey-Hunt Limited)
3924 27 St Ne, Calgary, AB, T1Y 5K7
(403) 248-3536
Emp Here 20
SIC 3444 Sheet Metalwork

D-U-N-S 24-757-4841   (BR)
BANK OF NOVA SCOTIA, THE
SCOTIABANK
2220 68 St Ne Suite 600, Calgary, AB, T1Y 6Y7
(403) 299-3090
Emp Here 20
SIC 6021 National commercial banks

D-U-N-S 20-300-5462   (BR)
BANK OF MONTREAL
BMO
2555 32 St Ne Suite 150, Calgary, AB, T1Y 7J6
(403) 234-1715
Emp Here 20
SIC 6021 National commercial banks

D-U-N-S 20-589-5027   (BR)
BANQUE TORONTO-DOMINION, LA
TD CANADA TRUST
(*Suby of* Toronto-Dominion Bank, The)
2045 34 St Ne, Calgary, AB, T1Y 6Z2
(403) 292-1254
Emp Here 20
SIC 6021 National commercial banks

D-U-N-S 24-363-3802   (BR)
BEST BUY CANADA LTD
BEST BUY
(*Suby of* Best Buy Co., Inc.)
3221 Sunridge Way Ne Suite 500, Calgary, AB, T1Y 7M4
(403) 717-1000
Emp Here 20
SIC 5999 Miscellaneous retail stores, nec

D-U-N-S 24-804-3411   (SL)
BRADSTREET IRONWORKS INC
(*Suby of* Canadian Test Case 168 Inc.)
75 Templehill Dr Ne Unit 7, Calgary, AB, T1Y 4C4

Emp Here 20   *Sales* 5,202,480
SIC 3533 Oil and gas field machinery
Pr Pr Carl Jones
   Peter Smith

D-U-N-S 25-000-6921   (BR)
CALGARY BOARD OF EDUCATION
CECIL SWANSON ELEMENTARY SCHOOL
4820 Rundlewood Dr Ne, Calgary, AB, T1Y 5V9
(403) 777-6690
Emp Here 45
SIC 8211 Elementary and secondary schools

D-U-N-S 20-590-8002   (BR)
CALGARY BOARD OF EDUCATION
MONTEREY PARK SCHOOL
7400 California Blvd Ne, Calgary, AB, T1Y 6R2
(403) 777-7233
Emp Here 40
SIC 8211 Elementary and secondary schools

D-U-N-S 20-713-1538   (BR)
CALGARY BOARD OF EDUCATION
PINERIDGE SCHOOL
1927 61 St Ne, Calgary, AB, T1Y 4W6
(403) 777-6750
Emp Here 30
SIC 8211 Elementary and secondary schools

D-U-N-S 25-011-7736   (BR)
CALGARY BOARD OF EDUCATION
LESTER B. PEARSON SENIOR HIGH SCHOOL
3020 52 St Ne, Calgary, AB, T1Y 5P4
(403) 280-6565
Emp Here 81
SIC 8211 Elementary and secondary schools

D-U-N-S 20-591-1766   (BR)
CALGARY BOARD OF EDUCATION
ANNIE FOOTE SCHOOL
6320 Temple Dr Ne, Calgary, AB, T1Y 5V5
(403) 777-6680
Emp Here 25
SIC 8211 Elementary and secondary schools

D-U-N-S 20-591-1691   (BR)
CALGARY BOARD OF EDUCATION
ANNIE GALE JUNIOR HIGH SCHOOL
577 Whiteridge Way Ne, Calgary, AB, T1Y 4S8
(403) 777-7680
Emp Here 25
SIC 8211 Elementary and secondary schools

D-U-N-S 25-269-6836   (BR)
CALGARY BOARD OF EDUCATION
DR GORDON HIGGINS JUNIOR HIGH SCHOOL
155 Rundlehill Dr Ne, Calgary, AB, T1Y 2W9
(403) 777-7060
Emp Here 40
SIC 8211 Elementary and secondary schools

D-U-N-S 25-269-8931   (BR)
CALGARY BOARD OF EDUCATION
CLARENCE SANSOM JUNIOR HIGH-SCHOOL
5840 24 Ave Ne, Calgary, AB, T1Y 6G4
(403) 777-7700
Emp Here 50
SIC 8211 Elementary and secondary schools

D-U-N-S 20-713-1637   (BR)
CALGARY BOARD OF EDUCATION
CHIEF JUSTICE MILVAIN ELEMENTARY SCHOOL
3428 42 St Ne, Calgary, AB, T1Y 6A3
(403) 777-6700
Emp Here 50
SIC 8211 Elementary and secondary schools

D-U-N-S 20-591-1741   (BR)
CALGARY BOARD OF EDUCATION
DOUGLAS HARKNESS COMMUNITY SCHOOL
6203 24 Ave Ne, Calgary, AB, T1Y 2C5
(403) 777-6720
Emp Here 25
SIC 8211 Elementary and secondary schools

D-U-N-S 20-591-1436   (BR)
CALGARY BOARD OF EDUCATION
RUNDLE SCHOOL
4120 Rundlehorn Dr Ne, Calgary, AB, T1Y 4W9
(403) 777-6760
Emp Here 25
SIC 8211 Elementary and secondary schools

D-U-N-S 20-574-8101   (BR)
CALGARY ROMAN CATHOLIC SEPARATE SCHOOL DISTRICT #1
ST. PATRICK SCHOOL
6006 Rundlehorn Dr Ne, Calgary, AB, T1Y 2X1
(403) 500-2076
Emp Here 21
SIC 8211 Elementary and secondary schools

D-U-N-S 25-450-4376   (BR)
CALGARY ROMAN CATHOLIC SEPARATE SCHOOL DISTRICT #1
ST. RUPERT SCHOOL
111 Rundlehill Dr Ne, Calgary, AB, T1Y 2W9
(403) 500-2044
Emp Here 25
SIC 8211 Elementary and secondary schools

D-U-N-S 20-294-0008   (BR)

CALGARY ROMAN CATHOLIC SEPARATE SCHOOL DISTRICT #1
SAINT ROSE OF LIMA JUNIOR HIGH SCHOOL
2419 50 St Ne, Calgary, AB, T1Y 1Z5
(403) 285-3800
Emp Here 34
SIC 8211 Elementary and secondary schools

D-U-N-S 20-034-2777   (BR)
CALGARY ROMAN CATHOLIC SEPARATE SCHOOL DISTRICT #1
ST. THOMAS MORE SCHOOL
6110 Temple Dr Ne, Calgary, AB, T1Y 5V4
(403) 500-2081
Emp Here 35
SIC 8211 Elementary and secondary schools

D-U-N-S 25-011-7348   (BR)
CALGARY ROMAN CATHOLIC SEPARATE SCHOOL DISTRICT #1
FATHER SCOLLEN ELEMENTARY JUNIOR HIGH SCHOOL
6839 Temple Dr Ne, Calgary, AB, T1Y 5N4
(403) 500-2088
Emp Here 35
SIC 8211 Elementary and secondary schools

D-U-N-S 20-028-4110   (BR)
CALGARY ROMAN CATHOLIC SEPARATE SCHOOL DISTRICT #1
ST. WILFRID SCHOOL
4225 44 Ave Ne, Calgary, AB, T1Y 4Y1
(403) 500-2077
Emp Here 35
SIC 8211 Elementary and secondary schools

D-U-N-S 20-549-3781   (SL)
CANADIAN CUSTOM CABLE INC
3823 29 St Ne, Calgary, AB, T1Y 6B5
(403) 250-2271
Emp Here 26   *Sales* 6,087,000
SIC 3496 Miscellaneous fabricated wire products
Pr Pr Steve Cunningham
Dir Jasdip Dhaliwal
   Colin Corasiniti

D-U-N-S 25-303-5877   (BR)
CANADIAN IMPERIAL BANK OF COMMERCE
CIBC
3070 Sunridge Blvd Ne, Calgary, AB, T1Y 7G6
(403) 221-6018
Emp Here 35
SIC 6021 National commercial banks

D-U-N-S 20-575-8563   (BR)
CANADIAN WESTERN BANK
2810 32 Ave Ne, Calgary, AB, T1Y 5J4
(403) 250-8838
Emp Here 22
SIC 6021 National commercial banks

D-U-N-S 25-287-8335   (HQ)
CANADREAM INC
CANADREAM CAMPERS
(*Suby of* Canadream Corporation)
2510 27 St Ne, Calgary, AB, T1Y 7G1
(403) 291-1000
Emp Here 30   *Emp Total* 122
Sales 4,613,520
SIC 7519 Utility trailer rental

D-U-N-S 20-302-5791   (BR)
CERIDIAN CANADA LTD
2618 Hopewell Pl Ne Suite 310, Calgary, AB, T1Y 7J2
(403) 262-6035
Emp Here 80
SIC 8721 Accounting, auditing, and book-keeping

D-U-N-S 25-315-4066   (BR)
COMPUGEN INC
3510 29 St Ne Suite 115, Calgary, AB, T1Y 7E5

(403) 571-4400
Emp Here 30
SIC 5045 Computers, peripherals, and software

D-U-N-S 20-034-5176   (BR)
CONNECT FIRST CREDIT UNION LTD
FIRST CALGARY FINANCIAL
2640 52 St Ne Suite 116, Calgary, AB, T1Y 3R6
(403) 736-4680
Emp Here 22
SIC 6062 State credit unions

D-U-N-S 25-287-5372   (BR)
COSTCO WHOLESALE CANADA LTD
COSTCO
(*Suby of* Costco Wholesale Corporation)
2853 32 St Ne, Calgary, AB, T1Y 6T7
(403) 299-1600
Emp Here 350
SIC 5099 Durable goods, nec

D-U-N-S 20-720-1922   (BR)
CREATIVE DOOR SERVICES LTD
3740 27 St Ne Suite 8, Calgary, AB, T1Y 5E2
(888) 621-3667
Emp Here 40
SIC 1751 Carpentry work

D-U-N-S 20-232-8352   (BR)
DIMENSION 3 HOSPITALITY CORPORATION
DAYS INN CALGARY AIRPORT
2799 Sunridge Way Ne, Calgary, AB, T1Y 7K7
(403) 250-3297
Emp Here 20
SIC 7011 Hotels and motels

D-U-N-S 20-715-8648   (BR)
EFW RADIOLOGY
2151 32 St Ne Suite 80, Calgary, AB, T1Y 7G3
(403) 209-3209
Emp Here 200
SIC 8071 Medical laboratories

D-U-N-S 24-340-0897   (BR)
FGL SPORTS LTD
SPORT-CHEK
2525 36 St Ne Unit 250a, Calgary, AB, T1Y 5T4
(403) 285-2435
Emp Here 40
SIC 5941 Sporting goods and bicycle shops

D-U-N-S 20-129-2471   (HQ)
FIELD AVIATION COMPANY INC
4300 26 St Ne Unit 125, Calgary, AB, T1Y 7H7
(403) 516-8200
Emp Here 85   *Emp Total* 2
Sales 27,027,031
SIC 1799 Special trade contractors, nec
Pr John Mactaggart
   Christina Friesen

D-U-N-S 20-174-3577   (BR)
GOVERNMENT OF THE PROVINCE OF ALBERTA
2675 36 St Ne, Calgary, AB, T1Y 6H6

Emp Here 35
SIC 8093 Specialty outpatient clinics, nec

D-U-N-S 20-270-9767   (BR)
GROUPE PAGES JAUNES CORP
YELLOW PAGES
2891 Sunridge Way Ne Suite 100, Calgary, AB, T1Y 7K7
(604) 268-4578
Emp Here 20
SIC 2741 Miscellaneous publishing

D-U-N-S 24-309-2736   (BR)
GROUPE PAGES JAUNES CORP
2891 Sunridge Way Ne Suite 230, Calgary, AB, T1Y 7K7

Emp Here 180
SIC 4899 Communication services, nec

D-U-N-S 20-645-1452   (BR)
HENRY SCHEIN CANADA, INC
4303 26 St Ne Suite 138, Calgary, AB, T1Y 7K2
(403) 640-1422
Emp Here 23
SIC 5047 Medical and hospital equipment

D-U-N-S 20-698-6429   (BR)
HUDSON'S BAY COMPANY
HOME OUTFITTERS
3333 Sunridge Way Ne, Calgary, AB, T1Y 7H5

Emp Here 100
SIC 5311 Department stores

D-U-N-S 25-485-8004   (BR)
HUDSON'S BAY COMPANY
BAY, THE
2525 36 St Ne, Calgary, AB, T1Y 5T4
(403) 261-0759
Emp Here 130
SIC 5311 Department stores

D-U-N-S 20-300-4994   (BR)
INDIGO BOOKS & MUSIC INC
CHAPTERS
(*Suby of* Indigo Books & Music Inc)
2555 32 St Ne Suite 500, Calgary, AB, T1Y 7J6
(403) 250-9171
Emp Here 202
SIC 5942 Book stores

D-U-N-S 20-825-1561   (BR)
KLOHN CRIPPEN BERGER LTD
IEG CONSULTANTS
(*Suby of* Klohn Crippen Berger Holdings Ltd)
2618 Hopewell Pl Ne Suite 500, Calgary, AB, T1Y 7J7
(403) 648-4244
Emp Here 90
SIC 8711 Engineering services

D-U-N-S 20-077-1269   (BR)
KONE INC
3510 29 St Ne Suite 115, Calgary, AB, T1Y 7E5
(403) 275-5650
Emp Here 36
SIC 1796 Installing building equipment

D-U-N-S 24-421-0535   (BR)
LIFEMARK HEALTH MANAGEMENT INC
LIFEMARK HEALTH MANAGEMENT INC
(*Suby of* Audax Group, L.P.)
2121 29 St Ne, Calgary, AB, T1Y 7H8
(403) 297-9500
Emp Here 65
SIC 8741 Management services

D-U-N-S 25-270-1446   (BR)
LOBLAWS INC
REAL CANADIAN SUPERSTORE
3575 20 Ave Ne, Calgary, AB, T1Y 6R3
(403) 280-8222
Emp Here 400
SIC 5411 Grocery stores

D-U-N-S 25-273-1690   (BR)
LONDON DRUGS LIMITED
3545 32 Ave Ne, Calgary, AB, T1Y 6M6
(403) 571-4931
Emp Here 100
SIC 5912 Drug stores and proprietary stores

D-U-N-S 25-091-4699   (BR)
LOWE'S COMPANIES CANADA, ULC
2909 Sunridge Way Ne, Calgary, AB, T1Y 7K7
(403) 277-0044
Emp Here 130
SIC 5211 Lumber and other building materials

D-U-N-S 25-290-7910   (BR)
MARK'S WORK WEARHOUSE LTD
3014 Sunridge Blvd Ne, Calgary, AB, T1Y 7G6
(403) 250-9942
Emp Here 25

SIC 5651 Family clothing stores

D-U-N-S 25-596-0734   (BR)
MATRIX LOGISTICS SERVICES LIMITED
2525 29 St Ne, Calgary, AB, T1Y 7B5
(403) 291-9292
Emp Here 180
SIC 4225 General warehousing and storage

D-U-N-S 20-038-3565   (BR)
MEDICENTRES CANADA INC
HORIZON MEDICENTRES
3508 32 Ave Ne Suite 401, Calgary, AB, T1Y 6J2
(403) 291-5589
Emp Here 20
SIC 8011 Offices and clinics of medical doctors

D-U-N-S 20-285-9260   (BR)
MEMORY EXPRESS INC
3305 32 St Ne, Calgary, AB, T1Y 5X7

Emp Here 42
SIC 5734 Computer and software stores

D-U-N-S 20-744-5268   (BR)
METROPOLITAN CALGARY FOUNDATION
GILCHRIST MANOR
3003 56 St Ne Suite 312, Calgary, AB, T1Y 4P5

Emp Here 20
SIC 8322 Individual and family services

D-U-N-S 20-037-8573   (SL)
MUSLIM COMMUNITY FOUNDATION OF CALGARY
CALGARY ISLAMIC SCHOOL
2612 37 Ave Ne, Calgary, AB, T1Y 5L2
(403) 219-0991
Emp Here 52   *Sales* 3,502,114
SIC 8211 Elementary and secondary schools

D-U-N-S 20-522-1179   (SL)
OYO GEO SPACE CANADA INC
(*Suby of* Geospace Technologies Corporation)
2735 37 Ave Ne, Calgary, AB, T1Y 5R8
(403) 250-9600
Emp Here 34   *Sales* 2,772,507
SIC 7359 Equipment rental and leasing, nec

D-U-N-S 24-003-9904   (BR)
OLD NAVY (CANADA) INC
(*Suby of* The Gap Inc)
2525 36 St Ne Suite 3, Calgary, AB, T1Y 5T4
(403) 590-9501
Emp Here 40
SIC 5651 Family clothing stores

D-U-N-S 24-357-0921   (BR)
PCC COMMUNICATIONS INC
(*Suby of* PCC Communications Inc)
4300 26 St Ne Suite 125, Calgary, AB, T1Y 7H7

Emp Here 20
SIC 4899 Communication services, nec

D-U-N-S 25-316-4339   (BR)
PASLEY, MAX ENTERPRISES LIMITED
MCDONALD'S RESTAURANTS
(*Suby of* Pasley, Max Enterprises Limited)
2740 32 Ave Ne, Calgary, AB, T1Y 5S5
(403) 291-0256
Emp Here 73
SIC 5812 Eating places

D-U-N-S 25-316-4107   (BR)
PASLEY, MAX ENTERPRISES LIMITED
MCDONALD'S RESTAURANTS 13861
(*Suby of* Pasley, Max Enterprises Limited)
1920 68 St, Calgary, AB, T1Y 6Y7
(403) 280-6388
Emp Here 90
SIC 5812 Eating places

D-U-N-S 20-354-1375   (BR)

PASLEY, MAX ENTERPRISES LIMITED
MCDONALD'S RESTAURANT
(*Suby* of Pasley, Max Enterprises Limited)
2665 Sunridge Way Ne, Calgary, AB, T1Y 7K7
(403) 663-6300
Emp Here 65
SIC 5812 Eating places

D-U-N-S 24-674-9410   (BR)
PATTERSON DENTAIRE CANADA INC
4152 27 St Ne Suite 112, Calgary, AB, T1Y 7J8
(403) 250-9838
Emp Here 50
SIC 5047 Medical and hospital equipment

D-U-N-S 20-316-6793   (SL)
PINEHILL MANAGEMENT CORP
CHEESECAKE CAFE, THE
2121 36 St Ne, Calgary, AB, T1Y 5S3

Emp Here 100   *Sales* 2,991,389
SIC 5812 Eating places

D-U-N-S 20-579-6415   (BR)
PITNEY BOWES OF CANADA LTD
(*Suby* of Pitney Bowes Inc.)
2150 29 St Ne Unit 30, Calgary, AB, T1Y 7G4
(403) 219-0536
Emp Here 40
SIC 5044 Office equipment

D-U-N-S 25-520-5775   (BR)
PRAIRIE LUBE LTD
MR LUBE
(*Suby* of Gruent Holdings Ltd)
3315 32 Ave Ne, Calgary, AB, T1Y 6M5
(403) 216-6973
Emp Here 20
SIC 5541 Gasoline service stations

D-U-N-S 24-300-0130   (BR)
PRINCESS AUTO LTD
2850 Hopewell Pl Ne, Calgary, AB, T1Y 7J7
(403) 250-1133
Emp Here 30
SIC 5085 Industrial supplies

D-U-N-S 20-825-5968   (SL)
RAM CARPET SERVICES LTD
RAM CLEANING SERVICES
3611 27 St Ne Suite 1, Calgary, AB, T1Y 5E4
(403) 291-1051
Emp Here 50   *Sales* 1,240,332
SIC 7217 Carpet and upholstery cleaning

D-U-N-S 24-441-2037   (HQ)
RAWLCO COMMUNICATIONS CAPITAL LTD
2723 37 Ave Ne Suite 220, Calgary, AB, T1Y 5R8
(403) 451-9893
Emp Here 50   *Emp Total* 80
Sales 17,079,840
SIC 4832 Radio broadcasting stations
Pr Pr Gordon Rawlinson

D-U-N-S 20-770-1686   (BR)
REHOBOTH A CHRISTIAN ASSOCIATION FOR THE MENTALLY HANDICAPPED OF ALBERTA
3505 29 St Ne Suite 106, Calgary, AB, T1Y 5W4
(403) 250-7333
Emp Here 100
SIC 8331 Job training and related services

D-U-N-S 20-070-4281   (BR)
ROYAL BANK OF CANADA
RBC
(*Suby* of Royal Bank Of Canada)
2640 52 St Ne Unit 100, Calgary, AB, T1Y 3R6
(403) 292-3355
Emp Here 38
SIC 6021 National commercial banks

D-U-N-S 20-532-4820   (BR)
SEARS CANADA INC

SUNRIDGE SEARS HOME STORE
3350 Sunridge Way Ne, Calgary, AB, T1Y 7K5
(403) 219-0320
Emp Here 30
SIC 5311 Department stores

D-U-N-S 24-007-1493   (SL)
SENTINEL PROTECTION SERVICES LTD
3132 26 St Ne Suite 335, Calgary, AB, T1Y 6Z1
(403) 237-8485
Emp Here 65   *Sales* 2,042,900
SIC 7381 Detective and armored car services

D-U-N-S 20-133-9467   (SL)
SIGNATURE INTERPRETIVE & TRANSLA-TIVE SERVICES LTD
4608 26 Ave Ne, Calgary, AB, T1Y 2R8
(403) 590-6382
Emp Here 51   *Sales* 2,626,585
SIC 7389 Business services, nec

D-U-N-S 25-521-7846   (BR)
SINIL RESTAURANTS LTD
DAIRY QUEEN
(*Suby* of Sinil Restaurants Ltd)
3709 26 Ave Ne, Calgary, AB, T1Y 4S3
(403) 285-3799
Emp Here 23
SIC 5812 Eating places

D-U-N-S 25-087-8634   (BR)
SLEEP COUNTRY CANADA INC
SLEEP COUNTRY WAREHOUSE 95
2777 23 Ave Ne Unit 31, Calgary, AB, T1Y 7L6
(403) 569-7717
Emp Here 50
SIC 5712 Furniture stores

D-U-N-S 25-622-6259   (BR)
SMITTY'S CANADA LIMITED
SMITTY'S FAMILY RESTAURANT
2620 32 St Ne Suite 2612, Calgary, AB, T1Y 7L8
(403) 285-5656
Emp Here 28
SIC 5812 Eating places

D-U-N-S 25-271-0702   (BR)
SOBEYS WEST INC
SAFEWAY, DIV OF
3550 32 Ave Ne Suite 286, Calgary, AB, T1Y 6J2
(403) 291-2035
Emp Here 190
SIC 5411 Grocery stores

D-U-N-S 20-860-0721   (BR)
SOURCE (BELL) ELECTRONICS INC, THE
SOURCE, THE
2525 36 St Ne Unit 155, Calgary, AB, T1Y 5T4
(403) 590-0433
Emp Here 25
SIC 5999 Miscellaneous retail stores, nec

D-U-N-S 20-078-0997   (HQ)
SOUTHERN MUSIC LTD
SML ENTERTAINMENT
3605 32 St Ne, Calgary, AB, T1Y 5Y9
(403) 291-1666
Emp Here 40   *Emp Total* 3
Sales 7,255,933
SIC 7359 Equipment rental and leasing, nec
Pr Pr Anthony Fisher
VP VP Otto Fisher
Dir Dean Fisher

D-U-N-S 24-493-7710   (SL)
SOUTHERN PROPERTY RENTALS LTD
SOUTHERN MUSIC, DIV OF
3605 32 St Ne, Calgary, AB, T1Y 5Y9
(403) 291-1666
Emp Here 60   *Sales* 3,811,504
SIC 7993 Coin-operated amusement devices

D-U-N-S 24-300-3472   (BR)
STANTEC CONSULTING LTD
STANTEC CONSULTING

2886 Sunridge Way Ne Suite 130, Calgary, AB, T1Y 7H9
(403) 245-5661
Emp Here 86
SIC 8711 Engineering services

D-U-N-S 25-483-9764   (BR)
STAPLES CANADA INC
STAPLES THE BUSINESS DEPOT
(*Suby* of Staples, Inc.)
3030 32 Ave Ne, Calgary, AB, T1Y 7A9
(403) 735-6336
Emp Here 50
SIC 5943 Stationery stores

D-U-N-S 25-186-2702   (BR)
STARBUCKS COFFEE CANADA, INC
(*Suby* of Starbucks Corporation)
2555 32 St Ne Suite 500, Calgary, AB, T1Y 7J6
(403) 219-3501
Emp Here 23
SIC 5812 Eating places

D-U-N-S 24-330-3968   (BR)
STUART OLSON CONSTRUCTION LTD
INDUSTRIAL CONSTRUCTORS DIVISION
3545 32 Ave Ne Unit 235, Calgary, AB, T1Y 6M6
(403) 520-6565
Emp Here 30
SIC 1522 Residential construction, nec

D-U-N-S 20-119-7642   (BR)
TDG FURNITURE INC
ASHLEY HOME FUNITURE HOME STORE
2930 32 Ave Ne, Calgary, AB, T1Y 5J4
(403) 250-3166
Emp Here 20
SIC 5712 Furniture stores

D-U-N-S 25-451-0589   (BR)
TIPPET-RICHARDSON LIMITED
T R WESTCAM
2905 37 Ave Ne, Calgary, AB, T1Y 5Z9
(403) 299-9700
Emp Here 40
SIC 4214 Local trucking with storage

D-U-N-S 25-315-5071   (BR)
TORONTO-DOMINION BANK, THE
TD BANK
(*Suby* of Toronto-Dominion Bank, The)
2045 34th St Ne, Calgary, AB, T1Y 6Z2
(403) 292-1400
Emp Here 150
SIC 6021 National commercial banks

D-U-N-S 24-554-2790   (BR)
URBAN SYSTEMS LTD
2716 Sunridge Way Ne Suite 101, Calgary, AB, T1Y 0A5
(403) 291-1193
Emp Here 63
SIC 8711 Engineering services

D-U-N-S 20-176-3880   (BR)
VALUE VILLAGE STORES, INC
SAVERS
(*Suby* of Savers, Inc.)
3405 34 St Ne, Calgary, AB, T1Y 6T6
(403) 291-3323
Emp Here 85
SIC 5399 Miscellaneous general merchandise

D-U-N-S 20-447-9406   (HQ)
VARIPERM (CANADA) LIMITED
(*Suby* of Nurco Holdings Ltd.)
3424 26 St Ne Suite 10, Calgary, AB, T1Y 4T7
(403) 250-7263
Emp Here 30   *Emp Total* 1
Sales 11,779,113
SIC 5082 Construction and mining machinery
Dir William Nurcombe
Pr Pr James Nurcombe

D-U-N-S 20-008-3835   (BR)
WALMART CANADA LOGISTICS ULC

EXCEL
3400 39 Ave Ne, Calgary, AB, T1Y 7J4
(403) 250-3648
Emp Here 900
SIC 4225 General warehousing and storage

D-U-N-S 20-334-5389   (BR)
WENDY'S RESTAURANTS OF CANADA INC
WENDY'S
(*Suby* of The Wendy's Company)
3232 Sunridge Blvd Ne, Calgary, AB, T1Y 7G6
(403) 250-8990
Emp Here 35
SIC 5812 Eating places

D-U-N-S 25-272-1204   (BR)
WESTMONT HOSPITALITY MANAGEMENT LIMITED
TRAVELODGE
(*Suby* of Westmont Hospitality Management Limited)
2750 Sunridge Blvd Ne, Calgary, AB, T1Y 3C2
(403) 291-1260
Emp Here 40
SIC 7011 Hotels and motels

D-U-N-S 24-320-1824   (BR)
WINNERS MERCHANTS INTERNATIONAL L.P.
WINNERS
(*Suby* of The TJX Companies Inc)
3351 20 Ave Ne, Calgary, AB, T1Y 7A8
(403) 285-4949
Emp Here 30
SIC 5651 Family clothing stores

D-U-N-S 20-860-4160   (BR)
WINNERS MERCHANTS INTERNATIONAL L.P.
HOMESENSE
(*Suby* of The TJX Companies Inc)
3221 Sunridge Way Ne Suite 400, Calgary, AB, T1Y 7M4
(403) 250-2461
Emp Here 25
SIC 5651 Family clothing stores

D-U-N-S 24-840-4055   (HQ)
YIKES ENTERPRISES LTD
TIM HORTONS
(*Suby* of Yikes Enterprises Ltd)
3508 32 Ave Ne Unit 500, Calgary, AB, T1Y 6J2
(403) 291-2925
Emp Here 40   *Emp Total* 110
Sales 3,720,996
SIC 5461 Retail bakeries

Calgary, AB T2A

D-U-N-S 25-359-5516   (BR)
3856011 CANADA INC
BLOOMSTAR BOUQUET
1108 53 Ave Suite 105, Calgary, AB, T2A 1V5
(403) 250-5667
Emp Here 25
SIC 5193 Flowers and florists supplies

D-U-N-S 25-173-2566   (BR)
A & W FOOD SERVICES OF CANADA INC
A & W
3120 17 Ave Se, Calgary, AB, T2A 0P9
(403) 273-1373
Emp Here 26
SIC 5812 Eating places

D-U-N-S 24-158-0760   (BR)
AGRA FOUNDATIONS LIMITED
416 Monument Pl Se, Calgary, AB, T2A 1X3
(403) 272-5531
Emp Here 60
SIC 1794 Excavation work

D-U-N-S 24-103-2155   (BR)
ALBERTA TREASURY BRANCHES

ATB FINANCIAL
229 33 St Ne Suite 400, Calgary, AB, T2A 4Y6
(403) 974-6850
Emp Here 900
SIC 8742 Management consulting services

D-U-N-S 20-581-3277 (BR)
ALBERTA TREASURY BRANCHES
ATB FINANCIAL
3620 17 Ave Se, Calgary, AB, T2A 0R9
(403) 297-6507
Emp Here 30
SIC 6036 Savings institutions, except federal

D-U-N-S 20-702-8858 (BR)
ALBION FISHERIES LTD
3320 14 Ave Ne Suite 5, Calgary, AB, T2A 6J4
(403) 235-4531
Emp Here 32
SIC 5146 Fish and seafoods

D-U-N-S 25-734-0521 (BR)
ALL-CAN EXPRESS LTD
ACE COURIER SERVICES
3016 10 Ave Ne Suite 122, Calgary, AB, T2A 6A3
(403) 235-6464
Emp Here 30
SIC 7389 Business services, nec

D-U-N-S 20-833-4206 (SL)
AMBASSADOR LIMOUSINE SERVICE
316 Meridian Rd Se, Calgary, AB, T2A 1X2
(403) 299-4910
Emp Here 50   *Sales* 1,751,057
SIC 4111 Local and suburban transit

D-U-N-S 24-157-9770 (BR)
ARMY & NAVY DEPT. STORE LIMITED
1107 33 St Ne Unit 1, Calgary, AB, T2A 6T2
(403) 248-6660
Emp Here 40
SIC 5311 Department stores

D-U-N-S 20-254-7977 (BR)
AUTOPRO AUTOMATION CONSULTANTS LTD
525 28 St Se Suite 360, Calgary, AB, T2A 6W9
(403) 569-6480
Emp Here 100
SIC 8711 Engineering services

D-U-N-S 24-013-3892 (BR)
BLACK & MCDONALD LIMITED
1071 26 St Ne, Calgary, AB, T2A 6K8
(403) 235-0335
Emp Here 30
SIC 1711 Plumbing, heating, air-conditioning

D-U-N-S 24-348-2239 (BR)
BREWERS' DISTRIBUTOR LTD
B D L
(*Suby of* Brewers' Distributor Ltd)
2930 Centre Ave Ne, Calgary, AB, T2A 4Y2
(403) 531-1050
Emp Here 50
SIC 5181 Beer and ale

D-U-N-S 20-824-4749 (BR)
BRINK'S CANADA LIMITED
BRINK'S
(*Suby of* The Brink's Company)
640 28 St Ne Unit 8, Calgary, AB, T2A 6R3
(403) 272-2259
Emp Here 160
SIC 7381 Detective and armored car services

D-U-N-S 20-245-3499 (BR)
BUY-LOW FOODS LTD
200 52 St Ne Suite 11, Calgary, AB, T2A 4K8

Emp Here 20
SIC 5411 Grocery stores

D-U-N-S 20-573-1201 (SL)
C. HEAD LIMITED
CANADIAN TIRE ASSOCIATE STORE
3516 8 Ave Ne Suite 326, Calgary, AB, T2A

6K5
(403) 248-6400
Emp Here 120   *Sales* 11,527,791
SIC 5251 Hardware stores
Pr Carl Head

D-U-N-S 24-353-3234 (BR)
CSG SECURITY CORPORATION
CHUBB SECURITY SYSTEMS
(*Suby of* United Technologies Corporation)
1470 28 St Ne Suite 7, Calgary, AB, T2A 7W6
(403) 233-9191
Emp Here 25
SIC 6211 Security brokers and dealers

D-U-N-S 20-303-9342 (BR)
CALGARY BOARD OF EDUCATION
RADISSON PARK SCHOOL
2805 Radcliffe Dr Se, Calgary, AB, T2A 0C8
(403) 777-8070
Emp Here 30
SIC 8211 Elementary and secondary schools

D-U-N-S 25-325-8396 (BR)
CALGARY BOARD OF EDUCATION
G W SKENE ELEMENTARY SCHOOL
6226 Penbrooke Dr Se, Calgary, AB, T2A 6M7
(403) 777-8150
Emp Here 30
SIC 8211 Elementary and secondary schools

D-U-N-S 20-713-1421 (BR)
CALGARY BOARD OF EDUCATION
FOREST LAWN HIGH SCHOOL
1304 44 St Se, Calgary, AB, T2A 1M8
(403) 272-6665
Emp Here 110
SIC 8211 Elementary and secondary schools

D-U-N-S 25-011-7587 (BR)
CALGARY BOARD OF EDUCATION
JAMES, JACK HIGH SCHOOL
5105 8 Ave Se, Calgary, AB, T2A 4M1
(403) 248-4054
Emp Here 70
SIC 8211 Elementary and secondary schools

D-U-N-S 20-591-1253 (BR)
CALGARY BOARD OF EDUCATION
ABBEYDALE ELEMENTARY SCHOOL
320 Abergale Dr Ne, Calgary, AB, T2A 6W2
(403) 777-6970
Emp Here 35
SIC 8211 Elementary and secondary schools

D-U-N-S 20-590-7673 (BR)
CALGARY BOARD OF EDUCATION
PATRICK AIRLIE SCHOOL
1520 39 St Se, Calgary, AB, T2A 1H9
(403) 777-8220
Emp Here 30
SIC 8211 Elementary and secondary schools

D-U-N-S 20-713-1389 (BR)
CALGARY BOARD OF EDUCATION
ERNEST MORROW JUNIOR SCHOOL
1212 47 St Se, Calgary, AB, T2A 1R3
(403) 777-7800
Emp Here 50
SIC 8211 Elementary and secondary schools

D-U-N-S 20-713-1181 (BR)
CALGARY BOARD OF EDUCATION
KEELER SCHOOL
4807 Forego Ave Se, Calgary, AB, T2A 2C4
(403) 777-8180
Emp Here 50
SIC 8211 Elementary and secondary schools

D-U-N-S 20-713-1520 (BR)
CALGARY BOARD OF EDUCATION
CAPPY SMART ELEMENTARY SCHOOL
5808 Madigan Dr Se, Calgary, AB, T2A 4P5
(403) 777-8110
Emp Here 50
SIC 8211 Elementary and secondary schools

D-U-N-S 25-011-2125 (BR)

CALGARY BOARD OF EDUCATION
BOB EDWARDS JUNIOR HIGH SCHOOL
4424 Marlborough Dr Ne, Calgary, AB, T2A 2Z5
(403) 777-7770
Emp Here 42
SIC 8211 Elementary and secondary schools

D-U-N-S 20-591-1717 (BR)
CALGARY BOARD OF EDUCATION
DR. GLADYS MCKELVIE EGBERT COMMUNITY SCHOOL
6033 Madigan Dr Ne, Calgary, AB, T2A 5G9
(403) 777-7780
Emp Here 25
SIC 8211 Elementary and secondary schools

D-U-N-S 20-591-1584 (BR)
CALGARY BOARD OF EDUCATION
CHRIS AKKERMAN ELEMENTARY SCHOOL
5004 Marbank Dr Ne, Calgary, AB, T2A 3J6
(403) 777-8120
Emp Here 58
SIC 8211 Elementary and secondary schools

D-U-N-S 25-452-8474 (BR)
CALGARY BOARD OF EDUCATION
SIR WILFRID LAURIER JUNIOR HIGH SCHOOL
819 32 St Se, Calgary, AB, T2A 0Y9
(403) 777-7370
Emp Here 37
SIC 8211 Elementary and secondary schools

D-U-N-S 20-713-1199 (BR)
CALGARY BOARD OF EDUCATION
MARLBOROUGH SCHOOL
4711 Maryvale Dr Ne, Calgary, AB, T2A 3A1
(403) 777-8190
Emp Here 50
SIC 8211 Elementary and secondary schools

D-U-N-S 20-591-1667 (BR)
CALGARY BOARD OF EDUCATION
PENBROOKE MEADOWS SCHOOL
5645 Pensacola Cres Se, Calgary, AB, T2A 2G4
(403) 777-8230
Emp Here 25
SIC 8211 Elementary and secondary schools

D-U-N-S 20-713-1462 (BR)
CALGARY BOARD OF EDUCATION
ROLAND MICHENER ELEMENTARY SCHOOL
5958 4 Ave Ne, Calgary, AB, T2A 4B1
(403) 777-8240
Emp Here 50
SIC 8211 Elementary and secondary schools

D-U-N-S 25-622-0666 (BR)
CALGARY CO-OPERATIVE ASSOCIATION LIMITED
FOREST LAWN CALGARY CO-OP, DIV
3330 17 Ave Se Suite 5, Calgary, AB, T2A 0P9
(403) 299-4461
Emp Here 250
SIC 5411 Grocery stores

D-U-N-S 20-027-4863 (BR)
CALGARY ROMAN CATHOLIC SEPARATE SCHOOL DISTRICT #1
ST. KATERI TEKAKWITHA SCHOOL
1005 Abbotsford Dr Ne, Calgary, AB, T2A 7N5
(403) 500-2090
Emp Here 40
SIC 8211 Elementary and secondary schools

D-U-N-S 20-043-6470 (BR)
CALGARY ROMAN CATHOLIC SEPARATE SCHOOL DISTRICT #1
HOLY FAMILY ELEMENTARY SCHOOL
904 32 St Se, Calgary, AB, T2A 0Z1
(403) 500-2054
Emp Here 20
SIC 8211 Elementary and secondary schools

D-U-N-S 20-034-2553 (BR)

CALGARY ROMAN CATHOLIC SEPARATE SCHOOL DISTRICT #1
ST. MARK ELEMENTARY SCHOOL
4589 Marbank Dr Ne, Calgary, AB, T2A 3V8
(403) 500-2068
Emp Here 30
SIC 8211 Elementary and secondary schools

D-U-N-S 25-450-4400 (BR)
CALGARY ROMAN CATHOLIC SEPARATE SCHOOL DISTRICT #1
ST. MARTHA SCHOOL
6020 4 Ave Ne, Calgary, AB, T2A 4B1
(403) 500-2074
Emp Here 50
SIC 8211 Elementary and secondary schools

D-U-N-S 20-169-8755 (BR)
CALGARY ROMAN CATHOLIC SEPARATE SCHOOL DISTRICT #1
ECOLE HOLY REDEEMER SCHOOL
708 47 St Se, Calgary, AB, T2A 1P8
(403) 500-2034
Emp Here 30
SIC 8211 Elementary and secondary schools

D-U-N-S 20-651-5152 (BR)
CALGARY ROMAN CATHOLIC SEPARATE SCHOOL DISTRICT #1
BISHOP KIDD SCHOOL
1420 28 St Se, Calgary, AB, T2A 0Y8
(403) 500-2052
Emp Here 27
SIC 8211 Elementary and secondary schools

D-U-N-S 20-028-4003 (BR)
CALGARY ROMAN CATHOLIC SEPARATE SCHOOL DISTRICT #1
HOLY TRINITY ELEMENTARY SCHOOL
1717 41 St Se, Calgary, AB, T2A 1L2
(403) 500-2032
Emp Here 22
SIC 8211 Elementary and secondary schools

D-U-N-S 20-588-8584 (BR)
CANADIAN IMPERIAL BANK OF COMMERCE
CIBC
122 17th Ave Sw, Calgary, AB, T2A 0R1
(403) 974-6371
Emp Here 20
SIC 6021 National commercial banks

D-U-N-S 20-588-8659 (BR)
CANADIAN IMPERIAL BANK OF COMMERCE
CIBC
200 52 St Ne Suite 2, Calgary, AB, T2A 4K8

Emp Here 20
SIC 6021 National commercial banks

D-U-N-S 24-098-8514 (HQ)
CARDTRONICS CANADA OPERATIONS INC
1420 28 St Ne Suite 6, Calgary, AB, T2A 7W6
(403) 207-1500
Emp Here 100   *Emp Total* 194
Sales 12,622,201
SIC 8741 Management services
Pr Pr Jeffrey J Smith

D-U-N-S 20-991-0132 (HQ)
CHECKER CABS LTD
CHECKER COURIER
316 Meridian Rd Se, Calgary, AB, T2A 1X2
(403) 299-4999
Emp Here 90   *Emp Total* 120
Sales 10,308,387
SIC 4212 Local trucking, without storage
Pr Pr Margaret Enders

D-U-N-S 24-390-6356 (SL)
CLOUDWERX DATA SOLUTIONS INC
1440 28 St Ne Suite 2, Calgary, AB, T2A 7W6

Emp Here 20   *Sales* 1,313,293

SIC 4813 Telephone communication, except radio

D-U-N-S 20-508-9159   (BR)
COAST HOTELS LIMITED
COAST PLAZA HOTEL
1316 33 St Ne, Calgary, AB, T2A 6B6
(403) 248-8888
Emp Here 50
SIC 7011 Hotels and motels

D-U-N-S 24-089-4634   (HQ)
COFFEE CONNECTION LTD, THE
EVEREST ENTERPRISES INTERNATIONAL
(*Suby of* Coffee Connection Ltd, The)
401 33 St Ne Unit 3, Calgary, AB, T2A 7R3
(403) 269-5977
Emp Here 35   *Emp Total* 54
Sales 2,772,507
SIC 7389 Business services, nec

D-U-N-S 25-452-7492   (BR)
CONFISERIES REGAL INC
112 28 St Se Suite 103, Calgary, AB, T2A 6J9
(403) 250-3701
Emp Here 20
SIC 5145 Confectionery

D-U-N-S 24-365-5805   (BR)
DOLLARAMA S.E.C.
DOLLARAMA
3800 Memorial Dr Ne Suite 1153, Calgary, AB, T2A 2K2
(403) 537-0338
Emp Here 20
SIC 5399 Miscellaneous general merchandise

D-U-N-S 20-641-1469   (BR)
DONG-PHUONG ORIENTAL MARKET LTD
LUCKY SUPERMARKET
4527 8 Ave Se Suite 237, Calgary, AB, T2A 0A7
(403) 569-0778
Emp Here 20
SIC 5411 Grocery stores

D-U-N-S 25-170-6701   (SL)
ELECTRIC FOODS INC
A & W RESTAURANT
3663 12 Ave Ne, Calgary, AB, T2A 7T1
(403) 248-7640
Emp Here 200   *Sales* 6,055,738
SIC 5812 Eating places
Pr Tyson Lefebvre

D-U-N-S 25-598-2159   (HQ)
EXECUTIVE MAT SERVICE LTD
(*Suby of* Executive Mat Service Ltd)
115 28 St Se Suite 6, Calgary, AB, T2A 5K4
(403) 720-5905
Emp Here 54   *Emp Total* 61
Sales 3,502,114
SIC 7218 Industrial launcerers

D-U-N-S 24-086-4264   (BR)
FABRICLAND DISTRIBUTORS (WESTERN) CORP
(*Suby of* Fabricland Distributors (Western) Corp)
495 36 St Ne Suite 104, Calgary, AB, T2A 6K3
(403) 248-8380
Emp Here 36
SIC 5949 Sewing, needlework, and piece goods

D-U-N-S 25-301-1886   (BR)
FABRICLAND PACIFIC/MIDWEST LIMITED
FABRICLAND
495 36 St Ne Suite 104, Calgary, AB, T2A 6K3
(403) 248-8380
Emp Here 26
SIC 5949 Sewing, needlework, and piece goods

D-U-N-S 25-624-8097   (SL)
FAMILIES MATTER SOCIETY OF CALGARY
FAMILIES MATTER
1440 52 St Ne Suite 158, Calgary, AB, T2A

4T8
(403) 205-5178
Emp Here 60   *Sales* 2,334,742
SIC 8322 Individual and family services

D-U-N-S 24-700-2728   (BR)
FARM BUSINESS CONSULTANTS INC
FBC
3015 5 Ave Ne Suite 150, Calgary, AB, T2A 6T8
(403) 735-6105
Emp Here 60
SIC 7291 Tax return preparation services

D-U-N-S 24-840-5466   (BR)
FEDERATED CO-OPERATIVES LIMITED
(*Suby of* Federated Co-Operatives Limited)
2626 10 Ave Ne, Calgary, AB, T2A 2M3
(403) 531-6665
Emp Here 300
SIC 5141 Groceries, general line

D-U-N-S 20-830-9609   (SL)
FOREST GROVE CARE CENTRE LTD
4726 8 Ave Se, Calgary, AB, T2A 0A8
(403) 272-9831
Emp Here 350   *Sales* 20,637,005
SIC 8051 Skilled nursing care facilities
Pr Jack King

D-U-N-S 25-518-9201   (BR)
FOUNTAIN TIRE LTD
615 Moraine Rd Ne, Calgary, AB, T2A 2P4
(403) 272-9763
Emp Here 24
SIC 5531 Auto and home supply stores

D-U-N-S 20-920-5066   (BR)
G&K SERVICES CANADA INC
(*Suby of* Cintas Corporation)
2925 10 Ave Ne Suite 7, Calgary, AB, T2A 5L4
(403) 272-4256
Emp Here 100
SIC 7219 Laundry and garment services, nec

D-U-N-S 24-914-4838   (SL)
GLC CONTROLS INC
3300 14 Ave Ne Suite 2, Calgary, AB, T2A 6J4

Emp Here 30   *Sales* 6,055,738
SIC 5063 Electrical apparatus and equipment
Pr Luke Beaudry

D-U-N-S 24-905-5633   (BR)
GOLDER ASSOCIATES LTD
2535 3 Ave Ne Suite 102, Calgary, AB, T2A 7W5
(403) 299-5600
Emp Here 550
SIC 8748 Business consulting, nec

D-U-N-S 20-047-0594   (BR)
GOVERNMENT OF THE PROVINCE OF ALBERTA
KEELER ELEMENTARY SCHOOL
4807 Forego Ave Se, Calgary, AB, T2A 2C4
(403) 777-8180
Emp Here 30
SIC 8211 Elementary and secondary schools

D-U-N-S 24-496-0324   (SL)
HILTAP FITTINGS LTD
HILTAP
(*Suby of* Dover Corporation)
3140 14 Ave Ne Unit 1, Calgary, AB, T2A 6J4
(403) 250-2986
Emp Here 22   *Sales* 2,918,428
SIC 3494 Valves and pipe fittings, nec

D-U-N-S 25-011-1044   (BR)
HOME DEPOT OF CANADA INC
HOME DEPOT
(*Suby of* The Home Depot Inc)
343 36 St Ne, Calgary, AB, T2A 7S9
(403) 248-3040
Emp Here 250
SIC 5251 Hardware stores

D-U-N-S 20-695-1910   (SL)

HOME IMPROVEMENT WAREHOUSE LTD, THE
2620 Centre Ave Ne, Calgary, AB, T2A 2L3
(403) 248-7333
Emp Here 26   *Sales* 5,275,400
SIC 5211 Lumber and other building materials
Pr Pr Michael Doyle
  Michael Doyle Jr
  Sheila Doyle
  Christine Salas

D-U-N-S 20-278-6968   (BR)
HONEYWELL LIMITED
HONEYWELL BUILDING SOLUTION
(*Suby of* Honeywell International Inc.)
2840 2 Ave Se, Calgary, AB, T2A 7X9
(403) 221-2200
Emp Here 50
SIC 3822 Environmental controls

D-U-N-S 25-011-1085   (BR)
KEG RESTAURANTS LTD
KEG STEAKHOUSE & BAR, THE
425 36 St Ne, Calgary, AB, T2A 6K3
(403) 235-5858
Emp Here 70
SIC 5812 Eating places

D-U-N-S 24-273-1453   (HQ)
KIGEP MANAGEMENT LTD
CALGARY INTEGRATED SERVICES
112 28 St Se Suite 110, Calgary, AB, T2A 6J9
(403) 283-4405
Emp Here 50   *Emp Total* 120
Sales 3,031,879
SIC 8322 Individual and family services

D-U-N-S 25-978-4908   (SL)
MANORRLEA SYSTEMS INC
3300 14 Ave Ne Unit 6, Calgary, AB, T2A 6J4
(403) 262-8550
Emp Here 360   *Sales* 14,135,040
SIC 7349 Building maintenance services, nec
Pr David Orr
Treas Patricia Orr

D-U-N-S 24-359-9292   (BR)
NATIONAL-OILWELL CANADA LTD
NATIONAL OILWELL VARCO
(*Suby of* National Oilwell Varco, Inc.)
1616 Meridian Rd Ne, Calgary, AB, T2A 2P1
(403) 569-2222
Emp Here 100
SIC 3533 Oil and gas field machinery

D-U-N-S 25-068-0485   (SL)
ORDMAN CORPORATION
SERVICEMASTER CALGARY DISASTER RESTORATION
920 26 St Ne, Calgary, AB, T2A 2M4
(403) 287-7700
Emp Here 50   *Sales* 5,197,506
SIC 1799 Special trade contractors, nec
Pr Pr Rob Ordman

D-U-N-S 20-013-6786   (BR)
P M ELECTRIC LTD
PM SIGNS & ELECTRIC
(*Suby of* P M Electric Ltd)
1501 Moraine Rd Ne, Calgary, AB, T2A 2P5
(403) 272-7460
Emp Here 20
SIC 3993 Signs and advertising specialties

D-U-N-S 25-316-4024   (BR)
PASLEY, MAX ENTERPRISES LIMITED
MCDONALD'S RESTAURANTS #14915
(*Suby of* Pasley, Max Enterprises Limited)
3835 Memorial Dr Ne, Calgary, AB, T2A 2K2
(403) 569-1754
Emp Here 60
SIC 5812 Eating places

D-U-N-S 25-316-3968   (BR)
PASLEY, MAX ENTERPRISES LIMITED
MCDONALD'S RESTAURANTS
(*Suby of* Pasley, Max Enterprises Limited)

3660 12 Ave Ne, Calgary, AB, T2A 6R4
(403) 273-1219
Emp Here 60
SIC 5812 Eating places

D-U-N-S 20-855-8879   (HQ)
PROSPECT HUMAN SERVICES SOCIETY
PROSPECT CALGARY
(*Suby of* Prospect Human Services Society)
915 33 St Ne, Calgary, AB, T2A 6T2
(403) 273-2822
Emp Here 75   *Emp Total* 120
Sales 23,411,840
SIC 5912 Drug stores and proprietary stores
Dir Debbie Spaudiling
CEO Melanie Mitra

D-U-N-S 25-521-6335   (BR)
RED LOBSTER HOSPITALITY LLC
RED LOBSTER RESTAURANTS
(*Suby of* Red Lobster Seafood Co., LLC)
312 35 St Ne, Calgary, AB, T2A 6S7
(403) 248-8111
Emp Here 120
SIC 5812 Eating places

D-U-N-S 25-944-9536   (BR)
REDBERRY FRANCHISING CORP
BURGER KING
4818 17 Ave Se, Calgary, AB, T2A 0V2
(403) 215-1012
Emp Here 30
SIC 5812 Eating places

D-U-N-S 24-806-2622   (BR)
ROTORK CONTROLS (CANADA) LTD
820 28 St Ne Unit 9, Calgary, AB, T2A 6K1
(403) 207-3020
Emp Here 20
SIC 3625 Relays and industrial controls

D-U-N-S 25-452-2600   (BR)
ROYAL BANK OF CANADA
RBC
(*Suby of* Royal Bank Of Canada)
5269 Memorial Dr Se Suite 1, Calgary, AB, T2A 4V1
(403) 292-2424
Emp Here 25
SIC 6021 National commercial banks

D-U-N-S 20-115-7430   (BR)
SMART TECHNOLOGIES ULC
1460 28 St Ne Suite 8, Calgary, AB, T2A 7W6

Emp Here 60
SIC 3823 Process control instruments

D-U-N-S 25-945-0351   (SL)
SCRAPBOOKER'S PARADISE LTD
2926 3 Ave Ne, Calgary, AB, T2A 6T7
(403) 229-0500
Emp Here 75   *Sales* 31,652,400
SIC 5111 Printing and writing paper
Pr Pr Leslie Lee
  Murray Lee

D-U-N-S 20-657-9786   (BR)
SEARS CANADA INC
3800 Memorial Dr Ne Suite 1600, Calgary, AB, T2A 2K2
(403) 273-2323
Emp Here 25
SIC 5311 Department stores

D-U-N-S 24-132-2457   (BR)
SMALL POTATOES URBAN DELIVERY INC
SPUD.CA
3200 14 Ave Ne Unit 3, Calgary, AB, T2A 6J4
(403) 615-3663
Emp Here 20
SIC 5431 Fruit and vegetable markets

D-U-N-S 24-136-7791   (BR)
SMITTY'S CANADA LIMITED
3800 Memorial Dr Ne Suite 1405, Calgary, AB, T2A 2K2
(403) 508-6931
Emp Here 30

SIC 5812 Eating places

D-U-N-S 25-271-0439   (BR)
SOBEYS WEST INC
399 36 St Ne, Calgary, AB, T2A 7R4
(403) 248-0848
Emp Here 150
SIC 5411 Grocery stores

D-U-N-S 25-271-0975   (BR)
SOBEYS WEST INC
SAFEWAY
1440 52 St Ne Suite 300, Calgary, AB, T2A 4T8
(403) 235-1437
Emp Here 77
SIC 5411 Grocery stores

D-U-N-S 20-860-0101   (BR)
SOURCE (BELL) ELECTRONICS INC, THE
SOURCE, THE
3800 Memorial Dr Ne Suite 1528, Calgary, AB, T2A 2K2
(403) 272-3088
Emp Here 25
SIC 5999 Miscellaneous retail stores, nec

D-U-N-S 24-340-5110   (BR)
STANLEY BLACK & DECKER CANADA CORPORATION
STANLEY SECURITY SYSTEMS
1305 33 St Ne Unit 13, Calgary, AB, T2A 5P1
(403) 250-7393
Emp Here 20
SIC 1731 Electrical work

D-U-N-S 24-101-2421   (BR)
STAPLES CANADA INC
STAPLES THE BUSINESS DEPOT
(*Suby of* Staples, Inc.)
565 36 St Ne Unit 121, Calgary, AB, T2A 6K3
(403) 204-3644
Emp Here 30
SIC 5943 Stationery stores

D-U-N-S 20-065-8958   (SL)
STOUGHTON FIRE PROTECTION LTD
620 Moraine Rd Ne, Calgary, AB, T2A 2P3
(403) 291-0291
Emp Here 65   *Sales* 3,283,232
SIC 7389 Business services, nec

D-U-N-S 20-940-4024   (BR)
T & T SUPERMARKET INC
999 36 St Ne Suite 800, Calgary, AB, T2A 7X6
(403) 569-6888
Emp Here 200
SIC 5411 Grocery stores

D-U-N-S 24-352-4027   (BR)
TELUS COMMUNICATIONS INC
2912 Memorial Dr Se Suite 200, Calgary, AB, T2A 6R1
(403) 387-4220
Emp Here 71
SIC 4899 Communication services, nec

D-U-N-S 25-519-7246   (HQ)
THERMON CANADA INC
THERMON HEAT TRACING
333 28 St Ne, Calgary, AB, T2A 7P4
(403) 273-5558
Emp Here 92   *Emp Total* 150
Sales 30,132,769
SIC 5063 E ectrical apparatus and equipment
Pr Dave Duval
   Richard L. Burdick
VP VP Bill Cunningham
   Mark Burdick

D-U-N-S 20-152-8804   (BR)
TRYLON TSF INC
3016 10 Ave Ne Suite 105, Calgary, AB, T2A 6A3
(403) 295-2206
Emp Here 20
SIC 1623 Water, sewer, and utility lines

D-U-N-S 24-118-5297   (BR)

UTC FIRE & SECURITY CANADA INC
UTC FIRE & SECURITY CANADA
(*Suby of* United Technologies Corporation)
Bay 8, Calgary, AB, T2A 7W6
(403) 253-9236
Emp Here 20
SIC 5063 Electrical apparatus and equipment

D-U-N-S 25-218-9857   (BR)
WAL-MART CANADA CORP
WALMART
3800 Memorial Dr Ne Suite 1100, Calgary, AB, T2A 2K2
(403) 235-2352
Emp Here 200
SIC 5311 Department stores

D-U-N-S 24-440-3325   (BR)
WENDY'S RESTAURANTS OF CANADA INC
WENDY'S
(*Suby of* The Wendy's Company)
475 36 St Ne, Calgary, AB, T2A 6K3
(403) 273-4740
Emp Here 45
SIC 5812 Eating places

D-U-N-S 24-160-3612   (BR)
WESTERN INVENTORY SERVICE LTD
WIS INTERNATIONAL
720 28 St Ne Suite 128, Calgary, AB, T2A 6R3
(403) 272-3850
Emp Here 80
SIC 7389 Business services, nec

D-U-N-S 25-272-5791   (BR)
WEYERHAEUSER COMPANY LIMITED
(*Suby of* Weyerhaeuser Company)
2719 3 Ave Ne, Calgary, AB, T2A 6H1

Emp Here 45
SIC 5031 Lumber, plywood, and millwork

Calgary, AB T2B

D-U-N-S 24-075-3215   (BR)
ALMADINA SCHOOL SOCIETY
ALMADINA LANGUAGE CHARTER ACADEMY
2031 Sable Dr Se, Calgary, AB, T2B 1R9
(403) 543-5074
Emp Here 30
SIC 8211 Elementary and secondary schools

D-U-N-S 20-267-6813   (BR)
ARMTEC LP
4300 50 Ave Se Suite 217, Calgary, AB, T2B 2T7
(403) 248-3171
Emp Here 150
SIC 3272 Concrete products, nec

D-U-N-S 25-685-3110   (BR)
BAKER HUGHES CANADA COMPANY
BAKER PETROLITE, DIV OF
(*Suby of* Baker Hughes, A GE Company)
5050 47 St Se, Calgary, AB, T2B 3S1
(403) 537-3850
Emp Here 50
SIC 2911 Petroleum refining

D-U-N-S 20-589-5001   (BR)
BANQUE TORONTO-DOMINION, LA
TD CANADA TRUST
(*Suby of* Toronto-Dominion Bank, The)
1804 36 St Se, Calgary, AB, T2B 0X6
(403) 299-3429
Emp Here 24
SIC 6021 National commercial banks

D-U-N-S 25-230-5164   (BR)
BRANDT TRACTOR LTD
3555 46 Ave Se, Calgary, AB, T2B 3B3
(403) 248-0018
Emp Here 35
SIC 5084 Industrial machinery and equipment

D-U-N-S 25-831-6728   (BR)
CHEP CANADA INC
4750 43 St Se Unit 134, Calgary, AB, T2B 3N3
(403) 236-1633
Emp Here 50
SIC 7359 Equipment rental and leasing, nec

D-U-N-S 25-107-9695   (HQ)
CTR REFRIGERATION AND FOOD STORE EQUIPMENT LTD
(*Suby of* CTR Refrigeration and Food Store Equipment Ltd)
4840 52 St Se, Calgary, AB, T2B 3R2
(403) 444-2877
Emp Here 20   *Emp Total* 50
Sales 4,377,642
SIC 1711 Plumbing, heating, air-conditioning

D-U-N-S 24-381-3271   (BR)
CALGARY BOARD OF EDUCATION
HAROLD W. RILEY ELEMENTARY SCHOOL
3743 Dover Ridge Dr Se, Calgary, AB, T2B 2E1
(403) 817-4000
Emp Here 20
SIC 8211 Elementary and secondary schools

D-U-N-S 25-011-7538   (BR)
CALGARY BOARD OF EDUCATION
IAN BAZALGETTE JUNIOR HIGH SCHOOL
3909 26 Ave Se, Calgary, AB, T2B 0C6
(403) 777-7360
Emp Here 45
SIC 8211 Elementary and secondary schools

D-U-N-S 20-590-7822   (BR)
CALGARY BOARD OF EDUCATION
ALMADINA CHARTER SCHOOL
2031 Sable Dr Se, Calgary, AB, T2B 1R9
(403) 543-5074
Emp Here 45
SIC 8211 Elementary and secondary schools

D-U-N-S 20-713-1256   (BR)
CALGARY BOARD OF EDUCATION
WEST DOVER SCHOOL
3113 30 Ave Se, Calgary, AB, T2B 0G9
(403) 777-8260
Emp Here 50
SIC 8211 Elementary and secondary schools

D-U-N-S 25-272-2939   (BR)
CALGARY ROMAN CATHOLIC SEPARATE SCHOOL DISTRICT #1
HOLY CROSS ELEMENTARY JUNIOR HIGH SCHOOL
3719 26 Ave Se, Calgary, AB, T2B 0C6
(403) 500-2033
Emp Here 35
SIC 8211 Elementary and secondary schools

D-U-N-S 20-036-3542   (BR)
CALGARY ROMAN CATHOLIC SEPARATE SCHOOL DISTRICT #1
ST. DAMIEN ELEMENTARY SCHOOL
3619 28 St Se, Calgary, AB, T2B 2J1
(403) 500-2073
Emp Here 25
SIC 8211 Elementary and secondary schools

D-U-N-S 20-814-4977   (BR)
CANADIAN TIRE CORPORATION, LIMITED
PARTSOURCE
1817 52 St Se Suite 714, Calgary, AB, T2B 2Y5
(403) 204-7854
Emp Here 23
SIC 5531 Auto and home supply stores

D-U-N-S 24-674-6531   (HQ)
CANEDA TRANSPORT LTD
4330 46 Ave Se, Calgary, AB, T2B 3N7
(403) 236-7900
Emp Here 55   *Emp Total* 5,515
Sales 8,682,323
SIC 4213 Trucking, except local
Pr Pr James Duncan
   Eileen Cowan

D-U-N-S 25-993-1954   (BR)
CONESTOGA COLD STORAGE (QUEBEC) LIMITED
4767 27 St Se, Calgary, AB, T2B 3M5
(403) 207-6766
Emp Here 20
SIC 4222 Refrigerated warehousing and storage

D-U-N-S 20-075-4604   (BR)
CUMMINS WESTERN CANADA LIMITED PARTNERSHIP
4887 35 St Se, Calgary, AB, T2B 3H6
(403) 569-1122
Emp Here 100
SIC 5084 Industrial machinery and equipment

D-U-N-S 20-345-4194   (SL)
FBM CANADA GSD, INC
(*Suby of* Foundation Building Materials, LLC)
5155 48 Ave Se, Calgary, AB, T2B 3S8
(403) 255-8157
Emp Here 45   *Sales* 11,174,638
SIC 5039 Construction materials, nec
  Reg Lillico

D-U-N-S 25-527-9192   (BR)
FEDERATED CO-OPERATIVES LIMITED
FOOD WAREHOUSE
(*Suby of* Federated Co-Operatives Limited)
3333 52 St Se, Calgary, AB, T2B 1N3
(403) 531-6684
Emp Here 130
SIC 5141 Groceries, general line

D-U-N-S 25-315-6392   (BR)
G.N. JOHNSTON EQUIPMENT CO. LTD
2880 45 Ave Se Unit 316, Calgary, AB, T2B 3M1
(403) 258-1221
Emp Here 40
SIC 5084 Industrial machinery and equipment

D-U-N-S 24-808-7249   (BR)
HARRIS STEEL ULC
HARRIS REBAR
(*Suby of* Nucor Corporation)
3208 52 St Se, Calgary, AB, T2B 1N2
(403) 272-8801
Emp Here 130
SIC 3441 Fabricated structural Metal

D-U-N-S 24-729-0401   (BR)
MMD SALES LTD
MARTIN MOTOR SPORTS
3444 44 Ave Se, Calgary, AB, T2B 3J9
(403) 301-0096
Emp Here 22
SIC 5551 Boat dealers

D-U-N-S 24-647-3755   (HQ)
NATIONAL MOTOR COACH SYSTEMS LTD
3606 50 Ave Se, Calgary, AB, T2B 2M7
(403) 240-1992
Emp Here 48   *Emp Total* 64
Sales 3,015,453
SIC 4142 Bus charter service, except local

D-U-N-S 20-732-6617   (BR)
PEPSICO CANADA ULC
FRITO LAY CANADA
(*Suby of* Pepsico, Inc.)
2867 45 Ave Se, Calgary, AB, T2B 3L8
(403) 571-9530
Emp Here 170
SIC 2096 Potato chips and similar snacks

D-U-N-S 24-684-3937   (SL)
PHASOR ENGINEERING INC
(*Suby of* Quanta Services, Inc.)
1829 54 St Se Suite 218, Calgary, AB, T2B 1N5
(403) 238-3695
Emp Here 24   *Sales* 2,512,128
SIC 8711 Engineering services

D-U-N-S 20-344-9376   (SL)
PRECISION MOUNTING TECHNOLOGIES

LTD
2322 49 Ave Se, Calgary, AB, T2B 3E3
(403) 216-5080
Emp Here 23   *Sales* 1,313,293
SIC 2511 Wood household furniture

D-U-N-S 24-368-5943   (SL)
REV ENGINEERING LTD
3236 50 Ave Se, Calgary, AB, T2B 3A3
(403) 287-0156
Emp Here 70   *Sales* 3,205,129
SIC 7629 Electrical repair shops

D-U-N-S 24-556-7255   (BR)
SMS EQUIPMENT INC
CONECO EQUIPMENT
3320 50 Ave Se, Calgary, AB, T2B 3J4
(403) 569-1109
Emp Here 25
SIC 5082 Construction and mining machinery

D-U-N-S 20-260-7404   (BR)
SIEMENS CANADA LIMITED
TURBOCARE CANADA
4920 43 St Se, Calgary, AB, T2B 3N3
(403) 279-2211
Emp Here 40
SIC 3625 Relays and industrial controls

D-U-N-S 24-346-1217   (SL)
T & C MOTOR HOTEL LTD
TOWN & COUNTRY MOTOR HOTEL
1825 50 St Se, Calgary, AB, T2B 1M6
(403) 272-9881
Emp Here 65   *Sales* 2,845,467
SIC 7011 Hotels and motels

D-U-N-S 20-333-6342   (BR)
TREE ISLAND INDUSTRIES LTD
TREE ISLAND INDUSTRIES CALGARY
2729 48 Ave Se, Calgary, AB, T2B 0M4
(403) 258-4242
Emp Here 42
SIC 3496 Miscellaneous fabricated wire products

D-U-N-S 20-011-0646   (BR)
UPS SCS, INC
UPS SUPPLY CHAIN SOLUTION
4807 47 St Se, Calgary, AB, T2B 3S5
(403) 387-0430
Emp Here 45
SIC 4731 Freight transportation arrangement

D-U-N-S 20-305-4510   (SL)
VARISYSTEMS INC
5304 Hubalta Rd Se, Calgary, AB, T2B 1T6
(403) 273-2111
Emp Here 150   *Sales* 30,342,994
SIC 3089 Plastics products, nec
  Richard Higdon

D-U-N-S 25-371-3960   (SL)
VERSA POWER SYSTEMS LTD
4852 52 St Se, Calgary, AB, T2B 3R2
(403) 204-6100
Emp Here 35   *Sales* 3,465,004
SIC 3621 Motors and generators

D-U-N-S 24-272-7378   (BR)
WASTE MANAGEMENT OF CANADA CORPORATION
(*Suby of* Waste Management, Inc.)
4668 25 St Se, Calgary, AB, T2B 3M2

Emp Here 112
SIC 4953 Refuse systems

D-U-N-S 20-927-4013   (BR)
WENDY'S RESTAURANTS OF CANADA INC
WENDY'S
(*Suby of* The Wendy's Company)
4605 25 St Se, Calgary, AB, T2B 3R9
(403) 272-7333
Emp Here 20
SIC 5812 Eating places

Calgary, AB T2C

D-U-N-S 25-271-8148   (BR)
1409096 ONTARIO LIMITED
PERI FORMWORK SYSTEMS
7505 48 St Se Suite 250, Calgary, AB, T2C 4C7
(780) 429-3676
Emp Here 35
SIC 7353 Heavy construction equipment rental

D-U-N-S 24-159-6782   (SL)
221449 ALBERTA LTD
ARTISTIC STAIRS
3504 80 Ave Se, Calgary, AB, T2C 1J3
(403) 279-5898
Emp Here 90   *Sales* 9,517,523
SIC 2431 Millwork
Pr Pr Bill Langen
  Cecil Hoffman

D-U-N-S 25-268-2901   (BR)
3618358 CANADA INC
ATS/CONCORDE TRANSPORTATION
5353 72 Ave Se Unit 49, Calgary, AB, T2C 4X6
(403) 279-5208
Emp Here 80
SIC 4212 Local trucking, without storage

D-U-N-S 24-325-0888   (SL)
725024 ALBERTA LTD
11158 42 St Se, Calgary, AB, T2C 0J9
(403) 279-7600
Emp Here 110   *Sales* 22,871,280
SIC 6712 Bank holding companies
Pr Pr Al Morrison

D-U-N-S 24-352-6360   (BR)
A. LASSONDE INC
LASSONDE WESTERN CANADA
(*Suby of* 3346625 Canada Inc)
7419 30 St Se, Calgary, AB, T2C 1N6
(403) 296-9350
Emp Here 55
SIC 2033 Canned fruits and specialties

D-U-N-S 20-336-9504   (BR)
ABB INC
PROCESS AUTOMATION OIL, GAS & PETROCHEMICAL
2 Smed Lane Suite 110, Calgary, AB, T2C 4T5
(403) 806-1700
Emp Here 135
SIC 5063 Electrical apparatus and equipment

D-U-N-S 24-300-1609   (BR)
ATS TRAFFIC-ALBERTA LTD
2807 58 Ave Se, Calgary, AB, T2C 0B4
(403) 236-9860
Emp Here 20
SIC 7353 Heavy construction equipment rental

D-U-N-S 20-551-7787   (BR)
ACRODEX INC
10524 42 St Se Suite 3, Calgary, AB, T2C 5C7
(403) 265-2667
Emp Here 30
SIC 5045 Computers, peripherals, and software

D-U-N-S 25-741-6529   (BR)
AECOM PRODUCTION SERVICES LTD
FLINT FIELD SERVICES LTD
9727 40 St Se, Calgary, AB, T2C 2P4
(403) 236-5611
Emp Here 100
SIC 3494 Valves and pipe fittings, nec

D-U-N-S 20-551-9858   (BR)
AINSWORTH INC
7304 30 St Se Suite 102, Calgary, AB, T2C 1W2
(403) 265-6750
Emp Here 60

SIC 1731 Electrical work

D-U-N-S 20-075-0826   (BR)
AIR LIQUIDE CANADA INC
3004 54 Ave Se, Calgary, AB, T2C 0A7
(403) 777-4700
Emp Here 75
SIC 5169 Chemicals and allied products, nec

D-U-N-S 25-230-7988   (BR)
ALL WEATHER WINDOWS LTD
8241 30 St Se Suite 1, Calgary, AB, T2C 1H7

Emp Here 40
SIC 2431 Millwork

D-U-N-S 24-442-4370   (BR)
ALLMAR INC
ALLMAR INTERNATIONAL
4910 76 Ave Se, Calgary, AB, T2C 2X2
(403) 236-2604
Emp Here 30
SIC 5072 Hardware

D-U-N-S 20-058-8650   (BR)
ALSTOM CANADA INC
ALSTOM TRANSPORT, DIV OF
(*Suby of* General Electric Company)
7550 Ogden Dale Rd Se Suite 200, Calgary, AB, T2C 4X9

Emp Here 400
SIC 4789 Transportation services, nec

D-U-N-S 24-086-3555   (SL)
ALTADORE GYMNASTIC CLUB
6303 30 St Se Suite 101, Calgary, AB, T2C 1R4
(403) 720-2711
Emp Here 55   *Sales* 2,188,821
SIC 7991 Physical fitness facilities

D-U-N-S 24-339-6582   (BR)
ALTALINK, L.P.
(*Suby of* Berkshire Hathaway Inc.)
7503 30 St Se, Calgary, AB, T2C 1V4
(403) 267-3400
Emp Here 30
SIC 4911 Electric services

D-U-N-S 24-928-9612   (HQ)
ARLYN ENTERPRISES LTD
BOSS LUBRICANTS
(*Suby of* Arlyn Enterprises Ltd)
6303 30 St Se Unit 112, Calgary, AB, T2C 1R4
(403) 279-2223
Emp Here 30   *Emp Total* 80
Sales 32,392,800
SIC 5172 Petroleum products, nec
Dir Murray Flegel
Pr Jarrett Flegel
Dir William K. Dickson

D-U-N-S 24-827-9650   (BR)
ARMTEC LP
ARMTEC
8916 48 St Se, Calgary, AB, T2C 2P9
(403) 279-8161
Emp Here 100
SIC 3312 Blast furnaces and steel mills

D-U-N-S 25-265-7473   (BR)
ARPAC STORAGE SYSTEMS CORPORATION
7220 44 St Se Suite 200, Calgary, AB, T2C 3A7
(403) 236-9066
Emp Here 40
SIC 5084 Industrial machinery and equipment

D-U-N-S 20-048-8190   (HQ)
ATOMIK INTERIORS INC
ATOMIK SPRAY SYSTEMS
(*Suby of* Atomik Interiors Inc)
4905 102 Ave Se Unit 19, Calgary, AB, T2C 2X7
(403) 215-5977
Emp Here 50   *Emp Total* 50
Sales 4,231,721

SIC 1742 Plastering, drywall, and insulation

D-U-N-S 20-641-0842   (SL)
BGI HOLDINGS INC
BOLDER GRAPHICS
5375 50 St Se Suite 3, Calgary, AB, T2C 3W1
(403) 299-9400
Emp Here 80   *Sales* 4,523,563
SIC 2731 Book publishing

D-U-N-S 25-097-6784   (HQ)
BJ TOOL SERVICES LTD
(*Suby of* BJ Services Company LLC)
7071 112 Ave Se, Calgary, AB, T2C 5A5
(403) 236-2815
Emp Here 60   *Emp Total* 2,600
Sales 54,054,062
SIC 3533 Oil and gas field machinery
  Delton A Campbell
Genl Mgr Randy Wallister
  William R. Stedman
  Ian Bootle
  Robert Jones
Dir Nicholas Kirton
Dir Douglas Freel
Dir Edward Dipaolo
Dir Robert A. Lehodey
  Blair J. Albers

D-U-N-S 24-523-7438   (SL)
BWI HOLDINGS INC
3915 61 Ave Se, Calgary, AB, T2C 1V5
(403) 255-2900
Emp Here 134   *Sales* 28,859,040
SIC 6712 Bank holding companies
Pr Jim Can
COO Branislav Javonic
CFO Bruce Milroy
VP Opers Michele Patrosh

D-U-N-S 25-832-3120   (BR)
BAKER HUGHES CANADA COMPANY
BJ PIPELINE INSPECTION SERVICES
(*Suby of* Baker Hughes, A GE Company)
4839 90 Ave Se Suite Frnt, Calgary, AB, T2C 2S8
(403) 531-5300
Emp Here 120
SIC 1389 Oil and gas field services, nec

D-U-N-S 25-977-8959   (HQ)
BAYER CROPSCIENCE INC
160 Quarry Park Blvd Se Suite 200, Calgary, AB, T2C 3G3
(403) 723-7400
Emp Here 120   *Emp Total* 115,200
Sales 36,122,667
SIC 2879 Agricultural chemicals, nec
Dir Paula Moore
Dir Kamel Beliazi
Dir Christian Lauterbach
Dir James Blome

D-U-N-S 20-801-3172   (BR)
BEAUTY SYSTEMS GROUP (CANADA) INC
MONARCH BEAUTY SUPPLY CO
5381 72 Ave Se Suite 54, Calgary, AB, T2C 4X6
(403) 236-7662
Emp Here 50
SIC 5087 Service establishment equipment

D-U-N-S 24-348-6920   (SL)
BECHT ENGINEERING CANADA LTD
4720 106 Ave Se Suite 210a, Calgary, AB, T2C 3G5
(403) 256-3575
Emp Here 35   *Sales* 3,210,271
SIC 8711 Engineering services

D-U-N-S 24-238-3800   (BR)
BELTERRA CORPORATION
9160 52 St Se, Calgary, AB, T2C 5A9
(403) 253-9333
Emp Here 25
SIC 5084 Industrial machinery and equipment

D-U-N-S 20-771-1149   (SL)

BENPRO TECHNOLOGIES CORPORATION
TRIPPLE D BENDING
4707 Glenmore Trail Se, Calgary, AB, T2C
2R9
(403) 255-2944
Emp Here 47   *Sales* 6,150,382
SIC 3499 Fabricated Metal products, nec

     D-U-N-S 25-318-8551   (BR)
BOART LONGYEAR CANADA
SDS DRILLING , DIV OF
4025 96 Ave Se, Calgary, AB, T2C 4T7
(403) 287-1460
Emp Here 25
SIC 1799 Special trade contractors, nec

     D-U-N-S 25-207-2509   (BR)
BRENNTAG CANADA INC
CALGARY TECH CENTRE
3124 54 Ave Se, Calgary, AB, T2C 0A8
(403) 720-5650
Emp Here 25
SIC 5169 Chemicals and allied products, nec

     D-U-N-S 20-065-2761   (BR)
BROCK CANADA INC
(Suby of Brock Canada Inc)
5401 53 St Se, Calgary, AB, T2C 4P6
(403) 203-0633
Emp Here 40
SIC 3999 Manufacturing industries, nec

     D-U-N-S 20-521-2079   (BR)
BROCK WHITE CANADA COMPANY, LLC
STEELS
4880 104 Ave Se, Calgary, AB, T2C 2H3
(403) 279-2710
Emp Here 60
SIC 5039 Construction materials, nec

     D-U-N-S 25-375-6605   (BR)
BUCKWOLD WESTERN LTD
BUCKWOLD WESTERN
6313 30 St Se, Calgary, AB, T2C 1R4
(403) 279-2636
Emp Here 30
SIC 5023 Homefurnishings

     D-U-N-S 24-426-4821   (BR)
BUY-LOW FOODS LTD
7100 44 St Se, Calgary, AB, T2C 2V7
(403) 236-6300
Emp Here 100
SIC 5411 Grocery stores

     D-U-N-S 20-966-3793   (BR)
C. KEAY INVESTMENTS LTD
OCEAN TRAILER
7288 84 St Se, Calgary, AB, T2C 4T6
(403) 720-7100
Emp Here 50
SIC 7519 Utility trailer rental

     D-U-N-S 20-178-6287   (BR)
C.D.M.V. INC
5375 50 St Se Suite 7, Calgary, AB, T2C 3W1

Emp Here 35
SIC 5047 Medical and hospital equipment

     D-U-N-S 25-236-6125   (SL)
**C.S.S. OFFICE FURNITURE SYSTEMS
SERVICE INC**
4920 72 Ave Se, Calgary, AB, T2C 4B5
(403) 720-3050
Emp Here 50   *Sales* 1,824,018
SIC 7641 Reupholstery and furniture repair

     D-U-N-S 24-347-5154   (BR)
CCS CONTRACTING LTD
2611 58 Ave Se Suite 677, Calgary, AB, T2C
0B4
(403) 215-4040
Emp Here 20
SIC 1761 Roofing, siding, and sheetMetal
work

     D-U-N-S 24-440-4182   (BR)

CP DISTRIBUTORS LTD
CP DISTRIBUTORS LTD.
3900 106 Ave Se Suite 29, Calgary, AB, T2C
5B6
(403) 253-2006
Emp Here 30
SIC 5031 Lumber, plywood, and millwork

     D-U-N-S 20-655-1223   (BR)
CALGARY BOARD OF EDUCATION
SHERWOOD SCHOOL
2011 66 Ave Se, Calgary, AB, T2C 1J4
(403) 777-7590
Emp Here 30
SIC 8211 Elementary and secondary schools

     D-U-N-S 20-713-1546   (BR)
CALGARY BOARD OF EDUCATION
BANTING & BEST SHERWOOD CAMPUS
1819 66 Ave Se, Calgary, AB, T2C 2K5
(403) 777-8650
Emp Here 60
SIC 8211 Elementary and secondary schools

     D-U-N-S 20-713-1751   (BR)
CALGARY BOARD OF EDUCATION
RIVERBEND ELEMENTARY SCHOOL
65 Rivervalley Dr Se, Calgary, AB, T2C 3Z7
(403) 777-6510
Emp Here 50
SIC 8211 Elementary and secondary schools

     D-U-N-S 25-622-0740   (BR)
CALGARY FASTENERS & TOOLS LTD
(Suby of 700635 Alberta Ltd)
4550 72 Ave Se, Calgary, AB, T2C 3Z2
(403) 279-7417
Emp Here 45
SIC 5085 Industrial supplies

     D-U-N-S 24-340-5052   (BR)
**CALGARY ROMAN CATHOLIC SEPARATE
SCHOOL DISTRICT #1**
ST. BROTHER ANDRE CENTRE
5 Avenue Sw Suite 1000, Calgary, AB, T2C
2V5
(403) 500-2000
Emp Here 20
SIC 8211 Elementary and secondary schools

     D-U-N-S 20-574-7491   (BR)
**CALGARY ROMAN CATHOLIC SEPARATE
SCHOOL DISTRICT #1**
ST. BERNADETTE SCHOOL
55 Lynndale Cres Se, Calgary, AB, T2C 0T8
(403) 500-2020
Emp Here 20
SIC 8211 Elementary and secondary schools

     D-U-N-S 24-156-8336   (BR)
CALMONT LEASING LTD
5475 53 St Se, Calgary, AB, T2C 4P6
(403) 279-8272
Emp Here 35
SIC 7513 Truck rental and leasing, no drivers

     D-U-N-S 20-078-6580   (BR)
CANWEL BUILDING MATERIALS LTD
CANWEL
9229 Barlow Trail Se, Calgary, AB, T2C 2N8
(403) 279-7108
Emp Here 20
SIC 5039 Construction materials, nec

     D-U-N-S 25-416-7216   (BR)
CANADA BREAD COMPANY, LIMITED
CANADA BREAD FROZEN BAKERY
4320 80 Ave Se, Calgary, AB, T2C 4N6
(403) 203-1675
Emp Here 165
SIC 2051 Bread, cake, and related products

     D-U-N-S 20-648-9747   (BR)
CANADA BREAD COMPANY, LIMITED
2425 52 Ave Se Suite 2, Calgary, AB, T2C 4X7
(403) 236-4505
Emp Here 50
SIC 5461 Retail bakeries

     D-U-N-S 20-012-3230   (BR)
**CANADA CARTAGE SYSTEM LIMITED
PARTNERSHIP**
CANADA CARTAGE
4700 102 Ave Se, Calgary, AB, T2C 2X8
(403) 296-0290
Emp Here 250
SIC 4213 Trucking, except local

     D-U-N-S 24-132-5690   (BR)
CANADIAN DEWATERING L.P.
8816 40 St Se, Calgary, AB, T2C 2P2
(403) 291-3313
Emp Here 30
SIC 5084 Industrial machinery and equipment

     D-U-N-S 20-303-9008   (BR)
CANADIAN DIABETES ASSOCIATION
NATIONAL DIABETES TRUST
3700 78 Ave Se Unit 240, Calgary, AB, T2C
2L8
(403) 509-0070
Emp Here 25
SIC 8699 Membership organizations, nec

     D-U-N-S 20-573-4242   (BR)
CANADIAN PACIFIC RAILWAY COMPANY
7550 Ogden Dale Rd Se, Calgary, AB, T2C
4X9

Emp Here 175
SIC 4011 Railroads, line-haul operating

     D-U-N-S 25-832-0696   (BR)
CANADIAN PACIFIC RAILWAY COMPANY
CPR
11020 52 St Se, Calgary, AB, T2C 4M2
(403) 203-8915
Emp Here 30
SIC 4011 Railroads, line-haul operating

     D-U-N-S 20-301-2195   (BR)
CANADIAN WESTERN BANK
CANADIAN WESTERN BANK & TRUST
6127 Barlow Trail Se, Calgary, AB, T2C 4W8
(403) 269-9882
Emp Here 20
SIC 6021 National commercial banks

     D-U-N-S 24-765-0786   (SL)
CANRIG DRILLING TECHNOLOGY LTD
5250 94 Ave Se Suite 5250, Calgary, AB, T2C
3Z3
(403) 279-3466
Emp Here 501   *Sales* 105,823,547
SIC 1389 Oil and gas field services, nec
Pr Chris Papouras

     D-U-N-S 24-853-3275   (BR)
CARPENTER CANADA CO
5800 36 St Se, Calgary, AB, T2C 2A9
(403) 279-2466
Emp Here 100
SIC 3089 Plastics products, nec

     D-U-N-S 25-450-0283   (HQ)
CASCADE CARRIERS L.P.
6111 Ogden Dale Rd Se, Calgary, AB, T2C
2A4
(403) 236-7110
Emp Here 40   *Emp Total* 5,515
Sales 7,536,384
SIC 4212 Local trucking, without storage
VP Opers Kevin James
Fin Ex Amy Wang
Opers Mgr Richard Schultz

     D-U-N-S 25-395-0323   (BR)
CASCADES CANADA ULC
CASCADES RECOVERY+
10351 46 St Se, Calgary, AB, T2C 2X9
(403) 243-5700
Emp Here 30
SIC 4953 Refuse systems

     D-U-N-S 24-337-2690   (BR)
CASCADES CANADA ULC
CASCADES TISSUE GROUP - CALGARY

4441 76 Ave Se, Calgary, AB, T2C 2G8
(403) 723-3750
Emp Here 24
SIC 2676 Sanitary paper products

     D-U-N-S 25-147-2452   (SL)
CATALYST LLP
200 Quarry Park Blvd Se Suite 250, Calgary,
AB, T2C 5E3
(403) 296-0082
Emp Here 60   *Sales* 2,626,585
SIC 8721 Accounting, auditing, and book-
keeping

     D-U-N-S 24-228-9614   (BR)
CERTAINTEED GYPSUM CANADA, INC
6715 Ogden Dale Rd Se, Calgary, AB, T2C
2A4
(403) 279-0916
Emp Here 20
SIC 3275 Gypsum products

     D-U-N-S 24-124-5567   (BR)
CERVUS CONTRACTORS EQUIPMENT LP
BOBCAT OF CALGARY
4403 112 Ave Se Suite Unit, Calgary, AB, T2C
5C5
(403) 243-2011
Emp Here 32
SIC 4213 Trucking, except local

     D-U-N-S 24-395-0644   (BR)
CERVUS EQUIPMENT CORPORATION
A.R. WILLIAMS MATERIALS HANDLING
5159 72 Ave Se, Calgary, AB, T2C 3H3
(403) 243-6011
Emp Here 30
SIC 8731 Commercial physical research

     D-U-N-S 25-362-4092   (BR)
CHAMPION TECHNOLOGIES ULC
6040 46 St Se, Calgary, AB, T2C 4P9
(403) 279-2835
Emp Here 70
SIC 5169 Chemicals and allied products, nec

     D-U-N-S 24-335-9051   (BR)
CLEMRO WESTERN (1996) LTD
SUPERIOR
5019 90 Ave Se Suite Frnt, Calgary, AB, T2C
2S9
(403) 279-3877
Emp Here 22
SIC 3532 Mining machinery

     D-U-N-S 24-616-7618   (SL)
CLOUGH ENERCORE LIMITED
115 Quarry Park Rd Se Suite 140, Calgary,
AB, T2C 5G9
(403) 523-2000
Emp Here 25   *Sales* 2,188,821
SIC 8711 Engineering services

     D-U-N-S 24-786-3921   (BR)
CLYDE UNION CANADA LIMITED
BROWN, DAVID UNION PUMPS
3525 62 Ave Se, Calgary, AB, T2C 1P5
(403) 236-8725
Emp Here 25
SIC 5084 Industrial machinery and equipment

     D-U-N-S 24-064-9009   (BR)
COASTAL PACIFIC XPRESS INC
4055 78 Ave Se, Calgary, AB, T2C 2J6
(403) 509-0144
Emp Here 50
SIC 5142 Packaged frozen goods

     D-U-N-S 25-733-9358   (BR)
COMMERCIAL EQUIPMENT CORP
COMMERCIAL TRUCK EQUIPMENT
11199 48 St Se, Calgary, AB, T2C 5H4
(403) 253-6421
Emp Here 30
SIC 5082 Construction and mining machinery

     D-U-N-S 20-176-2338   (BR)
**COMPAGNIE DES CHEMINS DE FER NA-
TIONAUX DU CANADA**

INTERMODAL
5310 27 St Se, Calgary, AB, T2C 1M7

Emp Here 46
SIC 4789 Transportation services, nec

D-U-N-S 20-554-5424 (SL)
COMPRESSCO CANADA INC
(Suby of Tetra Technologies, Inc.)
5050 76 Ave Se, Calgary, AB, T2C 2X2
(403) 279-5866
Emp Here 23   Sales 4,231,721
SIC 5084 Industrial machinery and equipment

D-U-N-S 20-521-9132 (BR)
CONSOLIDATED FASTFRATE INC
FASTFRATE
11440 54 St Se, Calgary, AB, T2C 4Y6
(403) 264-1687
Emp Here 75
SIC 4731 Freight transportation arrangement

D-U-N-S 24-317-2843 (HQ)
CONTINENTAL ALLOYS & SERVICES INC
(Suby of Reliance Steel & Aluminum Co.)
7520 114 Ave Se, Calgary, AB, T2C 4T3
(403) 216-5150
Emp Here 20   Emp Total 14,500
Sales 5,457,381
SIC 5084 Industrial machinery and equipment
Pr David Sapungis

D-U-N-S 25-100-5815 (BR)
CORIX INFRASTRUCTURE INC
CORIX WATER PRODUCTS
8515 48 St Se Suite 1a, Calgary, AB, T2C 2P8
(403) 203-4100
Emp Here 30
SIC 5083 Farm and garden machinery

D-U-N-S 25-974-1668 (BR)
COTT CORPORATION
COTT BEVERAGES
4810 76 Ave Se, Calgary, AB, T2C 2V2
(403) 279-6677
Emp Here 80
SIC 2086 Bottled and canned soft drinks

D-U-N-S 25-287-4300 (BR)
CRANE CARRIER (CANADA) LIMITED
ARCTIC TRUCK PARTS & SERVICE
(Suby of Illinois Tool Works Inc.)
7034 30 St Se, Calgary, AB, T2C 1N9
(403) 720-2910
Emp Here 24
SIC 5013 Motor vehicle supplies and new parts

D-U-N-S 24-299-9266 (BR)
CROWN METAL PACKAGING CANADA LP
(Suby of Crown Holdings Inc.)
4455 75 Ave Se, Calgary, AB, T2C 2K8
(403) 236-0241
Emp Here 120
SIC 3411 Metal cans

D-U-N-S 24-343-0571 (BR)
CURTISS-WRIGHT FLOW CONTROL COMPANY CANADA
DELTAVALVE CANADA, DIV OF
(Suby of Curtiss-Wright Corporation)
7712 56 St Se, Calgary, AB, T2C 4S9

Emp Here 25
SIC 3494 Valves and pipe fittings, nec

D-U-N-S 20-320-1459 (BR)
DEL EQUIPMENT LIMITED
3939 54 Ave Se Suite 12, Calgary, AB, T2C 2L2
(403) 236-9735
Emp Here 40
SIC 3713 Truck and bus bodies

D-U-N-S 24-715-5690 (HQ)
DATALOG TECHNOLOGY INC
(Suby of Datalog Technolcgy Inc)
10707 50 St Se, Calgary, AB, T2C 3E5

(403) 243-2024
Emp Here 296   Emp Total 300
Sales 62,476,413
SIC 1389 Oil and gas field services, nec
Pr Peter Huff
Dir Ian Underdown

D-U-N-S 25-485-8178 (BR)
DAVIDSON ENMAN LUMBER LIMITED
TRUSS DIVISION
9515 44 St Se, Calgary, AB, T2C 2P7
(403) 279-5525
Emp Here 100
SIC 2439 Structural wood members, nec

D-U-N-S 25-519-5463 (BR)
DIRECT LIMITED PARTNERSHIP
DIRECT TRANSPORT
5555 69 Ave Se Suite 121, Calgary, AB, T2C 4Y7
(403) 296-0291
Emp Here 100
SIC 4212 Local trucking, without storage

D-U-N-S 24-732-8784 (SL)
E.V. FYFE & ASSOCIATES LTD
5250 36 St Se, Calgary, AB, T2C 1P1
(403) 236-3822
Emp Here 50   Sales 3,939,878
SIC 4226 Special warehousing and storage, nec

D-U-N-S 24-310-4135 (BR)
ESIT CANADA ENTERPRISE SERVICES CO
ESIT CANADA ENTERPRISE SERVICES CO
(Suby of Dxc Technology Company)
2416 52 Ave Se Unit 1, Calgary, AB, T2C 4X7

Emp Here 40
SIC 3571 Electronic computers

D-U-N-S 20-802-7602 (BR)
ECCO HEATING PRODUCTS LTD
ECCO MANUFACTURING
11150 38 St Se Suite 23, Calgary, AB, T2C 2Z6
(403) 720-0895
Emp Here 50
SIC 5075 Warm air heating and air conditioning

D-U-N-S 20-440-4792 (BR)
ECCO HEATING PRODUCTS LTD
ECCO SUPPLY
11150 38 St Se Suite 11, Calgary, AB, T2C 2Z6
(403) 259-4344
Emp Here 70
SIC 5074 Plumbing and heating equipment and supplies (hydronics)

D-U-N-S 20-087-8130 (HQ)
ECONOMY CARRIERS LIMITED
SPECIAL COMODITIES, DIV OF
7100 44 St Se, Calgary, AB, T2C 2V7
(403) 720-5000
Emp Here 50   Emp Total 450
Sales 35,971,840
SIC 4213 Trucking, except local
Pr Pr Tom Fredericks
VP VP Donald Bietz
CFO Jim Davis

D-U-N-S 20-340-2115 (BR)
EDMONTON TRANSFER LTD
SOKIL TRANSPORTATION SERVICES
5402 44 St Se, Calgary, AB, T2C 4M8
(403) 279-8646
Emp Here 20
SIC 4731 Freight transportation arrangement

D-U-N-S 24-103-8376 (BR)
EMCO CORPORATION
7110 44 St Se, Calgary, AB, T2C 4Z3
(403) 252-6621
Emp Here 70
SIC 5074 Plumbing and heating equipment and supplies (hydronics)

D-U-N-S 24-309-6034 (BR)
EMERSON ELECTRIC CANADA LIMITED
EMERSON PROCESS MANAGEMENT
(Suby of Emerson Electric Co.)
110 Quarry Park Blvd Se Suite 200, Calgary, AB, T2C 3G3
(403) 258-6200
Emp Here 100
SIC 5063 Electrical apparatus and equipment

D-U-N-S 20-106-7639 (BR)
EMERSON ELECTRIC CANADA LIMITED
EMERSON PROCESS MANAGEMENT, DIV OF
(Suby of Emerson Electric Co.)
110 Quarry Park Blvd Se Suite 200, Calgary, AB, T2C 3G3
(403) 258-6200
Emp Here 200
SIC 8711 Engineering services

D-U-N-S 24-387-0271 (BR)
EVRAZ INC. NA CANADA
EVRAZ NORTH AMERICA
(Suby of EVRAZ PLC)
7201 Ogden Dale Rd Se, Calgary, AB, T2C 2A4
(403) 279-3351
Emp Here 500
SIC 3312 Blast furnaces and steel mills

D-U-N-S 25-388-7772 (BR)
EXALTA TRANSPORT CORP
5545 52 Ave Se, Calgary, AB, T2C 4M1
(403) 531-2550
Emp Here 40
SIC 4213 Trucking, except local

D-U-N-S 24-392-2994 (BR)
EXXONMOBIL CANADA LTD
EXXONMOBILE
(Suby of Exxon Mobil Corporation)
505 Quarry Park Blvd Se, Calgary, AB, T2C 5N1
(780) 956-8500
Emp Here 43
SIC 1311 Crude petroleum and natural gas

D-U-N-S 24-041-2069 (BR)
FASTENERS & FITTINGS INC
7803 35 St Se, Calgary, AB, T2C 1V3
(403) 279-2265
Emp Here 25
SIC 5072 Hardware

D-U-N-S 20-120-3077 (HQ)
FEDEX SUPPLY CHAIN DISTRIBUTION SYSTEM OF CANADA, INC
SYSTEME DE DISTRIBUTION DE LA CHAINE D'APPROVISIONNEMENT FEDEX DU CANADA
(Suby of Fedex Corporation)
6336 114 Ave Se, Calgary, AB, T2C 4T9
(800) 463-3339
Emp Here 20   Emp Total 169,000
Sales 106,376,701
SIC 4731 Freight transportation arrangement
Pr Arthur F. Smuck Iii
Sec Bradley R. Peacock
Treas Michael K. Fox
Genl Mgr Edward C. Klank Iii

D-U-N-S 20-052-9407 (HQ)
FLEXPIPE SYSTEMS INC
3501 54 Ave Se, Calgary, AB, T2C 0A9
(403) 503-0548
Emp Here 153   Emp Total 5,706
Sales 23,128,902
SIC 3498 Fabricated pipe and fittings
Pr Dame Broussard
VP Opers David Mccoll
Mfg Mgr Kevin Gartner
   Steve Guverra

D-U-N-S 24-299-9811 (BR)
FORT GARRY INDUSTRIES LTD
FGI
5350 72 Ave Se, Calgary, AB, T2C 4X5

(403) 236-9712
Emp Here 30
SIC 5012 Automobiles and other motor vehicles

D-U-N-S 24-928-0835 (SL)
FOUR STAR GRAVEL CONTRACTORS LTD
FOUR STAR GRAVEL & CONCRETE
(Suby of Plumb-Line Income Trust)
9816 44 St Se, Calgary, AB, T2C 2N4
(403) 236-1862
Emp Here 50   Sales 5,024,000
SIC 1794 Excavation work
Dir Marco Dedominicis
Dir Hoang Tran

D-U-N-S 20-282-2685 (BR)
FRONTIER POWER PRODUCTS LTD
10547 42 St Se, Calgary, AB, T2C 5B9
(403) 720-3735
Emp Here 23
SIC 3519 Internal combustion engines, nec

D-U-N-S 25-011-1218 (BR)
GARDEWINE GROUP INC
10612 24 St Se, Calgary, AB, T2C 4Z7
(403) 569-4011
Emp Here 55
SIC 4731 Freight transportation arrangement

D-U-N-S 24-013-5251 (BR)
GARLOCK OF CANADA LTD
FRANCE COMPRESSOR PRODUCTS
(Suby of Enpro Industries, Inc.)
7715 46 St Se, Calgary, AB, T2C 2Y5
(403) 253-4409
Emp Here 23
SIC 7699 Repair services, nec

D-U-N-S 25-325-3611 (BR)
GIBSON ENERGY ULC
CANWEST PROPANE
5205 76 Ave Se, Calgary, AB, T2C 3C6
(403) 236-3933
Emp Here 20
SIC 5172 Petroleum products, nec

D-U-N-S 24-330-1210 (BR)
GIENOW WINDOWS & DOORS INC
ARCHITECTURAL WINDOWS & DOORS
(Suby of H.I.G. Capital Inc.)
4315 61 Ave Se Unit 4, Calgary, AB, T2C 1Z6

Emp Here 58
SIC 2431 Millwork

D-U-N-S 24-355-3216 (HQ)
GIENOW WINDOWS & DOORS INC
(Suby of H.I.G. Capital Inc.)
7140 40 St Se, Calgary, AB, T2C 2B6
(403) 203-8200
Emp Here 600   Emp Total 2,519
Sales 79,155,636
SIC 2431 Millwork
Pr Pr Richard Boyer

D-U-N-S 20-695-7735 (HQ)
GLOBAL FLOW INC
(Suby of 1053384 Alberta Inc)
5796 40 St Se, Calgary, AB, T2C 2A1
(403) 528-4627
Emp Here 20   Emp Total 95
Sales 16,718,644
SIC 1389 Oil and gas field services, nec
Pr Pr Cam Marshall

D-U-N-S 20-178-4902 (BR)
GLOVER INTERNATIONAL TRUCKS LTD
ACE INTERNATIONAL TRUCK & ENGINE
(Suby of Glover International Trucks Ltd)
5425 90 Ave Se, Calgary, AB, T2C 4Z6
(403) 723-6666
Emp Here 50
SIC 5511 New and used car dealers

D-U-N-S 25-596-5113 (BR)
GOODFELLOW INC
5375 50 St Se Unit 11, Calgary, AB, T2C 3W1

(403) 252-9638
Emp Here 20
SIC 5031 Lumber, plywood, and millwork

D-U-N-S 25-763-4337   (BR)
GOVERNING COUNCIL OF THE SALVATION ARMY IN CANADA, THE
GOVERNING COUNCIL OF THE SALVATION ARMY IN CANADA, THE
2355 52 Ave Se Suite 29, Calgary, AB, T2C 4X7
(403) 287-9470
Emp Here 20
SIC 5932 Used merchandise stores

D-U-N-S 24-156-9107   (SL)
GRAND WEST ELECTRIC LTD
2408 91 Ave Se, Calgary, AB, T2C 5H2
(403) 291-2688
Emp Here 75   *Sales* 16,489,118
SIC 4931 Electric and other services combined
Pr Pr Anthony Dallazanna
Dir Gabe Rosati

D-U-N-S 25-386-0647   (BR)
H & R TRANSPORT LIMITED
4830 54 Ave Se, Calgary, AB, T2C 2Y8
(403) 720-8344
Emp Here 70
SIC 4213 Trucking, except local

D-U-N-S 24-570-4569   (BR)
HENRY SCHEIN CANADA, INC
HENRY SCHEIN ARCONA
5664 69 Ave Se Suite 106, Calgary, AB, T2C 5B1
(403) 279-9599
Emp Here 25
SIC 5047 Medical and hospital equipment

D-U-N-S 25-596-0221   (BR)
HI-WAY 9 EXPRESS LTD
5535 90 Ave Se, Calgary, AB, T2C 4Z6
(403) 237-7300
Emp Here 30
SIC 4212 Local trucking, without storage

D-U-N-S 24-158-5090   (BR)
HIGHLAND MOVING & STORAGE LTD
7115 48 St Se Suite 18, Calgary, AB, T2C 5A4
(403) 720-3222
Emp Here 40
SIC 4214 Local trucking with storage

D-U-N-S 24-336-4101   (BR)
HOOD PACKAGING CORPORATION
(*Suby of* Hood Packaging Corporation)
5615 44 St Se, Calgary, AB, T2C 1V2
(403) 236-8900
Emp Here 125
SIC 2674 Bags: uncoated paper and multiwall

D-U-N-S 20-271-9217   (SL)
ICONIC POWER SYSTEMS INC
11090 48 Ave Se, Calgary, AB, T2C 3E1
(403) 240-1233
Emp Here 60   *Sales* 5,253,170
SIC 1731 Electrical work
Pr Scott Ebner

D-U-N-S 24-346-7433   (BR)
INDEPENDENT COUNSELLING ENTERPRISES INC
(*Suby of* Independent Counselling Enterprises Inc)
4888 72 Ave Se, Calgary, AB, T2C 3Z2
(403) 219-0503
Emp Here 150
SIC 8322 Individual and family services

D-U-N-S 24-807-0054   (BR)
INGENIA POLYMERS CORP
3719 76 Ave Se, Calgary, AB, T2C 3K7
(403) 236-9333
Emp Here 38
SIC 2821 Plastics materials and resins

D-U-N-S 20-824-5865   (BR)

INGENIERIE CARMICHAEL LTEE
CARMICHAEL PERMAFROST
(*Suby of* Gestions Miller Carmichael Inc)
6504 30 St Se, Calgary, AB, T2C 1N4
(403) 255-3322
Emp Here 20
SIC 8711 Engineering services

D-U-N-S 24-312-7821   (BR)
INTEGRATED DISTRIBUTION SYSTEMS LIMITED PARTNERSHIP
WAJAX EQUIPMENT
5735 53 St Se, Calgary, AB, T2C 4V1
(403) 279-7278
Emp Here 65
SIC 6712 Bank holding companies

D-U-N-S 24-053-1272   (BR)
IRON MOUNTAIN CANADA OPERATIONS ULC
ARCHIVES IRON MOUNTAIN
5811 26 St Se Suite 15, Calgary, AB, T2C 1G3
(403) 531-2048
Emp Here 50
SIC 7389 Business services, nec

D-U-N-S 24-674-0344   (HQ)
JACOBS INDUSTRIAL SERVICES LTD
(*Suby of* Jacobs Engineering Group Inc.)
205 Quarry Park Blvd Se Suite 200, Calgary, AB, T2C 3E7
(403) 258-6899
Emp Here 25   *Emp Total* 64,000
Sales 145,921,400
SIC 7349 Building maintenance services, nec
Pr Earl J Mitchell
VP Opers N.L.H. Frederiksen
  Rejean J Thibeault

D-U-N-S 24-823-5827   (BR)
JOHN DEERE LANDSCAPES LTD
(*Suby of* Siteone Landscape Supply, Inc.)
9415 48 St Se, Calgary, AB, T2C 2R1
(403) 236-0102
Emp Here 20,000
SIC 1629 Heavy construction, nec

D-U-N-S 24-842-8885   (BR)
JOHN WATSON LIMITED
WATSON GLOVES
6155 46 St Se, Calgary, AB, T2C 5K6
(403) 279-2262
Emp Here 25
SIC 5136 Men's and boy's clothing

D-U-N-S 24-300-8794   (SL)
KEVCO PIPELINES LTD
5050 54 Ave Se, Calgary, AB, T2C 2Y8
(403) 279-5050
Emp Here 50   *Sales* 8,755,284
SIC 1623 Water, sewer, and utility lines
Pr Pr Kevin Dubetz
  Gloria Dubetz

D-U-N-S 24-068-0710   (BR)
KINDERSLEY TRANSPORT LTD
5515 98 Ave Se, Calgary, AB, T2C 4L1
(403) 279-8721
Emp Here 100
SIC 4213 Trucking, except local

D-U-N-S 20-594-1482   (SL)
KING'S TRANSFER VAN LINES (CALGARY) LTD
7803 35 St Se Unit G, Calgary, AB, T2C 1V3
(403) 730-5592
Emp Here 25   *Sales* 1,459,214
SIC 4214 Local trucking with storage

D-U-N-S 20-014-1864   (SL)
KOZUN EXPLORATION SERVICES LTD
5162 80 Ave Se Unit 20, Calgary, AB, T2C 2X3

Emp Here 30   *Sales* 31,148,800
SIC 1382 Oil and gas exploration services
Pr Pr Brian Kozun

D-U-N-S 24-806-8967   (HQ)

KUDU INDUSTRIES INC
(*Suby of* 563260 Alberta Ltd)
9112 40 St Se, Calgary, AB, T2C 2P3
(403) 279-5838
Emp Here 45   *Emp Total* 2
Sales 25,121,279
SIC 5084 Industrial machinery and equipment
Pr Pr Robert Mills
  Ray Mills

D-U-N-S 20-555-6959   (BR)
KVAERNER PROCESS SYSTEMS CANADA INC
3131 57 Ave Se, Calgary, AB, T2C 0B2
(403) 216-0750
Emp Here 40
SIC 8711 Engineering services

D-U-N-S 25-736-8225   (BR)
LAFARGE CANADA INC
9028 44 St Se Suite Lbby, Calgary, AB, T2C 2P6
(403) 292-9220
Emp Here 40
SIC 2891 Adhesives and sealants

D-U-N-S 24-116-3505   (BR)
LAFARGE CANADA INC
115 Quarry Park Rd Se Suite 300, Calgary, AB, T2C 5G9
(403) 225-5400
Emp Here 70
SIC 5032 Brick, stone, and related material

D-U-N-S 24-156-8989   (BR)
LARSON-JUHL CANADA INC
(*Suby of* Berkshire Hathaway Inc.)
3504 72 Ave Se Suite 6, Calgary, AB, T2C 1J9
(403) 279-8118
Emp Here 22
SIC 5023 Homefurnishings

D-U-N-S 24-827-0287   (BR)
LEGACY TRANSPORTATION SOLUTIONS INC
5505 72 Ave Se Unit 3, Calgary, AB, T2C 3C4
(403) 236-5903
Emp Here 40
SIC 4731 Freight transportation arrangement

D-U-N-S 24-855-2762   (BR)
LEHIGH HANSON MATERIALS LIMITED
2412 106 Ave Se, Calgary, AB, T2C 3W5
(403) 279-5531
Emp Here 80
SIC 5032 Brick, stone, and related material

D-U-N-S 24-343-0795   (BR)
LIVINGSTON TRANSPORTATION INC
4707 52 Ave Se, Calgary, AB, T2C 4N7
(403) 291-0620
Emp Here 20
SIC 4731 Freight transportation arrangement

D-U-N-S 24-204-9083   (BR)
LOBLAWS INC
WESTERN GROCERS
6810 40 St Se, Calgary, AB, T2C 2A5
(905) 459-2500
Emp Here 200
SIC 5411 Grocery stores

D-U-N-S 25-115-0827   (HQ)
LYNDEN INTERNATIONAL LOGISTICS CO
(*Suby of* Lynden Incorporated)
4441 76 Ave Se, Calgary, AB, T2C 2G8
(403) 279-2700
Emp Here 45   *Emp Total* 2,500
Sales 17,150,388
SIC 4225 General warehousing and storage
Pr David Richardson
  Kevin Gillies
Dir Opers Ray Tribe

D-U-N-S 24-320-9827   (SL)
MMR CANADA LIMITED
11083 48 St Se, Calgary, AB, T2C 1G8

---

(403) 720-9000
Emp Here 150   *Sales* 16,961,922
SIC 1731 Electrical work
  Michael Wilson
  William Mclin

D-U-N-S 20-051-0254   (SL)
MABRE PUMP INC
4451 54 Ave Se, Calgary, AB, T2C 2A2
(403) 720-4800
Emp Here 49   *Sales* 5,180,210
SIC 3569 General industrial machinery, nec
Pr Graeme Mcguire

D-U-N-S 25-389-1790   (SL)
MAGNUM DESIGNS CANADA (1998) INC
7120 Barlow Trail Se Suite Docks, Calgary, AB, T2C 2E1

Emp Here 60   *Sales* 7,507,300
SIC 2512 Upholstered household furniture
Pr Pr Ali Rahemtulla
VP VP Paul Ragon
  Pasquale Raviele

D-U-N-S 20-441-2449   (HQ)
MANTEI'S TRANSPORT LTD
8715 44 St Se, Calgary, AB, T2C 2P5
(403) 531-1600
Emp Here 60   *Emp Total* 750
Sales 7,879,756
SIC 4212 Local trucking, without storage
  Joseph Shannon
Pr Mark Shannon

D-U-N-S 24-597-6477   (BR)
MAPLE LEAF FOODS INC
4060 78 Ave Se, Calgary, AB, T2C 2L8
(403) 236-2000
Emp Here 50
SIC 2013 Sausages and other prepared meats

D-U-N-S 20-115-8198   (BR)
MATERIAUX DE CONSTRUCTION OLDCASTLE CANADA INC, LES
MATERIAUX DE CONSTRUCTION OLDCASTLE CANADA INC, LE
3601 72 Ave Se, Calgary, AB, T2C 2K3
(403) 279-2544
Emp Here 100
SIC 3211 Flat glass

D-U-N-S 25-266-8199   (BR)
MAXIM TRANSPORTATION SERVICES INC
MAXIM RENTALS & LEASING
6707 84 St Se, Calgary, AB, T2C 4T6
(403) 571-1275
Emp Here 35
SIC 7513 Truck rental and leasing, no drivers

D-U-N-S 20-291-3265   (BR)
MCCRUM'S DIRECT SALES LTD
MCCRUM'S OFFICE FURNISHINGS
5805 76 Ave Se Unit 5, Calgary, AB, T2C 5L8
(403) 259-4939
Emp Here 50
SIC 5712 Furniture stores

D-U-N-S 20-773-8852   (BR)
MCDONALD'S RESTAURANTS OF CANADA LIMITED
MCDONALD'S
(*Suby of* McDonald's Corporation)
5326 72 Ave Se, Calgary, AB, T2C 4X5
(403) 663-4390
Emp Here 30
SIC 5812 Eating places

D-U-N-S 20-809-3315   (BR)
MCINTYRE GROUP OFFICE SERVICES INC
4216 61 Ave Se Suite 34, Calgary, AB, T2C 1Z5
(403) 287-7779
Emp Here 70
SIC 1799 Special trade contractors, nec

D-U-N-S 24-330-0931   (BR)

METRIE CANADA LTD
SAUDER MOULDINGS CALGARY
5367 50 St Se, Calgary, AB, T2C 3W1
(403) 221-8141
Emp Here 100
SIC 2431 Millwork

D-U-N-S 25-741-7196   (BR)
MID-ARCTIC TRANSPORTATION CO. LTD
MATCO TRANSPORTATION SYSTEMS
5003 52 Ave Se, Calgary, AB, T2C 4N7
(403) 236-5010
Emp Here 20
SIC 4213 Trucking, except local

D-U-N-S 20-048-4884   (BR)
MOTION INDUSTRIES (CANADA), INC
(*Suby of* Genuine Parts Company)
4155 75 Ave Se Suite 16, Calgary, AB, T2C
2K8
(403) 236-5581
Emp Here 35
SIC 5085 Industrial supplies

D-U-N-S 24-438-8500   (BR)
MOUNTAIN PACIFIC TRANSPORT LTD
SHADOW LINES TRANSPORTATION GROUP
9315 40 St Se, Calgary, AB, T2C 2P4
(403) 279-8365
Emp Here 20
SIC 4213 Trucking, except local

D-U-N-S 24-379-7565   (BR)
NOV ENERFLOW ULC
NOV ENERFLOW
(*Suby of* National Oilwell Varco, Inc.)
8625 68 St Se, Calgary, AB, T2C 2R6
(403) 695-3189
Emp Here 80
SIC 3533 Oil and gas field machinery

D-U-N-S 20-177-3939   (BR)
NOV ENERFLOW ULC
NOV HYDRA RIG
4910 80 Ave Se, Calgary, AB, T2C 2X3
(403) 569-2222
Emp Here 150
SIC 1389 Oil and gas field services, nec

D-U-N-S 24-905-7217   (HQ)
NATCO CANADA, LTD
9423 Shepard Rd Se, Calgary, AB, T2C 4R6
(403) 203-2119
Emp Here 100   *Emp Total* 205
Sales 31,810,865
SIC 3443 Fabricated plate work (boiler shop)
Pr Pr James Crittall
Genl Mgr Ryan Chase
Dir Haimie Ledergerber
Michael J Mayer

D-U-N-S 25-538-2822   (HQ)
NATIONAL PROCESS EQUIPMENT INC
5409 74 Ave Se, Calgary, AB, T2C 3C9
(403) 219-0270
Emp Here 152   *Emp Total* 152
Sales 3,356,192
SIC 3561 Pumps and pumping equipment

D-U-N-S 20-077-3430   (BR)
OLD DUTCH FOODS LTD
HUMPTY DUMPTY OLD DUTCH FOODS
(*Suby of* Old Dutch Foods Ltd)
3103 54 Ave Se, Calgary, AB, T2C 0A9
(403) 279-2771
Emp Here 230
SIC 2096 Potato chips and similar snacks

D-U-N-S 24-858-3341   (BR)
OVERLAND WEST FREIGHT LINES LTD
9910 48 St Se, Calgary, AB, T2C 2R2
(403) 236-0912
Emp Here 25
SIC 4731 Freight transportation arrangement

D-U-N-S 24-675-2583   (BR)
PPG CANADA INC

(*Suby of* PPG Industries, Inc.)
4416 72 Ave Se Suite Side, Calgary, AB, T2C
2C1
(403) 279-8831
Emp Here 30
SIC 2851 Paints and allied products

D-U-N-S 24-616-7717   (SL)
PANAMOUNT INC
180 Quarry Park Blvd Se Suite 200, Calgary,
AB, T2C 3G3
(403) 258-1511
Emp Here 49   *Sales* 12,627,209
SIC 1522 Residential construction, nec
Dir Kerry Obrigewitsch

D-U-N-S 25-316-4263   (BR)
PASLEY, MAX ENTERPRISES LIMITED
MCDONALD'S RESTAURANTS
(*Suby of* Pasley, Max Enterprises Limited)
20 Riverglen Dr Se, Calgary, AB, T2C 3J3
(403) 236-4122
Emp Here 50
SIC 5812 Eating places

D-U-N-S 24-895-2603   (BR)
PENSKE TRUCK LEASING CANADA INC
(*Suby of* Penske Corporation)
6215 48 St Se, Calgary, AB, T2C 3J7
(403) 236-7165
Emp Here 30
SIC 7513 Truck rental and leasing, no drivers

D-U-N-S 24-004-1413   (BR)
PENSKE TRUCK LEASING CANADA INC
(*Suby of* Penske Corporation)
6215 48 St Se, Calgary, AB, T2C 3J7
(403) 236-7162
Emp Here 30
SIC 7359 Equipment rental and leasing, nec

D-U-N-S 25-364-3720   (BR)
PIONEER HI-BRED LIMITED
DUPONT WAREHOUSE
(*Suby of* E. I. Du Pont De Nemours and Com-
pany)
4444 72 Ave Se, Calgary, AB, T2C 2C1
(403) 531-4854
Emp Here 30
SIC 2824 Organic fibers, noncellulosic

D-U-N-S 24-273-0273   (BR)
PITTSBURGH GLASS WORKS, ULC
4416 72 Ave Se Suite Side, Calgary, AB, T2C
2C1
(403) 279-8831
Emp Here 35
SIC 5039 Construction materials, nec

D-U-N-S 24-009-8264   (BR)
PLATINUM ENERGY SERVICES ULC
TRINITY PLATINUM ENERGY SERVICES
7550 114 Ave Se, Calgary, AB, T2C 4T3
(403) 236-0530
Emp Here 50
SIC 3533 Oil and gas field machinery

D-U-N-S 20-773-8993   (BR)
PRAXAIR CANADA INC
PRAXAIR
(*Suby of* Praxair, Inc.)
8009 42 St Se, Calgary, AB, T2C 2T4
(403) 236-6511
Emp Here 50
SIC 3548 Welding apparatus

D-U-N-S 24-377-0398   (BR)
PRECISION DRILLING CORPORATION
ROSTEL INDUSTRIES, DIV OF
9699 Shepard Rd Se, Calgary, AB, T2C 4K5
(403) 720-3999
Emp Here 50
SIC 1381 Drilling oil and gas wells

D-U-N-S 24-341-5861   (BR)
PREMAY EQUIPMENT LP
8816 40 St Se, Calgary, AB, T2C 2P2

(403) 279-9775
Emp Here 65
SIC 4213 Trucking, except local

D-U-N-S 20-829-8372   (SL)
PROFESSIONAL EXCAVATORS LTD
10919 84 St Se, Calgary, AB, T2C 5A6
(403) 236-5686
Emp Here 60   *Sales* 4,377,642
SIC 1794 Excavation work

D-U-N-S 20-990-4205   (BR)
PRONGHORN CONTROLS LTD
4919 72 Ave Se Unit 101, Calgary, AB, T2C
3H3
(403) 720-2526
Emp Here 40
SIC 1389 Oil and gas field services, nec

D-U-N-S 25-990-5701   (HQ)
PRONGHORN CONTROLS LTD
(*Suby of* Pronghorn Controls Ltd)
4919 72 Ave Se Suite 101, Calgary, AB, T2C
3H3
(403) 720-2526
Emp Here 25   *Emp Total* 550
Sales 105,320,817
SIC 7629 Electrical repair shops
Pr Yves Tremblay
VP Opers Dean Toly
VP Fin Jason Boyd
Dir Peter Wesik

D-U-N-S 24-358-3114   (BR)
PRONGHORN CONTROLS LTD
4919 72 Ave Se Unit 101, Calgary, AB, T2C
3H3
(403) 292-0870
Emp Here 125
SIC 5084 Industrial machinery and equipment

D-U-N-S 20-771-6205   (BR)
QUINCAILLERIE RICHELIEU LTEE
RICHELIEU PANEL PRODUCTS
5211 52 St Se, Calgary, AB, T2C 4T2
(403) 203-2099
Emp Here 25
SIC 5072 Hardware

D-U-N-S 24-346-2041   (HQ)
RBS BULK SYSTEMS INC
(*Suby of* Reimer Consolidated Corp)
9910 48 St Se, Calgary, AB, T2C 2R2
(403) 248-1530
Emp Here 50   *Emp Total* 40
Sales 22,107,092
SIC 4213 Trucking, except local
Pr Pr Brian Murray
Donald S Reimer
Dir Anne Reimer

D-U-N-S 25-538-6385   (SL)
REGAL BEDDING LTD
5811 46 St Se, Calgary, AB, T2C 4Y5
(403) 236-7771
Emp Here 30   *Sales* 6,028,800
SIC 2515 Mattresses and bedsprings
Pr Pr Alykhan Sunderji
Rahim Sunderji

D-U-N-S 20-002-7444   (BR)
REIMER EXPRESS LINES LTD
ROADWAY EXPRESS
(*Suby of* Yrc Worldwide Inc.)
10120 52 St Se, Calgary, AB, T2C 4M2
(403) 279-0788
Emp Here 50
SIC 4213 Trucking, except local

D-U-N-S 24-700-1519   (BR)
REIMER EXPRESS LINES LTD
FAST AS FLITE
(*Suby of* Yrc Worldwide Inc.)
75 Dufferin Pl Se, Calgary, AB, T2C 4W3
(403) 279-0132
Emp Here 35
SIC 4213 Trucking, except local

D-U-N-S 20-321-7146   (BR)

RITE-WAY FENCING (2000) INC
7710 40 St Se, Calgary, AB, T2C 3S4
(403) 243-8733
Emp Here 49
SIC 1799 Special trade contractors, nec

D-U-N-S 25-265-9149   (SL)
ROBERTSON BRIGHT LTD
BREAKER ELECTRIC
6027 79 Ave Se Unit 1137, Calgary, AB, T2C
5P1
(403) 277-3077
Emp Here 35   *Sales* 3,064,349
SIC 1731 Electrical work

D-U-N-S 24-357-1127   (BR)
ROBINSON, B.A. CO. LTD
B.A. EXPRESS
5452 53 Ave Se, Calgary, AB, T2C 4R3
(403) 723-9030
Emp Here 31
SIC 5074 Plumbing and heating equipment
and supplies (hydronics)

D-U-N-S 20-174-8550   (BR)
ROSEDALE TRANSPORT LIMITED
ROSEDALE GROUP
4100 106 Ave Se Unit 2, Calgary, AB, T2C 5B6
(403) 259-6681
Emp Here 30
SIC 4225 General warehousing and storage

D-U-N-S 20-345-5621   (BR)
ROYAL CANADIAN LEGION, THE
OGDEN BRANCH NO 154
(*Suby of* Royal Canadian Legion, The)
2625 78 Ave Se, Calgary, AB, T2C 3B7

Emp Here 27
SIC 8641 Civic and social associations

D-U-N-S 24-314-7969   (BR)
RUSSEL METALS INC
5724 40 St Se, Calgary, AB, T2C 2A1
(403) 279-6600
Emp Here 100
SIC 3312 Blast furnaces and steel mills

D-U-N-S 24-765-1073   (BR)
RYDER TRUCK RENTAL CANADA LTD
(*Suby of* Ryder System, Inc.)
4830 54 Ave Se, Calgary, AB, T2C 2Y8
(403) 724-9343
Emp Here 22
SIC 7513 Truck rental and leasing, no drivers

D-U-N-S 20-124-7884   (BR)
S.L.H. TRANSPORT INC
5500 Dufferin Blvd Se, Calgary, AB, T2C 4Y2
(403) 720-2686
Emp Here 50
SIC 4213 Trucking, except local

D-U-N-S 20-108-5714   (SL)
SAFEGUARD SAFETY INC
4515 112 Ave Se, Calgary, AB, T2C 5C5
(403) 236-0752
Emp Here 34   *Sales* 6,030,906
SIC 3441 Fabricated structural Metal

D-U-N-S 24-982-9164   (BR)
SAFETY NET SECURITY LTD
3700 78 Ave Se Suite 200, Calgary, AB, T2C
2L8

Emp Here 30
SIC 7381 Detective and armored car services

D-U-N-S 20-030-4869   (SL)
SERVA GROUP (CANADA) ULC
7345 110 Ave Se, Calgary, AB, T2C 3B8
(403) 269-7847
Emp Here 42   *Sales* 24,988,376
SIC 3533 Oil and gas field machinery
Genl Mgr Ray Baker

D-U-N-S 25-415-9262   (SL)
SHAW PIPELINE SERVICES LTD

8010 40 St Se, Calgary, AB, T2C 2Y3
(403) 263-2255
Emp Here 20   *Sales* 2,407,703
SIC 1389 Oil and gas field services, nec

D-U-N-S 24-439-7444   (BR)
SHAWCOR LTD
SHAW PIPE PROTECTION
9229 Barlow Trail Se, Calgary, AB, T2C 2N8

Emp Here 100
SIC 1799 Special trade contractors, nec

D-U-N-S 24-654-5615   (BR)
SHRED-IT INTERNATIONAL ULC
SHRED-IT CALGARY
8009 57 St Se Suite 28, Calgary, AB, T2C 5K7
(403) 571-0777
Emp Here 40
SIC 7389 Business services, nec

D-U-N-S 20-599-3967   (HQ)
SIMARK CONTROLS LTD
(*Suby of* Simark Controls Ltd)
10509 46 St Se, Calgary, AB, T2C 5C2
(403) 236-0580
Emp Here 29   *Emp Total* 40
Sales 9,423,290
SIC 5084 Industrial machinery and equipment
Pr Pr Mark Wheeler
 Naresh Shankardass
 Perry Jamart
Dir George Rouault

D-U-N-S 25-114-7658   (BR)
SKYWAY CANADA LIMITED
6280 76 Ave Se Suite 20, Calgary, AB, T2C 5N5
(403) 276-6666
Emp Here 20
SIC 5082 Construction and mining machinery

D-U-N-S 24-157-1140   (BR)
SNAP-ON TOOLS OF CANADA LTD
(*Suby of* Snap-On Incorporated)
7403 48 St Se, Calgary, AB, T2C 4H6
(403) 720-0525
Emp Here 60
SIC 5072 Hardware

D-U-N-S 25-673-1902   (BR)
SOBEYS CAPITAL INCORPORATED
SOBEY'S WEST, DIV OF
7704 30 St Se, Calgary, AB, T2C 1M8
(403) 279-4483
Emp Here 260
SIC 5141 Groceries, general line

D-U-N-S 20-871-3425   (BR)
SOBEYS WEST INC
STORECARE
7505 48 St Se Suite 100, Calgary, AB, T2C 4C7

Emp Here 200
SIC 4225 General warehousing and storage

D-U-N-S 25-483-9491   (BR)
SOBEYS WEST INC
LUCERNE FOODS
3440 56 Ave Se, Calgary, AB, T2C 2C3
(403) 279-2555
Emp Here 550
SIC 2011 Meat packing plants

D-U-N-S 25-271-1056   (BR)
SOBEYS WEST INC
SAFEWAY
7740 18 St Se, Calgary, AB, T2C 2N5
(403) 236-0559
Emp Here 80
SIC 5411 Grocery stores

D-U-N-S 20-300-6853   (BR)
STANTEC CONSULTING LTD
37 Quarry Park Blvd Se Suite 200, Calgary, AB, T2C 5H9

(403) 252-3436
Emp Here 400
SIC 8711 Engineering services

D-U-N-S 25-498-9999   (BR)
STAPLES CANADA INC
STAPLES THE BUSINESS DEPOT
(*Suby of* Staples, Inc.)
3619 61 Ave Se Suite 100, Calgary, AB, T2C 4T8
(403) 509-2230
Emp Here 30
SIC 5943 Stationery stores

D-U-N-S 20-174-0276   (BR)
STARLINE MOVING SYSTEMS LTD
HIGHLAND MOVING
7115 48 St Se Unit 18, Calgary, AB, T2C 5A4
(403) 720-3222
Emp Here 40
SIC 4212 Local trucking, without storage

D-U-N-S 24-339-0171   (SL)
STEWART & STEVENSON CANADA INC
3111 Shepard Pl Se Suite 403, Calgary, AB, T2C 4P1
(403) 215-5300
Emp Here 100   *Sales* 50,155,933
SIC 3533 Oil and gas field machinery
Genl Mgr Jason Clark
Pr Pr Robert Hargrave

D-U-N-S 25-417-9732   (BR)
STRONGCO ENGINEERED SYSTEMS INC
STRONGCO EQUIPMENT
7923 54 St Se, Calgary, AB, T2C 4R7
(403) 216-1010
Emp Here 30
SIC 3541 Machine tools, Metal cutting type

D-U-N-S 20-188-6350   (BR)
SYSCO CANADA, INC
SYSCO FOOD SERVICES OF CALGARY
(*Suby of* Sysco Corporation)
4639 72 Ave Se, Calgary, AB, T2C 4H7
(403) 720-1300
Emp Here 350
SIC 5141 Groceries, general line

D-U-N-S 25-408-6028   (BR)
TDL GROUP CORP, THE
TIM HORTON REGIONAL OFFICE
7460 51 St Se, Calgary, AB, T2C 4B4
(403) 203-7400
Emp Here 100
SIC 5812 Eating places

D-U-N-S 20-558-1957   (HQ)
TIW WESTERN INC
(*Suby of* Canerector Inc)
7770 44 St Se, Calgary, AB, T2C 2L5
(403) 279-8310
Emp Here 55   *Emp Total* 3,000
Sales 42,451,185
SIC 3433 Heating equipment, except electric
Pr Pr Cecil Hawkins
 Amanda Hawkins
 Bill Nickel

D-U-N-S 24-929-6005   (SL)
TARPON ENERGY SERVICES(PROCESS SYSTEMS)LTD
7020 81 St Se, Calgary, AB, T2C 5B8
(403) 234-8647
Emp Here 50   *Sales* 9,120,088
SIC 5084 Industrial machinery and equipment
Pr Pr Wade Fleury

D-U-N-S 25-328-0564   (SL)
TECHWEST INC
5516 40 St Se Suite A, Calgary, AB, T2C 2A1
(403) 640-2124
Emp Here 26   *Sales* 6,407,837
SIC 3533 Oil and gas field machinery
Pr Pr Brian Krebs
 Barry Tanasychuk
 Darryl Tkachuk

D-U-N-S 20-530-5597   (SL)

TERVITA DRILLING AND CORING SERVICES LTD
(*Suby of* Tervita Corporation)
9919 Shepard Rd Se, Calgary, AB, T2C 3C5
(855) 837-8482
Emp Here 225   *Sales* 24,168,403
SIC 1081 Metal mining services
Pr Pr Garry Wegleitner

D-U-N-S 20-203-3382   (BR)
THERMO DESIGN INSULATION LTD
7124 Barlow Trail Se, Calgary, AB, T2C 2E1
(403) 720-8203
Emp Here 40
SIC 5211 Lumber and other building materials

D-U-N-S 24-395-9160   (HQ)
THERMO KING WESTERN (CALGARY) INC
(*Suby of* Thermo King Western (Calgary) Inc)
6213 29 St Se, Calgary, AB, T2C 1R3
(403) 236-1020
Emp Here 41   *Emp Total* 44
Sales 6,879,002
SIC 3713 Truck and bus bodies
Pr Pr Mitch Hancock

D-U-N-S 20-254-7738   (BR)
THYSSENKRUPP ELEVATOR (CANADA) LIMITED
THYSSEN DOVER ELEVATOR KRUPP
2419 52 Ave Se Unit 5, Calgary, AB, T2C 4X7
(403) 527-7284
Emp Here 40
SIC 1796 Installing building equipment

D-U-N-S 20-268-0075   (BR)
THYSSENKRUPP ELEVATOR (CANADA) LIMITED
THYSSENKRUPP ELEVATORS
2419 52 Ave Se Unit 5, Calgary, AB, T2C 4X7
(403) 259-4183
Emp Here 80
SIC 7699 Repair services, nec

D-U-N-S 24-308-4329   (BR)
TOTAL ENERGY SERVICES INC
BIDELL GAS COMPRESSION
6900 112 Ave Se, Calgary, AB, T2C 4Z1
(403) 235-5877
Emp Here 100
SIC 1382 Oil and gas exploration services

D-U-N-S 24-802-5970   (SL)
TRANS-OCEANIC HUMAN RESOURCES INC
5515 40 St Se, Calgary, AB, T2C 2A8

Emp Here 50   *Sales* 3,648,035
SIC 7361 Employment agencies

D-U-N-S 25-329-1751   (BR)
TROPHY FOODS INC
(*Suby of* Trophy Foods Inc)
6210 44 St Se, Calgary, AB, T2C 4L3
(403) 571-6887
Emp Here 100
SIC 5149 Groceries and related products, nec

D-U-N-S 24-362-8844   (BR)
TY-CROP MANUFACTURING LTD
PROPELL - OILFIELD EQUIPMENT INNOVATION
7211 110 Ave Se, Calgary, AB, T2C 3B8
(403) 724-9230
Emp Here 50
SIC 1389 Oil and gas field services, nec

D-U-N-S 25-330-4398   (BR)
UNIFIRST CANADA LTD
(*Suby of* Unifirst Corporation)
5728 35 St Se, Calgary, AB, T2C 2G3
(403) 279-2800
Emp Here 90
SIC 7213 Linen supply

D-U-N-S 25-413-8563   (SL)
UNIQUE SCAFFOLD INC
4750 104 Ave Se, Calgary, AB, T2C 2H3

(403) 203-3422
Emp Here 30   *Sales* 6,128,699
SIC 1799 Special trade contractors, nec
Pr Pr Jason Procyk
 William Procyk

D-U-N-S 24-104-6494   (BR)
UNITED RENTALS OF CANADA, INC
11447 42 St Se Suite Unit, Calgary, AB, T2C 2Y1
(403) 262-9998
Emp Here 20
SIC 7353 Heavy construction equipment rental

D-U-N-S 20-522-8083   (BR)
UNIVAR CANADA LTD
4220 78 Ave Se, Calgary, AB, T2C 2Z5
(403) 236-1713
Emp Here 60
SIC 5191 Farm supplies

D-U-N-S 24-006-7777   (BR)
VPC GROUP INC
VITAFOAM
(*Suby of* VPC Group Inc)
3220 56 Ave Se, Calgary, AB, T2C 0B1
(403) 279-2866
Emp Here 65
SIC 3069 Fabricated rubber products, nec

D-U-N-S 24-025-9288   (BR)
VARSTEEL LTD
VALUE STEEL & PIPE, DIV OF
55 Dufferin Pl Se, Calgary, AB, T2C 4W3
(403) 279-7030
Emp Here 65
SIC 5051 Metals service centers and offices

D-U-N-S 24-298-1843   (SL)
WARNER SHELTER SYSTEMS LIMITED
WSSL
9811 44 St Se, Calgary, AB, T2C 2P7
(403) 279-7662
Emp Here 50   *Sales* 2,188,821
SIC 2394 Canvas and related products

D-U-N-S 20-824-5167   (BR)
WESTCAN BULK TRANSPORT LTD
(*Suby of* The Kenan Advantage Group Inc)
3780 76 Ave Se, Calgary, AB, T2C 1J8
(403) 279-5505
Emp Here 143
SIC 4212 Local trucking, without storage

D-U-N-S 25-361-7807   (BR)
WESTCON PRECAST INC
(*Suby of* Zenco Alberta Ltd)
4412 54 Ave Se, Calgary, AB, T2C 2B9
(403) 279-2534
Emp Here 36
SIC 1791 Structural steel erection

D-U-N-S 25-217-7316   (SL)
WESTECH BUILDING PRODUCTS ULC
5201 64 Ave Se, Calgary, AB, T2C 4Z9
(403) 279-4497
Emp Here 180   *Sales* 28,746,516
SIC 3089 Plastics products, nec
 Mitchell H Gropper
Genl Mgr Glenn Syrowitz

D-U-N-S 24-807-1961   (BR)
WESTFAIR DRUGS LTD
3916 72 Ave Se, Calgary, AB, T2C 2E2
(403) 279-1600
Emp Here 120
SIC 5199 Nondurable goods, nec

D-U-N-S 20-178-1825   (BR)
WESTRIDGE CABINETS (1993) LTD
(*Suby of* Signal Hill Equity Partners Inc)
3953 112 Ave Se Suite 167, Calgary, AB, T2C 0J4
(403) 291-5022
Emp Here 40
SIC 2434 Wood kitchen cabinets

D-U-N-S 24-798-5476   (SL)

WHISTLER BREWING COMPANY LTD
5555 76 Ave Se Suite 1, Calgary, AB, T2C 4L8
(403) 720-4473
Emp Here 131   *Sales* 22,469,120
SIC 2082 Malt beverages
  Timothy A. Duffin

D-U-N-S 24-702-5901   (BR)
WILKINSON STEEL AND METALS INC
6125 51 St Se, Calgary, AB, T2C 3V2
(403) 236-0300
Emp Here 30
SIC 3599 Industrial machinery, nec

D-U-N-S 20-082-6779   (BR)
WOLSELEY CANADA INC
WOLSELEY MECHANICAL GROUP
(*Suby of* WOLSELEY PLC)
10775 42 St Se Unit 9, Calgary, AB, T2C 5B2
(403) 243-8790
Emp Here 70
SIC 5074 Plumbing and heating equipment and supplies (hydronics)

D-U-N-S 24-389-6730   (SL)
XL PERFORATING PARTNERSHIP
6060 86 Ave Se, Calgary, AB, T2C 4L7
(403) 255-7776
Emp Here 40   *Sales* 13,391,400
SIC 5169 Chemicals and allied products, nec
Genl Mgr Donald Mack

Calgary, AB T2E

D-U-N-S 25-366-1433   (BR)
1149318 ONTARIO INC
C.C.T. LOGISTIC SERVICES
(*Suby of* 1149318 Ontario Inc)
1726 25 Ave Ne Suite 2, Calgary, AB, T2E 7K1
(403) 717-2500
Emp Here 20
SIC 4214 Local trucking with storage

D-U-N-S 20-321-5025   (BR)
170TH C.T. GRILL INC
CHILI'S TEXAS GRILL
2480 37 Ave Ne, Calgary, AB, T2E 8S6
(403) 291-0520
Emp Here 50
SIC 5812 Eating places

D-U-N-S 25-417-3735   (SL)
369135 ALBERTA LTD
5438 11 St Ne Suite 212, Calgary, AB, T2E 7E9
(403) 295-0694
Emp Here 50   *Sales* 6,407,837
SIC 8713 Surveying services
Pr Pr Fred Welter

D-U-N-S 25-971-8252   (BR)
4513380 CANADA INC
LIVINGSTON INTERNATIONAL
1925 18 Ave Ne Suite 320, Calgary, AB, T2E 7T8
(403) 250-3753
Emp Here 20
SIC 4731 Freight transportation arrangement

D-U-N-S 20-297-3462   (SL)
550338 ALBERTA LIMITED
SERVICE MASTER OF CALGARY JMS
3530 11a St Ne Suite 1, Calgary, AB, T2E 6M7
(403) 250-7878
Emp Here 200   *Sales* 5,836,856
SIC 7349 Building maintenance services, nec
Pr Pr Malcom Sykes
  Zana Sykes

D-U-N-S 20-347-5269   (BR)
7-ELEVEN CANADA, INC
7-ELEVEN STORE #25349
311 16 Ave Ne, Calgary, AB, T2E 1K1
(403) 276-2111
Emp Here 20

SIC 5411 Grocery stores

D-U-N-S 25-385-5415   (SL)
704610 ALBERTA LTD
380 Mctavish Rd Ne Suite 3, Calgary, AB, T2E 7G5
(403) 735-3299
Emp Here 275   *Sales* 53,995,452
SIC 4581 Airports, flying fields, and services
Pr Pr John Binder
  Mike Dodd

D-U-N-S 25-776-9158   (SL)
A 1 DELIVERY SERVICES
2915 21 St Ne Unit 101, Calgary, AB, T2E 7T1

Emp Here 50   *Sales* 3,939,878
SIC 4212 Local trucking, without storage

D-U-N-S 24-160-5914   (HQ)
AGAT LABORATORIES LTD
AGAT
2905 12 St Ne, Calgary, AB, T2E 7J2
(403) 736-2000
Emp Here 130   *Emp Total* 575
Sales 77,529,465
SIC 8731 Commercial physical research
  John Desanti
  Allan Kostanuick

D-U-N-S 24-098-5247   (BR)
AGAT LABORATORIES LTD
CORE GEOLOGY BUILDING
3801 21 St Ne, Calgary, AB, T2E 6T5
(403) 299-2000
Emp Here 160
SIC 8734 Testing laboratories

D-U-N-S 20-827-6423   (BR)
ASM CANADA, INC
(*Suby of* Advantage Sales & Marketing Inc.)
5655 10 St Ne Suite 111, Calgary, AB, T2E 8W7
(403) 253-4488
Emp Here 30
SIC 5141 Groceries, general line

D-U-N-S 20-201-6015   (BR)
ATCO GAS AND PIPELINES LTD
4415 12 St Ne, Calgary, AB, T2E 4R1
(403) 245-7857
Emp Here 80
SIC 4923 Gas transmission and distribution

D-U-N-S 25-681-3247   (SL)
ABCO MAINTENANCE SYSTEMS INC
260 20 Ave Ne, Calgary, AB, T2E 1P9
(403) 293-5752
Emp Here 105   *Sales* 3,064,349
SIC 7349 Building maintenance services, nec

D-U-N-S 24-517-3570   (SL)
ACTION INTERNATIONAL MINISTRIES CORPORATION
3015 21 St Ne Unit A, Calgary, AB, T2E 7T1
(403) 204-1421
Emp Here 60   *Sales* 3,939,878
SIC 8661 Religious organizations

D-U-N-S 20-152-6568   (BR)
ACUREN GROUP INC
ACUREN GROUP
(*Suby of* Rockwood Service Corporation)
1411 25 Ave Ne Unit 3, Calgary, AB, T2E 7L6
(403) 291-3126
Emp Here 40
SIC 7389 Business services, nec

D-U-N-S 24-207-5690   (BR)
AERO AVIATION INC
393 Palmer Rd Ne Suite 59, Calgary, AB, T2E 7G4
(403) 250-3663
Emp Here 80
SIC 4581 Airports, flying fields, and services

D-U-N-S 20-106-7324   (BR)
AEROTEK ULC
7326 10 St Ne Suite 105, Calgary, AB, T2E

8W1
(403) 516-3600
Emp Here 28
SIC 7361 Employment agencies

D-U-N-S 25-535-9234   (BR)
AGRIFOODS INTERNATIONAL COOPERATIVE LTD
DAIRYWORLD FOODS
4215 12 St Ne, Calgary, AB, T2E 4P9
(403) 571-6400
Emp Here 350
SIC 2026 Fluid milk

D-U-N-S 20-152-8275   (BR)
AIR CANADA
AIR CANADA CARGO
8001 21 St Ne Unit B, Calgary, AB, T2E 8H2
(403) 221-2895
Emp Here 57
SIC 4512 Air transportation, scheduled

D-U-N-S 24-004-8442   (BR)
AIRSPRINT INC.
1910 Mccall Landng Ne, Calgary, AB, T2E 9B5
(403) 730-2344
Emp Here 50
SIC 4522 Air transportation, nonscheduled

D-U-N-S 20-106-8447   (HQ)
AIRPORT TERMINAL SERVICES CANADIAN COMPANY
8075 22 St Ne, Calgary, AB, T2E 7Z6
(403) 291-0965
Emp Here 25   *Emp Total* 1,900
Sales 151,977,138
SIC 4581 Airports, flying fields, and services
  Richard Hawes
Pr Pr Sally Leible
  John Tucker

D-U-N-S 20-831-1605   (HQ)
ALBERTA BEVERAGE CONTAINER RECYCLING CORPORATION
(*Suby of* Alberta Beverage Container Recycling Corporation)
901 57 Ave Ne Suite 8, Calgary, AB, T2E 8X9
(403) 264-0170
Emp Here 40   *Emp Total* 50
Sales 8,480,961
SIC 4953 Refuse systems
  Ken White
  Alain Maisonneube
  George Bowman
  Brian Feeney
  Sandra Banks
  Blair Patterson
  Jeff Shavchuk

D-U-N-S 24-364-7885   (BR)
ALBERTA TREASURY BRANCHES
ATB FINANCIAL
6715 8 St Ne Suite 144, Calgary, AB, T2E 7H7
(403) 541-4300
Emp Here 20
SIC 6036 Savings institutions, except federal

D-U-N-S 25-440-6028   (HQ)
ALEXANDRA COMMUNITY HEALTH CENTRE
THE ALEX COMMUNITY HEALTH CENTRE
(*Suby of* Alexandra Community Health Centre)
1318 Centre St Ne Suite 101, Calgary, AB, T2E 2R7
(403) 266-2622
Emp Here 28   *Emp Total* 80
Sales 4,815,406
SIC 8011 Offices and clinics of medical doctors

D-U-N-S 20-117-6752   (BR)
APPLIED INDUSTRIAL TECHNOLOGIES, LP
HYPOWER SYSTEMS
(*Suby of* Applied Industrial Technologies, Inc.)
4600 5 St Ne Suite 3, Calgary, AB, T2E 7C3

(403) 230-2428
Emp Here 20
SIC 5084 Industrial machinery and equipment

D-U-N-S 20-770-3377   (BR)
ASTRAL MEDIA RADIO INC
CKMX CJAY
(*Suby of* Astral Media Radio Inc)
1110 Centre St Ne Suite 300, Calgary, AB, T2E 2R2
(403) 242-1116
Emp Here 25
SIC 4832 Radio broadcasting stations

D-U-N-S 20-120-4562   (BR)
AVMAX GROUP INC
WESTERN AVIONICS
275 Palmer Rd Ne, Calgary, AB, T2E 7G4
(403) 250-2644
Emp Here 80
SIC 7622 Radio and television repair

D-U-N-S 24-685-4066   (BR)
AVMAX GROUP INC
MAINTENANCE, DIV OF
380 Mctavish Rd Ne, Calgary, AB, T2E 7G5
(403) 735-3299
Emp Here 80
SIC 4581 Airports, flying fields, and services

D-U-N-S 20-927-0680   (SL)
BTO VENTURES LTD
TOAD N TURTLE PUBHOUSE & GRILL
2475 27 Ave Ne, Calgary, AB, T2E 8M1
(403) 717-0670
Emp Here 60   *Sales* 1,824,018
SIC 5812 Eating places

D-U-N-S 24-839-9446   (BR)
BARTLE & GIBSON CO LTD
4300 21 St Ne, Calgary, AB, T2E 9A6
(403) 291-1099
Emp Here 35
SIC 5074 Plumbing and heating equipment and supplies (hydronics)

D-U-N-S 20-770-9457   (BR)
BELL HELICOPTER TEXTRON CANADA LIMITEE
BELL HELICOPTER
(*Suby of* Textron Inc.)
58 Aero Dr Ne Suite 101, Calgary, AB, T2E 8Z9
(403) 275-5876
Emp Here 21
SIC 3721 Aircraft

D-U-N-S 24-929-0933   (BR)
BELL MEDIA INC
CJAY 92
1110 Centre St Ne Suite 300, Calgary, AB, T2E 2R2
(403) 240-5850
Emp Here 60
SIC 4832 Radio broadcasting stations

D-U-N-S 25-104-2867   (BR)
BLACK PRESS GROUP LTD
CENTRAL WEB OFFSET, DIV OF
278 19 St Ne, Calgary, AB, T2E 8P7
(403) 730-8990
Emp Here 50
SIC 2711 Newspapers

D-U-N-S 25-414-6228   (SL)
BLUEWAVE ANTENNA SYSTEMS LTD
7015 8 St Ne, Calgary, AB, T2E 8A2
(403) 291-4422
Emp Here 35   *Sales* 2,553,625
SIC 4899 Communication services, nec

D-U-N-S 20-831-1589   (SL)
BOW CITY DELIVERY (1989) LTD
BOW CITY
1423 45 Ave Ne Bay Ctr, Calgary, AB, T2E 2P3
(403) 250-5329
Emp Here 76   *Sales* 3,866,917
SIC 7389 Business services, nec

D-U-N-S 24-982-1182   (SL)
BOWNESS BAKERY (ALBERTA) INC
4280 23 St Ne Suite 1, Calgary, AB, T2E 6X7
(403) 250-9760
Emp Here 70   *Sales* 3,648,035
SIC 2051 Bread, cake, and related products

D-U-N-S 24-156-3402   (SL)
C L CONSULTANTS LIMITED
DRILLTEL SYSTEMS
(*Suby of* Continental Laboratories (1985) Ltd)
3601 21 St Ne Suite A, Calgary, AB, T2E 6T5
(403) 250-3982
Emp Here 28   *Sales* 1,240,332
SIC 8999 Services, nec

D-U-N-S 20-327-8585   (BR)
CABELA'S RETAIL CANADA INC
CABELA'S
(*Suby of* Cabela's Incorporated)
851 64 Ave Ne, Calgary, AB, T2E 3B8
(403) 910-0200
Emp Here 150
SIC 5941 Sporting goods and bicycle shops

D-U-N-S 20-591-1329   (BR)
CALGARY BOARD OF EDUCATION
BUCHANAN ELEMENTARY SCHOOL
3717 Centre St Nw, Calgary, AB, T2E 2Y2
(403) 777-6260
Emp Here 25
SIC 8211 Elementary and secondary schools

D-U-N-S 20-591-1170   (BR)
CALGARY BOARD OF EDUCATION
TUXEDO PARK CAMPUS
130 28 Ave Ne, Calgary, AB, T2E 2A8
(403) 777-6330
Emp Here 25
SIC 8211 Elementary and secondary schools

D-U-N-S 20-591-1956   (BR)
CALGARY BOARD OF EDUCATION
STANLEY JONES ELEMENTARY SCHOOL
950 6 St Ne, Calgary, AB, T2E 8M3
(403) 777-6800
Emp Here 40
SIC 8211 Elementary and secondary schools

D-U-N-S 20-590-7863   (BR)
CALGARY BOARD OF EDUCATION
GREENVIEW ELEMENTARY
211 Mcknight Blvd Ne, Calgary, AB, T2E 5S7
(403) 253-9257
Emp Here 25
SIC 8211 Elementary and secondary schools

D-U-N-S 20-590-7913   (BR)
CALGARY BOARD OF EDUCATION
MAYLAND HEIGHTS SCHOOL
2324 Maunsell Dr Ne, Calgary, AB, T2E 6A2
(403) 777-6290
Emp Here 35
SIC 8211 Elementary and secondary schools

D-U-N-S 20-713-1033   (BR)
CALGARY BOARD OF EDUCATION
MOUNT VIEW ELEMENTARY SCHOOL
2004 4 St Ne, Calgary, AB, T2E 3T8
(403) 777-6300
Emp Here 20
SIC 8211 Elementary and secondary schools

D-U-N-S 20-713-1082   (BR)
CALGARY BOARD OF EDUCATION
VISTA HEIGHTS SCHOOL
2411 Vermillion St Ne, Calgary, AB, T2E 6J3
(403) 777-6000
Emp Here 20
SIC 8211 Elementary and secondary schools

D-U-N-S 20-713-1298   (BR)
CALGARY BOARD OF EDUCATION
COLONEL MACLEOD SCHOOL
1610 6 St Ne, Calgary, AB, T2E 3Y9
(403) 777-7500
Emp Here 34
SIC 8211 Elementary and secondary schools

D-U-N-S 25-325-4932   (BR)
CALGARY BOARD OF EDUCATION
BELFAST ELEMENTARY SCHOOL
1229 17a St Ne, Calgary, AB, T2E 4V4
(403) 777-6250
Emp Here 20
SIC 8211 Elementary and secondary schools

D-U-N-S 25-146-0978   (BR)
CALGARY BOARD OF EDUCATION
LANGEVIN ELEMENTARY SCHOOL
107 6a St Ne, Calgary, AB, T2E 0B7
(403) 777-7350
Emp Here 55
SIC 8211 Elementary and secondary schools

D-U-N-S 25-272-3440   (BR)
CALGARY BOARD OF EDUCATION
SIR JOHN FRANKLIN JUNIOR HIGH SCHOOL
2215 8 Ave Ne, Calgary, AB, T2E 0T7
(403) 777-7610
Emp Here 35
SIC 8211 Elementary and secondary schools

D-U-N-S 25-170-5398   (BR)
**CALGARY CATHOLIC IMMIGRATION SOCI-
ETY**
SETTLEMENT CENTRE, DIV OF
23 Mcdougall Crt Ne, Calgary, AB, T2E 8R3
(403) 262-8132
Emp Here 21
SIC 8322 Individual and family services

D-U-N-S 20-650-4065   (BR)
CALGARY CO-OPERATIVE ASSOCIATION LIMITED
CALGARY CO-OP
540 16 Ave Ne, Calgary, AB, T2E 1K4
(403) 299-4276
Emp Here 100
SIC 5411 Grocery stores

D-U-N-S 25-961-2984   (BR)
CALGARY FASTENERS & TOOLS LTD
(*Suby of* 700635 Alberta Ltd)
2211 32 Ave Ne, Calgary, AB, T2E 6Z3
(403) 291-9177
Emp Here 35
SIC 5085 Industrial supplies

D-U-N-S 20-574-7418   (BR)
CALGARY ROMAN CATHOLIC SEPARATE SCHOOL DISTRICT #1
ST. ALPHONSUS FINE ARTS SCHOOL
928 Radnor Ave Ne, Calgary, AB, T2E 5H5
(403) 500-2016
Emp Here 30
SIC 8211 Elementary and secondary schools

D-U-N-S 24-977-5276   (BR)
CALGARY ROMAN CATHOLIC SEPARATE SCHOOL DISTRICT #1
ST. ANGELA ELEMENTARY SCHOOL
231 6 St Ne, Calgary, AB, T2E 3Y1
(403) 500-2011
Emp Here 20
SIC 8211 Elementary and secondary schools

D-U-N-S 20-641-1279   (SL)
CALGARY SCOPE SOCIETY
219 18 St Se, Calgary, AB, T2E 6J5
(403) 509-0200
Emp Here 250   *Sales* 18,971,150
SIC 8322 Individual and family services
Fin Mgr Bob Gentals

D-U-N-S 20-128-7427   (HQ)
CAMERON FLOW SYSTEMS LTD
7944 10 St Ne, Calgary, AB, T2E 8W1
(403) 291-4814
Emp Here 52   *Emp Total* 160
Sales 23,566,306
SIC 3825 Instruments to measure electricity
  Warren Jale
  William C Lemmer

D-U-N-S 20-572-7196   (BR)

CANADA POST CORPORATION
5438 11 St Ne Suite 220, Calgary, AB, T2E 7E9
(403) 295-0694
Emp Here 20
SIC 4311 U.s. postal service

D-U-N-S 20-512-7462   (HQ)
CANADA TECH CORP
1437 47 Ave Ne Suite 105, Calgary, AB, T2E 6N7
(403) 232-1400
Emp Here 36   *Emp Total* 13,485
Sales 15,939,018
SIC 3533 Oil and gas field machinery
Pr Pr Cedric Doerksen
Opers Mgr Cory Parker

D-U-N-S 24-766-2034   (BR)
**CANADIAN BANK NOTE COMPANY, LIM-
ITED**
MCARA PRINTING
2507 12 St Ne Suite 105, Calgary, AB, T2E 7L5
(403) 250-9515
Emp Here 61
SIC 2759 Commercial printing, nec

D-U-N-S 25-776-9513   (BR)
CANADIAN CANCER SOCIETY
325 Manning Rd Ne Unit 200, Calgary, AB, T2E 2P5
(403) 205-3966
Emp Here 70
SIC 8399 Social services, nec

D-U-N-S 20-107-6549   (BR)
**CANADIAN CONTRACT CLEANING SPE-
CIALISTS, INC**
1420 40 Ave Ne Suite 3, Calgary, AB, T2E 6L1
(403) 259-5560
Emp Here 250
SIC 7349 Building maintenance services, nec

D-U-N-S 25-305-9331   (BR)
CANADIAN DIABETES ASSOCIATION
CALGARY & DISTRICT BRANCH
2323 32 Ave Ne Unit 204, Calgary, AB, T2E 6Z3
(403) 266-0620
Emp Here 20
SIC 8699 Membership organizations, nec

D-U-N-S 24-159-7160   (BR)
CANADIAN NATIONAL INSTITUTE FOR THE BLIND, THE
CNIB
(*Suby of* Canadian National Institute For The Blind, The)
15 Colonel Baker Pl Ne, Calgary, AB, T2E 4Z3
(403) 266-8831
Emp Here 35
SIC 8322 Individual and family services

D-U-N-S 24-677-8000   (BR)
CANADIAN NORTH INC
580 Palmer Rd Ne Suite 200, Calgary, AB, T2E 7R3
(403) 503-2310
Emp Here 150
SIC 4512 Air transportation, scheduled

D-U-N-S 24-297-8807   (BR)
CANON CANADA INC
2828 16 St Ne, Calgary, AB, T2E 7K7
(403) 717-2900
Emp Here 65
SIC 5044 Office equipment

D-U-N-S 24-417-2847   (BR)
CANPAR TRANSPORT L.P.
CANPAR CARRIER
(*Suby of* Canpar Transport L.P.)
707 Barlow Trail Se Unit D, Calgary, AB, T2E 8C2
(403) 235-6701
Emp Here 75
SIC 7389 Business services, nec

D-U-N-S 25-229-8609   (BR)
CANSEL SURVEY EQUIPMENT INC
CANSEL
(*Suby of* Cansel Survey Equipment Inc)
236 40 Ave Ne, Calgary, AB, T2E 2M7
(403) 243-1836
Emp Here 20
SIC 5049 Professional equipment, nec

D-U-N-S 24-854-9594   (SL)
CARDIOLOGY CONSULTANTS (CALGARY) INC
803 1 Ave Ne Suite 306, Calgary, AB, T2E 7C5
(403) 571-8600
Emp Here 60   *Sales* 3,648,035
SIC 8011 Offices and clinics of medical doctors

D-U-N-S 25-150-0625   (BR)
CAREWEST
*CAREWEST DR VERNON FANNING CEN-
TRE*
722 16 Ave Ne, Calgary, AB, T2E 6V7
(403) 230-6900
Emp Here 300
SIC 8052 Intermediate care facilities

D-U-N-S 20-976-5705   (BR)
CAREWEST
CAREWEST NICKLE HOUSE
950 Robert Rd Ne, Calgary, AB, T2E 7T4
(403) 520-6735
Emp Here 20
SIC 8051 Skilled nursing care facilities

D-U-N-S 20-744-3594   (SL)
CATERING HEADQUARTERS LTD
AN AFFAIR TO REMEMBER
3716 2 St Ne, Calgary, AB, T2E 3H7
(403) 245-5774
Emp Here 50   *Sales* 1,819,127
SIC 5812 Eating places

D-U-N-S 24-393-1933   (BR)
CHECKER CABS LTD
CHECKER COURIER
1726 25 Ave Ne Suite 2, Calgary, AB, T2E 7K1
(403) 974-1183
Emp Here 30
SIC 7389 Business services, nec

D-U-N-S 20-559-5213   (SL)
CHINESE CHRISTIAN WING KEI NURSING HOME ASSOCIATION
WING KEI CARE CENTER
1212 Centre St Ne, Calgary, AB, T2E 2R4
(403) 277-7433
Emp Here 260   *Sales* 12,250,277
SIC 8361 Residential care
Dir Evelyn Buckley
  Ester Lau
Dir Jacob Jung
Dir Leonard Lam
  Gus Chan
Dir Lyn Chow
Dir Donald Jung
  Brian Lee
  Vincent Leung
Dir Joseph Tse

D-U-N-S 25-289-9133   (BR)
CLIFTON ASSOCIATES LTD
2222 30 Ave Ne, Calgary, AB, T2E 7K9
(403) 263-2556
Emp Here 25
SIC 8742 Management consulting services

D-U-N-S 25-455-9669   (BR)
COCA-COLA REFRESHMENTS CANADA COMPANY
(*Suby of* The Coca-Cola Company)
3851 23 St Ne, Calgary, AB, T2E 6T2
(403) 291-3111
Emp Here 400
SIC 2086 Bottled and canned soft drinks

D-U-N-S 20-255-3038   (SL)

COCOCO CHOCOLATIERS INC
CHOCOLATERIE BERBARD CALLEBAUT
2320 2 Ave Se, Calgary, AB, T2E 6J9
(403) 265-5777
Emp Here 150   *Sales* 656,646
SIC 2066 Chocolate and cocoa products

D-U-N-S 25-384-4682   (SL)
COLTECH OPTRONICS INC
7879 8 St Ne Suite 103, Calgary, AB, T2E 8A2
(403) 516-2221
Emp Here 30   *Sales* 4,052,015
SIC 3089 Plastics products, nec

D-U-N-S 20-826-3368   (BR)
COMCARE (COMCARE) LIMITED
COMCARE HEALTH SERVICES
2323 32 Ave Ne Suite 212, Calgary, AB, T2E 6Z3
(403) 228-3877
Emp Here 140
SIC 7363 Help supply services

D-U-N-S 20-744-7764   (BR)
COMPAGNIE DE TELEPHONE BELL DU CANADA OU BELL CANADA, LA
BELL HELECOPTER TEXTRON
58 Aero Dr Ne Suite 101, Calgary, AB, T2E 8Z9

Emp Here 20
SIC 5088 Transportation equipment and supplies

D-U-N-S 24-244-9978   (BR)
CORE LABORATORIES CANADA LTD
2810 12 St Ne, Calgary, AB, T2E 7P7
(403) 250-4000
Emp Here 100
SIC 8734 Testing laboratories

D-U-N-S 24-554-1586   (BR)
CORRPRO CANADA, INC
(*Suby of* Aegion Corporation)
807 Manning Rd Ne Suite 200, Calgary, AB, T2E 7M8
(403) 235-6400
Emp Here 20
SIC 1389 Oil and gas field services, nec

D-U-N-S 25-450-0077   (BR)
CORUS MEDIA HOLDINGS INC
SHAW MEDIA INC
222 23 St Ne, Calgary, AB, T2E 7N2
(403) 235-7777
Emp Here 210
SIC 4833 Television broadcasting stations

D-U-N-S 25-266-9189   (BR)
CRAWFORD & COMPANY (CANADA) INC
CRAWFORD ADJUSTERS CANADA
(*Suby of* Crawford & Company)
3115 12 St Ne Suite 300, Calgary, AB, T2E 7J2
(403) 266-3933
Emp Here 50
SIC 6411 Insurance agents, brokers, and service

D-U-N-S 24-997-9311   (SL)
CULTURES UNITED LIMITED
PUSCH
1420 40 Ave Ne Suite 16, Calgary, AB, T2E 6L1
(403) 543-4999
Emp Here 57   *Sales* 5,757,536
SIC 5651 Family clothing stores
Pr Pr Hanif Panju
VP VP Rahim Panju

D-U-N-S 24-808-7124   (SL)
D.V.S. DRYWALL CONTRACTORS LTD
3920 Edmonton Trail Ne, Calgary, AB, T2E 3P6
(403) 276-8600
Emp Here 50   *Sales* 4,231,721
SIC 1742 Plastering, drywall, and insulation

D-U-N-S 20-988-9369   (BR)

DHL EXPRESS (CANADA) LTD
3000 15 St Ne, Calgary, AB, T2E 8V6
(403) 531-5900
Emp Here 120
SIC 7389 Business services, nec

D-U-N-S 25-484-4376   (BR)
DATA COMMUNICATIONS MANAGEMENT CORP
707 Barlow Trail Se Suite F, Calgary, AB, T2E 8C2

Emp Here 60
SIC 5112 Stationery and office supplies

D-U-N-S 25-766-6941   (BR)
DAWSON WALLACE CONSTRUCTION LTD
2015 32 Ave Ne Suite 28, Calgary, AB, T2E 6Z3
(403) 735-5988
Emp Here 20
SIC 1542 Nonresidential construction, nec

D-U-N-S 24-538-0345   (SL)
DELTA FACILITIES MAINTENANCE INC.
2000 Airport Rd Ne, Calgary, AB, T2E 6W5
(403) 250-7790
Emp Here 45   *Sales* 6,858,306
SIC 4581 Airports, flying fields, and services
Owner Diego Soto

D-U-N-S 24-156-7650   (BR)
DELTA HOTELS LIMITED
DELTA CALGARY AIRPORT HOTEL
2001 Airport Rd Ne, Calgary, AB, T2E 6Z8
(403) 291-2600
Emp Here 240
SIC 8741 Management services

D-U-N-S 24-088-7604   (BR)
DENCAN RESTAURANTS INC
DENNY'S RESTAURANT
(*Suby of* Northland Properties Corporation)
1804 19 St Ne Suite 11, Calgary, AB, T2E 4Y3
(403) 250-7177
Emp Here 55
SIC 5812 Eating places

D-U-N-S 24-318-6496   (BR)
DIVESTCO INC
1223 31 Ave Ne, Calgary, AB, T2E 7W1
(403) 237-9170
Emp Here 120
SIC 7371 Custom computer programming services

D-U-N-S 25-521-2367   (BR)
DOLLAR THRIFTY AUTOMOTIVE GROUP CANADA INC
DOLLAR THRIFTY
(*Suby of* Hertz Global Holdings, Inc.)
2000 Airport Rd Ne, Calgary, AB, T2E 6W5
(403) 291-4129
Emp Here 20
SIC 4119 Local passenger transportation, nec

D-U-N-S 25-991-4927   (BR)
DOLLAR THRIFTY AUTOMOTIVE GROUP CANADA INC
(*Suby of* Hertz Global Holdings, Inc.)
7904 22 St Ne, Calgary, AB, T2E 7H6
(403) 221-1962
Emp Here 65
SIC 7515 Passenger car leasing

D-U-N-S 20-065-7430   (BR)
DRIVING FORCE INC, THE
2332 23 St Ne, Calgary, AB, T2E 8N3
(403) 296-0777
Emp Here 25
SIC 7514 Passenger car rental

D-U-N-S 24-158-5280   (SL)
DUTCH PASTRY BOUTIQUE (CALGARY) LTD
DPB BAKING COMPANY
7440 10 St Ne, Calgary, AB, T2E 8W1

(403) 777-1221
Emp Here 25   *Sales* 1,313,293
SIC 2051 Bread, cake, and related products

D-U-N-S 20-128-8631   (HQ)
EAGLE CANADA, INC
(*Suby of* Dawson Geophysical Company)
7015 8 St Ne, Calgary, AB, T2E 8A2
(403) 781-1192
Emp Here 35   *Emp Total* 1,802
Sales 49,248,473
SIC 1382 Oil and gas exploration services
Pr Robert Wood

D-U-N-S 20-037-7690   (BR)
ELEMENT FLEET MANAGEMENT INC
PHH VEHICLE MANAGEMENT SERVICES
6815 8 St Ne Unit 240, Calgary, AB, T2E 7H7
(403) 262-8980
Emp Here 20
SIC 7515 Passenger car leasing

D-U-N-S 24-119-8662   (SL)
ENGEL'S BAKERIES LTD
4709 14 St Ne Unit 6, Calgary, AB, T2E 6S4
(403) 250-9560
Emp Here 70   *Sales* 3,648,035
SIC 2051 Bread, cake, and related products

D-U-N-S 25-416-0021   (SL)
ENMAX POWER SERVICES CORP
239 Mayland Pl Ne, Calgary, AB, T2E 7Z8
(403) 514-3000
Emp Here 493   *Sales* 235,736,022
SIC 4911 Electric services
Pr Pr Gary Holden
  Paul Dawson
  Robert Hawkesworth
  Dale Hodges
  Francis Leong
  H Tompson Macdonald

D-U-N-S 25-620-9867   (BR)
ENTERPRISE RENT-A-CAR CANADA COMPANY
(*Suby of* The Crawford Group Inc)
2335 78 Ave Ne, Calgary, AB, T2E 7L2
(403) 250-1395
Emp Here 200
SIC 7514 Passenger car rental

D-U-N-S 25-734-0893   (BR)
ENTERPRISE RENT-A-CAR CANADA COMPANY
CALGARY INTERNATIONAL AIRPORT
(*Suby of* The Crawford Group Inc)
2000 Airport Rd Ne, Calgary, AB, T2E 6W5
(403) 233-8021
Emp Here 20
SIC 7514 Passenger car rental

D-U-N-S 24-156-3329   (BR)
ESSILOR GROUPE CANADA INC
ESSILOR
3625 12 St Ne, Calgary, AB, T2E 6P4
(403) 250-1539
Emp Here 20
SIC 5995 Optical goods stores

D-U-N-S 24-320-1949   (BR)
EXOVA CANADA INC
(*Suby of* Exova, Inc.)
4605 12 St Ne, Calgary, AB, T2E 4R3

Emp Here 50
SIC 8731 Commercial physical research

D-U-N-S 20-107-2381   (BR)
EXPEDITORS CANADA INC
2340 Pegasus Way Ne Suite 123, Calgary, AB, T2E 8M5
(403) 265-9390
Emp Here 20
SIC 4731 Freight transportation arrangement

D-U-N-S 24-340-2604   (BR)
FGL SPORTS LTD
HOCKEY EXPERTS

901 64 Ave Ne Unit G1, Calgary, AB, T2E 7P4
(403) 274-6040
Emp Here 40
SIC 5941 Sporting goods and bicycle shops

D-U-N-S 20-183-6538   (SL)
FLYHT AEROSPACE SOLUTIONS LTD
1144 29 Ave Ne Suite 300e, Calgary, AB, T2E 7P1
(403) 250-9956
Emp Here 47   *Sales* 10,599,994
SIC 3812 Search and navigation equipment
  William T Tempany
CEO Thomas R. Schmutz
  Nola Heale
VP Sls David Perez
VP Opers Matieu Plamondon
  Douglas G Marlin
  Michael Brown
  Jack Olcott
  Paul Takalo
  John Belcher

D-U-N-S 24-341-0615   (BR)
FEDERAL EXPRESS CANADA CORPORATION
FEDERAL EXPRESS CANADA LTD
(*Suby of* Fedex Corporation)
24 Aero Dr Ne, Calgary, AB, T2E 8Z9
(800) 463-3339
Emp Here 250
SIC 7389 Business services, nec

D-U-N-S 25-522-0741   (BR)
FEDERATED INSURANCE COMPANY OF CANADA
2443 Pegasus Rd Ne, Calgary, AB, T2E 8C3
(403) 254-8500
Emp Here 40
SIC 6331 Fire, marine, and casualty insurance

D-U-N-S 25-539-3696   (BR)
FINNING INTERNATIONAL INC
FINNING POWER SYSTEMS
(*Suby of* Finning International Inc)
6735 11 St Ne, Calgary, AB, T2E 7H9
(403) 275-3340
Emp Here 20
SIC 7538 General automotive repair shops

D-U-N-S 24-458-8807   (BR)
FINNING INTERNATIONAL INC
FINNING POWER SYSTEMS
(*Suby of* Finning International Inc)
6700 9 St Ne, Calgary, AB, T2E 8K6
(403) 516-2800
Emp Here 30
SIC 7538 General automotive repair shops

D-U-N-S 25-146-3303   (BR)
FUJITEC CANADA, INC
49 Aero Dr Ne Unit 8, Calgary, AB, T2E 8Z9
(403) 730-5901
Emp Here 26
SIC 5084 Industrial machinery and equipment

D-U-N-S 25-957-0836   (BR)
G4S CASH SOLUTIONS (CANADA) LTD
5040 Skyline Way Ne, Calgary, AB, T2E 6V1
(403) 974-8350
Emp Here 100
SIC 7381 Detective and armored car services

D-U-N-S 25-449-9965   (BR)
GENERAL DYNAMICS LAND SYSTEMS - CANADA CORPORATION
(*Suby of* General Dynamics Corporation)
1020 68 Ave Ne, Calgary, AB, T2E 8P2
(403) 295-6700
Emp Here 503
SIC 7371 Custom computer programming services

D-U-N-S 20-695-0938   (SL)
GENESIS BUILDERS GROUP INC
POINTE GREY WAVERLY HOMES
3115 12 St Ne Suite 200, Calgary, AB, T2E 7J2

(403) 265-9237
Emp Here 25   *Sales* 5,173,950
SIC 1521 Single-family housing construction
Pr Pr Gobi Singh

D-U-N-S 24-685-2409   (BR)
GLOBAL FLOW INC
(*Suby of* 1053384 Alberta Inc)
2315 30 Ave Ne Suite 2, Calgary, AB, T2E 7C7
(403) 219-0488
Emp Here 40
SIC 1389 Oil and gas field services, nec

D-U-N-S 25-991-8118   (SL)
GOLDENCARE HOLDINGS LTD
HILTON GARDEN INN CALGARY AIRPORT
2335 Pegasus Rd Ne, Calgary, AB, T2E 8C3
(403) 717-1999
Emp Here 60   *Sales* 2,626,585
SIC 7011 Hotels and motels

D-U-N-S 24-017-0761   (BR)
GRAND & TOY LIMITED
WAREHOUSE DISTRIBUTION CENTRE
(*Suby of* Office Depot, Inc.)
37 Aero Dr Ne, Calgary, AB, T2E 8Z9
(403) 250-9700
Emp Here 160
SIC 5021 Furniture

D-U-N-S 20-297-2399   (BR)
HELIX ADVANCED COMMUNICATIONS & INFRASTRUCTURE, INC
WESTCAN WIRELESS
4001b 19 St Ne Suite 14, Calgary, AB, T2E 6X8
(403) 265-2355
Emp Here 20
SIC 5999 Miscellaneous retail stores, nec

D-U-N-S 25-678-5163   (HQ)
HUNTING ENERGY SERVICES (CANADA) LTD
5550 Skyline Way Ne, Calgary, AB, T2E 7Z7
(403) 543-4477
Emp Here 100   *Emp Total* 28
Sales 37,595,293
SIC 1389 Oil and gas field services, nec
Dir Dennis Proctor
Pr Pr Elmer Campbell

D-U-N-S 20-082-9179   (BR)
IBI GROUP
611 Meredith Rd Ne Suite 500, Calgary, AB, T2E 2W5
(403) 270-5600
Emp Here 100
SIC 8712 Architectural services

D-U-N-S 20-639-2651   (SL)
INNOVATIVE GLOBAL SOLUTIONS INC
320 19 St Se, Calgary, AB, T2E 6J6
(403) 204-1198
Emp Here 32   *Sales* 5,836,856
SIC 5136 Men's and boy's clothing
VP VP Clif Burnette

D-U-N-S 20-052-6536   (BR)
INOVA SYSTEMS CORPORATION
7236 10 St Ne, Calgary, AB, T2E 8X3
(403) 537-2100
Emp Here 75
SIC 3829 Measuring and controlling devices, nec

D-U-N-S 24-013-1086   (HQ)
INTERGRAPH CANADA LTD
1120 68 Ave Ne, Calgary, AB, T2E 8S5
(403) 569-5500
Emp Here 71   *Emp Total* 10
Sales 20,793,800
SIC 5045 Computers, peripherals, and software
 Halsey Wise
 Douglas Morrison
Pr Gerhard Sallinger
Treas Peter Thomson
Sr VP David Vance Lucas

Ex VP R Reid French Jr

D-U-N-S 20-365-8757   (BR)
JWP PUBLISHING LIMITED PARTNERSHIP
JUNE WARREN PUBLISHING
816 55 Ave Ne 2nd Fl, Calgary, AB, T2E 6Y4
(403) 265-3700
Emp Here 100
SIC 2721 Periodicals

D-U-N-S 24-358-2801   (SL)
JALCO INDUSTRIES INC
3801 19 St Ne, Calgary, AB, T2E 6S8
(403) 265-0911
Emp Here 40   *Sales* 7,129,801
SIC 7692 Welding repair
Pr Pr Garth Thompson
 Barry Schlinker
Mgr Jarrett Thompson
Mgr Craig Magas

D-U-N-S 24-271-9771   (SL)
JARVIS INTERIOR LTD
4615 8a St Ne, Calgary, AB, T2E 4J6
(403) 277-1444
Emp Here 52   *Sales* 4,450,603
SIC 1742 Plastering, drywall, and insulation

D-U-N-S 20-547-0342   (BR)
K-BRO LINEN SYSTEMS INC
1018 Mcdougall Rd Ne, Calgary, AB, T2E 8B8

Emp Here 100
SIC 7218 Industrial launderers

D-U-N-S 20-152-8325   (SL)
K. & W. OPTICAL (CALGARY) LIMITED
K W OPTICAL CALGARY
3625 12 St Ne, Calgary, AB, T2E 6P4
(403) 243-6133
Emp Here 25   *Sales* 3,502,114
SIC 3211 Flat glass

D-U-N-S 25-218-9626   (BR)
KAL TIRE LTD
2363 20 Ave Ne, Calgary, AB, T2E 8T1
(403) 291-2177
Emp Here 30
SIC 5531 Auto and home supply stores

D-U-N-S 24-332-4662   (HQ)
KENN BOREK AIR LTD
KBAL
290 Mctavish Rd Ne Suite 4, Calgary, AB, T2E 7G5
(403) 291-3300
Emp Here 200   *Emp Total* 160
Sales 44,785,177
SIC 4522 Air transportation, nonscheduled
Pr Pr Rosella Borek
VP VP Chris Vipond
Genl Mgr John Harmer

D-U-N-S 24-375-0093   (BR)
KUEHNE + NAGEL LTD
6835 8 St Ne, Calgary, AB, T2E 7H7
(403) 717-8620
Emp Here 40
SIC 4731 Freight transportation arrangement

D-U-N-S 25-571-2713   (BR)
LANDMARK HOMES (EDMONTON) INC
757 57 Ave Ne, Calgary, AB, T2E 8W6
(403) 212-1340
Emp Here 40
SIC 1521 Single-family housing construction

D-U-N-S 24-344-5462   (BR)
LIFEMARK HEALTH MANAGEMENT INC
LIFEMARK PHYSIOTHERAPY
(*Suby of* Audax Group, L.P.)
1221 Barlow Trail Se, Calgary, AB, T2E 6S2
(403) 569-8050
Emp Here 20
SIC 8741 Management services

D-U-N-S 20-051-8517   (BR)
LOBLAW COMPANIES LIMITED

WESTFAIR FOODS
3225 12 St Ne, Calgary, AB, T2E 7S9
(403) 291-7700
Emp Here 200
SIC 5411 Grocery stores

D-U-N-S 20-595-5847   (BR)
LOBLAWS INC
REAL CANADIAN WHOLESALE CLUB
2928 23 St Ne, Calgary, AB, T2E 8R7
(403) 291-2810
Emp Here 100
SIC 5141 Groceries, general line

D-U-N-S 20-353-2072   (SL)
MHVC CANADA ACQUISITION CORP
6727 9 St Ne, Calgary, AB, T2E 8R9
(403) 295-4781
Emp Here 75   *Sales* 4,523,563
SIC 7699 Repair services, nec

D-U-N-S 24-028-0839   (BR)
MI GROUP LTD, THE
7660 10 St Ne, Calgary, AB, T2E 8W1
(403) 730-1616
Emp Here 30
SIC 7389 Business services, nec

D-U-N-S 25-650-5876   (BR)
MARITIME TRAVEL INC
LEGROW'S TRAVEL
(*Suby of* Maritime Travel Inc)
1243 Mcknight Blvd Ne, Calgary, AB, T2E 5T1
(403) 292-7474
Emp Here 50
SIC 4724 Travel agencies

D-U-N-S 20-514-0572   (BR)
MAXXAM ANALYTICS INTERNATIONAL CORPORATION
MAXXAM
2021 41 Ave Ne, Calgary, AB, T2E 6P2
(403) 291-3077
Emp Here 150
SIC 8734 Testing laboratories

D-U-N-S 20-041-3479   (BR)
METROPOLITAN CALGARY FOUNDATION
SPRUCE LODGE
1055 Bow Valley Dr Ne, Calgary, AB, T2E 8A9
(403) 266-2630
Emp Here 20
SIC 8361 Residential care

D-U-N-S 24-826-0940   (BR)
METROPOLITAN FINE PRINTERS INC
RHINO PRINT SOLUTIONS
49 Aero Dr Ne Unit 6, Calgary, AB, T2E 8Z9
(403) 291-0405
Emp Here 26
SIC 2752 Commercial printing, lithographic

D-U-N-S 24-152-7035   (HQ)
MILNE & CRAIGHEAD, INC
CENTURY FREIGHT
3636 23 St Ne Suite 300, Calgary, AB, T2E 8Z5
(403) 263-7856
Emp Here 55   *Emp Total* 3,200
Sales 57,482,069
SIC 4731 Freight transportation arrangement
Pr Pr Darshan Kailly
 Allan R Kersch
 Gordon Bloom
Rgnl Mgr Dave Bosse

D-U-N-S 24-808-7793   (BR)
MOLSON CANADA 2005
(*Suby of* Molson Coors Brewing Company)
906 1 Ave Ne, Calgary, AB, T2E 0C5
(403) 233-1786
Emp Here 30
SIC 2082 Malt beverages

D-U-N-S 24-978-7763   (HQ)
MRS. WILLMAN'S BAKING LIMITED
4826 11 St Ne Unit 4, Calgary, AB, T2E 2W7

Emp Here 100   *Emp Total* 250
Sales 14,639,642
SIC 2051 Bread, cake, and related products
Pr Pr Winston Ho Fatt

D-U-N-S 20-104-2863   (BR)
NAV CANADA
7811 22 St Ne, Calgary, AB, T2E 5T3
(403) 216-7141
Emp Here 34
SIC 3812 Search and navigation equipment

D-U-N-S 20-698-0646   (BR)
NEWCAP INC
CIQX
1110 Centre St Ne Suite 100, Calgary, AB, T2E 2R2
(403) 736-1031
Emp Here 30
SIC 7922 Theatrical producers and services

D-U-N-S 24-073-7903   (BR)
NEWFOUNDLAND CAPITAL CORPORATION LIMITED
90.3 AMP RADIO
1110 Centre St Ne Suite 100, Calgary, AB, T2E 2R2
(403) 271-6366
Emp Here 22
SIC 4832 Radio broadcasting stations

D-U-N-S 24-492-1974   (BR)
NEWWAY CONCRETE FORMING LTD
NEWWAY CONCRETE STRUCTURES
427 38 Ave Ne Suite E, Calgary, AB, T2E 6R9
(403) 520-5211
Emp Here 50
SIC 1771 Concrete work

D-U-N-S 25-362-2468   (BR)
NORTH CARIBOO FLYING SERVICE LTD
NORTH CARIBOO AIR
600 Palmer Rd Ne, Calgary, AB, T2E 7R3
(403) 250-8694
Emp Here 60
SIC 4522 Air transportation, nonscheduled

D-U-N-S 20-117-4120   (HQ)
OIL LIFT TECHNOLOGY INC
(*Suby of* Dover Corporation)
19 Aero Dr Ne Unit 37, Calgary, AB, T2E 8Z9
(403) 291-5300
Emp Here 43   *Emp Total* 29,000
Sales 9,995,616
SIC 3533 Oil and gas field machinery
Pr Pr Vern Arthur Hult
 Dianne Crockett

D-U-N-S 25-581-4720   (BR)
OIL LIFT TECHNOLOGY INC
(*Suby of* Dover Corporation)
950 64 Ave Ne Unit 37, Calgary, AB, T2E 8S8
(403) 295-4370
Emp Here 50
SIC 3533 Oil and gas field machinery

D-U-N-S 24-311-1429   (BR)
OWEN & COMPANY LIMITED
KINGSDOWN MATTRESSES
2323 22 St Ne, Calgary, AB, T2E 8K8
(403) 219-3557
Emp Here 35
SIC 2515 Mattresses and bedsprings

D-U-N-S 25-452-2089   (BR)
PCL CONSTRUCTION MANAGEMENT INC
2882 11 St Ne, Calgary, AB, T2E 7S7
(403) 250-4800
Emp Here 145
SIC 8741 Management services

D-U-N-S 24-441-0015   (SL)
PDL MOBILITY LIMITED
2420 42 Ave Ne, Calgary, AB, T2E 7T6
(403) 291-5400
Emp Here 25   *Sales* 12,760,800
SIC 5999 Miscellaneous retail stores, nec
Pr Pr Marc Bombenon

D-U-N-S 25-452-2105 (BR)
PLH AVIATION SERVICES INC
2000 Airport Rd Ne Suite 124, Calgary, AB,
T2E 6W5
(403) 221-1920
Emp Here 50
SIC 5172 Petroleum products, nec

D-U-N-S 24-554-8201 (BR)
PANASONIC CANADA INC
PANASONIC/TECHNICS
6835 8 St Ne, Calgary, AB, T2E 7H7

Emp Here 30
SIC 5064 Electrical appliances, television and
radio

D-U-N-S 25-977-0964 (BR)
PARKER HANNIFIN CANADA
FLUID CONNECTOR GROUP (DIV OF)
3141 16 St Ne, Calgary, AB, T2E 7K8
(403) 291-9100
Emp Here 22
SIC 3593 Fluid power cylinders and actuators

D-U-N-S 20-077-4727 (SL)
PETERS' DRIVE INN
219 16 Ave Ne, Calgary, AB, T2E 1J9
(403) 277-2747
Emp Here 80   Sales 2,407,703
SIC 5812 Eating places

D-U-N-S 20-547-2157 (SL)
PHOENIX PRECISION LTD
2620 21 St Ne, Calgary, AB, T2E 7L3
(403) 291-3154
Emp Here 32   Sales 4,231,721
SIC 3491 Industrial valves

D-U-N-S 20-077-5336 (SL)
POCKAR MASONRY LTD
4632 5 St Ne, Calgary, AB, T2E 7C3
(403) 276-5591
Emp Here 65   Sales 4,742,446
SIC 1741 Masonry and other stonework

D-U-N-S 24-440-3630 (BR)
POSTMEDIA NETWORK INC
FLYER FORCE, THE
1058 72 Ave Ne, Calgary, AB, T2E 8V9
(403) 569-4744
Emp Here 50
SIC 7319 Advertising, nec

D-U-N-S 24-159-7723 (BR)
POSTMEDIA NETWORK INC
CALGARY HERALD, THE
215 16 St Se, Calgary, AB, T2E 7P5
(403) 235-7168
Emp Here 750
SIC 2711 Newspapers

D-U-N-S 25-136-0244 (BR)
PRAIRIE VIEW HOLDINGS LTD
BUDGET RENT-A-CAR OF CALGARY
(Suby of SM2 Holdings Ltd)
2000 Airport Rd Ne, Calgary, AB, T2E 6W5
(403) 221-1715
Emp Here 30
SIC 7514 Passenger car rental

D-U-N-S 24-350-1017 (BR)
PRECISION GEOMATICS INC
2816 11 St Ne Suite 102, Calgary, AB, T2E
7S7
(403) 250-1829
Emp Here 39
SIC 8713 Surveying services

D-U-N-S 25-065-3789 (BR)
PRISZM LP
KFC
1320 Edmonton Trail Ne, Calgary, AB, T2E
3K7
(403) 276-6235
Emp Here 50
SIC 5812 Eating places

D-U-N-S 20-299-2199 (BR)

PUROLATOR INC.
PUROLATOR INC
30 Aero Dr Ne, Calgary, AB, T2E 8Z9
(403) 516-6200
Emp Here 250
SIC 4731 Freight transportation arrangement

D-U-N-S 24-363-0790 (BR)
RGIS CANADA ULC
1935 32 Ave Ne Suite 130, Calgary, AB, T2E
7C8
(403) 291-6100
Emp Here 50
SIC 7389 Business services, nec

D-U-N-S 25-097-3021 (BR)
RAYTHEON CANADA LIMITED
(Suby of Raytheon Company)
838 55 Ave Ne, Calgary, AB, T2E 6Y4

Emp Here 45
SIC 3812 Search and navigation equipment

D-U-N-S 25-452-2550 (BR)
REID-BUILT HOMES LTD
2041 41 Ave Ne, Calgary, AB, T2E 6P2
(403) 250-3273
Emp Here 20
SIC 1521 Single-family housing construction

D-U-N-S 20-347-2709 (BR)
RELIABLE PARTS LTD
(Suby of Reliable Parts Ltd)
1058 72 Ave Ne, Calgary, AB, T2E 8V9
(403) 281-1863
Emp Here 20
SIC 5722 Household appliance stores

D-U-N-S 25-975-1907 (BR)
**RENFREW EDUCATIONAL SERVICES SO-
CIETY**
2050 21 St Ne, Calgary, AB, T2E 6S5
(403) 247-6200
Emp Here 23
SIC 8211 Elementary and secondary schools

D-U-N-S 20-645-5180 (BR)
ROTHMANS, BENSON & HEDGES INC
(Suby of Philip Morris International Inc.)
1245 34 Ave Ne Suite 6, Calgary, AB, T2E 6N4
(403) 250-9621
Emp Here 20
SIC 2111 Cigarettes

D-U-N-S 25-191-7241 (BR)
SKF CANADA LIMITED
SKF MAGNETIC BEARINGS
928 72 Ave Ne, Calgary, AB, T2E 8V9
(403) 232-9292
Emp Here 35
SIC 3568 Power transmission equipment, nec

D-U-N-S 24-364-3363 (BR)
SANMINA-SCI SYSTEMS (CANADA) INC
424 Aviation Rd Ne, Calgary, AB, T2E 8H6
(403) 295-5100
Emp Here 35
SIC 8748 Business consulting, nec

D-U-N-S 24-325-2553 (SL)
SAVM INC
3530 11a St Ne Suite 1, Calgary, AB, T2E 6M7
(403) 250-7878
Emp Here 100   Sales 17,438,720
SIC 6712 Bank holding companies
Pr Pr Malcom Sykes
Zana Sykes

D-U-N-S 24-859-4785 (BR)
SHANE HOLDINGS LTD
5661 7 St Ne, Calgary, AB, T2E 8V3
(403) 252-0995
Emp Here 77
SIC 1521 Single-family housing construction

D-U-N-S 25-290-8132 (HQ)
SHAW CABLESYSTEMS LIMITED
2400 32 Ave Ne, Calgary, AB, T2E 9A7

(403) 750-4500
Emp Here 100   Emp Total 14,000
Sales 58,806,324
SIC 4833 Television broadcasting stations
Ch Bd James Shaw Sr
Pr Pr Jim Shaw Jr
Dir Margot Micallef

D-U-N-S 24-360-1437 (HQ)
SHOEMAKER DRYWALL SUPPLIES LTD
7012 8 St Ne, Calgary, AB, T2E 8L8
(403) 291-1013
Emp Here 50   Emp Total 100
Sales 15,159,393
SIC 1742 Plastering, drywall, and insulation
Pr Pr Ryan Shoemaker
VP Fin Scott Friesen

D-U-N-S 24-354-8331 (BR)
**SHOPPERS HOME HEALTH CARE
(CANADA) INC**
SHOPPERS HOME HEALTH CARE
2720 12 St Ne Suite 1, Calgary, AB, T2E 7N4
(403) 250-2200
Emp Here 20
SIC 5912 Drug stores and proprietary stores

D-U-N-S 24-702-4870 (BR)
SIEMENS CANADA LIMITED
LANDIS, DIV OF
1930 Maynard Rd Se Unit 24, Calgary, AB,
T2E 6J8
(403) 259-3404
Emp Here 102
SIC 1711 Plumbing, heating, air-conditioning

D-U-N-S 20-213-4529 (BR)
SIEMENS CANADA LIMITED
1930 Maynard Rd Se Unit 24, Calgary, AB,
T2E 6J8
(403) 252-2278
Emp Here 240
SIC 3679 Electronic components, nec

D-U-N-S 25-614-6994 (BR)
SIEMENS CANADA LIMITED
FIRE SAFETY DIVISION
1930 Maynard Rd Se Unit 24, Calgary, AB,
T2E 6J8
(403) 624-9156
Emp Here 100
SIC 7382 Security systems services

D-U-N-S 25-519-1371 (BR)
SINCLAIR DENTAL CO. LTD
2135 32 Ave Ne Suite 8, Calgary, AB, T2E 6Z3
(403) 291-3611
Emp Here 25
SIC 5047 Medical and hospital equipment

D-U-N-S 24-852-9427 (BR)
SKY SERVICE F.B.O. INC.
575 Palmer Rd Ne, Calgary, AB, T2E 7G4
(403) 592-3706
Emp Here 50
SIC 4512 Air transportation, scheduled

D-U-N-S 24-030-3367 (BR)
SKYSERVICE BUSINESS AVIATION INC
575 Palmer Rd Ne, Calgary, AB, T2E 7G4
(403) 592-3700
Emp Here 80
SIC 7363 Help supply services

D-U-N-S 20-100-7791 (SL)
SMARTSYNCH LTD
1721 27 Ave Ne, Calgary, AB, T2E 7E1

Emp Here 47   Sales 5,202,480
SIC 3544 Special dies, tools, jigs, and fixtures
Pr Pat Hamilton

D-U-N-S 25-015-0885 (BR)
SOBEYS WEST INC
CANADA SAFEWAY 263
1818 Centre St Ne Suite 20, Calgary, AB, T2E
2S6
(403) 276-3328
Emp Here 150

SIC 5411 Grocery stores

D-U-N-S 20-109-8852 (HQ)
SOBEYS WEST INC
SAFEWAY
1020 64 Ave Ne, Calgary, AB, T2E 7V8
(403) 730-3500
Emp Here 600   Emp Total 125,000
Sales 4,182,909,892
SIC 5411 Grocery stores
Pr Pr Marc Poulin
VP Fin Clinton Keay
  Karin Mccaskill
  Francois Vimard
  Jane Mcdow

D-U-N-S 20-175-9433 (BR)
STAPLES CANADA INC
STAPLES THE BUSINESS DEPOT
(Suby of Staples, Inc.)
25 Aero Dr Ne Suite 4, Calgary, AB, T2E 8Z9
(403) 516-4022
Emp Here 30
SIC 5943 Stationery stores

D-U-N-S 25-919-5667 (HQ)
**STAR CHOICE TELEVISION NETWORK IN-
CORPORATED**
STAR CHOICE BUSINESS TELEVISION
2924 11 St Ne, Calgary, AB, T2E 7L7
(403) 538-4672
Emp Here 200   Emp Total 14,000
Sales 252,305,280
SIC 4841 Cable and other pay television ser-
vices
Pr Peter Bissonnette
VP Opers Brad Shaw

D-U-N-S 20-944-6116 (BR)
STARBUCKS COFFEE CANADA, INC
STARBUCKS COFFEE
(Suby of Starbucks Corporation)
951 General Ave Ne Suite 6, Calgary, AB, T2E
9E1
(403) 269-2006
Emp Here 20
SIC 5812 Eating places

D-U-N-S 20-826-3137 (HQ)
**STARTEC REFRIGERATION SERVICES
LTD**
(Suby of Cawthorn Investments Ltd)
7664 10 St Ne, Calgary, AB, T2E 8W1
(403) 295-5855
Emp Here 50   Emp Total 80
Sales 22,253,014
SIC 3563 Air and gas compressors
Pr Joel Cawthorn
  Kristi Cawthorn

D-U-N-S 24-983-9432 (BR)
**STARTEC REFRIGERATION SERVICES
LTD**
STARTEC REFRIGERATION AND COM-
PRESSION
(Suby of Cawthorn Investments Ltd)
7664 10 St Ne Suite 11, Calgary, AB, T2E
8W1
(403) 295-5855
Emp Here 50
SIC 7699 Repair services, nec

D-U-N-S 24-557-2941 (SL)
STRONGHOLD EXTERIORS LTD
(Suby of 1340133 Alberta Ltd)
2115 27 Ave Ne Suite 6, Calgary, AB, T2E 7E4
(403) 569-9150
Emp Here 50   Sales 11,975,520
SIC 1761 Roofing, siding, and sheetMetal
work
Dir Wayne Wilson
Dir Susan Leader
Dir Guy Bonnier

D-U-N-S 24-894-6261 (BR)
**STUART OLSON DOMINION CONSTRUC-
TION LTD**

DOMINION COMPANY
405 18 St Se, Calgary, AB, T2E 6J5

Emp Here 40
SIC 1541 Industrial buildings and warehouses

D-U-N-S 20-302-3747   (BR)
SWISSPORT CANADA INC
1601 Airport Rd Ne Suite 810, Calgary, AB,
T2E 6Z8
(403) 221-1660
Emp Here 150
SIC 4581 Airports, flying fields, and services

D-U-N-S 25-142-2069   (BR)
TELUS CORPORATION
2520 23 St Ne Suite 13, Calgary, AB, T2E 8L2
(403) 735-6600
Emp Here 70
SIC 4899 Communication services, nec

D-U-N-S 24-228-4441   (BR)
TELUS CORPORATION
TELUS COMMUNICATIONS
715 41 Ave Ne, Calgary, AB, T2E 3P8

Emp Here 100
SIC 4899 Communication services, nec

D-U-N-S 20-512-1655   (BR)
TERAGO NETWORKS INC
(*Suby of* TeraGo Inc)
300 Manning Rd Ne Suite 300, Calgary, AB,
T2E 8K4
(403) 668-5300
Emp Here 21
SIC 4813 Telephone communication, except
radio

D-U-N-S 20-812-5307   (SL)
TIM HORTONS
4015 Centre St Nw, Calgary, AB, T2E 2Y4
(403) 230-8999
Emp Here 55   *Sales* 1,678,096
SIC 5812 Eating places

D-U-N-S 20-965-2846   (SL)
TOPCO OILSITE PRODUCTS LTD
3401 19 St Ne Unit 5, Calgary, AB, T2E 6S8
(403) 219-0255
Emp Here 80   *Sales* 21,405,950
SIC 3533 Oil and gas field machinery
Pr Pr Alan Huehn

D-U-N-S 24-272-8343   (BR)
TORONTO-DOMINION BANK, THE
TD CANADA TRUST
(*Suby of* Toronto-Dominion Bank, The)
1216 Centre St Ne, Calgary, AB, T2E 2R4
(403) 230-2207
Emp Here 20
SIC 6021 National commercial banks

D-U-N-S 20-910-2651   (BR)
**TYCO INTEGRATED FIRE & SECURITY
CANADA, INC**
SIMPLEXGRINNELL
(*Suby of* Johnson Controls, Inc.)
615 18 St Se, Calgary, AB, T2E 3L9
(403) 569-4606
Emp Here 150
SIC 1731 Electrical work

D-U-N-S 20-702-7710   (BR)
UAP INC
NAPA AIRWAYS
(*Suby of* Genuine Parts Company)
2727 23 St Ne Suite 271, Calgary, AB, T2E
7M1
(403) 250-7334
Emp Here 30
SIC 5531 Auto and home supply stores

D-U-N-S 25-418-0417   (BR)
UNITED PARCEL SERVICE CANADA LTD
UPS
3650 12 St Ne Suite D, Calgary, AB, T2E 6N1

Emp Here 200

SIC 4731 Freight transportation arrangement

D-U-N-S 25-986-1292   (BR)
**VANCOUVER CAREER COLLEGE (BURN-
ABY) INC**
CDI COLLEGE
(*Suby of* Chung Family Holdings Inc)
805 Manning Rd Ne Suite 210, Calgary, AB,
T2E 7M8
(403) 571-8585
Emp Here 20
SIC 8211 Elementary and secondary schools

D-U-N-S 20-524-6411   (BR)
VARCO CANADA ULC
M D TOTCO
(*Suby of* National Oilwell Varco, Inc.)
2935 19 St Ne, Calgary, AB, T2E 7A2
(403) 264-9646
Emp Here 30
SIC 6792 Oil royalty traders

D-U-N-S 20-823-5569   (BR)
WSP CANADA INC
GENIVAR
405 18 St Se, Calgary, AB, T2E 6J5
(403) 248-9463
Emp Here 45
SIC 8711 Engineering services

D-U-N-S 25-218-9899   (BR)
WAL-MART CANADA CORP
1110 57 Ave Ne Suite 3013, Calgary, AB, T2E
9B7
(403) 730-0990
Emp Here 250
SIC 5311 Department stores

D-U-N-S 25-360-6966   (BR)
WEIR CANADA, INC
2715 18 St Ne, Calgary, AB, T2E 7E6
(403) 250-7000
Emp Here 40
SIC 8711 Engineering services

D-U-N-S 20-004-6279   (BR)
WENDY'S RESTAURANTS OF CANADA INC
WENDY'S
(*Suby of* The Wendy's Company)
1181 49 Ave Ne, Calgary, AB, T2E 8V2
(403) 730-5250
Emp Here 33
SIC 5812 Eating places

D-U-N-S 20-913-1437   (BR)
WESTJET AIRLINES LTD
5055 11 St Ne, Calgary, AB, T2E 8N4
(403) 735-2600
Emp Here 20
SIC 4512 Air transportation, scheduled

D-U-N-S 24-364-3637   (BR)
WESTJET AIRLINES LTD
21 Aerial Pl Ne, Calgary, AB, T2E 8X7
(403) 539-7070
Emp Here 20
SIC 4581 Airports, flying fields, and services

D-U-N-S 24-231-8111   (HQ)
WESTFAIR DRUGS LTD
3225 12 St Ne, Calgary, AB, T2E 7S9
(403) 291-7700
Emp Here 480   *Emp Total* 138,000
Sales 100,831,616
SIC 5912 Drug stores and proprietary stores
Sr VP Robert Balcom
VP Bradley Holland

D-U-N-S 24-329-0686   (BR)
WESTON BAKERIES LIMITED
MOISSON DOREE
906 1 Ave Ne, Calgary, AB, T2E 0C5
(403) 266-2279
Emp Here 50
SIC 2051 Bread, cake, and related products

D-U-N-S 24-088-9688   (BR)
WESTOWER COMMUNICATIONS LTD

3815 2 St Ne, Calgary, AB, T2E 3H8
(403) 226-2020
Emp Here 20
SIC 1623 Water, sewer, and utility lines

D-U-N-S 24-983-0514   (BR)
WESTWORLD COMPUTERS LTD
1000 Centre St Ne, Calgary, AB, T2E 7W6
(403) 221-9499
Emp Here 20
SIC 5734 Computer and software stores

D-U-N-S 20-829-0452   (HQ)
WINGENBACK INC
707 Barlow Trail Se, Calgary, AB, T2E 8C2
(403) 221-8120
Emp Here 55   *Emp Total* 180
Sales 16,961,922
SIC 3299 NonMetallic mineral products,
Pr Pr Wayne Wingenbach
VP VP Dennis Wingenbach

D-U-N-S 20-106-3323   (BR)
**WINNERS MERCHANTS INTERNATIONAL
L.P.**
WINNERS
(*Suby of* The TJX Companies Inc)
901 64 Ave Ne Suite F1, Calgary, AB, T2E 7P4
(403) 730-8387
Emp Here 35
SIC 5651 Family clothing stores

D-U-N-S 25-386-0753   (BR)
**WORKERS' COMPENSATION BOARD AL-
BERTA**
4311 12 St Ne Suite 150, Calgary, AB, T2E
4P9
(403) 517-6000
Emp Here 150
SIC 6331 Fire, marine, and casualty insurance

D-U-N-S 20-767-7352   (HQ)
**WYCLIFFE BIBLE TRANSLATORS OF
CANADA INC**
WYCLIFFE CANADA
(*Suby of* Wycliffe Bible Translators of Canada
Inc)
4316 10 St Ne, Calgary, AB, T2E 6K3
(403) 250-5411
Emp Here 70   *Emp Total* 470
Sales 14,824,217
SIC 7389 Business services, nec
Pr Roy Eyre
Ch Bd Jannice Moore
Fin Ex Don Buhler

D-U-N-S 25-409-1028   (BR)
YIKES ENTERPRISES LTD
TIM HORTONS
(*Suby of* Yikes Enterprises Ltd)
1341 32 Ave Ne, Calgary, AB, T2E 7Z5
(403) 291-2966
Emp Here 40
SIC 5812 Eating places

Calgary, AB T2G

D-U-N-S 24-346-9389   (SL)
1184892 ALBERTA LTD
RUTH'S CHRIS STEAK HOUSE
115 9 Ave Se Suite 294, Calgary, AB, T2G 0P5
(403) 246-3636
Emp Here 100   *Sales* 2,991,389
SIC 5812 Eating places

D-U-N-S 24-243-3741   (SL)
333 TRADING LTD
908 34 Ave Se, Calgary, AB, T2G 1V3
(403) 240-2540
Emp Here 49   *Sales* 9,517,760
SIC 2673 Bags: plastic, laminated, and
coated
Pr Ben Ng

D-U-N-S 25-521-3795   (SL)

517235 ALBERTA LTD
TEATRO
200 8 Ave Se, Calgary, AB, T2G 0K7
(403) 290-1012
Emp Here 50   *Sales* 1,532,175
SIC 5812 Eating places

D-U-N-S 25-266-0394   (BR)
A A A ALARM SYSTEMS LTD
A A A SECURITY SYSTEM
118 50 Ave Se, Calgary, AB, T2G 2A8
(403) 233-7454
Emp Here 50
SIC 5065 Electronic parts and equipment, nec

D-U-N-S 24-647-4662   (BR)
AB MAURI (CANADA) LIMITEE
FLEISHMANN'S YEAST
2201 15 St Se, Calgary, AB, T2G 3M3
(403) 265-4937
Emp Here 35
SIC 2099 Food preparations, nec

D-U-N-S 25-536-2097   (BR)
ABB INC
4411 6 St Se Unit 110, Calgary, AB, T2G 4E8
(403) 253-0271
Emp Here 90
SIC 8711 Engineering services

D-U-N-S 25-581-0517   (BR)
ADM AGRI-INDUSTRIES COMPANY
ADM MILLING DIV OF
(*Suby of* Archer-Daniels-Midland Company)
4002 Bonnybrook Rd Se, Calgary, AB, T2G
4M9
(403) 267-5600
Emp Here 85
SIC 2045 Prepared flour mixes and doughs

D-U-N-S 20-824-4830   (BR)
AON REED STENHOUSE INC
1100 1 St Se Suite 4fl, Calgary, AB, T2G 1B1
(403) 267-7010
Emp Here 150
SIC 6411 Insurance agents, brokers, and service

D-U-N-S 25-361-7716   (BR)
ACKLANDS - GRAINGER INC
AGI
(*Suby of* W.W. Grainger, Inc.)
4340 Manhattan Rd Se, Calgary, AB, T2G 4B2
(403) 243-4291
Emp Here 50
SIC 5085 Industrial supplies

D-U-N-S 24-298-3831   (SL)
ADAPTIVE ENGINEERING INC
4033 14 St Se, Calgary, AB, T2G 3K6
(403) 744-5120
Emp Here 498   *Sales* 42,390,167
SIC 3999 Manufacturing industries, nec
Pr Dave Smith
 Catherine Smith

D-U-N-S 24-297-9870   (SL)
ADRICO MACHINE WORKS LTD
(*Suby of* Panila Holdings Ltd)
1165j 44 Ave Se, Calgary, AB, T2G 4X4
(403) 243-7930
Emp Here 60   *Sales* 4,377,642
SIC 3599 Industrial machinery, nec

D-U-N-S 24-766-1929   (SL)
ALBERTA ONE-CALL CORPORATION
CALL BEFORE YOU DIG
4242 7 St Se Suite 104, Calgary, AB, T2G 2Y8
(403) 531-3700
Emp Here 48   *Sales* 6,933,120
SIC 4899 Communication services, nec
Pr Robert R. Chisholm
Treas Ken Hawrelko
 Boris Schurenko
 Taras Shwetz
 Andy Bowen
 Robert Chanasyk

Bruce Littke
Brian Mcconaghy

D-U-N-S 25-621-9429   (BR)
ALLSTATE INSURANCE COMPANY OF CANADA
4639 Manhattan Rd Se Suite 125, Calgary, AB, T2G 4B3
(403) 974-8700
Emp Here 50
SIC 6411 Insurance agents, brokers, and service

D-U-N-S 24-807-6478   (BR)
ALSCO CANADA CORPORATION
ALSCO UNIFORM & LINEN SERVICES
4080 Ogden Rd Se, Calgary, AB, T2G 4P7
(403) 265-7277
Emp Here 40
SIC 2269 Finishing plants, nec

D-U-N-S 20-521-4083   (BR)
ALSCO CANADA CORPORATION
ALSCO UNIFORM & LINEN SERVICE
4080 Ogden Rd Se, Calgary, AB, T2G 4P7
(403) 265-7277
Emp Here 65
SIC 7213 Linen supply

D-U-N-S 25-266-4032   (BR)
AXE MUSIC INC
4114 Macleod Trail Se, Calgary, AB, T2G 2R7
(403) 243-5200
Emp Here 24
SIC 5736 Musical instrument stores

D-U-N-S 20-588-2595   (BR)
BANQUE TORONTO-DOMINION, LA
TD CANADA TRUST
(*Suby of* Toronto-Dominion Bank, The)
305 Centre St Sw, Calgary, AB, T2G 2B9
(403) 292-1830
Emp Here 20
SIC 6021 National commercial banks

D-U-N-S 24-358-1415   (SL)
BLACKLINE SAFETY CORP
1215 13 St Se Suite 101, Calgary, AB, T2G 3J4
(403) 451-0327
Emp Here 115   *Sales* 6,147,310
SIC 3663 Radio and t.v. communications equipment
Cody Slater
Pr Pr Clark Swanson
CFO Shane Grennan
VP Barry Moore
VP Sls Sean Stinson
Kevin Meyers
Sls Dir Greg Rude
Michael Hayduk
John Finbow
Robert Herdman

D-U-N-S 20-831-7891   (HQ)
C.B. ENGINEERING LTD
5040 12a St Se, Calgary, AB, T2G 5K9
(403) 259-6220
Emp Here 35   *Emp Total* 2
Sales 8,244,559
SIC 5084 Industrial machinery and equipment
Pr Pr Craig R Bowyer
Heather Bowyer

D-U-N-S 20-558-9190   (SL)
C.R.A. COLLATERAL RECOVERY & ADMINISTRATION INC
1289 Highfield Cres Se Unit 109, Calgary, AB, T2G 5M2
(403) 240-3450
Emp Here 50   *Sales* 2,626,585
SIC 7381 Detective and armored car services

D-U-N-S 20-566-1684   (SL)
CALCON MANAGEMENT, L.P.
700 Centre St Se, Calgary, AB, T2G 5P6
(403) 537-4426
Emp Here 375   *Sales* 67,376,524

SIC 8741 Management services
Fin Ex Ross Salmon

D-U-N-S 20-791-4339   (BR)
CALGARY BOARD OF EDUCATION
PURCHASING SERVICES
3610 9 St Se, Calgary, AB, T2G 3C5

Emp Here 20
SIC 7389 Business services, nec

D-U-N-S 20-713-1264   (BR)
CALGARY BOARD OF EDUCATION
COLONEL WALKER COMMUNITY SCHOOL
1921 9 Ave Se, Calgary, AB, T2G 0V3
(403) 777-6780
Emp Here 28
SIC 8211 Elementary and secondary schools

D-U-N-S 20-590-8044   (BR)
CALGARY BOARD OF EDUCATION
DISCOVERING CHOICES SCHOOL
315 10 Ave Se Suite 206, Calgary, AB, T2G 0W2
(403) 268-3265
Emp Here 25
SIC 8211 Elementary and secondary schools

D-U-N-S 25-673-3502   (SL)
CALGARY COUNSELLING CENTRE
105 12 Ave Se Suite 100, Calgary, AB, T2G 1A1
(403) 265-4980
Emp Here 87   *Sales* 3,429,153
SIC 8322 Individual and family services

D-U-N-S 20-299-8816   (BR)
CALGARY EXHIBITION AND STAMPEDE LIMITED
MAVERICKS
1801 Big Four Trail Se, Calgary, AB, T2G 2W1
(403) 261-0108
Emp Here 40
SIC 5812 Eating places

D-U-N-S 24-119-7060   (HQ)
CALGARY FASTENERS & TOOLS LTD
1288 42 Ave Se Unit 1, Calgary, AB, T2G 5P1
(403) 287-5340
Emp Here 65   *Emp Total* 150
Sales 34,563,415
SIC 5085 Industrial supplies
Pr Pr Ronald Hall

D-U-N-S 24-714-9867   (HQ)
CALGARY JOHN HOWARD SOCIETY, THE
(*Suby of* Calgary John Howard Society, The)
917 9 Ave Se, Calgary, AB, T2G 0S5
(403) 266-4566
Emp Here 27   *Emp Total* 97
Sales 14,067,200
SIC 8322 Individual and family services
Ex Dir Gordon Sand
CFO Bette Thacker

D-U-N-S 20-913-4068   (BR)
CALGARY JOHN HOWARD SOCIETY, THE
(*Suby of* Calgary John Howard Society, The)
615 13 Ave Se, Calgary, AB, T2G 1C4
(403) 232-6388
Emp Here 20
SIC 8322 Individual and family services

D-U-N-S 20-867-4650   (BR)
CALGARY PARKING AUTHORITY
400 39 Ave Se, Calgary, AB, T2G 5P8
(403) 537-7012
Emp Here 100
SIC 7521 Automobile parking

D-U-N-S 24-159-9984   (HQ)
CALGARY PUBLIC LIBRARY
616 Macleod Trail Se, Calgary, AB, T2G 2M2
(403) 260-2712
Emp Here 150   *Emp Total* 10,000
Sales 47,945,600
SIC 8231 Libraries
Ch Bd Jamie Niessen

D-U-N-S 20-713-0761   (BR)
CALGARY ROMAN CATHOLIC SEPARATE SCHOOL DISTRICT #1
ST. ANNE ACADEMIC CENTRE
1010 21 Ave Se, Calgary, AB, T2G 1N2
(403) 500-2012
Emp Here 25
SIC 8211 Elementary and secondary schools

D-U-N-S 24-039-8698   (SL)
CALGARY SCIENTIFIC INC
1210 20 Ave Se Suite 208, Calgary, AB, T2G 1M8
(403) 270-7159
Emp Here 62   *Sales* 4,071,380
SIC 7374 Data processing and preparation

D-U-N-S 20-052-4838   (HQ)
CANADA BROKERLINK (ONTARIO) INC
4124 9 St Se Suite 100, Calgary, AB, T2G 3C4
(403) 209-6300
Emp Here 32   *Emp Total* 11,000
Sales 9,615,386
SIC 6411 Insurance agents, brokers, and service
Dir Guy Desjardins
Dir Roger Randall
Dir Tom Reid

D-U-N-S 24-380-9949   (BR)
CANADIAN LINEN AND UNIFORM SERVICE CO
(*Suby of* Ameripride Services, Inc.)
4525 Manilla Rd Se, Calgary, AB, T2G 4B6
(403) 243-8080
Emp Here 165
SIC 7213 Linen supply

D-U-N-S 24-578-4868   (BR)
CANADIAN MENTAL HEALTH ASSOCIATION, THE
(*Suby of* Canadian Mental Health Association, The)
105 12 Ave Se Suite 400, Calgary, AB, T2G 1A1
(403) 297-1700
Emp Here 70
SIC 8621 Professional organizations

D-U-N-S 24-106-1550   (SL)
CANADIAN OUTCOMES RESEARCH INSTITUTE
1212 1 St Se Suite 200, Calgary, AB, T2G 2H8

Emp Here 37   *Sales* 5,842,440
SIC 8699 Membership organizations, nec
Pr Linda Thorstad
VP Opers Angelica Miller
Ch Bd George Ghitan
V Ch Bd Bob Wyatt

D-U-N-S 24-103-9663   (BR)
CANADIAN PACIFIC RAILWAY COMPANY
ALYTH CAR DEPARTMENT
1702 30 Ave Se Suite 9, Calgary, AB, T2G 5S4
(403) 303-8766
Emp Here 72
SIC 4011 Railroads, line-haul operating

D-U-N-S 24-103-3401   (BR)
CANADIAN PACIFIC RAILWAY COMPANY
CPR
2881 Alyth Rd Se, Calgary, AB, T2G 5S3
(403) 303-8843
Emp Here 20
SIC 4011 Railroads, line-haul operating

D-U-N-S 24-156-8153   (BR)
CARRIER ENTERPRISE CANADA, L.P.
CARRIER ENTERPRISE CANADA, L.P
3201 Ogden Rd Se Suite 1, Calgary, AB, T2G 4N4
(403) 287-4800
Emp Here 20
SIC 5075 Warm air heating and air conditioning

D-U-N-S 20-078-6689   (BR)

CARRIER ENTERPRISE CANADA, L.P.
CARRIER ENTERPRISE CANADA, L.P
3201 Ogden Rd Se Suite 1, Calgary, AB, T2G 4N4
(403) 243-0233
Emp Here 20
SIC 5078 Refrigeration equipment and supplies

D-U-N-S 24-313-4942   (SL)
CENTENNIAL 2000 INC
4412 Manilla Rd Se Suite 1, Calgary, AB, T2G 4B7
(403) 214-0044
Emp Here 645   *Sales* 103,494,400
SIC 2011 Meat packing plants
Pr J R (Robert) Kalef

D-U-N-S 25-360-9309   (BR)
CINTAS CANADA LIMITED
SALLY FOURMY & ASSOCIATES
(*Suby of* Cintas Corporation)
1235 23 Ave Se, Calgary, AB, T2G 5S5
(403) 313-3889
Emp Here 120
SIC 7218 Industrial launderers

D-U-N-S 20-515-0456   (BR)
CITY OF CALGARY, THE
COMMUNITY & NEIGHBOURHOOD SERVICES
315 10 Ave Se Suite 101, Calgary, AB, T2G 0W2
(403) 268-5153
Emp Here 200
SIC 8399 Social services, nec

D-U-N-S 25-144-4394   (BR)
CITY OF CALGARY, THE
CALGARY ANIMAL SERVICES
2201 Portland St Se, Calgary, AB, T2G 4M7
(403) 268-1169
Emp Here 42
SIC 1623 Water, sewer, and utility lines

D-U-N-S 25-218-3066   (HQ)
CORE LABORATORIES CANADA LTD
SAYBOLT, DIV OF
125 9 Ave Se Suite 2100, Calgary, AB, T2G 0P6
(403) 269-2055
Emp Here 25   *Emp Total* 4,400
Sales 26,849,538
SIC 8734 Testing laboratories
Pr Pr Stephen Lee
Dir Brian Tofselmire

D-U-N-S 24-387-3820   (SL)
CRITICALCONTROL SOLUTIONS INC
410 10 Ave Se Suite 800, Calgary, AB, T2G 0R1
(403) 705-7500
Emp Here 65   *Sales* 9,329,057
SIC 7371 Custom computer programming services
Pr Pr Alykhan Mamdani
VP Opers Raymond South

D-U-N-S 20-341-2718   (SL)
DEANE HOUSE AT FORT CALGARY, THE
806 9 Ave Se, Calgary, AB, T2G 0S2
(403) 269-7747
Emp Here 60   *Sales* 1,824,018
SIC 5812 Eating places

D-U-N-S 24-158-9217   (BR)
DELTA HOTELS LIMITED
DELTA BOW VALLEY HOTEL
209 4 Ave Se, Calgary, AB, T2G 0C6
(403) 266-1980
Emp Here 260
SIC 8741 Management services

D-U-N-S 24-716-3975   (HQ)
DESA HOLDINGS LTD
DESA GLASS
3195 9 St Se, Calgary, AB, T2G 3C1

(403) 230-5011
Emp Here 110   Emp Total 1
Sales 13,192,606
SIC 2431 Millwork
Pr Pr Daniel Barker

D-U-N-S 20-040-7422   (BR)
DILLON CONSULTING LIMITED
(Suby of Dillon Consulting Inc)
334 11 Ave Se Suite 200, Calgary, AB, T2G
0Y2
(403) 215-8880
Emp Here 40
SIC 8748 Business consulting, nec

D-U-N-S 25-291-0310   (BR)
DIVERSIFIED TRANSPORTATION LTD
RED ARROW
205 9 Ave Se Suite 101, Calgary, AB, T2G
0R3
(403) 531-0350
Emp Here 70
SIC 4111 Local and suburban transit

D-U-N-S 25-505-6921   (HQ)
ENERFLEX LTD
ENERFLEX SERVICE
(Suby of Enerflex Ltd)
1331 Macleod Trail Se Suite 904, Calgary, AB,
T2G 0K3
(403) 387-6377
Emp Here 50   Emp Total 1,800
Sales 836,245,596
SIC 3563 Air and gas compressors
Pr Pr J. Blair Goertzen
   D. James Harbilas
Sr VP Greg Stewart
   Stephen Savidant
   Robert Boswell
   W. Byron Dunn
   Maureen Cormier Jackson
   H. Stanley Marshall
   Kevin Reinhart
   Michael Weill

D-U-N-S 25-521-1385   (BR)
**ENTERPRISE RENT-A-CAR CANADA COM-
PANY**
NATIONAL CAR RENTAL
(Suby of The Crawford Group Inc)
114 5 Ave Se, Calgary, AB, T2G 0E2
(403) 264-0424
Emp Here 75
SIC 7514 Passenger car rental

D-U-N-S 24-517-9569   (BR)
FOUNTAIN TIRE LTD
819 46 Ave Se, Calgary, AB, T2G 2A5
(403) 221-8473
Emp Here 45
SIC 5531 Auto and home supply stores

D-U-N-S 24-245-5546   (BR)
GATEWAY MECHANICAL SERVICES INC
4001 16a St Se, Calgary, AB, T2G 3T5
(403) 265-0010
Emp Here 100
SIC 1711 Plumbing, heating, air-conditioning

D-U-N-S 20-152-8481   (BR)
**GOVERNING COUNCIL OF THE SALVA-
TION ARMY IN CANADA, THE**
*GOVERNING COUNCIL OF THE SALVATION
ARMY IN CANADA, THE*
631 7 Ave Se, Calgary, AB, T2G 0J8

Emp Here 100
SIC 8322 Individual and family services

D-U-N-S 20-299-0540   (BR)
**GOVERNMENT OF THE PROVINCE OF AL-
BERTA**
OFFICE OF THE PUBLIC TRUSTEE, THE
411 1 St Se Suite 2100, Calgary, AB, T2G 4Y5
(403) 297-6541
Emp Here 38
SIC 6733 Trusts, nec

D-U-N-S 25-519-9986   (SL)
GREENPOINT SOFTWARE LTD
(Suby of Intuit Inc.)
1509 Centre St Sw Suite 600, Calgary, AB,
T2G 2E6
(403) 205-4848
Emp Here 26   Sales 2,544,288
SIC 7372 Prepackaged software

D-U-N-S 25-362-0355   (BR)
GUILLEVIN INTERNATIONAL CIE
GUILLEVIN INTERNATIONAL
4220a Blackfoot Trail Se, Calgary, AB, T2G
4E6
(403) 287-1680
Emp Here 30
SIC 3621 Motors and generators

D-U-N-S 25-270-0968   (BR)
HSBC BANK CANADA
111 3 Ave Se Suite 212, Calgary, AB, T2G 0B7
(403) 233-8303
Emp Here 25
SIC 6021 National commercial banks

D-U-N-S 24-350-2171   (BR)
HITACHI SOLUTIONS CANADA, LTD
308 11 Ave Se Suite 110, Calgary, AB, T2G
0Y2
(403) 265-4332
Emp Here 100
SIC 7372 Prepackaged software

D-U-N-S 20-299-2488   (SL)
HOLIDAY INN - MACLEOD TRAIL SOUTH
4206 Macleod Trail Se, Calgary, AB, T2G 2R7
(403) 287-2700
Emp Here 60   Sales 2,626,585
SIC 7011 Hotels and motels

D-U-N-S 20-268-0216   (BR)
HOOD PACKAGING CORPORATION
GLOPAK
(Suby of Hood Packaging Corporation)
1222 34 Ave Se, Calgary, AB, T2G 1V7
(403) 287-0450
Emp Here 70
SIC 2673 Bags: plastic, laminated, and
coated

D-U-N-S 25-359-7827   (HQ)
IHS ENERGY (CANADA) LTD
IHS
1331 Macleod Trail Se Suite 200, Calgary, AB,
T2G 0K3
(403) 532-8175
Emp Here 100   Sales 26,995,459
SIC 8741 Management services
Dir Chris Jones
Dir Vinod Kothari
Dir Stephen Green
Dir Michael Mccrory

D-U-N-S 20-310-0631   (HQ)
IHS GLOBAL CANADA LIMITED
1331 Macleod Trail Se Suite 200, Calgary, AB,
T2G 0K3
(403) 532-8175
Emp Here 25   Sales 5,977,132
SIC 7372 Prepackaged software
   Vinod Kothari
Sec Stephen Green
Genl Mgr Richard Walker

D-U-N-S 20-557-6791   (BR)
IKO INDUSTRIES LTD
ARMOROOF DIV OF
1600 42 Ave Se, Calgary, AB, T2G 5B5
(403) 265-6030
Emp Here 40
SIC 2952 Asphalt felts and coatings

D-U-N-S 24-368-5786   (SL)
ISTOCKPHOTO ULC
1240 20 Ave Se Suite 200, Calgary, AB, T2G
1M8
(403) 265-3062
Emp Here 130   Sales 5,791,440

SIC 7299 Miscellaneous personal service
VP VP Kjelti Kellough
   John J. Lapham Iii

D-U-N-S 20-337-1922   (HQ)
INNOVA GLOBAL LTD
4000 4 St Se Suite 222, Calgary, AB, T2G
2W3
(403) 292-7804
Emp Here 40   Emp Total 9
Sales 17,802,411
SIC 1541 Industrial buildings and warehouses
Pr Harry Wong

D-U-N-S 20-970-7046   (BR)
INTERNATIONAL FITNESS HOLDINGS INC
WORLD HEALTH CLUB
4344 Macleod Trail Sw, Calgary, AB, T2G 0A4
(403) 974-0300
Emp Here 27
SIC 7991 Physical fitness facilities

D-U-N-S 20-832-2172   (SL)
JAMES ELECTRIC MOTOR SERVICES LTD
4020 8 St Se, Calgary, AB, T2G 3A7
(403) 252-5477
Emp Here 42   Sales 7,660,874
SIC 5084 Industrial machinery and equipment
Pr Pr Douglas Rick James
   Theresa James

D-U-N-S 24-767-3320   (SL)
**KBM COMMERCIAL FLOOR COVERINGS
INC**
1260 26 Ave Se, Calgary, AB, T2G 5S2
(403) 274-5292
Emp Here 165   Sales 20,637,005
SIC 1752 Floor laying and floor work, nec
Pr Pr Mike Kulyk
   Beverley Ann Kulyk
Dir Barbara Bauer
Dir Kevin Kulyk
Dir Michael Kulyk

D-U-N-S 24-701-8849   (HQ)
LVM/HTES LTD
(Suby of LVM/HTES Ltd)
2806 Ogden Rd Se, Calgary, AB, T2G 4R7
(403) 255-3273
Emp Here 40   Emp Total 50
Sales 6,898,600
SIC 8711 Engineering services
   Rosaire Sauriol
   Jean-Pierre Sauriol

D-U-N-S 24-764-2759   (BR)
LEHIGH HANSON MATERIALS LIMITED
LEHIGH CEMENT
885 42 Ave Se Suite 222, Calgary, AB, T2G
1Y8
(403) 531-3000
Emp Here 40
SIC 2891 Adhesives and sealants

D-U-N-S 20-532-1388   (BR)
LIFEMARK HEALTH MANAGEMENT INC
LIFEMARK HEALTH CENTRE
(Suby of Audax Group, L.P.)
2225 Macleod Trail Se, Calgary, AB, T2G 5B6
(403) 221-8340
Emp Here 25
SIC 8741 Management services

D-U-N-S 25-993-3018   (SL)
LIGHTHOUSE CAMP SERVICES LTD
LIGHTHOUSE LOGISTICS, A DIV OF
(Suby of Icegate Holdings Inc.)
714 1 St Se Unit 300, Calgary, AB, T2G 2G8
(403) 265-5190
Emp Here 150   Sales 9,130,500
SIC 7011 Hotels and motels
Pr Dario Berloni

D-U-N-S 20-176-2965   (BR)
LILYDALE INC
LILYDALE POULTRY
2126 Hurst Rd Se, Calgary, AB, T2G 4M5

(403) 265-9010
Emp Here 375
SIC 2015 Poultry slaughtering and processing

D-U-N-S 25-521-8745   (BR)
LOYALTYONE, CO
LOYALTY GROUP, THE
1331 Macleod Trail Se, Calgary, AB, T2G 0K3
(403) 531-7750
Emp Here 24
SIC 7299 Miscellaneous personal service

D-U-N-S 25-096-9029   (BR)
**LUXURY HOTELS INTERNATIONAL OF
CANADA, ULC**
CALGARY MARRIOTT HOTEL
(Suby of Marriott International, Inc.)
110 9 Ave Se, Calgary, AB, T2G 5A6
(403) 266-7331
Emp Here 300
SIC 7011 Hotels and motels

D-U-N-S 20-328-7011   (BR)
MCF HOLDINGS LTD
MOUNTAIN CREEK FARMS
3410b Ogden Rd Se, Calgary, AB, T2G 4N5
(403) 290-0860
Emp Here 25
SIC 5154 Livestock

D-U-N-S 25-676-5389   (HQ)
MAINSTREET EQUITY CORP
(Suby of Mainstreet Equity Corp)
305 10 Ave Se, Calgary, AB, T2G 0W2
(403) 215-6060
Emp Here 250   Emp Total 350
Sales 76,725,903
SIC 6513 Apartment building operators
Pr Pr Bob Dhillon
   Johnny Lam
   Trina Cui
VP Opers Sheena Keslick
VP Darren Stewart
   John Irwin
   Joe Amantea
   Rich Grimaldi
   K.V. Dhillon
   Ron Anderson

D-U-N-S 24-948-5319   (BR)
MAXWELL PAPER CANADA INC
MAXWELL MEDIA PRODUCTS
421 Manitou Rd Se, Calgary, AB, T2G 4C2
(403) 216-8710
Emp Here 26
SIC 5112 Stationery and office supplies

D-U-N-S 25-521-2789   (BR)
MCCANN WORLDGROUP CANADA INC
MACLAREN MCCANN
(Suby of The Interpublic Group of Companies
Inc)
238 11 Ave Se Suite 100, Calgary, AB, T2G
0X8
(403) 269-6120
Emp Here 40
SIC 7311 Advertising agencies

D-U-N-S 20-914-1220   (BR)
MELOCHE MONNEX INC
(Suby of Toronto-Dominion Bank, The)
125 9 Ave Se Suite 1200, Calgary, AB, T2G
0P6
(403) 269-1112
Emp Here 160
SIC 6411 Insurance agents, brokers, and service

D-U-N-S 20-298-3743   (HQ)
MERCADO CAPITAL CORPORATION
(Suby of Westminster Savings Credit Union)
4411 6 St Se Suite 180, Calgary, AB, T2G 4E8
(403) 215-6117
Emp Here 22   Emp Total 400
Sales 3,855,100
SIC 6159 Miscellaneous business credit insti-
tutions

D-U-N-S 20-178-2013　(BR)
NATIONAL ENERGY EQUIPMENT INC
1350 42 Ave Se Bay Suite R, Calgary, AB,
T2G 4V6
(403) 735-1103
Emp Here 33
SIC 4925 Gas production and/or distribution

D-U-N-S 20-152-8465　(BR)
**NATURE CONSERVANCY OF CANADA,
THE**
1202 Centre St Se Suite 830, Calgary, AB,
T2G 5A5
(403) 262-1253
Emp Here 35
SIC 8999 Services, nec

D-U-N-S 24-359-5845　(SL)
NILE PROPERTIES (1988) LTD
BEST WESTERN CALGARY CENTRE INN
3630 Macleod Trail Se, Calgary, AB, T2G 2P9
(403) 287-3900
Emp Here 60　*Sales* 3,118,504
SIC 7011 Hotels and motels

D-U-N-S 20-286-3288　(BR)
NILSSON BROS. INC
XL FOODS
3410b Ogden Rd Se, Calgary, AB, T2G 4N5
(403) 290-0860
Emp Here 26
SIC 2011 Meat packing plants

D-U-N-S 24-766-2976　(SL)
NORWEST CORPORATION
(*Suby of* Norwest Corporation)
411 1 St Se Suite 2700, Calgary, AB, T2G 4Y5
(403) 237-7763
Emp Here 200　*Sales* 34,866,173
SIC 8748 Business consulting, nec
　Donovan Symonds
Pr Pr Joe Aiello
　Geoff Jordan
　Steve Cameron
　Craig Acott
VP VP Andrew Scrymgeour

D-U-N-S 24-494-9004　(SL)
O'DELL ELECTRIC LTD
3827 15a St Se, Calgary, AB, T2G 3N7
(403) 266-2935
Emp Here 130　*Sales* 11,476,321
SIC 1731 Electrical work
Pr Pr Randy O'dell
　Drew Woolsey

D-U-N-S 20-010-4107　(BR)
ORKIN CANADA CORPORATION
ORKIN PCO SERVICES
(*Suby of* Rollins, Inc.)
711 48th Ave Se Unit 12, Calgary, AB, T2G
4X2
(403) 236-2700
Emp Here 35
SIC 7342 Disinfecting and pest control services

D-U-N-S 20-521-1832　(HQ)
P.S.I. FLUID POWER LTD
4020 11a St Se, Calgary, AB, T2G 3H3
(403) 253-2236
Emp Here 25　*Emp Total* 11
Sales 14,592,140
SIC 5084 Industrial machinery and equipment
Pr Pr William George Lancaster
　Russell P Dueck
Dir Suzanne Edith Lancaster
Dir George Parker Lancaster
Dir Ross Sheldon Lancaster
Dir John Wylie Wood

D-U-N-S 20-047-9751　(BR)
**PACIFIC WESTERN TRANSPORTATION
LTD**
RED ARROW
205 9 Ave Se Suite 101, Calgary, AB, T2G
0R3

(403) 531-0355
Emp Here 20
SIC 4111 Local and suburban transit

D-U-N-S 25-316-4347　(BR)
PASLEY, MAX ENTERPRISES LIMITED
MCDONALD'S RESTAURANTS 10695
(*Suby of* Pasley, Max Enterprises Limited)
3912 Macleod Trail Se, Calgary, AB, T2G 2R5
(403) 243-7828
Emp Here 37
SIC 5812 Eating places

D-U-N-S 20-636-2691　(SL)
PECOFACET (CANADA) LIMITED
PECOFACET CANADA
(*Suby of* Parker-Hannifin Corporation)
1351 Hastings Cres Se, Calgary, AB, T2G 4C8
(403) 243-6700
Emp Here 29　*Sales* 5,370,756
SIC 3443 Fabricated plate work (boiler shop)
　Norman Hertzberg

D-U-N-S 24-379-7482　(SL)
PLUMBLINE CORPORATION
1212 34 Ave Se, Calgary, AB, T2G 1V7
(403) 569-4885
Emp Here 300　*Sales* 28,269,870
SIC 1741 Masonry and other stonework
　Paul Poscente
Pr Pr Marco Dedominicis

D-U-N-S 20-441-0229　(HQ)
PRAIRIE VIEW HOLDINGS LTD
BUDGET RENT-A-CAR OF CALGARY
140 6 Ave Se, Calgary, AB, T2G 0G2
(403) 232-4725
Emp Here 25　*Emp Total* 220
Sales 14,300,297
SIC 7514 Passenger car rental
Pr Pr Mohamed Ali
　Mithoo Gillani
　Shiraz Ali

D-U-N-S 20-123-0344　(SL)
REDPOINT MEDIA GROUP INC
AVENUE MAGAZINE, DIV OF
1900 11 St Se Suite 100, Calgary, AB, T2G
3G2
(403) 240-9055
Emp Here 60　*Sales* 4,377,642
SIC 2721 Periodicals

D-U-N-S 24-272-6610　(HQ)
**ROCKY CROSS CONSTRUCTION (CAL-
GARY) LIMITED**
444 42 Ave Se Suite 4, Calgary, AB, T2G 1Y4
(403) 253-2550
Emp Here 40　*Emp Total* 72
Sales 6,274,620
SIC 1799 Special trade contractors, nec
Pr Pr Rodger Cumberland

D-U-N-S 20-078-0229　(BR)
SSH BEDDING CANADA CO.
SIMMONS CANADA, DIV OF
(*Suby of* SSH Bedding Canada Co.)
3636 11a St Se, Calgary, AB, T2G 3H3
(403) 287-0600
Emp Here 120
SIC 2394 Canvas and related products

D-U-N-S 25-219-1044　(BR)
SAMUEL, SON & CO., LIMITED
ENCORE COILS
1401 17 Ave Se, Calgary, AB, T2G 1J9
(403) 531-0600
Emp Here 30
SIC 5051 Metals service centers and offices

D-U-N-S 24-786-2808　(BR)
SCHINDLER ELEVATOR CORPORATION
527 Manitou Rd Se, Calgary, AB, T2G 4C2
(403) 243-0715
Emp Here 50
SIC 1796 Installing building equipment

D-U-N-S 20-036-2494　(BR)

SHAW GMC CHEVROLET BUICK LTD
SUMMIT TRUCK
4620 Blackfoot Trail Se Suite 6, Calgary, AB,
T2G 4G2
(403) 243-6200
Emp Here 35
SIC 7515 Passenger car leasing

D-U-N-S 24-385-3376　(BR)
SHELL CANADA PRODUCTS
*SHELL CANADA PRODUCTS CALGARY LU-
BRICANTS AND GREASE PLANT*
2900 Alyth Rd Se, Calgary, AB, T2G 3W4
(403) 234-7534
Emp Here 40
SIC 2992 Lubricating oils and greases

D-U-N-S 25-687-5725　(BR)
SOBEYS WEST INC
MCDONALD CONSOLIDATED
203 42 Ave Se, Calgary, AB, T2G 1Y3
(403) 287-4048
Emp Here 130
SIC 4225 General warehousing and storage

D-U-N-S 24-598-2004　(HQ)
SOUTHLAND TRANSPORTATION LTD
823 Highfield Ave Se, Calgary, AB, T2G 4C7
(403) 287-1395
Emp Here 100　*Emp Total* 1,600
Sales 61,330,571
SIC 4151 School buses
Pr Michael Colborne
VP Thomas Jezersek

D-U-N-S 25-388-1429　(BR)
SPRINGWALL SLEEP PRODUCTS INC
4020 9 St Se Suite 6, Calgary, AB, T2G 3C4
(403) 287-0221
Emp Here 50
SIC 2515 Mattresses and bedsprings

D-U-N-S 24-417-2821　(HQ)
**STEINBOCK DEVELOPMENT CORPORA-
TION LTD**
PARK N JET
140 6 Ave Se, Calgary, AB, T2G 0G2
(403) 232-4725
Emp Here 45　*Emp Total* 220
Sales 875,528
SIC 7521 Automobile parking

D-U-N-S 20-772-8333　(BR)
SUREWAY METAL SYSTEMS LIMITED
SUREWAY METAL WAREHOUSE
1118 46 Ave Se, Calgary, AB, T2G 2A6
(403) 287-2742
Emp Here 55
SIC 1791 Structural steel erection

D-U-N-S 20-512-4261　(HQ)
TECK COAL LIMITED
205 9 Ave Se Suite 1000, Calgary, AB, T2G
0R3
(403) 767-8500
Emp Here 150　*Emp Total* 9,400
Sales 1,151,100,964
SIC 1221 Bituminous coal and lignite-surface
mining
Dir Peter C. Rozee
Dir Ronald A. Millos
Dir Robin B. Sheremeta

D-U-N-S 24-948-6002　(HQ)
TERVITA CORPORATION
(*Suby of* Tervita Corporation)
140 10 Ave Se Suite 1600, Calgary, AB, T2G
0R1
(403) 233-7565
Emp Here 800　*Emp Total* 4,000
Sales 573,835,906
SIC 8748 Business consulting, nec
　John Cooper
　Brad Dloughy
　Rob Dawson
　Grant Billing
　Kevin Walbridge

SHAW GMC CHEVROLET BUICK LTD

D-U-N-S 25-062-1422　(BR)
TIMBERTOWN BUILDING CENTRE LTD
TIMBERTOWN
230 42 Ave Se, Calgary, AB, T2G 1Y4
(403) 243-6500
Emp Here 20
SIC 5211 Lumber and other building materials

D-U-N-S 20-191-6983　(BR)
**TYCO INTEGRATED FIRE & SECURITY
CANADA, INC**
SIMPLEX GRINNELL
(*Suby of* Johnson Controls, Inc.)
431 Manitou Rd Se, Calgary, AB, T2G 4C2
(403) 287-3202
Emp Here 120
SIC 7389 Business services, nec

D-U-N-S 24-342-3998　(SL)
VAP HOLDINGS L.P.
4211 13a St Se, Calgary, AB, T2G 3J6
(403) 299-0844
Emp Here 300　*Sales* 48,594,550
SIC 2011 Meat packing plants
Pr Anthony Speteri

D-U-N-S 25-677-7277　(BR)
WBM OFFICE SYSTEMS INC
4411 6 St Se Unit 150, Calgary, AB, T2G 4E8
(403) 272-0707
Emp Here 22
SIC 5044 Office equipment

D-U-N-S 24-335-5547　(BR)
WSP CANADA INC
G NIVAR
1331 Macleod Trail Se Suite 805, Calgary, AB,
T2G 0K3
(403) 777-2477
Emp Here 14
SIC 1382 Oil and gas exploration services

D-U-N-S 24-118-7202　(BR)
**WESCLEAN EQUIPMENT & CLEANING
SUPPLIES LTD**
36 Highfield Cir Se, Calgary, AB, T2G 5N5
(403) 243-0677
Emp Here 21
SIC 5087 Service establishment equipment

D-U-N-S 24-677-7689　(SL)
**WESTERN LOUISEVILLE FIBERBOARD
INC**
WLF
4321 15 St Se, Calgary, AB, T2G 3M9
(403) 532-8700
Emp Here 27　*Sales* 5,748,207
SIC 2653 Corrugated and solid fiber boxes

D-U-N-S 20-076-8430　(BR)
WESTROCK COMPANY OF CANADA INC
(*Suby of* Westrock Company)
1115 34 Ave Se, Calgary, AB, T2G 1V5
(403) 214-5200
Emp Here 200
SIC 2653 Corrugated and solid fiber boxes

D-U-N-S 20-182-6190　(BR)
WOLSELEY CANADA INC
CRONKHITE SUPPLY
(*Suby of* WOLSELEY PLC)
3604 8 St Se Suite 403, Calgary, AB, T2G 3A7
(403) 287-2684
Emp Here 70
SIC 5074 Plumbing and heating equipment
and supplies (hydronics)

D-U-N-S 24-377-0109　(SL)
ISTOCKPHOTO L.P.
ISTOCKPHOTO
1240 20 Ave Se Suite 200, Calgary, AB, T2G
1M8
(403) 265-3062
Emp Here 130　*Sales* 4,304,681
SIC 7299 Miscellaneous personal service

Calgary, AB T2H

D-U-N-S 20-521-7698   (SL)
28 AUGUSTA FUND LTD
SMUGGLER'S INN
6920 Macleod Trail Se, Calgary, AB, T2H 0L3
(403) 259-3119
Emp Here 140   *Sales* 4,231,721
SIC 5812 Eating places

D-U-N-S 24-352-2393   (BR)
73559 ALBERTA LTD
5728 1 St Sw, Calgary, AB, T2H 0E2
(403) 252-7651
Emp Here 20
SIC 6512 Nonresidential building operators

D-U-N-S 20-108-9906   (BR)
ADP CANADA CO
ADP
(*Suby of* Automatic Data Processing, Inc.)
6025 11 St Se Suite 100, Calgary, AB, T2H
2Z2
(403) 258-5000
Emp Here 80
SIC 8721 Accounting, auditing, and book-keeping

D-U-N-S 20-048-7929   (BR)
ARAMARK CANADA LTD.
ARAMARK REFRESHMENT
625 77 Ave Se Unit 4, Calgary, AB, T2H 2B9
(403) 212-4800
Emp Here 36
SIC 7389 Business services, nec

D-U-N-S 25-100-7399   (SL)
ADVANCED MEASUREMENTS INC
(*Suby of* Key Energy Services, Inc.)
7110 Fisher Rd Se, Calgary, AB, T2H 0W3
(403) 571-7273
Emp Here 50   *Sales* 4,961,328
SIC 8711 Engineering services

D-U-N-S 20-278-3713   (BR)
AECOM CANADA LTD
6807 Railway St Se Suite 200, Calgary, AB,
T2H 2V6
(403) 254-3301
Emp Here 175
SIC 8711 Engineering services

D-U-N-S 25-538-7953   (HQ)
AECOM ENERGY SERVICES LTD
URS FLINT
6025 11 St Se Suite 240, Calgary, AB, T2H
2Z2
(403) 218-7100
Emp Here 40   *Emp Total* 87,000
Sales 1,663,465,288
SIC 1389 Oil and gas field services, nec
Pr William J. Lingard
 Paul Boechler
Dir Wayne Shaw
VP Sean Fitzgerald
Sr VP Glen Greenshields
Sr VP Deon Walsh
 Ray Sandhu
Sr VP Joel Jarding
VP Brad Mcfarlane
Sr VP Neil Wotton

D-U-N-S 25-261-8566   (SL)
AECON WATER INFRASTRUCTURE INC
7335 Flint Rd Se, Calgary, AB, T2H 1G3
(403) 770-1914
Emp Here 20   *Sales* 2,772,507
SIC 1629 Heavy construction, nec

D-U-N-S 25-219-9054   (BR)
AGRIUM INC
CARSELAND NITROGEN OPERATIONS
(*Suby of* Agrium Canada Partnership)
Gd, Calgary, AB, T2H 2P4
(403) 936-5821
Emp Here 145
SIC 2873 Nitrogenous fertilizers

D-U-N-S 25-236-1621   (BR)
ALBERTA TREASURY BRANCHES
ATB FINANCIAL
6455 Macleod Trail Sw Suite 264, Calgary, AB,
T2H 0K3
(403) 297-6503
Emp Here 35
SIC 6036 Savings institutions, except federal

D-U-N-S 24-722-6751   (BR)
ALBERTA TREASURY BRANCHES
ATB FINANCIAL
33 Heritage Meadows Way Se Suite 1200,
Calgary, AB, T2H 3B8
(403) 974-3599
Emp Here 27
SIC 6036 Savings institutions, except federal

D-U-N-S 24-894-4563   (BR)
ALLSTREAM BUSINESS INC
6101 6 St Se, Calgary, AB, T2H 1L9
(403) 258-8800
Emp Here 35
SIC 4899 Communication services, nec

D-U-N-S 24-290-6688   (SL)
BMP MECHANICAL LTD
6420 6a St Se Suite 110, Calgary, AB, T2H
2B7
(403) 816-4409
Emp Here 200   *Sales* 17,510,568
SIC 1711 Plumbing, heating, air-conditioning
Pr Pr Brad Shalagan

D-U-N-S 24-495-6397   (BR)
BAGOS BUN BAKERY LTD
SONS BAKERY
303 58 Ave Se Suite 3, Calgary, AB, T2H 0P3
(403) 252-3660
Emp Here 100
SIC 2051 Bread, cake, and related products

D-U-N-S 20-178-0983   (BR)
BANK OF NOVA SCOTIA, THE
SCOTIABANK
8706 Macleod Trail Se, Calgary, AB, T2H 0M4
(403) 221-6874
Emp Here 30
SIC 6021 National commercial banks

D-U-N-S 25-094-6428   (BR)
BEAUTY SYSTEMS GROUP (CANADA) INC
SALLY BEAUTY SUPPLY
5734 Burbank Cres Se, Calgary, AB, T2H 1Z6
(403) 253-9128
Emp Here 23
SIC 5999 Miscellaneous retail stores, nec

D-U-N-S 20-892-0855   (BR)
BEST BUY CANADA LTD
BEST BUY
(*Suby of* Best Buy Co., Inc.)
8180 11 St Se Unit 300, Calgary, AB, T2H 3B5
(403) 258-7975
Emp Here 50
SIC 5731 Radio, television, and electronic stores

D-U-N-S 24-554-2436   (BR)
BEST BUY CANADA LTD
FUTURE SHOP
(*Suby of* Best Buy Co., Inc.)
6909 Macleod Trail Sw, Calgary, AB, T2H 0L6

Emp Here 100
SIC 5734 Computer and software stores

D-U-N-S 24-321-2391   (BR)
BRICK WAREHOUSE LP, THE
THE BRICK
9 Heritage Meadows Way Se, Calgary, AB,
T2H 0A7
(403) 692-1100
Emp Here 50
SIC 5712 Furniture stores

D-U-N-S 20-563-3139   (BR)
CB PARTNERS CORPORATION

CLARK BUILDERS
7535 Flint Rd Se, Calgary, AB, T2H 1G3
(403) 253-0565
SIC 1542 Nonresidential construction, nec

D-U-N-S 24-554-7294   (BR)
CADILLAC FAIRVIEW CORPORATION LIMITED, THE
CHINOOK CENTRE
6455 Macleod Trail Sw Suite B1, Calgary, AB,
T2H 0K8
(403) 259-5241
Emp Here 35
SIC 6512 Nonresidential building operators

D-U-N-S 20-591-1493   (BR)
CALGARY BOARD OF EDUCATION
LE ROI DANIELS ELEMENTARY SCHOOL
47 Fyffe Rd Se, Calgary, AB, T2H 1B9
(403) 777-6420
Emp Here 4,030
SIC 8211 Elementary and secondary schools

D-U-N-S 25-269-4070   (BR)
CALGARY BOARD OF EDUCATION
FAIRVIEW JUNIOR HIGH SCHOOL
7840 Fairmount Dr Se, Calgary, AB, T2H 0Y1
(403) 777-7900
Emp Here 50
SIC 8211 Elementary and secondary schools

D-U-N-S 25-269-4369   (BR)
CALGARY BOARD OF EDUCATION
LORD BEAVERBROOK SENIOR HIGH SCHOOL
9019 Fairmount Dr Se, Calgary, AB, T2H 0Z4
(403) 259-5585
Emp Here 150
SIC 8211 Elementary and secondary schools

D-U-N-S 20-768-9373   (SL)
CALGARY GOLF AND COUNTRY CLUB
Elbow Dr & 50th Ave Sw, Calgary, AB, T2H
1Y3
(403) 243-3530
Emp Here 80   *Sales* 3,811,504
SIC 7997 Membership sports and recreation clubs

D-U-N-S 20-076-4520   (SL)
CALGARY ITALIAN BAKERY LTD
5310 5 St Se, Calgary, AB, T2H 1L2
(403) 255-3515
Emp Here 85   *Sales* 4,450,603
SIC 2051 Bread, cake, and related products

D-U-N-S 20-035-2107   (BR)
CALGARY ROMAN CATHOLIC SEPARATE SCHOOL DISTRICT #1
ECOLE ST. MATTHEW SCHOOL
416 83 Ave Se, Calgary, AB, T2H 1N3
(403) 500-2030
Emp Here 50
SIC 8211 Elementary and secondary schools

D-U-N-S 20-572-9952   (BR)
CANADA POST CORPORATION
6939 Fisher Rd Se, Calgary, AB, T2H 0W4
(403) 974-2645
Emp Here 20
SIC 4311 U.s. postal service

D-U-N-S 25-303-5927   (BR)
CANADIAN IMPERIAL BANK OF COMMERCE
CIBC
6200 Macleod Trail Sw, Calgary, AB, T2H 0K6
(403) 974-2744
Emp Here 80
SIC 6021 National commercial banks

D-U-N-S 25-622-0914   (BR)
CANADIAN WESTERN BANK
6606 Macleod Trail Sw, Calgary, AB, T2H 0K6
(403) 252-2299
Emp Here 30
SIC 6021 National commercial banks

D-U-N-S 20-768-3236   (BR)
CANEM SYSTEMS LTD
7110 Fairmount Dr Se, Calgary, AB, T2H 0X4
(403) 259-2221
Emp Here 25
SIC 1731 Electrical work

D-U-N-S 24-983-2593   (SL)
CARMANAH SIGNS INC
6025 12 St Se Suite 5, Calgary, AB, T2H 2K1
(403) 252-6047
Emp Here 30   *Sales* 1,824,018
SIC 3993 Signs and advertising specialties

D-U-N-S 24-156-5290   (BR)
CASCADES CANADA ULC
NORAMPAC-CALGARY, DIV OF
416 58 Ave Se, Calgary, AB, T2H 0P4
(403) 531-3800
Emp Here 160
SIC 2653 Corrugated and solid fiber boxes

D-U-N-S 24-314-3257   (HQ)
CELERO SOLUTIONS INC
(*Suby of* Celero Solutions Inc)
8500 Macleod Trail Se Suite 350n, Calgary,
AB, T2H 2N1
(403) 258-5900
Emp Here 100   *Emp Total* 300
Sales 53,430,054
SIC 8742 Management consulting services
Pr Bob Rezcka

D-U-N-S 20-232-5580   (BR)
CHANDOS CONSTRUCTION LTD
6170 12 St Se, Calgary, AB, T2H 2X2
(403) 640-0101
Emp Here 50
SIC 1542 Nonresidential construction, nec

D-U-N-S 25-448-8968   (BR)
CHEESECAKE CAFE & BAKERY INC, THE
CHEESECAKE CAFE, THE
7600 Macleod Trail Se, Calgary, AB, T2H 0L6
(403) 255-7443
Emp Here 50
SIC 5812 Eating places

D-U-N-S 20-791-4461   (BR)
CHILDREN'S PLACE (CANADA) LP, THE
6455 Macleod Trail Sw, Calgary, AB, T2H 0K3
(403) 255-3620
Emp Here 20
SIC 5641 Children's and infants' wear stores

D-U-N-S 25-386-1439   (BR)
CHRYSALIS: AN ALBERTA SOCIETY FOR CITIZENS WITH DISABILITIES
(*Suby of* Chrysalis: An Alberta Society For Citizens With Disabilities)
6020 1a St Sw Suite 7, Calgary, AB, T2H 0G3
(403) 258-1501
Emp Here 60
SIC 8331 Job training and related services

D-U-N-S 24-318-8104   (SL)
CIMARRON PROJECTS LTD
6025 11 St Se Suite 300, Calgary, AB, T2H
2Z2
(403) 252-3436
Emp Here 150   *Sales* 23,333,500
SIC 8711 Engineering services
Pr Ken Colvin

D-U-N-S 24-029-6264   (SL)
CINEPLEX DIGITAL MEDIA INC
ONSITE MEDIA NETWORK
6940 Fisher Rd Se Unit 200, Calgary, AB, T2H
0W3
(403) 264-4420
Emp Here 26   *Sales* 3,137,310
SIC 7311 Advertising agencies

D-U-N-S 20-776-0880   (BR)
CINEPLEX ODEON CORPORATION
SCOTIABANK THEATRE CHINOOK
6455 Macleod Trl Sw, Calgary, AB, T2H 0K4

(403) 212-8994
Emp Here 20
SIC 7832 Motion picture theaters, except drive-in

D-U-N-S 20-195-0529   (SL)
CLEANMAX INC
5925 12 St Se Suite 1, Calgary, AB, T2H 2M3
(403) 229-2406
Emp Here 60   *Sales* 1,751,057
SIC 7349 Building maintenance services, nec

D-U-N-S 24-322-2408   (BR)
CLUB MONACO CORP
CLUB MONACO
(*Suby of* Ralph Lauren Corporation)
6455 Macleod Trail Sw Unit 119, Calgary, AB, T2H 0K3
(403) 262-6507
Emp Here 20
SIC 5621 Women's clothing stores

D-U-N-S 25-372-1955   (BR)
COAST WHOLESALE APPLIANCES INC
(*Suby of* Coast Wholesale Appliances Inc)
6128 Centre St Se, Calgary, AB, T2H 0C4
(403) 243-8780
Emp Here 35
SIC 5064 Electrical appliances, television and radio

D-U-N-S 24-313-5279   (BR)
COMMUNITY NATURAL FOODS LTD
202 61 Ave Sw, Calgary, AB, T2H 0B4
(403) 541-0606
Emp Here 80
SIC 5411 Grocery stores

D-U-N-S 25-287-5299   (BR)
COSTCO WHOLESALE CANADA LTD
COSTCO
(*Suby of* Costco Wholesale Corporation)
99 Heritage Gate Se, Calgary, AB, T2H 3A7
(403) 313-7647
Emp Here 300
SIC 5099 Durable goods, nec

D-U-N-S 20-737-6034   (SL)
COURTESY CHRYSLER DODGE JEEP
125 Glendeer Cir Se, Calgary, AB, T2H 2S8
(403) 255-9100
Emp Here 200   *Sales* 72,960,700
SIC 5511 New and used car dealers

D-U-N-S 20-075-4224   (BR)
CRANE CANADA CO.
CRANE SUPPLY, DIV OF
(*Suby of* Crane Co.)
324 58 Ave Se, Calgary, AB, T2H 0P1
(403) 252-7811
Emp Here 37
SIC 5085 Industrial supplies

D-U-N-S 20-113-5139   (SL)
DMX MUSIC CANADA INC
DMX MUSIC
(*Suby of* Mood Media Corporation)
7260 12 St Se Suite 120, Calgary, AB, T2H 2S5
(403) 640-8525
Emp Here 32   *Sales* 1,751,057
SIC 7389 Business services, nec

D-U-N-S 20-832-2222   (BR)
DENCAN RESTAURANTS INC
DENNY'S RESTAURANT
(*Suby of* Northland Properties Corporation)
7215 Macleod Trail Sw, Calgary, AB, T2H 0L8
(403) 253-4818
Emp Here 49
SIC 5812 Eating places

D-U-N-S 24-615-8013   (BR)
DESJARDINS SECURITE FINANCIERE, COMPAGNIE D'ASSURANCE VIE
DESJARDINS FINANCIAL SECURITY
5920 1a St Sw Suite 203, Calgary, AB, T2H 0G3

(403) 265-9770
Emp Here 20
SIC 6311 Life insurance

D-U-N-S 24-339-8935   (BR)
DIVESTCO INC
FOCUS BUSINESS SOLUTIONS
1209 59 Ave Se Unit 150, Calgary, AB, T2H 2P6
(403) 255-5900
Emp Here 20
SIC 7379 Computer related services, nec

D-U-N-S 20-314-7210   (SL)
EC RESTAURANTS (CANADA) CORP
6001 1a St Sw Suite 200, Calgary, AB, T2H 0G5
(403) 263-4323
Emp Here 1,200   *Sales* 50,319,200
SIC 5812 Eating places
Fin Ex Daniel Joyce
  Andrea Erving

D-U-N-S 20-413-9419   (BR)
EXP SERVICES INC
7220 Fisher St Se Unit 375, Calgary, AB, T2H 2H8
(403) 509-3030
Emp Here 62
SIC 8711 Engineering services

D-U-N-S 20-195-9462   (BR)
EDDIE BAUER OF CANADA INC
(*Suby of* Golden Gate Capital LP)
6455 Macleod Trail Sw Suite 1229, Calgary, AB, T2H 0K8
(403) 262-6454
Emp Here 30
SIC 5651 Family clothing stores

D-U-N-S 24-554-7500   (BR)
EDMONTON GEAR CENTRE LTD
GEAR CENTRE, THE
7170 Blackfoot Trail Se, Calgary, AB, T2H 2M1
(403) 252-3880
Emp Here 28
SIC 7537 Automotive transmission repair shops

D-U-N-S 20-012-2542   (BR)
ELLISDON CONSTRUCTION SERVICES INC
7330 Fisher St Se Suite 300, Calgary, AB, T2H 2H8
(403) 259-6627
Emp Here 25
SIC 1541 Industrial buildings and warehouses

D-U-N-S 20-564-5315   (BR)
ENTERTAINMENT ONE GP LIMITED
VIDEO ONE
(*Suby of* 4384768 Canada Inc)
5023 4 St E, Calgary, AB, T2H 2A5
(403) 258-3880
Emp Here 20
SIC 5099 Durable goods, nec

D-U-N-S 20-075-7904   (HQ)
EXPLOSIVES LIMITED
YUKON EXPLOSIVES, A DIV
(*Suby of* G.L. Black Holdings Ltd)
5511 6 St Se, Calgary, AB, T2H 1L6
(403) 255-7776
Emp Here 30   *Emp Total* 2
Sales 20,825,471
SIC 5169 Chemicals and allied products, nec
Pr Pr Kenneth Black
Fin Ex Mike Grainger

D-U-N-S 24-368-3443   (BR)
FFCA CHARTER SCHOOL SOCIETY
FOUNDATION FOR THE FUTURE CHAPTER CHARTER SCHOOL
8710 Ancourt Rd Se, Calgary, AB, T2H 1V2
(403) 259-3175
Emp Here 35
SIC 8211 Elementary and secondary schools

D-U-N-S 24-733-5698   (BR)

FGL SPORTS LTD
SPORT CHEK CHINOOK CENTRE
6455 Macleod Trail Sw Unit L6, Calgary, AB, T2H 0K3
(403) 255-2161
Emp Here 50
SIC 5941 Sporting goods and bicycle shops

D-U-N-S 24-014-0822   (BR)
FABRICLAND PACIFIC/MIDWEST LIMITED
FABRICLAND
7130 Fisher Rd Se Suite 1, Calgary, AB, T2H 0W3
(403) 212-0097
Emp Here 24
SIC 5949 Sewing, needlework, and piece goods

D-U-N-S 25-684-8862   (BR)
FJORDS PROCESSING CANADA INC
KVAERNER PROCESS SYSTEMS, DIV OF
6835 Railway St Se, Calgary, AB, T2H 2V6
(403) 640-4230
Emp Here 100
SIC 3823 Process control instruments

D-U-N-S 20-064-7332   (HQ)
FLINT INFRASTRUCTURE SERVICES LTD
1209 59 Ave Se Suite 205, Calgary, AB, T2H 2P6
(403) 218-7113
Emp Here 200   *Emp Total* 87,000
Sales 70,042,272
SIC 1623 Water, sewer, and utility lines
Pr Brian Butlin

D-U-N-S 25-062-1661   (BR)
FOOT LOCKER CANADA CO.
FOOT LOCKER
6455 Macleod Trail Sw Suite 22, Calgary, AB, T2H 0K3
(403) 255-3641
Emp Here 30
SIC 5661 Shoe stores

D-U-N-S 24-916-0610   (BR)
FORENSIC INVESTIGATIONS CANADA INC
(*Suby of* Forensic Investigations Canada Inc)
7015 Macleod Trail Sw Suite 800, Calgary, AB, T2H 2K6
(403) 228-1170
Emp Here 35
SIC 7389 Business services, nec

D-U-N-S 20-122-9130   (BR)
G4S SECURE SOLUTIONS (CANADA) LTD
8180 Macleod Trail Se Suite 10, Calgary, AB, T2H 2B8
(403) 735-1141
Emp Here 31
SIC 7381 Detective and armored car services

D-U-N-S 25-595-5668   (BR)
GAP (CANADA) INC
GAP
(*Suby of* The Gap Inc)
6455 Macleod Trail Sw Suite 151, Calgary, AB, T2H 0K3
(403) 640-1305
Emp Here 150
SIC 5651 Family clothing stores

D-U-N-S 25-650-6007   (BR)
GAP (CANADA) INC
GAP
(*Suby of* The Gap Inc)
6455 Macleod Trail Sw Suite 210, Calgary, AB, T2H 0K3
(403) 640-1303
Emp Here 75
SIC 5651 Family clothing stores

D-U-N-S 20-065-1805   (BR)
GENERAL PAINT CORP
(*Suby of* The Sherwin-Williams Company)
7291 11 St Se, Calgary, AB, T2H 2S1
(403) 531-3450
Emp Here 20
SIC 2851 Paints and allied products

D-U-N-S 24-157-1736   (BR)
GENERAL SCRAP PARTNERSHIP
NAVAJO METALS
5857 12 St Se, Calgary, AB, T2H 2X9
(403) 252-7787
Emp Here 30
SIC 5093 Scrap and waste materials

D-U-N-S 25-386-6552   (HQ)
GREAT WEST KENWORTH LTD
(*Suby of* 334746 Alberta Inc)
5909 6 St Se, Calgary, AB, T2H 1L8
(403) 253-7555
Emp Here 95   *Emp Total* 2
Sales 84,459,473
SIC 5511 New and used car dealers
Pr Pr John Jeffrey (Jeff) Storwick
  Paul Storwick

D-U-N-S 24-339-8778   (BR)
GREGG DISTRIBUTORS LIMITED PARTNERSHIP
5755 11 St Se, Calgary, AB, T2H 1M7
(403) 253-6463
Emp Here 110
SIC 5085 Industrial supplies

D-U-N-S 24-099-3217   (BR)
GROUPE DE SECURITE GARDA INC, LE
8989 Macleod Trail Sw Suite 118, Calgary, AB, T2H 0M2
(403) 517-5899
Emp Here 510
SIC 7381 Detective and armored car services

D-U-N-S 25-010-3785   (BR)
H.B. GROUP INSURANCE MANAGEMENT LTD
8500 Macleod Trail Se Suite 220s, Calgary, AB, T2H 2N1
(403) 265-7211
Emp Here 25
SIC 6411 Insurance agents, brokers, and service

D-U-N-S 25-520-1410   (SL)
HOSPICE CALGARY SOCIETY
1245 70 Ave Se, Calgary, AB, T2H 2X8
(403) 206-9938
Emp Here 55   *Sales* 4,450,603
SIC 8069 Specialty hospitals, except psychiatric

D-U-N-S 20-191-7338   (BR)
HUDSON'S BAY COMPANY
HOME OUTFITTERS
33 Heritage Gate Se, Calgary, AB, T2H 3A7
(403) 538-0083
Emp Here 40
SIC 5311 Department stores

D-U-N-S 25-616-6828   (BR)
HUDSON'S BAY COMPANY
BAY, THE
6455 Macleod Trail Sw, Calgary, AB, T2H 0K3
(403) 255-6121
Emp Here 250
SIC 5311 Department stores

D-U-N-S 20-304-0258   (HQ)
IMT STANDEN'S LIMITED PARTNERSHIP
(*Suby of* IMT Corporation)
1222 58 Ave Se, Calgary, AB, T2H 2E9
(403) 258-7800
Emp Here 475   *Emp Total* 5
Sales 22,609,151
SIC 3493 Steel springs, except wire
Ch Bd Mel Svendson
Pr Dean Davenport
  Paul Takalo

D-U-N-S 25-116-5452   (BR)
ISL ENGINEERING AND LAND SERVICES LTD
6325 12 St Se Suite 1, Calgary, AB, T2H 2K1
(403) 254-0544
Emp Here 30
SIC 8711 Engineering services

D-U-N-S 24-532-8039   (BR)
ISL HOLDINGS INC
6325 12 St Se Unit 1, Calgary, AB, T2H 2K1
(403) 254-0544
Emp Here 40
SIC 8711 Engineering services

D-U-N-S 20-299-9947   (BR)
INDIGO BOOKS & MUSIC INC
CHAPTERS #964
(*Suby of* Indigo Books & Music Inc)
6455 Macleod Trail Sw Suite 21, Calgary, AB,
T2H 0K3
(403) 212-0090
Emp Here 20
SIC 5942 Book stores

D-U-N-S 24-343-7980   (HQ)
INTEGRATED COMMERCIAL INTERIORS INC
6120 11 St Se Suite 4, Calgary, AB, T2H 2L7

Emp Here 150   *Emp Total* 5
Sales 47,954,546
SIC 1542 Nonresidential construction, nec
Pr William Smith
 Keith Thomas
Dir Tom Redl
Dir Michael Leblanc
Dir Roger Babichuk

D-U-N-S 24-348-5351   (HQ)
INTERCARE CORPORATE GROUP INC
INTERCARE BRENTWOOD CARE CENTRE
(*Suby of* Intercare Corporate Group Inc)
211 Heritage Dr Se, Calgary, AB, T2H 1M9
(403) 252-1194
Emp Here 50   *Emp Total* 1,000
Sales 39,106,654
SIC 8322 Individual and family services
Pr David Ail

D-U-N-S 25-518-6934   (BR)
JBS CANADA INC
XL FOODS
(*Suby of* Tyson Foods, Inc.)
5101 11 St Se, Calgary, AB, T2H 1M7
(403) 258-3233
Emp Here 160
SIC 2011 Meat packing plants

D-U-N-S 24-354-7051   (BR)
JACOBS CANADA INC
(*Suby of* Jacobs Engineering Group Inc.)
6835 Railway St Se Suite 200, Calgary,
T2H 2V6
(403) 258-0554
Emp Here 245
SIC 8711 Engineering services

D-U-N-S 20-076-5162   (BR)
JOHNSON CONTROLS NOVA SCOTIA U.L.C.
SYSTEMS & SERVICES, DIV OF
(*Suby of* Johnson Controls, Inc.)
6046 12 St Se Suite 104, Calgary, AB, T2H 2X2
(403) 640-1700
Emp Here 50
SIC 1711 Plumbing, heating, air-conditioning

D-U-N-S 25-521-7044   (BR)
KEG RESTAURANTS LTD
KEG STEAKHOUSE & BAR, THE
7104 Macleod Trail Se, Calgary, AB, T2H 0L3
(403) 253-2534
Emp Here 103
SIC 5812 Eating places

D-U-N-S 24-517-2127   (SL)
KELLAM BERG ENGINEERING & SURVEYS LTD
KELLAM BERG
5800 1a St Sw, Calgary, AB, T2H 0G1
(403) 640-0900
Emp Here 50   *Sales* 4,961,328
SIC 8711 Engineering services

D-U-N-S 20-934-5722   (BR)
KONICA MINOLTA BUSINESS SOLUTIONS (CANADA) LTD
KONICA MINOLTA
1315 73 Ave Se, Calgary, AB, T2H 2X4
(403) 253-6485
Emp Here 20
SIC 5999 Miscellaneous retail stores, nec

D-U-N-S 25-230-2435   (SL)
L.J.B LIMITED
6999 11 St Se Suite 110, Calgary, AB, T2H 2S1
(403) 253-8200
Emp Here 60   *Sales* 8,763,660
SIC 5712 Furniture stores
Pr Stewart Bondar

D-U-N-S 24-367-4913   (BR)
LA-Z-BOY CANADA RETAIL, LTD
LA-Z-BOY FURNITURE GALLERIES
(*Suby of* La-Z-Boy Incorporated)
7300 11 St Se, Calgary, AB, T2H 2S9
(403) 259-1000
Emp Here 25
SIC 5712 Furniture stores

D-U-N-S 24-129-5331   (BR)
LABATT BREWING COMPANY LIMITED
700 58 Ave Se Suite 12, Calgary, AB, T2H 2E2
(403) 777-1610
Emp Here 20
SIC 2082 Malt beverages

D-U-N-S 25-361-8862   (BR)
LAFARGE CANADA INC
LAFARGE NORTH AMERICA
6920 13 St Se, Calgary, AB, T2H 3B1
(403) 292-9500
Emp Here 40
SIC 3272 Concrete products, nec

D-U-N-S 25-482-5961   (BR)
LEE VALLEY TOOLS LTD
7261 11 St Se, Calgary, AB, T2H 2S1
(403) 253-2066
Emp Here 30
SIC 5251 Hardware stores

D-U-N-S 20-112-7110   (BR)
LENNOX CANADA INC
HEAT CRAFT HEATING
7317 12 St Se Unit 2, Calgary, AB, T2H 2S6
(403) 252-4328
Emp Here 50
SIC 1711 Plumbing, heating, air-conditioning

D-U-N-S 24-354-4793   (BR)
LOBLAWS INC
REAL CANADIAN SUPERSTORE
20 Heritage Meadows Rd Se Unit, Calgary,
AB, T2H 3C1
(403) 692-6201
Emp Here 50
SIC 5411 Grocery stores

D-U-N-S 25-268-4964   (BR)
LOBLAWS INC
REAL CANADIAN WHOLESALE CLUB
222 58 Ave Se, Calgary, AB, T2H 0N9
(403) 255-5590
Emp Here 50
SIC 5141 Groceries, general line

D-U-N-S 20-076-7739   (BR)
LOCKERBIE & HOLE CONTRACTING LIMITED
LOCKERBIE & HOLE CONTRACTING - EDMONTON
7335 Flint Rd Se, Calgary, AB, T2H 1G3
(403) 571-2121
Emp Here 20
SIC 1711 Plumbing, heating, air-conditioning

D-U-N-S 25-021-9128   (BR)
LONDON DRUGS LIMITED
8330 Macleod Trail Se Suite 30, Calgary, AB,
T2H 2V2

(403) 571-4930
Emp Here 40
SIC 5912 Drug stores and proprietary stores

D-U-N-S 25-741-7071   (BR)
LONE STAR INC
LAND ROVER CALGARY
175 Glendeer Cir Se, Calgary, AB, T2H 2S8
(403) 255-1994
Emp Here 20
SIC 5511 New and used car dealers

D-U-N-S 20-076-5618   (BR)
LONG & MCQUADE LIMITED
LONG & MCQUADE MUSICAL INSTRUMENTS
225 58 Ave Se, Calgary, AB, T2H 0N8
(403) 244-5555
Emp Here 40
SIC 5736 Musical instrument stores

D-U-N-S 25-328-7171   (SL)
M.I. CABLE TECHNOLOGIES INC
5905 11 St Se Bay Suite 6, Calgary, AB, T2H 2A6
(403) 571-8266
Emp Here 33   *Sales* 4,937,631
SIC 3315 Steel wire and related products

D-U-N-S 25-290-7878   (BR)
MARK'S WORK WEARHOUSE LTD
MARK'S WORK WEARHOUSE #13
6636 Macleod Trail Sw, Calgary, AB, T2H 0K6
(403) 253-5708
Emp Here 30
SIC 5651 Family clothing stores

D-U-N-S 24-012-5070   (HQ)
MARK'S WORK WEARHOUSE LTD
L'EQUIPEUR
1035 64 Ave Se Suite 30, Calgary, AB, T2H 2J7
(403) 255-9220
Emp Here 382   *Emp Total* 12,356
Sales 257,186,468
SIC 5699 Miscellaneous apparel and accessory stores
Pr Stephen Wetmore
Sr VP Michael Strachan
Sec Karen Bentley
Sec Eleni Damianakis
Treas Candace Maclean
Asst Tr Debbie Champion
 Harry Taylor

D-U-N-S 25-290-8272   (BR)
MARK'S WORK WEARHOUSE LTD
MARK'S WORK WEARHOUSE 16
33 Heritage Meadows Way Se Unit S8, Calgary, AB, T2H 3B8
(403) 278-4885
Emp Here 20
SIC 5651 Family clothing stores

D-U-N-S 20-816-2011   (SL)
MASTER MECHANICAL PLUMBING & HEATING LTD
6025 12 St Se Suite 19, Calgary, AB, T2H 2K1
(403) 243-5880
Emp Here 50   *Sales* 4,377,642
SIC 1711 Plumbing, heating, air-conditioning

D-U-N-S 24-158-3319   (HQ)
MAVERICK LAND CONSULTANTS LTD
(*Suby of* Hma Land Services Ltd.)
6940 Fisher Rd Se Suite 310, Calgary, AB,
T2H 0W3
(403) 243-7833
Emp Here 29   *Emp Total* 15
Sales 5,107,249
SIC 1389 Oil and gas field services, nec
Pr Pr Brent Davidson

D-U-N-S 20-825-0563   (HQ)
MCGREGOR, DONALD INVESTMENTS LTD
ORANGE JULIUS
(*Suby of* McGregor, Donald Investments Ltd)
6455 Macleod Trail Sw Suite 607, Calgary, AB,

T2H 0K9
(403) 252-6023
Emp Here 24   *Emp Total* 54
Sales 1,605,135
SIC 5812 Eating places

D-U-N-S 20-260-0644   (BR)
MCMAN YOUTH, FAMILY AND COMMUNITY SERVICES ASSOCIATION
(*Suby of* McMan Youth, Family and Community Services Association)
6712 Fisher St Se Unit 80, Calgary, AB, T2H 2A7
(403) 508-7742
Emp Here 75
SIC 8641 Civic and social associations

D-U-N-S 25-315-1682   (BR)
MEDICENTRES CANADA INC
HERITAGE HILL MEDICENTRE
8180 Macleod Trail Se Suite 110, Calgary, AB,
T2H 2B8
(403) 259-3256
Emp Here 20
SIC 8011 Offices and clinics of medical doctors

D-U-N-S 24-318-8245   (BR)
MEMORY EXPRESS INC
120 58 Ave Se, Calgary, AB, T2H 0N7
(403) 253-5676
Emp Here 40
SIC 5734 Computer and software stores

D-U-N-S 20-856-5981   (BR)
MICHAELS OF CANADA, ULC
MICHAELS ARTS & CRAFTS
(*Suby of* The Michaels Companies Inc)
8180 11 St Se Unit 400, Calgary, AB, T2H 3B5
(403) 640-1633
Emp Here 30
SIC 5945 Hobby, toy, and game shops

D-U-N-S 24-983-7709   (BR)
MORNEAU SHEPELL LTD
SHEPPELL FGI DIV OF
(*Suby of* Morneau Shepell Inc)
5940 Macleod Trail Sw Suite 306, Calgary, AB,
T2H 2G4
(403) 355-3700
Emp Here 20
SIC 8999 Services, nec

D-U-N-S 20-232-4104   (BR)
MORRISON HERSHFIELD LIMITED
6807 Railway St Se Suite 300, Calgary, AB,
T2H 2V6
(403) 246-4500
Emp Here 100
SIC 8711 Engineering services

D-U-N-S 20-774-1708   (SL)
NATIONAL SPORTS DEVELOPMENT LTD
7475 Flint Rd Se, Calgary, AB, T2H 1G3
(403) 201-8788
Emp Here 74   *Sales* 5,579,750
SIC 7999 Amusement and recreation, nec
Dir Brian Strong

D-U-N-S 20-352-9391   (HQ)
NATURAL HEALTH SERVICES LTD
(*Suby of* Natural Health Services Ltd)
6120 2 St Se Unit A9a, Calgary, AB, T2H 2L8
(403) 680-9617
Emp Here 25   *Emp Total* 74
Sales 4,085,799
SIC 8093 Specialty outpatient clinics, nec

D-U-N-S 20-350-2919   (BR)
NATURAL HEALTH SERVICES LTD
(*Suby of* Natural Health Services Ltd)
5809 Macleod Trail Sw Suite 207, Calgary, AB,
T2H 0J9
(780) 885-6922
Emp Here 24
SIC 8093 Specialty outpatient clinics, nec

D-U-N-S 24-367-8161   (HQ)
NEWSWEST INC

5716 Burbank Rd Se, Calgary, AB, T2H 1Z4
(403) 253-8856
Emp Here 50　　　*Emp Total* 4
Sales 24,004,070
SIC 5192 Books, periodicals, and newspapers
Pr Pr Daniel Shapiro
　David Whelan
Dir Robert Campbell

D-U-N-S 24-786-7096　　　(BR)
NORSEMAN INC
CAMPERS VILLAGE DIV.
7208 Macleod Trail Se, Calgary, AB, T2H 0L9
(403) 252-3338
Emp Here 25
SIC 5941 Sporting goods and bicycle shops

D-U-N-S 20-994-3906　　　(BR)
**NORTHLAND PROPERTIES CORPORA-
TION**
*SANDMAN HOTEL & SUITES CALGARY
SOUTH*
(*Suby of* Northland Properties Corporation)
8001 11 St Se, Calgary, AB, T2H 0B8
(403) 252-7263
Emp Here 80
SIC 7011 Hotels and motels

D-U-N-S 24-803-4915　　　(BR)
ORICA CANADA INC
5511 6 St Se, Calgary, AB, T2H 1L6
(403) 212-6200
Emp Here 20
SIC 2892 Explosives

D-U-N-S 20-267-9986　　　(BR)
OTIS CANADA, INC
OTIS ELEVATORS
(*Suby of* United Technologies Corporation)
777 64 Ave Se Suite 7, Calgary, AB, T2H 2C3
(403) 244-1040
Emp Here 170
SIC 7699 Repair services, nec

D-U-N-S 25-533-4278　　　(SL)
OUTLAWS GROUP INC
OUTLAWS NIGHTCLUB
7400 Macleod Trail Se Suite 24, Calgary, AB,
T2H 0L9
(403) 255-4646
Emp Here 100　　　*Sales* 3,648,035
SIC 5813 Drinking places

D-U-N-S 20-317-2056　　　(BR)
**PACEKIDS SOCIETY FOR CHILDREN WITH
SPECIAL NEEDS**
5211 Macleod Trail Sw Suite 112, Calgary, AB,
T2H 0J3
(403) 234-7876
Emp Here 25
SIC 8322 Individual and family services

D-U-N-S 24-000-4791　　　(BR)
PALADIN SECURITY GROUP LTD
6455 Macleod Trail Sw Unit 701, Calgary, AB,
T2H 0K9
(403) 508-1888
Emp Here 100
SIC 7381 Detective and armored car services

D-U-N-S 25-316-4164　　　(BR)
PASLEY, MAX ENTERPRISES LIMITED
MCDONALD'S RESTAURANTS 1189
(*Suby of* Pasley, Max Enterprises Limited)
7212 Macleod Trail Se, Calgary, AB, T2H 0L9

Emp Here 50
SIC 5812 Eating places

D-U-N-S 24-118-0843　　　(BR)
PATTISON, JIM INDUSTRIES LTD
JIM PATTISON LEASE
1235 73 Ave Se, Calgary, AB, T2H 2X1
(403) 212-8900
Emp Here 30
SIC 7515 Passenger car leasing

D-U-N-S 20-651-4163　　　(BR)

PATTISON, JIM INDUSTRIES LTD
PATTISON SIGN GROUP DIV OF.
6304 6a St Se, Calgary, AB, T2H 2B7
(403) 258-0556
Emp Here 25
SIC 3993 Signs and advertising specialties

D-U-N-S 24-840-6381　　　(BR)
PETRIN MECHANICAL LTD
(*Suby of* Petrin Mechanical Ltd)
6445 10 St Se, Calgary, AB, T2H 2Z9
(403) 279-6881
Emp Here 50
SIC 1711 Plumbing, heating, air-conditioning

D-U-N-S 25-520-0099　　　(SL)
PHOENIX FENCE LTD
6204 2 St Se, Calgary, AB, T2H 1J4
(403) 259-5155
Emp Here 33　　　*Sales* 2,918,428
SIC 1799 Special trade contractors, nec

D-U-N-S 20-302-2731　　　(HQ)
**PLATINUM COMMUNICATIONS CORPORA-
TION**
550 71 Ave Se Suite 280, Calgary, AB, T2H
0S6
(403) 301-4590
Emp Here 40　　　*Emp Total* 800
Sales 7,945,034
SIC 4813 Telephone communication, except
radio
Pr Bernard Parkinson
CFO Katherine Kirkup
　Timothy Luttman
Sec Faralee Channin
　Cameron Henning

D-U-N-S 24-374-3288　　　(SL)
PRO-TRANS VENTURES INC
5920 1a St Sw Suite 520, Calgary, AB, T2H
0G3
(403) 452-7270
Emp Here 260　　　*Sales* 63,912,350
SIC 4213 Trucking, except local
Pr Pr Brian Murray
　Melinda Park
Dir David Criddle
Dir Sean Durfy
Dir Darby Kreitz
Dir Russel Marcoux
　A. Scott Hamilton
　Donald Black
Dir Douglas Davis
Dir Betty-Ann Heggie

D-U-N-S 25-521-8513　　　(BR)
RAYMOND SALONS LTD
HENNESSEY SALON & SPA
(*Suby of* Raymond Salons Ltd)
6455 Macleod Trail Sw Suite 141, Calgary, AB,
T2H 0K3
(403) 252-0522
Emp Here 20
SIC 7231 Beauty shops

D-U-N-S 25-452-2527　　　(BR)
RED LOBSTER HOSPITALITY LLC
RED LOBSTER RESTAURANTS
(*Suby of* Red Lobster Seafood Co., LLC)
6100 Macleod Trl Sw Suite 100, Calgary, AB,
T2H 0K5
(403) 252-8818
Emp Here 100
SIC 5812 Eating places

D-U-N-S 25-300-6308　　　(BR)
REDBERRY FRANCHISING CORP
BURGER KING
7110 Macleod Trail Se, Calgary, AB, T2H 0L3
(403) 216-8525
Emp Here 30
SIC 5812 Eating places

D-U-N-S 20-897-9849　　　(HQ)
**ROBYN'S TRANSPORTATION & DISTRIBU-
TION SERVICES LTD**
(*Suby of* Robyn's Transportation & Distribution

Services Ltd)
6404 Burbank Rd Se, Calgary, AB, T2H 2C2

Emp Here 131　　　*Emp Total* 160
Sales 27,975,600
SIC 4213 Trucking, except local
CFO David Donaldson
Pr Pr Robyn Jackson

D-U-N-S 24-734-1258　　　(BR)
ROYAL BANK OF CANADA
RBC
(*Suby of* Royal Bank Of Canada)
411 58 Ave Se, Calgary, AB, T2H 0P5
(403) 299-7420
Emp Here 25
SIC 6021 National commercial banks

D-U-N-S 20-104-4802　　　(BR)
ROYAL CANADIAN GOLF ASSOCIATION
RCGA GOLF CENTRE
7100 15 St Se, Calgary, AB, T2H 2Z8
(403) 640-3555
Emp Here 30
SIC 7992 Public golf courses

D-U-N-S 25-288-9324　　　(BR)
RUSSELL FOOD EQUIPMENT LIMITED
5707 4 St Se, Calgary, AB, T2H 1K8
(403) 253-1383
Emp Here 35
SIC 5046 Commercial equipment, nec

D-U-N-S 20-532-4846　　　(BR)
SEARS CANADA INC
6455 Macleod Trail Sw Suite 1000, Calgary,
AB, T2H 0K3

Emp Here 30
SIC 5311 Department stores

D-U-N-S 20-232-5689　　　(SL)
SHOOTING EDGE INC, THE
SHOOTING EDGE
77 Ave Bay Suite 510, Calgary, AB, T2H 1C3
(403) 720-4867
Emp Here 56　　　*Sales* 4,742,446
SIC 5941 Sporting goods and bicycle shops

D-U-N-S 20-116-9245　　　(SL)
SOUTH ALBERTA RIBS (2002) LTD
TONY ROMA'S
6712 Macleod Trail Se, Calgary, AB, T2H 0L3
(403) 301-7427
Emp Here 45　　　*Sales* 2,845,467
SIC 5812 Eating places

D-U-N-S 20-078-1169　　　(SL)
SOVEREIGN CASTINGS LTD
5110 5 St Se, Calgary, AB, T2H 1L1
(403) 252-1228
Emp Here 50
SIC 3321 Gray and ductile iron foundries

D-U-N-S 24-342-7510　　　(HQ)
**SOVEREIGN GENERAL INSURANCE COM-
PANY, THE**
6700 Macleod Trl Se Suite 140, Calgary, AB,
T2H 0L3
(403) 298-4200
Emp Here 75　　　*Emp Total* 4,567
Sales 262,046,595
SIC 6411 Insurance agents, brokers, and ser-
vice
　Rob Wesseling
VP Rod F. Bresciani
VP Herb Cline

D-U-N-S 20-299-7818　　　(BR)
SPRUNG INSTANT STRUCTURES LTD
6020 3 St Se, Calgary, AB, T2H 1K2
(403) 259-3696
Emp Here 40
SIC 3448 Prefabricated Metal buildings and
components

D-U-N-S 20-965-3265　　　(BR)
ST JOHN'S MUSIC LTD

105 58 Ave Se, Calgary, AB, T2H 0N8
(403) 265-6300
Emp Here 20
SIC 5736 Musical instrument stores

D-U-N-S 20-300-6838　　　(BR)
STANTEC CONSULTING LTD
1200 59 Ave Se Suite 150, Calgary, AB, T2H
2M4
(403) 216-2140
Emp Here 200
SIC 8711 Engineering services

D-U-N-S 25-986-1524　　　(BR)
STAPLES CANADA INC
STAPLES THE BUSINESS DEPOT
(*Suby of* Staples, Inc.)
321 61 Ave Sw Suite 3, Calgary, AB, T2H 2W7
(403) 259-6928
Emp Here 45
SIC 5943 Stationery stores

D-U-N-S 20-806-3920　　　(BR)
STARBUCKS COFFEE CANADA, INC
(*Suby of* Starbucks Corporation)
6455 Macleod Trail Sw Suite 178, Calgary, AB,
T2H 0K3
(403) 640-9846
Emp Here 20
SIC 5812 Eating places

D-U-N-S 20-625-1910　　　(BR)
STARBUCKS COFFEE CANADA, INC
DEERFOOT MEADOWS STARBUCKS
(*Suby of* Starbucks Corporation)
33 Heritage Meadows Way Se Suite 214, Cal-
gary, AB, T2H 3B8
(403) 253-4518
Emp Here 27
SIC 5812 Eating places

D-U-N-S 24-714-5659　　　(BR)
**SUN LIFE ASSURANCE COMPANY OF
CANADA**
5980 Centre St Se, Calgary, AB, T2H 0C1
(403) 266-2061
Emp Here 200
SIC 6311 Life insurance

D-U-N-S 24-562-1060　　　(BR)
**SUN LIFE FINANCIAL INVESTMENT SER-
VICES (CANADA) INC**
SUN LIFE FINANCIAL
5980 Centre St Se, Calgary, AB, T2H 0C1
(403) 266-2061
Emp Here 65
SIC 6411 Insurance agents, brokers, and ser-
vice

D-U-N-S 25-776-9844　　　(BR)
SUNCO DRYWALL LTD
(*Suby of* 464132 B.C. Ltd)
7835 Flint Rd Se, Calgary, AB, T2H 1G3
(403) 250-9701
Emp Here 80
SIC 1742 Plastering, drywall, and insulation

D-U-N-S 20-010-6511　　　(BR)
**SYNGENTA CROP PROTECTION CANADA,
INC**
6700 Macleod Trail Se Suite 300, Calgary, AB,
T2H 0L3
(403) 252-5867
Emp Here 30
SIC 5191 Farm supplies

D-U-N-S 20-567-9777　　　(BR)
TDG FURNITURE INC
ASHLEY FURNITURE HOME STORE
88 Heritage Gate Se, Calgary, AB, T2H 3A7
(403) 301-0100
Emp Here 20
SIC 3429 Hardware, nec

D-U-N-S 24-299-5942　　　(HQ)
TEMPCO DRILLING COMPANY INC
(*Suby of* Tempest Developments Ltd)
7015 Macleod Trail Sw Suite 410, Calgary, AB,

T2H 2K6
(403) 259-5533
Emp Here 52   *Emp Total* 10
Sales 15,029,904
SIC 1381 Drilling oil and gas wells
Pr Pr Thomas James Cascadden
   Ken D Weller

D-U-N-S 24-495-8880   (BR)
THURBER ENGINEERING LTD
THURBER ENGINEERING
180 7330 Fisher St Se, Calgary, AB, T2H 2H8
(403) 253-9217
Emp Here 41
SIC 8711 Engineering services

D-U-N-S 20-771-6908   (SL)
TIM HORTONS
5 Heritage Gate Se Unit 1, Calgary, AB, T2H 3A7
(403) 692-6629
Emp Here 60   *Sales* 2,042,900
SIC 5461 Retail bakeries

D-U-N-S 20-354-5892   (BR)
TRAIL APPLIANCES LTD
CALGARY HOME APPLIANCE
6880 11 St Se, Calgary, AB, T2H 2T9
(403) 253-5442
Emp Here 375
SIC 5722 Household appliance stores

D-U-N-S 24-674-0732   (BR)
TRANSCONTINENTAL PRINTING INC
5516 5 St Se, Calgary, AB, T2H 1L3
(403) 258-3788
Emp Here 420
SIC 2752 Commercial printing, lithographic

D-U-N-S 24-598-9579   (SL)
TRI-JAY CARPETS (1989)
7003 5 St Se Unit H, Calgary, AB, T2H 2G2
(403) 253-4441
Emp Here 40   *Sales* 6,594,250
SIC 5713 Floor covering stores
Pt Jack Van Deventer
Pt Al Becker

D-U-N-S 24-854-4520   (HQ)
TROTTER AND MORTON BUILDING TECH-NOLOGIES INC
5711 1 St Se, Calgary, AB, T2H 1H9
(403) 255-7535
Emp Here 345   *Emp Total* 1,150
Sales 129,937,650
SIC 1711 Plumbing, heating, air-conditioning
Pr Pr Michael Watson

D-U-N-S 24-337-9992   (BR)
TYCO INTEGRATED FIRE & SECURITY CANADA, INC
SIMPLEXGRINNELL
(*Suby of* Johnson Controls, Inc.)
401 Forge Rd Se, Calgary, AB, T2H 0S9

Emp Here 150
SIC 8748 Business consulting, nec

D-U-N-S 24-000-4452   (BR)
UAP INC
NAPA AUTOPARTS DIV OF
(*Suby of* Genuine Parts Company)
5530 3 St Se Suite 489, Calgary, AB, T2H 1J9
(403) 212-4600
Emp Here 80
SIC 5013 Motor vehicle supplies and new parts

D-U-N-S 24-523-7404   (BR)
UNITED FARMERS OF ALBERTA CO-OPERATIVE LIMITED
WHOLESALE SPORTS
25 Heritage Meadows Way Se, Calgary, AB, T2H 0A7
(403) 253-5566
Emp Here 125
SIC 5941 Sporting goods and bicycle shops

D-U-N-S 24-731-8561   (BR)
VALUE VILLAGE STORES, INC
(*Suby of* Savers, Inc.)
104 58 Ave Se Unit 10, Calgary, AB, T2H 0N7
(403) 255-5501
Emp Here 50
SIC 5399 Miscellaneous general merchandise

D-U-N-S 20-772-8697   (BR)
VECTOR ELECTRIC AND CONTROLS
VECTOR GROUP, THE
5919 3 St Se, Calgary, AB, T2H 1K3
(403) 290-1699
Emp Here 25
SIC 1731 Electrical work

D-U-N-S 20-349-9090   (SL)
VERTEX DOWNHOLE LTD
6806 Railway St Se, Calgary, AB, T2H 3A8
(403) 930-2742
Emp Here 20   *Sales* 1,459,214
SIC 7371 Custom computer programming ser-vices

D-U-N-S 24-807-1987   (BR)
VIPOND INC
VIPOND SYSTEM GROUP
6120 3 St Se Suite 13, Calgary, AB, T2H 1K4
(403) 253-6500
Emp Here 25
SIC 1711 Plumbing, heating, air-conditioning

D-U-N-S 25-146-8521   (BR)
WSP CANADA GROUP LIMITED
5151 3 St Se, Calgary, AB, T2H 2X6
(403) 269-7440
Emp Here 70
SIC 8711 Engineering services

D-U-N-S 24-606-1878   (BR)
WAL-MART CANADA CORP
7979 11 St Se Suite 1089, Calgary, AB, T2H 0B8
(403) 301-2051
Emp Here 40
SIC 5311 Department stores

D-U-N-S 25-948-2172   (BR)
WENDY'S RESTAURANTS OF CANADA INC
WENDY'S
(*Suby of* The Wendy's Company)
444 58 Ave Se Suite 112, Calgary, AB, T2H 0P4
(403) 259-5668
Emp Here 35
SIC 5812 Eating places

D-U-N-S 20-927-4021   (BR)
WENDY'S RESTAURANTS OF CANADA INC
(*Suby of* The Wendy's Company)
5 Heritage Gate Se Unit 2, Calgary, AB, T2H 3A7
(403) 258-2570
Emp Here 25
SIC 5812 Eating places

D-U-N-S 25-616-6679   (BR)
WENDY'S RESTAURANTS OF CANADA INC
WENDY'S
(*Suby of* The Wendy's Company)
7109 Macleod Trail Sw, Calgary, AB, T2H 0L8
(403) 253-5333
Emp Here 36
SIC 5812 Eating places

D-U-N-S 20-780-8234   (BR)
WENDY'S RESTAURANTS OF CANADA INC
WENDY'S
(*Suby of* The Wendy's Company)
8911 Bonaventure Dr Se, Calgary, AB, T2H 2Z5
(403) 252-5494
Emp Here 25
SIC 5812 Eating places

D-U-N-S 24-346-1548   (SL)
WEST ISLAND COLLEGE SOCIETY OF AL-BERTA

7410 Blackfoot Trail Se, Calgary, AB, T2H 1M5
(403) 444-0023
Emp Here 65   *Sales* 5,653,974
SIC 8211 Elementary and secondary schools

D-U-N-S 20-635-9085   (HQ)
WESTECH INDUSTRIAL LTD
5636 Burbank Cres Se, Calgary, AB, T2H 1Z6
(403) 252-8803
Emp Here 36   *Emp Total* 60
Sales 10,944,105
SIC 5084 Industrial machinery and equipment
Pr Pr Kenneth Lapp
   Jason Lapp
   Russ Lapp

D-U-N-S 24-098-8092   (BR)
WESTON BAKERIES LIMITED
MOISSON DOREE
5819 2 St Sw, Calgary, AB, T2H 0H3
(403) 259-1500
Emp Here 40
SIC 5149 Groceries and related products, nec

D-U-N-S 24-363-6748   (HQ)
WHOLESALE SPORTS CANADA LTD
WHOLESALE SPORTS
25 Heritage Meadows Way Se, Calgary, AB, T2H 0A7
(403) 253-5566
Emp Here 50   *Emp Total* 1,200
Sales 57,128,228
SIC 5699 Miscellaneous apparel and acces-sory stores
Dir Bob Chisholm
Dir Jim Laverick
Dir Peter Melnychuk
Dir Bob Nelson

D-U-N-S 24-004-2536   (BR)
WILLIAMS-SONOMA CANADA, INC
6455 Macleod Trail Sw Suite 106a, Calgary, AB, T2H 0K3
(403) 259-2100
Emp Here 25
SIC 5963 Direct selling establishments

D-U-N-S 25-062-1786   (BR)
WINNERS MERCHANTS INTERNATIONAL L.P.
WINNERS
(*Suby of* The TJX Companies Inc)
8228 Macleod Trail Se Suite 168, Calgary, AB, T2H 2B8
(403) 252-7678
Emp Here 45
SIC 5651 Family clothing stores

D-U-N-S 25-596-3894   (BR)
WOLSELEY CANADA INC
CRONKITE SUPPLIES, DIV OF
(*Suby of* WOLSELEY PLC)
5516 3 St Se, Calgary, AB, T2H 1J9
(403) 243-6614
Emp Here 25
SIC 5087 Service establishment equipment

D-U-N-S 24-327-8814   (HQ)
WORLEYPARSONS CANADA SERVICES LTD
WORLEYPARSONS MEG, DIV OF
8500 Macleod Tr Se, Calgary, AB, T2H 2N1
(403) 258-8000
Emp Here 3,000   *Emp Total* 24,500
Sales 413,030,523
SIC 8711 Engineering services
   Brian Janzen
   Randy Karren

D-U-N-S 20-281-2285   (SL)
ZAG BANK
6807 Railway St Se Unit 120, Calgary, AB, T2H 2V6
(403) 774-4253
Emp Here 56   *Sales* 4,109,024
SIC 6021 National commercial banks

Calgary, AB T2J

D-U-N-S 25-271-3839   (BR)
7-ELEVEN CANADA, INC
7-ELEVEN STORE #29510
9128 Macleod Trail Se, Calgary, AB, T2J 0P5
(403) 255-6540
Emp Here 20
SIC 5411 Grocery stores

D-U-N-S 24-956-8056   (HQ)
AGRIUM CANADA PARTNERSHIP
AGRIUM
(*Suby of* Agrium Canada Partnership)
13131 Lake Fraser Dr Se, Calgary, AB, T2J 7E8
(403) 225-7000
Emp Here 335   *Emp Total* 15,200
Sales 13,665,000,000
SIC 2873 Nitrogenous fertilizers
Pr Pr Chuck Magro
   Steve Douglas
Sr VP Henry Deans
Sr VP Susan Jones
Pers/VP Michael Webb
Ex VP Leslie O'donoghue
   Derek Pannell
   Maura Clark
   David Everitt
   Russell Girling

D-U-N-S 25-316-0345   (BR)
ALBERTA MOTOR ASSOCIATION
A M A
10816 Macleod Trail Se Suite 524, Calgary, AB, T2J 5N8
(403) 278-3530
Emp Here 40
SIC 4724 Travel agencies

D-U-N-S 25-014-1835   (BR)
BANQUE TORONTO-DOMINION, LA
TD FINANCIAL GROUP
(*Suby of* Toronto-Dominion Bank, The)
755 Lake Bonavista Dr Se, Calgary, AB, T2J 0N3
(403) 299-3400
Emp Here 21
SIC 6021 National commercial banks

D-U-N-S 20-991-3342   (BR)
BANQUE TORONTO-DOMINION, LA
TORONTO-DOMINION BANK, THE
(*Suby of* Toronto-Dominion Bank, The)
10816 Macleod Trail Se Suite 234, Calgary, AB, T2J 5N8
(403) 271-0202
Emp Here 30
SIC 6021 National commercial banks

D-U-N-S 24-681-5182   (BR)
CEDA INTERNATIONAL CORPORATION
11012 Macleod Trail Se Suite 500, Calgary, AB, T2J 6A5
(403) 253-3233
Emp Here 50
SIC 2819 Industrial inorganic chemicals, nec

D-U-N-S 20-713-1504   (BR)
CALGARY BOARD OF EDUCATION
PRINCE OF WALES ELEMENTARY SCHOOL
253 Parkland Way Se, Calgary, AB, T2J 3Y9
(403) 777-6880
Emp Here 30
SIC 8211 Elementary and secondary schools

D-U-N-S 20-591-1295   (BR)
CALGARY BOARD OF EDUCATION
WILLOW PARK SCHOOL
343 Willow Park Dr Se, Calgary, AB, T2J 0K7
(403) 777-6900
Emp Here 50
SIC 8211 Elementary and secondary schools

D-U-N-S 20-713-1215   (BR)

CALGARY BOARD OF EDUCATION
ANDREW SIBBALD ELEMENTARY SCHOOL
1711 Lake Bonavista Dr Se, Calgary, AB, T2J 2X9
(403) 777-6830
Emp Here 50
SIC 8211 Elementary and secondary schools

D-U-N-S 25-011-8544   (BR)
CALGARY BOARD OF EDUCATION
NICKLE JUNIOR HIGH
2500 Lake Bonavista Dr Se, Calgary, AB, T2J 2Y6
(403) 777-7720
Emp Here 50
SIC 8211 Elementary and secondary schools

D-U-N-S 20-713-1645   (BR)
CALGARY BOARD OF EDUCATION
WILMA HANSEN JUNIOR HGH SCHOOL
963 Queensland Dr Se, Calgary, AB, T2J 5E5
(403) 777-7430
Emp Here 50
SIC 8211 Elementary and secondary schools

D-U-N-S 25-269-6992   (BR)
CALGARY BOARD OF EDUCATION
R.T. ALDERMAN JR HIGH SCHOOL
725 Mapleton Dr Se, Calgary, AB, T2J 1S1
(403) 777-7520
Emp Here 53
SIC 8211 Elementary and secondary schools

D-U-N-S 20-713-1629   (BR)
CALGARY BOARD OF EDUCATION
DEER RUN ELEMENTARY SCHOOL
2127 146 Ave Se, Calgary, AB, T2J 6P8
(403) 777-6840
Emp Here 30
SIC 8211 Elementary and secondary schools

D-U-N-S 25-452-7120   (BR)
CALGARY BOARD OF EDUCATION
QUEENSLAND DOWNS ELEMENTARY
199 Queen Charlotte Way Se, Calgary, AB, T2J 4H9
(403) 777-6960
Emp Here 25
SIC 8211 Elementary and secondary schools

D-U-N-S 20-591-1964   (BR)
CALGARY BOARD OF EDUCATION
ACADIA ELEMENTARY SCHOOL
9603 5 St Se, Calgary, AB, T2J 1K4
(403) 777-8440
Emp Here 25
SIC 8211 Elementary and secondary schools

D-U-N-S 20-688-9037   (BR)
CALGARY BOARD OF EDUCATION
LAKE BONAVISTA ELEMENTARY SCHOOL
1015 120 Ave Se, Calgary, AB, T2J 2L1
(403) 777-6871
Emp Here 30
SIC 8211 Elementary and secondary schools

D-U-N-S 20-591-1725   (BR)
CALGARY BOARD OF EDUCATION
HAULTAIN MEMORIAL SCHOOL
605 Queensland Dr Se, Calgary, AB, T2J 4S8
(403) 777-6860
Emp Here 25
SIC 8211 Elementary and secondary schools

D-U-N-S 20-591-1055   (BR)
CALGARY BOARD OF EDUCATION
MAPLE RIDGE SCHOOL
10203 Maplemont Rd Se, Calgary, AB, T2J 1W3
(403) 777-6280
Emp Here 28
SIC 8211 Elementary and secondary schools

D-U-N-S 25-316-1145   (BR)
CALGARY CO-OPERATIVE ASSOCIATION LIMITED
CALGARY CO-OP
1221 Canyon Meadows Dr Se Suite 95, Cal-

gary, AB, T2J 6G2
(403) 299-4350
Emp Here 320
SIC 5411 Grocery stores

D-U-N-S 20-075-6521   (BR)
CALGARY PUBLIC LIBRARY
FISH CREEK LIBRARY
11161 Bonaventure Dr Se, Calgary, AB, T2J 6S1
(403) 221-2090
Emp Here 45
SIC 8231 Libraries

D-U-N-S 20-574-7616   (BR)
CALGARY ROMAN CATHOLIC SEPARATE SCHOOL DISTRICT #1
ST. BONIFACE SCHOOL
927 Lake Sylvan Dr Se, Calgary, AB, T2J 2P8
(403) 500-2060
Emp Here 21
SIC 8211 Elementary and secondary schools

D-U-N-S 20-574-8267   (BR)
CALGARY ROMAN CATHOLIC SEPARATE SCHOOL DISTRICT #1
ST. PHILIP ELEMENTARY SCHOOL
13825 Parkside Dr Se, Calgary, AB, T2J 5A8
(403) 500-2072
Emp Here 23
SIC 8211 Elementary and secondary schools

D-U-N-S 25-269-8899   (BR)
CALGARY ROMAN CATHOLIC SEPARATE SCHOOL DISTRICT #1
DON BOSCO SCHOOL
13615 Deer Ridge Dr Se, Calgary, AB, T2J 6S7
(403) 500-2057
Emp Here 50
SIC 8211 Elementary and secondary schools

D-U-N-S 20-713-0704   (BR)
CALGARY ROMAN CATHOLIC SEPARATE SCHOOL DISTRICT #1
SAINT ONAVENTURE SCHOOL
1710 Acadia Dr Se, Calgary, AB, T2J 3X8
(403) 271-5770
Emp Here 30
SIC 8211 Elementary and secondary schools

D-U-N-S 20-574-7731   (BR)
CALGARY ROMAN CATHOLIC SEPARATE SCHOOL DISTRICT #1
ST. CECILIA SCHOOL
610 Agate Cres Se, Calgary, AB, T2J 0Z3
(403) 500-2040
Emp Here 23
SIC 8211 Elementary and secondary schools

D-U-N-S 20-653-1647   (BR)
CONSEIL SCOLAIRE DU SUD DE L'ALBERTA
ECOLE DE LA SOURCE
360 94 Ave Se, Calgary, AB, T2J 0E8
(403) 255-6724
Emp Here 30
SIC 8211 Elementary and secondary schools

D-U-N-S 20-806-6550   (BR)
COUTTS, WILLIAM E. COMPANY, LIMITED
HALLMARK CARDS
(*Suby of* Hallmark Cards, Incorporated)
755 Lake Bonavista Dr Se Unit 173, Calgary, AB, T2J 0N3
(403) 278-7862
Emp Here 25
SIC 5947 Gift, novelty, and souvenir shop

D-U-N-S 24-298-9564   (SL)
DICK'S JANITORIAL SERVICE LTD
Gd, Calgary, AB, T2J 2T9
(403) 256-3070
Emp Here 70   *Sales* 2,042,900
SIC 7349 Building maintenance services, nec

D-U-N-S 25-622-1888   (BR)
EARL'S RESTAURANTS LTD

EARL WILLOW PARK
(*Suby of* Earl's Restaurants Ltd)
10640 Macleod Trail Se, Calgary, AB, T2J 0P8
(403) 278-7860
Emp Here 75
SIC 5812 Eating places

D-U-N-S 20-195-9470   (BR)
EDDIE BAUER OF CANADA INC
(*Suby of* Golden Gate Capital LP)
100 Anderson Rd Se Suite 306, Calgary, AB, T2J 3V1
(403) 278-6440
Emp Here 25
SIC 5699 Miscellaneous apparel and accessory stores

D-U-N-S 24-461-3233   (BR)
EVELINE VERAART HAIR LIMITED
EVELINE CHARLES SALON
(*Suby of* Eveline Veraart Hair Limited)
100 Anderson Rd Se Suite 273a, Calgary, AB, T2J 3V1
(403) 571-5666
Emp Here 39
SIC 7231 Beauty shops

D-U-N-S 24-340-2570   (BR)
FGL SPORTS LTD
SPORT CHEK SOUTHCENTRE MALL
100 Anderson Rd Se Unit 76, Calgary, AB, T2J 3V1
(403) 225-1411
Emp Here 40
SIC 5941 Sporting goods and bicycle shops

D-U-N-S 25-518-5787   (BR)
GAP (CANADA) INC
GAP
(*Suby of* The Gap Inc)
100 Anderson Rd Se Suite 239, Calgary, AB, T2J 3V1
(403) 278-7200
Emp Here 28
SIC 5651 Family clothing stores

D-U-N-S 24-529-8281   (BR)
GOODLIFE FITNESS CENTRES INC
13226 Macleod Trail Se, Calgary, AB, T2J 7E5
(403) 271-4348
Emp Here 30
SIC 7991 Physical fitness facilities

D-U-N-S 20-552-9667   (BR)
GOVERNMENT OF THE PROVINCE OF ALBERTA
10325 Bonaventure Dr Se, Calgary, AB, T2J 5R8
(403) 297-5028
Emp Here 30
SIC 8249 Vocational schools, nec

D-U-N-S 20-989-4708   (BR)
HUDSON'S BAY COMPANY
THE BAY SOUTH CENTRE
100 Anderson Rd Se, Calgary, AB, T2J 3V1
(403) 278-9520
Emp Here 170
SIC 5311 Department stores

D-U-N-S 25-741-6107   (BR)
INDIGO BOOKS & MUSIC INC
CHAPTERS
(*Suby of* Indigo Books & Music Inc)
9631 Macleod Trail Sw, Calgary, AB, T2J 0P6
(403) 212-1442
Emp Here 50
SIC 5942 Book stores

D-U-N-S 20-126-8526   (BR)
IVANHOE CAMBRIDGE INC
IVANHOE CAMBRIDGE INC
11012 Macleod Trail Se Suite 750, Calgary, AB, T2J 6A5
(403) 278-8588
Emp Here 50
SIC 6512 Nonresidential building operators

D-U-N-S 24-271-4186   (SL)

KOOPMAN RESOURCES, INC
UNIWORLD APPAREL INDUSTRIES
10919 Willowglen Pl Se, Calgary, AB, T2J 1R8
(403) 271-4564
Emp Here 100   *Sales* 79,521,842
SIC 1311 Crude petroleum and natural gas
Pr Pr Sharon Koopman
 Don Koopman

D-U-N-S 24-646-5942   (BR)
LAFARGE CANADA INC
LAFARGE AGGREGATES AND CONCRETE
10511 15 St Se, Calgary, AB, T2J 7H7
(403) 292-1555
Emp Here 200
SIC 1442 Construction sand and gravel

D-U-N-S 20-064-7035   (BR)
LIFEMARK HEALTH MANAGEMENT INC
CALGARY MANUAL THERAPY CENTRE
(*Suby of* Audax Group, L.P.)
9250 Macleod Trail Se Unit 1, Calgary, AB, T2J 0P5
(403) 974-0174
Emp Here 20
SIC 8741 Management services

D-U-N-S 24-017-4842   (BR)
LULULEMON ATHLETICA CANADA INC
LULULEMON
100 Anderson Rd Se Unit 146, Calgary, AB, T2J 3V1
(403) 313-4434
Emp Here 20
SIC 2339 Women's and misses' outerwear, nec

D-U-N-S 20-067-5473   (BR)
MAGASIN LAURA (P.V.) INC
MELANIE LYNE
100 Anderson Rd Se Unit 37, Calgary, AB, T2J 3V1
(403) 225-0880
Emp Here 25
SIC 5621 Women's clothing stores

D-U-N-S 25-316-3984   (BR)
PASLEY, MAX ENTERPRISES LIMITED
MCDONALD'S RESTAURANTS NO. 14916
(*Suby of* Pasley, Max Enterprises Limited)
9650 Macleod Trail Se, Calgary, AB, T2J 0P7
(403) 252-8929
Emp Here 20
SIC 5812 Eating places

D-U-N-S 25-316-4057   (BR)
PASLEY, MAX ENTERPRISES LIMITED
MCDONALD'S RESTAURANTS
(*Suby of* Pasley, Max Enterprises Limited)
9311 Macleod Trail Sw, Calgary, AB, T2J 0P6
(403) 253-2088
Emp Here 71
SIC 5812 Eating places

D-U-N-S 20-188-0932   (BR)
PASLEY, MAX ENTERPRISES LIMITED
MCDONALDS RESTAURANT
(*Suby of* Pasley, Max Enterprises Limited)
13780 Bow Bottom Trail Se, Calgary, AB, T2J 6T5
(403) 271-7411
Emp Here 70
SIC 5812 Eating places

D-U-N-S 20-105-7341   (BR)
RADIOLOGY CONSULTANTS ASSOCIATED
100 Anderson Rd Se Suite 177, Calgary, AB, T2J 3V1
(403) 777-3000
Emp Here 20
SIC 8011 Offices and clinics of medical doctors

D-U-N-S 25-287-9861   (BR)
RAYMOND SALONS LTD
HENNESSEY SALON
(*Suby of* Raymond Salons Ltd)

100 Anderson Rd Se Unit 509, Calgary, AB, T2J 3V1
(403) 263-9960
Emp Here 25
SIC 7231 Beauty shops

D-U-N-S 24-495-9292   (SL)
ROBERTSON, DR. DAVID D PROFESSIONAL CORPORATION
DEER VALLEY DENTAL CARE
1221 Canyon Meadows Dr Se Suite 30, Calgary, AB, T2J 6G2
(403) 271-6300
Emp Here 60   *Sales* 3,429,153
SIC 8021 Offices and clinics of dentists

D-U-N-S 25-622-5749   (BR)
ROYAL TRUST CORPORATION OF CANADA
(*Suby of* Royal Bank Of Canada)
755 Lake Bonavista Dr Se Suite 115, Calgary, AB, T2J 0N3
(403) 299-5040
Emp Here 20
SIC 6021 National commercial banks

D-U-N-S 25-520-0073   (BR)
SCM INSURANCE SERVICES INC
210 8826 Blackfoot Trail, Calgary, AB, T2J 3J1
(403) 228-5800
Emp Here 32
SIC 6411 Insurance agents, brokers, and service

D-U-N-S 20-938-0091   (BR)
SIR CORP
JACK ASTOR'S BAR AND GRILL
9823 Macleod Trail Sw, Calgary, AB, T2J 0P6
(403) 252-2246
Emp Here 50
SIC 5812 Eating places

D-U-N-S 25-622-5921   (BR)
SCHANKS INTERNATIONAL INC
SCHANKS ATHLETIC CLUB
(*Suby of* Schanks International Inc)
9627 Macleod Trail Sw, Calgary, AB, T2J 0P6
(403) 253-7300
Emp Here 50
SIC 5813 Drinking places

D-U-N-S 20-298-4303   (BR)
SEARS CANADA INC
100 Anderson Rd Se Suite 1, Calgary, AB, T2J 3V1
(403) 225-3536
Emp Here 300
SIC 5311 Department stores

D-U-N-S 20-302-3101   (SL)
SEVENTH LEVEL MANAGEMENT LTD
KELLER WILLIAMS REALTY SOUTH
11012 Macleod Trail Se Suite 600, Calgary, AB, T2J 6A5
(403) 837-1195
Emp Here 110   *Sales* 10,360,419
SIC 6531 Real estate agents and managers
Pr Pr Wayne Henuset

D-U-N-S 24-120-1417   (BR)
SHELTER CANADIAN PROPERTIES LIMITED
10325 Bonaventure Dr Se Suite 400, Calgary, AB, T2J 5R8
(403) 271-0041
Emp Here 30
SIC 6513 Apartment building operators

D-U-N-S 24-606-1944   (BR)
SOBEYS CAPITAL INCORPORATED
SOBEYS
9919 Fairmount Dr Se Suite 120, Calgary, AB, T2J 0S3

Emp Here 25
SIC 5141 Groceries, general line

D-U-N-S 25-271-0678   (BR)

SOBEYS WEST INC
755 Lake Bonavista Dr Se Suite 1, Calgary, AB, T2J 0N3
(403) 271-1616
Emp Here 80
SIC 5411 Grocery stores

D-U-N-S 25-271-0744   (BR)
SOBEYS WEST INC
SOUTHCENTRE SAFEWAY
11011 Bonaventure Dr Se, Calgary, AB, T2J 6S1
(403) 278-5225
Emp Here 120
SIC 5411 Grocery stores

D-U-N-S 25-271-0637   (BR)
SOBEYS WEST INC
CANADA SAFEWAY LIMITED
9737 Macleod Trail Sw, Calgary, AB, T2J 0P6
(403) 252-8199
Emp Here 138
SIC 5411 Grocery stores

D-U-N-S 24-517-2739   (SL)
SOCIETY FOR TREATMENT OF AUTISM (CALGARY REGION)
404 94 Ave Se, Calgary, AB, T2J 0E8
(403) 253-2291
Emp Here 140   *Sales* 15,018,480
SIC 8399 Social services, nec
Ex Dir David Mikkelsen
  Peter Johnson
  Joan Jakubec
  Myles Thurlow
  Ken Pidwysocki

D-U-N-S 24-701-4822   (SL)
STANLEY PARK INVESTMENTS LTD
HOLIDAY INN EXPRESS HOTEL & SUITES
12025 Lake Fraser Dr Se, Calgary, AB, T2J 7G5
(403) 225-3000
Emp Here 75   *Sales* 3,283,232
SIC 7011 Hotels and motels

D-U-N-S 20-506-1141   (BR)
STARBUCKS COFFEE CANADA, INC
(*Suby of* Starbucks Corporation)
9631 Macleod Trail Sw, Calgary, AB, T2J 0P6

Emp Here 20
SIC 5812 Eating places

D-U-N-S 24-320-0362   (BR)
TELUS CORPORATION
TELUS
907 Lake Bonavista Dr Se, Calgary, AB, T2J 0N5
(403) 530-3811
Emp Here 25
SIC 4812 Radiotelephone communication

D-U-N-S 25-315-5238   (BR)
TORONTO-DOMINION BANK, THE
TD BANK
(*Suby of* Toronto-Dominion Bank, The)
9737 Macleod Trail Sw Suite 200, Calgary, AB, T2J 0P6
(403) 299-3475
Emp Here 24
SIC 6021 National commercial banks

D-U-N-S 25-297-8192   (BR)
TOYS 'R' US (CANADA) LTD
TOYS 'R' US
(*Suby of* Toys "r" Us, Inc.)
10450 Macleod Trail Se, Calgary, AB, T2J 0P8
(403) 974-8686
Emp Here 30
SIC 5945 Hobby, toy, and game shops

D-U-N-S 25-679-0759   (SL)
VIRIDIAN INC
(*Suby of* Agrium Canada Partnership)
13131 Lake Fraser Dr Se, Calgary, AB, T2J 7E8
(403) 225-7000
Emp Here 200   *Sales* 135,488,020

SIC 2873 Nitrogenous fertilizers
  Bruce Waterman
  Ron A. Wilkinson

D-U-N-S 25-218-9816   (BR)
WAL-MART CANADA CORP
9650 Macleod Trail Se, Calgary, AB, T2J 0P7
(403) 258-3988
Emp Here 300
SIC 5311 Department stores

Calgary, AB T2K

D-U-N-S 25-314-8647   (BR)
ALBERTA HEALTH SERVICES
THORNHILL COMMUNITY HEALTH CENTRE
6617 Centre St Nw, Calgary, AB, T2K 4Y5
(403) 944-7500
Emp Here 30
SIC 8011 Offices and clinics of medical doctors

D-U-N-S 20-591-1865   (BR)
CALGARY BOARD OF EDUCATION
DR J K MULLOY ELEMENTARY SCHOOL
7440 10 St Nw, Calgary, AB, T2K 1H6
(403) 777-6640
Emp Here 25
SIC 8211 Elementary and secondary schools

D-U-N-S 20-713-1017   (BR)
CALGARY BOARD OF EDUCATION
HUNTINGTON HILLS ELEMENTARY SCHOOL
820 64 Ave Nw, Calgary, AB, T2K 0M5
(403) 777-6650
Emp Here 50
SIC 8211 Elementary and secondary schools

D-U-N-S 20-713-1405   (BR)
CALGARY BOARD OF EDUCATION
SIR JOHN A MCDONALD JUNIOR HIGH SCHOOL
6600 4 St Nw, Calgary, AB, T2K 1C6
(403) 777-7670
Emp Here 50
SIC 8211 Elementary and secondary schools

D-U-N-S 20-713-1447   (BR)
CALGARY BOARD OF EDUCATION
JAMES FOWLER HIGH SCHOOL
4004 4 St Nw, Calgary, AB, T2K 1A1
(403) 230-4743
Emp Here 50
SIC 8211 Elementary and secondary schools

D-U-N-S 20-713-1074   (BR)
CALGARY BOARD OF EDUCATION
THORNCLIFFE SCHOOL
5646 Thornton Rd Nw, Calgary, AB, T2K 3B9
(403) 777-6670
Emp Here 25
SIC 8211 Elementary and secondary schools

D-U-N-S 20-713-1314   (BR)
CALGARY BOARD OF EDUCATION
COLONEL IRVINE JUNIOR HIGH SCHOOL
412 Northmount Dr Nw, Calgary, AB, T2K 3H6
(403) 777-7280
Emp Here 50
SIC 8211 Elementary and secondary schools

D-U-N-S 20-713-1041   (BR)
CALGARY BOARD OF EDUCATION
NORTH HAVEN ELEMENTARY SCHOOL
4922 North Haven Dr Nw, Calgary, AB, T2K 2K2
(403) 777-6220
Emp Here 20
SIC 8211 Elementary and secondary schools

D-U-N-S 20-591-1444   (BR)
CALGARY BOARD OF EDUCATION
ALEX MUNRO ELEMENTARY SCHOOL

427 78 Ave Ne, Calgary, AB, T2K 0R9
(403) 777-6600
Emp Here 25
SIC 8211 Elementary and secondary schools

D-U-N-S 25-485-8384   (BR)
CALGARY BOARD OF EDUCATION
JOHN G DIEFENBAKER HIGH SCHOOL
6620 4 St Nw, Calgary, AB, T2K 1C2
(403) 274-2240
Emp Here 90
SIC 8211 Elementary and secondary schools

D-U-N-S 25-100-3018   (BR)
CALGARY BOARD OF EDUCATION
HIGHWOOD ELEMENTARY SCHOOL
11 Holmwood Ave Nw, Calgary, AB, T2K 2G5
(403) 777-6200
Emp Here 30
SIC 8211 Elementary and secondary schools

D-U-N-S 20-653-8592   (BR)
CALGARY BOARD OF EDUCATION
TRADITIONAL LEARNING CENTRE, THE
226 Northmount Dr Nw, Calgary, AB, T2K 3G5
(403) 777-6034
Emp Here 30
SIC 8211 Elementary and secondary schools

D-U-N-S 20-590-7764   (BR)
CALGARY BOARD OF EDUCATION
ROSEMONT ELEMENTARY SCHOOL
19n Rosevale Dr Nw, Calgary, AB, T2K 1N6
(403) 777-6230
Emp Here 22
SIC 8211 Elementary and secondary schools

D-U-N-S 25-011-2075   (BR)
CALGARY BOARD OF EDUCATION
CAMBRIAN HEIGHTS ELEMENTARY SCHOOL
640 Northmount Dr Nw, Calgary, AB, T2K 3J5
(403) 777-6150
Emp Here 30
SIC 8211 Elementary and secondary schools

D-U-N-S 20-591-1824   (BR)
CALGARY BOARD OF EDUCATION
CATHERINE NICOLS GUNN ELEMENTARY SCHOOL
6625 4 St Ne, Calgary, AB, T2K 5C7
(403) 777-6620
Emp Here 25
SIC 8211 Elementary and secondary schools

D-U-N-S 24-113-6030   (BR)
CALGARY ROMAN CATHOLIC SEPARATE SCHOOL DISTRICT #1
ST. HUBERT ELEMENTARY SCHOOL
320 72 Ave Ne, Calgary, AB, T2K 5J3
(403) 500-2067
Emp Here 30
SIC 8211 Elementary and secondary schools

D-U-N-S 20-574-6790   (BR)
CALGARY ROMAN CATHOLIC SEPARATE SCHOOL DISTRICT #1
CORPUS CHRISTI SCHOOL
5607 Thornton Rd Nw, Calgary, AB, T2K 3C1
(403) 295-1990
Emp Here 23
SIC 8211 Elementary and secondary schools

D-U-N-S 20-034-2546   (BR)
CALGARY ROMAN CATHOLIC SEPARATE SCHOOL DISTRICT #1
ST. HENRY ELEMENTARY SCHOOL
7423 10 St Nw, Calgary, AB, T2K 1H5
(403) 500-2059
Emp Here 21
SIC 8211 Elementary and secondary schools

D-U-N-S 20-713-0662   (BR)
CALGARY ROMAN CATHOLIC SEPARATE SCHOOL DISTRICT #1
ST. HELENA SCHOOL
320 64 Ave Nw, Calgary, AB, T2K 0L8

(403) 500-2049
Emp Here 50
SIC 8211 Elementary and secondary schools

D-U-N-S 20-831-5358   (SL)
CALGARY WINTER CLUB
4611 14 St Nw, Calgary, AB, T2K 1J7
(403) 289-0040
Emp Here 70   *Sales* 2,845,467
SIC 7997 Membership sports and recreation clubs

D-U-N-S 24-049-3853   (BR)
CANADIAN TIRE CORPORATION, LIMITED
PARTSOURCE
637 Goddard Ave Ne, Calgary, AB, T2K 6K1
(403) 274-5901
Emp Here 20
SIC 5531 Auto and home supply stores

D-U-N-S 25-763-2570   (SL)
DENCAN RESTAURANT INC
DENNY'S RESTAURANT
5015 4 St Ne, Calgary, AB, T2K 6K2
(403) 295-2504
Emp Here 70   *Sales* 2,115,860
SIC 5812 Eating places

D-U-N-S 24-359-1208   (BR)
LOBLAWS INC
REAL CANADIAN SUPERSTORE
7020 4 St Nw, Calgary, AB, T2K 1C4
(403) 516-8519
Emp Here 100
SIC 5411 Grocery stores

D-U-N-S 24-906-3348   (HQ)
MANTEI HOLDINGS LTD
(*Suby of* Mantei Holdings Ltd)
5935 6 St Ne, Calgary, AB, T2K 5R5
(403) 295-0028
Emp Here 43   *Emp Total* 55
Sales 6,085,920
SIC 2431 Millwork
Pr Pr Carey Mantei

D-U-N-S 25-316-4214   (BR)
PASLEY, MAX ENTERPRISES LIMITED
MCDONALD'S RESTAURANTS
(*Suby of* Pasley, Max Enterprises Limited)
6820 4 St Nw, Calgary, AB, T2K 1C2
(403) 295-1004
Emp Here 81
SIC 5812 Eating places

D-U-N-S 20-002-7980   (BR)
ROYAL BANK OF CANADA
RBC
(*Suby of* Royal Bank Of Canada)
728 Northmount Dr Nw Suite 17, Calgary, AB, T2K 3K2
(403) 292-2440
Emp Here 30
SIC 6021 National commercial banks

D-U-N-S 25-831-6983   (BR)
SOBEYS WEST INC
MACDONALDS CONSOLIDATED, DIV
215 42 Ave Se, Calgary, AB, T2K 0H3

Emp Here 95
SIC 5411 Grocery stores

D-U-N-S 25-364-9370   (BR)
SOBEYS WEST INC
THORNCLIFFE SAFEWAY
5607 4 St Nw, Calgary, AB, T2K 1B3
(403) 730-5080
Emp Here 100
SIC 5411 Grocery stores

D-U-N-S 20-296-5760   (BR)
SOBEYS WEST INC
SAFEWAY
215 42 Ave Se, Calgary, AB, T2K 0H3
(403) 730-3500
Emp Here 87
SIC 4225 General warehousing and storage

D-U-N-S 20-200-0068   (BR)
STATESMAN CORPORATION
STATESMAN LIFE CENTRE
6700 Hunterview Dr Nw, Calgary, AB, T2K 6K4
(403) 275-5667
Emp Here 40
SIC 8322 Individual and family services

D-U-N-S 25-366-8008   (BR)
WALLACE & CAREY INC
5445 8 St Ne,, Calgary, AB, T2K 5R9
(403) 275-7360
Emp Here 40
SIC 5194 Tobacco and tobacco products

Calgary, AB T2L

D-U-N-S 25-236-1431   (BR)
ALBERTA TREASURY BRANCHES
ATB FINANCIAL
3630 Brentwood Rd Nw, Calgary, AB, T2L 1K8
(403) 297-8164
Emp Here 25
SIC 6036 Savings institutions, except federal

D-U-N-S 20-591-1154   (BR)
CALGARY BOARD OF EDUCATION
BRENTWOOD ELEMENTARY
1231 Northmount Dr Nw, Calgary, AB, T2L 0C9
(403) 777-6130
Emp Here 55
SIC 8211 Elementary and secondary schools

D-U-N-S 20-591-1246   (BR)
CALGARY BOARD OF EDUCATION
CAPTAIN JOHN PALLISER ELEMENTARY SCHOOL
1484 Northmount Dr Nw, Calgary, AB, T2L 0G6
(403) 777-6170
Emp Here 25
SIC 8211 Elementary and secondary schools

D-U-N-S 20-519-3266   (BR)
CALGARY BOARD OF EDUCATION
SIR WINSTON CHURCHILL HIGH SCHOOL
5220 Northland Dr Nw, Calgary, AB, T2L 2J6
(403) 289-9241
Emp Here 140
SIC 8211 Elementary and secondary schools

D-U-N-S 20-713-1397   (BR)
CALGARY BOARD OF EDUCATION
SIMON FRAZER JUNIOR HIGH SCHOOL
5215 33 St Nw, Calgary, AB, T2L 1V3
(403) 777-7290
Emp Here 50
SIC 8211 Elementary and secondary schools

D-U-N-S 20-591-1386   (BR)
CALGARY BOARD OF EDUCATION
COLLINGWOOD ELEMENTARY SCHOOL
3826 Collingwood Dr Nw, Calgary, AB, T2L 0R6
(403) 777-6180
Emp Here 25
SIC 8211 Elementary and secondary schools

D-U-N-S 20-713-1371   (BR)
CALGARY BOARD OF EDUCATION
SENATOR PATRICK BURNS SCHOOL
2155 Chilcotin Rd Nw, Calgary, AB, T2L 0X2
(403) 777-7400
Emp Here 41
SIC 8211 Elementary and secondary schools

D-U-N-S 25-316-1426   (BR)
CALGARY CO-OPERATIVE ASSOCIATION LIMITED
BRENTWOOD CO-OP
4122 Brentwood Rd Nw Suite 4, Calgary, AB, T2L 1K8
(403) 299-4301
Emp Here 100

SIC 5411 Grocery stores

D-U-N-S 24-345-3029   (BR)
CALGARY PUBLIC LIBRARY
NOSE HILL LIBRARY
1530 Northmount Dr Nw, Calgary, AB, T2L 0G6
(403) 221-2030
Emp Here 32
SIC 8231 Libraries

D-U-N-S 20-580-7923   (BR)
CALGARY ROMAN CATHOLIC SEPARATE SCHOOL DISTRICT #1
SAINT FRANCIS HIGH SCHOOL (10-12)
877 Northmount Dr Nw, Calgary, AB, T2L 0A3
(403) 500-2026
Emp Here 150
SIC 8211 Elementary and secondary schools

D-U-N-S 20-103-8234   (BR)
CALGARY ROMAN CATHOLIC SEPARATE SCHOOL DISTRICT #1
ST. LUKE'S ELEMENTARY SCHOOL
1232 Northmount Dr Nw, Calgary, AB, T2L 0E1
(403) 500-2039
Emp Here 20
SIC 8211 Elementary and secondary schools

D-U-N-S 20-574-8028   (BR)
CALGARY ROMAN CATHOLIC SEPARATE SCHOOL DISTRICT #1
ST MARGARET SCHOOL
3320 Carol Dr Nw, Calgary, AB, T2L 0K7
(403) 500-2025
Emp Here 30
SIC 8211 Elementary and secondary schools

D-U-N-S 24-298-5935   (HQ)
COMPUTER MODELLING GROUP LTD
CMG
(*Suby of* Computer Modelling Group Ltd)
3710 33 St Nw, Calgary, AB, T2L 2M1
(403) 531-1300
Emp Here 45   *Emp Total* 203
Sales 57,164,512
SIC 7371 Custom computer programming services
Pr Pr Kenneth M. Dedeluk
  Sandra Balic
  Ryan Schneider
VP Rob Eastick
VP James Erdle
VP David Hicks
  Anjani Kumar
VP Long Nghiem
  John B. Zaozirny
  Judith Athaide

D-U-N-S 25-520-7482   (BR)
FOUNTAIN TIRE LTD
FOUNTAIN TIRE NORTHLAND
4911 Northland Dr Nw, Calgary, AB, T2L 2K3
(403) 286-3386
Emp Here 20
SIC 5531 Auto and home supply stores

D-U-N-S 20-106-3893   (BR)
HUDSON'S BAY COMPANY
HOME OUTFITTERS
5111 Northland Dr Nw Suite 555, Calgary, AB, T2L 2J8

Emp Here 60
SIC 5719 Miscellaneous homefurnishings

D-U-N-S 20-552-9469   (BR)
INNOTECH ALBERTA INC
ALBERTA INNOVATES-TECHNOLOGY FUTURES
3608 33 St Nw, Calgary, AB, T2L 2A6
(403) 210-5222
Emp Here 50
SIC 8733 Noncommercial research organizations

D-U-N-S 24-345-7017   (SL)

ROCKY MOUNTAIN COLLEGE A CENTRE FOR BIBLICAL STUDIES
ROCKY MOUNTAIN COLLEGE
4039 Brentwood Rd Nw, Calgary, AB, T2L 1L1
(403) 284-5100
Emp Here 50   *Sales* 3,283,232
SIC 8661 Religious organizations

D-U-N-S 25-018-8117   (BR)
ROYAL BANK OF CANADA
RBC
(*Suby of* Royal Bank Of Canada)
4820 Northland Dr Nw Ste 220, Calgary, AB, T2L 2L3
(403) 292-2477
Emp Here 60
SIC 6021 National commercial banks

D-U-N-S 25-616-7925   (BR)
ROYAL TRUST CORPORATION OF CANADA
(*Suby of* Royal Bank Of Canada)
4820 Northland Dr Nw Suite 220, Calgary, AB, T2L 2L3
(403) 299-5270
Emp Here 35
SIC 6021 National commercial banks

D-U-N-S 24-107-3472   (BR)
SOBEYS WEST INC
3636 Morley Tr Nw, Calgary, AB, T2L 1K8
(403) 289-9890
Emp Here 100
SIC 5411 Grocery stores

D-U-N-S 25-271-0900   (BR)
SOBEYS WEST INC
BRENTWOOD SAFEWAY
3636 Brentwood Rd Nw, Calgary, AB, T2L 1K8
(403) 289-1424
Emp Here 100
SIC 5411 Grocery stores

D-U-N-S 20-824-9847   (SL)
VECOVA
3304 33 St Nw, Calgary, AB, T2L 2A6
(403) 284-2231
Emp Here 350   *Sales* 21,296,635
SIC 8331 Job training and related services
Dir Leslie Tamagi
Dir Joan Lee
Dir Karyn Richardson
  Robert Sainsbury

D-U-N-S 25-218-9931   (BR)
WAL-MART CANADA CORP
5005 Northland Drive Nw, Calgary, AB, T2L 2K1
(403) 247-8585
Emp Here 320
SIC 5311 Department stores

D-U-N-S 24-412-5162   (BR)
WAL-MART CANADA CORP
WAL-MART
5005 Northland Dr Nw Suite 3011, Calgary, AB, T2L 2K1
(403) 288-0711
Emp Here 50
SIC 5311 Department stores

D-U-N-S 20-005-6161   (BR)
WENDY'S RESTAURANTS OF CANADA INC
WENDY'S
(*Suby of* The Wendy's Company)
4122 Brentwood Rd Nw, Calgary, AB, T2L 1K8
(403) 282-5216
Emp Here 36
SIC 5812 Eating places

D-U-N-S 20-136-3491   (BR)
WINNERS MERCHANTS INTERNATIONAL L.P.
WINNERS
(*Suby of* The TJX Companies Inc)
5111 Northland Dr Nw Suite 200, Calgary, AB, T2L 2J8

(403) 247-8100
Emp Here 90
SIC 5651 Family clothing stores

    D-U-N-S 20-806-2799   (BR)
YM INC. (SALES)
STITCHES
5111 Northland Dr Nw Unit 180, Calgary, AB,
T2L 2J8

Emp Here 25
SIC 5621 Women's clothing stores

Calgary, AB T2M

    D-U-N-S 24-598-4844   (SL)
337450 ALBERTA LTD
BOSTON PIZZA
2420 16 Ave Nw, Calgary, AB, T2M 0M5
(403) 289-6900
Emp Here 58   *Sales* 1,751,057
SIC 5812 Eating places

    D-U-N-S 25-783-2345   (BR)
ALBERTA TREASURY BRANCHES
MASTERCARD SECURITY DIV OF
217 16 Ave Nw Suite 200, Calgary, AB, T2M
0H5
(403) 974-5222
Emp Here 31
SIC 6036 Savings institutions, except federal

    D-U-N-S 24-335-1728   (SL)
CML INTERNATIONAL INC
414 16 Ave Nw Suite 414, Calgary, AB, T2M
0J1
(403) 203-8772
Emp Here 500   *Sales* 20,290,000
SIC 2396 Automotive and apparel trimmings
Fin Ex David Chan

    D-U-N-S 20-003-5173   (BR)
CALGARY BOARD OF EDUCATION
*ROSEDALE ELEMENTARY JUNIOR HIGH
SCHOOL*
905 13 Ave Nw, Calgary, AB, T2M 0G3
(403) 777-7530
Emp Here 24
SIC 8211 Elementary and secondary schools

    D-U-N-S 25-359-9039   (BR)
CALGARY BOARD OF EDUCATION
BALMORAL JUNIOR HIGH SCHOOL
220 16 Ave Nw, Calgary, AB, T2M 0H4
(403) 777-7330
Emp Here 25
SIC 8211 Elementary and secondary schools

    D-U-N-S 20-913-6659   (BR)
CALGARY BOARD OF EDUCATION
BRANTON JUNIOR HIGH SCHOOL
2103 20 St Nw, Calgary, AB, T2M 3W1
(403) 777-7440
Emp Here 45
SIC 8211 Elementary and secondary schools

    D-U-N-S 20-522-1760   (BR)
CALGARY BOARD OF EDUCATION
WILLIAM ABERHART SCHOOL
3009 Morley Trail Nw, Calgary, AB, T2M 4G9
(403) 289-2551
Emp Here 110
SIC 8211 Elementary and secondary schools

    D-U-N-S 20-591-1261   (BR)
CALGARY BOARD OF EDUCATION
BANFF TRAIL ELEMENTARY SCHOOL
3232 Cochrane Rd Nw, Calgary, AB, T2M 4J3
(403) 777-6120
Emp Here 25
SIC 8211 Elementary and secondary schools

    D-U-N-S 25-159-0089   (BR)
CALGARY BOARD OF EDUCATION
KING GEORGE SCHOOL
2108 10 St Nw, Calgary, AB, T2M 3M4

(403) 777-6210
Emp Here 30
SIC 8211 Elementary and secondary schools

    D-U-N-S 20-266-7569   (BR)
CALGARY BOARD OF EDUCATION
CRESCENT HEIGHTS HIGH SCHOOL
1019 1 St Nw, Calgary, AB, T2M 2S2
(403) 276-5521
Emp Here 120
SIC 8211 Elementary and secondary schools

    D-U-N-S 20-580-7949   (BR)
**CALGARY ROMAN CATHOLIC SEPARATE
SCHOOL DISTRICT #1**
*ST. JOSEPH ELEMENTARY & JUNIOR HIGH
SCHOOL*
2512 5 St Nw, Calgary, AB, T2M 3C7
(403) 500-2009
Emp Here 40
SIC 8211 Elementary and secondary schools

    D-U-N-S 20-030-7218   (BR)
**CALGARY ROMAN CATHOLIC SEPARATE
SCHOOL DISTRICT #1**
ST. PIUS SCHOOL
2312 18 St Nw, Calgary, AB, T2M 3T5
(403) 220-9556
Emp Here 21
SIC 8211 Elementary and secondary schools

    D-U-N-S 25-303-5752   (BR)
**CANADIAN IMPERIAL BANK OF COM-
MERCE**
CIBC
2015 16 Ave Nw, Calgary, AB, T2M 0M3
(403) 974-2734
Emp Here 30
SIC 6021 National commercial banks

    D-U-N-S 25-273-5345   (BR)
CITY OF CALGARY, THE
NORTH MOUNT PLEASANT ARTS CENTRE
523 27 Ave Nw, Calgary, AB, T2M 2H9
(403) 221-3682
Emp Here 40
SIC 8299 Schools and educational services,
nec

    D-U-N-S 25-522-1624   (BR)
EARL'S RESTAURANTS LTD
EARL'S
(*Suby of* Earl's Restaurants Ltd)
1110 16 Ave Nw, Calgary, AB, T2M 0K8
(403) 289-2566
Emp Here 100
SIC 5812 Eating places

    D-U-N-S 20-698-6221   (BR)
HOME DEPOT OF CANADA INC
(*Suby of* The Home Depot Inc)
1818 16 Ave Nw, Calgary, AB, T2M 0L8
(403) 284-7931
Emp Here 200
SIC 5251 Hardware stores

    D-U-N-S 25-086-0285   (BR)
KHATIJA INVESTMENTS LTD
*HAMPTONS INN & SUITES CALGARY UNI-
VERSITY NORTH WEST*
(*Suby of* Khatija Investments Ltd)
2231 Banff Trail Nw, Calgary, AB, T2M 4L2
(403) 289-9800
Emp Here 35
SIC 7011 Hotels and motels

    D-U-N-S 24-119-4810   (SL)
NICK'S STEAKHOUSE & PIZZA (1981) LTD
2430 Crowchild Trail Nw, Calgary, AB, T2M
4N5
(403) 282-9278
Emp Here 60   *Sales* 1,824,018
SIC 5812 Eating places

    D-U-N-S 25-315-1765   (BR)
PASLEY, MAX ENTERPRISES LIMITED
MCDONALD'S RESTAURANTS 17499
(*Suby of* Pasley, Max Enterprises Limited)

2320 16 Ave Nw, Calgary, AB, T2M 0M5
(403) 289-9050
Emp Here 64
SIC 5812 Eating places

    D-U-N-S 25-521-0395   (BR)
PHIL'S RESTAURANTS LTD
PHIL'S RESTAURANT
(*Suby of* Phil's Restaurants Ltd)
2312 16 Ave Nw, Calgary, AB, T2M 0M5
(403) 284-9696
Emp Here 35
SIC 5812 Eating places

    D-U-N-S 24-013-8180   (BR)
READ JONES CHRISTOFFERSEN LTD
RJC
1816 Crowchild Trail Nw Suite 500, Calgary,
AB, T2M 3Y7
(403) 283-5073
Emp Here 62
SIC 8711 Engineering services

    D-U-N-S 20-188-7093   (BR)
ROYAL HOST INC
BEST WESTERN VILLAGE PARK INN
1804 Crowchild Trail Nw, Calgary, AB, T2M
3Y7
(403) 289-0241
Emp Here 120
SIC 7011 Hotels and motels

    D-U-N-S 25-483-6448   (BR)
SODEXO CANADA LTD
1301 16 Ave Nw, Calgary, AB, T2M 0L4
(403) 284-8536
Emp Here 120
SIC 7349 Building maintenance services, nec

    D-U-N-S 24-716-8149   (SL)
SUNNY HOLDINGS LIMITED
ARBY'S
1140 16 Ave Nw, Calgary, AB, T2M 0K8

Emp Here 120   *Sales* 3,648,035
SIC 5812 Eating places

Calgary, AB T2N

    D-U-N-S 24-109-8123   (BR)
ALBERTA HEALTH SERVICES
FOOTHILLS HOSPITAL
1403 29 St Nw Suite 403, Calgary, AB, T2N
2T9
(403) 944-2068
Emp Here 100
SIC 8062 General medical and surgical hospitals

    D-U-N-S 25-314-8977   (BR)
ALBERTA HEALTH SERVICES
FOOTHILLS MEDICAL CENTRE
1403 29 St Nw Suite 1403, Calgary, AB, T2N
2T9
(403) 670-1110
Emp Here 6,000
SIC 8011 Offices and clinics of medical doctors

    D-U-N-S 25-768-6006   (BR)
ALBERTA HEALTH SERVICES
CALGARY ADDICTION YOUTH SERVICES
1005 17 Ave Nw, Calgary, AB, T2N 2E5
(403) 297-4664
Emp Here 40
SIC 8062 General medical and surgical hospi-
tals

    D-U-N-S 24-850-4768   (SL)
BFL CANADA INSURANCE SERVICES
1167 Kensington Cres Nw Suite 200, Calgary,
AB, T2N 1X7
(403) 451-4132
Emp Here 350   *Sales* 449,208,234
SIC 6311 Life insurance

Pr Barry Lorenzette

    D-U-N-S 20-572-2254   (BR)
BANK OF NOVA SCOTIA, THE
SCOTIABANK
1204 Kensington Rd Nw Suite 100, Calgary,
AB, T2N 3P5
(403) 974-7070
Emp Here 20
SIC 6021 National commercial banks

    D-U-N-S 25-620-9230   (BR)
BANK OF NOVA SCOTIA, THE
SCOTIABANK
1941 Uxbridge Dr Nw Suite 12, Calgary, AB,
T2N 2V2
(403) 221-6800
Emp Here 20
SIC 6021 National commercial banks

    D-U-N-S 25-622-0138   (BR)
BETHANY CARE SOCIETY
BETHANY CARE CENTRE CALGARY
916 18a St Nw Suite 3085, Calgary, AB, T2N
1C6
(403) 284-0161
Emp Here 500
SIC 8051 Skilled nursing care facilities

    D-U-N-S 20-713-1058   (BR)
CALGARY BOARD OF EDUCATION
QUEEN ELIZABETH HIGH SCHOOL
512 18 St Nw, Calgary, AB, T2N 2G5
(403) 777-6380
Emp Here 75
SIC 8211 Elementary and secondary schools

    D-U-N-S 20-713-0902   (BR)
CALGARY BOARD OF EDUCATION
*WOOD'S HOMES - WILLIAM TAYLOR
LEARNING CENTER*
805 37 St Nw, Calgary, AB, T2N 4N8
(403) 270-1751
Emp Here 50
SIC 8211 Elementary and secondary schools

    D-U-N-S 20-590-7848   (BR)
CALGARY BOARD OF EDUCATION
SUNNYSIDE SCHOOL
211 7 St Nw, Calgary, AB, T2N 1S2
(403) 777-6390
Emp Here 25
SIC 8211 Elementary and secondary schools

    D-U-N-S 25-325-8438   (BR)
CALGARY BOARD OF EDUCATION
UNIVERSITY ELEMENTARY SCHOOL
3035 Utah Dr Nw, Calgary, AB, T2N 3Z9
(403) 777-6240
Emp Here 28
SIC 8211 Elementary and secondary schools

    D-U-N-S 25-325-8479   (BR)
CALGARY BOARD OF EDUCATION
HILLHURST COMMUNITY SCHOOL
1418 7 Ave Nw, Calgary, AB, T2N 0Z2
(403) 777-6360
Emp Here 40
SIC 8211 Elementary and secondary schools

    D-U-N-S 20-591-1105   (BR)
CALGARY BOARD OF EDUCATION
LOUISE DEAN SCHOOL
120 23 St Nw, Calgary, AB, T2N 2P1
(403) 777-7630
Emp Here 25
SIC 8211 Elementary and secondary schools

    D-U-N-S 24-803-7124   (BR)
CALGARY BOARD OF EDUCATION
*QUEEN ELIZABETH ELEMENTARY
SCHOOL*
402 18 St Nw, Calgary, AB, T2N 2G5
(403) 777-6789
Emp Here 20
SIC 8211 Elementary and secondary schools

    D-U-N-S 20-713-0753   (BR)

CALGARY ROMAN CATHOLIC SEPARATE SCHOOL DISTRICT #1
ECOLE MADELEINE D'HOUETE
108 22 St Nw, Calgary, AB, T2N 2M8
(403) 500-2008
Emp Here 30
SIC 8211 Elementary and secondary schools

D-U-N-S 20-572-7162   (BR)
CANADA POST CORPORATION
1941 Uxbridge Dr Nw Suite 23, Calgary, AB, T2N 2V2
(403) 289-0202
Emp Here 20
SIC 4311 U.s. postal service

D-U-N-S 20-830-2141   (BR)
CANADIAN BROADCASTING CORPORATION
CBC/CBRT/CBR
1724 Westmount Blvd Nw, Calgary, AB, T2N 3G7
(403) 521-6000
Emp Here 160
SIC 4832 Radio broadcasting stations

D-U-N-S 24-012-3757   (BR)
DENTRIX INC
DENTRIX DENTALCARE
(*Suby of* Dentrix Inc)
1632 14 Ave Nw Suite 221, Calgary, AB, T2N 1M7
(403) 289-9908
Emp Here 20
SIC 8741 Management services

D-U-N-S 25-518-9474   (BR)
EXTENDICARE (CANADA) INC
EXTENDICARE HILLCREST
1512 8 Ave Nw, Calgary, AB, T2N 1C1
(403) 289-0236
Emp Here 120
SIC 8051 Skilled nursing care facilities

D-U-N-S 24-359-1463   (SL)
FNP ENGINEERING
1240 Kensington Rd Nw Suite 403, Calgary, AB, T2N 3P7
(403) 270-8833
Emp Here 100   *Sales* 15,116,050
SIC 8711 Engineering services
Pt Garry Mctighe
Pt Gerry Stebnicki
Pt Mahmood Rajan
Pt Kevin Lynch
Pt Mahendra Etwaroo
Pt Brad Fair
Pt Brad Currie
Pt Brian King
Pt Ravi Abraham
Pt Livio Barone

D-U-N-S 24-374-3841   (BR)
FRIENDS OF THE ALBERTA JUBILEE AUDITORIUM SOCIETY
JUBILEE AUDITORIUM SOCIETY
1415 14 Ave Nw, Calgary, AB, T2N 1M4
(403) 297-8001
Emp Here 60
SIC 8699 Membership organizations, nec

D-U-N-S 20-579-9989   (BR)
GOVERNMENT OF THE PROVINCE OF ALBERTA
CHILD AND USED ADVOCATE
301 14 St Nw Suite 406, Calgary, AB, T2N 2A1
(403) 297-8435
Emp Here 55
SIC 8399 Social services, nec

D-U-N-S 25-484-4574   (BR)
GOVERNMENT OF THE PROVINCE OF ALBERTA
ACCESS PROGRAM PERSONS WITH DEVELOPMENTAL DISABILITIES (PDD) INQUIRIES
535 37 St Nw, Calgary, AB, T2N 3C1

(403) 297-7096
Emp Here 21
SIC 8322 Individual and family services

D-U-N-S 20-112-2129   (BR)
GOVERNORS OF THE UNIVERSITY OF CALGARY, THE
MATERIALS MANAGEMENT
(*Suby of* Governors of the University of Calgary, The)
2500 University Dr Nw, Calgary, AB, T2N 1N4
(403) 220-5611
Emp Here 25
SIC 8211 Elementary and secondary schools

D-U-N-S 25-063-4300   (BR)
GOVERNORS OF THE UNIVERSITY OF CALGARY, THE
CAMPUS RECREATION
(*Suby of* Governors of the University of Calgary, The)
2500 University Dr Nw, Calgary, AB, T2N 1N4
(403) 220-7749
Emp Here 45
SIC 7997 Membership sports and recreation clubs

D-U-N-S 25-371-4687   (BR)
GOVERNORS OF THE UNIVERSITY OF CALGARY, THE
FACULTY OF MEDECINE
(*Suby of* Governors of the University of Calgary, The)
3330 Hospital Dr Nw Suite 3330, Calgary, AB, T2N 4N1

Emp Here 100
SIC 8733 Noncommercial research organizations

D-U-N-S 24-103-9416   (BR)
GOVERNORS OF THE UNIVERSITY OF CALGARY, THE
UNIVERSITY BOOKSTORE
(*Suby of* Governors of the University of Calgary, The)
2500 University Dr Nw Suite 250, Calgary, AB, T2N 1N4
(403) 220-5537
Emp Here 60
SIC 5942 Book stores

D-U-N-S 20-233-0143   (BR)
HEALTHCARE PROPERTIES HOLDINGS LTD
SUNNYHILL WELLNESS CENTRE
1402 8 Ave Nw Suite 171, Calgary, AB, T2N 1B9

Emp Here 30
SIC 8051 Skilled nursing care facilities

D-U-N-S 20-038-5040   (BR)
INTERCARE CORPORATE GROUP INC
BRENTWOOD CARE CENTER
(*Suby of* Intercare Corporate Group Inc)
2727 16 Ave Nw Suite 138, Calgary, AB, T2N 3Y6
(403) 289-2576
Emp Here 100
SIC 8051 Skilled nursing care facilities

D-U-N-S 20-874-5401   (BR)
KAL TIRE LTD
1616 14 Ave Nw, Calgary, AB, T2N 1M6
(587) 318-3044
Emp Here 27
SIC 5531 Auto and home supply stores

D-U-N-S 24-345-7041   (BR)
KEG RESTAURANTS LTD
KEG STEAKHOUSE & BAR, THE
1923 Uxbridge Dr Nw, Calgary, AB, T2N 2V2
(403) 282-0020
Emp Here 90
SIC 5812 Eating places

D-U-N-S 24-421-8108   (BR)
MOLSON COORS CANADA INC

(*Suby of* Molson Coors Brewing Company)
1400 Kensington Rd Nw Suite 100, Calgary, AB, T2N 3P9
(403) 806-1786
Emp Here 30
SIC 2082 Malt beverages

D-U-N-S 20-828-4869   (SL)
ROYAL CANADIAN LEGION NORTH CALGARY BRANCH (NO 264)
1910 Kensington Rd Nw, Calgary, AB, T2N 3R5
(403) 283-5264
Emp Here 70   *Sales* 5,034,288
SIC 8641 Civic and social associations

D-U-N-S 20-599-8065   (BR)
SEARS CANADA INC
1616 14 Ave Nw, Calgary, AB, T2N 1M6
(403) 289-7777
Emp Here 350
SIC 5311 Department stores

D-U-N-S 25-271-0934   (BR)
SOBEYS WEST INC
CANADA SAFEWAY LIMITED
410 10 St Nw, Calgary, AB, T2N 1V9
(403) 270-3054
Emp Here 110
SIC 5411 Grocery stores

D-U-N-S 25-138-3634   (BR)
SOBEYS WEST INC
SAFEWAY
1632 14 Ave Nw Unit 1846, Calgary, AB, T2N 1M7
(403) 210-0002
Emp Here 150
SIC 5411 Grocery stores

D-U-N-S 20-324-9664   (HQ)
UNIGLOBE BEACON TRAVEL LTD
(*Suby of* Uniglobe Beacon Travel Ltd)
1400 Kensington Rd Nw Suite 200, Calgary, AB, T2N 3P9
(877) 596-6860
Emp Here 55   *Emp Total* 66
Sales 21,913,200
SIC 4724 Travel agencies
Pr David Kruschell
COO Richard Gardner
CFO Anthony Johnston

D-U-N-S 24-440-3440   (BR)
WENDY'S RESTAURANTS OF CANADA INC
WENDY'S
(*Suby of* The Wendy's Company)
1927 Uxbridge Dr Nw, Calgary, AB, T2N 2V2
(403) 282-5831
Emp Here 27
SIC 5812 Eating places

Calgary, AB T2P

D-U-N-S 20-562-1415   (SL)
1140102 ALBERTA LTD
855 2 St Sw Suite 1800, Calgary, AB, T2P 4J8
(403) 645-2000
Emp Here 100   *Sales* 20,417,280
SIC 6712 Bank holding companies
Pr R William Oliver
VP Gerald H. Bietz
VP Paul A. Reimer
Anthony R. Dimaio
Sec Jeffery G. Paulson
Sec Racheal L. Desroches

D-U-N-S 20-123-2353   (SL)
1883865 ALBERTA LTD
KNOXVILLE'S TAVERN
840 9 Ave Sw, Calgary, AB, T2P 1L7
(403) 398-7623
Emp Here 80   *Sales* 2,918,428
SIC 5813 Drinking places

D-U-N-S 24-324-2521   (BR)
20 VIC MANAGEMENT INC
333 7 Ave Sw Suite 900, Calgary, AB, T2P 2Z1
(403) 441-4901
Emp Here 60
SIC 6531 Real estate agents and managers

D-U-N-S 25-987-0616   (SL)
817936 ALBERTA LTD
CEILI'S IRISH PUB & RESTAURANT
513 8 Ave Sw Suite 126, Calgary, AB, T2P 1G1
(403) 508-9999
Emp Here 100   *Sales* 2,991,389
SIC 5812 Eating places

D-U-N-S 20-844-8782   (SL)
995812 ALBERTA LTD
THE ROADHOUSE NIGHTCLUB
840 9 Ave Sw, Calgary, AB, T2P 1L7
(403) 398-7623
Emp Here 60   *Sales* 2,598,753
SIC 5813 Drinking places

D-U-N-S 20-354-3918   (SL)
AJM PETROLEUM CONSULTANTS, A PARTNERSHIP OF CORPORATIONS
425 1 St Sw Suite 600, Calgary, AB, T2P 3L8
(403) 648-3200
Emp Here 60   *Sales* 9,445,120
SIC 8748 Business consulting, nec
Robin Mann
Alan Ashton
Barry Ashton

D-U-N-S 24-848-3880   (BR)
AMEC FOSTER WHEELER AMERICAS LIMITED
AMEC
112 4 Ave Sw Suite 1000, Calgary, AB, T2P 0H3

Emp Here 50
SIC 8741 Management services

D-U-N-S 25-219-3719   (BR)
AMEC FOSTER WHEELER AMERICAS LIMITED
801 6 Ave Sw Suite 900, Calgary, AB, T2P 3W3
(403) 298-4170
Emp Here 1,000
SIC 8711 Engineering services

D-U-N-S 25-189-4437   (BR)
AMEC FOSTER WHEELER INC
801 6th Ave Sw Unit 900, Calgary, AB, T2P 3W3
(403) 298-4170
Emp Here 49
SIC 6719 Holding companies, nec

D-U-N-S 25-096-4772   (BR)
AMEC FOSTER WHEELER INC
AMEC ENGINEERING
801 6 Ave Sw Suite 900, Calgary, AB, T2P 3W3
(403) 298-4170
Emp Here 500
SIC 6712 Bank holding companies

D-U-N-S 25-235-7132   (HQ)
ATCO MIDSTREAM LTD
240 4 Ave Sw Suite 900, Calgary, AB, T2P 4H4
(403) 513-3700
Emp Here 74   *Emp Total* 7,860
Sales 31,096,857
SIC 4899 Communication services, nec
Dir Nancy C Southern
VP VP Marie Yan
Fin Ex Rob Harper
Arnold Macburnie

D-U-N-S 20-554-1456   (BR)
AECOM PRODUCTION SERVICES LTD
FLINT FIELD SERVICES LTD
300 5 Ave Sw Suite 700, Calgary, AB, T2P

3C4
(403) 218-7100
Emp Here 50
SIC 1389 Oil and gas field services, nec

D-U-N-S 20-304-6289   (BR)
AIR LIQUIDE CANADA INC
140 4 Ave Sw Suite 550, Calgary, AB, T2P 3N3
(403) 774-4320
Emp Here 35
SIC 2813 Industrial gases

D-U-N-S 24-948-8552   (HQ)
AKITA DRILLING LTD
(*Suby of* Akita Drilling Ltd)
333 7 Ave Sw Unit 1000, Calgary, AB, T2P 2Z1
(403) 292-7979
Emp Here 30   *Emp Total* 640
Sales 45,163,463
SIC 1382 Oil and gas exploration services
Pr Pr Karl Ruud
VP Fin Darcy Reynolds
Sr VP Raymond Coleman
  Fred Hensel
Sec Colin Dease
Prs Dir Craig Kushner
  Linda Southern-Heathcott
  Loraine Charlton
  Harish Mchan
  Dale Richardson

D-U-N-S 20-875-1201   (BR)
ALBERTA ELECTRIC SYSTEM OPERATOR
330 5 Ave Sw Suite 2500, Calgary, AB, T2P 0L4
(403) 539-2450
Emp Here 25
SIC 4911 Electric services

D-U-N-S 25-316-0428   (BR)
ALBERTA MOTOR ASSOCIATION
CAA/AMA
530 8 Ave Sw Suite 100, Calgary, AB, T2P 3S8
(403) 262-2345
Emp Here 20
SIC 8699 Membership organizations, nec

D-U-N-S 24-313-2953   (HQ)
ALTAGAS UTILITY GROUP INC
(*Suby of* AltaGas Holding Limited Partnership No. 1)
355 4 Ave Sw Suite 1700, Calgary, AB, T2P 0J1
(403) 806-3310
Emp Here 39   *Emp Total* 1
Sales 126,586,815
SIC 1311 Crude petroleum and natural gas
Pr Pr Patricia M. Newson
  David W. Cornhill
  Dennis A. Dawson
Dir Phillip R. Knoll
Dir Gerry M. Malin
Dir J. Bruce Petrie
  Jared B. Green

D-U-N-S 24-311-1148   (HQ)
ALTUS ENERGY SERVICES LTD
(*Suby of* Altus Energy Services Ltd)
222 3 Ave Sw Suite 740, Calgary, AB, T2P 0B4

Emp Here 200   *Emp Total* 440
Sales 98,771,840
SIC 1389 Oil and gas field services, nec
  Christopher Haslam
Pr Pr Frederick Moore
Sr VP Norman S. Denoon
Sr VP Darren K. Glover

D-U-N-S 25-678-7078   (HQ)
AMAYA (ALBERTA) INC
(*Suby of* Nyx Gaming Group Limited)
750 11 St Sw Suite 400, Calgary, AB, T2P 3N7

Emp Here 60   *Emp Total* 5
Sales 21,296,635
SIC 7371 Custom computer programming services
Pr Matt Davey
  Arthur Hamilton

D-U-N-S 25-676-9878   (HQ)
APACHE CANADA LTD
(*Suby of* Apache Corporation)
421 7 Ave Sw Suite 2800, Calgary, AB, T2P 4K9
(403) 261-1200
Emp Here 200   *Emp Total* 3,727
Sales 224,500,074
SIC 1382 Oil and gas exploration services
VP Rob Spitzer
VP Prd Al Buron

D-U-N-S 20-028-9788   (BR)
AQUA TERRE SOLUTIONS INC
AQUA TERRE
736 8 Ave Sw Suite 800, Calgary, AB, T2P 1H4
(403) 266-2555
Emp Here 30
SIC 8748 Business consulting, nec

D-U-N-S 24-059-2936   (BR)
ARBOR MEMORIAL SERVICES INC
17 Av Garden Rd Se, Calgary, AB, T2P 2G7
(403) 272-9824
Emp Here 22
SIC 7261 Funeral service and crematories

D-U-N-S 24-442-7258   (SL)
ARMSTRONG, DR C S PROFESSIONAL CORPORATION
ASSOCIATE CLINIC
401 9 Ave Sw Suite 320, Calgary, AB, T2P 3C5
(403) 221-4489
Emp Here 50   *Sales* 2,991,389
SIC 8011 Offices and clinics of medical doctors

D-U-N-S 20-821-6205   (BR)
ARNETT & BURGESS OIL FIELD CONSTRUCTION LIMITED
715 5 Ave Sw Suite 620, Calgary, AB, T2P 2X6
(403) 265-0900
Emp Here 50
SIC 4619 Pipelines, nec

D-U-N-S 25-686-6906   (SL)
ASPENTECH CANADA LTD
(*Suby of* Aspen Technology, Inc.)
205 5 Ave Sw Suite 3300, Calgary, AB, T2P 2V7
(403) 538-4781
Emp Here 250   *Sales* 50,927,900
SIC 7371 Custom computer programming services
Pr Greg O'neill

D-U-N-S 25-685-7087   (SL)
AUX SABLE CANADA LP
(*Suby of* Aux Sable Liquid Products, LP)
605 5 Ave Sw Suite 2800, Calgary, AB, T2P 3H5
(403) 508-5870
Emp Here 20   *Sales* 1,696,192
SIC 4899 Communication services, nec

D-U-N-S 20-824-6306   (BR)
AVIVA INSURANCE COMPANY OF CANADA
C G U INSURANCE
140 4 Ave Sw Suite 2400, Calgary, AB, T2P 3W4
(403) 750-0600
Emp Here 100
SIC 6331 Fire, marine, and casualty insurance

D-U-N-S 24-553-7410   (BR)
BDO CANADA LLP
903 8 Ave Sw Suite 620, Calgary, AB, T2P

0P7
(403) 232-0688
Emp Here 80
SIC 8721 Accounting, auditing, and book-keeping

D-U-N-S 24-997-7596   (BR)
BMO NESBITT BURNS INC
888 3 St Sw Suite 4100, Calgary, AB, T2P 5C5
(403) 260-9300
Emp Here 72
SIC 6211 Security brokers and dealers

D-U-N-S 20-519-7622   (BR)
BMO NESBITT BURNS INC
333 7 Ave Sw Suite 2200, Calgary, AB, T2P 2Z1
(403) 515-1500
Emp Here 40
SIC 6211 Security brokers and dealers

D-U-N-S 24-992-1979   (BR)
BMO NESBITT BURNS INC
NESBITT BURNS
525 8 Ave Sw Suite 3200, Calgary, AB, T2P 1G1
(403) 261-9550
Emp Here 100
SIC 6211 Security brokers and dealers

D-U-N-S 20-077-3919   (HQ)
BP CANADA ENERGY COMPANY
(*Suby of* BP P.L.C.)
240 4 Ave Sw, Calgary, AB, T2P 4H4
(403) 233-1313
Emp Here 2,100   *Emp Total* 84,700
Sales 1,473,295,415
SIC 1311 Crude petroleum and natural gas
Pr Pr Anne Drinkwater
VP Gerald K. Maxwell
VP Delwyn Robostan
VP Stephen Willis
VP Jeffrey Tanner
VP David Campbell
VP Tyler A Rimbey
VP Elizabeth Matheson
VP Mark Manser
Sr VP Macsen Jay Nuttall

D-U-N-S 25-326-1267   (HQ)
BAKER HUGHES CANADA COMPANY
BAKER ATLAS
(*Suby of* Baker Hughes, A GE Company)
401 9 Ave Sw Suite 1000, Calgary, AB, T2P 3C5
(403) 537-3400
Emp Here 200   *Emp Total* 33,000
Sales 200,641,925
SIC 5084 Industrial machinery and equipment
  Albert Lo
Pr Pr Alan J Keifer
Sec Sandra E Alford
  William D Marsh
Treas Jan Kees Van Galen

D-U-N-S 25-516-3156   (BR)
BAKER HUGHES CANADA COMPANY
BAKER OIL TOOLS
(*Suby of* Baker Hughes, A GE Company)
401 9 Ave Sw Suite 1300, Calgary, AB, T2P 3C5
(403) 537-3573
Emp Here 100
SIC 5169 Chemicals and allied products, nec

D-U-N-S 24-116-3653   (BR)
BANK OF NOVA SCOTIA, THE
SCOTIA CAPITAL
700 2 St Sw Suite 2000, Calgary, AB, T2P 2W1
(403) 221-6585
Emp Here 25
SIC 6021 National commercial banks

D-U-N-S 20-580-0795   (BR)
BANK OF NOVA SCOTIA, THE
SCOTIABANK
240 8 Ave Sw Suite 315, Calgary, AB, T2P

1B5
(403) 221-6401
Emp Here 20
SIC 6021 National commercial banks

D-U-N-S 20-152-8960   (BR)
BANK OF MONTREAL
BMO
350 7 Ave Sw Suite 900, Calgary, AB, T2P 3N9
(403) 503-7409
Emp Here 50
SIC 6021 National commercial banks

D-U-N-S 25-518-9219   (BR)
BANQUE NATIONALE DU CANADA
WELLINGTON WEST
450 1 St Sw Suite 2800, Calgary, AB, T2P 5H1
(403) 266-1116
Emp Here 80
SIC 8741 Management services

D-U-N-S 25-518-5274   (BR)
BANQUE NATIONALE DU CANADA
407 8 Ave Sw Suite 1000, Calgary, AB, T2P 1E5
(403) 294-4917
Emp Here 85
SIC 6021 National commercial banks

D-U-N-S 20-589-5399   (BR)
BANQUE TORONTO-DOMINION, LA
T D CANADA TRUST
(*Suby of* Toronto-Dominion Bank, The)
300 5 Ave Sw Suite 31, Calgary, AB, T2P 3C4
(403) 292-1012
Emp Here 40
SIC 6021 National commercial banks

D-U-N-S 20-589-4996   (BR)
BANQUE TORONTO-DOMINION, LA
TD CANADA TRUST
(*Suby of* Toronto-Dominion Bank, The)
317 7 Ave Sw Suite 180, Calgary, AB, T2P 2Y9
(403) 292-1221
Emp Here 20
SIC 6021 National commercial banks

D-U-N-S 20-589-5050   (BR)
BANQUE TORONTO-DOMINION, LA
TD BANK
(*Suby of* Toronto-Dominion Bank, The)
355 4 Ave Sw, Calgary, AB, T2P 0J1
(403) 292-1165
Emp Here 60
SIC 6021 National commercial banks

D-U-N-S 20-700-0246   (BR)
BANQUE DE DEVELOPPEMENT DU CANADA
BDC
444 7 Ave Sw Suite 110, Calgary, AB, T2P 0X8
(403) 292-5600
Emp Here 45
SIC 6141 Personal credit institutions

D-U-N-S 24-753-7538   (BR)
BANTREL CO.
(*Suby of* Bechtel Group, Inc.)
700 6 Ave Sw Suite 1400, Calgary, AB, T2P 0T8
(403) 290-5000
Emp Here 1,500
SIC 8711 Engineering services

D-U-N-S 24-336-5728   (SL)
BAY INTERNATIONAL CANADA ULC
140 4 Ave Sw Suite 2100, Calgary, AB, T2P 3N3
(403) 781-1110
Emp Here 50   *Sales* 13,797,200
SIC 1541 Industrial buildings and warehouses
Pr Pr Lawrence Berry
VP Fin Miguel Fuentes

D-U-N-S 24-702-0712   (SL)
BAYCOR INDUSTRIES LTD

404 6 Ave Sw Suite 300, Calgary, AB, T2P
0R9
(403) 294-0600
Emp Here 200   *Sales* 32,098,320
SIC 6211 Security brokers and dealers
Pr Pr Kevin R Baker

D-U-N-S 24-984-4952   (HQ)
BAYTEX ENERGY CORP
(*Suby of* Baytex Energy Corp)
520 3 Ave Sw Suite 2800, Calgary, AB, T2P
0R3
(587) 952-3000
Emp Here 147   *Emp Total* 252
Sales 576,993,366
SIC 1311 Crude petroleum and natural gas
Pr Pr Edward Lafehr
 Rodney Gray
 Richard Ramsay
 Geoffrey Darcy
Sr VP Brian Ector
VP Kendall Arthur
VP VP Murray Desrosiers
VP Ryan Johnson
VP Fin Chad Kalmakoff
VP Greg Sawchenko

D-U-N-S 24-381-9690   (BR)
BELL MEDIA INC
CKCE FM
535 7 Ave Sw, Calgary, AB, T2P 0Y4
(403) 508-2222
Emp Here 21
SIC 4832 Radio broadcasting stations

D-U-N-S 25-367-8874   (BR)
BELL MOBILITE INC
111 5 Ave Sw Suite 2100, Calgary, AB, T2P
3Y6

Emp Here 60
SIC 5065 Electronic parts and equipment, nec

D-U-N-S 20-017-0178   (BR)
**BENTALL KENNEDY (CANADA) LIMITED
PARTNERSHIP**
BENTALL REAL ESTATE SERVICES
112 4 Ave Sw Suite 1300, Calgary, AB, T2P
0H3
(403) 303-2400
Emp Here 70
SIC 6553 Cemetery subdividers and developers

D-U-N-S 20-082-6076   (BR)
BERLITZ CANADA INC
BERLITZ
237 4 Ave Sw Suite 103, Calgary, AB, T2P
4K3
(403) 265-3850
Emp Here 25
SIC 8299 Schools and educational services,
nec

D-U-N-S 24-356-9980   (SL)
BLACKFIRE EXPLORATION LTD
825 8 Ave Sw Suite 4150, Calgary, AB, T2P
2T4
(403) 289-7995
Emp Here 60   *Sales* 3,283,232
SIC 1481 NonMetallic mineral services

D-U-N-S 24-854-4363   (BR)
BLAKE, CASSELS & GRAYDON LLP
855 2 St Sw Suite 3500, Calgary, AB, T2P 4J8
(403) 260-9600
Emp Here 220
SIC 8111 Legal services

D-U-N-S 20-845-2602   (SL)
BONTERRA RESTAURANTS INC
BONTERRA TRATTARIA
101 6 St Sw Suite 120, Calgary, AB, T2P 5K7
(403) 262-8480
Emp Here 54   *Sales* 1,605,135
SIC 5812 Eating places

D-U-N-S 25-171-1560   (BR)

BORDEN LADNER GERVAIS LLP
BLG
(*Suby of* Borden Ladner Gervais LLP)
520 3 Ave Sw Suite 1900, Calgary, AB, T2P
0R3
(403) 232-9500
Emp Here 160
SIC 8111 Legal services

D-U-N-S 24-348-8124   (SL)
BOYCHUK ENERGY INC
440 2 Ave Sw Unit 1700, Calgary, AB, T2P
5E9
(403) 206-4122
Emp Here 30   *Sales* 4,240,481
SIC 4213 Trucking, except local

D-U-N-S 24-343-8140   (SL)
BOYD EXPLORATION CONSULTANTS LTD
BOYD PETRO SEARCH
800 6 Ave Sw Suite 1200, Calgary, AB, T2P
3G3
(403) 233-2455
Emp Here 20   *Sales* 1,130,795
SIC 8999 Services, nec

D-U-N-S 24-742-4398   (SL)
BOYKIW, DONALD
450 1 St Sw Suite 2500, Calgary, AB, T2P 5H1
(403) 260-7000
Emp Here 49   *Sales* 5,024,256
SIC 8111 Legal services

D-U-N-S 20-106-1616   (BR)
BROOKFIELD PROPERTIES LTD
335 8 Ave Sw Suite 800, Calgary, AB, T2P
1C9
(403) 266-8922
Emp Here 50
SIC 6531 Real estate agents and managers

D-U-N-S 20-038-1387   (BR)
BROOKFIELD PROPERTIES LTD
111 5 Ave Sw Suite 327, Calgary, AB, T2P
3Y6
(403) 265-2430
Emp Here 25
SIC 6531 Real estate agents and managers

D-U-N-S 20-747-6354   (HQ)
BUILDERS ENERGY SERVICES LTD
(*Suby of* Builders Energy Services Ltd)
250 2 St Sw Suite 1100, Calgary, AB, T2P 0C1
(403) 693-2378
Emp Here 40   *Emp Total* 750
Sales 166,184,880
SIC 1389 Oil and gas field services, nec
Pr Pr Garnet Amundson
 James Banister
 Verne Johnson
 Nicholas Kirton
 Frank Nieboer
 Michael Black

D-U-N-S 24-858-2061   (SL)
BURGENER KILPA TRICK DESIGN INTERNATIONAL
640 8 Ave Sw Suite 300, Calgary, AB, T2P
1G7
(403) 233-2525
Emp Here 50   *Sales* 6,832,640
SIC 8712 Architectural services

D-U-N-S 24-647-2328   (SL)
C & T RESOURCES LTD
C & T
520 5 Ave Sw Suite 1400, Calgary, AB, T2P
3R7
(403) 266-0930
Emp Here 25   *Sales* 23,009,920
SIC 1311 Crude petroleum and natural gas
Pr Pr Rahim Lakhoo

D-U-N-S 20-615-9683   (SL)
CASA ENERGY SERVICES CORP
630 8 Ave Sw Suite 500, Calgary, AB, T2P
1G6
(403) 264-4582
Emp Here 50   *Sales* 7,796,259

SIC 1389 Oil and gas field services, nec

D-U-N-S 24-323-9600   (BR)
CBRE LIMITED
CB RICHARD ELLIS MANAGEMENT SERVICES
530 8 Ave Sw Suite 500, Calgary, AB, T2P
3S8
(403) 536-1290
Emp Here 100
SIC 6531 Real estate agents and managers

D-U-N-S 24-667-5404   (BR)
CBRE LIMITED
530 8 Ave Sw Suite 500, Calgary, AB, T2P
3S8
(403) 263-4444
Emp Here 30
SIC 6531 Real estate agents and managers

D-U-N-S 20-013-4778   (SL)
CGG CANADA SERVICES LTD
CGG CSL
715 5 Ave Sw Suite 2200, Calgary, AB, T2P
2X6
(403) 205-6000
Emp Here 143   *Sales* 15,978,393
SIC 8713 Surveying services
 Kathleen Sendall

D-U-N-S 20-266-7296   (BR)
CH2M HILL CANADA LIMITED
(*Suby of* Ch2m Hill Companies, Ltd.)
800 6 Ave Sw Suite 1500, Calgary, AB, T2P
3G3

Emp Here 150
SIC 8711 Engineering services

D-U-N-S 25-266-4289   (BR)
CIBC MELLON TRUST COMPANY
333 7 Ave Sw Unit 600, Calgary, AB, T2P 2Z1
(403) 232-2400
Emp Here 33
SIC 6021 National commercial banks

D-U-N-S 25-293-9442   (BR)
CIBC WORLD MARKETS INC
855 2 St Sw Suite 900, Calgary, AB, T2P 4J7
(403) 260-0500
Emp Here 25
SIC 6211 Security brokers and dealers

D-U-N-S 25-366-9386   (BR)
CIBC WORLD MARKETS INC
250 6 Ave Sw, Calgary, AB, T2P 3H7
(403) 767-3587
Emp Here 100
SIC 6211 Security brokers and dealers

D-U-N-S 20-580-5265   (BR)
CIBC WORLD MARKETS INC
CIBC WOOD GUNDY
607 8 Ave Sw Suite 600, Calgary, AB, T2P
0A7
(403) 508-3200
Emp Here 200
SIC 6211 Security brokers and dealers

D-U-N-S 24-678-7985   (BR)
CIT FINANCIAL LTD
700 4 Ave Sw Suite 1070, Calgary, AB, T2P
3J4
(403) 265-5700
Emp Here 50
SIC 6153 Short-term business credit institutions, except agricultural

D-U-N-S 20-635-6102   (SL)
CMN CALGARY INC
335 8 Ave Sw Suite 1000, Calgary, AB, T2P
1C9
(403) 266-5544
Emp Here 70   *Sales* 6,566,463
SIC 6531 Real estate agents and managers
Pr Randy Fennessey
 Richard Schwann
 Carrie Stokes

D-U-N-S 25-104-9821   (HQ)
CNOOC CANADA ENERGY LTD.
801 7 Ave Sw, Calgary, AB, T2P 3P7
(403) 699-4000
Emp Here 350   *Sales* 187,370,091
SIC 1382 Oil and gas exploration services
VP Rick Beingessner

D-U-N-S 20-010-2387   (SL)
CP ENERGY MARKETING INC
505 2 St Sw Suite 84, Calgary, AB, T2P 1N8
(403) 717-4600
Emp Here 1,600   *Sales* 261,842,450
SIC 8711 Engineering services
 Stuart Anthony Lee
 Brian Tellef Vaasjo

D-U-N-S 24-025-3406   (BR)
CREIT MANAGEMENT L.P.
140 4 Ave Sw Suite 210, Calgary, AB, T2P
3N3
(403) 235-3443
Emp Here 22
SIC 6531 Real estate agents and managers

D-U-N-S 20-562-2546   (HQ)
CWC ENERGY SERVICES CORP
CWC
(*Suby of* Brookfield Capital Partners II L.P.)
205 5 Ave Sw Suite 610, Calgary, AB, T2P
2V7
(403) 264-2177
Emp Here 20   *Emp Total* 1,002
Sales 54,084,322
SIC 1382 Oil and gas exploration services
Pr Pr Duncan T. Au
 Craig Flint
VP Opers Paul Donohue
VP Opers Darwin Mcintyre
S&M/VP Bob Apps
S&M/VP Mike Dubois
 Jim Reid
 Gary L. Bentham
 Wade Mcgowan
 Daryl Austin

D-U-N-S 24-807-7117   (HQ)
CALGARY FAMILY SERVICE SOCIETY
(*Suby of* Calgary Family Service Society)
1000 8 Ave Sw Suite 200, Calgary, AB, T2P
3M7
(403) 205-5264
Emp Here 100   *Emp Total* 124
Sales 16,101,796
SIC 8322 Individual and family services
 Susan Mallon

D-U-N-S 25-622-0799   (BR)
CALGARY PARKING AUTHORITY
MCDOUGALL CENTRE
451 6 St Sw, Calgary, AB, T2P 4A2
(403) 264-4226
Emp Here 45
SIC 7521 Automobile parking

D-U-N-S 25-217-5856   (SL)
**CALGARY RAMADA DOWNTOWN LIMITED
PARTNERSHIP**
RAMADA HOTEL
708 8 Ave Sw, Calgary, AB, T2P 1H2
(403) 263-7600
Emp Here 100   *Sales* 4,377,642
SIC 7011 Hotels and motels

D-U-N-S 24-340-4899   (SL)
CALGARY TOWER FACILITIES LTD
101 9 Ave Sw, Calgary, AB, T2P 1J9
(403) 266-7171
Emp Here 100   *Sales* 2,991,389
SIC 5812 Eating places

D-U-N-S 20-152-8663   (BR)
CALGARY YOUNG MEN'S CHRISTIAN ASSOCIATION
YMCA
940 6 Ave Sw Suite 510, Calgary, AB, T2P 3T1
(403) 252-4206
Emp Here 20

SIC 7032 Sporting and recreational camps

D-U-N-S 25-325-9139   (SL)
CALTECH DESIGN INC
444 5 Ave Sw Suite 2350, Calgary, AB, T2P 2T8
(403) 216-2140
Emp Here 140   *Sales* 9,445,120
SIC 7389 Business services, nec
Pr Jim Floyd
VP VP Kelly Gerry
Garth Corsar
Gary Panasuik

D-U-N-S 24-853-4067   (SL)
CALVALLEY PETROLEUM INC
600 6 Ave Sw Suite 700, Calgary, AB, T2P 0S5
(403) 297-0490
Emp Here 114   *Sales* 92,960,000
SIC 1311 Crude petroleum and natural gas
Edmund Shimoon
Thomas E. Valentine
Gary Robertson
Thomas H. Skupa
Kenneth M. Stephenson
Nikolas Perrault
Bernard De Combret
Gerry Elms

D-U-N-S 25-456-0311   (BR)
CANACCORD GENUITY CORP
(*Suby of* Canaccord Genuity Group Inc)
450 1 St Sw Suite 2200, Calgary, AB, T2P 5H1
(403) 508-3800
Emp Here 80
SIC 6211 Security brokers and dealers

D-U-N-S 24-809-5770   (HQ)
CANADA IMPERIAL OIL LIMITED
(*Suby of* Exxon Mobil Corporation)
237 4 Ave Sw Suite 2480, Calgary, AB, T2P 0H6
(800) 567-3776
Emp Here 150   *Emp Total* 71,100
Sales 451 407,851
SIC 5172 Petroleum products, nec
Keith W Malverin

D-U-N-S 24-426-0423   (SL)
CANADIAN HORIZONS LAND INVEST-MENT CORPORATION
645 7 Ave Sw Suite 900, Calgary, AB, T2P 4G8
(403) 539-4814
Emp Here 45   *Sales* 14,300,297
SIC 6552 Subdividers and developers, nec
Pr Alan Baumann

D-U-N-S 20-700-6912   (BR)
CANADIAN IMPERIAL BANK OF COM-MERCE
CIBC
333 7 Ave Sw Suite 600, Calgary, AB, T2P 2Z1
(403) 232-2400
Emp Here 25
SIC 6021 National commercial banks

D-U-N-S 20-912-1412   (BR)
CANADIAN IMPERIAL BANK OF COM-MERCE
CIBC
309 8 Ave Sw Suite 1, Calgary, AB, T2P 1C6
(403) 974-1021
Emp Here 100
SIC 6021 National commercial banks

D-U-N-S 25-303-5679   (BR)
CANADIAN IMPERIAL BANK OF COM-MERCE
CIBC
717 7 Ave Sw, Calgary, AB, T2P 0Z3
(403) 974-2761
Emp Here 22
SIC 6021 National commercial banks

D-U-N-S 25-303-6412   (BR)
CANADIAN IMPERIAL BANK OF COM-

MERCE
CIBC
205 5 Ave Sw Suite 110, Calgary, AB, T2P 2V7
(403) 974-6326
Emp Here 20
SIC 6021 National commercial banks

D-U-N-S 24-347-2185   (BR)
CANADIAN NATIONAL STEEL CORPORA-TION
OSM TUBULAR CAMROSE
(*Suby of* EVRAZ PLC)
700 4 Ave Sw Suite 1060, Calgary, AB, T2P 3J4
(403) 263-2444
Emp Here 20
SIC 3317 Steel pipe and tubes

D-U-N-S 24-340-5292   (BR)
CANADIAN NATURAL RESOURCES LIM-ITED
324 8 Ave Sw Suite 1800, Calgary, AB, T2P 2Z2
(403) 517-6700
Emp Here 2,000
SIC 1311 Crude petroleum and natural gas

D-U-N-S 25-188-3054   (BR)
CANADIAN PACIFIC RAILWAY COMPANY
ROYAL CANADIAN PACIFIC, DIV OF
133 9 Ave Sw, Calgary, AB, T2P 2M3

Emp Here 25
SIC 4011 Railroads, line-haul operating

D-U-N-S 25-733-9978   (BR)
CANADIAN REAL ESTATE INVESTMENT TRUST
CREIT
140 4 Ave Sw Suite 210, Calgary, AB, T2P 3N3
(403) 235-3443
Emp Here 20
SIC 6531 Real estate agents and managers

D-U-N-S 25-316-0493   (BR)
CANADIAN WESTERN BANK
606 4 St Sw Suite 400, Calgary, AB, T2P 1T1
(403) 262-8700
Emp Here 30
SIC 6021 National commercial banks

D-U-N-S 24-647-5529   (SL)
CANPAR HOLDINGS LTD
144 4 Ave Sw Suite 400, Calgary, AB, T2P 3N4
(403) 221-0800
Emp Here 54   *Sales* 49,838,080
SIC 1311 Crude petroleum and natural gas
Russell J Hiscock
Peter Harrison
Pr Pr William Ingram
Thomas Mullane
Darren Gunderson

D-U-N-S 20-995-3157   (SL)
CANTAK CORPORATION
355 4 Ave Sw Suite 1050, Calgary, AB, T2P 0J1
(403) 269-5536
Emp Here 21   *Sales* 10,931,016
SIC 5051 Metals service centers and offices
Pr Pr C. Allan Cheng
Scott Gerla

D-U-N-S 20-699-7558   (HQ)
CANYON SERVICES GROUP INC
645 7 Ave Sw Suite 2900, Calgary, AB, T2P 4G8
(403) 266-0202
Emp Here 200   *Emp Total* 1,194
Sales 177,193,794
SIC 1389 Oil and gas field services, nec
Pr Pr Brad Fedora
VP Fin Barry Obrien
Todd Thue
VP Chuck Vozniak

VP Quentin Walker
Robert Skilnick
VP Todd Den Engelsen
Sls Dir David Westlund
Garnet Olson
Gord Haycraft

D-U-N-S 20-177-6379   (BR)
CARGILL LIMITED
440 2 Ave Sw Suite 200, Calgary, AB, T2P 5E9
(403) 218-1000
Emp Here 25
SIC 4924 Natural gas distribution

D-U-N-S 20-691-3514   (SL)
CARGILL POWER AND GAS MARKETS LTD
440 2 Ave Sw Suite 200, Calgary, AB, T2P 5E9
(403) 218-1000
Emp Here 25   *Sales* 10,650,880
SIC 4924 Natural gas distribution
Greg Page

D-U-N-S 20-522-6566   (BR)
CARLSON WAGONLIT CANADA
CARLSON WAGONLIP TRAVEL
645 7 Ave Sw Suite 350, Calgary, AB, T2P 4G8
(403) 508-3000
Emp Here 45
SIC 4724 Travel agencies

D-U-N-S 24-387-5593   (HQ)
CENOVUS ENERGY INC
(*Suby of* Cenovus Energy Inc)
500 Centre St Se, Calgary, AB, T2P 0M5
(403) 766-2000
Emp Here 1,386   *Emp Total* 2,775
Sales 820,960,832
SIC 1382 Oil and gas exploration services
Pr Pr Brian Ferguson
Ex VP Harbir Chhina
Ex VP Judy Fairburn
Ex VP Kieron Mcfadyen
Ex VP Robert Pease
Ex VP Al Reid
Ivor Ruste
Ex VP Drew Zieglgansberger
Patrick Daniel
Susan Dabarno

D-U-N-S 20-916-2325   (BR)
CENOVUS ENERGY MARKETING SER-VICES LTD
SIRC
(*Suby of* Cenovus Energy Inc)
421 7 Ave Sw, Calgary, AB, T2P 4K9
(403) 544-4485
Emp Here 30
SIC 1389 Oil and gas field services, nec

D-U-N-S 25-409-2646   (SL)
CENTURION ENERGY INTERNATIONAL INC
205 5 Ave Sw Suite 800, Calgary, AB, T2P 2V7
(403) 263-6002
Emp Here 42   *Sales* 37,378,560
SIC 1382 Oil and gas exploration services
Said S Arrata
M.N. Mike Zayat
VP VP A.D. Tony Anton
VP Greg Renwick

D-U-N-S 24-267-1415   (BR)
CHAMPION TECHNOLOGIES ULC
Gd Lcd 1, Calgary, AB, T2P 2G8
(403) 234-7881
Emp Here 50
SIC 5169 Chemicals and allied products, nec

D-U-N-S 20-441-2076   (HQ)
CHAMPION TECHNOLOGIES ULC
815 8 Ave Sw Suite 1400, Calgary, AB, T2P 3P2

(403) 234-7881
Emp Here 26   *Emp Total* 47,565
Sales 62,005,248
SIC 5169 Chemicals and allied products, nec
Dir Scott Knutson
Dir Karen Macpherson
Dir Richard Wong
Loren Ross
Dir John Johnson
Dir Steve Lindley

D-U-N-S 25-094-3925   (SL)
CHARLES TAYLOR CONSULTING SER-VICES (CANADA) INC
CHARLES TAYLOR ADJUSTING
321 6 Ave Sw Suite 910, Calgary, AB, T2P 3H3
(403) 266-3336
Emp Here 24   *Sales* 4,523,563
SIC 6411 Insurance agents, brokers, and ser-vice

D-U-N-S 24-962-8132   (SL)
CHEVRON RESOURCES LTD
(*Suby of* Chevron Corporation)
500 5 Ave Sw Suite 700, Calgary, AB, T2P 0L7
(403) 234-5000
Emp Here 250   *Sales* 216,264,506
SIC 1311 Crude petroleum and natural gas
Wayne Scott

D-U-N-S 25-681-8782   (SL)
CHICAGO CHOP HOUSE LTD, THE
604 8 Ave Sw, Calgary, AB, T2P 1G4

Emp Here 50   *Sales* 1,532,175
SIC 5812 Eating places

D-U-N-S 20-075-2798   (HQ)
CHURGIN, ARNOLD SHOES LIMITED
(*Suby of* Churgin, Arnold Shoes Limited)
227 8 Ave Sw, Calgary, AB, T2P 1B7
(403) 262-3366
Emp Here 22   *Emp Total* 65
Sales 3,939,878
SIC 5661 Shoe stores

D-U-N-S 24-418-4987   (BR)
CINEPLEX ODEON CORPORATION
EAU CLAIRE MARKET CINEMAS
200 Barclay Parade Sw Unit 90, Calgary, AB, T2P 4R5
(403) 263-3167
Emp Here 20
SIC 7832 Motion picture theaters, except drive-in

D-U-N-S 24-850-7084   (SL)
CITADEL WEST GENERAL PARTNER LTD
505 3 St Sw Suite 200, Calgary, AB, T2P 3E6
(403) 213-9716
Emp Here 300   *Sales* 38,885,760
SIC 6531 Real estate agents and managers
VP Stephen Taylor
Prin Kori Creighton

D-U-N-S 20-524-5876   (SL)
COASTAL ENERGY
520 5 Ave Sw Suite 1400, Calgary, AB, T2P 3R7
(403) 266-1930
Emp Here 25   *Sales* 21,579,334
SIC 1311 Crude petroleum and natural gas
Pt Rahim Lakhoo
Pt Azim Lakhoo
Pt Nazir Meghani
Pt Mahedi Meghani

D-U-N-S 20-245-9454   (BR)
CONOCOPHILLIPS WESTERN CANADA PARTNERSHIP
CONOCOPHILLIPS CANADA RESOURCES
401 9th Ave Sw, Calgary, AB, T2P 2H7
(403) 260-8000
Emp Here 1,700
SIC 1311 Crude petroleum and natural gas

D-U-N-S 20-051-8707   (HQ)

CONOCOPHILLIPS WESTERN CANADA PARTNERSHIP
CONOCOPHILLIPS CANADA
401 9 Ave Sw Suite 1600, Calgary, AB, T2P 3C5
(403) 233-4000
Emp Here 2,500   *Emp Total* 13,300
Sales 23,259,407,800
SIC 1382 Oil and gas exploration services
Genl Pt Brent Smolik

D-U-N-S 25-955-9425   (BR)
CONSEILLERS EN GESTION ET INFORMATIQUE CGI INC
CGI
444 7 Ave Sw Suite 200, Calgary, AB, T2P 0X8
(403) 218-8300
Emp Here 70
SIC 7371 Custom computer programming services

D-U-N-S 20-038-9570   (SL)
CORUS AUDIO & ADVERTISING SERVICES LTD
CORUS ENTERTAINMENT
630 3 Ave Sw Suite 501, Calgary, AB, T2P 4L4
(403) 716-6500
Emp Here 60   *Sales* 4,900,111
SIC 4832 Radio broadcasting stations

D-U-N-S 25-096-0879   (BR)
CORUS ENTERTAINMENT INC
CFGQ-FM
630 3 Ave Sw Suite 105, Calgary, AB, T2P 4L4
(403) 716-6500
Emp Here 100
SIC 7311 Advertising agencies

D-U-N-S 24-420-1203   (BR)
CORUS ENTERTAINMENT INC
CKRY-FM
630 3 Ave Sw Suite 501, Calgary, AB, T2P 4L4
(403) 716-6500
Emp Here 65
SIC 4832 Radio broadcasting stations

D-U-N-S 24-126-0384   (BR)
CUSHMAN & WAKEFIELD LTD
CUSHMAN & WAKEFIELD
(*Suby of* Cushman & Wakefield Holdings, Inc.)
111 5 Ave Sw Suite 1730, Calgary, AB, T2P 3Y6
(403) 261-1111
Emp Here 42
SIC 6531 Real estate agents and managers

D-U-N-S 24-393-1503   (SL)
DC ENERGY SERVICES LP
706 7 Ave Sw Suite 400, Calgary, AB, T2P 0Z1

Emp Here 20   *Sales* 7,362,000
SIC 1381 Drilling oil and gas wells
Genl Mgr Gerry Crowford
Opers Mgr Clint Galoury

D-U-N-S 20-075-9306   (HQ)
DNOW CANADA ULC
DISTRIBUTION NOW
(*Suby of* Now Inc.)
635 8 Ave Sw Unit 1800, Calgary, AB, T2P 3M3
(403) 531-5600
Emp Here 40   *Emp Total* 4,500
Sales 62,016,595
SIC 5084 Industrial machinery and equipment
Pr Pr Michael West
  Robert Mcclinton
  Derren Newell
  Michael Hogan
  John Kennedy
  Kjell-Erik Oestdahl
  Bradley Thompson
  Keith Turnbull

D-U-N-S 20-010-3377   (SL)
DO2 TECHNOLOGIES INC
(*Suby of* Automatic Data Processing, Inc.)

255 5 Ave Sw Suite 1000, Calgary, AB, T2P 3G6
(403) 205-2550
Emp Here 70   *Sales* 9,138,560
SIC 7372 Prepackaged software
Pr Pr Rod Munro
Ex VP Doug Spackman
Ex VP Deborah Close
Dir John Stewart
Dir Hayward Walls

D-U-N-S 25-539-4850   (HQ)
DAVID APLIN & ASSOCIATES INC
DAVID APLIN GROUP
(*Suby of* Pinellas Enterprises Inc)
700 2 St Sw Suite 3850, Calgary, AB, T2P 2W2
(403) 261-9000
Emp Here 150   *Emp Total* 5
Sales 39,577,818
SIC 7361 Employment agencies
  David Aplin
  Grace Elizabeth Aplin

D-U-N-S 20-934-9062   (BR)
DAVIS LLP
250 2 St Sw Suite 1000, Calgary, AB, T2P 0C1
(403) 296-4470
Emp Here 100
SIC 8111 Legal services

D-U-N-S 25-998-6792   (SL)
DEGOLYER AND MACNAUGHTON CANADA INC
(*Suby of* D&M Holding Inc.)
311 6 Ave Sw Suite 1430, Calgary, AB, T2P 3H2
(403) 266-8680
Emp Here 25   *Sales* 2,188,821
SIC 8711 Engineering services

D-U-N-S 20-341-1967   (BR)
DELOITTE LLP
850 2 St Sw Suite 700, Calgary, AB, T2P 0R8
(403) 267-1700
Emp Here 500
SIC 8721 Accounting, auditing, and bookkeeping

D-U-N-S 20-040-9113   (BR)
DENTONS CANADA LLP
(*Suby of* Dentons Canada LLP)
850 2 St Sw Suite 1500, Calgary, AB, T2P 0R8
(403) 268-7000
Emp Here 343
SIC 8111 Legal services

D-U-N-S 24-806-9940   (BR)
DESIGN GROUP STAFFING INC
DESIGN GROUP, THE
800 5 Ave Sw Suite 1500, Calgary, AB, T2P 3T6
(403) 233-2788
Emp Here 35
SIC 7361 Employment agencies

D-U-N-S 20-847-7898   (BR)
DEVENCORE LTEE
NEWMARK KNIGHT FRANK DEVENCORE
736 6 Ave Sw Suite 2020, Calgary, AB, T2P 3T7
(403) 265-9966
Emp Here 20
SIC 3531 Construction machinery

D-U-N-S 24-347-4053   (HQ)
DEVON CANADA CORPORATION
400 3 Ave Sw Suite 2000, Calgary, AB, T2P 4H2
(403) 232-7100
Emp Here 200   *Emp Total* 5,000
Sales 795,131,793
SIC 1311 Crude petroleum and natural gas
  J. Larry Nichols
Dir John Richels
Pr Rob Dutton
VP VP Thomas Mitchell
  Murray Brown

Treas Jeffrey Ritenour
  Chris R. Seasons
VP Fin VP Fin Jeff A. Agosta
Sec Janice A. Dobbs

D-U-N-S 25-313-9307   (BR)
DIRECT ENERGY MARKETING LIMITED
JUST DIRECT ENERGY
111 5 Ave Sw Suite 1000, Calgary, AB, T2P 3Y6
(403) 266-6393
Emp Here 300
SIC 1311 Crude petroleum and natural gas

D-U-N-S 20-920-7476   (SL)
DISTRESS CENTRE CALGARY
1010 8 Ave Sw Suite 300, Calgary, AB, T2P 1J2
(403) 266-1601
Emp Here 50   *Sales* 1,969,939
SIC 8322 Individual and family services

D-U-N-S 20-890-5005   (BR)
DIVERSITY TECHNOLOGIES CORPORATION
CANAMERA UNITED SUPPLY
800 6 Ave Sw Suite 360, Calgary, AB, T2P 3G3
(403) 265-4401
Emp Here 20
SIC 2899 Chemical preparations, nec

D-U-N-S 24-358-2199   (BR)
DIVINE HARDWOOD FLOORING LTD
235075 Ryan Rd Se, Calgary, AB, T2P 2G6

Emp Here 20
SIC 4225 General warehousing and storage

D-U-N-S 20-831-1068   (BR)
DOMINION OF CANADA GENERAL INSURANCE COMPANY, THE
(*Suby of* The Travelers Companies Inc)
777 8 Ave Sw Suite 1700, Calgary, AB, T2P 3R5
(403) 231-6600
Emp Here 100
SIC 6411 Insurance agents, brokers, and service

D-U-N-S 24-868-5901   (HQ)
DOW AGROSCIENCES CANADA INC
DAS
(*Suby of* The Dow Chemical Company)
450 1 St Sw Suite 2100, Calgary, AB, T2P 5H1
(403) 735-8800
Emp Here 55   *Emp Total* 56,000
Sales 25,362,500
SIC 2879 Agricultural chemicals, nec
Pr Jim Wispinski

D-U-N-S 24-014-2240   (BR)
DRAKE INTERNATIONAL INC
101 6 Ave Sw Suite 420, Calgary, AB, T2P 3P4
(403) 266-8971
Emp Here 30
SIC 7361 Employment agencies

D-U-N-S 24-906-9337   (HQ)
E.O.S. PIPELINE & FACILITIES INC
736 6 Ave Sw Suite 1205, Calgary, AB, T2P 3T7
(403) 232-8446
Emp Here 25   *Emp Total* 30
Sales 22,615,896
SIC 1623 Water, sewer, and utility lines
Pr Pr Dean Peterson

D-U-N-S 20-515-0225   (BR)
EMC CORPORATION OF CANADA
500 4 Ave Sw Suite 1410, Calgary, AB, T2P 2V6
(403) 263-9400
Emp Here 24
SIC 3577 Computer peripheral equipment, nec

D-U-N-S 20-767-0662   (HQ)

EOG RESOURCES CANADA INC
700 9 Ave Sw Suite 1300, Calgary, AB, T2P 3V4
(403) 297-9100
Emp Here 100   *Emp Total* 2,650
Sales 13,806,455,248
SIC 1311 Crude petroleum and natural gas
  Mark G Papa
Pr Pr Ed Segner
  Lawrence E Fenwick
Ex VP Gary Thomas
Dir Donald Greenfield

D-U-N-S 20-706-9134   (BR)
EPCOR UTILITIES INC
2 St Sw, Calgary, AB, T2P 1N8

Emp Here 90
SIC 4911 Electric services

D-U-N-S 24-125-1771   (BR)
ESIT CANADA ENTERPRISE SERVICES CO
ESIT CANADA ENTERPRISE SERVICES CO
(*Suby of* Dxc Technology Company)
240 4 Ave Sw Suite 500, Calgary, AB, T2P 4H4
(403) 508-4500
Emp Here 350
SIC 7379 Computer related services, nec

D-U-N-S 24-159-2203   (BR)
ESIT CANADA ENTERPRISE SERVICES CO
ESIT CANADA ENTERPRISE SERVICES CO
(*Suby of* Dxc Technology Company)
150 6 Ave Sw Suite 3600, Calgary, AB, T2P 3Y7

Emp Here 40
SIC 5045 Computers, peripherals, and software

D-U-N-S 24-161-0179   (BR)
ECONOMICAL MUTUAL INSURANCE COMPANY
ECONOMICAL INSURANCE GROUP
801 6 Ave Sw Suite 2700, Calgary, AB, T2P 3W2
(403) 265-8590
Emp Here 100
SIC 6331 Fire, marine, and casualty insurance

D-U-N-S 20-191-4905   (HQ)
ENBRIDGE INCOME FUND
425 1 St Sw Suite 3000, Calgary, AB, T2P 3L8
(403) 767-3642
Emp Here 269   *Emp Total* 10
Sales 303,297,630
SIC 4922 Natural gas transmission
  Ernest Roberts
Dir Richard Bird
Dir Laura Cillis
Dir Brian Frank
Dir George Lewis
Dir Bruce Waterman
Dir John Whelen

D-U-N-S 25-389-1246   (SL)
ENBRIDGE INTERNATIONAL INC
425 1 St Sw Suite 3000, Calgary, AB, T2P 3L8

Emp Here 25   *Sales* 2,334,742
SIC 8742 Management consulting services

D-U-N-S 24-598-8464   (HQ)
ENERPLUS GLOBAL ENERGY MANAGEMENT CO
333 7 Ave Sw Suite 3000, Calgary, AB, T2P 2Z1
(403) 298-2200
Emp Here 200   *Emp Total* 472
Sales 57,692,317
SIC 8741 Management services
Pr Pr Gordon Kerr
VP Fin VP Fin Robert J Waters
VP Fin Wayne T Foch

D-U-N-S 24-807-6390   (HQ)
ENSIGN DRILLING INC

400 5 Ave Sw Suite 1000, Calgary, AB, T2P 0L6
(403) 262-1361
Emp Here 75   *Emp Total* 3,718
Sales 948,861,850
SIC 1381 Drilling oil and gas wells
Pr Pr Robert Geddes
 Selby Porter
 Glenn Dagenais

D-U-N-S 24-523-2207   (SL)
EQUAL ENERGY CORP
500 4 Ave Sw Suite 2700, Calgary, AB, T2P 2V6
(403) 263-0262
Emp Here 40   *Sales* 36,724,900
SIC 1382 Oil and gas exploration services
Pr Pr Don Klapko
Dir John Brussa
Dir Peter Carpenter
Dir Michael E. Doyle
Dir Victor Dusik
Dir Roger Giovanetto
Dir Brian Illing

D-U-N-S 24-439-7568   (BR)
ERNST & YOUNG LLP
(*Suby of* Ernst & Young LLP)
440 2 Ave Sw Suite 1000, Calgary, AB, T2P 5E9
(403) 290-4100
Emp Here 200
SIC 8721 Accounting, auditing, and book-keeping

D-U-N-S 24-827-5831   (SL)
EXPAND ENERGY CORPORATION
404 6 Ave Sw Unit 645, Calgary, AB, T2P 0R9

Emp Here 20   *Sales* 22,478,640
SIC 1382 Oil and gas exploration services
Pr Russell Longley
Recvr Guy William Lynch Odhams

D-U-N-S 20-077-0873   (HQ)
EXXONMOBIL CANADA LTD
EMC
(*Suby of* Exxon Mobil Corporation)
237 4 Ave Sw, Calgary, AB, T2P 4K3
(403) 232-5300
Emp Here 500   *Emp Total* 71,100
Sales 669,706,265
SIC 1311 Crude petroleum and natural gas
Pr Pr Jerry Anderson
 Michael Morin
 Wayne Kubasek

D-U-N-S 20-119-7188   (SL)
EXXONMOBIL CANADA ENERGY
237 4 Ave Sw, Calgary, AB, T2P 4K3
(403) 260-7910
Emp Here 150   *Sales* 211,270,162
SIC 1382 Oil and gas exploration services
Genl Mgr Tim Cutt

D-U-N-S 24-099-2581   (BR)
FRHI HOTELS & RESORTS (CANADA) INC
133 9 Ave Sw, Calgary, AB, T2P 2M3
(403) 262-1234
Emp Here 300
SIC 7011 Hotels and motels

D-U-N-S 20-635-2890   (BR)
FAIRMONT HOTELS & RESORTS INC
FAIRMONT PALLISER, THE
133 9 Ave Sw, Calgary, AB, T2P 2M3
(403) 262-3473
Emp Here 375
SIC 7011 Hotels and motels

D-U-N-S 24-103-8632   (BR)
FAIRMONT HOTELS & RESORTS INC
PALLISER, THE
133 9 Ave Sw, Calgary, AB, T2P 2M3
(403) 262-1234
Emp Here 300
SIC 7011 Hotels and motels

D-U-N-S 25-063-1421   (BR)
FAIRMONT HOTELS & RESORTS INC
SHERATON SUITES CALGARY EAU CLAIRE
255 Barclay Parade Sw, Calgary, AB, T2P 5C2
(403) 266-7200
Emp Here 400
SIC 7011 Hotels and motels

D-U-N-S 20-773-8654   (BR)
FASKEN MARTINEAU DUMOULIN LLP
350 7 Ave Sw Suite 3400, Calgary, AB, T2P 3N9
(403) 261-5350
Emp Here 50
SIC 8111 Legal services

D-U-N-S 20-991-5610   (SL)
FEKETE ASSOCIATES INC
540 5 Ave Sw Suite 2000, Calgary, AB, T2P 0M2
(403) 213-4200
Emp Here 182   *Sales* 27,681,120
SIC 8711 Engineering services
Ch Bd Louis Mattar
Pr Pr David Dunn
VP VP Ed Ferguson

D-U-N-S 20-180-9212   (HQ)
FERUS INC
(*Suby of* The Energy & Minerals Group)
401 9 Ave Sw Suite 916, Calgary, AB, T2P 3C5
(403) 517-8777
Emp Here 50   *Emp Total* 2
Sales 2,707,034,375
SIC 4925 Gas production and/or distribution
Pr Richard Brown
 Joe Ladouceur
 John Raymond
VP Sean Lalani
Dir Jeff Ball
Dir Jeff Rawls
Dir Robert Rooney
Dir Henry Sykes
 Ronald Porter

D-U-N-S 20-321-6333   (BR)
FIDUCIAIRES DU FONDS DE PLACEMENT IMMOBILIER COMINAR, LES
FIDUCIAIRES DU FONDS DE PLACEMENT IMMOBILIER COMIN
700 2 St Sw Suite 400, Calgary, AB, T2P 2W1
(403) 296-2916
Emp Here 20
SIC 6719 Holding companies, nec

D-U-N-S 20-007-9767   (BR)
FIELD LLP
444 7 Ave Sw Suite 400, Calgary, AB, T2P 0X8
(403) 260-8500
Emp Here 80
SIC 8111 Legal services

D-U-N-S 20-306-3540   (BR)
FIERA CAPITAL CORPORATION
FIERA CAPITAL PRIVATE WEALTH
607 8 Ave Sw Suite 300, Calgary, AB, T2P 0A7
(403) 699-9000
Emp Here 20
SIC 6282 Investment advice

D-U-N-S 25-325-8412   (BR)
FINANCIERE BANQUE NATIONALE INC
NATIONAL BANK FINANCIAL
450 1 St Sw Suite 2800, Calgary, AB, T2P 5H1
(403) 531-8400
Emp Here 45
SIC 6211 Security brokers and dealers

D-U-N-S 24-023-9264   (BR)
FINANCIERE BANQUE NATIONALE INC
NATIONAL BANK FINANCIAL
450 1 St Sw Suite 2800, Calgary, AB, T2P 5H1
(403) 531-8400
Emp Here 65

SIC 6211 Security brokers and dealers

D-U-N-S 24-420-0304   (SL)
FIRCROFT (CANADA) LIMITED
205 5 Ave Sw Suite 3300, Calgary, AB, T2P 2V7
(403) 265-6960
Emp Here 20   *Sales* 17,338,854
SIC 1311 Crude petroleum and natural gas
Dir Julie Bowman

D-U-N-S 20-838-2494   (BR)
FIREMASTER OILFIELD SERVICES INC
441 5 Ave Sw Suite 570, Calgary, AB, T2P 2V1
(403) 266-1811
Emp Here 150
SIC 1389 Oil and gas field services, nec

D-U-N-S 20-200-0795   (BR)
FIRST NATIONAL FINANCIAL CORPORATION
800 5 Ave Sw Suite 600, Calgary, AB, T2P 3T6
(403) 509-0900
Emp Here 70
SIC 6162 Mortgage bankers and loan correspondents

D-U-N-S 20-989-5556   (HQ)
FOOTHILLS PIPE LINES LTD
450 1 St Sw, Calgary, AB, T2P 5H1
(403) 920-2000
Emp Here 44   *Emp Total* 7,165
Sales 8,463,441
SIC 4922 Natural gas transmission
 Dennis Mcconaghy
 Anthony Palmer
 David Kohlenberg
 Karl Johannson

D-U-N-S 20-955-2871   (SL)
FORT ENERGY CORP
444 7 Ave Sw Suite 1000, Calgary, AB, T2P 0X8
(403) 770-0333
Emp Here 20   *Sales* 18,666,800
SIC 1311 Crude petroleum and natural gas
Pr Pr John Baker
 Paul O'donoghue

D-U-N-S 25-700-6929   (SL)
FRACTION ENERGY SERVICES LTD
2900 255 5th Ave Sw, Calgary, AB, T2P 3G6
(403) 385-4300
Emp Here 150   *Sales* 27,633,407
SIC 1389 Oil and gas field services, nec
Pr Pr Brad Fedora

D-U-N-S 24-345-9984   (BR)
FRANKLIN TEMPLETON INVESTMENTS CORP
BISSETT INVESTMENT MANAGEMENT
(*Suby of* Franklin Resources, Inc.)
350 7 Ave Sw Suite 3000, Calgary, AB, T2P 3N9
(403) 266-4664
Emp Here 60
SIC 6282 Investment advice

D-U-N-S 25-097-2262   (SL)
FREEHOLD RESOURCES LTD
(*Suby of* Freehold Royalties Ltd)
144 4 Ave Sw Suite 400, Calgary, AB, T2P 3N4
(403) 221-0802
Emp Here 60   *Sales* 77,962,590
SIC 2911 Petroleum refining
Pr Pr William O Ingram
 David Sandmeyer
 Nolan Blades
 Harry Campbell
Dir Tullio Cedraschi
Dir Michael Maher
Dir Peter Harrison

D-U-N-S 25-292-0731   (BR)
FUJITSU CONSEIL (CANADA) INC
FUJITSU CONSULTING

606 4 St Sw Suite 1500, Calgary, AB, T2P 1T1

Emp Here 110
SIC 7379 Computer related services, nec

D-U-N-S 20-174-7388   (BR)
GDI SERVICES (CANADA) LP
400 3 Ave Sw, Calgary, AB, T2P 4H2
(403) 232-8402
Emp Here 350
SIC 7349 Building maintenance services, nec

D-U-N-S 25-998-4250   (BR)
GWL REALTY ADVISORS INC
530 8 Ave Sw Suite 1900, Calgary, AB, T2P 3S8
(403) 777-0410
Emp Here 50
SIC 6282 Investment advice

D-U-N-S 25-056-9886   (BR)
GAP (CANADA) INC
BANANA REPUBLIC
(*Suby of* The Gap Inc)
317 7 Ave Sw Unit 228, Calgary, AB, T2P 2Y9
(403) 264-8886
Emp Here 40
SIC 5651 Family clothing stores

D-U-N-S 24-334-8088   (SL)
GEMINI ENGINEERING LIMITED
GENSOLUTIONS
839 5 Ave Sw Suite 400, Calgary, AB, T2P 3C8
(403) 255-2916
Emp Here 120   *Sales* 15,258,880
SIC 8711 Engineering services
Pr Carl Johnson
 Marlene Quiring
CFO Robert Brookwell

D-U-N-S 24-854-7341   (BR)
GENERAL ELECTRIC CAPITAL CANADA
GE CAPITAL
(*Suby of* General Electric Company)
530 8 Ave Sw Suite 2120, Calgary, AB, T2P 3S8

Emp Here 25
SIC 6153 Short-term business credit institutions, except agricultural

D-U-N-S 20-280-1320   (BR)
GOLDMAN SACHS CANADA INC
(*Suby of* The Goldman Sachs Group Inc)
855 2 St Sw Suite 3835, Calgary, AB, T2P 4J8
(403) 233-3445
Emp Here 40
SIC 6211 Security brokers and dealers

D-U-N-S 20-579-8791   (BR)
GOVERNMENT OF THE PROVINCE OF ALBERTA
PROPERTY MANAGEMENT - CALGARY AND AREA
620 7 Ave Sw Rm 802, Calgary, AB, T2P 0Y8
(403) 297-6190
Emp Here 34
SIC 7349 Building maintenance services, nec

D-U-N-S 20-579-9062   (BR)
GOVERNMENT OF THE PROVINCE OF ALBERTA
CALGARY CROWN PROSECUTORS OFFICE, THE
332 6 Ave Sw Suite 600, Calgary, AB, T2P 0B2
(403) 297-8444
Emp Here 170
SIC 8111 Legal services

D-U-N-S 20-114-4453   (BR)
GOWLING WLG (CANADA) LLP
GOWLINGS
421 7 Ave Sw Unit 1600, Calgary, AB, T2P 4K9
(403) 298-1000
Emp Here 213

SIC 8111 Legal services

D-U-N-S 20-768-7757   (BR)
GRANT THORNTON LLP
CAPSERVCO
833 4 Ave Sw Suite 900, Calgary, AB, T2P 3T5
(403) 260-2500
Emp Here 40
SIC 8721 Accounting, auditing, and book-keeping

D-U-N-S 20-233-2230   (BR)
GREAT-WEST LIFE ASSURANCE COMPANY, THE
GROUP SALES AND SERVICES
300 5 Ave Sw Suite 1400, Calgary, AB, T2P 3C4
(403) 515-5900
Emp Here 60
SIC 6411 Insurance agents, brokers, and service

D-U-N-S 20-652-2562   (BR)
GREAT-WEST LIFE ASSURANCE COMPANY, THE
734 7 Ave Sw Suite 1101, Calgary, AB, T2P 3P8

Emp Here 36
SIC 6411 Insurance agents, brokers, and service

D-U-N-S 24-677-9115   (SL)
GRIZZLY OIL SANDS ULC
(*Suby of* Grizzly Holdings Inc)
605 5 Ave Sw Suite 2700, Calgary, AB, T2P 3H5
(403) 930-6400
Emp Here 45   *Sales* 38,918,188
SIC 1311 Crude petroleum and natural gas
CEO John Pears
Dir Mike Liddell
Dir Antony Lundy

D-U-N-S 20-082-9294   (BR)
GROUPE CONSEIL RES PUBLICA INC
NATIONAL PUBLIC RELATIONS CALGARY
(*Suby of* Groupe Conseil RES Publica Inc)
800 6 Ave Sw Suite 1600, Calgary, AB, T2P 3G3
(403) 531-0331
Emp Here 35
SIC 8743 Public relations services

D-U-N-S 20-769-9133   (HQ)
H & R BLOCK CANADA, INC
CASH BACK
(*Suby of* H&R Block, Inc.)
700 2 St Sw Suite 2600, Calgary, AB, T2P 2W2
(403) 254-8689
Emp Here 55   *Emp Total* 97,200
Sales 33,197,119
SIC 7291 Tax return preparation services
Rgnl VP Peter Bruno
Rgnl VP Renee Cillis
Sr VP Robert Luhen
Ex VP Todd Mccallum
VP Fin Terry Solomon
Dir Diane Barkley

D-U-N-S 24-702-9853   (BR)
HSBC BANK CANADA
407 8 Ave Sw, Calgary, AB, T2P 1E5
(403) 261-8910
Emp Here 30
SIC 6021 National commercial banks

D-U-N-S 25-095-0532   (BR)
HSBC SECURITIES (CANADA) INC
407 8 Ave Sw Suite 800, Calgary, AB, T2P 1E5
(403) 218-3838
Emp Here 25
SIC 6211 Security brokers and dealers

D-U-N-S 24-041-0576   (BR)
HALF, ROBERT CANADA INC

OFFICE TEAM
(*Suby of* Robert Half International Inc.)
888 3 St Sw Suite 4200, Calgary, AB, T2P 5C5
(403) 263-7266
Emp Here 40
SIC 7361 Employment agencies

D-U-N-S 25-375-1895   (BR)
HALF, ROBERT CANADA INC
ACCOUNTEMPS
(*Suby of* Robert Half International Inc.)
888 3 St Sw Suite 4200, Calgary, AB, T2P 5C5
(403) 410-6320
Emp Here 30
SIC 7361 Employment agencies

D-U-N-S 20-162-4314   (BR)
HALF, ROBERT CANADA INC
MANAGEMENT RESOURCES
(*Suby of* Robert Half International Inc.)
888 3 St Sw Suite 4200, Calgary, AB, T2P 5C5
(403) 264-5301
Emp Here 30
SIC 7361 Employment agencies

D-U-N-S 24-347-0069   (HQ)
HALLMARK TUBULARS LTD
HALLMARK TECHNICAL SERVICES DIV OF
308 4 Ave Sw Suite 400, Calgary, AB, T2P 0H7
(403) 266-3807
Emp Here 45   *Emp Total* 911
Sales 66,961,202
SIC 5051 Metals service centers and offices
Pr Henry Ewert
Ch Bd Dale Albert
S&M/VP Greg Northcott
VP John Palazeti
VP Opers Jim Mitchell
  Dean Kueber

D-U-N-S 25-293-6851   (BR)
HARRY ROSEN INC
HARRY ROSEN MENS WEAR
317 7 Ave Sw, Calgary, AB, T2P 2Y9
(403) 294-0992
Emp Here 20
SIC 5611 Men's and boys' clothing stores

D-U-N-S 20-181-7959   (HQ)
HARVEST OPERATIONS CORP
700 2nd St Sw Suite 1500, Calgary, AB, T2P 2W1
(403) 265-1178
Emp Here 250   *Sales* 212,500,009
SIC 1311 Crude petroleum and natural gas
Pr Pr Jeff Tooth
  Sungki Lee
  Taeheon Jang
VP Jon Lowes
VP Fin Grant Ukrainetz
VP Doug Walker
Sec Mark Tysowski
  Seungkook Lee
  Allan Buchignani
  Randall Henderson

D-U-N-S 24-369-8839   (BR)
HATCH CORPORATION
840 7 Ave Sw Suite 1250, Calgary, AB, T2P 3G2
(403) 269-9555
Emp Here 60
SIC 8711 Engineering services

D-U-N-S 25-313-9588   (HQ)
HAWORTH, LTD
222 5 Ave Sw Suite 112, Calgary, AB, T2P 0L1
(403) 203-6000
Emp Here 1,050   *Emp Total* 5,950
Sales 119,802,513
SIC 2542 Partitions and fixtures, except wood

D-U-N-S 20-525-8077   (BR)
HAYWOOD SECURITIES INC
808 1 St Sw Suite 301, Calgary, AB, T2P 1M9
(403) 509-1900
Emp Here 35

SIC 6211 Security brokers and dealers

D-U-N-S 20-986-8970   (BR)
HEENAN BLAIKIE S.E.N.C.R.L.
425 1 St Sw Unit 1200, Calgary, AB, T2P 3L8

Emp Here 52
SIC 8111 Legal services

D-U-N-S 24-139-1726   (BR)
HEENAN BLAIKIE S.E.N.C.R.L.
215 9 Ave Sw Suite 1900, Calgary, AB, T2P 1K3

Emp Here 50
SIC 8111 Legal services

D-U-N-S 24-125-8008   (BR)
HEWITT ASSOCIATES CORP
202 6 Ave Sw Suite 1700, Calgary, AB, T2P 2R9

Emp Here 35
SIC 8999 Services, nec

D-U-N-S 25-206-2427   (HQ)
HIGH ARCTIC ENERGY SERVICES LIMITED PARTNERSHIP
(*Suby of* High Arctic Energy Services Limited Partnership)
700 2 St Sw Suite 500, Calgary, AB, T2P 2W1
(403) 508-7836
Emp Here 100   *Emp Total* 450
Sales 122,865,819
SIC 1381 Drilling oil and gas wells
Ch Bd Michael Binnion
  Thomas Alford
  Brian Peters
  Dan Beaulieu
  Simon Batcup
  Steven Vasey
  Daniel Bordessa
  Joe Oliver
  Ember Shmitt

D-U-N-S 24-157-7816   (BR)
HOLT, RENFREW & CIE, LIMITEE
HOLT RENFREW
8 Ave Sw Unit 510, Calgary, AB, T2P 4H9
(403) 269-7341
Emp Here 120
SIC 5651 Family clothing stores

D-U-N-S 20-038-0694   (BR)
HOMEWOOD HEALTH INC
PALMWOOD HUMAN SOLUTIONS
407 2 St Sw Suite 400, Calgary, AB, T2P 2Y3
(403) 216-6347
Emp Here 30
SIC 8049 Offices of health practitioner

D-U-N-S 20-076-3720   (BR)
HUDSON'S BAY COMPANY
BAY, THE
200 8 Ave Sw, Calgary, AB, T2P 1B5
(403) 262-0345
Emp Here 450
SIC 5311 Department stores

D-U-N-S 20-913-4944   (BR)
IBM CANADA LIMITED
(*Suby of* International Business Machines Corporation)
639 5 Ave Sw Suite 2100, Calgary, AB, T2P 0M9

Emp Here 110
SIC 7371 Custom computer programming services

D-U-N-S 25-100-9445   (SL)
ICOM PRODUCTIONS INC
140 8 Ave Sw Suite 400, Calgary, AB, T2P 1B3
(403) 539-9276
Emp Here 60   *Sales* 5,399,092
SIC 8748 Business consulting, nec
Pr Gregory Surbey

D-U-N-S 25-094-6316   (SL)
IMV PROJECTS INC
500 5 Ave Sw Suite 1400, Calgary, AB, T2P 3L5
(403) 537-8811
Emp Here 400   *Sales* 116,456,320
SIC 8742 Management consulting services
Pr Pr Ivan Velev
  Kevin O'brien

D-U-N-S 24-016-4582   (HQ)
IMPERIAL OIL RESOURCES LIMITED
(*Suby of* Exxon Mobil Corporation)
237 4 Ave Sw Suite 4063, Calgary, AB, T2P 4K3
(800) 567-3776
Emp Here 1,500   *Emp Total* 71,100
Sales 1,154,019,392
SIC 1382 Oil and gas exploration services
Ch Bd Ch Bd Bruce March
VP Fin Paul Masschelin
Sr VP Glenn Scott
Sec Brian Livingston
  Eddie Lui
  Dave Wilis

D-U-N-S 24-807-3181   (BR)
IMPORT TOOL CORPORATION LTD
910 7 Ave Sw Suite 440, Calgary, AB, T2P 3N8
(403) 261-3032
Emp Here 65
SIC 8743 Public relations services

D-U-N-S 25-756-7227   (SL)
INPLAY OIL CORP
640 5 Ave Sw Suite 920, Calgary, AB, T2P 3G4

Emp Here 31   *Sales* 18,773,669
SIC 1381 Drilling oil and gas wells
Pr Pr Douglas Bartole
  Darren Dittmer
VP Gordon Reese
VP Kevin Yakiwchuk
VP Opers Thane Jensen
  Donald Cowie
  Craig Golinowski
  Dennis Nerland
  Stephen Nikiforuk
  Dale Shwed

D-U-N-S 25-322-0255   (BR)
INDIGO BOOKS & MUSIC INC
COLES THE BOOK PEOPLE
(*Suby of* Indigo Books & Music Inc)
317 7 Ave Sw, Calgary, AB, T2P 2Y9
(403) 263-7333
Emp Here 25
SIC 5942 Book stores

D-U-N-S 24-857-0751   (BR)
INFOSYS LIMITED
888 3 St Sw Suite 1000, Calgary, AB, T2P 5C5
(403) 444-6896
Emp Here 90
SIC 7379 Computer related services, nec

D-U-N-S 20-552-0609   (BR)
INTACT INSURANCE COMPANY
SURETY, DIV OF
321 6 Ave Sw Suite 1200, Calgary, AB, T2P 3H3
(403) 269-7961
Emp Here 900
SIC 6331 Fire, marine, and casualty insurance

D-U-N-S 20-919-5630   (BR)
INTERNATIONAL FITNESS HOLDINGS INC
WORLD HEALTH CLUB
217 7 Ave Sw, Calgary, AB, T2P 0X1
(403) 265-3444
Emp Here 35
SIC 7999 Amusement and recreation, nec

D-U-N-S 20-989-8774   (SL)
INTERNATIONAL HOTEL OF CALGARY LTD, THE

220 4 Ave Sw, Calgary, AB, T2P 0H5
(403) 265-9600
Emp Here 105   *Sales* 4,596,524
SIC 7011 Hotels and motels

D-U-N-S 25-315-8000   (BR)
**INVESTORS GROUP FINANCIAL SER-
VICES INC**
333 7 Ave Sw Suite 800, Calgary, AB, T2P 2Z1
(403) 284-0494
Emp Here 60
SIC 8742 Management consulting services

D-U-N-S 20-524-6130   (SL)
**JENSEN SHAWA SOLOMON DUGUID
HAWKES LLP**
JSS BARRISTERS
304 8 Ave Sw Suite 800, Calgary, AB, T2P
1C2
(403) 571-1520
Emp Here 51   *Sales* 4,377,642
SIC 8111 Legal services

D-U-N-S 20-138-6609   (SL)
JOEY TOMATO'S (EAU CLAIRE) INC
JOEY'S
208 Barclay Parade Sw, Calgary, AB, T2P 4R4
(403) 263-6336
Emp Here 100   *Sales* 2,991,389
SIC 5812 Eating places

D-U-N-S 24-027-8494   (BR)
JOHNSON INC
736 8 Ave Sw Suite 300, Calgary, AB, T2P
1H4
(403) 263-6424
Emp Here 50
SIC 6411 Insurance agents, brokers, and service

D-U-N-S 24-338-8241   (BR)
JONES BROWN INC
639 5 Ave Sw Suite 800, Calgary, AB, T2P
0M9
(403) 265-1920
Emp Here 25
SIC 6411 Insurance agents, brokers, and service

D-U-N-S 24-271-6991   (BR)
KPMG LLP
(*Suby of* KPMG LLP)
205 5 Ave Sw Suite 1200, Calgary, AB, T2P
2V7
(403) 691-8000
Emp Here 350
SIC 8721 Accounting, auditing, and book-
keeping

D-U-N-S 20-137-0827   (BR)
**KASIAN ARCHITECTURE INTERIOR DE-
SIGN AND PLANNING LTD**
1011 9 Ave Sw, Calgary, AB, T2P 1L3
(403) 265-2440
Emp Here 100
SIC 8712 Architectural services

D-U-N-S 20-304-4409   (SL)
KEANE COMPLETIONS CN CORP
435 4 Ave Sw Suite 380, Calgary, AB, T2P
2S6
(587) 390-0863
Emp Here 50   *Sales* 17,621,552
SIC 1381 Drilling oil and gas wells
VP VP Vince Kozak
Dir Greg Powell

D-U-N-S 25-096-3352   (HQ)
KEYERA CORP
(*Suby of* Keyera Corp)
144 4 Ave Sw Suite 600, Calgary, AB, T2P
3N4
(403) 205-8300
Emp Here 250   *Emp Total* 993
Sales 1,855,749,335
SIC 1389 Oil and gas field services, nec
Pr Pr David Smith
  Steven Kroeker

Sr VP Bradley Lock
Sr VP Dean Setoguchi
Sr VP Graham Balzun
VP Opers Jarrod Beztilny
VP Mike Freeman
VP VP Suzanne Hathaway
VP Engg Rick Koshman
Pers/VP Dion Kostiuk

D-U-N-S 24-523-1662   (SL)
KOCH EXPLORATION CANADA, L.P.
111 5 Ave Sw Suite 1500, Calgary, AB, T2P
3Y6
(403) 716-7800
Emp Here 23   *Sales* 18,459,057
SIC 1382 Oil and gas exploration services
Pr Dale Schlinsog

D-U-N-S 20-651-6572   (BR)
LSC LANGUAGE STUDIES CANADA LTD
LANGUAGE STUDIES CANADA
(*Suby of* LSC Language Studies Canada Ltd)
140 4 Ave Sw Suite 300, Calgary, AB, T2P
3N3

Emp Here 25
SIC 8299 Schools and educational services,
nec

D-U-N-S 20-594-2431   (SL)
LANDMARK GRAPHICS CANADA
645 7 Ave Sw Suite 1600, Calgary, AB, T2P
4G8
(403) 231-9300
Emp Here 50   *Sales* 3,648,035
SIC 7336 Commercial art and graphic design

D-U-N-S 24-827-4388   (SL)
**LAPRAIRIE WORKS OILFIELDS SERVICES
INC**
505 2 St Sw Suite 702, Calgary, AB, T2P 1N8
(403) 767-9942
Emp Here 70   *Sales* 9,922,655
SIC 1389 Oil and gas field services, nec
Pr Scott Laprairie
Sr VP Carl Laprairie
  Jim Feragen
VP Opers Reagan Laprairie
  Roachelle Laprairie
VP Opers Kelly Mcmanus
VP Cliff Laprairie

D-U-N-S 20-039-1808   (BR)
LAWSON LUNDELL LLP
205 5 Ave Sw Suite 3700, Calgary, AB, T2P
2V7
(403) 269-6900
Emp Here 21
SIC 8111 Legal services

D-U-N-S 24-344-5376   (BR)
LONDON LIFE INSURANCE COMPANY
605 5 Ave Sw, Calgary, AB, T2P 3H5
(403) 265-3733
Emp Here 45
SIC 6311 Life insurance

D-U-N-S 20-268-4056   (SL)
LONQUIST & CO. (CANADA) ULC
255 5 Ave Sw Suite 2360, Calgary, AB, T2P
3G6
(403) 451-4992
Emp Here 50   *Sales* 4,961,328
SIC 8711 Engineering services

D-U-N-S 24-673-4545   (HQ)
M-I DRILLING FLUIDS CANADA, INC
M-I SWACO, DIV OF
700 2 St Sw Suite 500, Calgary, AB, T2P 2W1
(403) 290-5300
Emp Here 50   *Emp Total* 350
Sales 76,270,320
SIC 1389 Oil and gas field services, nec
VP VP Robert Tilley
Dir Andrew Fisher
Dir James Webster
Fin Ex Wayne Burgess

D-U-N-S 20-119-7469   (SL)
MEG ENERGY CORP
3 Ave Sw Suite 600 25 Fl, Calgary, AB, T2P
0G5
(403) 770-0446
Emp Here 617   *Sales* 1,380,387,629
SIC 1311 Crude petroleum and natural gas
Pr Pr William Mccaffrey
  Eric Toews
  Don Moe
Sr VP Richard Sendall
Sr VP Chi-Tak Yee
VP VP Grant Borbridge
  John Nearing
VP John Rogers
VP Chris Sloof
VP Don Sutherland

D-U-N-S 25-452-2584   (BR)
**MACKIE RESEACH CAPITAL CORPORA-
TION**
140 4 Ave Sw Unit 1330, Calgary, AB, T2P
3N3
(403) 265-7400
Emp Here 30
SIC 6211 Security brokers and dealers

D-U-N-S 25-686-1436   (SL)
MANCAL ENERGY INC
530 8 Ave Sw Suite 1600, Calgary, AB, T2P
3S8
(403) 231-7680
Emp Here 20   *Sales* 21,579,334
SIC 1382 Oil and gas exploration services
Pr Pr Ross D.S. Douglas
  Douglas G Hittel

D-U-N-S 24-393-1792   (SL)
MANITOK ENERGY INC
444 7 Ave Sw Suite 700, Calgary, AB, T2P
0X8
(403) 984-1750
Emp Here 27   *Sales* 25,948,966
SIC 1311 Crude petroleum and natural gas
Pr Pr Massimo Geremia
Ex VP Gregory Vavra
VP Fin Robert Dion
  Tim Jerhoff
VP Donald Martin
VP Rodger Perry
  Cameron Vouri
  Bruno Geremia
  Keith Macleod
  Kenneth Mullen

D-U-N-S 20-894-8690   (SL)
MANPOWER PROFESSIONAL INC
MANPOWER SERVICES
734 7 Ave Sw Suite 120, Calgary, AB, T2P
3P8
(403) 269-6936
Emp Here 65   *Sales* 4,742,446
SIC 7361 Employment agencies

D-U-N-S 25-301-6984   (BR)
**MANUFACTURERS LIFE INSURANCE
COMPANY, THE**
MANULIFE FINANCIAL
855 2 St Sw Suite 2310, Calgary, AB, T2P 4J7

Emp Here 100
SIC 6311 Life insurance

D-U-N-S 20-829-6855   (BR)
MARSH CANADA LIMITED
(*Suby of* Marsh & McLennan Companies, Inc.)
222 3 Ave Sw Suite 1100, Calgary, AB, T2P
0B4
(403) 290-7900
Emp Here 200
SIC 6411 Insurance agents, brokers, and service

D-U-N-S 20-212-7705   (BR)
MASTER FLO VALVE INC
202 6 Ave Sw Suite 400, Calgary, AB, T2P
2R9

(403) 237-5557
Emp Here 25
SIC 3492 Fluid power valves and hose fittings

D-U-N-S 25-386-5372   (SL)
MATRIX GEOSERVICES LTD
808 4 Ave Sw Suite 600, Calgary, AB, T2P
3E8
(403) 294-0707
Emp Here 110   *Sales* 6,055,738
SIC 7374 Data processing and preparation
Pr Pr Mark Harrison
  Ying Cheung
  Lain Eng

D-U-N-S 24-786-2345   (BR)
MCCARTHY TETRAULT LLP
421 7 Ave Sw Suite 3300, Calgary, AB, T2P
4K9
(403) 260-3500
Emp Here 200
SIC 8111 Legal services

D-U-N-S 25-484-4673   (BR)
MCLENNAN ROSS LLP
350 7 Ave Sw Suite 1000, Calgary, AB, T2P
3N9
(403) 543-9120
Emp Here 60
SIC 8111 Legal services

D-U-N-S 24-595-6938   (BR)
MCMILLAN LLP
736 6 Ave Sw Suite 1900, Calgary, AB, T2P
3T7
(403) 531-4700
Emp Here 50
SIC 8111 Legal services

D-U-N-S 25-416-4544   (BR)
MERCER (CANADA) LIMITED
(*Suby of* Marsh & McLennan Companies, Inc.)
222 3 Ave Sw Suite 1200, Calgary, AB, T2P
0B4
(403) 269-4945
Emp Here 110
SIC 8999 Services, nec

D-U-N-S 20-966-6747   (BR)
MERRILL LYNCH CANADA INC
BANK OF AMERICA MERRILL LYNCH
(*Suby of* Bank of America Corporation)
255 5 Ave Sw Suite 2620, Calgary, AB, T2P
3G6
(403) 231-7300
Emp Here 22
SIC 6211 Security brokers and dealers

D-U-N-S 24-174-8982   (BR)
MICROSOFT CANADA INC
(*Suby of* Microsoft Corporation)
500 4 Ave Sw Suite 1900, Calgary, AB, T2P
2V6
(403) 296-6500
Emp Here 250
SIC 7371 Custom computer programming services

D-U-N-S 20-297-3082   (BR)
MILLER THOMSON LLP
MILTON MANAGEMENT
700 9 Ave Sw Suite 3000, Calgary, AB, T2P
3V4
(403) 298-2400
Emp Here 100
SIC 8111 Legal services

D-U-N-S 24-986-9665   (BR)
MILLS, BRYAN IRODESSO CORP
140 4 Ave Sw Suite 2240, Calgary, AB, T2P
3N3
(403) 503-0144
Emp Here 25
SIC 8748 Business consulting, nec

D-U-N-S 24-840-0467   (BR)
MONSTER WORLDWIDE CANADA INC
TMP WORLDWIDE
639 5 Ave Sw Suite 620, Calgary, AB, T2P
0M9

(403) 262-8055
Emp Here 20
SIC 7311 Advertising agencies

D-U-N-S 24-905-9700   (BR)
MORGUARD INVESTMENTS LIMITED
505 3 St Sw Suite 200, Calgary, AB, T2P 3E6
(403) 233-0274
Emp Here 33
SIC 6531 Real estate agents and managers

D-U-N-S 24-808-7769   (HQ)
NAL RESOURCES MANAGEMENT LIMITED
550 6 Ave Sw Suite 600, Calgary, AB, T2P 0S2
(403) 294-3600
Emp Here 220   *Emp Total* 34,000
Sales 40,627,172
SIC 8741 Management services
Pr Pr Kevin Stashin
Dir Kevin J.E Adolphe
Dir Jeffrey Smith
Dir William J Eeuwes
Dir Brian Lemke
Dir Donald Driscoll

D-U-N-S 24-849-9902   (HQ)
NCS MULTISTAGE INC
MONGOOSE
840 7 Ave Sw Suite 800, Calgary, AB, T2P 3G2
(403) 720-3236
Emp Here 41   *Emp Total* 200
Sales 10,568,262
SIC 1389 Oil and gas field services, nec
Pr Pr Robert Nipper
 Marty Stromquist
 Don Getzlaf

D-U-N-S 20-363-2398   (BR)
NOV ENERFLOW ULC
TUBOSCOPE CANADA
715 5 Ave Sw Suite 1700, Calgary, AB, T2P 2X6
(403) 216-5000
Emp Here 25
SIC 1389 Oil and gas field services, nec

D-U-N-S 25-678-0123   (HQ)
NOVA CHEMICALS CORPORATION
1000 7 Ave Sw Suite 1000, Calgary, AB, T2P 5L5
(403) 750-3600
Emp Here 50   *Emp Total* 2,700
Sales 295,490,835
SIC 2821 Plastics materials and resins
Pr Pr Todd Karran
 Julie Beck
Sr VP Chris Bezaire
Sr VP Naushad Jamani
VP Opers Arnel Santos
 Suhail Al Mazrouei
 Musabbeh Al Kaabi
 Abdulaziz Alhajri
 Mark Garrett
 Stephen Soules

D-U-N-S 24-894-7624   (SL)
NOVA PETROCHEMICALS LTD
1000 7 Ave Sw, Calgary, AB, T2P 5L5
(403) 750-3600
Emp Here 1,000   *Sales* 234,828,387
SIC 6712 Bank holding companies
Pr Walentin Mirosh
Sr VP Lawrence Macdonald
Sr VP Christopher Pappas
 Ron Kemle
 Jack Mustoe

D-U-N-S 25-519-7626   (SL)
NATIONAL PUBLIC RELATIONS (CANADA) INC
(*Suby of* Groupe Conseil RES Publica Inc)
800 6 Ave Sw Suite 1600, Calgary, AB, T2P 3G3
(403) 531-0331
Emp Here 20   *Sales* 1,824,018
SIC 8743 Public relations services

D-U-N-S 20-077-1913   (HQ)
NATIONAL-OILWELL CANADA LTD
NATIONAL OILWELL VARCO
(*Suby of* National Oilwell Varco, Inc.)
540 5 Ave Sw Suite 1100, Calgary, AB, T2P 0M2
(403) 294-4500
Emp Here 50   *Emp Total* 36,627
Sales 69,300,080
SIC 5084 Industrial machinery and equipment
Pr Scott Hauck
VP Brad Meyer
VP Kent Langstaff
Fin Ex Michael Collings

D-U-N-S 20-076-4934   (HQ)
NEXEN ENERGY ULC
801 7 Ave Sw Suite 2900, Calgary, AB, T2P 3P7
(403) 699-4000
Emp Here 300   *Sales* 1,937,370,362
SIC 1382 Oil and gas exploration services
Pr Kevin Reinhart
Ex VP Jim Arnold
Ex VP Ron Bailey
Ex VP Alan O'brien
VP Peter Addy
VP Pierre Alvarez
VP Patrick Mcveigh
VP Alistair Mooney
VP Quinn Wilson
VP Archie Kennedy

D-U-N-S 25-290-8371   (SL)
NEXEN PETROLEUM INTERNATIONAL LTD
801 7 Ave Sw Suite 2900, Calgary, AB, T2P 3P7
(403) 234-6700
Emp Here 111   *Sales* 88,270,977
SIC 1311 Crude petroleum and natural gas
VP VP Edward W Bogle
VP VP Patricia L Horsfall
VP VP Harry D Wasden
 John Patterson
 Laurence Murphy

D-U-N-S 25-143-1771   (BR)
NEXIENT LEARNING CANADA INC
POLAR BEAR CORPORATE SOLUTIONS
700 2 St Sw Suite 400, Calgary, AB, T2P 2W1
(403) 250-8686
Emp Here 20
SIC 8243 Data processing schools

D-U-N-S 25-230-9570   (HQ)
NINE ENERGY CANADA INC
INTEGRATED PRODUCTION SERVICES
(*Suby of* Nine Energy Service, Inc.)
840 7 Ave Sw Suite 1840, Calgary, AB, T2P 3G2
(403) 515-8410
Emp Here 30   *Emp Total* 800
Sales 48,372,944
SIC 1389 Oil and gas field services, nec
Pr John Geddes
VP VP Robert Duval
VP Fin Dennis Hassel
VP Opers Michael Taton
VP VP Nicholas Drake

D-U-N-S 24-376-2437   (SL)
NISKA GS HOLDINGS II, L.P.
607 8 Ave Sw Suite 400, Calgary, AB, T2P 0A7
(403) 513-8694
Emp Here 50   *Sales* 12,662,640
SIC 4922 Natural gas transmission
 David Pope

D-U-N-S 24-850-2937   (SL)
NORTH WEST REDWATER PARTNERSHIP
140 4 Ave Sw Suite 2800, Calgary, AB, T2P 3N3
(403) 398-0900
Emp Here 201   *Sales* 219,976,511
SIC 2911 Petroleum refining
Pr Chris Covert

D-U-N-S 20-068-9425   (SL)
NORTHCAN SURVEYS LTD
706 7 Ave Sw Suite 1070, Calgary, AB, T2P 0Z1
(403) 266-1046
Emp Here 50   *Sales* 4,961,328
SIC 8713 Surveying services

D-U-N-S 20-188-5030   (BR)
NORTHLAND PROPERTIES CORPORATION
SANDMAN HOTEL CALGARY CITY CENTRE
(*Suby of* Northland Properties Corporation)
888 7 Ave Sw, Calgary, AB, T2P 3J3
(403) 237-8626
Emp Here 60
SIC 7011 Hotels and motels

D-U-N-S 24-850-9072   (HQ)
NORTON ROSE CANADA LLP
400 3 Ave Sw Suite 3700, Calgary, AB, T2P 4H2
(403) 267-8222
Emp Here 300   *Emp Total* 1,000
Sales 707,580,160
SIC 8111 Legal services
Pt John Coleman

D-U-N-S 24-677-7820   (BR)
NORTON ROSE FULBRIGHT CANADA S.E.N.C.R.L., S.R.L.
400 3 Ave Sw Suite 3700, Calgary, AB, T2P 4H2
(403) 267-8222
Emp Here 20
SIC 8111 Legal services

D-U-N-S 24-678-9312   (BR)
OMICRON ARCHITECTURE ENGINEERING CONSTRUCTION LTD
OMICRON AEC
833 4 Ave Sw Suite 500, Calgary, AB, T2P 3T5
(403) 262-9733
Emp Here 40
SIC 8712 Architectural services

D-U-N-S 25-229-1133   (SL)
OMNILOGIC SYSTEMS COMPANY
833 4 Ave Sw Suite 900, Calgary, AB, T2P 3T5
(403) 232-6664
Emp Here 500   *Sales* 50,240,000
SIC 7379 Computer related services, nec
 Diane Horton

D-U-N-S 25-522-0931   (BR)
ONLINE ENTERPRISES INC
ONLINE BUSINESS SYSTEMS
(*Suby of* Online Enterprises Inc)
840 7 Ave Sw Suite 1710, Calgary, AB, T2P 3G2
(403) 265-8515
Emp Here 60
SIC 7379 Computer related services, nec

D-U-N-S 24-850-0378   (SL)
OPEN RANGE ENERGY CORP.
645 7 Ave Sw Unit 1100, Calgary, AB, T2P 4G8

Emp Here 20   *Sales* 39,093,261
SIC 1382 Oil and gas exploration services
Pr Pr Scott Dawson
Ex VP Gerald Costigan
Pr David Griffith
VP Opers Jamie Beninger
VP Opers Rob Mckechney
Fin Ex Mark Munro
Dir Kenneth Faircloth
Dir Dean Jensen
 Harley Winger
Dir Mike Seth

D-U-N-S 24-702-1363   (BR)
ORACLE CANADA ULC
(*Suby of* Oracle Corporation)
401 9 Ave Sw Suite 840, Calgary, AB, T2P 3C5

(403) 265-2622
Emp Here 34
SIC 7371 Custom computer programming services

D-U-N-S 25-196-0100   (BR)
OSLER, HOSKIN & HARCOURT LLP
450 1 St Sw Suite 2500, Calgary, AB, T2P 5H1
(403) 260-7000
Emp Here 130
SIC 8111 Legal services

D-U-N-S 20-772-7475   (BR)
OXFORD PROPERTIES GROUP INC
BOW VALLEY SQUARE
300-205 5 Ave Sw, Calgary, AB, T2P 2V7
(403) 261-0621
Emp Here 35
SIC 6512 Nonresidential building operators

D-U-N-S 20-213-7787   (BR)
OXFORD PROPERTIES GROUP INC
520 3 Ave Sw Suite 2900, Calgary, AB, T2P 0R3
(403) 206-6400
Emp Here 40
SIC 6531 Real estate agents and managers

D-U-N-S 20-694-6464   (SL)
P2 ENERGY SOLUTIONS ALBERTA ULC
639 5 Ave Sw Suite 2100, Calgary, AB, T2P 0M9
(403) 774-1000
Emp Here 120   *Sales* 15,321,747
SIC 7371 Custom computer programming services
Sr VP Bruce Macdonald
VP Sls Michael Danielewicz
VP VP Sherry Sturko

D-U-N-S 24-520-2382   (BR)
PEO CANADA LTD
DIVERSIFIED PAYROLL SOLUTIONS
805 5 Ave Sw Suite 100, Calgary, AB, T2P 0N6
(403) 237-5577
Emp Here 100
SIC 8721 Accounting, auditing, and bookkeeping

D-U-N-S 20-954-7848   (SL)
PHX ENERGY SERVICES CORP
250 2 St Sw Suite 1400, Calgary, AB, T2P 0C1
(403) 543-4466
Emp Here 529   *Sales* 109,763,768
SIC 1381 Drilling oil and gas wells
 John Hooks
Pr Mike Buker
 Cameron Ritchie
VP Opers Craig Brown
VP Sls Jeffery Shafer
VP Daniel Blanchard
 Randolph M Charron
 Myron Tetreault
 Judith J Athaide
 Lawrence (Larry) Hibbard

D-U-N-S 20-302-7037   (HQ)
PARKBRIDGE LIFESTYLE COMMUNITIES INC
500 4 Ave Sw Suite 1500, Calgary, AB, T2P 2V6
(403) 215-2100
Emp Here 25   *Emp Total* 60,000
Sales 171,864,198
SIC 6719 Holding companies, nec
Pr Andrew Blair
 Joseph F. Killi
 Walter Borthwick
 Ian Cockwell
 James Hankins
 Gary Perron
 David Richards
 Ken Cullen

D-U-N-S 20-990-3744   (BR)
PARLEE MCLAWS LLP
421 7 Ave Sw Unit 3300, Calgary, AB, T2P

4K9
(403) 294-7000
Emp Here 150
SIC 8111 Legal services

D-U-N-S 25-315-1849   (BR)
PASLEY, MAX ENTERPRISES LIMITED
MCDONALD'S RESTAURANTS
(*Suby of* Pasley, Max Enterprises Limited)
222 8 Ave Sw, Calgary, AB, T2P 1B5
(403) 265-8096
Emp Here 40
SIC 5812 Eating places

D-U-N-S 25-168-4221   (HQ)
PATTERSON-UTI DRILLING CO. CANADA
(*Suby of* Patterson-Uti Energy, Inc.)
734 7 Ave Sw Suite 720, Calgary, AB, T2P
3P8
(403) 269-2858
Emp Here 35   *Emp Total* 5,300
Sales 13,643,651
SIC 1381 Drilling oil and gas wells
 Cloyce Talbott
Ex VP John Brown
Sr VP Sr VP John Vollmer
 Douglas Wall

D-U-N-S 20-812-9697   (BR)
**PEMBINA INSTITUTE FOR APPROPRIATE
DEVELOPMENT**
(*Suby of* Pembina Institute for Appropriate Development)
608 7 St Sw Suite 200, Calgary, AB, T2P 1Z2

Emp Here 50
SIC 8748 Business consulting, nec

D-U-N-S 25-219-7710   (SL)
PENN WEST PETROLEUM
111 5 Ave Sw Suite 800, Calgary, AB, T2P
3Y6
(403) 777-2500
Emp Here 200   *Sales* 133,955,845
SIC 1311 Crude petroleum and natural gas

D-U-N-S 20-990-1248   (BR)
PERSONAL INSURANCE COMPANY, THE
*PERSONAL INSURANCE COMPANY OF
CANADA, THE*
855 2 St Sw Unit 710, Calgary, AB, T2P 4J7
(403) 265-5931
Emp Here 55
SIC 6331 Fire, marine, and casualty insurance

D-U-N-S 20-515-5331   (BR)
PETER KIEWIT INFRASTRUCTURE CO.
KIEWIT, PETER SONS CO.
(*Suby of* Peter Kiewit Sons', Inc.)
1000 7 Ave Sw Suite 500, Calgary, AB, T2P
5L5
(403) 693-8701
Emp Here 30
SIC 1611 Highway and street construction

D-U-N-S 20-599-9154   (SL)
PETRO-TECH PRINTING LTD
621 4 Ave Sw, Calgary, AB, T2P 0K2
(403) 266-1651
Emp Here 25   *Sales* 1,896,978
SIC 2752 Commercial printing, lithographic

D-U-N-S 20-282-8182   (SL)
**PETROCHINA INTERNATIONAL (CANADA)
TRADING LTD**
111 5 Ave Sw Suite 1750, Calgary, AB, T2P
3Y6
(587) 233-1200
Emp Here 150   *Sales* 46,621,887
SIC 4924 Natural gas distribution
 Shaolin Li
 Jie Wang

D-U-N-S 25-291-3046   (SL)
PETROCAPITA INCOME TRUST
717 7 Ave Sw Suite 1400, Calgary, AB, T2P
0Z3
(587) 393-3450
Emp Here 70   *Sales* 2,751,667

SIC 1382 Oil and gas exploration services

D-U-N-S 25-677-8903   (SL)
**PEYTO EXPLORATION & DEVELOPMENT
CORP**
600 3rd Ave Suite 300, Calgary, AB, T2P 0G5
(403) 261-6081
Emp Here 50   *Sales* 480,812,149
SIC 1382 Oil and gas exploration services
Pr Pr Darren Gee
 Kathy Turgeon
VP Prd Todd Burdick
VP Jean-Paul Lachance
VP Lee Curran
VP Timothy Louie
 Scott Robinson
VP David Thomas
 Stephen Chetner
 Donald Gray

D-U-N-S 20-112-1956   (SL)
PIPELINE MANAGEMENT INC
111 5 Ave Sw Suite 1400, Calgary, AB, T2P
3Y6
(403) 716-7600
Emp Here 100   *Sales* 68,478,750
SIC 1382 Oil and gas exploration services
VP VP Mark Ward

D-U-N-S 24-358-4757   (HQ)
PLAINS MIDSTREAM CANADA ULC
607 8 Ave Sw Suite 1400, Calgary, AB, T2P
0A7
(403) 298-2100
Emp Here 570   *Emp Total* 5,400
Sales 2,666,056,939
SIC 4612 Crude petroleum pipelines
Pr Pr David W Duckett
VP Fin Dave Craig
VP Opers Rick Jensen
 Greg L Armstrong
 Tim Moore
 Harry N Pefanis

D-U-N-S 24-378-2294   (SL)
**POLAR STAR CANADIAN OIL AND GAS,
INC**
700 4 Ave Sw Suite 1900, Calgary, AB, T2P
3J4
(403) 775-8061
Emp Here 30   *Sales* 22,617,817
SIC 1382 Oil and gas exploration services
 Kent Kufeldt
 Marina Mavrakis
 Marietta Moshiashvili
 David Tuer

D-U-N-S 25-344-6199   (SL)
PROCALL MARKETING INC
100 4 Ave Sw Unit 200, Calgary, AB, T2P 3N2
(403) 265-4014
Emp Here 50   *Sales* 2,626,585
SIC 7389 Business services, nec

D-U-N-S 25-792-1296   (BR)
PYRAMID CORPORATION
205 5 Ave Sw Suite 3300, Calgary, AB, T2P
2V7
(403) 205-3880
Emp Here 20
SIC 1731 Electrical work

D-U-N-S 25-329-7501   (SL)
QUADRUS DEVELOPMENT INC
IMPROVING
640 8 Ave Sw Suite 400, Calgary, AB, T2P
1G7
(403) 257-0850
Emp Here 50   *Sales* 3,648,035
SIC 7379 Computer related services, nec

D-U-N-S 20-273-2822   (SL)
QUALITAS OILFIELD SERVICES LTD
250 2 St Sw Suite 1400, Calgary, AB, T2P 0C1
(403) 543-4466
Emp Here 24   *Sales* 2,918,428
SIC 1389 Oil and gas field services, nec

D-U-N-S 24-308-7819   (SL)
RBC DEXIA INVESTORS SERVICES
335 8 Ave Sw, Calgary, AB, T2P 1C9
(403) 292-3978
Emp Here 32   *Sales* 6,492,800
SIC 6211 Security brokers and dealers
Owner Lori Warner

D-U-N-S 20-708-1576   (BR)
RBC DOMINION SECURITIES INC
(*Suby of* Royal Bank Of Canada)
333 7 Ave Sw Suite 1400, Calgary, AB, T2P
2Z1
(403) 266-9691
Emp Here 50
SIC 6211 Security brokers and dealers

D-U-N-S 24-364-5392   (HQ)
RGN ONTARIO LIMITED PARTNERSHIP
HQ A MEMBER OF THE REGUS GROUP
144 4 Ave Sw Suite 1200, Calgary, AB, T2P
3N4
(403) 716-3636
Emp Here 20   *Emp Total* 7,138
Sales 1,601,959
SIC 7389 Business services, nec

D-U-N-S 24-358-3817   (SL)
RPS ENERGY CANADA LTD
800 5 Ave Sw Suite 1400, Calgary, AB, T2P
3T6
(403) 265-7226
Emp Here 100   *Sales* 10,871,144
SIC 8711 Engineering services
Pr Peter Mulholland
Dir John Willams
Dir Gary Young

D-U-N-S 20-165-4824   (BR)
RWDI AIR INC
736 8 Ave Sw Suite 1000, Calgary, AB, T2P
1H4
(403) 232-6771
Emp Here 20
SIC 8711 Engineering services

D-U-N-S 25-359-7231   (BR)
RWDI GROUP INC
RWDI AIR
736 8 Ave Sw Suite 1000, Calgary, AB, T2P
1H4
(403) 232-6771
Emp Here 23
SIC 8711 Engineering services

D-U-N-S 25-521-3217   (BR)
RAYMOND JAMES (USA) LTD
(*Suby of* Raymond James Financial, Inc.)
525 8 Ave Sw Suite 161, Calgary, AB, T2P
1G1
(403) 221-0333
Emp Here 80
SIC 6211 Security brokers and dealers

D-U-N-S 24-320-3887   (HQ)
REALEX PROPERTIES CORP
(*Suby of* Dundee Real Estate Investment
Trust)
606 4 St Sw Suite 1200, Calgary, AB, T2P 1T1

Emp Here 20   *Emp Total* 1
Sales 7,016,633
SIC 6719 Holding companies, nec
Pr Pr Marc D Sardachuk
 Harold P Milavsky
 Joseph F Killi
 David V Richards
 Les Johannesen
 Bahaa Faltous
 Barry Emes
 Antonie Vanden Brink
 Gary E Perron
 Manfred Conrad

D-U-N-S 20-548-0218   (HQ)
**REPSOL CANADA ENERGY PARTNER-
SHIP**
888 3 St Sw Suite 2000, Calgary, AB, T2P 5C5

(403) 237-1234
Emp Here 200   *Emp Total* 2,312
Sales 582,591,190
SIC 1382 Oil and gas exploration services
Dir Jill Terakita-Jones

D-U-N-S 20-233-6496   (BR)
REVERA INC
EAU CLAIRE RETIREMENT RESIDENCE
301 7 St Sw, Calgary, AB, T2P 1Y6
(403) 269-3114
Emp Here 50
SIC 6513 Apartment building operators

D-U-N-S 20-087-1122   (SL)
RIVER CAFE
25 Prince'S Island Pk Sw, Calgary, AB, T2P
0R1
(403) 261-1915
Emp Here 50   *Sales* 1,532,175
SIC 5812 Eating places

D-U-N-S 20-591-6914   (BR)
**ROCKY VIEW SCHOOL DIVISION NO. 41,
THE**
CHESTERMERE HIGH SCHOOL
241078 Hwy 791, Calgary, AB, T2P 2G7
(403) 272-8868
Emp Here 60
SIC 8211 Elementary and secondary schools

D-U-N-S 20-036-3906   (BR)
ROGERS MEDIA INC
(*Suby of* Rogers Communications Inc)
535 7 Ave Sw, Calgary, AB, T2P 0Y4
(403) 250-9797
Emp Here 120
SIC 4832 Radio broadcasting stations

D-U-N-S 20-285-5383   (BR)
ROWAN WILLIAMS DAVIES & IRWIN INC
RWDI AIR
736 8 Ave Sw Suite 1000, Calgary, AB, T2P
1H4
(403) 232-6771
Emp Here 21
SIC 8711 Engineering services

D-U-N-S 20-740-7045   (BR)
ROYAL BANK OF CANADA
RBC
(*Suby of* Royal Bank Of Canada)
502 4 Ave Sw Suite 300, Calgary, AB, T2P 0J6

Emp Here 20
SIC 6021 National commercial banks

D-U-N-S 20-976-6638   (BR)
ROYAL BANK OF CANADA
COMMERCIAL MARKET
(*Suby of* Royal Bank Of Canada)
335 8th Ave Sw 11th Flr, Calgary, AB, T2P
2N4

Emp Here 20
SIC 6021 National commercial banks

D-U-N-S 25-179-5704   (SL)
S.I. SYSTEMS LTD
401 9 Ave Sw Suite 311, Calgary, AB, T2P
3C5
(403) 263-1200
Emp Here 25   *Sales* 5,399,092
SIC 8741 Management services
 Larry Fichtner
Pr Pr Derek Bullen
Dir Fin Brian Mckenzie
VP Fin Ken Krawic
VP Opers Chandra Ramasamy
VP Opers Jennifer Foster

D-U-N-S 24-419-1230   (HQ)
S.I. SYSTEMS PARTNERSHIP
(*Suby of* S.I. Systems Partnership)
401 9 Ave Sw Suite 311, Calgary, AB, T2P
3C5
(403) 450-5174
Emp Here 21   *Emp Total* 125
Sales 16,197,275

SIC 8741 Management services
Pr Derek Bullen
 Chandra Ramasamy
 Glenda Lewis

D-U-N-S 24-928-0934   (BR)
SAP CANADA INC
400 3 Ave Sw Suite 600, Calgary, AB, T2P
4H2
(403) 233-0985
Emp Here 70
SIC 7372 Prepackaged software

D-U-N-S 24-322-2622   (BR)
SAS INSTITUTE (CANADA) INC
(Suby of Sas Institute Inc.)
401 9 Ave Sw Suite 970, Calgary, AB, T2P
3C5
(403) 265-5177
Emp Here 30
SIC 7372 Prepackaged software

D-U-N-S 24-342-4079   (BR)
SCDA (2015) INC
639 5 Ave Sw Suite 1400, Calgary, AB, T2P
0M9
(403) 296-9400
Emp Here 95
SIC 6311 Life insurance

D-U-N-S 25-299-2763   (BR)
SCDA (2015) INC
STANDARD LIFE
639 5 Ave Sw, Calgary, AB, T2P 0M9

Emp Here 200
SIC 6531 Real estate agents and managers

D-U-N-S 20-747-4904   (SL)
SDR MANAGEMENT LTD
SILVER DRAGON RESTAURANT GROUP
205 Riverfront Ave Sw Suite 803, Calgary, AB,
T2P 5K4
(403) 261-9913
Emp Here 50   Sales 1,532,175
SIC 5812 Eating places

D-U-N-S 20-188-2532   (BR)
SNC-LAVALIN INC
HYDROCARBONS AND CHEMICALS DIVI-
SION
605 5 Ave Sw Suite 1400, Calgary, AB, T2P
3H5
(403) 294-2100
Emp Here 1,200
SIC 8711 Engineering services

D-U-N-S 24-391-3717   (BR)
SNC-LAVALIN INTERNATIONAL INC
605 5 Ave Sw Suite 1400, Calgary, AB, T2P
3H5
(403) 294-2100
Emp Here 500
SIC 8711 Engineering services

D-U-N-S 24-041-3182   (SL)
SAIPEM CANADA INC
SAIPEM CONSTRUCTION CANADA
530 8 Ave Sw Suite 2700, Calgary, AB, T2P
3S8
(403) 441-2793
Emp Here 800   Sales 205,238,449
SIC 1629 Heavy construction, nec
Pr Piero Cicalese
VP Amerigo Silvestri

D-U-N-S 24-314-3232   (SL)
SALT PLAINS STORAGE LLC
855 2 St Sw Unit 1200, Calgary, AB, T2P 4J7
(403) 513-8600
Emp Here 50   Sales 12,156,044
SIC 4922 Natural gas transmission
Pr Dave Pope
VP VP Paul Amirault
Fin Ex Darin Olson

D-U-N-S 24-929-8290   (BR)
SCOTIA CAPITAL INC
SCOTIA MCLEOD

119 6 Ave Sw Suite 300, Calgary, AB, T2P
0P8
(403) 298-4000
Emp Here 100
SIC 6211 Security brokers and dealers

D-U-N-S 24-087-2247   (HQ)
SEMCAMS ULC
(Suby of Semgroup Corporation)
520 3 Ave Sw Suite 700, Calgary, AB, T2P
0R3
(403) 536-3000
Emp Here 75   Emp Total 1,160
Sales 61,724,752
SIC 1389 Oil and gas field services, nec
VP VP David Williams
VP VP David Goose
VP Christopher Dutcher
VP Leanne Campbell
Prs Dir Jody Klotz
 Nancy Anderson

D-U-N-S 20-116-7587   (SL)
**SEMPRA ENERGY TRADING (CALGARY)
ULC**
(Suby of 1369202 Alberta ULC)
440 2 Ave Sw Suite 650, Calgary, AB, T2P
5E9
(403) 750-2450
Emp Here 20   Sales 16,768,000
SIC 6799 Investors, nec
Pr Pr Louis Draginov
Dir David Messer
VP VP Louis A Santore
 Ralph Todaro
Sec Michael A Goldstein
Sec Mara Kent

D-U-N-S 25-414-3415   (HQ)
SHAW CABLESYSTEMS G.P.
630 3 Ave Sw, Calgary, AB, T2P 4L4
(403) 750-4500
Emp Here 5,600   Emp Total 14,000
Sales 1,239,865,056
SIC 4841 Cable and other pay television ser-
vices
 J R Shaw
Pr Peter Bissonnette
Sr VP Michael D'avella
Sr VP Ken C. C. Stien
Ex VP James F Dinning

D-U-N-S 25-522-0113   (HQ)
SHAW PIPE PROTECTION LIMITED
333 7th Avenue Sw Unit 2200, Calgary, AB,
T2P 2Z1
(403) 263-2255
Emp Here 30   Emp Total 5,706
Sales 45,673,398
SIC 3479 Metal coating and allied services
Pr Pr William Buckley

D-U-N-S 24-785-2643   (BR)
SHELL CANADA LIMITED
JUMPING POUND COMPLEX
Gd, Calgary, AB, T2P 4V8
(403) 932-8200
Emp Here 90
SIC 4925 Gas production and/or distribution

D-U-N-S 25-357-5609   (HQ)
**SHELL ENERGY NORTH AMERICA
(CANADA) INC**
SHELL ENERGY
400 4 Ave Sw Suite 212, Calgary, AB, T2P 0J4
(403) 216-3600
Emp Here 100   Emp Total 93
Sales 74,161,292
SIC 4911 Electric services
 Arnold Macburnie
Dir James Chunn
Dir Nick Dimarzo

D-U-N-S 25-330-0602   (BR)
**SHERRITT INTERNATIONAL CORPORA-
TION**
425 1 St Sw Suite 2000, Calgary, AB, T2P 3L8

(403) 260-2900
Emp Here 60
SIC 3339 Primary nonferrous Metals, nec

D-U-N-S 20-350-6618   (BR)
SIERRA SYSTEMS GROUP INC
833 4 Ave Sw Ste 700, Calgary, AB, T2P 3T5
(403) 264-0955
Emp Here 50
SIC 7379 Computer related services, nec

D-U-N-S 25-365-8637   (SL)
**SINOCANADA PETROLEUM CORPORA-
TION**
444 7 Ave Sw Unit 800, Calgary, AB, T2P 0X8

Emp Here 100   Sales 41,797,400
SIC 5172 Petroleum products, nec
Pr Pngfei Yin

D-U-N-S 24-351-4960   (HQ)
SPECTRA ENERGY EMPRESS L.P.
425 1 St Sw Suite 2600, Calgary, AB, T2P 3L8
(403) 699-1999
Emp Here 20   Emp Total 7,733
Sales 14,986,142
SIC 8732 Commercial nonphysical research
Genl Mgr Peter Hoy

D-U-N-S 20-766-6850   (HQ)
SPROULE ASSOCIATES LIMITED
(Suby of Sproule Associates Limited)
140 4 Ave Sw Unit 900, Calgary, AB, T2P 3N3
(403) 294-5500
Emp Here 80   Emp Total 114
Sales 16,208,059
SIC 8711 Engineering services
Pr Pr R. Keith Macleod
Ex VP Harry J. Helwerda
 John L. Chipperfield
 Kevin Mcdonald

D-U-N-S 20-645-4068   (SL)
STAMPEDE PONTIAC BUICK (1988) LTD
STAMPEDE PONTIAC BUICK GMC
1110 9 Ave Sw, Calgary, AB, T2P 1M1

Emp Here 99   Sales 36,115,547
SIC 5511 New and used car dealers
Pr Pr David Bridarolli
 Mike Collinson

D-U-N-S 25-988-0359   (BR)
STARWOOD CANADA ULC
WESTIN CALGARY, THE
(Suby of Marriott International, Inc.)
320 4 Ave Sw, Calgary, AB, T2P 2S6
(403) 266-1611
Emp Here 500
SIC 7011 Hotels and motels

D-U-N-S 24-360-4779   (HQ)
STATOIL CANADA LTD
308 4 Ave Sw Suite 3600, Calgary, AB, T2P
0H7
(403) 234-0123
Emp Here 350   Emp Total 18,169
Sales 318,000,742
SIC 1311 Crude petroleum and natural gas
Pr Pr Stale Tungesvik
VP VP Heidi Wolden
Sec Patrizia Valle
Dir Verne Johnson
Dir Rob Adams
 Kurt Middleton

D-U-N-S 24-736-8769   (SL)
STONEHAM DRILLING INC
850 2 St Sw Suite 1020, Calgary, AB, T2P 0R8

Emp Here 20   Sales 7,608,750
SIC 1381 Drilling oil and gas wells
 Alex Macausland
 Dale Tremblay

D-U-N-S 20-250-9378   (SL)
STRATIFORM INC
620 8 Ave Sw Suite 200, Calgary, AB, T2P

1H9
(587) 747-7839
Emp Here 30   Sales 2,188,821
SIC 7379 Computer related services, nec

D-U-N-S 24-298-2742   (BR)
STREAM-FLO INDUSTRIES LTD
MASTER FLO
202 6 Ave Sw Suite 400, Calgary, AB, T2P
2R9
(403) 269-5531
Emp Here 25
SIC 3533 Oil and gas field machinery

D-U-N-S 24-012-6292   (BR)
**SUN LIFE ASSURANCE COMPANY OF
CANADA**
SUN LIFE FINANCIAL
140 4 Ave Sw Suite 1530, Calgary, AB, T2P
3N3
(403) 266-8959
Emp Here 90
SIC 6311 Life insurance

D-U-N-S 24-524-7171   (HQ)
**SUNCOR ENERGY PRODUCTS PARTNER-
SHIP**
150 6 Ave Sw, Calgary, AB, T2P 3Y7
(403) 296-8000
Emp Here 200   Emp Total 12,837
Sales 766,087,350
SIC 2911 Petroleum refining
 Steve Williams
Fin Ex Jonathan Mckenzie

D-U-N-S 24-354-2540   (SL)
SUNSHINE OILSANDS LTD
903 8 Ave Sw Unit 1020, Calgary, AB, T2P
0P7
(403) 984-1450
Emp Here 74   Sales 35,503
SIC 1311 Crude petroleum and natural gas

D-U-N-S 20-320-1702   (SL)
SUREPOINT HOLDINGS INC
800 6 Ave Sw Suite 950, Calgary, AB, T2P
3G3
(403) 532-4948
Emp Here 400   Sales 98,305,050
SIC 6712 Bank holding companies
 Kevin Mcbeth

D-U-N-S 20-270-3492   (SL)
SURGE GENERAL PARTNERSHIP
635 8 Ave Sw Suite 2100, Calgary, AB, T2P
3M3
(403) 930-1010
Emp Here 95   Sales 61,157,152
SIC 1382 Oil and gas exploration services
Pt Paul Colborne

D-U-N-S 24-618-0751   (SL)
SWIFT ENGINEERING INC
736 8 Ave Sw Suite 910, Calgary, AB, T2P
1H4
(403) 705-4800
Emp Here 20   Sales 1,751,057
SIC 8711 Engineering services

D-U-N-S 25-372-8448   (BR)
SYMANTEC (CANADA) CORPORATION
(Suby of Symantec Corporation)
100 4 Ave Sw Suite 1000, Calgary, AB, T2P
3N2
(403) 261-5400
Emp Here 100
SIC 4813 Telephone communication, except
radio

D-U-N-S 25-362-1940   (BR)
T.E. FINANCIAL CONSULTANTS LTD
T. E. WEALTHS
700 9 Ave Sw Suite 2230, Calgary, AB, T2P
3V4
(403) 233-8370
Emp Here 22
SIC 8742 Management consulting services

D-U-N-S 24-025-1624   (BR)

▲ Public Company   ■ Public Company Family Member   **HQ** Headquarters   **BR** Branch   **SL** Single Location

TD ASSET MANAGEMENT INC
T D WATERHOUSE PRIVATE INVESTMENT ADVICE
(*Suby of* Toronto-Dominion Bank, The)
324 8 Ave Sw Suite 1200, Calgary, AB, T2P 2Z2
(403) 299-8600
Emp Here 80
SIC 6282 Investment advice

D-U-N-S 20-255-5079 (BR)
TELUS COMMUNICATIONS INC
120 7 Ave Sw Suite 6, Calgary, AB, T2P 0W4

Emp Here 300
SIC 4899 Communication services, nec

D-U-N-S 20-010-7774 (HQ)
TSX VENTURE EXCHANGE INC
300 5 Ave Sw, Calgary, AB, T2P 3C4
(403) 218-2800
Emp Here 100　　　*Emp Total* 1,187
Sales 224,445,634
SIC 6231 Security and commodity exchanges
Dir Roy Hornyshin

D-U-N-S 25-416-6424 (SL)
TAYLOR GAS LIQUIDS LIMITED PARTNER-SHIP
TTLLP
800 5 Ave Sw Suite 2200, Calgary, AB, T2P 3T6
(403) 781-8181
Emp Here 28　　　*Sales* 44,211,200
SIC 1321 Natural gas liquids
Dir Robert (Bob) Pritchard
　David Schmunk
　Brad Mattson

D-U-N-S 20-293-1580 (SL)
TEKARRA PROJECT SERVICES LTD
131 9 Ave Sw Unit 20, Calgary, AB, T2P 1K1
(403) 984-6583
Emp Here 50　　　*Sales* 4,961,328
SIC 8711 Engineering services

D-U-N-S 24-997-5947 (SL)
TEKNICA OVERSEAS LTD
350 7 Ave Sw Suite 2700, Calgary, AB, T2P 3N9

Emp Here 74　　　*Sales* 3,356,192
SIC 8999 Services, nec

D-U-N-S 20-717-0932 (HQ)
TENARIS GLOBAL SERVICES (CANADA) INC
530 8 Ave Sw Suite 400, Calgary, AB, T2P 3S8
(403) 767-0100
Emp Here 74　　　*Sales* 13,686,766
SIC 3312 Blast furnaces and steel mills
Ch Bd Paolo Rocca
Pr Alberto Iperti
　Darren Flack

D-U-N-S 24-495-8724 (SL)
TERA ENVIRONMENTAL CONSULTANTS LTD
815 8 Ave Sw Suite 1100, Calgary, AB, T2P 3P2
(403) 265-2885
Emp Here 275　　　*Sales* 48,812,642
SIC 8748 Business consulting, nec
Pt Dean Mutrie
Pt Piers Fothergill

D-U-N-S 25-505-7028 (SL)
TIDAL ENERGY MARKETING INC
237 4 Ave Sw Suite 2000, Calgary, AB, T2P 4K3
(403) 205-7770
Emp Here 26　　　*Sales* 7,806,795
SIC 5172 Petroleum products, nec
Ch Bd Leigh Cruess
Pr James Lagadin

D-U-N-S 25-451-0548 (BR)

TORONTO-DOMINION BANK, THE
T D CANADA TRUST
(*Suby of* Toronto-Dominion Bank, The)
340 5 Ave Sw Suite 340, Calgary, AB, T2P 0L3
(403) 292-1100
Emp Here 40
SIC 6021 National commercial banks

D-U-N-S 24-776-5147 (BR)
TORYS LLP
4600 46fl 525 8 Ave Sw, Calgary, AB, T2P 1G1
(403) 776-3700
Emp Here 50
SIC 8111 Legal services

D-U-N-S 24-736-8512 (SL)
TOTAL CAPITAL CANADA LTD
240 4 Ave Sw Suite 2900, Calgary, AB, T2P 4H4
(403) 571-7599
Emp Here 50　　　*Sales* 35,862,791
SIC 1382 Oil and gas exploration services
Pr Pr Jean-Michel Dires

D-U-N-S 20-583-2061 (SL)
TOTAL E&P CANADA LTD
240 4 Ave Sw Suite 2900, Calgary, AB, T2P 4H4
(403) 571-7599
Emp Here 170　　　*Sales* 154,676,684
SIC 1311 Crude petroleum and natural gas
Pr Jean-Michel Gires
VP VP Gary Houston

D-U-N-S 25-977-4136 (SL)
TRANSZAP P2P CANADA, INC
OILDEX
(*Suby of* Transzap, Inc)
205 5 Ave Sw Suite 400, Calgary, AB, T2P 2V7
(403) 205-2550
Emp Here 65　　　*Sales* 7,223,109
SIC 7371 Custom computer programming services
Pr Lynn Taylor

D-U-N-S 20-920-3616 (BR)
TRAVERS FOOD SERVICE LTD
202 6 Ave Sw Suite 610, Calgary, AB, T2P 2R9

Emp Here 50
SIC 5812 Eating places

D-U-N-S 24-701-7288 (HQ)
TUCKER WIRELINE SERVICES CANADA INC
444 5 Ave Sw Suite 900, Calgary, AB, T2P 2T8
(403) 264-7040
Emp Here 37　　　*Emp Total* 181
Sales 28,454,673
SIC 1389 Oil and gas field services, nec
Pr Dave Jaellett
Dir Wayne Tucker
Dir Shawn Tucker

D-U-N-S 20-305-2253 (BR)
TUNDRA OIL & GAS LIMITED
715 5 Ave Sw Suite 1000, Calgary, AB, T2P 2X6
(403) 261-1876
Emp Here 44
SIC 1382 Oil and gas exploration services

D-U-N-S 25-290-9171 (SL)
UNIGLOBE BRAVO TRAVEL INC
600 6 Ave Sw Suite 1100, Calgary, AB, T2P 0S5
(403) 531-2400
Emp Here 25　　　*Sales* 7,103,258
SIC 4724 Travel agencies

D-U-N-S 24-318-5910 (BR)
UNIVERSAL GEOMATICS SOLUTIONS CORP.
910 7 Ave Sw Suite 1015, Calgary, AB, T2P 3N8
(403) 262-1306
Emp Here 20

SIC 7389 Business services, nec

D-U-N-S 25-315-3829 (HQ)
VALIANT TRUST COMPANY
606 4 St Sw Suite 310, Calgary, AB, T2P 1T1
(403) 233-2801
Emp Here 24　　　*Emp Total* 2,100
Sales 42,687,504
SIC 6021 National commercial banks
Pr Adrian Baker

D-U-N-S 25-150-2001 (BR)
VANCOUVER CAREER COLLEGE (BURN-ABY) INC
CDI COLLEGE
(*Suby of* Chung Family Holdings Inc)
800 5 Ave Sw Suite 100, Calgary, AB, T2P 3T6
(403) 232-6410
Emp Here 33
SIC 8211 Elementary and secondary schools

D-U-N-S 20-052-5140 (BR)
VARCO CANADA ULC
BRANDT
(*Suby of* National Oilwell Varco, Inc.)
715 5 Ave Sw Unit 1700, Calgary, AB, T2P 2X6
(403) 264-9646
Emp Here 40
SIC 1389 Oil and gas field services, nec

D-U-N-S 20-009-9810 (HQ)
VIDEON CABLESYSTEMS INC
D&D CABLE VISION
630 3 Ave Sw Suite 900, Calgary, AB, T2P 4L4
(403) 750-4500
Emp Here 900　　　*Emp Total* 14,000
Sales 227,587,200
SIC 4841 Cable and other pay television services
　Peter Bissonnette

D-U-N-S 24-324-7405 (BR)
WSP CANADA INC
717 7 Ave Sw Suite 1800, Calgary, AB, T2P 0Z3
(403) 263-8200
Emp Here 100
SIC 8713 Surveying services

D-U-N-S 24-851-3215 (BR)
WSP CANADA INC
GENIVAR
112 4 Ave Sw Suite 1000, Calgary, AB, T2P 0H3
(403) 266-2800
Emp Here 78
SIC 1382 Oil and gas exploration services

D-U-N-S 20-334-4143 (SL)
WATER STREET SPAGHETTI CORPORATION, THE
OLD SPAGHETTI FACTORY, THE
222 3 St Sw, Calgary, AB, T2P 1P9
(403) 263-7223
Emp Here 50　　　*Sales* 1,532,175
SIC 5812 Eating places

D-U-N-S 24-224-5608 (BR)
WENDY'S RESTAURANTS OF CANADA INC
WENDY'S
(*Suby of* The Wendy's Company)
111 5 Ave Sw, Calgary, AB, T2P 3Y6
(403) 290-0489
Emp Here 25
SIC 5812 Eating places

D-U-N-S 24-420-8018 (SL)
WESTERN CANADIAN OIL SANDS INC
707 7 Ave Sw Suite 400, Calgary, AB, T2P 3H6
(403) 232-1054
Emp Here 200　　　*Sales* 23,232,050
SIC 1382 Oil and gas exploration services
Pr Pr Errin Kimball
　Terry Lauder
Sec Darren Devine
Dir Joanne Finnerty

D-U-N-S 20-084-1604 (BR)
WINNERS MERCHANTS INTERNATIONAL L.P.
WINNERS
(*Suby of* The TJX Companies Inc)
128 8 Ave Sw, Calgary, AB, T2P 1B3
(403) 262-7606
Emp Here 40
SIC 5651 Family clothing stores

D-U-N-S 20-030-7358 (BR)
WOLVERTON SECURITIES LTD
335 8 Ave Sw Suite 2100, Calgary, AB, T2P 1C9

Emp Here 35
SIC 6211 Security brokers and dealers

D-U-N-S 24-598-8360 (BR)
WORLD WIDE CUSTOMS BROKERS LTD
Gd Lcd 1, Calgary, AB, T2P 2G8
(403) 538-3199
Emp Here 150
SIC 4731 Freight transportation arrangement

D-U-N-S 20-064-5633 (BR)
ZAYO CANADA INC
ALLSTREAM IT SERVICES, DIV OF
255 5 Ave Sw Suite 400, Calgary, AB, T2P 3G6
(403) 303-2000
Emp Here 30
SIC 4899 Communication services, nec

Calgary, AB T2R

D-U-N-S 24-680-2644 (SL)
1504953 ALBERTA LTD
HOTEL ARTS
119 12 Ave Sw, Calgary, AB, T2R 0G8
(403) 206-9565
Emp Here 80　　　*Sales* 3,502,114
SIC 7011 Hotels and motels

D-U-N-S 24-334-3253 (BR)
ATCO GAS AND PIPELINES LTD
ATCO GAS
1040 11 Ave Sw, Calgary, AB, T2R 0G3
(403) 245-7551
Emp Here 100
SIC 4923 Gas transmission and distribution

D-U-N-S 20-075-1055 (HQ)
ATCO GAS AND PIPELINES LTD
ATCO GAS, DIV OF
909 11 Ave Sw Suite 1200, Calgary, AB, T2R 1L7
(403) 245-7060
Emp Here 400　　　*Emp Total* 7,860
Sales 1,398,510,698
SIC 4923 Gas transmission and distribution
VP VP Patrick J House
　J A Campbell
　Ronald D Southern
　Craighton O Twa
　Basil K French
　William L Britton
　Nancy C Southern

D-U-N-S 20-291-3984 (SL)
ATCO POWER ALBERTA LTD
919 11 Ave Sw Suite 1400, Calgary, AB, T2R 1P3
(403) 209-6900
Emp Here 500　　　*Sales* 332,451,650
SIC 4911 Electric services
Pr John Ell

D-U-N-S 20-767-3559 (SL)
ADNAP ENTERPRISES LTD
PANDA CHILD CARE CENTRES
602 11 Ave Sw Suite 402, Calgary, AB, T2R 1J8

Emp Here 60　　　*Sales* 1,824,018

SIC 8351 Child day care services

D-U-N-S 24-761-9336   (BR)
ALBERTA HEALTH SERVICES
ADULT ADDICTION SERVICES
1177 11 Ave Sw Suite 200, Calgary, AB, T2R
1K9
(403) 297-3071
Emp Here 45
SIC 8322 Individual and family services

D-U-N-S 20-040-9535   (BR)
ALBERTA HEALTH SERVICES
STD CLINIC CALGARY, THE
1213 4 St Sw Suite 3223, Calgary, AB, T2R
0X7
(403) 955-6700
Emp Here 25
SIC 8093 Specialty outpatient clinics, nec

D-U-N-S 20-129-7251   (BR)
ALBERTA HEALTH SERVICES
SHELDON CHUMIR HEALTH CENTRE
1213 4 St Sw Suite 3223, Calgary, AB, T2R
0X7
(403) 532-6460
Emp Here 100
SIC 8011 Offices and clinics of medical doctors

D-U-N-S 20-578-2696   (BR)
ALBERTA TREASURY BRANCHES
ATB FINANCIAL
919 11 Ave Sw Suite 700, Calgary, AB, T2R
1P3
(403) 541-4119
Emp Here 400
SIC 6036 Savings institutions, except federal

D-U-N-S 24-348-1686   (SL)
BARLON ENGINEERING GROUP LTD, THE
TRACER SUPERVISION, DIV OF
340 12 Ave Sw Suite 1110, Calgary, AB, T2R
1L5
(403) 261-7097
Emp Here 50   *Sales* 4,961,328
SIC 8711 Engineering services

D-U-N-S 24-352-2443   (BR)
**BREWSTERS BREW PUB & BRASSERIE
(ALBERTA) INC**
BREWASTERS BREWING CO & RESTAURANT
834 11 Ave Sw, Calgary, AB, T2R 0E5
(403) 265-2739
Emp Here 50
SIC 5813 Drinking places

D-U-N-S 25-360-8772   (BR)
BROWNLEE LLP
396 11 Ave Sw Suite 700, Calgary, AB, T2R
0C5
(403) 232-8300
Emp Here 30
SIC 8111 Legal services

D-U-N-S 20-591-1089   (BR)
CALGARY BOARD OF EDUCATION
CONNAUGHT COMMUNITY SCHOOL
1121 12 Ave Sw, Calgary, AB, T2R 0J8
(403) 777-8560
Emp Here 25
SIC 8211 Elementary and secondary schools

D-U-N-S 24-011-9623   (BR)
CALGARY CATHOLIC IMMIGRATION SOCIETY
1111 11 Ave Sw Unit 111, Calgary, AB, T2R
0G5
(403) 262-2006
Emp Here 240
SIC 8322 Individual and family services

D-U-N-S 20-970-8317   (BR)
CALGARY URBAN PROJECT SOCIETY
ONE WORLD CHILD DEVELOPMENT CENTRE
622 11 Ave Sw, Calgary, AB, T2R 0E2

(403) 264-2217
Emp Here 22
SIC 8351 Child day care services

D-U-N-S 20-510-9478   (BR)
CANADIAN BLOOD SERVICES
737 13 Ave Sw, Calgary, AB, T2R 1J1
(403) 410-2650
Emp Here 50
SIC 8099 Health and allied services, nec

D-U-N-S 24-670-2430   (BR)
CANADIAN MEDICAL ASSOCIATION
(*Suby of* Canadian Medical Association)
708 11 Ave Sw Unit 300, Calgary, AB, T2R
0E4
(403) 244-8000
Emp Here 30
SIC 8621 Professional organizations

D-U-N-S 20-301-2224   (SL)
CASA ENERGY SERVICES CORP.
525 11 Ave Sw Suite 201, Calgary, AB, T2R
0C9
(403) 245-0029
Emp Here 250   *Sales* 94,855,750
SIC 1381 Drilling oil and gas wells
Pr Pr Ron Berg
  Dea Thomas
  Leonard David
  Quinn Douglas

D-U-N-S 25-094-2257   (SL)
**CATHOLIC FAMILY SERVICE OF CALGARY,
THE**
707 10 Ave Sw Suite 250, Calgary, AB, T2R
0B3
(403) 233-2360
Emp Here 80   *Sales* 3,137,310
SIC 8322 Individual and family services

D-U-N-S 24-023-5122   (SL)
**CONSOLIDATED REAL ESTATE SERVICES
INC**
602 12 Ave Sw Unit 500, Calgary, AB, T2R 1J3

Emp Here 40   *Sales* 6,969,360
SIC 6531 Real estate agents and managers
Pr Pr Richard Blair
VP VP Larry Beeston
Dir Arni Thornsteinson

D-U-N-S 20-318-3608   (BR)
DMG EVENTS (CANADA) INC
1333 8 St Sw Suite 302, Calgary, AB, T2R
1M6
(403) 209-3555
Emp Here 30
SIC 7389 Business services, nec

D-U-N-S 20-140-0293   (BR)
DMG EVENTS (CANADA) INC
302 1333 8 St, Calgary, AB, T2R 1M6
(403) 209-3555
Emp Here 24
SIC 7389 Business services, nec

D-U-N-S 24-330-7068   (SL)
DOCKTOR FREIGHT SOLUTIONS CORP
333 11 Ave Sw Suite 750, Calgary, AB, T2R
1L9
(403) 266-4131
Emp Here 40   *Sales* 7,396,450
SIC 4731 Freight transportation arrangement
Pr Pr G Ben Docktor
  Terry Andersen
VP Benjamin Docktor

D-U-N-S 20-251-8270   (BR)
EQUITABLE BANK
1333 8 St Sw Suite 600, Calgary, AB, T2R
1M6
(403) 440-1200
Emp Here 35
SIC 6021 National commercial banks

D-U-N-S 25-194-9319   (HQ)
FMC TECHNOLOGIES CANADA LTD
(*Suby of* Reliance Oilfield Services, LLC)

333 11 Ave Sw Suite 1000, Calgary, AB, T2R
1L9
(403) 262-4000
Emp Here 75   *Emp Total* 200
Sales 215,379,986
SIC 1389 Oil and gas field services, nec
  J. Kevin Delaney
Pr Pr Brad Gabel
Dir Harold R. Allsopp
Dir James C. Smith
Dir Robert M. Wilkinson
Dir Miles Lich
Dir Harry Knutson

D-U-N-S 20-152-8853   (BR)
**GOVERNMENT OF THE PROVINCE OF AL-
BERTA**
DISABILITIES SERVICE DIVISION
1520 4 St Sw Suite 600, Calgary, AB, T2R 1H5
(403) 297-5011
Emp Here 58
SIC 8322 Individual and family services

D-U-N-S 25-506-0055   (BR)
**GOVERNMENT OF THE PROVINCE OF AL-
BERTA**
TRAVEL ALBERTA
999 8 St Sw Suite 500, Calgary, AB, T2R 1J5
(403) 297-2700
Emp Here 20
SIC 4724 Travel agencies

D-U-N-S 20-578-8644   (BR)
**GREAT-WEST LIFE ASSURANCE COM-
PANY, THE**
CALGARY RESOURCE CENTER
906 12 Ave Sw Suite 300, Calgary, AB, T2R
1K7
(403) 262-2393
Emp Here 30
SIC 6311 Life insurance

D-U-N-S 20-638-7305   (SL)
GREENSMART MANUFACTURING LTD
GREENSMART
525 11 Ave Sw Suite 100, Calgary, AB, T2R
0C9

Emp Here 75   *Sales* 15,473,920
SIC 1521 Single-family housing construction
Pr Pr Greg Hammond

D-U-N-S 20-199-8338   (SL)
HEARTWORKS COMMUNICATIONS INC
THE OASIS WELLNESS CENTRE & SPA
880 16 Ave Sw, Calgary, AB, T2R 1J9
(403) 216-2747
Emp Here 55   *Sales* 1,824,018
SIC 7991 Physical fitness facilities

D-U-N-S 20-705-5596   (BR)
IA CLARINGTON INVESTMENTS INC
1414 8 St Sw, Calgary, AB, T2R 1J6
(403) 806-1078
Emp Here 20
SIC 6282 Investment advice

D-U-N-S 20-523-3955   (BR)
INTRIA ITEMS INC
TRANSIT 33409
301 11 Ave Sw, Calgary, AB, T2R 0C7

Emp Here 200
SIC 7374 Data processing and preparation

D-U-N-S 20-647-8625   (BR)
**INVESTORS GROUP FINANCIAL SER-
VICES INC**
1333 8 St Sw Suite 700, Calgary, AB, T2R
1M6
(403) 229-0555
Emp Here 60
SIC 8741 Management services

D-U-N-S 25-289-0868   (BR)
JWP PUBLISHING LIMITED PARTNERSHIP
NICKLE'S ENERGY GROUP
999 8 St Sw Suite 300, Calgary, AB, T2R 1N7

(403) 209-3500
Emp Here 44
SIC 2721 Periodicals

D-U-N-S 24-015-7917   (BR)
**JARDINE LLOYD THOMPSON CANADA
INC**
220 12 Ave Sw Suite 400, Calgary, AB, T2R
0E9
(403) 262-4605
Emp Here 70
SIC 6411 Insurance agents, brokers, and service

D-U-N-S 25-412-9141   (SL)
KAM AND RONSON MEDIA GROUP INC
815 10 Ave Sw Suite 210, Calgary, AB, T2R
0B4

Emp Here 20   *Sales* 7,255,776
SIC 5065 Electronic parts and equipment, nec
Pr Pr Kam Chak Man
Dir Gregory Hansen
Dir Wise Wong
Dir Sam Kwan
Dir John Wong
  Jane Leung

D-U-N-S 25-485-8202   (BR)
KHATIJA INVESTMENTS LTD
BEST WESTERN SUITES
(*Suby of* Khatija Investments Ltd)
1330 8 St Sw, Calgary, AB, T2R 1B6
(403) 228-6900
Emp Here 20
SIC 7011 Hotels and motels

D-U-N-S 25-311-0811   (BR)
LONDON LIFE INSURANCE COMPANY
LONDON LIFE ELVEDEN GROUP
227 11 Ave Sw Suite 500, Calgary, AB, T2R
1R9
(403) 261-4690
Emp Here 30
SIC 6311 Life insurance

D-U-N-S 20-435-4435   (HQ)
LOUIS DREYFUS COMPANY CANADA ULC
525 11 Ave Sw Suite 500, Calgary, AB, T2R
0C9
(403) 205-3322
Emp Here 25   *Emp Total* 35,890
Sales 96,413,736
SIC 5153 Grain and field beans
Pr Pr Brant Randles

D-U-N-S 25-281-5162   (BR)
MD MANAGEMENT LIMITED
MD FINANCIAL
(*Suby of* Canadian Medical Association)
708 11 Ave Sw Suite 300, Calgary, AB, T2R
0E4
(403) 244-8000
Emp Here 30
SIC 8741 Management services

D-U-N-S 25-681-1969   (HQ)
MATRIX SOLUTIONS INC
(*Suby of* Matrix Solutions Inc)
214 11 Ave Sw Suite 600, Calgary, AB, T2R
0K1
(403) 237-0606
Emp Here 300   *Emp Total* 500
Sales 70,188,193
SIC 8748 Business consulting, nec
  John Feick
CEO Robert Pockar

D-U-N-S 20-510-9973   (BR)
MCELHANNEY LAND SURVEYS LTD
999 8 St Sw Suite 450, Calgary, AB, T2R 1J5
(403) 245-4711
Emp Here 80
SIC 8713 Surveying services

D-U-N-S 24-118-4217   (BR)
MOUNTAIN EQUIPMENT CO-OPERATIVE
MOUNTAIN EQUIPMENT CO-OPERATIVE
830 10 Ave Sw, Calgary, AB, T2R 0A9

(403) 269-2420
Emp Here 80
SIC 5941 Sporting goods and bicycle shops

D-U-N-S 20-697-0977   (SL)
OILSANDS QUEST SASK INC
326 11 Ave Sw Suite 800, Calgary, AB, T2R 0C5

Emp Here 40   *Sales* 38,986,240
SIC 1382 Oil and gas exploration services
Pr Pr Christopher Hopkins
  Garth Wong
Recvr Harold Neil Narfson

D-U-N-S 20-353-6651   (SL)
PLATINUM ENERGY SERVICES ULC
333 11 Ave Sw Unit 400, Calgary, AB, T2R 1L9
(403) 264-6688
Emp Here 20   *Sales* 3,064,349
SIC 3443 Fabricated plate work (boiler shop)

D-U-N-S 25-506-8645   (HQ)
PURE TECHNOLOGIES LTD
(*Suby of* Pure Technologies Ltd)
705 11 Ave Sw Suite 300, Calgary, AB, T2R 0E3
(403) 266-6794
Emp Here 26   *Emp Total* 510
Sales 85,113,909
SIC 4899 Communication services, nec
Pr John Elliott
  Mark Holley
  Geoffrey Krause
Sr VP Michael Higgins
  Robert Budianto
Sr VP Michael Wrigglesworth
Sr VP Muthu Chandrasekaran
Sec Nicole Springer
  James Paulson
  Peter Paulson

D-U-N-S 20-830-7876   (BR)
ROYAL & SUN ALLIANCE INSURANCE COMPANY OF CANADA
RSA GROUP
326 11 Ave Sw Suite 300, Calgary, AB, T2R 0C5
(403) 233-6000
Emp Here 260
SIC 6331 Fire, marine, and casualty insurance

D-U-N-S 25-154-8764   (SL)
SABAL HOMES LIMITED PARTNERSHIP
1122 4 St Sw Suite 600, Calgary, AB, T2R 1M1
(403) 237-8555
Emp Here 75   *Sales* 15,623,300
SIC 1521 Single-family housing construction
Pr Pr Larry Fan
Dir Donna Fan
Dir Ken Lee

D-U-N-S 24-798-9606   (SL)
SMITH BITS
396 11 Ave Sw Suite 710, Calgary, AB, T2R 0C5

Emp Here 49   *Sales* 13,087,050
SIC 3533 Oil and gas field machinery
  Perry Genereux

D-U-N-S 20-075-6385   (HQ)
SMITH INTERNATIONAL CANADA LTD
396 11 Ave Sw Suite 710, Calgary, AB, T2R 0C5
(403) 264-6077
Emp Here 30   *Emp Total* 155
Sales 36,562,365
SIC 5084 Industrial machinery and equipment
Fin Ex Perry Genereux

D-U-N-S 25-079-8485   (BR)
SOBEYS WEST INC
CANADA SAFEWAY
813 11 Ave Sw, Calgary, AB, T2R 0E6
(403) 264-1375
Emp Here 250

SIC 5411 Grocery stores

D-U-N-S 24-343-1918   (BR)
SOVEREIGN GENERAL INSURANCE COMPANY, THE
550 11 Ave Sw Unit 900, Calgary, AB, T2R 1M7
(403) 781-1250
Emp Here 33
SIC 6411 Insurance agents, brokers, and service

D-U-N-S 20-010-4516   (BR)
SUNSHINE VILLAGE CORPORATION
550 11 Ave Sw Suite 400, Calgary, AB, T2R 1M7
(403) 705-4000
Emp Here 20
SIC 7389 Business services, nec

D-U-N-S 24-598-2652   (SL)
THE LAKE LOUISE SKI AREA LTD
1333 8 St Sw Suite 908, Calgary, AB, T2R 1M6
(403) 244-4449
Emp Here 600   *Sales* 35,337,600
SIC 7011 Hotels and motels
Pr Pr Charles Lock
  Derek Kwaskey
Dir Louise Lock

D-U-N-S 24-081-7499   (SL)
TOKER + ASSOCIATES ARCHITECTURE INDUSTRIAL DESIGN LTD
340 12 Ave Sw Unit 1180, Calgary, AB, T2R 1L5
(403) 245-3089
Emp Here 32   *Sales* 2,845,467
SIC 8712 Architectural services

D-U-N-S 20-990-0026   (SL)
TOMKINSON, D.N. INVESTMENTS LTD
340 12 Ave Sw Suite 900, Calgary, AB, T2R 1L5
(403) 269-8887
Emp Here 150   *Sales* 23,333,500
SIC 8713 Surveying services
Pr Pr Donald Tomkinson

D-U-N-S 20-768-2063   (SL)
TOOLE, P.J. & COTE REAL ESTATE LTD
309 10 Ave Sw, Calgary, AB, T2R 0A5
(403) 233-9638
Emp Here 250   *Sales* 31,705,680
SIC 6531 Real estate agents and managers
Pr Pr Patrick Toole
  Clair Cote
VP VP John Toole
  Wilfred Shalenko

D-U-N-S 20-890-4701   (BR)
TWIN BUTTE ENERGY LTD
396 11 Ave Sw Suite 410, Calgary, AB, T2R 0C5
(403) 215-2045
Emp Here 35
SIC 1381 Drilling oil and gas wells

D-U-N-S 24-915-5490   (BR)
WAWANESA LIFE INSURANCE COMPANY, THE
WAWANESA MUTUAL INSURANCE COMPANY
(*Suby of* Wawanesa Mutual Insurance Company, The)
708 11 Ave Sw Suite 600, Calgary, AB, T2R 0E4
(403) 536-9258
Emp Here 150
SIC 6311 Life insurance

D-U-N-S 25-207-5320   (BR)
WAWANESA MUTUAL INSURANCE COMPANY, THE
(*Suby of* Wawanesa Mutual Insurance Company, The)
708 11 Ave Sw Suite 600, Calgary, AB, T2R 0E4

(403) 266-8600
Emp Here 140
SIC 6331 Fire, marine, and casualty insurance

D-U-N-S 24-393-2485   (BR)
WORLEYPARSONS CANADA SERVICES LTD
540 12 Ave Sw, Calgary, AB, T2R 0H4
(403) 508-5300
Emp Here 300
SIC 8711 Engineering services

Calgary, AB T2S

D-U-N-S 24-271-8716   (SL)
4TH STREET ROSE RESTAURANT LTD
4TH STREET ROSE CATERING
2116 4 St Sw, Calgary, AB, T2S 1W7

Emp Here 50   *Sales* 1,532,175
SIC 5812 Eating places

D-U-N-S 25-218-8289   (SL)
599515 ALBERTA LTD
MELROSE CAFE & BAR
730 17 Ave Sw, Calgary, AB, T2S 0B7
(403) 228-3566
Emp Here 83   *Sales* 3,064,349
SIC 5813 Drinking places

D-U-N-S 20-810-1865   (HQ)
ALBERTA BALLET COMPANY, THE
(*Suby of* Alberta Ballet Company, The)
141 18 Ave Sw, Calgary, AB, T2S 0B8
(403) 228-4430
Emp Here 51   *Emp Total* 70
Sales 8,025,677
SIC 7922 Theatrical producers and services
Ex Dir Chris George
Ch Bd Larry Clausen
V Ch Bd George Goldhoff
Sec Frank Molnar
Treas Chandra Henry
Dir Kevin Krausert
Dir Ron Bryant
Dir John Masters

D-U-N-S 24-113-4837   (BR)
ALBERTA HEALTH SERVICES
ALBERTA CANCER CORRIDOR
2210 2 St Sw Suite 712, Calgary, AB, T2S 3C3
(403) 698-8020
Emp Here 23
SIC 8069 Specialty hospitals, except psychiatric

D-U-N-S 25-003-0202   (SL)
AVENTA TREATMENT FOUNDATION FOR WOMEN
610 25 Ave Sw, Calgary, AB, T2S 0L6
(403) 245-9050
Emp Here 52   *Sales* 2,042,900
SIC 8322 Individual and family services

D-U-N-S 20-713-1439   (BR)
CALGARY BOARD OF EDUCATION
WESTERN CANADA HIGH SCHOOL
641 17 Ave Sw, Calgary, AB, T2S 0B5
(403) 228-5363
Emp Here 125
SIC 8211 Elementary and secondary schools

D-U-N-S 20-591-1527   (BR)
CALGARY BOARD OF EDUCATION
ELBOYA ELEMENTARY JUNIOR HIGH SCHOOL
4804 6 St Sw, Calgary, AB, T2S 2N3
(403) 777-7760
Emp Here 40
SIC 8211 Elementary and secondary schools

D-U-N-S 20-713-1272   (BR)
CALGARY BOARD OF EDUCATION
RIDEAU PARK ELEMENTARY JUNIOR HIGH SCHOOL

829 Rideau Rd Sw, Calgary, AB, T2S 0S2
(403) 777-7480
Emp Here 50
SIC 8211 Elementary and secondary schools

D-U-N-S 20-974-4957   (BR)
CALGARY ROMAN CATHOLIC SEPARATE SCHOOL DISTRICT #1
OUR LADY OF LOURDES SCHOOL
1916 2 St Sw, Calgary, AB, T2S 1S3
(403) 500-2002
Emp Here 33
SIC 8211 Elementary and secondary schools

D-U-N-S 20-651-5145   (BR)
CALGARY ROMAN CATHOLIC SEPARATE SCHOOL DISTRICT #1
ST. MONICA SCHOOL
235 18 Ave Sw, Calgary, AB, T2S 0C2
(403) 500-2001
Emp Here 40
SIC 8211 Elementary and secondary schools

D-U-N-S 25-600-4276   (BR)
CALGARY ROMAN CATHOLIC SEPARATE SCHOOL DISTRICT #1
ST. MARY'S SENIOR HIGH SCHOOL
111 18 Ave Sw Suite 1, Calgary, AB, T2S 0B8
(403) 500-2024
Emp Here 85
SIC 8211 Elementary and secondary schools

D-U-N-S 20-152-1908   (BR)
CAN ALTA BINDERY CORP
(*Suby of* Can Alta Bindery Corp)
1711 4 St Sw Suite 407, Calgary, AB, T2S 1V8
(403) 245-8226
Emp Here 50
SIC 2789 Bookbinding and related work

D-U-N-S 24-068-4261   (BR)
EARL'S RESTAURANTS LTD
PIN PALACE
(*Suby of* Earl's Restaurants Ltd)
2401 4 St Sw, Calgary, AB, T2S 1X5
(403) 228-4141
Emp Here 100
SIC 5812 Eating places

D-U-N-S 20-232-3510   (BR)
ENTERPRISE UNIVERSAL INC
BOW RIVER PROPERTY MANAGEMENT & LEASING
2210 2 St Sw Unit B250, Calgary, AB, T2S 3C3
(403) 228-4431
Emp Here 106
SIC 6519 Real property lessors, nec

D-U-N-S 25-100-9007   (HQ)
FORTISALBERTA INC
320 17 Ave Sw, Calgary, AB, T2S 2V1
(403) 514-4000
Emp Here 1,000   *Emp Total* 8,000
Sales 423,253,715
SIC 4911 Electric services
Pr Pr Phonse Delaney
VP Curtis Eck
  Janine Sullivam
VP Opers Cam Aplin
Manager Rob Tisdale
VP Karl Bomhof
Sec Tamara Day
  Tracey Ball
  Bill Giebelhaus
  Susan Mackenzie

D-U-N-S 20-832-2438   (SL)
GLENCOE GOLF & COUNTRY CLUB, THE
(*Suby of* Glencoe Club, The)
636 29 Ave Sw, Calgary, AB, T2S 0P1
(403) 242-4019
Emp Here 35   *Sales* 1,386,253
SIC 7997 Membership sports and recreation clubs

D-U-N-S 24-376-3740   (BR)
HARVARD BROADCASTING INC

X 92.9 FM
255 17 Ave Sw Unit 400, Calgary, AB, T2S 2T8
(403) 670-0210
Emp Here 20
SIC 4832 Radio broadcasting stations

D-U-N-S 25-313-5263   (HQ)
HOPEWELL DEVELOPMENT CORPORATION
2020 4 St Sw Suite 410, Calgary, AB, T2S 1W3
(403) 232-8821
Emp Here 28   *Emp Total* 3
Sales 13,253,640
SIC 6552 Subdividers and developers, nec
Pr Pr Kevin Pshebniski
Dir Lawrence C K Fan
Dir Sanders Lee

D-U-N-S 20-823-4836   (SL)
LANMARK ENGINEERING INC
2424 4 St Sw Suite 340, Calgary, AB, T2S 2T4
(403) 536-7300
Emp Here 50   *Sales* 4,961,328
SIC 8711 Engineering services

D-U-N-S 24-033-2655   (SL)
MERCATO INTERNATIONAL LTD
2224 4 St Sw, Calgary, AB, T2S 1W9
(403) 263-5535
Emp Here 80   *Sales* 2,407,703
SIC 5812 Eating places

D-U-N-S 24-984-1487   (SL)
RAREMETHOD INTERACTIVE STUDIOS INC
RARE METHOD
1812 4 St Sw Suite 601, Calgary, AB, T2S 1W1

Emp Here 75   *Sales* 14,000,100
SIC 4899 Communication services, nec
Pr Pr Roger Jewett

D-U-N-S 20-350-1614   (SL)
RESPECT GROUP INC
540 21 Ave Sw Unit 8, Calgary, AB, T2S 0H1
(403) 249-2963
Emp Here 20   *Sales* 5,197,506
SIC 8322 Individual and family services

D-U-N-S 24-840-6068   (SL)
SHIP & ANCHOR PUB LTD
534 17 Ave Sw, Calgary, AB, T2S 0B1
(403) 245-3333
Emp Here 50   *Sales* 1,532,175
SIC 5812 Eating places

D-U-N-S 25-450-1273   (BR)
SHOPPERS DRUG MART CORPORATION
SHOPPERS DRUG MART
504 Elbow Dr Sw, Calgary, AB, T2S 2H6
(403) 228-3338
Emp Here 20
SIC 5912 Drug stores and proprietary stores

D-U-N-S 25-271-0868   (BR)
SOBEYS WEST INC
SAFEWAY
524 Elbow Dr Sw, Calgary, AB, T2S 2H6
(403) 228-6141
Emp Here 100
SIC 5411 Grocery stores

D-U-N-S 25-499-4858   (BR)
STARBUCKS COFFEE CANADA, INC
(*Suby of* Starbucks Corporation)
723 17 Ave Sw, Calgary, AB, T2S 0B6
(403) 209-2888
Emp Here 24
SIC 5812 Eating places

D-U-N-S 25-289-6246   (BR)
SUNCOR ENERGY INC
4 & 20 CAR WASH
1920 4 St Sw, Calgary, AB, T2S 1W3
(403) 228-6473
Emp Here 45

SIC 7542 Carwashes

Calgary, AB T2T

D-U-N-S 25-296-9712   (BR)
BANK OF NOVA SCOTIA, THE
SCOTIABANK
1401 17 Ave Sw, Calgary, AB, T2T 0C6
(403) 221-6821
Emp Here 24
SIC 6021 National commercial banks

D-U-N-S 20-591-1568   (BR)
CALGARY BOARD OF EDUCATION
ALTERNATIVE HIGH SCHOOL
5003 20 St Sw, Calgary, AB, T2T 5A5
(403) 777-7730
Emp Here 20
SIC 8211 Elementary and secondary schools

D-U-N-S 20-713-0936   (BR)
CALGARY BOARD OF EDUCATION
EARL GREY ELEMENTARY SCHOOL
845 Hillcrest Ave Sw, Calgary, AB, T2T 0Z1
(403) 777-8570
Emp Here 22
SIC 8211 Elementary and secondary schools

D-U-N-S 25-269-7032   (BR)
CALGARY BOARD OF EDUCATION
MOUNT ROYAL JUNIOR HIGH SCHOOL
2234 14 St Sw, Calgary, AB, T2T 3T3
(403) 777-7980
Emp Here 30
SIC 8211 Elementary and secondary schools

D-U-N-S 25-140-2061   (BR)
CALGARY BOARD OF EDUCATION
DR. CAKLEY SCHOOL
3904 20 St Sw, Calgary, AB, T2T 4Z9
(403) 777-8300
Emp Here 40
SIC 8211 Elementary and secondary schools

D-U-N-S 20-713-0910   (BR)
CALGARY BOARD OF EDUCATION
EMILY FOLLENBEE CENTRE SCHOOL
5139 14 St Sw, Calgary, AB, T2T 3W5
(403) 777-6980
Emp Here 50
SIC 8211 Elementary and secondary schools

D-U-N-S 20-591-1147   (BR)
CALGARY BOARD OF EDUCATION
WILLIAM REID SCHOOL
1216 36 Ave Sw, Calgary, AB, T2T 2E9
(403) 777-6940
Emp Here 20
SIC 8211 Elementary and secondary schools

D-U-N-S 20-591-1477   (BR)
CALGARY BOARD OF EDUCATION
ALTADORE ELEMENTARY SCHOOL
4506 16 St Sw, Calgary, AB, T2T 4H9
(403) 777-6910
Emp Here 20
SIC 8211 Elementary and secondary schools

D-U-N-S 20-590-7996   (BR)
CALGARY BOARD OF EDUCATION
RICHMOND SCHOOL
2701 22 St Sw, Calgary, AB, T2T 5G5
(403) 240-1470
Emp Here 25
SIC 8211 Elementary and secondary schools

D-U-N-S 20-036-2783   (BR)
CALGARY ROMAN CATHOLIC SEPARATE SCHOOL DISTRICT #1
ST. CHARLES CONGREGATED SCHOOL
2445 23 Ave Sw, Calgary, AB, T2T 0W3
(403) 249-8793
Emp Here 20
SIC 8211 Elementary and secondary schools

D-U-N-S 24-646-4952   (SL)
CENTURY 21 BAMBER REALTY LTD
1612 17 Ave Sw, Calgary, AB, T2T 0E3
(403) 875-4653
Emp Here 120   *Sales* 11,308,909
SIC 6531 Real estate agents and managers
Pr Pr George Bamber

D-U-N-S 25-367-4030   (SL)
GRIER CABINETS & DOORS INC
CAST FX
82 Ypres Green Sw, Calgary, AB, T2T 6M1

Emp Here 105   *Sales* 21,201,280
SIC 5211 Lumber and other building materials
Pr Pr Kenneth Grier
Dir Donald Robertson
Dir Melvin Grebinsky
Dir Christopher Dobbin
Dir Dale Hodgson

D-U-N-S 24-438-5522   (SL)
LYCEE LOUIS PASTEUR SOCIETY
4099 Garrison Blvd Sw, Calgary, AB, T2T 6G2
(403) 243-5420
Emp Here 60   *Sales* 4,012,839
SIC 8211 Elementary and secondary schools

D-U-N-S 25-523-3918   (BR)
MOXIE'S RESTAURANTS, LIMITED PARTNERSHIP
MOXIE'S CLASSIC GRILL
1331 17 Ave Sw, Calgary, AB, T2T 0C4

Emp Here 50
SIC 5812 Eating places

D-U-N-S 20-439-9810   (HQ)
PASLEY, MAX ENTERPRISES LIMITED
MCDONALD'S RESTAURANTS
(*Suby of* Pasley, Max Enterprises Limited)
1032 17 Ave Sw Suite 400, Calgary, AB, T2T 0A5
(403) 245-0846
Emp Here 20   *Emp Total* 3,000
Sales 124,595,200
SIC 5812 Eating places
 Max Pasley
Pr Gary Pasley
Pr Scott Pasley
 Helen Pasley
Dir Richard Bonnett

D-U-N-S 25-316-4172   (BR)
PASLEY, MAX ENTERPRISES LIMITED
MCDONALD'S RESTAURANT NO. 7559
(*Suby of* Pasley, Max Enterprises Limited)
1422 17 Ave Sw, Calgary, AB, T2T 0C3
(403) 245-4154
Emp Here 65
SIC 5812 Eating places

D-U-N-S 20-913-5479   (BR)
RUNDLE COLLEGE SOCIETY
4330 16 St Sw Suite 4416, Calgary, AB, T2T 4H9
(403) 250-2965
Emp Here 32
SIC 8211 Elementary and secondary schools

D-U-N-S 20-871-3367   (BR)
SOBEYS WEST INC
SAFEWAY
2425 34 Ave Sw, Calgary, AB, T2T 6E3
(403) 240-1098
Emp Here 50
SIC 5411 Grocery stores

D-U-N-S 20-642-4173   (BR)
STARBUCKS COFFEE CANADA, INC
STARBUCKS COFFEE COMPANY
(*Suby of* Starbucks Corporation)
3531 Garrison Gate Sw, Calgary, AB, T2T 6E4
(403) 685-4500
Emp Here 20
SIC 5812 Eating places

D-U-N-S 24-232-1474   (BR)

STATESMAN GROUP OF COMPANIES LTD, THE
2400 Sorrel Mews Sw, Calgary, AB, T2T 6H8
(403) 240-3636
Emp Here 50
SIC 8322 Individual and family services

D-U-N-S 25-413-9462   (SL)
STEEL INDUSTRIES LTD
909 17 Ave Sw 4th Flr, Calgary, AB, T2T 0A4
(866) 584-9653
Emp Here 194   *Sales* 18,281,183
SIC 3599 Industrial machinery, nec
Pr Pr Mark Rodacker
 Janet Rodacker

D-U-N-S 20-112-8985   (BR)
STERICYCLE COMMUNICATION SOLUTIONS, ULC
TIGERTEL COMMUNICATIONS
(*Suby of* Stericycle Communication Solutions, ULC)
1032 17 Ave Sw Suite 200, Calgary, AB, T2T 0A5
(403) 245-4434
Emp Here 35
SIC 4899 Communication services, nec

D-U-N-S 20-767-0670   (SL)
TOOLE PEET & CO LIMITED
TOOLE PEET INSURANCE
1135 17 Ave Sw, Calgary, AB, T2T 0B6
(403) 245-4366
Emp Here 75   *Sales* 9,746,560
SIC 6531 Real estate agents and managers
Pr Pr Laurence Toole

D-U-N-S 25-520-4596   (BR)
WENDY'S RESTAURANTS OF CANADA INC
WENDY'S
(*Suby of* The Wendy's Company)
1304 17 Ave Sw, Calgary, AB, T2T 0C3
(403) 245-0252
Emp Here 40
SIC 5812 Eating places

Calgary, AB T2V

D-U-N-S 25-314-9124   (BR)
ALBERTA HEALTH SERVICES
ROCKYVIEW GENERAL HOSPITAL
7007 14 St Sw, Calgary, AB, T2V 1P9
(403) 943-3000
Emp Here 2,500
SIC 8011 Offices and clinics of medical doctors

D-U-N-S 20-700-1285   (BR)
BANQUE TORONTO-DOMINION, LA
TORONTO-DOMINION BANK, THE
(*Suby of* Toronto-Dominion Bank, The)
1600 90 Ave Sw Suite C143, Calgary, AB, T2V 5A8
(403) 252-5352
Emp Here 20
SIC 6021 National commercial banks

D-U-N-S 24-441-2425   (HQ)
BANTREL CO.
(*Suby of* Bechtel Group, Inc.)
1201 Glenmore Trail Sw Suite 1061, Calgary, AB, T2V 4Y8
(403) 290-5000
Emp Here 2,525   *Emp Total* 52,700
Sales 342,039,762
SIC 8711 Engineering services
Pr Darrel Donly
VP Fin Kenneth L Baron
VP VP Douglas S Barth
VP Prd Mike Gordon
 Gerald Mulvany
VP VP Dan Michaud

D-U-N-S 20-267-4979   (BR)

BELL AND HOWELL CANADA LTD
(*Suby of* Bell and Howell Canada Ltd)
7620 Elbow Dr Sw, Calgary, AB, T2V 1K2
(403) 640-4214
Emp Here 20
SIC 5112 Stationery and office supplies

D-U-N-S 20-831-9665   (SL)
BEVERLY CENTRE INC, THE
1729 90 Ave Sw, Calgary, AB, T2V 4S1
(403) 253-8806
Emp Here 300   *Sales* 18,789,760
SIC 8051 Skilled nursing care facilities
Pr Hasmuth Patel

D-U-N-S 20-713-1322   (BR)
CALGARY BOARD OF EDUCATION
LOUIS RIEL ELEMENTARY & JUNIOR HIGH SCHOOL
9632 Oakfield Dr Sw, Calgary, AB, T2V 0L1
(403) 777-7650
Emp Here 45
SIC 8211 Elementary and secondary schools

D-U-N-S 25-130-7435   (BR)
CALGARY BOARD OF EDUCATION
HENRY WISE WOOD HIGH SCHOOL
910 75 Ave Sw, Calgary, AB, T2V 0S6
(403) 253-2261
Emp Here 130
SIC 8211 Elementary and secondary schools

D-U-N-S 25-269-8857   (BR)
CALGARY BOARD OF EDUCATION
JOHN WARE JUNIOR HIGH SCHOOL
10020 19 St Sw, Calgary, AB, T2V 1R2
(403) 777-7930
Emp Here 47
SIC 8211 Elementary and secondary schools

D-U-N-S 20-590-7905   (BR)
CALGARY BOARD OF EDUCATION
NELLIE MCCLUNG SCHOOL
2315 Palliser Dr Sw, Calgary, AB, T2V 3S4
(403) 777-8620
Emp Here 40
SIC 8211 Elementary and secondary schools

D-U-N-S 20-591-1196   (BR)
CALGARY BOARD OF EDUCATION
CHINOOK PARK ELEMENTARY SCHOOL
1312 75 Ave Sw, Calgary, AB, T2V 0S6
(403) 777-8480
Emp Here 50
SIC 8211 Elementary and secondary schools

D-U-N-S 20-591-1915   (BR)
CALGARY BOARD OF EDUCATION
WOODMAN JUNIOR HIGH
8706 Elbow Dr Sw, Calgary, AB, T2V 1L2
(403) 777-7490
Emp Here 64
SIC 8211 Elementary and secondary schools

D-U-N-S 20-591-1048   (BR)
CALGARY BOARD OF EDUCATION
EUGENE COSTE SCHOOL
10 Hillgrove Cres Sw, Calgary, AB, T2V 3K7
(403) 777-8511
Emp Here 25
SIC 8211 Elementary and secondary schools

D-U-N-S 24-716-6002   (SL)
CALGARY JEWISH ACADEMY, THE
6700 Kootenay St Sw, Calgary, AB, T2V 1P7
(403) 253-3992
Emp Here 50   *Sales* 1,532,175
SIC 8351 Child day care services

D-U-N-S 20-029-4382   (BR)
CALGARY ROMAN CATHOLIC SEPARATE SCHOOL DISTRICT #1
ST. BENEDICT SCHOOL
10340 19 St Sw, Calgary, AB, T2V 1R2
(403) 500-2053
Emp Here 38
SIC 8211 Elementary and secondary schools

D-U-N-S 25-272-3051   (BR)
CALGARY ROMAN CATHOLIC SEPARATE SCHOOL DISTRICT #1
ST. AUGUSTINE ELEMENTARY & JUNIOR HIGH SCHOOL
7112 7 St Sw, Calgary, AB, T2V 1E9
(403) 500-2022
Emp Here 40
SIC 8211 Elementary and secondary schools

D-U-N-S 25-121-0795   (BR)
CALGARY ROMAN CATHOLIC SEPARATE SCHOOL DISTRICT #1
BISHOP GRANDIN SENIOR HIGH SCHOOL
111 Haddon Rd Sw, Calgary, AB, T2V 2Y2
(403) 500-2047
Emp Here 110
SIC 8211 Elementary and secondary schools

D-U-N-S 20-209-3659   (BR)
CALGARY YOUNG MEN'S CHRISTIAN ASSOCIATION
YMCA HERITAGE
11 Haddon Rd Sw, Calgary, AB, T2V 2X8

Emp Here 120
SIC 8399 Social services, nec

D-U-N-S 20-572-7576   (BR)
CANADA POST CORPORATION
2580 Southland Dr Sw, Calgary, AB, T2V 4J8
(403) 246-1154
Emp Here 20
SIC 4311 U.s. postal service

D-U-N-S 20-806-6279   (BR)
COUTTS, WILLIAM E. COMPANY, LIMITED
HALLMARK CARDS
(*Suby of* Hallmark Cards, Incorporated)
1600 90 Ave Sw Unit A126, Calgary, AB, T2V 5A8

Emp Here 25
SIC 5947 Gift, novelty, and souvenir shop

D-U-N-S 24-335-5828   (BR)
DIVERSICARE CANADA MANAGEMENT SERVICES CO., INC
TRINITY LODGE
1111 Glenmore Trail Sw, Calgary, AB, T2V 4C9
(403) 253-7576
Emp Here 65
SIC 6513 Apartment building operators

D-U-N-S 24-790-3342   (SL)
HERITAGE LENDING GROUP LTD
6707 Elbow Dr Sw, Calgary, AB, T2V 0E3
(403) 255-5750
Emp Here 21   *Sales* 5,782,650
SIC 6162 Mortgage bankers and loan correspondents
Pr Christopher Chabel

D-U-N-S 24-392-5968   (BR)
INTERCARE CORPORATE GROUP INC
INTERCARE CHINOOK CARE CENTRE
(*Suby of* Intercare Corporate Group Inc)
1261 Glenmore Trail Sw, Calgary, AB, T2V 4Y8
(403) 252-0141
Emp Here 50
SIC 8322 Individual and family services

D-U-N-S 25-186-7081   (BR)
LIFEMARK HEALTH MANAGEMENT INC
LIFEMARK PHYSIOTHERAPY
(*Suby of* Audax Group, L.P.)
2000 Southland Dr Sw, Calgary, AB, T2V 4S4
(403) 252-8535
Emp Here 30
SIC 8741 Management services

D-U-N-S 25-521-5675   (BR)
PASLEY, MAX ENTERPRISES LIMITED
MCDONALD'S RESTAURANT
(*Suby of* Pasley, Max Enterprises Limited)
1600 90 Ave Sw Suite D267, Calgary, AB, T2V

5A8
(403) 258-3311
Emp Here 42
SIC 5812 Eating places

D-U-N-S 25-622-5137   (BR)
PHIL'S RESTAURANTS LTD
(*Suby of* Phil's Restaurants Ltd)
907 Glenmore Trail Sw, Calgary, AB, T2V 2H6
(403) 252-6061
Emp Here 30
SIC 5812 Eating places

D-U-N-S 25-321-4217   (BR)
REVERA INC
RENOIR RETIREMENT RESIDENCE
9229 16 St Sw, Calgary, AB, T2V 5H3
(403) 255-2105
Emp Here 160
SIC 8361 Residential care

D-U-N-S 25-271-0512   (BR)
SOBEYS WEST INC
SAFEWAY
1600 90 Ave Sw, Calgary, AB, T2V 5A8
(403) 255-2755
Emp Here 140
SIC 5411 Grocery stores

D-U-N-S 20-989-8170   (SL)
TRAVOIS HOLDINGS LTD
GLAMORGAN CARE CENTRE
8240 Collicutt St Sw, Calgary, AB, T2V 2X1
(403) 252-4445
Emp Here 260   *Sales* 16,277,760
SIC 8051 Skilled nursing care facilities
Pr Pr Carl Bond

D-U-N-S 25-522-5799   (BR)
VICTORIAN ORDER OF NURSES FOR CANADA
VON CALGARY DISTRICT
9705 Horton Rd Sw Suite 100, Calgary, AB, T2V 2X5
(403) 640-4765
Emp Here 150
SIC 8082 Home health care services

Calgary, AB T2W

D-U-N-S 24-043-2377   (SL)
300826 ALBERTA LTD
BOSTON PIZZA
10456 Southport Rd Sw, Calgary, AB, T2W 3M5

Emp Here 70   *Sales* 2,115,860
SIC 5812 Eating places

D-U-N-S 24-777-4214   (BR)
ALBERTA HEALTH SERVICES
DAVID THOMPSON HEALTH REGION
10101 Southport Rd Sw, Calgary, AB, T2W 3N2
(403) 943-1111
Emp Here 300
SIC 8011 Offices and clinics of medical doctors

D-U-N-S 20-568-5550   (BR)
ALBERTA HEALTH SERVICES
CALGARY FINANCE
10101 Southport Rd Sw, Calgary, AB, T2W 3N2
(403) 943-0755
Emp Here 600
SIC 8011 Offices and clinics of medical doctors

D-U-N-S 24-715-4305   (BR)
BANK OF MONTREAL
SOUTHWOOD CORNERS
10233 Elbow Dr Sw Suite 345, Calgary, AB, T2W 1E8
(403) 234-3844
Emp Here 20

SIC 6021 National commercial banks

D-U-N-S 20-713-1595   (BR)
CALGARY BOARD OF EDUCATION
WOODLANDS ELEMENTARY SCHOOL
88 Woodgreen Dr Sw, Calgary, AB, T2W 4W9
(403) 777-8640
Emp Here 50
SIC 8211 Elementary and secondary schools

D-U-N-S 20-713-1249   (BR)
CALGARY BOARD OF EDUCATION
CANYON MEADOWS ELEMENTARY SCHOOL
395 Canterbury Dr Sw, Calgary, AB, T2W 1J1
(403) 777-8600
Emp Here 30
SIC 8211 Elementary and secondary schools

D-U-N-S 24-971-7885   (BR)
CALGARY BOARD OF EDUCATION
SOUTHWOOD ELEMENTARY SCHOOL
898 Sylvester Cres Sw, Calgary, AB, T2W 0R7
(403) 259-3527
Emp Here 25
SIC 8211 Elementary and secondary schools

D-U-N-S 25-161-5100   (BR)
CALGARY BOARD OF EDUCATION
HAROLD PANABAKER JUNIOR HIGH SCHOOL
23 Sackville Dr Sw, Calgary, AB, T2W 0W3
(403) 777-7890
Emp Here 35
SIC 8211 Elementary and secondary schools

D-U-N-S 20-590-7897   (BR)
CALGARY BOARD OF EDUCATION
WILLIAM ROPER HULL SCHOOL
2266 Woodpark Ave Sw, Calgary, AB, T2W 2Z8
(403) 251-8022
Emp Here 80
SIC 8211 Elementary and secondary schools

D-U-N-S 20-913-5602   (BR)
CALGARY BOARD OF EDUCATION
WOODBINE SCHOOL
27 Woodfield Way Sw, Calgary, AB, T2W 5E1
(403) 777-8630
Emp Here 25
SIC 8211 Elementary and secondary schools

D-U-N-S 20-713-1496   (BR)
CALGARY BOARD OF EDUCATION
CEDARBRAE SCHOOL
10631 Oakfield Dr Sw, Calgary, AB, T2W 2T3
(403) 777-8610
Emp Here 50
SIC 8211 Elementary and secondary schools

D-U-N-S 20-590-7970   (BR)
CALGARY BOARD OF EDUCATION
ETHEL M JOHNSON SCHOOL
255 Sackville Dr Sw, Calgary, AB, T2W 0W7
(403) 777-8500
Emp Here 25
SIC 8211 Elementary and secondary schools

D-U-N-S 20-591-1162   (BR)
CALGARY BOARD OF EDUCATION
ROBERT WARREN JUNIOR HIGH SCHOOL
12424 Elbow Dr Sw, Calgary, AB, T2W 1H2
(403) 777-7690
Emp Here 25
SIC 8211 Elementary and secondary schools

D-U-N-S 20-713-1157   (BR)
CALGARY BOARD OF EDUCATION
BRAESIDE SCHOOL
1747 107 Ave Sw, Calgary, AB, T2W 0C3
(403) 777-8470
Emp Here 50
SIC 8211 Elementary and secondary schools

D-U-N-S 25-272-0834   (BR)
CALGARY ROMAN CATHOLIC SEPARATE SCHOOL DISTRICT #1

ST. CYRIL SCHOOL
2990 Cedarbrae Dr Sw, Calgary, AB, T2W 2N9
(403) 500-2070
Emp Here 30
SIC 8211 Elementary and secondary schools

D-U-N-S 20-574-7905   (BR)
CALGARY ROMAN CATHOLIC SEPARATE SCHOOL DISTRICT #1
ST. JUDE SCHOOL
730 Woodbine Blvd Sw, Calgary, AB, T2W 4W4
(403) 500-2084
Emp Here 20
SIC 8211 Elementary and secondary schools

D-U-N-S 25-272-2202   (BR)
CALGARY ROMAN CATHOLIC SEPARATE SCHOOL DISTRICT #1
ST. STEPHEN ELEMENTARY JUNIOR HIGH
10910 Elbow Dr Sw, Calgary, AB, T2W 1G6
(403) 500-2043
Emp Here 40
SIC 8211 Elementary and secondary schools

D-U-N-S 20-070-1832   (HQ)
CAREWEST
CAREWEST ROYAL PARK
10301 Southport Lane Sw, Calgary, AB, T2W 1S7
(403) 943-8140
Emp Here 50   Emp Total 35,000
Sales 110,528,000
SIC 8059 Nursing and personal care, nec
Ex Dir Dale Forbes

D-U-N-S 24-048-7624   (BR)
CATALYST CAPITAL GROUP INC, THE
PLANET ORGANIC MARKET
(Suby of Catalyst Capital Group Inc, The)
10233 Elbow Dr Sw Suite 100, Calgary, AB, T2W 1E8
(403) 252-2404
Emp Here 60
SIC 5149 Groceries and related products, nec

D-U-N-S 24-662-3982   (SL)
EVER READY SOLUTIONS LTD
ERS SECURITY
316 Cedarbrae Cres Sw, Calgary, AB, T2W 1Y4
(403) 451-9435
Emp Here 50   Sales 1,819,127
SIC 7381 Detective and armored car services

D-U-N-S 25-622-2134   (BR)
FABRICLAND PACIFIC/MIDWEST LIMITED
FABRICLAND
10233 Elbow Dr Sw Suite 110, Calgary, AB, T2W 1E8
(403) 271-8244
Emp Here 20
SIC 5949 Sewing, needlework, and piece goods

D-U-N-S 24-711-6580   (BR)
GOVERNMENT OF THE PROVINCE OF ALBERTA
CHILDREN AND YOUTH SERVICES
10233 Elbow Dr Sw, Calgary, AB, T2W 1E8
(403) 297-2049
Emp Here 50
SIC 8322 Individual and family services

D-U-N-S 24-982-1828   (BR)
LOBLAWS INC
REAL CANADIAN SUPERSTORE
10505 Southport Rd Sw Suite 1, Calgary, AB, T2W 3N2
(403) 225-6207
Emp Here 300
SIC 5411 Grocery stores

D-U-N-S 24-749-2929   (HQ)
MITSUBISHI HITACHI POWER SYSTEMS CANADA, LTD
10655 Southport Rd Sw Unit 460, Calgary, AB, T2W 4Y1

(403) 278-1881
Emp Here 34   Emp Total 335,244
Sales 93,462,657
SIC 3699 Electrical equipment and supplies, nec
Pr Pr Sheldon Myhre
VP Sls Robert Dueck
Lindy Antonini

D-U-N-S 25-366-5962   (BR)
MORGUARD INVESTMENTS LIMITED
10201 Southport Rd Sw Suite 108, Calgary, AB, T2W 4X9
(403) 253-8838
Emp Here 60
SIC 6531 Real estate agents and managers

D-U-N-S 24-627-0719   (BR)
MOXIE'S RESTAURANTS, LIMITED PARTNERSHIP
MOXIE'S CLASSIC GRILL
10606 Southport Rd Sw, Calgary, AB, T2W 3M5
(403) 225-9598
Emp Here 60
SIC 5812 Eating places

D-U-N-S 25-386-8962   (HQ)
SCOULAR CANADA LTD
(Suby of The Scoular Company)
10201 Southport Rd Sw Suite 1110, Calgary, AB, T2W 4X9
(403) 720-9050
Emp Here 20   Emp Total 801
Sales 173,250,200
SIC 6799 Investors, nec
Ch Bd David Faith
VP VP Roger Barber
VP VP John Heck

D-U-N-S 25-271-0355   (BR)
SOBEYS WEST INC
WOODBINE SAFEWAY
2525 Woodview Dr Sw Suite 280, Calgary, AB, T2W 4N4
(403) 238-1400
Emp Here 110
SIC 5411 Grocery stores

D-U-N-S 20-813-9217   (SL)
UPA CONSTRUCTION GROUP LIMITED PARTNERSHIP
10655 Southport Rd Sw Suite 700, Calgary, AB, T2W 4Y1
(403) 262-4440
Emp Here 50   Sales 13,665,280
SIC 1522 Residential construction, nec
Pr Richard Allen
Fin Ex Linda Bailey

Calgary, AB T2X

D-U-N-S 25-741-6024   (BR)
ATCO GAS AND PIPELINES LTD
ATCO GAS
383 Midpark Blvd Se, Calgary, AB, T2X 3C8
(403) 254-6200
Emp Here 70
SIC 4923 Gas transmission and distribution

D-U-N-S 20-554-8576   (BR)
AECOM CANADA LTD
340 Midpark Way Se Suite 300, Calgary, AB, T2X 1P1
(403) 270-9200
Emp Here 200
SIC 8711 Engineering services

D-U-N-S 24-104-6445   (BR)
ALBERTA HEALTH SERVICES
SOUTH CALGARY HEALTH CENTRE
31 Sunpark Plaza Se Suite 113, Calgary, AB, T2X 3W5
(403) 943-9300
Emp Here 500

SIC 8093 Specialty outpatient clinics, nec

D-U-N-S 24-121-1650   (BR)
BANK OF NOVA SCOTIA, THE
SCOTIA BANK
34 Midlake Blvd Se, Calgary, AB, T2X 2X7
(403) 221-6595
Emp Here 24
SIC 6021 National commercial banks

D-U-N-S 20-713-1769   (BR)
CALGARY BOARD OF EDUCATION
MIDSUN JUNIOR HIGH SCHOOL
660 Sunmills Dr Se, Calgary, AB, T2X 3R5
(403) 777-6430
Emp Here 52
SIC 8211 Elementary and secondary schools

D-U-N-S 20-590-7798   (BR)
CALGARY BOARD OF EDUCATION
SUNDANCE ELEMENTARY SCHOOL
200 Sunmills Dr Se, Calgary, AB, T2X 2N9
(403) 777-8690
Emp Here 40
SIC 8211 Elementary and secondary schools

D-U-N-S 20-034-4450   (BR)
CALGARY BOARD OF EDUCATION
FISH CREEK SCHOOL
1039 Suncastle Dr Se, Calgary, AB, T2X 2Z1
(403) 777-6400
Emp Here 40
SIC 8211 Elementary and secondary schools

D-U-N-S 20-655-0324   (BR)
CALGARY BOARD OF EDUCATION
MIDNAPORE SCHOOL
55 Midpark Rise Se, Calgary, AB, T2X 1L7
(403) 777-8680
Emp Here 35
SIC 8211 Elementary and secondary schools

D-U-N-S 20-574-6915   (BR)
CALGARY ROMAN CATHOLIC SEPARATE SCHOOL DISTRICT #1
FATHER JAMES WHELIHAN SCHOOL
70 Sunmills Dr Se, Calgary, AB, T2X 2R5
(403) 500-2087
Emp Here 50
SIC 8211 Elementary and secondary schools

D-U-N-S 20-713-0738   (BR)
CALGARY ROMAN CATHOLIC SEPARATE SCHOOL DISTRICT #1
BLESSED MOTHER THERESA SCHOOL
121 Midlake Blvd Se, Calgary, AB, T2X 1T7
(403) 500-2078
Emp Here 50
SIC 8211 Elementary and secondary schools

D-U-N-S 20-573-4028   (BR)
CANADIAN PACIFIC RAILWAY COMPANY
327 Chaparral Pl Se, Calgary, AB, T2X 3J9
(403) 201-3177
Emp Here 20
SIC 4011 Railroads, line-haul operating

D-U-N-S 24-229-7600   (HQ)
EECOL ELECTRIC ULC
63 Sunpark Dr Se, Calgary, AB, T2X 3V4
(403) 253-1952
Emp Here 25   Emp Total 650
Sales 130,526,692
SIC 5063 Electrical apparatus and equipment
Pr Darren Buium
VP Sls Kenneth Patola
Karleen Gobeil

D-U-N-S 24-410-7734   (HQ)
FLUOR CANADA LTD
(Suby of Fluor Corporation)
55 Sunpark Plaza Se, Calgary, AB, T2X 3R4
(403) 537-4000
Emp Here 1,900   Emp Total 61,551
Sales 282,941,595
SIC 8711 Engineering services
James Brittain
Dir Opers Peter Hatcher

Mgr Simon Nottingham

D-U-N-S 24-808-2687   (SL)
FLUOR CONSTRUCTORS CANADA LTD
(Suby of Fluor Corporation)
60 Sunpark Plaza Se, Calgary, AB, T2X 3Y2
(403) 537-4600
Emp Here 200   Sales 39,617,660
SIC 1541 Industrial buildings and warehouses
Pr Pr Richard Flinton
Mgr Rob Earle
Stephen Sanford
Treas C R Macdonald

D-U-N-S 24-228-6214   (BR)
HERSHEY CANADA INC
(Suby of Hershey Company)
14505 Bannister Rd Se Suite 101, Calgary, AB, T2X 3J3

Emp Here 25
SIC 5145 Confectionery

D-U-N-S 20-918-4576   (BR)
INVESTORS GROUP FINANCIAL SERVICES INC
51 Sunpark Dr Se Suite 201, Calgary, AB, T2X 3V4
(403) 256-5890
Emp Here 35
SIC 8741 Management services

D-U-N-S 25-976-0890   (BR)
RENFREW EDUCATIONAL SERVICES SOCIETY
75 Sunpark Dr Se, Calgary, AB, T2X 3V4
(403) 291-5038
Emp Here 400
SIC 8211 Elementary and secondary schools

D-U-N-S 24-961-8018   (BR)
REXALL PHARMACY GROUP LTD
REXALL
(Suby of McKesson Corporation)
290 Midpark Way Se Suite 120, Calgary, AB, T2X 1P1
(403) 254-9600
Emp Here 20
SIC 5912 Drug stores and proprietary stores

D-U-N-S 24-349-5590   (HQ)
SHAW WIN HOTEL LTD
(Suby of Shaw Win Hotel Ltd)
400 Midpark Way Se, Calgary, AB, T2X 3S4
(403) 514-0099
Emp Here 40   Emp Total 50
Sales 2,826,987
SIC 7011 Hotels and motels

Calgary, AB T2Y

D-U-N-S 20-933-6374   (SL)
668977 ALBERTA INC
BOSTON PIZZA
235 Shawville Blvd Se, Calgary, AB, T2Y 3H9
(403) 256-6999
Emp Here 80   Sales 2,407,703
SIC 5812 Eating places

D-U-N-S 20-029-2758   (HQ)
715639 ALBERTA LTD
A & W
(Suby of 715639 Alberta Ltd)
70 Shawville Blvd Se Suite 400, Calgary, AB, T2Y 2Z3
(403) 256-5681
Emp Here 35   Emp Total 70
Sales 2,115,860
SIC 5812 Eating places

D-U-N-S 20-005-6526   (BR)
BANQUE TORONTO-DOMINION, LA
TORONTO-DOMINION BANK, THE
(Suby of Toronto-Dominion Bank, The)
69 Shawville Blvd Se, Calgary, AB, T2Y 3P3

---

(403) 215-5670
Emp Here 21
SIC 6021 National commercial banks

D-U-N-S 20-643-1764   (BR)
BEST BUY CANADA LTD
FUTURE SHOP
(*Suby of* Best Buy Co., Inc.)
350 Shawville Blvd Se Unit 110, Calgary, AB,
T2Y 3S4
(403) 509-9120
Emp Here 100
SIC 5734 Computer and software stores

D-U-N-S 20-713-1819   (BR)
CALGARY BOARD OF EDUCATION
SOMERSET SCHOOL
150 Somerset Manor Sw, Calgary, AB, T2Y
4S2
(403) 777-7001
Emp Here 50
SIC 8211 Elementary and secondary schools

D-U-N-S 20-713-1603   (BR)
CALGARY BOARD OF EDUCATION
JANET JOHNSTON SCHOOL
224 Shawnessy Dr Sw, Calgary, AB, T2Y 1M1
(403) 777-8670
Emp Here 50
SIC 8211 Elementary and secondary schools

D-U-N-S 20-303-9359   (BR)
CALGARY BOARD OF EDUCATION
SAMUEL W. SHAW SCHOOL
115 Shannon Dr Sw, Calgary, AB, T2Y 0K6
(403) 777-6163
Emp Here 50
SIC 8211 Elementary and secondary schools

D-U-N-S 20-656-1057   (BR)
**CALGARY ROMAN CATHOLIC SEPARATE
SCHOOL DISTRICT #1**
*MSGR. J.J. O'BRIEN JUNIOR HIGH
SCHOOL*
99 Bridlewood Rd Sw, Calgary, AB, T2Y 4J5
(403) 500-2104
Emp Here 66
SIC 8211 Elementary and secondary schools

D-U-N-S 25-269-7115   (BR)
**CALGARY ROMAN CATHOLIC SEPARATE
SCHOOL DISTRICT #1**
*OUR LADY OF PEACE ELEMENTARY & JU-
NIOR HIGH SCHOOL*
14826 Millrise Hill Sw, Calgary, AB, T2Y 2B4
(403) 254-5446
Emp Here 60
SIC 8211 Elementary and secondary schools

D-U-N-S 20-713-0860   (BR)
**CALGARY ROMAN CATHOLIC SEPARATE
SCHOOL DISTRICT #1**
BISHOP O'BYRNE HIGH SCHOOL
333 Shawville Blvd Se Suite 500, Calgary, AB,
T2Y 4H3
(403) 500-2103
Emp Here 50
SIC 8211 Elementary and secondary schools

D-U-N-S 20-029-2634   (BR)
**CALGARY ROMAN CATHOLIC SEPARATE
SCHOOL DISTRICT #1**
FATHER DOUCET ELEMENTARY SCHOOL
65 Shannon Dr Sw, Calgary, AB, T2Y 2T5
(403) 500-2089
Emp Here 60
SIC 8211 Elementary and secondary schools

D-U-N-S 24-345-5982   (BR)
**CALGARY YOUNG MEN'S CHRISTIAN AS-
SOCIATION**
YMCA CALGARY
333 Shawville Blvd Se Suite 400, Calgary, AB,
T2Y 4H3

Emp Here 220
SIC 8322 Individual and family services

D-U-N-S 25-734-2253   (BR)

CARA OPERATIONS LIMITED
(*Suby of* Cara Holdings Limited)
265 Shawville Blvd Se, Calgary, AB, T2Y 3H9
(403) 254-1900
Emp Here 35
SIC 5812 Eating places

D-U-N-S 25-596-6103   (BR)
DAIRY QUEEN CANADA INC
215 Shawville Blvd Se, Calgary, AB, T2Y 3H9

Emp Here 50
SIC 8742 Management consulting services

D-U-N-S 20-772-6006   (SL)
EAST SIDE MARIO'S - SHAWNESSY
16061 Macleod Trail Se Unit 500, Calgary, AB,
T2Y 3S5
(403) 262-4326
Emp Here 50   *Sales* 1,532,175
SIC 5812 Eating places

D-U-N-S 24-442-2762   (SL)
GCA EDUCATIONAL SOCIETY
GLENMORE CHRISTIAN ACADEMY
16520 24 St Sw, Calgary, AB, T2Y 4W2
(403) 254-9050
Emp Here 60   *Sales* 4,012,839
SIC 8211 Elementary and secondary schools

D-U-N-S 24-049-3804   (BR)
GOLF TOWN LIMITED
GOLF TOWN
47 Shawville Blvd Se, Calgary, AB, T2Y 3P3
(403) 201-9301
Emp Here 40
SIC 5941 Sporting goods and bicycle shops

D-U-N-S 20-831-7453   (SL)
GREENGATE GARDEN CENTRES LTD
14111 Macleod Trail Sw, Calgary, AB, T2Y
1M6
(403) 256-1212
Emp Here 45   *Sales* 5,952,990
SIC 5992 Florists
Pr Pr Margaret Peggy Telford
VP VP Harrington Telford
    Shane Telford
    Derrik Telford
Genl Mgr Brad Hitching

D-U-N-S 20-003-3921   (BR)
HOME DEPOT OF CANADA INC
HOME DEPOT
(*Suby of* The Home Depot Inc)
390 Shawville Blvd Se, Calgary, AB, T2Y 3S4
(403) 201-5611
Emp Here 250
SIC 5251 Hardware stores

D-U-N-S 20-920-1495   (BR)
INDIGO BOOKS & MUSIC INC
CHAPTERS
(*Suby of* Indigo Books & Music Inc)
16061 Macleod Trail Se Unit 212, Calgary, AB,
T2Y 3S5
(403) 201-5660
Emp Here 50
SIC 5942 Book stores

D-U-N-S 24-392-5976   (BR)
INTERCARE CORPORATE GROUP INC
INTERCARE @ MILLRISE
(*Suby of* Intercare Corporate Group Inc)
14911 5 St Sw, Calgary, AB, T2Y 5B9
(403) 451-4211
Emp Here 50
SIC 8322 Individual and family services

D-U-N-S 25-087-6943   (BR)
LOBLAWS INC
REAL CANADIAN SUPERSTORE
15915 Macleod Trail Se Unit 100, Calgary, AB,
T2Y 3R9
(403) 254-3637
Emp Here 250
SIC 5411 Grocery stores

D-U-N-S 20-300-6676   (BR)
MARK'S WORK WEARHOUSE LTD
MARK'S WORK WEARHOUSE #19
350 Shawville Blvd Se Suite 240, Calgary, AB,
T2Y 3S4
(403) 201-4110
Emp Here 20
SIC 5651 Family clothing stores

D-U-N-S 25-860-4388   (BR)
PASLEY, MAX ENTERPRISES LIMITED
MCDONALD'S
(*Suby of* Pasley, Max Enterprises Limited)
250 Shawville Blvd Se Suite 10, Calgary, AB,
T2Y 2Z7
(403) 254-0310
Emp Here 50
SIC 5812 Eating places

D-U-N-S 20-813-0588   (SL)
PHOENIX GRILL LTD, THE
16061 Macleod Trail Se Suite 335, Calgary,
AB, T2Y 3S5
(403) 509-9111
Emp Here 80   *Sales* 2,407,703
SIC 5812 Eating places

D-U-N-S 20-700-6748   (BR)
REITMANS (CANADA) LIMITEE
85 Shawville Blvd Se Suite 510, Calgary, AB,
T2Y 3W5
(403) 254-5553
Emp Here 25
SIC 5621 Women's clothing stores

D-U-N-S 20-806-2294   (BR)
SOBEYS CAPITAL INCORPORATED
SOBEYS STORE 1117
2335 162 Ave Sw Suite 100, Calgary, AB, T2Y
4S6
(403) 873-0101
Emp Here 100
SIC 5411 Grocery stores

D-U-N-S 24-018-9683   (BR)
SOBEYS CAPITAL INCORPORATED
SOBEYS
150 Millrise Blvd Sw Unit 3109, Calgary, AB,
T2Y 5G7
(403) 873-5085
Emp Here 100
SIC 5411 Grocery stores

D-U-N-S 24-363-2010   (BR)
SOBEYS WEST INC
SHAWNESSEY SAFEWAY
70 Shawville Blvd Se, Calgary, AB, T2Y 2Z3
(403) 256-1401
Emp Here 150
SIC 5411 Grocery stores

D-U-N-S 24-523-0615   (BR)
SYMPHONY SENIOR LIVING INC
2220 162 Ave Sw Suite 210, Calgary, AB, T2Y
5E3
(403) 201-3555
Emp Here 100
SIC 8361 Residential care

D-U-N-S 25-498-2820   (BR)
WAL-MART CANADA CORP
310 Shawville Blvd Se Suite 100, Calgary, AB,
T2Y 3S4
(403) 201-5415
Emp Here 200
SIC 5311 Department stores

D-U-N-S 20-334-5371   (BR)
WENDY'S RESTAURANTS OF CANADA INC
WENDY'S
(*Suby of* The Wendy's Company)
303 Shawville Blvd Se Suite 410, Calgary, AB,
T2Y 3W6
(403) 254-4540
Emp Here 20
SIC 5812 Eating places

D-U-N-S 25-080-1768   (BR)
WINNERS MERCHANTS INTERNATIONAL

L.P.
WINNERS
(*Suby of* The TJX Companies Inc)
85 Shawville Blvd Se Suite 400, Calgary, AB,
T2Y 3W5
(403) 201-7460
Emp Here 40
SIC 5651 Family clothing stores

Calgary, AB T2Z

D-U-N-S 20-814-5016   (BR)
715639 ALBERTA LTD
A AND W
(*Suby of* 715639 Alberta Ltd)
4307 130 Ave Se Suite 190, Calgary, AB, T2Z
3V8
(403) 257-5337
Emp Here 25
SIC 5812 Eating places

D-U-N-S 25-365-1178   (BR)
ACOSTA CANADA CORPORATION
ACOSTA CANADA
(*Suby of* Acosta Inc.)
3445 114 Ave Se Suite 107, Calgary, AB, T2Z
0K6
(403) 236-5505
Emp Here 30
SIC 5141 Groceries, general line

D-U-N-S 24-132-5351   (BR)
BAKER HUGHES CANADA COMPANY
HUGHES CHRISTIANSON
(*Suby of* Baker Hughes, A GE Company)
4948 126 Ave Se Suite 27, Calgary, AB, T2Z
0A9
(403) 250-2111
Emp Here 40
SIC 1389 Oil and gas field services, nec

D-U-N-S 20-700-1202   (BR)
BANQUE TORONTO-DOMINION, LA
TORONTO-DOMINION BANK, THE
(*Suby of* Toronto-Dominion Bank, The)
4307 130 Ave Se Suite 20, Calgary, AB, T2Z
3V8
(403) 257-7120
Emp Here 20
SIC 6021 National commercial banks

D-U-N-S 24-392-6016   (BR)
BIRD CONSTRUCTION COMPANY LIMITED
BIRD CONSTRUCTION GROUP
12143 40 St Se Suite 106, Calgary, AB, T2Z
4E6
(403) 319-0470
Emp Here 30
SIC 1542 Nonresidential construction, nec

D-U-N-S 20-067-5523   (SL)
**BISHOP, DONALD H. PROFESSIONAL
CORPORATION**
BISHOP & ASSOCIATES
11410 27 St Se Unit 6, Calgary, AB, T2Z 3R6
(403) 974-3937
Emp Here 60   *Sales* 3,502,114
SIC 8042 Offices and clinics of optometrists

D-U-N-S 20-074-3243   (HQ)
BREWERS' DISTRIBUTOR LTD
B D L
(*Suby of* Brewers' Distributor Ltd)
11500 29 St Se Suite 101, Calgary, AB, T2Z
3W9
(800) 661-2337
Emp Here 75   *Emp Total* 700
Sales 66,394,237
SIC 4225 General warehousing and storage
Pr Garry Clermont
Dir Neil Sweeney
Dir Mike Ross
Dir Greg D'Abignon
Dir Charles Oliver
Dir Daren Hawrish

Dir John Aiken
Dir Linda Thomas
Dir Trent Carroll

D-U-N-S 20-705-8236   (BR)
CALGARY BOARD OF EDUCATION
DOUGLASDALE SCHOOL
400 Douglas Park Blvd Se, Calgary, AB, T2Z 4A3
(403) 777-6177
Emp Here 20
SIC 8211 Elementary and secondary schools

D-U-N-S 20-590-7681   (BR)
CALGARY BOARD OF EDUCATION
MCKENZIE LAKE ELEMENTRAY SCHOOL
16210 Mckenzie Lake Way Se, Calgary, AB, T2Z 1L7
(403) 777-6500
Emp Here 25
SIC 8211 Elementary and secondary schools

D-U-N-S 20-027-4343   (BR)
CALGARY ROMAN CATHOLIC SEPARATE SCHOOL DISTRICT #1
BLESSED CARDINAL NEWMAN ELEMENTARY & HIGH SCHOOL
16201 Mckenzie Lake Blvd Se, Calgary, AB, T2Z 2G7
(403) 500-2092
Emp Here 60
SIC 8211 Elementary and secondary schools

D-U-N-S 20-030-7432   (BR)
CALGARY ROMAN CATHOLIC SEPARATE SCHOOL DISTRICT #1
MSGR. JOHN S. SMITH SCHOOL
2919 Douglasdale Blvd Se, Calgary, AB, T2Z 2H9
(403) 500-2069
Emp Here 70
SIC 8211 Elementary and secondary schools

D-U-N-S 24-426-6842   (SL)
CANADIAN SAFETY INSPECTIONS INC
CSI CANADA SAFETY
3506 118 Ave Se Suite 106, Calgary, AB, T2Z 3X1
(780) 826-7642
Emp Here 120   *Sales* 14,786,875
SIC 8748 Business consulting, nec
Pr Dean Shaver
Fin Mgr Donna Shaver

D-U-N-S 24-317-9491   (BR)
CANADIAN WESTERN BANK
5222 130 Ave Se Suite 300, Calgary, AB, T2Z 0G4
(403) 257-8235
Emp Here 20
SIC 6021 National commercial banks

D-U-N-S 25-366-4973   (BR)
CARA OPERATIONS LIMITED
KELSEY'S RESTAURANT
(*Suby of* Cara Holdings Limited)
4307 130 Ave Se Unit 180, Calgary, AB, T2Z 3V8

Emp Here 60
SIC 5812 Eating places

D-U-N-S 20-699-5065   (BR)
CHRISTIAN AND MISSIONARY ALLIANCE IN CANADA, THE
FIRST ALLIANCE CHURCH
12345 40 St Se, Calgary, AB, T2Z 4E6
(403) 252-7572
Emp Here 50
SIC 8661 Religious organizations

D-U-N-S 25-142-1715   (BR)
CONSOLIDATED GYPSUM SUPPLY LTD
4140 120 Ave Se, Calgary, AB, T2Z 4H4
(403) 243-2633
Emp Here 40
SIC 5039 Construction materials, nec

D-U-N-S 24-669-0395   (BR)

DOLLARAMA S.E.C.
4307 130 Ave Se Suite 94, Calgary, AB, T2Z 3V8
(403) 726-1295
Emp Here 25
SIC 5331 Variety stores

D-U-N-S 25-170-6354   (BR)
DRIVE PRODUCTS INC
D S I DRIVE SYSTEMS
3939 54 Ave Se, Calgary, AB, T2Z 4V3
(403) 720-8033
Emp Here 20
SIC 5084 Industrial machinery and equipment

D-U-N-S 24-337-3458   (BR)
FGL SPORTS LTD
SPORT-CHEK
4307 130 Ave Se Unit 96, Calgary, AB, T2Z 3V8
(403) 257-8129
Emp Here 40
SIC 5941 Sporting goods and bicycle shops

D-U-N-S 24-417-1562   (BR)
FLYING J CANADA INC
FLYING J
1511 40th St Se, Calgary, AB, T2Z 4V6
(403) 720-5908
Emp Here 42
SIC 5541 Gasoline service stations

D-U-N-S 20-351-2199   (SL)
GRC FOOD SERVICES LTD
4988 126 Ave Se Suite 35, Calgary, AB, T2Z 0A9
(587) 353-0766
Emp Here 50   *Sales* 4,231,721
SIC 7032 Sporting and recreational camps

D-U-N-S 20-286-1233   (BR)
GRAHAM CONSTRUCTION AND ENGINEERING INC
10909 27 St Se, Calgary, AB, T2Z 3V9
(403) 253-1314
Emp Here 50
SIC 1542 Nonresidential construction, nec

D-U-N-S 24-552-6959   (HQ)
GRAHAM CONSTRUCTION AND ENGINEERING INC
GRACOM MASONRY, DIV OF
10840 27 St Se, Calgary, AB, T2Z 3R6
(403) 570-5000
Emp Here 80   *Emp Total* 1,200
Sales 44,092,176
SIC 1542 Nonresidential construction, nec
Tom Baxter
Pr Pr William Flaig
Treas Doug Bespalko
Ch Bd Brian Leuken
Dir Colin Anderson
Sec Simon Lee
    Mike Slapman

D-U-N-S 24-381-4055   (BR)
GRAHAM GROUP LTD
10909 27 St Se, Calgary, AB, T2Z 3V9
(403) 570-5000
Emp Here 30
SIC 6719 Holding companies, nec

D-U-N-S 20-903-8285   (SL)
GREAT WESTERN INTERIORS
G K PROJECTS
12221 44 St Se Unit 40, Calgary, AB, T2Z 4H3
(403) 217-1057
Emp Here 44   *Sales* 5,006,160
SIC 1742 Plastering, drywall, and insulation
Owner Gordon Kausche

D-U-N-S 20-954-6808   (SL)
GREG SAARI MERCHANDISING LTD
CANADIAN TIRE
4155 126 Ave Se, Calgary, AB, T2Z 0A1
(403) 257-4729
Emp Here 80   *Sales* 7,660,874
SIC 5251 Hardware stores

Pr Pr Gregory Saari

D-U-N-S 24-000-3041   (BR)
HOME DEPOT OF CANADA INC
(*Suby of* The Home Depot Inc)
5125 126 Ave Se, Calgary, AB, T2Z 0B2
(403) 257-8756
Emp Here 130
SIC 5251 Hardware stores

D-U-N-S 20-006-7239   (BR)
HUDSON'S BAY COMPANY
HOME OUTFITTERS
4916 130 Ave Se Unit 164, Calgary, AB, T2Z 0G4
(403) 216-4033
Emp Here 28
SIC 5311 Department stores

D-U-N-S 24-894-8275   (BR)
INTEGRATED DISTRIBUTION SYSTEMS LIMITED PARTNERSHIP
WAJAX POWER SYSTEMS
4343 114 Ave Se, Calgary, AB, T2Z 3M5
(403) 253-7601
Emp Here 100
SIC 5084 Industrial machinery and equipment

D-U-N-S 24-367-7296   (SL)
KARNALYTE RESOURCES INC
1140 27 St Se Unit 14, Calgary, AB, T2Z 3R6

Emp Here 21   *Sales* 8,104,029
SIC 3339 Primary nonferrous Metals, nec

D-U-N-S 25-114-7583   (BR)
LENNOX CANADA INC
CENTRAL AIRE HEATING & AIR CONDITIONING
(*Suby of* Lennox Canada Inc)
11500 35 St Se Suite 8002, Calgary, AB, T2Z 3W4
(403) 279-5757
Emp Here 50
SIC 1711 Plumbing, heating, air-conditioning

D-U-N-S 24-803-5144   (BR)
LOWE'S COMPANIES CANADA, ULC
13417 52 St Se, Calgary, AB, T2Z 0Z1
(403) 279-0450
Emp Here 100
SIC 5211 Lumber and other building materials

D-U-N-S 20-311-0978   (BR)
NCS MULTISTAGE INC
11929 40 St Se Suite 222, Calgary, AB, T2Z 4M8
(403) 862-3722
Emp Here 20
SIC 1389 Oil and gas field services, nec

D-U-N-S 24-034-4841   (SL)
NORTHERN ELECTRIC CANADA LTD
2850 107 Ave Se Suite 103, Calgary, AB, T2Z 3R7

Emp Here 43   *Sales* 5,104,320
SIC 1731 Electrical work
Pr Pr James C. Fiddler
VP VP Byron Mcquitty
    James L. Fiddler
Recvr Victor Paul Kroeger

D-U-N-S 25-013-1513   (HQ)
PINCHIN WEST LTD
(*Suby of* W.O.H.A Holdings Limited)
11505 35 St Se Suite 111, Calgary, AB, T2Z 4B1
(403) 250-5722
Emp Here 51   *Emp Total* 130
Sales 17,656,489
SIC 8748 Business consulting, nec
Pr Pr John Holland
VP VP Don Jakul
VP VP Steve Wilk
    Donald Pinchin

D-U-N-S 24-350-3252   (BR)
PRINCESS AUTO LTD

4143 114 Ave Se, Calgary, AB, T2Z 0H3
(403) 723-9904
Emp Here 30
SIC 5251 Hardware stores

D-U-N-S 20-298-7496   (BR)
RAYDON RENTALS LTD
CAT RENTAL STORE, THE
(*Suby of* Finning International Inc)
11560 42 St Se Suite 1, Calgary, AB, T2Z 4E1
(403) 640-4800
Emp Here 25
SIC 7353 Heavy construction equipment rental

D-U-N-S 24-346-5338   (BR)
REVERA INC
MCKENZIE TOWN CARE CENTRE
80 Promenade Way Se, Calgary, AB, T2Z 4G4
(403) 508-9808
Emp Here 150
SIC 8051 Skilled nursing care facilities

D-U-N-S 25-993-1517   (BR)
ROBINSON, C.H. COMPANY (CANADA) LTD
CALGARY TRANSPORTATION
3355 114 Ave Se Suite 105, Calgary, AB, T2Z 0K7
(403) 252-0808
Emp Here 20
SIC 4731 Freight transportation arrangement

D-U-N-S 20-161-7748   (BR)
SOBEYS CAPITAL INCORPORATED
SOBEYS MCKENZIE TOWNE MARKET
20 Mckenzie Towne Ave Se, Calgary, AB, T2Z 3S7
(403) 257-4343
Emp Here 150
SIC 5411 Grocery stores

D-U-N-S 20-337-3949   (SL)
SOUTH TRAIL CHRYSLER LTD
6103 130 Ave Se, Calgary, AB, T2Z 0N3
(587) 349-7272
Emp Here 80   *Sales* 15,467,668
SIC 5521 Used car dealers
    Michael Mcmanes

D-U-N-S 20-555-4152   (BR)
STAPLES CANADA INC
STAPLES THE BUSINESS DEPOT
(*Suby of* Staples, Inc.)
4307 130 Ave Se Unit 90, Calgary, AB, T2Z 3V8
(403) 257-8167
Emp Here 50
SIC 5943 Stationery stores

D-U-N-S 25-736-9660   (SL)
TENET MEDICAL ENGINEERING, INC
11979 40 St Se Unit 203, Calgary, AB, T2Z 4M3
(403) 571-0750
Emp Here 26   *Sales* 2,480,664
SIC 3842 Surgical appliances and supplies

D-U-N-S 20-864-6203   (SL)
TIM HORTONS
11488 24 St Se Suite 400, Calgary, AB, T2Z 4C9
(403) 236-3749
Emp Here 50   *Sales* 1,678,096
SIC 5461 Retail bakeries

D-U-N-S 24-022-2740   (BR)
TRICAN WELL SERVICE LTD
CALGARY R&D CENTRE
418 11979 40 St Se, Calgary, AB, T2Z 4M3
(403) 723-3688
Emp Here 1,500
SIC 1389 Oil and gas field services, nec

D-U-N-S 24-325-8303   (HQ)
TUNDRA PROCESS SOLUTIONS LTD
3200 118 Ave Se, Calgary, AB, T2Z 3X1

(403) 255-5222
Emp Here 80   *Emp Total* 51
Sales 36,122,667
SIC 5085 Industrial supplies
 Mike Miller
Pr Pr Dan Peet
VP Blaine Barnes
VP Sls Ashley Allers
VP Peter Mcaleer
 Iggy Domagaiski

D-U-N-S 25-095-0180   (BR)
VALARD CONSTRUCTION LTD
(*Suby of* Quanta Services, Inc.)
3595 114 Ave Se Suite 200, Calgary, AB, T2Z
3X2
(403) 279-1003
Emp Here 20
SIC 1623 Water, sewer, and utility lines

D-U-N-S 24-107-3597   (BR)
WAL-MART CANADA CORP
WALMART
4705 130 Ave Se, Calgary, AB, T2Z 4J2
(403) 726-0430
Emp Here 50
SIC 5311 Department stores

D-U-N-S 24-081-6285   (BR)
WINNERS MERCHANTS INTERNATIONAL L.P.
WINNERS
(*Suby of* The TJX Companies Inc)
4307 130 Ave Se Suite 100, Calgary, AB, T2Z
3V8
(587) 471-1522
Emp Here 40
SIC 5651 Family clothing stores

Calgary, AB T3A

D-U-N-S 20-589-5498   (BR)
BANQUE TORONTO-DOMINION, LA
TD CANADA TRUST
(*Suby of* Toronto-Dominion Bank, The)
5005 Dalhousie Dr Nw Suite 303, Calgary, AB,
T3A 5R8
(403) 543-7280
Emp Here 20
SIC 6021 National commercial banks

D-U-N-S 20-991-3581   (BR)
BANQUE TORONTO-DOMINION, LA
TORONTO-DOMINION BANK, THE
(*Suby of* Toronto-Dominion Bank, The)
4880 32 Ave Nw, Calgary, AB, T3A 4N7
(403) 299-3255
Emp Here 24
SIC 6021 National commercial banks

D-U-N-S 24-160-0873   (BR)
CADILLAC FAIRVIEW CORPORATION LIMITED, THE
MARKET MALL
3625 Shaganappi Trail Nw Unit 214, Calgary,
AB, T3A 0E2
(403) 286-8733
Emp Here 50
SIC 6512 Nonresidential building operators

D-U-N-S 20-713-1413   (BR)
CALGARY BOARD OF EDUCATION
H D CARTWRIGHT SCHOOL
5500 Dalhart Rd Nw, Calgary, AB, T3A 1V6
(403) 777-7420
Emp Here 50
SIC 8211 Elementary and secondary schools

D-U-N-S 20-590-7947   (BR)
CALGARY BOARD OF EDUCATION
TOM BAINS JUNIOR HIGH SCHOOL
250 Edgepark Blvd Nw, Calgary, AB, T3A 3S2
(403) 777-7190
Emp Here 53
SIC 8211 Elementary and secondary schools

D-U-N-S 20-591-1071   (BR)
CALGARY BOARD OF EDUCATION
HIDDEN VALLEY SCHOOL
10959 Hidden Valley Dr Nw, Calgary, AB, T3A
6J2
(403) 777-7236
Emp Here 25
SIC 8211 Elementary and secondary schools

D-U-N-S 20-713-1694   (BR)
CALGARY BOARD OF EDUCATION
EDGEMONT SCHOOL
55 Edgevalley Cir Nw, Calgary, AB, T3A 4X1
(403) 777-6340
Emp Here 50
SIC 8211 Elementary and secondary schools

D-U-N-S 20-044-8509   (BR)
CALGARY BOARD OF EDUCATION
VARSITY ACRES ELEMENTARY SCHOOL
4255 40 St Nw, Calgary, AB, T3A 0H7
(403) 777-6090
Emp Here 50
SIC 8211 Elementary and secondary schools

D-U-N-S 20-713-1090   (BR)
CALGARY BOARD OF EDUCATION
DALHOUSIE ELEMENTARY SCHOOL
4440 Dallyn St Nw, Calgary, AB, T3A 1K3
(403) 777-6030
Emp Here 50
SIC 8211 Elementary and secondary schools

D-U-N-S 20-591-1618   (BR)
CALGARY BOARD OF EDUCATION
MARION CARSON SCHOOL
5225 Varsity Dr Nw, Calgary, AB, T3A 1A7
(403) 777-6050
Emp Here 50
SIC 8211 Elementary and secondary schools

D-U-N-S 20-036-4383   (BR)
CALGARY BOARD OF EDUCATION
HAMPTONS SCHOOL
10330 Hamptons Blvd Nw, Calgary, AB, T3A
6G2
(403) 777-7300
Emp Here 20
SIC 8211 Elementary and secondary schools

D-U-N-S 25-273-5311   (BR)
CALGARY BOARD OF EDUCATION
F E OSBORNE JUNIOR HIGH SCHOOL
5315 Varsity Dr Nw, Calgary, AB, T3A 1A7
(403) 777-7540
Emp Here 40
SIC 8211 Elementary and secondary schools

D-U-N-S 20-127-3468   (BR)
CALGARY ROMAN CATHOLIC SEPARATE SCHOOL DISTRICT #1
ST. DOMINIC SCHOOL
4820 Dalhart Rd Nw, Calgary, AB, T3A 1C2
(403) 500-2058
Emp Here 32
SIC 8211 Elementary and secondary schools

D-U-N-S 20-713-0852   (BR)
CALGARY ROMAN CATHOLIC SEPARATE SCHOOL DISTRICT #1
ST. ELIZABETH SETON ELEMENTARY JUNIOR HIGH SCHOOL
10845 Hidden Valley Dr Nw, Calgary, AB, T3A
6K3
(403) 500-2105
Emp Here 20
SIC 8211 Elementary and secondary schools

D-U-N-S 25-269-4682   (BR)
CALGARY ROMAN CATHOLIC SEPARATE SCHOOL DISTRICT #1
ST VINCENT DE PAUL SCHOOL
4525 49 St Nw, Calgary, AB, T3A 0K4
(403) 500-2051
Emp Here 50
SIC 8211 Elementary and secondary schools

D-U-N-S 20-034-5481   (BR)

CALGARY ROMAN CATHOLIC SEPARATE SCHOOL DISTRICT #1
MOTHER MARY GREENE SCHOOL
115 Edenwold Dr Nw, Calgary, AB, T3A 3S8
(403) 241-8862
Emp Here 25
SIC 8211 Elementary and secondary schools

D-U-N-S 25-596-2326   (SL)
D B P ALBERTA INC
BOSTON PIZZA
5005 Dalhousie Dr Nw Suite 703, Calgary, AB,
T3A 5R8
(403) 288-1700
Emp Here 50   *Sales* 1,532,175
SIC 5812 Eating places

D-U-N-S 24-809-8915   (SL)
DEBRA'S HOTELS INC
RAMADA CROWCHILD INN
5353 Crowchild Trail Nw, Calgary, AB, T3A
1W9

Emp Here 80   *Sales* 4,523,179
SIC 7011 Hotels and motels

D-U-N-S 20-087-1130   (BR)
DENTRIX INC
(*Suby of* Dentrix Inc)
3625 Shaganappi Trail Nw Suite 218, Calgary,
AB, T3A 0E2
(403) 288-5500
Emp Here 20
SIC 8021 Offices and clinics of dentists

D-U-N-S 25-682-0226   (BR)
EARL'S RESTAURANTS LTD
(*Suby of* Earl's Restaurants Ltd)
5005 Dalhousie Dr Nw Suite 605, Calgary, AB,
T3A 5R8
(403) 247-1143
Emp Here 100
SIC 5812 Eating places

D-U-N-S 20-573-5868   (BR)
FLIGHT SHOPS INC, THE
3625 Shaganappi Trail Nw, Calgary, AB, T3A
0E2
(403) 247-7295
Emp Here 20
SIC 4724 Travel agencies

D-U-N-S 25-622-2555   (BR)
GAP (CANADA) INC
GAP
(*Suby of* The Gap Inc)
3625 Shaganappi Trail Nw, Calgary, AB, T3A
0E2
(403) 288-5188
Emp Here 85
SIC 5651 Family clothing stores

D-U-N-S 25-039-1497   (SL)
GIMBEL, DR. HOWARD V
GIMBEL EYE CENTRE
4935 40 Ave Nw Suite 450, Calgary, AB, T3A
2N1
(403) 286-3022
Emp Here 300   *Sales* 24,343,680
SIC 8011 Offices and clinics of medical doctors
Pt Howard V Gimbel
Pt Judy Gimbel

D-U-N-S 24-611-2796   (SL)
HAMPTONS GOLF COURSE LTD
69 Hamptons Dr Nw, Calgary, AB, T3A 5H7
(403) 239-8088
Emp Here 150   *Sales* 2,918,428
SIC 7999 Amusement and recreation, nec

D-U-N-S 20-635-8079   (BR)
HUDSON'S BAY COMPANY
3625 Shaganappi Trail Nw, Calgary, AB, T3A
0E2
(403) 286-1220
Emp Here 280
SIC 5311 Department stores

D-U-N-S 24-494-1886   (SL)
I CARE SERVICE LTD
GIMBLE EYE CENTER, THE
4935 40 Ave Nw Suite 450, Calgary, AB, T3A
2N1
(403) 286-3022
Emp Here 100   *Sales* 8,420,350
SIC 8011 Offices and clinics of medical doctors
Pr Pr Howard Gimbel
 Judy Gimbel

D-U-N-S 20-300-2170   (BR)
INDIGO BOOKS & MUSIC INC
CHAPTERS
(*Suby of* Indigo Books & Music Inc)
5005 Dalhousie Dr Nw Suite 171, Calgary, AB,
T3A 5R8
(403) 202-4600
Emp Here 45
SIC 5942 Book stores

D-U-N-S 25-063-2262   (BR)
LE CHATEAU INC
(*Suby of* Le Chateau Inc)
3625 Shaganappi Trail Nw, Calgary, AB, T3A
0E2
(403) 288-8110
Emp Here 23
SIC 5611 Men's and boys' clothing stores

D-U-N-S 25-270-1487   (BR)
LOBLAWS INC
REAL CANADIAN SUPERSTORE
5251 Country Hills Blvd Nw Suite 1575, Calgary, AB, T3A 5H8
(403) 241-4027
Emp Here 300
SIC 5411 Grocery stores

D-U-N-S 20-036-1645   (BR)
MAGASIN LAURA (P.V.) INC
LAURA CANADA
3625 Shaganappi Trail Nw, Calgary, AB, T3A
0E2
(403) 202-1424
Emp Here 40
SIC 5621 Women's clothing stores

D-U-N-S 25-629-2913   (BR)
MOXIE'S RESTAURANTS, LIMITED PARTNERSHIP
3625 Shaganappi Trail Nw, Calgary, AB, T3A
0E2
(403) 288-2663
Emp Here 130
SIC 5812 Eating places

D-U-N-S 20-949-9305   (BR)
SOBEYS WEST INC
SAFEWAY
3625 Shaganappi Trail Nw, Calgary, AB, T3A
0E2
(403) 286-5510
Emp Here 50
SIC 5411 Grocery stores

D-U-N-S 25-964-6578   (BR)
SOBEYS WEST INC
DALHOUSIE SAFEWAY
5005 Dalhousie Dr Nw Suite 291, Calgary, AB,
T3A 5R8
(403) 202-0425
Emp Here 50
SIC 5411 Grocery stores

D-U-N-S 25-499-0047   (BR)
STAPLES CANADA INC
STAPLES THE BUSINESS DEPOT
(*Suby of* Staples, Inc.)
3625 Shaganappi Trail Nw, Calgary, AB, T3A
0E2
(403) 247-2281
Emp Here 30
SIC 5943 Stationery stores

D-U-N-S 25-499-4734   (BR)
STARBUCKS COFFEE CANADA, INC
(*Suby of* Starbucks Corporation)

5005 Dalhousie Dr Nw Suite 195, Calgary, AB, T3A 5R8
(403) 202-1555
Emp Here 26
SIC 5812 Eating places

D-U-N-S 20-644-7430   (BR)
STARBUCKS COFFEE CANADA, INC
STARBUCKS COFFEE COMPANY #4399
(*Suby of* Starbucks Corporation)
5149 Country Hills Blvd Nw Suite 238, Calgary, AB, T3A 5K8
(403) 226-9867
Emp Here 20
SIC 5812 Eating places

D-U-N-S 20-700-5062   (BR)
TOMMY HILFIGER CANADA INC
TOMMY HILFIGER STORE
3625 Shaganappi Trail Nw, Calgary, AB, T3A 0E2

Emp Here 35
SIC 5136 Men's and boy's clothing

D-U-N-S 25-297-8713   (BR)
TOYS 'R' US (CANADA) LTD
TOYS 'R' US
(*Suby of* Toys "r" Us, Inc.)
3625 Shaganappi Trail Nw, Calgary, AB, T3A 0E2
(403) 974-8683
Emp Here 50
SIC 5945 Hobby, toy, and game shops

D-U-N-S 20-799-5239   (BR)
YM INC. (SALES)
BLUENOTES
3625 Shaganappi Trail Nw, Calgary, AB, T3A 0E2
(403) 286-1726
Emp Here 23
SIC 5621 Women's clothing stores

Calgary, AB T3B

D-U-N-S 20-591-1485   (BR)
CALGARY BOARD OF EDUCATION
*BELVEDERE-PARKWAY   ELEMENTARY
SCHOOL*
4631 85 St Nw, Calgary, AB, T3B 2R8
(403) 777-6010
Emp Here 25
SIC 8211 Elementary and secondary schools

D-U-N-S 24-971-8818   (BR)
CALGARY BOARD OF EDUCATION
SILVER SPRINGS ELEMENTARY
7235 Silver Mead Rd Nw, Calgary, AB, T3B 3V1
(403) 777-6070
Emp Here 20
SIC 8211 Elementary and secondary schools

D-U-N-S 20-713-1280   (BR)
CALGARY BOARD OF EDUCATION
THOMAS B RILEY JUNIOR HIGH SCHOOL
3915 69 St Nw, Calgary, AB, T3B 2J9
(403) 777-7260
Emp Here 50
SIC 8211 Elementary and secondary schools

D-U-N-S 25-485-7998   (BR)
CALGARY BOARD OF EDUCATION
BOWNESS HIGH SCHOOL
4627 77 St Nw, Calgary, AB, T3B 2N6
(403) 286-5092
Emp Here 85
SIC 8211 Elementary and secondary schools

D-U-N-S 20-591-1402   (BR)
CALGARY BOARD OF EDUCATION
BOWCROFT ELEMENTARY SCHOOL
3940 73 St Nw, Calgary, AB, T3B 2L9
(403) 777-6020
Emp Here 25

SIC 8211 Elementary and secondary schools

D-U-N-S 20-591-1758   (BR)
CALGARY BOARD OF EDUCATION
*RIVER VALLEY SCHOOL EARLY LEARNING
CAMPUS*
6305 33 Ave Nw, Calgary, AB, T3B 1K8
(403) 247-7771
Emp Here 50
SIC 8211 Elementary and secondary schools

D-U-N-S 20-813-1305   (SL)
CALGARY GYMNASTICS CENTRE
179 Canada Olympic Rd Sw, Calgary, AB, T3B 5R5
(403) 242-1171
Emp Here 80   *Sales* 4,377,642
SIC 7999 Amusement and recreation, nec

D-U-N-S 20-034-2561   (BR)
**CALGARY ROMAN CATHOLIC SEPARATE
SCHOOL DISTRICT #1**
ST. SYLVESTER ELEMENTARY SCHOOL
7318 Silver Springs Blvd Nw, Calgary, AB, T3B 4N1
(403) 500-2063
Emp Here 25
SIC 8211 Elementary and secondary schools

D-U-N-S 20-030-8109   (BR)
**CALGARY ROMAN CATHOLIC SEPARATE
SCHOOL DISTRICT #1**
*OUR LADY OF THE ASSUMPTION ELEMEN-
TARY JUNIOR HIGH SCHOOL*
7311 34 Ave Nw, Calgary, AB, T3B 1N5
(403) 500-2045
Emp Here 30
SIC 8211 Elementary and secondary schools

D-U-N-S 24-345-5685   (BR)
CAREWEST
CAREWEST COLOBEL BELCHER
1939 Veteran'S Way Nw, Calgary, AB, T3B 5Y8
(403) 944-7800
Emp Here 50
SIC 8361 Residential care

D-U-N-S 20-273-9223   (BR)
CHARTWELL MASTER CARE LP
*CHARTWELL COLONEL BELCHER RETIRE-
MENT RESIDENCE*
1945 Veteran'S Way Nw, Calgary, AB, T3B 5Y7
(587) 287-3937
Emp Here 30
SIC 6513 Apartment building operators

D-U-N-S 20-699-5420   (BR)
**CHRISTIAN AND MISSIONARY ALLIANCE
IN CANADA, THE**
ROCK POINT CHURCH
12 Bowridge Dr Nw, Calgary, AB, T3B 2T9
(403) 288-2674
Emp Here 35
SIC 8661 Religious organizations

D-U-N-S 20-653-1951   (BR)
FFCA CHARTER SCHOOL SOCIETY
FFCA HIGH SCHOOL
2116 Mackay Rd Nw, Calgary, AB, T3B 1C7
(403) 243-3316
Emp Here 40
SIC 8211 Elementary and secondary schools

D-U-N-S 25-484-4624   (BR)
**GOVERNMENT OF THE PROVINCE OF AL-
BERTA**
MEDICAL EXAMINER'S OFFICE
4070 Bowness Rd Nw, Calgary, AB, T3B 3R7
(403) 297-8123
Emp Here 25
SIC 8049 Offices of health practitioner

D-U-N-S 20-346-1285   (SL)
INN AT THE PARK INC
FOUR POINTS HOTEL SUITES
8220 Bowridge Cres Nw, Calgary, AB, T3B

2V1
(403) 288-4441
Emp Here 80   *Sales* 3,502,114
SIC 7011 Hotels and motels

D-U-N-S 20-861-0811   (BR)
INTERALIA INC
(*Suby of* Interalia Inc)
4110 79 St Nw, Calgary, AB, T3B 5C2
(403) 288-2706
Emp Here 50
SIC 3669 Communications equipment, nec

D-U-N-S 20-130-8900   (SL)
LODGE AT VALLEY RIDGE, THE
THE DIVERSICARE CANADA
11479 Valley Ridge Dr Nw Suite 332, Calgary, AB, T3B 5V5
(403) 286-4414
Emp Here 100
SIC 7041 Membership-basis organization ho-
tels

D-U-N-S 25-316-4388   (BR)
PASLEY, MAX ENTERPRISES LIMITED
MCDONALD'S RESTAURANTS #10418
(*Suby of* Pasley, Max Enterprises Limited)
8235 Bowridge Cres Nw, Calgary, AB, T3B 5A5
(403) 288-3203
Emp Here 70
SIC 5812 Eating places

D-U-N-S 24-771-7759   (SL)
**PATHWAYS COMMUNITY SERVICES AS-
SOCIATION**
6919 32 Ave Nw Suite 103, Calgary, AB, T3B 0K6
(403) 247-5003
Emp Here 40   *Sales* 12,073,680
SIC 8399 Social services, nec
Pr Peter Boland

D-U-N-S 25-098-9985   (BR)
REVERA INC
*RETIREMENT RESIDENCES REAL ESTATE
INVESTMENT TRUST*
5927 Bowness Rd Nw, Calgary, AB, T3B 0C7
(403) 288-2373
Emp Here 200
SIC 8051 Skilled nursing care facilities

D-U-N-S 20-859-4064   (BR)
SOBEYS WEST INC
5048 16 Ave Nw, Calgary, AB, T3B 0N3
(403) 288-3219
Emp Here 50
SIC 5411 Grocery stores

D-U-N-S 24-426-3187   (BR)
SURGICAL CENTRES INC
3127 Bowwood Dr Nw, Calgary, AB, T3B 2E7
(403) 288-9400
Emp Here 20
SIC 8011 Offices and clinics of medical doctors

D-U-N-S 25-627-5231   (BR)
WENDY'S RESTAURANTS OF CANADA INC
WENDY'S
(*Suby of* The Wendy's Company)
8435 Bowfort Rd Nw Suite 300, Calgary, AB, T3B 2V2
(403) 286-6660
Emp Here 27
SIC 5812 Eating places

D-U-N-S 20-860-4269   (BR)
**WINNERS MERCHANTS INTERNATIONAL
L.P.**
HOMESENSE
(*Suby of* The TJX Companies Inc)
4896 82 St Nw, Calgary, AB, T3B 2P7
(403) 288-2224
Emp Here 25
SIC 5651 Family clothing stores

D-U-N-S 20-082-9211   (BR)

WOOD'S HOMES SOCIETY
WOOD'S HOMES BOWNESS TREATMENT
9400 48 Ave Nw, Calgary, AB, T3B 2B2
(403) 247-6751
Emp Here 100
SIC 8361 Residential care

D-U-N-S 24-890-4687   (BR)
**WORLEYPARSONS CANADA SERVICES
LTD**
151 Canada Olympic Rd Sw Suite 500, Calgary, AB, T3B 6B7
(403) 247-0200
Emp Here 49
SIC 8711 Engineering services

Calgary, AB T3C

D-U-N-S 25-287-9564   (BR)
A & W FOOD SERVICES OF CANADA INC
A & W RESTAURANT
1320 14 St Sw, Calgary, AB, T3C 1C5
(403) 244-2761
Emp Here 25
SIC 5812 Eating places

D-U-N-S 25-325-8552   (BR)
CALGARY BOARD OF EDUCATION
WESTGATE ELEMENTARY SCHOOL
150 Westminster Dr Sw, Calgary, AB, T3C 2T3
(403) 777-8420
Emp Here 50
SIC 8211 Elementary and secondary schools

D-U-N-S 20-713-0985   (BR)
CALGARY BOARD OF EDUCATION
WILDWOOD SCHOOL
120 45 St Sw, Calgary, AB, T3C 2B3
(403) 777-8430
Emp Here 50
SIC 8211 Elementary and secondary schools

D-U-N-S 20-591-1279   (BR)
CALGARY BOARD OF EDUCATION
SPRUCE CLIFF ELEMENTARY SCHOOL
3405 Spruce Dr Sw, Calgary, AB, T3C 0A5
(403) 777-8410
Emp Here 25
SIC 8211 Elementary and secondary schools

D-U-N-S 20-713-0969   (BR)
CALGARY BOARD OF EDUCATION
ROSSCARROCK SCHOOL
1406 40 St Sw, Calgary, AB, T3C 1W7
(403) 777-8390
Emp Here 50
SIC 8211 Elementary and secondary schools

D-U-N-S 20-713-1744   (BR)
CALGARY BOARD OF EDUCATION
NATIONAL SPORT SCHOOL
3600 16 Ave Sw Suite 109, Calgary, AB, T3C 1A5
(403) 777-7329
Emp Here 20
SIC 8211 Elementary and secondary schools

D-U-N-S 25-272-0875   (BR)
CALGARY BOARD OF EDUCATION
VINCENT MASSEY SCHOOL
939 45 St Sw, Calgary, AB, T3C 2B9
(403) 777-7870
Emp Here 50
SIC 8211 Elementary and secondary schools

D-U-N-S 20-591-1626   (BR)
CALGARY BOARD OF EDUCATION
SUNALTA ELEMENTARY SCHOOL
536 Sonora Ave Sw, Calgary, AB, T3C 2J9
(403) 777-8590
Emp Here 25
SIC 8211 Elementary and secondary schools

D-U-N-S 20-165-4964   (BR)
CALGARY ROMAN CATHOLIC SEPARATE

SCHOOL DISTRICT #1
ST MICHAEL SCHOOL
4511 8 Ave Sw, Calgary, AB, T3C 0G9
(403) 500-2021
Emp Here 55
SIC 8211 Elementary and secondary schools

D-U-N-S 24-298-9358 (SL)
CALGARY SOCIETY FOR PERSONS WITH DISABILITIES
3410 Spruce Dr Sw, Calgary, AB, T3C 3A4
(403) 246-4450
Emp Here 65 *Sales* 3,064,349
SIC 8052 Intermediate care facilities

D-U-N-S 20-580-4516 (BR)
CANADA POST CORPORATION
1610 37 St Sw Suite 55, Calgary, AB, T3C 3P1
(403) 240-4473
Emp Here 20
SIC 4311 U.s. postal service

D-U-N-S 20-140-1507 (BR)
CANADIAN RED CROSS SOCIETY, THE
1305 11 Ave Sw, Calgary, AB, T3C 3P6
(403) 541-6100
Emp Here 40
SIC 8611 Business associations

D-U-N-S 20-244-9257 (BR)
CANADIAN RED CROSS SOCIETY, THE
1305 11 Ave Sw Suite 100, Calgary, AB, T3C 3P6
(403) 205-3448
Emp Here 100
SIC 8322 Individual and family services

D-U-N-S 24-810-4952 (BR)
CHINTZ & COMPANY DECORATIVE FUR-NISHINGS INC
1238 11 Ave Sw, Calgary, AB, T3C 0M4
(403) 245-3449
Emp Here 48
SIC 7389 Business services, nec

D-U-N-S 20-786-6562 (BR)
COMMUNITY NATURAL FOODS LTD
1304 10 Ave Sw, Calgary, AB, T3C 0J2
(403) 229-0164
Emp Here 200
SIC 5499 Miscellaneous food stores

D-U-N-S 24-035-4980 (BR)
DATA COMMUNICATIONS MANAGEMENT CORP
SUNDOG PRINTING, DIV OF
1311 9 Ave Sw Suite 300, Calgary, AB, T3C 0H9
(403) 272-7440
Emp Here 225
SIC 2759 Commercial printing, nec

D-U-N-S 24-552-6587 (BR)
EXTENDICARE INC
EXTENDICARE CEDARS VILLA
3330 8 Ave Sw, Calgary, AB, T3C 0E7
(403) 249-8915
Emp Here 220
SIC 8051 Skilled nursing care facilities

D-U-N-S 24-337-3383 (BR)
FGL SPORTS LTD
SPORT-CHEK
1200 37 St Sw Unit 54, Calgary, AB, T3C 1S2
(403) 249-4303
Emp Here 200
SIC 5941 Sporting goods and bicycle shops

D-U-N-S 25-313-9281 (HQ)
GREYHOUND CANADA TRANSPORTA-TION ULC
FIRSTGROUP AMERICA
877 Greyhound Way Sw, Calgary, AB, T3C 3V8
(403) 218-3000
Emp Here 350 *Emp Total* 120,475
Sales 167,792,819
SIC 4131 Intercity and rural bus transportation

Pr Pr Dave Leach
VP Fin Karim Lalani
Stuart Kendrick

D-U-N-S 20-635-7709 (SL)
GUNTHER'S BUILDING CENTER LTD
2100 10 Ave Sw, Calgary, AB, T3C 0K5
(403) 245-3311
Emp Here 22 *Sales* 9,143,680
SIC 5031 Lumber, plywood, and millwork
Pr Pr Peter Kockerbeck

D-U-N-S 24-983-7311 (SL)
LEXIN RESOURCES LTD
1207 11 Ave Sw Suite 300, Calgary, AB, T3C 0M5
(403) 237-9400
Emp Here 176 *Sales* 102,217,941
SIC 1382 Oil and gas exploration services
Pr Pr Edward W. Bogle
Ch Bd Adrian Loader
Randall Findlay
George Hickox Jr.
Michael Leffell
Glen Roane

D-U-N-S 20-828-2392 (HQ)
SANEAL CAMERA SUPPLIES LTD
SANEAL CAMERA
(Suby of Saneal Camera Supplies Ltd)
1402 11 Ave Sw, Calgary, AB, T3C 0M8
(403) 228-1865
Emp Here 20 *Emp Total* 60
Sales 3,210,271
SIC 5946 Camera and photographic supply stores

D-U-N-S 24-858-3374 (BR)
SHAW COMMUNICATIONS INC
1239 12 Ave Sw Suite 1101, Calgary, AB, T3C 3R8
(403) 750-4500
Emp Here 75
SIC 4841 Cable and other pay television ser-vices

D-U-N-S 20-771-6379 (BR)
SMITTY'S CANADA LIMITED
1200 37 St Sw Suite 7, Calgary, AB, T3C 1S2
(403) 249-1044
Emp Here 20
SIC 5812 Eating places

D-U-N-S 25-486-5637 (BR)
STAPLES CANADA INC
STAPLES THE BUSINESS DEPOT
(Suby of Staples, Inc.)
1215 9 Ave Sw, Calgary, AB, T3C 0H9
(403) 263-0200
Emp Here 30
SIC 5943 Stationery stores

D-U-N-S 20-512-2612 (BR)
VISTEK LTD
1231 10 Ave Sw, Calgary, AB, T3C 0J3
(403) 244-0333
Emp Here 30
SIC 5043 Photographic equipment and sup-plies

D-U-N-S 25-218-9774 (BR)
WAL-MART CANADA CORP
1212 37 St Sw Suite 3009, Calgary, AB, T3C 1S3
(403) 242-2205
Emp Here 250
SIC 5311 Department stores

D-U-N-S 24-440-3382 (BR)
WENDY'S RESTAURANTS OF CANADA INC
WENDY'S
(Suby of The Wendy's Company)
1720 37 St Sw, Calgary, AB, T3C 3R1
(403) 246-0065
Emp Here 25
SIC 5812 Eating places

Calgary, AB T3E

D-U-N-S 20-829-7176 (BR)
ALBERTA MOTOR ASSOCIATION
A M A
4700 17 Ave Sw, Calgary, AB, T3E 0E3
(403) 240-5300
Emp Here 180
SIC 4724 Travel agencies

D-U-N-S 20-947-3052 (BR)
ALBERTA MOTOR ASSOCIATION TRAVEL AGENCY LTD
AMA TRAVEL
4700 17 Ave Sw, Calgary, AB, T3E 0E3
(403) 240-5350
Emp Here 20
SIC 4725 Tour operators

D-U-N-S 20-002-9523 (BR)
BANK OF NOVA SCOTIA, THE
SCOTIABANK
6449 Crowchild Trail Sw, Calgary, AB, T3E 5R7
(403) 221-6846
Emp Here 20
SIC 6021 National commercial banks

D-U-N-S 20-298-7801 (BR)
BANK OF MONTREAL
BMO
5249 Richmond Rd Sw Suite 1, Calgary, AB, T3E 7C4
(403) 234-1886
Emp Here 71
SIC 6021 National commercial banks

D-U-N-S 25-269-4443 (BR)
CALGARY BOARD OF EDUCATION
LORD SHAUGHNESSY HIGH SCHOOL
2336 53 Ave Sw, Calgary, AB, T3E 1L2
(403) 243-4500
Emp Here 75
SIC 8211 Elementary and secondary schools

D-U-N-S 20-590-8010 (BR)
CALGARY BOARD OF EDUCATION
KILLARNEY SCHOOL
3008 33 St Sw, Calgary, AB, T3E 2T9
(403) 777-8360
Emp Here 20
SIC 8211 Elementary and secondary schools

D-U-N-S 20-012-3433 (BR)
CALGARY BOARD OF EDUCATION
CHINOOK LEARNING SERVICES
2519 Richmond Rd Sw Suite 168, Calgary, AB, T3E 4M2
(403) 777-7200
Emp Here 100
SIC 8221 Colleges and universities

D-U-N-S 20-713-0928 (BR)
CALGARY BOARD OF EDUCATION
JENNIE ELLIOTT SCHOOL
3031 Lindsay Dr Sw, Calgary, AB, T3E 6A9
(403) 777-8350
Emp Here 50
SIC 8211 Elementary and secondary schools

D-U-N-S 20-713-1363 (BR)
CALGARY BOARD OF EDUCATION
A.E. CROSS JUNIOR HIGH SCHOOL
3445 37 St Sw, Calgary, AB, T3E 3C2
(403) 777-7410
Emp Here 50
SIC 8211 Elementary and secondary schools

D-U-N-S 20-713-0951 (BR)
CALGARY BOARD OF EDUCATION
GLENBROOK ELEMENTARY SCHOOL
4725 33 Ave Sw, Calgary, AB, T3E 3V1
(403) 777-8320
Emp Here 24
SIC 8211 Elementary and secondary schools

D-U-N-S 20-713-0977 (BR)
CALGARY BOARD OF EDUCATION
SIR JAMES LOUGHEED ELEMENTARY SCHOOL
3519 36 Ave Sw, Calgary, AB, T3E 1C2
(403) 777-8400
Emp Here 50
SIC 8211 Elementary and secondary schools

D-U-N-S 25-011-2141 (BR)
CALGARY BOARD OF EDUCATION
CENTRAL MEMORIAL HIGH SCHOOL
5111 21 St Sw, Calgary, AB, T3E 1R9
(403) 243-8880
Emp Here 150
SIC 8211 Elementary and secondary schools

D-U-N-S 20-591-1550 (BR)
CALGARY BOARD OF EDUCATION
GLAMORGAN ELEMENTARY SCHOOL
50 Grafton Dr Sw, Calgary, AB, T3E 4W3
(403) 777-8310
Emp Here 25
SIC 8211 Elementary and secondary schools

D-U-N-S 20-034-2520 (BR)
CALGARY ROMAN CATHOLIC SEPARATE SCHOOL DISTRICT #1
ST. ANDREW SCHOOL
4331 41 Ave Sw, Calgary, AB, T3E 1G2
(403) 500-2031
Emp Here 23
SIC 8211 Elementary and secondary schools

D-U-N-S 25-269-4542 (BR)
CALGARY ROMAN CATHOLIC SEPARATE SCHOOL DISTRICT #1
BISHOP CARROLL HIGH SCHOOL
4624 Richard Rd Sw, Calgary, AB, T3E 6L1
(403) 500-2056
Emp Here 125
SIC 8211 Elementary and secondary schools

D-U-N-S 20-713-0654 (BR)
CALGARY ROMAN CATHOLIC SEPARATE SCHOOL DISTRICT #1
ST. GREGORY SCHOOL
5340 26 Ave Sw, Calgary, AB, T3E 0R6
(403) 500-2048
Emp Here 50
SIC 8211 Elementary and secondary schools

D-U-N-S 20-580-7873 (BR)
CALGARY ROMAN CATHOLIC SEPARATE SCHOOL DISTRICT #1
HOLY NAME SCHOOL
3011 35 St Sw, Calgary, AB, T3E 2Y7
(403) 500-2006
Emp Here 21
SIC 8211 Elementary and secondary schools

D-U-N-S 20-036-3807 (BR)
CALGARY ROMAN CATHOLIC SEPARATE SCHOOL DISTRICT #1
ST JAMES ELEMENTARY & JUNIOR HIGH SCHOOL
2227 58 Ave Sw, Calgary, AB, T3E 1N6
(403) 500-2035
Emp Here 33
SIC 8211 Elementary and secondary schools

D-U-N-S 20-913-1650 (BR)
CALGARY ROMAN CATHOLIC SEPARATE SCHOOL DISTRICT #1
ST. LEO CENTRE
6220 Lakeview Dr Sw, Calgary, AB, T3E 5T1
(403) 500-2000
Emp Here 65
SIC 8742 Management consulting services

D-U-N-S 25-314-8779 (BR)
CAREWEST
CAREWEST SARCEE
3504 Sarcee Rd Sw, Calgary, AB, T3E 2L3
(403) 686-8100
Emp Here 100
SIC 8051 Skilled nursing care facilities

▲ Public Company ■ Public Company Family Member **HQ** Headquarters **BR** Branch **SL** Single Location

D-U-N-S 24-673-9663　　(SL)
CENTURION MECHANICAL LTD
2509 Dieppe Ave Sw Unit 301, Calgary, AB,
T3E 7J9
(403) 452-6761
Emp Here 50　　*Sales* 4,377,642
SIC 1711 Plumbing, heating, air-conditioning

D-U-N-S 20-152-7384　　(SL)
CLEAR WATER ACADEMY FOUNDATION
2521 Dieppe Ave Sw, Calgary, AB, T3E 7J9
(403) 217-8448
Emp Here 400　　*Sales* 35,926,560
SIC 8211 Elementary and secondary schools
Ch Bd Kent Wang
　Randy Ritchie
　Bob Christianson
　William L. Britton
　Jon Budke
　Angelo F. Toselli
　Catherine M. Zentner
Prin Paul Hudec

D-U-N-S 20-035-2891　　(BR)
**CONSEIL SCOLAIRE CATHOLIQUE ET
FRANCOPHONE DU SUD DE L'ALBERTA**
ECOLE STE-MARGUERITE BOURGEOYS
(*Suby of* Conseil Scolaire Catholique et Francophone du Sud de l'Alberta)
4700 Richard Rd Sw, Calgary, AB, T3E 6L1
(403) 240-2007
Emp Here 25
SIC 8211 Elementary and secondary schools

D-U-N-S 20-010-0613　　(BR)
HUDSON'S BAY COMPANY
HOME OUTFITTERS DIV OF
3915 51 St Sw Unit 10, Calgary, AB, T3E 6N1
(403) 685-4394
Emp Here 50
SIC 5311 Department stores

D-U-N-S 25-946-6548　　(BR)
INTERNATIONAL FITNESS HOLDINGS INC
WORLD HEALTH
4604 37 St Sw Unit 20, Calgary, AB, T3E 3C9
(403) 240-1555
Emp Here 42
SIC 7991 Physical fitness facilities

D-U-N-S 25-315-8943　　(BR)
INVESTORS GROUP FINANCIAL SERVICES INC
37 Richard Way Sw Unit 100, Calgary, AB,
T3E 7M8
(403) 253-4840
Emp Here 130
SIC 8742 Management consulting services

D-U-N-S 24-880-7182　　(SL)
K L S CONTRACTING LTD
7 Glenbrook Pl Sw Suite 206, Calgary, AB,
T3E 6W4
(403) 240-3030
Emp Here 60　　*Sales* 4,377,642
SIC 1794 Excavation work

D-U-N-S 25-273-0981　　(BR)
LONDON DRUGS LIMITED
5255 Richmond Rd Sw Suite 300, Calgary,
AB, T3E 7C4
(403) 571-4932
Emp Here 100
SIC 5912 Drug stores and proprietary stores

D-U-N-S 25-316-4081　　(BR)
PASLEY, MAX ENTERPRISES LIMITED
MCDONALD'S RESTAURANTS
(*Suby of* Pasley, Max Enterprises Limited)
3611 17 Ave Sw, Calgary, AB, T3E 0B9
(403) 249-0780
Emp Here 62
SIC 5812 Eating places

D-U-N-S 24-418-5109　　(BR)
SODEXO CANADA LTD
SODEXO
4825 Mount Royal Gate Sw, Calgary, AB, T3E

6K6
(403) 240-6328
Emp Here 120
SIC 5812 Eating places

D-U-N-S 24-298-4698　　(BR)
XEROX CANADA LTD
(*Suby of* Xerox Corporation)
37 Richard Way Sw Suite 200, Calgary, AB,
T3E 7M8
(403) 260-8800
Emp Here 75
SIC 5044 Office equipment

Calgary, AB T3G

D-U-N-S 25-947-8535　　(BR)
1009833 ALBERTA LTD
PETLAND
40 Crowfoot Terr Nw, Calgary, AB, T3G 4J8
(403) 543-7969
Emp Here 20
SIC 5999 Miscellaneous retail stores, nec

D-U-N-S 25-090-6682　　(SL)
290756 ALBERTA LTD
HYUNDAI DEALERSHIP
710 Crowfoot Cres Nw, Calgary, AB, T3G 4S3
(403) 374-3374
Emp Here 60　　*Sales* 30,144,000
SIC 5511 New and used car dealers
Pr Pr Steven P Itzcovitch

D-U-N-S 24-338-6336　　(HQ)
586307 ALBERTA LTD
CROWFOOT LIQUOR STORE
(*Suby of* 580932 Alberta Ltd)
7422 Crowfoot Rd Nw Unit 201, Calgary, AB,
T3G 3N7
(403) 296-2200
Emp Here 40　　　*Emp Total* 1
Sales 13,132,926
SIC 5921 Liquor stores
Pr Terry Richardson

D-U-N-S 20-119-9374　　(HQ)
ABSOLUTE ENERGY SOLUTIONS INC
600 Crowfoot Cres Nw Suite 302, Calgary, AB,
T3G 0B4
(403) 266-5027
Emp Here 20　　　*Emp Total* 100
Sales 4,591,130
SIC 3533 Oil and gas field machinery

D-U-N-S 25-314-8720　　(BR)
ALBERTA HEALTH SERVICES
NORTHWEST HEALTH CENTRE
1829 Ranchlands Blvd Nw Suite 10, Calgary,
AB, T3G 2A7
(403) 239-6600
Emp Here 25
SIC 8011 Offices and clinics of medical doctors

D-U-N-S 20-028-9499　　(SL)
ARBOUR LAKE DENTAL CENTRE
150 Crowfoot Cres Nw Suite 224, Calgary, AB,
T3G 3T2
(403) 241-8808
Emp Here 50　　*Sales* 2,845,467
SIC 8021 Offices and clinics of dentists

D-U-N-S 24-440-2038　　(BR)
**ASSOCIATED ENGINEERING ALBERTA
LTD**
(*Suby of* Ashco Shareholders Inc)
600 Crowfoot Cres Nw Suite 400, Calgary,
T3G 0B4
(403) 262-4500
Emp Here 90
SIC 8711 Engineering services

D-U-N-S 25-522-5286　　(BR)
BANK OF NOVA SCOTIA, THE
SCOTIABANK

1829 Ranchlands Blvd Nw Suite 171, Calgary,
AB, T3G 2A7
(403) 221-6810
Emp Here 27
SIC 6021 National commercial banks

D-U-N-S 20-296-1850　　(BR)
BANK OF NOVA SCOTIA, THE
SCOTIABANK
8888 Country Hills Blvd Nw Suite 404, Calgary, AB, T3G 5T4
(403) 662-3270
Emp Here 20
SIC 6021 National commercial banks

D-U-N-S 20-567-7821　　(BR)
BANK OF MONTREAL
BMO
101 Crowfoot Way Nw, Calgary, AB, T3G 2R2
(403) 234-2896
Emp Here 30
SIC 6021 National commercial banks

D-U-N-S 20-589-5043　　(BR)
BANQUE TORONTO-DOMINION, LA
TD CANADA TRUST
(*Suby of* Toronto-Dominion Bank, The)
260 Crowfoot Cres Nw, Calgary, AB, T3G 3N5
(403) 299-3418
Emp Here 20
SIC 6021 National commercial banks

D-U-N-S 25-945-5350　　(BR)
**BREWSTERS BREW PUB & BRASSERIE
(ALBERTA) INC**
BREWSTERS BREWING CO & RESTAURANT
25 Crowfoot Terr Nw, Calgary, AB, T3G 4J8
(403) 208-2739
Emp Here 30
SIC 5812 Eating places

D-U-N-S 25-267-4416　　(BR)
CALGARY BOARD OF EDUCATION
ARBOUR LAKE SCHOOL
27 Arbour Crest Dr Nw, Calgary, AB, T3G 4H3
(403) 777-7310
Emp Here 70
SIC 8211 Elementary and secondary schools

D-U-N-S 20-591-1733　　(BR)
CALGARY BOARD OF EDUCATION
RANCHLANDS SCHOOL
610 Ranchlands Blvd Nw, Calgary, AB, T3G
2C5
(403) 777-6350
Emp Here 40
SIC 8211 Elementary and secondary schools

D-U-N-S 25-316-1061　　(BR)
**CALGARY CO-OPERATIVE ASSOCIATION
LIMITED**
CALGARY CO-OP
35 Crowfoot Way Nw, Calgary, AB, T3G 2L4
(403) 216-4500
Emp Here 320
SIC 5411 Grocery stores

D-U-N-S 20-574-8366　　(BR)
**CALGARY ROMAN CATHOLIC SEPARATE
SCHOOL DISTRICT #1**
ST. RITA SCHOOL
7811 Ranchview Dr Nw, Calgary, AB, T3G
2B3
(403) 500-2083
Emp Here 22
SIC 8211 Elementary and secondary schools

D-U-N-S 20-037-6791　　(BR)
**CALGARY ROMAN CATHOLIC SEPARATE
SCHOOL DISTRICT #1**
ST. MARIA GORETTI SCHOOL
375 Hawkstone Dr Nw, Calgary, AB, T3G 3T7
(403) 500-2099
Emp Here 22
SIC 8211 Elementary and secondary schools

D-U-N-S 20-713-0886　　(BR)

**CALGARY ROMAN CATHOLIC SEPARATE
SCHOOL DISTRICT #1**
ST. BRIGID SCHOOL
730 Citadel Way Nw, Calgary, AB, T3G 5S6
(403) 500-2113
Emp Here 52
SIC 8211 Elementary and secondary schools

D-U-N-S 25-094-2997　　(BR)
**CALGARY ROMAN CATHOLIC SEPARATE
SCHOOL DISTRICT #1**
ST. AMBROSE SCHOOL
1500 Arbour Lake Rd Nw, Calgary, AB, T3G
4X9
(403) 500-2100
Emp Here 50
SIC 8211 Elementary and secondary schools

D-U-N-S 25-677-7426　　(BR)
CALGARY YOUNG MEN'S CHRISTIAN ASSOCIATION
CROWFOOT YMCA
8100 John Laurie Blvd Nw, Calgary, AB, T3G
3S3
(403) 547-6576
Emp Here 250
SIC 8399 Social services, nec

D-U-N-S 20-589-6371　　(BR)
CANADA POST CORPORATION
7750 Ranchview Dr Nw, Calgary, AB, T3G
1Y9
(403) 239-6464
Emp Here 20
SIC 4311 U.s. postal service

D-U-N-S 24-342-8054　　(BR)
CARA OPERATIONS LIMITED
SWISS CHALET
(*Suby of* Cara Holdings Limited)
28 Crowfoot Cir Nw, Calgary, AB, T3G 2T3

Emp Here 40
SIC 5812 Eating places

D-U-N-S 20-069-0449　　(BR)
CARA OPERATIONS LIMITED
MONTANA'S COOKHOUSE
(*Suby of* Cara Holdings Limited)
112 Crowfoot Terr Nw, Calgary, AB, T3G 4J8
(403) 241-9740
Emp Here 45
SIC 5812 Eating places

D-U-N-S 25-310-6660　　(BR)
CINEPLEX ODEON CORPORATION
CINEPLEX CINEMA CROWFOOT CROSSING
91 Crowfoot Terr Nw, Calgary, AB, T3G 4J8
(403) 547-3316
Emp Here 50
SIC 7822 Motion picture and tape distribution

D-U-N-S 24-733-6332　　(SL)
DOUBLE B INVESTMENTS INC
BOSTON PIZZA CROWFOOT
140 Crowfoot Cres Nw, Calgary, AB, T3G 2W1
(403) 239-3333
Emp Here 50　　*Sales* 1,532,175
SIC 5812 Eating places

D-U-N-S 25-648-3132　　(HQ)
ELIZABETHS BAKERY LTD
TIM HORTONS
(*Suby of* Elizabeths Bakery Ltd)
79 Crowfoot Way Nw, Calgary, AB, T3G 2R2
(403) 239-2583
Emp Here 80　　　*Emp Total* 83
Sales 2,480,664
SIC 5812 Eating places

D-U-N-S 24-340-0293　　(BR)
FGL SPORTS LTD
SPORT MART
48 Crawford Cres, Calgary, AB, T3G 4J8
(403) 241-4803
Emp Here 30
SIC 5941 Sporting goods and bicycle shops

D-U-N-S 24-374-4237   (BR)
HUDSON'S BAY COMPANY
HOME OUTFITTERS
8888 Country Hills Blvd Nw Suite 600, Calgary, AB, T3G 5T4
(403) 974-7100
Emp Here 20
SIC 5311 Department stores

D-U-N-S 20-520-5292   (BR)
INDIGO BOOKS & MUSIC INC
CHAPTERS 906
(*Suby of* Indigo Books & Music Inc)
66 Crowfoot Terr Nw, Calgary, AB, T3G 4J8
(403) 208-8490
Emp Here 45
SIC 5942 Book stores

D-U-N-S 20-334-1677   (SL)
JOEY CROWFOOT
50 Crowfoot Way Nw, Calgary, AB, T3G 4C8
(403) 547-5639
Emp Here 160   *Sales* 4,815,406
SIC 5812 Eating places

D-U-N-S 25-435-2370   (BR)
MCI MEDICAL CLINICS (ALBERTA) INC
NOSE HILL CLINIC
(*Suby of* MCI Medical Clinics Inc)
1829 Ranchlands Blvd Nw Suite 137, Calgary, AB, T3G 2A7
(403) 239-8888
Emp Here 20
SIC 8011 Offices and clinics of medical doctors

D-U-N-S 25-570-5311   (BR)
MOORES THE SUIT PEOPLE INC
MOORES CLOTHING FOR MEN
(*Suby of* Tailored Brands, Inc.)
92 Crowfoot Terr Nw, Calgary, AB, T3G 4J8
(403) 247-9666
Emp Here 22
SIC 5611 Men's and boys' clothing stores

D-U-N-S 25-316-4305   (BR)
PASLEY, MAX ENTERPRISES LIMITED
MCDONALD'S RESTAURANTS
(*Suby of* Pasley, Max Enterprises Limited)
63 Crowfoot Way Nw, Calgary, AB, T3G 2R2
(403) 241-1785
Emp Here 70
SIC 5812 Eating places

D-U-N-S 20-734-4180   (BR)
PASLEY, MAX ENTERPRISES LIMITED
MCDONALD'S RESTAURANTS
(*Suby of* Pasley, Max Enterprises Limited)
8888 Country Hills Blvd Nw Suite 200, Calgary, AB, T3G 5T4
(403) 375-0845
Emp Here 20
SIC 5812 Eating places

D-U-N-S 25-271-1130   (BR)
SOBEYS WEST INC
SAFEWAY, DIV OF
99 Crowfoot Cres Nw, Calgary, AB, T3G 2L5
(403) 239-9000
Emp Here 200
SIC 5411 Grocery stores

D-U-N-S 25-304-6940   (BR)
SUN LIFE ASSURANCE COMPANY OF CANADA
CLARICA
600 Crowfoot Cres Nw Suite 300, Calgary, AB, T3G 0B4
(403) 231-8600
Emp Here 35
SIC 6311 Life insurance

D-U-N-S 20-860-5332   (BR)
TOWN SHOES LIMITED
SHOE COMPANY, THE
72 Crowfoot Terr Nw Suite 28, Calgary, AB, T3G 4J8

(403) 547-7777
Emp Here 25
SIC 5661 Shoe stores

D-U-N-S 20-916-2341   (BR)
WAL-MART CANADA CORP
8888 Country Hills Blvd Nw Suite 200, Calgary, AB, T3G 5T4
(403) 567-1502
Emp Here 375
SIC 5311 Department stores

Calgary, AB T3H

D-U-N-S 20-341-2502   (SL)
A SPLENDID AFFAIR
AFFINITY CATERING
10 Coachway Rd Sw Unit 143, Calgary, AB, T3H 1E5
(403) 228-6280
Emp Here 60   *Sales* 1,824,018
SIC 5812 Eating places

D-U-N-S 25-236-1514   (BR)
ALBERTA TREASURY BRANCHES
ATB FINANCIAL
601 Stewart Green Sw, Calgary, AB, T3H 3C8
(403) 297-3900
Emp Here 25
SIC 6036 Savings institutions, except federal

D-U-N-S 20-046-1106   (BR)
BELL MEDIA INC
CTV TELEVISION
80 Patina Rise Sw, Calgary, AB, T3H 2W4
(403) 240-5600
Emp Here 130
SIC 4833 Television broadcasting stations

D-U-N-S 20-713-1777   (BR)
CALGARY BOARD OF EDUCATION
BATTALION PARK SCHOOL
369 Sienna Park Dr Sw, Calgary, AB, T3H 4S2
(403) 777-7187
Emp Here 50
SIC 8211 Elementary and secondary schools

D-U-N-S 20-713-1710   (BR)
CALGARY BOARD OF EDUCATION
OLYMPIC HEIGHTS ELEMENTARY SCHOOL
875 Strathcona Dr Sw, Calgary, AB, T3H 2Z7
(403) 777-8370
Emp Here 65
SIC 8211 Elementary and secondary schools

D-U-N-S 25-485-8160   (SL)
CALGARY FRENCH & INTERNATIONAL SCHOOL SOCIETY, THE
CFIS LANGUAGE SCHOOLS
700 77 St Sw, Calgary, AB, T3H 5R1
(403) 240-1500
Emp Here 80   *Sales* 4,377,642
SIC 8299 Schools and educational services, nec

D-U-N-S 20-029-0570   (BR)
CALGARY ROMAN CATHOLIC SEPARATE SCHOOL DISTRICT #1
JOHN W. COSTELLO CATHOLIC SCHOOL
300 Strathcona Dr Sw, Calgary, AB, T3H 1N9
(403) 500-2003
Emp Here 48
SIC 8211 Elementary and secondary schools

D-U-N-S 24-840-7355   (SL)
CALGARY SOCIETY FOR EFFECTIVE EDUCATION OF LEARNING DISABLED
CALGARY ACADEMY
1677 93 St Sw, Calgary, AB, T3H 0R3
(403) 686-6444
Emp Here 128   *Sales* 11,869,650
SIC 8211 Elementary and secondary schools
Pr Peter Istvanffy
    James E Chaput
    George R Perry

    A Douglas Rogan
VP VP Jim Gray
Dir Ron Stanners
Dir Judy Copithorne
Dir John Howard
Dir Janet L'heureux

D-U-N-S 24-840-3909   (SL)
CALGARY WALDORF SCHOOL SOCIETY
CALGARY WALDORF SCHOOL
515 Cougar Ridge Dr Sw Suite 1, Calgary, AB, T3H 5G9
(403) 287-1868
Emp Here 50   *Sales* 3,356,192
SIC 8211 Elementary and secondary schools

D-U-N-S 20-069-0472   (BR)
CARA OPERATIONS LIMITED
MONTANA'S COOKHOUSE
(*Suby of* Cara Holdings Limited)
5622 Signal Hill Ctr Sw, Calgary, AB, T3H 3P8
(403) 217-1100
Emp Here 40
SIC 5812 Eating places

D-U-N-S 20-650-3349   (BR)
CAREWEST
6363 Simcoe Rd Sw, Calgary, AB, T3H 4M3
(403) 240-7950
Emp Here 88
SIC 8051 Skilled nursing care facilities

D-U-N-S 20-005-3663   (BR)
CINEPLEX ODEON CORPORATION
CINEPLEX CINEMAS WESTHILLS
165 Stewart Green Sw, Calgary, AB, T3H 3C8
(403) 246-5291
Emp Here 20
SIC 7832 Motion picture theaters, except drive-in

D-U-N-S 20-041-0368   (BR)
CONNECT FIRST CREDIT UNION LTD
FIRST CALGARY FINANCIAL
5735 Signal Hill Ctr Sw, Calgary, AB, T3H 3P8
(403) 736-4560
Emp Here 23
SIC 6062 State credit unions

D-U-N-S 25-571-0808   (BR)
HANSON RESTAURANTS INC
TACO BELL
(*Suby of* Hanson Restaurants Inc)
160 Stewart Green Sw, Calgary, AB, T3H 3C8

Emp Here 20
SIC 5812 Eating places

D-U-N-S 25-316-9353   (SL)
KNEBEL, MURRAY G. PROFESSIONAL CORPORATION
SIERRA CENTRE FOR DENTAL WELLNESS, THE
5982 Signal Hill Ctr Sw, Calgary, AB, T3H 3P8
(403) 297-9600
Emp Here 50   *Sales* 2,845,467
SIC 8021 Offices and clinics of dentists

D-U-N-S 25-522-7480   (BR)
LIFEMARK HEALTH MANAGEMENT INC
LIFEMARK PHYSIOTHERAPY
(*Suby of* Audax Group, L.P.)
2000 69 St Sw, Calgary, AB, T3H 4V7
(403) 240-0124
Emp Here 20
SIC 8741 Management services

D-U-N-S 25-792-1312   (BR)
LOBLAWS INC
REAL CANADIAN SUPERSTORE
5858 Signal Hill Ctr Sw Suite 1577, Calgary, AB, T3H 3P8
(403) 686-8035
Emp Here 200
SIC 5141 Groceries, general line

D-U-N-S 25-453-9471   (BR)
MOXIE'S RESTAURANTS, LIMITED PART-

NERSHIP
MOXIE'S WEST HILLS
120 Stewart Green Sw, Calgary, AB, T3H 3C8
(403) 246-0366
Emp Here 60
SIC 5812 Eating places

D-U-N-S 25-316-4180   (BR)
PASLEY, MAX ENTERPRISES LIMITED
MCDONALD'S RESTAURANTS
(*Suby of* Pasley, Max Enterprises Limited)
100 Stewart Green Sw Unit 100, Calgary, AB, T3H 3C8
(403) 246-1577
Emp Here 75
SIC 5812 Eating places

D-U-N-S 20-860-0515   (BR)
SOURCE (BELL) ELECTRONICS INC, THE
SOURCE, THE
5963 Signal Hill Ctr Sw, Calgary, AB, T3H 3P8

Emp Here 25
SIC 5999 Miscellaneous retail stores, nec

D-U-N-S 25-498-9353   (BR)
STAPLES CANADA INC
STAPLES THE BUSINESS DEPOT
(*Suby of* Staples, Inc.)
5662 Signal Hill Ctr Sw, Calgary, AB, T3H 3P8
(403) 217-7070
Emp Here 35
SIC 5943 Stationery stores

D-U-N-S 25-499-4916   (BR)
STARBUCKS COFFEE CANADA, INC
#4275
(*Suby of* Starbucks Corporation)
274 Stewart Green Sw, Calgary, AB, T3H 3C8
(403) 246-4100
Emp Here 25
SIC 5812 Eating places

D-U-N-S 20-038-9869   (BR)
STATESMAN CORPORATION
STATESMAN MANOR VILLAGE LIFE CENTER
1858 Sirocco Dr Sw Suite 312, Calgary, AB, T3H 3P7
(403) 249-7113
Emp Here 20
SIC 8699 Membership organizations, nec

D-U-N-S 20-860-5142   (BR)
TOWN SHOES LIMITED
SHOE COMPANY, THE
5657 Signal Hill Ctr Sw Unit 2, Calgary, AB, T3H 3P8
(403) 246-8666
Emp Here 25
SIC 5661 Shoe stores

D-U-N-S 20-232-5556   (SL)
WESTSIDE REGIONAL RECREATION SOCIETY
WESTSIDE RECREATION CENTRE
2000 69 St Sw, Calgary, AB, T3H 4V7
(403) 531-5875
Emp Here 100   *Sales* 10,838,427
SIC 7997 Membership sports and recreation clubs
    Tony Dimaio
Dir Joe Palin
    Norma-Jean Hogg

D-U-N-S 25-294-0473   (BR)
WINNERS MERCHANTS INTERNATIONAL L.P.
WINNERS
(*Suby of* The TJX Companies Inc)
5498 Signal Hill Ctr Sw, Calgary, AB, T3H 3P8
(403) 246-4999
Emp Here 100
SIC 5651 Family clothing stores

D-U-N-S 20-806-2765   (BR)
YM INC. (SALES)
STITCHES

5975 Signal Hill Ctr Sw Unit H4, Calgary, AB,
T3H 3P8
(403) 390-7985
Emp Here 25
SIC 5621 Women's clothing stores

Calgary, AB T3J

D-U-N-S 20-350-8288   (BR)
ATB SECURITES INC
3699 63 Ave Ne, Calgary, AB, T3J 0G7
(780) 619-7304
Emp Here 20
SIC 8742 Management consulting services

D-U-N-S 24-324-3628   (BR)
ADLER INSULATION 2005 LTD
(*Suby of* Adler Insulation 2005 Ltd)
3851 54 Ave Ne Suite 105, Calgary, AB, T3J
3W5
(403) 590-0758
Emp Here 50
SIC 1742 Plastering, drywall, and insulation

D-U-N-S 24-370-4991   (BR)
BANK OF NOVA SCOTIA, THE
SCOTIABANK
850 Saddletowne Cir Ne Suite 32, Calgary,
AB, T3J 0H5
(403) 299-6018
Emp Here 20
SIC 6021 National commercial banks

D-U-N-S 20-292-8073   (SL)
**CMP AUTOMOTIVE LIMITED PARTNER-
SHIP**
2307 Country Hills Blvd Ne, Calgary, AB, T3J
0R4
(403) 207-1006
Emp Here 190   *Sales* 19,275,500
SIC 7538 General automotive repair shops
Dir Richard Romeril

D-U-N-S 20-591-1212   (BR)
CALGARY BOARD OF EDUCATION
FALCONRIDGE ELEMENTARY SCHOOL
1331 Falconridge Dr Ne, Calgary, AB, T3J 1T4
(403) 777-6730
Emp Here 45
SIC 8211 Elementary and secondary schools

D-U-N-S 20-028-9051   (BR)
CALGARY BOARD OF EDUCATION
GEIGER, O. S. ELEMENTARY SCHOOL
100 Castlebrook Dr Ne, Calgary, AB, T3J 2J4
(403) 777-6950
Emp Here 35
SIC 8211 Elementary and secondary schools

D-U-N-S 20-043-9854   (BR)
CALGARY BOARD OF EDUCATION
TERRY FOX JUNIOR HIGH SCHOOL
139 Falshire Dr Ne, Calgary, AB, T3J 1P7
(403) 777-8800
Emp Here 45
SIC 8211 Elementary and secondary schools

D-U-N-S 20-591-1378   (BR)
CALGARY BOARD OF EDUCATION
CROSSING PARK SCHOOL
500 Martindale Blvd Ne, Calgary, AB, T3J
4W8
(403) 777-7195
Emp Here 70
SIC 8211 Elementary and secondary schools

D-U-N-S 20-713-1702   (BR)
CALGARY BOARD OF EDUCATION
GRANT MACEWAN ELEMENTARY SCHOOL
180 Falshire Dr Ne, Calgary, AB, T3J 3A5
(403) 777-6930
Emp Here 50
SIC 8211 Elementary and secondary schools

D-U-N-S 20-038-3128   (BR)

**CALGARY ROMAN CATHOLIC SEPARATE
SCHOOL DISTRICT #1**
*ST JOHN XXIII ELEMENTARY AND JUNIOR
HIGH SCHOOL*
1420 Falconridge Dr Ne, Calgary, AB, T3J 2C3
(403) 500-2080
Emp Here 55
SIC 8211 Elementary and secondary schools

D-U-N-S 20-574-7202   (BR)
**CALGARY ROMAN CATHOLIC SEPARATE
SCHOOL DISTRICT #1**
ST. JOHN PAUL 2ND SCHOOL
119 Castleridge Dr Ne, Calgary, AB, T3J 1P6
(403) 500-2085
Emp Here 25
SIC 8211 Elementary and secondary schools

D-U-N-S 20-037-4259   (BR)
**CALGARY ROMAN CATHOLIC SEPARATE
SCHOOL DISTRICT #1**
*MSGR. A.J. HETHERINGTON ELEMENTARY
SCHOOL*
4 Coral Springs Blvd Ne, Calgary, AB, T3J 3J3
(403) 500-2036
Emp Here 45
SIC 8211 Elementary and secondary schools

D-U-N-S 20-159-8200   (SL)
CAN WEST PROJECTS INC
85 Freeport Blvd Ne Suite 202, Calgary, AB,
T3J 4X8
(403) 261-8890
Emp Here 105   *Sales* 18,386,096
SIC 1623 Water, sewer, and utility lines
Pr Gord Brons
VP Wes Andrews

D-U-N-S 25-303-6578   (BR)
**CANADIAN IMPERIAL BANK OF COM-
MERCE**
CIBC
5242 Falsbridge Dr Ne, Calgary, AB, T3J 3G1
(403) 974-2787
Emp Here 30
SIC 6021 National commercial banks

D-U-N-S 25-449-0253   (SL)
**CEREBRAL PALSY ASSOCIATION IN AL-
BERTA**
3688 48 Ave Ne, Calgary, AB, T3J 5C8
(403) 543-1161
Emp Here 40   *Sales* 12,478,350
SIC 8322 Individual and family services
Ex Dir Janice Bushfield
Ch Bd Roland Offke

D-U-N-S 20-307-1444   (BR)
CITY OF CALGARY, THE
CALGARY TRANSIT
3910 54 Ave Ne, Calgary, AB, T3J 0C7
(403) 537-1613
Emp Here 85
SIC 4111 Local and suburban transit

D-U-N-S 20-831-5986   (SL)
CLASSIC MOVING & STORAGE LTD
PREMIERE VAN LINES
3950 52 Ave Ne, Calgary, AB, T3J 3X4
(403) 291-0250
Emp Here 50   *Sales* 2,845,467
SIC 4214 Local trucking with storage

D-U-N-S 24-394-1940   (BR)
**DATA COMMUNICATIONS MANAGEMENT
CORP**
DATA GROUP OF COMPANIES
5410 44 St Ne, Calgary, AB, T3J 3Z3
(403) 259-0054
Emp Here 70
SIC 2761 Manifold business forms

D-U-N-S 24-906-8677   (BR)
GAS DRIVE GLOBAL LP
10121 Barlow Trail Ne, Calgary, AB, T3J 3C6
(403) 291-3438
Emp Here 150

SIC 7699 Repair services, nec

D-U-N-S 24-358-5937   (BR)
GRAYBAR CANADA LIMITED
GRAYBAR WEST
(*Suby of* Graybar Electric Company, Inc.)
2765 48 Ave Ne Suite 105, Calgary, AB, T3J
5M9
(403) 250-5554
Emp Here 20
SIC 5112 Stationery and office supplies

D-U-N-S 20-177-4390   (BR)
LOBLAWS INC
55 Freeport Blvd Ne, Calgary, AB, T3J 4X9
(403) 567-4343
Emp Here 485
SIC 5141 Groceries, general line

D-U-N-S 25-363-1295   (BR)
LOBLAWS INC
REAL CANADIAN SUPERSTORE
3633 Westwinds Dr Ne Unit 100, Calgary, AB,
T3J 5K3
(403) 590-3347
Emp Here 100
SIC 5411 Grocery stores

D-U-N-S 20-798-7095   (BR)
**MOXIE'S RESTAURANTS, LIMITED PART-
NERSHIP**
SHARK CLUB BAR AND GRILL
31 Hopewell Way Ne, Calgary, AB, T3J 4V7
(403) 543-2600
Emp Here 30
SIC 5812 Eating places

D-U-N-S 20-798-5255   (BR)
**MOXIE'S RESTAURANTS, LIMITED PART-
NERSHIP**
MOXIE'S CLASSIC GRILL
25 Hopewell Way Ne, Calgary, AB, T3J 4V7
(403) 291-4636
Emp Here 120
SIC 5812 Eating places

D-U-N-S 25-316-4099   (BR)
PASLEY, MAX ENTERPRISES LIMITED
MCDONALD'S
(*Suby of* Pasley, Max Enterprises Limited)
5219 Falsbridge Dr Ne, Calgary, AB, T3J 3C1
(403) 293-4052
Emp Here 90
SIC 5812 Eating places

D-U-N-S 25-620-9776   (BR)
PRAIRIE VIEW HOLDINGS LTD
PARK & JET
(*Suby of* SM2 Holdings Ltd)
9707 Barlow Trail Ne, Calgary, AB, T3J 3C6
(403) 226-0010
Emp Here 25
SIC 7521 Automobile parking

D-U-N-S 25-976-0858   (BR)
**RENFREW EDUCATIONAL SERVICES SO-
CIETY**
265 Falshire Dr Ne, Calgary, AB, T3J 1T9
(403) 590-1948
Emp Here 24
SIC 8211 Elementary and secondary schools

D-U-N-S 20-070-4588   (BR)
ROYAL BANK OF CANADA
RBC
(*Suby of* Royal Bank Of Canada)
5445 Falsbridge Dr Ne, Calgary, AB, T3J 3E8
(403) 292-2400
Emp Here 20
SIC 6021 National commercial banks

D-U-N-S 20-058-9658   (BR)
SAPUTO INC
SAPUTO FOOD
5434 44 St Ne, Calgary, AB, T3J 3Z3
(403) 568-3800
Emp Here 175
SIC 4222 Refrigerated warehousing and stor-

age

D-U-N-S 25-359-9161   (BR)
SHAW COMMUNICATIONS INC
SHAW CABLE
4950 47 St Ne Suite 2, Calgary, AB, T3J 4T6
(403) 781-5116
Emp Here 65
SIC 4841 Cable and other pay television ser-
vices

D-U-N-S 24-363-3851   (BR)
SOBEYS WEST INC
SADDLERIDGE SAFEWAY
850 Saddletowne Cir Ne, Calgary, AB, T3J
0H5
(403) 293-1670
Emp Here 100
SIC 5411 Grocery stores

D-U-N-S 25-271-1015   (BR)
SOBEYS WEST INC
CASTLERIDGE SAFEWAY
55 Castleridge Blvd Ne, Calgary, AB, T3J 3J8
(403) 293-0321
Emp Here 150
SIC 5411 Grocery stores

D-U-N-S 24-439-2064   (BR)
SPICERS CANADA ULC
SPICERS
(*Suby of* CNG Canada Holding Inc.)
1845 104 Ave Ne Suite 181, Calgary, AB, T3J
0R2
(403) 351-5440
Emp Here 35
SIC 5111 Printing and writing paper

D-U-N-S 20-292-8057   (SL)
**SUNRIDGE NISSAN LIMITED PARTNER-
SHIP**
2307 Country Hills Blvd Ne, Calgary, AB, T3J
0R4
(403) 207-1006
Emp Here 65   *Sales* 6,594,250
SIC 7538 General automotive repair shops
Dir Richard Romeril

D-U-N-S 24-309-0516   (BR)
SYMCOR INC
3663 63 Ave Ne, Calgary, AB, T3J 0G6
(403) 806-5000
Emp Here 270
SIC 7389 Business services, nec

D-U-N-S 24-378-4126   (BR)
TOROMONT INDUSTRIES LTD
TOROMONT ENERGY
85 Freeport Blvd Ne Suite 102, Calgary, AB,
T3J 4X8
(403) 517-1300
Emp Here 48
SIC 5082 Construction and mining machinery

D-U-N-S 25-090-0347   (BR)
TRAFFIC TECH INC
(*Suby of* 2809664 Canada Inc)
1845 104 Ave Ne Suite 131, Calgary, AB, T3J
0R2
(403) 517-1119
Emp Here 30
SIC 4213 Trucking, except local

D-U-N-S 25-328-9938   (SL)
WASCANA BUILDING SERVICES LIMITED
113 Coral Shores Bay Ne, Calgary, AB, T3J
3J6
(403) 285-4842
Emp Here 89   *Sales* 3,118,504
SIC 7349 Building maintenance services, nec

D-U-N-S 25-676-6064   (HQ)
IMARKETING SOLUTIONS GROUP INC
(*Suby of* iMarketing Solutions Group Inc)
3710 Westwinds Dr Ne Unit 24, Calgary, AB,
T3J 5H3

Emp Here 500   *Emp Total* 2,000
Sales 72,942,550

SIC 8399 Social services, nec
Dir Andrew Langhorne
Pr Pr David Winograd
 Michael Davis
 Upkar Arora
Dir Jim Ambrose
Dir Michael Neuman
Dir Michael Platz
Dir Richard Reid

Calgary, AB T3K

D-U-N-S 25-530-0741   (SL)
725850 ALBERTA LTD
AMJ CAMPBELL COMMERCIAL
1881 120 Ave Ne, Calgary, AB, T3K 0S5
(403) 273-1220
Emp Here 35   Sales 3,580,850
SIC 4212 Local trucking, without storage

D-U-N-S 24-158-3236   (BR)
AMJ CAMPBELL INC
A M J CAMPBELL
1881 120 Ave Ne, Calgary, AB, T3K 0S5
(403) 273-1220
Emp Here 60
SIC 4213 Trucking, except local

D-U-N-S 20-198-8867   (SL)
ALAN ARSENAULT HOLDINGS LTD
TIM HORTONS
500 Country Hills Blvd Ne Unit 900, Calgary,
AB, T3K 5H2
(403) 226-9331
Emp Here 54   Sales 1,605,135
SIC 5812 Eating places

D-U-N-S 25-186-6166   (SL)
B.B. INVESTMENTS INC
BOSTON PIZZA 111
388 Country Hills Blvd Ne Suite 600, Calgary,
AB, T3K 5J6
(403) 226-7171
Emp Here 75   Sales 2,261,782
SIC 5812 Eating places

D-U-N-S 20-569-2267   (BR)
BANQUE TORONTO-DOMINION, LA
TORONTO-DOMINION BANK, THE
(Suby of Toronto-Dominion Bank, The)
8118 Beddington Blvd Nw, Calgary, AB, T3K
2R6
(403) 275-4033
Emp Here 23
SIC 6021 National commercial banks

D-U-N-S 20-650-3091   (BR)
BETHANY CARE SOCIETY
BETHANY HARVEST HILLS
19 Harvest Gold Manor Ne, Calgary, AB, T3K
4Y1
(403) 226-8200
Emp Here 100
SIC 8051 Skilled nursing care facilities

D-U-N-S 20-649-4812   (BR)
CALGARY BOARD OF EDUCATION
*BEDDINGTON HEIGHTS ELEMENTARY
SCHOOL*
95 Bermuda Rd Nw, Calgary, AB, T3K 2J6
(403) 777-6610
Emp Here 40
SIC 8211 Elementary and secondary schools

D-U-N-S 20-591-1360   (BR)
CALGARY BOARD OF EDUCATION
SIMONS VALLEY ELEMENTARY SCHOOL
375 Sandarac Dr Nw, Calgary, AB, T3K 4B2
(403) 777-6560
Emp Here 35
SIC 8211 Elementary and secondary schools

D-U-N-S 20-035-2347   (BR)
**CALGARY ROMAN CATHOLIC SEPARATE
SCHOOL DISTRICT #1**

MSGR. NEVILLE ANDERSON SCHOOL
327 Sandarac Dr Nw, Calgary, AB, T3K 4B2
(403) 500-2094
Emp Here 50
SIC 8211 Elementary and secondary schools

D-U-N-S 24-079-3179   (BR)
**CALGARY ROMAN CATHOLIC SEPARATE
SCHOOL DISTRICT #1**
ST. CLARE ELEMENTARY SCHOOL
12455 Coventry Hills Way Ne, Calgary, AB,
T3K 5Z4
(403) 500-2102
Emp Here 45
SIC 8211 Elementary and secondary schools

D-U-N-S 20-713-0829   (BR)
**CALGARY ROMAN CATHOLIC SEPARATE
SCHOOL DISTRICT #1**
ASCENSION OF OUR LORD SCHOOL
509 Harvest Hills Dr Ne, Calgary, AB, T3K
4G9
(403) 500-2075
Emp Here 50
SIC 8211 Elementary and secondary schools

D-U-N-S 24-810-1669   (SL)
COUNTRY HILLS GOLF CLUB
1334 Country Hills Blvd Nw, Calgary, AB, T3K
5A9
(403) 226-7777
Emp Here 65   Sales 2,626,585
SIC 7997 Membership sports and recreation
clubs

D-U-N-S 20-916-8199   (BR)
EMPIRE THEATRES LIMITED
MARIPLEX COMFECTIONS
388 Country Hills Blvd Ne Unit 300, Calgary,
AB, T3K 5J6
(403) 226-8685
Emp Here 75
SIC 7832 Motion picture theaters, except
drive-in

D-U-N-S 20-911-0068   (SL)
FRIENDLY TELECOM INC
CALGARY TELECOM
44 Berkshire Crt Nw, Calgary, AB, T3K 1Z5
(403) 243-6688
Emp Here 111   Sales 16,780,961
SIC 4899 Communication services, nec
Owner Brian Jerome

D-U-N-S 24-369-9910   (HQ)
HARMONY LOGISTICS CANADA INC
1724 115 Ave Ne, Calgary, AB, T3K 0P9
(403) 537-8996
Emp Here 148   Emp Total 498,459
Sales 31,883,826
SIC 4731 Freight transportation arrangement
Pr Pr Jim Gehr

D-U-N-S 25-169-9781   (BR)
HOME DEPOT OF CANADA INC
HOME DEPOT
(Suby of The Home Depot Inc)
388 Country Hills Blvd Ne Unit 100, Calgary,
AB, T3K 5J6
(403) 226-7500
Emp Here 200
SIC 5251 Hardware stores

D-U-N-S 20-515-9077   (BR)
LOBLAWS INC
REAL CANADIAN SUPERSTORE
100 Country Village Rd Ne Suite 1543, Cal-
gary, AB, T3K 5Z2
(403) 567-4219
Emp Here 350
SIC 5411 Grocery stores

D-U-N-S 25-273-1773   (BR)
LONDON DRUGS LIMITED
8120 Beddington Blvd Nw Unit 400, Calgary,
AB, T3K 2A8
(403) 571-4940
Emp Here 50

SIC 5912 Drug stores and proprietary stores

D-U-N-S 25-535-1017   (SL)
MICROHARD SYSTEMS INC
150 Country Hills Landng Nw Suite 101, Cal-
gary, AB, T3K 5P3
(403) 248-0028
Emp Here 50   Sales 9,234,824
SIC 3669 Communications equipment, nec
Pr Pr Hany Shenouda

D-U-N-S 24-375-6207   (SL)
**PUBLIC STORAGE CANADIAN PROPER-
TIES**
90 Country Hills Landng Nw, Calgary, AB, T3K
5P3
(403) 567-1193
Emp Here 50   Sales 6,531,200
SIC 4225 General warehousing and storage
Pr Pr David P. Singelyn
CFO Vincent R. Chan
Dir William E. Ardell
Dir Robert Bellany
Dir Roland A. Cardy

D-U-N-S 20-070-4604   (BR)
ROYAL BANK OF CANADA
RBC
(Suby of Royal Bank Of Canada)
8220 Centre St Ne Suite 111, Calgary, AB,
T3K 1J7
(403) 292-8292
Emp Here 44
SIC 6021 National commercial banks

D-U-N-S 25-271-0850   (BR)
SOBEYS WEST INC
BENNINGTON SAFEWAY
8120 Beddington Blvd Nw, Calgary, AB, T3K
2A8
(403) 295-6895
Emp Here 125
SIC 5411 Grocery stores

D-U-N-S 20-796-7204   (BR)
STAPLES CANADA INC
STAPLES THE BUSINESS DEPOT
(Suby of Staples, Inc.)
130 Country Village Rd Ne Unit 307, Calgary,
AB, T3K 6B8
(403) 509-3265
Emp Here 40
SIC 5943 Stationery stores

Calgary, AB T3L

D-U-N-S 20-653-3346   (SL)
BEARSPAW SCHOOL
253210 Bearspaw Rd, Calgary, AB, T3L 2S5
(403) 239-9607
Emp Here 50   Sales 3,356,192
SIC 8211 Elementary and secondary schools

D-U-N-S 20-653-4328   (BR)
CALGARY BOARD OF EDUCATION
SCENIC ACRES SCHOOL
50 Scurfield Way Nw, Calgary, AB, T3L 1T2
(403) 777-6193
Emp Here 20
SIC 8211 Elementary and secondary schools

D-U-N-S 20-013-0797   (BR)
**CALGARY ROMAN CATHOLIC SEPARATE
SCHOOL DISTRICT #1**
ST. BASIL SCHOOL
919 Tuscany Dr Nw, Calgary, AB, T3L 2T5
(403) 500-2108
Emp Here 57
SIC 8211 Elementary and secondary schools

D-U-N-S 24-361-7193   (BR)
HOME DEPOT OF CANADA INC
HOME DEPOT
(Suby of The Home Depot Inc)
5019 Nose Hill Dr Nw, Calgary, AB, T3L 0A2

(403) 241-4066
Emp Here 100
SIC 5251 Hardware stores

D-U-N-S 20-112-2277   (SL)
MGC GOLF INC
LYNX RIDGE GOLF CLUB
8 Lynx Ridge Blvd Nw, Calgary, AB, T3L 2M3
(403) 547-5969
Emp Here 60   Sales 2,553,625
SIC 7992 Public golf courses

D-U-N-S 20-647-3907   (BR)
REVERA INC
SCENIC ACRES RETIREMENT RESIDENCE
150 Scotia Landng Nw, Calgary, AB, T3L 2K1
(403) 208-0338
Emp Here 100
SIC 8322 Individual and family services

D-U-N-S 24-388-2664   (SL)
ROCKY MOUNTAIN ANALYTICAL INC
253147 Bearspaw Rd Unit A, Calgary, AB, T3L
2P5
(403) 241-4513
Emp Here 23   Sales 1,896,978
SIC 8071 Medical laboratories

D-U-N-S 20-806-2310   (BR)
SOBEYS CAPITAL INCORPORATED
SOBEYS
11300 Tuscany Blvd Nw Suite 2020, Calgary,
AB, T3L 2V7
(403) 375-0595
Emp Here 100
SIC 5411 Grocery stores

D-U-N-S 20-806-3805   (BR)
STARBUCKS COFFEE CANADA, INC
(Suby of Starbucks Corporation)
11300 Tuscany Blvd Nw, Calgary, AB, T3L
2V7
(403) 208-0203
Emp Here 34
SIC 5812 Eating places

Calgary, AB T3M

D-U-N-S 20-284-8719   (BR)
**ALL SENIORS CARE LIVING CENTRES
LTD**
*AUBURN HEIGHTS RETIREMENT RESI-
DENCE*
(Suby of All Seniors Care Holdings Inc)
21 Auburn Bay St Se Suite 428, Calgary, AB,
T3M 2A9
(403) 234-9695
Emp Here 90
SIC 6513 Apartment building operators

D-U-N-S 24-850-9502   (BR)
BANK OF NOVA SCOTIA, THE
SCOTIABANK
356 Cranston Rd Se Suite 5000, Calgary, AB,
T3M 0S9
(403) 221-6627
Emp Here 20
SIC 6021 National commercial banks

Calgary, AB T3N

D-U-N-S 24-363-9445   (BR)
**AVEDA TRANSPORTATION AND ENERGY
SERVICES INC**
FINNIE HAULING & STORAGE, DIV OF
2505 Country Hills Blvd Ne, Calgary, AB, T3N
1A6
(403) 226-0733
Emp Here 21
SIC 1389 Oil and gas field services, nec

D-U-N-S 24-091-6234   (BR)
DYNAMEX CANADA LIMITED

10725 25 St Ne Suite 116, Calgary, AB, T3N 0A4
(403) 235-8989
Emp Here 20
SIC 7389 Business services, nec

D-U-N-S 25-085-3231 (BR)
MICHENER-ALLEN AUCTIONEERING LTD
13090 Barlow Trail Ne, Calgary, AB, T3N 1A2
(403) 226-0405
Emp Here 27
SIC 7389 Business services, nec

D-U-N-S 25-452-2329 (BR)
POWER BATTERY SALES LTD
EAST PENN POWER BATTERY
10720 25 St Ne Unit 140, Calgary, AB, T3N 0A1
(403) 250-6640
Emp Here 20
SIC 5013 Motor vehicle supplies and new parts

Calgary, AB T3P

D-U-N-S 20-737-4893 (BR)
STARBUCKS COFFEE CANADA, INC
(*Suby of* Starbucks Corporation)
12294 Symons Valley Rd Nw Unit 103, Calgary, AB, T3P 0A3
(403) 516-0297
Emp Here 31
SIC 5812 Eating places

Calgary, AB T3R

D-U-N-S 20-713-1660 (BR)
CALGARY BOARD OF EDUCATION
WEST VIEW SECONDARY SCHOOL
12626 85 St Nw, Calgary, AB, T3R 1J3
(403) 662-3547
Emp Here 30
SIC 8211 Elementary and secondary schools

D-U-N-S 24-308-3586 (BR)
COSTCO WHOLESALE CANADA LTD
(*Suby of* Costco Wholesale Corporation)
11588 Sarcee Trail Nw Suite 543, Calgary, AB, T3R 0A1
(403) 516-3700
Emp Here 280
SIC 5099 Durable goods, nec

D-U-N-S 24-390-5820 (BR)
GOLF TOWN LIMITED
GOLF TOWN
11450 Sarcee Trail Nw, Calgary, AB, T3R 0A1
(403) 275-4100
Emp Here 40
SIC 5941 Sporting goods and bicycle shops

D-U-N-S 24-101-5259 (BR)
HOME DEPOT OF CANADA INC
HOME DEPOT
(*Suby of* The Home Depot Inc)
11320 Sarcee Trail Nw, Calgary, AB, T3R 0A1
(403) 374-3866
Emp Here 100
SIC 5211 Lumber and other building materials

D-U-N-S 20-553-7264 (BR)
MAPLE-REINDERS INC
32 Royal Vista Dr Nw Suite 205, Calgary, AB, T3R 0H9
(403) 216-1455
Emp Here 25
SIC 1541 Industrial buildings and warehouses

D-U-N-S 20-885-1704 (SL)
SOUTHERN ALBERTA FORENSIC PSYCHIATRY CENTRE
11333 85 St Nw, Calgary, AB, T3R 1J3

(403) 944-6800
Emp Here 50 *Sales* 2,991,389
SIC 8011 Offices and clinics of medical doctors

D-U-N-S 24-356-7943 (BR)
WINNERS MERCHANTS INTERNATIONAL L.P.
WINNERS
(*Suby of* The TJX Companies Inc)
11686 Sarcee Trail Nw, Calgary, AB, T3R 0A1
(403) 275-8228
Emp Here 50
SIC 5651 Family clothing stores

Calgary, AB T3S

D-U-N-S 24-578-5170 (BR)
ABB INC
9800 Endeavor Dr Se, Calgary, AB, T3S 0A1
(403) 252-7551
Emp Here 150
SIC 3621 Motors and generators

D-U-N-S 24-049-5130 (BR)
AECON TRANSPORTATION WEST LTD
9700 Endeavor Dr Se, Calgary, AB, T3S 0A1
(403) 293-9300
Emp Here 200
SIC 1611 Highway and street construction

D-U-N-S 20-110-2183 (HQ)
CHAMCO INDUSTRIES INC
(*Suby of* Chamco Industries Ltd)
8900 Venture Ave Se, Calgary, AB, T3S 0A2
(403) 777-1200
Emp Here 60 *Emp Total* 135
Sales 24,660,717
SIC 5084 Industrial machinery and equipment
Pr Pr Malcolm Cox
VP VP Don Carscadden
  Norrey Von Sturmer
  George St Clair
  Brian Blann
VP Grant Burton

D-U-N-S 24-715-6276 (SL)
CHARIOT EXPRESS LTD
9550 Enterprise Way Se, Calgary, AB, T3S 0A1
(403) 252-4047
Emp Here 60 *Sales* 4,742,446
SIC 4212 Local trucking, without storage

D-U-N-S 25-538-6047 (SL)
GATEWAY WEST LOGISTICS INC
9500 Venture Ave Se, Calgary, AB, T3S 0A1
(403) 720-9770
Emp Here 50 *Sales* 3,575,074
SIC 4231 Trucking terminal facilities

D-U-N-S 20-852-6199 (BR)
J. & R. HALL TRANSPORT INC
16 Technology Way Se, Calgary, AB, T3S 0B2
(403) 236-7758
Emp Here 25
SIC 4213 Trucking, except local

D-U-N-S 24-889-2841 (BR)
KNELSEN SAND & GRAVEL LTD
489 Exploration Ave Se, Calgary, AB, T3S 0B4
(403) 338-1911
Emp Here 20
SIC 5032 Brick, stone, and related material

D-U-N-S 20-852-6009 (BR)
LAFARGE CANADA INC
LAFARGE CONCRETE DIVISION
11321 85 St Se, Calgary, AB, T3S 0A3
(403) 239-6130
Emp Here 36
SIC 2891 Adhesives and sealants

D-U-N-S 20-772-6840 (BR)
LEAVITT MACHINERY AND RENTALS INC

55 Technology Way Se Unit 10, Calgary, AB, T3S 0B3
(403) 723-7555
Emp Here 20
SIC 7699 Repair services, nec

D-U-N-S 24-362-0940 (BR)
LOWER MAINLAND STEEL (1998) LTD
387 Exploration Ave Se, Calgary, AB, T3S 0A2
(403) 723-9930
Emp Here 20
SIC 1791 Structural steel erection

D-U-N-S 25-850-2819 (BR)
PETER KIEWIT INFRASTRUCTURE CO.
(*Suby of* Peter Kiewit Sons', Inc.)
9500 100 St Se, Calgary, AB, T3S 0A2

Emp Here 900
SIC 1611 Highway and street construction

D-U-N-S 20-566-6345 (SL)
RB2 ENERGY SERVICES INC
9550 114 Ave Se Suite 20, Calgary, AB, T3S 0A5
(403) 203-2344
Emp Here 34 *Sales* 3,724,879
SIC 8748 Business consulting, nec

D-U-N-S 20-078-0278 (BR)
SIMSON MAXWELL
467 Exploration Ave Se, Calgary, AB, T3S 0B4
(403) 252-8131
Emp Here 23
SIC 5084 Industrial machinery and equipment

D-U-N-S 25-361-4309 (BR)
STANDARD GENERAL INC
9660 Enterprise Way Se, Calgary, AB, T3S 0A1
(403) 255-1131
Emp Here 40
SIC 1611 Highway and street construction

Calgary, AB T3Z

D-U-N-S 20-233-5456 (SL)
EDGE SCHOOL FOR ATHLETES SOCIETY, THE
33055 Township Road 250, Calgary, AB, T3Z 1L4
(403) 247-9707
Emp Here 60 *Sales* 3,283,232
SIC 8299 Schools and educational services, nec

D-U-N-S 20-271-6960 (BR)
MEMORIAL GARDENS CANADA LIMITED
EDEN BROOK MEMORIAL GARDENS
17 Ave Sw, Calgary, AB, T3Z 3K2
(403) 217-3700
Emp Here 20
SIC 6531 Real estate agents and managers

D-U-N-S 20-588-5051 (BR)
ROCKY VIEW SCHOOL DIVISION NO. 41, THE
SPRINGBANK MIDDLE SCHOOL
244235 Range Road 33, Calgary, AB, T3Z 2E8
(403) 242-4456
Emp Here 43
SIC 8211 Elementary and secondary schools

D-U-N-S 20-653-6992 (BR)
ROCKY VIEW SCHOOL DIVISION NO. 41, THE
ELBOW VALLEY ELEMENTARY SCHOOL
244209 Range Road 33, Calgary, AB, T3Z 2E8
(403) 242-1117
Emp Here 50
SIC 8211 Elementary and secondary schools

D-U-N-S 20-030-7010 (BR)
ROCKY VIEW SCHOOL DIVISION NO. 41,

THE
SPRINGBANK COMMUNITY HIGH SCHOOL
32226 Springbank Rd, Calgary, AB, T3Z 2L9
(403) 246-4771
Emp Here 40
SIC 8211 Elementary and secondary schools

D-U-N-S 24-438-7221 (SL)
WILLCO TRANSPORTATION LTD
32023 Springbank Rd, Calgary, AB, T3Z 2E3
(403) 242-1176
Emp Here 60 *Sales* 1,678,096
SIC 4151 School buses

Calgary, AB T4C

D-U-N-S 24-855-2390 (HQ)
WESTFREIGHT SYSTEMS INC
6703 84 St Se, Calgary, AB, T4C 4T6
(403) 279-8388
Emp Here 26 *Emp Total* 25,438
Sales 4,012,839
SIC 4213 Trucking, except local

Calling Lake, AB T0G

D-U-N-S 20-134-6561 (BR)
MUNICIPAL DISTRICT OF OPPORTUNITY #17
MUNICIPAL DISTRICT OF OPPORTUNITY
Gd, Calling Lake, AB, T0G 0K0
(780) 331-2619
Emp Here 30
SIC 8399 Social services, nec

D-U-N-S 20-028-9085 (BR)
NORTHLAND SCHOOL DIVISION 61
CALLING LAKE SCHOOL
Gd, Calling Lake, AB, T0G 0K0
(780) 331-3774
Emp Here 25
SIC 8211 Elementary and secondary schools

Calmar, AB T0C

D-U-N-S 20-328-7180 (BR)
ACCEDE ENERGY SERVICES LTD
LATMANN EQUIPMENT
5022 42 Ave, Calmar, AB, T0C 0V0
(780) 985-4202
Emp Here 25
SIC 7353 Heavy construction equipment rental

D-U-N-S 25-267-1763 (BR)
BLACK GOLD REGIONAL DIVISION #18
CALMAR SECONDARY SCHOOL
5100 49th St, Calmar, AB, T0C 0V0
(780) 985-3515
Emp Here 45
SIC 8211 Elementary and secondary schools

Camrose, AB T4V

D-U-N-S 25-271-3359 (BR)
7-ELEVEN CANADA, INC
7-ELEVEN STORE #26140
5010 48 Ave, Camrose, AB, T4V 0J5
(780) 672-1126
Emp Here 20
SIC 5411 Grocery stores

D-U-N-S 24-509-7923 (BR)
ATCO GAS AND PIPELINES LTD
ATCO GAS AND PIPELINES LTD

4331 38 St, Camrose, AB, T4V 3P9
(780) 672-8804
Emp Here 20
SIC 4924 Natural gas distribution

D-U-N-S 24-101-0219   (BR)
ALBERTA HEALTH SERVICES
5015 50 Ave Suite 103, Camrose, AB, T4V
3P7
(780) 608-8611
Emp Here 30
SIC 8011 Offices and clinics of medical doctors

D-U-N-S 20-271-8461   (BR)
ALBERTA HEALTH SERVICES
CAMROSE HOME CARE
4615 56 St, Camrose, AB, T4V 4M5
(780) 679-2900
Emp Here 110
SIC 8059 Nursing and personal care, nec

D-U-N-S 25-231-7854   (BR)
ALBERTA TREASURY BRANCHES
ATB FINANCIAL
4887 50 St, Camrose, AB, T4V 1P6
(780) 672-3331
Emp Here 22
SIC 6036 Savings institutions, except federal

D-U-N-S 20-025-4774   (BR)
BATTLE RIVER REGIONAL DIVISION 31
CHESTER RONNING SCHOOL
6206 43 Ave, Camrose, AB, T4V 0A7
(780) 672-5588
Emp Here 36
SIC 8211 Elementary and secondary schools

D-U-N-S 20-028-4326   (BR)
BATTLE RIVER REGIONAL DIVISION 31
JACK STUART SCHOOL
200 Mount Pleasant Dr, Camrose, AB, T4V
4B5
(780) 672-0880
Emp Here 30
SIC 8211 Elementary and secondary schools

D-U-N-S 20-025-4782   (BR)
BATTLE RIVER REGIONAL DIVISION 31
SPARLING SCHOOL
5216 52 Ave, Camrose, AB, T4V 0X4
(780) 672-0106
Emp Here 25
SIC 8211 Elementary and secondary schools

D-U-N-S 20-710-5359   (BR)
BATTLE RIVER REGIONAL DIVISION 31
CAMROSE COMPOSITE HIGH SCHOOL
6205 48 Ave Suite 228, Camrose, AB, T4V
0K4
(780) 672-4416
Emp Here 50
SIC 8211 Elementary and secondary schools

D-U-N-S 20-025-4766   (BR)
BATTLE RIVER REGIONAL DIVISION 31
ECOLE SIFTON SCHOOL
4807 43 St, Camrose, AB, T4V 1A9
(780) 672-2980
Emp Here 30
SIC 8211 Elementary and secondary schools

D-U-N-S 20-020-2609   (BR)
BATTLE RIVER REGIONAL DIVISION 31
CHARLIE KILLAM SCHOOL
4809 46 St, Camrose, AB, T4V 1G8
(780) 672-7785
Emp Here 40
SIC 8211 Elementary and secondary schools

D-U-N-S 20-899-8757   (BR)
BORDER PAVING LTD
4217 41 St, Camrose, AB, T4V 3V8
(780) 672-3389
Emp Here 60
SIC 1611 Highway and street construction

D-U-N-S 25-969-9809   (SL)
CAMROSE ASSOCIATION FOR COMMU-

NITY LIVING
4604 57 St, Camrose, AB, T4V 2E7
(780) 672-0257
Emp Here 125   *Sales* 4,596,524
SIC 8361 Residential care

D-U-N-S 24-344-7161   (SL)
CAMROSE RESORT CASINO
3201 48 Ave, Camrose, AB, T4V 0K9
(780) 679-0904
Emp Here 50   *Sales* 2,188,821
SIC 7011 Hotels and motels

D-U-N-S 25-288-8706   (BR)
CANADA POST CORPORATION
4901 50 Ave, Camrose, AB, T4V 0S2
(780) 672-7332
Emp Here 26
SIC 4311 U.s. postal service

D-U-N-S 20-270-4219   (BR)
CARGILL LIMITED
GRAIN & OIL FEEDS SUPPLY CHAIN-
NORTH AMERICA
46450 Range Rd 200 Rr 1 Lcd Main, Camrose, AB, T4V 2M9
(780) 672-3815
Emp Here 50
SIC 5149 Groceries and related products, nec

D-U-N-S 24-396-9649   (BR)
CARGILL LIMITED
CARGILLL ANIMAL NUTRITION
46450 Range Rd 200, Camrose, AB, T4V 2M9

Emp Here 30
SIC 2048 Prepared feeds, nec

D-U-N-S 20-050-4426   (BR)
CITY OF CAMROSE, THE
CAMROSE GOLF COURSE
5105 66 St, Camrose, AB, T4V 1X3
(780) 672-2691
Emp Here 30
SIC 7992 Public golf courses

D-U-N-S 25-994-2399   (BR)
CITY OF CAMROSE, THE
CAMROSE EMERGENCY MEDICAL SER-
VICE
4907 49 St, Camrose, AB, T4V 1N3

Emp Here 24
SIC 4119 Local passenger transportation, nec

D-U-N-S 20-713-1884   (BR)
ELK ISLAND CATHOLIC SEPARATE RE-
GIONAL DIVISION NO. 41
ST PATRICK SCHOOL
4816 53 Ave, Camrose, AB, T4V 0Y2
(780) 672-2177
Emp Here 50
SIC 8211 Elementary and secondary schools

D-U-N-S 25-994-2506   (BR)
GLOVER INTERNATIONAL TRUCKS LTD
CAMROSE INTERNATIONAL
(*Suby of* Glover International Trucks Ltd)
3836 42 Ave, Camrose, AB, T4V 4B9
(780) 672-7396
Emp Here 20
SIC 7538 General automotive repair shops

D-U-N-S 24-375-3188   (BR)
GOVERNORS OF THE UNIVERSITY OF AL-
BERTA, THE
THE GOVERNORS OF THE UNIVERSITY
OF ALBERTA
4901 46 Ave, Camrose, AB, T4V 2R3
(780) 679-1100
Emp Here 20
SIC 8221 Colleges and universities

D-U-N-S 25-156-5073   (BR)
LOBLAWS INC
EXTRA FOODS
4920 48 St, Camrose, AB, T4V 4L5

Emp Here 45

SIC 5411 Grocery stores

D-U-N-S 24-686-0154   (BR)
MERIDIAN MANUFACTURING INC
4232 38 St, Camrose, AB, T4V 4B2
(780) 672-4516
Emp Here 170
SIC 3545 Machine tool accessories

D-U-N-S 24-004-3893   (SL)
NORSEMEN INN CAMROSE CORPORA-
TION
6505 48 Ave, Camrose, AB, T4V 3K3
(780) 672-9171
Emp Here 85   *Sales* 3,720,996
SIC 7011 Hotels and motels

D-U-N-S 25-174-5436   (BR)
RBC DOMINION SECURITIES INC
RBC INVESTMENTS
(*Suby of* Royal Bank Of Canada)
5102 50 Ave, Camrose, AB, T4V 0S7
(780) 672-8776
Emp Here 50
SIC 6282 Investment advice

D-U-N-S 24-342-1620   (BR)
RICHARDSON PIONEER LIMITED
PIONEER GRAIN
Gd Lcd Main, Camrose, AB, T4V 1X1
(780) 679-5230
Emp Here 20
SIC 5153 Grain and field beans

D-U-N-S 25-994-2530   (BR)
ROYAL BANK OF CANADA
RBC
(*Suby of* Royal Bank Of Canada)
5102 50 Ave, Camrose, AB, T4V 0S7
(780) 672-7751
Emp Here 25
SIC 6021 National commercial banks

D-U-N-S 24-206-5964   (BR)
SOBEYS WEST INC
6800 48 Ave Suite 200, Camrose, AB, T4V
4T1
(780) 672-1211
Emp Here 75
SIC 5411 Grocery stores

D-U-N-S 20-525-9141   (BR)
STAPLES CANADA INC
STAPLES THE BUSINESS DEPOT
(*Suby of* Staples, Inc.)
6800 48 Ave Suite 360, Camrose, AB, T4V
4T1
(780) 608-4100
Emp Here 20
SIC 5943 Stationery stores

D-U-N-S 25-315-4579   (BR)
TORONTO-DOMINION BANK, THE
TD BANK
(*Suby of* Toronto-Dominion Bank, The)
4888 50 St, Camrose, AB, T4V 1P7
(780) 672-7795
Emp Here 28
SIC 6021 National commercial banks

D-U-N-S 24-766-4956   (BR)
UNITED FARMERS OF ALBERTA CO-
OPERATIVE LIMITED
UFA
4904 39 St, Camrose, AB, T4V 2N7
(780) 672-1115
Emp Here 28
SIC 5191 Farm supplies

D-U-N-S 25-269-8170   (HQ)
VISION CREDIT UNION LTD.
(*Suby of* Vision Credit Union Ltd.)
5007 51 St, Camrose, AB, T4V 1S6
(780) 672-6341
Emp Here 22   *Emp Total* 95
Sales 18,666,800
SIC 6062 State credit unions
CEO Steve Friend

D-U-N-S 20-736-1739   (BR)
WAL-MART CANADA CORP
6800 48 Ave Unit 400, Camrose, AB, T4V 4T1
(780) 608-1211
Emp Here 200
SIC 5311 Department stores

Canmore, AB T1W

D-U-N-S 20-547-2132   (BR)
ALBERTA HEALTH SERVICES
CANMORE GENERAL HOSPITAL
1100 Hospital Pl, Canmore, AB, T1W 1N2
(403) 678-3769
Emp Here 250
SIC 6324 Hospital and medical service plans

D-U-N-S 25-952-6531   (BR)
ALPINE HELICOPTERS INC
CANMORE TOURISM OPERATIONS
(*Suby of* Intrawest Resorts Holdings, Inc.)
91 Bow Valley Trail, Canmore, AB, T1W 1N8
(403) 678-4802
Emp Here 25
SIC 4522 Air transportation, nonscheduled

D-U-N-S 24-160-2239   (BR)
BELLSTAR HOTELS & RESORTS LTD
ALCORNS
(*Suby of* Bellstar Hotels & Resorts Ltd)
107 Montane Rd Unit 100, Canmore, AB, T1W
3J2
(403) 678-9350
Emp Here 20
SIC 7011 Hotels and motels

D-U-N-S 25-538-5726   (SL)
CHIP REIT NO 29 OPERATIONS LIMITED
PARTNERSHIP
RADISSON HOTEL & CONFERENCE CEN-
TRE CANMORE
511 Bow Valley Trail, Canmore, AB, T1W 1N7
(403) 678-3625
Emp Here 50   *Sales* 2,188,821
SIC 7011 Hotels and motels

D-U-N-S 20-580-7444   (BR)
CANADIAN ROCKIES REGIONAL DIVISION
NO 12
CANMORE COLLEGIATE HIGH SCHOOL
1800 8 Ave Suite Unit, Canmore, AB, T1W
1Y2
(403) 678-6192
Emp Here 40
SIC 8211 Elementary and secondary schools

D-U-N-S 20-029-2998   (BR)
CANADIAN ROCKIES REGIONAL DIVISION
NO 12
LAWRENCE GRASSI MIDDLE SCHOOL
618 7 Ave Suite 12, Canmore, AB, T1W 2H5
(403) 678-6006
Emp Here 55
SIC 8211 Elementary and secondary schools

D-U-N-S 20-068-8062   (BR)
CANADIAN ROCKIES REGIONAL DIVISION
NO 12
CRPS TRANSPORTATION
618 7 Ave Suite 12, Canmore, AB, T1W 2H5
(403) 678-5545
Emp Here 30
SIC 4151 School buses

D-U-N-S 20-027-4335   (BR)
CANADIAN ROCKIES REGIONAL DIVISION
NO 12
ELIZABETH RUMMEL SCHOOL
1033 Cougar Creek Dr, Canmore, AB, T1W
1C8
(403) 678-6292
Emp Here 50
SIC 8211 Elementary and secondary schools

D-U-N-S 25-218-4163   (SL)

CHATEAU CANMORE RESORT INC
1720 Bow Valley Trail, Canmore, AB, T1W 2X3

Emp Here 90   Sales 5,425,920
SIC 7011 Hotels and motels
Dir Andre Muran
Dir Karamjeet Shargill

D-U-N-S 20-644-4379   (BR)
CHRIST THE REDEEMER CATHOLIC SEP-ARATE REGIONAL DIVISION NO. 3
OUR LADY OF THE SNOWS CATHOLIC ACADEMY
3100 Stewart Creek Dr Unit A, Canmore, AB, T1W 3M6
(403) 609-3699
Emp Here 35
SIC 8211 Elementary and secondary schools

D-U-N-S 25-146-5936   (BR)
FAIRMONT HOTELS & RESORTS INC
FAIRMONT STORE
102 Boulder Cres Suite 7, Canmore, AB, T1W 1L2
(403) 678-6866
Emp Here 50
SIC 5947 Gift, novelty, and souvenir shop

D-U-N-S 25-292-5003   (BR)
FAIRMONT HOTELS & RESORTS INC
101 Glacier Dr, Canmore, AB, T1W 1K8
(403) 678-5911
Emp Here 43
SIC 7211 Power laundries, family and commercial

D-U-N-S 20-807-5718   (SL)
GRAND CANADIAN RESORTS INC
91 Three Sisters Dr, Canmore, AB, T1W 3A1
(403) 678-0018
Emp Here 80   Sales 3,502,114
SIC 7011 Hotels and motels

D-U-N-S 20-282-4546   (SL)
H2 CANMORE LODGING LP
COAST CANMORE HOTEL & CONFERENCE CENTRE
511 Bow Valley Trail, Canmore, AB, T1W 1N7
(403) 678-3625
Emp Here 65   Sales 5,843,196
SIC 7011 Hotels and motels
Pr Pr Michael Hannan

D-U-N-S 25-092-8178   (BR)
JASPER INN INVESTMENTS LTD
RAMADA INN & SUITES CANMORE
1402 Bow Valley Trail, Canmore, AB, T1W 1N5
(403) 609-4656
Emp Here 50
SIC 7011 Hotels and motels

D-U-N-S 20-744-2187   (SL)
MOUNTAIN DEW INVESTMENTS LTD
CANMORE HOTEL
738 Main St, Canmore, AB, T1W 2B6

Emp Here 20   Sales 5,253,170
SIC 5921 Liquor stores
Dir Art Fopma
Dir Brian Evans
Dir Brian Twigg
Dir David Rencz

D-U-N-S 24-080-3663   (BR)
PRO-CON ROAD WORKS LTD
201a Casale Pl, Canmore, AB, T1W 3G2
(403) 678-7283
Emp Here 25
SIC 1771 Concrete work

D-U-N-S 25-174-8406   (BR)
ROYAL BANK OF CANADA
RBC
(Suby of Royal Bank Of Canada)
1000 Railway Ave, Canmore, AB, T1W 1P4
(403) 678-3180
Emp Here 20

SIC 6021 National commercial banks

D-U-N-S 24-382-3791   (SL)
SFJ HOSPITALITY INC
GRANDE ROCKIES RESORT
901 Mountain St, Canmore, AB, T1W 0C9
(403) 678-8880
Emp Here 50   Sales 2,188,821
SIC 7011 Hotels and motels

D-U-N-S 25-072-1776   (SL)
SILVERTIP GOLF COURSE LIMITED
2000 Silvertip Trail, Canmore, AB, T1W 3J4
(403) 678-1600
Emp Here 74   Sales 3,210,271
SIC 7992 Public golf courses

D-U-N-S 20-806-2328   (BR)
SOBEYS CAPITAL INCORPORATED
SOBEYS STORE
950 Railway Ave Suite 1127, Canmore, AB, T1W 1P4
(403) 678-6326
Emp Here 25
SIC 5411 Grocery stores

D-U-N-S 20-791-3810   (BR)
SOBEYS WEST INC
CANMORE SAFEWAY
1200 Railway Ave Unit 2244, Canmore, AB, T1W 1P4
(403) 609-4655
Emp Here 20
SIC 5411 Grocery stores

D-U-N-S 25-175-7001   (BR)
TOWN OF CANMORE
CANMORE RECREATION CENTRE
1900 8 Ave, Canmore, AB, T1W 1Y2
(403) 678-8920
Emp Here 38
SIC 7999 Amusement and recreation, nec

D-U-N-S 25-175-6995   (BR)
TOWN OF CANMORE
CANMORE FIRE RESCUE
1021 Railway Ave, Canmore, AB, T1W 1P3
(403) 678-6199
Emp Here 36
SIC 7389 Business services, nec

D-U-N-S 20-515-6339   (SL)
WILD BILL'S SALOON INC
WILD BILLS
737 Main St, Canmore, AB, T1W 2B2
(403) 762-0333
Emp Here 90   Sales 2,699,546
SIC 5812 Eating places

Cardston, AB T0K

D-U-N-S 25-325-8933   (BR)
ALBERTA HEALTH SERVICES
CARDSTON HEALTH CENTER
144 2nd St W, Cardston, AB, T0K 0K0
(403) 653-5234
Emp Here 166
SIC 8062 General medical and surgical hospitals

D-U-N-S 20-064-4271   (BR)
KAINAI BOARD OF EDUCATION
TATSIKIISAAPO'P MIDDLE SCHOOL
Gd, Cardston, AB, T0K 0K0
(403) 737-2846
Emp Here 25
SIC 8211 Elementary and secondary schools

D-U-N-S 20-949-9727   (BR)
LOBLAWS INC
EXTRA FOODS
120 2 St E, Cardston, AB, T0K 0K0
(403) 653-3341
Emp Here 100
SIC 5912 Drug stores and proprietary stores

D-U-N-S 20-711-3874   (BR)
WESTWIND SCHOOL DIVISION #74
CARDSTON JUNIOR HIGH SCHOOL
445 Main St, Cardston, AB, T0K 0K0
(403) 653-4991
Emp Here 20
SIC 8211 Elementary and secondary schools

D-U-N-S 20-711-3338   (BR)
WESTWIND SCHOOL DIVISION #74
CARDSTON ELEMENTARY SCHOOL
730 4th Ave W, Cardston, AB, T0K 0K0
(403) 653-4955
Emp Here 100
SIC 8211 Elementary and secondary schools

D-U-N-S 20-027-3923   (BR)
WESTWIND SCHOOL DIVISION #74
CARDSTON HIGH SCHOOL
145 4 Ave W, Cardston, AB, T0K 0K0
(403) 653-4951
Emp Here 20
SIC 8211 Elementary and secondary schools

D-U-N-S 20-711-3650   (BR)
WESTWIND SCHOOL DIVISION #74
HUTTERVILLE COLONY SCHOOL
445 Main St, Cardston, AB, T0K 0K0
(403) 758-6000
Emp Here 50
SIC 8211 Elementary and secondary schools

D-U-N-S 20-654-3394   (BR)
WESTWIND SCHOOL DIVISION #74
CARDSTON JUNIOR HIGH SCHOOL
430 5th Ave E, Cardston, AB, T0K 0K0
(403) 653-4958
Emp Here 25
SIC 8211 Elementary and secondary schools

Caroline, AB T0M

D-U-N-S 20-912-7690   (BR)
NAL RESOURCES MANAGEMENT LIMITED
NAL GAS TRUST
Gd, Caroline, AB, T0M 0M0

Emp Here 50
SIC 8741 Management services

D-U-N-S 25-686-7177   (BR)
SHELL CANADA LIMITED
Po Box 500, Caroline, AB, T0M 0M0
(403) 722-7000
Emp Here 130
SIC 1389 Oil and gas field services, nec

D-U-N-S 20-038-0041   (BR)
WILD ROSE SCHOOL DIVISION NO. 66
CAROLINE SCHOOL
(Suby of Wild Rose School Division No. 66)
5027 48th Ave, Caroline, AB, T0M 0M0
(403) 722-3833
Emp Here 35
SIC 8211 Elementary and secondary schools

Carseland, AB T0J

D-U-N-S 24-013-4254   (BR)
ORICA CANADA INC
3 Mount W Hwy 24, Carseland, AB, T0J 0M0
(403) 936-2350
Emp Here 57
SIC 5169 Chemicals and allied products, nec

Carstairs, AB T0M

D-U-N-S 20-653-2595   (BR)
CHINOOKS EDGE SCHOOL DIVISION NO.

73
HUGH SUTHERLAND SCHOOL
Gd, Carstairs, AB, T0M 0N0
(403) 337-3326
Emp Here 45
SIC 8211 Elementary and secondary schools

D-U-N-S 25-832-1553   (BR)
EXXONMOBIL CANADA LTD
(Suby of Exxon Mobil Corporation)
Gd, Carstairs, AB, T0M 0N0
(403) 337-3688
Emp Here 20
SIC 1311 Crude petroleum and natural gas

D-U-N-S 25-832-0449   (BR)
KAYCAN LTEE
KAYTEC VINYL
(Suby of Administration F.L.T. Ltee)
701 Highfield Dr, Carstairs, AB, T0M 0N0
(403) 337-3966
Emp Here 40
SIC 3089 Plastics products, nec

D-U-N-S 24-299-4440   (BR)
WESTVIEW CO-OPERATIVE ASSOCIATION LIMITED
CARSTAIRS MARKETPLACE COOP
400 10th Ave S, Carstairs, AB, T0M 0N0
(403) 337-3361
Emp Here 40
SIC 5411 Grocery stores

Caslan, AB T0A

D-U-N-S 20-713-5240   (BR)
NORTHERN LIGHTS SCHOOL DIVISION NO. 69
CASLAN SCHOOL
Gd, Caslan, AB, T0A 0R0
(780) 689-2118
Emp Here 20
SIC 8211 Elementary and secondary schools

Castor, AB T0C

D-U-N-S 20-082-7124   (BR)
APACHE CANADA LTD
(Suby of Apache Corporation)
5018 50 Ave, Castor, AB, T0C 0X0
(403) 882-3751
Emp Here 150
SIC 1311 Crude petroleum and natural gas

D-U-N-S 20-025-4873   (BR)
CLEARVIEW SCHOOL DIVISION #71
GUS WETTER SCHOOL
5301 51 Ave, Castor, AB, T0C 0X0
(403) 882-4475
Emp Here 35
SIC 8211 Elementary and secondary schools

D-U-N-S 20-828-7060   (SL)
OUR LADY OF THE ROSARY HOSPITAL
5402 47 St, Castor, AB, T0C 0X0
(403) 882-3434
Emp Here 70   Sales 4,888,367
SIC 8062 General medical and surgical hospitals

Cayley, AB T0L

D-U-N-S 20-970-9567   (SL)
HUTTERIAN BRETHREN CHURCH OF CAYLEY
CAYLEY COLONY
Gd, Cayley, AB, T0L 0P0
(403) 395-2125
Emp Here 50   Sales 3,283,232

SIC 8661 Religious organizations

Chauvin, AB T0B

D-U-N-S 24-274-5420   (SL)
BENOIT OILFIELD CONSTRUCTION (1997) LTD
302 Rupert St, Chauvin, AB, T0B 0V0
(780) 858-3794
Emp Here 50   Sales 8,755,284
SIC 1623 Water, sewer, and utility lines
Pr Pr Calvin Winterholt
 Daniel Delemont

Chestermere, AB T1X

D-U-N-S 20-713-0878   (BR)
CALGARY ROMAN CATHOLIC SEPARATE SCHOOL DISTRICT #1
ST. GABRIEL THE ARCHANGEL SCHOOL
197 Invermere Dr, Chestermere, AB, T1X 1M7
(403) 500-2110
Emp Here 50
SIC 8211 Elementary and secondary schools

D-U-N-S 20-264-4969   (BR)
LOBLAWS INC
ERIC'S NOFRILLS
100 Rainbow Rd Unit 301, Chestermere, AB, T1X 0V3
(403) 273-0111
Emp Here 50
SIC 5411 Grocery stores

D-U-N-S 20-591-6922   (BR)
ROCKY VIEW SCHOOL DIVISION NO. 41, THE
CHESTERMERE LAKE MIDDLE SCHOOL
128 West Lakeview Dr, Chestermere, AB, T1X 1J8
(403) 273-1343
Emp Here 41
SIC 8211 Elementary and secondary schools

D-U-N-S 20-655-0761   (BR)
ROCKY VIEW SCHOOL DIVISION NO. 41, THE
PRAIRIE WATERS ELEMENTARY SCHOOL
201 Invermere Dr, Chestermere, AB, T1X 1M6
(403) 285-6969
Emp Here 60
SIC 8211 Elementary and secondary schools

D-U-N-S 24-363-3844   (BR)
SOBEYS WEST INC
CHESTERMERE SAFEWAY
135 Chestermere Station Way Unit 100, Chestermere, AB, T1X 1V2
(403) 410-9700
Emp Here 165
SIC 5411 Grocery stores

D-U-N-S 24-502-5528   (BR)
TDL GROUP CORP, THE
TIM HORTONS
120 John Morris Way Suite 300, Chestermere, AB, T1X 1V3
(403) 248-0000
Emp Here 90
SIC 5812 Eating places

Clairmont, AB T0H

D-U-N-S 24-344-7153   (BR)
AECOM PRODUCTION SERVICES LTD
FLINT FIELD SERVICES LTD
10222 79 Ave Ss 55, Clairmont, AB, T0H 0W0
(780) 539-7111
Emp Here 60

SIC 4213 Trucking, except local

D-U-N-S 20-297-2548   (BR)
AECOM PRODUCTION SERVICES LTD
FLINT FIELD SERVICES LTD
10414 84 Ave Ss 55, Clairmont, AB, T0H 0W0
(780) 539-0069
Emp Here 100
SIC 1731 Electrical work

D-U-N-S 24-324-1606   (BR)
BAKER HUGHES CANADA COMPANY
(Suby of Baker Hughes, A GE Company)
8002 98 St Ss 55, Clairmont, AB, T0H 0W0
(780) 539-5210
Emp Here 20
SIC 1389 Oil and gas field services, nec

D-U-N-S 25-268-8999   (BR)
BAKER HUGHES CANADA COMPANY
BAKER OIL TOOLS
(Suby of Baker Hughes, A GE Company)
7002 96 St Ss 55, Clairmont, AB, T0H 0W0
(780) 538-9475
Emp Here 40
SIC 1389 Oil and gas field services, nec

D-U-N-S 24-890-2988   (BR)
BRANDT TRACTOR LTD
7301 102 St Ss 55, Clairmont, AB, T0H 0W0
(780) 532-3414
Emp Here 20
SIC 5084 Industrial machinery and equipment

D-U-N-S 20-999-0766   (BR)
BUILDERS ENERGY SERVICES LTD
BRAZEAU WELL SERVICING
(Suby of Builders Energy Services Ltd)
9020 99 St Ss 55, Clairmont, AB, T0H 0W0
(780) 539-5650
Emp Here 25
SIC 1381 Drilling oil and gas wells

D-U-N-S 20-542-7516   (BR)
CANADA POST CORPORATION
RED ROBIN MARKET
9922 102 Ave, Clairmont, AB, T0H 0W1
(780) 567-3848
Emp Here 20
SIC 4311 U.s. postal service

D-U-N-S 24-425-9110   (BR)
CANYON TECHNICAL SERVICES LTD
9102 102 St Ss 55 Suite 55, Clairmont, AB, T0H 0W0
(780) 357-2250
Emp Here 150
SIC 1389 Oil and gas field services, nec

D-U-N-S 20-786-5796   (BR)
CARON TRANSPORTATION SYSTEMS PARTNERSHIP
7502 98 St Ss 55, Clairmont, AB, T0H 0W0
(780) 539-0377
Emp Here 40
SIC 4213 Trucking, except local

D-U-N-S 20-517-7319   (BR)
CLEAN HARBORS INDUSTRIAL SERVICES CANADA, INC
PEAK ENERGY SERVICES
Gd, Clairmont, AB, T0H 0W0
(780) 567-2992
Emp Here 25
SIC 6712 Bank holding companies

D-U-N-S 20-086-0807   (BR)
FINNING INTERNATIONAL INC
FINNING CANADA
(Suby of Finning International Inc)
7601 99 St Ss 55, Clairmont, AB, T0H 0W0
(780) 831-2600
Emp Here 100
SIC 5082 Construction and mining machinery

D-U-N-S 20-979-3517   (HQ)
IPAC SERVICES CORPORATION
(Suby of IPAC Services Corporation)
8701 102 St Ss 55, Clairmont, AB, T0H 0W0

(780) 532-7350
Emp Here 100   Emp Total 350
Sales 79,155,636
SIC 1623 Water, sewer, and utility lines
Pr Pr Ron Ward
CFO Derrick Mysko

D-U-N-S 20-314-5875   (BR)
LOMAK BULK CARRIERS CORP
7402 98 St Ss 55, Clairmont, AB, T0H 0W0
(780) 532-5083
Emp Here 23
SIC 4212 Local trucking, without storage

D-U-N-S 20-744-6548   (BR)
PEACE WAPITI SCHOOL DIVISION NO.76
CLAIRMONT COMMUNITY SCHOOL
10407 97 St, Clairmont, AB, T0H 0W5
(780) 567-3553
Emp Here 49
SIC 8351 Child day care services

D-U-N-S 24-350-0266   (BR)
PETROWEST CONSTRUCTION LP
ROY LARSON CONSTRUCTION, DIV OF.
10226 84 Ave Ss 55 Suite 55, Clairmont, AB, T0H 0W0
(780) 830-3051
Emp Here 60
SIC 1389 Oil and gas field services, nec

D-U-N-S 20-114-4370   (BR)
PRECISION DRILLING CORPORATION
PRECISION RENTALS
7801 102 St Ss 55, Clairmont, AB, T0H 0W0
(780) 532-0788
Emp Here 20
SIC 1381 Drilling oil and gas wells

D-U-N-S 25-243-6089   (BR)
RED DEER IRONWORKS INC
RDI
10602 79 Ave Ss 55 Suite 6, Clairmont, AB, T0H 0W0
(780) 830-5474
Emp Here 25
SIC 1791 Structural steel erection

D-U-N-S 20-130-3836   (BR)
TRICAN WELL SERVICE LTD
TRICAN PARTNESHIP
9701 99 St Ss 55, Clairmont, AB, T0H 0W0
(780) 567-5200
Emp Here 250
SIC 1389 Oil and gas field services, nec

D-U-N-S 24-423-2885   (BR)
TRINIDAD DRILLING LTD
TRINIDAD WELL SERVICING
9021 99 St Ss 55, Clairmont, AB, T0H 0W0

Emp Here 20
SIC 1389 Oil and gas field services, nec

Claresholm, AB T0L

D-U-N-S 24-682-5314   (SL)
1430499 ALBERTA LTD
TIM HORTONS
29 Alberta Rd, Claresholm, AB, T0L 0T0
(403) 625-2546
Emp Here 53   Sales 1,605,135
SIC 5812 Eating places

D-U-N-S 25-123-7327   (BR)
ALBERTA HEALTH SERVICES
LANDER TREATMENT CENTER
221 42nd Ave W, Claresholm, AB, T0L 0T0
(403) 625-1395
Emp Here 36
SIC 8361 Residential care

D-U-N-S 25-000-5121   (BR)
LIVINGSTONE RANGE SCHOOL DIVISION NO 68
WEST MEADOW SCHOOL

5613 8th St W, Claresholm, AB, T0L 0T0
(403) 625-4464
Emp Here 30
SIC 8211 Elementary and secondary schools

D-U-N-S 20-711-3122   (BR)
LIVINGSTONE RANGE SCHOOL DIVISION NO 68
WILLOW CREEK COMPOSITE HIGH SCHOOL
628 55th Ave W, Claresholm, AB, T0L 0T0
(403) 625-3387
Emp Here 35
SIC 8211 Elementary and secondary schools

D-U-N-S 24-043-0728   (BR)
MAPLE LEAF FOODS INC
4149 3 St E, Claresholm, AB, T0L 0T0
(403) 625-3163
Emp Here 22
SIC 2048 Prepared feeds, nec

D-U-N-S 20-806-2336   (BR)
SOBEYS CAPITAL INCORPORATED
SOBEYS STORE 1118
1 St W Suite 4920, Claresholm, AB, T0L 0T0
(403) 625-2555
Emp Here 60
SIC 5411 Grocery stores

Cleardale, AB T0H

D-U-N-S 20-694-8460   (SL)
HUTTERIAN BRETHREN CHURCH OF CLEARDALE
CLEARDALE COLONY
Gd, Cleardale, AB, T0H 3Y0
(780) 685-2870
Emp Here 70   Sales 4,596,524
SIC 8661 Religious organizations

D-U-N-S 20-711-3320   (BR)
PEACE RIVER SCHOOL DIVISION 10
MENNO SIMONS SCHOOL
Bag 100, Cleardale, AB, T0H 3Y0
(780) 685-2340
Emp Here 50
SIC 8211 Elementary and secondary schools

Clive, AB T0C

D-U-N-S 20-072-4057   (BR)
WOLF CREEK SCHOOL DIVISION NO.72
CLIVE SCHOOL
5016 52 Ave, Clive, AB, T0C 0Y0
(403) 784-3354
Emp Here 30
SIC 8211 Elementary and secondary schools

Clyde, AB T0G

D-U-N-S 20-023-9577   (BR)
PEMBINA HILLS REGIONAL DIVISION 7
ELEANOR HALL SCHOOL
5402 50 St, Clyde, AB, T0G 0P0
(780) 348-5341
Emp Here 29
SIC 8211 Elementary and secondary schools

Coaldale, AB T1M

D-U-N-S 24-299-7575   (SL)
ADORA KITCHENS LTD
1112 18 Ave, Coaldale, AB, T1M 1N2
(403) 345-3118
Emp Here 58   Sales 3,356,192

SIC 2434 Wood kitchen cabinets

D-U-N-S 20-028-8194   (BR)
PALLISER REGIONAL DIVISION NO 26
EMERY. JENNIE ELEMENTARY SCHOOL
1101 22 Ave, Coaldale, AB, T1M 1N9
(403) 345-2403
Emp Here 60
SIC 8211 Elementary and secondary schools

D-U-N-S 20-711-4971   (BR)
PALLISER REGIONAL DIVISION NO 26
R I BAKER MIDDLE SCHOOL
2112 13 St, Coaldale, AB, T1M 1L7
(403) 345-3340
Emp Here 50
SIC 8211 Elementary and secondary schools

D-U-N-S 20-580-9903   (BR)
PALLISER REGIONAL DIVISION NO 26
KATE ANDREWS HIGH SCHOOL
2112 21 St, Coaldale, AB, T1M 1L9
(403) 345-3383
Emp Here 30
SIC 8211 Elementary and secondary schools

D-U-N-S 24-126-1226   (BR)
REHOBOTH A CHRISTIAN ASSOCIATION FOR THE MENTALLY HANDICAPPED OF ALBERTA
REHOBOTH CHRISTIAN MINISTRY
1km Hwy 845 N, Coaldale, AB, T1M 1N1
(403) 345-5199
Emp Here 140
SIC 2511 Wood household furniture

Coalhurst, AB T0L

D-U-N-S 20-830-2224   (BR)
CANADIAN PACIFIC RAILWAY COMPANY
CPR
Gd, Coalhurst, AB, T0L 0V0
(403) 329-7726
Emp Here 200
SIC 4011 Railroads, line-haul operating

D-U-N-S 20-029-2527   (BR)
PALLISER REGIONAL DIVISION NO 26
COALHURST ELEMENTARY SCHOOL
510 51 Ave, Coalhurst, AB, T0L 0V0
(403) 381-3330
Emp Here 46
SIC 8211 Elementary and secondary schools

Cochrane, AB T0S

D-U-N-S 25-314-8803   (BR)
ALBERTA HEALTH SERVICES
COCHRANE COMMUNITY HEALTH CENTRE
60 Grand Blvd, Cochrane, AB, T0S 0S4
(403) 851-6130
Emp Here 100
SIC 8062 General medical and surgical hospitals

Cochrane, AB T4C

D-U-N-S 24-859-0205   (SL)
4III INNOVATIONS INC
141 2 Ave, Cochrane, AB, T4C 2B9
(403) 800-3095
Emp Here 45   *Sales* 6,420,542
SIC 3699 Electrical equipment and supplies, nec
Pr Pr Kip Fyfe
Dir Janelle Chubey

D-U-N-S 25-073-7942   (BR)

ARAMARK MANAGEMENT SERVICES OF CANADA INC
ARAMARK
302 Quigley Dr, Cochrane, AB, T4C 1X9
(403) 932-6422
Emp Here 20
SIC 5312 Eating places

D-U-N-S 25-522-9056   (BR)
BETHANY CARE SOCIETY
302 Quigley Dr, Cochrane, AB, T4C 1X9
(403) 932-6422
Emp Here 150
SIC 8051 Skilled nursing care facilities

D-U-N-S 20-916-2358   (BR)
CALGARY ROMAN CATHOLIC SEPARATE SCHOOL DISTRICT #1
ST. TIMOTHY JUNIOR & SENIOR HIGH SCHOOL
501 Sunset Dr, Cochrane, AB, T4C 2K4
(403) 500-2106
Emp Here 30
SIC 8211 Elementary and secondary schools

D-U-N-S 20-713-0803   (BR)
CALGARY ROMAN CATHOLIC SEPARATE SCHOOL DISTRICT #1
HOLY SPIRIT CATHOLIC SCHOOL
129 Powell St, Cochrane, AB, T4C 1Y2
(403) 500-2065
Emp Here 30
SIC 8211 Elementary and secondary schools

D-U-N-S 20-303-4301   (BR)
CLEARSTREAM ENERGY SERVICES LIMITED PARTNERSHIP
INDUSTRIAL SERVICES - SOUTH REGION
141 2 Ave E, Cochrane, AB, T4C 2B9
(403) 932-9566
Emp Here 160
SIC 1389 Oil and gas field services, nec

D-U-N-S 24-075-4148   (BR)
CORPORATION OF THE TOWN OF COCHRANE
BIGHILL LEISURE POOL
201 5 Ave W, Cochrane, AB, T4C 1X3
(403) 851-2299
Emp Here 25
SIC 7999 Amusement and recreation, nec

D-U-N-S 20-305-2907   (BR)
DIRECT ENERGY MARKETING LIMITED
WILDCAT HILLS GAS PLANT
262130 Range Rd 54, Cochrane, AB, T4C 1A6
(403) 932-2241
Emp Here 45
SIC 1389 Oil and gas field services, nec

D-U-N-S 25-099-8630   (SL)
DYNASTREAM INNOVATIONS INC
100 Grande Blvd W Suite 201, Cochrane, AB, T4C 0S4
(403) 932-9292
Emp Here 78   *Sales* 4,231,721
SIC 8731 Commercial physical research

D-U-N-S 24-360-8192   (SL)
H&H NORWEST LIMITED
307 1 St E Unit 1, Cochrane, AB, T4C 1Z3

Emp Here 21   *Sales* 8,211,480
SIC 1542 Nonresidential construction, nec
Pr Pr Randy Halverson
VP VP John Hunter

D-U-N-S 20-870-7559   (BR)
HUDSON'S BAY COMPANY
FIELDS DOLLAR DEPOT
312 5 Ave W Suite 24, Cochrane, AB, T4C 2E3

Emp Here 25
SIC 5311 Department stores

D-U-N-S 25-986-7117   (BR)
LOBLAWS INC

EXTRA FOODS
210 5 Ave, Cochrane, AB, T4C 1X3
(403) 932-0402
Emp Here 100
SIC 5411 Grocery stores

D-U-N-S 24-442-5906   (BR)
PNR RAILWORKS INC
PACIFIC NORTHERN RAIL
325 Railway St E, Cochrane, AB, T4C 2C3
(403) 932-6966
Emp Here 30
SIC 1629 Heavy construction, nec

D-U-N-S 20-079-4274   (BR)
ROCKY VIEW SCHOOL DIVISION NO. 41, THE
MITFORD MIDDLE SCHOOL
110 Quigley Dr, Cochrane, AB, T4C 1Y1
(403) 932-4457
Emp Here 42
SIC 8211 Elementary and secondary schools

D-U-N-S 20-592-1195   (BR)
ROCKY VIEW SCHOOL DIVISION NO. 41, THE
BOW VALLEY HIGH SCHOOL
2000 River Heights Dr, Cochrane, AB, T4C 1Y8
(403) 932-9005
Emp Here 50
SIC 8211 Elementary and secondary schools

D-U-N-S 20-025-4964   (BR)
ROCKY VIEW SCHOOL DIVISION NO. 41, THE
ELIZABETH BARRETT SCHOOL
605 4 Ave N, Cochrane, AB, T4C 1Y5
(403) 932-3151
Emp Here 35
SIC 8211 Elementary and secondary schools

D-U-N-S 24-975-3534   (BR)
ROCKY VIEW SCHOOL DIVISION NO. 41, THE
COCHRANE HIGH SCHOOL
529 4 Ave N, Cochrane, AB, T4C 1Y6
(403) 932-2542
Emp Here 45
SIC 8211 Elementary and secondary schools

D-U-N-S 20-028-8558   (BR)
ROCKY VIEW SCHOOL DIVISION NO. 41, THE
MANACHABAN MIDDLE SCHOOL
724 Chiniki Dr, Cochrane, AB, T4C 1Y4
(403) 932-2215
Emp Here 36
SIC 8211 Elementary and secondary schools

D-U-N-S 20-591-7862   (BR)
ROCKY VIEW SCHOOL DIVISION NO. 41, THE
GLENVILLE SCHOOL
55 Glenpatrick Rd, Cochrane, AB, T4C 1X7
(403) 932-4922
Emp Here 55
SIC 8211 Elementary and secondary schools

D-U-N-S 20-086-6593   (BR)
ROYAL BANK OF CANADA
RBC
(*Suby of* Royal Bank Of Canada)
130 1st Ave W, Cochrane, AB, T4C 1A5
(403) 932-2231
Emp Here 26
SIC 6021 National commercial banks

D-U-N-S 20-152-9273   (BR)
SOBEYS CAPITAL INCORPORATED
COCHRANE IGA
305 1 St W, Cochrane, AB, T4C 1X8
(403) 932-3222
Emp Here 70
SIC 5411 Grocery stores

D-U-N-S 25-186-5879   (BR)
SOBEYS WEST INC

304 5 Ave W, Cochrane, AB, T4C 2A5
(403) 851-1290
Emp Here 20
SIC 5411 Grocery stores

D-U-N-S 20-078-2980   (BR)
SOUTHLAND TRANSPORTATION LTD
216 Griffin Rd E, Cochrane, AB, T4C 2B9
(403) 932-7100
Emp Here 100
SIC 4151 School buses

D-U-N-S 20-079-1333   (SL)
SPRAY LAKE SAWMILLS (1980) LTD
SPRAY LAKE SAWMILLS
305 Griffin Rd, Cochrane, AB, T4C 2C4
(403) 932-2234
Emp Here 200   *Sales* 32,133,419
SIC 2491 Wood preserving
Pr Pr Barry Mjolsness
Fin Mgr Cameron Worley

D-U-N-S 24-557-1224   (BR)
STARBUCKS COFFEE CANADA, INC
STARBUCKS
(*Suby of* Starbucks Corporation)
120 5 Ave W Suite 301, Cochrane, AB, T4C 0A4
(403) 932-9856
Emp Here 21
SIC 5812 Eating places

Cold Lake, AB T9M

D-U-N-S 20-064-2499   (BR)
ALBERTA HEALTH SERVICES
COLD LAKE COMMUNITY HEALTH SERVICE
4720 55 St, Cold Lake, AB, T9M 1V8
(780) 594-4404
Emp Here 45
SIC 8062 General medical and surgical hospitals

D-U-N-S 24-351-2618   (BR)
CUBIC FIELD SERVICES CANADA LIMITED
Gd, Cold Lake, AB, T9M 1P1
(780) 594-3970
Emp Here 60
SIC 5065 Electronic parts and equipment, nec

D-U-N-S 25-269-5374   (BR)
CURTIN, AUSTIN SALES LTD
CANADIAN TIRE 450
(*Suby of* Curtin, Austin Sales Ltd)
6703 51 St Suite 450, Cold Lake, AB, T9M 1Z9
(780) 594-3501
Emp Here 60
SIC 5531 Auto and home supply stores

D-U-N-S 20-561-9286   (BR)
DUCHARME MOTORS LTD
COLD LAKE FORD
3817 50 St, Cold Lake, AB, T9M 1K6
(780) 594-1000
Emp Here 50
SIC 5511 New and used car dealers

D-U-N-S 24-034-2480   (BR)
FLINT ENERGY SERVICES LTD.
Hwy 55 W, Cold Lake, AB, T9M 1P7
(780) 639-6034
Emp Here 150
SIC 1799 Special trade contractors, nec

D-U-N-S 24-115-3456   (BR)
L-3 COMMUNICATIONS MAS (CANADA) INC
(*Suby of* L3 Technologies, Inc.)
1 Hangar, Cold Lake, AB, T9M 2C1
(780) 594-3967
Emp Here 30
SIC 4581 Airports, flying fields, and services

D-U-N-S 25-063-9499   (BR)

LAKELAND CREDIT UNION LTD
5217 50 Ave, Cold Lake, AB, T9M 1P3
(780) 594-4011
Emp Here 20
SIC 6062 State credit unions

D-U-N-S 20-713-5901   (BR)
LAKELAND ROMAN CATHOLIC SEPARATE SCHOOL DISTRICT NO. 150
HOLY CROSS ELEMENTARY SCHOOL
Gd, Cold Lake, AB, T9M 0B9
(780) 594-0700
Emp Here 35
SIC 8211 Elementary and secondary schools

D-U-N-S 25-178-0284   (BR)
LAKELAND ROMAN CATHOLIC SEPARATE SCHOOL DISTRICT NO. 150
ASSUMPTION JUNIOR & SENIOR HIGH SCHOOL
5209 48 Ave, Cold Lake, AB, T9M 1S8
(780) 594-4050
Emp Here 40
SIC 8211 Elementary and secondary schools

D-U-N-S 25-174-6145   (BR)
LAKELAND ROMAN CATHOLIC SEPARATE SCHOOL DISTRICT NO. 150
ST DOMINIC ELEMENTARY SCHOOL
920 7 St, Cold Lake, AB, T9M 1M5
(780) 639-3520
Emp Here 35
SIC 8211 Elementary and secondary schools

D-U-N-S 20-591-7037   (BR)
NORTHERN LIGHTS SCHOOL DIVISION NO. 69
COLD LAKE ELEMENTARY SCHOOL
803 16 Ave, Cold Lake, AB, T9M 1M2
(780) 639-3107
Emp Here 40
SIC 8211 Elementary and secondary schools

D-U-N-S 20-646-9962   (BR)
NORTHERN LIGHTS SCHOOL DIVISION NO. 69
R A REYNOLDS SCHOOL
Gd, Cold Lake, AB, T9M 2C1

Emp Here 35
SIC 8211 Elementary and secondary schools

D-U-N-S 20-653-7156   (BR)
NORTHERN LIGHTS SCHOOL DIVISION NO. 69
GRAND CENTER HIGH SCHOOL
5533 48 Ave, Cold Lake, AB, T9M 1V7
(780) 594-5623
Emp Here 40
SIC 8211 Elementary and secondary schools

D-U-N-S 25-269-6588   (BR)
NORTHERN LIGHTS SCHOOL DIVISION NO. 69
GRAND CENTRE MIDDLE SCHOOL
5104 56 St, Cold Lake, AB, T9M 1R2
(780) 594-3832
Emp Here 20
SIC 8211 Elementary and secondary schools

D-U-N-S 20-713-5133   (BR)
NORTHERN LIGHTS SCHOOL DIVISION NO. 69
NELSON HEIGHTS SCHOOL
2035 5 Ave, Cold Lake, AB, T9M 1G7
(780) 639-3338
Emp Here 30
SIC 8211 Elementary and secondary schools

D-U-N-S 24-034-4122   (BR)
SOBEYS CAPITAL INCORPORATED
COLD LAKE FOODS
6403 51 St, Cold Lake, AB, T9M 1C8
(780) 594-3335
Emp Here 120
SIC 5411 Grocery stores

D-U-N-S 20-918-2471   (BR)

WAL-MART CANADA CORP
4702 43 Ave Suite 3640, Cold Lake, AB, T9M 1M9
(780) 840-2340
Emp Here 120
SIC 5311 Department stores

Coleman, AB T0K

D-U-N-S 24-311-1411   (BR)
BLUE FALLS MANUFACTURING LTD
ARTIC SPAS
(*Suby of* Spa Logic Inc)
3706 18 Ave, Coleman, AB, T0K 0M0
(403) 562-8008
Emp Here 90
SIC 3999 Manufacturing industries, nec

D-U-N-S 25-097-3468   (BR)
DEVON CANADA CORPORATION
Gd, Coleman, AB, T0K 0M0

Emp Here 30
SIC 1311 Crude petroleum and natural gas

D-U-N-S 20-711-2488   (BR)
LIVINGSTONE RANGE SCHOOL DIVISION NO 68
HORACE ALLEN SCHOOL
2002 76 St, Coleman, AB, T0K 0M0
(403) 563-3998
Emp Here 25
SIC 8211 Elementary and secondary schools

D-U-N-S 25-272-3010   (BR)
LIVINGSTONE RANGE SCHOOL DIVISION NO 68
CROWSNEST CONSOLIDATED HIGH SCHOOL
8901 20th Ave, Coleman, AB, T0K 0M0
(403) 563-5651
Emp Here 32
SIC 8211 Elementary and secondary schools

Condor, AB T0M

D-U-N-S 20-591-7052   (BR)
WILD ROSE SCHOOL DIVISION NO. 66
CONDOR ELEMENTARY SCHOOL
(*Suby of* Wild Rose School Division No. 66)
725 Condor Rd, Condor, AB, T0M 0P0
(403) 729-3868
Emp Here 20
SIC 8211 Elementary and secondary schools

Conklin, AB T0P

D-U-N-S 24-333-2702   (BR)
BP CANADA ENERGY COMPANY
(*Suby of* BP P.L.C.)
Gd, Conklin, AB, T0P 1H0
(780) 559-2236
Emp Here 30
SIC 1311 Crude petroleum and natural gas

D-U-N-S 24-399-5508   (BR)
ROBWEL MANUFACTURING INC
ROBWEL CONSTRUCTORS
135 Poplar Dr, Conklin, AB, T0P 1H1
(780) 559-2966
Emp Here 20
SIC 1389 Oil and gas field services, nec

D-U-N-S 20-321-3335   (BR)
UNITED RENTALS OF CANADA, INC
189 Northland Dr, Conklin, AB, T0P 1H1
(780) 559-0183
Emp Here 23
SIC 7353 Heavy construction equipment

rental

Consort, AB T0C

D-U-N-S 24-905-1749   (BR)
APACHE CANADA LTD
(*Suby of* Apache Corporation)
Gd, Consort, AB, T0C 1B0
(403) 577-3811
Emp Here 55
SIC 1382 Oil and gas exploration services

D-U-N-S 20-731-8051   (BR)
BONAVISTA ENERGY CORPORATION
Gd, Consort, AB, T0C 1B0
(403) 577-3777
Emp Here 70
SIC 1311 Crude petroleum and natural gas

D-U-N-S 20-025-4865   (BR)
PRAIRIE LAND REGIONAL DIVISION 25
CONSORT SCHOOL
5215 50 St, Consort, AB, T0C 1B0
(403) 577-3654
Emp Here 30
SIC 8211 Elementary and secondary schools

Coronation, AB T0C

D-U-N-S 20-030-0932   (BR)
CLEARVIEW SCHOOL DIVISION #71
CORONATION OUTREACH SCHOOL
4801 Norfolk Ave, Coronation, AB, T0C 1C0
(403) 578-3661
Emp Here 25
SIC 8211 Elementary and secondary schools

D-U-N-S 20-710-6969   (BR)
CLEARVIEW SCHOOL DIVISION #71
EAST OUTREACH SCHOOL
Gd, Coronation, AB, T0C 1C0
(403) 578-4475
Emp Here 50
SIC 8211 Elementary and secondary schools

County Of Grande Prairie No. 1, AB T8W

D-U-N-S 20-287-6827   (BR)
TOTAL OILFIELD RENTALS LIMITED PARTNERSHIP
61058 668 Hwy, County Of Grande Prairie No. 1, AB, T8W 5A9
(780) 532-1994
Emp Here 30
SIC 4213 Trucking, except local

Coutts, AB T0K

D-U-N-S 25-316-1988   (BR)
COLE INTERNATIONAL INC
107 1 Ave S, Coutts, AB, T0K 0N0
(403) 344-3855
Emp Here 22
SIC 4731 Freight transportation arrangement

Craigmyle, AB T0J

D-U-N-S 20-711-1548   (BR)
PRAIRIE LAND REGIONAL DIVISION 25
Gd, Craigmyle, AB, T0J 0T0

Emp Here 50

SIC 8211 Elementary and secondary schools

Cranford, AB T0K

D-U-N-S 20-549-5570   (SL)
ASHBROS ENTERPRISES LTD
4931 52 Ave, Cranford, AB, T0K 0R0
(403) 223-1888
Emp Here 80   *Sales* 16,130,550
SIC 1389 Oil and gas field services, nec
Pr Pr Randal (Randy) Miller
   Shannon Miller

Cremona, AB T0M

D-U-N-S 20-025-4915   (BR)
CHINOOKS EDGE SCHOOL DIVISION NO. 73
CREMONA SCHOOL
206 3rd St E, Cremona, AB, T0M 0R0
(403) 637-0077
Emp Here 40
SIC 8211 Elementary and secondary schools

Crooked Creek, AB T0H

D-U-N-S 20-710-1135   (BR)
PEACE WAPITI SCHOOL DIVISION NO.76
RIDGEVALLEY SCHOOL
Gd, Crooked Creek, AB, T0H 0Y0
(780) 957-3995
Emp Here 36
SIC 8211 Elementary and secondary schools

Crossfield, AB T0M

D-U-N-S 24-072-1287   (BR)
GREEN PRAIRIE INTERNATIONAL INC
34 Mccool Cres, Crossfield, AB, T0M 0S0
(403) 946-5567
Emp Here 20
SIC 5191 Farm supplies

D-U-N-S 24-700-7164   (SL)
HOCAN INDUSTRIES LTD
9 Laut Cres, Crossfield, AB, T0M 0S0
(403) 946-4440
Emp Here 26   *Sales* 4,617,412
SIC 3441 Fabricated structural Metal

D-U-N-S 20-115-3892   (HQ)
MAXFIELD INC
(*Suby of* Maxfield Group Inc)
1026 Western Dr, Crossfield, AB, T0M 0S0
(403) 946-5678
Emp Here 112   *Emp Total* 5
Sales 37,594,000
SIC 3533 Oil and gas field machinery
   Budi Setiawan
   Tony Giasson
   Horacio Abalos
   Raymond Smitke
   Allan Dolan

D-U-N-S 24-683-6147   (BR)
PLASTI-FAB LTD
718 Mccool St Gate E, Crossfield, AB, T0M 0S0
(403) 946-5622
Emp Here 55
SIC 2821 Plastics materials and resins

D-U-N-S 24-854-8067   (BR)
PLASTI-FAB LTD
802 Mccool St, Crossfield, AB, T0M 0S0

---

(403) 946-4576
Emp Here 100
SIC 2821 Plastics materials and resins

D-U-N-S 24-765-1123   (BR)
PLASTI-FAB LTD
POLYMER PLANT
Gd, Crossfield, AB, T0M 0S0
(403) 946-4576
Emp Here 20
SIC 2899 Chemical preparations, nec

D-U-N-S 20-025-4956   (BR)
ROCKY VIEW SCHOOL DIVISION NO. 41, THE
CROSSFIELD ELEMENTARY SCHOOL
1140 Mountain Ave, Crossfield, AB, T0M 0S0
(403) 946-5696
Emp Here 28
SIC 8211 Elementary and secondary schools

D-U-N-S 20-592-0163   (BR)
ROCKY VIEW SCHOOL DIVISION NO. 41, THE
W G MURDOCH SCHOOL
1020 Mountain Ave, Crossfield, AB, T0M 0S0
(403) 946-5665
Emp Here 35
SIC 8211 Elementary and secondary schools

D-U-N-S 25-094-6761   (BR)
VITERRA INC
AGRICORE UNITED
29340 Hwy 2a, Crossfield, AB, T0M 0S0
(403) 946-4311
Emp Here 20
SIC 4221 Farm product warehousing and storage

Daysland, AB T0B

D-U-N-S 25-236-3569   (BR)
ALBERTA HEALTH SERVICES
DAYSLAND HEALTH CENTRE
5920 51 Ave, Daysland, AB, T0B 1A0
(780) 374-3746
Emp Here 100
SIC 8062 General medical and surgical hospitals

D-U-N-S 20-710-5565   (BR)
BATTLE RIVER REGIONAL DIVISION 31
DAYSLAND SCHOOL
5210 50th St, Daysland, AB, T0B 1A0
(780) 374-3676
Emp Here 31
SIC 8211 Elementary and secondary schools

Delia, AB T0J

D-U-N-S 20-292-4762   (BR)
PRAIRIE LAND REGIONAL DIVISION 25
DELIA SCHOOL
205 3rd Ave N, Delia, AB, T0J 0W0
(403) 364-3777
Emp Here 20
SIC 8211 Elementary and secondary schools

Denwood, AB T0B

D-U-N-S 24-079-4581   (BR)
CUBIC FIELD SERVICES CANADA LIMITED
Gd, Denwood, AB, T0B 1B0
(780) 842-4180
Emp Here 25
SIC 4899 Communication services, nec

D-U-N-S 20-255-9100   (BR)
DEFENCE CONSTRUCTION (1951) LIM-

ITED
DEFENCE CONSTRUCTION CANADA
188 Buffalo Rd, Denwood, AB, T0B 1B0
(780) 842-1363
Emp Here 20
SIC 8741 Management services

Devon, AB T9G

D-U-N-S 25-135-6028   (BR)
BLACK GOLD REGIONAL DIVISION #18
JOHN MALAND HIGH SCHOOL
105 Athabasca Ave, Devon, AB, T9G 1A4
(780) 987-3709
Emp Here 3,025
SIC 8211 Elementary and secondary schools

D-U-N-S 25-116-9678   (BR)
BLACK GOLD REGIONAL DIVISION #18
RIVERVIEW MIDDLE SCHOOL
165 Athabasca Dr, Devon, AB, T9G 1A5
(780) 987-2204
Emp Here 35
SIC 8211 Elementary and secondary schools

D-U-N-S 25-092-2804   (BR)
BLACK GOLD REGIONAL DIVISION #18
ROBINA BAKER ELEMENTARY SCHOOL
1 Jasper Crt S, Devon, AB, T9G 1A2
(780) 987-3705
Emp Here 35
SIC 8211 Elementary and secondary schools

D-U-N-S 24-997-6127   (SL)
DEVON CHEVROLET LTD
7 Saskatchewan Ave W, Devon, AB, T9G 1B2
(780) 987-2433
Emp Here 34   *Sales* 17,081,600
SIC 5511 New and used car dealers
Pr Pr Brent T. Steckly

D-U-N-S 24-086-8935   (SL)
DEVON GOLF & CONFERENCE CENTRE
DEVON GOLF & C. C.
1130 River Valley, Devon, AB, T9G 1Z3
(780) 987-3477
Emp Here 68   *Sales* 2,699,546
SIC 7997 Membership sports and recreation clubs

D-U-N-S 20-551-9916   (BR)
FLINT ENERGY SERVICES LTD.
6 Well Head St, Devon, AB, T9G 1Z7

Emp Here 20
SIC 1623 Water, sewer, and utility lines

D-U-N-S 25-080-8537   (SL)
IRON EAGLE HOT OILING LTD
4 Saskatchewan Ave, Devon, AB, T9G 1E7
(780) 987-3520
Emp Here 23   *Sales* 23,840,924
SIC 1382 Oil and gas exploration services
Dir Edward Sautner
Dir Tina Sautner

D-U-N-S 24-841-4161   (HQ)
WAYLON TRANSPORT INC
(*Suby of* Anderson Trucking Service Inc)
2 Tool Push Ave, Devon, AB, T9G 2A2
(780) 987-5611
Emp Here 22   *Emp Total* 900
Sales 2,772,507
SIC 4213 Trucking, except local

Diamond City, AB T0K

D-U-N-S 20-099-9170   (BR)
AGROPUR COOPERATIVE
AGROPUR LETHBRIDGE
Gd, Diamond City, AB, T0K 0T0

(403) 381-4024
Emp Here 30
SIC 2022 Cheese; natural and processed

Didsbury, AB T0M

D-U-N-S 24-451-0835   (BR)
ACCREDITED SUPPORTS TO THE COMMUNITY
1709 15th Ave, Didsbury, AB, T0M 0W0
(403) 335-8671
Emp Here 100
SIC 8322 Individual and family services

D-U-N-S 25-194-3619   (BR)
ALBERTA HEALTH SERVICES
DIDSBURY DISTRICT HEALTH SERVICES
1210 20e Ave, Didsbury, AB, T0M 0W0
(403) 335-9393
Emp Here 250
SIC 8062 General medical and surgical hospitals

D-U-N-S 20-578-2381   (BR)
ALBERTA TREASURY BRANCHES
ATB FINANCIAL
1820 20 St, Didsbury, AB, T0M 0W0
(403) 335-3386
Emp Here 20
SIC 6036 Savings institutions, except federal

D-U-N-S 20-025-4923   (BR)
CHINOOKS EDGE SCHOOL DIVISION NO. 73
ROSS FORD ELEMENTARY SCHOOL
2016 23 St, Didsbury, AB, T0M 0W0
(403) 335-3234
Emp Here 50
SIC 8211 Elementary and secondary schools

D-U-N-S 20-591-6781   (BR)
CHINOOKS EDGE SCHOOL DIVISION NO. 73
WEST GLEN SCHOOL
2405 23 St, Didsbury, AB, T0M 0W0
(403) 335-8700
Emp Here 30
SIC 8211 Elementary and secondary schools

D-U-N-S 20-591-6740   (BR)
CHINOOKS EDGE SCHOOL DIVISION NO. 73
DIDSBURY HIGH SCHOOL
1515 15 Ave, Didsbury, AB, T0M 0W0
(403) 335-3356
Emp Here 25
SIC 8211 Elementary and secondary schools

D-U-N-S 25-230-2302   (SL)
CHRISTOPHER'S WELDING LTD
CWL
Gd, Didsbury, AB, T0M 0W0

Emp Here 60   *Sales* 11,354,240
SIC 1389 Oil and gas field services, nec
Pr Pr Christopher Overwater
 William Shaw

D-U-N-S 24-042-4556   (SL)
DIDSBURY DISTRICT HEALTH SERVICES
1210 20 Ave, Didsbury, AB, T0M 0W0
(403) 335-9393
Emp Here 243   *Sales* 16,926,882
SIC 8062 General medical and surgical hospitals

D-U-N-S 24-677-7846   (BR)
HARMATTAN GAS PROCESSING LIMITED PARTNERSHIP
ALTAGAS
Gd, Didsbury, AB, T0M 0W0
(403) 335-3321
Emp Here 65
SIC 1389 Oil and gas field services, nec

D-U-N-S 24-165-4078   (HQ)
PARKLAND AGRI SERVICES CORP
(*Suby of* Parkland Agri Services Corp)
Gd, Didsbury, AB, T0M 0W0
(403) 335-3055
Emp Here 26   *Emp Total* 32
Sales 8,932,560
SIC 5191 Farm supplies
Pr Pr Anthony Overwater
 Jim Pendergast
 Tom Reid

Donnelly, AB T0H

D-U-N-S 20-970-7769   (BR)
HIGH PRAIRIE SCHOOL DIVISION NO 48
G P VANIER JUNIOR & SENIOR SCHOOL
5504 Centennial Ave, Donnelly, AB, T0H 1G0
(780) 925-3959
Emp Here 30
SIC 8211 Elementary and secondary schools

Drayton Valley, AB T7A

D-U-N-S 20-690-8480   (HQ)
6518729 CANADA INC
3702 62 St, Drayton Valley, AB, T7A 1S1
(780) 542-5141
Emp Here 50   *Emp Total* 25,438
Sales 62,476,413
SIC 1389 Oil and gas field services, nec
Pr Alain Bedard
Fin Ex Dale Symon

D-U-N-S 20-080-0886   (BR)
AECOM PRODUCTION SERVICES LTD
FLINT FIELD SERVICES LTD
6242 56 Ave, Drayton Valley, AB, T7A 1T1
(780) 542-5348
Emp Here 25
SIC 4619 Pipelines, nec

D-U-N-S 25-231-7888   (BR)
ALBERTA TREASURY BRANCHES
ATB FINANCIAL
5017 51 Ave, Drayton Valley, AB, T7A 1S2
(780) 542-4406
Emp Here 20
SIC 6036 Savings institutions, except federal

D-U-N-S 20-437-5943   (BR)
BP CANADA ENERGY COMPANY
(*Suby of* BP P.L.C.)
24 48-07 W5 Gd Stn Main Gd Stn Main, Drayton Valley, AB, T7A 1T1
(780) 542-8100
Emp Here 50
SIC 4922 Natural gas transmission

D-U-N-S 20-114-6144   (SL)
BAILEY'S WELDING & CONSTRUCTION INC
6205 56 Ave, Drayton Valley, AB, T7A 1S5
(780) 542-3578
Emp Here 55   *Sales* 6,631,680
SIC 1799 Special trade contractors, nec
Pr Pr Dennis Bailey
 Rhonda Bailey

D-U-N-S 20-364-2210   (BR)
BELLATRIX EXPLORATION LTD
5516 Industrial Rd, Drayton Valley, AB, T7A 1R1
(403) 266-8670
Emp Here 85
SIC 1381 Drilling oil and gas wells

D-U-N-S 20-250-4452   (BR)
CASCADE ENERGY SERVICES L.P.
6209 56 Ave, Drayton Valley, AB, T7A 1R6
(780) 542-5958
Emp Here 20

SIC 4225 General warehousing and storage

D-U-N-S 24-103-9424   (BR)
CONOCOPHILLIPS WESTERN CANADA PARTNERSHIP
BURLINGTON RESOURCES
Gd Stn Main, Drayton Valley, AB, T7A 1T1

Emp Here 80
SIC 1311 Crude petroleum and natural gas

D-U-N-S 20-278-9723   (BR)
FOUNTAIN TIRE HOLDINGS LTD
FOUNTAIN TIRE DRAYTON VALLEY
55058 58 Ave, Drayton Valley, AB, T7A 1R7
(780) 542-4001
Emp Here 20
SIC 5531 Auto and home supply stores

D-U-N-S 20-884-1028   (BR)
KEYERA PARTNERSHIP
5211 Industrial Rd, Drayton Valley, AB, T7A 1R1
(780) 542-3770
Emp Here 55
SIC 1389 Oil and gas field services, nec

D-U-N-S 25-995-0041   (BR)
LAKEVIEW MANAGEMENT INC
LAKEVIEW INNS & SUITES
(Suby of Lakeview Management Inc)
4302 50 St, Drayton Valley, AB, T7A 1M4
(780) 542-3200
Emp Here 20
SIC 7011 Hotels and motels

D-U-N-S 20-852-5191   (BR)
LINCOLN COUNTY OILFIELD SERVICES LTD
5741 50a St, Drayton Valley, AB, T7A 1S8
(780) 542-6485
Emp Here 50
SIC 1389 Oil and gas field services, nec

D-U-N-S 20-253-5626   (BR)
LOBLAWS INC
EXTRA FOODS
5212 50 St, Drayton Valley, AB, T7A 1S6
(780) 542-2645
Emp Here 60
SIC 5411 Grocery stores

D-U-N-S 24-732-3124   (SL)
NELSON BROS. OILFIELD SERVICES 1997 LTD
(Suby of Nelson Bros. Oilfield Services Ltd)
5399 Jubilee Ave, Drayton Valley, AB, T7A 1R9
(780) 542-5777
Emp Here 35   Sales 5,030,400
SIC 1389 Oil and gas field services, nec
Pr Pr Donald Nelson
 Garry Nelson

D-U-N-S 25-362-5420   (BR)
OBSIDIAN ENERGY LTD
6521 50 Ave W, Drayton Valley, AB, T7A 1S1
(780) 542-8600
Emp Here 60
SIC 1311 Crude petroleum and natural gas

D-U-N-S 24-332-6931   (BR)
PEMBINA PIPELINE CORPORATION
PEMBINA PIPELINE
6113 50 Ave, Drayton Valley, AB, T7A 1R8
(780) 542-5341
Emp Here 50
SIC 4612 Crude petroleum pipelines

D-U-N-S 25-272-3291   (BR)
ST THOMAS AQUINAS ROMAN CATHOLIC SEPARATE REGIONAL DIVISION #38
ST ANTHONY SCHOOL
4921 43 St, Drayton Valley, AB, T7A 1P5
(780) 542-4396
Emp Here 30
SIC 8211 Elementary and secondary schools

D-U-N-S 24-353-0131   (BR)
TARPON ENERGY SERVICES LTD
4808 56 Ave Suite 6301, Drayton Valley, AB, T7A 0A7
(780) 514-7659
Emp Here 40
SIC 1389 Oil and gas field services, nec

D-U-N-S 25-230-1510   (BR)
TECHMATION ELECTRIC & CONTROLS LTD
5736 50a St, Drayton Valley, AB, T7A 1R7
(780) 542-2723
Emp Here 30
SIC 7629 Electrical repair shops

D-U-N-S 24-060-7080   (BR)
TRICAN WELL SERVICE LTD
7497 5 Hwy W Ste 22, Drayton Valley, AB, T7A 1S8
(780) 542-5331
Emp Here 40
SIC 1389 Oil and gas field services, nec

D-U-N-S 24-319-1074   (BR)
WAL-MART CANADA CORP
WALMART
5217 Power Centre Blvd, Drayton Valley, AB, T7A 0A5
(780) 514-3207
Emp Here 120
SIC 5311 Department stores

D-U-N-S 25-318-9591   (BR)
WASTE MANAGEMENT OF CANADA CORPORATION
(Suby of Waste Management, Inc.)
5450 55th St, Drayton Valley, AB, T7A 1R3
(780) 542-6764
Emp Here 40
SIC 4953 Refuse systems

D-U-N-S 25-684-2733   (BR)
WEYERHAEUSER COMPANY LIMITED
(Suby of Weyerhaeuser Company)
Gd Stn Main, Drayton Valley, AB, T7A 1T1
(780) 542-8000
Emp Here 500
SIC 2493 Reconstituted wood products

D-U-N-S 20-653-1993   (BR)
WILD ROSE SCHOOL DIVISION NO. 66
FRANK MADDOCK HIGH SCHOOL
(Suby of Wild Rose School Division No. 66)
4801 43 St Suite 4801, Drayton Valley, AB, T7A 1P4
(780) 542-4401
Emp Here 50
SIC 8211 Elementary and secondary schools

D-U-N-S 20-688-8807   (BR)
WILD ROSE SCHOOL DIVISION NO. 66
DRAYTON CHRISTIAN SCHOOL
(Suby of Wild Rose School Division No. 66)
4762 50 St, Drayton Valley, AB, T7A 1P1
(780) 542-7066
Emp Here 40
SIC 8211 Elementary and secondary schools

D-U-N-S 20-029-4655   (BR)
WILD ROSE SCHOOL DIVISION NO. 66
AURORA ELEMENTARY SCHOOL
(Suby of Wild Rose School Division No. 66)
3901 55 Ave, Drayton Valley, AB, T7A 1N9
(780) 542-9355
Emp Here 39
SIC 8211 Elementary and secondary schools

D-U-N-S 20-206-1805   (BR)
WILD ROSE SCHOOL DIVISION NO. 66
H W PICK UP JUNIOR HIGHSCHOOL
(Suby of Wild Rose School Division No. 66)
3505 58 Ave, Drayton Valley, AB, T7A 0B8
(780) 542-4495
Emp Here 50
SIC 8211 Elementary and secondary schools

Drumheller, AB T0J

D-U-N-S 25-316-7340   (BR)
ATCO ELECTRIC LTD
ATCO DRUMHELLER DIVISION
90 Railway Ave, Drumheller, AB, T0J 0Y0
(403) 823-1436
Emp Here 70
SIC 4911 Electric services

D-U-N-S 24-174-2035   (BR)
BAKER HUGHES CANADA COMPANY
(Suby of Baker Hughes, A GE Company)
4 Hy-Grade Cres, Drumheller, AB, T0J 0Y0

Emp Here 38
SIC 1389 Oil and gas field services, nec

D-U-N-S 24-334-2024   (BR)
BLACKWATCH ENERGY SERVICES OPERATING CORP
561 Premier Rd, Drumheller, AB, T0J 0Y0

Emp Here 28
SIC 1389 Oil and gas field services, nec

D-U-N-S 20-070-2699   (BR)
CANADIAN NATURAL RESOURCES LIMITED
Gd, Drumheller, AB, T0J 0Y0
(403) 787-3980
Emp Here 25
SIC 1311 Crude petroleum and natural gas

D-U-N-S 20-713-2072   (BR)
CHRIST THE REDEEMER CATHOLIC SEPARATE REGIONAL DIVISION NO. 3
ST ANTHONY'S SCHOOL
1000 North Dinosaur Trail, Drumheller, AB, T0J 0Y1
(403) 823-3485
Emp Here 42
SIC 8211 Elementary and secondary schools

D-U-N-S 20-573-3491   (BR)
COMPAGNIE DES CHEMINS DE FER NATIONAUX DU CANADA
COMPAGNIE DES CHEMINS DE FER NATIONAUX DU CANADA
Railroad Ave, Drumheller, AB, T0J 0Y0
(403) 823-7162
Emp Here 20
SIC 4011 Railroads, line-haul operating

D-U-N-S 20-787-5381   (SL)
DRUMHELLER AND DISTRICT SENIORS FOUNDATION
696 6 Ave E, Drumheller, AB, T0J 0Y5
(403) 823-3290
Emp Here 53   Sales 2,115,860
SIC 8322 Individual and family services

D-U-N-S 20-957-5088   (BR)
EOG RESOURCES CANADA INC
180 Riverside Dr E, Drumheller, AB, T0J 0Y4

Emp Here 30
SIC 1311 Crude petroleum and natural gas

D-U-N-S 24-319-9846   (BR)
GLOVER INTERNATIONAL TRUCKS LTD
(Suby of Glover International Trucks Ltd)
585 Premier Rd, Drumheller, AB, T0J 0Y1
(403) 823-6001
Emp Here 20
SIC 7699 Repair services, nec

D-U-N-S 25-118-8348   (BR)
GOLDEN HILLS SCHOOL DIVISION #75
DRUMHELLER COMPOSITE HIGH SCHOOL
450 17 St E, Drumheller, AB, T0J 0Y5
(403) 823-5171
Emp Here 44
SIC 8211 Elementary and secondary schools

D-U-N-S 25-118-8363   (BR)

D-U-N-S 25-118-8348   (BR)
GOLDEN HILLS SCHOOL DIVISION #75
GREEN TREE SCHOOL
1050 12 Ave Se Ss 7, Drumheller, AB, T0J 0Y7
(403) 823-5244
Emp Here 40
SIC 8211 Elementary and secondary schools

D-U-N-S 20-571-6173   (BR)
GOVERNMENT OF THE PROVINCE OF ALBERTA
HUMAN SERVICES ALBERTA WORKS
180 Riverside Dr E, Drumheller, AB, T0J 0Y4
(403) 823-1616
Emp Here 20
SIC 8399 Social services, nec

D-U-N-S 24-042-8714   (BR)
GOVERNMENT OF THE PROVINCE OF ALBERTA
ROYAL TYRRELL MUSEUM
Gdd, Drumheller, AB, T0J 0Y0
(403) 823-7707
Emp Here 65
SIC 8412 Museums and art galleries

D-U-N-S 20-635-9713   (HQ)
HI-WAY 9 EXPRESS LTD
711 Elgin Close, Drumheller, AB, T0J 0Y0
(403) 823-4242
Emp Here 35   Emp Total 5,515
Sales 28,153,158
SIC 4212 Local trucking, without storage
VP VP Reg Trentham
Fin Ex Shannon Wade
 Joe Hearn
 Virginia Rathberger
 Jerry Allen
 Graham Mcdonald

D-U-N-S 24-271-7882   (SL)
HUTTERIAN BRETHREN CHURCH OF STARLAND
STARLAND COLONY
Gd, Drumheller, AB, T0J 0Y0
(403) 772-3855
Emp Here 70   Sales 4,596,524
SIC 8661 Religious organizations

D-U-N-S 24-356-5269   (BR)
LOBLAW COMPANIES LIMITED
EXTRA FOODS
1252 Hwy 9 S, Drumheller, AB, T0J 0Y0
(403) 823-4795
Emp Here 20
SIC 5411 Grocery stores

D-U-N-S 24-024-1385   (BR)
MAC'S CONVENIENCE STORES INC
MAC'S CONVENIENCE STORES
175 South Railway Ave, Drumheller, AB, T0J 0Y6
(403) 823-2207
Emp Here 20
SIC 5411 Grocery stores

D-U-N-S 24-059-3439   (BR)
PRONGHORN CONTROLS LTD
601 9 St Sw, Drumheller, AB, T0J 0Y0
(403) 823-8426
Emp Here 40
SIC 1389 Oil and gas field services, nec

D-U-N-S 24-395-0768   (BR)
TECHMATION ELECTRIC & CONTROLS LTD
570 Premier Rd Bay, Drumheller, AB, T0J 0Y0
(403) 823-7410
Emp Here 25
SIC 4931 Electric and other services combined

D-U-N-S 24-647-4902   (BR)
W. RALSTON (CANADA) INC
1100 Railway Ave S, Drumheller, AB, T0J 0Y0
(403) 823-3468
Emp Here 75
SIC 3089 Plastics products, nec

▲ Public Company   ■ Public Company Family Member   **HQ** Headquarters   **BR** Branch   **SL** Single Location

D-U-N-S 24-319-6917   (BR)
WAL-MART CANADA CORP
WALMART
1801 South Railway Ave, Drumheller, AB, T0J 0Y0
(403) 820-7744
Emp Here 120
SIC 5311 Department stores

D-U-N-S 20-080-2775   (SL)
WESTERGARD MOTORS (DRUMHELLER) LTD
WESTERGARD MOTORS
1011 Hwy 9 S, Drumheller, AB, T0J 0Y0
(403) 823-2500
Emp Here 20   *Sales* 10,048,000
SIC 5511 New and used car dealers
Pr Pr James O'dwyer
Connie O'dwyer
Off Mgr Janice Kelm

Drumheller, AB T1A

D-U-N-S 24-421-7993   (BR)
ATCO ELECTRIC LTD
ATCO ELECTRIC
610 12th St Sw, Drumheller, AB, T1A 4T9
(403) 823-1428
Emp Here 63
SIC 4911 Electric services

Duchess, AB T0J

D-U-N-S 20-712-0309   (BR)
GRASSLANDS REGIONAL DIVISION 6
SPRINGSIDE COLONY SCHOOL
Gd, Duchess, AB, T0J 0Z0
(403) 378-4720
Emp Here 50
SIC 8211 Elementary and secondary schools

D-U-N-S 20-028-3336   (BR)
GRASSLANDS REGIONAL DIVISION 6
DUCHESS SCHOOL
315 Louise Ave, Duchess, AB, T0J 0Z0
(403) 378-4948
Emp Here 35
SIC 8211 Elementary and secondary schools

Duffield, AB T0E

D-U-N-S 24-493-8622   (BR)
PAUL BAND INDIAN RESERVE
PAUL BAND EDUCATION
Gd, Duffield, AB, T0E 0N0
(780) 892-2025
Emp Here 35
SIC 8211 Elementary and secondary schools

Dunmore, AB T1B

D-U-N-S 20-028-9895   (BR)
PRAIRIE ROSE SCHOOL DIVISION NO 8
EAGLE BUTTE HIGH SCHOOL
1150 Eagle Butte Rd, Dunmore, AB, T1B 0J3
(403) 528-1996
Emp Here 64
SIC 8211 Elementary and secondary schools

D-U-N-S 20-712-1448   (BR)
PRAIRIE ROSE SCHOOL DIVISION NO 8
MAYFIELD COLONY
918 2 Ave Suite 204, Dunmore, AB, T1B 0K3

Emp Here 50

SIC 8211 Elementary and secondary schools

Eckville, AB T0M

D-U-N-S 24-011-5902   (BR)
CONOCOPHILLIPS WESTERN CANADA PARTNERSHIP
Gd, Eckville, AB, T0M 0X0
(403) 746-8100
Emp Here 50
SIC 1382 Oil and gas exploration services

D-U-N-S 20-080-3344   (HQ)
ECKVILLE CO-OPERATIVE ASSOCIATION LIMITED, THE
(*Suby of* Eckville Co-Operative Association Limited, The)
4924 50 Ave, Eckville, AB, T0M 0X0
(403) 746-2102
Emp Here 32   *Emp Total* 40
Sales 6,531,200
SIC 5411 Grocery stores
Genl Mgr Shawn Adair

D-U-N-S 20-023-9890   (BR)
WOLF CREEK SCHOOL DIVISION NO.72
ECKVILLE ELEMENTARY SCHOOL
Gd, Eckville, AB, T0M 0X0
(403) 746-2297
Emp Here 22
SIC 8211 Elementary and secondary schools

Edberg, AB T0B

D-U-N-S 20-267-2791   (SL)
SIEMENS CONSTRUCTION INC
Gd, Edberg, AB, T0B 1J0
(780) 877-2478
Emp Here 30   *Sales* 7,381,120
SIC 1542 Nonresidential construction, nec
Pr Vernon Siemens

Edgerton, AB T0B

D-U-N-S 25-268-7967   (BR)
BUFFALO TRAIL PUBLIC SCHOOLS REGIONAL DIVISION NO. 28
EDGERTON PUBLIC SCHOOL
5216 53rd St, Edgerton, AB, T0B 1K0
(780) 755-3810
Emp Here 22
SIC 8211 Elementary and secondary schools

Edmonton, AB T2H

D-U-N-S 24-786-2113   (BR)
WORLEYPARSONSCORD LTD
8500 Macleod Trail Se Suite 400s, Edmonton, AB, T2H 2N1

Emp Here 35
SIC 8711 Engineering services

Edmonton, AB T4A

D-U-N-S 20-919-7024   (BR)
STILES' CLOTHIERS INC
322-261055 Crossiron Blvd, Edmonton, AB, T4A 0G3
(403) 452-6110
Emp Here 20
SIC 5611 Men's and boys' clothing stores

Edmonton, AB T5A

D-U-N-S 25-272-6302   (BR)
ALBERTA HEALTH SERVICES
NORTHEAST COMMUNITY HEALTH CENTRE
14007 50 St Nw, Edmonton, AB, T5A 5E4
(780) 342-4000
Emp Here 229
SIC 8062 General medical and surgical hospitals

D-U-N-S 25-236-1746   (BR)
ALBERTA TREASURY BRANCHES
ATB FINANCIAL
350 Manning Cross Nw, Edmonton, AB, T5A 5A1
(780) 422-6003
Emp Here 30
SIC 6036 Savings institutions, except federal

D-U-N-S 24-227-5352   (SL)
ALL-SIDE CONTRACTING LTD
12812 52 St Nw, Edmonton, AB, T5A 0B6
(780) 473-3959
Emp Here 50   *Sales* 4,961,328
SIC 1761 Roofing, siding, and sheetMetal work

D-U-N-S 20-589-4954   (BR)
BANQUE TORONTO-DOMINION, LA
TD CANADA TRUST
(*Suby of* Toronto-Dominion Bank, The)
13318 50 St Nw, Edmonton, AB, T5A 4Z8
(780) 456-8578
Emp Here 20
SIC 6021 National commercial banks

D-U-N-S 25-269-8675   (SL)
BATEMAN FOODS (1995) LTD
13504 Victoria Trail Nw, Edmonton, AB, T5A 5C9
(780) 432-1535
Emp Here 200   *Sales* 38,753,900
SIC 5411 Grocery stores
Pr Pr Michael Bateman
VP VP Deanne Bateman

D-U-N-S 24-879-9785   (SL)
CSB HOLDINGS LTD
12907 57 St Nw, Edmonton, AB, T5A 0E7
(780) 437-6188
Emp Here 125   *Sales* 19,992,000
SIC 6719 Holding companies, nec
Pr Pr Brent Komarnicki

D-U-N-S 25-303-5331   (BR)
CANADIAN IMPERIAL BANK OF COMMERCE
CIBC
13610 50 St Nw Suite 2769, Edmonton, AB, T5A 4Y3
(780) 473-3550
Emp Here 26
SIC 6021 National commercial banks

D-U-N-S 20-969-4637   (SL)
CHRISTIAN SENIOR CITIZENS HOME SOCIETY OF NORTHERN ALBERTA, THE
EMMANUEL HOME
13425 57 St Nw Suite 223, Edmonton, AB, T5A 2G1
(780) 478-2051
Emp Here 50   *Sales* 2,165,628
SIC 8361 Residential care

D-U-N-S 25-206-2476   (SL)
EARL'S RESTAURANT (CLAREVIEW) LTD
13330 50 St Nw, Edmonton, AB, T5A 4Z8
(780) 473-9008
Emp Here 150   *Sales* 4,523,563
SIC 5812 Eating places

D-U-N-S 20-028-3989   (BR)
EDMONTON CATHOLIC SEPARATE SCHOOL DISTRICT NO.7

ST. MARIA GORETTI CATHOLIC ELEMENTARY SCHOOL
(*Suby of* Edmonton Catholic Separate School District No.7)
4214 127 Ave Nw, Edmonton, AB, T5A 3K6
(780) 475-0158
Emp Here 45
SIC 8211 Elementary and secondary schools

D-U-N-S 20-028-3831   (BR)
EDMONTON CATHOLIC SEPARATE SCHOOL DISTRICT NO.7
ST. DOMINIC CATHOLIC ELEMENTARY SCHOOL
(*Suby of* Edmonton Catholic Separate School District No.7)
5804 144 Ave Nw, Edmonton, AB, T5A 1K5
(780) 475-5604
Emp Here 40
SIC 8211 Elementary and secondary schools

D-U-N-S 25-451-9002   (BR)
EDMONTON CATHOLIC SEPARATE SCHOOL DISTRICT NO.7
ST ELIZABETH SETON ELEMENTARY JUNIOR HIGH SCHOOL
(*Suby of* Edmonton Catholic Separate School District No.7)
3711 135 Ave Nw, Edmonton, AB, T5A 2V6
(780) 478-7751
Emp Here 50
SIC 8211 Elementary and secondary schools

D-U-N-S 20-592-1112   (BR)
EDMONTON SCHOOL DISTRICT NO. 7
BELMONT ELEMENTARY SCHOOL
3310 132a Ave Nw, Edmonton, AB, T5A 3T1
(780) 476-9590
Emp Here 20
SIC 8211 Elementary and secondary schools

D-U-N-S 20-027-3667   (BR)
EDMONTON SCHOOL DISTRICT NO. 7
HOMESTEADER ELEMENTARY SCHOOL
4455 128 Ave Nw, Edmonton, AB, T5A 3M9
(780) 478-1139
Emp Here 47
SIC 8211 Elementary and secondary schools

D-U-N-S 25-452-0539   (BR)
EDMONTON SCHOOL DISTRICT NO. 7
SIFTON ELEMENTARY SCHOOL
4305 134 Ave Nw, Edmonton, AB, T5A 3R5
(780) 476-7953
Emp Here 30
SIC 8211 Elementary and secondary schools

D-U-N-S 20-027-4038   (BR)
EDMONTON SCHOOL DISTRICT NO. 7
STEELE HEIGHTS JUNIOR HIGH SCHOOL
14607 59 St Nw, Edmonton, AB, T5A 1Y3
(780) 478-5319
Emp Here 42
SIC 8211 Elementary and secondary schools

D-U-N-S 20-029-2568   (BR)
EDMONTON SCHOOL DISTRICT NO. 7
YORK ACADEMIC SCHOOL
13915 61 St Nw, Edmonton, AB, T5A 1P3
(780) 476-6336
Emp Here 25
SIC 8211 Elementary and secondary schools

D-U-N-S 25-451-9721   (BR)
EDMONTON SCHOOL DISTRICT NO. 7
MCLEOD ELEMENTARY SCHOOL
14807 59 St Nw, Edmonton, AB, T5A 1Y3
(780) 478-2927
Emp Here 32
SIC 8211 Elementary and secondary schools

D-U-N-S 24-978-5338   (BR)
HOME DEPOT OF CANADA INC
HOME DEPOT
(*Suby of* The Home Depot Inc)
13304 50 St Nw, Edmonton, AB, T5A 4Z8
(780) 478-7133
Emp Here 120

SIC 5251 Hardware stores

D-U-N-S 24-781-5751   (BR)
INTERNATIONAL FITNESS HOLDINGS INC
WORLD HEALTH
13746 50 St Nw, Edmonton, AB, T5A 5J6
(780) 473-5549
Emp Here 40
SIC 7991 Physical fitness facilities

D-U-N-S 25-311-2668   (BR)
MCDONALD'S RESTAURANTS OF CANADA LIMITED
MCDONALD'S 7734
(*Suby of* McDonald's Corporation)
13504 Fort Rd Nw, Edmonton, AB, T5A 1C5
(780) 414-3316
Emp Here 46
SIC 5812 Eating places

D-U-N-S 20-810-3908   (BR)
REVERA LONG TERM CARE INC
MILLER CROSSING CARE CENTRE
14251 50 St Nw, Edmonton, AB, T5A 5J4
(780) 478-9212
Emp Here 170
SIC 8051 Skilled nursing care facilities

D-U-N-S 25-271-0801   (BR)
SOBEYS WEST INC
500 Manning Cross Nw, Edmonton, AB, T5A 5A1
(780) 475-2896
Emp Here 210
SIC 5411 Grocery stores

D-U-N-S 25-498-9494   (BR)
STAPLES CANADA INC
STAPLES THE BUSINESS DEPOT
(*Suby of* Staples, Inc.)
13118 50 St Nw, Edmonton, AB, T5A 5B5
(780) 472-7379
Emp Here 30
SIC 5943 Stationery stores

Edmonton, AB T5B

D-U-N-S 24-133-6663   (SL)
712934 ALBERTA LTD
AXE MUSIC
11931 Wayne Gretzky Dr, Edmonton, AB, T5B 1Z7
(780) 471-2001
Emp Here 50   *Sales* 4,331,255
SIC 5736 Musical instrument stores

D-U-N-S 25-236-1944   (BR)
ALBERTA TREASURY BRANCHES
ATB FINANCIAL
8804 118 Ave Nw, Edmonton, AB, T5B 0T4
(780) 427-4171
Emp Here 25
SIC 6036 Savings institutions, except federal

D-U-N-S 20-108-8379   (BR)
BANK OF NOVA SCOTIA, THE
SCOTIA BANK
8108 118 Ave Nw, Edmonton, AB, T5B 0S1
(780) 448-7735
Emp Here 21
SIC 6021 National commercial banks

D-U-N-S 20-069-0985   (HQ)
BEN CALF ROBE SOCIETY OF EDMONTON
(*Suby of* Ben Calf Robe Society Of Edmonton)
12046 77 St Nw, Edmonton, AB, T5B 2G7
(780) 477-6648
Emp Here 75   *Emp Total* 85
Sales 3,356,192
SIC 8322 Individual and family services

D-U-N-S 20-899-8468   (HQ)
CONCORDIA UNIVERSITY COLLEGE OF ALBERTA
CONCORDIA UNIVERSITY OF EDMONTON
7128 Ada Blvd Nw, Edmonton, AB, T5B 4E4

(780) 479-8481
Emp Here 300   *Emp Total* 150
Sales 43,225,925
SIC 8221 Colleges and universities
Pr Pr Gerald Krispin
VP Richard Willie
VP Fin VP Fin Richard Currie
 Martin Mueller
Dir Mark Damielson
Dir Ken Eifert
Dir Merv Fingas
Dir Al Gerdung
Dir Joel Haberstock
Dir Mark Hennig

D-U-N-S 20-066-5060   (SL)
DISTINCTIVE EMPLOYMENT COUNSELLING SERVICES
D.E.C.S.A.
11515 71 St Nw, Edmonton, AB, T5B 1W1
(780) 474-2500
Emp Here 65   *Sales* 3,064,349
SIC 8331 Job training and related services

D-U-N-S 20-712-8195   (BR)
EDMONTON CATHOLIC SEPARATE SCHOOL DISTRICT NO.7
ST. ALPHONSUS CATHOLIC ELEMENTARY SCHOOL
(*Suby of* Edmonton Catholic Separate School District No.7)
11624 81 St Nw, Edmonton, AB, T5B 2S2
(780) 477-2513
Emp Here 50
SIC 8211 Elementary and secondary schools

D-U-N-S 20-028-3849   (BR)
EDMONTON CATHOLIC SEPARATE SCHOOL DISTRICT NO.7
ST. GERARD CATHOLIC ELEMENTARY SCHOOL
(*Suby of* Edmonton Catholic Separate School District No.7)
12415 85 St Nw, Edmonton, AB, T5B 3H3
(780) 474-5208
Emp Here 21
SIC 8211 Elementary and secondary schools

D-U-N-S 24-025-5237   (BR)
EDMONTON MENNONITE CENTRE FOR NEWCOMERS
EMCN
8914 118 Ave Nw, Edmonton, AB, T5B 0T6
(780) 421-7400
Emp Here 25
SIC 8331 Job training and related services

D-U-N-S 25-364-2656   (BR)
EDMONTON NORTHLANDS
NORTHLAND PARK
7410 Borden Park Rd, Edmonton, AB, T5B 4W8
(780) 471-7278
Emp Here 250
SIC 7922 Theatrical producers and services

D-U-N-S 24-360-4811   (BR)
EDMONTON NORTHLANDS
NORTHLANDS SPECTRUM
7410 Borden Park Rd Nw, Edmonton, AB, T5B 0H8
(780) 471-7378
Emp Here 400
SIC 7999 Amusement and recreation, nec

D-U-N-S 24-318-6751   (BR)
EDMONTON NORTHLANDS
REXALL PLACE
7424 118 Ave Nw, Edmonton, AB, T5B 4M9
(780) 471-7210
Emp Here 2,100
SIC 7922 Theatrical producers and services

D-U-N-S 20-030-6830   (BR)
EDMONTON SCHOOL DISTRICT NO. 7
EASTGLEN HIGH SCHOOL
11430 68 St Nw, Edmonton, AB, T5B 1P1
(780) 479-1991
Emp Here 75

SIC 8211 Elementary and secondary schools

D-U-N-S 20-028-3484   (BR)
EDMONTON SCHOOL DISTRICT NO. 7
DELTON ELEMENTARY SCHOOL
12126 89 St Nw, Edmonton, AB, T5B 3W4
(780) 477-8742
Emp Here 30
SIC 8211 Elementary and secondary schools

D-U-N-S 20-712-5894   (BR)
EDMONTON SCHOOL DISTRICT NO. 7
PARKDALE SCHOOL
11648 85 St Nw, Edmonton, AB, T5B 3E5
(780) 474-5942
Emp Here 50
SIC 8211 Elementary and secondary schools

D-U-N-S 24-396-9128   (SL)
FABKO FOOD LTD
8715 126 Ave Nw, Edmonton, AB, T5B 1G8
(780) 471-1758
Emp Here 35   *Sales* 3,429,153
SIC 5421 Meat and fish markets

D-U-N-S 24-005-6291   (BR)
FLOFORM INDUSTRIES LTD
FLO-FORM COUNTER TOPS
7630 Yellowhead Trail Nw, Edmonton, AB, T5B 1G3
(780) 474-7999
Emp Here 60
SIC 2541 Wood partitions and fixtures

D-U-N-S 20-647-5662   (BR)
GREAT PACIFIC INDUSTRIES INC
SAVE-ON-FOODS
8124 112 Ave Nw, Edmonton, AB, T5B 4W4
(780) 471-6244
Emp Here 160
SIC 5411 Grocery stores

D-U-N-S 25-362-5644   (BR)
LENNOX CANADA INC
ROBS/ALBERTAN SERVICE EXPERT
(*Suby of* Lennox Canada Inc)
12235 Fort Rd Nw, Edmonton, AB, T5B 4H2
(780) 477-3261
Emp Here 43
SIC 1711 Plumbing, heating, air-conditioning

D-U-N-S 24-139-9521   (HQ)
LIFT BOSS INC
LIFT BOSS MATERIAL HANDLING GROUP
(*Suby of* Lift Boss Inc)
7912 Yellowhead Trail Nw, Edmonton, AB, T5B 1G3
(780) 474-9900
Emp Here 26   *Emp Total* 39
Sales 7,150,149
SIC 5084 Industrial machinery and equipment
 Andre Gagnon
 Dale Beatty
 Marc Tougas

D-U-N-S 20-276-9899   (BR)
PREMIUM BRANDS HOLDINGS CORPORATION
QUALITY FAST FOOD
12251 William Short Rd Nw, Edmonton, AB, T5B 2B7
(780) 474-5201
Emp Here 100
SIC 2099 Food preparations, nec

D-U-N-S 25-400-2454   (BR)
PREMIUM BRANDS OPERATING LIMITED PARTNERSHIP
GRIMM'S FINE FOODS
12130 68 St Nw, Edmonton, AB, T5B 1R1

Emp Here 60
SIC 2011 Meat packing plants

D-U-N-S 24-396-9854   (BR)
ROBYN'S TRANSPORTATION & DISTRIBUTION SERVICES LTD
(*Suby of* Robyn's Transportation & Distribution Services Ltd)

6805 Yellowhead Trail Nw, Edmonton, AB, T5B 4J9

Emp Here 30
SIC 4212 Local trucking, without storage

D-U-N-S 20-345-8476   (BR)
ROYAL CANADIAN LEGION, THE
NORWOOD BRANCH #178
(*Suby of* Royal Canadian Legion, The)
11150 82 St Nw Suite 178, Edmonton, AB, T5B 2V1
(780) 479-4277
Emp Here 20
SIC 8641 Civic and social associations

D-U-N-S 20-084-2151   (SL)
SANDS MOTOR HOTEL LTD
12340 Fort Rd Nw, Edmonton, AB, T5B 4H5
(780) 474-5476
Emp Here 50   *Sales* 2,188,821
SIC 7011 Hotels and motels

D-U-N-S 24-671-7946   (HQ)
SCANDINAVIAN BUILDING SERVICES LTD
(*Suby of* Scandinavian Building Services Ltd)
11651 71 St Nw, Edmonton, AB, T5B 1W3
(780) 477-3311
Emp Here 98   *Emp Total* 100
Sales 2,918,428
SIC 7349 Building maintenance services, nec

D-U-N-S 20-898-7263   (BR)
SOBEYS WEST INC
COLISEUM SAFEWAY
8118 118 Ave Nw, Edmonton, AB, T5B 0S1
(780) 461-4880
Emp Here 130
SIC 5411 Grocery stores

Edmonton, AB T5C

D-U-N-S 24-333-3593   (BR)
ARMY & NAVY DEPT. STORE LIMITED
ARMY & NAVY DEPT. STORE NO.12
100 Londonderry Mall Unit A, Edmonton, AB, T5C 3C8

Emp Here 75
SIC 5399 Miscellaneous general merchandise

D-U-N-S 24-523-4489   (BR)
BANQUE TORONTO-DOMINION, LA
TD BANK FINANCIAL GROUP
(*Suby of* Toronto-Dominion Bank, The)
36 Londonderry Mall Nw, Edmonton, AB, T5C 3C8
(780) 448-8630
Emp Here 33
SIC 6021 National commercial banks

D-U-N-S 20-712-7197   (BR)
EDMONTON CATHOLIC SEPARATE SCHOOL DISTRICT NO.7
FR. LEO GREEN SCHOOL
(*Suby of* Edmonton Catholic Separate School District No.7)
7512 144 Ave Nw, Edmonton, AB, T5C 2R7
(780) 476-0606
Emp Here 31
SIC 8211 Elementary and secondary schools

D-U-N-S 20-027-3675   (BR)
EDMONTON CATHOLIC SEPARATE SCHOOL DISTRICT NO.7
ST. VLADIMIR CATHOLIC ELEMENTARY SCHOOL
(*Suby of* Edmonton Catholic Separate School District No.7)
7510 132 Ave Nw, Edmonton, AB, T5C 2A9
(780) 476-4613
Emp Here 25
SIC 8211 Elementary and secondary schools

D-U-N-S 25-272-3259   (BR)

EDMONTON CATHOLIC SEPARATE SCHOOL DISTRICT NO.7
ST. FRANCIS ASSISI CATHOLIC ELEMENTARY SCHOOL
(*Suby of* Edmonton Catholic Separate School District No.7)
6614 129 Ave Nw, Edmonton, AB, T5C 1V7
(780) 476-7634
Emp Here 45
SIC 8211 Elementary and secondary schools

D-U-N-S 20-028-3583　　(BR)
EDMONTON SCHOOL DISTRICT NO. 7
JA FIFE ELEMENTARY SCHOOL
15004 76 St Nw, Edmonton, AB, T5C 1C2
(780) 476-0775
Emp Here 25
SIC 8211 Elementary and secondary schools

D-U-N-S 25-452-0166　　(BR)
EDMONTON SCHOOL DISTRICT NO. 7
PRINCETON ELEMENTARY SCHOOL
7720 130 Ave Nw, Edmonton, AB, T5C 1Y2
(780) 476-2344
Emp Here 25
SIC 8211 Elementary and secondary schools

D-U-N-S 20-028-3625　　(BR)
EDMONTON SCHOOL DISTRICT NO. 7
DELWOOD ELEMENTARY SCHOOL
7315 Delwood Rd Nw, Edmonton, AB, T5C 3A9
(780) 476-3969
Emp Here 43
SIC 8211 Elementary and secondary schools

D-U-N-S 20-651-6390　　(BR)
EDMONTON SCHOOL DISTRICT NO. 7
M E LAZERTE SENIOR HIGH SCHOOL
6804 144 Ave Nw, Edmonton, AB, T5C 3C7
(780) 408-9800
Emp Here 138
SIC 8211 Elementary and secondary schools

D-U-N-S 20-028-3534　　(BR)
EDMONTON SCHOOL DISTRICT NO. 7
KILDARE ELEMENTARY SCHOOL
7525 144 Ave Nw, Edmonton, AB, T5C 2R8
(780) 476-5675
Emp Here 45
SIC 8211 Elementary and secondary schools

D-U-N-S 20-028-3682　　(BR)
EDMONTON SCHOOL DISTRICT NO. 7
JOHN BARNETT ELEMENTARY SCHOOL
14840 72 St Nw, Edmonton, AB, T5C 3E5
(780) 478-1351
Emp Here 25
SIC 8211 Elementary and secondary schools

D-U-N-S 20-712-5266　　(BR)
EDMONTON SCHOOL DISTRICT NO. 7
LONDONDERRY JUNIOR HIGHSCHOOL
7104 144 Ave Nw, Edmonton, AB, T5C 2R4
(780) 473-4560
Emp Here 50
SIC 8211 Elementary and secondary schools

D-U-N-S 25-289-4894　　(BR)
EDMONTON SCHOOL DISTRICT NO. 7
BALWIN SCHOOL
7055 132 Ave Nw, Edmonton, AB, T5C 2A7
(780) 475-3646
Emp Here 40
SIC 8211 Elementary and secondary schools

D-U-N-S 24-807-5871　　(BR)
FABRICLAND PACIFIC/MIDWEST LIMITED
FABRICLAND
1 Londonderry Mall Nw Unit 202, Edmonton, AB, T5C 3C8
(780) 478-0435
Emp Here 22
SIC 5949 Sewing, needlework, and piece goods

D-U-N-S 20-179-8381　　(BR)
GREAT PACIFIC INDUSTRIES INC

SAVE-ON-FOODS
1 Londonderry Mall Nw, Edmonton, AB, T5C 3C8
(780) 473-7820
Emp Here 100
SIC 5411 Grocery stores

D-U-N-S 25-110-0012　　(BR)
HUDSON'S BAY COMPANY
BAY, THE
1 Londonderry Mall Nw Unit 86, Edmonton, AB, T5C 3C8
(780) 478-2931
Emp Here 132
SIC 5311 Department stores

D-U-N-S 25-316-7019　　(BR)
LILYDALE INC
LILYDALE HATCHERIES DIV
7503 127 Ave Nw, Edmonton, AB, T5C 1R9
(780) 475-6607
Emp Here 35
SIC 5144 Poultry and poultry products

D-U-N-S 20-080-5224　　(HQ)
LILYDALE INC
LILYDALE FOODS
7727 127 Ave Nw, Edmonton, AB, T5C 1R9
(780) 448-0990
Emp Here 300　　　*Emp Total* 600
Sales 640,230,143
SIC 5144 Poultry and poultry products
Pr Pr Ed Rodenburg
Pers/VP Jacques Pelletier
VP Fin Jeff Gresham
Div VP Mario Gonzalez
Div VP Dan Graham

D-U-N-S 20-860-1471　　(BR)
SOURCE (BELL) ELECTRONICS INC, THE
SOURCE, THE
250 Londonderry Mall Nw, Edmonton, AB, T5C 3C8
(780) 406-4706
Emp Here 25
SIC 5999 Miscellaneous retail stores, nec

D-U-N-S 24-582-3489　　(HQ)
ST MICHAEL'S EXTENDED CARE CENTRE SOCIETY
ST. MICHAEL'S HEALTH GROUP
(*Suby of* St Michael's Extended Care Centre Society)
7404 139 Ave Nw, Edmonton, AB, T5C 3H7
(780) 473-5621
Emp Here 374　　　*Emp Total* 375
Sales 22,050,499
SIC 8051 Skilled nursing care facilities
Pr Stan Fisher
　Wendy King

D-U-N-S 20-316-8534　　(SL)
ST. MICHAEL'S HEALTH GROUP
7406 139 Ave Nw, Edmonton, AB, T5C 3H7
(780) 472-4511
Emp Here 350　　　*Sales* 20,637,005
SIC 8051 Skilled nursing care facilities
Pr Pr Stan Fischer
Dir Fin Wendy King
　Ed Hladunewich
　Lubomyr Pastuszenko
　Melety Snihurowych
　Peter Kule

D-U-N-S 20-004-0611　　(BR)
WINNERS MERCHANTS INTERNATIONAL L.P.
WINNERS
(*Suby of* The TJX Companies Inc)
1 Londonderry Mall Nw, Edmonton, AB, T5C 3C8
(780) 456-5044
Emp Here 40
SIC 5651 Family clothing stores

Edmonton, AB T5E

D-U-N-S 20-120-5106　　(SL)
911640 ALBERTA LTD
GOOD BUDDY RESTAURANT
9499 137 Ave Nw Suite 239, Edmonton, AB, T5E 5R8
(780) 406-3838
Emp Here 50　　　*Sales* 1,532,175
SIC 5812 Eating places

D-U-N-S 25-236-1662　　(BR)
ALBERTA TREASURY BRANCHES
ATB FINANCIAL
12703 97 St Nw, Edmonton, AB, T5E 4C1
(780) 422-9438
Emp Here 25
SIC 6036 Savings institutions, except federal

D-U-N-S 20-059-4591　　(BR)
BANK OF NOVA SCOTIA, THE
SCOTIABANK
13150 97 St Nw, Edmonton, AB, T5E 4C6
(780) 448-7756
Emp Here 23
SIC 6021 National commercial banks

D-U-N-S 20-789-4697　　(BR)
BANQUE TORONTO-DOMINION, LA
TORONTO-DOMINION BANK, THE
(*Suby of* Toronto-Dominion Bank, The)
13711 93 St Nw, Edmonton, AB, T5E 5V6
(780) 475-6671
Emp Here 30
SIC 6021 National commercial banks

D-U-N-S 20-343-1911　　(SL)
CNLX CANADA INC
10229 127 Ave Nw, Edmonton, AB, T5E 0B9
(888) 888-5909
Emp Here 25　　　*Sales* 2,425,503
SIC 7359 Equipment rental and leasing, nec

D-U-N-S 20-143-5406　　(BR)
CAPITAL CARE GROUP INC
MCCONNELL PLACE NORTH
9113 144 Ave Nw, Edmonton, AB, T5E 6K2
(780) 496-2575
Emp Here 68
SIC 8051 Skilled nursing care facilities

D-U-N-S 20-573-2311　　(BR)
COMPAGNIE DES CHEMINS DE FER NATIONAUX DU CANADA
11709 127 Ave Nw, Edmonton, AB, T5E 0C9
(780) 472-3133
Emp Here 50
SIC 4011 Railroads, line-haul operating

D-U-N-S 20-573-2329　　(BR)
COMPAGNIE DES CHEMINS DE FER NATIONAUX DU CANADA
10229 127 Ave Nw, Edmonton, AB, T5E 0B9
(780) 472-3452
Emp Here 300
SIC 4011 Railroads, line-haul operating

D-U-N-S 20-573-2964　　(BR)
COMPAGNIE DES CHEMINS DE FER NATIONAUX DU CANADA
11703 127 Ave Nw, Edmonton, AB, T5E 0C9
(780) 472-3486
Emp Here 2,500
SIC 4011 Railroads, line-haul operating

D-U-N-S 25-094-4100　　(BR)
CONSEIL SCOLAIRE CENTRE-NORD
ECOLE PERE-LACOMBE
10715 131a Ave Nw, Edmonton, AB, T5E 0X4
(780) 478-9389
Emp Here 20
SIC 8211 Elementary and secondary schools

D-U-N-S 20-138-0891　　(BR)
EDMONTON CATHOLIC SEPARATE SCHOOL DISTRICT NO.7
ST. EDMUND CATHOLIC ELEMENTARY JUNIOR HIGH SCHOOL

(*Suby of* Edmonton Catholic Separate School District No.7)
11712 130 Ave Nw, Edmonton, AB, T5E 0V2
(780) 453-1596
Emp Here 50
SIC 8211 Elementary and secondary schools

D-U-N-S 20-028-8707　　(BR)
EDMONTON CATHOLIC SEPARATE SCHOOL DISTRICT NO.7
CARDINAL LEGER JUNIOR HIGH SCHOOL
(*Suby of* Edmonton Catholic Separate School District No.7)
8808 144 Ave Nw, Edmonton, AB, T5E 3G7
(780) 475-6262
Emp Here 29
SIC 8211 Elementary and secondary schools

D-U-N-S 20-068-2883　　(BR)
EDMONTON CATHOLIC SEPARATE SCHOOL DISTRICT NO.7
ST. MATTHEWS CATHOLIC ELEMENTARY SCHOOL
(*Suby of* Edmonton Catholic Separate School District No.7)
8735 132 Ave Nw, Edmonton, AB, T5E 0X7
(780) 473-6575
Emp Here 30
SIC 8211 Elementary and secondary schools

D-U-N-S 25-021-2479　　(BR)
EDMONTON CATHOLIC SEPARATE SCHOOL DISTRICT NO.7
ST. CECILIA JUNIOR HIGH SCHOOL
(*Suby of* Edmonton Catholic Separate School District No.7)
8830 132 Ave Nw, Edmonton, AB, T5E 0X8
(780) 476-7695
Emp Here 53
SIC 8211 Elementary and secondary schools

D-U-N-S 20-712-4327　　(BR)
EDMONTON SCHOOL DISTRICT NO. 7
EVANSDALE ELEMENTARY SCHOOL
9303 150 Ave Nw, Edmonton, AB, T5E 2N7
(780) 476-3331
Emp Here 50
SIC 8211 Elementary and secondary schools

D-U-N-S 25-452-0455　　(BR)
EDMONTON SCHOOL DISTRICT NO. 7
SCOTT ROBERTSON ELEMENTARY SCHOOL
13515 107 St Nw, Edmonton, AB, T5E 4W3
(780) 475-3565
Emp Here 100
SIC 8211 Elementary and secondary schools

D-U-N-S 20-028-3542　　(BR)
EDMONTON SCHOOL DISTRICT NO. 7
LAUDERDALE ELEMENTARY SCHOOL
10610 129 Ave Nw, Edmonton, AB, T5E 4V6
(780) 475-8737
Emp Here 25
SIC 8211 Elementary and secondary schools

D-U-N-S 25-272-3218　　(BR)
EDMONTON SCHOOL DISTRICT NO. 7
DICKINSFIELD JUNIOR HIGH
14320 88a St Nw, Edmonton, AB, T5E 6B6
(780) 476-4646
Emp Here 25
SIC 8211 Elementary and secondary schools

D-U-N-S 25-451-9556　　(BR)
EDMONTON SCHOOL DISTRICT NO. 7
KILLARNEY JUNIOR HIGH SCHOOL
13110 91 St Nw, Edmonton, AB, T5E 3P6
(780) 475-1737
Emp Here 25
SIC 8211 Elementary and secondary schools

D-U-N-S 20-208-3502　　(BR)
EDMONTON SCHOOL DISTRICT NO. 7
MAJOR GENERAL GRIESBACH SCHOOL
304 Griesbach School Rd Nw, Edmonton, AB, T5E 6R8

▲ Public Company　　■ Public Company Family Member　　**HQ** Headquarters　　**BR** Branch　　**SL** Single Location

(780) 456-9482
Emp Here 24
SIC 8211 Elementary and secondary schools

D-U-N-S 20-027-3659   (BR)
EDMONTON SCHOOL DISTRICT NO. 7
GLENGARRY ELEMENTARY SCHOOL
9211 135 Ave Nw, Edmonton, AB, T5E 1N7
(780) 476-5373
Emp Here 32
SIC 8211 Elementary and secondary schools

D-U-N-S 20-028-3450   (BR)
EDMONTON SCHOOL DISTRICT NO. 7
CALDER SCHOOL
12950 118 St Nw, Edmonton, AB, T5E 5L2
(780) 454-4313
Emp Here 25
SIC 8211 Elementary and secondary schools

D-U-N-S 24-340-2489   (BR)
FGL SPORTS LTD
SPORT MART
9499 137 Ave Nw Suite 1086, Edmonton, AB, T5E 5R8
(780) 478-5457
Emp Here 20
SIC 5941 Sporting goods and bicycle shops

D-U-N-S 24-003-9081   (BR)
LONDON DRUGS LIMITED
9450 137 Ave Nw Suite 120, Edmonton, AB, T5E 6C2
(780) 944-4521
Emp Here 50
SIC 5912 Drug stores and proprietary stores

D-U-N-S 25-018-8208   (BR)
ROYAL BANK OF CANADA
RBC
(*Suby of* Royal Bank Of Canada)
9499 137 Ave Nw Unit 1032, Edmonton, AB, T5E 5R8

Emp Here 20
SIC 6021 National commercial banks

D-U-N-S 25-266-5625   (BR)
SERVUS CREDIT UNION LTD
12809 82 St Nw, Edmonton, AB, T5E 2S9
(780) 496-2100
Emp Here 30
SIC 6062 State credit unions

D-U-N-S 20-871-3466   (BR)
SOBEYS WEST INC
NORTHGATE SAFEWAY
9499 137 Ave Nw Suite 200, Edmonton, AB, T5E 5R8
(780) 406-6455
Emp Here 70
SIC 5411 Grocery stores

D-U-N-S 25-297-7962   (BR)
TOYS 'R' US (CANADA) LTD
TOYS 'R' US
(*Suby of* Toys "r" Us, Inc.)
13029 97 St Nw, Edmonton, AB, T5E 4C4
(780) 944-9404
Emp Here 70
SIC 5945 Hobby, toy, and game shops

D-U-N-S 20-918-5847   (BR)
VANCOUVER CAREER COLLEGE (BURNABY) INC
CDI COLLEGE
(*Suby of* Chung Family Holdings Inc)
9450 137 Ave Unit 104, Edmonton, AB, T5E 6C2
(780) 478-7900
Emp Here 20
SIC 8211 Elementary and secondary schools

D-U-N-S 24-854-0890   (SL)
VENTA CARE CENTRE LTD
13525 102 St Nw, Edmonton, AB, T5E 4K3
(780) 476-6633
Emp Here 100   *Sales* 4,523,563
SIC 8051 Skilled nursing care facilities

D-U-N-S 20-199-2323   (BR)
WENDY'S RESTAURANTS OF CANADA INC
(*Suby of* The Wendy's Company)
9630 137 Ave Nw Suite 823, Edmonton, AB, T5E 6H7
(780) 475-9547
Emp Here 35
SIC 5812 Eating places

D-U-N-S 25-408-9279   (SL)
ZANE HOLDINGS LTD
ALBERTA HONDA
9525 127 Ave Nw, Edmonton, AB, T5E 6M7
(780) 474-7921
Emp Here 65   *Sales* 4,742,446
SIC 7538 General automotive repair shops

Edmonton, AB T5G

D-U-N-S 20-550-7622   (HQ)
ABL X-PRESS LTD
ABL XPERTECH
(*Suby of* ABL X-Press Ltd)
11560 120 St Nw, Edmonton, AB, T5G 2Y2
(780) 448-3673
Emp Here 40   *Emp Total* 60
Sales 9,914,160
SIC 4213 Trucking, except local
Pr Pr Allan Plummer
   Jason Plummer
   Brent Plummer

D-U-N-S 24-148-4083   (BR)
ALBERTA HEALTH SERVICES
GLENNROSE REHABLITATION HOSPITAL
10230 111 Ave Nw Suite 2e, Edmonton, AB, T5G 0B7
(780) 735-7999
Emp Here 1,000
SIC 8062 General medical and surgical hospitals

D-U-N-S 20-572-0043   (BR)
BANK OF MONTREAL
BMO
208 Kingsway Garden Mall Nw, Edmonton, AB, T5G 3A6
(780) 441-6528
Emp Here 20
SIC 6021 National commercial banks

D-U-N-S 20-867-7232   (BR)
CAPITAL CARE GROUP INC
10410 111 Ave Nw, Edmonton, AB, T5G 3A2
(780) 496-3200
Emp Here 225
SIC 8741 Management services

D-U-N-S 24-316-3974   (BR)
CITY OF EDMONTON
COMMUNITY SERVICES
12304 107 St Nw, Edmonton, AB, T5G 2S7
(780) 496-4270
Emp Here 150
SIC 7349 Building maintenance services, nec

D-U-N-S 20-712-8302   (BR)
EDMONTON CATHOLIC SEPARATE SCHOOL DISTRICT NO.7
ST. BASIL SCHOOL
(*Suby of* Edmonton Catholic Separate School District No.7)
10210 115 Ave Nw, Edmonton, AB, T5G 0L8
(780) 477-3584
Emp Here 40
SIC 8211 Elementary and secondary schools

D-U-N-S 24-060-5738   (BR)
EDMONTON JOHN HOWARD SOCIETY
101 STREET APARTMENTS
(*Suby of* Edmonton John Howard Society)
11908 101 St Nw, Edmonton, AB, T5G 2B9
(780) 471-4525
Emp Here 20
SIC 8361 Residential care

D-U-N-S 20-154-6855   (BR)
EDMONTON SCHOOL DISTRICT NO. 7
AMISKWACIY JUNIOR AND SENIOR HIGH SCHOOL
101 Airport Rd Nw, Edmonton, AB, T5G 3K2
(780) 424-1270
Emp Here 35
SIC 8211 Elementary and secondary schools

D-U-N-S 20-028-9614   (BR)
EDMONTON SCHOOL DISTRICT NO. 7
SPRUCE AVENUE ELEMENTARY-JR HIGH SCHOOL
11424 102 St Nw Suite 4, Edmonton, AB, T5G 2E7
(780) 479-0155
Emp Here 30
SIC 8211 Elementary and secondary schools

D-U-N-S 20-859-8172   (BR)
FGL SPORTS LTD
140 Kingsway Garden Mall Nw, Edmonton, AB, T5G 3A6
(780) 474-4082
Emp Here 25
SIC 5661 Shoe stores

D-U-N-S 20-920-3541   (BR)
GAP (CANADA) INC
GAP
(*Suby of* The Gap Inc)
243 Kingsway Garden Mall, Edmonton, AB, T5G 3A6
(780) 474-1622
Emp Here 30
SIC 5651 Family clothing stores

D-U-N-S 20-698-6460   (BR)
HUDSON'S BAY COMPANY
650 Kingsway Garden Mall Nw, Edmonton, AB, T5G 3E6
(780) 479-7100
Emp Here 100
SIC 5311 Department stores

D-U-N-S 20-016-3314   (HQ)
INSPECTIONS GROUP INC, THE
(*Suby of* Inspections Group Inc, The)
12010 111 Ave Nw, Edmonton, AB, T5G 0E6
(780) 454-5048
Emp Here 60   *Emp Total* 60
Sales 3,957,782
SIC 7389 Business services, nec

D-U-N-S 20-198-4940   (BR)
LAVTOR HOLDINGS (ALBERTA) LTD
SMITTY'S FAMILY RESTAURANT
1 Kingsway Garden Mall Nw Suite 555, Edmonton, AB, T5G 3A6

Emp Here 120
SIC 5812 Eating places

D-U-N-S 20-197-3968   (BR)
MCG RESTAURANTS LTD
MOXIE'S CLASSIC GRILL RESTAURANTS
(*Suby of* MCG Restaurants Ltd)
10628 Kingsway Nw, Edmonton, AB, T5G 0W8
(780) 944-0232
Emp Here 100
SIC 5812 Eating places

D-U-N-S 20-652-4568   (BR)
MAZDA CANADA INC
JARMAN MAZDA
9590 125a Ave Nw, Edmonton, AB, T5G 3E5

Emp Here 25
SIC 5013 Motor vehicle supplies and new parts

D-U-N-S 20-242-3062   (SL)
NITE TOURS INTERNATIONAL
SANDCASTLE TOURS
67 Airport Rd Nw, Edmonton, AB, T5G 0W6

Emp Here 25   *Sales* 5,982,777

SIC 4725 Tour operators
Owner Darin Feth

D-U-N-S 20-718-2259   (BR)
NORTHERN ALBERTA INSTITUTE OF TECHNOLOGY
NAIT
10504 Princess Elizabeth Ave Nw, Edmonton, AB, T5G 3K4
(780) 378-5060
Emp Here 500
SIC 8222 Junior colleges

D-U-N-S 20-802-6901   (BR)
NORTHERN ALBERTA INSTITUTE OF TECHNOLOGY
N.A.I.T
11311 120 St Nw Suite 131, Edmonton, AB, T5G 2Y1

Emp Here 30
SIC 8222 Junior colleges

D-U-N-S 24-274-5867   (BR)
OXFORD PROPERTIES GROUP INC
KINGSWAY MALL
320 Kingsway Garden Mall Nw Suite 320, Edmonton, AB, T5G 3A6
(780) 479-5955
Emp Here 35
SIC 6512 Nonresidential building operators

D-U-N-S 20-083-7250   (HQ)
PARK MEMORIAL LTD
9709 111 Ave Nw, Edmonton, AB, T5G 0B2
(780) 898-1329
Emp Here 48   *Emp Total* 55
Sales 4,012,839
SIC 7261 Funeral service and crematories

D-U-N-S 25-149-8994   (SL)
RGO OFFICE PRODUCTS EDMONTON LTD
11624 120 St Nw, Edmonton, AB, T5G 2Y2
(780) 413-6600
Emp Here 50   *Sales* 4,231,721
SIC 5943 Stationery stores

D-U-N-S 25-097-3237   (BR)
RHI CANADA INC
11210 120 St Nw, Edmonton, AB, T5G 0W5
(780) 452-0111
Emp Here 20
SIC 3297 Nonclay refractories

D-U-N-S 24-002-4968   (BR)
SEARS CANADA INC
SEARS
50 Kingsway Garden Mall Nw, Edmonton, AB, T5G 0Y3
(780) 479-8431
Emp Here 375
SIC 5311 Department stores

D-U-N-S 20-358-2015   (BR)
SERVUS CREDIT UNION LTD
11311 Kingsway Nw, Edmonton, AB, T5G 0X3
(780) 496-2142
Emp Here 60
SIC 6062 State credit unions

D-U-N-S 24-778-0047   (SL)
SONS OF PITCHES
11920 101 St Nw Suite 107, Edmonton, AB, T5G 2B9
(780) 233-1378
Emp Here 20   *Sales* 6,380,400
SIC 7941 Sports clubs, managers, and promoters
Prin Joe Whelen

D-U-N-S 20-588-1688   (BR)
VALUE VILLAGE STORES, INC
(*Suby of* Savers, Inc.)
11850 103 St Nw, Edmonton, AB, T5G 2J2
(780) 477-0025
Emp Here 30
SIC 5399 Miscellaneous general merchandise

D-U-N-S 20-199-2331   (BR)

WENDY'S RESTAURANTS OF CANADA INC
WENDY'S
(*Suby of* The Wendy's Company)
10107 111 Ave Nw, Edmonton, AB, T5G 0B5

Emp Here 25
SIC 5812 Eating places

D-U-N-S 20-806-2815   (BR)
YM INC. (SALES)
STITCHES
1 Kingsway Garden Mall Nw, Edmonton, AB, T5G 3A6
(780) 471-1737
Emp Here 20
SIC 5621 Women's clothing stores

Edmonton, AB T5H

D-U-N-S 24-584-4220   (HQ)
340107 ALBERTA LTD
SORRENTINO'S BISTRO BAR
(*Suby of* 340107 Alberta Ltd)
10665 109 St Nw, Edmonton, AB, T5H 3B5
(780) 474-6466
Emp Here 25   *Emp Total* 300
Sales 12,579,800
SIC 5812 Eating places
Pr Pr Carmelo Rago
 Maria Saccomanno

D-U-N-S 20-014-0429   (HQ)
595028 ALBERTA LTD
DOTS
(*Suby of* 595028 Alberta Ltd)
11825 105 Ave Nw, Edmonton, AB, T5H 0L9
(780) 421-7361
Emp Here 20   *Emp Total* 75
Sales 4,596,524
SIC 5621 Women's clothing stores

D-U-N-S 20-746-9797   (BR)
ALBERTA HEALTH SERVICES
EMERGENCY MEDICAL SERVICES
10539 105 St Nw, Edmonton, AB, T5H 2W8

Emp Here 350
SIC 8062 General medical and surgical hospitals

D-U-N-S 20-902-8377   (BR)
ALBERTA HEALTH SERVICES
COMMUNITY GERIATRIC PSYCHIATRY
11010 101 St Nw Suite 215, Edmonton, AB, T5H 4B9
(780) 424-4660
Emp Here 23
SIC 8062 General medical and surgical hospitals

D-U-N-S 24-393-5913   (BR)
AUDIO VISUAL SYSTEMS INTEGRATION INC
SHARP'S AUDIO VISUAL
10552 106 St Nw, Edmonton, AB, T5H 2X6
(780) 426-7454
Emp Here 25
SIC 5999 Miscellaneous retail stores, nec

D-U-N-S 24-001-6410   (HQ)
BISSELL CENTRE
(*Suby of* Bissell Centre)
10527 96 St Nw, Edmonton, AB, T5H 2H6
(780) 423-2285
Emp Here 40   *Emp Total* 75
Sales 7,208,141
SIC 8322 Individual and family services
Ex Dir Shelley Williams
 Earl Predy

D-U-N-S 25-231-7193   (BR)
BRICK WAREHOUSE LP, THE
BRICK WAREHOUSE, THE
10705 101 St Nw, Edmonton, AB, T5H 2S4

(780) 497-4900
Emp Here 60
SIC 5712 Furniture stores

D-U-N-S 20-081-1636   (BR)
CANADIAN LINEN AND UNIFORM SERVICE CO
CANADIAN DOORMAT AND MOP SERVICES
(*Suby of* Ameripride Services, Inc.)
8631 Stadium Rd Nw, Edmonton, AB, T5H 3W9
(780) 665-3905
Emp Here 115
SIC 7213 Linen supply

D-U-N-S 20-809-7121   (HQ)
CANADIAN URBAN MANAGEMENT LIMITED
(*Suby of* Canadian Urban Limited)
10572 105 St Nw, Edmonton, AB, T5H 2W7
(780) 424-7722
Emp Here 27   *Emp Total* 40
Sales 6,594,250
SIC 6531 Real estate agents and managers
 Donald G Horner
 David E Rostrup

D-U-N-S 20-919-1670   (BR)
CATHOLIC SOCIAL SERVICES
10709 105 St Nw, Edmonton, AB, T5H 2X3
(780) 424-3545
Emp Here 80
SIC 8399 Social services, nec

D-U-N-S 20-888-7757   (SL)
CHIMO YOUTH RETREAT CENTRE
10585 111 St Suite 103, Edmonton, AB, T5H 3E8
(780) 420-0324
Emp Here 80   *Sales* 3,137,310
SIC 8322 Individual and family services

D-U-N-S 25-072-3764   (BR)
CHINTZ & COMPANY DECORATIVE FURNISHINGS INC
10502 105 Ave Nw, Edmonton, AB, T5H 0K8
(780) 428-8181
Emp Here 35
SIC 5712 Furniture stores

D-U-N-S 24-417-4350   (BR)
DONG-PHUONG ORIENTAL MARKET LTD
LUCKY 97 SUPERMARKET
10725 97 St Nw, Edmonton, AB, T5H 2L9
(780) 424-8011
Emp Here 20
SIC 5411 Grocery stores

D-U-N-S 20-713-0175   (BR)
EDMONTON CATHOLIC SEPARATE SCHOOL DISTRICT NO.7
MOTHER THERESA CATHOLIC SCHOOL
(*Suby of* Edmonton Catholic Separate School District No.7)
9008 105a Ave Nw, Edmonton, AB, T5H 4P9
(780) 471-3631
Emp Here 38
SIC 8211 Elementary and secondary schools

D-U-N-S 25-400-1589   (BR)
EDMONTON CATHOLIC SEPARATE SCHOOL DISTRICT NO.7
ST. JOSEPH HIGH SCHOOL AND ASCENSION COLLEGIATE
(*Suby of* Edmonton Catholic Separate School District No.7)
10830 109 St Nw, Edmonton, AB, T5H 3C1
(780) 426-2010
Emp Here 100
SIC 8211 Elementary and secondary schools

D-U-N-S 20-712-9391   (BR)
EDMONTON CATHOLIC SEPARATE SCHOOL DISTRICT NO.7
FRESH START MILL WOODS SCHOOL
(*Suby of* Edmonton Catholic Separate School District No.7)
9624 108 Ave Nw, Edmonton, AB, T5H 1A4

(780) 944-2000
Emp Here 50
SIC 8211 Elementary and secondary schools

D-U-N-S 20-194-4175   (BR)
EDMONTON SCHOOL DISTRICT NO. 7
EDMONTON PUBLIC SCHOOL
10515 100 St Nw, Edmonton, AB, T5H 2R4
(780) 917-5150
Emp Here 250
SIC 8211 Elementary and secondary schools

D-U-N-S 20-712-4129   (BR)
EDMONTON SCHOOL DISTRICT NO. 7
VICTORIA SCHOOL
10210 108 Ave Nw Suite 123, Edmonton, AB, T5H 1A8
(780) 426-3010
Emp Here 100
SIC 8211 Elementary and secondary schools

D-U-N-S 20-712-4988   (BR)
EDMONTON SCHOOL DISTRICT NO. 7
JOHNNY MCDOUGAL SCHOOL
10930 107 St Nw, Edmonton, AB, T5H 2Z4
(780) 426-0205
Emp Here 50
SIC 8211 Elementary and secondary schools

D-U-N-S 20-712-6868   (BR)
EDMONTON SCHOOL DISTRICT NO. 7
10931 120 St Nw, Edmonton, AB, T5H 3P9
(780) 422-1937
Emp Here 50
SIC 8211 Elementary and secondary schools

D-U-N-S 24-353-7771   (HQ)
EPCOR DISTRIBUTION & TRANSMISSION INC
10423 101 St Nw Suite 2000, Edmonton, AB, T5H 0E8
(780) 412-3414
Emp Here 45   *Emp Total* 8,000
Sales 356,267,098
SIC 4911 Electric services
 Hugh John Bolton
 James Edward Clarke Carter
 Alexander Mackay
 Steven Emmanuel Matyas
 Allister John Mcphearson
 Douglas Harding Mitchell
 Robert Lawrence Philips
 Laurence Pollock
 Helen Katrina Sinclair
 Wesley Robert Twiss

D-U-N-S 24-274-4050   (BR)
GDI SERVICES (CANADA) LP
11041 105 Ave Nw Suite 201, Edmonton, AB, T5H 3Y1
(780) 428-9508
Emp Here 250
SIC 7349 Building maintenance services, nec

D-U-N-S 24-333-4120   (BR)
GOVERNING COUNCIL OF THE SALVATION ARMY IN CANADA, THE
GOVERNING COUNCIL OF THE SALVATION ARMY IN CANADA, THE
9611 102 Ave Nw, Edmonton, AB, T5H 0E5
(780) 429-4274
Emp Here 80
SIC 8322 Individual and family services

D-U-N-S 24-894-9364   (BR)
GOVERNING COUNCIL OF THE SALVATION ARMY IN CANADA, THE
SALVATION ARMY, THE
9618 101a Ave Nw, Edmonton, AB, T5H 0C7
(780) 423-2111
Emp Here 29
SIC 8399 Social services, nec

D-U-N-S 20-047-2376   (BR)
GOVERNING COUNCIL OF THE SALVATION ARMY IN CANADA, THE
GOVERNING COUNCIL OF THE SALVATION ARMY IN CANADA, THE
9620 101a Ave Nw, Edmonton, AB, T5H 0C7

(780) 424-9222
Emp Here 21
SIC 8322 Individual and family services

D-U-N-S 24-396-4996   (BR)
LAFARGE CANADA INC
8635 Stadium Rd Nw, Edmonton, AB, T5H 3X1
(780) 423-6161
Emp Here 450
SIC 3273 Ready-mixed concrete

D-U-N-S 20-322-6790   (BR)
LAFARGE CANADA INC
8635 Stadium Rd Nw, Edmonton, AB, T5H 3X1
(780) 423-6153
Emp Here 25
SIC 2891 Adhesives and sealants

D-U-N-S 20-083-2012   (HQ)
MCBAIN CAMERA LTD
(*Suby of* MCB Holdings Ltd)
10805 107 Ave Nw, Edmonton, AB, T5H 0W9
(780) 420-0404
Emp Here 30   *Emp Total* 75
Sales 4,815,406
SIC 5946 Camera and photographic supply stores

D-U-N-S 20-852-5290   (SL)
MCCALLUM PRINTING GROUP INC
BURKE MEDIA
11755 108 Ave Nw, Edmonton, AB, T5H 1B8
(780) 455-8885
Emp Here 90   *Sales* 4,523,563
SIC 2759 Commercial printing, nec

D-U-N-S 24-020-2825   (SL)
MERRICK'S FINE FOODS INC
FAT FRANK'S BIGGER BETTER BITE
10560 114 St Nw, Edmonton, AB, T5H 3J7
(780) 413-0278
Emp Here 50   *Sales* 1,532,175
SIC 5812 Eating places

D-U-N-S 20-069-1157   (BR)
NATIVE COUNSELLING SERVICES OF ALBERTA
STAN DANIELS HEALING CENTER
9516 101 Ave Nw, Edmonton, AB, T5H 0B3
(780) 495-3748
Emp Here 25
SIC 8361 Residential care

D-U-N-S 25-170-6362   (BR)
NATIVE COUNSELLING SERVICES OF ALBERTA
9330 104 Ave Nw, Edmonton, AB, T5H 4G7
(780) 423-2141
Emp Here 30
SIC 8111 Legal services

D-U-N-S 25-100-4974   (SL)
RED DEER RIBS LTD.
10544 114 St Nw, Edmonton, AB, T5H 3J7
(780) 429-1259
Emp Here 80   *Sales* 3,109,686
SIC 5812 Eating places

D-U-N-S 20-512-4006   (SL)
RIVER CITY ELECTRIC LTD
11306 107 Ave Nw, Edmonton, AB, T5H 0Y3
(780) 484-6676
Emp Here 50   *Sales* 4,377,642
SIC 1731 Electrical work

D-U-N-S 20-065-5087   (BR)
ROYAL BANK OF CANADA
RBC ROYAL BANK
(*Suby of* Royal Bank Of Canada)
10567 Kingsway Nw, Edmonton, AB, T5H 4K1
(780) 448-6112
Emp Here 25
SIC 6021 National commercial banks

D-U-N-S 25-288-9282   (BR)
RUSSELL FOOD EQUIPMENT LIMITED
10808 120 St Nw, Edmonton, AB, T5H 3P7

(780) 423-4221
Emp Here 47
SIC 5046 Commercial equipment, nec

D-U-N-S 24-627-9897   (SL)
SANTA MARIA GORETTI COMMUNITY CENTRE ASSOCIATION
S M G COMMUNITY CENTRE
11050 90 St Nw, Edmonton, AB, T5H 1S5
(780) 426-5026
Emp Here 50   *Sales* 2,699,546
SIC 7999 Amusement and recreation, nec

D-U-N-S 25-266-5708   (BR)
SERVUS CREDIT UNION LTD
10303 107 Ave Nw, Edmonton, AB, T5H 0V7
(780) 496-2133
Emp Here 20
SIC 6062 State credit unions

D-U-N-S 20-084-3753   (HQ)
SINCLAIR SUPPLY LTD
10914 120 St Nw, Edmonton, AB, T5H 3P7
(780) 452-3110
Emp Here 65   *Emp Total* 150
Sales 27,360,263
SIC 5075 Warm air heating and air conditioning
Pr Paul K. Lachambre

D-U-N-S 20-786-5523   (BR)
SOBEYS WEST INC
10930 82 St Nw, Edmonton, AB, T5H 1L8
(780) 433-6930
Emp Here 50
SIC 5411 Grocery stores

D-U-N-S 25-359-3990   (HQ)
TECHNICARE IMAGING LTD
TECHNICARE
(*Suby of* Technicare Imaging Ltd)
10924 119 St Nw, Edmonton, AB, T5H 3P5
(780) 424-7161
Emp Here 27   *Emp Total* 50
Sales 3,465,004
SIC 7384 Photofinish laboratories

D-U-N-S 24-321-2532   (SL)
TRAVEL ALBERTA IN-PROVINCE
10949 120 St Nw, Edmonton, AB, T5H 3R2
(780) 732-1627
Emp Here 30   *Sales* 9,234,824
SIC 4724 Travel agencies
Pr Jim Vincent

D-U-N-S 25-231-7185   (BR)
UNITED FURNITURE WAREHOUSE LP
12016 107 Ave Nw, Edmonton, AB, T5H 0Z2
(780) 452-7354
Emp Here 30
SIC 5712 Furniture stores

D-U-N-S 20-894-9701   (SL)
UNIVERSAL DENTAL LABORATORIES LTD
MILLCREEK UNIVERSAL CERAMICS
10735 107 Ave Nw Suite 400, Edmonton, AB, T5H 0W6
(780) 423-1009
Emp Here 65   *Sales* 3,793,956
SIC 8072 Dental laboratories

D-U-N-S 24-339-8083   (SL)
VISTEK WEST CALGARY INC
10569 109 St Nw, Edmonton, AB, T5H 3B1
(780) 484-0333
Emp Here 42   *Sales* 2,261,782
SIC 5946 Camera and photographic supply stores

D-U-N-S 25-733-3617   (BR)
WSP CANADA GROUP LIMITED
10576 113 St Nw Suite 200, Edmonton, AB, T5H 3H5
(780) 423-4123
Emp Here 30
SIC 8711 Engineering services

D-U-N-S 20-333-2429   (BR)
WEST CANADIAN DIGITAL IMAGING INC

10567 109 St Nw, Edmonton, AB, T5H 3B1
(780) 424-1000
Emp Here 40
SIC 2752 Commercial printing, lithographic

D-U-N-S 24-525-9796   (BR)
WEST CANADIAN INDUSTRIES GROUP LTD
10567 109 St Nw, Edmonton, AB, T5H 3B1
(780) 424-1000
Emp Here 40
SIC 2752 Commercial printing, lithographic

D-U-N-S 20-809-6917   (HQ)
WESTERN FOOD SERVICES LTD
(*Suby of* Western Food Services Ltd)
11000 Stadium Rd Nw Suite 114, Edmonton, AB, T5H 4E2
(780) 474-9733
Emp Here 20   *Emp Total* 120
Sales 3,648,035
SIC 5812 Eating places

D-U-N-S 24-004-2890   (SL)
WILDROSE VACATION INC
10582 116 St Nw, Edmonton, AB, T5H 3L7

Emp Here 30   *Sales* 7,150,149
SIC 4724 Travel agencies

Edmonton, AB T5J

D-U-N-S 25-147-6545   (SL)
3761258 CANADA INC
10180 101 St Nw Suite 310, Edmonton, AB, T5J 3S4
(780) 702-1432
Emp Here 130   *Sales* 23,333,500
SIC 7372 Prepackaged software
Pr Pr Ashif Mawji

D-U-N-S 24-392-4958   (BR)
4211596 CANADA INC
PPI FINANCIAL GROUP
(*Suby of* 4211596 Canada Inc)
10020 101a Ave Nw Suite 800, Edmonton, AB, T5J 3G2
(780) 423-6801
Emp Here 25
SIC 6411 Insurance agents, brokers, and service

D-U-N-S 20-069-3070   (BR)
4513380 CANADA INC
LIVINGSTON INTERNATIONAL
10060 Jasper Ave Nw Suite 950, Edmonton, AB, T5J 3R8
(780) 421-4351
Emp Here 20
SIC 4731 Freight transportation arrangement

D-U-N-S 24-067-4812   (BR)
AON CANADA INC
AON REED STENHOUSE
10025 102a Ave Nw Unit 700, Edmonton, AB, T5J 2Z2
(780) 423-1444
Emp Here 30
SIC 6411 Insurance agents, brokers, and service

D-U-N-S 25-305-0371   (BR)
AON REED STENHOUSE INC
10025 102a Ave Nw Suite 900, Edmonton, AB, T5J 0Y2
(780) 423-9801
Emp Here 85
SIC 6411 Insurance agents, brokers, and service

D-U-N-S 25-681-6349   (HQ)
ARC BUSINESS SOLUTIONS INC
(*Suby of* ARC Business Solutions Inc)
10088 102 Ave Nw Suite 2507, Edmonton, AB, T5J 2Z1

(780) 702-5022
Emp Here 50   *Emp Total* 64
Sales 4,669,485
SIC 7379 Computer related services, nec

D-U-N-S 24-227-0747   (BR)
ATCO ELECTRIC LTD
10080 Jasper Ave Nw, Edmonton, AB, T5J 1V9
(780) 420-7302
Emp Here 30
SIC 1623 Water, sewer, and utility lines

D-U-N-S 24-637-0934   (HQ)
ATCO ELECTRIC LTD
10035 105 St Nw, Edmonton, AB, T5J 2V6
(800) 668-2248
Emp Here 400   *Emp Total* 7,860
Sales 717,349,602
SIC 4911 Electric services
Nancy Southern
Ronald Southern
Loraine Charlton
James Simpson
Brian Bale

D-U-N-S 25-496-9439   (BR)
ATCO ELECTRIC LTD
ATCO POWER
10040 104 St Nw Suite 800, Edmonton, AB, T5J 0Z2
(780) 420-3859
Emp Here 25
SIC 1629 Heavy construction, nec

D-U-N-S 24-421-3075   (BR)
AIR CANADA
AIR CANADA CARGO
6th Ave N, Edmonton, AB, T5J 2T2
(780) 890-8121
Emp Here 33
SIC 4512 Air transportation, scheduled

D-U-N-S 24-014-5974   (BR)
ALBERTA DISTANCE LEARNING CENTRE
10055 106 St Nw Suite 300, Edmonton, AB, T5J 2Y2
(780) 452-4655
Emp Here 100
SIC 8211 Elementary and secondary schools

D-U-N-S 24-424-1571   (BR)
ALBERTA HEALTH SERVICES
FORENSIC ASSESSMENT & COMMUNITY SERVICES
104 Ave 100 St, Edmonton, AB, T5J 0K1

Emp Here 30
SIC 8322 Individual and family services

D-U-N-S 20-706-0745   (BR)
ALBERTA HEALTH SERVICES
CAPITAL HEALTH CENTRE
10030 107 St Nw Suite 700, Edmonton, AB, T5J 3E4
(780) 735-0986
Emp Here 700
SIC 8062 General medical and surgical hospitals

D-U-N-S 20-789-0059   (BR)
ALBERTA HEALTH SERVICES
ALBERTA ALCOHOL AND DRUG ABUSE
10302 107 St Nw, Edmonton, AB, T5J 1K2
(780) 427-4291
Emp Here 30
SIC 8062 General medical and surgical hospitals

D-U-N-S 24-000-9469   (BR)
ALBERTA HEALTH SERVICES
ACCOUNTS PAYABLE DEPT
10030 107 St Nw 14th Fl, Edmonton, AB, T5J 3E4
(403) 943-0845
Emp Here 30
SIC 8062 General medical and surgical hospitals

D-U-N-S 24-330-9051   (HQ)
ALBERTA INNOVATES - HEALTH SOLUTIONS
10104 103 Ave Nw Suite 1500, Edmonton, AB, T5J 0H8
(780) 423-5727
Emp Here 40   *Emp Total* 35,000
Sales 5,630,632
SIC 6111 Federal and federally sponsored credit agencies
Jacques Magnan

D-U-N-S 24-785-7725   (HQ)
ALBERTA TREASURY BRANCHES
ATB FINANCIAL
10020 100 St Nw Suite 2100, Edmonton, AB, T5J 0N3
(780) 408-7000
Emp Here 200   *Emp Total* 35,000
Sales 1,227,656,561
SIC 6036 Savings institutions, except federal
Pr Dave Mowat
Jim Mckillop
Ex VP Rob Bennett
Div Pres Sheldon Dyck
Sr VP Peggy Garrity
Ex VP Wellington Holbrook
Bob Mann
Ex VP Curtis Stange
Ex VP Ian Wild
VP Stuart Mckeller

D-U-N-S 20-578-2290   (BR)
ALBERTA TREASURY BRANCHES
ATB FINANCIAL
9888 Jasper Ave Nw Suite 100, Edmonton, AB, T5J 1P1
(780) 408-7500
Emp Here 20
SIC 6036 Savings institutions, except federal

D-U-N-S 24-391-4223   (HQ)
ASSOCIATED ENGINEERING ALBERTA LTD
(*Suby of* Ashco Shareholders Inc)
9888 Jasper Ave Suite 500, Edmonton, AB, T5J 5C6
(780) 451-7666
Emp Here 75   *Emp Total* 255
Sales 22,089,401
SIC 8711 Engineering services
Dir Gary T Hussey
Dir Herb R Kuehne
Dir R.H. Karius
Dir Alistar Black

D-U-N-S 25-979-6332   (HQ)
ATCO I-TEK BUSINESS SERVICES LTD
10035 105 St Nw, Edmonton, AB, T5J 1C8
(780) 420-7875
Emp Here 341   *Emp Total* 7,860
Sales 18,191,271
SIC 8721 Accounting, auditing, and bookkeeping
Pr Nancy Southern

D-U-N-S 20-571-8872   (BR)
AVIVA CANADA INC
10250 101 St Nw Suite 1700, Edmonton, AB, T5J 3P4
(780) 424-2300
Emp Here 20
SIC 8741 Management services

D-U-N-S 24-274-3128   (BR)
AVIVA INSURANCE COMPANY OF CANADA
AVIVA CANADA
10250 101 St Nw Suite 1700, Edmonton, AB, T5J 3P4
(780) 428-1822
Emp Here 100
SIC 6331 Fire, marine, and casualty insurance

D-U-N-S 24-032-6186   (BR)
BMO PRIVATE INVESTMENT COUNSEL INC
BMO HARRIS PRIVATE BANKING

10199 101 St Nw Suite 211, Edmonton, AB,
T5J 3Y4
(780) 408-0531
Emp Here 30
SIC 8742 Management consulting services

D-U-N-S 20-913-5453   (BR)
BANK OF NOVA SCOTIA, THE
SCOTIABANK
10050 Jasper Ave Nw, Edmonton, AB, T5J
1V7
(780) 448-7600
Emp Here 20
SIC 6021 National commercial banks

D-U-N-S 20-589-5365   (BR)
BANQUE TORONTO-DOMINION, LA
TD BANK
(*Suby of* Toronto-Dominion Bank, The)
10088 102 Ave Nw Suite 2601, Edmonton, AB,
T5J 2Z1
(780) 448-8156
Emp Here 30
SIC 6021 National commercial banks

D-U-N-S 20-852-5027   (BR)
BANQUE TORONTO-DOMINION, LA
TORONTO-DOMINION BANK, THE
(*Suby of* Toronto-Dominion Bank, The)
400 Edmonton City Centre Nw Suite 445, Ed-
monton, AB, T5J 4H5
(780) 415-7283
Emp Here 95
SIC 6021 National commercial banks

D-U-N-S 24-248-2128   (BR)
BELL MEDIA INC
CHBN FM THE BOUNCE
10212 Jasper Ave Nw, Edmonton, AB, T5J
5A3
(780) 424-2222
Emp Here 100
SIC 4832 Radio broadcasting stations

D-U-N-S 24-674-9014   (BR)
BENNETT JONES LLP
10020 100 St Nw Suite 3200, Edmonton, AB,
T5J 0N3
(780) 421-8133
Emp Here 50
SIC 8111 Legal services

D-U-N-S 20-651-6259   (BR)
BEST BUY CANADA LTD
FUTURE SHOP
(*Suby of* Best Buy Co., Inc.)
10304 109 St Nw, Edmonton, AB, T5J 1M3
(780) 498-5505
Emp Here 75
SIC 5731 Radio, television, and electronic
stores

D-U-N-S 24-643-2694   (SL)
BLUE TREE HOTELS GP ULC
WESTIN EDMONTON, THE
10135 100 St Nw, Edmonton, AB, T5J 0N7
(780) 426-3636
Emp Here 300   *Sales* 18,086,400
SIC 7011 Hotels and motels
Fin Ex Roula Haskett
Genl Mgr Catherine Mcdonald

D-U-N-S 25-290-0683   (BR)
CBRE LIMITED
10180 101 St Nw Suite 1220, Edmonton, AB,
T5J 3S4
(780) 424-5475
Emp Here 23
SIC 6531 Real estate agents and managers

D-U-N-S 20-580-9796   (BR)
CIBC WORLD MARKETS INC
CIBC WOOD GUNDY
10180 101 St Nw Suite 1800, Edmonton, AB,
T5J 3S4
(780) 429-8900
Emp Here 140
SIC 6211 Security brokers and dealers

D-U-N-S 24-332-5131   (SL)
CW EDMONTON INC
CUSHMAN & WAKEFIELD
10088 102 Ave Nw Unit 2700, Edmonton, AB,
T5J 2Z1
(780) 420-1177
Emp Here 50   *Sales* 4,742,446
SIC 6531 Real estate agents and managers

D-U-N-S 24-643-1365   (HQ)
CAIRO, FRANK ENTERPRISES LTD
(*Suby of* Cairo, Frank Enterprises Ltd)
10018 106 St Nw, Edmonton, AB, T5J 1G1
(780) 429-4407
Emp Here 96   *Emp Total* 100
Sales 1,969,939
SIC 7231 Beauty shops

D-U-N-S 20-302-3952   (BR)
CANACCORD GENUITY CORP
CANACCORD FINANCIAL
(*Suby of* Canaccord Genuity Group Inc)
10180 101 St Nw Suite 2700, Edmonton, AB,
T5J 3S4
(780) 408-1500
Emp Here 25
SIC 6211 Security brokers and dealers

D-U-N-S 24-700-0982   (BR)
**CANADIAN BROADCASTING CORPORA-
TION**
RADIO CANADA
123 Edmonton City Centre Nw, Edmonton,
AB, T5J 2Y8
(780) 468-7777
Emp Here 130
SIC 4833 Television broadcasting stations

D-U-N-S 25-012-1688   (BR)
**CANADIAN IMPERIAL BANK OF COM-
MERCE**
CIBC
10102 Jasper Ave Nw, Edmonton, AB, T5J
1W5
(780) 429-7744
Emp Here 80
SIC 6021 National commercial banks

D-U-N-S 25-090-8241   (BR)
CANADIAN UTILITIES LIMITED
ATCO ITEK
10035 105 St Nw, Edmonton, AB, T5J 1C8
(780) 420-7875
Emp Here 400
SIC 4911 Electric services

D-U-N-S 20-514-8344   (BR)
CANADIAN WESTERN BANK
10303 Jasper Ave Nw, Edmonton, AB, T5J
3N6
(780) 423-8801
Emp Here 40
SIC 6021 National commercial banks

D-U-N-S 24-398-0547   (BR)
CARMA DEVELOPERS LTD
10414 103 Ave Nw Suite 200, Edmonton, AB,
T5J 0J1
(780) 423-1910
Emp Here 40
SIC 6553 Cemetery subdividers and develop-
ers

D-U-N-S 20-302-2751   (SL)
**CASTLE ROCK RESEARCH CORPORA-
TION**
10180 101 St Nw Suite 2410, Edmonton, AB,
T5J 3S4
(780) 448-9619
Emp Here 30   *Sales* 3,502,114
SIC 2731 Book publishing

D-U-N-S 20-866-3794   (BR)
CENTURY HOSPITALITY GROUP LTD
LUX STEAKHOUSE & BAR
(*Suby of* Century Hospitality Group Ltd)
10155 102 St Nw Suite 2550, Edmonton, AB,
T5J 4G8

(780) 424-0400
Emp Here 20
SIC 5812 Eating places

D-U-N-S 24-838-9850   (SL)
CHATEAU LACOMBE HOTEL LTD
CROWNE PLAZA CHATEAU LACOMBE
(*Suby of* Allied Holdings Ltd)
10111 Bellamy Hill Nw, Edmonton, AB, T5J
1N7
(780) 428-6611
Emp Here 225   *Sales* 13,251,600
SIC 7011 Hotels and motels
Pr Pr Anthony Eng
  John Ellen

D-U-N-S 25-066-2624   (BR)
CITY OF EDMONTON
VICTORIA GOLF COURSE
12130 River Valley Rd, Edmonton, AB, T5J
2G7
(780) 496-4710
Emp Here 20
SIC 7992 Public golf courses

D-U-N-S 20-268-6408   (BR)
CITY OF EDMONTON
WASTE MANAGEMENT SERVICES
3 Sir Winston Churchill Sq Nw Suite 5, Edmon-
ton, AB, T5J 2C3
(780) 718-8941
Emp Here 500
SIC 4953 Refuse systems

D-U-N-S 20-643-1905   (BR)
CLARICA TRUSTCO INC
SUN LIFE FINANCIAL
10303 Jasper Ave Nw Suite 2928, Edmonton,
AB, T5J 3N6
(780) 424-8171
Emp Here 75
SIC 6411 Insurance agents, brokers, and ser-
vice

D-U-N-S 20-183-0424   (BR)
COAST HOTELS LIMITED
COAST EDMONTON PLAZA HOTEL
10155 105 St Nw, Edmonton, AB, T5J 1E2
(780) 425-2083
Emp Here 125
SIC 7011 Hotels and motels

D-U-N-S 25-977-6334   (BR)
**COMPAGNIE DE TELEPHONE BELL DU
CANADA OU BELL CANADA, LA**
10104 103 Ave Nw Suite 2800, Edmonton, AB,
T5J 0H8
(780) 409-6800
Emp Here 100
SIC 4899 Communication services, nec

D-U-N-S 20-081-1479   (BR)
COMSTOCK CANADA LTD
10180 101 St Nw Suite 1860, Edmonton, AB,
T5J 3S4

Emp Here 30
SIC 1731 Electrical work

D-U-N-S 24-928-7509   (BR)
**CONSEILLERS EN GESTION ET INFORMA-
TIQUE CGI INC**
CGI
10303 Jasper Ave Nw Suite 800, Edmonton,
AB, T5J 3N6
(780) 409-2200
Emp Here 350
SIC 7379 Computer related services, nec

D-U-N-S 20-539-6864   (BR)
CONSOLIDATED FASTFRATE INC
7725 101 St, Edmonton, AB, T5J 2M1
(780) 439-0061
Emp Here 100
SIC 4731 Freight transportation arrangement

D-U-N-S 20-514-9490   (BR)
CRAWFORD & COMPANY (CANADA) INC
(*Suby of* Crawford & Company)

10709 Jasper Ave Nw Suite 600, Edmonton,
AB, T5J 3N3
(780) 486-8000
Emp Here 30
SIC 6411 Insurance agents, brokers, and ser-
vice

D-U-N-S 24-318-6686   (BR)
**CRITICAL CONTROL ENERGY SERVICES
CORP**
10130 103 St Nw Suite 1500, Edmonton, AB,
T5J 3N9
(780) 423-3100
Emp Here 100
SIC 7371 Custom computer programming ser-
vices

D-U-N-S 20-005-7045   (BR)
CUSHMAN & WAKEFIELD LTD
CUSHMAN & WAKEFIELD EDMONTON
(*Suby of* Cushman & Wakefield Holdings, Inc.)
10088 102 Ave Suite 2700, Edmonton, AB,
T5J 2Z1
(780) 420-1177
Emp Here 60
SIC 6719 Holding companies, nec

D-U-N-S 20-112-3325   (BR)
DAVIS LLP
10060 Jasper Ave Nw Suite 1201, Edmonton,
AB, T5J 4E5
(780) 426-5330
Emp Here 70
SIC 8111 Legal services

D-U-N-S 25-359-6324   (BR)
DELOITTE LLP
10180 101 St Nw Suite 2000, Edmonton, AB,
T5J 4E4
(780) 421-3611
Emp Here 210
SIC 8721 Accounting, auditing, and book-
keeping

D-U-N-S 25-012-1829   (BR)
DELTA HOTELS LIMITED
DELTA EDMONTON CENTRE SUITE HOTEL
10222 102 St Nw, Edmonton, AB, T5J 4C5
(780) 429-3900
Emp Here 124
SIC 8741 Management services

D-U-N-S 20-195-8134   (SL)
DENNYS RESTAURANT
10803 104 Ave Nw, Edmonton, AB, T5J 4Z5
(780) 425-8408
Emp Here 50   *Sales* 1,532,175
SIC 5812 Eating places

D-U-N-S 24-880-6739   (BR)
DENTONS CANADA LLP
(*Suby of* Dentons Canada LLP)
10180 101 St Nw Suite 2900, Edmonton, AB,
T5J 3V5
(780) 423-7100
Emp Here 200
SIC 8111 Legal services

D-U-N-S 24-090-0472   (HQ)
DESIGN GROUP STAFFING INC
DESIGN GROUP STAFFING
10012 Jasper Ave Nw, Edmonton, AB, T5J
1R2
(780) 448-5850
Emp Here 80   *Emp Total* 150
Sales 27,720,032
SIC 7361 Employment agencies
Pr Pr Michael Duff
  Sharon Duff
  Damen Ng
Div Pres Matthew Williams
Div Pres Craig Brown
  Shelley Trenouth

D-U-N-S 24-031-8316   (BR)
DEVANEY, PATRICK V. INVESTMENTS LTD
ROSE & CROWN PUB
10235 101 St Nw Suite 195, Edmonton, AB,

T5J 3G1
(780) 426-7827
Emp Here 20
SIC 5813 Drinking places

D-U-N-S 24-498-0694   (BR)
DIALOG
10237 104 St Nw Suite 100, Edmonton, AB,
T5J 1B1
(780) 429-1580
Emp Here 80
SIC 8712 Architectural services

D-U-N-S 24-367-4368   (BR)
DIVERSIFIED TRANSPORTATION LTD
RED ARROW EXPRESS, DIV OF
10014 104 St Nw Unit 20, Edmonton, AB, T5J
0Z1
(780) 425-0820
Emp Here 100
SIC 4142 Bus charter service, except local

D-U-N-S 24-065-9813   (BR)
ECONOMICAL MUTUAL INSURANCE COMPANY
ECONOMICAL INSURANCE GROUP, THE
10250 101 St Nw Suite 1600, Edmonton, AB,
T5J 3P4
(780) 426-5925
Emp Here 52
SIC 6331 Fire, marine, and casualty insurance

D-U-N-S 24-343-4623   (BR)
EDGEWORTH PROPERTIES INC
(*Suby of* Edgeworth Ventures Inc)
10088 102 Ave Nw Suite 1905, Edmonton, AB,
T5J 2Z1

Emp Here 40
SIC 6552 Subdividers and developers, nec

D-U-N-S 20-234-4557   (SL)
EDMONTON CY LIMITED PARTNERSHIP
COURTYARD BY MARRIOTT
1 Thornton Crt Nw, Edmonton, AB, T5J 2E7
(780) 423-9999
Emp Here 70   *Sales* 3,064,349
SIC 7011 Hotels and motels

D-U-N-S 24-390-9520   (HQ)
EDMONTON ECONOMIC DEVELOPMENT CORPORATION
SHAW CONFERENCE CENTRE
9990 Jasper Ave Nw 3rd Fl, Edmonton, AB,
T5J 1P7
(780) 424-9191
Emp Here 75   *Emp Total* 8,000
Sales 43,046,813
SIC 7389 Business services, nec
Pr Brad Ferguson
   Corinne Ferguson
   Angela Fong
   John Babic
   Brian Baker
   Douglas Cox
   Jason Ding
   Joseph Doucet
   Sharilee Fossum
   Kris Hildebrand

D-U-N-S 20-561-9328   (BR)
EDMONTON ECONOMIC DEVELOPMENT CORPORATION
SHAW CONFERENCE CENTRE
9797 Jasper Ave Nw, Edmonton, AB, T5J 1N9
(780) 421-9797
Emp Here 400
SIC 7389 Business services, nec

D-U-N-S 24-384-6164   (HQ)
EDMONTON PUBLIC LIBRARY
(*Suby of* Edmonton Public Library)
7 Sir Winston Churchill Sq Nw Suite 5, Edmonton, AB, T5J 2V4
(780) 496-7050
Emp Here 50   *Emp Total* 600
Sales 38,182,400
SIC 8231 Libraries

Ch Bd Brent Mcdonough
V Ch Bd Carol Suddards

D-U-N-S 20-327-7546   (BR)
EDMONTON PUBLIC LIBRARY
STANLEY A MILNER LIBRARY
(*Suby of* Edmonton Public Library)
7 Sir Winston Churchill Sq Nw, Edmonton, AB,
T5J 2V4
(780) 496-7000
Emp Here 80
SIC 8231 Libraries

D-U-N-S 20-712-6520   (BR)
EDMONTON SCHOOL DISTRICT NO. 7
CENTER HIGH SCHOOL
10310 102 Ave Nw Suite 200, Edmonton, AB,
T5J 5A2
(780) 425-6753
Emp Here 200
SIC 8211 Elementary and secondary schools

D-U-N-S 20-800-2233   (BR)
ENBRIDGE PIPELINES INC
10201 Jasper Ave Nw, Edmonton, AB, T5J
3N7

Emp Here 1,000
SIC 4612 Crude petroleum pipelines

D-U-N-S 25-998-3302   (SL)
EPCOR POWER (WILLIAMS LAKE) LTD
10065 Jasper Ave Nw, Edmonton, AB, T5J
3B1
(780) 412-3191
Emp Here 750   *Sales* 482,554,560
SIC 4911 Electric services
Pr Pr Don Lowry
VP VP Kate Chisholm

D-U-N-S 24-330-8939   (BR)
ERNST & YOUNG INC
10020 100 St Nw Suite 2200, Edmonton, AB,
T5J 0N3
(780) 423-5811
Emp Here 60
SIC 8721 Accounting, auditing, and bookkeeping

D-U-N-S 24-097-8879   (BR)
FAIRMONT HOTELS & RESORTS INC
FAIRMONT HOTEL MACDONALD, THE
10065 100 St Nw, Edmonton, AB, T5J 0N6
(780) 424-5181
Emp Here 200
SIC 7011 Hotels and motels

D-U-N-S 25-683-5182   (SL)
FAS BENEFIT ADMINISTRATORS LTD
10154 - 108 St Nw, Edmonton, AB, T5J 1L3
(780) 452-5161
Emp Here 42   *Sales* 19,699,389
SIC 6726 Investment offices, nec
Pr Deb Petryk

D-U-N-S 25-293-2322   (BR)
FINANCIERE BANQUE NATIONALE INC
NATIONAL BANK FINANCIAL WEALTH MANAGEMENT
10180 101 St Nw Unit 3500, Edmonton, AB,
T5J 3S4
(780) 412-6600
Emp Here 36
SIC 6211 Security brokers and dealers

D-U-N-S 20-059-1852   (BR)
FORD CREDIT CANADA LIMITED
SALES BRANCH
(*Suby of* Ford Motor Company)
Gd Stn Main, Edmonton, AB, T5J 2G8
(877) 636-7346
Emp Here 29
SIC 6141 Personal credit institutions

D-U-N-S 24-065-7155   (BR)
FUJITSU CONSEIL (CANADA) INC
FUJITSU CONSULTING
10020 101a Ave Nw Suite 1500, Edmonton,
AB, T5J 3G2

(780) 423-2070
Emp Here 200
SIC 7376 Computer facilities management

D-U-N-S 20-179-6310   (SL)
GE FANUC AUTOMATION CANADA COMPANY
10235 101 St Nw, Edmonton, AB, T5J 3G1
(780) 420-2000
Emp Here 100   *Sales* 12,403,319
SIC 7372 Prepackaged software
Dir Sandra Cox

D-U-N-S 20-553-7058   (SL)
GLOBAL IQ INC
(*Suby of* Synteracthcr Holdings Corporation)
10230 Jasper Ave Nw Suite 4570, Edmonton,
AB, T5J 4P6
(780) 420-0633
Emp Here 50   *Sales* 3,486,617
SIC 8731 Commercial physical research

D-U-N-S 20-579-8957   (BR)
GOVERNMENT OF THE PROVINCE OF ALBERTA
PROSECUTOR'S OFFICE
10365 97 St Nw Suite 901, Edmonton, AB,
T5J 3W7
(780) 422-1111
Emp Here 150
SIC 8111 Legal services

D-U-N-S 20-579-9302   (BR)
GOVERNMENT OF THE PROVINCE OF ALBERTA
ALBERTA SENIORS AND COMMUNITY SUPPORT
10405 Jasper Ave Nw Suite 600, Edmonton,
AB, T5J 3N4
(780) 422-0105
Emp Here 125
SIC 8399 Social services, nec

D-U-N-S 25-092-3567   (BR)
GOVERNMENT OF THE PROVINCE OF ALBERTA
ENTERPRISE AND ADVANCED EDUCATION
10020 101a Ave Nw Suite 600, Edmonton, AB,
T5J 3G2
(780) 427-4498
Emp Here 100
SIC 8748 Business consulting, nec

D-U-N-S 20-734-4594   (BR)
GOVERNMENT OF THE PROVINCE OF ALBERTA
P D D (PERSONS WITH DEVELOPMENTAL DISSABILITIES)
10258 108 St Nw, Edmonton, AB, T5J 4Z7
(780) 427-2817
Emp Here 60
SIC 8322 Individual and family services

D-U-N-S 20-007-9783   (BR)
GOVERNMENT OF THE PROVINCE OF ALBERTA
ALBERTA LEARNING
10155 102 St Nw Suite 1109, Edmonton, AB,
T5J 4L4
(780) 427-8392
Emp Here 800
SIC 8999 Services, nec

D-U-N-S 20-579-7744   (BR)
GOVERNMENT OF THE PROVINCE OF ALBERTA
ALBERTA SENIOR AND COMMUNITY SUPPORT
10011 109 St Nw Suite 109, Edmonton, AB,
T5J 3S8
(780) 427-1177
Emp Here 25
SIC 8322 Individual and family services

D-U-N-S 24-703-0091   (BR)
GRANT THORNTON LLP
10060 Jasper Ave Nw Suite 1701, Edmonton,
AB, T5J 3R8

(780) 422-7114
Emp Here 120
SIC 8721 Accounting, auditing, and bookkeeping

D-U-N-S 20-108-3040   (BR)
GREAT PACIFIC INDUSTRIES INC
SAVE-ON-FOODS
10180 109 St Nw, Edmonton, AB, T5J 5B4
(780) 423-5678
Emp Here 180
SIC 5411 Grocery stores

D-U-N-S 24-002-4208   (BR)
GREAT-WEST LIFE ASSURANCE COMPANY, THE
10110 104 St Nw Suite 202, Edmonton, AB,
T5J 4R5
(780) 917-7776
Emp Here 80
SIC 6321 Accident and health insurance

D-U-N-S 24-853-5437   (BR)
HSBC BANK CANADA
10250 101 St Nw Suite 1530, Edmonton, AB,
T5J 3P4
(780) 428-1144
Emp Here 33
SIC 6021 National commercial banks

D-U-N-S 20-808-4954   (BR)
HSBC BANK CANADA
10561 Jasper Ave Nw, Edmonton, AB, T5J
1Z4
(780) 423-3563
Emp Here 60
SIC 6021 National commercial banks

D-U-N-S 24-449-1648   (BR)
HALF, ROBERT CANADA INC
ACCOUNTEMPS, DIV OF
(*Suby of* Robert Half International Inc.)
10180 101 St Nw Suite 1280, Edmonton, AB,
T5J 3S4
(780) 423-1466
Emp Here 25
SIC 7361 Employment agencies

D-U-N-S 25-686-9397   (BR)
HALF, ROBERT CANADA INC
(*Suby of* Robert Half International Inc.)
10180 101 St Nw Suite 1280, Edmonton, AB,
T5J 3S4
(780) 409-8780
Emp Here 30
SIC 7361 Employment agencies

D-U-N-S 24-449-2406   (BR)
HALF, ROBERT CANADA INC
(*Suby of* Robert Half International Inc.)
10180 101 St Nw Suite 1280, Edmonton, AB,
T5J 3S4
(780) 429-1750
Emp Here 25
SIC 7361 Employment agencies

D-U-N-S 20-082-4811   (BR)
HOLT, RENFREW & CIE, LIMITEE
HOLT RENFREW
10180 101 St Nw, Edmonton, AB, T5J 3S4
(780) 425-5300
Emp Here 95
SIC 5611 Men's and boys' clothing stores

D-U-N-S 20-644-6291   (SL)
HOSPITAL ACTIVITY BOOK FOR CHILDREN
10104 103 Ave Nw Suite 925, Edmonton, AB,
T5J 0H8
(780) 425-5335
Emp Here 50   *Sales* 2,918,428
SIC 2741 Miscellaneous publishing

D-U-N-S 20-179-1956   (BR)
HUDSON'S BAY COMPANY
HOME OUTFITTERS
220 Edmonton City Centre Nw, Edmonton,
AB, T5J 2Y9
(780) 701-0162
Emp Here 60

SIC 5651 Family clothing stores

D-U-N-S 24-003-6459   (BR)
IBI GROUP
10830 Jasper Ave Nw Suite 300, Edmonton, AB, T5J 2B3
(780) 428-4000
Emp Here 130
SIC 8712 Architectural services

D-U-N-S 25-989-6629   (BR)
IBM CANADA LIMITED
(*Suby of* International Business Machines Corporation)
10044 108 St Nw Suite 401, Edmonton, AB, T5J 3S7
(780) 642-4100
Emp Here 1,000
SIC 3571 Electronic computers

D-U-N-S 25-319-1654   (BR)
INDEPENDENT ORDER OF FORESTERS, THE
10235 101 St Nw Suite 1311, Edmonton, AB, T5J 3E8
(780) 425-2948
Emp Here 50
SIC 6311 Life insurance

D-U-N-S 20-651-6481   (BR)
INVESTORS GROUP FINANCIAL SERVICES INC
10060 Jasper Ave Nw Suite 2400, Edmonton, AB, T5J 3R8
(780) 448-1988
Emp Here 100
SIC 8741 Management services

D-U-N-S 20-353-2044   (SL)
JASPER AVENUE PIZZA LIMITED
BOSTON PIZZA
10620 Jasper Ave Nw, Edmonton, AB, T5J 2A3
(780) 423-2333
Emp Here 55   *Sales* 1,678,096
SIC 5812 Eating places

D-U-N-S 24-642-3230   (SL)
KBIM PORTABLE MACHINING LTD
Gd Stn Main, Edmonton, AB, T5J 2G8
(780) 463-0613
Emp Here 50   *Sales* 3,064,349
SIC 7699 Repair services, nec

D-U-N-S 24-671-2376   (BR)
KPMG INC
10125 102 St Nw, Edmonton, AB, T5J 3V8
(780) 429-7300
Emp Here 250
SIC 8721 Accounting, auditing, and book-keeping

D-U-N-S 25-301-5556   (BR)
KPMG LLP
K P M G MANAGEMENT CONSULTING
(*Suby of* KPMG LLP)
10125 102 St Nw, Edmonton, AB, T5J 3V8
(780) 429-7300
Emp Here 200
SIC 8721 Accounting, auditing, and book-keeping

D-U-N-S 20-180-8438   (BR)
KASIAN ARCHITECTURE INTERIOR DESIGN AND PLANNING LTD
10150 Jasper Ave Nw Suite 251, Edmonton, AB, T5J 1W4
(780) 990-0800
Emp Here 50
SIC 8712 Architectural services

D-U-N-S 24-125-2522   (SL)
KINGSTON ROSS PASNAK LLP
9888 Jasper Ave Nw Suite 1500, Edmonton, AB, T5J 5C6
(780) 424-3000
Emp Here 91   *Sales* 4,012,839
SIC 8721 Accounting, auditing, and book-keeping

D-U-N-S 20-899-2081   (BR)
LONDON LIFE INSURANCE COMPANY
FREEDOM 55 FINANCIAL
10250 101 St Nw Suite 1400, Edmonton, AB, T5J 3P4
(780) 428-8585
Emp Here 30
SIC 6311 Life insurance

D-U-N-S 24-336-3202   (BR)
LONG VIEW SYSTEMS CORPORATION
10180 101 St Nw Suite 1000, Edmonton, AB, T5J 3S4

Emp Here 22
SIC 7379 Computer related services, nec

D-U-N-S 24-389-2671   (BR)
MLT AIKINS LLP
10235 101 St Nw Suite 2200, Edmonton, AB, T5J 3G1
(780) 969-3500
Emp Here 20
SIC 8111 Legal services

D-U-N-S 25-562-1013   (BR)
MNP LLP
MNP
10104 103 Ave Nw Suite 400, Edmonton, AB, T5J 0H8
(780) 451-4406
Emp Here 50
SIC 8721 Accounting, auditing, and book-keeping

D-U-N-S 20-304-1900   (BR)
MNP LLP
10235 101 St Nw Suite 1600, Edmonton, AB, T5J 3G1
(780) 822-9420
Emp Here 225
SIC 8721 Accounting, auditing, and book-keeping

D-U-N-S 24-716-3918   (BR)
MACKAY & PARTNERS
(*Suby of* MacKay & Partners)
10010 106 St Nw Suite 705, Edmonton, AB, T5J 3L8
(780) 420-0626
Emp Here 20
SIC 8721 Accounting, auditing, and book-keeping

D-U-N-S 24-906-4619   (HQ)
MACLAB ENTERPRISES CORPORATION
MIDWEST PROPERTY MANAGEMENT
(*Suby of* Maclab Enterprises Corporation)
10205 100 Ave Nw Suite 3400, Edmonton, AB, T5J 4B5
(780) 420-4000
Emp Here 40   *Emp Total* 280
Sales 24,514,795
SIC 6513 Apartment building operators
J. Gregory Greenough
Sandy Mactaggart
Alastair Mactaggart
Marc De Labruyere
Pr Bruce Bentley

D-U-N-S 20-107-3736   (BR)
MALATEST, R. A. & ASSOCIATES LTD
10621 100 Ave Nw Suite 300, Edmonton, AB, T5J 0B3
(780) 448-9042
Emp Here 20
SIC 8732 Commercial nonphysical research

D-U-N-S 20-047-7045   (BR)
MARSH CANADA LIMITED
(*Suby of* Marsh & McLennan Companies, Inc.)
10180 101 St Nw Suite 680, Edmonton, AB, T5J 3S4
(780) 917-4850
Emp Here 25
SIC 6411 Insurance agents, brokers, and service

D-U-N-S 24-246-5396   (BR)

MARSH CANADA LIMITED
(*Suby of* Marsh & McLennan Companies, Inc.)
10180 101 St Suite 680, Edmonton, AB, T5J 3S4
(780) 917-4874
Emp Here 40
SIC 6411 Insurance agents, brokers, and service

D-U-N-S 20-810-0263   (HQ)
MAYFIELD INVESTMENTS LTD
MEDICINE HAT LODGE HOTEL
(*Suby of* Mayfield Investments Ltd)
10010 106 St Nw Suite 1005, Edmonton, AB, T5J 3L8
(780) 424-2921
Emp Here 50   *Emp Total* 200
Sales 12,174,000
SIC 7011 Hotels and motels
Pr Pr Howard Pechet

D-U-N-S 20-334-3913   (BR)
MCDONALD'S RESTAURANTS OF CANADA LIMITED
MCDONALD'S #8543
(*Suby of* McDonald's Corporation)
15 Edmonton City Centre Nw, Edmonton, AB, T5J 2Y7
(780) 414-8343
Emp Here 50
SIC 5812 Eating places

D-U-N-S 25-451-1751   (BR)
MELOCHE MONNEX ASSURANCE ET SERVICES FINANCIERS INC
MELOCHE MONNEX INSURANCE BROKERS
(*Suby of* Toronto-Dominion Bank, The)
10115 100a St Nw Suite 600, Edmonton, AB, T5J 2W2
(780) 429-1112
Emp Here 200
SIC 6411 Insurance agents, brokers, and service

D-U-N-S 24-345-6188   (BR)
MELOCHE MONNEX INC
(*Suby of* Toronto-Dominion Bank, The)
10025 102a Ave Nw Suite 2300, Edmonton, AB, T5J 2Z2
(800) 268-8955
Emp Here 200
SIC 6411 Insurance agents, brokers, and service

D-U-N-S 20-561-9419   (BR)
MILLER THOMSON LLP
10155 102 St Nw Suite 2700, Edmonton, AB, T5J 4G8
(780) 429-1751
Emp Here 150
SIC 8111 Legal services

D-U-N-S 20-297-2746   (SL)
MILTON MANAGEMENT
10155 102 St Nw Suite 2700, Edmonton, AB, T5J 4G8
(780) 429-1751
Emp Here 40   *Sales* 5,341,600
SIC 8741 Management services
Dennis Francis

D-U-N-S 20-589-9227   (BR)
NAV CANADA
Gd Stn Main, Edmonton, AB, T5J 2G8
(780) 890-4343
Emp Here 20
SIC 4899 Communication services, nec

D-U-N-S 20-895-0931   (BR)
NORDIC INSURANCE COMPANY OF CANADA, THE
ING INSURANCE COMPANY OF CANADA
10130 103 St Nw Unit 800, Edmonton, AB, T5J 3N9
(780) 945-5000
Emp Here 300
SIC 6411 Insurance agents, brokers, and service

vice
D-U-N-S 24-065-3121   (BR)
NORTEL NETWORKS LIMITED
10235 101 St Nw Suite 2200, Edmonton, AB, T5J 3G1

Emp Here 35
SIC 4899 Communication services, nec

D-U-N-S 24-341-6703   (BR)
NORTH CARIBOO FLYING SERVICE LTD
NORTH CARIBOO AIR
Airport Service Rd 9th Ave, Edmonton, AB, T5J 2T2
(780) 890-7600
Emp Here 33
SIC 4522 Air transportation, nonscheduled

D-U-N-S 24-807-3264   (BR)
NORTHBRIDGE COMMERCIAL INSURANCE CORPORATION
10707 100 Ave, Fl 10, Edmonton, AB, T5J 3M1
(780) 421-7890
Emp Here 23
SIC 6411 Insurance agents, brokers, and service

D-U-N-S 20-898-0961   (BR)
OMNICOM CANADA CORP
DDB CANADA
(*Suby of* Omnicom Group Inc.)
10025 102a Ave Nw Unit 1900, Edmonton, AB, T5J 2Z2
(780) 424-7000
Emp Here 30
SIC 7311 Advertising agencies

D-U-N-S 24-161-7021   (BR)
PEO CANADA LTD
10304 Jasper Ave Nw, Edmonton, AB, T5J 1Y7
(780) 429-9058
Emp Here 35
SIC 7361 Employment agencies

D-U-N-S 24-809-8600   (BR)
PLH AVIATION SERVICES INC
Gd, Edmonton, AB, T5J 2G8
(780) 890-4400
Emp Here 40
SIC 5172 Petroleum products, nec

D-U-N-S 24-331-8565   (HQ)
PEACE HILLS GENERAL INSURANCE COMPANY
PEACE HILLS INSURANCE
10709 Jasper Ave Nw Suite 300, Edmonton, AB, T5J 3N3
(780) 424-3986
Emp Here 117   *Emp Total* 20
Sales 14,446,219
SIC 6411 Insurance agents, brokers, and service
Pr Pr Diane Brickner
Marvin Yellowbird
Pat Buffalo
Victor Buffalo

D-U-N-S 25-327-0375   (SL)
PERSONAL SUPPORT & DEVELOPMENT NETWORK INC
P S D N
10621 100 Ave Nw Suite 560, Edmonton, AB, T5J 0B3
(780) 496-9224
Emp Here 40   *Sales* 5,579,750
SIC 8742 Management consulting services
Pr Pr Garry Rentz
Donna Rentz
Jill Dean

D-U-N-S 25-064-4341   (BR)
POSTMEDIA NETWORK INC
EDMONTON JOURNAL, THE
10006 101 St Nw, Edmonton, AB, T5J 0S1
(780) 429-5100
Emp Here 648

SIC 2711 Newspapers

D-U-N-S 25-995-4311   (BR)
PRICEWATERHOUSECOOPERS LLP
10088 102 Ave Nw Suite 1501, Edmonton, AB,
T5J 3N5
(780) 441-6700
Emp Here 200
SIC 8721 Accounting, auditing, and book-
keeping

D-U-N-S 24-395-6372   (BR)
RBC DOMINION SECURITIES INC
RBC DOMINION SECURITIES
(*Suby of* Royal Bank Of Canada)
10235 101 St Nw Suite 2400, Edmonton, AB,
T5J 3G1
(780) 428-0601
Emp Here 55
SIC 6211 Security brokers and dealers

D-U-N-S 20-153-7318   (BR)
RAYMOND JAMES (USA) LTD
(*Suby of* Raymond James Financial, Inc.)
10060 Jasper Ave Nw Suite 2300, Edmonton,
AB, T5J 3R8
(780) 414-2500
Emp Here 22
SIC 6211 Security brokers and dealers

D-U-N-S 20-195-4232   (BR)
REVERA INC
CHURCHILL RETIREMENT COMMUNITY,
THE
10015 103 Ave Nw Suite 1208, Edmonton, AB,
T5J 0H1
(780) 420-1222
Emp Here 80
SIC 8361 Residential care

D-U-N-S 20-143-4789   (BR)
REVERA INC
10264 100 St Nw, Edmonton, AB, T5J 5C2
(780) 988-7711
Emp Here 25
SIC 8741 Management services

D-U-N-S 24-254-8514   (BR)
RICOH CANADA INC
10150 Jasper Ave Nw Suite 163, Edmonton,
AB, T5J 1W4
(780) 930-7100
Emp Here 20
SIC 5044 Office equipment

D-U-N-S 20-084-0866   (BR)
RILEY'S REPRODUCTIONS & PRINTING
LTD
10180 108 St Nw, Edmonton, AB, T5J 1L3
(780) 413-6801
Emp Here 40
SIC 7334 Photocopying and duplicating ser-
vices

D-U-N-S 24-809-8121   (BR)
ROGERS COMMUNICATIONS INC
ROGERS WIRELESS
(*Suby of* Rogers Communications Inc)
10303 Jasper Ave Nw Suite 1950, Edmonton,
AB, T5J 3N6
(780) 429-1400
Emp Here 25
SIC 5999 Miscellaneous retail stores, nec

D-U-N-S 20-811-3258   (BR)
ROYAL BANK OF CANADA
RBC
(*Suby of* Royal Bank Of Canada)
10107 Jasper Ave Nw Suite 301, Edmonton,
AB, T5J 1W9
(780) 448-6611
Emp Here 30
SIC 6021 National commercial banks

D-U-N-S 20-087-8689   (BR)
ROYAL BANK OF CANADA
RBC
(*Suby of* Royal Bank Of Canada)
Gd Stn Main Edmonton, AB, T5J 2G8

(519) 821-5610
Emp Here 30
SIC 6021 National commercial banks

D-U-N-S 20-810-3440   (BR)
RUSSELL A. FARROW LIMITED
(*Suby of* Farrow Group Inc)
10310 Jasper Ave Nw Suite 500, Edmonton,
AB, T5J 2W4
(780) 423-5444
Emp Here 30
SIC 4731 Freight transportation arrangement

D-U-N-S 20-084-1864   (SL)
RUSSELL FOOD EQUIPMENT (EDMON-
TON) LIMITED
10225 106 St Nw, Edmonton, AB, T5J 1H5
(780) 423-4221
Emp Here 50   *Sales* 6,858,306
SIC 5046 Commercial equipment, nec

D-U-N-S 24-346-8928   (SL)
RUTH'S CHRIS STEAK HOUSE EDMON-
TON
10103 100 St Nw, Edmonton, AB, T5J 0N8
(780) 990-0123
Emp Here 90   *Sales* 2,699,546
SIC 5812 Eating places

D-U-N-S 24-125-8164   (BR)
SNC-LAVALIN INC
10235 101 St Nw Suite 608, Edmonton, AB,
T5J 3G1
(780) 426-1000
Emp Here 250
SIC 8711 Engineering services

D-U-N-S 20-720-7184   (BR)
SCOTIA CAPITAL INC
SCOTIA MCLEOD
10104 103 Ave Nw Suite 2000, Edmonton, AB,
T5J 0H8
(780) 497-3200
Emp Here 75
SIC 6211 Security brokers and dealers

D-U-N-S 24-961-0171   (BR)
SIERRA SYSTEMS GROUP INC
10104 103 Ave Nw Unit 1300, Edmonton, AB,
T5J 0H8
(780) 424-0852
Emp Here 81
SIC 7379 Computer related services, nec

D-U-N-S 24-609-4259   (BR)
SOBEYS CAPITAL INCORPORATED
SOBEYS JASPER # 104
10404 Jasper Ave Nw Suite 3023, Edmonton,
AB, T5J 1Z3
(780) 429-9922
Emp Here 73
SIC 5411 Grocery stores

D-U-N-S 25-341-7679   (BR)
SOBEYS WEST INC
1858230 82nd Ave, Edmonton, AB, T5J 2K2
(780) 469-9452
Emp Here 150
SIC 5411 Grocery stores

D-U-N-S 20-300-6861   (BR)
STANTEC CONSULTING LTD
10060 Jasper Ave Nw Suite 2001, Edmonton,
AB, T5J 3R8
(780) 229-1070
Emp Here 39
SIC 8711 Engineering services

D-U-N-S 20-644-6945   (BR)
STARBUCKS COFFEE CANADA, INC
(*Suby of* Starbucks Corporation)
10116 109 St Nw, Edmonton, AB, T5J 1M7
(780) 425-5133
Emp Here 28
SIC 5812 Eating places

D-U-N-S 24-115-9495   (BR)
SUN LIFE FINANCIAL TRUST INC
10123 99 T, Edmonton, AB, T5J 3H1

(780) 441-4474
Emp Here 20
SIC 6411 Insurance agents, brokers, and ser-
vice

D-U-N-S 25-361-1933   (BR)
SUNCOR ENERGY INC
EDMONTON REFINERY
Gd Stn Main, Edmonton, AB, T5J 2G8
(780) 410-5610
Emp Here 350
SIC 2911 Petroleum refining

D-U-N-S 20-554-7958   (BR)
SUTTON PLACE GRANDE LIMITED
THE SUTTON PLACE HOTEL EDMONTON
(*Suby of* Northland Properties Corporation)
10235 101 St Nw, Edmonton, AB, T5J 3E8
(780) 428-7111
Emp Here 150
SIC 7011 Hotels and motels

D-U-N-S 20-650-8090   (BR)
TELUS CORPORATION
10035 102 Ave Nw, Edmonton, AB, T5J 0E5
(780) 493-2998
Emp Here 20
SIC 4812 Radiotelephone communication

D-U-N-S 24-066-3377   (SL)
TECHNA-WEST ENGINEERING LTD
(*Suby of* Jacobs Engineering Group Inc.)
10010 106 St Nw Suite 600, Edmonton, AB,
T5J 3L8
(780) 451-4800
Emp Here 20   *Sales* 9,914,160
SIC 8711 Engineering services
Pr Pr Janko Misic
VP VP Mahary Gregory

D-U-N-S 25-677-5057   (HQ)
TELUS SERVICES INC
10020 100 St Nw Suite 100, Edmonton, AB,
T5J 0N5
(780) 493-7282
Emp Here 100   *Emp Total* 51,250
Sales 89,595,740
SIC 4899 Communication services, nec
Pr Pr Joseph Natale
VP Robert Mcfarlane

D-U-N-S 25-073-8275   (BR)
TICKETMASTER CANADA LP
10060 Jasper Ave Nw Suite 1800, Edmonton,
AB, T5J 3R8
(780) 447-6822
Emp Here 30
SIC 7999 Amusement and recreation, nec

D-U-N-S 25-315-5287   (BR)
TORONTO-DOMINION BANK, THE
TD BANK
(*Suby of* Toronto-Dominion Bank, The)
10004 Jasper Ave Nw Suite 500, Edmonton,
AB, T5J 1R3
(780) 448-8251
Emp Here 300
SIC 6021 National commercial banks

D-U-N-S 20-647-3717   (BR)
TRIOVEST REALTY ADVISORS INC
10025 Jasper Ave Nw Suite 48, Edmonton,
AB, T5J 2B8
(780) 990-1768
Emp Here 41
SIC 6519 Real property lessors, nec

D-U-N-S 24-345-7558   (BR)
UNIVERSITY OF LETHBRIDGE, THE
10707 100 Ave Nw Suite 1100, Edmonton, AB,
T5J 3M1
(780) 424-0425
Emp Here 100
SIC 8221 Colleges and universities

D-U-N-S 20-732-9066   (BR)
URBAN SYSTEMS LTD
10345 105 St Nw Suite 200, Edmonton, AB,
T5J 1E8

(780) 430-4041
Emp Here 70
SIC 8711 Engineering services

D-U-N-S 24-101-4583   (BR)
VANCOUVER CAREER COLLEGE (BURN-
ABY) INC
CDI COLLEGE
(*Suby of* Chung Family Holdings Inc)
10004 Jasper Ave Suite 200, Edmonton, AB,
T5J 1R3
(780) 424-6650
Emp Here 30
SIC 8221 Colleges and universities

D-U-N-S 20-715-5438   (BR)
WALTON INTERNATIONAL GROUP INC
10060 Jasper Ave Nw Suite 1450, Edmonton,
AB, T5J 3R8

Emp Here 20
SIC 6519 Real property lessors, nec

D-U-N-S 20-731-9455   (HQ)
XEROX BUSINESS SERVICES CANADA
INC.
(*Suby of* Xerox Corporation)
10117 Jasper Ave Nw Suite 101, Edmonton,
AB, T5J 1W8
(780) 421-8840
Emp Here 30   *Emp Total* 37,900
Sales 12,532,976
SIC 3674 Semiconductors and related devices
Dir John Butcher
Dir Michael Huerta
Dir Ernest D Mcnee

D-U-N-S 25-505-5543   (BR)
XEROX CANADA INC
(*Suby of* Xerox Corporation)
10180 101 St Nw Suite 1350, Edmonton, AB,
T5J 3S4
(780) 493-7800
Emp Here 100
SIC 5044 Office equipment

D-U-N-S 25-532-8247   (HQ)
ZAINUL & SHAZMA HOLDINGS (1997) LTD
HOLIDAY INN EXPRESS
(*Suby of* Zainul & Shazma Holdings (1997)
Ltd)
10080 Jasper Ave Nw Suite 900, Edmonton,
AB, T5J 1V9
(780) 702-5049
Emp Here 22   *Emp Total* 104
Sales 4,523,563
SIC 7011 Hotels and motels

D-U-N-S 20-205-4875   (BR)
IMARKETING SOLUTIONS GROUP INC
10025 106 St Nw Suite 200, Edmonton, AB,
T5J 1G4
(780) 482-5801
Emp Here 70
SIC 8399 Social services, nec

Edmonton, AB T5K

D-U-N-S 25-228-9699   (SL)
ABC HEAD START SOCIETY
9829 103 St Nw, Edmonton, AB, T5K 0X9
(780) 461-5353
Emp Here 130   *Sales* 7,101,500
SIC 8322 Individual and family services
Ex Dir Kathy Lenihan

D-U-N-S 24-347-9578   (BR)
ALBERTA HEALTH SERVICES
EDMONTON MENTAL HEALTH CLINIC
9942 108 St Nw, Edmonton, AB, T5K 2J5
(780) 342-7700
Emp Here 300
SIC 8062 General medical and surgical hospi-
tals

D-U-N-S 20-974-4726   (BR)

ALBERTA HEALTH SERVICES
CHARITAS HEALTH GROUP
11111 Jasper Ave Nw, Edmonton, AB, T5K 0L4
(780) 482-8111
Emp Here 100
SIC 8011 Offices and clinics of medical doctors

D-U-N-S 20-581-3145   (BR)
ALBERTA TREASURY BRANCHES
ATB FINANCIAL
11366 104 Ave Nw, Edmonton, AB, T5K 2W9
(780) 422-4800
Emp Here 20
SIC 6036 Savings institutions, except federal

D-U-N-S 20-589-4970   (BR)
BANQUE TORONTO-DOMINION, LA
TD CANADA TRUST
(*Suby of* Toronto-Dominion Bank, The)
11704 Jasper Ave Nw, Edmonton, AB, T5K 0N3
(780) 448-8480
Emp Here 20
SIC 6021 National commercial banks

D-U-N-S 24-582-9007   (SL)
BRUINSMA HOLDINGS LTD
10232 112 St Nw Suite 200, Edmonton, AB, T5K 1M4
(780) 421-4300
Emp Here 218   *Sales* 42,506,880
SIC 6712 Bank holding companies
Pr Pr Henry Bruinsma
  Theodore Bruinsma

D-U-N-S 25-303-5695   (BR)
CANADIAN IMPERIAL BANK OF COMMERCE
CIBC
11504 104 Ave Nw, Edmonton, AB, T5K 2S5
(780) 408-1183
Emp Here 22
SIC 6021 National commercial banks

D-U-N-S 20-308-7952   (BR)
CARA OPERATIONS LIMITED
KELSEY'S
(*Suby of* Cara Holdings Limited)
11736 104 Ave Nw, Edmonton, AB, T5K 2P3
(403) 217-7780
Emp Here 38
SIC 5812 Eating places

D-U-N-S 20-919-7602   (SL)
CARITAS HEALTH GROUP REHABILITATION MEDICINE
11111 Jasper Ave Nw Rm 2y08, Edmonton, AB, T5K 0L4
(780) 342-8163
Emp Here 50   *Sales* 2,858,628
SIC 8049 Offices of health practitioner

D-U-N-S 20-648-2445   (BR)
CRITICAL CONTROL ENERGY SERVICES CORP
10045 111 St Nw, Edmonton, AB, T5K 2M5
(780) 423-3100
Emp Here 100
SIC 8742 Management consulting services

D-U-N-S 24-643-3619   (BR)
EARL'S RESTAURANTS LTD
EARL'S TIN PALACE RESTAURANT
(*Suby of* Earl's Restaurants Ltd)
11830 Jasper Ave Nw, Edmonton, AB, T5K 0N7
(780) 488-6582
Emp Here 140
SIC 5812 Eating places

D-U-N-S 20-808-1919   (HQ)
EDMONTON CATHOLIC SEPARATE SCHOOL DISTRICT NO.7
EDMONTON CATHOLIC SCHOOLS
(*Suby of* Edmonton Catholic Separate School District No.7)

9807 106 St Nw Suite 7, Edmonton, AB, T5K 1C2
(780) 441-6000
Emp Here 120   *Emp Total* 3,500
Sales 398,305,864
SIC 8211 Elementary and secondary schools
Superintnt Joan Carr
  Barry Devlin
Ch Bd Debbie Engel
  Becky Kallal
Trst Cindy Olsen
Trst Rudy Arcilla
Trst Marilyn Bergstra
Trst Kara Pelech

D-U-N-S 20-031-8272   (BR)
EDMONTON SCHOOL DISTRICT NO. 7
OLIVER ELEMENTARY SCHOOL
10227 118 St Nw, Edmonton, AB, T5K 2V4
(780) 488-1221
Emp Here 30
SIC 8211 Elementary and secondary schools

D-U-N-S 20-028-3559   (BR)
EDMONTON SCHOOL DISTRICT NO. 7
9807 106 St Nw, Edmonton, AB, T5K 1C2
(780) 441-6000
Emp Here 200
SIC 8211 Elementary and secondary schools

D-U-N-S 25-451-1603   (BR)
FAMILY VISION CARE LTD
VISION MED
(*Suby of* Family Vision Care Ltd)
11208 104 Ave Nw, Edmonton, AB, T5K 2X4
(780) 421-0816
Emp Here 20
SIC 5995 Optical goods stores

D-U-N-S 20-028-8756   (BR)
GOVERNMENT OF THE PROVINCE OF ALBERTA
ERIC CORMACK CENTRE
9835 112 St Nw, Edmonton, AB, T5K 2E7
(780) 427-2764
Emp Here 100
SIC 8361 Residential care

D-U-N-S 20-536-9346   (BR)
GOVERNMENT OF THE PROVINCE OF ALBERTA
EMPLOYMENT AND IMMIGRATION
10808 99 Ave Nw, Edmonton, AB, T5K 0G5
(780) 422-7345
Emp Here 25
SIC 8742 Management consulting services

D-U-N-S 20-579-7637   (BR)
GOVERNMENT OF THE PROVINCE OF ALBERTA
SERVICE ALBERTA
8th Floor, Edmonton, AB, T5K 2J5
(780) 422-0017
Emp Here 24
SIC 8743 Public relations services

D-U-N-S 24-227-7494   (BR)
GOVERNMENT OF THE PROVINCE OF ALBERTA
ALBERTA TREASURY BOARD
9820 106 St Nw Suite 534, Edmonton, AB, T5K 2J6
(780) 427-3076
Emp Here 600
SIC 6289 Security and commodity service

D-U-N-S 20-571-5076   (BR)
GOVERNMENT OF THE PROVINCE OF ALBERTA
ALBERTA SUSTAINABLE RESOURCE DEV
9820 106 St Nw, Edmonton, AB, T5K 2J6
(780) 422-4106
Emp Here 60
SIC 7374 Data processing and preparation

D-U-N-S 24-077-8600   (BR)
HOPE MISSION SOCIETY
10336 114 St Nw, Edmonton, AB, T5K 1S3

(780) 453-3877
Emp Here 180
SIC 8399 Social services, nec

D-U-N-S 25-326-5417   (BR)
JOEY TOMATO'S KITCHENS INC
JOEY TOMATO'S RESTAURANT
(*Suby of* Joey Tomato's)
11228 Jasper Ave Nw, Edmonton, AB, T5K 2V2
(780) 420-1996
Emp Here 166
SIC 5812 Eating places

D-U-N-S 25-273-0908   (BR)
LONDON DRUGS LIMITED
11704 104 Ave Nw Suite 45, Edmonton, AB, T5K 2T6
(780) 944-4545
Emp Here 50
SIC 5912 Drug stores and proprietary stores

D-U-N-S 25-311-2189   (BR)
MCDONALD'S RESTAURANTS OF CANADA LIMITED
MCDONALD'S
(*Suby of* McDonald's Corporation)
11660 104 Ave Nw, Edmonton, AB, T5K 2T7
(780) 414-8405
Emp Here 67
SIC 5812 Eating places

D-U-N-S 20-747-7501   (SL)
NORTHERN LEAGUE IN EDMONTON, THE
EDMONTON CRACKER CAT, THE
10233 96 Ave Nw, Edmonton, AB, T5K 0A5
(780) 423-2255
Emp Here 37   *Sales* 8,828,245
SIC 7941 Sports clubs, managers, and promoters
Dir Dean Hengel

D-U-N-S 20-082-6159   (BR)
PINCHIN WEST LTD
(*Suby of* W.O.H.A Holdings Limited)
9707 110 St Nw Suite 200, Edmonton, AB, T5K 2L9
(780) 425-6600
Emp Here 25
SIC 8748 Business consulting, nec

D-U-N-S 20-921-5131   (SL)
ROSEDALE DEVELOPMENT CORP
ROSEDALE PARTNERSHIP
10103 111 St Nw Suite 105, Edmonton, AB, T5K 2Y1
(780) 426-7677
Emp Here 50   *Sales* 1,824,018
SIC 8361 Residential care

D-U-N-S 20-922-4489   (BR)
ROYAL BANK OF CANADA
RBC FINANCIAL GROUP
(*Suby of* Royal Bank Of Canada)
11604 104 Ave Nw Suite 3, Edmonton, AB, T5K 2T7
(780) 448-6340
Emp Here 22
SIC 6021 National commercial banks

D-U-N-S 24-020-4201   (BR)
SHAWN & ASSOCIATES MANAGEMENT LTD
9515 107 St Nw Suite 402, Edmonton, AB, T5K 2C1

Emp Here 20
SIC 6531 Real estate agents and managers

D-U-N-S 25-271-0413   (BR)
SOBEYS WEST INC
OLIVER SAFEWAY
11410 104 Ave Nw, Edmonton, AB, T5K 2S5
(780) 424-0666
Emp Here 175
SIC 5411 Grocery stores

D-U-N-S 20-192-0019   (HQ)
STANTEC ARCHITECTURE LTD

10160 112 St Nw, Edmonton, AB, T5K 2L6
(780) 917-7000
Emp Here 60   *Emp Total* 15,200
Sales 73,544,386
SIC 8712 Architectural services
VP VP Bruce Raber
  Stanis Ir Smith
  Robert J Gomes
  Alan Hartley

D-U-N-S 20-699-7707   (HQ)
STANTEC CONSULTING INTERNATIONAL LTD
10160 112 St Nw, Edmonton, AB, T5K 2L6
(780) 917-7000
Emp Here 250   *Emp Total* 15,200
Sales 180,577,733
SIC 8711 Engineering services
Pr Pr Robert J Gomes
VP Paul J.D. Alpern
VP John R. Adams
Sec Jennifer Al Addison
Treas Daniel J Lefaivre

D-U-N-S 25-415-9825   (HQ)
STANTEC CONSULTING LTD
10160 112 St Nw, Edmonton, AB, T5K 2L6
(780) 917-7000
Emp Here 1,400   *Emp Total* 15,200
Sales 1,665,546,860
SIC 8711 Engineering services
Pr Pr Robert J Gomes
Ex VP Richard K. Allen
Sec Kenna Houncaren
Treas Daniel J. Lefaivre

D-U-N-S 20-320-1769   (HQ)
STANTEC GEOMATICS LTD
10160 112 St Nw, Edmonton, AB, T5K 2L6
(780) 917-7000
Emp Here 100   *Emp Total* 15,200
Sales 180,577,733
SIC 8713 Surveying services
Pr Pr Robert Gomes

D-U-N-S 25-539-2698   (SL)
TAK INTERNATIONAL LTD
11507 100 Ave Nw, Edmonton, AB, T5K 2R2
(780) 482-1495
Emp Here 25   *Sales* 13,188,500
SIC 6231 Security and commodity exchanges
Pr Pr Brian Trendel
  Brenda Trendel

D-U-N-S 20-281-5726   (BR)
WSP CANADA INC
9925 109 St Nw Suite 1000, Edmonton, AB, T5K 2J8
(780) 466-6555
Emp Here 100
SIC 8713 Surveying services

D-U-N-S 24-134-3446   (SL)
WAMGREN LTD, THE
WAM DEVELOPMENT GROUP
10213 111 St Nw, Edmonton, AB, T5K 2V6
(780) 423-5525
Emp Here 20   *Sales* 7,294,080
SIC 6552 Subdividers and developers, nec

D-U-N-S 20-895-4685   (HQ)
WORKERS' COMPENSATION BOARD ALBERTA
WCB ALBERTA
9912 107 St Nw, Edmonton, AB, T5K 1G5
(780) 498-3999
Emp Here 500   *Emp Total* 35,000
Sales 1,277,955,398
SIC 6331 Fire, marine, and casualty insurance
Pr Pr Guy Kerr
  James Kindrake
Dir Alex Mcpherson
Dir Denis Herard
Dir Fred Nowicki

Edmonton, AB T5L

D-U-N-S 20-251-4550   (SL)
1471899 ALBERTA LTD
WOODWOORK & PUB INTERIORS
13040 148 St, Edmonton, AB, T5L 2H8
(780) 460-2399
Emp Here 28   *Sales* 5,180,210
SIC 1542 Nonresidential construction, nec
Pr Cory Brightwell

D-U-N-S 24-851-8003   (HQ)
324007 ALBERTA LTD
NILSSON BROS. LIVESTOCK EXCHANGE
13220 St Albert Trail Nw Suite 303, Edmonton,
AB, T5L 4W1
(780) 477-2233
Emp Here 30   *Emp Total* 1,400
Sales 29,139,200
SIC 7389 Business services, nec
Pr Pr Lee William Nilsson
Dir William T Grieve
Dir Brian Lynn Nilsson
 Patrick Bieleny

D-U-N-S 24-204-8978   (BR)
ACKLANDS - GRAINGER INC
WESTWARD TOOLS & EQUIPMENT, DIV OF
(*Suby of* W.W. Grainger, Inc.)
14360 123 Ave Nw, Edmonton, AB, T5L 2Y3
(780) 454-8180
Emp Here 75
SIC 5085 Industrial supplies

D-U-N-S 25-236-1985   (BR)
ALBERTA TREASURY BRANCHES
ATB FINANCIAL
13304 137 Ave Nw, Edmonton, AB, T5L 4Z6
(780) 427-7353
Emp Here 20
SIC 6036 Savings institutions, except federal

D-U-N-S 24-326-4822   (BR)
ALSCO CANADA CORPORATION
14710 123 Ave Nw, Edmonton, AB, T5L 2Y4
(780) 454-9641
Emp Here 100
SIC 7211 Power laundries, family and commercial

D-U-N-S 24-041-9445   (BR)
BRICK WAREHOUSE LP, THE
BRICK, THE
12222 137 Ave Nw Suite 101, Edmonton, AB,
T5L 4X5
(780) 472-4272
Emp Here 30
SIC 5712 Furniture stores

D-U-N-S 20-898-4294   (BR)
BRINK'S CANADA LIMITED
(*Suby of* The Brink's Company)
14680 134 Ave Nw, Edmonton, AB, T5L 4T4
(780) 453-5057
Emp Here 120
SIC 7381 Detective and armored car services

D-U-N-S 24-313-5204   (BR)
BUNGE CANADA
14711 128 Ave Nw, Edmonton, AB, T5L 3H3
(780) 452-4720
Emp Here 50
SIC 2079 Ecible fats and oils

D-U-N-S 24-393-9295   (SL)
**CAMPBELL SCIENTIFIC (CANADA) COR-
PORATION**
CSC
14532 131 Ave Nw, Edmonton, AB, T5L 4X4
(780) 454-2505
Emp Here 63   *Sales* 2,945,253
SIC 7629 Electrical repair shops

D-U-N-S 20-580-1520   (BR)
CANADA POST CORPORATION
12135 149 St Nw, Edmonton, AB, T5L 5H2
(780) 945-2600
Emp Here 20

SIC 4311 U.s. postal service

D-U-N-S 24-767-3627   (HQ)
CAPITAL PRINTING & FORMS INC
CAPITAL PRINTING & FORMS INK
(*Suby of* Capital Printing & Forms Inc)
14133 128a Ave Nw, Edmonton, AB, T5L 4P5
(780) 453-5039
Emp Here 51   *Emp Total* 55
Sales 4,012,839
SIC 5112 Stationery and office supplies

D-U-N-S 20-811-3985   (BR)
CARGILL LIMITED
ALBERTA TERMINALS
13020 127 Ave Nw, Edmonton, AB, T5L 4Z5
(780) 454-0475
Emp Here 23
SIC 5153 Grain and field beans

D-U-N-S 24-891-8786   (BR)
CARGILL LIMITED
CARGILL AGHORIZONS
13020 127 Ave Nw, Edmonton, AB, T5L 4Z5
(780) 454-0475
Emp Here 20
SIC 4221 Farm product warehousing and stor-
age

D-U-N-S 24-982-1919   (BR)
CERVUS CONTRACTORS EQUIPMENT LP
BOBCAT OF EDMONTON
14504 Yellowhead Trail Nw, Edmonton, AB,
T5L 3C5
(780) 447-4441
Emp Here 25
SIC 5082 Construction and mining machinery

D-U-N-S 24-044-6034   (BR)
CERVUS LP
SERVICE CONTRACTOR EQUIPMENT
14566 Yellowhead Trail Nw, Edmonton, AB,
T5L 3C5
(780) 448-4522
Emp Here 30
SIC 5999 Miscellaneous retail stores, nec

D-U-N-S 24-005-6010   (HQ)
CHRISTIAN CREDIT UNION LTD
(*Suby of* Christian Credit Union Ltd)
13504 142 St Nw, Edmonton, AB, T5L 4Z2
(780) 426-7165
Emp Here 28   *Emp Total* 33
Sales 6,282,240
SIC 6062 State credit unions
Pr Pr Johannes Bosch
CEO John Velkamp

D-U-N-S 20-896-2282   (HQ)
**CHRYSALIS: AN ALBERTA SOCIETY FOR
CITIZENS WITH DISABILITIES**
CHRYSALIS
(*Suby of* Chrysalis: An Alberta Society For
Citizens With Disabilities)
13325 St Albert Trail Nw, Edmonton, AB, T5L
4R3
(780) 454-9656
Emp Here 110   *Emp Total* 165
Sales 7,733,834
SIC 8331 Job training and related services
Ch Bd Lorri Martin
Ch Bd Mary Pat Barry
V Ch Bd Nancy Cumming
V Ch Bd Kim Dingler
V Ch Bd Garth Norris
Sec Allison Dennis
Dir Cathy Evanochko
Dir Lois Cassie
Dir Paul Brown
Dir Leona Colijn

D-U-N-S 24-103-9135   (BR)
**COMPAGNIE DES CHEMINS DE FER NA-
TIONAUX DU CANADA**
12646 124 St Nw, Edmonton, AB, T5L 0N9
(780) 472-3078
Emp Here 100
SIC 4111 Local and suburban transit

D-U-N-S 20-580-4912   (BR)
**COMPAGNIE DES CHEMINS DE FER NA-
TIONAUX DU CANADA**
C N RAIL
12103 127 Ave Nw, Edmonton, AB, T5L 4X7
(780) 472-3261
Emp Here 190
SIC 4011 Railroads, line-haul operating

D-U-N-S 24-854-9339   (SL)
CRUST CRAFT INC
13211 146 St Nw, Edmonton, AB, T5L 4S8
(780) 466-1333
Emp Here 70   *Sales* 2,407,703
SIC 5461 Retail bakeries

D-U-N-S 24-981-0706   (SL)
DSL INTERNATIONAL LTD
14520 128 Ave Nw, Edmonton, AB, T5L 3H6
(780) 452-7580
Emp Here 40   *Sales* 5,681,200
SIC 6712 Bank holding companies
Pr Rob Ryder

D-U-N-S 20-081-5694   (HQ)
DSL LTD
14520 128 Ave Nw, Edmonton, AB, T5L 3H6
(780) 452-7580
Emp Here 50   *Emp Total* 50
Sales 6,410,257
SIC 5078 Refrigeration equipment and sup-
plies
Pr Brian Tiedemann
Dir Michael Wilson
Dir Steven Rice
Dir Steven Barwick

D-U-N-S 24-702-9515   (HQ)
DENILLE INDUSTRIES LTD
AUBURN RENTALS
14440 Yellowhead Trail Nw, Edmonton, AB,
T5L 3C5
(780) 413-0900
Emp Here 62   *Emp Total* 65
Sales 5,617,974
SIC 7519 Utility trailer rental
Pr Pr Guy Bouvier

D-U-N-S 25-454-4927   (BR)
**EDMONTON   CATHOLIC   SEPARATE
SCHOOL DISTRICT NO.7**
*SIR JOHN THOMPSON CATHOLIC JUNIOR
HIGH SCHOOL*
(*Suby of* Edmonton Catholic Separate School
District No.7)
13525 132 Ave Nw, Edmonton, AB, T5L 3R6
(780) 454-9202
Emp Here 30
SIC 8211 Elementary and secondary schools

D-U-N-S 20-712-7411   (BR)
**EDMONTON   CATHOLIC   SEPARATE
SCHOOL DISTRICT NO.7**
*ST. ANGELA CATHLOIC ELEMENTARY
SCHOOL*
(*Suby of* Edmonton Catholic Separate School
District No.7)
13430 132a St Nw, Edmonton, AB, T5L 1S3
(780) 455-9743
Emp Here 50
SIC 8211 Elementary and secondary schools

D-U-N-S 20-154-8547   (BR)
**EDMONTON   CATHOLIC   SEPARATE
SCHOOL DISTRICT NO.7**
*ST. PIUS X CATHOLIC ELEMENTARY
SCHOOL*
(*Suby of* Edmonton Catholic Separate School
District No.7)
12214 128 St Nw, Edmonton, AB, T5L 1C5
(780) 453-3941
Emp Here 30
SIC 8211 Elementary and secondary schools

D-U-N-S 20-028-3567   (BR)
EDMONTON SCHOOL DISTRICT NO. 7
PRINCE CHARLES ELEMENTARY SCHOOL
12325 127 St Nw, Edmonton, AB, T5L 0Z9

(780) 455-5533
Emp Here 33
SIC 8211 Elementary and secondary schools

D-U-N-S 20-028-3492   (BR)
EDMONTON SCHOOL DISTRICT NO. 7
DOVERCOURT ELEMENTARY SCHOOL
13910 122 Ave Nw, Edmonton, AB, T5L 2W3
(780) 455-6171
Emp Here 30
SIC 8211 Elementary and secondary schools

D-U-N-S 25-267-6648   (BR)
EDMONTON SCHOOL DISTRICT NO. 7
YELLOWHEAD YOUTH CENTRE SCHOOL
12415 125 St Nw, Edmonton, AB, T5L 0T2
(780) 452-9381
Emp Here 22
SIC 8211 Elementary and secondary schools

D-U-N-S 20-154-7606   (BR)
EDMONTON SCHOOL DISTRICT NO. 7
MCARTHUR ELEMENTARY SCHOOL
13535 134 St Nw, Edmonton, AB, T5L 1W3
(780) 455-2728
Emp Here 20
SIC 8211 Elementary and secondary schools

D-U-N-S 20-154-6897   (BR)
EDMONTON SCHOOL DISTRICT NO. 7
ATHLONE ELEMENTARY SCHOOL
12940 129 St Nw, Edmonton, AB, T5L 1J3
(780) 455-5823
Emp Here 25
SIC 8211 Elementary and secondary schools

D-U-N-S 20-117-9947   (HQ)
ELITE SPORTSWEAR & AWARDS LTD
(*Suby of* Alberta Trophy Holdings Ltd)
14703 118 Ave Nw, Edmonton, AB, T5L 2M7
(780) 454-9775
Emp Here 100   *Emp Total* 5
Sales 10,725,223
SIC 5999 Miscellaneous retail stores, nec
Pr Pr Drew Schamehorn
 Harvey Bishop
Dir Bryan Thomas

D-U-N-S 20-736-9401   (BR)
EMCO CORPORATION
WHOLESALE HEATING SUPPLIES
14635 121a Ave Nw, Edmonton, AB, T5L 2T2
(780) 454-9551
Emp Here 30
SIC 5074 Plumbing and heating equipment
and supplies (hydronics)

D-U-N-S 20-990-3652   (BR)
EXCEL RESOURCES SOCIETY
KEDROS FURNITURE, DIV OF
11831 123 St Nw, Edmonton, AB, T5L 0G7
(780) 424-4366
Emp Here 40
SIC 8322 Individual and family services

D-U-N-S 20-617-2082   (BR)
FEDERATED CO-OPERATIVES LIMITED
(*Suby of* Federated Co-Operatives Limited)
12852 141 St Nw, Edmonton, AB, T5L 4N8

Emp Here 24
SIC 5141 Groceries, general line

D-U-N-S 20-537-9811   (HQ)
GATEWAY MECHANICAL SERVICES INC
SATELITE MECHANICAL SERVICES
14605 118 Ave Nw, Edmonton, AB, T5L 2M7
(780) 426-6055
Emp Here 60   *Emp Total* 300
Sales 30,643,494
SIC 1711 Plumbing, heating, air-conditioning
 Jackson Ohe
Pr Pr Mark Ohe

D-U-N-S 24-840-0889   (HQ)
GENESIS INTEGRATION INC
(*Suby of* 965591 Alberta Ltd)
14721 123 Ave Nw, Edmonton, AB, T5L 2Y6

(780) 455-3000
Emp Here 30   *Emp Total* 72
Sales 7,449,759
SIC 1731 Electrical work
Pr Pr Kelly Mccarthy
Ex VP Gabriel Gely

D-U-N-S 24-041-1772   (BR)
GOLF TOWN LIMITED
GOLF TOWN
13635 St Albert Trail Nw, Edmonton, AB, T5L
5E7
(780) 482-4653
Emp Here 50
SIC 5941 Sporting goods and bicycle shops

D-U-N-S 24-761-6381   (BR)
HELICOPTERES CANADIENS LIMITEE
CHL HELICOPTERS
12021 121 St Nw Suite 40, Edmonton, AB,
T5L 4H7
(780) 429-6900
Emp Here 30
SIC 4522 Air transportation, nonscheduled

D-U-N-S 25-688-2143   (BR)
HOME DEPOT OF CANADA INC
HOME DEPOT, THE
(*Suby of* The Home Depot Inc)
13360 137 Ave Nw, Edmonton, AB, T5L 5C9
(780) 472-4201
Emp Here 200
SIC 1521 Single-family housing construction

D-U-N-S 20-136-8714   (SL)
HORTON DISTRIBUTION SERVICES INC
14566 Yellowhead Trail Nw, Edmonton, AB,
T5L 3C5

Emp Here 73   *Sales* 24,343,680
SIC 4731 Freight transportation arrangement
Pr Trevor Horton

D-U-N-S 20-104-9371   (BR)
HUDSON'S BAY COMPANY
HOME OUTFITTERS
13554 137 Ave Nw, Edmonton, AB, T5L 5E9
(780) 456-8006
Emp Here 40
SIC 5719 Miscellaneous homefurnishings

D-U-N-S 24-351-6510   (HQ)
INOVATA FOODS CORP
(*Suby of* Pasta Mill Ltd, The)
12803 149 St Nw, Edmonton, AB, T5L 2J7
(780) 454-8665
Emp Here 70   *Emp Total* 3
Sales 26,046,970
SIC 2099 Food preparations, nec
Pr Pr Steve Parsons
  Jason Yohemas

D-U-N-S 20-039-1311   (BR)
IRON MOUNTAIN CANADA OPERATIONS ULC
ARCHIVES IRON MOUNTAIN
14410 121a Ave Nw, Edmonton, AB, T5L 4L2
(780) 466-7035
Emp Here 40
SIC 4226 Special warehousing and storage, nec

D-U-N-S 25-371-9678   (BR)
JYSK LINEN'N FURNITURE INC
JYSK BED-BATH-NORTH CITY CENTRE
13150 137 Ave Nw, Edmonton, AB, T5L 4Z6
(780) 457-5515
Emp Here 28
SIC 5712 Furniture stores

D-U-N-S 24-584-2109   (BR)
KAL TIRE LTD
14720 Yellowhead Trail Nw, Edmonton, AB,
T5L 3C5
(780) 451-5417
Emp Here 40
SIC 5531 Auto and home supply stores

D-U-N-S 20-866-3638   (SL)

KEG STEAKHOUSE AND BAR
SKYVIEW KEG
13960 137 Ave Nw, Edmonton, AB, T5L 5H1
(780) 472-0707
Emp Here 100   *Sales* 2,991,389
SIC 5812 Eating places

D-U-N-S 20-266-8609   (BR)
KRISTIAN ELECTRIC LTD
14236 121a Ave Nw, Edmonton, AB, T5L 4L2
(780) 444-6116
Emp Here 35
SIC 7699 Repair services, nec

D-U-N-S 24-392-3224   (BR)
LOBLAWS INC
SUPERSTORE
12350 137 Ave Nw, Edmonton, AB, T5L 4X6
(780) 406-3768
Emp Here 300
SIC 5411 Grocery stores

D-U-N-S 20-800-6861   (HQ)
MCG RESTAURANTS LTD
MOXIE'S CLASSIC GRILL RESTAURANTS
(*Suby of* MCG Restaurants Ltd)
13551 St Albert Trail Nw, Edmonton, AB, T5L
5E7
(780) 488-8492
Emp Here 20   *Emp Total* 150
Sales 4,523,563
SIC 5812 Eating places

D-U-N-S 25-113-4631   (HQ)
MTE LOGISTIX MANAGEMENT INC
(*Suby of* MTE Logistix Management Inc)
14627 128 Ave Nw, Edmonton, AB, T5L 3H3
(780) 944-9009
Emp Here 25   *Emp Total* 225
Sales 28,760,880
SIC 4225 General warehousing and storage
  Dennis Nolin
Pr Gerry Imbery
VP Fin Gloria Morhun

D-U-N-S 24-396-1125   (BR)
MARK'S WORK WEARHOUSE LTD
WORK WORLD
12222 137 Ave Nw Suite 121, Edmonton, AB,
T5L 4X5
(780) 478-6681
Emp Here 26
SIC 5699 Miscellaneous apparel and accessory stores

D-U-N-S 25-311-3039   (BR)
**MCDONALD'S   RESTAURANTS   OF
CANADA LIMITED**
MCDONALD'S #8251
(*Suby of* McDonald's Corporation)
14220 Yellowhead Trail Nw, Edmonton, AB,
T5L 3C2
(780) 414-8351
Emp Here 30
SIC 5812 Eating places

D-U-N-S 24-068-4550   (BR)
**MCMAN YOUTH, FAMILY AND COMMUNITY
SERVICES ASSOCIATION**
GROUP CARE
(*Suby of* McMan Youth, Family and Community Services Association)
11821 123 St Nw, Edmonton, AB, T5L 0G7
(780) 453-0449
Emp Here 35
SIC 8399 Social services, nec

D-U-N-S 20-974-4387   (BR)
MICHAELS OF CANADA, ULC
(*Suby of* The Michaels Companies Inc)
13640 137 Ave Nw, Edmonton, AB, T5L 5G6
(780) 456-4650
Emp Here 50
SIC 5945 Hobby, toy, and game shops

D-U-N-S 20-191-8385   (BR)
NAV CANADA
13335 127 St Nw, Edmonton, AB, T5L 1B5

(780) 413-5520
Emp Here 45
SIC 3812 Search and navigation equipment

D-U-N-S 20-063-7551   (HQ)
NELSON LUMBER COMPANY LTD
INTERCOAST TRUSS, DIV OF
12727 St Albert Trl Nw, Edmonton, AB, T5L
4H5
(780) 452-9151
Emp Here 100   *Emp Total* 400
Sales 69,733,206
SIC 5211 Lumber and other building materials
Pr Pr Dennis Patterson
  Brian Holterhus
  Robert Adria

D-U-N-S 24-042-9303   (BR)
OLD NAVY (CANADA) INC
(*Suby of* The Gap Inc)
13158 137 Ave, Edmonton, AB, T5L 5G6
(780) 478-4477
Emp Here 45
SIC 5651 Family clothing stores

D-U-N-S 25-986-5590   (BR)
PACIFIC WEST SYSTEMS SUPPLY LTD
PAC WEST
14735 Yellowhead Trail Nw, Edmonton, AB,
T5L 3C4
(780) 452-5202
Emp Here 27
SIC 5032 Brick, stone, and related material

D-U-N-S 24-982-4962   (SL)
PEARL VILLA HOMES LTD
14315 118 Ave Nw Suite 140, Edmonton, AB,
T5L 4S6
(780) 499-2337
Emp Here 100   *Sales* 4,742,446
SIC 8059 Nursing and personal care, nec

D-U-N-S 24-356-4817   (BR)
PRO INSUL LIMITED
14212 128 Ave Nw, Edmonton, AB, T5L 3H5
(780) 452-4724
Emp Here 20
SIC 1799 Special trade contractors, nec

D-U-N-S 24-391-3969   (SL)
PROGRESS LAND SERVICES LTD
14815 119 Ave Nw Suite 300, Edmonton, AB,
T5L 2N9
(780) 454-4717
Emp Here 42   *Sales* 106,408,320
SIC 6792 Oil royalty traders
  Bernard Tchir
Pr Elliott Friedrich
VP Phil Becker
VP Jason Svenningsen

D-U-N-S 20-360-1724   (BR)
QSR EDMONTON (2009) LTD
BURGER KING
(*Suby of* QSR Edmonton (2009) Ltd)
13338 137 Ave Nw, Edmonton, AB, T5L 4Z6
(780) 406-0486
Emp Here 20
SIC 5812 Eating places

D-U-N-S 20-870-9092   (BR)
SEARS CANADA INC
13932 137 Ave Nw, Edmonton, AB, T5L 5H1
(780) 456-5050
Emp Here 20
SIC 5399 Miscellaneous general merchandise

D-U-N-S 24-063-5925   (BR)
SHEPHERD'S CARE FOUNDATION
SHEPHERD'S CARE FOUNDATION KENSINGTON VILLAGE
12603 135 Ave Nw, Edmonton, AB, T5L 5B2
(780) 447-3840
Emp Here 200
SIC 8322 Individual and family services

D-U-N-S 24-887-9327   (BR)
SOBEYS CAPITAL INCORPORATED
13140 St Albert Trail Nw, Edmonton, AB, T5L

4P6
(780) 486-4800
Emp Here 100
SIC 5411 Grocery stores

D-U-N-S 24-701-8203   (BR)
SOBEYS WEST INC
14360 Yellowhead Trail Nw, Edmonton, AB,
T5L 3C5

Emp Here 20
SIC 5141 Groceries, general line

D-U-N-S 24-392-3059   (BR)
SOBEYS WEST INC
SAFEWAY
12950 137 Ave Nw, Edmonton, AB, T5L 4Y8
(780) 377-2402
Emp Here 120
SIC 5411 Grocery stores

D-U-N-S 20-514-2396   (BR)
STAPLES CANADA INC
STAPLES THE BUSINESS DEPOT
(*Suby of* Staples, Inc.)
13154 137 Ave Nw, Edmonton, AB, T5L 4Z6
(780) 447-4949
Emp Here 30
SIC 5943 Stationery stores

D-U-N-S 20-806-5339   (BR)
STARBUCKS COFFEE CANADA, INC
(*Suby of* Starbucks Corporation)
13682 137 Ave Nw, Edmonton, AB, T5L 4Z8
(780) 455-5302
Emp Here 22
SIC 5812 Eating places

D-U-N-S 20-084-4967   (HQ)
STEEL - CRAFT DOOR PRODUCTS LTD
(*Suby of* Mihalcheon Holdings Ltd)
13504 St Albert Trail Nw, Edmonton, AB, T5L
4P4
(780) 453-3761
Emp Here 200   *Emp Total* 2
Sales 41,806,481
SIC 3442 Metal doors, sash, and trim
Ex Dir Kimberly Mihalcheon

D-U-N-S 20-913-6121   (BR)
STUART OLSON INC
12836 146 St Nw, Edmonton, AB, T5L 2H7
(780) 454-3667
Emp Here 40
SIC 1711 Plumbing, heating, air-conditioning

D-U-N-S 20-082-6345   (SL)
SUNRISE BAKERY LTD
14728 119 Ave Nw, Edmonton, AB, T5L 2P2
(780) 454-5797
Emp Here 60   *Sales* 3,137,310
SIC 2051 Bread, cake, and related products

D-U-N-S 20-705-7956   (HQ)
SUPERIOR SAFETY CODES INC
(*Suby of* Superior Safety Codes Inc)
14613 134 Ave Nw, Edmonton, AB, T5L 4S9
(780) 489-4777
Emp Here 48   *Emp Total* 50
Sales 3,392,384
SIC 7389 Business services, nec

D-U-N-S 24-369-7260   (SL)
TAMARACK POWER PARTNERS
13155 146 St Nw, Edmonton, AB, T5L 4S8
(780) 455-4300
Emp Here 300   *Sales* 39,656,320
SIC 8711 Engineering services
Genl Mgr Bruce Van Heest

D-U-N-S 25-137-5981   (BR)
TLI CHO LANDTRAN TRANSPORT LTD
(*Suby of* Kluskus Holdings Ltd)
13120 Yellowhead Trail Nw, Edmonton, AB,
T5L 3C1
(780) 452-9414
Emp Here 30
SIC 4213 Trucking, except local

D-U-N-S 20-860-5456   (BR)
TOWN SHOES LIMITED
SHOE COMPANY, THE
13360 137 Ave Nw, Edmonton, AB, T5L 5C9
(780) 482-4803
Emp Here 25
SIC 5661 Shoe stores

D-U-N-S 20-065-5699   (BR)
TRANSPORT TFi 7 S.E.C
CANADIAN FREIGHTWAYS
14520 130 Ave Nw, Edmonton, AB, T5L 3M6
(780) 482-9483
Emp Here 150
SIC 4731 Freight transportation arrangement

D-U-N-S 24-422-6960   (SL)
UGL CANADA INC
14830 119 Ave Nw, Edmonton, AB, T5L 2P2

Emp Here 20   *Sales* 5,478,300
SIC 1541 Industrial buildings and warehouses
  Earl Bannister
  Philip Mirams
  Richard Leupen

D-U-N-S 25-002-8248   (BR)
VIA RAIL CANADA INC
EDMONTON VIA RAIL STATION
12360 121 St Nw, Edmonton, AB, T5L 5C3
(780) 448-2575
Emp Here 35
SIC 4111 Local and suburban transit

D-U-N-S 24-397-7543   (SL)
W.S.I. DOORS LTD
14425 118 Ave Nw, Edmonton, AB, T5L 2M7
(780) 454-1455
Emp Here 50   *Sales* 4,085,799
SIC 2431 Millwork

D-U-N-S 24-029-2693   (BR)
WFG SECURITIES OF CANADA INC
14315 118 Ave Nw Suite 148, Edmonton, AB,
T5L 4S6
(780) 451-2520
Emp Here 20
SIC 6321 Accident and health insurance

D-U-N-S 24-700-7412   (HQ)
WAYNE BUILDING PRODUCTS LTD
(*Suby of* Wayne Building Products Ltd)
12603 123 St Nw, Edmonton, AB, T5L 0H9
(780) 455-8929
Emp Here 24   *Emp Total* 30
Sales 6,274,620
SIC 5039 Construction materials, nec
Pr Pr Kevin Dale
Dir Dennis Dale

D-U-N-S 20-590-4068   (HQ)
WESTCAN WIRELESS
12540 129 St Nw, Edmonton, AB, T5L 4R4
(780) 451-2355
Emp Here 68   *Emp Total* 70
Sales 11,381,869
SIC 4899 Communication services, nec
Dir Rudy Dyck
  Wayne Mclean
Genl Mgr Craig Baker

D-U-N-S 20-860-4376   (BR)
**WINNERS MERCHANTS INTERNATIONAL
L.P.**
HOMESENSE
(*Suby of* The TJX Companies Inc)
13630 137 Ave Nw, Edmonton, AB, T5L 5G6
(780) 476-4041
Emp Here 25
SIC 5651 Family clothing stores

D-U-N-S 20-106-3521   (BR)
**WINNERS MERCHANTS INTERNATIONAL
L.P.**
WINNERS
(*Suby of* The TJX Companies Inc)
13546 137 Ave Nw, Edmonton, AB, T5L 5E9

(780) 478-5005
Emp Here 35
SIC 5651 Family clothing stores

Edmonton, AB T5M

D-U-N-S 24-335-4185   (BR)
ACKLANDS - GRAINGER INC
AGI
(*Suby of* W.W. Grainger, Inc.)
11708 167 St Nw, Edmonton, AB, T5M 3Z2
(780) 453-3684
Emp Here 300
SIC 5085 Industrial supplies

D-U-N-S 24-962-4875   (HQ)
ALL-WEST GLASS EDMONTON LTD
11638 156 St Nw, Edmonton, AB, T5M 3T5
(780) 451-6108
Emp Here 20   *Emp Total* 250
Sales 1,992,377
SIC 1793 Glass and glazing work

D-U-N-S 20-052-5421   (BR)
ALLDRITT DEVELOPMENT LIMITED
JETCO MECHANICAL
15035 114 Ave Nw, Edmonton, AB, T5M 2Z1
(780) 451-2732
Emp Here 120
SIC 1711 Plumbing, heating, air-conditioning

D-U-N-S 20-080-5737   (HQ)
ALLDRITT DEVELOPMENT LIMITED
SHAMROCK PROPERTY MANAGEMENT
14310 111 Ave Nw Suite 305, Edmonton, AB,
T5M 3Z7
(780) 453-5631
Emp Here 60   *Emp Total* 65
Sales 5,909,817
SIC 6512 Nonresidential building operators
  Stanley H Alldritt

D-U-N-S 24-281-8532   (BR)
ALLMAR INC
ALLMAR INTERNATIONAL
11641 151 St Nw, Edmonton, AB, T5M 4E6
(780) 447-1605
Emp Here 23
SIC 5039 Construction materials, nec

D-U-N-S 24-123-8398   (BR)
BANK OF NOVA SCOTIA, THE
SCOTIABANK
232 Westmount Shopping Center Nw Suite
232, Edmonton, AB, T5M 3L7
(780) 413-4330
Emp Here 26
SIC 6021 National commercial banks

D-U-N-S 20-360-4520   (SL)
BAYTEK DRYWALL & STUCCO LTD
14518 115a Ave Nw, Edmonton, AB, T5M 3C5
(780) 732-5316
Emp Here 50   *Sales* 4,231,721
SIC 1742 Plastering, drywall, and insulation

D-U-N-S 24-283-1618   (SL)
BINDERY OVERLOAD (EDMONTON) LTD
PROVINCIAL LAMINATING SUPPLIES
16815 117 Ave Nw Suite 110, Edmonton, AB,
T5M 3V6
(780) 484-9444
Emp Here 60   *Sales* 2,188,821
SIC 2789 Bookbinding and related work

D-U-N-S 24-339-7747   (BR)
CANWEL BUILDING MATERIALS LTD
BROADLEAF DISTRIBUTION
11553 154 St Nw, Edmonton, AB, T5M 3N7
(780) 452-5395
Emp Here 50
SIC 5039 Construction materials, nec

D-U-N-S 20-808-2024   (BR)
CANEM SYSTEMS LTD
11320 151 St Nw, Edmonton, AB, T5M 4A9

(780) 454-0381
Emp Here 140
SIC 1731 Electrical work

D-U-N-S 20-364-3515   (BR)
CITY OF EDMONTON
DRAINAGE DESIGN & CONSTRUCTION
14323 115 Ave Nw, Edmonton, AB, T5M 3B8
(780) 496-7900
Emp Here 100
SIC 1623 Water, sewer, and utility lines

D-U-N-S 20-362-2613   (SL)
**CLEAN HARBORS LODGING SERVICES
LTD**
14907 111 Ave Nw, Edmonton, AB, T5M 2P6
(780) 450-6526
Emp Here 20   *Sales* 5,827,840
SIC 5599 Automotive dealers, nec
Pr Pr Rodney Marlin
VP Gilbert Sanchez
CFO Jason Vandenberg

D-U-N-S 24-807-7257   (BR)
CLOVERDALE PAINT INC
15846 111 Ave Nw, Edmonton, AB, T5M 2R8
(780) 451-3830
Emp Here 25
SIC 2851 Paints and allied products

D-U-N-S 20-300-0075   (BR)
CO-OPERATORS GROUP LIMITED, THE
14310 111 Ave Nw Suite 500, Edmonton, AB,
T5M 3Z7
(780) 448-7000
Emp Here 70
SIC 6411 Insurance agents, brokers, and ser-
vice

D-U-N-S 20-081-4507   (HQ)
**CORMODE & DICKSON CONSTRUCTION
(1983) LTD**
11450 160 St Nw Unit 200, Edmonton, AB,
T5M 3Y7
(780) 701-9300
Emp Here 50   *Emp Total* 54
Sales 12,733,890
SIC 1541 Industrial buildings and warehouses
Pr Pr Berend Elzen

D-U-N-S 20-028-9416   (BR)
**EDMONTON   CATHOLIC   SEPARATE
SCHOOL DISTRICT NO.7**
*ST.   MARK   CATHOLIC   JUNIOR   HIGH
SCHOOL*
(*Suby of* Edmonton Catholic Separate School
District No.7)
11625 135 St Nw, Edmonton, AB, T5M 1L1
(780) 455-1684
Emp Here 35
SIC 8211 Elementary and secondary schools

D-U-N-S 20-553-3461   (BR)
EDMONTON GEAR CENTRE LTD
GEAR CENTRE, THE
14605 116 Ave Nw, Edmonton, AB, T5M 3E8
(780) 451-4040
Emp Here 30
SIC 5013 Motor vehicle supplies and new
parts

D-U-N-S 20-810-5056   (SL)
**EDMONTON REAL ESTATE BOARD CO-
OPERATIVE LISTING BUREAU LIMITED**
REALTORS ASSOCIATION OF EDMONTON
14220 112 Ave Nw, Edmonton, AB, T5M 2T8
(780) 451-6666
Emp Here 71   *Sales* 9,423,290
SIC 8611 Business associations
  Chris Mooney
Ex VP Ron Hutchinson
  Doug Singleton
  James Mabey
  Larry Westergard
  Darrell Cook
  Mike Eurchuk
  Rob Friele
  Greg Steele

D-U-N-S 24-394-4196   (SL)
**EDMONTON SPACE & SCIENCE FOUNDA-
TION**
TELUS WORLD OF SCIENCE-EDMONTON
11211 142 St Nw, Edmonton, AB, T5M 4A1
(780) 452-9100
Emp Here 130   *Sales* 9,922,655
SIC 8412 Museums and art galleries
VP Scott Henderson

D-U-N-S 24-246-0900   (BR)
FINNING INTERNATIONAL INC
(*Suby of* Finning International Inc)
16511 116 Ave Nw, Edmonton, AB, T5M 3V1
(780) 377-3321
Emp Here 50
SIC 4213 Trucking, except local

D-U-N-S 20-646-3726   (BR)
FLORISTS SUPPLY LTD
SWALLOWFIELD NURSERIES
(*Suby of* Floraco Holdings Inc)
14620 112 Ave Nw, Edmonton, AB, T5M 2T9
(780) 424-4576
Emp Here 28
SIC 5992 Florists

D-U-N-S 25-013-7072   (SL)
**GETTING READY FOR INCLUSION TODAY
(THE GRIT PROGRAM) SOCIETY OF ED-
MONTON**
GRIT PROGRAM, THE
14930 114 Ave Nw, Edmonton, AB, T5M 4G4
(780) 454-9910
Emp Here 75   *Sales* 2,261,782
SIC 8351 Child day care services

D-U-N-S 20-648-6685   (BR)
**GIBSON, R. W. CONSULTING SERVICES
LTD**
PAT'S DRIVELINE
14715 116 Ave Nw, Edmonton, AB, T5M 3E8
(780) 453-5105
Emp Here 20
SIC 3714 Motor vehicle parts and accessories

D-U-N-S 24-064-5622   (BR)
GRAND & TOY LIMITED
(*Suby of* Office Depot, Inc.)
11522 168 St Nw, Edmonton, AB, T5M 3T9
(780) 930-6910
Emp Here 80
SIC 5112 Stationery and office supplies

D-U-N-S 24-308-1598   (HQ)
GRIMSHAW TRUCKING LP
11510 151 St Nw, Edmonton, AB, T5M 3N6
(780) 414-2850
Emp Here 20   *Emp Total* 5,515
Sales 9,355,511
SIC 4212 Local trucking, without storage
Pr Joe Bogach
VP VP Gary Leddy
  Tom Hanna
  Curtis Timmer
  Craig Schmit

D-U-N-S 24-803-5474   (BR)
HOME DEPOT OF CANADA INC
HOME DEPOT
(*Suby of* The Home Depot Inc)
1 Westmount Shopping Ctr Nw Suite 604, Ed-
monton, AB, T5M 3L7
(780) 732-9225
Emp Here 80
SIC 5251 Hardware stores

D-U-N-S 24-359-5951   (BR)
**IRON MOUNTAIN CANADA OPERATIONS
ULC**
ARCHIVES IRON MOUNTAIN
14630 115a Ave Nw, Edmonton, AB, T5M 3C5
(780) 488-4333
Emp Here 20
SIC 4226 Special warehousing and storage,
nec

D-U-N-S 24-320-7789   (BR)

JOY GLOBAL (CANADA) LTD
P & H INDUSTRIAL SERVICES
15802 116 Ave Nw, Edmonton, AB, T5M 3S5
(780) 453-2407
Emp Here 60
SIC 7694 Armature rewinding shops

D-U-N-S 25-188-2218   (BR)
KAEFER INTEGRATED SERVICES LTD
15309 116 Ave Nw, Edmonton, AB, T5M 3Z5
(780) 484-4310
Emp Here 25
SIC 1799 Special trade contractors, nec

D-U-N-S 20-746-2367   (HQ)
KELLER CONSTRUCTION LTD
(*Suby of* Keller Management Inc)
11430 160 St Nw, Edmonton, AB, T5M 3Y7
(780) 484-1010
Emp Here 45   *Emp Total* 75
Sales 19,376,950
SIC 1542 Nonresidential construction, nec
Pr Pr John Cameron
Dir Christine Marchuk

D-U-N-S 25-996-8063   (BR)
LENNOX CANADA INC
MCKINLEY HEATING & AIR CONDITIONING
(DIV)
(*Suby of* Lennox Canada Inc)
11122 156 St Nw, Edmonton, AB, T5M 1Y1
(780) 474-1481
Emp Here 23
SIC 1711 Plumbing, heating, air-conditioning

D-U-N-S 20-101-8095   (BR)
LOBLAWS INC
REAL CANADIAN SUPERSTORE
14740 111 Ave Nw, Edmonton, AB, T5M 2P5
(780) 452-5411
Emp Here 150
SIC 5141 Groceries, general line

D-U-N-S 25-243-8176   (BR)
MACKIE TRANSPORTATION HOLDINGS INC
MACKIE MOVING SYSTEMS
11417 163 St Nw, Edmonton, AB, T5M 3Y3
(587) 881-0400
Emp Here 20
SIC 6712 Bank holding companies

D-U-N-S 24-358-2884   (BR)
MCELHANNEY CONSULTING SERVICES LTD
13455 114 Ave Suite 201, Edmonton, AB, T5M 4C4
(780) 451-3420
Emp Here 32
SIC 8748 Business consulting, nec

D-U-N-S 24-805-7080   (HQ)
NATIONAL CONCRETE ACCESSORIES CANADA INC
14760 116 Ave Nw, Edmonton, AB, T5M 3G1
(780) 451-1212
Emp Here 95   *Emp Total* 3
Sales 41,660,560
SIC 5032 Brick, stone, and related material
Pr Vince Butera
 Dan Walda
VP Marvin Ramsay
 Andrew Boulanger

D-U-N-S 24-348-6730   (BR)
PPG ARCHITECTURAL COATINGS CANADA INC
PPG ARCHITECTURAL COATINGS CANADA, INC
(*Suby of* PPG Industries, Inc.)
16660 114 Ave Nw, Edmonton, AB, T5M 3R8

Emp Here 22
SIC 3479 Metal coating and allied services

D-U-N-S 25-013-2404   (BR)
PACIFIC NORTHWEST MOVING (YUKON) LIMITED

PACIFIC NORTHWEST FREIGHT SYSTEM
14410 115 Ave Nw, Edmonton, AB, T5M 3B7
(780) 447-5110
Emp Here 30
SIC 4213 Trucking, except local

D-U-N-S 20-209-1984   (BR)
PENSKE TRUCK LEASING CANADA INC
PENSKE TRUCK RENTALS
(*Suby of* Penske Corporation)
15706 116 Ave Nw, Edmonton, AB, T5M 3S5
(780) 451-2686
Emp Here 21
SIC 7513 Truck rental and leasing, no drivers

D-U-N-S 25-505-5006   (BR)
PORTOLA PACKAGING CANADA LTD.
16230 112 Ave Nw, Edmonton, AB, T5M 2W1
(780) 451-9300
Emp Here 35
SIC 3089 Plastics products, nec

D-U-N-S 24-002-1345   (BR)
PRINCESS AUTO LTD
11150 163 St Nw, Edmonton, AB, T5M 3R5
(780) 483-0244
Emp Here 50
SIC 5251 Hardware stores

D-U-N-S 20-515-5406   (SL)
QUALITY CALL CARE SOLUTIONS INC
700 Westmount Ctr, Edmonton, AB, T5M 3L7

Emp Here 225   *Sales* 24,981,220
SIC 5399 Miscellaneous general merchandise
 Kathie Kinisky

D-U-N-S 25-326-5607   (SL)
RICHARDS JANITOR SERVICE INC
14602 116 Ave Nw Suite 4, Edmonton, AB, T5M 3E9
(780) 452-3995
Emp Here 60   *Sales* 1,751,057
SIC 7349 Building maintenance services, nec

D-U-N-S 24-805-4970   (BR)
RICOH CANADA INC
16011 116 Ave Nw, Edmonton, AB, T5M 3Y1
(780) 930-7100
Emp Here 60
SIC 5044 Office equipment

D-U-N-S 24-067-0844   (BR)
RYDER TRUCK RENTAL CANADA LTD
RYDER TRUCK LOGISTICS & TRANS-PORTATION
(*Suby of* Ryder System, Inc.)
11433 154 St Nw, Edmonton, AB, T5M 3N7
(780) 451-1894
Emp Here 24
SIC 7513 Truck rental and leasing, no drivers

D-U-N-S 25-453-9141   (BR)
S.L.H. TRANSPORT INC
14525 112 Ave Nw, Edmonton, AB, T5M 2V5
(780) 451-7543
Emp Here 80
SIC 4212 Local trucking, without storage

D-U-N-S 20-059-4385   (BR)
SMS EQUIPMENT INC
CONECO EQUIPMENT
16116 111 Ave Nw, Edmonton, AB, T5M 2S1
(780) 451-2630
Emp Here 160
SIC 5082 Construction and mining machinery

D-U-N-S 20-703-9160   (BR)
SAPUTO PRODUITS LAITIERS CANADA S.E.N.C.
(*Suby of* Saputo Produits Laitiers Canada S.E.N.C.)
16110 116 Ave Nw, Edmonton, AB, T5M 3V4
(780) 486-8400
Emp Here 370
SIC 5141 Groceries, general line

D-U-N-S 24-391-0304   (BR)
SCHINDLER ELEVATOR CORPORATION

15006 116 Ave Nw, Edmonton, AB, T5M 3T4
(780) 425-1043
Emp Here 30
SIC 1796 Installing building equipment

D-U-N-S 20-292-7526   (BR)
SCOTT LAND & LEASE LTD
11634 142 St Nw Suite 100, Edmonton, AB, T5M 1V4
(780) 428-2212
Emp Here 24
SIC 6211 Security brokers and dealers

D-U-N-S 24-331-2782   (BR)
SEALY CANADA LTD
(*Suby of* Tempur Sealy International, Inc.)
14550 112 Ave Nw, Edmonton, AB, T5M 2T9
(780) 452-3070
Emp Here 100
SIC 2515 Mattresses and bedsprings

D-U-N-S 25-185-8239   (BR)
SOBEYS WEST INC
CANADA SAFEWAY #838
601 Westmount Shopping Center, Edmonton, AB, T5M 3L7
(780) 451-1860
Emp Here 155
SIC 5411 Grocery stores

D-U-N-S 20-145-6154   (BR)
SOBEYS WEST INC
LUCERNE FOODS, DIV OF
11135 151 St Nw, Edmonton, AB, T5M 1X3
(780) 451-0817
Emp Here 100
SIC 2026 Fluid milk

D-U-N-S 20-714-2261   (SL)
ST GEORGE SCHOOL BOARD HELLENIC LANG SCHOOL
10831 124 St Nw, Edmonton, AB, T5M 0H4
(780) 452-1455
Emp Here 50   *Sales* 3,356,192
SIC 8211 Elementary and secondary schools

D-U-N-S 24-983-2577   (HQ)
STORDOR INVESTMENTS LTD
OVERHEAD DOOR COMPANY OF EDMON-TON
(*Suby of* 564967 Alberta Ltd)
11703 160 St Nw, Edmonton, AB, T5M 3Z3
(780) 451-0060
Emp Here 60   *Emp Total* 1
Sales 17,583,529
SIC 5211 Lumber and other building materials
Pr Pr John Rodney Storey

D-U-N-S 24-068-5354   (BR)
SUPREME OFFICE PRODUCTS LIMITED
SUPREME DISTRIBUTORS
(*Suby of* Placements Denis Latulippe Inc, Les)
16630 114 Ave Nw, Edmonton, AB, T5M 3R8
(780) 452-6312
Emp Here 64
SIC 5044 Office equipment

D-U-N-S 20-180-0146   (BR)
TRADER CORPORATION
TRADER PUBLICATION
11638 142 St Nw, Edmonton, AB, T5M 1V4
(780) 415-6800
Emp Here 35
SIC 2721 Periodicals

D-U-N-S 20-921-0736   (BR)
TYCO INTEGRATED FIRE & SECURITY CANADA, INC
SIMPLEXGRINNELL
(*Suby of* Johnson Controls, Inc.)
16447 117 Ave Nw, Edmonton, AB, T5M 3V3
(780) 930-1300
Emp Here 20
SIC 1731 Electrical work

D-U-N-S 25-064-5298   (BR)
UNITED PARCEL SERVICE CANADA LTD
UPS

11204 151 St Nw, Edmonton, AB, T5M 4A9
(800) 742-5877
Emp Here 80
SIC 7389 Business services, nec

D-U-N-S 20-028-8863   (BR)
VERSENT CORPORATION ULC
LASER QUEST
11271 170 St Nw, Edmonton, AB, T5M 0J1
(780) 424-2111
Emp Here 20
SIC 7929 Entertainers and entertainment groups

D-U-N-S 20-896-4866   (HQ)
WESCLEAN EQUIPMENT & CLEANING SUPPLIES LTD
11450 149 St Nw, Edmonton, AB, T5M 1W7
(780) 451-1533
Emp Here 54   *Emp Total* 11,956
Sales 21,012,682
SIC 5087 Service establishment equipment
Pr Pr Reid Toreson
 William Shepherd

D-U-N-S 24-786-2634   (SL)
WESTMOUNT RESTAURANT INC
BOSTON PIZZA
11320 Groat Rd Nw, Edmonton, AB, T5M 4E7
(780) 452-8585
Emp Here 60   *Sales* 1,824,018
SIC 5812 Eating places

Edmonton, AB T5N

D-U-N-S 24-858-3168   (BR)
ALBERTA MEDICAL ASSOCIATION
TOWARD OPTIMIZED PRACTICE
12204 106 Ave Nw Suite 300, Edmonton, AB, T5N 3Z1
(780) 482-0319
Emp Here 20
SIC 8621 Professional organizations

D-U-N-S 24-766-6837   (SL)
CANADIAN CORPS OF COMMISSION-AIRES (NORTHERN ALBERTA)
NORTHERN ALBERTA DIVISION
10633 124 St Nw Suite 101, Edmonton, AB, T5N 1S5
(780) 451-1974
Emp Here 1,800   *Sales* 72,370,867
SIC 7381 Detective and armored car services
Dir John D Slater

D-U-N-S 25-316-0691   (BR)
CANADIAN WESTERN BANK
12230 Jasper Ave Nw Suite 100, Edmonton, AB, T5N 3K3
(780) 424-4846
Emp Here 40
SIC 6021 National commercial banks

D-U-N-S 24-003-7481   (BR)
CERIDIAN CANADA LTD
10216 124 St Nw Suite 120, Edmonton, AB, T5N 4A3
(780) 702-8732
Emp Here 55
SIC 8721 Accounting, auditing, and book-keeping

D-U-N-S 24-066-2882   (SL)
COMPUTRONIX (CANADA) LTD
(*Suby of* H.W.L. Family Enterprises Inc)
10216 124 St Nw Suite 200, Edmonton, AB, T5N 4A3
(780) 454-3700
Emp Here 80   *Sales* 7,545,405
SIC 7371 Custom computer programming ser-vices
Pr Pr Harman Leusink
 James Den Otter

D-U-N-S 20-029-8086   (BR)

EDMONTON CATHOLIC SEPARATE SCHOOL DISTRICT NO.7
ST. VINCENT CATHOLIC ELEMENTARY SCHOOL
(Suby of Edmonton Catholic Separate School District No.7)
10530 138 St Nw, Edmonton, AB, T5N 2J6
(780) 452-4474
Emp Here 20
SIC 8211 Elementary and secondary schools

D-U-N-S 20-028-8426   (BR)
EDMONTON CATHOLIC SEPARATE SCHOOL DISTRICT NO.7
ST PAUL CATHOLIC ELEMENTARY SCHOOL
(Suby of Edmonton Catholic Separate School District No.7)
14410 96 Ave Nw, Edmonton, AB, T5N 0C7
(780) 452-1510
Emp Here 28
SIC 8211 Elementary and secondary schools

D-U-N-S 20-029-3137   (BR)
EDMONTON CATHOLIC SEPARATE SCHOOL DISTRICT NO.7
ARCHBISHOP MACDONALD HIGH SCHOOL
(Suby of Edmonton Catholic Separate School District No.7)
14219 109 Ave Nw, Edmonton, AB, T5N 1H5
(780) 451-1470
Emp Here 60
SIC 8211 Elementary and secondary schools

D-U-N-S 25-268-0947   (BR)
EDMONTON SCHOOL DISTRICT NO. 7
WESTMINSTER JR HIGH SCHOOL
13712 104 Ave Nw, Edmonton, AB, T5N 0W4
(780) 452-4343
Emp Here 40
SIC 8211 Elementary and secondary schools

D-U-N-S 24-397-5232   (SL)
EDMONTON SOCIETY FOR CHRISTIAN EDUCATION
14304 109 Ave Nw, Edmonton, AB, T5N 1H6
(780) 476-6281
Emp Here 150   *Sales* 13,898,650
SIC 8211 Elementary and secondary schools
Ex Dir Peter Buisman

D-U-N-S 20-299-4393   (SL)
FRONTIERS CHRISTIAN MINISTRIES INC
FRONTIERS
10216 124 St Nw Unit 215, Edmonton, AB, T5N 4A3
(780) 421-9090
Emp Here 45   *Sales* 4,071,380
SIC 8661 Religious organizations

D-U-N-S 20-259-6680   (BR)
GOVERNMENT OF THE PROVINCE OF ALBERTA
ALBERTA HUMAN SERVICE (CHILDREN SERVICE)
10408 124 St 5th Fl, Edmonton, AB, T5N 1R5
(780) 427-1511
Emp Here 25
SIC 8322 Individual and family services

D-U-N-S 24-110-8187   (BR)
GOVERNMENT OF THE PROVINCE OF ALBERTA
12323 Stony Plain Rd Nw Suite 500, Edmonton, AB, T5N 4B4
(780) 427-9190
Emp Here 75
SIC 8322 Individual and family services

D-U-N-S 20-065-9931   (BR)
GREATER EDMONTON FOUNDATION
10938 142 St Nw, Edmonton, AB, T5N 2P8
(780) 454-6350
Emp Here 50
SIC 8322 Individual and family services

D-U-N-S 20-177-2022   (BR)

H & R BLOCK CANADA, INC
H & R BLOCK
(Suby of H&R Block, Inc.)
10126 124 St Nw, Edmonton, AB, T5N 1P6
(780) 448-2100
Emp Here 25
SIC 7291 Tax return preparation services

D-U-N-S 20-934-9591   (BR)
JOHNSON INC
12220 Stony Plain Rd Nw Suite 301, Edmonton, AB, T5N 3Y4
(780) 465-7818
Emp Here 100
SIC 6331 Fire, marine, and casualty insurance

D-U-N-S 20-895-7993   (SL)
LLOYD SADD INSURANCE BROKERS LTD
10240 124 St Suite 700, Edmonton, AB, T5N 3W6
(780) 483-4544
Emp Here 80   *Sales* 7,223,109
SIC 6411 Insurance agents, brokers, and service
Pr Pr T Marshall Sadd
    Kevin Boyd

D-U-N-S 25-281-5204   (BR)
MD MANAGEMENT LIMITED
MD FINANCIAL
(Suby of Canadian Medical Association)
10339 124 St Nw Suite 300, Edmonton, AB, T5N 3W1
(780) 436-1333
Emp Here 30
SIC 6211 Security brokers and dealers

D-U-N-S 25-064-5306   (BR)
MOUNTAIN EQUIPMENT CO-OPERATIVE
MOUNTAIN EQUIPMENT CO-OPERATIVE
12328 102 Ave Nw, Edmonton, AB, T5N 0L9
(780) 488-6614
Emp Here 60
SIC 7699 Repair services, nec

D-U-N-S 24-998-1200   (BR)
PORTAGE LA PRAIRIE MUTUAL INSURANCE CO, THE
12220 Stony Plain Rd Nw Suite 310, Edmonton, AB, T5N 3Y4
(780) 423-3102
Emp Here 40
SIC 6331 Fire, marine, and casualty insurance

Edmonton, AB T5P

D-U-N-S 20-249-9666   (BR)
668824 ALBERTA LTD
VISIONS THE BEST NAME IN ELECTRONICS
10421 170 St Nw, Edmonton, AB, T5P 4T2
(780) 444-7007
Emp Here 20
SIC 5731 Radio, television, and electronic stores

D-U-N-S 24-425-1000   (BR)
ALBERTA JANITORIAL LTD
15557 Stony Plain Rd Nw Suite A, Edmonton, AB, T5P 3Z1
(780) 467-9202
Emp Here 25
SIC 7349 Building maintenance services, nec

D-U-N-S 24-398-1024   (SL)
B D L BUILDING SERVICES LTD
10515 170 St Nw, Edmonton, AB, T5P 4W2
(780) 486-4552
Emp Here 50   *Sales* 1,459,214
SIC 7349 Building maintenance services, nec

D-U-N-S 24-390-9108   (BR)
BANK OF MONTREAL
BMO
236 Mayfield Common Nw, Edmonton, AB,

T5P 4B3
(780) 441-6525
Emp Here 40
SIC 6021 National commercial banks

D-U-N-S 24-397-5182   (BR)
COMCARE (CANADA) LIMITED
COMCARE HEALTH SERVICES
10458 Mayfield Rd Nw Suite 200, Edmonton, AB, T5P 4P4
(780) 496-9430
Emp Here 50
SIC 7361 Employment agencies

D-U-N-S 20-637-8945   (SL)
DEFORD CONTRACTING INC
16720 109 Ave Nw Unit 16720, Edmonton, AB, T5P 4Y8
(780) 453-5841
Emp Here 100   *Sales* 14,134,935
SIC 1771 Concrete work
Pr Pr Anthony Deford
    Allan Owen

D-U-N-S 20-557-6049   (BR)
DIRECT ENERGY MARKETING LIMITED
16909 110 Ave Nw, Edmonton, AB, T5P 1G8
(780) 483-3056
Emp Here 20
SIC 1711 Plumbing, heating, air-conditioning

D-U-N-S 20-919-7479   (BR)
DRIVING FORCE INC, THE
16003 Stony Plain Rd Nw, Edmonton, AB, T5P 4A1
(780) 444-6611
Emp Here 50
SIC 7515 Passenger car leasing

D-U-N-S 25-168-5848   (BR)
EARL'S RESTAURANTS LTD
EARL'S
(Suby of Earl's Restaurants Ltd)
9961 170 St Nw, Edmonton, AB, T5P 4S2
(780) 481-2229
Emp Here 60
SIC 5812 Eating places

D-U-N-S 25-013-7353   (BR)
EDMONTON CATHOLIC SEPARATE SCHOOL DISTRICT NO.7
HOLY CROSS SCHOOL
(Suby of Edmonton Catholic Separate School District No.7)
15120 104 Ave Nw, Edmonton, AB, T5P 0R5
(780) 489-1981
Emp Here 40
SIC 8211 Elementary and secondary schools

D-U-N-S 25-013-8823   (BR)
EDMONTON CATHOLIC SEPARATE SCHOOL DISTRICT NO.7
OUR LADY OF PEACE CATHOLIC ELEMENTARY SCHOOL
(Suby of Edmonton Catholic Separate School District No.7)
15911 110 Ave Nw, Edmonton, AB, T5P 1G2
(780) 489-1222
Emp Here 25
SIC 8211 Elementary and secondary schools

D-U-N-S 20-028-3674   (BR)
EDMONTON SCHOOL DISTRICT NO. 7
YOUNGSTOWN SCHOOL
10330 163 St Nw, Edmonton, AB, T5P 3N5
(780) 489-4600
Emp Here 30
SIC 8211 Elementary and secondary schools

D-U-N-S 25-012-7453   (BR)
EDMONTON SCHOOL DISTRICT NO. 7
BRITANNIA JR HIGH SCHOOL
16018 104 Ave Nw, Edmonton, AB, T5P 0S3
(780) 489-5300
Emp Here 29
SIC 8211 Elementary and secondary schools

D-U-N-S 20-028-3666   (BR)
EDMONTON SCHOOL DISTRICT NO. 7

SHERWOOD ELEMENTARY SCHOOL
9550 152 St Nw, Edmonton, AB, T5P 0B9
(780) 489-2600
Emp Here 20
SIC 8211 Elementary and secondary schools

D-U-N-S 20-712-5357   (BR)
EDMONTON SCHOOL DISTRICT NO. 7
WESTLAWN JUNIOR HIGH SCHOOL
9520 165 St Nw, Edmonton, AB, T5P 3S4
(780) 484-3456
Emp Here 50
SIC 8211 Elementary and secondary schools

D-U-N-S 25-013-8401   (BR)
EDMONTON SCHOOL DISTRICT NO. 7
MEADOWLARK CHRISTIAN SCHOOL
9825 158 St Nw, Edmonton, AB, T5P 2X4
(780) 483-6476
Emp Here 40
SIC 8211 Elementary and secondary schools

D-U-N-S 20-072-6698   (BR)
EDMONTON SCHOOL DISTRICT NO. 7
MAYFIELD SCHOOL
10950 152 St Nw, Edmonton, AB, T5P 3C1
(780) 489-5100
Emp Here 65
SIC 8211 Elementary and secondary schools

D-U-N-S 20-028-3740   (BR)
EDMONTON SCHOOL DISTRICT NO. 7
BRIGHTVIEW ELEMENTARY SCHOOL
15425 106 Ave Nw, Edmonton, AB, T5P 0W3
(780) 484-6631
Emp Here 35
SIC 8211 Elementary and secondary schools

D-U-N-S 25-013-7270   (BR)
EDMONTON SCHOOL DISTRICT NO. 7
HIGH PARK ELEMENTARY SCHOOL
11031 154 St Nw, Edmonton, AB, T5P 2K2
(780) 489-1131
Emp Here 20
SIC 8211 Elementary and secondary schools

D-U-N-S 20-154-6160   (BR)
ELVES SPECIAL NEEDS SOCIETY
ELVES ADULT PROGRAM
(Suby of Elves Special Needs Society)
10419 159 St Nw, Edmonton, AB, T5P 3A6
(780) 481-5335
Emp Here 40
SIC 8322 Individual and family services

D-U-N-S 20-786-8105   (BR)
FINNING INTERNATIONAL INC
FINNING POWER SYSTEMS
(Suby of Finning International Inc)
16940 107 Ave Nw, Edmonton, AB, T5P 4C3
(780) 483-3499
Emp Here 45
SIC 7538 General automotive repair shops

D-U-N-S 20-555-0796   (BR)
FINNING INTERNATIONAL INC
FINNING CANADA
(Suby of Finning International Inc)
16830 107 Ave Nw, Edmonton, AB, T5P 4C3
(780) 930-4800
Emp Here 200
SIC 5082 Construction and mining machinery

D-U-N-S 20-515-5984   (BR)
GOLDER ASSOCIATES LTD
16820 107 Ave Nw, Edmonton, AB, T5P 4C3
(780) 483-3499
Emp Here 126
SIC 8711 Engineering services

D-U-N-S 25-065-1460   (BR)
GRANT MACEWAN UNIVERSITY
HAAR, JOHN L. THEATRE
10045 156 St Nw Rm 402, Edmonton, AB, T5P 2P7
(780) 497-4310
Emp Here 250
SIC 8299 Schools and educational services,

nec

D-U-N-S 24-962-9544   (BR)
GREAT PACIFIC INDUSTRIES INC
SAVE-ON-FOODS
360 Mayfield Common Nw, Edmonton, AB,
T5P 4B3
(780) 484-1088
Emp Here 160
SIC 5411 Grocery stores

D-U-N-S 25-625-7189   (BR)
HERBERS AUTO BODY REPAIR LTD
16929 107 Ave Nw, Edmonton, AB, T5P 4H7
(780) 486-3136
Emp Here 28
SIC 7532 Top and body repair and paint shops

D-U-N-S 24-149-6517   (SL)
INTEGRATED FINANCIAL GROUP INC
INDUSTRIAL ALLIANCE PACIFIC LIFE IN-SURANCE
10220 156 St Nw Suite 200, Edmonton, AB,
T5P 2R1
(780) 454-6505
Emp Here 50   *Sales* 4,523,563
SIC 6411 Insurance agents, brokers, and service

D-U-N-S 24-327-3836   (BR)
LONDON DRUGS LIMITED
14951 Stony Plain Rd Nw, Edmonton, AB, T5P
4W1
(780) 944-4522
Emp Here 100
SIC 5912 Drug stores and proprietary stores

D-U-N-S 25-315-1567   (BR)
MEDICENTRES CANADA INC
CASTLEDOWNS MEDICENTRE
10458 Mayfield Rd Nw Suite 204, Edmonton,
AB, T5P 4P4
(780) 483-7115
Emp Here 25
SIC 8011 Offices and clinics of medical doctors

D-U-N-S 24-065-2693   (BR)
MEMORIAL GARDENS CANADA LIMITED
WESTLAWN MEMORIAL GARDENS
10132 163 St Nw, Edmonton, AB, T5P 4X3
(780) 489-1602
Emp Here 25
SIC 6553 Cemetery subdividers and developers

D-U-N-S 24-767-7201   (BR)
NORSEMAN INC
CAMPERS VILLAGE DIV.
10951 170 St Nw, Edmonton, AB, T5P 4V6
(780) 484-2700
Emp Here 40
SIC 2394 Canvas and related products

D-U-N-S 20-573-8102   (BR)
ROYAL BANK OF CANADA
RBC
(*Suby of* Royal Bank Of Canada)
15103 Stony Plain Rd Nw Suite 5, Edmonton,
AB, T5P 3Y2

Emp Here 20
SIC 6021 National commercial banks

D-U-N-S 20-581-1834   (BR)
ROYAL LEPAGE LIMITED
ROYAL LEPAGE NORALTA
15057 Stony Plain Rd Nw Suite 200, Edmon-ton, AB, T5P 4W1
(780) 488-0000
Emp Here 49
SIC 6531 Real estate agents and managers

D-U-N-S 20-860-5431   (BR)
TOWN SHOES LIMITED
SHOE COMPANY, THE
318 Mayfield Common Nw, Edmonton, AB,
T5P 4B3

(780) 444-1441
Emp Here 25
SIC 5661 Shoe stores

D-U-N-S 24-966-0085   (SL)
UNITED WAY OF THE ALBERTA CAPITAL REGION
15132 Stony Plain Rd Nw, Edmonton, AB, T5P
3Y3
(780) 990-1000
Emp Here 55   *Sales* 20,893,320
SIC 8399 Social services, nec
Pr Anne Smith
Ch Bd William Bannister
Dir Barb Penney
 Joe Lavorato
Dir Robert Yager

D-U-N-S 20-154-9255   (BR)
VALUE VILLAGE STORES, INC
(*Suby of* Savers, Inc.)
204 Mayfield Common Nw, Edmonton, AB,
T5P 4B3
(780) 484-4177
Emp Here 45
SIC 5399 Miscellaneous general merchandise

D-U-N-S 24-086-9818   (SL)
WESTVIEW INN LTD
CONTINENTAL INN
16625 Stony Plain Rd Nw, Edmonton, AB, T5P
4A8
(780) 484-7751
Emp Here 100   *Sales* 4,377,642
SIC 7011 Hotels and motels

D-U-N-S 24-981-4039   (BR)
WINNERS MERCHANTS INTERNATIONAL L.P.
WINNERS
(*Suby of* The TJX Companies Inc)
300 Mayfield Common Nw, Edmonton, AB,
T5P 4B3
(780) 444-2445
Emp Here 60
SIC 5651 Family clothing stores

D-U-N-S 20-860-4491   (BR)
WINNERS MERCHANTS INTERNATIONAL L.P.
WINNERS
(*Suby of* The TJX Companies Inc)
300 Mayfield Common Nw, Edmonton, AB,
T5P 4B3
(780) 487-9042
Emp Here 25
SIC 5719 Miscellaneous homefurnishings

Edmonton, AB T5R

D-U-N-S 25-303-5570   (BR)
CANADIAN IMPERIAL BANK OF COM-MERCE
CIBC
15630 87 Ave Nw, Edmonton, AB, T5R 5W9
(780) 408-1202
Emp Here 35
SIC 6021 National commercial banks

D-U-N-S 25-091-1534   (BR)
CAPITAL CARE GROUP INC
CAPITAL CARE LYNNWOOD
8740 165 St Nw Suite 438, Edmonton, AB,
T5R 2R8
(780) 341-2300
Emp Here 500
SIC 8051 Skilled nursing care facilities

D-U-N-S 20-143-5422   (BR)
CAPITAL CARE GROUP INC
MCCONNELL PLACE WEST
8720 165 St Nw, Edmonton, AB, T5R 5Y8
(780) 413-4770
Emp Here 36
SIC 8059 Nursing and personal care, nec

D-U-N-S 20-026-1464   (BR)
CAPITAL CARE GROUP INC
LAURIER HOUSE
16815 88 Ave Nw Suite 119, Edmonton, AB,
T5R 5Y7
(780) 413-4712
Emp Here 100
SIC 8051 Skilled nursing care facilities

D-U-N-S 20-035-3360   (BR)
CITY OF EDMONTON
JASPER PLACE LEISURE CENTRE
9200 163 St Nw, Edmonton, AB, T5R 0A7
(780) 496-1411
Emp Here 30
SIC 8322 Individual and family services

D-U-N-S 20-028-9705   (BR)
EDMONTON CATHOLIC SEPARATE SCHOOL DISTRICT NO.7
ANNUNCIATION ELEMENTARY SCHOOL
(*Suby of* Edmonton Catholic Separate School
District No.7)
9325 165 St Nw, Edmonton, AB, T5R 2S5
(780) 484-4319
Emp Here 27
SIC 8211 Elementary and secondary schools

D-U-N-S 20-712-7304   (BR)
EDMONTON CATHOLIC SEPARATE SCHOOL DISTRICT NO.7
H. E. BERIAULT CATHOLIC JUNIOR HIGH SCHOOL
(*Suby of* Edmonton Catholic Separate School
District No.7)
8125 167 St Nw, Edmonton, AB, T5R 2T7
(780) 489-5490
Emp Here 50
SIC 8211 Elementary and secondary schools

D-U-N-S 25-013-8831   (BR)
EDMONTON CATHOLIC SEPARATE SCHOOL DISTRICT NO.7
OUR LADY VICTORIES CATHOLIC ELE-MENTARY SCHOOL
(*Suby of* Edmonton Catholic Separate School
District No.7)
7925 158 St Nw, Edmonton, AB, T5R 2B9
(780) 489-7630
Emp Here 20
SIC 8211 Elementary and secondary schools

D-U-N-S 20-028-3963   (BR)
EDMONTON CATHOLIC SEPARATE SCHOOL DISTRICT NO.7
ST. ROSE CATHOLIC JUNIOR HIGH SCHOOL
(*Suby of* Edmonton Catholic Separate School
District No.7)
8815 145 St Nw, Edmonton, AB, T5R 0T7
(780) 483-2695
Emp Here 25
SIC 8211 Elementary and secondary schools

D-U-N-S 20-027-3899   (BR)
EDMONTON CATHOLIC SEPARATE SCHOOL DISTRICT NO.7
ST. FRANCIS XAVIER HIGH SCHOOL
(*Suby of* Edmonton Catholic Separate School
District No.7)
9250 163 St Nw, Edmonton, AB, T5R 0A7
(780) 489-2571
Emp Here 95
SIC 8211 Elementary and secondary schools

D-U-N-S 25-533-7826   (BR)
EDMONTON SCHOOL DISTRICT NO. 7
PARKVIEW SCHOOL
14313 92 Ave Nw, Edmonton, AB, T5R 5B3
(780) 483-3415
Emp Here 45
SIC 8211 Elementary and secondary schools

D-U-N-S 25-013-8054   (BR)
EDMONTON SCHOOL DISTRICT NO. 7
LYNNWOOD ELEMENTARY SCHOOL
15451 84 Ave Nw, Edmonton, AB, T5R 3Y1

(780) 489-4500
Emp Here 24
SIC 8211 Elementary and secondary schools

D-U-N-S 20-020-2625   (BR)
EDMONTON SCHOOL DISTRICT NO. 7
PATRICIA HEIGHTS ELEMENTARY
16216 78 Ave Nw, Edmonton, AB, T5R 3E6
(780) 487-0550
Emp Here 23
SIC 8211 Elementary and secondary schools

D-U-N-S 20-028-3641   (BR)
EDMONTON SCHOOL DISTRICT NO. 7
ELMWOOD ELEMENTARY SCHOOL
16325 83 Ave Nw, Edmonton, AB, T5R 3V8
(780) 489-6749
Emp Here 50
SIC 8211 Elementary and secondary schools

D-U-N-S 20-592-0817   (BR)
EDMONTON SCHOOL DISTRICT NO. 7
AFTON SCHOOL OF THE ARTS
16604 91 Ave Nw Suite 7, Edmonton, AB, T5R
5A4
(780) 484-3263
Emp Here 40
SIC 8211 Elementary and secondary schools

D-U-N-S 25-013-8419   (BR)
EDMONTON SCHOOL DISTRICT NO. 7
MEADOWLARK ELEMENTARY SCHOOL
9150 160 St Nw, Edmonton, AB, T5R 2J2
(780) 489-5200
Emp Here 23
SIC 8211 Elementary and secondary schools

D-U-N-S 25-454-4372   (BR)
EDMONTON SCHOOL DISTRICT NO. 7
RIO TERRACE ELEMENTARY SCHOOL
7608 154 St Nw, Edmonton, AB, T5R 1R7
(780) 481-6866
Emp Here 20
SIC 8211 Elementary and secondary schools

D-U-N-S 20-712-4889   (BR)
EDMONTON SCHOOL DISTRICT NO. 7
LAURIER HEIGHTS SCHOOL
8210 142 St Nw, Edmonton, AB, T5R 0L9
(780) 483-5352
Emp Here 25
SIC 8211 Elementary and secondary schools

D-U-N-S 20-265-4182   (BR)
EDMONTON SCHOOL DISTRICT NO. 7
STRATFORD SCHOOL
8715 153 St Nw, Edmonton, AB, T5R 1P1
(780) 484-3381
Emp Here 30
SIC 8211 Elementary and secondary schools

D-U-N-S 25-013-7296   (BR)
EDMONTON SCHOOL DISTRICT NO. 7
HILLCREST JUNIOR HIGH SCHOOL
16400 80 Ave Nw, Edmonton, AB, T5R 3M6
(780) 489-2516
Emp Here 25
SIC 8211 Elementary and secondary schools

D-U-N-S 25-013-8427   (BR)
GREATER EDMONTON FOUNDATION
MEADOWLARK SENIOR CITIZENS LODGE
(*Suby of* Greater Edmonton Foundation)
8609 161 St Nw Suite 215, Edmonton, AB,
T5R 5X9
(780) 484-0581
Emp Here 20
SIC 8361 Residential care

D-U-N-S 24-387-3150   (BR)
LIFEMARK HEALTH MANAGEMENT INC
LIFEMARK HEALTH INSTITUTE
(*Suby of* Audax Group, L.P.)
154 Meadowlark Shopping Ctr Nw, Edmonton,
AB, T5R 5W9
(780) 429-4761
Emp Here 50
SIC 8741 Management services

D-U-N-S 20-064-4990   (BR)
MCDONALD'S RESTAURANTS OF CANADA LIMITED
MCDONALD'S
(*Suby of* McDonald's Corporation)
14920 87 Ave Nw, Edmonton, AB, T5R 4E8
(780) 414-8333
Emp Here 60
SIC 5812 Eating places

D-U-N-S 25-321-4530   (BR)
REVERA INC
CENTRAL PARK LODGES
8903 168 St Nw, Edmonton, AB, T5R 2V6
(780) 489-4931
Emp Here 100
SIC 8051 Skilled nursing care facilities

D-U-N-S 20-898-9129   (SL)
TREASURE'S LTD
14727 87 Ave Nw Suite 300, Edmonton, AB, T5R 4E5
(780) 452-4405
Emp Here 30   *Sales* 7,435,520
SIC 6411 Insurance agents, brokers, and service
Pr Pr Randy Treasure
Joanne Treasure

D-U-N-S 20-593-7592   (HQ)
VANAN FOODS LIMITED
SPRUCE GROVE I G A
(*Suby of* Vanan Foods Limited)
9106 142 St Nw, Edmonton, AB, T5R 0M7
(780) 483-1525
Emp Here 25   *Emp Total* 140
Sales 25,816,080
SIC 5411 Grocery stores
Pr Pr Andy Taschuk
Waine Van De Ligt
Gerrie Taschuk
Wendy Van De Ligt

Edmonton, AB T5S

D-U-N-S 24-961-5469   (SL)
2745925 CANADA INC
AMJ CAMPBELL VAN LINES-EDMONTON
18552 111 Ave Nw, Edmonton, AB, T5S 2V4
(780) 628-3291
Emp Here 50   *Sales* 3,378,379
SIC 4214 Local trucking with storage

D-U-N-S 20-719-0104   (BR)
487244 ALBERTA LTD
AUTO WEST SUPER STORE
10212 178 St Nw, Edmonton, AB, T5S 1H3
(780) 483-7516
Emp Here 20
SIC 5521 Used car dealers

D-U-N-S 20-703-2827   (HQ)
564438 ALBERTA LTD
(*Suby of* 564438 Alberta Ltd)
18043 111 Ave Nw, Edmonton, AB, T5S 2P2
(780) 453-3964
Emp Here 30   *Emp Total* 30
Sales 7,852,800
SIC 5085 Industrial supplies
Pr Pr Alfred Otto

D-U-N-S 24-840-7702   (SL)
AECOM CANADA LTD
18817 Stony Plain Rd Nw Suite 101, Edmonton, AB, T5S 0C2
(780) 486-7000
Emp Here 250   *Sales* 28,600,594
SIC 8711 Engineering services
Pr J.O. Kon
Al Salo

D-U-N-S 24-470-6730   (SL)
APX HOSPITALITY MANAGEMENT INC
18335 105 Ave Nw Suite 101, Edmonton, AB, T5S 2K9

(780) 484-1515
Emp Here 100   *Sales* 4,377,642
SIC 7011 Hotels and motels

D-U-N-S 24-227-4020   (BR)
ATCO GAS AND PIPELINES LTD
ATCO GAS
11751 186 St Nw, Edmonton, AB, T5S 2Y2
(780) 420-5719
Emp Here 60
SIC 1389 Oil and gas field services, nec

D-U-N-S 24-400-4768   (HQ)
ACRODEX INC
PCM CANADA
11420 170 St Nw, Edmonton, AB, T5S 1L7
(780) 426-4444
Emp Here 250   *Emp Total* 3,645
Sales 32,686,394
SIC 8731 Commercial physical research
Karim Amarshi
Barkat Chatur
Nazir Javer
Pr Pr Yasmin Jivraj
Jaferali Surmawala
Salma Rajwani
Nash Marani
Nadir Jivraj
Al-Karim Chatur
Salim Chatur

D-U-N-S 25-146-0572   (HQ)
ACUITY HOLDINGS, INC
ZEP MANUFACTURING COMPANY OF CANADA
(*Suby of* NM Z Parent Inc.)
11627 178 St Nw, Edmonton, AB, T5S 1N6
(780) 453-5800
Emp Here 68   *Emp Total* 2,300
Sales 21,669,328
SIC 2844 Toilet preparations
Pr Ralph Puertas
VP Al-Karim Hamir
VP Sls Andre Quennedille

D-U-N-S 25-678-9272   (BR)
ADWOOD MANUFACTURING LTD
ALBERTA BOARD COMPANY
(*Suby of* Adwood Manufacturing Ltd)
10604 205 St Nw, Edmonton, AB, T5S 1Z1
(780) 455-0912
Emp Here 30
SIC 5099 Durable goods, nec

D-U-N-S 20-539-5700   (BR)
AECOM CANADA LTD
SWAN HILLS TREATMENT CENTER
17203 103 Ave Nw, Edmonton, AB, T5S 1J4
(780) 488-6800
Emp Here 80
SIC 8711 Engineering services

D-U-N-S 24-158-0968   (HQ)
AECOM PRODUCTION SERVICES LTD
(*Suby of* Aecom Production Services Ltd)
18817 Stony Plain Rd, Edmonton, AB, T5S 0C2
(780) 486-7000
Emp Here 100   *Emp Total* 1,750
Sales 290,529,507
SIC 1389 Oil and gas field services, nec
Pr Bill Linguard
Terry Freeman

D-U-N-S 25-236-1712   (BR)
ALBERTA TREASURY BRANCHES
ATB FINANCIAL
17107 Stony Plain Rd Nw, Edmonton, AB, T5S 2M9
(780) 408-7474
Emp Here 30
SIC 6036 Savings institutions, except federal

D-U-N-S 25-235-1895   (HQ)
ALL WEATHER WINDOWS LTD
18550 118a Ave Nw, Edmonton, AB, T5S 2K7
(780) 468-2989
Emp Here 425   *Emp Total* 700
Sales 97,548,456

SIC 3442 Metal doors, sash, and trim
Pr Pr Gord Wiebe
VP Fin Roger Hutlet
Genl Mgr Richard Scott

D-U-N-S 20-050-2818   (SL)
ALLIANCE BUILDING MAINTENANCE LTD
18823 111 Ave Nw, Edmonton, AB, T5S 2X4
(780) 447-2574
Emp Here 105   *Sales* 3,064,349
SIC 7349 Building maintenance services, nec

D-U-N-S 24-997-7422   (BR)
ALLSTREAM BUSINESS INC
10638 178 St Nw, Edmonton, AB, T5S 1H4
(780) 486-1144
Emp Here 20
SIC 5065 Electronic parts and equipment, nec

D-U-N-S 20-080-5919   (SL)
ALPINE HEATING LTD
10333 174 St Nw, Edmonton, AB, T5S 1H1
(780) 469-0491
Emp Here 50   *Sales* 4,377,642
SIC 1711 Plumbing, heating, air-conditioning

D-U-N-S 20-123-1243   (SL)
ARAAM INC
HYPNOS CANADA
11616 178 St Nw, Edmonton, AB, T5S 2E6
(780) 444-1388
Emp Here 60   *Sales* 11,307,948
SIC 2515 Mattresses and bedsprings
Dir Feizal Chatur
Barkat Chatur
Pr Pr Farhan Chatur
Salim Chatur
Dir Al Karim Chatur

D-U-N-S 24-895-3200   (BR)
ARPAC STORAGE SYSTEMS CORPORATION
17847 111 Ave Nw, Edmonton, AB, T5S 2X3
(780) 454-8566
Emp Here 20
SIC 2542 Partitions and fixtures, except wood

D-U-N-S 20-176-3518   (SL)
BALON CONSTRUCTION LTD
18910 111 Ave Nw, Edmonton, AB, T5S 0B6

Emp Here 20   *Sales* 5,006,160
SIC 1542 Nonresidential construction, nec
Pr Pr Dennis Balon

D-U-N-S 20-555-8955   (BR)
BELFOR (CANADA) INC
BELFOR RESTORATION SERVICES
17408 116 Ave Nw, Edmonton, AB, T5S 2X2
(780) 455-5566
Emp Here 105
SIC 1799 Special trade contractors, nec

D-U-N-S 24-984-3970   (BR)
BELL MEDIA INC
CFBR-FM THE BEAR 100.3
18520 Stony Plain Rd Nw Suite 100, Edmonton, AB, T5S 1A8
(780) 435-1049
Emp Here 55
SIC 4832 Radio broadcasting stations

D-U-N-S 25-685-3284   (BR)
BELL MEDIA INC
CFRN TV
18520 Stony Plain Rd Nw Suite 100, Edmonton, AB, T5S 1A8
(780) 443-3322
Emp Here 100
SIC 4833 Television broadcasting stations

D-U-N-S 24-011-8591   (BR)
BEST BUY CANADA LTD
BEST BUY
(*Suby of* Best Buy Co., Inc.)
17539 Stony Plain Rd Nw, Edmonton, AB, T5S 2S1
(780) 443-6700
Emp Here 49

SIC 5731 Radio, television, and electronic stores

D-U-N-S 24-281-7690   (BR)
BLACK & MCDONALD LIMITED
10717 181 St Nw, Edmonton, AB, T5S 1N3
(780) 484-1141
Emp Here 48
SIC 1731 Electrical work

D-U-N-S 25-682-0127   (SL)
BOUNDARY-ABRASITEC PRODUCTS INC.
(*Suby of* 412962 Alberta Ltd.)
10740 181 St Nw, Edmonton, AB, T5S 1K8
(780) 486-2626
Emp Here 50   *Sales* 16,981,120
SIC 3532 Mining machinery
Pr Alex Tutschek

D-U-N-S 25-106-8854   (BR)
BRANDT TRACTOR LTD
10630 176 St Nw, Edmonton, AB, T5S 1M2
(780) 484-6613
Emp Here 120
SIC 5084 Industrial machinery and equipment

D-U-N-S 20-081-0075   (BR)
BREWS SUPPLY LTD
18003 111 Ave Nw Suite 452, Edmonton, AB, T5S 2P2
(780) 452-3730
Emp Here 20
SIC 5063 Electrical apparatus and equipment

D-U-N-S 24-327-7675   (BR)
BROCK WHITE CANADA COMPANY, LLC
21359 115 Ave Nw, Edmonton, AB, T5S 0K5
(780) 447-1774
Emp Here 40
SIC 5039 Construction materials, nec

D-U-N-S 24-398-7773   (BR)
CSG SECURITY CORPORATION
CHUBB SECURITY SYSTEMS
(*Suby of* United Technologies Corporation)
10118 175 St Nw, Edmonton, AB, T5S 1L1
(780) 423-3281
Emp Here 20
SIC 3699 Electrical equipment and supplies, nec

D-U-N-S 24-765-8776   (SL)
CALMONT TRUCK CENTRE LTD
VOLVO TRUCK CENTRE-EDMONTON
11403 174 St Nw, Edmonton, AB, T5S 2P4
(780) 451-2680
Emp Here 69   *Sales* 25,171,442
SIC 5511 New and used car dealers
Ch Bd Warren Soper
VP VP Lawrence Pudlowski
VP VP Grant Matula

D-U-N-S 20-922-6625   (BR)
CANADA BROKERLINK (ONTARIO) INC
17520 111 Ave Nw, Edmonton, AB, T5S 0A2
(780) 474-8911
Emp Here 30
SIC 6411 Insurance agents, brokers, and service

D-U-N-S 24-419-6023   (BR)
CANADIAN TIRE CORPORATION, LIMITED
PARTSOURCE
10103 175 St Nw, Edmonton, AB, T5S 1L9
(780) 489-5561
Emp Here 30
SIC 5531 Auto and home supply stores

D-U-N-S 25-316-0618   (BR)
CANADIAN WESTERN BANK
17603 100 Ave Nw, Edmonton, AB, T5S 2M1
(780) 484-7407
Emp Here 40
SIC 6021 National commercial banks

D-U-N-S 20-321-8243   (BR)
CARA OPERATIONS LIMITED
MILESTONE'S GRILL & BAR
(*Suby of* Cara Holdings Limited)

17115 100 Ave Nw, Edmonton, AB, T5S 1T9
(780) 641-2352
Emp Here 20
SIC 5812 Eating places

D-U-N-S 24-374-0763   (SL)
CARDONE INDUSTRIES ULC
(*Suby of* Cardone Industries, Inc.)
17803 111 Ave Nw, Edmonton, AB, T5S 2X3
(780) 444-5033
Emp Here 50   *Sales* 6,055,738
SIC 5013 Motor vehicle supplies and new parts
Mgr Morgan Lutz

D-U-N-S 25-680-3719   (HQ)
CATERPILLAR MINING CANADA ULC
18131 118 Ave Nw, Edmonton, AB, T5S 1M8

Emp Here 64   *Emp Total* 95,400
Sales 72,848,000
SIC 5082 Construction and mining machinery
Pr Pr Timothy Sullivan
Treas John Bosbous
 Craig Mackus
Dir Edward Nelson

D-U-N-S 20-311-3485   (BR)
CENTRAL WATER & EQUIPMENT SERVICES LTD
10642 178 St Nw Unit 101, Edmonton, AB, T5S 1H4

Emp Here 57
SIC 1389 Oil and gas field services, nec

D-U-N-S 24-516-3907   (BR)
CINTAS CANADA LIMITED
(*Suby of* Cintas Corporation)
17811 116 Ave Nw, Edmonton, AB, T5S 2J2
(780) 409-0610
Emp Here 50
SIC 7218 Industrial launderers

D-U-N-S 24-736-4248   (BR)
CITY OF EDMONTON
EDMONTON ENGINEERING SERVICES
11004 190 St Nw, Edmonton, AB, T5S 0G9
(780) 496-6770
Emp Here 82
SIC 7363 Help supply services

D-U-N-S 25-993-0670   (BR)
CIVEO PREMIUM CAMP SERVICES LTD
(*Suby of* Oil States International, Inc.)
17220 Stony Plain Rd Nw Suite 101, Edmonton, AB, T5S 1K6
(780) 733-4900
Emp Here 150
SIC 1522 Residential construction, nec

D-U-N-S 25-095-0482   (BR)
CLEARTECH INDUSTRIES LIMITED PARTNERSHIP
11750 180 St Nw, Edmonton, AB, T5S 1N7

Emp Here 60
SIC 5169 Chemicals and allied products, nec

D-U-N-S 24-827-0295   (SL)
CONCRETE INC
11240 199 St Nw, Edmonton, AB, T5S 2C6
(780) 930-4232
Emp Here 20   *Sales* 5,496,960
SIC 3272 Concrete products, nec
Pr Rui Veiga

D-U-N-S 20-719-4932   (SL)
CONERGY INC.
17815 111 Ave Nw, Edmonton, AB, T5S 2X3
(780) 489-3700
Emp Here 20   *Sales* 1,751,057
SIC 8711 Engineering services

D-U-N-S 20-547-6943   (BR)
CONEX BUSINESS SYSTEMS INC
TOSHIBA BUSINESS SOLUTIONS
18030 107 Ave Nw, Edmonton, AB, T5S 1P4

(780) 484-6116
Emp Here 50
SIC 5044 Office equipment

D-U-N-S 24-356-8024   (BR)
CONNECT LOGISTICS SERVICES INC
17115 118 Ave Nw, Edmonton, AB, T5S 2V3
(780) 458-4508
Emp Here 40
SIC 4226 Special warehousing and storage, nec

D-U-N-S 25-266-7969   (SL)
COWBOYS COUNTRY SALOON LTD
10102 180 St Nw, Edmonton, AB, T5S 1N4
(780) 444-3224
Emp Here 120   *Sales* 4,377,642
SIC 5813 Drinking places

D-U-N-S 20-145-3651   (HQ)
CRANE CARRIER (CANADA) LIMITED
CANADA POWERTRAIN, DIV OF
(*Suby of* Illinois Tool Works Inc.)
11523 186 St Nw, Edmonton, AB, T5S 2W6
(780) 443-2493
Emp Here 20   *Emp Total* 50,000
Sales 12,387,389
SIC 5013 Motor vehicle supplies and new parts
 Mark Ristow
 Mary Ann Spiegel
VP Roland Martel

D-U-N-S 20-512-7389   (BR)
CUMMINS WESTERN CANADA LIMITED PARTNERSHIP
11751 181 St Nw, Edmonton, AB, T5S 2K5
(780) 455-2151
Emp Here 100
SIC 5084 Industrial machinery and equipment

D-U-N-S 20-609-6948   (BR)
DHL EXPRESS (CANADA) LTD
10918 184 St Nw, Edmonton, AB, T5S 2N9
(780) 415-4011
Emp Here 200
SIC 7389 Business services, nec

D-U-N-S 20-849-3002   (SL)
DAYS INN SUITES WEST EDMONTON
10010 179a St Nw, Edmonton, AB, T5S 2T1
(780) 444-4440
Emp Here 100   *Sales* 4,377,642
SIC 7011 Hotels and motels

D-U-N-S 20-195-8118   (BR)
DENCAN RESTAURANTS INC
DENNY'S RESTAURANT
(*Suby of* Northland Properties Corporation)
17635 Stony Plain Rd Nw, Edmonton, AB, T5S 1E3
(780) 450-3663
Emp Here 30
SIC 5812 Eating places

D-U-N-S 20-592-7770   (BR)
DENCAN RESTAURANTS INC
DENNY'S RESTAURANT
(*Suby of* Northland Properties Corporation)
17635 Stony Plain Rd Nw Unit 6647, Edmonton, AB, T5S 1E3
(780) 487-3663
Emp Here 20
SIC 5812 Eating places

D-U-N-S 24-332-7434   (HQ)
DIAMOND INTERNATIONAL TRUCKS LTD
SOUTHSIDE INTERNATIONAL TRUCKS, DIV OF
17020 118 Ave Nw, Edmonton, AB, T5S 1S4
(780) 732-4468
Emp Here 75   *Emp Total* 1
Sales 47,116,450
SIC 5511 New and used car dealers
Pr Pr Don Macadam
 Scott Thresher

D-U-N-S 20-318-4127   (HQ)
DIAMOND SOFTWARE INC

DIAMOND MUNICIPAL SOLUTIONS
172 Street Nw, Edmonton, AB, T5S 0C9
(780) 944-1677
Emp Here 35   *Emp Total* 255
Sales 7,101,500
SIC 7379 Computer related services, nec
Pr Pr Ron Boudreau

D-U-N-S 20-810-5437   (BR)
DUCKS UNLIMITED CANADA
NATIVE PLANT SOLUTIONS
10720 178 St Nw Suite 200, Edmonton, AB, T5S 1J3
(780) 489-2203
Emp Here 20
SIC 8748 Business consulting, nec

D-U-N-S 25-399-5468   (SL)
EARTHWISE CONTRACTING LTD
20104 107 Ave Nw, Edmonton, AB, T5S 1W9
(780) 413-4235
Emp Here 45   *Sales* 5,253,170
SIC 1611 Highway and street construction
Pr Pr William (Bill) Dory
 Sandra Dory

D-U-N-S 25-090-3903   (BR)
ECCO HEATING PRODUCTS LTD
ECCO SUPPLY
11415 184 St Nw, Edmonton, AB, T5S 0H1
(780) 479-6055
Emp Here 55
SIC 3433 Heating equipment, except electric

D-U-N-S 20-010-7238   (BR)
EMCO CORPORATION
10930 184 St Nw Suite 745, Edmonton, AB, T5S 2P8
(780) 452-3626
Emp Here 70
SIC 5074 Plumbing and heating equipment and supplies (hydronics)

D-U-N-S 25-372-7226   (BR)
EMPIRE IRON WORKS LTD
21104 107 Ave Nw, Edmonton, AB, T5S 1X2
(780) 892-3773
Emp Here 30
SIC 3441 Fabricated structural Metal

D-U-N-S 20-123-2225   (SL)
ENVIROCLEAN BUILDING MAINTENANCE LTD
17233 109 Ave Nw Suite 101, Edmonton, AB, T5S 1H7
(780) 489-0500
Emp Here 80   *Sales* 2,334,742
SIC 7349 Building maintenance services, nec

D-U-N-S 20-270-4342   (BR)
EVER GREEN ECOLOGICAL SERVICES INC
20204 113 Ave Nw, Edmonton, AB, T5S 0G3
(780) 239-9419
Emp Here 80
SIC 4953 Refuse systems

D-U-N-S 20-081-9894   (HQ)
FABRIC CARE CLEANERS LTD
(*Suby of* Fabric Care Cleaners Ltd)
17520 108 Ave Nw, Edmonton, AB, T5S 1E8
(780) 483-7500
Emp Here 43   *Emp Total* 52
Sales 1,678,096
SIC 7219 Laundry and garment services, nec

D-U-N-S 20-122-7654   (BR)
FINNING INTERNATIONAL INC
FINNING CANADA
(*Suby of* Finning International Inc)
18131 118 Ave Nw, Edmonton, AB, T5S 1M8
(780) 930-4949
Emp Here 20
SIC 5082 Construction and mining machinery

D-U-N-S 24-000-4635   (BR)
FINNING INTERNATIONAL INC
FINNING CANADA
(*Suby of* Finning International Inc)

10910 170 St Nw, Edmonton, AB, T5S 1H6
(780) 483-1122
Emp Here 25
SIC 7359 Equipment rental and leasing, nec

D-U-N-S 24-628-9859   (BR)
FINNING INTERNATIONAL INC
FINNING (CANADA), DIV OF
(*Suby of* Finning International Inc)
10235 180 St Nw, Edmonton, AB, T5S 1C1
(780) 577-8988
Emp Here 35
SIC 5084 Industrial machinery and equipment

D-U-N-S 24-397-5521   (BR)
FISHER SCIENTIFIC COMPANY
(*Suby of* Thermo Fisher Scientific Inc.)
10720 178 St Nw, Edmonton, AB, T5S 1J3
(780) 486-8323
Emp Here 20
SIC 5049 Professional equipment, nec

D-U-N-S 20-799-2004   (SL)
FLATWORKS INDUSTRIES WEST LTD
CAPITAL CONCRETE
22230 115 Ave Nw, Edmonton, AB, T5S 2N7

Emp Here 20   *Sales* 5,595,120
SIC 5032 Brick, stone, and related material
Pr Mike Twombly

D-U-N-S 24-669-2396   (BR)
FORD CREDIT CANADA LIMITED
(*Suby of* Ford Motor Company)
10335 172 St Nw Suite 300, Edmonton, AB, T5S 1K9

Emp Here 75
SIC 8742 Management consulting services

D-U-N-S 24-067-8714   (BR)
FORD MOTOR COMPANY OF CANADA, LIMITED
FORD PARTS DISTRIBUTION CENTER
(*Suby of* Ford Motor Company)
11604 181 St Nw, Edmonton, AB, T5S 1M6
(780) 454-9621
Emp Here 150
SIC 5013 Motor vehicle supplies and new parts

D-U-N-S 24-090-4060   (HQ)
FOSTER PARK BROKERS INC
(*Suby of* Foster Park Brokers Inc)
17704 103 Ave Nw Suite 200, Edmonton, AB, T5S 1J9
(780) 489-4961
Emp Here 25   *Emp Total* 55
Sales 4,961,328
SIC 6411 Insurance agents, brokers, and service

D-U-N-S 20-075-9595   (HQ)
FULLER AUSTIN INC
11604 186 St Nw, Edmonton, AB, T5S 0C4
(780) 452-1701
Emp Here 25   *Emp Total* 586
Sales 41,580,048
SIC 1799 Special trade contractors, nec
VP Opers Ron Richards
VP Opers Perry Pugh

D-U-N-S 24-390-5320   (BR)
G.N. JOHNSTON EQUIPMENT CO. LTD
11204 184 St Nw, Edmonton, AB, T5S 2S6
(780) 483-7051
Emp Here 32
SIC 5084 Industrial machinery and equipment

D-U-N-S 20-082-4394   (BR)
GIENOW CANADA INC
PLY GEM CANADA
(*Suby of* Ply Gem Holdings, Inc.)
18703 111 Ave Nw Suite 11, Edmonton, AB, T5S 2X4
(780) 451-2590
Emp Here 30
SIC 3442 Metal doors, sash, and trim

D-U-N-S 24-766-9823   (BR)
GLENTEL INC
WIRELESS WAVES
10230 176 St Nw, Edmonton, AB, T5S 1L2
(780) 732-3400
Emp Here 40
SIC 4813 Telephone communication, except radio

D-U-N-S 24-983-3369   (SL)
GREENBORO HOMES LTD
10714 176 St Nw, Edmonton, AB, T5S 1G7
(780) 702-6192
Emp Here 45   *Sales* 9,030,720
SIC 1521 Single-family housing construction
Pr Tom Chisolm

D-U-N-S 24-584-0137   (BR)
GUILLEVIN INTERNATIONAL CIE
11220 180 St Nw, Edmonton, AB, T5S 2X5
(780) 453-1884
Emp Here 20
SIC 5063 Electrical apparatus and equipment

D-U-N-S 20-720-0049   (BR)
HILLMAN GROUP CANADA ULC, THE
PAPCO
11714 180 St Nw, Edmonton, AB, T5S 1N7
(780) 450-1346
Emp Here 20
SIC 3452 Bolts, nuts, rivets, and washers

D-U-N-S 20-179-3838   (BR)
HUDSON'S BAY COMPANY
HOME OUTFITTERS
17531 Stony Plain Rd Nw, Edmonton, AB, T5S 2S1
(780) 496-9354
Emp Here 50
SIC 5311 Department stores

D-U-N-S 20-179-6674   (BR)
INTRIA ITEMS INC
17509 106 Ave Nw, Edmonton, AB, T5S 1E7
(780) 408-1331
Emp Here 25
SIC 7374 Data processing and preparation

D-U-N-S 25-013-2446   (BR)
ITW CANADA INC
ITW INSULATION SYSTEMS CANADA, DIV OF
(*Suby of* Illinois Tool Works Inc.)
11240 184 St Nw, Edmonton, AB, T5S 2S6
(780) 484-2321
Emp Here 22
SIC 3443 Fabricated plate work (boiler shop)

D-U-N-S 24-906-7810   (BR)
ITW CANADA INVESTMENTS LIMITED PARTNERSHIP
HOBART FOOD EQUIPMENT GROUP
(*Suby of* Illinois Tool Works Inc.)
10609 172 Street Northwest, Edmonton, AB, T5S 1P1
(780) 486-2325
Emp Here 37
SIC 5046 Commercial equipment, nec

D-U-N-S 24-352-7335   (BR)
IMPACT SECURITY GROUP INC
10471 178 St Nw Suite 103, Edmonton, AB, T5S 1R5
(780) 485-6000
Emp Here 50
SIC 7381 Detective and armored car services

D-U-N-S 25-305-2864   (BR)
INNVEST PROPERTIES CORP
COMFORT INN WEST
(*Suby of* Innvest Properties Corp)
17610 100 Ave Nw, Edmonton, AB, T5S 1S9
(780) 484-4415
Emp Here 20
SIC 7011 Hotels and motels

D-U-N-S 25-094-4212   (HQ)
INSTALOANS INC
17631 103 Ave Nw, Edmonton, AB, T5S 1N8

(780) 408-5110
Emp Here 50   *Emp Total* 2,000
Sales 420,916,050
SIC 6141 Personal credit institutions
Pr Tim Latimer
    Marc Arcand

D-U-N-S 24-862-5282   (BR)
INTEGRATED DISTRIBUTION SYSTEMS LIMITED PARTNERSHIP
WAJAX EQUIPMENT
17604 105 Ave Nw, Edmonton, AB, T5S 1G4
(780) 483-6641
Emp Here 80
SIC 5084 Industrial machinery and equipment

D-U-N-S 24-027-5938   (BR)
JOHNSON INC
11120 178 St Nw, Edmonton, AB, T5S 1P2
(780) 483-0408
Emp Here 55
SIC 6331 Fire, marine, and casualty insurance

D-U-N-S 20-538-2799   (HQ)
KANE VETERINARY SUPPLIES LTD
WALCO CANADA ANIMAL HEALTH
11204 186 St Nw, Edmonton, AB, T5S 2W2
(780) 453-1516
Emp Here 68   *Emp Total* 7,000
Sales 14,300,297
SIC 5047 Medical and hospital equipment
Fin Ex Mark Panganiban
Dir Damian Olthoff
Dir Stephen Olsson
Dir Jon Kuehl
Dir Jeff Hyde
    Steve Olson

D-U-N-S 25-674-3428   (SL)
KIEWIT INDUSTRIAL CANADA CO.
(*Suby of* Peter Kiewit Sons', Inc.)
11211 Winterburn Rd Nw, Edmonton, AB, T5S 2B2
(780) 447-3509
Emp Here 20   *Sales* 2,772,507
SIC 1629 Heavy construction, nec

D-U-N-S 24-322-2291   (BR)
LAFARGE CANADA INC
21521 112 Ave Nw, Edmonton, AB, T5S 2T8
(780) 486-4050
Emp Here 35
SIC 1623 Water, sewer, and utility lines

D-U-N-S 20-771-6353   (BR)
LAVTOR HOLDINGS (ALBERTA) LTD
SMITTY'S FAMILY RESTAURANT
18310 Stony Plain Rd Nw, Edmonton, AB, T5S 1A7
(780) 483-6457
Emp Here 24
SIC 5812 Eating places

D-U-N-S 24-205-1352   (HQ)
LEASE LINK CANADA CORP
10471 178 St Nw Suite 205, Edmonton, AB, T5S 1R5
(780) 414-0616
Emp Here 25   *Emp Total* 18
Sales 11,119,482
SIC 6159 Miscellaneous business credit institutions
Pr James Jang
    Steve Passant
    Penny Thome
    Darren Brooks

D-U-N-S 20-722-5165   (BR)
LEAVITT MACHINERY AND RENTALS INC
LEAVITT MACHINERY
11015 186 St Nw, Edmonton, AB, T5S 2V5
(780) 451-7200
Emp Here 48
SIC 5084 Industrial machinery and equipment

D-U-N-S 24-950-1537   (BR)
LEE VALLEY TOOLS LTD
18403 104 Ave Nw, Edmonton, AB, T5S 2V8

(780) 444-6153
Emp Here 40
SIC 5251 Hardware stores

D-U-N-S 25-270-1453   (BR)
LOBLAWS INC
REAL CANADIAN SUPERSTORE 1573
17303 Stony Plain Rd Nw Suite 1573, Edmonton, AB, T5S 1B5
(780) 486-8452
Emp Here 320
SIC 5141 Groceries, general line

D-U-N-S 20-305-3780   (BR)
LOWE'S COMPANIES CANADA, ULC
10225 186 St Nw, Edmonton, AB, T5S 0G5
(780) 486-2508
Emp Here 145
SIC 5211 Lumber and other building materials

D-U-N-S 20-293-3896   (BR)
LYDALE CONSTRUCTION (1983) CO. LTD
17839 106a Ave Nw Unit 101, Edmonton, AB, T5S 1V8
(780) 822-1200
Emp Here 20
SIC 1521 Single-family housing construction

D-U-N-S 20-258-6434   (BR)
MMD SALES LTD
MARTIN MOTOR SPORTS WEST
17348 118 Ave Nw, Edmonton, AB, T5S 2L7
(780) 481-4000
Emp Here 50
SIC 5083 Farm and garden machinery

D-U-N-S 20-555-9623   (BR)
MTE LOGISTIX EDMONTON INC
BDL
11208 189 St Nw, Edmonton, AB, T5S 2V6
(780) 732-6525
Emp Here 150
SIC 4225 General warehousing and storage

D-U-N-S 20-337-9623   (BR)
MTE LOGISTIX EDMONTON INC
17374 116 Ave Nw, Edmonton, AB, T5S 2X2
(780) 341-4368
Emp Here 25
SIC 4225 General warehousing and storage

D-U-N-S 24-090-1892   (HQ)
MALTAIS GEOMATICS INC
(*Suby of* Maltais Geomatics Inc)
17011 105 Ave Nw, Edmonton, AB, T5S 1M5
(780) 483-2015
Emp Here 20   *Emp Total* 90
Sales 10,447,737
SIC 8713 Surveying services
Pr Pr Irwin Maltais
VP VP Bruce Gudim
    Milton Leinke

D-U-N-S 20-642-5147   (BR)
MALTAIS GEOMATICS INC
(*Suby of* Maltais Geomatics Inc)
17011 105 Ave Nw, Edmonton, AB, T5S 1M5
(780) 926-4123
Emp Here 30
SIC 8713 Surveying services

D-U-N-S 20-070-3697   (BR)
MCDONALD'S RESTAURANTS OF CANADA LIMITED
MCDONALD'S #8395
(*Suby of* McDonald's Corporation)
17720 100 Ave Nw, Edmonton, AB, T5S 1S9
(780) 414-8395
Emp Here 70
SIC 5812 Eating places

D-U-N-S 20-771-6304   (BR)
METRIE CANADA LTD
SAUDER DISTRIBUTORS EDMONTON
18150 109 Ave Nw, Edmonton, AB, T5S 2K2
(780) 454-9681
Emp Here 35
SIC 2431 Millwork

D-U-N-S 20-594-0844   (BR)
METRIE CANADA LTD
MOULDING & MILLWORK
18150 109 Ave Nw, Edmonton, AB, T5S 2K2
(780) 454-9681
Emp Here 25
SIC 5031 Lumber, plywood, and millwork

D-U-N-S 20-920-6353   (BR)
MID-ARCTIC TRANSPORTATION CO. LTD
MATCO
18151 107 Ave Nw, Edmonton, AB, T5S 1K4
(780) 484-8800
Emp Here 40
SIC 4213 Trucking, except local

D-U-N-S 20-192-7857   (BR)
MOORE CANADA CORPORATION
R.R. DONNELLEY
(*Suby of* R. R. Donnelley & Sons Company)
18330 102 Ave Nw, Edmonton, AB, T5S 2J9
(780) 452-5592
Emp Here 250
SIC 2761 Manifold business forms

D-U-N-S 20-318-2857   (BR)
NATIONAL ENERGY EQUIPMENT INC
17107 118 Ave Nw, Edmonton, AB, T5S 2V3
(780) 466-2171
Emp Here 30
SIC 1321 Natural gas liquids

D-U-N-S 20-138-7441   (BR)
NATIONAL ENERGY EQUIPMENT INC
GAS EQUIPMENT SUPPLIES
17107 118 Ave Nw, Edmonton, AB, T5S 2V3
(780) 468-4454
Emp Here 25
SIC 5075 Warm air heating and air conditioning

D-U-N-S 25-313-3490   (SL)
NEPTUNE CORING (WESTERN) LTD
21521 112 Ave Nw, Edmonton, AB, T5S 2T8
(780) 486-4050
Emp Here 30   *Sales* 3,502,114
SIC 1611 Highway and street construction

D-U-N-S 24-392-0337   (HQ)
NORTHERN INDUSTRIAL INSULATION CONTRACTORS INC
18910 111 Ave Nw, Edmonton, AB, T5S 0B6
(780) 483-1850
Emp Here 60   *Emp Total* 586
Sales 13,570,690
SIC 1799 Special trade contractors, nec
    Gary R Bardell
VP Opers Sheldon Dobish

D-U-N-S 20-083-6468   (BR)
OLD DUTCH FOODS LTD
HUMPTY DUMPTY OLD DUTCH FOODS
(*Suby of* Old Dutch Foods Ltd)
18027 114 Ave Nw, Edmonton, AB, T5S 1T8
(780) 453-2341
Emp Here 75
SIC 2096 Potato chips and similar snacks

D-U-N-S 20-913-6055   (BR)
ON SIDE RESTORATION SERVICES LTD
18547 104 Ave Nw, Edmonton, AB, T5S 2V8
(780) 497-7972
Emp Here 20
SIC 1771 Concrete work

D-U-N-S 20-438-1743   (BR)
OTIS CANADA, INC
(*Suby of* United Technologies Corporation)
10617 172 St Nw, Edmonton, AB, T5S 1P1
(780) 444-2900
Emp Here 45
SIC 3534 Elevators and moving stairways

D-U-N-S 20-594-3798   (HQ)
PAINE, J. R. & ASSOCIATES LTD
(*Suby of* Paine, J R Holdings Ltd)
17505 106 Ave Nw, Edmonton, AB, T5S 1E7

(780) 489-0700
Emp Here 60   *Emp Total* 2
Sales 7,441,991
SIC 8734 Testing laboratories
Pr Roman Stefaniw

D-U-N-S 24-395-2454   (SL)
PALS SURVEYS & ASSOCIATES LTD
10704 176 St Nw, Edmonton, AB, T5S 1G7
(780) 455-3177
Emp Here 130   *Sales* 23,110,400
SIC 8713 Surveying services
Pr Pr Larry Pals
  Peter John Jackson

D-U-N-S 24-928-7384   (BR)
PATTISON, JIM INDUSTRIES LTD
PATTISON OUTDOOR ADVERTISING
10707 178 St Nw, Edmonton, AB, T5S 1J6
(780) 669-7700
Emp Here 27
SIC 7312 Outdoor advertising services

D-U-N-S 20-206-9535   (SL)
PELICAN PRODUCTS ULC
(*Suby of* Pelican Products, Inc.)
10221 184 St Nw, Edmonton, AB, T5S 2J4
(780) 481-6076
Emp Here 27   *Sales* 5,370,756
SIC 2671 Paper; coated and laminated packaging
Genl Mgr Edwin Meyer
CEO Lynden Faulkner

D-U-N-S 20-112-9475   (HQ)
PETER KIEWIT INFRASTRUCTURE CO.
(*Suby of* Peter Kiewit Sons', Inc.)
11211 Winterburn Rd Nw, Edmonton, AB, T5S 2B2
(780) 447-3509
Emp Here 85   *Emp Total* 14,700
Sales 96,933,487
SIC 1611 Highway and street construction
Pr Pr Louis Chapdelaine
Dir Bruce E Grewcock
  Michael F Norton
VP VP Gregory D Dixon
Fin Ex Michael J Whetstine
VP Dan H Levert
VP Michael J Piechoski
VP Frank J Margitan
VP John W Neal

D-U-N-S 24-682-0000   (BR)
PLATINUM INVESTMENTS LTD
COURTYARD BY MARRIOTT EDMONTON WEST
(*Suby of* Platinum Investments Ltd)
10011 184 St Nw, Edmonton, AB, T5S 0C7
(780) 638-6070
Emp Here 50
SIC 7011 Hotels and motels

D-U-N-S 24-679-4387   (BR)
PLATINUM INVESTMENTS LTD
HAMPTON INN & SUITES, EDMONTON WEST
(*Suby of* Platinum Investments Ltd)
18304 100 Ave Nw, Edmonton, AB, T5S 2V2
(780) 484-7280
Emp Here 50
SIC 7011 Hotels and motels

D-U-N-S 20-692-2309   (HQ)
PLATINUM INVESTMENTS LTD
HILTON GARDEN INN
(*Suby of* Platinum Investments Ltd)
17610 Stony Plain Rd Nw, Edmonton, AB, T5S 1A2
(780) 443-2233
Emp Here 100   *Emp Total* 400
Sales 23,558,400
SIC 7011 Hotels and motels
Pr Ali Meghji

D-U-N-S 24-338-1550   (HQ)
PREMAY EQUIPMENT LP
11310 Winterburn Rd Nw, Edmonton, AB, T5S

2B5
(780) 447-5555
Emp Here 50   *Emp Total* 5,515
Sales 7,103,258
SIC 4213 Trucking, except local
Pr Duncan Cook

D-U-N-S 24-338-1568   (SL)
PREMAY PIPELINE HAULING L.P.
22703 112 Ave Nw, Edmonton, AB, T5S 2M4
(780) 447-3014
Emp Here 20   *Sales* 2,858,628
SIC 4213 Trucking, except local

D-U-N-S 25-454-4109   (BR)
PRIME FASTENERS LTD
10733 178 St Nw, Edmonton, AB, T5S 1J6
(780) 484-2218
Emp Here 20
SIC 5085 Industrial supplies

D-U-N-S 24-978-3465   (SL)
PUGWASH HOLDINGS LTD
INDEPENDENT JEWELLERS
11248 170 St Nw, Edmonton, AB, T5S 2X1
(780) 484-6342
Emp Here 50   *Sales* 2,772,507
SIC 5944 Jewelry stores

D-U-N-S 20-184-8533   (BR)
QSI INTERIORS LTD
10240 180 St Nw, Edmonton, AB, T5S 1E2
(780) 489-4462
Emp Here 100
SIC 1742 Plastering, drywall, and insulation

D-U-N-S 24-806-8082   (BR)
RTL- ROBINSON ENTERPRISES LTD
10821 209 St Nw, Edmonton, AB, T5S 1Z7

Emp Here 75
SIC 4213 Trucking, except local

D-U-N-S 24-265-8086   (HQ)
RAYDON RENTALS LTD
CAT THE RENTAL STORE
(*Suby of* Finning International Inc)
10235 180 Street Nw, Edmonton, AB, T5S 1C1
(780) 989-1301
Emp Here 30   *Emp Total* 11,900
Sales 32,248,629
SIC 7353 Heavy construction equipment rental
Pr Pr Harry Hoyer
Dir Joel Harrod
Dir Miles Hunt
Dir Steven Mandziuk
Dir David Parker

D-U-N-S 25-453-8705   (BR)
RED LOBSTER HOSPITALITY LLC
OLIVE GARDEN
(*Suby of* Red Lobster Seafood Co., LLC)
10121 171 St Nw, Edmonton, AB, T5S 1S6
(780) 484-0700
Emp Here 110
SIC 5812 Eating places

D-U-N-S 20-003-7492   (BR)
RED LOBSTER HOSPITALITY LLC
RED LOBSTER RESTAURANTS
(*Suby of* Red Lobster Seafood Co., LLC)
10111 171 St Nw, Edmonton, AB, T5S 1S6
(780) 484-0660
Emp Here 110
SIC 5812 Eating places

D-U-N-S 20-640-6154   (SL)
REDHILL SYSTEMS LTD
11458 Winterburn Rd Nw, Edmonton, AB, T5S 2Y3
(780) 472-9474
Emp Here 40   *Sales* 4,012,839
SIC 3613 Switchgear and switchboard apparatus

D-U-N-S 20-527-4637   (SL)
REFLEX MANUFACTURING LTD

17223 105 Ave Nw, Edmonton, AB, T5S 1H2
(780) 484-4002
Emp Here 35   *Sales* 6,201,660
SIC 3644 Noncurrent-carrying wiring devices
Pr Pr Gregory Triff
  Jason Meikle
VP VP Carole Triff

D-U-N-S 24-731-7407   (SL)
REMAI DURAND VENTURES INC
WEST HARVEST INN
17803 Stony Plain Rd Nw, Edmonton, AB, T5S 1B4
(780) 484-8000
Emp Here 60   *Sales* 2,626,585
SIC 7011 Hotels and motels

D-U-N-S 25-268-9831   (BR)
ROBINSON, B.A. CO. LTD
ROBINSON LIGHTING & BATH CENTRE
(*Suby of* Ross Group Inc)
18511 104 Ave Nw, Edmonton, AB, T5S 2V8
(780) 453-5714
Emp Here 50
SIC 5074 Plumbing and heating equipment and supplies (hydronics)

D-U-N-S 24-840-2836   (SL)
ROYAL WEST EDMONTON INN LTD
10010 178 St Nw, Edmonton, AB, T5S 1T3
(780) 484-6000
Emp Here 75   *Sales* 3,283,232
SIC 7011 Hotels and motels

D-U-N-S 24-858-2822   (BR)
SAPUTO PRODUITS LAITIERS CANADA S.E.N.C.
(*Suby of* Saputo Produits Laitiers Canada S.E.N.C.)
11235 186 St Nw, Edmonton, AB, T5S 2T7
(780) 483-4203
Emp Here 45
SIC 2022 Cheese; natural and processed

D-U-N-S 20-585-2549   (BR)
SHAW CABLESYSTEMS G.P.
10450 178 St Nw, Edmonton, AB, T5S 1S2
(780) 490-3555
Emp Here 600
SIC 4841 Cable and other pay television services

D-U-N-S 25-271-5586   (BR)
SHAW COMMUNICATIONS INC
SHAW CABLE
10450 178 St Nw, Edmonton, AB, T5S 1S2
(780) 490-3555
Emp Here 500
SIC 4841 Cable and other pay television services

D-U-N-S 20-174-5259   (BR)
SHAW WIN HOTEL LTD
WINGATE INN
(*Suby of* Shaw Win Hotel Ltd)
18220 100 Ave Nw, Edmonton, AB, T5S 2V2
(780) 443-1000
Emp Here 25
SIC 7011 Hotels and motels

D-U-N-S 24-128-2164   (BR)
SHOPPERS DRUG MART INC
EDMONTON REGIONAL OFFICE
17835 106a Ave Nw Suite 201, Edmonton, AB, T5S 1V8
(780) 484-3979
Emp Here 20
SIC 5912 Drug stores and proprietary stores

D-U-N-S 20-524-4325   (BR)
SHRED-IT INTERNATIONAL ULC
SHRED-IT EDMONTON
18603 111 Ave Nw, Edmonton, AB, T5S 2X4
(780) 444-8394
Emp Here 35
SIC 7389 Business services, nec

D-U-N-S 20-780-9885   (BR)
SIEMENS CANADA LIMITED

10310 176 St Nw, Edmonton, AB, T5S 1L3
(780) 452-3890
Emp Here 56
SIC 5063 Electrical apparatus and equipment

D-U-N-S 24-031-2152   (BR)
SPEEDY CREEK (1997) LTD
17724 102 Ave Nw, Edmonton, AB, T5S 1H5

Emp Here 600
SIC 5812 Eating places

D-U-N-S 24-971-1263   (BR)
STOCK TRANSPORTATION LTD
11454 Winterburn Rd Nw, Edmonton, AB, T5S 2Y3
(780) 451-9536
Emp Here 100
SIC 4151 School buses

D-U-N-S 20-318-3991   (SL)
STUART OLSON SPECIALTY FABRICATION INC
18023 111 Ave Nw, Edmonton, AB, T5S 2P2
(780) 509-4975
Emp Here 30   *Sales* 4,331,255
SIC 3498 Fabricated pipe and fittings

D-U-N-S 24-344-0679   (BR)
SUPERIOR PLUS LP
WINROC
10841 Winterburn Rd Nw, Edmonton, AB, T5S 2A9
(780) 447-3326
Emp Here 30
SIC 5039 Construction materials, nec

D-U-N-S 20-810-1998   (HQ)
SUPREME STEEL LP
SUPREME STEEL BRIDGE, DIV OF
(*Suby of* Leder Investments Ltd)
10457 184 St Nw, Edmonton, AB, T5S 1G1
(780) 483-3278
Emp Here 260   *Emp Total* 5
Sales 106,548,873
SIC 3441 Fabricated structural Metal
Pr Pr John Leder
  Sally Leder

D-U-N-S 25-334-9005   (HQ)
TECO-WESTINGHOUSE MOTORS (CANADA) INC
18060 109 Ave Nw, Edmonton, AB, T5S 2K2
(780) 444-8933
Emp Here 22   *Emp Total* 2,428
Sales 9,047,127
SIC 5063 Electrical apparatus and equipment
Pr Cheng-Hsiung Tang
  Fang Sheng Sun
  Sophia Chiu
  Sheng Chyuan Lin
Treas Li Chang

D-U-N-S 20-049-1913   (BR)
TOSHIBA OF CANADA LIMITED
TOSHIBA BUSINESS SYSTEMS
18030 107 Ave Nw, Edmonton, AB, T5S 1P4
(780) 484-6116
Emp Here 50
SIC 5999 Miscellaneous retail stores, nec

D-U-N-S 25-414-3506   (SL)
TRACER CANADA COMPANY
(*Suby of* Emerson Electric Co.)
11004 174 St Nw, Edmonton, AB, T5S 2P3

Emp Here 22   *Sales* 2,699,546
SIC 1389 Oil and gas field services, nec

D-U-N-S 25-524-6589   (BR)
TRANSX LTD
TRANSX LOGISTICS
19121 118a Ave Nw, Edmonton, AB, T5S 2J7
(780) 484-6434
Emp Here 20
SIC 4213 Trucking, except local

D-U-N-S 20-776-3335   (BR)
TYCO INTEGRATED FIRE & SECURITY

CANADA, INC
SIMPLEXGRINNELL, A DIV
(*Suby of* Johnson Controls, Inc.)
17402 116 Ave Nw, Edmonton, AB, T5S 2X2
(780) 452-5280
Emp Here 170
SIC 7389 Business services, nec

D-U-N-S 25-326-3503   (BR)
UAP INC
TW DISTRIBUTION CENTRE
(*Suby of* Genuine Parts Company)
18532 116 Ave Nw, Edmonton, AB, T5S 2W8
(780) 489-3300
Emp Here 47
SIC 5013 Motor vehicle supplies and new parts

D-U-N-S 24-327-8157   (BR)
UAP INC
UAP/NAPA DISTRIBUTION CENTRE
(*Suby of* Genuine Parts Company)
17310 111 Ave Nw Suite 239, Edmonton, AB, T5S 0A8
(780) 455-9151
Emp Here 70
SIC 5015 Motor vehicle parts, used

D-U-N-S 25-272-8076   (BR)
UAP INC
NAPA AUTO PARTS
(*Suby of* Genuine Parts Company)
17310 111 Ave Nw Suite 239, Edmonton, AB, T5S 0A8
(780) 451-3910
Emp Here 20
SIC 5013 Motor vehicle supplies and new parts

D-U-N-S 24-273-9829   (BR)
UTC FIRE & SECURITY CANADA INC
UTC FIRE & SECURITY CANADA
(*Suby of* United Technologies Corporation)
10118 175 St Nw, Edmonton, AB, T5S 1L1
(780) 452-6411
Emp Here 20
SIC 5063 Electrical apparatus and equipment

D-U-N-S 20-981-5880   (BR)
UNI-SELECT EASTERN INC
UNI-SELECT EASTERN INC
11754 170 St Nw, Edmonton, AB, T5S 1J7
(780) 452-2440
Emp Here 100
SIC 5013 Motor vehicle supplies and new parts

D-U-N-S 25-796-2662   (BR)
VITALAIRE CANADA INC
VITALAIRE HEALTHCARE
18244 102 Ave Nw, Edmonton, AB, T5S 1S7
(780) 944-0202
Emp Here 60
SIC 5169 Chemicals and allied products, nec

D-U-N-S 25-219-0293   (BR)
WAL-MART CANADA CORP
18521 Stony Plain Rd Nw Suite 3027, Edmonton, AB, T5S 2V9
(780) 487-8626
Emp Here 350
SIC 5311 Department stores

D-U-N-S 25-999-7849   (BR)
WALLACE & CAREY INC
18023 111 Ave Nw, Edmonton, AB, T5S 2P2
(780) 453-1507
Emp Here 40
SIC 5194 Tobacco and tobacco products

D-U-N-S 20-004-6436   (BR)
WENDY'S RESTAURANTS OF CANADA INC
WENDY'S
(*Suby of* The Wendy's Company)
17007 109 Ave Nw, Edmonton, AB, T5S 2H8
(780) 487-9701
Emp Here 20
SIC 5812 Eating places

D-U-N-S 25-451-0738   (BR)
WESTMONT HOSPITALITY MANAGEMENT LIMITED
TRAVELODGE
(*Suby of* Westmont Hospitality Management Limited)
18320 Stony Plain Rd Nw, Edmonton, AB, T5S 1A7
(780) 483-6031
Emp Here 30
SIC 7011 Hotels and motels

D-U-N-S 24-855-5349   (SL)
WINFIRE HOSPITALITY LTD
HOMEFIRE GRILL
18220 100 Ave Nw, Edmonton, AB, T5S 2V2
(780) 443-1000
Emp Here 65   *Sales* 2,845,467
SIC 7011 Hotels and motels

D-U-N-S 24-283-2012   (BR)
WOLSELEY CANADA INC
WOLSELEY MECHANICAL GROUP
(*Suby of* WOLSELEY PLC)
18404 116 Ave Nw, Edmonton, AB, T5S 2W8
(780) 452-0340
Emp Here 50
SIC 5074 Plumbing and heating equipment and supplies (hydronics)

Edmonton, AB T5T

D-U-N-S 24-319-8459   (BR)
7-ELEVEN CANADA, INC
7-ELEVEN STORE #33047
1017 Potter Greens Dr Nw, Edmonton, AB, T5T 6A4
(780) 443-2482
Emp Here 25
SIC 5411 Grocery stores

D-U-N-S 20-208-4880   (SL)
ALBERTA LIFE CARE LTD
LIFESTYLE OPTIONS
17203 99 Ave Nw, Edmonton, AB, T5T 6S5
(780) 433-2223
Emp Here 200   *Sales* 10,048,000
SIC 8361 Residential care
Genl Mgr Renate Sainsbury

D-U-N-S 25-068-9106   (BR)
ALBERTS RESTAURANTS LTD
TONY ROMA'S
(*Suby of* Alberts Restaurants Ltd)
1640 Burlington Ave, Edmonton, AB, T5T 3J7
(780) 444-3105
Emp Here 105
SIC 5812 Eating places

D-U-N-S 20-589-4939   (BR)
BANQUE TORONTO-DOMINION, LA
TD CANADA TRUST
(*Suby of* Toronto-Dominion Bank, The)
6655 178 St Nw Suite 120, Edmonton, AB, T5T 4J5
(780) 448-8360
Emp Here 20
SIC 6021 National commercial banks

D-U-N-S 20-104-7243   (BR)
BODY SHOP CANADA LIMITED, THE
BODY SHOP, THE
8882 170 St Nw Suite 1742, Edmonton, AB, T5T 4J2
(780) 481-1945
Emp Here 35
SIC 5999 Miscellaneous retail stores, nec

D-U-N-S 25-231-7672   (BR)
BRICK WAREHOUSE LP, THE
8770 170 St Suite 1480, Edmonton, AB, T5T 4M2
(780) 444-1000
Emp Here 60
SIC 5712 Furniture stores

D-U-N-S 25-452-0562   (BR)
CHANTELLE MANAGEMENT LTD
WATERFORD OF SUMMERLEA, THE
9395 172 St Nw Suite 224, Edmonton, AB, T5T 5S6
(780) 444-4545
Emp Here 50
SIC 8361 Residential care

D-U-N-S 20-966-6895   (BR)
CHARTWELL RETIREMENT RESIDENCES
CHARTWELL SENIORS HOUSING REAL ESTATE INVESTMENT TRUST
9612 172 St Nw Suite 112, Edmonton, AB, T5T 6C7
(780) 443-1234
Emp Here 40
SIC 8361 Residential care

D-U-N-S 25-064-6452   (BR)
CHIRO FOODS LIMITED
OUTBACK STEAKHOUSE
17118 90 Ave Nw, Edmonton, AB, T5T 4C8
(780) 438-8848
Emp Here 75
SIC 5812 Eating places

D-U-N-S 20-699-4910   (BR)
CHRISTIAN AND MISSIONARY ALLIANCE IN CANADA, THE
BEULAH ALLIANCE CHURCH
17504 98a Ave Nw, Edmonton, AB, T5T 5T8
(780) 486-4010
Emp Here 50
SIC 8661 Religious organizations

D-U-N-S 24-394-4352   (BR)
CINEPLEX ODEON CORPORATION
SCOTIABANK THEATRE WEST EDMONTON MALL
8882 170 St Nw Suite 3030, Edmonton, AB, T5T 4M2
(780) 444-2400
Emp Here 154
SIC 7832 Motion picture theaters, except drive-in

D-U-N-S 20-195-9454   (BR)
EDDIE BAUER OF CANADA INC
(*Suby of* Golden Gate Capital LP)
8882 170 St Nw Suite 2393, Edmonton, AB, T5T 4M2
(780) 444-1440
Emp Here 25
SIC 5699 Miscellaneous apparel and accessory stores

D-U-N-S 20-012-1148   (BR)
EDMONTON CATHOLIC SEPARATE SCHOOL DISTRICT NO.7
ST. MARTHA SCHOOL
(*Suby of* Edmonton Catholic Separate School District No.7)
7240 180 St Nw, Edmonton, AB, T5T 3B1
(780) 487-4594
Emp Here 25
SIC 8211 Elementary and secondary schools

D-U-N-S 20-028-4342   (BR)
EDMONTON CATHOLIC SEPARATE SCHOOL DISTRICT NO.7
OUR LADY OF PRAIRIES CATHOLIC ELEMENTARY SCHOOL
(*Suby of* Edmonton Catholic Separate School District No.7)
17655 64 Ave Nw, Edmonton, AB, T5T 4A6
(780) 481-0389
Emp Here 24
SIC 8211 Elementary and secondary schools

D-U-N-S 20-028-3997   (BR)
EDMONTON CATHOLIC SEPARATE SCHOOL DISTRICT NO.7
ST. BENEDICT CATHOLIC ELEMENTARY SCHOOL
(*Suby of* Edmonton Catholic Separate School District No.7)
18015 93 Ave Nw, Edmonton, AB, T5T 1X5

(780) 487-2733
Emp Here 40
SIC 8211 Elementary and secondary schools

D-U-N-S 20-028-3898   (BR)
EDMONTON CATHOLIC SEPARATE SCHOOL DISTRICT NO.7
ST. JUSTIN CATHOLIC ELEMENTARY SCHOOL
(*Suby of* Edmonton Catholic Separate School District No.7)
8405 175 St Nw, Edmonton, AB, T5T 0G9
(780) 487-2264
Emp Here 25
SIC 8211 Elementary and secondary schools

D-U-N-S 20-713-0506   (BR)
EDMONTON CATHOLIC SEPARATE SCHOOL DISTRICT NO.7
ARCHBISHOP OSCAR ROMERO CATHOLIC HIGH SCHOOL
(*Suby of* Edmonton Catholic Separate School District No.7)
17760 69 Ave Nw, Edmonton, AB, T5T 6X3
(780) 428-2705
Emp Here 50
SIC 8211 Elementary and secondary schools

D-U-N-S 20-712-6298   (BR)
EDMONTON SCHOOL DISTRICT NO. 7
WINTERBURN SCHOOL
9527 Winterburn Rd Nw, Edmonton, AB, T5T 5X9
(780) 447-3566
Emp Here 30
SIC 8211 Elementary and secondary schools

D-U-N-S 20-028-4276   (BR)
EDMONTON SCHOOL DISTRICT NO. 7
BELMEAD ELEMENTARY SCHOOL
9011 182 St Nw, Edmonton, AB, T5T 2Y9
(780) 481-3314
Emp Here 35
SIC 8211 Elementary and secondary schools

D-U-N-S 20-028-9200   (BR)
EDMONTON SCHOOL DISTRICT NO. 7
LYMBURN SCHOOL
18710 72 Ave Nw, Edmonton, AB, T5T 5E9
(780) 487-1777
Emp Here 32
SIC 8211 Elementary and secondary schools

D-U-N-S 20-028-3781   (BR)
EDMONTON SCHOOL DISTRICT NO. 7
ALDERGROVE SCHOOL
8525 182 St Nw, Edmonton, AB, T5T 1X1
(780) 487-5182
Emp Here 27
SIC 8211 Elementary and secondary schools

D-U-N-S 20-028-3708   (BR)
EDMONTON SCHOOL DISTRICT NO. 7
THORNCLIFFE COMMUNITY SCHOOL
8215 175 St Nw, Edmonton, AB, T5T 0G9
(780) 487-2061
Emp Here 25
SIC 8211 Elementary and secondary schools

D-U-N-S 20-712-5993   (BR)
EDMONTON SCHOOL DISTRICT NO. 7
CALLINGWOOD ELEMENTARY SCHOOL
17335 76 Ave Nw, Edmonton, AB, T5T 2B1
(780) 487-0727
Emp Here 50
SIC 8211 Elementary and secondary schools

D-U-N-S 20-857-9511   (BR)
ESTEE LAUDER COSMETICS LTD
MAC COSMETICS
8882 170 St Nw Suite 2339, Edmonton, AB, T5T 4M2
(780) 930-2166
Emp Here 20
SIC 5999 Miscellaneous retail stores, nec

D-U-N-S 20-859-8289   (BR)
FGL SPORTS LTD
ATHLETES WORLD

8882 170 St Nw Suite 2680, Edmonton, AB, T5T 4J2
(780) 484-7135
Emp Here 25
SIC 5661 Shoe stores

D-U-N-S 20-242-3658 (BR)
FGL SPORTS LTD
ATMOSPHERE
8882 170 St Nw Unit 2551, Edmonton, AB, T5T 4M2
(780) 487-5607
Emp Here 44
SIC 5941 Sporting goods and bicycle shops

D-U-N-S 20-338-3393 (BR)
FOOT LOCKER CANADA CO
FOOT LOCKER CANADA CO.
8882 170 St Nw Unit W L-111, Edmonton, AB, T5T 4M2
(780) 444-1398
Emp Here 40
SIC 5661 Shoe stores

D-U-N-S 25-064-6387 (BR)
FOOT LOCKER CANADA CO.
CHAMP'S SPORTS
8882 170 St, Edmonton, AB, T5T 4M2
(780) 444-1534
Emp Here 20
SIC 5699 Miscellaneous apparel and accessory stores

D-U-N-S 25-174-2870 (BR)
FOOT LOCKER CANADA CO.
FOOT LOCKER
8882 170 St Nw Suite 2297, Edmonton, AB, T5T 4M2
(780) 484-3161
Emp Here 28
SIC 5661 Shoe stores

D-U-N-S 24-354-4520 (BR)
FOREVER XXI ULC
8882 170 St Nw Unit 1205, Edmonton, AB, T5T 4J2
(780) 930-2014
Emp Here 20
SIC 5651 Family clothing stores

D-U-N-S 24-949-1481 (BR)
GAP (CANADA) INC
GAP
(*Suby of* The Gap Inc)
8882 170 St Nw Suite 1622, Edmonton, AB, T5T 4M2
(780) 444-1616
Emp Here 40
SIC 5651 Family clothing stores

D-U-N-S 20-002-9499 (BR)
GAP (CANADA) INC
BANANA REPUBLIC
(*Suby of* The Gap Inc)
8882 170 St Nw Suite 2568, Edmonton, AB, T5T 4M2
(780) 486-1266
Emp Here 30
SIC 5651 Family clothing stores

D-U-N-S 20-860-5803 (BR)
GLENTEL INC
WIRELESS WAVES
8882 170 St Nw Unit 2148, Edmonton, AB, T5T 4J2
(780) 444-9283
Emp Here 25
SIC 4813 Telephone communication, except radio

D-U-N-S 24-673-8561 (BR)
GROUPE ALDO INC, LE
ALDO ACCESSORIES
8882 170 St Nw Suite 1674, Edmonton, AB, T5T 4M2
(780) 484-2839
Emp Here 20
SIC 5661 Shoe stores

D-U-N-S 25-514-3166 (BR)
HOME DEPOT OF CANADA INC
HOME DEPOT
(*Suby of* The Home Depot Inc)
17404 99 Ave Nw, Edmonton, AB, T5T 5L5
(780) 486-6124
Emp Here 220
SIC 5251 Hardware stores

D-U-N-S 24-398-4564 (BR)
HUDSON'S BAY COMPANY
BAY, THE
8882 170 St Nw Suite 1001, Edmonton, AB, T5T 3J7
(780) 444-1550
Emp Here 150
SIC 5311 Department stores

D-U-N-S 25-066-6203 (BR)
INDIGO BOOKS & MUSIC INC
CHAPTERS STORE #920
(*Suby of* Indigo Books & Music Inc)
8882 170 St Nw Suite 1384, Edmonton, AB, T5T 4M2
(780) 444-2555
Emp Here 20
SIC 5942 Book stores

D-U-N-S 25-987-0277 (BR)
INDIGO BOOKS & MUSIC INC
CHAPTERS
(*Suby of* Indigo Books & Music Inc)
9952 170 St Nw, Edmonton, AB, T5T 6G7
(780) 487-6500
Emp Here 50
SIC 5942 Book stores

D-U-N-S 20-317-7048 (SL)
KEG RESTAURANTS LTD
9960 170 St Nw, Edmonton, AB, T5T 6G7
(780) 414-1114
Emp Here 100   *Sales* 2,991,389
SIC 5812 Eating places

D-U-N-S 25-290-8710 (BR)
MARK'S WORK WEARHOUSE LTD
MARK'S WORK WEARHOUSE 29
8882 170 St Nw Unit 1109, Edmonton, AB, T5T 3J7
(780) 444-1831
Emp Here 25
SIC 5651 Family clothing stores

D-U-N-S 24-809-2504 (BR)
NEWCAP INC
NEWCAP RADIO ALBERTA
2394 West Edmonton Mall, Edmonton, AB, T5T 4M2
(780) 432-3165
Emp Here 110
SIC 4832 Radio broadcasting stations

D-U-N-S 24-366-0557 (BR)
NEWCAP INC
BIG EARL RADIO
8882 170 St Nw Suite 2394, Edmonton, AB, T5T 4M2

Emp Here 75
SIC 4832 Radio broadcasting stations

D-U-N-S 20-197-6623 (SL)
OLD SPAGHETTI FACTORY (EDMONTON) LTD
OLD SPAGHETTI FACTORY, THE
8882 170 St Nw Suite 1632, Edmonton, AB, T5T 4M2
(780) 444-2181
Emp Here 100   *Sales* 2,991,389
SIC 5812 Eating places

D-U-N-S 20-315-7784 (BR)
SCHANKS INTERNATIONAL INC
SCHANKS SPORTS BAR
9927 178 St Nw, Edmonton, AB, T5T 6L8
(780) 444-2125
Emp Here 25
SIC 7997 Membership sports and recreation clubs

D-U-N-S 25-294-5290 (BR)
SEARS CANADA INC
8770 170 St Nw, Edmonton, AB, T5T 3J7
(780) 444-1450
Emp Here 234
SIC 5311 Department stores

D-U-N-S 25-266-5690 (BR)
SERVUS CREDIT UNION LTD
17010 90 Ave Nw Suite 148, Edmonton, AB, T5T 1L6
(780) 496-2300
Emp Here 20
SIC 6062 State credit unions

D-U-N-S 25-533-9632 (BR)
SOBEYS WEST INC
SAFEWAY
6655 178 St Nw Suite 600, Edmonton, AB, T5T 4J5
(780) 481-7646
Emp Here 200
SIC 5411 Grocery stores

D-U-N-S 24-363-2069 (BR)
SOBEYS WEST INC
GRANGE SAFEWAY
2534 Guardian Rd Nw, Edmonton, AB, T5T 1K8
(780) 490-0418
Emp Here 50
SIC 5411 Grocery stores

D-U-N-S 20-580-7709 (BR)
STAPLES CANADA INC
STAPLES THE BUSINESS DEPOT
(*Suby of* Staples, Inc.)
9580 170 St Nw Suite 41, Edmonton, AB, T5T 5R5
(780) 487-4949
Emp Here 30
SIC 5943 Stationery stores

D-U-N-S 25-362-7756 (BR)
T & T SUPERMARKET INC
8882 170 St Nw Suite 2580, Edmonton, AB, T5T 4M2
(780) 483-6638
Emp Here 80
SIC 5411 Grocery stores

D-U-N-S 20-709-3399 (BR)
TOMMY HILFIGER CANADA INC
8882 170 St Nw Suite 2560, Edmonton, AB, T5T 4M2
(780) 443-3999
Emp Here 30
SIC 5651 Family clothing stores

D-U-N-S 25-293-9293 (BR)
TOYS 'R' US (CANADA) LTD
TOYS 'R' US
(*Suby of* Toys "r" Us, Inc.)
9908 170 St Nw, Edmonton, AB, T5T 5L5
(780) 944-9414
Emp Here 51
SIC 5945 Hobby, toy, and game shops

D-U-N-S 20-205-4909 (BR)
W.O.W. HOSPITALITY CONCEPTS INC
JUBILATIONS DINNER THEATRE
8882 170 St Nw Suite 2553, Edmonton, AB, T5T 4M2
(780) 489-4289
Emp Here 30
SIC 7929 Entertainers and entertainment groups

D-U-N-S 20-004-7475 (BR)
WENDY'S RESTAURANTS OF CANADA INC
WENDY'S
(*Suby of* The Wendy's Company)
9598 170 St Nw, Edmonton, AB, T5T 5R5
(780) 484-2160
Emp Here 80
SIC 5812 Eating places

D-U-N-S 20-184-2965 (BR)
WINNERS MERCHANTS INTERNATIONAL

L.P.
WINNERS
(*Suby of* The TJX Companies Inc)
8882 170 St Nw, Edmonton, AB, T5T 4M2
(780) 444-0744
Emp Here 40
SIC 5651 Family clothing stores

D-U-N-S 20-806-2807 (BR)
YM INC. (SALES)
STITCHES
8882 170 St Nw Unit E-101, Edmonton, AB, T5T 4M2
(780) 481-1458
Emp Here 27
SIC 5621 Women's clothing stores

D-U-N-S 25-453-8457 (BR)
YOUNG MEN'S CHRISTIAN ASSOCIATION OF EDMONTON
JAMIE PLATZ
(*Suby of* Young Men's Christian Association of Edmonton)
7121 178 St Nw, Edmonton, AB, T5T 5T9
(780) 930-2311
Emp Here 125
SIC 8699 Membership organizations, nec

Edmonton, AB T5V

D-U-N-S 25-453-8721 (BR)
177293 CANADA LTD
PETRO-CANADA
15015 123 Ave Nw Suite 200, Edmonton, AB, T5V 1J7
(780) 453-5500
Emp Here 20
SIC 1311 Crude petroleum and natural gas

D-U-N-S 25-362-0124 (BR)
ACKLANDS - GRAINGER INC
AGI
(*Suby of* W.W. Grainger, Inc.)
15986 118 Ave Nw, Edmonton, AB, T5V 1C4
(780) 453-3071
Emp Here 40
SIC 5085 Industrial supplies

D-U-N-S 25-194-1472 (HQ)
AECON LOCKERBIE INDUSTRIAL INC
14940 121a Ave Nw, Edmonton, AB, T5V 1A3
(780) 452-1250
Emp Here 40   *Emp Total* 12,000
Sales 275,631,233
SIC 1542 Nonresidential construction, nec
Pr Pr James Hole
Dir Gordon Panas
Dir Darcy Trufyn
Dir Reid Drury
Dir Steve Mulherin
Dir Tom Sabourin

D-U-N-S 25-236-1803 (SL)
ALASKAN TECHNOLOGIES CORP
11810 152 St Nw, Edmonton, AB, T5V 1E3
(780) 447-2660
Emp Here 50   *Sales* 4,377,642
SIC 1711 Plumbing, heating, air-conditioning

D-U-N-S 24-674-9055 (BR)
ANIXTER CANADA INC
12354 184 St Nw, Edmonton, AB, T5V 0A5
(780) 452-8171
Emp Here 50
SIC 5051 Metals service centers and offices

D-U-N-S 25-088-2669 (BR)
B. & R. ECKEL'S TRANSPORT LTD
15911 132 Ave Nw, Edmonton, AB, T5V 1H8
(780) 447-5847
Emp Here 50
SIC 1389 Oil and gas field services, nec

D-U-N-S 24-732-5681 (BR)
BROCK WHITE CANADA COMPANY, LLC

STEELS
12959 156 St Nw, Edmonton, AB, T5V 0A2
(780) 451-1580
Emp Here 23
SIC 5039 Construction materials, nec

D-U-N-S 25-012-1456   (BR)
BUCKWOLD WESTERN LTD
12843 153 St Nw, Edmonton, AB, T5V 0B6
(780) 447-1539
Emp Here 22
SIC 5023 Homefurnishings

D-U-N-S 20-305-4866   (BR)
C. KEAY INVESTMENTS LTD
OCEAN TRAILER
15205 131 Ave Nw, Edmonton, AB, T5V 0A4
(780) 447-7373
Emp Here 45
SIC 7539 Automotive repair shops, nec

D-U-N-S 24-423-1945   (BR)
CAN-CELL INDUSTRIES INC
16355 130 Ave Nw, Edmonton, AB, T5V 1K5
(780) 453-3610
Emp Here 20
SIC 2621 Paper mills

D-U-N-S 20-071-1088   (BR)
CANADA BREAD COMPANY, LIMITED
12151 160 St Nw, Edmonton, AB, T5V 1M4
(780) 451-4663
Emp Here 200
SIC 2051 Bread, cake, and related products

D-U-N-S 24-562-0815   (BR)
CARMACKS ENTERPRISES LTD
13203 156 St, Edmonton, AB, T5V 1V2
(780) 451-9118
Emp Here 50
SIC 1629 Heavy construction, nec

D-U-N-S 20-745-8324   (SL)
CHRISTENSEN & MCLEAN ROOFING CO
16173 132 Ave Nw, Edmonton, AB, T5V 1H8
(780) 447-1672
Emp Here 50   *Sales* 4,961,328
SIC 1761 Roofing, siding, and sheetMetal
work

D-U-N-S 25-620-4710   (BR)
**CHRISTIAN LABOUR ASSOCIATION OF
CANADA**
14920 118 Ave Nw, Edmonton, AB, T5V 1B8
(780) 454-6181
Emp Here 75
SIC 8611 Business associations

D-U-N-S 24-784-3027   (BR)
CLEARTECH INDUSTRIES INC
12720 Inland Way Nw, Edmonton, AB, T5V
1K2
(780) 237-7450
Emp Here 125
SIC 2819 Industrial inorganic chemicals, nec

D-U-N-S 25-272-0610   (BR)
CLOVERDALE PAINT INC
16411 118 Ave Nw, Edmonton, AB, T5V 1H2
(780) 453-5700
Emp Here 25
SIC 2851 Paints and allied products

D-U-N-S 20-177-4200   (BR)
**COMPAGNIE DES CHEMINS DE FER NA-
TIONAUX DU CANADA**
CN INTERMODAL TERMINAL, DIV OF
12311 184 St Nw, Edmonton, AB, T5V 1T3
(780) 472-3863
Emp Here 35
SIC 4111 Local and suburban transit

D-U-N-S 24-350-8335   (BR)
COSTCO WHOLESALE CANADA LTD
COSTCO
(*Suby of* Costco Wholesale Corporation)
12450 149 St Nw Suite 154, Edmonton, AB,
T5V 1G9

(780) 453-8470
Emp Here 330
SIC 5099 Durable goods, nec

D-U-N-S 20-640-0090   (BR)
DIRECT LIMITED PARTNERSHIP
DIRECT INTEGRATED TRANSPORTATION
12915 151 St Nw, Edmonton, AB, T5V 1A7
(780) 452-7773
Emp Here 40
SIC 4212 Local trucking, without storage

D-U-N-S 20-014-7473   (BR)
EDMONTON GEAR CENTRE LTD
PDC
15729 118 Ave Nw, Edmonton, AB, T5V 1B7
(780) 452-2344
Emp Here 35
SIC 5084 Industrial machinery and equipment

D-U-N-S 24-357-9708   (SL)
**EDMONTON TRAILER MANUFACTURING
LTD**
16908 128a Ave Nw, Edmonton, AB, T5V 1K7
(403) 744-5120
Emp Here 706   *Sales* 161,316,108
SIC 3531 Construction machinery
Pr Pr Denis St. Andre
  Dirk Woestenenk
Fin Ex Brent Horn

D-U-N-S 20-081-9118   (BR)
ELECTRIC POWER EQUIPMENT LIMITED
15304 118 Ave Nw, Edmonton, AB, T5V 1C2
(780) 455-4194
Emp Here 25
SIC 3625 Relays and industrial controls

D-U-N-S 20-693-2043   (BR)
EMCO CORPORATION
EMCO WATERWORKS
15740 118 Ave Nw, Edmonton, AB, T5V 1C4
(780) 447-4800
Emp Here 20
SIC 5074 Plumbing and heating equipment
and supplies (hydronics)

D-U-N-S 24-387-3895   (SL)
EVEREADY HOLDINGS GP LTD
15817 121a Ave Nw, Edmonton, AB, T5V 1B1
(780) 451-6075
Emp Here 30   *Sales* 5,006,160
SIC 1389 Oil and gas field services, nec
Pr Rod Marlin
Dir Jason Vandenberg

D-U-N-S 24-004-4842   (BR)
FARM CREDIT CANADA
12040 149 St Nw, Edmonton, AB, T5V 1P2
(780) 495-4488
Emp Here 35
SIC 6159 Miscellaneous business credit institutions

D-U-N-S 25-368-2181   (BR)
FEDERATED CO-OPERATIVES LIMITED
TGP
(*Suby of* Federated Co-Operatives Limited)
13232 170 St Nw, Edmonton, AB, T5V 1M7
(780) 447-5700
Emp Here 100
SIC 5141 Groceries, general line

D-U-N-S 24-805-6509   (BR)
FORT GARRY INDUSTRIES LTD
FGI
16230 118 Ave Nw, Edmonton, AB, T5V 1C6
(780) 447-4422
Emp Here 70
SIC 5013 Motor vehicle supplies and new
parts

D-U-N-S 20-180-5103   (BR)
FOUNTAIN TIRE LTD
13520 156 St Nw, Edmonton, AB, T5V 1L3
(780) 463-2404
Emp Here 32
SIC 5014 Tires and tubes

D-U-N-S 20-898-2926   (SL)
GLENDALE GOLF & COUNTRY CLUB LTD
12410 199 St Nw, Edmonton, AB, T5V 1T8
(780) 447-3529
Emp Here 90   *Sales* 3,648,035
SIC 7997 Membership sports and recreation
clubs

D-U-N-S 24-703-0513   (BR)
GUILLEVIN INTERNATIONAL CIE
GIR DEL HYDRAULICS DIV OF
15304 131 Ave Nw, Edmonton, AB, T5V 0A1
(780) 483-1060
Emp Here 40
SIC 5084 Industrial machinery and equipment

D-U-N-S 20-044-2150   (HQ)
HEXION CANADA INC
12621 156 St Nw, Edmonton, AB, T5V 1E1
(780) 447-1270
Emp Here 103   *Emp Total* 180
Sales 19,699,389
SIC 2821 Plastics materials and resins
Pr William H. Carter
Sec Ellen German Berndt
Dir Dan Gouthro
Dir George F. Knight

D-U-N-S 24-879-8241   (HQ)
**INDEPENDENT COUNSELLING ENTER-
PRISES INC**
(*Suby of* Independent Counselling Enter-
prises Inc)
15055 118 Ave Nw, Edmonton, AB, T5V 1H9
(780) 454-9500
Emp Here 300   *Emp Total* 400
Sales 21,104,400
SIC 8322 Individual and family services
Pr Pr Michael Rutherford

D-U-N-S 20-852-5233   (BR)
INTERCITY PACKERS LTD
(*Suby of* Minto Industries Ltd)
13506 159 St Nw, Edmonton, AB, T5V 0C6
(780) 477-7373
Emp Here 50
SIC 5147 Meats and meat products

D-U-N-S 20-917-9683   (BR)
INTERCITY PACKERS LTD
(*Suby of* Minto Industries Ltd)
13503 163 St Nw, Edmonton, AB, T5V 0B5
(780) 477-7373
Emp Here 60
SIC 5147 Meats and meat products

D-U-N-S 20-066-0509   (BR)
JELD-WEN OF CANADA, LTD.
JELD-WEN MILLWORK DISTRIBUTION
12704 156 St Nw, Edmonton, AB, T5V 1K2

Emp Here 41
SIC 5039 Construction materials, nec

D-U-N-S 20-861-0019   (BR)
K-BRO LINEN SYSTEMS INC
15253 121a Ave Nw, Edmonton, AB, T5V 1N1
(780) 451-3131
Emp Here 400
SIC 7219 Laundry and garment services, nec

D-U-N-S 20-437-9903   (BR)
KUEHNE + NAGEL LTD
KN CUSTOMS BROKERS
12810 170 St Nw, Edmonton, AB, T5V 0A6
(780) 447-1370
Emp Here 35
SIC 4731 Freight transportation arrangement

D-U-N-S 25-194-6109   (BR)
LEHIGH HANSON MATERIALS LIMITED
INLAND CONCRETE
15015 123 Ave Nw Suite 100, Edmonton, AB,
T5V 1J7
(780) 423-6300
Emp Here 40
SIC 5032 Brick, stone, and related material

D-U-N-S 24-375-8278   (HQ)
LEHIGH HANSON MATERIALS LIMITED
LEHIGH CEMENT
12640 Inland Way Nw, Edmonton, AB, T5V
1K2
(780) 420-2500
Emp Here 150   *Emp Total* 54,132
Sales 124,033,190
SIC 2891 Adhesives and sealants
Pr Christopher Ward
VP Fin David Blackley

D-U-N-S 20-913-7681   (BR)
LOBLAWS INC
16104 121a Ave Nw, Edmonton, AB, T5V 1B2
(780) 451-7391
Emp Here 25
SIC 5141 Groceries, general line

D-U-N-S 25-234-3769   (HQ)
**LOCKERBIE & HOLE CONTRACTING LIM-
ITED**
14940 121a Ave Nw, Edmonton, AB, T5V 1A3
(780) 452-1250
Emp Here 40   *Emp Total* 12,000
Sales 51,975,060
SIC 1711 Plumbing, heating, air-conditioning
Pr Jeff Pigott

D-U-N-S 24-583-0153   (SL)
MAGAL MANUFACTURING LTD
14940 121a Ave Nw, Edmonton, AB, T5V 1A3
(780) 452-1250
Emp Here 75   *Sales* 20,497,920
SIC 1541 Industrial buildings and warehouses
Genl Mgr Harold Barson
  James D Hole

D-U-N-S 20-242-2882   (BR)
MAXIM TRANSPORTATION SERVICES INC
MAXIM TRANSPORTATION
13240 170 St Nw, Edmonton, AB, T5V 1M7
(780) 448-3830
Emp Here 20
SIC 7513 Truck rental and leasing, no drivers

D-U-N-S 20-270-9403   (BR)
**MAXIM TRUCK COLLISION & RECYCLING
LTD**
13240 170 St Nw, Edmonton, AB, T5V 1M7
(780) 448-3830
Emp Here 40
SIC 5521 Used car dealers

D-U-N-S 24-068-5024   (HQ)
MCKILLICAN CANADIAN INC
16420 118 Ave Nw, Edmonton, AB, T5V 1C8
(780) 453-3841
Emp Here 24   *Emp Total* 200
Sales 18,750,900
SIC 5039 Construction materials, nec
Pr Pr Gary Mckillican
  Lynn Mckillican

D-U-N-S 25-013-8377   (BR)
MCLEOD MERCANTILE LTD
MCLEOD WINDOW
15311 128 Ave Nw, Edmonton, AB, T5V 1A5
(780) 481-2575
Emp Here 30
SIC 3089 Plastics products, nec

D-U-N-S 20-734-5302   (BR)
**NORTHERN ALBERTA INSTITUTE OF
TECHNOLOGY**
12204 149 St Nw, Edmonton, AB, T5V 1A2
(780) 378-7200
Emp Here 100
SIC 8222 Junior colleges

D-U-N-S 25-370-5115   (SL)
**O.E.M. REMANUFACTURING COMPANY
INC**
(*Suby of* Finning International Inc)
13315 156 St Nw, Edmonton, AB, T5V 1V2
(780) 468-6220
Emp Here 350   *Sales* 35,168,000
SIC 7538 General automotive repair shops

Dir Norm Labonne

D-U-N-S 20-118-8955   (SL)
POLYTUBES INC
12160 160 St Nw, Edmonton, AB, T5V 1H5
(780) 453-2211
Emp Here 20   *Sales* 18,167,214
SIC 3088 Plastics plumbing fixtures
Pr Pr Robert D Miller
Neil Macdonald
Barb Brochu
Mary Mccaffery

D-U-N-S 25-064-4077   (BR)
PURE CANADIAN GAMING CORP
CASINOYELLOWHEAD
12464 153rd St, Edmonton, AB, T5V 3C5
(780) 424-9467
Emp Here 300
SIC 7999 Amusement and recreation, nec

D-U-N-S 20-272-6196   (BR)
REDROCK CAMPS INC
(*Suby of* Redrock Camps Inc)
12808 170 St Nw Unit 16, Edmonton, AB, T5V 0A6
(780) 452-0888
Emp Here 40
SIC 2411 Logging

D-U-N-S 24-367-7411   (HQ)
REGIONAL TIRE DISTRIBUTORS INC
RT DISTRIBUTORS
16408 121a Ave Nw, Edmonton, AB, T5V 1J9
(780) 483-1391
Emp Here 347   *Emp Total* 347
Sales 176,015,750
SIC 5014 Tires and tubes
Ch Bd Chris Fletchner
Pr Pr Michael Kustra

D-U-N-S 24-124-8280   (BR)
REIMER EXPRESS LINES LTD
YRC REIMER
(*Suby of* Yrc Worldwide Inc.)
16060 128 Ave Nw, Edmonton, AB, T5V 1B6
(780) 447-2434
Emp Here 200
SIC 4213 Trucking, except local

D-U-N-S 24-097-8648   (BR)
SERVUS CREDIT UNION LTD
14909 121a Ave Nw, Edmonton, AB, T5V 1P3
(780) 455-9500
Emp Here 20
SIC 6062 State credit unions

D-U-N-S 20-317-5877   (BR)
SHANAHAN'S LIMITED PARTNERSHIP
17439 129 Ave Nw, Edmonton, AB, T5V 0C1
(780) 489-5444
Emp Here 40
SIC 5932 Used merchandise stores

D-U-N-S 20-013-8464   (BR)
SIKA CANADA INC
16910 129 Ave Nw Suite 1, Edmonton, AB, T5V 1L1
(780) 453-3060
Emp Here 200
SIC 2891 Adhesives and sealants

D-U-N-S 24-972-0038   (BR)
SOBEYS CAPITAL INCORPORATED
SOBEYS
12910 156 St Nw, Edmonton, AB, T5V 1E9
(780) 447-1440
Emp Here 900
SIC 5141 Groceries, general line

D-U-N-S 24-672-6061   (HQ)
STARLINE MOVING SYSTEMS LTD
STARLINE OVERSEAS
15305 128 Ave Nw, Edmonton, AB, T5V 1A5
(780) 447-4242
Emp Here 30   *Emp Total* 350
Sales 2,845,467
SIC 4214 Local trucking with storage

D-U-N-S 25-012-1464   (BR)
SUPERIOR PLUS LP
SPECIALTY PRODUCTS AND INSULATION
12416 184 St Nw, Edmonton, AB, T5V 1T4
(780) 452-4966
Emp Here 45
SIC 5033 Roofing, siding, and insulation

D-U-N-S 24-335-3732   (BR)
TST SOLUTIONS L.P.
16750 129 Ave Nw, Edmonton, AB, T5V 1L1
(780) 447-1055
Emp Here 40
SIC 4213 Trucking, except local

D-U-N-S 20-354-3848   (HQ)
TETRA TECH CANADA INC
(*Suby of* Tetra Tech, Inc.)
14940 123 Ave Nw, Edmonton, AB, T5V 1B4
(780) 451-2121
Emp Here 500   *Emp Total* 16,000
Sales 413,030,523
SIC 8711 Engineering services
William R Brownlie
Robert J Sumsion
Richard A Lemmon

D-U-N-S 24-949-4170   (BR)
TIGER COURIER INC
15825 121a Ave Nw, Edmonton, AB, T5V 1B1
(780) 452-3777
Emp Here 20
SIC 7389 Business services, nec

D-U-N-S 24-677-1575   (BR)
TRAILER WIZARDS LTD
(*Suby of* Lions Gate Trailers Ltd)
12516 184 St Nw, Edmonton, AB, T5V 1T4
(780) 451-9015
Emp Here 20
SIC 7519 Utility trailer rental

D-U-N-S 24-000-6452   (BR)
TRIMAC TRANSPORTATION SERVICES LIMITED PARTNERSHIP
15410 Yellowhead Trail Nw, Edmonton, AB, T5V 1A1
(780) 447-1190
Emp Here 60
SIC 6722 Management investment, open-end

D-U-N-S 20-084-8810   (BR)
UNIVAR CANADA LTD
16911 118 Ave Nw, Edmonton, AB, T5V 1H3
(780) 452-6655
Emp Here 70
SIC 5169 Chemicals and allied products, nec

D-U-N-S 25-702-9384   (SL)
VALUE DRUG MART ASSOCIATES LTD
16504 121a Ave Nw, Edmonton, AB, T5V 1J9
(780) 453-1701
Emp Here 50   *Sales* 7,077,188
SIC 5912 Drug stores and proprietary stores

D-U-N-S 20-303-3907   (BR)
VICWEST INC
(*Suby of* Vicwest Inc)
15108 118 Ave Nw, Edmonton, AB, T5V 1B8
(780) 454-4477
Emp Here 50
SIC 3444 Sheet Metalwork

D-U-N-S 25-719-5669   (BR)
WASTE MANAGEMENT OF CANADA CORPORATION
(*Suby of* Waste Management, Inc.)
12707 170 St Nw, Edmonton, AB, T5V 1L9
(780) 447-2141
Emp Here 25
SIC 4953 Refuse systems

D-U-N-S 20-081-5132   (BR)
WOLSELEY CANADA INC
CRONKHITE SUPPLY, DIV OF
(*Suby of* WOLSELEY PLC)
12224 152 St Nw, Edmonton, AB, T5V 1S1
(780) 454-0481
Emp Here 25

SIC 5074 Plumbing and heating equipment and supplies (hydronics)

D-U-N-S 24-736-8637   (SL)
XS CARGO LIMITED PARTNERSHIP
15435 131 Ave Nw, Edmonton, AB, T5V 0A4
(780) 413-4296
Emp Here 300   *Sales* 18,752,347
SIC 7389 Business services, nec
CFO Ross Kelly

D-U-N-S 20-775-7253   (SL)
YELLOWHEAD MOTOR INN LTD
YELLOWHEAD MOTOR INN
15004 Yellowhead Trail Nw, Edmonton, AB, T5V 1A1
(780) 447-2400
Emp Here 75   *Sales* 3,283,232
SIC 7011 Hotels and motels

Edmonton, AB T5W

D-U-N-S 20-580-0803   (BR)
BANK OF NOVA SCOTIA, THE
SCOTIABANK
3210 118 Ave Nw Suite 166, Edmonton, AB, T5W 4W1

Emp Here 20
SIC 6021 National commercial banks

D-U-N-S 25-303-7139   (BR)
CANADIAN IMPERIAL BANK OF COMMERCE
CIBC
3924 118 Ave Nw, Edmonton, AB, T5W 0Z9
(780) 408-1125
Emp Here 40
SIC 6021 National commercial banks

D-U-N-S 20-913-7376   (BR)
CLARKE TRANSPORT INC
CLARKE TRANSPORT
12555 62 St Nw, Edmonton, AB, T5W 4W9
(780) 471-6336
Emp Here 30
SIC 4213 Trucking, except local

D-U-N-S 20-154-8430   (BR)
EDMONTON CATHOLIC SEPARATE SCHOOL DISTRICT NO.7
ST. BERNADETTE CATHOLIC ELEMENTARY SCHOOL
(*Suby of* Edmonton Catholic Separate School District No.7)
11917 40 St Nw, Edmonton, AB, T5W 2L1
(780) 474-4167
Emp Here 20
SIC 8211 Elementary and secondary schools

D-U-N-S 20-029-4473   (BR)
EDMONTON CATHOLIC SEPARATE SCHOOL DISTRICT NO.7
ST. LEO EDMONTON CATHOLIC ELEMENTARY SCHOOL
(*Suby of* Edmonton Catholic Separate School District No.7)
5412 121 Ave Nw, Edmonton, AB, T5W 1N9
(780) 477-3372
Emp Here 20
SIC 8211 Elementary and secondary schools

D-U-N-S 20-712-8633   (BR)
EDMONTON CATHOLIC SEPARATE SCHOOL DISTRICT NO.7
ST. NICHOLAS CATHOLIC ELEMENTARY SCHOOL
(*Suby of* Edmonton Catholic Separate School District No.7)
3643 115 Ave Nw, Edmonton, AB, T5W 0V1
(780) 474-3713
Emp Here 30
SIC 8211 Elementary and secondary schools

D-U-N-S 20-028-3872   (BR)

EDMONTON CATHOLIC SEPARATE SCHOOL DISTRICT NO.7
ST. JEROME CATHOLIC ELEMENTARY SCHOOL
(*Suby of* Edmonton Catholic Separate School District No.7)
3310 107 Ave Nw, Edmonton, AB, T5W 0C7
(780) 479-5847
Emp Here 20
SIC 8211 Elementary and secondary schools

D-U-N-S 25-000-4991   (BR)
EDMONTON CATHOLIC SEPARATE SCHOOL DISTRICT NO.7
BEN CALF ROBE - ST. CLARE ELEMENTARY JUNIOR HIGH SCHOOL
(*Suby of* Edmonton Catholic Separate School District No.7)
11833 64 St Nw, Edmonton, AB, T5W 4J2
(780) 471-2360
Emp Here 30
SIC 8211 Elementary and secondary schools

D-U-N-S 20-020-2617   (BR)
EDMONTON SCHOOL DISTRICT NO. 7
MONTROSE ELEMENTARY SCHOOL
11931 62 St Nw, Edmonton, AB, T5W 4C7
(780) 471-2358
Emp Here 20
SIC 8211 Elementary and secondary schools

D-U-N-S 20-029-2550   (BR)
EDMONTON SCHOOL DISTRICT NO. 7
RUNDLE SCHOOL
11005 34 St Nw, Edmonton, AB, T5W 1Y7
(780) 471-6100
Emp Here 34
SIC 8211 Elementary and secondary schools

D-U-N-S 25-020-1811   (BR)
EDMONTON SCHOOL DISTRICT NO. 7
ABBOTT ELEMENTARY SCHOOL
12045 34 St Nw, Edmonton, AB, T5W 1Z5
(780) 477-7310
Emp Here 35
SIC 8211 Elementary and secondary schools

D-U-N-S 20-064-2432   (BR)
EDMONTON SCHOOL DISTRICT NO. 7
ST. NICHOLAS JUNIOR HIGH SCHOOL
3643 115 Ave Nw, Edmonton, AB, T5W 0V1
(780) 474-3713
Emp Here 20
SIC 8211 Elementary and secondary schools

D-U-N-S 20-592-1070   (BR)
EDMONTON SCHOOL DISTRICT NO. 7
BEACON HEIGHTS SCHOOL
4610 121 Ave Nw, Edmonton, AB, T5W 1M8
(780) 479-4038
Emp Here 37
SIC 8211 Elementary and secondary schools

D-U-N-S 20-712-4772   (BR)
EDMONTON SCHOOL DISTRICT NO. 7
HIGHLANDS SCHOOL
11509 62 St Nw, Edmonton, AB, T5W 4C2
(780) 479-4206
Emp Here 20
SIC 8211 Elementary and secondary schools

D-U-N-S 24-810-3269   (SL)
FOUR PLUS FOOD MARKET LTD
BEVERLY GARDEN MARKET IGA
3425 118 Ave Nw, Edmonton, AB, T5W 0Z3
(780) 474-0931
Emp Here 75   *Sales* 9,849,695
SIC 5411 Grocery stores

D-U-N-S 20-811-1443   (SL)
HIGHLANDS GOLF CLUB
6603 Ada Blvd Nw, Edmonton, AB, T5W 4N5
(780) 474-4211
Emp Here 100   *Sales* 4,012,839
SIC 7997 Membership sports and recreation clubs

D-U-N-S 25-311-2585   (BR)

MCDONALD'S RESTAURANTS OF CANADA LIMITED
MCDONALD'S 8180
(*Suby of* McDonald's Corporation)
3004 118 Ave Nw, Edmonton, AB, T5W 4W3
(780) 477-5885
Emp Here 35
SIC 5812 Eating places

D-U-N-S 20-870-8920   (BR)
SEARS CANADA INC
4302 118 Ave Nw, Edmonton, AB, T5W 1A6
(780) 479-6890
Emp Here 20
SIC 5399 Miscellaneous general merchandise

D-U-N-S 25-271-0256   (BR)
SOBEYS WEST INC
3004 118 Ave Nw, Edmonton, AB, T5W 4W3
(780) 477-6923
Emp Here 82
SIC 5411 Grocery stores

Edmonton, AB T5X

D-U-N-S 20-772-6618   (BR)
340107 ALBERTA LTD
JOX SPORTS BAR & GRILL
(*Suby of* 340107 Alberta Ltd)
15327 97 St Nw, Edmonton, AB, T5X 5V3
(780) 476-6474
Emp Here 20
SIC 5812 Eating places

D-U-N-S 20-589-4947   (BR)
BANQUE TORONTO-DOMINION, LA
TD CANADA TRUST
(*Suby of* Toronto-Dominion Bank, The)
12645 142 Ave Nw, Edmonton, AB, T5X 5Y8
(780) 472-2400
Emp Here 20
SIC 6021 National commercial banks

D-U-N-S 20-340-7747   (BR)
BREWSTERS BREW PUB & BRASSERIE (ALBERTA) INC
BREWSTERS BREWING CO & RESTAURANT
15327 Castle Downs Rd Nw, Edmonton, AB, T5X 6C3
(780) 425-4677
Emp Here 30
SIC 5812 Eating places

D-U-N-S 20-021-7706   (BR)
EDMONTON CATHOLIC SEPARATE SCHOOL DISTRICT NO.7
ST CHARLES CATHOLIC ELEMENTARY
(*Suby of* Edmonton Catholic Separate School District No.7)
10423 172 Ave Nw, Edmonton, AB, T5X 4X4
(780) 456-5222
Emp Here 20
SIC 8211 Elementary and secondary schools

D-U-N-S 20-028-8814   (BR)
EDMONTON CATHOLIC SEPARATE SCHOOL DISTRICT NO.7
ST. LUCY CATHOLIC ELEMENTARY SCHOOL
(*Suby of* Edmonton Catholic Separate School District No.7)
11750 162 Ave Nw, Edmonton, AB, T5X 4L9
(780) 456-0053
Emp Here 26
SIC 8211 Elementary and secondary schools

D-U-N-S 20-028-3971   (BR)
EDMONTON CATHOLIC SEPARATE SCHOOL DISTRICT NO.7
ST. TIMOTHY CATHOLIC ELEMENTARY SCHOOL
(*Suby of* Edmonton Catholic Separate School District No.7)
14330 117 St Nw, Edmonton, AB, T5X 1S6

(780) 456-7375
Emp Here 30
SIC 8211 Elementary and secondary schools

D-U-N-S 20-030-0585   (BR)
EDMONTON CATHOLIC SEPARATE SCHOOL DISTRICT NO.7
BISHOP SAVARYN SCHOOL
(*Suby of* Edmonton Catholic Separate School District No.7)
16215 109 St Nw, Edmonton, AB, T5X 2R2
(780) 456-7837
Emp Here 31
SIC 8211 Elementary and secondary schools

D-U-N-S 20-028-4227   (BR)
EDMONTON SCHOOL DISTRICT NO. 7
ECOLE DUNLUCE SCHOOL
11735 162 Ave Nw, Edmonton, AB, T5X 4M6
(780) 456-9080
Emp Here 40
SIC 8211 Elementary and secondary schools

D-U-N-S 20-592-1047   (BR)
EDMONTON SCHOOL DISTRICT NO. 7
BATURYN ELEMENTARY SCHOOL
10603 172 Ave Nw, Edmonton, AB, T5X 4X4
(780) 456-6727
Emp Here 25
SIC 8211 Elementary and secondary schools

D-U-N-S 25-012-7644   (BR)
EDMONTON SCHOOL DISTRICT NO. 7
CAERNARVON SCHOOL
14820 118 St Nw, Edmonton, AB, T5X 1T4
(780) 456-7020
Emp Here 30
SIC 8211 Elementary and secondary schools

D-U-N-S 20-029-2592   (BR)
EDMONTON SCHOOL DISTRICT NO. 7
LORELEI ELEMENTARY SCHOOL
16230 103 St Nw, Edmonton, AB, T5X 3A9
(780) 456-4488
Emp Here 37
SIC 8211 Elementary and secondary schools

D-U-N-S 24-979-0577   (BR)
EDMONTON SCHOOL DISTRICT NO. 7
BUTTERWORTH, MARY SCHOOL
16315 109 St Nw, Edmonton, AB, T5X 2R2
(780) 476-1480
Emp Here 40
SIC 8211 Elementary and secondary schools

D-U-N-S 24-880-2712   (BR)
GOVERNING COUNCIL OF THE SALVATION ARMY IN CANADA, THE
GRACE MANOR
12510 140 Ave Nw, Edmonton, AB, T5X 6C4
(780) 454-5484
Emp Here 23
SIC 8361 Residential care

D-U-N-S 20-806-2344   (BR)
SOBEYS CAPITAL INCORPORATED
SOBEYS STORE 3132
15367 Castle Downs Rd Nw, Edmonton, AB, T5X 6C3
(780) 472-0100
Emp Here 160
SIC 5411 Grocery stores

D-U-N-S 20-040-0302   (BR)
YOUNG MEN'S CHRISTIAN ASSOCIATION OF EDMONTON
EDMONTON YMCA
(*Suby of* Young Men's Christian Association of Edmonton)
11510 153 Ave Nw, Edmonton, AB, T5X 6A3
(780) 476-9622
Emp Here 100
SIC 8322 Individual and family services

Edmonton, AB T5Y

D-U-N-S 24-345-0264   (BR)
ALBERTA HEALTH SERVICES
ALBERTA HOSPITAL EDMONTON
17480 Fort Rd Nw Suite 175, Edmonton, AB, T5Y 6A8
(780) 342-5555
Emp Here 400
SIC 8063 Psychiatric hospitals

D-U-N-S 24-520-4420   (BR)
DOLLARAMA S.E.C.
4278 137 Ave Nw Unit 1a, Edmonton, AB, T5Y 2W7
(780) 456-1810
Emp Here 30
SIC 5331 Variety stores

D-U-N-S 20-260-7453   (BR)
EDMONTON CATHOLIC SEPARATE SCHOOL DISTRICT NO.7
CARDINAL COLLINS HIGH SCHOOL ACADEMIC CENTRE
(*Suby of* Edmonton Catholic Separate School District No.7)
3802 139 Ave Nw, Edmonton, AB, T5Y 3G4
(780) 944-2002
Emp Here 30
SIC 8211 Elementary and secondary schools

D-U-N-S 20-027-3691   (BR)
EDMONTON CATHOLIC SEPARATE SCHOOL DISTRICT NO.7
ST BONAVENTURE CATHOLIC ELEMENTARY SCHOOL
(*Suby of* Edmonton Catholic Separate School District No.7)
3004 139 Ave Nw, Edmonton, AB, T5Y 1R9
(780) 476-7257
Emp Here 30
SIC 8211 Elementary and secondary schools

D-U-N-S 20-028-4334   (BR)
EDMONTON SCHOOL DISTRICT NO. 7
FRASER SCHOOL
14904 21 St Nw, Edmonton, AB, T5Y 2L6
(780) 472-0131
Emp Here 24
SIC 8211 Elementary and secondary schools

D-U-N-S 20-028-4250   (BR)
EDMONTON SCHOOL DISTRICT NO. 7
KIRKNESS ELEMENTARY SCHOOL
610 Kirkness Rd Nw, Edmonton, AB, T5Y 2K4
(780) 473-5924
Emp Here 27
SIC 8211 Elementary and secondary schools

D-U-N-S 20-068-2982   (BR)
EDMONTON SCHOOL DISTRICT NO. 7
BANNERMAN SCHOOL
14112 23 St Nw, Edmonton, AB, T5Y 2B9
(780) 478-7706
Emp Here 24
SIC 8211 Elementary and secondary schools

D-U-N-S 25-013-7692   (BR)
EDMONTON SCHOOL DISTRICT NO. 7
JOHN D BRACCO SCHOOL
3150 139 Ave Nw, Edmonton, AB, T5Y 2P7
(780) 475-1760
Emp Here 50
SIC 8211 Elementary and secondary schools

D-U-N-S 20-916-8173   (BR)
EMPIRE THEATRES LIMITED
4211 139 Ave Nw, Edmonton, AB, T5Y 2W8
(780) 473-8383
Emp Here 30
SIC 7832 Motion picture theaters, except drive-in

D-U-N-S 24-078-5985   (BR)
H & W PRODUCE CORPORATION
14083 Victoria Trail Nw, Edmonton, AB, T5Y 2B6
(780) 478-8780
Emp Here 60
SIC 5431 Fruit and vegetable markets

D-U-N-S 24-013-0802   (SL)
INNOVATIVE INTERIOR SYSTEMS
2050 227 Ave Ne, Edmonton, AB, T5Y 6H5
(780) 414-0637
Emp Here 50   *Sales* 2,626,585
SIC 7389 Business services, nec

D-U-N-S 24-391-8190   (BR)
MEMORIAL GARDENS CANADA LIMITED
EVERGREEN MEMORIAL GARDENS
16102 Fort Rd Nw, Edmonton, AB, T5Y 6A2
(780) 472-9007
Emp Here 20
SIC 6531 Real estate agents and managers

D-U-N-S 25-370-3623   (BR)
NORTH WEST COMPANY LP, THE
GIANT TIGER
14097 Victoria Trail Nw, Edmonton, AB, T5Y 2B6
(780) 472-7780
Emp Here 82
SIC 5411 Grocery stores

D-U-N-S 24-715-5018   (BR)
SOBEYS CAPITAL INCORPORATED
SOBEYS HOLLICK KENYON
5119 167 Ave Nw, Edmonton, AB, T5Y 0L2
(780) 478-4740
Emp Here 150
SIC 5411 Grocery stores

D-U-N-S 25-219-0053   (BR)
WAL-MART CANADA CORP
WAL-MART NORTHEAST
13703 40 St Nw Suite 3028, Edmonton, AB, T5Y 3B5
(780) 476-4460
Emp Here 300
SIC 5311 Department stores

Edmonton, AB T5Z

D-U-N-S 20-713-0282   (BR)
EDMONTON CATHOLIC SEPARATE SCHOOL DISTRICT NO.7
ST JOHN BOSCO CATHOLIC ELEMENTARY SCHOOL
(*Suby of* Edmonton Catholic Separate School District No.7)
7411 161a Ave Nw Suite 7411, Edmonton, AB, T5Z 3V4
(780) 471-3140
Emp Here 50
SIC 8211 Elementary and secondary schools

D-U-N-S 25-012-7271   (BR)
EDMONTON CATHOLIC SEPARATE SCHOOL DISTRICT NO.7
BISHOP GRESCHUK SCHOOL
(*Suby of* Edmonton Catholic Separate School District No.7)
17330 91 St Nw, Edmonton, AB, T5Z 3A1
(780) 472-2937
Emp Here 30
SIC 8211 Elementary and secondary schools

D-U-N-S 25-013-7841   (BR)
EDMONTON SCHOOL DISTRICT NO. 7
LAGO LINDO SCHOOL
17303 95 St Nw, Edmonton, AB, T5Z 2Z1
(780) 456-6980
Emp Here 35
SIC 8211 Elementary and secondary schools

D-U-N-S 25-289-0678   (BR)
GREAT PACIFIC INDUSTRIES INC
SAVE-ON-FOODS
9510 160 Ave Nw, Edmonton, AB, T5Z 3S5
(780) 472-7400
Emp Here 200
SIC 5411 Grocery stores

D-U-N-S 20-082-4386   (BR)
MCDONALD'S RESTAURANTS OF

CANADA LIMITED
MCDONALD'S
(*Suby of* McDonald's Corporation)
8770 170th St Unit 1592, Edmonton, AB, T5Z 2Y7

Emp Here 50
SIC 5812 Eating places

D-U-N-S 25-271-1080   (BR)
SOBEYS WEST INC
SAFEWAY
8720 156 Ave Nw, Edmonton, AB, T5Z 3B4
(780) 486-0584
Emp Here 120
SIC 5411 Grocery stores

Edmonton, AB T6A

D-U-N-S 24-983-8132   (BR)
ALBERTA CO-OP TAXI LINE LTD
(*Suby of* Alberta Co-Op Taxi Line Ltd)
5036 106 Ave Nw, Edmonton, AB, T6A 1E9
(780) 414-2698
Emp Here 50
SIC 4121 Taxicabs

D-U-N-S 20-028-3922   (BR)
EDMONTON   CATHOLIC   SEPARATE SCHOOL DISTRICT NO.7
ST GABRIEL CATHOLIC ELEMENTARY SCHOOL
(*Suby of* Edmonton Catholic Separate School District No.7)
5540 106 Ave Nw Suite 202, Edmonton, AB, T6A 1G3
(780) 466-0220
Emp Here 49
SIC 8211 Elementary and secondary schools

D-U-N-S 20-030-7093   (BR)
EDMONTON SCHOOL DISTRICT NO. 7
FULTON PLACE SCHOOL
10310 56 St Nw, Edmonton, AB, T6A 2J2
(780) 461-0051
Emp Here 30
SIC 8211 Elementary and secondary schools

D-U-N-S 20-592-0056   (BR)
EDMONTON SCHOOL DISTRICT NO. 7
TERRACE HEIGHTS ELEMENTARY
6859 100 Ave Nw, Edmonton, AB, T6A 0G3
(780) 450-2367
Emp Here 20
SIC 8211 Elementary and secondary schools

D-U-N-S 20-028-3468   (BR)
EDMONTON SCHOOL DISTRICT NO. 7
CAPILANO ELEMENTARY SCHOOL
10720 54 St Nw, Edmonton, AB, T6A 2H9
(780) 461-5890
Emp Here 25
SIC 8211 Elementary and secondary schools

D-U-N-S 20-028-3518   (BR)
EDMONTON SCHOOL DISTRICT NO. 7
GOLD BAR ELEMENTARY SCHOOL
10524 46 St Nw, Edmonton, AB, T6A 1Y3
(780) 466-4116
Emp Here 21
SIC 8211 Elementary and secondary schools

D-U-N-S 25-013-8393   (BR)
EDMONTON SCHOOL DISTRICT NO. 7
MCNALLY HIGH SCHOOL
8440 105 Ave Nw, Edmonton, AB, T6A 1B6
(780) 469-0442
Emp Here 100
SIC 8211 Elementary and secondary schools

D-U-N-S 25-013-7163   (BR)
EDMONTON SCHOOL DISTRICT NO. 7
HARDISTY ELEMENTARY JUNIOR HIGH SCHOOL
10534 62 St Nw, Edmonton, AB, T6A 2M3

(780) 469-0426
Emp Here 30
SIC 8211 Elementary and secondary schools

D-U-N-S 20-251-1465   (BR)
EPCOR WATER SERVICES INC
10977 50 St Nw, Edmonton, AB, T6A 2E9
(780) 969-8496
Emp Here 160
SIC 1629 Heavy construction, nec

D-U-N-S 24-732-0906   (SL)
M & V ENTERPRISES LTD
BOSTON PIZZA CAPILANO
5515 101 Ave Nw, Edmonton, AB, T6A 3Z7
(780) 465-0771
Emp Here 110   *Sales* 3,283,232
SIC 5812 Eating places

D-U-N-S 25-315-1609   (BR)
MEDICENTRES CANADA INC
CAPILANO MEDICENTRE
9945 50 St Nw, Edmonton, AB, T6A 0L4
(780) 468-2911
Emp Here 20
SIC 8011 Offices and clinics of medical doctors

D-U-N-S 24-128-6058   (BR)
SOBEYS WEST INC
SAFEWAY
5004 98 Ave Nw Unit 1062, Edmonton, AB, T6A 0A1
(780) 466-9001
Emp Here 20
SIC 5411 Grocery stores

D-U-N-S 20-860-1059   (BR)
SOURCE (BELL) ELECTRONICS INC, THE
SOURCE, THE
1042 Capilano Mall, Edmonton, AB, T6A 0A1

Emp Here 25
SIC 5999 Miscellaneous retail stores, nec

D-U-N-S 24-349-6952   (BR)
UNITED RENTALS OF CANADA, INC
4915 101 Ave Nw, Edmonton, AB, T6A 0L6
(780) 465-1411
Emp Here 20
SIC 7359 Equipment rental and leasing, nec

D-U-N-S 24-316-9096   (BR)
WAL-MART CANADA CORP
WALMART
5004 98 Ave Nw Suite 1, Edmonton, AB, T6A 0A1
(780) 466-2002
Emp Here 100
SIC 5311 Department stores

D-U-N-S 20-184-2916   (BR)
WINNERS MERCHANTS INTERNATIONAL L.P.
WINNERS
(*Suby of* The TJX Companies Inc)
5055 101 Ave Nw Unit 135, Edmonton, AB, T6A 0G7
(780) 490-0606
Emp Here 40
SIC 5651 Family clothing stores

Edmonton, AB T6B

D-U-N-S 20-640-6147   (BR)
1942675 ALBERTA LTD
GREAT WESTERN CONTAINERS
(*Suby of* 1942675 Alberta Ltd)
6943 68 Ave, Edmonton, AB, T6B 3E3
(780) 472-6806
Emp Here 20
SIC 5093 Scrap and waste materials

D-U-N-S 20-085-0287   (HQ)
316291 ALBERTA LTD
WESTERN ARCHRIB

(*Suby of* 377168 Alberta Ltd)
4315 92 Ave Nw, Edmonton, AB, T6B 3M7
(780) 465-9771
Emp Here 70   *Emp Total* 2
Sales 13,716,612
SIC 2439 Structural wood members, nec
Pr Pr Kent Fargey
    Joan Fargey

D-U-N-S 24-840-4709   (SL)
464161 ALBERTA LTD
HOLIDAY INN CONVENTION CENTRE
4520 76 Ave Nw, Edmonton, AB, T6B 0A5
(780) 468-5400
Emp Here 75   *Sales* 3,283,232
SIC 7011 Hotels and motels

D-U-N-S 20-245-8084   (HQ)
AGS FLEXITALLIC, INC
4340 78 Ave Nw, Edmonton, AB, T6B 3J5
(780) 466-5050
Emp Here 170   *Emp Total* 1
Sales 41,733,520
SIC 3053 Gaskets; packing and sealing devices
Pr Pr Jerry Lastovica Ii
Pr Pr Ken Berry

D-U-N-S 25-265-9511   (BR)
AMEC FOSTER WHEELER AMERICAS LIMITED
AMEC   ENVIRONMENT & INFRASTRACTURE, DIV OF
5681 70 St Nw, Edmonton, AB, T6B 3P6
(780) 436-2152
Emp Here 150
SIC 8711 Engineering services

D-U-N-S 20-104-5130   (BR)
ABSOLUTE ENERGY SOLUTIONS INC
ABSOLULTE COMPLETION TECHNOLOGIES
5710 36 St Nw, Edmonton, AB, T6B 3T2
(780) 440-9058
Emp Here 100
SIC 3545 Machine tool accessories

D-U-N-S 24-308-6878   (BR)
ABSOLUTE ENERGY SOLUTIONS INC
6312 50 St Nw, Edmonton, AB, T6B 2N7
(780) 469-7466
Emp Here 30
SIC 3533 Oil and gas field machinery

D-U-N-S 20-015-9080   (SL)
ALTEX INDUSTRIES INC
6831 42 St Nw, Edmonton, AB, T6B 2X1
(780) 468-6862
Emp Here 140   *Sales* 2,672,640
SIC 3443 Fabricated plate work (boiler shop)

D-U-N-S 25-271-0488   (BR)
BCB CORPORATE SERVICES LTD
MOTION INDUSTRY
5736 59 St Nw, Edmonton, AB, T6B 3L4
(780) 465-0821
Emp Here 23
SIC 5085 Industrial supplies

D-U-N-S 25-012-1472   (BR)
BURNCO ROCK PRODUCTS LTD
3867 92 Ave Nw, Edmonton, AB, T6B 3B4
(780) 414-8896
Emp Here 50
SIC 3273 Ready-mixed concrete

D-U-N-S 20-513-9095   (BR)
BAKER HUGHES CANADA COMPANY
PROCESS & PIPELINE SEVICES, DIV OF
(*Suby of* Baker Hughes, A GE Company)
9010 34 St Nw, Edmonton, AB, T6B 2V1
(780) 465-9495
Emp Here 75
SIC 1389 Oil and gas field services, nec

D-U-N-S 24-395-6539   (BR)
BAKER HUGHES CANADA COMPANY
HUGHES CHRISTENSEN CANADA, DIV OF

(*Suby of* Baker Hughes, A GE Company)
5119 67 Ave Nw, Edmonton, AB, T6B 2R8
(780) 434-8800
Emp Here 20
SIC 1389 Oil and gas field services, nec

D-U-N-S 20-580-0977   (BR)
BANK OF NOVA SCOTIA, THE
SCOTIABANK
6304 90 Ave Nw, Edmonton, AB, T6B 0P2
(780) 448-7860
Emp Here 20
SIC 6021 National commercial banks

D-U-N-S 25-328-1992   (BR)
BANTREL CO.
(*Suby of* Bechtel Group, Inc.)
4999 98 Ave Nw Unit 401, Edmonton, AB, T6B 2X3
(780) 462-5600
Emp Here 150
SIC 8711 Engineering services

D-U-N-S 24-393-9050   (SL)
BUFFALO INSPECTION SERVICES (2005) INC
3867 Roper Rd Nw, Edmonton, AB, T6B 3S5
(780) 486-7344
Emp Here 100   *Sales* 7,441,991
SIC 8734 Testing laboratories
Pr Bari Walsh

D-U-N-S 24-399-1171   (BR)
CCTF CORPORATION
5407 53 Ave Nw, Edmonton, AB, T6B 3G2
(780) 463-8700
Emp Here 40
SIC 5032 Brick, stone, and related material

D-U-N-S 24-273-9100   (BR)
CP DISTRIBUTORS LTD
CP DISTRIBUTORS LTD.
4715 Eleniak Rd Nw, Edmonton, AB, T6B 2N1
(780) 468-6754
Emp Here 35
SIC 5039 Construction materials, nec

D-U-N-S 24-026-3199   (SL)
CANADIAN   CONDOMINIUM   MANAGEMENT CORP
9440 49 St Nw Suite 230, Edmonton, AB, T6B 2M9
(780) 485-0505
Emp Here 30   *Sales* 22,086,000
SIC 1531 Operative builders
Pr Rod Osborne

D-U-N-S 24-331-6791   (BR)
CANPAR TRANSPORT L.P.
(*Suby of* Canpar Transport L.P.)
4635 92 Ave Nw, Edmonton, AB, T6B 2J4
(780) 465-4054
Emp Here 40
SIC 7389 Business services, nec

D-U-N-S 20-799-2038   (SL)
CAREFREE COACH & RV LTD
4510 51 Ave Nw, Edmonton, AB, T6B 2W2

Emp Here 45   *Sales* 13,188,500
SIC 5561 Recreational vehicle dealers
Pr Elmer Lastiwka
VP VP John Turgeon
Treas Darcy Turgeon
VP VP Phil Turgeon
Dir Laura Lastiwka

D-U-N-S 24-344-8680   (BR)
CENTENNIAL FOODSERVICE
5116 67 Ave Nw, Edmonton, AB, T6B 3N9
(780) 465-9991
Emp Here 60
SIC 5147 Meats and meat products

D-U-N-S 20-125-7248   (BR)
CONSEIL SCOLAIRE CENTRE-NORD
ECOLE SAINTE JEANNE D' ARC
8505 68a St Nw, Edmonton, AB, T6B 0J9

---

(780) 466-1800
Emp Here 34
SIC 8211 Elementary and secondary schools

D-U-N-S 25-149-8408   (BR)
CORE LABORATORIES CANADA LTD
PROMORE
5708 54 St Nw, Edmonton, AB, T6B 3G1
(780) 988-5105
Emp Here 30
SIC 1389 Oil and gas field services, nec

D-U-N-S 20-808-7577   (BR)
CORE LABORATORIES CANADA LTD
4777 93 Ave Nw, Edmonton, AB, T6B 2T6
(780) 468-2850
Emp Here 50
SIC 8731 Commercial physical research

D-U-N-S 20-617-3627   (HQ)
COWAN GRAPHICS INC
COWAN IMAGING GROUP
(*Suby of* Cowan Graphics Inc)
4864 93 Avenue Nw, Edmonton, AB, T6B 2P8
(780) 577-5700
Emp Here 85   *Emp Total* 110
Sales 5,472,053
SIC 2759 Commercial printing, nec
Pr Pr Blaine Macmillan
  Kevin Macmillan
  Muriel Jensen

D-U-N-S 25-624-9533   (BR)
CRANE, JOHN CANADA INC
POTTER SMITH'S GROUP
7123 Roper Rd Nw, Edmonton, AB, T6B 3K3
(780) 466-1338
Emp Here 40
SIC 3953 Marking devices

D-U-N-S 20-547-2173   (BR)
DH CORPORATION
5712 59 St Nw, Edmonton, AB, T6B 3L4
(780) 468-2646
Emp Here 50
SIC 6211 Security brokers and dealers

D-U-N-S 20-081-5645   (HQ)
DAAM GALVANIZING CO. LTD
DAAM GALVANIZING - EDMONTON
(*Suby of* DWP Co. Ltd)
9390 48 St Nw, Edmonton, AB, T6B 2R3
(780) 468-6868
Emp Here 70   *Emp Total* 1
Sales 11,524,275
SIC 3479 Metal coating and allied services
Pr Pr Darcy Pretula
  Dale Butterworth
  Pat Lauriks

D-U-N-S 24-364-7695   (BR)
DRECO ENERGY SERVICES ULC
NATIONAL OIL WELL
(*Suby of* National Oilwell Varco, Inc.)
7657 50 St Nw Suite 201, Edmonton, AB, T6B
2W9
(780) 944-3850
Emp Here 300
SIC 1389 Oil and gas field services, nec

D-U-N-S 20-553-5482   (BR)
DRYCO BUILDING SUPPLIES INC
7350 68 Ave Nw, Edmonton, AB, T6B 0A1
(780) 434-9481
Emp Here 30
SIC 5211 Lumber and other building materials

D-U-N-S 20-651-8388   (BR)
DYNAMEX CANADA LIMITED
7003 56 Ave Nw, Edmonton, AB, T6B 3L2
(780) 463-2422
Emp Here 30
SIC 7389 Business services, nec

D-U-N-S 24-642-7702   (BR)
E.C.S. ELECTRICAL CABLE SUPPLY LTD
7136 56 Ave Nw, Edmonton, AB, T6B 1E4
(780) 665-1158
Emp Here 20

SIC 5063 Electrical apparatus and equipment

D-U-N-S 20-154-8117   (BR)
**EDMONTON CATHOLIC SEPARATE
SCHOOL DISTRICT NO.7**
AUSTIN O'BRIEN CATHOLIC HIGH SCHOOL
(*Suby of* Edmonton Catholic Separate School
District No.7)
6110 95 Ave Nw, Edmonton, AB, T6B 1A5
(780) 466-3161
Emp Here 80
SIC 8211 Elementary and secondary schools

D-U-N-S 25-454-5148   (BR)
**EDMONTON CATHOLIC SEPARATE
SCHOOL DISTRICT NO.7**
*ST BRENDAN CATHOLIC ELEMENTARY
SCHOOL*
(*Suby of* Edmonton Catholic Separate School
District No.7)
5825 93a Ave Nw, Edmonton, AB, T6B 0X1
(780) 466-1281
Emp Here 20
SIC 8211 Elementary and secondary schools

D-U-N-S 20-028-3591   (BR)
EDMONTON SCHOOL DISTRICT NO. 7
WAVERLEY ELEMENTARY SCHOOL
6825 89 Ave Nw, Edmonton, AB, T6B 0N3
(780) 469-6682
Emp Here 48
SIC 8211 Elementary and secondary schools

D-U-N-S 20-712-5175   (BR)
EDMONTON SCHOOL DISTRICT NO. 7
OTTEWELL JUNIOR HIGH SCHOOL
9435 73 St Nw, Edmonton, AB, T6B 2A9
(780) 466-7331
Emp Here 50
SIC 8211 Elementary and secondary schools

D-U-N-S 20-712-5456   (BR)
EDMONTON SCHOOL DISTRICT NO. 7
KENWORTH JUNIOR HIGH SCHOOL
7005 89 Ave Nw, Edmonton, AB, T6B 0N3
(780) 466-2104
Emp Here 35
SIC 8211 Elementary and secondary schools

D-U-N-S 24-841-5317   (BR)
EMCO CORPORATION
WESTLUND INDUSTRIAL SUPPLY, DIV OF
4103 84 Ave Nw, Edmonton, AB, T6B 2Z3
(780) 463-7473
Emp Here 30
SIC 5084 Industrial machinery and equipment

D-U-N-S 24-674-9188   (BR)
ENERFLEX LTD.
PAMCO
4703 92 Ave Nw, Edmonton, AB, T6B 2J4
(780) 465-5371
Emp Here 31
SIC 7699 Repair services, nec

D-U-N-S 24-854-8513   (HQ)
FMC TECHNOLOGIES COMPANY
6703 68 Ave Nw, Edmonton, AB, T6B 3E3
(780) 468-9231
Emp Here 50   *Emp Total* 1
Sales 15,540,629
SIC 5084 Industrial machinery and equipment
Pr Pr John T. Gremp
  Jay A. Nutt
Ex VP Douglas J. Pferdehirt
  Maryann T. Seaman

D-U-N-S 20-809-9903   (BR)
G4S CASH SOLUTIONS (CANADA) LTD
SECURICOR CASH SERVICE
9373 47 St Nw, Edmonton, AB, T6B 2R7
(780) 465-9526
Emp Here 70
SIC 7381 Detective and armored car services

D-U-N-S 24-663-5135   (BR)
GFL ENVIRONMENTAL INC
GFL LIQUID WASTE DIVISION WEST -

HEAD OFFICE
4208 84 Ave Nw, Edmonton, AB, T6B 3N5
(780) 485-5000
Emp Here 25
SIC 4953 Refuse systems

D-U-N-S 24-522-4514   (BR)
GENERAL ELECTRIC CANADA COMPANY
GETSCO TECHNICAL SERVICES
(*Suby of* General Electric Company)
4421 Roper Rd Nw, Edmonton, AB, T6B 3S5
(780) 438-3280
Emp Here 40
SIC 3625 Relays and industrial controls

D-U-N-S 24-716-3116   (BR)
GENERAL ELECTRIC CANADA COMPANY
GE CANADA
(*Suby of* General Electric Company)
9449 49 St Nw, Edmonton, AB, T6B 2L8
(780) 440-7575
Emp Here 45
SIC 3625 Relays and industrial controls

D-U-N-S 20-579-7801   (BR)
**GOVERNMENT OF THE PROVINCE OF AL-
BERTA**
ALBERTA TRANSPORTATION
4999 98 Ave Nw, Edmonton, AB, T6B 2X3
(780) 427-8901
Emp Here 100
SIC 8742 Management consulting services

D-U-N-S 20-580-0415   (BR)
**GOVERNMENT OF THE PROVINCE OF AL-
BERTA**
*ALBERT INFRASTRUCTURE AND TRANS-
PORTATION*
4999 98 Ave Nw, Edmonton, AB, T6B 2X3
(780) 427-8901
Emp Here 75
SIC 8742 Management consulting services

D-U-N-S 24-325-0177   (BR)
**GOVERNMENT OF THE PROVINCE OF AL-
BERTA**
ALBERTA GEOLOGICAL SURVEY
4999 98 Ave Nw Suite 402, Edmonton, AB,
T6B 2X3
(780) 422-1927
Emp Here 70
SIC 8713 Surveying services

D-U-N-S 20-081-2782   (HQ)
HAGEMEYER CANADA INC
VALLEN
4810 92 Ave Nw, Edmonton, AB, T6B 2X4
(780) 468-3366
Emp Here 150   *Emp Total* 14
Sales 138,167,035
SIC 5085 Industrial supplies
Pr Dave Gabriel
Dir Paul Trudel
Dir Francois Poncet
Dir Marie-Christine Coisne
Dir Olivier Verley
Dir Franck Bruel
Dir Philippe De Moustier
Dir Francois Anquetil

D-U-N-S 25-475-1647   (HQ)
HARSCO CANADA CORPORATION
*PATENT CONSTRUCTION SYSTEMS
CANADA*
(*Suby of* Harsco Corporation)
7030 51 Ave Nw, Edmonton, AB, T6B 2P4
(780) 468-3292
Emp Here 20   *Emp Total* 9,400
Sales 6,237,007
SIC 1799 Special trade contractors, nec
Genl Mgr Martin Hayward

D-U-N-S 25-187-2698   (BR)
HELICAL PIER SYSTEMS LTD
4635 Eleniak Rd Nw, Edmonton, AB, T6B 2N1
(780) 440-3630
Emp Here 21
SIC 3312 Blast furnaces and steel mills

D-U-N-S 24-962-5310   (BR)
HI-WAY 9 EXPRESS LTD
6031 66a Ave Nw, Edmonton, AB, T6B 3R2
(780) 420-1062
Emp Here 47
SIC 4212 Local trucking, without storage

D-U-N-S 24-423-8809   (HQ)
**HORIZON NORTH CAMP & CATERING
PARTNERSHIP**
*HORIZON NORTH CAMPS & CATERING,
DIV OF*
5637 67 Ave Nw, Edmonton, AB, T6B 2R8
(780) 395-7300
Emp Here 25   *Emp Total* 2,004
Sales 10,741,512
SIC 5812 Eating places
Pr Robert German

D-U-N-S 20-052-8391   (SL)
HOWCO GROUP CANADA LTD
7504 52 St Nw, Edmonton, AB, T6B 2G3
(780) 439-6746
Emp Here 20   *Sales* 9,528,761
SIC 5051 Metals service centers and offices
Dir Jason Brezovski

D-U-N-S 20-213-2010   (BR)
IMPERIAL OIL LIMITED
(*Suby of* Exxon Mobil Corporation)
9210 34 St Nw, Edmonton, AB, T6B 2Y5
(780) 468-6587
Emp Here 20
SIC 2911 Petroleum refining

D-U-N-S 24-325-6968   (BR)
KONECRANES CANADA INC
3707 74 Ave Nw Suite 100, Edmonton, AB,
T6B 2T7
(780) 468-5321
Emp Here 20
SIC 3536 Hoists, cranes, and monorails

D-U-N-S 20-085-7514   (HQ)
LAIRD ELECTRIC INC
6707 59 St Nw, Edmonton, AB, T6B 3P8
(780) 450-9636
Emp Here 36   *Emp Total* 586
Sales 51,975,060
SIC 1731 Electrical work
Pr David Lemay
VP Opers Warren Stein
  Daryl Sands
Fin Ex Randy Morgan

D-U-N-S 20-270-1488   (BR)
LANDTRAN LOGISTICS INC
4715 90a Ave Nw, Edmonton, AB, T6B 2Y3
(780) 486-8607
Emp Here 50
SIC 4225 General warehousing and storage

D-U-N-S 24-839-1559   (HQ)
LANDTRAN SYSTEMS INC
9011 50 St Nw, Edmonton, AB, T6B 2Y2
(780) 468-4300
Emp Here 20   *Emp Total* 603
Sales 71,428,538
SIC 4212 Local trucking, without storage
Pr Pr John Assman
  James Maxwell

D-U-N-S 20-554-3452   (BR)
LEON'S FURNITURE LIMITED
4939 52 Ave Nw, Edmonton, AB, T6B 3L5
(780) 468-5511
Emp Here 30
SIC 5719 Miscellaneous homefurnishings

D-U-N-S 20-082-9752   (BR)
LEVITT-SAFETY LIMITED
NL TECHNOLOGIES
9241 48 St Nw, Edmonton, AB, T6B 2R9
(780) 461-8088
Emp Here 25
SIC 5084 Industrial machinery and equipment

D-U-N-S 20-328-9194   (HQ)

LIFTING SOLUTIONS INC
3710 78 Ave Nw, Edmonton, AB, T6B 3E5
(780) 784-7725
Emp Here 50   *Emp Total* 50
Sales 20,137,153
SIC 5051 Metals service centers and offices
Pr Pr David Labonte
  Greg Kauffman
  Douglas Freel
  Bill Slavin

D-U-N-S 24-352-5925   (BR)
LONKAR WELL TESTING LTD
(*Suby of* 1246607 Alberta Ltd)
4205 78 Ave Nw, Edmonton, AB, T6B 2N3
(780) 490-4243
Emp Here 40
SIC 1381 Drilling oil and gas wells

D-U-N-S 25-013-8070   (SL)
M & D DRAFTING LTD
3604 76 Ave Nw, Edmonton, AB, T6B 2N8
(780) 465-1520
Emp Here 75   *Sales* 3,793,956
SIC 7389 Business services, nec

D-U-N-S 25-593-6882   (BR)
MMD SALES LTD
MARTIN MOTOR SPORTS SOUTH
4630 51 Ave Nw, Edmonton, AB, T6B 2W2
(780) 438-2484
Emp Here 20
SIC 5261 Retail nurseries and garden stores

D-U-N-S 25-538-2228   (BR)
MAPLE-REINDERS INC
4050 69 Ave Nw, Edmonton, AB, T6B 2V2
(780) 465-5980
Emp Here 45
SIC 1542 Nonresidential construction, nec

D-U-N-S 24-731-1632   (BR)
MAXXAM ANALYTICS INTERNATIONAL CORPORATION
MAXXAM ANALYTICS
6744 50 St Nw, Edmonton, AB, T6B 3M9
(780) 378-8500
Emp Here 100
SIC 8734 Testing laboratories

D-U-N-S 24-028-1563   (BR)
MAXXAM ANALYTICS INTERNATIONAL CORPORATION
9331 48 St Nw, Edmonton, AB, T6B 2R4
(780) 468-3500
Emp Here 55
SIC 8731 Commercial physical research

D-U-N-S 25-532-3099   (HQ)
MEGA TECHNICAL HOLDINGS LTD
MEGA-TECH
(*Suby of* Mega Technical Holdings Ltd)
7116 67 St Nw, Edmonton, AB, T6B 3A6
(780) 438-9330
Emp Here 25   *Emp Total* 41
Sales 11,248,645
SIC 5999 Miscellaneous retail stores, nec
Pr Pr Robert Lindsay

D-U-N-S 24-808-2034   (HQ)
MET INC
UTT
(*Suby of* Met Inc)
5715 76 Ave Nw, Edmonton, AB, T6B 0A7
(780) 485-8500
Emp Here 50   *Emp Total* 300
Sales 56,972,160
SIC 8748 Business consulting, nec
Pr Pr Adrian Met

D-U-N-S 24-761-5276   (SL)
MILLENNIUM OILFLOW SYSTEMS & TECHNOLOGY INC
MOST OIL CANADA
(*Suby of* Next Equities Inc)
4640 Eleniak Rd, Edmonton, AB, T6B 2S1
(780) 468-1058
Emp Here 40   *Sales* 5,712,983

SIC 3533 Oil and gas field machinery
  Sami Mohammed
  Ch Bd Fred Atiq

D-U-N-S 25-146-5340   (HQ)
MONARCH TRANSPORT (1975) LTD
(*Suby of* Kluskus Holdings Ltd)
3464 78 Ave Nw, Edmonton, AB, T6B 2X9
(780) 440-6528
Emp Here 25   *Emp Total* 603
Sales 3,638,254
SIC 4212 Local trucking, without storage

D-U-N-S 24-351-9944   (BR)
MULTIPLE SCLEROSIS SOCIETY OF CANADA
MS SOCIETY
9405 50 St Nw Suite 150, Edmonton, AB, T6B 2T4
(780) 463-1190
Emp Here 32
SIC 8399 Social services, nec

D-U-N-S 20-915-1435   (BR)
NATIONAL-OILWELL CANADA LTD
NATIONAL OILWELL VARCO
(*Suby of* National Oilwell Varco, Inc.)
7127 56 Ave Nw, Edmonton, AB, T6B 3L2
(780) 465-0999
Emp Here 97
SIC 3533 Oil and gas field machinery

D-U-N-S 25-329-6743   (SL)
NORDIC MECHANICAL SERVICES LTD
(*Suby of* 619249 Alberta Ltd)
4143 78 Ave Nw, Edmonton, AB, T6B 2N3
(780) 469-7799
Emp Here 50   *Sales* 5,072,500
SIC 7623 Refrigeration service and repair
Pr Pr Jean-Louis Cloutier

D-U-N-S 20-083-5593   (HQ)
NORTHERN INDUSTRIAL CARRIERS LTD
NIC
(*Suby of* 321485 Alberta Ltd)
7823 34 St Nw, Edmonton, AB, T6B 2V5
(780) 465-0341
Emp Here 30   *Emp Total* 3
Sales 40,708,613
SIC 4213 Trucking, except local
Pr Pr Simon Sochatsky, Jr

D-U-N-S 24-336-3533   (BR)
PACKERS PLUS ENERGY SERVICES INC
4117 84 Ave Nw, Edmonton, AB, T6B 2Z3
(780) 440-3999
Emp Here 70
SIC 1382 Oil and gas exploration services

D-U-N-S 25-072-3707   (BR)
PAT'S DRIVE LINE SPECIALTY & MACHINE EDMONTON LTD
PAT'S DRIVE LINE
6811 50 St Nw, Edmonton, AB, T6B 3B7
(780) 466-7287
Emp Here 30
SIC 3714 Motor vehicle parts and accessories

D-U-N-S 24-283-7961   (BR)
PATTERSON DENTAIRE CANADA INC
6608 50 St Nw, Edmonton, AB, T6B 2N7
(780) 465-9041
Emp Here 35
SIC 5047 Medical and hospital equipment

D-U-N-S 24-904-6590   (BR)
PEMBRIDGE INSURANCE COMPANY
4999 98 Ave Nw Suite 108, Edmonton, AB, T6B 2X3
(780) 490-3000
Emp Here 63
SIC 6331 Fire, marine, and casualty insurance

D-U-N-S 25-688-1996   (BR)
PENTAIR VALVES & CONTROLS CANADA INC
TYCO FLOW CONTROL
(*Suby of* Johnson Controls, Inc.)
5538 48 St Nw, Edmonton, AB, T6B 2Z1

(780) 461-2228
Emp Here 60
SIC 5085 Industrial supplies

D-U-N-S 24-378-3870   (BR)
PERI FORMWORK SYSTEMS INC
PERI SCAFFOLD SERVICES, DIV OF
4839 74 Ave Nw, Edmonton, AB, T6B 2H5
(780) 432-7374
Emp Here 50
SIC 7353 Heavy construction equipment rental

D-U-N-S 25-115-4423   (BR)
PILLAR RESOURCE SERVICES INC
PILLAR OILFIELD PROJECTS
4155 84 Ave Nw, Edmonton, AB, T6B 2Z3
(780) 440-2212
Emp Here 100
SIC 1629 Heavy construction, nec

D-U-N-S 24-950-5975   (BR)
PRAXAIR CANADA INC
PRAXAIR DISTRIBUTION, DIV OF
(*Suby of* Praxair, Inc.)
6704 50 St Nw, Edmonton, AB, T6B 3M9
(780) 438-9141
Emp Here 34
SIC 5085 Industrial supplies

D-U-N-S 25-832-1348   (BR)
PRAXAIR CANADA INC
(*Suby of* Praxair, Inc.)
9501 34 St Nw, Edmonton, AB, T6B 2X6
(780) 449-0778
Emp Here 46
SIC 2813 Industrial gases

D-U-N-S 24-732-7646   (BR)
PRODUITS DE SECURITE NORTH LTEE
PRODUITS DE SECURITE NORTH LTEE
6303 Roper Rd Nw, Edmonton, AB, T6B 3G6
(780) 437-2641
Emp Here 22
SIC 3842 Surgical appliances and supplies

D-U-N-S 20-775-5232   (BR)
PROLINE PIPE EQUIPMENT INC
7141 67 St Nw, Edmonton, AB, T6B 3L7
(780) 465-6161
Emp Here 40   *Sales* 2,115,860
SIC 7389 Business services, nec

D-U-N-S 20-897-9237   (SL)
QUALITY FABRICATING & SUPPLY LIMITED
(*Suby of* Leder Investments Ltd)
3751 76 Ave Nw, Edmonton, AB, T6B 2S8
(780) 468-6762
Emp Here 30   *Sales* 7,754,640
SIC 3533 Oil and gas field machinery
Pr Pr John Leder
Sec Sally Leder

D-U-N-S 24-929-4612   (SL)
QUATTRO CAPITAL INC.
6907 36 St Nw, Edmonton, AB, T6B 2Z6
(780) 465-0341
Emp Here 260   *Sales* 61,694,720
SIC 6712 Bank holding companies
Sec Robert Day
Pr Venence Cote
  Kuldip Delhon
  Bruce Hammond

D-U-N-S 20-116-2133   (BR)
R.B.W. WASTE MANAGEMENT LTD
3907 69 Ave Nw, Edmonton, AB, T6B 3G4

Emp Here 35
SIC 4953 Refuse systems

D-U-N-S 24-701-8773   (HQ)
RTD QUALITY SERVICES INC
APPLUS RTD
5504 36 St Nw, Edmonton, AB, T6B 3P3
(780) 440-6600
Emp Here 50   *Emp Total* 20
Sales 14,379,767

SIC 7389 Business services, nec
Sec Denis Fourny
  Marcel Blinde
  Rob Van Doorn

D-U-N-S 24-702-5802   (HQ)
ROYAL CAMP SERVICES LTD
7111 67 St Nw, Edmonton, AB, T6B 3L7
(780) 463-8000
Emp Here 20   *Emp Total* 1
Sales 14,293,142
SIC 5812 Eating places
Pr Pr Daryl Rackel
Dir Larry Pickett
  David Dawyd
Dir Kevin Love
  Rod Streeper
Dir Darrell Streeper
Dir Lance Fisher

D-U-N-S 24-768-4041   (BR)
RUSSEL METALS INC
5730 72a Ave Nw, Edmonton, AB, T6B 3L1

Emp Here 35
SIC 5051 Metals service centers and offices

D-U-N-S 20-273-8167   (BR)
RUSSEL METALS INC
COMCO PIPE & SUPPLY COMPANY, DIV OF
4203 53 Ave Nw, Edmonton, AB, T6B 3P4
(780) 220-9994
Emp Here 30
SIC 5051 Metals service centers and offices

D-U-N-S 20-724-1659   (BR)
SCM INSURANCE SERVICES INC
CLAIMSPRO
4999 98 Ave Nw Suite 310, Edmonton, AB, T6B 2X3
(780) 466-6544
Emp Here 20
SIC 6411 Insurance agents, brokers, and service

D-U-N-S 24-023-4893   (BR)
SHEPHERD'S CARE FOUNDATION
OTTEWELL
6675 92 Ave Nw Suite 6, Edmonton, AB, T6B 0S3
(780) 490-7614
Emp Here 23
SIC 8051 Skilled nursing care facilities

D-U-N-S 20-898-7040   (HQ)
SHIPPERS SUPPLY INC
5219 47 St Nw, Edmonton, AB, T6B 3N4
(780) 444-7777
Emp Here 120   *Emp Total* 120
Sales 32,832,315
SIC 5113 Industrial and personal service paper
Pr Pr Ronald Brown

D-U-N-S 25-364-6244   (BR)
SHOPPERS HOME HEALTH CARE (CANADA) INC
SHOPPERS HOME HEALTH CARE
91 Ave Nw Suite 4619, Edmonton, AB, T6B 2M7
(780) 465-3310
Emp Here 33
SIC 5912 Drug stores and proprietary stores

D-U-N-S 25-453-9117   (BR)
SIEMENS CANADA LIMITED
6652 50 St Nw, Edmonton, AB, T6B 2N7
(780) 450-6762
Emp Here 200
SIC 8742 Management consulting services

D-U-N-S 20-205-4677   (BR)
SINCLAIR DENTAL CO. LTD
3844 53 Ave Nw, Edmonton, AB, T6B 3N7
(780) 440-1311
Emp Here 20
SIC 5047 Medical and hospital equipment

D-U-N-S 25-678-5007   (SL)

SKYWAY CANADA LTD
3408 76 Ave Nw, Edmonton, AB, T6B 2N8
(780) 413-8007
Emp Here 50   *Sales* 4,377,642
SIC 1799 Special trade contractors, nec

D-U-N-S 25-678-9280   (SL)
SOLOMON COATINGS LTD
6382 50 St Nw, Edmonton, AB, T6B 2N7
(780) 413-4545
Emp Here 67   *Sales* 4,888,367
SIC 7532 Top and body repair and paint shops

D-U-N-S 20-526-9504   (HQ)
TISI CANADA INC
TMS A DIV OF
3904 53 Ave Nw, Edmonton, AB, T6B 3N7
(780) 437-0860
Emp Here 26   *Emp Total* 7,400
Sales 2,772,507
SIC 8742 Management consulting services

D-U-N-S 24-331-2683   (BR)
TAIGA BUILDING PRODUCTS LTD
7605 67 St Nw, Edmonton, AB, T6B 1R4
(780) 466-4224
Emp Here 25
SIC 5031 Lumber, plywood, and millwork

D-U-N-S 24-055-6444   (BR)
TERRA CENTRE
TERRA CHILD & FAMILY SUPPORT CEN-TRE
9359 67a St Nw, Edmonton, AB, T6B 1R7
(780) 468-3218
Emp Here 30
SIC 8351 Child day care services

D-U-N-S 24-398-0653   (BR)
UAP INC
TRACTION
(*Suby of* Genuine Parts Company)
3404 78 Ave Nw Suite 561, Edmonton, AB,
T6B 2X9
(780) 465-8010
Emp Here 25
SIC 5013 Motor vehicle supplies and new parts

D-U-N-S 24-525-6776   (BR)
VARCO CANADA ULC
(*Suby of* National Oilwell Varco, Inc.)
7127 56 Ave Nw, Edmonton, AB, T6B 3L2
(780) 665-0200
Emp Here 100
SIC 7353 Heavy construction equipment rental

D-U-N-S 20-084-8992   (SL)
VET'S SHEET METAL LTD
6111 56 Ave Nw, Edmonton, AB, T6B 3E2
(780) 434-7476
Emp Here 45   *Sales* 5,088,577
SIC 1711 Plumbing, heating, air-conditioning
Pr Pr Sean Rayner

D-U-N-S 20-051-2445   (BR)
WASTE CONNECTIONS OF CANADA INC
BFI CANADA
3410 74 Ave, Edmonton, AB, T6B 2P7
(780) 464-9400
Emp Here 40
SIC 4953 Refuse systems

D-U-N-S 20-068-5642   (HQ)
WILKENING, HARV TRANSPORT LTD
WILKENING TRANSPORT
4205 76 Ave Nw, Edmonton, AB, T6B 2H7
(780) 466-9155
Emp Here 110   *Emp Total* 3
Sales 19,407,546
SIC 4213 Trucking, except local
Pr Pr Lily-Ann Siemens

D-U-N-S 20-505-5964   (SL)
WINDSHIELD SURGEONS LTD
ARNOLD WINDSHIELD DISTRIBUTORS
5203 82 Ave Nw, Edmonton, AB, T6B 2J6

(780) 466-9411
Emp Here 50   *Sales* 5,072,500
SIC 7536 Automotive glass replacement shops
Pr Pr Russell Lang
    Cynthia Lang

D-U-N-S 25-261-7246   (BR)
WORLEYPARSONS CANADA SERVICES LTD
COSYN TECHNOLOGY
9405 50 St Nw Suite 101, Edmonton, AB, T6B 2T4

Emp Here 700
SIC 8711 Engineering services

Edmonton, AB T6C

D-U-N-S 20-295-4371   (BR)
CONSEIL SCOLAIRE CENTRE-NORD
PADAGOGIQUS SCHOOL SERVICES
8627 91 St Nw Suite 3, Edmonton, AB, T6C 3N1
(780) 487-3200
Emp Here 20
SIC 8211 Elementary and secondary schools

D-U-N-S 24-971-3520   (BR)
CONSEIL SCOLAIRE CENTRE-NORD
ECOLE MAURICE-LAVALLEE
8828 95 St Nw, Edmonton, AB, T6C 4H9
(780) 465-6457
Emp Here 30
SIC 8211 Elementary and secondary schools

D-U-N-S 20-203-8456   (SL)
DAWNMARK HOLDINGS INC
CHANGES
9562 82 Ave Nw Suite 201, Edmonton, AB, T6C 0Z8
(780) 437-9866
Emp Here 100   *Sales* 4,677,755
SIC 8322 Individual and family services

D-U-N-S 20-028-3930   (BR)
EDMONTON CATHOLIC SEPARATE SCHOOL DISTRICT NO.7
ST JAMES CATHOLIC ELEMENTARY SCHOOL
(*Suby of* Edmonton Catholic Separate School District No.7)
7814 83 St Nw Suite 106, Edmonton, AB, T6C 2Y8
(780) 466-1247
Emp Here 23
SIC 8211 Elementary and secondary schools

D-U-N-S 20-310-4844   (BR)
EDMONTON SCHOOL DISTRICT NO. 7
AVONMORE ELEMENTARY SCHOOL
7835 76 Ave Nw, Edmonton, AB, T6C 2N1
(780) 466-2976
Emp Here 30
SIC 8211 Elementary and secondary schools

D-U-N-S 20-712-4657   (BR)
EDMONTON SCHOOL DISTRICT NO. 7
DONNAN SCHOOL
7803 87 St Nw, Edmonton, AB, T6C 3G6
(780) 466-8573
Emp Here 25
SIC 8211 Elementary and secondary schools

D-U-N-S 25-012-7396   (BR)
EDMONTON SCHOOL DISTRICT NO. 7
VIMY RIDGE ACADEMY
8205 90 Ave Nw, Edmonton, AB, T6C 1N8
(780) 465-5461
Emp Here 45
SIC 8211 Elementary and secondary schools

D-U-N-S 20-029-2584   (BR)
EDMONTON SCHOOL DISTRICT NO. 7
HOLYROOD SCHOOL
7920 94 Ave Nw, Edmonton, AB, T6C 1W4

(780) 466-2292
Emp Here 36
SIC 8211 Elementary and secondary schools

D-U-N-S 20-141-2892   (BR)
EDMONTON SCHOOL DISTRICT NO. 7
EDMONTON PUBLIC SCHOOL METRO CONTINUING EDUCATION
8205 90 Ave Nw, Edmonton, AB, T6C 1N8
(780) 428-1111
Emp Here 100
SIC 8211 Elementary and secondary schools

D-U-N-S 25-012-9640   (BR)
EXTENDICARE (CANADA) INC
EXTENDICARE HOLYROOD
8008 95 Ave Nw, Edmonton, AB, T6C 2T1
(780) 469-1307
Emp Here 100
SIC 8051 Skilled nursing care facilities

D-U-N-S 20-641-7136   (BR)
MCDONALD'S RESTAURANTS OF CANADA LIMITED
MCDONALD'S
(*Suby of* McDonald's Corporation)
8110 Argyll Rd Nw, Edmonton, AB, T6C 4B1
(780) 414-8525
Emp Here 30
SIC 5812 Eating places

D-U-N-S 20-775-8160   (HQ)
PURE CANADIAN GAMING CORP
CASINO ABS
7055 Argyll Rd Nw, Edmonton, AB, T6C 4A5
(780) 465-5377
Emp Here 100   *Emp Total* 1,100
Sales 59,754,813
SIC 7999 Amusement and recreation, nec
Pr Pr George Goldhoff
Dir Fin Lucy Papp
    Mark Mactadish
    Michael Lay
    Evan Hershberg

D-U-N-S 20-304-6359   (BR)
SEARS CANADA INC
SMALL PARCEL DELIVERY #1423
82 Ave 83rd St., Edmonton, AB, T6C 4E3
(780) 468-6611
Emp Here 20
SIC 5961 Catalog and mail-order houses

D-U-N-S 20-515-9184   (BR)
SOBEYS WEST INC
BONNIE DOON SAFEWAY
8330 82 Ave Nw, Edmonton, AB, T6C 0Y6
(780) 469-9464
Emp Here 160
SIC 5411 Grocery stores

D-U-N-S 24-228-4144   (SL)
ST THOMAS CENTRE DE SANTE
ST THOMAS HEALTH CENTER
8411 91 St Nw Suite 234, Edmonton, AB, T6C 1Z9
(780) 450-2987
Emp Here 110   *Sales* 4,012,839
SIC 8361 Residential care

D-U-N-S 24-627-8212   (BR)
VALUE VILLAGE STORES, INC
(*Suby of* Savers, Inc.)
8930 82 Ave Nw, Edmonton, AB, T6C 0Z3
(780) 468-1259
Emp Here 32
SIC 5399 Miscellaneous general merchandise

Edmonton, AB T6E

D-U-N-S 20-812-2825   (SL)
1133940 ALBERTA LTD
METTERA HOTEL ON WHYTE
(*Suby of* Westcorp Properties Inc)
10454 82 Ave Nw, Edmonton, AB, T6E 4Z7

(780) 465-8150
Emp Here 50   *Sales* 2,188,821
SIC 7011 Hotels and motels

D-U-N-S 20-518-3531   (SL)
252356 ALBERTA LTD
MOLLY MAID
9833 44 Ave Nw Suite 3, Edmonton, AB, T6E 5E3
(780) 452-5730
Emp Here 52   *Sales* 1,532,175
SIC 7349 Building maintenance services, nec

D-U-N-S 24-786-6270   (SL)
361680 ALBERTA LTD
CHIANTI CAFE & RESTAURANT
10501 82 Ave Nw, Edmonton, AB, T6E 2A3
(780) 439-9829
Emp Here 57   *Sales* 1,751,057
SIC 5812 Eating places

D-U-N-S 25-454-3374   (HQ)
470858 ALBERTA LTD
LUBE CITY
(*Suby of* 470858 Alberta Ltd)
5674 75 St Nw, Edmonton, AB, T6E 5X6
(780) 485-9905
Emp Here 65   *Emp Total* 75
Sales 4,523,563
SIC 7549 Automotive services, nec

D-U-N-S 20-772-6212   (SL)
483696 ALBERTA LTD
FIFE N'DEKEL
7921 Coronet Rd Nw, Edmonton, AB, T6E 4N7
(780) 465-4651
Emp Here 90   *Sales* 2,699,546
SIC 5812 Eating places

D-U-N-S 25-360-8723   (BR)
511670 ALBERTA LTD
CORAM CONSTRUCTION
4220 98 St Nw Suite 201, Edmonton, AB, T6E 6A1
(780) 466-1262
Emp Here 400
SIC 1542 Nonresidential construction, nec

D-U-N-S 20-063-7515   (BR)
668824 ALBERTA LTD
VISIONS ELECTRONICS
10133 34 Ave Nw, Edmonton, AB, T6E 6J8
(780) 438-6242
Emp Here 25
SIC 5731 Radio, television, and electronic stores

D-U-N-S 20-993-8401   (BR)
ABB INC
9418 39 Ave Nw, Edmonton, AB, T6E 5T9
(780) 447-4677
Emp Here 20
SIC 5063 Electrical apparatus and equipment

D-U-N-S 20-808-6108   (BR)
ARAMARK CANADA LTD.
ARAMARK REFRESHMENT SERVICES
9828 47 Ave Nw Suite 1, Edmonton, AB, T6E 5P3
(780) 438-3544
Emp Here 20
SIC 7389 Business services, nec

D-U-N-S 20-069-2791   (SL)
ACE BUILDING MAINTENANCE INC
8861 63 Ave Nw, Edmonton, AB, T6E 0E9
(780) 413-4537
Emp Here 85   *Sales* 2,480,664
SIC 7349 Building maintenance services, nec

D-U-N-S 24-003-9321   (BR)
ACKLANDS - GRAINGER INC
AGI
(*Suby of* W.W. Grainger, Inc.)
8468 Roper Rd Nw, Edmonton, AB, T6E 6W4
(780) 465-0511
Emp Here 20
SIC 5085 Industrial supplies

D-U-N-S 20-021-7870   (SL)
ACOUSTICAL CEILING & BUILDING MAIN-TENANCE LTD
ACOUSTICAL & TOTAL CLEANING SER-VICES
7940 Coronet Rd Nw, Edmonton, AB, T6E 4N8
(780) 496-9035
Emp Here 140   *Sales* 4,085,799
SIC 7349 Building maintenance services, nec

D-U-N-S 24-984-2345   (SL)
ACTION ELECTRICAL LTD
(*Suby of* Bunting Holdings Co Ltd)
7931 Coronet Rd Nw, Edmonton, AB, T6E 4N7
(780) 465-0792
Emp Here 75   *Sales* 8,834,400
SIC 1731 Electrical work
Pr Pr Donald Bunting
  Grace Bunting

D-U-N-S 20-546-5404   (HQ)
AGRA FOUNDATIONS LIMITED
7708 Wagner Rd Nw, Edmonton, AB, T6E 5B2
(780) 468-3392
Emp Here 125   *Emp Total* 254
Sales 18,823,861
SIC 1794 Excavation work
Pr Pr Derek Harris
  Charles Lammers

D-U-N-S 20-580-0456   (BR)
AIR LIQUIDE CANADA INC
10020 56 Ave Nw, Edmonton, AB, T6E 5Z2

Emp Here 115
SIC 2813 Industrial gases

D-U-N-S 20-080-4631   (BR)
AKHURST MACHINERY LIMITED
9615 63 Ave Nw, Edmonton, AB, T6E 0G2
(780) 435-3936
Emp Here 153
SIC 5084 Industrial machinery and equipment

D-U-N-S 20-811-1914   (BR)
ALBERTA BEVERAGE CONTAINER RECY-CLING CORPORATION
ABCRC
(*Suby of* Alberta Beverage Container Recycling Corporation)
9455 45 Ave Nw, Edmonton, AB, T6E 6B9
(780) 435-3640
Emp Here 30
SIC 3411 Metal cans

D-U-N-S 20-300-7161   (BR)
ALBERTA MOTOR ASSOCIATION
A M A
9520 42 Ave Nw, Edmonton, AB, T6E 5Y4
(780) 989-6230
Emp Here 400
SIC 8699 Membership organizations, nec

D-U-N-S 24-583-0906   (SL)
ALBERTA SPECIAL EVENT EQUIPMENT RENTALS & SALES LTD
SPECIAL EVENT RENTALS
6010 99 St Nw, Edmonton, AB, T6E 3P2
(780) 669-0179
Emp Here 60   *Sales* 4,815,406
SIC 7359 Equipment rental and leasing, nec

D-U-N-S 25-236-2041   (BR)
ALBERTA TREASURY BRANCHES
ATB FINANCIAL
8008 104 St Nw, Edmonton, AB, T6E 4E2
(780) 427-4162
Emp Here 60
SIC 6036 Savings institutions, except federal

D-U-N-S 24-091-3632   (SL)
ALBERTA URBAN MUNICIPALITIES ASSO-CIATION
AUMA
10507 Saskatchewan Dr Nw, Edmonton, AB, T6E 4S1

(780) 409-4319
Emp Here 52   *Sales* 7,656,480
SIC 8741 Management services
Pr Pr Lloyd Bertschi
VP VP Darren Aldous
VP VP Ric Mciver
VP VP Helene Rice
VP VP Glenn Taylor
VP VP Dave Thiele
Dir Karen Ann Bertamini
Dir Bob Clark
Dir Linda Osinchuk
Dir Reg Pointe

D-U-N-S 20-307-2223   (BR)
ALBERTS RESTAURANTS LTD
ALBERTS FAMILY RESTAURANT
(*Suby of* Alberts Restaurants Ltd)
5107 99 St Nw, Edmonton, AB, T6E 5B7

Emp Here 20
SIC 5812 Eating places

D-U-N-S 20-743-7740   (HQ)
ALCO GAS & OIL PRODUCTION EQUIP-MENT LTD
5203 75 St Nw, Edmonton, AB, T6E 5S5
(780) 465-9061
Emp Here 122   *Emp Total* 5
Sales 28,499,658
SIC 3533 Oil and gas field machinery
Ex VP David Higgins
Pr Pr Robert Taubner

D-U-N-S 20-159-0478   (SL)
ALTAIR CONTRACTING ULC
9464 51 Ave Nw, Edmonton, AB, T6E 5A6
(780) 465-5363
Emp Here 50   *Sales* 35,279,107
SIC 1742 Plastering, drywall, and insulation
Pr Lionel Williams
Treas Lori A Pickell

D-U-N-S 20-080-6586   (HQ)
ARGUS MACHINE CO. LTD
(*Suby of* Argus Machine Co. Ltd)
5820 97 St Nw Suite 5720, Edmonton, AB, T6E 3J1
(780) 434-9451
Emp Here 60   *Emp Total* 150
Sales 38,173,750
SIC 3494 Valves and pipe fittings, nec
Pr Pr Kris Mauthe

D-U-N-S 20-594-0034   (BR)
ARMY & NAVY DEPT. STORE LIMITED
10411 82 Ave Nw Suite 5, Edmonton, AB, T6E 2A1
(780) 433-5503
Emp Here 30
SIC 5311 Department stores

D-U-N-S 24-710-3463   (BR)
AUTOPRO AUTOMATION CONSULTANTS LTD
4208 97 St Nw Suite 203, Edmonton, AB, T6E 5Z9
(780) 733-7550
Emp Here 30
SIC 8711 Engineering services

D-U-N-S 24-221-8733   (SL)
B. GINGRAS ENTERPRISES LTD
BEE CLEAN
4505 101 St Nw, Edmonton, AB, T6E 5C6
(780) 435-3355
Emp Here 2,000   *Sales* 81,160,000
SIC 7349 Building maintenance services, nec
Pr Pr Brian Gingras

D-U-N-S 24-582-9015   (BR)
BDO CANADA LLP
EDMONTON ACCOUNTING
9897 34 Ave Nw, Edmonton, AB, T6E 5X9
(780) 461-8000
Emp Here 26
SIC 8721 Accounting, auditing, and book-keeping

D-U-N-S 20-970-9294   (BR)
BANQUE TORONTO-DOMINION, LA
TORONTO-DOMINION BANK, THE
(*Suby of* Toronto-Dominion Bank, The)
10864 82 Ave Nw, Edmonton, AB, T6E 2B3
(780) 448-8450
Emp Here 20
SIC 6021 National commercial banks

D-U-N-S 20-589-4905   (BR)
BANQUE TORONTO-DOMINION, LA
TD CANADA TRUST
(*Suby of* Toronto-Dominion Bank, The)
10864 82 Ave Nw, Edmonton, AB, T6E 2B3
(780) 448-8435
Emp Here 20
SIC 6021 National commercial banks

D-U-N-S 20-080-8350   (SL)
BEE BELL HEALTH BAKERY INC
10416 80 Ave Nw, Edmonton, AB, T6E 5T7

Emp Here 80   *Sales* 2,699,546
SIC 5461 Retail bakeries

D-U-N-S 25-106-0208   (SL)
BIOPAK LIMITED
7824 51 Ave Nw, Edmonton, AB, T6E 6W2

Emp Here 80   *Sales* 15,077,264
SIC 2023 Dry, condensed and evaporated dairy products
Pr Pr Bret Smith

D-U-N-S 20-876-8478   (BR)
BISSELL CENTRE
(*Suby of* Bissell Centre)
9238 34 Ave Nw, Edmonton, AB, T6E 5P2
(780) 440-1883
Emp Here 20
SIC 8322 Individual and family services

D-U-N-S 24-861-1790   (HQ)
BROCK CANADA INC
(*Suby of* Brock Canada Inc)
8925 62 Ave Nw, Edmonton, AB, T6E 5L2
(780) 465-9016
Emp Here 40   *Emp Total* 800
Sales 131,839,985
SIC 1389 Oil and gas field services, nec
Pr Willi Hamm

D-U-N-S 24-642-6407   (HQ)
CAN ALTA BINDERY CORP
(*Suby of* Can Alta Bindery Corp)
8445 Davies Rd Nw, Edmonton, AB, T6E 4N3
(780) 466-9973
Emp Here 47   *Emp Total* 50
Sales 4,231,721
SIC 5943 Stationery stores

D-U-N-S 24-003-7374   (BR)
CAN-AM GEOMATICS CORP
7909 51 Ave Nw Suite 110, Edmonton, AB, T6E 5L9
(780) 468-5900
Emp Here 30
SIC 8713 Surveying services

D-U-N-S 24-810-5181   (SL)
CAN-DER CONSTRUCTION LTD
5410 97 St Nw, Edmonton, AB, T6E 5C1
(780) 436-2980
Emp Here 75   *Sales* 20,598,400
SIC 1522 Residential construction, nec
Pr Pr Peter Dirksen
  Greg Christenson

D-U-N-S 20-065-5046   (BR)
CANADA BREAD COMPANY, LIMITED
ADRIAN'S BAKERY
9850 62 Ave Nw, Edmonton, AB, T6E 0E3

Emp Here 70
SIC 2051 Bread, cake, and related products

D-U-N-S 20-573-4200   (BR)
CANADIAN PACIFIC RAILWAY COMPANY

7935 Gateway Blvd Nw, Edmonton, AB, T6E 3X8
(780) 414-2320
Emp Here 20
SIC 4011 Railroads, line-haul operating

D-U-N-S 24-098-4919   (BR)
CANADIAN PACIFIC RAILWAY COMPANY
CPR
7935 Gateway Blvd Nw, Edmonton, AB, T6E 3X8
(780) 414-2305
Emp Here 108
SIC 4011 Railroads, line-haul operating

D-U-N-S 24-962-3141   (BR)
CANADIAN PACIFIC RAILWAY COMPANY
CPR
10155 39 Ave Nw, Edmonton, AB, T6E 6C8
(780) 463-6550
Emp Here 20
SIC 4011 Railroads, line-haul operating

D-U-N-S 20-573-4275   (BR)
CANADIAN PACIFIC RAILWAY COMPANY
CANADIAN PACIFIC RAILWAY
7710 100 St Nw, Edmonton, AB, T6E 4X7
(780) 414-2308
Emp Here 30
SIC 4011 Railroads, line-haul operating

D-U-N-S 20-081-2287   (HQ)
CARLSON BODY SHOP SUPPLY LTD
5308 97 St Nw, Edmonton, AB, T6E 5W5
(780) 438-0808
Emp Here 20   *Emp Total* 15
Sales 6,055,738
SIC 5013 Motor vehicle supplies and new parts
Dir Sumio (Chris) Kikuchi
Pr Pr Robert (Rob) Neale
Dir Brian Tod
  Gordon Milford

D-U-N-S 20-794-9020   (BR)
CENTRAL LABORATORY FOR VETERI-NARIANS LTD
8131 Roper Rd Nw, Edmonton, AB, T6E 6S4
(780) 437-8808
Emp Here 25
SIC 8734 Testing laboratories

D-U-N-S 25-971-9383   (BR)
CERVUS EQUIPMENT CORPORATION
A.R. WILLIAMS MATERIALS HANDLING
9412 51 Ave Nw, Edmonton, AB, T6E 5A6
(780) 432-6262
Emp Here 36
SIC 8731 Commercial physical research

D-U-N-S 24-399-0298   (HQ)
CESSCO FABRICATION & ENGINEERING LIMITED
(*Suby of* Canerector Inc)
7310 99 St Nw, Edmonton, AB, T6E 3R8
(780) 433-9531
Emp Here 100   *Emp Total* 3,000
Sales 11,308,909
SIC 3499 Fabricated Metal products, nec
Pr Burke Oswald
  Amanda Hawkins

D-U-N-S 24-599-8927   (BR)
CHAMCO INDUSTRIES LTD
(*Suby of* Chamco Industries Ltd)
9515 51 Ave Nw, Edmonton, AB, T6E 4W8
(780) 438-8076
Emp Here 22
SIC 5084 Industrial machinery and equipment

D-U-N-S 20-073-9808   (BR)
CITY OF EDMONTON
KINSMAN SPORTS CENTER, THE
9100 Walterdale Hill Nw Suite 102, Edmonton, AB, T6E 2V3
(780) 496-7330
Emp Here 70
SIC 7389 Business services, nec

D-U-N-S 25-366-0732   (BR)
COLE INTERNATIONAL INC
8657 51 Ave Nw Suite 310, Edmonton, AB, T6E 6A8
(780) 437-1936
Emp Here 45
SIC 4731 Freight transportation arrangement

D-U-N-S 20-081-3889   (HQ)
COMMERCIAL BEARING SERVICE (1966) LTD.
(*Suby of* Genuine Parts Company)
4203 95 St Nw Suite 1966, Edmonton, AB, T6E 5R6
(780) 432-1611
Emp Here 125   *Emp Total* 40,000
Sales 57,605,692
SIC 5085 industrial supplies
Pr Pr Jim Barker

D-U-N-S 20-316-6850   (BR)
COMMERCIAL EQUIPMENT CORP
COMMERCIAL TRUCK EQUIPMENT
9111 41 Ave Nw, Edmonton, AB, T6E 6M5
(780) 486-5151
Emp Here 50
SIC 7389 Business services, nec

D-U-N-S 24-850-8140   (SL)
COMPRESSOR PRODUCTS INTERNA-TIONAL CANADA INC
CPI SERVICE
(*Suby of* Enpro Industries, Inc.)
6308 Davies Rd Nw, Edmonton, AB, T6E 4M9
(780) 468-5145
Emp Here 50   *Sales* 3,064,349
SIC 7699 Repair services, nec

D-U-N-S 24-025-4552   (BR)
CONVERGINT TECHNOLOGIES LTD
(*Suby of* Convergint Technologies LLC)
10017 56 Ave Nw, Edmonton, AB, T6E 5L7
(780) 452-9800
Emp Here 24
SIC 8748 Business consulting, nec

D-U-N-S 20-718-4578   (HQ)
CORIX CONTROL SOLUTIONS LIMITED PARTNERSHIP
8803 58 Ave Nw, Edmonton, AB, T6E 5X1
(780) 465-2939
Emp Here 40   *Emp Total* 2,500
Sales 14,983,031
SIC 1389 Oil and gas field services, nec
Pr Pr Brett Hodson
VP VP Randy Helgren

D-U-N-S 20-339-7778   (BR)
CORUS ENTERTAINMENT INC
CHED-AM
5204 84 St Nw, Edmonton, AB, T6E 5N8
(780) 440-6300
Emp Here 105
SIC 7299 Miscellaneous personal service

D-U-N-S 20-138-2046   (BR)
CUNNINGHAM TRANSPORT (1986) LTD
(*Suby of* Cunningham Transport (1986) Ltd)
9340 62 Ave Nw, Edmonton, AB, T6E 0C9
(780) 435-3070
Emp Here 70
SIC 4151 School buses

D-U-N-S 24-290-8478   (SL)
DALMAC OILFIELD SERVICES INC
4934 89 St Nw, Edmonton, AB, T6E 5K1
(780) 988-8510
Emp Here 20   *Sales* 40,226,180
SIC 1389 Oil and gas field services, nec
Pr Pr John Babic
 John Beasley

D-U-N-S 20-970-6829   (HQ)
DERRICK CONCRETE CUTTING & CON-STRUCTION LTD
(*Suby of* Derrick Concrete Cutting & Construction Ltd)
5815 99 St Nw, Edmonton, AB, T6E 3N8

(780) 436-7934
Emp Here 40   *Emp Total* 50
Sales 5,653,974
SIC 1799 Special trade contractors, nec
Pr Pr Ed Moroz

D-U-N-S 20-922-9520   (BR)
DIGITEX CANADA INC
9943 109 St, Edmonton, AB, T6E 5P3
(780) 442-2770
Emp Here 20
SIC 5044 Office equipment

D-U-N-S 20-081-6742   (HQ)
DIVERSIFIED TRANSPORTATION LTD
RED ARROW EXPRESS, DIV OF
8351 Mcintyre Rd Nw, Edmonton, AB, T6E 5J7
(780) 468-6771
Emp Here 100   *Emp Total* 1,600
Sales 18,969,782
SIC 4142 Bus charter service, except local
Pr Pr Bob Colborne
 William Hamilton
VP Rick Colborne
 Michael Colborne

D-U-N-S 20-875-0807   (BR)
DOVER CORPORATION (CANADA) LIM-ITED
ALBERTA OIL TOOL
(*Suby of* Dover Corporation)
9530 60 Ave Nw, Edmonton, AB, T6E 0C1
(780) 434-8566
Emp Here 100
SIC 7699 Repair services, nec

D-U-N-S 25-012-1928   (BR)
DRECO ENERGY SERVICES ULC
NATIONAL OILWELL DRECO
(*Suby of* National Oilwell Varco, Inc.)
3620 93 St Nw, Edmonton, AB, T6E 5N3
(780) 722-2339
Emp Here 400
SIC 3533 Oil and gas field machinery

D-U-N-S 24-701-6595   (HQ)
DRESSER-RAND CANADA, ULC
9330 45 Ave Nw, Edmonton, AB, T6E 6S1
(780) 436-0604
Emp Here 45   *Emp Total* 351,000
Sales 12,987,005
SIC 5085 Industrial supplies
 Derek Hosking

D-U-N-S 20-963-8530   (BR)
DYAND MECHANICAL SYSTEMS INC
WOOD & ENERGY STORE
4146 99 St Nw, Edmonton, AB, T6E 3N5
(780) 430-0194
Emp Here 50
SIC 1711 Plumbing, heating, air-conditioning

D-U-N-S 24-330-1355   (SL)
E & M INTERIORS INC
PARADISE CARPETS
3651 99 St Nw, Edmonton, AB, T6E 6K5
(780) 437-1957
Emp Here 50   *Sales* 4,815,406
SIC 1752 Floor laying and floor work, nec

D-U-N-S 25-998-7035   (BR)
EXP SERVICES INC
EXP GLOBAL
8616 51 Ave Nw Unit 101, Edmonton, AB, T6E 6E6
(780) 435-3662
Emp Here 45
SIC 8711 Engineering services

D-U-N-S 20-712-9722   (BR)
EDMONTON CATHOLIC SEPARATE SCHOOL DISTRICT NO.7
FRESH START OUTREACH HIGH SCHOOL
(*Suby of* Edmonton Catholic Separate School District No.7)
10425 84 Ave Nw, Edmonton, AB, T6E 2H3
(780) 433-8100
Emp Here 50

SIC 8211 Elementary and secondary schools

D-U-N-S 20-070-7144   (BR)
EDMONTON   CATHOLIC   SEPARATE SCHOOL DISTRICT NO.7
J.H.F. PICARD SCHOOL
(*Suby of* Edmonton Catholic Separate School District No.7)
7055 99 St Nw, Edmonton, AB, T6E 3R4
(780) 433-4251
Emp Here 50
SIC 8211 Elementary and secondary schools

D-U-N-S 25-327-1209   (SL)
EDMONTON ROCKERS ATHLETIC, THE
6840 88 St Nw, Edmonton, AB, T6E 5H6
(780) 461-7625
Emp Here 50   *Sales* 2,042,900
SIC 7991 Physical fitness facilities

D-U-N-S 20-591-8332   (BR)
EDMONTON SCHOOL DISTRICT NO. 7
MILL CREEK ELEMENTARY SCHOOL
9735 80 Ave Nw, Edmonton, AB, T6E 1S8
(780) 433-5746
Emp Here 20
SIC 8211 Elementary and secondary schools

D-U-N-S 20-154-7705   (BR)
EDMONTON SCHOOL DISTRICT NO. 7
OLD SCONA ACADEMIC HIGH SCHOOL
10523 84 Ave Nw, Edmonton, AB, T6E 2H5
(780) 433-0627
Emp Here 26
SIC 8211 Elementary and secondary schools

D-U-N-S 25-013-7213   (BR)
EDMONTON SCHOOL DISTRICT NO. 7
HAZELDEAN ELEMENTARY SCHOOL
6715 97 St Nw, Edmonton, AB, T6E 3J9
(780) 433-7583
Emp Here 55
SIC 8211 Elementary and secondary schools

D-U-N-S 20-712-6629   (BR)
EDMONTON SCHOOL DISTRICT NO. 7
ACADEMY OF KING EDWARD, THE
8525 101 St Nw, Edmonton, AB, T6E 3Z4
(780) 439-1368
Emp Here 20
SIC 8211 Elementary and secondary schools

D-U-N-S 25-454-5205   (BR)
EDMONTON SCHOOL DISTRICT NO. 7
STRATHCONA COMPOSITE HIGH SCHOOL
10450 72 Ave Nw, Edmonton, AB, T6E 0Z6
(780) 439-3957
Emp Here 84
SIC 8211 Elementary and secondary schools

D-U-N-S 20-591-9850   (BR)
EDMONTON SCHOOL DISTRICT NO. 7
KING EDWARD SCHOOL
8530 101 St Nw, Edmonton, AB, T6E 3Z5
(780) 439-2491
Emp Here 20
SIC 8211 Elementary and secondary schools

D-U-N-S 20-209-4012   (BR)
EDMONTON SCHOOL DISTRICT NO. 7
W P WAGNER SCHOOL
6310 Wagner Rd Nw, Edmonton, AB, T6E 4N5
(780) 469-1315
Emp Here 130
SIC 8211 Elementary and secondary schools

D-U-N-S 25-683-0126   (SL)
EDMONTON STEEL PLATE LTD
(*Suby of* Gusse Holdings Limited)
5545 89 St Nw, Edmonton, AB, T6E 5W9
(780) 468-6722
Emp Here 130   *Sales* 52,385,783
SIC 5051 Metals service centers and offices
Pr Larry Gusse
Dir Adelle Gusse

D-U-N-S 20-081-9100   (HQ)
ELECTRIC MOTOR SERVICE LIMITED
(*Suby of* 507518 Alberta Ltd)

8835 60 Ave Nw, Edmonton, AB, T6E 6L9
(780) 496-9300
Emp Here 50   *Emp Total* 65
Sales 5,977,132
SIC 7694 Armature rewinding shops
Pr Pr Robert Knickle
 David Ash
 Jacqueline Knickle

D-U-N-S 25-366-5947   (SL)
ELOG LTD
3907 98 St Nw Suite 109, Edmonton, AB, T6E 6M3
(780) 414-0199
Emp Here 200   *Sales* 37,637,950
SIC 7371 Custom computer programming services
Pr Pr Manoranjan Sahu
Dir Alka Sahu

D-U-N-S 25-192-4080   (BR)
EMERSON ELECTRIC CANADA LIMITED
EMERSON PROCESS MANAGEMENT
(*Suby of* Emerson Electric Co.)
4112 91a St Nw, Edmonton, AB, T6E 5V2
(780) 450-3600
Emp Here 150
SIC 3533 Oil and gas field machinery

D-U-N-S 24-091-5959   (BR)
EMERSON ELECTRIC CANADA LIMITED
FISHER ROSEMONT SERVICE
(*Suby of* Emerson Electric Co.)
4112 91a St Nw, Edmonton, AB, T6E 5V2
(780) 450-3600
Emp Here 30
SIC 7699 Repair services, nec

D-U-N-S 20-691-9495   (BR)
ENERFLEX LTD.
CFX ENGINE CONTROLS AND ACCES-SORIES
8235 Wagner Rd Nw, Edmonton, AB, T6E 4N6

Emp Here 40
SIC 3563 Air and gas compressors

D-U-N-S 20-779-1299   (SL)
EVENT PLANNING HEADQUARTERS
AMMAR, JOE
6010 99 St Nw, Edmonton, AB, T6E 3P2
(780) 435-2211
Emp Here 70   *Sales* 2,334,742
SIC 7299 Miscellaneous personal service

D-U-N-S 20-179-7912   (BR)
EXALTA TRANSPORT CORP
4174 95 St Nw, Edmonton, AB, T6E 6H5
(780) 490-1112
Emp Here 20
SIC 4213 Trucking, except local

D-U-N-S 20-636-8771   (HQ)
FACTOR FORMS WEST LTD
(*Suby of* B J Baker & Sons Holdings Ltd)
8411 Mcintyre Rd Nw, Edmonton, AB, T6E 6G3
(780) 468-1111
Emp Here 90   *Emp Total* 165
Sales 7,587,913
SIC 5112 Stationery and office supplies
Pr Pr Greg Drechsler

D-U-N-S 25-961-0533   (BR)
FRONTIER POWER PRODUCTS LTD
9204 37 Ave Nw, Edmonton, AB, T6E 5L4
(780) 455-2260
Emp Here 30
SIC 3519 Internal combustion engines, nec

D-U-N-S 25-205-8458   (BR)
G4S SECURE SOLUTIONS (CANADA) LTD
9618 42 Ave Nw Suite 110, Edmonton, AB, T6E 5Y4
(780) 423-4444
Emp Here 150
SIC 7381 Detective and armored car services

D-U-N-S 24-978-6617   (BR)

GRAHAM GROUP LTD
GRAHAM INDUSTRIAL SERVICES AT J V
8404 Mcintyre Rd Nw, Edmonton, AB, T6E
6V3
(780) 430-9600
Emp Here 130
SIC 1541 Industrial buildings and warehouses

D-U-N-S 24-344-6163   (SL)
GREAT CANADIAN RENOVATION & CON-STRUCTION CORPORATION
GREAT CANADIAN FRAMING
9310 62 Ave Nw, Edmonton, AB, T6E 0C9
(780) 449-6991
Emp Here 50   *Sales* 9,611,756
SIC 1521 Single-family housing construction
Pr Pr Curt Beyer
Fin Ex Linda Playfair

D-U-N-S 20-015-6367   (BR)
GREAT PACIFIC INDUSTRIES INC
SAVE-ON-FOODS
10368 78 Ave Nw, Edmonton, AB, T6E 6T2
(780) 438-0385
Emp Here 140
SIC 5411 Grocery stores

D-U-N-S 20-008-2472   (BR)
HERBERS AUTO BODY REPAIR LTD
6804 75 St Nw, Edmonton, AB, T6E 5A9
(780) 468-3020
Emp Here 20
SIC 7532 Top and body repair and paint shops

D-U-N-S 20-852-5365   (SL)
HI SIGNS THE FATH GROUP LTD
9570 58 Ave Nw, Edmonton, AB, T6E 0B6
(780) 468-6181
Emp Here 50   *Sales* 3,064,349
SIC 3993 Signs and advertising specialties

D-U-N-S 24-343-7022   (BR)
HI-KALIBRE EQUIPMENT LIMITED
NORALTA POLY, DIV OF
7705 Coronet Rd Nw, Edmonton, AB, T6E
4N7
(780) 485-5813
Emp Here 25
SIC 3069 Fabricated rubber products, nec

D-U-N-S 24-331-0984   (HQ)
ISL ENGINEERING AND LAND SERVICES LTD
7909 51 Ave Nw Suite 100, Edmonton, AB,
T6E 5L9
(780) 438-9000
Emp Here 156   *Emp Total* 210
Sales 32,571,038
SIC 8711 Engineering services
Pr Pr Gary Mack

D-U-N-S 24-807-7885   (SL)
INOTEC COATINGS AND HYDRAULICS INC
4263 95 St Nw, Edmonton, AB, T6E 5R6
(780) 461-8333
Emp Here 110   *Sales* 10,347,900
SIC 3471 Plating and polishing
Garry Knull

D-U-N-S 24-320-3606   (BR)
INTEGRATED DISTRIBUTION SYSTEMS LIMITED PARTNERSHIP
WAJAX POWER SYSTEMS
10025 51 Ave Nw, Edmonton, AB, T6E 0A8
(780) 437-8200
Emp Here 135
SIC 5084 Industrial machinery and equipment

D-U-N-S 25-315-7556   (BR)
INVESTORS GROUP FINANCIAL SER-VICES INC
8905 51 Ave Nw Unit 102, Edmonton, AB, T6E
5J3
(780) 468-1658
Emp Here 40
SIC 8742 Management consulting services

D-U-N-S 24-101-7826   (BR)
IRON MOUNTAIN CANADA OPERATIONS

ULC
ARCHIVES IRON MOUNTAIN
3905 101 St Nw, Edmonton, AB, T6E 0A4
(780) 466-7272
Emp Here 30
SIC 4226 Special warehousing and storage, nec

D-U-N-S 24-522-8036   (BR)
IRWIN, DICK GROUP LTD, THE
MILLWOODS HONDA
9688 34 Ave Nw, Edmonton, AB, T6E 6S9
(780) 463-7888
Emp Here 35
SIC 5511 New and used car dealers

D-U-N-S 24-068-5776   (SL)
JAVA JIVE MERCHANTS LTD
COFFEE FACTORY, THE
9929 77 Ave Nw, Edmonton, AB, T6E 1M6

Emp Here 50   *Sales* 9,942,100
SIC 5149 Groceries and related products, nec
Pr Pr Michael Ould
Linda Ould

D-U-N-S 20-082-6998   (SL)
JET-LUBE OF CANADA LTD
(Suby of Csw Industrials, Inc.)
3820 97 St Nw, Edmonton, AB, T6E 5S8
(780) 463-7441
Emp Here 20   *Sales* 1,240,332
SIC 7549 Automotive services, nec

D-U-N-S 20-734-6607   (HQ)
JIM PATTISON BROADCAST GROUP LIM-ITED PARTNERSHIP
JIM PATTISON BROADCAST GROUP
(Suby of Jim Pattison Broadcast Group Lim-ited Partnership)
9894 42 Ave Suite 102, Edmonton, AB, T6E
5V5
(780) 433-7877
Emp Here 50   *Emp Total* 340
Sales 27,798,706
SIC 4832 Radio broadcasting stations
Pr Rod Schween
Genl Mgr Jamie Wall

D-U-N-S 20-799-9793   (SL)
KADON ELECTRO MECHANICAL SER-VICES LTD
4808 87 St Nw Suite 140, Edmonton, AB, T6E
5W3
(780) 466-4470
Emp Here 50   *Sales* 3,064,349
SIC 7699 Repair services, nec

D-U-N-S 25-272-9488   (BR)
KEG RESTAURANTS LTD
KEG STEAKHOUSE & BAR, THE
8020 105 St Nw, Edmonton, AB, T6E 4Z4
(780) 432-7494
Emp Here 90
SIC 5812 Eating places

D-U-N-S 25-986-5509   (BR)
KEYSTONE AUTOMOTIVE INDUSTRIES ON INC
CROSS CANADA AUTO BODY (WEST)
8221 Mcintyre Rd Nw, Edmonton, AB, T6E
5J7
(780) 448-1901
Emp Here 30
SIC 5013 Motor vehicle supplies and new parts

D-U-N-S 25-831-7601   (BR)
LABATT BREWING COMPANY LIMITED
LABATT BREWERIES WESTERN CANADA
10119 45 Ave Nw, Edmonton, AB, T6E 0G8
(780) 436-6060
Emp Here 170
SIC 2082 Malt beverages

D-U-N-S 20-353-4032   (BR)
LANSDOWNE HOLDINGS LTD
BOSTON PIZZA

10854 82 Ave Nw, Edmonton, AB, T6E 2B3
(780) 433-3151
Emp Here 50
SIC 5812 Eating places

D-U-N-S 25-236-2090   (BR)
LEADING BRANDS OF CANADA, INC
NORTH AMERICAN BOTTLING
(Suby of Leading Brands, Inc)
4104 99 St Nw, Edmonton, AB, T6E 3N5
(780) 435-2746
Emp Here 50
SIC 2033 Canned fruits and specialties

D-U-N-S 25-677-5313   (SL)
LIGHTS ALIVE LTD
3809 98 St Nw, Edmonton, AB, T6E 5V4
(780) 438-6624
Emp Here 30   *Sales* 8,147,280
SIC 5063 Electrical apparatus and equipment
Pr Pr Xinxin Shan

D-U-N-S 20-724-0990   (BR)
LILYDALE INC
LILYDALE FOODS
9620 56 Ave Nw, Edmonton, AB, T6E 0B3
(780) 435-3944
Emp Here 30
SIC 5144 Poultry and poultry products

D-U-N-S 20-174-5242   (BR)
LOBLAWS INC
REAL CANADIAN WHOLESALE CLUB
6904 99 St Nw, Edmonton, AB, T6E 6G1
(780) 431-1090
Emp Here 60
SIC 5141 Groceries, general line

D-U-N-S 20-178-3847   (BR)
LOBLAWS INC
SUNSPUN FOOD SERVICE
9910 69 Ave Nw, Edmonton, AB, T6E 6G1

Emp Here 100
SIC 5141 Groceries, general line

D-U-N-S 25-092-7337   (BR)
LULULEMON ATHLETICA CANADA INC
LULULEMON
10558 82 Ave Nw, Edmonton, AB, T6E 2A4
(780) 435-9363
Emp Here 20
SIC 2339 Women's and misses' outerwear, nec

D-U-N-S 24-337-0876   (SL)
MARBLE RESTAURANTS LTD
PIZZA HUT
9054 51 Ave Nw Suite 200, Edmonton, AB,
T6E 5X4
(780) 462-5755
Emp Here 200   *Sales* 7,821,331
SIC 5812 Eating places
Pr Pr Shamez Jivraj
Aly Jivraj
Dir Mohamed Jivraj

D-U-N-S 25-311-2700   (BR)
MCDONALD'S RESTAURANTS OF CANADA LIMITED
MCDONALD'S
(Suby of McDonald's Corporation)
3404 99 St Nw, Edmonton, AB, T6E 5X5
(780) 463-0302
Emp Here 50
SIC 5812 Eating places

D-U-N-S 25-373-8595   (HQ)
MCMATT INVESTMENTS LTD
MCDONALD'S RESTAURANTS
(Suby of McMatt Investments Ltd)
10305 80 Ave Nw, Edmonton, AB, T6E 1T8
(780) 414-8445
Emp Here 35   *Emp Total* 140
Sales 4,231,721
SIC 5812 Eating places

D-U-N-S 20-083-3168   (BR)

MIDWEST SURVEYS INC
MIDWEST CONSULTING
9830 42 Ave Nw Unit 102, Edmonton, AB, T6E
5V5
(780) 433-6411
Emp Here 50
SIC 8713 Surveying services

D-U-N-S 25-012-1621   (BR)
NCS INTERNATIONAL CO.
NORAMCO
4130 101 St Nw, Edmonton, AB, T6E 0A5
(780) 468-5678
Emp Here 30
SIC 5063 Electrical apparatus and equipment

D-U-N-S 20-913-1163   (BR)
NATIONAL-OILWELL CANADA LTD
DOWNHOLE TOOLS
(Suby of National Oilwell Varco, Inc.)
3550 93 St Nw, Edmonton, AB, T6E 5N3
(780) 465-9500
Emp Here 300
SIC 3533 Oil and gas field machinery

D-U-N-S 25-955-9508   (BR)
NATIONAL-OILWELL CANADA LTD
NATIONAL-OILWELL VARCO
(Suby of National Oilwell Varco, Inc.)
6415 75 St Nw, Edmonton, AB, T6E 0T3
(780) 944-3850
Emp Here 200
SIC 3533 Oil and gas field machinery

D-U-N-S 20-181-2364   (BR)
NATIONAL-OILWELL CANADA LTD
(Suby of National Oilwell Varco, Inc.)
9120 34a Ave Nw, Edmonton, AB, T6E 5P4
(780) 414-7602
Emp Here 100
SIC 5084 Industrial machinery and equipment

D-U-N-S 24-089-0496   (BR)
NATIONAL-OILWELL CANADA LTD
DOWNHOLE TOOLS, DIV
(Suby of National Oilwell Varco, Inc.)
3660 93 St Nw, Edmonton, AB, T6E 5N3

Emp Here 30
SIC 7699 Repair services, nec

D-U-N-S 25-451-9515   (BR)
NEWCAP INC
EDMONTON RADIO GROUP
4752 99 St Nw Suite 2394, Edmonton, AB,
T6E 5H5
(780) 437-4996
Emp Here 50
SIC 4832 Radio broadcasting stations

D-U-N-S 24-002-9173   (BR)
NORWESCO INDUSTRIES (1983) LTD
9510 39 Ave Nw, Edmonton, AB, T6E 5T9
(780) 437-5440
Emp Here 40
SIC 5084 Industrial machinery and equipment

D-U-N-S 20-191-7437   (SL)
ORBIS ENGINEERING FIELD SERVICES LTD
9404 41 Ave Nw Suite 300, Edmonton, AB,
T6E 6G8
(780) 988-1455
Emp Here 50   *Sales* 6,407,837
SIC 8711 Engineering services
Pr Pr Doug Mortimer

D-U-N-S 24-982-4780   (HQ)
PCL CONSTRUCTION MANAGEMENT INC
5400 99 St Nw, Edmonton, AB, T6E 3P4
(780) 733-6000
Emp Here 200   *Emp Total* 16,380
Sales 83,333,346
SIC 8741 Management services
Pr Pr Alan Kuysters
Dir Robert Holmberg

D-U-N-S 24-982-4707   (SL)
PCL CONSTRUCTORS NORTHERN INC

9915 56 Ave Nw Suite 1, Edmonton, AB, T6E 5L7
(780) 733-6000
Emp Here 20   *Sales* 5,173,950
SIC 1542 Nonresidential construction, nec
Pr Pr Rob Otway

D-U-N-S 24-642-7017   (HQ)
PCL INDUSTRIAL CONSTRUCTORS INC
9915 56 Ave Nw, Edmonton, AB, T6E 5L7
(780) 733-5500
Emp Here 100   *Emp Total* 16,380
Sales 635,135,233
SIC 1541 Industrial buildings and warehouses
Pr Gary Truhn

D-U-N-S 20-560-3231   (SL)
PCL INDUSTRIAL MANAGEMENT INC
5404 99 St Nww, Edmonton, AB, T6E 3N7
(780) 733-5700
Emp Here 35   *Sales* 3,898,130
SIC 8742 Management consulting services

D-U-N-S 20-555-7346   (SL)
PCL INTRACON POWER INC
9915 56 Ave Nw, Edmonton, AB, T6E 5L7
(780) 733-5300
Emp Here 400   *Sales* 48,696,000
SIC 1731 Electrical work
Pr Pr Chris Pullen
Dir Brent Holdner

D-U-N-S 20-732-6583   (BR)
PACIFIC RADIATOR MFG. LTD
9625 45 Ave Nw Suite 205, Edmonton, AB, T6E 5Z8
(780) 435-7684
Emp Here 20
SIC 3433 Heating equipment, except electric

D-U-N-S 20-844-5754   (BR)
PEPSICO CANADA ULC
FRITO LAY CANADA
(*Suby of* Pepsico, Inc.)
4110 101 St Nw, Edmonton, AB, T6E 0A5
(780) 577-2150
Emp Here 20
SIC 2096 Potato chips and similar snacks

D-U-N-S 20-721-0188   (BR)
PITNEY BOWES OF CANADA LTD
(*Suby of* Pitney Bowes Inc.)
9636 51 Ave Nw Suite 104, Edmonton, AB, T6E 6A5
(780) 433-2562
Emp Here 25
SIC 5044 Office equipment

D-U-N-S 20-539-0438   (SL)
PLAINSMAN MFG. INC
8305 Mcintyre Rd Nw, Edmonton, AB, T6E 5J7
(780) 496-9800
Emp Here 53   *Sales* 13,192,606
SIC 3533 Oil and gas field machinery
Pr Pr Lee Makelki
VP VP Larry Makelki

D-U-N-S 24-928-7947   (BR)
POLYBOTTLE GROUP LIMITED
(*Suby of* Cerberus Capital Management, L.P.)
6008 75 St Nw, Edmonton, AB, T6E 2W6
(780) 468-6019
Emp Here 70
SIC 5085 Industrial supplies

D-U-N-S 25-679-1211   (SL)
PRAIRIE NORTH CONST. LTD
4936 87 St Nw Suite 280, Edmonton, AB, T6E 5W3
(780) 463-3363
Emp Here 75   *Sales* 11,307,948
SIC 1611 Highway and street construction
Pr Pr F Craig Robertson
D Alvin Spray

D-U-N-S 20-083-9082   (HQ)
PRICE, GORDON MUSIC LTD
MOTHERS MUSIC

(*Suby of* Price, Gordon Music Ltd)
10828 82 Ave Nw, Edmonton, AB, T6E 2B3
(780) 439-0007
Emp Here 21   *Emp Total* 54
Sales 3,939,878
SIC 5736 Musical instrument stores

D-U-N-S 24-981-4112   (SL)
PROFESSIONAL GROUP INC, THE
PROFESSIONAL REALTY GROUP, THE DIV OF
9222 51 Ave Nw, Edmonton, AB, T6E 5L8
(780) 439-9818
Emp Here 68   *Sales* 8,842,240
SIC 6531 Real estate agents and managers
Pr Pr Russel Robideau
  Helen D Robideau

D-U-N-S 25-082-4786   (BR)
PUMPS & PRESSURE INC
(*Suby of* Pumps & Pressure Inc)
8632 Coronet Rd Nw, Edmonton, AB, T6E 4P3
(780) 430-9359
Emp Here 40
SIC 5084 Industrial machinery and equipment

D-U-N-S 20-313-3426   (SL)
RC PARTNERSHIP LTD
8812 60 Ave Nw, Edmonton, AB, T6E 6A6
(780) 462-3301
Emp Here 175   *Sales* 17,753,750
SIC 7538 General automotive repair shops
Pr Pr Ryan Giese
Dir Corrie King

D-U-N-S 24-764-6545   (BR)
RAYDON RENTALS LTD
THE CAT RENTAL STORE
(*Suby of* Finning International Inc)
4750 101 St Nw, Edmonton, AB, T6E 5G9
(780) 455-2005
Emp Here 30
SIC 7353 Heavy construction equipment rental

D-U-N-S 24-854-9495   (SL)
REDCO CONSTRUCTION LTD
REDCO RESTORATION SPECIALISTS
8105 Davies Rd Nw, Edmonton, AB, T6E 4N1
(780) 466-1820
Emp Here 40   *Sales* 7,724,992
SIC 1771 Concrete work
Pr Pr Dennis Coulson
  Ralph Ewel

D-U-N-S 20-720-3233   (BR)
RINGBALL CORPORATION
VANGUARD STEEL
7606 Mcintyre Rd Nw, Edmonton, AB, T6E 6Z1
(780) 465-3311
Emp Here 20
SIC 5051 Metals service centers and offices

D-U-N-S 25-137-0078   (BR)
RITE-WAY FENCING (2000) INC
8625 63 Ave Nw, Edmonton, AB, T6E 0E8
(780) 440-4300
Emp Here 25
SIC 5039 Construction materials, nec

D-U-N-S 25-454-4547   (SL)
ROHIT DEVELOPMENTS LTD
(*Suby of* Rohit Holdings Ltd)
9636 51 Ave Nw, Edmonton, AB, T6E 6A5
(780) 436-9015
Emp Here 84   *Sales* 23,232,050
SIC 1522 Residential construction, nec
Pr Pr Radhe Gupta

D-U-N-S 20-296-2403   (BR)
ROSENAU TRANSPORT LTD
(*Suby of* Mid-Nite Sun Transportation Ltd)
5805 98 St Nw, Edmonton, AB, T6E 3L4
(780) 431-0594
Emp Here 100
SIC 4213 Trucking, except local

D-U-N-S 20-070-4554   (BR)
ROYAL BANK OF CANADA
RBC
(*Suby of* Royal Bank Of Canada)
10843 82 Ave Nw, Edmonton, AB, T6E 2B2
(780) 448-6900
Emp Here 25
SIC 6021 National commercial banks

D-U-N-S 24-715-2507   (BR)
ROYAL BANK OF CANADA
ROYAL FINANCIAL GROUP
(*Suby of* Royal Bank of Canada)
9042 51 Ave Nw, Edmonton, AB, T6E 5X4
(780) 448-6845
Emp Here 20
SIC 6021 National commercial banks

D-U-N-S 24-905-1137   (BR)
RUSSEL METALS INC
7016 99 St Nw, Edmonton, AB, T6E 3R3
(780) 439-2051
Emp Here 90
SIC 5051 Metals service centers and offices

D-U-N-S 20-438-0224   (BR)
RYERSON CANADA, INC
7945 Coronet Rd Nw, Edmonton, AB, T6E 4N7
(780) 469-0402
Emp Here 50
SIC 5051 Metals service centers and offices

D-U-N-S 24-984-1896   (BR)
SGI CANADA INSURANCE SERVICES LTD
4220 98 St Nw Suite 303, Edmonton, AB, T6E 6A1
(780) 435-1488
Emp Here 55
SIC 6411 Insurance agents, brokers, and service

D-U-N-S 24-327-7068   (HQ)
SAN FRANCISCO GIFTS LTD
SAN DIEGO GIFTS
9762 54 Ave Nw, Edmonton, AB, T6E 0A9

Emp Here 80   *Emp Total* 80
Sales 51,975,060
SIC 5947 Gift, novelty, and souvenir shop
Pr Pr Barry Slawsky

D-U-N-S 25-097-1009   (BR)
SCOTT BUILDERS INC
(*Suby of* Scott Builders Inc)
9835 60 Ave Nw, Edmonton, AB, T6E 0C6
(780) 463-4565
Emp Here 30
SIC 1541 Industrial buildings and warehouses

D-U-N-S 20-793-6902   (SL)
SECURITY OFFICER CAREER COLLEGE
8055 Coronet Rd Nw, Edmonton, AB, T6E 4N7

Emp Here 600   *Sales* 117,792,000
SIC 6211 Security brokers and dealers
Mgr Tom Hill
CFO Freddy Ramsoondar

D-U-N-S 25-137-1571   (SL)
SERENITY FAMILY SERVICE SOCIETY
SERENITY FUNERAL SERVICE
5311 91 St Nw Suite 7, Edmonton, AB, T6E 6E2
(780) 450-0101
Emp Here 50   *Sales* 5,072,500
SIC 7261 Funeral service and crematories
Dir Gary Howele

D-U-N-S 24-390-4658   (SL)
SILKROAD TECHNOLOGY, CANADA INC.
(*Suby of* Silkroad Technology, Inc.)
9618 42 Ave Nw Suite 202, Edmonton, AB, T6E 5Y4
(780) 421-8374
Emp Here 23   *Sales* 1,678,096
SIC 7372 Prepackaged software

D-U-N-S 20-115-9563   (HQ)
SIMSON MAXWELL
8750 58 Ave Nw, Edmonton, AB, T6E 6G6
(780) 434-6431
Emp Here 40   *Emp Total* 100
Sales 28,413,033
SIC 5084 Industrial machinery and equipment
Dir Daryl Kruper
Dir Brad Kruper

D-U-N-S 20-742-6805   (BR)
SINCLAIR SUPPLY LTD
6243 88 St Nw, Edmonton, AB, T6E 5T4
(780) 465-9551
Emp Here 20
SIC 1711 Plumbing, heating, air-conditioning

D-U-N-S 20-084-4512   (BR)
SPARTAN CONTROLS LTD
STERLING VALVE AUTOMATION, DIV. OF
8403 51 Ave Nw, Edmonton, AB, T6E 5L9
(780) 468-5463
Emp Here 200
SIC 5085 Industrial supplies

D-U-N-S 20-793-6910   (BR)
SPARTAN CONTROLS LTD
8403 51 Ave Nw, Edmonton, AB, T6E 5L9
(780) 468-5463
Emp Here 25
SIC 5999 Miscellaneous retail stores, nec

D-U-N-S 25-140-2202   (BR)
STARBUCKS COFFEE CANADA, INC
SCONA MARKET STARBUCKS
(*Suby of* Starbucks Corporation)
10380 78 Ave Nw, Edmonton, AB, T6E 6T2
(780) 430-6950
Emp Here 20
SIC 5812 Eating places

D-U-N-S 20-905-7327   (SL)
STEELE SECURITY & INVESTIGATION SERVICE DIVISION OF UNITED PROTECTIONS
UNITED PROTECTIONS
8055 Coronet Rd Nw, Edmonton, AB, T6E 4N7

Emp Here 100   *Sales* 4,052,015
SIC 7381 Detective and armored car services

D-U-N-S 24-426-1769   (SL)
STEEPLEJACK MANAGEMENT CORPORATION
(*Suby of* Brock Canada Inc)
8925 62 Ave Nw, Edmonton, AB, T6E 5L2
(780) 465-9016
Emp Here 50   *Sales* 5,399,092
SIC 8741 Management services
Pr Willi Hamm

D-U-N-S 24-715-7381   (SL)
TARANI REBUILDERS INC
9210 60 Ave Nw, Edmonton, AB, T6E 0C1
(780) 437-2575
Emp Here 20   *Sales* 3,137,310
SIC 3714 Motor vehicle parts and accessories

D-U-N-S 24-961-7846   (SL)
TEMPO ALBERTA ELECTRICAL CONTRACTORS CO LTD
TEMPO ELECTRIC
9625 60 Ave Nw Unit 20, Edmonton, AB, T6E 5N1
(780) 448-2877
Emp Here 50   *Sales* 4,377,642
SIC 1731 Electrical work

D-U-N-S 24-839-9024   (BR)
THURBER ENGINEERING LTD
9636 51 Ave Nw Suite 200, Edmonton, AB, T6E 6A5
(780) 438-1460
Emp Here 100
SIC 8711 Engineering services

D-U-N-S 25-451-0696   (BR)
TIMBERTOWN BUILDING CENTRE LTD

4840 99 St Nw, Edmonton, AB, T6E 3N6
(780) 435-4747
Emp Here 20
SIC 5211 Lumber and other building materials

D-U-N-S 24-395-3650   (BR)
TOROMONT INDUSTRIES LTD
CIMCO REFRIGERATION
5909 83 St Nw, Edmonton, AE, T6E 4Y3
(780) 468-1490
Emp Here 35
SIC 3585 Refrigeration and heating equipment

D-U-N-S 25-361-0612   (BR)
TOROMONT INDUSTRIES LTD
TOROMONT ENERGY SERVICES
8835 53 Ave Nw, Edmonton, AB, T6E 5E9
(780) 485-0690
Emp Here 31
SIC 7699 Repair services, nec

D-U-N-S 24-394-9542   (BR)
TRAIL APPLIANCES LTD
CALGARY HOME APPLIANCE
9880 47 Ave Nw, Edmonton, AB, T6E 5P3
(780) 434-9414
Emp Here 60
SIC 5722 Household appliance stores

D-U-N-S 24-584-9476   (HQ)
TRAVERS FOOD SERVICE LTD
ARAMARK REMOTE SERVICES
9647 45 Ave Nw, Edmonton, AB, T6E 5Z8
(780) 437-5665
Emp Here 40   *Emp Total* 266,500
Sales 11,684,880
SIC 5812 Eating places
Pr John Dampf

D-U-N-S 24-328-3215   (HQ)
TRI-SERVICE OILFIELD MANUFACTURING LTD
(*Suby of* Kuchar, Wally Investments Inc)
9545 58 Ave Nw, Edmonton, AB, T6E 0B8
(780) 434-9596
Emp Here 20   *Emp Total* 2
Sales 7,660,874
SIC 3533 Oil and gas field machinery
Pr Pr John De Moissac
  Christopher Kuchar

D-U-N-S 25-094-7504   (BR)
UNIFIRST CANADA LTD
(*Suby of* Unifirst Corporation)
3691 98 St Nw, Edmonton, AB, T6E 5N2
(780) 423-0384
Emp Here 80
SIC 7213 Linen supply

D-U-N-S 24-065-6033   (HQ)
VALARD CONSTRUCTION LTD
(*Suby of* Quanta Services, Inc.)
4209 99 St Nw Suite 301, Edmonton, AB, T6E 5V7
(780) 436-9876
Emp Here 100   *Emp Total* 28,100
Sales 122,573,976
SIC 1623 Water, sewer, and utility lines
  Victor Budzinski
Pr Pr Adam Budzinski
VP VP Phillip Seeley

D-U-N-S 20-176-2916   (BR)
VALUE VILLAGE STORES, INC
SAVERS
(*Suby of* Savers, Inc.)
10127 34 Ave Nw, Edmonton, AB, T6E 6J8
(780) 414-5859
Emp Here 50
SIC 5399 Miscellaneous general merchandise

D-U-N-S 20-918-9070   (BR)
WATERGROUP COMPANIES INC
CULLIGAN
(*Suby of* Clayton, Dubilier & Rice, Inc.)
4150 101 St Nw, Edmonton, AB, T6E 0A5

(780) 489-5502
Emp Here 50
SIC 5963 Direct selling establishments

D-U-N-S 20-811-3019   (BR)
WAWANESA MUTUAL INSURANCE COMPANY, THE
(*Suby of* Wawanesa Mutual Insurance Company, The)
8657 51 Ave Nw Suite 100, Edmonton, AB, T6E 6A8
(780) 469-5700
Emp Here 119
SIC 6331 Fire, marine, and casualty insurance

D-U-N-S 24-327-3406   (BR)
WEIR CANADA, INC
WEIR OIL & GAS
4737 97 St Nw, Edmonton, AB, T6E 5W2
(780) 438-1122
Emp Here 25
SIC 5084 Industrial machinery and equipment

D-U-N-S 20-199-2349   (BR)
WENDY'S RESTAURANTS OF CANADA INC
WENDY'S
(*Suby of* The Wendy's Company)
10195 34 Ave Nw, Edmonton, AB, T6E 6J8
(780) 462-7560
Emp Here 30
SIC 5812 Eating places

D-U-N-S 24-066-1710   (BR)
WESTERN INVENTORY SERVICE LTD
9750 51 Ave Nw Suite 208, Edmonton, AB, T6E 0A6
(780) 457-4477
Emp Here 60
SIC 7389 Business services, nec

D-U-N-S 20-616-9500   (BR)
WESTERN MATERIALS HANDLING & EQUIPMENT LTD
5927 86 St Nw Suite 25, Edmonton, AB, T6E 2X4
(780) 465-6417
Emp Here 60
SIC 3537 Industrial trucks and tractors

D-U-N-S 24-806-9270   (BR)
WILKINSON STEEL AND METALS INC
9525 60 Ave Nw, Edmonton, AB, T6E 0C3
(780) 434-8441
Emp Here 70
SIC 5051 Metals service centers and offices

D-U-N-S 24-360-1395   (BR)
WOLSELEY INDUSTRIAL CANADA INC
MERIDIAN SPECIALTIES
(*Suby of* WOLSELEY PLC)
3780 98 St Nw, Edmonton, AB, T6E 6B4
(780) 468-7161
Emp Here 40
SIC 5085 Industrial supplies

D-U-N-S 24-396-2776   (BR)
WORLEYPARSONS CANADA SERVICES LTD
WORLEYPARSONS EDMONTON
5008 86 St Nw Suite 120, Edmonton, AB, T6E 5S2
(780) 440-5300
Emp Here 1,200
SIC 8711 Engineering services

Edmonton, AB T6G

D-U-N-S 20-867-4395   (BR)
ARAMARK CANADA LTD.
ARAMARK MANAGED SERVICES
125 University Campus Nw, Edmonton, AB, T6G 2H6
(780) 492-5800
Emp Here 100
SIC 5812 Eating places

D-U-N-S 20-268-7190   (BR)
ALBERTA HEALTH SERVICES
ALBERTA HEALTH SERVICES, EDM CLI-NENG
8440 112 St Nw, Edmonton, AB, T6G 2B7
(780) 616-6215
Emp Here 25
SIC 8731 Commercial physical research

D-U-N-S 20-109-0599   (BR)
BANK OF MONTREAL
BMO
11160 87 Ave Nw, Edmonton, AB, T6G 0Y2
(780) 441-6580
Emp Here 25
SIC 6021 National commercial banks

D-U-N-S 24-332-6246   (SL)
BAXANDALL DRUGS LTD
SHOPPERS DRUG MART #312
8210 109 St Nw, Edmonton, AB, T6G 1C8
(780) 433-3121
Emp Here 50   *Sales* 9,840,650
SIC 5912 Drug stores and proprietary stores
Pr Pr Randy Baxandall
  Salwa Baxandall

D-U-N-S 24-997-8446   (HQ)
BUNCHES FLOWER COMPANY
(*Suby of* Bunches Flower Company)
7108 109 St Nw, Edmonton, AB, T6G 1B8
(780) 447-5359
Emp Here 57   *Emp Total* 60
Sales 3,811,504
SIC 5992 Florists

D-U-N-S 25-300-1820   (BR)
CANADIAN IMPERIAL BANK OF COMMERCE
CIBC
8207 112 St Nw, Edmonton, AB, T6G 2L9
(780) 432-1620
Emp Here 20
SIC 6021 National commercial banks

D-U-N-S 20-334-3228   (BR)
EARL'S RESTAURANTS LTD
EARL'S
(*Suby of* Earl's Restaurants Ltd)
8629 112 St Nw, Edmonton, AB, T6G 1K8
(780) 408-3914
Emp Here 130
SIC 5812 Eating places

D-U-N-S 25-289-4936   (BR)
EDMONTON SCHOOL DISTRICT NO. 7
MCKERNAN SCHOOL
11330 76 Ave Nw, Edmonton, AB, T6G 0K1
(780) 435-4163
Emp Here 45
SIC 8211 Elementary and secondary schools

D-U-N-S 20-030-7085   (BR)
EDMONTON SCHOOL DISTRICT NO. 7
GARNEAU ELEMENTARY SCHOOL
10925 87 Ave Nw, Edmonton, AB, T6G 0X4
(780) 433-1390
Emp Here 30
SIC 8211 Elementary and secondary schools

D-U-N-S 24-397-4110   (SL)
FACULTY CLUB OF THE UNIVERSITY OF ALBERTA EDMONTON, THE
11435 Saskatchewan Dr Nw, Edmonton, AB, T6G 2G9
(780) 492-4231
Emp Here 75   *Sales* 2,261,782
SIC 5812 Eating places

D-U-N-S 24-227-5050   (BR)
GOVERNORS OF THE UNIVERSITY OF ALBERTA, THE
THE GOVERNORS OF THE UNIVERSITY OF ALBERTA
63 University Campus Nw Suite 751, Edmonton, AB, T6G 2H1
(780) 492-4413
Emp Here 25

SIC 8221 Colleges and universities

D-U-N-S 20-051-0738   (BR)
GOVERNORS OF THE UNIVERSITY OF ALBERTA, THE
THE GOVERNORS OF THE UNIVERSITY OF ALBERTA
144 University Campus Nw, Edmonton, AB, T6G 2R3
(780) 492-4668
Emp Here 30
SIC 8741 Management services

D-U-N-S 25-070-3733   (BR)
GOVERNORS OF THE UNIVERSITY OF ALBERTA, THE
THE GOVERNORS OF THE UNIVERSITY OF ALBERTA
45 University Campus Nw Rm 410, Edmonton, AB, T6G 2P5
(780) 492-2131
Emp Here 700
SIC 8731 Commercial physical research

D-U-N-S 24-345-0587   (BR)
GOVERNORS OF THE UNIVERSITY OF ALBERTA, THE
THE GOVERNORS OF THE UNIVERSITY OF ALBERTA
115 St 87 Ave, Edmonton, AB, T6G 2H9
(780) 492-3570
Emp Here 40
SIC 7999 Amusement and recreation, nec

D-U-N-S 25-065-4167   (BR)
GOVERNORS OF THE UNIVERSITY OF ALBERTA, THE
THE GOVERNORS OF THE UNIVERSITY OF ALBERTA
8900 114 St Nw, Edmonton, AB, T6G 2V2
(780) 492-4241
Emp Here 100
SIC 8742 Management consulting services

D-U-N-S 25-166-1088   (BR)
GOVERNORS OF THE UNIVERSITY OF ALBERTA, THE
THE GOVERNORS OF THE UNIVERSITY OF ALBERTA
11227 Saskatchewan Dr Unit E344, Edmonton, AB, T6G 2G2
(780) 492-3254
Emp Here 400
SIC 8731 Commercial physical research

D-U-N-S 24-953-7536   (BR)
GOVERNORS OF THE UNIVERSITY OF ALBERTA, THE
UNVERSITY OF ALBERTA
11315 87 Ave Nw Suite 519, Edmonton, AB, T6G 2T9
(780) 433-5624
Emp Here 50
SIC 8221 Colleges and universities

D-U-N-S 25-093-4812   (BR)
GOVERNORS OF THE UNIVERSITY OF ALBERTA, THE
THE GOVERNORS OF THE UNIVERSITY OF ALBERTA
51 University Campus Nw Suite 632, Edmonton, AB, T6G 2G1
(780) 492-3396
Emp Here 200
SIC 8221 Colleges and universities

D-U-N-S 20-536-3349   (BR)
GOVERNORS OF THE UNIVERSITY OF ALBERTA, THE
CENTER FOR HEALTH PROMOTIONS STUDIES
11405 87 Ave Nw Suite 3 300, Edmonton, AB, T6G 1C9
(780) 492-8211
Emp Here 30
SIC 8732 Commercial nonphysical research

D-U-N-S 24-387-4422   (BR)

GOVERNORS OF THE UNIVERSITY OF AL-BERTA, THE
THE GOVERNORS OF THE UNIVERSITY OF ALBERTA
5 Humanities Ctr Unit 6, Edmonton, AB, T6G 2E5
(780) 492-2787
Emp Here 100
SIC 8221 Colleges and universities

D-U-N-S 25-685-4209   (BR)
GOVERNORS OF THE UNIVERSITY OF AL-BERTA, THE
THE GOVERNORS OF THE UNIVERSITY OF ALBERTA
125 University Campus Nw, Edmonton, AB, T6G 2H6
(780) 492-7275
Emp Here 60
SIC 7521 Automobile parking

D-U-N-S 24-132-2986   (BR)
GOVERNORS OF THE UNIVERSITY OF AL-BERTA, THE
THE GOVERNORS OF THE UNIVERSITY OF ALBERTA
132 University Campus Nw, Edmonton, AB, T6G 2R7
(780) 407-6503
Emp Here 30
SIC 8221 Colleges and universities

D-U-N-S 20-913-1536   (BR)
GOVERNORS OF THE UNIVERSITY OF AL-BERTA, THE
THE GOVERNORS OF THE UNIVERSITY OF ALBERTA
131 University Campus Nw, Edmonton, AB, T6G 2H7
(780) 492-3575
Emp Here 80
SIC 8221 Colleges and universities

D-U-N-S 24-329-5156   (BR)
GOVERNORS OF THE UNIVERSITY OF AL-BERTA, THE
THE GOVERNORS OF THE UNIVERSITY OF ALBERTA
66 University Campus Nw, Edmonton, AB, T6G 2J7
(780) 492-3101
Emp Here 50
SIC 5812 Eating places

D-U-N-S 20-875-0229   (BR)
GOVERNORS OF THE UNIVERSITY OF AL-BERTA, THE
THE GOVERNORS OF THE UNIVERSITY OF ALBERTA
1 University Campus Nw, Edmonton, AB, T6G 2E1
(780) 492-2175
Emp Here 50
SIC 8221 Colleges and universities

D-U-N-S 20-553-7009   (BR)
GOVERNORS OF THE UNIVERSITY OF AL-BERTA, THE
THE GOVERNORS OF THE UNIVERSITY OF ALBERTA
52 University Campus Nw, Edmonton, AB, T6G 2J8
(780) 492-3790
Emp Here 400
SIC 8231 Libraries

D-U-N-S 20-058-8296   (BR)
MEDICAL IMAGING CONSULTANTS
8215 112 St Nw Suite 700, Edmonton, AB, T6G 2C8
(780) 432-1121
Emp Here 100
SIC 8011 Offices and clinics of medical doctors

D-U-N-S 20-039-2590   (SL)
NATIONAL PHOENIX 1984 FIREARMS IN-FORMATION AND COMMUNICATION AS-SOCIATION
NATIONAL FIREARMS ASSOCIATION
8540 109 St Nw Suite 7, Edmonton, AB, T6G 1E6
(780) 439-1394
Emp Here 305   *Sales* 16,490,880
SIC 7997 Membership sports and recreation clubs
Pr Blair Hagen

D-U-N-S 24-346-8670   (BR)
PRISZM LP
KFC
8517 109 St Nw, Edmonton, AB, T6G 1E4

Emp Here 20
SIC 5812 Eating places

D-U-N-S 24-121-6329   (BR)
THE GOVERNORS OF THE UNIVERSITY OF ALBERTA
11 University Campus Nw Suite 405, Edmonton, AB, T6G 2E9
(780) 492-9400
Emp Here 20
SIC 8733 Noncommercial research organizations

D-U-N-S 20-535-7465   (BR)
THE GOVERNORS OF THE UNIVERSITY OF ALBERTA
FACULTY OF EDUCATION
106 University Campus Nw Suite 6, Edmonton, AB, T6G 2G5
(780) 492-3751
Emp Here 25
SIC 8221 Colleges and universities

D-U-N-S 25-481-5582   (BR)
THE GOVERNORS OF THE UNIVERSITY OF ALBERTA
DEPT OF HOUSING & FOOD SERVICES
125 University Campus Nw, Edmonton, AB, T6G 2H6
(780) 492-9400
Emp Here 169
SIC 8221 Colleges and universities

D-U-N-S 20-317-1277   (BR)
THE GOVERNORS OF THE UNIVERSITY OF ALBERTA
FACULTY OF LAW
91 University Campus Nw Suite 128, Edmonton, AB, T6G 2H5
(780) 492-0046
Emp Here 100
SIC 8221 Colleges and universities

D-U-N-S 25-064-9159   (BR)
THE GOVERNORS OF THE UNIVERSITY OF ALBERTA
CANADIAN INSTITUTE OF UKRAINIAN STUDIES, DIV OF
430 Pembina Hall University Of Alberta, Edmonton, AB, T6G 2H8
(780) 492-2972
Emp Here 22
SIC 8221 Colleges and universities

D-U-N-S 20-917-5541   (BR)
THE GOVERNORS OF THE UNIVERSITY OF ALBERTA
CENTER FOR HEALTH MEDICINE
8308 114 St Nw Suite 2105, Edmonton, AB, T6G 2V2
(780) 492-9400
Emp Here 20
SIC 8221 Colleges and universities

D-U-N-S 20-184-8459   (BR)
THE GOVERNORS OF THE UNIVERSITY OF ALBERTA
RESEARCH SERVICES
8625 112 St Nw Suite 222, Edmonton, AB, T6G 1K8
(780) 492-5787
Emp Here 100
SIC 8733 Noncommercial research organiza-

tions

D-U-N-S 20-535-7978   (BR)
THE GOVERNORS OF THE UNIVERSITY OF ALBERTA
54 University Campus Nw, Edmonton, AB, T6G 2E6
(780) 492-4776
Emp Here 25
SIC 8221 Colleges and universities

D-U-N-S 24-227-8484   (BR)
THE GOVERNORS OF THE UNIVERSITY OF ALBERTA
DEPARTMENT OF CHEMICAL AND MATERI-ALS ENGINEERING
21 University Campus Nw, Edmonton, AB, T6G 2G6
(780) 492-8423
Emp Here 50
SIC 8221 Colleges and universities

D-U-N-S 20-515-2775   (BR)
THE GOVERNORS OF THE UNIVERSITY OF ALBERTA
DEPARTMENT OF SCIENCE
32 University Campus Nw Suite 1, Edmonton, AB, T6G 2E3
(780) 492-3111
Emp Here 50
SIC 8221 Colleges and universities

D-U-N-S 24-627-9996   (SL)
UPPER CRUST CATERERS LTD
UPPER CRUST CAFE
10909 86 Ave Nw, Edmonton, AB, T6G 0W8
(780) 758-5599
Emp Here 75   *Sales* 2,261,782
SIC 5812 Eating places

D-U-N-S 20-004-7277   (BR)
WENDY'S RESTAURANTS OF CANADA INC
WENDY'S
(*Suby of* The Wendy's Company)
8427 112 St Nw, Edmonton, AB, T6G 1K5
(780) 434-6608
Emp Here 28
SIC 5812 Eating places

D-U-N-S 24-367-4590   (HQ)
WESTCORP PROPERTIES INC
(*Suby of* Westcorp Properties Inc)
8215 112 St Nw Suite 200, Edmonton, AB, T6G 2C8

Emp Here 35   *Emp Total* 450
Sales 57,030,960
SIC 6531 Real estate agents and managers
Pr Pr Phillip Milroy

Edmonton, AB T6H

D-U-N-S 25-505-7184   (SL)
A.M.A. INSURANCE AGENCY LTD
10310 39a Ave, Edmonton, AB, T6H 5X9
(780) 430-5555
Emp Here 32   *Sales* 3,465,004
SIC 6411 Insurance agents, brokers, and service

D-U-N-S 25-505-7226   (HQ)
ALBERTA MOTOR ASSOCIATION TRAVEL AGENCY LTD
AMA TRAVEL
10310 39a Ave, Edmonton, AB, T6H 5X9
(780) 430-5555
Emp Here 50   *Emp Total* 1,500
Sales 53,626,115
SIC 4724 Travel agencies
Pr Pr Don Smitten
VP Fin Doug Creighton
Genl Mgr Michelle Chimko

D-U-N-S 20-920-6858   (BR)
ALBERTS RESTAURANTS LTD

ALBERTS FAMILY RESTAURANT
(*Suby of* Alberts Restaurants Ltd)
10362 51 Ave Nw, Edmonton, AB, T6H 5X6
(780) 437-7081
Emp Here 75
SIC 5812 Eating places

D-U-N-S 24-582-6540   (HQ)
ALCO INC
6925 104 St Nw, Edmonton, AB, T6H 2L5
(780) 435-3502
Emp Here 60   *Emp Total* 5
Sales 49,102,551
SIC 3541 Machine tools, Metal cutting type
*   Robert Taubner

D-U-N-S 25-296-9670   (BR)
BANK OF NOVA SCOTIA, THE
SCOTIABANK
6304 104 St Nw, Edmonton, AB, T6H 2K9

Emp Here 20
SIC 6021 National commercial banks

D-U-N-S 20-044-7352   (BR)
CAPITAL CARE GROUP INC
CAPITAL CARE GRANDVIEW
6215 124 St Nw, Edmonton, AB, T6H 3V1
(780) 496-7100
Emp Here 300
SIC 8051 Skilled nursing care facilities

D-U-N-S 20-649-8292   (BR)
COMMERCE CORNELL LTEE
111 St 51st Ave Unit 5, Edmonton, AB, T6H 4M6
(780) 437-9406
Emp Here 60
SIC 5137 Women's and children's clothing

D-U-N-S 20-048-8018   (BR)
CORUS MEDIA HOLDINGS INC
SHAW MEDIA INC
5325 Allard Way Nw, Edmonton, AB, T6H 5B8
(780) 436-1250
Emp Here 200
SIC 7822 Motion picture and tape distribution

D-U-N-S 20-341-0167   (BR)
DELTA HOTELS LIMITED
TRAVELODGE EDMONTON SOUTH
10320 45 Ave Nw, Edmonton, AB, T6H 5K3
(780) 436-9770
Emp Here 50
SIC 7011 Hotels and motels

D-U-N-S 20-699-9174   (BR)
DELTA HOTELS LIMITED
DELTA EDMONTON SOUTH HOTEL AND CONFERENCE CENTER
4404 Gateway Blvd Nw, Edmonton, AB, T6H 5C2
(780) 434-6415
Emp Here 200
SIC 7011 Hotels and motels

D-U-N-S 20-712-9284   (BR)
EDMONTON   CATHOLIC   SEPARATE SCHOOL DISTRICT NO.7
ST. MONICA CATHOLIC ELEMENTARY SCHOOL
(*Suby of* Edmonton Catholic Separate School District No.7)
14710 53 Ave Nw, Edmonton, AB, T6H 4C6
(780) 436-7888
Emp Here 50
SIC 8211 Elementary and secondary schools

D-U-N-S 20-712-4434   (BR)
EDMONTON SCHOOL DISTRICT NO. 7
ALLENDALE JUNIOR HIGH SCHOOL
6415 106 St Nw, Edmonton, AB, T6H 2V5
(780) 434-6756
Emp Here 40
SIC 8211 Elementary and secondary schools

D-U-N-S 25-013-8583   (BR)
EDMONTON SCHOOL DISTRICT NO. 7

MOUNT PLEASANT ELEMENTARY SCHOOL
10541 60a Ave Nw, Edmonton, AB, T6H 1K4
(780) 434-6766
Emp Here 25
SIC 8211 Elementary and secondary schools

D-U-N-S 20-102-3830   (BR)
EDMONTON SCHOOL DISTRICT NO. 7
BROOKSIDE ELEMENTARY SCHOOL
5504 143 St Nw, Edmonton, AB, T6H 4E5
(780) 434-0464
Emp Here 25
SIC 8211 Elementary and secondary schools

D-U-N-S 20-069-3377   (BR)
EDMONTON SCHOOL DISTRICT NO. 7
TEVEI MILLER HERITAGE SCHOOL
6240 113 St Nw, Edmonton, AB, T6H 3L2
(780) 436-0465
Emp Here 80
SIC 8211 Elementary and secondary schools

D-U-N-S 20-069-3385   (BR)
EDMONTON SCHOOL DISTRICT NO. 7
GRANDVIEW HEIGHTS SCHOOL
6225 127 St Nw, Edmonton, AB, T6H 3W8
(780) 434-1502
Emp Here 20
SIC 8211 Elementary and secondary schools

D-U-N-S 25-013-8179   (BR)
EDMONTON SCHOOL DISTRICT NO. 7
MALMO SCHOOL
4716 115 St Nw, Edmonton, AB, T6H 3N8
(780) 434-1362
Emp Here 20
SIC 8211 Elementary and secondary schools

D-U-N-S 25-013-7858   (BR)
EDMONTON SCHOOL DISTRICT NO. 7
LANSDOWNE SCHOOL
12323 51 Ave Nw, Edmonton, AB, T6H 0M6
(780) 434-3160
Emp Here 21
SIC 8211 Elementary and secondary schools

D-U-N-S 20-712-5670   (BR)
EDMONTON SCHOOL DISTRICT NO. 7
RIVERBEND JUNIOR HIGH SCHOOL
14820 53 Ave Nw, Edmonton, AB, T6H 4C6
(780) 434-7914
Emp Here 50
SIC 8211 Elementary and secondary schools

D-U-N-S 25-073-4662   (BR)
EDMONTON SCHOOL DISTRICT NO. 7
ALBERTA SCHOOL FOR THE DEAF
6240 113 St Nw, Edmonton, AB, T6H 3L2
(780) 439-3323
Emp Here 42
SIC 8211 Elementary and secondary schools

D-U-N-S 20-293-6402   (BR)
EDMONTON SCHOOL DISTRICT NO. 7
AVALON SCHOOL
5425 114 St Nw, Edmonton, AB, T6H 3M1
(780) 434-8402
Emp Here 35
SIC 8211 Elementary and secondary schools

D-U-N-S 25-013-7932   (BR)
EDMONTON SCHOOL DISTRICT NO. 7
LENDRUM SCHOOL
11330 54 Ave Nw, Edmonton, AB, T6H 0V7
(780) 434-3588
Emp Here 24
SIC 8211 Elementary and secondary schools

D-U-N-S 20-028-3633   (BR)
EDMONTON SCHOOL DISTRICT NO. 7
MCKEE ELEMENTARY SCHOOL
10725 51 Ave Nw, Edmonton, AB, T6H 0L3
(780) 435-7140
Emp Here 25
SIC 8211 Elementary and secondary schools

D-U-N-S 20-746-2151   (HQ)
FAIRMONT ELECTROPLATING (1990) LTD

(Suby of Edmonton Electro-Plating Ltd)
5625 103a St Nw, Edmonton, AB, T6H 2J6
(780) 434-1495
Emp Here 48   Emp Total 7
Sales 6,125,139
SIC 3471 Plating and polishing
Pr Pr Anton Petovar
  Frederick Petovar
Treas David Petrovar

D-U-N-S 20-509-7186   (BR)
GOVERNMENT OF THE PROVINCE OF AL-BERTA
CHIEF MEDICAL EXAMINER OFFICE
7007 116 St Nw, Edmonton, AB, T6H 5R8

Emp Here 25
SIC 8049 Offices of health practitioner

D-U-N-S 20-969-7163   (BR)
GOVERNMENT OF THE PROVINCE OF AL-BERTA
LIVESTOCK AIR QUALITY SPECIALIST
7000 113 St Nw Suite 3, Edmonton, AB, T6H 5T6
(780) 427-4215
Emp Here 25
SIC 8399 Social services, nec

D-U-N-S 20-120-9728   (BR)
GOVERNMENT OF THE PROVINCE OF AL-BERTA
DEPARTMENT OF INFRASTRUCTURE
6950 113 St Nw, Edmonton, AB, T6H 5V7
(780) 427-3900
Emp Here 400
SIC 7389 Business services, nec

D-U-N-S 25-064-9233   (BR)
GOVERNORS OF THE UNIVERSITY OF AL-BERTA, THE
THE GOVERNORS OF THE UNIVERSITY OF ALBERTA
6403 105 St Nw, Edmonton, AB, T6H 2N8

Emp Here 250
SIC 8221 Colleges and universities

D-U-N-S 25-194-1225   (BR)
HOME DEPOT OF CANADA INC
HOME DEPOT
(Suby of The Home Depot Inc)
6725 104 St Nw, Edmonton, AB, T6H 2L3
(780) 431-4743
Emp Here 200
SIC 5251 Hardware stores

D-U-N-S 20-616-4931   (BR)
HUDSON'S BAY COMPANY
BAY, THE
150 Southgate Shopping Ctr Nw, Edmonton, AB, T6H 4M7
(780) 435-9211
Emp Here 110
SIC 5311 Department stores

D-U-N-S 24-804-7941   (BR)
ITALIAN CENTRE SHOP SOUTH LTD
5028 104a St Nw, Edmonton, AB, T6H 6A2
(780) 989-4869
Emp Here 100
SIC 5411 Grocery stores

D-U-N-S 25-093-3301   (BR)
IVANHOE CAMBRIDGE II INC.
IVANHOE CAMBRIDGE
5015 111 St Nw Suite 51, Edmonton, AB, T6H 4M6
(780) 435-3721
Emp Here 50
SIC 6512 Nonresidential building operators

D-U-N-S 20-066-4113   (BR)
KUMON CANADA INC
RIVERBEND KUMON MATH & READING CENTRE
5607 Riverbend Rd Nw, Edmonton, AB, T6H 5K4

(780) 433-5182
Emp Here 33
SIC 8211 Elementary and secondary schools

D-U-N-S 24-392-3281   (BR)
LOBLAWS INC
REAL CANADIAN SUPERSTORE, THE
4821 Calgary Trail Nw Suite 1570, Edmonton, AB, T6H 5W8
(780) 430-2797
Emp Here 400
SIC 5411 Grocery stores

D-U-N-S 25-092-7329   (BR)
LULULEMON ATHLETICA CANADA INC
LULULEMON
223a 109 St, Edmonton, AB, T6H 3B9
(780) 471-1200
Emp Here 30
SIC 5699 Miscellaneous apparel and accessory stores

D-U-N-S 20-974-4585   (BR)
MATRIX SOLUTIONS INC
6325 Gateway Blvd Nw Suite 142, Edmonton, AB, T6H 5H6
(780) 490-6830
Emp Here 30
SIC 8748 Business consulting, nec

D-U-N-S 20-197-2952   (BR)
MCDONALD'S RESTAURANTS OF CANADA LIMITED
MCDONALD'S 8618
(Suby of McDonald's Corporation)
6104 109 St Nw, Edmonton, AB, T6H 1M2
(780) 414-8428
Emp Here 35
SIC 5812 Eating places

D-U-N-S 25-315-1526   (BR)
MEDICENTRES CANADA INC
CALGARY TRAIL MEDICENTRE
10407 51 Ave Nw Suite 1, Edmonton, AB, T6H 0K4
(780) 436-8071
Emp Here 25
SIC 8011 Offices and clinics of medical doctors

D-U-N-S 24-018-9915   (SL)
RAWLCO RADIO LTD
MAGIC 99
5241 Calgary Trail Nw Suite 700, Edmonton, AB, T6H 5G8
(780) 433-7877
Emp Here 20   Sales 1,696,192
SIC 4899 Communication services, nec

D-U-N-S 25-287-9143   (BR)
RAYMOND SALONS LTD
HENNESSEY SALONS
(Suby of Raymond Salons Ltd)
5015 111 St Nw Suite 458, Edmonton, AB, T6H 4M6
(780) 436-1515
Emp Here 25
SIC 7231 Beauty shops

D-U-N-S 25-287-9184   (BR)
RAYMOND SALONS LTD
HENNESSEY
(Suby of Raymond Salons Ltd)
100 Southgate Shopping Ctr Nw, Edmonton, AB, T6H 4M8

Emp Here 30
SIC 7231 Beauty shops

D-U-N-S 24-962-0063   (BR)
RAYMOND SALONS LTD
HENNESSEY SALON AND SPA
(Suby of Raymond Salons Ltd)
100 Southgate Shopping Ctr Nw Unit 458, Edmonton, AB, T6H 4M8
(780) 435-0286
Emp Here 31
SIC 7231 Beauty shops

D-U-N-S 25-321-4498   (BR)
REVERA INC
SOUTH TERRACE CONTINUING CARE CENTRE
5905 112 St Nw, Edmonton, AB, T6H 3J4
(780) 434-1451
Emp Here 50
SIC 8051 Skilled nursing care facilities

D-U-N-S 25-066-9009   (BR)
REXALL PHARMACY GROUP LTD
SOUTHGATE REXALL DRUG STORE
(Suby of McKesson Corporation)
5015 111 St Nw, Edmonton, AB, T6H 4M6
(780) 434-0451
Emp Here 20
SIC 5912 Drug stores and proprietary stores

D-U-N-S 20-303-0569   (BR)
SEARS CANADA INC
SEARS STORE 1429
5015 111 St Nw Unit 100, Edmonton, AB, T6H 4M6
(780) 438-2098
Emp Here 200
SIC 5311 Department stores

D-U-N-S 20-974-8727   (BR)
SODEXO CANADA LTD
DALTONS CONFERENCE CENTRE
4485 Gateway Blvd Nw, Edmonton, AB, T6H 5C3
(780) 431-1100
Emp Here 20
SIC 5812 Eating places

D-U-N-S 20-543-6392   (BR)
STAPLES CANADA INC
STAPLES THE BUSINESS DEPOT
(Suby of Staples, Inc.)
6510 Gateway Blvd Nw Suite 142, Edmonton, AB, T6H 5Z5
(780) 414-1601
Emp Here 30
SIC 5943 Stationery stores

D-U-N-S 24-005-3041   (SL)
T. T. P. INVESTMENTS LTD
SAWMILL RESTAURANT & LOUNGE
4810 Calgary Trail Nw, Edmonton, AB, T6H 5H5
(780) 463-4499
Emp Here 70   Sales 2,115,860
SIC 5812 Eating places

D-U-N-S 24-349-5756   (SL)
TOUCH CANADA BROADCASTING INC
5316 Calgary Trail Nw, Edmonton, AB, T6H 4J8
(780) 469-5200
Emp Here 65   Sales 4,851,006
SIC 4832 Radio broadcasting stations

D-U-N-S 20-321-5590   (BR)
WEST FRASER MILLS LTD
ALBERTA PLYWOOD
6325 Gateway Blvd Nw Suite 140, Edmonton, AB, T6H 5H6
(780) 468-3311
Emp Here 20
SIC 2421 Sawmills and planing mills, general

D-U-N-S 24-281-9399   (HQ)
WESTERN CRYSTAL GLASS LTD
6424 Gateway Blvd Nw, Edmonton, AB, T6H 2H9
(780) 436-8780
Emp Here 20   Emp Total 5
Sales 16,785,360
SIC 5039 Construction materials, nec
Treas Terry Bean
Pr Edwin Bean
Dir Robert Edwards
Dir Harry Mann
Dir Gerhart Tillner

Edmonton, AB T6J

D-U-N-S 20-002-5083   (BR)
170TH C.T. GRILL INC
CHILIS TEXAS GRILL
10333 34 Ave Nw, Edmonton, AB, T6J 6V1
(780) 430-0606
Emp Here 100
SIC 5812 Eating places

D-U-N-S 24-807-8800   (SL)
23RD AVENUE PIZZA LTD
BOSTON PIZZA
11023 23 Ave Nw, Edmonton, AB, T6J 6P9
(780) 435-5005
Emp Here 60   *Sales* 1,824,018
SIC 5812 Eating places

D-U-N-S 25-538-5940   (SL)
710712 ALBERTA INC
GATEWAY RECREATION CENTRE
3414 Gateway Blvd Nw Suite 406, Edmonton,
AB, T6J 6R5
(780) 435-1922
Emp Here 50   *Sales* 1,507,726
SIC 7933 Bowling centers

D-U-N-S 25-408-6374   (SL)
742718 ALBERTA LTD
HOLIDAY INN THE PALACE
4235 Gateway Blvd Nw, Edmonton, AB, T6J
5H2
(780) 438-1222
Emp Here 78   *Sales* 3,429,153
SIC 7011 Hotels and motels

D-U-N-S 24-232-2613   (BR)
ALBERTA HEALTH SERVICES
ST JOSEPHS AUXILIARY HOSPITAL
10707 29 Ave Nw, Edmonton, AB, T6J 6W1
(780) 430-9110
Emp Here 200
SIC 8062 General medical and surgical hospitals

D-U-N-S 20-903-1876   (BR)
ALBERTA HEALTH SERVICES
TWIN BROOKS PUBLIC HEALTH CENTRE
1110 113 St Nw, Edmonton, AB, T6J 7J4
(780) 342-1560
Emp Here 30
SIC 8621 Professional organizations

D-U-N-S 24-079-5257   (BR)
BANQUE TORONTO-DOMINION, LA
TORONTO-DOMINION BANK, THE
(*Suby of* Toronto-Dominion Bank, The)
4108 Calgary Trail Nw, Edmonton, AB, T6J
6Y6
(780) 434-6481
Emp Here 20
SIC 6021 National commercial banks

D-U-N-S 20-589-4889   (BR)
BANQUE TORONTO-DOMINION, LA
TD CANADA TRUST
(*Suby of* Toronto-Dominion Bank, The)
2325 111 St Nw, Edmonton, AB, T6J 5E5
(780) 448-8282
Emp Here 20
SIC 6021 National commercial banks

D-U-N-S 25-270-0984   (BR)
BEST BUY CANADA LTD
FUTURE SHOP
(*Suby of* Best Buy Co., Inc.)
3451 Calgary Trail Nw, Edmonton, AB, T6J
6Z2

Emp Here 100
SIC 5731 Radio, television, and electronic stores

D-U-N-S 20-029-0430   (BR)
CARA OPERATIONS LIMITED
(*Suby of* Cara Holdings Limited)
3203 Calgary Trail Nw, Edmonton, AB, T6J

5X8
(780) 477-9402
Emp Here 40
SIC 5812 Eating places

D-U-N-S 20-789-4044   (BR)
CHIRO FOODS LIMITED
A & W RESTAURANT
4130 Calgary Trail Nw Suite 606, Edmonton,
AB, T6J 6Y6
(780) 438-3102
Emp Here 21
SIC 5812 Eating places

D-U-N-S 20-912-7658   (BR)
DENCAN RESTAURANTS INC
DENNY'S RESTAURANT
(*Suby of* Northland Properties Corporation)
3604 Gateway Blvd Nw, Edmonton, AB, T6J
7A9
(780) 438-3663
Emp Here 50
SIC 5812 Eating places

D-U-N-S 20-028-9812   (BR)
**EDMONTON CATHOLIC SEPARATE
SCHOOL DISTRICT NO.7**
*ST. BONIFACE CATHOLIC ELEMENTARY
SCHOOL*
(*Suby of* Edmonton Catholic Separate School
District No.7)
11810 40 Ave Nw, Edmonton, AB, T6J 0R9
(780) 434-0294
Emp Here 25
SIC 8211 Elementary and secondary schools

D-U-N-S 20-029-3194   (BR)
**EDMONTON CATHOLIC SEPARATE
SCHOOL DISTRICT NO.7**
*ST. AUGUSTINE CATHOLIC ELEMENTARY
SCHOOL*
(*Suby of* Edmonton Catholic Separate School
District No.7)
3808 106 St Nw, Edmonton, AB, T6J 1A5
(780) 435-4949
Emp Here 30
SIC 8211 Elementary and secondary schools

D-U-N-S 20-028-3864   (BR)
**EDMONTON CATHOLIC SEPARATE
SCHOOL DISTRICT NO.7**
*ST. STANISLAUS CATHOLIC ELEMENTARY
SCHOOL*
(*Suby of* Edmonton Catholic Separate School
District No.7)
3855 114 St Nw, Edmonton, AB, T6J 1M3
(780) 434-0295
Emp Here 23
SIC 8211 Elementary and secondary schools

D-U-N-S 20-028-4169   (BR)
**EDMONTON CATHOLIC SEPARATE
SCHOOL DISTRICT NO.7**
*ST TERESA CATHOLIC ELEMENTARY
SCHOOL*
(*Suby of* Edmonton Catholic Separate School
District No.7)
11350 25 Ave Nw, Edmonton, AB, T6J 5B1
(780) 437-6022
Emp Here 43
SIC 8211 Elementary and secondary schools

D-U-N-S 25-013-8021   (BR)
**EDMONTON CATHOLIC SEPARATE
SCHOOL DISTRICT NO.7**
LOUIS ST. LAURENT SCHOOL
(*Suby of* Edmonton Catholic Separate School
District No.7)
11230 43 Ave Nw, Edmonton, AB, T6J 0X8
(780) 435-3964
Emp Here 82
SIC 8211 Elementary and secondary schools

D-U-N-S 20-591-9991   (BR)
EDMONTON SCHOOL DISTRICT NO. 7
SWEET GRASS ELEMENTARY SCHOOL
11351 31 Ave Nw, Edmonton, AB, T6J 4T6

(780) 437-0366
Emp Here 24
SIC 8211 Elementary and secondary schools

D-U-N-S 20-592-0148   (BR)
EDMONTON SCHOOL DISTRICT NO. 7
*VERNON BARFORD JUNIOR HIGH
SCHOOL*
32 Fairway Dr Nw, Edmonton, AB, T6J 2C1
(780) 413-2211
Emp Here 40
SIC 8211 Elementary and secondary schools

D-U-N-S 20-028-3716   (BR)
EDMONTON SCHOOL DISTRICT NO. 7
DUGGAN ELEMENTARY SCHOOL
10616 36a Ave Nw, Edmonton, AB, T6J 0C9
(780) 434-0319
Emp Here 22
SIC 8211 Elementary and secondary schools

D-U-N-S 20-352-9768   (BR)
EDMONTON SCHOOL DISTRICT NO. 7
RICHARD SECORD ELEMENTARY
4025 117 St Nw, Edmonton, AB, T6J 1T4
(780) 436-9839
Emp Here 40
SIC 8211 Elementary and secondary schools

D-U-N-S 20-028-4219   (BR)
EDMONTON SCHOOL DISTRICT NO. 7
KEHEEWIN ELEMENTARY SCHOOL
1910 105 St Nw, Edmonton, AB, T6J 5J8
(780) 438-3874
Emp Here 28
SIC 8211 Elementary and secondary schools

D-U-N-S 20-609-7516   (BR)
EDMONTON SCHOOL DISTRICT NO. 7
NICHOLSON, GEORGE P SCHOOL
1120 113 St Nw, Edmonton, AB, T6J 7J4
(780) 439-9314
Emp Here 30
SIC 8211 Elementary and secondary schools

D-U-N-S 20-742-6409   (BR)
EDMONTON SCHOOL DISTRICT NO. 7
*HARRY AINLAY COMPOSITE HIGH
SCHOOL*
4350 111 St Nw, Edmonton, AB, T6J 1E8
(780) 413-2700
Emp Here 150
SIC 8211 Elementary and secondary schools

D-U-N-S 20-028-3807   (BR)
EDMONTON SCHOOL DISTRICT NO. 7
STEINHAUER ELEMENTARY SCHOOL
10717 32a Ave Nw, Edmonton, AB, T6J 4A6
(780) 437-1080
Emp Here 25
SIC 8211 Elementary and secondary schools

D-U-N-S 20-154-7960   (BR)
EDMONTON SCHOOL DISTRICT NO. 7
WESTBROOK ELEMENTARY SCHOOL
11915 40 Ave Nw, Edmonton, AB, T6J 0S1
(780) 438-4200
Emp Here 35
SIC 8211 Elementary and secondary schools

D-U-N-S 20-029-2535   (BR)
EDMONTON SCHOOL DISTRICT NO. 7
GREENFIELD ELEMENTARY SCHOOL
3735 114 St Nw, Edmonton, AB, T6J 2G6
(780) 434-8581
Emp Here 36
SIC 8211 Elementary and secondary schools

D-U-N-S 20-913-6642   (BR)
EDMONTON SCHOOL DISTRICT NO. 7
D.S. MACKENZIE SCHOOL
4020 106 St Nw, Edmonton, AB, T6J 1A6
(780) 438-9103
Emp Here 35
SIC 8211 Elementary and secondary schools

D-U-N-S 24-340-2455   (BR)
FGL SPORTS LTD
SPORT-CHEK SOUTH PARK CENTRE

3803 Calgary Trail Nw Unit 190, Edmonton,
AB, T6J 5M8
(780) 435-8488
Emp Here 50
SIC 5941 Sporting goods and bicycle shops

D-U-N-S 24-391-2891   (BR)
GOODLIFE FITNESS CENTRES INC
3803 Calgary Trail Nw Unit 180, Edmonton,
AB, T6J 5M8
(780) 466-4124
Emp Here 35
SIC 7991 Physical fitness facilities

D-U-N-S 24-929-5130   (BR)
GREAT PACIFIC INDUSTRIES INC
SAVE-ON-FOODS
3361 Calgary Trail Nw, Edmonton, AB, T6J
6V1
(780) 437-3322
Emp Here 230
SIC 5411 Grocery stores

D-U-N-S 25-064-8219   (BR)
INDIGO BOOKS & MUSIC INC
CHAPTERS
(*Suby of* Indigo Books & Music Inc)
3227 Calgary Trail Nw, Edmonton, AB, T6J
5X8
(780) 431-9694
Emp Here 50
SIC 5942 Book stores

D-U-N-S 24-803-6043   (BR)
JYSK LINEN'N FURNITURE INC
JYSK LINEN'N FURNITURE INC
3803 Calgary Trail Nw Unit 500, Edmonton,
AB, T6J 5M8
(780) 701-1791
Emp Here 20
SIC 5712 Furniture stores

D-U-N-S 24-915-9443   (BR)
KITCHEN CRAFT OF CANADA
2866 Calgary Trail Nw Suite 2862, Edmonton,
AB, T6J 6V7
(780) 465-6531
Emp Here 70
SIC 5031 Lumber, plywood, and millwork

D-U-N-S 25-318-1663   (BR)
**MCDONALD'S RESTAURANTS OF
CANADA LIMITED**
MCDONALD'S
(*Suby of* McDonald's Corporation)
2323 111 St Nw, Edmonton, AB, T6J 5E5

Emp Here 80
SIC 5812 Eating places

D-U-N-S 25-311-2460   (BR)
**MCDONALD'S RESTAURANTS OF
CANADA LIMITED**
MCDONALD'S #8377
(*Suby of* McDonald's Corporation)
11007 23 Ave Nw, Edmonton, AB, T6J 6P9
(780) 414-8377
Emp Here 70
SIC 5812 Eating places

D-U-N-S 24-323-4304   (BR)
MEDICAL IMAGING CONSULTANTS
2377 111 St Nw Suite 201, Edmonton, AB,
T6J 5E5
(780) 450-1500
Emp Here 20
SIC 8011 Offices and clinics of medical doctors

D-U-N-S 25-315-1914   (BR)
MEDICENTRES CANADA INC
2041 111 St Nw, Edmonton, AB, T6J 4V9
(780) 438-2306
Emp Here 20
SIC 8011 Offices and clinics of medical doctors

D-U-N-S 25-064-7203   (BR)
MOORES THE SUIT PEOPLE INC

MOORES CLOTHING FOR MEN
(Suby of Tailored Brands, Inc.)
3279 Calgary Trail Nw Suite 3281, Edmonton,
AB, T6J 5X8
(780) 439-1818
Emp Here 20
SIC 5611 Men's and boys' clothing stores

D-U-N-S 25-453-8812   (BR)
RED LOBSTER HOSPITALITY LLC
RED LOBSTER RESTAURANTS
(Suby of Red Lobster Seafood Co., LLC)
4111 Calgary Trl Nw, Edmonton, AB, T6J 6S6
(780) 436-8510
Emp Here 80
SIC 5812 Eating places

D-U-N-S 25-453-8697   (BR)
RED LOBSTER HOSPITALITY LLC
OLIVE GARDEN RESTAURANT
(Suby of Red Lobster Seafood Co., LLC)
4110 Calgary Trl Nw, Edmonton, AB, T6J 6Y6
(780) 437-3434
Emp Here 110
SIC 5812 Eating places

D-U-N-S 24-731-1749   (SL)
**RED ROBIN RESTAURANT (WHITEMUD
LANDING) LTD**
RED ROBIN
4211 106 St Nw Unit 230, Edmonton, AB, T6J
6P3
(780) 438-2473
Emp Here 70   Sales 2,115,860
SIC 5812 Eating places

D-U-N-S 25-453-8903   (BR)
ROYAL LEPAGE LIMITED
ROYAL LEPAGE NORALTA
3018 Calgary Trail Nw, Edmonton, AB, T6J
6V4
(780) 915-4980
Emp Here 65
SIC 6531 Real estate agents and managers

D-U-N-S 20-069-3542   (BR)
SHELL CANADA LIMITED
SHELL CANADA
2203 110 St Nw, Edmonton, AB, T6J 6P4
(780) 435-8319
Emp Here 20
SIC 5541 Gasoline service stations

D-U-N-S 20-362-3686   (BR)
SOBEYS CAPITAL INCORPORATED
HERITAGE SOBEYS
2011 111 St Nw, Edmonton, AB, T6J 4V9
(780) 435-1166
Emp Here 150
SIC 5411 Grocery stores

D-U-N-S 20-806-2351   (BR)
SOBEYS CAPITAL INCORPORATED
SOBEYS STORE# 3107
2011 111 St Nw, Edmonton, AB, T6J 4V9
(780) 435-1224
Emp Here 25
SIC 5411 Grocery stores

D-U-N-S 20-871-3540   (BR)
SOBEYS WEST INC
2304 109 St Nw, Edmonton, AB, T6J 3S8
(780) 430-4278
Emp Here 130
SIC 5411 Grocery stores

D-U-N-S 25-498-9247   (BR)
STAPLES CANADA INC
STAPLES THE BUSINESS DEPOT
(Suby of Staples, Inc.)
4122 Calgary Trail Nw, Edmonton, AB, T6J
6Y6
(780) 433-4554
Emp Here 50
SIC 5943 Stationery stores

D-U-N-S 25-297-8473   (BR)
TOYS 'R' US (CANADA) LTD

TOYS 'R' US
(Suby of Toys "r" Us, Inc.)
3940 Gateway Blvd Nw, Edmonton, AB, T6J
7A9
(780) 944-9424
Emp Here 50
SIC 5961 Catalog and mail-order houses

D-U-N-S 25-294-0754   (BR)
**WINNERS MERCHANTS INTERNATIONAL
L.P.**
WINNERS
(Suby of The TJX Companies Inc)
3355 Calgary Trail Nw, Edmonton, AB, T6J
6V1
(780) 440-4490
Emp Here 58
SIC 5651 Family clothing stores

D-U-N-S 20-860-4483   (BR)
**WINNERS MERCHANTS INTERNATIONAL
L.P.**
HOMESENSE
(Suby of The TJX Companies Inc)
3411 Calgary Trail Nw, Edmonton, AB, T6J
6Z2
(780) 485-8843
Emp Here 25
SIC 5651 Family clothing stores

Edmonton, AB T6K

D-U-N-S 20-572-2411   (BR)
BANK OF NOVA SCOTIA, THE
SCOTIABANK
2331 66 St Nw Suite 119, Edmonton, AB, T6K
4B4
(780) 448-7960
Emp Here 30
SIC 6021 National commercial banks

D-U-N-S 20-589-5449   (BR)
BANQUE TORONTO-DOMINION, LA
TD CANADA TRUST
(Suby of Toronto-Dominion Bank, The)
133 Millbourne Shopping Centre Nw, Edmon-
ton, AB, T6K 3L6
(780) 462-4625
Emp Here 20
SIC 6021 National commercial banks

D-U-N-S 20-029-0562   (BR)
**EDMONTON CATHOLIC SEPARATE
SCHOOL DISTRICT NO.7**
ST. CLEMENT ELEMENTARY JUNIOR HIGH
SCHOOL
(Suby of Edmonton Catholic Separate School
District No.7)
7620 Mill Woods Road South Nw, Edmonton,
AB, T6K 2P7
(780) 462-3806
Emp Here 48
SIC 8211 Elementary and secondary schools

D-U-N-S 20-910-1372   (BR)
**EDMONTON CATHOLIC SEPARATE
SCHOOL DISTRICT NO.7**
HOLY TRINITY CATHOLIC HIGH SCHOOL
(Suby of Edmonton Catholic Separate School
District No.7)
7007 28 Ave Nw, Edmonton, AB, T6K 4A5
(780) 462-5777
Emp Here 50
SIC 8211 Elementary and secondary schools

D-U-N-S 20-028-4284   (BR)
**EDMONTON CATHOLIC SEPARATE
SCHOOL DISTRICT NO.7**
FRERE ANTOINE CATHOLIC ELEMENTARY
SCHOOL
(Suby of Edmonton Catholic Separate School
District No.7)
2850 Mill Woods Rd Nw, Edmonton, AB, T6K
4A1

(780) 463-2957
Emp Here 40
SIC 8211 Elementary and secondary schools

D-U-N-S 20-028-3906   (BR)
**EDMONTON CATHOLIC SEPARATE
SCHOOL DISTRICT NO.7**
ST ELIZABETH CATHOLIC ELEMENTARY
SCHOOL
(Suby of Edmonton Catholic Separate School
District No.7)
7712 36 Ave Nw, Edmonton, AB, T6K 1H7
(780) 462-7022
Emp Here 22
SIC 8211 Elementary and secondary schools

D-U-N-S 20-591-9280   (BR)
EDMONTON SCHOOL DISTRICT NO. 7
SATOO ELEMENTARY SCHOOL
8515 17 Ave Nw Ste N, Edmonton, AB, T6K
2C7
(780) 462-5125
Emp Here 20
SIC 8211 Elementary and secondary schools

D-U-N-S 20-647-3964   (BR)
EDMONTON SCHOOL DISTRICT NO. 7
J PERCY PAGE
2707 Mill Woods Rd Nw, Edmonton, AB, T6K
4A6
(780) 462-3322
Emp Here 75
SIC 8211 Elementary and secondary schools

D-U-N-S 20-591-7474   (BR)
EDMONTON SCHOOL DISTRICT NO. 7
EKOTA SCHOOL
1395 Knottwood Road East Nw, Edmonton,
AB, T6K 2P5
(780) 462-5112
Emp Here 20
SIC 8211 Elementary and secondary schools

D-U-N-S 20-028-3765   (BR)
EDMONTON SCHOOL DISTRICT NO. 7
MALCOLM TWEDDLE ELEMENTARY
SCHOOL
2340 Millbourne Road West Nw, Edmonton,
AB, T6K 1Y9
(780) 462-3270
Emp Here 25
SIC 8211 Elementary and secondary schools

D-U-N-S 25-013-8492   (BR)
EDMONTON SCHOOL DISTRICT NO. 7
MENISA ELEMENTARY SCHOOL
933 Knottwood Road South Nw, Edmonton,
AB, T6K 3Y9
(780) 463-8474
Emp Here 20
SIC 8211 Elementary and secondary schools

D-U-N-S 20-028-3724   (BR)
EDMONTON SCHOOL DISTRICT NO. 7
GRACE MARTIN ELEMENTARY SCHOOL
8210 36 Ave Nw, Edmonton, AB, T6K 0C7
(780) 462-7121
Emp Here 25
SIC 8211 Elementary and secondary schools

D-U-N-S 20-651-6135   (BR)
EDMONTON SCHOOL DISTRICT NO. 7
MILLWOODS CHRISTIAN ELEMENTARY-
JUNIOR HIGH SCHOOL
8704 Mill Woods Rd Nw, Edmonton, AB, T6K
3J3
(780) 462-2627
Emp Here 40
SIC 8211 Elementary and secondary schools

D-U-N-S 20-028-3773   (BR)
EDMONTON SCHOOL DISTRICT NO. 7
LEE RIDGE ELEMENTARY SCHOOL
440 Millbourne Road East Nw, Edmonton, AB,
T6K 1Y8
(780) 462-3230
Emp Here 30
SIC 8211 Elementary and secondary schools

D-U-N-S 20-592-0098   (BR)
EDMONTON SCHOOL DISTRICT NO. 7
TIPASKAN ELEMENTARY SCHOOL
1200 Lakewood Road North Nw, Edmonton,
AB, T6K 4A3
(780) 462-5031
Emp Here 40
SIC 8211 Elementary and secondary schools

D-U-N-S 25-013-8526   (BR)
EDMONTON SCHOOL DISTRICT NO. 7
MEYONOHK ELEMENTARY SCHOOL
1850 Lakewood Road South Nw, Edmonton,
AB, T6K 3Y5
(780) 463-7627
Emp Here 30
SIC 8211 Elementary and secondary schools

D-U-N-S 20-712-5787   (BR)
EDMONTON SCHOOL DISTRICT NO. 7
EDITH ROGERS SCHOOL
8308 Mill Woods Rd Nw, Edmonton, AB, T6K
1Y7
(780) 462-3310
Emp Here 50
SIC 8211 Elementary and secondary schools

D-U-N-S 25-012-8808   (BR)
EDMONTON SCHOOL DISTRICT NO. 7
DAN KNOTT SCHOOL
1434 80 St Nw, Edmonton, AB, T6K 2C6
(780) 462-7954
Emp Here 36
SIC 8211 Elementary and secondary schools

D-U-N-S 20-070-2533   (BR)
GRANT MACEWAN UNIVERSITY
SOUTH CAMPUS
7319 29 Ave Nw Suite 311, Edmonton, AB,
T6K 2P1
(780) 497-4040
Emp Here 50
SIC 8222 Junior colleges

D-U-N-S 24-392-9031   (BR)
MCMATT INVESTMENTS LTD
MCDONALD'S
4202 66 St Nw, Edmonton, AB, T6K 4A2
(780) 414-8369
Emp Here 50
SIC 5812 Eating places

D-U-N-S 20-119-7683   (BR)
MEDICAL IMAGING CONSULTANTS
TAWA IMAGING CENTRE
3017 66 St Nw Suite 200, Edmonton, AB, T6K
4B2
(780) 450-9729
Emp Here 30
SIC 8011 Offices and clinics of medical doctors

D-U-N-S 24-731-3943   (SL)
MILLWOODS PENTACOSTAL ASSEMBLY
MILL WOODS ASSEMBLY
2225 66 St Nw, Edmonton, AB, T6K 4E6
(780) 462-1515
Emp Here 50   Sales 3,283,232
SIC 8661 Religious organizations

D-U-N-S 24-065-0796   (BR)
SOBEYS WEST INC
SAFEWAY
2331 66 St Nw Suite 341, Edmonton, AB, T6K
4B4
(780) 450-8180
Emp Here 120
SIC 5411 Grocery stores

D-U-N-S 25-271-1049   (BR)
SOBEYS WEST INC
MILLBOURNE SAFEWAY
100 Millbourne Shopping Centre Nw, Edmon-
ton, AB, T6K 3L6
(780) 462-4424
Emp Here 90
SIC 5411 Grocery stores

Edmonton, AB T6L

D-U-N-S 25-236-1860   (BR)
ALBERTA TREASURY BRANCHES
ATB FINANCIAL
5331 23 Ave Nw, Edmonton, AB, T6L 7G4
(780) 422-2600
Emp Here 25
SIC 6159 Miscellaneous business credit institutions

D-U-N-S 25-013-7361   (BR)
EDMONTON CATHOLIC SEPARATE SCHOOL DISTRICT NO.7
HOLY FAMILY SCHOOL
(Suby of Edmonton Catholic Separate School District No.7)
1710 Mill Woods Road East Nw, Edmonton, AB, T6L 5C5
(780) 463-8858
Emp Here 55
SIC 8211 Elementary and secondary schools

D-U-N-S 20-712-8856   (BR)
EDMONTON CATHOLIC SEPARATE SCHOOL DISTRICT NO.7
ST. RICHARD CATHOLIC ELEMENTARY SCHOOL
(Suby of Edmonton Catholic Separate School District No.7)
5704 Mill Woods Road South Nw, Edmonton, AB, T6L 3K9
(780) 463-5976
Emp Here 25
SIC 8211 Elementary and secondary schools

D-U-N-S 20-127-5620   (BR)
EDMONTON CATHOLIC SEPARATE SCHOOL DISTRICT NO.7
ST. KATERI CATHOLIC ELEMENTARY SCHOOL
(Suby of Edmonton Catholic Separate School District No.7)
3807 41 Ave Nw, Edmonton, AB, T6L 6M3
(780) 440-3322
Emp Here 32
SIC 8211 Elementary and secondary schools

D-U-N-S 20-028-4359   (BR)
EDMONTON CATHOLIC SEPARATE SCHOOL DISTRICT NO.7
MARY HANLEY CATHOLIC ELEMENTARY SCHOOL
(Suby of Edmonton Catholic Separate School District No.7)
3330 37 St Nw, Edmonton, AB, T6L 5X1
(780) 461-2551
Emp Here 35
SIC 8211 Elementary and secondary schools

D-U-N-S 20-028-4177   (BR)
EDMONTON CATHOLIC SEPARATE SCHOOL DISTRICT NO.7
JOHN PAUL I SCHOOL
(Suby of Edmonton Catholic Separate School District No.7)
5675 38 Ave Nw, Edmonton, AB, T6L 2Z1
(780) 462-6448
Emp Here 25
SIC 8211 Elementary and secondary schools

D-U-N-S 20-209-3527   (BR)
EDMONTON SCHOOL DISTRICT NO. 7
JULIA KINISKI SCHOOL
4304 41 Ave Nw, Edmonton, AB, T6L 5Y6
(780) 462-4622
Emp Here 30
SIC 8211 Elementary and secondary schools

D-U-N-S 20-029-3293   (BR)
EDMONTON SCHOOL DISTRICT NO. 7
T. D. BAKER JUNIOR HIGH SCHOOL
1750 Mill Woods Road East Nw, Edmonton, AB, T6L 5C5
(780) 462-5496
Emp Here 47

SIC 8211 Elementary and secondary schools

D-U-N-S 20-027-4046   (BR)
EDMONTON SCHOOL DISTRICT NO. 7
KATE CHEGWIN SCHOOL
3119 48 St Nw, Edmonton, AB, T6L 6P5
(780) 469-0470
Emp Here 40
SIC 8211 Elementary and secondary schools

D-U-N-S 20-591-7136   (BR)
EDMONTON SCHOOL DISTRICT NO. 7
DALY GROVE SCHOOL
1888 37 St Nw, Edmonton, AB, T6L 2R2
(780) 450-1532
Emp Here 20
SIC 8211 Elementary and secondary schools

D-U-N-S 20-913-8119   (BR)
EDMONTON SCHOOL DISTRICT NO. 7
WEINLOS SCHOOL
2911 48 St Nw, Edmonton, AB, T6L 5T7
(780) 462-5261
Emp Here 30
SIC 8211 Elementary and secondary schools

D-U-N-S 20-591-8365   (BR)
EDMONTON SCHOOL DISTRICT NO. 7
MINCHAU ELEMENTARY SCHOOL
3615 Mill Woods Road East Nw, Edmonton, AB, T6L 5X2
(780) 461-0616
Emp Here 20
SIC 8211 Elementary and secondary schools

D-U-N-S 25-454-4703   (BR)
EDMONTON SCHOOL DISTRICT NO. 7
SAKAW ELEMENTARY SCHOOL
5730 11a Ave Nw, Edmonton, AB, T6L 3A9
(780) 463-1854
Emp Here 25
SIC 8211 Elementary and secondary schools

D-U-N-S 25-013-7015   (BR)
EDMONTON SCHOOL DISTRICT NO. 7
GREENVIEW ELEMENTARY SCHOOL
5904 38 Ave Nw, Edmonton, AB, T6L 3P5
(780) 462-0660
Emp Here 35
SIC 8211 Elementary and secondary schools

D-U-N-S 25-325-3108   (BR)
EDMONTON SCHOOL DISTRICT NO. 7
BISSET ELEMENTARY SCHOOL
3020 37 St Nw, Edmonton, AB, T6L 5X1
(780) 450-6536
Emp Here 30
SIC 8211 Elementary and secondary schools

D-U-N-S 25-013-8518   (BR)
EDMONTON SCHOOL DISTRICT NO. 7
MEYOKUMIN ELEMENTARY SCHOOL
5703 19a Ave Nw, Edmonton, AB, T6L 4J8
(780) 463-8409
Emp Here 40
SIC 8211 Elementary and secondary schools

D-U-N-S 20-030-7077   (BR)
EDMONTON SCHOOL DISTRICT NO. 7
POLLARD MEADOWS SCHOOL
1751 48 St Nw, Edmonton, AB, T6L 3J6
(780) 463-8680
Emp Here 30
SIC 8211 Elementary and secondary schools

D-U-N-S 20-802-8410   (BR)
MCDONALD'S RESTAURANTS OF CANADA LIMITED
MCDONALD'S #8449
(Suby of McDonald's Corporation)
5360 23 Ave Nw, Edmonton, AB, T6L 6X2
(780) 414-8449
Emp Here 100
SIC 5812 Eating places

D-U-N-S 25-315-1633   (BR)
MEDICENTRES CANADA INC
MILL WOODS MEDICENTRE
6426 28 Ave Nw, Edmonton, AB, T6L 6N3

(780) 462-3491
Emp Here 24
SIC 8011 Offices and clinics of medical doctors

D-U-N-S 20-976-5903   (SL)
P D G (MILLWOODS GOOD SAMARITAN)
101 Youville Drive East Nw, Edmonton, AB, T6L 7A4
(780) 485-0816
Emp Here 119   Sales 4,669,485
SIC 8322 Individual and family services

D-U-N-S 20-736-9450   (BR)
SOBEYS CAPITAL INCORPORATED
5011 23 Ave Nw, Edmonton, AB, T6L 7G5
(780) 485-6622
Emp Here 180
SIC 5411 Grocery stores

D-U-N-S 20-199-2307   (BR)
WENDY'S RESTAURANTS OF CANADA INC
WENDY'S
(Suby of The Wendy's Company)
6510 28 Ave Nw, Edmonton, AB, T6L 6N3
(780) 450-1427
Emp Here 25
SIC 5812 Eating places

Edmonton, AB T6M

D-U-N-S 20-154-8281   (BR)
EDMONTON CATHOLIC SEPARATE SCHOOL DISTRICT NO.7
GOOD SHEPHERD SCHOOL
(Suby of Edmonton Catholic Separate School District No.7)
18111 57 Ave Nw, Edmonton, AB, T6M 1W1
(780) 444-4299
Emp Here 37
SIC 8211 Elementary and secondary schools

D-U-N-S 20-028-4268   (BR)
EDMONTON SCHOOL DISTRICT NO. 7
CENTENNIAL SCHOOL
17420 57 Ave Nw, Edmonton, AB, T6M 1K4
(780) 481-5590
Emp Here 21
SIC 8211 Elementary and secondary schools

D-U-N-S 20-265-3986   (BR)
EDMONTON SCHOOL DISTRICT NO. 7
BESSIE NICHOLS SCHOOL
189 Hemingway Rd Nw, Edmonton, AB, T6M 2Z7
(780) 444-1922
Emp Here 30
SIC 8211 Elementary and secondary schools

D-U-N-S 20-712-6389   (BR)
EDMONTON SCHOOL DISTRICT NO. 7
MICHAEL A KOSTEK SCHOOL
5303 190 St Nw, Edmonton, AB, T6M 2L2
(780) 489-7277
Emp Here 50
SIC 8211 Elementary and secondary schools

D-U-N-S 20-029-4598   (BR)
EDMONTON SCHOOL DISTRICT NO. 7
S BRUCE SMITH JUNIOR HIGH SCHOOL
5545 184 St Nw, Edmonton, AB, T6M 2L9
(780) 444-4946
Emp Here 50
SIC 8211 Elementary and secondary schools

D-U-N-S 24-025-7902   (BR)
SOBEYS CAPITAL INCORPORATED
SOBEY'S HAWKSTONE
18370 Lessard Rd Nw Suite 3073, Edmonton, AB, T6M 2W8
(780) 441-3502
Emp Here 60
SIC 5411 Grocery stores

Edmonton, AB T6N

D-U-N-S 20-272-7509   (BR)
A.R. THOMSON GROUP
10030 31 Ave Nw, Edmonton, AB, T6N 1G4
(780) 450-8080
Emp Here 100
SIC 3053 Gaskets; packing and sealing devices

D-U-N-S 24-377-3145   (BR)
ABB INC
9604 31 Ave Nw, Edmonton, AB, T6N 1C4
(780) 466-1676
Emp Here 25
SIC 7629 Electrical repair shops

D-U-N-S 24-789-7106   (BR)
ADIDAS CANADA LIMITED
1409 99 St Nw Suite 103, Edmonton, AB, T6N 0B4
(780) 440-1446
Emp Here 20
SIC 5091 Sporting and recreation goods

D-U-N-S 25-409-3685   (HQ)
ALBERTA BOILERS SAFETY ASSOCIATION (ABSA)
ABSA THE PRESSURE EQUIPMENT SAFETY AUTHORITY
(Suby of Alberta Boilers Safety Association (ABSA))
9410 20 Ave Nw, Edmonton, AB, T6N 0A4
(780) 437-9100
Emp Here 60   Emp Total 91
Sales 4,523,563
SIC 7389 Business services, nec

D-U-N-S 20-113-3589   (BR)
ALSTOM CANADA INC
(Suby of General Electric Company)
9623 25 Ave Nw, Edmonton, AB, T6N 1H7
(780) 447-4660
Emp Here 50
SIC 4911 Electric services

D-U-N-S 20-910-2180   (BR)
BEST BUY CANADA LTD
BEST BUY
(Suby of Best Buy Co., Inc.)
9931 19 Ave Nw, Edmonton, AB, T6N 1M4
(780) 431-6700
Emp Here 50
SIC 5999 Miscellaneous retail stores, nec

D-U-N-S 25-452-2386   (BR)
CANADIAN STANDARDS ASSOCIATION
1707 94 St Nw, Edmonton, AB, T6N 1E6
(780) 490-2035
Emp Here 40
SIC 8734 Testing laboratories

D-U-N-S 24-552-9743   (BR)
CARA OPERATIONS LIMITED
MILESTONE'S GRILL & BAR
(Suby of Cara Holdings Limited)
1708 99 St Nw, Edmonton, AB, T6N 1M5
(780) 469-9013
Emp Here 60
SIC 5812 Eating places

D-U-N-S 20-338-0811   (BR)
CINEPLEX ENTERTAINMENT LIMITED PARTNERSHIP
THE REC ROOM
1725 99 St Nw, Edmonton, AB, T6N 1M5
(587) 585-3760
Emp Here 300
SIC 7999 Amusement and recreation, nec

D-U-N-S 20-004-3284   (BR)
CINEPLEX ODEON CORPORATION
CINEPLEX CINEMAS SOUTH EDMONTON
1525 99 St Nw, Edmonton, AB, T6N 1K5
(780) 436-8585
Emp Here 95
SIC 7832 Motion picture theaters, except

drive-in

D-U-N-S 20-081-3673 (BR)
COCA-COLA REFRESHMENTS CANADA COMPANY
(*Suby of* The Coca-Cola Company)
9621 27 Ave Nw, Edmonton, AB, T6N 1E7
(780) 450-2653
Emp Here 200
SIC 2024 Ice cream and frozen deserts

D-U-N-S 25-370-7970 (BR)
COSTCO WHOLESALE CANADA LTD
(*Suby of* Costco Wholesale Corporation)
2616 91 St Nw, Edmonton, AB, T6N 1N2
(780) 577-1201
Emp Here 50
SIC 5099 Durable goods, nec

D-U-N-S 20-003-8628 (BR)
EQUIPEMENTS SPORTIFS PRO HOCKEY LIFE INC, LES
1412 99 St Nw, Edmonton, AB, T6N 0A8
(780) 409-8395
Emp Here 30
SIC 5941 Sporting goods and bicycle shops

D-U-N-S 24-785-9747 (SL)
FOREVER IN DOUGH INC
BOSTON PIZZA
9804 22 Ave Nw, Edmonton, AB, T6N 1L1
(780) 463-9086
Emp Here 75   *Sales* 2,261,782
SIC 5812 Eating places

D-U-N-S 25-222-2430 (BR)
GAP (CANADA) INC
GAP OUTLET
(*Suby of* The Gap Inc)
1414 Parsons Rd Nw, Edmonton, AB, T6N 0B5
(780) 468-4848
Emp Here 30
SIC 5651 Family clothing stores

D-U-N-S 20-552-1896 (BR)
GENERAL ELECTRIC CANADA COMPANY
BENTLY NEVADA
(*Suby of* General Electric Company)
9403 17 Ave Nw, Edmonton, AB, T6N 1J1
(780) 439-4000
Emp Here 23
SIC 3625 Relays and industrial controls

D-U-N-S 24-390-5788 (BR)
GOLF TOWN LIMITED
GOLF TOWN
1940 99 St Nw, Edmonton, AB, T6N 1K9
(780) 988-6000
Emp Here 50
SIC 5941 Sporting goods and bicycle shops

D-U-N-S 25-090-2509 (BR)
HERBERS AUTO BODY REPAIR LTD
2721 Parsons Rd Nw, Edmonton, AB, T6N 1B8
(780) 440-1055
Emp Here 25
SIC 7538 General automotive repair shops

D-U-N-S 25-514-3208 (BR)
HOME DEPOT OF CANADA INC
HOME DEPOT
(*Suby of* The Home Depot Inc)
2020 101 St Nw, Edmonton, AB, T6N 1J2

Emp Here 200
SIC 1522 Residential construction, nec

D-U-N-S 20-059-7826 (BR)
HUDSON'S BAY COMPANY
HOME OUTFITTERS
9738 19 Ave Nw, Edmonton, AB, T6N 1K6
(780) 414-5850
Emp Here 25
SIC 5311 Department stores

D-U-N-S 20-651-7588 (BR)
IKEA LIMITED

IKEA LIMITED
1311 102 St Nw, Edmonton, AB, T6N 1M3
(780) 433-6000
Emp Here 300
SIC 5712 Furniture stores

D-U-N-S 20-143-3385 (BR)
INDIGO BOOKS & MUSIC INC
INDIGO
(*Suby of* Indigo Books & Music Inc)
1837 99 St Nw, Edmonton, AB, T6N 1K8
(780) 432-4488
Emp Here 25
SIC 5942 Book stores

D-U-N-S 25-235-7496 (HQ)
INLAND INDUSTRIAL SUPPLY LTD
(*Suby of* Inland Industrial Supply Ltd)
9949 29a Ave Nw, Edmonton, AB, T6N 1A9
(780) 413-0029
Emp Here 44   *Emp Total* 50
Sales 12,532,976
SIC 5085 Industrial supplies
Pr Pr Gordon Dixon

D-U-N-S 24-333-1316 (BR)
KEG RESTAURANTS LTD
KEG STEAKHOUSE & BAR, THE
1631 102 St Nw, Edmonton, AB, T6N 1M3

Emp Here 112
SIC 5812 Eating places

D-U-N-S 25-832-1074 (BR)
KONICA MINOLTA BUSINESS SOLUTIONS (CANADA) LTD
KONICA MINOLTA
9651 25 Ave Nw, Edmonton, AB, T6N 1H7
(780) 465-6232
Emp Here 95
SIC 5044 Office equipment

D-U-N-S 20-059-8857 (BR)
LOBLAWS INC
REAL CANADIAN-SUPERSTORES
9711 23 Ave Nw, Edmonton, AB, T6N 1K7
(780) 490-3935
Emp Here 100
SIC 5141 Groceries, general line

D-U-N-S 20-305-4119 (BR)
LOWE'S COMPANIES CANADA, ULC
10141 13 Ave Nw, Edmonton, AB, T6N 0B6
(780) 430-1344
Emp Here 140
SIC 5211 Lumber and other building materials

D-U-N-S 20-644-2720 (BR)
MARK'S WORK WEARHOUSE LTD
WORK WORLD
1404 99 St Nw, Edmonton, AB, T6N 0A8
(780) 468-6793
Emp Here 40
SIC 5699 Miscellaneous apparel and accessory stores

D-U-N-S 24-014-0793 (SL)
MONTANA'S COOKHOUSE SALOON
1720 99 St Nw, Edmonton, AB, T6N 1M5
(780) 466-8520
Emp Here 90   *Sales* 2,699,546
SIC 5812 Eating places

D-U-N-S 20-981-5422 (BR)
NEWLY WEDS FOODS CO.
NEWLY WEDS FOODS
9110 23 Ave Nw, Edmonton, AB, T6N 1H9
(780) 414-9500
Emp Here 120
SIC 2099 Food preparations, nec

D-U-N-S 24-701-0486 (BR)
NIKE CANADA CORP
(*Suby of* Nike, Inc.)
9743 19 Ave Nw, Edmonton, AB, T6N 1N5
(780) 409-8244
Emp Here 33
SIC 5091 Sporting and recreation goods

D-U-N-S 20-693-2068 (SL)
OPM (SOUTH EDMONTON) LTD
1820 99 St Nw, Edmonton, AB, T6N 1M5
(780) 989-5898
Emp Here 50   *Sales* 1,532,175
SIC 5812 Eating places

D-U-N-S 20-104-4984 (BR)
POSTMEDIA NETWORK INC
FLYER FORCE
9303 28 Ave Nw, Edmonton, AB, T6N 1N1
(780) 436-8050
Emp Here 50
SIC 7319 Advertising, nec

D-U-N-S 24-337-5156 (BR)
PRECISION DRILLING CORPORATION
PRECISION CAMP SERVICES
3050 Parsons Rd Nw Suite 1, Edmonton, AB, T6N 1B1
(780) 431-3484
Emp Here 50
SIC 1381 Drilling oil and gas wells

D-U-N-S 25-363-7078 (BR)
PRECISION DRILLING CORPORATION
COLUMBIA OILFIELD SUPPLY
9280 25 Ave Nw, Edmonton, AB, T6N 1E1
(780) 437-5110
Emp Here 40
SIC 1381 Drilling oil and gas wells

D-U-N-S 20-793-6936 (SL)
PRESTIGE TRANSPORTATION LTD
PRESTIGE LIMOUSINE
(*Suby of* Agio Investments Ltd)
10135 31 Ave Nw, Edmonton, AB, T6N 1C2
(780) 462-4444
Emp Here 120   *Sales* 5,827,840
SIC 4111 Local and suburban transit
Pr Pr Philip Strong

D-U-N-S 20-921-1338 (BR)
PUROLATOR INC.
PUROLATOR INC
3104 97 St Nw, Edmonton, AB, T6N 1K3
(780) 408-2420
Emp Here 110
SIC 7389 Business services, nec

D-U-N-S 25-370-7947 (BR)
RANCHO REALTY (EDMONTON) LTD
QUALICO DEVELOPMENT WEST
3203 93 St Nw Suite 300, Edmonton, AB, T6N 0B2
(780) 463-1126
Emp Here 80
SIC 6553 Cemetery subdividers and developers

D-U-N-S 24-005-0443 (BR)
RANCHO REALTY SERVICES (MANITOBA) LTD
RANCHO REALTY SERVICES EDMONTON
3203 93 St Nw Suite 200, Edmonton, AB, T6N 0B2
(780) 463-2132
Emp Here 37
SIC 6531 Real estate agents and managers

D-U-N-S 20-594-5173 (HQ)
ROSENAU TRANSPORT LTD
(*Suby of* Mid-Nite Sun Transportation Ltd)
2950 Parsons Rd Nw Unit 200, Edmonton, AB, T6N 1B1
(780) 431-2877
Emp Here 35   *Emp Total* 330
Sales 92,725,174
SIC 4213 Trucking, except local
Pr Pr Carl Rosenau
Dir Rodney Rosenau
VP Timothy Rosenau
Dir Valerie Stevenson
Dir Ken Rosenau
Treas Patricia Young

D-U-N-S 24-599-8158 (BR)
SHOEMAKER DRYWALL SUPPLIES LTD

10050 29a Ave Nw, Edmonton, AB, T6N 1A8
(780) 463-7413
Emp Here 25
SIC 5032 Brick, stone, and related material

D-U-N-S 20-716-1964 (BR)
STAPLES CANADA INC
STAPLES THE BUSINESS DEPOT
(*Suby of* Staples, Inc.)
1960 101 St Nw, Edmonton, AB, T6N 1K1
(780) 414-0361
Emp Here 35
SIC 5943 Stationery stores

D-U-N-S 24-643-4943 (BR)
STARBUCKS COFFEE CANADA, INC
STARBUCKS
(*Suby of* Starbucks Corporation)
1751 102 St Nw, Edmonton, AB, T6N 0B1
(780) 490-6599
Emp Here 24
SIC 5812 Eating places

D-U-N-S 25-085-5681 (SL)
SWISS CHALET
2203 99 St Nw, Edmonton, AB, T6N 1J7
(780) 988-2233
Emp Here 50   *Sales* 1,532,175
SIC 5812 Eating places

D-U-N-S 24-423-5938 (BR)
SYNCRUDE CANADA LTD
EDMONTON RESEARCH CENTRE
9421 17 Ave Nw, Edmonton, AB, T6N 1H4
(780) 970-6800
Emp Here 100
SIC 8731 Commercial physical research

D-U-N-S 20-700-5187 (BR)
TOMMY HILFIGER CANADA INC
TOMMY HILLFIGER OUTLET
1907 99 St Nw, Edmonton, AB, T6N 1M7
(780) 465-6936
Emp Here 30
SIC 5136 Men's and boy's clothing

D-U-N-S 20-860-5449 (BR)
TOWN SHOES LIMITED
SHOE COMPANY, THE
2022 99 St Nw, Edmonton, AB, T6N 1L3
(780) 433-4466
Emp Here 25
SIC 5661 Shoe stores

D-U-N-S 24-582-8199 (HQ)
WIKA INSTRUMENTS LTD
3103 Parsons Rd Nw, Edmonton, AB, T6N 1C8
(780) 438-6662
Emp Here 133   *Emp Total* 9,000
Sales 37,422,043
SIC 3823 Process control instruments
Pr Pr Dave Wannamaker
 Matt Matia

D-U-N-S 25-218-9972 (BR)
WAL-MART CANADA CORP
1203 Parsons Rd Nw Suite 3029, Edmonton, AB, T6N 0A9
(780) 461-1509
Emp Here 365
SIC 5311 Department stores

D-U-N-S 24-224-5632 (BR)
WENDY'S RESTAURANTS OF CANADA INC
WENDY'S
(*Suby of* The Wendy's Company)
1850 102 St Nw Unit 2, Edmonton, AB, T6N 1N3
(780) 461-6967
Emp Here 25
SIC 5812 Eating places

D-U-N-S 25-684-6114 (BR)
WENZEL DOWNHOLE TOOLS LTD
MANUFACTURING / SALES FACILITIES
3115 93 St Nw, Edmonton, AB, T6N 1L7
(780) 440-4220
Emp Here 120

▲ Public Company   ■ Public Company Family Member   **HQ** Headquarters   **BR** Branch   **SL** Single Location

SIC 3533 Oil and gas field machinery

D-U-N-S 24-852-0954   (BR)
WESTPOWER EQUIPMENT LTD
SPARTCO
9930 29a Ave Nw, Edmonton, AB, T6N 1A8
(780) 485-0310
Emp Here 20
SIC 7699 Repair services, nec

D-U-N-S 20-806-2823   (BR)
YM INC. (SALES)
STITCHES
1974 99 St Nw Unit 9 5a, Edmonton, AB, T6N 1K9
(780) 485-9494
Emp Here 25
SIC 5621 Women's clothing stores

D-U-N-S 24-418-6446   (BR)
ZEDI INC
1855 94 St Nw Suite 101, Edmonton, AB, T6N 1E6
(780) 701-3000
Emp Here 70
SIC 1731 Electrical work

Edmonton, AB T6P

D-U-N-S 24-808-1564   (BR)
1942675 ALBERTA LTD
GREAT WESTERN CONTAINERS
(*Suby of* 1942675 Alberta Ltd)
1912 66 Ave Nw, Edmonton, AB, T6P 1M4
(780) 440-2222
Emp Here 70
SIC 3412 Metal barrels, drums, and pails

D-U-N-S 24-384-9325   (HQ)
993106 ALBERTA LTD
(*Suby of* 993106 Alberta Ltd)
1444 78 Ave Nw, Edmonton, AB, T6P 1L7
(780) 438-5930
Emp Here 40   *Emp Total* 200
Sales 320,953,850
SIC 5172 Petroleum products, nec
Pr Pr Parker Mclean
Dir Kim Mclean

D-U-N-S 20-321-5272   (BR)
A. M. CASTLE & CO. (CANADA) INC
CASTLE METALS
(*Suby of* A. M. Castle & Co.)
2503 84 Ave Nw, Edmonton, AB, T6P 1K1
(780) 417-4130
Emp Here 21
SIC 5541 Gasoline service stations

D-U-N-S 24-928-3763   (HQ)
AFD PETROLEUM LTD
(*Suby of* 993106 Alberta Ltd)
1444 78 Ave Nw, Edmonton, AB, T6P 1L7
(780) 438-5930
Emp Here 32   *Emp Total* 200
Sales 16,853,922
SIC 5172 Petroleum products, nec
Pr Pr Parker Mclean

D-U-N-S 20-537-7989   (HQ)
ATS TRAFFIC-ALBERTA LTD
9015 14 St Nw, Edmonton, AB, T6P 0C9
(780) 440-4114
Emp Here 75   *Emp Total* 76
Sales 7,189,883
SIC 3993 Signs and advertising specialties
Pr Pr Lorne Hooper
  Laine Hooper
  Prosper Boisvert

D-U-N-S 24-598-1329   (HQ)
ACUREN GROUP INC
(*Suby of* Rockwood Service Corporation)
7450 18 St Nw, Edmonton, AB, T6P 1N8

(780) 440-2131
Emp Here 300   *Emp Total* 3,009
Sales 88,444,227
SIC 8734 Testing laboratories
Pr Pr Kenneth Stankievech
  Peter Scannell

D-U-N-S 25-447-3460   (BR)
AEVITAS INC
7722 9 St Nw, Edmonton, AB, T6P 1L6
(780) 440-1825
Emp Here 40
SIC 4953 Refuse systems

D-U-N-S 24-283-8365   (SL)
ALBERTA ASPHALT ENTERPRISES INC
6450 27 St Nw, Edmonton, AB, T6P 1M6
(780) 469-9999
Emp Here 25   *Sales* 2,188,821
SIC 1799 Special trade contractors, nec

D-U-N-S 24-906-8149   (BR)
APPLIED INDUSTRIAL TECHNOLOGIES, LP
HYPOWER SYSTEMS, DIV OF
(*Suby of* Applied Industrial Technologies, Inc.)
8620 18 St Nw, Edmonton, AB, T6P 1K5
(780) 464-5528
Emp Here 23
SIC 5084 Industrial machinery and equipment

D-U-N-S 25-975-2025   (SL)
BROWN & ROOT INDUSTRIAL SERVICES CANADA CORPORATION
BROWN & ROOT
(*Suby of* Brown & Root Industrial Services, LLC of Delaware)
3300 76 Ave Nw Bldg B, Edmonton, AB, T6P 1J4
(780) 577-4440
Emp Here 60   *Sales* 18,491,125
SIC 1629 Heavy construction, nec
  Andy Dupuy
  Robin Campeau
  Lee Barnett
Sec Jeff Jenkins
Dir Bart Turner
Dir Peter Hall

D-U-N-S 24-352-2310   (BR)
CWS INDUSTRIES (MFG) CORP
CWS INDUSTRIES (MFG) CORP.
7622 18 St Nw, Edmonton, AB, T6P 1Y6
(780) 469-9185
Emp Here 102
SIC 3545 Machine tool accessories

D-U-N-S 24-338-1618   (HQ)
CANADIAN DEWATERING L.P.
8350 1 St Nw, Edmonton, AB, T6P 1X2
(780) 400-2260
Emp Here 50   *Emp Total* 5,515
Sales 54,140,688
SIC 5084 Industrial machinery and equipment
Pr Pr Dale Marchand
VP Shaun Fielding
VP Acctg Mary Ellen Vandusen

D-U-N-S 20-809-6982   (HQ)
DFI CORPORATION
DFI
2404 51 Ave Nw, Edmonton, AB, T6P 0E4
(780) 466-5237
Emp Here 78   *Emp Total* 120
Sales 12,038,516
SIC 3312 Blast furnaces and steel mills
Pr Pr David Alexander Freeland
  Jane Freeland
Dir Sean Freeland

D-U-N-S 20-082-1007   (BR)
DNOW CANADA ULC
(*Suby of* Now Inc.)
2603 76 Ave Nw, Edmonton, AB, T6P 1P6
(780) 944-1000
Emp Here 100
SIC 5085 Industrial supplies

D-U-N-S 20-178-0884   (BR)

DIVERSEY CANADA, INC
(*Suby of* Sealed Air Corporation)
2020 84 Ave Nw, Edmonton, AB, T6P 1K2

Emp Here 30
SIC 2842 Polishes and sanitation goods

D-U-N-S 24-353-7334   (BR)
ECL GROUP OF COMPANIES LTD
ECL TRANSPORTATION FREIGHT DIVISION
2303 51 Ave Nw, Edmonton, AB, T6P 0B5

Emp Here 50
SIC 4212 Local trucking, without storage

D-U-N-S 20-808-8138   (BR)
ECONOMY CARRIERS LIMITED
10502 17 St Nw, Edmonton, AB, T6P 1P4

Emp Here 60
SIC 4213 Trucking, except local

D-U-N-S 25-528-0984   (BR)
ECONOMY CARRIERS LIMITED
STARFIELD TERMINALS
1810 66 Ave Nw, Edmonton, AB, T6P 1M4

Emp Here 50
SIC 4213 Trucking, except local

D-U-N-S 25-616-6919   (BR)
EDMONTON KENWORTH LTD
PACLEASE
2210 91 Ave Nw, Edmonton, AB, T6P 1K9
(780) 464-1212
Emp Here 25
SIC 7513 Truck rental and leasing, no drivers

D-U-N-S 20-107-6291   (BR)
EMCO CORPORATION
3011 101 Ave Nw, Edmonton, AB, T6P 1X7
(780) 440-7333
Emp Here 100
SIC 5074 Plumbing and heating equipment and supplies (hydronics)

D-U-N-S 25-389-3911   (HQ)
F I OILFIELD SERVICES CANADA ULC
2880 64 Ave Nw, Edmonton, AB, T6P 1W6
(780) 463-3333
Emp Here 35   *Emp Total* 800
Sales 19,115,703
SIC 1389 Oil and gas field services, nec
Genl Mgr Gord Robb

D-U-N-S 24-804-9855   (BR)
FLINT ENERGY SERVICES LTD.
FLINT GLOBAL POLY
3052 84 Ave Nw, Edmonton, AB, T6P 1K3
(780) 449-4567
Emp Here 35
SIC 3084 Plastics pipe

D-U-N-S 25-974-1320   (BR)
FLOWSERVE CANADA CORP
(*Suby of* Flowserve Corporation)
9044 18 St Nw Suite 1, Edmonton, AB, T6P 1K6
(780) 449-4850
Emp Here 20
SIC 3714 Motor vehicle parts and accessories

D-U-N-S 20-065-1854   (BR)
GIBSON ENERGY ULC
10534 17 St Nw, Edmonton, AB, T6P 1P4
(780) 449-9350
Emp Here 50
SIC 5172 Petroleum products, nec

D-U-N-S 24-583-6713   (HQ)
HIGH LINE ELECTRICAL CONSTRUCTORS LTD
(*Suby of* High Line Electrical Constructors Ltd)
7212 8 St Nw, Edmonton, AB, T6P 1V1
(780) 452-8900
Emp Here 75   *Emp Total* 190
Sales 21,485,101

SIC 1731 Electrical work
Pr Pr Scott Hutton
  Tony Broadhurst
  Chris Rauschning
  Tim Ashton

D-U-N-S 24-533-7733   (HQ)
JACOBS INDUSTRIAL SERVICES
(*Suby of* Jacobs Engineering Group Inc.)
1104 70 Ave Nw, Edmonton, AB, T6P 1P5
(780) 468-2533
Emp Here 25   *Emp Total* 64,000
Sales 145,921,400
SIC 7349 Building maintenance services, nec
Pr Earl Mitchell

D-U-N-S 20-576-0882   (HQ)
KBR INDUSTRIAL CANADA CO.
3300 76 Ave Nw, Edmonton, AB, T6P 1J4
(780) 468-1341
Emp Here 998   *Emp Total* 27,500
Sales 198,161,261
SIC 1541 Industrial buildings and warehouses
Pr Pr Christian Brown
  William Pohl

D-U-N-S 20-637-9984   (BR)
KINDER MORGAN CANADA INC
1680 101a Ave Nw, Edmonton, AB, T6P 1X1
(780) 449-5900
Emp Here 50
SIC 4612 Crude petroleum pipelines

D-U-N-S 20-070-4158   (BR)
MAPLE LEAF FOODS INC
MAPLE LEAF POULTRY
2619 91 Ave Nw, Edmonton, AB, T6P 1S3
(780) 467-6022
Emp Here 380
SIC 2015 Poultry slaughtering and processing

D-U-N-S 25-329-1165   (BR)
NEWALTA CORPORATION
6110 27 St Nw, Edmonton, AB, T6P 1Y5
(780) 440-6780
Emp Here 20
SIC 4953 Refuse systems

D-U-N-S 20-776-2118   (BR)
NEXEO SOLUTIONS CANADA CORP
(*Suby of* Nexeo Solutions, Inc.)
1720 106 Ave Nw, Edmonton, AB, T6P 1X9
(780) 417-9385
Emp Here 20
SIC 5033 Roofing, siding, and insulation

D-U-N-S 20-895-2440   (HQ)
PSL PARTITION SYSTEMS LTD
PARTITION SYSTEMS
(*Suby of* PSL Partition Systems Ltd)
1105 70 Ave Nw, Edmonton, AB, T6P 1N5
(780) 465-0001
Emp Here 45   *Emp Total* 61
SIC 3275 Gypsum products

D-U-N-S 24-329-4605   (HQ)
PE BEN OILFIELD SERVICES LP
4510 17 St Nw, Edmonton, AB, T6P 1X5
(780) 440-4425
Emp Here 30   *Emp Total* 5,515
Sales 57,432,441
SIC 1389 Oil and gas field services, nec
VP VP Darryl Esch
Fin Ex Nimal Kumarasinghe

D-U-N-S 24-314-7399   (BR)
PEMBINA PIPELINE CORPORATION
10503 17 St Nw, Edmonton, AB, T6P 1R2
(780) 467-8841
Emp Here 35
SIC 4612 Crude petroleum pipelines

D-U-N-S 25-064-4895   (BR)
PRAXAIR CANADA INC
(*Suby of* Praxair, Inc.)
9020 24 St Nw, Edmonton, AB, T6P 1X8
(905) 803-1600
Emp Here 20

SIC 5169 Chemicals and allied products, nec

D-U-N-S 20-105-7072   (SL)
PRINCE GEORGE WAREHOUSING CO LTD
2840 76 Ave Nw, Edmonton, AB, T6P 1J4
(780) 465-8466
Emp Here 100   *Sales* 17,652,300
SIC 4213 Trucking, except local
Herbert Assman
Pr John Assman
VP Elie Musa

D-U-N-S 25-315-6079   (SL)
PROECO CORPORATION
7722 9 St Nw, Edmonton, AB, T6P 1L6
(780) 440-1825
Emp Here 26   *Sales* 3,429,153
SIC 4953 Refuse systems

D-U-N-S 20-269-5078   (SL)
REVOLUTION ENVIRONMENTAL SOLU-TIONS ACQUISITION GP INC
TERRAPURE ENVIRONMENTAL
6110 27 St Nw, Edmonton, AB, T6P 1Y5
(780) 450-7664
Emp Here 900   *Sales* 63,230,276
SIC 8731 Commercial physical research
Pr Pr Todd Moser
VP VP Darren Zwicker

D-U-N-S 25-314-9496   (BR)
REVOLUTION ENVIRONMENTAL SOLU-TIONS LP
TERRAPURE ENVIRONMENTAL
(*Suby of* Revolution Environmental Solutions LP)
6024 27 St Nw, Edmonton, AB, T6P 1Y5
(780) 440-4100
Emp Here 21
SIC 4953 Refuse systems

D-U-N-S 24-064-0060   (BR)
ROLF C. HAGEN INC
8770 24 St Nw, Edmonton, AB, T6P 1X8

Emp Here 65
SIC 5199 Nondurable goods, nec

D-U-N-S 24-337-5669   (BR)
RUSSEL METALS INC
COMCO PIPE & SUPPLY
2165 70 Ave Nw, Edmonton, AB, T6P 0B4
(780) 468-1115
Emp Here 25
SIC 5051 Metals service centers and offices

D-U-N-S 24-310-3392   (BR)
RUSSEL METALS INC
2471 76 Avenue Nw, Edmonton, AB, T6P 1P6
(780) 440-0779
Emp Here 40
SIC 3444 Sheet Metalwork

D-U-N-S 25-329-6180   (BR)
RUSSEL METALS INC
COMCO PIPE & SUPPLY COMPANY, DIV OF
5910 17 St Nw, Edmonton, AB, T6P 1S5
(780) 440-2000
Emp Here 50
SIC 5051 Metals service centers and offices

D-U-N-S 25-626-4037   (BR)
SHAW PIPE PROTECTION LIMITED
10275 21 St Nw, Edmonton, AB, T6P 1P3
(780) 467-5501
Emp Here 80
SIC 3479 Metal coating and allied services

D-U-N-S 20-919-0219   (BR)
SHAWCOR LTD
1201 76 Ave Nw, Edmonton, AB, T6P 1P2
(780) 490-1321
Emp Here 40
SIC 1389 Oil and gas field services, nec

D-U-N-S 24-929-8860   (BR)
SHAWCOR LTD
GUARDIAN, DIV OF
950 78 Ave Nw, Edmonton, AB, T6P 1L7

(780) 440-1444
Emp Here 49
SIC 1389 Oil and gas field services, nec

D-U-N-S 24-283-1576   (HQ)
SOLAR TURBINES CANADA LTD
2510 84 Ave Nw, Edmonton, AB, T6P 1K3
(780) 464-8900
Emp Here 25   *Emp Total* 95,400
Sales 6,596,303
SIC 5084 Industrial machinery and equipment
Genl Mgr Larry Woods
Pr Charles J Swiniarski
Herb Zechel
Sec Jacquiline Loaiza
Treas Daniel Boylan
David Esbeck
Dir Stephen A Gosselin

D-U-N-S 20-697-3435   (BR)
SPECIALIZED RIGGING SERVICES LTD
(*Suby of* Specialized Rigging Services Ltd)
233 91 Ave Unit 1, Edmonton, AB, T6P 1L1
(780) 449-3052
Emp Here 30
SIC 1541 Industrial buildings and warehouses

D-U-N-S 24-786-1651   (BR)
STRONGCO ENGINEERED SYSTEMS INC
STRONGCO EQUIPMENT
2820 84 Ave Nw, Edmonton, AB, T6P 1P7
(780) 948-3515
Emp Here 42
SIC 7353 Heavy construction equipment rental

D-U-N-S 25-148-2113   (SL)
SUREWAY CONSTRUCTION MANAGE-MENT LTD
(*Suby of* 482842 Alberta Ltd)
7331 18 St Nw, Edmonton, AB, T6P 1P9
(780) 440-2121
Emp Here 20   *Sales* 2,772,507
SIC 8741 Management services

D-U-N-S 20-705-3807   (BR)
SUREWAY CONTRACTING LTD
YELLOWHEAD AGGREGATES DIV OF
7331 18 St Nw, Edmonton, AB, T6P 1P9
(780) 449-4617
Emp Here 20
SIC 5032 Brick, stone, and related material

D-U-N-S 24-280-9911   (BR)
TISI CANADA INC
TEAM INDUSTRIAL SERVICES
8525 18 St Nw, Edmonton, AB, T6P 1K4
(780) 467-8070
Emp Here 30
SIC 3398 Metal heat treating

D-U-N-S 20-641-6427   (BR)
TAIGA BUILDING PRODUCTS LTD
10120 17 St Nw, Edmonton, AB, T6P 1V8
(780) 417-8306
Emp Here 30
SIC 5031 Lumber, plywood, and millwork

D-U-N-S 24-089-8064   (BR)
TRANS AM PIPING PRODUCTS LTD
1711 66 Ave Nw, Edmonton, AB, T6P 1Y9
(780) 440-4567
Emp Here 45
SIC 5051 Metals service centers and offices

D-U-N-S 24-064-7719   (BR)
TRANSX LTD
BIG HORN TRANSPORT
2451 76 Ave Nw, Edmonton, AB, T6P 1P6
(780) 461-1166
Emp Here 50
SIC 4213 Trucking, except local

D-U-N-S 24-676-8027   (BR)
TRANSPORT TFI 8 S.E.C.
UTL TRANSPORTATION SERVICES
2840 76 Ave Nw, Edmonton, AB, T6P 1J4
(780) 454-0761
Emp Here 20

SIC 4213 Trucking, except local

D-U-N-S 20-719-7786   (BR)
UNITED FARMERS OF ALBERTA CO-OPERATIVE LIMITED
UFA
6510 20 St Nw, Edmonton, AB, T6P 1Z2
(780) 450-0000
Emp Here 60
SIC 5172 Petroleum products, nec

D-U-N-S 24-559-2204   (BR)
WITHERS L.P.
POLEGE OILFIELD HAULING, DIV OF
903 76 Ave Nw, Edmonton, AB, T6P 1P2
(780) 440-2840
Emp Here 50
SIC 4213 Trucking, except local

Edmonton, AB T6R

D-U-N-S 20-580-1579   (BR)
CANADA POST CORPORATION
584 Riverbend Sq Nw, Edmonton, AB, T6R 2E3
(780) 439-9778
Emp Here 20
SIC 4311 U.s. postal service

D-U-N-S 20-029-2659   (BR)
EDMONTON CATHOLIC SEPARATE SCHOOL DISTRICT NO.7
ST. MARY CATHOLIC ELEMENTARY SCHOOL
(*Suby of* Edmonton Catholic Separate School District No.7)
490 Rhatigan Road East Nw, Edmonton, AB, T6R 2E2
(780) 988-6577
Emp Here 49
SIC 8211 Elementary and secondary schools

D-U-N-S 20-713-0068   (BR)
EDMONTON CATHOLIC SEPARATE SCHOOL DISTRICT NO.7
ARCHBISHOP JOSEPH MACNEIL SCHOOL
(*Suby of* Edmonton Catholic Separate School District No.7)
750 Leger Way Nw, Edmonton, AB, T6R 3H4
(780) 471-4218
Emp Here 35
SIC 8211 Elementary and secondary schools

D-U-N-S 20-591-7276   (BR)
EDMONTON SCHOOL DISTRICT NO. 7
EARL EUXTON ELEMENTARY SCHOOL
250 Rhatigan Road East Nw, Edmonton, AB, T6R 2H7
(780) 435-1577
Emp Here 40
SIC 8211 Elementary and secondary schools

D-U-N-S 20-063-7523   (BR)
MCDONALD'S RESTAURANTS OF CANADA LIMITED
MCDONALD'S
(*Suby of* McDonald's Corporation)
494 Riverbend Sq Nw, Edmonton, AB, T6R 2E3
(780) 414-8403
Emp Here 70
SIC 5812 Eating places

D-U-N-S 25-315-1757   (BR)
MEDICENTRES CANADA INC
RIVERBEND MEDICENTRE
600 Riverbend Sq Nw, Edmonton, AB, T6R 2E3
(780) 434-7234
Emp Here 20
SIC 8011 Offices and clinics of medical doctors

D-U-N-S 25-234-9543   (HQ)
PETROCORP GROUP INC

(*Suby of* Petrocorp Group Inc)
14032 23 Ave Nw Suite 166, Edmonton, AB, T6R 3L6
(780) 910-9436
Emp Here 90   *Emp Total* 300
Sales 33,923,844
SIC 1731 Electrical work
Pr Pr Larry Patriquin
Randy Fries
James Snowdon
VP Opers Ashley Hope
Martin Bernholtz
Garry Wetsch

D-U-N-S 20-806-2369   (BR)
SOBEYS CAPITAL INCORPORATED
SOBEYS
2430 Rabbit Hill Rd Nw, Edmonton, AB, T6R 3B5
(780) 989-1610
Emp Here 180
SIC 5411 Grocery stores

D-U-N-S 25-271-0215   (BR)
SOBEYS WEST INC
SAFEWAY
576 Riverbend Sq Nw Suite 802, Edmonton, AB, T6R 2E3
(780) 434-6124
Emp Here 150
SIC 5411 Grocery stores

D-U-N-S 20-806-5289   (BR)
STARBUCKS COFFEE CANADA, INC
STARBUCKS
(*Suby of* Starbucks Corporation)
14239 23 Ave Nw, Edmonton, AB, T6R 3E7
(780) 433-3331
Emp Here 30
SIC 5812 Eating places

D-U-N-S 24-342-6140   (SL)
WELL RESOURCES INC
(*Suby of* The Well Corporation)
3919 149a St Nw, Edmonton, AB, T6R 1J8
(780) 430-7789
Emp Here 238   *Sales* 16,867,689
SIC 8731 Commercial physical research
Pr Pr Keng Chung

Edmonton, AB T6S

D-U-N-S 24-382-1407   (BR)
543077 ALBERTA LTD
SIL INDUSTRIAL MINERALS
305 116 Ave Nw, Edmonton, AB, T6S 1G3
(780) 467-2627
Emp Here 50
SIC 5032 Brick, stone, and related material

D-U-N-S 24-003-8997   (BR)
AIR PRODUCTS CANADA LTD
(*Suby of* Air Products and Chemicals, Inc.)
720 Petroleum Way Nw, Edmonton, AB, T6S 1H5
(780) 417-1957
Emp Here 20
SIC 1311 Crude petroleum and natural gas

D-U-N-S 25-321-4282   (BR)
ALLIED SYSTEMS (CANADA) COMPANY
12210 17 St Ne, Edmonton, AB, T6S 1A6
(780) 472-6641
Emp Here 59
SIC 4213 Trucking, except local

D-U-N-S 24-525-7139   (BR)
CEDA FIELD SERVICES LP
2220 119 Ave Ne, Edmonton, AB, T6S 1B3
(780) 478-1048
Emp Here 30
SIC 7699 Repair services, nec

D-U-N-S 20-580-4920   (BR)
COMPAGNIE DES CHEMINS DE FER NA-

TIONAUX DU CANADA
CN RAIL
12310 17 St Ne, Edmonton, AB, T6S 1A7
(780) 472-6869
Emp Here 20
SIC 4011 Railroads, line-haul operating

D-U-N-S 25-314-3770   (BR)
GEORGIA-PACIFIC CANADA LP
(*Suby of* Koch Industries, Inc.)
403 118a Ave Ne, Edmonton, AB, T6S 1C6
(780) 472-6631
Emp Here 50
SIC 3299 NonMetallic mineral products,

D-U-N-S 25-986-3715   (BR)
KEYERA CORP
(*Suby of* Keyera Corp)
1250 Hayter Rd Nw, Edmonton, AB, T6S 1A2
(780) 414-7417
Emp Here 30
SIC 1389 Oil and gas field services, nec

D-U-N-S 25-105-3807   (BR)
MASTERFEEDS INC
1903 121 Ave Ne, Edmonton, AB, T6S 1B2
(780) 472-6600
Emp Here 20
SIC 2048 Prepared feeds, nec

D-U-N-S 24-063-5326   (BR)
OC CANADA HOLDINGS COMPANY
OWEN CORNING
831 Hayter Rd Nw, Edmonton, AB, T6S 1A1
(780) 472-6644
Emp Here 130
SIC 5033 Roofing, siding, and insulation

D-U-N-S 20-538-8457   (BR)
PARK DEROCHIE INC
(*Suby of* Industrial Construction Investments
Inc)
11850 28 St Ne, Edmonton, AB, T6S 1G6
(780) 478-4688
Emp Here 250
SIC 1721 Painting and paper hanging

D-U-N-S 20-251-5078   (BR)
SUEZ CANADA WASTE SERIVCES INC
SENA WASTE SERVICES
13111 Meridian St Suite 600, Edmonton, AB,
T6S 1G9
(780) 472-9966
Emp Here 55
SIC 4953 Refuse systems

D-U-N-S 20-058-7587   (BR)
SUEZ CANADA WASTE SERIVCES INC
13111 Meridian St Ne Suite 500, Edmonton,
AB, T6S 1G9
(780) 472-9966
Emp Here 81
SIC 2875 Fertilizers, mixing only

D-U-N-S 25-093-4739   (BR)
SUNCOR ENERGY INC
801 Petroleum Way Nw, Edmonton, AB, T6S
1H5
(780) 410-5681
Emp Here 500
SIC 2911 Petroleum refining

D-U-N-S 20-001-4004   (BR)
TERVITA CORPORATION
(*Suby of* Tervita Corporation)
12311 17 St Ne, Edmonton, AB, T6S 1A7
(780) 456-1444
Emp Here 60
SIC 1629 Heavy construction, nec

D-U-N-S 20-440-1012   (HQ)
WESTCAN BULK TRANSPORT LTD
WESTCAN FREIGHT SYSTEMS
(*Suby of* The Kenan Advantage Group Inc)
12110 17 St Ne, Edmonton, AB, T6S 1A5
(780) 472-6951
Emp Here 300   *Emp Total* 4,923
Sales 60,984,070

SIC 4212 Local trucking, without storage
Pr Pr Tom Kenny

D-U-N-S 20-348-4498   (BR)
WORLEYPARSONSCORD LTD
WORLEYPARSONSCORD LTD.
2455 130 Ave Ne, Edmonton, AB, T6S 0A4
(780) 440-6942
Emp Here 150
SIC 1623 Water, sewer, and utility lines

Edmonton, AB T6T

D-U-N-S 24-359-6397   (BR)
BANK OF NOVA SCOTIA, THE
SCOTIABANK
3804 17 St Nw, Edmonton, AB, T6T 0C2
(780) 448-7711
Emp Here 20
SIC 6021 National commercial banks

D-U-N-S 20-713-0399   (BR)
**EDMONTON CATHOLIC SEPARATE
SCHOOL DISTRICT NO.7**
*FATHER MICHAEL TROY CATHOLIC JU-
NIOR HIGH SCHOOL*
(*Suby of* Edmonton Catholic Separate School
District No.7)
3630 23 St Nw, Edmonton, AB, T6T 1W7
(780) 471-1962
Emp Here 25
SIC 8211 Elementary and secondary schools

D-U-N-S 20-154-7937   (BR)
EDMONTON SCHOOL DISTRICT NO. 7
VELMA E BAKER SCHOOL
2845 43a Ave Nw, Edmonton, AB, T6T 1J9
(780) 440-4088
Emp Here 35
SIC 8211 Elementary and secondary schools

D-U-N-S 24-361-7235   (BR)
HOME DEPOT OF CANADA INC
HOME DEPOT
(*Suby of* The Home Depot Inc)
4430 17 St Nw, Edmonton, AB, T6T 0B4
(780) 577-3575
Emp Here 100
SIC 5251 Hardware stores

D-U-N-S 24-385-2451   (BR)
LOBLAWS INC
REAL CANADIAN SUPERSTORE
4410 17 St Nw, Edmonton, AB, T6T 0C1
(780) 450-2041
Emp Here 300
SIC 5411 Grocery stores

D-U-N-S 20-197-2937   (BR)
MCMATT INVESTMENTS LTD
MCDONALD'S
3841 34 St Nw, Edmonton, AB, T6T 1K9
(780) 414-8370
Emp Here 50
SIC 5812 Eating places

D-U-N-S 24-609-4408   (BR)
SOBEYS CAPITAL INCORPORATED
3819 34 St Nw, Edmonton, AB, T6T 1K9
(780) 463-8383
Emp Here 49
SIC 5411 Grocery stores

D-U-N-S 24-313-5774   (BR)
**WINNERS MERCHANTS INTERNATIONAL
L.P.**
WINNERS
(*Suby of* The TJX Companies Inc)
2058 38 Ave Nw, Edmonton, AB, T6T 0B9
(780) 461-0030
Emp Here 30
SIC 5651 Family clothing stores

Edmonton, AB T6V

D-U-N-S 20-714-0521   (SL)
EDMONTON ISLAMIC SCHOOL SOCIETY
EDMONTON ISLAMIC SCHOOL
14525 127 St Nw, Edmonton, AB, T6V 0B3
(780) 472-7309
Emp Here 50   *Sales* 3,356,192
SIC 8211 Elementary and secondary schools

D-U-N-S 20-082-7087   (HQ)
HIGHLAND MOVING & STORAGE LTD
THE MOVER
157 Ave Nw Suite 14490, Edmonton, AB, T6V
0K8
(780) 453-6777
Emp Here 75   *Emp Total* 350
Sales 5,399,092
SIC 4214 Local trucking with storage
 Donald Kachur

D-U-N-S 20-897-8486   (BR)
LEON'S FURNITURE LIMITED
*LEON'S FURNITURE WAREHOUSE &
SHOWROOM*
13730 140 St Nw, Edmonton, AB, T6V 1J8
(780) 456-4455
Emp Here 120
SIC 5712 Furniture stores

D-U-N-S 25-318-1234   (BR)
**MCDONALD'S RESTAURANTS OF
CANADA LIMITED**
MCDONALD'S 8457
(*Suby of* McDonald's Corporation)
14003 127 St Nw, Edmonton, AB, T6V 1E7
(780) 414-8457
Emp Here 58
SIC 5812 Eating places

Edmonton, AB T6W

D-U-N-S 24-733-7116   (HQ)
FOUNTAIN TIRE LTD
1006 103a St Sw Suite 103, Edmonton, AB,
T6W 2P6
(780) 464-3700
Emp Here 200   *Emp Total* 1,804
Sales 194,586,187
SIC 5531 Auto and home supply stores
Dir Brent Hesje
 Brian Hesje
 David Janzen
VP Pat Witiw
 Nelson Tonn

D-U-N-S 24-803-5490   (BR)
HOME DEPOT OF CANADA INC
HOME DEPOT
(*Suby of* The Home Depot Inc)
6218 Currents Dr Nw, Edmonton, AB, T6W
0L8
(780) 989-7460
Emp Here 100
SIC 5251 Hardware stores

D-U-N-S 24-953-1633   (BR)
JAYMAN BUILT LTD
5083 Windermere Blvd Sw Suite 102, Edmonton, AB, T6W 0J5
(780) 481-6666
Emp Here 50
SIC 1521 Single-family housing construction

D-U-N-S 20-737-7987   (BR)
STARBUCKS COFFEE CANADA, INC
(*Suby of* Starbucks Corporation)
961 James Mowatt Trail Sw, Edmonton, AB,
T6W 1S4
(780) 435-3081
Emp Here 23
SIC 5812 Eating places

D-U-N-S 20-896-2068   (SL)

Edmonton, AB T6V

**WINDERMERE GOLF AND COUNTRY
CLUB**
19110 Ellerslie Rd Sw, Edmonton, AB, T6W
1A5
(780) 988-5501
Emp Here 60   *Sales* 2,858,628
SIC 7997 Membership sports and recreation
clubs

Edmonton, AB T6X

D-U-N-S 24-376-5109   (BR)
AECON CONSTRUCTION GROUP INC
AECON INFRASTRUCTURE
1003 Ellwood Rd Sw Suite 301, Edmonton,
AB, T6X 0B3

Emp Here 100
SIC 1541 Industrial buildings and warehouses

D-U-N-S 25-315-4108   (BR)
COMPUGEN INC
2627 Ellwood Dr Sw Suite 102, Edmonton,
AB, T6X 0P7
(780) 448-2525
Emp Here 50
SIC 5045 Computers, peripherals, and soft-
ware

D-U-N-S 20-718-4586   (BR)
COMPUGEN SYSTEMS LTD
2627 Ellwood Dr Sw Suite 102, Edmonton,
AB, T6X 0P7
(780) 448-2525
Emp Here 60
SIC 7372 Prepackaged software

D-U-N-S 20-203-8357   (SL)
CROSSROADS FAMILY SERVICES INC
1207 91 St Sw Unit 201, Edmonton, AB, T6X
1E9
(780) 430-7715
Emp Here 55   *Sales* 2,042,900
SIC 8361 Residential care

D-U-N-S 24-966-8658   (BR)
**DATA COMMUNICATIONS MANAGEMENT
CORP**
DATA GROUP OF COMPANIES
9503 12 Ave Sw, Edmonton, AB, T6X 0C3
(780) 462-9700
Emp Here 130
SIC 5112 Stationery and office supplies

D-U-N-S 20-875-0567   (SL)
**DUNCAN SABINE COLLYER PARTNERS
LLP**
DSCP
Gd, Edmonton, AB, T6X 0P6
(780) 414-0364
Emp Here 100   *Sales* 4,377,642
SIC 8721 Accounting, auditing, and book-
keeping

D-U-N-S 20-166-1220   (HQ)
ERIKS INDUSTRIAL SERVICES LP
9748 12 Ave Sw, Edmonton, AB, T6X 0J5
(780) 437-1260
Emp Here 51   *Emp Total* 60,800
Sales 21,304,524
SIC 5085 Industrial supplies
VP Ryan Antoniadis

D-U-N-S 20-712-6181   (BR)
EDMONTON SCHOOL DISTRICT NO. 7
ELLERSLIE CAMPUS NORTH
521 66 St Sw, Edmonton, AB, T6X 1A3
(780) 988-5556
Emp Here 40
SIC 8211 Elementary and secondary schools

D-U-N-S 24-859-2276   (SL)
**FOUR POINTS BY SHERATON EDMONTON
GATEWAY**
10010 12 Ave Sw, Edmonton, AB, T6X 0P9

▲ Public Company   ■ Public Company Family Member   **HQ** Headquarters   **BR** Branch   **SL** Single Location

(780) 801-4000
Emp Here 100 *Sales* 4,377,642
SIC 7011 Hotels and motels

D-U-N-S 24-809-8139 (BR)
GIENOW WINDOWS & DOORS INC
(*Suby of* H.I.G. Capital Inc.)
9704 12 Ave Sw, Edmonton, AB, T6X 0J5
(780) 450-8000
Emp Here 30
SIC 2431 Millwork

D-U-N-S 24-761-1192 (BR)
JOHN DEERE CANADA ULC
9832 12 Ave Sw, Edmonton, AB, T6X 0J5
(780) 638-6750
Emp Here 30
SIC 5083 Farm and garden machinery

D-U-N-S 24-392-9536 (SL)
MILLS NISSAN LTD
GO NISSAN
1275 101 St Sw, Edmonton, AB, T6X 1A1
(780) 463-5700
Emp Here 33 *Sales* 12,038,516
SIC 5511 New and used car dealers
Pr Pr Lance Mills

D-U-N-S 24-344-5454 (BR)
MORRISON HERSHFIELD LIMITED
1603 91 St Sw Suite 300, Edmonton, AB, T6X 0W8
(780) 483-5200
Emp Here 45
SIC 8711 Engineering services

D-U-N-S 24-826-3001 (BR)
MOTION INDUSTRIES (CANADA), INC
(*Suby of* Genuine Parts Company)
9860 12 Ave Sw, Edmonton, AB, T6X 0J5
(780) 466-6501
Emp Here 35
SIC 5085 Industrial supplies

D-U-N-S 20-807-8253 (HQ)
NORTHWEST HYDRAULIC CONSULTANTS LTD
(*Suby of* Northwest Hydraulic Consultants Ltd)
9819 12 Ave Sw, Edmonton, AB, T6X 0E3
(780) 436-5868
Emp Here 25 *Emp Total* 125
Sales 17,904,251
SIC 8711 Engineering services
Pr Pr Herbert Wiebe
Gerald Mutter
Dir Michael H Okun

D-U-N-S 24-381-5318 (HQ)
WILLBROS CONSTRUCTION SERVICES (CANADA) LP
WILLBROS CANADA
1103 95 St Sw Suite 201, Edmonton, AB, T6X 0P8
(403) 817-2265
Emp Here 466 *Emp Total* 3,579
Sales 223,492,758
SIC 1623 Water, sewer, and utility lines
Pr Pr Michael Fournier
Lorri Pinder

D-U-N-S 24-733-2760 (HQ)
ZCL COMPOSITES INC
(*Suby of* ZCL Composites Inc)
1420 Parsons Rd Sw, Edmonton, AB, T6X 1M5
(780) 466-6648
Emp Here 80 *Emp Total* 573
Sales 136,185,656
SIC 3299 NonMetallic mineral products,
Pr Pr Ronald Bachmeier
Kathy Demuth
Rene Aldana
Anthony Franceschini
D. Bruce Bentley
Diane Brickner
Leonard Cornez
Darcy Morris

Ralph Young

Edmonton, AB T9E

D-U-N-S 20-746-4301 (BR)
GOVERNMENT OF THE PROVINCE OF ALBERTA
AIR TRANSPORTATION SERVICE
3759 60 Ave E Hangar 3 Edmonton International Airport, Edmonton, AB, T9E 0V4
(780) 427-7343
Emp Here 25
SIC 4111 Local and suburban transit

D-U-N-S 24-859-9016 (SL)
HUDSON DUFRY - EDMONTON
Po Box 9898, Edmonton, AB, T9E 0V3
(780) 890-7263
Emp Here 100 *Sales* 6,380,400
SIC 5441 Candy, nut, and confectionery stores
Genl Mgr Dave Neil

Edson, AB T7E

D-U-N-S 20-578-2456 (BR)
ALBERTA TREASURY BRANCHES
ATB FINANCIAL
313 50 St W, Edson, AB, T7E 1T8
(780) 723-5571
Emp Here 23
SIC 6036 Savings institutions, except federal

D-U-N-S 20-070-2418 (BR)
BP CANADA ENERGY COMPANY
(*Suby of* BP P.L.C.)
5310 4 Ave, Edson, AB, T7E 1L4
(780) 723-3604
Emp Here 35
SIC 1311 Crude petroleum and natural gas

D-U-N-S 24-296-6757 (BR)
BLUEWAVE ENERGY LTD
7539 1a Ave, Edson, AB, T7E 1X6
(780) 712-6111
Emp Here 23
SIC 5541 Gasoline service stations

D-U-N-S 20-303-4376 (BR)
CLEARSTREAM ENERGY SERVICES LIMITED PARTNERSHIP
FABRICATION
22 53304 Range Rd 170 Mizera Subd, Edson, AB, T7E 1T6
(780) 723-4237
Emp Here 60
SIC 1389 Oil and gas field services, nec

D-U-N-S 25-764-1050 (BR)
ENERFLEX LTD.
SYNTECH ENERFLEX
(*Suby of* Enerflex Ltd)
4439 2 Ave, Edson, AB, T7E 1C1
(780) 723-2173
Emp Here 20
SIC 3563 Air and gas compressors

D-U-N-S 24-905-0998 (HQ)
ERNIE O 'S RESTAURANT & PUB (EDSON) INC
(*Suby of* Ernie O 's Restaurant & Pub (Edson) Inc)
4404 5 Ave, Edson, AB, T7E 1B7
(780) 723-3500
Emp Here 35 *Emp Total* 95
Sales 2,845,467
SIC 5812 Eating places

D-U-N-S 24-068-2047 (BR)
FLINT ENERGY SERVICES LTD.
FLINT FIELD SERVICES
Gd Stn Main, Edson, AB, T7E 1T1

Emp Here 25
SIC 1623 Water, sewer, and utility lines

D-U-N-S 20-293-7798 (BR)
FORMULA POWELL L.P.
Gd Stn Main, Edson, AB, T7E 1T1
(780) 712-6110
Emp Here 50
SIC 4213 Trucking, except local

D-U-N-S 20-713-0894 (BR)
GRANDE YELLOWHEAD PUBLIC SCHOOL DIVISION 77
WESTHAVEN ELEMENTARY SCHOOL
1205 Westhaven Dr Suite 1, Edson, AB, T7E 1S6
(780) 723-3397
Emp Here 35
SIC 8211 Elementary and secondary schools

D-U-N-S 25-014-4417 (BR)
GRANDE YELLOWHEAD PUBLIC SCHOOL DIVISION 77
PARKLAND COMPOSITE HIGH SCHOOL
4630 12 Ave, Edson, AB, T7E 1S7
(780) 723-6035
Emp Here 52
SIC 8211 Elementary and secondary schools

D-U-N-S 20-713-0050 (BR)
GRANDE YELLOWHEAD PUBLIC SCHOOL DIVISION 77
ECOLE PINE GROVE SCHOOL
4619 12 Ave, Edson, AB, T7E 1S7
(780) 723-3992
Emp Here 50
SIC 8211 Elementary and secondary schools

D-U-N-S 20-837-9508 (BR)
HUSKY OIL OPERATIONS LIMITED
5964 3 Ave, Edson, AB, T7E 1R8
(780) 723-6945
Emp Here 25
SIC 1311 Crude petroleum and natural gas

D-U-N-S 20-085-2903 (SL)
LINFORD FOODS LTD
EDSON I G A
Gd Stn Main, Edson, AB, T7E 1T1
(780) 723-3753
Emp Here 100 *Sales* 38,383,360
SIC 5411 Grocery stores
Evelyn Linford
Ken Linford
Keith Linford

D-U-N-S 20-105-3597 (BR)
LIVING WATERS CATHOLIC REGIONAL DIVISION NO.42
VANIER COMMUNITY CATHOLIC SCHOOL
831 56 St, Edson, AB, T7E 0A3
(780) 723-6612
Emp Here 35
SIC 8211 Elementary and secondary schools

D-U-N-S 20-852-5019 (BR)
MCMAN YOUTH, FAMILY AND COMMUNITY SERVICES ASSOCIATION
(*Suby of* McMan Youth, Family and Community Services Association)
4926 1st Ave, Edson, AB, T7E 1V7
(780) 712-7677
Emp Here 40
SIC 8322 Individual and family services

D-U-N-S 20-016-3868 (BR)
PRAIRIE MINES & ROYALTY ULC
(*Suby of* Westmoreland Coal Company)
Gd, Edson, AB, T7E 1W1
(780) 794-8100
Emp Here 500
SIC 1221 Bituminous coal and lignite-surface mining

D-U-N-S 24-082-3331 (BR)
PYRAMID CORPORATION
5933 4 Ave, Edson, AB, T7E 1L9

(780) 723-2887
Emp Here 20
SIC 1731 Electrical work

D-U-N-S 25-329-6883 (BR)
REPSOL OIL & GAS CANADA INC
5 Ave, Edson, AB, T7E 1T1
(780) 723-9800
Emp Here 70
SIC 1382 Oil and gas exploration services

D-U-N-S 24-041-4404 (BR)
STINGER WELLHEAD PROTECTION (CANADA) INCORPORATED
174 27 St, Edson, AB, T7E 1N9

Emp Here 30
SIC 1389 Oil and gas field services, nec

D-U-N-S 20-702-9146 (BR)
SUNCOR ENERGY INC
SUNCOR ENERGY
Gd Stn Main, Edson, AB, T7E 1T1
(780) 693-7300
Emp Here 30
SIC 2911 Petroleum refining

D-U-N-S 20-085-4248 (SL)
SUNDANCE FOREST INDUSTRIES LTD
Gd Stn Main, Edson, AB, T7E 1T1
(780) 723-3977
Emp Here 240 *Sales* 31,349,760
SIC 2421 Sawmills and planing mills, general
Rodney Goldie
John Huey
Joseph Zhou
Shawn Liu
Yang Shu

D-U-N-S 24-319-5000 (BR)
WAL-MART CANADA CORP
WALMART
5750 2 Ave, Edson, AB, T7E 0A1
(780) 723-6357
Emp Here 120
SIC 5311 Department stores

Elk Point, AB T0A

D-U-N-S 24-391-4744 (HQ)
E-CAN OILFIELD SERVICES LP
5113 46 St, Elk Point, AB, T0A 1A0
(780) 724-4018
Emp Here 270 *Emp Total* 5,515
Sales 77,182,964
SIC 1389 Oil and gas field services, nec
VP VP Clifford Smith
Karen Bjornstad
Opers Mgr Steve Penz
Walt Czuroski
Shawn Cousins

D-U-N-S 24-615-3162 (BR)
K+S SEL WINDSOR LTEE
CANADIAN SALT COMPANY
Gd, Elk Point, AB, T0A 1A0
(780) 724-4180
Emp Here 100
SIC 1479 Chemical and fertilizer mining

D-U-N-S 20-088-3577 (BR)
K+S SEL WINDSOR LTEE
WINDSOR SALT
Hwy 646, Elk Point, AB, T0A 1A0
(780) 724-3745
Emp Here 50
SIC 2899 Chemical preparations, nec

D-U-N-S 20-519-8703 (BR)
NEWALTA CORPORATION
Gd, Elk Point, AB, T0A 1A0
(780) 724-4333
Emp Here 22
SIC 4953 Refuse systems

D-U-N-S 20-023-9668 (BR)

ST. PAUL EDUCATION REGIONAL DIVISION NO 1
ELK POINT ELEMENTARY SCHOOL
5410 50 St, Elk Point, AB, T0A 1A0
(780) 724-3880
Emp Here 38
SIC 8211 Elementary and secondary schools

D-U-N-S 20-591-7607   (BR)
ST. PAUL EDUCATION REGIONAL DIVISION NO 1
F G MILLER HIGH SCHOOL
5218 51st St, Elk Point, AB, T0A 1A0
(780) 724-3966
Emp Here 35
SIC 8211 Elementary and secondary schools

D-U-N-S 20-085-3554   (BR)
ST. PAUL AND DISTRICT CO-OPERATIVE ASSOCIATION LIMITED
ST. PAUL AND DISTRICT CO-OPERATIVE ASSOCIATION LIMITED
4901 50th Ave, Elk Point, AB, T0A 1A0
(780) 724-3895
Emp Here 30
SIC 5411 Grocery stores

D-U-N-S 20-209-1836   (BR)
TERVITA CORPORATION
CCS MIDSTREAM SERVICES
(*Suby of* Tervita Corporation)
140-10 Ave S E Unit 500, Elk Point, AB, T0A 1A0
(780) 724-3002
Emp Here 21
SIC 1389 Oil and gas field services, nec

Evansburg, AB T0E

D-U-N-S 20-651-6937   (BR)
ALBERTA HEALTH SERVICES
EVANSBURG DISTRICT HEALTH CENTRE
5225 50 St, Evansburg, AB, T0E 0T0
(780) 727-2288
Emp Here 35
SIC 8093 Specialty outpatient clinics, nec

D-U-N-S 25-172-5792   (BR)
GRANDE YELLOWHEAD PUBLIC SCHOOL DIVISION 77
GRAND TRUNK HIGH SCHOOL
4707 46 Ave, Evansburg, AB, T0E 0T0
(780) 727-3925
Emp Here 20
SIC 8211 Elementary and secondary schools

D-U-N-S 20-569-2242   (BR)
ROYAL BANK OF CANADA
RBC
(*Suby of* Royal Bank Of Canada)
5119 50th St, Evansburg, AB, T0E 0T0
(780) 727-3566
Emp Here 20
SIC 6021 National commercial banks

Exshaw, AB T0L

D-U-N-S 20-063-4900   (BR)
CALGARY YOUNG MEN'S CHRISTIAN ASSOCIATION
Y M C A
Gd, Exshaw, AB, T0L 2C0
(403) 673-3858
Emp Here 200
SIC 8621 Professional organizations

D-U-N-S 20-028-4052   (BR)
CANADIAN ROCKIES REGIONAL DIVISION NO 12
EXSHAW SCHOOL
27 Mount Allan Dr, Exshaw, AB, T0L 2C0

(403) 673-3656
Emp Here 32
SIC 8211 Elementary and secondary schools

D-U-N-S 20-957-5195   (BR)
GRAYMONT WESTERN CANADA INC
Gd, Exshaw, AB, T0L 2C0
(403) 673-3595
Emp Here 60
SIC 3274 Lime

D-U-N-S 20-085-4644   (BR)
LAFARGE CANADA INC
Hwy 1a, Exshaw, AB, T0L 2C0
(403) 673-3815
Emp Here 150
SIC 2891 Adhesives and sealants

Fairview, AB T0H

D-U-N-S 24-121-6535   (BR)
ALBERTA HEALTH SERVICES
FAIRVIEW HEALTH COMPLEX
10628 100th St, Fairview, AB, T0H 1L0
(780) 835-6100
Emp Here 100
SIC 8062 General medical and surgical hospitals

D-U-N-S 20-897-2729   (BR)
DEVON CANADA CORPORATION
10924 92nd Ave, Fairview, AB, T0H 1L0

Emp Here 115
SIC 1382 Oil and gas exploration services

D-U-N-S 20-153-7755   (BR)
FLINT ENERGY SERVICES LTD.
10211 98 St, Fairview, AB, T0H 1L0

Emp Here 120
SIC 1389 Oil and gas field services, nec

D-U-N-S 25-192-4593   (BR)
FRESON MARKET LTD
IGA
(*Suby of* Altamart Investments (1993) Ltd)
10905 101 Ave,, Fairview, AB, T0H 1L0
(780) 835-2716
Emp Here 30
SIC 5411 Grocery stores

D-U-N-S 20-747-1694   (BR)
GRANDE PRAIRIE CATHOLIC SCHOOL DISTRICT 28
ST THOMAS MORE SCHOOL
10208 114 St, Fairview, AB, T0H 1L0
(780) 835-2245
Emp Here 25
SIC 8211 Elementary and secondary schools

D-U-N-S 24-676-8050   (BR)
INNVEST PROPERTIES CORP
COMFORT INN
(*Suby of* Innvest Properties Corp)
11232 101 Ave, Fairview, AB, T0H 1L0
(780) 835-4921
Emp Here 50
SIC 7011 Hotels and motels

D-U-N-S 20-029-4036   (BR)
PEACE RIVER SCHOOL DIVISION 10
E E OLIVER ELEMENTARY SCHOOL
11204 104 Ave, Fairview, AB, T0H 1L0
(780) 835-2225
Emp Here 41
SIC 8211 Elementary and secondary schools

D-U-N-S 20-037-3293   (BR)
PEACE RIVER SCHOOL DIVISION 10
FAIRVIEW HIGH SCHOOL
10317 106 St, Fairview, AB, T0H 1L0
(780) 835-5421
Emp Here 35
SIC 8211 Elementary and secondary schools

D-U-N-S 24-376-7154   (BR)
PRAIRIECOAST EQUIPMENT INC
11520 101 Ave, Fairview, AB, T0H 1L0
(780) 835-4440
Emp Here 25
SIC 5083 Farm and garden machinery

D-U-N-S 24-766-3586   (SL)
SENEY HOLDINGS LTD
H & R BLOCK
10404 110 St, Fairview, AB, T0H 1L0
(780) 835-2929
Emp Here 120   *Sales* 5,579,750
SIC 7291 Tax return preparation services
Pr Donald Seney
VP VP James Seney

D-U-N-S 24-227-4962   (BR)
TRANSCANADA PIPELINES LIMITED
Gd, Fairview, AB, T0H 1L0
(780) 835-8107
Emp Here 20
SIC 4619 Pipelines, nec

Falher, AB T0H

D-U-N-S 20-043-6496   (BR)
HIGH PRAIRIE SCHOOL DIVISION NO 48
ROUTHIER SCHOOL
134 Central Ave Ne, Falher, AB, T0H 1M0
(780) 837-2114
Emp Here 38
SIC 8211 Elementary and secondary schools

D-U-N-S 24-032-4785   (BR)
PENN WEST PETROLEUM LTD
GIROUXVILLE PLANT
Gd, Falher, AB, T0H 1M0
(780) 837-2929
Emp Here 100
SIC 2911 Petroleum refining

D-U-N-S 25-316-7951   (SL)
TWILIGHT HUTTERIAN BRETHREN
TWILIGHT COLONY
Gd, Falher, AB, T0H 1M0

Emp Here 140   *Sales* 8,857,893
SIC 7389 Business services, nec
Pr Pr John B Wipf
 Sam Entz
Sec Paul M Wipf
Dir Peter M Entz
Dir Elias Wipf
Dir Paul A Wipf
Dir Lawrence K Entz

Falun, AB T0C

D-U-N-S 20-260-1175   (BR)
WETASKIWIN REGIONAL PUBLIC SCHOOLS
FALUN ELEMENTARY SCHOOL
(*Suby of* Wetaskiwin Regional Public Schools)
Gd, Falun, AB, T0C 1H0
(780) 352-2898
Emp Here 40
SIC 8211 Elementary and secondary schools

D-U-N-S 25-135-4817   (BR)
WETASKIWIN REGIONAL PUBLIC SCHOOLS
PIGEON LAKE REGIONAL SCHOOL
(*Suby of* Wetaskiwin Regional Public Schools)
Gd, Falun, AB, T0C 1H0
(780) 352-4916
Emp Here 43
SIC 8211 Elementary and secondary schools

Foisy, AB T0A

D-U-N-S 20-058-8064   (BR)
CANADIAN NATURAL RESOURCES LIMITED
ANADARKO
Gd, Foisy, AB, T0A 1E0

Emp Here 30
SIC 1311 Crude petroleum and natural gas

Foremost, AB T0K

D-U-N-S 25-194-1498   (BR)
ENCANA CORPORATION
ENCANA RESOURCES
Gd, Foremost, AB, T0K 0X0
(403) 868-2403
Emp Here 35
SIC 1382 Oil and gas exploration services

Forestburg, AB T0B

D-U-N-S 20-025-4840   (BR)
BATTLE RIVER REGIONAL DIVISION 31
FORESTBURG SCHOOL
4914 46 Ave, Forestburg, AB, T0B 1N0
(780) 582-3792
Emp Here 34
SIC 8211 Elementary and secondary schools

D-U-N-S 24-786-2964   (BR)
PRAIRIE MINES & ROYALTY ULC
(*Suby of* Westmoreland Coal Company)
Gd, Forestburg, AB, T0B 1N0
(403) 884-3000
Emp Here 100
SIC 1221 Bituminous coal and lignite-surface mining

Fort Mackay, AB T0P

D-U-N-S 20-189-2127   (BR)
BANK OF MONTREAL
BMO
Gd, Fort Mackay, AB, T0P 1C0
(780) 762-3500
Emp Here 20
SIC 6021 National commercial banks

Fort Macleod, AB T0L

D-U-N-S 25-266-4321   (BR)
BOUVRY EXPORTS CALGARY LTD
Gd, Fort Macleod, AB, T0L 0Z0
(403) 553-4431
Emp Here 110
SIC 2011 Meat packing plants

D-U-N-S 25-967-1311   (BR)
EXTENDICARE (CANADA) INC
EXTENDICARE FORT MACLEOD
654 29th St, Fort Macleod, AB, T0L 0Z0
(403) 553-3955
Emp Here 75
SIC 8051 Skilled nursing care facilities

D-U-N-S 25-484-4442   (SL)
FORT MACLEOD HOSPITAL
FORT MACLEOD HEALTH CENTER
744 26th St, Fort Macleod, AB, T0L 0Z0
(403) 553-4487
Emp Here 50   *Sales* 3,502,114
SIC 8062 General medical and surgical hospitals

D-U-N-S 24-476-7955 (BR)
GOVERNMENT OF THE PROVINCE OF AL-BERTA
HEALTH CARE CENTRE
744 26th St, Fort Macleod, AB, T0L 0Z0
(403) 553-5300
Emp Here 150
SIC 8062 General medical and surgical hospitals

D-U-N-S 24-042-8755 (SL)
HUTTERIAN BRETHREN CHURCH OF EWELME COLONY
Gd, Fort Macleod, AB, T0L 0Z0
(403) 553-2606
Emp Here 85   *Sales* 5,617,974
SIC 8661 Religious organizations
Pr Pr Peter Walter
George Hofer
Darius Walter
Dir Elias Walter
Dir Kenneth Hofer

D-U-N-S 20-028-3278 (BR)
LIVINGSTONE RANGE SCHOOL DIVISION NO 68
W A DAY ELEMENTARY SCHOOL
521 26th St, Fort Macleod, AB, T0L 0Z0
(403) 553-3362
Emp Here 28
SIC 8211 Elementary and secondary schools

D-U-N-S 20-027-3634 (BR)
LIVINGSTONE RANGE SCHOOL DIVISION NO 68
G R DAVIS SCHOOL
410 20th St, Fort Macleod, AB, T0L 0Z0

Emp Here 21
SIC 8211 Elementary and secondary schools

D-U-N-S 20-711-2801 (BR)
LIVINGSTONE RANGE SCHOOL DIVISION NO 68
FP WALSH SCHOOL
538 16 St, Fort Macleod, AB, T0L 0Z0
(403) 553-4411
Emp Here 50
SIC 8211 Elementary and secondary schools

D-U-N-S 25-082-6096 (BR)
LOBLAWS INC
EXTRA FOODS #9010
1906 8th Ave, Fort Macleod, AB, T0L 0Z0
(403) 553-7900
Emp Here 52
SIC 5411 Grocery stores

D-U-N-S 25-124-0941 (BR)
VOLKER STEVIN CONTRACTING LTD.
Junction Hwy 2 Secondary Rd, Fort Macleod, AB, T0L 0Z0
(403) 553-4225
Emp Here 30
SIC 1611 Highway and street construction

Fort Mcmurray, AB T9H

D-U-N-S 24-325-8345 (SL)
580799 ALBERTA LTD
316 Mackay Cres, Fort Mcmurray, AB, T9H 4E4
(780) 791-5477
Emp Here 260   *Sales* 60,270,240
SIC 6712 Bank holding companies
Pr Pr Alphonse Hutchings

D-U-N-S 25-684-5009 (BR)
7-ELEVEN CANADA, INC
7-ELEVEN STORE #32252
10002 Franklin Ave, Fort Mcmurray, AB, T9H 2K6
(780) 715-0781
Emp Here 24
SIC 5411 Grocery stores

D-U-N-S 24-207-0816 (BR)
AMEC FOSTER WHEELER AMERICAS LIMITED
AMEC EARTH & ENVIRONMENTAL, DIV OF
10204 Centennial Dr, Fort Mcmurray, AB, T9H 1Y5
(780) 791-0848
Emp Here 32
SIC 8711 Engineering services

D-U-N-S 25-316-7621 (BR)
ATCO ELECTRIC LTD
190 Mackay Cres, Fort Mcmurray, AB, T9H 4W8

Emp Here 40
SIC 4911 Electric services

D-U-N-S 24-715-4888 (BR)
ATCO STRUCTURES & LOGISTICS LTD
121 Signal Rd, Fort Mcmurray, AB, T9H 4N6
(780) 714-6773
Emp Here 20
SIC 7519 Utility trailer rental

D-U-N-S 25-947-6844 (BR)
ACKLANDS - GRAINGER INC
AGI
(*Suby* of W.W. Grainger, Inc.)
284 Macdonald Cres Suite 200, Fort Mcmurray, AB, T9H 4B6
(780) 743-3344
Emp Here 50
SIC 5085 Industrial supplies

D-U-N-S 20-581-3137 (BR)
ALBERTA TREASURY BRANCHES
ATB FINANCIAL
11 Haineault St, Fort Mcmurray, AB, T9H 1R8
(780) 790-3300
Emp Here 20
SIC 6036 Savings institutions, except federal

D-U-N-S 25-995-3958 (HQ)
ALBIAN SANDS ENERGY INC
Gd Lcd Main, Fort Mcmurray, AB, T9H 3E2
(780) 713-4400
Emp Here 420   *Emp Total* 93
Sales 173,062,780
SIC 1382 Oil and gas exploration services
Dir John C Abbott
Dir Steve T Hutchinson
Dir Stephen D.L. Reynish

D-U-N-S 25-947-6398 (BR)
ALUMA SYSTEMS INC
(*Suby* of Clayton, Dubilier & Rice, Inc.)
Gd Lcd Main, Fort Mcmurray, AB, T9H 3E2
(780) 790-4852
Emp Here 650
SIC 1799 Special trade contractors, nec

D-U-N-S 24-378-8804 (SL)
ATHABASCA CHIPEWYAN EMPIRE INDUSTRIAL SERVICES LTD
ACE INDUSTRIAL SERVICES
125b Macdonald Cres, Fort Mcmurray, AB, T9H 4B3
(780) 743-9739
Emp Here 50   *Sales* 4,377,642
SIC 1799 Special trade contractors, nec

D-U-N-S 20-787-2347 (BR)
B.G.E. SERVICE & SUPPLY LTD
305 Macdonald Cres Suite 4, Fort Mcmurray, AB, T9H 4B7
(780) 743-2998
Emp Here 20
SIC 5085 Industrial supplies

D-U-N-S 25-954-5051 (BR)
BANK OF NOVA SCOTIA, THE
SCOTIABANK
9541 Franklin Ave, Fort Mcmurray, AB, T9H 3Z7
(780) 743-3386
Emp Here 36
SIC 6021 National commercial banks

D-U-N-S 20-567-3721 (BR)
BANK OF MONTREAL
BMO
9920 Franklin Ave, Fort Mcmurray, AB, T9H 2K5
(780) 790-6992
Emp Here 25
SIC 6021 National commercial banks

D-U-N-S 24-421-1475 (SL)
BOREALIS MECHANICAL LTD
330 Mackenzie Blvd, Fort Mcmurray, AB, T9H 4C4
(780) 792-2660
Emp Here 20   *Sales* 1,751,057
SIC 1711 Plumbing, heating, air-conditioning

D-U-N-S 25-788-2357 (BR)
BRANDT TRACTOR LTD
360 Mackenzie Blvd Suite 5, Fort Mcmurray, AB, T9H 4C4
(780) 791-6635
Emp Here 20
SIC 5084 Industrial machinery and equipment

D-U-N-S 24-395-8204 (BR)
BRICK WAREHOUSE LP, THE
BRICK, THE
19 Riedel St Suite 110, Fort Mcmurray, AB, T9H 5P8
(780) 743-5777
Emp Here 25
SIC 5712 Furniture stores

D-U-N-S 24-394-9898 (HQ)
C. B. S. CONSTRUCTION LTD
CBS
(*Suby* of C. B. S. Construction Ltd)
150 Mackay Cres, Fort Mcmurray, AB, T9H 4W8
(780) 743-1810
Emp Here 300   *Emp Total* 350
Sales 47,862,219
SIC 1629 Heavy construction, nec
Pr Pr Garry Fizzell

D-U-N-S 24-525-1272 (BR)
CEDA INTERNATIONAL CORPORATION
CEDA-REACTOR
180 Maclennan Cres, Fort Mcmurray, AB, T9H 4E8
(780) 791-0707
Emp Here 40
SIC 2819 Industrial inorganic chemicals, nec

D-U-N-S 20-743-4239 (BR)
CAISSEN WATER TECHNOLOGIES INC
381 Mackenzie Blvd, Fort Mcmurray, AB, T9H 5E2

Emp Here 25
SIC 3589 Service industry machinery, nec

D-U-N-S 25-288-9142 (BR)
CANADA POST CORPORATION
FORT MCMURRAY POST OFFICE
9521 Franklin Ave Suite 160, Fort Mcmurray, AB, T9H 3Z7
(780) 880-3323
Emp Here 60
SIC 4311 U.s. postal service

D-U-N-S 20-569-2499 (BR)
CANADIAN IMPERIAL BANK OF COMMERCE
CIBC
8553 Manning Ave, Fort Mcmurray, AB, T9H 3N7
(780) 743-3312
Emp Here 25
SIC 6021 National commercial banks

D-U-N-S 20-291-6045 (BR)
CANADIAN NATURAL RESOURCES LIMITED
HORIZON OIL SANDS
Hwy 63, Fort Mcmurray, AB, T9H 5N4
(780) 828-2500
Emp Here 4,500

SIC 1311 Crude petroleum and natural gas

D-U-N-S 20-065-7315 (BR)
CARMACKS ENTERPRISES LTD
CARMACKS INDUSTRIES
Gd Lcd Main, Fort Mcmurray, AB, T9H 3E2

Emp Here 100
SIC 1611 Highway and street construction

D-U-N-S 24-399-6915 (SL)
CHRISTINA RIVER ENTERPRISES LIMITED PARTNERSHIP
Gd Lcd Main, Fort Mcmurray, AB, T9H 3E2
(780) 334-2446
Emp Here 135   *Sales* 13,205,887
SIC 2448 Wood pallets and skids
Pr Maxine Butt

D-U-N-S 25-962-3502 (BR)
CIVEO CROWN CAMP SERVICES LTD
PTI LODGE
(*Suby* of Oil States International, Inc.)
Gd Lcd Main, Fort Mcmurray, AB, T9H 3E2

Emp Here 20
SIC 5812 Eating places

D-U-N-S 20-069-4060 (BR)
CIVEO PREMIUM CAMP SERVICES LTD
PTI LODGE
(*Suby* of Oil States International, Inc.)
10020 Franklin Ave Suite 207, Fort Mcmurray, AB, T9H 2K6

Emp Here 47
SIC 7011 Hotels and motels

D-U-N-S 24-378-7285 (BR)
CLEAN HARBORS ENERGY AND INDUSTRIAL SERVICES CORP.
26 Airport Rd, Fort Mcmurray, AB, T9H 5B4
(780) 743-0222
Emp Here 300
SIC 7349 Building maintenance services, nec

D-U-N-S 20-329-4756 (SL)
CLEARWATER ENERGY SERVICES LP
355 Mackenzie Blvd, Fort Mcmurray, AB, T9H 5E2
(780) 743-2171
Emp Here 25   *Sales* 4,961,328
SIC 1541 Industrial buildings and warehouses

D-U-N-S 25-539-0965 (BR)
CORPORATE VENTURES INC
PODOLLAN INNS
(*Suby* of Corporate Ventures Inc)
10131 Franklin Ave, Fort Mcmurray, AB, T9H 2K8
(780) 762-0227
Emp Here 60
SIC 7011 Hotels and motels

D-U-N-S 24-370-9719 (SL)
CREEBURN LAKE LODGE LIMITED PARTNERSHIP
Gd, Fort Mcmurray, AB, T9H 3E2
(780) 788-2310
Emp Here 50   *Sales* 2,188,821
SIC 7011 Hotels and motels

D-U-N-S 25-162-7998 (HQ)
DENESOLINE ENVIRONMENT LIMITED PARTNERSHIP
(*Suby* of Denesoline Environment Limited Partnership)
9816 Hardin St Unit 333, Fort Mcmurray, AB, T9H 4K3
(780) 791-7788
Emp Here 265   *Emp Total* 270
Sales 10,177,153
SIC 7349 Building maintenance services, nec
Pr Pr Archie Cyprien
Fin Ex Kevin Anderson

D-U-N-S 25-951-7530 (BR)
DIVERSIFIED TRANSPORTATION LTD

8030 Golcsky Ave, Fort Mcmurray, AB, T9H 1V5
(780) 790-3960
Emp Here 100
SIC 4111 Local and suburban transit

D-U-N-S 25-954-4989   (BR)
DIVERSIFIED TRANSPORTATION LTD
120 Maclennan Cres, Fort Mcmurray, AB, T9H 4E8
(780) 743-2244
Emp Here 250
SIC 4142 Bus charter service, except local

D-U-N-S 24-523-3114   (BR)
DOLEMO DEVELOPMENT CORPORATION
STONEBRIDGE HOTEL - FORT MCMURRAY
(*Suby of* Bulova Developments Inc)
9713 Harcin St, Fort Mcmurray, AB, T9H 1L2
(780) 743-3301
Emp Here 50
SIC 7011 Hotels and motels

D-U-N-S 20-875-1011   (BR)
ENBRIDGE PIPELINES (ATHABASCA) INC
341 Mackenzie Blvd Unit 8, Fort Mcmurray, AB, T9H 4C5
(780) 788-2051
Emp Here 30
SIC 4619 Pipelines, nec

D-U-N-S 24-337-3490   (BR)
FGL SPORTS LTD
SPORT-CHEK CLEARWATER LANDING
19 Riedel St Unit 102, Fort Mcmurray, AB, T9H 5P8
(780) 747-7010
Emp Here 30
SIC 5941 Sporting goods and bicycle shops

D-U-N-S 25-538-2475   (SL)
FMR MECHANICAL ELECTRICAL INC
330 Mackenzie Blvd, Fort Mcmurray, AB, T9H 4C4
(780) 791-9283
Emp Here 39   *Sales* 3,378,379
SIC 7623 Refrigeration service and repair

D-U-N-S 24-282-7855   (BR)
FINNING INTERNATIONAL INC
FINNING (CANADA)
(*Suby of* Finning International Inc)
118 Macdonald Cres, Fort Mcmurray, AB, T9H 4B2
(780) 743-2218
Emp Here 150
SIC 5082 Construction and mining machinery

D-U-N-S 24-784-5121   (BR)
FLINT ENERGY SERVICES LTD.
150 Macdonald Cres, Fort Mcmurray, AB, T9H 4B2
(780) 588-2425
Emp Here 40
SIC 1389 Oil and gas field services, nec

D-U-N-S 20-267-1223   (BR)
FLUOR CANADA LTD
(*Suby of* Fluor Corporation)
9816 Hardin St Suite 300, Fort Mcmurray, AB, T9H 4K3
(780) 790-6002
Emp Here 40
SIC 8711 Engineering services

D-U-N-S 20-020-3581   (BR)
FORT MCMURRAY CATHOLIC BOARD OF EDUCATION
FATHER JA TURCOTTE SCHOOL
8553 Franklin Ave, Fort Mcmurray, AB, T9H 2J5
(780) 799-5772
Emp Here 50
SIC 8211 Elementary and secondary schools

D-U-N-S 20-025-9443   (BR)
FORT MCMURRAY CATHOLIC BOARD OF EDUCATION

GOOD SHEPHERD SCHOOL
211 Beacon Hill Dr, Fort Mcmurray, AB, T9H 2R1
(780) 799-5763
Emp Here 30
SIC 8211 Elementary and secondary schools

D-U-N-S 20-024-4601   (BR)
FORT MCMURRAY CATHOLIC BOARD OF EDUCATION
ST PAUL'S SCHOOL
429 Ross Haven Dr, Fort Mcmurray, AB, T9H 3P3
(780) 799-5760
Emp Here 40
SIC 8211 Elementary and secondary schools

D-U-N-S 20-712-7858   (BR)
FORT MCMURRAY CATHOLIC BOARD OF EDUCATION
FATHER MERCREDI HIGH SCHOOL
455 Silin Forest Rd, Fort Mcmurray, AB, T9H 4V6
(780) 799-5725
Emp Here 50
SIC 8211 Elementary and secondary schools

D-U-N-S 20-027-3709   (BR)
FORT MCMURRAY CATHOLIC BOARD OF EDUCATION
ST GABRIEL SCHOOL
585 Signal Rd, Fort Mcmurray, AB, T9H 4V3
(780) 799-7650
Emp Here 40
SIC 8211 Elementary and secondary schools

D-U-N-S 20-552-3710   (SL)
FORT MCMURRAY PIZZA LTD
BOSTON PIZZA
10202 Macdonald Ave, Fort Mcmurray, AB, T9H 1T4
(780) 743-5056
Emp Here 100   *Sales* 2,991,389
SIC 5812 Eating places

D-U-N-S 20-028-4128   (BR)
FORT MCMURRAY PUBLIC SCHOOL DISTRICT #2833
WESTVIEW SCHOOL
407 Wolverine Dr, Fort Mcmurray, AB, T9H 4S6
(780) 791-3121
Emp Here 50
SIC 8211 Elementary and secondary schools

D-U-N-S 20-712-1869   (BR)
FORT MCMURRAY PUBLIC SCHOOL DISTRICT #2833
DR K A CLARK ELEMENTARY SCHOOL
8453 Franklin Ave, Fort Mcmurray, AB, T9H 2J2
(780) 743-2444
Emp Here 75
SIC 8211 Elementary and secondary schools

D-U-N-S 25-325-7570   (BR)
FORT MCMURRAY PUBLIC SCHOOL DISTRICT #2833
WESTWOOD COMMUNITY HIGH SCHOOL
221 Tundra Dr, Fort Mcmurray, AB, T9H 4Z7
(780) 791-1986
Emp Here 65
SIC 8211 Elementary and secondary schools

D-U-N-S 20-712-3683   (BR)
FORT MCMURRAY PUBLIC SCHOOL DISTRICT #2833
GREELY ROAD SCHOOL
109 Greely Rd, Fort Mcmurray, AB, T9H 4V4
(780) 791-7470
Emp Here 30
SIC 8211 Elementary and secondary schools

D-U-N-S 20-712-2693   (BR)
FORT MCMURRAY PUBLIC SCHOOL DISTRICT #2833
BEACON HILL SCHOOL
210 Beacon Hill Dr, Fort Mcmurray, AB, T9H

2R1
(780) 743-8722
Emp Here 30
SIC 8211 Elementary and secondary schools

D-U-N-S 25-155-2568   (BR)
FORT MCMURRAY PUBLIC SCHOOL DISTRICT #2833
THICKWOOD HEIGHTS SCHOOL
96 Silin Forest Rd, Fort Mcmurray, AB, T9H 3A1
(780) 743-8417
Emp Here 38
SIC 8211 Elementary and secondary schools

D-U-N-S 25-014-4581   (BR)
FORT MCMURRAY PUBLIC SCHOOL DISTRICT #2833
FORT MCMURRAY COMPOSITE HIGH SCHOOL
9803 King St, Fort Mcmurray, AB, T9H 1L3

Emp Here 45
SIC 8211 Elementary and secondary schools

D-U-N-S 25-153-6942   (SL)
FOUR C'S MILLWORK LTD
330 Mackenzie Blvd, Fort Mcmurray, AB, T9H 4C4
(780) 791-0955
Emp Here 20   *Sales* 2,918,428
SIC 5211 Lumber and other building materials

D-U-N-S 24-334-5480   (BR)
GAMEHOST INC
BOOM TOWN CASINO
9825 Hardin St, Fort Mcmurray, AB, T9H 4G9
(780) 790-9739
Emp Here 100
SIC 7999 Amusement and recreation, nec

D-U-N-S 24-578-5303   (BR)
GIBSON ENERGY ULC
CANWEST PROPANE
235 Macalpine Cres Suite 1a, Fort Mcmurray, AB, T9H 4A5
(780) 715-1001
Emp Here 30
SIC 5172 Petroleum products, nec

D-U-N-S 20-205-5104   (BR)
GOVERNMENT OF THE PROVINCE OF ALBERTA
NORTHEAST CHILD AND FAMILY SERVICE AUTHORITY
9915 Franklin Ave, Fort Mcmurray, AB, T9H 2K4
(780) 743-7416
Emp Here 20
SIC 8399 Social services, nec

D-U-N-S 20-194-4167   (BR)
GOVERNMENT OF THE PROVINCE OF ALBERTA
SUSTAINABLE RESOURCES DEVELOPMENT
9915 Franklin Ave, Fort Mcmurray, AB, T9H 2K4
(780) 743-7125
Emp Here 30
SIC 7389 Business services, nec

D-U-N-S 25-155-8805   (BR)
GREAT PACIFIC INDUSTRIES INC
SAVE-ON-FOODS
8406 Franklin Ave, Fort Mcmurray, AB, T9H 2J3
(780) 791-4077
Emp Here 100
SIC 5411 Grocery stores

D-U-N-S 20-028-8845   (BR)
HARVARD BROADCASTING INC
9904 Franklin Ave, Fort Mcmurray, AB, T9H 2K5
(780) 791-0103
Emp Here 25
SIC 4841 Cable and other pay television services

D-U-N-S 24-683-3482   (BR)
HOLLOWAY LODGING LIMITED PARTNERSHIP
RADISSON HOTEL & SUITES
435 Gregoire Dr, Fort Mcmurray, AB, T9H 4K7

Emp Here 30
SIC 7011 Hotels and motels

D-U-N-S 25-270-0711   (BR)
INTEGRATED DISTRIBUTION SYSTEMS LIMITED PARTNERSHIP
WAJAX EQUIPMENT
(*Suby of* Integrated Distribution Systems Limited Partnership)
255 Macalpine Cres, Fort Mcmurray, AB, T9H 4A5
(780) 791-6447
Emp Here 40
SIC 5084 Industrial machinery and equipment

D-U-N-S 20-321-6544   (BR)
INTEGRATED DISTRIBUTION SYSTEMS LIMITED PARTNERSHIP
WAJAX POWER SYSTEMS
430 Macalpine Cres, Fort Mcmurray, AB, T9H 4B1
(780) 743-6252
Emp Here 30
SIC 5084 Industrial machinery and equipment

D-U-N-S 24-255-2185   (BR)
JACOBS INDUSTRIAL SERVICES LTD
(*Suby of* Jacobs Engineering Group Inc.)
Gd, Fort Mcmurray, AB, T9H 5B7
(780) 790-8060
Emp Here 30
SIC 7349 Building maintenance services, nec

D-U-N-S 20-269-4399   (BR)
JAPAN CANADA OIL SANDS LIMITED
JACOS
Gd Lcd Main, Fort Mcmurray, AB, T9H 3E2
(780) 799-4000
Emp Here 60
SIC 1311 Crude petroleum and natural gas

D-U-N-S 24-174-1045   (BR)
KAL TIRE LTD
Gd Lcd Main, Fort Mcmurray, AB, T9H 3E2
(780) 790-0101
Emp Here 30
SIC 5531 Auto and home supply stores

D-U-N-S 24-373-7959   (SL)
KIEWIT CONSTRUCTION CANADA CO
9707 Franklin Ave Suite 206, Fort Mcmurray, AB, T9H 2K1

Emp Here 25   *Sales* 6,832,640
SIC 1541 Industrial buildings and warehouses
Dir Richard Colf

D-U-N-S 24-599-8208   (BR)
LAFARGE CANADA INC
Gd Lcd Main, Fort Mcmurray, AB, T9H 3E2
(780) 743-8655
Emp Here 50
SIC 5999 Miscellaneous retail stores, nec

D-U-N-S 20-703-0086   (BR)
LAIRD ELECTRIC INC
225 Macdonald Cres, Fort Mcmurray, AB, T9H 4B5
(780) 743-2595
Emp Here 20
SIC 1731 Electrical work

D-U-N-S 20-718-5302   (SL)
LANDING TRAIL PETROLEUM CO
253 Gregoire Dr Unit 311, Fort Mcmurray, AB, T9H 4G7
(780) 799-2772
Emp Here 540   *Sales* 118,969,920
SIC 1389 Oil and gas field services, nec
Pr Charles Iggulden

D-U-N-S 24-350-8509   (BR)

LEAVITT MACHINERY AND RENTALS INC
275 Macalpine Cres, Fort Mcmurray, AB, T9H 4Y4
(780) 790-9387
Emp Here 30
SIC 7359 Equipment rental and leasing, nec

D-U-N-S 24-350-3310   (BR)
LIEBHERR-CANADA LTD
98 Wilson Dr, Fort Mcmurray, AB, T9H 0A1
(780) 791-2967
Emp Here 40
SIC 5082 Construction and mining machinery

D-U-N-S 25-960-0070   (BR)
LOBLAWS INC
REAL CANADIAN SUPERSTORE
9 Haineault St, Fort Mcmurray, AB, T9H 1R8
(780) 790-3827
Emp Here 240
SIC 5411 Grocery stores

D-U-N-S 20-522-3444   (BR)
MNP LLP
9707 Main St, Fort Mcmurray, AB, T9H 1T5
(780) 791-9000
Emp Here 38
SIC 8721 Accounting, auditing, and book-keeping

D-U-N-S 24-328-1136   (SL)
MACDONALD ISLAND PARK CORPORA-TION
151 Macdonald Dr, Fort Mcmurray, AB, T9H 5C5
(780) 791-0070
Emp Here 45   *Sales* 1,824,018
SIC 7997 Membership sports and recreation clubs

D-U-N-S 25-290-8595   (BR)
MARK'S WORK WEARHOUSE LTD
MARK'S WORK WEARHOUSE #37
19 Riedel St Suite 200, Fort Mcmurray, AB, T9H 5P8
(780) 791-5151
Emp Here 30
SIC 5699 Miscellaneous apparel and accessory stores

D-U-N-S 24-681-9937   (BR)
MCDONALD'S   RESTAURANTS   OF CANADA LIMITED
MCDONALD'S
(*Suby of* McDonald's Corporation)
450 Gregoire Dr, Fort Mcmurray, AB, T9H 3R2
(780) 791-0551
Emp Here 80
SIC 5812 Eating places

D-U-N-S 20-197-2945   (BR)
MCDONALD'S   RESTAURANTS   OF CANADA LIMITED
MCDONALD'S
(*Suby of* McDonald's Corporation)
96 Signal Rd, Fort Mcmurray, AB, T9H 5G4
(780) 790-9157
Emp Here 57
SIC 5812 Eating places

D-U-N-S 20-197-3034   (BR)
MCDONALD'S   RESTAURANTS   OF CANADA LIMITED
MCDONALD'S
(*Suby of* McDonald's Corporation)
2 Hospital St, Fort Mcmurray, AB, T9H 5E4
(780) 715-2050
Emp Here 20
SIC 5812 Eating places

D-U-N-S 20-069-4052   (BR)
MCMAN YOUTH, FAMILY AND COMMUNITY SERVICES ASSOCIATION
(*Suby of* McMan Youth, Family and Community Services Association)
9916 Manning Ave, Fort Mcmurray, AB, T9H 2B9

(780) 743-1110
Emp Here 40
SIC 8322 Individual and family services

D-U-N-S 24-283-4356   (SL)
MCMURRAY SERV-U EXPEDITING LTD
350 Macalpine Cres Suite 2, Fort Mcmurray, AB, T9H 4A8
(780) 791-3530
Emp Here 35   *Sales* 2,772,507
SIC 4212 Local trucking, without storage

D-U-N-S 25-065-6162   (SL)
MCRAY'S ROAD HOUSE GRILL
606 Signal Rd, Fort Mcmurray, AB, T9H 4Z4
(780) 790-1135
Emp Here 80   *Sales* 2,858,628
SIC 5812 Eating places

D-U-N-S 25-670-5930   (BR)
MIDWEST CONSTRUCTORS LTD
242 Macalpine Cres Unit 4a, Fort Mcmurray, AB, T9H 4A6
(780) 791-0090
Emp Here 25
SIC 1791 Structural steel erection

D-U-N-S 24-042-9220   (BR)
MYSHAK CRANE AND RIGGING LTD
(*Suby of* Myshak Equipment Ltd)
135 Mackay Cres, Fort Mcmurray, AB, T9H 4C9
(780) 791-9222
Emp Here 20
SIC 7389 Business services, nec

D-U-N-S 25-677-6915   (SL)
NEEGAN TECHNICAL SERVICES LTD
Gd Lcd Main, Fort Mcmurray, AB, T9H 3E2
(780) 715-2444
Emp Here 50   *Sales* 2,626,585
SIC 7389 Business services, nec

D-U-N-S 20-325-1962   (BR)
NORALTA LODGE LTD
BUFFALO LODGE
7210 Cliff Ave,Suite 7202, Fort Mcmurray, AB, T9H 1A1
(780) 791-3334
Emp Here 75
SIC 7041 Membership-basis organization hotels

D-U-N-S 25-950-9958   (BR)
NORTH   AMERICAN   CONSTRUCTION GROUP INC
NORTH AMERICAN MINING DIVISION
Po Box 6639 Stn Main, Fort Mcmurray, AB, T9H 5N4
(780) 791-1997
Emp Here 300
SIC 1629 Heavy construction, nec

D-U-N-S 24-041-4289   (BR)
NORTHVIEW APARTMENT REAL ESTATE INVESTMENT TRUST
NORTHERN PROPERTY REIT
117 Stroud Bay Suite 118, Fort Mcmurray, AB, T9H 4Y8
(780) 790-0806
Emp Here 30
SIC 6531 Real estate agents and managers

D-U-N-S 24-349-3264   (BR)
PALADIN SECURITY GROUP LTD
604 Signal Rd, Fort Mcmurray, AB, T9H 4Z4
(780) 743-1422
Emp Here 100
SIC 7381 Detective and armored car services

D-U-N-S 24-341-5911   (BR)
PREMAY EQUIPMENT LP
135 Mackay Cres, Fort Mcmurray, AB, T9H 4C9
(780) 743-6214
Emp Here 20
SIC 4213 Trucking, except local

D-U-N-S 24-050-6746   (BR)
PYRAMID CORPORATION

130 Mackenzie King Rd, Fort Mcmurray, AB, T9H 4L2
(780) 743-8801
Emp Here 40
SIC 1731 Electrical work

D-U-N-S 20-349-7552   (BR)
RAYDON RENTALS LTD
CAT RENTALS
(*Suby of* Finning International Inc)
905 Memorial Dr, Fort Mcmurray, AB, T9H 3G6
(780) 743-5217
Emp Here 30
SIC 7359 Equipment rental and leasing, nec

D-U-N-S 25-947-6182   (BR)
ROYAL BANK OF CANADA
RBC
(*Suby of* Royal Bank Of Canada)
8540 Manning Ave, Fort Mcmurray, AB, T9H 5G2
(780) 743-3327
Emp Here 30
SIC 6021 National commercial banks

D-U-N-S 24-761-9377   (BR)
SGS CANADA INC
235 Macdonald Cres, Fort Mcmurray, AB, T9H 4B5
(780) 791-6454
Emp Here 200
SIC 8734 Testing laboratories

D-U-N-S 25-014-0761   (BR)
SMS EQUIPMENT INC
CONECO EQUIPMENT, DIV OF
310 Mackenzie Blvd, Fort Mcmurray, AB, T9H 4C4
(780) 791-0616
Emp Here 50
SIC 5082 Construction and mining machinery

D-U-N-S 25-999-0542   (BR)
SMS EQUIPMENT INC
CONECO EQUIPMENT
22k Highway 63 North, Fort Mcmurray, AB, T9H 3G2
(780) 743-2622
Emp Here 600
SIC 5082 Construction and mining machinery

D-U-N-S 20-191-8864   (BR)
SAWRIDGE ENTERPRISES LTD
SAWRIDGE INN & CONFERENCE CENTRE
530 Mackenzie Blvd, Fort Mcmurray, AB, T9H 4C8
(780) 791-7900
Emp Here 100
SIC 7011 Hotels and motels

D-U-N-S 20-867-7323   (BR)
SHAW CABLESYSTEMS G.P.
208 Beacon Hill Dr Suite 200, Fort Mcmurray, AB, T9H 2R1
(780) 714-5355
Emp Here 25
SIC 4841 Cable and other pay television services

D-U-N-S 25-712-1277   (BR)
SHAW COMMUNICATIONS INC
208 Beacon Hill Dr Suite 200, Fort Mcmurray, AB, T9H 2R1
(780) 743-3717
Emp Here 25
SIC 4841 Cable and other pay television services

D-U-N-S 24-538-0790   (BR)
SOBEYS CAPITAL INCORPORATED
SOBEYS
19 Riedel St Unit 300, Fort Mcmurray, AB, T9H 5P8
(780) 791-1550
Emp Here 50
SIC 5411 Grocery stores

D-U-N-S 25-271-0728   (BR)

SOBEYS WEST INC
THICKWOOD SAFEWAY
131 Signal Rd, Fort Mcmurray, AB, T9H 4N6
(780) 791-3909
Emp Here 84
SIC 5411 Grocery stores

D-U-N-S 25-271-0769   (BR)
SOBEYS WEST INC
9601 Franklin Ave, Fort Mcmurray, AB, T9H 2J8
(780) 790-1988
Emp Here 80
SIC 5411 Grocery stores

D-U-N-S 25-954-5358   (SL)
SPARKSMAN TRANSPORTATION LTD
8030 Golosky Ave, Fort Mcmurray, AB, T9H 1V5
(780) 790-3960
Emp Here 68   *Sales* 1,896,978
SIC 4151 School buses

D-U-N-S 20-590-3391   (BR)
STAHL PETERBILT INC
340 Mackenzie Blvd, Fort Mcmurray, AB, T9H 4C4
(780) 715-3627
Emp Here 20
SIC 5084 Industrial machinery and equipment

D-U-N-S 25-082-5692   (BR)
STAPLES CANADA INC
STAPLES THE BUSINESS DEPOT
(*Suby of* Staples, Inc.)
8544 Manning Ave, Fort Mcmurray, AB, T9H 5G2
(780) 799-8100
Emp Here 30
SIC 5943 Stationery stores

D-U-N-S 24-398-3418   (BR)
SUNCOR ENERGY INC
OIL SANDS GROUP
Gd, Fort Mcmurray, AB, T9H 3E3
(780) 713-7163
Emp Here 2,300
SIC 1311 Crude petroleum and natural gas

D-U-N-S 20-803-4384   (BR)
SUNCOR ENERGY INC
Gd Lcd Main, Fort Mcmurray, AB, T9H 3E2
(780) 743-1382
Emp Here 30
SIC 1311 Crude petroleum and natural gas

D-U-N-S 20-853-0977   (BR)
SUNCOR ENERGY INC
Gd, Fort Mcmurray, AB, T9H 3E2
(780) 743-6411
Emp Here 500
SIC 1311 Crude petroleum and natural gas

D-U-N-S 24-034-1722   (SL)
SURMONT SAND & GRAVEL LTD
431 Mackenzie Blvd, Fort Mcmurray, AB, T9H 4C5
(780) 743-2533
Emp Here 60   *Sales* 8,828,245
SIC 5211 Lumber and other building materials
Pr Pr David Laboucane

D-U-N-S 24-009-5286   (BR)
TISI CANADA INC
235 Macalpine Cres Unit 9, Fort Mcmurray, AB, T9H 4A5
(780) 715-1648
Emp Here 50
SIC 7363 Help supply services

D-U-N-S 20-300-9972   (SL)
TSG ENERGY SERVICES LTD
311 253 Gregoire Dr, Fort Mcmurray, AB, T9H 4G7
(780) 799-2772
Emp Here 600   *Sales* 135,695,376
SIC 1623 Water, sewer, and utility lines
Pr Pr Charles Iggulden

D-U-N-S 25-153-2370   (BR)
TERRACON GEOTECHNIQUE LTD
8212 Manning Ave, Fort Mcmurray, AB, T9H 1V9
(780) 743-9343
Emp Here 220
SIC 8711 Engineering services

D-U-N-S 25-998-6193   (BR)
TERVITA CORPORATION
(*Suby of* Tervita Corporation)
8130 Fraser Ave, Fort Mcmurray, AB, T9H 1W6
(780) 714-3372
Emp Here 25
SIC 8748 Business consulting, nec

D-U-N-S 25-315-4819   (BR)
TORONTO-DOMINION BANK, THE
TD BANK
(*Suby of* Toronto-Dominion Bank, The)
8600 Franklin Ave Suite 504, Fort Mcmurray, AB, T9H 4G8
(780) 743-2261
Emp Here 21
SIC 6021 National commercial banks

D-U-N-S 20-834-2555   (SL)
TRIPLE A GENERAL CONTRACTING
380 Mackenzie Blvd Unit 2f, Fort Mcmurray, AB, T9H 4C4
(780) 715-0208
Emp Here 28   *Sales* 5,782,650
SIC 1521 Single-family housing construction
Pt Michael Hanrahan
Pt Harold Brown

D-U-N-S 24-028-4088   (BR)
UNIFIED SYSTEMS GROUP INC
8112 Manning Ave, Fort Mcmurray, AB, T9H 1V7
(780) 743-3117
Emp Here 20
SIC 1731 Electrical work

D-U-N-S 24-369-5553   (BR)
UNITED FARMERS OF ALBERTA CO-OPERATIVE LIMITED
SPRUCELAND LUMBER DIV OF
Gd Lcd Main, Fort Mcmurray, AB, T9H 3E2
(780) 791-3232
Emp Here 36
SIC 5211 Lumber and other building materials

D-U-N-S 25-273-3241   (BR)
UNITED FURNITURE WAREHOUSE LP
441 Gregoire Dr, Fort Mcmurray, AB, T9H 4K7
(780) 791-1888
Emp Here 20
SIC 5712 Furniture stores

D-U-N-S 20-069-7345   (SL)
UNITED GLASS CABS
8222 Fraser Ave, Fort Mcmurray, AB, T9H 1W8
(780) 790-2891
Emp Here 95   *Sales* 3,378,379
SIC 4121 Taxicabs

D-U-N-S 25-947-6711   (BR)
VOICE CONSTRUCTION LTD
200 Macdonald Cres, Fort Mcmurray, AB, T9H 4B2
(780) 790-0981
Emp Here 500
SIC 1794 Excavation work

D-U-N-S 25-236-7800   (BR)
WSP CANADA INC
GENIVAR
9905 Sutherland St, Fort Mcmurray, AB, T9H 1V3
(780) 743-3969
Emp Here 20
SIC 8711 Engineering services

D-U-N-S 25-498-2945   (BR)
WAL-MART CANADA CORP
2 Hospital St, Fort Mcmurray, AB, T9H 5E4

(780) 790-6012
Emp Here 190
SIC 5311 Department stores

D-U-N-S 24-325-9293   (SL)
WAPOSE MEDICAL SERVICES INC
431 Mackenzie Blvd Suite 12, Fort Mcmurray, AB, T9H 4C5
(780) 714-6654
Emp Here 50   *Sales* 3,638,254
SIC 7363 Help supply services

Fort Mcmurray, AB T9J

D-U-N-S 20-713-2148   (BR)
CONSEIL SCOLAIRE CENTRE-NORD
BOREAL CENTER
312 Abasand Dr, Fort Mcmurray, AB, T9J 1B2
(780) 791-0200
Emp Here 50
SIC 8211 Elementary and secondary schools

D-U-N-S 20-712-6744   (BR)
FORT MCMURRAY CATHOLIC BOARD OF EDUCATION
FATHER BEAUREGARD SCHOOL
255 Athabasca Ave Suite 167, Fort Mcmurray, AB, T9J 1G7
(780) 790-9065
Emp Here 50
SIC 8211 Elementary and secondary schools

Fort Mcmurray, AB T9K

D-U-N-S 20-742-7373   (BR)
ACUREN GROUP INC
(*Suby of* Rockwood Service Corporation)
240 Taiganova Cres Unit 2, Fort Mcmurray, AB, T9K 0T4
(780) 790-1776
Emp Here 200
SIC 8711 Engineering services

D-U-N-S 25-951-7589   (BR)
ALUMA SYSTEMS INC
(*Suby of* Clayton, Dubilier & Rice, Inc.)
925 Memorial Dr, Fort Mcmurray, AB, T9K 0K4
(780) 743-5011
Emp Here 40
SIC 5082 Construction and mining machinery

D-U-N-S 24-736-1491   (BR)
AMECO SERVICES INC
1025 Memorial Dr, Fort Mcmurray, AB, T9K 0K4
(780) 588-2400
Emp Here 30
SIC 7359 Equipment rental and leasing, nec

D-U-N-S 20-840-2292   (BR)
BAKER HUGHES CANADA COMPANY
BJ PROCESS & PIPELINE SERVICES DIV
(*Suby of* Baker Hughes, A GE Company)
805 Memorial Dr Unit 3, Fort Mcmurray, AB, T9K 0K4
(780) 799-3327
Emp Here 30
SIC 1623 Water, sewer, and utility lines

D-U-N-S 24-367-4319   (BR)
BANK OF NOVA SCOTIA, THE
SCOTIABANK
287 Powder Dr, Fort Mcmurray, AB, T9K 0M3

Emp Here 20
SIC 6021 National commercial banks

D-U-N-S 20-735-3223   (BR)
CUMMINS WESTERN CANADA LIMITED PARTNERSHIP
300 Taiganova Cres, Fort Mcmurray, AB, T9K 0T4

(780) 791-6836
Emp Here 35
SIC 7538 General automotive repair shops

D-U-N-S 20-712-8955   (BR)
FORT MCMURRAY CATHOLIC BOARD OF EDUCATION
SISTER MARY PHILLIPS
177 Dickins Dr, Fort Mcmurray, AB, T9K 1M3
(780) 799-5720
Emp Here 50
SIC 8211 Elementary and secondary schools

D-U-N-S 25-014-4912   (BR)
FORT MCMURRAY CATHOLIC BOARD OF EDUCATION
ST ANNE SCHOOL
101 Brett Dr, Fort Mcmurray, AB, T9K 1V1
(780) 799-5752
Emp Here 55
SIC 8211 Elementary and secondary schools

D-U-N-S 25-153-1497   (BR)
FORT MCMURRAY PUBLIC SCHOOL DISTRICT #2833
TIMBERLEA PUBLIC SCHOOL
107 Brett Dr, Fort Mcmurray, AB, T9K 1V1
(780) 743-5771
Emp Here 95
SIC 8211 Elementary and secondary schools

D-U-N-S 25-155-2576   (BR)
FORT MCMURRAY PUBLIC SCHOOL DISTRICT #2833
ECOLE DICKINSFIELD SCHOOL
201 Dickins Dr, Fort Mcmurray, AB, T9K 1M9
(780) 791-6990
Emp Here 60
SIC 8211 Elementary and secondary schools

D-U-N-S 25-153-6926   (BR)
FORT MCMURRAY PUBLIC SCHOOL DISTRICT #2833
FORT MCMURRAY CHRISTIAN SCHOOL
190 Tamarack Way, Fort Mcmurray, AB, T9K 1A1
(780) 743-1079
Emp Here 20
SIC 8211 Elementary and secondary schools

D-U-N-S 25-360-1090   (BR)
JOY GLOBAL (CANADA) LTD
P & H MINDPRO SERVICES
965 Memorial Dr, Fort Mcmurray, AB, T9K 0K4
(780) 791-4016
Emp Here 50
SIC 5082 Construction and mining machinery

D-U-N-S 25-947-6174   (BR)
LEHIGH HANSON MATERIALS LIMITED
580 Memorial Dr, Fort Mcmurray, AB, T9K 0N9
(780) 743-2180
Emp Here 20
SIC 5032 Brick, stone, and related material

D-U-N-S 24-388-8521   (SL)
LEON'S HEAVY EQUIPMENT LTD
100 Real Martin Dr Suite 14, Fort Mcmurray, AB, T9K 2S1
(780) 715-0648
Emp Here 20   *Sales* 5,024,000
SIC 5084 Industrial machinery and equipment
Pr Pr Leon Arsenault

D-U-N-S 24-206-8299   (BR)
LOBLAWS INC
DRUG STORE PHARMACIE
251 Powder Dr, Fort Mcmurray, AB, T9K 2W6
(780) 788-1402
Emp Here 50
SIC 5912 Drug stores and proprietary stores

D-U-N-S 24-853-6252   (SL)
MIDLITE CONSTRUCTION LTD
135 Boreal Ave, Fort Mcmurray, AB, T9K 0T4
(780) 714-6559
Emp Here 100   *Sales* 17,510,568
SIC 1623 Water, sewer, and utility lines

Pr Pr Rocky Buksa

D-U-N-S 24-851-6622   (BR)
SAFWAY SERVICES CANADA, ULC
SAFEWAY SREVICES CANADA, INC (FT. MCMURRAY-ALBIAN)
(*Suby of* Safway Group Holding LLC)
1005 Memorial Dr Unit 3, Fort Mcmurray, AB, T9K 0K4
(780) 791-6473
Emp Here 650
SIC 1799 Special trade contractors, nec

D-U-N-S 25-056-9308   (BR)
SOBEYS CAPITAL INCORPORATED
THICKWOOD GARDEN MARKET I G A
210 Thickwood Blvd, Fort Mcmurray, AB, T9K 1X9
(780) 743-9339
Emp Here 100
SIC 5411 Grocery stores

D-U-N-S 20-830-4543   (BR)
STARBUCKS COFFEE CANADA, INC
(*Suby of* Starbucks Corporation)
112 Riverstone Ridge Unit 107, Fort Mcmurray, AB, T9K 1S6
(780) 743-6331
Emp Here 23
SIC 5812 Eating places

D-U-N-S 24-056-6658   (BR)
THOMPSON BROS. (CONSTR.) LTD
685 Memorial Dr, Fort Mcmurray, AB, T9K 0K4
(780) 715-3422
Emp Here 60
SIC 1629 Heavy construction, nec

D-U-N-S 24-445-0958   (BR)
UNITED RENTALS OF CANADA, INC
RSC EQUIPMENT RENTALS
140 Taiganova Cres, Fort Mcmurray, AB, T9K 0T4
(780) 743-9555
Emp Here 43
SIC 7353 Heavy construction equipment rental

D-U-N-S 24-033-5625   (BR)
YOUNG MEN'S CHRISTIAN ASSOCIATION OF EDMONTON
YMCA BIRCHWOOD CHILD DEVELOPMENT CENTER
(*Suby of* Young Men's Christian Association of Edmonton)
190 Tamarack Way, Fort Mcmurray, AB, T9K 1A1
(780) 790-9532
Emp Here 21
SIC 7011 Hotels and motels

Fort Saskatchewan, AB T8L

D-U-N-S 24-714-9933   (SL)
301726 ALBERTA LTD
BOSTON PIZZA
8751 94 St, Fort Saskatchewan, AB, T8L 4P7
(780) 998-9999
Emp Here 85   *Sales* 2,553,625
SIC 5812 Eating places

D-U-N-S 20-316-9461   (BR)
AGF - REBAR INC
186 Sturgeon Way, Fort Saskatchewan, AB, T8L 2N9
(780) 998-5565
Emp Here 20
SIC 3449 Miscellaneous Metalwork

D-U-N-S 24-542-8037   (BR)
ACCESS PIPELINE INC
88 Ave, Fort Saskatchewan, AB, T8L 2S9
(780) 997-0499
Emp Here 30
SIC 4789 Transportation services, nec

D-U-N-S 25-181-2392   (BR)
AGRIUM INC
(*Suby of* Agrium Canada Partnership)
11751 River Rd, Fort Saskatchewan, AB, T8L
4J1
(780) 998-6911
Emp Here 50
SIC 2873 Nitrogenous fertilizers

D-U-N-S 25-170-0480   (BR)
AIR LIQUIDE CANADA INC
AIR LIQUIDE
55522 Route 214, Fort Saskatchewan, AB,
T8L 3T2
(780) 992-1077
Emp Here 25
SIC 2813 Industrial gases

D-U-N-S 25-014-5059   (BR)
ALBERTA HEALTH SERVICES
FORT SASKATCHEWAN HEALTH CENTRE
9430 95 St, Fort Saskatchewan, AB, T8L 1R8
(780) 998-2256
Emp Here 120
SIC 8062 General medical and surgical hospitals

D-U-N-S 20-919-4872   (BR)
ALBERTA HEALTH SERVICES
FORT SASKATCHEWAN HEALTH UNIT
10420 98 Ave Suite 121, Fort Saskatchewan,
AB, T8L 2N6

Emp Here 40
SIC 8062 General medical and surgical hospitals

D-U-N-S 20-573-9365   (BR)
ALBERTA TREASURY BRANCHES
ATB FINANCIAL
9964 99 Ave, Fort Saskatchewan, AB, T8L
4G8
(780) 998-5161
Emp Here 20
SIC 6036 Savings institutions, except federal

D-U-N-S 25-316-0352   (BR)
BP CANADA ENERGY COMPANY
(*Suby of* BP P.L.C.)
11010 126th St, Fort Saskatchewan, AB, T8L
2T2
(780) 992-2700
Emp Here 75
SIC 1311 Crude petroleum and natural gas

D-U-N-S 25-288-9183   (BR)
CANADA POST CORPORATION
10004 103 St, Fort Saskatchewan, AB, T8L
2E1
(780) 992-6000
Emp Here 26
SIC 4311 U.s. postal service

D-U-N-S 25-303-6016   (BR)
CANADIAN IMPERIAL BANK OF COMMERCE
CIBC
9903 101 St, Fort Saskatchewan, AB, T8L 1V6
(780) 998-2261
Emp Here 20
SIC 6021 National commercial banks

D-U-N-S 25-014-0878   (BR)
DOW AGROSCIENCES CANADA INC
DOW
(*Suby of* The Dow Chemical Company)
127 Sturgeon Cres, Fort Saskatchewan, AB,
T8L 2N9
(780) 998-4833
Emp Here 20
SIC 2879 Agricultural chemicals, nec

D-U-N-S 24-025-2556   (SL)
DOW CENTENNIAL CENTRE
8700 84 St, Fort Saskatchewan, AB, T8L 4P5
(780) 992-6266
Emp Here 50   *Sales* 2,699,546
SIC 7999 Amusement and recreation, nec

D-U-N-S 20-085-8033   (BR)
DOW CHEMICAL CANADA ULC
(*Suby of* The Dow Chemical Company)
Gd, Fort Saskatchewan, AB, T8L 2P4
(780) 998-8000
Emp Here 800
SIC 2899 Chemical preparations, nec

D-U-N-S 25-156-5248   (BR)
ELK ISLAND CATHOLIC SEPARATE REGIONAL DIVISION NO. 41
OUR LADY OF THE CATHOLIC ANGEL SCHOOL
9622 Sherridon Dr, Fort Saskatchewan, AB,
T8L 1W7
(780) 998-3716
Emp Here 29
SIC 8211 Elementary and secondary schools

D-U-N-S 25-165-4620   (BR)
ELK ISLAND CATHOLIC SEPARATE REGIONAL DIVISION NO. 41
POPE JOHN XXIII CATHOLIC SCHOOL
9526 89 St, Fort Saskatchewan, AB, T8L 2X7
(780) 998-7777
Emp Here 29
SIC 8211 Elementary and secondary schools

D-U-N-S 25-014-5133   (BR)
ELK ISLAND CATHOLIC SEPARATE REGIONAL DIVISION NO. 41
JOHN PAUL II HIGH SCHOOL
9975 93 Ave, Fort Saskatchewan, AB, T8L
1N5
(780) 992-0889
Emp Here 30
SIC 8211 Elementary and secondary schools

D-U-N-S 25-000-5071   (BR)
ELK ISLAND PUBLIC SCHOOLS REGIONAL DIVISION NO. 14
FORT SASKATCHEWAN ELEMENTARY
(*Suby of* Elk Island Public Schools Regional
Division No. 14)
9802 101 St, Fort Saskatchewan, AB, T8L 1V4
(780) 998-7771
Emp Here 35
SIC 8211 Elementary and secondary schools

D-U-N-S 20-020-2807   (BR)
ELK ISLAND PUBLIC SCHOOLS REGIONAL DIVISION NO. 14
WIN FERGUSON COMMUNITY SCHOOL
9529 89 St, Fort Saskatchewan, AB, T8L 1J2
(780) 998-1441
Emp Here 35
SIC 8211 Elementary and secondary schools

D-U-N-S 25-016-0058   (BR)
ELK ISLAND PUBLIC SCHOOLS REGIONAL DIVISION NO. 14
FORT SASKATCHEWAN HIGH SCHOOL
(*Suby of* Elk Island Public Schools Regional
Division No. 14)
10002 97 Ave, Fort Saskatchewan, AB, T8L
1R2
(780) 998-3751
Emp Here 43
SIC 8211 Elementary and secondary schools

D-U-N-S 20-709-8513   (BR)
ELK ISLAND PUBLIC SCHOOLS REGIONAL DIVISION NO. 14
FORT SASKATCHEWAN JUNIOR SCHOOL
9607 Sherridon Dr, Fort Saskatchewan, AB,
T8L 1W5
(780) 998-3741
Emp Here 27
SIC 8211 Elementary and secondary schools

D-U-N-S 20-709-9578   (BR)
ELK ISLAND PUBLIC SCHOOLS REGIONAL DIVISION NO. 14
NEXT STEP FORT SASKATCHEWAN
9807 108 St, Fort Saskatchewan, AB, T8L 2J2
(780) 992-0101
Emp Here 50
SIC 8211 Elementary and secondary schools

D-U-N-S 20-705-0704   (BR)
ELK ISLAND PUBLIC SCHOOLS REGIONAL DIVISION NO. 14
JAMES MOWAT SCHOOL
9625 82 St, Fort Saskatchewan, AB, T8L 3T6
(780) 992-1272
Emp Here 32
SIC 8211 Elementary and secondary schools

D-U-N-S 20-709-8612   (BR)
ELK ISLAND PUBLIC SCHOOLS REGIONAL DIVISION NO. 14
ECOLE RUDOLPH HENNIG SCHOOL
9512 92 St, Fort Saskatchewan, AB, T8L 1L7
(780) 998-2216
Emp Here 50
SIC 8211 Elementary and secondary schools

D-U-N-S 24-806-4206   (SL)
ENERGY & CHEMICAL WORKERS UNION LOCAL 530
ENERGY & CEP
10208 99 Ave, Fort Saskatchewan, AB, T8L
1Y1
(780) 998-2074
Emp Here 605   *Sales* 88,120,960
SIC 8631 Labor organizations
Pr Leonard Morin
Treas Jim Woodland
VP Shea Turner

D-U-N-S 24-905-3166   (SL)
FORT SASKATCHEWAN FAST-FOOD ENTERPRISES LTD
DAIRY QUEEN
9910 99 Ave, Fort Saskatchewan, AB, T8L
4G8
(780) 998-0880
Emp Here 55   *Sales* 1,678,096
SIC 5812 Eating places

D-U-N-S 24-087-4045   (BR)
GEMINI CORPORATION
KINETIC
11232 87 Ave, Fort Saskatchewan, AB, T8L
2S4
(780) 998-5460
Emp Here 25
SIC 1799 Special trade contractors, nec

D-U-N-S 20-571-7973   (BR)
GOVERNMENT OF THE PROVINCE OF ALBERTA
*EDMONTON & AREA CHILD AND FAMILY
SERVICES REGION 6*
2-9401 86 Ave, Fort Saskatchewan, AB, T8L
0C6
(780) 992-6700
Emp Here 20
SIC 8322 Individual and family services

D-U-N-S 24-343-4177   (BR)
HARRIS STEEL ULC
HARRIS REBAR
(*Suby of* Nucor Corporation)
11215 87 Ave, Fort Saskatchewan, AB, T8L
2S3
(780) 992-0777
Emp Here 150
SIC 3499 Fabricated Metal products, nec

D-U-N-S 24-325-2215   (BR)
HORTON CBI, LIMITED
55116 Hwy 825, Fort Saskatchewan, AB, T8L
2T4
(780) 998-2800
Emp Here 20
SIC 1791 Structural steel erection

D-U-N-S 20-898-0276   (BR)
KEYERA PARTNERSHIP
12310 River Rd, Fort Saskatchewan, AB, T8L
2T2
(780) 998-3791
Emp Here 26
SIC 1321 Natural gas liquids

D-U-N-S 24-645-2689   (BR)
LAKEVIEW MANAGEMENT INC

10115 88 Ave, Fort Saskatchewan, AB, T8L
4K1
(780) 998-7888
Emp Here 20
SIC 7011 Hotels and motels

D-U-N-S 20-644-5673   (HQ)
OERLIKON METCO (CANADA) INC
10108 114 St, Fort Saskatchewan, AB, T8L
4R1
(780) 992-5100
Emp Here 66   *Emp Total* 130
Sales 8,609,363
SIC 3399 Primary Metal products
VP VP Gerald Deck
  Neil Marshall
  Friedrich Herold
  Marc Hamacher

D-U-N-S 20-251-1259   (BR)
PLAINS MIDSTREAM CANADA ULC
*PLAINS   MIDSTREAM   FORT
SASKATCHEWAN*
11010 125 St, Fort Saskatchewan, AB, T8L
2T2
(780) 992-2700
Emp Here 70
SIC 4225 General warehousing and storage

D-U-N-S 25-965-0075   (BR)
PRAIRIE EMERGENCY MEDICAL SYSTEMS INC
10099 93 Ave, Fort Saskatchewan, AB, T8L
1N5
(780) 998-4466
Emp Here 45
SIC 4119 Local passenger transportation, nec

D-U-N-S 20-919-7198   (BR)
PYRAMID CORPORATION
11201 84 Ave, Fort Saskatchewan, AB, T8L
4L1
(780) 992-1399
Emp Here 20
SIC 1731 Electrical work

D-U-N-S 20-959-6290   (SL)
RDVC INVESTMENTS LTD
SUPER 8 HOTEL
8750 84 St, Fort Saskatchewan, AB, T8L 4P5
(780) 998-2898
Emp Here 50   *Sales* 2,188,821
SIC 7011 Hotels and motels

D-U-N-S 20-969-5469   (SL)
RIVERCREST LODGE NURSING HOME LTD
RIVERCREST CARE CENTRE
10104 101 Ave, Fort Saskatchewan, AB, T8L
2A5
(780) 998-2425
Emp Here 75   *Sales* 3,429,153
SIC 8051 Skilled nursing care facilities

D-U-N-S 20-580-6131   (BR)
ROYAL BANK OF CANADA
RBC
(*Suby of* Royal Bank Of Canada)
9916 102 St, Fort Saskatchewan, AB, T8L
2C3
(780) 998-3721
Emp Here 20
SIC 6021 National commercial banks

D-U-N-S 20-116-8643   (HQ)
SAFWAY SERVICES CANADA, ULC
(*Suby of* Safway Group Holding LLC)
11237 87 Ave, Fort Saskatchewan, AB, T8L
2S3
(780) 992-1929
Emp Here 23   *Emp Total* 7,300
Sales 4,669,485
SIC 1799 Special trade contractors, nec

D-U-N-S 24-397-9382   (BR)
SHELL CANADA LIMITED
SCOTFORD COMPLEX
55522 Range Road 214, Fort Saskatchewan,
AB, T8L 4A4

(780) 992-3600
Emp Here 250
SIC 2911 Petroleum refining

D-U-N-S 24-381-6571   (BR)
SHERRITT INTERNATIONAL CORPORATION
SHERRITT TECHNOLOGIES, DIV OF
8301 113 St, Fort Saskatchewan, AB, T8L 4K7
(780) 992-8081
Emp Here 54
SIC 3339 Primary nonferrous Metals, nec

D-U-N-S 25-746-4008   (BR)
SHERRITT INTERNATIONAL CORPORATION
MOA NICKLE S.A. DIV OF
10101 114 St, Fort Saskatchewan, AB, T8L 2T3
(780) 992-7000
Emp Here 600
SIC 3339 Primary nonferrous Metals, nec

D-U-N-S 24-394-6014   (SL)
SMITH & NEPHEW (ALBERTA) INC
10102 114 St, Fort Saskatchewan, AB, T8L 3W4
(780) 992-5500
Emp Here 40   *Sales* 3,866,917
SIC 3842 Surgical appliances and supplies

D-U-N-S 20-640-1783   (BR)
SOBEYS CAPITAL INCORPORATED
SOBEYS PHARMACY
10004 99 Ave, Fort Saskatchewan, AB, T8L 3Y1
(780) 998-5429
Emp Here 100
SIC 5411 Grocery stores

D-U-N-S 24-363-2085   (BR)
SOBEYS WEST INC
SAFEWAY FORT SASKATCHEWAN
9450 86 Ave, Fort Saskatchewan, AB, T8L 4P4
(780) 998-4065
Emp Here 50
SIC 5411 Grocery stores

D-U-N-S 24-327-8269   (BR)
STAPLES CANADA INC
STAPLES THE BUSINESS DEPOT
(*Suby of* Staples, Inc.)
9410 86 St Suite 107, Fort Saskatchewan, AB, T8L 2R1
(780) 992-6012
Emp Here 30
SIC 5943 Stationery stores

D-U-N-S 20-017-8564   (BR)
STARBUCKS COFFEE CANADA, INC
(*Suby of* Starbucks Corporation)
9378 Southfort Dr Suite 101, Fort Saskatchewan, AB, T8L 0C5
(780) 589-4430
Emp Here 20
SIC 5812 Eating places

D-U-N-S 20-736-2505   (BR)
WAL-MART CANADA CORP
9551 87 Ave, Fort Saskatchewan, AB, T8L 4N3
(780) 998-3633
Emp Here 200
SIC 5311 Department stores

Fort Vermilion, AB T0H

D-U-N-S 20-711-5515   (BR)
FORT VERMILION SCHOOL DIVISON 52
ST MARY'S ELEMENTARY SCHOOL
(*Suby of* Fort Vermilion School Divison 52)
4611 River Rd, Fort Vermilion, AB, T0H 1N0
(780) 927-3201
Emp Here 25
SIC 8211 Elementary and secondary schools

Fox Creek, AB T0H

D-U-N-S 20-828-5580   (SL)
770970 ALBERTA LTD
3 BOYS TANK/VAC
315 St E, Fox Creek, AB, T0H 1P0
(780) 622-2273
Emp Here 22   *Sales* 7,382,110
SIC 4212 Local trucking, without storage
Pr Pr Christopher Mckennitt
   James Mckennitt

D-U-N-S 25-230-3565   (BR)
ERNIE O 'S RESTAURANT & PUB (EDSON) INC
ERNIE O'S RESTAURANT AND PUB
(*Suby of* Ernie O 's Restaurant & Pub (Edson) Inc)
1042 Highway Ave, Fox Creek, AB, T0H 1P0
(780) 622-3600
Emp Here 30
SIC 5812 Eating places

D-U-N-S 20-350-9351   (SL)
FOX CREEK DEVELOPMENTS 2011 LTD
BEST WESTERN PLUS
313 1 Ave, Fox Creek, AB, T0H 1P0
(780) 548-3338
Emp Here 50   *Sales* 2,188,821
SIC 7011 Hotels and motels

D-U-N-S 24-930-0203   (BR)
FRESON MARKET LTD
IGA
(*Suby of* Altamart Investments (1993) Ltd)
13 Commercial Crt, Fox Creek, AB, T0H 1P0
(780) 622-3779
Emp Here 30
SIC 5411 Grocery stores

D-U-N-S 20-965-8405   (BR)
GOVERNMENT OF THE PROVINCE OF ALBERTA
FOX CREEK HEALTH CARE CENTER
600 Third St, Fox Creek, AB, T0H 1P0
(780) 622-3545
Emp Here 30
SIC 8062 General medical and surgical hospitals

D-U-N-S 25-110-6043   (BR)
NORTHERN GATEWAY REGIONAL DIVISION #10
FOX CREEK SCHOOL
501 8th St, Fox Creek, AB, T0H 1P0
(780) 622-2234
Emp Here 50
SIC 8211 Elementary and secondary schools

D-U-N-S 20-574-5263   (BR)
SEMCAMS ULC
(*Suby of* Semgroup Corporation)
Gd, Fox Creek, AB, T0H 1P0
(780) 622-6200
Emp Here 20
SIC 1389 Oil and gas field services, nec

Fox Lake, AB T0H

D-U-N-S 25-271-4779   (BR)
NORTH WEST COMPANY LP, THE
NORTHERN STAR
Gd, Fox Lake, AB, T0H 1R0
(780) 659-3920
Emp Here 24
SIC 5411 Grocery stores

Galahad, AB T0B

D-U-N-S 20-654-9854   (BR)
ALBERTA HEALTH SERVICES
GALAHAD CARE CENTRE
102 Lady Helen Ave, Galahad, AB, T0B 1R0
(780) 583-3788
Emp Here 40
SIC 8051 Skilled nursing care facilities

Gibbons, AB T0A

D-U-N-S 24-369-2287   (BR)
EVONIK CANADA INC
22010 Secondary Hwy 643 E, Gibbons, AB, T0A 1N4
(780) 992-3300
Emp Here 48
SIC 2869 Industrial organic chemicals, nec

D-U-N-S 20-655-0142   (BR)
STURGEON SCHOOL DIVISION #24
LANNING TRAIL SCHOOL
5325 37th Ave, Gibbons, AB, T0A 1N4
(780) 923-2898
Emp Here 37
SIC 8211 Elementary and secondary schools

D-U-N-S 20-020-3425   (BR)
STURGEON SCHOOL DIVISION #24
GIBBONS SCHOOL
4908 51 Ave, Gibbons, AB, T0A 1N4
(780) 923-2240
Emp Here 30
SIC 8211 Elementary and secondary schools

Glendon, AB T0A

D-U-N-S 20-713-4920   (BR)
NORTHERN LIGHTS SCHOOL DIVISION NO. 69
GLENDON SCHOOL
20 1st St Nw, Glendon, AB, T0A 1P0
(780) 635-3881
Emp Here 30
SIC 8211 Elementary and secondary schools

Glenwood, AB T0K

D-U-N-S 25-366-6648   (BR)
ALIMENTS SAPUTO LIMITEE
SAPUTO
82 Main Ave Sw, Glenwood, AB, T0K 2R0
(403) 626-3691
Emp Here 30
SIC 2023 Dry, condensed and evaporated dairy products

D-U-N-S 25-092-3062   (BR)
SAPUTO PRODUITS LAITIERS CANADA S.E.N.C.
(*Suby of* Saputo Produits Laitiers Canada S.E.N.C.)
82 Main Ave Sw, Glenwood, AB, T0K 2R0
(403) 626-3691
Emp Here 28
SIC 2023 Dry, condensed and evaporated dairy products

D-U-N-S 24-054-7708   (BR)
WESTWIND SCHOOL DIVISION #74
GLENWOOD SCHOOL
151 2nd St Nw, Glenwood, AB, T0K 2R0
(403) 626-3611
Emp Here 20
SIC 8211 Elementary and secondary schools

Goodfish Lake, AB T0A

D-U-N-S 24-390-5650   (HQ)
GOODFISH DRYCLEANING CORP
GOODFISH LAKE SEWING & GARMENT, DIV OF
Gd, Goodfish Lake, AB, T0A 1R0
(780) 636-2863
Emp Here 90   *Emp Total* 110
Sales 9,995,616
SIC 2326 Men's and boy's work clothing
VP Sandy Jackson
Pr Tommy Houle
   Randy Cardinal
   Greg Sparklingeyes
   Agnes Bull
   Ernest Jackson
   Leslie Cardinal
   James Jackson

D-U-N-S 20-592-0270   (BR)
WHITE FISH LAKE BAND #128
PAKAN ELEMENTARY & JUNIOR HIGH SCHOOL
Gd, Goodfish Lake, AB, T0A 1R0
(780) 636-2525
Emp Here 37
SIC 8211 Elementary and secondary schools

Gordondale, AB T0H

D-U-N-S 20-292-7500   (BR)
CANADIAN NATURAL RESOURCES LIMITED
Gd, Gordondale, AB, T0H 1V0
(780) 353-3984
Emp Here 27
SIC 1311 Crude petroleum and natural gas

Grande Cache, AB T0E

D-U-N-S 25-372-2466   (BR)
GRANDE CACHE COAL CORPORATION
Gd, Grande Cache, AB, T0E 0Y0
(780) 827-4646
Emp Here 200
SIC 1221 Bituminous coal and lignite-surface mining

D-U-N-S 25-094-5540   (BR)
GRANDE YELLOWHEAD PUBLIC SCHOOL DIVISION 77
GRANDE CACHE COMMUNITY HIGH SCHOOL
10601 Shand Ave, Grande Cache, AB, T0E 0Y0
(780) 827-3502
Emp Here 30
SIC 8211 Elementary and secondary schools

D-U-N-S 20-713-1009   (BR)
GRANDE YELLOWHEAD PUBLIC SCHOOL DIVISION 77
SHELDON COATES SCHOOL
11080 Swann Dr, Grande Cache, AB, T0E 0Y0
(780) 827-4343
Emp Here 20
SIC 8211 Elementary and secondary schools

D-U-N-S 25-156-3557   (BR)
GRANDE YELLOWHEAD PUBLIC SCHOOL DIVISION 77
SUMMITVIEW MIDDLE SCHOOL
10402 Hoppe Ave, Grande Cache, AB, T0E 0Y0
(780) 827-3820
Emp Here 25
SIC 8211 Elementary and secondary schools

D-U-N-S 20-799-0321   (BR)
MILNER POWER INC

---

1 Power Plant, Grande Cache, AB, T0E 0Y0
(780) 827-7100
Emp Here 70
SIC 1629 Heavy construction, nec

D-U-N-S 20-029-2626   (BR)
NORTHLAND SCHOOL DIVISION 61
SUSA CREEK SCHOOL
Gd, Grande Cache, AB, T0E 0Y0
(780) 827-3919
Emp Here 20
SIC 8211 Elementary and secondary schools

D-U-N-S 25-272-5718   (BR)
WEYERHAEUSER COMPANY LIMITED
(*Suby of* Weyerhaeuser Company)
Gd, Grande Cache, AB, T0E 0Y0

Emp Here 150
SIC 2421 Sawmills and planing mills, general

Grande Prairie, AB T8V

D-U-N-S 25-184-0492   (BR)
1009833 ALBERTA LTD
PETLAND
10310 108a St, Grande Prairie, AB, T8V 7M1
(780) 513-4409
Emp Here 25
SIC 5999 Miscellaneous retail stores, nec

D-U-N-S 24-222-3225   (BR)
1063967 ALBERTA CORPORATION
WENDY'S RESTAURANT
(*Suby of* 1063967 Alberta Corporation)
10007 99 Ave, Grande Prairie, AB, T8V 0R7
(780) 538-3828
Emp Here 26
SIC 5812 Eating places

D-U-N-S 20-773-1170   (SL)
1073946 ALBERTA LTD
NORTHMED SAFETY SERVICES
12002 101 Ave Suite 101, Grande Prairie, AB,
T8V 8B1
(780) 882-8800
Emp Here 30   *Sales* 10,246,450
SIC 8322 Individual and family services
Pr Heather Tscaja

D-U-N-S 25-182-3464   (BR)
599681 SASKATCHEWAN LTD
BRANDT TRACTOR
9101 116 St, Grande Prairie, AB, T8V 6S7
(780) 532-3414
Emp Here 50
SIC 7699 Repair services, nec

D-U-N-S 25-360-9275   (BR)
6518729 CANADA INC
Gd, Grande Prairie, AB, T8V 2Z7

Emp Here 30
SIC 4213 Trucking, except local

D-U-N-S 20-558-6618   (SL)
911 INDUSTRIAL RESPONSE INC
11025 89 Ave Unit 120, Grande Prairie, AB,
T8V 5B9
(780) 933-9111
Emp Here 30   *Sales* 10,246,450
SIC 8322 Individual and family services
Dir Tanya Johnson

D-U-N-S 24-337-5560   (BR)
AGAT LABORATORIES LTD
AGAT
10203 123 St Unit B, Grande Prairie, AB, T8V
8B7
(780) 402-2050
Emp Here 20
SIC 8734 Testing laboratories

D-U-N-S 25-185-1721   (BR)
ALS CANADA LTD
ENVIRO-TEST LABORATORIES, DIV OF

9505 111 St, Grande Prairie, AB, T8V 5W1
(780) 539-5196
Emp Here 26
SIC 8731 Commercial physical research

D-U-N-S 25-686-7672   (BR)
ATCO ELECTRIC LTD
ATCO ELECTRIC
9717 97 Ave, Grande Prairie, AB, T8V 6L9
(780) 538-7032
Emp Here 280
SIC 4911 Electric services

D-U-N-S 25-267-1433   (BR)
ATCO GAS AND PIPELINES LTD
ATCO GAS
8801 112 St, Grande Prairie, AB, T8V 6A4
(780) 539-2400
Emp Here 50
SIC 4924 Natural gas distribution

D-U-N-S 24-274-2575   (BR)
ACKLANDS - GRAINGER INC
AGI
(*Suby of* W.W. Grainger, Inc.)
11537 95 Ave, Grande Prairie, AB, T8V 5P7
(780) 532-5541
Emp Here 20
SIC 5085 Industrial supplies

D-U-N-S 24-683-7871   (SL)
ADVANCED SAFETY PARAMEDICS INC
9728 101 Ave Unit 204, Grande Prairie, AB,
T8V 5B6

Emp Here 46   *Sales* 5,909,817
SIC 1389 Oil and gas field services, nec

D-U-N-S 25-762-0856   (BR)
ALBERTA HEALTH SERVICES
NORTHERN ADDICTION CENTRE
11333 106 St, Grande Prairie, AB, T8V 6T7
(780) 538-5210
Emp Here 50
SIC 8062 General medical and surgical hospitals

D-U-N-S 24-343-0829   (BR)
ALBERTA HEALTH SERVICES
10409 98 St, Grande Prairie, AB, T8V 2E8
(780) 538-7100
Emp Here 20
SIC 8062 General medical and surgical hospitals

D-U-N-S 25-948-0424   (BR)
ALBERTA HEALTH SERVICES
EMS
10710 97 St, Grande Prairie, AB, T8V 7G6
(780) 538-1253
Emp Here 70
SIC 4119 Local passenger transportation, nec

D-U-N-S 25-316-0105   (BR)
ALBERTA MOTOR ASSOCIATION
A M A
11401 99 St, Grande Prairie, AB, T8V 2H6
(780) 532-4421
Emp Here 32
SIC 8699 Membership organizations, nec

D-U-N-S 20-299-0953   (SL)
ALL PEACE PROTECTION LTD
APP PARKING
11117 100 St Suite 202, Grande Prairie, AB,
T8V 2N2
(780) 538-1166
Emp Here 150   *Sales* 4,669,485
SIC 7381 Detective and armored car services

D-U-N-S 24-967-1587   (SL)
ALL-EQUIPMENT LTD
CUSTOM TRUCK PARTS/CTP DISTRIBUTORS
11426 97 Ave, Grande Prairie, AB, T8V 5Z5
(780) 538-2211
Emp Here 58   *Sales* 9,521,520
SIC 5013 Motor vehicle supplies and new parts

Mgr Steven Darr
Dir Gordon Watt
Dir Charles Grubisich

D-U-N-S 20-245-5304   (BR)
ALLIANCE PIPELINE LTD
10944 92 Ave, Grande Prairie, AB, T8V 6B5
(780) 402-3102
Emp Here 23
SIC 4922 Natural gas transmission

D-U-N-S 25-360-0720   (BR)
ALTUS GEOMATICS LIMITED PARTNERSHIP
ALTUS GROUP
11417 91 Ave, Grande Prairie, AB, T8V 5Z3
(780) 532-6793
Emp Here 20
SIC 8713 Surveying services

D-U-N-S 25-316-0550   (BR)
BP CANADA ENERGY COMPANY
SOUTH WAPITI GAS PLANT
(*Suby of* BP P.L.C.)
9909 102 St Suite 214, Grande Prairie, AB,
T8V 2V4
(780) 354-2226
Emp Here 35
SIC 1311 Crude petroleum and natural gas

D-U-N-S 24-011-8047   (BR)
BADGER DAYLIGHTING LTD
8930 111 St Suite 123, Grande Prairie, AB,
T8V 4W1
(780) 538-2777
Emp Here 24
SIC 1389 Oil and gas field services, nec

D-U-N-S 25-297-0116   (BR)
BANK OF NOVA SCOTIA, THE
SCOTIABANK
9834 100 Ave, Grande Prairie, AB, T8V 0T8
(780) 532-9250
Emp Here 20
SIC 6021 National commercial banks

D-U-N-S 25-764-2165   (BR)
BANK OF MONTREAL
BMO
10705 West Side Dr, Grande Prairie, AB, T8V
8J4
(780) 538-8150
Emp Here 25
SIC 6021 National commercial banks

D-U-N-S 24-806-2580   (HQ)
BARON OILFIELD SUPPLY
9515 108 St, Grande Prairie, AB, T8V 5R7
(780) 532-5661
Emp Here 130   *Emp Total* 120
Sales 30,625,693
SIC 5084 Industrial machinery and equipment
Pr Pr Barry Smith
Dir H.A. Side

D-U-N-S 25-183-6706   (BR)
BEST BUY CANADA LTD
FUTURE SHOP
(*Suby of* Best Buy Co., Inc.)
11120 100 Ave, Grande Prairie, AB, T8V 7L2

Emp Here 50
SIC 5731 Radio, television, and electronic stores

D-U-N-S 20-068-3238   (BR)
BEST FACILITIES SERVICES LTD
A & A SERVICE COMPANY
Gd, Grande Prairie, AB, T8V 2Z7
(780) 532-3508
Emp Here 30
SIC 7349 Building maintenance services, nec

D-U-N-S 24-377-0331   (BR)
BLUEWAVE ENERGY LTD
NEUFELD PETROLEUM & PROPANE
14125 99 St Suite 101, Grande Prairie, AB,
T8V 7G2

(780) 814-6111
Emp Here 50
SIC 5541 Gasoline service stations

D-U-N-S 25-231-7227   (BR)
BRICK WAREHOUSE LP, THE
11345 104 Ave, Grande Prairie, AB, T8V 0N7
(780) 538-2525
Emp Here 30
SIC 5712 Furniture stores

D-U-N-S 25-288-9084   (BR)
CANADA POST CORPORATION
GRANDE PRAIRIE POST OFFICE
11524 84 Ave, Grande Prairie, AB, T8V 3B5
(780) 831-0203
Emp Here 100
SIC 4311 U.s. postal service

D-U-N-S 24-643-2314   (BR)
CANADIAN IMPERIAL BANK OF COMMERCE
CIBC
9933 100 Ave, Grande Prairie, AB, T8V 0V1
(780) 538-8300
Emp Here 30
SIC 6021 National commercial banks

D-U-N-S 20-189-2135   (BR)
CANADIAN NATURAL RESOURCES LIMITED
9705 97 St, Grande Prairie, AB, T8V 8B9
(780) 831-7475
Emp Here 200
SIC 1311 Crude petroleum and natural gas

D-U-N-S 20-547-2116   (BR)
CANADIAN WESTERN BANK
11226 100 Ave, Grande Prairie, AB, T8V 7L2
(780) 831-1888
Emp Here 22
SIC 6021 National commercial banks

D-U-N-S 24-418-4995   (BR)
CINEPLEX ODEON CORPORATION
CINEPLEX CINEMAS GRANDE PRAIRIE
10330 109 St, Grande Prairie, AB, T8V 7X3
(780) 513-5534
Emp Here 40
SIC 7832 Motion picture theaters, except drive-in

D-U-N-S 25-970-4336   (BR)
CITY OF GRANDE PRAIRIE, THE
CRYSTAL CENTRE
10017 99 Ave, Grande Prairie, AB, T8V 0R7
(780) 539-4009
Emp Here 70
SIC 7997 Membership sports and recreation clubs

D-U-N-S 24-519-2310   (BR)
CITY OF GRANDE PRAIRIE, THE
DAVE BARR COMMUNITY CENTRE
9535 Prairie Rd, Grande Prairie, AB, T8V 6G5
(780) 538-0469
Emp Here 20
SIC 7999 Amusement and recreation, nec

D-U-N-S 24-803-2455   (BR)
CITY OF GRANDE PRAIRIE, THE
CITY OF GRANDE PRAIRIE, THE
9839 103 Ave Unit 101, Grande Prairie, AB,
T8V 6M7
(780) 532-3580
Emp Here 20
SIC 8231 Libraries

D-U-N-S 20-884-5425   (BR)
CLEAN HARBORS INDUSTRIAL SERVICES CANADA, INC
Gd, Grande Prairie, AB, T8V 6L4

Emp Here 30
SIC 7353 Heavy construction equipment rental

D-U-N-S 20-918-0590   (BR)
CONNECTING CARE (2000) INC

GARDENS, THE
(Suby of Connecting Care (2000) Inc)
10402 111 St Suite 411, Grande Prairie, AB, T8V 8G4
(780) 539-5538
Emp Here 30
SIC 8322 Individual and family services

D-U-N-S 20-809-2200   (BR)
CONOCOPHILLIPS WESTERN CANADA PARTNERSHIP
CONOCCPHILLIPS CANADA RESOURCES
9701 116 St, Grande Prairie, AB, T8V 6H6
(780) 539-3007
Emp Here 25
SIC 1381 Drilling oil and gas wells

D-U-N-S 25-524-6696   (BR)
COSTCO WHOLESALE CANADA LTD
COSTCO
(Suby of Costco Wholesale Corporation)
9901 116 St, Grande Prairie, AB, T8V 6H6
(780) 538-2911
Emp Here 200
SIC 5099 Durable goods, nec

D-U-N-S 24-020-5158   (SL)
CUTTING EDGE MASONRY LTD
11307 100 St, Grande Prairie, AB, T8V 2N4
(780) 538-3686
Emp Here 55   *Sales* 4,012,839
SIC 1741 Masonry and other stonework

D-U-N-S 25-014-0944   (BR)
DC ENERGY SERVICES INC
(Suby of DC Energy Group Inc)
Gd Lcd Main, Grande Prairie, AB, T8V 2Z7

Emp Here 20
SIC 7353 Heavy construction equipment rental

D-U-N-S 20-720-2284   (SL)
DAVCO SOLUTIONS INC
Gd Lcd Main, Grande Prairie, AB, T8V 2Z7
(780) 532-1850
Emp Here 50   *Sales* 4,331,255
SIC 3599 Industrial machinery, nec

D-U-N-S 24-394-7301   (BR)
DEVON CANADA CORPORATION
9601 116 St Unit 101, Grande Prairie, AB, T8V 5W3

Emp Here 100
SIC 1382 Oil and gas exploration services

D-U-N-S 24-523-3122   (BR)
DOLEMO DEVELOPMENT CORPORATION
STONEBRIDGE HOTEL - GRANDE PRAIRIE
(Suby of Eulova Developments Inc)
12102 100 St, Grande Prairie, AB, T8V 5P1
(780) 539-5561
Emp Here 50
SIC 7011 Hotels and motels

D-U-N-S 20-191-2172   (BR)
DOVER CORPORATION (CANADA) LIMITED
COMPRESSOR COMPONET A DIV OF
(Suby of Dover Corporation)
11405 86 Ave, Grande Prairie, AB, T8V 6Z6

Emp Here 20
SIC 3599 Industrial machinery, nec

D-U-N-S 25-014-5505   (SL)
EARLS MARKET SQUARE LTD
EARL'S RESTAURANT
9825 100 St, Grande Prairie, AB, T8V 6X3
(780) 538-3275
Emp Here 85   *Sales* 2,553,625
SIC 5812 Eating places

D-U-N-S 25-775-5058   (BR)
ENERGETIC SERVICES INC
13701 99 St, Grande Prairie, AB, T8V 7N9
(780) 532-9195
Emp Here 30

SIC 1389 Oil and gas field services, nec

D-U-N-S 25-181-8555   (BR)
F I OILFIELD SERVICES CANADA ULC
8909 154 Ave, Grande Prairie, AB, T8V 2B7
(780) 539-9313
Emp Here 20
SIC 1389 Oil and gas field services, nec

D-U-N-S 24-684-4281   (SL)
FYI EYE CARE SERVICE AND PRODUCTS INC
FYI DOCTORS
1211 99 St, Grande Prairie, AB, T8V 6X9
(780) 532-2969
Emp Here 1,000   *Sales* 78,626,160
SIC 8042 Offices and clinics of optometrists
Pr Allen Ulsifer

D-U-N-S 25-764-1381   (BR)
FIREMASTER OILFIELD SERVICES INC
12138 101 Ave, Grande Prairie, AB, T8V 8A9
(780) 539-4400
Emp Here 33
SIC 1389 Oil and gas field services, nec

D-U-N-S 20-048-5360   (BR)
FIRSTCANADA ULC
SCHOOL BUSES
11456 97 Ave, Grande Prairie, AB, T8V 5Z5
(780) 532-3545
Emp Here 50
SIC 4151 School buses

D-U-N-S 20-628-7653   (BR)
FRESON MARKET LTD
FRESON BROS
(Suby of Altamart Investments (1993) Ltd)
8038 100 St, Grande Prairie, AB, T8V 6H7
(780) 539-0760
Emp Here 60
SIC 5411 Grocery stores

D-U-N-S 25-775-1768   (BR)
FRESON MARKET LTD
IGA
(Suby of Altamart Investments (1993) Ltd)
11417 99 St, Grande Prairie, AB, T8V 2H6
(780) 532-2920
Emp Here 76
SIC 5411 Grocery stores

D-U-N-S 24-333-7826   (BR)
GAMEHOST INC
GREAT NORTHERN CASINO
10910 104 Ave, Grande Prairie, AB, T8V 7R2
(780) 539-4454
Emp Here 50
SIC 7999 Amusement and recreation, nec

D-U-N-S 24-334-8468   (BR)
GAMEHOST INC
SERVICE PLUS INNS & SUITES
10810 107a Ave, Grande Prairie, AB, T8V 7A9
(780) 538-3900
Emp Here 20
SIC 7011 Hotels and motels

D-U-N-S 24-887-0730   (BR)
GAS DRIVE GLOBAL LP
INERFLEX
8410 113 St, Grande Prairie, AB, T8V 6T9
(780) 539-5974
Emp Here 25
SIC 7699 Repair services, nec

D-U-N-S 25-314-7060   (BR)
GIBSON ENERGY ULC
9502 42 Ave, Grande Prairie, AB, T8V 5N3
(780) 539-4427
Emp Here 100
SIC 5172 Petroleum products, nec

D-U-N-S 24-001-2880   (HQ)
GOLD STAR TRANSPORT (1975) LTD
11002 89 Ave, Grande Prairie, AB, T8V 4W4
(780) 532-0773
Emp Here 30   *Emp Total* 500
Sales 19,407,546

SIC 4213 Trucking, except local
Jack Charles
Genl Mgr Bob Munro

D-U-N-S 25-764-5176   (BR)
GOVERNING COUNCIL OF THE SALVATION ARMY IN CANADA, THE
GOVERNING COUNCIL OF THE SALVATION ARMY IN CANADA, THE
9525 83 Ave, Grande Prairie, AB, T8V 6V1
(780) 538-2848
Emp Here 30
SIC 8322 Individual and family services

D-U-N-S 20-657-5594   (BR)
GOVERNMENT OF THE PROVINCE OF ALBERTA
ALBERTA JUSTICE
10260 99 St, Grande Prairie, AB, T8V 2H4
(780) 538-5340
Emp Here 25
SIC 8111 Legal services

D-U-N-S 20-153-7706   (BR)
GOVERNMENT OF THE PROVINCE OF ALBERTA
GRANDE PRAIRIE REGIONAL COLLEGE
10726 106 Ave, Grande Prairie, AB, T8V 4C4
(780) 539-2057
Emp Here 600
SIC 8221 Colleges and universities

D-U-N-S 25-014-5513   (BR)
GRANDE PRAIRIE CATHOLIC SCHOOL DISTRICT 28
ST GERARD CATHOLIC SCHOOL
9724 88 Ave, Grande Prairie, AB, T8V 0B7
(780) 532-5398
Emp Here 40
SIC 8211 Elementary and secondary schools

D-U-N-S 25-182-8497   (BR)
GRANDE PRAIRIE CATHOLIC SCHOOL DISTRICT 28
ST PATRICK CATHOLIC SCHOOL
7810 Poplar Dr, Grande Prairie, AB, T8V 4T8
(780) 539-7434
Emp Here 40
SIC 8211 Elementary and secondary schools

D-U-N-S 20-037-3285   (BR)
GRANDE PRAIRIE CATHOLIC SCHOOL DISTRICT 28
ST CLEMENT CATHOLIC SCHOOL
9636 109 Ave, Grande Prairie, AB, T8V 1R2
(780) 532-4698
Emp Here 35
SIC 8211 Elementary and secondary schools

D-U-N-S 20-023-9304   (BR)
GRANDE PRAIRIE PUBLIC SCHOOL DISTRICT #2357
GRANDE PRAIRIE COMPOSITE HIGH SCHOOL
(Suby of Grande Prairie Public School District #2357)
11202 104 St Suite 2357, Grande Prairie, AB, T8V 2Z1
(780) 532-7721
Emp Here 100
SIC 8211 Elementary and secondary schools

D-U-N-S 25-269-7347   (BR)
GRANDE PRAIRIE PUBLIC SCHOOL DISTRICT #2357
CRYSTAL PARK SCHOOL
(Suby of Grande Prairie Public School District #2357)
9351 116 Ave, Grande Prairie, AB, T8V 6L5
(780) 830-3384
Emp Here 145
SIC 8211 Elementary and secondary schools

D-U-N-S 20-592-0858   (BR)
GRANDE PRAIRIE PUBLIC SCHOOL DISTRICT #2357
ALEXANDER FORBES SCHOOL
(Suby of Grande Prairie Public School District

#2357)
7240 Poplar Dr, Grande Prairie, AB, T8V 5A6
(780) 532-1365
Emp Here 50
SIC 8211 Elementary and secondary schools

D-U-N-S 25-181-6393   (BR)
GRANDE PRAIRIE PUBLIC SCHOOL DISTRICT #2357
PARKSIDE ELEMENTARY SCHOOL
(Suby of Grande Prairie Public School District #2357)
9617 91a Ave, Grande Prairie, AB, T8V 0G7
(780) 532-7429
Emp Here 26
SIC 8211 Elementary and secondary schools

D-U-N-S 25-181-6377   (BR)
GRANDE PRAIRIE PUBLIC SCHOOL DISTRICT #2357
SWANAVON ELEMENTARY SCHOOL
(Suby of Grande Prairie Public School District #2357)
8908 100 St, Grande Prairie, AB, T8V 2K4
(780) 830-3416
Emp Here 30
SIC 8211 Elementary and secondary schools

D-U-N-S 25-181-6369   (BR)
GRANDE PRAIRIE PUBLIC SCHOOL DISTRICT #2357
AVONDALE ELEMENTARY SCHOOL
(Suby of Grande Prairie Public School District #2357)
10213 99 St Suite 2357, Grande Prairie, AB, T8V 2H3
(780) 532-4491
Emp Here 35
SIC 8211 Elementary and secondary schools

D-U-N-S 20-023-9312   (BR)
GRANDE PRAIRIE PUBLIC SCHOOL DISTRICT #2357
HILLSIDE COMMUNITY SCHOOL
(Suby of Grande Prairie Public School District #2357)
9410 106 Ave, Grande Prairie, AB, T8V 1H8
(780) 532-0743
Emp Here 35
SIC 8211 Elementary and secondary schools

D-U-N-S 20-003-9134   (BR)
GREAT PACIFIC INDUSTRIES INC
SAVE-ON-FOODS
10819 106 Ave, Grande Prairie, AB, T8V 7X1
(780) 402-2522
Emp Here 150
SIC 5411 Grocery stores

D-U-N-S 25-522-9452   (BR)
GREAT-WEST LIFE ASSURANCE COMPANY, THE
10134 97 Ave Suite 203, Grande Prairie, AB, T8V 7X6
(780) 532-2818
Emp Here 20
SIC 6411 Insurance agents, brokers, and service

D-U-N-S 20-104-1766   (BR)
HI-PRO FEEDS LP
CHAMPION OATS PROCESSORS
(Suby of Hi-Pro Feeds LP)
12805 97b St, Grande Prairie, AB, T8V 6K1
(780) 532-3151
Emp Here 23
SIC 5999 Miscellaneous retail stores, nec

D-U-N-S 20-359-3207   (BR)
HOLLOWAY LODGING LIMITED PARTNERSHIP
BEST WESTERN HOTEL & SUITES
10745 117 Ave, Grande Prairie, AB, T8V 7N6
(780) 402-2378
Emp Here 20
SIC 7011 Hotels and motels

D-U-N-S 20-514-9326   (BR)

HOME DEPOT OF CANADA INC
HOME DEPOT
(*Suby of* The Home Depot Inc)
11222 103 Ave, Grande Prairie, AB, T8V 7H1
(780) 831-3160
Emp Here 100
SIC 5211 Lumber and other building materials

D-U-N-S 24-357-1093   (BR)
HORIZON NORTH LOGISTICS INC
10320 140 Ave Suite 102, Grande Prairie, AB,
T8V 8A4
(780) 830-5333
Emp Here 80
SIC 4731 Freight transportation arrangement

D-U-N-S 20-837-9557   (BR)
HUSKY OIL OPERATIONS LIMITED
9805 97 St Suite 104, Grande Prairie, AB, T8V
8B9
(780) 513-5610
Emp Here 30
SIC 1311 Crude petroleum and natural gas

D-U-N-S 20-867-5129   (BR)
INDEPENDENT COUNSELLING ENTER-PRISES INC
(*Suby of* Independent Counselling Enter-prises Inc)
11402 100 St Suite 202, Grande Prairie, AB,
T8V 2N5
(780) 402-8556
Emp Here 50
SIC 8399 Social services, nec

D-U-N-S 20-918-6803   (BR)
INTEGRATED DISTRIBUTION SYSTEMS LIMITED PARTNERSHIP
WAJAX POWER SYSTEMS
10906 97 Ave, Grande Prairie, AB, T8V 3J8
(780) 532-2396
Emp Here 24
SIC 5084 Industrial machinery and equipment

D-U-N-S 20-302-1865   (BR)
INVESTORS GROUP FINANCIAL SER-VICES INC
11012 100 St Suite 109, Grande Prairie, AB,
T8V 2N1
(780) 532-3366
Emp Here 20
SIC 8741 Management services

D-U-N-S 24-009-2101   (BR)
ISOLATION EQUIPMENT SERVICES INC
12925 97b St, Grande Prairie, AB, T8V 6K1
(780) 402-3060
Emp Here 75
SIC 3533 Oil and gas field machinery

D-U-N-S 20-923-0866   (BR)
JIM PATTISON BROADCAST GROUP LIM-ITED PARTNERSHIP
BIG COUNTRY XXFM
(*Suby of* Jim Pattison Broadcast Group Lim-ited Partnership)
9817 101 Ave Suite 202, Grande Prairie, AB,
T8V 0X6
(780) 532-0840
Emp Here 25
SIC 4832 Radio broadcasting stations

D-U-N-S 24-059-3751   (BR)
JYSK LINEN'N FURNITURE INC
10502 109a St Unit 103, Grande Prairie, AB,
T8V 7Y3
(780) 882-7925
Emp Here 20
SIC 5712 Furniture stores

D-U-N-S 20-970-8148   (HQ)
KAEFER INTEGRATED SERVICES LTD
10006 101 Ave Unit 201, Grande Prairie, AB,
T8V 0Y1
(780) 539-5367
Emp Here 26   *Emp Total* 27,874
Sales 19,261,625
SIC 1799 Special trade contractors, nec
Michael Woloszyn

Norm Guindon

D-U-N-S 20-594-3475   (HQ)
KEN SARGENT GMC BUICK LTD
12308 100 St, Grande Prairie, AB, T8V 4H7
(780) 532-8865
Emp Here 66   *Emp Total* 95
Sales 41,146,923
SIC 5511 New and used car dealers
Pr Pr Ken Sargent

D-U-N-S 25-270-1131   (BR)
LOBLAWS INC
REAL CANADIAN SUPERSTORE
12225 99 St Suite 1544, Grande Prairie, AB,
T8V 6X9
(780) 831-3827
Emp Here 275
SIC 5411 Grocery stores

D-U-N-S 25-273-1732   (BR)
LONDON DRUGS LIMITED
10820 104b Ave, Grande Prairie, AB, T8V 7L6
(780) 538-3700
Emp Here 70
SIC 5912 Drug stores and proprietary stores

D-U-N-S 20-803-0341   (BR)
LONDON DRUGS LIMITED
10820 104b Ave Suite 34, Grande Prairie, AB,
T8V 7L6
(780) 538-3717
Emp Here 70
SIC 5912 Drug stores and proprietary stores

D-U-N-S 20-298-4774   (BR)
MNP LLP
MYERS NORRIS PENNY
9909 102 St Suite 7, Grande Prairie, AB, T8V
2V4
(780) 831-1700
Emp Here 70
SIC 8721 Accounting, auditing, and book-keeping

D-U-N-S 25-183-7282   (HQ)
MAJESTIC OILFIELD SERVICES INC
9201 148 Ave, Grande Prairie, AB, T8V 7W1
(780) 513-2655
Emp Here 20   *Emp Total* 5,515
Sales 5,763,895
SIC 1389 Oil and gas field services, nec
VP Opers Lona Gies

D-U-N-S 20-270-3674   (BR)
MANITOULIN TRANSPORT INC
8601 115 St, Grande Prairie, AB, T8V 6Y6
(780) 538-1441
Emp Here 25
SIC 4213 Trucking, except local

D-U-N-S 25-505-9768   (BR)
MCELHANNEY LAND SURVEYS LTD
(*Suby of* McElhanney Land Surveys Ltd)
9928 111 Ave, Grande Prairie, AB, T8V 4C3
(780) 532-0633
Emp Here 32
SIC 8713 Surveying services

D-U-N-S 25-367-6951   (BR)
NABORS DRILLING CANADA LIMITED
NABORS PRODUCTION SERVICES, DIV OF
Hwy 40 W, Grande Prairie, AB, T8V 3A1

Emp Here 200
SIC 1389 Oil and gas field services, nec

D-U-N-S 25-261-4656   (BR)
NORBORD INC
6700 Hwy 40 S, Grande Prairie, AB, T8V 6Y9
(780) 831-2500
Emp Here 200
SIC 2493 Reconstituted wood products

D-U-N-S 20-897-4162   (BR)
NORTHERN CABLEVISION LTD
(*Suby of* Persona Communications Inc)
9823 116 Ave, Grande Prairie, AB, T8V 4B4

(780) 532-4949
Emp Here 25
SIC 4841 Cable and other pay television ser-vices

D-U-N-S 25-192-3827   (HQ)
NORTHERN METALIC SALES (G.P.) LTD
9708 108 St, Grande Prairie, AB, T8V 4E2
(780) 539-9555
Emp Here 60   *Emp Total* 120
Sales 11,307,948
SIC 5251 Hardware stores
Pr Pr Ken Sargent
Dir Gene Bombier

D-U-N-S 24-700-5283   (BR)
NORTRUX INC
11401 96 Ave, Grande Prairie, AB, T8V 5M3
(780) 532-1290
Emp Here 20
SIC 5012 Automobiles and other motor vehi-cles

D-U-N-S 24-355-3232   (BR)
PARKLAND FUEL CORPORATION
WIEBE TRANSPORT
14605 97 St, Grande Prairie, AB, T8V 7B6
(780) 538-2212
Emp Here 20
SIC 5541 Gasoline service stations

D-U-N-S 24-355-3182   (BR)
PARKLAND FUEL CORPORATION
WIEBE TRANSPORT
14605 97 St, Grande Prairie, AB, T8V 7B6
(780) 538-2212
Emp Here 20
SIC 5172 Petroleum products, nec

D-U-N-S 20-556-2981   (BR)
PE BEN OILFIELD SERVICES LP
Rr 3 Lcd Main, Grande Prairie, AB, T8V 5N3
(780) 539-3642
Emp Here 20
SIC 1389 Oil and gas field services, nec

D-U-N-S 20-710-3628   (BR)
PEACE WAPITI SCHOOL DIVISION NO.76
PEACE WAPITI ACADEMY
11410 104 St, Grande Prairie, AB, T8V 2Z1
(780) 513-9504
Emp Here 50
SIC 8211 Elementary and secondary schools

D-U-N-S 20-023-9270   (BR)
PEACE WAPITI SCHOOL DIVISION NO.76
HARRY BALFOUR SCHOOL
10815 104 St, Grande Prairie, AB, T8V 6R2
(780) 532-9276
Emp Here 62
SIC 8211 Elementary and secondary schools

D-U-N-S 24-312-3796   (BR)
PHOENIX INSURANCE GROUP GRANDE PRAIRIE INC
HUB INTERNATIONAL PHOENIX INSURACE BROKERS
9909 102 St 4th Fl, Grande Prairie, AB, T8V
2V4
(780) 513-5300
Emp Here 42
SIC 6411 Insurance agents, brokers, and ser-vice

D-U-N-S 24-424-4849   (SL)
POWERSTROKE WELL CONTROL LTD
Gd Stn Main, Grande Prairie, AB, T8V 2Z7
(780) 539-0102
Emp Here 35   *Sales* 12,858,960
SIC 1381 Drilling oil and gas wells
Pr Tim Dewald
VP VP Ron Walker

D-U-N-S 25-267-4551   (BR)
PRINCESS AUTO LTD
13601 100 St, Grande Prairie, AB, T8V 4H4
(780) 539-1550
Emp Here 24
SIC 5013 Motor vehicle supplies and new

parts

D-U-N-S 24-391-8781   (BR)
R.E.D. HOLDINGS INC
MCDONALD'S
11469 100 Ave, Grande Prairie, AB, T8V 5M6
(780) 513-2330
Emp Here 20
SIC 5812 Eating places

D-U-N-S 24-319-8533   (BR)
RAINBOW TRANSPORT (1974) LTD
MANITOLIN RAINBOW
(*Suby of* Rainbow Transport (1974) Ltd)
8601 115 St, Grande Prairie, AB, T8V 6Y6
(780) 538-1441
Emp Here 30
SIC 4213 Trucking, except local

D-U-N-S 24-368-7303   (SL)
RAND-BRO ENTERPRISES LTD
PIZZA HUT
12520 100 St, Grande Prairie, AB, T8V 4H8
(780) 538-1991
Emp Here 60   *Sales* 1,824,018
SIC 5812 Eating places

D-U-N-S 20-296-1731   (BR)
RAYDON RENTALS LTD
CAT RENTAL STORE, THE
(*Suby of* Finning International Inc)
9501 116 St Suite 201, Grande Prairie, AB,
T8V 5W3
(780) 513-1245
Emp Here 20
SIC 7353 Heavy construction equipment rental

D-U-N-S 20-086-2670   (HQ)
RENTCO EQUIPMENT LTD
RENTCO'S TOOL SHED
(*Suby of* Peace Foods Ltd)
11437 97 Ave, Grande Prairie, AB, T8V 5R8
(780) 539-7860
Emp Here 37   *Emp Total* 100
Sales 9,840,650
SIC 7353 Heavy construction equipment rental
Pr Pr George Shields

D-U-N-S 25-184-0641   (BR)
ROCKWELL SERVICING INC
ENSIGN ROCKWELL SERVICING
14011 97 St, Grande Prairie, AB, T8V 7B6
(780) 539-6736
Emp Here 50
SIC 1389 Oil and gas field services, nec

D-U-N-S 20-128-0034   (BR)
ROYAL BANK OF CANADA
RBC
(*Suby of* Royal Bank Of Canada)
10102 100 Ave, Grande Prairie, AB, T8V 0V5
(780) 538-6590
Emp Here 20
SIC 6021 National commercial banks

D-U-N-S 20-917-9907   (BR)
ROYAL CANADIAN LEGION, THE
(*Suby of* Royal Canadian Legion, The)
9912 101 Ave Suite 54, Grande Prairie, AB,
T8V 0X8
(780) 532-3110
Emp Here 20
SIC 8641 Civic and social associations

D-U-N-S 25-451-7709   (SL)
S & T ALLARD FOOD LTD
TIM HORTONS
10206 100 St Suite 640, Grande Prairie, AB,
T8V 3K1
(780) 532-6660
Emp Here 125   *Sales* 3,793,956
SIC 5812 Eating places

D-U-N-S 25-678-3366   (BR)
SMS EQUIPMENT INC
CONECO EQUIPMENT
9116 108 St, Grande Prairie, AB, T8V 4C8

(780) 532-9410
Emp Here 32
SIC 5082 Construction and mining machinery

D-U-N-S 25-294-5332   (BR)
SEARS CANADA INC
12429 99 St, Grande Prairie, AB, T8V 6Y5
(780) 513-5270
Emp Here 60
SIC 5311 Department stores

D-U-N-S 20-514-4756   (BR)
SERVUS CREDIT UNION LTD
GRANDE PRAIRIE BRANCH
9930 99 Ave, Grande Prairie, AB, T8V 0R5
(780) 831-2928
Emp Here 25
SIC 6062 State credit unions

D-U-N-S 25-182-3720   (BR)
SHARK CLUBS OF CANADA INC
SHARK CLUB
9898 99 St, Grande Prairie, AB, T8V 2H2
(780) 513-5450
Emp Here 90
SIC 5813 Drinking places

D-U-N-S 20-316-1232   (BR)
SHOCK TRAUMA AIR RESCUE SOCIETY
STARS
10911 123 St Suite 10911, Grande Prairie, AB, T8V 7Z3
(780) 830-7000
Emp Here 42
SIC 4522 Air transportation, nonscheduled

D-U-N-S 25-325-6408   (SL)
SILVERBIRCH HOTELS AND RESORTS LIMITED PARTNERSHIP
11201 100 Ave, Grande Prairie, AB, T8V 5M6
(780) 539-6000
Emp Here 106   *Sales* 6,492,800
SIC 7011 Hotels and motels
Dir Robert O'neill

D-U-N-S 20-811-7635   (SL)
SILVERTIP PRODUCTION SERVICES LTD
11309 98 Ave, Grande Prairie, AB, T8V 5A5
(780) 882-7707
Emp Here 30   *Sales* 5,173,950
SIC 1389 Oil and gas field services, nec
Pr Frederick Dankwerth
VP VP Aidan Kelly
Treas Kenneth Charney

D-U-N-S 25-271-1007   (BR)
SOBEYS WEST INC
NORTHGATE SAFEWAY
9925 114 Ave, Grande Prairie, AB, T8V 4A9
(780) 532-1627
Emp Here 120
SIC 5411 Grocery stores

D-U-N-S 24-644-1799   (BR)
SOBEYS WEST INC
8060 100 St, Grande Prairie, AB, T8V 6H7
(780) 833-8620
Emp Here 20
SIC 5411 Grocery stores

D-U-N-S 20-914-5544   (BR)
STAHL PETERBILT INC
12020 101 Ave, Grande Prairie, AB, T8V 8B1
(780) 539-9991
Emp Here 25
SIC 5084 Industrial machinery and equipment

D-U-N-S 25-766-5281   (BR)
STAPLES CANADA INC
STAPLES THE BUSINESS DEPOT
(*Suby of* Staples, Inc.)
10160 108 St, Grande Prairie, AB, T8V 7B1
(780) 814-6020
Emp Here 45
SIC 5943 Stationery stores

D-U-N-S 20-806-5404   (BR)
STARBUCKS COFFEE CANADA, INC
(*Suby of* Starbucks Corporation)

10948 100 Ave, Grande Prairie, AB, T8V 7G5
(780) 832-4857
Emp Here 20
SIC 5812 Eating places

D-U-N-S 24-391-6681   (BR)
SUN LIFE ASSURANCE COMPANY OF CANADA
CLARICA
10104 97 Ave Suite 103, Grande Prairie, AB, T8V 7X6
(780) 532-2388
Emp Here 50
SIC 6311 Life insurance

D-U-N-S 24-344-0513   (BR)
SUPERIOR PLUS LP
ERCO WORLDWIDE
Gd Lcd Main, Grande Prairie, AB, T8V 2Z7
(780) 539-7200
Emp Here 25
SIC 2819 Industrial inorganic chemicals, nec

D-U-N-S 24-348-8934   (BR)
TARPON ENERGY SERVICES LTD
SYNTEX-ENERFLEX
11418 91 Ave, Grande Prairie, AB, T8V 6K6
(780) 539-9696
Emp Here 120
SIC 1389 Oil and gas field services, nec

D-U-N-S 20-986-9192   (BR)
TOROMONT INDUSTRIES LTD
11537 97 Ave, Grande Prairie, AB, T8V 5R9

Emp Here 27
SIC 7699 Repair services, nec

D-U-N-S 25-979-0509   (BR)
UNITED FARMERS OF ALBERTA CO-OPERATIVE LIMITED
UFA
15602 101 St, Grande Prairie, AB, T8V 0P2
(780) 532-1281
Emp Here 50
SIC 5191 Farm supplies

D-U-N-S 24-377-0430   (BR)
VALARD CONSTRUCTION LTD
(*Suby of* Quanta Services, Inc.)
14310 97 St, Grande Prairie, AB, T8V 7B7
(780) 539-4750
Emp Here 250
SIC 1623 Water, sewer, and utility lines

D-U-N-S 20-242-3815   (BR)
WSP CANADA INC
10070 117 Ave, Grande Prairie, AB, T8V 7S4
(780) 538-2667
Emp Here 21
SIC 8748 Business consulting, nec

D-U-N-S 25-183-6656   (BR)
WSP CANADA INC
FOCUS INTEC, DIV OF
10127 120 Ave, Grande Prairie, AB, T8V 8H8
(780) 539-3222
Emp Here 75
SIC 8732 Commercial nonphysical research

D-U-N-S 25-498-2986   (BR)
WAL-MART CANADA CORP
WALMART
11050 103 Ave, Grande Prairie, AB, T8V 7H1
(780) 513-3740
Emp Here 200
SIC 5311 Department stores

D-U-N-S 24-948-9741   (BR)
WEYERHAEUSER COMPANY LIMITED
(*Suby of* Weyerhaeuser Company)
Gd Stn Main, Grande Prairie, AB, T8V 3A9
(780) 539-8500
Emp Here 650
SIC 5031 Lumber, plywood, and millwork

D-U-N-S 20-184-3179   (BR)
WINNERS MERCHANTS INTERNATIONAL L.P.

WINNERS
(*Suby of* The TJX Companies Inc)
10502 109a St Unit 101, Grande Prairie, AB, T8V 7Y3
(780) 402-9797
Emp Here 24
SIC 5651 Family clothing stores

D-U-N-S 20-303-5167   (BR)
WINNERS MERCHANTS INTERNATIONAL L.P.
HOMESENSE
(*Suby of* The TJX Companies Inc)
11517 Westgate Dr Suite 117, Grande Prairie, AB, T8V 3B1
(780) 532-1508
Emp Here 30
SIC 5651 Family clothing stores

Grande Prairie, AB T8W

D-U-N-S 24-337-1908   (BR)
CITY OF GRANDE PRAIRIE, THE
COCA-COLA CENTRE
6 Knowledge Way, Grande Prairie, AB, T8W 2V9
(780) 513-5252
Emp Here 27
SIC 7999 Amusement and recreation, nec

D-U-N-S 20-549-9259   (BR)
CLEAN HARBORS CANADA, INC
DOUBLE R DRILLING
9805 42nd Ave, Grande Prairie, AB, T8W 1A8
(780) 532-0011
Emp Here 25
SIC 1389 Oil and gas field services, nec

D-U-N-S 24-067-1768   (BR)
EMCO CORPORATION
11905 99 Ave, Grande Prairie, AB, T8W 0C7
(780) 532-3363
Emp Here 30
SIC 5074 Plumbing and heating equipment and supplies (hydronics)

D-U-N-S 20-334-2373   (BR)
ERNIE'S SPORTS (S3) INC
S3 BOARD SHOP
(*Suby of* Ernie's Sports (S3) Inc)
9815 116 St, Grande Prairie, AB, T8W 0C7
(780) 814-5372
Emp Here 20
SIC 5941 Sporting goods and bicycle shops

D-U-N-S 25-269-5853   (BR)
GRANDE PRAIRIE CATHOLIC SCHOOL DISTRICT 28
ST KATERI MISSION CATHOLIC SCHOOL
7906 Mission Heights Dr, Grande Prairie, AB, T8W 1H3
(780) 539-4280
Emp Here 50
SIC 8211 Elementary and secondary schools

D-U-N-S 25-182-4173   (BR)
GRANDE PRAIRIE CATHOLIC SCHOOL DISTRICT 28
ST JOSEPH CATHOLIC HIGH SCHOOL
10520 68 Ave, Grande Prairie, AB, T8W 2P1
(780) 532-7779
Emp Here 60
SIC 8211 Elementary and secondary schools

D-U-N-S 25-183-3554   (BR)
GRANDE PRAIRIE PUBLIC SCHOOL DISTRICT #2357
ASPEN GROVE SCHOOL
(*Suby of* Grande Prairie Public School District #2357)
9720 63 Ave, Grande Prairie, AB, T8W 1K3
(780) 538-3009
Emp Here 25
SIC 8211 Elementary and secondary schools

D-U-N-S 20-710-5789   (BR)
GRANDE PRAIRIE PUBLIC SCHOOL DISTRICT #2357
MONTROSE JUNIOR HIGH
(*Suby of* Grande Prairie Public School District #2357)
6431 98 St, Grande Prairie, AB, T8W 2H3
(780) 532-8861
Emp Here 40
SIC 8211 Elementary and secondary schools

D-U-N-S 20-713-9119   (BR)
GRANDE PRAIRIE PUBLIC SCHOOL DISTRICT #2357
GRANDE PRAIRIE CHRISTIAN SCHOOL
(*Suby of* Grande Prairie Public School District #2357)
8202 110 St, Grande Prairie, AB, T8W 1M3
(780) 539-4566
Emp Here 20
SIC 8211 Elementary and secondary schools

D-U-N-S 20-294-0870   (BR)
LOBLAWS INC
NO FRILLS
10702 83 Ave, Grande Prairie, AB, T8W 0G9
(780) 538-2362
Emp Here 100
SIC 5411 Grocery stores

D-U-N-S 25-290-8512   (BR)
MARK'S WORK WEARHOUSE LTD
WORK WORLD
9821 116 St, Grande Prairie, AB, T8W 0C7
(780) 532-9233
Emp Here 20
SIC 5651 Family clothing stores

D-U-N-S 25-766-6727   (SL)
MAYFAIR PERSONNEL (NORTHERN) LTD
MAYFAIR BUSINESS COLLEGE
11039 78 Ave Suite 102, Grande Prairie, AB, T8W 2J7
(780) 539-5090
Emp Here 50   *Sales* 3,648,035
SIC 7361 Employment agencies

D-U-N-S 24-353-1113   (HQ)
PCC COMMUNICATIONS INC
(*Suby of* PCC Communications Inc)
78 Ave Bay Suite 10821, Grande Prairie, AB, T8W 2L2
(780) 402-8092
Emp Here 30   *Emp Total* 140
Sales 30,646,400
SIC 4899 Communication services, nec
Dir Glen Boyd
Dir Phil Sarozek

D-U-N-S 20-876-8932   (BR)
PEMBINA PIPELINE CORPORATION
8111 110 St, Grande Prairie, AB, T8W 6T2
(780) 539-5700
Emp Here 30
SIC 4612 Crude petroleum pipelines

D-U-N-S 25-362-0348   (BR)
WESTERN STAR TRUCKS (NORTH) LTD
WESTERN STAR AND FREIGHT LINER TRUCK OF GRANDE PRAIRE
7802 110 St, Grande Prairie, AB, T8W 1M3
(780) 513-2236
Emp Here 25
SIC 5511 New and used car dealers

Grande Prairie, AB T8X

D-U-N-S 20-922-9306   (BR)
CALFRAC WELL SERVICES LTD
13401 97 St, Grande Prairie, AB, T8X 1S8
(780) 402-3125
Emp Here 300
SIC 1389 Oil and gas field services, nec

D-U-N-S 25-183-5083   (BR)

FMC TECHNOLOGIES CANADA LTD
(*Suby of* Reliance Oilfield Services, LLC)
15402 91 St, Grande Prairie, AB, T8X 0B2
(780) 513-2811
Emp Here 200
SIC 1389 Oil and gas field services, nec

D-U-N-S 24-524-1695   (BR)
FORMER RESTORATION L.P.
FIRSTONSITE RESTORATION
15001 89 St, Grande Prairie, AB, T8X 0J2
(780) 539-1900
Emp Here 100
SIC 1799 Special trade contractors, nec

D-U-N-S 25-183-6375   (BR)
GRANDE PRAIRIE CATHOLIC SCHOOL DISTRICT 28
HOLY CROSS CATHOLIC SCHOOL
11011 90 St, Grande Prairie, AB, T8X 1J7
(780) 538-0077
Emp Here 45
SIC 8211 Elementary and secondary schools

D-U-N-S 20-710-7959   (BR)
GRANDE PRAIRIE PUBLIC SCHOOL DISTRICT #2357
MACKLIN, I. V. PUBLIC SCHOOL
(*Suby of* Grande Prairie Public School District #2357)
8876 108 Ave, Grande Prairie, AB, T8X 1N7
(780) 513-3391
Emp Here 50
SIC 8211 Elementary and secondary schools

D-U-N-S 20-874-9304   (BR)
NATIONAL-OILWELL CANADA LTD
NATIONAL OILWELL DOWNHOLE TOOLS
(*Suby of* National Oilwell Varco, Inc.)
15402 91 St, Grande Prairie, AB, T8X 0B2
(780) 539-9366
Emp Here 24
SIC 7353 Heavy construction equipment rental

D-U-N-S 25-014-1132   (BR)
NELSON LUMBER COMPANY LTD
15603 94 St, Grande Prairie, AB, T8X 0B9
(780) 532-5454
Emp Here 50
SIC 5211 Lumber and other building materials

D-U-N-S 20-997-0305   (BR)
PETROWEST TRANSPORTATION LP
MURTRON HAULING, DIV OF
9201 163 Ave, Grande Prairie, AB, T8X 0B6
(780) 402-0383
Emp Here 75
SIC 1382 Oil and gas exploration services

D-U-N-S 24-343-5844   (SL)
PRO-PIPE MANUFACTURING LTD
15201 91 St, Grande Prairie, AB, T8X 0B3
(780) 830-0955
Emp Here 30   *Sales* 5,173,950
SIC 1389 Oil and gas field services, nec
Pr Pr Mike Esfarjani

Grande Prairie, AB T9E

D-U-N-S 20-317-1145   (SL)
AERO MAG 2000 (YEG) INC
4123 39 St E, Grande Prairie, AB, T9E 0V4
(780) 890-7273
Emp Here 65   *Sales* 4,158,760
SIC 1721 Painting and paper hanging

D-U-N-S 24-054-0109   (BR)
BBE EXPEDITING LTD
BBE
3724 47 Ave E, Grande Prairie, AB, T9E 0V4
(780) 890-8611
Emp Here 30
SIC 4731 Freight transportation arrangement

D-U-N-S 20-206-1946   (BR)
ENTERPRISE RENT-A-CAR CANADA COMPANY
EDMONTON INTERNATIONAL AIRPORT
(*Suby of* The Crawford Group Inc)
1000 Airport Rd Suite 1, Grande Prairie, AB, T9E 0V3
(780) 980-2338
Emp Here 25
SIC 7514 Passenger car rental

D-U-N-S 20-720-9164   (HQ)
MORNINGSTAR AIR EXPRESS INC
3759 60 Ave E, Grande Prairie, AB, T9E 0V4
(780) 453-3022
Emp Here 30   *Emp Total* 3
Sales 11,308,909
SIC 4522 Air transportation, nonscheduled
 Donald A Wheaton
Pr Pr Bill Mcgoey
 Kim Ward

D-U-N-S 20-058-8338   (BR)
NAV CANADA
4396 34 St E, Grande Prairie, AB, T9E 0V4
(780) 890-8360
Emp Here 420
SIC 4581 Airports, flying fields, and services

D-U-N-S 25-359-3370   (BR)
SHOCK TRAUMA AIR RESCUE SOCIETY
STARS
1519 35 Ave E Suite 100, Grande Prairie, AB, T9E 0V6
(780) 890-3131
Emp Here 87
SIC 4522 Air transportation, nonscheduled

Granum, AB T0L

D-U-N-S 20-656-7724   (BR)
GOVERNMENT OF THE PROVINCE OF ALBERTA
GRANUM PUBLIC LIBRARY
310 Railway Ave, Granum, AB, T0L 1A0
(403) 687-3912
Emp Here 20
SIC 8231 Libraries

Grassland, AB T0A

D-U-N-S 24-568-0140   (BR)
CLEAN HARBORS ENERGY AND INDUSTRIAL SERVICES CORP.
Gd, Grassland, AB, T0A 1V0

Emp Here 22
SIC 7349 Building maintenance services, nec

Grassy Lake, AB T0K

D-U-N-S 20-591-6906   (BR)
BOARD OF TRUSTEES OF HORIZON SCHOOL DIVISION NO 67
CHAMBERLAIN SCHOOL
Gd, Grassy Lake, AB, T0K 0Z0
(403) 655-2211
Emp Here 20
SIC 8211 Elementary and secondary schools

Grimshaw, AB T0H

D-U-N-S 24-392-0469   (BR)
ALBERTA HEALTH SERVICES
GRIMSHAW BERWYN & COMMUNITY

HEALTH CENTRE
5621 Wilcox Rd, Grimshaw, AB, T0H 1W0
(780) 332-6500
Emp Here 60
SIC 8062 General medical and surgical hospitals

D-U-N-S 24-764-3013   (BR)
HOLY FAMILY CATHOLIC REGIONAL DIVISION 37
HOLY FAMILY SCHOOL
5002 47 St, Grimshaw, AB, T0H 1W0
(780) 332-4550
Emp Here 24
SIC 8211 Elementary and secondary schools

D-U-N-S 20-280-1663   (BR)
MULLEN TRUCKING L.P.
MULLEN TRUCKING L.P
Cor Hwy 2 & Hwy Suite 35, Grimshaw, AB, T0H 1W0
(780) 332-3940
Emp Here 30
SIC 4213 Trucking, except local

D-U-N-S 20-023-9403   (BR)
PEACE RIVER SCHOOL DIVISION 10
GRIMSHAW JR & SR HIGH SCHOOL
4702 51 St, Grimshaw, AB, T0H 1W0
(780) 332-4075
Emp Here 33
SIC 8211 Elementary and secondary schools

D-U-N-S 20-023-9445   (BR)
PEACE RIVER SCHOOL DIVISION 10
KENNEDY ELEMENTARY SCHOOL
4612 50 St, Grimshaw, AB, T0H 1W0
(780) 332-4066
Emp Here 35
SIC 8211 Elementary and secondary schools

Grouard, AB T0G

D-U-N-S 24-389-6193   (BR)
NORTHERN LAKES COLLEGE
64 Mission St, Grouard, AB, T0G 1C0
(780) 751-3200
Emp Here 20
SIC 8222 Junior colleges

D-U-N-S 20-029-2667   (BR)
NORTHLAND SCHOOL DIVISION 61
GROUARD NORTHLAND SCHOOL
4th Ave Ne, Grouard, AB, T0G 1C0
(780) 751-3772
Emp Here 20
SIC 8211 Elementary and secondary schools

Gunn, AB T0E

D-U-N-S 20-713-1678   (BR)
NORTHERN GATEWAY REGIONAL DIVISION #10
RIDGE VALLEY SCHOOL
3202 Township Rd 564 Hwy 33, Gunn, AB, T0E 1A0
(780) 967-5754
Emp Here 50
SIC 8211 Elementary and secondary schools

Hanna, AB T0J

D-U-N-S 25-316-7142   (BR)
ATCO ELECTRIC LTD
ATCO POWER
Gd, Hanna, AB, T0J 1P0
(403) 854-5141
Emp Here 100
SIC 4911 Electric services

D-U-N-S 20-043-8344   (BR)
ACADIA FOUNDATION
HANNA LODGE
501 5 St W Suite 17, Hanna, AB, T0J 1P0
(403) 854-3288
Emp Here 25
SIC 8361 Residential care

D-U-N-S 24-346-5346   (BR)
ALBERTA HEALTH SERVICES
HANNA HEALTH CENTRE
904 Centre St N, Hanna, AB, T0J 1P0
(403) 854-3331
Emp Here 150
SIC 8062 General medical and surgical hospitals

D-U-N-S 20-052-1222   (BR)
ALBERTA POWER (2000) LTD
ATCO TOWER SHEERNESS
Gd, Hanna, AB, T0J 1P0
(403) 854-5100
Emp Here 100
SIC 4911 Electric services

D-U-N-S 20-578-2407   (BR)
ALBERTA TREASURY BRANCHES
ATB FINANCIAL
232 2 Ave W, Hanna, AB, T0J 1P0
(403) 854-4404
Emp Here 20
SIC 6036 Savings institutions, except federal

D-U-N-S 25-614-8172   (BR)
FRESON MARKET LTD
IGA
(*Suby of* Altamart Investments (1993) Ltd)
602 2nd Ave W, Hanna, AB, T0J 1P0
(403) 854-3553
Emp Here 31
SIC 5411 Grocery stores

D-U-N-S 25-701-1734   (BR)
GREYHOUND CANADA TRANSPORTATION ULC
CANADA GREY MOTOR INN
616 2nd Ave W, Hanna, AB, T0J 1P0
(403) 854-4471
Emp Here 25
SIC 4111 Local and suburban transit

D-U-N-S 20-870-7641   (BR)
HUDSON'S BAY COMPANY
FIELDS STORES
602 2 Ave W, Hanna, AB, T0J 1P0
(403) 854-5814
Emp Here 25
SIC 5311 Department stores

D-U-N-S 20-711-2058   (BR)
PRAIRIE LAND REGIONAL DIVISION 25
HAND HILL COLONY SCHOOL
Gd, Hanna, AB, T0J 1P0

Emp Here 50
SIC 8211 Elementary and secondary schools

D-U-N-S 20-711-2165   (BR)
PRAIRIE LAND REGIONAL DIVISION 25
HANNA PRIMARY SCHOOL
618 1st St E, Hanna, AB, T0J 1P0
(403) 854-3694
Emp Here 22
SIC 8211 Elementary and secondary schools

D-U-N-S 25-266-8009   (HQ)
PRAIRIE LAND REGIONAL DIVISION 25
(*Suby of* Prairie Land Regional Division 25)
101 Palliser Trail, Hanna, AB, T0J 1P0
(403) 854-2803
Emp Here 20   *Emp Total* 680
Sales 23,248,365
SIC 8211 Elementary and secondary schools
Superintnt Wes Neumeier
Ch Bd Edward Brinkman

D-U-N-S 25-272-1113   (BR)
PRAIRIE LAND REGIONAL DIVISION 25

J.C. CHARYK HANNA SCHOOL
(*Suby of* Prairie Land Regional Division 25)
801 4th St W, Hanna, AB, T0J 1P0
(403) 854-3642
Emp Here 45
SIC 8211 Elementary and secondary schools

D-U-N-S 25-678-7383   (BR)
PRAIRIE MINES & ROYALTY ULC
(*Suby of* Westmoreland Coal Company)
Gd, Hanna, AB, T0J 1P0
(403) 854-5200
Emp Here 100
SIC 1221 Bituminous coal and lignite-surface mining

D-U-N-S 24-042-5504   (SL)
STEWART DRUGS HANNA (1984) LTD
PHARMASAVE 354
610 2nd Ave W, Hanna, AB, T0J 1P0
(403) 854-4154
Emp Here 50   *Sales* 6,201,660
SIC 5411 Grocery stores
Pr Pr Calvin Warnock
  Sherry Warnock

Hardisty, AB T0B

D-U-N-S 25-594-4266   (BR)
ALBERTA HEALTH SERVICES
HARDISTY HEALTH CENTRE
4531 47 Ave, Hardisty, AB, T0B 1V0
(780) 888-3742
Emp Here 50
SIC 8011 Offices and clinics of medical doctors

D-U-N-S 25-384-5242   (BR)
ENBRIDGE PIPELINES INC
Gd, Hardisty, AB, T0B 1V0
(780) 888-3520
Emp Here 24
SIC 4612 Crude petroleum pipelines

D-U-N-S 24-522-3995   (BR)
GIBSON ENERGY ULC
Rr 95 Hwy 13, Hardisty, AB, T0B 1V0
(780) 888-8200
Emp Here 50
SIC 5172 Petroleum products, nec

Hay Lakes, AB T0B

D-U-N-S 25-115-5859   (BR)
BATTLE RIVER REGIONAL DIVISION 31
HAY LAKES SCHOOL
Gd, Hay Lakes, AB, T0B 1W0
(780) 878-3368
Emp Here 20
SIC 8211 Elementary and secondary schools

Heinsburg, AB T0A

D-U-N-S 20-023-9676   (BR)
ST. PAUL EDUCATION REGIONAL DIVISION NO 1
HEINSBURG COMMUNITY SCHOOL
Gd, Heinsburg, AB, T0A 1X0
(780) 943-3913
Emp Here 30
SIC 8211 Elementary and secondary schools

High Level, AB T0H

D-U-N-S 20-021-3952   (SL)

725961 ALBERTA LIMITED
FLAMINGO INN
9802 97 St Ss 1, High Level, AB, T0H 1Z0
(780) 926-8844
Emp Here 60   *Sales* 2,626,585
SIC 7011 Hotels and motels

D-U-N-S 24-802-5582   (SL)
941624 ALBERTA LTD
BEST WESTERN MIRAGE HOTEL & RESORT
9616 Hwy 58, High Level, AB, T0H 1Z0
(780) 821-1000
Emp Here 50   *Sales* 2,188,821
SIC 7011 Hotels and motels

D-U-N-S 24-928-8275   (BR)
ATCO ELECTRIC LTD
Gd, High Level, AB, T0H 1Z0
(780) 926-4491
Emp Here 29
SIC 4911 Electric services

D-U-N-S 24-001-7553   (BR)
ALBERTA ENERGY REGULATOR
AER
9808 100 Ave Ss 1 Suite 205, High Level, AB, T0H 1Z0
(780) 926-5399
Emp Here 25
SIC 8611 Business associations

D-U-N-S 25-300-2265   (BR)
CANADIAN IMPERIAL BANK OF COMMERCE
CIBC
10004 100 Ave Ss 1, High Level, AB, T0H 1Z0
(780) 926-2211
Emp Here 21
SIC 6021 National commercial banks

D-U-N-S 24-330-6227   (BR)
CLEAN HARBORS ENERGY AND INDUSTRIAL SERVICES CORP.
10493 92 St Ss 1, High Level, AB, T0H 1Z0
(780) 926-3248
Emp Here 30
SIC 7349 Building maintenance services, nec

D-U-N-S 24-333-0495   (HQ)
DECHANT CONSTRUCTION LTD
(*Suby of* Dechant Construction Ltd)
11004 97 St Ss 1, High Level, AB, T0H 1Z0
(780) 926-4411
Emp Here 160   *Emp Total* 200
Sales 30,154,528
SIC 1611 Highway and street construction
  Alphonse Dechant
Pr Pr Daniel Dechant
  Doug Dechant
  Wayne Dechant

D-U-N-S 20-699-8929   (BR)
FEDERATED CO-OPERATIVES LIMITED
TGP
(*Suby of* Federated Co-Operatives Limited)
10300 103 Ave, High Level, AB, T0H 1Z0
(780) 926-2231
Emp Here 46
SIC 5141 Groceries, general line

D-U-N-S 25-107-0579   (BR)
FORT VERMILION SCHOOL DIVISON 52
FLORENCE MACDOUGALL COMMUNITY SCHOOL
(*Suby of* Fort Vermilion School Divison 52)
10802 Rainbow Blvd, High Level, AB, T0H 1Z0
(780) 926-2331
Emp Here 42
SIC 8211 Elementary and secondary schools

D-U-N-S 25-191-5856   (BR)
FORT VERMILION SCHOOL DIVISON 52
HIGH LEVEL PUBLIC SCHOOL
(*Suby of* Fort Vermilion School Divison 52)
9701 105 Ave Ss 1, High Level, AB, T0H 1Z0
(780) 926-3706
Emp Here 40

SIC 8211 Elementary and secondary schools

D-U-N-S 20-591-9512   (BR)
FORT VERMILION SCHOOL DIVISON 52
SPIRIT OF THE NORTH COMMUNITY SCHOOL
(*Suby of* Fort Vermilion School Divison 52)
10801 102 St Ss 1, High Level, AB, T0H 1Z0
(780) 841-7200
Emp Here 30
SIC 8211 Elementary and secondary schools

D-U-N-S 24-905-6573   (BR)
FOUR WINDS HOTELS MANAGEMENT CORP
FOUR WINDS CENTRE LIQUOR STORE
10302 97 St, High Level, AB, T0H 1Z0
(780) 926-3736
Emp Here 30
SIC 5813 Drinking places

D-U-N-S 25-992-7861   (BR)
GEMINI HELICOPTERS INC
Gd, High Level, AB, T0H 1Z0
(780) 926-5558
Emp Here 30
SIC 4522 Air transportation, nonscheduled

D-U-N-S 20-174-5036   (BR)
TOLKO INDUSTRIES LTD
HIGH LEVEL LUMBER DIVISION
11401 92 St Ss 1 Suite 1, High Level, AB, T0H 1Z0
(780) 926-3781
Emp Here 220
SIC 2421 Sawmills and planing mills, general

High Prairie, AB T0G

D-U-N-S 24-385-7898   (BR)
BUCHANAN, GORDON ENTERPRISES LTD
BUCHANAN LUMBER DIV OF
1 Railway Ave, High Prairie, AB, T0G 1E0
(780) 523-4544
Emp Here 175
SIC 2421 Sawmills and planing mills, general

D-U-N-S 20-280-0616   (BR)
DEVON CANADA CORPORATION
DEVON
4340 Pleasantview Dr, High Prairie, AB, T0G 1E0

Emp Here 25
SIC 1389 Oil and gas field services, nec

D-U-N-S 24-097-8630   (SL)
EMERALD TRUCKING ENTERPRISES (2005) LTD
36-74 17-5 Nw, High Prairie, AB, T0G 1E0
(780) 523-3909
Emp Here 150   *Sales* 13,852,236
SIC 4231 Trucking terminal facilities
Pr Conan Ochran
Dir John Geddes
  Linda Williscroft

D-U-N-S 25-451-0944   (BR)
FEDERATED CO-OPERATIVES LIMITED
HIGH PRAIRIE SUPER A FOODS
(*Suby of* Federated Co-Operatives Limited)
4920 53 Ave, High Prairie, AB, T0G 1E0
(780) 523-3430
Emp Here 20
SIC 5411 Grocery stores

D-U-N-S 24-702-0803   (BR)
FRESON MARKET LTD
(*Suby of* Altamart Investments (1993) Ltd)
5032 53rd Ave, High Prairie, AB, T0G 1E0
(780) 523-3253
Emp Here 75
SIC 5411 Grocery stores

D-U-N-S 20-703-9053   (BR)

GOVERNMENT OF THE PROVINCE OF ALBERTA
PEACE COUNTRY HEALTH
4620 53 Ave, High Prairie, AB, T0G 1E0
(780) 523-6450
Emp Here 350
SIC 8399 Social services, nec

D-U-N-S 20-297-1748   (SL)
HEALTH REGION 8
4620 53rd Ave, High Prairie, AB, T0G 1E0

Emp Here 45   *Sales* 6,282,240
SIC 8742 Management consulting services
Prin Kate Butler

D-U-N-S 24-000-1842   (SL)
HEART RIVER HOUSING
4600 Pleasant View Dr, High Prairie, AB, T0G 1E0
(780) 523-5282
Emp Here 70   *Sales* 9,434,850
SIC 6514 Dwelling operators, except apartments
  Patricia Billings

D-U-N-S 20-086-3970   (BR)
HIGH PRAIRIE SCHOOL DIVISION NO 48
PRAIRIE RIVER JUNIOR HIGH SCHOOL
5006 56th Ave, High Prairie, AB, T0G 1E0
(780) 523-4418
Emp Here 25
SIC 8211 Elementary and secondary schools

D-U-N-S 20-023-9452   (BR)
HIGH PRAIRIE SCHOOL DIVISION NO 48
HIGH PRAIRIE ELEMENTARY
5701 48th St, High Prairie, AB, T0G 1E0
(780) 523-4531
Emp Here 42
SIC 8211 Elementary and secondary schools

D-U-N-S 25-090-6070   (BR)
HIGH PRAIRIE SCHOOL DIVISION NO 48
E W PRATT HIGH SCHOOL
5650 50th St, High Prairie, AB, T0G 1E0
(780) 523-3813
Emp Here 25
SIC 8211 Elementary and secondary schools

D-U-N-S 20-713-1835   (BR)
HOLY FAMILY CATHOLIC REGIONAL DIVISION 37
ST ANDREW'S SCHOOL
4718 53 Ave, High Prairie, AB, T0G 1E0
(780) 523-4595
Emp Here 65
SIC 8211 Elementary and secondary schools

D-U-N-S 20-712-0044   (BR)
NORTHLAND SCHOOL DIVISION 61
BISHOP ROUTHIER SCHOOL
Gd, High Prairie, AB, T0G 1E0
(780) 523-2216
Emp Here 25
SIC 8211 Elementary and secondary schools

D-U-N-S 25-316-8793   (BR)
TOLKO INDUSTRIES LTD
HIGH PRAIRIE DIVISION
Hwy 2 W, High Prairie, AB, T0G 1E0
(780) 523-2101
Emp Here 178
SIC 2631 Paperboard mills

High Prairie, AB T8A

D-U-N-S 20-642-5774   (BR)
AMEC FOSTER WHEELER AMERICAS LIMITED
AMEC EARTH & ENVIRONMENTAL, DIV OF
4208 55 Ave, High Prairie, AB, T8A 3X5
(780) 523-4842
Emp Here 20

SIC 8711 Engineering services

High River, AB T1V

D-U-N-S 24-885-6093   (SL)
ARP AUTOMATION CONTROLS INC
80042 475 Ave E Unit 200, High River, AB,
T1V 1M3
(403) 652-7130
Emp Here 25   Sales 3,866,917
SIC 3625 Relays and industrial controls

D-U-N-S 20-890-4230   (BR)
ALBERTA HEALTH SERVICES
HIGH RIVER GENERAL HOSPITAL
560 9 Ave Sw, High River, AB, T1V 1B3
(403) 652-2200
Emp Here 300
SIC 8062 General medical and surgical hospitals

D-U-N-S 20-107-6507   (BR)
**CANADIAN CONTRACT CLEANING SPE-
CIALISTS, INC**
603 10 Ave Se, High River, AB, T1V 1K2

Emp Here 102
SIC 7349 Building maintenance services, nec

D-U-N-S 24-734-1571   (BR)
CARGILL LIMITED
CARGILL FOODS
472 Avenue & Hwy Suite 2a, High River, AB,
T1V 1P4
(403) 652-4688
Emp Here 2,000
SIC 2011 Meat packing plants

D-U-N-S 20-713-2106   (BR)
**CHRIST THE REDEEMER CATHOLIC SEP-
ARATE REGIONAL DIVISION NO. 3**
NOTRE DAME COLLEGIATE
1500 High Country Dr Nw, High River, AB, T1V
1T7
(403) 652-2231
Emp Here 30
SIC 8211 Elementary and secondary schools

D-U-N-S 20-713-2080   (BR)
**CHRIST THE REDEEMER CATHOLIC SEP-
ARATE REGIONAL DIVISION NO. 3**
HOLY SPIRIT ACADEMY
4 21 St Se, High River, AB, T1V 2A1
(403) 652-2889
Emp Here 40
SIC 8211 Elementary and secondary schools

D-U-N-S 25-316-1590   (BR)
FOOTHILLS SCHOOL DIVISION NO. 38
JOE CLARK SCHOOL
1208 9 Ave Se, High River, AB, T1V 1L2
(403) 652-2020
Emp Here 32
SIC 8211 Elementary and secondary schools

D-U-N-S 25-269-8956   (BR)
FOOTHILLS SCHOOL DIVISION NO. 38
SPITZEE ELEMENTARY SCHOOL
409 Macleod Trail Sw, High River, AB, T1V
1B5
(403) 652-2376
Emp Here 30
SIC 8211 Elementary and secondary schools

D-U-N-S 20-710-7967   (BR)
FOOTHILLS SCHOOL DIVISION NO. 38
EDUCATION PLUS
1204 10 St, High River, AB, T1V 2B9

Emp Here 50
SIC 8211 Elementary and secondary schools

D-U-N-S 20-654-9995   (BR)
FOOTHILLS SCHOOL DIVISION NO. 38
HIGHWOOD HIGH SCHOOL

12th Ave S, High River, AB, T1V 1S1
(403) 652-5500
Emp Here 45
SIC 8211 Elementary and secondary schools

D-U-N-S 20-735-2720   (BR)
FORTISALBERTA INC
Gd, High River, AB, T1V 1M2
(403) 652-4810
Emp Here 25
SIC 4911 Electric services

D-U-N-S 24-027-8478   (BR)
GOLDEN WEST BROADCASTING LTD
EAGLE, THE
11 5 Ave Se, High River, AB, T1V 1G2
(403) 995-9611
Emp Here 30
SIC 4832 Radio broadcasting stations

D-U-N-S 24-158-8391   (SL)
HI-CAL HOLDINGS LTD
HERITAGE INN
1104 11 Ave Se, High River, AB, T1V 1P2
(403) 652-3834
Emp Here 50   Sales 2,188,821
SIC 7011 Hotels and motels

D-U-N-S 20-514-7882   (BR)
LOBLAWS INC
EXTRA FOODS
1103 18 St Se, High River, AB, T1V 2A9
(403) 652-8654
Emp Here 100
SIC 5141 Groceries, general line

D-U-N-S 24-518-6259   (SL)
MESKEN CONTRACTING LIMITED
CORDY OILFIELD SERVICES, DIV OF
12 Ave & Centre St Se, High River, AB, T1V
1M5
(403) 652-2345
Emp Here 25   Sales 4,158,005
SIC 1611 Highway and street construction

D-U-N-S 20-292-8086   (BR)
ROCKY MOUNTAIN DEALERSHIPS INC
ROCKY MOUNTAIN EQUIPMENT
710 24 St Se, High River, AB, T1V 0B3
(403) 652-7944
Emp Here 23
SIC 5083 Farm and garden machinery

D-U-N-S 25-270-0109   (BR)
**UNITED FARMERS OF ALBERTA CO-
OPERATIVE LIMITED**
U F A
2006 10 Ave Se, High River, AB, T1V 2A6
(403) 652-2733
Emp Here 20
SIC 5999 Miscellaneous retail stores, nec

D-U-N-S 25-329-5836   (HQ)
WESTERN FINANCIAL GROUP INC
(Suby of Western Financial Group Inc)
1010 24 St Se, High River, AB, T1V 2A7
(403) 652-2663
Emp Here 119   Emp Total 1,700
Sales 1,689,259,087
SIC 6311 Life insurance
Pr Pr Scott A. Tannas
Jim Dinning
Ex VP Catherine A. Rogers
Dir Robert Herdman
Dir Doug Buchanan
Dir Sylvie Paquette
Dir Normand Desautels
Dir Stephane Achard
Dir Pierre Mathieu
Dir Karen Radford

Hines Creek, AB T0H

D-U-N-S 24-274-9778   (BR)
CANADIAN FOREST PRODUCTS LTD

CANFOR
Gd, Hines Creek, AB, T0H 2A0

Emp Here 120
SIC 2421 Sawmills and planing mills, general

D-U-N-S 20-023-9387   (BR)
PEACE RIVER SCHOOL DIVISION 10
HINES CREEK COMPOSITE SCHOOL
331 Government Rd W, Hines Creek, AB, T0H
2A0
(780) 494-3510
Emp Here 22
SIC 8211 Elementary and secondary schools

D-U-N-S 25-178-2132   (SL)
VERN BASNETT CONSULTING LTD
BASNETT TRUCK SERVICE
203 Government Rd, Hines Creek, AB, T0H
2A0
(780) 494-3006
Emp Here 55   Sales 4,377,642
SIC 4212 Local trucking, without storage

D-U-N-S 20-086-8693   (SL)
ZAVISHA SAWMILLS LTD
324 Zavisha St, Hines Creek, AB, T0H 2A0
(780) 494-3333
Emp Here 50   Sales 4,742,446
SIC 2421 Sawmills and planing mills, general

Hinton, AB T7V

D-U-N-S 25-236-1217   (BR)
ALBERTA TREASURY BRANCHES
ATB FINANCIAL
207 Pembina Ave, Hinton, AB, T7V 2B3
(780) 865-2294
Emp Here 24
SIC 6036 Savings institutions, except federal

D-U-N-S 20-637-7749   (SL)
**ATHABASCA VALLEY HOTEL ENTER-
PRISES INC**
ATHABASCA VALLEY HOTEL
124 Athabasca Ave, Hinton, AB, T7V 2A5
(780) 865-2241
Emp Here 50   Sales 1,824,018
SIC 5813 Drinking places

D-U-N-S 24-227-2412   (BR)
BAKER HUGHES CANADA COMPANY
PUMPING SERVICES
(Suby of Baker Hughes, A GE Company)
522 East River Rd, Hinton, AB, T7V 2G3

Emp Here 40
SIC 1389 Oil and gas field services, nec

D-U-N-S 20-336-9314   (SL)
CANADIAN TIRE ASSOCIATE STORE
868 Carmichael Lane, Hinton, AB, T7V 1Y6
(780) 865-6198
Emp Here 35   Sales 5,024,256
SIC 5531 Auto and home supply stores

D-U-N-S 20-537-6601   (SL)
CARDINAL RIVER COALS LTD
Gd, Hinton, AB, T7V 1V5
(780) 692-5100
Emp Here 350   Sales 154,968,527
SIC 1221 Bituminous coal and lignite-surface
mining
Pr James Gardiner
Dir Fin Ronald Millos

D-U-N-S 20-573-2683   (BR)
**COMPAGNIE DES CHEMINS DE FER NA-
TIONAUX DU CANADA**
COMPAGNIE DES CHEMINS DE FER NA-
TIONAUX DU CANADA
260 Carmichael Ln, Hinton, AB, T7V 1T4
(780) 865-4999
Emp Here 20
SIC 4011 Railroads, line-haul operating

D-U-N-S 20-027-3717   (BR)
**EVERGREEN CATHOLIC SEPARATE RE-
GIONAL DIVISION 2**
GERARD REDMOND COMMUNITY
CATHOLIC SCHOOL
174 Maligne Dr, Hinton, AB, T7V 1J4
(780) 865-2820
Emp Here 40
SIC 8211 Elementary and secondary schools

D-U-N-S 24-391-8141   (BR)
FRESON MARKET LTD
IGA
(Suby of Altamart Investments (1993) Ltd)
632 Carmichael Lane, Hinton, AB, T7V 1S8
(780) 865-3061
Emp Here 40
SIC 5411 Grocery stores

D-U-N-S 25-824-1157   (BR)
FRESON MARKET LTD
IGA
(Suby of Altamart Investments (1993) Ltd)
108 Athabasca Ave Unit 1, Hinton, AB, T7V
2A5
(780) 865-4801
Emp Here 50
SIC 5411 Grocery stores

D-U-N-S 20-650-6938   (BR)
**GOOD SAMARITAN SOCIETY, THE (A
LUTHERAN SOCIAL SERVICE ORGANIZA-
TION)**
1290 Switzer Dr Suite 120, Hinton, AB, T7V
2E9
(780) 865-5926
Emp Here 50
SIC 8059 Nursing and personal care, nec

D-U-N-S 20-917-9873   (BR)
**GRANDE YELLOWHEAD PUBLIC SCHOOL
DIVISION 77**
ECOLE MOUNTAIN VIEW SCHOOL
141 Macleod Ave, Hinton, AB, T7V 1T6
(780) 865-2628
Emp Here 39
SIC 8211 Elementary and secondary schools

D-U-N-S 25-289-4969   (BR)
**GRANDE YELLOWHEAD PUBLIC SCHOOL
DIVISION 77**
HARRY COLLINGE HIGHSCHOOL
158 Sunwapta Dr, Hinton, AB, T7V 1E9
(780) 865-3714
Emp Here 50
SIC 8211 Elementary and secondary schools

D-U-N-S 20-713-0670   (BR)
**GRANDE YELLOWHEAD PUBLIC SCHOOL
DIVISION 77**
CRESCENT VALLEY SCHOOL
213 Tamarack Ave, Hinton, AB, T7V 1T7
(780) 865-2569
Emp Here 35
SIC 8211 Elementary and secondary schools

D-U-N-S 20-719-6606   (BR)
INSTALOANS INC
183 Pembina Ave, Hinton, AB, T7V 2B2
(780) 817-3880
Emp Here 50
SIC 6141 Personal credit institutions

D-U-N-S 24-351-6171   (SL)
MOUNTAIN VIEW RESTAURANT INC
BOSTON PIZZA
506 Carmichael Lane Suite 100, Hinton, AB,
T7V 1S8
(780) 817-2400
Emp Here 50   Sales 1,532,175
SIC 5812 Eating places

D-U-N-S 24-077-9616   (BR)
SOBEYS WEST INC
SAFEWAY FOOD & DRUG
900 Carmichael Lane Suite 500, Hinton, AB,
T7V 1Y6
(780) 865-5978
Emp Here 50

SIC 5411 Grocery stores

D-U-N-S 24-025-5468   (BR)
TECK COAL LIMITED
CARDINAL RIVER OPERATIONS
Gd Stn Main, Hinton, AB, T7V 1T9
(780) 692-5100
Emp Here 335
SIC 1221 Bituminous coal and lignite-surface
mining

D-U-N-S 20-789-3756   (BR)
**TRIMAC TRANSPORTATION SERVICES
LIMITED PARTNERSHIP**
301 Kelley Rd, Hinton, AB, T7V 1H2
(780) 865-7599
Emp Here 27
SIC 6722 Management investment, open-end

D-U-N-S 25-297-6030   (BR)
WAL-MART CANADA CORP
900 Carmichael Lane Suite 100, Hinton, AB,
T7V 1Y6
(780) 865-1421
Emp Here 110
SIC 5311 Department stores

D-U-N-S 24-962-1749   (BR)
WEST FRASER MILLS LTD
HINTON WOOD PRODUCTS
99 West River Rd, Hinton, AB, T7V 1Y7
(780) 865-8900
Emp Here 240
SIC 5211 Lumber and other building materials

D-U-N-S 25-120-8492   (SL)
ZAINUL & SHAZMA HOLDINGS (1997) LTD
HOLIDAY INN HINTON
393 Gregg Ave, Hinton, AB, T7V 1N1
(780) 865-3321
Emp Here 65   *Sales* 2,845,467
SIC 7011 Hotels and motels

Hobbema, AB T0C

D-U-N-S 20-120-9249   (SL)
**KASOHKOWEW CHILD WELLNESS SOCI-
ETY**
Gd, Hobbema, AB, T0C 1N0

Emp Here 55   *Sales* 2,826,987
SIC 8322 Individual and family services

D-U-N-S 20-591-7540   (BR)
**MIYO WAHKOHTOWIN COMMUNITY EDU-
CATION AUTHORITY**
*ERMINESKiN JUNIOR AND SENIOR HIGH
SCHOOL*
1 School House Rd, Hobbema, AB, T0C 1N0
(780) 585-3931
Emp Here 48
SIC 8211 Elementary and secondary schools

D-U-N-S 25-122-8490   (SL)
**MUSKWACHEES AMBULANCE AUTHOR-
ITY LTD**
Gd, Hobbema, AB, T0C 1N0
(780) 585-4001
Emp Here 61   *Sales* 3,137,310
SIC 4119 Local passenger transportation, nec

D-U-N-S 20-005-4588   (BR)
PEACE HILLS TRUST COMPANY
Gd, Hobbema, AB, T0C 1N0
(780) 585-3013
Emp Here 20
SIC 6021 National commercial banks

D-U-N-S 24-736-1350   (BR)
**SAMSON CREE NATION CHIEF AND
COUNCIL**
SAMSON DAY CARE CENTRE
Gd, Hobbema, AB, T0C 1N0
(780) 585-3930
Emp Here 27

SIC 8351 Child day care services

D-U-N-S 20-296-0485   (BR)
**SAMSON CREE NATION CHIEF AND
COUNCIL**
SAMSON GROCERY STORE
Gd, Hobbema, AB, T0C 1N0
(780) 585-3793
Emp Here 20
SIC 5411 Grocery stores

Holden, AB T0B

D-U-N-S 20-710-4915   (BR)
BATTLE RIVER REGIONAL DIVISION 31
HOLDEN SCHOOL
5335 50 Ave, Holden, AB, T0B 2C0
(780) 688-3858
Emp Here 50
SIC 8211 Elementary and secondary schools

Hussar, AB T0J

D-U-N-S 24-359-0176   (BR)
CHINOOK CREDIT UNION LTD
111 Centre St, Hussar, AB, T0J 1S0
(403) 787-3733
Emp Here 22
SIC 6062 State credit unions

Hythe, AB T0H

D-U-N-S 24-155-6120   (BR)
DEVON CANADA CORPORATION
20 Gas Plant Suite 8, Hythe, AB, T0H 2C0

Emp Here 25
SIC 1389 Oil and gas field services, nec

D-U-N-S 20-939-7046   (BR)
**GOVERNMENT OF THE PROVINCE OF AL-
BERTA**
HYTHE CONTINUING CARE CENTRE
10307 100 St, Hythe, AB, T0H 2C0
(780) 356-3818
Emp Here 40
SIC 8051 Skilled nursing care facilities

D-U-N-S 24-786-3863   (SL)
**PEACE LAND FABRICATING AND SUPPLY
LTD**
FOREMOST GRANDE PRAIRIE
Hwy 43, Hythe, AB, T0H 2C0
(780) 356-2200
Emp Here 30   *Sales* 5,763,895
SIC 3533 Oil and gas field machinery
Pr Pat Breen
Dir Warren Barker
Dir Mike Strilchuk

D-U-N-S 20-023-9288   (BR)
PEACE WAPITI SCHOOL DIVISION NO.76
HYTHE REGIONAL JUNIOR HIGH SCHOOL
10108 104 Ave, Hythe, AB, T0H 2C0

Emp Here 25
SIC 8211 Elementary and secondary schools

D-U-N-S 20-023-9296   (BR)
PEACE WAPITI SCHOOL DIVISION NO.76
HYTHE ELEMENTARY SCHOOL
10108 104 Ave, Hythe, AB, T0H 2C0
(780) 356-2778
Emp Here 20
SIC 8211 Elementary and secondary schools

Innisfail, AB T4G

D-U-N-S 25-231-7789   (BR)
ALBERTA TREASURY BRANCHES
ATB FINANCIAL
4962 50th St, Innisfail, AB, T4G 1S7
(403) 227-3350
Emp Here 30
SIC 6036 Savings institutions, except federal

D-U-N-S 20-104-2665   (BR)
BANK OF NOVA SCOTIA, THE
SCOTIABANK
4949 50 St, Innisfail, AB, T4G 1S7
(403) 227-0158
Emp Here 25
SIC 6021 National commercial banks

D-U-N-S 20-029-3863   (BR)
**CHINOOKS EDGE SCHOOL DIVISION NO.
73**
*?COLE JOHN WILSON ELEMENTARY
SCHOOL*
4457 51 Ave, Innisfail, AB, T4G 1A7
(403) 227-3292
Emp Here 45
SIC 8211 Elementary and secondary schools

D-U-N-S 20-654-9961   (BR)
**CHINOOKS EDGE SCHOOL DIVISION NO.
73**
INNISFAIL JUNIOR SENIOR HIGH SCHOOL
4459 51 Avenue, Innisfail, AB, T4G 1W4
(403) 227-3244
Emp Here 50
SIC 8211 Elementary and secondary schools

D-U-N-S 20-710-2810   (BR)
**CHINOOKS EDGE SCHOOL DIVISION NO.
73**
ECOLE INNINSFAIL MIDDLE SCHOOL
4501 52 Ave, Innisfail, AB, T4G 1A7
(403) 227-0060
Emp Here 39
SIC 8211 Elementary and secondary schools

D-U-N-S 24-963-4817   (HQ)
JOHNS MANVILLE CANADA INC
(*Suby of* Berkshire Hathaway Inc.)
5301 42 Ave, Innisfail, AB, T4G 1A2
(403) 227-7100
Emp Here 200   *Emp Total* 331,000
Sales 21,888,210
SIC 3299 NonMetallic mineral products,
Genl Mgr Jim Wilson

D-U-N-S 24-356-5285   (BR)
LOBLAW COMPANIES LIMITED
EXTRA FOODS
5080 43 Ave, Innisfail, AB, T4G 1Y9
(403) 227-5037
Emp Here 20
SIC 5411 Grocery stores

D-U-N-S 25-368-7495   (BR)
LOBLAWS INC
EXTRA FOODS
5040 43 Ave, Innisfail, AB, T4G 1Y9
(403) 227-4138
Emp Here 50
SIC 5411 Grocery stores

D-U-N-S 20-077-3026   (HQ)
NWP INDUSTRIES INC
(*Suby of* TerraVest Capital Inc)
4017 60 Ave, Innisfail, AB, T4G 1S9
(403) 227-4100
Emp Here 112   *Emp Total* 427
Sales 21,136,524
SIC 3443 Fabricated plate work (boiler shop)
Pr *Pr* Deborah Debelser
Sec George Den Haan
VP Marvin Debelser

D-U-N-S 20-280-2591   (HQ)
NWP INDUSTRIES LP
(*Suby of* TerraVest Capital Inc)
4017 60 Ave, Innisfail, AB, T4G 1S9

(403) 227-4100
Emp Here 20   *Emp Total* 427
Sales 35,044,680
SIC 3443 Fabricated plate work (boiler shop)
Pr *Pr* Mitch Debelser

D-U-N-S 20-175-3873   (BR)
NESTLE CANADA INC
NESTLE PURINA PET CARE DIV OF
5128 54 St, Innisfail, AB, T4G 1S1
(403) 227-3777
Emp Here 80
SIC 2047 Dog and cat food

D-U-N-S 20-296-5158   (SL)
NOSSACK GOURMET FOODS LTD
5804 37 St, Innisfail, AB, T4G 1S8
(403) 346-5006
Emp Here 50   *Sales* 6,969,360
SIC 2099 Food preparations, nec
Pr Karsten Nossack

D-U-N-S 20-710-4261   (BR)
**RED DEER CATHOLIC REGIONAL DIVI-
SION NO. 39**
ST MARGUERETTE BOURGEOYS
4453 51 Ave, Innisfail, AB, T4G 1A7
(403) 227-2123
Emp Here 30
SIC 8211 Elementary and secondary schools

Irma, AB T0B

D-U-N-S 20-970-1523   (SL)
**HUTTERIAN BRETHREN CHURCH OF
HOLT**
HOLT COLONY
Gd, Irma, AB, T0B 2H0
(780) 754-2175
Emp Here 80   *Sales* 5,253,170
SIC 8661 Religious organizations
Dir Jacob Tschetter

Irricana, AB T0M

D-U-N-S 24-417-3738   (SL)
**HUTTERIAN BRETHREN CHURCH OF
TSCHETTER**
Gd, Irricana, AB, T0M 1B0
(403) 935-2362
Emp Here 67   *Sales* 4,377,642
SIC 8661 Religious organizations

Irvine, AB T0J

D-U-N-S 20-712-0655   (BR)
PRAIRIE ROSE SCHOOL DIVISION NO 8
HUTTERIAN BRETHREN SCHOOL
Gd, Irvine, AB, T0J 1V0

Emp Here 50
SIC 8211 Elementary and secondary schools

D-U-N-S 20-653-2645   (BR)
PRAIRIE ROSE SCHOOL DIVISION NO 8
IRVINE SCHOOL
89 Brock St, Irvine, AB, T0J 1V0
(403) 834-3783
Emp Here 35
SIC 8211 Elementary and secondary schools

Jasper, AB T0E

D-U-N-S 20-645-3487   (BR)
ALBERTA HEALTH SERVICES
JASPER SETON HEALTHCARE CENTRE

---

518 Robson St, Jasper, AB, T0E 1E0
(780) 852-4395
Emp Here 110
SIC 8621 Professional organizations

D-U-N-S 20-745-4562   (SL)
ATHABASCA MOTOR HOTEL (1972) LTD
510 Patricia St, Jasper, AB, T0E 1E0
(780) 852-3386
Emp Here 50   *Sales* 2,188,821
SIC 7011 Hotels and motels

D-U-N-S 20-656-9852   (BR)
CANADIAN PACIFIC RAILWAY COMPANY
FAIRMONT JASPER PARK LODGE, THE
1 Old Lodge Rd, Jasper, AB, T0E 1E0
(780) 852-6406
Emp Here 800
SIC 7011 Hotels and motels

D-U-N-S 25-159-4503   (BR)
COAST HOTELS LIMITED
COAST PYRAMID LAKE RESORT
Gd, Jasper, AB, T0E 1E0
(780) 852-4900
Emp Here 30
SIC 7011 Hotels and motels

D-U-N-S 25-770-6317   (BR)
EARL'S RESTAURANTS LTD
(*Suby of* Earl's Restaurants Ltd)
600 Patricia St 2nd Fl, Jasper, AB, T0E 1E0
(780) 852-2393
Emp Here 40
SIC 5812 Eating places

D-U-N-S 25-362-6634   (BR)
FAIRMONT HOTELS & RESORTS INC
FAIRMONT JASPER PARK LODGE
1 Lodge Rd, Jasper, AB, T0E 1E0
(780) 852-3301
Emp Here 550
SIC 7011 Hotels and motels

D-U-N-S 25-056-7849   (BR)
FEDERATED CO-OPERATIVES LIMITED
TGP
(*Suby of* Federated Co-Operatives Limited)
601 Patricia St, Jasper, AB, T0E 1E0
(780) 852-3200
Emp Here 21
SIC 5411 Grocery stores

D-U-N-S 25-157-3366   (BR)
GRANDE YELLOWHEAD PUBLIC SCHOOL DIVISION 77
JASPER ELEMENTARY SCHOOL
300 Elm Ave, Jasper, AB, T0E 1E0
(780) 852-4447
Emp Here 28
SIC 8211 Elementary and secondary schools

D-U-N-S 20-115-2902   (BR)
JAS DAY INVESTMENTS LTD
MOUNTAIN PARK LODGES
(*Suby of* Jas Day Investments Ltd)
94 Geikie St, Jasper, AB, T0E 1E0
(780) 852-4431
Emp Here 75
SIC 7011 Hotels and motels

D-U-N-S 24-331-3541   (HQ)
JAS DAY INVESTMENTS LTD
LOBSTICK LODGE
(*Suby of* Jas Day Investments Ltd)
94 Gielke St, Jasper, AB, T0E 1E0
(780) 852-4431
Emp Here 40   *Emp Total* 70
Sales 3,638,254
SIC 7011 Hotels and motels

D-U-N-S 24-676-7318   (BR)
JAS DAY INVESTMENTS LTD
CHATEAU JASPER
(*Suby of* Jas Day Investments Ltd)
96 Geikie St, Jasper, AB, T0E 1E0
(780) 852-5644
Emp Here 100

SIC 7011 Hotels and motels

D-U-N-S 24-399-9158   (BR)
JAS DAY INVESTMENTS LTD
MARMOT LODGE
(*Suby of* Jas Day Investments Ltd)
86 Connaught Dr, Jasper, AB, T0E 1E0
(780) 852-4471
Emp Here 40
SIC 7011 Hotels and motels

D-U-N-S 20-953-4614   (SL)
JASPER PHYSIOTHERAPY & HEALTH CENTER
622 Connaught Dr, Jasper, AB, T0E 1E0
(780) 852-2262
Emp Here 67   *Sales* 3,210,271
SIC 8049 Offices of health practitioner

D-U-N-S 25-206-4696   (BR)
MALIGNE LODGE LTD
TONQUIN INN
(*Suby of* Maligne Lodge Ltd)
100 Juniper St, Jasper, AB, T0E 1E0
(780) 852-4987
Emp Here 50
SIC 7011 Hotels and motels

D-U-N-S 24-396-5910   (BR)
SAWRIDGE ENTERPRISES LTD
76 Connaught Dr, Jasper, AB, T0E 1E0
(780) 852-5111
Emp Here 55
SIC 7011 Hotels and motels

D-U-N-S 20-746-1146   (SL)
SUNWAPTA FALLS RESORT LTD
SUNWAPTA FALLS ROCKY AND MOUNTAIN LODGE
Gd, Jasper, AB, T0E 1E0
(780) 852-4852
Emp Here 60   *Sales* 2,626,585
SIC 7011 Hotels and motels

Kananaskis, AB T0L

D-U-N-S 25-952-6309   (BR)
TIM HORTON CHILDREN'S FOUNDATION, INC
TIM HORTON CHILDREN'S RANCH
Gd, Kananaskis, AB, T0L 2H0
(403) 673-2494
Emp Here 75
SIC 7032 Sporting and recreational camps

D-U-N-S 24-345-5966   (BR)
VOLKER STEVIN CONTRACTING LTD.
Gd, Kananaskis, AB, T0L 2H0
(403) 591-7124
Emp Here 50
SIC 1611 Highway and street construction

Kathyrn, AB T0M

D-U-N-S 20-912-4515   (BR)
ROCKY VIEW SCHOOL DIVISION NO. 41, THE
KATHRYN SCHOOL
Gd, Kathryn, AB, T0M 1E0
(403) 935-4291
Emp Here 26
SIC 8211 Elementary and secondary schools

Kikino, AB T0A

D-U-N-S 20-029-3327   (BR)
NORTHERN LIGHTS SCHOOL DIVISION NO. 69
KIKINO ELEMENTARY SCHOOL

Gd, Kikino, AB, T0A 2B0
(780) 623-3153
Emp Here 20
SIC 8211 Elementary and secondary schools

Killam, AB T0B

D-U-N-S 20-030-8166   (BR)
BATTLE RIVER REGIONAL DIVISION 31
KILLAM PUBLIC SCHOOL
5017 49 Ave, Killam, AB, T0B 2L0
(780) 385-3690
Emp Here 25
SIC 8211 Elementary and secondary schools

Kinuso, AB T0G

D-U-N-S 25-176-7729   (BR)
HIGH PRAIRIE SCHOOL DIVISION NO 48
KINUSO SCHOOL
500 Kinuso Ave, Kinuso, AB, T0G 1K0
(780) 775-3694
Emp Here 39
SIC 8211 Elementary and secondary schools

Kitscoty, AB T0B

D-U-N-S 20-028-9077   (BR)
BUFFALO TRAIL PUBLIC SCHOOLS REGIONAL DIVISION NO. 28
KITSCOTY JUNIOR & SENIOR HIGH SCHOOL
5110 51 St, Kitscoty, AB, T0B 2P0
(780) 846-2121
Emp Here 23
SIC 8211 Elementary and secondary schools

La Crete, AB T0H

D-U-N-S 20-776-0497   (HQ)
CRETE TRANSPORT 79 LTD, LA
9706 99th St, La Crete, AB, T0H 2H0
(780) 928-3989
Emp Here 22   *Emp Total* 25,438
Sales 5,763,895
SIC 4213 Trucking, except local
Pr Pr Jake Fehr
 David Fehr
 George Fehr
 Andrew Fehr

D-U-N-S 20-029-7104   (BR)
FORT VERMILION SCHOOL DIVISON 52
RIDGEVIEW CENTRAL SCHOOL
(*Suby of* Fort Vermilion School Divison 52)
10402 94 Ave, La Crete, AB, T0H 2H0
(780) 928-3100
Emp Here 28
SIC 8211 Elementary and secondary schools

D-U-N-S 20-023-9486   (BR)
FORT VERMILION SCHOOL DIVISON 52
SAND HILLS ELEMENTARY SCHOOL
(*Suby of* Fort Vermilion School Divison 52)
10202 94 Ave, La Crete, AB, T0H 2H0
(780) 928-3947
Emp Here 35
SIC 8211 Elementary and secondary schools

D-U-N-S 20-029-7096   (BR)
FORT VERMILION SCHOOL DIVISON 52
HILL CREST COMMUNITY SCHOOL
(*Suby of* Fort Vermilion School Divison 52)
Gd, La Crete, AB, T0H 2H0

(780) 928-3632
Emp Here 24
SIC 8211 Elementary and secondary schools

D-U-N-S 20-027-4251   (BR)
FORT VERMILION SCHOOL DIVISON 52
LACRETE PUBLIC SCHOOL
(*Suby of* Fort Vermilion School Divison 52)
Gd, La Crete, AB, T0H 2H0
(780) 928-3913
Emp Here 29
SIC 8211 Elementary and secondary schools

D-U-N-S 24-840-8882   (BR)
UNITED FARMERS OF ALBERTA CO-OPERATIVE LIMITED
U F A
Hwy 697, La Crete, AB, T0H 2H0
(780) 928-3088
Emp Here 21
SIC 5031 Lumber, plywood, and millwork

Lac La Biche, AB T0A

D-U-N-S 25-996-7479   (BR)
ALBERTA HEALTH SERVICES
CADZOW, WILLIAM J HEALTH CENTRE
9110 93rd St, Lac La Biche, AB, T0A 2C0
(780) 623-4404
Emp Here 185
SIC 8062 General medical and surgical hospitals

D-U-N-S 24-367-5266   (BR)
COMPAGNIE DES CHEMINS DE FER NATIONAUX DU CANADA
ATHABASCA NORTHERN DIVISION
9804 99th Ave, Lac La Biche, AB, T0A 2C0

Emp Here 30
SIC 4731 Freight transportation arrangement

D-U-N-S 20-655-2262   (BR)
GOVERNMENT OF THE PROVINCE OF ALBERTA
YOUTH ASSESSMENT CENTRE
9540 94 Ave, Lac La Biche, AB, T0A 2C0
(780) 623-5266
Emp Here 30
SIC 8999 Services, nec

D-U-N-S 20-616-7728   (SL)
LAC LA BICHE TRANSPORT LTD
555 Tower Rd, Lac La Biche, AB, T0A 2C0
(780) 623-4711
Emp Here 80   *Sales* 8,539,920
SIC 4212 Local trucking, without storage
Pr Pr Gerald Wowk
VP VP Randy Wowk
 Steven Wowk

D-U-N-S 20-556-2072   (BR)
LOBLAWS INC
EXTRA FOODS
10527 101 Ave, Lac La Biche, AB, T0A 2C0
(780) 623-6400
Emp Here 50
SIC 5411 Grocery stores

D-U-N-S 20-023-9619   (BR)
NORTHERN LIGHTS SCHOOL DIVISION NO. 69
J A WILLIAMS HIGH SCHOOL
90108 103 St, Lac La Biche, AB, T0A 2C0
(780) 623-4271
Emp Here 50
SIC 8211 Elementary and secondary schools

D-U-N-S 25-269-7107   (BR)
NORTHERN LIGHTS SCHOOL DIVISION NO. 69
DR SWIFT MIDDLE SCHOOL
10140 104 St, Lac La Biche, AB, T0A 2C0
(780) 623-4129
Emp Here 35

SIC 8211 Elementary and secondary schools

D-U-N-S 20-592-0130   (BR)
NORTHERN LIGHTS SCHOOL DIVISION NO. 69
VERA M WELSH ELEMENTARY SCHOOL
9912 103 St, Lac La Biche, AB, T0A 2C0
(780) 623-4672
Emp Here 42
SIC 8211 Elementary and secondary schools

D-U-N-S 20-021-1998   (BR)
NORTHERN LIGHTS SCHOOL DIVISION NO. 69
CENTRAL ELEMENTARY SCHOOL
103109 102 Ave, Lac La Biche, AB, T0A 2C0
(780) 623-2075
Emp Here 30
SIC 8211 Elementary and secondary schools

Lacombe, AB T4L

D-U-N-S 25-484-5035   (BR)
AGRICULTURE FINANCIAL SERVICES CORPORATION
AFSC
5030 51 St, Lacombe, AB, T4L 1W8
(403) 782-4641
Emp Here 35
SIC 6159 Miscellaneous business credit institutions

D-U-N-S 25-217-9759   (HQ)
AGRICULTURE FINANCIAL SERVICES CORPORATION
AFSC
5718 56 Ave, Lacombe, AB, T4L 1B1
(403) 782-8200
Emp Here 300   *Emp Total* 35,000
Sales 792,475,111
SIC 6159 Miscellaneous business credit institutions
Pr Pr Brad Klak
Ch Bd H.D. Haney

D-U-N-S 25-325-8578   (BR)
ALBERTA HEALTH SERVICES
LACOMBE HOSPITAL & CARE CENTRE
5430 47 Ave, Lacombe, AB, T4L 1G8
(403) 782-3336
Emp Here 200
SIC 8062 General medical and surgical hospitals

D-U-N-S 20-260-1063   (BR)
ALBERTA HEALTH SERVICES
LACOMBE COMMUNITY HEALTH CENTRE
5010 51 St, Lacombe, AB, T4L 1W2
(403) 782-6535
Emp Here 30
SIC 8062 General medical and surgical hospitals

D-U-N-S 25-272-5841   (BR)
CANADA POST CORPORATION
5120 51 Ave Lacombe, AB, T4L 1J5
(403) 782-6006
Emp Here 21
SIC 4311 U.s. postal service

D-U-N-S 20-771-1511   (SL)
CROWN JEWEL INVESTMENTS LTD
BOSTON PIZZA
5846 Highway 2a, Lacombe, AB, T4L 2G5
(403) 782-9938
Emp Here 50   *Sales* 1,532,175
SIC 5812 Eating places

D-U-N-S 20-969-7239   (BR)
GOVERNMENT OF THE PROVINCE OF ALBERTA
CORPORATE MANAGEMENT
5718 56 Ave, Lacombe, AB, T4L 1B1
(403) 782-8309
Emp Here 700

SIC 6331 Fire, marine, and casualty insurance

D-U-N-S 25-096-7437   (SL)
LACOMBE FOUNDATION
LACOMBE SENIOR CITIZENS LODGE
4508 C And E Trail, Lacombe, AB, T4L 1V9
(403) 782-4118
Emp Here 50   *Sales* 1,824,018
SIC 8361 Residential care

D-U-N-S 24-161-2134   (SL)
LETO STEAK & SEAFOOD HOUSE LTD
LETO'S
4944 Highway 2a, Lacombe, AB, T4L 1J9
(403) 782-4647
Emp Here 60   *Sales* 1,824,018
SIC 5812 Eating places

D-U-N-S 20-514-8369   (BR)
LOBLAWS INC
EXTRA FOODS 9032
5700 Highway 2a, Lacombe, AB, T4L 1A3
(403) 782-7332
Emp Here 80
SIC 5141 Groceries, general line

D-U-N-S 24-087-8660   (BR)
RED DEER CO-OP LIMITED
LACOMBE CO-OP, DIV OF
5842 Highway 2a Unit 1, Lacombe, AB, T4L 2G5
(403) 782-6200
Emp Here 50
SIC 5411 Grocery stores

D-U-N-S 24-616-7972   (BR)
SOBEYS CAPITAL INCORPORATED
SOBEYS
5110 Highway 2a, Lacombe, AB, T4L 1Y7
(403) 782-7871
Emp Here 25
SIC 5411 Grocery stores

D-U-N-S 20-087-4568   (SL)
WEIDNER MOTORS LIMITED
WEIDNER CHEVROLET
5640 Highway 2a, Lacombe, AB, T4L 1A3
(403) 782-3626
Emp Here 30   *Sales* 15,217,500
SIC 5511 New and used car dealers
Pr Pr David Weidner
VP VP Robert Weidner
Fin Ex Bill Wright

D-U-N-S 24-348-5229   (BR)
WOLF CREEK SCHOOL DIVISION NO.72
TRANSPORTATION SERVICES DIVISION
5226 56 Ave, Lacombe, AB, T4L 2H4
(403) 783-3473
Emp Here 25
SIC 4151 School buses

D-U-N-S 20-710-1697   (BR)
WOLF CREEK SCHOOL DIVISION NO.72
LACOMBE JUNIOR HIGHSCHOOL
5830 50 St, Lacombe, AB, T4L 1G5
(403) 782-3812
Emp Here 50
SIC 8211 Elementary and secondary schools

D-U-N-S 20-592-0627   (BR)
WOLF CREEK SCHOOL DIVISION NO.72
ECOLE LACOMBE UPPER ELEMENTARY SCHOOL
5414 50 St, Lacombe, AB, T4L 1G4
(403) 782-7410
Emp Here 20
SIC 8211 Elementary and secondary schools

D-U-N-S 25-272-0859   (BR)
WOLF CREEK SCHOOL DIVISION NO.72
LACOMBE COMPOSITE HIGH SCHOOL
(*Suby of* Wolf Creek School Division No.72)
5628 56 Ave, Lacombe, AB, T4L 1G6
(403) 782-6615
Emp Here 65
SIC 8211 Elementary and secondary schools

D-U-N-S 20-047-0578   (BR)

WOLF CREEK SCHOOL DIVISION NO.72
ECKVILLE JUNIOR SENIOR HIGH SCHOOL
5303 50 St, Lacombe, AB, T4L 1H7
(403) 746-2236
Emp Here 20
SIC 8211 Elementary and secondary schools

D-U-N-S 20-027-4855   (BR)
WOLF CREEK SCHOOL DIVISION NO.72
J S MCCORMICK ELEM SCHOOL
5424 50 St, Lacombe, AB, T4L 1G2
(403) 782-3096
Emp Here 64
SIC 8211 Elementary and secondary schools

D-U-N-S 20-710-1788   (BR)
WOLF CREEK SCHOOL DIVISION NO.72
TERRACE RIDGE SCHOOL
6739 C And E Trail, Lacombe, AB, T4L 2P2
(403) 782-0050
Emp Here 30
SIC 8211 Elementary and secondary schools

Lake Louise, AB T0L

D-U-N-S 25-293-2587   (BR)
ATLIFIC INC
LAKE LOUISE INN
(*Suby of* 3376290 Canada Inc)
210 Village Rd, Lake Louise, AB, T0L 1E0
(403) 522-3791
Emp Here 150
SIC 7011 Hotels and motels

D-U-N-S 24-701-0812   (BR)
FAIRMONT HOTELS & RESORTS INC
FAIRMONT CHATEAU LAKE LOUISE, THE
111 Lake Louise Dr, Lake Louise, AB, T0L 1E0
(403) 522-1818
Emp Here 800
SIC 7011 Hotels and motels

D-U-N-S 24-376-9119   (SL)
LAKE LOUISE SKI AREA LTD, THE
1 Whitehorn Rd, Lake Louise, AB, T0L 1E0
(403) 522-3555
Emp Here 100   *Sales* 4,377,642
SIC 7011 Hotels and motels

D-U-N-S 20-829-6574   (BR)
RESORTS OF THE CANADIAN ROCKIES INC
LAKE LOUISE SKI AREA
1 Whait Horn Rd, Lake Louise, AB, T0L 1E0
(403) 522-3555
Emp Here 150
SIC 7999 Amusement and recreation, nec

D-U-N-S 20-087-5052   (SL)
SKI CLUB OF THE CANADIAN ROCKIES LIMITED, THE
POST HOTEL
200 Pipestone Rd, Lake Louise, AB, T0L 1E0
(403) 522-3989
Emp Here 110   *Sales* 4,815,406
SIC 7011 Hotels and motels

Lamont, AB T0B

D-U-N-S 24-586-4876   (SL)
ALL STEEL BUILDERS LIMITED
Gd, Lamont, AB, T0B 2R0

Emp Here 40   *Sales* 6,087,000
SIC 1791 Structural steel erection
Prin Joe Childs

D-U-N-S 20-771-5587   (SL)
COUNTRY OF LAMONT FOUNDATION
LAMONT HEALTH CARE CENTER
5216 53 St, Lamont, AB, T0B 2R0

---

(780) 895-2211
Emp Here 50   *Sales* 3,502,114
SIC 8062 General medical and surgical hospitals

D-U-N-S 20-023-9783   (BR)
ELK ISLAND PUBLIC SCHOOLS REGIONAL DIVISION NO. 14
LAMONT ELEMENTARY SCHOOL
4723 50 Ave, Lamont, AB, T0B 2R0
(780) 895-2269
Emp Here 26
SIC 8211 Elementary and secondary schools

D-U-N-S 20-327-7405   (BR)
HELICAL PIER SYSTEMS LTD
HPS
195043 Hwy 29, Lamont, AB, T0B 2R0
(780) 895-2130
Emp Here 25
SIC 3312 Blast furnaces and steel mills

Lancaster Park, AB T0A

D-U-N-S 20-034-9020   (BR)
STURGEON SCHOOL DIVISION #24
GUTHRIE SCHOOL
Gd, Lancaster Park, AB, T0A 2H0
(780) 973-3111
Emp Here 55
SIC 8211 Elementary and secondary schools

Langdon, AB T0J

D-U-N-S 20-710-7405   (BR)
ROCKY VIEW SCHOOL DIVISION NO. 41, THE
LANGDON SCHOOL
17 Brander Ave, Langdon, AB, T0J 1X2
(403) 936-4579
Emp Here 50
SIC 8211 Elementary and secondary schools

Lavoy, AB T0B

D-U-N-S 20-259-8421   (BR)
RICHARDSON PIONEER LIMITED
Gd, Lavoy, AB, T0B 2S0
(780) 658-2408
Emp Here 20
SIC 5153 Grain and field beans

Leduc, AB T9E

D-U-N-S 20-112-1519   (BR)
402909 ALBERTA LTD
BIG RIG COLLISION
(*Suby of* 402909 Alberta Ltd)
8224 Sparrow Cres, Leduc, AB, T9E 8B7

Emp Here 50
SIC 7532 Top and body repair and paint shops

D-U-N-S 25-625-5795   (HQ)
487244 ALBERTA LTD
AUTOWORLD SUPERSTORE
(*Suby of* 487244 Alberta Ltd)
6217 50 St, Leduc, AB, T9E 7A9
(780) 986-9665
Emp Here 60   *Emp Total* 85
Sales 41,718,000
SIC 5511 New and used car dealers
Pr Pr Don Lewicki
  Lorne Isfeld
  Valerie Lewicki

D-U-N-S 24-346-3010   (BR)
ALBERTA HEALTH SERVICES
LEDUC COMMUNITY HOSPITAL
4210 48 St, Leduc, AB, T9E 5Z3
(780) 986-7711
Emp Here 500
SIC 8062 General medical and surgical hospitals

D-U-N-S 25-236-2025   (BR)
ALBERTA TREASURY BRANCHES
ATB FINANCIAL
4821 50 Ave, Leduc, AB, T9E 6X6
(780) 986-2226
Emp Here 31
SIC 6036 Savings institutions, except federal

D-U-N-S 20-083-8381   (HQ)
ALTAGAS UTILITIES INC
(*Suby of* AltaGas Holding Limited Partnership No. 1)
5509 45 St, Leduc, AB, T9E 6T6
(780) 986-5215
Emp Here 70   *Emp Total* 1
Sales 156,143,915
SIC 4923 Gas transmission and distr bution
Pr Pr Lorne M Heikkinen
  David Cornhill
Dir Patricia Newson
Dir Opers Earl Tuele
  Peter Whalley

D-U-N-S 24-275-2525   (BR)
BAKER HUGHES CANADA COMPANY
CENTRILIFT
(*Suby of* Baker Hughes, A GE Company)
7016 45 St, Leduc, AB, T9E 7E7
(780) 986-5559
Emp Here 100
SIC 5084 Industrial machinery and equipment

D-U-N-S 25-595-3077   (BR)
BANK OF NOVA SCOTIA, THE
SCOTIABANK
5419 50 St, Leduc, AB, T9E 6Z7
(780) 986-4441
Emp Here 20
SIC 6021 National commercial banks

D-U-N-S 20-024-1425   (BR)
BLACK GOLD REGIONAL DIVISION #18
?COLE CORINTHIA PARK SCHOOL
127 Corinthia Dr Suite 1, Leduc, AB, T9E 7J2
(780) 986-8404
Emp Here 35
SIC 8211 Elementary and secondary schools

D-U-N-S 20-027-4707   (BR)
BLACK GOLD REGIONAL DIVISION #18
LINSFORD PARK SCHOOL
4502 51 St, Leduc, AB, T9E 7J7
(780) 986-8474
Emp Here 25
SIC 8211 Elementary and secondary schools

D-U-N-S 24-129-7048   (BR)
BLACK GOLD REGIONAL DIVISION #18
BLACK GOLD REGIONAL SCHOOLS
4412 48 St, Leduc, AB, T9E 7J3
(780) 986-2184
Emp Here 30
SIC 8211 Elementary and secondary schools

D-U-N-S 20-709-7317   (BR)
BLACK GOLD REGIONAL DIVISION #18
WILLOW PARK SCHOOL
5212 52 St, Leduc, AB, T9E 6V6
(780) 986-8456
Emp Here 30
SIC 8211 Elementary and secondary schools

D-U-N-S 25-014-6578   (BR)
BLACK GOLD REGIONAL DIVISION #18
LEDUC ESTATES SCHOOL
95 Alton Dr, Leduc, AB, T9E 5K4
(780) 986-6750
Emp Here 27
SIC 8211 Elementary and secondary schools

D-U-N-S 25-014-6339   (BR)
BLACK GOLD REGIONAL DIVISION #18
EAST ELEMENTARY SCHOOL
4503 45 St Suite 1, Leduc, AB, T9E 7K4
(780) 986-8421
Emp Here 26
SIC 8211 Elementary and secondary schools

D-U-N-S 20-028-8723   (BR)
BLACK GOLD REGIONAL DIVISION #18
CALEDONIA PARK SCHOOL
3206 Coady Blvd, Leduc, AB, T9E 7J8
(780) 986-7888
Emp Here 40
SIC 8211 Elementary and secondary schools

D-U-N-S 25-014-6552   (BR)
BLACK GOLD REGIONAL DIVISION #18
LEDUC COMPOSITE HIGH SCHOOL
4308 50 St, Leduc, AB, T9E 6K8
(780) 986-2248
Emp Here 70
SIC 8211 Elementary and secondary schools

D-U-N-S 24-853-7946   (BR)
BRENNTAG CANADA INC
6628 45 St, Leduc, AB, T9E 7C9
(780) 986-4544
Emp Here 32
SIC 5169 Chemicals and allied products, nec

D-U-N-S 20-273-6492   (BR)
CANADA COLORS AND CHEMICALS LIMITED
CCC PLASTICS
7106 42 St, Leduc, AB, T9E 0R8
(780) 224-3841
Emp Here 20
SIC 5169 Chemicals and allied products, nec

D-U-N-S 20-280-4753   (SL)
CHAD SMOKESHOPE 420 LTD.
5111 50 St, Leduc, AB, T9E 6X3
(780) 986-8560
Emp Here 30   *Sales* 13,594,300
SIC 5194 Tobacco and tobacco products
Dir Chad Wentworth
Dir Jessica Wentworth

D-U-N-S 24-890-4471   (BR)
CLEAN HARBORS ENERGY AND INDUSTRIAL SERVICES CORP.
3902 77 Ave, Leduc, AB, T9E 0B6
(780) 980-1868
Emp Here 500
SIC 7349 Building maintenance services, nec

D-U-N-S 24-322-2127   (BR)
CLEAN HARBORS SURFACE RENTALS PARTNERSHIP
3902 77 Ave, Leduc, AB, T9E 0B6
(780) 980-1868
Emp Here 75
SIC 1389 Oil and gas field services, nec

D-U-N-S 24-017-4891   (BR)
DOLLARAMA S.E.C.
5309 Discovery Way Unit 1, Leduc, AB, T9E 8N4
(780) 986-9666
Emp Here 25
SIC 5331 Variety stores

D-U-N-S 20-919-7404   (BR)
DRIVING FORCE INC, THE
DRIVING FORCE
8336 Sparrow Crescent, Leduc, AB, T9E 8B7
(780) 980-2672
Emp Here 20
SIC 7514 Passenger car rental

D-U-N-S 24-861-4351   (BR)
ENERFLEX LTD.
3905 Allard Ave, Leduc, AB, T9E 0R8
(780) 980-8855
Emp Here 45
SIC 3563 Air and gas compressors

D-U-N-S 20-293-5011   (BR)

D-U-N-S 25-014-6339 (BR)
ENSIGN DRILLING PARTNERSHIP
ENSIGN DEPARTURE DIRECTIONAL SERVICES, DIV OF
8009 39 St Suite 106, Leduc, AB, T9E 0B3
(780) 980-3900
Emp Here 30
SIC 1381 Drilling oil and gas wells

D-U-N-S 24-738-9518   (BR)
ENTERPRISE RENT-A-CAR CANADA COMPANY
ENTERPRISE RENT-A-CAR
(*Suby of* The Crawford Group Inc)
3912 84 Ave Suite 309, Leduc, AB, T9E 8M6
(780) 986-4705
Emp Here 20
SIC 7514 Passenger car rental

D-U-N-S 24-715-2085   (BR)
EXTENDICARE (CANADA) INC
EXTENDICARE LEDUC
4309 50 St, Leduc, AB, T9E 6K6
(780) 986-2245
Emp Here 75
SIC 8051 Skilled nursing care facilities

D-U-N-S 25-156-4845   (BR)
FLOWSERVE CANADA CORP
(*Suby of* Flowserve Corporation)
4405 70 Ave, Leduc, AB, T9E 7E6
(780) 986-7100
Emp Here 30
SIC 3561 Pumps and pumping equipment

D-U-N-S 24-043-4501   (SL)
FORCE INSPECTION SERVICES INC
7500a 43 St, Leduc, AB, T9E 7E8
(780) 955-2370
Emp Here 50   *Sales* 3,118,504
SIC 7389 Business services, nec

D-U-N-S 25-290-6888   (HQ)
GE OIL & GAS ESP (CANADA), LTD
(*Suby of* General Electric Company)
3917 81 Ave, Leduc, AB, T9E 8S6
(780) 986-9816
Emp Here 35   *Emp Total* 295,017
Sales 7,296,070
SIC 5084 Industrial machinery and equipment
Pr Pr Gareth Ford

D-U-N-S 24-807-2522   (SL)
GOOSEBERRY'S RESTAURANT LTD
5230 50 Ave, Leduc, AB, T9E 6V2
(780) 986-1600
Emp Here 65   *Sales* 1,969,939
SIC 5812 Eating places

D-U-N-S 24-702-5943   (BR)
HARRIS STEEL ULC
HARRIS REBAR
(*Suby of* Nucor Corporation)
6613 44 St, Leduc, AB, T9E 7E5
(780) 986-7055
Emp Here 45
SIC 3441 Fabricated structural Metal

D-U-N-S 24-089-8841   (SL)
KUNY'S   LEATHER   MANUFACTURING COMPANY LTD
5901 44a St, Leduc, AB, T9E 7B8
(780) 986-1151
Emp Here 100   *Sales* 4,596,524
SIC 5948 Luggage and leather goods stores

D-U-N-S 25-594-4969   (BR)
LEDUC FOUNDATION
PLANEVIEW MANOR PLACE
(*Suby of* Leduc Foundation)
5105 52 St, Leduc, AB, T9E 8P1
(780) 980-0524
Emp Here 35
SIC 8322 Individual and family services

D-U-N-S 20-899-7775   (SL)
LEDUC GOLF & COUNTRY CLUB
5725 Black Gold Dr, Leduc, AB, T9E 0B8
(780) 986-4653
Emp Here 50   *Sales* 2,042,900

SIC 7997 Membership sports and recreation clubs

D-U-N-S 25-597-1178   (BR)
LEDUC, CITY OF
LEDUC REACREATION CENTRE
4330 Black Gold Dr Suite 101, Leduc, AB, T9E 3C3
(780) 980-7120
Emp Here 50
SIC 8322 Individual and family services

D-U-N-S 20-515-5828   (BR)
LOBLAWS INC
NO FRILLS
3915 50 St, Leduc, AB, T9E 6R3
(780) 980-8212
Emp Here 75
SIC 5411 Grocery stores

D-U-N-S 20-040-0690   (BR)
MNP LLP
5019 49 Ave Suite 200, Leduc, AB, T9E 6T5
(780) 986-2626
Emp Here 21
SIC 8721 Accounting, auditing, and bookkeeping

D-U-N-S 20-957-4628   (SL)
MARKING SERVICES CANADA LTD
3902 81 Ave, Leduc, AB, T9E 0C3
(780) 986-8480
Emp Here 25   *Sales* 2,553,625
SIC 2679 Converted paper products, nec

D-U-N-S 24-334-6363   (BR)
NATIONAL-OILWELL CANADA LTD
NATIONAL OILWELL VARCO
(*Suby of* National Oilwell Varco, Inc.)
6621 45 St, Leduc, AB, T9E 7E3
(780) 980-1490
Emp Here 200
SIC 5084 Industrial machinery and equipment

D-U-N-S 20-922-6823   (BR)
NEWALTA CORPORATION
3901 84 Ave, Leduc, AB, T9E 8M5
(780) 980-6665
Emp Here 20
SIC 4953 Refuse systems

D-U-N-S 24-715-8546   (SL)
NISKU TRUCK STOP LTD
NISKU TRUCK STOP
8020 Sparrow Dr Suite 201, Leduc, AB, T9E 7G3
(780) 986-5312
Emp Here 150   *Sales* 27,190,320
SIC 5541 Gasoline service stations
Pr Pr Bob Sparrow
Dir Murrey Sparrow

D-U-N-S 20-334-9345   (SL)
NORTH WEST CRANE ENTERPRISES LTD
7015 Sparrow Dr, Leduc, AB, T9E 7L1
(780) 980-2227
Emp Here 30   *Sales* 3,898,130
SIC 7389 Business services, nec

D-U-N-S 20-074-3149   (BR)
PNF HOLDINGS LIMITED
PARK'N FLY
(*Suby of* PNF Holdings Limited)
8410 43 St, Leduc, AB, T9E 7E9
(780) 986-9090
Emp Here 20
SIC 7521 Automobile parking

D-U-N-S 24-767-7537   (BR)
PEACE HILLS INVESTMENTS LTD
DENHAM INN & SUITES
5207 50 Ave, Leduc, AB, T9E 6V3
(780) 986-2241
Emp Here 100
SIC 7011 Hotels and motels

D-U-N-S 24-004-3062   (BR)
PEAVEY INDUSTRIES LIMITED
PEAVEY MART

5301 Discovery Way, Leduc, AB, T9E 8N4
(780) 980-1800
Emp Here 21
SIC 5251 Hardware stores

D-U-N-S 24-865-0447   (BR)
PUMPS & PRESSURE INC
3813 82 Ave, Leduc, AB, T9E 0K2
(780) 980-9294
Emp Here 50
SIC 5084 Industrial machinery and equipment

D-U-N-S 20-210-4977   (SL)
REMAI KORPACH VENTURES INC
EXECUTIVE ROYAL INN LEDUC
8450 Sparrow Dr, Leduc, AB, T9E 7G4
(780) 986-1840
Emp Here 50   *Sales* 2,188,821
SIC 7011 Hotels and motels

D-U-N-S 24-086-2516   (BR)
ROYAL BANK OF CANADA
RBC
(*Suby of* Royal Bank Of Canada)
10 Leduc Towne Ctr, Leduc, AB, T9E 7K6
(780) 986-2266
Emp Here 23
SIC 6021 National commercial banks

D-U-N-S 25-234-4817   (SL)
SCHWAB CHEVROLET BUICK GMC LTD
6503 Sparrow Dr, Leduc, AB, T9E 7C7
(780) 986-2277
Emp Here 50   *Sales* 3,648,035
SIC 7538 General automotive repair shops

D-U-N-S 25-271-0652   (BR)
SOBEYS WEST INC
SAFEWAY #801
6112 50 St Suite 6112, Leduc, AB, T9E 6N7
(780) 986-0390
Emp Here 132
SIC 5411 Grocery stores

D-U-N-S 24-338-8258   (BR)
ST THOMAS AQUINAS ROMAN CATHOLIC SEPARATE REGIONAL DIVISION #38
CHRIST THE KING JUNIOR & SENIOR HIGH SCHOOL
3511 Rollyview Rd, Leduc, AB, T9E 6N4
(780) 986-6859
Emp Here 40
SIC 8211 Elementary and secondary schools

D-U-N-S 24-014-2203   (BR)
STAPLES CANADA INC
STAPLES THE BUSINESS DEPOT
(*Suby of* Staples, Inc.)
5305 Discovery Way Suite 274, Leduc, AB, T9E 8N4
(780) 980-4336
Emp Here 28
SIC 5943 Stationery stores

D-U-N-S 20-733-1930   (BR)
TECHMATION ELECTRIC & CONTROLS LTD
3923 81 Ave Suite 101, Leduc, AB, T9E 8S6
Emp Here 20
SIC 1731 Electrical work

D-U-N-S 25-687-1922   (BR)
UMICORE CANADA INC
7820 43 St, Leduc, AB, T9E 7E8
(780) 980-7350
Emp Here 25
SIC 3674 Semiconductors and related devices

D-U-N-S 20-552-3751   (SL)
UNDERHILL FOOD SERVICES LTD
MCDONALDS
6504 Sparrow Dr, Leduc, AB, T9E 6T9
(780) 986-5323
Emp Here 80   *Sales* 2,858,628
SIC 5812 Eating places

D-U-N-S 20-826-0273   (HQ)
VARCO CANADA ULC

(*Suby of* National Oilwell Varco, Inc.)
6621 45 St, Leduc, AB, T9E 7E3
(780) 986-6063
Emp Here 90   *Emp Total* 36,627
Sales 24,861,404
SIC 7353 Heavy construction equipment rental
Pr Clay Williams
   Glen Arnelien
   Dwight W Retting
Sec Vincent J Gillespie
VP VP Daniel Molinaro
VP David J Keener
Sec Raymond W Chang
Acct Mgr Sharon Durling

D-U-N-S 20-918-2521   (BR)
WAL-MART CANADA CORP
Hwy 2nd And 50 Ave, Leduc, AB, T9E 2A1
(780) 986-7574
Emp Here 150
SIC 5311 Department stores

D-U-N-S 25-186-2678   (BR)
WHITE SPOT LIMITED
WHITE SPOT RESTAURANT
5230 50 Ave, Leduc, AB, T9E 6V2
(780) 980-1394
Emp Here 40
SIC 5812 Eating places

Legal, AB T0G

D-U-N-S 20-713-2130   (BR)
CONSEIL SCOLAIRE CENTRE-NORD
ECOLE CITADELLE
5111 46 St, Legal, AB, T0G 1L0
(780) 961-3557
Emp Here 20
SIC 8211 Elementary and secondary schools

D-U-N-S 25-677-7772   (BR)
GREATER ST. ALBERT CATHOLIC REGIONAL DIVISION NO. 29
LEGAL SCHOOL
5122 46th St, Legal, AB, T0G 1L0
(780) 961-3791
Emp Here 25
SIC 8211 Elementary and secondary schools

D-U-N-S 20-895-6532   (SL)
LEGAL ALFALFA PRODUCTS LTD
ALFATEC
57420 Range Road 252 A, Legal, AB, T0G 1L0
(780) 961-3958
Emp Here 35   *Sales* 7,623,009
SIC 2048 Prepared feeds, nec
Pr Pr Maurice Schayes
   Robert Chauvet
   Dennis Devolder

D-U-N-S 20-120-7797   (SL)
RUBBER TECH. INTERNATIONAL LTD
Gd, Legal, AB, T0G 1L0
(780) 961-3229
Emp Here 100   *Sales* 16,739,250
SIC 5199 Nondurable goods, nec
Pr Pr Alan Champagne

Leslieville, AB T0M

D-U-N-S 20-023-9874   (BR)
WILD ROSE SCHOOL DIVISION NO. 66
LESLIEVILLE ELEMENTARY SCHOOL
(*Suby of* Wild Rose School Division No. 66)
Hwy 761 3rd St, Leslieville, AB, T0M 1H0
(403) 729-3830
Emp Here 22
SIC 8211 Elementary and secondary schools

Lethbridge, AB T1H

D-U-N-S 25-956-2767   (BR)
A & W FOOD SERVICES OF CANADA INC
A & W RESTAURANT
1250 2a Ave N, Lethbridge, AB, T1H 0E3
(403) 381-3444
Emp Here 34
SIC 5812 Eating places

D-U-N-S 20-799-4877   (BR)
ATCO GAS AND PIPELINES LTD
410 Stafford Dr N, Lethbridge, AB, T1H 2A9
(403) 380-5400
Emp Here 60
SIC 4922 Natural gas transmission

D-U-N-S 20-520-8861   (BR)
AECOM CANADA LTD
514 Stafford Dr N Suite 200, Lethbridge, AB, T1H 2B2
(403) 329-1678
Emp Here 55
SIC 8711 Engineering services

D-U-N-S 20-297-2415   (BR)
BAYER CROPSCIENCE INC
3106 9 Ave N Suite 10, Lethbridge, AB, T1H 5E5
(403) 329-0706
Emp Here 20
SIC 2879 Agricultural chemicals, nec

D-U-N-S 25-959-8423   (BR)
BELL MEDIA INC
CFCN-TV CHANNEL 3
640 13 St N, Lethbridge, AB, T1H 2S8
(403) 329-3644
Emp Here 28
SIC 4833 Television broadcasting stations

D-U-N-S 25-137-0714   (BR)
CALGARY PETERBILT LTD
PEWTERBILT LETHBRIDGE
(*Suby of* Calgary Peterbilt Ltd)
4110 18 Ave N, Lethbridge, AB, T1H 6N7
(403) 328-0500
Emp Here 24
SIC 5012 Automobiles and other motor vehicles

D-U-N-S 24-972-0835   (SL)
CARDTRONICS CANADA, LTD
(*Suby of* Cardtronics PLC)
1530 33 St N Unit 3, Lethbridge, AB, T1H 5H3
(403) 327-2162
Emp Here 22   *Sales* 11,595,360
SIC 6099 Functions related to deposit banking
Pr Pr Michael H. Clinard
Pr Pr Michael Keller
Dir Chris Brewstar

D-U-N-S 24-928-0256   (BR)
COCA-COLA REFRESHMENTS CANADA COMPANY
(*Suby of* The Coca-Cola Company)
2920 9 Ave N, Lethbridge, AB, T1H 5E4
(403) 328-8891
Emp Here 25
SIC 5149 Groceries and related products, nec

D-U-N-S 25-168-7190   (BR)
CORUS MEDIA HOLDINGS INC
SHAW MEDIA INC
1401 28 St N, Lethbridge, AB, T1H 6H9
(403) 327-1521
Emp Here 30
SIC 4833 Television broadcasting stations

D-U-N-S 20-090-0587   (SL)
COX, G W CONSTRUCTION LTD
1210 31 St N, Lethbridge, AB, T1H 5J8
(403) 328-1346
Emp Here 65   *Sales* 4,742,446
SIC 1794 Excavation work

D-U-N-S 20-830-2562   (SL)
D A ELECTRIC LTD
220 31 St N, Lethbridge, AB, T1H 3Z3
(403) 328-4849
Emp Here 50   *Sales* 4,377,642
SIC 1731 Electrical work

D-U-N-S 20-522-0320   (BR)
FINNING INTERNATIONAL INC
(*Suby of* Finning International Inc)
4204 5 Ave N, Lethbridge, AB, T1H 5S4
(403) 328-3366
Emp Here 35
SIC 5082 Construction and mining machinery

D-U-N-S 24-174-5541   (BR)
GOVERNMENT OF THE PROVINCE OF ALBERTA
SOUTHWEST ALBERTA CHILD & FAMILY SERVICES
3305 18 Ave N Suite 107, Lethbridge, AB, T1H 5S1
(403) 381-5543
Emp Here 200
SIC 8322 Individual and family services

D-U-N-S 20-653-3973   (BR)
GOVERNMENT OF THE PROVINCE OF ALBERTA
SOUTHWEST ALBERTA CHILD AND FAMILY SERVICES, SIFTON FAMILY AND YOUTH SERVICES
528 Stafford Dr N, Lethbridge, AB, T1H 2B2
(403) 381-5411
Emp Here 45
SIC 8322 Individual and family services

D-U-N-S 25-014-9564   (BR)
GREAT PACIFIC INDUSTRIES INC
SAVE-ON-FOODS
1112 2a Ave N, Lethbridge, AB, T1H 0E3
(403) 380-6000
Emp Here 250
SIC 5411 Grocery stores

D-U-N-S 25-964-9937   (BR)
GREEN ACRES FOUNDATION HOUSING FOR SENIORS
GREEN ACRES FOUNDATION HOUSING FOR SENIORS
1431 16 Ave N Suite 47, Lethbridge, AB, T1H 4B9
(403) 328-9422
Emp Here 30
SIC 8322 Individual and family services

D-U-N-S 20-711-8410   (BR)
HOLY SPIRIT ROMAN CATHOLIC SEPARATE REGIONAL DIVISION NO 4
SAINT PAUL SCHOOL
(*Suby of* Holy Spirit Roman Catholic Separate Regional Division No 4)
1212 12 Ave N, Lethbridge, AB, T1H 6W1
(403) 328-0611
Emp Here 50
SIC 8211 Elementary and secondary schools

D-U-N-S 24-272-6032   (HQ)
HOLY SPIRIT ROMAN CATHOLIC SEPARATE REGIONAL DIVISION NO 4
HOLY SPIRIT SEPARATE SCHOOLS
(*Suby of* Holy Spirit Roman Catholic Separate Regional Division No 4)
620 12b St N, Lethbridge, AB, T1H 2L7
(403) 327-9555
Emp Here 50   *Emp Total* 295
Sales 27,129,600
SIC 8211 Elementary and secondary schools
Superintnt Christopher Smeaton

D-U-N-S 20-820-1322   (SL)
HUNTER CONSTRUCTION
3626 14 Ave N, Lethbridge, AB, T1H 6E7
(403) 380-6159
Emp Here 30   *Sales* 5,284,131
SIC 1521 Single-family housing construction

D-U-N-S 24-416-3812   (BR)

KAWNEER COMPANY CANADA LIMITED
(*Suby of* Arconic Inc.)
4000 18 Ave N Suite Side, Lethbridge, AB,
T1H 5S8
(403) 320-7755
Emp Here 300
SIC 3442 Metal doors, sash, and trim

D-U-N-S 24-673-1897   (BR)
LAFARGE CANADA INC
530 9 Ave N, Lethbridge, AB, T1H 1E4
(403) 332-6200
Emp Here 35
SIC 1442 Construction sand and gravel

D-U-N-S 25-014-7493   (HQ)
LETHBRIDGE FAMILY SERVICES
(*Suby of* Lethbridge Family Services)
1107 2a Ave N, Lethbridge, AB, T1H 0E6
(403) 327-5724
Emp Here 195   *Emp Total* 270
Sales 14,233,200
SIC 8322 Individual and family services
Ex Dir Francis Bogle
Pr Hazel Mitchell
Treas Bruce Tait

D-U-N-S 20-088-0102   (SL)
LETHBRIDGE IRON WORKS COMPANY LIMITED
LETHIRON
720 32 St N, Lethbridge, AB, T1H 5K5
(403) 329-4242
Emp Here 130
SIC 3321 Gray and ductile iron foundries

D-U-N-S 20-825-8848   (SL)
LETHBRIDGE NORTHERN IRRIGATION DISTRICT
LNID
334 13 St N, Lethbridge, AB, T1H 2R8
(403) 327-3302
Emp Here 35   *Sales* 7,979,779
SIC 4971 Irrigation systems
Genl Mgr Alan Harrold
John Vandenberg
Jack Puurveen
Brian Nauta
Martin Van Diemen
Klaas Slomp

D-U-N-S 20-336-6955   (BR)
LETHBRIDGE SCHOOL DISTRICT NO. 51
WILSON MIDDLE SCHOOL
2003 9 Ave N, Lethbridge, AB, T1H 1J3
(403) 329-3144
Emp Here 75
SIC 8211 Elementary and secondary schools

D-U-N-S 20-029-7781   (BR)
LETHBRIDGE SCHOOL DISTRICT NO. 51
WINSTON CHURCHILL HIGH SCHOOL
1605 15 Ave N, Lethbridge, AB, T1H 1W4
(403) 328-4723
Emp Here 78
SIC 8211 Elementary and secondary schools

D-U-N-S 20-028-3302   (BR)
LETHBRIDGE SCHOOL DISTRICT NO. 51
WESTMINSTER SCHOOL
402 18 St N, Lethbridge, AB, T1H 3G4
(403) 327-4169
Emp Here 43
SIC 8211 Elementary and secondary schools

D-U-N-S 20-711-7123   (BR)
LETHBRIDGE SCHOOL DISTRICT NO. 51
GALVRAITH ELEMENTARY SCHOOL
1801 8a Ave N, Lethbridge, AB, T1H 1C5
(403) 327-3653
Emp Here 50
SIC 8211 Elementary and secondary schools

D-U-N-S 20-028-4193   (BR)
LETHBRIDGE SCHOOL DISTRICT NO. 51
PARK MEADOWS ELEMENTARY SCHOOL
50 Meadowlark Blvd N, Lethbridge, AB, T1H 4J4

(403) 328-9965
Emp Here 38
SIC 8211 Elementary and secondary schools

D-U-N-S 20-038-5958   (BR)
LETHBRIDGE, CITY OF
LETHBRIDGE TRANSIT
619 4 Ave N, Lethbridge, AB, T1H 0K4
(403) 320-3885
Emp Here 120
SIC 4111 Local and suburban transit

D-U-N-S 25-677-4670   (SL)
LOGIC INSULATION LTD
1217 39 St N, Lethbridge, AB, T1H 6Y8
(403) 328-7755
Emp Here 32   *Sales* 4,669,485
SIC 5211 Lumber and other building materials

D-U-N-S 24-118-0934   (BR)
MAPLE LEAF FOODS INC
MAPLE LEAF POTOTOES, DIV OF
2720 2a Ave N, Lethbridge, AB, T1H 5B4
(403) 380-9900
Emp Here 120
SIC 5148 Fresh fruits and vegetables

D-U-N-S 20-308-4389   (HQ)
MERIDIAN MANUFACTURING INC
3125 24 Ave N, Lethbridge, AB, T1H 5G2
(403) 320-7070
Emp Here 150   *Emp Total* 1,700
Sales 98,496,945
SIC 3545 Machine tool accessories
Pr Paul Cunningham
Russell Edwards
VP Opers Victor Holodryga
Sr VP Bernie Thiessen
Sr VP Gary Edwards
Sr VP Kevin Edwards
VP VP Edna Edwards
S&M/VP Glen Friesen
VP Fin Mike Froese
Margaret Morgan

D-U-N-S 25-832-0720   (BR)
NORMERICA INC
112 30 St N, Lethbridge, AB, T1H 3Z1

Emp Here 30
SIC 3295 Minerals, ground or treated

D-U-N-S 24-341-8436   (BR)
ON SIDE RESTORATION SERVICES LTD
410 26 St N, Lethbridge, AB, T1H 3W2
(403) 394-2980
Emp Here 20
SIC 1771 Concrete work

D-U-N-S 20-711-5523   (BR)
PALLISER REGIONAL DIVISION NO 26
HOFMAN SCHOOL
3305 18 Ave N Suite 101, Lethbridge, AB, T1H 5S1
(403) 328-4111
Emp Here 50
SIC 8211 Elementary and secondary schools

D-U-N-S 25-316-4149   (BR)
PASLEY, MAX ENTERPRISES LIMITED
MCDONALD'S RESTAURANTS #13846
(*Suby of* Pasley, Max Enterprises Limited)
444 Mayor Magrath Dr N, Lethbridge, AB, T1H 6H7
(403) 328-0050
Emp Here 60
SIC 5812 Eating places

D-U-N-S 25-014-1405   (BR)
PEPSICO CANADA ULC
HOSTESS FRITO-LAY
(*Suby of* Pepsico, Inc.)
2200 31 St N, Lethbridge, AB, T1H 5K8
(403) 380-5775
Emo Here 250
SIC 2096 Potato chips and similar snacks

D-U-N-S 24-647-3839   (HQ)
REHABILITATION SOCIETY OF SOUTH-

WESTERN ALBERTA
(*Suby of* Rehabilitation Society of Southwestern Alberta)
1610 29 St N, Lethbridge, AB, T1H 5L3
(403) 317-4880
Emp Here 65   *Emp Total* 80
Sales 3,793,956
SIC 8331 Job training and related services

D-U-N-S 24-618-2468   (BR)
RICHARDSON OILSEED LIMITED
2415 2a Ave N, Lethbridge, AB, T1H 6P5
(403) 329-5500
Emp Here 200
SIC 3556 Food products machinery

D-U-N-S 25-154-1850   (BR)
ROCKY CROSS CONSTRUCTION (CALGARY) LIMITED
432 13 St N, Lethbridge, AB, T1H 2S2
(403) 327-2575
Emp Here 20
SIC 1799 Special trade contractors, nec

D-U-N-S 24-517-5336   (SL)
ROEST ACOUSTICS LTD
1235 36 St N, Lethbridge, AB, T1H 6L5
(403) 394-9185
Emp Here 50   *Sales* 4,231,721
SIC 1742 Plastering, drywall, and insulation

D-U-N-S 20-743-2274   (BR)
SOBEYS CAPITAL INCORPORATED
327 Bluefox Blvd N, Lethbridge, AB, T1H 6T3
(403) 320-5154
Emp Here 100
SIC 5411 Grocery stores

D-U-N-S 20-005-5023   (BR)
SOBEYS WEST INC
131 22 St N, Lethbridge, AB, T1H 3R6
(403) 328-5501
Emp Here 50
SIC 2032 Canned specialties

D-U-N-S 25-271-0389   (BR)
SOBEYS WEST INC
PARK MEADOWS SAFEWAY
1702 23 St N, Lethbridge, AB, T1H 5B3
(403) 320-2231
Emp Here 80
SIC 5411 Grocery stores

D-U-N-S 20-068-7551   (BR)
SOCIETY FOR CHRISTIAN EDUCATION IN SOUTHERN ALBERTA, THE
IMMANUEL CHRISTIAN ELEMENTARY
2010 5 Ave N, Lethbridge, AB, T1H 0N5
(403) 317-7860
Emp Here 35
SIC 8211 Elementary and secondary schools

D-U-N-S 24-345-9005   (HQ)
SOUTHLAND TRAILER CORP
LETHBRIDGE TRUCK EQUIPMENT, DIV OF
1405 41 St N, Lethbridge, AB, T1H 6G3
(403) 327-8212
Emp Here 120   *Emp Total* 1
Sales 21,136,524
SIC 3715 Truck trailers
Pr Monty Sailer

D-U-N-S 24-495-6256   (HQ)
TIMBER-TECH TRUSS INC
(*Suby of* Murphy Five Investments Ltd)
1405 31 St N, Lethbridge, AB, T1H 5G8
(403) 328-5499
Emp Here 40   *Emp Total* 4
Sales 9,193,048
SIC 2439 Structural wood members, nec
Pr Derrill Murphy
Mary Pearl Murphy
Dir Brian Peters
Dir Kelly Skauge
Dir Wendy Going

D-U-N-S 25-562-5253   (BR)
UNITED FARMERS OF ALBERTA CO-

OPERATIVE LIMITED
U F A LETHBRIDGE FARM SUPPLY
2905 2 Ave N, Lethbridge, AB, T1H 6M1
(403) 328-5531
Emp Here 30
SIC 5999 Miscellaneous retail stores, nec

D-U-N-S 25-685-0280   (BR)
VARSTEEL LTD
2900 5 Ave N, Lethbridge, AB, T1H 6K3
(403) 329-0233
Emp Here 100
SIC 5051 Metals service centers and offices

D-U-N-S 25-387-6270   (BR)
VOLKER STEVIN CONTRACTING LTD.
VOLKER STEVIN HIGHWAY
4004 6 Ave N, Lethbridge, AB, T1H 6W4
(403) 320-4920
Emp Here 200
SIC 1611 Highway and street construction

D-U-N-S 24-345-6758   (BR)
WAL-MART CANADA CORP
3195 26 Ave N Suite 1078, Lethbridge, AB, T1H 5P3
(403) 380-6722
Emp Here 400
SIC 5311 Department stores

D-U-N-S 24-381-2182   (BR)
WASTE CONNECTIONS OF CANADA INC
BFI CANADA
703 32 St N, Lethbridge, AB, T1H 5H5
(403) 328-6355
Emp Here 30
SIC 4953 Refuse systems

D-U-N-S 25-133-4264   (BR)
WAWANESA MUTUAL INSURANCE COMPANY, THE
(*Suby of* Wawanesa Mutual Insurance Company, The)
234 22 St N, Lethbridge, AB, T1H 3R7
(403) 329-4655
Emp Here 30
SIC 6331 Fire, marine, and casualty insurance

D-U-N-S 20-178-0157   (HQ)
WOODHAVEN CAPITAL CORP
3125 24 Ave N, Lethbridge, AB, T1H 5G2
(403) 320-7070
Emp Here 150   *Emp Total* 1,700
Sales 41,085,544
SIC 6712 Bank holding companies
Pr Pr Paul Cunningham

Lethbridge, AB T1J

D-U-N-S 24-906-5590   (HQ)
512844 ALBERTA LTD
(*Suby of* Stimson, Derek Holdings Ltd)
3939 1 Ave S, Lethbridge, AB, T1J 4P8
(403) 327-3154
Emp Here 50   *Emp Total* 3
Sales 24,406,321
SIC 6712 Bank holding companies
Pr Pr Derek Stimson
Susan Stimson-Kasun

D-U-N-S 25-316-4115   (BR)
AMEC FOSTER WHEELER AMERICAS LIMITED
740 4 Ave S Suite 210, Lethbridge, AB, T1J 0N9
(403) 329-1467
Emp Here 30
SIC 8711 Engineering services

D-U-N-S 20-830-3214   (BR)
AGRICULTURE FINANCIAL SERVICES CORPORATION
AFSC
905 4 Ave S Suite 200, Lethbridge, AB, T1J 0P4

(403) 381-5474
Emp Here 25
SIC 6411 Insurance agents, brokers, and service

D-U-N-S 24-372-1185   (BR)
ALBERTA HEALTH SERVICES
CHINOOK REGIONAL HOSPITAL
960 19 St S Suite 110, Lethbridge, AB, T1J 1W5
(403) 388-6009
Emp Here 100
SIC 8062 General medical and surgical hospitals

D-U-N-S 20-041-0145   (BR)
ALBERTA HEALTH SERVICES
CHILDREN'S AUDIOLOGY AND ALLIED HEALTH SERVICES
200 5 Ave S Rm A252, Lethbridge, AB, T1J 4L1
(403) 329-5255
Emp Here 32
SIC 8011 Offices and clinics of medical doctors

D-U-N-S 20-068-7619   (BR)
ALBERTA HEALTH SERVICES
COMMUNITY CARE LETHBRIDGE
200 4 Ave S Suite 110, Lethbridge, AB, T1J 4C9
(403) 388-6700
Emp Here 150
SIC 8099 Health and allied services, nec

D-U-N-S 24-518-0096   (BR)
ALBERTA MOTOR ASSOCIATION
A M A
120 Scenic Dr S, Lethbridge, AB, T1J 4R4
(403) 328-1181
Emp Here 25
SIC 4724 Travel agencies

D-U-N-S 24-418-6438   (BR)
ALBERTA NEWSPAPER GROUP INC
LETHBRIDGE HERALD
504 7 St S, Lethbridge, AB, T1J 2H1
(403) 328-4411
Emp Here 20
SIC 2711 Newspapers

D-U-N-S 25-236-1993   (BR)
ALBERTA TREASURY BRANCHES
A T B FINANCIAL
727 4 Ave S, Lethbridge, AB, T1J 0P1
(403) 381-5431
Emp Here 25
SIC 6036 Savings institutions, except federal

D-U-N-S 25-236-2033   (BR)
ALBERTA TREASURY BRANCHES
ATB FINANCIAL
601 Mayor Magrath Dr S, Lethbridge, AB, T1J 4M5
(403) 382-4388
Emp Here 44
SIC 6036 Savings institutions, except federal

D-U-N-S 25-266-3703   (BR)
ASSOCIATED ENGINEERING ALBERTA LTD
(*Suby of* Ashco Shareholders Inc)
400 4 Ave S Suite 1001, Lethbridge, AB, T1J 4E1
(403) 329-1404
Emp Here 23
SIC 8711 Engineering services

D-U-N-S 24-346-8477   (SL)
BALOG AUCTION SERVICES INC
Gd Lcd Main, Lethbridge, AB, T1J 3Y2
(403) 320-1980
Emp Here 45   *Sales* 52,551,100
SIC 5154 Livestock
Pr Pr Robert C Balog

D-U-N-S 20-002-8053   (BR)
BANK OF NOVA SCOTIA, THE
SCOTIABANK

702 3 Ave S, Lethbridge, AB, T1J 0H6
(403) 382-3300
Emp Here 32
SIC 6021 National commercial banks

D-U-N-S 20-535-6228   (BR)
BANK OF MONTREAL
BMO
606 4 Ave S, Lethbridge, AB, T1J 0N7
(403) 382-3200
Emp Here 20
SIC 6021 National commercial banks

D-U-N-S 24-416-2889   (HQ)
BIGELOW FOWLER CLINIC
(*Suby of* Bigelow Fowler Clinic)
1605 9 Ave S, Lethbridge, AB, T1J 1W2
(403) 327-3121
Emp Here 45   *Emp Total* 64
Sales 3,866,917
SIC 8011 Offices and clinics of medical doctors

D-U-N-S 24-553-2189   (SL)
CAMPBELL ASSOCIATES (LETHBRIDGE) LIMITED
CAMPBELL CLINIC
430 Mayor Magrath Dr S Suite 1, Lethbridge, AB, T1J 3M1
(403) 328-8101
Emp Here 52   *Sales* 3,137,310
SIC 8011 Offices and clinics of medical doctors

D-U-N-S 25-288-9423   (BR)
CANADA POST CORPORATION
704 4 Ave S, Lethbridge, AB, T1J 0N8
(403) 382-4604
Emp Here 115
SIC 4311 U.s. postal service

D-U-N-S 24-646-2527   (BR)
CANADIAN IMPERIAL BANK OF COMMERCE
CIBC
701 4 Ave S, Lethbridge, AB, T1J 0P1
(403) 382-2000
Emp Here 65
SIC 6021 National commercial banks

D-U-N-S 20-136-8342   (BR)
CANADIAN LINEN AND UNIFORM SERVICE CO
CANADIAN LINEN AND UNIFORM SERVICE CO
(*Suby of* Ameripride Services, Inc.)
1818 3 Ave S, Lethbridge, AB, T1J 0L5
(403) 328-2321
Emp Here 63
SIC 7213 Linen supply

D-U-N-S 20-903-2726   (BR)
CANADIAN UNION OF POSTAL WORKERS
CUPW
Gd Lcd Main, Lethbridge, AB, T1J 3Y2

Emp Here 120
SIC 8631 Labor organizations

D-U-N-S 25-217-8397   (BR)
CHANTELLE MANAGEMENT LTD
CAVELL, EDITH CARE CENTRE
1255 5 Ave S, Lethbridge, AB, T1J 0V6
(403) 328-6631
Emp Here 120
SIC 8051 Skilled nursing care facilities

D-U-N-S 20-087-7546   (SL)
CITY PACKERS LTD
915 43 St S, Lethbridge, AB, T1J 4W2

Emp Here 60   *Sales* 9,739,200
SIC 2011 Meat packing plants
Pr Pr Paul Adams

D-U-N-S 20-766-5548   (HQ)
DRAFFIN, R. PHARMACY (1970) LTD
DRAFFIN'S PHARMASAVE NO. 369 & 356

(*Suby of* Draffin, R. Pharmacy (1970) Ltd)
200 4 Ave S, Lethbridge, AB, T1J 4C9
(403) 327-3364
Emp Here 24   *Emp Total* 30
Sales 5,693,280
SIC 5912 Drug stores and proprietary stores
Pr Pr Rodney Draffin
   Martha Draffin
Opers Mgr Michael Ramsdell

D-U-N-S 24-840-1572   (SL)
EARL'S RESTAURANT (LETHBRIDGE) LTD
203 13 St S, Lethbridge, AB, T1J 4M2
(403) 320-7677
Emp Here 55   *Sales* 1,678,096
SIC 5812 Eating places

D-U-N-S 24-340-2711   (BR)
FGL SPORTS LTD
SPORT CHEK PARK PLACE SHOPPING CENTRE
501 1 Ave S Unit Bo1, Lethbridge, AB, T1J 4L9
(403) 329-3318
Emp Here 75
SIC 5941 Sporting goods and bicycle shops

D-U-N-S 25-987-1366   (BR)
GAP (CANADA) INC
GAP
(*Suby of* The Gap Inc)
501 1 Ave S, Lethbridge, AB, T1J 4L9
(403) 320-6956
Emp Here 20
SIC 5651 Family clothing stores

D-U-N-S 25-014-9556   (BR)
GOVERNING COUNCIL OF THE SALVATION ARMY IN CANADA, THE
GOVERNING COUNCIL OF THE SALVATION ARMY IN CANADA, THE
1249 3 Ave S, Lethbridge, AB, T1J 0K1
(403) 328-2860
Emp Here 30
SIC 5932 Used merchandise stores

D-U-N-S 20-299-0326   (BR)
H & R BLOCK CANADA, INC
(*Suby of* H&R Block, Inc.)
1218 3 Ave S, Lethbridge, AB, T1J 0J9
(403) 329-3632
Emp Here 50
SIC 7291 Tax return preparation services

D-U-N-S 20-711-8501   (BR)
HOLY SPIRIT ROMAN CATHOLIC SEPARATE REGIONAL DIVISION NO 4
ST FRANCIS JUNIOR HIGHSCHOOL
(*Suby of* Holy Spirit Roman Catholic Separate Regional Division No 4)
333 18 St S, Lethbridge, AB, T1J 3E5
(403) 327-3402
Emp Here 50
SIC 8211 Elementary and secondary schools

D-U-N-S 25-269-4724   (BR)
HOLY SPIRIT ROMAN CATHOLIC SEPARATE REGIONAL DIVISION NO 4
CATHOLIC CENTRAL HIGH SCHOOL
(*Suby of* Holy Spirit Roman Catholic Separate Regional Division No 4)
405 18 St S, Lethbridge, AB, T1J 3E5
(403) 327-4596
Emp Here 60
SIC 8211 Elementary and secondary schools

D-U-N-S 20-711-8261   (BR)
HOLY SPIRIT ROMAN CATHOLIC SEPARATE REGIONAL DIVISION NO 4
ECOLE ST MARY SCHOOL
(*Suby of* Holy Spirit Roman Catholic Separate Regional Division No 4)
422 20 St S, Lethbridge, AB, T1J 2V5
(403) 327-3098
Emp Here 50
SIC 8211 Elementary and secondary schools

D-U-N-S 25-301-2744   (BR)

HUDSON'S BAY COMPANY
BAY, THE
200 4 Ave S Suite 200, Lethbridge, AB, T1J 4C9
(403) 329-3131
Emp Here 100
SIC 5311 Department stores

D-U-N-S 25-301-5408   (BR)
KPMG LLP
K P M G
(*Suby of* KPMG LLP)
400 4 Ave S Suite 500, Lethbridge, AB, T1J 4E1
(403) 380-5700
Emp Here 45
SIC 8721 Accounting, auditing, and bookkeeping

D-U-N-S 20-300-0422   (SL)
LETHBRIDGE COMMUNITY OUT OF SCHOOL ASSOCIATION
ITS A BLAST PROGRAM
811 5 Ave S, Lethbridge, AB, T1J 0V2
(403) 320-3988
Emp Here 60   *Sales* 2,334,742
SIC 8322 Individual and family services

D-U-N-S 20-711-7305   (BR)
LETHBRIDGE SCHOOL DISTRICT NO. 51
SENATOR BUCHANAN ELEMENTARY SCHOOL
1101 7 Ave S, Lethbridge, AB, T1J 1K4
(403) 327-7321
Emp Here 50
SIC 8211 Elementary and secondary schools

D-U-N-S 25-090-6013   (BR)
LETHBRIDGE SCHOOL DISTRICT NO. 51
ALLAN WATSON HIGH SCHOOL
433 15 St S, Lethbridge, AB, T1J 2Z4
(403) 327-3945
Emp Here 26
SIC 8211 Elementary and secondary schools

D-U-N-S 20-653-1928   (BR)
LETHBRIDGE SCHOOL DISTRICT NO. 51
FLEETWOOD-BAWDEN ELEMENTARY SCHOOL
1222 9 Ave S, Lethbridge, AB, T1J 1V4
(403) 327-5818
Emp Here 35
SIC 8211 Elementary and secondary schools

D-U-N-S 20-711-7693   (BR)
LETHBRIDGE SCHOOL DISTRICT NO. 51
910 4 Ave S Suite 200, Lethbridge, AB, T1J 0P6

Emp Here 50
SIC 8211 Elementary and secondary schools

D-U-N-S 20-711-8089   (BR)
LETHBRIDGE SCHOOL DISTRICT NO. 51
OUT REACH HIGH SCHOOL
817 4 Ave S, Lethbridge, AB, T1J 0P3

Emp Here 24
SIC 8211 Elementary and secondary schools

D-U-N-S 20-003-5165   (BR)
LETHBRIDGE SCHOOL DISTRICT NO. 51
GENERAL STEWART SCHOOL
215 Corvette Cres S, Lethbridge, AB, T1J 3X6
(403) 328-1201
Emp Here 20
SIC 8211 Elementary and secondary schools

D-U-N-S 20-040-9717   (BR)
LETHBRIDGE, CITY OF
LETHBRIDGE REGIONAL LANDFILL
910 4 Ave S, Lethbridge, AB, T1J 0P6
(403) 329-7367
Emp Here 40
SIC 4953 Refuse systems

D-U-N-S 24-808-0251   (BR)
LONDON DRUGS LIMITED

905 1 Ave S Suite 110, Lethbridge, AB, T1J
4M7
(403) 320-8899
Emp Here 100
SIC 5912 Drug stores and proprietary stores

D-U-N-S 25-451-2429   (BR)
MNP LLP
MNP
3425 2 Ave S Suite 1, Lethbridge, AB, T1J 4V1
(403) 380-1600
Emp Here 130
SIC 8721 Accounting, auditing, and book-
keeping

D-U-N-S 25-267-6697   (HQ)
MPE ENGINEERING LTD
714 5 Ave S Suite 300, Lethbridge, AB, T1J
0V1
(403) 329-3442
Emp Here 50   *Emp Total* 1
Sales 12,695,162
SIC 8711 Engineering services
Pr Pr Ronald Hust
Dir Randy Boras
Dir Peter Brouwer
Dir Daniel Parker
Dir Douglas Mickey
Dir Gerald Veldman
Dir Gordon Ayers
Dir Michael Breunig
Dir Myles Kasun

D-U-N-S 20-048-5816   (BR)
MAPLE LEAF FOODS INC
MAPLE LEAF PORK
4141 1 Ave S, Lethbridge, AB, T1J 4P8
(403) 328-1756
Emp Here 200
SIC 2011 Meat packing plants

D-U-N-S 25-124-1535   (BR)
**MCMAN YOUTH, FAMILY AND COMMUNITY
SERVICES ASSOCIATION**
MCMAN
(*Suby of* McMan Youth, Family and Commu-
nity Services Association)
517 4 Ave S Unit 203, Lethbridge, AB, T1J
0N4
(403) 328-2488
Emp Here 40
SIC 8322 Individual and family services

D-U-N-S 25-014-1504   (BR)
**MOXIE'S RESTAURANTS, LIMITED PART-
NERSHIP**
MOXIE'S RESTAURANT
1621 3 Ave S, Lethbridge, AB, T1J 0L1
(403) 320-1102
Emp Here 100
SIC 5812 Eating places

D-U-N-S 25-316-4446   (BR)
**NORTHLAND PROPERTIES CORPORA-
TION**
SANDMAN HOTEL LETHBRIDGE
(*Suby of* Northland Properties Corporation)
421 Mayor Magrath Dr S, Lethbridge, AB, T1J
3L8
(403) 320-8055
Emp Here 40
SIC 7011 Hotels and motels

D-U-N-S 20-826-5918   (BR)
PARRISH & HEIMBECKER, LIMITED
*NEW-LIFE MILLS - LETHBRIDGE FEED
MILL*
(*Suby of* Parrish & Heimbecker, Limited)
1301 2 Ave S, Lethbridge, AB, T1J 0E8
(403) 328-6622
Emp Here 65
SIC 5153 Grain and field beans

D-U-N-S 25-316-4016   (BR)
PASLEY, MAX ENTERPRISES LIMITED
MCDONALD'S
(*Suby of* Pasley, Max Enterprises Limited)
217 3 Ave S, Lethbridge, AB, T1J 4L6

(403) 328-8844
Emp Here 86
SIC 5812 Eating places

D-U-N-S 20-197-2879   (BR)
PASLEY, MAX ENTERPRISES LIMITED
MCDONALD'S
(*Suby of* Pasley, Max Enterprises Limited)
550 University Dr W Suite 31, Lethbridge, AB,
T1J 4T3
(403) 380-2228
Emp Here 73
SIC 5812 Eating places

D-U-N-S 20-922-9439   (BR)
PATTISON, JIM INDUSTRIES LTD
B-93 FM CJBZ
401 Mayor Magrath Dr S, Lethbridge, AB, T1J
3L8
(403) 394-9300
Emp Here 30
SIC 4832 Radio broadcasting stations

D-U-N-S 24-060-5605   (BR)
PIONEER HI-BRED PRODUCTION LTD
(*Suby of* E. I. Du Pont De Nemours and Com-
pany)
Gd Lcd Main, Lethbridge, AB, T1J 3Y2
(403) 327-6135
Emp Here 30
SIC 3556 Food products machinery

D-U-N-S 25-965-4085   (BR)
PURE CANADIAN GAMING CORP
CASINO LETHBRIDGE
1251 3 Ave S, Lethbridge, AB, T1J 0K1
(403) 381-9467
Emp Here 275
SIC 7999 Amusement and recreation, nec

D-U-N-S 25-293-7461   (BR)
RBC DOMINION SECURITIES INC
(*Suby of* Royal Bank Of Canada)
204 1 Ave S, Lethbridge, AB, T1J 0A4

Emp Here 22
SIC 6211 Security brokers and dealers

D-U-N-S 24-042-8417   (SL)
REGENT RESTAURANT INC
1255 3 Ave S, Lethbridge, AB, T1J 0K1
(403) 328-7800
Emp Here 50   *Sales* 1,532,175
SIC 5812 Eating places

D-U-N-S 24-858-2103   (BR)
ROCKY MOUNTAIN DEALERSHIPS INC
ROCKY MOUNTAIN EQUIPMENT
3939 1 Ave S, Lethbridge, AB, T1J 4P8
(403) 327-3154
Emp Here 100
SIC 5082 Construction and mining machinery

D-U-N-S 24-949-8429   (BR)
ROGERS MEDIA INC
ROCK 106 CJRX
(*Suby of* Rogers Communications Inc)
1015 3 Ave S, Lethbridge, AB, T1J 0J3
(403) 331-1067
Emp Here 29
SIC 4832 Radio broadcasting stations

D-U-N-S 20-646-3440   (BR)
SEARS CANADA INC
401 1 Ave S, Lethbridge, AB, T1J 4L8

Emp Here 150
SIC 5311 Department stores

D-U-N-S 25-986-4577   (BR)
SOBEYS CAPITAL INCORPORATED
THIRD AVENUE GARDEN MARKET IGA
721 3 Ave S, Lethbridge, AB, T1J 4C3

Emp Here 50
SIC 5411 Grocery stores

D-U-N-S 20-871-3458   (BR)
SOBEYS WEST INC

550 University Dr W Suite 1, Lethbridge, AB,
T1J 4T3
(403) 329-6382
Emp Here 50
SIC 5411 Grocery stores

D-U-N-S 20-699-7822   (BR)
STANTEC CONSULTING LTD
220 4 St S Suite 290, Lethbridge, AB, T1J 4J7
(403) 329-3344
Emp Here 35
SIC 8711 Engineering services

D-U-N-S 20-790-7697   (BR)
STAPLES CANADA INC
STAPLES THE BUSINESS DEPOT
(*Suby of* Staples, Inc.)
501 1 Ave S Suite 118, Lethbridge, AB, T1J
4L9
(403) 317-4530
Emp Here 55
SIC 5943 Stationery stores

D-U-N-S 20-506-0465   (BR)
STARBUCKS COFFEE CANADA, INC
(*Suby of* Starbucks Corporation)
701 1 Ave S, Lethbridge, AB, T1J 4V7
(403) 329-9091
Emp Here 20
SIC 5812 Eating places

D-U-N-S 25-304-7104   (BR)
**SUN LIFE ASSURANCE COMPANY OF
CANADA**
SUN LIFE FINANCIAL
404 Scenic Dr S, Lethbridge, AB, T1J 4S3
(403) 328-3306
Emp Here 40
SIC 6311 Life insurance

D-U-N-S 20-646-1246   (BR)
TELUS COMMUNICATIONS INC
808 4 Ave S, Lethbridge, AB, T1J 0P2
(403) 382-2555
Emp Here 50
SIC 4899 Communication services, nec

D-U-N-S 25-297-8044   (BR)
TOYS 'R' US (CANADA) LTD
TOYS 'R' US
(*Suby of* Toys "r" Us, Inc.)
225 1 Ave S, Lethbridge, AB, T1J 4P2
(403) 328-3677
Emp Here 35
SIC 5945 Hobby, toy, and game shops

D-U-N-S 20-829-8802   (HQ)
VARSTEEL LTD
VALUE STEEL & PIPE, DIV OF
220 4 St S Suite 330, Lethbridge, AB, T1J 4J7
(403) 320-1953
Emp Here 35   *Emp Total* 200
Sales 171,165,802
SIC 5051 Metals service centers and offices
Pr Pr Gerald Varzari

D-U-N-S 25-979-4113   (BR)
WE CARE HEALTH SERVICES INC
400 4 Ave S Suite 411, Lethbridge, AB, T1J
4E1
(403) 380-4441
Emp Here 49
SIC 8741 Management services

D-U-N-S 24-578-0630   (HQ)
**WILBUR-ELLIS COMPANY OF CANADA
LIMITED**
WECO
(*Suby of* Wilbur-Ellis Holdings, Inc.)
Gd Lcd Main, Lethbridge, AB, T1J 3Y2
(403) 328-3311
Emp Here 25   *Emp Total* 4,600
Sales 10,433,380
SIC 5191 Farm supplies
Pr Robert Fullerton
Dir Brent Quinton

D-U-N-S 25-987-1515   (BR)

**WINNERS MERCHANTS INTERNATIONAL
L.P.**
WINNERS
(*Suby of* The TJX Companies Inc)
501 1 Ave S Unit 2, Lethbridge, AB, T1J 4L9
(403) 320-6677
Emp Here 30
SIC 5651 Family clothing stores

D-U-N-S 24-011-7937   (HQ)
YOUNG PARKYN MCNAB LLP
(*Suby of* Young Parkyn McNab LLP)
530 8 St S Suite 100, Lethbridge, AB, T1J 2J8
(403) 382-6800
Emp Here 50   *Emp Total* 84
Sales 3,648,035
SIC 8721 Accounting, auditing, and book-
keeping

Lethbridge, AB T1K

D-U-N-S 20-588-2587   (BR)
BANQUE TORONTO-DOMINION, LA
TD CANADA TRUST
(*Suby of* Toronto-Dominion Bank, The)
2033 Mayor Magrath Dr S, Lethbridge, AB,
T1K 2S2
(403) 381-5030
Emp Here 20
SIC 6021 National commercial banks

D-U-N-S 24-064-8373   (BR)
BIGELOW FOWLER CLINIC
(*Suby of* Bigelow Fowler Clinic)
30 Jerry Potts Blvd W, Lethbridge, AB, T1K
5M5
(403) 381-8444
Emp Here 25
SIC 8093 Specialty outpatient clinics, nec

D-U-N-S 20-798-4449   (BR)
BOSTON PIZZA INTERNATIONAL INC
BOSTON PIZZA
2041 Mayor Magrath Dr S, Lethbridge, AB,
T1K 2S2
(403) 327-4590
Emp Here 50
SIC 5812 Eating places

D-U-N-S 25-231-7300   (BR)
BRICK WAREHOUSE LP, THE
3727 Mayor Magrath Dr S, Lethbridge, AB,
T1K 8A8
(403) 320-2900
Emp Here 30
SIC 5712 Furniture stores

D-U-N-S 24-143-9723   (SL)
CHINESE SENIORS SOCIETY
35 Coachwood Rd W, Lethbridge, AB, T1K
6B7
(403) 328-3138
Emp Here 40   *Sales* 12,478,350
SIC 8322 Individual and family services
Treas Wally Lee
Genl Mgr Kulie Yip

D-U-N-S 25-482-9591   (BR)
COSTCO WHOLESALE CANADA LTD
COSTCO
(*Suby of* Costco Wholesale Corporation)
3200 Mayor Magrath Dr S, Lethbridge, AB,
T1K 6Y6
(403) 320-8917
Emp Here 200
SIC 5099 Durable goods, nec

D-U-N-S 25-014-1330   (BR)
EXTENDICARE INC
EXTENDICARE FAIRMONT
115 Fairmont Blvd S, Lethbridge, AB, T1K 5V2
(403) 320-0120
Emp Here 140
SIC 8051 Skilled nursing care facilities

D-U-N-S 25-676-4408   (BR)
HOLY SPIRIT ROMAN CATHOLIC SEPA-RATE REGIONAL DIVISION NO 4
CHILDREN OF ST MARTHA ELEMENTARY SCHOOL
(*Suby of* Holy Spirit Roman Catholic Separate Regional Division No 4)
206 Mcmaster Blvd W, Lethbridge, AB, T1K 4R3
(403) 381-8111
Emp Here 27
SIC 8211 Elementary and secondary schools

D-U-N-S 20-711-8188   (BR)
HOLY SPIRIT ROMAN CATHOLIC SEPA-RATE REGIONAL DIVISION NO 4
OUR LADY OF THE ASSUMPTION
(*Suby of* Holy Spirit Roman Catholic Separate Regional Division No 4)
2219 14 Ave S, Lethbridge, AB, T1K 0V6
(403) 327-5028
Emp Here 30
SIC 8211 Elementary and secondary schools

D-U-N-S 25-014-6750   (BR)
HOLY SPIRIT ROMAN CATHOLIC SEPA-RATE REGIONAL DIVISION NO 4
FATHER LEONARD VAN TIGHEM SCHOOL
(*Suby of* Holy Spirit Roman Catholic Separate Regional Division No 4)
25 Stoney Cres W, Lethbridge, AB, T1K 6V5
(403) 381-0953
Emp Here 45
SIC 8211 Elementary and secondary schools

D-U-N-S 20-176-7154   (BR)
HOME DEPOT OF CANADA INC
HOME DEPOT
(*Suby of* The Home Depot Inc)
3708 Maycr Magrath Dr S, Lethbridge, AB, T1K 7V1
(403) 331-3581
Emp Here 150
SIC 5251 Hardware stores

D-U-N-S 25-415-5435   (SL)
KILMAR ENTERPRISES LTD
PIZZA HUT
1358 Mayor Magrath Dr S, Lethbridge, AB, T1K 2R2
(403) 320-6600
Emp Here 52   *Sales* 1,532,175
SIC 5812 Eating places

D-U-N-S 20-826-3426   (SL)
LETHBRIDGE COUNTRY CLUB
101 Country Club Rd, Lethbridge, AB, T1K 7N9
(403) 327-6900
Emp Here 90   *Sales* 3,648,035
SIC 7997 Membership sports and recreation clubs

D-U-N-S 20-852-6280   (BR)
LETHBRIDGE FAMILY SERVICES
1410 Mayor Magrath Dr S Suite 106, Lethbridge, AB, T1K 2R3
(403) 317-4624
Emp Here 200
SIC 8361 Residential care

D-U-N-S 20-028-4185   (BR)
LETHBRIDGE SCHOOL DISTRICT NO. 51
NICHOLAS   SHERAN   COMMUNITY SCHOOL
380 Laval Blvd W, Lethbridge, AB, T1K 3Y2
(403) 381-1244
Emp Here 42
SIC 8211 Elementary and secondary schools

D-U-N-S 20-711-7214   (BR)
LETHBRIDGE SCHOOL DISTRICT NO. 51
GILBERT PATERSON MIDDLE SCHOOL
2109 12 Ave S Suite 51, Lethbridge, AB, T1K 0P1
(403) 329-0125
Emp Here 50
SIC 8211 Elementary and secondary schools

D-U-N-S 20-653-1621   (BR)
LETHBRIDGE SCHOOL DISTRICT NO. 51
ECOLE AGNES DAVIDSON SCHOOL
2103 20 St S, Lethbridge, AB, T1K 2G7
(403) 328-5153
Emp Here 22
SIC 8211 Elementary and secondary schools

D-U-N-S 20-711-7628   (BR)
LETHBRIDGE SCHOOL DISTRICT NO. 51
MIKE MELTON HORSE SCHOOL
155 Jerry Potts Blvd W, Lethbridge, AB, T1K 6G8
(403) 381-2211
Emp Here 50
SIC 8211 Elementary and secondary schools

D-U-N-S 20-027-3642   (BR)
LETHBRIDGE SCHOOL DISTRICT NO. 51
LAKEVIEW SCHOOL
1129 Henderson Lake Blvd S, Lethbridge, AB, T1K 3B6
(403) 328-5454
Emp Here 42
SIC 8211 Elementary and secondary schools

D-U-N-S 24-766-3797   (BR)
LETHBRIDGE SCHOOL DISTRICT NO. 51
DR GERALD B PROBE ELEMENTARY SCHOOL
120 Rocky Mountain Blvd W, Lethbridge, AB, T1K 7J2
(403) 381-3103
Emp Here 50
SIC 8211 Elementary and secondary schools

D-U-N-S 20-652-3735   (BR)
LETHBRIDGE SCHOOL DISTRICT NO. 51
G.S. LAKIE MIDDLE SCHOOL
50 Blackfoot Blvd W, Lethbridge, AB, T1K 7N7
(403) 327-3465
Emp Here 40
SIC 8211 Elementary and secondary schools

D-U-N-S 20-068-7668   (BR)
LETHBRIDGE, CITY OF
ENMAX CENTRE
2510 Scenic Dr S, Lethbridge, AB, T1K 7V7
(403) 320-4040
Emp Here 50
SIC 7999 Amusement and recreation, nec

D-U-N-S 24-336-7005   (BR)
LOBLAWS INC
REAL CANADIAN WHOLESALE CLUB
1706 Mayor Magrath Dr S, Lethbridge, AB, T1K 2R5
(403) 320-2368
Emp Here 40
SIC 5411 Grocery stores

D-U-N-S 20-101-9374   (BR)
LOBLAWS INC
REAL CANADIAN WHOLESALE CLUB, THE
1706 Mayor Magrath Dr S, Lethbridge, AB, T1K 2R5
(403) 320-2607
Emp Here 70
SIC 5141 Groceries, general line

D-U-N-S 20-589-2271   (BR)
NAV CANADA
417 Stubb Ross Rd Suite 209, Lethbridge, AB, T1K 7N3
(403) 317-4545
Emp Here 20
SIC 4899 Communication services, nec

D-U-N-S 24-598-7532   (BR)
PASLEY, MAX ENTERPRISES LIMITED
MCDONALD'S RESTAURANT #20785
(*Suby of* Pasley, Max Enterprises Limited)
2430 Fairway Plaza Rd S, Lethbridge, AB, T1K 6Z3
(403) 329-1919
Emp Here 60
SIC 5812 Eating places

D-U-N-S 25-316-4065   (BR)

PASLEY, MAX ENTERPRISES LIMITED
MCDONALD'S RESTAURANTS #29103
(*Suby of* Pasley, Max Enterprises Limited)
3700 Mayor Magrath Dr S, Lethbridge, AB, T1K 7T6
(403) 320-2899
Emp Here 60
SIC 5812 Eating places

D-U-N-S 20-975-2901   (BR)
ROMA RIBS LTD
TONY ROMA'S A PLACE FOR RIBS
(*Suby of* Roma Ribs Ltd)
3716 Mayor Magrath Dr S, Lethbridge, AB, T1K 7V1

Emp Here 47
SIC 5812 Eating places

D-U-N-S 25-020-0722   (BR)
SOBEYS WEST INC
2750 Fairway Plaza Rd S, Lethbridge, AB, T1K 6Z3
(403) 328-8444
Emp Here 180
SIC 5411 Grocery stores

D-U-N-S 24-418-5117   (BR)
SODEXO CANADA LTD
SODEXO
4401 University Dr W, Lethbridge, AB, T1K 3M4
(403) 329-2491
Emp Here 50
SIC 5812 Eating places

D-U-N-S 24-337-5545   (BR)
TDG FURNITURE INC
ASHLEY FURNITURE HOMESTORE
3732 Mayor Magrath Dr S, Lethbridge, AB, T1K 7V1
(403) 320-4528
Emp Here 20
SIC 5712 Furniture stores

D-U-N-S 24-426-0381   (BR)
TOLLCORP RESTAURANTS
WENDY'S
3120 Fairway St S, Lethbridge, AB, T1K 6T9
(403) 327-6700
Emp Here 50
SIC 5812 Eating places

D-U-N-S 20-745-5804   (BR)
UNIVERSITY OF LETHBRIDGE, THE
UNIVERSITY OF LETHBRIDGE STUDENT'S UNION
4401 University Dr W Suite 180, Lethbridge, AB, T1K 3M4
(403) 329-2222
Emp Here 49
SIC 8641 Civic and social associations

D-U-N-S 20-776-2928   (BR)
UNIVERSITY OF LETHBRIDGE, THE
RECREATION SERVICES
4401 University Dr W Suite 180, Lethbridge, AB, T1K 3M4
(403) 329-2706
Emp Here 30
SIC 7999 Amusement and recreation, nec

D-U-N-S 25-534-0978   (BR)
VALUE VILLAGE STORES, INC
(*Suby of* Savers, Inc.)
1616 Mayor Magrath Dr S, Lethbridge, AB, T1K 2R5
(403) 320-5358
Emp Here 76
SIC 5399 Miscellaneous general merchandise

D-U-N-S 25-219-0095   (BR)
WAL-MART CANADA CORP
VISION CENTER AT WALMART
3700 Mayor Magrath Dr S Suite 3048, Lethbridge, AB, T1K 7T6
(403) 328-6277
Emp Here 150

SIC 5311 Department stores

Linden, AB T0M

D-U-N-S 24-345-5438   (BR)
ALBERTA HEALTH SERVICES
LINDEN NURSING HOME
700 Nursing Home Rd, Linden, AB, T0M 1J0
(403) 546-3966
Emp Here 80
SIC 8051 Skilled nursing care facilities

D-U-N-S 20-710-9930   (BR)
GOLDEN HILLS SCHOOL DIVISION #75
DR ELLIOTT COMMUNITY SCHOOL
215 1 St Se, Linden, AB, T0M 1J0
(403) 546-3863
Emp Here 25
SIC 8211 Elementary and secondary schools

D-U-N-S 24-786-1875   (BR)
RIDLEY INC
FEED RITE
700 1 Ave Nw, Linden, AB, T0M 1J0

Emp Here 27
SIC 2048 Prepared feeds, nec

Lloydminster, AB S9V

D-U-N-S 20-088-5106   (BR)
WESTCAN BULK TRANSPORT LTD
(*Suby of* The Kenan Advantage Group Inc)
5406 59 Ave, Lloydminster, AB, S9V 0Y2
(780) 875-8471
Emp Here 30
SIC 2911 Petroleum refining

Lloydminster, AB T9V

D-U-N-S 24-350-9150   (BR)
1942675 ALBERTA LTD
GREAT WESTERN CONTAINERS
(*Suby of* 1942675 Alberta Ltd)
5408 52 Ave, Lloydminster, AB, T9V 2T5
(780) 875-4421
Emp Here 40
SIC 3412 Metal barrels, drums, and pails

D-U-N-S 20-184-6511   (SL)
516447 ALBERTA LTD
DAVID'S STEAK HOUSE
5501 44 St, Lloydminster, AB, T9V 0B1
(780) 875-3809
Emp Here 50   *Sales* 1,532,175
SIC 5812 Eating places

D-U-N-S 25-978-3967   (SL)
524986 SASKATCHEWAN LTD
TROPICAL INN
5621 44 St, Lloydminster, AB, T9V 0B2
(780) 875-7000
Emp Here 65   *Sales* 2,845,467
SIC 7011 Hotels and motels

D-U-N-S 24-916-0318   (BR)
ADM AGRI-INDUSTRIES COMPANY
ADM MILLING COMPANY
(*Suby of* Archer-Daniels-Midland Company)
4805 62 Ave, Lloydminster, AB, T9V 2J7
(780) 875-5554
Emp Here 60
SIC 2079 Edible fats and oils

D-U-N-S 25-316-7753   (BR)
ATCO ELECTRIC LTD
6208 48 St, Lloydminster, AB, T9V 2G1
(780) 871-5624
Emp Here 40

▲ Public Company   ■ Public Company Family Member   **HQ** Headquarters   **BR** Branch   **SL** Single Location

SIC 4911 Electric services

D-U-N-S 20-063-8161   (HQ)
AGLAND CORP
AGLAND
(*Suby of* Agland Corp)
Hwy 16, Lloydminster, AB, T9V 3A2
(780) 875-4471
Emp Here 70   *Emp Total* 95
Sales 26,667,911
SIC 5083 Farm and garden machinery
Pr Pr Kenneth Garnet Kay
 Cameron William Kay
 Robert C. Christie
Dir Richard B. Walker
Dir Robert Benning
Dir Vernon Kay
Dir Darren Lindsay
Dir Brian Coutts

D-U-N-S 20-789-0091   (BR)
BAKER HUGHES CANADA COMPANY
(*Suby of* Baker Hughes, A GE Company)
5101 65 St, Lloydminster, AB, T9V 2E8
(780) 875-6181
Emp Here 60
SIC 1389 Oil and gas field services, nec

D-U-N-S 25-506-4883   (SL)
BORDER CITY BUILDING CENTRE LTD
HOME HARDWARE BUILDING CENTRE
2802 50 Ave, Lloydminster, AB, T9V 2S3
(780) 875-7762
Emp Here 50   *Sales* 4,815,406
SIC 5251 Hardware stores

D-U-N-S 25-148-8292   (BR)
CWC ENERGY SERVICES CORP
TRINIDAD WELL SERVICING
(*Suby of* Brookfield Capital Partners II L.P.)
3606 50 Ave, Lloydminster, AB, T9V 0V7
(780) 875-4259
Emp Here 40
SIC 1389 Oil and gas field services, nec

D-U-N-S 24-227-3105   (BR)
CANADIAN NATURAL RESOURCES LIMITED
6603 44 St, Lloydminster, AB, T9V 2X1
(780) 871-7800
Emp Here 30
SIC 1311 Crude petroleum and natural gas

D-U-N-S 25-967-6484   (BR)
CHAMPION TECHNOLOGIES ULC
5201 63 St, Lloydminster, AB, T9V 2E7
(780) 875-7488
Emp Here 24
SIC 5169 Chemicals and allied products, nec

D-U-N-S 24-967-7311   (BR)
DEVON CANADA CORPORATION
5208 62 St, Lloydminster, AB, T9V 2E4
(780) 875-9837
Emp Here 65
SIC 1311 Crude petroleum and natural gas

D-U-N-S 20-588-3635   (BR)
EDMONTON KENWORTH LTD
KENWORTH OF LLOYDMINSTER
6101 63 Ave, Lloydminster, AB, T9V 3T6
(780) 871-0950
Emp Here 50
SIC 5511 New and used car dealers

D-U-N-S 24-977-2026   (BR)
FGL SPORTS LTD
SPORT CHEK LLOYDMINSTER POWER CENTRE
7501 44 St Unit 102, Lloydminster, AB, T9V 0X9
(780) 872-5246
Emp Here 20
SIC 5941 Sporting goods and bicycle shops

D-U-N-S 20-065-1425   (BR)
FLINT ENERGY SERVICES LTD.
URS FLINT

4206 59 Ave Suite 5701, Lloydminster, AB, T9V 2V4
(780) 875-1885
Emp Here 30
SIC 7389 Business services, nec

D-U-N-S 25-361-8466   (BR)
GIBSON ENERGY ULC
CANWEST PROPANE
5503 63 Ave, Lloydminster, AB, T9V 3T8
(780) 808-2400
Emp Here 50
SIC 5172 Petroleum products, nec

D-U-N-S 20-013-9397   (HQ)
GRIT INDUSTRIES INC
A-FIRE BURNER SYSTEMS
(*Suby of* Sand Control Systems Ltd)
10-50-1-4 Airport Rd Nw, Lloydminster, AB, T9V 3A5
(780) 875-5577
Emp Here 65   *Emp Total* 20
Sales 8,857,893
SIC 3433 Heating equipment, except electric
Pr Pr Wayne King
 Tom Anweiler

D-U-N-S 24-803-5508   (BR)
HOME DEPOT OF CANADA INC
HOME DEPOT
(*Suby of* The Home Depot Inc)
7705 44 St, Lloydminster, AB, T9V 0X9
(780) 870-9420
Emp Here 80
SIC 5251 Hardware stores

D-U-N-S 20-861-0076   (BR)
HUSKY OIL OPERATIONS LIMITED
5650 52 St, Lloydminster, AB, T9V 0R7

Emp Here 800
SIC 1311 Crude petroleum and natural gas

D-U-N-S 20-788-6297   (BR)
INVESTORS GROUP FINANCIAL SERVICES INC
4204 70 Ave, Lloydminster, AB, T9V 2X3

Emp Here 25
SIC 8742 Management consulting services

D-U-N-S 20-027-3725   (BR)
LLOYDMINSTER ROMAN CATHOLIC SCHOOL BOARD
ST JOSEPH'S ELEMENTARY SCHOOL
(*Suby of* LLoydminster Roman Catholic School Board)
5706 27 St, Lloydminster, AB, T9V 2B8
(780) 875-2442
Emp Here 25
SIC 8211 Elementary and secondary schools

D-U-N-S 20-713-0464   (BR)
LLOYDMINSTER ROMAN CATHOLIC SCHOOL BOARD
ST MARY'S ELEMENTARY SCHOOL
(*Suby of* LLoydminster Roman Catholic School Board)
5207 42 St, Lloydminster, AB, T9V 1M8
(780) 808-8600
Emp Here 50
SIC 8211 Elementary and secondary schools

D-U-N-S 20-600-3915   (SL)
LEYEN OIL WELL SERVICING LTD
6302 53 Ave, Lloydminster, AB, T9V 2E2
(403) 265-6361
Emp Here 300   *Sales* 67,261,350
SIC 1389 Oil and gas field services, nec
Pr Pr Glenn Dagenais

D-U-N-S 24-617-2626   (BR)
LLOYDMINSTER AND DISTRICT CO-OPERATIVE LIMITED
(*Suby of* Lloydminster And District Co-Operative Limited)
5002 18 St, Lloydminster, AB, T9V 1V4

(780) 872-7000
Emp Here 22
SIC 5541 Gasoline service stations

D-U-N-S 20-028-8491   (BR)
LLOYDMINSTER SCHOOL DIVISION NO 99
LLOYDMINSTER COMPREHENSIVE HIGH SCHOOL
(*Suby of* Lloydminster School Division No 99)
5615 42 St, Lloydminster, AB, T9V 0A2
(780) 875-5513
Emp Here 75
SIC 8211 Elementary and secondary schools

D-U-N-S 20-713-2023   (BR)
LLOYDMINSTER SCHOOL DIVISION NO 99
RENDALL PARK ELEMENTARY SCHOOL
(*Suby of* Lloydminster School Division No 99)
3401 57 Ave, Lloydminster, AB, T9V 2K6
(780) 875-7278
Emp Here 52
SIC 8211 Elementary and secondary schools

D-U-N-S 20-713-2015   (BR)
LLOYDMINSTER SCHOOL DIVISION NO 99
LLOYDMINSTER PUBLIC SCHOOL
(*Suby of* Lloydminster School Division No 99)
4812 56 Ave, Lloydminster, AB, T9V 0Z6
(780) 875-3112
Emp Here 50
SIC 8211 Elementary and secondary schools

D-U-N-S 24-114-7776   (HQ)
LLOYDMINSTER SCHOOL DIVISION NO 99
LLOYDMINSTER PUBLIC SCHOOL DIVISION
(*Suby of* Lloydminster School Division No 99)
5017 46 St Suite 99, Lloydminster, AB, T9V 1R4
(780) 875-5541
Emp Here 25   *Emp Total* 375
Sales 34,464,640
SIC 8211 Elementary and secondary schools
Treas Jack Klamont
Dir Michael Diachuk

D-U-N-S 20-713-1991   (BR)
LLOYDMINSTER SCHOOL DIVISION NO 99
BARR COLONY SCHOOL
(*Suby of* Lloydminster School Division No 99)
3103 52 Ave, Lloydminster, AB, T9V 1M9
(780) 875-4054
Emp Here 40
SIC 8211 Elementary and secondary schools

D-U-N-S 25-015-5652   (BR)
LLOYDMINSTER SCHOOL DIVISION NO 99
QUEEN ELIZABETH SCHOOL
(*Suby of* Lloydminster School Division No 99)
5512 51 Ave, Lloydminster, AB, T9V 0Y7
(780) 875-5090
Emp Here 30
SIC 8211 Elementary and secondary schools

D-U-N-S 25-483-0086   (BR)
LLOYDMINSTER SCHOOL DIVISION NO 99
BISHOP LLOYD MIDDLE SCHOOL
(*Suby of* Lloydminster School Division No 99)
5524 31 St, Lloydminster, AB, T9V 1W1
(780) 875-6239
Emp Here 45
SIC 8211 Elementary and secondary schools

D-U-N-S 20-076-5597   (BR)
LLOYDMINSTER, CITY OF
LLOYDMINSTER LEISURE CENTER
(*Suby of* Lloydminster, City of)
2902 58 Ave, Lloydminster, AB, T9V 1X8
(780) 875-4497
Emp Here 46
SIC 7999 Amusement and recreation, nec

D-U-N-S 25-014-9614   (BR)
LOBLAWS INC
REAL CANADIAN SUPERSTORES
5031 44 St, Lloydminster, AB, T9V 0A6
(780) 871-8000
Emp Here 200

SIC 5411 Grocery stores

D-U-N-S 25-290-8439   (BR)
MARK'S WORK WEARHOUSE LTD
4107 80 Ave Suite 113, Lloydminster, AB, T9V 0X9
(780) 875-1221
Emp Here 20
SIC 5651 Family clothing stores

D-U-N-S 20-203-9710   (BR)
MCELHANNEY ASSOCIATES LAND SURVEYING LTD
MCELHANNEY ASSOCIATES
5704 44 St Suite 116, Lloydminster, AB, T9V 2A1
(780) 875-8857
Emp Here 25
SIC 8732 Commercial nonphysical research

D-U-N-S 20-352-3506   (BR)
MCELHANNEY CONSULTING SERVICES LTD
5704 44 St Suite 116, Lloydminster, AB, T9V 2A1
(780) 875-8857
Emp Here 20
SIC 8713 Surveying services

D-U-N-S 20-589-2354   (BR)
NAV CANADA
Gd Rpo 10, Lloydminster, AB, T9V 2H2

Emp Here 20
SIC 4899 Communication services, nec

D-U-N-S 24-364-7638   (BR)
NOV ENERFLOW ULC
NOV TUBOSCOPE
Gd, Lloydminster, AB, T9V 3E5
(780) 875-5566
Emp Here 45
SIC 1389 Oil and gas field services, nec

D-U-N-S 24-310-5801   (BR)
NATIONAL-OILWELL CANADA LTD
NATIONAL OILWELL VARCO
(*Suby of* National Oilwell Varco, Inc.)
6452 66 St, Lloydminster, AB, T9V 3T6
(780) 875-5504
Emp Here 300
SIC 5084 Industrial machinery and equipment

D-U-N-S 25-596-0684   (BR)
NATIONAL-OILWELL CANADA LTD
NATIONAL OILWELL VARCO
(*Suby of* National Oilwell Varco, Inc.)
Gd Rpo 10, Lloydminster, AB, T9V 2H2

Emp Here 100
SIC 5084 Industrial machinery and equipment

D-U-N-S 24-330-1269   (BR)
NEWCAP INC
LLOYD FM
5026 50 St, Lloydminster, AB, T9V 1P3
(780) 875-3321
Emp Here 70
SIC 4832 Radio broadcasting stations

D-U-N-S 20-852-5753   (BR)
NINE ENERGY CANADA INC
Site 2 Reinhart Industrial Park, Lloydminster, AB, T9V 3B4

Emp Here 35
SIC 1389 Oil and gas field services, nec

D-U-N-S 20-139-0619   (BR)
NINE ENERGY CANADA INC
INTEGRATED PRODUCTION SERVICES
Gd Rpo 10, Lloydminster, AB, T9V 2H2

Emp Here 27
SIC 1389 Oil and gas field services, nec

D-U-N-S 25-260-5860   (HQ)
NORALTA TECHNOLOGIES INC
(*Suby of* Noralta Technologies Inc)

6010b 50 Ave, Lloydminster, AB, T9V 2T9
(780) 875-6777
Emp Here 42   *Emp Total* 77
Sales 3,551,629
SIC 7629 Electrical repair shops

D-U-N-S 25-569-5785   (BR)
PEAVEY INDUSTRIES LIMITED
PEAVEY MART
6206 44 St, Lloydminster, AB, T9V 1V9
(780) 875-5589
Emp Here 20
SIC 5251 Hardware stores

D-U-N-S 20-706-9969   (BR)
PRINCESS AUTO LTD
7920 44th St, Lloydminster, AB, T9V 3A7
(780) 872-5704
Emp Here 35
SIC 7218 Industrial launderers

D-U-N-S 20-571-4814   (BR)
PUROLATOR LTD
PUROLATOR INC
5010 51 St, Lloydminster, AB, T9V 0P4
(780) 871-5855
Emp Here 20
SIC 4731 Freight transportation arrangement

D-U-N-S 24-347-4595   (BR)
PYRAMID CORPORATION
6304 56 St, Lloydminster, AB, T9V 3T7
(780) 875-6644
Emp Here 90
SIC 1731 Electrical work

D-U-N-S 24-915-6530   (SL)
R & D PLUMBING & HEATING LTD
6305 43 St, Lloydminster, AB, T9V 2W9
(780) 875-9435
Emp Here 55   *Sales* 4,815,406
SIC 1711 Plumbing, heating, air-conditioning

D-U-N-S 24-914-0252   (BR)
REMAI HOLDINGS II LTD
WEST HARVEST INN
(*Suby of* Remai Holdings II Ltd)
5620 44 St, Lloydminster, AB, T9V 0B6
(780) 875-6113
Emp Here 54
SIC 7011 Hotels and motels

D-U-N-S 25-616-5952   (BR)
ROYAL BANK OF CANADA
RBC
(*Suby of* Royal Bank Of Canada)
4716 50 Ave, Lloydminster, AB, T9V 0W4
(780) 871-5800
Emp Here 30
SIC 6021 National commercial banks

D-U-N-S 25-294-6702   (BR)
SEARS CANADA INC
5211 44 St Suite 121, Lloydminster, AB, T9V 0A7
(780) 875-1111
Emp Here 75
SIC 5311 Department stores

D-U-N-S 24-811-6480   (BR)
SERVUS CREDIT UNION LTD
5012 49 St, Lloydminster, AB, T9V 0K2
(780) 875-4434
Emp Here 30
SIC 6062 State credit unions

D-U-N-S 20-806-2385   (BR)
SOBEYS CAPITAL INCORPORATED
SOBEYS STORE 3170
4227 75 Ave, Lloydminster, AB, T9V 2X4
(780) 871-0955
Emp Here 130
SIC 5411 Grocery stores

D-U-N-S 25-569-5942   (BR)
SOBEYS CAPITAL INCORPORATED
SOBEYS
4227 75 Ave, Lloydminster, AB, T9V 2X4

(780) 875-3215
Emp Here 150
SIC 5411 Grocery stores

D-U-N-S 25-271-0686   (BR)
SOBEYS WEST INC
LLOYDMINSTER SAFEWAY
5211 44 St, Lloydminster, AB, T9V 0A7
(780) 875-3448
Emp Here 75
SIC 5411 Grocery stores

D-U-N-S 20-105-0320   (BR)
STAPLES CANADA INC
STAPLES THE BUSINESS DEPOT
(*Suby of* Staples, Inc.)
4219 75 Ave, Lloydminster, AB, T9V 2X4
(780) 808-2010
Emp Here 55
SIC 5943 Stationery stores

D-U-N-S 20-864-5999   (SL)
TIM HORTONS
4301 75 Ave, Lloydminster, AB, T9V 2X4
(780) 808-2600
Emp Here 50   *Sales* 1,678,096
SIC 5461 Retail bakeries

D-U-N-S 25-417-4162   (BR)
TRICAN WELL SERVICE LTD
6013 52 Ave, Lloydminster, AB, T9V 2S7
(780) 875-7327
Emp Here 50
SIC 1389 Oil and gas field services, nec

D-U-N-S 24-844-4577   (BR)
UAP INC
NAPA
(*Suby of* Genuine Parts Company)
5205 65 St, Lloydminster, AB, T9V 2E8
(780) 875-7712
Emp Here 35
SIC 5013 Motor vehicle supplies and new parts

D-U-N-S 20-172-9303   (BR)
WAL-MART CANADA CORP
4210 70 Ave Suite 3168, Lloydminster, AB, T9V 2X3
(780) 875-4777
Emp Here 200
SIC 5311 Department stores

D-U-N-S 24-428-1598   (BR)
WATERFLOOD SERVICE & SALES LTD
2 County Energie Rd N, Lloydminster, AB, T9V 2E9
(780) 875-7638
Emp Here 22
SIC 5084 Industrial machinery and equipment

D-U-N-S 24-717-7215   (SL)
WAYSIDE MANAGEMENT LTD
BEST WESTERN WAYSIDE INN & SUITE
5411 44 St, Lloydminster, AB, T9V 0A9
(780) 875-4404
Emp Here 75   *Sales* 3,283,232
SIC 7011 Hotels and motels

D-U-N-S 20-270-4057   (HQ)
WEATHERFORD ARTIFICIAL LIFT SYSTEMS CANADA LTD
BMW PRODUCTS & SERVICES
4206 59 Ave, Lloydminster, AB, T9V 2V4
(780) 875-2730
Emp Here 230   *Emp Total* 250
Sales 39,982,464
SIC 1389 Oil and gas field services, nec
Geoffrey Inose
Burt M Martin

Longview, AB T0L

D-U-N-S 20-710-7629   (BR)
FOOTHILLS SCHOOL DIVISION NO. 38
LONGVIEW SCHOOL

101 Morrison Rd, Longview, AB, T0L 1H0
(403) 601-1753
Emp Here 50
SIC 8211 Elementary and secondary schools

Lundbreck, AB T0K

D-U-N-S 20-025-5011   (BR)
LIVINGSTONE RANGE SCHOOL DIVISION NO 68
LIVINGSTONE SCHOOL
215 Robinson Ave, Lundbreck, AB, T0K 1H0
(403) 628-3897
Emp Here 27
SIC 7389 Business services, nec

Magrath, AB T0K

D-U-N-S 20-829-3431   (SL)
NEW ELMSPRING HUTTERIAN BRETHEREN
Gd, Magrath, AB, T0K 1J0
(403) 758-3255
Emp Here 71   *Sales* 4,669,485
SIC 8661 Religious organizations

D-U-N-S 20-653-4344   (BR)
WESTWIND SCHOOL DIVISION #74
MAGRATH ELEMENTARY SCHOOL
41 Center St S, Magrath, AB, T0K 1J0
(403) 758-3367
Emp Here 51
SIC 8211 Elementary and secondary schools

D-U-N-S 20-711-3437   (BR)
WESTWIND SCHOOL DIVISION #74
MAGRATH JUNIOR SENIOR HIGH SCHOOL
41 Center St S, Magrath, AB, T0K 1J0
(403) 758-3366
Emp Here 40
SIC 8211 Elementary and secondary schools

Mallaig, AB T0A

D-U-N-S 20-713-1934   (BR)
ST. PAUL EDUCATION REGIONAL DIVISION NO 1
MALLAIG SCHOOL
3110 1 St E, Mallaig, AB, T0A 2K0
(780) 635-3858
Emp Here 31
SIC 8211 Elementary and secondary schools

Manning, AB T0H

D-U-N-S 25-316-0634   (BR)
BP CANADA ENERGY COMPANY
(*Suby of* BP P.L.C.)
Gd, Manning, AB, T0H 2M0
(780) 836-3364
Emp Here 25
SIC 1311 Crude petroleum and natural gas

D-U-N-S 25-166-8224   (BR)
HOLY FAMILY CATHOLIC REGIONAL DIVISION 37
ROSARY SCHOOL
(*Suby of* Holy Family Catholic Regional Division 37)
505 River St, Manning, AB, T0H 2M0
(780) 836-3625
Emp Here 20
SIC 8211 Elementary and secondary schools

D-U-N-S 20-021-1980   (BR)

Peace River School Division 10

PEACE RIVER SCHOOL DIVISION 10
MANNING ELEMENTARY SCHOOL
603 3 St Se, Manning, AB, T0H 2M0
(780) 836-3532
Emp Here 20
SIC 8211 Elementary and secondary schools

D-U-N-S 25-192-8685   (BR)
PEACE RIVER SCHOOL DIVISION 10
PAUL ROWE JUNIOR SENIOR HIGH SCHOOL
501 4th Ave Ne, Manning, AB, T0H 2M0
(780) 836-3397
Emp Here 24
SIC 8211 Elementary and secondary schools

Mannville, AB T0B

D-U-N-S 25-136-7371   (BR)
BUFFALO TRAIL PUBLIC SCHOOLS REGIONAL DIVISION NO. 28
MANNVILLE SCHOOL
5002 52nd Ave, Mannville, AB, T0B 2W0
(780) 763-3615
Emp Here 27
SIC 8211 Elementary and secondary schools

Manyberries, AB T0K

D-U-N-S 20-837-9896   (SL)
BONAVISTA PETROLEUM LTD
Gd, Manyberries, AB, T0K 1L0
(403) 868-3789
Emp Here 20   *Sales* 13,424,769
SIC 1311 Crude petroleum and natural gas

Marwayne, AB T0B

D-U-N-S 20-023-9841   (BR)
BUFFALO TRAIL PUBLIC SCHOOLS REGIONAL DIVISION NO. 28
MARWAYNE JUBILEE SCHOOL
105 2 St S, Marwayne, AB, T0B 2X0
(780) 847-3930
Emp Here 35
SIC 8211 Elementary and secondary schools

Mayerthorpe, AB T0E

D-U-N-S 25-091-1641   (BR)
ALBERTA HEALTH SERVICES
MAYERTHORPE HEALTHCARE CENTRE
4417 45th St, Mayerthorpe, AB, T0E 1N0
(780) 786-2261
Emp Here 100
SIC 8062 General medical and surgical hospitals

D-U-N-S 20-578-2522   (BR)
ALBERTA TREASURY BRANCHES
ATB FINANCIAL
4910 50 St, Mayerthorpe, AB, T0E 1N0
(780) 786-2207
Emp Here 20
SIC 6036 Savings institutions, except federal

D-U-N-S 25-820-9626   (BR)
EXTENDICARE INC
EXTENDICARE MAYERTHORPE
4706 54 St, Mayerthorpe, AB, T0E 1N0
(780) 786-2211
Emp Here 75
SIC 8051 Skilled nursing care facilities

D-U-N-S 25-139-5901   (BR)

NORTHERN GATEWAY REGIONAL DIVISION #10
ELSON, ELMER ELEMENTARY SCHOOL
4215 Geinger Ave, Mayerthorpe, AB, T0E 1N0
(780) 786-2268
Emp Here 20
SIC 8211 Elementary and secondary schools

D-U-N-S 20-088-0248   (BR)
NORTHERN GATEWAY REGIONAL DIVISION #10
MAYERTHORPE JUNIOR SENIOR HIGH SCHOOL
5310 50th Ave, Mayerthorpe, AB, T0E 1N0
(780) 786-2624
Emp Here 23
SIC 8211 Elementary and secondary schools

D-U-N-S 25-066-2319   (BR)
UNITED FARMERS OF ALBERTA CO-OPERATIVE LIMITED
UFA
4606 42 Ave Nw, Mayerthorpe, AB, T0E 1N0
(780) 786-4451
Emp Here 20
SIC 5999 Miscellaneous retail stores, nec

Mclennan, AB T0H

D-U-N-S 20-896-1268   (BR)
ALBERTA HEALTH SERVICES
SACRED HEART COMMUNITY HEALTH CENTRE
350 3rd Ave Nw, Mclennan, AB, T0H 2L0
(780) 324-3730
Emp Here 180
SIC 8062 General medical and surgical hospitals

D-U-N-S 20-714-0976   (BR)
NORTHERN LAKES COLLEGE
MCLENNAN CAMPUS
107 1st St E, Mclennan, AB, T0H 2L0
(780) 324-3737
Emp Here 20
SIC 8222 Junior colleges

Medicine Hat, AB T0K

D-U-N-S 20-712-1158   (BR)
PRAIRIE ROSE SCHOOL DIVISION NO 8
FOREMOST SCHOOL
302 Main St, Medicine Hat, AB, T0K 0X0
(403) 867-3843
Emp Here 30
SIC 8211 Elementary and secondary schools

Medicine Hat, AB T1A

D-U-N-S 25-364-7911   (BR)
ADM AGRI-INDUSTRIES COMPANY
OGILVIE ADM MILLING
(*Suby of* Archer-Daniels-Midland Company)
1222 Allowance Ave Se, Medicine Hat, AB, T1A 3H1

Emp Here 60
SIC 2041 Flour and other grain mill products

D-U-N-S 24-338-8381   (BR)
ARGO SALES INC
ARGO SALES ULC
925 23 St Sw, Medicine Hat, AB, T1A 8R1
(403) 526-3142
Emp Here 75
SIC 3443 Fabricated plate work (boiler shop)

D-U-N-S 25-316-0394   (BR)

BP CANADA ENERGY COMPANY
(*Suby of* BP P.L.C.)
Gd Lcd 1, Medicine Hat, AB, T1A 7E4
(403) 529-2361
Emp Here 72
SIC 1311 Crude petroleum and natural gas

D-U-N-S 24-098-7763   (BR)
BANQUE TORONTO-DOMINION, LA
TORONTO-DOMINION BANK, THE
(*Suby of* Toronto-Dominion Bank, The)
601 3 St Se, Medicine Hat, AB, T1A 0H4
(403) 528-6300
Emp Here 35
SIC 6021 National commercial banks

D-U-N-S 20-766-3535   (HQ)
CALLAGHAN INN LIMITED
LODGE MOTEL IN TABER, THE
(*Suby of* Callinn Holdings Inc)
954 7 St Sw, Medicine Hat, AB, T1A 7R7
(403) 527-8844
Emp Here 72   *Emp Total* 4
Sales 6,784,769
SIC 7011 Hotels and motels
Pr Pr Frank Callaghan
  Theresa Callaghan
  Gordon Callaghan
VP VP Clay Callaghan

D-U-N-S 20-535-9313   (BR)
CANADIAN IMPERIAL BANK OF COMMERCE
CIBC
501 3 St Se, Medicine Hat, AB, T1A 0H2
(403) 528-6100
Emp Here 20
SIC 6021 National commercial banks

D-U-N-S 24-271-3568   (BR)
CANADIAN PACIFIC RAILWAY COMPANY
PACIFIC RAILWAY
402 North Railway St Se, Medicine Hat, AB, T1A 2Z2
(403) 528-5008
Emp Here 300
SIC 4011 Railroads, line-haul operating

D-U-N-S 20-702-4832   (BR)
CANADIAN WELLHEAD ISOLATION CORPORATION
2319 10 Ave Sw Suite A, Medicine Hat, AB, T1A 8G2

Emp Here 25
SIC 1389 Oil and gas field services, nec

D-U-N-S 24-785-9481   (SL)
CARE CABS LTD
232 Maple Ave Se, Medicine Hat, AB, T1A 3A4
(403) 529-2211
Emp Here 65   *Sales* 1,969,939
SIC 4121 Taxicabs

D-U-N-S 20-641-2673   (BR)
ENERPLUS CORPORATION
906 16 St Sw, Medicine Hat, AB, T1A 8A4
(403) 504-1560
Emp Here 25
SIC 1311 Crude petroleum and natural gas

D-U-N-S 24-984-1958   (SL)
EVANGELICAL HOUSING SOCIETY OF ALBERTA
CHINOOK VILLAGE
2801 13 Ave Se, Medicine Hat, AB, T1A 3R1
(403) 526-6951
Emp Here 60   *Sales* 8,038,400
SIC 6514 Dwelling operators, except apartments
Pr Pr Phil Horch
Ch Bd Al Widmer
Fin Mgr Kim Coullard

D-U-N-S 25-994-3173   (BR)
G4S SECURE SOLUTIONS (CANADA) LTD
525 4 St Se, Medicine Hat, AB, T1A 0K7

(403) 526-2001
Emp Here 200
SIC 7381 Detective and armored car services

D-U-N-S 20-841-6623   (SL)
GYP-TEC DRYWALL
1922 16 Ave Se, Medicine Hat, AB, T1A 3T3
(403) 527-3777
Emp Here 50   *Sales* 4,231,721
SIC 1742 Plastering, drywall, and insulation

D-U-N-S 20-830-2497   (HQ)
I-XL LTD
(*Suby of* I-XL Ltd)
525 2 St Se, Medicine Hat, AB, T1A 0C5
(403) 526-5501
Emp Here 100   *Emp Total* 300
Sales 63,694,691
SIC 3251 Brick and structural clay tile
Pr Pr Clayton Sissons
VP VP Graham Sissons
VP VP Malcolm Sissons
VP Fin VP Fin Quentin Brehmer

D-U-N-S 20-088-8980   (HQ)
I.XL INDUSTRIES LTD
(*Suby of* I-XL Ltd)
612 Porcelain Ave Se, Medicine Hat, AB, T1A 8S4
(403) 526-5901
Emp Here 80   *Emp Total* 300
Sales 53,042,429
SIC 3251 Brick and structural clay tile
Pr Pr Malcolm Sissons
  Clayton Sissons
VP Fin Quentin Brehmer
  Thomas Sissons
  Graham Sissons
Dir Paul Sissons

D-U-N-S 20-257-4356   (SL)
JOUJAN BROTHERS FLOORING INC
CASH & CARRY CARPETS
941 South Railway St Se Unit 3, Medicine Hat, AB, T1A 2W3
(403) 528-8008
Emp Here 78   *Sales* 1,100,991
SIC 5713 Floor covering stores

D-U-N-S 25-963-2644   (BR)
LEHIGH HANSON MATERIALS LIMITED
821 17 St Sw, Medicine Hat, AB, T1A 4X9
(403) 527-1303
Emp Here 25
SIC 5032 Brick, stone, and related material

D-U-N-S 24-124-9957   (BR)
MNP LLP
666 4 St Se, Medicine Hat, AB, T1A 0K9
(403) 548-2105
Emp Here 50
SIC 8721 Accounting, auditing, and bookkeeping

D-U-N-S 25-965-7377   (BR)
MCMAN YOUTH, FAMILY AND COMMUNITY SERVICES ASSOCIATION
MCMAN YOUTH SERVICES
(*Suby of* McMan Youth, Family and Community Services Association)
941 South Railway St Se Unit 4, Medicine Hat, AB, T1A 2W3
(403) 527-1588
Emp Here 40
SIC 8399 Social services, nec

D-U-N-S 20-028-3401   (BR)
MEDICINE HAT CATHOLIC BOARD OF EDUCATION
ST. FRANCIS XAVIER SCHOOL
318 8 St Ne, Medicine Hat, AB, T1A 5R6
(403) 527-7223
Emp Here 20
SIC 8211 Elementary and secondary schools

D-U-N-S 25-015-6551   (HQ)
MEDICINE HAT CATHOLIC BOARD OF EDUCATION

MEDICINE HAT CATHOLIC SEPARATE REGIONAL DIVISION NO.20
(*Suby of* Medicine Hat Catholic Board of Education)
1251 1 Ave Sw Suite 20, Medicine Hat, AB, T1A 8B4
(403) 527-2292
Emp Here 100   *Emp Total* 350
Sales 32,254,080
SIC 8211 Elementary and secondary schools
Ch Bd Stan Aberle
VP Jody Churla
Treas Greg Macpherson
Superintnt David Leahy

D-U-N-S 20-027-4814   (BR)
MEDICINE HAT CATHOLIC BOARD OF EDUCATION
ST LOUIS SCHOOL
861 4 St Se, Medicine Hat, AB, T1A 0L5
(403) 527-7411
Emp Here 25
SIC 8211 Elementary and secondary schools

D-U-N-S 25-015-6478   (BR)
MEDICINE HAT CATHOLIC BOARD OF EDUCATION
MCCOY HIGH SCHOOL
(*Suby of* Medicine Hat Catholic Board of Education)
202 8 St Ne, Medicine Hat, AB, T1A 5R6
(403) 527-8161
Emp Here 50
SIC 8211 Elementary and secondary schools

D-U-N-S 20-712-3303   (BR)
MEDICINE HAT CATHOLIC SEPARATE REGIONAL DIVISION NO. 20
ST MARY'S SCHOOL
(*Suby of* Medicine Hat Catholic Separate Regional Division No. 20)
155 11 St Sw, Medicine Hat, AB, T1A 4S2
(403) 527-7616
Emp Here 45
SIC 8211 Elementary and secondary schools

D-U-N-S 20-712-3386   (BR)
MEDICINE HAT CATHOLIC SEPARATE REGIONAL DIVISION NO. 20
ST MICHAEL SCHOOL
(*Suby of* Medicine Hat Catholic Separate Regional Division No. 20)
865 Black Blvd Nw, Medicine Hat, AB, T1A 7B5
(403) 527-7242
Emp Here 35
SIC 8211 Elementary and secondary schools

D-U-N-S 24-345-7942   (SL)
MEDICINE HAT EXHIBITION & STAMPEDE CO LTD
2055 21 Ave Se, Medicine Hat, AB, T1A 7N1
(403) 527-1234
Emp Here 80   *Sales* 4,377,642
SIC 7999 Amusement and recreation, nec

D-U-N-S 20-712-2370   (BR)
MEDICINE HAT SCHOOL DISTRICT NO. 76
ECOLE CONNAUGHT SCHOOL
101 8 St Sw, Medicine Hat, AB, T1A 4L5
(403) 526-2392
Emp Here 29
SIC 8211 Elementary and secondary schools

D-U-N-S 20-712-2487   (BR)
MEDICINE HAT SCHOOL DISTRICT NO. 76
CRESTWOOD SCHOOL
2300 19 Ave Se, Medicine Hat, AB, T1A 3X5
(403) 527-2257
Emp Here 50
SIC 8211 Elementary and secondary schools

D-U-N-S 25-165-9140   (BR)
MEDICINE HAT SCHOOL DISTRICT NO. 76
ALEXANDRA JUNIOR HIGH SCHOOL
477 6 St Se, Medicine Hat, AB, T1A 1H4
(403) 527-8571
Emp Here 40

SIC 8211 Elementary and secondary schools

D-U-N-S 20-072-8173   (BR)
MEDICINE HAT SCHOOL DISTRICT NO. 76
RIVER HEIGHTS ELEMENTARY SCHOOL
301 6 Ave Sw, Medicine Hat, AB, T1A 5A8
(403) 527-3730
Emp Here 30
SIC 8211 Elementary and secondary schools

D-U-N-S 25-000-5170   (BR)
MEDICINE HAT SCHOOL DISTRICT NO. 76
CRESCENT HEIGHTS HIGH SCHOOL
1201 Division Ave N, Medicine Hat, AB, T1A
5Y8
(403) 527-6641
Emp Here 90
SIC 8211 Elementary and secondary schools

D-U-N-S 25-015-6023   (BR)
MEDICINE HAT SCHOOL DISTRICT NO. 76
HERALD ELEMENTARY SCHOOL
301 5 St Sw, Medicine Hat, AB, T1A 4G5
(403) 526-4477
Emp Here 40
SIC 8211 Elementary and secondary schools

D-U-N-S 20-712-2586   (BR)
MEDICINE HAT SCHOOL DISTRICT NO. 76
ELM STREET SCHOOL
1001 Elm St Se, Medicine Hat, AB, T1A 1C2
(403) 526-3528
Emp Here 25
SIC 8211 Elementary and secondary schools

D-U-N-S 20-296-1327   (BR)
MEDICINE HAT SCHOOL DISTRICT NO. 76
VINCENT MASSEY SCHOOL
901 Hargrave Way Nw, Medicine Hat, AB, T1A
6Y8
(403) 527-3750
Emp Here 30
SIC 8211 Elementary and secondary schools

D-U-N-S 20-029-3780   (BR)
MEDICINE HAT SCHOOL DISTRICT NO. 76
WEBSTER NIBLOCK SCHOOL
909 4 Ave Ne, Medicine Hat, AB, T1A 6B6
(403) 527-4541
Emp Here 25
SIC 8211 Elementary and secondary schools

D-U-N-S 20-712-2701   (BR)
MEDICINE HAT SCHOOL DISTRICT NO. 76
MEDICINE HAT HIGH SCHOOL
200 7 St Sw, Medicine Hat, AB, T1A 4K1
(403) 527-3371
Emp Here 70
SIC 8211 Elementary and secondary schools

D-U-N-S 20-712-2818   (BR)
MEDICINE HAT SCHOOL DISTRICT NO. 76
RIVERSIDE ELEMENTARY SCHOOL
201 2 St Nw Medicine Hat, AB, T1A 6J4
(403) 526-3793
Emp Here 50
SIC 8211 Elementary and secondary schools

D-U-N-S 20-036-4219   (BR)
MEDICINE HAT, CITY OF
*DEPARTMENT OF PARKS AND RECRE-
ATION*
88 Kipling St Se, Medicine Hat, AB, T1A 1Y3
(403) 529-8333
Emp Here 100
SIC 7389 Business services, nec

D-U-N-S 25-314-1303   (BR)
MEDICINE HAT, CITY OF
*CITY OF MEDICINE HAT FIRE AND MAN-
AGEMENT SERVICES*
440 Maple Ave Se, Medicine Hat, AB, T1A 0L3
(403) 529-8282
Emp Here 20
SIC 7389 Business services, nec

D-U-N-S 24-336-5496   (BR)
MEDICINE HAT, CITY OF
NATURAL GAS AND PETROLEUM RE-

SOURCES
364 Kipling St Se, Medicine Hat, AB, T1A 1Y4
(403) 529-8248
Emp Here 148
SIC 4925 Gas production and/or distribution

D-U-N-S 24-078-6678   (BR)
MEDICINE HAT, CITY OF
CULTURAL DEVELOPMENT
401 1 St Se, Medicine Hat, AB, T1A 8W2
(403) 502-8580
Emp Here 35
SIC 8412 Museums and art galleries

D-U-N-S 24-972-0707   (BR)
MIDWEST SURVEYS INC
1825 Bomford Cres Sw Suite 100, Medicine
Hat, AB, T1A 5E8
(403) 527-2944
Emp Here 50
SIC 8713 Surveying services

D-U-N-S 24-715-2945   (HQ)
**NUTTER'S BULK & NATURAL FOODS
(MEDICINE HAT) LTD**
(*Suby of* Nutter's Bulk & Natural Foods
(Medicine Hat) Ltd)
1601 Dunmore Rd Se Suite 107, Medicine
Hat, AB, T1A 1Z8
(800) 665-5122
Emp Here 25   *Emp Total* 75
Sales 3,648,035
SIC 5499 Miscellaneous food stores

D-U-N-S 25-007-7422   (BR)
PEMBINA PIPELINE CORPORATION
PEMBINA PIPELINE
Gd Lcd 1, Medicine Hat, AB, T1A 7E4
(403) 838-8384
Emp Here 26
SIC 1311 Crude petroleum and natural gas

D-U-N-S 25-321-4613   (BR)
REVERA INC
RIVERVIEW CARE CENTRE
603 Prospect Dr Sw, Medicine Hat, AB, T1A
4C2
(403) 527-5531
Emp Here 150
SIC 8051 Skilled nursing care facilities

D-U-N-S 25-994-3108   (BR)
ROYAL BANK OF CANADA
ROYAL BANK
(*Suby of* Royal Bank Of Canada)
580 3 St Se, Medicine Hat, AB, T1A 0H3
(403) 528-6400
Emp Here 40
SIC 6021 National commercial banks

D-U-N-S 20-803-6793   (BR)
ROYAL HOST INC
TRAVELODGE MEDICINE HAT
1100 Redcliff Dr Sw, Medicine Hat, AB, T1A
5E5
(403) 527-2275
Emp Here 30
SIC 7011 Hotels and motels

D-U-N-S 25-271-0660   (BR)
SOBEYS WEST INC
DIVISION AVENUE SAFEWAY
615 Division Ave S, Medicine Hat, AB, T1A
2J9
(403) 504-2920
Emp Here 50
SIC 5411 Grocery stores

D-U-N-S 25-271-0272   (BR)
SOBEYS WEST INC
SAFEWAY
97 8 St Nw, Medicine Hat, AB, T1A 6N9

Emp Here 52
SIC 5411 Grocery stores

D-U-N-S 24-518-4478   (SL)
SOUTH COUNTRY VILLAGE
1720 Bell St Sw, Medicine Hat, AB, T1A 5G1

(403) 526-2002
Emp Here 150   *Sales* 7,362,000
SIC 8361 Residential care
Sheila Greenstein
Roy Weiss

D-U-N-S 24-357-5763   (BR)
SPECTRA ENERGY EMPRESS L.P.
Gd Lcd 1, Medicine Hat, AB, T1A 7E4
(403) 838-8317
Emp Here 70
SIC 4922 Natural gas transmission

D-U-N-S 25-250-0504   (BR)
UAP INC
TRACTION HEAVY DUTY PARTS
(*Suby of* Genuine Parts Company)
2111 9 Ave Sw, Medicine Hat, AB, T1A 8M9
(403) 526-2244
Emp Here 50
SIC 5013 Motor vehicle supplies and new
parts

D-U-N-S 25-361-8326   (BR)
WSP CANADA INC
623 4 St Se Suite 302, Medicine Hat, AB, T1A
0L1
(403) 527-3707
Emp Here 53
SIC 8713 Surveying services

Medicine Hat, AB T1B

D-U-N-S 24-995-9040   (BR)
BEST BUY CANADA LTD
FUTURE SHOP
(*Suby of* Best Buy Co., Inc.)
3292 Dunmore Rd Se Unit 600, Medicine Hat,
AB, T1B 2R4
(403) 527-0982
Emp Here 50
SIC 5731 Radio, television, and electronic
stores

D-U-N-S 20-539-2207   (BR)
CANADA POST CORPORATION
MEDICINE HAT MALL P.O.
3292 Dunmore Rd Se, Medicine Hat, AB, T1B
2R4
(403) 526-1426
Emp Here 40
SIC 4311 U.s. postal service

D-U-N-S 25-303-6206   (BR)
**CANADIAN IMPERIAL BANK OF COM-
MERCE**
*CANADIAN IMPERIAL BANK OF COM-
MERCE*
3292 Dunmore Rd Se Suite 113, Medicine
Hat, AB, T1B 2R4
(403) 528-6145
Emp Here 50
SIC 6021 National commercial banks

D-U-N-S 20-334-3236   (BR)
EARL'S RESTAURANTS LTD
(*Suby of* Earl's Restaurants Ltd)
3215 Dunmore Rd Se Suite G, Medicine Hat,
AB, T1B 2H2
(403) 528-3275
Emp Here 40
SIC 5812 Eating places

D-U-N-S 25-015-5744   (HQ)
EXALTA TRANSPORT CORP
1849 30 St Sw, Medicine Hat, AB, T1B 3N6
(403) 526-5961
Emp Here 25   *Emp Total* 100
Sales 19,407,546
SIC 4213 Trucking, except local
Pr Pr John Finn
VP VP Ronald A Brimacombe
Treas Debbie Ziegenhagel

D-U-N-S 24-337-3235   (BR)
FGL SPORTS LTD

SPORT CHEK CARRY POWER CENTRE
3214 Dunmore Rd Se Unit 100, Medicine Hat,
AB, T1B 2X2
(403) 526-5614
Emp Here 40
SIC 5941 Sporting goods and bicycle shops

D-U-N-S 24-818-3076   (BR)
FINNING INTERNATIONAL INC
FINNING (CANADA), DIV OF
(*Suby of* Finning International Inc)
1791 30 St Sw, Medicine Hat, AB, T1B 3N5
(403) 525-4100
Emp Here 35
SIC 5084 Industrial machinery and equipment

D-U-N-S 24-346-5544   (BR)
**GOOD SAMARITAN SOCIETY, THE (A
LUTHERAN SOCIAL SERVICE ORGANIZA-
TION)**
GOOD SAMARITAN SOCIETY, THE
550 Spruce Way Se, Medicine Hat, AB, T1B
4P1
(403) 528-5050
Emp Here 140
SIC 8699 Membership organizations, nec

D-U-N-S 20-304-2098   (BR)
**GOVERNING COUNCIL OF THE SALVA-
TION ARMY IN CANADA, THE**
*GOVERNING COUNCIL OF THE SALVATION
ARMY IN CANADA, THE*
164 Stratton Way Se, Medicine Hat, AB, T1B
3R3
(403) 527-2474
Emp Here 50
SIC 8661 Religious organizations

D-U-N-S 25-241-7154   (BR)
HELICAL PIER SYSTEMS LTD
3378 15 Ave Sw, Medicine Hat, AB, T1B 3W5
(403) 580-3700
Emp Here 37
SIC 3312 Blast furnaces and steel mills

D-U-N-S 20-698-6189   (BR)
HOME DEPOT OF CANADA INC
(*Suby of* The Home Depot Inc)
1851 Strachan Rd Se, Medicine Hat, AB, T1B
4V7
(403) 581-4300
Emp Here 100
SIC 5251 Hardware stores

D-U-N-S 25-301-2629   (BR)
HUDSON'S BAY COMPANY
BAY
3292 Dunmore Rd Se Suite F7, Medicine Hat,
AB, T1B 2R4
(403) 526-7888
Emp Here 80
SIC 5311 Department stores

D-U-N-S 25-270-1099   (BR)
LOBLAWS INC
REAL CANADIAN SUPERSTORE 1550
1792 Trans Canada Way Se Suite 1550,
Medicine Hat, AB, T1B 4C6
(403) 528-5727
Emp Here 260
SIC 5411 Grocery stores

D-U-N-S 24-841-5408   (BR)
MAYFIELD INVESTMENTS LTD
MEDICINE HAT LODGE HOTEL
(*Suby of* Mayfield Investments Ltd)
1051 Ross Glen Dr Se, Medicine Hat, AB, T1B
3T8
(403) 502-8185
Emp Here 220
SIC 7011 Hotels and motels

D-U-N-S 25-134-7134   (BR)
**MEDICINE HAT CATHOLIC BOARD OF ED-
UCATION**
MOTHER TERESA SCHOOL
(*Suby of* Medicine Hat Catholic Board of Edu-
cation)

235 Cameron Rd Se, Medicine Hat, AB, T1B 2Z2
(403) 529-2000
Emp Here 23
SIC 8211 Elementary and secondary schools

D-U-N-S 20-712-3691   (BR)
MEDICINE HAT CATHOLIC SEPARATE RE-GIONAL DIVISION NO. 20
MOTHER TERESA SCHOOL
(*Suby of* Medicine Hat Catholic Separate Regional Division No. 20)
235 Cameron Rd Se, Medicine Hat, AB, T1B 2Z2
(403) 529-2000
Emp Here 50
SIC 8211 Elementary and secondary schools

D-U-N-S 20-712-3485   (BR)
MEDICINE HAT CATHOLIC SEPARATE RE-GIONAL DIVISION NO. 20
ST PATRICK SCHOOL
(*Suby of* Medicine Hat Catholic Separate Regional Division No. 20)
241 Stratton Way Se, Medicine Hat, AB, T1B 3Z2
(403) 527-1177
Emp Here 45
SIC 8211 Elementary and secondary schools

D-U-N-S 20-712-3907   (BR)
MEDICINE HAT CATHOLIC SEPARATE RE-GIONAL DIVISION NO. 20
NOTRE DAME ACADEMY
(*Suby of* Medicine Hat Catholic Separate Regional Division No. 20)
646 Spruce Way Se, Medicine Hat, AB, T1B 4X3
(403) 527-5118
Emp Here 35
SIC 8211 Elementary and secondary schools

D-U-N-S 20-088-8998   (HQ)
MEDICINE HAT CO-OP LIMITED
(*Suby of* Medicine Hat Co-Op Limited)
3030 13 Ave Se Suite 100, Medicine Hat, AB, T1B 1E3
(403) 528-6604
Emp Here 100   *Emp Total* 237
Sales 183,738,893
SIC 5411 Grocery stores
Ch Bd Rodger Vizbar
Genl Mgr Methodious Rodych
Fin Ex Michael Jamieson

D-U-N-S 20-712-3196   (BR)
MEDICINE HAT SCHOOL DISTRICT NO. 76
GEORGE DAVIDSON SCHOOL
155 Sprague Way Se, Medicine Hat, AB, T1B 3L5
(403) 529-1555
Emp Here 45
SIC 8211 Elementary and secondary schools

D-U-N-S 20-712-3097   (BR)
MEDICINE HAT SCHOOL DISTRICT NO. 76
ROSS GLEN SCHOOL
48 Ross Glen Rd Se, Medicine Hat, AB, T1B 3A8
(403) 529-2960
Emp Here 35
SIC 8211 Elementary and secondary schools

D-U-N-S 25-015-7310   (BR)
MEDICINE HAT SCHOOL DISTRICT NO. 76
SOUTHVIEW COMMUNITY SCHOOL
2425 Southview Dr Se, Medicine Hat, AB, T1B 1E8
(403) 526-4495
Emp Here 41
SIC 8211 Elementary and secondary schools

D-U-N-S 20-334-4010   (SL)
MOXIE'S RESTAURANTS INC
3090 Dunmore Rd Se, Medicine Hat, AB, T1B 2X2
(403) 528-8628
Emp Here 85   *Sales* 2,553,625
SIC 5812 Eating places

D-U-N-S 20-734-8058   (BR)
MURRAY CHEVROLET OLDSMOBILE CADILLAC LTD
1270 Trans Canada Way Se, Medicine Hat, AB, T1B 1J5
(403) 527-1141
Emp Here 100
SIC 7532 Top and body repair and paint shops

D-U-N-S 20-715-1999   (BR)
ON SIDE RESTORATION SERVICES LTD
3371 17 Ave Sw, Medicine Hat, AB, T1B 4B1
(403) 528-6470
Emp Here 20
SIC 1771 Concrete work

D-U-N-S 24-929-3549   (SL)
PAD-CAR MECHANICAL LTD
3271 17 Ave Sw, Medicine Hat, AB, T1B 4B1
(403) 528-3353
Emp Here 52   *Sales* 4,523,563
SIC 1711 Plumbing, heating, air-conditioning

D-U-N-S 20-700-6680   (BR)
REITMANS (CANADA) LIMITEE
3201 13 Ave Se, Medicine Hat, AB, T1B 1E2
(403) 526-5813
Emp Here 25
SIC 5621 Women's clothing stores

D-U-N-S 25-179-2925   (BR)
REVERA INC
MEADOWLANDS RETIREMENT RESI-DENCE
223 Park Meadows Dr Se Suite 127, Medicine Hat, AB, T1B 4K7
(403) 504-5123
Emp Here 80
SIC 6513 Apartment building operators

D-U-N-S 24-928-5743   (SL)
SALVATION ARMY MEDICINE HAT CORPS, THE
164 Stratton Way Se, Medicine Hat, AB, T1B 3R3
(403) 527-2474
Emp Here 50   *Sales* 3,283,232
SIC 8661 Religious organizations

D-U-N-S 25-294-5373   (BR)
SEARS CANADA INC
SEARS
3292 Dunmore Rd Se, Medicine Hat, AB, T1B 2R4
(403) 526-5552
Emp Here 140
SIC 5311 Department stores

D-U-N-S 20-920-5306   (BR)
SERVUS CREDIT UNION LTD
3150 13 Ave Se Suite 101, Medicine Hat, AB, T1B 1E3
(403) 528-6540
Emp Here 40
SIC 6062 State credit unions

D-U-N-S 25-451-2486   (SL)
SHOOTING STAR EVENTS INC
54 Taylor Cres Se, Medicine Hat, AB, T1B 3X6
(403) 527-2345
Emp Here 50   *Sales* 1,532,175
SIC 5812 Eating places

D-U-N-S 24-805-4744   (SL)
SLEEPING BAY BUILDING CORP
MEDICINE HAT MALL
3292 Dunmore Rd Se Suite F7, Medicine Hat, AB, T1B 2R4
(403) 526-4888
Emp Here 50   *Sales* 4,596,524
SIC 6512 Nonresidential building operators

D-U-N-S 20-949-9255   (BR)
SOBEYS WEST INC
MEDICINE HAT SAFEWAY
3292 Dunmore Rd Se Suite 139, Medicine Hat, AB, T1B 2R4
(403) 526-7778
Emp Here 50

SIC 5411 Grocery stores

D-U-N-S 25-499-0039   (BR)
STAPLES CANADA INC
STAPLES THE BUSINESS DEPOT
(*Suby of* Staples, Inc.)
1910 Strachan Rd Se Suite 113, Medicine Hat, AB, T1B 4K4
(403) 504-2460
Emp Here 30
SIC 5943 Stationery stores

D-U-N-S 24-673-1061   (SL)
TOT-EM TRANSPORTATION MEDICINE HAT LTD
3314 17 Ave Sw, Medicine Hat, AB, T1B 4B2
(403) 527-6986
Emp Here 70   *Sales* 1,969,939
SIC 4151 School buses

D-U-N-S 20-924-5518   (SL)
TRIPLE ANGLE ENTERPRISES LTD
PERKINS FAMILY RESTAURANT & BAKERY
2301 Trans Canada Way Se, Medicine Hat, AB, T1B 4E9
(403) 527-9311
Emp Here 50   *Sales* 1,532,175
SIC 5812 Eating places

D-U-N-S 25-498-2861   (BR)
WAL-MART CANADA CORP
2051 Strachan Rd Se, Medicine Hat, AB, T1B 0G4
(403) 504-4410
Emp Here 218
SIC 5311 Department stores

D-U-N-S 20-199-2372   (BR)
WENDY'S RESTAURANTS OF CANADA INC
WENDY'S
(*Suby of* The Wendy's Company)
2375 Trans Canada Way Se, Medicine Hat, AB, T1B 4E9
(403) 529-0600
Emp Here 25
SIC 5812 Eating places

D-U-N-S 20-184-1694   (BR)
WINNERS MERCHANTS INTERNATIONAL L.P.
WINNERS
(*Suby of* The TJX Companies Inc)
3201 13 Ave Se Unit 105, Medicine Hat, AB, T1B 1E2
(403) 527-8238
Emp Here 40
SIC 5651 Family clothing stores

Medicine Hat, AB T1C

D-U-N-S 24-376-9952   (BR)
BIG COUNTRY ENERGY SERVICES LIMITED PARTNERSHIP
1010 Brier Park Dr Nw, Medicine Hat, AB, T1C 1Z7
(403) 529-6444
Emp Here 100
SIC 1623 Water, sewer, and utility lines

D-U-N-S 24-354-4066   (BR)
COSTCO WHOLESALE CANADA LTD
COSTCO
(*Suby of* Costco Wholesale Corporation)
2350 Box Springs Blvd Nw Box Suite 593, Medicine Hat, AB, T1C 0C8
(403) 581-5700
Emp Here 160
SIC 5099 Durable goods, nec

D-U-N-S 20-192-3062   (BR)
CRITERION CATALYSTS & TECHNOLO-GIES CANADA, INC
2159 Brier Park Pl Nw, Medicine Hat, AB, T1C 1S7
(403) 527-4400
Emp Here 63

SIC 2819 Industrial inorganic chemicals, nec

D-U-N-S 24-674-9147   (BR)
ENERFLEX LTD.
PAMCO, DIV OF
1269 Brier Park Dr Nw, Medicine Hat, AB, T1C 1T1

Emp Here 40
SIC 5084 Industrial machinery and equipment

D-U-N-S 20-599-7562   (BR)
GOODYEAR CANADA INC
(*Suby of* The Goodyear Tire & Rubber Company)
1271 12 St Nw, Medicine Hat, AB, T1C 1W8
(403) 527-3353
Emp Here 340
SIC 3011 Tires and inner tubes

D-U-N-S 25-506-8876   (BR)
MAPLE LEAF FOODS INC
1950 Brier Park Rd Nw, Medicine Hat, AB, T1C 1V3
(403) 527-5600
Emp Here 22
SIC 2048 Prepared feeds, nec

D-U-N-S 20-352-4103   (SL)
QINETIQ GROUP CANADA INC
QINETIQ TARGET SYSTEMS
1735 Brier Park Rd Nw Unit 3, Medicine Hat, AB, T1C 1V5
(403) 528-8782
Emp Here 45   *Sales* 9,703,773
SIC 3728 Aircraft parts and equipment, nec
Peter Longstaff
Corrissa Dale

D-U-N-S 20-938-2105   (BR)
TRANSCANADA PIPELINES SERVICES LTD
1702 Brier Park Cres Nw Suite A, Medicine Hat, AB, T1C 1T9
(403) 529-4387
Emp Here 22
SIC 4619 Pipelines, nec

Milk River, AB T0K

D-U-N-S 20-919-6596   (BR)
ALBERTA HEALTH SERVICES
MILK RIVER GENERAL HOSPITAL
517 Center E, Milk River, AB, T0K 1M0
(403) 647-3500
Emp Here 40
SIC 8062 General medical and surgical hospitals

D-U-N-S 20-591-7532   (BR)
BOARD OF TRUSTEES OF HORIZON SCHOOL DIVISION NO 67
ERLE RIVERS HIGH SCHOOL
205 5th Ave, Milk River, AB, T0K 1M0
(403) 647-3665
Emp Here 20
SIC 8211 Elementary and secondary schools

D-U-N-S 24-767-4138   (SL)
RIVER ROAD COLONY
Gd, Milk River, AB, T0K 1M0
(403) 344-4433
Emp Here 65   *Sales* 5,559,741
SIC 8661 Religious organizations

Millarville, AB T0L

D-U-N-S 20-568-7424   (BR)
ASPLUNDH CANADA ULC
(*Suby of* Asplundh Tree Expert Co.)
Gd, Millarville, AB, T0L 1K0

Emp Here 20

SIC 5191 Farm supplies

Millet, AB T0C

D-U-N-S 20-029-3723   (BR)
WETASKIWIN REGIONAL PUBLIC SCHOOLS
MILLET SCHOOL
(*Suby of* Wetaskiwin Regional Public Schools)
4528 51 St, Millet, AB, T0C 1Z0
(780) 387-4696
Emp Here 30
SIC 8211 Elementary and secondary schools

D-U-N-S 20-591-9017   (BR)
WETASKIWIN REGIONAL PUBLIC SCHOOLS
GRIFFITHS-SCOTT MIDDLE SCHOOL
(*Suby of* Wetaskiwin Regional Public Schools)
4612 51 St, Millet, AB, T0C 1Z0
(780) 387-4101
Emp Here 20
SIC 8211 Elementary and secondary schools

Mirror, AB T0B

D-U-N-S 24-011-4392   (BR)
APACHE CANADA LTD
(*Suby of* Apache Corporation)
Gd, Mirror, AB, T0B 3C0
(403) 788-2350
Emp Here 23
SIC 1311 Crude petroleum and natural gas

Morinville, AB T8R

D-U-N-S 24-082-3778   (BR)
ALBERTA HEALTH SERVICES
ASPEN HOUSE
9706 100 Ave, Morinville, AB, T8R 1T2
(780) 939-7482
Emp Here 50
SIC 8322 Individual and family services

D-U-N-S 20-028-4367   (SL)
ALEXANDER FIRST NATIONS EDUCATION AUTHORITY
KIPOHTAKAW EDUCATION CENTRE
Gd, Morinville, AB, T8R 1A1
(780) 939-3551
Emp Here 50   *Sales* 3,356,192
SIC 8211 Elementary and secondary schools

D-U-N-S 25-677-1403   (BR)
GREATER ST. ALBERT CATHOLIC REGIONAL DIVISION NO. 29
NOTRE DAME ELEMENTARY SCHOOL
9719 Morinville Dr, Morinville, AB, T8R 1M1
(780) 939-4020
Emp Here 42
SIC 8211 Elementary and secondary schools

D-U-N-S 25-015-7419   (BR)
GREATER ST. ALBERT CATHOLIC REGIONAL DIVISION NO. 29
MORINVILLE COMMUNITY HIGH SCHOOL
9506 100 Ave, Morinville, AB, T8R 1P6
(780) 939-6891
Emp Here 50
SIC 8211 Elementary and secondary schools

D-U-N-S 20-713-4201   (BR)
GREATER ST. ALBERT CATHOLIC REGIONAL DIVISION NO. 29
G.H. PRIMEAU MIDDLE SCHOOL
811 Grandin Dr, Morinville, AB, T8R 1L7
(780) 939-3593
Emp Here 50
SIC 8211 Elementary and secondary schools

D-U-N-S 25-677-1387   (BR)
GREATER ST. ALBERT CATHOLIC REGIONAL DIVISION NO. 29
GEORGES P. VANIER SCHOOL
10020 101 Ave, Morinville, AB, T8R 1L5

Emp Here 45
SIC 8211 Elementary and secondary schools

D-U-N-S 25-364-3886   (BR)
LOBLAWS INC
EXTRA FOODS
8901 100 St, Morinville, AB, T8R 1V5
(780) 939-2915
Emp Here 60
SIC 5411 Grocery stores

D-U-N-S 25-269-4435   (BR)
RADCO FOOD STORES LTD
MORINVILLE SOBEYS
(*Suby of* Radco Food Stores Ltd)
10003 100 St, Morinville, AB, T8R 1R5
(780) 939-4418
Emp Here 150
SIC 5411 Grocery stores

D-U-N-S 20-806-2393   (BR)
SOBEYS CAPITAL INCORPORATED
SOBEYS STORE# 5068
10003 100 St, Morinville, AB, T8R 1R5
(780) 939-2209
Emp Here 73
SIC 5411 Grocery stores

D-U-N-S 24-042-6028   (BR)
TRAVERS FOOD SERVICE LTD
ARAMARK REMOTE SERVICES
9903 90 Ave, Morinville, AB, T8R 1K7

Emp Here 25
SIC 5812 Eating places

Morrin, AB T0J

D-U-N-S 20-736-7694   (BR)
CONOCOPHILLIPS WESTERN CANADA PARTNERSHIP
CONOCOPHILLIPS CANADA
Gd, Morrin, AB, T0J 2B0
(403) 772-3778
Emp Here 25
SIC 1381 Drilling oil and gas wells

D-U-N-S 25-269-4609   (BR)
PRAIRIE LAND REGIONAL DIVISION 25
MORRIN SCHOOL
(*Suby of* Prairie Land Regional Division 25)
2nd Ave Main St W, Morrin, AB, T0J 2B0
(403) 772-3838
Emp Here 25
SIC 8211 Elementary and secondary schools

Mundare, AB T0B

D-U-N-S 20-709-9461   (BR)
ELK ISLAND PUBLIC SCHOOLS REGIONAL DIVISION NO. 14
MUNDARE SCHOOL
5201 Sawchuk St, Mundare, AB, T0B 3H0
(780) 764-3962
Emp Here 25
SIC 8211 Elementary and secondary schools

D-U-N-S 24-522-6394   (SL)
MARY IMMACULATE HOSPITAL (MUNDARE) FOUNDATION
Gd, Mundare, AB, T0B 3H0
(780) 764-3730
Emp Here 60   *Sales* 2,699,546
SIC 8051 Skilled nursing care facilities

Myrnam, AB T0B

D-U-N-S 20-020-4100   (BR)
ST. PAUL EDUCATION REGIONAL DIVISION NO 1
MYRNAM SCHOOL
5015 50 St, Myrnam, AB, T0B 3K0
(780) 366-3801
Emp Here 20
SIC 8211 Elementary and secondary schools

Nanton, AB T0L

D-U-N-S 20-028-4318   (BR)
LIVINGSTONE RANGE SCHOOL DIVISION NO 68
A B DALEY COMMUNITY SCHOOL
2409 24th Ave, Nanton, AB, T0L 1R0
(403) 646-3161
Emp Here 20
SIC 8211 Elementary and secondary schools

D-U-N-S 20-028-3286   (BR)
LIVINGSTONE RANGE SCHOOL DIVISION NO 68
J T FOSTER SCHOOL
2501 22 St, Nanton, AB, T0L 1R0
(403) 646-2264
Emp Here 21
SIC 7389 Business services, nec

Neerlandia, AB T0G

D-U-N-S 25-103-0649   (BR)
PEMBINA HILLS REGIONAL DIVISION 7
NEERLANDIA PUBLIC CHRISTIAN SCHOOL
4915 50 St, Neerlandia, AB, T0G 1R0
(780) 674-5581
Emp Here 20
SIC 8211 Elementary and secondary schools

New Dayton, AB T0K

D-U-N-S 20-829-3720   (SL)
NEW ROCKPORT HUTTERIAN BRETHREN
Gd, New Dayton, AB, T0K 1P0
(403) 733-2122
Emp Here 50   *Sales* 2,626,585
SIC 7389 Business services, nec

New Norway, AB T0B

D-U-N-S 20-710-4584   (BR)
BATTLE RIVER REGIONAL DIVISION 31
NEW NORWAY SCHOOL
808 2nd Ave, New Norway, AB, T0B 3L0
(780) 855-3936
Emp Here 30
SIC 8211 Elementary and secondary schools

New Sarepta, AB T0B

D-U-N-S 20-029-3749   (BR)
BLACK GOLD REGIONAL DIVISION #18
NEW SAREPTA COMMUNITY HIGH SCHOOL
5150 Centre St, New Sarepta, AB, T0B 3M0
(780) 941-3924
Emp Here 27
SIC 8211 Elementary and secondary schools

D-U-N-S 20-709-7424   (BR)
BLACK GOLD REGIONAL DIVISION #18
NEW SAREPTA ELEMENTARY SCHOOL
5051 2 St S, New Sarepta, AB, T0B 3M0
(780) 941-3927
Emp Here 25
SIC 8211 Elementary and secondary schools

Nisku, AB T6E

D-U-N-S 25-360-2056   (SL)
LEDCOR FABRICATION INC
LEDCOR INDUSTRIES DIV
101 41 Ave Sw, Nisku, AB, T6E 4T2
(780) 955-1400
Emp Here 200   *Sales* 28,846,158
SIC 3498 Fabricated pipe and fittings
Pr Pr Ron Stevenson
 Jim Logan
Ex VP Rod Neys

Nisku, AB T9E

D-U-N-S 20-426-0764   (HQ)
ACR GROUP INC
ACCURATE RIVER PRODUCTS
511 12 Ave, Nisku, AB, T9E 7N8
(780) 955-2802
Emp Here 56   *Emp Total* 600
Sales 17,904,251
SIC 3069 Fabricated rubber products, nec
Pr Pr L. Grant Burton

D-U-N-S 20-294-2983   (BR)
ADESA AUCTIONS CANADA CORPORATION
ADESA EDMONTON
1701 9 St, Nisku, AB, T9E 8M8
(780) 955-4400
Emp Here 130
SIC 5012 Automobiles and other motor vehicles

D-U-N-S 25-686-8548   (BR)
ATCO ELECTRIC LTD
NISKU DISTRIBUTION CENTRE
1006 15 Ave, Nisku, AB, T9E 7S5
(780) 955-6200
Emp Here 50
SIC 4911 Electric services

D-U-N-S 24-400-4479   (BR)
AKITA DRILLING LTD
(*Suby of* Akita Drilling Ltd)
2302 8 St, Nisku, AB, T9E 7Z2
(780) 955-6700
Emp Here 600
SIC 1381 Drilling oil and gas wells

D-U-N-S 20-689-5018   (SL)
ALEGRO PROJECTS AND FABRICATION LTD.
1201 8 St, Nisku, AB, T9E 7M3
(780) 955-0266
Emp Here 80   *Sales* 6,797,150
SIC 7692 Welding repair
Pr Pr Armin Haut
VP Brett Burgess

D-U-N-S 24-283-2483   (BR)
ARGO SALES INC
ARGO SALES ULC
655 30 Ave, Nisku, AB, T9E 0R4
(780) 955-8660
Emp Here 40
SIC 5084 Industrial machinery and equipment

D-U-N-S 24-011-7734   (BR)
ARGUS MACHINE CO. LTD
(*Suby of* Argus Machine Co. Ltd)
2327 5 St, Nisku, AB, T9E 8H7

(780) 955-9314
Emp Here 63
SIC 3599 Industrial machinery, nec

D-U-N-S 25-993-0600   (BR)
BAKER HUGHES CANADA COMPANY
BAKER ATLAS
(*Suby of* Baker Hughes, A GE Company)
402 22 Ave, Nisku, AB, T9E 7W8
(780) 955-3033
Emp Here 55
SIC 1389 Oil and gas field services, nec

D-U-N-S 25-623-8353   (BR)
BAKER HUGHES CANADA COMPANY
BAKER HUGHES INTEQ, DIV OF
(*Suby of* Baker Hughes, A GE Company)
1201 8 St, Nisku, AB, T9E 7M3
(780) 955-2020
Emp Here 30
SIC 5084 Industrial machinery and equipment

D-U-N-S 24-385-0695   (SL)
BORETS CANADA LTD
BORETS-WEATHERFORD
2305 8 St, Nisku, AB, T9E 7Z3
(780) 955-4795
Emp Here 71   *Sales* 16,773,456
SIC 5084 Industrial machinery and equipment
Pr Philip Fouillard
 Sergey Alehkin

D-U-N-S 24-939-1939   (HQ)
CARMACKS ENTERPRISES LTD
701 25 Ave, Nisku, AB, T9E 0C1
(780) 955-5545
Emp Here 50   *Emp Total* 254
Sales 236,551,590
SIC 1611 Highway and street construction
Pr Pr Keith James

D-U-N-S 25-992-8216   (SL)
CASSADY ENGINEERING LTD
2314 5 St, Nisku, AB, T9E 7W9
(780) 955-3780
Emp Here 50   *Sales* 4,961,328
SIC 8711 Engineering services

D-U-N-S 20-084-4025   (HQ)
CHEMCO ELECTRICAL CONTRACTORS LTD
(*Suby of* Balm Management Enterprises Ltd)
3135 4 St, Nisku, AB, T9E 8L1
(780) 436-9570
Emp Here 120   *Emp Total* 2
Sales 359,893,194
SIC 1731 Electrical work
Pr Pr Brian Halina
Ex VP Terry Milot
 Todd Halina
 Jill Halina

D-U-N-S 24-064-8055   (SL)
CIVEO MODULAR STRUCTURES LTD
(*Suby of* Oil States International, Inc.)
1507 8 St, Nisku, AB, T9E 7S7
(780) 955-7366
Emp Here 300   *Sales* 123,971,900
SIC 3448 Prefabricated Metal buildings and components
 Mark Menard

D-U-N-S 24-133-7828   (BR)
CLEAN HARBORS CANADA, INC
1102 6 St, Nisku, AB, T9E 7N7
(780) 955-8788
Emp Here 30
SIC 7353 Heavy construction equipment rental

D-U-N-S 24-949-5789   (BR)
DRECO ENERGY SERVICES ULC
NATIONAL OIL WELL VARCO
(*Suby of* National Oilwell Varco, Inc.)
506 17 Ave, Nisku, AB, T9E 7T1
(780) 955-5451
Emp Here 140
SIC 3533 Oil and gas field machinery

D-U-N-S 24-857-2252   (BR)
DRECO ENERGY SERVICES ULC
NATIONAL OILWELL VARCO
(*Suby of* National Oilwell Varco, Inc.)
1505 4 St, Nisku, AB, T9E 7M9
(780) 955-8929
Emp Here 60
SIC 3533 Oil and gas field machinery

D-U-N-S 24-715-2143   (BR)
ENFORM CANADA
1020 20 Ave, Nisku, AB, T9E 7Z6
(780) 955-7770
Emp Here 28
SIC 8299 Schools and educational services, nec

D-U-N-S 24-890-4208   (BR)
ESSENTIAL ENERGY SERVICES LTD
ESSENTIAL WELL SERVICE
1203 - 4 St, Nisku, AB, T9E 7L3
(780) 955-5961
Emp Here 20
SIC 1389 Oil and gas field services, nec

D-U-N-S 24-399-7491   (HQ)
FRANK FLAMAN SALES LTD
(*Suby of* Flaman, Frank Investments Ltd)
2310 Sparrow Dr, Nisku, AB, T9E 8A2
(780) 955-3400
Emp Here 41   *Emp Total* 50
Sales 6,347,581
SIC 5999 Miscellaneous retail stores, nec
Pr Pr Frank Flaman

D-U-N-S 24-324-1051   (BR)
GISBORNE FIRE PROTECTION ALBERTA LTD
1201 6 St, Nisku, AB, T9E 7P1
(780) 447-3830
Emp Here 24
SIC 1711 Plumbing, heating, air-conditioning

D-U-N-S 25-367-9096   (BR)
GISBORNE INDUSTRIAL CONSTRUCTION LTD
GISBORNE FIRE PROTECTION
1201 6 St, Nisku, AB, T9E 7P1
(780) 955-0509
Emp Here 100
SIC 1541 Industrial buildings and warehouses

D-U-N-S 20-747-7477   (BR)
HALLMARK TUBULARS LTD
HALLMARK INTEGRATED TUBULAR SERVICES
1201 10 St, Nisku, AB, T9E 8L6
(780) 955-7955
Emp Here 60
SIC 5051 Metals service centers and offices

D-U-N-S 20-298-8403   (SL)
IMPACT OILFIELD SUPPLY INC
(*Suby of* Genuine Parts Company)
2714 5 St, Nisku, AB, T9E 0H1
(780) 466-7484
Emp Here 20   *Sales* 4,331,255
SIC 5082 Construction and mining machinery

D-U-N-S 20-003-2089   (HQ)
IRONLINE COMPRESSION LIMITED PARTNERSHIP
700 15 Ave, Nisku, AB, T9E 7S2
(780) 955-0700
Emp Here 45   *Emp Total* 109
Sales 43,805,850
SIC 7699 Repair services, nec
Dir Timothy Kelley
Pr Pr Stephen Owen
 Hootan Yaghoobzadeh

D-U-N-S 24-423-2919   (SL)
J.V. DRIVER FABRICATORS INC
706 25 Ave, Nisku, AB, T9E 0G6
(780) 955-4282
Emp Here 100   *Sales* 14,134,935
SIC 3312 Blast furnaces and steel mills
Genl Mgr Corey Callahan

D-U-N-S 24-684-3288   (SL)
JL FILTRATION INC
A DIVISION OF CLEAN HARBORS
1102 6 St, Nisku, AB, T9E 7N7
(780) 955-8789
Emp Here 24   *Sales* 4,887,220
SIC 3569 General industrial machinery, nec

D-U-N-S 24-000-6085   (BR)
KIK OPERATING PARTNERSHIP
1202 8 St, Nisku, AB, T9E 7M1

Emp Here 20
SIC 2842 Polishes and sanitation goods

D-U-N-S 20-053-3326   (SL)
LAKOTA DRILLING INC
1704 5 St, Nisku, AB, T9E 8P8
(780) 955-7535
Emp Here 600   *Sales* 148,408,960
SIC 6712 Bank holding companies
Pr Pr Elson Mcdougald

D-U-N-S 24-802-2449   (SL)
LEADING MANUFACTURING GROUP INC
LMG
(*Suby of* Leading Manufacturing Group Holdings Inc)
2313 8 St, Nisku, AB, T9E 7Z3
(780) 955-8895
Emp Here 70   *Sales* 10,871,144
SIC 3443 Fabricated plate work (boiler shop)
Pr Pr Lee Gottschlich

D-U-N-S 24-855-4151   (HQ)
LINK SUSPENSIONS OF CANADA, LIMITED PARTNERSHIP
601 18 Ave, Nisku, AB, T9E 7T7
(780) 955-2859
Emp Here 50   *Emp Total* 180
Sales 4,815,406
SIC 3842 Surgical appliances and supplies

D-U-N-S 20-083-0313   (SL)
LUFKIN INDUSTRIES CANADA ULC
(*Suby of* General Electric Company)
1107 8a St, Nisku, AB, T9E 7R3
(780) 955-7566
Emp Here 106   *Sales* 2,772,003
SIC 3561 Pumps and pumping equipment

D-U-N-S 24-364-7455   (HQ)
NDT SYSTEMS & SERVICES (CANADA) INC
604 19 Ave, Nisku, AB, T9E 7W1
(780) 955-8611
Emp Here 22   *Emp Total* 160
Sales 3,502,114
SIC 1389 Oil and gas field services, nec

D-U-N-S 25-498-3414   (BR)
NOV ENERFLOW ULC
TUBOSCOPE CANADA
2201 9 St, Nisku, AB, T9E 7Z7
(780) 955-7675
Emp Here 75
SIC 1389 Oil and gas field services, nec

D-U-N-S 24-732-5723   (BR)
NOV ENERFLOW ULC
NOVTUBOSCOPE
2304a 8 St, Nisku, AB, T9E 7Z2
(780) 955-2924
Emp Here 60
SIC 3479 Metal coating and allied services

D-U-N-S 25-368-4211   (BR)
NOV ENERFLOW ULC
TUBOSCOPE CANADA
2203 9 St Suite 2201, Nisku, AB, T9E 7Z7
(780) 955-2901
Emp Here 30
SIC 1389 Oil and gas field services, nec

D-U-N-S 25-367-6878   (BR)
NABORS DRILLING CANADA LIMITED
NABORS DRILLING
902 20 Ave, Nisku, AB, T9E 7Z6

(780) 955-2381
Emp Here 140
SIC 1381 Drilling oil and gas wells

D-U-N-S 24-347-6764   (BR)
NATIONAL-OILWELL CANADA LTD
NATIONAL OILWELL VARCO
(*Suby of* National Oilwell Varco, Inc.)
1507 4 St, Nisku, AB, T9E 7M9
(780) 955-8828
Emp Here 51
SIC 5084 Industrial machinery and equipment

D-U-N-S 24-005-2381   (SL)
NISKU PRINTERS (1980) LTD
2002 8 St Suite 7, Nisku, AB, T9E 7Y8

Emp Here 50   *Sales* 5,104,320
SIC 2752 Commercial printing, lithographic
Pr Pr Peter Fargey
 Gwen Fargey

D-U-N-S 25-680-6548   (SL)
O.J. PIPELINES CANADA
RMS WELDING SYSTEMS, DIV OF
(*Suby of* Quanta Services, Inc.)
1409 4 St, Nisku, AB, T9E 7M9
(780) 955-3900
Emp Here 200   *Sales* 35,021,136
SIC 1623 Water, sewer, and utility lines
Pr Pr David Kavanaugh

D-U-N-S 25-074-9421   (BR)
PRECISION DRILLING CORPORATION
PRECISION DRILLING
1513 8 St, Nisku, AB, T9E 7S7
(780) 955-7922
Emp Here 55
SIC 1381 Drilling oil and gas wells

D-U-N-S 20-651-6986   (BR)
PRECISION DRILLING CORPORATION
PRECISION DRILLING
807 25 Ave, Nisku, AB, T9E 7Z4
(780) 955-7011
Emp Here 35
SIC 1381 Drilling oil and gas wells

D-U-N-S 25-136-0103   (HQ)
R.B.W. WASTE MANAGEMENT LTD
RB WILLLIAM INDUSTRIAL SUPPLY
3280 10 St, Nisku, AB, T9E 1E7
(780) 438-2183
Emp Here 38   *Emp Total* 65
Sales 6,583,508
SIC 4953 Refuse systems
Pr Pr Rick Williams
 Lynn Williams

D-U-N-S 24-853-7177   (BR)
RECOCHEM INC.
CONSUMER DIVISION
604 22 Ave, Nisku, AB, T9E 7X6
(780) 955-2644
Emp Here 65
SIC 2899 Chemical preparations, nec

D-U-N-S 20-084-0221   (HQ)
RED-L DISTRIBUTORS LTD
3675 13 St, Nisku, AB, T9E 1C5
(780) 437-2630
Emp Here 60   *Emp Total* 2
Sales 21,304,524
SIC 5085 Industrial supplies
Dir Michael Ludwig
Pr Jamie Ludwig
 Guy Ludwig
VP VP Rick Lafrance
VP VP Ronald Petryk

D-U-N-S 24-365-8957   (SL)
RELIANCE INDUSTRIAL INVESTMENTS LTD
606 19 Ave, Nisku, AB, T9E 7W1
(780) 955-7115
Emp Here 64   *Sales* 11,025,249
SIC 6712 Bank holding companies
Dir Georg Eger

Dir Michael Sirois

D-U-N-S 24-336-8433   (BR)
RELIANCE INDUSTRIAL PRODUCTS ULC
MECHANICAL DIVISION
(*Suby of* Applied Industrial Technologies, Inc.)
602 19 Ave, Nisku, AB, T9E 7W1
(780) 955-2042
Emp Here 20
SIC 1711 Plumbing, heating, air-conditioning

D-U-N-S 24-962-7043   (HQ)
RELIANCE INDUSTRIAL PRODUCTS ULC
(*Suby of* Applied Industrial Technologies, Inc.)
606 19 Ave, Nisku, AB, T9E 7W1
(780) 955-7115
Emp Here 150   *Emp Total* 5,569
Sales 96,964,770
SIC 5085 Industrial supplies
Pr Pr Michael Sirois
 Leo Farley
 Georg Eger

D-U-N-S 24-318-6645   (BR)
RIG SHOP LIMITED, THE
2107 5 St, Nisku, AB, T9E 7X4

Emp Here 30
SIC 1799 Special trade contractors, nec

D-U-N-S 20-733-8497   (BR)
RITCHIE BROS. AUCTIONEERS INCORPO-RATED
1500 Sparrow Dr, Nisku, AB, T9E 8H6
(780) 955-2486
Emp Here 30
SIC 7389 Business services, nec

D-U-N-S 24-204-9877   (BR)
ROCKWELL SERVICING INC
ENSIGN ROCKWELL SERVICING
2105 8 St, Nisku, AB, T9E 7Z1
(780) 955-7066
Emp Here 80
SIC 1389 Oil and gas field services, nec

D-U-N-S 24-354-8380   (BR)
SAMUEL, SON & CO., LIMITED
OMEGA JCIST
1709 8 St, Nisku, AB, T9E 7S8
(780) 955-7516
Emp Here 80
SIC 5051 Metals service centers and offices

D-U-N-S 24-702-9168   (BR)
SHAWCOR LTD
SHAWCOR NISKU NORTH
950 30 Ave, Nisku, AB, T9E 0S2
(780) 955-3380
Emp Here 45
SIC 1389 Oil and gas field services, nec

D-U-N-S 24-322-0493   (BR)
SUREPOINT SERVICES INC
(*Suby of* Wynnchurch Capital, Ltd.)
1211 8a St, Nisku, AB, T9E 7R3
(780) 955-3939
Emp Here 100
SIC 5084 Industrial machinery and equipment

D-U-N-S 24-397-3864   (HQ)
TIW CANADA LTD
(*Suby of* Dril-Quip, Inc.)
507 12 Ave, Nisku, AB, T9E 7N8
(780) 955-2510
Emp Here 28   *Emp Total* 2,179
Sales 7,263,340
SIC 3533 Oil and gas field machinery
Pr Pr Stephen R. Pearce
Genl Mgr Al Ricalton
 Britt Braddick
 Chandler Washington

D-U-N-S 24-387-8597   (BR)
TIW WESTERN INC
(*Suby of* Canerector Inc)
1012 16 Ave, Nisku, AB, T9E 0A9
(780) 979-0500
Emp Here 40

SIC 3433 Heating equipment, except electric

D-U-N-S 25-507-4247   (BR)
TARPON ENERGY SERVICES LTD
1409 6 St, Nisku, AB, T9E 7M7
(780) 955-2787
SIC 1389 Oil and gas field services, nec

D-U-N-S 24-928-6915   (HQ)
TIGER CALCIUM SERVICES INC
15 Ave Suite 603, Nisku, AB, T9E 7M6
(403) 955-5004
Emp Here 25   *Emp Total* 14
Sales 14,119,891
SIC 1499 Miscellaneous nonMetallic minerals, except fuels
Pr Pr Clark Sazwan
 Brandy Deford
 Richard Kolodziej
 Shilo Sazwan
Sec Rod Senst
 Rob Wildeman

D-U-N-S 20-280-2471   (BR)
TRICAN WELL SERVICE LTD
TRICAN PRODUCTION SERVICES
2305 5a St, Nisku, AB, T9E 8G6
(780) 955-5675
Emp Here 88
SIC 1389 Oil and gas field services, nec

D-U-N-S 24-814-4243   (BR)
TRINIDAD DRILLING LTD
3059 4 St, Nisku, AB, T9E 8L1
(780) 955-2340
Emp Here 40
SIC 1381 Drilling oil and gas wells

D-U-N-S 25-193-8064   (BR)
VARSTEEL LTD
602 13 Ave, Nisku, AB, T9E 7P6
(780) 955-1953
Emp Here 20
SIC 5051 Metals service centers and offices

D-U-N-S 24-374-1316   (BR)
VICTORY RIG EQUIPMENT CORPORATION
1511 10 St, Nisku, AB, T9E 8C5
(780) 955-4711
Emp Here 40
SIC 3569 General industrial machinery, nec

D-U-N-S 24-714-7788   (HQ)
W.F. WELDING & OVERHEAD CRANES LTD
(*Suby of* Camber Corporation)
705 23 Ave, Nisku, AB, T9E 7Y5
(780) 955-7671
Emp Here 84   *Emp Total* 80
Sales 15,540,629
SIC 5084 Industrial machinery and equipment
Pr Pr Brad Chrystian

Niton Junction, AB T0E

D-U-N-S 25-156-3532   (BR)
GRANDE YELLOWHEAD PUBLIC SCHOOL DIVISION 77
NITON CENTRAL SCHOOL
4706 46 Ave, Niton Junction, AB, T0E 1S0
(780) 795-3782
Emp Here 22
SIC 8211 Elementary and secondary schools

Nobleford, AB T0L

D-U-N-S 24-818-2649   (BR)
AG GROWTH INTERNATIONAL INC
EDWARDS GROUP
215 Barons St, Nobleford, AB, T0L 1S0
(403) 320-5585
Emp Here 100

SIC 3523 Farm machinery and equipment

D-U-N-S 20-089-3790   (SL)
NIEBOER FARM SUPPLIES (1977) LTD
233016 Hwy 519, Nobleford, AB, T0L 1S0
(403) 824-3404
Emp Here 30   *Sales* 6,493,502
SIC 5083 Farm and garden machinery
 William Nieboer
Pr Kevin Nieboer
Dir Pearl Nieboer

D-U-N-S 20-711-5291   (BR)
PALLISER REGIONAL DIVISION NO 26
NOBLEFORD CENTRAL SCHOOL
418 Hwy Ave, Nobleford, AB, T0L 1S0
(403) 824-3817
Emp Here 28
SIC 8211 Elementary and secondary schools

Okotoks, AB T1S

D-U-N-S 20-255-5780   (SL)
945575 ALBERTA LTD
BOSTON PIZZA
10 Southridge Dr, Okotoks, AB, T1S 1N1
(403) 995-0224
Emp Here 75   *Sales* 2,261,782
SIC 5812 Eating places

D-U-N-S 24-025-3232   (BR)
ALBERTA HEALTH SERVICES
OKOTOKS HEALTH AND WELLNESS CEN-TRE
11 Cimarron Common, Okotoks, AB, T1S 2E9
(403) 995-2600
Emp Here 100
SIC 8093 Specialty outpatient clinics, nec

D-U-N-S 20-584-9826   (BR)
CANADA POST CORPORATION
27 Mcrae St, Okotoks, AB, T1S 1A0
(403) 938-4233
Emp Here 30
SIC 4311 U.s. postal service

D-U-N-S 20-030-6384   (BR)
CHRIST THE REDEEMER CATHOLIC SEP-ARATE REGIONAL DIVISION NO. 3
ECOLE GOOD SHEPHERD SCHOOL
52 Robinson Dr Suite 1, Okotoks, AB, T1S 2A3
(403) 938-4318
Emp Here 72
SIC 8211 Elementary and secondary schools

D-U-N-S 20-707-9513   (BR)
CHRIST THE REDEEMER CATHOLIC SEP-ARATE REGIONAL DIVISION NO. 3
ST MARY'S SCHOOL
42 Cimarron Trail, Okotoks, AB, T1S 2A8
(403) 938-8048
Emp Here 70
SIC 8211 Elementary and secondary schools

D-U-N-S 20-713-2064   (BR)
CHRIST THE REDEEMER CATHOLIC SEP-ARATE REGIONAL DIVISION NO. 3
JOHN PAULL II COLLEGIATE
53 Cimarron Dr Suite 1, Okotoks, AB, T1S 2A6
(403) 938-4600
Emp Here 50
SIC 8211 Elementary and secondary schools

D-U-N-S 25-119-1961   (BR)
CHRIST THE REDEEMER CATHOLIC SEP-ARATE REGIONAL DIVISION NO. 3
OKOTOKS HOME SCHOOLING
(*Suby of* Christ The Redeemer Catholic Separate Regional Division No. 3)
53 Cimarron Dr Suite 1, Okotoks, AB, T1S 2A6
(403) 938-8046
Emp Here 25
SIC 8249 Vocational schools, nec

D-U-N-S 24-369-4028   (BR)
CHRIST THE REDEEMER CATHOLIC SEP-ARATE REGIONAL DIVISION NO. 3
HOLY TRINITY ACADEMY
338072 32 St E, Okotoks, AB, T1S 1A2
(403) 938-2477
Emp Here 65
SIC 8211 Elementary and secondary schools

D-U-N-S 24-319-2965   (SL)
FOOTHILLS COUNTRY HOSPICE SOCIETY
Gd, Okotoks, AB, T1S 1A3
(403) 995-4673
Emp Here 50   *Sales* 4,012,839
SIC 8069 Specialty hospitals, except psychiatric

D-U-N-S 20-710-8296   (BR)
FOOTHILLS SCHOOL DIVISION NO. 38
FOOTHILLS COMPOSITE HIGH SCHOOL AND ALBERTA HIGH SCHOOL OF FINE ARTS
229 Woodhaven Dr, Okotoks, AB, T1S 2A7
(403) 938-6116
Emp Here 80
SIC 8211 Elementary and secondary schools

D-U-N-S 20-710-7736   (BR)
FOOTHILLS SCHOOL DIVISION NO. 38
ECOLE ELEMENTAIRE PERCY PEGLER SCHOOL
69 Okotoks Dr, Okotoks, AB, T1S 2B1
(403) 938-3865
Emp Here 50
SIC 8211 Elementary and secondary schools

D-U-N-S 25-272-2244   (BR)
FOOTHILLS SCHOOL DIVISION NO. 38
BIG ROCK SCHOOL
33 Hunter'S Gate, Okotoks, AB, T1S 2A4
(403) 938-6666
Emp Here 32
SIC 8211 Elementary and secondary schools

D-U-N-S 25-269-4583   (BR)
FOOTHILLS SCHOOL DIVISION NO. 38
OKOTOKS JUNIOR HIGH SCHOOL
1 Pacific Dr, Okotoks, AB, T1S 2A9
(403) 938-4426
Emp Here 55
SIC 8211 Elementary and secondary schools

D-U-N-S 24-858-9918   (HQ)
HI-PRO FEEDS LP
TROUW NUTRITION
Hwy 2a 306 Ave, Okotoks, AB, T1S 1A2
(403) 938-8350
Emp Here 150   *Emp Total* 60,800
Sales 40,712,071
SIC 5999 Miscellaneous retail stores, nec
 Daren Kennett
 Mark Knief
VP Mfg Jeff Dykstra

D-U-N-S 24-364-7240   (BR)
HOME DEPOT OF CANADA INC
HOME DEPOT
(*Suby of* The Home Depot Inc)
101 Southbank Blvd Unit 10, Okotoks, AB, T1S 0G1
(403) 995-4710
Emp Here 150
SIC 5211 Lumber and other building materials

D-U-N-S 25-194-0581   (BR)
MBG BUILDINGS INC
Gd, Okotoks, AB, T1S 1A2
(403) 262-9020
Emp Here 20
SIC 1541 Industrial buildings and warehouses

D-U-N-S 20-700-6649   (BR)
REITMANS (CANADA) LIMITEE
201 Southridge Dr Unit 315, Okotoks, AB, T1S 2E1
(403) 995-1872
Emp Here 25
SIC 5621 Women's clothing stores

D-U-N-S 25-094-6493   (BR)
SHELL CANADA LIMITED
SHELL
61 Riverside Dr, Okotoks, AB, T1S 1M3
(403) 938-3227
Emp Here 20
SIC 5541 Gasoline service stations

D-U-N-S 20-806-2401   (BR)
SOBEYS CAPITAL INCORPORATED
SOBEYS STORE 1130
201 Southridge Dr Suite 700, Okotoks, AB,
T1S 2E1
(403) 995-4088
Emp Here 185
SIC 5411 Grocery stores

D-U-N-S 24-363-3869   (BR)
SOBEYS WEST INC
OKOTOKS SAFEWAY
610 Big Rock Lane, Okotoks, AB, T1S 1L2
(403) 938-9341
Emp Here 150
SIC 5411 Grocery stores

D-U-N-S 20-880-4224   (BR)
SOUTHLAND TRANSPORTATION LTD
117 Stockton Pt, Okotoks, AB, T1S 1H8
(403) 938-3966
Emp Here 49
SIC 4151 School buses

D-U-N-S 20-806-3961   (BR)
STARBUCKS COFFEE CANADA, INC
STARBUCKS COFFEE
(*Suby of* Starbucks Corporation)
201 Southridge Dr Unit 111, Okotoks, AB, T1S
2E1
(403) 995-1924
Emp Here 25
SIC 5812 Eating places

D-U-N-S 25-119-4270   (SL)
TOMANICK GROUP, THE
BOSTON PIZZA OKOTOKS 149
10 Southridge Dr, Okotoks, AB, T1S 1N1
(403) 995-0224
Emp Here 75   *Sales* 2,685,378
SIC 5812 Eating places

D-U-N-S 24-160-1157   (BR)
WENDY'S RESTAURANTS OF CANADA INC
(*Suby of* The Wendy's Company)
18 Southridge Dr Suite 6877, Okotoks, AB,
T1S 1N1
(403) 995-2552
Emp Here 28
SIC 5812 Eating places

D-U-N-S 24-088-5160   (SL)
WESTERN WHEEL PUBLISHING LTD, THE
*OKOTOKS WESTERN WHEEL NEWSPA-
PER*
9 Mcrae St, Okotoks, AB, T1S 2A2
(403) 938-6397
Emp Here 25   *Sales* 28,589,440
SIC 2711 Newspapers
Pr Paul Rockley

D-U-N-S 25-518-8120   (BR)
WOODRIDGE FORD LINCOLN LTD
WOODRIDGE OF OKOTOKS
4 Westland Rd, Okotoks, AB, T1S 1N1
(403) 938-2222
Emp Here 30
SIC 5511 New and used car dealers

Olds, AB T4H

D-U-N-S 20-574-2419   (SL)
876350 ALBERTA LTD
BOSTON PIZZA
4520 46 St, Olds, AB, T4H 1A1
(403) 556-7988
Emp Here 50   *Sales* 1,532,175

SIC 5812 Eating places

D-U-N-S 20-828-4109   (BR)
ALBERTA HEALTH SERVICES
OLDS HOSPITAL & CARE CENTRE
3901 57 Ave, Olds, AB, T4H 1T4
(403) 556-3381
Emp Here 230
SIC 8062 General medical and surgical hospi-
tals

D-U-N-S 24-075-2696   (BR)
BAYTEX ENERGY CORP
(*Suby of* Baytex Energy Corp)
4526 49 Ave Suite 7, Olds, AB, T4H 1A4
(403) 556-3174
Emp Here 23
SIC 1382 Oil and gas exploration services

D-U-N-S 24-356-5624   (BR)
CANADIAN TIRE CORPORATION, LIMITED
6900 46 St Unit 600, Olds, AB, T4H 0A2
(403) 556-9949
Emp Here 20
SIC 5531 Auto and home supply stores

D-U-N-S 25-064-9139   (BR)
CERVUS LP
AGRO OLDS JOHN DEERE
4310 50 Ave, Olds, AB, T4H 1A5
(403) 556-6961
Emp Here 20
SIC 5999 Miscellaneous retail stores, nec

D-U-N-S 20-025-4931   (BR)
**CHINOOKS EDGE SCHOOL DIVISION NO.
73**
ECHOLE OLDS ELEMENTARY SCHOOL
5413 53 St, Olds, AB, T4H 1S9
(403) 556-8477
Emp Here 50
SIC 8211 Elementary and secondary schools

D-U-N-S 20-027-4319   (BR)
**CHINOOKS EDGE SCHOOL DIVISION NO.
73**
ECOLE DEER MEADOW SCHOOL
5411 61 Ave, Olds, AB, T4H 1T2
(403) 556-1003
Emp Here 40
SIC 8211 Elementary and secondary schools

D-U-N-S 24-299-1912   (BR)
HI-PRO FEEDS LP
(*Suby of* Hi-Pro Feeds LP)
5902 48 Ave, Olds, AB, T4H 1V1
(403) 556-3395
Emp Here 20
SIC 5999 Miscellaneous retail stores, nec

D-U-N-S 25-073-8861   (HQ)
MOUNTAIN VIEW PUBLISHING INC
OLDS ALBERTAN, THE
5021 51 St, Olds, AB, T4H 1P6
(403) 556-7510
Emp Here 30   *Emp Total* 200
Sales 3,575,074
SIC 5192 Books, periodicals, and newspapers

D-U-N-S 20-028-8186   (SL)
OLDS KOINONIA CHRISTIAN SCHOOL
Gd Stn Main, Olds, AB, T4H 1R4
(403) 556-4038
Emp Here 50   *Sales* 3,356,192
SIC 8211 Elementary and secondary schools

D-U-N-S 25-999-9787   (BR)
PENGROWTH ENERGY CORPORATION
OLDS OPERATIONS
(*Suby of* Pengrowth Energy Corporation)
Gd, Olds, AB, T4H 1T8
(403) 556-3424
Emp Here 45
SIC 1311 Crude petroleum and natural gas

D-U-N-S 24-082-1566   (BR)
PETROCORP GROUP INC
5321 49 Ave, Olds, AB, T4H 1G3

Emp Here 20
SIC 7699 Repair services, nec

D-U-N-S 20-920-5264   (BR)
PLAINS MIDSTREAM CANADA ULC
4810 45 St, Olds, AB, T4H 1S5
(403) 556-3366
Emp Here 20
SIC 4619 Pipelines, nec

D-U-N-S 24-905-4461   (BR)
PREMIER HORTICULTURE LTEE
4803 60 St, Olds, AB, T4H 1V1
(403) 556-7328
Emp Here 26
SIC 5159 Farm-product raw materials, nec

D-U-N-S 20-648-4110   (BR)
SOBEYS CAPITAL INCORPORATED
SOBEYS
6700 46 St Suite 300, Olds, AB, T4H 0A2
(403) 556-3113
Emp Here 100
SIC 5411 Grocery stores

D-U-N-S 24-632-0720   (BR)
**TECHMATION ELECTRIC & CONTROLS
LTD**
4250 47 Ave, Olds, AB, T4H 1T9
(403) 556-1517
Emp Here 30
SIC 1731 Electrical work

D-U-N-S 24-599-1950   (BR)
WAL-MART CANADA CORP
WALMART
6900 46 St Unit 400, Olds, AB, T4H 0A2
(403) 556-3844
Emp Here 50
SIC 5311 Department stores

D-U-N-S 25-507-5772   (BR)
WESTWARD PRODUCTS LTD
5901 48 Ave, Olds, AB, T4H 1V1
(403) 556-7100
Emp Here 52
SIC 3523 Farm machinery and equipment

Onoway, AB T0E

D-U-N-S 24-345-6147   (BR)
ALBERTA HEALTH SERVICES
ONOWAY COMMUNITY HEALTH
4919 Lac St, Onoway, AB, T0E 1V0
(780) 967-4136
Emp Here 37
SIC 8062 General medical and surgical hospi-
tals

D-U-N-S 25-724-3477   (BR)
**GOVERNMENT OF THE PROVINCE OF AL-
BERTA**
ASPEN HEALTH SERVICES
4919 Lac Suite Anne, Onoway, AB, T0E 1V0
(780) 967-4440
Emp Here 30
SIC 8011 Offices and clinics of medical doc-
tors

D-U-N-S 25-289-5131   (BR)
**NORTHERN GATEWAY REGIONAL DIVI-
SION #10**
ONOWAY JUNIOR/SENIOR HIGH SCHOOL
4704 Lac Ste Anne Trail N, Onoway, AB, T0E
1V0
(780) 967-2271
Emp Here 60
SIC 8211 Elementary and secondary schools

D-U-N-S 25-111-2454   (BR)
**NORTHERN GATEWAY REGIONAL DIVI-
SION #10**
ONOWAY ELEMENTARY SCHOOL
5108 Lac Ste-Anne Trail, Onoway, AB, T0E
1V0

(780) 967-5209
Emp Here 40
SIC 8211 Elementary and secondary schools

Oyen, AB T0J

D-U-N-S 24-422-4338   (BR)
ACADIA FOUNDATION
OYEN SENIORS LODGE
310 2nd St W, Oyen, AB, T0J 2J0
(403) 664-3661
Emp Here 26
SIC 8361 Residential care

D-U-N-S 25-317-0765   (BR)
ALBERTA HEALTH SERVICES
BIG COUNTRY HOSPITAL
312 3 St E, Oyen, AB, T0J 2J0
(403) 664-3528
Emp Here 110
SIC 8062 General medical and surgical hospi-
tals

D-U-N-S 20-712-0960   (BR)
PRAIRIE ROSE SCHOOL DIVISION NO 8
SOUTH CENTRAL HIGH SCHOOL
Gd, Oyen, AB, T0J 2J0
(403) 664-3644
Emp Here 50
SIC 8211 Elementary and secondary schools

D-U-N-S 20-025-5003   (BR)
PRAIRIE ROSE SCHOOL DIVISION NO 8
OYEN PUBLIC SCHOOL
107 4 Ave E, Oyen, AB, T0J 2J0
(403) 664-3733
Emp Here 22
SIC 8211 Elementary and secondary schools

Paddle Prairie, AB T0H

D-U-N-S 20-027-4830   (BR)
NORTHLAND SCHOOL DIVISION 61
PADDLE PRAIRIE SCHOOL
Gd, Paddle Prairie, AB, T0H 2W0
(780) 981-2124
Emp Here 25
SIC 8211 Elementary and secondary schools

Paradise Valley, AB T0B

D-U-N-S 25-268-7843   (BR)
**BUFFALO TRAIL PUBLIC SCHOOLS RE-
GIONAL DIVISION NO. 28**
E.H. WALTER SCHOOL
310 Park Ave, Paradise Valley, AB, T0B 3R0
(780) 745-2277
Emp Here 25
SIC 8211 Elementary and secondary schools

Patricia, AB T0J

D-U-N-S 25-361-5546   (BR)
**GOVERNMENT OF THE PROVINCE OF AL-
BERTA**
DINOSAUR PROVINCIAL PARK
Gd, Patricia, AB, T0J 2K0
(403) 378-4342
Emp Here 30
SIC 7996 Amusement parks

Peace River, AB T8S

D-U-N-S 25-686-7714   (BR)
ATCO ELECTRIC LTD
ATCO ELECTRIC
7902 104th Ave, Peace River, AB, T8S 1T9
(780) 624-6701
Emp Here 50
SIC 4911 Electric services

D-U-N-S 25-110-4246   (BR)
ALBERTA HEALTH SERVICES
PEACE REGION EMS
Lot 18 Peace River Airport, Peace River, AB, T8S 1Z1

Emp Here 20
SIC 4119 Local passenger transportation, nec

D-U-N-S 20-578-2704   (BR)
ALBERTA TREASURY BRANCHES
ETB FINANCIAL
9904 100 Ave, Peace River, AB, T8S 1S2
(780) 618-3282
Emp Here 20
SIC 6036 Savings institutions, except federal

D-U-N-S 25-182-4371   (BR)
CLEAN HARBORS ENERGY AND INDUS-TRIAL SERVICES CORP.
Gd Stn Ma n, Peace River, AB, T8S 1V8
(780) 624-1440
Emp Here 25
SIC 7699 Repair services, nec

D-U-N-S 24-810-3012   (BR)
DAISHOWA-MARUBENI INTERNATIONAL LTD
PEACE RIVER PULP DIVISION
Gd, Peace River, AB, T8S 1V7
(780) 624-7000
Emp Here 340
SIC 2611 Pulp mills

D-U-N-S 20-089-5902   (BR)
FINNING INTERNATIONAL INC
FINNING (CANADA), A DIV
(*Suby of* Finning International Inc)
8710 87th Ave, Peace River, AB, T8S 1S2
(780) 624-1550
Emp Here 60
SIC 5082 Construction and mining machinery

D-U-N-S 24-616-0951   (BR)
FIRSTCANADA ULC
10401 75 St, Peace River, AB, T8S 1R2
(780) 624-3538
Emp Here 20
SIC 4151 School buses

D-U-N-S 24-360-1486   (BR)
FRESON MARKET LTD
(*Suby of* Altamart Investments (1993) Ltd)
7900 99 Ave, Peace River, AB, T8S 1Y7
(780) 624-7673
Emp Here 75
SIC 5411 Grocery stores

D-U-N-S 24-702-9325   (BR)
GOLD STAR TRANSPORT (1975) LTD
ARROW TRANSPORTATION SYSTEMS
Gd Stn Main Peace River, AB, T8S 1V8
(780) 624-4444
Emp Here 70
SIC 4212 Local trucking, without storage

D-U-N-S 25-960-6242   (BR)
GOVERNMENT OF THE PROVINCE OF AL-BERTA
ALBERTA EMPLOYMENT & IMMIGRATION
9621 96 Ave Room 112 Provincial Building, Peace River, AB, T8S 1T4
(780) 624-6193
Emp Here 27
SIC 8399 Social services, nec

D-U-N-S 20-028-4045   (BR)
HOLY FAMILY CATHOLIC REGIONAL DIVI-SION 37
GOOD SHEPHERD SCHOOL

9810 71 Ave, Peace River, AB, T8S 1R4
(780) 624-3432
Emp Here 50
SIC 8211 Elementary and secondary schools

D-U-N-S 20-515-5570   (BR)
LOBLAWS INC
KRIS' NOFRILLS
7613 100 Ave, Peace River, AB, T8S 1M5
(780) 618-2465
Emp Here 75
SIC 5411 Grocery stores

D-U-N-S 20-576-5063   (BR)
MNP LLP
9913 98 Ave, Peace River, AB, T8S 1J5
(780) 624-3252
Emp Here 20
SIC 8721 Accounting, auditing, and book-keeping

D-U-N-S 25-943-7671   (BR)
NORTHERN ALBERTA INSTITUTE OF TECHNOLOGY
NAIT
8106 99 Ave, Peace River, AB, T8S 1V9
(780) 618-2600
Emp Here 20
SIC 8221 Colleges and universities

D-U-N-S 20-023-9429   (BR)
PEACE RIVER SCHOOL DIVISION 10
T A NORRIS MIDDLE SCHOOL
8701 95 St, Peace River, AB, T8S 1R6
(780) 624-3144
Emp Here 35
SIC 8211 Elementary and secondary schools

D-U-N-S 20-023-9437   (BR)
PEACE RIVER SCHOOL DIVISION 10
SPRINGFIELD ELEMENTARY SCHOOL
7701 99 St, Peace River, AB, T8S 1R4
(780) 624-2143
Emp Here 32
SIC 8211 Elementary and secondary schools

D-U-N-S 25-015-7765   (BR)
PEACE RIVER SCHOOL DIVISION 10
PEACE RIVER HIGH SCHOOL
10001 91 Ave, Peace River, AB, T8S 1Z5
(780) 624-4221
Emp Here 30
SIC 8211 Elementary and secondary schools

D-U-N-S 20-885-3569   (BR)
PEACE RIVER, TOWN OF
PEACE REGIONAL POOL
7201 98 St, Peace River, AB, T8S 1E2
(780) 624-3720
Emp Here 26
SIC 7999 Amusement and recreation, nec

D-U-N-S 24-807-1532   (SL)
PEACE VALLEY INNS LTD
SMITTY'S RESTAURANT
9609 101 St, Peace River, AB, T8S 1J6
(780) 624-3141
Emp Here 60   *Sales* 1,824,018
SIC 5812 Eating places

D-U-N-S 20-085-8822   (BR)
RAINBOW TRANSPORT (1974) LTD
(*Suby of* Rainbow Transport (1974) Ltd)
9700 74 St, Peace River, AB, T8S 1T3
(780) 624-1377
Emp Here 20
SIC 4731 Freight transportation arrangement

D-U-N-S 24-672-1237   (BR)
SHELL CANADA LIMITED
100 St, Peace River, AB, T8S 1V8
(780) 624-6800
Emp Here 90
SIC 1311 Crude petroleum and natural gas

D-U-N-S 25-106-4952   (SL)
STRATA OIL & GAS INC
10010 - 98 St, Peace River, AB, T8S 1T3

(403) 237-5443
Emp Here 172   *Sales* 115,204,945
SIC 1311 Crude petroleum and natural gas
Trevor Newton
VP Opers Dave Mahowich
Michael Ranger

D-U-N-S 24-025-2572   (BR)
TARPON ENERGY SERVICES LTD
8013 102 Ave, Peace River, AB, T8S 1M6
(780) 624-0900
Emp Here 40
SIC 1389 Oil and gas field services, nec

D-U-N-S 24-599-1984   (BR)
WAL-MART CANADA CORP
WALMART
9701 78 St, Peace River, AB, T8S 0A3
(780) 624-8911
Emp Here 50
SIC 5311 Department stores

Peerless Lake, AB T0G

D-U-N-S 20-591-2962   (BR)
NORTHLAND SCHOOL DIVISION 61
PEERLESS LAKE SCHOOL
Gd, Peerless Lake, AB, T0G 2W0
(780) 869-3832
Emp Here 25
SIC 8211 Elementary and secondary schools

Penhold, AB T0M

D-U-N-S 20-573-1305   (BR)
CANADA POST CORPORATION
1220 Windsor Ave, Penhold, AB, T0M 1R0
(403) 886-2450
Emp Here 20
SIC 4311 U.s. postal service

D-U-N-S 20-591-9223   (BR)
CHINOOKS EDGE SCHOOL DIVISION NO. 73
JESSIE DUNCAN ELEMENTARY SCHOOL
Gd, Penhold, AB, T0M 1R0
(403) 886-2233
Emp Here 20
SIC 8211 Elementary and secondary schools

Picture Butte, AB T0K

D-U-N-S 25-676-4481   (BR)
HOLY SPIRIT ROMAN CATHOLIC SEPA-RATE REGIONAL DIVISION NO 4
ST CATHERINE'S SCHOOL
(*Suby of* Holy Spirit Roman Catholic Separate Regional Division No 4)
300 7 St N, Picture Butte, AB, T0K 1V0
(403) 732-4359
Emp Here 25
SIC 8211 Elementary and secondary schools

D-U-N-S 25-415-2341   (BR)
PALLISER REGIONAL DIVISION NO 26
PALLISER REGIONAL SCHOOLS PICTURE BUTTE HIGH SCHOOL
401 Rogers Ave, Picture Butte, AB, T0K 1V0
(403) 732-4404
Emp Here 35
SIC 8211 Elementary and secondary schools

D-U-N-S 25-269-6950   (BR)
PALLISER REGIONAL DIVISION NO 26
DOROTHY DALGLIESH SCHOOL
400 6th St N, Picture Butte, AB, T0K 1V0
(403) 732-5636
Emp Here 34
SIC 8211 Elementary and secondary schools

Pincher Creek, AB T0K

D-U-N-S 25-273-5378   (BR)
ALBERTA HEALTH SERVICES
PINCHER CREEK HOSPITAL
1222 Bev Mclachlin Dr, Pincher Creek, AB, T0K 1W0
(403) 627-1234
Emp Here 100
SIC 8062 General medical and surgical hospi-tals

D-U-N-S 25-231-7482   (BR)
ALBERTA TREASURY BRANCHES
PINCHER CREEK LOCATION
769 Main St, Pincher Creek, AB, T0K 1W0
(403) 627-3304
Emp Here 21
SIC 6036 Savings institutions, except federal

D-U-N-S 24-085-4906   (BR)
ENERSUL LIMITED PARTNERSHIP
Gd, Pincher Creek, AB, T0K 1W0
(403) 627-2675
Emp Here 27
SIC 1389 Oil and gas field services, nec

D-U-N-S 24-442-5898   (BR)
FIRSTCANADA ULC
AIRPORTER BUS SERVICE
921 Davidson Ave, Pincher Creek, AB, T0K 1W0
(403) 627-3060
Emp Here 30
SIC 4151 School buses

D-U-N-S 24-043-8700   (BR)
GOOD SAMARITAN SOCIETY, THE (A LUTHERAN SOCIAL SERVICE ORGANIZA-TION)
VISTA VILLAGE
1240 Ken Thornton Blvd, Pincher Creek, AB, T0K 1W0
(403) 627-1900
Emp Here 50
SIC 8361 Residential care

D-U-N-S 20-711-9038   (BR)
HOLY SPIRIT ROMAN CATHOLIC SEPA-RATE REGIONAL DIVISION NO 4
ST MICHAEL'S SCHOOL
(*Suby of* Holy Spirit Roman Catholic Separate Regional Division No 4)
864 Christie Ave, Pincher Creek, AB, T0K 1W0
(403) 627-3488
Emp Here 40
SIC 8211 Elementary and secondary schools

D-U-N-S 24-442-4222   (SL)
HUTTERIAN BRETHREN OF PINCHER CREEK AS A CHURCH, THE
Gd, Pincher Creek, AB, T0K 1W0
(403) 627-4021
Emp Here 74   *Sales* 4,888,367
SIC 8661 Religious organizations

D-U-N-S 20-294-0750   (BR)
LIVINGSTONE RANGE SCHOOL DIVISION NO 68
MATTHEW HALTON HIGH SCHOOL
945 Davidson Ave, Pincher Creek, AB, T0K 1W0
(403) 627-4414
Emp Here 31
SIC 8211 Elementary and secondary schools

D-U-N-S 25-990-0397   (BR)
PHARMX REXALL DRUG STORES (AL-BERTA) LTD
HIGA'S REXALL
789 Main St, Pincher Creek, AB, T0K 1W0
(403) 627-3195
Emp Here 20
SIC 5912 Drug stores and proprietary stores

D-U-N-S 24-272-6115   (BR)
SHELL CANADA LIMITED
SHELL WATERTON COMPLEX
Po Box 1088, Pincher Creek, AB, T0K 1W0
(403) 627-7200
Emp Here 150
SIC 1311 Crude petroleum and natural gas

D-U-N-S 24-133-2860   (BR)
SOBEYS CAPITAL INCORPORATED
819 Main St, Pincher Creek, AB, T0K 1W0
Emp Here 45
SIC 5411 Grocery stores

D-U-N-S 24-330-0535   (BR)
WAL-MART CANADA CORP
1100 Table Mountain Rd, Pincher Creek, AB,
T0K 1W0
(403) 627-1790
Emp Here 200
SIC 5311 Department stores

Plamondon, AB T0A

D-U-N-S 20-029-3251   (BR)
**NORTHERN LIGHTS SCHOOL DIVISION
NO. 69**
ECOLE PLAMONDON SCHOOL
9814 100 St, Plamondon, AB, T0A 2T0
(780) 798-3840
Emp Here 40
SIC 8211 Elementary and secondary schools

Ponoka, AB T4J

D-U-N-S 20-719-9642   (BR)
ALBERTA HEALTH SERVICES
CENTENNIAL CENTRE, THE
Gd Stn Main, Ponoka, AB, T4J 1R9
(403) 783-7600
Emp Here 900
SIC 8011 Offices and clinics of medical doctors

D-U-N-S 24-351-8326   (BR)
ALBERTA HEALTH SERVICES
PONOKA HOSPITAL & CARE CENTRE
5800 57 Ave, Ponoka, AB, T4J 1P1
(403) 783-3341
Emp Here 200
SIC 8062 General medical and surgical hospitals

D-U-N-S 20-271-8487   (BR)
ALBERTA HEALTH SERVICES
PONOKA COMMUNITY HEALTH CENTRE
5900 Highway 2a, Ponoka, AB, T4J 1P5
(403) 783-4491
Emp Here 25
SIC 8011 Offices and clinics of medical doctors

D-U-N-S 24-308-9997   (BR)
BIG COUNTRY ENERGY SERVICES LIMITED PARTNERSHIP
6709 44 Ave, Ponoka, AB, T4J 1J8
Emp Here 100
SIC 1623 Water, sewer, and utility lines

D-U-N-S 20-513-7966   (BR)
CANADIAN IMPERIAL BANK OF COMMERCE
CIBC
5002 50 St, Ponoka, AB, T4J 1R7
(403) 783-5581
Emp Here 20
SIC 6021 National commercial banks

D-U-N-S 24-359-0168   (BR)
CERVUS LP

6610 46 Ave, Ponoka, AB, T4J 1J8
(403) 783-3337
Emp Here 25
SIC 5083 Farm and garden machinery

D-U-N-S 20-273-0243   (BR)
ENCANA CORPORATION
Gd Stn Main, Ponoka, AB, T4J 1R9
Emp Here 30
SIC 1382 Oil and gas exploration services

D-U-N-S 25-290-9932   (BR)
ENCANA CORPORATION
ENCANA RESOURCES
4205 Highway 2a, Ponoka, AB, T4J 1V9
(403) 783-4929
Emp Here 57
SIC 1382 Oil and gas exploration services

D-U-N-S 25-361-0257   (BR)
GEMINI FIELD SOLUTIONS LTD
4100 67 St, Ponoka, AB, T4J 1J8
(403) 783-3365
Emp Here 140
SIC 7692 Welding repair

D-U-N-S 24-643-6919   (SL)
HUTTERIAN BRETHREN CHURCH OF FERRYBANK
FERRYBANK COLONY
Gd, Ponoka, AB, T4J 1R9
(403) 783-2259
Emp Here 70   *Sales* 5,457,381
SIC 8661 Religious organizations

D-U-N-S 20-283-3349   (BR)
LKQ CANADA AUTO PARTS INC
LKQ ALBERTA
430054 Don Laing Busine Pk Rr 4 Stn Main,
Ponoka, AB, T4J 1R4
(403) 783-5189
Emp Here 20
SIC 5531 Auto and home supply stores

D-U-N-S 20-969-4942   (SL)
NORTHCOTT LODGE NURSING HOME LTD
NORTHCOTT CARE CENTRE
4209 48 Ave, Ponoka, AB, T4J 1P4
(403) 783-4764
Emp Here 60   *Sales* 2,699,546
SIC 8051 Skilled nursing care facilities

D-U-N-S 20-798-6428   (BR)
PHARMX REXALL DRUG STORES (ALBERTA) LTD
REXALL
4502 50 St, Ponoka, AB, T4J 1J5
(403) 783-5568
Emp Here 30
SIC 5912 Drug stores and proprietary stores

D-U-N-S 25-482-5441   (BR)
ST THOMAS AQUINAS ROMAN CATHOLIC SEPARATE REGIONAL DIVISION #38
ST AUGUSTINE SCHOOL
5520 45 Ave Cres, Ponoka, AB, T4J 1N6
(403) 704-1155
Emp Here 50
SIC 8211 Elementary and secondary schools

D-U-N-S 24-375-3469   (BR)
VITERRA INC
VITERRA
6701 44 Ave, Ponoka, AB, T4J 1J8
(403) 783-6037
Emp Here 20
SIC 4221 Farm product warehousing and storage

D-U-N-S 25-766-5075   (BR)
WENDY'S RESTAURANTS OF CANADA INC
WENDY'S
(*Suby of* The Wendy's Company)
4750 Highway 2a, Ponoka, AB, T4J 1K3
(403) 783-6338
Emp Here 30
SIC 5812 Eating places

D-U-N-S 20-200-1363   (BR)
WOLF CREEK SCHOOL DIVISION NO.72
DIAMOND WILLOW MIDDLE SCHOOL
5510 48 Ave, Ponoka, AB, T4J 1N7
Emp Here 30
SIC 8211 Elementary and secondary schools

D-U-N-S 20-297-1755   (BR)
WOLF CREEK SCHOOL DIVISION NO.72
PONOKA COMPOSITE HIGHSCHOOL
6002 54 Ave, Ponoka, AB, T4J 1N9
(403) 783-4411
Emp Here 50
SIC 8211 Elementary and secondary schools

D-U-N-S 20-710-1598   (BR)
WOLF CREEK SCHOOL DIVISION NO.72
PONOKA ELEMENTARY SCHOOL
5004 54 St, Ponoka, AB, T4J 1N8
(403) 783-3583
Emp Here 50
SIC 8211 Elementary and secondary schools

D-U-N-S 20-710-1994   (BR)
WOLF CREEK SCHOOL DIVISION NO.72
PONOKA OUTREACH SCHOOL
Gd Stn Main, Ponoka, AB, T4J 1R9
(403) 783-5464
Emp Here 20
SIC 8211 Elementary and secondary schools

D-U-N-S 25-496-4109   (HQ)
WOLF CREEK SCHOOL DIVISION NO.72
WOLF CREEK PUBLIC SCHOOL
(*Suby of* Wolf Creek School Division No.72)
6000 Highway 2a, Ponoka, AB, T4J 1P6
(403) 783-3473
Emp Here 45   *Emp Total* 1,000
Sales 92,039,680
SIC 8211 Elementary and secondary schools
Treas Joe Henderson
Superintnt Larry Jacobs

Provost, AB T0B

D-U-N-S 20-897-0012   (BR)
ALBERTA HEALTH SERVICES
PROVOST HEALTH CENTRE
5002 54 Ave, Provost, AB, T0B 3S0
(780) 753-2291
Emp Here 100
SIC 8062 General medical and surgical hospitals

D-U-N-S 20-578-2738   (BR)
ALBERTA TREASURY BRANCHES
ATB FINANCIAL
5013 50th St, Provost, AB, T0B 3S0
(780) 753-2247
Emp Here 20
SIC 6036 Savings institutions, except federal

D-U-N-S 20-020-7178   (BR)
BUFFALO TRAIL PUBLIC SCHOOLS REGIONAL DIVISION NO. 28
PROVOST PUBLIC SCHOOL
4504 52 Ave, Provost, AB, T0B 3S0
(780) 753-6824
Emp Here 50
SIC 8211 Elementary and secondary schools

D-U-N-S 24-377-7906   (BR)
CLEAN HARBORS ENERGY AND INDUSTRIAL SERVICES CORP.
3605 57 Ave, Provost, AB, T0B 3S0
(780) 753-6149
Emp Here 20
SIC 7349 Building maintenance services, nec

D-U-N-S 25-315-1542   (BR)
PYRAMID CORPORATION
5519 36 St, Provost, AB, T0B 3S0
(780) 753-4700
Emp Here 20

SIC 1731 Electrical work

D-U-N-S 20-279-9867   (BR)
TRICAN WELL SERVICE LTD
TRICAN OILWELL SERVICE
25 Wheatland Cres, Provost, AB, T0B 3S0
Emp Here 21
SIC 1389 Oil and gas field services, nec

D-U-N-S 24-802-6648   (BR)
WITHERS L.P.
LEACHMAN OILFIELD TRUCKING, DIV OF
Gd, Provost, AB, T0B 3S0
(780) 753-2976
Emp Here 40
SIC 4213 Trucking, except local

Rainbow Lake, AB T0H

D-U-N-S 25-316-7035   (BR)
AECOM PRODUCTION SERVICES LTD
FLINT FIELD SERVICES LTD
53 Imperial Dr, Rainbow Lake, AB, T0H 2Y0
(780) 956-3941
Emp Here 25
SIC 1629 Heavy construction, nec

D-U-N-S 20-577-1491   (BR)
FORT VERMILION SCHOOL DIVISON 52
RAINBOW LAKE SCHOOL
(*Suby of* Fort Vermilion School Divison 52)
2 Neander Cres, Rainbow Lake, AB, T0H 2Y0
(780) 956-3851
Emp Here 30
SIC 8211 Elementary and secondary schools

D-U-N-S 24-075-5723   (BR)
HARVEST OPERATIONS CORP
Gd, Rainbow Lake, AB, T0H 2Y0
(780) 956-3771
Emp Here 23
SIC 1311 Crude petroleum and natural gas

D-U-N-S 25-971-6314   (BR)
HUSKY OIL OPERATIONS LIMITED
Hwy 58 W, Rainbow Lake, AB, T0H 2Y0
(780) 956-8000
Emp Here 175
SIC 1311 Crude petroleum and natural gas

D-U-N-S 20-169-8458   (SL)
NORTHGATE CONTRACTORS INC
41 Home Rd, Rainbow Lake, AB, T0H 2Y0
(780) 448-9222
Emp Here 40   *Sales* 5,275,400
SIC 6531 Real estate agents and managers
Pr Pr Sid Braaksma

Ralston, AB T0J

D-U-N-S 25-174-8596   (BR)
PRAIRIE ROSE SCHOOL DIVISION NO 8
RALSTON SCHOOL
17 Dugway St, Ralston, AB, T0J 2N0
(403) 544-3535
Emp Here 21
SIC 8211 Elementary and secondary schools

Raymond, AB T0K

D-U-N-S 25-483-4906   (BR)
GOVERNMENT OF THE PROVINCE OF ALBERTA
GOVERNMENT OF THE PROVINCE OF ALBERTA
150 N 400 E, Raymond, AB, T0K 2S0
(403) 752-5411
Emp Here 100

SIC 8062 General medical and surgical hospitals

D-U-N-S 20-711-4310　　(BR)
WESTWIND SCHOOL DIVISION #74
MILFORD SCHOOL
Gd, Raymond, AB, T0K 2S0
(403) 752-4014
Emp Here 50
SIC 8211 Elementary and secondary schools

D-U-N-S 20-911-5083　　(BR)
WESTWIND SCHOOL DIVISION #74
RAYMOND SENIOR HIGH SCHOOL
65w 100 N, Raymond, AB, T0K 2S0
(403) 752-3381
Emp Here 20
SIC 8211 Elementary and secondary schools

D-U-N-S 20-711-4534　　(BR)
WESTWIND SCHOOL DIVISION #74
RAYMOND HIGH SCHOOL
65 W 100 N, Raymond, AB, T0K 2S0
(403) 752-3348
Emp Here 50
SIC 8211 Elementary and secondary schools

D-U-N-S 20-588-3858　　(BR)
WESTWIND SCHOOL DIVISION #74
RAYMOND ELEMENTARY SCHOOL
145 N 200 W, Raymond, AB, T0K 2S0
(403) 752-3004
Emp Here 75
SIC 8211 Elementary and secondary schools

Red Deer, AB T4E

D-U-N-S 24-802-1219　　(BR)
V.D.M. TRUCKING SERVICE LTD
37428 Range Road 273, Red Deer, AB, T4E 0A1

Emp Here 20
SIC 4213 Trucking, except local

Red Deer, AB T4N

D-U-N-S 25-136-8940　　(BR)
287706 ALBERTA LTD
STANFORD INN
4707 50 St, Red Deer, AB, T4N 1X3

Emp Here 30
SIC 7011 Hotels and motels

D-U-N-S 25-268-5698　　(SL)
341-7777 TAXI LTD
ALBERTA GOLD TAXI
4819 48 Ave Unit 280, Red Deer, AB, T4N 3T2
(403) 341-7777
Emp Here 85　　*Sales* 2,553,625
SIC 4121 Taxicabs

D-U-N-S 25-538-3762　　(SL)
633515 ALBERTA LTD
LOCKHART OILFIELD SERVICES
4422 33a St, Red Deer, AB, T4N 0N8
(403) 347-7861
Emp Here 34　　*Sales* 5,985,550
SIC 1389 Oil and gas field services, nec
Pr Pr Kevin Lockhart
Myriam Lockhart

D-U-N-S 25-271-3516　　(BR)
7-ELEVEN CANADA, INC
7-ELEVEN STORE #26940
5925 54 Ave, Red Deer, AB, T4N 4M7
(403) 343-7111
Emp Here 20
SIC 5411 Grocery stores

D-U-N-S 25-947-4971　　(BR)

AGRIFOODS INTERNATIONAL COOPERATIVE LTD
5410 50 Ave, Red Deer, AB, T4N 4B5
(403) 357-3861
Emp Here 100
SIC 2021 Creamery butter

D-U-N-S 24-674-9337　　(BR)
AGRIUM INC
(*Suby of* Agrium Canada Partnership)
Gd Stn Postal Box Ctr, Red Deer, AB, T4N 5E6
(403) 885-4010
Emp Here 31
SIC 2873 Nitrogenous fertilizers

D-U-N-S 24-731-6839　　(SL)
AIRFLO HEATING & AIR CONDITIONING LTD
6013 48 Ave, Red Deer, AB, T4N 3V5
(403) 340-3866
Emp Here 30　　*Sales* 2,626,585
SIC 1711 Plumbing, heating, air-conditioning

D-U-N-S 20-058-4253　　(BR)
ALBERTA HEALTH SERVICES
TEEN/YOUNG ADULT SEXUAL HEALTH CLINIC
4755 49 St Unit 2, Red Deer, AB, T4N 1T6
(403) 346-8336
Emp Here 53
SIC 8093 Specialty outpatient clinics, nec

D-U-N-S 25-367-5862　　(BR)
ALBERTA HEALTH SERVICES
MENTAL HEALTH SERVICES
4920 51 St Suite 202, Red Deer, AB, T4N 6K8
(403) 340-5103
Emp Here 75
SIC 8093 Specialty outpatient clinics, nec

D-U-N-S 25-764-2181　　(BR)
ALBERTA HEALTH SERVICES
RED DEER NURSING HOME
4736 30 St, Red Deer, AB, T4N 5H8

Emp Here 100
SIC 8051 Skilled nursing care facilities

D-U-N-S 24-160-2002　　(BR)
ALBERTA HEALTH SERVICES
RED DEER REGIONAL HOSPITAL CENTRE
3942 50a Ave, Red Deer, AB, T4N 4E7
(403) 343-4422
Emp Here 3,000
SIC 8062 General medical and surgical hospitals

D-U-N-S 25-236-1910　　(BR)
ALBERTA TREASURY BRANCHES
ATB FINANCIAL
4919 59 St Suite 101, Red Deer, AB, T4N 6C9
(403) 340-5384
Emp Here 20
SIC 6036 Savings institutions, except federal

D-U-N-S 25-236-1878　　(BR)
ALBERTA TREASURY BRANCHES
ATB FINANCIAL
4911 51 St Suite 100, Red Deer, AB, T4N 6V4
(403) 340-5130
Emp Here 25
SIC 6159 Miscellaneous business credit institutions

D-U-N-S 25-777-0073　　(SL)
ASPIRE SPECIAL NEEDS RESOURCE SOCIETY
4826 47 St, Red Deer, AB, T4N 1R2
(403) 340-2606
Emp Here 70　　*Sales* 2,772,507
SIC 8322 Individual and family services

D-U-N-S 25-037-5813　　(SL)
ASSOCIATE CLINIC
4705 48 Ave, Red Deer, AB, T4N 3T1
(403) 346-2057
Emp Here 50　　*Sales* 3,863,549
SIC 8011 Offices and clinics of medical doc-

tors

D-U-N-S 25-960-0666　　(BR)
BANK OF NOVA SCOTIA, THE
SCOTIABANK
4421 50 Ave, Red Deer, AB, T4N 3Z5
(403) 340-4794
Emp Here 25
SIC 6021 National commercial banks

D-U-N-S 25-776-9992　　(BR)
BANK OF NOVA SCOTIA, THE
SCOTIABANK
5002 50 St, Red Deer, AB, T4N 1Y3
(403) 340-4780
Emp Here 25
SIC 6021 National commercial banks

D-U-N-S 20-710-3297　　(BR)
BOARD OF TRUSTEES OF THE RED DEER PUBLIC SCHOOL DISTRICT NO. 104, THE
NORTH COLLEGE HIGHSCHOOL
5704 50 St, Red Deer, AB, T4N 6V6
(403) 342-2170
Emp Here 50
SIC 8211 Elementary and secondary schools

D-U-N-S 20-003-5124　　(BR)
BOARD OF TRUSTEES OF THE RED DEER PUBLIC SCHOOL DISTRICT NO. 104, THE
ECOLE ORIOLE PARK SCHOOL
5 Oldbury St, Red Deer, AB, T4N 5A8
(403) 347-3731
Emp Here 30
SIC 8211 Elementary and secondary schools

D-U-N-S 20-003-5116　　(BR)
BOARD OF TRUSTEES OF THE RED DEER PUBLIC SCHOOL DISTRICT NO. 104, THE
WELSH, JOSEPH ELEMENTARY SCHOOL
4401 37 Ave, Red Deer, AB, T4N 2T5
(403) 346-6377
Emp Here 30
SIC 8211 Elementary and secondary schools

D-U-N-S 20-003-5090　　(BR)
BOARD OF TRUSTEES OF THE RED DEER PUBLIC SCHOOL DISTRICT NO. 104, THE
FAIRVIEW ELEMENTARY SCHOOL
5901 55 St, Red Deer, AB, T4N 7C8
(403) 343-8780
Emp Here 25
SIC 8211 Elementary and secondary schools

D-U-N-S 20-710-3404　　(BR)
BOARD OF TRUSTEES OF THE RED DEER PUBLIC SCHOOL DISTRICT NO. 104, THE
4720 49 St, Red Deer, AB, T4N 1T7
(403) 340-3200
Emp Here 50
SIC 8211 Elementary and secondary schools

D-U-N-S 20-003-5082　　(BR)
BOARD OF TRUSTEES OF THE RED DEER PUBLIC SCHOOL DISTRICT NO. 104, THE
ANNIE L GAETZ ELEMENTARY SCHOOL
32 Mitchell Ave, Red Deer, AB, T4N 0L6
(403) 347-5660
Emp Here 30
SIC 8211 Elementary and secondary schools

D-U-N-S 25-273-5394　　(BR)
BOARD OF TRUSTEES OF THE RED DEER PUBLIC SCHOOL DISTRICT NO. 104, THE
LINDSAY THURBER COMPREHENSIVE HIGH SCHOOL
4204 58 St, Red Deer, AB, T4N 2L6
(403) 347-1171
Emp Here 160
SIC 8211 Elementary and secondary schools

D-U-N-S 25-454-8811　　(BR)
BOARD OF TRUSTEES OF THE RED DEER PUBLIC SCHOOL DISTRICT NO. 104, THE
EASTVIEW MIDDLE SCHOOL
3929 40 Ave, Red Deer, AB, T4N 2W5
(403) 343-2455
Emp Here 70

SIC 8211 Elementary and secondary schools

D-U-N-S 20-710-3743　　(BR)
BOARD OF TRUSTEES OF THE RED DEER PUBLIC SCHOOL DISTRICT NO. 104, THE
GATEWAY CHRISTIAN SCHOOL
5205 48 Ave, Red Deer, AB, T4N 6X3
(403) 346-5795
Emp Here 40
SIC 8211 Elementary and secondary schools

D-U-N-S 20-039-3739　　(BR)
BOARD OF TRUSTEES OF THE RED DEER PUBLIC SCHOOL DISTRICT NO. 104, THE
GRANDVIEW ELEMENTARY SCHOOL
4145 46 St, Red Deer, AB, T4N 3C5
(403) 346-3223
Emp Here 30
SIC 8211 Elementary and secondary schools

D-U-N-S 20-003-5132　　(BR)
BOARD OF TRUSTEES OF THE RED DEER PUBLIC SCHOOL DISTRICT NO. 104, THE
WEST PARK ELEMENTARY SCHOOL
3814 55 Ave, Red Deer, AB, T4N 4N3
(403) 343-1838
Emp Here 35
SIC 8211 Elementary and secondary schools

D-U-N-S 20-710-3099　　(BR)
BOARD OF TRUSTEES OF THE RED DEER PUBLIC SCHOOL DISTRICT NO. 104, THE
56 Holt St, Red Deer, AB, T4N 6A6
(403) 343-3288
Emp Here 50
SIC 8211 Elementary and secondary schools

D-U-N-S 20-710-2885　　(BR)
BOARD OF TRUSTEES OF THE RED DEER PUBLIC SCHOOL DISTRICT NO. 104, THE
G W SMITH SCHOOL
17 Springfield Ave, Red Deer, AB, T4N 0C6
(403) 346-3838
Emp Here 30
SIC 8211 Elementary and secondary schools

D-U-N-S 20-025-4709　　(BR)
BOARD OF TRUSTEES OF THE RED DEER PUBLIC SCHOOL DISTRICT NO. 104, THE
ECOLE MOUNTVIEW SCHOOL
4331 34 St, Red Deer, AB, T4N 0N9
(403) 346-5765
Emp Here 25
SIC 8211 Elementary and secondary schools

D-U-N-S 20-025-4691　　(BR)
BOARD OF TRUSTEES OF THE RED DEER PUBLIC SCHOOL DISTRICT NO. 104, THE
ECOLE CENTRAL MIDDLE SCHOOL
5121 48 Ave, Red Deer, AB, T4N 6X3
(403) 346-4397
Emp Here 40
SIC 8211 Elementary and secondary schools

D-U-N-S 20-025-4717　　(BR)
BOARD OF TRUSTEES OF THE RED DEER PUBLIC SCHOOL DISTRICT NO. 104, THE
WEST PARK MIDDLE SCHOOL
3310 55 Ave, Red Deer, AB, T4N 4N1
(403) 347-8911
Emp Here 30
SIC 8211 Elementary and secondary schools

D-U-N-S 20-572-9143　　(BR)
CANADA POST CORPORATION
4909 50 St, Red Deer, AB, T4N 1X8

Emp Here 20
SIC 4311 U.s. postal service

D-U-N-S 20-245-5197　　(BR)
CANADIAN BLOOD SERVICES
5020 68 St Suite 5, Red Deer, AB, T4N 7B4
(403) 309-3378
Emp Here 40
SIC 8099 Health and allied services, nec

D-U-N-S 25-316-0451　　(BR)
CANADIAN WESTERN BANK

4822 51 Ave, Red Deer, AB, T4N 4H3
(403) 341-4000
Emp Here 21
SIC 6021 National commercial banks

D-U-N-S 24-373-4733   (BR)
CANYON TECHNICAL SERVICES LTD
28042 Hwy 11 Unit 322, Red Deer, AB, T4N 5H3
(403) 309-0505
Emp Here 120
SIC 1389 Oil and gas field services, nec

D-U-N-S 24-346-3002   (BR)
CATHOLIC SOCIAL SERVICES
5104 48 Ave, Red Deer, AB, T4N 3T8
(403) 347-8844
Emp Here 500
SIC 8361 Residential care

D-U-N-S 25-273-5618   (BR)
CHINOOKS EDGE SCHOOL DIVISION NO. 73
RIVER GLEN SCHOOL
4210 59 St, Red Deer, AB, T4N 2M9
(403) 346-4755
Emp Here 30
SIC 8211 Elementary and secondary schools

D-U-N-S 20-555-2610   (BR)
CHOICES IN COMMUNITY LIVING INC
WEST PARK LODGE, THE
(*Suby of* Choices in Community Living Inc)
5715 41 Street Cres, Red Deer, AB, T4N 1B3
(403) 343-7471
Emp Here 25
SIC 8741 Management services

D-U-N-S 25-783-6502   (BR)
CITY OF RED DEER, THE
RECREATION, PARKS AND CULTURE
4501 47a Ave, Red Deer, AB, T4N 6Z6

Emp Here 20
SIC 7999 Amusement and recreation, nec

D-U-N-S 20-919-6968   (BR)
CITY OF RED DEER, THE
IT SERVICES
4914 48 Ave, Red Deer, AB, T4N 3T3
(403) 342-8392
Emp Here 30
SIC 4813 Telephone communication, except radio

D-U-N-S 20-041-0038   (BR)
CITY OF RED DEER, THE
ENVIRONMENTAL SERVICES
Gd, Red Deer, AB, T4N 3T4
(403) 342-8750
Emp Here 50
SIC 4953 Refuse systems

D-U-N-S 20-956-3076   (BR)
COMPAGNIE DES CHEMINS DE FER NATIONAUX DU CANADA
4647 61 St, Red Deer, AB, T4N 2R2
(403) 443-2350
Emp Here 100
SIC 4011 Railroads, line-haul operating

D-U-N-S 24-906-5392   (BR)
DOW CHEMICAL CANADA ULC
ALBERTA OPERATIONS, PRENTISS SITE
(*Suby of* The Dow Chemical Company)
Gd, Red Deer, AB, T4N 6N1
(403) 885-7000
Emp Here 202
SIC 2899 Chemical preparations, nec

D-U-N-S 20-063-4843   (BR)
DYNALIFEDX
5002 55 St Suite 101, Red Deer, AB, T4N 7A4
(403) 347-3588
Emp Here 30
SIC 8071 Medical laboratories

D-U-N-S 25-014-1876   (BR)
EAST CENTRAL ALBERTA CATHOLIC

SEPERATE SCHOOLS REGIONAL DIVISION NO 16
ST. THOMAS AQUINAS SCHOOL
4403 52 Ave, Red Deer, AB, T4N 6S4
(780) 753-6838
Emp Here 24
SIC 8211 Elementary and secondary schools

D-U-N-S 25-274-2804   (BR)
EMCO CORPORATION
4605 61 St, Red Deer, AB, T4N 6Z2
(403) 346-7300
Emp Here 25
SIC 5074 Plumbing and heating equipment and supplies (hydronics)

D-U-N-S 24-340-2596   (BR)
FGL SPORTS LTD
SPORT CHEK PARKLAND MALL
4747 67 St Unit 150, Red Deer, AB, T4N 6H3
(403) 346-1244
Emp Here 40
SIC 5941 Sporting goods and bicycle shops

D-U-N-S 25-169-1358   (HQ)
FUTURE AG INC
(*Suby of* Future AG Inc)
37337 Burnt Lake Trail Unit 69, Red Deer, AB, T4N 5G1
(403) 343-6101
Emp Here 21   *Emp Total* 39
Sales 10,931,016
SIC 5083 Farm and garden machinery
Genl Mgr Larry Watt
Pr Pr Josef Felder

D-U-N-S 20-152-8895   (BR)
GOVERNMENT OF THE PROVINCE OF ALBERTA
ADDICTION AND MENTAL HEALTH SERVICES
4733 49 St, Red Deer, AB, T4N 1T6
(403) 340-5466
Emp Here 100
SIC 8093 Specialty outpatient clinics, nec

D-U-N-S 20-587-2828   (BR)
GOVERNMENT OF THE PROVINCE OF ALBERTA
GOVERNMENT OF THE PROVINCE OF ALBERTA
4920 51 St Suite 103, Red Deer, AB, T4N 6K8
(403) 340-5180
Emp Here 20
SIC 8322 Individual and family services

D-U-N-S 25-272-4075   (BR)
GREAT PACIFIC INDUSTRIES INC
SAVE-ON-FOODS
6720 52 Ave, Red Deer, AB, T4N 4K9
(403) 343-7744
Emp Here 150
SIC 5411 Grocery stores

D-U-N-S 20-744-1676   (SL)
HAMILL'S DRIVE INN LTD
HAMILL'S DAIRY QUEEN BRAZIER
4202 50 Ave, Red Deer, AB, T4N 3Z3
(403) 346-3518
Emp Here 50   *Sales* 1,532,175
SIC 5812 Eating places

D-U-N-S 24-029-2131   (SL)
IP FABRICATIONS LTD
6835 52 Ave, Red Deer, AB, T4N 4L2
(403) 343-1797
Emp Here 51   *Sales* 4,450,603
SIC 1799 Special trade contractors, nec

D-U-N-S 24-420-4603   (SL)
INEOS CANADA COMPANY
Gd Stn Postal Box Ctr, Red Deer, AB, T4N 5E6
(403) 314-4500
Emp Here 86   *Sales* 14,899,517
SIC 6712 Bank holding companies
Dir Robert Learman
 Barry Mackenzie
Fin Ex Gary Cole

D-U-N-S 20-544-9817   (BR)
INVESTORS GROUP FINANCIAL SERVICES INC
4909 49 St Suite 200, Red Deer, AB, T4N 1V1
(403) 343-7030
Emp Here 50
SIC 8741 Management services

D-U-N-S 24-324-1069   (BR)
K & C SILVICULTURE LTD
Gd Stn Postal Box Ctr Box, Red Deer, AB, T4N 5E6

Emp Here 26
SIC 5261 Retail nurseries and garden stores

D-U-N-S 24-809-2595   (BR)
KAL TIRE LTD
5030 67 St, Red Deer, AB, T4N 2R6
(403) 346-4124
Emp Here 38
SIC 5531 Auto and home supply stores

D-U-N-S 24-807-2365   (BR)
KAL TIRE LTD
KAL SPRING & STEERING
6719 52 Ave, Red Deer, AB, T4N 4K8
(403) 343-2255
Emp Here 30
SIC 5531 Auto and home supply stores

D-U-N-S 24-982-1745   (BR)
LOBLAWS INC
REAL CANADIAN SUPERSTORE
5016 51 Ave, Red Deer, AB, T4N 4H5
(403) 350-3531
Emp Here 200
SIC 5411 Grocery stores

D-U-N-S 24-802-8404   (BR)
MEGLOBAL CANADA INC
Hwy 597 Prentiss Rd, Red Deer, AB, T4N 6N1
(403) 885-7000
Emp Here 100
SIC 5169 Chemicals and allied products, nec

D-U-N-S 25-318-5748   (BR)
MORNEAU SHEPELL LTD
SHEPPELL FGI DIV OF
(*Suby of* Morneau Shepell Inc)
4808 50 St Suite 50, Red Deer, AB, T4N 1X5

Emp Here 30
SIC 8999 Services, nec

D-U-N-S 24-125-6275   (BR)
NEWCAP INC
4920 59 St, Red Deer, AB, T4N 2N1
(403) 343-1170
Emp Here 50
SIC 4832 Radio broadcasting stations

D-U-N-S 20-090-3961   (SL)
NORTHWEST MOTORS (RED DEER) LIMITED
3115 50 Ave, Red Deer, AB, T4N 3X8
(403) 346-2035
Emp Here 65   *Sales* 23,712,228
SIC 5511 New and used car dealers
Pr Pr Graham Moore
 Fred Moore
 Brent Moore
Dir Daniel T. Moore
Dir Ruth M. Moore
Dir Joanne K. Moore
Dir Isabelle Moore
Dir Laura Moore
Dir Carla Moore

D-U-N-S 24-599-3704   (SL)
OGILVIE, BRIAN HOLDING LTD
88 Howarth St Suite 5, Red Deer, AB, T4N 6V9
(403) 342-6307
Emp Here 67   *Sales* 12,459,520
SIC 5541 Gasoline service stations
Pr Pr Brian Ogilvie

D-U-N-S 25-217-5500   (SL)
PARKLAND COMMUNITY LIVING AND SUPPORTS SOCIETY
PARKLAND C.L.A.S.S.
6010 45 Ave, Red Deer, AB, T4N 3M4
(403) 347-3333
Emp Here 600   *Sales* 28,760,880
SIC 8322 Individual and family services
Ex Dir Phillip Stephan

D-U-N-S 25-316-4297   (BR)
PASLEY, MAX ENTERPRISES LIMITED
MCDONALD'S RESTAURANTS 7031
(*Suby of* Pasley, Max Enterprises Limited)
7149 50 Ave, Red Deer, AB, T4N 4E4
(403) 342-2226
Emp Here 80
SIC 5812 Eating places

D-U-N-S 25-315-1807   (BR)
PASLEY, MAX ENTERPRISES LIMITED
MCDONALD'S RESTAURANTS
(*Suby of* Pasley, Max Enterprises Limited)
4840 52 Ave, Red Deer, AB, T4N 6Y8
(403) 347-7171
Emp Here 42
SIC 5812 Eating places

D-U-N-S 24-905-8082   (BR)
PHIL'S RESTAURANTS LTD
PHIL'S PANCAKE HOUSE
(*Suby of* Phil's Restaurants Ltd)
4312 49 Ave, Red Deer, AB, T4N 3W6
(403) 347-1220
Emp Here 30
SIC 5812 Eating places

D-U-N-S 24-906-1888   (HQ)
PIPER CREEK FOUNDATION
(*Suby of* Piper Creek Foundation)
4901 48 St Suite 402, Red Deer, AB, T4N 6M4
(403) 343-1077
Emp Here 66   *Emp Total* 76
Sales 2,772,507
SIC 8361 Residential care

D-U-N-S 20-636-5322   (SL)
PRAIRIE BUS LINES LTD
5310 54 St, Red Deer, AB, T4N 6M1
(403) 342-6390
Emp Here 90   *Sales* 2,553,625
SIC 4151 School buses

D-U-N-S 20-027-3881   (BR)
RED DEER CATHOLIC REGIONAL DIVISION NO. 39
ST MARTIN DE PORRES SCHOOL
3911 57a Ave, Red Deer, AB, T4N 4T1
(403) 347-5650
Emp Here 30
SIC 8211 Elementary and secondary schools

D-U-N-S 20-652-8270   (BR)
RED DEER CATHOLIC REGIONAL DIVISION NO. 39
ST GABRIEL CYBER SCHOOL
2014915 54th St, Red Deer, AB, T4N 2G7
(403) 314-9382
Emp Here 20
SIC 8211 Elementary and secondary schools

D-U-N-S 20-710-3966   (BR)
RED DEER CATHOLIC REGIONAL DIVISION NO. 39
ECOLE CAMILLE J. LAROUGE SCHOOL
5530 42a Ave, Red Deer, AB, T4N 3A8
(403) 347-7830
Emp Here 50
SIC 8211 Elementary and secondary schools

D-U-N-S 20-028-8939   (BR)
RED DEER CATHOLIC REGIONAL DIVISION NO. 39
MARYVIEW SCHOOL
3829 39 St, Red Deer, AB, T4N 0Y6
(403) 347-1455
Emp Here 27
SIC 8211 Elementary and secondary schools

D-U-N-S 20-070-3200   (BR)
RED DEER CATHOLIC REGIONAL DIVISION NO. 39
ST PATRICKS COMMUNITY SCHOOL
56 Holt St Suite 1, Red Deer, AB, T4N 6A6
(403) 343-3238
Emp Here 45
SIC 8211 Elementary and secondary schools

D-U-N-S 20-025-4725   (BR)
RED DEER CATHOLIC REGIONAL DIVISION NO. 39
ST THOMAS AQUINAS MIDDLE SCHOOL
3821 39 St, Red Deer, AB, T4N 0Y6
(403) 346-8951
Emp Here 30
SIC 8211 Elementary and secondary schools

D-U-N-S 25-497-3076   (HQ)
RED DEER CATHOLIC REGIONAL DIVISION NO. 39
(*Suby of* Red Deer Catholic Regional Division No. 39)
5210 61 St, Red Deer, AB, T4N 6N8
(403) 343-1055
Emp Here 20   *Emp Total* 500
Sales 46,019,840
SIC 8211 Elementary and secondary schools
Superintnt Paulette Hanna
Treas Roderic Steeves

D-U-N-S 24-854-2854   (SL)
RED DEER CHILD CARE SOCIETY
5571 45 St Unit 2, Red Deer, AB, T4N 1L2
(403) 347-7973
Emp Here 100   *Sales* 2,991,389
SIC 8351 Child day care services

D-U-N-S 24-333-9616   (BR)
RED DEER CO-OP LIMITED
HOME AND GARDEN CENTRE
4738 Riverside Dr, Red Deer, AB, T4N 2N7
(403) 341-5600
Emp Here 70
SIC 5399 Miscellaneous general merchandise

D-U-N-S 20-830-8114   (SL)
RED DEER GOLF AND COUNTRY CLUB LIMITED, THE
4500 Fountain Dr, Red Deer, AB, T4N 6W8
(403) 347-5441
Emp Here 69   *Sales* 2,772,507
SIC 7997 Membership sports and recreation clubs

D-U-N-S 25-092-3534   (BR)
RICOH CANADA INC
GRAYCON I.T.
5208 53 Ave, Red Deer, AB, T4N 5K2
(403) 352-2202
Emp Here 20
SIC 7379 Computer related services, nec

D-U-N-S 25-453-9943   (BR)
ROYAL LEPAGE LIMITED
ROYAL LEPAGE RED DEER REAL ESTATE
3608 50 Ave Suite 6, Red Deer, AB, T4N 3Y6
(403) 346-8900
Emp Here 40
SIC 6531 Real estate agents and managers

D-U-N-S 25-777-0792   (BR)
ROYAL TRUST CORPORATION OF CANADA
RBC
(*Suby of* Royal Bank Of Canada)
4943 50 St, Red Deer, AB, T4N 1Y1
(403) 340-7200
Emp Here 20
SIC 6021 National commercial banks

D-U-N-S 24-982-5902   (BR)
SAPUTO INC
ARMSTRONG CHEEES
5410 50 Ave, Red Deer, AB, T4N 4B5
(403) 357-3855
Emp Here 30
SIC 2021 Creamery butter

D-U-N-S 24-622-9491   (BR)
SEARS CANADA INC
5423 57 St Suite 516, Red Deer, AB, T4N 2K8
(403) 343-6650
Emp Here 30
SIC 5311 Department stores

D-U-N-S 20-725-5253   (BR)
SERVUS CREDIT UNION LTD
4901 48 St Suite 201, Red Deer, AB, T4N 6M4
(403) 342-5533
Emp Here 300
SIC 6062 State credit unions

D-U-N-S 20-725-5345   (BR)
SERVUS CREDIT UNION LTD
NORTH HILL BRANCH
6757 50 Ave, Red Deer, AB, T4N 4C9
(403) 343-8955
Emp Here 20
SIC 6062 State credit unions

D-U-N-S 20-248-5624   (BR)
SHAWN & ASSOCIATES MANAGEMENT LTD
EDON MANAGEMENT SHAWN AND ASSOCIATES
4920 51 St Suite 304, Red Deer, AB, T4N 6K8

Emp Here 20
SIC 6531 Real estate agents and managers

D-U-N-S 25-271-0504   (BR)
SOBEYS WEST INC
PORT O'CALL SAFEWAY
4408 50 Ave, Red Deer, AB, T4N 3Z6
(403) 346-1886
Emp Here 100
SIC 5411 Grocery stores

D-U-N-S 20-200-8475   (BR)
SODEXO CANADA LTD
212 Medley Dr, Red Deer, AB, T4N 6A1
(403) 340-7870
Emp Here 35
SIC 5963 Direct selling establishments

D-U-N-S 20-860-3543   (BR)
SOURCE (BELL) ELECTRONICS INC, THE
SOURCE, THE
4747 67 St Suite 464, Red Deer, AB, T4N 6H3
(403) 314-4430
Emp Here 25
SIC 5999 Miscellaneous retail stores, nec

D-U-N-S 24-785-2486   (SL)
SOUTH HILL HOLDINGS INC
BOSTON PIZZA #137
3215 50 Ave, Red Deer, AB, T4N 3Y1
(403) 343-7777
Emp Here 65   *Sales* 1,969,939
SIC 5812 Eating places

D-U-N-S 24-313-5782   (BR)
STAPLES CANADA INC
STAPLES THE BUSINESS DEPOT
(*Suby of* Staples, Inc.)
4747 67 St Unit 211, Red Deer, AB, T4N 6H3
(403) 314-3085
Emp Here 30
SIC 5943 Stationery stores

D-U-N-S 25-593-5830   (BR)
STARBUCKS COFFEE CANADA, INC
(*Suby of* Starbucks Corporation)
37400 Hwy 2 Unit 144a, Red Deer, AB, T4N 1E3
(403) 340-0396
Emp Here 27
SIC 5812 Eating places

D-U-N-S 24-948-4114   (SL)
SUNRISE RESIDENTIAL SERVICES LTD
Gd, Red Deer, AB, T4N 5E2
(403) 346-3422
Emp Here 50   *Sales* 1,824,018
SIC 8361 Residential care

D-U-N-S 24-384-2791   (BR)

TDL GROUP CORP, THE
TIM HORTONS
6721 50 Ave Suite 7, Red Deer, AB, T4N 4C9

Emp Here 45
SIC 5812 Eating places

D-U-N-S 25-315-0817   (BR)
TORONTO-DOMINION BANK, THE
TD CANADA TRUST
(*Suby of* Toronto-Dominion Bank, The)
4902 50 Ave, Red Deer, AB, T4N 4A8
(403) 340-7400
Emp Here 50
SIC 6021 National commercial banks

D-U-N-S 20-740-7730   (BR)
WAL-MART CANADA CORP
6375 50 Ave, Red Deer, AB, T4N 4C7
(403) 346-6650
Emp Here 200
SIC 5311 Department stores

D-U-N-S 25-762-1680   (BR)
WENDY'S RESTAURANTS OF CANADA INC
WENDY'S
(*Suby of* The Wendy's Company)
6781 50 Ave, Red Deer, AB, T4N 4C9
(403) 343-1071
Emp Here 30
SIC 5812 Eating places

Red Deer, AB T4P

D-U-N-S 24-553-0340   (SL)
313679 ALBERTA LTD
MOE, GARY SATURN
7620 50 Ave, Red Deer, AB, T4P 2A8
(403) 340-2224
Emp Here 24   *Sales* 22,826,250
SIC 5511 New and used car dealers
Pr Pr Gary Moe

D-U-N-S 20-874-0337   (BR)
392268 ALBERTA LTD
C.A.R.S. RV AND MARINE
7414 50 Ave, Red Deer, AB, T4P 1X7
(403) 347-3300
Emp Here 26
SIC 5521 Used car dealers

D-U-N-S 25-764-2702   (SL)
406421 ALBERTA LTD
8133 Edgar Industrial Close, Red Deer, AB, T4P 3R4
(403) 340-9825
Emp Here 100   *Sales* 35,243,105
SIC 1381 Drilling oil and gas wells
Pr Pr Jed Wood

D-U-N-S 25-764-2090   (BR)
477599 ALBERTA LTD
CASH CASINO PLACE
6350 67 St Suite 1, Red Deer, AB, T4P 3L7
(403) 346-3339
Emp Here 25
SIC 7999 Amusement and recreation, nec

D-U-N-S 25-678-7334   (BR)
A.R. THOMSON GROUP
7621 Edgar Industrial Dr Suite 3, Red Deer, AB, T4P 3R2
(403) 341-4511
Emp Here 20
SIC 5085 Industrial supplies

D-U-N-S 25-004-3619   (BR)
ATCO GAS AND PIPELINES LTD
ATCO GAS
7590 Edgar Industrial Dr, Red Deer, AB, T4P 3R2
(403) 357-5200
Emp Here 40
SIC 4924 Natural gas distribution

D-U-N-S 20-515-8921   (BR)

AECOM PRODUCTION SERVICES LTD
FLINT FIELD SERVICES LTD
4747 78a St Close, Red Deer, AB, T4P 2G9
(403) 342-6280
Emp Here 30
SIC 7389 Business services, nec

D-U-N-S 24-524-9920   (BR)
BADGER DAYLIGHTING LTD
6740 65 Ave Suite 403, Red Deer, AB, T4P 1A5
(403) 343-0303
Emp Here 20
SIC 1389 Oil and gas field services, nec

D-U-N-S 20-191-8773   (BR)
BAKER HUGHES CANADA COMPANY
(*Suby of* Baker Hughes, A GE Company)
7880 Edgar Industrial Drive, Red Deer, AB, T4P 3R2
(403) 340-3015
Emp Here 300
SIC 1389 Oil and gas field services, nec

D-U-N-S 20-789-3723   (BR)
BAKER HUGHES CANADA COMPANY
(*Suby of* Baker Hughes, A GE Company)
4940 81 St Suite 4, Red Deer, AB, T4P 3V3
(403) 341-7575
Emp Here 40
SIC 1389 Oil and gas field services, nec

D-U-N-S 20-191-7767   (BR)
BAKER HUGHES CANADA COMPANY
COILED TUBING DISTRICT, DIV OF
(*Suby of* Baker Hughes, A GE Company)
4089 77 St, Red Deer, AB, T4P 2T3
(403) 357-1401
Emp Here 180
SIC 1389 Oil and gas field services, nec

D-U-N-S 24-732-9030   (BR)
BAKER HUGHES CANADA COMPANY
BAKER OIL TOOLS, DIV OF
(*Suby of* Baker Hughes, A GE Company)
8009 Edgar Industrial Cres, Red Deer, AB, T4P 3S2
(403) 340-3500
Emp Here 50
SIC 5084 Industrial machinery and equipment

D-U-N-S 20-591-3432   (BR)
BOARD OF TRUSTEES OF THE RED DEER PUBLIC SCHOOL DISTRICT NO. 104, THE
ASPEN HEIGHTS ELEMENTARY SCHOOL
5869 69 Street Dr, Red Deer, AB, T4P 1C3
(403) 347-2581
Emp Here 25
SIC 8211 Elementary and secondary schools

D-U-N-S 20-591-3440   (BR)
BOARD OF TRUSTEES OF THE RED DEER PUBLIC SCHOOL DISTRICT NO. 104, THE
GLENDALE MIDDLE SCHOOL
6375 77 St, Red Deer, AB, T4P 3E9
(403) 340-3100
Emp Here 35
SIC 8211 Elementary and secondary schools

D-U-N-S 20-047-1261   (BR)
BOARD OF TRUSTEES OF THE RED DEER PUBLIC SCHOOL DISTRICT NO. 104, THE
NORMANDEAU SCHOOL
61 Noble Ave, Red Deer, AB, T4P 2C4
(403) 342-0727
Emp Here 35
SIC 8211 Elementary and secondary schools

D-U-N-S 20-283-0915   (BR)
BOARD OF TRUSTEES OF THE RED DEER PUBLIC SCHOOL DISTRICT NO. 104, THE
BOARD OF TRUSTEES OF THE RED DEER PUBLIC SCHOOL DISTRICT NO. 104, THE
300 Timothy Dr, Red Deer, AB, T4P 0L1
(403) 348-0050
Emp Here 32
SIC 8211 Elementary and secondary schools

D-U-N-S 25-680-8213   (BR)

BRANDT TRACTOR LTD
101 Burnt Park Dr, Red Deer, AB, T4P 0J7
(403) 343-7557
Emp Here 36
SIC 5084 Industrial machinery and equipment

D-U-N-S 25-777-0016   (BR)
CEB INVESTMENTS INC
BER-MAC
7659 Edgar Industrial Dr Suite 4, Red Deer,
AB, T4P 3R2
(403) 347-0077
Emp Here 24
SIC 1389 Oil and gas field services, nec

D-U-N-S 20-208-3858   (BR)
CALFRAC WELL SERVICES LTD
7310 Edgar Industrial Dr, Red Deer, AB, T4P
3R2
(403) 340-3569
Emp Here 100
SIC 1381 Drilling oil and gas wells

D-U-N-S 24-346-5460   (BR)
CALKINS CONSULTING INC
TIM HORTONS
6620 Orr Dr, Red Deer, AB, T4P 3V8
(403) 341-3561
Emp Here 35
SIC 5812 Eating places

D-U-N-S 20-894-6488   (BR)
**CANADIAN CONTRACT CLEANING SPE-
CIALISTS, INC**
7550 40 Ave, Red Deer, AB, T4P 2H8
(403) 348-8440
Emp Here 75
SIC 7349 Building maintenance services, nec

D-U-N-S 25-094-3255   (BR)
CANADIAN PACIFIC RAILWAY COMPANY
CPR
6867 Edgar Industrial Dr, Red Deer, AB, T4P
3R2
(403) 346-2189
Emp Here 60
SIC 4011 Railroads, line-haul operating

D-U-N-S 25-766-5091   (BR)
CANEM SYSTEMS LTD
7483 49 Ave, Red Deer, AB, T4P 1N1
(403) 347-1266
Emp Here 40
SIC 1731 Electrical work

D-U-N-S 20-040-9881   (BR)
CITY OF RED DEER, THE
RED DEER ELECTRIC LIGHT & POWER
DEPT
7721 40 Ave, Red Deer, AB, T4P 0K2
(403) 342-8274
Emp Here 39
SIC 4911 Electric services

D-U-N-S 20-246-7838   (BR)
**CLEAN HARBORS ENERGY AND INDUS-
TRIAL SERVICES CORP.**
7750 Edgar Industrial Dr, Red Deer, AB, T4P
3R2
(403) 342-1102
Emp Here 45
SIC 1389 Oil and gas field services, nec

D-U-N-S 20-645-8804   (BR)
**CONOCOPHILLIPS CANADA RESOURCES
CORP**
6759 65 Ave Unit 4, Red Deer, AB, T4P 1X5

Emp Here 40
SIC 1311 Crude petroleum and natural gas

D-U-N-S 20-740-7573   (SL)
COSMOS I BOTTLE DEPOT
7428 49 Ave Suite 1, Red Deer, AB, T4P 1M2
(403) 342-2034
Emp Here 90   Sales 4,523,563
SIC 7389 Business services, nec

D-U-N-S 24-345-5151   (BR)

DHL EXPRESS (CANADA) LTD
6660 Taylor Dr Suite 108, Red Deer, AB, T4P
1Y3

Emp Here 39
SIC 7389 Business services, nec

D-U-N-S 24-676-0636   (SL)
**ESSENTIAL COIL AND STIMULATION SER-
VICES LTD**
7755 Edgar Industrial Dr, Red Deer, AB, T4P
3R2
(403) 347-6717
Emp Here 30   Sales 3,720,996
SIC 1389 Oil and gas field services, nec

D-U-N-S 24-502-1162   (BR)
ESSENTIAL ENERGY SERVICES LTD
ESSENTIAL WELL SERVICE
77 Queensgate Cres, Red Deer, AB, T4P 0R2
(403) 314-3090
Emp Here 40
SIC 1389 Oil and gas field services, nec

D-U-N-S 25-999-2829   (BR)
EXTENDICARE INC
EXTENDICARE MICHENER HILL
12 Michener Blvd Suite 3609, Red Deer, AB,
T4P 0M1
(403) 348-0340
Emp Here 400
SIC 8051 Skilled nursing care facilities

D-U-N-S 20-440-2275   (BR)
FINNING INTERNATIONAL INC
FINNING CANADA
(Suby of Finning International Inc)
6740 67 Ave, Red Deer, AB, T4P 1A9
(403) 347-1106
Emp Here 60
SIC 5082 Construction and mining machinery

D-U-N-S 24-041-3542   (BR)
FLEET BRAKE PARTS & SERVICE LTD
4841 78 St, Red Deer, AB, T4P 1N5
(403) 343-8771
Emp Here 23
SIC 7538 General automotive repair shops

D-U-N-S 20-028-8921   (BR)
FORT GARRY INDUSTRIES LTD
FGI
170 Queens Dr, Red Deer, AB, T4P 0R5
(403) 343-1383
Emp Here 22
SIC 5531 Auto and home supply stores

D-U-N-S 24-012-6813   (SL)
FREIGHTLINER OF RED DEER INC
8046 Edgar Industrial Cres, Red Deer, AB,
T4P 3R3
(403) 309-8225
Emp Here 45   Sales 16,416,158
SIC 5511 New and used car dealers
Pr Pr Don Patterson

D-U-N-S 20-522-1286   (BR)
GATX RAIL CANADA CORPORATION
CORPORATION GATX RAIL CANADA
4310 77 St, Red Deer, AB, T4P 3P7
(403) 347-6700
Emp Here 65
SIC 4789 Transportation services, nec

D-U-N-S 24-951-9880   (BR)
GAS DRIVE GLOBAL LP
8036 Edgar Industrial Green Suite 57, Red
Deer, AB, T4P 3S2
(403) 341-3900
Emp Here 45
SIC 7699 Repair services, nec

D-U-N-S 24-379-8290   (HQ)
GLOVER INTERNATIONAL TRUCKS LTD
(Suby of Glover International Trucks Ltd)
226 Queens Dr, Red Deer, AB, T4P 0V8
(403) 346-5525
Emp Here 50   Emp Total 50
Sales 4,711,645

SIC 7538 General automotive repair shops

D-U-N-S 24-174-7521   (BR)
**GRANT PRODUCTION TESTING SERVICES
LTD**
(Suby of Grant Corporation)
6750 Golden West Ave, Red Deer, AB, T4P
1A8
(403) 314-0042
Emp Here 100
SIC 8748 Business consulting, nec

D-U-N-S 20-919-8212   (BR)
**GREGG DISTRIBUTORS LIMITED PART-
NERSHIP**
5141 76a Street Close, Red Deer, AB, T4P
3M2
(403) 341-3100
Emp Here 34
SIC 3531 Construction machinery

D-U-N-S 20-708-9504   (BR)
HI-WAY 9 EXPRESS LTD
4120 78 St Cres Suite 4120, Red Deer, AB,
T4P 3E3
(403) 342-4266
Emp Here 90
SIC 4212 Local trucking, without storage

D-U-N-S 20-321-6601   (BR)
**INTEGRATED DISTRIBUTION SYSTEMS
LIMITED PARTNERSHIP**
WAJAX POWER SYSTEMS
7980 Edgar Industrial Dr, Red Deer, AB, T4P
3R2
(403) 346-8981
Emp Here 25
SIC 5084 Industrial machinery and equipment

D-U-N-S 20-347-0240   (BR)
KAL TIRE LTD
8050 49 Ave, Red Deer, AB, T4P 2V7
(403) 347-8851
Emp Here 35
SIC 5531 Auto and home supply stores

D-U-N-S 25-770-3744   (BR)
LOBLAWS INC
REAL CANADIAN WHOLESALE CLUB
6350 67 St Unit 15, Red Deer, AB, T4P 3L7
(403) 347-4533
Emp Here 30
SIC 5141 Groceries, general line

D-U-N-S 20-181-1028   (BR)
MCCOY CORPORATION
FARR CANADA, DIV OF
7911 Edgar Industrial Dr, Red Deer, AB, T4P
3R2
(780) 453-3277
Emp Here 90
SIC 3533 Oil and gas field machinery

D-U-N-S 24-142-8882   (SL)
**MICHENER, ROLAND RECREATION CEN-
TER**
MICHENER SERVICES
2 Michener Rd, Red Deer, AB, T4P 0J9
(403) 340-5785
Emp Here 50   Sales 2,699,546
SIC 7999 Amusement and recreation, nec

D-U-N-S 25-533-4062   (BR)
NABORS DRILLING CANADA LIMITED
NABORS PRODUCTION SERVICES
8112 Edgar Industrial Dr, Red Deer, AB, T4P
3R2
(403) 346-0441
Emp Here 125
SIC 1389 Oil and gas field services, nec

D-U-N-S 25-764-2645   (SL)
NORTH HILL HOLDINGS INC
BOSTON PIZZA
7494 50 Ave, Red Deer, AB, T4P 1X7
(403) 342-4446
Emp Here 50   Sales 1,532,175
SIC 5812 Eating places

D-U-N-S 25-996-6398   (BR)
OLYMEL S.E.C.
FLAMINGO
7550 40 Ave, Red Deer, AB, T4P 2H8
(403) 343-8700
Emp Here 50
SIC 2013 Sausages and other prepared
meats

D-U-N-S 24-125-8727   (BR)
ON SIDE RESTORATION SERVICES LTD
7480 49 Ave Cres, Red Deer, AB, T4P 1X8
(403) 340-8884
Emp Here 20
SIC 1799 Special trade contractors, nec

D-U-N-S 24-716-4411   (SL)
PARKLAND COLORPRESS LTD
PROLIFIC GRAPHICS
7449 49 Ave, Red Deer, AB, T4P 1N2
(403) 340-8100
Emp Here 26   Sales 1,969,939
SIC 2752 Commercial printing, lithographic

D-U-N-S 24-321-8174   (BR)
PENTAGON OPTIMIZATION SERVICES INC
(Suby of General Electric Company)
7700 76 St Close Unit 220, Red Deer, AB, T4P
4G6
(403) 347-6277
Emp Here 25
SIC 1389 Oil and gas field services, nec

D-U-N-S 20-917-8727   (BR)
PRINCESS AUTO LTD
6833 66 St, Red Deer, AB, T4P 3T5
(403) 342-6181
Emp Here 40
SIC 5251 Hardware stores

D-U-N-S 20-048-1856   (BR)
PROLIFIC GRAPHICS INC
PROLIFIC GROUP OF GRAPHIC ARTS
COMPANIES, THE
7449 49 Ave, Red Deer, AB, T4P 1N2
(403) 340-8100
Emp Here 35
SIC 2752 Commercial printing, lithographic

D-U-N-S 25-681-2025   (HQ)
PUMPS & PRESSURE INC
(Suby of Pumps & Pressure Inc)
7018 Johnstone Dr, Red Deer, AB, T4P 3Y6
(403) 340-3666
Emp Here 50   Emp Total 115
Sales 29,217,600
SIC 5084 Industrial machinery and equipment
Pr Pr John Tremain
Dir Dale Cripps
Sandra Tremain
Dir Wes Gyori

D-U-N-S 20-262-1785   (HQ)
**QUINN'S RENTAL SERVICES (CANADA)
INC**
7739 Edgar Industrial Dr, Red Deer, AB, T4P
3R2
(403) 346-0770
Emp Here 40   Emp Total 50
Sales 5,182,810
SIC 7353 Heavy construction equipment
rental
Dir Douglas Quinn

D-U-N-S 20-710-3859   (BR)
**RED DEER CATHOLIC REGIONAL DIVI-
SION NO. 39**
ST THERESA OF AVILA SCHOOL
190 Glendale Blvd, Red Deer, AB, T4P 2P7
(403) 346-0505
Emp Here 40
SIC 8211 Elementary and secondary schools

D-U-N-S 20-049-0113   (SL)
RED FLAME INDUSTRIES INC
6736 71 St, Red Deer, AB, T4P 3Y7
(403) 343-2012
Emp Here 35   Sales 5,653,974

SIC 1389 Oil and gas field services, nec
Pr Pr Jared Sayers

D-U-N-S 20-342-2019   (BR)
RUSSEL METALS INC
ALBERTA INDUSTRIAL METALS
4821 78 St, Red Deer, AB, T4P 1N5
(403) 343-1452
Emp Here 27
SIC 4225 General warehousing and storage

D-U-N-S 24-702-0126   (SL)
S.J. SULEMAN INVESTMENTS LTD
HOLIDAY INN 67 STREET
6500 67 St, Red Deer, AB, T4P 1A2
(403) 342-6567
Emp Here 54   *Sales* 2,334,742
SIC 7011 Hotels and motels

D-U-N-S 25-766-6107   (HQ)
SPM FLOW CONTROL LTD
8060 Edgar Industrial Cres Unit A, Red Deer,
AB, T4P 3R3
(403) 341-3410
Emp Here 25   *Emp Total* 13,245
Sales 6,055,738
SIC 1389 Oil and gas field services, nec
Dir Craig Ralston
Pr Gavin Nicol

D-U-N-S 24-982-9149   (BR)
SAFETY BOSS INC
8118 49 Ave Close, Red Deer, AB, T4P 2V5
(780) 831-2910
Emp Here 25
SIC 1389 Oil and gas field services, nec

D-U-N-S 24-159-4449   (HQ)
SCOTT BUILDERS INC
(*Suby of* Scott Builders Inc)
8105 49 Ave, Red Deer, AB, T4P 2V5
(403) 343-7270
Emp Here 50   *Emp Total* 75
Sales 14,883,983
SIC 1541 Industrial buildings and warehouses
Pr Scot Rutherford
Ch Bd Ralph Ward
VP Hans Te Stroete
Terry Bolen
Murray Cunningham

D-U-N-S 24-141-6812   (BR)
**STERLING WESTERN STAR TRUCKS AL-
BERTA LTD**
7690 Edgar Industrial Crt, Red Deer, AB, T4P
4E2
(403) 314-1919
Emp Here 21
SIC 7538 General automotive repair shops

D-U-N-S 24-352-0330   (BR)
**TECHMATION ELECTRIC & CONTROLS
LTD**
8034 Edgar Industrial Cres, Red Deer, AB,
T4P 3R3
(403) 341-3558
Emp Here 50
SIC 7629 Electrical repair shops

D-U-N-S 24-523-8386   (BR)
TERVITA CORPORATION
HAZCO ENVIRONMENTAL SERVICES
(*Suby of* Tervita Corporation)
8149 Edgar Industrial Close, Red Deer, AB,
T4P 3R4
(403) 346-4550
Emp Here 50
SIC 8748 Business consulting, nec

D-U-N-S 24-125-6762   (BR)
TRINIDAD DRILLING LTD
TRINIDAD WELL SERVICING
6763 76 St, Red Deer, AB, T4P 3R7
(403) 314-0771
Emp Here 45
SIC 1381 Drilling oil and gas wells

D-U-N-S 25-977-9036   (BR)
TROJAN SAFETY SERVICES LTD

7669 Edgar Industrial Crt Unit 3, Red Deer,
AB, T4P 4E2
(403) 309-3025
Emp Here 20
SIC 7353 Heavy construction equipment
rental

D-U-N-S 20-295-4327   (BR)
WEIR CANADA, INC
WEIR OIL & GAS
8060 Edgar Industrial Cres Unit A, Red Deer,
AB, T4P 3R3
(403) 341-3410
Emp Here 40
SIC 7699 Repair services, nec

Red Deer, AB T4R

D-U-N-S 20-197-8686   (BR)
1009833 ALBERTA LTD
PETLAND
5250 22 St Suite 100, Red Deer, AB, T4R 2T4
(403) 309-4800
Emp Here 35
SIC 5999 Miscellaneous retail stores, nec

D-U-N-S 25-417-0129   (SL)
733644 ALBERTA LTD
RUSTY PELICAN
2079 50 Ave, Red Deer, AB, T4R 1Z4
(403) 986-4312
Emp Here 55   *Sales* 1,678,096
SIC 5812 Eating places

D-U-N-S 20-209-8690   (BR)
ALBERTS RESTAURANTS LTD
TONY ROMA'S
(*Suby of* Alberts Restaurants Ltd)
5250 22 St Suite 60, Red Deer, AB, T4R 2T4
(403) 358-3223
Emp Here 55
SIC 5812 Eating places

D-U-N-S 20-589-5472   (BR)
BANQUE TORONTO-DOMINION, LA
TD CANADA TRUST
(*Suby of* Toronto-Dominion Bank, The)
5001 19 St Unit 500, Red Deer, AB, T4R 3R1
(403) 342-4700
Emp Here 20
SIC 6021 National commercial banks

D-U-N-S 20-641-4604   (BR)
BEST BUY CANADA LTD
FUTURE SHOP
(*Suby of* Best Buy Co., Inc.)
5250 22 St Suite 110, Red Deer, AB, T4R 2T4

Emp Here 50
SIC 5731 Radio, television, and electronic
stores

D-U-N-S 25-371-6989   (BR)
BEST BUY CANADA LTD
BEST BUY
(*Suby of* Best Buy Co., Inc.)
5001 19 St Unit 800, Red Deer, AB, T4R 3R1
(403) 314-5645
Emp Here 100
SIC 5731 Radio, television, and electronic
stores

D-U-N-S 24-986-2868   (BR)
BETHANY CARE SOCIETY
99 College Cir, Red Deer, AB, T4R 0M3
(403) 357-3700
Emp Here 300
SIC 8322 Individual and family services

D-U-N-S 20-116-8254   (BR)
BLACK PRESS GROUP LTD
RED DEER ADVOCATE
2950 Bremner Ave, Red Deer, AB, T4R 1M9
(403) 343-2400
Emp Here 150

SIC 2711 Newspapers

D-U-N-S 24-040-4363   (BR)
**BOARD OF TRUSTEES OF THE RED DEER
PUBLIC SCHOOL DISTRICT NO. 104, THE**
*MATTIE   MCCULLOGH   ELEMENTARY
SCHOOL*
26 Lawford Ave, Red Deer, AB, T4R 3L6
(403) 343-8958
Emp Here 30
SIC 8211 Elementary and secondary schools

D-U-N-S 25-269-7479   (BR)
**BOARD OF TRUSTEES OF THE RED DEER
PUBLIC SCHOOL DISTRICT NO. 104, THE**
HUNTING HILLS HIGH SCHOOL
150 Lockwood Ave, Red Deer, AB, T4R 2M4
(403) 342-6655
Emp Here 120
SIC 8211 Elementary and secondary schools

D-U-N-S 24-971-9071   (BR)
BOOTLEGGER CLOTHING INC
BOOTLEGGER
4900 Molly Bannister Dr Unit 113, Red Deer,
AB, T4R 1N9
(403) 346-2170
Emp Here 20
SIC 5651 Family clothing stores

D-U-N-S 25-231-7425   (BR)
BRICK WAREHOUSE LP, THE
BRICK, THE
5111 22 St Suite 7, Red Deer, AB, T4R 2K1
(403) 340-2000
Emp Here 40
SIC 5712 Furniture stores

D-U-N-S 20-038-8606   (BR)
CARA OPERATIONS LIMITED
KELSEY'S
(*Suby of* Cara Holdings Limited)
1935 50 Ave, Red Deer, AB, T4R 1Z4

Emp Here 40
SIC 5812 Eating places

D-U-N-S 20-706-9175   (BR)
CARA OPERATIONS LIMITED
MONTANA'S COOKHOUSE
(*Suby of* Cara Holdings Limited)
2004 50 Ave Unit 195, Red Deer, AB, T4R 3A2
(403) 352-0030
Emp Here 20
SIC 5812 Eating places

D-U-N-S 24-949-7157   (BR)
CORUS MEDIA HOLDINGS INC
SHAW MEDIA INC
2840 Bremner Ave, Red Deer, AB, T4R 1M9

Emp Here 38
SIC 4833 Television broadcasting stations

D-U-N-S 20-914-9207   (BR)
DENCAN RESTAURANTS INC
DENNY'S RESTAURANT
(*Suby of* Northland Properties Corporation)
2940 50 Ave Ste 81, Red Deer, AB, T4R 1M4
(403) 348-5040
Emp Here 50
SIC 5812 Eating places

D-U-N-S 24-517-5278   (SL)
EARLS RESTAURANT (RED DEER) LTD
EARLS PLACE
2111 50 Ave, Red Deer, AB, T4R 1Z4
(403) 342-4055
Emp Here 75   *Sales* 2,261,782
SIC 5812 Eating places

D-U-N-S 24-118-8416   (BR)
FABRICLAND PACIFIC/MIDWEST LIMITED
FABRICLAND
2119 50 Ave Unit 2, Red Deer, AB, T4R 1Z4
(403) 343-1277
Emp Here 20
SIC 5949 Sewing, needlework, and piece

goods

D-U-N-S 25-141-2490   (BR)
GAP (CANADA) INC
GAP
(*Suby of* The Gap Inc)
4900 Molly Bannister Dr Suite 165, Red Deer,
AB, T4R 1N9
(403) 314-4050
Emp Here 32
SIC 5651 Family clothing stores

D-U-N-S 24-391-5688   (BR)
GOLF TOWN LIMITED
5111 22 St Unit 6, Red Deer, AB, T4R 2K1
(403) 341-9898
Emp Here 25
SIC 5941 Sporting goods and bicycle shops

D-U-N-S 25-372-6897   (BR)
GREAT PACIFIC INDUSTRIES INC
SAVE-ON-FOODS
3020 22 St Suite 300, Red Deer, AB, T4R 3J5
(403) 309-0520
Emp Here 150
SIC 5411 Grocery stores

D-U-N-S 20-105-8281   (BR)
HOME DEPOT OF CANADA INC
HOME DEPOT
(*Suby of* The Home Depot Inc)
2030 50 Ave, Red Deer, AB, T4R 3A2
(403) 358-7550
Emp Here 130
SIC 5251 Hardware stores

D-U-N-S 20-645-4340   (BR)
HUDSON'S BAY COMPANY
BAY, THE
4900 Molly Bannister Dr, Red Deer, AB, T4R
1N9
(403) 347-2211
Emp Here 120
SIC 5311 Department stores

D-U-N-S 20-520-6696   (BR)
INDIGO BOOKS & MUSIC INC
CHAPTERS 924
(*Suby of* Indigo Books & Music Inc)
5250 22 St Unit 10, Red Deer, AB, T4R 2T4
(403) 309-2427
Emp Here 30
SIC 5942 Book stores

D-U-N-S 24-439-1108   (BR)
LONDON DRUGS LIMITED
50 Mclean St Unite 109, Red Deer, AB, T4R
1W7
(403) 342-1242
Emp Here 50
SIC 5912 Drug stores and proprietary stores

D-U-N-S 20-884-1143   (BR)
MASTERPIECE INC
3100 22 St, Red Deer, AB, T4R 3N7
(403) 341-5522
Emp Here 40
SIC 6513 Apartment building operators

D-U-N-S 20-936-2354   (SL)
NORTHERN APPLE RESTAURANTS INC
APPLEBEE'S GRILL & BAR
5250 22 St Suite 50, Red Deer, AB, T4R 2T4

Emp Here 140   *Sales* 5,693,280
SIC 5812 Eating places
Genl Mgr Mark Mcisaac
Pr Pr Samuel Wong

D-U-N-S 25-138-8880   (BR)
**NORTHLAND   PROPERTIES   CORPORA-
TION**
SANDMAN HOTEL RED DEER
(*Suby of* Northland Properties Corporation)
2818 50 Ave, Red Deer, AB, T4R 1M4
(403) 343-7400
Emp Here 25
SIC 7011 Hotels and motels

D-U-N-S 20-738-1752   (BR)
PASLEY, MAX ENTERPRISES LIMITED
MCDONALD'S RESTAURANTS
(*Suby of* Pasley, Max Enterprises Limited)
3020 22 St Ste 800, Red Deer, AB, T4R 3J5
(403) 341-7819
Emp Here 60
SIC 5812 Eating places

D-U-N-S 25-316-4255   (BR)
PASLEY, MAX ENTERPRISES LIMITED
MCDONALD'S RESTAURANTS #7186
(*Suby of* Pasley, Max Enterprises Limited)
2502 50 Ave, Red Deer, AB, T4R 1M3
(403) 347-1700
Emp Here 50
SIC 5812 Eating places

D-U-N-S 20-152-8903   (BR)
PATTISON, JIM BROADCAST GROUP LTD
PATTISON, JIM BROADCASTING
2840 Bremner Ave, Red Deer, AB, T4R 1M9
(403) 343-0700
Emp Here 38
SIC 4832 Radio broadcasting stations

D-U-N-S 25-289-7095   (BR)
PEAVEY INDUSTRIES LIMITED
PEAVEY MART
2410 50 Ave, Red Deer, AB, T4R 1M3
(403) 346-6402
Emp Here 30
SIC 5251 Hardware stores

D-U-N-S 20-069-0928   (BR)
RED DEER CATHOLIC REGIONAL DIVISION NO. 39
ECO SECONDAIRE NOTREDAME
50 Lees St, Red Deer, AB, T4R 2P6
(403) 342-4800
Emp Here 20
SIC 8211 Elementary and secondary schools

D-U-N-S 20-030-1419   (BR)
RED DEER CATHOLIC REGIONAL DIVISION NO. 39
HOLY FAMILY SCHOOL
69 Douglas Ave, Red Deer, AB, T4R 2L3
(403) 341-3777
Emp Here 42
SIC 8211 Elementary and secondary schools

D-U-N-S 20-981-6193   (BR)
RED DEER CATHOLIC REGIONAL DIVISION NO. 39
ST FRANCIS OF ASSISI MIDDLE SCHOOL
321 Lindsay Ave, Red Deer, AB, T4R 3M1
(403) 314-1449
Emp Here 35
SIC 8211 Elementary and secondary schools

D-U-N-S 20-029-4457   (BR)
RED DEER CATHOLIC REGIONAL DIVISION NO. 39
ST ELIZABETH SETON SCHOOL
35 Addinell Ave, Red Deer, AB, T4R 1V5
(403) 343-6017
Emp Here 50
SIC 8211 Elementary and secondary schools

D-U-N-S 20-798-7988   (BR)
SOBEYS CAPITAL INCORPORATED
SOBEYS
2110 50 Ave, Red Deer, AB, T4R 2K1
(403) 348-0848
Emp Here 100
SIC 5411 Grocery stores

D-U-N-S 24-523-0607   (BR)
SYMPHONY SENIOR LIVING INC
3100 22 St Suite 205, Red Deer, AB, T4R 3N7
(403) 341-5522
Emp Here 20
SIC 8322 Individual and family services

D-U-N-S 24-523-0425   (BR)
SYMPHONY SENIOR LIVING INC
10 Inglewood Dr Suite 315, Red Deer, AB,

T4R 0L2
(403) 346-1134
Emp Here 20
SIC 8741 Management services

D-U-N-S 24-041-9015   (SL)
TANKSAFE INC
4136 39139 Hwy Suite 2a, Red Deer, AB, T4R 2M2
(403) 343-8265
Emp Here 40   *Sales* 8,623,250
SIC 3443 Fabricated plate work (boiler shop)
Wayne Bowd
Pr Pr Reinhardt Schuetz

D-U-N-S 25-297-6758   (BR)
TOYS 'R' US (CANADA) LTD
TOYS 'R' US
(*Suby of* Toys "r" Us, Inc.)
4900 Molly Bannister Dr Suite 171, Red Deer, AB, T4R 1N9
(403) 341-8760
Emp Here 22
SIC 5945 Hobby, toy, and game shops

D-U-N-S 25-770-5210   (BR)
VALUE VILLAGE STORES, INC
VALUE VILLAGE 2028
(*Suby of* Savers, Inc.)
2235 50 Ave, Red Deer, AB, T4R 1M7
(403) 343-3000
Emp Here 40
SIC 5399 Miscellaneous general merchandise

D-U-N-S 20-552-2316   (BR)
WAL-MART CANADA CORP
2010 50 Ave Suite 3194, Red Deer, AB, T4R 3A2
(403) 358-5842
Emp Here 300
SIC 5311 Department stores

D-U-N-S 25-770-5384   (BR)
WENDY'S RESTAURANTS OF CANADA INC
(*Suby of* The Wendy's Company)
2410 50 Ave, Red Deer, AB, T4R 1M3
(403) 346-9466
Emp Here 35
SIC 5812 Eating places

D-U-N-S 20-106-3281   (BR)
WINNERS MERCHANTS INTERNATIONAL L.P.
WINNERS
(*Suby of* The TJX Companies Inc)
5001 19 St Suite 700, Red Deer, AB, T4R 3R1
(403) 340-1717
Emp Here 40
SIC 5651 Family clothing stores

D-U-N-S 24-319-4433   (BR)
ZAINUL & SHAZMA HOLDINGS (1997) LTD
HOLIDAY INN EXPRESS
2803 50 Ave, Red Deer, AB, T4R 1H1
(403) 343-2112
Emp Here 22
SIC 7011 Hotels and motels

Red Deer, AB T4S

D-U-N-S 20-190-5523   (BR)
UNITED FARMERS OF ALBERTA CO-OPERATIVE LIMITED
STIRDON BETKER UFA
28042 Hwy 11, Red Deer, AB, T4S 2L4

Emp Here 40
SIC 5191 Farm supplies

Red Deer County, AB T4E

D-U-N-S 20-068-2768   (BR)

A & W FOOD SERVICES OF CANADA INC
A & W
121 Leva Ave, Red Deer County, AB, T4E 1B2
(403) 343-6893
Emp Here 40
SIC 5812 Eating places

D-U-N-S 20-296-6016   (BR)
A.R. THOMSON GROUP
215 Clearview Dr, Red Deer County, AB, T4E 0A1
(403) 341-4511
Emp Here 50
SIC 5085 Industrial supplies

D-U-N-S 20-454-8969   (SL)
AUTUMN ENTERPRISES INC
GASOLINE ALLEY HARLEY-DAVIDSON
(*Suby of* 1453078 Alberta Ltd)
37473 Highway 2, Red Deer County, AB, T4E 1B3
(403) 341-3040
Emp Here 38   *Sales* 8,932,560
SIC 5571 Motorcycle dealers
Pr Pr Grant Murray Price

D-U-N-S 24-418-5026   (BR)
CINEPLEX ODEON CORPORATION
GALAXY CINEMAS RED DEER
357 Liberty Ave, Red Deer County, AB, T4E 0A5
(403) 348-5074
Emp Here 60
SIC 7832 Motion picture theaters, except drive-in

D-U-N-S 20-702-3495   (BR)
CLEAN HARBORS INDUSTRIAL SERVICES CANADA, INC
102-113 Clearskye Way, Red Deer County, AB, T4E 0A1
(403) 346-8265
Emp Here 60
SIC 3533 Oil and gas field machinery

D-U-N-S 25-524-6647   (BR)
COSTCO WHOLESALE CANADA LTD
COSTCO
(*Suby of* Costco Wholesale Corporation)
37400 Highway 2 Unit 162, Red Deer County, AB, T4E 1B9
(403) 340-3736
Emp Here 130
SIC 5099 Durable goods, nec

D-U-N-S 24-646-8847   (SL)
GLENN'S RESTAURANT LTD
GLENN'S FAMILY RESTAURANT
125 Leva Ave Unit 5, Red Deer County, AB, T4E 1B2
(403) 346-5448
Emp Here 65   *Sales* 1,969,939
SIC 5812 Eating places

D-U-N-S 20-086-8573   (BR)
LAVTOR HOLDINGS (ALBERTA) LTD
HUSKY & SMITTYS RESTAURANT
37438 Highway 2, Red Deer County, AB, T4E 1B2

Emp Here 70
SIC 5812 Eating places

D-U-N-S 24-330-3505   (HQ)
OPTIMA CAPITAL PARTNERS INC
(*Suby of* Optima Capital Partners Inc)
96 Poplar St Suite 100, Red Deer County, AB, T4E 1B4

Emp Here 20   *Emp Total* 50
Sales 7,632,865
SIC 6712 Bank holding companies
Pr Pr Gerard Hermary

D-U-N-S 20-064-2390   (BR)
ROSENAU TRANSPORT LTD
(*Suby of* Mid-Nite Sun Transportation Ltd)
28042 Hwy 11 Suite 286, Red Deer County, AB, T4E 1A5

(403) 341-2340
Emp Here 24
SIC 4731 Freight transportation arrangement

D-U-N-S 20-544-8488   (BR)
STAPLES CANADA INC
STAPLES/BUSINESS DEPOT
(*Suby of* Staples, Inc.)
37400 Hwy 2 Suite 150d, Red Deer County, AB, T4E 1B9
(403) 357-1760
Emp Here 30
SIC 5943 Stationery stores

D-U-N-S 20-090-5339   (SL)
ULTRA SALES AND SERVICE LTD
UNCLE BEN'S R.V. & AUTO
29 Petrolia Dr, Red Deer County, AB, T4E 1B3
(403) 347-5546
Emp Here 30   *Sales* 19,896,665
SIC 5561 Recreational vehicle dealers
Pr Pr Robert Janko
Andrew Janko

D-U-N-S 24-224-5442   (BR)
WENDY'S RESTAURANTS OF CANADA INC
(*Suby of* The Wendy's Company)
37444 Highway 2 Suite 2, Red Deer County, AB, T4E 1B2
(403) 341-5432
Emp Here 25
SIC 5812 Eating places

D-U-N-S 25-206-1858   (HQ)
WESTRIDGE CABINETS (1993) LTD
(*Suby of* Signal Hill Equity Partners Inc)
41237400 Highway 2, Red Deer County, AB, T4E 1B9
(403) 342-6671
Emp Here 240   *Emp Total* 300
Sales 20,790,024
SIC 2434 Wood kitchen cabinets
Pr Ron Goss

Red Deer County, AB T4G

D-U-N-S 25-678-3044   (SL)
RAINBOW COLONY FARMING CO LTD
HUTTERIAN BRETHREN CHURCH OF RAINBOW
26052 Township Road 350, Red Deer County, AB, T4G 0M4
(403) 227-6465
Emp Here 57   *Sales* 4,417,880
SIC 8661 Religious organizations

Red Deer County, AB T4S

D-U-N-S 24-025-2002   (BR)
CALGARY PETERBILT LTD
(*Suby of* Calgary Peterbilt Ltd)
27 Burnt Lake Cres, Red Deer County, AB, T4S 0K6
(403) 342-5100
Emp Here 70
SIC 5511 New and used car dealers

D-U-N-S 24-522-0244   (BR)
CERVUS EQUIPMENT CORPORATION
A.R. WILLIAMS MATERIALS HANDLING
280 Burnt Park Dr Unit 10, Red Deer County, AB, T4S 0K7
(403) 346-9011
Emp Here 30
SIC 8731 Commercial physical research

D-U-N-S 20-051-6636   (BR)
CORE LABORATORIES CANADA LTD
OWEN OIL TOOLS
39139 Highway 2a Unit 5409, Red Deer County, AB, T4S 2B3

(403) 340-1017
Emp Here 150
SIC 1389 Oil and gas field services, nec

D-U-N-S 20-702-3263   (BR)
ENHANCED PETROLEUM SERVICES PARTNERSHIP
ENHANCED DRILL SYSTEMS
(*Suby of* Enhanced Petroleum Services Partnership)
39139 Highway 2a Suite 5398, Red Deer County, AB, T4S 2B3
(403) 314-1564
Emp Here 30
SIC 1381 Drilling oil and gas wells

D-U-N-S 20-174-7123   (BR)
ENVIROSORT INC
4229 Hewlett Dr, Red Deer County, AB, T4S 2B3
(403) 342-7823
Emp Here 30
SIC 4953 Refuse systems

D-U-N-S 24-962-4719   (BR)
LAFARGE CANADA INC
4120 Henry St, Red Deer County, AB, T4S 2B3
(403) 346-1644
Emp Here 40
SIC 3273 Ready-mixed concrete

D-U-N-S 20-965-7159   (BR)
LEON'S FURNITURE LIMITED
LEON'S FURNITURE WAREHOUSE & SHOWROOM
10 Mckenzie Dr, Red Deer County, AB, T4S 2H4
(403) 340-0234
Emp Here 40
SIC 5712 Furniture stores

D-U-N-S 20-733-6525   (BR)
NOV ENERFLOW ULC
NOV TUBOSCOPE
4040 Industry Ave, Red Deer County, AB, T4S 2B3
(403) 343-8100
Emp Here 20
SIC 1389 Oil and gas field services, nec

D-U-N-S 24-348-2069   (BR)
NINE ENERGY CANADA INC
IPS WIREL!NE, DIV OF
37337 Burnt Lake Trail Unit 30, Red Deer County, AB, T4S 2K5
(403) 340-4218
Emp Here 160
SIC 1389 Oil and gas field services, nec

D-U-N-S 20-892-1531   (BR)
PRECISION DRILLING CORPORATION
PRECISION RENTALS
27240 Township Road 392, Red Deer County, AB, T4S 1X5
(403) 342-4250
Emp Here 25
SIC 1381 Drilling oil and gas wells

D-U-N-S 20-978-9036   (BR)
PRECISION DRILLING CORPORATION
PRECISION WELL SERVICING
27240 Township Road 392, Red Deer County, AB, T4S 1X5
(403) 346-8922
Emp Here 65
SIC 1381 Drilling oil and gas wells

D-U-N-S 25-000-8174   (BR)
ROCKWELL SERVICING INC
ENSIGN ROCKWELL SERVICING
39139 Highway 2a Suite 4212, Red Deer County, AB, T4S 2A3
(403) 346-6175
Emp Here 50
SIC 1389 Oil and gas field services, nec

D-U-N-S 24-849-9266   (SL)
ROTATING ENERGY SERVICES CA CORP

39139 Highway 2a Suite 4016, Red Deer County, AB, T4S 2A8
(403) 358-5577
Emp Here 20   *Sales* 12,344,510
SIC 4911 Electric services
Dir John Carlson
    Kim Gray
Dir Jason Tymko

D-U-N-S 25-191-0824   (BR)
TOROMONT INDUSTRIES LTD
TOROMONT ENERGY SERVICES
39139 Highway 2a Unit 5304, Red Deer County, AB, T4S 2B3

Emp Here 20
SIC 1389 Oil and gas field services, nec

D-U-N-S 24-552-5191   (BR)
UNITED FARMERS OF ALBERTA CO-OPERATIVE LIMITED
UFA
204 Burnt Lake, Red Deer County, AB, T4S 2L4

Emp Here 40
SIC 5191 Farm supplies

Redcliff, AB T0J

D-U-N-S 25-677-9414   (BR)
AECOM PRODUCTION SERVICES LTD
FLINT FIELD SERVICES LTD
1901 Highway Ave Ne, Redcliff, T0J 2P0
(403) 548-3190
Emp Here 350
SIC 1623 Water, sewer, and utility lines

D-U-N-S 20-191-7809   (BR)
BAKER HUGHES CANADA COMPANY
PUMPING SERVICES, DIV OF
(*Suby of* Baker Hughes, A GE Company)
1901 Broadway Ave Ne, Redcliff, AB, T0J 2P0

Emp Here 250
SIC 1389 Oil and gas field services, nec

D-U-N-S 24-857-9562   (BR)
BAKER HUGHES INC
(*Suby of* Baker Hughes, A GE Company)
1901 Broadway Ave Ne, Redcliff, AB, T0J 2P0

Emp Here 300
SIC 3533 Oil and gas field machinery

D-U-N-S 24-104-6460   (BR)
CANADIAN SUB-SURFACE ENERGY SERVICES CORP
(*Suby of* Reliance Oilfield Services, LLC)
Gd, Redcliff, AB, T0J 2P0
(403) 529-1388
Emp Here 30
SIC 8322 Individual and family services

D-U-N-S 24-009-7001   (BR)
FLINT ENERGY SERVICES LTD.
URS FLINT
1901 Highway Ave Se, Redcliff, AB, T0J 2P0

Emp Here 210
SIC 8742 Management consulting services

D-U-N-S 24-806-2762   (SL)
GVN STRUCTURES INC
1611 Broadway Ave E Suite 1, Redcliff, AB, T0J 2P0
(403) 548-3100
Emp Here 35   *Sales* 6,931,267
SIC 1541 Industrial buildings and warehouses
Pr Pr Bruce Vine
Dir Larry Becker

D-U-N-S 20-966-6382   (BR)
NATIONAL-OILWELL CANADA LTD
(*Suby of* National Oilwell Varco, Inc.)

1451 Hwy Ave Se, Redcliff, AB, T0J 2P0
(403) 548-8121
Emp Here 25
SIC 5082 Construction and mining machinery

D-U-N-S 25-135-8495   (BR)
PATTISON, JIM INDUSTRIES LTD
CHAT RADIO 94.5 FM
10 Boundary Rd Se, Redcliff, AB, T0J 2P0
(403) 548-8282
Emp Here 80
SIC 4832 Radio broadcasting stations

D-U-N-S 20-712-2081   (BR)
PRAIRIE ROSE SCHOOL DIVISION NO 8
ISABEL F COX SCHOOL
339 3rd St Se, Redcliff, AB, T0J 2P0
(403) 548-3449
Emp Here 41
SIC 8211 Elementary and secondary schools

D-U-N-S 20-655-0241   (BR)
PRAIRIE ROSE SCHOOL DIVISION NO 8
MARGARET WOODING SCHOOL
401 8th Ave Se, Redcliff, AB, T0J 2P0
(403) 548-7516
Emp Here 23
SIC 8211 Elementary and secondary schools

D-U-N-S 20-920-4390   (BR)
PRECISION DRILLING CORPORATION
PRECISION RENTALS
111 Elbow Dr Ne, Redcliff, AB, T0J 2P0
(403) 526-4111
Emp Here 20
SIC 1381 Drilling oil and gas wells

D-U-N-S 25-315-1583   (BR)
PYRAMID CORPORATION
170 Saskatchewan Dr Ne, Redcliff, AB, T0J 2P0
(403) 527-2585
Emp Here 30
SIC 1731 Electrical work

D-U-N-S 25-096-8005   (BR)
ROSENAU TRANSPORT LTD
(*Suby of* Mid-Nite Sun Transportation Ltd)
1860 Broadway Ave Ne, Redcliff, AB, T0J 2P0
(403) 548-6704
Emp Here 20
SIC 4213 Trucking, except local

D-U-N-S 20-867-5178   (BR)
TARPON ENERGY SERVICES LTD
1711 Broadway Ave Ne Suite 3, Redcliff, AB, T0J 2P0
(403) 529-9666
Emp Here 40
SIC 3825 Instruments to measure electricity

Redwater, AB T0A

D-U-N-S 20-795-0259   (BR)
AGRIUM INC
(*Suby of* Agrium Canada Partnership)
Gd, Redwater, AB, T0A 2W0
(780) 998-6111
Emp Here 350
SIC 2873 Nitrogenous fertilizers

D-U-N-S 20-702-4311   (BR)
ALBERTA HEALTH SERVICES
REDWATER HEALTH CENTRE
4812 58 St, Redwater, AB, T0A 2W0
(780) 942-3932
Emp Here 60
SIC 8011 Offices and clinics of medical doctors

D-U-N-S 20-745-2913   (BR)
PYRAMID CORPORATION
4806 44 St, Redwater, AB, T0A 2W0
(780) 942-2225
Emp Here 25

SIC 1731 Electrical work

D-U-N-S 20-021-8282   (BR)
STURGEON SCHOOL DIVISION #24
REDWATER SCHOOL
5023 50 Ave, Redwater, AB, T0A 2W0
(780) 942-3625
Emp Here 35
SIC 8211 Elementary and secondary schools

D-U-N-S 20-591-8720   (BR)
STURGEON SCHOOL DIVISION #24
OCHRE PARK SCHOOL
5024 Okotoks Rd, Redwater, AB, T0A 2W0
(780) 942-2902
Emp Here 27
SIC 8211 Elementary and secondary schools

D-U-N-S 20-090-6113   (SL)
TARTAN INDUSTRIAL CONTRACTORS LTD
5007 48 Ave, Redwater, AB, T0A 2W0
(780) 942-3802
Emp Here 20   *Sales* 5,006,160
SIC 1389 Oil and gas field services, nec
Pr Pr Darrell Howell

D-U-N-S 24-101-4492   (BR)
TRANSCANADA PIPELINES LIMITED
REDWATER POWER PLANT
Gd, Redwater, AB, T0A 2W0

Emp Here 20
SIC 4922 Natural gas transmission

Rimbey, AB T0C

D-U-N-S 24-158-7567   (SL)
HUTTERIAN BRETHREN CHURCH OF LEEDALE
LEEDALE COLONY
Rr 4, Rimbey, AB, T0C 2J0
(403) 843-6681
Emp Here 60   *Sales* 3,939,878
SIC 8661 Religious organizations

D-U-N-S 24-342-3741   (BR)
KEYERA PARTNERSHIP
RIMBEY GAS PLANT
Gd, Rimbey, AB, T0C 2J0
(403) 843-7100
Emp Here 77
SIC 1311 Crude petroleum and natural gas

D-U-N-S 25-770-3959   (BR)
RIMOKA HOUSING FOUNDATION
PARKLAND MANOR
4906 54th Ave, Rimbey, AB, T0C 2J0
(403) 843-2376
Emp Here 30
SIC 8361 Residential care

D-U-N-S 20-591-9165   (BR)
WOLF CREEK SCHOOL DIVISION NO.72
RIMBEY ELEMENTARY SCHOOL
5302 52nd St, Rimbey, AB, T0C 2J0
(403) 843-3751
Emp Here 20
SIC 8211 Elementary and secondary schools

Rocky Mountain House, AB T4T

D-U-N-S 20-315-2616   (SL)
1597823 ALBERTA LTD
Hwy 11 Range Rd 70, Rocky Mountain House, AB, T4T 1A7
(403) 845-3072
Emp Here 400   *Sales* 95,117,040
SIC 6712 Bank holding companies
Dir Mervyn Pidherney
Dir Earlyne Pidherney

D-U-N-S 25-482-9385   (BR)

ALBERTA HEALTH SERVICES
ROCKY MOUNTAIN HOUSE HEALTH CENTER
5016 52 Ave Suite 1, Rocky Mountain House, AB, T4T 1T2
(403) 845-3347
Emp Here 200
SIC 8062 General medical and surgical hospitals

D-U-N-S 25-231-7409   (BR)
ALBERTA TREASURY BRANCHES
ATB FINANCIAL
4515 52 Ave, Rocky Mountain House, AB, T4T 1A6
(403) 844-2004
Emp Here 22
SIC 6036 Savings institutions, except federal

D-U-N-S 25-792-6402   (BR)
CEB INVESTMENTS INC
ABB BER-MAC
4435 45th Ave, Rocky Mountain House, AB, T4T 1T1
(403) 845-5404
Emp Here 28
SIC 1731 Electrical work

D-U-N-S 24-346-2918   (SL)
COPE, ROCKY MOUNTAIN HOUSE SOCIETY FOR PERSONS WITH DISABILITIES
4940 50 Ave, Rocky Mountain House, AB, T4T 1A8
(403) 845-4080
Emp Here 80   *Sales* 13,695,750
SIC 8399 Social services, nec
Ex Dir Laurel Ponich

D-U-N-S 20-539-9673   (BR)
CANADA POST CORPORATION
4912 47 Ave, Rocky Mountain House, AB, T4T 1V3
(403) 845-3606
Emp Here 20
SIC 4311 U.s. postal service

D-U-N-S 24-342-4111   (BR)
DEVON CANADA CORPORATION
Gd Stn Main, Rocky Mountain House, AB, T4T 1T1
(403) 845-2831
Emp Here 25
SIC 1382 Oil and gas exploration services

D-U-N-S 20-291-7126   (BR)
DIRECT ENERGY MARKETING LIMITED
CENTRICA ENERGY
Gd Stn Main, Rocky Mountain House, AB, T4T 1T1
(403) 844-5000
Emp Here 45
SIC 1311 Crude petroleum and natural gas

D-U-N-S 20-733-3357   (BR)
ENERFLEX LTD.
4915 44 St, Rocky Mountain House, AB, T4T 1A7
(403) 845-4666
Emp Here 25
SIC 3563 Air and gas compressors

D-U-N-S 20-706-1081   (BR)
FLINT FIELD SERVICES LTD
44a St Suite 4908, Rocky Mountain House, AB, T4T 1B6
(403) 845-3832
Emp Here 20
SIC 8742 Management consulting services

D-U-N-S 24-033-6367   (BR)
GOOD SAMARITAN SOCIETY, THE (A LUTHERAN SOCIAL SERVICE ORGANIZATION)
5615 60 St, Rocky Mountain House, AB, T4T 1W2
(403) 845-6033
Emp Here 20
SIC 8059 Nursing and personal care, nec

D-U-N-S 20-303-3803   (BR)
GOVERNMENT OF THE PROVINCE OF ALBERTA
CENTRAL REGION CHILD & FAMILY SERVICES
4919 51 St, Rocky Mountain House, AB, T4T 1A7
(403) 845-8290
Emp Here 20
SIC 8322 Individual and family services

D-U-N-S 25-957-5132   (BR)
KEYERA PARTNERSHIP
Gd Stn Main, Rocky Mountain House, AB, T4T 1T1
(403) 845-8100
Emp Here 50
SIC 2813 Industrial gases

D-U-N-S 24-356-5277   (BR)
LOBLAW COMPANIES LIMITED
EXTRA FOODS
5520 46 St Suite 640, Rocky Mountain House, AB, T4T 1X1
(403) 846-4700
Emp Here 20
SIC 5411 Grocery stores

D-U-N-S 20-272-9484   (BR)
QUINN CONTRACTING LTD
QUINN CONSTRUCTION
4315 49th Ave, Rocky Mountain House, AB, T4T 1A9
(403) 845-1003
Emp Here 65
SIC 1389 Oil and gas field services, nec

D-U-N-S 20-069-8566   (BR)
RED DEER CATHOLIC REGIONAL DIVISION NO. 39
ST MATTHEW SCHOOL
5735 58 St Suite 1, Rocky Mountain House, AB, T4T 1S2
(403) 345-2836
Emp Here 53
SIC 8211 Elementary and secondary schools

D-U-N-S 25-809-4101   (BR)
SOBEYS CAPITAL INCORPORATED
SOBEYS ROCKY MOUNTAIN HOUSE
5427 52 Ave, Rocky Mountain House, AB, T4T 1S9
(403) 845-3371
Emp Here 110
SIC 5411 Grocery stores

D-U-N-S 20-806-2419   (BR)
SOBEYS CAPITAL INCORPORATED
SOBEYS STORE# 3149
4419 52 Ave, Rocky Mountain House, AB, T4T 1A3
(403) 846-0038
Emp Here 125
SIC 5411 Grocery stores

D-U-N-S 20-704-4814   (BR)
TRANSCANADA PIPELINES LIMITED
4931 45 St, Rocky Mountain House, AB, T4T 1E1
(403) 845-1209
Emp Here 20
SIC 4924 Natural gas distribution

D-U-N-S 20-699-8648   (BR)
WEST FRASER TIMBER CO. LTD
WEST FRASER LVL
Gd Stn Main, Rocky Mountain House, AB, T4T 1T1
(403) 845-5522
Emp Here 190
SIC 5031 Lumber, plywood, and millwork

D-U-N-S 20-710-1549   (BR)
WILD ROSE SCHOOL DIVISION NO. 66
WEST CENTRAL HIGH SCHOOL
(*Suby of* Wild Rose School Division No. 66)
5506 50 St Suite 1, Rocky Mountain House, AB, T4T 1W7

(403) 845-3711
Emp Here 60
SIC 8211 Elementary and secondary schools

D-U-N-S 20-087-3540   (BR)
WILD ROSE SCHOOL DIVISION NO. 66
LOCHEARN ELEMENTARY SCHOOL
(*Suby of* Wild Rose School Division No. 66)
5416 54 St, Rocky Mountain House, AB, T4T 1S6
(403) 845-3721
Emp Here 43
SIC 8211 Elementary and secondary schools

D-U-N-S 20-086-5579   (HQ)
WILD ROSE SCHOOL DIVISION NO. 66
AURORA ELEMENTARY SCHOOL
(*Suby of* Wild Rose School Division No. 66)
4912 43 St, Rocky Mountain House, AB, T4T 1P4
(403) 845-3376
Emp Here 25   *Emp Total* 680
Sales 58,707,097
SIC 8211 Elementary and secondary schools
Ch Bd Keith Warren
Treas Gaordon Majeran
Superintnt Brian Celli

D-U-N-S 20-653-1688   (BR)
WILD ROSE SCHOOL DIVISION NO. 66
ECOLE ROCKY ELEMENTARY SCHOOL
(*Suby of* Wild Rose School Division No. 66)
4703 50 Ave, Rocky Mountain House, AB, T4T 1S4
(403) 845-3541
Emp Here 40
SIC 8211 Elementary and secondary schools

D-U-N-S 24-854-6376   (SL)
WILDERNESS VILLAGE CAMPGROUND ASSOCIATION
WILDERNESS VILLAGE RESORT
Se 14 4008 W 5, Rocky Mountain House, AB, T4T 1A9
(403) 845-2145
Emp Here 55   *Sales* 1,605,135
SIC 7033 Trailer parks and campsites

D-U-N-S 20-583-9124   (SL)
X-CALIBUR PIPELINE AND UTILITY LOCATION INC
X-CALIBUR GROUND DISTURBANCE SOLUTIONS
4407 45a Ave, Rocky Mountain House, AB, T4T 1T1
(403) 844-8662
Emp Here 75   *Sales* 15,159,393
SIC 1389 Oil and gas field services, nec
Pr Pr Jason Quintal
Genl Mgr Lindsay Quintal

Rocky View County, AB T1X

D-U-N-S 20-804-1413   (BR)
CANXPRESS DISTRIBUTION LTD
51st Ave 61 Se Bldg No. 285115, Rocky View County, AB, T1X 0K3
(403) 265-6563
Emp Here 20
SIC 4212 Local trucking, without storage

D-U-N-S 20-547-0839   (HQ)
CLEAN HARBORS ENERGY AND INDUSTRIAL SERVICES CORP.
235133 Ryan Rd, Rocky View County, AB, T1X 0K1
(403) 236-9891
Emp Here 30   *Emp Total* 12,400
Sales 17,325,020
SIC 7349 Building maintenance services, nec
Pr Pr Rod Marlin
Dir Kirk Calvert
Dir Bert Holtby

D-U-N-S 24-357-3164   (BR)
ENTREC CORPORATION

235132 84 St Se, Rocky View County, AB, T1X 0K1
(403) 777-1644
Emp Here 60
SIC 4213 Trucking, except local

D-U-N-S 24-791-6351   (BR)
FLYNN CANADA LTD
285221 Kleysen Way, Rocky View County, AB, T1X 0K1
(403) 720-8155
Emp Here 100
SIC 1761 Roofing, siding, and sheetMetal work

D-U-N-S 20-799-0826   (SL)
FOOTHILLS READY MIX INC
285135 Duff Dr, Rocky View County, AB, T1X 0K1
(403) 723-2225
Emp Here 55   *Sales* 11,159,500
SIC 3273 Ready-mixed concrete
Dir David Blackley
Sec Sandi Parks

D-U-N-S 20-556-2601   (SL)
IRON HORSE EARTHWORKS INC
235090 Wrangler Dr, Rocky View County, AB, T1X 0K3
(403) 217-2711
Emp Here 50   *Sales* 4,711,645
SIC 1794 Excavation work

D-U-N-S 24-160-9320   (HQ)
LUFF INDUSTRIES LTD
235010 Wrangler Rd, Rocky View County, AB, T1X 0K3
(403) 279-3555
Emp Here 86   *Emp Total* 2
Sales 156,961,193
SIC 3535 Conveyors and conveying equipment
Pr Pr Luigi Fasoli
Valerie Fasoli

D-U-N-S 24-344-5827   (BR)
PHOENIX TECHNOLOGY SERVICES INC
JAG (OILFIELD) RENTALS
285119 Bluegrass Dr, Rocky View County, AB, T1X 0P5
(403) 236-1394
Emp Here 50
SIC 7353 Heavy construction equipment rental

D-U-N-S 25-315-1666   (BR)
PYRAMID CORPORATION
235038 Wrangler Rd, Rocky View County, AB, T1X 0K3
(403) 720-0505
Emp Here 30
SIC 1731 Electrical work

D-U-N-S 20-768-0851   (BR)
ROSENAU TRANSPORT LTD
(*Suby of* Mid-Nite Sun Transportation Ltd)
234180 Wrangler Rd, Rocky View County, AB, T1X 0K2
(403) 279-4800
Emp Here 75
SIC 4212 Local trucking, without storage

D-U-N-S 24-016-5142   (BR)
TAIGA BUILDING PRODUCTS LTD
285230 Kleysen Way, Rocky View County, AB, T1X 0K1
(403) 279-0926
Emp Here 40
SIC 5031 Lumber, plywood, and millwork

D-U-N-S 24-702-0282   (BR)
TRANSX LTD
TRANSX LOGISTICS
285115 61 Av Se, Rocky View County, AB, T1X 0K3
(403) 236-9300
Emp Here 90
SIC 4213 Trucking, except local

D-U-N-S 24-325-5606   (HQ)
TREO DRILLING SERVICES L.P.
285160 Kleysen Way, Rocky View County, AB, T1X 0K1
(403) 723-8600
Emp Here 430   Emp Total 5,515
Sales 178,274,456
SIC 1381 Drilling oil and gas wells
Pr Rod Schmidt
VP Steve Bogstie

D-U-N-S 24-272-9408   (BR)
WASTE CONNECTIONS OF CANADA INC
BFI CANADA
285122 Bluegrass Dr, Rocky View County, AB, T1X 0P5
(403) 236-3883
Emp Here 85
SIC 4953 Refuse systems

Rocky View County, AB T4A

D-U-N-S 24-379-0008   (HQ)
AM-GAS SERVICES INC
261064 Wagon Wheel Cres, Rocky View County, AB, T4A 0E2
(403) 984-9830
Emp Here 47   Emp Total 11
Sales 6,785,345
SIC 3564 Blowers and fans
   Kelly Meston
Pr Pr January Mckee
   Dennis Scboe

D-U-N-S 25-687-8141   (HQ)
CANADREAM CORPORATION
CANADREAM RV RENTALS & SALES
292154 Crosspointe Dr, Rocky View County, AB, T4A 0V2
(403) 291-1000
Emp Here 45   Sales 10,506,341
SIC 7519 Utility trailer rental
Pr Pr Brian Gronberg
   Kariann Burmaster
   Blaine Nicholson
   Gerald Wood
   Scott Graham
   Louis Trouchet

D-U-N-S 24-747-2249   (BR)
COSTCO WHOLESALE CANADA LTD
COSTCO STORE#1076
(Suby of Costco Wholesale Corporation)
293020 Crossiron Common Suite 300, Rocky View County, AB, T4A 0J6
(403) 516-5050
Emp Here 280
SIC 5099 Durable goods, nec

D-U-N-S 20-268-3942   (BR)
GORDON FOOD SERVICE CANADA LTD
GFS CALGARY
290212 Township Road 261, Rocky View County, AB, T4A 0V6
(403) 235-8555
Emp Here 380
SIC 5141 Groceries, general line

D-U-N-S 24-803-5037   (BR)
LOWE'S COMPANIES CANADA, ULC
261199 Crossiron Blvd Unit 300, Rocky View County, AB, T4A 0J6
(403) 567-7440
Emp Here 160
SIC 5211 Lumber and other building materials

D-U-N-S 24-890-1204   (BR)
ROCKY MOUNTAIN DEALERSHIPS INC
ROCKY MOUNTAIN EQUIPMENT
260180 Writing Creek Cres, Rocky View County, AB, T4A 0M9
(403) 513-7000
Emp Here 850
SIC 5082 Construction and mining machinery

D-U-N-S 24-853-1212   (HQ)
SKYLINE BUILDING SYSTEMS INC
261185 Wagon Wheel Way, Rocky View County, AB, T4A 0E2
(403) 277-0700
Emp Here 24   Emp Total 400
Sales 7,449,759
SIC 5039 Construction materials, nec
Pr Trevor Kent

D-U-N-S 24-558-4029   (SL)
UNITED HORSEMEN OF ALBERTA INC
CENTURY DOWNS RACETRACK & CASINO
260 Century Downs Dr, Rocky View County, AB, T4A 0V5
(587) 349-7777
Emp Here 50
SIC 7948 Racing, including track operation

D-U-N-S 24-685-8729   (BR)
WALMART CANADA LOGISTICS ULC
261039 Wagon Wheel Cres, Rocky View County, AB, T4A 0E2
(403) 295-8364
Emp Here 280
SIC 4225 General warehousing and storage

Rockyford, AB T0J

D-U-N-S 24-715-5807   (SL)
HUTTERIAN BRETHREN CHURCH OF ROSEBUD
ROSEBUD COLONY
Gd, Rockyford, AB, T0J 2R0
(403) 533-2205
Emp Here 94   Sales 6,201,660
SIC 8661 Religious organizations
Pr Pr George Hofer
   Dan Hofer

Rycroft, AB T0H

D-U-N-S 20-709-9149   (BR)
PEACE WAPITI SCHOOL DIVISION NO.76
RYCROFT SCHOOL
5208 45 Ave, Rycroft, AB, T0H 3A0
(780) 765-3830
Emp Here 20
SIC 8211 Elementary and secondary schools

D-U-N-S 20-519-5618   (BR)
RICHARDSON INTERNATIONAL LIMITED
PIONEER GRAIN
Gd Lcd Main, Rycroft, AB, T0H 3A0
(780) 765-2270
Emp Here 22
SIC 5153 Grain and field beans

D-U-N-S 24-343-2536   (BR)
RICHARDSON PIONEER LIMITED
PIONEER GRAIN
Gd, Rycroft, AB, T0H 3A0
(780) 765-2000
Emp Here 20
SIC 5261 Retail nurseries and garden stores

D-U-N-S 20-329-5043   (SL)
TECHNISAND CANADA SALES LTD
(Suby of Fairmount Santrol Holdings Inc.)
781069 Range Rd 52, Rycroft, AB, T0H 3A0
Emp Here 40   Sales 3,769,316
SIC 2891 Adhesives and sealants

Saddle Lake, AB T0A

D-U-N-S 24-678-3190   (BR)
HEALTH CANADA

CANADA HEALTH & WELFARE
Gd, Saddle Lake, AB, T0A 3T0
(780) 726-3838
Emp Here 25
SIC 8011 Offices and clinics of medical doctors

Sangudo, AB T0E

D-U-N-S 20-573-1545   (BR)
CANADA POST CORPORATION
5017 51st Ave, Sangudo, AB, T0E 2A0
(780) 785-2223
Emp Here 20
SIC 4311 U.s. postal service

Seba Beach, AB T0E

D-U-N-S 20-591-9322   (BR)
PARKLAND SCHOOL DIVISION NO. 70
SEBA BEACH SCHOOL
53112 Hwy 31, Seba Beach, AB, T0E 2B0
(780) 797-3733
Emp Here 20
SIC 8211 Elementary and secondary schools

Sedgewick, AB T0B

D-U-N-S 20-074-4829   (HQ)
ARNETT & BURGESS OIL FIELD CONSTRUCTION LIMITED
4510 50 St, Sedgewick, AB, T0B 4C0
(780) 384-4050
Emp Here 50   Emp Total 50
Sales 10,395,012
SIC 1623 Water, sewer, and utility lines
Pr Pr Tom Arnett

D-U-N-S 20-710-5466   (BR)
BATTLE RIVER REGIONAL DIVISION 31
CENTRAL HIGH SCHOOL
5101 50 Ave, Sedgewick, AB, T0B 4C0
(780) 384-3817
Emp Here 50
SIC 8211 Elementary and secondary schools

D-U-N-S 24-365-0699   (BR)
BEAVER FOUNDATION
VIALTA LODGE
(Suby of Beaver Foundation)
5128 57 Ave, Sedgewick, AB, T0B 4C0
(780) 336-3353
Emp Here 20
SIC 8361 Residential care

Seven Persons, AB T0K

D-U-N-S 25-414-4975   (BR)
PRAIRIE ROSE SCHOOL DIVISION NO 8
SEVEN PERSONS SCHOOL
24 3 Ave, Seven Persons, AB, T0K 1Z0
(403) 832-3732
Emp Here 30
SIC 8211 Elementary and secondary schools

Sexsmith, AB T0H

D-U-N-S 25-313-1247   (BR)
ENCANA CORPORATION
ENCANA OIL & GAS
Gd, Sexsmith, AB, T0H 3C0

(780) 568-4444
Emp Here 40
SIC 1311 Crude petroleum and natural gas

D-U-N-S 25-000-5204   (BR)
GRANDE PRAIRIE CATHOLIC SCHOOL DISTRICT 28
ST MARY'S SCHOOL
9001 103 St, Sexsmith, AB, T0H 3C0
(780) 568-3631
Emp Here 30
SIC 8211 Elementary and secondary schools

D-U-N-S 20-037-3277   (BR)
PEACE WAPITI SCHOOL DIVISION NO.76
SEXSMITH SECONDARY SCHOOL
9401 99 Ave, Sexsmith, AB, T0H 3C0
(780) 568-3642
Emp Here 35
SIC 8211 Elementary and secondary schools

Sherwood Park, AB T8A

D-U-N-S 24-390-4935   (SL)
297943 ALBERTA LTD
FRANKLIN'S INN
2016 Sherwood Dr Suite 15, Sherwood Park, AB, T8A 3X3
(780) 467-1234
Emp Here 50   Sales 2,188,821
SIC 7011 Hotels and motels

D-U-N-S 24-399-7835   (BR)
AECON CONSTRUCTION AND MATERIALS LIMITED
AECON INDUSTRIAL WESTERN
53367 Range Road 232, Sherwood Park, AB, T8A 4V2
(780) 416-5700
Emp Here 200
SIC 1629 Heavy construction, nec

D-U-N-S 20-317-1798   (BR)
ARROW RELOAD SYSTEMS INC
53309 Range Road 232, Sherwood Park, AB, T8A 4V2
(780) 464-4640
Emp Here 465
SIC 4789 Transportation services, nec

D-U-N-S 25-516-1879   (BR)
BANK OF NOVA SCOTIA, THE
SCOTIABANK
993 Fir St Suite 15, Sherwood Park, AB, T8A 4N5
(780) 467-2276
Emp Here 26
SIC 6021 National commercial banks

D-U-N-S 20-572-5240   (BR)
CANADA POST CORPORATION
1080 Strathcona Dr, Sherwood Park, AB, T8A 0Z7
(780) 449-2040
Emp Here 20
SIC 4311 U.s. postal service

D-U-N-S 20-303-3170   (BR)
CARA OPERATIONS LIMITED
KELSEY'S
(Suby of Cara Holdings Limited)
975 Broadmoor Blvd Suite 42, Sherwood Park, AB, T8A 5W9
(780) 944-0202
Emp Here 40
SIC 5812 Eating places

D-U-N-S 24-418-5000   (BR)
CINEPLEX ODEON CORPORATION
GALAXY CINEMAS
2020 Sherwood Dr Suite 3146, Sherwood Park, AB, T8A 3H9
(780) 416-0152
Emp Here 60
SIC 7832 Motion picture theaters, except drive-in

D-U-N-S 24-000-6689   (BR)
COMPAGNIE DES CHEMINS DE FER NA-TIONAUX DU CANADA
CN OIL & GAS SERVICE CENTRE
53307 Range Road 232, Sherwood Park, AB, T8A 4V2

Emp Here 20
SIC 4111 Local and suburban transit

D-U-N-S 24-000-3863   (SL)
CONMAR JANITORIAL CO. LTD
50 Ridgeview Crt, Sherwood Park, AB, T8A 6B4
(780) 441-5459
Emp Here 75   Sales 2,598,753
SIC 7349 Building maintenance services, nec

D-U-N-S 25-626-3955   (BR)
DENCAN RESTAURANTS INC
DENNY'S RESTAURANT
(Suby of Northland Properties Corporation)
975 Broadmoor Blvd Unit 44, Sherwood Park, AB, T8A 5W9
(780) 467-7893
Emp Here 50
SIC 5812 Eating places

D-U-N-S 25-261-4649   (SL)
DRAGON SANDBLASTING & PAINTING (2001) LTD
53323 Range Road 232, Sherwood Park, AB, T8A 4V2
(780) 472-6969
Emp Here 50   Sales 4,146,248
SIC 1721 Painting and paper hanging

D-U-N-S 24-828-2944   (BR)
EDLEUN, INC
EDUCATION LEARNING UNIVERSE
20 Main Blvd, Sherwood Park, AB, T8A 3W8
(780) 417-3444
Emp Here 30
SIC 8351 Child day care services

D-U-N-S 20-162-4587   (BR)
ELK ISLAND CATHOLIC SEPARATE RE-GIONAL DIVISION NO. 41
ARCHBISHOP JORDAN HIGH SCHOOL
2021 Brentwood Blvd, Sherwood Park, AB, T8A 0X2
(780) 467-2121
Emp Here 20
SIC 8211 Elementary and secondary schools

D-U-N-S 25-015-8219   (BR)
ELK ISLAND CATHOLIC SEPARATE RE-GIONAL DIVISION NO. 41
ECOLE OUR LADY OF PERPETUAL HELP SCHOOL
273 Fir St, Sherwood Park, AB, T8A 2G7
(780) 467-5631
Emp Here 42
SIC 8211 Elementary and secondary schools

D-U-N-S 25-269-5903   (BR)
ELK ISLAND CATHOLIC SEPARATE RE-GIONAL DIVISION NO. 41
JEAN VANIER CATHOLIC SCHOOL
109 Georgian Way, Sherwood Park, AB, T8A 3K9
(780) 467-3633
Emp Here 35
SIC 8211 Elementary and secondary schools

D-U-N-S 25-015-8102   (BR)
ELK ISLAND CATHOLIC SEPARATE RE-GIONAL DIVISION NO. 41
MADONNA CATHOLIC SCHOOL
15 Main Blvd, Sherwood Park, AB, T8A 3N3
(780) 467-7972
Emp Here 32
SIC 8211 Elementary and secondary schools

D-U-N-S 20-069-3864   (BR)
ELK ISLAND CATHOLIC SEPARATE RE-GIONAL DIVISION NO. 41
ST THERESA CATHOLIC SCHOOL

2021 Brentwood Blvd, Sherwood Park, AB, T8A 0X2
(780) 464-4001
Emp Here 45
SIC 8211 Elementary and secondary schools

D-U-N-S 25-015-7864   (BR)
ELK ISLAND CATHOLIC SEPARATE RE-GIONAL DIVISION NO. 41
KEARNS, FATHER KENNETH SCHOOL
8 Sancpiper Dr, Sherwood Park, AB, T8A 0B6
(780) 467-7135
Emp Here 40
SIC 8211 Elementary and secondary schools

D-U-N-S 25-065-2708   (BR)
ELK ISLAND PUBLIC SCHOOLS RE-GIONAL DIVISION NO. 14
WESTBORO ELEMENTARY SCHOOL
(Suby of Elk Island Public Schools Regional Division No. 14)
1078 Strathcona Dr, Sherwood Park, AB, T8A 0Z9
(780) 467-7751
Emp Here 42
SIC 8211 Elementary and secondary schools

D-U-N-S 25-015-9076   (BR)
ELK ISLAND PUBLIC SCHOOLS RE-GIONAL DIVISION NO. 14
SALISBURY COMPOSITE HIGH SCHOOL
(Suby of Elk Island Public Schools Regional Division No. 14)
20 Festival Way, Sherwood Park, AB, T8A 4Y1
(780) 467-8816
Emp Here 100
SIC 8211 Elementary and secondary schools

D-U-N-S 20-023-9734   (BR)
ELK ISLAND PUBLIC SCHOOLS RE-GIONAL DIVISION NO. 14
CAMPBELLTOWN ELEMENTARY SCHOOL
271 Conifer St, Sherwood Park, AB, T8A 1M4
(780) 467-5143
Emp Here 38
SIC 8211 Elementary and secondary schools

D-U-N-S 20-023-9767   (BR)
ELK ISLAND PUBLIC SCHOOLS RE-GIONAL DIVISION NO. 14
WES HOSFORD ELEMENTARY SCHOOL
207 Granada Blvd, Sherwood Park, AB, T8A 3R5
(780) 464-1711
Emp Here 45
SIC 8211 Elementary and secondary schools

D-U-N-S 25-267-1771   (BR)
ELK ISLAND PUBLIC SCHOOLS RE-GIONAL DIVISION NO. 14
CLOVER BAR JUNIOR HIGH SCHOOL
(Suby of Elk Island Public Schools Regional Division No. 14)
50 Main Blvd, Sherwood Park, AB, T8A 0R2
(780) 467-2295
Emp Here 48
SIC 8211 Elementary and secondary schools

D-U-N-S 25-015-9225   (BR)
ELK ISLAND PUBLIC SCHOOLS RE-GIONAL DIVISION NO. 14
SHERWOOD HEIGHTS JUNIOR HIGH SCHOOL
(Suby of Elk Island Public Schools Regional Division No. 14)
241 Fir St, Sherwood Park, AB, T8A 2G6
(780) 467-5930
Emp Here 50
SIC 8211 Elementary and secondary schools

D-U-N-S 20-709-9677   (BR)
ELK ISLAND PUBLIC SCHOOLS RE-GIONAL DIVISION NO. 14
NEXT STEP OUTREACH
1020 Sherwood Dr Suite 130, Sherwood Park, AB, T8A 2G4
(780) 464-1899
Emp Here 40

SIC 8211 Elementary and secondary schools

D-U-N-S 20-709-8810   (BR)
ELK ISLAND PUBLIC SCHOOLS RE-GIONAL DIVISION NO. 14
BRENTWOOD ELEMENTARY
28 Heron Rd, Sherwood Park, AB, T8A 0H2
(780) 467-5591
Emp Here 50
SIC 8211 Elementary and secondary schools

D-U-N-S 20-709-8703   (BR)
ELK ISLAND PUBLIC SCHOOLS RE-GIONAL DIVISION NO. 14
FRHAYPHORNE JUNIOR HIGH SCHOOL
300 Colwill Blvd, Sherwood Park, AB, T8A 5R7
(780) 467-3800
Emp Here 50
SIC 8211 Elementary and secondary schools

D-U-N-S 20-709-9255   (BR)
ELK ISLAND PUBLIC SCHOOLS RE-GIONAL DIVISION NO. 14
GLENN ALLEN ELEMENTARY SCHOOL
106 Georgian Way, Sherwood Park, AB, T8A 2V9
(780) 467-5519
Emp Here 35
SIC 8211 Elementary and secondary schools

D-U-N-S 20-028-4136   (BR)
ELK ISLAND PUBLIC SCHOOLS RE-GIONAL DIVISION NO. 14
WOODBRIDGE FARMS SCHOOL
1127 Parker Dr, Sherwood Park, AB, T8A 4E5
(780) 464-3330
Emp Here 35
SIC 8211 Elementary and secondary schools

D-U-N-S 20-023-9742   (BR)
ELK ISLAND PUBLIC SCHOOLS RE-GIONAL DIVISION NO. 14
PINE STREET SCHOOL
133 Pine St, Sherwood Park, AB, T8A 1H2
(780) 467-2246
Emp Here 35
SIC 8211 Elementary and secondary schools

D-U-N-S 20-709-9032   (BR)
ELK ISLAND PUBLIC SCHOOLS RE-GIONAL DIVISION NO. 14
MILLS HAVEN ELEMENTARY.
73 Main Blvd, Sherwood Park, AB, T8A 0R1
(780) 467-5556
Emp Here 50
SIC 8211 Elementary and secondary schools

D-U-N-S 25-089-1330   (BR)
FGL SPORTS LTD
SPORT CHEK SHERWOOD PARK MALL
2020 Sherwood Dr Unit 15, Sherwood Park, AB, T8A 3H9
(780) 467-4712
Emp Here 40
SIC 5941 Sporting goods and bicycle shops

D-U-N-S 24-928-5461   (BR)
GENERAL MILLS CANADA CORPORATION
(Suby of General Mills, Inc.)
246 Cree Rd, Sherwood Park, AB, T8A 3X8
(780) 464-1544
Emp Here 50
SIC 2041 Flour and other grain mill products

D-U-N-S 25-184-5561   (BR)
GOODLIFE FITNESS CENTRES INC
2020 Sherwood Dr Unit 300, Sherwood Park, AB, T8A 3H9
(780) 416-5464
Emp Here 30
SIC 7991 Physical fitness facilities

D-U-N-S 25-832-2577   (SL)
HOOD TECHNICAL CONSULTANTS LTD
HOOD TECH
150 Chippewa Rd Suite 258, Sherwood Park, AB, T8A 6A2

(780) 416-4663
Emp Here 50   Sales 6,898,600
SIC 8711 Engineering services
Pr Pr Donald Quist

D-U-N-S 20-048-5290   (HQ)
HORTON CBI, LIMITED
261 Seneca Rd, Sherwood Park, AB, T8A 4G6
(780) 410-2760
Emp Here 250   Emp Total 43,841
Sales 38,981,295
SIC 1791 Structural steel erection
Pr Pr Marc Beauregard
VP VP Kim Tsang
Karl Thiessen
Sec Bridget Toms
Treas Jonathan Cahwoon

D-U-N-S 20-965-7993   (BR)
INDIGO BOOKS & MUSIC INC
CHAPTERS
(Suby of Indigo Books & Music Inc)
2020 Sherwood Dr Suite 104, Sherwood Park, AB, T8A 3H9
(780) 449-3331
Emp Here 28
SIC 5942 Book stores

D-U-N-S 25-218-5111   (BR)
LOCKERBIE & HOLE CONTRACTING LIMITED
LOCKERBIE & HOLE CONTRACTING - SHERWOOD PARK
53367 Range Road 232, Sherwood Park, AB, T8A 4V2

Emp Here 300
SIC 1711 Plumbing, heating, air-conditioning

D-U-N-S 25-218-0542   (BR)
LOCKERBIE & HOLE CONTRACTING LIMITED
LOCKERBIE & HOLE CONSTRUCTION
53367 Range Road 232, Sherwood Park, AB, T8A 4V2
(780) 416-5700
Emp Here 70
SIC 1711 Plumbing, heating, air-conditioning

D-U-N-S 25-015-8136   (BR)
MCDONALD'S   RESTAURANTS   OF CANADA LIMITED
MCDONALD'S RESTAURANT
(Suby of McDonald's Corporation)
1 Kaska Rd, Sherwood Park, AB, T8A 4E7
(780) 449-6221
Emp Here 55
SIC 5812 Eating places

D-U-N-S 20-800-6986   (BR)
MCDONALD'S   RESTAURANTS   OF CANADA LIMITED
MCDONALD'S
(Suby of McDonald's Corporation)
950 Ordze Rd, Sherwood Park, AB, T8A 4L8
(780) 467-6490
Emp Here 75
SIC 5812 Eating places

D-U-N-S 20-142-7569   (SL)
MILLENNIUM INSURANCE CORPORATION
(Suby of Firstcan Management Inc)
340 Sioux Rd, Sherwood Park, AB, T8A 3X6
(780) 467-1500
Emp Here 60   Sales 5,399,092
SIC 6411 Insurance agents, brokers, and service
Aaron Perdue
Donald Wheaton
Pr Pr William G Wheaton
Dir Donald A Wheaton
Dir Denis Brown
Dir Dennis Erker
Dir Stephen Laird
Dir Kim Ward

D-U-N-S 20-859-9147   (BR)
PACIFIC LINK COMMUNICATIONS INC

BELL WORLD
2020 Sherwood Dr Unit 16a, Sherwood Park, AB, T8A 3H9
(780) 464-3914
Emp Here 25
SIC 5999 Miscellaneous retail stores, nec

D-U-N-S 24-983-9903　　(SL)
PANDA REALTY INC
COLDWELL BANKER
2016 Sherwood Dr, Sherwood Park, AB, T8A 3X3

Emp Here 185　　*Sales* 24,246,550
SIC 6531 Real estate agents and managers
Dir Tom Darby
　John Fisher
　Sherry Belcourt
　Ken Hartenberger
　Lynn Scrima
　Brian Vane

D-U-N-S 25-271-0330　　(BR)
SOBEYS WEST INC
SHERWOOD SAFEWAY
2020 Sherwood Dr, Sherwood Park, AB, T8A 3H9
(780) 467-3037
Emp Here 140
SIC 5411 Grocery stores

D-U-N-S 25-014-9820　　(BR)
SOBEYS WEST INC
985 Fir St, Sherwood Park, AB, T8A 4N5
(780) 467-0177
Emp Here 175
SIC 5411 Grocery stores

D-U-N-S 20-860-3584　　(BR)
SOURCE (BELL) ELECTRONICS INC, THE
SOURCE, THE
2020 Sherwood Dr Suite 104, Sherwood Park, AB, T8A 3H9
(780) 416-1140
Emp Here 25
SIC 5999 Miscellaneous retail stores, nec

D-U-N-S 24-871-9853　　(SL)
SPIFFY CLEAN INC
165 Seneca Rd, Sherwood Park, AB, T8A 4G6
(780) 467-5584
Emp Here 30　　*Sales* 5,284,131
SIC 1521 Single-family housing construction

D-U-N-S 25-243-7210　　(BR)
STARBUCKS COFFEE CANADA, INC
STARBUCKS
(*Suby of* Starbucks Corporation)
1000 Alder Ave Unit 25, Sherwood Park, AB, T8A 2G2
(780) 467-2836
Emp Here 30
SIC 5812 Eating places

D-U-N-S 25-451-1173　　(BR)
SUNCOR ENERGY INC
SUNCOR SOCIAL CLUB
241 Kaska Rd, Sherwood Park, AB, T8A 4E8
(780) 449-2100
Emp Here 100
SIC 4613 Refined petroleum pipelines

D-U-N-S 25-505-3639　　(BR)
SYSTEMATIX CONSULTANTS INC
SYSTEMATIX
2016 Sherwood Dr Suite 15, Sherwood Park, AB, T8A 3X3
(780) 416-4337
Emp Here 55
SIC 7379 Computer related services, nec

D-U-N-S 25-315-0619　　(BR)
TORONTO-DOMINION BANK, THE
TD BANK FINANCIAL GROUP
(*Suby of* Toronto-Dominion Bank, The)
2020 Sherwood Dr Suite 30, Sherwood Park, AB, T8A 3H9
(780) 449-9300
Emp Here 30

SIC 6021 National commercial banks

D-U-N-S 24-520-8244　　(SL)
ULTIMA HOLDINGS LTD
BOSTON PIZZA
967 Ordze Rd, Sherwood Park, AB, T8A 4L7
(780) 467-2223
Emp Here 50　　*Sales* 1,532,175
SIC 5812 Eating places

D-U-N-S 20-321-0448　　(SL)
WILLBROS PSS MIDSTREAM (CANADA) L.P.
261 Seneca Rd, Sherwood Park, AB, T8A 4G6
(780) 400-4200
Emp Here 100　　*Sales* 22,615,896
SIC 1623 Water, sewer, and utility lines
CFO Michael Jurcevic

D-U-N-S 24-395-1118　　(HQ)
WOWU FACTOR DESSERTS LTD
(*Suby of* WowU Factor Desserts Ltd)
152 Cree Rd, Sherwood Park, AB, T8A 3X8
(780) 464-0303
Emp Here 35　　*Emp Total* 55
Sales 4,764,381
SIC 2053 Frozen bakery products, except bread

Sherwood Park, AB T8B

D-U-N-S 20-578-2621　　(BR)
ALBERTA TREASURY BRANCHES
ATB FINANCIAL
201 Wye Rd, Sherwood Park, AB, T8B 1N1
(780) 449-6770
Emp Here 20
SIC 6036 Savings institutions, except federal

D-U-N-S 25-516-8452　　(BR)
CHIRO FOODS LIMITED
A & W RESTAURANTS
99 Wye Rd Suite 43, Sherwood Park, AB, T8B 1M1
(780) 449-3366
Emp Here 20
SIC 5812 Eating places

D-U-N-S 25-015-7831　　(HQ)
ELK ISLAND PUBLIC SCHOOLS REGIONAL DIVISION NO. 14
(*Suby of* Elk Island Public Schools Regional Division No. 14)
683 Wye Rd, Sherwood Park, AB, T8B 1N2
(780) 464-3477
Emp Here 160　　*Emp Total* 1,400
Sales 128,815,360
SIC 8211 Elementary and secondary schools
Ch Bd Paul Dolynny
V Ch Bd Glen Buchan
Sec Brian Smith
Trst Mae Adamyk
Trst W.H. Gordon
Trst Lynn Patterson
Trst Lisa Brower
Trst Bonnie Riddell
Trst Pat Mclauchlan
Trst Lois Byers

D-U-N-S 20-706-4416　　(BR)
ELK ISLAND PUBLIC SCHOOLS REGIONAL DIVISION NO. 14
COLCHESTER ELEMENTARY SCHOOL
23358 Township Road 520 Suite 520, Sherwood Park, AB, T8B 1G5
(780) 467-5940
Emp Here 26
SIC 8211 Elementary and secondary schools

D-U-N-S 25-498-2788　　(BR)
WAL-MART CANADA CORP
239 Wye Rd, Sherwood Park, AB, T8B 1N1
(780) 464-2105
Emp Here 263

SIC 5311 Department stores

D-U-N-S 20-199-2356　　(BR)
WENDY'S RESTAURANTS OF CANADA INC
WENDY'S
(*Suby of* The Wendy's Company)
198 Ordze Ave, Sherwood Park, AB, T8B 1M6
(780) 467-3924
Emp Here 25
SIC 5812 Eating places

Sherwood Park, AB T8C

D-U-N-S 25-065-3151　　(BR)
ELK ISLAND PUBLIC SCHOOLS REGIONAL DIVISION NO. 14
FULTONVALE ELEMENTARY JUNIOR HIGH SCHOOL
(*Suby of* Elk Island Public Schools Regional Division No. 14)
52029 Range Road 224, Sherwood Park, AB, T8C 1B5
(780) 922-3058
Emp Here 30
SIC 8211 Elementary and secondary schools

D-U-N-S 25-360-2460　　(SL)
NB DEVELOPMENTS LTD
51055 Range Road 222 Suite 222, Sherwood Park, AB, T8C 1J6
(780) 922-2327
Emp Here 55　　*Sales* 2,188,821
SIC 7997 Membership sports and recreation clubs

Sherwood Park, AB T8G

D-U-N-S 20-024-1052　　(BR)
MEMORIAL GARDENS CANADA LIMITED
GLENWOOD MEMORIAL GARDENS
52356 Range Road 210 Suite 232, Sherwood Park, AB, T8G 1A6
(780) 467-0971
Emp Here 20
SIC 6553 Cemetery subdividers and developers

Sherwood Park, AB T8H

D-U-N-S 25-099-9430　　(HQ)
3033441 NOVA SCOTIA COMPANY
ALLIED FITTING CANADA
172 Turbo Dr, Sherwood Park, AB, T8H 2J6
(780) 464-7774
Emp Here 30　　*Emp Total* 80
Sales 7,733,834
SIC 5085 Industrial supplies
Pr Pr Marc Herstein

D-U-N-S 20-868-5339　　(HQ)
A & B RAIL SERVICES LTD
FRONTLINE CIVIL MANAGEMENT
(*Suby of* Universal Rail Systems Inc)
50 Strathmoor Dr Suite 200, Sherwood Park, AB, T8H 2B6
(780) 449-7699
Emp Here 45　　*Emp Total* 10
Sales 13,716,612
SIC 1629 Heavy construction, nec
Pr Pr Paul H Brum
Dir Fin Troy Hilliker
Dir Daniel Jacques
Dir Neil Johansen
Dir Paul Rowe

D-U-N-S 20-069-7865　　(BR)
ALBERTA HEALTH SERVICES
STRATHCONA COUNTY HEALTH CENTER

2 Brower Dr, Sherwood Park, AB, T8H 1V4
(780) 342-4600
Emp Here 100
SIC 8093 Specialty outpatient clinics, nec

D-U-N-S 25-236-1951　　(BR)
ALBERTA TREASURY BRANCHES
ATB FINANCIAL
550 Baseline Rd Unit 100, Sherwood Park, AB, T8H 2G8
(780) 464-4444
Emp Here 25
SIC 6036 Savings institutions, except federal

D-U-N-S 20-030-7507　　(BR)
ALBERTS RESTAURANTS LTD
ALBERTS HOMESTEAD GRILL
(*Suby of* Alberts Restaurants Ltd)
26 Strathmoor Dr, Sherwood Park, AB, T8H 2B6

Emp Here 50
SIC 5812 Eating places

D-U-N-S 24-398-1842　　(SL)
BELVEDERE GOLF & COUNTRY CLUB
51418 Hwy 21 S, Sherwood Park, AB, T8H 2T2
(780) 467-2025
Emp Here 80　　*Sales* 3,210,271
SIC 7997 Membership sports and recreation clubs

D-U-N-S 24-089-0520　　(SL)
BORZA INSPECTIONS LTD
(*Suby of* Aegion Corporation)
140 Portage Close, Sherwood Park, AB, T8H 2W2
(780) 416-0999
Emp Here 40　　*Sales* 7,101,500
SIC 1389 Oil and gas field services, nec
Dir Delton Gray

D-U-N-S 25-272-5924　　(BR)
CANADA POST CORPORATION
SHERWOOD PARK POST OFFICE
26 Cranford Way, Sherwood Park, AB, T8H 0W7

Emp Here 55
SIC 4311 U.s. postal service

D-U-N-S 20-588-8733　　(BR)
CANADIAN IMPERIAL BANK OF COMMERCE
CIBC
590 Baseline Rd Suite 160, Sherwood Park, AB, T8H 1Y4
(780) 417-7677
Emp Here 20
SIC 6021 National commercial banks

D-U-N-S 20-315-5742　　(BR)
CANADIAN SPECIALTY METALS ULC
ASA ALLOYS
20 Challenger Cres, Sherwood Park, AB, T8H 2R1
(780) 416-6422
Emp Here 20
SIC 5051 Metals service centers and offices

D-U-N-S 20-555-8104　　(BR)
CHAMPION TECHNOLOGIES ULC
2300 Premier Way, Sherwood Park, AB, T8H 2L2
(780) 417-2720
Emp Here 25
SIC 8731 Commercial physical research

D-U-N-S 24-312-3002　　(BR)
COSTCO WHOLESALE CANADA LTD
(*Suby of* Costco Wholesale Corporation)
2201 Broadmoor Blvd, Sherwood Park, AB, T8H 0A1
(780) 410-2521
Emp Here 200
SIC 5099 Durable goods, nec

D-U-N-S 24-418-8236　　(BR)

▲ **Public Company**　　■ **Public Company Family Member**　　**HQ** Headquarters　　**BR** Branch　　**SL** Single Location

CRANE CARRIER (CANADA) LIMITED
ARCTIC TRUCK PARTS & SERVICE
(*Suby of* Illinois Tool Works Inc.)
63 Strathmoor Dr, Sherwood Park, AB, T8H
0C1
(780) 416-4444
Emp Here 29
SIC 5013 Motor vehicle supplies and new
parts

D-U-N-S 20-713-1918   (BR)
ELK ISLAND CATHOLIC SEPARATE RE-GIONAL DIVISION NO. 41
HOLY SPIRIT CATHOLIC SCHOOL
151 Crimson Dr, Sherwood Park, AB, T8H
2R2
(780) 416-9526
Emp Here 50
SIC 8211 Elementary and secondary schools

D-U-N-S 20-709-9891   (BR)
ELK ISLAND PUBLIC SCHOOLS RE-GIONAL DIVISION NO. 14
LAKE LAND RIDGE SCHOOL
101 Crimson Dr, Sherwood Park, AB, T8H 2P1
(780) 416-9018
Emp Here 50
SIC 8211 Elementary and secondary schools

D-U-N-S 20-743-3850   (BR)
FLINT ENERGY SERVICES LTD.
FLINT FABRICATION AND MODULARIZA-TION
2899 Broadmoor Blvd Suite 100, Sherwood
Park, AB, T8H 1B5
(780) 416-3400
Emp Here 40
SIC 3498 Fabricated pipe and fittings

D-U-N-S 25-328-6496   (SL)
FLINT FABRICATION AND MODULARIZA-TION LTD
180 Strathmoor Dr, Sherwood Park, AB, T8H
2B7
(780) 416-3501
Emp Here 115   *Sales* 22,992,828
SIC 3443 Fabricated plate work (boiler shop)
Kerri Beuk
Donald Nehajowich

D-U-N-S 20-945-3831   (BR)
FLYING J CANADA INC
FLYING J TRAVEL PLAZA
50 Pembina Rd Suite 10, Sherwood Park, AB,
T8H 2G9
(780) 416-2035
Emp Here 20
SIC 4725 Tour operators

D-U-N-S 25-015-0893   (BR)
GREAT PACIFIC INDUSTRIES INC
SAVE-ON-FOODS
60 Broadway Blvd, Sherwood Park, AB, T8H
2A2
(780) 449-7208
Emp Here 280
SIC 5411 Grocery stores

D-U-N-S 20-177-5041   (BR)
HOME DEPOT OF CANADA INC
HOME DEPOT
(*Suby of* The Home Depot Inc)
390 Baseline Rd Suite 200, Sherwood Park,
AB, T8H 1X1
(780) 417-7875
Emp Here 150
SIC 5251 Hardware stores

D-U-N-S 24-322-3497   (BR)
HONEYWELL LIMITED
(*Suby of* Honeywell International Inc.)
2181 Premier Way Suite 160, Sherwood Park,
AB, T8H 2V1
(780) 410-0010
Emp Here 40
SIC 3822 Environmental controls

D-U-N-S 25-092-8608   (SL)

HUNTER POWER SYSTEMS INC
Gd, Sherwood Park, AB, T8H 2T1
(780) 718-9105
Emp Here 50   *Sales* 5,653,974
SIC 1731 Electrical work
Pr Pr Bill Willcox
VP VP Barbara Willcox

D-U-N-S 24-071-3136   (BR)
JOEY TOMATO'S KITCHENS INC
JOEY RESTAURANT
222 Baseline Rd Unit 250, Sherwood Park,
AB, T8H 1S8
(780) 449-1161
Emp Here 150
SIC 5812 Eating places

D-U-N-S 24-344-3400   (BR)
KAL TIRE LTD
27 Strathmoor Dr, Sherwood Park, AB, T8H
0C1
(780) 417-9500
Emp Here 35
SIC 5531 Auto and home supply stores

D-U-N-S 20-333-6305   (BR)
LEHIGH HANSON MATERIALS LIMITED
INLAND CONCRETE
301 Petroleum Way, Sherwood Park, AB, T8H
2G2
(780) 417-6776
Emp Here 50
SIC 5032 Brick, stone, and related material

D-U-N-S 25-148-1800   (BR)
LOBLAWS INC
REAL CANADIAN SUPERSTORE
410 Baseline Rd Suite 100, Sherwood Park,
AB, T8H 2A7
(780) 417-5212
Emp Here 300
SIC 5411 Grocery stores

D-U-N-S 25-518-8476   (BR)
**MCDONALD'S   RESTAURANTS   OF
CANADA LIMITED**
MCDONALD'S RESTAURANTS
(*Suby of* McDonald's Corporation)
590 Baseline Rd Suite 200, Sherwood Park,
AB, T8H 1Y4
(780) 417-2801
Emp Here 49
SIC 5812 Eating places

D-U-N-S 20-798-4837   (BR)
**MCDONALD'S   RESTAURANTS   OF
CANADA LIMITED**
MCDONALD'S
(*Suby of* McDonald's Corporation)
22 Strathmoor Dr, Sherwood Park, AB, T8H
2B6
(780) 417-7304
Emp Here 20
SIC 5812 Eating places

D-U-N-S 20-809-6198   (HQ)
OPUS STEWART WEIR LTD
STEWART WEIR GROUP
2121 Premier Way Suite 140, Sherwood Park,
AB, T8H 0B8
(780) 410-2580
Emp Here 119   *Sales* 21,396,400
SIC 8713 Surveying services
Pr Pr Ronald Mcgaffin
Brian Pearse
Frank Meashaw
Paul Dixon

D-U-N-S 24-330-2614   (BR)
PIONEER ENVIRO GROUP LTD
2055 Premier Way Suite 121, Sherwood Park,
AB, T8H 0G2
(780) 464-2184
Emp Here 20
SIC 8748 Business consulting, nec

D-U-N-S 20-736-1218   (BR)
PRIME RESTAURANTS INC

EAST SIDE MARIOS
(*Suby of* Cara Holdings Limited)
270 Baseline Rd Suite 200, Sherwood Park,
AB, T8H 1R4

Emp Here 50
SIC 5812 Eating places

D-U-N-S 24-378-3987   (BR)
QM LP
15 Turbo Dr, Sherwood Park, AB, T8H 2J6
(780) 467-8881
Emp Here 60
SIC 1795 Wrecking and demolition work

D-U-N-S 24-773-0356   (BR)
REXALL PHARMACY GROUP LTD
REXALL DRUG STORE 7233
(*Suby of* McKesson Corporation)
101 Bremner Dr Suite 5, Sherwood Park, AB,
T8H 0M5

Emp Here 20
SIC 5912 Drug stores and proprietary stores

D-U-N-S 25-515-9196   (BR)
ROYAL BANK OF CANADA
ROYAL BANK FINANCIAL GROUP
(*Suby of* Royal Bank Of Canada)
390 Baseline Rd Suite 160, Sherwood Park,
AB, T8H 1X1
(780) 449-7700
Emp Here 38
SIC 6021 National commercial banks

D-U-N-S 20-352-1112   (SL)
SPV MOTORS GP INC
SHERWOOD PARK VOLKSWAGEN
2365 Broadmoor Blvd, Sherwood Park, AB,
T8H 1N1
(780) 400-4800
Emp Here 22   *Sales* 8,025,677
SIC 5511 New and used car dealers
Steven Landry
Christopher Burrows

D-U-N-S 24-064-4815   (BR)
SERVUS CREDIT UNION LTD
800 Bethel Dr, Sherwood Park, AB, T8H 2N4
(780) 449-7760
Emp Here 25
SIC 6062 State credit unions

D-U-N-S 25-485-8806   (SL)
SHERWOOD PARK FOODS LTD
SOBEYS LAKELAND RIDGE
590 Baseline Rd Suite 100, Sherwood Park,
AB, T8H 1Y4

Emp Here 328   *Sales* 63,804,800
SIC 5411 Grocery stores
Pr Pr Dave Lukawenko

D-U-N-S 20-645-8999   (BR)
SOBEYS CAPITAL INCORPORATED
SOBEYS
590 Baseline Rd Unit 100, Sherwood Park,
AB, T8H 1Y4
(780) 417-0419
Emp Here 150
SIC 5411 Grocery stores

D-U-N-S 25-689-5228   (BR)
STAPLES CANADA INC
STAPLES THE BUSINESS DEPOT
(*Suby of* Staples, Inc.)
390 Baseline Rd Unit 350, Sherwood Park,
AB, T8H 1X1
(780) 417-7510
Emp Here 40
SIC 5943 Stationery stores

D-U-N-S 25-626-0431   (BR)
STRATHCONA COUNTY
STRATHCONA FAMILY & COMMUNITY SER-VICES
(*Suby of* Strathcona County)
2755 Broadmoor Blvd Suite 276, Sherwood

Park, AB, T8H 2W7
(780) 464-4044
Emp Here 47
SIC 8399 Social services, nec

D-U-N-S 24-345-6006   (BR)
STRATHCONA COUNTY
*MILLENNIUM   PLACE   STRATHCONA
COUNTY*
(*Suby of* Strathcona County)
2000 Premier Way, Sherwood Park, AB, T8H
2G4
(780) 416-3300
Emp Here 250
SIC 7999 Amusement and recreation, nec

D-U-N-S 25-626-4045   (BR)
TDL GROUP CORP, THE
TIM HORTONS
222 Baseline Rd Suite 340, Sherwood Park,
AB, T8H 1S8
(780) 467-0803
Emp Here 25
SIC 5812 Eating places

D-U-N-S 20-772-8507   (BR)
TDL GROUP CORP, THE
TIM HORTONS
240 590th Baseline Rd, Sherwood Park, AB,
T8H 1Y4

Emp Here 25
SIC 5812 Eating places

D-U-N-S 20-340-7663   (BR)
VALUE VILLAGE STORES, INC
(*Suby of* Savers, Inc.)
270 Baseline Rd Unit 280, Sherwood Park,
AB, T8H 1R4
(780) 449-0024
Emp Here 50
SIC 5399 Miscellaneous general merchandise

D-U-N-S 24-349-7760   (HQ)
VERTEX RESOURCE SERVICES LTD
(*Suby of* Vertex Resource Group Ltd)
2055 Premier Way Suite 121, Sherwood Park,
AB, T8H 0G2
(780) 464-3295
Emp Here 200   *Emp Total* 5
Sales 92,806,010
SIC 1542 Nonresidential construction, nec
Ch Bd Brian Butlin
Pr Pr Terry Stephenson
Ex VP Jason Clemett

D-U-N-S 24-860-4659   (BR)
WSP CANADA INC
GENIVAR
2693 Broadmoor Blvd Suite 132, Sherwood
Park, AB, T8H 0G1
(780) 410-6740
Emp Here 85
SIC 8711 Engineering services

D-U-N-S 20-860-4467   (BR)
**WINNERS MERCHANTS INTERNATIONAL
L.P.**
HOMESENSE
(*Suby of* The TJX Companies Inc)
390 Baseline Rd Suite 346, Sherwood Park,
AB, T8H 1X1
(780) 417-4124
Emp Here 25
SIC 5651 Family clothing stores

D-U-N-S 20-199-3016   (BR)
**WINNERS MERCHANTS INTERNATIONAL
L.P.**
WINNERS
(*Suby of* The TJX Companies Inc)
5000 Emerald Dr Unit 375, Sherwood Park,
AB, T8H 0P5
(780) 417-0480
Emp Here 35
SIC 5651 Family clothing stores

Sibbald, AB T0J

D-U-N-S 24-271-9847   (SL)
PRAIRIEVIEW COLONY
Gd, Sibbald, AB, T0J 3E0
(403) 676-2230
Emp Here 57   *Sales* 3,720,996
SIC 8661 Religious organizations

Siksika, AB T0J

D-U-N-S 24-345-0926   (BR)
SIKSIKA BOARD OF EDUCATION
CHIEF OLD SUN ELEMENTARY SCHOOL
Gd, Siksika, AB, T0J 3W0
(403) 734-5300
Emp Here 42
SIC 8211 Elementary and secondary schools

D-U-N-S 20-073-9949   (BR)
SIKSIKA BOARD OF EDUCATION
CROWFOOT SCHOOL
Gd, Siksika, AB, T0J 3W0
(403) 734-5320
Emp Here 27
SIC 8211 Elementary and secondary schools

D-U-N-S 20-591-9421   (BR)
SIKSIKA BOARD OF EDUCATION
SIKSIKA HIGH SCHOOL
Gd, Siksika, AB, T0J 3W0
(403) 734-5400
Emp Here 25
SIC 8211 Elementary and secondary schools

Slave Lake, AB T0G

D-U-N-S 25-314-7284   (BR)
ATCO ELECTRIC LTD
104 Birch Rd, Slave Lake, AB, T0G 2A0
(780) 849-7622
Emp Here 30
SIC 4911 Electric services

D-U-N-S 25-316-0675   (BR)
BP CANADA ENERGY COMPANY
(*Suby of* BP P.L.C.)
Gd, Slave Lake, AB, T0G 2A0

Emp Here 20
SIC 1311 Crude petroleum and natural gas

D-U-N-S 24-148-7946   (BR)
BUILDERS ENERGY SERVICES LTD
(*Suby of* Builders Energy Services Ltd)
Gd, Slave Lake, AB, T0G 2A0
(780) 849-2342
Emp Here 20
SIC 5251 Hardware stores

D-U-N-S 20-140-1564   (BR)
E CONSTRUCTION LTD
224 Balsam Rd Ne, Slave Lake, AB, T0G 2A0
(780) 849-2265
Emp Here 30
SIC 1611 Highway and street construction

D-U-N-S 24-352-8945   (HQ)
ENTERPRISE ENERGY SERVICES INC
900 8 St Nw Ss 1, Slave Lake, AB, T0G 2A1
(780) 849-3865
Emp Here 40   *Emp Total* 40
Sales 8,038,400
SIC 4619 Pipelines, nec
Pr Pr Leonard Jaroszuk
    Desmond O'kell
    Kevin Spitzmacher
    Ron Ingram
    Nick Demare
    Fredy Ramsoonar

D-U-N-S 25-506-8637   (SL)
GWN PIZZA CORP
BOSTON PIZZA
604 Main St S Ss 3, Slave Lake, AB, T0G 2A3
(780) 849-9699
Emp Here 50   *Sales* 1,532,175
SIC 5812 Eating places

D-U-N-S 24-584-6530   (SL)
HEAVY EQUIPMENT REPAIR LTD
404 Balsam Rd, Slave Lake, AB, T0G 2A0
(780) 849-3768
Emp Here 50   *Sales* 3,638,254
SIC 7699 Repair services, nec

D-U-N-S 25-269-6349   (BR)
HIGH PRAIRIE SCHOOL DIVISION NO 48
E G WAHLSTROM SCHOOL
228 4 Ave Nw Ss 1, Slave Lake, AB, T0G 2A1
(780) 849-3539
Emp Here 50
SIC 8211 Elementary and secondary schools

D-U-N-S 25-117-4892   (BR)
HIGH PRAIRIE SCHOOL DIVISION NO 48
MICHENER, ROLAND SECONDARY SCHOOL
106 7 St Se Ss 3, Slave Lake, AB, T0G 2A3
(780) 849-3064
Emp Here 50
SIC 8211 Elementary and secondary schools

D-U-N-S 20-030-6798   (BR)
HIGH PRAIRIE SCHOOL DIVISION NO 48
C J SCHURTER ELEMENTARY SCHOOL
300 6 Ave Ne Ss 2, Slave Lake, AB, T0G 2A2
(780) 849-4344
Emp Here 40
SIC 8211 Elementary and secondary schools

D-U-N-S 25-014-9929   (BR)
HUSKY OIL OPERATIONS LIMITED
HUSKY ENERGY
208 Caribou Trail Nw, Slave Lake, AB, T0G 2A0
(780) 849-2276
Emp Here 72
SIC 1311 Crude petroleum and natural gas

D-U-N-S 20-027-4624   (BR)
LIVING WATERS CATHOLIC REGIONAL DIVISION NO.42
ST MARY OF THE LAKE SCHOOL
409 6 St Sw, Slave Lake, AB, T0G 2A4
(780) 849-5244
Emp Here 25
SIC 8211 Elementary and secondary schools

D-U-N-S 25-270-1594   (BR)
LOBLAWS INC
TIM'S NOSRILLS
100 Main St S Suite 790, Slave Lake, AB, T0G 2A3
(780) 849-2369
Emp Here 45
SIC 5141 Groceries, general line

D-U-N-S 24-880-7380   (HQ)
MAX FUEL DISTRIBUTORS LTD
PETRO-CANADA WHOLSALE MARKETING
(*Suby of* Max Fuel Distributors Ltd)
701 12 Ave Ne, Slave Lake, AB, T0G 2A2
(780) 849-3820
Emp Here 25   *Emp Total* 50
Sales 17,527,319
SIC 5171 Petroleum bulk stations and terminals
Pr Pr Ingo Von Wackerbarth

D-U-N-S 20-437-2650   (BR)
PYRAMID CORPORATION
400 Birch Rd Ne, Slave Lake, AB, T0G 2A0
(780) 849-2789
Emp Here 30
SIC 1731 Electrical work

D-U-N-S 24-807-0872   (HQ)
SLAVE LAKE PULP CORPORATION
Gd, Slave Lake, AB, T0G 2A0

(780) 849-7777
Emp Here 100   *Emp Total* 7,900
Sales 5,110,881
SIC 2611 Pulp mills
Genl Mgr Peter Rippon
    Vince Parrot
Pr Henry Ketchum Iii
VP Gerry Miller
Dir Fin Martti Solin

D-U-N-S 20-091-5361   (SL)
VANDERWELL CONTRACTORS (1971) LTD
3 River Dr E, Slave Lake, AB, T0G 2A0
(780) 849-3824
Emp Here 160   *Sales* 19,600,443
SIC 2421 Sawmills and planing mills, general
Pr Pr Robert Vanderwell
Genl Mgr Kenneth Vanderwell

D-U-N-S 24-019-1721   (BR)
WAL-MART CANADA CORP
WALMART
1500 Main St Sw, Slave Lake, AB, T0G 2A4
(780) 849-9579
Emp Here 120
SIC 5311 Department stores

D-U-N-S 24-522-0111   (BR)
WEST FRASER MILLS LTD
ALBERTA PLYWOOD
Gd, Slave Lake, AB, T0G 2A0
(780) 849-4145
Emp Here 180
SIC 2421 Sawmills and planing mills, general

Smoky Lake, AB T0A

D-U-N-S 20-299-9764   (BR)
ALBERTA HEALTH SERVICES
SMOKY LAKE COMMUNITY HEALTH SERVICES
4212 55 Ave, Smoky Lake, AB, T0A 3C0
(780) 656-2030
Emp Here 25
SIC 8062 General medical and surgical hospitals

D-U-N-S 20-133-7420   (BR)
ASPEN VIEW PUBLIC SCHOOL DIVISION NO. 78
H A KOSTASH SCHOOL
(*Suby of* Aspen View Public School Division No. 78)
5019 50 St, Smoky Lake, AB, T0A 3C0
(780) 656-3820
Emp Here 40
SIC 8211 Elementary and secondary schools

Spirit River, AB T0H

D-U-N-S 24-643-3718   (SL)
379778 ALBERTA CORPORATION
WOODLAND ENTERPRISES
Gd, Spirit River, AB, T0H 3G0
(780) 765-2496
Emp Here 35   *Sales* 6,028,800
SIC 1389 Oil and gas field services, nec
Pr Pr Dale Wood
Off Mgr Lyn Wood

D-U-N-S 20-578-2480   (BR)
ALBERTA TREASURY BRANCHES
ATB FINANCIAL
4518 50 St, Spirit River, AB, T0H 3G0
(780) 864-3650
Emp Here 20
SIC 6036 Savings institutions, except federal

D-U-N-S 24-030-8549   (BR)
BIRCHCLIFF ENERGY LTD
5605 Hwy 49, Spirit River, AB, T0H 3G0

(780) 864-4624
Emp Here 40
SIC 2911 Petroleum refining

D-U-N-S 25-055-8665   (BR)
GRANDE SPIRIT FOUNDATION
PLEASANT VIEW LODGE
5230 44 Ave, Spirit River, AB, T0H 3G0
(780) 864-3766
Emp Here 20
SIC 8361 Residential care

D-U-N-S 24-125-0237   (BR)
PEACE WAPITI SCHOOL DIVISION NO.76
PEACE ACADEMY OF VIRTUAL EDUCATION
4201 50 St, Spirit River, AB, T0H 3G0
(780) 864-3741
Emp Here 20
SIC 8211 Elementary and secondary schools

D-U-N-S 20-867-7349   (BR)
PEACE WAPITI SCHOOL DIVISION NO.76
SPIRIT REGIONAL ACADEMY
4501 46 St, Spirit River, AB, T0H 3G0
(780) 864-3696
Emp Here 30
SIC 8211 Elementary and secondary schools

D-U-N-S 20-209-8336   (BR)
SPECTRA ENERGY MIDSTREAM CORPORATION
GORDONDALE GAS PLANT
Gd, Spirit River, AB, T0H 3G0
(780) 864-3125
Emp Here 24
SIC 1389 Oil and gas field services, nec

Spring Coulee, AB T0K

D-U-N-S 20-653-4559   (BR)
WESTWIND SCHOOL DIVISION #74
SPRING VALLEY COLONY SCHOOL
Gd, Spring Coulee, AB, T0K 2C0
(403) 758-0006
Emp Here 40
SIC 8299 Schools and educational services, nec

Springbrook, AB T4S

D-U-N-S 24-767-6802   (BR)
AIRSPRAY (1967) LTD
AIRSPRAY TANKERS
2160 Airport Dr, Springbrook, AB, T4S 2E8
(403) 886-4088
Emp Here 60
SIC 7389 Business services, nec

Spruce Grove, AB T7X

D-U-N-S 24-274-0884   (BR)
AMEC FOSTER WHEELER AMERICAS LIMITED
AMEC FOSTER WHEELER AMERICAS LIMITED
7 Mcleod Ave Suite 112, Spruce Grove, AB, T7X 4B8
(780) 571-8075
Emp Here 25
SIC 8711 Engineering services

D-U-N-S 25-831-4236   (BR)
ATCO STRUCTURES & LOGISTICS LTD
ATCO STUCTURES
30 Alberta Ave, Spruce Grove, AB, T7X 4A9
(780) 962-3111
Emp Here 20
SIC 3448 Prefabricated Metal buildings and

components

D-U-N-S 25-236-1548   (BR)
ALBERTA TREASURY BRANCHES
ATB FINANCIAL
16 Mcleod Ave, Spruce Grove, AB, T7X 3Y1
(780) 962-6000
Emp Here 26
SIC 6036 Savings institutions, except federal

D-U-N-S 24-905-7878   (BR)
BLCO ENTERPRISES LTD
K F C
(*Suby of* BLCO Enterprises Ltd)
170 Highway 16a, Spruce Grove, AB, T7X 3X3
(780) 962-4822
Emp Here 25
SIC 5812 Eating places

D-U-N-S 20-588-2538   (BR)
BANQUE TORONTO-DOMINION, LA
TD CANADA TRUST
(*Suby of* Toronto-Dominion Bank, The)
100 Jennifer Heil Way Ste 10, Spruce Grove, AB, T7X 4B8
(780) 962-0404
Emp Here 20
SIC 6021 National commercial banks

D-U-N-S 25-206-0389   (BR)
BEE MAID HONEY LIMITED
ALBERTA HONEY PRODUCERS COOPERATIVE
70 Alberta Ave, Spruce Grove, AB, T7X 3B1
(780) 962-5573
Emp Here 30
SIC 2099 Food preparations, nec

D-U-N-S 20-337-0507   (BR)
CAM TRAN CO. LTD
120 Diamond Ave, Spruce Grove, AB, T7X 3B2
(780) 948-8703
Emp Here 20
SIC 3533 Oil and gas field machinery

D-U-N-S 25-272-6005   (BR)
CANADA POST CORPORATION
SPRUCE GROVE PO
360 Saskatchewan Ave, Spruce Grove, AB, T7X 0G6
(780) 962-4419
Emp Here 30
SIC 4311 U.s. postal service

D-U-N-S 24-701-6603   (BR)
CIVEO PREMIUM CAMP SERVICES LTD
(*Suby of* Oil States International, Inc.)
220 Diamond Ave, Spruce Grove, AB, T7X 3B5
(780) 962-8169
Emp Here 50
SIC 7519 Utility trailer rental

D-U-N-S 24-821-3113   (SL)
COPPERLINE EXCAVATING LTD
375 Saskatchewan Ave, Spruce Grove, AB, T7X 3A1
(780) 968-3805
Emp Here 80   *Sales* 8,244,559
SIC 1796 Installing building equipment
Pr Jamie Black

D-U-N-S 24-633-2709   (BR)
DOLLARAMA S.E.C.
187 Highway 16a Unit 104, Spruce Grove, AB, T7X 4P9
(780) 960-8455
Emp Here 24
SIC 5331 Variety stores

D-U-N-S 24-043-3599   (SL)
ELIZABETHAN CATERING SERVICES LTD
55 Alberta Ave, Spruce Grove, AB, T7X 4B9
(780) 962-3663
Emp Here 100   *Sales* 2,991,389
SIC 5812 Eating places

D-U-N-S 20-297-3173   (BR)

EVERGREEN CATHOLIC SEPARATE REGIONAL DIVISION 2
ST JOSEPH'S CATHOLIC SCHOOL
195 Weston Dr, Spruce Grove, AB, T7X 1V1
(780) 962-8788
Emp Here 45
SIC 8211 Elementary and secondary schools

D-U-N-S 20-028-8202   (BR)
EVERGREEN CATHOLIC SEPARATE REGIONAL DIVISION 2
ST. MARGUERITE CATHOLIC SCHOOL
395 Grove Dr, Spruce Grove, AB, T7X 2Y7
(780) 962-8787
Emp Here 36
SIC 8211 Elementary and secondary schools

D-U-N-S 25-373-0782   (BR)
EVERGREEN CATHOLIC SEPARATE REGIONAL DIVISION 2
ST. THOMAS AQUINAS CATHOLIC HIGH SCHOOL
381 Grove Dr Suite 110, Spruce Grove, AB, T7X 2Y9
(780) 962-1585
Emp Here 40
SIC 8211 Elementary and secondary schools

D-U-N-S 20-746-2677   (BR)
FORTISALBERTA INC
FORTISALBERTA
250 Diamond Ave, Spruce Grove, AB, T7X 2Y8
(780) 962-7705
Emp Here 30
SIC 4911 Electric services

D-U-N-S 20-637-9476   (BR)
GOVERNMENT OF THE PROVINCE OF ALBERTA
HEALTH SERVICES
Gd Lcd Main, Spruce Grove, AB, T7X 3A1
(780) 470-5440
Emp Here 30
SIC 8011 Offices and clinics of medical doctors

D-U-N-S 24-001-3755   (SL)
GROUP FIVE INVESTORS LTD
GROVE MOTOR INN
Gd Lcd Main, Spruce Grove, AB, T7X 3A1
(780) 962-5000
Emp Here 100   *Sales* 4,377,642
SIC 7011 Hotels and motels

D-U-N-S 20-091-2996   (SL)
GROVE PONTIAC BUICK GMC LTD
Highway 16a W, Spruce Grove, AB, T7X 3B2

Emp Here 60   *Sales* 28,269,870
SIC 5511 New and used car dealers
Pr Pr Gerard Levasseur
Dir Helga Levassuer
Dir Gerard P. Levasseur

D-U-N-S 25-365-8629   (BR)
HOME DEPOT OF CANADA INC
HOME DEPOT
(*Suby of* The Home Depot Inc)
168 Highway 16a, Spruce Grove, AB, T7X 3X3
(780) 960-5600
Emp Here 100
SIC 5251 Hardware stores

D-U-N-S 25-142-0493   (BR)
LOBLAWS INC
REAL CANADIAN SUPERSTORE
100 Jennifer Heil Way Suite 10, Spruce Grove, AB, T7X 4B8
(780) 960-7400
Emp Here 375
SIC 5411 Grocery stores

D-U-N-S 25-166-1286   (BR)
MAGIC LANTERN THEATRES LTD
LANDMARK CINEMA SPURCE GROVE
130 Century Cross, Spruce Grove, AB, T7X 0C8

(780) 962-9553
Emp Here 30
SIC 7832 Motion picture theaters, except drive-in

D-U-N-S 25-087-2132   (BR)
PARKLAND SCHOOL DIVISION NO. 70
ECOLE BROXTON PARK SCHOOL
505 Mcleod Ave Suite 505, Spruce Grove, AB, T7X 2Y5
(780) 962-0212
Emp Here 108
SIC 8211 Elementary and secondary schools

D-U-N-S 20-578-1722   (BR)
PARKLAND SCHOOL DIVISION NO. 70
WOODHAVEN JUNIOR HIGH SCHOOL
475 King St, Spruce Grove, AB, T7X 0A4
(780) 962-2626
Emp Here 47
SIC 8211 Elementary and secondary schools

D-U-N-S 20-655-1355   (BR)
PARKLAND SCHOOL DIVISION NO. 70
SPRUCE GROVE COMPOSITE HIGH SCHOOL
1000 Calahoo Rd, Spruce Grove, AB, T7X 2T7
(780) 962-0800
Emp Here 100
SIC 8211 Elementary and secondary schools

D-U-N-S 20-023-9569   (BR)
PARKLAND SCHOOL DIVISION NO. 70
BROOKWOOD EARLY SCHOOL
460 King St, Spruce Grove, AB, T7X 2T6
(780) 962-3942
Emp Here 51
SIC 8211 Elementary and secondary schools

D-U-N-S 25-016-1569   (BR)
PARKLAND SCHOOL DIVISION NO. 70
MILLGROVE ELEMENTARY SCHOOL
851 Calahoo Rd, Spruce Grove, AB, T7X 2M1
(780) 962-6122
Emp Here 25
SIC 8211 Elementary and secondary schools

D-U-N-S 24-049-3762   (SL)
PREMIUM TESTING & SERVICES LTD
Gd, Spruce Grove, AB, T7X 2T5

Emp Here 50   *Sales* 7,796,259
SIC 1389 Oil and gas field services, nec

D-U-N-S 25-625-5498   (BR)
ROYAL BANK OF CANADA
RBC
(*Suby of* Royal Bank Of Canada)
112 King St, Spruce Grove, AB, T7X 0J6
(780) 962-2872
Emp Here 25
SIC 6021 National commercial banks

D-U-N-S 20-087-6345   (BR)
SOBEYS CAPITAL INCORPORATED
11 Westway Rd, Spruce Grove, AB, T7X 3X3
(780) 962-4121
Emp Here 100
SIC 5411 Grocery stores

D-U-N-S 25-271-0264   (BR)
SOBEYS WEST INC
94 Mcleod Ave, Spruce Grove, AB, T7X 1R2
(780) 962-9183
Emp Here 120
SIC 5411 Grocery stores

D-U-N-S 24-643-8139   (SL)
SPRUCE GROVE PIZZA LTD
BOSTON PIZZA
201 Calahoo Rd, Spruce Grove, AB, T7X 1R1
(780) 962-0224
Emp Here 85   *Sales* 3,031,879
SIC 5812 Eating places

D-U-N-S 20-176-2783   (BR)
TRANSCANADA PIPELINES LIMITED
425 Diamond Ave, Spruce Grove, AB, T7X

4C5
(780) 962-7300
Emp Here 100
SIC 4922 Natural gas transmission

D-U-N-S 20-895-0527   (BR)
UNITED FARMERS OF ALBERTA CO-OPERATIVE LIMITED
U F A
200 Diamond Ave, Spruce Grove, AB, T7X 3A8
(780) 962-2282
Emp Here 28
SIC 5191 Farm supplies

D-U-N-S 24-399-4605   (SL)
ZELL INDUSTRIES INC
27224 Township Road 524, Spruce Grove, AB, T7X 3R6
(780) 962-8099
Emp Here 50   *Sales* 7,101,500
SIC 2411 Logging
Pr Pr Les Zeller

Spruce Grove, AB T7Y

D-U-N-S 20-029-0695   (BR)
PARKLAND SCHOOL DIVISION NO. 70
GRAMINIA COMMUNITY SCHOOL
51101 Range Road 271, Spruce Grove, AB, T7Y 1G7
(780) 963-5035
Emp Here 55
SIC 8211 Elementary and secondary schools

Spruce View, AB T0M

D-U-N-S 20-023-9924   (BR)
CHINOOKS EDGE SCHOOL DIVISION NO. 73
SPRUCE VIEW SCHOOL
1 Hwy 54, Spruce View, AB, T0M 1V0
(403) 728-3459
Emp Here 30
SIC 8211 Elementary and secondary schools

St Paul, AB T0A

D-U-N-S 20-029-0356   (BR)
ALBERTA HEALTH SERVICES
ST PAUL'S COMMUNITY HEALTH SERVICES
5610 50 Ave, St Paul, AB, T0A 3A1
(780) 645-3396
Emp Here 30
SIC 8062 General medical and surgical hospitals

D-U-N-S 24-346-4422   (BR)
ALBERTA HEALTH SERVICES
ST THERESE HEALTH CENTRE
4713 48 Ave, St Paul, AB, T0A 3A3
(780) 645-3331
Emp Here 200
SIC 8062 General medical and surgical hospitals

D-U-N-S 20-048-0148   (BR)
EAST CENTRAL FRANCOPHONE EDUCATION REGION NO. 3
ECOLE DU SOMMET
4609 40 St, St Paul, AB, T0A 3A2
(780) 645-1949
Emp Here 20
SIC 8211 Elementary and secondary schools

D-U-N-S 25-121-2619   (BR)
EXTENDICARE INC
EXTENDICARE ST. PAUL

4614 47 Ave, St Paul, AB, T0A 3A3
(780) 645-3375
Emp Here 120
SIC 8051 Skilled nursing care facilities

D-U-N-S 24-227-1463   (BR)
GOVERNMENT OF THE PROVINCE OF AL-BERTA
5025 49 Ave, St Paul, AB, T0A 3A4
(780) 645-6210
Emp Here 120
SIC 8741 Management services

D-U-N-S 24-417-4004   (BR)
LOBLAWS INC
EXTRA FOODS
5701 50 Ave, St Paul, AB, T0A 3A1
(780) 645-7030
Emp Here 50
SIC 5411 Grocery stores

D-U-N-S 24-344-9118   (BR)
PORTAGE COLLEGE
5025 49 Ave, St Paul, AB, T0A 3A4

Emp Here 30
SIC 8221 Colleges and universities

D-U-N-S 24-339-8802   (BR)
SERVUS CREDIT UNION LTD
4738 50 Ave, St Paul, AB, T0A 3A0
(780) 645-3357
Emp Here 23
SIC 6062 State credit unions

D-U-N-S 20-091-0412   (HQ)
SMYL MOTORS LTD
5015 44 St Ss 2, St Paul, AB, T0A 3A2
(780) 645-4414
Emp Here 37   *Emp Total* 3
Sales 17,145,765
SIC 5511 New and used car dealers
Pr Pr Bernard Smyl
  Henry Smyl
  George Smyl

D-U-N-S 25-971-8476   (BR)
ST PAUL, TOWN OF
ST PAUL AQUATIC CENTER
4702 53 St Ss 4, St Paul, AB, T0A 3A0
(780) 645-3388
Emp Here 20
SIC 7999 Amusement and recreation, nec

D-U-N-S 20-655-1686   (BR)
ST. PAUL EDUCATION REGIONAL DIVISION NO 1
ST. PAUL ELEMENTARY SCHOOL ECOLE ELEMENTARY
4313 48 Ave Suite 1, St Paul, AB, T0A 3A3
(780) 645-3537
Emp Here 60
SIC 8211 Elementary and secondary schools

D-U-N-S 20-591-9835   (BR)
ST. PAUL EDUCATION REGIONAL DIVISION NO 1
ST PAUL REGIONAL HIGH SCHOOL
4701 44 St, St Paul, AB, T0A 3A3
(780) 645-4491
Emp Here 50
SIC 8211 Elementary and secondary schools

D-U-N-S 20-029-7567   (BR)
ST. PAUL EDUCATION REGIONAL DIVISION NO 1
GLEN AVON SCHOOL
5201 50 Ave, St Paul, AB, T0A 3A0
(780) 645-3237
Emp Here 77
SIC 8211 Elementary and secondary schools

D-U-N-S 25-174-6046   (BR)
ST. PAUL EDUCATION REGIONAL DIVISION NO 1
RACETTE JUNIOR HIGH SCHOOL
4638 50 Ave, St Paul, AB, T0A 3A2
(780) 645-3571
Emp Here 45

SIC 8211 Elementary and secondary schools

D-U-N-S 20-790-7713   (SL)
SUNNYSIDE MANOR
MD OF ST PAUL FOUNDATION
4522 47 Ave Suite 24, St Paul, AB, T0A 3A3
(780) 645-3530
Emp Here 50   *Sales* 1,824,018
SIC 8361 Residential care

St. Albert, AB T8N

D-U-N-S 24-521-7351   (SL)
293967 ALBERTA LTD
TIM HORTONS
470 St Albert Rd Suite 20, St. Albert, AB, T8N 5J9
(780) 458-6884
Emp Here 70   *Sales* 2,115,860
SIC 5812 Eating places

D-U-N-S 25-634-8483   (BR)
340107 ALBERTA LTD
SORRENTINO'S BISTRO BAR
(*Suby of* 340107 Alberta Ltd)
595 St Albert Trail, St. Albert, AB, T8N 6G5
(780) 459-1411
Emp Here 40
SIC 5812 Eating places

D-U-N-S 20-651-7463   (BR)
ATCO GAS AND PIPELINES LTD
DIVISION OF ATCO GAS
23 Boudreau Rd, St. Albert, AB, T8N 7P6

Emp Here 25
SIC 4924 Natural gas distribution

D-U-N-S 24-399-2278   (SL)
ACCESS PLUMBING & HEATING LTD
215 Carnegie Dr Unit 5, St. Albert, AB, T8N 5B1
(780) 459-5999
Emp Here 50   *Sales* 4,377,642
SIC 1711 Plumbing, heating, air-conditioning

D-U-N-S 24-356-5376   (BR)
ALBERTA HEALTH SERVICES
STURGEON COMMUNITY HOSPITAL
201 Boudreau Rd, St. Albert, AB, T8N 6C4
(780) 418-8200
Emp Here 50
SIC 8062 General medical and surgical hospitals

D-U-N-S 25-530-8439   (BR)
ATHABASCA UNIVERSITY
CENTRE FOR INNOVATIVE MANAGEMENT
22 Sir Winston Churchill Ave Unit 301, St. Albert, AB, T8N 1B4
(780) 459-1144
Emp Here 45
SIC 8249 Vocational schools, nec

D-U-N-S 25-515-9212   (BR)
BANK OF NOVA SCOTIA, THE
SCOTIABANK
138 Gradin Park Plaza, St. Albert, AB, T8N 1B4

Emp Here 26
SIC 6021 National commercial banks

D-U-N-S 24-342-2008   (BR)
CARA OPERATIONS LIMITED
MONTANA'S COOKHOUSE
(*Suby of* Cara Holdings Limited)
445 St Albert Trail Suite 10, St. Albert, AB, T8N 6T9
(780) 458-7770
Emp Here 70
SIC 5812 Eating places

D-U-N-S 25-516-0020   (BR)
CHIRO FOODS LIMITED
A & W RESTAURANT

2 Hebert Rd Suite 100, St. Albert, AB, T8N 5T8
(780) 460-2060
Emp Here 20
SIC 5812 Eating places

D-U-N-S 20-205-4768   (BR)
CONSEIL SCOLAIRE CENTRE-NORD
ECOLE LA MISSION
46 Heritage Dr, St. Albert, AB, T8N 7J5
(780) 459-9568
Emp Here 20
SIC 8211 Elementary and secondary schools

D-U-N-S 25-676-8979   (SL)
COX MECHANICAL LTD
65 Corriveau Ave, St. Albert, AB, T8N 5A3
(780) 459-2530
Emp Here 55   *Sales* 4,815,406
SIC 1711 Plumbing, heating, air-conditioning

D-U-N-S 25-655-8909   (BR)
CRUISESHIPCENTERS INTERNATIONAL INC
CRUISESHIPCENTERS
(*Suby of* Cruiseshipcenters International Inc)
340 St Albert Rd Unit 140, St. Albert, AB, T8N 7C8
(780) 460-5727
Emp Here 20
SIC 4724 Travel agencies

D-U-N-S 24-340-0970   (BR)
FGL SPORTS LTD
SPORT CHEK ST. ALBERT CENTRE
375 St Albert Trail Suite 103, St. Albert, AB, T8N 3K8
(780) 460-0220
Emp Here 50
SIC 5941 Sporting goods and bicycle shops

D-U-N-S 24-805-4756   (BR)
FOUNTAIN TIRE LTD
220 Carnegie Dr Suite 208, St. Albert, AB, T8N 5A7
(780) 418-3418
Emp Here 30
SIC 5531 Auto and home supply stores

D-U-N-S 24-853-4711   (BR)
GOODYEAR CANADA INC
(*Suby of* The Goodyear Tire & Rubber Company)
220 Carnegie Dr, St. Albert, AB, T8N 5B1

Emp Here 40
SIC 5531 Auto and home supply stores

D-U-N-S 20-553-0327   (BR)
GREAT PACIFIC INDUSTRIES INC
SAVE-ON-FOODS
740 St Albert Trail, St. Albert, AB, T8N 7H5
(780) 419-2065
Emp Here 140
SIC 5411 Grocery stores

D-U-N-S 25-677-1338   (BR)
GREATER ST. ALBERT CATHOLIC REGIONAL DIVISION NO. 29
ST ALBERT CATHOLIC HIGH SCHOOL
33 Malmo Ave, St. Albert, AB, T8N 1L5
(780) 459-7781
Emp Here 56
SIC 8211 Elementary and secondary schools

D-U-N-S 25-677-1254   (BR)
GREATER ST. ALBERT CATHOLIC REGIONAL DIVISION NO. 29
JJ NEARING CATHOLIC ELEMENTARY SCHOOL
196 Deer Ridge Dr, St. Albert, AB, T8N 6T6
(780) 418-6330
Emp Here 38
SIC 8211 Elementary and secondary schools

D-U-N-S 25-677-1320   (BR)
GREATER ST. ALBERT CATHOLIC REGIONAL DIVISION NO. 29
VINCENT J MALONEY CATHOLIC JUNIOR

HIGH SCHOOL
20 Mont Clare Pl, St. Albert, AB, T8N 1K9
(780) 458-1113
Emp Here 40
SIC 8211 Elementary and secondary schools

D-U-N-S 25-016-2500   (BR)
GREATER ST. ALBERT CATHOLIC REGIONAL DIVISION NO. 29
ECOLE SECONDAIRE SAINTE-MARGUERITE D'YOUVILLE
51 Boudreau Rd, St. Albert, AB, T8N 6B7
(780) 459-5702
Emp Here 31
SIC 8211 Elementary and secondary schools

D-U-N-S 25-677-1312   (BR)
GREATER ST. ALBERT CATHOLIC REGIONAL DIVISION NO. 29
VITAL GRANDIN SCHOOL
39 Sunset Blvd, St. Albert, AB, T8N 0N6
(780) 459-7734
Emp Here 50
SIC 8211 Elementary and secondary schools

D-U-N-S 20-713-4318   (BR)
GREATER ST. ALBERT CATHOLIC REGIONAL DIVISION NO. 29
ST. GABRIEL STORE FRONT SCHOOL
39 Sunset Blvd, St. Albert, AB, T8N 0N6
(780) 459-6616
Emp Here 20
SIC 8211 Elementary and secondary schools

D-U-N-S 25-677-1239   (BR)
GREATER ST. ALBERT CATHOLIC REGIONAL DIVISION NO. 29
ALBERT LACOMBE ELEMENTARY SCHOOL
50 Gainsborough Ave, St. Albert, AB, T8N 0W5
(780) 459-4478
Emp Here 38
SIC 8211 Elementary and secondary schools

D-U-N-S 25-016-5784   (BR)
GREATER ST. ALBERT CATHOLIC REGIONAL DIVISION NO. 29
NEIL M ROSS CATHOLIC SCHOOL
60 Woodlands Rd, St. Albert, AB, T8N 3X3
(780) 459-1244
Emp Here 42
SIC 8211 Elementary and secondary schools

D-U-N-S 25-269-4062   (BR)
GREATER ST. ALBERT CATHOLIC REGIONAL DIVISION NO. 29
RICHARD S FOWLER JUNIOR HIGH SCHOOL
65 Sir Winston Churchill Ave, St. Albert, AB, T8N 0G5
(780) 459-2644
Emp Here 35
SIC 8211 Elementary and secondary schools

D-U-N-S 25-677-1270   (BR)
GREATER ST. ALBERT CATHOLIC REGIONAL DIVISION NO. 29
ECOLE MARIE POBURAN
100 Sir Winston Churchill Ave, St. Albert, AB, T8N 5Y2
(780) 458-1112
Emp Here 30
SIC 8211 Elementary and secondary schools

D-U-N-S 25-677-1262   (BR)
GREATER ST. ALBERT CATHOLIC REGIONAL DIVISION NO. 29
ECOLE FATHER JAN
15 Mission Ave, St. Albert, AB, T8N 1H6
(780) 458-3300
Emp Here 31
SIC 8211 Elementary and secondary schools

D-U-N-S 20-713-4094   (BR)
GREATER ST. ALBERT CATHOLIC REGIONAL DIVISION NO. 29
BERTHA KENNEDY SCHOOL
175 Larose Dr, St. Albert, AB, T8N 2G7

(780) 458-6101
Emp Here 32
SIC 8211 Elementary and secondary schools

D-U-N-S 24-090-5521   (SL)
HOLE'S GREENHOUSES & GARDENS LTD
101 Riel Dr, St. Albert, AB, T8N 3X4
(780) 651-7355
Emp Here 50   *Sales* 3,118,504
SIC 5992 Florists

D-U-N-S 24-014-3474   (BR)
HOME DEPOT OF CANADA INC
(*Suby of* The Home Depot Inc)
750 St Albert Trail, St. Albert, AB, T8N 7H5
(780) 458-4026
Emp Here 100
SIC 5251 Hardware stores

D-U-N-S 25-301-2348   (BR)
HUDSON'S BAY COMPANY
375 St Albert Trail Suite 300, St. Albert, AB, T8N 3K8
(780) 458-5800
Emp Here 110
SIC 5311 Department stores

D-U-N-S 20-966-9998   (BR)
INDIGO BOOKS & MUSIC INC
CHAPTERS
(*Suby of* Indigo Books & Music Inc)
445 St Albert Trail Suite 30, St. Albert, AB, T8N 6T9
(780) 419-7114
Emp Here 25
SIC 5942 Book stores

D-U-N-S 24-703-0125   (SL)
JAMISON NEWSPAPERS INC
25 Chisholm Ave Unit 10, St. Albert, AB, T8N 5A5
(780) 460-5500
Emp Here 100   *Sales* 10,742,551
SIC 2711 Newspapers
Pr Pr Donald Jamison
Dir Mary Jamison
Dir Paula Jamison
Dir Sarah Jamison

D-U-N-S 24-091-0976   (SL)
JENSEN ROOFING LTD
4 Rowland Cres, St. Albert, AB, T8N 4B3
(780) 459-5561
Emp Here 50   *Sales* 4,961,328
SIC 1761 Roofing, siding, and sheetMetal work

D-U-N-S 25-148-1842   (BR)
LOBLAWS INC
REAL CANADIAN SUPERSTORE
101 St Albert Rd Suite 1, St. Albert, AB, T8N 6L5
(780) 418-6818
Emp Here 200
SIC 5399 Miscellaneous general merchandise

D-U-N-S 25-609-2164   (BR)
LONDON DRUGS LIMITED
LONDON DRUGS
19 Bellerose Dr Suite 10, St. Albert, AB, T8N 5E1
(780) 944-4548
Emp Here 90
SIC 5912 Drug stores and proprietary stores

D-U-N-S 25-318-1358   (BR)
MCDONALD'S RESTAURANTS OF CANADA LIMITED
MCDONALD'S #8458
(*Suby of* McDonald's Corporation)
10 Galarneau Pl, St. Albert, AB, T8N 2Y3
(780) 460-4488
Emp Here 50
SIC 5812 Eating places

D-U-N-S 25-014-9887   (BR)
MCDONALD'S RESTAURANTS OF CANADA LIMITED
MCDONALD'S RESTAURANTS

(*Suby of* McDonald's Corporation)
369 St Albert Trail, St. Albert, AB, T8N 0R1
(780) 458-1121
Emp Here 55
SIC 5812 Eating places

D-U-N-S 25-310-9565   (BR)
MCDONALD'S RESTAURANTS OF CANADA LIMITED
MCDONALD'S
(*Suby of* McDonald's Corporation)
700 St Albert Trail, St. Albert, AB, T8N 7A5
(780) 460-4640
Emp Here 50
SIC 5812 Eating places

D-U-N-S 20-590-2690   (BR)
MEDICAL IMAGING CONSULTANTS
200 Boudreau Rd Suite 102, St. Albert, AB, T8N 6B9
(780) 459-1266
Emp Here 25
SIC 8071 Medical laboratories

D-U-N-S 20-538-5362   (SL)
PRO-WESTERN PLASTICS LTD
30 Riel Dr, St. Albert, AB, T8N 3Z7
(780) 459-4491
Emp Here 160   *Sales* 33,963,360
SIC 3089 Plastics products, nec
Pr Pr Paul Lacroix
  David Lacroix
  Michael Lacroix
VP Opers Real Chamberland
S&M/VP Greg Karbonik

D-U-N-S 24-396-7429   (SL)
ROSE BUILDING MAINTENANCE LTD
7 St Anne St Suite 223, St. Albert, AB, T8N 2X4
(780) 459-4146
Emp Here 75   *Sales* 2,188,821
SIC 7349 Building maintenance services, nec

D-U-N-S 25-654-5849   (BR)
SECOND CUP LTD, THE
SECOND CUP, THE
19 Bellerose Dr Suite 30, St. Albert, AB, T8N 5E1
(780) 458-8163
Emp Here 23
SIC 5812 Eating places

D-U-N-S 25-516-2232   (BR)
SERVUS CREDIT UNION LTD
565 St Albert Trail, St. Albert, AB, T8N 6G5
(780) 460-3260
Emp Here 20
SIC 6062 State credit unions

D-U-N-S 24-330-4065   (BR)
SOBEYS CAPITAL INCORPORATED
SOBEYS
392 St Albert Rd, St. Albert, AB, T8N 5J9
(780) 459-5909
Emp Here 100
SIC 5411 Grocery stores

D-U-N-S 25-271-0496   (BR)
SOBEYS WEST INC
ST ALBERT/INGLEWOOD SAFEWAY
395 St Albert Trail, St. Albert, AB, T8N 5Z9
(780) 458-3620
Emp Here 250
SIC 5411 Grocery stores

D-U-N-S 25-271-0538   (BR)
SOBEYS WEST INC
SAFEWAY, DIV OF
2 Hebert Rd Suite 300, St. Albert, AB, T8N 5T8
(780) 460-9356
Emp Here 180
SIC 5411 Grocery stores

D-U-N-S 24-421-1277   (BR)
ST. ALBERT PUBLIC SCHOOL DISTRICT NO. 5565
KANE, PAUL HIGH SCHOOL

12 Cunningham Rd, St. Albert, AB, T8N 2E9
(780) 459-4405
Emp Here 85
SIC 8211 Elementary and secondary schools

D-U-N-S 20-008-2654   (BR)
ST. ALBERT PUBLIC SCHOOL DISTRICT NO. 5565
KEENOOSHAYO SCHOOL
40 Woodlands Rd, St. Albert, AB, T8N 3X3
(780) 459-3114
Emp Here 30
SIC 8211 Elementary and secondary schools

D-U-N-S 25-016-7434   (BR)
ST. ALBERT PUBLIC SCHOOL DISTRICT NO. 5565
SIR ALEXANDER MACKENZIE SCHOOL
61 Sir Winston Churchill Ave, St. Albert, AB, T8N 0G5
(780) 459-4467
Emp Here 50
SIC 8211 Elementary and secondary schools

D-U-N-S 20-713-3989   (BR)
ST. ALBERT PUBLIC SCHOOL DISTRICT NO. 5565
LORNE AKINS JUNIOR HIGH SCHOOL
4 Fairview Blvd, St. Albert, AB, T8N 2G1
(780) 460-3728
Emp Here 50
SIC 8211 Elementary and secondary schools

D-U-N-S 20-008-2696   (BR)
ST. ALBERT PUBLIC SCHOOL DISTRICT NO. 5565
WILLIAM D CUTS JUNIOR HIGH SCHOOL
149 Larose Dr, St. Albert, AB, T8N 2X7
(780) 458-8585
Emp Here 27
SIC 8211 Elementary and secondary schools

D-U-N-S 20-008-2647   (BR)
ST. ALBERT PUBLIC SCHOOL DISTRICT NO. 5565
BELLEROSE COMPOSITE HIGH SCHOOL
49 Giroux Rd, St. Albert, AB, T8N 6N4
(780) 460-8490
Emp Here 90
SIC 8211 Elementary and secondary schools

D-U-N-S 20-008-2670   (BR)
ST. ALBERT PUBLIC SCHOOL DISTRICT NO. 5565
RONALD HARVEY ELEMENTARY SCHOOL
15 Langley Ave, St. Albert, AB, T8N 1S4
(780) 459-5541
Emp Here 35
SIC 8211 Elementary and secondary schools

D-U-N-S 25-016-7186   (BR)
ST. ALBERT PUBLIC SCHOOL DISTRICT NO. 5565
ROBERT RUNDLE ELEMENTARY SCHOOL
50 Grosvenor Blvd Suite A, St. Albert, AB, T8N 0X6
(780) 459-4475
Emp Here 30
SIC 8211 Elementary and secondary schools

D-U-N-S 20-008-2688   (BR)
ST. ALBERT PUBLIC SCHOOL DISTRICT NO. 5565
WILD ROSE ELEMENTARY SCHOOL
58 Grenfell Ave, St. Albert, AB, T8N 2Z9
(780) 460-3737
Emp Here 28
SIC 8211 Elementary and secondary schools

D-U-N-S 20-008-2662   (BR)
ST. ALBERT PUBLIC SCHOOL DISTRICT NO. 5565
NICKERSON, LEO ELEMENTARY SCHOOL
10 Sycamore Ave, St. Albert, AB, T8N 0K3
(780) 459-4426
Emp Here 51
SIC 8211 Elementary and secondary schools

D-U-N-S 25-020-1910   (BR)
ST. ALBERT, CITY OF
ST ALBERT FIRE SERVICES
18 Sir Winston Churchill Ave, St. Albert, AB, T8N 2W5
(780) 459-7021
Emp Here 80
SIC 7389 Business services, nec

D-U-N-S 25-498-9312   (BR)
STAPLES CANADA INC
STAPLES THE BUSINESS DEPOT
(*Suby of* Staples, Inc.)
445 St Albert Trail Unit 40, St. Albert, AB, T8N 6T9
(780) 418-3650
Emp Here 50
SIC 5943 Stationery stores

D-U-N-S 20-019-2649   (BR)
STARBUCKS COFFEE CANADA, INC
(*Suby of* Starbucks Corporation)
5 Giroux Rd Unit 510, St. Albert, AB, T8N 6J8
(780) 458-2364
Emp Here 25
SIC 5812 Eating places

D-U-N-S 25-858-0364   (BR)
STURGEON FOUNDATION
NORTH RIDGE LODGE
21 Mont Clare Pl Suite 213, St. Albert, AB, T8N 5Z4
(780) 460-0445
Emp Here 20
SIC 8361 Residential care

D-U-N-S 20-746-2508   (SL)
STURGEON HOTEL LTD
ST. ALBERT INN & SUITES
156 St Albert Trail Suite 10, St. Albert, AB, T8N 0P5
(780) 459-5551
Emp Here 105   *Sales* 4,596,524
SIC 7011 Hotels and motels

D-U-N-S 20-591-9926   (BR)
STURGEON SCHOOL DIVISION #24
STURGEON HEIGHTS SCHOOL
50 Hogan Rd, St. Albert, AB, T8N 3X7
(780) 459-3990
Emp Here 35
SIC 8211 Elementary and secondary schools

D-U-N-S 25-096-5241   (BR)
TORONTO-DOMINION BANK, THE
TD CANADA TRUST
(*Suby of* Toronto-Dominion Bank, The)
11 Inglewood Dr Suite 1, St. Albert, AB, T8N 5E2

Emp Here 30
SIC 6021 National commercial banks

D-U-N-S 20-778-6588   (BR)
UNITED RENTALS OF CANADA, INC
UNITED RENTAL
23 Renault Cres, St. Albert, AB, T8N 4B7
(780) 458-2700
Emp Here 30
SIC 6159 Miscellaneous business credit institutions

D-U-N-S 25-219-0210   (BR)
WAL-MART CANADA CORP
700 St Albert Trail Suite 3087, St. Albert, AB, T8N 7A5
(780) 458-1629
Emp Here 300
SIC 5311 Department stores

D-U-N-S 25-609-5944   (BR)
WENDY'S RESTAURANTS OF CANADA INC
WENDY'S
(*Suby of* The Wendy's Company)
470 St Albert Trail Unit 10, St. Albert, AB, T8N 5J9
(780) 459-9690
Emp Here 21
SIC 5812 Eating places

D-U-N-S 20-048-5279   (HQ)
WESTCON PRECAST INC
19 Riel Dr. St. Albert, AB, T8N 3Z2
(780) 459-6695
Emp Here 20   *Emp Total* 50
Sales 10,141,537
SIC 3272 Concrete products, nec
Pr Pr Zennie Andrusiw
 Cory Andrusiw
Dir Jason Andrusiw
Dir Robin Andrusiw

D-U-N-S 25-153-5998   (SL)
WILCO CONTRACTORS NORTHWEST INC
205 Carnegie Dr Unit 108, St. Albert, AB, T8N 5B2
(780) 447-1199
Emp Here 180   *Sales* 24,149,992
SIC 8742 Management consulting services
Dir Arthur Maat

D-U-N-S 20-926-8270   (SL)
WILDE HOSPITALITY GROUP LTD
SWISS CHALET 1954
140 St Albert Trail Suite 700, St. Albert, AB, T8N 7C8
(780) 458-5313
Emp Here 50   *Sales* 1,532,175
SIC 5812 Eating places

D-U-N-S 25-079-1670   (BR)
WINNERS MERCHANTS INTERNATIONAL L.P.
WINNERS
(*Suby of* The TJX Companies Inc)
375 St Albert Trail Suite 191, St. Albert, AB, T8N 3K8
(780) 418-6363
Emp Here 35
SIC 5651 Family clothing stores

Stand Off, AB T0L

D-U-N-S 20-781-0123   (BR)
GOVERNMENT OF THE PROVINCE OF ALBERTA
KAINAI BOARD OF EDUCATION
Gd, Stand Off, AB, T0L 1Y0
(403) 737-3966
Emp Here 170
SIC 8211 Elementary and secondary schools

D-U-N-S 20-068-6454   (BR)
KAINAI BOARD OF EDUCATION
TATFIKIISAAPO'P MIDDLE SCHOOL
Gd, Stand Off, AB, T0L 1Y0
(403) 737-2946
Emp Here 28
SIC 8211 E ementary and secondary schools

D-U-N-S 20-653-4286   (BR)
KAINAI BOARD OF EDUCATION
SAIPOYI COMMUNITY SCHOOL
Po Box 240, Stand Off, AB, T0L 1Y0
(403) 737-3772
Emp Here 45
SIC 8211 Elementary and secondary schools

Standard, AB T0J

D-U-N-S 20-025-9476   (BR)
GOLDEN HILLS SCHOOL DIVISION #75
STANDARD SCHOOL
121 9 Ave E. Standard, AB, T0J 3G0
(403) 644-3791
Emp Here 20
SIC 8211 Elementary and secondary schools

D-U-N-S 25-127-0831   (BR)
HUSKY OIL OPERATIONS LIMITED
HUSKY ENERGY
Gd, Standard, AB, T0J 3G0

---

(403) 644-3855
Emp Here 45
SIC 1311 Crude petroleum and natural gas

Stettler, AB T0C

D-U-N-S 24-495-0101   (SL)
284734 ALBERTA LTD
C J ENTERPRISES
4701 42 St, Stettler, AB, T0C 2L0
(403) 742-1102
Emp Here 53   *Sales* 14,608,800
SIC 1541 Industrial buildings and warehouses
Pr Pr Doug Cumberland
 Grace Stewart
Dir Al Mattie

D-U-N-S 24-329-3607   (BR)
CERVUS LP
AGRO STETTLER
Hwy 12 W, Stettler, AB, T0C 2L0
(403) 742-4427
Emp Here 30
SIC 5999 Miscellaneous retail stores, nec

D-U-N-S 20-025-4832   (BR)
CLEARVIEW SCHOOL DIVISION #71
STETTLER ELEMENTARY SCHOOL
4808 54 St, Stettler, AB, T0C 2L2
(403) 742-2235
Emp Here 50
SIC 8211 Elementary and secondary schools

D-U-N-S 20-025-4824   (BR)
CLEARVIEW SCHOOL DIVISION #71
STETTLER MIDDLE SCHOOL
4814 54 St, Stettler, AB, T0C 2L2

Emp Here 30
SIC 8211 Elementary and secondary schools

D-U-N-S 20-025-4816   (BR)
CLEARVIEW SCHOOL DIVISION #71
WM HAY COMPOSITE HIGH SCHOOL
5411 50 Ave, Stettler, AB, T0C 2L2
(403) 742-3466
Emp Here 40
SIC 8211 Elementary and secondary schools

D-U-N-S 25-140-9306   (BR)
COUNTY STETTLER HOUSING AUTHORITY, THE
611 50th Ave, Stettler, AB, T0C 2L1
(403) 742-9220
Emp Here 110
SIC 6513 Apartment building operators

D-U-N-S 20-280-0541   (SL)
DNR PRESSURE WELDING LTD
(*Suby of* Quanta Services, Inc.)
Gd, Stettler, AB, T0C 2L0
(403) 742-2859
Emp Here 55   *Sales* 6,695,700
SIC 1799 Special trade contractors, nec
Pr Aaron Nixon
VP Ryan Nixon
VP Noel Nixon

D-U-N-S 20-554-4377   (SL)
DVN OILFIELD SERVICES LTD
4604 40 St, Stettler, AB, T0C 2L0
(403) 740-2517
Emp Here 35   *Sales* 6,128,699
SIC 1623 Water, sewer, and utility lines
Pr Darren Nichaus

D-U-N-S 20-248-5632   (BR)
DEVON CANADA CORPORATION
Gd, Stettler, AB, T0C 2L0
(403) 574-2125
Emp Here 20
SIC 1311 Crude petroleum and natural gas

D-U-N-S 25-998-8194   (BR)
EMPIRE IRON WORKS LTD
PETRO FIELD INDUSTRY

4102 44 Ave, Stettler, AB, T0C 2L0
(403) 742-6121
Emp Here 80
SIC 3713 Truck and bus bodies

D-U-N-S 24-763-4814   (BR)
KEYERA ENERGY LTD
NEVIS GAS PLANT
Gd, Stettler, AB, T0C 2L0
(403) 742-7200
Emp Here 33
SIC 5541 Gasoline service stations

D-U-N-S 20-245-9488   (BR)
LOBLAWS INC
EXTRA FOODS
5701 47 Ave, Stettler, AB, T0C 2L0
(403) 742-9186
Emp Here 60
SIC 5411 Grocery stores

D-U-N-S 24-972-1200   (BR)
PEAVEY INDUSTRIES LIMITED
PEAVEY MART
6610 50 Ave, Stettler, AB, T0C 2L2
(403) 742-5600
Emp Here 20
SIC 5251 Hardware stores

D-U-N-S 24-734-1217   (BR)
ROYAL BANK OF CANADA
RBC
(*Suby of* Royal Bank Of Canada)
4920 51 Ave Ss 2, Stettler, AB, T0C 2L2
(403) 742-2382
Emp Here 25
SIC 6021 National commercial banks

D-U-N-S 25-770-4635   (BR)
SOBEYS CAPITAL INCORPORATED
STETTLER SOBEYS
4607 50 St, Stettler, AB, T0C 2L0
(403) 742-5025
Emp Here 88
SIC 5411 Grocery stores

D-U-N-S 20-547-8840   (HQ)
STRAD COMPRESSION AND PRODUCTION SERVICES LTD
Hwy 12 W, Stettler, AB, T0C 2L0
(403) 742-6900
Emp Here 36   *Emp Total* 139
Sales 7,937,920
SIC 7699 Repair services, nec
Pr Brady Flett
 Wayne Long

D-U-N-S 24-961-5774   (SL)
TKS CONTROLS LTD
4605 41 St, Stettler, AB, T0C 2L0
(403) 740-4071
Emp Here 22   *Sales* 5,579,750
SIC 5084 Industrial machinery and equipment
Dir Brad Syson
Dir Brent Kranzler
Dir Glenn Kobi

D-U-N-S 25-269-9871   (BR)
UNITED FARMERS OF ALBERTA CO-OPERATIVE LIMITED
STETTLER FARM SUPPLY STORE
7007 50th Ave Nw, Stettler, AB, T0C 2L1
(403) 742-3426
Emp Here 20
SIC 5083 Farm and garden machinery

D-U-N-S 24-025-9833   (BR)
WAL-MART CANADA CORP
WALMART
4724 70th St, Stettler, AB, T0C 2L1
(403) 742-4404
Emp Here 120
SIC 5311 Department stores

D-U-N-S 20-919-2025   (BR)
WESTERN CANADA LOTTERY CORPORATION
6910 50 Ave, Stettler, AB, T0C 2L0

---

(403) 742-3504
Emp Here 25
SIC 7999 Amusement and recreation, nec

Stirling, AB T0K

D-U-N-S 25-616-5598   (SL)
HUTTERIAN BRETHREN CHURCH OF WOLF CREEK
Gd, Stirling, AB, T0K 2E0
(403) 756-2180
Emp Here 60   *Sales* 3,939,878
SIC 8661 Religious organizations

D-U-N-S 20-711-4757   (BR)
WESTWIND SCHOOL DIVISION #74
STIRLING SCHOOL
426 3 St, Stirling, AB, T0K 2E0
(403) 756-3355
Emp Here 35
SIC 8211 Elementary and secondary schools

Stony Plain, AB T7Z

D-U-N-S 24-356-5368   (BR)
ALBERTA HEALTH SERVICES
WESTVIEW HEALTH CENTRE
4405 South Park Dr, Stony Plain, AB, T7Z 2M7
(780) 968-3600
Emp Here 640
SIC 8062 General medical and surgical hospitals

D-U-N-S 25-236-1589   (BR)
ALBERTA TREASURY BRANCHES
ATB FINANCIAL
5014 50 St, Stony Plain, AB, T7Z 1T2
(780) 963-2214
Emp Here 20
SIC 6211 Security brokers and dealers

D-U-N-S 24-733-5938   (BR)
BORDER PAVING LTD
Gd, Stony Plain, AB, T7Z 1W1
(780) 967-3330
Emp Here 70
SIC 1611 Highway and street construction

D-U-N-S 25-118-4958   (SL)
BOSTON PIZZA
70 Boulder Blvd, Stony Plain, AB, T7Z 1V7
(780) 963-5006
Emp Here 60   *Sales* 1,824,018
SIC 5812 Eating places

D-U-N-S 25-288-9092   (BR)
CANADA POST CORPORATION
STONY PLAIN POST OFFICE
5305 50 St, Stony Plain, AB, T7Z 1A0
(780) 963-2867
Emp Here 23
SIC 4311 U.s. postal service

D-U-N-S 25-516-1465   (BR)
GOOD SAMARITAN SOCIETY, THE (A LUTHERAN SOCIAL SERVICE ORGANIZATION)
GOOD SAMARITAN CARE CENTRE
5600 50 St, Stony Plain, AB, T7Z 1B1
(780) 963-2261
Emp Here 50
SIC 8051 Skilled nursing care facilities

D-U-N-S 24-962-0881   (BR)
JASPER INN INVESTMENTS LTD
STONY CONVENTION INN
4620 48 St, Stony Plain, AB, T7Z 1L4
(780) 963-7810
Emp Here 60
SIC 7011 Hotels and motels

D-U-N-S 24-904-9909   (BR)

JASPER INN INVESTMENTS LTD
RAMADA INN & SUITES
3301 43 Ave, Stony Plain, AB, T7Z 1L1
(780) 963-0222
Emp Here 45
SIC 7011 Hotels and motels

D-U-N-S 20-911-0985   (BR)
NORQUEST COLLEGE
3201 43 Ave, Stony Plain, AB, T7Z 1L1
(780) 968-6489
Emp Here 100
SIC 8221 Colleges and universities

D-U-N-S 20-029-0059   (BR)
PARKLAND SCHOOL DIVISION NO. 70
FOREST GREEN SCHOOL
5210 45 St, Stony Plain, AB, T7Z 1R5
(780) 963-7366
Emp Here 35
SIC 8211 Elementary and secondary schools

D-U-N-S 25-485-8624   (BR)
PARKLAND SCHOOL DIVISION NO. 70
MUIR LAKE SCHOOL
53422 Secondary Hwy Suite 779, Stony Plain, AB, T7Z 1Y5
(780) 963-3535
Emp Here 45
SIC 8211 Elementary and secondary schools

D-U-N-S 20-642-8893   (BR)
PARKLAND SCHOOL DIVISION NO. 70
BLUEBERRY COMMUNITY SCHOOL
20 Parkland Drive Range Road, Stony Plain, AB, T7Z 1Y6
(780) 963-3625
Emp Here 53
SIC 8211 Elementary and secondary schools

D-U-N-S 20-653-3338   (BR)
PARKLAND SCHOOL DIVISION NO. 70
MERIDIAN HEIGHTS SCHOOL
4119 43 St, Stony Plain, AB, T7Z 1R2
(780) 963-2289
Emp Here 55
SIC 8211 Elementary and secondary schools

D-U-N-S 25-183-6016   (BR)
TERVITA CORPORATION
(*Suby of* Tervita Corporation)
946 Boulder Blvd, Stony Plain, AB, T7Z 0E6
(780) 963-1484
Emp Here 20
SIC 8748 Business consulting, nec

D-U-N-S 20-267-3831   (BR)
THYS INVESTMENTS LTD
MCDONALD'S
(*Suby of* Thys Investments Ltd)
4201 South Park Dr, Stony Plain, AB, T7Z 1L1
(780) 968-6441
Emp Here 50
SIC 5812 Eating places

Strathmore, AB T1P

D-U-N-S 20-933-6473   (SL)
BOSTON PIZZA
800 Pine Rd Suite 114, Strathmore, AB, T1P 0A2
(403) 934-0017
Emp Here 50   *Sales* 1,532,175
SIC 5812 Eating places

D-U-N-S 20-971-6955   (BR)
CALGARY CO-OPERATIVE ASSOCIATION LIMITED
CALGARY CO-OP
320 2nd St, Strathmore, AB, T1P 1K1
(403) 934-3121
Emp Here 130
SIC 5411 Grocery stores

D-U-N-S 24-012-0878   (BR)

CHINOOK CREDIT UNION LTD
100 2nd Ave, Strathmore, AB, T1P 1K1
(403) 934-3358
Emp Here 20
SIC 6062 State credit unions

D-U-N-S 25-081-2463   (BR)
DOLLARAMA S.E.C.
100 Ranch Market Suite 105e, Strathmore, AB, T1P 0A8
(403) 934-6351
Emp Here 32
SIC 5331 Variety stores

D-U-N-S 24-324-0145   (BR)
ENCANA CORPORATION
601 Westmount Rd, Strathmore, AB, T1P 1W8
(403) 934-6108
Emp Here 20
SIC 1382 Oil and gas exploration services

D-U-N-S 20-711-0607   (BR)
GOLDEN HILLS SCHOOL DIVISION #75
ROSEBUD RIVER SCHOOL
435b Hwy 1, Strathmore, AB, T1P 1J4
(403) 901-9266
Emp Here 50
SIC 8211 Elementary and secondary schools

D-U-N-S 20-301-0272   (BR)
GOLDEN HILLS SCHOOL DIVISION #75
STRATHMORE HIGH SCHOOL
100 Brent Blvd, Strathmore, AB, T1P 1V2
(403) 934-3135
Emp Here 65
SIC 8211 Elementary and secondary schools

D-U-N-S 20-710-9385   (BR)
GOLDEN HILLS SCHOOL DIVISION #75
BRENTWOOD ELEMENTARY SCHOOL
95 Brentwood Dr W, Strathmore, AB, T1P 1E3
(403) 934-5013
Emp Here 45
SIC 8211 Elementary and secondary schools

D-U-N-S 24-027-5664   (BR)
GOLDEN HILLS SCHOOL DIVISION #75
CROWTHER MEMORIAL JUNIOR HIGH SCHOOL
190 Brent Blvd, Strathmore, AB, T1P 1T4
(403) 901-1410
Emp Here 50
SIC 8211 Elementary and secondary schools

D-U-N-S 20-029-3335   (BR)
GOLDEN HILLS SCHOOL DIVISION #75
WESTMOUNT ELEMENTARY SCHOOL
220 Wheatland Trail, Strathmore, AB, T1P 1B2
(403) 934-3041
Emp Here 50
SIC 8211 Elementary and secondary schools

D-U-N-S 20-867-4783   (BR)
GOLDEN HILLS SCHOOL DIVISION #75
WHEATLAND ELEMENTARY SCHOOL
220 Brent Blvd, Strathmore, AB, T1P 1K6
(403) 934-3318
Emp Here 45
SIC 8211 Elementary and secondary schools

D-U-N-S 20-710-9054   (BR)
GOLDEN HILLS SCHOOL DIVISION #75
ROSEBUD RIVER SCHOOL
435a Hwy 1 Suite 1, Strathmore, AB, T1P 1J4

Emp Here 50
SIC 8211 Elementary and secondary schools

D-U-N-S 20-299-9335   (BR)
GOVERNMENT OF THE PROVINCE OF ALBERTA
ATB FINANCIAL
100 Ranch Market Suite 109, Strathmore, AB, T1P 0A8
(403) 934-8816
Emp Here 25
SIC 8742 Management consulting services

D-U-N-S 20-915-3381   (BR)

LOBLAWS INC
TINA'S NOFRILLS
900 Pine Rd Suite 101, Strathmore, AB, T1P 0A2
(403) 934-6510
Emp Here 60
SIC 5411 Grocery stores

D-U-N-S 25-085-3777   (SL)
MEZZE MANAGEMENT LTD
STRATHMORE STATION RESTAURANT & PUB
380 Ridge Rd, Strathmore, AB, T1P 1B5
(403) 934-0000
Emp Here 52   *Sales* 1,532,175
SIC 5812 Eating places

D-U-N-S 24-616-8020   (BR)
SOBEYS CAPITAL INCORPORATED
SOBEYS
100 Ranch Market Suite 100, Strathmore, AB, T1P 0A8
(403) 934-4512
Emp Here 25
SIC 5411 Grocery stores

D-U-N-S 25-269-9137   (SL)
STRATHMORE GOLF CLUB
80 Wheatland Trail, Strathmore, AB, T1P 1A5
(403) 934-3925
Emp Here 50   *Sales* 2,042,900
SIC 7997 Membership sports and recreation clubs

D-U-N-S 25-269-9673   (BR)
UNITED FARMERS OF ALBERTA CO-OPERATIVE LIMITED
STRATHMORE FARM SUPPLY STORE
58 Slater Rd, Strathmore, AB, T1P 1J3
(403) 934-6684
Emp Here 20
SIC 5083 Farm and garden machinery

D-U-N-S 24-319-5158   (BR)
WAL-MART CANADA CORP
WAL-MART
200 Ranch Market, Strathmore, AB, T1P 0A8
(403) 934-9776
Emp Here 120
SIC 5311 Department stores

D-U-N-S 25-999-4986   (BR)
WESTERN FEEDLOTS LTD
Gd Stn Main, Strathmore, AB, T1P 1J5

Emp Here 20
SIC 5191 Farm supplies

D-U-N-S 20-646-1766   (SL)
WESTERN IRRIGATION DISTRICT
900 Pine Rd Unit 105, Strathmore, AB, T1P 0A2
(403) 934-3542
Emp Here 30   *Sales* 5,250,594
SIC 4971 Irrigation systems
 Dan Shute
 Henry Colpoys
Dir Doug Brown
Dir Rick Page
Dir Don Kathol
Dir Grant Klaiber
 Lucie Montford

Strome, AB T0B

D-U-N-S 20-710-5797   (BR)
BATTLE RIVER REGIONAL DIVISION 31
STROME SCHOOL
Gd, Strome, AB, T0B 4H0
(780) 376-3504
Emp Here 50
SIC 8211 Elementary and secondary schools

Sturgeon County, AB T8G

D-U-N-S 24-327-4305   (SL)
POUNDMAKER'S LODGE TREATMENT CENTRES (THE SOCIETY)
25108 Poundmaker Rd, Sturgeon County, AB, T8G 2A2
(780) 458-1884
Emp Here 60   *Sales* 2,826,987
SIC 8361 Residential care

Sturgeon County, AB T8L

D-U-N-S 25-696-9598   (SL)
C T REINFORCING STEEL CO ALBERTA LTD
55202 Sh 825 Unit 186, Sturgeon County, AB, T8L 5C1
(780) 998-5565
Emp Here 49   *Sales* 9,434,850
SIC 3441 Fabricated structural Metal
Genl Mgr Meloudy Miller

Sturgeon County, AB T8R

D-U-N-S 20-713-3229   (BR)
STURGEON SCHOOL DIVISION #24
CAMILLA SCHOOL
26500 Hwy 44 Suite 146, Sturgeon County, AB, T8R 0J3
(780) 939-2074
Emp Here 45
SIC 8211 Elementary and secondary schools

Sturgeon County, AB T8T

D-U-N-S 20-023-9585   (BR)
STURGEON SCHOOL DIVISION #24
NAMAO SCHOOL
24400 Hwy 37 Unit 2, Sturgeon County, AB, T8T 0E9
(780) 973-9191
Emp Here 45
SIC 8211 Elementary and secondary schools

Sturgeon County, AB T8W

D-U-N-S 24-338-1584   (HQ)
WITHERS L.P.
WITHERS TRUCKING
3602 93 St, Sturgeon County, AB, T8W 5A8
(780) 539-5347
Emp Here 35   *Emp Total* 5,515
Sales 13,513,516
SIC 4213 Trucking, except local
 Keith Withers

Sundre, AB T0M

D-U-N-S 20-778-1910   (BR)
ALBERTA HEALTH SERVICES
SUNDRE HOSPITAL & CARE CENTRE
709 1 St Ne, Sundre, AB, T0M 1X0
(403) 638-3033
Emp Here 100
SIC 8062 General medical and surgical hospitals

D-U-N-S 20-588-4062   (BR)
CHINOOKS EDGE SCHOOL DIVISION NO. 73

SUNDRE HIGH SCHOOL
102 Second Ave Nw, Sundre, AB, T0M 1X0
(403) 638-4545
Emp Here 35
SIC 8211 Elementary and secondary schools

D-U-N-S 20-591-6765   (BR)
CHINOOKS EDGE SCHOOL DIVISION NO. 73
RIVER VALLEY SCHOOL
310 Centre St N Unit 1, Sundre, AB, T0M 1X0
(403) 638-3939
Emp Here 70
SIC 8211 Elementary and secondary schools

D-U-N-S 24-119-4448   (SL)
MILLARD TRUCKING LTD
Rd Industrial Park W, Sundre, AB, T0M 1X0
(403) 638-4500
Emp Here 50   *Sales* 3,939,878
SIC 4212 Local trucking, without storage

Swan Hills, AB T0G

D-U-N-S 25-325-4098   (BR)
ALBERTA HEALTH SERVICES
SWAN HILLS HEALTHCARE CENTRE
29 Freeman Dr, Swan Hills, AB, T0G 2C0
(780) 333-7000
Emp Here 35
SIC 8011 Offices and clinics of medical doctors

D-U-N-S 25-456-6110   (BR)
APACHE CANADA LTD
(*Suby of* Apache Corporation)
Gd, Swan Hills, AB, T0G 2C0

Emp Here 30
SIC 5541 Gasoline service stations

D-U-N-S 20-741-7515   (BR)
DEVON CANADA CORPORATION
Gd, Swan Hills, AB, T0G 2C0
(780) 333-7800
Emp Here 75
SIC 5172 Petroleum products, nec

D-U-N-S 20-650-3539   (BR)
PEMBINA HILLS REGIONAL DIVISION 7
SWAN HILLS SCHOOL
4707 Ravine Dr, Swan Hills, AB, T0G 2C0
(780) 333-4471
Emp Here 35
SIC 8211 Elementary and secondary schools

D-U-N-S 25-507-2175   (BR)
PENGROWTH ENERGY CORPORATION
JUDY CREEK OPERATIONS
(*Suby of* Pengrowth Energy Corporation)
Po Box 390, Swan Hills, AB, T0G 2C0
(780) 333-7100
Emp Here 100
SIC 1311 Crude petroleum and natural gas

D-U-N-S 24-337-5800   (BR)
SUEZ CANADA WASTE SERIVCES INC
SWAN HILLS TREATMENT CENTRE
10000 Chrystina Lake Rd, Swan Hills, AB, T0G 2C0
(780) 391-7303
Emp Here 110
SIC 4953 Refuse systems

Sylvan Lake, AB T4S

D-U-N-S 20-128-6551   (BR)
ALBERTA HEALTH SERVICES
SYLVAN LAKE COMMUNITY HEALTH CENTRE
4602 49 Ave, Sylvan Lake, AB, T4S 1M7

(403) 887-2242
Emp Here 30
SIC 8322 Individual and family services

D-U-N-S 24-369-9175   (BR)
BANK OF NOVA SCOTIA, THE
SCOTIABANK
10 Hewlett Park Landng Unit 13a, Sylvan Lake, AB, T4S 2J3
(403) 887-1340
Emp Here 20
SIC 6021 National commercial banks

D-U-N-S 24-036-5036   (BR)
BETHANY CARE SOCIETY
BETHANY SYLVAN LAKE
4700 47 Ave Suite 16, Sylvan Lake, AB, T4S 2M3
(403) 887-8687
Emp Here 70
SIC 8051 Skilled nursing care facilities

D-U-N-S 25-483-9913   (SL)
BIG MOO ICE CREAM PARLOURS, THE
4603 Lakeshore Dr, Sylvan Lake, AB, T4S 1C3
(403) 887-5533
Emp Here 60   *Sales* 2,480,664
SIC 5451 Dairy products stores

D-U-N-S 25-021-4053   (BR)
CHINOOKS EDGE SCHOOL DIVISION NO. 73
ECOLE STEFFIE WOIMA ELEMENTARY SCHOOL
4720 45 Ave, Sylvan Lake, AB, T4S 1A5
(403) 887-3088
Emp Here 44
SIC 8211 Elementary and secondary schools

D-U-N-S 20-653-1969   (BR)
CHINOOKS EDGE SCHOOL DIVISION NO. 73
ECOLE FOX RUN SCHOOL
2 Falcon Ridge Dr, Sylvan Lake, AB, T4S 2H1
(403) 887-0491
Emp Here 45
SIC 8211 Elementary and secondary schools

D-U-N-S 25-021-3782   (BR)
CHINOOKS EDGE SCHOOL DIVISION NO. 73
ECOLE H J CODY SCHOOL
4520 50 St, Sylvan Lake, AB, T4S 1A4
(403) 887-2412
Emp Here 45
SIC 8211 Elementary and secondary schools

D-U-N-S 20-895-0113   (SL)
DELTA ENERGY LTD
DELTA OILFIELD
16 Industrial Dr, Sylvan Lake, AB, T4S 1P4

Emp Here 50   *Sales* 7,852,800
SIC 1611 Highway and street construction
Pr Pr Frank Wilson
  Lynne Wilson

D-U-N-S 20-190-0201   (SL)
KGH MECHANICAL SYSTEMS LTD
11 Erickson Cres, Sylvan Lake, AB, T4S 1P5

Emp Here 50   *Sales* 6,028,800
SIC 1711 Plumbing, heating, air-conditioning
Pr Pr Kevin Halsey
  Carrie Halsey

D-U-N-S 20-514-8401   (BR)
LOBLAWS INC
NO FRILLS
70 Hewlett Park Landng Suite 9076, Sylvan Lake, AB, T4S 2J3
(403) 887-1302
Emp Here 50
SIC 5411 Grocery stores

D-U-N-S 24-254-6195   (BR)
NABORS DRILLING CANADA LIMITED
NABORS PRODUCTION SERVICES

33 Schenk Ind. Rd Suite 2008, Sylvan Lake, AB, T4S 2J9
(403) 887-0744
Emp Here 70
SIC 1389 Oil and gas field services, nec

D-U-N-S 20-152-9257   (BR)
RED DEER CATHOLIC REGIONAL DIVISION NO. 39
MOTHER TERESA SCHOOL
79 Old Boomer Rd, Sylvan Lake, AB, T4S 1Z4
(403) 887-6371
Emp Here 45
SIC 8211 Elementary and secondary schools

D-U-N-S 24-599-2008   (BR)
WAL-MART CANADA CORP
WALMART
3420 47 Ave, Sylvan Lake, AB, T4S 0B6
(403) 887-7590
Emp Here 150
SIC 5311 Department stores

D-U-N-S 25-362-3581   (BR)
WESTWINN GROUP ENTERPRISES INC
HARBERCRAFT
6 Erickson Cres, Sylvan Lake, AB, T4S 1P5

Emp Here 30
SIC 3732 Boatbuilding and repairing

Taber, AB T1G

D-U-N-S 24-808-7574   (BR)
ALBERTA HEALTH SERVICES
PUBLIC COMMUNITY HEALTH
5011 50 Ave E Wing, Taber, AB, T1G 1N9
(403) 223-7230
Emp Here 25
SIC 8011 Offices and clinics of medical doctors

D-U-N-S 25-174-2417   (SL)
AMLOG CANADA, INC
(*Suby of* Yucaipa Companies LLC)
Hwy 3, Taber, AB, T1G 2C6
(403) 223-8833
Emp Here 28   *Sales* 2,626,585
SIC 4222 Refrigerated warehousing and storage

D-U-N-S 20-028-9622   (BR)
BOARD OF TRUSTEES OF HORIZON SCHOOL DIVISION NO 67
L T WESTLAKE SCHOOL
5310 42 Ave, Taber, AB, T1G 1B6
(403) 223-2487
Emp Here 26
SIC 8211 Elementary and secondary schools

D-U-N-S 20-711-9319   (BR)
BOARD OF TRUSTEES OF HORIZON SCHOOL DIVISION NO 67
DR HAMMAN SCHOOL
4820 56 Ave, Taber, AB, T1G 1H4
(403) 223-2988
Emp Here 25
SIC 8211 Elementary and secondary schools

D-U-N-S 20-653-8477   (BR)
BOARD OF TRUSTEES OF HORIZON SCHOOL DIVISION NO 67
CENTRAL SCHOOL
5412 54 St, Taber, AB, T1G 1L5
(403) 223-2170
Emp Here 30
SIC 8211 Elementary and secondary schools

D-U-N-S 20-046-0850   (BR)
BOARD OF TRUSTEES OF HORIZON SCHOOL DIVISION NO 67
WR MYERS HIGH SCHOOL
5511a 54 St, Taber, AB, T1G 1L5
(403) 223-2292
Emp Here 50

SIC 8211 Elementary and secondary schools

D-U-N-S 20-922-9975   (BR)
BUILDERS ENERGY SERVICES LTD
CIRCLE D TRANSPORT
(*Suby of* Builders Energy Services Ltd)
6002 64 St, Taber, AB, T1G 1Z3

Emp Here 30
SIC 1389 Oil and gas field services, nec

D-U-N-S 20-794-6729   (BR)
FIRSTCANADA ULC
FIRST STUDENT
6304b 52 St, Taber, AB, T1G 1J7
(403) 223-5670
Emp Here 110
SIC 4151 School buses

D-U-N-S 20-711-8675   (BR)
HOLY SPIRIT ROMAN CATHOLIC SEPARATE REGIONAL DIVISION NO 4
ST MARY'S SCHOOL
(*Suby of* Holy Spirit Roman Catholic Separate Regional Division No 4)
5427 50 St, Taber, AB, T1G 1M2
(403) 223-3165
Emp Here 26
SIC 8211 Elementary and secondary schools

D-U-N-S 20-088-2350   (BR)
HOLY SPIRIT ROMAN CATHOLIC SEPARATE REGIONAL DIVISION NO 4
ST PATRICK'S SCHOOL
(*Suby of* Holy Spirit Roman Catholic Separate Regional Division No 4)
5302 48 St, Taber, AB, T1G 1H3
(403) 223-3352
Emp Here 25
SIC 8211 Elementary and secondary schools

D-U-N-S 24-439-7527   (BR)
LANTIC INC
5405 64 St, Taber, AB, T1G 2C4
(403) 223-3535
Emp Here 115
SIC 5149 Groceries and related products, nec

D-U-N-S 24-014-5540   (BR)
PEPSICO CANADA ULC
HOSTESS FRITO-LAY
(*Suby of* Pepsico, Inc.)
5904 54 Ave, Taber, AB, T1G 1X3
(403) 223-3574
Emp Here 200
SIC 2096 Potato chips and similar snacks

D-U-N-S 20-368-5383   (BR)
PRONGHORN CONTROLS LTD
5910a 52 Ave, Taber, AB, T1G 1W8
(403) 223-8811
Emp Here 20
SIC 7629 Electrical repair shops

D-U-N-S 25-359-6563   (BR)
SOBEYS WEST INC
LUCERNE FOODS
5115 57 St, Taber, AB, T1G 1X1

Emp Here 50
SIC 2033 Canned fruits and specialties

D-U-N-S 24-011-9789   (BR)
SOBEYS WEST INC
LUCERNE FOODS, DIV OF
4926 46 Ave, Taber, AB, T1G 2A4
(403) 223-5749
Emp Here 120
SIC 5411 Grocery stores

D-U-N-S 20-040-7513   (BR)
SOCIETY FOR CHRISTIAN EDUCATION IN SOUTHERN ALBERTA, THE
TABER CHRISTIAN SCHOOL
4809 60 Ave, Taber, AB, T1G 1E9
(403) 223-4550
Emp Here 20
SIC 8211 Elementary and secondary schools

D-U-N-S 20-877-2959   (BR)
TARPON ENERGY SERVICES LTD
6410 53 St, Taber, AB, T1G 2A2
(403) 223-4415
Emp Here 28
SIC 1389 Oil and gas field services, nec

D-U-N-S 24-854-3514   (BR)
UNIFIRST CANADA LTD
(*Suby of* Unifirst Corporation)
5702 60 St, Taber, AB, T1G 2B3
(403) 223-2182
Emp Here 45
SIC 7218 Industrial launderers

D-U-N-S 25-073-1494   (BR)
VITERRA INC
VITERRA
Gd, Taber, AB, T1G 2E5
(403) 223-2772
Emp Here 20
SIC 4221 Farm product warehousing and storage

D-U-N-S 24-319-5018   (BR)
WAL-MART CANADA CORP
WALMART
4500 64 St Suite 1, Taber, AB, T1G 0A4
(403) 223-3458
Emp Here 101
SIC 5311 Department stores

D-U-N-S 24-827-1079   (HQ)
WELL-TECH ENERGY SERVICES INC
6006 58 St, Taber, AB, T1G 2B8
(403) 223-4244
Emp Here 60   *Emp Total* 51
Sales 10,335,823
SIC 1389 Oil and gas field services, nec
Pr Pr Brad Lockhart
 Ken Shelstad
 Jeff Lockhart
Dir Brandon Harker

D-U-N-S 20-875-3785   (BR)
WESTERN FINANCIAL GROUP INC
5300 47 Ave, Taber, AB, T1G 1R1
(403) 223-8123
Emp Here 20
SIC 6411 Insurance agents, brokers, and service

Thorhild, AB T0A

D-U-N-S 20-656-0760   (BR)
ASPEN VIEW PUBLIC SCHOOL DIVISION NO. 78
THORHILD CENTRAL SCHOOL
(*Suby of* Aspen View Public School Division No. 78)
Half Apt Mile, Thorhild, AB, T0A 3J0
(780) 398-3610
Emp Here 30
SIC 8211 Elementary and secondary schools

Thorsby, AB T0C

D-U-N-S 20-205-5138   (BR)
BLACK GOLD REGIONAL DIVISION #18
THORSBY ELEMENTARY SCHOOL
5303 48 Ave, Thorsby, AB, T0C 2P0
(780) 789-3776
Emp Here 25
SIC 8211 Elementary and secondary schools

D-U-N-S 25-206-2823   (HQ)
BLUE FALLS MANUFACTURING LTD
ARCTIC SPAS
(*Suby of* Spa Logic Inc)
4549 52 St, Thorsby, AB, T0C 2P0

(780) 789-2626
Emp Here 120   *Emp Total* 126
Sales 12,038,516
SIC 3999 Manufacturing industries, nec
Pr Pr Darcy Amendt
Dir Brent Macklin
Dir Opers Dennis Kellner

D-U-N-S 25-976-3563   (BR)
WESTOWER COMMUNICATIONS LTD
4933 46th St, Thorsby, AB, T0C 2P0
(780) 789-2375
Emp Here 80
SIC 1623 Water, sewer, and utility lines

Three Hills, AB T0M

D-U-N-S 25-272-2988   (BR)
GOLDEN HILLS SCHOOL DIVISION #75
THREE HILLS SCHOOL
400 6 Ave S, Three Hills, AB, T0M 2A0
(403) 443-5335
Emp Here 61
SIC 8211 Elementary and secondary schools

Tofield, AB T0B

D-U-N-S 20-037-3301   (BR)
BATTLE RIVER REGIONAL DIVISION 31
TOFIELD SCHOOL
4824 58th Ave, Tofield, AB, T0B 4J0
(780) 662-3133
Emp Here 50
SIC 8211 Elementary and secondary schools

D-U-N-S 20-075-0466   (BR)
BEAVER FOUNDATION
TOFIELD LODGE
(*Suby of* Beaver Foundation)
5824 50th St, Tofield, AB, T0B 4J0
(780) 662-3477
Emp Here 29
SIC 8361 Residential care

Trochu, AB T0M

D-U-N-S 25-436-3083   (BR)
CERVUS LP
102 1st Avenue N, Trochu, AB, T0M 2C0
(403) 442-3982
Emp Here 30
SIC 5999 Miscellaneous retail stores, nec

D-U-N-S 24-104-5181   (BR)
CONOCOPHILLIPS WESTERN CANADA PARTNERSHIP
CONOCOPHILLIPS CANADA
Gd, Trochu, AB, T0M 2C0
(403) 442-4244
Emp Here 22
SIC 1311 Crude petroleum and natural gas

D-U-N-S 24-904-6749   (SL)
COVENANT HEALTH ST MARY'S TROCHU
451 Dechaueney Ave, Trochu, AB, T0M 2C0
(403) 442-3955
Emp Here 72   *Sales* 3,283,232
SIC 8051 Skilled nursing care facilities

D-U-N-S 20-025-4998   (BR)
GOLDEN HILLS SCHOOL DIVISION #75
TROCHU VALLEY SCHOOL
211 School Rd, Trochu, AB, T0M 2C0
(403) 442-3872
Emp Here 28
SIC 8211 Elementary and secondary schools

D-U-N-S 20-711-0383   (BR)
GOLDEN HILLS SCHOOL DIVISION #75

TROCHU VALLEY SCHOOL
102 School Rd, Trochu, AB, T0M 2C0

Emp Here 35
SIC 8211 Elementary and secondary schools

Tsuu T'Ina, AB T2W

D-U-N-S 24-807-3397   (SL)
TSUU T'INA MECHANICAL SERVICES LTD
9911 Chula Blvd Sw Suite 250, Tsuu T'Ina, AB, T2W 6H6
(403) 251-7695
Emp Here 40   *Sales* 6,973,235
SIC 5541 Gasoline service stations
 Jerry Simon

Tsuu T'Ina, AB T3E

D-U-N-S 24-682-6650   (SL)
SONCO GAMING LIMITED PARTNERSHIP
GREY EAGLE CASINO & BINGO
377 Grey Eagle Dr, Tsuu T'Ina, AB, T3E 3X8
(403) 385-3777
Emp Here 400   *Sales* 28,081,404
SIC 7999 Amusement and recreation, nec
Genl Mgr Martin Brickstock
 Britt Gudmundson

Turner Valley, AB T0L

D-U-N-S 25-316-1871   (BR)
FOOTHILLS SCHOOL DIVISION NO. 38
TURNER VALLEY SCHOOL
114 Royal Ave Nw, Turner Valley, AB, T0L 2A0
(403) 938-7359
Emp Here 21
SIC 8211 Elementary and secondary schools

D-U-N-S 25-363-7482   (BR)
ROYAL BANK OF CANADA
RBC ROYAL BANK
(*Suby of* Royal Bank Of Canada)
Sunset Blvd Suite &, Turner Valley, AB, T0L 2A0
(403) 933-4364
Emp Here 250
SIC 6021 National commercial banks

Two Hills, AB T0B

D-U-N-S 20-713-1975   (BR)
ST. PAUL EDUCATION REGIONAL DIVISION NO 1
TWO HILLS MENONITE SCHOOL
4801 Diefen Baker Ave, Two Hills, AB, T0B 4K0
(780) 657-2434
Emp Here 30
SIC 8211 Elementary and secondary schools

D-U-N-S 20-023-9791   (BR)
ST. PAUL EDUCATION REGIONAL DIVISION NO 1
TWO HILLS SCHOOL
4806 51 Ave, Two Hills, AB, T0B 4K0
(780) 657-3383
Emp Here 28
SIC 7389 Business services, nec

D-U-N-S 24-701-7627   (BR)
STELMASCHUK, W. J. AND ASSOCIATES LTD
Gd, Two Hills, AB, T0B 4K0
(780) 657-3307
Emp Here 25

SIC 8322 Individual and family services

Valleyview, AB T0H

D-U-N-S 20-028-4037   (BR)
HOLY FAMILY CATHOLIC REGIONAL DIVISION 37
ST STEPHEN'S CATHOLIC SCHOOL
4301 51st Ave, Valleyview, AB, T0H 3N0
(780) 524-3562
Emp Here 35
SIC 8211 Elementary and secondary schools

D-U-N-S 20-870-7633   (BR)
HUDSON'S BAY COMPANY
FIELDS STORES
5001 50th Ave, Valleyview, AB, T0H 3N0
(780) 524-2500
Emp Here 25
SIC 5311 Department stores

D-U-N-S 20-023-9338   (BR)
NORTHERN GATEWAY REGIONAL DIVISION #10
HARRY GRAY ELEMENTARY SCHOOL
5013 48 St, Valleyview, AB, T0H 3N0
(780) 524-3433
Emp Here 20
SIC 8211 Elementary and secondary schools

D-U-N-S 20-915-1492   (BR)
NORTHERN GATEWAY REGIONAL DIVISION #10
TRANSPORTATION DEPARTMENT
5102 49 St, Valleyview, AB, T0H 3N0
(780) 524-3833
Emp Here 20
SIC 4151 School buses

D-U-N-S 20-023-9346   (BR)
NORTHERN GATEWAY REGIONAL DIVISION #10
OSCAR ADOLPSON PRIMARY SCHOOL
5201 48 St, Valleyview, AB, T0H 3N0
(780) 524-3144
Emp Here 25
SIC 8211 Elementary and secondary schools

D-U-N-S 20-029-3970   (BR)
NORTHERN GATEWAY REGIONAL DIVISION #10
HILLSIDE JUNIOR SENIOR HIGH SCHOOL
4701 52 Ave, Valleyview, AB, T0H 3N0
(780) 524-3277
Emp Here 31
SIC 8211 Elementary and secondary schools

D-U-N-S 20-703-8931   (BR)
PEMBINA PIPELINE CORPORATION
4807 36th Ave, Valleyview, AB, T0H 3N0
(780) 524-3392
Emp Here 27
SIC 4612 Crude petroleum pipelines

D-U-N-S 20-775-5448   (BR)
REXALL PHARMACY GROUP LTD
MEDICINE BOTTLE REXALL
(*Suby of* McKesson Corporation)
4705 50 Ave, Valleyview, AB, T0H 3N0
(780) 524-3508
Emp Here 21
SIC 5912 Drug stores and proprietary stores

D-U-N-S 20-029-7179   (BR)
STURGEON LAKE CREE NATION
STURGEON LAKE SCHOOL
Gd, Valleyview, AB, T0H 3N0
(780) 524-4590
Emp Here 25
SIC 8211 Elementary and secondary schools

Vauxhall, AB T0K

D-U-N-S 20-292-7427   (BR)
BOARD OF TRUSTEES OF HORIZON SCHOOL DIVISION NO 67
VAUXHALL SCHOOL
623 5th Ave N, Vauxhall, AB, T0K 2K0
(403) 654-2145
Emp Here 32
SIC 8211 Elementary and secondary schools

D-U-N-S 20-655-2007   (BR)
BOARD OF TRUSTEES OF HORIZON SCHOOL DIVISION NO 67
VAUXHALL ELEMENTARY SCHOOL
423 7 St N, Vauxhall, AB, T0K 2K0
(403) 654-2422
Emp Here 37
SIC 8211 Elementary and secondary schools

D-U-N-S 20-646-0156   (SL)
BOW RIVER IRRIGATION DISTRICT
704 7 Ave N, Vauxhall, AB, T0K 2K0
(403) 654-2111
Emp Here 50   *Sales* 3,116,830
SIC 4971 Irrigation systems

Vegreville, AB T9C

D-U-N-S 20-889-9067   (BR)
ATCO ELECTRIC LTD
6502 55th Ave, Vegreville, AB, T9C 1R7
(780) 632-5973
Emp Here 60
SIC 4911 Electric services

D-U-N-S 25-370-3243   (BR)
AGRITRAC EQUIPMENT LTD
(*Suby of* Agritrac Equipment Ltd)
6425 55 Ave, Vegreville, AB, T9C 1T5
(780) 632-6677
Emp Here 20
SIC 5999 Miscellaneous retail stores, nec

D-U-N-S 20-578-2530   (BR)
ALBERTA TREASURY BRANCHES
A T B FINANCIAL
4931 50th St Gd, Vegreville, AB, T9C 1V5
(780) 632-2340
Emp Here 20
SIC 6036 Savings institutions, except federal

D-U-N-S 24-414-0963   (SL)
BUHLER EZEE-ON, INC
5110 62 St, Vegreville, AB, T9C 1N6
(780) 632-2126
Emp Here 85   *Sales* 271,612,600
SIC 3523 Farm machinery and equipment
Pr Dmitry Lyubimov
VP Maxim Loktionov
Genl Mgr Leo Turko

D-U-N-S 24-325-2967   (BR)
CARILLION CANADA INC
14403 16 Hwy, Vegreville, AB, T9C 1V5
(780) 632-5063
Emp Here 20
SIC 1611 Highway and street construction

D-U-N-S 20-713-1900   (BR)
ELK ISLAND CATHOLIC SEPARATE RE-GIONAL DIVISION NO. 41
SAINT MARY'S CATHOLIC SCHOOL
4434 53 St, Vegreville, AB, T9C 1A1
(780) 632-3934
Emp Here 50
SIC 8211 Elementary and secondary schools

D-U-N-S 20-028-4540   (BR)
ELK ISLAND CATHOLIC SEPARATE RE-GIONAL DIVISION NO. 41
ST MARTIN SCHOOL
4314 54a Ave, Vegreville, AB, T9C 1C8
(780) 632-2266
Emp Here 27

SIC 8211 Elementary and secondary schools

D-U-N-S 25-269-6000   (BR)
ELK ISLAND PUBLIC SCHOOLS RE-GIONAL DIVISION NO. 14
VEGREVILLE COMPOSITE HIGH SCHOOL
(*Suby of* Elk Island Public Schools Regional Division No. 14)
6426 55 Ave, Vegreville, AB, T9C 1S5
(780) 632-3341
Emp Here 45
SIC 8211 Elementary and secondary schools

D-U-N-S 24-089-4456   (BR)
ELK ISLAND PUBLIC SCHOOLS RE-GIONAL DIVISION NO. 14
NEXT STEP OUTREACH SCHOOL VEGRE-VILLE
4908 50 Ave, Vegreville, AB, T9C 1V5
(780) 632-7998
Emp Here 25
SIC 8211 Elementary and secondary schools

D-U-N-S 25-269-1217   (BR)
ELK ISLAND PUBLIC SCHOOLS RE-GIONAL DIVISION NO. 14
A L HORTON ELEMENTARY SCHOOL
(*Suby of* Elk Island Public Schools Regional Division No. 14)
5037 48 Ave, Vegreville, AB, T9C 1L8
(780) 632-3113
Emp Here 40
SIC 8211 Elementary and secondary schools

D-U-N-S 20-068-3287   (BR)
GOVERNMENT OF THE PROVINCE OF AL-BERTA
VEGREVILLE AQUATIC & FITNESS CEN-TRE
4509 48 St, Vegreville, AB, T9C 1K8
(780) 632-6403
Emp Here 25
SIC 7999 Amusement and recreation, nec

D-U-N-S 20-086-8979   (BR)
INNOTECH ALBERTA INC
ALBERTA INNOVATES-TECHNOLOGY FU-TURES
75th St Hwy 16a, Vegreville, AB, T9C 1T4
(780) 632-8211
Emp Here 150
SIC 8733 Noncommercial research organizations

D-U-N-S 20-515-5539   (BR)
LOBLAWS INC
EXTRA FOODS
4734 50 Ave Suite 3958, Vegreville, AB, T9C 1L1
(780) 603-2600
Emp Here 75
SIC 5411 Grocery stores

D-U-N-S 20-860-6918   (BR)
PORTAGE COLLEGE
5005 50 Ave, Vegreville, AB, T9C 1T1
(780) 632-6301
Emp Here 250
SIC 8221 Colleges and universities

D-U-N-S 24-377-5124   (BR)
TERRAVEST INDUSTRIES LIMITED PART-NERSHIP
R.J.V. GAS FIELD SERVICES
5234 52 Ave, Vegreville, AB, T9C 1A3
(780) 632-7668
Emp Here 25
SIC 1389 Oil and gas field services, nec

D-U-N-S 20-789-1198   (SL)
VEGREVILLE ASSOCIATION FOR LIVING IN DIGNITY
4843 49 St, Vegreville, AB, T9C 1K7
(780) 632-2418
Emp Here 50   *Sales* 1,969,939
SIC 8322 Individual and family services

D-U-N-S 24-882-0446   (BR)

VEGREVILLE, TOWN OF
VEGREVILLE FIRE HALL
5100 60 St, Vegreville, AB, T9C 1N6
(780) 632-2254
Emp Here 20
SIC 4119 Local passenger transportation, nec

D-U-N-S 24-330-0550   (BR)
WAL-MART CANADA CORP
6809 16a Hwy W, Vegreville, AB, T9C 0A2
(780) 632-6016
Emp Here 200
SIC 5311 Department stores

D-U-N-S 25-021-5712   (SL)
WEBB'S MACHINERY (VEGREVILLE) LTD
(*Suby of* Webb, Geo. C. & Sons (1980) Ltd)
5342 50 Ave, Vegreville, AB, T9C 1M3
(780) 632-6772
Emp Here 24   *Sales* 2,261,782
SIC 5999 Miscellaneous retail stores, nec

Vermilion, AB T9X

D-U-N-S 25-360-7980   (BR)
324007 ALBERTA LTD
NILSSON BROTHERS LIVESTOCK EX-CHANGE
(*Suby of* 400369 Alberta Ltd)
Gd Stn Main, Vermilion, AB, T9X 2C1
(780) 853-5372
Emp Here 25
SIC 5154 Livestock

D-U-N-S 25-236-3726   (BR)
ALBERTA HEALTH SERVICES
VERMILION HEALTH CARE CENTRE
5720 50 Ave, Vermilion, AB, T9X 1K7
(780) 853-5305
Emp Here 180
SIC 8062 General medical and surgical hospitals

D-U-N-S 20-951-2735   (BR)
B. & R. ECKEL'S TRANSPORT LTD
4837 40 St, Vermilion, AB, T9X 1H6
(780) 853-5368
Emp Here 32
SIC 4213 Trucking, except local

D-U-N-S 25-174-8281   (BR)
BUFFALO TRAIL PUBLIC SCHOOLS RE-GIONAL DIVISION NO. 28
VERMILION ELEMENTARY SCHOOL
4837 44 St, Vermilion, AB, T9X 1G3
(780) 853-5444
Emp Here 35
SIC 8211 Elementary and secondary schools

D-U-N-S 20-918-5813   (BR)
BUFFALO TRAIL PUBLIC SCHOOLS RE-GIONAL DIVISION NO. 28
JR ROBSON SCHOOL
5102 46 St, Vermilion, AB, T9X 1G5
(780) 853-4177
Emp Here 30
SIC 8211 Elementary and secondary schools

D-U-N-S 20-066-6118   (BR)
EAST CENTRAL ALBERTA CATHOLIC SEPERATE SCHOOLS REGIONAL DIVI-SION NO 16
ST JEROME'S SEPARATE SCHOOL
4820 46 St, Vermilion, AB, T9X 1G2
(780) 853-5251
Emp Here 30
SIC 8211 Elementary and secondary schools

D-U-N-S 20-655-2031   (SL)
EAST CENTRAL HEALTH AND PUBLIC HEATH HOMECARE AND REHABILITATION
4701 52 St Suite 11, Vermilion, AB, T9X 1J9
(780) 853-5270
Emp Here 45   *Sales* 5,803,882
SIC 8621 Professional organizations

D-U-N-S 20-026-9876   (BR)
LEADING MANUFACTURING GROUP HOLDINGS INC
(*Suby of* Leading Manufacturing Group Holdings Inc)
3801 48 Ave, Vermilion, AB, T9X 1G9
(780) 854-0004
Emp Here 100
SIC 3443 Fabricated plate work (boiler shop)

D-U-N-S 24-004-2200   (SL)
VERMILION CREDIT UNION LTD
5019 50 Ave, Vermilion, AB, T9X 1A7
(780) 853-2822
Emp Here 29   *Sales* 5,681,200
SIC 6062 State credit unions
Brnch Mgr David Eremko
 Larry Bingham
 Maxine Sweeney

D-U-N-S 20-365-7957   (SL)
WEBB'S FORD LTD
(*Suby of* Webb, Geo. C. & Sons (1980) Ltd)
4802 50 St, Vermilion, AB, T9X 1M3
(780) 853-2841
Emp Here 26   *Sales* 12,760,800
SIC 5511 New and used car dealers
Pr Pr Robert C Jacobson

Viking, AB T0B

D-U-N-S 20-710-5243   (BR)
BATTLE RIVER REGIONAL DIVISION 31
VIKING SCHOOL
5503 51 St, Viking, AB, T0B 4N0
(780) 336-3352
Emp Here 30
SIC 8211 Elementary and secondary schools

D-U-N-S 25-969-6961   (BR)
EXTENDICARE INC
EXTENDICARE VIKING
5020 57th Ave, Viking, AB, T0B 4N0
(780) 336-4790
Emp Here 80
SIC 8051 Skilled nursing care facilities

Vilna, AB T0A

D-U-N-S 20-023-9627   (BR)
ASPEN VIEW PUBLIC SCHOOL DIVISION NO. 78
VILNA SCHOOL
(*Suby of* Aspen View Public School Division No. 78)
5014 52 Ave, Vilna, AB, T0A 3L0
(780) 636-1406
Emp Here 35
SIC 8211 Elementary and secondary schools

Vulcan, AB T0L

D-U-N-S 20-070-3648   (BR)
CONOCOPHILLIPS WESTERN CANADA PARTNERSHIP
CONOCOPHILLIPS CANADA RESOURCES
Gd, Vulcan, AB, T0L 2B0
(403) 897-3030
Emp Here 30
SIC 1311 Crude petroleum and natural gas

D-U-N-S 20-699-6477   (BR)
EXTENDICARE INC
EXTENDICARE VULCAN
715 2nd Ave S, Vulcan, AB, T0L 2B0
(403) 485-2022
Emp Here 26
SIC 8051 Skilled nursing care facilities

D-U-N-S 20-003-5140 (BR)
PALLISER REGIONAL DIVISION NO 26
VULCAN PRAIRIEVIEW ELEMENTARY SCHOOL
305 6 Ave S, Vulcan, AB, T0L 2B0
(403) 485-2074
Emp Here 39
SIC 8211 Elementary and secondary schools

D-U-N-S 20-711-7016 (BR)
PALLISER REGIONAL DIVISION NO 26
VULCAN OUTREACH SCHOOL
102b 1 St Sout, Vulcan, AB, T0L 2B0
(403) 485-6180
Emp Here 50
SIC 8211 Elementary and secondary schools

D-U-N-S 20-270-5815 (BR)
SEARS CANADA INC
215 Centre St, Vulcan, AB, T0L 2B0

Emp Here 50
SIC 5399 Miscellaneous general merchandise

Vulcan, AB T1J

D-U-N-S 20-037-7823 (BR)
PALLISER REGIONAL DIVISION NO 26
COUNTY CENTRAL HIGH SCHOOL
504 4 Ave S, Vulcan, AB, T1J 0N5
(403) 485-2223
Emp Here 25
SIC 7389 Business services, nec

Wabasca, AB T0G

D-U-N-S 25-267-7133 (BR)
ALBERTA HEALTH SERVICES
WABASCA DESMARAIS GENERAL HOSPI-TAL
881 Mistassiny Rd, Wabasca, AB, T0G 2K0
(780) 891-3007
Emp Here 35
SIC 8062 General medical and surgical hospitals

D-U-N-S 24-344-8540 (BR)
E-CAN OILFIELD SERVICES LP
Gd, Wabasca, AB, T0G 2K0
(780) 891-3771
Emp Here 50
SIC 1389 Oil and gas field services, nec

D-U-N-S 24-764-9283 (BR)
NORTHLAND SCHOOL DIVISION 61
MISTASSINIY SCHOOL
750 Mistassiniy Lane, Wabasca, AB, T0G 0T0
(780) 891-3949
Emp Here 25
SIC 8211 Elementary and secondary schools

D-U-N-S 20-023-9528 (BR)
NORTHLAND SCHOOL DIVISION 61
ST THERESA SCHOOL
2753 Neewatim Dr, Wabasca, AB, T0G 2K0
(780) 891-3833
Emp Here 60
SIC 8211 Elementary and secondary schools

Wainwright, AB T9W

D-U-N-S 24-345-8804 (BR)
AECOM CANADA LTD
1718 23rd Ave, Wainwright, AB, T9W 1T2
(780) 842-4220
Emp Here 100
SIC 7692 Welding repair

D-U-N-S 24-372-2779 (BR)

AECOM CANADA LTD
1910 15 Ave, Wainwright, AB, T9W 1L2
(780) 842-6188
Emp Here 50
SIC 1623 Water, sewer, and utility lines

D-U-N-S 25-236-3643 (BR)
ALBERTA HEALTH SERVICES
WAINWRIGHT HEALTH CENTER
530 6 Ave, Wainwright, AB, T9W 1R6
(780) 842-1539
Emp Here 200
SIC 8062 General medical and surgical hospitals

D-U-N-S 20-710-0699 (BR)
BUFFALO TRAIL PUBLIC SCHOOLS RE-GIONAL DIVISION NO. 28
WAINWRIGHT ELEMENTARY SCHOOL
905 10 St, Wainwright, AB, T9W 2R6
(780) 842-3361
Emp Here 50
SIC 8211 Elementary and secondary schools

D-U-N-S 20-710-0798 (BR)
BUFFALO TRAIL PUBLIC SCHOOLS RE-GIONAL DIVISION NO. 28
WAINWRIGHT HIGHSCHOOL
800 6 St, Wainwright, AB, T9W 2R5
(780) 842-4481
Emp Here 50
SIC 8211 Elementary and secondary schools

D-U-N-S 24-671-2541 (BR)
BUNGE CANADA
1101 4 Ave, Wainwright, AB, T9W 1H1
(780) 842-6154
Emp Here 29
SIC 2076 Vegetable oil mills, nec

D-U-N-S 25-629-0362 (BR)
CATHOLIC SOCIAL SERVICES
1037 2 Ave Suite A, Wainwright, AB, T9W 1K7
(780) 842-6899
Emp Here 35
SIC 8361 Residential care

D-U-N-S 20-573-3350 (BR)
COMPAGNIE DES CHEMINS DE FER NA-TIONAUX DU CANADA
1001 1 Ave Suite A, Wainwright, AB, T9W 1S5
(780) 842-4111
Emp Here 20
SIC 4011 Railroads, line-haul operating

D-U-N-S 25-073-2047 (BR)
EAST CENTRAL ALBERTA CATHOLIC SEPERATE SCHOOLS REGIONAL DIVI-SION NO 16
BLESSED SACRAMENT SCHOOL
1321 4 Ave, Wainwright, AB, T9W 2R7
(780) 342-3808
Emp Here 31
SIC 8211 Elementary and secondary schools

D-U-N-S 20-092-6350 (BR)
EASTALTA CO-OP LTD
1027 3 Ave, Wainwright, AB, T9W 1T6
(780) 842-3678
Emp Here 62
SIC 5399 Miscellaneous general merchandise

D-U-N-S 25-133-4728 (SL)
KING, TREVOR OILFIELD SERVICES LTD
Po Box 3353 Stn Main, Wainwright, AB, T9W 1T3

Emp Here 45 *Sales* 7,800,460
SIC 1389 Oil and gas field services, nec
Pr Pr Trevor King
 Lynn King

D-U-N-S 20-211-1261 (BR)
LOBLAWS INC
EXTRA FOODS
2601 14 Ave, Wainwright, AB, T9W 1V5
(780) 806-5100
Emp Here 40

SIC 5411 Grocery stores

D-U-N-S 25-317-1540 (BR)
OBSIDIAN ENERGY LTD
PENN WEST PETROLEUM LTD
Gd, Wainwright, AB, T9W 1M3
(780) 842-4677
Emp Here 40
SIC 1311 Crude petroleum and natural gas

D-U-N-S 24-785-5406 (SL)
WAINWRIGHT GOLF AND COUNTRY CLUB
1505a 2 St, Wainwright, AB, T9W 1L5
(780) 842-3046
Emp Here 50 *Sales* 2,188,821
SIC 7992 Public golf courses

D-U-N-S 24-330-0568 (BR)
WAL-MART CANADA CORP
2901 13 Ave Suite 1062, Wainwright, AB, T9W 0A2
(780) 842-3144
Emp Here 200
SIC 5311 Department stores

Warburg, AB T0C

D-U-N-S 20-913-1502 (BR)
BLACK GOLD REGIONAL DIVISION #18
WARBURG SCHOOL
5412 50 St, Warburg, AB, T0C 2T0
(780) 848-2822
Emp Here 36
SIC 8211 Elementary and secondary schools

D-U-N-S 25-831-8534 (BR)
PRAIRIE MINES & ROYALTY ULC
(Suby of Westmoreland Coal Company)
Gd, Warburg, AB, T0C 2T0
(780) 848-7786
Emp Here 81
SIC 1221 Bituminous coal and lignite-surface mining

D-U-N-S 25-329-6842 (BR)
REPSOL OIL & GAS CANADA INC
Gd, Warburg, AB, T0C 2T0
(780) 848-2100
Emp Here 36
SIC 1382 Oil and gas exploration services

Warner, AB T0K

D-U-N-S 20-711-9715 (BR)
BOARD OF TRUSTEES OF HORIZON SCHOOL DIVISION NO 67
WARNER SCHOOL
409 3rd Ave, Warner, AB, T0K 2L0
(403) 642-3931
Emp Here 20
SIC 8211 Elementary and secondary schools

Wembley, AB T0H

D-U-N-S 24-335-7386 (BR)
PETROWEST CIVIL SERVICES LP
R BEE CRUSHING
Gd, Wembley, AB, T0H 3S0
(780) 942-2434
Emp Here 25
SIC 1422 Crushed and broken limestone

Westlock, AB T7P

D-U-N-S 25-169-1523 (HQ)
AGRITRAC EQUIPMENT LTD

(Suby of Agritrac Equipment Ltd)
11140 100 St, Westlock, AB, T7P 2C3
(780) 349-3720
Emp Here 43 *Emp Total* 75
Sales 9,847,040
SIC 5999 Miscellaneous retail stores, nec
Pr Pr Michael Karczmarczyk
 Curtis Borduzak

D-U-N-S 25-119-8289 (BR)
ALBERTA HEALTH SERVICES
ASPEN HEALTH SERVICES
10024 107 Ave, Westlock, AB, T7P 2E3
(780) 349-3316
Emp Here 30
SIC 8062 General medical and surgical hospitals

D-U-N-S 25-764-3239 (BR)
ALBERTA HEALTH SERVICES
WESTLOCK CONTINUING CARE CENTRE
10203 96 St Suite 137, Westlock, AB, T7P 2R3
(780) 349-3306
Emp Here 103
SIC 8062 General medical and surgical hospitals

D-U-N-S 25-236-2017 (BR)
ALBERTA TREASURY BRANCHES
ATB FINANCIAL
10532 100 Ave, Westlock, AB, T7P 2J9
(780) 349-4481
Emp Here 20
SIC 6036 Savings institutions, except federal

D-U-N-S 24-345-7483 (BR)
APACHE CANADA LTD
(Suby of Apache Corporation)
10011 106 St Unit 204, Westlock, AB, T7P 2K3
(780) 307-3800
Emp Here 25
SIC 1382 Oil and gas exploration services

D-U-N-S 24-331-2204 (BR)
CHAMPION FEED SERVICES LTD
9415 109 St, Westlock, AB, T7P 2M6
(780) 349-5886
Emp Here 40
SIC 2048 Prepared feeds, nec

D-U-N-S 25-014-1892 (BR)
EVERGREEN CATHOLIC SEPARATE RE-GIONAL DIVISION 2
SAINT MARY SCHOOL
9916 97 St, Westlock, AB, T7P 2G2
(780) 349-3644
Emp Here 30
SIC 8211 Elementary and secondary schools

D-U-N-S 20-697-5687 (BR)
LOBLAWS INC
EXTRA FOODS
10851 100 St, Westlock, AB, T7P 2R5
(780) 349-7040
Emp Here 80
SIC 5431 Fruit and vegetable markets

D-U-N-S 24-680-6017 (BR)
MMD SALES LTD
MARTIN DEERLINE
10803 100 St, Westlock, AB, T7P 2R7
(780) 349-3391
Emp Here 38
SIC 5083 Farm and garden machinery

D-U-N-S 20-713-2809 (BR)
PEMBINA HILLS REGIONAL DIVISION 7
R F STAPLES SECONDARY SCHOOL
10015 104 St, Westlock, AB, T7P 1T8
(780) 349-4454
Emp Here 50
SIC 8211 Elementary and secondary schools

D-U-N-S 20-049-1327 (BR)
PEMBINA HILLS REGIONAL DIVISION 7
WESTLOCK ELEMENTARY SCHOOL
10515 106a St, Westlock, AB, T7P 2E7

---

(780) 349-3385
Emp Here 60
SIC 8211 Elementary and secondary schools

D-U-N-S 20-732-6633   (BR)
PENTAGON FARM CENTRE LTD
(*Suby of* Pentagon Farm Centre Ltd)
592 Highway 44 S, Westlock, AB, T7P 2P1
(780) 349-3113
Emp Here 50
SIC 5999 Miscellaneous retail stores, nec

D-U-N-S 25-429-5442   (BR)
ROCKY MOUNTAIN DEALERSHIPS INC
ROCKY MOUNTAIN EQUIPMENT
11140 100 St, Westlock, AB, T7P 2C3
(780) 349-3720
Emp Here 30
SIC 5082 Construction and mining machinery

D-U-N-S 25-741-5299   (BR)
TOWN OF WESTLOCK
AQUATIC CENTRE
10450 106a St, Westlock, AB, T7P 2E5
(780) 349-6677
Emp Here 20
SIC 7999 Amusement and recreation, nec

D-U-N-S 20-092-8208   (SL)
TRIPLE J LIVESTOCK LTD
9004 110a St, Westlock, AB, T7P 2N4
(780) 349-3153
Emp Here 46   *Sales* 38,596,210
SIC 5154 Livestock
Pr Pr Gary Jarvis

D-U-N-S 24-809-8436   (SL)
WESTLOCK FOUNDATION
SMITHFIELD LODGE
10203 97 St, Westlock, AB, T7P 2H1
(780) 349-4123
Emp Here 68   *Sales* 2,480,664
SIC 8361 Residential care

D-U-N-S 25-372-8893   (BR)
WINNERS MERCHANTS INTERNATIONAL L.P.
WINNERS
(*Suby of* The TJX Companies Inc)
10200 102 Ave, Westlock, AB, T7P 2H9
(780) 420-1801
Emp Here 40
SIC 5651 Family clothing stores

Wetaskiwin, AB T9A

D-U-N-S 24-086-9115   (BR)
ALBERTA HEALTH SERVICES
CROSSROADS HEALTH REGION
6910 47 St, Wetaskiwin, AB, T9A 3N3
(780) 361-7100
Emp Here 500
SIC 8062 General medical and surgical hospitals

D-U-N-S 24-385-7906   (BR)
ALBERTA HEALTH SERVICES
CROSSROADS HEALTH REGION
5610 40 Ave, Wetaskiwin, AB, T9A 3E4

Emp Here 400
SIC 8069 Specialty hospitals, except psychiatric

D-U-N-S 20-789-6783   (BR)
BANQUE TORONTO-DOMINION, LA
TORONTO-DOMINION BANK, THE
(*Suby of* Toronto-Dominion Bank, The)
5002 50 Ave, Wetaskiwin, AB, T9A 0S4
(780) 361-5200
Emp Here 22
SIC 6021 National commercial banks

D-U-N-S 25-288-9258   (BR)
CANADA POST CORPORATION
WETASKIWIN POST OFFICE

4811 51 St, Wetaskiwin, AB, T9A 1L1

Emp Here 20
SIC 4311 U.s. postal service

D-U-N-S 25-560-8655   (BR)
CATHOLIC SOCIAL SERVICES
5206 51 Ave, Wetaskiwin, AB, T9A 0V4
(780) 352-5535
Emp Here 200
SIC 8361 Residential care

D-U-N-S 24-642-7306   (SL)
DOPKO FOOD SERVICES LTD
MCDONALD'S RESTAURANTS
5517 37a Ave, Wetaskiwin, AB, T9A 3A5
(780) 986-5322
Emp Here 87   *Sales* 2,626,585
SIC 5812 Eating places

D-U-N-S 20-939-7020   (BR)
DUNCAN CRAIG LLP
4725 56 St Suite 103, Wetaskiwin, AB, T9A 3M2
(780) 352-1662
Emp Here 140
SIC 8111 Legal services

D-U-N-S 24-481-6729   (BR)
HARRIS STEEL ULC
FISHER & LUDLOW, DIV OF
(*Suby of* Nucor Corporation)
4609 64 Ave, Wetaskiwin, AB, T9A 2S7
(780) 352-9171
Emp Here 50
SIC 3446 Architectural Metalwork

D-U-N-S 24-399-0546   (BR)
HOME HARDWARE STORES LIMITED
HOME HARDWARE DISTRIBUTION CENTRE
6410 36 St, Wetaskiwin, AB, T9A 3B6
(780) 352-1984
Emp Here 396
SIC 5211 Lumber and other building materials

D-U-N-S 24-391-4798   (BR)
LOBLAWS INC
NO FRILLS
5217 50 Ave, Wetaskiwin, AB, T9A 0S7
(780) 352-8402
Emp Here 50
SIC 5411 Grocery stores

D-U-N-S 24-058-0253   (SL)
MANLUK INDUSTRIES (2008) INC
MANLUK GLOBAL MANUFACTURING SOLUTIONS
(*Suby of* 1418856 Alberta Ltd)
4815 42 Ave, Wetaskiwin, AB, T9A 2P6
(780) 352-5522
Emp Here 160   *Sales* 22,540,562
SIC 3494 Valves and pipe fittings, nec
Pr Pr Frank Luebke
Dir Manfred Luebke

D-U-N-S 20-635-6151   (SL)
PEACE HILLS BINGO ASSOCIATION
4708 57 St, Wetaskiwin, AB, T9A 2B7
(780) 352-2137
Emp Here 25   *Sales* 8,217,450
SIC 8399 Social services, nec
Mgr Jeannie Mcguire

D-U-N-S 25-595-1386   (BR)
ROYAL BANK OF CANADA
ROYAL BANK
(*Suby of* Royal Bank Of Canada)
4916 50 Ave, Wetaskiwin, AB, T9A 3P8
(780) 352-6011
Emp Here 20
SIC 6021 National commercial banks

D-U-N-S 20-345-8526   (BR)
ROYAL CANADIAN LEGION, THE
ROYAL CANADIAN LEGION #86
(*Suby of* Royal Canadian Legion, The)
5003 52 Ave, Wetaskiwin, AB, T9A 0W9

(780) 352-2662
Emp Here 28
SIC 8641 Civic and social associations

D-U-N-S 20-980-0593   (BR)
SOBEYS CAPITAL INCORPORATED
4703 50 St, Wetaskiwin, AB, T9A 1J6
(780) 352-2227
Emp Here 100
SIC 5411 Grocery stores

D-U-N-S 20-296-1566   (BR)
ST THOMAS AQUINAS ROMAN CATHOLIC SEPARATE REGIONAL DIVISION #38
SACRED HEART SCHOOL
4419 52 Ave, Wetaskiwin, AB, T9A 2X7
(780) 352-5533
Emp Here 40
SIC 8211 Elementary and secondary schools

D-U-N-S 24-422-6879   (SL)
STADUS FOOD SERVICE LTD
MCDONALD'S
5517 37a Ave, Wetaskiwin, AB, T9A 3A5
(780) 352-3103
Emp Here 165   *Sales* 6,898,600
SIC 5812 Eating places
Pr Pr Sidney Johnson

D-U-N-S 24-767-8899   (SL)
WATER TOWER RESTAURANT (2000) LTD
BOSTON PIZZA
5527a 49 Ave, Wetaskiwin, AB, T9A 0R5
(780) 352-9235
Emp Here 50   *Sales* 1,532,175
SIC 5812 Eating places

D-U-N-S 25-625-9953   (BR)
WENDY'S RESTAURANTS OF CANADA INC
WENDY'S
(*Suby of* The Wendy's Company)
4912 56 St, Wetaskiwin, AB, T9A 1V8
(780) 352-9350
Emp Here 42
SIC 5812 Eating places

D-U-N-S 20-704-1182   (BR)
WETASKIWIN REGIONAL PUBLIC SCHOOLS
CENTENNIAL ELEMENTARY SCHOOL
(*Suby of* Wetaskiwin Regional Public Schools)
5310 55 Ave, Wetaskiwin, AB, T9A 1A5
(780) 352-5088
Emp Here 29
SIC 8211 Elementary and secondary schools

D-U-N-S 20-268-6804   (BR)
WETASKIWIN REGIONAL PUBLIC SCHOOLS
ROSEBRIER COMMUNITY SCHOOL
(*Suby of* Wetaskiwin Regional Public Schools)
Rr 2 Lcd Main, Wetaskiwin, AB, T9A 1W9
(780) 352-3168
Emp Here 25
SIC 8211 Elementary and secondary schools

D-U-N-S 24-619-4125   (BR)
WETASKIWIN REGIONAL PUBLIC SCHOOLS
PARKDALE SCHOOL
(*Suby of* Wetaskiwin Regional Public Schools)
4107 54 St, Wetaskiwin, AB, T9A 1S8
(780) 352-4594
Emp Here 30
SIC 8211 Elementary and secondary schools

D-U-N-S 20-028-4243   (BR)
WETASKIWIN REGIONAL PUBLIC SCHOOLS
NORWOOD ELEMENTARY SCHOOL
(*Suby of* Wetaskiwin Regional Public Schools)
5505 44 St, Wetaskiwin, AB, T9A 2Z8
(780) 352-3782
Emp Here 36
SIC 8211 Elementary and secondary schools

D-U-N-S 20-260-1217   (BR)
WETASKIWIN REGIONAL PUBLIC SCHOOLS

WETASKIWIN COMPOSITE HIGHSCHOOL
(*Suby of* Wetaskiwin Regional Public Schools)
4619 50 Ave, Wetaskiwin, AB, T9A 0R6
(780) 352-2295
Emp Here 80
SIC 8211 Elementary and secondary schools

Whitecourt, AB T7S

D-U-N-S 24-880-4148   (SL)
330626 ALBERTA LTD
WHITE COURT IGA
4802 51 St Suite 1, Whitecourt, AB, T7S 1R9
(780) 778-5900
Emp Here 105   *Sales* 19,493,120
SIC 5411 Grocery stores
Pr Pr Ken Linford
 Keith Linford
 Ron Linford
 Evelyn Linford
 Brian Linford

D-U-N-S 25-327-3742   (SL)
508173 ALBERTA LTD
DYNAMIC AMUSEMENTS
5016 50 Ave, Whitecourt, AB, T7S 1S8
(780) 778-6656
Emp Here 33   *Sales* 5,376,850
SIC 5411 Grocery stores
Pr Pr James E Rennie
VP VP James S Rennie

D-U-N-S 24-853-8647   (SL)
825173 ABERTA LTD
TAG'S FOOD & GAS
Gd Stn Main, Whitecourt, AB, T7S 1S1
(780) 778-6611
Emp Here 65   *Sales* 1,969,939
SIC 5812 Eating places

D-U-N-S 24-345-6139   (BR)
ALBERTA HEALTH SERVICES
WHITECOURT HEALTH CARE CENTRE
20 Sunset Blvd, Whitecourt, AB, T7S 1M8
(780) 778-2285
Emp Here 100
SIC 8062 General medical and surgical hospitals

D-U-N-S 25-680-6555   (BR)
ALBERTA TREASURY BRANCHES
ATB FINANCIAL
5115 50 Ave, Whitecourt, AB, T7S 1S8
(780) 778-2442
Emp Here 20
SIC 6036 Savings institutions, except federal

D-U-N-S 24-324-1614   (BR)
BAKER HUGHES CANADA COMPANY
(*Suby of* Baker Hughes, A GE Company)
3804 38 Ave, Whitecourt, AB, T7S 0A2

Emp Here 45
SIC 1389 Oil and gas field services, nec

D-U-N-S 20-286-1548   (BR)
BIG COUNTRY ENERGY SERVICES LIMITED PARTNERSHIP
3905 35 St Suite 3, Whitecourt, AB, T7S 0A2
(780) 706-2141
Emp Here 100
SIC 1623 Water, sewer, and utility lines

D-U-N-S 24-617-8284   (BR)
FMC TECHNOLOGIES CANADA LTD
(*Suby of* Reliance Oilfield Services, LLC)
3720 33 St, Whitecourt, AB, T7S 0A2
(780) 778-8445
Emp Here 30
SIC 1389 Oil and gas field services, nec

D-U-N-S 24-628-9867   (BR)
FIRSTCANADA ULC
CARDINAL COACH LINE
3531 37 Ave, Whitecourt, AB, T7S 0C3

(780) 778-2850
Emp Here 50
SIC 4151 School buses

D-U-N-S 24-309-1639   (SL)
FOUR NORTH VENTURES LTD
MCDONALD'S
4111 Kepler St, Whitecourt, AB, T7S 0A3
(780) 779-2710
Emp Here 50   *Sales* 1,532,175
SIC 5812 Eating places

D-U-N-S 25-216-8638   (BR)
GOLD STAR TRANSPORT (1975) LTD
Gd, Whitecourt, AB, T7S 1S1

Emp Here 20
SIC 4212 Local trucking, without storage

D-U-N-S 25-943-8307   (BR)
LIVING WATERS CATHOLIC REGIONAL DIVISION NO.42
ST MARY SCHOOL
(*Suby of* Living Waters Catholic Regional Division No.42)
5630 Mink Creek Rd, Whitecourt, AB, T7S 1M9
(780) 778-2050
Emp Here 36
SIC 8211 Elementary and secondary schools

D-U-N-S 20-713-1926   (BR)
LIVING WATERS CATHOLIC REGIONAL DIVISION NO.42
ST. JOSEPH SCHOOL
3804 47 St, Whitecourt, AB, T7S 1M8
(780) 778-2345
Emp Here 50
SIC 8211 Elementary and secondary schools

D-U-N-S 20-736-9195   (BR)
MCMAN YOUTH, FAMILY AND COMMUNITY SERVICES ASSOCIATION
(*Suby of* McMan Youth, Family and Community Services Association)
5115 49 St Suite 208, Whitecourt, AB, T7S 1N7
(780) 778-3290
Emp Here 25
SIC 8399 Social services, nec

D-U-N-S 25-483-1563   (BR)
MILLAR WESTERN FOREST PRODUCTS LTD
WHITECOURT PULP DIVISION
5501 50 Ave, Whitecourt, AB, T7S 1N9
(780) 778-2036
Emp Here 130
SIC 2611 Pulp mills

D-U-N-S 24-330-5075   (BR)
MILLAR WESTERN INDUSTRIES LTD
WHITECOURT WOOD PRODUCT DIVISION
5004 52 St, Whitecourt, AB, T7S 1N2
(780) 778-2221
Emp Here 250
SIC 2421 Sawmills and planing mills, general

D-U-N-S 25-267-1060   (BR)
NORTHERN GATEWAY REGIONAL DIVISION #10
PERCY BAXTER SCHOOL
1 Mink Creek Rd, Whitecourt, AB, T7S 1S2
(780) 778-3898
Emp Here 47
SIC 8211 Elementary and secondary schools

D-U-N-S 25-021-9292   (BR)
NORTHERN GATEWAY REGIONAL DIVISION #10
PAT HARDY PRIMARY SCHOOL
35 Feero Dr, Whitecourt, AB, T7S 1M8
(780) 778-6266
Emp Here 45
SIC 8211 Elementary and secondary schools

D-U-N-S 20-713-2114   (BR)
NORTHERN GATEWAY REGIONAL DIVISION #10

HILLTOP HIGH SCHOOL
71 Sunset Blvd, Whitecourt, AB, T7S 1N1
(780) 778-2446
Emp Here 50
SIC 8211 Elementary and secondary schools

D-U-N-S 24-764-4532   (BR)
NORTHERN GATEWAY REGIONAL DIVISION #10
WHITECOURT CENTRAL ELEMENTARY SCHOOL
4807 53 Ave, Whitecourt, AB, T7S 1N2
(780) 778-2136
Emp Here 50
SIC 8211 Elementary and secondary schools

D-U-N-S 20-802-7420   (BR)
PEMBINA PIPELINE CORPORATION
3470 33 St, Whitecourt, AB, T7S 0A2
(780) 778-3903
Emp Here 25
SIC 4612 Crude petroleum pipelines

D-U-N-S 20-088-0271   (SL)
SCOTT SAFETY SUPPLY SERVICES LTD
5012 Caxton St W, Whitecourt, AB, T7S 0A6
(780) 778-3389
Emp Here 50   *Sales* 4,742,446
SIC 5999 Miscellaneous retail stores, nec

D-U-N-S 20-084-9441   (BR)
SEMCAMS ULC
(*Suby of* Semgroup Corporation)
Gd Stn Main, Whitecourt, AB, T7S 1S1
(780) 778-7800
Emp Here 75
SIC 1389 Oil and gas field services, nec

D-U-N-S 24-805-4855   (BR)
STRAD ENERGY SERVICES LTD
STRAD OIL FIELD RENTALS
2974 37 Ave, Whitecourt, AB, T7S 0E4
(780) 778-2552
Emp Here 27
SIC 4213 Trucking, except local

D-U-N-S 20-584-6806   (HQ)
STRAD OILFIELD RENTALS LTD
5910 45 Ave, Whitecourt, AB, T7S 0B8
(780) 778-2552
Emp Here 22   *Emp Total* 139
Sales 2,918,428
SIC 7353 Heavy construction equipment rental

D-U-N-S 24-317-8865   (BR)
TARPON ENERGY SERVICES LTD
Bay 1, Whitecourt, AB, T7S 0A2
(780) 778-3249
Emp Here 30
SIC 1389 Oil and gas field services, nec

D-U-N-S 24-041-3703   (BR)
TRYTON TOOL SERVICES LTD
3421 41 Ave, Whitecourt, AB, T7S 0A9
(780) 706-2555
Emp Here 40
SIC 1389 Oil and gas field services, nec

D-U-N-S 24-030-8408   (BR)
WAL-MART CANADA CORP
5005 Dahl Dr, Whitecourt, AB, T7S 1X6
(780) 706-3323
Emp Here 200
SIC 5311 Department stores

D-U-N-S 24-808-3420   (BR)
WEST FRASER TIMBER CO. LTD
ALBERTA NEWSPRINT
9 Km W Of Whitecourt Hwy Suite 43, Whitecourt, AB, T7S 1P9
(780) 778-7000
Emp Here 200
SIC 2621 Paper mills

Winfield, AB T0C

D-U-N-S 20-912-8672   (BR)
ALBERTA HEALTH SERVICES
Gd, Winfield, AB, T0C 2X0
(780) 682-4755
Emp Here 50
SIC 8062 General medical and surgical hospitals

D-U-N-S 20-981-5997   (BR)
SENIORS HOMES & COMMUNITY HOUSING WETASKIWIN
WESTPINE LODGE
Gd, Winfield, AB, T0C 2X0
(780) 682-3960
Emp Here 22
SIC 8322 Individual and family services

D-U-N-S 20-790-4751   (BR)
WETASKIWIN REGIONAL PUBLIC SCHOOLS
WINFIELD SCHOOL
(*Suby of* Wetaskiwin Regional Public Schools)
Gd, Winfield, AB, T0C 2X0
(780) 682-3856
Emp Here 20
SIC 8211 Elementary and secondary schools

Worsley, AB T0H

D-U-N-S 20-021-6666   (BR)
PEACE RIVER SCHOOL DIVISION 10
WORSLEY CENTRAL SCHOOL
216 Alberta Ave, Worsley, AB, T0H 3W0
(780) 685-3842
Emp Here 20
SIC 8211 Elementary and secondary schools

Youngstown, AB T0J

D-U-N-S 20-510-2630   (BR)
GOVERNMENT OF THE PROVINCE OF ALBERTA
YOUNGSTOWN HOME
304 3 St E, Youngstown, AB, T0J 3P0

Emp Here 45
SIC 8361 Residential care

Zama City, AB T0H

D-U-N-S 20-088-3242   (BR)
APACHE CANADA LTD
(*Suby of* Apache Corporation)
958 Beach Rd, Zama City, AB, T0H 4E0
(780) 683-8000
Emp Here 50
SIC 2911 Petroleum refining

100 Mile House, BC V0K
Cariboo County

D-U-N-S 25-098-5413   (SL)
CANADA'S LOG PEOPLE INC
5467 Tatton Stn. Rd Rr 1, 100 Mile House,
BC, V0K 2E1
(250) 791-5222
Emp Here 27   *Sales* 5,398,800
SIC 1521 Single-family housing construction
Dir Theo Wiering
Pr Pr Jill Wiering

D-U-N-S 20-993-9995   (BR)
GREAT PACIFIC INDUSTRIES INC
SAVE-ON-FOODS
157 Cariboo Hwy Suite 97, 100 Mile House,
BC, V0K 2E0
(250) 395-2543
Emp Here 100
SIC 5411 Grocery stores

D-U-N-S 25-844-1625   (BR)
INTERIOR HEALTH AUTHORITY
*INTERIOR HOME HEALTH SUPPORT SER-
VICE*
555 Cedar Ave, 100 Mile House, BC, V0K 2E0
(250) 395-7634
Emp Here 30
SIC 8062 General medical and surgical hospi-
tals

D-U-N-S 25-786-8703   (BR)
INTERIOR ROADS LTD
220 Exeter Rd, 100 Mile House, BC, V0K 2E0
(250) 395-2117
Emp Here 20
SIC 1611 Highway and street construction

D-U-N-S 20-333-3856   (BR)
NORBORD INC
995 Exeter Stn Rd, 100 Mile House, BC, V0K
2E0
(250) 395-6200
Emp Here 140
SIC 2435 Hardwood veneer and plywood

D-U-N-S 25-148-3707   (BR)
NORBORD INDUSTRIES INC
EXCO INDUSTRIES
350 Exeter Truck Rd, 100 Mile House, BC,
V0K 2E0
(250) 395-6240
Emp Here 40
SIC 3553 Woodworking machinery

D-U-N-S 25-832-4110   (BR)
ROYAL BANK OF CANADA
RBC
(Suby of Royal Bank Of Canada)
200 Birch Ave, 100 Mile House, BC, V0K 2E0
(250) 395-7460
Emp Here 32
SIC 6021 National commercial banks

D-U-N-S 20-975-4246   (BR)
**SCHOOL DISTRICT NO 27 (CARIBOO-
CHILCOTIN)**
BUS INFORMATION
330 Exeter Truck Rte, 100 Mile House, BC,
V0K 2E0
(250) 395-2230
Emp Here 30
SIC 4151 School buses

D-U-N-S 25-269-6364   (BR)
**SCHOOL DISTRICT NO 27 (CARIBOO-
CHILCOTIN)**
100 MILE HOUSE ELEMENTARY SCHOOL
145 Birch Ave S, 100 Mile House, BC, V0K
2E0
(250) 395-3685
Emp Here 35
SIC 8211 Elementary and secondary schools

D-U-N-S 20-292-4549   (BR)

**SCHOOL DISTRICT NO 27 (CARIBOO-
CHILCOTIN)**
100 MILE JUNIOR SECONDARY SCHOOL
485 Cedar Ave, 100 Mile House, BC, V0K 2E0

Emp Here 30
SIC 8211 Elementary and secondary schools

D-U-N-S 20-713-2734   (BR)
**SCHOOL DISTRICT NO 27 (CARIBOO-
CHILCOTIN)**
100 MILE ELEMENTARY SCHOOL
145 Birch Ave S, 100 Mile House, BC, V0K
2E0
(250) 395-2258
Emp Here 35
SIC 8211 Elementary and secondary schools

D-U-N-S 20-641-5023   (BR)
**SCHOOL DISTRICT NO 27 (CARIBOO-
CHILCOTIN)**
*PETER SKENE OGDEN SECONDARY
SCHOOL*
200 7th St, 100 Mile House, BC, V0K 2E0
(250) 395-2461
Emp Here 45
SIC 8211 Elementary and secondary schools

D-U-N-S 25-271-7053   (BR)
SOBEYS WEST INC
CANADA SAFEWAY
535 Caribou Hwy S, 100 Mile House, BC, V0K
2E0
(250) 395-4952
Emp Here 70
SIC 5411 Grocery stores

D-U-N-S 20-700-0253   (BR)
WEST FRASER TIMBER CO. LTD
100 MILE LUMBER
910 Exeter Rd, 100 Mile House, BC, V0K 2E0
(250) 395-8200
Emp Here 230
SIC 5031 Lumber, plywood, and millwork

108 Mile Ranch, BC V0K
Cariboo County

D-U-N-S 24-493-3701   (SL)
HILLS HEALTH & GUEST RANCH LTD, THE
HILLS HEALTH RANCH, THE
4871 Cariboo Hwy Suite 97, 108 Mile Ranch,
BC, V0K 2Z0
(250) 791-5225
Emp Here 60   *Sales* 2,626,585
SIC 7011 Hotels and motels

150 Mile House, BC V0K
Cariboo County

D-U-N-S 20-713-2742   (BR)
**SCHOOL DISTRICT NO 27 (CARIBOO-
CHILCOTIN)**
150 MILE ELEMENTARY SCHOOL
3081 Cariboo Hwy 97 Ctr, 150 Mile House,
BC, V0K 2G0
(250) 296-3356
Emp Here 30
SIC 8211 Elementary and secondary schools

70 Mile House, BC V0K
Thompson - Nicola County

D-U-N-S 20-165-4089   (BR)
WEST FRASER MILLS LTD
CHASM SAWMILLS
1020 Chasm Rd, 70 Mile House, BC, V0K 2K0
(250) 459-2229
Emp Here 200

SIC 2421 Sawmills and planing mills, general

Abbotsford, BC V2S
Central Fraser-Val County

D-U-N-S 25-654-1533   (SL)
446784 B.C. LTD
WE CARE HOME HEALTH SERVICES
2291 West Railway St Suite B, Abbotsford,
BC, V2S 2E3
(604) 864-9682
Emp Here 75   *Sales* 2,918,428
SIC 8322 Individual and family services

D-U-N-S 25-183-8702   (SL)
ABBOTSFORD RESTAURANTS LTD
KEG IN THE VALLEY
2142 West Railway St, Abbotsford, BC, V2S
2E2
(604) 855-9893
Emp Here 80   *Sales* 2,407,703
SIC 5812 Eating places

D-U-N-S 24-597-1911   (BR)
APLIN & MARTIN CONSULTANTS LTD
33230 Old Yale Rd Suite 101, Abbotsford, BC,
V2S 2J5

Emp Here 95
SIC 8711 Engineering services

D-U-N-S 20-649-8383   (BR)
ASSANTE FINANCIAL MANAGEMENT LTD
ASSANTE WEALTH MANAGEMENT
33386 South Fraser Way Suite 101, Abbots-
ford, BC, V2S 2B5
(604) 852-1804
Emp Here 20
SIC 8741 Management services

D-U-N-S 20-714-9188   (HQ)
AVENUE MACHINERY CORP
(Suby of Avenue Machinery Corp)
1521 Sumas Way, Abbotsford, BC, V2S 8M9
(604) 792-4111
Emp Here 35   *Emp Total* 55
Sales 11,965,555
SIC 5083 Farm and garden machinery
Pr Tim Drake

D-U-N-S 20-589-5159   (BR)
BANQUE TORONTO-DOMINION, LA
TD CANADA TRUST
(Suby of Toronto-Dominion Bank, The)
2130 Sumas Way, Abbotsford, BC, V2S 2C7
(604) 870-3950
Emp Here 20
SIC 6021 National commercial banks

D-U-N-S 24-318-8260   (BR)
BLACK PRESS GROUP LTD
ABBOTSFORD NEWS, THE
34375 Gladys Ave, Abbotsford, BC, V2S 2H5
(604) 853-1144
Emp Here 130
SIC 2711 Newspapers

D-U-N-S 25-978-7331   (BR)
BRICK WAREHOUSE LP, THE
2067 Sumas Way, Abbotsford, BC, V2S 8H6
(604) 504-1771
Emp Here 25
SIC 5712 Furniture stores

D-U-N-S 25-316-5633   (BR)
**BRITISH COLUMBIA AUTOMOBILE ASSO-
CIATION**
33310 South Fraser Way, Abbotsford, BC, V2S
2B4
(604) 855-0530
Emp Here 25
SIC 8699 Membership organizations, nec

D-U-N-S 25-019-7936   (BR)
**BRITISH COLUMBIA HYDRO AND POWER
AUTHORITY**

BC HYDRO
916 Riverside Rd, Abbotsford, BC, V2S 7N9
(604) 854-8483
Emp Here 50
SIC 4911 Electric services

D-U-N-S 20-589-7304   (BR)
CANADIAN PACIFIC RAILWAY COMPANY
CPR
63 West Railway Ave, Abbotsford, BC, V2S
8H9
(604) 944-5706
Emp Here 20
SIC 4011 Railroads, line-haul operating

D-U-N-S 24-166-3603   (HQ)
CENTRAL VALLEY TAXI LTD
CENTRAL VALLEY TAXI
(Suby of Central Valley Taxi Ltd)
1643 Salton Rd, Abbotsford, BC, V2S 7P2
(604) 859-1111
Emp Here 42   *Emp Total* 50
Sales 1,532,175
SIC 4121 Taxicabs

D-U-N-S 24-420-5832   (BR)
CITY OF ABBOTSFORD
ABBOTSFORD CENTRE
33800 King Rd Suite 100, Abbotsford, BC,
V2S 8H8
(604) 743-5000
Emp Here 20
SIC 7999 Amusement and recreation, nec

D-U-N-S 24-233-8379   (BR)
CLARA INDUSTRIAL SERVICES LIMITED
(Suby of Clara Industrial Services Limited)
34613 Vye Rd, Abbotsford, BC, V2S 8J7
(604) 859-8608
Emp Here 30
SIC 1721 Painting and paper hanging

D-U-N-S 25-184-5707   (BR)
CORIX INFRASTRUCTURE INC
CORIX WATER PRODUCTS
3175 Turner St, Abbotsford, BC, V2S 7T9
(604) 850-0441
Emp Here 27
SIC 5074 Plumbing and heating equipment
and supplies (hydronics)

D-U-N-S 25-287-5695   (BR)
COSTCO WHOLESALE CANADA LTD
(Suby of Costco Wholesale Corporation)
1127 Sumas Way, Abbotsford, BC, V2S 8H2
(604) 850-3458
Emp Here 200
SIC 5099 Durable goods, nec

D-U-N-S 20-802-8303   (BR)
EARL'S RESTAURANTS LTD
(Suby of Earl's Restaurants Ltd)
32900 South Fraser Way Suite 1, Abbotsford,
BC, V2S 5A1

Emp Here 100
SIC 5812 Eating places

D-U-N-S 20-040-2308   (BR)
FARM CREDIT CANADA
FARM CREDIT
1520 Mccallum Rd Suite 200, Abbotsford, BC,
V2S 8A3
(604) 870-2417
Emp Here 32
SIC 6159 Miscellaneous business credit insti-
tutions

D-U-N-S 20-075-9129   (BR)
FRASER HEALTH AUTHORITY
ABBOTSFORD HEALTH PROTECTION
2776 Bourquin Cres W Suite 207, Abbotsford,
BC, V2S 6A4
(604) 870-7900
Emp Here 24
SIC 8062 General medical and surgical hospi-
tals

D-U-N-S 24-677-8042   (BR)

FRESHWATER FISHERIES SOCIETY OF BC
FRASER VALLEY TROUT HATCHERY
34345 Vye Rd, Abbotsford, BC, V2S 7P6
(604) 504-4709
Emp Here 33
SIC 8699 Membership organizations, nec

D-U-N-S 24-128-5951   (BR)
GAP (CANADA) INC
GAP
(*Suby of* The Gap Inc)
32900 South Fraser Way Suite 201, Abbotsford, BC, V2S 5A1
(604) 859-7700
Emp Here 20
SIC 5651 Family clothing stores

D-U-N-S 20-860-5704   (BR)
GLENTEL INC
WIRELESS WAVES
32900 South Fraser Way Unit 3k, Abbotsford, BC, V2S 5A1
(604) 852-9283
Emp Here 25
SIC 4813 Telephone communication, except radio

D-U-N-S 20-126-7775   (BR)
GOLDER ASSOCIATES LTD
2190 West Railway St Suite 300, Abbotsford, BC, V2S 2E2
(604) 850-8786
Emp Here 24
SIC 8711 Engineering services

D-U-N-S 24-000-4379   (BR)
GREAT PACIFIC INDUSTRIES INC
SAVE-ON-FOODS
2140 Sumas Way, Abbotsford, BC, V2S 2C7
(604) 504-4453
Emp Here 180
SIC 5411 Grocery stores

D-U-N-S 20-179-6161   (BR)
HOME DEPOT OF CANADA INC
HOME DEPOT
(*Suby of* The Home Depot Inc)
1956 Vedder Way, Abbotsford, BC, V2S 8K1
(604) 851-4400
Emp Here 150
SIC 5211 Lumber and other building materials

D-U-N-S 25-301-2587   (BR)
HUDSON'S BAY COMPANY
32900 South Fraser Way Suite 2, Abbotsford, BC, V2S 5A1
(604) 853-7711
Emp Here 100
SIC 5311 Department stores

D-U-N-S 20-105-5949   (BR)
HUDSON'S BAY COMPANY
HOME OUTFITTERS STORE 5157
1425 Sumas Way Unit 106, Abbotsford, BC, V2S 8M9
(604) 855-7506
Emp Here 30
SIC 5311 Department stores

D-U-N-S 25-325-9626   (BR)
INVESTORS GROUP FINANCIAL SERVICES INC
2001 Mccallum Rd Suite 101, Abbotsford, BC, V2S 3N5
(604) 853-8111
Emp Here 40
SIC 8741 Management services

D-U-N-S 24-367-3584   (BR)
JOHNSON CONTROLS L.P.
32900 Marshall Rd, Abbotsford, BC, V2S 0C2
(604) 851-4979
Emp Here 30
SIC 1731 Electrical work

D-U-N-S 24-030-9542   (BR)
KAL TIRE LTD
975 Coutts Way, Abbotsford, BC, V2S 7M2

(604) 853-5981
Emp Here 20
SIC 5531 Auto and home supply stores

D-U-N-S 25-616-3965   (BR)
LOBLAWS INC
EXTRA FOODS
32900 South Fraser Way Suite 3, Abbotsford, BC, V2S 5A1
(604) 859-6501
Emp Here 100
SIC 5411 Grocery stores

D-U-N-S 24-248-0846   (SL)
MATSQUI-SUMAS-ABBOTSFORD GENERAL HOSPITAL SOCIETY
M S A GENERAL HOSPITAL
32900 Marshall Rd, Abbotsford, BC, V2S 0C2
(604) 851-4700
Emp Here 1,100   *Sales* 102,969,840
SIC 8062 General medical and surgical hospitals
Ch Bd John Koot
Treas Lucas Henry

D-U-N-S 25-483-1787   (BR)
MENNONITE BENEVOLENT SOCIETY
MENNO HOME
32910 Brundige Ave Suite 257, Abbotsford, BC, V2S 1N2
(604) 853-2411
Emp Here 200
SIC 8059 Nursing and personal care, nec

D-U-N-S 25-992-3035   (BR)
MENNONITE CENTRAL COMMITTEE CANADA
MCC SUPPORTIVE CARE SERVICES
2776 Bourquin Cres W Suite 103, Abbotsford, BC, V2S 6A4
(604) 850-6608
Emp Here 350
SIC 8399 Social services, nec

D-U-N-S 20-919-3650   (BR)
OMSTEAD FOODS LIMITED
1925 Riverside Rd, Abbotsford, BC, V2S 4J8

Emp Here 80
SIC 2037 Frozen fruits and vegetables

D-U-N-S 20-748-0273   (BR)
PANAGO PIZZA INC
3033 Immel St Unit 510, Abbotsford, BC, V2S 6S2
(604) 504-4930
Emp Here 20
SIC 5812 Eating places

D-U-N-S 20-646-4658   (BR)
PENTECOSTAL ASSEMBLIES OF CANADA, THE
CHRISTIAN LIFE COMMUNITY CHURCH
35131 Straiton Rd, Abbotsford, BC, V2S 7Z1
(604) 853-4166
Emp Here 25
SIC 8661 Religious organizations

D-U-N-S 24-354-4272   (BR)
PREMIER TECH HOME & GARDEN INC
1050 Riverside Rd, Abbotsford, BC, V2S 7P6
(604) 850-9641
Emp Here 20
SIC 3494 Valves and pipe fittings, nec

D-U-N-S 25-545-4676   (BR)
PROSPERA CREDIT UNION
33655 Essendene Ave Suite 20, Abbotsford, BC, V2S 2G5
(604) 853-3317
Emp Here 25
SIC 6062 State credit unions

D-U-N-S 25-370-3086   (BR)
REXALL PHARMACY GROUP LTD
CLAYBURN REXALL DRUGSTORE
(*Suby of* McKesson Corporation)
3033 Immel St Suite 150, Abbotsford, BC, V2S 6S2

Emp Here 23
SIC 5912 Drug stores and proprietary stores

D-U-N-S 20-428-2487   (HQ)
RITCHIE-SMITH FEEDS INC
33777 Enterprise Ave, Abbotsford, BC, V2S 7T9
(604) 859-7128
Emp Here 70   *Emp Total* 140
Sales 29,452,534
SIC 2048 Prepared feeds, nec
Pr Pr Richard Reimer
  Frederick Fleming
  Kenneth Mackenzie
  Kenneth Warkentin

D-U-N-S 20-309-3203   (SL)
ROBERTSON, DOWNE & MULLALLY
33695 South Fraser Way Suite 301, Abbotsford, BC, V2S 2C1
(604) 853-0774
Emp Here 55   *Sales* 4,742,446
SIC 8111 Legal services

D-U-N-S 20-002-5695   (BR)
ROYAL BANK OF CANADA
RBC
(*Suby of* Royal Bank Of Canada)
32900 South Fraser Way Suite 142, Abbotsford, BC, V2S 5A1
(604) 853-8384
Emp Here 33
SIC 6021 National commercial banks

D-U-N-S 24-639-8796   (BR)
SAPUTO INC
SAPUTO FOODS
1799 Riverside Rd Suite 48, Abbotsford, BC, V2S 4J8
(604) 853-2225
Emp Here 100
SIC 5143 Dairy products, except dried or canned

D-U-N-S 20-591-4224   (BR)
SCHOOL DISTRICT NO 34 (ABBOTSFORD)
DR THOMAS A SWIFT ELEMENTARY SCHOOL
34800 Mierau St, Abbotsford, BC, V2S 5Y4
(604) 850-1615
Emp Here 25
SIC 8211 Elementary and secondary schools

D-U-N-S 20-591-4208   (BR)
SCHOOL DISTRICT NO 34 (ABBOTSFORD)
ABBOTSFORD VIRTUAL SCHOOL
33952 Pine St, Abbotsford, BC, V2S 2P3
(604) 859-6726
Emp Here 25
SIC 8211 Elementary and secondary schools

D-U-N-S 20-591-3994   (BR)
SCHOOL DISTRICT NO 34 (ABBOTSFORD)
MCMILLAN ELEMENTARY
34830 Oakhill Dr, Abbotsford, BC, V2S 7R3
(604) 859-0126
Emp Here 35
SIC 8211 Elementary and secondary schools

D-U-N-S 20-072-1871   (BR)
SCHOOL DISTRICT NO 34 (ABBOTSFORD)
CHIEF DAN GEORGE MIDDLE SCHOOL
32877 Old Riverside Rd, Abbotsford, BC, V2S 8K2
(604) 852-9616
Emp Here 45
SIC 8211 Elementary and secondary schools

D-U-N-S 25-136-8460   (BR)
SCHOOL DISTRICT NO 34 (ABBOTSFORD)
YALE SECONDARY SCHOOL
34620 Old Yale Rd, Abbotsford, BC, V2S 7S6
(604) 853-0778
Emp Here 100
SIC 8211 Elementary and secondary schools

D-U-N-S 25-113-6388   (BR)
SCHOOL DISTRICT NO 34 (ABBOTSFORD)

ALEXANDER ELEMENTARY SCHOOL
2250 Lobban Rd, Abbotsford, BC, V2S 3W1
(604) 859-3167
Emp Here 20
SIC 8211 Elementary and secondary schools

D-U-N-S 20-591-4182   (BR)
SCHOOL DISTRICT NO 34 (ABBOTSFORD)
JACKSON ELEMENTARY SCHOOL
33165 King Rd, Abbotsford, BC, V2S 7Z9
(604) 859-5826
Emp Here 25
SIC 8211 Elementary and secondary schools

D-U-N-S 20-076-0507   (BR)
SCHOOL DISTRICT NO 34 (ABBOTSFORD)
MARGARETT STENERSEN EMENTERAY SCHOOL
3060 Old Clayburn Rd, Abbotsford, BC, V2S 4H3
(604) 859-3151
Emp Here 25
SIC 8211 Elementary and secondary schools

D-U-N-S 25-014-8293   (BR)
SCHOOL DISTRICT NO 34 (ABBOTSFORD)
ROBERT BATEMAN SECONDARY SCHOOL
35045 Exbury Ave, Abbotsford, BC, V2S 7L1
(604) 864-0220
Emp Here 90
SIC 8211 Elementary and secondary schools

D-U-N-S 20-657-0629   (BR)
SCHOOL DISTRICT NO 34 (ABBOTSFORD)
CLAYBURN MIDDLE SCHOOL
35139 Laburnum Ave, Abbotsford, BC, V2S 8N3
(604) 504-7007
Emp Here 50
SIC 8211 Elementary and secondary schools

D-U-N-S 20-591-4216   (BR)
SCHOOL DISTRICT NO 34 (ABBOTSFORD)
WILLIAM A FRASER MIDDLE SCHOOL
34695 Blatchford Way, Abbotsford, BC, V2S 6M6
(604) 859-6794
Emp Here 57
SIC 8211 Elementary and secondary schools

D-U-N-S 20-591-4174   (BR)
SCHOOL DISTRICT NO 34 (ABBOTSFORD)
GODSON ELEMENTARY SCHOOL
33130 Bevan Ave, Abbotsford, BC, V2S 1T6
(604) 853-8374
Emp Here 25
SIC 8211 Elementary and secondary schools

D-U-N-S 20-043-8476   (BR)
SCHOOL DISTRICT NO 34 (ABBOTSFORD)
ABBOTSFORD MIDDLE SCHOOL
33231 Bevan Ave, Abbotsford, BC, V2S 0A9
(604) 859-7125
Emp Here 70
SIC 8211 Elementary and secondary schools

D-U-N-S 25-096-1653   (BR)
SEARS CANADA INC
32900 South Fraser Way, Abbotsford, BC, V2S 5A1
(604) 504-5574
Emp Here 200
SIC 5311 Department stores

D-U-N-S 20-884-1796   (BR)
SERVICEMASTER OF CANADA LIMITED
(*Suby of* ServiceMaster Global Holdings, Inc.)
34100 South Fraser Way Unit 1, Abbotsford, BC, V2S 2C6
(604) 853-8779
Emp Here 28
SIC 7349 Building maintenance services, nec

D-U-N-S 25-571-0212   (BR)
SMITTY'S CANADA LIMITED
SMITTY'S FAMILY RESTAURANT
1965 Sumas Way, Abbotsford, BC, V2S 4L5
(604) 853-1911
Emp Here 30

SIC 5812 Eating places

D-U-N-S 24-193-3097   (BR)
SODEXO CANADA LTD
SODEXO
33844 King Rd, Abbotsford, BC, V2S 7M8
(604) 854-4531
Emp Here 22
SIC 5812 Eating places

D-U-N-S 25-995-8056   (BR)
STARBUCKS COFFEE CANADA, INC
(*Suby of* Starbucks Corporation)
1399 Sumas Way Unit 100, Abbotsford, BC, V2S 8M9
(604) 864-6035
Emp Here 20
SIC 5812 Eating places

D-U-N-S 25-315-1005   (BR)
TORONTO-DOMINION BANK, THE
T D BANK FINANCIAL GROUP
(*Suby of* Toronto-Dominion Bank, The)
32817 South Fraser Way, Abbotsford, BC, V2S 2A6
(604) 870-2200
Emp Here 36
SIC 6021 National commercial banks

D-U-N-S 25-452-8698   (HQ)
TOWNSHIP TRANSIT SERVICES INC
CENTRAL FRASER VALLEY BUS LINE
(*Suby of* Township Transit Services Inc)
1125 Riverside Rd, Abbotsford, BC, V2S 7P1
(604) 854-2960
Emp Here 25   *Emp Total* 75
Sales 2,626,585
SIC 4111 Local and suburban transit

D-U-N-S 24-856-5939   (SL)
VALLEY BERRIES INC
34372 Industrial Way, Abbotsford, BC, V2S 7M6

Emp Here 60   *Sales* 2,845,467
SIC 2033 Canned fruits and specialties

D-U-N-S 20-105-9701   (BR)
VAN BELLE NURSERY INC
CLAYBURN SITE
4262 Wright St, Abbotsford, BC, V2S 7Y8

Emp Here 35
SIC 5193 Flowers and florists supplies

D-U-N-S 24-027-7462   (BR)
WFG SECURITIES OF CANADA INC
WORLD FINANCIAL GROUP
34314 Marshall Rd Suite 206, Abbotsford, BC, V2S 1L9
(604) 851-5806
Emp Here 20
SIC 8741 Management services

D-U-N-S 25-296-4994   (BR)
WAL-MART CANADA CORP
1812 Vedder Way Suite 3019, Abbotsford, BC, V2S 8K1
(604) 854-3575
Emp Here 270
SIC 5311 Department stores

D-U-N-S 20-703-5911   (BR)
WASTE CONNECTIONS OF CANADA INC
PROGRESSIVE   WASTE   SOLUTIONS CANADA INC
34321 Industrial Way, Abbotsford, BC, V2S 7M6
(604) 857-1990
Emp Here 100
SIC 4953 Refuse systems

D-U-N-S 20-508-9530   (BR)
WINNERS MERCHANTS INTERNATIONAL L.P.
WINNERS
(*Suby of* The TJX Companies Inc)
1335 Sumas Way Unit 100, Abbotsford, BC, V2S 8H2

(604) 556-7558
Emp Here 40
SIC 5651 Family clothing stores

Abbotsford, BC V2T
Central Fraser-Val County

D-U-N-S 24-798-0857   (SL)
277702 BRITISH COLUMBIA LTD
WOODWORKS
(*Suby of* 630377 B.C. Ltd)
2320 Peardonville Rd, Abbotsford, BC, V2T 6J8
(604) 850-7414
Emp Here 50   *Sales* 2,918,428
SIC 2511 Wood household furniture

D-U-N-S 24-134-4170   (SL)
625009 B.C. LTD
PACIFIC R.I.M. SERVICES
30435 Progressive Way Unit 1, Abbotsford, BC, V2T 6Z1

Emp Here 60   *Sales* 15,521,850
SIC 1542 Nonresidential construction, nec
Pr Pr Dwayne Stewart
Prin Phil Goddard

D-U-N-S 24-009-5328   (SL)
ABBOTSFORD SECURITY SERVICES
1ST SECURE
2669 Langdon St Suite 201, Abbotsford, BC, V2T 3L3
(604) 870-4731
Emp Here 100   *Sales* 3,137,310
SIC 7381 Detective and armored car services

D-U-N-S 20-093-2457   (SL)
ABBOTSFORD TAXI LTD
30950 Wheel Ave Suite 502, Abbotsford, BC, V2T 6G7
(604) 859-5251
Emp Here 60   *Sales* 1,824,018
SIC 4121 Taxicabs

D-U-N-S 25-627-5769   (BR)
ALDERGROVE FOODS LTD
A & W
(*Suby of* Aldergrove Foods Ltd)
32520 South Fraser Way, Abbotsford, BC, V2T 1X5
(604) 850-1012
Emp Here 34
SIC 5812 Eating places

D-U-N-S 24-345-6071   (BR)
BC HOUSING MANAGEMENT COMMIS-SION
BC ASSESSMENT AUTHORITY
31935 South Fraser Way Suite 240, Abbotsford, BC, V2T 5N7
(604) 850-5900
Emp Here 50
SIC 6531 Real estate agents and managers

D-U-N-S 25-316-9817   (HQ)
BE PRESSURE SUPPLY INC
30585 Progressive Way, Abbotsford, BC, V2T 6W3
(604) 850-6662
Emp Here 85   *Emp Total* 100
Sales 18,624,397
SIC 3589 Service industry machinery, nec
Susan Lois Braber

D-U-N-S 20-296-1285   (BR)
BAKER NEWBY LLP
BAKER NEWBY
2955 Gladwin Rd Suite 200, Abbotsford, BC, V2T 5T4
(604) 852-3646
Emp Here 50
SIC 8111 Legal services

D-U-N-S 20-002-8079   (BR)
BANQUE TORONTO-DOMINION, LA

TORONTO-DOMINION BANK, THE
(*Suby of* Toronto-Dominion Bank, The)
32435 South Fraser Way Suite 1, Abbotsford, BC, V2T 1X4
(604) 850-5921
Emp Here 30
SIC 6021 National commercial banks

D-U-N-S 24-956-9096   (HQ)
BETHESDA CHRISTIAN ASSOCIATION
(*Suby of* Bethesda Christian Association)
2975 Gladwin Rd Suite 105, Abbotsford, BC, V2T 5T4
(604) 850-6604
Emp Here 348   *Emp Total* 350
Sales 21,300,720
SIC 8322 Individual and family services
Pr Pr Michael Blok
Hugh Noort

D-U-N-S 24-328-9220   (SL)
BRADBURYS RESTAURANTS (1994) LTD
A B C FAMILY RESTAURANT
32080 Marshall Rd, Abbotsford, BC, V2T 1A1
(604) 854-3344
Emp Here 60   *Sales* 1,824,018
SIC 5812 Eating places

D-U-N-S 24-760-6114   (HQ)
BROOKSIDE FOODS LTD
(*Suby of* Hershey Company)
3899 Mt Lehman Rd, Abbotsford, BC, V2T 5W5
(604) 607-7665
Emp Here 60   *Emp Total* 17,980
Sales 21,523,407
SIC 5149 Groceries and related products, nec
Denis Mcguire
Pr Kenneth Shaver
J Hugh Wiebe

D-U-N-S 24-825-8824   (SL)
BROOKSIDE FRUIT COMPANY
(*Suby of* Hershey Company)
3889 Mt Lehman Rd, Abbotsford, BC, V2T 5W5
(604) 607-6650
Emp Here 50   *Sales* 4,711,645
SIC 2064 Candy and other confectionery products

D-U-N-S 20-137-0330   (BR)
CANACCORD GENUITY CORP
CANACCORD CAPITAL CORPORATION
(*Suby of* Canaccord Genuity Group Inc)
32071 South Fraser Way Suite 2, Abbotsford, BC, V2T 1W3
(604) 504-1504
Emp Here 24
SIC 6211 Security brokers and dealers

D-U-N-S 25-616-9277   (BR)
CANADIAN IMPERIAL BANK OF COM-MERCE
CIBC
32041 South Fraser Way, Abbotsford, BC, V2T 1W3
(604) 870-3123
Emp Here 30
SIC 6021 National commercial banks

D-U-N-S 25-616-7990   (BR)
CARA OPERATIONS LIMITED
SWISS CHALET ROTISSERIE & GRILL
(*Suby of* Cara Holdings Limited)
32470 South Fraser Way Unit 1, Abbotsford, BC, V2T 1X3

Emp Here 30
SIC 5812 Eating places

D-U-N-S 25-831-8765   (BR)
CITY OF ABBOTSFORD
ABBOTSFORD FIRE RESCUE SERVICE
32270 George Ferguson Way, Abbotsford, BC, V2T 2L1
(604) 853-3566
Emp Here 200

SIC 7389 Business services, nec

D-U-N-S 25-616-3635   (BR)
CITY OF ABBOTSFORD
MATSQUI RECREATION CENTRE
3106 Clearbrook Rd, Abbotsford, BC, V2T 4N6
(604) 855-0500
Emp Here 100
SIC 7999 Amusement and recreation, nec

D-U-N-S 25-094-8320   (BR)
CLEARBROOK GRAIN & MILLING COM-PANY LIMITED
33833 Entreprise St, Abbotsford, BC, V2T 4X3
(604) 853-5901
Emp Here 22
SIC 2048 Prepared feeds, nec

D-U-N-S 24-309-9327   (BR)
COLUMBIA KITCHEN CABINETS LTD
COLUMBIA COUNTER TOPS, DIV OF
(*Suby of* Columbia Kitchen Cabinets Ltd)
2210 Mason St, Abbotsford, BC, V2T 6C5
(604) 850-0371
Emp Here 50
SIC 2541 Wood partitions and fixtures

D-U-N-S 24-363-5831   (BR)
EAGLEWEST TRUCK AND CRANE INC
EAGLEWEST TOWER CRANES, DIV OF
2170 Carpenter St, Abbotsford, BC, V2T 6B4
(877) 577-4474
Emp Here 30
SIC 5084 Industrial machinery and equipment

D-U-N-S 25-408-5830   (SL)
ECOTEX SERVICE CORPORATION
2448 Townline Rd, Abbotsford, BC, V2T 6L6
(604) 850-3111
Emp Here 60   *Sales* 1,824,018
SIC 7211 Power laundries, family and com-mercial

D-U-N-S 25-150-2118   (BR)
ENTERPRISE RENT-A-CAR CANADA COM-PANY
ENTERPRISE RENT-A-CAR
(*Suby of* The Crawford Group Inc)
103-30125 Automall Dr, Abbotsford, BC, V2T 6Y9
(604) 855-5282
Emp Here 25
SIC 7514 Passenger car rental

D-U-N-S 24-374-1308   (BR)
FLEXIFORCE CANADA INC
FLEXIFORCE CANADA INC
2285 Queen St Suite 105, Abbotsford, BC, V2T 6J3
(604) 854-8788
Emp Here 40
SIC 5211 Lumber and other building materials

D-U-N-S 20-988-2120   (BR)
FLYNN CANADA LTD
2234 Carpenter St, Abbotsford, BC, V2T 6B4

Emp Here 30
SIC 1761 Roofing, siding, and sheetMetal work

D-U-N-S 25-267-7034   (SL)
FOURTH-RITE CONSTRUCTION (1994) LTD
2609 Progressive Way Suite B, Abbotsford, BC, V2T 6H8
(604) 850-7684
Emp Here 60   *Sales* 9,922,655
SIC 1522 Residential construction, nec
Pr Pr Mike Kuhn
Geoff Wade

D-U-N-S 24-899-2075   (SL)
FRASER VALLEY INDUSTRIES LTD
30781 Simpson Rd Suite 201, Abbotsford, BC, V2T 6X4
(604) 852-8125
Emp Here 30   *Sales* 2,480,664
SIC 2431 Millwork

▲ Public Company   ■ Public Company Family Member   **HQ** Headquarters   **BR** Branch   **SL** Single Location

D-U-N-S 20-875-1409   (BR)
FRASER VALLEY REGIONAL LIBRARY DISTRICT
CLEARBROOK LIBRARY
32320 George Ferguson Way, Abbotsford, BC, V2T 6N4
(604) 859-7814
Emp Here 20
SIC 8231 Libraries

D-U-N-S 25-140-1006   (SL)
IMAGE PLUS
CLEARBROOK PLAZA
31935 South Fraser Way Unit 104, Abbotsford, BC, V2T 5N7
(604) 504-7222
Emp Here 50   *Sales* 2,918,428
SIC 7384 Photofinish laboratories

D-U-N-S 24-881-8387   (SL)
JONET CONSTRUCTION LTD
1777 Townline Rd, Abbotsford, BC, V2T 6E2
(604) 850-1288
Emp Here 50   *Sales* 4,714,758
SIC 1799 Special trade contractors, nec

D-U-N-S 25-500-0127   (SL)
K & R POULTRY LTD
FARM FED, DIV OF
31171 Peardonville Rd Unit 2, Abbotsford, BC, V2T 6K6
(604) 850-5808
Emp Here 84   *Sales* 15,905,433
SIC 2015 Poultry slaughtering and processing
Pr Pr Kenneth Huttema
  Robert Vane

D-U-N-S 20-957-0647   (BR)
KPMG INC
32575 Simon Ave, Abbotsford, BC, V2T 4W6
(604) 857-2269
Emp Here 55
SIC 8721 Accounting, auditing, and bookkeeping

D-U-N-S 24-069-9231   (BR)
KAL TIRE LTD
31180 Peardonville Rd, Abbotsford, BC, V2T 6K6
(604) 854-1161
Emp Here 23
SIC 5531 Auto and home supply stores

D-U-N-S 24-068-5391   (SL)
KLASSIC CATERING LTD
30455 Progressive Way Suite 1, Abbotsford, BC, V2T 6W3
(604) 864-8250
Emp Here 50   *Sales* 1,532,175
SIC 5812 Eating places

D-U-N-S 20-075-0362   (BR)
LAFARGE CANADA INC
31601 Walmsley Ave, Abbotsford, BC, V2T 6G5
(604) 856-8313
Emp Here 80
SIC 5032 Brick, stone, and related material

D-U-N-S 20-218-7048   (SL)
LILYDALE COOP INCORPORATED
31894 Marshall Rd, Abbotsford, BC, V2T 5Z9
(604) 857-1261
Emp Here 200   *Sales* 13,251,600
SIC 3269 Pottery products, nec
Manager Gregg Marshalsay
Mgr Gerry Beadle

D-U-N-S 24-535-0822   (BR)
LILYDALE INC
LILYDALE FOODS
31894 Marshall Pl Suite 5, Abbotsford, BC, V2T 5Z9
(604) 850-2633
Emp Here 166
SIC 2015 Poultry slaughtering and processing

D-U-N-S 24-899-1432   (BR)
LONDON DRUGS LIMITED

32700 South Fraser Way Suite 26, Abbotsford, BC, V2T 4M5
(604) 852-0936
Emp Here 100
SIC 5912 Drug stores and proprietary stores

D-U-N-S 25-621-2267   (SL)
M A & T J HOLDINGS LTD
TIM HORTONS
30340 Automall Dr, Abbotsford, BC, V2T 5M1
(604) 857-7733
Emp Here 70   *Sales* 2,115,860
SIC 5812 Eating places

D-U-N-S 25-088-4483   (SL)
M.D. TRANSPORT CO. LTD
1683 Mt Lehman Rd, Abbotsford, BC, V2T 6H6
(604) 850-1818
Emp Here 40   *Sales* 11,282,616
SIC 4213 Trucking, except local
Pr Pr Major Dhillon

D-U-N-S 20-733-8802   (SL)
MCDONALD'S
2532 Clearbrook Rd, Abbotsford, BC, V2T 2Y4
(604) 870-5360
Emp Here 65   *Sales* 1,969,939
SIC 5812 Eating places

D-U-N-S 24-355-7241   (HQ)
PNR RAILWORKS INC
PNR
2595 Deacon St, Abbotsford, BC, V2T 6L4
(604) 850-9166
Emp Here 40   *Emp Total* 5,742
Sales 18,884,272
SIC 1629 Heavy construction, nec
Pr Jamey Craig
VP Opers Peter Pearce
Sec Jeff Loewen
Dir John August
Dir Jeffrey Levey

D-U-N-S 25-366-5137   (BR)
POSTMEDIA NETWORK INC
ABBOTSFORD TIMES
30887 Peardonville Rd Suite 1, Abbotsford, BC, V2T 6K2

Emp Here 30
SIC 2711 Newspapers

D-U-N-S 20-562-8139   (BR)
RBC DOMINION SECURITIES INC
(*Suby of* Royal Bank Of Canada)
31975 South Fraser Way, Abbotsford, BC, V2T 1V5
(604) 855-5349
Emp Here 20
SIC 6282 Investment advice

D-U-N-S 24-004-7183   (BR)
RAYMOND JAMES (USA) LTD
(*Suby of* Raymond James Financial, Inc.)
2881 Garden St Unit 200, Abbotsford, BC, V2T 4X1
(604) 855-0654
Emp Here 20
SIC 6211 Security brokers and dealers

D-U-N-S 20-122-7894   (BR)
REITMANS (CANADA) LIMITEE
REITMANS
32700 South Fraser Way Unit 55, Abbotsford, BC, V2T 4M5
(604) 870-8929
Emp Here 25
SIC 5621 Women's clothing stores

D-U-N-S 25-408-5590   (BR)
ROYAL BANK OF CANADA
RBC ROYAL BANK
(*Suby of* Royal Bank Of Canada)
31975 South Fraser Way, Abbotsford, BC, V2T 1V5
(604) 855-5349
Emp Here 35

SIC 6021 National commercial banks

D-U-N-S 20-591-4240   (BR)
SCHOOL DISTRICT NO 34 (ABBOTSFORD)
CLEARBROOK ELEMENTARY SCHOOL
3614 Clearbrook Rd, Abbotsford, BC, V2T 6N3
(604) 859-5348
Emp Here 35
SIC 8211 Elementary and secondary schools

D-U-N-S 20-591-4158   (BR)
SCHOOL DISTRICT NO 34 (ABBOTSFORD)
SELF POPLAR TRADITIONAL ELEMENTARY SCHOOL
32746 Huntingdon Rd, Abbotsford, BC, V2T 5Z1
(604) 853-1845
Emp Here 25
SIC 8211 Elementary and secondary schools

D-U-N-S 20-072-3307   (BR)
SCHOOL DISTRICT NO 34 (ABBOTSFORD)
SAYERS, HARRY ELEMENTARY SCHOOL
31321 Blueridge Dr, Abbotsford, BC, V2T 6W2
(604) 852-9665
Emp Here 43
SIC 8211 Elementary and secondary schools

D-U-N-S 20-591-4133   (BR)
SCHOOL DISTRICT NO 34 (ABBOTSFORD)
DORMICK PARK ELEMENTARY SCHOOL
32161 Dormick Ave, Abbotsford, BC, V2T 1J6
(604) 859-3712
Emp Here 25
SIC 8211 Elementary and secondary schools

D-U-N-S 20-591-4141   (BR)
SCHOOL DISTRICT NO 34 (ABBOTSFORD)
BAKERVIEW ELEMENTARY SCHOOL
32622 Marshall Rd, Abbotsford, BC, V2T 4A2
(604) 852-1250
Emp Here 25
SIC 8211 Elementary and secondary schools

D-U-N-S 20-026-9285   (BR)
SCHOOL DISTRICT NO 34 (ABBOTSFORD)
DAVE KANDAL ELEMENTARY SCHOOL
3551 Crestview Ave, Abbotsford, BC, V2T 6T5
(604) 856-7342
Emp Here 30
SIC 8211 Elementary and secondary schools

D-U-N-S 20-591-4042   (BR)
SCHOOL DISTRICT NO 34 (ABBOTSFORD)
CENTENNIAL PARK ELEMENTARY
2527 Gladwin Rd, Abbotsford, BC, V2T 3N8
(604) 853-9148
Emp Here 25
SIC 8211 Elementary and secondary schools

D-U-N-S 20-654-8575   (BR)
SCHOOL DISTRICT NO 34 (ABBOTSFORD)
EUGENE REIMER MIDDLE SCHOOL
3433 Firhill Dr, Abbotsford, BC, V2T 6X6
(604) 504-5343
Emp Here 60
SIC 8211 Elementary and secondary schools

D-U-N-S 20-980-1260   (BR)
SCHOOL DISTRICT NO 34 (ABBOTSFORD)
JOHN MACLURE COMMUNITY SCHOOL
2990 Oriole Cres, Abbotsford, BC, V2T 4E1
(604) 853-1246
Emp Here 30
SIC 8211 Elementary and secondary schools

D-U-N-S 20-591-4059   (BR)
SCHOOL DISTRICT NO 34 (ABBOTSFORD)
STANLEY ELEMENTARY SCHOOL
2580 Stanley St, Abbotsford, BC, V2T 2R4
(604) 850-6657
Emp Here 25
SIC 8211 Elementary and secondary schools

D-U-N-S 20-044-6636   (BR)
SCHOOL DISTRICT NO 34 (ABBOTSFORD)
DR ROBERTA BONDAR ELEMENTARY
32717 Chilcotin Dr, Abbotsford, BC, V2T 5S5

(604) 864-8572
Emp Here 20
SIC 8211 Elementary and secondary schools

D-U-N-S 25-288-5207   (BR)
SCHOOL DISTRICT NO 34 (ABBOTSFORD)
W.J. MOUAT SECONDARY SCHOOL
32355 Mouat Dr, Abbotsford, BC, V2T 4E9
(604) 853-7191
Emp Here 120
SIC 8211 Elementary and secondary schools

D-U-N-S 20-591-4091   (BR)
SCHOOL DISTRICT NO 34 (ABBOTSFORD)
ABBOTSFORD TRADITIONAL MIDDLE SCHOOL
2272 Windsor St, Abbotsford, BC, V2T 6M1
(604) 850-7029
Emp Here 25
SIC 8211 Elementary and secondary schools

D-U-N-S 20-043-9284   (BR)
SCHOOL DISTRICT NO 34 (ABBOTSFORD)
ABBOTSFORD CONTINUING EDUCATION SECONDARY SCHOOL
32622 Marshall Rd, Abbotsford, BC, V2T 4A2
(604) 859-7820
Emp Here 45
SIC 8211 Elementary and secondary schools

D-U-N-S 20-591-4117   (BR)
SCHOOL DISTRICT NO 34 (ABBOTSFORD)
RICKHANSEN SECONDARY SCHOOL
31150 Blueridge Dr, Abbotsford, BC, V2T 5R2
(604) 864-0011
Emp Here 80
SIC 8211 Elementary and secondary schools

D-U-N-S 20-591-4109   (BR)
SCHOOL DISTRICT NO 34 (ABBOTSFORD)
BLUE JAY ELEMENTARY SCHOOL
30995 Southern Dr, Abbotsford, BC, V2T 6X5
(604) 852-0802
Emp Here 25
SIC 8211 Elementary and secondary schools

D-U-N-S 24-806-5310   (BR)
SERVICE CORPORATION INTERNATIONAL (CANADA) LIMITED
WOODLAWN FUNERAL HOME
2310 Clearbrook Rd, Abbotsford, BC, V2T 2X5
(604) 853-2643
Emp Here 20
SIC 7261 Funeral service and crematories

D-U-N-S 20-717-0361   (BR)
SHAW COMMUNICATIONS INC
31450 Marshall Rd, Abbotsford, BC, V2T 6B1
(604) 850-2517
Emp Here 30
SIC 4841 Cable and other pay television services

D-U-N-S 25-616-7172   (BR)
SOBEYS WEST INC
LUCERNE FOODS
31122 South Fraser Way, Abbotsford, BC, V2T 6L5
(604) 854-1191
Emp Here 150
SIC 5142 Packaged frozen goods

D-U-N-S 25-271-0991   (BR)
SOBEYS WEST INC
32500 South Fraser Way Unit 100, Abbotsford, BC, V2T 4W1
(604) 852-3558
Emp Here 150
SIC 5411 Grocery stores

D-U-N-S 25-498-9965   (BR)
STAPLES CANADA INC
STAPLES THE BUSINESS DEPOT
(*Suby of* Staples, Inc.)
32500 South Fraser Way Suite 110, Abbotsford, BC, V2T 4W1
(604) 870-3440
Emp Here 30

▲ Public Company   ■ Public Company Family Member   **HQ** Headquarters   **BR** Branch   **SL** Single Location

SIC 5943 Stationery stores

D-U-N-S 20-371-6449   (HQ)
TNT CRANE & RIGGING CANADA INC
STAMPEDE CRANE & RIGGING
(*Suby of* TNT Crane & Rigging Canada Inc)
2190 Carpenter St, Abbotsford, BC, V2T 6B4
(800) 667-2215
Emp Here 20   *Emp Total* 50
Sales 4,764,381
SIC 7353 Heavy construction equipment rental

D-U-N-S 24-154-9120   (SL)
VALLEY RACQUETS CENTRE INC
2814 Gladwin Rd, Abbotsford, BC, V2T 4S8
(604) 859-1331
Emp Here 50   *Sales* 2,042,900
SIC 7997 Membership sports and recreation clubs

D-U-N-S 24-767-5572   (BR)
VALUE VILLAGE STORES, INC
(*Suby of* Savers, Inc.)
31970 South Fraser Way, Abbotsford, BC, V2T 1V6
(604) 850-3712
Emp Here 30
SIC 5399 Miscellaneous general merchandise

D-U-N-S 25-621-2432   (BR)
WENDY'S RESTAURANTS OF CANADA INC
WENDY'S
(*Suby of* The Wendy's Company)
32733 South Fraser Way, Abbotsford, BC, V2T 3S3
(604) 853-0911
Emp Here 30
SIC 5812 Eating places

D-U-N-S 25-620-1336   (BR)
WENDY'S RESTAURANTS OF CANADA INC
WENDY'S # 6530
(*Suby of* The Wendy's Company)
30340 Automall Dr, Abbotsford, BC, V2T 5M1
(604) 857-5336
Emp Here 40
SIC 5812 Eating places

D-U-N-S 20-978-9556   (BR)
WESTJET AIRLINES LTD
RS & ASSOCIATES
30440 Liberator Ave Unit 7, Abbotsford, BC, V2T 6H5
(604) 504-7786
Emp Here 25
SIC 4512 Air transportation, scheduled

D-U-N-S 20-980-1062   (BR)
WORKERS' COMPENSATION BOARD OF BRITISH COLUMBIA
WORKSASEBC
2774 Trethewey St, Abbotsford, BC, V2T 3R1
(604) 556-2000
Emp Here 67
SIC 6331 Fire, marine, and casualty insurance

Abbotsford, BC V3G
Central Fraser-Val County

D-U-N-S 20-713-9044   (SL)
ABBOTSFORD CHRISTIAN ELEMENTARY SCHOOL
3939 Old Clayburn Rd, Abbotsford, BC, V3G 1J9
(604) 850-2694
Emp Here 50   *Sales* 3,356,192
SIC 8211 Elementary and secondary schools

D-U-N-S 25-570-9081   (BR)
OCEANS RETAIL INVESTMENTS INC
PETRO CANADA
2054 Whatcom Rd Suite 1, Abbotsford, BC, V3G 2K8
(604) 850-8951
Emp Here 36

SIC 5541 Gasoline service stations

D-U-N-S 20-713-3161   (BR)
SCHOOL DISTRICT NO 34 (ABBOTSFORD)
AUGUSTON ELEMENTARY SCHOOL
36367 Stephen Leacock Dr, Abbotsford, BC, V3G 2Z6
(604) 557-0422
Emp Here 50
SIC 8211 Elementary and secondary schools

D-U-N-S 20-026-8980   (BR)
SCHOOL DISTRICT NO 34 (ABBOTSFORD)
SANDY HILL ELEMENTARY SCHOOL
3836 Old Clayburn Rd, Abbotsford, BC, V3G 2Z5
(604) 850-7131
Emp Here 30
SIC 8211 Elementary and secondary schools

D-U-N-S 20-591-3986   (BR)
SCHOOL DISTRICT NO 34 (ABBOTSFORD)
MOUNTAIN ELEMENTARY
2299 Mountain Dr, Abbotsford, BC, V3G 1E6
(604) 852-7299
Emp Here 25
SIC 8211 Elementary and secondary schools

D-U-N-S 20-026-8998   (BR)
SCHOOL DISTRICT NO 34 (ABBOTSFORD)
UPPER SUMAS ELEMENTARY SCHOOL
36321 Vye Rd, Abbotsford, BC, V3G 1Z5
(604) 852-3900
Emp Here 23
SIC 8211 Elementary and secondary schools

Abbotsford, BC V4X
Central Fraser-Val County

D-U-N-S 25-818-1692   (BR)
FRASERWAY RV LIMITED PARTNERSHIP
TRAVELHOME
2866 Mt Lehman Rd, Abbotsford, BC, V4X 2N6
(604) 853-1566
Emp Here 30
SIC 5561 Recreational vehicle dealers

D-U-N-S 24-048-6626   (BR)
LAFARGE CANADA INC
1080 Bradner Rd, Abbotsford, BC, V4X 1H8
(604) 856-5521
Emp Here 25
SIC 5032 Brick, stone, and related material

D-U-N-S 20-641-5544   (SL)
MCDONALD'S RESTAURANTS
3230 Mt Lehman Rd Unit 100, Abbotsford, BC, V4X 2M9
(604) 857-7990
Emp Here 61   *Sales* 1,824,018
SIC 5812 Eating places

D-U-N-S 20-591-4075   (BR)
SCHOOL DISTRICT NO 34 (ABBOTSFORD)
ABERDEEN ELEMENTARY SCHOOL
2975 Bradner Rd, Abbotsford, BC, V4X 1K6
(604) 856-5137
Emp Here 25
SIC 8211 Elementary and secondary schools

D-U-N-S 20-713-3096   (BR)
SCHOOL DISTRICT NO 34 (ABBOTSFORD)
MATSQUI ELEMENTARY
33661 Elizabeth Ave, Abbotsford, BC, V4X 1T4
(604) 826-8181
Emp Here 20
SIC 8211 Elementary and secondary schools

D-U-N-S 20-591-4083   (BR)
SCHOOL DISTRICT NO 34 (ABBOTSFORD)
DUNACH ELEMENTARY SCHOOL
30357 Downes Rd, Abbotsford, BC, V4X 1Z8
(604) 856-2186
Emp Here 25

SIC 8211 Elementary and secondary schools

D-U-N-S 20-591-4034   (BR)
SCHOOL DISTRICT NO 34 (ABBOTSFORD)
ROSS ELEMENTARY
2451 Ross Rd, Abbotsford, BC, V4X 1J3
(604) 856-6079
Emp Here 25
SIC 8211 Elementary and secondary schools

D-U-N-S 24-014-5248   (BR)
STARBUCKS COFFEE CANADA, INC
STARBUCKS
(*Suby of* Starbucks Corporation)
3250 Mt Lehman Rd, Abbotsford, BC, V4X 2M9
(604) 856-2531
Emp Here 20
SIC 5812 Eating places

D-U-N-S 20-251-1713   (BR)
WESTBROOK FLORAL LTD
29349 58 Ave, Abbotsford, BC, V4X 2G1
(604) 626-4343
Emp Here 50
SIC 5193 Flowers and florists supplies

Agassiz, BC V0M

D-U-N-S 24-321-1609   (SL)
0773278 B.C LTD
HEMLOCK RESORT
20955 Hemlock Valley Rd, Agassiz, BC, V0M 1A1
(604) 797-6882
Emp Here 50   *Sales* 2,188,821
SIC 7011 Hotels and motels

D-U-N-S 25-086-9310   (BR)
A & W FOOD SERVICES OF CANADA INC
A & W RESTAURANT
7211 Morrow Rd, Agassiz, BC, V0M 1A0
(604) 796-2070
Emp Here 32
SIC 5812 Eating places

D-U-N-S 24-898-9394   (BR)
BRITCO LP
1825 Tower Dr, Agassiz, BC, V0M 1A2
(604) 796-2257
Emp Here 95
SIC 2452 Prefabricated wood buildings

D-U-N-S 25-985-2341   (SL)
LEYEN HOLDINGS LTD
GLENWOOD CARE CENTRE
1458 Glenwood Dr, Agassiz, BC, V0M 1A3
(604) 796-9202
Emp Here 60   *Sales* 2,188,821
SIC 8361 Residential care

D-U-N-S 25-912-4709   (BR)
RIMEX SUPPLY LTD
2995 Cameron Rd, Agassiz, BC, V0M 1A1
(604) 796-5502
Emp Here 70
SIC 3714 Motor vehicle parts and accessories

D-U-N-S 20-713-2965   (BR)
SCHOOL DISTRICT 78
AGASSIZ ELEMENTARY & SECONDARY SCHOOL
7110 Cheam Ave, Agassiz, BC, V0M 1A0
(604) 796-2238
Emp Here 40
SIC 8211 Elementary and secondary schools

D-U-N-S 20-009-6530   (BR)
SCHOOL DISTRICT 78
KENT ELEMENTARY SCHOOL
7285 Mccullough Rd, Agassiz, BC, V0M 1A2
(604) 796-2164
Emp Here 35
SIC 8211 Elementary and secondary schools

D-U-N-S 25-660-1170   (BR)

SIC 8211 Elementary and secondary schools

D-U-N-S 20-591-4034   (BR)
SEABIRD ISLAND INDIAN BAND
2895 Chowat Rd Rr 2, Agassiz, BC, V0M 1A2
(604) 796-2177
Emp Here 150
SIC 8299 Schools and educational services, nec

Ainsworth Hot Springs, BC V0G
Central Kootenay County

D-U-N-S 24-150-3283   (SL)
AINSWORTH HOT SPRINGS LTD
AINSWORTH HOT SPRINGS RESORT
3609 Highway 31, Ainsworth Hot Springs, BC, V0G 1A0
(250) 229-4212
Emp Here 60   *Sales* 2,626,585
SIC 7011 Hotels and motels

Aiyansh, BC V0J
Kitimat - Stikine County

D-U-N-S 24-658-8578   (HQ)
NISGA'S VALLEY HEALTH AUTHORITY
(*Suby of* Nisga's Valley Health Authority)
4920 Tait Ave, Aiyansh, BC, V0J 1A0
(250) 633-5000
Emp Here 32   *Emp Total* 65
Sales 4,231,721
SIC 8093 Specialty outpatient clinics, nec

D-U-N-S 20-713-6446   (BR)
SCHOOL DISTRICT 92 NISGA'A
SCHOOL DISTRICT NO. 92 (NISGA'A)
5000 Skadeen Ave, Aiyansh, BC, V0J 1A0
(250) 633-2225
Emp Here 50
SIC 8211 Elementary and secondary schools

Aldergrove, BC V4W
Greater Vancouver County

D-U-N-S 24-099-3845   (SL)
ADVANCED INTEGRATION TECHNOLOGY CANADA INC
AIT
(*Suby of* Advanced Integration Technology, LP)
3168 262 St Suite 100, Aldergrove, BC, V4W 2Z6
(604) 856-8939
Emp Here 25   *Sales* 4,244,630
SIC 3812 Search and navigation equipment

D-U-N-S 25-650-2063   (SL)
AUTUMN INVESTMENTS LTD
WHITE SPOT RESTAURANTS
3070 264 St Suite B, Aldergrove, BC, V4W 3E1
(604) 856-0344
Emp Here 55   *Sales* 1,992,377
SIC 5812 Eating places

D-U-N-S 20-034-9608   (BR)
BOARD OF EDUCATION OF SCHOOL DISTRICT NO. 35 (LANGLEY)
SHORTREED COMMUNITY SCHOOL
(*Suby of* Board of Education of School District No. 35 (Langley))
27330 28 Ave, Aldergrove, BC, V4W 3K1
(604) 856-4167
Emp Here 37
SIC 8211 Elementary and secondary schools

D-U-N-S 20-033-6639   (BR)
BOARD OF EDUCATION OF SCHOOL DISTRICT NO. 35 (LANGLEY)
COGHLAN FUNDAMENTAL ELEMENTARY SCHOOL

(*Suby of* Board of Education of School District No. 35 (Langley))
4452 256 St, Aldergrove, BC, V4W 1J3
(604) 856-8539
Emp Here 20
SIC 8211 Elementary and secondary schools

D-U-N-S 20-034-9251   (BR)
BOARD OF EDUCATION OF SCHOOL DISTRICT NO. 35 (LANGLEY)
PARKSIDE CENTENNIAL ELEMENTARY SCHOOL
(*Suby of* Board of Education of School District No. 35 (Langley))
3300 270 St, Aldergrove, BC, V4W 3H2
(604) 856-7775
Emp Here 40
SIC 8211 Elementary and secondary schools

D-U-N-S 25-650-9928   (BR)
CREDIT UNION CENTRAL OF CANADA
ALDERGROVE CREDIT UNION
2941 272 St, Aldergrove, BC, V4W 3R3
(604) 856-7724
Emp Here 85
SIC 6062 State credit unions

D-U-N-S 25-082-5783   (BR)
GREAT PACIFIC INDUSTRIES INC
SAVE-ON-FOODS
26310 Fraser Hwy Unit 100, Aldergrove, BC, V4W 2Z7
(604) 607-6550
Emp Here 150
SIC 5411 Grocery stores

D-U-N-S 25-068-3851   (BR)
LANGLEY, CORPORATION OF THE TOWNSHIP OF
ALDERGROVE KINSMEN COMMUNITY CENTRE
26770 29 Ave Suite A, Aldergrove, BC, V4W 3B8
(604) 856-2899
Emp Here 25
SIC 8322 Individual and family services

D-U-N-S 25-363-8498   (BR)
LOBLAWS INC
EXTRA FOOD
3100 272 St Suite 1, Aldergrove, BC, V4W 3N7
(604) 856-5101
Emp Here 33
SIC 5411 Grocery stores

D-U-N-S 20-296-6289   (BR)
OTTER FARM & HOME CO-OPERATIVE
OTTER CO-OP
3548 248 St Suite 3548, Aldergrove, BC, V4W 1Y7
(604) 607-6903
Emp Here 50
SIC 5191 Farm supplies

D-U-N-S 24-073-3816   (BR)
SCHOOL DISTRICT NO. 35 (LANGLEY)
ALDERGROVE COMMUNITY SECONDARY SCHOOL
26850 29 Ave, Aldergrove, BC, V4W 3C1
(604) 856-2521
Emp Here 80
SIC 8211 Elementary and secondary schools

D-U-N-S 20-030-6277   (BR)
SCHOOL DISTRICT NO. 35 (LANGLEY)
NORTH OTTER ELEMENTARY SCHOOL
5370 248 St, Aldergrove, BC, V4W 1A7
(604) 856-3355
Emp Here 28
SIC 8211 Elementary and secondary schools

D-U-N-S 20-713-3278   (BR)
SCHOOL DISTRICT NO. 35 (LANGLEY)
BETTY GILBERT ELEMENTARY SCHOOL
26845 27 Ave, Aldergrove, BC, V4W 3E6
(604) 856-8178
Emp Here 40

SIC 8211 Elementary and secondary schools

D-U-N-S 25-015-0117   (BR)
SOBEYS WEST INC
CANADA SAFEWAY # 165
27566 Fraser Hwy, Aldergrove, BC, V4W 3N5
(604) 857-1351
Emp Here 100
SIC 5411 Grocery stores

Anahim Lake, BC V0L
Cariboo County

D-U-N-S 24-422-9519   (BR)
WEST CHILCOTIN FOREST PRODUCTS LTD
ANAHIM LAKE SAWMILL
21841 Hwy 20, Anahim Lake, BC, V0L 1C0

Emp Here 50
SIC 2421 Sawmills and planing mills, general

Armstrong, BC V0E
North Okanagan County

D-U-N-S 24-034-1586   (BR)
ASKEW'S FOOD SERVICE LTD
3305 Smith Dr Unit 8, Armstrong, BC, V0E 1B1
(250) 546-3039
Emp Here 40
SIC 5411 Grocery stores

D-U-N-S 24-345-0702   (BR)
INTERIOR HEALTH AUTHORITY
PLEASANT VALLEY HEALTH CENTRE
3800 Patten Dr, Armstrong, BC, V0E 1B2
(250) 546-4707
Emp Here 40
SIC 8062 General medical and surgical hospitals

D-U-N-S 20-713-6438   (BR)
NORTH OKANAGAN SHUSWAP SCHOOL DISTRICT 83
HIGHLAND PARK ELEMENTARY SCHOOL
3200 Wood Ave, Armstrong, BC, V0E 1B0
(250) 546-8723
Emp Here 30
SIC 8211 Elementary and secondary schools

D-U-N-S 20-024-4726   (BR)
NORTH OKANAGAN SHUSWAP SCHOOL DISTRICT 83
PLEASANT VALLEY SECONDARY SCHOOL
2365 Pleasant Valley Rd, Armstrong, BC, V0E 1B2
(250) 546-3114
Emp Here 80
SIC 8211 Elementary and secondary schools

D-U-N-S 25-100-2846   (BR)
NORTH OKANAGAN SHUSWAP SCHOOL DISTRICT 83
LEN WOOD MIDDLE SCHOOL
3700 Patten Dr, Armstrong, BC, V0E 1B2
(250) 546-3476
Emp Here 40
SIC 8211 Elementary and secondary schools

D-U-N-S 24-373-6303   (HQ)
ROGERS FOODS LTD
4420 Larkin Cross Rd, Armstrong, BC, V0E 1B6
(250) 546-8744
Emp Here 70   *Emp Total* 6,324
Sales 109,441,050
SIC 2041 Flour and other grain mill products
Pr Pr Victor Bell
Dir Arthur Hara
  Robert Banno
VP Joe Girdner

Brent Henderson

D-U-N-S 24-207-5682   (BR)
TOLKO INDUSTRIES LTD
844 Otter Lake Cross Rd, Armstrong, BC, V0E 1B6
(250) 546-3171
Emp Here 550
SIC 2421 Sawmills and planing mills, general

Ashcroft, BC V0K
Thompson - Nicola County

D-U-N-S 25-216-8679   (BR)
ARROW TRANSPORTATION SYSTEMS INC
925 Mesa Vista Dr, Ashcroft, BC, V0K 1A0
(250) 453-9411
Emp Here 20
SIC 4212 Local trucking, without storage

D-U-N-S 20-015-8660   (BR)
I.G. MACHINE & FIBERS LTD
3745 Barnes Lake Rd, Ashcroft, BC, V0K 1A0
(250) 453-9015
Emp Here 50
SIC 3444 Sheet Metalwork

D-U-N-S 25-481-5228   (BR)
INTERIOR HEALTH AUTHORITY
ASHCROFT HOSPITAL AND COMMUNITY HEALTH CARE CENTRE
700 Elm St, Ashcroft, BC, V0K 1A0
(250) 453-2211
Emp Here 60
SIC 8062 General medical and surgical hospitals

D-U-N-S 20-294-2967   (SL)
KOPPERS ASHCROFT INC
1425 Evans Rd, Ashcroft, BC, V0K 1A0
(250) 453-2221
Emp Here 40   *Sales* 4,377,642
SIC 3312 Blast furnaces and steel mills

D-U-N-S 20-590-8432   (BR)
SCHOOL DISTRICT #74 (GOLD TRAIL)
ASHCROFT SECONDARY SCHOOL
435 Ranch Rd, Ashcroft, BC, V0K 1A0
(250) 453-9144
Emp Here 20
SIC 8211 Elementary and secondary schools

D-U-N-S 20-713-2874   (BR)
SCHOOL DISTRICT #74 (GOLD TRAIL)
GOLD TRAIL LEARNING PROGRAM
711 Hill St, Ashcroft, BC, V0K 1A0
(250) 453-9050
Emp Here 50
SIC 8211 Elementary and secondary schools

Atlin, BC V0W
Stikine Region County

D-U-N-S 20-572-4342   (BR)
BRITISH COLUMBIA HYDRO AND POWER AUTHORITY
BC HYDRO
Main St, Atlin, BC, V0W 1A0
(250) 651-7526
Emp Here 20
SIC 4911 Electric services

Baldonnel, BC V0C
Peace River - Laird County

D-U-N-S 20-026-8618   (BR)
SCHOOL DISTRICT NO. 60 (PEACE RIVER NORTH)
BALDONNEL ELEMENTARY SCHOOL

5836 Baldonnel Rd, Baldonnel, BC, V0C 1C6
(250) 789-3396
Emp Here 20
SIC 8211 Elementary and secondary schools

Balfour, BC V0G
Central Kootenay County

D-U-N-S 24-312-1972   (BR)
WESTERN PACIFIC MARINE LTD
7721 Upper Balfour Rd, Balfour, BC, V0G 1C0
(250) 229-5650
Emp Here 60
SIC 4482 Ferries

Bamfield, BC V0R
Alberni - Clayoquot County

D-U-N-S 24-787-0652   (BR)
UNIVERSITY OF BRITISH COLUMBIA, THE
WESTERN CANADIAN UNIVERSITIES MARINE SCIENCES SOCIETY
100 Pachena Rd, Bamfield, BC, V0R 1B0
(250) 728-3301
Emp Here 40
SIC 8733 Noncommercial research organizations

Barriere, BC V0E
Thompson - Nicola County

D-U-N-S 25-316-5344   (BR)
BLACK PRESS GROUP LTD
NORTH THOMPSON STAR JOURNAL
359 Borthwick Ave, Barriere, BC, V0E 1E0
(250) 672-5611
Emp Here 25
SIC 2711 Newspapers

D-U-N-S 20-975-5169   (BR)
SCHOOL DISTRICT 73 (KAMLOOPS/THOMPSON)
BARRIERE SECONDARY SCHOOL
845 Barriere Town, Barriere, BC, V0E 1E0
(250) 672-9943
Emp Here 20
SIC 8211 Elementary and secondary schools

D-U-N-S 20-713-2635   (BR)
SCHOOL DISTRICT 73 (KAMLOOPS/THOMPSON)
BARRIERE ELEMENTARY SCHOOL
4475 Airfield Rd, Barriere, BC, V0E 1E0
(250) 672-9916
Emp Here 30
SIC 8211 Elementary and secondary schools

Bear Lake, BC V0J
Fraser-Fort George County

D-U-N-S 24-824-3222   (BR)
CANADIAN FOREST PRODUCTS LTD
POLAR, DIV
36654 Hart Hwy, Bear Lake, BC, V0J 3G0
(250) 972-4700
Emp Here 140
SIC 2421 Sawmills and planing mills, general

Bella Bella, BC V0T
Central Coast County

D-U-N-S 24-071-8346   (SL)
BELLA BELLA COMMUNITY SCHOOL SO-

CIETY
Gd, Bella Bella, BC, V0T 1Z0
(250) 957-2323
Emp Here 60   *Sales* 4,012,839
SIC 8211 Elementary and secondary schools

D-U-N-S 24-337-1395   (BR)
VANCOUVER COASTAL HEALTH AUTHOR-ITY
LARGE, RW MEMORIAL HOSPITAL
Gd, Bella Bella, BC, V0T 1Z0
(250) 957-2314
Emp Here 50
SIC 8051 Skilled nursing care facilities

Bella Coola, BC V0T
Central Coast County

D-U-N-S 20-591-4299   (BR)
SCHOOL DISTRICT 49 CENTRAL COAST
BELLA COOLA ELEMENTARY SCHOOL
(*Suby of* School District 49 Central Coast)
808 Mackay St, Bella Coola, BC, V0T 1C0
(250) 799-5556
Emp Here 25
SIC 8211 Elementary and secondary schools

Black Creek, BC V9J
Comox - Strathcona County

D-U-N-S 25-485-7840   (BR)
SCHOOL DISTRICT NO. 71 (COMOX VAL-LEY)
MIRACLE BEACH ELEMENTARY SCHOOL
8763 Paulsen Rd, Black Creek, BC, V9J 1J8
(250) 337-5114
Emp Here 20
SIC 8211 Elementary and secondary schools

Blue River, BC V0E
Thompson - Nicola County

D-U-N-S 20-573-3210   (BR)
COMPAGNIE DES CHEMINS DE FER NA-TIONAUX DU CANADA
7876 Hwy 5, Blue River, BC, V0E 1J0
(250) 828-6376
Emp Here 20
SIC 4011 Railroads, line-haul operating

Bowen Island, BC V0N
Greater Vancouver County

D-U-N-S 20-075-4393   (BR)
SCHOOL DISTRICT NO. 45 (WEST VAN-COUVER)
BOWEN ISLAND ELEMENTARY SCHOOL
1041 Mount Gardner Rd, Bowen Island, BC, V0N 1G2
(604) 947-9337
Emp Here 35
SIC 8211 Elementary and secondary schools

Bowser, BC V0R
Nanaimo County

D-U-N-S 25-111-2306   (BR)
SCHOOL DISTRICT NO 69 (QUALICUM)
BOWSER ELEMENTARY SCHOOL
4830 Faye Rd, Bowser, BC, V0R 1G0
(250) 757-8487
Emp Here 24

SIC 8211 Elementary and secondary schools

Brackendale, BC V0N
Squamish - Lillooet County

D-U-N-S 24-454-9135   (BR)
SCHOOL DISTRICT NO. 44 (NORTH VAN-COUVER)
NORTH VANCOUVER OUTDOOR SCHOOL
(*Suby of* School District No. 44 (North Van-couver))
2 Paradise Valley Rd, Brackendale, BC, V0N 1H0
(604) 898-5422
Emp Here 29
SIC 8299 Schools and educational services, nec

D-U-N-S 20-034-2611   (BR)
SCHOOL DISTRICT NO. 48 (HOWE SOUND)
BRACKENDALE ELEMENTARY SCHOOL
42000 Government Rd, Brackendale, BC, V0N 1H0
(604) 898-3651
Emp Here 32
SIC 8211 Elementary and secondary schools

D-U-N-S 20-043-6553   (BR)
SCHOOL DISTRICT NO. 48 (HOWE SOUND)
DON ROSS MIDDLE SCHOOL
42091 Ross Rd, Brackendale, BC, V0N 1H0
(604) 898-3671
Emp Here 35
SIC 8211 Elementary and secondary schools

Brentwood Bay, BC V8M
Capital County

D-U-N-S 20-650-1178   (SL)
BRENTWOOD BAY LODGE LTD
BRENTWOOD BAY RESORT & SPA
849 Verdier Ave, Brentwood Bay, BC, V8M 1C5
(250) 544-2079
Emp Here 90   *Sales* 2,991,389
SIC 7991 Physical fitness facilities

D-U-N-S 20-713-5612   (BR)
SCHOOL DISTRICT 63 (SAANICH)
BRENTWOOD ELEMENTARY SCHOOL
7085 Wallace Dr, Brentwood Bay, BC, V8M 1P9
(250) 652-3996
Emp Here 30
SIC 8211 Elementary and secondary schools

D-U-N-S 20-015-5583   (BR)
SCHOOL DISTRICT 63 (SAANICH)
BAYSIDE MIDDLE SCHOOL
1101 Newton Pl, Brentwood Bay, BC, V8M 1G3
(250) 652-1135
Emp Here 75
SIC 8211 Elementary and secondary schools

Buick, BC V0C
Peace River - Laird County

D-U-N-S 20-713-5380   (BR)
SCHOOL DISTRICT NO. 60 (PEACE RIVER NORTH)
BUICK CREEK ELEMENTARY & JUNIOR SECONDARY SCHOOL
15263 Buick Ck, Buick, BC, V0C 2R0
(250) 630-2231
Emp Here 50
SIC 8211 Elementary and secondary schools

Burnaby, BC V3J
Greater Vancouver County

D-U-N-S 20-591-2210   (BR)
BURNABY SCHOOL BOARD DISTRICT 41
LINDHURST ELEMENTARY SCHOOL
9847 Lyndhurst St, Burnaby, BC, V3J 1E9
(604) 664-8751
Emp Here 25
SIC 8211 Elementary and secondary schools

D-U-N-S 20-654-2008   (BR)
BURNABY SCHOOL BOARD DISTRICT 41
CAMERON ELEMENTARY SCHOOL
9540 Erickson Dr, Burnaby, BC, V3J 1M9

Emp Here 40
SIC 8211 Elementary and secondary schools

D-U-N-S 20-591-2202   (BR)
BURNABY SCHOOL BOARD DISTRICT 41
BURNABY MOUNTAIN SECONDARY SCHOOL
8800 Eastlake Dr, Burnaby, BC, V3J 7X5

Emp Here 150
SIC 8211 Elementary and secondary schools

D-U-N-S 24-337-3417   (BR)
FGL SPORTS LTD
SPORT-CHEK LOUGHEED MALL
9855 Austin Rd Unit 102, Burnaby, BC, V3J 1N4
(604) 415-5150
Emp Here 40
SIC 5941 Sporting goods and bicycle shops

D-U-N-S 20-860-5654   (BR)
GLENTEL INC
WIRELESS WAVES
9855 Austin Rd Suite 218, Burnaby, BC, V3J 1N4
(604) 444-9283
Emp Here 25
SIC 4813 Telephone communication, except radio

D-U-N-S 20-197-1020   (BR)
LONDON DRUGS LIMITED
PHOTO & ELECTRONICS
9855 Austin Rd Unit 101, Burnaby, BC, V3J 1N4
(604) 448-4825
Emp Here 20
SIC 5912 Drug stores and proprietary stores

D-U-N-S 25-318-1820   (BR)
MCDONALD'S RESTAURANTS OF CANADA LIMITED
MCDONALD'S RESTAURANTS OF CANADA LIMITED
(*Suby of* McDonald's Corporation)
9855 Austin Rd Unit 300, Burnaby, BC, V3J 1N5
(604) 718-1140
Emp Here 40
SIC 5812 Eating places

D-U-N-S 24-535-0996   (SL)
RED ROBIN RESTAURANT (BURNABY) LTD
9628 Cameron St, Burnaby, BC, V3J 1M2
(604) 421-7266
Emp Here 70   *Sales* 2,512,128
SIC 5812 Eating places

D-U-N-S 20-059-0128   (BR)
SEARS CANADA INC
SEARS OUTLET STORE
9850 Austin Rd, Burnaby, BC, V3J 7B3

Emp Here 80
SIC 5311 Department stores

D-U-N-S 25-271-6931   (BR)
SOBEYS WEST INC

SAFEWAY PHARMACY
9855 Austin Rd, Burnaby, BC, V3J 1N4
(604) 420-8091
Emp Here 125
SIC 5411 Grocery stores

D-U-N-S 20-506-0879   (BR)
STARBUCKS COFFEE CANADA, INC
STARBUCKS
(*Suby of* Starbucks Corporation)
9855 Austin Rd Suite 215a, Burnaby, BC, V3J 1N4
(604) 415-5336
Emp Here 20
SIC 5812 Eating places

D-U-N-S 25-730-9633   (BR)
WAL-MART CANADA CORP
9855 Austin Rd Suite 300, Burnaby, BC, V3J 1N5
(604) 421-0661
Emp Here 325
SIC 5311 Department stores

D-U-N-S 20-997-2061   (BR)
WEST 49 GROUP INC
OFF THE WALL
9855 Austin Rd Suite 248, Burnaby, BC, V3J 1N4
(604) 420-8778
Emp Here 20
SIC 5651 Family clothing stores

D-U-N-S 25-663-1367   (BR)
WHITE SPOT LIMITED
WHITE SPOT RESTAURANT
4075 North Rd, Burnaby, BC, V3J 1S3
(604) 421-4620
Emp Here 75
SIC 5812 Eating places

Burnaby, BC V3N
Greater Vancouver County

D-U-N-S 25-415-9304   (HQ)
406106 ALBERTA INC
AM PM SERVICE
(*Suby of* 675843 Alberta Inc)
6741 Cariboo Rd Suite 101, Burnaby, BC, V3N 4A3
(604) 421-5677
Emp Here 40   *Emp Total* 200
Sales 27,360,263
SIC 5044 Office equipment
Pr Pr John Chan
Dir Karen Chan
Dir Kathy Lau
Dir Ken Tjia

D-U-N-S 24-996-2135   (HQ)
429149 B.C. LTD
QUILTS ETC
8168 Glenwood Dr, Burnaby, BC, V3N 5E9
(604) 549-2000
Emp Here 35   *Emp Total* 250
Sales 30,862,376
SIC 5719 Miscellaneous homefurnishings
Pr Pr Howard Haugom
Jixin Xu

D-U-N-S 20-108-4274   (HQ)
A.B.C. RECYCLING LTD
(*Suby of* A.B.C. Holdings Ltd)
8081 Meadow Ave, Burnaby, BC, V3N 2V9
(604) 522-9727
Emp Here 20   *Emp Total* 60
Sales 28,846,158
SIC 5093 Scrap and waste materials
Genl Mgr David Yochlowitz
Pr Pr Harold Yochlowitz
Sec Melvyn Yochlowitz
 Dirk Odenwald

D-U-N-S 24-000-8800   (BR)
BLACK PRESS GROUP LTD

VANPRESS PRINTERS
8325 Riverbend Crt, Burnaby, BC, V3N 5E7
(604) 636-8020
Emp Here 60
SIC 2711 Newspapers

D-U-N-S 25-756-9939   (BR)
BURNABY SCHOOL BOARD DISTRICT 41
ARMSTRONG ELEMENTARY SCHOOL
8757 Armstrong Ave, Burnaby, BC, V3N 2H8

Emp Here 50
SIC 8211 Elementary and secondary schools

D-U-N-S 20-591-2178   (BR)
BURNABY SCHOOL BOARD DISTRICT 41
STRIDE AVENUE COMMUNITY SCHOOL
7014 Stride Ave, Burnaby, BC, V3N 1T4
(604) 527-0444
Emp Here 50
SIC 8211 Elementary and secondary schools

D-U-N-S 20-026-9095   (BR)
BURNABY SCHOOL BOARD DISTRICT 41
TWELFTH AVENUE ELEMENTARY SCHOOL
7622 12th Ave, Burnaby, BC, V3N 2K1

Emp Here 40
SIC 8211 Elementary and secondary schools

D-U-N-S 24-513-7273   (BR)
BURNABY SCHOOL BOARD DISTRICT 41
BYRNE CREEK SECONDARY SCHOOL
7777 18th St, Burnaby, BC, V3N 5E5

Emp Here 85
SIC 8211 Elementary and secondary schools

D-U-N-S 20-875-3934   (BR)
BURNABY SCHOOL BOARD DISTRICT 41
CARIBOO HILL SECONDARY SCHOOL
8580 16th Ave, Burnaby, BC, V3N 1S6

Emp Here 80
SIC 8211 Elementary and secondary schools

D-U-N-S 20-026-9087   (BR)
BURNABY SCHOOL BOARD DISTRICT 41
EDMONDS COMMUNITY SCHOOL
7651 18th Ave, Burnaby, BC, V3N 1J1

Emp Here 50
SIC 8211 Elementary and secondary schools

D-U-N-S 20-713-4508   (BR)
BURNABY SCHOOL BOARD DISTRICT 41
TAYLOR PARK ELEMENTARY SCHOOL
7590 Mission Ave, Burnaby, BC, V3N 5C7
(604) 664-8226
Emp Here 50
SIC 8211 Elementary and secondary schools

D-U-N-S 20-026-9103   (BR)
BURNABY SCHOOL BOARD DISTRICT 41
SECOND STREET COMMUNITY SCHOOL
7502 2nd St, Burnaby, BC, V3N 3R5
(604) 664-8819
Emp Here 45
SIC 8211 Elementary and secondary schools

D-U-N-S 20-512-9005   (SL)
CHRISTMAS NATURAL FOODS (WHOLE-SALERS) LTD
5589 Trapp Ave App Ave, Burnaby, BC, V3N 0B2
(604) 524-9964
Emp Here 20   Sales 1,094,411
SIC 5499 Miscellaneous food stores

D-U-N-S 25-011-1432   (BR)
CLARKE TRANSPORT INC
CLARKE TRANSPORT
8246 Willard St, Burnaby, BC, V3N 4S2
(604) 526-4499
Emp Here 60
SIC 4213 Trucking, except local

D-U-N-S 25-012-0185   (HQ)

ENVIROTEST SYSTEMS (B.C.) LTD
ENVIROTEST CANADA
(Suby of Envirotest Systems (B.C.) Ltd)
6741 Cariboo Rd Suite 207, Burnaby, BC, V3N 4A3
(604) 436-2640
Emp Here 50   Emp Total 250
Sales 12,111,476
SIC 7389 Business services, nec
 Edward R. Theobald
 Daniel Jennings

D-U-N-S 24-419-8276   (SL)
GENERAL FUSION INC
3680 Bonneville Pl Suite 106, Burnaby, BC, V3N 4T5
(604) 420-0920
Emp Here 60   Sales 3,283,232
SIC 8731 Commercial physical research

D-U-N-S 20-725-5519   (BR)
GULF AND FRASER FISHERMEN'S CREDIT UNION
G&F FINANCIAL GROUP
7375 Kingsway, Burnaby, BC, V3N 3B5
(604) 419-8888
Emp Here 175
SIC 6062 State credit unions

D-U-N-S 24-826-0247   (BR)
JFC INTERNATIONAL (CANADA) INC
8289 North Fraser Way Suite 102, Burnaby, BC, V3N 0B9
(604) 521-7556
Emp Here 20
SIC 5141 Groceries, general line

D-U-N-S 20-315-4919   (SL)
NEMO PRODUCTIONS - CAN, INC
8035 Glenwood Dr, Burnaby, BC, V3N 5C8

Emp Here 700   Sales 119,755,200
SIC 7829 Motion picture distribution services
 Arthur Evrensel
Dir John Martin Willhite

D-U-N-S 20-800-5926   (SL)
NORWEGIAN OLD PEOPLE'S HOME AS-SOCIATION
NORMANNA REST HOME
7725 4th St, Burnaby, BC, V3N 5B6
(604) 522-5812
Emp Here 100   Sales 3,648,035
SIC 8361 Residential care

D-U-N-S 24-132-6763   (BR)
PIONEER COMMUNITY LIVING ASSOCIA-TION
MILLERS WAY
7710 15th Ave, Burnaby, BC, V3N 1W5
(604) 526-9316
Emp Here 20
SIC 8093 Specialty outpatient clinics, nec

D-U-N-S 25-800-3433   (BR)
ROMAN CATHOLIC ARCHDIOCESE OF VANCOUVER, THE
ST THOMAS MORE COLLEGIATE
(Suby of Roman Catholic Archdiocese of Van-couver, The)
7450 12th Ave, Burnaby, BC, V3N 2K1
(604) 521-1801
Emp Here 45
SIC 8211 Elementary and secondary schools

D-U-N-S 25-809-6056   (BR)
ROMAN CATHOLIC ARCHDIOCESE OF VANCOUVER, THE
OUR LADY OF MERCY SCHOOL
(Suby of Roman Catholic Archdiocese of Van-couver, The)
7481 10th Ave, Burnaby, BC, V3N 2S1
(604) 526-7121
Emp Here 20
SIC 8211 Elementary and secondary schools

D-U-N-S 24-000-5368   (BR)
SHOPPERS HOME HEALTH CARE

(CANADA) INC
SHOPPERS HOME HEALTH CARE
8289 North Fraser Way Suite 101, Burnaby, BC, V3N 0B9
(778) 328-8300
Emp Here 40
SIC 7699 Repair services, nec

D-U-N-S 24-120-6028   (SL)
SNOW CAP ENTERPRISES LTD
5698 Trapp Ave Suite 564, Burnaby, BC, V3N 5G4
(604) 515-3202
Emp Here 130   Sales 4,450,603
SIC 5461 Retail bakeries

D-U-N-S 20-003-7443   (BR)
SOBEYS WEST INC
7650 18th St, Burnaby, BC, V3N 4K3
(604) 524-4491
Emp Here 20
SIC 2026 Fluid milk

D-U-N-S 25-999-7450   (BR)
UPPER CANADA FOREST PRODUCTS LTD
UPPER CANADA
5768 Trapp Ave App Ave, Burnaby, BC, V3N 5G4
(604) 522-3334
Emp Here 30
SIC 5031 Lumber, plywood, and millwork

D-U-N-S 25-985-6524   (BR)
VALUE VILLAGE STORES, INC
VALUE VILLAGE STORE 24
(Suby of Savers, Inc.)
7350 Edmonds St, Burnaby, BC, V3N 1A8
(604) 540-4066
Emp Here 40
SIC 5399 Miscellaneous general merchandise

D-U-N-S 24-027-8205   (BR)
WFG SECURITIES OF CANADA INC
WORLD FINANCIAL GROUP INSURANCE AGENCY OF CANADA
7501 6th St, Burnaby, BC, V3N 3M2

Emp Here 20
SIC 8742 Management consulting services

D-U-N-S 25-734-1412   (BR)
WESTERN WAFFLES CORP
7018 14th Ave, Burnaby, BC, V3N 1Z2
(604) 524-2540
Emp Here 70
SIC 2052 Cookies and crackers

D-U-N-S 24-227-4413   (HQ)
WESTKEY GRAPHICS LTD
KEYSTONE BUSINESS FORMS
(Suby of Westkey Graphics Ltd)
8315 Riverbend Crt, Burnaby, BC, V3N 5E7
(604) 549-2350
Emp Here 112   Emp Total 137
Sales 13,860,016
SIC 5943 Stationery stores
Pr Alfie Karmal
VP Fin Greg Don
Dir Robert Tite
Treas Donald Klein

Burnaby, BC V5A
Greater Vancouver County

D-U-N-S 24-343-2023   (SL)
0725671 B.C. LTD
3600 Bainbridge Ave, Burnaby, BC, V5A 4X2
(604) 606-1903
Emp Here 45   Sales 6,674,880
SIC 6712 Bank holding companies
Pr Stuart Mclauglin

D-U-N-S 24-773-0224   (BR)
ALS CANADA LTD
ALS ENVIRONMENTAL

8081 Lougheed Hwy Suite 100, Burnaby, BC, V5A 1W9
(778) 370-3150
Emp Here 200
SIC 8071 Medical laboratories

D-U-N-S 24-366-0847   (HQ)
AECOM CANADA LTD
3292 Production Way, Burnaby, BC, V5A 4R4
(604) 444-6400
Emp Here 100   Emp Total 87,000
Sales 595,894,063
SIC 8742 Management consulting services
Pr Tom Bishop
 Bob Foran
Ex VP Doug Allingham
 Nathan Schauerte

D-U-N-S 20-183-7585   (BR)
AQUATERRA CORPORATION
POLARIS WATER CO, DIV OF
3600 Bainbridge Ave, Burnaby, BC, V5A 4X2
(604) 606-1903
Emp Here 55
SIC 5149 Groceries and related products, nec

D-U-N-S 24-314-6052   (SL)
BOLD EVENT CREATIVE INC
7570 Conrad St, Burnaby, BC, V5A 2H7
(604) 437-7677
Emp Here 50   Sales 4,231,721
SIC 3999 Manufacturing industries, nec

D-U-N-S 25-011-1309   (BR)
BRICK WAREHOUSE LP, THE
BRICK, THE
3100 Production Way Suite 103, Burnaby, BC, V5A 4R4
(604) 415-4900
Emp Here 300
SIC 5712 Furniture stores

D-U-N-S 20-713-4409   (BR)
BURNABY SCHOOL BOARD DISTRICT 41
SEAFORTH ELEMENTARY SCHOOL
7881 Government Rd, Burnaby, BC, V5A 2C9

Emp Here 50
SIC 8211 Elementary and secondary schools

D-U-N-S 20-713-4383   (BR)
BURNABY SCHOOL BOARD DISTRICT 41
MONTECITO ELEMENTARY SCHOOL
2176 Duthie Ave, Burnaby, BC, V5A 2S2
(604) 664-8766
Emp Here 25
SIC 8211 Elementary and secondary schools

D-U-N-S 20-713-4466   (BR)
BURNABY SCHOOL BOARD DISTRICT 41
FOREST GROVE ELEMENTARY SCHOOL
8525 Forest Grove Dr, Burnaby, BC, V5A 4H5

Emp Here 35
SIC 8211 Elementary and secondary schools

D-U-N-S 24-514-5144   (BR)
CANADIAN UTILITY CONSTRUCTION CORP
(Suby of Quanta Services, Inc.)
7950 Venture St, Burnaby, BC, V5A 1V3
(604) 415-3463
Emp Here 80
SIC 1623 Water, sewer, and utility lines

D-U-N-S 25-095-9707   (BR)
CANPAR TRANSPORT L.P.
(Suby of Canpar Transport L.P.)
8399 Eastlake Dr, Burnaby, BC, V5A 4W2
(604) 421-3452
Emp Here 110
SIC 4731 Freight transportation arrangement

D-U-N-S 20-515-7154   (BR)
CARDINAL HEALTH CANADA INC
(Suby of Cardinal Health, Inc.)
8590 Baxter Pl, Burnaby, BC, V5A 4T2

(604) 421-8588
Emp Here 30
SIC 3845 Electromedical equipment

D-U-N-S 24-678-6409   (BR)
CORUS MEDIA HOLDINGS INC
SHAW MEDIA INC
7850 Enterprise St, Burnaby, BC, V5A 1V7
(604) 420-2288
Emp Here 20
SIC 4833 Television broadcasting stations

D-U-N-S 25-195-5886   (BR)
COSTCO WHOLESALE CANADA LTD
(*Suby of* Costco Wholesale Corporation)
3550 Brighton Ave Suite 51, Burnaby, BC, V5A 4W3
(604) 420-2668
Emp Here 250
SIC 5099 Durable goods, nec

D-U-N-S 20-918-8978   (HQ)
DOLPHIN DELIVERY LTD
DOLPHIN TRANSPORT
(*Suby of* Dolphin Delivery (1985) Ltd)
4201 Lozells Ave, Burnaby, BC, V5A 2Z4
(604) 421-1115
Emp Here 100   *Emp Total* 450
Sales 19,772,350
SIC 4212 Local trucking, without storage
Pr Pr William Morris Peter

D-U-N-S 24-957-6679   (SL)
DOLPHIN DISTRIBUTION LTD
(*Suby of* Dolphin Delivery (1985) Ltd)
4201 Lozells Ave, Burnaby, BC, V5A 2Z4
(604) 421-7059
Emp Here 50   *Sales* 9,054,720
SIC 4212 Local trucking, without storage
Pr Pr William Morris Peter

D-U-N-S 20-111-0822   (BR)
ECCO HEATING PRODUCTS LTD
ECCO SUPPLY
7959 Enterprise St, Burnaby, BC, V5A 1V5
(604) 420-4323
Emp Here 35
SIC 5075 Warm air heating and air conditioning

D-U-N-S 25-012-2306   (BR)
GE MULTILIN
(*Suby of* General Electric Company)
8525 Baxter Pl Suite 100, Burnaby, BC, V5A 4V7
(604) 421-8700
Emp Here 40
SIC 5065 Electronic parts and equipment, nec

D-U-N-S 24-124-7837   (BR)
GENERAL ELECTRIC CANADA COMPANY
GE HEALTHCARE
(*Suby of* General Electric Company)
8525 Baxter Pl Suite 100, Burnaby, BC, V5A 4V7
(604) 451-3200
Emp Here 20
SIC 5047 Medical and hospital equipment

D-U-N-S 24-370-4033   (HQ)
GOLDEN BOY FOODS LTD
GOLDEN BOY
7725 Lougheed Hwy, Burnaby, BC, V5A 4V8
(604) 433-2200
Emp Here 220   *Emp Total* 8,700
Sales 46,767,809
SIC 2068 Salted and roasted nuts and seeds
CEO Paul Henderson
VP Opers Ali Rezaei
  Brian Irving
VP Gord Love

D-U-N-S 20-554-0250   (BR)
GOLDEN BOY FOODS LTD
3151 Lake City Way, Burnaby, BC, V5A 3A3
(604) 421-4500
Emp Here 200
SIC 4226 Special warehousing and storage,

nec

D-U-N-S 24-797-2235   (SL)
HAZMASTERS ENVIRONMENTAL CONTROLS INC
3131 Underhill Ave, Burnaby, BC, V5A 3C8
(604) 420-0025
Emp Here 40   *Sales* 10,145,000
SIC 5084 Industrial machinery and equipment
Pr Pr Randal Myers
  Thomas Bowen

D-U-N-S 24-135-3887   (HQ)
HITCHCO DISTRIBUTORS LTD
HITCH COMPANY, THE
(*Suby of* Hitchco Distributors Ltd)
7832 Enterprise St, Burnaby, BC, V5A 1V7

Emp Here 25   *Emp Total* 40
Sales 6,313,604
SIC 5013 Motor vehicle supplies and new parts
Pr Pr Glyn Evans

D-U-N-S 24-994-9991   (BR)
IMPERIAL OIL LIMITED
ESSO PETROLEUM
(*Suby of* Exxon Mobil Corporation)
3100 Underhill Ave, Burnaby, BC, V5A 3C6
(604) 444-7700
Emp Here 40
SIC 2911 Petroleum refining

D-U-N-S 25-385-7841   (BR)
KEYCORP INC
OPTIMAL SEVICES GROUP
7860 Venture St, Burnaby, BC, V5A 1V3
(604) 325-1252
Emp Here 30
SIC 7378 Computer maintenance and repair

D-U-N-S 20-733-8513   (BR)
KEYSTONE AUTOMOTIVE INDUSTRIES ON INC
CROSS CANADA
7069 Winston St, Burnaby, BC, V5A 2G7
(604) 420-6988
Emp Here 25
SIC 5013 Motor vehicle supplies and new parts

D-U-N-S 24-930-5442   (HQ)
MICROSEMI STORAGE SOLUTIONS LTD
MICROSEMI ISRAEL STORAGE SOLUTIONS
8555 Baxter Pl Suite 105, Burnaby, BC, V5A 4V7
(604) 415-6000
Emp Here 300   *Emp Total* 4,400
Sales 167,152,964
SIC 3661 Telephone and telegraph apparatus
Pr Jim Peterson
VP Gregory Aasen

D-U-N-S 20-699-7145   (BR)
NORDION INC
MDS LABORATORIES, DIV OF
8590 Baxter Pl, Burnaby, BC, V5A 4T2
(604) 421-8588
Emp Here 25
SIC 8071 Medical laboratories

D-U-N-S 24-373-0939   (BR)
NOVADAQ TECHNOLOGIES INC
8329 Eastlake Dr Unit 101, Burnaby, BC, V5A 4W2
(604) 232-9861
Emp Here 80
SIC 8731 Commercial physical research

D-U-N-S 25-369-9094   (BR)
OMSTEAD FOODS LIMITED
SNOWCREST PACKERS
3676 Bainbridge Ave, Burnaby, BC, V5A 2T4

Emp Here 35
SIC 2037 Frozen fruits and vegetables

D-U-N-S 20-061-4497   (BR)
OPTIQUE NIKON CANADA INC
NIKON OPTICAL CANADA INC
2999 Underhill Ave Unit 103, Burnaby, BC, V5A 3C2
(604) 713-7400
Emp Here 25
SIC 5995 Optical goods stores

D-U-N-S 24-367-9433   (BR)
OWEN & COMPANY LIMITED
KINGSDOWN CANADA
8651 Eastlake Dr, Burnaby, BC, V5A 4T7
(604) 421-9203
Emp Here 20
SIC 5712 Furniture stores

D-U-N-S 25-013-1471   (BR)
P.S. PRODUCTION SERVICES LTD
P S PRODUCTION SERVICES
8301 Eastlake Dr, Burnaby, BC, V5A 4W2
(604) 434-4008
Emp Here 30
SIC 7819 Services allied to motion pictures

D-U-N-S 24-819-9734   (BR)
PATTISON, JIM INDUSTRIES LTD
NESTERS MARKET
9000 University High St, Burnaby, BC, V5A 0C1
(604) 298-1522
Emp Here 50
SIC 5411 Grocery stores

D-U-N-S 20-358-7399   (SL)
PEREGRINE PLASTICS LTD
PEREGRINE RETAIL DESIGN MANUFACTURING
3131 Production Way, Burnaby, BC, V5A 3H1
(604) 251-3174
Emp Here 50   *Sales* 3,356,192
SIC 2541 Wood partitions and fixtures

D-U-N-S 20-621-3571   (HQ)
PICO OF CANADA LTD
(*Suby of* Pico of Canada Ltd)
7590 Conrad St, Burnaby, BC, V5A 2H7
(604) 438-7571
Emp Here 22   *Emp Total* 44
Sales 5,326,131
SIC 5013 Motor vehicle supplies and new parts
Pr Pr Ron Grieve
  Monica Grosser

D-U-N-S 24-899-6373   (BR)
POSTMEDIA NETWORK INC
7850 Enterprise St, Burnaby, BC, V5A 1V7
(604) 420-2288
Emp Here 250
SIC 4833 Television broadcasting stations

D-U-N-S 25-131-5131   (BR)
POSTMEDIA NETWORK INC
BURNABY NOW
3430 Brighton Ave Suite 201a, Burnaby, BC, V5A 3H4
(604) 444-3451
Emp Here 45
SIC 2711 Newspapers

D-U-N-S 20-648-5851   (SL)
RECORD NEW WESTMINSTER, THE
RECORD, THE
3430 Brighton Ave Suite 201a, Burnaby, BC, V5A 3H4
(604) 444-3451
Emp Here 50   *Sales* 4,937,631
SIC 2711 Newspapers

D-U-N-S 20-213-4347   (BR)
SAPUTO PRODUITS LAITIERS CANADA S.E.N.C.
(*Suby of* Saputo Produits Laitiers Canada S.E.N.C.)
6800 Lougheed Hwy Suite 3, Burnaby, BC, V5A 1W2
(604) 420-6611
Emp Here 500

SIC 2023 Dry, condensed and evaporated dairy products

D-U-N-S 20-177-8151   (BR)
SEARS CANADA INC
2820 Underhill Ave, Burnaby, BC, V5A 0A2
(604) 415-9512
Emp Here 350
SIC 7389 Business services, nec

D-U-N-S 24-852-0947   (BR)
SIMON FRASER UNIVERSITY
TEACHING AND LEARNING CENTRE
8888 University Dr Suite Edb, Burnaby, BC, V5A 1S6
(778) 782-3910
Emp Here 43
SIC 8221 Colleges and universities

D-U-N-S 20-075-8865   (BR)
SIMON FRASER UNIVERSITY
PSYCHOLOGY DEPARTMENT
8888 University Dr Suite 3000, Burnaby, BC, V5A 1S6
(604) 291-3354
Emp Here 70
SIC 8742 Management consulting services

D-U-N-S 20-797-8610   (HQ)
SKY-HI SCAFFOLDING LTD
(*Suby of* Northstar Scaffold Services Inc)
3195 Production Way, Burnaby, BC, V5A 3H2
(604) 291-7245
Emp Here 35   *Emp Total* 250
Sales 6,128,699
SIC 1799 Special trade contractors, nec
Pr Pr Kevin Lottis
Sec Lynn Perlstrom
  James Johnson

D-U-N-S 20-109-2533   (HQ)
SULZER PUMPS (CANADA) INC
4129 Lozells Ave, Burnaby, BC, V5A 2Z5
(604) 415-7800
Emp Here 100   *Emp Total* 139
Sales 3,638,254
SIC 3561 Pumps and pumping equipment

D-U-N-S 20-116-4308   (HQ)
TARGET PRODUCTS LTD
QUIKRETE
8535 Eastlake Dr, Burnaby, BC, V5A 4T7
(604) 444-3620
Emp Here 30   *Emp Total* 150
Sales 36,209,292
SIC 3272 Concrete products, nec
Asst Cont Brenda Matthews
Pr Pr James Winchester
Dir John Winchester
Dir Dennis Winchester

D-U-N-S 24-339-6020   (BR)
TRANSPORT TFI 3 L.P.
HIGHLAND TRANSPORT
7867 Express St Suite 212, Burnaby, BC, V5A 1S7
(604) 415-9226
Emp Here 20
SIC 4213 Trucking, except local

D-U-N-S 24-346-4489   (BR)
TRANSPORT TFI 7 S.E.C
CANADIAN FREIGHTWAYS
7867 Express St, Burnaby, BC, V5A 1S7
(604) 420-2030
Emp Here 130
SIC 4213 Trucking, except local

D-U-N-S 20-427-0631   (BR)
UTC FIRE & SECURITY CANADA
EDWARDS PART OF GE SECURITY CANADA
(*Suby of* United Technologies Corporation)
7989 Enterprise St, Burnaby, BC, V5A 1V5
(604) 420-4436
Emp Here 40
SIC 5063 Electrical apparatus and equipment

D-U-N-S 20-588-0651   (HQ)
UNDERHILL GEOMATICS LTD
(*Suby of* Underhill Geomatics Ltd)
3430 Brighton Ave Suite 210a, Burnaby, BC,
V5A 3H4
(604) 687-6866
Emp Here 28   *Emp Total* 50
Sales 4,961,328
SIC 8713 Surveying services

D-U-N-S 20-116-1064   (BR)
UNI-SELECT INC
UNI-SELECT PACIFIC
8000 Winston St, Burnaby, BC, V5A 2H5

Emp Here 60
SIC 5013 Motor vehicle supplies and new
parts

D-U-N-S 24-390-1779   (BR)
VECIMA NETWORKS INC
*SPECTRUM SIGNAL PROCESSING BY
VECIMA*
2700 Production Way Suite 300, Burnaby, BC,
V5A 4X1
(604) 421-5422
Emp Here 50
SIC 7371 Custom computer programming services

D-U-N-S 24-776-6413   (BR)
**WESCLEAN EQUIPMENT & CLEANING
SUPPLIES LTD**
4082 Mcconnell Crt, Burnaby, BC, V5A 3L8
(604) 421-7150
Emp Here 25
SIC 5087 Service establishment equipment

D-U-N-S 20-735-6549   (BR)
WESTKEY GRAPHICS LTD
(*Suby of* Westkey Graphics Ltd)
3212 Lake City Way, Burnaby, BC, V5A 3A4
(604) 421-7778
Emp Here 120
SIC 5734 Computer and software stores

D-U-N-S 24-029-5030   (BR)
WILLIAM F. WHITE INTERNATIONAL INC
8363 Lougheed Hwy Unit 100, Burnaby, BC,
V5A 1X3
(604) 253-5050
Emp Here 40
SIC 7922 Theatrical producers and services

Burnaby, BC V5B
Greater Vancouver County

D-U-N-S 24-372-4283   (BR)
ALLMAR INC
ALLMAR INTERNATIONAL
3085 Norland Ave, Burnaby, BC, V5B 3A9
(604) 299-7531
Emp Here 30
SIC 5039 Construction materials, nec

D-U-N-S 25-677-1197   (BR)
ALLSTREAM BUSINESS INC
M T S ALL STREAM
6150 Lougheed Hwy, Burnaby, BC, V5B 2Z9
(604) 421-0505
Emp Here 25
SIC 5065 Electronic parts and equipment, nec

D-U-N-S 20-993-1203   (SL)
ANDERSON WATTS LTD
6336 Darnley St, Burnaby, BC, V5B 3B1
(604) 291-7751
Emp Here 35   *Sales* 9,120,088
SIC 5141 Groceries, general line
Pr Pr John Smithson
  Edward C. Anderson
  Thomas K. Watts

D-U-N-S 24-011-5001   (BR)
BD CANADA LTD

COBS BREAD
6558 Hastings St Unit 141, Burnaby, BC, V5B
1S2
(604) 205-6937
Emp Here 21
SIC 5461 Retail bakeries

D-U-N-S 20-713-4334   (BR)
BURNABY SCHOOL BOARD DISTRICT 41
BRENTWOOD PARK SCHOOL
1455 Delta Ave, Burnaby, BC, V5B 3G4

Emp Here 50
SIC 8211 Elementary and secondary schools

D-U-N-S 20-591-2038   (BR)
BURNABY SCHOOL BOARD DISTRICT 41
SPERLING ELEMENTARY SCHOOL
2200 Sperling Ave, Burnaby, BC, V5B 4K7

Emp Here 35
SIC 8211 Elementary and secondary schools

D-U-N-S 20-713-4326   (BR)
BURNABY SCHOOL BOARD DISTRICT 41
EXOL AUBURY ELEMETARY SCHOOL
1075 Stratford Ave, Burnaby, BC, V5B 3X9

Emp Here 50
SIC 8211 Elementary and secondary schools

D-U-N-S 25-013-1737   (BR)
BURNABY SCHOOL BOARD DISTRICT 41
PARKCREST ELEMENTARY SCHOOL
6055 Halifax St, Burnaby, BC, V5B 2P4
(604) 664-8794
Emp Here 25
SIC 8211 Elementary and secondary schools

D-U-N-S 20-713-4342   (BR)
BURNABY SCHOOL BOARD DISTRICT 41
CAPITOL HILL ELEMENTARY SCHOOL
350 Holdom Ave, Burnaby, BC, V5B 3V1
(604) 664-8637
Emp Here 50
SIC 8211 Elementary and secondary schools

D-U-N-S 20-591-2160   (BR)
BURNABY SCHOOL BOARD DISTRICT 41
LOCKDALE COMMUNITY SCHOOL
6990 Aubrey St, Burnaby, BC, V5B 2E5

Emp Here 40
SIC 8211 Elementary and secondary schools

D-U-N-S 20-713-4441   (BR)
BURNABY SCHOOL BOARD DISTRICT 41
WESTRIDGE ELEMENTARY SCHOOL
510 Duncan Ave, Burnaby, BC, V5B 4L9

Emp Here 50
SIC 8211 Elementary and secondary schools

D-U-N-S 25-011-9021   (BR)
BURNABY SCHOOL BOARD DISTRICT 41
BURNABY NORTH SECONDARY SCHOOL
751 Hammarskjold Dr Rm 115, Burnaby, BC,
V5B 4A1

Emp Here 200
SIC 8211 Elementary and secondary schools

D-U-N-S 24-682-9105   (HQ)
CASCADE AQUA-TECH LTD
(*Suby of* Cascade Aqua-Tech Ltd)
3215 Norland Ave Suite 100, Burnaby, BC,
V5B 3A9
(604) 291-6101
Emp Here 30   *Emp Total* 52
Sales 15,116,050
SIC 5169 Chemicals and allied products, nec
Pr David Metzler
Dir Ranada Pritchard
Dir Neil Pritchard

D-U-N-S 20-068-3402   (BR)
**CATHOLIC INDEPENDENT SCHOOLS OF
VANCOUVER ARCHDIOCESE, THE**

HOLY CROSS ELEMENTARY SCHOOL
1450 Delta Ave, Burnaby, BC, V5B 3G2
(604) 299-3530
Emp Here 20
SIC 8211 Elementary and secondary schools

D-U-N-S 25-702-9587   (BR)
CITY OF BURNABY
C.G. BROWN MEMORIAL POOL
3702 Kensington Ave, Burnaby, BC, V5B 4Z6
(604) 299-9374
Emp Here 30
SIC 7999 Amusement and recreation, nec

D-U-N-S 25-485-6552   (BR)
CITY OF BURNABY
COPELAND, BILL SPORTS CENTRE
3676 Kensington Ave, Burnaby, BC, V5B 4Z6
(604) 291-1261
Emp Here 50
SIC 7999 Amusement and recreation, nec

D-U-N-S 25-719-1585   (SL)
**D.S.R.F. DOWN SYNDROME RESEARCH
FOUNDATION**
DOWN SYNDROME RESEARCH FOUNDATION
1409 Sperling Ave, Burnaby, BC, V5B 4J8
(604) 444-3773
Emp Here 20   *Sales* 5,889,600
SIC 8322 Individual and family services
  Dan Lewin
Dir Jason Brooks
Dir George Klukas
  Joel Whittemore

D-U-N-S 24-695-0695   (BR)
GUILLEVIN INTERNATIONAL CIE
5344 Lougheed Hwy, Burnaby, BC, V5B 2Z8
(604) 438-8661
Emp Here 34
SIC 5063 Electrical apparatus and equipment

D-U-N-S 20-587-9406   (SL)
JONES FOOD STORE EQUIPMENT LTD
2896 Norland Ave, Burnaby, BC, V5B 3A6
(604) 294-6321
Emp Here 50   *Sales* 4,334,713
SIC 5078 Refrigeration equipment and supplies

D-U-N-S 24-322-3083   (BR)
LAFARGE CANADA INC
KASK BROS. READY MIX DIV OF
7500 Barnet Hwy, Burnaby, BC, V5B 2A9
(604) 294-3286
Emp Here 45
SIC 5999 Miscellaneous retail stores, nec

D-U-N-S 24-826-3506   (SL)
LEXSPAN LIMITED PARTNERSHIP
LNS SERVICES
3111 Norland Ave, Burnaby, BC, V5B 3A9
(604) 205-9600
Emp Here 20   *Sales* 2,425,503
SIC 1796 Installing building equipment

D-U-N-S 20-867-2451   (BR)
PENSKE TRUCK LEASING CANADA INC
(*Suby of* Penske Corporation)
2916 Norland Ave, Burnaby, BC, V5B 3A6
(604) 294-1351
Emp Here 45
SIC 7513 Truck rental and leasing, no drivers

D-U-N-S 24-492-7166   (HQ)
QUARTECH SYSTEMS LIMITED
(*Suby of* Quartech Systems Limited)
2160 Springer Ave Suite 200, Burnaby, BC,
V5B 3M7
(604) 291-9686
Emp Here 50   *Emp Total* 100
Sales 16,019,593
SIC 7371 Custom computer programming services
Pr Pr David Marshall
Dir Paul Huffington
  William O'brien

D-U-N-S 24-291-3374   (SL)
ROLLS-RIGHT INDUSTRIES LTD
ROLLS-RIGHT TRUCKING
2864 Norland Ave, Burnaby, BC, V5B 3A6
(604) 298-0077
Emp Here 53   *Sales* 2,991,389
SIC 4214 Local trucking with storage

D-U-N-S 25-691-8228   (BR)
ROYAL BANK OF CANADA
RBC
(*Suby of* Royal Bank Of Canada)
6570 Hastings St, Burnaby, BC, V5B 1S2
(604) 665-5925
Emp Here 30
SIC 6021 National commercial banks

D-U-N-S 20-183-5266   (SL)
**SANTAFIORA PIETRE INTERNATIONAL
INC**
5338 Goring St, Burnaby, BC, V5B 3A3
(604) 430-8037
Emp Here 20   *Sales* 5,782,650
SIC 5032 Brick, stone, and related material
Pr Pr Maurizio Grande
Dir Greg Charalambous
Dir Marco Guigobono

D-U-N-S 24-153-6341   (BR)
SHELL CANADA LIMITED
201 Kensington Ave, Burnaby, BC, V5B 4B2
(604) 298-2484
Emp Here 50
SIC 5172 Petroleum products, nec

D-U-N-S 25-003-6399   (BR)
SOBEYS WEST INC
SAFEWAY
6564 Hastings St, Burnaby, BC, V5B 1S2
(604) 291-0118
Emp Here 100
SIC 5411 Grocery stores

D-U-N-S 20-944-5183   (BR)
STARBUCKS COFFEE CANADA, INC
STARBUCKS COFFEE CO
(*Suby of* Starbucks Corporation)
6568 Hastings St Suite 101, Burnaby, BC, V5B
1S2
(604) 205-9044
Emp Here 25
SIC 5812 Eating places

D-U-N-S 24-137-7092   (BR)
WOLSELEY CANADA INC
WOLSELEY MECHANICAL GROUP
(*Suby of* WOLSELEY PLC)
5950 Kingsland Dr, Burnaby, BC, V5B 4W7
(604) 294-3473
Emp Here 30
SIC 5074 Plumbing and heating equipment
and supplies (hydronics)

Burnaby, BC V5C
Greater Vancouver County

D-U-N-S 25-314-5841   (BR)
20 VIC MANAGEMENT INC
BRENTWOOD TOWN CENTER
4567 Lougheed Hwy Suite 260, Burnaby, BC,
V5C 3Z6
(604) 299-0606
Emp Here 42
SIC 6512 Nonresidential building operators

D-U-N-S 25-696-7761   (SL)
423027 BC LTD
BOSTON PIZZA
4219a Lougheed Hwy Unit A, Burnaby, BC,
V5C 3Y6
(604) 299-7600
Emp Here 50   *Sales* 1,532,175
SIC 5812 Eating places

D-U-N-S 24-898-9295   (HQ)

A.G. PROFESSIONAL HAIR CARE PRODUCTS LTD
A.G. HAIR COSMETICS
3765 William St, Burnaby, BC, V5C 3H8
(604) 294-8870
Emp Here 57   *Emp Total* 60
Sales 5,034,288
SIC 2844 Toilet preparations
Pr Pr John Davis
 Charlotte Davis

D-U-N-S 25-055-2585   (BR)
A.G. PROFESSIONAL HAIR CARE PRODUCTS LTD
A G PROFESSIONAL HAIR CARE PRODUCTS
(*Suby of* Amalfi Holdings Ltd)
3765 William St, Burnaby, BC, V5C 3H8
(604) 294-8870
Emp Here 50
SIC 5122 Drugs, proprietaries, and sundries

D-U-N-S 24-033-7188   (BR)
AMEC FOSTER WHEELER AMERICAS LIMITED
AMEC EARTH & ENVIRONMENTAL, DIV OF
4445 Lougheed Hwy Suite 600, Burnaby, BC, V5C 0E4
(604) 294-3811
Emp Here 90
SIC 8711 Engineering services

D-U-N-S 25-883-9877   (BR)
ACCENT INNS INC
BLUE RIDGE INN
3777 Henning Dr, Burnaby, BC, V5C 6N5
(604) 473-5000
Emp Here 60
SIC 7011 Hotels and motels

D-U-N-S 20-573-0237   (BR)
ACKLANDS - GRAINGER INC
AGI
(*Suby of* W.W. Grainger, Inc.)
2475 Douglas Rd, Burnaby, BC, V5C 5A9
(604) 299-1212
Emp Here 50
SIC 5085 Industrial supplies

D-U-N-S 20-797-6531   (SL)
ACTION LINE HOUSING SOCIETY
SEATON VILLA
3755 Mcgill St, Burnaby, BC, V5C 1M2
(604) 291-0607
Emp Here 85   *Sales* 3,137,310
SIC 8361 Residential care

D-U-N-S 24-786-8081   (BR)
AEROTEK ULC
4321 Still Creek Dr Suite 150, Burnaby, BC, V5C 6S7
(604) 293-8000
Emp Here 50
SIC 7361 Employment agencies

D-U-N-S 25-910-3810   (BR)
ALCATEL-LUCENT CANADA INC
4190 Still Creek Dr Suite 3140, Burnaby, BC, V5C 6C6
(604) 430-3600
Emp Here 20
SIC 4899 Communication services, nec

D-U-N-S 24-101-1456   (BR)
ALLTECK LINE CONTRACTORS INC
(*Suby of* Quanta Services, Inc.)
4940 Still Creek Ave, Burnaby, BC, V5C 4E4
(604) 294-8172
Emp Here 35
SIC 1623 Water, sewer, and utility lines

D-U-N-S 24-370-5886   (SL)
ANTON'S PASTA LTD
4260 Hastings St, Burnaby, BC, V5C 2J6
(604) 299-6636
Emp Here 64   *Sales* 1,896,978
SIC 5812 Eating places

D-U-N-S 20-864-6468   (BR)
ARIVLE ENTERPRISES LTD
TIM HORTONS
4512 Lougheed Hwy, Burnaby, BC, V5C 3Z4
(604) 294-0471
Emp Here 20
SIC 5812 Eating places

D-U-N-S 24-824-8395   (BR)
AUDIO VISUAL SYSTEMS INTEGRATION INC
SHARP'S AUDIO VISUAL
3830 1st Ave, Burnaby, BC, V5C 3W1
(604) 877-1400
Emp Here 40
SIC 5999 Miscellaneous retail stores, nec

D-U-N-S 20-572-1207   (BR)
BANK OF MONTREAL
BMO
4567 Lougheed Hwy Suite 72, Burnaby, BC, V5C 4A1
(604) 665-6660
Emp Here 20
SIC 6021 National commercial banks

D-U-N-S 25-014-1843   (BR)
BANQUE TORONTO-DOMINION, LA
TD BANK FINANCIAL GROUP
(*Suby of* Toronto-Dominion Bank, The)
1933 Willingdon Ave Suite 2, Burnaby, BC, V5C 5J3
(604) 654-3939
Emp Here 50
SIC 6021 National commercial banks

D-U-N-S 20-696-2206   (SL)
BLUE CASTLE GAMES INC
4401 Still Creek Dr Unit 300, Burnaby, BC, V5C 6G9
(604) 299-5626
Emp Here 80   *Sales* 9,411,930
SIC 7372 Prepackaged software
Pr Rob Barrett
Dir Daniel Brady

D-U-N-S 20-328-8217   (BR)
BURNABY PUBLIC LIBRARY
4595 Albert St, Burnaby, BC, V5C 2G6
(604) 299-8955
Emp Here 20
SIC 8231 Libraries

D-U-N-S 25-165-4851   (BR)
BURNABY SCHOOL BOARD DISTRICT 41
ALPHA SECONDARY SCHOOL
4600 Parker St, Burnaby, BC, V5C 3E2

Emp Here 90
SIC 8211 Elementary and secondary schools

D-U-N-S 20-713-4391   (BR)
BURNABY SCHOOL BOARD DISTRICT 41
ROSSER ELEMENTARY SCHOOL
4375 Pandora St, Burnaby, BC, V5C 2B6

Emp Here 30
SIC 8211 Elementary and secondary schools

D-U-N-S 25-012-0680   (BR)
BURNABY SCHOOL BOARD DISTRICT 41
GILMORE COMMUNITY ELEMENTARY SCHOOL
50 Gilmore Ave, Burnaby, BC, V5C 4P5

Emp Here 45
SIC 8211 Elementary and secondary schools

D-U-N-S 20-803-8224   (HQ)
CBV COLLECTION SERVICES LTD
CBV COLLECTIONS
4664 Lougheed Hwy Unit 20, Burnaby, BC, V5C 5T5
(604) 687-4559
Emp Here 275   *Emp Total* 6
Sales 31,271,661
SIC 7322 Adjustment and collection services
Pr Pr Robert Richards

CEO Bryan Waters

D-U-N-S 20-276-1904   (SL)
CFSW LNG CONSTRUCTORS
4321 Still Creek Dr Suite 600, Burnaby, BC, V5C 6S7
(604) 603-4734
Emp Here 20   *Sales* 5,088,577
SIC 1541 Industrial buildings and warehouses
 Oliver Munar

D-U-N-S 25-749-4559   (SL)
CRI CREDIT GROUP SERVICES INC
CRI CANADA
4185 Still Creek Dr Unit 350a, Burnaby, BC, V5C 6G9
(604) 438-7785
Emp Here 30   *Sales* 2,699,546
SIC 6411 Insurance agents, brokers, and service

D-U-N-S 25-300-2455   (BR)
CSG SECURITY CORPORATION
(*Suby of* United Technologies Corporation)
3997 Henning Dr Suite 101, Burnaby, BC, V5C 6N5
(604) 681-7364
Emp Here 35
SIC 3699 Electrical equipment and supplies, nec

D-U-N-S 25-127-8248   (BR)
CACTUS RESTAURANTS LTD
CACTUS CLUB CAFE
4219 Lougheed Hwy, Burnaby, BC, V5C 3Y6

Emp Here 125
SIC 5812 Eating places

D-U-N-S 25-415-2648   (BR)
CANADIAN LINEN AND UNIFORM SERVICE CO
QUEBEC LINGE
(*Suby of* Ameripride Services, Inc.)
2750 Gilmore Ave, Burnaby, BC, V5C 4T9
(778) 331-6200
Emp Here 160
SIC 7213 Linen supply

D-U-N-S 25-707-6802   (BR)
CARA OPERATIONS LIMITED
SWISS CHALET
(*Suby of* Cara Holdings Limited)
3860 Lougheed Hwy, Burnaby, BC, V5C 6N4

Emp Here 50
SIC 5812 Eating places

D-U-N-S 25-665-9350   (BR)
CARTER CHEVROLET CADILLAC BUICK GMC BURNABY LTD
CARTER BODY SHOPS
2460 Alpha Ave, Burnaby, BC, V5C 5L6
(604) 291-2311
Emp Here 27
SIC 7532 Top and body repair and paint shops

D-U-N-S 24-787-0405   (BR)
CHEVRON CANADA LIMITED
(*Suby of* Chevron Corporation)
355 Willingdon Ave N, Burnaby, BC, V5C 1X4
(604) 257-4040
Emp Here 200
SIC 2911 Petroleum refining

D-U-N-S 25-087-2751   (BR)
CITY OF BURNABY
EILEEN DAILLY LEISURE POOL AND FITNESS CENTRE
240 Willingdon Ave, Burnaby, BC, V5C 5E9
(604) 298-7946
Emp Here 100
SIC 7999 Amusement and recreation, nec

D-U-N-S 20-058-9732   (BR)
COAST MOUNTAIN BUS COMPANY LTD
CMBC
3855 Kitchener St Suite 420, Burnaby, BC,

V5C 3L8
(604) 205-6111
Emp Here 350
SIC 4111 Local and suburban transit

D-U-N-S 25-901-2813   (SL)
COBBETT & COTTON LAW CORPORATION
410 Carleton Ave Suite 300, Burnaby, BC, V5C 6P6
(604) 299-6251
Emp Here 52   *Sales* 4,450,603
SIC 8111 Legal services

D-U-N-S 24-031-9384   (SL)
CRELOGIX ACCEPTANCE CORPORATION
4445 Lougheed Hwy Suite 900, Burnaby, BC, V5C 0E4
(604) 293-1131
Emp Here 45   *Sales* 21,377,485
SIC 6153 Short-term business credit institutions, except agricultural
Pr Pr Dennis Holmes
VP David Lynde
VP Mike Mckay

D-U-N-S 20-994-0613   (BR)
DHL EXPRESS (CANADA) LTD
5499 Regent St, Burnaby, BC, V5C 4H4

Emp Here 80
SIC 4215 Courier services, except by air

D-U-N-S 24-851-9980   (BR)
DENNISON AUTO LTD
4780 Hastings St, Burnaby, BC, V5C 2K7
(604) 294-2111
Emp Here 35
SIC 5511 New and used car dealers

D-U-N-S 24-457-2095   (SL)
DESTINATION AUTO VENTURE INC
DESTINATION CHRYSLER JEEP DODGE NORTHSHORE
4278 Lougheed Hwy, Burnaby, BC, V5C 3Y5
(604) 291-8122
Emp Here 100   *Sales* 50,240,000
SIC 5511 New and used car dealers
Pr Pr Aziz Ahamed

D-U-N-S 20-110-9592   (HQ)
DOUGLAS LIGHTING CONTROLS INC
(*Suby of* Douglas Lighting Controls Inc)
4455 Juneau St, Burnaby, BC, V5C 4C4
(604) 873-4800
Emp Here 40   *Emp Total* 60
Sales 4,596,524
SIC 3625 Relays and industrial controls

D-U-N-S 20-913-8143   (BR)
DYNAMEX CANADA LIMITED
2808 Ingleton Ave, Burnaby, BC, V5C 6G7
(604) 432-7700
Emp Here 50
SIC 7389 Business services, nec

D-U-N-S 25-710-0065   (BR)
EARL'S RESTAURANTS LTD
EARL'S BRIDGE PARK
(*Suby of* Earl's Restaurants Ltd)
3850 Lougheed Hwy, Burnaby, BC, V5C 6N4
(604) 291-1019
Emp Here 100
SIC 5812 Eating places

D-U-N-S 25-386-8640   (SL)
ELECTRIC MAIL COMPANY INC, THE
(*Suby of* J2 Global, Inc.)
3999 Henning Dr Suite 300, Burnaby, BC, V5C 6P9

Emp Here 22   *Sales* 1,459,214
SIC 4899 Communication services, nec

D-U-N-S 25-295-2262   (BR)
FEDERAL EXPRESS CANADA CORPORATION
FEDERAL EXPRESS CANADA LTD
(*Suby of* Fedex Corporation)

4270 Dawson St, Burnaby, BC, V5C 4B1
(800) 463-3339
Emp Here 119
SIC 7389 Business services, nec

D-U-N-S 25-087-2637 (BR)
FITCITY SPORTS CORPORATION
FITCITY FOR WOMEN
(*Suby of* Fitcity Sports Corporation)
4664 Lougheed Hwy Suite 150, Burnaby, BC,
V5C 5T5

Emp Here 40
SIC 7991 Physical fitness facilities

D-U-N-S 24-104-1735 (HQ)
FORTINET TECHNOLOGIES (CANADA) ULC
(*Suby of* Fortinet, Inc.)
4190 Still Creek Dr Unit 400, Burnaby, BC,
V5C 6C6
(604) 430-1297
Emp Here 180   *Emp Total* 4,665
Sales 16,458,769
SIC 7379 Computer related services, nec
Pr Pr Michael Xie
  Hongwei Li
  Hanfen Gua Crawford

D-U-N-S 25-360-3666 (BR)
FORTISBC ENERGY INC
3700 2nd Ave, Burnaby, BC, V5C 6S4
(604) 293-8506
Emp Here 30
SIC 4923 Gas transmission and distribution

D-U-N-S 24-672-4843 (BR)
GWIL INDUSTRIES INC
GWIL CRANE SERVICE
5337 Regent St, Burnaby, BC, V5C 4H4
(604) 291-9401
Emp Here 40
SIC 7353 Heavy construction equipment rental

D-U-N-S 24-137-5708 (BR)
GOVERNING COUNCIL OF THE SALVA-TION ARMY IN CANADA, THE
GOVERNING COUNCIL OF THE SALVATION ARMY IN CANADA, THE
3833 Henning Dr Suite 103, Burnaby, BC, V5C
6N5
(604) 299-3908
Emp Here 30
SIC 8741 Management services

D-U-N-S 20-104-3200 (BR)
GREAT PACIFIC INDUSTRIES INC
SAVE-ON-FOODS
4399 Lougheed Hwy Suite 996, Burnaby, BC,
V5C 3Y7
(604) 298-8412
Emp Here 110
SIC 5411 Grocery stores

D-U-N-S 25-270-3087 (BR)
HSBC BANK CANADA
HSBC
4106 Hastings St, Burnaby, BC, V5C 2J4
(604) 294-9431
Emp Here 20
SIC 6021 National commercial banks

D-U-N-S 20-321-9951 (SL)
HUB INTERNATIONAL INSURANCE BRO-KERS
4350 Still Creek Dr Suite 400, Burnaby, BC,
V5C 0G5
(604) 293-1481
Emp Here 170   *Sales* 15,321,747
SIC 6411 Insurance agents, brokers, and service
Pr Tina Osen

D-U-N-S 25-931-8350 (BR)
HOLLAND IMPORTS INC
SAMONA INTERNATIONAL
3905 1st Ave Suite 200, Burnaby, BC, V5C

3W3
(604) 298-4484
Emp Here 25
SIC 5072 Hardware

D-U-N-S 25-366-9055 (BR)
HOLLAND IMPORTS INC
SUMMIT TOLLS
3905 1st Ave, Burnaby, BC, V5C 3W3
(604) 294-1743
Emp Here 30
SIC 5251 Hardware stores

D-U-N-S 25-012-2165 (BR)
HOME DEPOT OF CANADA INC
HOME DEPOT
(*Suby of* The Home Depot Inc)
3950 Henning Dr, Burnaby, BC, V5C 6M2
(604) 294-3077
Emp Here 250
SIC 5251 Hardware stores

D-U-N-S 20-727-3587 (SL)
INDIANLIFE FOOD CORPORATION
3835 2nd Ave, Burnaby, BC, V5C 3W7
(604) 205-9176
Emp Here 55   *Sales* 4,742,446
SIC 2032 Canned specialties

D-U-N-S 25-689-6614 (SL)
J.W. RESEARCH LTD
3823 Henning Dr Suite 104, Burnaby, BC, V5C
6P3
(604) 291-1877
Emp Here 200   *Sales* 37,536,500
SIC 8743 Public relations services
Pr Pr Alan Wilson
VP VP Robert Ruterford

D-U-N-S 24-837-8952 (BR)
KEG RESTAURANTS LTD
KEG STEAKHOUSE & BAR, THE
4510 Still Creek Ave, Burnaby, BC, V5C 0B5
(604) 294-4626
Emp Here 60
SIC 5812 Eating places

D-U-N-S 25-613-8009 (BR)
KERRISDALE REALTY LTD
PRUDENTIAL UNITED REALTY
4567 Lougheed Hwy, Burnaby, BC, V5C 3Z6
(604) 437-9431
Emp Here 70
SIC 6531 Real estate agents and managers

D-U-N-S 25-215-8605 (HQ)
KITO CANADA INC
3815 1st Ave Suite 309, Burnaby, BC, V5C
3V6
(888) 322-5486
Emp Here 20   *Emp Total* 2,433
Sales 15,392,973
SIC 5084 Industrial machinery and equipment
Pr Pr Marc Premont
Dir Yoshio Kito

D-U-N-S 25-655-5293 (BR)
KONICA MINOLTA BUSINESS SOLUTIONS (CANADA) LTD
KONICA MINOLTA
4170 Still Creek Dr Suite 100, Burnaby, BC,
V5C 6C6
(604) 855-4899
Emp Here 20
SIC 5999 Miscellaneous retail stores, nec

D-U-N-S 24-888-0973 (SL)
LEMMER SPRAY SYSTEMS (BC) LTD
4141 Grandview Hwy, Burnaby, BC, V5C 4J1
(604) 430-3216
Emp Here 35   *Sales* 8,927,600
SIC 5084 Industrial machinery and equipment
Pr Pr Thomas Lemmer

D-U-N-S 24-760-7658 (BR)
MCDONALD'S RESTAURANTS OF CANADA LIMITED
MCDONALD'S #8341

(*Suby of* McDonald's Corporation)
4410 Still Creek Dr, Burnaby, BC, V5C 6C6
(604) 718-1090
Emp Here 100
SIC 5812 Eating places

D-U-N-S 25-318-1796 (BR)
MCDONALD'S RESTAURANTS OF CANADA LIMITED
MCDONALD'S 8784
(*Suby of* McDonald's Corporation)
4805 Hastings St, Burnaby, BC, V5C 2L1
(604) 718-1015
Emp Here 80
SIC 5812 Eating places

D-U-N-S 20-861-1553 (BR)
MCDONALD'S RESTAURANTS OF CANADA LIMITED
MCDONALD'S
(*Suby of* McDonald's Corporation)
4400 Still Creek Dr, Burnaby, BC, V5C 6C6
(604) 294-2181
Emp Here 85
SIC 5812 Eating places

D-U-N-S 24-372-8540 (BR)
MORGUARD CORPORATION
ACCURATE DOOR & HARDWARE
5134 Still Creek Ave, Burnaby, BC, V5C 4E4
(604) 299-8914
Emp Here 20
SIC 3442 Metal doors, sash, and trim

D-U-N-S 25-371-1634 (BR)
MORRISON HERSHFIELD LIMITED
4321 Still Creek Dr Unit 310, Burnaby, BC,
V5C 6S7
(604) 454-0402
Emp Here 50
SIC 8711 Engineering services

D-U-N-S 25-662-0436 (BR)
N R S WESTBURN REALTY LTD
COLDWELL BANKER WESTBURN
4259 Hastings St, Burnaby, BC, V5C 2J5
(604) 240-2215
Emp Here 50
SIC 6531 Real estate agents and managers

D-U-N-S 25-079-6208 (BR)
OLYMPIA TILE INTERNATIONAL INC
2350 Willingdon Ave, Burnaby, BC, V5C 5J6
(604) 294-2244
Emp Here 30
SIC 5032 Brick, stone, and related material

D-U-N-S 20-153-1964 (BR)
PANASONIC CANADA INC
PANASONIC DOCUMENT SYSTEMS DI-RECT
4175 Dawson St, Burnaby, BC, V5C 4B3

Emp Here 30
SIC 5731 Radio, television, and electronic stores

D-U-N-S 24-394-3995 (BR)
PATTISON, JIM INDUSTRIES LTD
JIM PATTISON LEASE
4937 Regent St, Burnaby, BC, V5C 4H4
(604) 433-4743
Emp Here 30
SIC 7515 Passenger car leasing

D-U-N-S 25-483-1902 (BR)
PETER KIEWIT INFRASTRUCTURE CO.
KIEWIT, PETER INFRASTRUCTURE
(*Suby of* Peter Kiewit Sons', Inc.)
4350 Still Creek Dr Suite 310, Burnaby, BC,
V5C 0G5
(604) 629-5419
Emp Here 80
SIC 1629 Heavy construction, nec

D-U-N-S 25-009-9129 (HQ)
POSABILITIES ASSOCIATION OF BRITISH COLUMBIA

(*Suby of* Posabilities Association Of British
Columbia)
4664 Lougheed Hwy Unit 240, Burnaby, BC,
V5C 5T5
(604) 299-4001
Emp Here 50   *Emp Total* 600
Sales 23,648,301
SIC 8322 Individual and family services
  Fernando Coelho
Pr Pr Celso A. A. Boscariol
VP VP Sid Mindess
VP VP Paul Girardi
  Chris Chris
  Paul Van Koll
Dir Stuart Carmichael
Dir Linda Eaves
Dir Anita Lee
Dir Helen Premia

D-U-N-S 20-986-8137 (SL)
PRIME GRAPHIC RESOURCES LTD
STILL CREEK PRESS
3988 Still Creek Ave, Burnaby, BC, V5C 6N9
(604) 437-5800
Emp Here 70   *Sales* 3,502,114
SIC 2759 Commercial printing, nec

D-U-N-S 25-710-4232 (BR)
REGENCY AUTO INVESTMENTS INC
REGENCY TOYOTA BURNABY
4278 Lougheed Hwy, Burnaby, BC, V5C 3Y5
(604) 879-8411
Emp Here 40
SIC 5521 Used car dealers

D-U-N-S 25-505-6483 (BR)
REIMER EXPRESS LINES LTD
FAST AS FLITE
(*Suby of* Yrc Worldwide Inc.)
3985 Still Creek Ave, Burnaby, BC, V5C 4E2
(604) 433-3321
Emp Here 150
SIC 4213 Trucking, except local

D-U-N-S 20-296-2242 (BR)
ROBINSON, C.H. COMPANY (CANADA) LTD
4445 Lougheed Hwy Suite 400, Burnaby, BC,
V5C 0E4
(604) 298-6767
Emp Here 37
SIC 4213 Trucking, except local

D-U-N-S 25-705-2845 (BR)
ROYAL BANK OF CANADA
ROYAL BANK FINANCIAL GROUP
(*Suby of* Royal Bank Of Canada)
4382 Hastings St, Burnaby, BC, V5C 2J9
(604) 665-5900
Emp Here 23
SIC 6021 National commercial banks

D-U-N-S 20-733-7374 (BR)
SCM INSURANCE SERVICES INC
CLAIMSPRO
3999 Henning Dr Suite 101, Burnaby, BC, V5C
6P9
(604) 684-1581
Emp Here 30
SIC 6411 Insurance agents, brokers, and service

D-U-N-S 20-917-6106 (HQ)
SAYANI INVESTMENTS LTD
EXECUTIVE INN HOTELS
(*Suby of* Sayani Investments Ltd)
4201 Lougheed Hwy, Burnaby, BC, V5C 3Y6
(604) 278-5555
Emp Here 40   *Emp Total* 100
Sales 4,377,642
SIC 7011 Hotels and motels

D-U-N-S 25-094-6688 (BR)
SEARS CANADA INC
SEARS
4567 Lougheed Hwy Suite 100, Burnaby, BC,
V5C 3Z7

(604) 299-5511
Emp Here 300
SIC 5311 Department stores

D-U-N-S 24-777-8608   (BR)
SHOPPERS DRUG MART INC
3999 Henning Dr Unit 400, Burnaby, BC, V5C 6P9
(604) 296-4400
Emp Here 30
SIC 8741 Management services

D-U-N-S 25-364-9339   (BR)
SOBEYS WEST INC
SAFEWAY
4440 Hastings St Suite E, Burnaby, BC, V5C 2K2
(604) 205-7497
Emp Here 175
SIC 5411 Grocery stores

D-U-N-S 25-498-9403   (BR)
STAPLES CANADA INC
STAPLES THE BUSINESS DEPOT
(*Suby of* Staples, Inc.)
4265 Lougheed Hwy Suite 84, Burnaby, BC, V5C 3Y6
(604) 320-6800
Emp Here 40
SIC 5943 Stationery stores

D-U-N-S 24-696-4316   (HQ)
TFG FINANCIAL CORPORATION
4180 Lougheed Hwy Suite 500, Burnaby, BC, V5C 6A7
(604) 473-3844
Emp Here 20   *Emp Total* 65
Sales 5,630,632
SIC 6159 Miscellaneous business credit institutions
Pr Pr Dennis Holmes
  James Case
  Roberto Cortese

D-U-N-S 25-011-1549   (BR)
THYSSENKRUPP ELEVATOR (CANADA) LIMITED
THYSSENKRUPP ELEVATOR
2303 Douglas Rd, Burnaby, BC, V5C 5A9
(604) 294-2209
Emp Here 50
SIC 1796 Installing building equipment

D-U-N-S 24-957-0003   (BR)
TIERRA SOL CERAMIC TILE LTD
4121 Halifax St, Burnaby, BC, V5C 3X3
(604) 435-5400
Emp Here 25
SIC 5032 Brick, stone, and related material

D-U-N-S 25-080-9555   (BR)
UNITED RENTALS OF CANADA, INC
5175 Regent St, Burnaby, BC, V5C 4H4
(604) 299-5888
Emp Here 24
SIC 7353 Heavy construction equipment rental

D-U-N-S 20-587-0533   (BR)
VANCOUVER CITY SAVINGS CREDIT UNION
VANCITY CREDIT UNION
4302 Hastings St, Burnaby, BC, V5C 2J9
(604) 877-7062
Emp Here 20
SIC 6062 State credit unions

D-U-N-S 20-262-4417   (BR)
VANCOUVER COASTAL HEALTH AUTHORITY
1795 Willingdon Ave, Burnaby, BC, V5C 6E3
(604) 297-9226
Emp Here 20
SIC 8062 General medical and surgical hospitals

D-U-N-S 24-446-4897   (HQ)
WELCO LUMBER CORP
(*Suby of* August Corporate Partners Inc)

4445 Lougheed Hwy Suite 1001, Burnaby, BC, V5C 0E4
(604) 732-1411
Emp Here 31   *Emp Total* 30
Sales 12,038,516
SIC 5031 Lumber, plywood, and millwork
Pr Pr Bradley Johansen
  Brian Elcock
  Michael Thelin

D-U-N-S 24-798-2705   (SL)
WEST COAST SIGHTSEEING LTD
2350 Beta Ave, Burnaby, BC, V5C 5M8
(604) 451-1600
Emp Here 150   *Sales* 3,575,074
SIC 4141 Local bus charter service

D-U-N-S 25-717-3336   (BR)
WESTERN INVENTORY SERVICE LTD
WIS INTERNATIONAL
4199 Lougheed Hwy Suite 201, Burnaby, BC, V5C 3Y6
(604) 473-9200
Emp Here 25
SIC 7389 Business services, nec

D-U-N-S 25-944-6706   (BR)
WHITE SPOT LIMITED
WHITE SPOT RESTAURANT
4129 Lougheed Hwy, Burnaby, BC, V5C 3Y6
(604) 299-4423
Emp Here 70
SIC 5812 Eating places

D-U-N-S 20-106-3232   (BR)
WINNERS MERCHANTS INTERNATIONAL L.P.
WINNERS
(*Suby of* The TJX Companies Inc)
1899 Rosser Ave Unit 100, Burnaby, BC, V5C 6R5
(604) 294-0117
Emp Here 35
SIC 5651 Family clothing stores

D-U-N-S 20-646-4443   (BR)
WORLEYPARSONS CANADA SERVICES LTD
4321 Still Creek Dr Suite 600, Burnaby, BC, V5C 6S7
(604) 298-1616
Emp Here 176
SIC 8711 Engineering services

Burnaby, BC V5E
Greater Vancouver County

D-U-N-S 20-013-3721   (BR)
428675 BC LTD
BOARDWALK GAMING
(*Suby of* 428675 BC Ltd)
7155 Kingsway Suite 300, Burnaby, BC, V5E 2V1

Emp Here 30
SIC 7999 Amusement and recreation, nec

D-U-N-S 24-248-0994   (SL)
528728 BC LTD
CANADA WAY CARE CENTRE
7195 Canada Way, Burnaby, BC, V5E 3R7

Emp Here 80   *Sales* 3,648,035
SIC 8051 Skilled nursing care facilities

D-U-N-S 25-287-9044   (BR)
A & W FOOD SERVICES OF CANADA INC
A & W
6535 Kingsway, Burnaby, BC, V5E 1E1
(604) 433-6212
Emp Here 25
SIC 5812 Eating places

D-U-N-S 24-129-7162   (BR)
BOSA PROPERTIES INC

7155 Kingsway Suite 1200, Burnaby, BC, V5E 2V1
(604) 412-0313
Emp Here 100
SIC 6531 Real estate agents and managers

D-U-N-S 25-919-7655   (BR)
BURNABY PUBLIC LIBRARY
TOMMY DOUGLAS BRANCH
7311 Kingsway, Burnaby, BC, V5E 1G8
(604) 522-3971
Emp Here 20
SIC 8231 Libraries

D-U-N-S 25-013-1190   (BR)
BURNABY SCHOOL BOARD DISTRICT 41
MORLEY ELEMENTARY SCHOOL
7355 Morley St, Burnaby, BC, V5E 2K1

Emp Here 45
SIC 8211 Elementary and secondary schools

D-U-N-S 20-591-2137   (BR)
BURNABY SCHOOL BOARD DISTRICT 41
BUCKINGHAM ELEMENTARY SCHOOL
6066 Buckingham Ave, Burnaby, BC, V5E 2A4
(604) 664-8616
Emp Here 25
SIC 8211 Elementary and secondary schools

D-U-N-S 20-591-2152   (BR)
BURNABY SCHOOL BOARD DISTRICT 41
BRANTFORD ELEMENTARY SCHOOL
6512 Brantford Ave, Burnaby, BC, V5E 2S1
(604) 664-8603
Emp Here 20
SIC 8211 Elementary and secondary schools

D-U-N-S 20-588-3353   (BR)
CANADA POST CORPORATION
7155 Kingsway Ste 302, Burnaby, BC, V5E 2V1
(604) 525-1571
Emp Here 20
SIC 4311 U.s. postal service

D-U-N-S 25-166-2557   (BR)
CATHOLIC INDEPENDENT SCHOOLS OF VANCOUVER ARCHDIOCESE, THE
ST FRANCIS DE SALES SCHOOL
6656 Balmoral St, Burnaby, BC, V5E 1J1
(604) 435-5311
Emp Here 30
SIC 8211 Elementary and secondary schools

D-U-N-S 20-860-8153   (SL)
D.M.S. MECHANICAL LTD
D.M.S. PLUMBING HEATING AND AIR CONDITIONING
7449 Conway Ave Unit 104, Burnaby, BC, V5E 2P7
(604) 291-8919
Emp Here 50   *Sales* 4,377,642
SIC 1711 Plumbing, heating, air-conditioning

D-U-N-S 20-732-1063   (BR)
ESSILOR GROUPE CANADA INC
7541 Conway Ave Suite 5, Burnaby, BC, V5E 2P7
(604) 437-5300
Emp Here 100
SIC 3851 Ophthalmic goods

D-U-N-S 25-401-9763   (BR)
ESSILOR NETWORK IN CANADA INC
7541 Conway Ave Suite 5, Burnaby, BC, V5E 2P7
(604) 437-5333
Emp Here 100
SIC 5049 Professional equipment, nec

D-U-N-S 24-579-2379   (HQ)
GISBORNE FIRE PROTECTION ALBERTA LTD
7476 Hedley Ave, Burnaby, BC, V5E 2P9
(604) 520-7300
Emp Here 60   *Emp Total* 400
Sales 11,779,200
SIC 1711 Plumbing, heating, air-conditioning

Pr Pr James Sawers
  Leslie Maivs

D-U-N-S 20-016-8073   (HQ)
GISBORNE INDUSTRIAL CONSTRUCTION LTD
7476 Hedley Ave, Burnaby, BC, V5E 2P9
(604) 520-7300
Emp Here 45   *Emp Total* 400
Sales 80,000,400
SIC 1541 Industrial buildings and warehouses
Pr Pr Rae Clarkson
  Les Maivs
Dir James Sawers

D-U-N-S 25-369-4277   (BR)
GREAT PACIFIC INDUSTRIES INC
SAVE-ON-FOODS
7155 Kingsway Unit 200, Burnaby, BC, V5E 2V1
(604) 540-1368
Emp Here 180
SIC 5411 Grocery stores

D-U-N-S 20-623-1052   (HQ)
ME-N-EDS PIZZA PARLOUR LTD
(*Suby of* Me-N-Eds Pizza Parlour Ltd)
7110 Hall Ave, Burnaby, BC, V5E 3B1
(604) 521-8881
Emp Here 30   *Emp Total* 60
Sales 1,824,018
SIC 5812 Eating places

D-U-N-S 20-911-6367   (SL)
NEW VISTA SOCIETY, THE
7550 Rosewood St Suite 235, Burnaby, BC, V5E 3Z3
(604) 521-7764
Emp Here 200   *Sales* 10,145,000
SIC 8361 Residential care
Pr Sonja Alton
VP VP Nan Blackmore
Treas Art Kube
Dir Fin Gord Mcnaughton

D-U-N-S 20-299-8113   (BR)
OPENROAD AUTO GROUP LIMITED
MIDDLEGATE HONDA
6984 Kingsway, Burnaby, BC, V5E 1E6
(604) 525-4667
Emp Here 50
SIC 5511 New and used car dealers

D-U-N-S 20-291-0188   (BR)
SOLOTECH QUEBEC INC
7475 Hedley Ave Suite 205, Burnaby, BC, V5E 2R1
(604) 620-9220
Emp Here 25
SIC 5099 Durable goods, nec

D-U-N-S 24-360-9810   (BR)
TROTTER AND MORTON BUILDING TECHNOLOGIES INC
TROTTER AND MORTON BUILDING TECHNOLOGIES INC
5151 Canada Way Unit 200, Burnaby, BC, V5E 3N1
(604) 525-4499
Emp Here 20
SIC 1711 Plumbing, heating, air-conditioning

D-U-N-S 20-102-1151   (HQ)
WESTERN BELTING & HOSE (1986) LTD
(*Suby of* W.B.H. Holding Ltd)
6468 Beresford St, Burnaby, BC, V5E 1B6
(604) 451-4133
Emp Here 25   *Emp Total* 50
Sales 11,779,113
SIC 5084 Industrial machinery and equipment
Pr Pr David Bennett
Genl Mgr Victor Loski

Burnaby, BC V5G
Greater Vancouver County

D-U-N-S 25-316-2663   (BR)
AECOM CANADA LTD
3001 Wayburne Dr Unit 275, Burnaby, BC,
V5G 4W3

Emp Here 50
SIC 8711 Engineering services

D-U-N-S 24-957-1951   (BR)
AECOM CANADA LTD
6400 Roberts St Suite 490, Burnaby, BC, V5G
4C9
(604) 299-4144
Emp Here 20
SIC 8748 Business consulting, nec

D-U-N-S 20-587-3797   (HQ)
ALLIANCE MERCANTILE INC
3451 Wayburne Dr, Burnaby, BC, V5G 3L1
(604) 299-3566
Emp Here 45   *Emp Total* 2
Sales 44,378,700
SIC 5023 Homefurnishings
Pr Pr Douglas Bell

D-U-N-S 25-363-7284   (BR)
AMER SPORTS CANADA INC
ARC'TERYX EQUIPMENT DIV.
4250 Manor St, Burnaby, BC, V5G 1B2
(604) 454-9900
Emp Here 290
SIC 3949 Sporting and athletic goods, nec

D-U-N-S 24-558-6490   (HQ)
ASSOCIATED ENGINEERING (B.C.) LTD
(*Suby of* Ashco Shareholders Inc)
4940 Canada Way Suite 300, Burnaby, BC,
V5G 4M5
(604) 293-1411
Emp Here 100   *Emp Total* 255
Sales 29,306,432
SIC 8711 Engineering services
Ch Bd Ch Bd Kerry Rudd
VP VP Martin Jobke
Sec Donna Bonk

D-U-N-S 25-737-0981   (BR)
ASSOCIATED ENGINEERING GROUP LTD
ASSOCIATED ENGINEERING (BC)
(*Suby of* Ashco Shareholders Inc)
4940 Canada Way Suite 300, Burnaby, BC,
V5G 4M5
(604) 293-1411
Emp Here 140
SIC 8711 Engineering services

D-U-N-S 20-307-2848   (BR)
**AUTOPRO AUTOMATION CONSULTANTS
LTD**
4370 Dominion St Suite 600, Burnaby, BC,
V5G 4L7
(604) 419-4350
Emp Here 35
SIC 8711 Engineering services

D-U-N-S 20-702-6381   (BR)
**BC GOVERNMENT AND SERVICE EM-
PLOYEES' UNION**
4925 Canada Way, Burnaby, BC, V5G 1M1
(604) 215-1499
Emp Here 100
SIC 8631 Labor organizations

D-U-N-S 20-353-6701   (BR)
BSM TECHNOLOGIES LTD
4299 Canada Way Suite 215, Burnaby, BC,
V5G 1H3
(866) 287-0135
Emp Here 82
SIC 3699 Electrical equipment and supplies,
nec

D-U-N-S 20-713-4367   (BR)
BURNABY SCHOOL BOARD DISTRICT 41
DOUGLAS ROAD ELEMENTARY SCHOOL
4861 Canada Way, Burnaby, BC, V5G 1L7

Emp Here 50

SIC 8211 Elementary and secondary schools

D-U-N-S 25-012-0698   (BR)
BURNABY SCHOOL BOARD DISTRICT 41
GILPIN ELEMENTARY SCHOOL
5490 Eglinton St, Burnaby, BC, V5G 2B2
(604) 664-8712
Emp Here 25
SIC 8211 Elementary and secondary schools

D-U-N-S 25-013-0531   (BR)
BURNABY SCHOOL BOARD DISTRICT 41
LAKEVIEW ELEMENTARY SCHOOL
5325 Kincaid St, Burnaby, BC, V5G 1W2
(604) 664-8735
Emp Here 25
SIC 8211 Elementary and secondary schools

D-U-N-S 20-072-6094   (BR)
BURNABY SCHOOL BOARD DISTRICT 41
*BURNABY   CENTRAL   SECONDARY
SCHOOL*
4939 Canada Way, Burnaby, BC, V5G 1M1

Emp Here 110
SIC 8211 Elementary and secondary schools

D-U-N-S 20-978-9895   (BR)
BURNABY SCHOOL BOARD DISTRICT 41
SCHCU EDUCATION CENTRE
4041 Canada Way, Burnaby, BC, V5G 1G6
(604) 296-6915
Emp Here 50
SIC 7389 Business services, nec

D-U-N-S 20-591-2053   (BR)
BURNABY SCHOOL BOARD DISTRICT 41
INMAN ELEMENTARY SCHOOL
3963 Brandon St, Burnaby, BC, V5G 2P6

Emp Here 55
SIC 8211 Elementary and secondary schools

D-U-N-S 20-713-4359   (BR)
BURNABY SCHOOL BOARD DISTRICT 41
*CASCADE   HEIGHTS   ELEMENTARY
SCHOOL*
4343 Smith Ave, Burnaby, BC, V5G 2V5

Emp Here 50
SIC 8211 Elementary and secondary schools

D-U-N-S 25-216-3076   (BR)
**CANADIAN UNION OF PUBLIC EMPLOY-
EES**
*CUPE BRITISH COLUMBIA REGIONAL OF-
FICE*
4940 Canada Way Suite 500, Burnaby, BC,
V5G 4T3
(604) 291-1940
Emp Here 80
SIC 8631 Labor organizations

D-U-N-S 24-643-9558   (SL)
CENTURA (VANCOUVER) LIMITED
CENTURA FLOOR & WALL FASHIONS
(*Suby of* Centura Limited)
4616 Canada Way, Burnaby, BC, V5G 1K5
(604) 298-8453
Emp Here 25   *Sales* 5,180,210
SIC 5032 Brick, stone, and related material
Pr Pr Brian Cowie
VP Fin Peter Donath
Gen Mgr Mike Macaulay

D-U-N-S 24-360-1411   (BR)
**CHARTWELL SENIORS HOUSING REAL
ESTATE INVESTMENT TRUST**
CARLETON GARDENS
4125 Canada Way, Burnaby, BC, V5G 1G9
(604) 438-8224
Emp Here 35
SIC 8051 Skilled nursing care facilities

D-U-N-S 25-723-5051   (BR)
CITY OF BURNABY
SHADBOLT CENTRE FOR THE ARTS
6450 Deer Lake Ave, Burnaby, BC, V5G 2J3

(604) 291-6864
Emp Here 30
SIC 8322 Individual and family services

D-U-N-S 25-696-6581   (BR)
CITY OF BURNABY
BURNABY VILLAGE MUSEUM
6501 Deer Lake Ave, Burnaby, BC, V5G 3T6
(604) 297-4565
Emp Here 50
SIC 8412 Museums and art galleries

D-U-N-S 20-179-9694   (BR)
**CONSEILLERS EN GESTION ET INFORMA-
TIQUE CGI INC**
CGI
4601 Canada Way Suite 201, Burnaby, BC,
V5G 4X7
(604) 420-0108
Emp Here 25
SIC 7379 Computer related services, nec

D-U-N-S 24-536-3486   (SL)
DANIA HOME SOCIETY
4279 Norland Ave, Burnaby, BC, V5G 3Z6
(604) 299-1370
Emp Here 100   *Sales* 3,648,035
SIC 8361 Residential care

D-U-N-S 25-282-2531   (BR)
**DESJARDINS SECURITE FINANCIERE,
COMPAGNIE D'ASSURANCE VIE**
DESJARDINS FINANCIAL SERVICES
4400 Dominion St Suite 500, Burnaby, BC,
V5G 4G3
(604) 685-9099
Emp Here 20
SIC 6311 Life insurance

D-U-N-S 20-733-6418   (BR)
EXP SERVICES INC
3001 Wayburne Dr Suite 275, Burnaby, BC,
V5G 4W3
(604) 874-1245
Emp Here 80
SIC 8711 Engineering services

D-U-N-S 24-825-1589   (HQ)
ELECTRONIC ARTS (CANADA) INC
EA SPORTS
(*Suby of* Electronic Arts Inc.)
4330 Sanderson Way, Burnaby, BC, V5G 4X1
(604) 456-3600
Emp Here 20   *Emp Total* 8,800
Sales 144,681,068
SIC 7371 Custom computer programming ser-
vices
Sr VP V Paul Lee
  Lawrence Probst Iii
  Stanton Mckee
  Ruth Kennedy
Dir Donald Mattrick

D-U-N-S 25-124-0727   (BR)
EMCO CORPORATION
3140 Gilmore Divers, Burnaby, BC, V5G 3B4
(604) 713-2200
Emp Here 30
SIC 5074 Plumbing and heating equipment
and supplies (hydronics)

D-U-N-S 24-761-2471   (BR)
EMCO CORPORATION
ENSUITE, THE
3139 Sumner Ave, Burnaby, BC, V5G 3E3
(604) 412-2830
Emp Here 60
SIC 5074 Plumbing and heating equipment
and supplies (hydronics)

D-U-N-S 24-548-3842   (SL)
EXCELLERIS TECHNOLOGIES INC
3500 Gilmore Way Suite 200, Burnaby, BC,
V5G 4W7
(604) 566-8420
Emp Here 30   *Sales* 1,678,096
SIC 7376 Computer facilities management

D-U-N-S 25-412-3896   (BR)

*FINNISH CANADIAN REST HOME ASSOCI-
ATION*
FINNISH MANOR, DIV OF
(*Suby of* Finnish Canadian Rest Home Asso-
ciation)
3460 Kalyk Ave, Burnaby, BC, V5G 3B2
(604) 434-2666
Emp Here 65
SIC 8361 Residential care

D-U-N-S 24-678-3752   (BR)
FRASER HEALTH AUTHORITY
BC COMMUNITY CARE
4946 Canada Way Suite 300, Burnaby, BC,
V5G 4H7
(604) 918-7683
Emp Here 50
SIC 8062 General medical and surgical hospi-
tals

D-U-N-S 20-646-1357   (BR)
FRASER HEALTH AUTHORITY
BURNABY HOSPITAL
3935 Kincaid St, Burnaby, BC, V5G 2X6
(604) 434-3992
Emp Here 1,800
SIC 8062 General medical and surgical hospi-
tals

D-U-N-S 24-694-5653   (SL)
**GENTLE CARE DRAPERY & CARPET
CLEANERS LTD**
COIT SERVICES
3755 Wayburne Dr, Burnaby, BC, V5G 3L1
(604) 296-4000
Emp Here 80   *Sales* 2,042,900
SIC 7217 Carpet and upholstery cleaning

D-U-N-S 25-002-4874   (BR)
HSBC BANK CANADA
3555 Gilmore Way Suite 300, Burnaby, BC,
V5G 4S1
(604) 273-1961
Emp Here 65
SIC 6021 National commercial banks

D-U-N-S 24-134-5292   (BR)
HSBC BANK CANADA
3555 Gilmore Way Suite 399, Burnaby, BC,
V5G 4S1
(604) 216-2270
Emp Here 55
SIC 6162 Mortgage bankers and loan corre-
spondents

D-U-N-S 20-555-7890   (BR)
**MAXXAM ANALYTICS INTERNATIONAL
CORPORATION**
MAXXAM ANALYTICS
4606 Canada Way, Burnaby, BC, V5G 1K5
(604) 734-7276
Emp Here 350
SIC 8734 Testing laboratories

D-U-N-S 24-983-6052   (SL)
MINDFIELD RPO GROUP INC
3480 Gilmore Way, Burnaby, BC, V5G 4Y1
(604) 899-4473
Emp Here 50   *Sales* 3,648,035
SIC 7361 Employment agencies

D-U-N-S 24-335-9028   (BR)
MONERIS SOLUTIONS CORPORATION
ERNEX
4259 Canada Way Suite 225, Burnaby, BC,
V5G 1H1
(604) 415-1500
Emp Here 65
SIC 7372 Prepackaged software

D-U-N-S 25-090-5189   (BR)
MRS. WILLMAN'S BAKING LIMITED
3732 Canada Way, Burnaby, BC, V5G 1G4

Emp Here 25
SIC 2051 Bread, cake, and related products

D-U-N-S 20-699-7103   (BR)

▲ Public Company   ■ Public Company Family Member   **HQ** Headquarters   **BR** Branch   **SL** Single Location

NORDION INC
MDS DIAGNOSTIC SERVICES
3680 Gilmore Way, Burnaby, BC, V5G 4V8
(604) 431-5005
Emp Here 800
SIC 8071 Medical laboratories

    D-U-N-S 20-575-8808   (BR)
PITNEY BOWES OF CANADA LTD
(*Suby of* Pitney Bowes Inc.)
3001 Wayburne Dr Suite 125, Burnaby, BC,
V5G 4W3
(778) 328-8900
Emp Here 75
SIC 5044 Office equipment

    D-U-N-S 25-366-3884   (HQ)
POLYCOM CANADA LTD
3605 Gilmore Way Suite 200, Burnaby, BC,
V5G 4X5
(604) 453-9400
Emp Here 55   *Emp Total* 3,451
Sales 7,660,874
SIC 5065 Electronic parts and equipment, nec
   Robert Hagert

    D-U-N-S 24-418-6958   (SL)
PREMIER DIVERSIFIED HOLDINGS INC
3185 Willingdon Green Suite 301, Burnaby,
BC, V5G 4P3
(604) 678-9115
Emp Here 50   *Sales* 1,003,393
SIC 3829 Measuring and controlling devices,
nec

    D-U-N-S 20-338-4284   (SL)
SEQUEL NATURALS ULC
VEGA
3001 Wayburne Dr Unit 101, Burnaby, BC,
V5G 4W3
(604) 945-3133
Emp Here 20   *Sales* 2,845,467
SIC 5149 Groceries and related products, nec

    D-U-N-S 20-297-3959   (BR)
TELUS CORPORATION
3500 Gilmore Way Suite 2, Burnaby, BC, V5G
4W7
(604) 415-2500
Emp Here 200
SIC 4899 Communication services, nec

    D-U-N-S 24-101-3809   (BR)
TELE-MOBILE COMPANY
TELUS MOBILITY
4519 Canada Way Suite 2, Burnaby, BC, V5G
4S4
(604) 291-2355
Emp Here 200
SIC 4899 Communication services, nec

    D-U-N-S 25-719-4605   (BR)
TRADER CORPORATION
HOMEBASE MEDIA
3555 Gilmore Way 1 West, Burnaby, BC, V5G
0B3
(604) 540-4455
Emp Here 200
SIC 2721 Periodicals

    D-U-N-S 24-354-1633   (SL)
UNITED WAY OF THE LOWER MAINLAND
4543 Canada Way, Burnaby, BC, V5G 4T4
(604) 294-8929
Emp Here 46   *Sales* 24,696,894
SIC 8399 Social services, nec
Pr Michael Mcknight
Ch Bd Steve Hunt
V Ch Bd Jane Peverett
Treas John Delucchi
Dir Amber Hockin
Dir Anna Lilly
Dir Catherine Warren
Dir Damon Williams
Dir Debra Hewson
Dir George Davison

    D-U-N-S 25-758-2197   (SL)

WILLINGDON CHURCH
4812 Willingdon Ave, Burnaby, BC, V5G 3H6
(604) 435-5544
Emp Here 50   *Sales* 3,283,232
SIC 8661 Religious organizations

    D-U-N-S 24-387-8837   (BR)
XPO LOGISTICS CANADA INC
4400 Dominion St Suite 280, Burnaby, BC,
V5G 4G3
(604) 638-6500
Emp Here 26
SIC 4731 Freight transportation arrangement

    D-U-N-S 20-052-8698   (SL)
XENON PHARMACEUTICALS INC
3650 Gilmore Way, Burnaby, BC, V5G 4W8
(604) 484-3300
Emp Here 88   *Sales* 1,803,000
SIC 8731 Commercial physical research

Burnaby, BC V5H
Greater Vancouver County

    D-U-N-S 20-916-5302   (BR)
1075992 ALBERTA LTD
HOLIDAY INN EXPRESS METRO TOWN
(*Suby of* 1075992 Alberta Ltd)
4405 Central Blvd, Burnaby, BC, V5H 4M3
(604) 438-1881
Emp Here 50
SIC 7011 Hotels and motels

    D-U-N-S 25-902-2762   (BR)
ADP CANADA CO
ADP DEALER SERVICES
(*Suby of* Automatic Data Processing, Inc.)
4720 Kingsway Suite 500, Burnaby, BC, V5H
4N2
(604) 431-2700
Emp Here 130
SIC 8721 Accounting, auditing, and book-
keeping

    D-U-N-S 24-676-9025   (SL)
AISCENT TECHNOLOGIES INC
4720 Kingsway Suite 2600, Burnaby, BC, V5H
4N2
(778) 374-1720
Emp Here 100   *Sales* 48,531,840
SIC 3699 Electrical equipment and supplies,
nec
Dir Richard Du

    D-U-N-S 20-805-3686   (SL)
ANDERSON, PAT AGENCIES LTD
(*Suby of* P.G. Anderson Holdings Ltd)
4680 Kingsway Suite 200, Burnaby, BC, V5H
4L9
(604) 430-8887
Emp Here 24   *Sales* 7,263,840
SIC 6411 Insurance agents, brokers, and ser-
vice
Pr Pr Patrick Anderson
VP VP Paul Towriss

    D-U-N-S 20-189-7696   (BR)
BEST BUY CANADA LTD
FUTURE SHOP
(*Suby of* Best Buy Co., Inc.)
6200 Mckay Ave Unit 144, Burnaby, BC, V5H
4L7
(604) 434-3844
Emp Here 78
SIC 5999 Miscellaneous retail stores, nec

    D-U-N-S 24-363-2135   (BR)
BEST BUY CANADA LTD
BEST BUY
(*Suby of* Best Buy Co., Inc.)
4805 Kingsway, Burnaby, BC, V5H 4T6
(778) 452-2250
Emp Here 20
SIC 5731 Radio, television, and electronic
stores

    D-U-N-S 25-723-3189   (BR)
BOUTIQUE JACOB INC
JACOB
(*Suby of* Boutique Jacob Inc)
4700 Kingsway Suite 2135, Burnaby, BC, V5H
4M1
Emp Here 30
SIC 5621 Women's clothing stores

    D-U-N-S 20-591-2087   (BR)
BURNABY SCHOOL BOARD DISTRICT 41
CHAFFEY-BURKE ELEMENTARY SCHOOL
4404 Sardis St, Burnaby, BC, V5H 1K7

Emp Here 80
SIC 8211 Elementary and secondary schools

    D-U-N-S 25-013-0945   (BR)
BURNABY SCHOOL BOARD DISTRICT 41
*ECOLE MARLBOROUGH ELEMENTARY
SCHOOL*
6060 Marlborough Ave, Burnaby, BC, V5H 3L7
(604) 296-9021
Emp Here 77
SIC 8211 Elementary and secondary schools

    D-U-N-S 20-189-8678   (BR)
CH2M HILL CANADA LIMITED
VBC
(*Suby of* Ch2m Hill Companies, Ltd.)
4720 Kingsway Suite 2100, Burnaby, BC, V5H
4N2
(604) 684-3282
Emp Here 100
SIC 8711 Engineering services

    D-U-N-S 25-325-9089   (SL)
CJW CONSULTANTS INC
*CINNAMON JANG WILLOUGHBY & COM-
PANY*
4720 Kingsway Suite 900, Burnaby, BC, V5H
4N2
(604) 435-4317
Emp Here 50   *Sales* 2,188,821
SIC 8721 Accounting, auditing, and book-
keeping

    D-U-N-S 25-011-9112   (SL)
CACTUS RESTAURANTS LTD
CACTUS CLUB
4653 Kingsway, Burnaby, BC, V5H 2B3
(604) 431-8448
Emp Here 55   *Sales* 1,678,096
SIC 5812 Eating places

    D-U-N-S 25-288-8953   (BR)
CANADA POST CORPORATION
6025 Sussex St, Burnaby, BC, V5H 3C2
(604) 482-4299
Emp Here 70
SIC 4311 U.s. postal service

    D-U-N-S 25-016-9133   (BR)
**CANADIAN IMPERIAL BANK OF COM-
MERCE**
CIBC
4755 Kingsway, Burnaby, BC, V5H 4W2
(604) 665-1379
Emp Here 40
SIC 6021 National commercial banks

    D-U-N-S 24-011-4814   (BR)
CHILDREN'S PLACE (CANADA) LP, THE
CHILDREN'S PLACE, THE
4700 Kingsway Suite 1211, Burnaby, BC, V5H
4M1
(604) 430-6030
Emp Here 35
SIC 5641 Children's and infants' wear stores

    D-U-N-S 24-418-2882   (BR)
CINEPLEX ODEON CORPORATION
SILVERCITY METROPOLIS
4700 Kingsway Suite M4, Burnaby, BC, V5H
4M1
(604) 435-7474
Emp Here 20

SIC 7832 Motion picture theaters, except
drive-in

    D-U-N-S 24-345-9497   (BR)
CITY OF BURNABY
BURNABY PARKS & RECREATION
6533 Nelson Ave, Burnaby, BC, V5H 0C2
(604) 439-5510
Emp Here 200
SIC 8322 Individual and family services

    D-U-N-S 25-011-1507   (BR)
DENCAN RESTAURANTS INC
DENNY'S RESTAURANT
(*Suby of* Northland Properties Corporation)
5605 Kingsway, Burnaby, BC, V5H 2G4
(604) 434-9016
Emp Here 37
SIC 5812 Eating places

    D-U-N-S 20-645-2489   (SL)
DIGIFACTS SYNDICATE
4720 Kingsway Suite 900, Burnaby, BC, V5H
4N2
(604) 435-4317
Emp Here 52   *Sales* 2,685,378
SIC 8721 Accounting, auditing, and book-
keeping

    D-U-N-S 25-319-5291   (BR)
DON MICHAEL HOLDINGS INC
ROOTS
4700 Kingsway Suite 1119, Burnaby, BC, V5H
4M1
(604) 435-5554
Emp Here 20
SIC 5651 Family clothing stores

    D-U-N-S 20-153-4794   (BR)
EARL'S RESTAURANTS LTD
EARL'S
(*Suby of* Earl's Restaurants Ltd)
4361 Kingsway, Burnaby, BC, V5H 1Z9
(604) 432-7329
Emp Here 40
SIC 5812 Eating places

    D-U-N-S 25-714-8247   (BR)
FGL SPORTS LTD
ATHLETES WORLD
4700 Kingsway Suite 1150, Burnaby, BC, V5H
4M1
(604) 436-1001
Emp Here 30
SIC 5699 Miscellaneous apparel and accessory stores

    D-U-N-S 25-506-0527   (BR)
FGL SPORTS LTD
SPORT CHEK
6200 Mckay Ave Suite 128, Burnaby, BC, V5H
4L7
(604) 433-1115
Emp Here 30
SIC 5941 Sporting goods and bicycle shops

    D-U-N-S 20-331-8204   (BR)
FAIRWEATHER LTD
4700 Kingsway Suite 2187, Burnaby, BC, V5H
4M1
(604) 227-1044
Emp Here 20
SIC 5621 Women's clothing stores

    D-U-N-S 20-863-0603   (BR)
GAP (CANADA) INC
BANANA REPUBLIC
(*Suby of* The Gap Inc)
4800 Kingsway Suite 221, Burnaby, BC, V5H
4J2
(604) 438-7900
Emp Here 60
SIC 5651 Family clothing stores

    D-U-N-S 25-736-2053   (BR)
GAP (CANADA) INC
GAP
(*Suby of* The Gap Inc)
4700 Kingsway Suite 2138, Burnaby, BC, V5H

4M1
(604) 431-6559
Emp Here 75
SIC 5651 Family clothing stores

D-U-N-S 24-787-2021   (BR)
GREAT PACIFIC INDUSTRIES INC
SAVE-ON-FOODS
6200 Mckay Ave Suite 120, Burnaby, BC, V5H
4L7
(604) 433-3760
Emp Here 380
SIC 5411 Grocery stores

D-U-N-S 25-712-3653   (SL)
GREATER VANCOUVER REGIONAL DISTRICT, THE
METRO VANCOUVER
4330 Kingsway, Burnaby, BC, V5H 4G7
(604) 451-6575
Emp Here 1,500   *Sales* 276,479,329
SIC 8741 Management services
Johnny Carline
Sec Paulette Vetleson
James (Jim) Rusnak
Lois Jackson
Richard Wolton

D-U-N-S 25-068-4370   (BR)
GROUPE ALDO INC, LE
4700 Kingsway Suite 2300, Burnaby, BC, V5H
4M1
(604) 430-6364
Emp Here 20
SIC 5661 Shoe stores

D-U-N-S 24-614-0024   (BR)
H. & C. MANAGEMENT CONSULTANTS LTD
FITNESS WORLD
(*Suby of* H. & C. Management Consultants
Ltd)
5500 Kingsway, Burnaby, BC, V5H 2G2
(604) 435-3385
Emp Here 20
SIC 7991 Physical fitness facilities

D-U-N-S 25-270-3046   (BR)
HSBC BANK CANADA
HSBC
5210 Kingsway, Burnaby, BC, V5H 2E9
(604) 438-6411
Emp Here 30
SIC 6021 National commercial banks

D-U-N-S 25-327-7446   (HQ)
HEMMERA ENVIROCHEM INC
4730 Kingsway 18 Fl, Burnaby, BC, V5H 0C6
(604) 669-0424
Emp Here 100   *Emp Total* 2
Sales 27,286,907
SIC 8748 Business consulting, nec
Pr Pr Paul Hemsley
Dir Shawn Cornett
Dir Jeff Devins
Dir Jim Stewart

D-U-N-S 25-684-1248   (SL)
HILTON VANCOUVER METROTOWN
6083 Mckay Ave, Burnaby, BC, V5H 2W7
(604) 438-1200
Emp Here 156   *Sales* 6,858,306
SIC 7011 Hotels and motels
Genl Mgr Ed Jaskula

D-U-N-S 24-040-3118   (BR)
HUDSON'S BAY COMPANY
HOME OUTFITTERS
4800 Kingsway Suite 118, Burnaby, BC, V5H
4J2
(604) 629-0144
Emp Here 376
SIC 5719 Miscellaneous homefurnishings

D-U-N-S 25-301-2306   (BR)
HUDSON'S BAY COMPANY
BAY, THE
4850 Kingsway, Burnaby, BC, V5H 4P2

(604) 436-1196
Emp Here 200
SIC 5311 Department stores

D-U-N-S 25-831-1430   (SL)
I.W.A. FOREST INDUSTRY PENSION & PLAN
3777 Kingsway Suite 2100, Burnaby, BC, V5H
3Z7
(604) 433-6310
Emp Here 50   *Sales* 5,399,092
SIC 8742 Management consulting services
Genl Mgr Robert Bishoff

D-U-N-S 20-087-4670   (BR)
INDIGO BOOKS & MUSIC INC
CHAPTERS
(*Suby of* Indigo Books & Music Inc)
4700 Kingsway Unit 1174, Burnaby, BC, V5H
4M1
(604) 431-0463
Emp Here 50
SIC 5942 Book stores

D-U-N-S 25-315-7432   (BR)
INVESTORS GROUP FINANCIAL SERVICES INC
INVESTORS GROUP
5945 Kathleen Ave Suite 900, Burnaby, BC,
V5H 4J7
(604) 431-0117
Emp Here 45
SIC 8741 Management services

D-U-N-S 20-104-9272   (BR)
IVANHOE CAMBRIDGE INC
IVANHOE CAMBRIDGE INC
4720 Kingsway Suite 604, Burnaby, BC, V5H
4N2
(604) 438-4715
Emp Here 50
SIC 6512 Nonresidential building operators

D-U-N-S 25-713-4486   (BR)
IVANHOE CAMBRIDGE INC
EATON CENTRE METROTOWN
4729 Kingsway Suite 604, Burnaby, BC, V5H
2C3
(604) 438-4715
Emp Here 20
SIC 8741 Management services

D-U-N-S 25-014-1819   (BR)
KPMG LLP
KPMG
(*Suby of* KPMG LLP)
4720 Kingsway Suite 2400, Burnaby, BC, V5H
4N2
(604) 527-3600
Emp Here 150
SIC 8721 Accounting, auditing, and bookkeeping

D-U-N-S 25-068-4446   (BR)
KAMEI ROYALE JAPANESE RESTAURANT LTD
TAISHO RESTAURANT
(*Suby of* Kamei Royale Japanese Restaurant
Ltd)
4700 Kingsway Suite 15e, Burnaby, BC, V5H
4M1

Emp Here 50
SIC 5812 Eating places

D-U-N-S 24-029-1047   (SL)
LAMBETH HOLDINGS LTD
BEST WESTERN KINGS INN
5411 Kingsway, Burnaby, BC, V5H 2G1
(604) 438-1383
Emp Here 65   *Sales* 2,845,467
SIC 7011 Hotels and motels

D-U-N-S 20-005-6047   (BR)
LOBLAWS INC
DISPLAY FIXTURES
5335 Kingsway, Burnaby, BC, V5H 2G1

Emp Here 36

SIC 5141 Groceries, general line

D-U-N-S 24-311-0509   (BR)
LONDON DRUGS LIMITED
4970 Kingsway, Burnaby, BC, V5H 2E2
(604) 448-4806
Emp Here 100
SIC 5912 Drug stores and proprietary stores

D-U-N-S 25-303-9440   (BR)
LONDON LIFE INSURANCE COMPANY
FREEDOM 55 QUADRUS
4710 Kingsway Suite 2238, Burnaby, BC, V5H
4M2
(604) 438-1232
Emp Here 40
SIC 6311 Life insurance

D-U-N-S 20-197-1194   (BR)
LORDCO PARTS LTD
LORDCO AUTO PARTS
5459 Kingsway, Burnaby, BC, V5H 2G1
(604) 412-9970
Emp Here 43
SIC 5531 Auto and home supply stores

D-U-N-S 24-161-7641   (BR)
LULULEMON ATHLETICA CANADA INC
LULULEMON
4800 Kingsway Unit 318, Burnaby, BC, V5H
4J2
(604) 430-4659
Emp Here 35
SIC 2339 Women's and misses' outerwear,
nec

D-U-N-S 25-450-4905   (BR)
MANCHU WOK (CANADA) INC
4820 Kingsway Unit 343, Burnaby, BC, V5H
4P1
(604) 439-9637
Emp Here 28
SIC 5812 Eating places

D-U-N-S 25-318-1952   (BR)
MCDONALD'S RESTAURANTS OF CANADA LIMITED
MCDONALD'S
(*Suby of* McDonald's Corporation)
4700 Kingsway Suite 1160, Burnaby, BC, V5H
4M1
(604) 718-1005
Emp Here 95
SIC 5812 Eating places

D-U-N-S 24-850-5187   (HQ)
MERIDIAN ONECAP CREDIT CORP
MERIDIAN ONECAP
4710 Kingsway Suite 1500, Burnaby, BC, V5H
4M2
(604) 646-2247
Emp Here 25   *Emp Total* 1,250
Sales 8,974,166
SIC 6159 Miscellaneous business credit institutions
Pr Pr Joe Laleggia
VP Mark Cannon
VP Robert Murphy
VP Sls Bob Mormina
VP Acctg Lui Spizzirri

D-U-N-S 20-648-5588   (BR)
MULTIPLE SCLEROSIS SOCIETY OF CANADA
*MULTIPLE SCLEROSIS SOCIETY OF
CANADA BC DIVISION*
4330 Kingsway Suite 1501, Burnaby, BC, V5H
4G7
(604) 689-3144
Emp Here 25
SIC 8399 Social services, nec

D-U-N-S 25-011-9633   (BR)
PATTISON, JIM INDUSTRIES LTD
JIM PATTISON SUZUKI
5400 Kingsway, Burnaby, BC, V5H 2E9
(604) 629-1800
Emp Here 45

SIC 5511 New and used car dealers

D-U-N-S 25-696-6110   (BR)
PRISZM LP
KFC
5094 Kingsway, Burnaby, BC, V5H 2E7
(604) 433-2220
Emp Here 21
SIC 5812 Eating places

D-U-N-S 24-449-7587   (BR)
RGIS CANADA ULC
5172 Kingsway Suite 310, Burnaby, BC, V5H
2E8
(604) 439-9222
Emp Here 49
SIC 7389 Business services, nec

D-U-N-S 24-503-1091   (HQ)
RLG INTERNATIONAL INC.
(*Suby of* RLG International Inc.)
4710 Kingsway Suite 2800, Burnaby, BC, V5H
4M2
(604) 669-7178
Emp Here 31   *Emp Total* 245
Sales 43,252,901
SIC 8741 Management services
Pr Pr Keith Cross
Dir Richard Mazur
Brad Farrow
Dave Helewka

D-U-N-S 20-709-2631   (BR)
ROGERS COMMUNICATIONS INC
ROGERS SHARED OPERATIONS
(*Suby of* Rogers Communications Inc)
4710 Kingsway Suite 1600, Burnaby, BC, V5H
4W4
(604) 431-1400
Emp Here 400
SIC 4899 Communication services, nec

D-U-N-S 20-115-9530   (BR)
SEARS CANADA INC
4750 Kingsway, Burnaby, BC, V5H 2C2
(604) 433-3211
Emp Here 290
SIC 5311 Department stores

D-U-N-S 24-797-8849   (BR)
SECURITAS CANADA LIMITED
5172 Kingsway Suite 270, Burnaby, BC, V5H
2E8
(604) 454-3600
Emp Here 300
SIC 7381 Detective and armored car services

D-U-N-S 24-350-3534   (SL)
SITA
4789 Kingsway Unit 500, Burnaby, BC, V5H
0A3
(604) 453-1050
Emp Here 53   *Sales* 4,591,130
SIC 7379 Computer related services, nec

D-U-N-S 25-064-9928   (BR)
STANTEC CONSULTING LTD
4730 Kingsway Suite 500, Burnaby, BC, V5H
0C6
(604) 436-3014
Emp Here 350
SIC 8748 Business consulting, nec

D-U-N-S 20-806-4514   (BR)
STARBUCKS COFFEE CANADA, INC
(*Suby of* Starbucks Corporation)
4700 Kingsway Suite 2255, Burnaby, BC, V5H
4M1
(604) 436-2500
Emp Here 30
SIC 5812 Eating places

D-U-N-S 25-499-1821   (BR)
STARBUCKS COFFEE CANADA, INC
STARBUCKS
(*Suby of* Starbucks Corporation)
4700 Kingsway Suite 1174, Burnaby, BC, V5H
4M1

(604) 431-9996
Emp Here 25
SIC 5812 Eating places

D-U-N-S 20-580-6255   (BR)
SUN LIFE ASSURANCE COMPANY OF CANADA
CLARICA
4720 Kingsway Suite 720, Burnaby, BC, V5H 4N2
(604) 438-5528
Emp Here 20
SIC 6311 Life insurance

D-U-N-S 25-718-5199   (BR)
T & T SUPERMARKET INC
METROTOWN STORE
4800 Kingsway Suite 147, Burnaby, BC, V5H 4J2
(604) 436-4881
Emp Here 150
SIC 5411 Grocery stores

D-U-N-S 25-297-8440   (BR)
TOYS 'R' US (CANADA) LTD
TOYS 'R' US
(*Suby of* Toys "r" Us, Inc.)
4800 Kingsway, Burnaby, BC, V5H 4J2
(604) 668-8330
Emp Here 50
SIC 5945 Hobby, toy, and game shops

D-U-N-S 24-042-8552   (HQ)
VFA CANADA CORPORATION
(*Suby of* VFA Canada Corporation)
4211 Kingsway Suite 400, Burnaby, BC, V5H 1Z6
(604) 685-3757
Emp Here 24   *Emp Total* 51
Sales 5,545,013
SIC 8748 Business consulting, nec
    Susan Anson
Off Mgr Lynda Gabriel

D-U-N-S 20-587-0582   (BR)
VANCOUVER CITY SAVINGS CREDIT UNION
VANCITY CREDIT UNION
6100 Mckay Ave Suite 120a, Burnaby, BC, V5H 4L6

Emp Here 20
SIC 6062 State credit unions

D-U-N-S 20-863-4634   (SL)
WILLINGDON PARK HOSPITAL LTD
WILLINGDON CARE CENTRE
4435 Grange St, Burnaby, BC, V5H 1P4
(604) 433-2455
Emp Here 100   *Sales* 4,523,563
SIC 8051 Skilled nursing care facilities

D-U-N-S 24-313-6160   (BR)
WINNERS MERCHANTS INTERNATIONAL L.P.
WINNERS
(*Suby of* The TJX Companies Inc)
4700 Kingsway Unit 604, Burnaby, BC, V5H 4M1
(604) 430-3457
Emp Here 70
SIC 5651 Family clothing stores

Burnaby, BC V5J
Greater Vancouver County

D-U-N-S 24-362-6525   (BR)
3856011 CANADA INC
BLOOMSTAR BOUQUET
8560 Roseberry Ave Unit 1, Burnaby, BC, V5J 3N3
(604) 412-9760
Emp Here 20
SIC 5992 Florists

D-U-N-S 24-750-5100   (BR)

ABB INC
3731 North Fraser Way Suite 600, Burnaby, BC, V5J 5J2
(604) 434-2454
Emp Here 30
SIC 3823 Process control instruments

D-U-N-S 25-723-2090   (BR)
ADIDAS CANADA LIMITED
3771 North Fraser Way Suite 7, Burnaby, BC, V5J 5G5
(604) 420-6646
Emp Here 20
SIC 5091 Sporting and recreation goods

D-U-N-S 20-138-9835   (BR)
ALSTOM CANADA INC
(*Suby of* General Electric Company)
731 North Fraser Way Suite 550, Burnaby, BC, V5J 5J2
(604) 412-2849
Emp Here 35
SIC 3621 Motors and generators

D-U-N-S 20-912-9498   (BR)
ARLA FOODS INC
7525 Lowland Dr, Burnaby, BC, V5J 5L1
(604) 437-8561
Emp Here 41
SIC 5143 Dairy products, except dried or canned

D-U-N-S 20-108-8226   (SL)
ARMATURE ELECTRIC LIMITED
3811 North Fraser Way, Burnaby, BC, V5J 5J2
(604) 879-6141
Emp Here 50   *Sales* 4,377,642
SIC 1731 Electrical work

D-U-N-S 24-696-5107   (HQ)
AUTOGAS PROPANE LTD
(*Suby of* A-1 Industrial Propane Holdings Ltd)
5605 Byrne Rd, Burnaby, BC, V5J 3J1
(604) 433-4900
Emp Here 40   *Emp Total* 4
Sales 10,798,184
SIC 5984 Liquefied petroleum gas dealers
Pr Pr Robert Good
    Jamie Good
    Bill Good

D-U-N-S 24-312-0367   (SL)
BARE SPORTS CANADA LTD
HUISH OUTDOORS
3711 North Fraser Way Suite 50, Burnaby, BC, V5J 5J2
(604) 235-2630
Emp Here 90   *Sales* 13,716,612
SIC 3069 Fabricated rubber products, nec
Pr Pr Gerry May
    Jorma Kallio
    Neil Melliship

D-U-N-S 24-034-5314   (SL)
BROADWAY ROOFING CO LTD
7430 Lowland Dr Suite 400, Burnaby, BC, V5J 5A4
(604) 439-9107
Emp Here 40   *Sales* 5,088,577
SIC 1761 Roofing, siding, and sheetMetal work

D-U-N-S 20-713-4458   (BR)
BURNABY SCHOOL BOARD DISTRICT 41
WINDSOR ELEMENTARY SCHOOL
6166 Imperial St, Burnaby, BC, V5J 1G5

Emp Here 50
SIC 8211 Elementary and secondary schools

D-U-N-S 20-713-4417   (BR)
BURNABY SCHOOL BOARD DISTRICT 41
SUNCREST ELEMENTARY SCHOOL
3883 Rumble St, Burnaby, BC, V5J 1Z5
(604) 664-8862
Emp Here 50
SIC 8211 Elementary and secondary schools

D-U-N-S 20-034-0425   (BR)
BURNABY SCHOOL BOARD DISTRICT 41
MAYWOOD COMMUNITY SCHOOL
4567 Imperial St, Burnaby, BC, V5J 1B7

Emp Here 60
SIC 8211 Elementary and secondary schools

D-U-N-S 25-011-9526   (BR)
BURNABY SCHOOL BOARD DISTRICT 41
CLINTON ELEMENTARY SCHOOL
5858 Clinton St, Burnaby, BC, V5J 2M3
(604) 664-8660
Emp Here 40
SIC 8211 Elementary and secondary schools

D-U-N-S 20-713-4474   (BR)
BURNABY SCHOOL BOARD DISTRICT 41
SOUTH SLOPE ELEMENTARY SCHOOL
4446 Watling St, Burnaby, BC, V5J 5H3

Emp Here 65
SIC 8211 Elementary and secondary schools

D-U-N-S 25-011-9070   (BR)
BURNABY SCHOOL BOARD DISTRICT 41
BURNABY SOUTH SECONDARY SCHOOL
5455 Rumble St, Burnaby, BC, V5J 2B7

Emp Here 250
SIC 8211 Elementary and secondary schools

D-U-N-S 25-013-1315   (BR)
BURNABY SCHOOL BOARD DISTRICT 41
NELSON ELEMENTARY SCHOOL
4850 Irmin St, Burnaby, BC, V5J 1Y2

Emp Here 40
SIC 8211 Elementary and secondary schools

D-U-N-S 25-195-4871   (BR)
CH2M HILL ENERGY CANADA LTD
(*Suby of* Ch2m Hill Companies, Ltd.)
4599 Tillicum St, Burnaby, BC, V5J 3J9

Emp Here 75
SIC 8711 Engineering services

D-U-N-S 24-386-8440   (HQ)
CANDA SIX FORTUNE ENTERPRISE CO. LTD
8138 North Fraser Way, Burnaby, BC, V5J 0E7
(604) 432-9000
Emp Here 40   *Emp Total* 138,000
Sales 5,763,895
SIC 5149 Groceries and related products, nec
    Tina Lee
Pr Cindy Lee
    Robert Balcom
    Sarah Davis
    Grant Froese
    Peter Mclaughlin
    Deborah Morshead
    Robert Stassen
    Irene Tsui

D-U-N-S 24-162-5839   (HQ)
CERTIFIED GENERAL ACCOUNTANTS ASSOCIATION OF CANADA
CGA CANADA
(*Suby of* Certified General Accountants Association of Canada)
4200 North Fraser Way Suite 100, Burnaby, BC, V5J 5K7
(604) 408-6660
Emp Here 117   *Emp Total* 125
Sales 17,621,552
SIC 8621 Professional organizations
    Tony Ducie
V Ch Bd Terry Leblanc

D-U-N-S 20-558-2666   (SL)
CITADEL COMMERCE CORP
(*Suby of* ESI Entertainment Systems Inc)
8610 Glenlyon Pky Unit 130, Burnaby, BC, V5J 0B6
(604) 299-6924
Emp Here 95   *Sales* 12,403,319

SIC 7372 Prepackaged software
Pr Pr Michael Meeks
    Ian Franks
Dir Mary Betts
VP Opers Colin Ramsay
VP Ivan Metalnikov
Fin Ex Patti Nakashima

D-U-N-S 20-584-4335   (SL)
COLUMBIA VALVE & FITTING LTD
SWAGELOK CANADA
8678 Greenall Ave Suite 117, Burnaby, BC, V5J 3M6
(604) 629-9355
Emp Here 20   *Sales* 5,376,850
SIC 5085 Industrial supplies
Pr Pr James Crozier

D-U-N-S 25-977-4115   (SL)
COMTOWER SERVICES INC
7590 Lowland Dr, Burnaby, BC, V5J 5A4
(604) 436-5755
Emp Here 25   *Sales* 5,197,506
SIC 1623 Water, sewer, and utility lines

D-U-N-S 20-333-2432   (BR)
CREATION TECHNOLOGIES LP
8997 Fraserton Crt Suite 102, Burnaby, BC, V5J 5H8
(604) 430-4336
Emp Here 400
SIC 3679 Electronic components, nec

D-U-N-S 25-414-4983   (SL)
DNA DATA NETWORKING AND ASSEMBLIES LTD
8057 North Fraser Way, Burnaby, BC, V5J 5M8
(604) 439-1099
Emp Here 70
SIC 3678 Electronic connectors

D-U-N-S 24-797-4322   (BR)
ELECTRO SONIC INC
(*Suby of* Electro Sonic Inc)
5489 Byrne Rd Suite 173, Burnaby, BC, V5J 3J1
(604) 273-2911
Emp Here 21
SIC 5065 Electronic parts and equipment, nec

D-U-N-S 24-376-3690   (BR)
EPIC PRODUCTION TECHNOLOGIES (CANADA SALES) INC
(*Suby of* Epic Production Technologies (Canada Sales) Inc)
3771 Marine Way, Burnaby, BC, V5J 5A7

Emp Here 20
SIC 7812 Motion picture and video production

D-U-N-S 24-977-1986   (BR)
FGL SPORTS LTD
SPORT CHEK BIG BEND CROSSING
5771 Marine Way Unit 600, Burnaby, BC, V5J 0A6
(778) 329-9381
Emp Here 20
SIC 5941 Sporting goods and bicycle shops

D-U-N-S 24-795-4949   (SL)
FEMO CONSTRUCTION LTD
8555 Greenall Ave Suite 1, Burnaby, BC, V5J 3M8
(604) 254-3999
Emp Here 200   *Sales* 21,888,210
SIC 1771 Concrete work
Pr Pr Emilio Zanna

D-U-N-S 20-006-6541   (BR)
GRAND & TOY LIMITED
(*Suby of* Office Depot, Inc.)
4560 Tillicum St, Burnaby, BC, V5J 5L4
(604) 324-5151
Emp Here 110
SIC 5943 Stationery stores

D-U-N-S 24-345-9463   (BR)
GREAT PACIFIC INDUSTRIES INC

PRICE SMART FOODS
7501 Market Cross, Burnaby, BC, V5J 0A3
(604) 433-4816
Emp Here 150
SIC 5411 Grocery stores

D-U-N-S 24-825-6844   (SL)
HEMLOCK EXPRESS (VANCOUVER) LTD
(*Suby of* Hemlock Printers Ltd)
7050 Buller Ave, Burnaby, BC, V5J 4S4
(604) 439-2456
Emp Here 20   *Sales* 1,532,175
SIC 2752 Commercial printing, lithographic

D-U-N-S 20-576-1448   (HQ)
HOULE ELECTRIC LIMITED
5050 North Fraser Way, Burnaby, BC, V5J 0H1
(604) 434-2681
Emp Here 60   *Emp Total* 300
Sales 31,185,036
SIC 1731 Electrical work
Pr Pr Robert Lashin
VP VP Dennis Carlow
Rois Rizzo
Shawn Boyd
Wayne Nielsen

D-U-N-S 20-298-3008   (SL)
HUDSON PLATING AND COATING CO. LTD
HUDSON POWDER COATING
3750 North Fraser Way Suite 102, Burnaby, BC, V5J 5G1
(604) 430-8384
Emp Here 50   *Sales* 4,523,179
SIC 3479 Metal coating and allied services

D-U-N-S 25-543-4854   (BR)
INTERTEK TESTING SERVICES (ITS) CANADA LTD
CALEB BRETT CANADA
9000 Bill Fox Way Suite 105, Burnaby, BC, V5J 5J3
(604) 454-9011
Emp Here 35
SIC 8099 Health and allied services, nec

D-U-N-S 24-345-8697   (BR)
INTERWEST RESTAURANTS INC
WENDY'S RESTAURANTS OF CANADA
5970 Kingsway, Burnaby, BC, V5J 1H2
(604) 437-9911
Emp Here 30
SIC 5812 Eating places

D-U-N-S 20-112-2822   (BR)
IRON MOUNTAIN CANADA OPERATIONS ULC
ARCHIVES IRON MOUNTAIN
8825 Northbrook Crt, Burnaby, BC, V5J 5J1
(604) 451-0618
Emp Here 60
SIC 4226 Special warehousing and storage, nec

D-U-N-S 20-116-3938   (HQ)
JAY DEE ESS INVESTMENTS LTD
HAMPTON HOUSE FOODS, DIV OF
7542 Gilley Ave, Burnaby, BC, V5J 4X5
(604) 430-1173
Emp Here 100   *Emp Total* 6,000
Sales 56,690,464
SIC 2015 Poultry slaughtering and processing
Pr Pr Blair Shier
Sultan Thiara
Treas Kim Bortnak
Ron Toigo
Peter Toigo

D-U-N-S 24-848-0043   (SL)
KARDIUM INC
8518 Glenlyon Pky Suite 155, Burnaby, BC, V5J 0B6
(604) 248-8891
Emp Here 40   *Sales* 2,699,546
SIC 8731 Commercial physical research

D-U-N-S 24-366-1431   (BR)
LIVANOVA CANADA CORP

5005 North Fraser Way, Burnaby, BC, V5J 5M1
(604) 412-5650
Emp Here 250
SIC 3841 Surgical and medical instruments

D-U-N-S 25-561-2520   (SL)
LIVART FURNITURE CANADA CO. LTD
5618 Imperial St, Burnaby, BC, V5J 1E9
(778) 318-2191
Emp Here 50   *Sales* 3,465,004
SIC 2511 Wood household furniture

D-U-N-S 20-047-1329   (SL)
LYNCH BUS LINES LTD
4687 Byrne Rd, Burnaby, BC, V5J 3H6
(604) 439-0842
Emp Here 60   *Sales* 1,678,096
SIC 4151 School buses

D-U-N-S 20-799-8287   (SL)
MAIL-O-MATIC SERVICES LIMITED
7550 Lowland Dr, Burnaby, BC, V5J 5A4
(604) 439-9668
Emp Here 55   *Sales* 2,772,507
SIC 7331 Direct mail advertising services

D-U-N-S 24-724-5269   (SL)
MANDEVILLE GARDEN CENTER LTD
(*Suby of* Summerwinds Garden Centers, Inc.)
4746 Marine Dr, Burnaby, BC, V5J 3G6
(604) 434-4118
Emp Here 35   *Sales* 5,690,935
SIC 5261 Retail nurseries and garden stores
Walter C. Minnick
Dir John Jozwik
Dir William J. Mcfetridge
Dir Grant K. Weaver

D-U-N-S 20-425-5566   (HQ)
MCLAREN, P. D. LIMITED
5069 Beresford St, Burnaby, BC, V5J 1H8
(604) 437-0616
Emp Here 20   *Emp Total* 50
Sales 5,653,974
SIC 1799 Special trade contractors, nec
Pr Pr Philip Douglas Mclaren
John Briggs

D-U-N-S 25-453-1080   (SL)
MEDI-TRAN SERVICES (1993) LTD
MTS LOGISTICS
7125 Curragh Ave, Burnaby, BC, V5J 4V6
(604) 872-5293
Emp Here 50   *Sales* 2,626,585
SIC 7389 Business services, nec

D-U-N-S 24-899-2463   (HQ)
MEDIACO THE PRESENTATION COMPANY INC
(*Suby of* Mediaco The Presentation Company Inc)
4595 Tillicum St, Burnaby, BC, V5J 5K9
(604) 871-1000
Emp Here 35   *Emp Total* 305
Sales 31,756,487
SIC 7359 Equipment rental and leasing, nec
Pr Pr Kevin Leinbach
James Brett

D-U-N-S 25-977-4156   (BR)
MOTT ELECTRIC GENERAL PARTNERSHIP
MTI
(*Suby of* Mott Electric General Partnership)
7590 Lowland Dr, Burnaby, BC, V5J 5A4
(604) 436-5755
Emp Here 45
SIC 1541 Industrial buildings and warehouses

D-U-N-S 24-368-3427   (HQ)
MOTT ELECTRIC GENERAL PARTNERSHIP
MTI
(*Suby of* Mott Electric General Partnership)
4599 Tillicum St Suite 100, Burnaby, BC, V5J 3J9

(604) 522-5757
Emp Here 30   *Emp Total* 250
Sales 21,888,210
SIC 1731 Electrical work
Pt Dan Mott
Pt Robert Brett
Pt Graham Trafford

D-U-N-S 25-387-9019   (SL)
MUSTANG SURVIVAL ULC
(*Suby of* Maui Acquisition Corp.)
7525 Lowland Dr, Burnaby, BC, V5J 5L1
(604) 270-8631
Emp Here 350   *Sales* 63,236,323
SIC 3069 Fabricated rubber products, nec
Pr Sean Mccarthy
CEO James (Jim) Hartt

D-U-N-S 20-426-1523   (BR)
OLD DUTCH FOODS LTD
HUMPTY DUMPTY OLD DUTCH FOODS
(*Suby of* Old Dutch Foods Ltd)
7800 Fraser Park Dr, Burnaby, BC, V5J 5L8
(604) 430-9955
Emp Here 30
SIC 2096 Potato chips and similar snacks

D-U-N-S 24-070-8180   (BR)
OPTIQUE NIKON CANADA INC
5542 Short St, Burnaby, BC, V5J 1L9
(604) 713-7400
Emp Here 30
SIC 5049 Professional equipment, nec

D-U-N-S 24-837-6683   (BR)
ORKIN CANADA CORPORATION
ORKIN PCO
(*Suby of* Rollins, Inc.)
7061 Gilley Ave, Burnaby, BC, V5J 4X1
(604) 434-6641
Emp Here 40
SIC 7342 Disinfecting and pest control services

D-U-N-S 25-314-6351   (SL)
PARAMOUNT PRODUCTION SUPPORT INC
8015 North Fraser Way, Burnaby, BC, V5J 5M8
(604) 294-9660
Emp Here 39   *Sales* 2,188,821
SIC 7819 Services allied to motion pictures

D-U-N-S 24-881-8056   (SL)
PRESIDENT CANADA SYNDICATES INC
PRESIDENT CANADA GROUP
3888 North Fraser Way Suite 8, Burnaby, BC, V5J 5H6
(604) 432-9848
Emp Here 30   *Sales* 12,344,510
SIC 6553 Cemetery subdividers and developers
Pr Pr Jack Lee
Yung-Kwei Lu
Ching-Feng Wu
Chin-Tsu Lee

D-U-N-S 24-359-8831   (BR)
PROTECTION INCENDIE VIKING INC
VIKING FIRE PROTECTION
7885 North Fraser Way Unit 140, Burnaby, BC, V5J 5M7
(604) 324-7122
Emp Here 25
SIC 8711 Engineering services

D-U-N-S 24-797-9446   (BR)
RINGBALL CORPORATION
7880 Fraser Park Dr, Burnaby, BC, V5J 5L8
(604) 294-3461
Emp Here 25
SIC 5085 Industrial supplies

D-U-N-S 24-421-5039   (SL)
RITCHIE BROS. AUCTIONEERS (INTERNATIONAL) LTD
9500 Glenlyon Pky Suite 300, Burnaby, BC, V5J 0C6
(778) 331-5500
Emp Here 50   *Sales* 5,630,632

SIC 5999 Miscellaneous retail stores, nec
Dir Robert Mackay
Dir Peter Blake

D-U-N-S 25-099-0108   (BR)
SECURITE POLYGON INC
VIKING FIRE PROTECTION
7885 North Fraser Way Unit 140, Burnaby, BC, V5J 5M7
(604) 324-7122
Emp Here 50
SIC 1623 Water, sewer, and utility lines

D-U-N-S 20-187-4810   (BR)
SERVICES KAMTECH INC
3700 North Fraser Way Suite 220, Burnaby, BC, V5J 5H4

Emp Here 30
SIC 1541 Industrial buildings and warehouses

Burns Lake, BC V0J
Bulkley - Nechako County

D-U-N-S 20-590-5008   (BR)
BOARD OF EDUCATION OF SCHOOL DISTRICT NO. 91 (NECHAKO LAKE), THE
GRASSY PLAINS ELEMENTARY JUNIOR SECONDARY SCHOOL
34310 Keefes Landing Rd, Burns Lake, BC, V0J 1E4
(250) 694-3396
Emp Here 25
SIC 8211 Elementary and secondary schools

D-U-N-S 20-034-0938   (BR)
BOARD OF EDUCATION OF SCHOOL DISTRICT NO. 91 (NECHAKO LAKE), THE
DECKER LAKE ELEMENTARY SCHOOL
6710 Decker Lake Frontage Rd, Burns Lake, BC, V0J 1E1
(250) 698-7301
Emp Here 20
SIC 8211 Elementary and secondary schools

D-U-N-S 24-561-7175   (BR)
BOARD OF EDUCATION OF SCHOOL DISTRICT NO. 91 (NECHAKO LAKE), THE
LAKES DISTRICT SECONDARY SCHOOL
685 Hwy 16 W, Burns Lake, BC, V0J 1E0
(250) 692-7733
Emp Here 51
SIC 8211 Elementary and secondary schools

D-U-N-S 20-590-4977   (BR)
BOARD OF EDUCATION OF SCHOOL DISTRICT NO. 91 (NECHAKO LAKE), THE
WILLIAM KONKIN ELEMENTARY SCHOOL
Gd, Burns Lake, BC, V0J 1E0
(250) 692-3146
Emp Here 32
SIC 8211 Elementary and secondary schools

D-U-N-S 24-345-5339   (BR)
COLLEGE OF NEW CALEDONIA, THE
LAKES DISTRICT CAMPUS
(*Suby of* College Of New Caledonia, The)
545 Hwy 16, Burns Lake, BC, V0J 1E0
(250) 692-1700
Emp Here 50
SIC 8221 Colleges and universities

D-U-N-S 24-333-9624   (SL)
HAMPTON LUMBER MILLS - CANADA, LTD
Gd, Burns Lake, BC, V0J 1E0
(250) 692-7177
Emp Here 350   *Sales* 70,593,280
SIC 6712 Bank holding companies
Dir Steve Zika

D-U-N-S 20-733-9230   (BR)
LOBLAWS INC
REAL CANADIAN WHOLESALE CLUB
221 Hwy 16, Burns Lake, BC, V0J 1E0

(250) 692-1981
Emp Here 20
SIC 5141 Groceries, general line

D-U-N-S 20-875-3280   (BR)
NORTHERN HEALTH AUTHORITY
LAKE DISTRICT HOSPITAL
741 Ctr St, Burns Lake, BC, V0J 1E0
(250) 692-2400
Emp Here 200
SIC 6324 Hospital and medical service plans

D-U-N-S 20-333-3422   (BR)
PINNACLE RENEWABLE ENERGY INC
22975 Hwy 16 E, Burns Lake, BC, V0J 1E3
(250) 562-5562
Emp Here 65
SIC 2499 Wood products, nec

Cache Creek, BC V0K
Thompson - Nicola County

D-U-N-S 20-057-0401   (BR)
GRAYMONT WESTERN CANADA INC
Gd, Cache Creek, BC, V0K 1H0
(250) 457-6291
Emp Here 30
SIC 3274 Lime

D-U-N-S 25-453-2161   (BR)
WASTECH SERVICES LTD
S Trans-Canada Hwy, Cache Creek, BC, V0K 1H0
(250) 457-6464
Emp Here 50
SIC 4953 Refuse systems

Campbell River, BC V9H
Comox - Strathcona County

D-U-N-S 20-591-6013   (BR)
BOARD OF EDUCATION SCHOOL DISTRICT 72 (CAMPBELL RIVER), THE
GEORGIA PARK ELEMENTARY SCHOOL
678 Hudson Rd, Campbell River, BC, V9H 1T4
(250) 923-0735
Emp Here 28
SIC 8211 Elementary and secondary schools

D-U-N-S 25-416-8818   (BR)
BOARD OF EDUCATION SCHOOL DISTRICT 72 (CAMPBELL RIVER), THE
OCEAN GROVE ELEMENTARY SCHOOL
3773 Mclelan Rd, Campbell River, BC, V9H 1K2
(250) 923-4266
Emp Here 20
SIC 8211 Elementary and secondary schools

D-U-N-S 24-859-1625   (BR)
QUINSAM COAL CORPORATION
5800 Argonaut Rd, Campbell River, BC, V9H 1P3
(250) 286-3224
Emp Here 50
SIC 1222 Bituminous coal-underground mining

Campbell River, BC V9W
Comox - Strathcona County

D-U-N-S 25-296-9019   (BR)
BANK OF NOVA SCOTIA, THE
SCOTIABANK
961 Alder St, Campbell River, BC, V9W 2R1
(250) 286-4350
Emp Here 22
SIC 6021 National commercial banks

D-U-N-S 25-289-2393   (BR)

BLACK PRESS GROUP LTD
CAMPBELL RIVER MIRROR
250 Dogwood St Suite 104, Campbell River, BC, V9W 2X9
(250) 287-9227
Emp Here 25
SIC 2711 Newspapers

D-U-N-S 20-031-1756   (BR)
BOARD OF EDUCATION SCHOOL DISTRICT 72 (CAMPBELL RIVER), THE
TIMBERLINE SECONDARY SCHOOL
1681 Dogwood St S, Campbell River, BC, V9W 8C1

Emp Here 65
SIC 8211 Elementary and secondary schools

D-U-N-S 24-974-6603   (BR)
BOARD OF EDUCATION SCHOOL DISTRICT 72 (CAMPBELL RIVER), THE
CARIHI HIGH SECONDARY SCHOOL
350 Dogwood St, Campbell River, BC, V9W 2X9
(250) 286-6282
Emp Here 60
SIC 8211 Elementary and secondary schools

D-U-N-S 20-033-7413   (BR)
BOARD OF EDUCATION SCHOOL DISTRICT 72 (CAMPBELL RIVER), THE
ECOLE PHOENIX MIDDLE SCHOOL
400 7th Ave, Campbell River, BC, V9W 3Z9
(250) 287-8346
Emp Here 70
SIC 8211 Elementary and secondary schools

D-U-N-S 20-034-0847   (BR)
BOARD OF EDUCATION SCHOOL DISTRICT 72 (CAMPBELL RIVER), THE
SANDOWNE ELEMENTARY SCHOOL
699 Sandowne Dr, Campbell River, BC, V9W 5G9
(250) 923-4248
Emp Here 30
SIC 8211 Elementary and secondary schools

D-U-N-S 20-591-5981   (BR)
BOARD OF EDUCATION SCHOOL DISTRICT 72 (CAMPBELL RIVER), THE
CEDAR ELEMENTARY
261 Cedar St, Campbell River, BC, V9W 2V3
(250) 287-8335
Emp Here 30
SIC 8211 Elementary and secondary schools

D-U-N-S 24-974-6611   (BR)
BOARD OF EDUCATION SCHOOL DISTRICT 72 (CAMPBELL RIVER), THE
CAMPBELLTON ELEMENTARY SCHOOL
2175 Campbell River Rd, Campbell River, BC, V9W 4N8

Emp Here 28
SIC 8211 Elementary and secondary schools

D-U-N-S 25-485-7766   (BR)
BOARD OF EDUCATION SCHOOL DISTRICT 72 (CAMPBELL RIVER), THE
PINECREST ELEMENTARY SCHOOL
300 Birch St S, Campbell River, BC, V9W 2S1
(250) 287-8805
Emp Here 45
SIC 8211 Elementary and secondary schools

D-U-N-S 20-027-0473   (BR)
BOARD OF EDUCATION SCHOOL DISTRICT 72 (CAMPBELL RIVER), THE
PENFIELD ELEMENTARY SCHOOL
525 Hilchey Rd, Campbell River, BC, V9W 6S3
(250) 923-4251
Emp Here 25
SIC 8211 Elementary and secondary schools

D-U-N-S 20-591-5973   (BR)
BOARD OF EDUCATION SCHOOL DISTRICT 72 (CAMPBELL RIVER), THE

ECOLE WILLOW POINT ELEMENTARY
250 Larwood Rd, Campbell River, BC, V9W 1S4
(250) 923-4311
Emp Here 30
SIC 8211 Elementary and secondary schools

D-U-N-S 25-313-4548   (BR)
BRITISH COLUMBIA HYDRO AND POWER AUTHORITY
BC HYDRO
1105 Evergreen Rd, Campbell River, BC, V9W 3S1
(250) 286-8700
Emp Here 22
SIC 4911 Electric services

D-U-N-S 20-786-4583   (SL)
BROWN, BARRIE PONTIAC BUICK GMC LTD
2700 Island Hwy, Campbell River, BC, V9W 2H5
(250) 287-7272
Emp Here 26   *Sales* 13,188,500
SIC 5511 New and used car dealers
Pr Barrie Brown

D-U-N-S 20-580-1405   (BR)
CANADA POST CORPORATION
1090 Ironwood St, Campbell River, BC, V9W 5P0
(250) 287-9124
Emp Here 60
SIC 4311 U.s. postal service

D-U-N-S 25-089-8715   (SL)
CANADIAN SURF BOAT MFG. INC
Gd, Campbell River, BC, V9W 5B6
(250) 287-6421
Emp Here 50   *Sales* 3,638,254
SIC 3732 Boatbuilding and repairing

D-U-N-S 25-817-5561   (BR)
CANADIAN UNION OF POSTAL WORKERS
CUPW
1090 Ironwood St, Campbell River, BC, V9W 5P7

Emp Here 60
SIC 8631 Labor organizations

D-U-N-S 20-623-6507   (SL)
CHOO KIN ENTERPRISES LTD
SEYMOUR PEOPLE DRUG MART #174
984 Shoppers Row, Campbell River, BC, V9W 2C5
(250) 287-8311
Emp Here 54   *Sales* 7,660,874
SIC 5912 Drug stores and proprietary stores
Pr Pr Victor Choo
  Judith Choo

D-U-N-S 25-936-2408   (BR)
COAST HOTELS LIMITED
COAST DISCOVERY INN & MARINA
975 Shoppers Row, Campbell River, BC, V9W 2C4
(250) 287-9225
Emp Here 75
SIC 7011 Hotels and motels

D-U-N-S 25-902-3950   (BR)
COAST REALTY GROUP LTD
COAST REALTY (CAMPBELL RIVER)
1211 Cypress St, Campbell River, BC, V9W 2Z3
(250) 830-8088
Emp Here 20
SIC 6531 Real estate agents and managers

D-U-N-S 25-129-3809   (BR)
COMOX VALLEY REGIONAL DISTRICT
STRATHCONA GARDENS RECREATION
225 Dogwood St S, Campbell River, BC, V9W 8C8
(250) 287-9234
Emp Here 88
SIC 7999 Amusement and recreation, nec

D-U-N-S 20-064-2853   (BR)
FIRSTCANADA ULC
509 13th Ave, Campbell River, BC, V9W 4G7
(250) 287-7151
Emp Here 30
SIC 4141 Local bus charter service

D-U-N-S 24-804-3098   (SL)
GTA GOLF
500 Colwyn St Suite 58, Campbell River, BC, V9W 5J2
(250) 255-8897
Emp Here 120   *Sales* 5,717,257
SIC 7997 Membership sports and recreation clubs
Ch Bd Spencer Basha

D-U-N-S 25-155-9787   (BR)
GREAT CANADIAN RAILTOUR COMPANY LTD
(*Suby of* Armstrong Hospitality Group Ltd)
509 13th Ave, Campbell River, BC, V9W 4G7
(250) 287-7151
Emp Here 27
SIC 4111 Local and suburban transit

D-U-N-S 25-270-3129   (BR)
HSBC BANK CANADA
1000 Shoppers Row, Campbell River, BC, V9W 2C6
(250) 286-0011
Emp Here 25
SIC 6021 National commercial banks

D-U-N-S 24-803-7306   (BR)
HOME DEPOT OF CANADA INC
HOME DEPOT
(*Suby of* The Home Depot Inc)
1482 Island Hwy, Campbell River, BC, V9W 8C9
(250) 286-5400
Emp Here 50
SIC 5251 Hardware stores

D-U-N-S 24-986-7792   (BR)
INLAND KENWORTH LTD
INLAND KENWORTH
2900n Island Hwy, Campbell River, BC, V9W 2H5
(250) 287-8878
Emp Here 31
SIC 5084 Industrial machinery and equipment

D-U-N-S 24-620-1990   (BR)
INLAND KENWORTH LTD
INLAND KENWORTH
2470n Island Hwy, Campbell River, BC, V9W 2H1
(250) 287-8878
Emp Here 28
SIC 5012 Automobiles and other motor vehicles

D-U-N-S 24-995-7689   (SL)
ISLAND PIPELINES CONSTRUCTION (B.C. CANADA) CORP
Gd Stn A, Campbell River, BC, V9W 4Z8
(250) 923-4468
Emp Here 164   *Sales* 33,032,960
SIC 1623 Water, sewer, and utility lines
Pr Pr Percy Baxandall

D-U-N-S 25-148-7583   (BR)
LOBLAWS INC
REAL CANADIAN SUPERSTORE
1424 Island Hwy Suite 1524, Campbell River, BC, V9W 8C9
(250) 830-2736
Emp Here 200
SIC 5399 Miscellaneous general merchandise

D-U-N-S 25-042-1518   (SL)
MACNEILL, DR PHILIP M
ALDER MEDICAL CENTER
277 Evergreen Rd, Campbell River, BC, V9W 5Y4
(250) 287-7441
Emp Here 50   *Sales* 3,863,549

SIC 8011 Offices and clinics of medical doctors

D-U-N-S 20-094-1367   (SL)
MARSHALL, STEVE MOTORS (1996) LTD
STEVE MARSHALL FORD
2300 N Island Hwy, Campbell River, BC, V9W 2G8
(250) 287-9171
Emp Here 75   *Sales* 27,360,263
SIC 5511 New and used car dealers
Pr Pr Steve Marshall

D-U-N-S 25-165-1188   (SL)
MOXIE'S CLASSIC GRILL
1360 Island Hwy, Campbell River, BC, V9W 8C9
(250) 830-1500
Emp Here 50   *Sales* 1,532,175
SIC 5812 Eating places

D-U-N-S 20-040-5210   (BR)
NORTH ISLAND COLLEGE
1685 Dogwood St S, Campbell River, BC, V9W 8C1
(250) 923-9700
Emp Here 200
SIC 8221 Colleges and universities

D-U-N-S 20-581-4002   (HQ)
NYRSTAR MYRA FALLS LTD.
1 Boliden Mine St, Campbell River, BC, V9W 5E2
(250) 287-9271
Emp Here 379   *Emp Total* 380
Sales 24,688,154
SIC 1481 NonMetallic mineral services
Pr Pr John Galassini
Sec Sara Smith

D-U-N-S 24-855-9734   (BR)
PLAYTIME COMMUNITY GAMING CENTRES INC
111 St. Ann'S Rd, Campbell River, BC, V9W 4C5
(250) 286-1442
Emp Here 60
SIC 8322 Individual and family services

D-U-N-S 25-019-0428   (BR)
ROYAL BANK OF CANADA
RBC
(*Suby of* Royal Bank Of Canada)
1290 Shoppers Row, Campbell River, BC, V9W 2C8
(250) 286-5500
Emp Here 24
SIC 6021 National commercial banks

D-U-N-S 25-417-4022   (SL)
SEYMOUR PACIFIC DEVELOPMENTS LTD
920 Alder St, Campbell River, BC, V9W 2P8
(250) 286-8045
Emp Here 150   *Sales* 38,541,256
SIC 1522 Residential construction, nec
Pr Pr Krisjan Daniel Mailman

D-U-N-S 25-689-5186   (BR)
STAPLES CANADA INC
STAPLES THE BUSINESS DEPOT
(*Suby of* Staples, Inc.)
1440 Island Hwy, Campbell River, BC, V9W 8C9
(250) 286-4390
Emp Here 30
SIC 5943 Stationery stores

D-U-N-S 24-337-1791   (BR)
THE CITY OF CAMPBELL RIVER
SPORTSPLEX
(*Suby of* The City Of Campbell River)
1800 Alder St S, Campbell River, BC, V9W 7J1
(250) 923-7911
Emp Here 24
SIC 8322 Individual and family services

D-U-N-S 25-896-1614   (SL)
UNCLE RAY'S RESTAURANT CO. LTD

MCDONALD'S RESTAURANT
1361 16th Ave, Campbell River, BC, V9W 2C9
(250) 287-2631
Emp Here 100   *Sales* 2,991,389
SIC 5812 Eating places

D-U-N-S 20-705-5174   (BR)
VANCOUVER ISLAND HEALTH AUTHORITY
CAMPBELL RIVER HEALTH UNIT
1100 Island Hwy Unit 200, Campbell River, BC, V9W 8C6
(250) 850-2110
Emp Here 27
SIC 8011 Offices and clinics of medical doctors

D-U-N-S 24-581-8260   (BR)
WAL-MART CANADA CORP
WALMART
1477 Island Hwy, Campbell River, BC, V9W 8E5
(250) 287-3631
Emp Here 50
SIC 5311 Department stores

D-U-N-S 20-914-7094   (BR)
WESTERN FOREST PRODUCTS INC
TIMBERLANDS CORPORATE OFFICE
1334 Island Hwy Suite 118, Campbell River, BC, V9W 8C9
(250) 286-3767
Emp Here 40
SIC 2611 Pulp mills

D-U-N-S 25-129-6752   (BR)
WHITE SPOT LIMITED
WHITE SPOT RESTAURANT
1329 Island Hwy, Campbell River, BC, V9W 8C2
(250) 287-9350
Emp Here 38
SIC 5812 Eating places

Canyon, BC V0B
Central Kootenay County

D-U-N-S 25-676-7591   (BR)
SCHOOL DISTRICT NO. 8 (KOOTENAY LAKE)
CANYON-LISTER ELEMENTARY SCHOOL
(*Suby of* School District No. 8 (Kootenay Lake))
4575 Canyon-Lister Rd, Canyon, BC, V0B 1C1
(250) 428-4161
Emp Here 20
SIC 8211 Elementary and secondary schools

Castlegar, BC V1N
Central Kootenay County

D-U-N-S 25-627-1503   (BR)
A & W FOOD SERVICES OF CANADA INC
A & W RESTAURANTS
1982 Columbia Ave, Castlegar, BC, V1N 2W7
(250) 365-4990
Emp Here 35
SIC 5812 Eating places

D-U-N-S 25-288-9456   (BR)
CANADA POST CORPORATION
CASTLEGAR PO
1011 4th St, Castlegar, BC, V1N 2B1
(250) 365-7237
Emp Here 50
SIC 4311 U.s. postal service

D-U-N-S 25-016-8945   (BR)
CANADIAN IMPERIAL BANK OF COMMERCE
CIBC

1801 Columbia Ave, Castlegar, BC, V1N 3Y2
(250) 365-3325
Emp Here 25
SIC 6021 National commercial banks

D-U-N-S 25-126-6508   (BR)
CHANTELLE MANAGEMENT LTD
CASTLEVIEW CARE CENTRE
2300 14th Ave, Castlegar, BC, V1N 4A6
(250) 365-7277
Emp Here 50
SIC 8361 Residential care

D-U-N-S 25-626-0845   (BR)
GOLDER ASSOCIATES LTD
201 Columbia Ave, Castlegar, BC, V1N 1A8
(250) 365-0344
Emp Here 20
SIC 8711 Engineering services

D-U-N-S 25-362-2971   (BR)
INTERIOR HEALTH AUTHORITY
CASTLEGAR MENTAL HEALTH
709 10th St, Castlegar, BC, V1N 2H7
(250) 365-4300
Emp Here 100
SIC 8062 General medical and surgical hospitals

D-U-N-S 24-030-2869   (SL)
KALAWSKY PONTIAC BUICK G M C (1989) LTD
(*Suby of* Kalawsky Management Services Ltd)
1700 Columbia Ave, Castlegar, BC, V1N 2W4
(250) 365-2155
Emp Here 25   *Sales* 12,560,000
SIC 5511 New and used car dealers
Pr Pr Neil Kalawsky
VP VP Darlene Kalawsky

D-U-N-S 20-108-0751   (SL)
KALESNIKOFF LUMBER CO. LTD
2090 3a Hwy, Castlegar, BC, V1N 4N1
(250) 399-4211
Emp Here 100   *Sales* 9,484,891
SIC 2421 Sawmills and planing mills, general
Pr Pr Kenneth Kalesnikoff

D-U-N-S 24-897-1053   (BR)
NORTHLAND PROPERTIES CORPORATION
SANDMAN HOTEL
(*Suby of* Northland Properties Corporation)
1944 Columbia Ave, Castlegar, BC, V1N 2W7
(250) 365-8444
Emp Here 45
SIC 7011 Hotels and motels

D-U-N-S 20-034-6349   (BR)
SCHOOL DISTRICT # 20 (KOOTENAY-COLUMBIA)
STANLEY HUMPHRIES SECONDARY
720 7th Ave, Castlegar, BC, V1N 1R5
(250) 365-7735
Emp Here 40
SIC 8211 Elementary and secondary schools

D-U-N-S 25-100-3034   (BR)
SCHOOL DISTRICT # 20 (KOOTENAY-COLUMBIA)
KINNAIRD ELEMENTARY SCHOOL
(*Suby of* School District # 20 (Kootenay-Columbia))
2273 10th Ave, Castlegar, BC, V1N 2Z8
(250) 365-8478
Emp Here 35
SIC 8211 Elementary and secondary schools

D-U-N-S 25-480-7977   (BR)
SCHOOL DISTRICT # 20 (KOOTENAY-COLUMBIA)
TWIN RIVERS ELEMENTARY SCHOOL
(*Suby of* School District # 20 (Kootenay-Columbia))
649 7th Ave, Castlegar, BC, V1N 1R6
(250) 365-8465
Emp Here 30

SIC 8211 Elementary and secondary schools

D-U-N-S 24-233-3511   (BR)
SCHOOL DISTRICT # 20 (KOOTENAY-COLUMBIA)
BLUEBERRY CREEK COMMUNITY SCHOOL
200 Centre Ave, Castlegar, BC, V1N 3B9
(250) 365-7201
Emp Here 30
SIC 8222 Junior colleges

D-U-N-S 25-003-6621   (BR)
SOBEYS WEST INC
SAFEWAY
1721 Columbia Ave, Castlegar, BC, V1N 2W6
(250) 365-7771
Emp Here 60
SIC 5411 Grocery stores

D-U-N-S 20-790-3746   (BR)
TELUS COMMUNICATIONS INC
TELUS BC
2229 14th Ave, Castlegar, BC, V1N 3X5
(250) 365-2191
Emp Here 50
SIC 4813 Telephone communication, except radio

D-U-N-S 20-690-3531   (SL)
ZELLSTOFF CELGAR LIMITED
1921 Arrow Lakes Dr, Castlegar, BC, V1N 3H9
(250) 365-7211
Emp Here 420   *Sales* 18,021,293
SIC 2611 Pulp mills
Pr Pr Jimmy Lee
David M Gandossi

Castlegar, BC V1R
Central Kootenay County

D-U-N-S 24-351-2279   (BR)
BRITISH COLUMBIA HYDRO AND POWER AUTHORITY
BC HYDRO
601 18 St, Castlegar, BC, V1R 4L2
(250) 365-4550
Emp Here 20
SIC 4911 Electric services

Cawston, BC V0X
Okanagn-Similkameen County

D-U-N-S 20-713-2387   (BR)
SCHOOL DISTRICT NO. 53 (OKANAGAN SIMILKAMEEN)
CAWSTON PRIMARY SCHOOL
517 School Rd, Cawston, BC, V0X 1C1
(250) 499-5617
Emp Here 25
SIC 8211 Elementary and secondary schools

Celista, BC V0E
Columbia - Shuswap County

D-U-N-S 20-590-9869   (BR)
NORTH OKANAGAN SHUSWAP SCHOOL DISTRICT 83
NORTH SHUSAP ELEMENTARY SCHOOL
5437 Meadow Creek Rd, Celista, BC, V0E 1M6
(250) 955-2214
Emp Here 25
SIC 8211 Elementary and secondary schools

Charlie Lake, BC V0C
Peace River - Laird County

D-U-N-S 24-350-0308   (BR)
PETROWEST CONSTRUCTION LP
QUIGLEY CONTRACTING, DIV OF
Gd, Charlie Lake, BC, V0C 1H0
(250) 787-0254
Emp Here 35
SIC 1381 Drilling oil and gas wells

D-U-N-S 20-026-8527   (BR)
SCHOOL DISTRICT NO. 60 (PEACE RIVER NORTH)
CHARLIE LAKE ELEMENTARY SCHOOL
52 Alaska Hwy, Charlie Lake, BC, V0C 1H0
(250) 785-2025
Emp Here 35
SIC 8211 Elementary and secondary schools

Chase, BC V0E
Thompson - Nicola County

D-U-N-S 24-724-9717   (BR)
INTERFOR CORPORATION
ADAMS LAKE LUMBER
9200 Holding Rd Suite 2, Chase, BC, V0E 1M2
(250) 679-3234
Emp Here 200
SIC 2421 Sawmills and planing mills, general

D-U-N-S 25-482-7801   (BR)
INTERIOR HEALTH AUTHORITY
CHASE HEALTH CENTRE
825 Thompson Ave, Chase, BC, V0E 1M0
(250) 679-2899
Emp Here 30
SIC 8062 General medical and surgical hospitals

D-U-N-S 20-915-8211   (BR)
SCHOOL DISTRICT 73 (KAMLOOPS/THOMPSON)
CHASE SECONDARY SCHOOL
420 Cottonwood Rd, Chase, BC, V0E 1M0
(250) 679-3218
Emp Here 25
SIC 8211 Elementary and secondary schools

D-U-N-S 20-027-0564   (BR)
SCHOOL DISTRICT 73 (KAMLOOPS/THOMPSON)
HALDANE ELEMENTARY SCHOOL
530 Cottonwood Ave, Chase, BC, V0E 1M0
(250) 679-3269
Emp Here 25
SIC 8211 Elementary and secondary schools

D-U-N-S 24-899-2265   (SL)
SKWLAX INVESTMENTS INC
TALKING ROCK RESORT & QUAAOUT LODGE
1663 Little Shuswap Lake Rd Rr 2, Chase, BC, V0E 1M2
(250) 679-3090
Emp Here 38   *Sales* 1,992,377
SIC 7011 Hotels and motels

Chemainus, BC V0R
Cowichan Valley County

D-U-N-S 20-339-6028   (BR)
COASTAL COMMUNITY CREDIT UNION
CHEMAINUS CREDIT UNION
9781 Willow St, Chemainus, BC, V0R 1K0
(250) 246-4704
Emp Here 25
SIC 6062 State credit unions

D-U-N-S 20-797-0653   (BR)
SCHOOL DISTRICT NO. 79 (COWICHAN VALLEY)
CHEMAINUS ALTERNATE SCHOOL
9796 Willow St, Chemainus, BC, V0R 1K0
(250) 246-4040
Emp Here 20
SIC 8211 Elementary and secondary schools

D-U-N-S 20-590-8218   (BR)
SCHOOL DISTRICT NO. 79 (COWICHAN VALLEY)
CHEMAINUS SECONDARY SCHOOL
9947 Daniel St, Chemainus, BC, V0R 1K1
(250) 246-4711
Emp Here 45
SIC 8211 Elementary and secondary schools

D-U-N-S 20-590-8093   (BR)
SCHOOL DISTRICT NO. 79 (COWICHAN VALLEY)
CHEMAINUS ELEMENTARY COMMUNITY SCHOOL
3172 Garner St, Chemainus, BC, V0R 1K2
(250) 246-3522
Emp Here 30
SIC 8211 Elementary and secondary schools

D-U-N-S 20-561-3768   (BR)
WESTERN FOREST PRODUCTS INC
VALUE ADDED REMAN
9469 Trans Canada Hwy, Chemainus, BC, V0R 1K4
(250) 246-1566
Emp Here 75
SIC 2611 Pulp mills

D-U-N-S 25-366-8859   (BR)
WESTERN FOREST PRODUCTS INC
CHEMAINUS SAWMILL
2860 Victoria St, Chemainus, BC, V0R 1K0
(250) 246-3221
Emp Here 190
SIC 2611 Pulp mills

Chetwynd, BC V0C
Peace River - Laird County

D-U-N-S 25-592-9333   (BR)
7-ELEVEN CANADA, INC
7-ELEVEN STORE #32104
5001 Access Rd S, Chetwynd, BC, V0C 1J0
(250) 788-3710
Emp Here 28
SIC 5411 Grocery stores

D-U-N-S 20-821-0984   (SL)
DUZ CHO CONSTRUCTION LP
4821 Access Rd S, Chetwynd, BC, V0C 1J0
(250) 788-3120
Emp Here 50   *Sales* 9,423,290
SIC 4619 Pipelines, nec
Dir Arlene Salones

D-U-N-S 24-388-1450   (BR)
PEACE RIVER REGIONAL DISTRICT
4552 Access Rd N, Chetwynd, BC, V0C 1J0
(250) 788-2214
Emp Here 35
SIC 7999 Amusement and recreation, nec

D-U-N-S 20-033-3586   (BR)
SCHOOL DISTRICT #59 PEACE RIVER SOUTH
CHETWYND SECONDARY SCHOOL
5000 46th St, Chetwynd, BC, V0C 1J0
(250) 788-2267
Emp Here 47
SIC 8211 Elementary and secondary schools

D-U-N-S 20-027-0895   (BR)
SCHOOL DISTRICT #59 PEACE RIVER SOUTH
WINDREM ELEMENTARY SCHOOL
5004 46th St, Chetwynd, BC, V0C 1J0
(250) 788-2528
Emp Here 20

SIC 8211 Elementary and secondary schools

D-U-N-S 20-026-8543   (BR)
SCHOOL DISTRICT #59 PEACE RIVER SOUTH
LITTLE PRAIRIE ELEMENTARY SCHOOL
4200 51st Ave, Chetwynd, BC, V0C 1J0
(250) 788-1924
Emp Here 30
SIC 8211 Elementary and secondary schools

D-U-N-S 24-066-8665   (BR)
WEST FRASER MILLS LTD
CHETWYND FOREST INDUSTRIES
3598 Fraser St W, Chetwynd, BC, V0C 1J0
(250) 788-2686
Emp Here 200
SIC 2421 Sawmills and planing mills, general

D-U-N-S 20-325-1509   (BR)
WESTCOAST ENERGY INC
SPECTRA ENERGY
4528 44 Ave, Chetwynd, BC, V0C 1J0
(250) 788-4700
Emp Here 100
SIC 4922 Natural gas transmission

Chilliwack, BC V2P

D-U-N-S 20-031-9692   (BR)
AGROPUR COOPERATIVE
NATREL
47582 Yale Rd, Chilliwack, BC, V2P 7N1

Emp Here 30
SIC 5143 Dairy products, except dried or canned

D-U-N-S 25-296-9050   (BR)
BANK OF NOVA SCOTIA, THE
SCOTIABANK
46059 Yale Rd, Chilliwack, BC, V2P 2M1
(604) 702-3250
Emp Here 30
SIC 6021 National commercial banks

D-U-N-S 25-642-5638   (BR)
BANK OF MONTREAL
BANK OF MONTREAL
46115 Yale Rd, Chilliwack, BC, V2P 2P2
(604) 792-1971
Emp Here 22
SIC 6021 National commercial banks

D-U-N-S 24-129-6263   (BR)
BLACK PRESS GROUP LTD
CHILLIWACK PROGRESS, THE
45860 Spadina Ave, Chilliwack, BC, V2P 6H9
(604) 702-5550
Emp Here 25
SIC 2711 Newspapers

D-U-N-S 24-426-3534   (SL)
CSH HAMPTON HOUSE INC
CHARTWELL SELECT HAMPTON HOUSE RETIREMENT COMMUNITY
45555 Hodgins Ave Unit 223, Chilliwack, BC, V2P 1P3
(604) 703-1982
Emp Here 20   *Sales* 729,607
SIC 8361 Residential care

D-U-N-S 25-126-4925   (SL)
CSH LYNNWOOD INC
LYNNWOOD RETIREMENT RESIDENCE
9168 Corbould St Suite 224, Chilliwack, BC, V2P 8A1
(604) 792-0689
Emp Here 30   *Sales* 1,299,377
SIC 8361 Residential care

D-U-N-S 25-288-9530   (BR)
CANADA POST CORPORATION
CHILLIWACK POST OFFICE
46229 Yale Rd, Chilliwack, BC, V2P 2P4

(604) 795-1604
Emp Here 43
SIC 4311 U.s. postal service

D-U-N-S 25-622-8248   (BR)
CANADIAN IMPERIAL BANK OF COMMERCE
CIBC
9245 Young Rd, Chilliwack, BC, V2P 4R3
(604) 702-3130
Emp Here 40
SIC 6021 National commercial banks

D-U-N-S 25-450-5886   (BR)
CATHOLIC INDEPENDENT SCHOOLS OF VANCOUVER ARCHDIOCESE, THE
ST MARY'S SCHOOL
8909 Mary St, Chilliwack, BC, V2P 4J4
(604) 792-7715
Emp Here 30
SIC 8211 Elementary and secondary schools

D-U-N-S 25-082-5734   (HQ)
CHILLIWACK COMMUNITY SERVICES
(Suby of Chilliwack Community Services)
45938 Wellington Ave, Chilliwack, BC, V2P 2C7
(604) 792-4267
Emp Here 26   *Emp Total* 120
Sales 14,770,560
SIC 8399 Social services, nec
Ex Dir James Challman
Dir Opers Suzanne Cameron

D-U-N-S 20-623-7885   (SL)
CHILLIWACK TAXI LTD
45877 Hocking Ave, Chilliwack, BC, V2P 1B5
(604) 795-9177
Emp Here 85   *Sales* 2,553,625
SIC 4121 Taxicabs

D-U-N-S 20-713-3356   (SL)
DAIRY BOY SALES LTD
DAIRY QUEEN
9055 Young Rd, Chilliwack, BC, V2P 4R3
(604) 792-8531
Emp Here 58   *Sales* 1,751,057
SIC 5812 Eating places

D-U-N-S 24-858-5742   (BR)
DEVRY GREENHOUSES (1989) LTD
DEVRY GREENHOUSES LTD
10074 Reeves Rd, Chilliwack, BC, V2P 6H4
(604) 794-3874
Emp Here 50
SIC 5261 Retail nurseries and garden stores

D-U-N-S 25-782-1777   (BR)
EDENVALE RESTORATION SPECIALISTS LTD
8465 Harvard Pl Suite 5, Chilliwack, BC, V2P 7Z5
(604) 795-4884
Emp Here 200
SIC 1542 Nonresidential construction, nec

D-U-N-S 25-217-1608   (BR)
FRASER HEALTH AUTHORITY
PARKHOLM PLACE
9090 Newman Rd, Chilliwack, BC, V2P 3Z8
(604) 792-7121
Emp Here 20
SIC 8322 Individual and family services

D-U-N-S 25-451-4839   (BR)
FRASER HEALTH AUTHORITY
CHILLIWACK HEALTH UNIT
45470 Menholm Rd, Chilliwack, BC, V2P 1M2
(604) 702-4900
Emp Here 150
SIC 8011 Offices and clinics of medical doctors

D-U-N-S 20-134-5357   (BR)
FRASER HEALTH AUTHORITY
CHILLIWACK MENTAL HEALTH CENTRE
45470 Menholm Rd, Chilliwack, BC, V2P 1M2
(604) 702-4860
Emp Here 30

SIC 8093 Specialty outpatient clinics, nec

D-U-N-S 25-082-4349   (BR)
FRASER VALLEY REGIONAL LIBRARY DISTRICT
45860 First Ave, Chilliwack, BC, V2P 7K1
(604) 792-1941
Emp Here 20
SIC 8231 Libraries

D-U-N-S 20-040-2498   (BR)
GOVERNING COUNCIL OF THE SALVATION ARMY IN CANADA, THE
GOVERNING COUNCIL OF THE SALVATION ARMY IN CANADA, THE
46420 Brooks Ave, Chilliwack, BC, V2P 1C5
(604) 792-0311
Emp Here 50
SIC 8661 Religious organizations

D-U-N-S 24-724-5293   (BR)
GREAT PACIFIC INDUSTRIES INC
PRICE SMART FOODS
46020 Yale Rd, Chilliwack, BC, V2P 7V2
(604) 792-7520
Emp Here 200
SIC 5411 Grocery stores

D-U-N-S 25-270-3160   (BR)
HSBC BANK CANADA
9345 Main St, Chilliwack, BC, V2P 4M3
(604) 795-9181
Emp Here 40
SIC 6021 National commercial banks

D-U-N-S 24-803-7298   (BR)
HOME DEPOT OF CANADA INC
HOME DEPOT
(Suby of The Home Depot Inc)
8443 Eagle Landing Pky Unit 100, Chilliwack, BC, V2P 0E2
(604) 703-1502
Emp Here 50
SIC 5251 Hardware stores

D-U-N-S 25-301-5804   (BR)
KPMG LLP
KPMG
(Suby of KPMG LLP)
9123 Mary St Suite 200, Chilliwack, BC, V2P 4H7
(604) 793-4700
Emp Here 20
SIC 8721 Accounting, auditing, and book-keeping

D-U-N-S 25-273-1435   (BR)
LORDCO PARTS LTD
LORDCO AUTO PARTS
45771 Yale Rd, Chilliwack, BC, V2P 2N5
(604) 792-1999
Emp Here 30
SIC 5531 Auto and home supply stores

D-U-N-S 24-136-5865   (BR)
MNP LLP
45780 Yale Rd Unit 1, Chilliwack, BC, V2P 2N4
(604) 792-1915
Emp Here 25
SIC 8721 Accounting, auditing, and book-keeping

D-U-N-S 25-892-8407   (BR)
MCDONALD'S RESTAURANTS OF CANADA LIMITED
MCDONALD'S
(Suby of McDonald's Corporation)
45816 Yale Rd, Chilliwack, BC, V2P 2N7
(604) 795-5911
Emp Here 100
SIC 5812 Eating places

D-U-N-S 24-367-2250   (SL)
NETHERLANDS REFORMED CONGREGATION OF CHILLIWACK, THE
TIMOTHY CHRISTIAN SCHOOL
50420 Castleman Rd, Chilliwack, BC, V2P 6H4

(604) 792-9945
Emp Here 75   Sales 6,898,600
SIC 8661 Religious organizations
Dir Pieter Van Ruitenburg
Dir Gerard Hofman
Dir Frank Les
Dir Gert Kuipers
Dir Ed Maljaars
Dir Johan Proos
 Wim Neels
Dir Neil Stam
Dir Martin Zwartbol
Dir Henk Rozendaall

D-U-N-S 20-094-7489   (SL)
PIONEER BUILDING SUPPLIES LTD
PIONEER TIM-BR MART
45754 Yale Rd, Chilliwack, BC, V2P 2N4
(604) 795-7238
Emp Here 43   Sales 6,274,620
SIC 5211 Lumber and other building materials
 John Giesbrecht
Pr Pr Barry Giesbrecht
 Beatrice Giesbrecht
 Shirley Giesbrecht
 Donna Giesbrecht
 Wendy Murphy
 Randall Giesbrecth

D-U-N-S 20-177-8730   (BR)
POSTMEDIA NETWORK INC
CHILLIWACK TIMES NEWSPAPER
45951 Trethewey Ave Unit 101, Chilliwack, BC, V2P 1K4
(604) 792-9117
Emp Here 20
SIC 2711 Newspapers

D-U-N-S 25-616-5853   (BR)
PROSPERA CREDIT UNION
45820 Wellington Ave, Chilliwack, BC, V2P 2C9

Emp Here 20
SIC 6062 State credit unions

D-U-N-S 24-335-3989   (BR)
ROGERS MEDIA INC
(Suby of Rogers Communications Inc)
46167 Yale Rd Suite 309, Chilliwack, BC, V2P 2P2
(604) 795-5711
Emp Here 20
SIC 4832 Radio broadcasting stations

D-U-N-S 20-713-2981   (BR)
SCHOOL DISTRICT NO 33 CHILLIWACK
EAST CHILLIWACK ELEMENTARY SCHOOL
49190 Chilliwack Central Rd, Chilliwack, BC, V2P 6H3
(604) 794-7533
Emp Here 20
SIC 8211 Elementary and secondary schools

D-U-N-S 25-082-5924   (BR)
SCHOOL DISTRICT NO 33 CHILLIWACK
CHILLIWAKE MIDDLE SCHOOL
46354 Yale Rd, Chilliwack, BC, V2P 2R1
(604) 795-5781
Emp Here 50
SIC 8211 Elementary and secondary schools

D-U-N-S 25-539-4306   (BR)
SCHOOL DISTRICT NO 33 CHILLIWACK
FRASER VALLEY DISTANCE EDUCATION SCHOOL
49520 Prairie Central Rd Suite 33, Chilliwack, BC, V2P 6H3
(604) 701-4910
Emp Here 60
SIC 8249 Vocational schools, nec

D-U-N-S 25-676-4549   (BR)
SCHOOL DISTRICT NO 33 CHILLIWACK
STUDENT SERVICES, DIV OF
8430 Cessna Dr, Chilliwack, BC, V2P 7K4
(604) 792-2515
Emp Here 35

SIC 8322 Individual and family services

D-U-N-S 25-539-4389   (BR)
SCHOOL DISTRICT NO 33 CHILLIWACK
ROBERTSON ELEMENTARY
46106 Southlands Cres, Chilliwack, BC, V2P 1B1
(604) 795-5312
Emp Here 30
SIC 8211 Elementary and secondary schools

D-U-N-S 25-539-4660   (BR)
SCHOOL DISTRICT NO 33 CHILLIWACK
STRATHCONA ELEMENTARY SCHOOL
46375 Strathcona Rd, Chilliwack, BC, V2P 3T1
(604) 792-9301
Emp Here 40
SIC 8211 Elementary and secondary schools

D-U-N-S 25-539-4579   (BR)
SCHOOL DISTRICT NO 33 CHILLIWACK
MCCAMMON TRADITIONAL ELEMENTARY SCHOOL
9601 Hamilton St, Chilliwack, BC, V2P 3X4
(604) 795-7000
Emp Here 32
SIC 8211 Elementary and secondary schools

D-U-N-S 25-538-8001   (BR)
SCHOOL DISTRICT NO 33 CHILLIWACK
A.D. RUNDLE MIDDLE SCHOOL
45660 Hocking Ave, Chilliwack, BC, V2P 1B3
(604) 792-4257
Emp Here 40
SIC 8211 Elementary and secondary schools

D-U-N-S 25-538-7888   (BR)
SCHOOL DISTRICT NO 33 CHILLIWACK
CHILLIWACK SECONDARY SCHOOL
46363 Yale Rd, Chilliwack, BC, V2P 2P8
(604) 795-7295
Emp Here 92
SIC 8211 Elementary and secondary schools

D-U-N-S 25-539-4330   (BR)
SCHOOL DISTRICT NO 33 CHILLIWACK
BERNARD ELEMENTARY SCHOOL
45465 Bernard Ave, Chilliwack, BC, V2P 1H6
(604) 795-7840
Emp Here 37
SIC 8211 Elementary and secondary schools

D-U-N-S 25-676-4424   (BR)
SCHOOL DISTRICT NO 33 CHILLIWACK
CHILLIWAK SCHOOL DISTRICT 33
8430 Cessna Dr, Chilliwack, BC, V2P 7K4
(604) 792-1321
Emp Here 40
SIC 8211 Elementary and secondary schools

D-U-N-S 25-539-4371   (BR)
SCHOOL DISTRICT NO 33 CHILLIWACK
CHILLIWACK CENTRAL ELEMENTARY SCHOOL
9435 Young Rd, Chilliwack, BC, V2P 4S7
(604) 792-8537
Emp Here 40
SIC 8211 Elementary and secondary schools

D-U-N-S 25-539-4538   (BR)
SCHOOL DISTRICT NO 33 CHILLIWACK
F.G. LEARY ELEMENTARY SCHOOL
9320 Walden St, Chilliwack, BC, V2P 7Y2
(604) 792-1281
Emp Here 21
SIC 8211 Elementary and secondary schools

D-U-N-S 25-539-4546   (BR)
SCHOOL DISTRICT NO 33 CHILLIWACK
LITTLE MOUNTAIN ELEMENTARY SCHOOL
9900 Carleton St, Chilliwack, BC, V2P 6E5
(604) 792-0681
Emp Here 45
SIC 8211 Elementary and secondary schools

D-U-N-S 25-271-1155   (BR)
SOBEYS WEST INC
CHILLIWACK SAFEWAY

45850 Yale Rd, Chilliwack, BC, V2P 2N9
(604) 795-6428
Emp Here 63
SIC 5411 Grocery stores

D-U-N-S 25-642-6149   (BR)
TORONTO-DOMINION BANK, THE
TD CANADA TRUST
(Suby of Toronto-Dominion Bank, The)
46017 Yale Rd, Chilliwack, BC, V2P 2M1
(604) 795-9166
Emp Here 20
SIC 6021 National commercial banks

D-U-N-S 24-042-6176   (BR)
YOUNG MEN'S CHRISTIAN ASSOCIATION OF GREATER VANCOUVER
CHILLIWACK FAMILY YMCA, THE
45844 Hocking Ave, Chilliwack, BC, V2P 1B4
(604) 792-3371
Emp Here 75
SIC 7999 Amusement and recreation, nec

Chilliwack, BC V2R

D-U-N-S 25-329-4748   (SL)
3992 BC INC
MACDONALD'S
45225 Luckakuck Way, Chilliwack, BC, V2R 3C7
(604) 858-5512
Emp Here 69   Sales 2,512,128
SIC 5812 Eating places

D-U-N-S 24-064-3387   (BR)
A & W FOOD SERVICES OF CANADA INC
8249 Eagle Landing Pky Unit 500, Chilliwack, BC, V2R 0P9
(604) 392-1128
Emp Here 20
SIC 5812 Eating places

D-U-N-S 20-321-7294   (BR)
CARA OPERATIONS LIMITED
SWISS CHALET
(Suby of Cara Holdings Limited)
8249 Eagle Landing Pky Suite 600, Chilliwack, BC, V2R 0P9
(604) 701-3480
Emp Here 20
SIC 5812 Eating places

D-U-N-S 24-066-3976   (BR)
CITY OF CHILLIWACK
TWIN RINKS ICE ARENA
5725 Tyson Rd, Chilliwack, BC, V2R 3R6
(604) 793-2904
Emp Here 20
SIC 7999 Amusement and recreation, nec

D-U-N-S 20-937-0407   (SL)
COOKIES GRILL
44335 Yale Rd Suite 3a, Chilliwack, BC, V2R 4H2
(604) 792-0444
Emp Here 69   Sales 2,334,742
SIC 5461 Retail bakeries

D-U-N-S 25-620-1237   (BR)
EARL'S RESTAURANTS LTD
(Suby of Earl's Restaurants Ltd)
45583 Luckakuck Way, Chilliwack, BC, V2R 1A3
(604) 858-3360
Emp Here 60
SIC 5812 Eating places

D-U-N-S 20-860-5696   (BR)
GLENTEL INC
WIRELESS WAVES
44585 Luckakuck Way, Chilliwack, BC, V2R 3C7
(604) 824-7144
Emp Here 25
SIC 4813 Telephone communication, except

radio

D-U-N-S 25-300-2372   (BR)
INNVEST PROPERTIES CORP
COMFORT INN
(*Suby of* Innvest Properties Corp)
45405 Luckakuck Way, Chilliwack, BC, V2R
3C7
(604) 858-0636
Emp Here 20
SIC 7011 Hotels and motels

D-U-N-S 25-360-1298   (BR)
JOHNSTON PACKERS LTD
5828 Promontory Rd, Chilliwack, BC, V2R
4M4
(604) 858-4882
Emp Here 100
SIC 2011 Meat packing plants

D-U-N-S 24-314-2606   (BR)
KAL TIRE LTD
KAL TIRE RETREAD PLANT
43850 Progress Way Unit 2, Chilliwack, BC,
V2R 0C3
(604) 701-6153
Emp Here 35
SIC 5531 Auto and home supply stores

D-U-N-S 24-640-3976   (SL)
LICKMAN TRAVEL CENTRE INC
BEST WESTERN RAINBOW COUNTRY INN
43971 Industrial Way Suite 2, Chilliwack,
BC, V2R 3A4
(604) 795-3828
Emp Here 80   *Sales* 3,502,114
SIC 7011 Hotels and motels

D-U-N-S 25-651-9141   (SL)
MANSFIELD FOODS #3 - 611 LTD
WHITE SPOT
45373 Luckakuck Way, Chilliwack, BC, V2R
3C7
(604) 858-0616
Emp Here 50   *Sales* 1,819,127
SIC 5812 Eating places

D-U-N-S 20-212-7333   (BR)
**MASONITE INTERNATIONAL CORPORA-
TION**
(*Suby of* Masonite International Corporation)
41916 Yarrow Central Rd, Chilliwack, BC, V2R
5E7
(604) 823-6223
Emp Here 135
SIC 2431 Millwork

D-U-N-S 24-631-2933   (BR)
PRAIRIECOAST EQUIPMENT INC
44158 Progress Way, Chilliwack, BC, V2R
0W3
(250) 544-8010
Emp Here 250
SIC 5083 Farm and garden machinery

D-U-N-S 25-646-3092   (BR)
PRISZM LP
KFC
45367 Luckakuck Way, Chilliwack, BC, V2R
3C7
(604) 858-3799
Emp Here 29
SIC 5812 Eating places

D-U-N-S 24-555-0616   (BR)
PROSPERA CREDIT UNION
7565 Vedder Rd, Chilliwack, BC, V2R 4E8
(604) 858-7080
Emp Here 35
SIC 6062 State credit unions

D-U-N-S 25-170-5240   (HQ)
QSR SERVICES CORP
BURGER KING
(*Suby of* QSR Services Corp)
45625 Luckakuck Way, Chilliwack, BC, V2R
1A3
(604) 858-4148
Emp Here 30   *Emp Total* 50
Sales 1,532,175

SIC 5812 Eating places

D-U-N-S 25-370-5396   (BR)
ROGERS FOODS LTD
44360 Simpson Rd, Chilliwack, BC, V2R 4B7
(604) 824-6260
Emp Here 25
SIC 2041 Flour and other grain mill products

D-U-N-S 20-512-0082   (SL)
SARDIS EXPLOSIVES (2000) LTD
WESTERN EXPLOSIVES
6890 Lickman Rd, Chilliwack, BC, V2R 4A9
(604) 858-6919
Emp Here 20   *Sales* 6,219,371
SIC 5169 Chemicals and allied products, nec

D-U-N-S 25-539-4736   (BR)
SCHOOL DISTRICT NO 33 CHILLIWACK
VEDDER ELEMENTARY SCHOOL
45850 Promontory Rd, Chilliwack, BC, V2R
5Z5
(604) 858-4759
Emp Here 50
SIC 8211 Elementary and secondary schools

D-U-N-S 25-538-7920   (BR)
SCHOOL DISTRICT NO 33 CHILLIWACK
MOUNT SLESSE MIDDLE SCHOOL
5871 Tyson Rd, Chilliwack, BC, V2R 3R6
(604) 824-7481
Emp Here 60
SIC 8211 Elementary and secondary schools

D-U-N-S 25-538-7938   (BR)
SCHOOL DISTRICT NO 33 CHILLIWACK
SARDIS SECONDARY SCHOOL
45460 Stevenson Rd, Chilliwack, BC, V2R
2Z6
(604) 858-9424
Emp Here 120
SIC 8211 Elementary and secondary schools

D-U-N-S 25-539-4629   (BR)
SCHOOL DISTRICT NO 33 CHILLIWACK
SARDIS ELEMENTARY SCHOOL
45775 Manuel Rd, Chilliwack, BC, V2R 2E6
(604) 858-7145
Emp Here 46
SIC 8211 Elementary and secondary schools

D-U-N-S 25-539-4702   (BR)
SCHOOL DISTRICT NO 33 CHILLIWACK
UNSWORTH ELEMENTARY
5621 Unsworth Rd, Chilliwack, BC, V2R 4B6
(604) 858-4510
Emp Here 45
SIC 8211 Elementary and secondary schools

D-U-N-S 25-539-4652   (BR)
SCHOOL DISTRICT NO 33 CHILLIWACK
WATSON ELEMENTARY SCHOOL
45305 Watson Rd, Chilliwack, BC, V2R 2H5
(604) 858-9477
Emp Here 30
SIC 8211 Elementary and secondary schools

D-U-N-S 20-713-3039   (BR)
SCHOOL DISTRICT NO 33 CHILLIWACK
*PROMONTORY HEIGHTS ELEMENTARY
SCHOOL*
46200 Stoneview Dr, Chilliwack, BC, V2R 5W8
(604) 824-4885
Emp Here 50
SIC 8211 Elementary and secondary schools

D-U-N-S 20-713-2999   (BR)
SCHOOL DISTRICT NO 33 CHILLIWACK
EVANS ELEMENTARY SCHOOL
7600 Evans Rd, Chilliwack, BC, V2R 1L2
(604) 858-3057
Emp Here 27
SIC 8211 Elementary and secondary schools

D-U-N-S 25-000-6053   (BR)
SCHOOL DISTRICT NO 33 CHILLIWACK
YARROW COMMUNITY SCHOOL
4605 Wilson Rd, Chilliwack, BC, V2R 5C4

(604) 823-4408
Emp Here 28
SIC 8211 Elementary and secondary schools

D-U-N-S 25-676-4507   (BR)
SCHOOL DISTRICT NO 33 CHILLIWACK
TRANSPORTATION DEPARTMENT
44877 Yale Rd, Chilliwack, BC, V2R 4H3
(604) 792-4327
Emp Here 54
SIC 4151 School buses

D-U-N-S 24-139-3953   (BR)
SCHOOL DISTRICT NO 33 CHILLIWACK
GW GRAHAM SECONDARY SCHOOL
45955 Thomas Rd, Chilliwack, BC, V2R 0B5
(604) 847-0772
Emp Here 50
SIC 8211 Elementary and secondary schools

D-U-N-S 20-591-4539   (BR)
SCHOOL DISTRICT NO 33 CHILLIWACK
TYSON ELEMENTARY SCHOOL
45170 South Sumas Rd, Chilliwack, BC, V2R
1W9
(604) 858-2111
Emp Here 33
SIC 8211 Elementary and secondary schools

D-U-N-S 25-294-6553   (BR)
SEARS CANADA INC
45585 Luckakuck Way, Chilliwack, BC, V2R
1A1
(604) 858-5211
Emp Here 180
SIC 5311 Department stores

D-U-N-S 25-271-7293   (BR)
SOBEYS WEST INC
45610 Luckakuck Way, Chilliwack, BC, V2R
1A2
(604) 858-8115
Emp Here 60
SIC 5411 Grocery stores

D-U-N-S 20-525-9422   (BR)
STAPLES CANADA INC
STAPLES THE BUSINESS DEPOT
(*Suby of* Staples, Inc.)
7491 Vedder Rd Suite 101, Chilliwack, BC,
V2R 6E7
(604) 824-8474
Emp Here 30
SIC 5943 Stationery stores

D-U-N-S 20-514-3378   (BR)
STREAM INTERNATIONAL CANADA ULC
SOLECTRON GLOBAL SERVICES
(*Suby of* Convergys Corporation)
7955 Evans Rd, Chilliwack, BC, V2R 5R7
(604) 702-5100
Emp Here 1,100
SIC 7389 Business services, nec

D-U-N-S 20-979-0422   (BR)
**TRIMAC TRANSPORTATION SERVICES
LIMITED PARTNERSHIP**
8510 Aitken Rd, Chilliwack, BC, V2R 3W8

Emp Here 250
SIC 4213 Trucking, except local

D-U-N-S 25-361-0117   (BR)
TROY LIFE & FIRE SAFETY LTD
*UPPER VALLEY FIRE PROTECTION, DIV
OF*
43775 Industrial Way, Chilliwack, BC, V2R 4L2

Emp Here 100
SIC 1711 Plumbing, heating, air-conditioning

D-U-N-S 24-374-0990   (BR)
UNIVERSITY OF THE FRASER VALLEY
UCFV
45190 Caen Ave, Chilliwack, BC, V2R 0N3
(604) 792-0025
Emp Here 600
SIC 8221 Colleges and universities

D-U-N-S 20-934-8577   (BR)

VALUE VILLAGE STORES, INC
(*Suby of* Savers, Inc.)
45150 Luckakuck Way Suite 1, Chilliwack, BC,
V2R 3C7
(604) 847-0667
Emp Here 40
SIC 5399 Miscellaneous general merchandise

D-U-N-S 25-627-5827   (BR)
**VANCOUVER CITY SAVINGS CREDIT
UNION**
VANCITY CREDIT UNION
45617 Luckakuck Way, Chilliwack, BC, V2R
1A3
(604) 824-8300
Emp Here 20
SIC 6062 State credit unions

D-U-N-S 20-015-2200   (BR)
VANTAGE FOODS INC
8200 Brannick Pl, Chilliwack, BC, V2R 0E9
(604) 795-4774
Emp Here 150
SIC 2011 Meat packing plants

D-U-N-S 24-858-6013   (BR)
VISSCHER LUMBER INC
VISSCHER SPECIALTY PRODUCTS
44565 Yale Rd Unit 6, Chilliwack, BC, V2R
4H2
(604) 858-3375
Emp Here 40
SIC 5031 Lumber, plywood, and millwork

D-U-N-S 25-498-2598   (BR)
WAL-MART CANADA CORP
45610 Luckakuck Way Unit 200, Chilliwack,
BC, V2R 1A2
(604) 858-5100
Emp Here 150
SIC 5311 Department stores

D-U-N-S 25-643-0083   (BR)
WENDY'S RESTAURANTS OF CANADA INC
WENDY'S
(*Suby of* The Wendy's Company)
7615 Vedder Rd, Chilliwack, BC, V2R 4E8
(604) 858-2323
Emp Here 35
SIC 5812 Eating places

D-U-N-S 20-013-7045   (SL)
WESTFORM MANUFACTURING INC
6435 Lickman Rd, Chilliwack, BC, V2R 4A9
(604) 858-7134
Emp Here 36   *Sales* 4,900,111
SIC 3444 Sheet Metalwork

D-U-N-S 25-416-0476   (HQ)
WESTFORM METALS INC
6435 Lickman Rd, Chilliwack, BC, V2R 4A9
(604) 858-7134
Emp Here 62   *Emp Total* 150
Sales 9,009,010
SIC 3444 Sheet Metalwork
Dir Christopher Visscher
Dir Art Dekker
Pr Peter L. Visscher
Dir Peter Visscher
Dir Theodore Visscher
Dir Leonard Visscher

Clearwater, BC V0E
Thompson - Nicola County

D-U-N-S 20-517-4662   (BR)
INTERIOR HEALTH AUTHORITY
DR ER HELMCKEN MEMORIAL HOSPITAL
640 Park Dr, Clearwater, BC, V0E 1N1
(250) 674-2244
Emp Here 100
SIC 8062 General medical and surgical hospi-
tals

D-U-N-S 20-714-3058   (SL)

RUTTAN ENTERPRISES LTD
WELLS GRAY INN
Gd, Clearwater, BC, V0E 1N0
(250) 674-2340
Emp Here 50   *Sales* 2,188,821
SIC 7011 Hotels and motels

D-U-N-S 20-860-8948   (BR)
SCHOOL   DISTRICT   73   (KAM-LOOPS/THOMPSON)
CLEARWATER SECONDARY SCHOOL
440 Murtle Cres, Clearwater, BC, V0E 1N1

Emp Here 20
SIC 8211 Elementary and secondary schools

D-U-N-S 20-064-5146   (BR)
SCHOOL   DISTRICT   73   (KAM-LOOPS/THOMPSON)
RAFT RIVER ELEMENTARY SCHOOL
801 Clearwater Village Rd, Clearwater, BC, V0E 1N1
(250) 674-2218
Emp Here 30
SIC 8211 Elementary and secondary schools

Clinton, BC V0K
Thompson - Nicola County

D-U-N-S 20-590-8473   (BR)
SCHOOL DISTRICT #74 (GOLD TRAIL)
DAVID STODDART SECONDARY SCHOOL
1203 Cariboo Ave, Clinton, BC, V0K 1K0
(250) 459-2219
Emp Here 25
SIC 8211 Elementary and secondary schools

Cobble Hill, BC V0R
Cowichan Valley County

D-U-N-S 20-031-5864   (BR)
SCHOOL DISTRICT NO. 79 (COWICHAN VALLEY)
BENCH ELEMENTARY SCHOOL
1501 Cowichan Bay Rd, Cobble Hill, BC, V0R 1L0
(250) 743-5552
Emp Here 40
SIC 8211 Elementary and secondary schools

D-U-N-S 20-991-8130   (BR)
SCHOOL DISTRICT NO. 79 (COWICHAN VALLEY)
COBBLE HILL ELEMENTARY SCHOOL
3642 Learning Way, Cobble Hill, BC, V0R 1L2
(250) 709-7607
Emp Here 20
SIC 8211 Elementary and secondary schools

D-U-N-S 24-355-7829   (BR)
VICTORIA TRUSS (2007) LTD
3605 Cobble Hill Rd Rr 1, Cobble Hill, BC, V0R 1L5
(250) 743-9922
Emp Here 50
SIC 2439 Structural wood members, nec

Coldstream, BC V1B
North Okanagan County

D-U-N-S 20-357-5238   (BR)
PINNACLE RENEWABLE ENERGY INC
9900 School Rd, Coldstream, BC, V1B 3C7
(250) 542-1720
Emp Here 30
SIC 2499 Wood products, nec

D-U-N-S 20-713-2452   (BR)
SCHOOL DISTRICT NO 22 (VERNON)

KIDSTON ELEMENTARY SCHOOL
12101 Linden Dr, Coldstream, BC, V1B 2H3
(250) 542-5351
Emp Here 50
SIC 8211 Elementary and secondary schools

D-U-N-S 20-713-2445   (BR)
SCHOOL DISTRICT NO 22 (VERNON)
KALAMALKA SECONDARY
7900 Mcclounie Rd, Coldstream, BC, V1B 1P8
(250) 545-1396
Emp Here 50
SIC 8211 Elementary and secondary schools

D-U-N-S 20-713-2429   (BR)
SCHOOL DISTRICT NO 22 (VERNON)
COLDSTEAM ELEMENTARY SCHOOL
10104 Kalamalka Rd, Coldstream, BC, V1B 1L7
(250) 545-0597
Emp Here 40
SIC 8211 Elementary and secondary schools

D-U-N-S 20-713-2437   (BR)
SCHOOL DISTRICT NO 22 (VERNON)
LAVINGTON ELEMENTARY SCHOOL
9715 School Rd, Coldstream, BC, V1B 3G4
(250) 545-1710
Emp Here 20
SIC 8211 Elementary and secondary schools

D-U-N-S 24-787-0926   (BR)
TOLKO INDUSTRIES LTD
LAVINGTON PLANER DIVISION
6200 Jeffers Dr, Coldstream, BC, V1B 3G4
(250) 545-4992
Emp Here 200
SIC 2421 Sawmills and planing mills, general

Comox, BC V9M
Comox - Strathcona County

D-U-N-S 20-197-9973   (BR)
KELLAND FOODS LTD
QUALITY FOODS
1220 Guthrie Rd, Comox, BC, V9M 4A6
(250) 890-1005
Emp Here 120
SIC 5411 Grocery stores

D-U-N-S 20-733-8471   (BR)
LOBLAWS INC
EXTRA FOODS # 8579
215 Port Augusta St, Comox, BC, V9M 3M9
(250) 339-7651
Emp Here 70
SIC 5411 Grocery stores

D-U-N-S 20-591-5411   (BR)
SCHOOL DISTRICT NO. 71 (COMOX VALLEY)
ASPEN PARK ELEMENTARY SCHOOL
2250 Bolt Ave, Comox, BC, V9M 4E7
(250) 890-0944
Emp Here 25
SIC 8211 Elementary and secondary schools

D-U-N-S 20-027-0366   (BR)
SCHOOL DISTRICT NO. 71 (COMOX VALLEY)
VILLAGE PARK ELEMENTARY SCHOOL
566 Linshart Rd, Comox, BC, V9M 2K8

Emp Here 30
SIC 8211 Elementary and secondary schools

D-U-N-S 20-713-6131   (BR)
SCHOOL DISTRICT NO. 71 (COMOX VALLEY)
AECOLE   ROBB   ROAD   ELEMENTARY SCHOOL
1909 Robb Ave, Comox, BC, V9M 2C9
(250) 339-6864
Emp Here 30
SIC 8211 Elementary and secondary schools

D-U-N-S 25-485-7691   (BR)
SCHOOL DISTRICT NO. 71 (COMOX VALLEY)
HIGHLAND SECONDARY SCHOOL
750 Pritchard Rd, Comox, BC, V9M 3S8
(250) 339-3617
Emp Here 60
SIC 8211 Elementary and secondary schools

D-U-N-S 25-134-7720   (BR)
SCHOOL DISTRICT NO. 71 (COMOX VALLEY)
BROOKLYN ELEMENTARY SCHOOL
1475 Noel Ave, Comox, BC, V9M 3H8

Emp Here 30
SIC 8211 Elementary and secondary schools

D-U-N-S 20-713-6032   (BR)
SCHOOL DISTRICT NO. 71 (COMOX VALLEY)
BROOKLYN ELEMENTARY-CAPE LAZO
1290 Guthrie Rd, Comox, BC, V9M 4G2
(250) 339-2232
Emp Here 32
SIC 8211 Elementary and secondary schools

D-U-N-S 24-335-0365   (BR)
SLEGG DEVELOPMENTS LTD
554 Anderton Rd, Comox, BC, V9M 2J6
(250) 339-2207
Emp Here 35
SIC 5211 Lumber and other building materials

D-U-N-S 20-957-3047   (HQ)
ST JOSEPH'S GENERAL HOSPITAL
UPPER   ISLAND   GERIATRIC   OUTREACH PROGRAM
(*Suby of* St Joseph's General Hospital)
2137 Comox Ave, Comox, BC, V9M 1P2
(250) 339-1451
Emp Here 900   *Emp Total* 1,100
Sales 76,535,774
SIC 8062 General medical and surgical hospitals
Pr Pr Michael Pontus

Coquitlam, BC V3B
Greater Vancouver County

D-U-N-S 25-297-1049   (BR)
BANK OF NOVA SCOTIA, THE
SCOTIABANK
2929 Barnet Hwy Suite 2308, Coquitlam, BC, V3B 5R5
(604) 927-7075
Emp Here 25
SIC 6021 National commercial banks

D-U-N-S 24-492-3496   (BR)
BEST BUY CANADA LTD
BEST BUY
(*Suby of* Best Buy Co., Inc.)
1135 Pinetree Way, Coquitlam, BC, V3B 7K5
(604) 468-5500
Emp Here 50
SIC 5731 Radio, television, and electronic stores

D-U-N-S 25-231-7151   (BR)
BRICK WAREHOUSE LP, THE
3000 Lougheed Hwy Suite 122, Coquitlam, BC, V3B 1C5
(604) 941-0808
Emp Here 50
SIC 5712 Furniture stores

D-U-N-S 24-595-0758   (BR)
BRITISH COLUMBIA AUTOMOBILE ASSOCIATION
BCAA TRAVE
2773 Barnet Hwy Suite 50, Coquitlam, BC, V3B 1C2
(604) 268-5750
Emp Here 20

SIC 6411 Insurance agents, brokers, and service

D-U-N-S 20-650-3992   (BR)
CANADIAN IMPERIAL BANK OF COMMERCE
CIBC
3000 Lincoln Ave, Coquitlam, BC, V3B 7L9
(604) 927-2767
Emp Here 35
SIC 6036 Savings institutions, except federal

D-U-N-S 24-081-5154   (BR)
CARA OPERATIONS LIMITED
MONTANA'S COOKHOUSE
(*Suby of* Cara Holdings Limited)
2929 Barnet Hwy Suite 1046, Coquitlam, BC, V3B 5R5
(604) 472-7772
Emp Here 30
SIC 5812 Eating places

D-U-N-S 20-076-4012   (BR)
COQUITLAM PUBLIC LIBRARY
CITY CENTRE LIBRARY
(*Suby of* Coquitlam Public Library)
3001 Burlington Dr, Coquitlam, BC, V3B 6X1
(604) 927-3560
Emp Here 20
SIC 8231 Libraries

D-U-N-S 24-337-3227   (BR)
FGL SPORTS LTD
SPORT CHEK COQUITLAM CENTRE
2929 Barnet Hwy Unit 1400, Coquitlam, BC, V3B 5R5
(604) 464-5122
Emp Here 40
SIC 5941 Sporting goods and bicycle shops

D-U-N-S 24-977-2786   (BR)
FGL SPORTS LTD
ATMOSPHERE
2929 Barnet Hwy Unit 1048, Coquitlam, BC, V3B 5R5
(604) 945-9511
Emp Here 25
SIC 5941 Sporting goods and bicycle shops

D-U-N-S 20-026-8949   (BR)
FRIENDSHIP FOOD COMPANY LTD, THE
A & W FAMILY RESTAURANT
(*Suby of* Friendship Food Company Ltd, The)
2991 Lougheed Hwy Suite 10, Coquitlam, BC, V3B 6J6
(604) 464-8953
Emp Here 25
SIC 5812 Eating places

D-U-N-S 20-349-1084   (BR)
GAP (CANADA) INC
GAP
(*Suby of* The Gap Inc)
2929 Barnet Hwy Suite 2830, Coquitlam, BC, V3B 5R5
(604) 472-0101
Emp Here 40
SIC 5651 Family clothing stores

D-U-N-S 24-194-6289   (BR)
GOLF TOWN LIMITED
GOLF TOWN
2929 Barnet Hwy Unit 2142, Coquitlam, BC, V3B 5R5
(604) 944-7976
Emp Here 35
SIC 5941 Sporting goods and bicycle shops

D-U-N-S 24-696-5032   (BR)
GREAT PACIFIC INDUSTRIES INC
SAVE-ON-FOODS
2991 Lougheed Hwy Suite 6, Coquitlam, BC, V3B 6J6
(604) 552-1772
Emp Here 300
SIC 5411 Grocery stores

D-U-N-S 24-979-7440   (BR)
HUDSON'S BAY COMPANY

THE BAY
2929 Barnet Hwy Suite 100, Coquitlam, BC,
V3B 5R9
(604) 468-4453
Emp Here 160
SIC 5311 Department stores

D-U-N-S 20-650-6649　　　(BR)
INVESTORS GROUP FINANCIAL SERVICES INC
2963 Glen Dr Suite 305, Coquitlam, BC, V3B
2P7
(604) 941-4697
Emp Here 30
SIC 6211 Security brokers and dealers

D-U-N-S 24-624-3245　　　(BR)
KEG RESTAURANTS LTD
KEG STEAKHOUSE & BAR, THE
2991 Lougheed Hwy Unit 130, Coquitlam, BC,
V3B 6J6
(604) 464-5340
Emp Here 90
SIC 5812 Eating places

D-U-N-S 20-555-7668　　　(BR)
LOBLAWS INC
REAL CANADIAN SUPERSTORE
3000 Lougheed Hwy Suite 205, Coquitlam,
BC, V3B 1C5
(604) 468-6735
Emp Here 200
SIC 5411 Grocery stores

D-U-N-S 24-247-7180　　　(BR)
LONDON DRUGS LIMITED
2929 Barnet Hwy Unit 1030, Coquitlam, BC,
V3B 5R5
(604) 464-3322
Emp Here 20
SIC 5912 Drug stores and proprietary stores

D-U-N-S 24-244-6805　　　(BR)
MORGUARD INVESTMENTS LIMITED
COQUITLAM CENTRE, THE
2929 Barnet Hwy Suite 2201, Coquitlam, BC,
V3B 5R5
(604) 464-1511
Emp Here 25
SIC 6512 Nonresidential building operators

D-U-N-S 25-613-3489　　　(BR)
REVERA INC
PARKWOOD MANOR
1142 Dufferin St Suite 353, Coquitlam, BC,
V3B 6V4
(604) 941-7651
Emp Here 40
SIC 8361 Residential care

D-U-N-S 24-915-2711　　　(BR)
ROMA RIBS LTD
TONY ROMA'S A PLACE FOR RIBS
(*Suby of* Roma Ribs Ltd)
3025 Lougheed Hwy Suite 650, Coquitlam,
BC, V3B 6S2

Emp Here 40
SIC 5812 Eating places

D-U-N-S 20-576-2300　　　(BR)
SCHOOL DISTRICT NO. 43 (COQUITLAM)
LEIGH ELEMENTARY SCHOOL
1230 Soball St, Coquitlam, BC, V3B 3H7
(604) 941-8661
Emp Here 29
SIC 8211 Elementary and secondary schools

D-U-N-S 20-713-4722　　　(BR)
SCHOOL DISTRICT NO. 43 (COQUITLAM)
GLENEAGLE SECONDARY SCHOOL
1195 Lansdowne Dr, Coquitlam, BC, V3B 7Y8
(604) 464-5793
Emp Here 103
SIC 8211 Elementary and secondary schools

D-U-N-S 20-034-8758　　　(BR)
SCHOOL DISTRICT NO. 43 (COQUITLAM)
PINETREE SECONDARY SCHOOL

3000 Pinewood Ave, Coquitlam, BC, V3B 7Y7
(604) 464-2513
Emp Here 150
SIC 8211 Elementary and secondary schools

D-U-N-S 20-713-4698　　　(BR)
SCHOOL DISTRICT NO. 43 (COQUITLAM)
WALTON ELEMENTAY SCHOOL
2960 Walton Ave, Coquitlam, BC, V3B 6V6
(604) 941-1962
Emp Here 50
SIC 8211 Elementary and secondary schools

D-U-N-S 20-590-6329　　　(BR)
SCHOOL DISTRICT NO. 43 (COQUITLAM)
GLENN ELEMENTARY SCHOOL
3064 Glen Dr, Coquitlam, BC, V3B 2P9
(604) 464-6608
Emp Here 50
SIC 8211 Elementary and secondary schools

D-U-N-S 25-294-6595　　　(BR)
SEARS CANADA INC
2929 Barnet Hwy Suite 300, Coquitlam, BC,
V3B 5R5
(604) 464-8600
Emp Here 150
SIC 5311 Department stores

D-U-N-S 25-094-3388　　　(BR)
SOBEYS WEST INC
3051 Lougheed Hwy Suite 100, Coquitlam,
BC, V3B 1C6
(604) 941-6894
Emp Here 300
SIC 5411 Grocery stores

D-U-N-S 25-795-9676　　　(SL)
SUTTON GROUP 1ST WEST REALTY INC
3030 Lincoln Ave Suite 118, Coquitlam, BC,
V3B 6B4

Emp Here 49　　　*Sales* 6,118,560
SIC 6531 Real estate agents and managers
Brnch Mgr Len Ashton

D-U-N-S 25-718-3962　　　(BR)
WHITE SPOT LIMITED
3025 Lougheed Hwy Suite 500, Coquitlam,
BC, V3B 6S2
(604) 942-9224
Emp Here 80
SIC 5812 Eating places

D-U-N-S 20-106-2911　　　(BR)
**WINNERS MERCHANTS INTERNATIONAL
L.P.**
WINNERS
(*Suby of* The TJX Companies Inc)
3000 Lougheed Hwy Suite 114, Coquitlam,
BC, V3B 1C5
(604) 468-2210
Emp Here 35
SIC 5651 Family clothing stores

Coquitlam, BC V3C
Greater Vancouver County

D-U-N-S 24-761-6873　　　(SL)
BRITISH COLUMBIA MENTAL HEALTH SOCIETY
RIVERVIEW HOSPITAL
2601 Lougheed Hwy, Coquitlam, BC, V3C 4J2
(604) 524-7000
Emp Here 1,700　　　*Sales* 164,712,480
SIC 8063 Psychiatric hospitals
Pr Leslie Arnold

D-U-N-S 20-362-0369　　　(BR)
**CHRISTIAN AND MISSIONARY ALLIANCE
IN CANADA, THE**
COQUITLAM ALLIANCE CHURCH
2601 Spuraway Ave, Coquitlam, BC, V3C 2C4
(604) 464-6744
Emp Here 20

SIC 8661 Religious organizations

D-U-N-S 25-021-9532　　　(HQ)
FORENSIC PSYCHIATRIC SERVICES COMMISSION
70 Colony Farm Rd, Coquitlam, BC, V3C 5X9
(604) 524-7700
Emp Here 400　　　*Emp Total* 10,000
Sales 48,491,040
SIC 8063 Psychiatric hospitals
CEO Leslie M Arnold

D-U-N-S 24-345-9547　　　(BR)
FRASER HEALTH AUTHORITY
TRI CITY HOME HEALTH
2601 Lougheed Hwy Unit 6, Coquitlam, BC,
V3C 4J2
(604) 777-7300
Emp Here 200
SIC 8742 Management consulting services

D-U-N-S 20-000-3007　　　(BR)
JUST LADIES FITNESS LTD
3000 Christmas Way, Coquitlam, BC, V3C
2M2
(604) 945-5135
Emp Here 20
SIC 7991 Physical fitness facilities

D-U-N-S 25-273-1518　　　(BR)
LORDCO PARTS LTD
LORDCO AUTO PARTS
1024 Westwood St, Coquitlam, BC, V3C 3L5
(604) 942-7354
Emp Here 38
SIC 5531 Auto and home supply stores

D-U-N-S 20-013-2269　　　(SL)
MARQUEE HOTELS LTD
HILTON GARDEN INN
2857 Mara Dr, Coquitlam, BC, V3C 5L3
(604) 506-2336
Emp Here 50　　　*Sales* 2,826,987
SIC 7011 Hotels and motels

D-U-N-S 20-590-6303　　　(BR)
SCHOOL DISTRICT NO. 43 (COQUITLAM)
RANCH PARK ELEMENTARY SCHOOL
2701 Spuraway Ave, Coquitlam, BC, V3C 2C4
(604) 464-6684
Emp Here 25
SIC 8211 Elementary and secondary schools

D-U-N-S 25-757-0028　　　(BR)
SCHOOL DISTRICT NO. 43 (COQUITLAM)
RIVERVIEW PARK ELEMENTARY SCHOOL
700 Clearwater Way, Coquitlam, BC, V3C 6A3
(604) 945-7004
Emp Here 28
SIC 8211 Elementary and secondary schools

Coquitlam, BC V3E
Greater Vancouver County

D-U-N-S 20-261-2735　　　(SL)
1630 PARKWAY GOLF COURSE LTD
WESTWOOD PLATEAU
3251 Plateau Blvd, Coquitlam, BC, V3E 3B8
(604) 945-4007
Emp Here 50　　　*Sales* 2,598,753
SIC 7992 Public golf courses

D-U-N-S 20-261-2750　　　(SL)
3251 PLATEAU GOLF COURSE LTD
3251 Plateau Blvd, Coquitlam, BC, V3E 3B8
(604) 945-4007
Emp Here 50　　　*Sales* 2,188,821
SIC 7992 Public golf courses

D-U-N-S 20-713-4706　　　(BR)
SCHOOL DISTRICT NO. 43 (COQUITLAM)
PINETREE WAY ELEMENTARY SCHOOL
1420 Pinetree Way, Coquitlam, BC, V3E 6A3
(604) 945-7011
Emp Here 50

SIC 8211 Elementary and secondary schools

D-U-N-S 20-292-8029　　　(BR)
SCHOOL DISTRICT NO. 43 (COQUITLAM)
SCOTT CREEK MIDDLE SCHOOL
1240 Lansdowne Dr, Coquitlam, BC, V3E 3E7
(604) 945-0156
Emp Here 70
SIC 8211 Elementary and secondary schools

D-U-N-S 20-647-6611　　　(BR)
SCHOOL DISTRICT NO. 43 (COQUITLAM)
EAGLE RIDGE ELEMENTARY SCHOOL
1215 Falcon Dr, Coquitlam, BC, V3E 1X9
(604) 464-5848
Emp Here 30
SIC 8211 Elementary and secondary schools

D-U-N-S 20-648-4920　　　(BR)
SCHOOL DISTRICT NO. 43 (COQUITLAM)
HAMPTON PARK ELEMENTARY SCHOOL
1760 Paddock Dr, Coquitlam, BC, V3E 3N8
(604) 464-2549
Emp Here 30
SIC 8211 Elementary and secondary schools

D-U-N-S 20-713-4730　　　(BR)
SCHOOL DISTRICT NO. 43 (COQUITLAM)
SUMMIT MIDDLE SCHOOL
1450 Parkway Blvd, Coquitlam, BC, V3E 3L2
(604) 944-8273
Emp Here 50
SIC 8211 Elementary and secondary schools

D-U-N-S 20-590-6204　　　(BR)
SCHOOL DISTRICT NO. 43 (COQUITLAM)
NESTOR ELEMENTARY SCHOOL
1266 Nestor St, Coquitlam, BC, V3E 2A4
(604) 464-9422
Emp Here 35
SIC 8211 Elementary and secondary schools

D-U-N-S 20-034-7511　　　(BR)
SCHOOL DISTRICT NO. 43 (COQUITLAM)
BRAMBLEWOOD ELEMENTARY SCHOOL
2875 Panorama Dr, Coquitlam, BC, V3E 2S7
(604) 552-0313
Emp Here 30
SIC 8211 Elementary and secondary schools

D-U-N-S 20-590-6220　　　(BR)
SCHOOL DISTRICT NO. 43 (COQUITLAM)
*PANORAMA HEIGHTS ELEMENTARY
SCHOOL*
1455 Johnson St, Coquitlam, BC, V3E 2T1
(604) 944-4840
Emp Here 25
SIC 8211 Elementary and secondary schools

D-U-N-S 24-319-8327　　　(BR)
VALUE VILLAGE STORES, INC
(*Suby of* Savers, Inc.)
2739 Barnet Hwy, Coquitlam, BC, V3E 1K9
(604) 464-9179
Emp Here 50
SIC 5399 Miscellaneous general merchandise

D-U-N-S 25-485-7055　　　(BR)
WESBILD HOLDINGS LTD
*WESTWOOD PLATEAU GOLF & COUNTRY
CLUB*
(*Suby of* Inwest Investments Ltd)
3251 Plateau Blvd, Coquitlam, BC, V3E 3B8
(604) 945-4007
Emp Here 200
SIC 7997 Membership sports and recreation
clubs

Coquitlam, BC V3H
Greater Vancouver County

D-U-N-S 25-301-3783　　　(BR)
U-HAUL CO. (CANADA) LTD
U HAUL REPAIR
(*Suby of* Amerco)

2534 Barnet Hwy, Coquitlam, BC, V3H 1W3
(604) 461-2455
Emp Here 20
SIC 7519 Utility trailer rental

Coquitlam, BC V3J
Greater Vancouver County

D-U-N-S 20-572-9531   (BR)
CANADA POST CORPORATION
552 Clarke Rd Unit 107, Coquitlam, BC, V3J
3X5
(604) 936-7255
Emp Here 20
SIC 4311 U.s. postal service

D-U-N-S 25-288-8615   (BR)
CANADA POST CORPORATION
1029 Ridgeway Ave, Coquitlam, BC, V3J 1S6

Emp Here 44
SIC 4311 U.s. postal service

D-U-N-S 25-017-0263   (BR)
**CANADIAN IMPERIAL BANK OF COM-
MERCE**
*CANADIAN IMPERIAL BANK OF COM-
MERCE*
552 Clarke Rd Unit 403, Coquitlam, BC, V3J
3X5
(604) 933-2133
Emp Here 21
SIC 6021 National commercial banks

D-U-N-S 20-914-4943   (BR)
**CATHOLIC INDEPENDENT SCHOOLS OF
VANCOUVER ARCHDIOCESE, THE**
QUEEN OF ALL SAINTS SCHOOL
1405 Como Lake Ave, Coquitlam, BC, V3J
3P4
(604) 931-9071
Emp Here 20
SIC 8211 Elementary and secondary schools

D-U-N-S 24-491-3539   (SL)
COQUITLAM COLLEGE INC
516 Brookmere Ave, Coquitlam, BC, V3J 1W9
(604) 939-6633
Emp Here 65   *Sales* 9,344,640
SIC 8221 Colleges and universities
Pr Pr Tom Tait
 Donald Homer

D-U-N-S 24-137-4065   (HQ)
COQUITLAM PUBLIC LIBRARY
(*Suby of* Coquitlam Public Library)
575 Poirier St, Coquitlam, BC, V3J 6A9
(604) 937-4141
Emp Here 45   *Emp Total* 90
Sales 4,158,760
SIC 8231 Libraries

D-U-N-S 24-569-3598   (BR)
**JOHNSTON, MEIER INSURANCE AGEN-
CIES LTD**
*JOHNSTON MEIER INSURANCE AGEN-
CIES GROUP*
1944 Como Lake Ave, Coquitlam, BC, V3J
3R3
(604) 937-3601
Emp Here 20
SIC 6411 Insurance agents, brokers, and ser-
vice

D-U-N-S 25-318-1283   (BR)
**MCDONALD'S   RESTAURANTS   OF
CANADA LIMITED**
MCDONALD'S #8023
(*Suby of* McDonald's Corporation)
515 North Rd, Coquitlam, BC, V3J 1N7
(604) 937-4690
Emp Here 60
SIC 5812 Eating places

D-U-N-S 25-811-7498   (BR)

ROYAL BANK OF CANADA
ROYAL BANK FINANCIAL GROUP
(*Suby of* Royal Bank Of Canada)
1962 Como Lake Ave, Coquitlam, BC, V3J
3R3
(604) 927-5633
Emp Here 30
SIC 6021 National commercial banks

D-U-N-S 25-757-0051   (BR)
SCHOOL DISTRICT NO. 43 (COQUITLAM)
BAKER DRIVE ELEMENTARY SCHOOL
885 Baker Dr, Coquitlam, BC, V3J 6W9
(604) 461-5323
Emp Here 20
SIC 8211 Elementary and secondary schools

D-U-N-S 25-013-9425   (BR)
SCHOOL DISTRICT NO. 43 (COQUITLAM)
DR CHARLES BEST SECONDARY SCHOOL
2525 Como Lake Ave, Coquitlam, BC, V3J
3R8
(604) 461-5581
Emp Here 85
SIC 8211 Elementary and secondary schools

D-U-N-S 25-026-3597   (BR)
SCHOOL DISTRICT NO. 43 (COQUITLAM)
WINSLOW CENTRE
1100 Winslow Ave Suite 43, Coquitlam, BC,
V3J 2G3
(604) 936-0491
Emp Here 60
SIC 8211 Elementary and secondary schools

D-U-N-S 20-047-0677   (BR)
SCHOOL DISTRICT NO. 43 (COQUITLAM)
HARBOUR VIEW ELEMENTARY SCHOOL
960 Lillian St, Coquitlam, BC, V3J 5C7
(604) 936-1494
Emp Here 27
SIC 8211 Elementary and secondary schools

D-U-N-S 25-266-8090   (BR)
SCHOOL DISTRICT NO. 43 (COQUITLAM)
COMO LAKE MIDDLE SCHOOL
1121 King Albert Ave, Coquitlam, BC, V3J 1X8
(604) 936-1451
Emp Here 54
SIC 8211 Elementary and secondary schools

D-U-N-S 20-713-4672   (BR)
SCHOOL DISTRICT NO. 43 (COQUITLAM)
PORTER STREET ELEMENTARY SCHOOL
728 Porter St, Coquitlam, BC, V3J 5B4
(604) 936-4296
Emp Here 36
SIC 8211 Elementary and secondary schools

D-U-N-S 20-047-0719   (BR)
SCHOOL DISTRICT NO. 43 (COQUITLAM)
ROY STIBBS ELEMENTARY SCHOOL
600 Fairview St, Coquitlam, BC, V3J 4A7
(604) 939-2486
Emp Here 34
SIC 8211 Elementary and secondary schools

D-U-N-S 25-066-1980   (BR)
SCHOOL DISTRICT NO. 43 (COQUITLAM)
BANTING MIDDLE SCHOOL
820 Banting St, Coquitlam, BC, V3J 4J4
(604) 939-9247
Emp Here 51
SIC 8211 Elementary and secondary schools

D-U-N-S 20-026-9020   (BR)
SCHOOL DISTRICT NO. 43 (COQUITLAM)
MILLER PARK COMMUNITY SCHOOL
800 Egmont Ave, Coquitlam, BC, V3J 4J8
(604) 936-0245
Emp Here 40
SIC 8211 Elementary and secondary schools

D-U-N-S 20-590-6261   (BR)
SCHOOL DISTRICT NO. 43 (COQUITLAM)
HILLCREST MIDDLE SCHOOL
2161 Regan Ave, Coquitlam, BC, V3J 3C5
(604) 936-4237
Emp Here 60

SIC 8211 Elementary and secondary schools

D-U-N-S 20-590-6246   (BR)
SCHOOL DISTRICT NO. 43 (COQUITLAM)
PARKLAND ELEMENTARY SCHOOL
1563 Regan Ave, Coquitlam, BC, V3J 3B7
(604) 939-1151
Emp Here 35
SIC 8211 Elementary and secondary schools

D-U-N-S 20-590-6428   (BR)
SCHOOL DISTRICT NO. 43 (COQUITLAM)
MOUNTAIN VIEW ELEMENTARY
740 Smith Ave, Coquitlam, BC, V3J 4E7
(604) 936-7288
Emp Here 27
SIC 8211 Elementary and secondary schools

D-U-N-S 20-034-6257   (BR)
SCHOOL DISTRICT NO. 43 (COQUITLAM)
CABE ALTERNATE SECONDARY SCHOOL
1411 Foster Ave, Coquitlam, BC, V3J 2N1
(604) 939-4522
Emp Here 30
SIC 8211 Elementary and secondary schools

D-U-N-S 24-249-9937   (BR)
SCHOOL DISTRICT NO. 43 (COQUITLAM)
CENTENNIAL SECONDARY SCHOOL
570 Poirier St, Coquitlam, BC, V3J 6A8
(604) 936-7205
Emp Here 110
SIC 8211 Elementary and secondary schools

D-U-N-S 25-271-6972   (BR)
SOBEYS WEST INC
580 Clarke Rd, Coquitlam, BC, V3J 0G4

Emp Here 70
SIC 5411 Grocery stores

D-U-N-S 20-806-5040   (BR)
STARBUCKS COFFEE CANADA, INC
(*Suby of* Starbucks Corporation)
1980 Como Lake Ave Suite A, Coquitlam, BC,
V3J 3R3
(604) 937-7781
Emp Here 20
SIC 5812 Eating places

D-U-N-S 25-174-3415   (BR)
VALUE VILLAGE STORES, INC
VALUE VILLAGE STORES
(*Suby of* Savers, Inc.)
552 Clarke Rd Unit 301, Coquitlam, BC, V3J
3X5
(604) 937-7087
Emp Here 40
SIC 5399 Miscellaneous general merchandise

D-U-N-S 25-170-7741   (SL)
WOODBRIDGE ENTERPRISES LTD
MCDONALD'S
531 Clarke Rd, Coquitlam, BC, V3J 3X4
(604) 936-4222
Emp Here 70   *Sales* 2,115,860
SIC 5812 Eating places

Coquitlam, BC V3K
Greater Vancouver County

D-U-N-S 20-562-8345   (SL)
AIM HOLDING TRUST
(*Suby of* Art In Motion Income Fund)
2000 Brigantine Dr, Coquitlam, BC, V3K 7B5
(604) 525-3900
Emp Here 500   *Sales* 102,536,320
SIC 6712 Bank holding companies
 Gary Peters

D-U-N-S 24-030-3834   (HQ)
AMPCO MANUFACTURERS INC
AMPCO GRAFIX DIV OF
(*Suby of* AMG Holdings Inc)
9 Burbidge St Suite 101, Coquitlam, BC, V3K

7B2
(604) 472-3800
Emp Here 95   *Emp Total* 104
Sales 7,103,258
SIC 2759 Commercial printing, nec
Pr Pr Dann Konkin
 Tanya Vermeulen

D-U-N-S 24-129-7568   (BR)
AMPCO MANUFACTURERS INC
(*Suby of* AMG Holdings Inc)
9 Burbidge St Unit 101, Coquitlam, BC, V3K
7B2

Emp Here 120
SIC 2759 Commercial printing, nec

D-U-N-S 25-360-1546   (SL)
ART IN MOTION LIMITED PARTNERSHIP
ART IN MOTION
2000 Hartley Ave, Coquitlam, BC, V3K 6W5
(604) 525-3900
Emp Here 250   *Sales* 41,297,280
SIC 5199 Nondurable goods, nec
 Allan Achternichuk

D-U-N-S 25-727-6485   (BR)
BANK OF NOVA SCOTIA, THE
SCOTIABANK
465 North Rd, Coquitlam, BC, V3K 3V9
(604) 933-3300
Emp Here 20
SIC 6021 National commercial banks

D-U-N-S 25-483-1829   (SL)
BURQUITLAM CARE SOCIETY
BURQUITLAM LIONS CARE CENTRE
560 Sydney Ave, Coquitlam, BC, V3K 6A4
(604) 939-6485
Emp Here 85   *Sales* 3,866,917
SIC 8051 Skilled nursing care facilities

D-U-N-S 20-942-3875   (BR)
CACTUS RESTAURANTS LTD
CACTUS CLUB CAFE
101 Schoolhouse St Suite 110, Coquitlam,
BC, V3K 4X8
(604) 777-0440
Emp Here 50
SIC 5812 Eating places

D-U-N-S 20-569-5377   (BR)
CANADIAN WESTERN BANK
101 Schoolhouse St Suite 310, Coquitlam,
BC, V3K 4X8
(604) 540-8829
Emp Here 28
SIC 6021 National commercial banks

D-U-N-S 25-485-7386   (SL)
CARTIER HOUSE CARE CENTRE LTD
1419 Cartier Ave, Coquitlam, BC, V3K 2C6
(604) 939-4654
Emp Here 85   *Sales* 3,137,310
SIC 8361 Residential care

D-U-N-S 20-900-8585   (BR)
**CATHOLIC INDEPENDENT SCHOOLS OF
VANCOUVER ARCHDIOCESE, THE**
OUR LADY OF FATIMA SCHOOL
315 Walker St, Coquitlam, BC, V3K 4C7
(604) 936-4228
Emp Here 38
SIC 8211 Elementary and secondary schools

D-U-N-S 20-005-1469   (BR)
CINEPLEX ODEON CORPORATION
SILVERCITY COQUITLAM
170 Schoolhouse St, Coquitlam, BC, V3K 6V6
(604) 523-2911
Emp Here 20
SIC 7832 Motion picture theaters, except
drive-in

D-U-N-S 25-451-0035   (BR)
**COCA-COLA REFRESHMENTS CANADA
COMPANY**
(*Suby of* The Coca-Cola Company)

2450 United Blvd Suite D, Coquitlam, BC, V3K 6G2

Emp Here 25
SIC 5149 Groceries and related products, nec

D-U-N-S 24-312-3122   (SL)
COQUITLAM INN AND CONVENTION CENTRE LTD
BEST WESTERN COQUITLAM
319 North Rd, Coquitlam, BC, V3K 3V8
(604) 931-9011
Emp Here 50   Sales 2,188,821
SIC 7011 Hotels and motels

D-U-N-S 25-003-0756   (BR)
COQUITLAM, CITY OF
PLACE DES ARTS
1120 Brunette Ave, Coquitlam, BC, V3K 1G2
(604) 664-1636
Emp Here 92
SIC 8299 Schools and educational services, nec

D-U-N-S 25-937-2886   (BR)
DENCAN RESTAURANTS INC
DENNY'S RESTAURANT
(Suby of Northland Properties Corporation)
500 Austin Ave, Coquitlam, BC, V3K 3M7
(604) 939-6545
Emp Here 50
SIC 5812 Eating places

D-U-N-S 24-788-3056   (SL)
DYNAMIC RESCUE SYSTEMS INC
63a Clipper St, Coquitlam, BC, V3K 6X2
(604) 522-0228
Emp Here 50   Sales 2,261,782
SIC 8999 Services, nec

D-U-N-S 20-074-2539   (BR)
ENVIROTEST SYSTEMS (B.C.) LTD
AIRCARE PROGRAM
1316 United Blvd, Coquitlam, BC, V3K 6Y2

Emp Here 25
SIC 8734 Testing laboratories

D-U-N-S 24-341-2165   (BR)
EXECUTIVE HOTELS GENERAL PARTNERSHIP
EXECUTIVE HOTELS & RESORTS
405 North Rd, Coquitlam, BC, V3K 3V9
(604) 936-9399
Emp Here 100
SIC 7011 Hotels and motels

D-U-N-S 25-902-7373   (BR)
FIRSTCANADA ULC
FIRST STUDENT CANADA
1640 Booth Ave, Coquitlam, BC, V3K 1B9
(604) 255-3555
Emp Here 35
SIC 4151 School buses

D-U-N-S 25-676-4846   (SL)
GFR PHARMA LTD
65 North Bend St Unit 65, Coquitlam, BC, V3K 6N9
(604) 460-8440
Emp Here 110   Sales 4,888,367
SIC 2833 Medicinals and botanicals

D-U-N-S 20-059-3544   (BR)
GREAT CANADIAN CASINOS INC
HARD ROCK CASINO
2080 United Blvd Suite D, Coquitlam, BC, V3K 6W3
(604) 523-6888
Emp Here 250
SIC 7999 Amusement and recreation, nec

D-U-N-S 25-536-4614   (HQ)
GREAT CANADIAN GAMING CORPORATION
(Suby of Great Canadian Gaming Corporation)
95 Schooner St, Coquitlam, BC, V3K 7A8

(604) 303-1000
Emp Here 250   Emp Total 5,600
Sales 418,934,928
SIC 7999 Amusement and recreation, nec
Pr Pr Rod Baker
    Terrance Doyle
VP Opers Craig Demarta
VP Opers Raj Mutti
Ex VP Walter Soo
VP Chuck Keeling
VP Jackie Gorton
    Peter Meredith
    Neil Baker
    Larry Campbell

D-U-N-S 25-696-3489   (BR)
HSBC BANK CANADA
405 North Rd Suite 1, Coquitlam, BC, V3K 3V9
(604) 939-8366
Emp Here 20
SIC 6021 National commercial banks

D-U-N-S 25-514-3216   (BR)
HOME DEPOT OF CANADA INC
HOME DEPOT
(Suby of The Home Depot Inc)
1900 United Blvd Suite D, Coquitlam, BC, V3K 6Z1
(604) 540-6277
Emp Here 200
SIC 5251 Hardware stores

D-U-N-S 20-584-1831   (BR)
INSURANCE CORPORATION OF BRITISH COLUMBIA
ICBC CENTRAL ESTIMATING FACILITY
1575 Hartley Ave, Coquitlam, BC, V3K 6Z7
(604) 777-4627
Emp Here 120
SIC 6331 Fire, marine, and casualty insurance

D-U-N-S 24-948-3058   (HQ)
JOEY TOMATO'S KITCHENS INC
JOEY TOMATO'S RESTAURANT
550 Lougheed Hwy, Coquitlam, BC, V3K 3S3
(604) 939-3077
Emp Here 50   Emp Total 513
Sales 45,718,400
SIC 5812 Eating places
Pr Pr Jeff Fuller
VP Peter Upton
    Leroy Fuller

D-U-N-S 25-050-4321   (BR)
JORDANS INTERIORS LTD
JORDANS RUGS
1539 United Blvd Suite D, Coquitlam, BC, V3K 6Y7
(604) 522-9855
Emp Here 20
SIC 5712 Furniture stores

D-U-N-S 25-316-4941   (BR)
JORDANS RUGS LTD
JORDANS INTERIORS
1539 United Blvd Suite D, Coquitlam, BC, V3K 6Y7
(604) 522-9852
Emp Here 25
SIC 5713 Floor covering stores

D-U-N-S 24-448-6254   (BR)
KAL TIRE LTD
1851 Lougheed Hwy, Coquitlam, BC, V3K 3T7
(604) 524-1166
Emp Here 23
SIC 5531 Auto and home supply stores

D-U-N-S 20-428-1885   (BR)
KAO CANADA INC
1580 Brigantine Dr Unit 110, Coquitlam, BC, V3K 7C1

Emp Here 30
SIC 5131 Piece goods and notions

D-U-N-S 24-135-3668   (BR)
LAFARGE CANADA INC

VALLEY RITE MIX
22 Leeder St, Coquitlam, BC, V3K 6P2
(604) 856-8313
Emp Here 20
SIC 5032 Brick, stone, and related material

D-U-N-S 20-774-6129   (BR)
LAFARGE CANADA INC
LAFARGE
22 Leeder St, Coquitlam, BC, V3K 6P2
(604) 527-7739
Emp Here 20
SIC 3273 Ready-mixed concrete

D-U-N-S 20-914-8282   (BR)
LEE VALLEY TOOLS LTD
1401 United Blvd, Coquitlam, BC, V3K 6Y7
(604) 515-8896
Emp Here 20
SIC 5251 Hardware stores

D-U-N-S 25-618-7428   (BR)
LOBLAWS INC
REAL CANADIAN-SUPERSTORES
1301 Lougheed Hwy, Coquitlam, BC, V3K 6P9
(604) 520-8339
Emp Here 300
SIC 5411 Grocery stores

D-U-N-S 20-795-5605   (BR)
MAPLE LEAF FOODS INC
68 Brigantine Dr, Coquitlam, BC, V3K 6Z6

Emp Here 50
SIC 2013 Sausages and other prepared meats

D-U-N-S 20-809-5286   (SL)
MAYDAY CLEANING SERVICES INC
910 Tupper Ave Unit 6, Coquitlam, BC, V3K 1A5
(604) 540-8801
Emp Here 50   Sales 4,377,642
SIC 1799 Special trade contractors, nec

D-U-N-S 25-366-1144   (BR)
MCDONALD'S RESTAURANTS OF CANADA LIMITED
MCDONALD'S #8657
(Suby of McDonald's Corporation)
1095 Woolridge St, Coquitlam, BC, V3K 7A9
(604) 718-1170
Emp Here 50
SIC 5812 Eating places

D-U-N-S 24-029-5162   (BR)
ME-N-EDS PIZZA PARLOUR LTD
(Suby of Me-N-Eds Pizza Parlour Ltd)
1121 Austin Ave, Coquitlam, BC, V3K 3P4
(604) 931-2468
Emp Here 20
SIC 5812 Eating places

D-U-N-S 24-844-5491   (SL)
MOTOSEL INDUSTRIAL GROUP INC
204 Cayer St Unit 407, Coquitlam, BC, V3K 5B1
(604) 629-8733
Emp Here 20   Sales 5,982,777
SIC 5172 Petroleum products, nec
Pr Morteza Irantour
Dir David Mah

D-U-N-S 24-477-3461   (HQ)
NCS INTERNATIONAL CO.
NATIONAL CABLE SPECIALIST, DIV OF
70 Glacier St, Coquitlam, BC, V3K 5Y9
(604) 472-6980
Emp Here 25   Emp Total 150
Sales 32,102,708
SIC 5063 Electrical apparatus and equipment
    Robert J. Bouchard
VP VP Gary Mcneil

D-U-N-S 24-886-9877   (SL)
PACIFIC MAINLAND HOLDINGS LTD
LOUGHEED ACURA
1288 Lougheed Hwy, Coquitlam, BC, V3K 6S4

(604) 522-6140
Emp Here 34   Sales 12,403,319
SIC 5511 New and used car dealers
Pr Pr Jimmy Chiang

D-U-N-S 24-762-1303   (SL)
POINT FOUR SYSTEMS INC
16 Fawcett Rd Unit 103, Coquitlam, BC, V3K 6X9
(604) 759-2114
Emp Here 22   Sales 4,012,839
SIC 5084 Industrial machinery and equipment

D-U-N-S 25-384-4617   (HQ)
PRIMELINE FOOD PARTNERS LTD
PJB-PRIMELINE
1580 Brigantine Dr Suite 200, Coquitlam, BC, V3K 7C1
(604) 526-1788
Emp Here 20   Emp Total 2
Sales 7,296,070
SIC 5141 Groceries, general line
Pr Pr Grant Christopher Huxtable

D-U-N-S 20-568-0189   (BR)
PRINCESS AUTO LTD
15d King Edward St, Coquitlam, BC, V3K 4S8
(604) 777-0735
Emp Here 25
SIC 5251 Hardware stores

D-U-N-S 25-665-8303   (BR)
PROCRANE INC
STERLING CRANE
(Suby of Berkshire Hathaway Inc.)
10 Burbidge St, Coquitlam, BC, V3K 5Y5
(604) 468-0222
Emp Here 20
SIC 7353 Heavy construction equipment rental

D-U-N-S 20-115-2980   (HQ)
RELIABLE PARTS LTD
(Suby of Reliable Parts Ltd)
85 North Bend St, Coquitlam, BC, V3K 6N1
(604) 941-1355
Emp Here 54   Emp Total 160
Sales 11,673,712
SIC 5722 Household appliance stores
Pr Pr Douglas Loughran
VP VP Phil Orazietti
    Theresa Loughran

D-U-N-S 20-044-2502   (BR)
SAYANI INVESTMENTS LTD
EXECUTIVE PLAZA
(Suby of Sayani Investments Ltd)
405 North Rd, Coquitlam, BC, V3K 3V9
(604) 936-9399
Emp Here 100
SIC 7011 Hotels and motels

D-U-N-S 24-325-6984   (BR)
SCAN DESIGNS LTD
1655 Brigantine Dr, Coquitlam, BC, V3K 7B4
(604) 524-3447
Emp Here 30
SIC 5712 Furniture stores

D-U-N-S 20-590-6345   (BR)
SCHOOL DISTRICT NO. 43 (COQUITLAM)
COQUITLAM CONTINUING EDUCATION
380 Montgomery St, Coquitlam, BC, V3K 5G2
(604) 936-4261
Emp Here 25
SIC 8211 Elementary and secondary schools

D-U-N-S 25-013-9581   (BR)
SCHOOL DISTRICT NO. 43 (COQUITLAM)
MAILLARD MIDDLE SCHOOL
1300 Rochester Ave, Coquitlam, BC, V3K 2X5
(604) 931-3574
Emp Here 50
SIC 8211 Elementary and secondary schools

D-U-N-S 25-757-0044   (BR)
SCHOOL DISTRICT NO. 43 (COQUITLAM)
ALDERSON ELEMENTARY SCHOOL
825 Gauthier Ave, Coquitlam, BC, V3K 7C4

(604) 939-8301
Emp Here 32
SIC 8211 Elementary and secondary schools

D-U-N-S 25-454-5783   (BR)
SCHOOL DISTRICT NO. 43 (COQUITLAM)
MONTGOMERY MIDDLE SCHOOL
1900 Edgewood Ave, Coquitlam, BC, V3K 2Y1
(604) 939-7367
Emp Here 58
SIC 8211 Elementary and secondary schools

D-U-N-S 20-590-6360   (BR)
SCHOOL DISTRICT NO. 43 (COQUITLAM)
ROCHESTER ELEMENTARY SCHOOL
411 Schoolhouse St, Coquitlam, BC, V3K 4Y7
(604) 939-4624
Emp Here 25
SIC 8211 Elementary and secondary schools

D-U-N-S 25-013-9631   (BR)
SCHOOL DISTRICT NO. 43 (COQUITLAM)
SUWA'LKH SCHOOL
1432 Brunette Ave, Coquitlam, BC, V3K 1G5
(604) 523-6011
Emp Here 24
SIC 8211 Elementary and secondary schools

D-U-N-S 20-590-6279   (BR)
SCHOOL DISTRICT NO. 43 (COQUITLAM)
MUNDY ROAD ELEMENTARY SCHOOL
2200 Austin Ave, Coquitlam, BC, V3K 3S1
(604) 936-4271
Emp Here 25
SIC 8211 Elementary and secondary schools

D-U-N-S 20-713-4615   (BR)
SCHOOL DISTRICT NO. 43 (COQUITLAM)
CAPE HORN ELEMENTARY SCHOOL
155 Finnigan St, Coquitlam, BC, V3K 5J2
(604) 526-4428
Emp Here 50
SIC 8211 Elementary and secondary schools

D-U-N-S 20-047-0685   (BR)
SCHOOL DISTRICT NO. 43 (COQUITLAM)
LORD BADEN-POWELL ELEMENTARY SCHOOL
450 Joyce St, Coquitlam, BC, V3K 4G4
(604) 936-1436
Emp Here 30
SIC 8211 Elementary and secondary schools

D-U-N-S 20-268-1917   (BR)
SERVICES D'ESSAIS INTERTEK AN LTEE
1500 Brigantine Dr, Coquitlam, BC, V3K 7C1
(604) 520-3321
Emp Here 50
SIC 8734 Testing laboratories

D-U-N-S 20-975-5235   (BR)
SHRED-IT INTERNATIONAL ULC
SHRED-IT VANCOUVER
1650 Brigantine Dr Unit 300, Coquitlam, BC, V3K 7B5
(604) 444-4044
Emp Here 50
SIC 7389 Business services, nec

D-U-N-S 20-427-6679   (HQ)
SKEANS ENGINEERING & MACHINERY LTD
SKEANS COMPRESSED AIR PRODUCTS
(*Suby of* Skeans Engineering & Machinery Ltd)
1900 Brigantine Dr, Coquitlam, BC, V3K 7B5
(604) 777-4247
Emp Here 30   *Emp Total* 41
Sales 9,705,989
SIC 5084 Industrial machinery and equipment
VP VP Chris Skeans
   Tim Skeans
Dir Tony Skeans
Pr Pr John Skeans

D-U-N-S 25-015-0174   (BR)
SOBEYS WEST INC
CANADA SAFEWAY 76

1033 Austin Ave, Coquitlam, BC, V3K 3P2
(604) 939-2850
Emp Here 100
SIC 5411 Grocery stores

D-U-N-S 20-956-3683   (SL)
SOCIETE FOYER MAILLARD
FOYER MAILLARD
1010 Alderson Ave, Coquitlam, BC, V3K 1W1
(604) 937-5578
Emp Here 70   *Sales* 2,553,625
SIC 8361 Residential care

D-U-N-S 20-511-8573   (BR)
SONY OF CANADA LTD
SONY STORES, THE
65 North Bend St, Coquitlam, BC, V3K 6N9

Emp Here 65
SIC 7629 Electrical repair shops

D-U-N-S 25-873-8533   (BR)
STAPLES CANADA INC
BUSINESS DEPOT/STAPLES
(*Suby of* Staples, Inc.)
1220 Seguin Dr, Coquitlam, BC, V3K 6W8
(604) 517-2100
Emp Here 40
SIC 5943 Stationery stores

D-U-N-S 24-344-0422   (BR)
SUPERIOR PLUS LP
51 Glacier St, Coquitlam, BC, V3K 5Y6
(604) 552-8700
Emp Here 40
SIC 5984 Liquefied petroleum gas dealers

D-U-N-S 24-061-5849   (HQ)
SURFWOOD SUPPLY (1964) LTD
(*Suby of* Boma Industries Ltd)
98 Fawcett Rd, Coquitlam, BC, V3K 6V5

Emp Here 39   *Emp Total* 65
Sales 1,678,096
SIC 3561 Pumps and pumping equipment

D-U-N-S 24-134-8101   (SL)
THERMO KING OF BRITISH COLUMBIA INC
68 Fawcett Rd, Coquitlam, BC, V3K 6V5
(604) 526-4414
Emp Here 50   *Sales* 3,648,035
SIC 7623 Refrigeration service and repair

D-U-N-S 25-297-8523   (BR)
TOYS 'R' US (CANADA) LTD
TOYS 'R' US
(*Suby of* Toys "r" Us, Inc.)
1110 Lougheed Hwy, Coquitlam, BC, V3K 6S4
(604) 654-4775
Emp Here 60
SIC 5945 Hobby, toy, and game shops

D-U-N-S 20-512-1481   (BR)
TREE OF LIFE CANADA ULC
(*Suby of* Kehe Distributors, LLC)
91 Glacier St, Coquitlam, BC, V3K 5Z1
(604) 941-8502
Emp Here 60
SIC 5141 Groceries, general line

D-U-N-S 25-483-6638   (HQ)
UNI-SELECT PACIFIC INC
91 Glacier St, Coquitlam, BC, V3K 5Z1
(604) 472-4900
Emp Here 50   *Emp Total* 2,597
Sales 15,175,826
SIC 5013 Motor vehicle supplies and new parts
Dir Henry Buckley
Dir Eric Bussieres

D-U-N-S 25-646-8844   (SL)
VANHOUTTE COFFEE SERVICES LTD
9 Burbidge St Suite 120, Coquitlam, BC, V3K 7B2
(604) 552-5452
Emp Here 60   *Sales* 3,064,349

SIC 7389 Business services, nec

D-U-N-S 25-372-4371   (BR)
VEOLIA ES CANADA SERVICES INDUSTRIELS INC
VEOLIA ENVIRONMENTAL SERVICES
10 King Edward St Suite 400, Coquitlam, BC, V3K 4S8
(604) 525-5261
Emp Here 30
SIC 7699 Repair services, nec

D-U-N-S 25-362-8291   (BR)
WASTE MANAGEMENT OF CANADA CORPORATION
VANCOUVER HAULING
(*Suby of* Waste Management, Inc.)
2330 United Blvd, Coquitlam, BC, V3K 6S1
(604) 520-7963
Emp Here 30
SIC 4953 Refuse systems

D-U-N-S 20-117-1667   (SL)
WELSH, FRED LTD
94 Glacier Street Suite 201, Coquitlam, BC, V3K 6B2
(604) 942-0012
Emp Here 50   *Sales* 4,377,642
SIC 1711 Plumbing, heating, air-conditioning

D-U-N-S 20-005-2368   (BR)
WENDY'S RESTAURANTS OF CANADA INC
WENDY'S
(*Suby of* The Wendy's Company)
100 Schoolhouse St Suite 101, Coquitlam, BC, V3K 6V9
(604) 520-6528
Emp Here 30
SIC 5812 Eating places

D-U-N-S 20-117-3903   (HQ)
WHITE & PETERS LTD
1368 United Blvd Unit 101, Coquitlam, BC, V3K 6Y2
(604) 526-4641
Emp Here 20   *Emp Total* 15
Sales 7,296,070
SIC 5013 Motor vehicle supplies and new parts
Pr Pr Sumio Kikuchi
   Mort Hall
VP VP Rob Neale
   Martin Gifford

D-U-N-S 25-098-3194   (BR)
WILLIAMS MOVING & STORAGE (B.C.) LTD
(*Suby of* Williams Moving & Storage (B.C.) Ltd)
26 Fawcett Rd, Coquitlam, BC, V3K 6X9

Emp Here 30
SIC 4214 Local trucking with storage

D-U-N-S 20-117-4562   (HQ)
WILLIAMS MOVING & STORAGE (B.C.) LTD
WILLIAMS MOVING INTERNATIONAL
(*Suby of* Williams Moving & Storage (B.C.) Ltd)
2401 United Blvd, Coquitlam, BC, V3K 5X9

Emp Here 75   *Emp Total* 300
Sales 22,050,499
SIC 4214 Local trucking with storage
Pr Pr George Williams Jr
   Glenn Thomsen
   Verna Williams
Fin Ex Ernie Klassen

D-U-N-S 20-184-3062   (BR)
WINNERS MERCHANTS INTERNATIONAL L.P.
HOMESENSE
(*Suby of* The TJX Companies Inc)
101 Schoolhouse St Unit 260, Coquitlam, BC, V3K 4X8
(604) 523-2210
Emp Here 40
SIC 5651 Family clothing stores

D-U-N-S 20-199-3107   (BR)
WINNERS MERCHANTS INTERNATIONAL L.P.
WINNERS
(*Suby of* The TJX Companies Inc)
101 Schoolhouse St, Coquitlam, BC, V3K 4X8
(604) 524-2602
Emp Here 40
SIC 5651 Family clothing stores

Courtenay, BC V9J
Comox - Strathcona County

D-U-N-S 20-713-6081   (BR)
SCHOOL DISTRICT NO. 71 (COMOX VALLEY)
VANIER SCHOOL
4830 Headquarters Rd, Courtenay, BC, V9J 1P2
(250) 338-9262
Emp Here 50
SIC 8211 Elementary and secondary schools

D-U-N-S 20-087-0645   (BR)
SCHOOL DISTRICT NO. 71 (COMOX VALLEY)
HUBAND PARK ELEMENTARY SCHOOL
5120 Mottishaw Rd, Courtenay, BC, V9J 1L5
(250) 338-6596
Emp Here 42
SIC 8211 Elementary and secondary schools

D-U-N-S 20-591-5460   (BR)
SCHOOL DISTRICT NO. 71 (COMOX VALLEY)
SANDWICK ALTERNATE SCHOOL
2947 Rennison Rd, Courtenay, BC, V9J 1M1
(250) 334-2520
Emp Here 25
SIC 8211 Elementary and secondary schools

D-U-N-S 25-914-1133   (BR)
SCOUTS CANADA
5200 Comox Logging Rd, Courtenay, BC, V9J 1P9

Emp Here 45
SIC 8641 Civic and social associations

Courtenay, BC V9N
Comox - Strathcona County

D-U-N-S 24-363-4933   (SL)
ARG SERVICES INC
1130 21st St, Courtenay, BC, V9N 2B8

Emp Here 25   *Sales* 5,376,850
SIC 3443 Fabricated plate work (boiler shop)
Owner Rick Agee

D-U-N-S 25-296-9175   (BR)
BANK OF NOVA SCOTIA, THE
SCOTIABANK
392 5th St, Courtenay, BC, V9N 1K1
(250) 703-4800
Emp Here 28
SIC 6021 National commercial banks

D-U-N-S 20-104-2749   (BR)
BANK OF MONTREAL
BMO
585 England Ave, Courtenay, BC, V9N 2N2
(250) 334-3181
Emp Here 20
SIC 6021 National commercial banks

D-U-N-S 20-977-6827   (BR)
BEST BUY CANADA LTD
FUTURE SHOP
(*Suby of* Best Buy Co., Inc.)
3245 Cliffe Ave Suite 1, Courtenay, BC, V9N 2L9

---

(250) 334-9791
Emp Here 50
SIC 5731 Radio, television, and electronic stores

D-U-N-S 25-289-2351   (BR)
BLACK PRESS GROUP LTD
COMOX VALLEY RECORD
765 Mcphee Ave, Courtenay, BC, V9N 2Z7
(250) 338-5811
Emp Here 25
SIC 2711 Newspapers

D-U-N-S 20-302-1139   (BR)
BRITISH COLUMBIA HYDRO AND POWER AUTHORITY
BC HYDRO
330 Lerwick Rd, Courtenay, BC, V9N 9E5
(250) 897-7402
Emp Here 25
SIC 4911 Electric services

D-U-N-S 20-572-8228   (BR)
CANADA POST CORPORATION
333 Hunt Pl, Courtenay, BC, V9N 1G0
(250) 334-9423
Emp Here 20
SIC 4311 U.s. postal service

D-U-N-S 25-017-0495   (BR)
CANADIAN IMPERIAL BANK OF COMMERCE
CIBC
825 Cliffe Ave, Courtenay, BC, V9N 2J8
(250) 338-6751
Emp Here 35
SIC 6021 National commercial banks

D-U-N-S 20-563-2719   (BR)
CENTRAL BUILDERS' SUPPLY P.G. LIMITED
HOME HARDWARE BUILDING CENTRE
610 Anderton Ave, Courtenay, BC, V9N 2H3
(250) 334-4416
Emp Here 49
SIC 1541 Industrial buildings and warehouses

D-U-N-S 20-797-8490   (BR)
CORPORATION OF THE CITY OF COURTENAY, THE
COURTENAY RECREATION CENTRE
489 Old Island Hwy, Courtenay, BC, V9N 3P5
(250) 338-5371
Emp Here 80
SIC 7999 Amusement and recreation, nec

D-U-N-S 24-448-4465   (SL)
COURTENAY LODGE LTD
BEST WESTERN THE WESTERLY HOTEL, DIV OF
1590 Cliffe Ave, Courtenay, BC, V9N 2K4
(250) 338-7741
Emp Here 75   *Sales* 4,240,481
SIC 7011 Hotels and motels

D-U-N-S 25-977-4607   (SL)
GABRIELLA'S KITCHEN INC
910 Fitzgerald Ave Unit 301, Courtenay, BC, V9N 2R5
(250) 334-3209
Emp Here 50   *Sales* 7,150,149
SIC 5149 Groceries and related products, nec
Dir Margot Micallef
Pr Pr Vincent Micallef
   Christopher Fenn

D-U-N-S 25-155-1800   (BR)
GOVERNING COUNCIL OF THE SALVATION ARMY IN CANADA, THE
GOVERNING COUNCIL OF THE SALVATION ARMY IN CANADA, THE
2966 Kilpatrick Ave Suite 12, Courtenay, BC, V9N 8P1
(250) 338-8151
Emp Here 30
SIC 5932 Used merchandise stores

D-U-N-S 20-095-2695   (BR)
GREAT PACIFIC INDUSTRIES INC

OVERWAITEA FOODS
2701 Cliffe Ave, Courtenay, BC, V9N 2L8

Emp Here 150
SIC 5411 Grocery stores

D-U-N-S 20-556-2270   (BR)
HOME DEPOT OF CANADA INC
HOME DEPOT
(*Suby of* The Home Depot Inc)
388 Lerwick Rd, Courtenay, BC, V9N 9E5
(250) 334-5400
Emp Here 151
SIC 5211 Lumber and other building materials

D-U-N-S 25-272-7284   (BR)
INSURANCE CORPORATION OF BRITISH COLUMBIA
I C B C
505 Crown Isle Blvd, Courtenay, BC, V9N 9W1
(250) 338-7731
Emp Here 29
SIC 6331 Fire, marine, and casualty insurance

D-U-N-S 25-315-8505   (BR)
INVESTORS GROUP FINANCIAL SERVICES INC
1599 Cliffe Ave Suite 22, Courtenay, BC, V9N 2K6
(250) 338-7811
Emp Here 25
SIC 8741 Management services

D-U-N-S 25-153-3709   (BR)
JOHN HOWARD SOCIETY OF NORTH ISLAND, THE
1455 Cliffe Ave, Courtenay, BC, V9N 2K6
(250) 338-7341
Emp Here 28
SIC 8399 Social services, nec

D-U-N-S 24-291-6310   (SL)
KINGFISHER INN LTD
KINGFISHER OCEANSIDE RESORT & SPA
4330 Island Hwy S, Courtenay, BC, V9N 9R9
(250) 338-1323
Emp Here 70   *Sales* 3,064,349
SIC 7011 Hotels and motels

D-U-N-S 20-949-9008   (BR)
LOBLAWS INC
REAL CANADIAN SUPERSTORE
757 Ryan Rd, Courtenay, BC, V9N 3R6
(250) 334-6900
Emp Here 300
SIC 5912 Drug stores and proprietary stores

D-U-N-S 20-874-4537   (BR)
LORDCO PARTS LTD
LORDCO AUTO PARTS
2401 Cliffe Ave Unit 1, Courtenay, BC, V9N 2L5
(250) 338-6266
Emp Here 30
SIC 5531 Auto and home supply stores

D-U-N-S 24-620-2337   (BR)
O.K. INDUSTRIES LTD
TAYCO PAVING CO, DIV OF
801a 29th St, Courtenay, BC, V9N 7Z5
(250) 338-7251
Emp Here 20
SIC 1611 Highway and street construction

D-U-N-S 20-863-6282   (SL)
RIVERHOUSE ENTERPRISES LTD
OLD HOUSE RESTAURANT, THE
1760 Riverside Lane, Courtenay, BC, V9N 8C7

Emp Here 55   *Sales* 1,678,096
SIC 5812 Eating places

D-U-N-S 25-912-5730   (BR)
ROYAL BANK OF CANADA
RBC
(*Suby of* Royal Bank Of Canada)
1015 Ryan Rd, Courtenay, BC, V9N 3R6

(250) 334-6150
Emp Here 26
SIC 6021 National commercial banks

D-U-N-S 24-318-0432   (BR)
SAPUTO INC
DAIRYLAND FLUID
743 28th St, Courtenay, BC, V9N 7P4
(250) 334-3143
Emp Here 25
SIC 2026 Fluid milk

D-U-N-S 20-713-6057   (BR)
SCHOOL DISTRICT NO. 71 (COMOX VALLEY)
QUEENEESH ELEMENTARY SCHOOL
2345 Mission Rd Suite 171, Courtenay, BC, V9N 9H1
(250) 338-1481
Emp Here 50
SIC 8211 Elementary and secondary schools

D-U-N-S 20-713-6040   (BR)
SCHOOL DISTRICT NO. 71 (COMOX VALLEY)
COURTENAY ELEMENTARY SCHOOL
1540 Mcphee Ave, Courtenay, BC, V9N 3A5
(250) 338-5396
Emp Here 40
SIC 8211 Elementary and secondary schools

D-U-N-S 20-713-6123   (BR)
SCHOOL DISTRICT NO. 71 (COMOX VALLEY)
MARK ISFELD SCHOOL
1551 Lerwick Rd, Courtenay, BC, V9N 9B5
(250) 334-2428
Emp Here 110
SIC 8211 Elementary and secondary schools

D-U-N-S 20-591-5478   (BR)
SCHOOL DISTRICT NO. 71 (COMOX VALLEY)
PUNTLEDGE PARK ELEMENTARY SCHOOL
401 Willemar Ave, Courtenay, BC, V9N 3L3
(250) 334-4495
Emp Here 25
SIC 8211 Elementary and secondary schools

D-U-N-S 24-614-5085   (BR)
SCHOOL DISTRICT NO. 71 (COMOX VALLEY)
SCHOOL DISTRICT NO 71 MAINTENANCE
2963 Vanier Dr, Courtenay, BC, V9N 5Y2
(250) 338-7475
Emp Here 45
SIC 7349 Building maintenance services, nec

D-U-N-S 20-027-0390   (BR)
SCHOOL DISTRICT NO. 71 (COMOX VALLEY)
VALLEY VIEW ELEMENTARY SCHOOL
2300 Valley View Dr, Courtenay, BC, V9N 9A3
(250) 897-0343
Emp Here 40
SIC 8211 Elementary and secondary schools

D-U-N-S 20-030-5899   (BR)
SCHOOL DISTRICT NO. 71 (COMOX VALLEY)
ARDEN ELEMENTARY SCHOOL
3040 Lake Trail Rd, Courtenay, BC, V9N 9M1
(250) 334-3191
Emp Here 40
SIC 8211 Elementary and secondary schools

D-U-N-S 20-713-6099   (BR)
SCHOOL DISTRICT NO. 71 (COMOX VALLEY)
LAKE TRAIL MIDDLE SCHOOL
805 Willemar Ave, Courtenay, BC, V9N 3L7
(250) 334-3168
Emp Here 50
SIC 8211 Elementary and secondary schools

D-U-N-S 20-556-0571   (BR)
STAPLES CANADA INC
STAPLES THE BUSINESS DEPOT

(*Suby of* Staples, Inc.)
3299 Cliffe Ave Unit 2, Courtenay, BC, V9N 2L9
(250) 334-8357
Emp Here 30
SIC 5943 Stationery stores

D-U-N-S 20-003-5749   (BR)
VALUE VILLAGE STORES, INC
(*Suby of* Savers, Inc.)
360 Old Island Hwy, Courtenay, BC, V9N 3P3
(250) 334-3085
Emp Here 40
SIC 5399 Miscellaneous general merchandise

D-U-N-S 20-512-5755   (BR)
VANCOUVER ISLAND INSURANCENTRES INC
364 8th St Unit 109, Courtenay, BC, V9N 1N3
(250) 338-1401
Emp Here 20
SIC 6411 Insurance agents, brokers, and service

D-U-N-S 24-073-6665   (BR)
WINNERS MERCHANTS INTERNATIONAL L.P.
WINNERS
(*Suby of* The TJX Companies Inc)
3199 Cliffe Ave, Courtenay, BC, V9N 2L9
(250) 703-0161
Emp Here 35
SIC 5651 Family clothing stores

D-U-N-S 25-893-5162   (BR)
WORKERS' COMPENSATION BOARD OF BRITISH COLUMBIA
WORKSAFE BC
801 30th St, Courtenay, BC, V9N 8G6
(250) 334-8701
Emp Here 50
SIC 6331 Fire, marine, and casualty insurance

Cranbrook, BC V1C
East Kootenay County

D-U-N-S 25-321-0330   (BR)
BDO CANADA LLP
CRANBROOK ACCOUNTING
35 10th Ave S, Cranbrook, BC, V1C 2M9
(250) 426-4285
Emp Here 21
SIC 8721 Accounting, auditing, and bookkeeping

D-U-N-S 25-288-8698   (BR)
CANADA POST CORPORATION
CANADA POST
101 10th Ave S, Cranbrook, BC, V1C 2N1
(250) 426-8266
Emp Here 40
SIC 4311 U.s. postal service

D-U-N-S 25-998-6649   (BR)
CANADIAN FOREST PRODUCTS LTD
1000 Industrial Road 1, Cranbrook, BC, V1C 4C6
(250) 426-6241
Emp Here 2,500
SIC 2421 Sawmills and planing mills, general

D-U-N-S 25-003-6415   (BR)
CANADIAN IMPERIAL BANK OF COMMERCE
CIBC
919 Baker St, Cranbrook, BC, V1C 1A4
(800) 465-2422
Emp Here 25
SIC 6021 National commercial banks

D-U-N-S 20-988-9781   (BR)
CULLEN DIESEL POWER LTD
DETROIT DIESEL ALLISON
601 Industrial Road 3, Cranbrook, BC, V1C 4E1

(250) 426-8271
Emp Here 22
SIC 7699 Repair services, nec

D-U-N-S 25-072-6700   (BR)
DENCAN RESTAURANTS INC
DENNY'S RESTAURANT
(*Suby of* Northland Properties Corporation)
405 Cranbrook St N, Cranbrook, BC, V1C 3R5
(250) 426-8866
Emp Here 30
SIC 5812 Eating places

D-U-N-S 25-620-1138   (BR)
EMIL ANDERSON CONSTRUCTION CO. LTD
EMIL ANDERSON CONSTRUCTION CO LTD
1425 Industrial Road 2, Cranbrook, BC, V1C 5X5
(250) 426-7716
Emp Here 20
SIC 1611 Highway and street construction

D-U-N-S 20-230-4353   (SL)
FW GREEN HOME, THE
NURSES OFFICE
1700 4th St S, Cranbrook, BC, V1C 6E1
(250) 426-8016
Emp Here 100   *Sales* 4,742,446
SIC 8059 Nursing and personal care, nec

D-U-N-S 20-095-4147   (BR)
FINNING INTERNATIONAL INC
FINNING CANADA
(*Suby of* Finning International Inc)
815 Cranbrook St N, Cranbrook, BC, V1C 3S2
(250) 489-6631
Emp Here 30
SIC 5082 Construction and mining machinery

D-U-N-S 25-267-8560   (BR)
GREAT PACIFIC INDUSTRIES INC
SAVE-ON-FOODS
505 Victoria Ave N, Cranbrook, BC, V1C 6S3
(250) 489-3461
Emp Here 120
SIC 5411 Grocery stores

D-U-N-S 25-270-3202   (BR)
HSBC BANK CANADA
928 Baker St, Cranbrook, BC, V1C 1A5
(250) 426-7221
Emp Here 24
SIC 6021 National commercial banks

D-U-N-S 24-361-7227   (BR)
HOME DEPOT OF CANADA INC
HOME DEPOT
(*Suby of* The Home Depot Inc)
2000 Mcphee Rd, Cranbrook, BC, V1C 0A3
(250) 420-4250
Emp Here 100
SIC 5251 Hardware stores

D-U-N-S 20-047-3234   (BR)
INLAND KENWORTH LTD
INLAND KENWORTH
816 Industrial Road 1, Cranbrook, BC, V1C 4C6
(250) 426-6205
Emp Here 30
SIC 5531 Auto and home supply stores

D-U-N-S 24-517-3638   (SL)
INN OF THE SOUTH HOTEL (1986) LTD
HERITAGE INN HOTEL & CONVENTION CENTRE
803 Cranbrook St N, Cranbrook, BC, V1C 3S2
(250) 489-4301
Emp Here 65   *Sales* 2,845,467
SIC 7011 Hotels and motels

D-U-N-S 25-272-7326   (BR)
INSURANCE CORPORATION OF BRITISH COLUMBIA
I C B C
126 Briar Ave Nw, Cranbrook, BC, V1C 5S3
(250) 426-5246
Emp Here 20

SIC 6331 Fire, marine, and casualty insurance

D-U-N-S 24-930-4650   (BR)
INTERIOR HEALTH AUTHORITY
EAST KOOTENAY REGIONAL HOSPITAL
13 24th Ave N, Cranbrook, BC, V1C 3H9
(250) 426-5281
Emp Here 50
SIC 8062 General medical and surgical hospitals

D-U-N-S 25-937-9410   (BR)
KTUNAXA NATION COUNCIL
CHILD & FAMILY SERVICES SOCIETY
7472 Mission Rd, Cranbrook, BC, V1C 7E5
(250) 489-4563
Emp Here 35
SIC 8322 Individual and family services

D-U-N-S 20-556-1298   (BR)
LOBLAWS INC
SUPERSTORE THE REAL CANADIAN
2100 17th St N Suite 1553, Cranbrook, BC, V1C 7J1
(250) 420-2118
Emp Here 200
SIC 5411 Grocery stores

D-U-N-S 25-777-1840   (BR)
LORDCO PARTS LTD
LORDCO AUTO PARTS
2201 Cranbrook St N, Cranbrook, BC, V1C 5M6
(250) 417-0888
Emp Here 28
SIC 5531 Auto and home supply stores

D-U-N-S 25-108-7235   (BR)
MAINROAD EAST KOOTENAY CONTRACTING LTD
258 Industrial Road F, Cranbrook, BC, V1C 6N8
(250) 417-4624
Emp Here 100
SIC 1611 Highway and street construction

D-U-N-S 20-527-9438   (BR)
NAV CANADA
9380 Airport Access Rd, Cranbrook, BC, V1C 7E4
(250) 426-3814
Emp Here 20
SIC 4581 Airports, flying fields, and services

D-U-N-S 24-325-8022   (SL)
PRAIRIE HOLDINGS INC
4201 Echo Field Rd, Cranbrook, BC, V1C 7B6
(250) 489-0776
Emp Here 40   *Sales* 5,681,200
SIC 2411 Logging
Pr Pr Jake Blackmore
VP VP Shane Palmer
Hyrum Blackmore

D-U-N-S 25-140-2863   (SL)
QUAD CITY BUILDING MATERIALS LTD
HOME HARDWARE BUILDING CENTRE
1901 Mcphee Rd, Cranbrook, BC, V1C 7J2
(250) 426-6288
Emp Here 50   *Sales* 4,815,406
SIC 5251 Hardware stores

D-U-N-S 25-018-7911   (BR)
SCHOOL DISTRICT NO 5 (SOUTHEAST KOOTENAY)
PINEWOOD ELEMENTARY SCHOOL
40 Pinewood Ave, Cranbrook, BC, V1C 5X8
(250) 426-6201
Emp Here 20
SIC 8211 Elementary and secondary schools

D-U-N-S 20-511-9170   (BR)
SCHOOL DISTRICT NO 5 (SOUTHEAST KOOTENAY)
HIGHLANDS ELEMENTARY SCHOOL
3300 7th St S, Cranbrook, BC, V1C 5G3
(250) 489-4391
Emp Here 30
SIC 8211 Elementary and secondary schools

D-U-N-S 25-818-9018   (BR)
SCHOOL DISTRICT NO 5 (SOUTHEAST KOOTENAY)
LAURIE MIDDLE SCHOOL
1808 2nd St S, Cranbrook, BC, V1C 1C5
(250) 426-5291
Emp Here 46
SIC 8211 Elementary and secondary schools

D-U-N-S 20-713-2163   (BR)
SCHOOL DISTRICT NO 5 (SOUTHEAST KOOTENAY)
KOOTENAY ORCHARDS ELEMENTARY
1301 20th Ave S Suite 1, Cranbrook, BC, V1C 6N5
(250) 426-8551
Emp Here 20
SIC 8211 Elementary and secondary schools

D-U-N-S 20-592-0692   (BR)
SCHOOL DISTRICT NO 5 (SOUTHEAST KOOTENAY)
PARKLAND MIDDLE SCHOOL
1115 2nd Ave S, Cranbrook, BC, V1C 2B4
(250) 426-3327
Emp Here 30
SIC 8211 Elementary and secondary schools

D-U-N-S 20-653-4989   (BR)
SCHOOL DISTRICT NO 5 (SOUTHEAST KOOTENAY)
STEEPLES ELEMENTARY SCHOOL
700 24th Ave N, Cranbrook, BC, V1C 5P6
(250) 426-3352
Emp Here 25
SIC 8211 Elementary and secondary schools

D-U-N-S 25-453-2369   (BR)
SCHOOL DISTRICT NO 5 (SOUTHEAST KOOTENAY)
GORDON TERRACE ELEMENTARY SCHOOL
1200 5th Ave S, Cranbrook, BC, V1C 2H1
(250) 426-8248
Emp Here 30
SIC 8211 Elementary and secondary schools

D-U-N-S 25-154-1512   (BR)
SCHOOL DISTRICT NO 5 (SOUTHEAST KOOTENAY)
MOUNT BAKER SENIOR SECONDARY SCHOOL
940 Industrial Road 1 Suite 1, Cranbrook, BC, V1C 4C6
(250) 426-4201
Emp Here 80
SIC 8211 Elementary and secondary schools

D-U-N-S 24-442-1897   (HQ)
SELKIRK SIGNS & SERVICES LTD
(*Suby of* Selkirk Signs & Services Ltd)
421 Patterson St W, Cranbrook, BC, V1C 6T3
(250) 489-3321
Emp Here 40   *Emp Total* 75
Sales 4,523,563
SIC 3993 Signs and advertising specialties

D-U-N-S 25-140-9876   (SL)
SEM RESORT LIMITED PARTNERSHIP BY GENERAL PARTNER
ST EUGENE GOLF RESORT AND CASINO
7648 Mission Rd, Cranbrook, BC, V1C 7E5
(250) 420-2000
Emp Here 100   *Sales* 5,928,320
SIC 7992 Public golf courses
Max Dressler

D-U-N-S 25-272-0123   (BR)
SOBEYS WEST INC
SAFEWAY, DIV OF
1200 Baker St, Cranbrook, BC, V1C 1A8
(250) 417-0221
Emp Here 130
SIC 5411 Grocery stores

D-U-N-S 20-793-0897   (BR)
STAPLES CANADA INC
STAPLE THE BUSINESS DEPOT

(*Suby of* Staples, Inc.)
1500 Cranbrook St N Unit 43, Cranbrook, BC, V1C 3S8
(250) 417-2346
Emp Here 30
SIC 5943 Stationery stores

D-U-N-S 20-875-3314   (BR)
STELMASCHUK, W. J. AND ASSOCIATES LTD
KOOTENAY EAST YOUTH PROGRAM
2001 Industrial Road 2, Cranbrook, BC, V1C 6H3
(250) 426-3387
Emp Here 26
SIC 8322 Individual and family services

D-U-N-S 25-269-6240   (HQ)
TERRIM PROPERTIES LTD
FAIRWEATHER BINGO
(*Suby of* Terrim Properties Ltd)
1850 2nd St N Suite 106, Cranbrook, BC, V1C 5A2
(250) 489-5160
Emp Here 45   *Emp Total* 55
Sales 3,863,549
SIC 7999 Amusement and recreation, nec

D-U-N-S 24-317-1829   (BR)
WAL-MART CANADA CORP
WALMART
2100 Willowbrook Dr Suite 3183, Cranbrook, BC, V1C 7H2
(250) 489-3202
Emp Here 185
SIC 5311 Department stores

D-U-N-S 25-828-4454   (BR)
WALTER, B & D TRUCKING LTD
WALTERS TRUCKING
900 Industrial Road 2, Cranbrook, BC, V1C 4P8
(250) 426-0590
Emp Here 50
SIC 4213 Trucking, except local

D-U-N-S 20-003-8300   (BR)
WASTE MANAGEMENT OF CANADA CORPORATION
(*Suby of* Waste Management, Inc.)
2000 17th St N, Cranbrook, BC, V1C 7G2

Emp Here 30
SIC 4953 Refuse systems

D-U-N-S 25-372-9016   (BR)
WINNERS MERCHANTS INTERNATIONAL L.P.
WINNERS
(*Suby of* The TJX Companies Inc)
1500 Cranbrook St N, Cranbrook, BC, V1C 3S8
(250) 417-0949
Emp Here 30
SIC 5651 Family clothing stores

Crawford Bay, BC V0B
Central Kootenay County

D-U-N-S 25-676-7625   (BR)
SCHOOL DISTRICT NO. 8 (KOOTENAY LAKE)
CRAWFORD BAY ELEMENTARY-SECONDARY SCHOOL
(*Suby of* School District No. 8 (Kootenay Lake))
16230 Wadds Rd, Crawford Bay, BC, V0B 1E0
(250) 227-9218
Emp Here 25
SIC 8211 Elementary and secondary schools

Crescent Valley, BC V0G
Central Kootenay County

D-U-N-S 25-676-7583   (BR)
SCHOOL DISTRICT NO. 8 (KOOTENAY LAKE)
BRENT KENNEDY ELEMENTARY SCHOOL
(*Suby of* School District No. 8 (Kootenay Lake))
1092 Hwy 6, Crescent Valley, BC, V0G 1H0
(250) 359-5011
Emp Here 25
SIC 8211 Elementary and secondary schools

Creston, BC V0B
Central Kootenay County

D-U-N-S 25-827-0693   (BR)
GREAT PACIFIC INDUSTRIES INC
OVERWAITEA FOOD GROUP
1000 Northwest Blvd Suite 3, Creston, BC, V0B 1G6
(250) 428-0030
Emp Here 70
SIC 5411 Grocery stores

D-U-N-S 24-494-6471   (SL)
INTERIOR HEALTH CRESTON VALLEY HOSPITAL
CRESTON VALLEY HOSPITAL
312 15 Ave N, Creston, BC, V0B 1G0
(250) 428-2286
Emp Here 450   *Sales* 42,110,640
SIC 8062 General medical and surgical hospitals
Eleanor Sander

D-U-N-S 20-096-3064   (SL)
J.H. HUSCROFT LTD
(*Suby of* Huscroft, Ken Ltd)
922 32 Ave S, Creston, BC, V0B 1G1
(250) 428-7106
Emp Here 100   *Sales* 9,484,891
SIC 2421 Sawmills and planing mills, general
Pr Pr Justin Storm
Dir Irwin Kenneth Huscroft
Dir Gwendclyn Telling
Dir Charles Kevin Huscroft

D-U-N-S 25-084-9957   (BR)
LOBLAWS INC
EXTRA FOODS
1501 Cook St, Creston, BC, V0B 1G0
(250) 402-6020
Emp Here 60
SIC 5411 Grocery stores

D-U-N-S 20-719-0260   (BR)
SCHOOL DISTRICT NO. 8 (KOOTENAY LAKE)
CRESTON EDUCATION CENTRE
617 11 Ave S, Creston, BC, V0B 1G3
(250) 428-2217
Emp Here 20
SIC 8211 Elementary and secondary schools

D-U-N-S 25-676-7963   (BR)
SCHOOL DISTRICT NO. 8 (KOOTENAY LAKE)
MAINTENANCE DEPT (CRESTON)
(*Suby of* School District No. 8 (Kootenay Lake))
1427 Northwest Blvd, Creston, BC, V0B 1G6
(250) 428-5329
Emp Here 25
SIC 4151 School buses

D-U-N-S 25-676-4655   (BR)
SCHOOL DISTRICT NO. 8 (KOOTENAY LAKE)
ADAM ROBERTSON ELEMENTARY SCHOOL
(*Suby of* School District No. 8 (Kootenay Lake))
421 9 Ave N, Creston, BC, V0B 1G4

(250) 428-2051
Emp Here 39
SIC 8211 Elementary and secondary schools

D-U-N-S 25-273-5576   (BR)
SCHOOL DISTRICT NO. 8 (KOOTENAY LAKE)
PRINCE CHARLES SECONDARY SCHOOL
(*Suby of* School District No. 8 (Kootenay Lake))
223 18 Ave S, Creston, BC, V0B 1G5
(250) 428-2274
Emp Here 60
SIC 8211 Elementary and secondary schools

D-U-N-S 20-994-0068   (BR)
YELLOWHEAD ROAD & BRIDGE (KOOTENAY) LTD
YRB
600 Helen St Suite 6, Creston, BC, V0B 1G6
(250) 428-7606
Emp Here 25
SIC 3531 Construction machinery

Crofton, BC V0R
Cowichan Valley County

D-U-N-S 20-327-4774   (BR)
CATALYST PAPER CORPORATION
CROFTON MILL
8541 Hay Road N, Crofton, BC, V0R 1R0
(250) 246-6100
Emp Here 578
SIC 2621 Paper mills

Cultus Lake, BC V2R

D-U-N-S 25-539-4496   (BR)
SCHOOL DISTRICT NO 33 CHILLIWACK
CULTUS LAKE COMMUNITY SCHOOL
71 Sunnyside Blvd, Cultus Lake, BC, V2R 5B5
(604) 858-6266
Emp Here 23
SIC 8211 Elementary and secondary schools

Cumberland, BC V0R
Comox - Strathcona County

D-U-N-S 20-655-1207   (BR)
SCHOOL DISTRICT NO. 71 (COMOX VALLEY)
CUMBERLAND COMMUNITY SCHOOL
2674 Windermere Ave, Cumberland, BC, V0R 1S0
(250) 336-8511
Emp Here 25
SIC 8211 Elementary and secondary schools

D-U-N-S 20-591-5445   (BR)
SCHOOL DISTRICT NO. 71 (COMOX VALLEY)
CUMBERLAND ELEMENTARY SCHOOL
2644 Ulverston Ave, Cumberland, BC, V0R 1S0

Emp Here 38
SIC 8211 Elementary and secondary schools

D-U-N-S 20-031-5880   (BR)
SCHOOL DISTRICT NO. 71 (COMOX VALLEY)
CUMBERLAND JUNIOR SECONDARY SCHOOL
Po Box 430, Cumberland, BC, V0R 1S0
(250) 336-8511
Emp Here 25
SIC 8211 Elementary and secondary schools

D-U-N-S 24-136-8323   (BR)

Vancouver Island Health Authority

VANCOUVER ISLAND HEALTH AUTHORITY
CUMBERLAND HEALTH CENTRE
2696 Windermere St, Cumberland, BC, V0R 1S0
(250) 336-2087
Emp Here 85
SIC 8011 Offices and clinics of medical doctors

D'Arcy, BC V0N
Squamish - Lillooet County

D-U-N-S 20-713-4896   (BR)
SCHOOL DISTRICT NO. 48 (HOWE SOUND)
BLACKWATER CREEK ELEMENTARY SCHOOL
Gd, D'Arcy, BC, V0N 1L0
(604) 452-3330
Emp Here 50
SIC 8211 Elementary and secondary schools

Dawson Creek, BC V1G
Peace River - Laird County

D-U-N-S 24-786-9258   (SL)
356746 HOLDINGS INC
GEORGE DAWSON INN
11705 8 St, Dawson Creek, BC, V1G 4N9

Emp Here 60   *Sales* 2,626,585
SIC 7011 Hotels and motels

D-U-N-S 24-713-7339   (BR)
CALFRAC WELL SERVICES LTD
709 106 Ave, Dawson Creek, BC, V1G 4V9
(250) 782-2529
Emp Here 20
SIC 1389 Oil and gas field services, nec

D-U-N-S 25-288-8730   (BR)
CANADA POST CORPORATION
DAWSON CREEK MAIL PROCESSING PLANT
11622 7 St, Dawson Creek, BC, V1G 4R8
(250) 782-2322
Emp Here 40
SIC 4311 U.s. postal service

D-U-N-S 25-518-8583   (BR)
CANADIAN UNION OF POSTAL WORKERS
C U P W
11622 7 St, Dawson Creek, BC, V1G 4R8
(250) 782-1882
Emp Here 45
SIC 8631 Labor organizations

D-U-N-S 24-916-2129   (BR)
CORPORATION OF THE CITY OF DAWSON CREEK
MEMORIAL ARENA
1310 106 Ave, Dawson Creek, BC, V1G 2P1
(250) 782-2229
Emp Here 20
SIC 7999 Amusement and recreation, nec

D-U-N-S 24-396-4707   (SL)
DUFOUR, R ENTERPRISES LTD
R DUFOUR
1505 97 Ave, Dawson Creek, BC, V1G 1N6
(250) 782-7084
Emp Here 48   *Sales* 8,014,550
SIC 4213 Trucking, except local
Pr Pr Richard Dufour
Carol Dufour

D-U-N-S 24-627-7537   (SL)
GEAR-O-RAMA SUPPLY LTD
9300 Golf Course Rd, Dawson Creek, BC, V1G 4E9
(250) 782-8126
Emp Here 25   *Sales* 9,120,088

SIC 5511 New and used car dealers
Pr Pr Richard Hackworth
Andreas Schurmann
Barrie Beddel

D-U-N-S 24-340-1309   (BR)
GLACIER MEDIA INC
DAWSON CREEK DAILY
901 100 Ave, Dawson Creek, BC, V1G 1W2
(250) 782-4888
Emp Here 26
SIC 2711 Newspapers

D-U-N-S 24-098-3551   (SL)
INLAND AUTO CENTRE LTD
11600 8 St, Dawson Creek, BC, V1G 4R7
(250) 782-5507
Emp Here 32   *Sales* 16,076,800
SIC 5511 New and used car dealers
Pr Pr James Inkster

D-U-N-S 24-095-8304   (HQ)
LAWRENCE MEAT PACKING CO. LTD
BUTCHER BLOCK, THE
(*Suby of* Lawrence Meat Packing Co. Ltd)
11088 4th St, Dawson Creek, BC, V1G 4H8
(250) 782-5111
Emp Here 20   *Emp Total* 75
Sales 19,188,664
SIC 5147 Meats and meat products
Pr Pr Joseph Lafond
Jerry Lafond
Maurice Lafond
Irene Lafond

D-U-N-S 24-397-3237   (SL)
PAVLIS TRUCKING LTD
Gd Stn Main, Dawson Creek, BC, V1G 4E6
(250) 782-9819
Emp Here 41   *Sales* 5,180,210
SIC 1389 Oil and gas field services, nec
Pr Pr Richard Pavlis

D-U-N-S 25-289-6840   (BR)
PEAVEY INDUSTRIES LIMITED
PEAVEY MART
1300 Alaska Ave, Dawson Creek, BC, V1G 1Z3
(250) 782-4056
Emp Here 20
SIC 5251 Hardware stores

D-U-N-S 20-004-4456   (BR)
ROYAL BANK OF CANADA
RBC
(*Suby of* Royal Bank Of Canada)
10324 10 St, Dawson Creek, BC, V1G 3T6
(250) 782-9441
Emp Here 20
SIC 6021 National commercial banks

D-U-N-S 20-026-8576   (BR)
SCHOOL DISTRICT #59 PEACE RIVER SOUTH
ECOLE FRANK ROSS ELEMENTARY
1000 92 Ave, Dawson Creek, BC, V1G 1C1
(250) 782-5206
Emp Here 50
SIC 8211 Elementary and secondary schools

D-U-N-S 25-454-6112   (BR)
SCHOOL DISTRICT #59 PEACE RIVER SOUTH
SOUTH PEACE SECONDARY SCHOOL
10808 15 St, Dawson Creek, BC, V1G 3Z3
(250) 782-5585
Emp Here 63
SIC 8211 Elementary and secondary schools

D-U-N-S 20-591-3507   (BR)
SCHOOL DISTRICT #59 PEACE RIVER SOUTH
CRESCENT PARK ELEMENTARY SCHOOL
9300 17 St, Dawson Creek, BC, V1G 4A6
(250) 782-8412
Emp Here 25
SIC 8211 Elementary and secondary schools

D-U-N-S 20-034-0276   (BR)
SCHOOL DISTRICT #59 PEACE RIVER SOUTH
DISTRICT RESOURCE CENTRE
10701 10 St, Dawson Creek, BC, V1G 3V2
(250) 782-6336
Emp Here 100
SIC 8211 Elementary and secondary schools

D-U-N-S 20-591-3499   (BR)
SCHOOL DISTRICT #59 PEACE RIVER SOUTH
CANALTA AFTER-SCHOOL CARE
1901 110 Ave, Dawson Creek, BC, V1G 2W6
(250) 782-8403
Emp Here 25
SIC 8211 Elementary and secondary schools

D-U-N-S 20-591-3481   (BR)
SCHOOL DISTRICT #59 PEACE RIVER SOUTH
TREMBLAY ELEMENTARY SCHOOL
11311 13a St, Dawson Creek, BC, V1G 3X8
(250) 782-8147
Emp Here 25
SIC 8211 Elementary and secondary schools

D-U-N-S 24-363-2044   (BR)
SOBEYS WEST INC
DAWSON CREEK SAFEWAY
11200 8 St, Dawson Creek, BC, V1G 3R4
(250) 782-9561
Emp Here 50
SIC 5411 Grocery stores

D-U-N-S 25-578-1411   (SL)
SOUTH PEACE HUTTERIAN BRETHREN CHURCH
SOUTH PEACE COLONY
13204 Mckinnon Way, Dawson Creek, BC, V1G 4H7

Emp Here 130   *Sales* 11,025,249
SIC 8661 Religious organizations
Dir Peter Tschetter
Dir Mike K. Tschetter
Dir Jonathon Tschetter
Dir Ben Tschetter
Dir Mike Hofer

D-U-N-S 24-129-8806   (BR)
WAL-MART CANADA CORP
600 Highway 2, Dawson Creek, BC, V1G 0A4
(250) 719-0128
Emp Here 100
SIC 5311 Department stores

D-U-N-S 20-272-5081   (BR)
WESTERN FINANCIAL GROUP INC
1020 104 Ave, Dawson Creek, BC, V1G 4Y8
(250) 782-4505
Emp Here 20
SIC 6311 Life insurance

Dawson Creek, BC V1T
Peace River - Laird County

D-U-N-S 25-097-3633   (BR)
DAWSON CO-OPERATIVE UNION
10020 Parkhill Dr, Dawson Creek, BC, V1T 3P8
(250) 782-3371
Emp Here 20
SIC 5211 Lumber and other building materials

Dease Lake, BC V0C
Stikine Region County

D-U-N-S 24-350-5807   (BR)
LAKES DISTRICT MAINTENANCE LTD
(*Suby of* Lakes District Maintenance Ltd)
Gd, Dease Lake, BC, V0C 1L0

(250) 771-3000
Emp Here 40
SIC 1611 Highway and street construction

D-U-N-S 20-114-4024   (SL)
SPATSIZI REMOTE SERVICES CORPORATION
(*Suby of* Tahltan Nation Development Corporation)
Gd, Dease Lake, BC, V0C 1L0
(250) 771-5484
Emp Here 160   *Sales* 4,815,406
SIC 5812 Eating places

D-U-N-S 24-726-1522   (HQ)
TAHLTAN NATION DEVELOPMENT CORPORATION
(*Suby of* Tahltan Nation Development Corporation)
Hwy 37 N, Dease Lake, BC, V0C 1L0
(250) 771-5482
Emp Here 50   *Emp Total* 85
Sales 12,815,674
SIC 1611 Highway and street construction
 Keith Marrion
Pr Pr William Adsit

Delta, BC V3M
Greater Vancouver County

D-U-N-S 24-161-7992   (HQ)
0429746 B.C. LTD
THE ORIGINAL CAKERIE
(*Suby of* O.C. Holdings '87 Inc)
1345 Cliveden Ave, Delta, BC, V3M 6C7
(604) 515-4555
Emp Here 280   *Emp Total* 350
Sales 171,777,573
SIC 5142 Packaged frozen goods
Pr Pr Dave Hood
 Doug Mcfetridge

D-U-N-S 25-686-8639   (BR)
ARAMARK CANADA LTD.
ARAMARK MANAGED SERVICES
1585 Cliveden Ave Unit 1, Delta, BC, V3M 6M1
(604) 521-5727
Emp Here 20
SIC 5962 Merchandising machine operators

D-U-N-S 25-816-9119   (BR)
ABELL PEST CONTROL INC
207669 Ribley St, Delta, BC, V3M 6L9
(604) 421-6619
Emp Here 25
SIC 7342 Disinfecting and pest control services

D-U-N-S 25-310-9482   (BR)
ABREY ENTERPRISES INC
MCDONALD'S
1285 Cliveden Ave, Delta, BC, V3M 6M3
(604) 718-1125
Emp Here 30
SIC 5812 Eating places

D-U-N-S 24-977-2992   (HQ)
AIRGAS CANADA INC
634 Derwent Way, Delta, BC, V3M 5P8
(604) 520-0355
Emp Here 30   *Emp Total* 1,107
Sales 7,223,109
SIC 5169 Chemicals and allied products, nec
Ch Bd Peter Mccausland
VP VP Michael Molinini

D-U-N-S 20-108-5644   (HQ)
AKHURST MACHINERY LIMITED
1669 Foster'S Way, Delta, BC, V3M 6S7
(604) 540-1430
Emp Here 35   *Emp Total* 80
Sales 18,451,146
SIC 5084 Industrial machinery and equipment
Pr Pr Eric Stebner

 Brian Akhurst
 Bruce Akhurst

D-U-N-S 24-514-0270   (HQ)
BELTERRA CORPORATION
1609 Derwent Way, Delta, BC, V3M 6K8
(604) 540-1950
Emp Here 40   *Emp Total* 39,914
Sales 50,675,684
SIC 5085 Industrial supplies
Pr Pr Donald Latham
Rgnl VP Roger Pelat
Rgnl VP Mike Lake
Rgnl VP Scott Matheson
Rgnl VP Brian Martin

D-U-N-S 24-695-7716   (BR)
CHEP CANADA INC
559 Annance Crt Suite 2, Delta, BC, V3M 6Y7
(604) 520-2583
Emp Here 50
SIC 7359 Equipment rental and leasing, nec

D-U-N-S 24-535-5201   (HQ)
CIPA LUMBER CO. LTD
DELTA PANEL, DIV OF
797 Carlisle Rd, Delta, BC, V3M 5P4
(604) 523-2250
Emp Here 120   *Emp Total* 98,673
Sales 12,257,398
SIC 2436 Softwood veneer and plywood
Pastor Toshihiro Matsuki
Dir Akihiko Yoshioka

D-U-N-S 20-192-7790   (BR)
CANADA BREAD COMPANY, LIMITED
WORLD AUTHENTIC BAKING COMPMAY DIV.
669 Ridley Pl Suite 101, Delta, BC, V3M 6Y9
(604) 526-4700
Emp Here 43
SIC 2051 Bread, cake, and related products

D-U-N-S 20-553-3586   (BR)
CERTAINTEED GYPSUM CANADA, INC
1070 Derwent Way, Delta, BC, V3M 5R1
(604) 527-1405
Emp Here 80
SIC 3275 Gypsum products

D-U-N-S 24-558-5575   (SL)
CHEWTERS CHOCOLATES (1992) INC
1648 Derwent Way, Delta, BC, V3M 6R9
(604) 515-7117
Emp Here 50   *Sales* 259,875
SIC 2066 Chocolate and cocoa products

D-U-N-S 20-799-7292   (BR)
CLARIANT (CANADA) INC
1081 Cliveden Ave, Delta, BC, V3M 5V1
(604) 517-0561
Emp Here 50
SIC 2865 Cyclic crudes and intermediates

D-U-N-S 20-317-1210   (BR)
COASTLAND WOOD INDUSTRIES LTD
COASTLAND WOOD INDUSTRIES, DIV. OF
755 Belgrave Way, Delta, BC, V3M 5R8
(604) 516-0355
Emp Here 40
SIC 2431 Millwork

D-U-N-S 25-417-1317   (BR)
CONCORD TRANSPORTATION INC
1659 Foster'S Way, Delta, BC, V3M 6S7
(604) 524-8811
Emp Here 40
SIC 4213 Trucking, except local

D-U-N-S 25-400-2074   (BR)
CREATIVE DOOR SERVICES LTD
1678 Foster'S Way Unit 3, Delta, BC, V3M 6S6
(604) 524-8444
Emp Here 40
SIC 1751 Carpentry work

D-U-N-S 24-310-7617   (HQ)
CRYOPAK INDUSTRIES (2007) ULC

1053 Derwent Way, Delta, BC, V3M 5R4
(604) 515-7977
Emp Here 45   *Emp Total* 75
Sales 6,274,620
SIC 3822 Environmental controls
Genl Mgr Raj Gill
Fin Ex Alexandra Borisova
Pr Pr Maurice Barakat
 Jay H Schafrann
Treas Tony Spina
 Nareem Schafrann

D-U-N-S 24-134-8986   (SL)
DBC MARINE SAFETY SYSTEMS LTD
1689 Cliveden Ave, Delta, BC, V3M 6V5
(604) 278-3221
Emp Here 50   *Sales* 3,064,349
SIC 3732 Boatbuilding and repairing

D-U-N-S 20-108-9927   (HQ)
DAVIS WIRE INDUSTRIES LTD
960 Derwent Way, Delta, BC, V3M 5R1
(604) 525-3622
Emp Here 35   *Emp Total* 1
Sales 7,660,874
SIC 3496 Miscellaneous fabricated wire products
 David Lloyd

D-U-N-S 20-251-3537   (BR)
DIRECT LIMITED PARTNERSHIP
DIRECT DISTRIBUTION CENTRES
1005 Derwent Way, Delta, BC, V3M 5R4
(778) 846-4466
Emp Here 20
SIC 4225 General warehousing and storage

D-U-N-S 20-325-3695   (SL)
FLUXWERX ILLUMINATION INC
FLUXWERX
(*Suby of* Lumenpulse Inc)
1364 Cliveden Ave, Delta, BC, V3M 6K2
(604) 549-9379
Emp Here 45   *Sales* 4,523,563
SIC 3648 Lighting equipment, nec

D-U-N-S 25-622-2464   (BR)
FRASERWAY RV LIMITED PARTNERSHIP
747 Cliveden Pl, Delta, BC, V3M 6C7
(604) 527-1102
Emp Here 60
SIC 3716 Motor homes

D-U-N-S 20-108-2786   (BR)
G.N. JOHNSTON EQUIPMENT CO. LTD
JOHNSON EQUIPMENT
581 Chester Rd Suite 105, Delta, BC, V3M 6G7
(604) 524-0361
Emp Here 70
SIC 5084 Industrial machinery and equipment

D-U-N-S 24-446-1679   (SL)
GOLDEN WEST BAKERY LTD
GOLDEN WEST BAKING COMPANY
1111 Derwent Way, Delta, BC, V3M 5R4
(604) 525-2491
Emp Here 90   *Sales* 3,064,349
SIC 5461 Retail bakeries

D-U-N-S 20-267-0100   (BR)
GREATER VANCOUVER REGIONAL DISTRICT
ANNACIS ISLAND WASTE WATER TREATMENT PLANT
1299 Derwent Way, Delta, BC, V3M 5V9
(604) 525-5681
Emp Here 92
SIC 4953 Refuse systems

D-U-N-S 20-557-5512   (HQ)
GREEN LINE HOSE & FITTINGS (B.C.) LTD
1477 Derwent Way, Delta, BC, V3M 6N3
(604) 525-6800
Emp Here 160   *Emp Total* 200
Sales 34,875,215
SIC 5085 Industrial supplies
Pr Andrew Dunham

D-U-N-S 24-979-6137   (BR)
HENRY SCHEIN CANADA, INC
1619 Foster'S Way, Delta, BC, V3M 6S7
(604) 527-8888
Emp Here 120
SIC 5047 Medical and hospital equipment

D-U-N-S 25-203-0861   (BR)
I.C.T.C. HOLDINGS CORPORATION
HERO INDUSTRIES, DIV OF
720 Eaton Way, Delta, BC, V3M 6J9
(604) 522-6543
Emp Here 45
SIC 3563 Air and gas compressors

D-U-N-S 25-100-3406   (BR)
ITW CANADA INVESTMENTS LIMITED PARTNERSHIP
HOBART FOOD EQUIPMENT GROUP
(*Suby of* Illinois Tool Works Inc.)
1668 Derwent Way Unit 10, Delta, BC, V3M 6R9
(604) 522-1070
Emp Here 20
SIC 3589 Service industry machinery, nec

D-U-N-S 20-586-3012   (SL)
IDEAL WELDERS LTD
660 Caldew St, Delta, BC, V3M 5S2
(604) 525-5558
Emp Here 85   *Sales* 13,381,072
SIC 3498 Fabricated pipe and fittings
Pr Pr R. James Longo

D-U-N-S 20-178-4522   (BR)
INDUSTRIES RAD INC
INDUSTRIES RAD INC
1610 Derwent Way Unit 16, Delta, BC, V3M 6W1

Emp Here 100
SIC 3751 Motorcycles, bicycles and parts

D-U-N-S 25-357-4438   (SL)
INNOVATIVE MANUFACTURING INC
861 Derwent Way Suite 877, Delta, BC, V3M 5R4
(604) 522-2811
Emp Here 37   *Sales* 8,014,550
SIC 5198 Faints, varnishes, and supplies
Pr Pr Craig Anderson
 Ivan Wirch
Dir Marjory Anderson

D-U-N-S 25-937-8594   (BR)
KINDERSLEY TRANSPORT LTD
(*Suby of* EKS Holdings Ltd)
660 Aldford Ave, Delta, BC, V3M 6X1
(604) 522-4002
Emp Here 50
SIC 4213 Trucking, except local

D-U-N-S 24-796-0763   (BR)
KONE INC
1488 Cliveden Ave, Delta, BC, V3M 6L9
(604) 777-5663
Emp Here 75
SIC 1799 Special trade contractors, nec

D-U-N-S 24-024-6694   (HQ)
LOCHER EVERS INTERNATIONAL INC
456 Humber Pl, Delta, BC, V3M 6A5
(604) 523-5100
Emp Here 75   *Emp Total* 170
Sales 47,990,305
SIC 4731 Freight transportation arrangement
 Chris Locher
 Greg Locher
 Peter Broerken

D-U-N-S 24-639-4811   (BR)
LOCHER EVERS INTERNATIONAL INC
LOCHER EVERS INTERNATIONAL
456 Humber Pl, Delta, BC, V3M 6A5
(604) 525-0577
Emp Here 90
SIC 4225 General warehousing and storage

D-U-N-S 24-000-9501   (BR)

MARK ANTHONY GROUP INC
465 Fraserview Pl, Delta, BC, V3M 6H4
(604) 519-5370
Emp Here 100
SIC 2084 Wines, brandy, and brandy spirits

D-U-N-S 20-509-4881   (HQ)
MASON LIFT LTD
(*Suby of* Dinat Resources Ltd)
1605 Cliveden Ave, Delta, BC, V3M 6P7
(604) 517-5600
Emp Here 61   *Emp Total* 125
Sales 13,492,850
SIC 7359 Equipment rental and leasing, nec
Pr Pr D. George Peles
 Jennifer Peles

D-U-N-S 20-264-8192   (BR)
NFI DOMINION CANADA, ULC
DOMINION WAREHOUSING & DISTRIBUTION SERVICES LTD
1020 Derwent Way, Delta, BC, V3M 5R1
(778) 383-6405
Emp Here 20
SIC 4225 General warehousing and storage

D-U-N-S 24-371-1033   (HQ)
NATIONAL SIGNCORP INVESTMENTS LTD
SIGNCORP
(*Suby of* National Signcorp Investments Ltd)
1471 Derwent Way, Delta, BC, V3M 6N2
(604) 525-4300
Emp Here 45   *Emp Total* 60
Sales 3,648,035
SIC 3993 Signs and advertising specialties

D-U-N-S 24-329-9877   (SL)
NIRADIA ENTERPRISES INC
460 Fraserview Pl, Delta, BC, V3M 6H4
(604) 523-6188
Emp Here 60   *Sales* 10,753,700
SIC 6712 Bank holding companies
Pr Guerrino Nichele

D-U-N-S 24-289-9243   (BR)
PATTERSON DENTAIRE CANADA INC
1105 Cliveden Ave, Delta, BC, V3M 6G9

Emp Here 50
SIC 5047 Medical and hospital equipment

D-U-N-S 20-867-2618   (BR)
PLASTI-FAB LTD
679 Aldford Ave, Delta, BC, V3M 5P5
(604) 526-2771
Emp Here 30
SIC 3086 Plastics foam products

D-U-N-S 24-995-6103   (BR)
PRAXAIR CANADA INC
(*Suby of* Praxair, Inc.)
1470 Derwent Way, Delta, BC, V3M 6H9
(604) 527-0700
Emp Here 100
SIC 5169 Chemicals and allied products, nec

D-U-N-S 24-008-8328   (BR)
QUALITY INSERTIONS LTD
1487 Lindsey Pl, Delta, BC, V3M 6V1

Emp Here 45
SIC 7319 Advertising, nec

D-U-N-S 24-503-6801   (SL)
RAUTE CANADA LTD
1633 Cliveden Ave, Delta, BC, V3M 6V5
(604) 524-6611
Emp Here 100   *Sales* 14,569,600
SIC 3569 General industrial machinery, nec
Pr Pr Bruce Alexander
S&M/VP Martin Murphy
VP Opers Ray Tyler
 Peter Gibson
Dir Fin Greg Holtus

D-U-N-S 24-867-1851   (BR)
RUSSEL METALS INC
A.J. FORSYTH

830 Carlisle Rd, Delta, BC, V3M 5P4
(604) 525-0544
Emp Here 100
SIC 5051 Metals service centers and offices

D-U-N-S 20-868-1049   (BR)
RYDER TRUCK RENTAL CANADA LTD
RYDER CANADA
(*Suby of* Ryder System, Inc.)
1699 Cliveden Ave, Delta, BC, V3M 6V5
(604) 515-1688
Emp Here 25
SIC 7513 Truck rental and leasing, no drivers

D-U-N-S 25-094-7132   (HQ)
SSAB SWEDISH STEEL LTD
SSAB HARDOX, DIV OF
1031 Cliveden Ave, Delta, BC, V3M 5V1
(604) 526-3700
Emp Here 21   *Emp Total* 50
Sales 19,144,147
SIC 5051 Metals service centers and offices
Pr Pr Louis Bolen
Dir Olof Martinsson
 Peter Tang

D-U-N-S 24-750-5449   (BR)
SSH BEDDING CANADA CO.
SIMMONS CANADA, DIV OF
(*Suby of* SSH Bedding Canada Co.)
927 Derwent Way, Delta, BC, V3M 5R4

Emp Here 80
SIC 2394 Canvas and related products

D-U-N-S 24-446-9920   (BR)
SAMUEL, SON & CO., LIMITED
SAMUEL STRAPPING SYSTEMS
1365 Derwent Way, Delta, BC, V3M 5V9
(604) 521-3700
Emp Here 40
SIC 5051 Metals service centers and offices

D-U-N-S 20-294-4252   (BR)
SONOCO CANADA CORPORATION
(*Suby of* Sonoco Products Company)
1388 Cliveden Ave, Delta, BC, V3M 6K2
(604) 526-7888
Emp Here 20
SIC 2655 Fiber cans, drums, and similar products

D-U-N-S 25-613-5328   (BR)
TIGER COURIER INC
(*Suby of* EKS Holdings Ltd)
660 Aldford Ave, Delta, BC, V3M 6X1
(604) 522-0804
Emp Here 22
SIC 7389 Business services, nec

D-U-N-S 20-109-9249   (BR)
TOROMONT INDUSTRIES LTD
CIMCO REFRIGERATION
1095 Cliveden Ave, Delta, BC, V3M 6G9
(604) 525-8899
Emp Here 35
SIC 1711 Plumbing, heating, air-conditioning

D-U-N-S 24-980-6472   (BR)
TRANSCONTINENTAL PRINTING INC
TRANSCONTINENTAL PRINTING
725 Hampstead Close, Delta, BC, V3M 6R6
(604) 540-2333
Emp Here 200
SIC 2752 Commercial printing, lithographic

D-U-N-S 25-370-2245   (BR)
TYCO INTEGRATED FIRE & SECURITY CANADA, INC
SIMPLEXGRINNELL
(*Suby of* Johnson Controls, Inc.)
1485 Lindsey Pl, Delta, BC, V3M 6V1
(604) 515-8872
Emp Here 98
SIC 7389 Business services, nec

D-U-N-S 20-209-0994   (BR)
UNILEVER CANADA INC

GOOD HURMOR-BREYERS CANADA
1460 Cliveden Ave, Delta, BC, V3M 6L9
(604) 519-0600
Emp Here 20
SIC 5143 Dairy products, except dried or canned

D-U-N-S 20-793-2950   (BR)
UNITED PARCEL SERVICE CANADA LTD
UPS
790 Belgrave Way, Delta, BC, V3M 5R9
(604) 528-4254
Emp Here 300
SIC 7389 Business services, nec

D-U-N-S 24-956-8866   (BR)
VPC GROUP INC
VITAFOAM   PRODUCTS   WESTERN CANADA
(*Suby of* VPC Group Inc)
927 Derwent Way Suite 400, Delta, BC, V3M 5R4
(604) 540-0530
Emp Here 20
SIC 3069 Fabricated rubber products, nec

D-U-N-S 24-424-7222   (SL)
W. S. NICHOLLS WESTERN CONSTRUCTION LTD
(*Suby of* Southwest Gas Holdings, Inc.)
851 Derwent Way, Delta, BC, V3M 5R4
(604) 521-2004
Emp Here 20   *Sales* 2,991,389
SIC 1521 Single-family housing construction

D-U-N-S 24-357-2836   (BR)
WEYERHAEUSER COMPANY LIMITED
ILEVEL
(*Suby of* Weyerhaeuser Company)
1272 Derwent Way, Delta, BC, V3M 5R1
(604) 526-4665
Emp Here 190
SIC 2421 Sawmills and planing mills, general

D-U-N-S 25-412-8853   (BR)
WHITEWATER WEST INDUSTRIES LTD
PRIME PLAY SYSTEMS, A DIV
1418 Cliveden Ave, Delta, BC, V3M 6L9

Emp Here 60
SIC 3949 Sporting and athletic goods, nec

Delta, BC V4C
Greater Vancouver County

D-U-N-S 24-244-7449   (BR)
BOYS AND GIRLS CLUB COMMUNITY SERVICES OF DELTA/RICHMOND
HILLSIDE CLUB
(*Suby of* Boys And Girls Club Community Services Of Delta/Richmond)
11393 84 Ave, Delta, BC, V4C 2L9
(604) 596-9595
Emp Here 25
SIC 8322 Individual and family services

D-U-N-S 25-316-5393   (BR)
BRITISH COLUMBIA AUTOMOBILE ASSOCIATION
7343 120 St, Delta, BC, V4C 6P5
(604) 268-5900
Emp Here 25
SIC 8699 Membership organizations, nec

D-U-N-S 25-954-8238   (BR)
CACTUS RESTAURANTS LTD
CACTUS CLUB CAFE
7907 120 St, Delta, BC, V4C 6P6
(604) 591-1707
Emp Here 50
SIC 5812 Eating places

D-U-N-S 24-173-9676   (BR)
COAST CAPITAL SAVINGS CREDIT UNION
8445 120 St, Delta, BC, V4C 6R2

(604) 517-7100
Emp Here 20
SIC 6062 State credit unions

D-U-N-S 20-794-4898   (BR)
CORPORATION OF DELTA, THE
SUNGOD RECREATION CENTRE
7815 112 St, Delta, BC, V4C 4V9
(604) 952-3075
Emp Here 100
SIC 7999 Amusement and recreation, nec

D-U-N-S 25-944-7704   (BR)
CORPORATION OF DELTA, THE
NORTH DELTA RECREATION CENTRE
11415 84 Ave, Delta, BC, V4C 2L9
(604) 595-8400
Emp Here 40
SIC 7999 Amusement and recreation, nec

D-U-N-S 25-616-0060   (BR)
DELTA CEDAR PRODUCTS LTD
SUNBURY CEDAR SALES
10008 River Rd, Delta, BC, V4C 2R3
(604) 583-9100
Emp Here 40
SIC 5211 Lumber and other building materials

D-U-N-S 20-031-6565   (BR)
DELTA SCHOOL DISTRICT NO.37
DELVIEW SECONDARY SCHOOL
9111 116 St, Delta, BC, V4C 5W8
(604) 594-5491
Emp Here 50
SIC 8211 Elementary and secondary schools

D-U-N-S 20-591-2996   (BR)
DELTA SCHOOL DISTRICT NO.37
RICHARDSON ELEMENTARY SCHOOL
11339 83 Ave, Delta, BC, V4C 7B9
(604) 596-7481
Emp Here 50
SIC 8211 Elementary and secondary schools

D-U-N-S 20-591-2988   (BR)
DELTA SCHOOL DISTRICT NO.37
CHALMERS ELEMENTARY SCHOOL
11315 75 Ave, Delta, BC, V4C 1H4
(604) 594-5437
Emp Here 25
SIC 8211 Elementary and secondary schools

D-U-N-S 25-013-9839   (BR)
DELTA SCHOOL DISTRICT NO.37
GRAY ELEMENTARY SCHOOL
10855 80 Ave, Delta, BC, V4C 1W4
(604) 594-2474
Emp Here 40
SIC 8211 Elementary and secondary schools

D-U-N-S 20-591-3093   (BR)
DELTA SCHOOL DISTRICT NO.37
JARVIS SCHOOL
7670 118 St, Delta, BC, V4C 6G8
(604) 594-3484
Emp Here 45
SIC 8211 Elementary and secondary schools

D-U-N-S 20-591-3101   (BR)
DELTA SCHOOL DISTRICT NO.37
DELTA BROOKE ELEMENTARY
8718 Delwood Dr, Delta, BC, V4C 3Z9
(604) 583-6668
Emp Here 25
SIC 8211 Elementary and secondary schools

D-U-N-S 25-116-9124   (BR)
DELTA SCHOOL DISTRICT NO.37
BURNSVIEW SECONDARY SCHOOL
7658 112 St, Delta, BC, V4C 4V8
(604) 594-0491
Emp Here 55
SIC 8211 Elementary and secondary schools

D-U-N-S 25-013-9862   (BR)
DELTA SCHOOL DISTRICT NO.37
HELLINGS ELEMENTARY SCHOOL
11655 86 Ave, Delta, BC, V4C 2X5
(604) 596-1701
Emp Here 53

SIC 8211 Elementary and secondary schools

D-U-N-S 20-591-3119   (BR)
DELTA SCHOOL DISTRICT NO.37
DEVON GARDENS ELEMENTARY SCHOOL
8884 Russell Dr, Delta, BC, V4C 4P8
(604) 581-6185
Emp Here 35
SIC 8211 Elementary and secondary schools

D-U-N-S 20-005-5205   (BR)
DELTA SCHOOL DISTRICT NO.37
DELVIEW ADULT LEARNING CENTRE
9115 116 St, Delta, BC, V4C 5W8
(604) 594-6100
Emp Here 100
SIC 8211 Elementary and secondary schools

D-U-N-S 20-048-8356   (BR)
DELTA SCHOOL DISTRICT NO.37
SANDS SECONDARY SCHOOL
10840 82 Ave, Delta, BC, V4C 2B3
(604) 594-3474
Emp Here 60
SIC 8211 Elementary and secondary schools

D-U-N-S 25-013-9961   (BR)
DELTA SCHOOL DISTRICT NO.37
NORTH DELTA SENIOR SECONDARY SCHOOL
11447 82 Ave, Delta, BC, V4C 5J6
(604) 596-7471
Emp Here 86
SIC 8211 Elementary and secondary schools

D-U-N-S 20-591-3028   (BR)
DELTA SCHOOL DISTRICT NO.37
GIBSON ELEMENTARY
11451 90 Ave, Delta, BC, V4C 3H3
(604) 594-7588
Emp Here 40
SIC 8211 Elementary and secondary schools

D-U-N-S 25-013-9896   (BR)
DELTA SCHOOL DISTRICT NO.37
MCCLOSKEY ELEMENTARY SCHOOL
11531 80 Ave, Delta, BC, V4C 1X5
(604) 596-9554
Emp Here 35
SIC 8211 Elementary and secondary schools

D-U-N-S 25-714-1648   (BR)
DELTASSIST FAMILY & COMMUNITY SERVICES SOCIETY
DELTASSIST FAMILY & COMMUNITY
9097 120 St, Delta, BC, V4C 6R7
(604) 594-3455
Emp Here 35
SIC 8322 Individual and family services

D-U-N-S 20-651-7224   (BR)
FRASER HEALTH AUTHORITY
11245 84 Ave Suite 101, Delta, BC, V4C 2L9
(604) 507-5400
Emp Here 100
SIC 8062 General medical and surgical hospitals

D-U-N-S 20-555-7700   (BR)
LOBLAWS INC
REAL CANADIAN SUPERSTORE
8195 120 St, Delta, BC, V4C 6P7
(604) 592-5218
Emp Here 322
SIC 5411 Grocery stores

D-U-N-S 25-800-3409   (BR)
ROMAN CATHOLIC ARCHDIOCESE OF VANCOUVER, THE
IMMACULATE CONCEPTION SCHOOL
(*Suby of* Roman Catholic Archdiocese of Vancouver, The)
8840 119 St, Delta, BC, V4C 6M4
(604) 596-6116
Emp Here 40
SIC 8211 Elementary and secondary schools

D-U-N-S 25-893-0296   (BR)
STAPLES CANADA INC

STAPLES THE BUSINESS DEPOT
(*Suby of* Staples, Inc.)
7315 120 St, Delta, BC, V4C 6P5
(604) 501-7820
Emp Here 40
SIC 5943 Stationery stores

D-U-N-S 20-997-3507   (BR)
THRIFT MAGIC LP
TALIZE
11930 88 Ave, Delta, BC, V4C 3C8
(604) 599-6116
Emp Here 50
SIC 5932 Used merchandise stores

D-U-N-S 24-773-0273   (BR)
TRYLON TSF INC
9563 Gunderson Rd, Delta, BC, V4C 4R9

Emp Here 20
SIC 4899 Communication services, nec

D-U-N-S 20-589-5803   (BR)
VANCOUVER CITY SAVINGS CREDIT UNION
VANCITY CREDIT UNION
7211 120 St, Delta, BC, V4C 6P5
(604) 877-7193
Emp Here 25
SIC 6062 State credit unions

Delta, BC V4E
Greater Vancouver County

D-U-N-S 20-591-3036   (BR)
DELTA SCHOOL DISTRICT NO.37
PINEWOOD ELEMENTARY SCHOOL
11777 Pinewood Dr, Delta, BC, V4E 3E9
(604) 597-8353
Emp Here 25
SIC 8211 Elementary and secondary schools

D-U-N-S 20-591-3002   (BR)
DELTA SCHOOL DISTRICT NO.37
HEATH ELEMENTARY SCHOOL
11364 72 Ave, Delta, BC, V4E 1Y5
(604) 596-1508
Emp Here 35
SIC 8211 Elementary and secondary schools

D-U-N-S 25-071-6446   (BR)
DELTA SCHOOL DISTRICT NO.37
SCAQUAM SECONDARY SCHOOL
11584 Lyon Rd, Delta, BC, V4E 2K4
(604) 591-6166
Emp Here 85
SIC 8211 Elementary and secondary schools

D-U-N-S 20-047-0669   (BR)
DELTA SCHOOL DISTRICT NO.37
SUNSHINE HILLS ELEMENTARY SCHOOL
11285 Bond Blvd, Delta, BC, V4E 1N3
(604) 594-8491
Emp Here 51
SIC 8211 Elementary and secondary schools

D-U-N-S 24-593-8691   (BR)
GREAT PACIFIC INDUSTRIES INC
SAVE-ON-FOODS
7015 120 St Suite 963, Delta, BC, V4E 2A9
(604) 596-2944
Emp Here 250
SIC 5411 Grocery stores

D-U-N-S 25-318-1598   (BR)
MCDONALD'S RESTAURANTS OF CANADA LIMITED
MCDONALD'S 8075
(*Suby of* McDonald's Corporation)
7005 120 St, Delta, BC, V4E 2A9
(604) 592-1330
Emp Here 85
SIC 5812 Eating places

D-U-N-S 25-262-6882   (SL)

NORTHCREST CARE CENTRE LTD
6771 120 St, Delta, BC, V4E 2A7
(604) 597-7878
Emp Here 75   *Sales* 3,429,153
SIC 8051 Skilled nursing care facilities

D-U-N-S 25-015-0190   (BR)
ROYAL BANK OF CANADA
RBC
(*Suby of* Royal Bank Of Canada)
7157 120 St, Delta, BC, V4E 2A9
(604) 665-0484
Emp Here 28
SIC 6021 National commercial banks

D-U-N-S 25-015-0216   (BR)
SOBEYS WEST INC
CANADA SAFEWAY # 14
6401 120 St, Delta, BC, V4E 3G3
(604) 596-5634
Emp Here 175
SIC 5411 Grocery stores

Delta, BC V4G
Greater Vancouver County

D-U-N-S 25-194-9293   (SL)
501070 BC LTD
AMJ CAMPBELL INTERNATIONAL/ALLPORTS INTERNATIONAL MOVERS
9924 River Rd, Delta, BC, V4G 1B5
(604) 940-8410
Emp Here 20   *Sales* 5,024,256
SIC 4731 Freight transportation arrangement
Kevin Brown

D-U-N-S 20-553-1689   (BR)
AMPACET CANADA COMPANY
(*Suby of* Ampacet Corporation)
7763 Progress Way, Delta, BC, V4G 1A3

Emp Here 20
SIC 2816 Inorganic pigments

D-U-N-S 20-100-1984   (BR)
BACB HOLDINGS LTD
7228 Progress Way Suite 15, Delta, BC, V4G 1H2
(778) 785-1534
Emp Here 45
SIC 4789 Transportation services, nec

D-U-N-S 24-850-6995   (SL)
BC STEVENS COMPANY
8188 Swenson Way, Delta, BC, V4G 1J6
(604) 634-3088
Emp Here 51   *Sales* 10,347,900
SIC 5047 Medical and hospital equipment
Ex VP Rod Hilliard
Dir Scott Baker
Opers Mgr Mike Wheatley
Dir Laura Bailey

D-U-N-S 25-714-9328   (BR)
BERRY & SMITH TRUCKING LTD
8208 Swenson Way Unit 100, Delta, BC, V4G 1J6
(604) 582-1244
Emp Here 40
SIC 4212 Local trucking, without storage

D-U-N-S 20-646-4567   (BR)
BUCKWOLD WESTERN LTD
10207 Nordel Crt, Delta, BC, V4G 1J9
(604) 583-2355
Emp Here 34
SIC 5023 Homefurnishings

D-U-N-S 20-317-0188   (BR)
CANADIAN ALLIANCE TERMINALS INC
7510 Hopcott Rd Suite 10, Delta, BC, V4G 1B6
(604) 270-6077
Emp Here 20

SIC 4225 General warehousing and storage

D-U-N-S 25-710-8290   (BR)
CANADREAM INC
CANADREAM CAMPERS
(*Suby of* Canadream Corporation)
7119 River Rd, Delta, BC, V4G 1A9
(604) 940-2171
Emp Here 38
SIC 7519 Utility trailer rental

D-U-N-S 25-930-0051   (HQ)
CASCADIA METALS LTD
7630 Berg Rd, Delta, BC, V4G 1G4
(604) 946-3890
Emp Here 75   *Emp Total* 135
Sales 43,052,675
SIC 5051 Metals service centers and offices
Pr Pr Earl William Ritchie
Dir Florence Ritchie

D-U-N-S 20-114-0659   (HQ)
DAMCO DISTRIBUTION CANADA INC
8400 River Rd, Delta, BC, V4G 1B5
(604) 940-1357
Emp Here 115   *Emp Total* 3
Sales 63,149,698
SIC 4731 Freight transportation arrangement
Dir John Crewson
Dir Nick Taro
Dir David R Cardin

D-U-N-S 24-778-5694   (BR)
EBCO INDUSTRIES LTD
8510 River Rd, Delta, BC, V4G 1B5
(604) 946-4900
Emp Here 50
SIC 3728 Aircraft parts and equipment, nec

D-U-N-S 24-445-4302   (BR)
EMPIRE IRON WORKS LTD
7501 Vantage Way, Delta, BC, V4G 1C9
(604) 946-5515
Emp Here 45
SIC 3441 Fabricated structural Metal

D-U-N-S 24-247-0086   (HQ)
FPI FIREPLACE PRODUCTS INTERNATIONAL LTD
(*Suby of* FPI Fireplace Products International Ltd)
6988 Venture St, Delta, BC, V4G 1H4
(604) 946-5155
Emp Here 300   *Emp Total* 400
Sales 36,480,350
SIC 3433 Heating equipment, except electric
 Robert Little
Pr Pr Anthony Woodruff
VP Opers Tracy Zomar
Dir Fin Mino Padda

D-U-N-S 24-760-8607   (BR)
FLOCOR INC
MUELLER FLOW CONTROLS
(*Suby of* Entreprises Mirca Inc, Les)
7168 Progress Way, Delta, BC, V4G 1J2
(604) 940-1449
Emp Here 30
SIC 5085 Industrial supplies

D-U-N-S 25-236-3924   (BR)
FOUNTAIN TIRE LTD
AUTOMOTIVE TECHNICIAN
7993 Progress Way, Delta, BC, V4G 1A3
(604) 940-6388
Emp Here 20
SIC 5531 Auto and home supply stores

D-U-N-S 25-369-0069   (BR)
FUJIFILM CANADA INC
6805 Dennett Pl Unit 200, Delta, BC, V4G 1N4

Emp Here 22
SIC 5946 Camera and photographic supply stores

D-U-N-S 24-456-4795   (SL)
GENFOR MACHINERY INC

8320 River Rd, Delta, BC, V4G 1B5
(604) 946-6911
Emp Here 90   *Sales* 12,275,450
SIC 3553 Woodworking machinery
Pr Ross Chapman
 Fred Chapman

D-U-N-S 24-378-2286   (BR)
GREAT LITTLE BOX COMPANY LTD, THE
PARROT LABEL
7533 Progress Way, Delta, BC, V4G 1E7

Emp Here 25
SIC 5113 Industrial and personal service paper

D-U-N-S 24-327-1660   (HQ)
INTEPLAST BAGS AND FILMS CORPORATION
7503 Vantage Pl, Delta, BC, V4G 1A5
(604) 946-5431
Emp Here 35   *Emp Total* 7,400
Sales 16,961,922
SIC 2673 Bags: plastic, laminated, and coated
Pr Pr Joe Chen
VP Ben Tseng
VP VP Robert H Wang
Treas Joseph Wang
Manager Gordon Sedawie
 Tony Cosman
 John Ding-E Young

D-U-N-S 20-325-2788   (BR)
JJM CONSTRUCTION LTD
8218 River Way, Delta, BC, V4G 1C4
(604) 946-0978
Emp Here 49
SIC 1611 Highway and street construction

D-U-N-S 20-104-4281   (BR)
LYNDEN INTERNATIONAL LOGISTICS CO
(*Suby of* Lynden Incorporated)
7403 Progress Way, Delta, BC, V4G 1E7
(604) 940-4116
Emp Here 25
SIC 4225 General warehousing and storage

D-U-N-S 24-866-6620   (HQ)
MARPOLE TRANSPORT LIMITED
(*Suby of* R B R Holdings Inc)
7086 Brown St, Delta, BC, V4G 1G8
(604) 940-7000
Emp Here 30   *Emp Total* 2
Sales 11,600,751
SIC 4213 Trucking, except local
Pr Pr Bhajan (Pudge) Bawa
 John Ross Grant
 Suhkdave S. Lashman
 Sarban Bawa

D-U-N-S 20-150-6297   (SL)
MCRAE'S ENVIRONMENTAL SERVICES LTD
MCRAE'S SPEC LIQUID WASTE
7783 Progress Way, Delta, BC, V4G 1A3
(604) 434-8313
Emp Here 50   *Sales* 3,648,035
SIC 1794 Excavation work

D-U-N-S 24-849-3178   (BR)
NU-GRO LTD
AGRIUM ADVANCED
(*Suby of* Agrium Canada Partnership)
7430 Hopcott Rd, Delta, BC, V4G 1B6
(604) 940-0290
Emp Here 50
SIC 5191 Farm supplies

D-U-N-S 25-496-9736   (BR)
PPG ARCHITECTURAL COATINGS CANADA INC
PPG ARCHITECTURAL COATINGS CANADA, INC
(*Suby of* PPG Industries, Inc.)
7560 Vantage Way Suite 1, Delta, BC, V4G 1H1

(604) 940-0433
Emp Here 35
SIC 2851 Paints and allied products

D-U-N-S 25-721-4288   (BR)
PEPSICO CANADA ULC
FRITO LAY
(*Suby of* Pepsico, Inc.)
7762 Progress Way Unit 5, Delta, BC, V4G 1A4

Emp Here 58
SIC 5145 Confectionery

D-U-N-S 25-385-0333   (BR)
QUADRA CHIMIE LTEE
7930 Vantage Way, Delta, BC, V4G 1A8
(604) 940-2313
Emp Here 25
SIC 5169 Chemicals and allied products, nec

D-U-N-S 25-849-8401   (HQ)
QUALITY MOVE MANAGEMENT INC
ALLIED INTERNATIONAL OF VANCOUVER
(*Suby of* Quality Move Management Inc)
7979 82 St, Delta, BC, V4G 1L7
(604) 952-3650
Emp Here 30   *Emp Total* 85
Sales 4,231,721
SIC 7389 Business services, nec

D-U-N-S 20-802-1402   (HQ)
RADION LABORATORIES LTD
BOWERS MEDICAL SUPPLY
(*Suby of* Northwest Medical Group Ltd)
7198 Progress Way, Delta, BC, V4G 1J2
(604) 946-7712
Emp Here 40   *Emp Total* 5
Sales 9,484,891
SIC 5047 Medical and hospital equipment
Pr Pr Francis Bowers
 Brittany Bowers

D-U-N-S 20-059-0367   (BR)
RYDER TRUCK RENTAL CANADA LTD
(*Suby of* Ryder System, Inc.)
9960 River Way, Delta, BC, V4G 1M9
(604) 588-1145
Emp Here 60
SIC 4225 General warehousing and storage

D-U-N-S 25-979-7348   (BR)
SAFETY-KLEEN CANADA INC.
7803 Progress Way, Delta, BC, V4G 1A3
(604) 952-4700
Emp Here 24
SIC 5172 Petroleum products, nec

D-U-N-S 24-340-5359   (BR)
SAPUTO PRODUITS LAITIERS CANADA S.E.N.C.
(*Suby of* Saputo Produits Laitiers Canada S.E.N.C.)
7307 76 St, Delta, BC, V4G 1E6
(604) 946-5611
Emp Here 50
SIC 2022 Cheese; natural and processed

D-U-N-S 24-369-7349   (SL)
SCIENTEK TECHNOLOGY CORPORATION
SCIENTEK HOSPITAL LABORATORY
8235 Swenson Way, Delta, BC, V4G 1J5
(604) 940-8084
Emp Here 28   *Sales* 3,205,129
SIC 3842 Surgical appliances and supplies

D-U-N-S 24-413-0220   (SL)
SONIC ENCLOSURES LTD
7127 Honeyman St, Delta, BC, V4G 1E2
(604) 946-6100
Emp Here 45   *Sales* 7,545,460
SIC 3448 Prefabricated Metal buildings and components
Pr Matei Ghelesel
Dir Stan King

D-U-N-S 25-236-6950   (BR)
STEVENS COMPANY LIMITED, THE
8188 Swenson Way, Delta, BC, V4G 1J6

(604) 634-3088
Emp Here 65
SIC 5047 Medical and hospital equipment

D-U-N-S 20-994-4636   (BR)
SUPREMEX INC
SUPREMEX
(*Suby of* Supremex Inc)
8189 River Way, Delta, BC, V4G 1L2
(604) 940-4488
Emp Here 35
SIC 2677 Envelopes

D-U-N-S 20-333-6664   (BR)
TRAILER WIZARDS LTD
(*Suby of* Lions Gate Trailers Ltd)
10387 Nordel Crt, Delta, BC, V4G 1J9
(604) 464-2220
Emp Here 30
SIC 7519 Utility trailer rental

D-U-N-S 24-898-7950   (SL)
UNIFILLER SYSTEMS INC
7621 Macdonald Rd, Delta, BC, V4G 1N3
(604) 940-2233
Emp Here 80   *Sales* 3,486,617
SIC 5461 Retail bakeries

D-U-N-S 25-612-4298   (BR)
VSL CANADA LTD
HARRIS REBAR
(*Suby of* Nucor Corporation)
7690 Vantage Way, Delta, BC, V4G 1A7

Emp Here 40
SIC 3449 Miscellaneous Metalwork

D-U-N-S 24-133-4606   (HQ)
VALMONT WC ENGINEERING GROUP LTD
7984 River Rd, Delta, BC, V4G 1E3
(604) 946-1256
Emp Here 80   *Emp Total* 10,552
Sales 15,686,551
SIC 5211 Lumber and other building materials
 Ted Brockman

D-U-N-S 20-773-8027   (BR)
VANCOUVER COASTAL HEALTH AUTHORITY
TILBURY LAUNDRY FACILITY
7781 Vantage Way, Delta, BC, V4G 1A6

Emp Here 80
SIC 7219 Laundry and garment services, nec

D-U-N-S 25-371-1519   (BR)
VARSTEEL LTD
DOMINION PIPE & PILING
8500 River Rd Unit 6, Delta, BC, V4G 1B5
(604) 946-2717
Emp Here 40
SIC 5051 Metals service centers and offices

D-U-N-S 25-415-6078   (HQ)
WESTERN TANK & LINING LTD
(*Suby of* Western Tank & Lining Ltd)
7192 Vantage Way, Delta, BC, V4G 1K7
(604) 241-9487
Emp Here 42   *Emp Total* 44
Sales 6,785,345
SIC 3443 Fabricated plate work (boiler shop)
 Kim Biehl
 Micah Cohen
 Chris Calvez

D-U-N-S 20-799-0326   (SL)
ZODIAC HURRICANE TECHNOLOGIES INC
7830 Vantage Way, Delta, BC, V4G 1A7
(604) 940-2999
Emp Here 114   *Sales* 14,466,392
SIC 3732 Boatbuilding and repairing
 Jean Jacques Arignon
 Sandra Kyle
S&M/VP Ernie Hammond

Delta, BC V4K
Greater Vancouver County

D-U-N-S 24-931-2323   (SL)
323416 B.C. LTD
DELTA TOWN & COUNTRY INN
6005 17a Hwy, Delta, BC, V4K 5B8
(604) 946-4404
Emp Here 65   *Sales* 2,845,467
SIC 7011 Hotels and motels

D-U-N-S 25-359-4659   (BR)
AECON LOCKERBIE INDUSTRIAL INC
6425 River Rd, Delta, BC, V4K 5B9
(604) 521-3322
Emp Here 30
SIC 3443 Fabricated plate work (boiler shop)

D-U-N-S 20-047-1360   (BR)
**CATHOLIC INDEPENDENT SCHOOLS OF
VANCOUVER ARCHDIOCESE, THE**
SACRED HEART SCHOOL
3900 Arthur Dr, Delta, BC, V4K 3N5
(604) 946-2611
Emp Here 40
SIC 8211 Elementary and secondary schools

D-U-N-S 25-019-3307   (BR)
DELTA SCHOOL DISTRICT NO.37
DELTA SECONDARY SCHOOL
4615 51 St, Delta, BC, V4K 2V8
(604) 946-4194
Emp Here 100
SIC 8211 Elementary and secondary schools

D-U-N-S 20-591-3051   (BR)
DELTA SCHOOL DISTRICT NO.37
HOLLY ELEMENTARY SCHOOL
4625 62 St, Delta, BC, V4K 3L8
(604) 946-0218
Emp Here 25
SIC 8211 Elementary and secondary schools

D-U-N-S 20-591-7359   (BR)
DELTA SCHOOL DISTRICT NO.37
LADNER ELEMENTARY SCHOOL
5016 44 Ave, Delta, BC, V4K 1C1
(604) 946-4158
Emp Here 40
SIC 8211 Elementary and secondary schools

D-U-N-S 20-047-0651   (BR)
DELTA SCHOOL DISTRICT NO.37
HAWTHORNE ELEMENTARY SCHOOL
5160 Central Ave, Delta, BC, V4K 2H2
(604) 946-7601
Emp Here 25
SIC 8211 Elementary and secondary schools

D-U-N-S 20-794-9814   (BR)
DELTA SCHOOL DISTRICT NO.37
DISTRICT RESOURCE CENTRE
4750 57 St, Delta, BC, V4K 3C9
(604) 946-3150
Emp Here 20
SIC 8211 Elementary and secondary schools

D-U-N-S 20-097-8463   (BR)
DELTA SCHOOL DISTRICT NO.37
PORT GUICHON ELEMENTARY SCHOOL
4381 46a St, Delta, BC, V4K 2M2
(604) 946-0321
Emp Here 25
SIC 8211 Elementary and secondary schools

D-U-N-S 25-752-7689   (SL)
DELTA VIEW HABILITATION CENTRE LTD
9341 Burns Dr, Delta, BC, V4K 3N3
(604) 501-6700
Emp Here 79   *Sales* 3,939,878
SIC 7389 Business services, nec

D-U-N-S 20-860-8294   (SL)
**DELTA VIEW LIFE ENRICHMENT CENTRES
LTD**
9341 Burns Dr, Delta, BC, V4K 3N3
(604) 501-6700
Emp Here 100   *Sales* 4,523,563
SIC 8052 Intermediate care facilities

D-U-N-S 20-731-7228   (BR)
**GOVERNMENT OF THE PROVINCE OF
BRITISH COLUMBIA**
DELTA HOSPITAL
5800 Mountain View Blvd, Delta, BC, V4K 3V6
(604) 946-1121
Emp Here 250
SIC 8062 General medical and surgical hospitals

D-U-N-S 25-071-6073   (BR)
GREAT PACIFIC INDUSTRIES INC
SAVE-ON-FOODS
5186 Ladner Trunk Rd Suite 936, Delta, BC,
V4K 1W3
(604) 946-5251
Emp Here 167
SIC 5411 Grocery stores

D-U-N-S 25-633-0770   (BR)
KIN'S FARM LTD
KIN'S FARMER'S MARKET
5227 Ladner Trunk Rd, Delta, BC, V4K 1W4
(604) 940-0733
Emp Here 21
SIC 5411 Grocery stores

D-U-N-S 24-153-0872   (SL)
**NORTH AMERICA INDIAN MISSION OF
CANADA**
NAIM MINISTRIES
5027 47a Ave Suite 200, Delta, BC, V4K 1T9

Emp Here 80   *Sales* 7,304,400
SIC 8661 Religious organizations
Ex Dir William Tarter
Dir Opers Tim Higginbotham
Dir Fin Shelley Vaters

D-U-N-S 24-311-1163   (BR)
SJR FOOD SERVICES LTD
MCDONALD'S RESTAURANTS
(*Suby of* SJR Food Services Ltd)
5776 Ladner Trunk Rd, Delta, BC, V4K 1X6
(604) 940-3770
Emp Here 30
SIC 5812 Eating places

D-U-N-S 25-499-1490   (BR)
STARBUCKS COFFEE CANADA, INC
(*Suby of* Starbucks Corporation)
5263 Ladner Trunk Rd, Delta, BC, V4K 1W4
(604) 940-8394
Emp Here 23
SIC 5812 Eating places

Delta, BC V4L
Greater Vancouver County

D-U-N-S 20-571-9425   (BR)
BANK OF MONTREAL
BMO
1206 56 St, Delta, BC, V4L 2A4
(604) 668-1412
Emp Here 20
SIC 6021 National commercial banks

D-U-N-S 20-194-3888   (SL)
COAST TSAWWASSEN INN
1665 56 St, Delta, BC, V4L 2B2
(604) 943-8221
Emp Here 50   *Sales* 2,188,821
SIC 7011 Hotels and motels

D-U-N-S 20-703-2462   (BR)
JACE HOLDINGS LTD
THRIFTY FOODS
1270 56 St, Delta, BC, V4L 2A4
(604) 948-9210
Emp Here 170
SIC 5411 Grocery stores

D-U-N-S 24-062-1958   (HQ)
SJR FOOD SERVICES LTD
MCDONALD'S RESTAURANTS

(*Suby of* SJR Food Services Ltd)
1835 56 St Unit 44, Delta, BC, V4L 2M1
(604) 948-3630
Emp Here 80   *Emp Total* 80
Sales 2,407,703
SIC 5812 Eating places

D-U-N-S 24-312-3788   (SL)
**TSAWWASSEN INDEPENDENT SCHOOL
SOCIETY**
SOUTH POINT ACADEMY
1900 56 St, Delta, BC, V4L 2B1
(604) 948-8826
Emp Here 50   *Sales* 3,356,192
SIC 8211 Elementary and secondary schools

D-U-N-S 20-717-2748   (SL)
WATERFORD AT WINDSOR WOODS, THE
1345 56 St Suite 221, Delta, BC, V4L 2P9
(604) 943-5954
Emp Here 54   *Sales* 2,115,860
SIC 8322 Individual and family services

Delta, BC V4M
Greater Vancouver County

D-U-N-S 20-794-5424   (BR)
CANADA POST CORPORATION
DELTA POST OFFICE
5432 12 Ave, Delta, BC, V4M 2B3
(604) 943-4747
Emp Here 25
SIC 4311 U.s. postal service

D-U-N-S 25-020-0193   (BR)
CORPORATION OF DELTA, THE
DELTA PARKS AND RECREATION
5575 9 Ave, Delta, BC, V4M 1W1
(604) 952-3005
Emp Here 30
SIC 7999 Amusement and recreation, nec

D-U-N-S 20-591-3085   (BR)
DELTA SCHOOL DISTRICT NO.37
SOUTH DELTA SECONDARY SCHOOL
750 53 St, Delta, BC, V4M 3B7
(604) 943-7407
Emp Here 100
SIC 8211 Elementary and secondary schools

D-U-N-S 25-453-7236   (BR)
DELTA SCHOOL DISTRICT NO.37
CLIFF DRIVE ELEMENTARY SCHOOL
5025 12 Ave, Delta, BC, V4M 2A7
(604) 943-2244
Emp Here 30
SIC 8211 Elementary and secondary schools

D-U-N-S 20-088-6013   (BR)
DELTA SCHOOL DISTRICT NO.37
ENGLISH BLUFF ELEMENTARY SCHOOL
402 English Bluff Rd, Delta, BC, V4M 2N2
(604) 943-0201
Emp Here 25
SIC 8211 Elementary and secondary schools

D-U-N-S 20-591-3077   (BR)
DELTA SCHOOL DISTRICT NO.37
SOUTH PARK ELEMENTARY SCHOOL
735 Gilchrist Dr, Delta, BC, V4M 3L4
(604) 943-1105
Emp Here 25
SIC 8211 Elementary and secondary schools

Denny Island, BC V0T
Central Coast County

D-U-N-S 24-658-3090   (BR)
SHEARWATER MARINE LIMITED
SHEARWATER MARINE GROUP
(*Suby of* Shearwater Marine Limited)
1 Shearwater Rd, Denny Island, BC, V0T 1B0

(250) 957-2305
Emp Here 40
SIC 7011 Hotels and motels

Dewdney, BC V0M

D-U-N-S 20-913-6287   (BR)
SCHOOL DISTRICT #75 (MISSION)
DEWDNEY ELEMENTARY SCHOOL
37151 Hawkins Pickle, Dewdney, BC, V0M
1H0
(604) 826-2516
Emp Here 23
SIC 8211 Elementary and secondary schools

D-U-N-S 20-185-1792   (BR)
STAVE LAKE CEDAR MILLS INC
8653 River Rd S, Dewdney, BC, V0M 1H0
(604) 826-0219
Emp Here 25
SIC 2429 Special product sawmills, nec

Duncan, BC V9L
Cowichan Valley County

D-U-N-S 25-236-1027   (SL)
458890 B.C. LTD
DUNCAN WHITE SPOT
101 Trans Canada Hwy, Duncan, BC, V9L 3P8
(250) 748-5151
Emp Here 80   *Sales* 2,407,703
SIC 5812 Eating places

D-U-N-S 25-087-8311   (SL)
ADAMS 22 HOLDINGS LTD
TIM HORTONS
2628 Beverly St, Duncan, BC, V9L 5C7
(250) 709-2205
Emp Here 50   *Sales* 1,678,096
SIC 5461 Retail bakeries

D-U-N-S 25-296-8342   (BR)
BANK OF NOVA SCOTIA, THE
SCOTIABANK
435 Trunk Rd, Duncan, BC, V9L 2P5
(250) 715-3850
Emp Here 25
SIC 6021 National commercial banks

D-U-N-S 25-289-2153   (BR)
BLACK PRESS GROUP LTD
COWICHAN NEWS LEADER PICTORIAL
5380 Trans Canada Hwy Unit 2, Duncan, BC,
V9L 6W4

Emp Here 30
SIC 2711 Newspapers

D-U-N-S 20-651-8016   (SL)
BOW MEL CHRYSLER LTD
461 Trans Canada Hwy, Duncan, BC, V9L 3R7
(250) 748-8144
Emp Here 28   *Sales* 10,214,498
SIC 5511 New and used car dealers
Fin Ex Connie Johnston
Dir Todd Blumel

D-U-N-S 25-313-4829   (BR)
**BRITISH COLUMBIA HYDRO AND POWER
AUTHORITY**
DUNCAN DISTRICT OFFICE
6494 Norcross Rd, Duncan, BC, V9L 6C1
(250) 746-3807
Emp Here 20
SIC 4911 Electric services

D-U-N-S 20-845-3196   (BR)
**BRITISH COLUMBIA HYDRO AND POWER
AUTHORITY**
B C HYDRO
7056 Bell Mckinnon Rd, Duncan, BC, V9L 6B5
(250) 701-4600
Emp Here 50

SIC 4911 Electric services

D-U-N-S 25-288-8813   (BR)
CANADA POST CORPORATION
191 Ingram St, Duncan, BC, V9L 1N8
(250) 746-4523
Emp Here 50
SIC 4311 U.s. postal service

D-U-N-S 24-711-1482   (BR)
CANADIAN MENTAL HEALTH ASSOCIATION, THE
(Suby of Canadian Mental Health Association, The)
51 Trunk Rd, Duncan, BC, V9L 2N7
(250) 746-5512
Emp Here 30
SIC 8621 Professional organizations

D-U-N-S 25-117-7853   (BR)
COWICHAN TRIBES
LE'LUM'UY'LH DAY CARE
5588 River Rd, Duncan, BC, V9L 6V9
(250) 746-5966
Emp Here 22
SIC 8351 Child day care services

D-U-N-S 25-119-7026   (BR)
COWICHAN TRIBES
LALUM'UTUL SMUNEEN CHILD & FAMILY SERVICES
5766 Allenby Rd, Duncan, BC, V9L 5J1
(250) 746-1002
Emp Here 27
SIC 8399 Social services, nec

D-U-N-S 25-745-3894   (BR)
COWICHAN VALLEY REGIONAL DISTRICT
ISLAND SAVINGS CENTER
2687 James St, Duncan, BC, V9L 2X5
(250) 748-7529
Emp Here 60
SIC 8322 Individual and family services

D-U-N-S 24-678-4180   (BR)
EMERGENCY AND HEALTH SERVICES COMMISSION
BC MENTAL HEALTH
3088 Gibbins Rd, Duncan, BC, V9L 1E8
(250) 709-3040
Emp Here 30
SIC 8093 Specialty outpatient clinics, nec

D-U-N-S 20-809-2754   (HQ)
GLOBAL TRANSITION CONSULTING INC
(Suby of Global Transition Consulting Inc)
80 Station St Suite 301, Duncan, BC, V9L 1M4
(250) 748-9880
Emp Here 29   Emp Total 49
Sales 7,304 400
SIC 8742 Management consulting services
Pr Ann Norris

D-U-N-S 20-044-8705   (BR)
GOVERNMENT OF THE PROVINCE OF BRITISH COLUMBIA
BC MIN CHILD & FAM DEV
161 Fourth St, Duncan, BC, V9L 5J8
(250) 715-2725
Emp Here 40
SIC 8399 Social services, nec

D-U-N-S 20-917-0054   (BR)
GOVERNMENT OF THE PROVINCE OF BRITISH COLUMBIA
COMMUNITY LIVING BC DUNCAN
116 Queens Rd Suite 101, Duncan, BC, V9L 2W6
(250) 715-2830
Emp Here 25
SIC 8399 Social services, nec

D-U-N-S 24-803-7280   (BR)
HOME DEPOT OF CANADA INC
HOME DEPOT
(Suby of The Home Depot Inc)
2980 Drinkwater Rd Unit 1, Duncan, BC, V9L 6C6

(250) 737-2360
Emp Here 80
SIC 5251 Hardware stores

D-U-N-S 25-272-7094   (BR)
INSURANCE CORPORATION OF BRITISH COLUMBIA
ICBC
5151 Polkey Rd, Duncan, BC, V9L 6W3
(250) 748-3121
Emp Here 21
SIC 6331 Fire, marine, and casualty insurance

D-U-N-S 20-349-0185   (BR)
ISLAND SAVINGS CREDIT UNION
(Suby of Island Savings Credit Union)
89 Evans St, Duncan, BC, V9L 1P5
(250) 746-4171
Emp Here 50
SIC 8742 Management consulting services

D-U-N-S 24-034-0661   (HQ)
ISLAND SAVINGS CREDIT UNION
ISLAND SAVINGS, A DIVISION OF FIRST WEST CREDIT UNION
(Suby of Island Savings Credit Union)
499 Canada Ave Suite 300, Duncan, BC, V9L 1T7
(250) 748-4728
Emp Here 45   Emp Total 300
Sales 54,843,548
SIC 6062 State credit unions
VP Fin VP Fin Fred Zdan
Sr VP Randy Bertsch
VP Fin Jeff Wood
William Mccreadie
Dir Pearl Graham
Dir John Richmond
Dir Sheila Service

D-U-N-S 25-681-6562   (SL)
KHOWUTZUN MUSTIMUHW CONTRACTORS LIMITED PARTNERSHIP
(Suby of Khowutzun Development Corp)
200 Cowichan Way, Duncan, BC, V9L 6P4
(250) 746-8350
Emp Here 40   Sales 9,030,720
SIC 1521 Single-family housing construction
Pr Harvey Alphonse

D-U-N-S 25-270-1529   (BR)
LOBLAWS INC
REAL CANADIAN SUPERSTORE 1563
291 Cowichan Way Suite 1563, Duncan, BC, V9L 6P5
(250) 746-0529
Emp Here 250
SIC 5141 Groceries, general line

D-U-N-S 24-331-8107   (BR)
MNP LLP
372 Coronation Ave Suite 200, Duncan, BC, V9L 2T3
(250) 748-3761
Emp Here 25
SIC 8721 Accounting, auditing, and bookkeeping

D-U-N-S 25-318-1481   (BR)
MCDONALD'S   RESTAURANTS   OF CANADA LIMITED
MCDONALD'S
(Suby of McDonald's Corporation)
5883 Trans Canada Hwy, Duncan, BC, V9L 3R9
(250) 715-2370
Emp Here 100
SIC 5812 Eating places

D-U-N-S 20-180-2795   (BR)
NOVA PACIFIC CARE INC
WEDGEWOOD HOUSE
256 Government St, Duncan, BC, V9L 1A4
(250) 746-9808
Emp Here 22
SIC 8322 Individual and family services

D-U-N-S 20-918-6076   (BR)
O.K. INDUSTRIES LTD

DUNCAN PAVING
6357 Lake Cowichan Hwy, Duncan, BC, V9L 3Y2
(250) 748-2531
Emp Here 35
SIC 1611 Highway and street construction

D-U-N-S 25-507-1060   (SL)
PACIFIC ENERGY FIREPLACE PRODUCTS LTD
2975 Allenby Rd, Duncan, BC, V9L 6V8
(250) 748-1184
Emp Here 100   Sales 9,120,088
SIC 3433 Heating equipment, except electric
Pr Pr Paul Erickson

D-U-N-S 24-126-0111   (BR)
PANAGO PIZZA INC
180 Central Rd Suite 9, Duncan, BC, V9L 4X3
(250) 709-3200
Emp Here 22
SIC 5812 Eating places

D-U-N-S 20-573-8250   (BR)
ROYAL BANK OF CANADA
RBC
(Suby of Royal Bank Of Canada)
395 Trunk Rd, Duncan, BC, V9L 2P4
(250) 746-2400
Emp Here 20
SIC 6021 National commercial banks

D-U-N-S 24-245-0153   (SL)
SACPYR INVESTMENTS LTD
BEST WESTERN COWICHAN VALLEY INN
6474 Trans Canada Hwy, Duncan, BC, V9L 6C6
(250) 748-2722
Emp Here 59   Sales 2,553,625
SIC 7011 Hotels and motels

D-U-N-S 20-713-5711   (BR)
SCHOOL DISTRICT NO. 79 (COWICHAN VALLEY)
ALEX AITKEN ELEMENTARY SCHOOL
2494 Roome Rd, Duncan, BC, V9L 4L2
(250) 748-8724
Emp Here 50
SIC 8211 Elementary and secondary schools

D-U-N-S 20-713-5737   (BR)
SCHOOL DISTRICT NO. 79 (COWICHAN VALLEY)
MT PREBOST MIDDLE SCHOOL
6177 Somenos Rd, Duncan, BC, V9L 4E7
(250) 746-7187
Emp Here 50
SIC 8211 Elementary and secondary schools

D-U-N-S 20-047-0826   (BR)
SCHOOL DISTRICT NO. 79 (COWICHAN VALLEY)
DRINKWATER ELEMENTARY SCHOOL
6236 Lane Rd, Duncan, BC, V9L 4E3
(250) 748-9232
Emp Here 20
SIC 8211 Elementary and secondary schools

D-U-N-S 25-139-1421   (BR)
SCHOOL DISTRICT NO. 79 (COWICHAN VALLEY)
KOWHEMUN ELEMENTARY SCHOOL
2918 Cliffs Rd, Duncan, BC, V9L 1C5
(250) 746-7845
Emp Here 30
SIC 8211 Elementary and secondary schools

D-U-N-S 25-117-4900   (BR)
SCHOOL DISTRICT NO. 79 (COWICHAN VALLEY)
MAPLE BAY ELEMENTARY SCHOOL
1500 Donnay Dr, Duncan, BC, V9L 5R4
(250) 746-7541
Emp Here 30
SIC 8211 Elementary and secondary schools

D-U-N-S 20-590-8143   (BR)
SCHOOL DISTRICT NO. 79 (COWICHAN

VALLEY)
5265 Polkey Rd, Duncan, BC, V9L 6W3

Emp Here 25
SIC 8211 Elementary and secondary schools

D-U-N-S 20-590-8069   (BR)
SCHOOL DISTRICT NO. 79 (COWICHAN VALLEY)
QUAMICHAN MIDDLE SCHOOL
2515 Beverly St, Duncan, BC, V9L 3A5
(250) 746-6168
Emp Here 25
SIC 8211 Elementary and secondary schools

D-U-N-S 20-590-8176   (BR)
SCHOOL DISTRICT NO. 79 (COWICHAN VALLEY)
2557 Beverly St, Duncan, BC, V9L 2X3
(250) 748-0321
Emp Here 25
SIC 8621 Professional organizations

D-U-N-S 20-017-6043   (BR)
STARBUCKS COFFEE CANADA, INC
(Suby of Starbucks Corporation)
2755 Beverly St, Duncan, BC, V9L 6X2
(250) 737-1077
Emp Here 20
SIC 5812 Eating places

D-U-N-S 20-506-0614   (BR)
STARBUCKS COFFEE CANADA, INC
(Suby of Starbucks Corporation)
350 Trunk Rd Suite 1, Duncan, BC, V9L 2P6
(250) 746-9394
Emp Here 25
SIC 5812 Eating places

D-U-N-S 20-275-6672   (SL)
SUNRIDGE SENIORS COMMUNITY PARTNERSHIP
361 Bundock Ave, Duncan, BC, V9L 3P1
(250) 748-8048
Emp Here 50   Sales 2,334,742
SIC 8059 Nursing and personal care, nec

D-U-N-S 20-735-2027   (BR)
VANCOUVER ISLAND HEALTH AUTHORITY
MARGARET MOSS HEALTH CENTER
675 Canada Ave, Duncan, BC, V9L 1T9
(250) 709-3050
Emp Here 30
SIC 8011 Offices and clinics of medical doctors

D-U-N-S 25-140-8969   (BR)
VANCOUVER ISLAND HEALTH AUTHORITY
COWICHAN DISTRICT HOSPITAL
3045 Gibbins Rd, Duncan, BC, V9L 1E5
(250) 709-3000
Emp Here 4,500
SIC 8011 Offices and clinics of medical doctors

D-U-N-S 20-994-1165   (BR)
VANCOUVER ISLAND HEALTH AUTHORITY
CAIRNSMORE PLACE
250 Cairnsmore St, Duncan, BC, V9L 4H2
(250) 715-1955
Emp Here 60
SIC 8011 Offices and clinics of medical doctors

D-U-N-S 25-297-7624   (BR)
WAL-MART CANADA CORP
3020 Drinkwater Rd, Duncan, BC, V9L 6C6
(250) 748-2566
Emp Here 100
SIC 5311 Department stores

D-U-N-S 24-672-6780   (SL)
WEN DUNCAN FOODS LTD
WENDY'S
5845 Trans Canada Hwy, Duncan, BC, V9L

3R9
(250) 748-3424
Emp Here 55   *Sales* 1,678,096
SIC 5812 Eating places

Egmont, BC V0N
Sunshine Coast County

D-U-N-S 20-799-9231   (BR)
LAFARGE CANADA INC
Gd, Egmont, BC, V0N 1N0
(604) 883-2615
Emp Here 20
SIC 1442 Construction sand and gravel

Elkford, BC V0B
East Kootenay County

D-U-N-S 25-909-8903   (BR)
DSR HOLDINGS LTD
LEYDEN BUS LINES
(*Suby of* DSR Holdings Ltd)
7 Water St, Elkford, BC, V0B 1H0

Emp Here 60
SIC 4111 Local and suburban transit

D-U-N-S 25-680-1788   (SL)
GREENHILLS MINE JOINT VENTURE
Gd, Elkford, BC, V0B 1H0
(250) 865-3097
Emp Here 460   *Sales* 271,061,920
SIC 1221 Bituminous coal and lignite-surface mining
Genl Mgr Pat Koski

D-U-N-S 20-645-3685   (BR)
SCHOOL DISTRICT NO 5 (SOUTHEAST KOOTENAY)
ELKFORD SECONDARY SCHOOL
2500 Balmer Dr, Elkford, BC, V0B 1H0
(250) 865-4674
Emp Here 21
SIC 8211 Elementary and secondary schools

D-U-N-S 25-454-6682   (BR)
SCHOOL DISTRICT NO 5 (SOUTHEAST KOOTENAY)
ROCKY MOUNTAIN ELEMENTARY SCHOOL
2500a Balmer Dr, Elkford, BC, V0B 1H0
(250) 865-4625
Emp Here 25
SIC 8211 Elementary and secondary schools

D-U-N-S 24-320-8423   (BR)
TECK COAL LIMITED
FORDING RIVER OPERATIONS
Gd, Elkford, BC, V0B 1H0
(250) 865-2271
Emp Here 520
SIC 1221 Bituminous coal and lignite-surface mining

Enderby, BC V0E
North Okanagan County

D-U-N-S 20-804-1959   (BR)
INTERIOR HEALTH AUTHORITY
ENDERBY COMMUNITY HEALTH CENTRE
707 3rd Ave, Enderby, BC, V0E 1V0
(250) 838-2450
Emp Here 20
SIC 8093 Specialty outpatient clinics, nec

D-U-N-S 20-027-0986   (BR)
NORTH OKANAGAN SHUSWAP SCHOOL DISTRICT 83
M V BEATTIE ELEMENTARY SCHOOL
1308 Sicamous St, Enderby, BC, V0E 1V0

(250) 838-6434
Emp Here 40
SIC 8211 Elementary and secondary schools

D-U-N-S 25-186-9558   (BR)
NORTH OKANAGAN SHUSWAP SCHOOL DISTRICT 83
A L FORTUNE SECONDARY SCHOOL
500 Bass Ave, Enderby, BC, V0E 1V2
(250) 838-6431
Emp Here 40
SIC 8211 Elementary and secondary schools

D-U-N-S 20-194-9323   (BR)
NORTH OKANAGAN SHUSWAP SCHOOL DISTRICT 83
ASHTON CREEK ELEMENTARY
11 Rands Rd, Enderby, BC, V0E 1V5
(250) 838-7087
Emp Here 20
SIC 8211 Elementary and secondary schools

D-U-N-S 24-897-3497   (SL)
QUILAKWA INVESTMENTS LTD
QUILAKWA GALLERY & SUPER SAVE GAS
(*Suby of* Splatsin)
5655 Hwy 97a Rr 3, Enderby, BC, V0E 1V3
(250) 838-9422
Emp Here 30   *Sales* 3,502,114
SIC 5411 Grocery stores

Erickson, BC V0B
Central Kootenay County

D-U-N-S 25-676-7633   (BR)
SCHOOL DISTRICT NO. 8 (KOOTENAY LAKE)
ERICKSON ELEMENTARY SCHOOL
(*Suby of* School District No. 8 (Kootenay Lake))
3523 Hwy 3, Erickson, BC, V0B 1K0
(250) 428-2363
Emp Here 20
SIC 8211 Elementary and secondary schools

Errington, BC V0R
Nanaimo County

D-U-N-S 20-713-5984   (BR)
SCHOOL DISTRICT NO 69 (QUALICUM)
ERRINGTON ELEMENTARY SCHOOL
1390 Sairdowne Rd, Errington, BC, V0R 1V0
(250) 248-8446
Emp Here 25
SIC 8211 Elementary and secondary schools

Falkland, BC V0E
Columbia - Shuswap County

D-U-N-S 20-027-0978   (BR)
NORTH OKANAGAN SHUSWAP SCHOOL DISTRICT 83
FALKLAND ELEMENTARY SCHOOL
5732 Tuktakmain St, Falkland, BC, V0E 1W0
(250) 379-2320
Emp Here 20
SIC 8211 Elementary and secondary schools

Fernie, BC V0B
East Kootenay County

D-U-N-S 24-298-2288   (SL)
357672 B.C. LTD
PARK PLACE LODGE
742 Hwy 3 Rr 5, Fernie, BC, V0B 1M5

(250) 423-6871
Emp Here 85   *Sales* 3,720,996
SIC 7011 Hotels and motels

D-U-N-S 24-351-6163   (SL)
BOSTON PIZZA
1602 7th Ave, Fernie, BC, V0B 1M0
(250) 423-2634
Emp Here 50   *Sales* 1,532,175
SIC 5812 Eating places

D-U-N-S 20-020-1874   (BR)
CORPORATION OF THE CITY OF FERNIE
FERNIE FIRE RESCUE
692 3rd Ave, Fernie, BC, V0B 1M0
(250) 423-4226
Emp Here 27
SIC 7389 Business services, nec

D-U-N-S 24-028-9053   (BR)
GOLDEN LIFE MANAGEMENT CORP
ROCKY MOUNTAIN VILLAGE
55 Cokato Rd Suite 206, Fernie, BC, V0B 1M4
(250) 423-4214
Emp Here 80
SIC 8059 Nursing and personal care, nec

D-U-N-S 20-556-1215   (BR)
GREAT PACIFIC INDUSTRIES INC
OVERWAITEA FOOD GROUP
792 2nd Ave, Fernie, BC, V0B 1M0
(250) 423-4607
Emp Here 50
SIC 5411 Grocery stores

D-U-N-S 24-419-6205   (SL)
HAYES, J.A. HOLDINGS LTD
CANADIAN TIRE
1791 9th Ave, Fernie, BC, V0B 1M5
(250) 423-4222
Emp Here 40   *Sales* 6,313,604
SIC 5531 Auto and home supply stores
Pr Jason Hayes

D-U-N-S 24-312-6856   (BR)
INTERIOR HEALTH AUTHORITY
ELK VALLEY HOSPITAL
1501 5 Ave, Fernie, BC, V0B 1M0
(250) 423-4453
Emp Here 100
SIC 8062 General medical and surgical hospitals

D-U-N-S 20-914-9165   (BR)
LOBLAWS INC
1792 9th Ave, Fernie, BC, V0B 1M0
(250) 423-7387
Emp Here 45
SIC 5411 Grocery stores

D-U-N-S 20-191-5464   (BR)
RESORTS OF THE CANADIAN ROCKIES INC
KELSEY'S RESTAURANT
5339 Fernie Ski Hill Rd Rr 6, Fernie, BC, V0B 1M6
(250) 423-2444
Emp Here 70
SIC 5812 Eating places

D-U-N-S 20-031-1772   (BR)
SCHOOL DISTRICT NO 5 (SOUTHEAST KOOTENAY)
FERNIE SECONDARY SCHOOL
102 Fairway Dr, Fernie, BC, V0B 1M5
(250) 423-4471
Emp Here 50
SIC 8211 Elementary and secondary schools

Field, BC V0A
Columbia - Shuswap County

D-U-N-S 25-123-7442   (BR)
CANADIAN ROCKY MOUNTAIN RESORTS LTD
EMERALD LAKE LODGE

Gd, Field, BC, V0A 1G0
(250) 343-6418
Emp Here 74
SIC 7011 Hotels and motels

Fort Nelson, BC V0C
Peace River - Laird County

D-U-N-S 25-272-6823   (BR)
FINNING INTERNATIONAL INC
FINNING CANADA, A DIV
(*Suby of* Finning International Inc)
295 Alaska Hwy, Fort Nelson, BC, V0C 1R0
(250) 774-8000
Emp Here 20
SIC 5082 Construction and mining machinery

D-U-N-S 20-951-2594   (BR)
FORMULA POWELL L.P.
308 Alaska Hwy, Fort Nelson, BC, V0C 1R0
(250) 774-6100
Emp Here 40
SIC 4213 Trucking, except local

D-U-N-S 20-280-3578   (BR)
IMPERIAL OIL LIMITED
EXXON MOBIL
(*Suby of* Exxon Mobil Corporation)
Mi 293 Alaska Hwy, Fort Nelson, BC, V0C 1R0
(250) 774-3151
Emp Here 20
SIC 2911 Petroleum refining

D-U-N-S 24-397-5781   (BR)
KOS OILFIELD TRANSPORTATION LTD
293 Alaska Hwy, Fort Nelson, BC, V0C 1R0

Emp Here 40
SIC 1381 Drilling oil and gas wells

D-U-N-S 24-231-0162   (BR)
LAKEVIEW MANAGEMENT INC
LAKEVIEW INN AND SUITES
4507 50th Ave, Fort Nelson, BC, V0C 1R0
(250) 233-5001
Emp Here 20
SIC 7011 Hotels and motels

D-U-N-S 20-653-1936   (BR)
SCHOOL DISTRICT #81 (FORT NELSON)
FORT NELSON SECONDARY SCHOOL
5419 Simpson Trail, Fort Nelson, BC, V0C 1R0
(250) 774-6958
Emp Here 40
SIC 8211 Elementary and secondary schools

D-U-N-S 20-003-5231   (BR)
SCHOOL DISTRICT #81 (FORT NELSON)
CARLSON, G W ELEMENTARY SCHOOL
Gd, Fort Nelson, BC, V0C 1R0
(250) 774-6941
Emp Here 30
SIC 8211 Elementary and secondary schools

D-U-N-S 25-678-2020   (BR)
SCHOOL DISTRICT #81 (FORT NELSON)
R.L. ANGUS ELEMENTARY SCHOOL
5501 Mountain View Dr, Fort Nelson, BC, V0C 1R0
(250) 774-2738
Emp Here 25
SIC 8211 Elementary and secondary schools

Fort St. James, BC V0J
Bulkley - Nechako County

D-U-N-S 20-027-0747   (BR)
BOARD OF EDUCATION OF SCHOOL DISTRICT NO. 91 (NECHAKO LAKE), THE
DAVID HOY ELEMENTARY SCHOOL
12 Ave E, Fort St. James, BC, V0J 1P0

---

(250) 996-8237
Emp Here 30
SIC 8211 Elementary and secondary schools

D-U-N-S 20-027-0762 (BR)
BOARD OF EDUCATION OF SCHOOL DIS-TRICT NO. 91 (NECHAKO LAKE), THE
FORT ST JAMES SECONDARY SCHOOL
450 Douglas St, Fort St. James, BC, V0J 1P0
(250) 996-7126
Emp Here 52
SIC 8211 Elementary and secondary schools

D-U-N-S 20-919-3445 (BR)
CONIFEX INC
300 Takla Rd, Fort St. James, BC, V0J 1P0
(250) 996-3241
Emp Here 200
SIC 2421 Sawmills and planing mills, general

D-U-N-S 25-267-8727 (BR)
GREAT PACIFIC INDUSTRIES INC
OVERWAITEA FOOD GROUP
488 Stuart Dr, Fort St. James, BC, V0J 1P0
(250) 996-8333
Emp Here 28
SIC 5411 Grocery stores

D-U-N-S 20-796-9643 (BR)
NORTHERN HEALTH AUTHORITY
STUART LAKE HOSPITAL
600 Stuart Dr E, Fort St. James, BC, V0J 1P0
(250) 996-8201
Emp Here 35
SIC 8062 General medical and surgical hospitals

D-U-N-S 24-329-3834 (SL)
TANIZUL TIMBER LTD
Gd, Fort St. James, BC, V0J 1P0
(250) 648-3221
Emp Here 24 *Sales* 1,047,991
SIC 5099 Durable goods, nec

Fort St. John, BC V1J
Peace River - Laird County

D-U-N-S 24-390-4765 (BR)
AECOM PRODUCTION SERVICES LTD
FLINT FIELD SERVICES LTD
8320 89a St, Fort St. John, BC, V1J 4H6
(250) 787-9092
Emp Here 50
SIC 1389 Oil and gas field services, nec

D-U-N-S 20-914-5452 (BR)
AECOM PRODUCTION SERVICES LTD
FLINT FIELD SERVICES LTD
9507 Alaska Rd, Fort St. John, BC, V1J 1A3
(250) 787-7878
Emp Here 25
SIC 1731 Electrical work

D-U-N-S 24-802-6580 (HQ)
AVENTUR ENERGY CORP
(*Suby of* Aventur Energy Corp)
10493 Alder Cres, Fort St. John, BC, V1J 4M7
(250) 787-7093
Emp Here 25 *Emp Total* 50
Sales 351,653
SIC 1389 Oil and gas field services, nec

D-U-N-S 25-592-8806 (BR)
BAILEY HELICOPTERS LTD
6219 242 Rd, Fort St. John, BC, V1J 4M6
(250) 785-2518
Emp Here 25
SIC 4522 Air transportation, nonscheduled

D-U-N-S 25-296-8748 (BR)
BANK OF NOVA SCOTIA, THE
SCOTIABANK
9915 100 St, Fort St. John, BC, V1J 3Y3
(250) 262-5150
Emp Here 22
SIC 6021 National commercial banks

D-U-N-S 24-284-2680 (BR)
BRANDT TRACTOR LTD
48 Alaska Hwy, Fort St. John, BC, V1J 4J1
(250) 785-6762
Emp Here 22
SIC 5082 Construction and mining machinery

D-U-N-S 24-335-8509 (BR)
BRITISH COLUMBIA HYDRO AND POWER AUTHORITY
BC HYDRO
9228 100 Ave, Fort St. John, BC, V1J 1X7
(250) 267-5187
Emp Here 20
SIC 4911 Electric services

D-U-N-S 25-288-8854 (BR)
CANADA POST CORPORATION
10139 101 Ave, Fort St. John, BC, V1J 2B4
(250) 785-4625
Emp Here 36
SIC 4311 U.s. postal service

D-U-N-S 20-740-0974 (BR)
CANADIAN FOREST PRODUCTS LTD
CANFOR
9312 259 Rd Lcd Main, Fort St. John, BC, V1J 4M6
(250) 787-3600
Emp Here 200
SIC 5031 Lumber, plywood, and millwork

D-U-N-S 20-913-8077 (BR)
CANADIAN IMPERIAL BANK OF COM-MERCE
CIBC
9959 100 Ave, Fort St. John, BC, V1J 1Y4
(250) 785-8101
Emp Here 25
SIC 6021 National commercial banks

D-U-N-S 20-034-5846 (BR)
CANADIAN NATURAL RESOURCES LIM-ITED
9900 100 Ave Suite 220, Fort St. John, BC, V1J 5S7
(250) 785-3085
Emp Here 50
SIC 1311 Crude petroleum and natural gas

D-U-N-S 20-609-2731 (SL)
CASCADE SERVICES LTD
9619 81 Ave, Fort St. John, BC, V1J 6P6
(250) 785-0236
Emp Here 130 *Sales* 27,695,850
SIC 1389 Oil and gas field services, nec
Dir Ken Wagner
Genl Mgr Doug Marquardt

D-U-N-S 20-253-8224 (SL)
CHEBUCTO VENTURES CORP
TIM HORTONS
8911 117 Ave, Fort St. John, BC, V1J 6B8
(250) 787-7501
Emp Here 88 *Sales* 3,118,504
SIC 5812 Eating places

D-U-N-S 20-877-3338 (BR)
CLEAN HARBORS INDUSTRIAL SERVICES CANADA, INC
6715 85th Ave, Fort St. John, BC, V1J 4J3
(250) 785-8500
Emp Here 30
SIC 1382 Oil and gas exploration services

D-U-N-S 25-516-3024 (BR)
CORRPRO CANADA, INC
(*Suby of* Aegion Corporation)
8607 101 St, Fort St. John, BC, V1J 5K4
(250) 787-9100
Emp Here 1,500
SIC 8711 Engineering services

D-U-N-S 25-453-1619 (BR)
DEVON CANADA CORPORATION
DEVON CANADA
10514 87 Ave, Fort St. John, BC, V1J 5K7

Emp Here 80

SIC 1382 Oil and gas exploration services

D-U-N-S 24-523-3106 (BR)
DOLEMO DEVELOPMENT CORPORATION
STONEBRIDGE HOTEL - FORT ST JOHN
(*Suby of* Bulova Developments Inc)
9223 100 St, Fort St. John, BC, V1J 3X3
(250) 263-6880
Emp Here 50
SIC 7011 Hotels and motels

D-U-N-S 24-336-6619 (SL)
FSJ L.A.N.D. TRANSPORT LP
8140 Alaska Rd, Fort St. John, BC, V1J 4H8
(250) 785-8935
Emp Here 380 *Sales* 83,043,360
SIC 1389 Oil and gas field services, nec
VP Bruce Mullen

D-U-N-S 24-906-5632 (BR)
FINNING INTERNATIONAL INC
FINNING CANADA
(*Suby of* Finning International Inc)
10755 Finning Frontage Rd, Fort St. John, BC, V1J 4H6
(250) 787-7761
Emp Here 50
SIC 5082 Construction and mining machinery

D-U-N-S 20-096-6430 (SL)
FORT MOTORS LTD
11104 Alaska Rd, Fort St. John, BC, V1J 5T5

Emp Here 56 *Sales* 27,484,800
SIC 5511 New and used car dealers
Pr Pr Brian Gentles

D-U-N-S 24-702-2965 (SL)
G & G PIZZA INC
BOSTON PIZZA
9824 100 St, Fort St. John, BC, V1J 3Y1
(250) 787-0455
Emp Here 55 *Sales* 1,992,377
SIC 5812 Eating places

D-U-N-S 24-085-3072 (BR)
GOLDER ASSOCIATES LTD
10628 Peck Lane, Fort St. John, BC, V1J 4M7
(250) 785-9281
Emp Here 20
SIC 8748 Business consulting, nec

D-U-N-S 25-267-8768 (BR)
GREAT PACIFIC INDUSTRIES INC
OVERWAITEA FOOD GROUP
10345 100 St, Fort St. John, BC, V1J 3Z2
(250) 785-2985
Emp Here 90
SIC 5411 Grocery stores

D-U-N-S 20-852-9011 (BR)
GRIMES WELL SERVICING LTD
8011 93 St, Fort St. John, BC, V1J 6X1
(250) 787-9264
Emp Here 50
SIC 1381 Drilling oil and gas wells

D-U-N-S 24-368-7105 (BR)
HELICAL PIER SYSTEMS LTD
PEACE LAND PILING
6362 265 Rd, Fort St. John, BC, V1J 4H7
(250) 785-4491
Emp Here 25
SIC 3312 Blast furnaces and steel mills

D-U-N-S 24-350-0019 (BR)
HOERBIGER (CANADA) LTD
9304 111 St, Fort St. John, BC, V1J 7J5
(250) 785-4602
Emp Here 21
SIC 3599 Industrial machinery, nec

D-U-N-S 24-089-6407 (BR)
INLAND KENWORTH LTD
INLAND KENWORTH
Gd Lcd Main, Fort St. John, BC, V1J 4H5
(250) 785-6105
Emp Here 66
SIC 5012 Automobiles and other motor vehi-

cles

D-U-N-S 24-375-5894 (BR)
INTEROUTE CONSTRUCTION LTD
DGS ASTRO PAVING
9503 79th Ave, Fort St. John, BC, V1J 4J3
(250) 787-7283
Emp Here 100
SIC 1611 Highway and street construction

D-U-N-S 25-678-7961 (BR)
JAMES WESTERN STAR TRUCK & TRAILER LTD
9604 112 St, Fort St. John, BC, V1J 7H2
(250) 785-1475
Emp Here 35
SIC 5084 Industrial machinery and equipment

D-U-N-S 24-398-3087 (BR)
JORDAN ENTERPRISES LIMITED
QUALITY INN NORTHERN GRAND HOTEL
9830 100 Ave, Fort St. John, BC, V1J 1Y5
(250) 787-0521
Emp Here 100
SIC 7011 Hotels and motels

D-U-N-S 25-761-9585 (BR)
LOBLAWS INC
SUNSPUN SHOPPING SERVICE
9116 107 St, Fort St. John, BC, V1J 6E3
(250) 262-2000
Emp Here 50
SIC 5411 Grocery stores

D-U-N-S 20-301-5482 (SL)
MACRO PIPELINES INC
6807 100 Ave, Fort St. John, BC, V1J 4J2
(250) 785-0033
Emp Here 100 *Sales* 14,592,140
SIC 4619 Pipelines, nec
Pr Pr Frank Miles
Dir Mike Nielsen

D-U-N-S 20-966-3975 (BR)
MCCOY CORPORATION
REAL MCCOY SERVICE CENTER, THE
9604 112 St, Fort St. John, BC, V1J 7H2
(250) 261-6700
Emp Here 25
SIC 7699 Repair services, nec

D-U-N-S 24-332-5263 (BR)
MCELHANNEY ASSOCIATES LAND SUR-VEYING LTD
MCELHANNEY LAND SURVEYORS
8808 72 St, Fort St. John, BC, V1J 6M2
(250) 787-0356
Emp Here 600
SIC 8713 Surveying services

D-U-N-S 24-806-8348 (SL)
MURRAY CHEVROLET PONTIAC BUICK GMC FORT ST. JOHN
11204 Alaska Rd, Fort St. John, BC, V1J 5T5
(250) 787-7280
Emp Here 65 *Sales* 32,656,000
SIC 5511 New and used car dealers
Pr Clark Lang

D-U-N-S 20-527-9453 (BR)
NAV CANADA
Gd, Fort St. John, BC, V1J 4H5
(250) 787-0175
Emp Here 20
SIC 4581 Airports, flying fields, and services

D-U-N-S 20-302-0094 (BR)
NCSG CRANE & HEAVY HAUL SERVICES LTD
6720 87a Ave, Fort St. John, BC, V1J 0B4
(250) 787-0930
Emp Here 25
SIC 7353 Heavy construction equipment rental

D-U-N-S 25-058-0404 (BR)
NEWALTA CORPORATION
6228 249 Rd, Fort St. John, BC, V1J 4J3

(250) 789-3051
Emp Here 20
SIC 4953 Refuse systems

D-U-N-S 20-280-3313   (BR)
NINE ENERGY CANADA INC
IPS
9404 73 Ave, Fort St. John, BC, V1J 4H7
(250) 785-4210
Emp Here 111
SIC 1389 Oil and gas field services, nec

D-U-N-S 24-089-7124   (BR)
NORTHERN LIGHTS COLLEGE
9820 120 Ave, Fort St. John, BC, V1J 6K1
(250) 785-6981
Emp Here 50
SIC 8222 Junior colleges

D-U-N-S 24-322-1384   (SL)
PATCH POINT LIMITED PARTNERSHIP
Site 7 Comp 16 Ss 2 Lcd Main, Fort St. John,
BC, V1J 4M7
(250) 787-0787
Emp Here 150   *Sales* 28,507,450
SIC 1629 Heavy construction, nec
 Richard Kuzyk
 Len Torgerson
Rgnl Mgr Wayne Baron
 Kevin Dawley
 Peter Venables
 Michael Hellman

D-U-N-S 25-149-2013   (BR)
PEMBINA PIPELINE CORPORATION
10919 89 Ave, Fort St. John, BC, V1J 6V2
(250) 785-6791
Emp Here 25
SIC 4612 Crude petroleum pipelines

D-U-N-S 20-845-2776   (BR)
PENN WEST PETROLEUM LTD
10511 100 Ave, Fort St. John, BC, V1J 1Z1
(250) 785-8363
Emp Here 40
SIC 2911 Petroleum refining

D-U-N-S 20-775-7381   (BR)
PETROWEST CIVIL SERVICES LP
S.O.S. OILFIELD SAFETY
8223 93 St, Fort St. John, BC, V1J 6X1
(250) 787-0969
Emp Here 20
SIC 1422 Crushed and broken limestone

D-U-N-S 24-805-1307   (BR)
POMEROY LODGING LP
FORT ST. JOHN POMEROY INN & SUITES
9320 Alaska Rd, Fort St. John, BC, V1J 6L5
(250) 262-3030
Emp Here 50
SIC 7011 Hotels and motels

D-U-N-S 25-517-6273   (BR)
PYRAMID CORPORATION
12051 242 Rd, Fort St. John, BC, V1J 4M7
(250) 787-2511
Emp Here 40
SIC 1731 Electrical work

D-U-N-S 24-929-8696   (SL)
RHYASON CONTRACTING LTD
7307 Bipa Rd E, Fort St. John, BC, V1J 4M6
(250) 785-0515
Emp Here 80   *Sales* 14,008,454
SIC 1623 Water, sewer, and utility lines
Pr Pr Greg Rhyason
Mgr Robin Cant

D-U-N-S 25-523-0260   (BR)
ROYAL BANK OF CANADA
RBC
(*Suby of* Royal Bank Of Canada)
10312 100 St, Fort St. John, BC, V1J 3Z1
(250) 787-0681
Emp Here 43
SIC 6021 National commercial banks

D-U-N-S 25-098-9191   (BR)

SCHOOL DISTRICT NO. 60 (PEACE RIVER NORTH)
DUNCAN CRAN ELEMENTARY SCHOOL
8130 89 Ave, Fort St. John, BC, V1J 5S5
(250) 787-0417
Emp Here 35
SIC 8211 Elementary and secondary schools

D-U-N-S 25-288-4721   (BR)
SCHOOL DISTRICT NO. 60 (PEACE RIVER NORTH)
DR KEARNEY JUNIOR SECONDARY SCHOOL
10723 92 St, Fort St. John, BC, V1J 3J4
(250) 785-8378
Emp Here 40
SIC 8211 Elementary and secondary schools

D-U-N-S 20-713-5331   (BR)
SCHOOL DISTRICT NO. 60 (PEACE RIVER NORTH)
FT ST JOHN CENTRAL SCHOOL
10215 99 Ave, Fort St. John, BC, V1J 1V5
(250) 785-4511
Emp Here 50
SIC 8211 Elementary and secondary schools

D-U-N-S 20-127-4961   (BR)
SCHOOL DISTRICT NO. 60 (PEACE RIVER NORTH)
STUDENT SUPPORT SERVICES
10112 105 Ave, Fort St. John, BC, V1J 4S4
(250) 262-6000
Emp Here 30
SIC 8748 Business consulting, nec

D-U-N-S 20-026-8626   (BR)
SCHOOL DISTRICT NO. 60 (PEACE RIVER NORTH)
CLEARVIEW ELEMENTARY JR SEC-ONDARY SCHOOL
10716 97 Ave, Fort St. John, BC, V1J 6L7
(250) 785-1577
Emp Here 27
SIC 8211 Elementary and secondary schools

D-U-N-S 20-656-2477   (BR)
SCHOOL DISTRICT NO. 60 (PEACE RIVER NORTH)
NORTH PEACE SECONDARY SCHOOL
9304 86 St, Fort St. John, BC, V1J 6L9
(250) 785-4429
Emp Here 75
SIC 8211 Elementary and secondary schools

D-U-N-S 20-591-3374   (BR)
SCHOOL DISTRICT NO. 60 (PEACE RIVER NORTH)
BERC BOWES JUNIOR SECONDARY SCHOOL
9816 106 St, Fort St. John, BC, V1J 4E6
(250) 785-6717
Emp Here 40
SIC 8211 Elementary and secondary schools

D-U-N-S 20-030-6301   (BR)
SCHOOL DISTRICT NO. 60 (PEACE RIVER NORTH)
ROBERT OGILVIE ELEMENTARY SCHOOL
9907 86 St, Fort St. John, BC, V1J 3G4
(250) 785-3704
Emp Here 42
SIC 8211 Elementary and secondary schools

D-U-N-S 20-713-5398   (BR)
SCHOOL DISTRICT NO. 60 (PEACE RIVER NORTH)
JUNIOR ALTERNATE SCHOOL
10511 99 Ave, Fort St. John, BC, V1J 1V6
(250) 261-5660
Emp Here 50
SIC 8211 Elementary and secondary schools

D-U-N-S 20-591-3358   (BR)
SCHOOL DISTRICT NO. 60 (PEACE RIVER NORTH)
C M FINCH ELEMENTARY SCHOOL
10904 106 Ave, Fort St. John, BC, V1J 4G3

(250) 785-8580
Emp Here 30
SIC 8211 Elementary and secondary schools

D-U-N-S 20-165-2307   (BR)
SCHOOL DISTRICT NO. 60 (PEACE RIVER NORTH)
BERT AMBROSE SCHOOL
9616 115 Ave, Fort St. John, BC, V1J 2Y1
(250) 785-2321
Emp Here 30
SIC 8211 Elementary and secondary schools

D-U-N-S 25-154-5414   (BR)
SCHOOL DISTRICT NO. 60 (PEACE RIVER NORTH)
ALWIN HOLLAND ELEMENTARY SCHOOL
10615 96 St, Fort St. John, BC, V1J 3R3
(250) 785-6125
Emp Here 30
SIC 8211 Elementary and secondary schools

D-U-N-S 20-512-3875   (BR)
SHELL CANADA LIMITED
6814 Airport Rd Rr 1 Lcd Main, Fort St. John,
BC, V1J 4M6
(250) 785-2854
Emp Here 40
SIC 1382 Oil and gas exploration services

D-U-N-S 20-358-7139   (BR)
SOBEYS WEST INC
SAFEWAY
9123 100 Ave, Fort St. John, BC, V1J 1X6
(250) 261-5477
Emp Here 50
SIC 5411 Grocery stores

D-U-N-S 24-335-8491   (BR)
STAPLES CANADA INC
STAPLES THE BUSINESS DEPOT
(*Suby of* Staples, Inc.)
9600 93 Ave Suite 3010, Fort St. John, BC,
V1J 5Z2
(250) 794-3000
Emp Here 20
SIC 5943 Stationery stores

D-U-N-S 24-616-6883   (BR)
STONEWATER GROUP OF FRANCHISES
MR MIKE STEAKHOUSE
(*Suby of* Stonewater Group Of Franchises)
9324 Alaska Rd, Fort St. John, BC, V1J 6L5
(250) 262-4151
Emp Here 80
SIC 5812 Eating places

D-U-N-S 24-685-7291   (BR)
SUNCOR ENERGY INC
11527 Alaska Rd, Fort St. John, BC, V1J 6N2
(250) 787-8200
Emp Here 100
SIC 2911 Petroleum refining

D-U-N-S 24-340-2414   (BR)
SWANBERG BROS TRUCKING LP
(*Suby of* Swanberg Bros Trucking LP)
Gd Lcd Main, Fort St. John, BC, V1J 4H5
(250) 785-6975
Emp Here 60
SIC 4212 Local trucking, without storage

D-U-N-S 25-899-0597   (BR)
TARPON ENERGY SERVICES LTD
SYNTECH ENERFLEX
10459 Struce St, Fort St. John, BC, V1J 4M7
(250) 785-9072
Emp Here 32
SIC 1389 Oil and gas field services, nec

D-U-N-S 20-280-3487   (BR)
TECHMATION ELECTRIC & CONTROLS LTD
8708 107 St, Fort St. John, BC, V1J 5R6
(250) 261-6532
Emp Here 20
SIC 1389 Oil and gas field services, nec

D-U-N-S 24-334-8278   (BR)

TELFORD SERVICES GROUP, INC
HYLAND 2000 INDUSTRIES
8819 101 St, Fort St. John, BC, V1J 5K4

Emp Here 20
SIC 1389 Oil and gas field services, nec

D-U-N-S 24-732-0641   (BR)
TRANS PEACE CONSTRUCTION (1987) LTD
BUTLER BUILDING & OILFIELD INSULA-TION
7315 93 Ave, Fort St. John, BC, V1J 1C8
(250) 785-6926
Emp Here 25
SIC 1389 Oil and gas field services, nec

D-U-N-S 20-743-1920   (BR)
TRICAN WELL SERVICE LTD
11003 91 Ave, Fort St. John, BC, V1J 6G7
(250) 787-8881
Emp Here 30
SIC 1389 Oil and gas field services, nec

D-U-N-S 20-046-9729   (BR)
WSP CANADA INC
FOCUS SURVEYS
10716 100 Ave, Fort St. John, BC, V1J 1Z3
(250) 787-0300
Emp Here 100
SIC 8713 Surveying services

D-U-N-S 20-515-7147   (BR)
WAL-MART CANADA CORP
WALMART
9007 96a St, Fort St. John, BC, V1J 7B6
(250) 261-5544
Emp Here 300
SIC 5311 Department stores

Fraser Lake, BC V0J
Bulkley - Nechako County

D-U-N-S 20-713-5034   (BR)
BOARD OF EDUCATION OF SCHOOL DIS-TRICT NO. 91 (NECHAKO LAKE), THE
FRASER LAKE ELEMENTARY SECONDARY
110 Chowsunket St, Fraser Lake, BC, V0J 1S0
(250) 699-6233
Emp Here 50
SIC 8211 Elementary and secondary schools

D-U-N-S 24-152-6698   (BR)
WEST FRASER MILLS LTD
FRASER LAKE SAWMILLS
6626 Highway 16 E, Fraser Lake, BC, V0J 1S0
(250) 699-6235
Emp Here 250
SIC 2621 Paper mills

Fruitvale, BC V0G
Kootenay Boundary County

D-U-N-S 25-820-5731   (BR)
SCHOOL DISTRICT # 20 (KOOTENAY-COLUMBIA)
FRUITVALE ELEMENTARY SCHOOL
(*Suby of* School District # 20 (Kootenay-Columbia))
1867 Columbia Gardens Rd, Fruitvale, BC,
V0G 1L0
(250) 367-7541
Emp Here 39
SIC 8211 Elementary and secondary schools

Gabriola, BC V0R
Nanaimo County

D-U-N-S 20-031-5872   (BR)

SCHOOL DISTRICT NO. 68 (NANAIMO-LADYSMITH)
GABRIOLA ELEMENTARY SCHOOL
680 North Rd, Gabriola, BC, V0R 1X0
(250) 247-9342
Emp Here 25
SIC 8211 Elementary and secondary schools

Garibaldi Highlands, BC V0N
Squamish - Lillooet County

D-U-N-S 20-918-6832   (SL)
A. J. FOREST PRODUCTS LTD
59952 Squamish Valley Rd, Garibaldi Highlands, BC, V0N 1T0
(604) 898-3712
Emp Here 24   *Sales* 2,261,782
SIC 2421 Sawmills and planing mills, general

D-U-N-S 20-713-6495   (BR)
CONSEIL SCOLAIRE FRANCOPHONE DE LA COLOMBIE BRITANNIQUE
GARIBALDI HIGHLANDS ELEMENTARY SCHOOL
2590 Portree Way, Garibaldi Highlands, BC, V0N 1T0
(604) 898-3688
Emp Here 50
SIC 8211 Elementary and secondary schools

D-U-N-S 20-064-5203   (BR)
SCHOOL DISTRICT NO. 48 (HOWE SOUND)
MAMQUAM ELEMENTARY
40266 Government Rd, Garibaldi Highlands, BC, V0N 1T0
(604) 898-3601
Emp Here 38
SIC 8211 Elementary and secondary schools

D-U-N-S 20-591-3606   (BR)
SCHOOL DISTRICT NO. 48 (HOWE SOUND)
GARIBALDI HIGHLANDS ELEMENTARY SCHOOL
2590 Portree Way, Garibaldi Highlands, BC, V0N 1T0
(604) 898-3688
Emp Here 25
SIC 8211 Elementary and secondary schools

D-U-N-S 25-260-1232   (SL)
SEA TO SKY HOTEL INC
BEST WESTERN SEA TO SKY HOTEL
Gd, Garibaldi Highlands, BC, V0N 1T0
(604) 898-4874
Emp Here 60   *Sales* 2,626,585
SIC 7011 Hotels and motels

Genelle, BC V0G
Kootenay Boundary County

D-U-N-S 25-965-0786   (BR)
EMCON SERVICES INC
5555 Hwy 22 Genelle, BC, V0G 1G0
(250) 693-5609
Emp Here 100
SIC 1611 Highway and street construction

Gibsons, BC V0N
Sunshine Coast County

D-U-N-S 20-622-7167   (HQ)
GIBSONS BUILDING SUPPLIES LTD
924 Highway 101, Gibsons, BC, V0N 1V7
(604) 886-8141
Emp Here 38   *Emp Total* 2
Sales 10,135,137
SIC 5211 Lumber and other building materials
Pr Pr Barrie Reeves
Dir Marion Reeves

D-U-N-S 20-591-5692   (BR)
SCHOOL DISTRICT NO. 46 (SUNSHINE COAST)
CEDARGROVE ELEMENTARY SCHOOL
1196 Chaster Rd, Gibsons, BC, V0N 1V4
(604) 886-7818
Emp Here 25
SIC 8211 Elementary and secondary schools

D-U-N-S 20-043-8179   (BR)
SCHOOL DISTRICT NO. 46 (SUNSHINE COAST)
GIBSONS ELEMENTARY SCHOOL
783 School Rd, Gibsons, BC, V0N 1V9
(604) 886-2612
Emp Here 44
SIC 8211 Elementary and secondary schools

D-U-N-S 20-976-7065   (BR)
SCHOOL DISTRICT NO. 46 (SUNSHINE COAST)
857 Henry Rd, Gibsons, BC, V0N 1V2
(604) 886-9870
Emp Here 70
SIC 7349 Building maintenance services, nec

D-U-N-S 25-125-9842   (BR)
UNIFOR
CEP LOCAL 1119
1045 Gibsons Way, Gibsons, BC, V0N 1V4
(604) 886-2722
Emp Here 530
SIC 8631 Labor organizations

Gold River, BC V0P
Comox - Strathcona County

D-U-N-S 25-121-0084   (BR)
GOVERNMENT OF THE PROVINCE OF BRITISH COLUMBIA
LIQUOR DISTRIBUTION 55, DIV OF
375 Nimpkish Plz, Gold River, BC, V0P 1G0
(250) 283-2919
Emp Here 20
SIC 5921 Liquor stores

D-U-N-S 20-591-4794   (BR)
SCHOOL DISTRICT #84 (VANCOUVER ISLAND WEST)
GOLD RIVER SECONDARY SCHOOL
201 Muchalat Dr, Gold River, BC, V0P 1G0
(250) 283-2538
Emp Here 30
SIC 8211 Elementary and secondary schools

D-U-N-S 20-033-7959   (BR)
SCHOOL DISTRICT #84 (VANCOUVER ISLAND WEST)
RAY WATKINS ELEMENTARY SCHOOL
500 Trumpeter Dr, Gold River, BC, V0P 1G0
(250) 283-2220
Emp Here 28
SIC 8211 Elementary and secondary schools

D-U-N-S 24-553-6987   (BR)
WESTERN FOREST PRODUCTS INC
NOOTKA SOUND DRYLAND
300 Western Dr, Gold River, BC, V0P 1G0
(250) 283-2961
Emp Here 175
SIC 2611 Pulp mills

Golden, BC V0A
Columbia - Shuswap County

D-U-N-S 20-086-4010   (BR)
BOARD OF EDUCATION OF SCHOOL DISTRICT NO. 06 (ROCKY MOUNTAIN), THE
LADY GREY ELEMENTARY SCHOOL
620 9th St S, Golden, BC, V0A 1H0
(250) 344-6317
Emp Here 35

SIC 8211 Elementary and secondary schools

D-U-N-S 20-561-9716   (BR)
BOARD OF EDUCATION OF SCHOOL DISTRICT NO. 06 (ROCKY MOUNTAIN), THE
GOLDEN ZONE OFFICE
812 14th St S, Golden, BC, V0A 1H0
(250) 344-5068
Emp Here 20
SIC 8211 Elementary and secondary schools

D-U-N-S 20-590-5040   (BR)
BOARD OF EDUCATION OF SCHOOL DISTRICT NO. 06 (ROCKY MOUNTAIN), THE
GOLDEN SECONDARY SCHOOL
1500 9th St S, Golden, BC, V0A 1H0
(250) 344-2201
Emp Here 50
SIC 8211 Elementary and secondary schools

D-U-N-S 20-034-0623   (BR)
BOARD OF EDUCATION OF SCHOOL DISTRICT NO. 06 (ROCKY MOUNTAIN), THE
SCHOOL DISTRICT NO. 6 (ROCKY MOUNTAIN)
1000 14th Ave S, Golden, BC, V0A 1H0
(250) 344-5513
Emp Here 30
SIC 8211 Elementary and secondary schools

D-U-N-S 20-713-2239   (BR)
BOARD OF EDUCATION OF SCHOOL DISTRICT NO. 06 (ROCKY MOUNTAIN), THE
GOLDEN ALTERNATE SCHOOL
1500 9 St S, Golden, BC, V0A 1H0

Emp Here 50
SIC 8211 Elementary and secondary schools

D-U-N-S 20-797-2782   (BR)
COLLEGE OF THE ROCKIES
1305 9th St N Rr 2, Golden, BC, V0A 1H2
(250) 344-5901
Emp Here 40
SIC 8221 Colleges and universities

D-U-N-S 25-267-8966   (BR)
GREAT PACIFIC INDUSTRIES INC
OVERWAITEA FOOD GROUP
1020 10th Ave S, Golden, BC, V0A 1H0
(250) 344-5315
Emp Here 55
SIC 5411 Grocery stores

D-U-N-S 20-968-8071   (BR)
H M C SERVICES INC
521 Golden Donald Upper Rd, Golden, BC, V0A 1H1
(250) 344-5009
Emp Here 20
SIC 1611 Highway and street construction

D-U-N-S 24-657-6917   (BR)
HUBER DEVELOPMENT LTD
PRESTIGE MOUNTAINSIDE RESORT
1049 Trans Canada Hwy W, Golden, BC, V0A 1H2
(250) 344-7990
Emp Here 25
SIC 7011 Hotels and motels

D-U-N-S 25-629-7573   (BR)
HUBER DEVELOPMENT LTD
PRESTIGE HOTELS AND RESORT
1049 Trans Canada Hwy W, Golden, BC, V0A 1H2
(250) 344-7990
Emp Here 20
SIC 7011 Hotels and motels

D-U-N-S 25-365-1335   (BR)
LOUISIANA-PACIFIC CANADA LTD
LOUISIANA-PACIFIC BUILDING PRODUCTS
(*Suby of* Louisiana-Pacific Corporation)
1221 10th Ave N, Golden, BC, V0A 1H2
(250) 344-8800
Emp Here 300
SIC 2436 Softwood veneer and plywood

SIC 8211 Elementary and secondary schools

D-U-N-S 20-803-6314   (BR)
SOBEYS CAPITAL INCORPORATED
GOLDEN SOBEYS
624 9 Ave N, Golden, BC, V0A 1H0
(250) 344-2361
Emp Here 50
SIC 5411 Grocery stores

Grand Forks, BC V0H
Kootenay Boundary County

D-U-N-S 20-994-0100   (BR)
BUY-LOW FOODS LTD
7370 4th St, Grand Forks, BC, V0H 1H0
(250) 442-5560
Emp Here 28
SIC 5411 Grocery stores

D-U-N-S 25-267-8800   (BR)
GREAT PACIFIC INDUSTRIES INC
OVERWAITEA FOOD GROUP
441 Central Ave, Grand Forks, BC, V0H 1H0
(250) 442-2778
Emp Here 62
SIC 5411 Grocery stores

D-U-N-S 24-761-1390   (BR)
INTERIOR HEALTH AUTHORITY
HARDY VIEW LODGE
7649 22nd St, Grand Forks, BC, V0H 1H2
(250) 443-2146
Emp Here 50
SIC 8062 General medical and surgical hospitals

D-U-N-S 25-506-8223   (BR)
ROXUL INC
WESTERN FACILITY
6526 Industrial Pkwy, Grand Forks, BC, V0H 1H0
(250) 442-5253
Emp Here 180
SIC 3296 Mineral wool

D-U-N-S 20-688-8757   (BR)
SCHOOL DISTRICT 51 BOUNDARY
DR D A PERLEY ELEMENTARY SCHOOL
1200 Central Ave, Grand Forks, BC, V0H 1H0
(250) 442-2135
Emp Here 40
SIC 8211 Elementary and secondary schools

D-U-N-S 20-590-5149   (BR)
SCHOOL DISTRICT 51 BOUNDARY
JOHN A HUTTON ELEMENTARY SCHOOL
2575 75th Ave, Grand Forks, BC, V0H 1H2
(250) 442-8275
Emp Here 30
SIC 8211 Elementary and secondary schools

D-U-N-S 20-917-9600   (BR)
SCHOOL DISTRICT 51 BOUNDARY
GRANDFOLKS SECONDARY SCHOOL
131 Central Ave, Grand Forks, BC, V0H 1H0
(250) 442-8285
Emp Here 53
SIC 8211 Elementary and secondary schools

Grindrod, BC V0E
North Okanagan County

D-U-N-S 24-369-9733   (BR)
RITCHIE-SMITH FEEDS INC
SURE CROP FEEDS
6863 Hwy 97 N, Grindrod, BC, V0E 1Y0
(250) 838-6855
Emp Here 30
SIC 2048 Prepared feeds, nec

▲ Public Company   ■ Public Company Family Member   **HQ** Headquarters   **BR** Branch   **SL** Single Location

Hagensborg, BC V0T
Central Coast County

D-U-N-S 20-713-4938 (BR)
SCHOOL DISTRICT 49 CENTRAL COAST
*SIR ALEXANDER MCKENSIE SECONDARY
SCHOOL*
(*Suby of* School District 49 Central Coast)
1961 Mackenzie Hwy, Hagensborg, BC, V0T
1H0
(250) 982-2355
Emp Here 22
SIC 8211 Elementary and secondary schools

D-U-N-S 20-913-1221 (BR)
SCHOOL DISTRICT 49 CENTRAL COAST
CENTRAL COAST SCHOOL DISTRICT 49
(*Suby of* School District 49 Central Coast)
1962 Hwy 20, Hagensborg, BC, V0T 1H0
(250) 982-2691
Emp Here 25
SIC 8211 Elementary and secondary schools

Halfmoon Bay, BC V0N
Sunshine Coast County

D-U-N-S 20-591-5775 (BR)
**SCHOOL DISTRICT NO. 46 (SUNSHINE
COAST)**
HALFMOON BAY ELEMENTARY SCHOOL
8086 Northwood Rd, Halfmoon Bay, BC, V0N
1Y1
(604) 885-2318
Emp Here 25
SIC 8211 Elementary and secondary schools

Harrison Mills, BC V0M

D-U-N-S 20-034-7438 (SL)
PRETTY ESTATES LTD
*SANDPIPER GOLF CLUB/ROWENAS INN
ON THE RIVER*
14282 Morris Valley Rd, Harrison Mills, BC,
V0M 1L0
(604) 796-1000
Emp Here 75   *Sales* 4,565,250
SIC 7011 Hotels and motels

Hazelton, BC V0J
Kitimat - Stikine County

D-U-N-S 20-653-7354 (BR)
**COAST MOUNTAINS BOARD OF EDUCA-
TION SCHOOL DISTRICT NO. 82**
JOHN FIELD ELEMENTARY SCHOOL
3990 John Field Rd, Hazelton, BC, V0J 1Y0
(250) 842-5313
Emp Here 20
SIC 8211 Elementary and secondary schools

D-U-N-S 24-561-5401 (BR)
**COAST MOUNTAINS BOARD OF EDUCA-
TION SCHOOL DISTRICT NO. 82**
HAZELTON SECONDARY SCHOOLS
2725 62 Hwy Rr 1, Hazelton, BC, V0J 1Y0
(250) 842-5214
Emp Here 50
SIC 8211 Elementary and secondary schools

D-U-N-S 24-594-8224 (BR)
DISTRICT OF KITIMAT
*AMBULANCE   SERVICE   BRITISH
COLUMBIA*
2510 62 Hwy, Hazelton, BC, V0J 1Y1
(250) 842-5655
Emp Here 20
SIC 4119 Local passenger transportation, nec

D-U-N-S 20-344-1407 (SL)

GITXSAN SAFETY SERVICES INC
(*Suby of* Gitxsan Development Corporation)
1650 Cmineca St, Hazelton, BC, V0J 1Y0
(250) 842-6780
Emp Here 80   *Sales* 1,127,820
SIC 8748 Business consulting, nec

D-U-N-S 20-069-4656 (HQ)
**UNITED CHURCH HEALTH SERVICES SO-
CIETY, THE**
HAZELTON COMMUNITY HEALTH
(*Suby of* United Church Health Services Soci-
ety, The)
2510 62 Hwy, Hazelton, BC, V0J 1Y1
(250) 842-5556
Emp Here 51   *Emp Total* 66
Sales 4,304,681
SIC 8093 Specialty outpatient clinics, nec

Heffley Creek, BC V0E
Thompson - Nicola County

D-U-N-S 20-180-7182 (SL)
19959 YUKON INC
DELTA SUN PEAKS RESORT
3240 Village Way, Heffley Creek, BC, V0E 1Z1
(250) 578-6000
Emp Here 80   *Sales* 3,502,114
SIC 7011 Hotels and motels

Hixon, BC V0K
Fraser-Fort George County

D-U-N-S 20-105-3030 (SL)
DUNKLEY LUMBER LTD
(*Suby of* Novak Bros Contracting Ltd)
17000 Dunkley Rd Rr 1, Hixon, BC, V0K 1S1
(250) 998-4421
Emp Here 280   *Sales* 34,300,776
SIC 2421 Sawmills and planing mills, general
Pr Pr Henry Novak
 Anton (Tony) Novak
 Joe Novak

Holberg, BC V0N
Mount Waddington County

D-U-N-S 24-128-2099 (BR)
WESTERN FOREST PRODUCTS INC
HOLBERG FOREST OPERATION
1 Main St, Holberg, BC, V0N 1Z0
(250) 288-3362
Emp Here 100
SIC 2611 Pulp mills

Hope, BC V0X

D-U-N-S 20-573-3327 (BR)
**COMPAGNIE DES CHEMINS DE FER NA-
TIONAUX DU CANADA**
945 5th Ave, Hope, BC, V0X 1L0
(604) 869-5304
Emp Here 20
SIC 4011 Railroads, line-haul operating

D-U-N-S 25-654-0006 (BR)
COOPER MARKET LTD
COOPER'S FOODS
559 Old Hope Princeton Way, Hope, BC, V0X
1L4
(604) 869-3663
Emp Here 40
SIC 5411 Grocery stores

D-U-N-S 25-816-1678 (BR)

EMIL ANDERSON MAINTENANCE CO. LTD
1313 6th Ave, Hope, BC, V0X 1L4
(604) 869-7171
Emp Here 20
SIC 1611 Highway and street construction

D-U-N-S 20-992-2657 (BR)
FRASER HEALTH AUTHORITY
FRASER CANYON HOSPITAL
1275 7th Ave, Hope, BC, V0X 1L4
(604) 869-5656
Emp Here 130
SIC 8011 Offices and clinics of medical doc-
tors

D-U-N-S 20-037-7609 (BR)
FRASER VALLEY REGIONAL DISTRICT
*HOPE AND DISTRICT RECREATION AND
CULTURAL SERVICES*
1005 6th Ave, Hope, BC, V0X 1L4
(604) 869-2304
Emp Here 33
SIC 7999 Amusement and recreation, nec

D-U-N-S 25-685-2443 (BR)
NESTLE CANADA INC
NESTLE WATERS CANADA DIV
66700 Othello Rd, Hope, BC, V0X 1L1
(604) 860-4888
Emp Here 75
SIC 5149 Groceries and related products, nec

D-U-N-S 25-399-8082 (SL)
PASS CONSTRUCTION CO. LTD
1148 6th Ave Rr 4, Hope, BC, V0X 1L4

Emp Here 150   *Sales* 27,898,750
SIC 6712 Bank holding companies
 Gil Jacobs
Pr Pr Robert Hazel
Dir Chad Northcot

D-U-N-S 24-939-1905 (SL)
ROLLY'S RESTAURANT
Gd, Hope, BC, V0X 1L0
(604) 869-7448
Emp Here 50   *Sales* 1,532,175
SIC 5812 Eating places

D-U-N-S 20-591-4851 (BR)
SCHOOL DISTRICT 78
HOPE SECONDARY SCHOOL
444 Stuart St, Hope, BC, V0X 1L0
(604) 869-9971
Emp Here 30
SIC 8211 Elementary and secondary schools

D-U-N-S 20-021-6617 (BR)
SCHOOL DISTRICT 78
COQUIHALLA ELEMENTARY SCHOOL
455 6th Ave, Hope, BC, V0X 1L0
(604) 869-9904
Emp Here 30
SIC 8211 Elementary and secondary schools

D-U-N-S 20-591-4844 (BR)
SCHOOL DISTRICT 78
C. E. BARRY INTERMEDIATE SCHOOL
444 Queen, Hope, BC, V0X 1L0

Emp Here 25
SIC 8211 Elementary and secondary schools

Hornby Island, BC V0R
Comox - Strathcona County

D-U-N-S 20-541-6477 (BR)
CANADA POST CORPORATION
HORNBY ISLAND CO OP STORE
5875 Central, Hornby Island, BC, V0R 1Z0
(250) 335-1121
Emp Here 20
SIC 4311 U.s. postal service

Houston, BC V0J
Bulkley - Nechako County

D-U-N-S 20-511-9779 (BR)
CANADIAN FOREST PRODUCTS LTD
CANFOR
1397 Morice River Forest Service Rd Rr 1,
Houston, BC, V0J 1Z1
(250) 845-5200
Emp Here 350
SIC 2421 Sawmills and planing mills, general

D-U-N-S 20-700-6573 (BR)
FINNING INTERNATIONAL INC
FINNING (CANADA)
(*Suby of* Finning International Inc)
Hwy 16 W, Houston, BC, V0J 1Z0
(250) 845-2213
Emp Here 50
SIC 5082 Construction and mining machinery

D-U-N-S 20-965-2838 (BR)
HUCKLEBERRY MINES LTD
Gd, Houston, BC, V0J 1Z0
(604) 517-4223
Emp Here 220
SIC 1021 Copper ores

D-U-N-S 24-682-9337 (BR)
INLAND KENWORTH
PARKER PACIFIC
226 Nadina Ave, Houston, BC, V0J 1Z0
(250) 845-2333
Emp Here 25
SIC 5511 New and used car dealers

D-U-N-S 20-357-5220 (BR)
PINNACLE RENEWABLE ENERGY INC
Gd, Houston, BC, V0J 1Z0
(250) 845-5254
Emp Here 20
SIC 2499 Wood products, nec

D-U-N-S 24-995-4942 (SL)
**PLEASANT VALLEY REMANUFACTURING
LTD**
3 Km Morice River Rd, Houston, BC, V0J 1Z0
(250) 845-7585
Emp Here 40   *Sales* 3,793,956
SIC 2421 Sawmills and planing mills, general

D-U-N-S 20-716-8795 (BR)
**SCHOOL DISTRICT NO. 54 (BULKLEY VAL-
LEY)**
SILVERTHORNE ELEMENTARY SCHOOL
3455 13th Street, Houston, BC, V0J 1Z0
(250) 845-2228
Emp Here 20
SIC 8211 Elementary and secondary schools

D-U-N-S 20-069-4672 (BR)
**SMITHERS SCHOOL BOARD DISTRICT #54
(BULKLEY VALLEY)**
HOUSTON SECONDARY SCHOOL
(*Suby of* Smithers School Board District #54
(Bulkley Valley))
1771 Hungerford Dr, Houston, BC, V0J 1Z0
(250) 845-7217
Emp Here 45
SIC 8211 Elementary and secondary schools

D-U-N-S 25-000-5758 (BR)
**SMITHERS SCHOOL BOARD DISTRICT #54
(BULKLEY VALLEY)**
TWAIN SULLIVAN ELEMENTARY
(*Suby of* Smithers School Board District #54
(Bulkley Valley))
1771 Hungerford Dr, Houston, BC, V0J 1Z0
(250) 845-2227
Emp Here 20
SIC 8211 Elementary and secondary schools

D-U-N-S 20-700-0337 (BR)
WEST FRASER MILLS LTD
Gd, Houston, BC, V0J 1Z0

---

(250) 845-2322
Emp Here 300
SIC 2621 Paper mills

Hudson'S Hope, BC V0C

D-U-N-S 20-572-4375   (BR)
BRITISH COLUMBIA HYDRO AND POWER AUTHORITY
BC HYDRO
20632 Peace Canyon Rd, Hudson'S Hope, BC, V0C 1V0
(250) 783-7400
Emp Here 20
SIC 4911 Electric services

D-U-N-S 20-713-5349   (BR)
SCHOOL DISTRICT NO. 60 (PEACE RIVER NORTH)
HUDSON'S HOPE SCHOOL
10441 Holland, Hudson'S Hope, BC, V0C 1V0
(250) 783-9994
Emp Here 35
SIC 8211 Elementary and secondary schools

Invermere, BC V0A
East Kootenay County

D-U-N-S 20-917-9766   (BR)
BOARD OF EDUCATION OF SCHOOL DISTRICT NO. 06 (ROCKY MOUNTAIN), THE
DAVID THOMPSON SECONDARY SCHOOL
1535 14th St Suite 4, Invermere, BC, V0A 1K4
(250) 342-9213
Emp Here 78
SIC 8211 Elementary and secondary schools

D-U-N-S 20-156-0740   (BR)
BOARD OF EDUCATION OF SCHOOL DISTRICT NO. 06 (ROCKY MOUNTAIN), THE
LAIRD, J ALFRED ELEMENTARY SCHOOL
1202 13th Ave, Invermere, BC, V0A 1K4
(250) 342-6232
Emp Here 25
SIC 8211 Elementary and secondary schools

D-U-N-S 20-317-0550   (BR)
CANADIAN TIRE CORPORATION, LIMITED
480 Sarah Rd, Invermere, BC, V0A 1K3
(250) 342-4433
Emp Here 49
SIC 5531 Auto and home supply stores

D-U-N-S 24-336-1412   (BR)
CORPORATION OF THE DISTRICT OF INVERMERE, THE
INVERMERE FIRE/RESCUE
626 4th St, Invermere, BC, V0A 1K0
(250) 342-3200
Emp Here 30
SIC 7389 Business services, nec

D-U-N-S 20-870-7526   (BR)
HUDSON'S BAY COMPANY
FIELDS STORES
516 13th Ave Rr 4, Invermere, BC, V0A 1K0
(250) 341-6173
Emp Here 25
SIC 5311 Department stores

D-U-N-S 24-554-0984   (BR)
INTERIOR HEALTH AUTHORITY
INVERMERE & DISTRICT HOSPITAL
850 10 Ave, Invermere, BC, V0A 1K0
(250) 342-9201
Emp Here 70
SIC 8062 General medical and surgical hospitals

D-U-N-S 24-040-6673   (BR)
NOHELS GROUP INC
4854 Athalmer Rd, Invermere, BC, V0A 1K3

---

(250) 342-8849
Emp Here 50
SIC 1629 Heavy construction, nec

Jaffray, BC V0B
East Kootenay County

D-U-N-S 25-534-0036   (BR)
BUL RIVER MINERAL CORPORATION
BUL RIVER MINERAL
Gd, Jaffray, BC, V0B 1T0
(250) 429-3711
Emp Here 50
SIC 1081 Metal mining services

D-U-N-S 20-713-2171   (BR)
SCHOOL DISTRICT NO 5 (SOUTHEAST KOOTENAY)
JAFFRAY SCHOOL
7355 Village Loop Rd, Jaffray, BC, V0B 1T0
(250) 429-3211
Emp Here 50
SIC 8211 Elementary and secondary schools

Jordan River, BC V9Z
Capital County

D-U-N-S 25-917-1577   (BR)
WESTERN FOREST PRODUCTS INC
JORDAN RIVER FOREST OPERATION
11793 West Coast Rd, Jordan River, BC, V9Z 1L1

Emp Here 21
SIC 2611 Pulp mills

Kamloops, BC V1S
Thompson - Nicola County

D-U-N-S 24-957-2892   (BR)
COCA-COLA REFRESHMENTS CANADA COMPANY
(*Suby of* The Coca-Cola Company)
1484 Iron Mask Rd, Kamloops, BC, V1S 1C7
(250) 374-7389
Emp Here 40
SIC 5149 Groceries and related products, nec

D-U-N-S 25-287-5778   (BR)
COSTCO WHOLESALE CANADA LTD
COSTCO
(*Suby of* Costco Wholesale Corporation)
1675 Versatile Dr, Kamloops, BC, V1S 1W7
(250) 374-5336
Emp Here 240
SIC 5099 Durable goods, nec

D-U-N-S 25-792-6857   (HQ)
DAWNAL QUICK SERVE LTD
MCDONALD'S RESTAURANT
(*Suby of* Dawnal Quick Serve Ltd)
1465 Trans Canada Hwy W, Kamloops, BC, V1S 1A1
(250) 374-1922
Emp Here 80   *Emp Total* 250
Sales 7,514,952
SIC 5812 Eating places
Pr Pr Al Gozda

D-U-N-S 24-340-2703   (BR)
FGL SPORTS LTD
ATMOSPHERE
1320 Trans Canada Hwy W Unit Y0500, Kamloops, BC, V1S 1J2
(250) 314-1602
Emp Here 75
SIC 5941 Sporting goods and bicycle shops

D-U-N-S 20-860-5563   (BR)

GLENTEL INC
WIRELESS WAVES
1320 Trans Canada Hwy W, Kamloops, BC, V1S 1J2
(250) 372-1868
Emp Here 25
SIC 4899 Communication services, nec

D-U-N-S 25-301-2462   (BR)
HUDSON'S BAY COMPANY
BAY, THE
1320 Trans Canada Hwy W Suite 300, Kamloops, BC, V1S 1J1
(250) 372-8271
Emp Here 100
SIC 5311 Department stores

D-U-N-S 20-913-4535   (SL)
INLAND GLASS & ALUMINUM LIMITED
1820 Kryczka Pl, Kamloops, BC, V1S 1S4
(250) 374-7306
Emp Here 50   *Sales* 3,648,035
SIC 1793 Glass and glazing work

D-U-N-S 24-727-4561   (BR)
INTEGRATED DISTRIBUTION SYSTEMS LIMITED PARTNERSHIP
WAJAX EQUIPMENT
1880 Kryczka Pl, Kamloops, BC, V1S 1S4
(250) 374-5055
Emp Here 20
SIC 5084 Industrial machinery and equipment

D-U-N-S 25-603-7094   (HQ)
INTEGRATED PROACTION CORP
IPAC
(*Suby of* Integrated Proaction Corp)
1425 Hugh Allan Dr, Kamloops, BC, V1S 1J3
(250) 828-7977
Emp Here 35   *Emp Total* 50
Sales 2,626,585
SIC 7389 Business services, nec

D-U-N-S 24-839-0890   (SL)
KAMLOOPS TOWNE LODGE LTD
1250 Rogers Way, Kamloops, BC, V1S 1N5
(250) 828-6660
Emp Here 50   *Sales* 2,188,821
SIC 7011 Hotels and motels

D-U-N-S 24-656-6202   (BR)
KINDER MORGAN CANADA INC
2355 Trans Canada Hwy W, Kamloops, BC, V1S 1A7
(250) 371-4000
Emp Here 40
SIC 4612 Crude petroleum pipelines

D-U-N-S 20-027-1067   (BR)
SCHOOL DISTRICT 73 (KAMLOOPS/THOMPSON)
ABERDEEN ELEMENTARY SCHOOL
2191 Van Horne Dr, Kamloops, BC, V1S 1L9
(250) 372-5844
Emp Here 32
SIC 8211 Elementary and secondary schools

D-U-N-S 24-345-9570   (BR)
SEARS CANADA INC
1320 Trans Canada Hwy W Suite 275, Kamloops, BC, V1S 1J2
(250) 374-6611
Emp Here 200
SIC 5311 Department stores

Kamloops, BC V2B
Thompson - Nicola County

D-U-N-S 25-481-3249   (BR)
COOPER MARKET LTD
COOPER'S FOODS
3435 Westsyde Rd Suite 18, Kamloops, BC, V2B 7H1
(250) 579-5414
Emp Here 30

SIC 5411 Grocery stores

D-U-N-S 25-773-0192   (BR)
COOPER MARKET LTD
1800 Tranquille Rd Unit 38, Kamloops, BC, V2B 3L9
(250) 376-5757
Emp Here 70
SIC 5411 Grocery stores

D-U-N-S 24-383-7817   (BR)
DAWNAL QUICK SERVE LTD
MCDONALD'S
661 Fortune Dr, Kamloops, BC, V2B 2K7
(250) 376-0222
Emp Here 100
SIC 5812 Eating places

D-U-N-S 25-903-2431   (BR)
DENCAN RESTAURANTS INC
DENNY'S RESTAURANT
(*Suby of* Northland Properties Corporation)
898 Tranquille Rd Suite 77, Kamloops, BC, V2B 3J4
(250) 554-4480
Emp Here 45
SIC 5812 Eating places

D-U-N-S 25-451-0167   (BR)
GOVERNING COUNCIL OF THE SALVATION ARMY IN CANADA, THE
GOVERNING COUNCIL OF THE SALVATION ARMY IN CANADA, THE
344 Poplar St, Kamloops, BC, V2B 4B8
(250) 554-1611
Emp Here 20
SIC 8661 Religious organizations

D-U-N-S 24-777-0092   (SL)
HIGH COUNTRY HEALTH CARE INC
1800 Tranquille Rd Suite 18, Kamloops, BC, V2B 3L9
(250) 376-7417
Emp Here 50   *Sales* 1,969,939
SIC 8322 Individual and family services

D-U-N-S 24-381-1457   (BR)
INLAND RESTAURANTS (KELOWNA) LTD
WENDY'S
(*Suby of* Inland Restaurants (Kelowna) Ltd)
800 Fortune Dr Unit 6500, Kamloops, BC, V2B 2L5
(250) 376-4155
Emp Here 35
SIC 5812 Eating places

D-U-N-S 20-968-8154   (HQ)
INTERIOR COMMUNITY SERVICES
FAMILY THERAPY CENTRE
(*Suby of* Interior Community Services)
765 Tranquille Rd, Kamloops, BC, V2B 3J3
(250) 376-3511
Emp Here 46   *Emp Total* 50
Sales 3,575,074
SIC 8641 Civic and social associations

D-U-N-S 24-309-1688   (BR)
INTERIOR HEALTH AUTHORITY
APPLE LANE TERTIARY MENTAL HEALTH GERIATRIC UNIT
945 Southill St Unit 200, Kamloops, BC, V2B 7Z9
(250) 554-5590
Emp Here 76
SIC 8062 General medical and surgical hospitals

D-U-N-S 25-369-3402   (BR)
INTERIOR SAVINGS CREDIT UNION
430 Tranquille Rd Suite 100, Kamloops, BC, V2B 3H1
(250) 376-6255
Emp Here 30
SIC 6062 State credit unions

D-U-N-S 25-746-4644   (BR)
JUUSOLA, JACK SALES LTD
CANADIAN TIRE 356
944 8th St, Kamloops, BC, V2B 2X5

---

(250) 376-2013
Emp Here 30
SIC 5531 Auto and home supply stores

D-U-N-S 20-299-2876 (BR)
NAV CANADA
3100 Aviation Way, Kamloops, BC, V2B 7W1
(250) 376-6547
Emp Here 45
SIC 4899 Communication services, nec

D-U-N-S 25-955-1620 (SL)
RKL FOODS LTD
A & W RESTAURANTS
750 Fortune Dr Suite 7a, Kamloops, BC, V2B 2L2
(250) 376-6632
Emp Here 60   *Sales* 1,824,018
SIC 5812 Eating places

D-U-N-S 24-493-1804 (BR)
ROYAL BANK OF CANADA
RBC
(*Suby of* Royal Bank Of Canada)
789 Fortune Dr, Kamloops, BC, V2B 2L3
(250) 376-8822
Emp Here 30
SIC 6021 National commercial banks

D-U-N-S 20-027-0549 (BR)
SCHOOL DISTRICT 73 (KAM-LOOPS/THOMPSON)
BERT EDWARDS ELEMENTARY SCHOOL
711 Windsor Ave, Kamloops, BC, V2B 2B7
(250) 376-2205
Emp Here 30
SIC 8211 Elementary and secondary schools

D-U-N-S 25-107-8176 (BR)
SCHOOL DISTRICT 73 (KAM-LOOPS/THOMPSON)
WESTSYDE SECONDARY SCHOOL
855 Bebek Rd, Kamloops, BC, V2B 6P2
(250) 579-9271
Emp Here 55
SIC 8211 Elementary and secondary schools

D-U-N-S 25-825-7310 (BR)
SCHOOL DISTRICT 73 (KAM-LOOPS/THOMPSON)
PARKCREST ELEMENTARY SCHOOL
2170 Parkcrest Ave, Kamloops, BC, V2B 4Y1
(250) 554-2368
Emp Here 33
SIC 8211 Elementary and secondary schools

D-U-N-S 20-024-4742 (BR)
SCHOOL DISTRICT 73 (KAM-LOOPS/THOMPSON)
ARTHUR STEVENSON ELEMENTARY
2890 Bank Rd, Kamloops, BC, V2B 6Y7
(250) 579-9284
Emp Here 26
SIC 8211 Elementary and secondary schools

D-U-N-S 20-027-0606 (BR)
SCHOOL DISTRICT 73 (KAM-LOOPS/THOMPSON)
WESTSYDE ELEMENTARY SCHOOL
3550 Westsyde Rd, Kamloops, BC, V2B 7H4

Emp Here 20
SIC 8211 Elementary and secondary schools

D-U-N-S 25-015-2477 (BR)
SCHOOL DISTRICT 73 (KAM-LOOPS/THOMPSON)
KAY BINGHAM ELEMENTARY SCHOOL
950 Southill St, Kamloops, BC, V2B 5M2
(250) 376-5586
Emp Here 30
SIC 8211 Elementary and secondary schools

D-U-N-S 25-015-1503 (BR)
SCHOOL DISTRICT 73 (KAM-LOOPS/THOMPSON)
GEORGE HILLIARD ELEMENTARY SCHOOL

985 Holt St, Kamloops, BC, V2B 5H1
(250) 376-7253
Emp Here 25
SIC 8211 Elementary and secondary schools

D-U-N-S 20-026-8733 (BR)
SCHOOL DISTRICT 73 (KAM-LOOPS/THOMPSON)
DAVID THOMPSON ELEMENTARY SCHOOL
1051 Pine Springs Rd, Kamloops, BC, V2B 7W3
(250) 579-9228
Emp Here 31
SIC 8211 Elementary and secondary schools

D-U-N-S 20-653-2819 (BR)
SCHOOL DISTRICT 73 (KAM-LOOPS/THOMPSON)
A E PERRY ELEMENTARY
1380 Sherbrooke Ave, Kamloops, BC, V2B 1W9
(250) 376-6224
Emp Here 25
SIC 8211 Elementary and secondary schools

D-U-N-S 20-156-7752 (BR)
SCHOOL DISTRICT 73 (KAM-LOOPS/THOMPSON)
ARTHUR HATTON ELEMENTARY SCHOOL
315 Chestnut Ave, Kamloops, BC, V2B 1L4
(250) 376-7217
Emp Here 31
SIC 8211 Elementary and secondary schools

D-U-N-S 20-027-1414 (BR)
SCHOOL DISTRICT 73 (KAM-LOOPS/THOMPSON)
BROCKLEHURST MIDDLE SCHOOL
985 Windbreak St, Kamloops, BC, V2B 5P5
(250) 376-1232
Emp Here 65
SIC 8211 Elementary and secondary schools

D-U-N-S 25-015-2204 (BR)
SCHOOL DISTRICT 73 (KAM-LOOPS/THOMPSON)
JOHN TODD ELEMENTARY
435 Mcgowan Ave, Kamloops, BC, V2B 2P2
(250) 376-7231
Emp Here 28
SIC 8211 Elementary and secondary schools

D-U-N-S 25-015-2329 (BR)
SCHOOL DISTRICT 73 (KAM-LOOPS/THOMPSON)
TWIN RIVERS EDUCATION CENTER
985 Holt St, Kamloops, BC, V2B 5H1
(250) 554-3438
Emp Here 31
SIC 8211 Elementary and secondary schools

D-U-N-S 20-652-3719 (BR)
SHAW COMMUNICATIONS INC
SHAW CABLE
180 Briar Ave, Kamloops, BC, V2B 1C1
(250) 312-7104
Emp Here 30
SIC 7389 Business services, nec

D-U-N-S 24-593-9764 (BR)
SOBEYS WEST INC
750 Fortune Dr, Kamloops, BC, V2B 2L2
(250) 376-4129
Emp Here 160
SIC 5411 Grocery stores

D-U-N-S 24-380-0013 (BR)
SUPERIOR PLUS LP
WINROC
660 Kingston Ave, Kamloops, BC, V2B 2C8
(250) 376-5781
Emp Here 20
SIC 5039 Construction materials, nec

D-U-N-S 25-520-7586 (BR)
WHITE SPOT LIMITED
675 Tranquille Rd Unit 669, Kamloops, BC, V2B 3H7

(778) 470-5581
Emp Here 25
SIC 5812 Eating places

Kamloops, BC V2C
Thompson - Nicola County

D-U-N-S 25-218-7521 (SL)
A.R.M. HOLDINGS INC
1962 Glenwood Dr, Kamloops, BC, V2C 4G4
(250) 372-5479
Emp Here 220   *Sales* 24,416,640
SIC 7359 Equipment rental and leasing, nec
  Case Van Diemen
  Robert Wills

D-U-N-S 24-750-0523 (BR)
AMEC FOSTER WHEELER AMERICAS LIMITED
AMEC EARTH & ENVIRONMENTAL, DIV OF
913 Laval Cres, Kamloops, BC, V2C 5P4
(250) 374-1347
Emp Here 20
SIC 8711 Engineering services

D-U-N-S 25-482-8213 (BR)
ACCENT INNS INC
ACCENT INNS
1325 Columbia St W, Kamloops, BC, V2C 6P4
(250) 374-8877
Emp Here 25
SIC 7011 Hotels and motels

D-U-N-S 25-113-6610 (SL)
ACRES ENTERPRISES LTD
971 Camosun Cres, Kamloops, BC, V2C 6G1
(250) 372-7456
Emp Here 65   *Sales* 20,720,839
SIC 6553 Cemetery subdividers and developers
Pr Pr Jason Paige

D-U-N-S 25-887-7422 (BR)
ALL-CAN EXPRESS LTD
A. C. E. COURIER SERVICE
775 Laval Cres, Kamloops, BC, V2C 5P2
(250) 828-1311
Emp Here 30
SIC 7389 Business services, nec

D-U-N-S 20-864-2371 (BR)
ARROW TRANSPORTATION SYSTEMS INC
1805 Mission Flats Rd, Kamloops, BC, V2C 1A9
(250) 374-6715
Emp Here 100
SIC 4212 Local trucking, without storage

D-U-N-S 20-008-0674 (BR)
ARROW TRANSPORTATION SYSTEMS INC
970 Mcmaster Way Suite 400, Kamloops, BC, V2C 6K2
(250) 374-3831
Emp Here 20
SIC 4212 Local trucking, without storage

D-U-N-S 20-015-3950 (SL)
AUDIOTECH HEALTHCARE CORPORATION
175 2nd Ave Suite 760, Kamloops, BC, V2C 5W1
(250) 372-5847
Emp Here 30   *Sales* 6,087,000
SIC 5047 Medical and hospital equipment
Pr Osvaldo Iadarola
Dir Daniel Allen
Dir Gerald Mill
  Grant Robertson
Dir Glen Martin
  James T Gillis

D-U-N-S 24-152-7167 (BR)
BDO CANADA LLP
272 Victoria St Suite 300, Kamloops, BC, V2C 1Z6

(778) 257-1486
Emp Here 28
SIC 8721 Accounting, auditing, and bookkeeping

D-U-N-S 25-296-8425 (BR)
BANK OF NOVA SCOTIA, THE
SCOTIABANK
276 Victoria St, Kamloops, BC, V2C 2A2
(250) 314-3950
Emp Here 29
SIC 6021 National commercial banks

D-U-N-S 20-700-1525 (BR)
BANQUE TORONTO-DOMINION, LA
TORONTO-DOMINION BANK, THE
(*Suby of* Toronto-Dominion Bank, The)
500 Notre Dame Dr Suite 500, Kamloops, BC, V2C 6T6
(250) 314-3000
Emp Here 20
SIC 6021 National commercial banks

D-U-N-S 25-537-9521 (BR)
BRICK WAREHOUSE LP, THE
1689 Trans Canada Hwy E, Kamloops, BC, V2C 3Z5
(250) 314-1115
Emp Here 40
SIC 5712 Furniture stores

D-U-N-S 25-316-5799 (BR)
BRITISH COLUMBIA AUTOMOBILE ASSOCIATION
BCAA
500 Notre Dame Dr Suite 400, Kamloops, BC, V2C 6T6
(250) 852-4600
Emp Here 23
SIC 8699 Membership organizations, nec

D-U-N-S 25-366-1367 (BR)
CANADA POST CORPORATION
CAMOSUN POSTAL OUTLET
970 Camosun Cres, Kamloops, BC, V2C 6G2
(250) 374-1879
Emp Here 120
SIC 4311 U.s. postal service

D-U-N-S 25-786-6228 (BR)
CANADIAN CANCER SOCIETY
141 Victoria St Suite 214, Kamloops, BC, V2C 1Z5
(250) 374-9188
Emp Here 49
SIC 8399 Social services, nec

D-U-N-S 24-657-3398 (BR)
CANADIAN IMPERIAL BANK OF COMMERCE
CIBC BANKING CENTRE
304 Victoria St, Kamloops, BC, V2C 2A5
(250) 314-3188
Emp Here 60
SIC 6021 National commercial banks

D-U-N-S 20-880-2202 (BR)
CANADIAN PACIFIC RAILWAY COMPANY
CPR
2855 Thompson Dr, Kamloops, BC, V2C 4L7

Emp Here 50
SIC 4011 Railroads, line-haul operating

D-U-N-S 20-903-2346 (BR)
CANADIAN UNION OF PUBLIC EMPLOYEES
CUPE LOCAL 3500
736b Seymour St, Kamloops, BC, V2C 2H3
(250) 377-8446
Emp Here 20
SIC 8631 Labor organizations

D-U-N-S 20-655-2676 (BR)
COOPER MARKET LTD
2101 Trans Canada Hwy E Unit 9, Kamloops, BC, V2C 4A6
(250) 374-4343
Emp Here 20

SIC 5411 Grocery stores

D-U-N-S 24-414-0344 (BR)
CULLEN DIESEL POWER LTD
9925 Dallas Dr, Kamloops, BC, V2C 6T4
(250) 573-4450
Emp Here 30
SIC 7538 General automotive repair shops

D-U-N-S 20-734-8728 (BR)
DAWNAL QUICK SERVE LTD
MCDONALD'S
301 Victoria St, Kamloops, BC, V2C 2A3
(250) 314-6493
Emp Here 30
SIC 5812 Eating places

D-U-N-S 25-773-1968 (BR)
DAWNAL QUICK SERVE LTD
MCDONALD'S RESTAURANTS
(*Suby of* Dawnal Quick Serve Ltd)
500 Notre Dame Dr Unit 800, Kamloops, BC,
V2C 6T6
(250) 314-3686
Emp Here 80
SIC 5812 Eating places

D-U-N-S 20-280-2500 (BR)
DENCAN RESTAURANTS INC
DENNY'S RESTAURANT
(*Suby of* Northland Properties Corporation)
570 Columbia St Unit 6852, Kamloops, BC,
V2C 2V1
(250) 374-6369
Emp Here 45
SIC 5812 Eating places

D-U-N-S 25-014-9176 (BR)
EARL'S RESTAURANTS LTD
EARL'1
(*Suby of* Earl's Restaurants Ltd)
1210 Summit Dr Suite 800, Kamloops, BC,
V2C 6M1
(250) 372-3275
Emp Here 75
SIC 5812 Eating places

D-U-N-S 25-771-6605 (SL)
EXCEL PERSONNEL INC
418 St Paul St Suite 200, Kamloops, BC, V2C
2J6
(250) 374-3853
Emp Here 60   *Sales* 4,377,642
SIC 7361 Employment agencies

D-U-N-S 20-006-7429 (BR)
FABRICLAND PACIFIC/MIDWEST LIMITED
FABRICLAND
2121 Trans Canada Hwy E, Kamloops, BC,
V2C 4A6
(250) 374-3360
Emp Here 100
SIC 5949 Sewing, needlework, and piece
goods

D-U-N-S 20-798-4043 (BR)
FEDERATED CO-OPERATIVES LIMITED
TGP
(*Suby of* Federated Co-Operatives Limited)
945 Laval Cres, Kamloops, BC, V2C 5P4
(250) 372-2043
Emp Here 20
SIC 5411 Grocery stores

D-U-N-S 24-762-1089 (BR)
FINNING INTERNATIONAL INC
FINNING (CANADA), A DIV
(*Suby of* Finning International Inc)
1764 Kelly Douglas Rd, Kamloops, BC, V2C
5S4
(250) 372-9552
Emp Here 130
SIC 5082 Construction and mining machinery

D-U-N-S 24-353-4141 (BR)
FINNING INTERNATIONAL INC
FINNING CANADA, DIV OF
(*Suby of* Finning International Inc)
1967 Trans Canada Hwy E Suite 25, Kam-

loops, BC, V2C 4A4
(250) 852-7500
Emp Here 34
SIC 5082 Construction and mining machinery

D-U-N-S 25-849-5365 (BR)
GOLDER ASSOCIATES LTD
929 Mcgill Rd, Kamloops, BC, V2C 6E9
(250) 828-6116
Emp Here 20
SIC 8711 Engineering services

D-U-N-S 25-267-8842 (BR)
GREAT PACIFIC INDUSTRIES INC
SAVE-ON-FOODS
1210 Summit Dr Suite 100, Kamloops, BC,
V2C 6M1
(250) 374-6685
Emp Here 250
SIC 5411 Grocery stores

D-U-N-S 25-014-9218 (BR)
**GREYHOUND CANADA TRANSPORTA-
TION ULC**
725 Notre Dame Dr, Kamloops, BC, V2C 5N8
(250) 374-1226
Emp Here 35
SIC 4131 Intercity and rural bus transportation

D-U-N-S 20-097-9755 (BR)
INLAND KENWORTH LTD
INLAND KENWORTH
865 Notre Dame Dr, Kamloops, BC, V2C 5N8
(250) 374-4406
Emp Here 50
SIC 5511 New and used car dealers

D-U-N-S 24-309-1159 (BR)
INTERIOR HEALTH AUTHORITY
*KAMLOOPS HOME AND COMMUNITY
CARE*
450 Lansdowne St Unit 37, Kamloops, BC,
V2C 1Y3
(250) 851-7900
Emp Here 110
SIC 8062 General medical and surgical hospi-
tals

D-U-N-S 24-309-1092 (BR)
INTERIOR HEALTH AUTHORITY
*HILLSIDE COMMUNITY CARE HEALTH
SERVICES*
450 Lansdowne St Unit 37, Kamloops, BC,
V2C 1Y3
(250) 374-5111
Emp Here 80
SIC 8062 General medical and surgical hospi-
tals

D-U-N-S 20-177-9704 (BR)
INTERIOR HEALTH AUTHORITY
ROYAL INLAND HOSPITAL
311 Columbia St, Kamloops, BC, V2C 2T1
(250) 374-5111
Emp Here 800
SIC 8062 General medical and surgical hospi-
tals

D-U-N-S 20-921-2278 (BR)
INTERIOR HEALTH AUTHORITY
*KAMLOOPS HEALTH PROTECTION OF-
FICE*
519 Columbia St, Kamloops, BC, V2C 2T8
(250) 851-7300
Emp Here 100
SIC 8062 General medical and surgical hospi-
tals

D-U-N-S 25-315-8182 (BR)
**INVESTORS GROUP FINANCIAL SER-
VICES INC**
741 Sahali Terr Suite 100, Kamloops, BC, V2C
6X7
(250) 372-2955
Emp Here 25
SIC 8741 Management services

D-U-N-S 25-773-9649 (SL)

J.D. FOODS LTD
WHITE SPOT RESTAURANT KAMLOOPS
555 Notre Dame Dr Suite 1, Kamloops, BC,
V2C 1E6
(250) 374-4973
Emp Here 50   *Sales* 1,532,175
SIC 5812 Eating places

D-U-N-S 24-310-7153 (BR)
JHAJ HOLDINGS LTD
WEST-CAN SAFETY & INDUSTRIAL
(*Suby of* JHAJ Holdings Ltd)
874 Notre Dame Dr, Kamloops, BC, V2C 6L5
(250) 372-1991
Emp Here 20
SIC 5531 Auto and home supply stores

D-U-N-S 25-269-6513 (SL)
K.A.M. 1200 HOLDINGS LTD
SUBWAY SANDWICHES & SALADS #7764
1203 Summit Dr Suite C, Kamloops, BC, V2C
6C5
(250) 374-7821
Emp Here 60   *Sales* 1,824,018
SIC 5812 Eating places

D-U-N-S 24-824-1440 (BR)
KPMG LLP
(*Suby of* KPMG LLP)
206 Seymour St Suite 200, Kamloops, BC,
V2C 6P5
(250) 372-5581
Emp Here 85
SIC 8721 Accounting, auditing, and book-
keeping

D-U-N-S 24-311-1200 (BR)
KAL TIRE LTD
1870 Kelly Douglas Rd Suite 401, Kamloops,
BC, V2C 5S5
(250) 374-2273
Emp Here 20
SIC 3011 Tires and inner tubes

D-U-N-S 20-980-5055 (SL)
KAMLOOPS THIS WEEK PAPER
KAMLOOPS THIS WEEK
1365b Dalhousie Dr, Kamloops, BC, V2C 5P6
(250) 374-7467
Emp Here 60   *Sales* 4,961,328
SIC 2711 Newspapers

D-U-N-S 20-067-1233 (BR)
**KAMLOOPS, THE CORPORATION OF THE
CITY OF**
CANADA GAMES AQUATIC CENTRE
910 Mcgill Rd, Kamloops, BC, V2C 6N6
(250) 828-3655
Emp Here 100
SIC 7999 Amusement and recreation, nec

D-U-N-S 20-040-4924 (BR)
**KAMLOOPS, THE CORPORATION OF THE
CITY OF**
*ENGINEERING DEVELOPMENT AND ENGI-
NEERING SERVICES*
105 Seymour St, Kamloops, BC, V2C 2C6
(250) 828-3311
Emp Here 40
SIC 8748 Business consulting, nec

D-U-N-S 20-922-7706 (BR)
KEG RESTAURANTS LTD
KEG STEAKHOUSE & BAR, THE
500 Lorne St, Kamloops, BC, V2C 1W3
(250) 374-5347
Emp Here 60
SIC 5812 Eating places

D-U-N-S 25-136-9393 (BR)
LOBLAWS INC
REAL CANADIAN SUPERSTORE
910 Columbia St W Suite 1522, Kamloops,
BC, V2C 1L2
(250) 371-6418
Emp Here 300
SIC 5411 Grocery stores

D-U-N-S 25-273-1385 (BR)
LONDON DRUGS LIMITED
450 Lansdowne St Suite 68, Kamloops, BC,
V2C 1Y3
(250) 372-0028
Emp Here 100
SIC 5912 Drug stores and proprietary stores

D-U-N-S 25-267-8939 (BR)
LORDCO PARTS LTD
LORDCO AUTO PARTS
940 Notre Dame Dr, Kamloops, BC, V2C 6J2
(250) 374-9912
Emp Here 30
SIC 5531 Auto and home supply stores

D-U-N-S 24-579-0902 (SL)
MJB MGMT CORP
MAIR JENSEN BLAIR LLP
275 Lansdowne St Suite 700, Kamloops, BC,
V2C 6H6
(250) 374-3161
Emp Here 50   *Sales* 5,791,440
SIC 8111 Legal services
Sr Pt Richard Jensen
Pt Robert Adkin
Pt David Mcdougall
Pt J Barry Carter
Pt Dennis Coates
Pt Jim Mccreight
Pt Darren Paulsen
Pt Marlene Harrison
Pt Michael J Sutherland
Pt Murray Weeres

D-U-N-S 25-771-7652 (SL)
MCDONALD'S RESTAURANTS LTD
1751 Trans Canada Hwy E, Kamloops, BC,
V2C 3Z6
(250) 374-1718
Emp Here 80   *Sales* 2,407,703
SIC 5812 Eating places

D-U-N-S 20-352-7239 (BR)
NORTHAM BEVERAGES LTD
965 Mcgill Pl, Kamloops, BC, V2C 6N9
(250) 851-2543
Emp Here 87
SIC 2085 Distilled and blended liquors

D-U-N-S 20-917-9030 (BR)
PANAGO PIZZA INC
1350 Summit Dr Unit 1, Kamloops, BC, V2C
1T8
(250) 851-2250
Emp Here 27
SIC 5812 Eating places

D-U-N-S 25-360-0027 (HQ)
PATTISON, JIM BROADCAST GROUP LTD
COUNTRY 95.5 FM
460 Pemberton Terr, Kamloops, BC, V2C 1T5
(250) 372-3322
Emp Here 60   *Emp Total* 33,000
Sales 34,061,520
SIC 4832 Radio broadcasting stations
Pr Rick Arnish

D-U-N-S 25-325-7232 (BR)
PATTISON, JIM INDUSTRIES LTD
BROADCAST CENTER
460 Pemberton Terr, Kamloops, BC, V2C 1T5
(250) 372-3322
Emp Here 60
SIC 4832 Radio broadcasting stations

D-U-N-S 20-097-7759 (BR)
POSTMEDIA NETWORK INC
KAMLOOPS DAILY NEWS, THE
393 Seymour St, Kamloops, BC, V2C 6P6
(250) 371-6152
Emp Here 80
SIC 2711 Newspapers

D-U-N-S 25-453-9448 (BR)
PRISZM LP
PIZZA HUT
470 Columbia St, Kamloops, BC, V2C 2T5

(250) 372-2733
Emp Here 24
SIC 5812 Eating places

D-U-N-S 25-792-6741   (BR)
PRISZM LP
KFC
555 Notre Dame Dr Suite B, Kamloops, BC,
V2C 1E6
(250) 374-6534
Emp Here 28
SIC 5812 Eating places

D-U-N-S 25-232-1612   (BR)
RICOH CANADA INC
971 Laval Cres, Kamloops, BC, V2C 5P4
(604) 293-9700
Emp Here 90
SIC 5044 Office equipment

D-U-N-S 25-767-5681   (HQ)
RJAMES MANAGEMENT GROUP LTD
WESTERN STAR FREIGHTLINER DIV OF
(*Suby of* Rjames Management Group Ltd)
2072 Falcon Rd, Kamloops, BC, V2C 4J3
(250) 374-1431
Emp Here 50   *Emp Total* 100
Sales 47,116,450
SIC 5511 New and used car dealers
Robert James

D-U-N-S 25-771-5615   (BR)
ROYAL BANK OF CANADA
RBC
(*Suby of* Royal Bank Of Canada)
186 Victoria St, Kamloops, BC, V2C 5R3
(250) 371-1500
Emp Here 100
SIC 6021 National commercial banks

D-U-N-S 20-970-9653   (BR)
SCHOOL DISTRICT 73 (KAM-LOOPS/THOMPSON)
965 Notre Dame Dr, Kamloops, BC, V2C 5P8
(250) 851-4420
Emp Here 70
SIC 8211 Elementary and secondary schools

D-U-N-S 20-653-4179   (BR)
SCHOOL DISTRICT 73 (KAM-LOOPS/THOMPSON)
RL CLEMITSON ELEMENTARY
5990 Todd Rd, Kamloops, BC, V2C 5B7
(250) 573-3227
Emp Here 25
SIC 8211 Elementary and secondary schools

D-U-N-S 20-156-7869   (BR)
SCHOOL DISTRICT 73 (KAM-LOOPS/THOMPSON)
SA-HALI SECONDARY SCHOOL
255 Arrowstone Dr, Kamloops, BC, V2C 1P8
(250) 374-0861
Emp Here 65
SIC 8211 Elementary and secondary schools

D-U-N-S 20-713-2577   (BR)
SCHOOL DISTRICT 73 (KAM-LOOPS/THOMPSON)
LLOYD GEORGE ELEMENTARY SCHOOL
830 Pine St, Kamloops, BC, V2C 3A1
(250) 374-3174
Emp Here 50
SIC 8211 Elementary and secondary schools

D-U-N-S 20-033-7652   (BR)
SCHOOL DISTRICT 73 (KAM-LOOPS/THOMPSON)
BEATTIE SCHOOL OF THE ARTS
492 Mcgill Rd, Kamloops, BC, V2C 1M3
(250) 374-0608
Emp Here 30
SIC 8211 Elementary and secondary schools

D-U-N-S 20-713-2585   (BR)
SCHOOL DISTRICT 73 (KAM-LOOPS/THOMPSON)
MARION SCHILLING ELEMENTARY

SCHOOL
2200 Park Dr, Kamloops, BC, V2C 4P6
(250) 372-2027
Emp Here 30
SIC 8211 Elementary and secondary schools

D-U-N-S 20-034-0920   (BR)
SCHOOL DISTRICT 73 (KAM-LOOPS/THOMPSON)
SOUTH KAMLOOPS SECONDARY SCHOOL
821 Munro St, Kamloops, BC, V2C 3E9
(250) 374-1405
Emp Here 130
SIC 8211 Elementary and secondary schools

D-U-N-S 25-820-5830   (BR)
SCHOOL DISTRICT 73 (KAM-LOOPS/THOMPSON)
DALLAS ELEMENTARY SCHOOL
296 Harper Rd, Kamloops, BC, V2C 4Z2
(250) 573-3261
Emp Here 25
SIC 8211 Elementary and secondary schools

D-U-N-S 25-815-1273   (BR)
SCHOOL DISTRICT 73 (KAM-LOOPS/THOMPSON)
BUS GARAGE
710 Mcgill Rd, Kamloops, BC, V2C 0A2
(250) 372-5853
Emp Here 86
SIC 4173 Bus terminal and service facilities

D-U-N-S 24-593-9772   (BR)
SOBEYS WEST INC
SAHALI SAFEWAY
945 Columbia St W, Kamloops, BC, V2C 1L5
(250) 372-1994
Emp Here 50
SIC 5411 Grocery stores

D-U-N-S 20-714-3046   (SL)
ST ANN SCHOOL BOARD ACADEMY
205 Columbia St, Kamloops, BC, V2C 2S7
(250) 372-5452
Emp Here 50   *Sales* 3,356,192
SIC 8211 Elementary and secondary schools

D-U-N-S 25-611-2272   (BR)
STARBUCKS COFFEE CANADA, INC
STARBUCKS
(*Suby of* Starbucks Corporation)
1967 Trans Canada Hwy E Unit 90c, Kam-
loops, BC, V2C 4A4
(250) 314-4120
Emp Here 25
SIC 5812 Eating places

D-U-N-S 25-316-8363   (BR)
SUN LIFE ASSURANCE COMPANY OF CANADA
275 Lansdowne St Suite 600, Kamloops, BC,
V2C 6H6
(250) 374-5308
Emp Here 20
SIC 6311 Life insurance

D-U-N-S 20-086-8433   (SL)
THOMPSON HEALTH REGION
KAMLOOPS MENTAL HEALTH CENTRE
311 Columbia St, Kamloops, BC, V2C 2T1
(250) 314-2784
Emp Here 2,000   *Sales* 182,407,100
SIC 8093 Specialty outpatient clinics, nec
Dir Mike Wolfram
Ch Bd Berthe Hall

D-U-N-S 24-314-8421   (SL)
THOMPSON RIVER VENEER PRODUCTS LIMITED
8405 Dallas Dr, Kamloops, BC, V2C 6X2
(250) 573-6002
Emp Here 55   *Sales* 4,815,406
SIC 2436 Softwood veneer and plywood

D-U-N-S 25-315-1336   (BR)
TORONTO-DOMINION BANK, THE
TD CANADA TRUST

(*Suby of* Toronto-Dominion Bank, The)
301 Victoria St Suite 102, Kamloops, BC, V2C
2A3
(250) 314-5035
Emp Here 23
SIC 6021 National commercial banks

D-U-N-S 25-056-8334   (BR)
TOYS 'R' US (CANADA) LTD
TOYS 'R' US #3558
(*Suby of* Toys "r" Us, Inc.)
500 Notre Dame Dr Unit 100, Kamloops, BC,
V2C 6T6
(250) 851-8250
Emp Here 37
SIC 5945 Hobby, toy, and game shops

D-U-N-S 25-684-1131   (SL)
VS VISUAL STATEMENT INC
VISUAL STATEMENT
(*Suby of* Trimble Inc.)
175 2nd Ave Suite 900, Kamloops, BC, V2C
5W1
(250) 828-0383
Emp Here 21   *Sales* 1,819,127
SIC 7372 Prepackaged software

D-U-N-S 25-771-8486   (SL)
VALUE VILLAGE STORES, INC
(*Suby of* Savers, Inc.)
444 Seymour St, Kamloops, BC, V2C 2G6
(250) 374-6609
Emp Here 40
SIC 5399 Miscellaneous general merchandise

Kamloops, BC V2E
Thompson - Nicola County

D-U-N-S 20-303-3394   (BR)
CARA OPERATIONS LIMITED
KELSEY'S
(*Suby of* Cara Holdings Limited)
1055 Hillside Dr Unit 600, Kamloops, BC, V2E
2S5
(250) 314-0714
Emp Here 45
SIC 5812 Eating places

D-U-N-S 20-177-5082   (BR)
HOME DEPOT OF CANADA INC
HOME DEPOT
(*Suby of* The Home Depot Inc)
1020 Hillside Dr, Kamloops, BC, V2E 2N1
(250) 371-4300
Emp Here 150
SIC 5251 Hardware stores

D-U-N-S 25-080-7344   (BR)
INDIGO BOOKS & MUSIC INC
CHAPTERS
(*Suby of* Indigo Books & Music Inc)
1395 Hillside Dr Suite 4, Kamloops, BC, V2E
2R7
(250) 377-8468
Emp Here 35
SIC 5942 Book stores

D-U-N-S 20-982-2159   (BR)
MICHAELS OF CANADA, ULC
(*Suby of* The Michaels Companies Inc)
1055 Hillside Dr Suite 200, Kamloops, BC,
V2E 2S5
(250) 571-1066
Emp Here 40
SIC 5945 Hobby, toy, and game shops

D-U-N-S 25-128-5706   (BR)
SCHOOL DISTRICT 73 (KAM-LOOPS/THOMPSON)
JUNIPER RIDGE ELEMENTARY SCHOOL
2540 Qu'Appelle Blvd, Kamloops, BC, V2E
2E9
(250) 374-2305
Emp Here 32
SIC 8211 Elementary and secondary schools

D-U-N-S 20-713-2619   (BR)
SCHOOL DISTRICT 73 (KAM-LOOPS/THOMPSON)
SOUTH SAHALI ELEMENTARY SCHOOL
1585 Summit Dr, Kamloops, BC, V2E 1E9
(250) 374-2451
Emp Here 26
SIC 8211 Elementary and secondary schools

D-U-N-S 25-825-7278   (BR)
SCHOOL DISTRICT 73 (KAM-LOOPS/THOMPSON)
SUMMIT ELEMENTARY SCHOOL
425 Monarch Crt, Kamloops, BC, V2E 1Y3
(250) 372-1224
Emp Here 24
SIC 8211 Elementary and secondary schools

D-U-N-S 20-066-0087   (BR)
SCHOOL DISTRICT 73 (KAM-LOOPS/THOMPSON)
MCGOWN PARK ELEMENTARY
2080 Tremerton Dr, Kamloops, BC, V2E 2S2
(250) 374-4545
Emp Here 25
SIC 8211 Elementary and secondary schools

D-U-N-S 25-080-1693   (BR)
STAPLES CANADA INC
STAPLES THE BUSINESS DEPOT
(*Suby of* Staples, Inc.)
1395 Hillside Dr Suite 1, Kamloops, BC, V2E
2R7
(250) 377-4550
Emp Here 35
SIC 5943 Stationery stores

D-U-N-S 24-314-0584   (BR)
WAL-MART CANADA CORP
1055 Hillside Dr Unit 100, Kamloops, BC, V2E
2S5
(250) 374-1591
Emp Here 300
SIC 5311 Department stores

Kamloops, BC V2H
Thompson - Nicola County

D-U-N-S 24-887-7425   (BR)
BRANDT TRACTOR LTD
499 Chilcotin Rd, Kamloops, BC, V2H 1G4
(250) 374-2115
Emp Here 20
SIC 5082 Construction and mining machinery

D-U-N-S 20-733-3670   (BR)
COMPAGNIE DES CHEMINS DE FER NA-TIONAUX DU CANADA
309 Cn Rd, Kamloops, BC, V2H 1K3
(250) 828-6331
Emp Here 375
SIC 4111 Local and suburban transit

D-U-N-S 20-508-9415   (BR)
DOUGLAS LAKE CATTLE COMPANY
DOUGLAS LAKE EQUIPMENT
519 Mt Paul Way, Kamloops, BC, V2H 1A9
(250) 828-6788
Emp Here 20
SIC 5999 Miscellaneous retail stores, nec

D-U-N-S 20-508-9456   (BR)
DOUGLAS LAKE CATTLE COMPANY
DOUGLAS LAKE EQUIPMENT
706 Carrier St, Kamloops, BC, V2H 1G2
(250) 851-2044
Emp Here 23
SIC 5083 Farm and garden machinery

D-U-N-S 20-514-7908   (BR)
FOUNTAIN TIRE LTD
FOUNTAIN TIRE TRUCK CENTRE BRANCH F105
916 Yellowhead Hwy, Kamloops, BC, V2H 1A2

(250) 851-7600
Emp Here 22
SIC 5531 Auto and home supply stores

D-U-N-S 25-999-4531   (BR)
GREAT CANADIAN RAIL TOUR COMPANY LTD
GREAT CANADIAN RAILTOUR COMPANY LTD
(*Suby of* Armstrong Hospitality Group Ltd)
525 Cn Rd, Kamloops, BC, V2H 1K3
(250) 314-3998
Emp Here 150
SIC 4725 Tour operators

D-U-N-S 20-747-1488   (BR)
KAL TIRE LTD
788 Mt Paul Way, Kamloops, BC, V2H 1B5
(250) 374-6258
Emp Here 27
SIC 5531 Auto and home supply stores

D-U-N-S 25-215-8688   (BR)
LAFARGE CANADA INC
9750 Shuswap Rd, Kamloops, BC, V2H 1T4
(250) 573-6405
Emp Here 35
SIC 3241 Cement, hydraulic

D-U-N-S 20-309-9309   (BR)
NORCAN FLUID POWER LTD
728 Tagish St, Kamloops, BC, V2H 1B7
(250) 372-3933
Emp Here 20
SIC 2869 Industrial organic chemicals, nec

D-U-N-S 20-653-7800   (BR)
SCHOOL DISTRICT 73 (KAMLOOPS/THOMPSON)
RAYLEIGH ELEMENTARY
306 Puett Ranch Rd, Kamloops, BC, V2H 1M9
(250) 578-7229
Emp Here 20
SIC 8211 Elementary and secondary schools

D-U-N-S 20-879-6628   (BR)
TOLKO INDUSTRIES LTD
HEFFLEY CREEK, DIVISION OF
6275 Old Hwy 5, Kamloops, BC, V2H 1T8
(250) 578-7212
Emp Here 200
SIC 2435 Hardwood veneer and plywood

D-U-N-S 25-384-6554   (HQ)
VALLEY ROADWAYS LTD
(*Suby of* Kluskus Holdings Ltd)
1115 Chief Louis Way, Kamloops, BC, V2H 1J8
(250) 374-3467
Emp Here 39   *Emp Total* 603
Sales 4,815,406
SIC 4213 Trucking, except local

D-U-N-S 20-098-2791   (BR)
VAN-KAM FREIGHTWAYS LTD
682 Sarcee St W, Kamloops, BC, V2H 1E5
(250) 372-2235
Emp Here 52
SIC 4212 Local trucking, without storage

Kaslo, BC V0G
Central Kootenay County

D-U-N-S 20-867-6499   (BR)
INTERIOR HEALTH AUTHORITY
KASLO PRIMARY HEALTH CENTRE
673 A Ave, Kaslo, BC, V0G 1M0
(250) 353-2296
Emp Here 50
SIC 8062 General medical and surgical hospitals

D-U-N-S 25-676-7674   (BR)
SCHOOL DISTRICT NO. 8 (KOOTENAY LAKE)
J.V. HUMPHRIES SCHOOL

(*Suby of* School District No. 8 (Kootenay Lake))
500 Sixth St, Kaslo, BC, V0G 1M0
(250) 353-2227
Emp Here 50
SIC 8211 Elementary and secondary schools

D-U-N-S 20-655-2072   (SL)
VICTORIAN COMMUNITY HEALTH CENTRE OF KASLO
673 A Ave, Kaslo, BC, V0G 1M0
(250) 353-2211
Emp Here 50   *Sales* 1,969,939
SIC 8322 Individual and family services

Kelowna, BC V1P
Central Okanagan County

D-U-N-S 25-175-0501   (BR)
BOARD OF EDUCATION OF SCHOOL DISTRICT NO. 23 (CENTRAL OKANAGAN), THE
BLACK MOUNTAIN ELEMENTARY SCHOOL
1650 Gallagher Rd, Kelowna, BC, V1P 1G7
(250) 765-1955
Emp Here 30
SIC 8211 Elementary and secondary schools

D-U-N-S 20-168-9531   (SL)
P & D LOGGIN
2335 Highway 33 E, Kelowna, BC, V1P 1H2

Emp Here 40   *Sales* 5,496,960
SIC 2411 Logging
Owner Dennis Pilon

Kelowna, BC V1V
Central Okanagan County

D-U-N-S 24-076-4824   (BR)
ARAMARK CANADA LTD.
ARAMARK MANAGED SERVICES
3333 University Way Suite 124, Kelowna, BC, V1V 1V7
(250) 807-9208
Emp Here 25
SIC 5812 Eating places

D-U-N-S 20-713-2502   (BR)
BOARD OF EDUCATION OF SCHOOL DISTRICT NO. 23 (CENTRAL OKANAGAN), THE
DR KNOX MIDDLE SCHOOL
121 Drysdale Blvd, Kelowna, BC, V1V 2X9
(250) 870-5130
Emp Here 50
SIC 8211 Elementary and secondary schools

D-U-N-S 20-713-2528   (BR)
BOARD OF EDUCATION OF SCHOOL DISTRICT NO. 23 (CENTRAL OKANAGAN), THE
NORTH GLENMORE ELEMENTARY SCHOOL
125 Snowsell St N, Kelowna, BC, V1V 2E3

Emp Here 50
SIC 8211 Elementary and secondary schools

D-U-N-S 20-591-5502   (BR)
BOARD OF EDUCATION OF SCHOOL DISTRICT NO. 23 (CENTRAL OKANAGAN), THE
NORTH GLENMORE ELEMENTARY SCHOOL
125 Snowsell St N, Kelowna, BC, V1V 2E3
(250) 870-5128
Emp Here 40
SIC 8211 Elementary and secondary schools

D-U-N-S 25-174-5915   (BR)
BOARD OF EDUCATION OF SCHOOL DIS-

TRICT NO. 23 (CENTRAL OKANAGAN), THE
WATSON ROAD ELEMENTARY SCHOOL
475 Yates Rd, Kelowna, BC, V1V 1R3
(250) 762-4495
Emp Here 25
SIC 8211 Elementary and secondary schools

D-U-N-S 25-988-7602   (BR)
H.Y. LOUIE CO. LIMITED
IGA #169
1940 Kane Rd Suite 101, Kelowna, BC, V1V 2J9
(250) 868-3009
Emp Here 30
SIC 5411 Grocery stores

D-U-N-S 24-164-7411   (HQ)
KELOWNA FLIGHTCRAFT AIR CHARTER LTD
(*Suby of* Rainmaker Industries Inc)
5655 Airport Way Suite 1, Kelowna, BC, V1V 1S1
(250) 491-5500
Emp Here 500   *Emp Total* 5
Sales 104,831,760
SIC 4512 Air transportation, scheduled
 Barry Lapointe
Pr Pr Tracy Medve

D-U-N-S 20-586-0885   (HQ)
KON KAST PRODUCTS (2005) LTD
(*Suby of* Kon Kast Products (2005) Ltd)
1313 Innovation Dr, Kelowna, BC, V1V 3B3
(250) 765-1423
Emp Here 40   *Emp Total* 42
Sales 11,869,650
SIC 3272 Concrete products, nec
Pr Pr William Smeltzer
 Ian Smeltzer
 Tony Vicaretti

D-U-N-S 20-841-4511   (SL)
LITTCO ENTERPRISES LTD
LITTCO INSULATION & DRYWALL
3314 Appaloosa Rd Unit 1, Kelowna, BC, V1V 2W5
(250) 765-6444
Emp Here 50   *Sales* 4,231,721
SIC 1742 Plastering, drywall, and insulation

D-U-N-S 25-387-5041   (BR)
MAPLE-REINDERS INC
225 Lougheed Rd, Kelowna, BC, V1V 2M1
(250) 765-8892
Emp Here 52
SIC 1541 Industrial buildings and warehouses

D-U-N-S 20-812-4979   (SL)
OKANAGAN GENERAL PARTNERSHIP
MONTANA KAMLOOPS
3333 University Way, Kelowna, BC, V1V 1V7
(250) 807-9851
Emp Here 75   *Sales* 2,685,378
SIC 5812 Eating places

D-U-N-S 20-863-2489   (SL)
PIER MAC PETROLEUM INSTALLATION LTD
3185 Via Centrale Unit 4, Kelowna, BC, V1V 2A7
(250) 765-3155
Emp Here 20   *Sales* 8,539,920
SIC 6553 Cemetery subdividers and developers
Pr Pr Douglas Macnaughton
Off Mgr Vickie Barron

D-U-N-S 24-660-4313   (BR)
UNIVERSITY OF BRITISH COLUMBIA, THE
OKANAGAN CAMPUS
3333 University Way Suite 324, Kelowna, BC, V1V 1V7
(250) 807-8000
Emp Here 20
SIC 8221 Colleges and universities

D-U-N-S 20-812-5257   (HQ)

WGP-225 HOLDINGS LTD
TIM HORTONS
(*Suby of* WGP-225 Holdings Ltd)
1936 Kane Rd, Kelowna, BC, V1V 2J9
(250) 712-0919
Emp Here 55   *Emp Total* 85
Sales 2,553,625
SIC 5812 Eating places

Kelowna, BC V1W
Central Okanagan County

D-U-N-S 24-673-5260   (BR)
AECOM CANADA LTD
SWAN HILLS TREATMENT CENTER
3275 Lakeshore Rd Suite 201, Kelowna, BC, V1W 3S9
(250) 762-3727
Emp Here 40
SIC 8711 Engineering services

D-U-N-S 24-316-6837   (BR)
BANK OF NOVA SCOTIA, THE
SCOTIABANK
3275 Lakeshore Rd Suite 100, Kelowna, BC, V1W 3S9
(250) 712-3075
Emp Here 21
SIC 6021 National commercial banks

D-U-N-S 25-150-4197   (BR)
BOARD OF EDUCATION OF SCHOOL DISTRICT NO. 23 (CENTRAL OKANAGAN), THE
ANNE MCCLYMONT ELEMENTARY
4489 Lakeshore Rd, Kelowna, BC, V1W 1W9
(250) 870-5133
Emp Here 40
SIC 8211 Elementary and secondary schools

D-U-N-S 25-156-5131   (BR)
BOARD OF EDUCATION OF SCHOOL DISTRICT NO. 23 (CENTRAL OKANAGAN), THE
DOROTHEA WALKER ELEMENTARY SCHOOL
4346 Gordon Dr, Kelowna, BC, V1W 1S5
(250) 870-5138
Emp Here 40
SIC 8211 Elementary and secondary schools

D-U-N-S 25-163-5074   (BR)
BOARD OF EDUCATION OF SCHOOL DISTRICT NO. 23 (CENTRAL OKANAGAN), THE
SOUTH KELOWNA ELEMENTARY
4176 Spiers Rd, Kelowna, BC, V1W 4B5
(250) 861-1122
Emp Here 25
SIC 8211 Elementary and secondary schools

D-U-N-S 20-713-2494   (BR)
BOARD OF EDUCATION OF SCHOOL DISTRICT NO. 23 (CENTRAL OKANAGAN), THE
CASORSO ELEMENTARY SCHOOL
3675 Casorso Rd, Kelowna, BC, V1W 3E1
(250) 870-5135
Emp Here 50
SIC 8211 Elementary and secondary schools

D-U-N-S 20-177-0471   (BR)
BOARD OF EDUCATION OF SCHOOL DISTRICT NO. 23 (CENTRAL OKANAGAN), THE
K L O MIDDLE SCHOOL
3130 Gordon Dr, Kelowna, BC, V1W 3M4
(250) 870-5106
Emp Here 75
SIC 8211 Elementary and secondary schools

D-U-N-S 25-156-7384   (SL)
CRC CANADIAN RETIREMENT CORPORATION
4390 Gallaghers Dr E, Kelowna, BC, V1W 3Z8

---

(250) 860-9013
Emp Here 30   *Sales* 6,129,280
SIC 1521 Single-family housing construction
Pr Pr Caleb Chan
Donald Lee
Tom Chan

D-U-N-S 25-366-5368   (BR)
CONSEIL SCOLAIRE FRANCOPHONE DE LA COLOMBIE BRITANNIQUE
ECOLE DE L'ANSE AU SABLE
675 Lequime Rd, Kelowna, BC, V1W 1A3
(250) 764-2771
Emp Here 20
SIC 8211 Elementary and secondary schools

D-U-N-S 25-485-6503   (BR)
COOPER MARKET LTD
COOPER'S FOODS
3155 Lakeshore Rd Unit 45, Kelowna, BC, V1W 3S9
(250) 860-0608
Emp Here 60
SIC 5411 Grocery stores

D-U-N-S 25-301-5523   (BR)
KPMG LLP
(*Suby of* KPMG LLP)
3200 Richter St Suite 200, Kelowna, BC, V1W 5K9
(250) 979-7150
Emp Here 30
SIC 8721 Accounting, auditing, and book-keeping

D-U-N-S 25-163-3178   (BR)
KELOWNA SOCIETY FOR CHRISTIAN EDUCATION
3285 Gordon Dr, Kelowna, BC, V1W 3N4
(250) 861-5432
Emp Here 30
SIC 8211 Elementary and secondary schools

D-U-N-S 25-910-0311   (SL)
MANTEO BEACH CLUB LTD
MANTEO RESORT
3766 Lakeshore Rd, Kelowna, BC, V1W 3L4
(250) 860-1031
Emp Here 100   *Sales* 4,377,642
SIC 7011 Hotels and motels

D-U-N-S 25-130-6023   (SL)
MCT & T FOODS DBA INC
MCDONALD'S RESTAURANTS
3100 Lakeshore Rd, Kelowna, BC, V1W 3T1
(250) 860-3450
Emp Here 50   *Sales* 1,532,175
SIC 5812 Eating places

D-U-N-S 24-127-4559   (BR)
PATTISON, JIM BROADCAST GROUP LTD
Q 103.1
3805 Lakeshore Rd, Kelowna, BC, V1W 3K6
(250) 762-3331
Emp Here 32
SIC 4832 Radio broadcasting stations

D-U-N-S 20-722-8482   (BR)
STARBUCKS COFFEE CANADA, INC
STARBUCKS COFFEE COMPANY
(*Suby of* Starbucks Corporation)
3151 Lakeshore Rd Suite 55, Kelowna, BC, V1W 3S9
(250) 762-6273
Emp Here 25
SIC 5812 Eating places

D-U-N-S 24-371-5331   (SL)
SUTHERLAND HILLS REST HOME LTD
3081 Hall Rd, Kelowna, BC, V1W 2R5
(250) 860-2330
Emp Here 80   *Sales* 3,648,035
SIC 8051 Skilled nursing care facilities

D-U-N-S 20-166-5994   (SL)
WILD APPLE GRILL
3762 Lakeshore Rd, Kelowna, BC, V1W 3L4
(250) 860-4488
Emp Here 50   *Sales* 1,824,018

SIC 5813 Drinking places

D-U-N-S 24-812-8964   (BR)
YMCA-YWCA OF THE CENTRAL OKANAGAN
H2O ADVENTURES + FITNESS CENTRE
4075 Gordon Dr, Kelowna, BC, V1W 5J2
(250) 764-4040
Emp Here 140
SIC 7997 Membership sports and recreation clubs

Kelowna, BC V1X
Central Okanagan County

D-U-N-S 24-044-7586   (BR)
668824 ALBERTA LTD
VISIONS THE BEST NAME IN ELECTRONICS
2463 Highway 97 N Suite 155, Kelowna, BC, V1X 4J2
(250) 762-5900
Emp Here 20
SIC 7539 Automotive repair shops, nec

D-U-N-S 25-157-6922   (BR)
ARO INC
ARO COLLECTION PACIFIQUE
405 Highway 33 W, Kelowna, BC, V1X 1Y2
(250) 762-7070
Emp Here 40
SIC 7322 Adjustment and collection services

D-U-N-S 20-868-3854   (SL)
BLACK MOUNTAIN PHARMACY (1979) LTD
BLACK MOUNTAIN IDA PHARMACY
590 Highway 33 W Unit 11, Kelowna, BC, V1X 6A8
(250) 860-1707
Emp Here 21   *Sales* 2,991,389
SIC 5912 Drug stores and proprietary stores

D-U-N-S 25-932-6080   (BR)
BLACK PRESS GROUP LTD
CALENDAR, THE
2495 Enterprise Way, Kelowna, BC, V1X 7K2
(250) 766-4688
Emp Here 75
SIC 2711 Newspapers

D-U-N-S 25-174-5527   (BR)
BOARD OF EDUCATION OF SCHOOL DISTRICT NO. 23 (CENTRAL OKANAGAN), THE
SOUTH RUTLAND ELEMENTARY SCHOOL
200 Mallach Rd, Kelowna, BC, V1X 2W5
(250) 870-5113
Emp Here 31
SIC 8211 Elementary and secondary schools

D-U-N-S 20-653-4245   (BR)
BOARD OF EDUCATION OF SCHOOL DISTRICT NO. 23 (CENTRAL OKANAGAN), THE
RUTLAND ELEMENTARY SCHOOL
620 Webster Rd, Kelowna, BC, V1X 4V5

Emp Here 40
SIC 8211 Elementary and secondary schools

D-U-N-S 25-157-0230   (BR)
BOARD OF EDUCATION OF SCHOOL DISTRICT NO. 23 (CENTRAL OKANAGAN), THE
SPRING VALLEY ELEMENTARY SCHOOL
470 Ziprick Rd, Kelowna, BC, V1X 4H4
(250) 870-5119
Emp Here 30
SIC 8211 Elementary and secondary schools

D-U-N-S 25-156-3656   (BR)
BOARD OF EDUCATION OF SCHOOL DISTRICT NO. 23 (CENTRAL OKANAGAN), THE
QUIGLEY ELEMENTARY SCHOOL

705 Kitch Rd, Kelowna, BC, V1X 5V8
(250) 870-5134
Emp Here 35
SIC 8211 Elementary and secondary schools

D-U-N-S 25-156-4902   (BR)
BOARD OF EDUCATION OF SCHOOL DISTRICT NO. 23 (CENTRAL OKANAGAN), THE
BELGO ELEMENTARY SCHOOL
125 Adventure Rd, Kelowna, BC, V1X 1N3

Emp Here 30
SIC 8211 Elementary and secondary schools

D-U-N-S 25-164-4464   (BR)
BOARD OF EDUCATION OF SCHOOL DISTRICT NO. 23 (CENTRAL OKANAGAN), THE
ELLISON ELEMENTARY SCHOOL
3735 Parkdale Rd, Kelowna, BC, V1X 6K9

Emp Here 25
SIC 8211 Elementary and secondary schools

D-U-N-S 25-150-3777   (BR)
BOARD OF EDUCATION OF SCHOOL DISTRICT NO. 23 (CENTRAL OKANAGAN), THE
RUTLAND SENIOR SECONDARY SCHOOL
705 Rutland Rd N, Kelowna, BC, V1X 3B6
(250) 870-5134
Emp Here 100
SIC 8211 Elementary and secondary schools

D-U-N-S 25-156-4282   (BR)
BOARD OF EDUCATION OF SCHOOL DISTRICT NO. 23 (CENTRAL OKANAGAN), THE
SPRINGVALLEY MIDDLE SCHOOL
350 Ziprick Rd, Kelowna, BC, V1X 4H3
(250) 870-5111
Emp Here 60
SIC 8211 Elementary and secondary schools

D-U-N-S 25-156-3623   (BR)
BOARD OF EDUCATION OF SCHOOL DISTRICT NO. 23 (CENTRAL OKANAGAN), THE
PEARSON ROAD ELEMENTARY SCHOOL
700 Pearson Rd, Kelowna, BC, V1X 5H8

Emp Here 53
SIC 8211 Elementary and secondary schools

D-U-N-S 25-231-7268   (BR)
BRICK WAREHOUSE LP, THE
BRICK, THE
948 Mccurdy Rd Suite 100, Kelowna, BC, V1X 2P7
(250) 765-2220
Emp Here 75
SIC 5712 Furniture stores

D-U-N-S 25-310-7940   (BR)
BRINK'S CANADA LIMITED
(*Suby of* The Brink's Company)
1516 Keehn Rd Suite 107, Kelowna, BC, V1X 5T3
(250) 862-3244
Emp Here 20
SIC 7381 Detective and armored car services

D-U-N-S 24-001-8940   (BR)
CACTUS RESTAURANTS LTD
CACTUS CLUB CAFE
1575 Banks Rd Suite 200, Kelowna, BC, V1X 7Y8
(250) 763-6752
Emp Here 120
SIC 5812 Eating places

D-U-N-S 24-931-2463   (SL)
CAMCO CUTTING TOOLS LTD
KENNAMETAL CAMCO
(*Suby of* Kennametal Inc.)
124 Adams Rd Suite 101, Kelowna, BC, V1X 7R2

Emp Here 21   *Sales* 5,626,880
SIC 5085 Industrial supplies
Fin Ex Jackie Patridge

D-U-N-S 20-303-3402   (BR)
CARA OPERATIONS LIMITED
KELSEY'S
(*Suby of* Cara Holdings Limited)
1500 Banks Rd Unit 400, Kelowna, BC, V1X 7Y1
(250) 861-7888
Emp Here 20
SIC 5812 Eating places

D-U-N-S 20-867-6788   (BR)
CASCADES CANADA ULC
CASCADES RECOVERY+
144 Cambro Rd Unit A, Kelowna, BC, V1X 7T3
(250) 491-2242
Emp Here 40
SIC 2611 Pulp mills

D-U-N-S 20-585-8777   (BR)
CINTAS CANADA LIMITED
CINTAS-THE UNIFORM PEOPLE
(*Suby of* Cintas Corporation)
2325 Norris Rd S, Kelowna, BC, V1X 8G7
(250) 491-9400
Emp Here 73
SIC 7213 Linen supply

D-U-N-S 25-999-1487   (BR)
COCA-COLA REFRESHMENTS CANADA COMPANY
(*Suby of* The Coca-Cola Company)
406 Old Vernon Rd Suite 100, Kelowna, BC, V1X 4R2
(250) 491-3414
Emp Here 100
SIC 2086 Bottled and canned soft drinks

D-U-N-S 20-802-0040   (BR)
COOPER MARKET LTD
COOPER'S FOODS
301 Highway 33 W Unit 10, Kelowna, BC, V1X 1X8
(250) 765-5690
Emp Here 100
SIC 5411 Grocery stores

D-U-N-S 25-287-5257   (BR)
COSTCO WHOLESALE CANADA LTD
COSTCO
(*Suby of* Costco Wholesale Corporation)
2479 Highway 97 N, Kelowna, BC, V1X 4J2
(250) 868-9515
Emp Here 250
SIC 5099 Durable goods, nec

D-U-N-S 24-033-1090   (SL)
CROSSROAD TREATMENT CENTRE SOCIETY
123 Franklyn Rd, Kelowna, BC, V1X 6A9
(250) 860-4001
Emp Here 65   *Sales* 2,553,625
SIC 8322 Individual and family services

D-U-N-S 24-798-2200   (BR)
FABRICLAND PACIFIC/MIDWEST LIMITED
FABRICLAND
2455 Highway 97 N, Kelowna, BC, V1X 4J2

Emp Here 30
SIC 5949 Sewing, needlework, and piece goods

D-U-N-S 24-317-2652   (BR)
GRAHAM GROUP LTD
184 Adams Rd Unit 101, Kelowna, BC, V1X 7R2
(250) 765-6662
Emp Here 30
SIC 1542 Nonresidential construction, nec

D-U-N-S 20-098-5000   (HQ)
GROWERS SUPPLY COMPANY LIMITED
(*Suby of* Okanagan Similkameen Cooperative Growers Association)

2605 Acland Rd, Kelowna, BC, V1X 7J4
(250) 765-4500
Emp Here 21   *Emp Total* 10
Sales 12,907,140
SIC 5191 Farm supplies
Pr Pr David Sloan
Mae Shannon

D-U-N-S 25-171-5637   (BR)
HOME DEPOT OF CANADA INC
HOME DEPOT
(*Suby of* The Home Depot Inc)
2515 Enterprise Way, Kelowna, BC, V1X 7K2
(250) 979-4501
Emp Here 150
SIC 5251 Hardware stores

D-U-N-S 20-698-6825   (BR)
HUDSON'S BAY COMPANY
HOME OUTFITTERS
1500 Banks Rd Unit 102, Kelowna, BC, V1X 7Y1
(250) 860-9052
Emp Here 40
SIC 5311 Department stores

D-U-N-S 20-927-3411   (BR)
INLAND RESTAURANTS (KAMLOOPS) LTD
WENDY'S
130 Hollywood Rd S, Kelowna, BC, V1X 3S9
(250) 868-3311
Emp Here 24
SIC 5812 Eating places

D-U-N-S 25-369-5746   (BR)
INTERIOR HEALTH AUTHORITY
REID'S CORNER REGIONAL SERVICES
2355 Acland Rd Suite 101, Kelowna, BC, V1X 7X9
(250) 491-6300
Emp Here 100
SIC 8062 General medical and surgical hospitals

D-U-N-S 25-014-9416   (BR)
INTERIOR SAVINGS CREDIT UNION
185 Futland Rd S, Kelowna, BC, V1X 2Z3
(250) 469-6575
Emp Here 26
SIC 6062 State credit unions

D-U-N-S 20-266-9771   (BR)
LOBLAWS INC
REAL CANADIAN SUPERSTORE, THE
2280 Baron Rd Suite 1564, Kelowna, BC, V1X 7W3
(250) 717-2536
Emp Here 200
SIC 5411 Grocery stores

D-U-N-S 25-408-7182   (BR)
METSO MINERALS CANADA INC
2281 Hunter Rd, Kelowna, BC, V1X 7C5
(250) 861-5501
Emp Here 21
SIC 8711 Engineering services

D-U-N-S 24-732-6028   (SL)
NORELCO CABINETS LTD
CUCINA DEL RE CABINETRY, DIV OF
205 Adams Rd, Kelowna, BC, V1X 7R1
(250) 765-2121
Emp Here 65   *Sales* 4,900,111
SIC 2434 Wood kitchen cabinets

D-U-N-S 20-956-7747   (SL)
OAKRIDGE ACCOUNTING SERVICES LTD
2604 Enterprise Way Unit 1, Kelowna, BC, V1X 7Y5
(250) 712-3800
Emp Here 86   *Sales* 3,793,956
SIC 8721 Accounting, auditing, and bookkeeping

D-U-N-S 20-893-2942   (BR)
ORKIN CANADA CORPORATION
ORKIN PEST CONTROL
(*Suby of* Rollins, Inc.)
3677 Highway 97 N Unit 107, Kelowna, BC,

V1X 5C3
(250) 624-9555
Emp Here 26
SIC 7342 Disinfecting and pest control services

D-U-N-S 25-190-0283   (BR)
ORKIN CANADA CORPORATION
PCO SERVICES
(*Suby of* Rollins, Inc.)
Unit 3 , 3190 Sexsmith Rd, Kelowna, BC, V1X 7S6
(250) 765-3714
Emp Here 38
SIC 7342 Disinfecting and pest control services

D-U-N-S 24-009-9445   (BR)
ORKIN CANADA CORPORATION
ORKIN PCO SERVICES
(*Suby of* Rollins, Inc.)
3677 Highway 97 N Suite 107, Kelowna, BC, V1X 5C3
(250) 765-3714
Emp Here 26
SIC 7342 Disinfecting and pest control services

D-U-N-S 24-342-2347   (BR)
P R HOTELS LTD
FAIRFIELD INN & SUITESSM BY MARRIOTT KELOWNA
(*Suby of* P R Hotels Ltd)
1655 Powick Rd, Kelowna, BC, V1X 4L1
(250) 763-2800
Emp Here 20
SIC 7011 Hotels and motels

D-U-N-S 25-320-8946   (BR)
PUROLATOR INC.
PUROLATOR INC
613 Adams Rd, Kelowna, BC, V1X 7R9
(250) 765-9422
Emp Here 21
SIC 7389 Business services, nec

D-U-N-S 24-778-4408   (HQ)
RAYBURN'S MARINE WORLD LTD
2330 Enterprise Way, Kelowna, BC, V1X 4H7
(250) 860-4232
Emp Here 35   *Emp Total* 36
Sales 6,055,738
SIC 5551 Boat dealers
Pr Pr Dale Koepke

D-U-N-S 25-944-0183   (BR)
RJAMES MANAGEMENT GROUP LTD
(*Suby of* Rjames Management Group Ltd)
150 Edwards Rd, Kelowna, BC, V1X 7J5
(250) 765-5555
Emp Here 35
SIC 5511 New and used car dealers

D-U-N-S 25-656-4097   (BR)
ROYAL BANK OF CANADA
RBC
(*Suby of* Royal Bank Of Canada)
301 Highway 33 W Unit 48, Kelowna, BC, V1X 1X8
(250) 765-7761
Emp Here 20
SIC 6021 National commercial banks

D-U-N-S 20-180-5913   (SL)
SPRING VALLEY CARE CENTRE LTD
355 Terai Crt Suite 220, Kelowna, BC, V1X 5X6
(250) 979-6000
Emp Here 120   *Sales* 7,913,100
SIC 8059 Nursing and personal care, nec
Pr Pr Altaf Jina
Jenny Jina

D-U-N-S 25-498-9593   (BR)
STAPLES CANADA INC
STAPLES THE BUSINESS DEPOT
(*Suby of* Staples, Inc.)
2339 Highway 97 N Suite 430, Kelowna, BC,

V1X 4H9
(250) 979-7920
Emp Here 30
SIC 5943 Stationery stores

D-U-N-S 24-020-5810   (BR)
STARBUCKS COFFEE CANADA, INC
STARBUCKS COFFEE
(*Suby of* Starbucks Corporation)
2709 Highway 97 N, Kelowna, BC, V1X 4J8
(250) 860-7632
Emp Here 23
SIC 5812 Eating places

D-U-N-S 20-187-3929   (SL)
TOTAL RESTORATION SERVICES INC
707 Finns Rd, Kelowna, BC, V1X 5B7
(250) 491-3828
Emp Here 50   *Sales* 1,708,160
SIC 7217 Carpet and upholstery cleaning

D-U-N-S 25-653-5089   (BR)
VALUE VILLAGE STORES, INC
(*Suby of* Savers, Inc.)
190 Aurora Cres, Kelowna, BC, V1X 7M3
(250) 491-1356
Emp Here 40
SIC 5399 Miscellaneous general merchandise

D-U-N-S 24-141-9324   (BR)
WAL-MART CANADA CORP
1555 Banks Rd, Kelowna, BC, V1X 7Y8
(250) 860-8811
Emp Here 150
SIC 5311 Department stores

D-U-N-S 24-839-3753   (BR)
WASTE CONNECTIONS OF CANADA INC
BFI CANADA
150 Campion St Unit 4, Kelowna, BC, V1X 7S8
(250) 765-0565
Emp Here 22
SIC 4953 Refuse systems

D-U-N-S 25-656-2042   (BR)
WENDCORP HOLDINGS INC
WENDY'S OLD FASHIONED HAMBURG
2330 Highway 97 N Suite 220, Kelowna, BC, V1X 4H8
(250) 768-8988
Emp Here 45
SIC 5812 Eating places

D-U-N-S 25-711-6152   (BR)
WILPAT INDUSTRIES LTD
DAIRY QUEEN
(*Suby of* Wilpat Industries Ltd)
570 Highway 33 W, Kelowna, BC, V1X 7K8
(250) 765-9477
Emp Here 28
SIC 5812 Eating places

D-U-N-S 20-860-4178   (BR)
WINNERS MERCHANTS INTERNATIONAL L.P.
HOMESENSE
(*Suby of* The TJX Companies Inc)
1575 Banks Rd Suite 400, Kelowna, BC, V1X 7Y8
(250) 763-6002
Emp Here 25
SIC 5651 Family clothing stores

Kelowna, BC V1Y
Central Okanagan County

D-U-N-S 24-316-3768   (SL)
ABOUGOUSH COLLISION INC
BOYD AUTOBODY AND GLASS
1960 Dayton St, Kelowna, BC, V1Y 7W6
(250) 868-2693
Emp Here 61   *Sales* 4,377,642
SIC 7532 Top and body repair and paint shops

D-U-N-S 25-630-9758   (BR)

ACCENT INNS INC
BLUE RIDGE INN
1140 Harvey Ave, Kelowna, BC, V1Y 6E7
(250) 862-8888
Emp Here 20
SIC 7011 Hotels and motels

D-U-N-S 20-182-3973   (BR)
ANDREW PELLER LIMITED
1125 Richter St, Kelowna, BC, V1Y 2K6
(250) 762-3332
Emp Here 70
SIC 5921 Liquor stores

D-U-N-S 20-703-0359   (BR)
ARAMARK ENTERTAINMENT SERVICES (CANADA) INC
1223 Water St, Kelowna, BC, V1Y 9V1
(250) 979-0878
Emp Here 125
SIC 8742 Management consulting services

D-U-N-S 25-654-1657   (SL)
ARC PROGRAMS LTD
513 Bernard Ave, Kelowna, BC, V1Y 6N9
(250) 763-2977
Emp Here 50   *Sales* 1,824,018
SIC 8361 Residential care

D-U-N-S 20-297-6051   (BR)
BC CANCER FOUNDATION
BRITISH COLUMBIA CANCER FOUNDATION
399 Royal Ave, Kelowna, BC, V1Y 5L3
(250) 712-3900
Emp Here 250
SIC 8069 Specialty hospitals, except psychiatric

D-U-N-S 25-321-0579   (BR)
BDO CANADA LLP
KELOWNA ACCOUNTING
1631 Dickson Ave Suite 400, Kelowna, BC, V1Y 0B5
(250) 763-6700
Emp Here 48
SIC 8721 Accounting, auditing, and bookkeeping

D-U-N-S 25-295-8772   (BR)
BANK OF NOVA SCOTIA, THE
SCOTIABANK
488 Bernard Ave, Kelowna, BC, V1Y 6N7
(250) 712-4055
Emp Here 32
SIC 6021 National commercial banks

D-U-N-S 25-604-9545   (BR)
BANK OF MONTREAL
BMO
1141 Harvey Ave, Kelowna, BC, V1Y 6E8
(250) 861-1660
Emp Here 30
SIC 6021 National commercial banks

D-U-N-S 20-002-9903   (BR)
BANQUE TORONTO-DOMINION, LA
TORONTO-DOMINION BANK, THE
(*Suby of* Toronto-Dominion Bank, The)
1950 Harvey Ave Suite 150, Kelowna, BC, V1Y 8J8
(250) 762-4142
Emp Here 25
SIC 6021 National commercial banks

D-U-N-S 20-700-0477   (BR)
BANQUE DE DEVELOPPEMENT DU CANADA
BDC
313 Bernard Ave, Kelowna, BC, V1Y 6N6
(250) 470-4802
Emp Here 30
SIC 6141 Personal credit institutions

D-U-N-S 20-702-3578   (BR)
BELL MEDIA INC
CKBL & CHSU BULLET 1150
435 Bernard Ave Suite 300, Kelowna, BC, V1Y

6N8
(250) 860-8600
Emp Here 50
SIC 4832 Radio broadcasting stations

D-U-N-S 25-150-4270   (BR)
BOARD OF EDUCATION OF SCHOOL DISTRICT NO. 23 (CENTRAL OKANAGAN), THE
A. S. MATHESON ELEMENTARY SCHOOL
2090 Gordon Dr, Kelowna, BC, V1Y 3H9

Emp Here 40
SIC 8211 Elementary and secondary schools

D-U-N-S 25-151-0541   (BR)
BOARD OF EDUCATION OF SCHOOL DISTRICT NO. 23 (CENTRAL OKANAGAN), THE
KELOWNA SECONDARY
1079 Raymer Ave, Kelowna, BC, V1Y 4Z7
(250) 870-5105
Emp Here 130
SIC 8211 Elementary and secondary schools

D-U-N-S 20-713-2510   (BR)
BOARD OF EDUCATION OF SCHOOL DISTRICT NO. 23 (CENTRAL OKANAGAN), THE
GLENMORE ELEMENTARY
960 Glenmore Dr, Kelowna, BC, V1Y 4P1

Emp Here 50
SIC 8211 Elementary and secondary schools

D-U-N-S 20-713-2478   (BR)
BOARD OF EDUCATION OF SCHOOL DISTRICT NO. 23 (CENTRAL OKANAGAN), THE
BANKHEAD ELEMENTARY SCHOOL
1280 Wilson Ave, Kelowna, BC, V1Y 6Y6

Emp Here 50
SIC 8211 Elementary and secondary schools

D-U-N-S 20-713-2544   (BR)
BOARD OF EDUCATION OF SCHOOL DISTRICT NO. 23 (CENTRAL OKANAGAN), THE
MCWILLIAM CENTRE
580 Doyle Ave, Kelowna, BC, V1Y 7V1

Emp Here 50
SIC 8211 Elementary and secondary schools

D-U-N-S 20-236-1981   (BR)
BOYD GROUP INC, THE
BOYD AUTOBODY & GLASS
1960a Dayton St, Kelowna, BC, V1Y 7W6
(250) 868-2693
Emp Here 30
SIC 7532 Top and body repair and paint shops

D-U-N-S 25-067-5790   (BR)
BRITISH COLUMBIA AUTOMOBILE ASSOCIATION
BCAA KELOWNA 82
1470 Harvey Ave Suite 18, Kelowna, BC, V1Y 9K8
(250) 870-4900
Emp Here 25
SIC 8699 Membership organizations, nec

D-U-N-S 25-288-8938   (BR)
CANADA POST CORPORATION
530 Gaston Ave, Kelowna, BC, V1Y 0A5
(250) 762-2118
Emp Here 50
SIC 4311 U.s. postal service

D-U-N-S 20-026-8691   (BR)
CANADIAN BLOOD SERVICES
1865 Dilworth Dr Suite 103, Kelowna, BC, V1Y 9T1
(250) 717-5244
Emp Here 30
SIC 8099 Health and allied services, nec

D-U-N-S 24-657-3356   (BR)
CANADIAN IMPERIAL BANK OF COMMERCE
CIBC
328 Bernard Ave Ste 2, Kelowna, BC, V1Y 6N5
(250) 763-6611
Emp Here 50
SIC 6021 National commercial banks

D-U-N-S 25-970-0771   (BR)
CANADIAN IMPERIAL BANK OF COMMERCE
CIBC
2107 Harvey Ave, Kelowna, BC, V1Y 9X4
(250) 470-1650
Emp Here 50
SIC 6021 National commercial banks

D-U-N-S 24-760-2811   (BR)
CANADIAN MENTAL HEALTH ASSOCIATION, THE
KELOWNA DISTRICT BRANCH
(*Suby of* Canadian Mental Health Association, The)
504 Sutherland Ave, Kelowna, BC, V1Y 5X1
(250) 861-3644
Emp Here 30
SIC 8621 Professional organizations

D-U-N-S 20-860-9151   (BR)
CANADIAN NORTHERN SHIELD INSURANCE COMPANY
CNS
1633 Ellis St Suite 400, Kelowna, BC, V1Y 2A8
(250) 712-1236
Emp Here 22
SIC 6411 Insurance agents, brokers, and service

D-U-N-S 25-316-0121   (BR)
CANADIAN WESTERN BANK
1674 Bertram St Suite 100, Kelowna, BC, V1Y 9G4
(250) 862-8008
Emp Here 20
SIC 6021 National commercial banks

D-U-N-S 25-657-0102   (SL)
CAPRI INTERCITY FINANCIAL CORP
1835 Gordon Dr Suite 204, Kelowna, BC, V1Y 3H5
(250) 860-2426
Emp Here 49   *Sales* 4,377,642
SIC 6411 Insurance agents, brokers, and service

D-U-N-S 24-343-1355   (BR)
CARA OPERATIONS LIMITED
SWISS CHALET
(*Suby of* Cara Holdings Limited)
1455 Harvey Ave Suite 1475, Kelowna, BC, V1Y 6E9
(250) 762-6362
Emp Here 40
SIC 5812 Eating places

D-U-N-S 24-938-8950   (SL)
CHELTON TECHNOLOGIES CANADA LIMITED
(*Suby of* COBHAM PLC)
1925 Kirschner Rd Suite 14, Kelowna, BC, V1Y 4N7
(250) 763-2232
Emp Here 160   *Sales* 27,200,281
SIC 3663 Radio and t.v. communications equipment
Fin Ex Mark Phillips
Pr Steve Brunsden

D-U-N-S 24-823-9493   (BR)
CINEPLEX ODEON CORPORATION
FAMOUS PLAYERS ORCHARD PLAZA 5
1876 Cooper Rd Suite 160, Kelowna, BC, V1Y 9N6
(250) 860-1611
Emp Here 20

SIC 7832 Motion picture theaters, except drive-in

D-U-N-S 24-320-3556   (BR)
COAST HOTELS LIMITED
COAST CAPRI HOTEL, THE
1171 Harvey Ave, Kelowna, BC, V1Y 6E8
(250) 860-6060
Emp Here 50
SIC 7011 Hotels and motels

D-U-N-S 25-652-8498   (SL)
COLDWELL BANKER HORIZON REALTY LTD
COLDWELL BANKER HORIZON REALTY
1470 Harvey Ave Suite 14, Kelowna, BC, V1Y 9K8
(250) 860-7500
Emp Here 49   *Sales* 6,184,080
SIC 6531 Real estate agents and managers
Prin Christina Raho

D-U-N-S 24-234-1121   (BR)
COLLIERS MACAULAY NICOLLS INC
546 Leon Ave Unit 304, Kelowna, BC, V1Y 6J6
(250) 763-2300
Emp Here 30
SIC 6531 Real estate agents and managers

D-U-N-S 20-284-6093   (BR)
DAVIDSTEA INC
DAVIDSTEA
2271 Harvey Ave, Kelowna, BC, V1Y 6H2
(250) 862-1331
Emp Here 20
SIC 5499 Miscellaneous food stores

D-U-N-S 20-937-1975   (BR)
DENCAN RESTAURANTS INC
DENNY'S RESTAURANT
(*Suby of* Northland Properties Corporation)
2130 Harvey Ave, Kelowna, BC, V1Y 6G8
(250) 860-1133
Emp Here 20
SIC 5812 Eating places

D-U-N-S 20-072-9825   (BR)
DIVERSICARE CANADA MANAGEMENT SERVICES CO., INC
HAWTHORN PARK
867 K.L.O. Rd, Kelowna, BC, V1Y 9G5
(250) 861-6636
Emp Here 100
SIC 8361 Residential care

D-U-N-S 20-919-3655   (SL)
DOAK SHIRREFF LLP
537 Leon Ave Suite 200, Kelowna, BC, V1Y 2A9
(250) 763-4345
Emp Here 52   *Sales* 4,450,603
SIC 8111 Legal services

D-U-N-S 20-055-7416   (SL)
DYCK'S DRUGS (1994) LTD
DYCK'S MEDICINE CENTER
1460 St. Paul St, Kelowna, BC, V1Y 2E6
(250) 762-3333
Emp Here 30   *Sales* 5,693,280
SIC 5912 Drug stores and proprietary stores
Pr Doug Patterson

D-U-N-S 24-329-5321   (SL)
EARL'S ON TOP RESTAURANT LTD
211 Bernard Ave, Kelowna, BC, V1Y 6N2
(250) 763-2777
Emp Here 100   *Sales* 2,991,389
SIC 5812 Eating places

D-U-N-S 24-340-1028   (BR)
FGL SPORTS LTD
SPORT-CHEK
2271 Harvey Ave Unit 1410, Kelowna, BC, V1Y 6H2
(250) 860-7669
Emp Here 70
SIC 5941 Sporting goods and bicycle shops

D-U-N-S 24-527-3052   (BR)

FARM BUSINESS CONSULTANTS INC
FBC
1690 Water St Suite 200, Kelowna, BC, V1Y 8T8

Emp Here 50
SIC 7291 Tax return preparation services

D-U-N-S 20-296-0563   (BR)
FARRIS, VAUGHAN, WILLS & MURPHY LLP
(*Suby of* Farris, Vaughan, Wills & Murphy LLP)
1631 Dickson Ave Suite 1800, Kelowna, BC, V1Y 0B5
(250) 861-5332
Emp Here 31
SIC 8111 Legal services

D-U-N-S 20-108-3169   (HQ)
FORTISBC INC
1975 Springfield Rd Suite 100, Kelowna, BC, V1Y 7V7
(604) 576-7000
Emp Here 80   *Emp Total* 8,000
Sales 266,642,023
SIC 4911 Electric services
Pr Pr Michael Mulcahy
  Roger A. Dall'antonia
  Doyle Sam
  Ian Lorimer
VP Cynthia Des Brisay
  Douglas L. Stout
VP Dennis Swanson
VP Diane Roy
Pers/VP Jody Drope
  Brenda Eaton

D-U-N-S 24-374-3775   (BR)
FORTISBC INC
2076 Enterprise Way Suite 200, Kelowna, BC, V1Y 6H7
(250) 469-8000
Emp Here 50
SIC 4911 Electric services

D-U-N-S 20-298-9166   (SL)
FORTISBC PACIFIC HOLDINGS INC
1975 Springfield Rd Suite 100, Kelowna, BC, V1Y 7V7
(250) 469-8000
Emp Here 2,000   *Sales* 1,286,779,440
SIC 4911 Electric services
Pr John Walker
VP Fin Michele Leeners

D-U-N-S 25-853-0724   (BR)
GOLDER ASSOCIATES LTD
1755 Springfield Rd Suite 220, Kelowna, BC, V1Y 5V5
(250) 860-8424
Emp Here 40
SIC 8748 Business consulting, nec

D-U-N-S 24-497-1719   (SL)
GOLDWING INVESTMENTS (SASKATOON) LIMITED
BINGO KELOWNA
1585 Springfield Rd, Kelowna, BC, V1Y 5V5
(250) 860-9577
Emp Here 60   *Sales* 3,283,232
SIC 7999 Amusement and recreation, nec

D-U-N-S 25-186-7768   (BR)
GOODLIFE FITNESS CENTRES INC
GOODLIFE FITNESS
1835 Gordon Dr Unit 119, Kelowna, BC, V1Y 3H4
(250) 868-3788
Emp Here 30
SIC 7991 Physical fitness facilities

D-U-N-S 24-371-6982   (BR)
GOVERNING COUNCIL OF THE SALVATION ARMY IN CANADA, THE
GOVERNING COUNCIL OF THE SALVATION ARMY IN CANADA, THE
1447 Ellis St, Kelowna, BC, V1Y 2A3
(250) 762-5182
Emp Here 20

SIC 5932 Used merchandise stores

D-U-N-S 20-739-1843   (BR)
GOVERNMENT OF THE PROVINCE OF BRITISH COLUMBIA
LIQUOR STORE
1835 Dilworth Dr Suite 109, Kelowna, BC, V1Y 9T1
(250) 861-7339
Emp Here 70
SIC 5921 Liquor stores

D-U-N-S 20-272-1945   (BR)
GRAND OKANAGAN RESORT LIMITED PARTNERSHIP
GRAND CKANAGAN RESORT
(*Suby of* Grand Okanagan Resort Limited Partnership)
1310 Water St, Kelowna, BC, V1Y 9P3
(250) 868-5629
Emp Here 20
SIC 7991 Physical fitness facilities

D-U-N-S 20-860-9201   (BR)
GRANT THORNTON LLP
CAPSERVCO
1633 Ellis St Suite 200, Kelowna, V1Y 2A8
(250) 712-6800
Emp Here 75
SIC 8721 Accounting, auditing, and bookkeeping

D-U-N-S 24-797-8547   (BR)
GREAT PACIFIC INDUSTRIES INC
SAVE-ON-FOODS
1876 Cooper Rd Suite 101, Kelowna, BC, V1Y 9N6
(250) 860-1444
Emp Here 130
SIC 5411 Grocery stores

D-U-N-S 24-681-4131   (BR)
HSBC BANK CANADA
1950 Cooper Rd, Kelowna, BC, V1Y 8K5
(250) 762-2811
Emp Here 22
SIC 6021 National commercial banks

D-U-N-S 25-270-3244   (BR)
HSBC BANK CANADA
384 Bernard Ave, Kelowna, BC, V1Y 6N5
(250) 763-3939
Emp Here 30
SIC 6021 National commercial banks

D-U-N-S 24-204-2625   (BR)
HUBER DEVELOPMENT LTD
PRESTIGE HOTELS
1675 Abbott St, Kelowna, BC, V1Y 8S3
(250) 860-7900
Emp Here 35
SIC 7011 Hotels and motels

D-U-N-S 25-301-2264   (BR)
HUDSON'S BAY COMPANY
2271 Harvey Ave Suite 1415, Kelowna, BC, V1Y 6H3
(250) 860-2483
Emp Here 175
SIC 5311 Department stores

D-U-N-S 24-309-3718   (BR)
INTERIOR HEALTH AUTHORITY
COMMUNITY CARE HEALTH CARE SERVICES
1860 Dayton St Unit 102, Kelowna, BC, V1Y 7W6
(250) 870-5852
Emp Here 27
SIC 8093 Specialty outpatient clinics, nec

D-U-N-S 20-939-0447   (BR)
INTERIOR HEALTH AUTHORITY
DAVID LLOYD JONES HOME
934 Bernard Ave, Kelowna, BC, V1Y 6P8
(250) 762-2706
Emp Here 84
SIC 8062 General medical and surgical hospi-

tals

D-U-N-S 20-317-3591   (BR)
INTERIOR HEALTH AUTHORITY
COTTONWOODS CARE CENTRE
2255 Ethel St, Kelowna, BC, V1Y 2Z9
(250) 862-4100
Emp Here 478
SIC 8062 General medical and surgical hospitals

D-U-N-S 20-875-3470   (BR)
INTERIOR HEALTH AUTHORITY
CAPRI COMMUNITY HEALTH CENTRE
1835 Gordon Dr Suite 118, Kelowna, BC, V1Y 3H4
(250) 980-1400
Emp Here 200
SIC 8062 General medical and surgical hospitals

D-U-N-S 20-802-4559   (BR)
INTERIOR HEALTH AUTHORITY
1340 Ellis St, Kelowna, BC, V1Y 9N1
(250) 862-4205
Emp Here 20
SIC 8093 Specialty outpatient clinics, nec

D-U-N-S 24-457-9397   (BR)
INTERIOR HEALTH AUTHORITY
THREE LINKS MANOR
1449 Kelglen Cres, Kelowna, BC, V1Y 8P4
(250) 763-2585
Emp Here 80
SIC 8062 General medical and surgical hospitals

D-U-N-S 24-309-1118   (BR)
INTERIOR HEALTH AUTHORITY
CENTRAL OKANAGAN HOSPICE HOUSE
2035 Ethel St, Kelowna, BC, V1Y 2Z6
(250) 862-4126
Emp Here 200
SIC 8062 General medical and surgical hospitals

D-U-N-S 24-394-7988   (BR)
INTERIOR HEALTH AUTHORITY
1620 Dickson Ave Unit B3, Kelowna, V1Y 9Y2
(250) 870-5874
Emp Here 50
SIC 8062 General medical and surgical hospitals

D-U-N-S 25-630-1698   (BR)
INTERIOR SAVINGS CREDIT UNION
2071 Harvey Ave, Kelowna, BC, V1Y 8M1
(250) 860-7400
Emp Here 27
SIC 6062 State credit unions

D-U-N-S 25-315-7275   (BR)
INVESTORS GROUP FINANCIAL SERVICES INC
INVESTORS GROUP
1628 Dickson Ave Suite 100, Kelowna, BC, V1Y 9X1
(250) 762-3329
Emp Here 75
SIC 8742 Management consulting services

D-U-N-S 25-357-4180   (SL)
KELOWNA COMMUNITY RESOURCES SOCIETY
1735 Dolphin Ave Suite 120, Kelowna, BC, V1Y 8A6
(250) 763-8008
Emp Here 50   *Sales* 1,969,939
SIC 8322 Individual and family services

D-U-N-S 24-492-8289   (SL)
KELOWNA TRINITY BAPTIST CHURCH
TRINITY BAPTIST
1905 Springfield Rd, Kelowna, BC, V1Y 7V7
(250) 860-3273
Emp Here 51   *Sales* 3,356,192
SIC 8661 Religious organizations

D-U-N-S 25-839-4329   (SL)
LIFESTYLE EQUITY SOCIETY
1726 Dolphin Ave Suite 305, Kelowna, BC, V1Y 9R9
(250) 869-0186
Emp Here 50   *Sales* 1,824,018
SIC 8361 Residential care

D-U-N-S 25-159-1517   (BR)
LOBLAWS INC
EXTRA FOODS
1835 Gordon Dr Suite 136, Kelowna, BC, V1Y 3H4
(250) 861-1525
Emp Here 40
SIC 5912 Drug stores and proprietary stores

D-U-N-S 20-166-6638   (SL)
LODGING COMPANY RESERVATIONS LTD, THE
510 Bernard Ave Suite 200, Kelowna, BC, V1Y 6P1
(250) 979-3939
Emp Here 55   *Sales* 2,845,467
SIC 7389 Business services, nec

D-U-N-S 25-604-2201   (BR)
LORDCO PARTS LTD
LORDCO AUTO PARTS
1656 Dilworth Dr, Kelowna, BC, V1Y 7V3
(250) 763-3621
Emp Here 35
SIC 5531 Auto and home supply stores

D-U-N-S 20-867-6879   (BR)
MNP LLP
1628 Dickson Ave Suite 600, Kelowna, BC, V1Y 9X1
(250) 763-8919
Emp Here 50
SIC 8721 Accounting, auditing, and bookkeeping

D-U-N-S 25-653-3639   (BR)
NETWORC HEALTH INC
LIFE MARK HEALTH CENTRE
(*Suby of* Networc Health Inc)
1634 Harvey Ave Unit 104, Kelowna, BC, V1Y 6G2
(250) 860-0171
Emp Here 50
SIC 8093 Specialty outpatient clinics, nec

D-U-N-S 25-116-8535   (BR)
NEWCAP INC
1601 Bertram St, Kelowna, BC, V1Y 2G5
(250) 869-8102
Emp Here 20
SIC 4832 Radio broadcasting stations

D-U-N-S 24-162-9468   (SL)
NORTHERN AIRBORNE TECHNOLOGY LTD
(*Suby of* COBHAM PLC)
1925 Kirschner Rd Suite 14, Kelowna, BC, V1Y 4N7
(250) 763-2232
Emp Here 40   *Sales* 5,690,935
SIC 3663 Radio and t.v. communications equipment
   Kenneth Veitch
   Raymond Lewis

D-U-N-S 25-316-4842   (BR)
NORTHLAND PROPERTIES CORPORATION
SANDMAN HOTEL & SUITES KELOWNA
(*Suby of* Northland Properties Corporation)
2130 Harvey Ave, Kelowna, BC, V1Y 6G8
(250) 860-6409
Emp Here 80
SIC 7011 Hotels and motels

D-U-N-S 25-630-1862   (SL)
O'BRYAN'S, KELLY NEIGHBOURHOOD RESTAURANT (2000) LTD
262 Bernard Ave, Kelowna, BC, V1Y 6N4
(250) 861-1338
Emp Here 50   *Sales* 1,532,175

SIC 5812 Eating places

D-U-N-S 20-734-0139   (BR)
OK BUILDERS SUPPLIES LTD
1095 Ellis St, Kelowna, BC, V1Y 1Z3
(250) 762-2422
Emp Here 25
SIC 5211 Lumber and other building materials

D-U-N-S 20-336-9533   (BR)
OKANAGAN COLLEGE
CONTINUING STUDIES
1000 K.L.O. Rd Unit A108, Kelowna, V1Y 4X8
(250) 862-5480
Emp Here 200
SIC 7371 Custom computer programming services

D-U-N-S 25-841-8664   (BR)
OKANAGAN REGIONAL LIBRARY DISTRICT
KELOWNA BRANCH OF THE OKANAGAN REGIONAL LIBRARY
1380 Ellis St, Kelowna, BC, V1Y 2A2
(250) 762-2800
Emp Here 40
SIC 8231 Libraries

D-U-N-S 25-656-3107   (BR)
OLD NAVY (CANADA) INC
(*Suby of* The Gap Inc)
2271 Harvey Ave Ste 877, Kelowna, BC, V1Y 6H2
(250) 860-0151
Emp Here 28
SIC 5651 Family clothing stores

D-U-N-S 25-267-4353   (BR)
PRINCESS AUTO LTD
1920 Spall Rd, Kelowna, BC, V1Y 4R1
(250) 860-6191
Emp Here 45
SIC 5999 Miscellaneous retail stores, nec

D-U-N-S 25-986-9600   (SL)
QUALITY GREENS LTD
1889 Spall Rd Unit 101, Kelowna, BC, V1Y 4R2
(250) 763-8200
Emp Here 48   *Sales* 5,681,200
SIC 5431 Fruit and vegetable markets
Pr Pr Chris Holmes
   Lisa Taylor-Holmes

D-U-N-S 24-566-0902   (BR)
RBC DOMINION SECURITIES INC
(*Suby of* Royal Bank Of Canada)
1708 Dolphin Ave Suite 1100, Kelowna, BC, V1Y 9S4
(250) 395-4259
Emp Here 25
SIC 6282 Investment advice

D-U-N-S 25-086-4204   (BR)
RG PROPERTIES LTD
1223 Water St Suite 102, Kelowna, BC, V1Y 9V1
(250) 979-0888
Emp Here 150
SIC 7999 Amusement and recreation, nec

D-U-N-S 25-656-4089   (BR)
RTM OPERATING COMPANY OF CANADA INC
ARBY'S OF CANADA
(*Suby of* Roark Capital Group Inc.)
2070 Harvey Ave Suite 16, Kelowna, BC, V1Y 8P8
(250) 763-0006
Emp Here 40
SIC 5812 Eating places

D-U-N-S 25-157-4539   (BR)
RAYMOND JAMES (USA) LTD
(*Suby of* Raymond James Financial, Inc.)
1726 Dolphin Ave Suite 500, Kelowna, BC, V1Y 9R9

(250) 979-2700
Emp Here 26
SIC 6211 Security brokers and dealers

D-U-N-S 20-708-9850   (BR)
REVERA INC
DORCHESTER RETIREMENT RESIDENCE, THE
863 Leon Ave Suite 204, Kelowna, BC, V1Y 9V4
(250) 860-0725
Emp Here 30
SIC 6513 Apartment building operators

D-U-N-S 25-630-9386   (BR)
ROYAL BANK OF CANADA
ROYAL BANK FINANCIAL GROUP
(*Suby of* Royal Bank Of Canada)
1840 Cooper Rd, Kelowna, BC, V1Y 8K5
(250) 860-3727
Emp Here 26
SIC 6021 National commercial banks

D-U-N-S 24-019-1275   (BR)
S C RESTORATIONS LTD
1025 Trench Pl, Kelowna, BC, V1Y 9Y4
(250) 763-1556
Emp Here 100
SIC 7299 Miscellaneous personal service

D-U-N-S 25-652-8589   (BR)
SCOTIA CAPITAL INC
SCOTIA MCLEOD
1620 Dickson Ave Suite 600, Kelowna, BC, V1Y 9Y2
(250) 868-5500
Emp Here 20
SIC 6211 Security brokers and dealers

D-U-N-S 25-656-2257   (SL)
SLIZEK INC
ADVOCARE HEALTH SERVICES
1450 St. Paul St, Kelowna, BC, V1Y 2E6
(250) 861-3446
Emp Here 100   *Sales* 4,815,406
SIC 8049 Offices of health practitioner

D-U-N-S 20-300-7059   (BR)
STANTEC ARCHITECTURE LTD
1620 Dickson Ave Suite 400, Kelowna, BC, V1Y 9Y2
(250) 860-3225
Emp Here 21
SIC 8712 Architectural services

D-U-N-S 25-147-4953   (BR)
STANTEC CONSULTING LTD
1620 Dickson Ave Suite 400, Kelowna, BC, V1Y 9Y2
(250) 860-3225
Emp Here 21
SIC 8711 Engineering services

D-U-N-S 20-300-7216   (BR)
STANTEC GEOMATICS LTD
1620 Dickson Ave Suite 400, Kelowna, BC, V1Y 9Y2
(250) 860-3225
Emp Here 21
SIC 8713 Surveying services

D-U-N-S 20-506-0598   (BR)
STARBUCKS COFFEE CANADA, INC
(*Suby of* Starbucks Corporation)
2271 Harvey Ave Suite 1264, Kelowna, BC, V1Y 6H2
(250) 762-8851
Emp Here 24
SIC 5812 Eating places

D-U-N-S 24-228-2296   (BR)
SYSTEMES CANADIEN KRONOS INC
(*Suby of* Kronos Parent Corporation)
1060 Manhattan Dr Suite 200, Kelowna, BC, V1Y 9X9
(250) 763-0034
Emp Here 20
SIC 7371 Custom computer programming services

D-U-N-S 20-294-6559   (BR)
TEC THE EDUCATION COMPANY INC
CENTER FOR ARTS & TECHNOLOGY OKANAGAN
1632 Dickson Ave Suite 100, Kelowna, BC, V1Y 7T2
(250) 860-2787
Emp Here 75
SIC 8222 Junior colleges

D-U-N-S 25-748-6217   (BR)
TETRA TECH CANADA INC
(*Suby of* Tetra Tech, Inc.)
1715 Dickson Ave Suite 150, Kelowna, BC, V1Y 9G6
(250) 862-4832
Emp Here 42
SIC 8711 Engineering services

D-U-N-S 20-191-8377   (BR)
THYSSENKRUPP ELEVATOR (CANADA) LIMITED
THYSSENKRUPP ELEVATOR
1891 Springfield Rd Suite 205, Kelowna, BC, V1Y 5V5
(250) 763-2804
Emp Here 22
SIC 1796 Installing building equipment

D-U-N-S 25-297-8754   (BR)
TOYS 'R' US (CANADA) LTD
TOYS 'R' US
(*Suby of* Toys "r" Us, Inc.)
2020 Harvey Ave, Kelowna, BC, V1Y 8J8
(250) 362-8697
Emp Here 20
SIC 5945 Hobby, toy, and game shops

D-U-N-S 24-390-0359   (BR)
TRAVELBRANDS INC
TRAVELBRANDS INC
2067 Enterprise Way, Kelowna, BC, V1Y 8R6
(250) 861-8000
Emp Here 50
SIC 4724 Travel agencies

D-U-N-S 24-014-8853   (SL)
TROIKA DEVELOPMENT INC
(*Suby of* Troika Ventures Inc)
1856 Ambrosi Rd Suite 114, Kelowna, BC, V1Y 4R9
(250) 869-4945
Emp Here 40   *Sales* 12,478,350
SIC 8399 Social services, nec
Pr Renee Wasylyk
Bradley (Brad) Klassen
Brian Wall

D-U-N-S 25-862-2273   (BR)
URBAN SYSTEMS LTD
1353 Ellis St Unit 304, Kelowna, BC, V1Y 1Z9
(250) 762-2517
Emp Here 400
SIC 8711 Engineering services

D-U-N-S 24-370-8559   (HQ)
VALLEY MEDICAL LABORATORIES
(*Suby of* Valley Medical Laboratories)
537 Leon Ave Suite 105, Kelowna, BC, V1Y 2A9
(250) 763-4813
Emp Here 20   *Emp Total* 57
Sales 4,596,524
SIC 8071 Medical laboratories

D-U-N-S 20-513-9715   (BR)
VANCOUVER CAREER COLLEGE (BURNABY) INC
VANCOUVER CAREER COLLEGE
(*Suby of* Chung Family Holdings Inc)
1649 Pandosy St, Kelowna, BC, V1Y 1P6
(250) 763-5800
Emp Here 27
SIC 8221 Colleges and universities

D-U-N-S 25-813-2471   (BR)
VITALAIRE CANADA INC
VILALAIRE HEATHCARE/SANTE

1980 Springfield Rd, Kelowna, BC, V1Y 5V7
(250) 862-2350
Emp Here 20
SIC 5047 Medical and hospital equipment

D-U-N-S 20-864-6922   (BR)
WGP-225 HOLDINGS LTD
TIM HORTONS
(*Suby of* WGP-225 Holdings Ltd)
1901 Harvey Ave, Kelowna, BC, V1Y 6G5
(250) 869-0855
Emp Here 50
SIC 5812 Eating places

D-U-N-S 20-735-2225   (BR)
WSP CANADA GROUP LIMITED
MMM GEOMATICS BC
540 Leon Ave, Kelowna, BC, V1Y 6J6
(250) 869-1334
Emp Here 30
SIC 8711 Engineering services

D-U-N-S 24-842-4801   (SL)
WATERPLAY SOLUTIONS CORP
1451 Ellis St Unit B, Kelowna, BC, V1Y 2A3
(250) 712-3393
Emp Here 60   *Sales* 10,214,498
SIC 4941 Water supply
Lisa Neilson

D-U-N-S 20-749-3008   (HQ)
WILPAT INDUSTRIES LTD
DAIRY QUEEN
(*Suby of* Wilpat Industries Ltd)
1740 Gordon Dr, Kelowna, BC, V1Y 3H2
(250) 762-5452
Emp Here 30   *Emp Total* 120
Sales 3,648,035
SIC 5812 Eating places

D-U-N-S 20-199-3099   (BR)
WINNERS MERCHANTS INTERNATIONAL L.P.
WINNERS
(*Suby of* The TJX Companies Inc)
1835 Gordon Dr, Kelowna, BC, V1Y 3H4
(250) 860-0267
Emp Here 40
SIC 5651 Family clothing stores

D-U-N-S 25-898-6991   (BR)
WORKERS' COMPENSATION BOARD OF BRITISH COLUMBIA
WORKSAFE BC
2045 Enterprise Way Unit 110, Kelowna, BC, V1Y 9T5
(250) 717-4301
Emp Here 50
SIC 6331 Fire, marine, and casualty insurance

D-U-N-S 20-308-7507   (BR)
YM INC. (SALES)
URBAN PLANET
2271 Harvey Ave, Kelowna, BC, V1Y 6H2
(250) 712-0362
Emp Here 30
SIC 5621 Women's clothing stores

Kelowna, BC V4V
Central Okanagan County

D-U-N-S 24-387-4927   (SL)
ARMORWORKS ENTERPRISES CANADA, ULC
(*Suby of* Armorworks, Inc)
8775 Jim Bailey Cres Suite B2, Kelowna, BC, V4V 2L7
(250) 766-0145
Emp Here 45   *Sales* 4,961,328
SIC 3499 Fabricated Metal products, nec

D-U-N-S 24-400-2382   (SL)
HOLIDAY PARK RESORT LTD
415 Commonwealth Rd Unit 1, Kelowna, BC, V4V 1P4

(250) 766-4255
Emp Here 50   *Sales* 2,188,821
SIC 7011 Hotels and motels

D-U-N-S 20-960-6867   (SL)
HOLIDAY PARK RV & CONDO RESORT LTD
415 Commonwealth Rd Unit 1, Kelowna, BC, V4V 1P4
(250) 766-4255
Emp Here 60   *Sales* 2,626,585
SIC 7011 Hotels and motels

D-U-N-S 20-867-6952   (BR)
TOLKO INDUSTRIES LTD
LAKE COUNTRY DIVISION
400 Beaver Lake Rd, Kelowna, BC, V4V 1S5
(250) 766-1207
Emp Here 35
SIC 5031 Lumber, plywood, and millwork

D-U-N-S 24-333-5226   (BR)
VARSTEEL LTD
280 Bubna Rd, Kelowna, BC, V4V 2N4
(250) 766-5222
Emp Here 20
SIC 5051 Metals service centers and offices

D-U-N-S 24-990-9334   (BR)
WASTE MANAGEMENT OF CANADA CORPORATION
(*Suby of* Waste Management, Inc.)
350 Beaver Lake Rd, Kelowna, BC, V4V 1S5
(250) 766-9100
Emp Here 75
SIC 4953 Refuse systems

Kimberley, BC V1A
East Kootenay County

D-U-N-S 25-836-0031   (BR)
BOARD OF EDUCATION OF SCHOOL DISTRICT NO. 06 (ROCKY MOUNTAIN), THE
SCHOOL DISTRICT NO 6 (KIMBERLEY) SCHOOL BUS OPERATION
8676 95a Hwy, Kimberley, BC, V1A 3M3
(250) 427-2268
Emp Here 20
SIC 4151 School buses

D-U-N-S 20-031-6326   (BR)
BOARD OF EDUCATION OF SCHOOL DISTRICT NO. 06 (ROCKY MOUNTAIN), THE
SELKIRK SECONDARY SCHOOL
405 Halpin St, Kimberley, BC, V1A 2H1
(250) 427-4827
Emp Here 50
SIC 8211 Elementary and secondary schools

D-U-N-S 20-590-5057   (BR)
BOARD OF EDUCATION OF SCHOOL DISTRICT NO. 06 (ROCKY MOUNTAIN), THE
BLARCHMONT ELEMENTARY SCHOOL
1850 Warren Ave, Kimberley, BC, V1A 1S1

Emp Here 25
SIC 8211 Elementary and secondary schools

D-U-N-S 20-590-5115   (BR)
BOARD OF EDUCATION OF SCHOOL DISTRICT NO. 06 (ROCKY MOUNTAIN), THE
MCKIM MIDDLE SCHOOL
689 Rotary Dr, Kimberley, BC, V1A 1E4
(250) 427-2283
Emp Here 30
SIC 8211 Elementary and secondary schools

D-U-N-S 25-267-8669   (BR)
GREAT PACIFIC INDUSTRIES INC
OVERWAITEA FOOD GROUP
1545 Warren Ave, Kimberley, BC, V1A 1R4
(250) 427-2313
Emp Here 40
SIC 5411 Grocery stores

D-U-N-S 25-620-7374   (SL)
INTERIOR HEALTH KIMBERLY SPECIAL

CARE HOME
KIMBERLEY SPECIAL CARE HOME
386 2nd Ave, Kimberley, BC, V1A 2Z8
(250) 427-4807
Emp Here 80   *Sales* 2,918,428
SIC 8361 Residential care

D-U-N-S 20-846-3112   (BR)
KOOTENAY SAVINGS CREDIT UNION
200 Wallinger Ave, Kimberley, BC, V1A 1Z1
(250) 427-2288
Emp Here 20
SIC 6062 State credit unions

D-U-N-S 25-680-5896   (BR)
RESORTS OF THE CANADIAN ROCKIES INC
KIMBERLEY ALPINE RESORT
301 North Star Blvd, Kimberley, BC, V1A 2Y5
(250) 427-4881
Emp Here 200
SIC 7011 Hotels and motels

D-U-N-S 25-770-7273   (BR)
RESORTS OF THE CANADIAN ROCKIES INC
TRICKLE CREEK GOLF RESORT
500 Jerry Sorenson Way, Kimberley, BC, V1A 2Y6
(250) 427-5171
Emp Here 60
SIC 7999 Amusement and recreation, nec

D-U-N-S 20-194-8044   (BR)
RESORTS OF THE CANADIAN ROCKIES INC
TRICKLE CREEK LODGE, THE
500 Sternwinder Dr, Kimberley, BC, V1A 2Y6
(250) 427-5175
Emp Here 52
SIC 7011 Hotels and motels

Kitimat, BC V8C
Kitimat - Stikine County

D-U-N-S 25-288-8979   (BR)
CANADA POST CORPORATION
CITY CENTRE P O
450 City Centre, Kitimat, BC, V8C 1T0
(250) 632-6722
Emp Here 20
SIC 4311 U.s. postal service

D-U-N-S 25-128-6159   (BR)
COAST MOUNTAINS BOARD OF EDUCATION SCHOOL DISTRICT NO. 82
KILDALA ELEMENTARY SCHOOL
803 Columbia Ave E, Kitimat, BC, V8C 1V7
(250) 632-6194
Emp Here 32
SIC 8211 Elementary and secondary schools

D-U-N-S 25-129-6034   (BR)
COAST MOUNTAINS BOARD OF EDUCATION SCHOOL DISTRICT NO. 82
NECHAKO ELEMENTARY SCHOOL
61 Nightingale St, Kitimat, BC, V8C 1M9
(250) 632-2912
Emp Here 25
SIC 8211 Elementary and secondary schools

D-U-N-S 24-773-1115   (BR)
DISTRICT OF KITIMAT
AMBULANCE   SERVICE   BRITISH COLUMBIA
1101 Kingfisher Ave S Suite 1304, Kitimat, BC, V8C 2N4
(250) 632-8940
Emp Here 21
SIC 4119 Local passenger transportation, nec

D-U-N-S 20-575-3833   (BR)
GREAT PACIFIC INDUSTRIES INC
OVERWAITEA FOOD GROUP
535 Mountainview Sq Suite 34, Kitimat, BC,

V8C 2N1
(250) 632-7262
Emp Here 90
SIC 5411 Grocery stores

D-U-N-S 25-823-3212   (SL)
KITIMAT CHILD DEVELOPMENT CENTRE ASSOCIATION
1515 Kingfisher Ave N, Kitimat, BC, V8C 1S5
(250) 632-3144
Emp Here 50   *Sales* 1,819,127
SIC 8351 Child day care services

D-U-N-S 25-191-7332   (BR)
NORTHERN HEALTH AUTHORITY
KITIMAT GENERAL HOSPITAL
920 Lahakas Blvd S, Kitimat, BC, V8C 2S3
(250) 632-2121
Emp Here 150
SIC 8062 General medical and surgical hospitals

D-U-N-S 24-137-2655   (BR)
RIO TINTO ALCAN INC
ALCAN PRIMARY METAL GROUP, DIV OF
(*Suby of* RIO TINTO PLC)
1 Smelter Site Rd, Kitimat, BC, V8C 2H2
(250) 639-8000
Emp Here 2,000
SIC 3334 Primary aluminum

D-U-N-S 25-887-8024   (BR)
ROYAL BANK OF CANADA
RBC
(*Suby of* Royal Bank Of Canada)
378 City Centre, Kitimat, BC, V8C 1T6
(250) 639-9281
Emp Here 23
SIC 6021 National commercial banks

D-U-N-S 20-295-0759   (BR)
THE BOARD OF EDUCATION OF SCHOOL DISTRICT #82 (COAST MOUNTAIN)
MOUNT ELIZABETH SECONDARY SCHOOL
1491 Kingfisher Ave N, Kitimat, BC, V8C 1E9
(250) 632-6174
Emp Here 80
SIC 8211 Elementary and secondary schools

Lac La Hache, BC V0K
Cariboo County

D-U-N-S 20-713-2668   (BR)
SCHOOL DISTRICT NO 27 (CARIBOO-CHILCOTIN)
LAC LA HACHE ELEMENTARY SCHOOL
Gd, Lac La Hache, BC, V0K 1T0
(250) 396-7230
Emp Here 50
SIC 8211 Elementary and secondary schools

Ladysmith, BC V9G
Cowichan Valley County

D-U-N-S 24-334-6744   (BR)
AGROPUR COOPERATIVE
ISLAND FARMS DAIRIES, DIV OF
13269 Simpson Rd, Ladysmith, BC, V9G 1H8
(250) 245-7978
Emp Here 40
SIC 5143 Dairy products, except dried or canned

D-U-N-S 24-050-6001   (SL)
ARBUTUS WEST ENTERPRISES LTD
TIM HORTONS
Gd Stn Main, Ladysmith, BC, V9G 1B9
(250) 245-2303
Emp Here 50   *Sales* 1,532,175
SIC 5812 Eating places

D-U-N-S 20-104-2327   (BR)

BLACK PRESS GROUP LTD
LADYSMITH PRESS
940 Oyster Bay Dr, Ladysmith, BC, V9G 1G3
(250) 245-0350
Emp Here 70
SIC 2711 Newspapers

D-U-N-S 20-552-5913   (BR)
CORPORATION OF THE TOWN OF LADY-SMITH
LADYSMITH FIRE RESCUE
Gd Stn Main, Ladysmith, BC, V9G 1B9
(250) 245-6436
Emp Here 32
SIC 7389 Business services, nec

D-U-N-S 24-504-5851   (SL)
E. MADILL OFFICE COMPANY (2001) LTD
MADILL - THE OFFICE COMPANY
1300 Rocky Creek Rd, Ladysmith, BC, V9G 1K4
(250) 245-3455
Emp Here 34   *Sales* 21,511,980
SIC 5943 Stationery stores

D-U-N-S 25-910-0931   (BR)
MCDONALD'S   RESTAURANTS   OF CANADA LIMITED
MCDONALD'S
(*Suby of* McDonald's Corporation)
370 Davis Rd Suite 1, Ladysmith, BC, V9G 1T9
(250) 245-7560
Emp Here 41
SIC 5812 Eating places

D-U-N-S 25-486-2071   (BR)
SCHOOL DISTRICT NO. 68 (NANAIMO-LADYSMITH)
LADYSMITH SECONDARY SCHOOL
710 6th Ave, Ladysmith, BC, V9G 1A1
(250) 245-3043
Emp Here 80
SIC 8211 Elementary and secondary schools

D-U-N-S 25-453-6717   (BR)
SCHOOL DISTRICT NO. 68 (NANAIMO-LADYSMITH)
WATERLOO ELEMENTARY SCHOOL
3519 Hallberg Rd, Ladysmith, BC, V9G 1K1

Emp Here 20
SIC 8211 Elementary and secondary schools

D-U-N-S 25-485-7907   (BR)
SCHOOL DISTRICT NO. 68 (NANAIMO-LADYSMITH)
LADYSMITH PRIMARY SCHOOL
510 6 Ave, Ladysmith, BC, V9G 1B9
(250) 245-3912
Emp Here 30
SIC 8211 Elementary and secondary schools

D-U-N-S 25-092-4107   (BR)
SCHOOL DISTRICT NO. 68 (NANAIMO-LADYSMITH)
NORTH OYSTER ELEMENTARY SCHOOL
13470 Cedar Rd, Ladysmith, BC, V9G 1H6
(250) 245-3330
Emp Here 20
SIC 8211 Elementary and secondary schools

D-U-N-S 25-271-7350   (BR)
SOBEYS WEST INC
370 Davis Rd, Ladysmith, BC, V9G 1T9
(250) 245-2033
Emp Here 40
SIC 5411 Grocery stores

D-U-N-S 25-359-4576   (BR)
VANCOUVER ISLAND HEALTH AUTHOR-ITY
LADYSMITH COMMUNITY HEALTH CEN-TRE
1111 4th Ave, Ladysmith, BC, V9G 1A1
(250) 739-5777
Emp Here 20
SIC 8011 Offices and clinics of medical doc-

tors

Lake Country, BC V4V

D-U-N-S 20-919-9467   (BR)
COOPER MARKET LTD
9522 Main St Unit 10, Lake Country, BC, V4V 2L9
(250) 766-9009
Emp Here 40
SIC 5411 Grocery stores

D-U-N-S 25-630-1706   (BR)
INTERIOR SAVINGS CREDIT UNION
9522 Main St Suite 30, Lake Country, BC, V4V 2L9
(250) 766-3663
Emp Here 21
SIC 6062 State credit unions

D-U-N-S 20-792-5178   (BR)
MCDONALD'S   RESTAURANTS   OF CANADA LIMITED
MCDONALD'S 8739
(*Suby of* McDonald's Corporation)
9522 Main St Unit 20, Lake Country, BC, V4V 2L9
(250) 766-1228
Emp Here 38
SIC 5812 Eating places

Lake Cowichan, BC V0R
Cowichan Valley County

D-U-N-S 20-713-5794   (BR)
SCHOOL DISTRICT NO. 79 (COWICHAN VALLEY)
A B GREENWELL PRIMARY
109 Hammond, Lake Cowichan, BC, V0R 2G0

Emp Here 50
SIC 8211 Elementary and secondary schools

D-U-N-S 20-713-5810   (BR)
SCHOOL DISTRICT NO. 79 (COWICHAN VALLEY)
PALSSON ELEMENTARY SCHOOL
9 Grosskleg Way, Lake Cowichan, BC, V0R 2G0
(250) 749-6691
Emp Here 30
SIC 8211 Elementary and secondary schools

D-U-N-S 25-015-4937   (BR)
SCHOOL DISTRICT NO. 79 (COWICHAN VALLEY)
LAKE COWICHAN SCHOOL
190 South Shore Rd, Lake Cowichan, BC, V0R 2G0
(250) 749-6634
Emp Here 43
SIC 8211 Elementary and secondary schools

Langley, BC V1M
Greater Vancouver County

D-U-N-S 20-511-7505   (BR)
AFA FOREST PRODUCTS INC
19822 101 Ave, Langley, BC, V1M 3G6
(604) 513-4850
Emp Here 24
SIC 5039 Construction materials, nec

D-U-N-S 20-698-0455   (BR)
ACOSTA CANADA CORPORATION
ACOSTA CANADA
(*Suby of* Acosta Inc.)
9440 202 St Unit 100, Langley, BC, V1M 4A6
(604) 881-1414
Emp Here 30

SIC 5141 Groceries, general line

D-U-N-S 20-971-1071   (BR)
BC BIOMEDICAL LABORATORIES LTD
20999 88 Ave Suite 102, Langley, BC, V1M 2C9
(604) 882-0426
Emp Here 20
SIC 8071 Medical laboratories

D-U-N-S 25-288-7856   (SL)
BELMONT GOLF COURSE LTD
(*Suby of* Hazelmere Golf and Tennis Club Ltd)
22555 Telegraph Trail, Langley, BC, V1M 3S4
(604) 888-9898
Emp Here 20   *Sales* 1,105,280
SIC 7997 Membership sports and recreation clubs

D-U-N-S 24-995-8687   (BR)
BEST BUY CANADA LTD
(*Suby of* Best Buy Co., Inc.)
19890 92a Ave, Langley, BC, V1M 3A9
(604) 419-5500
Emp Here 150
SIC 5999 Miscellaneous retail stores, nec

D-U-N-S 20-034-7859   (BR)
BOARD OF EDUCATION OF SCHOOL DISTRICT NO. 35 (LANGLEY)
TOPHAM ELEMENTARY SCHOOL
(*Suby of* Board of Education of School District No. 35 (Langley))
21555 91 Ave, Langley, BC, V1M 3Z3
(604) 888-6111
Emp Here 30
SIC 8211 Elementary and secondary schools

D-U-N-S 20-034-9277   (BR)
BOARD OF EDUCATION OF SCHOOL DISTRICT NO. 35 (LANGLEY)
DOROTHY PEACOCK ELEMENTARY SCHOOL
(*Suby of* Board of Education of School District No. 35 (Langley))
20292 91a Ave, Langley, BC, V1M 2G2
(604) 513-8000
Emp Here 40
SIC 8211 Elementary and secondary schools

D-U-N-S 20-028-4425   (BR)
BOARD OF EDUCATION OF SCHOOL DISTRICT NO. 35 (LANGLEY)
ALEX HOPE ELEMENTARY
(*Suby of* Board of Education of School District No. 35 (Langley))
21150 85 Ave, Langley, BC, V1M 2M4
(604) 888-7109
Emp Here 45
SIC 8211 Elementary and secondary schools

D-U-N-S 20-179-4323   (BR)
BOARD OF EDUCATION OF SCHOOL DISTRICT NO. 35 (LANGLEY)
LANGLEY FINE ARTS SCHOOL
(*Suby of* Board of Education of School District No. 35 (Langley))
9096 Trattle St Gd Stn Fort Langley, Langley, BC, V1M 2S6
(604) 888-3113
Emp Here 70
SIC 8211 Elementary and secondary schools

D-U-N-S 20-267-7246   (BR)
BRENNTAG CANADA INC
20333 102b Ave, Langley, BC, V1M 3H1
(604) 513-9009
Emp Here 27
SIC 5169 Chemicals and allied products, nec

D-U-N-S 25-731-4211   (BR)
BRIDGESTONE CANADA INC
20146 100a Ave, Langley, BC, V1M 3G2
(604) 530-4162
Emp Here 21
SIC 5014 Tires and tubes

D-U-N-S 20-620-2806   (HQ)

BRITISH PACIFIC TRANSPORT LTD
SHADOW LINES
9975 199b St, Langley, BC, V1M 3G4
(604) 888-2976
Emp Here 35   *Emp Total* 60
Sales 5,326,131
SIC 4213 Trucking, except local
Pr Pr Robert W Reid
 Keith Mcguiness

D-U-N-S 25-813-2869   (BR)
BUY-LOW FOODS LTD
WESTCOAST PRODUCE WHOLESALERS, DIV OF
19676 Telegraph Trail, Langley, BC, V1M 3E5
(604) 888-1121
Emp Here 1,500
SIC 5141 Groceries, general line

D-U-N-S 25-365-3554   (BR)
CANADIAN HERITAGE
FORT LANGLEY NATIONAL HISTORIC SITE
23433 Mavis Ave, Langley, BC, V1M 2R5
(604) 513-4779
Emp Here 25
SIC 8412 Museums and art galleries

D-U-N-S 20-256-1549   (BR)
CINEPLEX ODEON CORPORATION
CINEPLEX CINEMAS LANGLEY
20090 91a Ave, Langley, BC, V1M 3Y9
(604) 513-8747
Emp Here 20
SIC 7832 Motion picture theaters, except drive-in

D-U-N-S 20-749-0996   (SL)
COLLINS MANUFACTURING CO. LTD
9835 199a St Suite 5, Langley, BC, V1M 2X7
(604) 888-2812
Emp Here 60   *Sales* 9,329,057
SIC 3713 Truck and bus bodies
Pr Pr Mike Sondergaard

D-U-N-S 25-944-0261   (BR)
DENCAN RESTAURANTS INC
DENNY'S RESTAURANT
(*Suby of* Northland Properties Corporation)
8855 202 St Unit 7034, Langley, BC, V1M 2N9
(604) 888-6073
Emp Here 35
SIC 5812 Eating places

D-U-N-S 25-688-6565   (SL)
DINAMAC HOLDINGS LTD
Gd, Langley, BC, V1M 2M3
(604) 513-0388
Emp Here 50   *Sales* 3,210,271
SIC 1721 Painting and paper hanging

D-U-N-S 20-273-1014   (BR)
DRIVING FORCE INC, THE
9522 200 St, Langley, BC, V1M 3A6
(604) 881-9559
Emp Here 20
SIC 7514 Passenger car rental

D-U-N-S 24-339-3233   (BR)
ECP L.P.
ENGINEERED COATED PRODUCTS
19680 94a Ave, Langley, BC, V1M 3B7
(604) 513-1266
Emp Here 65
SIC 2671 Paper; coated and laminated packaging

D-U-N-S 24-373-8718   (BR)
EMERGENCY AND HEALTH SERVICES COMMISSION
HEALTHLINK BC
9440 202 St, Langley, BC, V1M 4A6
(604) 215-8103
Emp Here 100
SIC 8099 Health and allied services, nec

D-U-N-S 20-786-3346   (SL)
FELXIA CORPORATION
19680 94a Ave, Langley, BC, V1M 3B7

(604) 513-1266
Emp Here 49   *Sales* 25,058,150
SIC 2621 Paper mills
Brnch Mgr Brigit Stefani

D-U-N-S 24-329-1432   (BR)
FUCHS LUBRICANTS CANADA LTD
19829 99a Ave Unit A, Langley, BC, V1M 3G4
(604) 888-1552
Emp Here 22
SIC 2992 Lubricating oils and greases

D-U-N-S 24-552-0838   (SL)
HERITAGE STEEL SALES LTD
(*Suby of* Myer Salit Limited)
9718 197b St, Langley, BC, V1M 3G3
(604) 888-1414
Emp Here 20   *Sales* 4,377,642
SIC 3449 Miscellaneous Metalwork

D-U-N-S 24-980-4899   (BR)
INTEGRATED DISTRIBUTION SYSTEMS LIMITED PARTNERSHIP
WAJAX EQUIPMENT
9087 198 St, Langley, BC, V1M 3B1
(604) 513-2216
Emp Here 42
SIC 5084 Industrial machinery and equipment

D-U-N-S 25-018-4983   (BR)
JAY DEE ESS INVESTMENTS LTD
9696 199a St, Langley, BC, V1M 2X7
(604) 882-4721
Emp Here 200
SIC 2015 Poultry slaughtering and processing

D-U-N-S 25-270-2683   (BR)
KAL TIRE LTD
COMMERCIAL VEHICLE
20140 98 Ave, Langley, BC, V1M 3G1
(604) 882-3911
Emp Here 50
SIC 5531 Auto and home supply stores

D-U-N-S 24-980-0897   (SL)
L.J.D. PROPERTIES LTD
19935 96 Ave, Langley, BC, V1M 3C7
(604) 888-8083
Emp Here 60   *Sales* 2,188,821
SIC 5813 Drinking places

D-U-N-S 25-806-9285   (BR)
LTP SPORTS GROUP INC
VEET INDUSTRIES, A DIV
9552 198 St, Langley, BC, V1M 3C8

Emp Here 30
SIC 7389 Business services, nec

D-U-N-S 20-328-4166   (BR)
MAPLE-REINDERS INC
9440 202 St Suite 216, Langley, BC, V1M 4A6
(604) 546-0255
Emp Here 33
SIC 1542 Nonresidential construction, nec

D-U-N-S 25-654-8504   (BR)
MCKILLICAN CANADIAN INC
20233 100a Ave, Langley, BC, V1M 3X6
(604) 513-8122
Emp Here 20
SIC 5039 Construction materials, nec

D-U-N-S 24-881-8569   (BR)
MEADOW GARDENS GOLF COURSE (1979) LTD
FORT LANGLEY GOLF COURSE
9782 Mckinnon Cres, Langley, BC, V1M 3V6
(604) 888-5911
Emp Here 30
SIC 7992 Public golf courses

D-U-N-S 25-732-9607   (BR)
METRIE CANADA LTD
MOULDINGS & MILLWORK
19950 101 Ave, Langley, BC, V1M 3G6
(604) 882-5500
Emp Here 50

SIC 2431 Millwork

D-U-N-S 24-310-7711   (SL)
MITSUI HOMES CANADA INC
19707 94a Ave, Langley, BC, V1M 2R1
(604) 882-8415
Emp Here 80   *Sales* 87,611,700
SIC 4731 Freight transportation arrangement
Pr Hiroshi Kuratsu
Sr VP Tatsuya Suzuki
VP Douglas Smith

D-U-N-S 20-065-5194   (SL)
MUTUAL MATERIAL LANGLEY LTD
19675 98 Ave, Langley, BC, V1M 2X5
(604) 888-0555
Emp Here 30   *Sales* 1,896,978
SIC 3281 Cut stone and stone products

D-U-N-S 20-911-7407   (HQ)
NORCAN FLUID POWER LTD
19650 Telegraph Trail, Langley, BC, V1M 3E5
(604) 881-7877
Emp Here 20   *Emp Total* 190
Sales 6,712,384
SIC 7699 Repair services, nec
 Bill Dix

D-U-N-S 20-918-7926   (BR)
NORSEMAN INC
9080 196a St Unit 80, Langley, BC, V1M 3B4
(604) 888-9155
Emp Here 30
SIC 2394 Canvas and related products

D-U-N-S 25-747-8008   (BR)
PARSONS CANADA LTD
19890 92a Ave, Langley, BC, V1M 3A9
(604) 513-1000
Emp Here 45
SIC 8748 Business consulting, nec

D-U-N-S 24-995-4074   (BR)
RHI CANADA INC
9080 196a St Unit 60, Langley, BC, V1M 3B4

Emp Here 20
SIC 3297 Nonclay refractories

D-U-N-S 24-311-1155   (SL)
RJMB RESTAURANTS LTD
MCDONALD'S RESTAURANT
20394 88 Ave, Langley, BC, V1M 2Y6
(604) 881-6220
Emp Here 110   *Sales* 3,283,232
SIC 5812 Eating places

D-U-N-S 20-746-3147   (BR)
RAYDON RENTALS LTD
CAT RENTAL STORE, THE
(*Suby of* Finning International Inc)
9565 198 St, Langley, BC, V1M 3B8
(604) 888-5787
Emp Here 25
SIC 7353 Heavy construction equipment rental

D-U-N-S 20-802-8563   (HQ)
REGAL BELOIT CANADA ULC
THOMSON POWER SYSTEMS
(*Suby of* Regal Beloit Corporation)
9087a 198 St, Langley, BC, V1M 3B1
(604) 888-0110
Emp Here 133   *Emp Total* 23,000
Sales 14,206,516
SIC 3625 Relays and industrial controls
Pt Henry Knueppel

D-U-N-S 20-125-9731   (SL)
RITE-WAY METALS LTD
20058 92a Ave, Langley, BC, V1M 3A4
(604) 882-7557
Emp Here 35   *Sales* 6,493,502
SIC 1542 Nonresidential construction, nec
Pr Pr Donald Mccarthy
 Todd Collins

D-U-N-S 20-175-2685   (BR)

SCI LOGISTICS LTD
9087b 198 St Suite 210, Langley, BC, V1M 3B1
(604) 888-3170
Emp Here 50
SIC 8741 Management services

D-U-N-S 25-725-6248   (BR)
SAMUEL, SON & CO., LIMITED
SAMUEL SPECIALTY
9087c 198 St Unit 300, Langley, BC, V1M 3B1
(604) 882-0429
Emp Here 40
SIC 5051 Metals service centers and offices

D-U-N-S 25-451-5950   (BR)
SCHOOL DISTRICT NO. 35 (LANGLEY)
WALNUT GROVE SECONDARY SCHOOL
8919 Walnut Grove Dr, Langley, BC, V1M 2N7
(604) 882-0220
Emp Here 140
SIC 8211 Elementary and secondary schools

D-U-N-S 20-713-3260   (BR)
SCHOOL DISTRICT NO. 35 (LANGLEY)
ALEX HOPE ELEMENTARY SCHOOL
21150 85 Ave, Langley, BC, V1M 2M4
(604) 888-7109
Emp Here 50
SIC 8211 Elementary and secondary schools

D-U-N-S 20-027-8674   (BR)
SCHOOL DISTRICT NO. 35 (LANGLEY)
GORDON GREENWOOD ELEMENTARY
9175 206 St, Langley, BC, V1M 2X2
(604) 882-0114
Emp Here 38
SIC 8211 Elementary and secondary schools

D-U-N-S 20-030-6285   (BR)
SCHOOL DISTRICT NO. 35 (LANGLEY)
WEST LANGLEY ELEMENTARY
9403 212 St, Langley, BC, V1M 1M1
(604) 888-6444
Emp Here 35
SIC 8211 Elementary and secondary schools

D-U-N-S 20-027-1075   (BR)
SCHOOL DISTRICT NO. 35 (LANGLEY)
KENNEDY JAMES ELEMENTARY SCHOOL
9060 212 St, Langley, BC, V1M 2B7
(604) 888-5257
Emp Here 58
SIC 8211 Elementary and secondary schools

D-U-N-S 24-073-6025   (SL)
SHAWOOD LUMBER INC
(*Suby of* Shaw Production Way Holdings Inc)
20039 96 Ave, Langley, BC, V1M 3C6
(604) 538-2227
Emp Here 49   *Sales* 4,742,446
SIC 2499 Wood products, nec

D-U-N-S 25-769-2277   (SL)
SPORTSPLEX MANAGEMENT LTD
20165 91a Ave Unit 100, Langley, BC, V1M 3A2
(604) 882-1611
Emp Here 50   *Sales* 2,699,546
SIC 7999 Amusement and recreation, nec

D-U-N-S 24-557-1364   (BR)
STARBUCKS COFFEE CANADA, INC
STARBUCKS
(*Suby of* Starbucks Corporation)
20159 88 Ave, Langley, BC, V1M 0A4
(604) 455-0393
Emp Here 30
SIC 5812 Eating places

D-U-N-S 25-215-8092   (SL)
TMS TRANSPORTATION MANAGEMENT SERVICES LTD
TMS
9975 199b St, Langley, BC, V1M 3G4
(604) 882-2550
Emp Here 100   *Sales* 19,600,443
SIC 6712 Bank holding companies

Pr Pr Robert Benedict
Dietmar Krause
Lawrence Flint
Allan Benedict

D-U-N-S 20-325-2192   (BR)
TRAILER WIZARDS LTD
(*Suby of* Lions Gate Trailers Ltd)
20289 102 Ave, Langley, BC, V1M 4B4
(604) 464-2220
Emp Here 30
SIC 7519 Utility trailer rental

D-U-N-S 24-640-0899   (BR)
TRIMAC TRANSPORTATION SERVICES LIMITED PARTNERSHIP
9930 197 St, Langley, BC, V1M 3G5
(604) 888-2002
Emp Here 50
SIC 6722 Management investment, open-end

D-U-N-S 20-922-4588   (BR)
UAP INC
NAPA AUTO PARTS
(*Suby of* Genuine Parts Company)
9325 200 St Unit 100, Langley, BC, V1M 3A7
(604) 513-9458
Emp Here 150
SIC 5013 Motor vehicle supplies and new parts

D-U-N-S 24-825-0359   (BR)
UNIFIRST CANADA LTD
(*Suby of* Unifirst Corporation)
9189 196a St, Langley, BC, V1M 3B5
(604) 888-8119
Emp Here 80
SIC 7213 Linen supply

D-U-N-S 20-552-6986   (BR)
VITALAIRE CANADA INC
VITALAIRE HEALTHCARE
9087 198 St Suite 201, Langley, BC, V1M 3B1
(604) 881-0214
Emp Here 20
SIC 8082 Home health care services

D-U-N-S 25-731-8311   (BR)
WENDY'S RESTAURANTS OF CANADA INC
(*Suby of* The Wendy's Company)
19875 96 Ave Unit 2, Langley, BC, V1M 3C7
(604) 513-2253
Emp Here 30
SIC 5812 Eating places

D-U-N-S 20-117-1790   (HQ)
WESCO INDUSTRIES LTD
9663 199a St Unit 1, Langley, BC, V1M 2X7
(604) 881-3000
Emp Here 24   *Emp Total* 16
Sales 7,236,445
SIC 5085 Industrial supplies
Allison Arai
David Arai
Pr Pr Kaz Arai

D-U-N-S 20-959-0108   (HQ)
YOKOHAMA TIRE (CANADA) INC
9325 200 St Suite 500, Langley, BC, V1M 3A7
(604) 546-9656
Emp Here 30   *Emp Total* 24,761
Sales 7,296,070
SIC 5531 Auto and home supply stores
Pr Pr Eric Dedoyard
Fin Ex Lawrence Kumar
Naoki Takeda

Langley, BC V2Y
Greater Vancouver County

D-U-N-S 20-767-0089   (SL)
AERO TURBINE SUPPORT LTD
5225 216 St Suite 18a, Langley, BC, V2Y 2N3

Emp Here 20   *Sales* 3,064,349

SIC 4581 Airports, flying fields, and services

D-U-N-S 25-321-0496   (BR)
BDO CANADA LLP
LANGLEY ACCOUNTING
19916 64 Ave Suite 220, Langley, BC, V2Y 1A2
(604) 534-8691
Emp Here 50
SIC 8721 Accounting, auditing, and book-keeping

D-U-N-S 20-700-0204   (BR)
BANQUE DE DEVELOPPEMENT DU CANADA
6424 200 St Suite 101b, Langley, BC, V2Y 2T3
(604) 532-5151
Emp Here 40
SIC 6141 Personal credit institutions

D-U-N-S 24-011-8617   (BR)
BEST BUY CANADA LTD
BEST BUY
(*Suby of* Best Buy Co., Inc.)
20202 66 Ave Suite 3f, Langley, BC, V2Y 1P3
(604) 530-7787
Emp Here 50
SIC 5731 Radio, television, and electronic stores

D-U-N-S 20-651-8743   (BR)
BOARD OF EDUCATION OF SCHOOL DISTRICT NO. 35 (LANGLEY)
MAINTENANCE
(*Suby of* Board of Education of School District No. 35 (Langley))
20260 64 Ave, Langley, BC, V2Y 1N3
(604) 534-3294
Emp Here 70
SIC 8211 Elementary and secondary schools

D-U-N-S 20-526-2970   (BR)
BRICK WAREHOUSE LP, THE
20020 Willowbrook Dr Suite 400, Langley, BC, V2Y 2T4
(604) 539-3900
Emp Here 30
SIC 5712 Furniture stores

D-U-N-S 24-826-3472   (HQ)
BRITCO LP
21690 Smith Cres Glover Rd, Langley, BC, V2Y 2R1
(604) 888-2000
Emp Here 59   *Emp Total* 322
Sales 110,973,225
SIC 2452 Prefabricated wood buildings
Pr Mike Ridley

D-U-N-S 25-532-9435   (BR)
CANADA BREAD COMPANY, LIMITED
DEMPSTER BREAD, DIV OF
6350 203 St, Langley, BC, V2Y 1L9
(604) 532-8200
Emp Here 280
SIC 2051 Bread, cake, and related products

D-U-N-S 25-372-0742   (BR)
COSTCO WHOLESALE CANADA LTD
COSTCO WHOLESALE
(*Suby of* Costco Wholesale Corporation)
20499 64 Ave, Langley, BC, V2Y 1N5
(604) 539-8900
Emp Here 250
SIC 5099 Durable goods, nec

D-U-N-S 24-360-0660   (BR)
CRESTWOOD ENGINEERING COMPANY LTD
TCS
6252 205 St, Langley, BC, V2Y 1N7
(604) 532-8024
Emp Here 20
SIC 7539 Automotive repair shops, nec

D-U-N-S 24-446-9805   (BR)
DELOITTE LLP
8621 201 St Suite 600, Langley, BC, V2Y 0G9

(604) 534-7477
Emp Here 50
SIC 8721 Accounting, auditing, and book-keeping

D-U-N-S 25-116-1261   (SL)
EARLS RESTAURANT (LANGLEY) LTD
EARLS RESTAURANT LANGLEY
6339 200 St Suite 600, Langley, BC, V2Y 1A2
(604) 534-8750
Emp Here 50   *Sales* 1,532,175
SIC 5812 Eating places

D-U-N-S 20-852-9409   (SL)
EVANGELICAL FREE CHURCH OF CANADA MISSION
7600 Glover Rd, Langley, BC, V2Y 1Y1
(604) 513-2183
Emp Here 70   *Sales* 4,596,524
SIC 8661 Religious organizations

D-U-N-S 24-491-9312   (SL)
FOCUS ON THE FAMILY (CANADA) ASSOCIATION
19946 80a Ave, Langley, BC, V2Y 0J8
(604) 455-7900
Emp Here 70   *Sales* 2,772,507
SIC 8322 Individual and family services

D-U-N-S 24-316-1796   (BR)
FRASER HEALTH AUTHORITY
8521 198a St, Langley, BC, V2Y 0A1
(604) 455-1300
Emp Here 400
SIC 8742 Management consulting services

D-U-N-S 20-178-2435   (BR)
GRANT THORNTON LLP
8700 200 St Suite 320, Langley, BC, V2Y 0G4
(604) 455-2600
Emp Here 20
SIC 8721 Accounting, auditing, and book-keeping

D-U-N-S 24-000-4411   (BR)
GREAT PACIFIC INDUSTRIES INC
SAVE-ON-FOODS
20255 64 Ave Suite 1, Langley, BC, V2Y 1M9
(604) 532-5833
Emp Here 150
SIC 5411 Grocery stores

D-U-N-S 20-064-2598   (BR)
H. & C. MANAGEMENT CONSULTANTS LTD
FITNESS WORLD
(*Suby of* H. & C. Management Consultants Ltd)
19925 Willowbrook Dr Suite 200, Langley, BC, V2Y 1A7
(604) 533-3113
Emp Here 25
SIC 7991 Physical fitness facilities

D-U-N-S 25-734-0711   (BR)
HOME DEPOT OF CANADA INC
HOME DEPOT
(*Suby of* The Home Depot Inc)
6550 200 St, Langley, BC, V2Y 1P2
(604) 514-1788
Emp Here 250
SIC 5251 Hardware stores

D-U-N-S 20-107-1102   (BR)
HUDSON'S BAY COMPANY
HOME OUTFITTERS
20202 66 Ave Suite F1, Langley, BC, V2Y 1P3
(604) 539-8673
Emp Here 30
SIC 5712 Furniture stores

D-U-N-S 20-798-0033   (BR)
ISL ENGINEERING AND LAND SERVICES LTD
20338 65 Ave Suite 301, Langley, BC, V2Y 2X3
(604) 530-2288
Emp Here 25
SIC 8712 Architectural services

D-U-N-S 20-651-7331 (BR)
INVIS INC
(*Suby of* Invis Inc)
20434 64 Ave Suite 200, Langley, BC, V2Y 1N4
(604) 308-1528
Emp Here 25
SIC 6162 Mortgage bankers and loan correspondents

D-U-N-S 25-653-1872 (BR)
JOHNSTON, MEIER INSURANCE AGENCIES LTD
JOHNSTON MEIER INSURANCE AGENCIES GROUP
19978 72 Ave Unit 101, Langley, BC, V2Y 1R7
(604) 533-0333
Emp Here 20
SIC 6411 Insurance agents, brokers, and service

D-U-N-S 24-377-0208 (BR)
LANGLEY, CORPORATION OF THE TOWNSHIP OF
LANGLEY EVENTS CENTRE
7888 200 St, Langley, BC, V2Y 3J4
(604) 532-3595
Emp Here 50
SIC 7999 Amusement and recreation, nec

D-U-N-S 24-337-1122 (BR)
LANGLEY, CORPORATION OF THE TOWNSHIP OF
TOWNSHIP OF LANGLEY FIRE DEPARTMENT
22170 50 Ave, Langley, BC, V2Y 2V4
(604) 532-7500
Emp Here 190
SIC 7389 Business services, nec

D-U-N-S 20-914-2681 (BR)
MCDONALD'S RESTAURANTS OF CANADA LIMITED
MCDONALD'S #8583
(*Suby of* McDonald's Corporation)
20020 Willowbrook Dr Suite 100, Langley, BC, V2Y 2T4
(604) 539-4620
Emp Here 60
SIC 5812 Eating places

D-U-N-S 24-072-0156 (BR)
OLD NAVY (CANADA) INC
(*Suby of* The Gap Inc)
20202 66 Ave Suite 210, Langley, BC, V2Y 1P3
(604) 539-8559
Emp Here 40
SIC 5651 Family clothing stores

D-U-N-S 25-809-7914 (HQ)
PACIFIC DEVELOPMENTAL PATHWAYS LTD
(*Suby of* Pacific Developmental Pathways Ltd)
20434 64 Ave Unit 109, Langley, BC, V2Y 1N4
(604) 533-3602
Emp Here 20   *Emp Total* 57
Sales 2,261,782
SIC 8322 Individual and family services

D-U-N-S 20-118-2859 (BR)
PENTECOSTAL ASSEMBLIES OF CANADA, THE
CHRISTIAN LIFE ASSEMBLY
21277 56 Ave, Langley, BC, V2Y 1M3
(604) 530-7538
Emp Here 72
SIC 8661 Religious organizations

D-U-N-S 25-733-9143 (BR)
PEPPERS, SAMMY J GOURMET GRILL AND BAR
19925 Willowbrook Dr Suite 101, Langley, BC, V2Y 1A7
(604) 514-0224
Emp Here 75
SIC 5812 Eating places

D-U-N-S 20-349-2983 (SL)
POLMAR ENTERPRISES LTD
TIM HORTONS
20020 Willowbrook Dr Suite 200, Langley, BC, V2Y 2T4
(604) 530-4910
Emp Here 50   *Sales* 1,532,175
SIC 5812 Eating places

D-U-N-S 25-733-4433 (BR)
PRISZM LP
KFC
19971 64 Ave, Langley, BC, V2Y 1G9
(604) 530-2032
Emp Here 20
SIC 5812 Eating places

D-U-N-S 25-124-0495 (BR)
ROYAL BANK OF CANADA
RBC
(*Suby of* Royal Bank Of Canada)
19888 Willowbrook Dr, Langley, BC, V2Y 1K9
(604) 533-6800
Emp Here 60
SIC 6021 National commercial banks

D-U-N-S 20-034-6067 (BR)
SCHOOL DISTRICT NO. 35 (LANGLEY)
WILLOUGHBY ELEMENTARY SCHOOL
20766 80 Ave, Langley, BC, V2Y 1X6
(604) 888-6033
Emp Here 45
SIC 8211 Elementary and secondary schools

D-U-N-S 20-591-5932 (BR)
SCHOOL DISTRICT NO. 35 (LANGLEY)
R E MOUNTAIN SECONDARY SCHOOL
7755 202a St, Langley, BC, V2Y 1W4
(604) 888-3033
Emp Here 70
SIC 8211 Elementary and secondary schools

D-U-N-S 25-019-9973 (BR)
SCHOOL DISTRICT NO. 35 (LANGLEY)
LANGLEY MEADOWS COMMUNITY SCHOOL
2244 Willoughby Way, Langley, BC, V2Y 1C1
(604) 530-4101
Emp Here 50
SIC 8211 Elementary and secondary schools

D-U-N-S 20-033-6746 (BR)
SCHOOL DISTRICT NO. 35 (LANGLEY)
LANGLEY SECONDARY SCHOOL
21405 56 Ave, Langley, BC, V2Y 2N1
(604) 534-7155
Emp Here 100
SIC 8211 Elementary and secondary schools

D-U-N-S 25-271-1072 (BR)
SOBEYS WEST INC
WILLOWBROOK SAFEWAY
6153 200 St, Langley, BC, V2Y 1A2
(604) 530-6131
Emp Here 280
SIC 5411 Grocery stores

D-U-N-S 24-174-1284 (BR)
SODEXO CANADA LTD
7600 Glover Rd, Langley, BC, V2Y 1Y1
(604) 513-2009
Emp Here 80
SIC 5812 Eating places

D-U-N-S 25-898-7155 (BR)
STAPLES CANADA INC
STAPLES THE BUSINESS DEPOT
(*Suby of* Staples, Inc.)
20055 Willowbrook Dr Suite 200, Langley, BC, V2Y 2T5
(604) 514-2160
Emp Here 30
SIC 5943 Stationery stores

D-U-N-S 20-281-5767 (BR)
TAPP LABEL LTD
6270 205 St, Langley, BC, V2Y 1N7

(604) 513-4119
Emp Here 25
SIC 2759 Commercial printing, nec

D-U-N-S 24-348-5567 (BR)
TORBRAM ELECTRIC SUPPLY CORPORATION
6360 202 St Suite 103, Langley, BC, V2Y 1N2
(604) 539-9331
Emp Here 90
SIC 5063 Electrical apparatus and equipment

D-U-N-S 20-275-9648 (SL)
UTOPIA DAY SPAS & SALONS LTD
SPA UTOPIA & SALON
20486 64 Ave Suite 110, Langley, BC, V2Y 2V5
(604) 539-8772
Emp Here 90   *Sales* 3,863,549
SIC 7991 Physical fitness facilities

D-U-N-S 20-589-5738 (BR)
VANCOUVER CITY SAVINGS CREDIT UNION
VANCITY CREDIT UNION
20055 Willowbrook Dr Suite 100, Langley, BC, V2Y 2T5
(604) 877-7233
Emp Here 20
SIC 6062 State credit unions

D-U-N-S 24-360-0900 (BR)
VECTOR AEROSPACE HELICOPTER SERVICES INC
5225 216 St Suite 102, Langley, BC, V2Y 2N3
(604) 514-0388
Emp Here 400
SIC 4581 Airports, flying fields, and services

D-U-N-S 20-187-9975 (BR)
WAL-MART CANADA CORP
WALMART TIRE & LUBE EXPRESS
20202 66 Ave, Langley, BC, V2Y 1P3
(604) 539-5210
Emp Here 175
SIC 5531 Auto and home supply stores

Langley, BC V2Z
Greater Vancouver County

D-U-N-S 20-645-5078 (BR)
BOARD OF EDUCATION OF SCHOOL DISTRICT NO. 35 (LANGLEY)
JAMES HILL ELEMENTARY
(*Suby of* Board of Education of School District No. 35 (Langley))
22144 Old Yale Rd Suite 11, Langley, BC, V2Z 1B5
(604) 532-1181
Emp Here 20
SIC 8211 Elementary and secondary schools

D-U-N-S 20-027-0648 (BR)
BOARD OF EDUCATION OF SCHOOL DISTRICT NO. 35 (LANGLEY)
GLENWOOD ELEMENTARY SCHOOL
(*Suby of* Board of Education of School District No. 35 (Langley))
20785 24 Ave, Langley, BC, V2Z 2B4
(604) 534-4644
Emp Here 25
SIC 8211 Elementary and secondary schools

D-U-N-S 20-914-4935 (BR)
BOARD OF EDUCATION OF SCHOOL DISTRICT NO. 35 (LANGLEY)
JAMES HILL ELEMENTARY
(*Suby of* Board of Education of School District No. 35 (Langley))
22144 Old Yale Rd, Langley, BC, V2Z 1B5
(604) 530-0251
Emp Here 30
SIC 8211 Elementary and secondary schools

D-U-N-S 20-027-0655 (BR)

BOARD OF EDUCATION OF SCHOOL DISTRICT NO. 35 (LANGLEY)
PETERSON ROAD ELEMENTARY SCHOOL
(*Suby of* Board of Education of School District No. 35 (Langley))
23422 47 Ave, Langley, BC, V2Z 2S3
(604) 534-7904
Emp Here 35
SIC 8211 Elementary and secondary schools

D-U-N-S 20-589-2024 (BR)
GREATER VANCOUVER REGIONAL DISTRICT
EAST AREA PARKS
1558 200 St, Langley, BC, V2Z 1W5
(604) 530-4983
Emp Here 60
SIC 7999 Amusement and recreation, nec

D-U-N-S 25-902-6383 (BR)
H.Y. LOUIE CO. LIMITED
IGA 51
2410 200 St, Langley, BC, V2Z 1X1
(604) 530-7013
Emp Here 20
SIC 5411 Grocery stores

D-U-N-S 20-034-7289 (BR)
LANGLEY CHRISTIAN SCHOOL SOCIETY
LANGLEY CHRISTIAN MIDDLE AND HIGH SCHOOL
22702 48 Ave, Langley, BC, V2Z 2T6
(604) 533-0839
Emp Here 46
SIC 8211 Elementary and secondary schools

D-U-N-S 20-087-5867 (BR)
LANGLEY, CORPORATION OF THE TOWNSHIP OF
4700 224 St, Langley, BC, V2Z 1N4
(604) 532-7300
Emp Here 250
SIC 6111 Federal and federally sponsored credit agencies

D-U-N-S 20-309-0365 (SL)
MCMULLAN, RICHARD W LAW CORPORATION
CAMPBELL BURTIN & MCMULLAN
4769 222 St Suite 200, Langley, BC, V2Z 3C1
(604) 533-3821
Emp Here 50   *Sales* 4,304,681
SIC 8111 Legal services

D-U-N-S 24-974-8260 (BR)
SCHOOL DISTRICT NO. 35 (LANGLEY)
D W POPPY SECONDARY SCHOOL
23752 52 Ave, Langley, BC, V2Z 2P3
(604) 530-2151
Emp Here 90
SIC 8211 Elementary and secondary schools

D-U-N-S 25-453-3276 (BR)
SCHOOL DISTRICT NO. 35 (LANGLEY)
NOEL BOOTH ELEMENTARY SCHOOL
20202 35 Ave, Langley, BC, V2Z 1A2
(604) 530-9747
Emp Here 30
SIC 8211 Elementary and secondary schools

D-U-N-S 20-027-8633 (BR)
SCHOOL DISTRICT NO. 35 (LANGLEY)
WIX-BROWN ELEMENTARY SCHOOL
23851 24 Ave, Langley, BC, V2Z 3A3
(604) 534-5633
Emp Here 33
SIC 8211 Elementary and secondary schools

D-U-N-S 20-862-3368 (SL)
UNDERCOVER WEAR FASHIONS & LINGERIE
4888 236 St, Langley, BC, V2Z 2S5

Emp Here 200   *Sales* 12,532,976
SIC 5632 Women's accessory and specialty stores
Owner Yvonne Habart

Langley, BC V3A
Greater Vancouver County

D-U-N-S 20-004-9265   (SL)
APPLEWOOD MOTORS INC
APPLEWOOD KIA
19764 Langley Bypass, Langley, BC, V3A 7B1
(604) 533-7881
Emp Here 50   *Sales* 49,080,000
SIC 5511 New and used car dealers
Pr Pr Darren Graham

D-U-N-S 25-362-4589   (BR)
ARMY & NAVY DEPT. STORE LIMITED
5501 204 St Unit 100, Langley, BC, V3A 5N8
(604) 514-1774
Emp Here 50
SIC 5311 Department stores

D-U-N-S 25-494-8032   (BR)
BURNCO ROCK PRODUCTS LTD
19779 56 Ave, Langley, BC, V3A 3X8
(604) 534-3700
Emp Here 24
SIC 3273 Ready-mixed concrete

D-U-N-S 25-528-6221   (BR)
BANK OF NOVA SCOTIA, THE
SCOTIABANK
20555 56 Ave Unit 101, Langley, BC, V3A 3Y9
(604) 532-6750
Emp Here 33
SIC 6021 National commercial banks

D-U-N-S 20-514-2180   (BR)
BEST BUY CANADA LTD
FUTURE SHOP
(*Suby of* Best Buy Co., Inc.)
20150 Langley Bypass Suite 90, Langley, BC, V3A 9J8

Emp Here 55
SIC 5731 Radio, television, and electronic stores

D-U-N-S 25-019-6946   (BR)
BOARD OF EDUCATION OF SCHOOL DIS-TRICT NO. 35 (LANGLEY)
H.D. STAFFORD SECONDARY SCHOOL
(*Suby of* Board of Education of School District No. 35 (Langley))
20441 Grade Cres, Langley, BC, V3A 4J8
(604) 534-9285
Emp Here 50
SIC 8211 Elementary and secondary schools

D-U-N-S 20-027-3683   (BR)
BOARD OF EDUCATION OF SCHOOL DIS-TRICT NO. 35 (LANGLEY)
SIMONDS ELEMENTARY SCHOOL
(*Suby of* Board of Education of School District No. 35 (Langley))
20190 48 Ave, Langley, BC, V3A 3L4
(604) 530-5151
Emp Here 30
SIC 8211 Elementary and secondary schools

D-U-N-S 20-717-1237   (BR)
BOARD OF EDUCATION OF SCHOOL DIS-TRICT NO. 35 (LANGLEY)
SPECIAL SERVICES
(*Suby of* Board of Education of School District No. 35 (Langley))
4875 222 St, Langley, BC, V3A 3Z7
(604) 532-0188
Emp Here 40
SIC 8211 Elementary and secondary schools

D-U-N-S 20-028-4441   (BR)
BOARD OF EDUCATION OF SCHOOL DIS-TRICT NO. 35 (LANGLEY)
BROOKSWOOD SECONDARY SCHOOL
(*Suby of* Board of Education of School District No. 35 (Langley))
20902 37a Ave, Langley, BC, V3A 5N2

(604) 530-2141
Emp Here 100
SIC 8211 Elementary and secondary schools

D-U-N-S 20-027-0663   (BR)
BOARD OF EDUCATION OF SCHOOL DIS-TRICT NO. 35 (LANGLEY)
NICOMEKL ELEMENTARY SCHOOL
(*Suby of* Board of Education of School District No. 35 (Langley))
20050 53 Ave, Langley, BC, V3A 3T9
(604) 533-1468
Emp Here 35
SIC 8211 Elementary and secondary schools

D-U-N-S 20-027-0671   (BR)
BOARD OF EDUCATION OF SCHOOL DIS-TRICT NO. 35 (LANGLEY)
ALICE BROWN ELEMENTARY SCHOOL
(*Suby of* Board of Education of School District No. 35 (Langley))
20011 44 Ave, Langley, BC, V3A 6L8
(604) 534-0744
Emp Here 30
SIC 8211 Elementary and secondary schools

D-U-N-S 25-761-6904   (BR)
BOOTLEGGER CLOTHING INC
BOOTLEGGER
19705 Fraser Hwy Suite 219, Langley, BC, V3A 7E9
(604) 534-6410
Emp Here 20
SIC 5621 Women's clothing stores

D-U-N-S 20-860-4772   (BR)
BOUTIQUE LA VIE EN ROSE INC
BOUTIQUE LA VIE EN ROSE INC
20150 Langley Bypass Unit 10, Langley, BC, V3A 9J8
(604) 539-0257
Emp Here 25
SIC 5632 Women's accessory and specialty stores

D-U-N-S 25-316-5591   (BR)
BRITISH COLUMBIA AUTOMOBILE ASSO-CIATION
B C A A
20190 Langley Bypass Unit 10, Langley, BC, V3A 9J9
(604) 268-5950
Emp Here 25
SIC 8699 Membership organizations, nec

D-U-N-S 24-135-3817   (BR)
BUY-LOW FOODS LTD
4121 200 St, Langley, BC, V3A 1K8
(604) 533-1823
Emp Here 40
SIC 5411 Grocery stores

D-U-N-S 24-067-6382   (BR)
CANLAN ICE SPORTS CORP
CANLAN ICE SPORTS LANGLEY TWIN RINKS
5700 Langley Bypass, Langley, BC, V3A 8L7
(604) 532-8946
Emp Here 30
SIC 7999 Amusement and recreation, nec

D-U-N-S 20-923-9776   (BR)
CARA OPERATIONS LIMITED
MILESTONE'S GRILL & BAR
(*Suby of* Cara Holdings Limited)
20075 Langley Bypass, Langley, BC, V3A 8R6
(604) 514-9000
Emp Here 40
SIC 5812 Eating places

D-U-N-S 20-139-6558   (SL)
CARA RESTAURANTS
MONTANA'S COOK HOUSE
20100 Langley Bypass, Langley, BC, V3A 9J7
(604) 532-6799
Emp Here 60   *Sales* 1,824,018
SIC 5812 Eating places

D-U-N-S 24-316-8833   (BR)

CARRIER ENTERPRISE CANADA, L.P.
CARRIER ENTERPRISE CANADA, L.P
20350 Langley Bypass Suite 200, Langley, BC, V3A 5E7
(604) 539-4650
Emp Here 20
SIC 5075 Warm air heating and air condition-ing

D-U-N-S 24-343-0522   (BR)
CORIX INFRASTRUCTURE INC
CORIX WATER PRODUCTS
20239 Logan Ave Unit 100, Langley, BC, V3A 4L5
(604) 539-9399
Emp Here 50
SIC 5085 Industrial supplies

D-U-N-S 24-378-2385   (BR)
CORIX WATER SYSTEMS INC
20239 Logan Ave Unit 100, Langley, BC, V3A 4L5
(604) 539-9399
Emp Here 30
SIC 3589 Service industry machinery, nec

D-U-N-S 20-099-4853   (SL)
CROSS & NORMAN (1986) LTD
LANGLEY VOLKSWAGEN
20027 Fraser Hwy, Langley, BC, V3A 4E4
(604) 534-7927
Emp Here 23   *Sales* 8,390,481
SIC 5511 New and used car dealers
Pr Pr Bruce Norman
    Janet Norman

D-U-N-S 24-139-9257   (SL)
DARMAN RECYCLING CO INC
20408 102b Ave, Langley, BC, V3A 4R5
(604) 882-8597
Emp Here 35   *Sales* 5,457,381
SIC 4953 Refuse systems
Pr Darcy Gill
VP VP Manjit Gill

D-U-N-S 20-303-9797   (BR)
DAVID'S BRIDAL CANADA INC
20070 Langley Bypass Suite 10, Langley, BC, V3A 9J7
(604) 533-7240
Emp Here 20
SIC 5621 Women's clothing stores

D-U-N-S 25-960-1847   (BR)
ECCO HEATING PRODUCTS LTD
ECCO SUPPLY
19700 Landmark Way, Langley, BC, V3A 7Z5
(604) 530-2748
Emp Here 25
SIC 3444 Sheet Metalwork

D-U-N-S 20-802-5866   (BR)
ECCO HEATING PRODUCTS LTD
ECCO MANUFACTURING
19860 Fraser Hwy, Langley, BC, V3A 4C9
(604) 530-4151
Emp Here 100
SIC 3567 Industrial furnaces and ovens

D-U-N-S 24-337-3391   (BR)
FGL SPORTS LTD
COAST MOUNTAIN SPORTS
20150 Langley Bypass Unit 60, Langley, BC, V3A 9J8
(604) 530-1404
Emp Here 25
SIC 5941 Sporting goods and bicycle shops

D-U-N-S 24-989-5942   (BR)
FRASER HEALTH AUTHORITY
LANGLEY MENTAL HEALTH AND SUB-STANCE USE SERVICES
20300 Fraser Hwy Suite 305, Langley, BC, V3A 4E6
(604) 514-7940
Emp Here 33
SIC 8093 Specialty outpatient clinics, nec

D-U-N-S 24-342-0184   (BR)

FRASERWAY RV LIMITED PARTNERSHIP
FRASERWAY RV
20467 Langley Bypass, Langley, BC, V3A 5E8
(604) 530-3030
Emp Here 20
SIC 5561 Recreational vehicle dealers

D-U-N-S 24-995-0270   (SL)
GILLEY RESTAURANTS LTD
WHITE SPOT RESTAURANTS 609
19651 Fraser Hwy, Langley, BC, V3A 4C6
(604) 534-1222
Emp Here 70   *Sales* 2,115,860
SIC 5812 Eating places

D-U-N-S 20-860-5662   (BR)
GLENTEL INC
WIRELESS WAVES
19705 Fraser Hwy Suite 114a, Langley, BC, V3A 7E9
(604) 534-5666
Emp Here 25
SIC 4813 Telephone communication, except radio

D-U-N-S 20-731-6824   (BR)
GOLF TOWN LIMITED
GOLF TOWN
20150 Langley Bypass Unit 110, Langley, BC, V3A 9J8
(604) 539-9320
Emp Here 25
SIC 5941 Sporting goods and bicycle shops

D-U-N-S 24-335-0050   (BR)
GOVERNING COUNCIL OF THE SALVA-TION ARMY IN CANADA, THE
GOVERNING COUNCIL OF THE SALVATION ARMY IN CANADA, THE
19868 Langley Bypass, Langley, BC, V3A 4Y1

Emp Here 45
SIC 8322 Individual and family services

D-U-N-S 24-023-7755   (BR)
GOVERNING COUNCIL OF THE SALVA-TION ARMY IN CANADA, THE
GOVERNING COUNCIL OF THE SALVATION ARMY IN CANADA, THE
5787 Langley Bypass, Langley, BC, V3A 0A9
(604) 514-7375
Emp Here 70
SIC 8399 Social services, nec

D-U-N-S 20-528-5617   (SL)
GRAND CONSTRUCTION LTD
4539 210a St, Langley, BC, V3A 8Z3
(604) 530-1931
Emp Here 40   *Sales* 10,347,900
SIC 1542 Nonresidential construction, nec
    Andrew Guran
Dir Eric Guran

D-U-N-S 24-309-9686   (BR)
GREAT PACIFIC INDUSTRIES INC
PRICESMART FOODS
20151 Fraser Hwy Suite 100, Langley, BC, V3A 4E4
(604) 533-2911
Emp Here 250
SIC 5411 Grocery stores

D-U-N-S 25-270-3285   (BR)
HSBC BANK CANADA
20045 Langley Bypass, Langley, BC, V3A 8R6
(604) 530-5331
Emp Here 30
SIC 6021 National commercial banks

D-U-N-S 25-301-2421   (BR)
HUDSON'S BAY COMPANY
19705 Fraser Hwy Suite 320, Langley, BC, V3A 7E9
(604) 530-8434
Emp Here 170
SIC 5311 Department stores

D-U-N-S 25-943-7358   (BR)

INDIGO BOOKS & MUSIC INC
CHAPTERS
(*Suby of* Indigo Books & Music Inc)
20015 Langley Bypass Suite 115, Langley,
BC, V3A 8R6
(604) 514-8663
Emp Here 45
SIC 5942 Book stores

D-U-N-S 25-272-7474   (BR)
INSURANCE CORPORATION OF BRITISH
COLUMBIA
I C B C
6000 Production Way, Langley, BC, V3A 6L5
(604) 530-7111
Emp Here 100
SIC 6331 Fire, marine, and casualty insurance

D-U-N-S 24-370-6405   (BR)
KWANTLEN POLYTECHNIC UNIVERSITY
20901 Langley Bypass, Langley, BC, V3A 8G9
(604) 599-2100
Emp Here 300
SIC 8222 Junior colleges

D-U-N-S 24-551-6612   (SL)
LAIKA ENTERPRISES LTD
A B C FAMILY RESTAURANT
5978 Glover Rd, Langley, BC, V3A 4H9
(604) 530-1322
Emp Here 55   *Sales* 1,678,096
SIC 5812 Eating places

D-U-N-S 25-095-1506   (SL)
LAMI GLASS PRODUCTS, LLC
20350 Langley Bypass Suite 100, Langley,
BC, V3A 5E7

Emp Here 30   *Sales* 4,231,721
SIC 3211 Flat glass

D-U-N-S 24-345-5214   (BR)
LANGLEY, CITY OF
FRASER VALLEY REGIONAL LIBRARY
20399 Douglas Cres, Langley, BC, V3A 4B3
(604) 514-2850
Emp Here 20
SIC 8231 Libraries

D-U-N-S 25-622-0252   (BR)
LANGLEY, CORPORATION OF THE TOWN-
SHIP OF
BLAIR, W C RECREATION CENTRE
22200 Fraser Hwy, Langley, BC, V3A 7T2
(604) 533-6170
Emp Here 50
SIC 7999 Amusement and recreation, nec

D-U-N-S 25-107-4720   (BR)
LENNOX CANADA INC
GANDY INSTALLATIONS
(*Suby of* Lennox Canada Inc)
20202 Industrial Ave, Langley, BC, V3A 4K7
(604) 534-5555
Emp Here 35
SIC 1711 Plumbing, heating, air-conditioning

D-U-N-S 25-273-1591   (BR)
LORDCO PARTS LTD
LORDCO AUTO PARTS
5825 200 St, Langley, BC, V3A 1M7
(604) 533-6607
Emp Here 30
SIC 5531 Auto and home supply stores

D-U-N-S 25-910-0923   (BR)
MCDONALD'S   RESTAURANTS   OF
CANADA LIMITED
MCDONALD'S #8572
(*Suby of* McDonald's Corporation)
21558 Fraser Hwy, Langley, BC, V3A 8R2
(604) 514-5470
Emp Here 74
SIC 5812 Eating places

D-U-N-S 25-318-2067   (BR)
MCDONALD'S   RESTAURANTS   OF
CANADA LIMITED

MCDONALD'S #8187
(*Suby of* McDonald's Corporation)
19780 Fraser Hwy, Langley, BC, V3A 4C9
(604) 514-1820
Emp Here 110
SIC 5812 Eating places

D-U-N-S 25-685-2054   (BR)
NEUFELD INVESTMENTS LTD
HIGHLAND LODGE
20619 Eastleigh Cres, Langley, BC, V3A 4C3

Emp Here 30
SIC 8361 Residential care

D-U-N-S 24-882-3692   (SL)
NEW DIRECTIONS VOCATIONAL TESTING
AND COUNSELLING
20570 56 Ave, Langley, BC, V3A 3Z1

Emp Here 50   *Sales* 1,969,939
SIC 8322 Individual and family services

D-U-N-S 20-800-9019   (SL)
NEWLANDS GOLF & COUNTRY CLUB LTD
21025 48 Ave, Langley, BC, V3A 3M3
(604) 534-3205
Emp Here 150   *Sales* 4,961,328
SIC 7299 Miscellaneous personal service

D-U-N-S 20-789-9811   (SL)
OLIVE GARDEN ITALIAN RESTAURANT
20080 Langley Bypass, Langley, BC, V3A 9J7
(604) 514-3499
Emp Here 130   *Sales* 3,939,878
SIC 5812 Eating places

D-U-N-S 20-333-4057   (BR)
PARTY CITY CANADA INC
(*Suby of* Party City Canada Inc)
20150 Langley Bypass Unit 20 & 30, Langley,
BC, V3A 9J8
(604) 534-1623
Emp Here 30
SIC 5947 Gift, novelty, and souvenir shop

D-U-N-S 20-955-4778   (BR)
PENTECOSTAL   ASSEMBLIES   OF
CANADA, THE
OPEN DOOR JAPANESE PENTECOSTAL
CHURCH
20411 Douglas Cres, Langley, BC, V3A 4B6
(604) 533-2232
Emp Here 21
SIC 8661 Religious organizations

D-U-N-S 20-655-7386   (SL)
PIVOT POINT CONSULTING
20644 Eastleigh Cres Suite 304, Langley, BC,
V3A 4C4
(604) 531-4544
Emp Here 50   *Sales* 1,969,939
SIC 8322 Individual and family services

D-U-N-S 25-989-2131   (BR)
PRINCESS GROUP INC
PRINCESS AUTO
19878 Langley Bypass Unit 150, Langley, BC,
V3A 4Y1
(604) 534-9554
Emp Here 40
SIC 5085 Industrial supplies

D-U-N-S 25-986-7943   (BR)
RFGOP RESTAURANT HOLDINGS LTD
BURGER KING 3918
(*Suby of* RFGOP Restaurant Holdings Ltd)
19996 Fraser Hwy, Langley, BC, V3A 4E3
(604) 530-0884
Emp Here 23
SIC 5812 Eating places

D-U-N-S 25-019-7613   (BR)
SCHOOL DISTRICT NO. 35 (LANGLEY)
H. D. STAFFORD
20441 Grade Cres, Langley, BC, V3A 4J8
(604) 534-9285
Emp Here 60

SIC 8211 Elementary and secondary schools

D-U-N-S 20-591-5924   (BR)
SCHOOL DISTRICT NO. 35 (LANGLEY)
DOUGLAS PARK COMMUNITY SCHOOL
5409 206 St, Langley, BC, V3A 2C5
(604) 533-4491
Emp Here 25
SIC 8211 Elementary and secondary schools

D-U-N-S 20-026-8881   (BR)
SCHOOL DISTRICT NO. 35 (LANGLEY)
LANGLEY   EDUCATION   SECONDARY
SCHOOL
20216 Fraser Hwy Suite 215, Langley, BC,
V3A 4E6
(604) 534-7155
Emp Here 40
SIC 8211 Elementary and secondary schools

D-U-N-S 20-591-5866   (BR)
SCHOOL DISTRICT NO. 35 (LANGLEY)
APEX SECONDARY
20060 Fraser Hwy, Langley, BC, V3A 4E5

Emp Here 25
SIC 8211 Elementary and secondary schools

D-U-N-S 20-713-3252   (BR)
SCHOOL DISTRICT NO. 35 (LANGLEY)
UPLANDS ELEMENTARY SCHOOL
4471 207a St, Langley, BC, V3A 5V8
(604) 533-1285
Emp Here 25
SIC 8211 Elementary and secondary schools

D-U-N-S 20-027-0630   (BR)
SCHOOL DISTRICT NO. 35 (LANGLEY)
BLACKLOCK FINE ART'S ELEMENTRY
SCHOOL
5100 206 St, Langley, BC, V3A 2E5
(604) 530-3188
Emp Here 25
SIC 8211 Elementary and secondary schools

D-U-N-S 20-713-3195   (BR)
SCHOOL DISTRICT NO. 35 (LANGLEY)
BRADSHAW ELEMENTARY SCHOOL
3920 198 St, Langley, BC, V3A 1E1

Emp Here 50
SIC 8211 Elementary and secondary schools

D-U-N-S 20-713-3203   (BR)
SCHOOL DISTRICT NO. 35 (LANGLEY)
ELY FUNDAMENTAL ELEMENTARY
21250 42 Ave, Langley, BC, V3A 8K6
(604) 530-9973
Emp Here 50
SIC 8211 Elementary and secondary schools

D-U-N-S 20-713-3286   (BR)
SCHOOL DISTRICT NO. 35 (LANGLEY)
3786 208 St, Langley, BC, V3A 4X7
(604) 534-7891
Emp Here 150
SIC 8211 Elementary and secondary schools

D-U-N-S 20-713-3187   (BR)
SCHOOL DISTRICT NO. 35 (LANGLEY)
BELMONT ELEMENTARY SCHOOL
20390 40 Ave, Langley, BC, V3A 2X1
(604) 533-3641
Emp Here 50
SIC 8211 Elementary and secondary schools

D-U-N-S 20-591-5874   (BR)
SCHOOL DISTRICT NO. 35 (LANGLEY)
LANGLEY FUNDAMENTAL MIDDLE AND
SECONDARY SCHOOL
21250 42 Ave, Langley, BC, V3A 8K6
(604) 534-7779
Emp Here 32
SIC 8211 Elementary and secondary schools

D-U-N-S 24-206-5956   (BR)
SOBEYS WEST INC
LANGLEY SAFEWAY

20871 Fraser Hwy, Langley, BC, V3A 4G7
(604) 534-4363
Emp Here 150
SIC 5411 Grocery stores

D-U-N-S 24-957-2942   (HQ)
SPECIALTY POLYMER COATINGS INC
(*Suby of* RPM International Inc.)
20529 62 Ave Suite 104, Langley, BC, V3A
8R4
(604) 514-9711
Emp Here 27   *Emp Total* 14,318
Sales 8,171,598
SIC 2851 Paints and allied products
Jane Lang
Pr Pr George R Alliston
Sharon Alliston
Christopher Alliston
Robert Alliston

D-U-N-S 20-806-4571   (BR)
STARBUCKS COFFEE CANADA, INC
(*Suby of* Starbucks Corporation)
20151 Fraser Hwy, Langley, BC, V3A 4E4
(604) 533-7015
Emp Here 25
SIC 5812 Eating places

D-U-N-S 24-760-9993   (SL)
TEAM MANUFACTURING LTD
THEISSEN TEAM USA
(*Suby of* Thiessen Equipment Ltd)
20131 Logan Ave, Langley, BC, V3A 4L5
(604) 514-8326
Emp Here 45   *Sales* 14,323,401
SIC 3532 Mining machinery
Pr Pr Lawrence Thiessen

D-U-N-S 20-864-6260   (SL)
TIM HORTONS
20270 Logan Ave, Langley, BC, V3A 4L6
(604) 530-4909
Emp Here 50   *Sales* 1,532,175
SIC 5812 Eating places

D-U-N-S 20-860-5159   (BR)
TOWN SHOES LIMITED
SHOE COMPANY, THE
20150 Langley Bypass Suite 40, Langley, BC,
V3A 9J8
(604) 539-9992
Emp Here 25
SIC 5661 Shoe stores

D-U-N-S 25-297-8630   (BR)
TOYS 'R' US (CANADA) LTD
TOYS 'R' US
(*Suby of* Toys "r" Us, Inc.)
19705 Fraser Hwy Suite 100, Langley, BC,
V3A 7E9
(604) 534-8607
Emp Here 45
SIC 5945 Hobby, toy, and game shops

D-U-N-S 25-715-2009   (SL)
TRAVELAND R.V. RENTALS LTD
CANDAN R.V. CENTER
20257 Langley Bypass, Langley, BC, V3A 6K9
(604) 532-8128
Emp Here 25   *Sales* 4,888,367
SIC 5571 Motorcycle dealers

D-U-N-S 25-451-0241   (BR)
VALUE VILLAGE STORES, INC
VALUE VILLAGE
(*Suby of* Savers, Inc.)
20501 56 Ave, Langley, BC, V3A 3Y9
(604) 533-1663
Emp Here 30
SIC 5399 Miscellaneous general merchandise

D-U-N-S 20-185-1107   (BR)
VECTOR AEROSPACE CORPORATION
VECTOR AEROSPACE HELICOPTER SER-
VICES
5947 206a St Suite 101b, Langley, BC, V3A
8M1

(604) 514-0388
Emp Here 100
SIC 7699 Repair services, nec

   D-U-N-S 24-333-7776   (BR)
VECTOR AEROSPACE HELICOPTER SER-VICES INC
5947 206a St Suite 101b, Langley, BC, V3A 8M1
(604) 514-0388
Emp Here 100
SIC 4581 Airports, flying fields, and services

   D-U-N-S 24-334-8823   (BR)
VECTOR AEROSPACE HELICOPTER SER-VICES INC
5947 206a St Suite 101b, Langley, BC, V3A 8M1
(604) 514-0388
Emp Here 100
SIC 4581 Airports, flying fields, and services

   D-U-N-S 24-309-7867   (BR)
WGI WESTMAN GROUP INC
WESTMAN STEEL INDUSTRIES
5741 Production Way, Langley, BC, V3A 4N5
(604) 532-0203
Emp Here 20
SIC 5084 Industrial machinery and equipment

   D-U-N-S 24-882-3403   (BR)
WELDCO-BEALES MFG. ALBERTA LTD
WELDCO-BEALES MANUFACTURING
5770 Production Way, Langley, BC, V3A 4N4
(604) 533-8933
Emp Here 120
SIC 3531 Construction machinery

   D-U-N-S 25-948-7957   (BR)
WENDY'S RESTAURANTS OF CANADA INC
WENDY'S
(*Suby of* The Wendy's Company)
19644 Fraser Hwy, Langley, BC, V3A 4C5
(604) 533-2143
Emp Here 27
SIC 5812 Eating places

   D-U-N-S 20-048-6301   (BR)
WINNERS MERCHANTS INTERNATIONAL L.P.
WINNERS
(*Suby of* The TJX Companies Inc)
20150 Langley Bypass Suite 100, Langley, BC, V3A 9J8
(604) 532-0377
Emp Here 50
SIC 5651 Family clothing stores

   D-U-N-S 20-860-4194   (BR)
WINNERS MERCHANTS INTERNATIONAL L.P.
HOMESENSE
(*Suby of* The TJX Companies Inc)
20015 Langley Bypass, Langley, BC, V3A 8R6
(604) 532-0325
Emp Here 25
SIC 5651 Family clothing stores

Langley, BC V4W
Greater Vancouver County

   D-U-N-S 24-357-0574   (HQ)
3090723 NOVA SCOTIA LIMITED
ALLIED WINDOWS
(*Suby of* 3090723 Nova Scotia Limited)
5690 268 St, Langley, BC, V4W 3X4

Emp Here 115   *Emp Total* 120
Sales 22,478,640
SIC 3442 Metal doors, sash, and trim
Crdt Mgr Sharon Mcgee
Fin Ex Dave Clifford
Pr Pr Guy Wonnacott

   D-U-N-S 25-012-2272   (HQ)

ALLTECK LINE CONTRACTORS INC
(*Suby of* Quanta Services, Inc.)
5363 273a St, Langley, BC, V4W 3Z4
(604) 857-6600
Emp Here 50   *Emp Total* 28,100
Sales 46,604,304
SIC 1623 Water, sewer, and utility lines
Pr Keith Sones
 Robin Lucas
VP David Hill
 Mike Scott
 Doug Allen
Treas Nicholas Grindstaff

   D-U-N-S 24-508-6314   (BR)
AMICO CANADA INC
AMICO ISG VANCOUVER
(*Suby of* Gibraltar Industries, Inc.)
27475 52 Ave, Langley, BC, V4W 4B2
(604) 607-1475
Emp Here 20
SIC 3499 Fabricated Metal products, nec

   D-U-N-S 24-357-2869   (BR)
CANWEL BUILDING MATERIALS LTD
5350 275 St, Langley, BC, V4W 0C1
(604) 607-6888
Emp Here 30
SIC 5039 Construction materials, nec

   D-U-N-S 25-417-8189   (BR)
CINTAS CANADA LIMITED
(*Suby of* Cintas Corporation)
5293 272 St, Langley, BC, V4W 1P1
(604) 857-2281
Emp Here 160
SIC 7218 Industrial launderers

   D-U-N-S 20-554-0235   (BR)
EV LOGISTICS
EV LOGISTICS PERISHABLES
(*Suby of* EV Logistics)
5111 272 St, Langley, BC, V4W 3Z2
(604) 857-6750
Emp Here 260
SIC 4225 General warehousing and storage

   D-U-N-S 20-111-5789   (HQ)
FG DELI GROUP LTD
27101 56 Ave, Langley, BC, V4W 3Y4
(604) 607-7426
Emp Here 250   *Emp Total* 4,507
Sales 48,423,431
SIC 2011 Meat packing plants
Pr Pr Henning Freybe
 Sven Freybe

   D-U-N-S 24-373-4936   (SL)
FREYBE GOURMET CHEF LTD
5451 275 St, Langley, BC, V4W 3X8
(604) 856-5221
Emp Here 42   *Sales* 3,064,349
SIC 2038 Frozen specialties, nec

   D-U-N-S 24-354-3274   (BR)
HARDWOODS SPECIALTY PRODUCTS LP
27321 58 Cres, Langley, BC, V4W 3W7
(604) 856-1111
Emp Here 20
SIC 5031 Lumber, plywood, and millwork

   D-U-N-S 24-394-9331   (SL)
IEM INDUSTRIAL ELECTRIC MFG. (CANADA) INC
IEM CANADA
27353 58 Cres Unit 201, Langley, BC, V4W 3W7
(866) 302-9836
Emp Here 23   *Sales* 4,596,524
SIC 5063 Electrical apparatus and equipment

   D-U-N-S 20-305-3558   (BR)
INLAND KENWORTH LTD
INLAND KENWORTH
26820 Gloucester Way, Langley, BC, V4W 3V6
(604) 607-8555
Emp Here 27

SIC 5082 Construction and mining machinery

   D-U-N-S 24-360-1163   (BR)
INLAND KENWORTH LTD
INLAND KENWORTH
26770 Gloucester Way, Langley, BC, V4W 3V6
(604) 607-0300
Emp Here 23
SIC 7699 Repair services, nec

   D-U-N-S 25-974-4811   (SL)
INTERNATIONAL PLAY COMPANY INC
IPLAYCO
27353 58 Cres Unit 215, Langley, BC, V4W 3W7
(604) 607-1111
Emp Here 49   *Sales* 4,158,760
SIC 3949 Sporting and athletic goods, nec

   D-U-N-S 20-280-7269   (BR)
JELD-WEN OF CANADA, LTD.
4916 272 St, Langley, BC, V4W 0A3
(604) 857-6500
Emp Here 40
SIC 5031 Lumber, plywood, and millwork

   D-U-N-S 25-655-5756   (HQ)
MTF MAINLAND DISTRIBUTORS INC
MTF PRICE MATTERS
(*Suby of* MVF Investment Fund Inc)
26868 56 Ave Unit 101, Langley, BC, V4W 1N9
(604) 626-4465
Emp Here 40   *Emp Total* 200
Sales 21,202,403
SIC 5399 Miscellaneous general merchandise
Pr Pr Mark Funk
Dir Opers Norman Dyck
Dir Fin James Huth

   D-U-N-S 25-290-6516   (SL)
MADE-RITE MEAT PRODUCTS INC
26656 56 Ave, Langley, BC, V4W 3X5
(604) 607-8844
Emp Here 65   *Sales* 2,845,467
SIC 2013 Sausages and other prepared meats

   D-U-N-S 24-125-7927   (BR)
MASONITE INTERNATIONAL CORPORATION
(*Suby of* Masonite International Corporation)
26977 56 Ave, Langley, BC, V4W 3Y2
(604) 626-4555
Emp Here 20
SIC 2431 Millwork

   D-U-N-S 20-563-4251   (BR)
MATERIAUX DE CONSTRUCTION OLD-CASTLE CANADA INC, LES
OLDCASTLE BUILDING ENVELOPE
5075 275 St, Langley, BC, V4W 0A8
(604) 607-1300
Emp Here 130
SIC 3211 Flat glass

   D-U-N-S 25-216-7705   (BR)
MOORE, BENJAMIN & CO., LIMITED
(*Suby of* Berkshire Hathaway Inc.)
26680 Gloucester Way, Langley, BC, V4W 3V6
(604) 857-0600
Emp Here 25
SIC 2851 Paints and allied products

   D-U-N-S 25-098-1594   (SL)
PACIFIC COAST DISTRIBUTION LTD
27433 52 Ave, Langley, BC, V4W 4B2
(604) 888-8489
Emp Here 55   *Sales* 11,418,135
SIC 4731 Freight transportation arrangement
Pr Pr Ted Pozniak

   D-U-N-S 20-958-6429   (HQ)
ROPAK CANADA INC
CAPILANO, DIV OF
(*Suby of* Stone Canyon Industries LLC)
5850 272 St, Langley, BC, V4W 3Z1

(604) 857-1177
Emp Here 150   *Emp Total* 2,708
Sales 85,145,137
SIC 3089 Plastics products, nec
Pr Greg Toft
 David A. Williams
VP VP James R. Dobell
Dir Douglas Hugh Macdonald

   D-U-N-S 20-270-4201   (BR)
SCI LOGISTICS LTD
SCI WHITE GLOVE
26868 56 Ave Unit 109, Langley, BC, V4W 1N9
(604) 857-5051
Emp Here 30
SIC 8741 Management services

   D-U-N-S 25-413-8464   (SL)
STUYVER'S BAKESTUDIO
27353 58 Cres Unit 101, Langley, BC, V4W 3W7
(604) 607-7760
Emp Here 60   *Sales* 3,137,310
SIC 2051 Bread, cake, and related products

   D-U-N-S 24-010-7758   (BR)
TDL GROUP CORP, THE
TIM HORTON REGIONAL OFFICE
26585 Gloucester Way, Langley, BC, V4W 3S8
(604) 857-5430
Emp Here 25
SIC 5812 Eating places

   D-U-N-S 24-641-5830   (SL)
TITAN CONSTRUCTION COMPANY LIMITED
27355 Gloucester Way Unit 1a, Langley, BC, V4W 3Z8
(604) 856-8888
Emp Here 30   *Sales* 5,909,817
SIC 1541 Industrial buildings and warehouses
 Richard Coleman

   D-U-N-S 20-288-6248   (BR)
UNIFIED ALLOYS (EDMONTON) LTD
26835 Gloucester Way, Langley, BC, V4W 3Y3
(604) 607-6750
Emp Here 35
SIC 5051 Metals service centers and offices

   D-U-N-S 24-047-3483   (BR)
WATTS WATER TECHNOLOGIES (CANADA) INC
(*Suby of* Watts Water Technologies, Inc.)
27049 Gloucester Way, Langley, BC, V4W 3Y3

Emp Here 33
SIC 3494 Valves and pipe fittings, nec

Lantzville, BC V0R
Nanaimo County

   D-U-N-S 20-170-9164   (SL)
GARNONS, J WILLIAMS LTD
7393 Lantzville Rd, Lantzville, BC, V0R 2H0
(250) 390-5056
Emp Here 65   *Sales* 3,064,349
SIC 8059 Nursing and personal care, nec

   D-U-N-S 20-653-4377   (BR)
SCHOOL DISTRICT NO. 68 (NANAIMO-LADYSMITH)
SEAVIEW ELEMENTARY SCHOOL
7000 Lantzville School Rd, Lantzville, BC, V0R 2H0
(250) 390-4022
Emp Here 38
SIC 8211 Elementary and secondary schools

Lazo, BC V0R
Comox - Strathcona County

D-U-N-S 20-965-2523   (BR)
**DEFENCE CONSTRUCTION (1951) LIM-
ITED**
DEFENCE CONSTRUCTION CANADA
Gd, Lazo, BC, V0R 2K0
(250) 339-2721
Emp Here 20
SIC 1541 Industrial buildings and warehouses

D-U-N-S 20-655-5448   (BR)
**SCHOOL DISTRICT NO. 71 (COMOX VAL-
LEY)**
AIRPORT ELEMENTARY SCHOOL
1475 Salmonberry, Lazo, BC, V0R 2K0
(250) 339-3732
Emp Here 30
SIC 8211 Elementary and secondary schools

Lillooet, BC V0K
Squamish - Lillooet County

D-U-N-S 24-403-0164   (BR)
BUY-LOW FOODS LTD
155 Main St, Lillooet, BC, V0K 1V0
(250) 256-7922
Emp Here 60
SIC 5411 Grocery stores

D-U-N-S 20-990-4478   (BR)
INTERIOR HEALTH AUTHORITY
LILOOET HOSPITAL & HEALTH CENTER
951 Murray St, Lillooet, BC, V0K 1V0
(250) 256-1300
Emp Here 80
SIC 8062 General medical and surgical hospi-
tals

D-U-N-S 25-591-6090   (BR)
INTERIOR ROADS LTD
429 Main St, Lillooet, BC, V0K 1V0
(250) 256-7411
Emp Here 30
SIC 1611 Highway and street construction

D-U-N-S 20-333-4172   (BR)
SAVONA SPECIALTY PLYWOOD CO. LTD
530 Main St, Lillooet, BC, V0K 1V0
(250) 256-5200
Emp Here 40
SIC 2435 Hardwood veneer and plywood

D-U-N-S 25-020-4286   (BR)
SCHOOL DISTRICT #74 (GOLD TRAIL)
LILLOOET SECONDARY SCHOOL
920 Columbia St, Lillooet, BC, V0K 1V0
(250) 256-4274
Emp Here 40
SIC 8211 Elementary and secondary schools

D-U-N-S 20-590-8424   (BR)
SCHOOL DISTRICT #74 (GOLD TRAIL)
CAYOOSH ELEMENTARY SCHOOL
351 6th Ave, Lillooet, BC, V0K 1V0
(250) 256-4212
Emp Here 25
SIC 8211 Elementary and secondary schools

D-U-N-S 20-747-0381   (BR)
THOMPSON RIVERS UNIVERSITY
155 Main St Suite 10, Lillooet, BC, V0K 1V0
(250) 256-4296
Emp Here 20
SIC 8221 Colleges and universities

Lions Bay, BC V0N
Greater Vancouver County

D-U-N-S 25-143-8685   (SL)
**FURRY CREEK GOLF & COUNTRY CLUB
INC**
150 Country Club Rd, Lions Bay, BC, V0N 2E0

(604) 896-2216
Emp Here 120   *Sales* 5,180,210
SIC 7992 Public golf courses
Genl Mgr Sarah Cruse

D-U-N-S 20-688-1851   (BR)
**GOVERNMENT OF THE PROVINCE OF
BRITISH COLUMBIA**
BC AMBULANCE SERVICE
410 Centre Rd, Lions Bay, BC, V0N 2E0
(604) 921-9203
Emp Here 25
SIC 4119 Local passenger transportation, nec

Lumby, BC V0E
North Okanagan County

D-U-N-S 24-397-8348   (BR)
GORMAN BROS. LUMBER LTD
53 Dure Meadow Rd, Lumby, BC, V0E 2G7
(250) 547-9296
Emp Here 20
SIC 2499 Wood products, nec

D-U-N-S 25-829-4297   (BR)
SCHOOL DISTRICT NO 22 (VERNON)
J W INGLIS ELEMENTARY SCHOOL
2287 Schuswap Ave, Lumby, BC, V0E 2G0
(250) 547-9231
Emp Here 35
SIC 8211 Elementary and secondary schools

D-U-N-S 25-811-9775   (BR)
SCHOOL DISTRICT NO 22 (VERNON)
CHARLES BLOOM SECONDARY SCHOOL
1894 Glencaird, Lumby, BC, V0E 2G0
(250) 547-2191
Emp Here 40
SIC 8211 Elementary and secondary schools

Lytton, BC V0K
Thompson - Nicola County

D-U-N-S 20-590-8416   (BR)
SCHOOL DISTRICT #74 (GOLD TRAIL)
LYTTON ELEMENTARY SCHOOL
270 7th St, Lytton, BC, V0K 1Z0
(250) 455-2215
Emp Here 25
SIC 8211 Elementary and secondary schools

Mackenzie, BC V0J
Fraser-Fort George County

D-U-N-S 20-027-0861   (BR)
**BOARD OF EDUCATION OF SCHOOL DIS-
TRICT NO. 57 (PRINCE GEORGE), THE**
MACKENZIE ELEMENTARY SCHOOL
(*Suby of* Board of Education of School District
No. 57 (Prince George), The)
32 Heather Cres, Mackenzie, BC, V0J 2C0

Emp Here 30
SIC 8211 Elementary and secondary schools

D-U-N-S 20-027-0812   (BR)
**BOARD OF EDUCATION OF SCHOOL DIS-
TRICT NO. 57 (PRINCE GEORGE), THE**
MORFEE ELEMENTARY
(*Suby of* Board of Education of School District
No. 57 (Prince George), The)
310 Nechako Dr, Mackenzie, BC, V0J 2C0
(250) 997-6340
Emp Here 25
SIC 8211 Elementary and secondary schools

D-U-N-S 20-033-3685   (BR)
**BOARD OF EDUCATION OF SCHOOL DIS-
TRICT NO. 57 (PRINCE GEORGE), THE**

MACKENZIE SECONDARY SCHOOL
(*Suby of* Board of Education of School District
No. 57 (Prince George), The)
500 Skeena Dr, Mackenzie, BC, V0J 2C0
(250) 997-6510
Emp Here 33
SIC 8211 Elementary and secondary schools

D-U-N-S 20-522-3626   (BR)
CANADIAN FOREST PRODUCTS LTD
CANFOR MACKENZIE DIVISION
Mill Rd, Mackenzie, BC, V0J 2C0
(250) 997-3271
Emp Here 200
SIC 2421 Sawmills and planing mills, general

D-U-N-S 25-792-7657   (BR)
DISTRICT OF MACKENZIE
MACKENZIE RECREATION COMPLEX
400 Skeena Dr, Mackenzie, BC, V0J 2C0
(250) 997-5283
Emp Here 30
SIC 7999 Amusement and recreation, nec

D-U-N-S 20-875-3231   (BR)
LOMAK BULK CARRIERS CORP
1401 Mill Rd, Mackenzie, BC, V0J 2C0

Emp Here 45
SIC 4213 Trucking, except local

D-U-N-S 20-986-7873   (BR)
LOMAK BULK CARRIERS CORP
1150 Airport Rd, Mackenzie, BC, V0J 2C0

Emp Here 24
SIC 4213 Trucking, except local

D-U-N-S 25-841-6890   (BR)
NORTHERN HEALTH AUTHORITY
MACKENZIE DISTRICTL HOSPITAL
45 Centennial, Mackenzie, BC, V0J 2C0
(250) 997-3263
Emp Here 55
SIC 8051 Skilled nursing care facilities

Malahat, BC V0R
Cowichan Valley County

D-U-N-S 20-346-1439   (SL)
1946338 ONTARIO LIMITED
VILLA EYRIE RESORT
600 Ebadora Ln, Malahat, BC, V0R 2L0
(250) 856-0188
Emp Here 65   *Sales* 2,845,467
SIC 7011 Hotels and motels

Malakwa, BC V0E
Columbia - Shuswap County

D-U-N-S 24-167-6985   (SL)
EAGLE RIVER INDUSTRIES INC
4872a Lybarger Rd, Malakwa, BC, V0E 2J0

Emp Here 75   *Sales* 9,234,824
SIC 2421 Sawmills and planing mills, general
Fin Ex Diana Gould
Pr Pr Peter Wise

D-U-N-S 25-365-1095   (BR)
LOUISIANA-PACIFIC CANADA LTD
LP MALAKWA DIV OF
(*Suby of* Louisiana-Pacific Corporation)
4872 Lybarger Rd, Malakwa, BC, V0E 2J0
(250) 836-3100
Emp Here 30
SIC 2421 Sawmills and planing mills, general

Maple Ridge, BC V2W
Greater Vancouver County

D-U-N-S 24-956-9815   (SL)
**ANDERSEN PACIFIC FOREST PRODUCTS
LTD**
9730 287 St, Maple Ridge, BC, V2W 1L1
(604) 462-7316
Emp Here 50   *Sales* 4,742,446
SIC 2421 Sawmills and planing mills, general

D-U-N-S 24-726-3262   (SL)
ELK WOOD SPECIALTIES LTD
23347 Mckay Ave, Maple Ridge, BC, V2W 1B9
(604) 467-0911
Emp Here 33   *Sales* 3,137,310
SIC 2421 Sawmills and planing mills, general

D-U-N-S 20-026-8865   (BR)
**SCHOOL DISTRICT NO 42 (MAPLE RIDGE-
PITT MEADOWS)**
KANAKA CREEK ELEMENTARY SCHOOL
11120 234a St, Maple Ridge, BC, V2W 1C8
(604) 467-9050
Emp Here 50
SIC 8211 Elementary and secondary schools

D-U-N-S 24-027-6308   (BR)
**SCHOOL DISTRICT NO 42 (MAPLE RIDGE-
PITT MEADOWS)**
*ROBERTSON, SAMUEL TECHNICAL SEC-
ONDARY SCHOOL*
10445 245 St Suite 10445, Maple Ridge, BC,
V2W 2G4
(604) 466-8409
Emp Here 75
SIC 8211 Elementary and secondary schools

D-U-N-S 20-590-9893   (BR)
**SCHOOL DISTRICT NO 42 (MAPLE RIDGE-
PITT MEADOWS)**
ALBION ELEMENTARY SCHOOL
10031 240 St, Maple Ridge, BC, V2W 1G2
(604) 463-4848
Emp Here 41
SIC 8211 Elementary and secondary schools

D-U-N-S 20-095-9914   (HQ)
STAVE LAKE CEDAR MILLS INC
9393 287 St, Maple Ridge, BC, V2W 1L1
(604) 462-8266
Emp Here 30   *Emp Total* 150
Sales 3,283,232
SIC 2429 Special product sawmills, nec

D-U-N-S 25-170-3674   (SL)
TWIN RIVER CEDAR PRODUCTS LTD
9393 287 St, Maple Ridge, BC, V2W 1L1
(604) 462-0909
Emp Here 50   *Sales* 4,742,446
SIC 2421 Sawmills and planing mills, general

Maple Ridge, BC V2X
Greater Vancouver County

D-U-N-S 24-503-1372   (BR)
BANK OF MONTREAL
BMO
22410 Lougheed Hwy, Maple Ridge, BC, V2X
2T6
(604) 463-2444
Emp Here 20
SIC 6021 National commercial banks

D-U-N-S 20-589-5142   (BR)
BANQUE TORONTO-DOMINION, LA
TD CANADA TRUST
(*Suby of* Toronto-Dominion Bank, The)
20398 Dewdney Trunk Rd Unit 200, Maple
Ridge, BC, V2X 3E3
(604) 460-2925
Emp Here 20
SIC 6021 National commercial banks

D-U-N-S 20-589-5167   (BR)

BANQUE TORONTO-DOMINION, LA
TD CANADA TRUST
(*Suby of* Toronto-Dominion Bank, The)
22709 Lougheed Hwy Unit 560, Maple Ridge, BC, V2X 2V5
(604) 466-6800
Emp Here 20
SIC 6021 National commercial banks

D-U-N-S 25-288-9050   (BR)
CANADA POST CORPORATION
20800 Lougheed Hwy, Maple Ridge, BC, V2X 2R3
(604) 463-3651
Emp Here 70
SIC 4311 U.s. postal service

D-U-N-S 24-343-1702   (BR)
CARA OPERATIONS LIMITED
SWISS CHALET
(*Suby of* Cara Holdings Limited)
20395 Lougheed Hwy Suite 680, Maple Ridge, BC. V2X 2P9

Emp Here 50
SIC 5812 Eating places

D-U-N-S 24-171-3119   (BR)
CHARTWELL SENIORS HOUSING REAL ESTATE INVESTMENT TRUST
12275 224 St, Maple Ridge, BC, V2X 6H5
(604) 466-8602
Emp Here 40
SIC 8322 Individual and family services

D-U-N-S 24-931-3545   (SL)
CORPORATE CLEANING SERVICES LTD
20285 Stewart Cres Suite 402, Maple Ridge, BC, V2X 8G1
(604) 465-4699
Emp Here 34   *Sales* 2,115,860
SIC 7217 Carpet and upholstery cleaning

D-U-N-S 24-837-4845   (SL)
E-ONE MOLI ENERGY (CANADA) LIMITED
20000 Stewart Cres, Maple Ridge, BC, V2X 9E7
(604) 466-6654
Emp Here 65   *Sales* 5,284,131
SIC 3691 Storage batteries
Pr Stephen Pither

D-U-N-S 20-800-7653   (SL)
EPIC FOOD SERVICES INC
TIM HORTONS
22987 Dewdney Trunk Rd, Maple Ridge, BC, V2X 3K8
(604) 466-0671
Emp Here 55   *Sales* 1,896,978
SIC 5461 Retail bakeries

D-U-N-S 25-021-1257   (BR)
FRASER HEALTH AUTHORITY
RIDGE MEADOWS HOSPITAL
11666 Laity St, Maple Ridge, BC, V2X 5A3
(604) 463-4111
Emp Here 1,000
SIC 8062 General medical and surgical hospitals

D-U-N-S 24-683-2716   (BR)
FRASER HEALTH AUTHORITY
MAPLE RIDGE TREATMENT CENTRE
22269 Callaghan Ave, Maple Ridge, BC, V2X 2E2
(604) 467-3471
Emp Here 60
SIC 8093 Specialty outpatient clinics, nec

D-U-N-S 20-707-4233   (BR)
FRASER HEALTH AUTHORITY
ENVIRONMENTAL HEALTH UNIT
22470 Dewdney Trunk Rd Suite 400, Maple Ridge, BC, V2X 5Z6
(604) 476-7053
Emp Here 44
SIC 8062 General medical and surgical hospitals

D-U-N-S 24-000-5806   (BR)
GREAT PACIFIC INDUSTRIES INC
SAVE-ON-FOODS
22703 Lougheed Hwy Suite 935, Maple Ridge, BC, V2X 2V5
(604) 463-3329
Emp Here 285
SIC 5411 Grocery stores

D-U-N-S 25-685-0371   (BR)
GREAT PACIFIC INDUSTRIES INC
SAVE-ON-FOODS
20395 Lougheed Hwy Suite 300, Maple Ridge, BC, V2X 2P9
(604) 465-8606
Emp Here 280
SIC 5411 Grocery stores

D-U-N-S 25-658-2438   (BR)
HSBC BANK CANADA
11955 224 St, Maple Ridge, BC, V2X 6B4
(604) 467-1131
Emp Here 30
SIC 6021 National commercial banks

D-U-N-S 25-272-7359   (BR)
INSURANCE CORPORATION OF BRITISH COLUMBIA
ICBC
22811 Dewdney Trunk Rd, Maple Ridge, BC, V2X 9J7
(604) 463-3999
Emp Here 50
SIC 6331 Fire, marine, and casualty insurance

D-U-N-S 24-331-8099   (BR)
MNP LLP
INTERNATIONAL AIRLINE TECHNICAL POOL
11939 224 St Suite 201, Maple Ridge, BC, V2X 6B2
(604) 463-8831
Emp Here 20
SIC 8721 Accounting, auditing, and bookkeeping

D-U-N-S 24-930-8982   (SL)
MAPLE RIDGE COMMUNITY GAMING CENTRE
22366 119 Ave, Maple Ridge, BC, V2X 2Z3

Emp Here 57   *Sales* 3,064,349
SIC 7999 Amusement and recreation, nec

D-U-N-S 24-455-0711   (SL)
MAPLE RIDGE STEAK HOUSE LTD
KEG, THE
(*Suby of* Argus Holdings Ltd)
20640 Dewdney Trunk Rd, Maple Ridge, BC, V2X 3E5
(604) 465-8911
Emp Here 70   *Sales* 2,115,860
SIC 5812 Eating places

D-U-N-S 24-441-6413   (BR)
MCDONALD'S RESTAURANTS OF CANADA LIMITED
MCDONALDS - MAPLE RIDGE
(*Suby of* McDonald's Corporation)
22780 Lougheed Hwy, Maple Ridge, BC, V2X 2V6
(604) 463-7858
Emp Here 80
SIC 5812 Eating places

D-U-N-S 20-773-8001   (BR)
METRIE CANADA LTD
MOULDING & MILLWORK
20142 113b Ave, Maple Ridge, BC, V2X 0Y9
(604) 460-0070
Emp Here 50
SIC 2431 Millwork

D-U-N-S 25-811-7449   (BR)
ROYAL BANK OF CANADA
RBC
(*Suby of* Royal Bank Of Canada)
11855 224 St, Maple Ridge, BC, V2X 6B1

(604) 501-7180
Emp Here 25
SIC 6021 National commercial banks

D-U-N-S 20-590-9984   (BR)
SCHOOL DISTRICT NO 42 (MAPLE RIDGE-PITT MEADOWS)
MAPLE RIDGE ELEMENTARY
20820 River Rd, Maple Ridge, BC, V2X 1Z7
(604) 467-5551
Emp Here 25
SIC 8211 Elementary and secondary schools

D-U-N-S 20-590-9950   (BR)
SCHOOL DISTRICT NO 42 (MAPLE RIDGE-PITT MEADOWS)
HARRY HOOGE ELEMENTARY
12280 230 St, Maple Ridge, BC, V2X 0P6
(604) 463-0866
Emp Here 35
SIC 8211 Elementary and secondary schools

D-U-N-S 20-591-0040   (BR)
SCHOOL DISTRICT NO 42 (MAPLE RIDGE-PITT MEADOWS)
GOLDEN EARS ELEMENTARY
23124 118 Ave, Maple Ridge, BC, V2X 2N1
(604) 463-9513
Emp Here 50
SIC 8211 Elementary and secondary schools

D-U-N-S 20-126-7528   (BR)
SCHOOL DISTRICT NO 42 (MAPLE RIDGE-PITT MEADOWS)
THOMAS HANEY SECONDARY SCHOOL
23000 116 Ave, Maple Ridge, BC, V2X 0T8
(604) 463-2001
Emp Here 60
SIC 8211 Elementary and secondary schools

D-U-N-S 25-266-8728   (BR)
SCHOOL DISTRICT NO 42 (MAPLE RIDGE-PITT MEADOWS)
WESTVIEW SECONDARY SCHOOL
20905 Wicklund Ave, Maple Ridge, BC, V2X 8E8
(604) 467-3481
Emp Here 110
SIC 8211 Elementary and secondary schools

D-U-N-S 25-453-3664   (BR)
SCHOOL DISTRICT NO 42 (MAPLE RIDGE-PITT MEADOWS)
MAPLE RIDGE SECONDARY SCHOOL
21911 122 Ave, Maple Ridge, BC, V2X 3X2
(604) 463-4175
Emp Here 150
SIC 8211 Elementary and secondary schools

D-U-N-S 25-538-5676   (BR)
SCHOOL DISTRICT NO 42 (MAPLE RIDGE-PITT MEADOWS)
HAMMOND ELEMENTARY SCHOOL
11520 203 St, Maple Ridge, BC, V2X 4T6
(604) 460-1136
Emp Here 35
SIC 8211 Elementary and secondary schools

D-U-N-S 20-590-9976   (BR)
SCHOOL DISTRICT NO 42 (MAPLE RIDGE-PITT MEADOWS)
RIVERSIDE ELEMENTARY SCHOOL
20575 Thorne Ave, Maple Ridge, BC, V2X 9A6
(604) 465-2322
Emp Here 45
SIC 8211 Elementary and secondary schools

D-U-N-S 25-021-0929   (BR)
SCHOOL DISTRICT NO 42 (MAPLE RIDGE-PITT MEADOWS)
LAITY VIEW ELEMENTARY SCHOOL
21023 123 Ave, Maple Ridge, BC, V2X 4B5
(604) 463-7108
Emp Here 50
SIC 8211 Elementary and secondary schools

D-U-N-S 24-103-7527   (BR)
SCHOOL DISTRICT NO 42 (MAPLE RIDGE-

PITT MEADOWS)
COMMUNITY EDUCATION ARTHUR PEAKE CENTER
23125 116 Ave, Maple Ridge, BC, V2X 0G8
(604) 466-6555
Emp Here 40
SIC 8211 Elementary and secondary schools

D-U-N-S 20-039-3804   (BR)
SCHOOL DISTRICT NO 42 (MAPLE RIDGE-PITT MEADOWS)
ALOUETTE ELEMENTARY SCHOOL
22155 Isaac Cres, Maple Ridge, BC, V2X 0V9
(604) 463-8730
Emp Here 40
SIC 8211 Elementary and secondary schools

D-U-N-S 20-590-9992   (BR)
SCHOOL DISTRICT NO 42 (MAPLE RIDGE-PITT MEADOWS)
GLENWOOD ELEMENTARY
21410 Glenwood Ave, Maple Ridge, BC, V2X 3P6
(604) 463-6512
Emp Here 25
SIC 8211 Elementary and secondary schools

D-U-N-S 20-590-9943   (BR)
SCHOOL DISTRICT NO 42 (MAPLE RIDGE-PITT MEADOWS)
FAIRVIEW ELEMENTARY
12209 206 St, Maple Ridge, BC, V2X 1T8
(604) 465-9331
Emp Here 25
SIC 8211 Elementary and secondary schools

D-U-N-S 20-591-0008   (BR)
SCHOOL DISTRICT NO 42 (MAPLE RIDGE-PITT MEADOWS)
MOUNT CRESCENT ELEMENTARY
21821 122 Ave, Maple Ridge, BC, V2X 3X2
(604) 463-9257
Emp Here 25
SIC 8211 Elementary and secondary schools

D-U-N-S 20-591-0057   (BR)
SCHOOL DISTRICT NO 42 (MAPLE RIDGE-PITT MEADOWS)
YENNADON ELEMENTARY SCHOOL
23347 128 Ave, Maple Ridge, BC, V2X 4R9
(604) 463-8871
Emp Here 50
SIC 8211 Elementary and secondary schools

D-U-N-S 20-590-9935   (BR)
SCHOOL DISTRICT NO 42 (MAPLE RIDGE-PITT MEADOWS)
ERIC LANGTON ELEMENTARY
12138 Edge St, Maple Ridge, BC, V2X 6G8
(604) 463-3810
Emp Here 40
SIC 8211 Elementary and secondary schools

D-U-N-S 20-532-5249   (BR)
SEARS CANADA INC
20475 Lougheed Hwy Suite 10, Maple Ridge, BC, V2X 9B6
(604) 460-8077
Emp Here 30
SIC 5722 Household appliance stores

D-U-N-S 24-684-6732   (BR)
SIMPSON STRONG-TIE CANADA LIMITED
(*Suby of* Simpson Manufacturing Co., Inc.)
11476 Kingston St, Maple Ridge, BC, V2X 0Y5
(604) 465-0296
Emp Here 50
SIC 3496 Miscellaneous fabricated wire products

D-U-N-S 25-087-6679   (BR)
SOBEYS WEST INC
SAFEWAY STORE #0198
20201 Lougheed Hwy Suite 300, Maple Ridge, BC, V2X 2P6
(604) 460-7200
Emp Here 150

SIC 5411 Grocery stores

D-U-N-S 20-860-3782   (BR)
SOURCE (BELL) ELECTRONICS INC, THE
SOURCE, THE
11900 Haney Pl Suite 127, Maple Ridge, BC,
V2X 8R9
(604) 466-1690
Emp Here 25
SIC 5999 Miscellaneous retail stores, nec

D-U-N-S 25-370-1551   (BR)
STAPLES CANADA INC
STAPLES THE BUSINESS DEPOT
(*Suby of* Staples, Inc.)
20050 Lougheed Hwy, Maple Ridge, BC, V2X
0P5
(604) 465-3429
Emp Here 20
SIC 5943 Stationery stores

D-U-N-S 20-806-4548   (BR)
STARBUCKS COFFEE CANADA, INC
STARBUCKS COFFEE
(*Suby of* Starbucks Corporation)
22645 Dewdney Trunk Rd Unit 100, Maple
Ridge, BC, V2X 3K1
(604) 463-1320
Emp Here 25
SIC 5812 Eating places

D-U-N-S 24-322-2523   (BR)
VALUE VILLAGE STORES, INC
(*Suby of* Savers, Inc.)
11998 207 St Unit 4, Maple Ridge, BC, V2X
1X7
(604) 463-6053
Emp Here 40
SIC 5399 Miscellaneous general merchandise

D-U-N-S 20-589-5795   (BR)
**VANCOUVER CITY SAVINGS CREDIT
UNION**
VANCITY CREDIT UNION
22824 Lougheed Hwy Suite 29, Maple Ridge,
BC, V2X 2V6
(604) 877-7293
Emp Here 20
SIC 6062 State credit unions

D-U-N-S 20-153-2053   (BR)
WENDY'S RESTAURANTS OF CANADA INC
WENDY'S
(*Suby of* The Wendy's Company)
20201 Lougheed Hwy Suite 100, Maple
Ridge, BC, V2X 2P6
(604) 460-8183
Emp Here 32
SIC 5812 Eating places

Maple Ridge, BC V4R
Greater Vancouver County

D-U-N-S 25-499-2043   (SL)
MEADOWRIDGE SCHOOL SOCIETY
MEADOWRIDGE SCHOOL
12224 240 St, Maple Ridge, BC, V4R 1N1
(604) 467-4444
Emp Here 60   *Sales* 4,012,839
SIC 8211 Elementary and secondary schools

D-U-N-S 20-591-0065   (BR)
**SCHOOL DISTRICT NO 42 (MAPLE RIDGE-
PITT MEADOWS)**
*WEBSTER'S CORNER ELEMENTARY
SCHOOL*
25554 Dewdney Trunk Rd, Maple Ridge, BC,
V4R 1X9
(604) 462-7595
Emp Here 25
SIC 8211 Elementary and secondary schools

D-U-N-S 25-020-9129   (BR)
**SCHOOL DISTRICT NO 42 (MAPLE RIDGE-
PITT MEADOWS)**

GARIBALDI SECONDARY SCHOOL
24789 Dewdney Trunk Rd, Maple Ridge, BC,
V4R 1X2
(604) 463-6287
Emp Here 80
SIC 8211 Elementary and secondary schools

D-U-N-S 25-020-4922   (BR)
**SCHOOL DISTRICT NO 42 (MAPLE RIDGE-
PITT MEADOWS)**
BLUE MOUNTAIN ELEMENTARY SCHOOL
12153 248 St, Maple Ridge, BC, V4R 1J3
(604) 463-6414
Emp Here 20
SIC 8211 Elementary and secondary schools

D-U-N-S 20-294-0313   (BR)
**SCHOOL DISTRICT NO 42 (MAPLE RIDGE-
PITT MEADOWS)**
*ALEXANDER ROBINSON ELEMENTARY
SCHOOL*
11849 238b St, Maple Ridge, BC, V4R 2T8
(604) 463-3035
Emp Here 60
SIC 8211 Elementary and secondary schools

D-U-N-S 20-968-8865   (BR)
**SCHOOL DISTRICT NO 42 (MAPLE RIDGE-
PITT MEADOWS)**
23889 Dewdney Trunk Rd, Maple Ridge, BC,
V4R 1W1
(604) 463-8918
Emp Here 40
SIC 8211 Elementary and secondary schools

Masset, BC V0T
Skeena-Qn-Charlotte County

D-U-N-S 25-451-6008   (BR)
**BOARD OF EDUCATION OF SCHOOL DIS-
TRICT NO. 50 (HAIDA GWAII), THE**
TAHAYGHEN ELEMENTARY SCHOOL
2151 Tahayghen Dr, Masset, BC, V0T 1M0
(250) 626-5572
Emp Here 30
SIC 8211 Elementary and secondary schools

D-U-N-S 20-033-3784   (BR)
**BOARD OF EDUCATION OF SCHOOL DIS-
TRICT NO. 50 (HAIDA GWAII), THE**
*GEORGE M DAWFON SECONDARY
SCHOOL*
1647 Collison St, Masset, BC, V0T 1M0
(250) 626-5522
Emp Here 20
SIC 8211 Elementary and secondary schools

Mcbride, BC V0J
Fraser-Fort George County

D-U-N-S 20-655-0266   (SL)
MCBRIDE & DISTRICT HOSPITAL
1136 5th Ave, Mcbride, BC, V0J 2E0

Emp Here 60   *Sales* 4,158,760
SIC 8062 General medical and surgical hospitals

D-U-N-S 25-912-6464   (BR)
**NORTHLAND PROPERTIES CORPORA-
TION**
SANDMAN INNS MCBRIDE
(*Suby of* Northland Properties Corporation)
1051 Frontage St Se, Mcbride, BC, V0J 2E0
(250) 569-2285
Emp Here 20
SIC 7011 Hotels and motels

Mcleese Lake, BC V0L
Cariboo County

D-U-N-S 20-335-3359   (BR)
GIBRALTAR MINES LTD
10251 Gibraltar Mine Rd, Mcleese Lake, BC,
V0L 1P0
(250) 297-6211
Emp Here 50
SIC 1081 Metal mining services

Merritt, BC V1K
Thompson - Nicola County

D-U-N-S 20-152-2856   (BR)
ASPEN PLANERS LTD
2399 Quilchena Ave, Merritt, BC, V1K 1B8
(250) 378-9266
Emp Here 200
SIC 2421 Sawmills and planing mills, general

D-U-N-S 25-267-8701   (BR)
COOPER MARKET LTD
1700 Garcia St Unit 1700, Merritt, BC, V1K
1B8
(250) 378-5564
Emp Here 80
SIC 5411 Grocery stores

D-U-N-S 20-765-1592   (SL)
COQUIHALLA / GILLIS HOUSE
3451 Voght St, Merritt, BC, V1K 1C6
(250) 378-3271
Emp Here 49   *Sales* 9,193,048
SIC 8322 Individual and family services
Owner Lillie Scott

D-U-N-S 25-775-1792   (BR)
DAWNAL QUICK SERVE LTD
MCDONALD'S RESTAURANTS
(*Suby of* Dawnal Quick Serve Ltd)
3360 Airport Rd, Merritt, BC, V1K 1M5
(250) 378-2170
Emp Here 45
SIC 5812 Eating places

D-U-N-S 20-917-2316   (BR)
**GOVERNMENT OF THE PROVINCE OF
BRITISH COLUMBIA**
PROBATION OFFICE
Gd Stn Main, Merritt, BC, V1K 1B7
(250) 378-9355
Emp Here 25
SIC 8322 Individual and family services

D-U-N-S 24-206-6889   (SL)
**MURRAY CHEVROLET PONTIAC BUICK
GMC MERRITT LIMITED PARTNERSHIP**
MURRAY GM MERRITT
2049 Nicola Ave, Merritt, BC, V1K 1B8
(250) 378-9255
Emp Here 28   *Sales* 10,214,498
SIC 5511 New and used car dealers
Genl Pt Scott Robertson
 Jason Leech

D-U-N-S 20-713-2908   (BR)
**SCHOOL DISTRICT NO 58 (NICOLA-
SIMILKAMEEN)**
*MERRITT CENTRAL ELEMENTARY
SCHOOL*
1501 Voght St, Merritt, BC, V1K 1B8
(250) 378-9931
Emp Here 50
SIC 8211 Elementary and secondary schools

D-U-N-S 25-269-6323   (BR)
**SCHOOL DISTRICT NO 58 (NICOLA-
SIMILKAMEEN)**
MERRITT SECONDARY SCHOOL
(*Suby of* School District No 58 (Nicola-
Similkameen))
1561 Champman St, Merritt, BC, V1K 1B8
(250) 378-5131
Emp Here 49

SIC 8211 Elementary and secondary schools

D-U-N-S 20-591-6260   (BR)
**SCHOOL DISTRICT NO 58 (NICOLA-
SIMILKAMEEN)**
KENGARD LEARNING CENTRE
2475 Merritt, Merritt, BC, V1K 0A1
(250) 378-4245
Emp Here 25
SIC 8211 Elementary and secondary schools

D-U-N-S 20-591-6294   (BR)
**SCHOOL DISTRICT NO 58 (NICOLA-
SIMILKAMEEN)**
MERRITT BENCH ELEMENTARY
3441 Grimmet St, Merritt, BC, V1K 1M3
(250) 378-2528
Emp Here 25
SIC 8211 Elementary and secondary schools

D-U-N-S 20-030-5626   (BR)
**SCHOOL DISTRICT NO 58 (NICOLA-
SIMILKAMEEN)**
DIAMOND VALE ELEMENTARY SCHOOL
2675 Coldwater Ave, Merritt, BC, V1K 1B2
(250) 378-2514
Emp Here 25
SIC 8211 Elementary and secondary schools

D-U-N-S 25-803-4362   (BR)
SHAW COMMUNICATIONS INC
SHAW CABLE
Gd Stn Main, Merritt, BC, V1K 1B7
(250) 378-2568
Emp Here 30
SIC 4833 Television broadcasting stations

D-U-N-S 24-824-4766   (BR)
TOLKO INDUSTRIES LTD
NICOLA VALLEY DIVISION
1750 Lindley Creek Rd, Merritt, BC, V1K 0A2

Emp Here 200
SIC 2421 Sawmills and planing mills, general

D-U-N-S 20-981-7183   (BR)
VSA HIGHWAY MAINTENANCE LTD
2925 Pooley Ave, Merritt, BC, V1K 1C2
(250) 315-0166
Emp Here 100
SIC 1611 Highway and street construction

D-U-N-S 24-319-5083   (BR)
WAL-MART CANADA CORP
WALMART
3900 Crawford Ave Suite 100, Merritt, BC, V1K
0A4
(250) 315-1366
Emp Here 120
SIC 5311 Department stores

Midway, BC V0H
Kootenay Boundary County

D-U-N-S 20-713-2304   (BR)
SCHOOL DISTRICT 51 BOUNDARY
*BOUNDARY CENTRAL SECONDARY
SCHOOL*
355 5th Ave, Midway, BC, V0H 1M0
(250) 449-2224
Emp Here 50
SIC 8211 Elementary and secondary schools

Mill Bay, BC V0R
Cowichan Valley County

D-U-N-S 25-855-0367   (BR)
COWICHAN VALLEY REGIONAL DISTRICT
KERRY PARK RECREATION CENTER
1035 Shawnigan-Mill Bay Rd, Mill Bay, BC,
V0R 2P2
(250) 743-9211
Emp Here 30

SIC 7999 Amusement and recreation, nec

D-U-N-S 25-177-3818   (BR)
ISLAND SAVINGS CREDIT UNION
(*Suby of* Island Savings Credit Union)
2720 Mill Bay Rd, Mill Bay, BC, V0R 2P1
(250) 743-5534
Emp Here 30
SIC 6062 State credit unions

D-U-N-S 20-191-3287   (BR)
JACE HOLDINGS LTD
THRIFTY FOODS
2720 Mill Bay Rd, Mill Bay, BC, V0R 2P1
(250) 743-3261
Emp Here 100
SIC 5411 Grocery stores

D-U-N-S 20-994-5625   (SL)
MILL BAY PHARMACY LTD
PHARMASAVE
2720 Mill Eay Rd Suite 230, Mill Bay, BC, V0R
2P1

Emp Here 38   *Sales* 5,399,092
SIC 5912 Drug stores and proprietary stores
Pr Pr Heather Skoretz

D-U-N-S 20-819-2711   (BR)
RUSKIN CONSTRUCTION LTD
(*Suby of* Northern Linkwell Construction Ltd)
1451 Trowsse Rd, Mill Bay, BC, V0R 2P4
(250) 360-0672
Emp Here 25
SIC 1541 Industrial buildings and warehouses

D-U-N-S 20-034-4948   (BR)
SCHOOL DISTRICT NO. 79 (COWICHAN VALLEY)
GEORGE BONNER MIDDLE SCHOOL
3060 Cobble Hill Rd, Mill Bay, BC, V0R 2P3
(250) 743-5571
Emp Here 40
SIC 8211 Elementary and secondary schools

D-U-N-S 20-034-7339   (BR)
SCHOOL DISTRICT NO. 79 (COWICHAN VALLEY)
FRANCES-KELSEY SECONDARY SCHOOL
953 Shawnigan-Mill Bay Rd, Mill Bay, BC, V0R
2P2
(250) 743-6916
Emp Here 80
SIC 8211 Elementary and secondary schools

Mission, BC V2V

D-U-N-S 20-589-5100   (BR)
BANQUE TORONTO-DOMINION, LA
TD CANADA TRUST
(*Suby of* Toronto-Dominion Bank, The)
32555 London Ave Suite 140, Mission, BC,
V2V 6M7
(604) 820-5600
Emp Here 20
SIC 6021 National commercial banks

D-U-N-S 20-147-7168   (BR)
BLACK BOND BOOKS LTD
EDU KIDS (DIV OF)
(*Suby of* Black Bond Books Ltd)
32555 London Ave Suite 344, Mission, BC,
V2V 6M7

Emp Here 619
SIC 5942 Book stores

D-U-N-S 25-288-9035   (BR)
CANADA POST CORPORATION
33191 1st Ave, Mission, BC, V2V 1G5
(604) 826-6034
Emp Here 30
SIC 4311 U.s. postal service

D-U-N-S 20-786-5812   (BR)
CHARTWELL MASTER CARE LP

CARRINGTON HOUSE RESSIDENCE AND SUITES
32700 Seventh Ave, Mission, BC, V2V 2C1
(604) 826-4747
Emp Here 25
SIC 6513 Apartment building operators

D-U-N-S 24-418-2767   (BR)
CINEPLEX ODEON CORPORATION
SILVERCITY MISSION
32555 London Ave Suite 1407, Mission, BC,
V2V 6M7
(604) 820-2733
Emp Here 49
SIC 7832 Motion picture theaters, except drive-in

D-U-N-S 24-051-9566   (BR)
CONSEIL SCOLAIRE FRANCOPHONE DE LA COLOMBIE BRITANNIQUE
ECOLE DES DEUX-RIVES
7674 Stave Lake St, Mission, BC, V2V 4G4
(604) 820-5710
Emp Here 42
SIC 8211 Elementary and secondary schools

D-U-N-S 24-174-0906   (BR)
FRASER HEALTH AUTHORITY
33070 5th Ave Suite 101, Mission, BC, V2V
1V5
(604) 814-5600
Emp Here 20
SIC 8062 General medical and surgical hospitals

D-U-N-S 25-268-0087   (BR)
GREAT PACIFIC INDUSTRIES INC
SAVE-ON-FOODS
32555 London Ave Suite 400, Mission, BC,
V2V 6M7
(604) 826-9564
Emp Here 245
SIC 5411 Grocery stores

D-U-N-S 20-000-3015   (BR)
JUST LADIES FITNESS LTD
32646 Logan Ave, Mission, BC, V2V 6C7
(604) 820-9008
Emp Here 20
SIC 7991 Physical fitness facilities

D-U-N-S 25-685-0421   (BR)
LOBLAWS INC
REAL CANADIAN SUPERSTORE
32136 Lougheed Hwy Suite 1559, Mission,
BC, V2V 1A4
(604) 820-6436
Emp Here 50
SIC 5912 Drug stores and proprietary stores

D-U-N-S 24-150-5114   (BR)
LORDCO PARTS LTD
LORDCO AUTO PARTS
32885 London Ave, Mission, BC, V2V 6M7
(604) 826-7121
Emp Here 35
SIC 5531 Auto and home supply stores

D-U-N-S 24-248-9243   (HQ)
MISSION ASSOCIATION FOR COMMUNITY LIVING
(*Suby of* Mission Association For Community Living)
33345 2nd Ave, Mission, BC, V2V 1K4
(604) 826-9080
Emp Here 120   *Emp Total* 121
Sales 4,450,603
SIC 8361 Residential care

D-U-N-S 24-446-2636   (SL)
PLEASANT VIEW HOUSING SOCIETY 1980
PLEASANT VIEW CARE HOME
7540 Hurd St Unit 101, Mission, BC, V2V 3H9
(604) 826-2176
Emp Here 100   *Sales* 4,742,446
SIC 8051 Skilled nursing care facilities

D-U-N-S 25-236-2181   (SL)
QUALITY ASSURED AUTO BODY SERVICE

LIMITED
7077 Mershon St, Mission, BC, V2V 2Y6
(604) 299-4414
Emp Here 110   *Sales* 10,956,600
SIC 7532 Top and body repair and paint shops
Genl Mgr Gordon Grant

D-U-N-S 25-782-1397   (BR)
ROYAL BANK OF CANADA
RBC
(*Suby of* Royal Bank Of Canada)
33114 1st Ave, Mission, BC, V2V 1G4
(604) 824-4700
Emp Here 22
SIC 6021 National commercial banks

D-U-N-S 20-590-8952   (BR)
SCHOOL DISTRICT #75 (MISSION)
HILLSIDE ELEMENTARY
33621 Best Ave, Mission, BC, V2V 5Z3
(604) 826-4187
Emp Here 25
SIC 8211 Elementary and secondary schools

D-U-N-S 20-590-8978   (BR)
SCHOOL DISTRICT #75 (MISSION)
HATZIT ELEMENTARY SCHOOL
8465 Draper St, Mission, BC, V2V 5V6
(604) 826-2481
Emp Here 25
SIC 8211 Elementary and secondary schools

D-U-N-S 20-590-8846   (BR)
SCHOOL DISTRICT #75 (MISSION)
DURIEU ELEMENTARY SCHOOL
11620 Seux Rd, Mission, BC, V2V 4J1

Emp Here 25
SIC 8211 Elementary and secondary schools

D-U-N-S 20-590-8879   (BR)
SCHOOL DISTRICT #75 (MISSION)
WEST HEIGHTS ELEMENTARY SCHOOL
32065 Van Velzen Ave, Mission, BC, V2V 2G6
(604) 826-6401
Emp Here 28
SIC 8211 Elementary and secondary schools

D-U-N-S 20-590-8895   (BR)
SCHOOL DISTRICT #75 (MISSION)
CHERRY HILL ELEMENTARY SCHOOL
32557 Best Ave, Mission, BC, V2V 2S5
(604) 826-9239
Emp Here 20
SIC 8211 Elementary and secondary schools

D-U-N-S 20-047-0859   (BR)
SCHOOL DISTRICT #75 (MISSION)
RICHARD'S ELEMENTARY
33419 Cherry Ave, Mission, BC, V2V 2V5
(604) 826-2834
Emp Here 44
SIC 8211 Elementary and secondary schools

D-U-N-S 20-590-8911   (BR)
SCHOOL DISTRICT #75 (MISSION)
ALBERT MCMAHON ELEMENTARY SCHOOL
32865 Cherry Ave, Mission, BC, V2V 2V1
(604) 826-0274
Emp Here 25
SIC 8211 Elementary and secondary schools

D-U-N-S 20-043-9748   (BR)
SCHOOL DISTRICT #75 (MISSION)
ECOLE CHRISTINE MORRISON ELEMENTARY
32611 Mcrae Ave, Mission, BC, V2V 2L8
(604) 826-6528
Emp Here 35
SIC 8211 Elementary and secondary schools

D-U-N-S 20-590-8960   (BR)
SCHOOL DISTRICT #75 (MISSION)
MISSION CENTRAL ELEMENTARY SCHOOL
7466 Welton St, Mission, BC, V2V 6L4
(604) 826-1414
Emp Here 25

SIC 8211 Elementary and secondary schools

D-U-N-S 20-590-8903   (BR)
SCHOOL DISTRICT #75 (MISSION)
CEDAR VALLEY SCHOOL
32811 Dewdney Trunk Rd, Mission, BC, V2V
6X6

Emp Here 25
SIC 8211 Elementary and secondary schools

D-U-N-S 20-575-8589   (BR)
SCHOOL DISTRICT #75 (MISSION)
HERITAGE PARK SECONDARY SCHOOL
33700 Prentis Ave Suite 1000, Mission, BC,
V2V 7B1
(604) 820-4587
Emp Here 50
SIC 8211 Elementary and secondary schools

D-U-N-S 20-590-8945   (BR)
SCHOOL DISTRICT #75 (MISSION)
WINDEBANK ELEMENTARY SCHOOL
33570 Eleventh Ave, Mission, BC, V2V 6Z2
(604) 826-2213
Emp Here 25
SIC 8211 Elementary and secondary schools

D-U-N-S 20-299-3916   (BR)
SCHOOL DISTRICT #75 (MISSION)
HATZIC SECONDARY SCHOOL
34800 Dewdney Trunk Rd Suite 1, Mission,
BC, V2V 5V6
(604) 826-3651
Emp Here 75
SIC 8211 Elementary and secondary schools

D-U-N-S 20-299-3999   (BR)
SCHOOL DISTRICT #75 (MISSION)
MISSION SECONDARY SCHOOL
32939 7th Ave, Mission, BC, V2V 2C5
(604) 826-7191
Emp Here 100
SIC 8211 Elementary and secondary schools

D-U-N-S 20-981-6722   (BR)
SCHOOL DISTRICT #75 (MISSION)
33919 Dewdney Trunk Rd Suite 75, Mission,
BC, V2V 6Y4
(604) 826-7375
Emp Here 25
SIC 7349 Building maintenance services, nec

D-U-N-S 24-327-8327   (BR)
STAPLES CANADA INC
STAPLES THE BUSINESS DEPOT
(*Suby of* Staples, Inc.)
32555 London Ave Unit 900, Mission, BC, V2V
6M7
(604) 814-3850
Emp Here 30
SIC 5943 Stationery stores

D-U-N-S 20-806-4852   (BR)
STARBUCKS COFFEE CANADA, INC
(*Suby of* Starbucks Corporation)
32555 London Ave Unit 370, Mission, BC, V2V
6M7
(604) 820-0025
Emp Here 21
SIC 5812 Eating places

D-U-N-S 24-392-7233   (SL)
STARLINER TRANSPORT (1981) LTD
STARLINER
32916 Mission Way, Mission, BC, V2V 5X9
(604) 820-0523
Emp Here 65   *Sales* 10,797,600
SIC 4213 Trucking, except local
Pr Pr Rene Savoie
Treas David Savoie

D-U-N-S 24-656-6236   (BR)
UNIVERSITY OF THE FRASER VALLEY
33700 Prentis Ave Suite 1000, Mission, BC,
V2V 7B1
(604) 557-7603
Emp Here 50
SIC 8221 Colleges and universities

D-U-N-S 24-886-9687   (SL)
V. I. P. SOAP PRODUCTS LTD
32859 Mission Way, Mission, BC, V2V 6E4
(604) 820-8665
Emp Here 60   *Sales* 1,472,627
SIC 2841 Soap and other detergents

D-U-N-S 25-664-9216   (BR)
WAL-MART CANADA CORP
WALMART PHARMACIES
31956 Lougheed Hwy Suite 1119, Mission, BC, V2V 0C6
(604) 820-0048
Emp Here 150
SIC 5311 Department stores

Mission, BC V4S

D-U-N-S 20-590-8853   (BR)
SCHOOL DISTRICT #75 (MISSION)
SILVERDALE ELEMENTARY SCHOOL
29715 Donatelli Ave, Mission, BC, V4S 1H6
(604) 826-2526
Emp Here 20
SIC 8211 Elementary and secondary schools

D-U-N-S 25-414-8703   (SL)
SILVER CREEK PREMIUM PRODUCTS LTD
(*Suby of* Mission Shake & Shingle Ltd)
7250 Nelson St, Mission, BC, V4S 1H3
(604) 826-5971
Emp Here 40   *Sales* 5,030,400
SIC 2429 Special product sawmills, nec
Pr Pr Amarjit Brar
  Preetpal Brar

Nakusp, BC V0G
Central Kootenay County

D-U-N-S 24-558-7431   (SL)
682523 ALBERTA LTD
KUSKANAX LODGE
(*Suby of* Intrawest Resorts Holdings, Inc.)
515 Broadway Dr, Nakusp, BC, V0G 1R0
(250) 265-3618
Emp Here 40   *Sales* 1,751,057
SIC 7011 Hotels and motels

D-U-N-S 20-024-4668   (BR)
ARROW LAKES SCHOOL DISTRICT #10
NAKUSP ELEMENTARY SCHOOL
(*Suby of* Arrow Lakes School District #10)
403 23 Hwy N, Nakusp, BC, V0G 1R0
(250) 265-3731
Emp Here 25
SIC 8211 Elementary and secondary schools

D-U-N-S 24-373-2229   (BR)
ARROW LAKES SCHOOL DISTRICT #10
NAKUSP SECONDARY SCHOOL
(*Suby of* Arrow Lakes School District #10)
619 4th St, Nakusp, BC, V0G 1R0
(250) 265-3668
Emp Here 28
SIC 8211 Elementary and secondary schools

D-U-N-S 20-572-4276   (BR)
BRITISH COLUMBIA HYDRO AND POWER AUTHORITY
BC HYDRO
92 7th Ave W, Nakusp, BC, V0G 1R0
(250) 265-2239
Emp Here 20
SIC 4911 Electric services

D-U-N-S 25-059-1641   (BR)
CANADIAN MOUNTAIN HOLIDAYS LIMITED PARTNERSHIP
KOOTENAY HELICOPTER SKIING
(*Suby of* Intrawest Resorts Holdings, Inc.)
515 Broadway Dr, Nakusp, BC, V0G 1R0

(250) 265-3121
Emp Here 30
SIC 7011 Hotels and motels

D-U-N-S 25-268-0202   (BR)
GREAT PACIFIC INDUSTRIES INC
OVERWAITEA FOOD GROUP
510 Broadway St, Nakusp, BC, V0G 1R0
(250) 265-3662
Emp Here 40
SIC 5411 Grocery stores

D-U-N-S 24-031-2462   (BR)
INTERIOR HEALTH AUTHORITY
ARROW LAKES HOSPITAL
97 1st Ave E, Nakusp, BC, V0G 1R0
(250) 265-3622
Emp Here 30
SIC 8062 General medical and surgical hospitals

D-U-N-S 20-591-6443   (BR)
SCHOOL DISTRICT NO 10
NAKUSP SECONDARY SCHOOL
619 4th St Nw, Nakusp, BC, V0G 1R0
(250) 265-3668
Emp Here 25
SIC 8211 Elementary and secondary schools

Nanaimo, BC V9R
Nanaimo County

D-U-N-S 25-506-2044   (SL)
434870 B.C. LTD
HUB CITY FISHERIES
262 Southside Dr, Nanaimo, BC, V9R 6Z5
(250) 753-4135
Emp Here 30   *Sales* 4,961,328
SIC 2092 Fresh or frozen packaged fish

D-U-N-S 20-650-3463   (SL)
490892 B.C. LTD
HOWARD JOHNSON HARBOURSIDE HOTEL
1 Terminal Ave N, Nanaimo, BC, V9R 5R4
(250) 753-3051
Emp Here 65   *Sales* 2,845,467
SIC 7011 Hotels and motels

D-U-N-S 25-958-1106   (BR)
ALL-CAN EXPRESS LTD
ACE COURIER SERVICES
85 Tenth St, Nanaimo, BC, V9R 6R6
(250) 741-1422
Emp Here 20
SIC 7389 Business services, nec

D-U-N-S 25-392-9962   (BR)
ALSCO CANADA CORPORATION
ALSCO UNIFORM & LINEN SERVICE
91 Comox Rd, Nanaimo, BC, V9R 3H7
(250) 754-4464
Emp Here 50
SIC 7213 Linen supply

D-U-N-S 25-100-4354   (HQ)
BOYS AND GIRLS CLUBS OF CENTRAL VANCOUVER ISLAND
BGCCVI
(*Suby of* Boys and Girls Clubs of Central Vancouver Island)
20 Fifth St, Nanaimo, BC, V9R 1M7
(250) 754-3215
Emp Here 28   *Emp Total* 82
Sales 3,210,271
SIC 8322 Individual and family services

D-U-N-S 24-657-3364   (BR)
CANADIAN IMPERIAL BANK OF COMMERCE
CIBC
650 Terminal Ave Suite 66, Nanaimo, BC, V9R 5E2
(250) 716-2060
Emp Here 45

SIC 6021 National commercial banks

D-U-N-S 24-348-2796   (BR)
CATALYST PAPER CORPORATION
65 Front St Suite 201, Nanaimo, BC, V9R 5H9
(250) 734-8000
Emp Here 45
SIC 2621 Paper mills

D-U-N-S 20-803-5191   (BR)
CITY OF NANAIMO
NANAIMO AQUATIC CENTER
741 Third St, Nanaimo, BC, V9R 7B2
(250) 755-7574
Emp Here 50
SIC 7999 Amusement and recreation, nec

D-U-N-S 24-344-5314   (BR)
CITY OF NANAIMO
GREATER NANAIMO WATER DISTRICT
455 Wallace St, Nanaimo, BC, V9R 5J6
(250) 755-4428
Emp Here 50
SIC 4941 Water supply

D-U-N-S 20-075-6190   (BR)
CITY OF NANAIMO
ENGINEERING DEPARTMENT
238 Franklyn St, Nanaimo, BC, V9R 2X4
(250) 755-4409
Emp Here 30
SIC 7389 Business services, nec

D-U-N-S 24-578-5597   (BR)
COAST HOTELS LIMITED
COAST BASTION INN
11 Bastion St, Nanaimo, BC, V9R 6E4
(250) 753-6601
Emp Here 90
SIC 7011 Hotels and motels

D-U-N-S 24-616-7097   (BR)
COASTAL COMMUNITY CREDIT UNION
59 Wharf St Unit 220, Nanaimo, BC, V9R 2X3
(250) 716-2331
Emp Here 100
SIC 6062 State credit unions

D-U-N-S 25-133-7986   (BR)
COASTAL COMMUNITY CREDIT UNION
SOUTHGATE COMMUNITY BRANCH
50 Tenth St Suite 111, Nanaimo, BC, V9R 6L1

Emp Here 20
SIC 6062 State credit unions

D-U-N-S 25-893-1377   (BR)
COASTAL COMMUNITY CREDIT UNION
59 Wharf St Suite 111, Nanaimo, BC, V9R 2X3
(888) 741-1010
Emp Here 20
SIC 6062 State credit unions

D-U-N-S 24-626-2005   (SL)
COASTAL COMMUNITY INSURANCE SERVICES 2007 LTD
59 Wharf St Suite 220, Nanaimo, BC, V9R 2X3

Emp Here 30   *Sales* 29,840,926
SIC 6311 Life insurance
Pr Robert Buckley

D-U-N-S 24-551-0888   (HQ)
COMOX VALLEY DISTRIBUTION LTD
(*Suby of* Reimer Consolidated Corp)
140 Tenth St, Nanaimo, BC, V9R 6Z5
(250) 754-7773
Emp Here 64   *Emp Total* 40
Sales 11,892,594
SIC 4213 Trucking, except local
Pr Pr Ken Hiebert

D-U-N-S 25-680-0699   (BR)
DAVEY TREE EXPERT CO. OF CANADA, LIMITED
DAVEY TREE SERVICES
13 Victoria Cres Suite 20, Nanaimo, BC, V9R 5B9

(250) 755-1288
Emp Here 150
SIC 5261 Retail nurseries and garden stores

D-U-N-S 25-831-7478   (SL)
E & N RAILWAY COMPANY (1998) LTD
(*Suby of* Genesee & Wyoming Inc.)
7 Port Way, Nanaimo, BC, V9R 5L3
(250) 754-9222
Emp Here 20   *Sales* 10,652,250
SIC 4011 Railroads, line-haul operating
Sr VP Tom Schlosser

D-U-N-S 20-198-1797   (HQ)
GARDEN CITY WAREHOUSING & DISTRIBUTION LTD
RICHARDSON FOODS GROUP
839 Old Victoria Rd, Nanaimo, BC, V9R 5Z9
(250) 754-5447
Emp Here 43   *Emp Total* 2
Sales 14,373,258
SIC 5141 Groceries, general line
Pr Pr Tom Richardson
Genl Mgr James Richardson
Fin Ex John Bannerman

D-U-N-S 24-456-0454   (BR)
GOVERNING COUNCIL OF THE SALVATION ARMY IN CANADA, THE
GOVERNING COUNCIL OF THE SALVATION ARMY IN CANADA, THE
505 Eighth St, Nanaimo, BC, V9R 1B5
(250) 753-8834
Emp Here 60
SIC 8322 Individual and family services

D-U-N-S 20-589-2917   (BR)
GOVERNMENT OF THE PROVINCE OF BRITISH COLUMBIA
MINISTRY OF CHILDREN AND FAMILY DEVELOPMENT
190 Wallace St Suite 301, Nanaimo, BC, V9R 5B1
(250) 741-5701
Emp Here 23
SIC 8399 Social services, nec

D-U-N-S 25-822-8097   (BR)
GREAT CANADIAN CASINOS INC
CASINO NANAIMO
(*Suby of* Great Canadian Gaming Corporation)
620 Terminal Ave, Nanaimo, BC, V9R 5E2
(250) 753-3033
Emp Here 200
SIC 7999 Amusement and recreation, nec

D-U-N-S 24-695-3731   (BR)
INSURANCE CORPORATION OF BRITISH COLUMBIA
ICBC
6460 Applecroix Rd, Nanaimo, BC, V9R 6E6
(250) 390-4511
Emp Here 44
SIC 6331 Fire, marine, and casualty insurance

D-U-N-S 25-181-5098   (BR)
JACE HOLDINGS LTD
THRIFTY FOODS NANAIMO
650 Terminal Ave Unit 3, Nanaimo, BC, V9R 5E2
(250) 754-6273
Emp Here 100
SIC 5411 Grocery stores

D-U-N-S 25-098-9910   (BR)
KELLAND FOODS LTD
QUALITY FOODS
530 Fifth St Suite 100, Nanaimo, BC, V9R 1P1
(250) 754-6012
Emp Here 35
SIC 5411 Grocery stores

D-U-N-S 20-874-4560   (BR)
LORDCO PARTS LTD
LORDCO AUTO PARTS
140 Terminal Ave Suite 1, Nanaimo, BC, V9R 5C5

---

(250) 753-1711
Emp Here 22
SIC 5531 Auto and home supply stores

D-U-N-S 20-177-6361   (BR)
MNP LLP
96 Wallace St, Nanaimo, BC, V9R 0E2
(250) 753-8251
Emp Here 40
SIC 8721 Accounting, auditing, and book-keeping

D-U-N-S 24-823-8594   (SL)
N & S HOTEL GROUP INC
BEST WESTERN DORCHESTER HOTEL, THE
70 Church St, Nanaimo, BC, V9R 5H4
(250) 754-6835
Emp Here 50   *Sales* 2,188,821
SIC 7011 Hotels and motels

D-U-N-S 25-850-8779   (SL)
NANAIMO ASSOCIATION FOR COMMU-NITY LIVING
NACL
96 Cavan St Suite 201, Nanaimo, BC, V9R 2V1
(250) 741-0224
Emp Here 110   *Sales* 15,574,400
SIC 8611 Business associations
Ex Dir Graham Morry
Pr Pr Kathleen Haegith

D-U-N-S 20-590-8325   (BR)
SCHOOL DISTRICT NO. 68 (NANAIMO-LADYSMITH)
HAREWOOD SCHOOL
505 Howard Ave, Nanaimo, BC, V9R 3S5

Emp Here 25
SIC 8211 Elementary and secondary schools

D-U-N-S 20-590-8226   (BR)
SCHOOL DISTRICT NO. 68 (NANAIMO-LADYSMITH)
10 Strickland St, Nanaimo, BC, V9R 4R9
(250) 753-4012
Emp Here 25
SIC 8211 Elementary and secondary schools

D-U-N-S 20-048-3001   (BR)
SCHOOL DISTRICT NO. 68 (NANAIMO-LADYSMITH)
PAULINE HAARER SCHOOL
400 Campbell St, Nanaimo, BC, V9R 3G7
(250) 754-2722
Emp Here 22
SIC 8211 Elementary and secondary schools

D-U-N-S 25-182-7846   (BR)
SCHOOL DISTRICT NO. 68 (NANAIMO-LADYSMITH)
CHASE RIVER ELEMENTARY SCHOOL
1503 Cranberry Ave, Nanaimo, BC, V9R 6R7
(250) 754-6983
Emp Here 20
SIC 8211 Elementary and secondary schools

D-U-N-S 20-713-5976   (BR)
SCHOOL DISTRICT NO. 68 (NANAIMO-LADYSMITH)
DISTRICT ADMINISTRATION CENTRE
395 Wakesiah Ave, Nanaimo, BC, V9R 3K6
(250) 754-5521
Emp Here 50
SIC 8211 Elementary and secondary schools

D-U-N-S 20-590-8259   (BR)
SCHOOL DISTRICT NO. 68 (NANAIMO-LADYSMITH)
FAIRVIEW COMMUNITY SCHOOL
205 Howard Ave, Nanaimo, BC, V9R 3R3
(250) 753-3418
Emp Here 25
SIC 8211 Elementary and secondary schools

D-U-N-S 20-199-7785   (BR)
SCHOOL DISTRICT NO. 68 (NANAIMO-LADYSMITH)

BAYVIEW ELEMENTARY SCHOOL
140 View St, Nanaimo, BC, V9R 4N6
(250) 754-3231
Emp Here 27
SIC 8211 Elementary and secondary schools

D-U-N-S 20-713-5885   (BR)
SCHOOL DISTRICT NO. 68 (NANAIMO-LADYSMITH)
MOUNTAIN VIEW SCHOOL
2480 East Wellington Rd, Nanaimo, BC, V9R 6V6
(250) 753-2831
Emp Here 30
SIC 8211 Elementary and secondary schools

D-U-N-S 20-590-8374   (BR)
SCHOOL DISTRICT NO. 68 (NANAIMO-LADYSMITH)
JUNIOR LEARNING ALTERNATIVES
897 Harbour View St, Nanaimo, BC, V9R 4V4

Emp Here 20
SIC 8211 Elementary and secondary schools

D-U-N-S 20-713-5893   (BR)
SCHOOL DISTRICT NO. 68 (NANAIMO-LADYSMITH)
PARK AVENUE COMMUNITY SCHOOL
395 Eighth St, Nanaimo, BC, V9R 1A9
(250) 754-5591
Emp Here 37
SIC 8211 Elementary and secondary schools

D-U-N-S 24-089-4829   (BR)
STERICYCLE COMMUNICATION SOLU-TIONS, ULC
TIGERTEL
(*Suby of* Stericycle Communication Solutions, ULC)
235 Bastion St Suite 205, Nanaimo, BC, V9R 3A3
(250) 386-1166
Emp Here 35
SIC 7389 Business services, nec

D-U-N-S 24-137-7050   (SL)
TILLICUM LELUM ABORIGINAL SOCIETY
927 Haliburton St, Nanaimo, BC, V9R 6N4
(250) 753-6578
Emp Here 60   *Sales* 3,283,232
SIC 8299 Schools and educational services, nec

D-U-N-S 20-293-7384   (BR)
TIMBERWEST FOREST COMPANY
648 Terminal Ave Suite 201, Nanaimo, BC, V9R 5E2
(250) 716-3700
Emp Here 40
SIC 2411 Logging

D-U-N-S 25-999-9753   (BR)
TRIMAC TRANSPORTATION SERVICES LIMITED PARTNERSHIP
125 Tenth St, Nanaimo, BC, V9R 6Z5
(250) 754-0085
Emp Here 20
SIC 6722 Management investment, open-end

D-U-N-S 25-948-6835   (BR)
VALUE VILLAGE STORES, INC
VALUE VILLAGE
(*Suby of* Savers, Inc.)
530 Fifth St Suite 101, Nanaimo, BC, V9R 1P1
(250) 741-0803
Emp Here 30
SIC 5399 Miscellaneous general merchandise

D-U-N-S 25-893-1385   (BR)
VAN-KAM FREIGHTWAYS LTD
1151 Milton St, Nanaimo, BC, V9R 2M2
(250) 723-3733
Emp Here 25
SIC 4212 Local trucking, without storage

D-U-N-S 24-957-5614   (SL)
WEN HARBOURSIDE FOODS LTD
WENDY'S

660 Terminal Ave, Nanaimo, BC, V9R 5E2
(250) 754-0705
Emp Here 55   *Sales* 1,678,096
SIC 5812 Eating places

D-U-N-S 24-348-5823   (BR)
WESTERN FOREST PRODUCTS INC
NANAIMO SAWMILL
31 Port Way, Nanaimo, BC, V9R 5L5
(250) 755-4600
Emp Here 130
SIC 2611 Pulp mills

D-U-N-S 24-060-7940   (BR)
WESTERN FOREST PRODUCTS INC
DUKE POINT SAWMILL
500 Duke Pt Rd, Nanaimo, BC, V9R 1K1
(250) 722-2533
Emp Here 200
SIC 2611 Pulp mills

Nanaimo, BC V9S
Nanaimo County

D-U-N-S 25-131-1460   (BR)
7-ELEVEN CANADA, INC
7-ELEVEN STORE #20926
1602 Bowen Rd, Nanaimo, BC, V9S 1G6
(250) 753-4233
Emp Here 20
SIC 5411 Grocery stores

D-U-N-S 24-313-5881   (BR)
ALLNORTH CONSULTANTS LIMITED
20 Townsite Rd, Nanaimo, BC, V9S 5T7
(250) 753-7472
Emp Here 25
SIC 8742 Management consulting services

D-U-N-S 20-834-5749   (SL)
ASPIN ROOFING & GUTTERS LTD
ASPIN HOME SERVICES
2210 Petersen Pl, Nanaimo, BC, V9S 4N5

Emp Here 40   *Sales* 5,478,300
SIC 1761 Roofing, siding, and sheetMetal work
Pr Donovan Aspin

D-U-N-S 24-535-1358   (BR)
BANQUE TORONTO-DOMINION, LA
TD CANADA TRUST
(*Suby of* Toronto-Dominion Bank, The)
1150 Terminal Ave N Suite 1, Nanaimo, BC, V9S 5L6
(250) 754-7731
Emp Here 35
SIC 6021 National commercial banks

D-U-N-S 25-901-4306   (BR)
BELFOR (CANADA) INC
BELFOR PROPERTY RESTORATION
2301a Mccullough Rd, Nanaimo, BC, V9S 4M9
(250) 756-9333
Emp Here 25
SIC 1799 Special trade contractors, nec

D-U-N-S 25-137-9947   (BR)
BLACK PRESS GROUP LTD
NANAIMO NEWS BULLETIN
777b Poplar St, Nanaimo, BC, V9S 2H7
(250) 753-3707
Emp Here 30
SIC 2711 Newspapers

D-U-N-S 20-852-9110   (BR)
BRITISH COLUMBIA FERRY SERVICES INC
BC FERRIES
1904 East Wellington Rd, Nanaimo, BC, V9S 5X6
(250) 753-2214
Emp Here 23
SIC 4482 Ferries

D-U-N-S 20-713-6503   (BR)
CONSEIL SCOLAIRE FRANCOPHONE DE LA COLOMBIE BRITANNIQUE
ECOLE OCEANE
1951 Estevan Rd, Nanaimo, BC, V9S 3Y9
(250) 714-0761
Emp Here 20
SIC 8211 Elementary and secondary schools

D-U-N-S 24-718-1472   (SL)
FORESIGHT CONSTRUCTORS LTD
1610d Northfield Rd, Nanaimo, BC, V9S 3A7

Emp Here 22   *Sales* 5,681,200
SIC 1542 Nonresidential construction, nec
Pr G Wayne Anderson
Sec Gayle Anderson

D-U-N-S 25-132-1477   (BR)
FORTISBC ENERGY INC
2220 Dorman Rd, Nanaimo, BC, V9S 5W2
(250) 751-8300
Emp Here 44
SIC 4923 Gas transmission and distribution

D-U-N-S 24-593-8709   (BR)
GREAT PACIFIC INDUSTRIES INC
SAVE-ON-FOODS
1501 Estevan Rd Suite 949, Nanaimo, BC, V9S 3Y3

Emp Here 70
SIC 5411 Grocery stores

D-U-N-S 25-960-7281   (BR)
INLAND KENWORTH LTD
INLAND KENWORTH
2365 Northfield Rd, Nanaimo, BC, V9S 3C3
(250) 758-5288
Emp Here 33
SIC 5511 New and used car dealers

D-U-N-S 24-855-4628   (BR)
KELLAND FOODS LTD
QUALITY FOODS
2220 Bowen Rd Suite 7, Nanaimo, BC, V9S 1H9
(250) 758-3733
Emp Here 40
SIC 5411 Grocery stores

D-U-N-S 25-485-9358   (SL)
KIWANIS VILLAGE LODGE
1221 Kiwanis Cres, Nanaimo, BC, V9S 5Y1
(250) 753-6471
Emp Here 100   *Sales* 4,523,563
SIC 8051 Skilled nursing care facilities

D-U-N-S 24-337-2021   (BR)
LONDON LIFE INSURANCE COMPANY
FREEDOM 55 FINANCIAL
1150 Terminal Ave N Unit 30, Nanaimo, BC, V9S 5L6
(250) 753-9955
Emp Here 23
SIC 8742 Management consulting services

D-U-N-S 20-515-6800   (BR)
MCELHANNEY CONSULTING SERVICES LTD
MCELHANNEY
1351 Estevan Rd Unit 1, Nanaimo, BC, V9S 3Y3
(250) 716-3336
Emp Here 20
SIC 8711 Engineering services

D-U-N-S 20-100-6376   (HQ)
NANAIMO REALTY CO LTD
ROYAL LEPAGE-NANAIMO REALTY
(*Suby of* Great National Investments Ltd)
2000 Island Hwy N Suite 275, Nanaimo, BC, V9S 5W3
(250) 713-0494
Emp Here 50   *Emp Total* 3
Sales 5,617,974
SIC 6531 Real estate agents and managers
Pr Pr Barry Clark

Dir Allan Lupton
Dir Ted Lewis

D-U-N-S 24-165-6289   (SL)
NANAIMO TRAVELLERS LODGE SOCIETY
1298 Nelson St, Nanaimo, BC, V9S 2K5
(250) 758-4676
Emp Here 110   *Sales* 4,012,839
SIC 8361 Residential care

D-U-N-S 25-913-8170   (BR)
POSTMEDIA NETWORK INC
NANAIMO DAILY NEWS
2575 Mccullough Rd Suite B1, Nanaimo, BC,
V9S 5W5

Emp Here 200
SIC 2711 Newspapers

D-U-N-S 25-215-6625   (BR)
RUSSEL METALS INC
A J FORSYTH
1950 East Wellington Rd, Nanaimo, BC, V9S
5V2
(250) 753-1555
Emp Here 22
SIC 5051 Metals service centers and offices

D-U-N-S 20-790-7424   (BR)
SCHOOL DISTRICT NO. 68 (NANAIMO-LADYSMITH)
WOODLAND SECONDARY SCHOOL
1270 Strathmore St, Nanaimo, BC, V9S 2L9
(250) 753-2271
Emp Here 75
SIC 8211 Elementary and secondary schools

D-U-N-S 25-181-4612   (BR)
SCHOOL DISTRICT NO. 68 (NANAIMO-LADYSMITH)
BRECHIN ELEMENTARY SCHOOL
510 Millstone Ave, Nanaimo, BC, V9S 5A9
(250) 754-7523
Emp Here 22
SIC 8211 Elementary and secondary schools

D-U-N-S 20-713-5869   (BR)
SCHOOL DISTRICT NO. 68 (NANAIMO-LADYSMITH)
1111 Dufferin Cres, Nanaimo, BC, V9S 2B5
(250) 740-3500
Emp Here 50
SIC 8211 Elementary and secondary schools

D-U-N-S 25-181-5270   (BR)
SCHOOL DISTRICT NO. 68 (NANAIMO-LADYSMITH)
PRINCESS ANNE SCHOOL
1951 Estevan Rd, Nanaimo, BC, V9S 3Y9
(250) 754-5442
Emp Here 20
SIC 8211 Elementary and secondary schools

D-U-N-S 20-713-5919   (BR)
SCHOOL DISTRICT NO. 68 (NANAIMO-LADYSMITH)
QUARTERWAY ELEMENTARY SCHOOL
1632 Bowen Rd, Nanaimo, BC, V9S 1G6
(250) 754-6845
Emp Here 50
SIC 8211 Elementary and secondary schools

D-U-N-S 25-181-9520   (BR)
SCHOOL DISTRICT NO. 68 (NANAIMO-LADYSMITH)
FOREST PARK ELEMENTARY SCHOOL
2050 Latimer Rd, Nanaimo, BC, V9S 2W5
(250) 758-6892
Emp Here 30
SIC 8211 Elementary and secondary schools

D-U-N-S 20-100-7267   (BR)
SHERET, ANDREW LIMITED
SPLASHES
(*Suby of* Sheret, Andrew Holdings Limited)
2545 Mccullough Rd, Nanaimo, BC, V9S 4M9
(250) 758-7383
Emp Here 30

SIC 5074 Plumbing and heating equipment
and supplies (hydronics)

D-U-N-S 25-498-9510   (BR)
STAPLES CANADA INC
STAPLES/BUSINESS DEPOT
(*Suby of* Staples, Inc.)
2000 Island Hwy N Suite 100, Nanaimo, BC,
V9S 5W3
(250) 751-7770
Emp Here 25
SIC 5943 Stationery stores

D-U-N-S 24-343-9929   (BR)
SUPERIOR PLUS LP
SUPERIOR PROPANE
2585 Mccullough Rd, Nanaimo, BC, V9S 4M9
(250) 739-2573
Emp Here 20
SIC 5984 Liquefied petroleum gas dealers

D-U-N-S 20-321-6395   (BR)
WHITE SPOT LIMITED
130 Terminal Ave N, Nanaimo, BC, V9S 4J3
(250) 754-2241
Emp Here 60
SIC 5812 Eating places

Nanaimo, BC V9T
Nanaimo County

D-U-N-S 25-070-7718   (BR)
A & W FOOD SERVICES OF CANADA INC
A & W RESTAURANTS
5800 Turner Rd Suite 701, Nanaimo, BC, V9T
6J4
(250) 756-4076
Emp Here 30
SIC 5812 Eating places

D-U-N-S 20-700-0519   (BR)
BANQUE DE DEVELOPPEMENT DU CANADA
BDC
6581 Aulds Rd Unit 500, Nanaimo, BC, V9T
6J6
(250) 754-0247
Emp Here 30
SIC 6141 Personal credit institutions

D-U-N-S 20-698-6270   (BR)
BEST BUY CANADA LTD
FUTURE SHOP
(*Suby of* Best Buy Co., Inc.)
3200 Island Hwy N Unit 87, Nanaimo, BC, V9T
1W1
(250) 729-8632
Emp Here 50
SIC 5731 Radio, television, and electronic
stores

D-U-N-S 25-231-7342   (BR)
BRICK WAREHOUSE LP, THE
BRICK, THE
6361 Hammond Bay Rd, Nanaimo, BC, V9T
5Y1
(250) 390-3999
Emp Here 25
SIC 5712 Furniture stores

D-U-N-S 25-316-5674   (BR)
BRITISH COLUMBIA AUTOMOBILE ASSOCIATION
BCAA
6581 Aulds Rd Suite 400, Nanaimo, BC, V9T
6J6
(250) 390-7700
Emp Here 26
SIC 8699 Membership organizations, nec

D-U-N-S 25-131-6972   (BR)
CACTUS RESTAURANTS LTD
CACTUS CLUB CAFE
5800 Turner Rd Unit 8, Nanaimo, BC, V9T 6J4
(250) 729-0011
Emp Here 40

SIC 5812 Eating places

D-U-N-S 25-316-0246   (BR)
CANADIAN WESTERN BANK
6475 Metral Dr Unit 101, Nanaimo, BC, V9T
2L9
(250) 390-0088
Emp Here 27
SIC 6021 National commercial banks

D-U-N-S 25-181-5262   (BR)
CANEM SYSTEMS LTD
4386 Boban Dr Suite 9b, Nanaimo, BC, V9T
6A7
(250) 751-7760
Emp Here 40
SIC 1731 Electrical work

D-U-N-S 20-644-4437   (BR)
CARA OPERATIONS LIMITED
MONTANA'S COOKHOUSE
(*Suby of* Cara Holdings Limited)
4715 Rutherford Rd, Nanaimo, BC, V9T 5S5
(250) 758-2388
Emp Here 60
SIC 5812 Eating places

D-U-N-S 24-797-8109   (BR)
COCA-COLA REFRESHMENTS CANADA COMPANY
(*Suby of* The Coca-Cola Company)
4148 Mostar Rd, Nanaimo, BC, V9T 6C9
(250) 756-2788
Emp Here 35
SIC 5149 Groceries and related products, nec

D-U-N-S 25-132-1790   (SL)
EARL'S RESTAURANT (NANAIMO) LTD
2980 Island Hwy N Unit 100, Nanaimo, BC,
V9T 5V4

Emp Here 56   *Sales* 1,678,096
SIC 5812 Eating places

D-U-N-S 24-000-5640   (BR)
EDDIE BAUER OF CANADA INC
(*Suby of* Golden Gate Capital LP)
6631 Island Hwy N Suite 80, Nanaimo, BC,
V9T 4T7
(250) 390-9388
Emp Here 20
SIC 5699 Miscellaneous apparel and accessory stores

D-U-N-S 24-337-3516   (BR)
FGL SPORTS LTD
SPORT-CHEK WOODGROVE CENTRE
6631 Island Hwy N Unit 126, Nanaimo, BC,
V9T 4T7
(250) 390-1581
Emp Here 40
SIC 5941 Sporting goods and bicycle shops

D-U-N-S 24-391-7023   (BR)
FRESHPOINT VANCOUVER, LTD
FRESHPOINT NANAIMO
(*Suby of* Sysco Corporation)
4911 Wellington Rd, Nanaimo, BC, V9T 2H5
(250) 758-0191
Emp Here 40
SIC 5148 Fresh fruits and vegetables

D-U-N-S 24-726-1050   (BR)
FRESHPOINT VANCOUVER, LTD
PACIFIC PRODUCE
(*Suby of* Sysco Corporation)
4911 Wellington Rd, Nanaimo, BC, V9T 2H5
(250) 758-0191
Emp Here 50
SIC 5141 Groceries, general line

D-U-N-S 25-959-4364   (BR)
G4S CASH SOLUTIONS (CANADA) LTD
SECURICOR CASH SERVICES
4300 Wellington Rd Suite 301, Nanaimo, BC,
V9T 2H3
(250) 751-8563
Emp Here 50
SIC 7381 Detective and armored car services

D-U-N-S 20-798-4050   (BR)
GALAXY ENTERTAINMENT INC
GALAXY NANAIMO
4750 Rutherford Rd Suite 213, Nanaimo, BC,
V9T 4K6
(250) 729-8012
Emp Here 30
SIC 7832 Motion picture theaters, except
drive-in

D-U-N-S 25-362-3623   (BR)
GAP (CANADA) INC
GAP
(*Suby of* The Gap Inc)
6631 Island Hwy N Suite 110, Nanaimo, BC,
V9T 4T7
(250) 390-6886
Emp Here 30
SIC 5651 Family clothing stores

D-U-N-S 25-267-8651   (BR)
GREAT PACIFIC INDUSTRIES INC
OVERWAITEA FOOD GROUP
3200 Island Hwy N, Nanaimo, BC, V9T 1W1
(250) 751-1414
Emp Here 160
SIC 5411 Grocery stores

D-U-N-S 20-169-6163   (BR)
GREAT PACIFIC INDUSTRIES INC
SAVE ON FOODS
4750 Rutherford Rd Suite 175, Nanaimo, BC,
V9T 4K6
(250) 758-5741
Emp Here 50
SIC 5411 Grocery stores

D-U-N-S 25-822-9715   (BR)
HSBC BANK CANADA
6551 Aulds Rd Suite 101, Nanaimo, BC, V9T
6K2
(250) 390-0668
Emp Here 27
SIC 6021 National commercial banks

D-U-N-S 24-168-4534   (SL)
HAMMOND BAY HOLDINGS LTD
3164 Barons Rd, Nanaimo, BC, V9T 4B5
(250) 751-1777
Emp Here 40   *Sales* 5,496,960
SIC 2411 Logging

D-U-N-S 25-514-2770   (BR)
HOME DEPOT OF CANADA INC
HOME DEPOT
(*Suby of* The Home Depot Inc)
6555 Metral Dr, Nanaimo, BC, V9T 2L9
(250) 390-7663
Emp Here 230
SIC 5251 Hardware stores

D-U-N-S 25-094-6563   (BR)
HUDSON'S BAY COMPANY
6631 Island Hwy N Suite 1a, Nanaimo, BC,
V9T 4T7
(250) 390-3141
Emp Here 130
SIC 5311 Department stores

D-U-N-S 25-315-7911   (BR)
INVESTORS GROUP FINANCIAL SERVICES INC
5070 Uplands Dr Suite 101, Nanaimo, BC,
V9T 6N1
(250) 729-0904
Emp Here 35
SIC 8741 Management services

D-U-N-S 24-397-1251   (HQ)
ISLAND RADIO LTD
(*Suby of* Jim Pattison Broadcast Group Limited Partnership)
4550 Wellington Rd, Nanaimo, BC, V9T 2H3
(250) 758-1131
Emp Here 20   *Emp Total* 340
Sales 2,553,625
SIC 4832 Radio broadcasting stations

D-U-N-S 24-088-5173   (BR)

JYSK LINEN'N FURNITURE INC
JYSK LINEN'N FURNITURE INC
3200 Island Hwy N Suite 85, Nanaimo, BC,
V9T 1W1
(250) 758-2590
Emp Here 30
SIC 5712 Furniture stores

D-U-N-S 20-798-4613   (BR)
MARK'S WORK WEARHOUSE LTD
WORK WORLD
6334 Metral Dr, Nanaimo, BC, V9T 2L8
(250) 390-1793
Emp Here 25
SIC 5699 Miscellaneous apparel and accessory stores

D-U-N-S 24-802-1268   (SL)
MIDISLAND HOLDINGS LTD
FAIRWAY MARKET GROCERY
4750 Rutherford Rd Suite 103, Nanaimo, BC,
V9T 4K6
(250) 729-2611
Emp Here 45   *Sales* 7,362,000
SIC 5411 Grocery stores
Mgr Randy Richter

D-U-N-S 25-320-8987   (BR)
PUROLATOR INC.
PUROLATOR INC
3607 Shenton Rd, Nanaimo, BC, V9T 2H1
(250) 751-8810
Emp Here 40
SIC 4731 Freight transportation arrangement

D-U-N-S 25-165-7326   (BR)
ROYAL BANK OF CANADA
RBC
(*Suby of* Royal Bank Of Canada)
6631 Island Hwy N Suite 246, Nanaimo, BC,
V9T 4T7
(250) 390-4311
Emp Here 44
SIC 6021 National commercial banks

D-U-N-S 25-181-2871   (BR)
SCHOOL DISTRICT NO. 68 (NANAIMO-LADYSMITH)
WELLINGTON SECONDARY SCHOOL
3135 Mexicana Rd, Nanaimo, BC, V9T 2W8
(250) 758-9191
Emp Here 85
SIC 8211 Elementary and secondary schools

D-U-N-S 20-713-5851   (BR)
SCHOOL DISTRICT NO. 68 (NANAIMO-LADYSMITH)
DEPARTURE BAY ELEMENTARY SCHOOL
3004 Departure Bay Rd, Nanaimo, BC, V9T
1B4
(250) 758-6541
Emp Here 50
SIC 8211 Elementary and secondary schools

D-U-N-S 20-713-5968   (BR)
SCHOOL DISTRICT NO. 68 (NANAIMO-LADYSMITH)
TOAL TYEE ELEMENTARY SCHOOL
2280 Sun Valley Dr, Nanaimo, BC, V9T 6P1
(250) 729-0450
Emp Here 50
SIC 8211 Elementary and secondary schools

D-U-N-S 20-713-5877   (BR)
SCHOOL DISTRICT NO. 68 (NANAIMO-LADYSMITH)
MOUNT BENSON ELEMENTARY SCHOOL
4355 Jingle Pot Rd, Nanaimo, BC, V9T 5P4

Emp Here 50
SIC 8211 Elementary and secondary schools

D-U-N-S 20-713-5927   (BR)
SCHOOL DISTRICT NO. 68 (NANAIMO-LADYSMITH)
ROCK CITY ELEMENTARY SCHOOL
3741 Departure Bay Rd, Nanaimo, BC, V9T
1C5

(250) 758-2434
Emp Here 35
SIC 8211 Elementary and secondary schools

D-U-N-S 25-183-2986   (BR)
SCHOOL DISTRICT NO. 68 (NANAIMO-LADYSMITH)
UPLANDS PARK SCHOOL
3821 Stronach Dr, Nanaimo, BC, V9T 3X4
(250) 758-3252
Emp Here 40
SIC 8211 Elementary and secondary schools

D-U-N-S 25-181-9231   (BR)
SCHOOL DISTRICT NO. 68 (NANAIMO-LADYSMITH)
HAMMOND BAY ELEMENTARY SCHOOL
1025 Morningside Dr, Nanaimo, BC, V9T 1N5
(250) 758-5711
Emp Here 30
SIC 8211 Elementary and secondary schools

D-U-N-S 25-186-1811   (BR)
SCHOOL DISTRICT NO. 68 (NANAIMO-LADYSMITH)
RANDERSON RIDGE SCHOOL
6021 Nelson Rd, Nanaimo, BC, V9T 5N7
(250) 758-5076
Emp Here 25
SIC 8211 Elementary and secondary schools

D-U-N-S 20-030-0510   (BR)
SCHOOL DISTRICT NO. 68 (NANAIMO-LADYSMITH)
RUTHERFORD ELEMENTARY SCHOOL
5840 Hammond Bay Rd, Nanaimo, BC, V9T
5N3
(250) 758-5331
Emp Here 40
SIC 8211 Elementary and secondary schools

D-U-N-S 20-100-7309   (BR)
SEARS CANADA INC
4750 Rutherford Rd, Nanaimo, BC, V9T 4K6
(250) 756-4111
Emp Here 175
SIC 5311 Department stores

D-U-N-S 25-848-7883   (BR)
SECURIGUARD SERVICES LIMITED
WEST GUARD SECURITY
2520 Bowen Rd Suite 205, Nanaimo, BC, V9T
3L3
(250) 756-4452
Emp Here 180
SIC 7381 Detective and armored car services

D-U-N-S 25-893-0080   (BR)
SLEGG LIMITED PARTNERSHIP
SLEGG CONSTRUCTION
4950 Jordan Ave, Nanaimo, BC, V9T 2H8
(250) 758-8329
Emp Here 100
SIC 5031 Lumber, plywood, and millwork

D-U-N-S 20-860-3816   (BR)
SOURCE (BELL) ELECTRONICS INC, THE
SOURCE, THE
6631 Island Hwy N Unit 374, Nanaimo, BC,
V9T 4T7
(250) 390-1693
Emp Here 25
SIC 5999 Miscellaneous retail stores, nec

D-U-N-S 25-498-9254   (BR)
STAPLES CANADA INC
STAPLES
(*Suby of* Staples, Inc.)
6581 Aulds Rd Suite 100, Nanaimo, BC, V9T
6J6
(250) 390-5900
Emp Here 35
SIC 5943 Stationery stores

D-U-N-S 20-944-5613   (BR)
STARBUCKS COFFEE CANADA, INC
STARBUCKS
(*Suby of* Starbucks Corporation)
3200 Island Hwy N Suite 120c, Nanaimo, BC,

V9T 1W1
(250) 758-5955
Emp Here 21
SIC 5812 Eating places

D-U-N-S 20-336-6658   (BR)
STARBUCKS COFFEE CANADA, INC
(*Suby of* Starbucks Corporation)
6334 Metral Dr, Nanaimo, BC, V9T 2L8
(250) 390-9861
Emp Here 20
SIC 5812 Eating places

D-U-N-S 20-194-8986   (BR)
TETRA TECH CANADA INC
(*Suby of* Tetra Tech, Inc.)
4376 Boban Dr Suite 1, Nanaimo, BC, V9T
6A7
(250) 756-2256
Emp Here 25
SIC 8711 Engineering services

D-U-N-S 25-297-7889   (BR)
TOYS 'R' US (CANADA) LTD
TOYS 'R' US
(*Suby of* Toys "r" Us, Inc.)
6631 Island Hwy N, Nanaimo, BC, V9T 4T7
(250) 390-1993
Emp Here 33
SIC 5945 Hobby, toy, and game shops

D-U-N-S 20-065-5426   (BR)
UNITED RENTALS OF CANADA, INC
2530 Kenworth Rd, Nanaimo, BC, V9T 3Y4
(250) 758-3911
Emp Here 20
SIC 7353 Heavy construction equipment rental

D-U-N-S 20-647-0390   (BR)
VANCOUVER ISLAND HEALTH AUTHORITY
NANAIMO REGIONAL GENERAL HOSPITAL
6475 Metral Dr Suite 300, Nanaimo, BC, V9T
2L9
(250) 755-7691
Emp Here 56
SIC 8011 Offices and clinics of medical doctors

D-U-N-S 24-308-9898   (BR)
WFG SECURITIES OF CANADA INC
3260 Norwell Dr Suite 200, Nanaimo, BC, V9T
1X5
(250) 751-7595
Emp Here 30
SIC 6411 Insurance agents, brokers, and service

D-U-N-S 25-294-7460   (BR)
WAL-MART CANADA CORP
6801 Island Hwy N Suite 3059, Nanaimo, BC,
V9T 6N8
(250) 758-0343
Emp Here 250
SIC 5311 Department stores

D-U-N-S 25-988-7826   (BR)
WINNERS MERCHANTS INTERNATIONAL L.P.
WINNERS
(*Suby of* The TJX Companies Inc)
6631 Island Hwy N Suite 147, Nanaimo, BC,
V9T 4T7
(250) 751-0308
Emp Here 36
SIC 5651 Family clothing stores

D-U-N-S 20-920-0562   (BR)
WORKERS' COMPENSATION BOARD OF BRITISH COLUMBIA
WORKSAFE BC
4980 Wills Rd, Nanaimo, BC, V9T 6C6
(604) 273-2266
Emp Here 100
SIC 6331 Fire, marine, and casualty insurance

Nanaimo, BC V9V
Nanaimo County

D-U-N-S 24-762-0016   (SL)
A.M.L. HOLDINGS LTD
WOODGROVE CHRYSLER DODGE
6800 Island Hwy N, Nanaimo, BC, V9V 1A3
(250) 390-3031
Emp Here 29   *Sales* 14,569,600
SIC 5511 New and used car dealers
Pr Pr Gordon Heys
Off Mgr Helen Thingelstad

D-U-N-S 25-288-9555   (BR)
COSTCO WHOLESALE CANADA LTD
(*Suby of* Costco Wholesale Corporation)
6700 Island Hwy N Suite 155, Nanaimo, BC,
V9V 1K8
(250) 390-3231
Emp Here 20
SIC 5099 Durable goods, nec

D-U-N-S 24-202-6602   (BR)
HUDSON'S BAY COMPANY
HBC HOME OUTFITTERS
6950 Island Hwy N Unit 200, Nanaimo, BC,
V9V 1W3
(250) 390-1479
Emp Here 20
SIC 5963 Direct selling establishments

D-U-N-S 20-004-0744   (BR)
INDIGO BOOKS & MUSIC INC
CHAPTERS
(*Suby of* Indigo Books & Music Inc)
6670 Mary Ellen Dr, Nanaimo, BC, V9V 1T7
(250) 390-0380
Emp Here 35
SIC 5942 Book stores

D-U-N-S 20-570-8121   (BR)
LORDCO PARTS LTD
LORDCO AUTO PARTS
6580a Island Hwy N Suite A, Nanaimo, BC,
V9V 1K8
(250) 390-9232
Emp Here 20
SIC 5531 Auto and home supply stores

D-U-N-S 20-197-3356   (BR)
MICHAELS OF CANADA, ULC
MICHAELS ARTS & CRAFTS
(*Suby of* The Michaels Companies Inc)
6677 Mary Ellen Dr, Nanaimo, BC, V9V 1T7
(250) 390-5309
Emp Here 30
SIC 5945 Hobby, toy, and game shops

D-U-N-S 20-584-7127   (BR)
NANAIMO SENIORS VILLAGE VENTURES LTD
6085 Uplands Dr, Nanaimo, BC, V9V 1T8
(250) 760-2325
Emp Here 200
SIC 6513 Apartment building operators

D-U-N-S 20-713-5950   (BR)
SCHOOL DISTRICT NO. 68 (NANAIMO-LADYSMITH)
DOVER BAY SECONDARY SCHOOL
6135 Mcgirr Rd, Nanaimo, BC, V9V 1M1
(250) 756-4595
Emp Here 125
SIC 8211 Elementary and secondary schools

D-U-N-S 20-590-8333   (BR)
SCHOOL DISTRICT NO. 68 (NANAIMO-LADYSMITH)
FRANK J NEY ELEMENTARY SCHOOL
5301 Williamson Rd, Nanaimo, BC, V9V 1L1
(250) 729-8045
Emp Here 25
SIC 8211 Elementary and secondary schools

D-U-N-S 20-713-5935   (BR)
SCHOOL DISTRICT NO. 68 (NANAIMO-LADYSMITH)

MCGIRR ELEMENTARY SCHOOL
6199 Mcgirr Rd, Nanaimo, BC, V9V 1C7
(250) 758-8946
Emp Here 50
SIC 8211 Elementary and secondary schools

Nanaimo, BC V9X
Nanaimo County

D-U-N-S 25-070-9748   (BR)
49TH PARALLEL GROCERY LIMITED
1824 Cedar Rd, Nanaimo, BC, V9X 1H9
(250) 722-7010
Emp Here 50
SIC 5411 Grocery stores

D-U-N-S 25-093-2733   (BR)
CASCADES CANADA ULC
CASCADES RECOVERY+
800 Maughan Rd, Nanaimo, BC, V9X 1J2
(250) 722-3396
Emp Here 150
SIC 4953 Refuse systems

D-U-N-S 25-671-5905   (BR)
CHEMTRADE ELECTROCHEM INC
CANEXUS CORPORATION
1200 Macphee Rd, Nanaimo, BC, V9X 1J2
(250) 722-2212
Emp Here 22
SIC 2899 Chemical preparations, nec

D-U-N-S 24-888-1260   (SL)
COPCAN CONTRACTING LTD
1920 Balsam Rd, Nanaimo, BC, V9X 1T5
(250) 754-7260
Emp Here 45   Sales 3,898,130
SIC 1794 Excavation work

D-U-N-S 20-700-6771   (BR)
FINNING INTERNATIONAL INC
(Suby of Finning International Inc)
1922 Schoolhouse Rd, Nanaimo, BC, V9X
1T4
(250) 753-2441
Emp Here 20
SIC 5082 Construction and mining machinery

D-U-N-S 20-194-8929   (BR)
LAFARGE CANADA INC
HUB CITY PAVING
61 Nanaimo River Rd, Nanaimo, BC, V9X 1S5
(250) 754-2195
Emp Here 50
SIC 1611 Highway and street construction

D-U-N-S 24-957-6307   (HQ)
MAYCO MIX LTD
1125 Cedar Rd, Nanaimo, BC, V9X 1K9
(250) 722-0064
Emp Here 26   Emp Total 54,132
Sales 9,411,930
SIC 5032 Brick, stone, and related material
Doug Blender

D-U-N-S 20-595-1317   (SL)
PR AQUA SUPPLIES LTD
PR AQUA
(Suby of In-Situ, Inc.)
1631 Harold Rd, Nanaimo, BC, V9X 1T4
(250) 754-4844
Emp Here 30   Sales 4,596,524
SIC 3069 Fabricated rubber products, nec

D-U-N-S 25-070-3840   (BR)
REGIONAL DISTRICT OF NANAIMO
REGIONAL LANDFILL
1105 Cedar Rd, Nanaimo, BC, V9X 1K9
(250) 722-2044
Emp Here 35
SIC 1629 Heavy construction, nec

D-U-N-S 20-002-7204   (BR)
SCHOOL DISTRICT NO. 68 (NANAIMO-LADYSMITH)

NORTH SEEDER INTERMEDIETE SCHOOL
2215 Gould Rd W, Nanaimo, BC, V9X 1J9
(250) 722-2722
Emp Here 35
SIC 8211 Elementary and secondary schools

D-U-N-S 20-713-5943   (BR)
SCHOOL DISTRICT NO. 68 (NANAIMO-LADYSMITH)
SOUTH WELLINGTON SCHOOL
1536 Morden Rd, Nanaimo, BC, V9X 1S2

Emp Here 20
SIC 8211 Elementary and secondary schools

D-U-N-S 24-227-7759   (BR)
SCHOOL DISTRICT NO. 68 (NANAIMO-LADYSMITH)
CINNABAR VALLEY ELEMENTARY
SCHOOL
1800 Richardson Rd, Nanaimo, BC, V9X 1C9
(250) 716-1030
Emp Here 30
SIC 8211 Elementary and secondary schools

D-U-N-S 20-004-8002   (BR)
SCHOOL DISTRICT NO. 68 (NANAIMO-LADYSMITH)
CEDAR COMMUNITY SECONDARY
SCHOOL
1640 Macmillan Rd, Nanaimo, BC, V9X 1L9
(250) 722-2414
Emp Here 60
SIC 8211 Elementary and secondary schools

Nanoose Bay, BC V9P
Nanaimo County

D-U-N-S 20-543-7325   (HQ)
AVIAWEST RESORTS INC
(Suby of Aviawest Resorts Inc)
1600 Stroulger Rd Unit 1, Nanoose Bay, BC,
V9P 9B7
(250) 468-7121
Emp Here 286   Emp Total 300
Sales 17,668,800
SIC 7011 Hotels and motels
Dir Lawrence J. Pearson
Pr Pr Andrew Pearson
 Susan Lee Pearson
Dir James L. Pearson

D-U-N-S 25-124-2160   (BR)
KELLAND FOODS LTD
QUALITY FOODS (NANOOSE)
2443 Collins Cres Unit 1, Nanoose Bay, BC,
V9P 9A1
(250) 468-7131
Emp Here 23
SIC 5411 Grocery stores

D-U-N-S 24-898-4171   (SL)
PACIFIC SHORES RESORT & SPA LTD
1600 Stroulger Rd Unit 1, Nanoose Bay, BC,
V9P 9B7
(250) 468-7121
Emp Here 100   Sales 5,889,600
SIC 7011 Hotels and motels
Pr Pr Andy Pearson
Treas Lawrence Pearson

D-U-N-S 20-086-4507   (BR)
SCHOOL DISTRICT NO 69 (QUALICUM)
NANOOSE BAY ELEMENTRY SCHOOL
2875 Northwest Bay Rd, Nanoose Bay, BC,
V9P 9E6
(250) 468-7414
Emp Here 33
SIC 8211 Elementary and secondary schools

D-U-N-S 20-070-1998   (BR)
SUNCOR ENERGY INC
NANOOSE PETRO-CANADA
2345 Island Hwy E, Nanoose Bay, BC, V9P
9E2

---

(250) 468-7441
Emp Here 25
SIC 5541 Gasoline service stations

Naramata, BC V0H
Okanagn-Similkameen County

D-U-N-S 25-485-6735   (BR)
SCHOOL DISTRICT NO 67 (OKANAGAN SKAHA)
NARAMATA SCHOOL
3660 8th St, Naramata, BC, V0H 1N0
(250) 770-7688
Emp Here 25
SIC 8211 Elementary and secondary schools

Nelson, BC V1L
Central Kootenay County

D-U-N-S 20-572-2684   (BR)
BANK OF NOVA SCOTIA, THE
SCOTIABANK
502 Baker St Suite 5, Nelson, BC, V1L 4H9
(250) 354-5590
Emp Here 20
SIC 6021 National commercial banks

D-U-N-S 25-523-5038   (BR)
BANK OF MONTREAL
BMO
298 Baker St, Nelson, BC, V1L 4H3
(250) 352-5321
Emp Here 22
SIC 6021 National commercial banks

D-U-N-S 25-288-8680   (BR)
CANADA POST CORPORATION
514 Vernon St, Nelson, BC, V1L 4E7
(250) 352-3538
Emp Here 34
SIC 4311 U.s. postal service

D-U-N-S 25-370-6576   (SL)
GEEKS ON THE WAY INC
1099 South Poplar St, Nelson, BC, V1L 2J3
(800) 875-5017
Emp Here 50   Sales 3,648,035
SIC 7378 Computer maintenance and repair

D-U-N-S 25-267-8743   (BR)
GREAT PACIFIC INDUSTRIES INC
SAVE-ON-FOODS
1200 Lakeside Dr, Nelson, BC, V1L 5Z3
(250) 352-7617
Emp Here 125
SIC 5411 Grocery stores

D-U-N-S 25-620-4553   (BR)
HUBER DEVELOPMENT LTD
PRESTIGE LAKESIDE RESORT & CONVEN-
TION CENTRE
701 Lakeside Dr, Nelson, BC, V1L 6G3
(250) 352-7222
Emp Here 100
SIC 7011 Hotels and motels

D-U-N-S 20-867-6465   (BR)
INTERIOR HEALTH AUTHORITY
COMMUNITY CARE SERVICES
905 Gordon St, Nelson, BC, V1L 3L8
(250) 352-1401
Emp Here 93
SIC 8062 General medical and surgical hospi-
tals

D-U-N-S 24-362-5352   (BR)
INTERIOR HEALTH AUTHORITY
KOOTENAY LAKE HOSPITAL
3 View St Suite 426, Nelson, BC, V1L 2V1
(250) 352-3111
Emp Here 100
SIC 8062 General medical and surgical hospi-
tals

D-U-N-S 24-009-0964   (BR)
INTERIOR HEALTH AUTHORITY
NELSON MENTAL HEALTH & SUBSTAN-
CIES
333 Victoria St 2nd Floor, Nelson, BC, V1L
4K3
(250) 505-7248
Emp Here 35
SIC 8062 General medical and surgical hospi-
tals

D-U-N-S 25-902-8074   (SL)
KOOTENAY SCHOOL OF THE ARTS AT SELKIRK COLLEGE
KOOTENAY SCHOOL OF THE ARTS
606 Victoria St, Nelson, BC, V1L 4K9
(250) 352-2821
Emp Here 50   Sales 2,699,546
SIC 8299 Schools and educational services,
nec

D-U-N-S 20-555-9706   (BR)
LOBLAWS INC
REAL CANADIAN WHOLESALE CLUB
402 Lakeside Dr, Nelson, BC, V1L 6B9
(250) 352-2930
Emp Here 40
SIC 5141 Groceries, general line

D-U-N-S 24-773-2121   (SL)
MADBURN ENTERPRISES LTD
610 Railway St Suite A, Nelson, BC, V1L 1H4

Emp Here 49   Sales 9,646,080
SIC 3827 Optical instruments and lenses
Pr David Duncan

D-U-N-S 20-100-8687   (SL)
MAGLIO BUILDING CENTRE LTD
(Suby of Louis Maglio Holdings Ltd)
29 Government Rd, Nelson, BC, V1L 4L9
(250) 352-6661
Emp Here 40   Sales 5,836,856
SIC 5211 Lumber and other building materials
Dir Antonio Maglio
Pr Pr Dominic Maglio

D-U-N-S 24-247-1274   (SL)
MARBOR HOLDINGS LTD
HERITAGE INN
422 Vernon St, Nelson, BC, V1L 4E5
(250) 352-5331
Emp Here 80   Sales 4,869,600
SIC 7011 Hotels and motels

D-U-N-S 25-623-3594   (BR)
ROYAL BANK OF CANADA
RBC
(Suby of Royal Bank Of Canada)
401 Baker St, Nelson, BC, V1L 4H7
(250) 354-4111
Emp Here 25
SIC 6021 National commercial banks

D-U-N-S 25-676-4572   (HQ)
SCHOOL DISTRICT NO. 8 (KOOTENAY LAKE)
(Suby of School District No. 8 (Kootenay
Lake))
570 Johnstone Rd, Nelson, BC, V1L 6J2
(250) 352-6681
Emp Here 30   Emp Total 500
Sales 43,158,668
SIC 8211 Elementary and secondary schools

D-U-N-S 25-676-7666   (BR)
SCHOOL DISTRICT NO. 8 (KOOTENAY LAKE)
HUME ELEMENTARY SCHOOL
(Suby of School District No. 8 (Kootenay
Lake))
310 Nelson Ave, Nelson, BC, V1L 2M8
(250) 352-3186
Emp Here 23
SIC 8211 Elementary and secondary schools

D-U-N-S 25-676-7724   (BR)
SCHOOL DISTRICT NO. 8 (KOOTENAY

LAKE)
MAINTENANCE DEPT (NELSON)
(*Suby of* School District No. 8 (Kootenay
Lake))
90 Lakeside Dr, Nelson, BC, V1L 6B9
(250) 354-4871
Emp Here 20
SIC 7349 Building maintenance services, nec

D-U-N-S 25-676-7872   (BR)
**SCHOOL DISTRICT NO. 8 (KOOTENAY
LAKE)**
TRAFALGAR MIDDLE SCHOOL
(*Suby of* School District No. 8 (Kootenay
Lake))
1201 Josephine St, Nelson, BC, V1L 1X8
(250) 352-5591
Emp Here 60
SIC 8211 Elementary and secondary schools

D-U-N-S 25-676-7708   (BR)
**SCHOOL DISTRICT NO. 8 (KOOTENAY
LAKE)**
L.V. ROGERS SECONDARY SCHOOL
(*Suby of* School District No. 8 (Kootenay
Lake))
1004 Cottonwood St, Nelson, BC, V1L 3W2
(250) 352-5538
Emp Here 60
SIC 8211 Elementary and secondary schools

D-U-N-S 25-294-7387   (BR)
WAL-MART CANADA CORP
1000 Lakeside Dr, Nelson, BC, V1L 5Z4
(250) 352-3782
Emp Here 166
SIC 5311 Department stores

D-U-N-S 20-727-9287   (SL)
**WEST KOOTENAY SOCIAL ENTERPRISE
SOCIETY**
542 Baker St Suite 204, Nelson, BC, V1L 4H9
(250) 352-1942
Emp Here 50   *Sales* 1,459,214
SIC 7349 Building maintenance services, nec

D-U-N-S 25-893-5170   (BR)
**WORKERS' COMPENSATION BOARD OF
BRITISH COLUMBIA**
WORKSAFE BRITISH COLUMBIA
524 Kootenay St, Nelson, BC, V1L 6B4
(250) 354-5700
Emp Here 30
SIC 6331 Fire, marine, and casualty insurance

New Denver, BC V0G
Central Kootenay County

D-U-N-S 20-033-7892   (BR)
ARROW LAKES SCHOOL DISTRICT #10
*LUCERNE ELEMENTARY SECONDARY
SCHOOL*
(*Suby of* Arrow Lakes School District #10)
604 7th Ave, New Denver, BC, V0G 1S0
(250) 358-7222
Emp Here 25
SIC 8211 Elementary and secondary schools

D-U-N-S 25-591-2099   (BR)
INTERIOR HEALTH AUTHORITY
SLOCAN COMMUNITY HEALTH CENTRE
401 Galena Ave, New Denver, BC, V0G 1S0
(250) 358-7911
Emp Here 71
SIC 8062 General medical and surgical hospitals

New Hazelton, BC V0J
Kitimat - Stikine County

D-U-N-S 20-736-5763   (BR)
HUDSON'S BAY COMPANY

FIELDS STORES
4633 10th Ave, New Hazelton, BC, V0J 2J0

Emp Here 25
SIC 5311 Department stores

New Westminster, BC V3L
Greater Vancouver County

D-U-N-S 20-792-4841   (BR)
ABREY ENTERPRISES INC
MCDONALD'S RESTAURANT
515 Sixth St, New Westminster, BC, V3L 3B9
(604) 718-1172
Emp Here 30
SIC 5812 Eating places

D-U-N-S 20-101-1699   (BR)
ARMY & NAVY DEPT. STORE LIMITED
502 Columbia St, New Westminster, BC, V3L
1B1
(604) 526-4661
Emp Here 100
SIC 5311 Department stores

D-U-N-S 24-594-3931   (HQ)
AVOCETTE TECHNOLOGIES INC
(*Suby of* Avocette Technologies Inc)
610 Sixth St Suite 202, New Westminster, BC,
V3L 3C2
(604) 395-6000
Emp Here 60   *Emp Total* 100
Sales 11,673,712
SIC 7371 Custom computer programming services
Pr Pr Scott Ross
  Mitchell Mgai

D-U-N-S 24-136-9875   (BR)
BANK OF MONTREAL
BMO
610 Sixth Ave Suite 125, New Westminster,
BC, V3L 3C2
(604) 665-3770
Emp Here 100
SIC 6021 National commercial banks

D-U-N-S 20-732-8332   (BR)
BANQUE TORONTO-DOMINION, LA
TORONTO-DOMINION BANK, THE
(*Suby of* Toronto-Dominion Bank, The)
610 Sixth St Suite 237, New Westminster, BC,
V3L 3C2
(604) 654-5394
Emp Here 25
SIC 6021 National commercial banks

D-U-N-S 20-591-5676   (BR)
**BOARD OF SCHOOL TRUSTEES OF
SCHOOL DISTRICT #40 (NEW WEST-
MINSTER), THE**
F W HOWEY ELEMENTARY SCHOOL
91 Courtney Cres, New Westminster, BC, V3L
4M1
(604) 517-6020
Emp Here 25
SIC 8211 Elementary and secondary schools

D-U-N-S 20-031-5740   (BR)
**BOARD OF SCHOOL TRUSTEES OF
SCHOOL DISTRICT #40 (NEW WEST-
MINSTER), THE**
*HERBERT SPENCER ELEMENTARY
SCHOOL*
605 Second St, New Westminster, BC, V3L
5R9
(604) 517-6030
Emp Here 50
SIC 8211 Elementary and secondary schools

D-U-N-S 20-034-7040   (BR)
**BOARD OF SCHOOL TRUSTEES OF
SCHOOL DISTRICT #40 (NEW WEST-
MINSTER), THE**
RICHARD MCBRIDE ELEMENTARY

SCHOOL
331 Richmond St, New Westminster, BC, V3L
4B7
(604) 517-6090
Emp Here 45
SIC 8211 Elementary and secondary schools

D-U-N-S 20-294-0495   (BR)
**BOARD OF SCHOOL TRUSTEES OF
SCHOOL DISTRICT #40 (NEW WEST-
MINSTER), THE**
ECOLE GLENBROOK MIDDLE SCHOOL
701 Park Cres, New Westminster, BC, V3L
5V4
(604) 517-5940
Emp Here 50
SIC 8211 Elementary and secondary schools

D-U-N-S 24-346-7425   (BR)
BREWERS' DISTRIBUTOR LTD
ENTERPRISE PACIFIC BREWER
(*Suby of* Brewers' Distributor Ltd)
109 Braid St Suite 101, New Westminster, BC,
V3L 5H4
(604) 664-2300
Emp Here 300
SIC 2082 Malt beverages

D-U-N-S 20-572-4201   (BR)
**BRITISH COLUMBIA HYDRO AND POWER
AUTHORITY**
BC HYDRO
Gd Stn Main, New Westminster, BC, V3L 4X8
(604) 528-1600
Emp Here 20
SIC 4911 Electric services

D-U-N-S 24-248-9685   (BR)
CANADA POST CORPORATION
24 Ovens Ave, New Westminster, BC, V3L
1Z2
(604) 522-8050
Emp Here 100
SIC 4311 U.s. postal service

D-U-N-S 24-778-1925   (BR)
CANADIAN FOREST PRODUCTS LTD
PANEL & FIBER, DIV OF
430 Canfor Ave, New Westminster, BC, V3L
5G2
(604) 521-9650
Emp Here 140
SIC 2421 Sawmills and planing mills, general

D-U-N-S 20-052-3616   (HQ)
COAST MOUNTAIN BUS COMPANY LTD
CMBC
287 Nelson'S Crt Suite 700, New Westminster, BC, V3L 0E7
(778) 375-6400
Emp Here 300   *Emp Total* 5,500
Sales 187,436,038
SIC 4111 Local and suburban transit
  Doug Kelsey
Pr Haydn Acheson
Sec Kristin Dacre
Dir Fin Donald Mclellan

D-U-N-S 25-140-5973   (BR)
**CORPORATION OF THE CITY OF NEW
WESTMINSTER**
ELECTRICAL AND DESIGN OFFICE
905 First St, New Westminster, BC, V3L 2J1
(604) 527-4528
Emp Here 30
SIC 4931 Electric and other services combined

D-U-N-S 24-174-1193   (BR)
**CORPORATION OF THE CITY OF NEW
WESTMINSTER**
GLENBROOK FIRE HALL
1 Sixth Ave E, New Westminster, BC, V3L 4G6
(604) 519-1000
Emp Here 100
SIC 7389 Business services, nec

D-U-N-S 25-069-0096   (BR)

D-U-N-S 25-069-0096   (BR)
**CORPORATION OF THE CITY OF NEW
WESTMINSTER**
CANADA GAMES POOL
65 Sixth Ave E, New Westminster, BC, V3L
4G6
(604) 526-4281
Emp Here 90
SIC 7999 Amusement and recreation, nec

D-U-N-S 24-881-7116   (BR)
**GOVERNING COUNCIL OF THE SALVA-
TION ARMY IN CANADA, THE**
*GOVERNING COUNCIL OF THE SALVATION
ARMY IN CANADA, THE*
409 Blair Ave, New Westminster, BC, V3L 4A4
(604) 522-7033
Emp Here 130
SIC 8361 Residential care

D-U-N-S 20-055-5154   (BR)
H & R BLOCK CANADA, INC
(*Suby of* H&R Block, Inc.)
622 Sixth St Suite 36, New Westminster, BC,
V3L 3C3
(604) 931-3481
Emp Here 20
SIC 7291 Tax return preparation services

D-U-N-S 25-026-2870   (BR)
HSBC BANK CANADA
HSBC
504 Sixth St, New Westminster, BC, V3L 3B4
(604) 524-9751
Emp Here 22
SIC 6021 National commercial banks

D-U-N-S 25-818-2906   (BR)
HON'S WUN-TUN HOUSE LTD
(*Suby of* Hon's Wun-Tun House Ltd)
408 Sixth St, New Westminster, BC, V3L 3B2
(604) 520-6661
Emp Here 28
SIC 5812 Eating places

D-U-N-S 24-493-4055   (SL)
**KIWANIS CARE SOCIETY (1979) OF NEW
WESTMINSTER**
KIWANIS CARE CENTRE
35 Clute St, New Westminster, BC, V3L 1Z5
(604) 525-6471
Emp Here 75   *Sales* 3,429,153
SIC 8051 Skilled nursing care facilities

D-U-N-S 25-366-7760   (BR)
**LAND TITLE & SURVEY AUTHORITY OF
BRITISH COLUMBIA**
88 Sixth St, New Westminster, BC, V3L 5B3
(604) 660-2595
Emp Here 35
SIC 6541 Title abstract offices

D-U-N-S 24-566-6870   (SL)
PRISAL HOLDINGS LTD
228 Sixth St, New Westminster, BC, V3L 3A4
(604) 525-2611
Emp Here 50   *Sales* 1,532,175
SIC 5812 Eating places

D-U-N-S 24-456-5495   (SL)
ROYAL TOWERS HOTEL INC
PLANCY'S BAR & GRILL
140 Sixth St, New Westminster, BC, V3L 2Z9
(604) 524-4689
Emp Here 93   *Sales* 4,085,799
SIC 7011 Hotels and motels

D-U-N-S 25-271-7343   (BR)
SOBEYS WEST INC
800 Mcbride Blvd, New Westminster, BC, V3L
2B8

Emp Here 50
SIC 5411 Grocery stores

D-U-N-S 25-271-7384   (BR)
SOBEYS WEST INC
ROYAL CITY SAFEWAY
610 Sixth St Unit 198, New Westminster, BC,
V3L 3C2

▲ Public Company   ■ Public Company Family Member   **HQ** Headquarters   **BR** Branch   **SL** Single Location

(604) 520-5937
Emp Here 180
SIC 5411 Grocery stores

D-U-N-S 24-346-7391   (BR)
SOUTH COAST BRITISH COLUMBIA TRANSPORTATION AUTHORITY
TRANSIT POLICE
287 Nelson'S Crt Suite 300, New Westminster, BC, V3L 0E7
(604) 515-8300
Emp Here 175
SIC 4111 Local and suburban transit

D-U-N-S 20-506-0838   (BR)
STARBUCKS COFFEE CANADA, INC
(*Suby of* Starbucks Corporation)
800 Mcbride Blvd Suite 21, New Westminster, BC, V3L 2B8
(604) 525-5277
Emp Here 20
SIC 5812 Eating places

D-U-N-S 25-524-6597   (BR)
TRANSX LTD
TRANSX LOGISTICS
25 Capilano Way, New Westminster, BC, V3L 5G3
(604) 540-5572
Emp Here 50
SIC 4213 Trucking, except local

D-U-N-S 25-809-1677   (BR)
WENDY'S RESTAURANTS OF CANADA INC
WENDY'S
(*Suby of* The Wendy's Company)
715 Sixth St, New Westminster, BC, V3L 3C6
(604) 522-1134
Emp Here 35
SIC 5812 Eating places

D-U-N-S 25-366-8818   (BR)
WESTERN FOREST PRODUCTS INC
Gd Stn Main, New Westminster, BC, V3L 4X8
(250) 734-4700
Emp Here 300
SIC 2621 Paper mills

D-U-N-S 24-995-1393   (BR)
YOUNG MEN'S CHRISTIAN ASSOCIATION OF GREATER VANCOUVER
YMCA CARDIAC REHABILITATION PROGRAM
245 Columbia St E Suite 208, New Westminster, BC, V3L 3W4
(604) 521-5801
Emp Here 20
SIC 8011 Offices and clinics of medical doctors

New Westminster, BC V3M
Greater Vancouver County

D-U-N-S 20-713-4300   (BR)
BOARD OF SCHOOL TRUSTEES OF SCHOOL DISTRICT #40 (NEW WESTMINSTER), THE
QUEENSBOROUGH MIDDLE SCHOOL
833 Salter St, New Westminster, BC, V3M 6G8
(604) 517-6040
Emp Here 50
SIC 8211 Elementary and secondary schools

D-U-N-S 20-591-5668   (BR)
BOARD OF SCHOOL TRUSTEES OF SCHOOL DISTRICT #40 (NEW WESTMINSTER), THE
NEW WESTMINISTER SECONDARY SCHOOL
835 Eighth St, New Westminster, BC, V3M 3S9
(604) 517-6220
Emp Here 40
SIC 8211 Elementary and secondary schools

D-U-N-S 25-014-9044   (BR)
BOARD OF SCHOOL TRUSTEES OF SCHOOL DISTRICT #40 (NEW WESTMINSTER), THE
LORD KELVIN ELEMENTARY SCHOOL
1010 Hamilton St, New Westminster, BC, V3M 2M9
(604) 517-6060
Emp Here 60
SIC 8211 Elementary and secondary schools

D-U-N-S 20-653-4112   (BR)
BOARD OF SCHOOL TRUSTEES OF SCHOOL DISTRICT #40 (NEW WESTMINSTER), THE
QUEEN ELIZABETH COMMUNITY SCHOOL
921 Salter St, New Westminster, BC, V3M 6G8
(604) 517-6080
Emp Here 30
SIC 8211 Elementary and secondary schools

D-U-N-S 24-103-7501   (BR)
CAPSERVCO LIMITED PARTNERSHIP
(*Suby of* CapServCo Limited Partnership)
628 Sixth Ave, New Westminster, BC, V3M 6Z1
(604) 521-3761
Emp Here 35
SIC 8721 Accounting, auditing, and bookkeeping

D-U-N-S 20-651-5269   (BR)
CORPORATION OF THE CITY OF NEW WESTMINSTER
QUEEN'S PARK ARENA
600 Eighth St, New Westminster, BC, V3M 3S2
(604) 777-5111
Emp Here 30
SIC 7999 Amusement and recreation, nec

D-U-N-S 24-619-2202   (BR)
GATEWAY CASINOS & ENTERTAINMENT INC
STARLIGHT CASINO
350 Gifford St Suite 1, New Westminster, BC, V3M 7A3
(604) 777-2946
Emp Here 600
SIC 7011 Hotels and motels

D-U-N-S 24-202-8707   (BR)
HATCH CORPORATION
2201 Marine Dr, New Westminster, BC, V3M 2H4

Emp Here 60
SIC 8711 Engineering services

D-U-N-S 20-698-6908   (BR)
HUDSON'S BAY COMPANY
HOME OUTFITTERS
805 Boyd St, New Westminster, BC, V3M 5X2
(604) 525-7362
Emp Here 100
SIC 5311 Department stores

D-U-N-S 20-570-6091   (BR)
INSURANCE CORPORATION OF BRITISH COLUMBIA
ICBC
747 Boyd St, New Westminster, BC, V3M 5X2
(604) 525-3671
Emp Here 25
SIC 6331 Fire, marine, and casualty insurance

D-U-N-S 20-864-6450   (SL)
INTERWEST RESTAURANTS PARTNERSHIP
TIM HORTONS, DIVISION OF
805 Boyd St Suite 100, New Westminster, BC, V3M 5X2
(604) 515-0132
Emp Here 50   *Sales* 1,532,175
SIC 5812 Eating places

D-U-N-S 24-456-1668   (BR)
KEG RESTAURANTS LTD

KEG STEAKHOUSE & BAR, THE
800 Columbia St, New Westminster, BC, V3M 1B8

Emp Here 50
SIC 5812 Eating places

D-U-N-S 20-087-3045   (BR)
KRUGER PRODUCTS L.P.
1625 Fifth Ave, New Westminster, BC, V3M 1Z7
(604) 520-0851
Emp Here 400
SIC 2621 Paper mills

D-U-N-S 24-976-2501   (BR)
LONDON DRUGS LIMITED
60 Tenth St, New Westminster, BC, V3M 3X3
(604) 524-1326
Emp Here 100
SIC 5912 Drug stores and proprietary stores

D-U-N-S 24-827-4099   (BR)
LOWE'S COMPANIES CANADA, ULC
1085 Tanaka Crt, New Westminster, BC, V3M 0G2
(604) 527-7239
Emp Here 175
SIC 5211 Lumber and other building materials

D-U-N-S 20-919-2645   (SL)
NOR PAC MARKETING LTD
960 Quayside Dr Suite 206, New Westminster, BC, V3M 6G2
(604) 736-3133
Emp Here 50   *Sales* 2,626,585
SIC 7389 Business services, nec

D-U-N-S 25-685-6402   (SL)
PARASUN TECHNOLOGIES INC
(*Suby of* Uniserve Communications Corporation)
628 Sixth Ave Suite 300, New Westminster, BC, V3M 6Z1
(604) 357-0057
Emp Here 141   *Sales* 22,398,935
SIC 4813 Telephone communication, except radio
Pr Pr Steven Macdonald
 Barry Carlson
VP Opers Paul Needham
VP Sls Mike Schmidt
Fin Ex Anne Wong

D-U-N-S 25-977-3950   (BR)
PARSONS INC
DELCAN
604 Columbia St Suite 400, New Westminster, BC, V3M 1A5
(604) 525-9333
Emp Here 25
SIC 8711 Engineering services

D-U-N-S 24-839-6830   (SL)
PROBYN LOG LTD
628 Sixth Ave Suite 500, New Westminster, BC, V3M 6Z1
(604) 526-8545
Emp Here 30   *Sales* 1,678,096
SIC 7389 Business services, nec

D-U-N-S 25-715-3825   (SL)
PROCARE HEALTH SERVICES INC
624 Columbia St Suite 201, New Westminster, BC, V3M 1A5
(604) 525-1234
Emp Here 100   *Sales* 4,815,406
SIC 8049 Offices of health practitioner

D-U-N-S 25-954-7966   (BR)
RBC DOMINION SECURITIES INC
(*Suby of* Royal Bank Of Canada)
960 Quayside Dr Suite 201, New Westminster, BC, V3M 6G2
(604) 257-7400
Emp Here 36
SIC 6211 Security brokers and dealers

D-U-N-S 24-178-7741   (BR)

SCM INSURANCE SERVICES INC
CLAIMSPRO
668 Carnarvon St Suite 303, New Westminster, BC, V3M 5Y6
(604) 519-6070
Emp Here 20
SIC 6411 Insurance agents, brokers, and service

D-U-N-S 20-796-7055   (BR)
SLEEP COUNTRY CANADA INC
805 Boyd St Suite 100, New Westminster, BC, V3M 5X2
(604) 515-9711
Emp Here 1,000
SIC 5712 Furniture stores

D-U-N-S 24-930-8115   (BR)
SMIT MARINE CANADA INC
713 Columbia St Suite 617, New Westminster, BC, V3M 1B2
(604) 255-1133
Emp Here 27
SIC 4492 Towing and tugboat service

D-U-N-S 20-428-1380   (BR)
SOBEYS WEST INC
800 Carnarvon St Suite 220, New Westminster, BC, V3M 0G3
(604) 522-2019
Emp Here 140
SIC 5411 Grocery stores

D-U-N-S 24-777-7733   (HQ)
SOUTHERN RAILWAY OF BRITISH COLUMBIA LIMITED
SRY
2102 River Dr, New Westminster, BC, V3M 6S3
(604) 521-1966
Emp Here 170   *Emp Total* 5
Sales 91,028,981
SIC 4011 Railroads, line-haul operating
Pr Frank J Butzelaar
Dir William Brodsky

D-U-N-S 25-536-1297   (SL)
STAR OF FORTUNE GAMING MANAGEMENT (B.C.) CORP
ROYAL CITY STAR RIVERBOAT CASINO
788 Quayside Dr, New Westminster, BC, V3M 6Z6
(604) 412-0166
Emp Here 350   *Sales* 25,619,760
SIC 7999 Amusement and recreation, nec
Pr Pr David Gadhia
 Graham Nash

D-U-N-S 24-309-2553   (BR)
UNIVERSAL PROTECTION SERVICE OF CANADA CO
LEGACY UNIVERSAL PROTECTION SERVICE
(*Suby of* Universal Protection Gp, LLC)
627 Columbia St Suite 200a, New Westminster, BC, V3M 1A7
(604) 522-5550
Emp Here 100
SIC 7381 Detective and armored car services

D-U-N-S 25-535-7469   (SL)
WS LEASING LTD
(*Suby of* Westminster Savings Credit Union)
960 Quayside Dr Suite 403, New Westminster, BC, V3M 6G2
(604) 528-3802
Emp Here 25   *Sales* 3,298,152
SIC 7515 Passenger car leasing

D-U-N-S 24-207-5229   (SL)
WAL-MART CANADA CORP
805 Boyd St, New Westminster, BC, V3M 5X2
(604) 524-1291
Emp Here 25
SIC 5311 Department stores

D-U-N-S 25-507-1755   (SL)
WESTERN LEGAL INFORMATION SER-

VICES INC
620 Royal Ave Suite 10, New Westminster, BC, V3M 1J2

Emp Here 114   Sales 13,594,300
SIC 8111 Legal services
Genl Mgr Shelley Williams

D-U-N-S 20-865-7304   (HQ)
WESTMINSTER SAVINGS CREDIT UNION
(Suby of Westminster Savings Credit Union)
960 Quayside Dr Suite 108, New Westminster, BC, V3M 6G2
(604) 517-0100
Emp Here 60   Emp Total 400
Sales 1,135,655
SIC 6062 State credit unions

North Saanich, BC V8L
Capital County

D-U-N-S 25-153-7981   (BR)
AVISCAR INC
(Suby of Avis Budget Group, Inc.)
1640 Electra Blvd Suite 131, North Saanich, BC, V8L 5V4
(250) 656-6033
Emp Here 25
SIC 7514 Passenger car rental

D-U-N-S 24-567-4601   (BR)
CAPITAL REGIONAL DISTRICT
PANORAMA RECREATION CENTRE
1885 Forest Park Dr, North Saanich, BC, V8L 4A3
(250) 656-7271
Emp Here 20
SIC 8322 Individual and family services

D-U-N-S 25-093-5116   (BR)
JACE HOLDINGS LTD
THRIFTY FOODS
1893 Mills Rd, North Saanich, BC, V8L 5S9
(250) 483-1709
Emp Here 300
SIC 5141 Groceries, general line

D-U-N-S 20-035-7536   (BR)
SCHOOL DISTRICT 63 (SAANICH)
DEEP COVE ELEMENTARY SCHOOL
10975 West Saanich Rd, North Saanich, BC, V8L 5P6
(250) 656-7254
Emp Here 30
SIC 8211 Elementary and secondary schools

D-U-N-S 20-032-8602   (BR)
SCHOOL DISTRICT 63 (SAANICH)
MCTAVISH ELEMENTARY SCHOOL
1720 Mctavish Rd, North Saanich, BC, V8L 5T9

Emp Here 20
SIC 8211 Elementary and secondary schools

D-U-N-S 20-352-3667   (SL)
VIH AEROSPACE INC
1962 Canso Rd, North Saanich, BC, V8L 5V5
(250) 656-3987
Emp Here 39   Sales 5,909,817
SIC 4581 Airports, flying fields, and services
Pr Kenneth Norie

North Vancouver, BC V7G
Greater Vancouver County

D-U-N-S 20-713-4839   (BR)
SCHOOL DISTRICT NO. 44 (NORTH VANCOUVER)
DOROTHY LYNAS ELEMENTARY SCHOOL
(Suby of School District No. 44 (North Vancouver))

4000 Inlet Cres, North Vancouver, BC, V7G 2R2
(604) 903-3430
Emp Here 50
SIC 8211 Elementary and secondary schools

D-U-N-S 20-713-4821   (BR)
SCHOOL DISTRICT NO. 44 (NORTH VANCOUVER)
SHERWOOD PARK ELEMENTARY
(Suby of School District No. 44 (North Vancouver))
4085 Dollar Rd, North Vancouver, BC, V7G 1A5
(604) 903-3810
Emp Here 50
SIC 8211 Elementary and secondary schools

D-U-N-S 20-591-0875   (BR)
SCHOOL DISTRICT NO. 44 (NORTH VANCOUVER)
COVE CLIFF ELEMENTARY SCHOOL
(Suby of School District No. 44 (North Vancouver))
1818 Banbury Rd, North Vancouver, BC, V7G 1W4
(604) 903-3420
Emp Here 40
SIC 8211 Elementary and secondary schools

North Vancouver, BC V7H
Greater Vancouver County

D-U-N-S 20-429-3906   (HQ)
ALS CANADA LTD
ALS GROUP
2103 Dollarton Hwy, North Vancouver, BC, V7H 0A7
(604) 984-0221
Emp Here 353   Emp Total 13,485
Sales 10,586,479
SIC 8734 Testing laboratories
Tammy Moore
VP Jill Bridgman
VP Lisa Droppo
VP David Taylor
Ch Bd Genevieve Bertrand
Dir Heather Durham
Dir Nick Egarhos
Dir Ronald Foerster
Dir Angela Genge
Dir Anne Marie Giannetti

D-U-N-S 24-515-1295   (HQ)
AMER SPORTS CANADA INC
ARC'TERYX EQUIPMENT DIV.
2220 Dollarton Hwy Unit 110, North Vancouver, BC, V7H 1A8
(604) 960-3001
Emp Here 1,000   Emp Total 8,526
Sales 1,137,238,431
SIC 5091 Sporting and recreation goods
VP VP Paul S Mckeown
VP VP Paul Blanchette
David Deasley

D-U-N-S 25-142-3893   (BR)
CHEMTRADE ELECTROCHEM INC
CANEXUS CORPORATION
100 Amherst Ave, North Vancouver, BC, V7H 1S4
(604) 924-2828
Emp Here 167
SIC 2899 Chemical preparations, nec

D-U-N-S 20-703-5564   (BR)
CHEMTRADE ELECTROCHEM INC
CANEXUS CORPORATION
100 Amherst Ave, North Vancouver, BC, V7H 1S4
(604) 929-1107
Emp Here 167
SIC 2812 Alkalies and chlorine

D-U-N-S 20-108-5354   (HQ)
E-Z-RECT MANUFACTURING LTD
ALLIED ENGINEERING, DIV OF
(Suby of Kingswood Capital Corporation)
94 Riverside Dr, North Vancouver, BC, V7H 2M6
(604) 929-1214
Emp Here 60   Emp Total 10
Sales 5,544,006
SIC 2542 Partitions and fixtures, except wood
Pr Pr George Gilbert
Joseph Segal
VP VP Gary Segal
Dir Mannie Druker

D-U-N-S 24-029-9321   (SL)
MILES INDUSTRIES LTD
VALOR FIREPLACES
2255 Dollarton Hwy Suite 190, North Vancouver, BC, V7H 3B1
(604) 984-3496
Emp Here 55   Sales 4,742,446
SIC 3429 Hardware, nec

D-U-N-S 20-106-8371   (BR)
REVOLUTION ENVIRONMENTAL SOLUTIONS LP
TERRAPURE ENVIRONMENTAL
(Suby of Revolution Environmental Solutions LP)
130 Forester St, North Vancouver, BC, V7H 2M9
(604) 929-1283
Emp Here 50
SIC 5093 Scrap and waste materials

D-U-N-S 25-073-5446   (BR)
SCHOOL DISTRICT NO. 44 (NORTH VANCOUVER)
WINDSOR SECONDARY SCHOOL
(Suby of School District No. 44 (North Vancouver))
931 Broadview Dr, North Vancouver, BC, V7H 2E9
(604) 903-3700
Emp Here 110
SIC 8211 Elementary and secondary schools

D-U-N-S 24-321-1328   (BR)
SCHOOL DISTRICT NO. 44 (NORTH VANCOUVER)
PLYMOUTH ELEMENTARY SCHOOL
(Suby of School District No. 44 (North Vancouver))
919 Tollcross Rd, North Vancouver, BC, V7H 2G3

Emp Here 30
SIC 8211 Elementary and secondary schools

D-U-N-S 20-020-2716   (BR)
SCHOOL DISTRICT NO. 44 (NORTH VANCOUVER)
SEYMOUR HEIGHTS ELEMENTARY SCHOOL
(Suby of School District No. 44 (North Vancouver))
2640 Carnation St, North Vancouver, BC, V7H 1H5
(604) 903-3760
Emp Here 30
SIC 8211 Elementary and secondary schools

D-U-N-S 20-020-2641   (BR)
SCHOOL DISTRICT NO. 44 (NORTH VANCOUVER)
BLUERIDGE ELEMENTARY SCHOOL
(Suby of School District No. 44 (North Vancouver))
2650 Bronte Dr, North Vancouver, BC, V7H 1M4
(604) 903-3250
Emp Here 35
SIC 8211 Elementary and secondary schools

D-U-N-S 25-271-7061   (BR)
SOBEYS WEST INC
1175 Mt Seymour Rd, North Vancouver, BC, V7H 2Y4

(604) 924-1302
Emp Here 100
SIC 5411 Grocery stores

D-U-N-S 24-344-0455   (BR)
SUPERIOR PLUS LP
100 Forester St, North Vancouver, BC, V7H 1W4
(604) 929-2331
Emp Here 33
SIC 2819 Industrial inorganic chemicals, nec

North Vancouver, BC V7J
Greater Vancouver County

D-U-N-S 20-040-1805   (SL)
ANGEL RESTORATION INC
ANGEL RESTORATION & DESASTER CLEANUP
1484 Rupert St, North Vancouver, BC, V7J 1E9
(604) 984-7575
Emp Here 60   Sales 2,334,742
SIC 8322 Individual and family services

D-U-N-S 20-913-6548   (HQ)
CAPILANO UNIVERSITY
2055 Purcell Way Suite 284, North Vancouver, BC, V7J 3H5
(604) 986-1911
Emp Here 797   Emp Total 60,000
Sales 31,559,191
SIC 8221 Colleges and universities
Pr Kris Bulcroft
VP Richard Gale
VP Cindy Turner

D-U-N-S 20-520-8460   (SL)
CENTRE BAY YACHT STATION LTD
1103 Heritage Blvd, North Vancouver, BC, V7J 3G8
(604) 986-0010
Emp Here 100   Sales 18,018,021
SIC 6719 Holding companies, nec
Pr Ray Ordano

D-U-N-S 25-310-6447   (BR)
CINEPLEX ODEON CORPORATION
CINEPLEX CINEMAS PARK & TILFORD
333 Brooksbank Ave Unit 200, North Vancouver, BC, V7J 3S8
(604) 904-2359
Emp Here 25
SIC 7832 Motion picture theaters, except drive-in

D-U-N-S 20-573-2295   (BR)
COMPAGNIE DES CHEMINS DE FER NATIONAUX DU CANADA
1155 Cotton Dr, North Vancouver, BC, V7J 1B9
(604) 665-5452
Emp Here 20
SIC 4011 Railroads, line-haul operating

D-U-N-S 20-573-2712   (SL)
FERGUSON MOVING (1990) LTD
FERGUSON MOVING & STORAGE
1584 Columbia St, North Vancouver, BC, V7J 1A4
(604) 922-2212
Emp Here 50   Sales 3,939,878
SIC 4212 Local trucking, without storage

D-U-N-S 24-798-0907   (BR)
GREAT PACIFIC INDUSTRIES INC
SAVE-ON-FOODS
333 Brooksbank Ave Suite 200, North Vancouver, BC, V7J 3S8
(604) 983-3033
Emp Here 389
SIC 5411 Grocery stores

D-U-N-S 20-192-0720   (BR)
GREAT PACIFIC INDUSTRIES INC
SAVE-ON-FOODS

1199 Lynn Valley Rd Suite 1221, North Vancouver, BC, V7J 3H2
(604) 980-4857
Emp Here 150
SIC 5411 Grocery stores

D-U-N-S 24-205-7664   (SL)
GROSVENOR PARK IMPACT PRODUCTIONS INC
555 Brooksbank Ave, North Vancouver, BC, V7J 3S5

Emp Here 300   *Sales* 31,509,360
SIC 7812 Motion picture and video production
Dir Donald Arthur Starr

D-U-N-S 20-189-8876   (BR)
HONEYWELL LIMITED
(*Suby of* Honeywell International Inc.)
500 Brooksbank Ave, North Vancouver, BC, V7J 3S4
(604) 980-3421
Emp Here 250
SIC 2679 Converted paper products, nec

D-U-N-S 24-566-6730   (SL)
J. R. TRORY & COMPANY LTD
TRORY CONSTRUCTION SPECIALTY
1443 Crown St, North Vancouver, BC, V7J 1G4
(604) 980-5074
Emp Here 50   *Sales* 4,377,642
SIC 1799 Special trade contractors, nec

D-U-N-S 25-148-1750   (BR)
LOBLAWS INC
REAL CANADIAN SUPERSTORE
333 Seymour Blvd Suite 1560, North Vancouver, BC, V7J 2J4
(604) 904-5537
Emp Here 350
SIC 5411 Grocery stores

D-U-N-S 20-646-0672   (BR)
LONG & MCQUADE LIMITED
LONG & MCQUADE MUSICAL INSTRUMENTS
1363 Main St, North Vancouver, BC, V7J 1C4
(604) 986-3118
Emp Here 20
SIC 5736 Musical instrument stores

D-U-N-S 20-875-3025   (BR)
NORTH VANCOUVER RECREATION COMMISSION
KAREN MAGNUSSEN RECREATIONAL CENTER
(*Suby of* North Vancouver Recreation Commission)
2300 Kirkstone Rd, North Vancouver, BC, V7J 3M3
(604) 984-4484
Emp Here 50
SIC 7999 Amusement and recreation, nec

D-U-N-S 24-330-5328   (SL)
OLYMPIC BROADCASTING SERVICES VANCOUVER LTD
555 Brooksbank Ave Unit 210, North Vancouver, BC, V7J 3S5

Emp Here 100   *Sales* 12,560,000
SIC 7812 Motion picture and video production
Pr Pr Manolo Romero
Nancy Lee
Ned Blum

D-U-N-S 24-980-3560   (SL)
OLYMPIC INTERNATIONAL SERVICE AGENCY LTD
344 Harbour Ave, North Vancouver, BC, V7J 2E9
(604) 986-1400
Emp Here 35   *Sales* 2,553,625
SIC 7623 Refrigeration service and repair

D-U-N-S 24-887-6955   (SL)
ROBINSON, KEN & SONS (1978) LTD

LITTLE CAESARS PIZZA
1254 Lynn Valley Rd, North Vancouver, BC, V7J 2A3
(604) 990-2910
Emp Here 62   *Sales* 1,896,978
SIC 5812 Eating places

D-U-N-S 20-536-1749   (BR)
ROYAL BANK OF CANADA
RBC
(*Suby of* Royal Bank Of Canada)
1501 Lynn Valley Rd, North Vancouver, BC, V7J 2B1
(604) 981-7880
Emp Here 20
SIC 6021 National commercial banks

D-U-N-S 24-724-1086   (SL)
SACRE CONSULTANTS LTD
SACRE-DAVEY INNOVATIONS
315 Mountain Hwy, North Vancouver, BC, V7J 2K7
(604) 983-0305
Emp Here 50   *Sales* 4,961,328
SIC 8711 Engineering services

D-U-N-S 20-591-0867   (BR)
SCHOOL DISTRICT NO. 44 (NORTH VANCOUVER)
EASTVIEW ELEMENTARY SCHOOL
(*Suby of* School District No. 44 (North Vancouver))
1801 Mountain Hwy, North Vancouver, BC, V7J 2M7
(604) 903-3520
Emp Here 40
SIC 8211 Elementary and secondary schools

D-U-N-S 20-713-4813   (BR)
SCHOOL DISTRICT NO. 44 (NORTH VANCOUVER)
ROSS ROAD ELEMENTARY
(*Suby of* School District No. 44 (North Vancouver))
2875 Bushnell Pl, North Vancouver, BC, V7J 2Y9
(604) 903-3750
Emp Here 45
SIC 8211 Elementary and secondary schools

D-U-N-S 20-020-2690   (BR)
SCHOOL DISTRICT NO. 44 (NORTH VANCOUVER)
LYNNMOUR COMMUNITY SCHOOL
(*Suby of* School District No. 44 (North Vancouver))
800 Forsman Ave, North Vancouver, BC, V7J 2G6
(604) 903-3590
Emp Here 30
SIC 8211 Elementary and secondary schools

D-U-N-S 25-271-7020   (BR)
SOBEYS WEST INC
LYNN VALLEY SAFEWAY
1170 27th St E, North Vancouver, BC, V7J 1S1
(604) 988-7095
Emp Here 85
SIC 5411 Grocery stores

D-U-N-S 20-944-5019   (BR)
STARBUCKS COFFEE CANADA, INC
STARBUCKS COFFEE CO
(*Suby of* Starbucks Corporation)
333 Brooksbank Ave Suite 510, North Vancouver, BC, V7J 3S8
(604) 986-4255
Emp Here 30
SIC 5812 Eating places

D-U-N-S 20-307-3510   (BR)
SUNRISE NORTH SENIOR LIVING LTD
(*Suby of* Welltower Inc.)
980 Lynn Valley Rd, North Vancouver, BC, V7J 3V7
(604) 904-1226
Emp Here 100

SIC 8361 Residential care

D-U-N-S 24-312-8667   (SL)
SUNSHINE CABS LIMITED
1465 Rupert St, North Vancouver, BC, V7J 1G1
(604) 987-3333
Emp Here 80   *Sales* 2,407,703
SIC 4121 Taxicabs

D-U-N-S 20-052-2808   (SL)
T MACRAE FAMILY SALES LTD
CANADIAN TIRE
1350 Main St Suite 601, North Vancouver, BC, V7J 1C6
(604) 982-9101
Emp Here 140   *Sales* 51,072,490
SIC 5014 Tires and tubes
Pr Pr Todd Macrae

D-U-N-S 25-612-6707   (HQ)
TOTAL SAFETY SERVICES INC
PACIFIC ENVIRONMENTAL CONSULTING
(*Suby of* Total Safety U.S., Inc.)
1336 Main St, North Vancouver, BC, V7J 1C3

Emp Here 40   *Emp Total* 1,560
Sales 5,399,092
SIC 8748 Business consulting, nec
Genl Mgr David Mcconnach

D-U-N-S 24-683-6261   (BR)
VANCOUVER COASTAL HEALTH AUTHORITY
CEDARVIEW LODGE
1200 Cedar Village Close, North Vancouver, BC, V7J 3P3
(604) 904-6400
Emp Here 20
SIC 8062 General medical and surgical hospitals

D-U-N-S 25-613-1715   (BR)
WENDY'S RESTAURANTS OF CANADA INC
WENDY'S
(*Suby of* The Wendy's Company)
1488 Main St, North Vancouver, BC, V7J 1C8
(604) 986-1770
Emp Here 36
SIC 5812 Eating places

D-U-N-S 20-117-3325   (HQ)
WESTERN STEVEDORING COMPANY LIMITED
15 Mountain Hwy, North Vancouver, BC, V7J 2J9
(604) 904-2800
Emp Here 400   *Emp Total* 12,002
Sales 94,232,900
SIC 4491 Marine cargo handling
Pr Pr Brad Eshleman
VP Opers Dave Lucas
Dir Jon Hemingway
Dir Mark Knudsen
Dir Jhon Aldaya

D-U-N-S 20-552-9758   (BR)
WESTERN STEVEDORING COMPANY LIMITED
95 Brooksbank Ave, North Vancouver, BC, V7J 2B9
(604) 983-4700
Emp Here 20
SIC 4491 Marine cargo handling

D-U-N-S 25-714-4493   (BR)
WHITE SPOT LIMITED
WHITE SPOT RESTAURANT
333 Brooksbank Ave Suite 1100, North Vancouver, BC, V7J 3S8
(604) 988-6717
Emp Here 90
SIC 5812 Eating places

D-U-N-S 20-004-3276   (BR)
WINNERS MERCHANTS INTERNATIONAL L.P.
WINNERS

(*Suby of* The TJX Companies Inc)
1199 Lynn Valley Rd, North Vancouver, BC, V7J 3H2
(604) 990-8230
Emp Here 20
SIC 5651 Family clothing stores

North Vancouver, BC V7K
Greater Vancouver County

D-U-N-S 25-612-7275   (SL)
NORTH SHORE DISABILITY RESOURCE CENTRE ASSOCIATION
NSDRC
3158 Mountain Hwy, North Vancouver, BC, V7K 2H5
(604) 985-5371
Emp Here 250   *Sales* 12,681,250
SIC 8361 Residential care
Ex Dir Elizabeth Barnett
Lucy Goncalves
Sally Scott
Janet Kuan
Hin Lee
Dir John Newman
Dir Anita Dadson

D-U-N-S 20-298-9310   (BR)
SCHOOL DISTRICT NO. 44 (NORTH VANCOUVER)
ARGYLE SECONDARY SCHOOL
(*Suby of* School District No. 44 (North Vancouver))
1131 Frederick Rd, North Vancouver, BC, V7K 1J3
(604) 903-3300
Emp Here 100
SIC 8211 Elementary and secondary schools

D-U-N-S 20-591-1022   (BR)
SCHOOL DISTRICT NO. 44 (NORTH VANCOUVER)
BOUNDARY ELEMENTARY SCHOOL
(*Suby of* School District No. 44 (North Vancouver))
750 26th St E, North Vancouver, BC, V7K 1A4
(604) 903-3260
Emp Here 25
SIC 8211 Elementary and secondary schools

D-U-N-S 20-591-0859   (BR)
SCHOOL DISTRICT NO. 44 (NORTH VANCOUVER)
UPPER LYNN ELEMENTARY SCHOOL
(*Suby of* School District No. 44 (North Vancouver))
1540 Coleman St, North Vancouver, BC, V7K 1W8
(604) 903-3820
Emp Here 30
SIC 8211 Elementary and secondary schools

D-U-N-S 20-591-0941   (BR)
SCHOOL DISTRICT NO. 44 (NORTH VANCOUVER)
LYN VALLEY ELEMENTARY SCHOOL
(*Suby of* School District No. 44 (North Vancouver))
3207 Institute Rd, North Vancouver, BC, V7K 3E5
(604) 903-3620
Emp Here 25
SIC 8211 Elementary and secondary schools

D-U-N-S 20-020-2666   (BR)
SCHOOL DISTRICT NO. 44 (NORTH VANCOUVER)
FROMME ELEMENTARY SCHOOL
(*Suby of* School District No. 44 (North Vancouver))
3657 Fromme Rd, North Vancouver, BC, V7K 2E6

Emp Here 30
SIC 8211 Elementary and secondary schools

North Vancouver, BC V7L
Greater Vancouver County

D-U-N-S 20-272-6894   (BR)
COAST MOUNTAIN BUS COMPANY LTD
NORTH VANCOUVER BUS DEPOT
536 3rd St E, North Vancouver, BC, V7L 1G5

Emp Here 250
SIC 4111 Local and suburban transit

D-U-N-S 25-145-3031   (BR)
POSTMEDIA NETWORK INC
NORTH SHORE NEWS
126 15th St E Suite 100, North Vancouver, BC,
V7L 2P9
(604) 985-2131
Emp Here 70
SIC 2711 Newspapers

D-U-N-S 24-595-2866   (BR)
RICHARDSON INTERNATIONAL LIMITED
375 Low Level Rd, North Vancouver, BC, V7L
1A7
(604) 987-8855
Emp Here 94
SIC 5153 Grain and field beans

D-U-N-S 20-027-1430   (BR)
SCHOOL DISTRICT NO. 44 (NORTH VAN-COUVER)
SUTHERLAND SECONDARY SCHOOL
(*Suby of* School District No. 44 (North Van-couver))
1860 Sutherland Ave, North Vancouver, BC,
V7L 4C2
(604) 903-3500
Emp Here 85
SIC 8211 Elementary and secondary schools

D-U-N-S 20-713-4797   (BR)
SCHOOL DISTRICT NO. 44 (NORTH VAN-COUVER)
QUEENSBURY ELEMENTARY SCHOOL
(*Suby of* School District No. 44 (North Van-couver))
2020 Moody Ave, North Vancouver, BC, V7L
3V3
(604) 903-3730
Emp Here 30
SIC 8211 Elementary and secondary schools

D-U-N-S 20-713-4805   (BR)
SCHOOL DISTRICT NO. 44 (NORTH VAN-COUVER)
RIDGEWAY ELEMENTARY
(*Suby of* School District No. 44 (North Van-couver))
420 8th St E, North Vancouver, BC, V7L 1Z5

Emp Here 50
SIC 8211 Elementary and secondary schools

D-U-N-S 20-591-0974   (BR)
SCHOOL DISTRICT NO. 44 (NORTH VAN-COUVER)
RIDGEWAY SCHOOL
(*Suby of* School District No. 44 (North Van-couver))
420 8th St E, North Vancouver, BC, V7L 1Z5
(604) 903-3740
Emp Here 25
SIC 8211 Elementary and secondary schools

D-U-N-S 20-591-0982   (BR)
SCHOOL DISTRICT NO. 44 (NORTH VAN-COUVER)
(*Suby of* School District No. 44 (North Van-couver))
440 Hendry Ave, North Vancouver, BC, V7L
4C5
(604) 903-3366
Emp Here 25
SIC 8211 Elementary and secondary schools

D-U-N-S 20-591-0842   (BR)

SCHOOL DISTRICT NO. 44 (NORTH VAN-COUVER)
KEITH LYNN ALTERNATE SCHOOL
(*Suby of* School District No. 44 (North Van-couver))
1290 Shavington St, North Vancouver, BC,
V7L 1L2

Emp Here 25
SIC 8211 Elementary and secondary schools

D-U-N-S 20-591-1030   (BR)
SCHOOL DISTRICT NO. 44 (NORTH VAN-COUVER)
BROOKSBANK ELEMENTARY SCHOOL
(*Suby of* School District No. 44 (North Van-couver))
980 13th St E, North Vancouver, BC, V7L 2N2
(604) 903-3280
Emp Here 25
SIC 8211 Elementary and secondary schools

D-U-N-S 20-020-7186   (BR)
SCHOOL DISTRICT NO. 44 (NORTH VAN-COUVER)
RIDGEWAY ANNEX
(*Suby of* School District No. 44 (North Van-couver))
450 5th St E, North Vancouver, BC, V7L 1M2

Emp Here 20
SIC 8211 Elementary and secondary schools

D-U-N-S 20-913-2955   (BR)
SODEXO CANADA LTD
LIENS GATE HOSPITAL
231 15th St E, North Vancouver, BC, V7L 2L7
(604) 984-3753
Emp Here 50
SIC 5812 Eating places

D-U-N-S 20-035-3519   (BR)
VANCOUVER COASTAL HEALTH
NORTH SHORE HEALTH REGION
231 15th St E, North Vancouver, BC, V7L 2L7
(604) 988-3131
Emp Here 100
SIC 8062 General medical and surgical hospi-tals

D-U-N-S 24-344-9589   (SL)
WASHINGTON YACHTING GROUP ULC
3 St. Andrews Ave, North Vancouver, BC, V7L
3K7
(604) 990-8400
Emp Here 60   *Sales* 6,690,536
SIC 3731 Shipbuilding and repairing
Genl Mgr Denis Larose
Pr Lawrence Simkins

North Vancouver, BC V7M
Greater Vancouver County

D-U-N-S 24-310-4247   (SL)
281558 B.C. LTD
ANDREAS STEAK & LOBSTER
153 16th St W, North Vancouver, BC, V7M 1T3
(604) 985-0414
Emp Here 60   *Sales* 1,824,018
SIC 5812 Eating places

D-U-N-S 20-922-7086   (SL)
BCR PROPERTIES LTD
221 Esplanade W Suite 600, North Vancouver,
BC, V7M 3J3
(604) 678-4701
Emp Here 30   *Sales* 3,378,379
SIC 6719 Holding companies, nec

D-U-N-S 24-796-9926   (BR)
BLUESHORE FINANCIAL CREDIT UNION
1100 Lonsdale Ave Suite 101, North Vancou-ver, BC, V7M 2H1
(604) 903-2660
Emp Here 25

SIC 6062 State credit unions

D-U-N-S 25-360-5125   (BR)
BRITISH COLUMBIA INSTITUTE OF TECH-NOLOGY, THE
BRITISH COLUMBIA INSTITUTE OF TECH-NOLOGY FACULTY AND STAFF ASSOCIA-TION
265 Esplanade W, North Vancouver, BC, V7M
1A5
(604) 453-4100
Emp Here 30
SIC 8222 Junior colleges

D-U-N-S 24-658-3371   (BR)
CANADIAN IMPERIAL BANK OF COM-MERCE
CIBC
1601 Lonsdale Ave, North Vancouver, BC,
V7M 2J5
(604) 981-2402
Emp Here 50
SIC 6021 National commercial banks

D-U-N-S 20-650-3018   (BR)
**CATHOLIC INDEPENDENT SCHOOLS OF
VANCOUVER ARCHDIOCESE, THE**
ST. THOMAS AQUINAS HIGH SCHOOL
541 Keith Rd W, North Vancouver, BC, V7M
1M5
(604) 987-4431
Emp Here 50
SIC 8211 Elementary and secondary schools

D-U-N-S 25-696-4073   (BR)
CINEPLEX ODEON CORPORATION
LANDMARK CINEMAS ESPLANADE
200 Esplanade W, North Vancouver, BC, V7M
1A4
(604) 983-2762
Emp Here 20
SIC 7832 Motion picture theaters, except
drive-in

D-U-N-S 24-791-5015   (BR)
**CRUISESHIPCENTERS INTERNATIONAL
INC**
EXPEDIA CRUSIE SHIP CENTRE
(*Suby of* Cruiseshipcenters International Inc)
110 Esplanade W, North Vancouver, BC, V7M
1A2
(604) 985-7447
Emp Here 25
SIC 4724 Travel agencies

D-U-N-S 24-311-9948   (SL)
FAMILY SERVICES OF THE NORTH SHORE
255 1st St W Suite 101, North Vancouver, BC,
V7M 3G8
(604) 988-5281
Emp Here 50   *Sales* 1,969,939
SIC 8322 Individual and family services

D-U-N-S 24-125-9741   (BR)
IGM FINANCIAL INC
INVESTOR'S GROUP
1200 Lonsdale Ave Suite 200, North Vancou-ver, BC, V7M 3H6
(604) 986-1200
Emp Here 40
SIC 6719 Holding companies, nec

D-U-N-S 20-864-2157   (HQ)
**INSURANCE CORPORATION OF BRITISH
COLUMBIA**
ICBC
151 Esplanade W Suite 135, North Vancouver,
BC, V7M 3H9
(604) 661-2800
Emp Here 1,500   *Emp Total* 60,000
Sales 3,797,134,051
SIC 6331 Fire, marine, and casualty insurance
Pr Pr Mark Blucher
VP Steve Crombie
VP Barbara Meens
VP Brian Jarvis
CFO Geri Prior
T.Richard Turner

T. Michael Porter
Paul G Haggis
Jatinder S Rai
Carol Brown

D-U-N-S 25-506-1830   (SL)
KEITH PANEL SYSTEMS CO., LTD
KPS
(*Suby of* Keith Plumbing & Heating Co. Ltd)
40 Gostick Pl Suite 1, North Vancouver, BC,
V7M 3G3
(604) 987-4499
Emp Here 100   *Sales* 12,907,140
SIC 8712 Architectural services
Pr Pr Paul Myers

D-U-N-S 20-794-5965   (HQ)
KEITH PLUMBING & HEATING CO. LTD
(*Suby of* Keith Plumbing & Heating Co. Ltd)
40 Gostick Pl Unit 1, North Vancouver, BC,
V7M 3G3
(604) 988-5241
Emp Here 205   *Emp Total* 330
Sales 28,892,437
SIC 1711 Plumbing, heating, air-conditioning
Pr Pr Paul Myers

D-U-N-S 25-612-6004   (BR)
**MCDONALD'S   RESTAURANTS   OF
CANADA LIMITED**
MCDONALD'S
(*Suby of* McDonald's Corporation)
2001 Lonsdale Ave, North Vancouver, BC,
V7M 2K4
(604) 987-6815
Emp Here 34
SIC 5812 Eating places

D-U-N-S 20-918-9083   (SL)
NAIRNE, DAVID & ASSOCIATES LTD
171 Esplanade W Suite 250, North Vancouver,
BC, V7M 3J9
(604) 984-3503
Emp Here 50   *Sales* 4,961,328
SIC 8711 Engineering services

D-U-N-S 24-372-6775   (SL)
NORTH SHORE HEALTH REGION
NORTH SHORE HOME SUPPORT SERVICE
132 Esplanade W, North Vancouver, BC, V7M
1A2
(604) 986-7111
Emp Here 345   *Sales* 18,257,760
SIC 8322 Individual and family services
Dir Sandra Edelman

D-U-N-S 24-367-8844   (BR)
**NORTHWEST HYDRAULIC CONSULTANTS
LTD**
N H C
(*Suby of* Northwest Hydraulic Consultants
Ltd)
30 Gostick Pl, North Vancouver, BC, V7M 3G3
(604) 980-6011
Emp Here 40
SIC 8711 Engineering services

D-U-N-S 20-622-4602   (SL)
OLYMPIC INDUSTRIES, INC
(*Suby of* Fctg Holdings, Inc.)
221 Esplanade W Suite 402, North Vancouver,
BC, V7M 3J8
(604) 985-2115
Emp Here 35   *Sales* 10,506,341
SIC 5031 Lumber, plywood, and millwork
Pr Gerry Pankratz
Dir David Smith
Dir Craig Johnston

D-U-N-S 20-020-3144   (BR)
SCHOOL DISTRICT NO. 44 (NORTH VAN-COUVER)
WESTVIEW ELEMENTARY SCHOOL
(*Suby of* School District No. 44 (North Van-couver))
641 17th St W Suite 101, North Vancouver,
BC, V7M 0A1

---

(604) 903-3840
Emp Here 35
SIC 8211 Elementary and secondary schools

D-U-N-S 20-591-0925   (BR)
SCHOOL DISTRICT NO. 44 (NORTH VAN-COUVER)
QUEEN MARY ELEMENTARY SCHOOL
(*Suby of* School District No. 44 (North Vancouver))
230 Keith Rd W, North Vancouver, BC, V7M 1L8
(604) 903-3720
Emp Here 60
SIC 8211 Elementary and secondary schools

D-U-N-S 20-805-0401   (HQ)
SCHOOL DISTRICT NO. 44 (NORTH VAN-COUVER)
NORTH VANCOUVER SCHOOL DISTRICT
(*Suby of* School District No. 44 (North Vancouver))
2121 Lonsdale Ave, North Vancouver, BC, V7M 2K6
(604) 903-3444
Emp Here 800   *Emp Total* 1,980
Sales 140,539,433
SIC 8211 Elementary and secondary schools
Superintnt John Lewis

D-U-N-S 20-591-0891   (BR)
SCHOOL DISTRICT NO. 44 (NORTH VAN-COUVER)
CARSON GRAHAM SECONDARY SCHOOL
(*Suby of* School District No. 44 (North Vancouver))
2145 Jones Ave, North Vancouver, BC, V7M 2W7
(604) 903-3555
Emp Here 25
SIC 8211 Elementary and secondary schools

D-U-N-S 25-271-6980   (BR)
SOBEYS WEST INC
LONSDALE SAFEWAY
1300 Lonsdale Ave, North Vancouver, BC, V7M 2H8

Emp Here 120
SIC 5411 Grocery stores

D-U-N-S 25-485-7196   (BR)
TORONTO-DOMINION BANK, THE
T D BANK FINANCIAL GROUP
(*Suby of* Toronto-Dominion Bank, The)
1400 Lonsdale Ave, North Vancouver, BC, V7M 2J1
(604) 981-5600
Emp Here 20
SIC 6021 National commercial banks

D-U-N-S 20-981-6805   (BR)
VANCOUVER COASTAL HEALTH AUTHOR-ITY
ASSESSMENT AND TREATMENT SER-VICES
145 17th St W Suite 250, North Vancouver, BC, V7M 3G4

Emp Here 50
SIC 8093 Specialty outpatient clinics, nec

D-U-N-S 25-613-5682   (BR)
WHITE SPOT LIMITED
WHITE SPOT RESTAURANT
2205 Lonsdale Ave, North Vancouver, BC, V7M 2K8
(604) 987-0024
Emp Here 53
SIC 5812 Eating places

D-U-N-S 20-702-9245   (BR)
WORLEYPARSONS CANADA SERVICES LTD
233 1st St W, North Vancouver, BC, V7M 1B3
(604) 985-6488
Emp Here 200
SIC 8711 Engineering services

North Vancouver, BC V7N
Greater Vancouver County

D-U-N-S 20-038-5461   (BR)
CONSEIL SCOLAIRE FRANCOPHONE DE LA COLOMBIE BRITANNIQUE
ECOLE ANDRE-PIOLAT
380 Kings Rd W, North Vancouver, BC, V7N 2L9
(778) 340-1034
Emp Here 20
SIC 8211 Elementary and secondary schools

D-U-N-S 24-696-2026   (BR)
MAPLE LEAF FOODS INC
4030 St. Georges Ave, North Vancouver, BC, V7N 1W8

Emp Here 20
SIC 2011 Meat packing plants

D-U-N-S 20-030-5832   (BR)
PIKE, JIM LTD
MCDONALD'S
(*Suby of* Pike, Jim Ltd)
2601 Westview Dr Suite 600, North Vancouver, BC, V7N 3X3
(604) 985-0203
Emp Here 40
SIC 5812 Eating places

D-U-N-S 20-713-4789   (BR)
SCHOOL DISTRICT NO. 44 (NORTH VAN-COUVER)
CARISBROOKE ELEMENTARY SCHOOL
(*Suby of* School District No. 44 (North Vancouver))
510 Carisbrooke Rd E, North Vancouver, BC, V7N 1N5
(604) 903-3380
Emp Here 50
SIC 8211 Elementary and secondary schools

D-U-N-S 20-020-2682   (BR)
SCHOOL DISTRICT NO. 44 (NORTH VAN-COUVER)
LARSON ELEMENTARY SCHOOL
(*Suby of* School District No. 44 (North Vancouver))
2605 Larson Rd, North Vancouver, BC, V7N 3W4
(604) 903-3570
Emp Here 42
SIC 8211 Elementary and secondary schools

D-U-N-S 20-914-5486   (BR)
SCHOOL DISTRICT NO. 44 (NORTH VAN-COUVER)
BEALMORAL JUNIOR SECONDARY
(*Suby of* School District No. 44 (North Vancouver))
3365 Mahon Ave, North Vancouver, BC, V7N 3T7

Emp Here 70
SIC 8211 Elementary and secondary schools

D-U-N-S 20-020-2658   (BR)
SCHOOL DISTRICT NO. 44 (NORTH VAN-COUVER)
BRAEMAR ELEMENTARY SCHOOL
(*Suby of* School District No. 44 (North Vancouver))
3600 Mahon Ave, North Vancouver, BC, V7N 3T6
(604) 903-3270
Emp Here 45
SIC 8211 Elementary and secondary schools

D-U-N-S 25-836-2441   (BR)
SOBEYS WEST INC
WESTVIEW SAFEWAY
2601 Westview Dr Unit 780, North Vancouver, BC, V7N 3X4
(604) 988-4476
Emp Here 20

SIC 5411 Grocery stores

D-U-N-S 25-229-8468   (SL)
TEJAZZ MANAGEMENT SERVICES INC
CORPORATE CLASSICS CATERERS
4238 St. Pauls Ave, North Vancouver, BC, V7N 1T5
(604) 986-9475
Emp Here 100   *Sales* 2,991,389
SIC 5812 Eating places

D-U-N-S 24-808-1494   (SL)
TIC AGENCIES LTD
2609 Westview Dr Suite 300, North Vancouver, BC, V7N 4M2

Emp Here 75   *Sales* 9,128,880
SIC 6411 Insurance agents, brokers, and service
Pr Ruth Simons

North Vancouver, BC V7P
Greater Vancouver County

D-U-N-S 20-588-2934   (BR)
BANQUE TORONTO-DOMINION, LA
TD CANADA TRUST
(*Suby of* Toronto-Dominion Bank, The)
1315 Marine Dr, North Vancouver, BC, V7P 3E5
(604) 984-4282
Emp Here 20
SIC 6021 National commercial banks

D-U-N-S 25-453-7509   (BR)
CACTUS RESTAURANTS LTD
CACTUS CLUB CAFE
1598 Pemberton Ave, North Vancouver, BC, V7P 2S2
(604) 986-5776
Emp Here 50
SIC 5812 Eating places

D-U-N-S 20-537-9717   (BR)
CANADA POST CORPORATION
949 3rd St W Suite 105, North Vancouver, BC, V7P 3P7

Emp Here 21
SIC 4311 U.s. postal service

D-U-N-S 20-702-8833   (BR)
COMPAGNIE DES CHEMINS DE FER NA-TIONAUX DU CANADA
CN RAIL
1777 1st St W, North Vancouver, BC, V7P 3T5
(604) 984-5524
Emp Here 85
SIC 4789 Transportation services, nec

D-U-N-S 20-038-1957   (BR)
CORPORATION OF THE DISTRICT OF WEST VANCOUVER, THE
BLUE BUS
221 Lloyd Ave, North Vancouver, BC, V7P 3M2
(604) 985-7777
Emp Here 100
SIC 4111 Local and suburban transit

D-U-N-S 20-584-4822   (HQ)
DAYTON & KNIGHT LTD
889 Harbourside Dr Suite 210, North Vancouver, BC, V7P 3S1
(604) 990-4800
Emp Here 50   *Sales* 9,009,010
SIC 8748 Business consulting, nec
Pr Sean P Brophy
VP Harlan Kelly
CFO John Boyle
COO Jack Lee

D-U-N-S 25-069-4544   (BR)
DENCAN RESTAURANTS INC
DENNY'S RESTAURANT
(*Suby of* Northland Properties Corporation)

2050 Marine Dr, North Vancouver, BC, V7P 1V7
(604) 980-8210
Emp Here 40
SIC 5812 Eating places

D-U-N-S 20-547-3700   (SL)
DIAMANTS STORNOWAY (CANADA) INC, LES
DIAMANTS ASHTON (CANADA)
(*Suby of* Stornoway Diamond Corporation)
980 1st St W Suite 116, North Vancouver, BC, V7P 3N4
(604) 983-7750
Emp Here 21   *Sales* 2,252,253
SIC 1481 NonMetallic mineral services

D-U-N-S 20-804-1350   (SL)
E. E. C. INDUSTRIES LIMITED
(*Suby of* E. E. C. Holdings Ltd)
1237 Welch St, North Vancouver, BC, V7P 1B3
(604) 986-5633
Emp Here 67   *Sales* 4,085,799
SIC 3993 Signs and advertising specialties

D-U-N-S 25-682-0317   (SL)
EARL'S MEDICINE HAT LTD
949 3rd St W, North Vancouver, BC, V7P 3P7
(604) 984-4606
Emp Here 49   *Sales* 7,444,399
SIC 6712 Bank holding companies
Pr Stan Fuller

D-U-N-S 24-448-4473   (HQ)
EARL'S RESTAURANTS LTD
EARL'S
(*Suby of* Earl's Restaurants Ltd)
949 3rd St W Suite 108b, North Vancouver, BC, V7P 3P7
(604) 984-4606
Emp Here 50   *Emp Total* 150
Sales 4,523,563
SIC 5812 Eating places

D-U-N-S 24-525-0100   (BR)
ENBALA POWER NETWORKS INC
930 1st St W Suite 211, North Vancouver, BC, V7P 3N4
(604) 998-8900
Emp Here 20
SIC 4911 Electric services

D-U-N-S 24-958-1794   (HQ)
FDM SOFTWARE LTD
(*Suby of* Aptean, Inc.)
949 3rd St W Suite 113, North Vancouver, BC, V7P 3P7
(604) 986-9941
Emp Here 27   *Emp Total* 2,469
Sales 2,261,782
SIC 7372 Prepackaged software

D-U-N-S 25-640-0409   (BR)
HONDA CANADA INC
PACIFIC HONDA
816 Automall Dr, North Vancouver, BC, V7P 3R8
(604) 984-0331
Emp Here 80
SIC 5511 New and used car dealers

D-U-N-S 24-342-4160   (BR)
INTRAWEST ULC
INTRAWEST CENTRAL RESERVATIONS
(*Suby of* Intrawest Resorts Holdings, Inc.)
788 Harbourside Dr Suite 100, North Vancouver, BC, V7P 3R7
(604) 904-7135
Emp Here 200
SIC 7011 Hotels and motels

D-U-N-S 24-378-8358   (SL)
KM CANADA MARINE TERMINAL LIMITED PARTNERSHIP
KINDER MORGAN
1995 1st St W, North Vancouver, BC, V7P 1A8
(604) 985-3177
Emp Here 24   *Sales* 3,648,035

▲ Public Company   ■ Public Company Family Member   **HQ** Headquarters   **BR** Branch   **SL** Single Location

SIC 4491 Marine cargo handling

D-U-N-S 20-705-8632   (SL)
KEG RESTAURANT
PARK ROYAL KEG
800 Marine Dr, North Vancouver, BC, V7P 1R8

Emp Here 100   *Sales* 2,991,389
SIC 5812 Eating places

D-U-N-S 20-799-9335   (HQ)
LEVETT AUTO METAL LTD
(*Suby of* Levett Auto Metal Ltd)
183 Pemberton Ave, North Vancouver, BC, V7P 2R4
(604) 985-7195
Emp Here 30   *Emp Total* 50
Sales 3,575,074
SIC 7532 Top and body repair and paint shops

D-U-N-S 20-547-4245   (BR)
LEVETT AUTO METAL LTD
WESTERN BUS PARTS & SERVICE (DIV)
(*Suby of* Levett Auto Metal Ltd)
95 Philip Ave, North Vancouver, BC, V7P 2V5
(604) 980-4844
Emp Here 35
SIC 5013 Motor vehicle supplies and new parts

D-U-N-S 25-273-1096   (BR)
LORDCO PARTS LTD
LORDCO AUTO PARTS
1500 Fell Ave, North Vancouver, BC, V7P 3E7
(604) 984-0277
Emp Here 20
SIC 5531 Auto and home supply stores

D-U-N-S 25-318-2117   (BR)
MCDONALD'S   RESTAURANTS   OF CANADA LIMITED
MCDONALD'S #8486
(*Suby of* McDonald's Corporation)
925 Marine Dr, North Vancouver, BC, V7P 1S2
(604) 985-6757
Emp Here 75
SIC 5812 Eating places

D-U-N-S 25-318-2158   (BR)
MCDONALD'S   RESTAURANTS   OF CANADA LIMITED
MCDONALD'S #8045
(*Suby of* McDonald's Corporation)
1219 Marine Dr, North Vancouver, BC, V7P 1T3
(604) 904-4390
Emp Here 95
SIC 5812 Eating places

D-U-N-S 24-372-8425   (BR)
MERCEDES-BENZ CANADA INC
1375 Marine Dr, North Vancouver, BC, V7P 3E5
(604) 984-7780
Emp Here 40
SIC 5511 New and used car dealers

D-U-N-S 25-146-2511   (SL)
MORREY AUTO GROUP LTD
MORREY MAZDA
818 Automall Dr, North Vancouver, BC, V7P 3R8
(604) 984-9211
Emp Here 35   *Sales* 17,178,000
SIC 5511 New and used car dealers
Pr Steve Morrey

D-U-N-S 25-712-5310   (BR)
NORTH SHORE PARTS & INDUSTRIAL SUPPLIES LTD
850 1st St W, North Vancouver, BC, V7P 1A2
(604) 985-1113
Emp Here 20
SIC 5013 Motor vehicle supplies and new parts

D-U-N-S 25-360-5059   (BR)
OPENROAD AUTO GROUP LIMITED

828 Automall Dr, North Vancouver, BC, V7P 3R8
(604) 929-6736
Emp Here 30
SIC 5511 New and used car dealers

D-U-N-S 25-015-0299   (BR)
RFGOP RESTAURANT HOLDINGS LTD
BURGER KING 3739
(*Suby of* RFGOP Restaurant Holdings Ltd)
1493 Marine Dr, North Vancouver, BC, V7P 1T5

Emp Here 30
SIC 5812 Eating places

D-U-N-S 24-683-3164   (SL)
RED ROBIN RESTAURANT (CAPILANO) LTD
801 Marine Dr Suite 100, North Vancouver, BC, V7P 3K6

Emp Here 100   *Sales* 2,991,389
SIC 5812 Eating places

D-U-N-S 25-144-5565   (BR)
SCHOOL DISTRICT NO. 44 (NORTH VANCOUVER)
LEO MARSHALL CURRICULUM CENTRE
(*Suby of* School District No. 44 (North Vancouver))
810 21st St W, North Vancouver, BC, V7P 2C1
(604) 903-3798
Emp Here 20
SIC 8999 Services, nec

D-U-N-S 20-713-4854   (BR)
SCHOOL DISTRICT NO. 44 (NORTH VANCOUVER)
LUCAS CENTER CONTINUING EDUCATION
(*Suby of* School District No. 44 (North Vancouver))
2132 Hamilton Ave, North Vancouver, BC, V7P 2M3
(604) 903-3333
Emp Here 50
SIC 8211 Elementary and secondary schools

D-U-N-S 20-975-6373   (BR)
SCHOOL DISTRICT NO. 44 (NORTH VANCOUVER)
NORTH VANCOUVER CONTINUING EDUCATION EMPLOYMENT SERVICES DIVISION
(*Suby of* School District No. 44 (North Vancouver))
935 Marine Dr Suite 304, North Vancouver, BC, V7P 1S3

Emp Here 20
SIC 8331 Job training and related services

D-U-N-S 20-047-0768   (BR)
SCHOOL DISTRICT NO. 44 (NORTH VANCOUVER)
CAPILANO ELEMENTARY SCHOOL
(*Suby of* School District No. 44 (North Vancouver))
1230 20th St W, North Vancouver, BC, V7P 2B9
(604) 903-3370
Emp Here 35
SIC 8211 Elementary and secondary schools

D-U-N-S 20-027-0036   (BR)
SCHOOL DISTRICT NO. 44 (NORTH VANCOUVER)
NORGATE COMMUNITY SCHOOL
(*Suby of* School District No. 44 (North Vancouver))
1295 Sowden St, North Vancouver, BC, V7P 1L9
(604) 903-3680
Emp Here 30
SIC 8211 Elementary and secondary schools

D-U-N-S 25-294-6512   (BR)
SEARS CANADA INC

943 Marine Dr, North Vancouver, BC, V7P 1S1
(604) 985-7722
Emp Here 200
SIC 5311 Department stores

D-U-N-S 25-613-1160   (BR)
STAPLES CANADA INC
STAPLES THE BUSINESS DEPOT
(*Suby of* Staples, Inc.)
1999 Marine Dr, North Vancouver, BC, V7P 3J3
(604) 990-2900
Emp Here 40
SIC 5943 Stationery stores

D-U-N-S 20-506-0952   (BR)
STARBUCKS COFFEE CANADA, INC
STARBUCKS
(*Suby of* Starbucks Corporation)
1276 Marine Dr, North Vancouver, BC, V7P 1T2
(604) 987-1191
Emp Here 35
SIC 5812 Eating places

D-U-N-S 20-587-0327   (BR)
VANCOUVER CITY SAVINGS CREDIT UNION
VANCITY CREDIT UNION
1290 Marine Dr, North Vancouver, BC, V7P 1T2
(604) 877-7000
Emp Here 20
SIC 8742 Management consulting services

D-U-N-S 25-714-3321   (BR)
WAL-MART CANADA CORP
925 Marine Dr Suite 3057, North Vancouver, BC, V7P 1S2
(604) 984-6830
Emp Here 200
SIC 5311 Department stores

North Vancouver, BC V7R
Greater Vancouver County

D-U-N-S 20-364-3309   (BR)
AMICA MATURE LIFESTYLES INC
AMICA AT EDGEMONT VILLAGE
3225 Highland Blvd, North Vancouver, BC, V7R 0A3
(604) 929-6361
Emp Here 70
SIC 8361 Residential care

D-U-N-S 20-748-1029   (SL)
CAPILANO HEIGHTS RESTAURANT CO. LTD
CAPILANO HEIGHTS CHINESE RESTAURANT
5020 Capilano Rd, North Vancouver, BC, V7R 4K7
(604) 987-9511
Emp Here 50   *Sales* 2,130,450
SIC 5812 Eating places

D-U-N-S 24-764-3328   (SL)
CAPILANO SUSPENSION BRIDGE LTD
3735 Capilano Rd Suite 1889, North Vancouver, BC, V7R 4J1
(604) 985-7474
Emp Here 49   *Sales* 11,673,712
SIC 4724 Travel agencies
Pr Pr Nancy Stibbard

D-U-N-S 20-285-0921   (SL)
RIVERSIDE RETIREMENT CENTRE LTD
BROCKLEHURST GEMSTONE CARE CENTRE
4315 Skyline Dr, North Vancouver, BC, V7R 3G9
(604) 307-1104
Emp Here 250   *Sales* 12,681,250
SIC 8361 Residential care
CEO Mary Mcdougall

D-U-N-S 20-020-2674   (BR)
SCHOOL DISTRICT NO. 44 (NORTH VANCOUVER)
HIGHLANDS ELEMENTARY SCHOOL
(*Suby of* School District No. 44 (North Vancouver))
3150 Colwood Dr, North Vancouver, BC, V7R 2R6
(604) 903-3540
Emp Here 40
SIC 8211 Elementary and secondary schools

D-U-N-S 20-591-0834   (BR)
SCHOOL DISTRICT NO. 44 (NORTH VANCOUVER)
HANDSWORTH SECONDARY SCHOOL
(*Suby of* School District No. 44 (North Vancouver))
1044 Edgewood Rd, North Vancouver, BC, V7R 1Y7
(604) 903-3600
Emp Here 80
SIC 8211 Elementary and secondary schools

D-U-N-S 20-020-2708   (BR)
SCHOOL DISTRICT NO. 44 (NORTH VANCOUVER)
MONTROYAL ELEMENTARY SCHOOL
(*Suby of* School District No. 44 (North Vancouver))
5310 Sonora Dr, North Vancouver, BC, V7R 3V8
(604) 903-3650
Emp Here 45
SIC 8211 Elementary and secondary schools

D-U-N-S 20-591-0990   (BR)
SCHOOL DISTRICT NO. 44 (NORTH VANCOUVER)
CANYON HEIGHTS ELEMENTARY SCHOOL
(*Suby of* School District No. 44 (North Vancouver))
4501 Highland Blvd, North Vancouver, BC, V7R 3A2
(604) 903-3290
Emp Here 35
SIC 8211 Elementary and secondary schools

D-U-N-S 20-506-0218   (BR)
STARBUCKS COFFEE CANADA, INC
(*Suby of* Starbucks Corporation)
3127 Edgemont Blvd, North Vancouver, BC, V7R 2N7
(604) 985-8750
Emp Here 20
SIC 5812 Eating places

Okanagan Falls, BC V0H
Okanagn-Similkameen County

D-U-N-S 20-713-2353   (BR)
SCHOOL DISTRICT NO. 53 (OKANAGAN SIMILKAMEEN)
OKANAGAN FALLS ELEMENTARY SCHOOL
1141 Cedar St, Okanagan Falls, BC, V0H 1R0
(250) 497-5414
Emp Here 39
SIC 8211 Elementary and secondary schools

Oliver, BC V0H
Okanagn-Similkameen County

D-U-N-S 20-296-0910   (BR)
ANDREW PELLER LIMITED
400 Covert Pl, Oliver, BC, V0H 1T5
(250) 485-8538
Emp Here 40
SIC 2084 Wines, brandy, and brandy spirits

D-U-N-S 25-136-5334   (SL)
BURROWING OWL VINEYARDS LTD
BURROWING OWL ESTATE WINERY

100 Burrowing Owl Pl, Oliver, BC, V0H 1T0
(250) 498-0620
Emp Here 55   *Sales* 1,605,135
SIC 2084 Wines, brandy, and brandy spirits

D-U-N-S 24-345-4246   (SL)
FAIRVIEW MOUNTAIN GOLF CLUB
13105 334 Ave, Oliver, BC, V0H 1T0
(250) 498-3777
Emp Here 50   *Sales* 2,042,900
SIC 7997 Membership sports and recreation clubs

D-U-N-S 20-844-4658   (SL)
HESTER CREEK ESTATE WINERY LTD
877 Rd 8, Oliver, BC, V0H 1T1
(250) 498-4435
Emp Here 20   *Sales* 5,253,170
SIC 5921 Liquor stores
Curtis Garland
Pr Pr David Livingstone

D-U-N-S 25-812-5293   (BR)
INTERIOR HEALTH AUTHORITY
SUNNYBANK RETIREMENT CENTRE
6553 Park Dr, Oliver, BC, V0H 1T4
(250) 498-4951
Emp Here 48
SIC 8062 General medical and surgical hospitals

D-U-N-S 24-348-2093   (BR)
INTERIOR HEALTH AUTHORITY
SOUTH OKANAGAN GENERAL HOSPITAL
911 Mckinney Rd, Oliver, BC, V0H 1T3
(250) 498-5000
Emp Here 200
SIC 8062 General medical and surgical hospitals

D-U-N-S 25-823-1844   (BR)
INTERIOR SAVINGS CREDIT UNION
6287 Main St, Oliver, BC, V0H 1T0
(250) 498-3457
Emp Here 25
SIC 6062 State credit unions

D-U-N-S 24-026-1987   (BR)
MARK ANTHONY PROPERTIES LTD
MISSION HILL FAMILY ESTATE
7151 Sibco Landfill, Oliver, BC, V0H 1T0
(250) 485-4400
Emp Here 200
SIC 6531 Real estate agents and managers

D-U-N-S 25-316-6151   (BR)
OKANAGAN COLLEGE
OLIVER-OSOYOOS CENTRE
9315 350th Ave, Oliver, BC, V0H 1T0
(250) 498-6264
Emp Here 41
SIC 8221 Colleges and universities

D-U-N-S 20-047-0610   (BR)
SCHOOL DISTRICT NO. 53 (OKANAGAN SIMILKAMEEN)
TUC EL NUIT ELEMENTARY SCHOOL
6648 Park Dr, Oliver, BC, V0H 1T4
(250) 498-3415
Emp Here 30
SIC 8211 Elementary and secondary schools

D-U-N-S 20-038-4605   (BR)
SCHOOL DISTRICT NO. 53 (OKANAGAN SIMILKAMEEN)
SOUTHERN OKANAGAN SECONDARY SCHOOL
6140 Gala St, Oliver, BC, V0H 1T0
(250) 498-4931
Emp Here 60
SIC 8211 Elementary and secondary schools

D-U-N-S 20-865-3741   (SL)
SOUTHERN OKANAGAN ASSOCIATION FOR INGTERGRATED COMMUNITY LIVING
38246 93 Ave, Oliver, BC, V0H 1T0
(250) 498-0309
Emp Here 50   *Sales* 1,824,018

SIC 8361 Residential care

D-U-N-S 24-536-8816   (SL)
SUNNYBANK RETIREMENT HOME
Gd, Oliver, BC, V0H 1T0
(250) 498-4951
Emp Here 71   *Sales* 3,118,504
SIC 8361 Residential care

Osoyoos, BC V0H
Okanagn-Similkameen County

D-U-N-S 20-590-9760   (BR)
SCHOOL DISTRICT NO. 53 (OKANAGAN SIMILKAMEEN)
OSOYOOS ELEMENTARY SCHOOL
8507 68th Ave, Osoyoos, BC, V0H 1V0
(250) 498-3468
Emp Here 25
SIC 8211 Elementary and secondary schools

D-U-N-S 20-713-2361   (BR)
SCHOOL DISTRICT NO. 53 (OKANAGAN SIMILKAMEEN)
OSOYOOS SECONDARY SCHOOL
5800 115th St, Osoyoos, BC, V0H 1V4
(250) 485-4433
Emp Here 35
SIC 8211 Elementary and secondary schools

D-U-N-S 24-041-3463   (SL)
SPIRIT RIDGE VINEYARD RESORT INC
SPIRIT RIDGE VINEYARD RESORT & SPA
(*Suby of* Bellstar Hotels & Resorts Ltd)
1200 Rancher Creek Rd, Osoyoos, BC, V0H 1V6
(250) 495-5445
Emp Here 70   *Sales* 3,064,349
SIC 7011 Hotels and motels

Parksville, BC V9P
Nanaimo County

D-U-N-S 24-578-5241   (BR)
BANK OF MONTREAL
PARKSVILLE BRANCH
220 Island Hwy W Suite 1, Parksville, BC, V9P 2P3
(250) 248-5711
Emp Here 20
SIC 6021 National commercial banks

D-U-N-S 20-590-0678   (BR)
BANQUE TORONTO-DOMINION, LA
TORONTO-DOMINION BANK, THE
(*Suby of* Toronto-Dominion Bank, The)
115 Alberni Hwy, Parksville, BC, V9P 2G9
(250) 248-7329
Emp Here 20
SIC 6021 National commercial banks

D-U-N-S 20-949-2607   (BR)
BEKINS MOVING & STORAGE (CANADA) LTD
Gd, Parksville, BC, V9P 2G2
(250) 248-8805
Emp Here 20
SIC 4212 Local trucking, without storage

D-U-N-S 24-995-0783   (BR)
BLACK PRESS GROUP LTD
PARKSVILLE QUALICUM BEACH NEWS
154 Middleton Ave Suite 4, Parksville, BC, V9P 2H2
(250) 248-4341
Emp Here 25
SIC 2711 Newspapers

D-U-N-S 20-513-3932   (BR)
CENTRAL BUILDERS' SUPPLY P.G. LIMITED
HOME BUILDING CENTER

1395 Island Hwy W, Parksville, BC, V9P 1Y8
(250) 752-5565
Emp Here 60
SIC 5211 Lumber and other building materials

D-U-N-S 20-734-2051   (BR)
COASTAL COMMUNITY CREDIT UNION
1400 Alberni Hwy, Parksville, BC, V9P 2N6
(250) 248-3275
Emp Here 35
SIC 6062 State credit unions

D-U-N-S 20-864-5973   (SL)
ELM STREET RESTAURANTS INC
TIM HORTONS
494 Island Hwy W, Parksville, BC, V9P 1H2
(250) 248-0094
Emp Here 54   *Sales* 1,605,135
SIC 5812 Eating places

D-U-N-S 25-289-0918   (BR)
GREAT PACIFIC INDUSTRIES INC
SAVE-ON-FOODS
826 Island Hwy W Suite 20, Parksville, BC, V9P 2B7
(250) 248-8944
Emp Here 100
SIC 5411 Grocery stores

D-U-N-S 20-732-3002   (SL)
MCM FOOD SERVICES INC
MCDONALDS RESTAURANT
310 Island Hwy W, Parksville, BC, V9P 1K8
(250) 248-8885
Emp Here 65   *Sales* 1,969,939
SIC 5812 Eating places

D-U-N-S 20-573-8458   (BR)
ROYAL BANK OF CANADA
ROYAL BANK OF CANADA
(*Suby of* Royal Bank Of Canada)
152 S Alberni Hwy, Parksville, BC, V9P 2G5
(250) 248-8321
Emp Here 20
SIC 6021 National commercial banks

D-U-N-S 20-713-6008   (BR)
SCHOOL DISTRICT NO 69 (QUALICUM)
WINCHELSEA ELEMENTARY SCHOOLS
140 Renz Rd, Parksville, BC, V9P 2H2
(250) 248-3296
Emp Here 35
SIC 8211 Elementary and secondary schools

D-U-N-S 20-591-2806   (BR)
SCHOOL DISTRICT NO 69 (QUALICUM)
OCEANSIDE MIDDLE SCHOOL
980 Wright Rd, Parksville, BC, V9P 2B3
(250) 248-4662
Emp Here 25
SIC 8211 Elementary and secondary schools

D-U-N-S 20-591-2772   (BR)
SCHOOL DISTRICT NO 69 (QUALICUM)
PARKSVILLE ELEMENTARY SCHOOL
330 Craig St, Parksville, BC, V9P 1L4

Emp Here 50
SIC 8211 Elementary and secondary schools

D-U-N-S 25-485-7873   (BR)
SCHOOL DISTRICT NO 69 (QUALICUM)
ECOLE BALLENAS SECONDARY SCHOOL
135 N Pym Rd, Parksville, BC, V9P 2H4
(250) 248-5721
Emp Here 90
SIC 8211 Elementary and secondary schools

D-U-N-S 25-155-3806   (BR)
SCHOOL DISTRICT NO 69 (QUALICUM)
SPRINGWOOD MIDDLE SCHOOL
450 Despard Ave, Parksville, BC, V9P 2G3
(250) 248-2038
Emp Here 40
SIC 8211 Elementary and secondary schools

D-U-N-S 24-694-6305   (SL)
SCHOONER COVE HOLDINGS LTD

SCHOONER COVE RESORT HOTEL & MARINA
Gd Stn Main, Parksville, BC, V9P 2G2

Emp Here 70   *Sales* 3,064,349
SIC 7011 Hotels and motels

D-U-N-S 24-345-6311   (BR)
VANCOUVER ISLAND HEALTH AUTHORITY
TRILLIUM LODGE
Gd, Parksville, BC, V9P 2G2
(250) 947-8230
Emp Here 150
SIC 8011 Offices and clinics of medical doctors

D-U-N-S 20-086-9845   (BR)
VANCOUVER ISLAND HEALTH AUTHORITY
HOME & COMMUNITY CARE SERVICES
180 Mccarter St Suite 100, Parksville, BC, V9P 2H3
(250) 731-1315
Emp Here 175
SIC 7389 Business services, nec

D-U-N-S 24-194-0050   (BR)
WASTE CONNECTIONS OF CANADA INC
BFI CANADA
1151 Herring Gull Way, Parksville, BC, V9P 1R2
(250) 758-5360
Emp Here 30
SIC 4953 Refuse systems

D-U-N-S 20-976-7610   (BR)
WASTE CONNECTIONS OF CANADA INC
1151 Herring Gull Way, Parksville, BC, V9P 1R2
(250) 248-8109
Emp Here 35
SIC 4953 Refuse systems

Peachland, BC V0H
Central Okanagan County

D-U-N-S 25-811-9791   (BR)
BOARD OF EDUCATION OF SCHOOL DISTRICT NO. 23 (CENTRAL OKANAGAN), THE
PEACHLAND ELEMENTARY & PRIMARY SCHOOL
5486 Clements Cres, Peachland, BC, V0H 1X5
(250) 870-5122
Emp Here 25
SIC 8211 Elementary and secondary schools

Pemberton, BC V0N
Squamish - Lillooet County

D-U-N-S 20-645-5045   (SL)
PEMBERTON VALLEY SUPERMARKET
7438 Prospect St Rr 1, Pemberton, BC, V0N 2L1
(604) 894-2009
Emp Here 45   *Sales* 7,362,000
SIC 5411 Grocery stores
Owner Robert Adams

D-U-N-S 20-645-5441   (BR)
SCHOOL DISTRICT NO. 48 (HOWE SOUND)
PEMBERTON SECONDARY SCHOOL
1400 Oak St, Pemberton, BC, V0N 2L0
(604) 894-6318
Emp Here 30
SIC 8211 Elementary and secondary schools

D-U-N-S 20-043-6546   (BR)
SCHOOL DISTRICT NO. 48 (HOWE SOUND)
SIGNAL HILL ELEMENTARY SCHOOL

1410 Portage Rd, Pemberton, BC, V0N 2L1
(604) 894-6378
Emp Here 70
SIC 8211 Elementary and secondary schools

D-U-N-S 25-843-8597   (BR)
SEA TO SKY COMMUNITY HEALTH COUNCIL
PEMBERTON HEALTH CENTRE
(*Suby of* Vancouver Coastal Health Authority)
1403 Portage Rd, Pemberton, BC, V0N 2L0
(604) 894-6633
Emp Here 29
SIC 8011 Offices and clinics of medical doctors

Pender Island, BC V0N
Capital County

D-U-N-S 20-590-7392   (BR)
SCHOOL DISTRICT NO. 64 (GULF ISLANDS)
PENDER ISLANDS ELEMENTARY SECONDARY SCHOOL
5714 Canal Rd, Pender Island, BC, V0N 2M1
(250) 629-3711
Emp Here 25
SIC 8211 Elementary and secondary schools

Penticton, BC V2A
Okanagn-Similkameen County

D-U-N-S 20-911-8884   (SL)
A.C.M.C.J. HOLDINGS LTD
HAVEN HILL RETIREMENT CENTRE
415 Haven Hill Rd, Penticton, BC, V2A 4E9
(250) 492-2600
Emp Here 54   *Sales* 1,969,939
SIC 8361 Residential care

D-U-N-S 25-142-7076   (BR)
ASTRAL MEDIA RADIO INC
CKOR AM
(*Suby of* Astral Media Radio Inc)
33 Carmi Ave, Penticton, BC, V2A 3G4
(250) 492-2800
Emp Here 20
SIC 4832 Radio broadcasting stations

D-U-N-S 25-363-8555   (BR)
BANK OF MONTREAL
BMO
195 Main St Suite 201, Penticton, BC, V2A 6K1
(250) 492-4240
Emp Here 34
SIC 6021 National commercial banks

D-U-N-S 20-588-2629   (BR)
BANQUE TORONTO-DOMINION, LA
TD CANADA TRUST
(*Suby of* Toronto-Dominion Bank, The)
2210 Main St Suite 130, Penticton, BC, V2A 5H8
(250) 770-2333
Emp Here 20
SIC 6021 National commercial banks

D-U-N-S 25-922-9607   (BR)
BANQUE TORONTO-DOMINION, LA
TORONTO-DOMINION BANK, THE
(*Suby of* Toronto-Dominion Bank, The)
390 Main St, Penticton, BC, V2A 5C3
(250) 492-0145
Emp Here 21
SIC 6021 National commercial banks

D-U-N-S 24-337-9281   (BR)
BLACK PRESS GROUP LTD
PENTICTON WESTERN NEWS
2250 Camrose St, Penticton, BC, V2A 8R1

(250) 492-0444
Emp Here 40
SIC 2711 Newspapers

D-U-N-S 25-325-2761   (BR)
BRITISH COLUMBIA AUTOMOBILE ASSOCIATION
CAA BRITISH COLUMBIA
2100 Main St Unit 100, Penticton, BC, V2A 5H7
(250) 487-2450
Emp Here 21
SIC 8699 Membership organizations, nec

D-U-N-S 25-288-8805   (BR)
CANADA POST CORPORATION
PENTICTON POSTAL OUTLET
56 Industrial Ave W, Penticton, BC, V2A 6M2
(250) 492-5717
Emp Here 60
SIC 4311 U.s. postal service

D-U-N-S 25-786-6236   (BR)
CANADIAN CANCER SOCIETY
74 Wade Ave E Unit 103, Penticton, BC, V2A 8M4
(250) 490-9681
Emp Here 30
SIC 8399 Social services, nec

D-U-N-S 20-914-0933   (BR)
CANADIAN IMPERIAL BANK OF COMMERCE
CIBC
295 Main St, Penticton, BC, V2A 5B1
(250) 770-3333
Emp Here 40
SIC 6021 National commercial banks

D-U-N-S 20-075-5598   (BR)
CANADIAN RED CROSS SOCIETY, THE
216 Hastings Ave Suite 130, Penticton, BC, V2A 2V6
(250) 493-7533
Emp Here 20
SIC 8621 Professional organizations

D-U-N-S 20-104-2116   (BR)
CONTINENTAL NEWSPAPERS (CANADA) LTD
PENTICTON HERALD
186 Nanaimo Ave W Suite 101, Penticton, BC, V2A 1N4
(250) 493-6737
Emp Here 20
SIC 2711 Newspapers

D-U-N-S 25-603-9348   (BR)
DENCAN RESTAURANTS INC
DENNY'S RESTAURANT
(*Suby of* Northland Properties Corporation)
939 Burnaby Ave, Penticton, BC, V2A 1G7
(250) 490-9390
Emp Here 30
SIC 5812 Eating places

D-U-N-S 20-026-8725   (BR)
DIVERSICARE CANADA MANAGEMENT SERVICES CO., INC
CONCORDE ASSISTED LIVING
3235 Skaha Lake Rd, Penticton, BC, V2A 6G5
(250) 490-8800
Emp Here 30
SIC 8051 Skilled nursing care facilities

D-U-N-S 24-069-0305   (BR)
EMERGENCY AND HEALTH SERVICES COMMISSION
BC AMBULANCE
1475 Fairview Rd Suite 90, Penticton, BC, V2A 7W5
(250) 493-2108
Emp Here 24
SIC 4119 Local passenger transportation, nec

D-U-N-S 24-019-2133   (BR)
FGL SPORTS LTD
SPORT CHEK PEACHTREE SQUARE
2701 Skaha Lake Rd Unit 101, Penticton, BC,

V2A 9B8
(250) 276-8370
Emp Here 42
SIC 5941 Sporting goods and bicycle shops

D-U-N-S 20-174-8972   (BR)
FORTISBC ENERGY INC
444 Okanagan Ave E, Penticton, BC, V2A 3K3
(250) 490-2626
Emp Here 25
SIC 4923 Gas transmission and distribution

D-U-N-S 25-267-8784   (BR)
GREAT PACIFIC INDUSTRIES INC
OVERWAITEA FOOD GROUP
2111 Main St Suite 100, Penticton, BC, V2A 6W6
(250) 492-2011
Emp Here 75
SIC 5411 Grocery stores

D-U-N-S 25-018-4611   (BR)
HSBC BANK CANADA
HSBC
201 Main St, Penticton, BC, V2A 5B1
(250) 492-2704
Emp Here 30
SIC 6021 National commercial banks

D-U-N-S 25-301-2504   (BR)
HUDSON'S BAY COMPANY
BAY, THE
2111 Main St Suite 160, Penticton, BC, V2A 6V1
(250) 493-1900
Emp Here 120
SIC 5311 Department stores

D-U-N-S 25-163-3863   (BR)
INLAND CONTRACTING LTD
150 Industrial Pl, Penticton, BC, V2A 7C8
(250) 493-6791
Emp Here 20
SIC 5084 Industrial machinery and equipment

D-U-N-S 24-369-2357   (HQ)
INLAND CONTRACTING LTD
INLAND EQUIPMENT SALES
716 Okanagan Ave E, Penticton, BC, V2A 3K6
(250) 492-2626
Emp Here 45   *Emp Total* 50
Sales 5,836,856
SIC 1611 Highway and street construction
Pr David Kampe

D-U-N-S 25-596-7945   (BR)
INLAND KENWORTH LTD
INLAND KENWORTH
1690 Fairview Rd, Penticton, BC, V2A 6A8
(250) 492-3939
Emp Here 22
SIC 5084 Industrial machinery and equipment

D-U-N-S 25-003-7520   (BR)
INSURANCE CORPORATION OF BRITISH COLUMBIA
I C B C
90 Industrial Ave E, Penticton, BC, V2A 3H8
(250) 493-4181
Emp Here 23
SIC 6331 Fire, marine, and casualty insurance

D-U-N-S 20-825-3463   (BR)
INVESTORS GROUP FINANCIAL SERVICES INC
INVESTORS GROUP MORTGAGE SERVICES
300 Riverside Dr Suite 206, Penticton, BC, V2A 9C9
(250) 492-8806
Emp Here 24
SIC 8742 Management consulting services

D-U-N-S 25-604-0874   (BR)
KELDON ELECTRIC & DATA LTD
380 Okanagan Ave E Suite 101, Penticton, BC, V2A 8N3
(250) 493-7177
Emp Here 25

SIC 1731 Electrical work

D-U-N-S 20-213-2580   (BR)
LOBLAWS INC
REAL CANADIAN WHOLESALE CLUB
200 Carmi Ave, Penticton, BC, V2A 3G5
(250) 493-5888
Emp Here 100
SIC 5141 Groceries, general line

D-U-N-S 20-333-6268   (BR)
LOBLAWS INC
REAL CANADIAN SUPERSTORE
2210 Main St Suite 100, Penticton, BC, V2A 5H8
(250) 487-7700
Emp Here 200
SIC 5411 Grocery stores

D-U-N-S 25-372-3241   (BR)
MCDONALD'S RESTAURANTS OF CANADA LIMITED
MCDONALD'S
(*Suby of* McDonald's Corporation)
1804 Main St, Penticton, BC, V2A 5H3
(250) 493-0826
Emp Here 60
SIC 5812 Eating places

D-U-N-S 25-195-9482   (SL)
NOR-MAR INDUSTRIES LTD
682 Okanagan Ave E, Penticton, BC, V2A 3K6
(250) 492-7866
Emp Here 68   *Sales* 3,429,153
SIC 7389 Business services, nec

D-U-N-S 24-351-6841   (SL)
OSPREY CARE PENTICTON INC
HAMLETS AT PENTICTON
103 Duncan Ave W, Penticton, BC, V2A 2Y3
(250) 490-8503
Emp Here 150   *Sales* 9,521,520
SIC 8059 Nursing and personal care, nec
Andre Van Ryk
Dir Kasey Vandongen

D-U-N-S 24-390-5119   (SL)
PARKER MOTORS (1946) LTD
1765 Main St, Penticton, BC, V2A 5H1
(250) 492-2839
Emp Here 47   *Sales* 23,612,800
SIC 5511 New and used car dealers
Janet Parker
VP Colin Parker

D-U-N-S 24-362-5618   (BR)
PATTISON, JIM INDUSTRIES LTD
PATTISON SIGN GROUP DIV OF
165 Waterloo Ave, Penticton, BC, V2A 7J3
(250) 492-4522
Emp Here 100
SIC 3993 Signs and advertising specialties

D-U-N-S 24-750-4046   (SL)
PENTICTON COURTYARD INN LTD
RAMADA INN & SUITES PENTICTON
1050 Eckhardt Ave W, Penticton, BC, V2A 2C3
(250) 492-8926
Emp Here 80   *Sales* 3,502,114
SIC 7011 Hotels and motels

D-U-N-S 25-538-2939   (BR)
PRISZM LP
KFC
1897 Main St, Penticton, BC, V2A 5H2
(250) 492-0003
Emp Here 25
SIC 5812 Eating places

D-U-N-S 20-590-5313   (BR)
SCHOOL DISTRICT NO 67 (OKANAGAN SKAHA)
K V R MIDDLE SCHOOL
300 Jermyn Ave, Penticton, BC, V2A 2E1
(250) 770-7600
Emp Here 38
SIC 8211 Elementary and secondary schools

D-U-N-S 25-815-1216   (BR)

SCHOOL DISTRICT NO 67 (OKANAGAN SKAHA)
CARMI ELEMENTARY SCHOOL
400 Carmi Ave, Penticton, BC, V2A 3G5
(250) 770-7697
Emp Here 30
SIC 8211 Elementary and secondary schools

D-U-N-S 20-590-5263   (BR)
SCHOOL DISTRICT NO 67 (OKANAGAN SKAHA)
PENTICTON SECONDARY SCHOOL
158 Eckhardt Ave E, Penticton, BC, V2A 1Z3
(250) 770-7750
Emp Here 25
SIC 8211 Elementary and secondary schools

D-U-N-S 20-718-5864   (BR)
SCHOOL DISTRICT NO 67 (OKANAGAN SKAHA)
PRINCESS MARGARET SECONDARY SCHOOL
120 Green Ave W, Penticton, BC, V2A 3T1
(250) 770-7620
Emp Here 70
SIC 8211 Elementary and secondary schools

D-U-N-S 25-975-3341   (BR)
SEVCON MANUFACTURING INC
LEE LYNN WOOD PRODUCTS DIV OF
(*Suby of* Sevcon Manufacturing Inc)
325 Dawson Ave, Penticton, BC, V2A 3N5

Emp Here 64
SIC 2431 Millwork

D-U-N-S 20-612-0722   (BR)
SHERET, ANDREW LIMITED
SPLASHES BATH & KITCHEN CENTRE
(*Suby of* Sheret, Andrew Holdings Limited)
324 Duncan Ave W, Penticton, BC, V2A 7N1
(250) 493-9369
Emp Here 20
SIC 5074 Plumbing and heating equipment and supplies (hydronics)

D-U-N-S 25-498-9874   (BR)
STAPLES CANADA INC
STAPLES/BUSINESS DEPOT
(*Suby of* Staples, Inc.)
102 Warren Ave E Suite 100, Penticton, BC, V2A 8X3
(250) 770-2990
Emp Here 30
SIC 5943 Stationery stores

D-U-N-S 20-865-2867   (HQ)
VALLEY COMFORT SYSTEMS INC
BLAZE KING
1290 Commercial Way, Penticton, BC, V2A 3H5
(250) 493-7444
Emp Here 60   *Emp Total* 20
Sales 13,600,141
SIC 3585 Refrigeration and heating equipment
Pr Pr Alan Murphy
Opers Mgr Gray Cameron
Fin Ex Andrew Hofer

D-U-N-S 24-558-5877   (BR)
VALLEY FIRST CREDIT UNION
2111 Main St Suite 135, Penticton, BC, V2A 6W6
(250) 493-7773
Emp Here 20
SIC 6062 State credit unions

D-U-N-S 24-370-5399   (HQ)
VALLEY KING FOODS INC
BURGER KING
(*Suby of* Valley King Foods Inc)
1717 Main St, Penticton, BC, V2A 5G9
(250) 493-8411
Emp Here 20   *Emp Total* 85
Sales 3,031,879
SIC 5812 Eating places

D-U-N-S 24-246-9484   (BR)
WAL-MART CANADA CORP
275 Green Ave W Suite 135, Penticton, BC, V2A 7J2
(250) 493-6681
Emp Here 250
SIC 5311 Department stores

D-U-N-S 20-000-4336   (BR)
WHITE SPOT LIMITED
WHITE SPOT RESTAURANT
1770 Main St Unit 101, Penticton, BC, V2A 5G8
(250) 492-0038
Emp Here 36
SIC 5812 Eating places

D-U-N-S 24-313-5923   (BR)
WINNERS MERCHANTS INTERNATIONAL L.P.
WINNERS
(*Suby of* The TJX Companies Inc)
2210 Main St, Penticton, BC, V2A 5H8
(250) 487-1141
Emp Here 40
SIC 5651 Family clothing stores

Pitt Meadows, BC V3Y

D-U-N-S 20-917-6598   (SL)
458291 BC LTD
JOLLY COACHMAN PUB
19167 Ford Rd, Pitt Meadows, BC, V3Y 2B6
(604) 465-9237
Emp Here 50   *Sales* 1,532,175
SIC 5812 Eating places

D-U-N-S 20-588-9004   (BR)
CANADIAN PACIFIC RAILWAY COMPANY
CPR
17900 Kennedy Rd, Pitt Meadows, BC, V3Y 1Z1
(604) 469-4300
Emp Here 20
SIC 4011 Railroads, line-haul operating

D-U-N-S 24-337-3532   (BR)
FGL SPORTS LTD
SPORT-CHEK
19800 Lougheed Hwy Unit 405, Pitt Meadows, BC, V3Y 2W1
(604) 460-6612
Emp Here 50
SIC 5941 Sporting goods and bicycle shops

D-U-N-S 25-217-8314   (SL)
GOLDEN EAGLE GOLF COURSES INC
GOLDEN EAGLE GOLF CLUB
21770 Ladner Rd, Pitt Meadows, BC, V3Y 1Z1
(604) 460-1871
Emp Here 90   *Sales* 3,866,917
SIC 7992 Public golf courses

D-U-N-S 20-553-5318   (SL)
HOWE PRECISION INDUSTRIAL INC
11718 Harris Rd, Pitt Meadows, BC, V3Y 1Y6
(604) 460-2892
Emp Here 130   *Sales* 34,594,450
SIC 3823 Process control instruments
Pr Yukun Du
Sec Lina Hao

D-U-N-S 25-670-6508   (BR)
HUDSON'S BAY COMPANY
FIELDS STORE
19150 Lougheed Hwy Suite 129, Pitt Meadows, BC, V3Y 2H6

Emp Here 25
SIC 5311 Department stores

D-U-N-S 20-155-9692   (BR)
LAFARGE CANADA INC
PITT RIVER QUARRIES
16101 Rannie Rd, Pitt Meadows, BC, V3Y 1Z1

(604) 465-4114
Emp Here 30
SIC 1481 NonMetallic mineral services

D-U-N-S 25-368-7248   (BR)
LOBLAWS INC
REAL CANADIAN SUPERSTORE
19800 Lougheed Hwy Suite 201, Pitt Meadows, BC, V3Y 2W1
(604) 460-4319
Emp Here 350
SIC 5411 Grocery stores

D-U-N-S 20-557-6007   (BR)
PRT GROWING SERVICES LTD
HYBRID NURSERIES
12682 Woolridge Rd, Pitt Meadows, BC, V3Y 1Z1
(604) 465-6276
Emp Here 20
SIC 5261 Retail nurseries and garden stores

D-U-N-S 24-363-3562   (BR)
PETER KIEWIT INFRASTRUCTURE CO.
(*Suby of* Peter Kiewit Sons', Inc.)
17949 Kennedy Rd, Pitt Meadows, BC, V3Y 1Z1
(604) 460-2550
Emp Here 65
SIC 1629 Heavy construction, nec

D-U-N-S 20-590-9927   (BR)
SCHOOL DISTRICT NO 42 (MAPLE RIDGE-PITT MEADOWS)
DAVIE JONES ELEMENTARY SCHOOL
12030 Blakely Rd, Pitt Meadows, BC, V3Y 1J6
(604) 465-9908
Emp Here 35
SIC 8211 Elementary and secondary schools

D-U-N-S 20-590-9919   (BR)
SCHOOL DISTRICT NO 42 (MAPLE RIDGE-PITT MEADOWS)
PITT MEADOWS ELEMENTARY SCHOOL
11941 Harris Rd, Pitt Meadows, BC, V3Y 2B5
(604) 465-5828
Emp Here 40
SIC 8211 Elementary and secondary schools

D-U-N-S 20-158-0516   (BR)
SCHOOL DISTRICT NO 42 (MAPLE RIDGE-PITT MEADOWS)
EDITH MC DERMOTT ELEMENTARY
12178 Bonson Rd, Pitt Meadows, BC, V3Y 2L5
(604) 460-9993
Emp Here 50
SIC 8211 Elementary and secondary schools

D-U-N-S 20-590-9968   (BR)
SCHOOL DISTRICT NO 42 (MAPLE RIDGE-PITT MEADOWS)
HIGHLAND PARK ELEMENTARY
18961 Advent Rd, Pitt Meadows, BC, V3Y 2G4
(604) 465-6737
Emp Here 25
SIC 8211 Elementary and secondary schools

D-U-N-S 20-294-8126   (BR)
SCHOOL DISTRICT NO 42 (MAPLE RIDGE-PITT MEADOWS)
PITT MEADOWS SECONDARY SCHOOL
19438 116b Ave, Pitt Meadows, BC, V3Y 1G1
(604) 465-7141
Emp Here 85
SIC 8211 Elementary and secondary schools

D-U-N-S 24-014-2476   (BR)
WINNERS MERCHANTS INTERNATIONAL L.P.
HOMESENSE
(*Suby of* The TJX Companies Inc)
19800 Lougheed Hwy Suite 160, Pitt Meadows, BC, V3Y 2W1
(604) 465-4330
Emp Here 80
SIC 5651 Family clothing stores

Port Alberni, BC V9Y
Alberni - Clayoquot County

D-U-N-S 20-589-5191   (BR)
BANQUE TORONTO-DOMINION, LA
TD CANADA TRUST
(*Suby of* Toronto-Dominion Bank, The)
3008 3rd Ave, Port Alberni, BC, V9Y 2A5
(250) 720-4810
Emp Here 20
SIC 6021 National commercial banks

D-U-N-S 24-152-9981   (BR)
BRITISH COLUMBIA HYDRO AND POWER AUTHORITY
BC HYDRO
4820 Wallace St, Port Alberni, BC, V9Y 3Y2
(250) 724-2711
Emp Here 27
SIC 4911 Electric services

D-U-N-S 25-119-8883   (BR)
BUY-LOW FOODS LTD
4647 Johnston Rd, Port Alberni, BC, V9Y 5M5
(250) 723-4811
Emp Here 55
SIC 5411 Grocery stores

D-U-N-S 20-539-4500   (BR)
CANADA POST CORPORATION
PORT ALBERNI POST OFFICE
3737 10th Ave, Port Alberni, BC, V9Y 4W5
(250) 724-1442
Emp Here 60
SIC 4311 U.s. postal service

D-U-N-S 25-288-8763   (BR)
CANADA POST CORPORATION
5262 Argyle St Unit F, Port Alberni, BC, V9Y 1T9
(250) 723-5411
Emp Here 43
SIC 4311 U.s. postal service

D-U-N-S 25-021-1604   (BR)
CANADIAN IMPERIAL BANK OF COMMERCE
CIBC
2995 3rd Ave, Port Alberni, BC, V9Y 2A6
(250) 720-2300
Emp Here 25
SIC 6021 National commercial banks

D-U-N-S 25-538-4117   (BR)
CATALYST PAPER CORPORATION
PORT ALBERNI MILL
4000 Stamp Ave, Port Alberni, BC, V9Y 5J7
(250) 723-2161
Emp Here 324
SIC 2621 Paper mills

D-U-N-S 24-593-6133   (HQ)
COULSON AIRCRANE LTD
(*Suby of* Coulson Forest Products Limited)
4890 Cherry Creek Rd, Port Alberni, BC, V9Y 8E9
(250) 723-8118
Emp Here 20   *Emp Total* 500
Sales 34,206,543
SIC 4522 Air transportation, nonscheduled
Pr Pr Wayne Coulson

D-U-N-S 25-939-6406   (BR)
COULSON AIRCRANE LTD
(*Suby of* Coulson Forest Products Limited)
7500 Airport Rd, Port Alberni, BC, V9Y 8Y9
(250) 723-8100
Emp Here 20
SIC 4522 Air transportation, nonscheduled

D-U-N-S 20-342-3736   (BR)
DITIDAHT FIRST NATION
DITIDAHT COMMUNITY SCHOOL
Gd, Port Alberni, BC, V9Y 7M3
(250) 745-3223
Emp Here 20

SIC 8211 Elementary and secondary schools

D-U-N-S 20-544-8256   (BR)
FAIRWAY HOLDINGS (1994) LTD
WEST PORT FOOD
3737 10th Ave, Port Alberni, BC, V9Y 4W5
(250) 724-1442
Emp Here 50
SIC 5411 Grocery stores

D-U-N-S 24-995-6186   (SL)
FRANKLIN FOREST PRODUCTS LTD
4536 Glenwood Dr, Port Alberni, BC, V9Y 4P8
(250) 724-1166
Emp Here 45   *Sales* 5,791,440
SIC 2421 Sawmills and planing mills, general
Pr Pr Patrick Mckay
   Gary Reed

D-U-N-S 24-244-9536   (SL)
G. D. P. INVESTMENTS LTD
BEST WESTERN BARCLAY HOTEL
4277 Stamp Ave, Port Alberni, BC, V9Y 7X8
(250) 724-7171
Emp Here 50   *Sales* 2,188,821
SIC 7011 Hotels and motels

D-U-N-S 25-384-9244   (BR)
KELLAND FOODS LTD
QUALITY FOODS, DIV OF
2943 10th Ave, Port Alberni, BC, V9Y 2N5
(250) 723-3397
Emp Here 100
SIC 5411 Grocery stores

D-U-N-S 20-713-9093   (SL)
LIGHTHOUSE CHRISTIAN ACADEMY SO-CIETY, THE
Gd Lcd Main, Port Alberni, BC, V9Y 7M3
(250) 723-7382
Emp Here 50   *Sales* 4,334,713
SIC 8211 Elementary and secondary schools

D-U-N-S 24-417-4301   (BR)
LOBLAWS INC
EXTRA FOODS
3455 Johnston Rd, Port Alberni, BC, V9Y 8K1
(250) 723-1624
Emp Here 50
SIC 5411 Grocery stores

D-U-N-S 20-104-4237   (SL)
MARS CONTRACTING CO. LTD
3213 Kingsway Ave, Port Alberni, BC, V9Y 3B3
(250) 724-3351
Emp Here 50   *Sales* 5,107,249
SIC 2411 Logging
Pr Pr Larry Mackenzie
   Wendy Mackenzie

D-U-N-S 20-975-5243   (BR)
NAVY LEAGUE OF CANADA, THE
4210 Cedarwood St, Port Alberni, BC, V9Y 4A6
(250) 723-7442
Emp Here 49
SIC 8641 C vic and social associations

D-U-N-S 25-314-7664   (BR)
NORTH ISLAND COLLEGE
PORT ALBERNI REGIONAL CAMPUS, DIV OF
3699 Roger St, Port Alberni, BC, V9Y 8E3
(250) 724-8711
Emp Here 50
SIC 8221 Colleges and universities

D-U-N-S 20-311-0671   (SL)
NU BODY EQUIPMENT SALES LTD
5211 Compton Rd, Port Alberni, BC, V9Y 7B5
(778) 552-4540
Emp Here 54   *Sales* 6,274,620
SIC 3845 Electromedical equipment
Pr Pr Amanda Hall

D-U-N-S 24-030-7934   (BR)
POSTMEDIA NETWORK INC
ALBERNI VALLEY TIMES

4918 Napier St, Port Alberni, BC, V9Y 3H5

Emp Here 30
SIC 2711 Newspapers

D-U-N-S 25-806-6596   (BR)
ROYAL BANK OF CANADA
ROYAL BANK FINANCIAL GROUP
(*Suby of* Royal Bank Of Canada)
2925 3rd Ave, Port Alberni, BC, V9Y 2A6

Emp Here 22
SIC 6021 National commercial banks

D-U-N-S 25-288-5124   (BR)
SCHOOL DISTRICT #70 (ALBERNI) SCHOOL BOARD
ALBERNI DISTRICT SECONDARY SCHOOL
4000 Burde St, Port Alberni, BC, V9Y 3L6
(250) 724-3284
Emp Here 110
SIC 8211 Elementary and secondary schools

D-U-N-S 20-592-0775   (BR)
SCHOOL DISTRICT #70 (ALBERNI) SCHOOL BOARD
WOOD ELEMENTARY SCHOOL
4111 Wood Ave, Port Alberni, BC, V9Y 5E8
(250) 724-1132
Emp Here 20
SIC 8211 Elementary and secondary schools

D-U-N-S 20-027-0481   (BR)
SCHOOL DISTRICT #70 (ALBERNI) SCHOOL BOARD
ECOLE ALBERNI ELEMENTARY SCHOOL
4645 Helen St, Port Alberni, BC, V9Y 6P6
(250) 724-0623
Emp Here 30
SIC 8211 Elementary and secondary schools

D-U-N-S 25-011-6548   (BR)
SCHOOL DISTRICT #70 (ALBERNI) SCHOOL BOARD
GILL ELEMENTARY SCHOOL
5520 Beaver Creek Rd, Port Alberni, BC, V9Y 8X6
(250) 723-9311
Emp Here 20
SIC 8211 Elementary and secondary schools

D-U-N-S 25-117-6582   (BR)
SCHOOL DISTRICT #70 (ALBERNI) SCHOOL BOARD
JOHN HOWITT ELEMENTARY SCHOOL
3867 Marpole St, Port Alberni, BC, V9Y 6Y3
(250) 723-7521
Emp Here 20
SIC 8211 Elementary and secondary schools

D-U-N-S 25-120-7395   (BR)
SCHOOL DISTRICT #70 (ALBERNI) SCHOOL BOARD
EIGHTH AVENUE ELEMENTARY SCHOOL
2941 8th Ave, Port Alberni, BC, V9Y 2K5
(250) 723-7631
Emp Here 20
SIC 8211 Elementary and secondary schools

D-U-N-S 25-919-6228   (BR)
SCHOOL DISTRICT #70 (ALBERNI) SCHOOL BOARD
ERIC J DUNN MIDDLE SCHOOL
3500 Argyle St, Port Alberni, BC, V9Y 3A8
(250) 723-7522
Emp Here 45
SIC 8249 Vocational schools, nec

D-U-N-S 25-117-6897   (BR)
SCHOOL DISTRICT #70 (ALBERNI) SCHOOL BOARD
MAQUINNA ELEMENTARY SCHOOL
3881 Bruce St, Port Alberni, BC, V9Y 1J6
(250) 724-0512
Emp Here 30
SIC 8211 Elementary and secondary schools

D-U-N-S 20-713-6016   (BR)

SCHOOL DISTRICT #70 (ALBERNI) SCHOOL BOARD
NEILL MIDDLE SCHOOL
5055 Compton Rd, Port Alberni, BC, V9Y 7B5
(250) 723-8151
Emp Here 33
SIC 8211 Elementary and secondary schools

D-U-N-S 25-120-7411   (BR)
SCHOOL DISTRICT #70 (ALBERNI) SCHOOL BOARD
VAST CENTRE
4152 Redford St Suite 202, Port Alberni, BC, V9Y 3R5
(250) 723-3744
Emp Here 30
SIC 8211 Elementary and secondary schools

D-U-N-S 25-271-1114   (BR)
SOBEYS WEST INC
PORT ALBERNI SAFEWAY
3756 10th Ave, Port Alberni, BC, V9Y 4W6
(250) 723-6212
Emp Here 50
SIC 5411 Grocery stores

D-U-N-S 20-641-6914   (BR)
TANDEM FOODS INC
MCDONALD'S RESTAURANTS
(*Suby of* Tandem Foods Inc)
4152 Redford St, Port Alberni, BC, V9Y 3R5
(250) 723-4747
Emp Here 49
SIC 5812 Eating places

D-U-N-S 25-965-7120   (BR)
VANCOUVER ISLAND HEALTH AUTHOR-ITY
PORT ALBERNI CHILD, YOUTH & FAMILY HEALTH UNIT
4227 6th Ave, Port Alberni, BC, V9Y 4N1
(250) 731-1315
Emp Here 50
SIC 8011 Offices and clinics of medical doctors

D-U-N-S 24-319-5034   (BR)
WAL-MART CANADA CORP
3355 Johnston Rd, Port Alberni, BC, V9Y 8K1
(250) 720-0912
Emp Here 120
SIC 5311 Department stores

D-U-N-S 25-893-3456   (SL)
WESTCOAST NATIVE HEALTH CARE SO-CIETY
TSAWAAYUUS RAINBOW GARDENS
6151 Russell Pl, Port Alberni, BC, V9Y 7W3
(250) 724-5655
Emp Here 60   *Sales* 2,699,546
SIC 8051 Skilled nursing care facilities

D-U-N-S 25-366-4163   (BR)
WESTERN FOREST PRODUCTS INC
SOMASS SAWMILL
3500 Harbour Rd, Port Alberni, BC, V9Y 3G3
(250) 720-4600
Emp Here 60
SIC 2611 Pulp mills

D-U-N-S 20-869-5903   (BR)
WESTERN FOREST PRODUCTS INC
ALBERNI PACIFIC SAWMILL
2500 1st Ave, Port Alberni, BC, V9Y 8H7
(250) 724-7438
Emp Here 300
SIC 2611 Pulp mills

D-U-N-S 24-336-4671   (BR)
WINDSOR BUILDING SUPPLIES LTD
WINDSOR PLYWOOD PORT ALBERNI
4740 Tebo Ave, Port Alberni, BC, V9Y 8B1
(250) 724-5751
Emp Here 20
SIC 5211 Lumber and other building materials

Port Alice, BC V0N
Mount Waddington County

D-U-N-S 24-070-3798   (HQ)
NEUCEL SPECIALTY CELLULOSE LTD
300 Marine Drive, Port Alice, BC, V0N 2N0
(250) 284-3331
Emp Here 30   *Emp Total* 375
Sales 63,111,006
SIC 3081 Unsupported plastics film and sheet
Pr Wanli Zhao

Port Coquitlam, BC V3B
Greater Vancouver County

D-U-N-S 24-841-0925   (BR)
1009833 ALBERTA LTD
PETLAND
1097 Nicola Ave Suite 110, Port Coquitlam, BC, V3B 8B2
(604) 464-9770
Emp Here 25
SIC 5999 Miscellaneous retail stores, nec

D-U-N-S 24-069-2145   (SL)
372831 BC LTD
ARMS PUB
3261 Coast Meridian Rd, Port Coquitlam, BC, V3B 3N3
(604) 941-4711
Emp Here 50   *Sales* 3,064,349
SIC 5621 Women's clothing stores

D-U-N-S 25-095-4393   (SL)
APPLE AMERICAN
APPLEBEE'S NEIGHBORHOOD GRILL
2325 Ottawa St Suite 300, Port Coquitlam, BC, V3B 8A4

Emp Here 58   *Sales* 1,751,057
SIC 5812 Eating places

D-U-N-S 25-314-1360   (BR)
CANADIAN PACIFIC RAILWAY COMPANY
PACIFIC STEEL GANG
2080 Lougheed Hwy, Port Coquitlam, BC, V3B 4H3
(604) 944-5816
Emp Here 50
SIC 4011 Railroads, line-haul operating

D-U-N-S 24-162-9448   (BR)
CATALYST CAPITAL GROUP INC, THE
PLANET ORGANIC MARKET
(*Suby of* Catalyst Capital Group Inc, The)
2755 Lougheed Hwy Suite 10, Port Coquitlam, BC, V3B 5Y9
(403) 288-6700
Emp Here 30
SIC 5149 Groceries and related products, nec

D-U-N-S 25-059-5980   (BR)
CATHOLIC INDEPENDENT SCHOOLS OF VANCOUVER ARCHDIOCESE, THE
ARCHBISHOP CARNEY REGIONAL SEC-ONDARY SCHOOL
1335 Dominion Ave, Port Coquitlam, BC, V3B 8G7
(604) 942-7465
Emp Here 55
SIC 8211 Elementary and secondary schools

D-U-N-S 20-153-2178   (BR)
CONSEIL SCOLAIRE FRANCOPHONE DE LA COLOMBIE BRITANNIQUE
ECOLE DES PIONNIERS
3550 Wellington St, Port Coquitlam, BC, V3B 3Y5
(604) 552-7915
Emp Here 40
SIC 8211 Elementary and secondary schools

D-U-N-S 25-831-4426   (BR)
COSTCO WHOLESALE CANADA LTD

COSTCO
(*Suby of* Costco Wholesale Corporation)
2370 Ottawa St Suite 255, Port Coquitlam, BC, V3B 7Z1
(604) 552-2228
Emp Here 300
SIC 5099 Durable goods, nec

D-U-N-S 20-003-9118   (BR)
GREAT PACIFIC INDUSTRIES INC
SAVE-ON-FOODS
2385 Ottawa St, Port Coquitlam, BC, V3B 8A4
(604) 464-9984
Emp Here 120
SIC 5411 Grocery stores

D-U-N-S 25-270-0653   (BR)
HSBC BANK CANADA
2755 Lougheed Hwy Suite 41, Port Coquitlam, BC, V3B 5Y9
(604) 464-6444
Emp Here 40
SIC 6021 National commercial banks

D-U-N-S 20-209-2446   (BR)
HOME DEPOT OF CANADA INC
HOME DEPOT
(*Suby of* The Home Depot Inc)
1069 Nicola Ave, Port Coquitlam, BC, V3B 8B2
(604) 468-3360
Emp Here 200
SIC 5251 Hardware stores

D-U-N-S 25-664-6183   (SL)
HOPE DISTRIBUTION & SALES INC
CANADIAN TIRE
2125 Hawkins St Suite 609, Port Coquitlam, BC, V3B 0G6
(604) 468-6951
Emp Here 60   *Sales* 4,304,681
SIC 5311 Department stores

D-U-N-S 24-027-6886   (BR)
HUDSON'S BAY COMPANY
HOME OUTFITTERS
985 Nicola Ave Suite 105, Port Coquitlam, BC, V3B 8B2
(604) 464-9506
Emp Here 32
SIC 5399 Miscellaneous general merchandise

D-U-N-S 25-318-0392   (BR)
LONDON LIFE INSURANCE COMPANY
FREEDOM 55 FINANCIAL GROUP
2755 Lougheed Hwy Suite 410, Port Coquitlam, BC, V3B 5Y9

Emp Here 20
SIC 6311 Life insurance

D-U-N-S 25-898-9060   (BR)
LONG & MCQUADE LIMITED
LONG & MCQUADE MUSICAL INSTRUMENTS
1360 Dominion Ave, Port Coquitlam, BC, V3B 8G7
(604) 464-1011
Emp Here 40
SIC 5736 Musical instrument stores

D-U-N-S 25-310-9243   (BR)
MCDONALD'S   RESTAURANTS   OF CANADA LIMITED
MCDONALD'S #21548
(*Suby of* McDonald's Corporation)
2330 Ottawa St, Port Coquitlam, BC, V3B 7Z1
(604) 552-6380
Emp Here 50
SIC 5812 Eating places

D-U-N-S 24-776-6033   (SL)
NOLEX ENTERPRISES LTD
INTERNATIONAL HOUSE OF PANCAKES #308
(*Suby of* Dineequity, Inc.)
2755 Lougheed Hwy Unit 42, Port Coquitlam, BC, V3B 5Y9

(604) 941-5345
Emp Here 30   *Sales* 875,528
SIC 5812 Eating places

D-U-N-S 20-646-5119   (BR)
PATTISON, JIM INDUSTRIES LTD
JIM PATTISON HYUNDAI COQUITLAM
2385 Ottawa St Unit B, Port Coquitlam, BC, V3B 8A4
(604) 552-1700
Emp Here 20
SIC 5511 New and used car dealers

D-U-N-S 20-590-6337   (BR)
SCHOOL DISTRICT NO. 43 (COQUITLAM)
KWAYHQUITLUM MIDDLE SCHOOL
3280 Flint St, Port Coquitlam, BC, V3B 4J2
(604) 942-1524
Emp Here 70
SIC 8211 Elementary and secondary schools

D-U-N-S 20-590-6352   (BR)
SCHOOL DISTRICT NO. 43 (COQUITLAM)
IRVINE ELEMENTARY SCHOOL
3862 Wellington St, Port Coquitlam, BC, V3B 3Z4
(604) 941-3408
Emp Here 42
SIC 8211 Elementary and secondary schools

D-U-N-S 20-713-4748   (BR)
SCHOOL DISTRICT NO. 43 (COQUITLAM)
BLAKEBURN ELEMENTARY SCHOOL
1040 Riverside Dr, Port Coquitlam, BC, V3B 8A7
(604) 944-9037
Emp Here 50
SIC 8211 Elementary and secondary schools

D-U-N-S 25-777-2855   (BR)
SCHOOL DISTRICT NO. 43 (COQUITLAM)
JAMES PARK ELEMENTARY SCHOOL
1761 Westminster Ave, Port Coquitlam, BC, V3B 1E5
(604) 942-6658
Emp Here 30
SIC 8211 Elementary and secondary schools

D-U-N-S 25-757-0002   (BR)
SCHOOL DISTRICT NO. 43 (COQUITLAM)
CEDAR DRIVE ELEMENTARY SCHOOL
3150 Cedar Dr, Port Coquitlam, BC, V3B 3C3
(604) 941-3481
Emp Here 31
SIC 8211 Elementary and secondary schools

D-U-N-S 20-047-0735   (BR)
SCHOOL DISTRICT NO. 43 (COQUITLAM)
LINCOLN ELEMENTARY SCHOOL
1019 Fernwood Ave, Port Coquitlam, BC, V3B 5A8
(604) 941-6144
Emp Here 25
SIC 8211 Elementary and secondary schools

D-U-N-S 25-451-3286   (BR)
SCHOOL DISTRICT NO. 43 (COQUITLAM)
TERRY FOX SECONDARY SCHOOL
1260 Riverwood Gate, Port Coquitlam, BC, V3B 7Z5
(604) 941-5401
Emp Here 95
SIC 8211 Elementary and secondary schools

D-U-N-S 20-037-4028   (BR)
SCHOOL DISTRICT NO. 43 (COQUITLAM)
MINNEKHADA MIDDLE SCHOOL
1390 Laurier Ave, Port Coquitlam, BC, V3B 2B8
(604) 942-0261
Emp Here 60
SIC 8211 Elementary and secondary schools

D-U-N-S 20-033-7868   (BR)
SCHOOL DISTRICT NO. 43 (COQUITLAM)
MAPLE CREEK MIDDLE SCHOOL
3700 Hastings St, Port Coquitlam, BC, V3B 5K7
(604) 464-8581
Emp Here 70

SIC 8211 Elementary and secondary schools

D-U-N-S 20-026-8907   (BR)
SCHOOL DISTRICT NO. 43 (COQUITLAM)
BIRCHLAND ELEMENTARY SCHOOL
1331 Fraser Ave, Port Coquitlam, BC, V3B 1M5
(604) 941-3428
Emp Here 20
SIC 8211 Elementary and secondary schools

D-U-N-S 20-026-8931   (BR)
SCHOOL DISTRICT NO. 43 (COQUITLAM)
WESTWOOD ELEMENTARY SCHOOL
3610 Hastings St, Port Coquitlam, BC, V3B 4N6
(604) 464-2421
Emp Here 30
SIC 8211 Elementary and secondary schools

Port Coquitlam, BC V3C
Greater Vancouver County

D-U-N-S 25-360-5158   (BR)
ADCO POWER LTD
SIMSON-MAXWELL
1605 Kebet Way, Port Coquitlam, BC, V3C 5W9
(604) 941-1002
Emp Here 50
SIC 4911 Electric services

D-U-N-S 25-231-6849   (BR)
BARTLE & GIBSON CO LTD
1458 Mustang Pl, Port Coquitlam, BC, V3C 6L2
(604) 941-7318
Emp Here 50
SIC 5074 Plumbing and heating equipment and supplies (hydronics)

D-U-N-S 24-418-0035   (BR)
BREWERS' DISTRIBUTOR LTD
(*Suby of* Brewers' Distributor Ltd)
1711 Kingsway Ave, Port Coquitlam, BC, V3C 0B6
(604) 927-4055
Emp Here 1,200
SIC 5181 Beer and ale

D-U-N-S 20-291-6599   (BR)
CANADA DRAYAGE INC
1375 Kingsway Ave, Port Coquitlam, BC, V3C 1S2
(604) 364-1454
Emp Here 40
SIC 4212 Local trucking, without storage

D-U-N-S 25-288-8888   (BR)
CANADA POST CORPORATION
PORT COQUITLAM DELIVERY CENTRE
1628 Industrial Ave, Port Coquitlam, BC, V3C 6N3
(604) 942-9112
Emp Here 100
SIC 4311 U.s. postal service

D-U-N-S 24-825-2249   (SL)
CANADIAN ELECTRO DRIVES (2009) LTD
CANADIAN ELECTRO DRIVES
1538 Kebet Way, Port Coquitlam, BC, V3C 5M5
(604) 468-8788
Emp Here 20   *Sales* 18,657,676
SIC 5063 Electrical apparatus and equipment
Pr Pr Keith Salchenberger
VP John Mcgill

D-U-N-S 20-588-8519   (BR)
CANADIAN PACIFIC RAILWAY COMPANY
CPR
1118 Coutts Way, Port Coquitlam, BC, V3C 6B6
(604) 944-7427
Emp Here 20
SIC 4011 Railroads, line-haul operating

D-U-N-S 24-558-9155   (SL)
DESIGN ROOFING & SHEET METAL LTD
1385 Kingsway Ave, Port Coquitlam, BC, V3C 1S2
(604) 944-2977
Emp Here 50   *Sales* 4,961,328
SIC 1761 Roofing, siding, and sheetMetal work

D-U-N-S 20-530-9458   (SL)
DUSO'S ENTERPRISES LTD
DUSO'S FINE FOODS
1625 Kebet Way Suite 200, Port Coquitlam, BC, V3C 5W9
(604) 464-8101
Emp Here 26   *Sales* 3,064,349
SIC 2098 Macaroni and spaghetti

D-U-N-S 24-363-1335   (SL)
DYNAMIC INSTALLATIONS INC
1225 Kingsway Ave Unit 3112, Port Coquitlam, BC, V3C 1S2
(604) 464-7695
Emp Here 50   *Sales* 5,909,817
SIC 3462 Iron and steel forgings
Pr Pr Luke Pretty

D-U-N-S 25-219-6522   (SL)
EAGLE RIDGE MECHANICAL CONTRACTING LTD
1515 Broadway St Suite 116, Port Coquitlam, BC, V3C 6M2
(604) 941-1071
Emp Here 50   *Sales* 4,377,642
SIC 1711 Plumbing, heating, air-conditioning

D-U-N-S 25-820-3165   (BR)
EARL'S RESTAURANTS LTD
EARL'S PORT COQUITLAM
(*Suby of* Earl's Restaurants Ltd)
2850 Shaughnessy St Suite 5100, Port Coquitlam, BC, V3C 6K5
(604) 941-1733
Emp Here 200
SIC 5812 Eating places

D-U-N-S 25-274-3042   (BR)
EMCO CORPORATION
1585 Kebet Way, Port Coquitlam, BC, V3C 6L5
(604) 464-6975
Emp Here 25
SIC 5074 Plumbing and heating equipment and supplies (hydronics)

D-U-N-S 20-104-6307   (HQ)
ESCO LIMITED
(*Suby of* Esco Corporation)
1855 Kingsway Ave, Port Coquitlam, BC, V3C 1T1
(604) 942-7261
Emp Here 190   *Emp Tctal* 5,200
Sales 51,291,372
SIC 3325 Steel foundries, nec
Pr Larry Huget

D-U-N-S 24-695-2394   (SL)
GILLNETTER PUB CO (1989) LTD
1864 Argue St, Port Coquitlam, BC, V3C 5K4
(604) 941-5599
Emp Here 50   *Sales* 1,824,018
SIC 5813 Drinking places

D-U-N-S 20-273-6591   (SL)
GLASTECH GLAZING CONTRACTORS LTD
1613 Kebet Way, Port Coquitlam, BC, V3C 5W9
(604) 941-9115
Emp Here 140   *Sales* 10,214,498
SIC 1793 Glass and glazing work
Pr Pr Warren Elmer
Mark Degoutiere

D-U-N-S 20-104-6489   (SL)
HARKEN TOWING CO. LTD
1990 Argue St, Port Coquitlam, BC, V3C 5K4
(604) 942-8511
Emp Here 70   *Sales* 4,231,721
SIC 7549 Automotive services, nec

D-U-N-S 25-072-9779   (BR)
INTERWRAP INC
1650 Broadway St Suite 101, Port Coquitlam, BC, V3C 2M8

Emp Here 130
SIC 3069 Fabricated rubber products, nec

D-U-N-S 24-931-7843   (HQ)
IOTRON INDUSTRIES CANADA INC
(Suby of Iotron Industries Canada Inc)
1425 Kebet Way, Port Coquitlam, BC, V3C 6L3
(604) 945-8838
Emp Here 20   Emp Total 65
Sales 6,219,371
SIC 8734 Testing laboratories
Lloyd Scott
John Macxay
Sol Rauch
Bruce Hynds
Norman Mack Ritchie

D-U-N-S 20-288-6560   (BR)
JYSK LINEN'N FURNITURE INC
1435 Broadway St, Port Coquitlam, BC, V3C 6L6
(604) 472-0722
Emp Here 50
SIC 5712 Furniture stores

D-U-N-S 20-915-3030   (HQ)
KONGSBERG MESOTECH LTD
1598 Kebet Way, Port Coquitlam, BC, V3C 5M5
(604) 464-8144
Emp Here 52   Emp Total 52
Sales 16,541,360
SIC 3812 Search and navigation equipment
Pr Nader Fiahi
Karen O'grady

D-U-N-S 25-321-7632   (BR)
LEVITT-SAFETY LIMITED
FIRE CODE PLUS
1611 Broadway St Unit 106, Port Coquitlam, BC, V3C 2M7
(604) 464-6332
Emp Here 20
SIC 5087 Service establishment equipment

D-U-N-S 24-620-0943   (BR)
LILYDALE INC
1910 Kingsway Ave, Port Coquitlam, BC, V3C 1S7
(604) 941-4041
Emp Here 400
SIC 2015 Poultry slaughtering and processing

D-U-N-S 24-164-6306   (SL)
MILLERS LANDING PUB LTD
CAT AND FiDDLE SPORTS BAR
1979 Brown St, Port Coquitlam, BC, V3C 2N4
(604) 941-8822
Emp Here 75   Sales 2,772,507
SIC 5813 Drinking places

D-U-N-S 25-110-0343   (BR)
POSTMEDIA NETWORK INC
VANNET DISTRIBUTION
1525 Broadway St Unit 115, Port Coquitlam, BC, V3C 6P6

Emp Here 50
SIC 2711 Newspapers

D-U-N-S 20-175-2602   (BR)
PRODUITS STANDARD INC
1680 Broadway St Suite 101, Port Coquitlam, BC, V3C 2M8
(604) 945-4550
Emp Here 20
SIC 7349 Building maintenance services, nec

D-U-N-S 20-281-5106   (BR)
RECOCHEM INC.
CONSUMER DIVISION
1745 Kingsway Ave, Port Coquitlam, BC, V3C 4P2

(604) 941-9404
Emp Here 45
SIC 2899 Chemical preparations, nec

D-U-N-S 20-700-6607   (BR)
REITMANS (CANADA) LIMITEE
2850 Shaughnessy St Suite 2103, Port Coquitlam, BC, V3C 6K5

Emp Here 25
SIC 5621 Women's clothing stores

D-U-N-S 20-003-4192   (BR)
ROYAL BANK OF CANADA
RBC
(Suby of Royal Bank Of Canada)
2581 Shaughnessy St, Port Coquitlam, BC, V3C 3G3
(604) 927-5500
Emp Here 25
SIC 6021 National commercial banks

D-U-N-S 24-391-1257   (HQ)
RYDER CONTAINER TERMINALS
(Suby of Ryder Container Terminals)
1275 Kingsway Ave, Port Coquitlam, BC, V3C 1S2
(604) 941-0266
Emp Here 90   Emp Total 115
Sales 33,660,800
SIC 4731 Freight transportation arrangement
Christopher Woodward

D-U-N-S 24-561-3539   (BR)
SMS EQUIPMENT INC
CONECO EQUIPMENT
1923 Mclean Ave, Port Coquitlam, BC, V3C 1N1
(604) 941-6611
Emp Here 50
SIC 5082 Construction and mining machinery

D-U-N-S 20-157-2091   (BR)
SCHOOL DISTRICT NO. 43 (COQUITLAM)
HAZEL TREMBATH ELEMENTARY SCHOOL
1278 Confederation Dr, Port Coquitlam, BC, V3C 6L9
(604) 941-0517
Emp Here 30
SIC 8211 Elementary and secondary schools

D-U-N-S 25-757-0010   (BR)
SCHOOL DISTRICT NO. 43 (COQUITLAM)
CITADEL MIDDLE SCHOOL
1265 Citadel Dr, Port Coquitlam, BC, V3C 5X6
(604) 945-6187
Emp Here 50
SIC 8211 Elementary and secondary schools

D-U-N-S 20-033-7587   (BR)
SCHOOL DISTRICT NO. 43 (COQUITLAM)
KILMER ELEMENTARY SCHOOL
1575 Knappen St, Port Coquitlam, BC, V3C 2P8
(604) 941-3401
Emp Here 35
SIC 8211 Elementary and secondary schools

D-U-N-S 20-705-0100   (BR)
SCHOOL DISTRICT NO. 43 (COQUITLAM)
MAINTAINANCE SHOP
1982 Kingsway Ave, Port Coquitlam, BC, V3C 1S5
(604) 941-5643
Emp Here 80
SIC 8211 Elementary and secondary schools

D-U-N-S 20-020-8705   (BR)
SCHOOL DISTRICT NO. 43 (COQUITLAM)
RIVERSIDE SECONDARY SCHOOL
2215 Reeve St, Port Coquitlam, BC, V3C 6K8
(604) 941-6053
Emp Here 130
SIC 8211 Elementary and secondary schools

D-U-N-S 20-979-0158   (BR)
SCHOOL DISTRICT NO. 43 (COQUITLAM)
CASTLE PARK ELEMENTARY SCHOOL
1144 Confederation Dr, Port Coquitlam, BC,

V3C 6P1
(604) 468-8620
Emp Here 35
SIC 8211 Elementary and secondary schools

D-U-N-S 20-590-6287   (BR)
SCHOOL DISTRICT NO. 43 (COQUITLAM)
CENTRAL COMMUNITY ELEMENTARY SCHOOL
2260 Central Ave, Port Coquitlam, BC, V3C 1V8
(604) 941-0355
Emp Here 25
SIC 8211 Elementary and secondary schools

D-U-N-S 20-020-1528   (BR)
SCHOOL DISTRICT NO. 43 (COQUITLAM)
PITT RIVER MIDDLE SCHOOL
2070 Tyner St, Port Coquitlam, BC, V3C 2Z1
(604) 464-0207
Emp Here 50
SIC 8211 Elementary and secondary schools

D-U-N-S 20-713-4649   (BR)
SCHOOL DISTRICT NO. 43 (COQUITLAM)
MARY HILL ELEMENTARY SCHOOL
1890 Humber Cres, Port Coquitlam, BC, V3C 2V7
(604) 942-0264
Emp Here 40
SIC 8211 Elementary and secondary schools

D-U-N-S 25-195-6124   (BR)
SEARS CANADA INC
1488 Coast Meridian Rd, Port Coquitlam, BC, V3C 6P7
(604) 468-5149
Emp Here 150
SIC 5399 Miscellaneous general merchandise

D-U-N-S 25-664-1838   (BR)
SOBEYS WEST INC
SHAUGHNESSY SAFEWAY
2850 Shaughnessy St Suite 1100, Port Coquitlam, BC, V3C 6K5
(604) 945-7018
Emp Here 50
SIC 5411 Grocery stores

D-U-N-S 20-734-1012   (BR)
STARBUCKS COFFEE CANADA, INC
STARBUCKS
(Suby of Starbucks Corporation)
2564 Shaughnessy St Suite 101, Port Coquitlam, BC, V3C 3G4
(604) 552-0674
Emp Here 50
SIC 5812 Eating places

D-U-N-S 20-294-4963   (BR)
STERICYCLE, ULC
1407 Kebet Way Unit 100, Port Coquitlam, BC, V3C 6L3
(604) 552-1011
Emp Here 30
SIC 4953 Refuse systems

D-U-N-S 24-345-0041   (BR)
SYSCO CANADA, INC
SYSCO VANCOUVER
(Suby of Sysco Corporation)
1346 Kingsway Ave, Port Coquitlam, BC, V3C 6G4
(604) 944-4410
Emp Here 500
SIC 5141 Groceries, general line

D-U-N-S 20-735-8909   (BR)
WENDY'S RESTAURANTS OF CANADA INC
WENDY'S INTERWEST RESTAURANT
(Suby of The Wendy's Company)
1320 Kingsway Ave, Port Coquitlam, BC, V3C 6P4
(604) 468-8840
Emp Here 40
SIC 5812 Eating places

D-U-N-S 20-117-3192   (SL)
WESTERN SCALE CO LTD

1670 Kingsway Ave, Port Coquitlam, BC, V3C 3Y9
(604) 941-3474
Emp Here 55   Sales 3,210,271
SIC 3596 Scales and balances, except laboratory

D-U-N-S 25-190-5803   (SL)
ZCL DUALAM INC
(Suby of ZCL Composites Inc)
1620 Kingsway Ave, Port Coquitlam, BC, V3C 3Y9

Emp Here 35   Sales 2,512,128
SIC 3732 Boatbuilding and repairing

Port Hardy, BC V0N
Mount Waddington County

D-U-N-S 20-798-0108   (BR)
BRITISH COLUMBIA FERRY SERVICES INC
BC FERRIES
6800 Hwy 19, Port Hardy, BC, V0N 2P0
(877) 223-8778
Emp Here 29
SIC 4482 Ferries

D-U-N-S 25-316-9908   (SL)
CARD'S AQUACULTURE PRODUCTS (B.C.) LTD
(Suby of Badinotti Net Services Canada Ltd)
8300 Bing Rd, Port Hardy, BC, V0N 2P0

Emp Here 25   Sales 8,420,350
SIC 2399 Fabricated textile products, nec
Pr Pr Rod Card
Opers Mgr David Craig

D-U-N-S 25-329-1553   (BR)
MARINE HARVEST CANADA INC
(Suby of Marine Harvest North America Inc)
7200 Cohoe Rd, Port Hardy, BC, V0N 2P0
(250) 949-9699
Emp Here 150
SIC 2091 Canned and cured fish and seafoods

D-U-N-S 24-750-0432   (BR)
PACIFIC COASTAL AIRLINES LIMITED
(Suby of Pacific Coastal Airlines Limited)
3675 Byng Rd, Port Hardy, BC, V0N 2P0
(250) 949-6353
Emp Here 20
SIC 4512 Air transportation, scheduled

D-U-N-S 20-591-2269   (BR)
SCHOOL DISTRICT NO 85 (VANCOUVER ISLAND NORTH)
EAGLE VIEW ELEMENTARY SCHOOL
9050 Seaview St, Port Hardy, BC, V0N 2P0
(250) 949-6418
Emp Here 25
SIC 8211 Elementary and secondary schools

D-U-N-S 25-266-8801   (BR)
SCHOOL DISTRICT NO 85 (VANCOUVER ISLAND NORTH)
PORT HARDY SECONDARY SCHOOL
9350 Granfell St, Port Hardy, BC, V0N 2P0
(250) 949-7443
Emp Here 40
SIC 8211 Elementary and secondary schools

D-U-N-S 25-325-8677   (BR)
VANCOUVER ISLAND HEALTH AUTHORITY
EAGLE RIDGE MANOR
9120 Grandville St, Port Hardy, BC, V0N 2P0
(250) 902-6043
Emp Here 57
SIC 8011 Offices and clinics of medical doctors

D-U-N-S 24-348-4636   (BR)

VANCOUVER ISLAND HEALTH AUTHORITY
PORT HARDY HEALTH UNIT
7070 Market St, Port Hardy, BC, V0N 2P0
(250) 902-6071
Emp Here 20
SIC 8011 Offices and clinics of medical doctors

D-U-N-S 24-552-4418   (SL)
WALKUS, JAMES FISHING CO. LTD
Gd, Port Hardy, BC, V0N 2P0
(250) 949-7223
Emp Here 50   *Sales* 4,231,721
SIC 7032 Sporting and recreational camps

Port Mcneill, BC V0N
Mount Waddington County

D-U-N-S 25-071-3716   (SL)
ENGLEWOOD PACKING COMPANY LTD
Gd, Port Mcneill, BC, V0N 2R0

Emp Here 130   *Sales* 16,600,320
SIC 2091 Canned and cured fish and seafoods
Pr Pr Don Millerd

D-U-N-S 24-087-2767   (SL)
ORCA SAND & GRAVEL LTD
6505 Island Hwy, Port Mcneill, BC, V0N 2R0
(604) 628-3353
Emp Here 20   *Sales* 1,824,018
SIC 1442 Construction sand and gravel

D-U-N-S 20-035-7098   (BR)
SCHOOL DISTRICT NO 85 (VANCOUVER ISLAND NORTH)
SUNSET ELEMENTARY SCHOOL
2433 Mountainview Cres, Port Mcneill, BC, V0N 2R0
(250) 956-4434
Emp Here 35
SIC 8211 Elementary and secondary schools

D-U-N-S 20-591-2228   (BR)
SCHOOL DISTRICT NO 85 (VANCOUVER ISLAND NORTH)
NORTH ISLAND SECONDARY SCHOOL
2071 Mcneill Rd, Port Mcneill, BC, V0N 2R0
(250) 956-3394
Emp Here 25
SIC 8211 Elementary and secondary schools

D-U-N-S 24-032-4137   (SL)
SIMPSON PRIVATE HOSPITAL 1968 LTD
8838 Glover Rd, Port Mcneill, BC, V0N 2R0
(604) 888-0711
Emp Here 45   *Sales* 5,072,500
SIC 8069 Specialty hospitals, except psychiatric
Pr Pr Ernie Beaudin

D-U-N-S 24-311-7301   (HQ)
WEST COAST HELICOPTERS MAINTENANCE AND CONTRACTING LTD
WEST COAST HELICOPTERS
(*Suby* of 600690 British Columbia Ltd)
1011 Airport Rd, Port Mcneill, BC, V0N 2R0
(250) 956-2244
Emp Here 20   *Emp Total* 35
Sales 6,858,306
SIC 4522 Air transportation, nonscheduled
Pr Pr Granger Avery
Peter Barratt
Terrence Dean Eissfeldt

Port Mellon, BC V0N
Sunshine Coast County

D-U-N-S 20-739-0589   (BR)
INTERFOR CORPORATION

Pt Mellon Hwy, Port Mellon, BC, V0N 2S0
(604) 884-5300
Emp Here 40
SIC 2411 Logging

Port Moody, BC V3H
Greater Vancouver County

D-U-N-S 24-228-1009   (BR)
177293 CANADA LTD
PETRO-CANADA
Gd, Port Moody, BC, V3H 3E1
(604) 933-2641
Emp Here 20
SIC 1311 Crude petroleum and natural gas

D-U-N-S 20-852-9235   (BR)
BRITISH COLUMBIA HYDRO AND POWER AUTHORITY
BC HYDRO
Gd, Port Moody, BC, V3H 3C8
(604) 469-6100
Emp Here 25
SIC 4911 Electric services

D-U-N-S 25-288-8920   (BR)
CANADA POST CORPORATION
PORT MOODY DEPOT
45 Mary St, Port Moody, BC, V3H 9X9
(604) 936-5515
Emp Here 31
SIC 4311 U.s. postal service

D-U-N-S 20-282-1666   (BR)
CERTISPEC SERVICES INC
2813 Murray St, Port Moody, BC, V3H 1X3
(604) 469-9180
Emp Here 64
SIC 8734 Testing laboratories

D-U-N-S 20-097-7387   (BR)
IMPERIAL OIL LIMITED
(*Suby* of Exxon Mobil Corporation)
2225 Ioco Rd, Port Moody, BC, V3H 3C8
(604) 469-8300
Emp Here 20
SIC 2911 Petroleum refining

D-U-N-S 20-136-6163   (BR)
IRWIN, DICK GROUP LTD, THE
WESTWOOD HONDA
2400 Barnet Hwy, Port Moody, BC, V3H 1W3
(604) 461-0633
Emp Here 50
SIC 5511 New and used car dealers

D-U-N-S 20-353-3851   (BR)
IRWIN, DICK GROUP LTD, THE
WESTWOOD HONDA PARTS & ACCESSORIES
2400 Barnet Hwy, Port Moody, BC, V3H 1W3
(604) 461-3326
Emp Here 60
SIC 5511 New and used car dealers

D-U-N-S 20-646-6596   (SL)
JON WOOD
ROYAL LEPAGE SHOWCASE PLUS
3137 St Johns St, Port Moody, BC, V3H 2C8

Emp Here 80   *Sales* 7,514,952
SIC 6531 Real estate agents and managers
Mgr Paul Degraaf

D-U-N-S 20-173-8895   (SL)
REICHHOLD INDUSTRIES LIMITED
50 Douglas St, Port Moody, BC, V3H 3L9
(604) 939-1181
Emp Here 40   *Sales* 16,416,158
SIC 2821 Plastics materials and resins
Dir Lee Forester

D-U-N-S 25-128-5847   (BR)
SCHOOL DISTRICT NO. 43 (COQUITLAM)
MOUNTAIN MEADOWS ELEMENTARY

999 Noons Creek Dr, Port Moody, BC, V3H 4N3
(604) 469-2238
Emp Here 20
SIC 8211 Elementary and secondary schools

D-U-N-S 20-653-2710   (BR)
SCHOOL DISTRICT NO. 43 (COQUITLAM)
ASPENWOOD ELEMENTARY SCHOOL
2001 Panorama Dr, Port Moody, BC, V3H 5G8
(604) 461-7680
Emp Here 33
SIC 8211 Elementary and secondary schools

D-U-N-S 25-756-9970   (BR)
SCHOOL DISTRICT NO. 43 (COQUITLAM)
PLEASANTSIDE ELEMENTARY SCHOOL
195 Barber St, Port Moody, BC, V3H 3A8
(604) 469-9288
Emp Here 23
SIC 8211 Elementary and secondary schools

D-U-N-S 25-756-9996   (BR)
SCHOOL DISTRICT NO. 43 (COQUITLAM)
SEA VIEW COMMUNITY SCHOOL
1215 Cecile Dr, Port Moody, BC, V3H 1N2
(604) 936-9991
Emp Here 26
SIC 8211 Elementary and secondary schools

D-U-N-S 25-266-8017   (BR)
SCHOOL DISTRICT NO. 43 (COQUITLAM)
MOODY MIDDLE SCHOOL
3115 St Johns St, Port Moody, BC, V3H 2C6
(604) 461-7384
Emp Here 30
SIC 8211 Elementary and secondary schools

D-U-N-S 25-745-6327   (BR)
SCHOOL DISTRICT NO. 43 (COQUITLAM)
PORT MOODY SECONDARY SCHOOL
300 Albert St, Port Moody, BC, V3H 2M5
(604) 939-6656
Emp Here 125
SIC 8211 Elementary and secondary schools

D-U-N-S 20-713-4623   (BR)
SCHOOL DISTRICT NO. 43 (COQUITLAM)
ECOLE GLENAYRE ELEMENTARY SCHOOL
495 Glencoe Dr, Port Moody, BC, V3H 1G6
(604) 939-9214
Emp Here 50
SIC 8211 Elementary and secondary schools

D-U-N-S 20-156-9881   (BR)
SCHOOL DISTRICT NO. 43 (COQUITLAM)
SEAVIEW COMMUNITY SCHOOL
1215 Cecile Dr, Port Moody, BC, V3H 1N2
(604) 936-9991
Emp Here 21
SIC 8351 Child day care services

D-U-N-S 20-713-4763   (BR)
SCHOOL DISTRICT NO. 43 (COQUITLAM)
HERITAGE WOODS SECONDARY SCHOOL
1300 David Ave, Port Moody, BC, V3H 5K6
(604) 461-8679
Emp Here 100
SIC 8211 Elementary and secondary schools

D-U-N-S 25-926-4588   (BR)
SCHOOL DISTRICT NO. 43 (COQUITLAM)
HERITAGE MOUNTAIN ELEMENTARY SCHOOL
125 Ravine Dr, Port Moody, BC, V3H 4Z1
(604) 469-6407
Emp Here 30
SIC 8211 Elementary and secondary schools

D-U-N-S 20-104-8485   (BR)
SUNCOR ENERGY INC
1154 Glenayre Dr, Port Moody, BC, V3H 1J7
(604) 933-3000
Emp Here 55
SIC 5171 Petroleum bulk stations and terminals

Pouce Coupe, BC V0C
Peace River - Laird County

D-U-N-S 20-978-2361   (BR)
CARIBOU ROAD SERVICES LTD
CRS
5201 52nd Ave, Pouce Coupe, BC, V0C 2C0
(250) 786-5440
Emp Here 80
SIC 5082 Construction and mining machinery

D-U-N-S 20-287-5761   (SL)
KIKINAW ENERGY SERVICES LTD
12069 207 Rd, Pouce Coupe, BC, V0C 2C0
(250) 787-0152
Emp Here 80   *Sales* 6,930,008
SIC 7363 Help supply services

D-U-N-S 20-650-3414   (SL)
POUCE COUPE CARE HOME
5216 50 Ave, Pouce Coupe, BC, V0C 2C0

Emp Here 50   *Sales* 2,334,742
SIC 8059 Nursing and personal care, nec

Powell River, BC V8A
Powell River County

D-U-N-S 25-297-0439   (BR)
BANK OF NOVA SCOTIA, THE
SCOTIABANK
7030 Alberni St, Powell River, BC, V8A 2C3
(604) 485-3175
Emp Here 20
SIC 6021 National commercial banks

D-U-N-S 20-064-2804   (BR)
BOARD OF SCHOOL TRUSTEE OF SCHOOL DISTRICT NO. 47 (POWELL RIVER)
BOARD OF SCHOOL TRUSTEE OF SCHOOL DISTRICT NO. 47 (POWELLL RIVER)
7105 Nootka St, Powell River, BC, V8A 5E3
(604) 485-2756
Emp Here 40
SIC 8211 Elementary and secondary schools

D-U-N-S 20-030-5840   (BR)
BOARD OF SCHOOL TRUSTEE OF SCHOOL DISTRICT NO. 47 (POWELL RIVER)
BOARD OF SCHOOL TRUSTEE OF SCHOOL DISTRICT NO. 47 (POWELLL RIVER)
7312 Abbotsford St, Powell River, BC, V8A 2G5
(604) 485-6164
Emp Here 30
SIC 8211 Elementary and secondary schools

D-U-N-S 20-034-7842   (BR)
BOARD OF SCHOOL TRUSTEE OF SCHOOL DISTRICT NO. 47 (POWELL RIVER)
BOARD OF SCHOOL TRUSTEE OF SCHOOL DISTRICT NO. 47 (POWELLL RIVER)
5400 Marine Ave, Powell River, BC, V8A 2L6
(604) 483-3171
Emp Here 80
SIC 8211 Elementary and secondary schools

D-U-N-S 20-027-0085   (BR)
BOARD OF SCHOOL TRUSTEE OF SCHOOL DISTRICT NO. 47 (POWELLL RIVER)
GRIEF POINT ELEMENTARY SCHOOL
6960 Quesnel St, Powell River, BC, V8A 1J2
(604) 485-5660
Emp Here 30
SIC 8211 Elementary and secondary schools

D-U-N-S 20-027-0721 (BR)
BOARD OF SCHOOL TRUSTEE OF SCHOOL DISTRICT NO. 47 (POWERLL RIVER)
HENDERSON ELEMENTARY SCHOOL
5506 Willow Ave, Powell River, BC, V8A 4P4
(604) 483-9162
Emp Here 25
SIC 8211 Elementary and secondary schools

D-U-N-S 20-027-0739 (BR)
BOARD OF SCHOOL TRUSTEE OF SCHOOL DISTRICT NO. 47 (POWERLL RIVER)
JAMES THOMSON ELEMENTARY SCHOOL
6388 Sutherland Ave, Powell River, BC, V8A 4W4
(604) 483-3191
Emp Here 20
SIC 8211 Elementary and secondary schools

D-U-N-S 25-288-9001 (BR)
CANADA POST CORPORATION
4812 Joyce Ave, Powell River, BC, V8A 3B8
(604) 485-0281
Emp Here 34
SIC 4311 U.s. postal service

D-U-N-S 24-347-2458 (BR)
CATALYST PAPER CORPORATION
POWELL RIVER MILL
5775 Ash Ave, Powell River, BC, V8A 4R3
(604) 483-3722
Emp Here 441
SIC 2621 Paper mills

D-U-N-S 24-060-0705 (BR)
COAST REALTY GROUP LTD
4766 Joyce Ave, Powell River, BC, V8A 3B6
(604) 414-7441
Emp Here 30
SIC 6531 Real estate agents and managers

D-U-N-S 20-065-9477 (SL)
PEAK PUBLISHING LTD
POWELL RIVER PEAK
4400 Marine Ave Unit 102, Powell River, BC, V8A 2K1
(604) 485-5313
Emp Here 25   *Sales* 2,042,900
SIC 2711 Newspapers

D-U-N-S 25-651-4068 (BR)
ROYAL BANK OF CANADA
RBC
(*Suby of* Royal Bank Of Canada)
7035 Barnet St Suite 101, Powell River, BC, V8A 1Z9
(604) 485-7991
Emp Here 24
SIC 6021 National commercial banks

D-U-N-S 25-271-7327 (BR)
SOBEYS WEST INC
SAFEWAY DIV OF
7040 Barnet St, Powell River, BC, V8A 2A1
(604) 485-4244
Emp Here 80
SIC 5411 Grocery stores

D-U-N-S 24-455-5061 (BR)
VANCOUVER COASTAL HEALTH AUTHORITY
OLIVE DEVAUD RESIDENCE
7105 Kemano St, Powell River, BC, V8A 1L8
(604) 485-9868
Emp Here 205
SIC 8361 Residential care

D-U-N-S 25-964-0514 (BR)
VANCOUVER ISLAND UNIVERSITY
7085 Nootka St Unit 100, Powell River, BC, V8A 3C6
(604) 485-8043
Emp Here 50
SIC 8221 Colleges and universities

D-U-N-S 25-294-7866 (BR)
WAL-MART CANADA CORP

WAL-MART
7100 Alberni St Suite 23, Powell River, BC, V8A 5K9
(604) 485-9811
Emp Here 110
SIC 5311 Department stores

Prespatou, BC V0C

D-U-N-S 20-653-4062 (BR)
SCHOOL DISTRICT NO. 60 (PEACE RIVER NORTH)
PRESPATOU SCHOOL
22113 Triad Rd, Prespatou, BC, V0C 2S0
(250) 630-2241
Emp Here 26
SIC 8211 Elementary and secondary schools

Prince George, BC V2K
Fraser-Fort George County

D-U-N-S 20-194-5784 (BR)
ANDRITZ AUTOMATION LTD
556 North Nechako Rd Suite 205, Prince George, BC, V2K 1A1
(250) 564-3381
Emp Here 30
SIC 8748 Business consulting, nec

D-U-N-S 20-027-0846 (BR)
BOARD OF EDUCATION OF SCHOOL DISTRICT NO. 57 (PRINCE GEORGE), THE
HART HIGHLANDS ELEMENTARY SCHOOL
(*Suby of* Board of Education of School District No. 57 (Prince George), The)
2233 Sussex Lane, Prince George, BC, V2K 3J1
(250) 962-9211
Emp Here 25
SIC 8211 Elementary and secondary schools

D-U-N-S 20-027-0770 (BR)
BOARD OF EDUCATION OF SCHOOL DISTRICT NO. 57 (PRINCE GEORGE), THE
AUSTIN ROAD ELEMENTARY SCHOOL
(*Suby of* Board of Education of School District No. 57 (Prince George), The)
4543 Austin Rd W, Prince George, BC, V2K 2H9
Emp Here 40
SIC 8211 Elementary and secondary schools

D-U-N-S 25-415-4685 (BR)
BOARD OF EDUCATION OF SCHOOL DISTRICT NO. 57 (PRINCE GEORGE), THE
CEDARS CHRISTIAN SCHOOL
(*Suby of* Board of Education of School District No. 57 (Prince George), The)
701 North Nechako Rd, Prince George, BC, V2K 1A2
(250) 564-0707
Emp Here 25
SIC 8211 Elementary and secondary schools

D-U-N-S 20-591-4497 (BR)
BOARD OF EDUCATION OF SCHOOL DISTRICT NO. 57 (PRINCE GEORGE), THE
HEATHER PARK MIDDLE SCHOOL
(*Suby of* Board of Education of School District No. 57 (Prince George), The)
7151 Heather Park Rd, Prince George, BC, V2K 5Y3
(250) 962-1811
Emp Here 60
SIC 8211 Elementary and secondary schools

D-U-N-S 20-230-6135 (BR)
BOARD OF EDUCATION OF SCHOOL DISTRICT NO. 57 (PRINCE GEORGE), THE
EDGEWOOD ELEMENTARY SCHOOL
(*Suby of* Board of Education of School District

No. 57 (Prince George), The)
4440 Craig Dr, Prince George, BC, V2K 3P5
(250) 562-5381
Emp Here 30
SIC 8211 Elementary and secondary schools

D-U-N-S 20-034-2629 (BR)
BOARD OF EDUCATION OF SCHOOL DISTRICT NO. 57 (PRINCE GEORGE), THE
SPRINGWOOD ELEMENTARY SCHOOL
(*Suby of* Board of Education of School District No. 57 (Prince George), The)
4600 Zral Rd, Prince George, BC, V2K 5X9
(250) 962-6966
Emp Here 22
SIC 8211 Elementary and secondary schools

D-U-N-S 25-484-1265 (BR)
BOARD OF EDUCATION OF SCHOOL DISTRICT NO. 57 (PRINCE GEORGE), THE
KELLY ROAD SECONDARY SCHOOL
(*Suby of* Board of Education of School District No. 57 (Prince George), The)
4540 Handlen Rd, Prince George, BC, V2K 2J8
(250) 962-9271
Emp Here 130
SIC 8211 Elementary and secondary schools

D-U-N-S 24-365-8882 (BR)
CANADIAN FOREST PRODUCTS LTD
CANFOR-NORTHWOOD PULP MILL
5353 Northwood Pulpmill Rd, Prince George, BC, V2K 5R8
(250) 962-3828
Emp Here 20
SIC 2421 Sawmills and planing mills, general

D-U-N-S 20-810-7628 (SL)
CENTRAL INTERIOR PIPING & MAINTENANCE LTD
CIP
7405 Hart Hwy Suite 1, Prince George, BC, V2K 3B1
(250) 962-7405
Emp Here 50   *Sales* 4,377,642
SIC 1799 Special trade contractors, nec

D-U-N-S 20-555-8260 (BR)
CLEAN HARBORS ENERGY AND INDUSTRIAL SERVICES CORP.
405 Mcaloney Rd Suite 1, Prince George, BC, V2K 4L2
(250) 563-5882
Emp Here 20
SIC 7349 Building maintenance services, nec

D-U-N-S 20-915-4371 (BR)
DIVERSIFIED TRANSPORTATION LTD
PACIFIC WESTERN TRANSPORTATION
391 North Nechako Rd, Prince George, BC, V2K 4K8
(250) 563-5431
Emp Here 113
SIC 4142 Bus charter service, except local

D-U-N-S 24-313-1823 (SL)
EXCEL TRANSPORTATION ALBERTA INC
333 Ongman Rd, Prince George, BC, V2K 4K9
(250) 563-7356
Emp Here 250   *Sales* 25,537,116
SIC 4212 Local trucking, without storage
Pr Roy Dondale

D-U-N-S 20-361-4102 (SL)
GEOTECH DRILLING SERVICES AFRICA LTD
5052 Hartway Dr, Prince George, BC, V2K 5B7
(250) 962-9041
Emp Here 100   *Sales* 2,366,864
SIC 1781 Water well drilling

D-U-N-S 25-771-7918 (BR)
GOLDEN ARCH FOOD SERVICES LTD
MCDONALD'S
(*Suby of* Golden Arch Food Services Ltd)

6777 Hart Hwy, Prince George, BC, V2K 3A5
(250) 962-8281
Emp Here 20
SIC 5812 Eating places

D-U-N-S 20-921-2260 (BR)
HUSKY ENERGY INC
2542 Prince George Pulpmill Rd, Prince George, BC, V2K 5P5
(250) 960-2500
Emp Here 80
SIC 1311 Crude petroleum and natural gas

D-U-N-S 25-107-9299 (SL)
LHEIT LIT'EN DEVELOPMENT CORPORATION
(*Suby of* Lheidli T'enneh Band)
1041 Whenun Rd, Prince George, BC, V2K 5X8
(250) 963-8451
Emp Here 22   *Sales* 1,167,371
SIC 7999 Amusement and recreation, nec

D-U-N-S 20-510-2791 (HQ)
NORTHERN LINEN SUPPLY LTD
NORTHERN LINEN & UNIFORM SUPPLY
(*Suby of* Northern Linen Supply Ltd)
3902 Kenworth Rd E, Prince George, BC, V2K 1P2
(250) 962-6900
Emp Here 50   *Emp Total* 51
Sales 1,459,214
SIC 7216 Drycleaning plants, except rugs

D-U-N-S 24-724-0146 (BR)
PACIFIC WESTERN BREWING COMPANY LTD
641 North Nechako Rd, Prince George, BC, V2K 4M4
(250) 562-2424
Emp Here 50
SIC 2082 Malt beverages

D-U-N-S 25-320-8748 (BR)
PUROLATOR INC.
PUROLATOR INC
429 Mcaloney Rd, Prince George, BC, V2K 4L2
(800) 528-0858
Emp Here 20
SIC 4731 Freight transportation arrangement

D-U-N-S 20-818-7448 (BR)
RUSKIN CONSTRUCTION LTD
(*Suby of* Northern Linkwell Construction Ltd)
2011 Pg Pulp Mill Road, Prince George, BC, V2K 5P5
(604) 331-1032
Emp Here 50
SIC 1541 Industrial buildings and warehouses

Prince George, BC V2L
Fraser-Fort George County

D-U-N-S 25-771-7462 (BR)
A & W FOOD SERVICES OF CANADA INC
A & W RESTAURANTS
1716 20th Ave, Prince George, BC, V2L 4B8
(250) 564-2311
Emp Here 25
SIC 5812 Eating places

D-U-N-S 20-304-2619 (BR)
AWG NORTHERN INDUSTRIES INC
ALL-WEST GLASS PRINCE GEORGE
1011 Victoria St, Prince George, BC, V2L 0C8
(250) 563-1555
Emp Here 35
SIC 8741 Management services

D-U-N-S 20-267-7894 (SL)
AMCO WHOLESALE
(*Suby of* Northern Hardware & Furniture Co., Ltd)
1030 2nd Ave, Prince George, BC, V2L 3A9

(250) 564-4451
Emp Here 45   *Sales* 5,559,741
SIC 5251 Hardware stores
Owner Kelly Green

D-U-N-S 20-873-2458   (SL)
AUTOCANADA NORTHLAND MOTORS GP INC
NORTHLAND HYUNDAI
2021 Highway 16 W, Prince George, BC, V2L 0A4
(250) 564-6663
Emp Here 28   *Sales* 10,214,498
SIC 5511 New and used car dealers
Pr Steven Landry

D-U-N-S 25-297-0231   (BR)
BANK OF NOVA SCOTIA, THE
SCOTIABANK
390 Victoria St, Prince George, BC, V2L 4X4
(250) 960-4700
Emp Here 25
SIC 6021 National commercial banks

D-U-N-S 24-114-5684   (BR)
BANQUE TORONTO-DOMINION, LA
TORONTO-DOMINION BANK, THE
(*Suby of* Toronto-Dominion Bank, The)
400 Victoria St Suite 390, Prince George, BC, V2L 2J7
(250) 614-2950
Emp Here 25
SIC 6021 National commercial banks

D-U-N-S 20-621-9032   (BR)
BEKINS MOVING & STORAGE (CANADA) LTD
BEKINS CANTINS
551 1st Ave, Prince George, BC, V2L 2Y2
(250) 563-0371
Emp Here 50
SIC 4213 Trucking, except local

D-U-N-S 20-030-5659   (BR)
BOARD OF EDUCATION OF SCHOOL DISTRICT NO. 57 (PRINCE GEORGE), THE
RON BRENT ELEMENTARY SCHOOL
(*Suby of* Board of Education of School District No. 57 (Prince George), The)
1401 17th Ave, Prince George, BC, V2L 3Z2
(250) 562-2737
Emp Here 38
SIC 8211 Elementary and secondary schools

D-U-N-S 20-713-5158   (BR)
BOARD OF EDUCATION OF SCHOOL DISTRICT NO. 57 (PRINCE GEORGE), THE
CARNEY HILL ELEMENTARY SCHOOL
(*Suby of* Board of Education of School District No. 57 (Prince George), The)
2579 Victoria St, Prince George, BC, V2L 2M3
(250) 562-4843
Emp Here 30
SIC 8211 Elementary and secondary schools

D-U-N-S 25-361-8524   (BR)
BOARD OF EDUCATION OF SCHOOL DISTRICT NO. 57 (PRINCE GEORGE), THE
VAN BIEN ELEMENTARY SHOOL
(*Suby of* Board of Education of School District No. 57 (Prince George), The)
311 Wilson Cres, Prince George, BC, V2L 4P8
(250) 563-1062
Emp Here 27
SIC 8211 Elementary and secondary schools

D-U-N-S 24-152-8645   (HQ)
BOARD OF EDUCATION OF SCHOOL DISTRICT NO. 57 (PRINCE GEORGE), THE
(*Suby of* Board of Education of School District No. 57 (Prince George), The)
2100 Ferry Ave, Prince George, BC, V2L 4R5
(250) 561-6800
Emp Here 120   *Emp Total* 2,300
Sales 198,454,487
SIC 8211 Elementary and secondary schools
Treas Bryan Mix
Superintnt Dick Chamber

D-U-N-S 20-591-4364   (BR)
BOARD OF EDUCATION OF SCHOOL DISTRICT NO. 57 (PRINCE GEORGE), THE
ECOLE DUSHCESS PARK SECONDAIRE
(*Suby of* Board of Education of School District No. 57 (Prince George), The)
747 Winnipeg St, Prince George, BC, V2L 2V3
(250) 563-7124
Emp Here 100
SIC 8211 Elementary and secondary schools

D-U-N-S 20-747-8483   (BR)
CANADIAN FOREST PRODUCTS LTD
5162 Northwood Pulp Mill Rd, Prince George, BC, V2L 4W2
(250) 962-3500
Emp Here 200
SIC 2421 Sawmills and planing mills, general

D-U-N-S 25-785-5387   (BR)
CANADIAN IMPERIAL BANK OF COMMERCE
CIBC BANKING CENTRE
1410 3rd Ave, Prince George, BC, V2L 3G2
(250) 614-6444
Emp Here 30
SIC 6021 National commercial banks

D-U-N-S 25-015-0059   (BR)
CENTRAL 1 CREDIT UNION
SPRUCE CREDIT UNION
(*Suby of* Central 1 Credit Union)
879 Victoria St, Prince George, BC, V2L 2K7
(250) 562-5415
Emp Here 40
SIC 6062 State credit unions

D-U-N-S 24-859-1856   (SL)
CHU - CHO ENTERPRISES LTD
1157 5th Ave Suite 202, Prince George, BC, V2L 3L1

Emp Here 80   *Sales* 8,826,150
SIC 4212 Local trucking, without storage
Owner Tsaw Keh Dene
Dir Dennis Izony

D-U-N-S 20-779-0614   (BR)
CINEPLEX ODEON CORPORATION
FAMOUS PLAYERS 6
1600 15th Ave Suite 172, Prince George, BC, V2L 3X3
(250) 612-3993
Emp Here 20
SIC 7832 Motion picture theaters, except drive-in

D-U-N-S 24-346-7292   (BR)
COAST HOTELS LIMITED
COAST HOTELS AND RESORTS
770 Brunswick St, Prince George, BC, V2L 2C2
(250) 563-0121
Emp Here 130
SIC 7011 Hotels and motels

D-U-N-S 24-946-8265   (BR)
COCA-COLA REFRESHMENTS CANADA COMPANY
(*Suby of* The Coca-Cola Company)
405 2nd Ave, Prince George, BC, V2L 2Z6
(250) 562-1289
Emp Here 49
SIC 5149 Groceries and related products, nec

D-U-N-S 24-074-3112   (BR)
DELOITTE LLP
DELOITTE
299 Victoria St Suite 500, Prince George, BC, V2L 5B8
(250) 564-1111
Emp Here 40
SIC 8721 Accounting, auditing, and bookkeeping

D-U-N-S 24-325-6927   (BR)
DEVON TRANSPORT LTD
BUDGET RENT-A-CAR

955 1st Ave, Prince George, BC, V2L 2Y4
(250) 564-7072
Emp Here 50
SIC 7514 Passenger car rental

D-U-N-S 20-596-7990   (SL)
DHILLON FOOD SERVICES LTD
WHITE SPOT RESTAURANT
820 Victoria St, Prince George, BC, V2L 5P1
(250) 563-2331
Emp Here 80   *Sales* 2,407,703
SIC 5812 Eating places

D-U-N-S 25-766-1657   (BR)
FGL SPORTS LTD
ATMOSPHERE
1600 15th Ave Suite 195, Prince George, BC, V2L 3X3
(250) 563-9914
Emp Here 25
SIC 5941 Sporting goods and bicycle shops

D-U-N-S 25-858-4267   (SL)
FAMILY YOUNG MEN'S CHRISTIAN ASSOCIATION OF PRINCE GEORGE
PRINCE GEORGE YMCA
2020 Massey Dr, Prince George, BC, V2L 4V7
(250) 563-2483
Emp Here 65   *Sales* 2,626,585
SIC 7991 Physical fitness facilities

D-U-N-S 20-210-8382   (BR)
G4S CASH SOLUTIONS (CANADA) LTD
2344 Queensway, Prince George, BC, V2L 1M7
(250) 562-8818
Emp Here 40
SIC 7381 Detective and armored car services

D-U-N-S 20-583-6802   (BR)
GLACIER MEDIA INC
PRINCE GEORGE CITIZENS NEWSPAPER
150 Brunswick St, Prince George, BC, V2L 2B3
(250) 562-6666
Emp Here 100
SIC 2711 Newspapers

D-U-N-S 25-320-4721   (HQ)
GOLDEN ARCH FOOD SERVICES LTD
MCDONALD'S
(*Suby of* Golden Arch Food Services Ltd)
2001 Victoria St, Prince George, BC, V2L 2L8
(250) 563-2287
Emp Here 100   *Emp Total* 320
Sales 12,438,743
SIC 5812 Eating places
Pr Dean O'connor

D-U-N-S 20-105-6447   (BR)
GREAT PACIFIC INDUSTRIES INC
SAVE-ON-FOODS
1600 15th Ave Suite 100, Prince George, BC, V2L 3X3
(250) 564-4525
Emp Here 180
SIC 5411 Grocery stores

D-U-N-S 24-310-6242   (SL)
GREAT STEAK HOUSE INC, THE
KEG RESTAURANT
582 George St, Prince George, BC, V2L 1R7
(250) 563-1768
Emp Here 150   *Sales* 4,523,563
SIC 5812 Eating places

D-U-N-S 25-774-5257   (BR)
H & R BLOCK CANADA, INC
(*Suby of* H&R Block, Inc.)
1262 3rd Ave, Prince George, BC, V2L 3E7
(250) 564-0344
Emp Here 40
SIC 7291 Tax return preparation services

D-U-N-S 25-216-6913   (BR)
HSBC BANK CANADA
299 Victoria St Unit 110, Prince George, BC, V2L 5B8

(250) 564-9800
Emp Here 30
SIC 6021 National commercial banks

D-U-N-S 24-958-0382   (BR)
HUDSON'S BAY COMPANY
BAY, THE
1600 15th Ave Suite 140, Prince George, BC, V2L 3X3
(250) 563-0211
Emp Here 90
SIC 5311 Department stores

D-U-N-S 24-292-6038   (BR)
HUSKY OIL OPERATIONS LIMITED
HUSKY ENERGY
2542 Pg Pulpmill Rd, Prince George, BC, V2L 4V4
(250) 960-2500
Emp Here 79
SIC 2911 Petroleum refining

D-U-N-S 25-315-7580   (BR)
INVESTORS GROUP FINANCIAL SERVICES INC
299 Victoria St Suite 900, Prince George, BC, V2L 5B8
(250) 564-2310
Emp Here 25
SIC 8742 Management consulting services

D-U-N-S 25-300-5771   (BR)
KPMG LLP
KPMG
(*Suby of* KPMG LLP)
177 Victoria St Suite 400, Prince George, BC, V2L 5R8
(250) 563-7151
Emp Here 40
SIC 8721 Accounting, auditing, and bookkeeping

D-U-N-S 24-696-0199   (HQ)
L.E.J. INTERNATIONAL TRUCKS LTD
1951 1st Ave, Prince George, BC, V2L 2Y8
(250) 563-0478
Emp Here 26   *Emp Total* 12,400
Sales 2,042,900
SIC 4212 Local trucking, without storage

D-U-N-S 25-273-4454   (BR)
LANDTRAN SYSTEMS INC
BYERS TRANSPORTATION SYSTEMS
(*Suby of* Kluskus Holdings Ltd)
1633 1st Ave, Prince George, BC, V2L 2Y8
(250) 564-1122
Emp Here 25
SIC 4213 Trucking, except local

D-U-N-S 20-105-6132   (HQ)
NORTHERN HARDWARE & FURNITURE CO., LTD
AMCO WHOLESALE
(*Suby of* Northern Hardware & Furniture Co., Ltd)
1386 3rd Ave, Prince George BC, V2L 3E9
(250) 563-7161
Emp Here 45   *Emp Total* 55
Sales 5,253,170
SIC 5251 Hardware stores
Pr Pr Kelly Green
Sec Hilliard Clare

D-U-N-S 24-272-4565   (SL)
PRINCE GEORGE GOLF & CURLING CLUB
2515 Recreation Pl, Prince George, BC, V2L 4S1
(250) 563-0357
Emp Here 70   *Sales* 2,845,467
SIC 7997 Membership sports and recreation clubs

D-U-N-S 20-860-8591   (BR)
PRINCE GEORGE NATIVE FRIENDSHIP CENTRE SOCIETY
EMPLOYMENT SERVICES UNIT
1600 3rd Ave Suite 21, Prince George, BC, V2L 3G6

(250) 564-3568
Emp Here 150
SIC 8399 Social services, nec

D-U-N-S 24-153-2514   (SL)
REGIONAL SECURITY SERVICES LTD
190 Victoria St, Prince George, BC, V2L 2J2
(250) 562-1215
Emp Here 70   *Sales* 2,188,821
SIC 7381 Detective and armored car services

D-U-N-S 20-736-6464   (BR)
SHAW COMMUNICATIONS INC
2519 Queensway, Prince George, BC, V2L 1N1
(250) 614-7300
Emp Here 50
SIC 4841 Cable and other pay television services

D-U-N-S 25-414-4710   (HQ)
SPATIAL MAPPING LTD
(*Suby of* Industrial Forestry Service Ltd)
484 2nd Ave Suite 200, Prince George, BC, V2L 2Z7
(250) 564-1928
Emp Here 20   *Emp Total* 75
Sales 1,559,252
SIC 7389 Business services, nec

D-U-N-S 25-778-3969   (BR)
STAPLES CANADA INC
STAPLES THE BUSINESS DEPOT
(*Suby of* Staples, Inc.)
1600 15th Ave Suite 206, Prince George, BC, V2L 3X3
(250) 614-4270
Emp Here 30
SIC 5943 Stationery stores

D-U-N-S 25-174-3365   (BR)
VALUE VILLAGE STORES, INC
VALUE VILLAGE
(*Suby of* Savers, Inc.)
1666 Spruce St, Prince George, BC, V2L 2R2
(250) 561-0311
Emp Here 35
SIC 5399 Miscellaneous general merchandise

D-U-N-S 25-793-2269   (BR)
WESTERN INVENTORY SERVICE LTD
WIS INTERNATIONAL
575 Quebec St Rm 203, Prince George, BC, V2L 1W6
(250) 562-6628
Emp Here 20
SIC 7389 Business services, nec

D-U-N-S 20-105-6629   (SL)
WINTON GLOBAL LUMBER LTD
1850 River Rd, Prince George, BC, V2L 5S8

Emp Here 375   *Sales* 47,902,080
SIC 2421 Sawmills and planing mills, general
Pr Pr Mike Low
Dir William Stuart
Dir Gordon Anderson

D-U-N-S 25-887-6747   (BR)
WORKERS' COMPENSATION BOARD OF BRITISH COLUMBIA
WORKERS' COMPENSATION BOARD
1066 Vancouver St, Prince George, BC, V2L 5M4
(250) 563-9264
Emp Here 100
SIC 6331 Fire, marine, and casualty insurance

Prince George, BC V2M
Fraser-Fort George County

D-U-N-S 24-897-6227   (HQ)
ALLEN, LARRY HOLDINGS (1997) LTD
DAIRY QUEEN
(*Suby of* Allen, Larry Holdings (1997) Ltd)
1924 3rd Ave, Prince George, BC, V2M 1G7

(250) 564-4103
Emp Here 25   *Emp Total* 50
Sales 1,532,175
SIC 5812 Eating places

D-U-N-S 20-591-4380   (BR)
BOARD OF EDUCATION OF SCHOOL DISTRICT NO. 57 (PRINCE GEORGE), THE
QUEENSEN ELEMENTARY SCHOOL
(*Suby of* Board of Education of School District No. 57 (Prince George), The)
251 Ogilvie St S, Prince George, BC, V2M 3M4
(250) 562-1161
Emp Here 35
SIC 8211 Elementary and secondary schools

D-U-N-S 20-027-0853   (BR)
BOARD OF EDUCATION OF SCHOOL DISTRICT NO. 57 (PRINCE GEORGE), THE
HERITAGE ELEMENTARY SCHOOL
(*Suby of* Board of Education of School District No. 57 (Prince George), The)
257 Anderson St, Prince George, BC, V2M 6C1
(250) 562-5384
Emp Here 45
SIC 8211 Elementary and secondary schools

D-U-N-S 24-345-6329   (BR)
BOARD OF EDUCATION OF SCHOOL DISTRICT NO. 57 (PRINCE GEORGE), THE
PRINCE GEORGE SECONDARY SCHOOL
(*Suby of* Board of Education of School District No. 57 (Prince George), The)
2901 Griffiths Ave, Prince George, BC, V2M 2S7
(250) 562-6441
Emp Here 140
SIC 8211 Elementary and secondary schools

D-U-N-S 20-713-5190   (BR)
BOARD OF EDUCATION OF SCHOOL DISTRICT NO. 57 (PRINCE GEORGE), THE
FOOTHILLS ELEMENTARY SCHOOL
(*Suby of* Board of Education of School District No. 57 (Prince George), The)
4375 Eaglenest Cres, Prince George, BC, V2M 4Y5
(250) 562-2862
Emp Here 30
SIC 8211 Elementary and secondary schools

D-U-N-S 20-027-0804   (BR)
BOARD OF EDUCATION OF SCHOOL DISTRICT NO. 57 (PRINCE GEORGE), THE
LAKEWOOD JR SECONDARY SCHOOL
(*Suby of* Board of Education of School District No. 57 (Prince George), The)
4131 Rainbow Dr, Prince George, BC, V2M 3W3
(250) 562-1164
Emp Here 55
SIC 8211 Elementary and secondary schools

D-U-N-S 20-230-6150   (BR)
BOARD OF EDUCATION OF SCHOOL DISTRICT NO. 57 (PRINCE GEORGE), THE
HIGHGLEN MONTESSORI ELEMENTARY SCHOOL
(*Suby of* Board of Education of School District No. 57 (Prince George), The)
290 Voyageur Dr, Prince George, BC, V2M 4P2
(250) 964-7743
Emp Here 40
SIC 8211 Elementary and secondary schools

D-U-N-S 20-027-0820   (BR)
BOARD OF EDUCATION OF SCHOOL DISTRICT NO. 57 (PRINCE GEORGE), THE
SPRUCELAND ELEMENTARY SCHOOL
(*Suby of* Board of Education of School District No. 57 (Prince George), The)
3805 Rainbow Dr, Prince George, BC, V2M 3W2
(250) 563-4208
Emp Here 27

SIC 8211 Elementary and secondary schools

D-U-N-S 20-026-8816   (BR)
BOARD OF EDUCATION OF SCHOOL DISTRICT NO. 57 (PRINCE GEORGE), THE
HARWIN ELEMENTARY SCHOOL
(*Suby of* Board of Education of School District No. 57 (Prince George), The)
1193 Harper St, Prince George, BC, V2M 2X1
(250) 562-1773
Emp Here 30
SIC 8211 Elementary and secondary schools

D-U-N-S 20-296-1152   (BR)
BOARD OF EDUCATION OF SCHOOL DISTRICT NO. 57 (PRINCE GEORGE), THE
DP TODD SECONDARY SCHOOL
(*Suby of* Board of Education of School District No. 57 (Prince George), The)
4444 Hill Ave, Prince George, BC, V2M 5V9
(250) 562-9525
Emp Here 63
SIC 8211 Elementary and secondary schools

D-U-N-S 20-860-8526   (BR)
CITY OF PRINCE GEORGE
1770 Monroe St, Prince George, BC, V2M 7A4
(250) 561-7542
Emp Here 50
SIC 7999 Amusement and recreation, nec

D-U-N-S 25-901-3514   (BR)
DENCAN RESTAURANTS INC
DENNY'S RESTAURANT
(*Suby of* Northland Properties Corporation)
1650 Central St E, Prince George, BC, V2M 3C2
(250) 562-6723
Emp Here 55
SIC 5812 Eating places

D-U-N-S 24-551-6539   (SL)
EARL'S RESTAURANTS LTD
EARL'S PLACE
1440 Central St E, Prince George, BC, V2M 3C1
(250) 562-1527
Emp Here 75   *Sales* 2,261,782
SIC 5812 Eating places

D-U-N-S 24-291-3382   (SL)
ESTHER'S INN LTD
1151 Commercial Cres, Prince George, BC, V2M 6W6
(250) 564-3311
Emp Here 100   *Sales* 4,377,642
SIC 7011 Hotels and motels

D-U-N-S 24-343-7378   (BR)
FGL SPORTS LTD
SPORT MART
795 Central St W, Prince George, BC, V2M 3C6
(250) 563-8889
Emp Here 20
SIC 5941 Sporting goods and bicycle shops

D-U-N-S 25-267-8867   (BR)
GREAT PACIFIC INDUSTRIES INC
SAVE-ON-FOODS
555 Central St W, Prince George, BC, V2M 3C6
(250) 563-8112
Emp Here 50
SIC 5411 Grocery stores

D-U-N-S 24-366-3643   (BR)
JIM PATTISON BROADCAST GROUP LIMITED PARTNERSHIP
CKPG
(*Suby of* Jim Pattison Broadcast Group Limited Partnership)
1810 3rd Ave Fl 2, Prince George, BC, V2M 1G4
(250) 564-8861
Emp Here 50
SIC 4832 Radio broadcasting stations

D-U-N-S 20-792-1821   (BR)

SIC 8211 Elementary and secondary schools

KAL TIRE LTD
1073 Central St W, Prince George, BC, V2M 3C9
(250) 562-2105
Emp Here 20
SIC 5531 Auto and home supply stores

D-U-N-S 24-682-7885   (SL)
KONA DRUGS LTD
SHOPPERS DRUG MART
737 Central St W, Prince George, BC, V2M 3C6
(250) 562-2311
Emp Here 60   *Sales* 8,463,441
SIC 5912 Drug stores and proprietary stores
Pr Pr Donald Eisbrenner
  Linda Eisbrenner

D-U-N-S 20-956-7585   (SL)
LAKEWOOD DENTAL SERVICES LTD
4122 15th Ave, Prince George, BC, V2M 1V9
(250) 562-5551
Emp Here 60   *Sales* 3,429,153
SIC 8021 Offices and clinics of dentists

D-U-N-S 20-210-8457   (BR)
MOXIE'S RESTAURANTS, LIMITED PARTNERSHIP
MOXIE'S CLASIC GROW RESTAURANT
1804 Central St E, Prince George, BC, V2M 3C3
(250) 564-4700
Emp Here 75
SIC 5812 Eating places

D-U-N-S 24-385-7575   (BR)
NORTHERN HEALTH AUTHORITY
RAINBOW INTERMEDIATE CARE HOME
1000 Liard Dr, Prince George, BC, V2M 3Z3
(250) 649-7293
Emp Here 300
SIC 8361 Residential care

D-U-N-S 24-974-8427   (BR)
NORTHLAND PROPERTIES CORPORATION
SANDMAN HOTEL & SUITES PRINCE GEORGE
(*Suby of* Northland Properties Corporation)
1650 Central St E, Prince George, BC, V2M 3C2
(250) 563-8131
Emp Here 25
SIC 7011 Hotels and motels

D-U-N-S 24-980-2497   (BR)
REDBERRY FRANCHISING CORP
BURGER KING
1023 Central St W, Prince George, BC, V2M 3C9
(250) 561-8700
Emp Here 28
SIC 5812 Eating places

D-U-N-S 24-537-1773   (BR)
VISTA RADIO LTD
CIRX
1940 3rd Ave, Prince George, BC, V2M 1G7
(250) 564-2524
Emp Here 30
SIC 4832 Radio broadcasting stations

D-U-N-S 20-302-1246   (BR)
WESTERN FINANCIAL GROUP (NETWORK) INC
FOURNIER AGENCY
790 Central St E, Prince George, BC, V2M 3B7
(250) 565-4924
Emp Here 20
SIC 6411 Insurance agents, brokers, and service

D-U-N-S 24-957-7628   (BR)
YCS HOLDINGS LTD
Y C S HOLDINGS LTD
4955 Sandberg Rd, Prince George, BC, V2M 7B4

Emp Here 20
SIC 1611 Highway and street construction

Prince George, BC V2N
Fraser-Fort George County

D-U-N-S 20-322-0686   (SL)
0947951 BC LTD.
UNIVERSAL MATS
7677 Pacific St, Prince George, BC, V2N 5S4
(250) 961-8851
Emp Here 50   *Sales* 3,378,379
SIC 7218 Industrial launderers

D-U-N-S 24-033-5216   (BR)
AMEC FOSTER WHEELER AMERICAS LIMITED
AMEC EARTH & ENVIRONMENTAL, DIV OF
3456 Opie Cres, Prince George, BC, V2N 2P9
(250) 564-3243
Emp Here 20
SIC 8711 Engineering services

D-U-N-S 24-324-0061   (BR)
ARMTEC LP
ARMTEC
2001 Industrial Way, Prince George, BC, V2N 5S6
(250) 561-0017
Emp Here 20
SIC 3312 Blast furnaces and steel mills

D-U-N-S 25-486-0588   (BR)
BANDSTRA TRANSPORTATION SYSTEMS LTD
9499 Milwaukee Way, Prince George, BC, V2N 5T3
(250) 562-6621
Emp Here 30
SIC 4212 Local trucking, without storage

D-U-N-S 24-897-8033   (BR)
BELTERRA CORPORATION
BELTERRA
2247 Quinn St S, Prince George, BC, V2N 2X4
(250) 562-1245
Emp Here 25
SIC 5085 Industrial supplies

D-U-N-S 20-304-3810   (BR)
BEST BUY CANADA LTD
FUTURE SHOP
(*Suby of* Best Buy Co., Inc.)
3900 Walls Ave Suite 701, Prince George, BC, V2N 4L4
(250) 561-2277
Emp Here 60
SIC 5731 Radio, television, and electronic stores

D-U-N-S 20-591-4356   (BR)
BOARD OF EDUCATION OF SCHOOL DISTRICT NO. 57 (PRINCE GEORGE), THE
BLACKBURN ELEMENTARY SCHOOL
(*Suby of* Board of Education of School District No. 57 (Prince George), The)
2222 Blackburn South Rd, Prince George, BC, V2N 6C1
(250) 963-7060
Emp Here 25
SIC 8211 Elementary and secondary schools

D-U-N-S 25-483-1555   (BR)
BOARD OF EDUCATION OF SCHOOL DISTRICT NO. 57 (PRINCE GEORGE), THE
JOHN MCINNIS SECONDARY SCHOOL
(*Suby of* Board of Education of School District No. 57 (Prince George), The)
3400 Westwood Dr, Prince George, BC, V2N 1S1
(250) 562-4321
Emp Here 30
SIC 8211 Elementary and secondary schools

D-U-N-S 20-591-4422   (BR)
BOARD OF EDUCATION OF SCHOOL DISTRICT NO. 57 (PRINCE GEORGE), THE
PINEWOOD ELEMENTARY SCHOOL
(*Suby of* Board of Education of School District No. 57 (Prince George), The)
4140 Campbell Ave, Prince George, BC, V2N 3A9
(250) 562-5388
Emp Here 25
SIC 8211 Elementary and secondary schools

D-U-N-S 20-230-6176   (BR)
BOARD OF EDUCATION OF SCHOOL DISTRICT NO. 57 (PRINCE GEORGE), THE
PEDEN HILL ELEMENTARY
(*Suby of* Board of Education of School District No. 57 (Prince George), The)
3500 Westwood Dr, Prince George, BC, V2N 1S1
(250) 562-5822
Emp Here 30
SIC 8211 Elementary and secondary schools

D-U-N-S 20-230-9022   (BR)
BOARD OF EDUCATION OF SCHOOL DISTRICT NO. 57 (PRINCE GEORGE), THE
COLLEGE HEIGHTS SECONDARY SCHOOL
(*Suby of* Board of Education of School District No. 57 (Prince George), The)
6180 Domano Blvd, Prince George, BC, V2N 3Z4
(250) 964-4431
Emp Here 20
SIC 8211 Elementary and secondary schools

D-U-N-S 25-486-0679   (BR)
BOARD OF EDUCATION OF SCHOOL DISTRICT NO. 57 (PRINCE GEORGE), THE
PINEVIEW ELEMENTARY SCHOOL
(*Suby of* Board of Education of School District No. 57 (Prince George), The)
8515 Old Cariboo Hwy, Prince George, BC, V2N 5X5
(250) 963-7259
Emp Here 25
SIC 8211 Elementary and secondary schools

D-U-N-S 20-039-3150   (BR)
BOARD OF EDUCATION OF SCHOOL DISTRICT NO. 57 (PRINCE GEORGE), THE
VANWAY ELEMENTARY SCHOOL
(*Suby of* Board of Education of School District No. 57 (Prince George), The)
4509 Highway 16 W, Prince George, BC, V2N 5M8
(250) 964-6422
Emp Here 33
SIC 8211 Elementary and secondary schools

D-U-N-S 20-064-2572   (BR)
BOARD OF EDUCATION OF SCHOOL DISTRICT NO. 57 (PRINCE GEORGE), THE
SOUTHRIDGE SCHOOL
(*Suby of* Board of Education of School District No. 57 (Prince George), The)
7300 Southridge Ave, Prince George, BC, V2N 4Y6
(250) 964-3544
Emp Here 30
SIC 8211 Elementary and secondary schools

D-U-N-S 20-026-8840   (BR)
BOARD OF EDUCATION OF SCHOOL DISTRICT NO. 57 (PRINCE GEORGE), THE
BEAVERLY ELEMENTARY SCHOOL
(*Suby of* Board of Education of School District No. 57 (Prince George), The)
9777 Western Rd, Prince George, BC, V2N 6M9
(250) 964-9311
Emp Here 24
SIC 8211 Elementary and secondary schools

D-U-N-S 20-027-0796   (BR)
BOARD OF EDUCATION OF SCHOOL DISTRICT NO. 57 (PRINCE GEORGE), THE
COLLEGE HEIGHTS ELEMENTARY

SCHOOL
(*Suby of* Board of Education of School District No. 57 (Prince George), The)
5410 Cowart Rd, Prince George, BC, V2N 1Z2
(250) 964-4408
Emp Here 30
SIC 8211 Elementary and secondary schools

D-U-N-S 20-027-0838   (BR)
BOARD OF EDUCATION OF SCHOOL DISTRICT NO. 57 (PRINCE GEORGE), THE
WESTWOOD ELEMENTARY SCHOOL
(*Suby of* Board of Education of School District No. 57 (Prince George), The)
2633 Vanier Dr, Prince George, BC, V2N 1V1
(250) 562-3076
Emp Here 41
SIC 8211 Elementary and secondary schools

D-U-N-S 20-713-5216   (BR)
BOARD OF EDUCATION OF SCHOOL DISTRICT NO. 57 (PRINCE GEORGE), THE
MALASPINA ELEMENTARY SCHOOL
(*Suby of* Board of Education of School District No. 57 (Prince George), The)
7900 Malaspina Ave, Prince George, BC, V2N 4A9
(250) 964-9874
Emp Here 30
SIC 8211 Elementary and secondary schools

D-U-N-S 24-367-8505   (BR)
BRANDT TRACTOR LTD
1049 Great St, Prince George, BC, V2N 2K8
(250) 562-1151
Emp Here 30
SIC 5084 Industrial machinery and equipment

D-U-N-S 25-774-0456   (BR)
BRICK WAREHOUSE LP, THE
BRICK, THE
2454 Ferry Ave, Prince George, BC, V2N 0B1
(250) 614-8080
Emp Here 22
SIC 5712 Furniture stores

D-U-N-S 25-325-2720   (BR)
BRITISH COLUMBIA AUTOMOBILE ASSOCIATION
B C A A
2324 Ferry Ave Suite 100, Prince George, BC, V2N 0B1
(250) 649-2399
Emp Here 25
SIC 8699 Membership organizations, nec

D-U-N-S 20-572-4193   (BR)
BRITISH COLUMBIA HYDRO AND POWER AUTHORITY
BC HYDRO
3333 22nd Ave, Prince George, BC, V2N 1B4
(250) 561-4800
Emp Here 20
SIC 4911 Electric services

D-U-N-S 20-568-7978   (BR)
CANADA POST CORPORATION
9598 Penn Rd, Prince George, BC, V2N 5T6
(250) 562-5241
Emp Here 20
SIC 4311 U.s. postal service

D-U-N-S 20-575-4554   (BR)
CANADA POST CORPORATION
3505 15th Ave, Prince George, BC, V2N 0E8
(250) 563-4422
Emp Here 100
SIC 4311 U.s. postal service

D-U-N-S 20-039-1162   (BR)
CANADIAN BLOOD SERVICES
2277 Westwood Dr, Prince George, BC, V2N 4V6
(250) 563-2560
Emp Here 26
SIC 8099 Health and allied services, nec

D-U-N-S 25-097-3885   (BR)

CANADIAN FOREST PRODUCTS LTD
CANFOR PULP
2533 Prince George Pulpmill Rd, Prince George, BC, V2N 2K3
(250) 561-3981
Emp Here 250
SIC 2421 Sawmills and planing mills, general

D-U-N-S 20-175-2834   (BR)
CANADIAN FOREST PRODUCTS LTD
PRINCE GEORGE PULP & PAPER
2789 Pulp Mill Rd, Prince George, BC, V2N 2K3
(250) 563-0161
Emp Here 400
SIC 2421 Sawmills and planing mills, general

D-U-N-S 25-148-5272   (BR)
CANADIAN IMPERIAL BANK OF COMMERCE
CIBC
3055 Massey Dr Suite 233, Prince George, BC, V2N 2S9
(250) 614-6400
Emp Here 20
SIC 6021 National commercial banks

D-U-N-S 24-000-8297   (BR)
CARRIER FOREST PRODUCTS LTD
12200 Willow Cale Forest Rd, Prince George, BC, V2N 7A8
(250) 963-9664
Emp Here 30
SIC 2421 Sawmills and planing mills, general

D-U-N-S 20-911-8223   (HQ)
COLLEGE OF NEW CALEDONIA, THE
CNC
(*Suby of* College Of New Caledonia, The)
3330 22nd Ave, Prince George, BC, V2N 1P8
(250) 562-2131
Emp Here 800   *Emp Total* 1,000
Sales 134,281,883
SIC 8221 Colleges and universities
Pr Henry Reiser
 Penny Fahlman
 Bruce Sutherland
V Ch Bd Ray Jerow

D-U-N-S 24-104-5926   (BR)
COMPAGNIE DES CHEMINS DE FER NATIONAUX DU CANADA
CN RAILWAY
1108 Industrial Way, Prince George, BC, V2N 5S1
(250) 561-4190
Emp Here 750
SIC 4111 Local and suburban transit

D-U-N-S 24-354-8943   (BR)
COSTCO WHOLESALE CANADA LTD
(*Suby of* Costco Wholesale Corporation)
2555 Range Rd Suite 158, Prince George, BC, V2N 4G8
(250) 561-1176
Emp Here 200
SIC 5099 Durable goods, nec

D-U-N-S 20-902-5738   (BR)
DUCKS UNLIMITED CANADA
7813 Renison Pl, Prince George, BC, V2N 3J2
(250) 964-3825
Emp Here 300
SIC 8999 Services, nec

D-U-N-S 24-394-7533   (SL)
EX-CEL ACOUSTICS LTD
4162 Cowart Rd, Prince George, BC, V2N 6H9
(250) 563-4181
Emp Here 50   *Sales* 4,231,721
SIC 1742 Plastering, drywall, and insulation

D-U-N-S 24-337-3342   (BR)
FGL SPORTS LTD
SPORT-CHEK PINE CENTRE
3115 Massey Dr Suite 152, Prince George, BC, V2N 2S9

---

(250) 561-3002
Emp Here 40
SIC 5941 Sporting goods and bicycle shops

D-U-N-S 24-683-2687   (BR)
FINNING INTERNATIONAL INC
FINNING (CANADA), A DIV
(*Suby of* Finning International Inc)
1100 Pacific St, Prince George, BC, V2N 5S3
(250) 563-0331
Emp Here 90
SIC 5082 Construction and mining machinery

D-U-N-S 20-860-5977   (BR)
GLENTEL INC
WIRELESS WAVES
3055 Massey Dr, Prince George, BC, V2N 2S9
(250) 561-2360
Emp Here 25
SIC 4813 Telephone communication, except radio

D-U-N-S 20-176-7311   (BR)
HOME DEPOT OF CANADA INC
HOME DEPOT
(*Suby of* The Home Depot Inc)
5959 O'Grady Rd, Prince George, BC, V2N 6Z5
(250) 906-3610
Emp Here 150
SIC 5251 Hardware stores

D-U-N-S 20-105-4483   (HQ)
INLAND DIESEL LTD
FREIGHTLINER PRINCE GEORGE
(*Suby of* Inland Diesel Ltd)
1015 Great St, Prince George, BC, V2N 2K8

Emp Here 35   *Emp Total* 55
Sales 26,994,000
SIC 5511 New and used car dealers
Tom Coffey
Pr Pr Glenn Latimer

D-U-N-S 20-917-0539   (BR)
INLAND KENWORTH LTD
INLAND KENWORTH
1995 Quinn St S, Prince George, BC, V2N 2X2
(250) 562-8171
Emp Here 40
SIC 7538 General automotive repair shops

D-U-N-S 24-368-7233   (BR)
INSURANCE CORPORATION OF BRITISH COLUMBIA
I C B C
4001 15th Ave, Prince George, BC, V2N 2X3
(250) 562-4311
Emp Here 65
SIC 6331 Fire, marine, and casualty insurance

D-U-N-S 25-995-3693   (BR)
INTEGRATED DISTRIBUTION SYSTEMS LIMITED PARTNERSHIP
WAJAX EQUIPMENT
(*Suby of* Integrated Distribution Systems Limited Partnership)
1140 Pacific St, Prince George, BC, V2N 5S3
(250) 562-7321
Emp Here 25
SIC 5084 Industrial machinery and equipment

D-U-N-S 25-836-1120   (BR)
JAZZ AVIATION LP
CARGO OFFICE
3900 Grumman Rd Unit 8, Prince George, BC, V2N 4M6
(250) 963-3300
Emp Here 20
SIC 4512 Air transportation, scheduled

D-U-N-S 20-801-1648   (BR)
KAL TIRE LTD
750 Boundary Rd, Prince George, BC, V2N 5T2
(250) 561-1525
Emp Here 30
SIC 5531 Auto and home supply stores

D-U-N-S 20-795-5704   (BR)
LOBLAWS INC
REAL CANADIAN SUPERSTORE, THE
2155 Ferry Ave, Prince George, BC, V2N 5E8
(250) 960-1300
Emp Here 300
SIC 5411 Grocery stores

D-U-N-S 20-197-1178   (BR)
LORDCO PARTS LTD
LORDCO AUTO PARTS
3463 22nd Ave, Prince George, BC, V2N 1B4
(250) 612-0223
Emp Here 38
SIC 5531 Auto and home supply stores

D-U-N-S 25-839-8635   (BR)
MANITOULIN TRANSPORTATION
BANDSTRA TRANSPORTATION
9499 Milwaukee Way, Prince George, BC, V2N 5T3
(250) 563-9138
Emp Here 90
SIC 4212 Local trucking, without storage

D-U-N-S 20-298-7124   (BR)
NAV CANADA
4141 Airport Rd Suite 2, Prince George, BC, V2N 4M6
(250) 963-7689
Emp Here 26
SIC 4899 Communication services, nec

D-U-N-S 24-826-7028   (SL)
NORTHERN INDUSTRIAL CONSTRUCTION GROUP INC
1416 Santa Fe Rd, Prince George, BC, V2N 5T5
(250) 562-6660
Emp Here 300   *Sales* 80,000,400
SIC 1541 Industrial buildings and warehouses
Pr Pr Jeffrey Houghton

D-U-N-S 24-030-3180   (SL)
NORTHERN STEEL LTD
(*Suby of* Canerector Inc)
9588 Milwaukee Way, Prince George, BC, V2N 5T3
(250) 561-1121
Emp Here 50   *Sales* 7,733,834
SIC 3443 Fabricated plate work (boiler shop)
Pr Pr Fritz Hausot

D-U-N-S 25-991-9090   (HQ)
PEROXYCHEM CANADA LTD
(*Suby of* Jpmorgan Chase & Co.)
2147 Pg Pulp Mill Rd, Prince George, BC, V2N 2S6
(250) 561-4200
Emp Here 50   *Emp Total* 243,355
Sales 12,474,014
SIC 2819 Industrial inorganic chemicals, nec
Pr James A. Mcclung
VP Theodore H. Laws
VP Randall (Randy) S. Ellis
VP Joseph H. Netherland
Steven H Shapiro
Dir Michael J Matymish
Dir Charlotte M Smith
Dir Robert Service

D-U-N-S 20-489-1261   (BR)
PINNACLE RENEWABLE ENERGY INC
8545 Willow Cale Rd, Prince George, BC, V2N 6Z9
(250) 562-5562
Emp Here 25
SIC 5099 Durable goods, nec

D-U-N-S 25-774-2221   (BR)
PRAXAIR CANADA INC
PRAXAIR MEDIGAS
(*Suby of* Praxair, Inc.)
1601 Central St W, Prince George, BC, V2N 1P6
(250) 563-3641
Emp Here 20
SIC 5541 Gasoline service stations

D-U-N-S 20-700-6623   (BR)
REITMANS (CANADA) LIMITEE
6007 Southridge Ave, Prince George, BC, V2N 6Z4

Emp Here 25
SIC 5621 Women's clothing stores

D-U-N-S 20-785-8478   (BR)
ROMAN CATHOLIC EPISCOPAL CORPORATION OF PRINCE RUPERT, THE
IMMACULATE CONCEPTION SCHOOL
3285 Cathedral Ave, Prince George, BC, V2N 6R4
(250) 964-4362
Emp Here 20
SIC 8211 Elementary and secondary schools

D-U-N-S 25-774-3237   (BR)
ROYAL BANK OF CANADA
RBC
(*Suby of* Royal Bank Of Canada)
3161 Massey Dr Unit 57, Prince George, BC, V2N 2S9
(250) 960-4540
Emp Here 20
SIC 6021 National commercial banks

D-U-N-S 20-328-5940   (SL)
ROYAL LEPAGE PRINCE GEORGE
3166 Massey Dr, Prince George, BC, V2N 2S9
(250) 564-4488
Emp Here 40   *Sales* 5,104,320
SIC 6531 Real estate agents and managers
Mgr Jim Mcneal

D-U-N-S 24-881-2844   (HQ)
RUSKIN CONSTRUCTION LTD
(*Suby of* Northern Linkwell Construction Ltd)
2011 Pg Pulp Mill Rd, Prince George, BC, V2N 2K3
(250) 563-2800
Emp Here 20   *Emp Total* 245
Sales 91,054,954
SIC 1622 Bridge, tunnel, and elevated highway construction
Pr Pr Andrew Purdey

D-U-N-S 25-832-0589   (BR)
RUSSEL METALS INC
AJ FORSYTH
990 Industrial Way, Prince George, BC, V2N 5S1
(250) 563-1274
Emp Here 50
SIC 5051 Metals service centers and offices

D-U-N-S 20-992-1865   (BR)
SEARS CANADA INC
3199 Massey Dr, Prince George, BC, V2N 3M7
(250) 564-8111
Emp Here 225
SIC 5311 Department stores

D-U-N-S 24-174-6382   (BR)
SODEXO CANADA LTD
SODEXO
3333 University Way, Prince George, BC, V2N 4Z9

Emp Here 25
SIC 7349 Building maintenance services, nec

D-U-N-S 20-018-3952   (BR)
STARBUCKS COFFEE CANADA, INC
(*Suby of* Starbucks Corporation)
3161 Massey Dr Suite 101, Prince George, BC, V2N 2S9
(250) 562-4272
Emp Here 20
SIC 5812 Eating places

D-U-N-S 20-105-2214   (BR)
TRANSPORT TFI 7 S.E.C
CANADIAN FREIGHTWAYS
3851 22nd Ave, Prince George, BC, V2N 1B5
(250) 563-0375
Emp Here 47

SIC 4213 Trucking, except local

D-U-N-S 24-766-8536   (BR)
TRIMAC TRANSPORTATION SERVICES LIMITED PARTNERSHIP
9355 Penn Rd, Prince George, BC, V2N 5T6
(250) 561-1363
Emp Here 35
SIC 4213 Trucking, except local

D-U-N-S 25-107-6147   (BR)
WAJAX INDUSTRIAL COMPONENTS LIMITED PARTNERSHIP
WAJAX INDUSTRIAL COMPONENTS
901 Great St, Prince George, BC, V2N 5R7
(250) 562-1334
Emp Here 26
SIC 5084 Industrial machinery and equipment

D-U-N-S 24-027-0780   (BR)
WAL-MART CANADA CORP
6565 Southridge Ave Suite 3651, Prince George, BC, V2N 6Z4
(250) 906-3203
Emp Here 200
SIC 5311 Department stores

D-U-N-S 20-105-8914   (BR)
WILLIAMS MOVING & STORAGE (B.C.) LTD
(*Suby of* Williams Moving & Storage (B.C.) Ltd)
9545 Milwaukee Way, Prince George, BC, V2N 5T3
(250) 563-8814
Emp Here 25
SIC 4214 Local trucking with storage

D-U-N-S 20-003-8953   (BR)
WINNERS MERCHANTS INTERNATIONAL L.P.
WINNERS
(*Suby of* The TJX Companies Inc)
3900 Walls Ave Suite 101, Prince George, BC, V2N 4L4
(250) 562-9465
Emp Here 25
SIC 5651 Family clothing stores

D-U-N-S 20-562-8402   (BR)
WOLFTEK INDUSTRIES INC
5018 Continental Way, Prince George, BC, V2N 5S5
(250) 562-7543
Emp Here 30
SIC 3499 Fabricated Metal products, nec

D-U-N-S 25-968-5605   (SL)
WOOD WHEATON HONDA
2500 Range Rd, Prince George, BC, V2N 0C3
(250) 562-9391
Emp Here 30   *Sales* 15,217,500
SIC 5511 New and used car dealers
Owner Craig Wood

Prince Rupert, BC V8J
Skeena-Qn-Charlotte County

D-U-N-S 24-798-4990   (BR)
AQUILINI INVESTMENT GROUP INC
HIGHLINER PLAZA HOTEL & CONFERENCE CENTER
815 1st Ave W, Prince Rupert, BC, V8J 1B3
(250) 624-9060
Emp Here 30
SIC 7011 Hotels and motels

D-U-N-S 25-116-5478   (BR)
BRITISH COLUMBIA FERRY SERVICES INC
BC FERRIES
Gd Stn Main, Prince Rupert, BC, V8J 3P3
(250) 624-9627
Emp Here 20
SIC 4482 Ferries

D-U-N-S 24-137-0720   (BR)
CANADIAN FISHING COMPANY LIMITED, THE
121 George Hills Way, Prince Rupert, BC, V8J 1A3
(250) 624-6726
Emp Here 100
SIC 2091 Canned and cured fish and seafoods

D-U-N-S 25-786-9297   (BR)
CANADIAN UNION OF POSTAL WORKERS
CUPW
Gd Stn Main, Prince Rupert, BC, V8J 3P3
(250) 627-7233
Emp Here 20
SIC 8631 Labor organizations

D-U-N-S 25-984-7440   (BR)
CINEPLEX ODEON CORPORATION
FAMOUS PLAYERS PRINCE RUPERT
525 2nd Ave W Suite 683, Prince Rupert, BC, V8J 1G9
(250) 624-6770
Emp Here 20
SIC 7832 Motion picture theaters, except drive-in

D-U-N-S 20-034-4930   (BR)
CORPORATION OF THE CITY OF PRINCE RUPERT
PUBLIC WORKS
221 Wantage Rd, Prince Rupert, BC, V8J 4R1
(250) 624-6795
Emp Here 60
SIC 7549 Automotive services, nec

D-U-N-S 25-361-2287   (BR)
CORPORATION OF THE CITY OF PRINCE RUPERT
CITYWEST
248 3rd Ave W, Prince Rupert, BC, V8J 1L1
(250) 627-0941
Emp Here 35
SIC 4899 Communication services, nec

D-U-N-S 20-105-9441   (SL)
CREST HOTEL LTD
222 1st Ave W, Prince Rupert, BC, V8J 1A8
(250) 624-6771
Emp Here 75   *Sales* 3,283,232
SIC 7011 Hotels and motels

D-U-N-S 24-445-7073   (BR)
FIRSTCANADA ULC
COASTAL BUS LINES FARWEST BUS LINE
225 2nd Ave W, Prince Rupert, BC, V8J 1G4
(250) 624-3343
Emp Here 25
SIC 4142 Bus charter service, except local

D-U-N-S 24-374-4005   (BR)
GOVERNMENT OF THE PROVINCE OF BRITISH COLUMBIA
BC AMBULANCE SERVICE
1301 Summit Ave, Prince Rupert, BC, V8J 4K5
(250) 624-2233
Emp Here 20
SIC 4119 Local passenger transportation, nec

D-U-N-S 25-957-5587   (BR)
HARBOUR AIR LTD
HARBOUR AIR SEAPLANES
Gd Stn Main, Prince Rupert, BC, V8J 3P3

Emp Here 20
SIC 4512 Air transportation, scheduled

D-U-N-S 24-032-6504   (BR)
MCMILLAN, J.S. FISHERIES LTD
Gd Stn Main, Prince Rupert, BC, V8J 3P3
(250) 624-2146
Emp Here 100
SIC 2092 Fresh or frozen packaged fish

D-U-N-S 25-364-7838   (BR)
NORTHERN HEALTH AUTHORITY

PRINCE RUPERT REGIONAL HOSPITAL
1305 Summit Ave, Prince Rupert, BC, V8J 2A6
(250) 624-2171
Emp Here 350
SIC 8062 General medical and surgical hospitals

D-U-N-S 25-887-7349   (BR)
NORTHWEST COMMUNITY COLLEGE
NWCC
353 5th St, Prince Rupert, BC, V8J 3L6
(250) 624-6054
Emp Here 40
SIC 8221 Colleges and universities

D-U-N-S 24-491-3935   (SL)
PRINCE RUPERT PORT AUTHORITY
PORT OF PRINCE RUPERT
215 Cow Bay Rd Suite 200, Prince Rupert, BC, V8J 1A2
(250) 627-8899
Emp Here 30   *Sales* 4,523,563
SIC 4491 Marine cargo handling

D-U-N-S 20-713-4995   (BR)
PRINCE RUPERT SCHOOL DISTRICT 52
ECOLE WESTVIEW
2000 2nd Ave W, Prince Rupert, BC, V8J 1J8

Emp Here 25
SIC 8211 Elementary and secondary schools

D-U-N-S 25-901-4538   (BR)
PRINCE RUPERT SCHOOL DISTRICT 52
ANNUNCIATION SCHOOL
627 5th Ave W, Prince Rupert, BC, V8J 1V1
(250) 624-5873
Emp Here 25
SIC 8211 Elementary and secondary schools

D-U-N-S 20-591-3713   (BR)
PRINCE RUPERT SCHOOL DISTRICT 52
PINE RIDGE ELEMENTARY SCHOOL
1700 Sloan Ave, Prince Rupert, BC, V8J 2B6
(250) 627-7054
Emp Here 30
SIC 8211 Elementary and secondary schools

D-U-N-S 20-591-3721   (BR)
PRINCE RUPERT SCHOOL DISTRICT 52
SEAL COVE ELEMENTARY
1725 8th Ave E, Prince Rupert, BC, V8J 2N9
(250) 624-6361
Emp Here 25
SIC 8211 Elementary and secondary schools

D-U-N-S 20-713-4987   (BR)
PRINCE RUPERT SCHOOL DISTRICT 52
PRINCE RUPERT SECONDARY SCHOOL
417 9th Ave W, Prince Rupert, BC, V8J 2S9
(250) 624-6757
Emp Here 50
SIC 8211 Elementary and secondary schools

D-U-N-S 20-034-6521   (BR)
PRINCE RUPERT SCHOOL DISTRICT 52
ROOSEVELT PARK COMMUNITY SCHOOL
800 Summit Ave, Prince Rupert, BC, V8J 3W2
(250) 624-6126
Emp Here 40
SIC 8211 Elementary and secondary schools

D-U-N-S 20-713-5000   (BR)
PRINCE RUPERT SCHOOL DISTRICT 52
634 6th Ave E, Prince Rupert, BC, V8J 1X1
(250) 627-0772
Emp Here 500
SIC 8211 Elementary and secondary schools

D-U-N-S 20-106-0779   (SL)
RUPERT CLEANERS & LAUNDRY LTD
ULTRAPURE PURIFIED WATER
340 Mcbride St, Prince Rupert, BC, V8J 3G2
(250) 624-9601
Emp Here 50   *Sales* 2,845,467
SIC 7218 Industrial launderers

D-U-N-S 20-713-4631   (BR)
SCHOOL DISTRICT NO. 43 (COQUITLAM)
IOCO SCHOOL
101 1st Ave E, Prince Rupert, BC, V8J 3X4
(604) 469-9151
Emp Here 50
SIC 8211 Elementary and secondary schools

D-U-N-S 25-901-4157   (BR)
YCS HOLDINGS LTD
Y C S HOLDINGS LTD
161 Mishaw Rd, Prince Rupert, BC, V8J 3Y1
(250) 624-5814
Emp Here 20
SIC 1611 Highway and street construction

Princeton, BC V0X
Okanagn-Similkameen County

D-U-N-S 25-267-8941   (BR)
GREAT PACIFIC INDUSTRIES INC
OVERWAITEA FOOD GROUP
247 Bridge St, Princeton, BC, V0X 1W0
(250) 295-6322
Emp Here 30
SIC 5411 Grocery stores

D-U-N-S 25-773-9490   (SL)
KTW HOLDINGS LTD
VALLEYVIEW MOHAWK
580 Highway W, Princeton, BC, V0X 1W0
(250) 372-0451
Emp Here 30   *Sales* 5,579,750
SIC 5541 Gasoline service stations
Pr Pr Al Knowles
  Lois Knowles

D-U-N-S 20-591-6310   (BR)
SCHOOL DISTRICT NO 58 (NICOLA-SIMILKAMEEN)
VERMILION FORKS ELEMENTARY SCHOOL
99 Ridgewood Dr, Princeton, BC, V0X 1W0
(250) 295-6642
Emp Here 30
SIC 8211 Elementary and secondary schools

D-U-N-S 20-591-6252   (BR)
SCHOOL DISTRICT NO 58 (NICOLA-SIMILKAMEEN)
PRINCETON SECONDARY SCHOOL
201 Old Merritt Hwy, Princeton, BC, V0X 1W0
(250) 295-3218
Emp Here 25
SIC 8211 Elementary and secondary schools

D-U-N-S 20-993-9227   (BR)
SCHOOL DISTRICT NO 58 (NICOLA-SIMILKAMEEN)
170 Vermilion, Princeton, BC, V0X 1W0
(250) 295-6914
Emp Here 20
SIC 8211 Elementary and secondary schools

D-U-N-S 24-639-8770   (BR)
WEYERHAEUSER COMPANY LIMITED
(*Suby of Weyerhaeuser Company*)
201 Old Hedley Rd, Princeton, BC, V0X 1W0
(250) 295-3281
Emp Here 250
SIC 2421 Sawmills and planing mills, general

Qualicum Beach, BC V9K
Nanaimo County

D-U-N-S 25-795-3679   (BR)
CANADIAN CANCER SOCIETY
172 2 Ave W, Qualicum Beach, BC, V9K 1T7

Emp Here 75
SIC 8399 Social services, nec

D-U-N-S 20-034-6430   (BR)
REGIONAL DISTRICT OF NANAIMO
RAVENSONG AQUATIC CENTRE
737 Jones St, Qualicum Beach, BC, V9K 1S4
(250) 752-5014
Emp Here 40
SIC 7999 Amusement and recreation, nec

D-U-N-S 25-485-7717   (BR)
SCHOOL DISTRICT NO 69 (QUALICUM)
QUALICUM SECONDARY SCHOOL
266 Village Way, Qualicum Beach, BC, V9K 1L1
(250) 752-5651
Emp Here 60
SIC 8211 Elementary and secondary schools

D-U-N-S 25-154-0340   (BR)
SCHOOL DISTRICT NO 69 (QUALICUM)
QUALICUM BEACH ELEMENTARY
744 Primrose St, Qualicum Beach, BC, V9K 1S3
(250) 752-6989
Emp Here 40
SIC 8211 Elementary and secondary schools

D-U-N-S 25-165-5478   (BR)
SCHOOL DISTRICT NO 69 (QUALICUM)
ARROWVIEW ELEMENTARY SCHOOL
650 Bennett Rd, Qualicum Beach, BC, V9K 1N1
(250) 752-3875
Emp Here 34
SIC 8211 Elementary and secondary schools

D-U-N-S 20-027-0937   (BR)
SCHOOL DISTRICT NO 69 (QUALICUM)
QUALICUM BEACH MIDDLE SCHOOL
699 Claymore Rd, Qualicum Beach, BC, V9K 2T6
(250) 752-9212
Emp Here 43
SIC 8211 Elementary and secondary schools

D-U-N-S 24-518-5926   (BR)
SILVERADO LAND CORP
CROWN MANSION
292 Crescent Rd E, Qualicum Beach, BC, V9K 0A5
(250) 752-5776
Emp Here 60
SIC 6513 Apartment building operators

D-U-N-S 25-937-4379   (BR)
VANCOUVER ISLAND HEALTH AUTHORITY
EAGLE PARK HEALTH CARE FACILITY
777 Jones St, Qualicum Beach, BC, V9K 2L1
(250) 947-8220
Emp Here 130
SIC 8011 Offices and clinics of medical doctors

Queen Charlotte, BC V0T
Skeena-Qn-Charlotte County

D-U-N-S 20-086-7492   (BR)
BOARD OF EDUCATION OF SCHOOL DISTRICT NO. 50 (HAIDA GWAII), THE
QUEEN CHARLOTTE SECONDARY SCHOOL
701 Oceanview Dr, Queen Charlotte, BC, V0T 1S1
(250) 559-8822
Emp Here 25
SIC 8211 Elementary and secondary schools

D-U-N-S 24-346-4323   (BR)
NORTHERN HEALTH AUTHORITY
QUEEN CHARLOTTE ISLANDS GENERAL HOSPITAL
3211 Third Ave, Queen Charlotte, BC, V0T 1S1
(250) 559-4300
Emp Here 150

▲ Public Company   ■ Public Company Family Member   **HQ** Headquarters   **BR** Branch   **SL** Single Location

SIC 8062 General medical and surgical hospitals

Quesnel, BC V2J
Cariboo County

D-U-N-S 24-881-8015   (HQ)
A.B.C. ALLEN BUSINESS COMMUNICATIONS LTD
ABC COMMUNICATIONS
(Suby of A.B.C. Allen Business Communications Ltd)
248 Reid St, Quesnel, BC, V2J 2M2
(250) 992-1230
Emp Here 35   *Emp Total* 50
Sales 4,742,446
SIC 4812 Radiotelephone communication

D-U-N-S 25-216-8711   (BR)
ARROW TRANSPORTATION SYSTEMS INC
75 Star Rd N, Quesnel, BC, V2J 5K2
(250) 992-8103
Emp Here 60
SIC 4212 Local trucking, without storage

D-U-N-S 25-288-8599   (BR)
CANADA POST CORPORATION
346 Reid St, Quesnel, V2J 2M4
(250) 992-2200
Emp Here 48
SIC 4311 U.s. postal service

D-U-N-S 20-592-1724   (BR)
CANADIAN CANCER SOCIETY
QUESNEL UNIT
332 Front St, Quesnel, BC, V2J 2K3

Emp Here 36
SIC 8399 Social services, nec

D-U-N-S 24-151-3845   (BR)
CANADIAN FOREST PRODUCTS LTD
1920 Brownmiller Rd, Quesnel, BC, V2J 6S1

Emp Here 200
SIC 5031 Lumber, plywood, and millwork

D-U-N-S 25-901-0502   (BR)
COLLEGE OF NEW CALEDONIA, THE
(Suby of College Of New Caledonia, The)
100 Campus Way, Quesnel, BC, V2J 7K1
(250) 991-7500
Emp Here 100
SIC 8222 Junior colleges

D-U-N-S 20-364-6344   (SL)
FOOTHILLS FOREST PRODUCTS INC
1751 Quesnel-Hixon Rd, Quesnel, BC, V2J 5Z5
(250) 991-0254
Emp Here 100   *Sales* 10,944,105
SIC 2426 Hardwood dimension and flooring mills

D-U-N-S 20-106-3872   (BR)
GREAT PACIFIC INDUSTRIES INC
SAVE-ON-FOODS
155 Malcolm Dr Suite 7, Quesnel, BC, V2J 3K2
(250) 992-8718
Emp Here 85
SIC 5411 Grocery stores

D-U-N-S 20-870-7591   (BR)
HUDSON'S BAY COMPANY
FIELDS STORES
155 Malcolm Dr Suite 12, Quesnel, BC, V2J 3K2

Emp Here 25
SIC 5311 Department stores

D-U-N-S 20-866-0977   (BR)
INLAND KENWORTH LTD
INLAND KENWORTH
3150 Hwy 97 N, Quesnel, BC, V2J 5Y9

(250) 992-7256
Emp Here 20
SIC 5012 Automobiles and other motor vehicles

D-U-N-S 20-699-1247   (BR)
KATES' PHARMACY LTD
SHOPPERS DRUG MART # 213
225 St Laurent Ave, Quesnel, BC, V2J 2C8
(250) 992-2214
Emp Here 32
SIC 5912 Drug stores and proprietary stores

D-U-N-S 25-364-3845   (BR)
LOBLAWS INC
EXTRA FOODS
2335 Maple Dr E, Quesnel, BC, V2J 7J6
(250) 747-2803
Emp Here 130
SIC 5411 Grocery stores

D-U-N-S 25-359-6415   (BR)
NORTHERN HEALTH AUTHORITY
BAKER, G.R. MEMORIAL HOSPITAL
543 Front St, Quesnel, BC, V2J 2K7
(250) 985-5600
Emp Here 350
SIC 8062 General medical and surgical hospitals

D-U-N-S 24-761-9807   (BR)
PINNACLE RENEWABLE ENERGY INC
4252 Dog Prairie Rd, Quesnel, BC, V2J 6K9
(250) 747-1714
Emp Here 25
SIC 2499 Wood products, nec

D-U-N-S 24-617-8466   (BR)
PRIMA ENTERPRISES LTD
QUESNEL DAY PROGRAM
2391 Quesnel-Hydraulic Rd, Quesnel, BC, V2J 4H4
(250) 747-3844
Emp Here 30
SIC 4953 Refuse systems

D-U-N-S 25-838-7778   (SL)
QUESNEL CRAFTERS SOCIETY
CARIBOO KEEPSAKES
102 Carson Ave, Quesnel, BC, V2J 2A8
(250) 991-0419
Emp Here 65   *Sales* 3,575,074
SIC 5947 Gift, novelty, and souvenir shop

D-U-N-S 24-880-0968   (BR)
QUESNEL, CITY OF
500 Barlow Ave, Quesnel, BC, V2J 2C4
(250) 992-7125
Emp Here 27
SIC 7999 Amusement and recreation, nec

D-U-N-S 20-002-2080   (BR)
ROYAL BANK OF CANADA
RBC
(Suby of Royal Bank Of Canada)
201 St Laurent Ave, Quesnel, BC, V2J 2C8
(250) 992-2127
Emp Here 31
SIC 6021 National commercial banks

D-U-N-S 20-199-7728   (BR)
SHARK CLUBS OF CANADA INC
940 Chew Ave, Quesnel, BC, V2J 6R8
(250) 747-0311
Emp Here 27
SIC 5812 Eating places

D-U-N-S 25-775-5983   (BR)
SHAW COMMUNICATIONS INC
SHAW CABLE
156 Front St, Quesnel, V2J 2K1
(250) 979-6565
Emp Here 50
SIC 4841 Cable and other pay television services

D-U-N-S 24-536-7818   (BR)
TOLKO INDUSTRIES LTD
QUEST WOOD DIVISION

1879 Brownmiller Rd, Quesnel, BC, V2J 6R9
(250) 992-1700
Emp Here 250
SIC 2421 Sawmills and planing mills, general

D-U-N-S 24-654-9997   (BR)
WAL-MART CANADA CORP
WALMART QUESNEL
890 Rita Rd, Quesnel, BC, V2J 7J3
(250) 747-4464
Emp Here 140
SIC 5311 Department stores

D-U-N-S 24-113-5735   (BR)
WEST FRASER MILLS LTD
QUESNEL MILL PLYWOOD
1000 Plywood Rd, Quesnel, BC, V2J 3J5
(250) 991-7619
Emp Here 300
SIC 2421 Sawmills and planing mills, general

D-U-N-S 20-269-9047   (BR)
WEST FRASER MILLS LTD
QUESNEL PLYWOOD
2000 Plywood Rd, Quesnel, BC, V2J 5W1
(250) 992-5511
Emp Here 300
SIC 2435 Hardwood veneer and plywood

D-U-N-S 24-694-5703   (BR)
WEST FRASER MILLS LTD
EUROCAN PULP & PAPER, DIV OF
1250 Brownmiller Rd, Quesnel, BC, V2J 6P5
(250) 992-9244
Emp Here 450
SIC 5031 Lumber, plywood, and millwork

D-U-N-S 20-189-2028   (BR)
WEST FRASER TIMBER CO. LTD
QUESNEL RIVER PULP
1000 Finning Rd, Quesnel, BC, V2J 6A1
(250) 992-8919
Emp Here 130
SIC 2611 Pulp mills

D-U-N-S 20-300-6382   (BR)
WEST FRASER TIMBER CO. LTD
WEST FRASER
1250 Brownmiller Rd, Quesnel, BC, V2J 6P5
(250) 992-9244
Emp Here 500
SIC 5031 Lumber, plywood, and millwork

D-U-N-S 20-038-1486   (BR)
YCS HOLDINGS LTD
Y C S HOLDINGS LTD
Gd Lcd Main, Quesnel, BC, V2J 3J1
(250) 992-9033
Emp Here 20
SIC 1611 Highway and street construction

D-U-N-S 24-681-5898   (SL)
YESNABY INVESTMENTS LTD
MCDONALD'S RESTAURANT
105 North Star Rd, Quesnel, BC, V2J 5K2
(250) 992-6868
Emp Here 100   *Sales* 2,991,389
SIC 5812 Eating places

Radium Hot Springs, BC V0A
East Kootenay County

D-U-N-S 25-155-3434   (BR)
RADIUM RESORT INC
SPRINGS GOLF PRO SHOP
7565 Columbia Ave, Radium Hot Springs, BC, V0A 1M0
(250) 347-6200
Emp Here 50
SIC 5941 Sporting goods and bicycle shops

Revelstoke, BC V0E
Columbia - Shuswap County

D-U-N-S 24-061-3463   (SL)
BARTON INSURANCE BROKERS LTD
103 East 1 St Suite 101, Revelstoke, BC, V0E 2S0
(250) 837-5211
Emp Here 100   *Sales* 12,478,350
SIC 6411 Insurance agents, brokers, and service
Pr Edward Woodcock

D-U-N-S 20-106-5190   (SL)
BERUSCHI ENTERPRISES LTD
REGENT INN
112 1 St E, Revelstoke, BC, V0E 2S0
(250) 837-2107
Emp Here 65   *Sales* 2,845,467
SIC 7011 Hotels and motels

D-U-N-S 24-126-4808   (BR)
BRITISH COLUMBIA HYDRO AND POWER AUTHORITY
BC HYDRO
1200 Powerhouse Rd, Revelstoke, BC, V0E 2S0
(250) 814-6600
Emp Here 25
SIC 4911 Electric services

D-U-N-S 25-839-6381   (BR)
CANADIAN MOUNTAIN HOLIDAYS LIMITED PARTNERSHIP
THE GOTHIC
(Suby of Intrawest Resorts Holdings, Inc.)
Highway 23 N, Revelstoke, BC, V0E 2S0
(250) 837-4245
Emp Here 20
SIC 7011 Hotels and motels

D-U-N-S 24-120-7211   (BR)
CANADIAN PACIFIC RAILWAY COMPANY
CPR
420 Victoria Rd, Revelstoke, BC, V0E 2S0
(250) 837-8236
Emp Here 50
SIC 4111 Local and suburban transit

D-U-N-S 24-272-4359   (BR)
CANADIAN PACIFIC RAILWAY COMPANY
CPR
127 Track St E, Revelstoke, BC, V0E 2S0
(250) 837-8253
Emp Here 400
SIC 4731 Freight transportation arrangement

D-U-N-S 20-645-7801   (BR)
CANADIAN PACIFIC RAILWAY COMPANY
CPR
420 Victoria Rd, Revelstoke, BC, V0E 2S0
(250) 837-8229
Emp Here 300
SIC 4011 Railroads, line-haul operating

D-U-N-S 20-288-2978   (SL)
COMMUNITY CONNECTIONS (REVELSTOKE) SOCIETY
314 2nd St E, Revelstoke, BC, V0E 2S0
(250) 837-2062
Emp Here 50   *Sales* 1,969,939
SIC 8322 Individual and family services

D-U-N-S 20-992-3127   (BR)
COOPER MARKET LTD
COOPER'S FOODS
555 Victoria St, Revelstoke, BC, V0E 2S0
(250) 837-4372
Emp Here 60
SIC 5411 Grocery stores

D-U-N-S 25-939-7305   (BR)
DENCAN RESTAURANTS INC
DENNY'S RESTAURANT
(Suby of Northland Properties Corporation)
1891 Fraser Dr, Revelstoke, BC, V0E 2S0
(250) 837-2034
Emp Here 50
SIC 5812 Eating places

D-U-N-S 20-555-9581   (BR)
H M C SERVICES INC
723 Hwy 23 S, Revelstoke, BC, V0E 2S0
(250) 837-3136
Emp Here 50
SIC 1611 Highway and street construction

D-U-N-S 25-316-4768   (BR)
**NORTHLAND PROPERTIES CORPORA-
TION**
SANDMAN HOTEL REVELSTROKE
(*Suby of* Northland Properties Corporation)
1901 Laforme Blvd, Revelstoke, BC, V0E 2S0
(250) 837-5271
Emp Here 20
SIC 7011 Hotels and motels

D-U-N-S 20-295-1950   (BR)
REVELSTOKE, CITY OF
PUBLIC WORKS
1200 Victoris St E, Revelstoke, BC, V0E 2S0
(250) 837-2001
Emp Here 45
SIC 1611 Highway and street construction

D-U-N-S 24-034-3079   (SL)
TIL-VAN HOLDINGS LTD
FRONTIER MOTEL & RESTAURANT
122 Hwy 23 N, Revelstoke, BC, V0E 2S0
(250) 837-5119
Emp Here 50   *Sales* 1,532,175
SIC 5812 Eating places

Richmond, BC V6V
Greater Vancouver County

D-U-N-S 24-313-2164   (SL)
0203114 B.C. LTD
3031 Viking Way Suite 210, Richmond, BC,
V6V 1W1
(604) 270-7728
Emp Here 130   *Sales* 20,087,100
SIC 8711 Engineering services
Pr Pr Mike Cantor
Treas Jim Noon

D-U-N-S 20-218-3252   (BR)
1371185 ONTARIO INC
3389 No. 6 Rd, Richmond, BC, V6V 1P6

Emp Here 140
SIC 5045 Computers, peripherals, and software

D-U-N-S 25-485-7071   (BR)
7-ELEVEN CANADA, INC
7-ELEVEN FOOD CENTER
3531 Viking Way Unit 7, Richmond, BC, V6V
1W1
(604) 273-2008
Emp Here 100
SIC 5411 Grocery stores

D-U-N-S 20-250-5459   (BR)
9134417 CANADA INC
VERSACOLD LOGISTICS SERVICES
3231 No. 6 Rd, Richmond, BC, V6V 1P6
(604) 258-0370
Emp Here 40
SIC 4222 Refrigerated warehousing and storage

D-U-N-S 20-327-4506   (BR)
9134417 CANADA INC
VERSACOLD LOGISTICS SERVICES
3371 No. 6 Rd, Richmond, BC, V6V 1P6
(604) 258-0354
Emp Here 20
SIC 6153 Short-term business credit institutions, except agricultural

D-U-N-S 25-956-0233   (SL)
AEROINFO SYSTEMS INC
*COMMERCIAL AVIATION SERVICES (CAS),
DIV OF*

(*Suby of* The Boeing Company)
13575 Commerce Pky Unit 200, Richmond,
BC, V6V 2L1
(604) 232-4200
Emp Here 31   *Sales* 2,772,003
SIC 7371 Custom computer programming services

D-U-N-S 24-350-8848   (BR)
AEROTEK ULC
13575 Commerce Pky Suite 150, Richmond,
BC, V6V 2L1
(604) 412-3500
Emp Here 100
SIC 7361 Employment agencies

D-U-N-S 24-353-2210   (BR)
AIR LIQUIDE CANADA INC
23231 Fraserwood Way, Richmond, BC, V6V
3B3
(604) 677-4427
Emp Here 41
SIC 2813 Industrial gases

D-U-N-S 24-647-7376   (HQ)
ALLSCRIPTS CANADA CORPORATION
13888 Wireless Way Suite 110, Richmond,
BC, V6V 0A3
(604) 273-4900
Emp Here 80   *Emp Total* 6,900
Sales 15,321,747
SIC 7372 Prepackaged software
Pr Pr Robert L Hawkins

D-U-N-S 24-311-3896   (SL)
APPLIED BIOLOGICAL MATERIALS INC
ABM
1-3671 Viking Way, Richmond, BC, V6V 2J5
(604) 247-2416
Emp Here 60   *Sales* 3,898,130
SIC 8731 Commercial physical research

D-U-N-S 24-369-5855   (SL)
ARODAL SERVICES LTD
2631 Viking Way Suite 248, Richmond, BC,
V6V 3B5
(604) 274-0477
Emp Here 100   *Sales* 2,918,428
SIC 7349 Building maintenance services, nec

D-U-N-S 25-094-5763   (SL)
ARROW MARINE SERVICES LTD
11580 Mitchell Rd, Richmond, BC, V6V 1T7

Emp Here 25   *Sales* 1,992,377
SIC 4493 Marinas

D-U-N-S 20-032-2670   (BR)
ARROW SPEED CONTROLS LIMITED
13851 Bridgeport Rd, Richmond, BC, V6V 1J6
(604) 321-4033
Emp Here 50
SIC 8742 Management consulting services

D-U-N-S 20-113-0226   (HQ)
**BAKEMARK INGREDIENTS CANADA LIM-
ITED**
BAKEMARK CANADA
2480 Viking Way, Richmond, BC, V6V 1N2
(604) 303-1700
Emp Here 50   *Sales* 21,523,407
SIC 5149 Groceries and related products, nec
Pr Jim Parker
VP VP Rick Barnes
VP Dave Ford

D-U-N-S 25-015-0489   (BR)
**BALL PACKAGING PRODUCTS CANADA
CORP**
1700 No. 6 Rd, Richmond, BC, V6V 1W3

Emp Here 45
SIC 3411 Metal cans

D-U-N-S 25-297-0736   (BR)
BANK OF NOVA SCOTIA, THE
SCOTIABANK
13340 Smallwood Pl Suite 205, Richmond,

BC, V6V 1W8
(800) 663-9215
Emp Here 40
SIC 6021 National commercial banks

D-U-N-S 20-713-3849   (BR)
**BOARD OF EDUCATION SCHOOL DIS-
TRICT #38 (RICHMOND)**
H J CAMBIE SECONDARY SCHOOL
4151 Jacombs Rd, Richmond, BC, V6V 1N7

Emp Here 75
SIC 8211 Elementary and secondary schools

D-U-N-S 20-590-6501   (BR)
**BOARD OF EDUCATION SCHOOL DIS-
TRICT #38 (RICHMOND)**
MITCHELL ELEMENTARY SCHOOL
12091 Cambie Rd, Richmond, BC, V6V 1G5
(604) 668-6225
Emp Here 35
SIC 8211 Elementary and secondary schools

D-U-N-S 20-026-9830   (BR)
**BOARD OF EDUCATION SCHOOL DIS-
TRICT #38 (RICHMOND)**
HAMILTON ELEMENTARY SCHOOL
5180 Smith Dr, Richmond, BC, V6V 2W5
(604) 668-6514
Emp Here 40
SIC 8211 Elementary and secondary schools

D-U-N-S 20-249-7467   (HQ)
BOOTLEGGER CLOTHING INC
4460 Jacombs Rd, Richmond, BC, V6V 2C5
(604) 276-8400
Emp Here 50   *Emp Total* 3,000
Sales 6,055,738
SIC 5621 Women's clothing stores
Conrad Ledrew
Gerry Bachynski

D-U-N-S 24-839-5113   (SL)
BRIGHTER MECHANICAL LIMITED
21000 Westminster Hwy Suite 2140, Rich-
mond, BC, V6V 2S9
(604) 279-0901
Emp Here 65   *Sales* 5,690,935
SIC 1711 Plumbing, heating, air-conditioning
Dir Robert Vincent
Dir Edward Mcdowall

D-U-N-S 25-327-6703   (SL)
BROADCOM CANADA LTD
13711 International Pl Unit 200, Richmond,
BC, V6V 2Z8
(604) 233-8500
Emp Here 80   *Sales* 12,156,044
SIC 7371 Custom computer programming ser-
vices
Henry Samueli

D-U-N-S 20-264-4613   (BR)
BUILDDIRECT.COM TECHNOLOGIES INC
13333 Vulcan Way Unit 10, Richmond, BC,
V6V 1K4
(604) 318-8169
Emp Here 30
SIC 4225 General warehousing and storage

D-U-N-S 20-012-5792   (SL)
C2 MEDIA CANADA ULC
C2 MEDIA
14291 Burrows Rd, Richmond, BC, V6V 1K9
(604) 270-4000
Emp Here 62   *Sales* 3,064,349
SIC 2759 Commercial printing, nec

D-U-N-S 20-299-3130   (SL)
CTC LOGISTICS (CANADA) INC
14351 Burrows Rd Suite 130, Richmond, BC,
V6V 1K9
(604) 278-6366
Emp Here 50   *Sales* 17,246,500
SIC 4731 Freight transportation arrangement
Pr Pr Yonglong Li

D-U-N-S 25-414-1260   (SL)
CANCAP PHARMACEUTICAL LTD

13111 Vanier Pl Unit 180, Richmond, BC, V6V
2J1
(604) 278-2188
Emp Here 35   *Sales* 4,961,328
SIC 5912 Drug stores and proprietary stores

D-U-N-S 24-324-6704   (SL)
CANADIAN BLIND MANUFACTURING INC
5900 No. 6 Rd Unit 110, Richmond, BC, V6V
1Z1
(604) 304-3476
Emp Here 33   *Sales* 5,180,210
SIC 2591 Drapery hardware and window
blinds and shades
Pr Pr Laurence Segal

D-U-N-S 24-364-9188   (BR)
CANADIAN STANDARDS ASSOCIATION
CSA INTERNATIONAL
13799 Commerce Pky, Richmond, BC, V6V
2N9
(604) 273-4581
Emp Here 90
SIC 8734 Testing laboratories

D-U-N-S 24-375-6496   (BR)
CANEM SYSTEMS LTD
1600 Valmont Way Suite 100, Richmond, BC,
V6V 1Y4
(604) 273-1131
Emp Here 87
SIC 1731 Electrical work

D-U-N-S 24-275-0461   (BR)
CASCADES CANADA ULC
3300 Viking Way, Richmond, BC, V6V 1N6
(604) 273-7321
Emp Here 140
SIC 2653 Corrugated and solid fiber boxes

D-U-N-S 24-344-8656   (BR)
CENTENNIAL FOODSERVICE
12759 Vulcan Way Unit 108, Richmond, BC,
V6V 3C8
(604) 273-5261
Emp Here 90
SIC 2011 Meat packing plants

D-U-N-S 20-735-2472   (BR)
CITY TRANSFER INC
14271 River Rd, Richmond, BC, V6V 1L3

Emp Here 25
SIC 4212 Local trucking, without storage

D-U-N-S 24-456-1148   (BR)
COINAMATIC CANADA INC
12753 Vulcan Way Unit 185, Richmond, BC,
V6V 3C8
(604) 270-8441
Emp Here 40
SIC 7215 Coin-operated laundries and clean-
ing

D-U-N-S 20-573-2642   (BR)
**COMPAGNIE DES CHEMINS DE FER NA-
TIONAUX DU CANADA**
CN
2491 No. 8 Rd, Richmond, BC, V6V 1S2
(604) 665-5425
Emp Here 20
SIC 4011 Railroads, line-haul operating

D-U-N-S 25-505-9891   (BR)
COMPUGEN INC
13151 Vanier Pl Suite 130, Richmond, BC,
V6V 2J1
(604) 801-5500
Emp Here 60
SIC 5045 Computers, peripherals, and soft-
ware

D-U-N-S 20-320-1553   (BR)
CORIX INFRASTRUCTURE INC
1128 Burdette St, Richmond, BC, V6V 2Z3
(604) 273-4987
Emp Here 50
SIC 1623 Water, sewer, and utility lines

D-U-N-S 24-314-1632   (BR)
DHL GLOBAL FORWARDING (CANADA) INC
13091 Vanier Pl Suite 230, Richmond, BC, V6V 2J1
(604) 207-8100
Emp Here 25
SIC 4731 Freight transportation arrangement

D-U-N-S 25-616-4138   (BR)
DATA COMMUNICATIONS MANAGEMENT CORP
23220 Fraserwood Way, Richmond, BC, V6V 3C7
(604) 525-2055
Emp Here 30
SIC 5112 Stationery and office supplies

D-U-N-S 24-996-8728   (HQ)
DATAWAVE SYSTEMS INC
(*Suby of* Incomm Holdings, Inc.)
13575 Commerce Pky Suite 110, Richmond, BC, V6V 2L1
(604) 295-1800
Emp Here 65   *Emp Total* 884
Sales 8,974,166
SIC 4813 Telephone communication, except radio
  Joshua Emanuel
  Div VP William Turner
  VP Sls Larry Wetzel
  VP Sls Bob Stanchina
  Debbie Camoia

D-U-N-S 20-806-8080   (HQ)
DEELEY, FRED IMPORTS LTD.
DEELEY HARLEY-DAVIDSON CANADA
(*Suby of* Fred Deeley Limited)
13500 Verdun Pl, Richmond, BC, V6V 1V2
(604) 273-5421
Emp Here 30   *Emp Total* 6
Sales 89,728,640
SIC 5012 Automobiles and other motor vehicles
  Donald A. James
  Pr Pr Malcolm H. Hunter
  Ex VP John Patrick Hanna
  Sr VP Sr VP Bremner Green

D-U-N-S 20-187-5031   (SL)
DISCOVER ENERGY CORP
13511 Crestwood Pl Unit 4 & 5, Richmond, BC, V6V 2E9
(778) 776-3288
Emp Here 21   *Sales* 33,145,555
SIC 5013 Motor vehicle supplies and new parts
  Sang Nam
  Pr Pr Darwin Sauer
  Dean Smurthwaitz

D-U-N-S 24-798-4982   (SL)
EBCO METAL FINISHING LIMITED PARTNERSHIP
15200 Knox Way, Richmond, BC, V6V 3A6
(604) 244-1500
Emp Here 70   *Sales* 4,888,367
SIC 3479 Metal coating and allied services

D-U-N-S 20-798-3979   (BR)
ENTERPRISE RENT-A-CAR CANADA COMPANY
(*Suby of* The Crawford Group Inc)
13460 Smallwood Pl Suite 110, Richmond, BC, V6V 1W3
(604) 278-8865
Emp Here 40
SIC 7514 Passenger car rental

D-U-N-S 20-081-5848   (BR)
ETHAN ALLEN (CANADA) INC
ETHAN ALLEN
2633 Sweden Way Unit 170, Richmond, BC, V6V 2Z6
(604) 821-1191
Emp Here 20
SIC 5712 Furniture stores

D-U-N-S 20-267-9622   (BR)
FINNING INTERNATIONAL INC
FINNING POWER SYSTEMS
(*Suby of* Finning International Inc)
15100 River Rd Suite 120, Richmond, BC, V6V 3B2
(604) 231-3900
Emp Here 150
SIC 1796 Installing building equipment

D-U-N-S 20-650-8025   (BR)
FUJITEC CANADA, INC
3511 Viking Way Unit 7, Richmond, BC, V6V 1W1
(604) 276-9904
Emp Here 60
SIC 7699 Repair services, nec

D-U-N-S 20-384-8804   (SL)
G-III APPAREL CANADA ULC
13551 Commerce Pky Unit 100, Richmond, BC, V6V 2L1
(604) 231-0400
Emp Here 40   *Sales* 3,465,004
SIC 2389 Apparel and accessories, nec

D-U-N-S 24-369-9225   (BR)
GWL REALTY ADVISORS INC
13575 Commerce Pky Ave Suite 150, Richmond, BC, V6V 2L1
(604) 586-1400
Emp Here 21
SIC 6282 Investment advice

D-U-N-S 24-313-6926   (SL)
GLENMORE PRINTING LTD
13751 Mayfield Pl Unit 150, Richmond, BC, V6V 2G9
(604) 273-6323
Emp Here 50   *Sales* 2,945,253
SIC 2759 Commercial printing, nec

D-U-N-S 24-931-7975   (SL)
GRAND HALE MARINE PRODUCTS COMPANY LIMITED
11551 Twigg Pl, Richmond, BC, V6V 2Y2
(604) 325-9393
Emp Here 150   *Sales* 54,720,525
SIC 5146 Fish and seafoods
  Pr Pr Reginald Cheung
  VP VP Francis Cheung
  Pandora Cheung

D-U-N-S 20-734-5690   (BR)
GREAT PACIFIC INDUSTRIES INC
PRICESMART FOODS
23200 Gilley Rd Unit 100, Richmond, BC, V6V 2L6
(604) 522-8608
Emp Here 50
SIC 5411 Grocery stores

D-U-N-S 24-996-8157   (SL)
HAZCO ENVIRONMENTAL SERVICES
(*Suby of* Tervita Corporation)
13511 Vulcan Way, Richmond, BC, V6V 1K4
(604) 214-7000
Emp Here 100   *Sales* 10,931,016
SIC 4959 Sanitary services, nec
  Dir Gregory Campbell
  Dir Gary Smith
  Mark Geiger

D-U-N-S 25-313-8853   (BR)
HOME DEPOT OF CANADA INC
HOME DEPOT
(*Suby of* The Home Depot Inc)
2700 Sweden Way, Richmond, BC, V6V 2W8
(604) 303-7360
Emp Here 250
SIC 5251 Hardware stores

D-U-N-S 20-861-1371   (BR)
HONDA CANADA FINANCE INC
13711 International Pl Suite 110, Richmond, BC, V6V 2Z8
(604) 278-9250
Emp Here 20

SIC 6159 Miscellaneous business credit institutions

D-U-N-S 20-800-7476   (BR)
HONDA CANADA INC
13240 Worster Crt, Richmond, BC, V6V 2B8
(604) 278-6504
Emp Here 60
SIC 5012 Automobiles and other motor vehicles

D-U-N-S 20-735-2621   (BR)
IBM CANADA LIMITED
(*Suby of* International Business Machines Corporation)
13511 Crestwood Pl Suite 1, Richmond, BC, V6V 2E9
(604) 244-2100
Emp Here 35
SIC 7374 Data processing and preparation

D-U-N-S 20-171-6724   (SL)
JENSEN HUGHES CONSULTING CANADA LTD
13900 Maycrest Way Unit 135, Richmond, BC, V6V 3E2
(604) 295-4000
Emp Here 20   *Sales* 12,695,162
SIC 8711 Engineering services
  Ex VP Peter Senez

D-U-N-S 24-359-7684   (BR)
JMAX GLOBAL DISTRIBUTORS INC
GAULTS APPAREL DIV OF
3960 Jacombs Rd Suite 150, Richmond, BC, V6V 1Y6

Emp Here 50
SIC 5137 Women's and children's clothing

D-U-N-S 20-531-0886   (BR)
JOINTS ETANCHES R.B. INC, LES
FLUID SEAL
13680 Bridgeport Rd Suite 5, Richmond, BC, V6V 1V3
(604) 278-6808
Emp Here 25
SIC 5085 Industrial supplies

D-U-N-S 24-503-5977   (BR)
KNOWLEDGE FIRST FINANCIAL INC.
ROBSON AGENCY
20800 Westminster Hwy Suite 1203, Richmond, BC, V6V 2W3
(604) 276-0500
Emp Here 40
SIC 8299 Schools and educational services, nec

D-U-N-S 25-229-8369   (BR)
KONICA MINOLTA BUSINESS SOLUTIONS (CANADA) LTD
KONICA MINOLTA
21500 Westminster Hwy, Richmond, BC, V6V 2V1
(604) 276-1611
Emp Here 75
SIC 5044 Office equipment

D-U-N-S 20-645-7173   (SL)
LAPORTE MOVING & STORAGE SYSTEMS LIMITED
14571 Burrows Rd, Richmond, BC, V6V 1K9
(604) 276-2216
Emp Here 50   *Sales* 2,845,467
SIC 4214 Local trucking with storage

D-U-N-S 24-365-9385   (BR)
LEHIGH HANSON MATERIALS LIMITED
13980 Mitchell Rd, Richmond, BC, V6V 1M8
(604) 324-8191
Emp Here 31
SIC 5032 Brick, stone, and related material

D-U-N-S 25-972-5716   (BR)
LEON'S FURNITURE LIMITED
2633 Sweden Way Unit 110, Richmond, BC, V6V 2Z6

(604) 214-2440
Emp Here 34
SIC 5712 Furniture stores

D-U-N-S 24-846-7623   (HQ)
MDA GEOSPATIAL SERVICES INC
13800 Commerce Pky, Richmond, BC, V6V 2J3
(604) 244-0400
Emp Here 85   *Emp Total* 3,220
Sales 8,390,481
SIC 7335 Commercial photography
  Bernard Clark
  Pr John Hornsby
  Anil Wirasekara
  Daniel Freidmann
  Gordon Thiessen

D-U-N-S 20-059-0417   (HQ)
MACDONALD, DETTWILER AND ASSOCIATES CORPORATION
MDA
13800 Commerce Pky, Richmond, BC, V6V 2J3
(604) 278-3411
Emp Here 150   *Emp Total* 3,220
Sales 16,112,269
SIC 7999 Amusement and recreation, nec
  Pr Pr Daniel Friedmann
  Anil Wirasekara

D-U-N-S 24-375-2974   (BR)
MARINE CANADA ACQUISITION LIMITED PARTNERSHIP
SEASTAR SOLUTIONS
3831 No. 6 Rd, Richmond, BC, V6V 1P6
(604) 270-6899
Emp Here 20
SIC 3492 Fluid power valves and hose fittings

D-U-N-S 24-362-4918   (BR)
MATRIX LOGISTICS SERVICES LIMITED
3751 Viking Way, Richmond, BC, V6V 1W1
(778) 296-4070
Emp Here 25
SIC 4225 General warehousing and storage

D-U-N-S 25-612-0908   (BR)
MCDONALD'S RESTAURANTS OF CANADA LIMITED
MCDONALD'S 8521
(*Suby of* McDonald's Corporation)
2760 Sweden Way, Richmond, BC, V6V 2X1
(604) 718-1150
Emp Here 70
SIC 5812 Eating places

D-U-N-S 20-038-6485   (BR)
MERCEDES-BENZ CANADA INC
5691 Parkwood Way, Richmond, BC, V6V 2M6
(604) 278-7662
Emp Here 25
SIC 5511 New and used car dealers

D-U-N-S 25-975-4919   (BR)
MING PAO NEWSPAPERS (CANADA) LIMITED
5368 Parkwood Pl, Richmond, BC, V6V 2N1
(604) 231-8998
Emp Here 125
SIC 2711 Newspapers

D-U-N-S 25-481-4775   (BR)
MOUNTAIN EQUIPMENT CO-OPERATIVE
13333 Vulcan Way Suite 11, Richmond, BC, V6V 1K4

Emp Here 40
SIC 5399 Miscellaneous general merchandise

D-U-N-S 20-050-8609   (SL)
NEOVASC MEDICAL INC
PERFORMANCE MEDICAL DEVICES
13700 Mayfield Pl Suite 2135, Richmond, BC, V6V 2E4
(604) 270-4344
Emp Here 25   *Sales* 2,188,821
SIC 3841 Surgical and medical instruments

D-U-N-S 25-928-7787   (BR)
NEXEO SOLUTIONS CANADA CORP
(*Suby of* Nexeo Solutions, Inc.)
2060 Viceroy Pl Suite 100, Richmond, BC,
V6V 1Y9
(800) 563-3435
Emp Here 25
SIC 5169 Chemicals and allied products, nec

D-U-N-S 24-246-0616   (HQ)
NORSAT INTERNATIONAL INC
4020 Viking Way Suite 110, Richmond, BC,
V6V 2L4
(604) 821-2800
Emp Here 70   *Emp Total* 6,754
Sales 25,755,127
SIC 3669 Communications equipment, nec
Pr Pr Amiee Chan
  Arthur Chin

D-U-N-S 20-178-6089   (BR)
OPENROAD AUTO GROUP LIMITED
RICHMOND LEXUS
5631 Parkwood Way, Richmond, BC, V6V
2M6
(604) 273-5533
Emp Here 35
SIC 5511 New and used car dealers

D-U-N-S 25-362-6295   (BR)
OPENROAD AUTO GROUP LIMITED
OPENROAD HYUNDAI RICHMOND
5571 Parkwood Way, Richmond, BC, V6V
2M7
(604) 606-9033
Emp Here 26
SIC 5511 New and used car dealers

D-U-N-S 24-837-7574   (SL)
PPC INTERNATIONAL INC
PROPLUS PROFESSIONAL CLEANERS
12811 Clarke Pl Unit 120, Richmond, BC, V6V
2H9
(604) 278-8369
Emp Here 50   *Sales* 1,240,332
SIC 7217 Carpet and upholstery cleaning

D-U-N-S 24-345-3867   (SL)
PRIME BUILDING MAINTENANCE LTD
12800 Bathgate Way Unit 13, Richmond, BC,
V6V 1Z4
(604) 270-7766
Emp Here 80   *Sales* 2,334,742
SIC 7349 Building maintenance services, nec

D-U-N-S 25-217-0733   (BR)
QUINCAILLERIE RICHELIEU LTEE
RICHELIEU HARDWARE
12851 Rowan Pl Unit 150, Richmond, BC,
V6V 2K5
(604) 278-4821
Emp Here 30
SIC 5072 Hardware

D-U-N-S 24-362-1443   (BR)
RAY-MONT LOGISTIQUES CANADA INC
15900 River Rd, Richmond, BC, V6V 1L5
(604) 244-0200
Emp Here 20
SIC 4731 Freight transportation arrangement

D-U-N-S 24-000-6093   (SL)
**RICHMOND INTERNATIONAL TECHNOL-
OGY CORP**
DR. BATTERY
4460 Jacombs Rd Suite 102, Richmond, BC,
V6V 2C5
(604) 273-8248
Emp Here 40   *Sales* 8,025,677
SIC 5063 Electrical apparatus and equipment
Pr Kei Yip Huen
  Fan Chun
  Ricky Ho

D-U-N-S 24-313-3696   (SL)
RICHMOND YACHTS CO
RICHMOND YACHTS
23591 Dyke Rd, Richmond, BC, V6V 1E3

Emp Here 154   *Sales* 14,203,000
SIC 4493 Marinas
Pr Pr Donald Davis
  Warren Hutson
VP Opers Keith Kiselback

D-U-N-S 20-294-6732   (BR)
RICHMOND, CITY OF
CAMBIE COMMUNITY CENTRE
12800 Cambie Rd, Richmond, BC, V6V 0A9
(604) 233-8399
Emp Here 100
SIC 8322 Individual and family services

D-U-N-S 24-681-6151   (BR)
ROTHMANS, BENSON & HEDGES INC
(*Suby of* Philip Morris International Inc.)
4311 Viking Way Suite 170, Richmond, BC,
V6V 2K9
(604) 273-7200
Emp Here 31
SIC 5194 Tobacco and tobacco products

D-U-N-S 24-342-6512   (BR)
STT ENVIRO CORP
STANCO PROJECTS, DIV OF
3031 Viking Way Suite 210, Richmond, BC,
V6V 1W1
(604) 273-6441
Emp Here 50
SIC 3295 Minerals, ground or treated

D-U-N-S 24-798-9523   (BR)
SAFWAY SERVICES CANADA, ULC
(*Suby of* Safway Group Holding LLC)
11211 Twigg Pl, Richmond, BC, V6V 3C9
(604) 294-2753
Emp Here 25
SIC 1799 Special trade contractors, nec

D-U-N-S 25-486-9456   (BR)
SIEMENS CANADA LIMITED
4011 Viking Way Suite 150, Richmond, BC,
V6V 2K9
(604) 233-1700
Emp Here 70
SIC 5047 Medical and hospital equipment

D-U-N-S 24-724-4882   (HQ)
SKANA FOREST PRODUCTS LTD
(*Suby of* J.C. Beveridge Equities Ltd)
20800 Westminster Hwy Suite 1303, Rich-
mond, BC, V6V 2W3
(604) 273-5441
Emp Here 20   *Emp Total* 14
Sales 8,575,885
SIC 5031 Lumber, plywood, and millwork
Pr Pr John Christopher Beveridge

D-U-N-S 25-899-0514   (BR)
STAPLES CANADA INC
STAPLES THE BUSINESS DEPOT
(*Suby of* Staples, Inc.)
2780 Sweden Way Suite 110, Richmond, BC,
V6V 2X1
(604) 303-7850
Emp Here 40
SIC 5943 Stationery stores

D-U-N-S 20-944-5225   (BR)
STARBUCKS COFFEE CANADA, INC
(*Suby of* Starbucks Corporation)
12571 Bridgeport Rd Unit 110, Richmond, BC,
V6V 1J4
(604) 279-9328
Emp Here 20
SIC 5812 Eating places

D-U-N-S 24-355-3109   (BR)
STUART OLSON CONSTRUCTION LTD
BUILDINGS DIVISION
13777 Commerce Pky Suite 300, Richmond,
BC, V6V 2X3
(604) 273-7765
Emp Here 125
SIC 1522 Residential construction, nec

D-U-N-S 24-646-0885   (BR)

SUN CHEMICAL LIMITED
13800 Vulcan Way, Richmond, BC, V6V 1K6
(604) 273-3791
Emp Here 20
SIC 5085 Industrial supplies

D-U-N-S 24-336-2626   (BR)
TECHNOLOGIES METAFORE INC
MICROAGE COMPUTER CENTRES
4320 Viking Way Unit 130, Richmond, BC,
V6V 2L4
(604) 270-3555
Emp Here 30
SIC 7373 Computer integrated systems de-
sign

D-U-N-S 24-363-8488   (HQ)
TELDON MEDIA GROUP INC
TELDON PRINT MEDIA, DIV OF
(*Suby of* Teldon Media Group Inc)
12751 Vulcan Way Suite 100, Richmond, BC,
V6V 3C8
(604) 231-3454
Emp Here 50   *Emp Total* 300
Sales 29,212,199
SIC 2752 Commercial printing, lithographic
Pr Pr Michael Mcadam
Dir Volker Wagner

D-U-N-S 24-101-4500   (BR)
TERVITA CORPORATION
(*Suby of* Tervita Corporation)
13511 Vulcan Way Unit 160, Richmond, BC,
V6V 1K4
(604) 214-7000
Emp Here 60
SIC 1389 Oil and gas field services, nec

D-U-N-S 20-115-9787   (HQ)
THOMAS SKINNER & SON LIMITED
13880 Vulcan Way, Richmond, BC, V6V 1K6
(604) 276-2131
Emp Here 50   *Emp Total* 2
Sales 21,656,275
SIC 5084 Industrial machinery and equipment
Pr Pr Paul Krainer
  Vincent Khoo

D-U-N-S 24-838-4174   (SL)
TRIMSEAL PLASTICS LTD
3511 Jacombs Rd, Richmond, BC, V6V 1Z8
(604) 278-3803
Emp Here 75   *Sales* 4,450,603
SIC 2782 Blankbooks and looseleaf binders

D-U-N-S 24-838-6567   (BR)
TYCO ELECTRONICS CANADA ULC
13120 Vanier Pl Suite 110, Richmond, BC,
V6V 2J2
(604) 276-8611
Emp Here 23
SIC 5065 Electronic parts and equipment, nec

D-U-N-S 24-566-5260   (SL)
UNITED LOCK-BLOCK LTD
13171 Mitchell Rd, Richmond, BC, V6V 1M7
(604) 325-9161
Emp Here 30   *Sales* 6,128,699
SIC 3272 Concrete products, nec
Pr Pr James Drew
  Janet Drew

D-U-N-S 25-195-5266   (BR)
URBAN SYSTEMS LTD
13353 Commerce Pky Unit 2163, Richmond,
BC, V6V 3A1
(604) 736-6336
Emp Here 45
SIC 8711 Engineering services

D-U-N-S 24-367-2420   (HQ)
VERSACOLD LOGISTICS CANADA INC
VERSACOLD LOGISTICS SERVICES
3371 No 6 Rd, Richmond, BC, V6V 1P6
(604) 258-0350
Emp Here 50   *Emp Total* 1
Sales 56,544,543
SIC 4222 Refrigerated warehousing and stor-

age
Pr Doug Harrison
  Michele (Mike) Arcamone
Sr VP Sr VP Jim Macintosh
Sr VP Sr VP Sandro Caccaro
Sr VP Sr VP Richard Tremblay
  Roger Rees
S&M/VP Mark Dienesch
Sr VP Laurie Wright
Sr VP Bala Puvitharan
Sr VP Sr VP Marcelo Bohm

D-U-N-S 24-313-3220   (HQ)
VOESTALPINE NORTRAK LTD
5500 Parkwood Way, Richmond, BC, V6V
2M4
(604) 273-3030
Emp Here 132   *Emp Total* 47,186
Sales 20,825,471
SIC 3312 Blast furnaces and steel mills
Dir Eddie Pienhopf
Dir Allan Tuningley

D-U-N-S 20-453-6361   (BR)
VOESTALPINE NORTRAK LTD
5500 Parkwood Way, Richmond, BC, V6V
2M4
(604) 231-3358
Emp Here 60
SIC 3312 Blast furnaces and steel mills

D-U-N-S 24-897-7183   (BR)
WAINBEE LIMITED
2231 Vauxhall Pl, Richmond, BC, V6V 1Z5
(604) 278-4288
Emp Here 20
SIC 5084 Industrial machinery and equipment

D-U-N-S 24-887-7334   (HQ)
WARTSILA CANADA, INCORPORATED
WARTSILA CANADA INCORPOREE
1771 Savage Rd, Richmond, BC, V6V 1R1
(604) 244-8181
Emp Here 80   *Emp Total* 18,332
Sales 11,746,673
SIC 3731 Shipbuilding and repairing
Ch Bd Tomas Ronn
Pr Rumi Mistry
Dir Aaron Gordon Bresnahan
Dir Guido Barbazza

D-U-N-S 24-593-8188   (SL)
**WESTCOAST CONTEMPO FASHIONS LIM-
ITED**
MAC & JAC
100-13551 Commerce Pky, Richmond, BC,
V6V 2L1
(604) 231-0400
Emp Here 30   *Sales* 14,983,031
SIC 5137 Women's and children's clothing
Pr Pr Eric Karls
VP Lelani Karls

D-U-N-S 25-484-6736   (BR)
WESTROCK COMPANY OF CANADA INC
IMAGE PAC GRAPHICS
(*Suby of* Westrock Company)
13160 Vanier Pl Suite 190, Richmond, BC,
V6V 2J2
(604) 214-7040
Emp Here 23
SIC 7336 Commercial art and graphic design

D-U-N-S 24-318-0564   (BR)
WEXXAR PACKAGING INC
WEXXAR/BEL
14211 Burrows Rd Unit 1, Richmond, BC, V6V
1K9
(604) 270-0811
Emp Here 80
SIC 3565 Packaging machinery

D-U-N-S 20-735-0815   (BR)
WORLDPAC CANADA INC
(*Suby of* Advance Auto Parts, Inc.)
13480 Crestwood Pl Unit 120, Richmond, BC,
V6V 2K1

(604) 248-1059
Emp Here 40
SIC 5531 Auto and home supply stores

Richmond, BC V6W
Greater Vancouver County

D-U-N-S 20-309-0683   (BR)
7922825 CANADA INC
NETRICOM
651 Fraserwood Pl Unit 210, Richmond, BC, V6W 1J3
(604) 247-4001
Emp Here 30
SIC 4899 Communication services, nec

D-U-N-S 20-656-0968   (BR)
ADESA AUCTIONS CANADA CORPORATION
ADESA VANCOUVER
7111 No. 8 Rd, Richmond, BC, V6W 1L9
(604) 232-4403
Emp Here 225
SIC 5012 Automobiles and other motor vehicles

D-U-N-S 24-762-1048   (BR)
ANIXTER CANADA INC
18371 Blundell Rd, Richmond, BC, V6W 1L8
(604) 276-0366
Emp Here 30
SIC 5051 Metals service centers and offices

D-U-N-S 24-346-7276   (BR)
AQUATERRA CORPORATION
CANADIAN SPRINGS
6560 Mcmillan Way, Richmond, BC, V6W 1L2
(604) 232-7600
Emp Here 100
SIC 5149 Groceries and related products, nec

D-U-N-S 20-646-7073   (BR)
AQUATERRA CORPORATION
CANADIAN SPRINGS WATER COMPANY
6560 Mcmillan Way, Richmond, BC, V6W 1L2
(604) 232-7610
Emp Here 100
SIC 5963 Direct selling establishments

D-U-N-S 24-696-5776   (BR)
ARMTEC LP
ARMTEC
7900 Nelson Rd, Richmond, BC, V6W 1G4
(604) 278-9766
Emp Here 150
SIC 3312 Blast furnaces and steel mills

D-U-N-S 24-838-3499   (BR)
BIRD CONSTRUCTION COMPANY LIMITED
6900 Graybar Rd Suite 2370, Richmond, BC, V6W 0A5
(604) 271-4600
Emp Here 100
SIC 1542 Nonresidential construction, nec

D-U-N-S 20-256-1598   (BR)
CINEPLEX ODEON CORPORATION
SILVERCITY RIVERPORT
14211 Entertainment Blvd, Richmond, BC, V6W 1K4
(604) 277-5993
Emp Here 20
SIC 7832 Motion picture theaters, except drive-in

D-U-N-S 20-255-4606   (BR)
COCA-COLA REFRESHMENTS CANADA COMPANY
(*Suby of* The Coca-Cola Company)
7200 Nelson Rd, Richmond, BC, V6W 1G4
(416) 424-6000
Emp Here 150
SIC 4225 General warehousing and storage

D-U-N-S 24-174-6135   (HQ)
COMMERCIAL LOGISTICS INC

16133 Blundell Rd, Richmond, BC, V6W 0A3
(604) 276-1300
Emp Here 60   *Emp Total* 280
Sales 33,276,240
SIC 4731 Freight transportation arrangement
Pr Dennis Chrismas

D-U-N-S 20-332-4574   (SL)
COUNTRY MEADOWS GOLF COURSE LTD
ROOSTERTAIL GRILL
8482 No. 6 Rd, Richmond, BC, V6W 1E2
(604) 241-4653
Emp Here 50   *Sales* 2,188,821
SIC 7992 Public golf courses

D-U-N-S 24-373-8734   (BR)
DUECK CHEVROLET BUICK CADILLAC GMC LIMITED
DUECK GM
12100 Featherstone Way, Richmond, BC, V6W 1K9
(604) 273-1311
Emp Here 50
SIC 5511 New and used car dealers

D-U-N-S 24-457-0966   (HQ)
E.C.S. ELECTRICAL CABLE SUPPLY LTD
6900 Graybar Rd Unit 3135, Richmond, BC, V6W 0A5
(604) 207-1500
Emp Here 25   *Emp Total* 90
Sales 27,460,157
SIC 5063 Electrical apparatus and equipment
  Mohamed Mohseni
Pr Gordon Thursfield

D-U-N-S 25-290-7472   (BR)
EXPEDITORS CANADA INC
21320 Gordon Way Suite 200, Richmond, BC, V6W 1J8
(604) 244-8543
Emp Here 31
SIC 4731 Freight transportation arrangement

D-U-N-S 24-163-1985   (SL)
GEMINI PACKAGING LTD
12071 Jacobson Way Unit 150, Richmond, BC, V6W 1L5
(604) 278-3455
Emp Here 50   *Sales* 1,021,450
SIC 2841 Soap and other detergents

D-U-N-S 20-537-0153   (BR)
GIENOW WINDOWS & DOORS INC
ARCHITECTUAL WINDOWS AND DOORS
(*Suby of* H.I.G. Capital Inc.)
21300 Gordon Way Suite 178, Richmond, BC, V6W 1M2
(604) 233-0477
Emp Here 36
SIC 2431 Millwork

D-U-N-S 24-383-8633   (BR)
HARRIS STEEL ULC
HARRIS REBAR
(*Suby of* Nucor Corporation)
7440 Nelson Rd, Richmond, BC, V6W 1G4
(604) 244-0575
Emp Here 40
SIC 3449 Miscellaneous Metalwork

D-U-N-S 20-178-8747   (BR)
HUDSON'S BAY COMPANY
VANCOUVER LOGISTICS CENTER
18111 Blundell Rd, Richmond, BC, V6W 1L8
(604) 249-3000
Emp Here 400
SIC 4225 General warehousing and storage

D-U-N-S 24-361-9236   (HQ)
ILLEN PRODUCTS LTD
IMPRINT PLUS
(*Suby of* Illen Products Ltd)
21320 Gordon Way Unit 260, Richmond, BC, V6W 1J8
(604) 278-7147
Emp Here 56   *Emp Total* 58
Sales 4,961,328

SIC 3999 Manufacturing industries, nec

D-U-N-S 25-219-6951   (BR)
INGRAM MICRO INC
7451 Nelson Rd, Richmond, BC, V6W 1L7
(604) 247-1275
Emp Here 120
SIC 5045 Computers, peripherals, and software

D-U-N-S 24-153-4122   (SL)
NICKELS CUSTOM CABINETS LTD
NICHELS CABINETS
6760 Graybar Rd, Richmond, BC, V6W 1J1
(604) 270-8080
Emp Here 50   *Sales* 2,918,428
SIC 2434 Wood kitchen cabinets

D-U-N-S 20-880-9314   (SL)
NORTHERN CARTAGE LTD
18111 Blundell Rd, Richmond, BC, V6W 1L8

Emp Here 53   *Sales* 4,158,760
SIC 4212 Local trucking, without storage

D-U-N-S 20-713-6060   (SL)
PANABODE INTERNATIONAL LTD
6311 Graybar Rd, Richmond, BC, V6W 1H3
(604) 270-7891
Emp Here 25   *Sales* 3,283,232
SIC 2452 Prefabricated wood buildings

D-U-N-S 24-684-6849   (HQ)
PRIMESOURCE BUILDING PRODUCTS CANADA CORPORATION
(*Suby of* Primesource Building Products, Inc.)
7431 Nelson Rd Suite 110, Richmond, BC, V6W 1G3
(604) 231-0473
Emp Here 30   *Emp Total* 1,200
Sales 50,131,903
SIC 5085 Industrial supplies
Rgnl Mgr Michael Gibson
CEO Mona Zinman
Pr Ken Fishbein
  Jerry Kegley

D-U-N-S 20-131-8308   (BR)
SCI LOGISTICS LTD
12291 Riverside Way, Richmond, BC, V6W 1K8
(604) 272-3177
Emp Here 30
SIC 4731 Freight transportation arrangement

D-U-N-S 20-590-6527   (BR)
SCHOOL DISTRICT NO. 43 (COQUITLAM)
SIDAWAY ELEMENTARY SCHOOL
12600 Blundell Rd, Richmond, BC, V6W 1B3
(604) 668-6466
Emp Here 25
SIC 8211 Elementary and secondary schools

D-U-N-S 20-270-2585   (BR)
T & T SUPERMARKET INC
22031 Fraserwood Way, Richmond, BC, V6W 1J5
(604) 276-9889
Emp Here 20
SIC 4225 General warehousing and storage

D-U-N-S 24-980-1127   (BR)
TECH DATA CANADA CORPORATION
7415 Nelson Rd Suite 115, Richmond, BC, V6W 1G3
(604) 270-3296
Emp Here 35
SIC 5045 Computers, peripherals, and software

D-U-N-S 24-594-9581   (HQ)
TOYO TIRE CANADA INC.
TOYO TIRES
7791 Nelson Rd Unit 120, Richmond, BC, V6W 1G3
(604) 304-1941
Emp Here 33   *Emp Total* 11,333
Sales 9,268,886
SIC 5531 Auto and home supply stores

Pr Pr Shoji Hirao
Sec Shabbir Mohammad
  Matsaru Oda

D-U-N-S 24-797-3605   (BR)
UPS SCS, INC
UPS SUPPLY TEAM SOLUTIONS
7451 Nelson Rd, Richmond, BC, V6W 1L7
(604) 270-9449
Emp Here 80
SIC 4731 Freight transportation arrangement

D-U-N-S 24-314-1178   (BR)
VOLKSWAGEN GROUP CANADA INC
21720 Fraserwood Way, Richmond, BC, V6W 1J6
(604) 233-9000
Emp Here 50
SIC 5013 Motor vehicle supplies and new parts

Richmond, BC V6X
Greater Vancouver County

D-U-N-S 20-177-9209   (BR)
3499481 CANADA INC
SUPER PET DIV OF
4551 No. 3 Rd, Richmond, BC, V6X 2C3
(604) 214-1306
Emp Here 26
SIC 5999 Miscellaneous retail stores, nec

D-U-N-S 24-803-2562   (BR)
ABB INC
VENTYX, DIV
10651 Shellbridge Way, Richmond, BC, V6X 2W8
(604) 207-6000
Emp Here 170
SIC 7372 Prepackaged software

D-U-N-S 24-029-3639   (HQ)
AZ TRADING CO. LTD
AZ HOME AND GIFTS
(*Suby of* AZ Trading Co. Ltd)
7080 River Rd Suite 223, Richmond, BC, V6X 1X5
(604) 214-3600
Emp Here 37   *Emp Total* 50
Sales 2,772,507
SIC 5947 Gift, novelty, and souvenir shop

D-U-N-S 25-714-9369   (BR)
ACCENT INNS INC
ACCENT INN HOTEL
10551 St. Edwards Dr, Richmond, BC, V6X 3L8
(604) 273-3311
Emp Here 60
SIC 7011 Hotels and motels

D-U-N-S 20-864-1225   (HQ)
AVERY WEIGH-TRONIX
(*Suby of* Illinois Tool Works Inc.)
9111 River Dr, Richmond, BC, V6X 1Z1
(604) 273-9401
Emp Here 36   *Emp Total* 50,000
Sales 2,918,428
SIC 3596 Scales and balances, except laboratory

D-U-N-S 24-838-7425   (SL)
BANDSTRA MOVING SYSTEMS LTD
9920 River Dr Unit 135, Richmond, BC, V6X 3S3
(604) 273-5111
Emp Here 20   *Sales* 1,167,371
SIC 4214 Local trucking with storage

D-U-N-S 20-514-7312   (BR)
BANDSTRA TRANSPORTATION SYSTEMS LTD
9920 River Dr Unit 135, Richmond, BC, V6X 3S3
(604) 270-4440
Emp Here 20

SIC 4213 Trucking, except local

D-U-N-S 20-709-6517   (BR)
BANK OF MONTREAL
BMO
3880 No. 3 Rd Suite 100, Richmond, BC, V6X 2C1
(604) 668-1388
Emp Here 20
SIC 6021 National commercial banks

D-U-N-S 25-975-2632   (SL)
BLUNDELL INDUSTRIES LTD
11351 River Rd, Richmond, BC, V6X 1Z6
(604) 270-3300
Emp Here 70   *Sales* 13,391,400
SIC 6712 Bank holding companies
Pr Pr Ian Tak Yen Law
  Anita Law
VP Fin Russ Kitaura

D-U-N-S 20-026-9921   (BR)
BOARD OF EDUCATION SCHOOL DISTRICT #38 (RICHMOND)
R C TALMEY ELEMENTARY SCHOOL
9500 Kilby Dr, Richmond, BC, V6X 3N2
(604) 668-6275
Emp Here 20
SIC 8211 Elementary and secondary schools

D-U-N-S 25-019-9429   (BR)
BOARD OF EDUCATION SCHOOL DISTRICT #38 (RICHMOND)
ROBERT J TAIT ELEMENTARY SCHOOL
10071 Finlayson Dr, Richmond, BC, V6X 1W7
(604) 668-6444
Emp Here 40
SIC 8211 Elementary and secondary schools

D-U-N-S 20-202-7426   (BR)
BOARD OF EDUCATION SCHOOL DISTRICT #38 (RICHMOND)
TOMSETT ELEMENTARY SCHOOL
9671 Odlin Rd, Richmond, BC, V6X 1E1
(604) 668-6448
Emp Here 31
SIC 8211 Elementary and secondary schools

D-U-N-S 25-231-7466   (BR)
BRICK WAREHOUSE LP, THE
BRICK, THE
3100 St. Edwards Dr Unit 150, Richmond, BC, V6X 4C4
(604) 270-8829
Emp Here 25
SIC 5712 Furniture stores

D-U-N-S 20-914-1733   (BR)
BRITISH COLUMBIA AUTOMOBILE ASSOCIATION
BCAA
5951 No. 3 Rd Unit 180, Richmond, BC, V6X 2E3
(604) 268-5850
Emp Here 20
SIC 8621 Professional organizations

D-U-N-S 20-190-5150   (SL)
BUDGET BRAKE & MUFFLER
4280 No. 3 Rd Suite 120, Richmond, BC, V6X 2C2
(604) 273-1288
Emp Here 100   *Sales* 10,145,000
SIC 7533 Auto exhaust system repair shops
Pr Pr Phil Murray

D-U-N-S 25-717-4110   (BR)
CACTUS RESTAURANTS LTD
CACTUS CLUB
5500 No. 3 Rd, Richmond, BC, V6X 2C8
(604) 244-9969
Emp Here 80
SIC 5812 Eating places

D-U-N-S 25-288-9159   (BR)
CANADA POST CORPORATION
RICHMOND DELIVERY CENTER
7680 River Rd, Richmond, BC, V6X 3K0

(604) 273-3743
Emp Here 240
SIC 4311 U.s. postal service

D-U-N-S 24-696-3011   (HQ)
CHOYS HOLDINGS INCORPORATED
FRESH CHOICE FOOD DISTRIBUTION & SERVICES
(*Suby of* Top Management Incorporated)
4751 Shell Rd Suite 2, Richmond, BC, V6X 3H4
(604) 270-6882
Emp Here 40   *Emp Total* 2
Sales 12,085,616
SIC 5147 Meats and meat products
Pr Pr George Choy
  Cecelia Choy

D-U-N-S 25-697-1920   (SL)
CHUNG KEE NOODLE SHOP LTD
MAK'S NOODLE RESTAURANT
8291 Alexandra Rd Suite 185, Richmond, BC, V6X 1C3
(604) 231-8141
Emp Here 50   *Sales* 1,532,175
SIC 5812 Eating places

D-U-N-S 25-287-5216   (BR)
COSTCO WHOLESALE CANADA LTD
(*Suby of* Costco Wholesale Corporation)
9151 Bridgeport Rd Suite 54, Richmond, BC, V6X 3L9
(604) 270-3647
Emp Here 400
SIC 5099 Durable goods, nec

D-U-N-S 24-825-5440   (HQ)
DELTA TOUR AND TRAVEL SERVICES (CANADA) INC
DELTA TOUR VANCOUVER
5611 Cooney Rd Suite 160, Richmond, BC, V6X 3J6
(604) 233-0081
Emp Here 20   *Emp Total* 900
Sales 5,982,777
SIC 4724 Travel agencies
Pr Pr Eric Li
Opers Mgr Kelvin Chu

D-U-N-S 24-887-7151   (SL)
DYNAMIC FACILITY SERVICES LTD
4651 Shell Rd Suite 140, Richmond, BC, V6X 3M3
(604) 273-1619
Emp Here 275   *Sales* 11,052,800
SIC 7349 Building maintenance services, nec
Pr Pr Mukhtar Olak
  Mohan Olak

D-U-N-S 25-514-1384   (BR)
EXECUTIVE HOTELS GENERAL PARTNERSHIP
EXECUTIVE AIRPORT PLAZA
7311 Westminster Hwy, Richmond, BC, V6X 1A3
(604) 278-5555
Emp Here 200
SIC 7011 Hotels and motels

D-U-N-S 20-748-4122   (SL)
FJORD PACIFIC MARINE INDUSTRIES LTD.
2400 Simpson Rd, Richmond, BC, V6X 2P9
(604) 270-3393
Emp Here 75   *Sales* 11,454,720
SIC 2091 Canned and cured fish and seafoods
Genl Mgr Don Pollard

D-U-N-S 25-534-8252   (SL)
GLOBAL COMMERCE DEVELOPMENT INC
11611 Bridgeport Rd, Richmond, BC, V6X 1T5
(604) 278-8688
Emp Here 100   *Sales* 19,794,560
SIC 5149 Groceries and related products, nec
  Anne Chong-Hill
  Richard Breakell
  John Burgis
  Lawrence Hill

D-U-N-S 25-365-1319   (BR)
GREAT CANADIAN CASINOS INC
RIVER ROCK CASINO RESORT
(*Suby of* Great Canadian Gaming Corporation)
8811 River Rd, Richmond, BC, V6X 3P8
(604) 247-8900
Emp Here 450
SIC 7999 Amusement and recreation, nec

D-U-N-S 25-268-0160   (BR)
GREAT PACIFIC INDUSTRIES INC
SAVE-ON-FOODS
8200 Ackroyd Rd, Richmond, BC, V6X 1B5
(604) 278-3229
Emp Here 300
SIC 5411 Grocery stores

D-U-N-S 25-612-3076   (BR)
GULF AND FRASER FISHERMEN'S CREDIT UNION
G&F FINANCIAL GROUP
7971 Westminster Hwy, Richmond, BC, V6X 1A4
(604) 419-8888
Emp Here 20
SIC 6062 State credit unions

D-U-N-S 24-681-4081   (BR)
HSBC BANK CANADA
4380 No. 3 Rd Suite 1010, Richmond, BC, V6X 3V7
(604) 270-8711
Emp Here 45
SIC 6021 National commercial banks

D-U-N-S 20-918-6451   (SL)
HANSEN INDUSTRIES LTD
2871 Olafsen Ave, Richmond, BC, V6X 2R4
(604) 278-2223
Emp Here 55   *Sales* 6,201,660
SIC 3469 Metal stampings, nec
  Edwin Beange

D-U-N-S 20-105-5907   (BR)
HUDSON'S BAY COMPANY
HOME OUTFITTERS
5300 No. 3 Rd Unit 101, Richmond, BC, V6X 2X9
(604) 248-0475
Emp Here 60
SIC 5311 Department stores

D-U-N-S 25-697-1870   (SL)
IMPERIAL SECURITY AND PROTECTION SERVICES LTD
4871 Shell Rd Suite 2255, Richmond, BC, V6X 3Z6
(604) 231-9973
Emp Here 50   *Sales* 1,532,175
SIC 7381 Detective and armored car services

D-U-N-S 25-571-3240   (BR)
INDIGO BOOKS & MUSIC INC
CHAPTERS BOOK STORE
(*Suby of* Indigo Books & Music Inc)
8171 Ackroyd Rd Suite 180, Richmond, BC, V6X 3K1

Emp Here 40
SIC 5942 Book stores

D-U-N-S 20-554-9913   (BR)
INSURANCE CORPORATION OF BRITISH COLUMBIA
DRIVERS SERVICES OFFICE
5740 Minoru Blvd, Richmond, BC, V6X 2A9
(604) 232-4350
Emp Here 25
SIC 6331 Fire, marine, and casualty insurance

D-U-N-S 24-166-2287   (SL)
INTERNATIONAL STAGE LINES INC
4171 Vanguard Rd, Richmond, BC, V6X 2P6
(604) 270-6135
Emp Here 100   *Sales* 4,742,446
SIC 4142 Bus charter service, except local

D-U-N-S 25-069-2183   (SL)

D-U-N-S 25-365-1319   (BR)
INTERNATIONAL VINEYARD INC
4631 Shell Rd Suite 165, Richmond, BC, V6X 3M4
(604) 303-5778
Emp Here 50   *Sales* 4,304,681
SIC 2032 Canned specialties

D-U-N-S 25-095-8980   (SL)
INTERTECH BUILDING SERVICES LTD
10451 Shellbridge Way Suite 201, Richmond, BC, V6X 2W8
(604) 270-3478
Emp Here 54   *Sales* 1,605,135
SIC 7349 Building maintenance services, nec

D-U-N-S 24-980-0806   (BR)
INVESTORS GROUP FINANCIAL SERVICES INC
INVESTORS FINANCIAL SERVICES PLANNING CENTRE
5811 Cooney Rd Suite 100, Richmond, BC, V6X 3M1
(604) 270-7700
Emp Here 60
SIC 8741 Management services

D-U-N-S 24-372-4549   (HQ)
JTB INTERNATIONAL (CANADA) LTD
JTB CANADA
8899 Odlin Cres, Richmond, BC, V6X 3Z7
(604) 276-0300
Emp Here 50   *Emp Total* 26,646
Sales 18,469,648
SIC 4725 Tour operators
Pr Pr Hiroyuki Kitagawa
Ex Dir Isao Onaga
  Andrew Shimizu
Acctg Dir Amyn Khimji
Dir Chiemi Nishinari
Genl Mgr Toru Tsuthie

D-U-N-S 24-392-7159   (BR)
KAL TIRE LTD
2633 No. 5 Rd, Richmond, BC, V6X 2S8
(604) 278-9181
Emp Here 20
SIC 5531 Auto and home supply stores

D-U-N-S 25-186-1134   (SL)
LZB ENTERPRISES LTD
LA-Z-BOY FURNITURE GALLERIES
3100 St. Edwards Dr Suite 110, Richmond, BC, V6X 4C4
(604) 248-0330
Emp Here 70   *Sales* 11,058,050
SIC 5712 Furniture stores
Pr Pr Gerald Miller
  Mariann Miller

D-U-N-S 25-713-6358   (SL)
LEGENDARY CANADIAN ENTERPRISES LTD
FISHERMAN'S TERRACE SEAFOOD RESTAURANT
4151 Hazelbridge Way Unit 3580, Richmond, BC, V6X 4J7
(604) 303-9739
Emp Here 50   *Sales* 1,532,175
SIC 5812 Eating places

D-U-N-S 25-187-7171   (BR)
LOBLAWS INC
REAL CANADIAN SUPERSTORE
4651 No. 3 Rd Suite 1557, Richmond, BC, V6X 2C4
(604) 233-2418
Emp Here 100
SIC 5141 Groceries, general line

D-U-N-S 25-273-1021   (BR)
LONDON DRUGS LIMITED
5951 No. 3 Rd, Richmond, BC, V6X 2E3
(604) 278-4521
Emp Here 70
SIC 5912 Drug stores and proprietary stores

D-U-N-S 25-273-0973   (BR)
LORDCO PARTS LTD

LORDCO AUTO PARTS
5355 No. 3 Rd, Richmond, BC, V6X 2C7
(604) 276-1866
Emp Here 25
SIC 5531 Auto and home supply stores

D-U-N-S 24-640-1095 (HQ)
M T K AUTO WEST LTD
AUTO WEST BMW
(Suby of M T K Auto West Ltd)
10780 Cambie Rd, Richmond, BC, V6X 1K8
(604) 233-0700
Emp Here 20 Emp Total 160
Sales 80,384,000
SIC 5511 New and used car dealers
Pr Pr Joachim Neumann
  Pete Sargent
  Leonard Fong

D-U-N-S 24-424-1654 (BR)
M T K AUTO WEST LTD
MINI RICHMOND
(Suby of M T K Auto West Ltd)
10700 Cambie Rd Suite 410, Richmond, BC,
V6X 1K8
(604) 233-0700
Emp Here 20
SIC 5511 New and used car dealers

D-U-N-S 20-188-1690 (BR)
MANUFACTURERS LIFE INSURANCE COMPANY, THE
MANULIFE FINANCIAL
4671 No. 3 Rd Suite 110, Richmond, BC, V6X 2C3
(604) 273-6388
Emp Here 60
SIC 6411 Insurance agents, brokers, and service

D-U-N-S 20-792-5160 (BR)
MCDONALD'S RESTAURANTS OF CANADA LIMITED
MCDONALD'S
(Suby of McDonald's Corporation)
10700 Cambie Rd Suite 115, Richmond, BC, V6X 1K8
(604) 718-1023
Emp Here 60
SIC 5812 Eating places

D-U-N-S 25-318-1747 (BR)
MCDONALD'S RESTAURANTS OF CANADA LIMITED
MCDONALD'S
(Suby of McDonald's Corporation)
8191 Alderbridge Way, Richmond, BC, V6X 3A9
(604) 718-1088
Emp Here 85
SIC 5812 Eating places

D-U-N-S 24-370-9003 (SL)
MENNONITE INTERMEDIATE CARE HOME SOCIETY OF RICHMOND
PINEGROVE PLACE
11331 Mellis Dr, Richmond, BC, V6X 1L8
(604) 278-1296
Emp Here 105 Sales 4,815,406
SIC 8051 Skilled nursing care facilities

D-U-N-S 20-029-2444 (BR)
MOXIE'S RESTAURANTS, LIMITED PARTNERSHIP
MOXIE CLASSIC GRILL
3233 St. Edwards Dr, Richmond, BC, V6X 3K9
(604) 303-1111
Emp Here 50
SIC 5812 Eating places

D-U-N-S 25-107-6493 (BR)
MULTIPLE REALTY LTD
9780 Cambie Rd Unit 110, Richmond, BC, V6X 1K4
(604) 273-8555
Emp Here 70
SIC 6531 Real estate agents and managers

D-U-N-S 25-831-4012 (BR)
NIPPON EXPRESS CANADA LTD
7360 River Rd, Richmond, BC, V6X 1X6
(604) 278-6084
Emp Here 22
SIC 4731 Freight transportation arrangement

D-U-N-S 20-114-8694 (BR)
NORTHLAND PROPERTIES CORPORATION
SANDMAN SIGNATURE VANCOUVER AIRPORT HOTEL & RESORT
(Suby of Northland Properties Corporation)
10251 St. Edwards Dr, Richmond, BC, V6X 2M9
(604) 278-9611
Emp Here 50
SIC 7011 Hotels and motels

D-U-N-S 24-804-0128 (HQ)
PAPER EXCELLENCE CANADA HOLDINGS CORPORATION
10551 Shellbridge Way Suite 95, Richmond, BC, V6X 2W8
(604) 232-2453
Emp Here 50 Emp Total 114
Sales 4,888,367
SIC 2611 Pulp mills

D-U-N-S 24-974-6553 (BR)
PENTECOSTAL ASSEMBLIES OF CANADA, THE
RICHMOND PENTECOSTAL CHURCH
9300 Westminster Hwy, Richmond, BC, V6X 1B1
(604) 278-3191
Emp Here 23
SIC 8661 Religious organizations

D-U-N-S 20-014-7176 (HQ)
PHELPS APARTMENT LAUNDRIES LTD
LAUNDRY PEOPLE
3640 No. 4 Rd Suite 1, Richmond, BC, V6X 2L7
(604) 257-8200
Emp Here 28 Emp Total 170
Sales 11,877,360
SIC 7359 Equipment rental and leasing, nec
  William Ung
Pr Pr Stanley Saibil
  Ellen Pan
  Conchita Ung

D-U-N-S 24-137-0782 (HQ)
PHELPS LEASING LTD
BUDGET RENT-A-CAR
3640 No. 4 Rd, Richmond, BC, V6X 2L7
(604) 257-8230
Emp Here 20 Emp Total 170
Sales 6,128,699
SIC 7514 Passenger car rental
Pr Pr William (Bill) Ung
  Olen Pan
  Conafita Ung

D-U-N-S 20-189-7555 (BR)
POSTMEDIA NETWORK INC
COLLEGE PRINTERS
7280 River Rd Suite 110, Richmond, BC, V6X 1X5

Emp Here 90
SIC 7374 Data processing and preparation

D-U-N-S 20-152-2880 (BR)
POSTMEDIA NETWORK INC
RICHMOND NEWS
5731 No. 3 Rd, Richmond, BC, V6X 2C9
(604) 270-8031
Emp Here 25
SIC 2711 Newspapers

D-U-N-S 24-326-4053 (BR)
PREMIUM BRANDS OPERATING LIMITED PARTNERSHIP
GRIMM'S FINE FOODS
7680 Alderbridge Way, Richmond, BC, V6X 2A2

(604) 717-6000
Emp Here 180
SIC 2013 Sausages and other prepared meats

D-U-N-S 20-562-7172 (BR)
RBC DOMINION SECURITIES INC
DOMINION SECURITIES
(Suby of Royal Bank Of Canada)
5811 Cooney Rd Suite 401, Richmond, BC, V6X 3M1
(604) 718-3000
Emp Here 33
SIC 6282 Investment advice

D-U-N-S 20-702-7439 (SL)
RAYMOND-CBE MACHINERY INC
11788 River Rd Suite 118, Richmond, BC, V6X 1Z7

Emp Here 103 Sales 2,261,782
SIC 3561 Pumps and pumping equipment

D-U-N-S 25-715-4815 (BR)
ROYAL BANK OF CANADA
RBC
(Suby of Royal Bank Of Canada)
8171 Ackroyd Rd Suite 1950, Richmond, BC, V6X 3K1
(604) 668-4997
Emp Here 27
SIC 6021 National commercial banks

D-U-N-S 25-716-5241 (BR)
ROYCO HOTELS & RESORTS LTD
TRAVELODGE HOTEL VANCOUVER AIRPORT
3071 St Edwards Dr, Richmond, BC, V6X 3K4
(604) 278-5155
Emp Here 40
SIC 7011 Hotels and motels

D-U-N-S 25-714-9906 (BR)
S.U.C.C.E.S.S. (ALSO KNOWN AS UNITED CHINESE COMMUNITY ENRICHMENT SERVICES SOCIETY)
S U C C E S S
8191 Westminster Hwy Unit 300, Richmond, BC, V6X 1A7
(604) 270-0077
Emp Here 20
SIC 8399 Social services, nec

D-U-N-S 24-456-3672 (SL)
SUNCREST CABINETS INC
4651 Vanguard Rd, Richmond, BC, V6X 2P7
(604) 278-3445
Emp Here 50 Sales 4,334,713
SIC 2541 Wood partitions and fixtures

D-U-N-S 25-648-3629 (BR)
T & T SUPERMARKET INC
8181 Cambie Rd Suite 1000, Richmond, BC, V6X 3X9

Emp Here 80
SIC 5411 Grocery stores

D-U-N-S 20-913-8390 (BR)
T & T SUPERMARKET INC
3700 No. 3 Rd Suite 1000, Richmond, BC, V6X 3X2
(604) 276-8808
Emp Here 150
SIC 5411 Grocery stores

D-U-N-S 20-278-4963 (SL)
TECHART WOODWORKS LTD
11220 Voyageur Way Unit 10, Richmond, BC, V6X 3E1
(604) 276-2282
Emp Here 600 Sales 63,324,509
SIC 2431 Millwork
Pr Pr Cheong Kong To

D-U-N-S 24-682-4804 (SL)
TETRA TECH OGD INC
(Suby of Tetra Tech, Inc.)
10851 Shellbridge Way Suite 100, Richmond,

BC, V6X 2W8
(604) 270-7728
Emp Here 160 Sales 28,600,594
SIC 8711 Engineering services
Pr Colin Craig
VP VP James Mcpherson

D-U-N-S 24-974-6439 (BR)
TORONTO-DOMINION BANK, THE
TD CANADA TRUST
(Suby of Toronto-Dominion Bank, The)
5300 No. 3 Rd Unit 626, Richmond, BC, V6X 2X9
(604) 273-0821
Emp Here 30
SIC 6021 National commercial banks

D-U-N-S 24-695-6437 (SL)
TOURLAND TRAVEL LTD
8899 Odlin Cres, Richmond, BC, V6X 3Z7
(604) 276-9592
Emp Here 45 Sales 10,725,223
SIC 4725 Tour operators
  Isao Onaga
  Hideo Nishi
  Gordon M. Craig

D-U-N-S 20-913-8762 (BR)
TOYS 'R' US (CANADA) LTD
TOYS 'R' US
(Suby of Toys "r" Us, Inc.)
5300 No. 3 Rd Suite 314, Richmond, BC, V6X 2X9
(604) 654-4790
Emp Here 45
SIC 5945 Hobby, toy, and game shops

D-U-N-S 25-054-5100 (HQ)
VANCOUVER AIRPORT CENTRE LIMITED
VANCOUVER AIRPORT MARRIOTT HOTEL
(Suby of Larco Investments Ltd)
7571 Westminster Hwy, Richmond, BC, V6X 1A3
(604) 276-2112
Emp Here 120 Emp Total 50
Sales 8,755,284
SIC 7011 Hotels and motels
Pr Pr Amin Lalji
  Vazir Kara

D-U-N-S 24-421-5500 (BR)
VANCOUVER AIRPORT CENTRE LIMITED
HILTON
(Suby of Larco Investments Ltd)
5911 Minoru Blvd, Richmond, BC, V6X 4C7
(604) 273-6336
Emp Here 110
SIC 7011 Hotels and motels

D-U-N-S 20-587-0467 (BR)
VANCOUVER CITY SAVINGS CREDIT UNION
VANCITY CREDIT UNION
5900 No. 3 Rd Suite 100, Richmond, BC, V6X 3P7
(604) 877-7263
Emp Here 20
SIC 6062 State credit unions

D-U-N-S 20-117-0966 (SL)
WALLACE SIGN-CRAFTERS WEST LIMITED
WALLACE NEON
2771 Simpson Rd, Richmond, BC, V6X 3H6

Emp Here 30 Sales 5,681,200
SIC 5046 Commercial equipment, nec
Pr Pr Don Armitage
  Joan Macdonald
Dir Ethel Armitage

D-U-N-S 25-710-4695 (BR)
WENDY'S RESTAURANTS OF CANADA INC
WENDY'S
(Suby of The Wendy's Company)
4700 No. 3 Rd, Richmond, BC, V6X 3C2

Emp Here 37

SIC 5812 Eating places

D-U-N-S 25-482-9948   (BR)
WHITE SPOT LIMITED
WHITE SPOT RESTAURANT
5880 No. 3 Rd, Richmond, BC, V6X 2E1
(604) 273-1556
Emp Here 75
SIC 5812 Eating places

D-U-N-S 20-106-2879   (BR)
WINNERS MERCHANTS INTERNATIONAL L.P.
WINNERS
(*Suby of* The TJX Companies Inc)
5300 No. 3 Rd Suite 856, Richmond, BC, V6X 2X9
(604) 279-9466
Emp Here 35
SIC 5651 Family clothing stores

Richmond, BC V6Y
Greater Vancouver County

D-U-N-S 25-110-1127   (BR)
BANK OF NOVA SCOTIA, THE
SCOTIABANK
6300 No. 3 Rd, Richmond, BC, V6Y 2B3
(604) 668-3079
Emp Here 45
SIC 6021 National commercial banks

D-U-N-S 20-589-5308   (BR)
BANQUE TORONTO-DOMINION, LA
TD CANADA TRUST
(*Suby of* Toronto-Dominion Bank, The)
6020 No. 3 Rd, Richmond, BC, V6Y 2B3
(604) 606-0700
Emp Here 20
SIC 6021 National commercial banks

D-U-N-S 20-713-3898   (BR)
BOARD OF EDUCATION SCHOOL DISTRICT #38 (RICHMOND)
RC PALMER SECONDARY SCHOOL
8160 St. Albans Rd, Richmond, BC, V6Y 2K9
(604) 668-6288
Emp Here 50
SIC 8211 Elementary and secondary schools

D-U-N-S 20-044-0753   (BR)
BOARD OF EDUCATION SCHOOL DISTRICT #38 (RICHMOND)
HOWARD DE BECK ELEMENTARY SCHOOL
8600 Ash St, Richmond, BC, V6Y 2S3
(604) 668-6281
Emp Here 25
SIC 8211 Elementary and secondary schools

D-U-N-S 20-713-3971   (BR)
BOARD OF EDUCATION SCHOOL DISTRICT #38 (RICHMOND)
ANDERSON ELEMENTARY SCHOOL
9460 Alberta Rd, Richmond, BC, V6Y 1T6
(604) 214-6629
Emp Here 50
SIC 8211 Elementary and secondary schools

D-U-N-S 20-044-6982   (BR)
BOARD OF EDUCATION SCHOOL DISTRICT #38 (RICHMOND)
RICHMOND SECONDARY
7171 Minoru Blvd, Richmond, BC, V6Y 1Z3
(604) 668-6400
Emp Here 97
SIC 8211 Elementary and secondary schools

D-U-N-S 20-713-3922   (BR)
BOARD OF EDUCATION SCHOOL DISTRICT #38 (RICHMOND)
FERRIS ELEMENTARY SCHOOL
7520 Sunnymede Cres, Richmond, BC, V6Y 2V8
(604) 668-6538
Emp Here 50

SIC 8211 Elementary and secondary schools

D-U-N-S 20-653-8832   (BR)
BOARD OF EDUCATION SCHOOL DISTRICT #38 (RICHMOND)
WILLIAM COOK ELEMENTARY SCHOOL
8600 Cook Rd, Richmond, BC, V6Y 1V7
(604) 668-6454
Emp Here 50
SIC 8211 Elementary and secondary schools

D-U-N-S 25-977-6651   (BR)
CIK TELECOM INC
6490 Euswell St, Richmond, BC, V6Y 2E9
(604) 628-3877
Emp Here 20
SIC 4899 Communication services, nec

D-U-N-S 24-578-2453   (BR)
CANADIAN IMPERIAL BANK OF COMMERCE
CIBC
6011 No. 3 Rd, Richmond, BC, V6Y 2B2
(604) 665-6106
Emp Here 50
SIC 6021 National commercial banks

D-U-N-S 25-104-2909   (HQ)
CHINA SHIPPING (CANADA) AGENCY CO. LTD
CHINA SHIPPING
8100 Granville Ave Unit 730, Richmond, BC, V6Y 3T6

Emp Here 31   *Emp Total* 7,546
Sales 4,908,000
SIC 7359 Equipment rental and leasing, nec

D-U-N-S 25-072-6536   (BR)
CINEPLEX ODEON CORPORATION
RICHMOND CENTRE CINEMA
6551 No. 3 Rd Suite 1702, Richmond, BC, V6Y 2B6

Emp Here 30
SIC 7832 Motion picture theaters, except drive-in

D-U-N-S 20-914-0974   (BR)
EARL'S RESTAURANTS LTD
(*Suby of* Earl's Restaurants Ltd)
5300 3 Rd Nw Suite 304, Richmond, BC, V6Y 1X9
(604) 303-9702
Emp Here 70
SIC 5812 Eating places

D-U-N-S 25-714-9807   (BR)
GAP (CANADA) INC
GAPKIDS
(*Suby of* The Gap Inc)
6551 No. 3 Rd Suite 1928, Richmond, BC, V6Y 2B6
(604) 270-6412
Emp Here 33
SIC 5651 Family clothing stores

D-U-N-S 20-368-3730   (BR)
GAP (CANADA) INC
BANANA REPUBLIC
(*Suby of* The Gap Inc)
6551 No. 3 Rd Suite 1640, Richmond, BC, V6Y 2B6

Emp Here 40
SIC 5651 Family clothing stores

D-U-N-S 25-689-7166   (BR)
GAP (CANADA) INC
GAP
(*Suby of* The Gap Inc)
6551 No. 3 Rd Suite 1924, Richmond, BC, V6Y 2B6
(604) 270-6747
Emp Here 35
SIC 5651 Family clothing stores

D-U-N-S 24-334-2826   (BR)
GOVERNING COUNCIL OF THE SALVA-

TION ARMY IN CANADA, THE
GOVERNING COUNCIL OF THE SALVATION ARMY IN CANADA, THE
6460 No. 4 Rd, Richmond, BC, V6Y 2S9
(604) 207-1212
Emp Here 20
SIC 8322 Individual and family services

D-U-N-S 25-270-0695   (BR)
HSBC BANK CANADA
HSBC
6168 No. 3 Rd, Richmond, BC, V6Y 2B3
(604) 276-8700
Emp Here 50
SIC 6021 National commercial banks

D-U-N-S 20-574-2042   (BR)
HUDSON'S BAY COMPANY
BAY, THE
6060 Minoru Blvd Suite 100, Richmond, BC, V6Y 1Y2
(604) 273-3844
Emp Here 310
SIC 5311 Department stores

D-U-N-S 20-347-1540   (BR)
KIN'S HOLDINGS LTD
KIN'S FARM MARKET
6060 Minoru Blvd Unit 1460, Richmond, BC, V6Y 2V7
(604) 214-0253
Emp Here 25
SIC 5431 Fruit and vegetable markets

D-U-N-S 24-724-9589   (SL)
MASTER HUNG BBQ & WON TON
8780 Blundell Rd Suite 140, Richmond, BC, V6Y 3Y8
(604) 272-3813
Emp Here 35   *Sales* 5,496,960
SIC 2098 Macaroni and spaghetti

D-U-N-S 20-657-9653   (BR)
OLD NAVY (CANADA) INC
(*Suby of* The Gap Inc)
6551 No. 3 Rd Suite 1410, Richmond, BC, V6Y 2B6
(604) 303-6700
Emp Here 30
SIC 5651 Family clothing stores

D-U-N-S 25-287-9267   (BR)
RAYMOND SALONS LTD
RAYMOND-HENNESSEY SALON & SPA RICHMOND CENTRE
(*Suby of* Raymond Salons Ltd)
6551 No. 3 Rd Suite 1450, Richmond, BC, V6Y 2B6
(604) 482-3262
Emp Here 26
SIC 7231 Beauty shops

D-U-N-S 24-345-9539   (BR)
RICHMOND HOSPITAL, THE
MINORU RESIDENCE
6111 Minoru Blvd, Richmond, BC, V6Y 1Y4
(604) 244-5300
Emp Here 200
SIC 8059 Nursing and personal care, nec

D-U-N-S 24-502-9657   (HQ)
RICHMOND PUBLIC LIBRARY BOARD
(*Suby of* Richmond Public Library Board)
7700 Minoru Gate Suite 100, Richmond, BC, V6Y 1R8
(604) 231-6422
Emp Here 75   *Emp Total* 109
Sales 6,502,070
SIC 8231 Libraries
Sec Greg Buss

D-U-N-S 20-569-9981   (BR)
RICHMOND, CITY OF
LIBRARY OF RICHMOND
7700 Minoru Gate Suite 100, Richmond, BC, V6Y 1R8
(604) 231-6401
Emp Here 20
SIC 8231 Libraries

D-U-N-S 20-590-6634   (BR)
SCHOOL DISTRICT NO. 43 (COQUITLAM)
WD FERRIS ELEMENTARY SCHOOL
7520 Sunnymede Cres, Richmond, BC, V6Y 2V8
(604) 668-6538
Emp Here 25
SIC 8211 Elementary and secondary schools

D-U-N-S 20-590-6667   (BR)
SCHOOL DISTRICT NO. 43 (COQUITLAM)
GENERAL CURRIE ELEMENTARY SCHOOL
8220 General Currie Rd, Richmond, BC, V6Y 1M1

Emp Here 40
SIC 8211 Elementary and secondary schools

D-U-N-S 24-174-0161   (BR)
SODEXO CANADA LTD
6111 Minoru Blvd, Richmond, BC, V6Y 1Y4
(604) 244-5314
Emp Here 35
SIC 5812 Eating places

D-U-N-S 20-860-3964   (BR)
SOURCE (BELL) ELECTRONICS INC, THE
SOURCE, THE
6551 No. 3 Rd Suite 1236a, Richmond, BC, V6Y 2B6
(604) 273-1475
Emp Here 25
SIC 5999 Miscellaneous retail stores, nec

D-U-N-S 25-314-1998   (BR)
STAPLES CANADA INC
STAPLES THE BUSINESS DEPOT
(*Suby of* Staples, Inc.)
6390 No. 3 Rd Suite 1, Richmond, BC, V6Y 2B3
(604) 270-9599
Emp Here 30
SIC 5943 Stationery stores

D-U-N-S 20-700-4735   (BR)
TOMMY HILFIGER CANADA INC
TOMMY HILFIGER STORE
6551 No. 3 Rd Suite 500, Richmond, BC, V6Y 2B7

Emp Here 30
SIC 5651 Family clothing stores

D-U-N-S 25-710-7342   (BR)
WHITE SPOT LIMITED
WHITE SPOT RESTAURANT
6551 No. 3 Rd Suite 1902, Richmond, BC, V6Y 2B6
(604) 278-3911
Emp Here 50
SIC 5812 Eating places

Richmond, BC V7A
Greater Vancouver County

D-U-N-S 24-939-0162   (SL)
0037264 BC LTD
11388 No. 5 Rd Suite 110, Richmond, BC, V7A 4E7
(604) 279-8484
Emp Here 75   *Sales* 3,793,956
SIC 7331 Direct mail advertising services

D-U-N-S 20-012-1155   (BR)
ACR GROUP INC
ACR RUBBER
12771 No. 5 Rd, Richmond, BC, V7A 4E9
(604) 274-9955
Emp Here 37
SIC 3069 Fabricated rubber products, nec

D-U-N-S 25-116-1972   (BR)
ACUREN GROUP INC
(*Suby of* Rockwood Service Corporation)
12271 Horseshoe Way, Richmond, BC, V7A 4V4

▲ Public Company   ■ Public Company Family Member   **HQ** Headquarters   **BR** Branch   **SL** Single Location

(604) 275-3800
Emp Here 90
SIC 3821 Laboratory apparatus and furniture

D-U-N-S 24-594-8612   (BR)
APEX COMMUNICATIONS INC
APEX WIRELESS
(*Suby of* Apex Communications Inc)
11666 Steveston Hwy Suite 3120, Richmond, BC, V7A 5J3
(604) 274-3300
Emp Here 20
SIC 5999 Miscellaneous retail stores, nec

D-U-N-S 20-713-3914   (BR)
BOARD OF EDUCATION SCHOOL DISTRICT #38 (RICHMOND)
THOMAS KIDD
10851 Shell Rd, Richmond, BC, V7A 3W6
(604) 668-6602
Emp Here 20
SIC 8211 Elementary and secondary schools

D-U-N-S 20-034-0862   (BR)
BOARD OF EDUCATION SCHOOL DISTRICT #38 (RICHMOND)
HUGH MCROBERTS SECONDARY SCHOOL
8980 Williams Rd, Richmond, BC, V7A 1G6
(604) 668-6600
Emp Here 100
SIC 8211 Elementary and secondary schools

D-U-N-S 20-026-9962   (BR)
BOARD OF EDUCATION SCHOOL DISTRICT #38 (RICHMOND)
ERRINGTON, J. T. ELEMENTARY SCHOOL
9831 Herbert Rd, Richmond, BC, V7A 1T6
(604) 668-6699
Emp Here 20
SIC 8211 Elementary and secondary schools

D-U-N-S 20-713-3948   (BR)
BOARD OF EDUCATION SCHOOL DISTRICT #38 (RICHMOND)
7700 Alouette Dr, Richmond, BC, V7A 1S1
(604) 668-6692
Emp Here 50
SIC 8211 Elementary and secondary schools

D-U-N-S 20-713-3856   (BR)
BOARD OF EDUCATION SCHOOL DISTRICT #38 (RICHMOND)
DANIEL WOODWARD ELEMENTARY
10300 Seacote Rd, Richmond, BC, V7A 4B2
(604) 668-7810
Emp Here 50
SIC 8211 Elementary and secondary schools

D-U-N-S 20-034-1035   (BR)
BOARD OF EDUCATION SCHOOL DISTRICT #38 (RICHMOND)
WALTER LEE ELEMENTARY SCHOOL
9491 Ash St, Richmond, BC, V7A 2T7
(604) 668-6269
Emp Here 30
SIC 8211 Elementary and secondary schools

D-U-N-S 20-713-3930   (BR)
BOARD OF EDUCATION SCHOOL DISTRICT #38 (RICHMOND)
WILLIAM BRIDGE ELEMENTARY
10400 Leonard Rd, Richmond, BC, V7A 2N5
(604) 668-6236
Emp Here 40
SIC 8211 Elementary and secondary schools

D-U-N-S 20-590-6493   (BR)
BOARD OF EDUCATION SCHOOL DISTRICT #38 (RICHMOND)
KINGSWOOD ELEMENTARY
11511 King Rd, Richmond, BC, V7A 3B5
(604) 668-6280
Emp Here 25
SIC 8211 Elementary and secondary schools

D-U-N-S 20-033-3628   (BR)
BOARD OF EDUCATION SCHOOL DISTRICT #38 (RICHMOND)

MATHEW MCNAIR SECONDARY SCHOOL
9500 No. 4 Rd, Richmond, BC, V7A 2Y9
(604) 668-6575
Emp Here 85
SIC 8211 Elementary and secondary schools

D-U-N-S 24-372-3074   (BR)
CANADIAN TIRE CORPORATION, LIMITED
CANADIAN TIRE
11388 Steveston Hwy, Richmond, BC, V7A 5J5
(604) 271-6651
Emp Here 50
SIC 5531 Auto and home supply stores

D-U-N-S 24-340-2943   (BR)
COAST MOUNTAIN BUS COMPANY LTD
CMBC
11133 Coppersmith Way, Richmond, BC, V7A 5E8
(604) 277-7787
Emp Here 443
SIC 4142 Bus charter service, except local

D-U-N-S 20-213-4388   (HQ)
CROWN CORRUGATED COMPANY
BOXMASTER, DIV OF
13911 Garden City Rd, Richmond, BC, V7A 2S5
(604) 277-7111
Emp Here 210   *Emp Total* 1,540
Sales 66,175,355
SIC 2653 Corrugated and solid fiber boxes
Pr Pr Joseph Beers
VP VP John Combatti
Dir Fraser Macfadyen
  Ted Lodge
Treas Ernest Conrads
Dir Dale Stahl

D-U-N-S 25-168-3397   (BR)
GORDON FOOD SERVICE CANADA LTD
GFS BRITISH COLOMBIA
12411 Horseshoe Way, Richmond, BC, V7A 4X6
(604) 277-7740
Emp Here 50
SIC 5141 Groceries, general line

D-U-N-S 20-514-1211   (HQ)
LONDON DRUGS LIMITED
12251 Horseshoe Way, Richmond, BC, V7A 4X5
(604) 272-7400
Emp Here 350   *Emp Total* 4,500
Sales 991,025,188
SIC 5912 Drug stores and proprietary stores
Ch Bd Brandt Louie
Pr Wynne Powell
VP Clint Mahlman
Dir Laird Miller

D-U-N-S 25-105-9564   (SL)
MDMI TECHNOLOGIES INC
12051 Horseshoe Way Unit 110, Richmond, BC, V7A 4V4

Emp Here 65   *Sales* 7,754,640
SIC 3841 Surgical and medical instruments
Pr Pr Jim Elliott
Fin Ex Richard Everest
  Rodney Elliott
Sec John Heroux

D-U-N-S 24-995-8984   (BR)
MAKITA CANADA INC
11771 Hammersmith Way, Richmond, BC, V7A 5H6
(604) 272-3104
Emp Here 25
SIC 5072 Hardware

D-U-N-S 20-792-3843   (BR)
MARK'S WORK WEARHOUSE LTD
11380 Steveston Hwy Suite 120, Richmond, BC, V7A 5J5
(604) 241-4016
Emp Here 20

SIC 5651 Family clothing stores

D-U-N-S 20-117-7040   (BR)
ORGANIKA HEALTH PRODUCTS INC
11880 Machrina Way, Richmond, BC, V7A 4V1

Emp Here 30
SIC 5149 Groceries and related products, nec

D-U-N-S 20-793-2224   (SL)
PACIFIC LINK RETAIL GROUP
TIM HORTONS
11320 Steveston Hwy Suite 110, Richmond, BC, V7A 5J5
(604) 277-8467
Emp Here 60   *Sales* 1,824,018
SIC 5812 Eating places

D-U-N-S 25-218-7653   (HQ)
PORTOLA PACKAGING CANADA LTD.
12431 Horseshoe Way, Richmond, BC, V7A 4X6
(604) 272-5000
Emp Here 64   *Emp Total* 9,600
Sales 16,416,158
SIC 2821 Plastics materials and resins
VP Fin Kevin Happer

D-U-N-S 20-577-2408   (SL)
RICHMOND CHRISTIAN SCHOOL ASSOCIATION
10200 No. 5 Rd, Richmond, BC, V7A 4E5
(604) 272-5720
Emp Here 140   *Sales* 12,985,600
SIC 8211 Elementary and secondary schools
Prin Roger Grose
Mgr Aza Nakagawa

D-U-N-S 24-309-1105   (SL)
RICHMOND COUNTRY CLUB
9100 Steveston Hwy, Richmond, BC, V7A 1M5
(604) 277-3141
Emp Here 100   *Sales* 4,012,839
SIC 7997 Membership sports and recreation clubs

D-U-N-S 20-653-2694   (BR)
RICHMOND, CITY OF
JAMES WHITESIDE ELEMENTARY
9282 Williams Rd, Richmond, BC, V7A 1H1
(604) 668-6209
Emp Here 30
SIC 8211 Elementary and secondary schools

D-U-N-S 25-126-8587   (BR)
ROYAL BANK OF CANADA
RBC
(*Suby of* Royal Bank Of Canada)
10111 No. 3 Rd Suite 125, Richmond, BC, V7A 1W6
(604) 665-8132
Emp Here 25
SIC 6021 National commercial banks

D-U-N-S 24-694-3021   (BR)
RYERSON CANADA, INC
12311 Horseshoe Way, Richmond, BC, V7A 4X6
(604) 272-2422
Emp Here 30
SIC 5051 Metals service centers and offices

D-U-N-S 24-723-9965   (SL)
SARIHAN HOLDINGS LTD.
ALDILA BOUTIQUE
12240 Horseshoe Way Suite 14, Richmond, BC, V7A 4X9

Emp Here 50   *Sales* 5,535,750
SIC 5621 Women's clothing stores
Pr Pr Hasan Sarihan
  Gulay Sarihan

D-U-N-S 25-079-4922   (BR)
SOBEYS WEST INC
BROADMOOR SAFEWAY
10151 No. 3 Rd Unit 100, Richmond, BC, V7A

4R6
(604) 271-8678
Emp Here 50
SIC 5411 Grocery stores

D-U-N-S 20-806-4449   (BR)
STARBUCKS COFFEE CANADA, INC
(*Suby of* Starbucks Corporation)
11688 Steveston Hwy Suite 1166, Richmond, BC, V7A 1N6
(604) 241-5900
Emp Here 30
SIC 5812 Eating places

D-U-N-S 24-838-1105   (SL)
STEVESTON RESTAURANTS LTD
KEG SOUTH RICHMOND
11151 No. 5 Rd, Richmond, BC, V7A 4E8
(604) 272-1399
Emp Here 100   *Sales* 3,551,629
SIC 5812 Eating places

D-U-N-S 24-761-4423   (HQ)
T L D COMPUTERS INC
12251 Horseshoe Way Unit 100, Richmond, BC, V7A 4V4
(604) 272-6000
Emp Here 50   *Emp Total* 4,500
Sales 6,639,424
SIC 5734 Computer and software stores
Pr Pr G. Wynne Powell
  Brandt Louie
Sr VP Clint Mahlman
  Laird Miller
  John Matyus
  Nick Curalli

D-U-N-S 24-245-4473   (BR)
TFI FOODS LTD
11231 Dyke Rd Suite 120, Richmond, BC, V7A 0A1
(604) 231-9966
Emp Here 22
SIC 5146 Fish and seafoods

D-U-N-S 25-685-3235   (BR)
TECK RESOURCES LIMITED
12380 Horseshoe Way, Richmond, BC, V7A 4Z1
(778) 296-4900
Emp Here 80
SIC 8731 Commercial physical research

D-U-N-S 20-702-3032   (SL)
VERY JAZZROO ENTERPRISES INCORPORATED
HOSPITALITY DESIGNS
11720 Horseshoe Way, Richmond, BC, V7A 4V5
(604) 248-1806
Emp Here 68   *Sales* 4,304,681
SIC 2599 Furniture and fixtures, nec

D-U-N-S 20-790-5154   (HQ)
WESTERN PROTECTION ALLIANCE INC
(*Suby of* Western Protection Alliance Inc)
11771 Horseshoe Way Unit 1, Richmond, BC, V7A 4V4
(604) 271-7475
Emp Here 85   *Emp Total* 85
Sales 2,626,585
SIC 7381 Detective and armored car services

D-U-N-S 20-273-3085   (HQ)
WISMETTAC ASIAN FOODS, INC
11388 No. 5 Rd Suite 130, Richmond, BC, V7A 4E7
(604) 303-8620
Emp Here 60   *Emp Total* 3
Sales 31,373,101
SIC 5141 Groceries, general line
Pr Hitoshi Hashimoto
Dir Toshiyuki Nishikawa

Richmond, BC V7B
Greater Vancouver County

D-U-N-S 24-507-6810   (BR)
AIR NORTH PARTNERSHIP
AIR NORTH, YUKON'S AIRLINE
4840 Miller Rd Unit 100, Richmond, BC, V7B
1K7
(604) 279-0330
Emp Here 20
SIC 4512 Air transportation, scheduled

D-U-N-S 24-214-6327   (BR)
AIR NORTH PARTNERSHIP
1 3rd Suite 3135, Richmond, BC, V7B 1Y7
(604) 207-1165
Emp Here 120
SIC 4512 Air transportation, scheduled

D-U-N-S 24-838-9272   (BR)
**BRITISH COLUMBIA INSTITUTE OF TECH-
NOLOGY, THE**
AREOSPACE AND TECHNOLOGY CAMPUS
3800 Cessna Dr, Richmond, BC, V7B 0A1
(604) 419-3777
Emp Here 50
SIC 8222 Junior colleges

D-U-N-S 20-426-2356   (HQ)
BUDGET RENT-A-CAR OF B.C. LTD
BUDGET RENT-A-CAR
(*Suby of* Sea Gull Leasing Ltd)
3840 Mcdonald Rd, Richmond, BC, V7B 1L8
(604) 668-7000
Emp Here 70   *Emp Total* 2
Sales 19,788,909
SIC 7514 Passenger car rental
Sydney Belzberg
Pr Paul Ung

D-U-N-S 24-421-6276   (SL)
CHC HELICOPTERS CANADA INC
4740 Agar Dr, Richmond, BC, V7B 1A3
(604) 276-7500
Emp Here 200   *Sales* 131,985,906
SIC 4522 Air transportation, nonscheduled
Pr Pr William Amelio
COO Peter Bartolotta
VP Anthony Dinota

D-U-N-S 24-292-4785   (HQ)
CLS CATERING SERVICES LTD
3560 Jericho Rd, Richmond, BC, V7B 1C2
(604) 273-4438
Emp Here 270   *Emp Total* 123,287
Sales 16,270,236
SIC 5812 Eating places
Dir Opers David Wainman

D-U-N-S 25-831-9433   (BR)
CARA OPERATIONS LIMITED
(*Suby of* Cara Holdings Limited)
6260 Miller Rd, Richmond, BC, V7B 1B3
(604) 278-9144
Emp Here 600
SIC 5812 Eating places

D-U-N-S 20-860-7528   (BR)
CENTRAL MOUNTAIN AIR LTD
4180 Agar Dr, Richmond, BC, V7B 1A3
(604) 207-0130
Emp Here 100
SIC 4512 Air transportation, scheduled

D-U-N-S 24-696-4803   (BR)
COLE INTERNATIONAL INC
COLE FREIGHT
3820 Cessna Dr Suite 220, Richmond, BC,
V7B 0A2
(604) 273-5161
Emp Here 28
SIC 4731 Freight transportation arrangement

D-U-N-S 24-558-8843   (BR)
DHL EXPRESS (CANADA) LTD
101-5000 Miller Rd, Richmond, BC, V7B 1K6

Emp Here 50
SIC 4731 Freight transportation arrangement

D-U-N-S 25-167-2259   (BR)
DAY & ROSS INC
SAMEDAY WORLDWIDE
3511 Jericho Rd, Richmond, BC, V7B 1M3
(604) 231-1450
Emp Here 50
SIC 4213 Trucking, except local

D-U-N-S 24-357-2450   (BR)
DELTA HOTELS LIMITED
DELTA VANCOUVER AIRPORT HOTEL
3500 Cessna Dr, Richmond, BC, V7B 1C7
(604) 278-1241
Emp Here 240
SIC 8741 Management services

D-U-N-S 25-115-0058   (BR)
DILLON CONSULTING LIMITED
(*Suby of* Dillon Consulting Inc)
3820 Cessna Dr Suite 510, Richmond, BC,
V7B 0A2
(604) 278-7847
Emp Here 25
SIC 8742 Management consulting services

D-U-N-S 25-314-2376   (BR)
**DOLLAR THRIFTY AUTOMOTIVE GROUP
CANADA INC**
THRIFTY CAR RENTALS
(*Suby of* Hertz Global Holdings, Inc.)
3826 Mcdonald Rd, Richmond, BC, V7B 1L8
(604) 606-1695
Emp Here 55
SIC 7513 Truck rental and leasing, no drivers

D-U-N-S 20-979-0059   (BR)
**ENTERPRISE RENT-A-CAR CANADA COM-
PANY**
(*Suby of* The Crawford Group Inc)
3866 Mcdonald Rd, Richmond, BC, V7B 1L8
(604) 273-7341
Emp Here 70
SIC 7514 Passenger car rental

D-U-N-S 24-308-4477   (BR)
FAIRMONT HOTELS & RESORTS INC
FAIRMONT VANCOUVER AIRPORT HOTEL
3111 Grant Mcconachie Way, Richmond, BC,
V7B 0A6
(604) 207-5200
Emp Here 400
SIC 7011 Hotels and motels

D-U-N-S 24-797-4249   (BR)
**FEDERAL EXPRESS CANADA CORPORA-
TION**
FEDERAL EXPRESS CANADA LTD
(*Suby of* Fedex Corporation)
3151 Aylmer Rd, Richmond, BC, V7B 1L5
(800) 463-3339
Emp Here 300
SIC 7389 Business services, nec

D-U-N-S 24-129-3708   (BR)
HARBOUR AIR LTD
HARBOUR AIR SEAPLANES
4680 Cowley Cres, Richmond, BC, V7B 1C1
(604) 274-1277
Emp Here 25
SIC 4512 Air transportation, scheduled

D-U-N-S 20-573-2613   (HQ)
HIGHLAND HELICOPTERS LTD
(*Suby of* Wescan Turbo Helicopters Ltd)
4240 Agar Dr, Richmond, BC, V7B 1A3
(604) 273-6161
Emp Here 25   *Emp Total* 3
Sales 9,140,591
SIC 4522 Air transportation, nonscheduled
April Lee O'brien
Robert Henry Jens
Kenneth Rudolph Jens
Pr Pr Audrey Diane Rendall

D-U-N-S 25-360-2171   (BR)
I.M.P. GROUP LIMITED
PACIFIC AVIONICS
4200 Cowley Cres, Richmond, BC, V7B 1B8

Emp Here 30
SIC 4581 Airports, flying fields, and services

D-U-N-S 20-867-7059   (BR)
KELOWNA FLIGHTCRAFT LTD
3611 Jericho Rd Suite 142, Richmond, BC,
V7B 1M3
(604) 303-3611
Emp Here 20
SIC 4512 Air transportation, scheduled

D-U-N-S 25-676-5256   (SL)
MTU MAINTENANCE CANADA LTD
6020 Russ Baker Way, Richmond, BC, V7B
1B4
(604) 233-5700
Emp Here 300   *Sales* 96,751
SIC 7699 Repair services, nec

D-U-N-S 20-273-1584   (BR)
**MCDONALD'S   RESTAURANTS   OF
CANADA LIMITED**
MCDONALD'S
(*Suby of* McDonald's Corporation)
6086 Russ Baker Way Suite 6020, Richmond,
BC, V7B 1B4
(604) 718-1013
Emp Here 25
SIC 5812 Eating places

D-U-N-S 24-881-5110   (SL)
MILLER ROAD HOLDINGS LTD
PARK N FLY
6380 Miller Rd, Richmond, BC, V7B 1B3
(604) 270-9395
Emp Here 80   *Sales* 1,094,411
SIC 7521 Automobile parking

D-U-N-S 24-132-4545   (BR)
NORTHERN THUNDERBIRD AIR INC
5360 Airport Rd S, Richmond, BC, V7B 1B4
(604) 232-9211
Emp Here 30
SIC 4581 Airports, flying fields, and services

D-U-N-S 24-716-5426   (HQ)
PACIFIC COASTAL AIRLINES LIMITED
(*Suby of* Pacific Coastal Airlines Limited)
4440 Cowley Cres Suite 204, Richmond, BC,
V7B 1B8
(604) 232-3391
Emp Here 110   *Emp Total* 200
Sales 34,145,608
SIC 4512 Air transportation, scheduled
Dir Daryl Smith
Pr Quetin Smith
Dir Ian Harris
Dir Fin David Rossi

D-U-N-S 24-015-9863   (BR)
PANTOS LOGISTICS CANADA INC
5000 Miller Rd Unit 2010, Richmond, BC, V7B
1K9
(604) 278-0511
Emp Here 30
SIC 4731 Freight transportation arrangement

D-U-N-S 25-216-3324   (HQ)
PINNACLE RENEWABLE ENERGY INC
3600 Lysander Lane Suite 350, Richmond,
BC, V7B 1C3
(604) 270-9613
Emp Here 20   *Emp Total* 1,318
Sales 19,626,428
SIC 2499 Wood products, nec
Dir Robert Mccurdy
Pr Leroy Reitsma
VP Prd Scott Bax
VP Sls Vaughan Bassett

D-U-N-S 20-585-6073   (HQ)
RUTHERFORD, WILLIAM L (BC) LTD
RUTHERFORD TERMINALS
(*Suby of* Rutherford, William L. Limited)
6086 Russ Baker Way Suite 125, Richmond,
BC, V7B 1B4

(604) 273-8611
Emp Here 33   *Emp Total* 188
Sales 8,098,638
SIC 4731 Freight transportation arrangement
Larry Wiseman
Pr Pr Romas Krilavicius
VP VP Barton Ramsay

D-U-N-S 25-304-7344   (BR)
**SUN LIFE ASSURANCE COMPANY OF
CANADA**
CLARICA LIFE FINANCIAL
3600 Lysander Ln Suite 120, Richmond, BC,
V7B 1C3
(604) 279-2388
Emp Here 40
SIC 6311 Life insurance

D-U-N-S 20-270-3575   (BR)
SWISSPORT CANADA HANDLING INC
4840 Miller Rd Unit 120, Richmond, BC, V7B
1K7
(604) 273-8856
Emp Here 20
SIC 4512 Air transportation, scheduled

D-U-N-S 20-852-3972   (BR)
SWISSPORT CANADA INC
Gd, Richmond, BC, V7B 1Y4
(604) 303-4550
Emp Here 750
SIC 4581 Airports, flying fields, and services

D-U-N-S 20-979-0380   (BR)
VANCOUVER AIRPORT AUTHORITY
*VANCOUVER INTERNATIONAL AIRPORT
AUTHORITY*
4900 North Service Rd, Richmond, BC, V7B
1L8
(604) 276-6594
Emp Here 50
SIC 4581 Airports, flying fields, and services

D-U-N-S 24-751-1632   (SL)
WDFG VANCOUVER LP
WORLD DUTY FREE GROUP
Gd, Richmond, BC, V7B 1W2
(604) 243-1708
Emp Here 200   *Sales* 16,416,158
SIC 5399 Miscellaneous general merchandise
Prs Mgr Debbie Mckinley
CEO Freda Cheung

D-U-N-S 20-980-1344   (BR)
WEST COAST AIR LTD
5220 Airport Rd S, Richmond, BC, V7B 1B4

Emp Here 100
SIC 4512 Air transportation, scheduled

D-U-N-S 24-344-3590   (BR)
WESTJET AIRLINES LTD
3880 Grant Mcconachie Way Suite 4130,
Richmond, BC, V7B 0A5
(604) 249-1165
Emp Here 200
SIC 4512 Air transportation, scheduled

D-U-N-S 25-050-5005   (BR)
**YALETOWN   BREWING   COMPANY   &
RESTAURANT CORP**
FLYING BEAVER BAR AND GRILL
4760 Inglis Dr, Richmond, BC, V7B 1W4
(604) 273-0278
Emp Here 45
SIC 5812 Eating places

Richmond, BC V7C
Greater Vancouver County

D-U-N-S 20-713-3864   (BR)
**BOARD OF EDUCATION SCHOOL DIS-
TRICT #38 (RICHMOND)**
MCKAY ELEMENTARY SCHOOL
7360 Lombard Rd, Richmond, BC, V7C 3N1

(604) 668-6470
Emp Here 50
SIC 8211 Elementary and secondary schools

D-U-N-S 20-653-7883   (BR)
BOARD OF EDUCATION SCHOOL DIS-TRICT #38 (RICHMOND)
BRIGHOUSE ELEMENTARY SCHOOL
6800 Azure Rd, Richmond, BC, V7C 2S8
(604) 668-6522
Emp Here 35
SIC 8211 Elementary and secondary schools

D-U-N-S 25-128-5904   (BR)
BOARD OF EDUCATION SCHOOL DIS-TRICT #38 (RICHMOND)
BLUNDELL ELEMENTARY SCHOOL
6480 Blundell Rd, Richmond, BC, V7C 1H8
(604) 668-6562
Emp Here 30
SIC 8211 Elementary and secondary schools

D-U-N-S 20-123-4387   (HQ)
BOSLEY'S PET FOOD PLUS INC
6751 Westminster Hwy Suite 140, Richmond, BC, V7C 4V4

Emp Here 20   *Emp Total* 550
Sales 12,330,358
SIC 5999 Miscellaneous retail stores, nec
Pr Pr Kenneth Almond
Michael Woodward

D-U-N-S 20-915-2854   (BR)
DARE FOODS LIMITED
6751 Elmbridge Way, Richmond, BC, V7C 4N1
(604) 233-1117
Emp Here 100
SIC 2051 Bread, cake, and related products

D-U-N-S 20-647-8294   (BR)
GOVERNMENT OF THE PROVINCE OF BRITISH COLUMBIA
BRITISH COLUMBIA COMPENSATION BOARD
6951 Westminster Hwy, Richmond, BC, V7C 1C6
(604) 273-2266
Emp Here 3,200
SIC 6331 Fire, marine, and casualty insurance

D-U-N-S 25-485-6016   (BR)
H. & C. MANAGEMENT CONSULTANTS LTD
FITNESS WORLD
(*Suby of* H. & C. Management Consultants Ltd)
7011 Elmbridge Way, Richmond, BC, V7C 4V5
(604) 278-3831
Emp Here 25
SIC 7991 Physical fitness facilities

D-U-N-S 25-126-8553   (BR)
KIN'S FARM LTD
KIN'S FARM MARKET
8120 No. 2 Rd Suite 176, Richmond, BC, V7C 5J8
(604) 275-1401
Emp Here 20
SIC 5411 Grocery stores

D-U-N-S 24-031-7420   (SL)
PENTEL STATIONERY OF CANADA LIM-ITED
5900 No. 2 Rd Suite 140, Richmond, BC, V7C 4R9
(604) 270-1566
Emp Here 21   *Sales* 2,079,002
SIC 5112 Stationery and office supplies

D-U-N-S 20-115-1610   (SL)
QUILCHENA GOLF & COUNTRY CLUB
3551 Granville Ave, Richmond, BC, V7C 1C8
(604) 277-1101
Emp Here 100   *Sales* 4,012,839
SIC 7997 Membership sports and recreation clubs

D-U-N-S 20-569-9999   (BR)
RICHMOND, CITY OF
6960 Gilbert Rd, Richmond, BC, V7C 3V4
(604) 303-2734
Emp Here 20
SIC 7389 Business services, nec

D-U-N-S 20-590-6675   (BR)
SCHOOL DISTRICT NO. 43 (COQUITLAM)
JAMES GILMORE ELEMENTARY
8380 Elsmore Rd, Richmond, BC, V7C 2A1
(604) 668-6268
Emp Here 39
SIC 8211 Elementary and secondary schools

D-U-N-S 24-363-3885   (BR)
SOBEYS WEST INC
SEAFAIR SAFEWAY
8671 No. 1 Rd, Richmond, BC, V7C 1V2
(604) 241-4013
Emp Here 65
SIC 5411 Grocery stores

D-U-N-S 25-499-1516   (BR)
STARBUCKS COFFEE CANADA, INC
(*Suby of* Starbucks Corporation)
8100 No. 2 Rd Suite 130, Richmond, BC, V7C 5J9
(604) 241-7842
Emp Here 26
SIC 5812 Eating places

D-U-N-S 25-843-6138   (BR)
STERICYCLE COMMUNICATION SOLU-TIONS, ULC
(*Suby of* Stericycle Communication Solutions, ULC)
6011 Westminster Hwy Unit 212, Richmond, BC, V7C 4V4
(604) 244-9166
Emp Here 32
SIC 7389 Business services, nec

Richmond, BC V7E
Greater Vancouver County

D-U-N-S 25-612-5142   (SL)
BENCHMARK LAW CORP
9471 Kirkmond Cres, Richmond, BC, V7E 1M7
(604) 786-7724
Emp Here 49   *Sales* 5,024,256
SIC 8111 Legal services

D-U-N-S 20-713-3997   (BR)
BOARD OF EDUCATION SCHOOL DIS-TRICT #38 (RICHMOND)
MCMATH SECONDARY SCHOOL
4251 Garry St, Richmond, BC, V7E 2T9
(604) 718-4050
Emp Here 80
SIC 8211 Elementary and secondary schools

D-U-N-S 25-012-0896   (BR)
BOARD OF EDUCATION SCHOOL DIS-TRICT #38 (RICHMOND)
MANOAH STEVES ELEMENTARY SCHOOL
10111 4th Ave, Richmond, BC, V7E 1V5
(604) 668-6660
Emp Here 45
SIC 8211 Elementary and secondary schools

D-U-N-S 25-929-4262   (BR)
BOARD OF EDUCATION SCHOOL DIS-TRICT #38 (RICHMOND)
WESTWIND ELEMENTARY SCHOOL
11371 Kingfisher Dr, Richmond, BC, V7E 4Y6
(604) 668-6497
Emp Here 36
SIC 8211 Elementary and secondary schools

D-U-N-S 20-914-0180   (BR)
BOARD OF EDUCATION SCHOOL DIS-TRICT #38 (RICHMOND)
STEVESTON LONDON SECONDARY

SCHOOL
6600 Williams Rd, Richmond, BC, V7E 1K5
(604) 668-6668
Emp Here 75
SIC 8211 Elementary and secondary schools

D-U-N-S 20-590-6469   (BR)
BOARD OF EDUCATION SCHOOL DIS-TRICT #38 (RICHMOND)
JAMES MCKINNEY ELEMENTARY SCHOOL
10451 Lassam Rd, Richmond, BC, V7E 2C2
(604) 668-6133
Emp Here 25
SIC 8211 Elementary and secondary schools

D-U-N-S 20-980-0957   (BR)
BOARD OF EDUCATION SCHOOL DIS-TRICT #38 (RICHMOND)
BOYD SECONDARY SCHOOL
9200 No. 1 Rd, Richmond, BC, V7E 6L5

Emp Here 81
SIC 8211 Elementary and secondary schools

D-U-N-S 20-713-3955   (BR)
BOARD OF EDUCATION SCHOOL DIS-TRICT #38 (RICHMOND)
WOWK ELEMENTARY
5380 Woodwards Rd, Richmond, BC, V7E 1H1
(604) 668-6198
Emp Here 50
SIC 8211 Elementary and secondary schools

D-U-N-S 20-026-9996   (BR)
BOARD OF EDUCATION SCHOOL DIS-TRICT #38 (RICHMOND)
JOHN G. DIEFENBAKER ELEMENTARY SCHOOL
4511 Hermitage Dr, Richmond, BC, V7E 4T1
(604) 668-6639
Emp Here 30
SIC 8211 Elementary and secondary schools

D-U-N-S 25-128-5920   (BR)
BOARD OF EDUCATION SCHOOL DIS-TRICT #38 (RICHMOND)
TOMEKICHI ELEMENTARY SCHOOL
5100 Brunswick Dr, Richmond, BC, V7E 6K9
(604) 668-7844
Emp Here 45
SIC 8211 Elementary and secondary schools

D-U-N-S 20-027-0002   (BR)
BOARD OF EDUCATION SCHOOL DIS-TRICT #38 (RICHMOND)
LORD BYNG ELEMENTARY SCHOOL
3711 Georgia St, Richmond, BC, V7E 6M3
(604) 668-6649
Emp Here 40
SIC 8211 Elementary and secondary schools

D-U-N-S 24-070-2332   (SL)
GOLDFINGER JEWELRY INC
SHANE MANUFACTURING CO
Gd, Richmond, BC, V7E 3E6
(604) 275-0061
Emp Here 500   *Sales* 85,508,480
SIC 8733 Noncommercial research organiza-tions
Pr Pr Shane Sheehan
VP VP Diane Sheehan

D-U-N-S 20-259-3641   (SL)
MASTER HOSPITALITY RESOURCES LTD
3580 Moncton St Unit 212, Richmond, BC, V7E 3A4
(604) 278-3024
Emp Here 70   *Sales* 2,334,742
SIC 7299 Miscellaneous personal service

D-U-N-S 20-988-1940   (BR)
RICHMOND, CITY OF
WEST RICHMOND COMMUNITY CENTRE
9180 No. 1 Rd, Richmond, BC, V7E 6L5
(604) 238-8400
Emp Here 120
SIC 8322 Individual and family services

D-U-N-S 20-322-7525   (SL)
TRUSTING INVESTMENT & CONSULTING CO., LTD
10891 Hogarth Dr, Richmond, BC, V7E 3Z9
(778) 321-7399
Emp Here 120   *Sales* 26,275,550
SIC 6719 Holding companies, nec
Pr Liang Ji Zhuang

D-U-N-S 20-795-5675   (BR)
VANCOUVER COASTAL HEALTH AUTHOR-ITY
RICHMOND LIONS MANOR
11771 Fentiman Pl, Richmond, BC, V7E 3M4

Emp Here 120
SIC 8051 Skilled nursing care facilities

Roberts Creek, BC V0N
Sunshine Coast County

D-U-N-S 24-975-0340   (BR)
SCHOOL DISTRICT NO. 46 (SUNSHINE COAST)
ROBERTS CREEK ELEMENTARY SCHOOL
1088 Roberts Creek Rd, Roberts Creek, BC, V0N 2W0
(604) 885-3481
Emp Here 35
SIC 8211 Elementary and secondary schools

Rose Prairie, BC V0C
Peace River - Laird County

D-U-N-S 20-978-0951   (BR)
SCHOOL DISTRICT NO. 60 (PEACE RIVER NORTH)
UPPER PINE SCHOOL
16242 Rose Prairie, Rose Prairie, BC, V0C 2H0
(250) 827-3691
Emp Here 24
SIC 8211 Elementary and secondary schools

Rosedale, BC V0X

D-U-N-S 25-638-2516   (BR)
COUNTRY GARDEN LTD
TRILLIUM RESTAURANT, & BLOOMER
52892 Bunker Rd, Rosedale, BC, V0X 1X1

Emp Here 20
SIC 5812 Eating places

D-U-N-S 25-500-6850   (HQ)
EMIL ANDERSON MAINTENANCE CO. LTD
CONSTRUCTION
51160 Sache St, Rosedale, BC, V0X 1X0
(604) 794-7414
Emp Here 100   *Emp Total* 100
Sales 18,677,939
SIC 1611 Highway and street construction
Robert J. Hasell
Pr Pr Mike Jacobs

D-U-N-S 20-591-4521   (BR)
SCHOOL DISTRICT NO 33 CHILLIWACK
ROSEDALE ELEMENTARY
10125 Mcgrath Rd, Rosedale, BC, V0X 1X2

Emp Here 20
SIC 8211 Elementary and secondary schools

D-U-N-S 25-538-7961   (BR)
SCHOOL DISTRICT NO 33 CHILLIWACK
ROSEDALE MIDDLE SCHOOL
50850 Yale Rd, Rosedale, BC, V0X 1X2
(604) 794-7124
Emp Here 30

SIC 8211 Elementary and secondary schools

Rossland, BC V0G
Kootenay Boundary County

D-U-N-S 24-838-3911 (BR)
ANNABLE FOODS LTD
FERRARO FOODS
2027 Columbia Ave, Rossland, BC, V0G 1Y0
(250) 362-5206
Emp Here 35
SIC 5411 Grocery stores

D-U-N-S 25-811-9718 (BR)
SCHOOL DISTRICT # 20 (KOOTENAY-COLUMBIA)
ROSSLAND SECONDARY SCHOOL
(*Suby of* School District # 20 (Kootenay-Columbia))
2390 Jubilee St, Rossland, BC, V0G 1Y0
(250) 362-7388
Emp Here 35
SIC 8211 Elementary and secondary schools

D-U-N-S 20-713-2262 (BR)
SCHOOL DISTRICT # 20 (KOOTENAY-COLUMBIA)
MACLEAN ELEMENTARY SCHOOL
2160 St Paul, Rossland, BC, V0G 1Y0
(250) 362-9059
Emp Here 50
SIC 8211 Elementary and secondary schools

Royston, BC V0R
Comox - Strathcona County

D-U-N-S 20-068-3626 (BR)
SCHOOL DISTRICT NO. 71 (COMOX VALLEY)
ROYSTON ELEMENTARY SCHOOL
3830 Warren Ave, Royston, BC, V0R 2V0
(250) 334-2161
Emp Here 20
SIC 8211 Elementary and secondary schools

Saanichton, BC V8M
Capital County

D-U-N-S 24-839-2011 (SL)
AQUA-LUNG CANADA LTD
6820 Kirkpatrick Cres, Saanichton, BC, V8M 1Z9
(250) 652-5881
Emp Here 36   *Sales* 2,631,580
SIC 5091 Sporting and recreation goods

D-U-N-S 20-808-3225 (BR)
BALMORAL INVESTMENTS LTD
QUALITY INN
(*Suby of* Balmoral Investments Ltd)
2476 Mount Newton Cross Rd, Saanichton, BC, V8M 2B8
(250) 652-1146
Emp Here 100
SIC 7011 Hotels and motels

D-U-N-S 20-787-5928 (BR)
BEKINS MOVING & STORAGE (CANADA) LTD
6598 Bryn Rd, Saanichton, BC, V8M 1X6
(250) 544-2245
Emp Here 30
SIC 4214 Local trucking with storage

D-U-N-S 24-099-1104 (BR)
BRINK'S CANADA LIMITED
(*Suby of* The Brink's Company)
6721 Butler Cres Suite 6, Saanichton, BC, V8M 1Z7

(250) 544-2016
Emp Here 30
SIC 7381 Detective and armored car services

D-U-N-S 20-955-4695 (BR)
CELLFOR INC
6772 Oldfield Rd Suite 200, Saanichton, BC, V8M 2A3
(250) 507-3649
Emp Here 50
SIC 7389 Business services, nec

D-U-N-S 24-594-5225 (SL)
CENTRAL COAST POWER CORPORATION
629 Senanus Dr, Saanichton, BC, V8M 1S6
(250) 544-4985
Emp Here 20   *Sales* 13,162,880
SIC 4911 Electric services
Pr Pr Anthony Knott

D-U-N-S 24-517-0076 (SL)
COASTAL CONSTRUCTION
2003 Hovey Rd, Saanichton, BC, V8M 1V8

Emp Here 41   *Sales* 7,915,564
SIC 1521 Single-family construction
Owner Brad Johnson

D-U-N-S 20-188-2151 (BR)
FLYNN CANADA LTD
6836 Kirkpatrick Cres Unit 1, Saanichton, BC, V8M 1Z9
(250) 652-0599
Emp Here 20
SIC 1761 Roofing, siding, and sheetMetal work

D-U-N-S 20-927-4419 (SL)
GAR-DON ENTERPRISES LTD
WHITE SPOT RESTAURANTS
2401 Mount Newton Cross Rd, Saanichton, BC, V8M 1T8

Emp Here 70   *Sales* 2,115,860
SIC 5812 Eating places

D-U-N-S 24-621-1064 (BR)
HOULE ELECTRIC LIMITED
2661 Keating Crossroad Suite 300 A, Saanichton, BC, V8M 2A5
(250) 388-5665
Emp Here 70
SIC 1731 Electrical work

D-U-N-S 24-376-9937 (BR)
JACE HOLDINGS LTD
THRIFTY KITCHENS
6772 Kirkpatrick Cres, Saanichton, BC, V8M 1Z9
(250) 483-1616
Emp Here 100
SIC 5411 Grocery stores

D-U-N-S 24-454-9671 (HQ)
M.D. CHARLTON CO. LTD
2200 Keating Cross Rd Suite E, Saanichton, BC, V8M 2A6
(250) 652-5266
Emp Here 20   *Emp Total* 60
Sales 7,441,991
SIC 5049 Professional equipment, nec
Pr Pr Alec Rossa
  Joan Rossa

D-U-N-S 25-414-2425 (SL)
MICROTEK INTERNATIONAL INC
(*Suby of* Pfizer Inc.)
6761 Kirkpatrick Cres, Saanichton, BC, V8M 1Z8

Emp Here 20   *Sales* 1,094,411
SIC 8731 Commercial physical research

D-U-N-S 24-154-0855 (HQ)
P. & R. REPAIRS LTD
P & R WESTERN STAR TRUCKS
(*Suby of* P. & R. Repairs Ltd)
2005 Keating Cross Rd, Saanichton, BC, V8M 2A5

(250) 652-9139
Emp Here 55   *Emp Total* 60
Sales 4,742,446
SIC 4212 Local trucking, without storage

D-U-N-S 20-119-4859 (SL)
PARKER, JOHNSTON LIMITED
6791 Oldfield Road, Saanichton, BC, V8M 2A2
(250) 382-9181
Emp Here 50   *Sales* 4,961,328
SIC 1761 Roofing, siding, and sheetMetal work

D-U-N-S 20-041-4881 (BR)
SAANICH INDIAN SCHOOL BOARD
LAU WELNEW TRIBAL SCHOOL
7449 West Saanich Rd, Saanichton, BC, V8M 1R7
(250) 652-1811
Emp Here 25
SIC 8211 Elementary and secondary schools

D-U-N-S 25-134-8066 (BR)
SCHOOL DISTRICT 63 (SAANICH)
SAANICHTON ELEMENTARY SCHOOL
1649 Mount Newton Cross Rd, Saanichton, BC, V8M 1L1
(250) 652-4042
Emp Here 35
SIC 8211 Elementary and secondary schools

D-U-N-S 20-713-5679 (BR)
SCHOOL DISTRICT 63 (SAANICH)
STELLY'S SECONDARY SCHOOL
1627 Stellys Cross Rd, Saanichton, BC, V8M 1S8
(250) 652-4401
Emp Here 100
SIC 8211 Elementary and secondary schools

D-U-N-S 20-554-2439 (BR)
SHERWOOD INDUSTRIES LTD
6845 Kirkpatrick Cres, Saanichton, BC, V8M 1Z8
(250) 652-6080
Emp Here 100
SIC 2499 Wood products, nec

D-U-N-S 20-296-3823 (BR)
SLEGG LIMITED PARTNERSHIP
SLEGG CONSTRUCTION MATERIALS
2046 Keating Cross Rd, Saanichton, BC, V8M 2A6
(250) 652-1130
Emp Here 38
SIC 5031 Lumber, plywood, and millwork

D-U-N-S 24-797-0304 (SL)
SPECIFIC MECHANICAL SYSTEMS LTD
6848 Kirkpatrick Cres, Saanichton, BC, V8M 1Z9
(250) 652-2111
Emp Here 75   *Sales* 9,894,455
SIC 3556 Food products machinery
Pr Pr Philip Zacharias
  William Cummings
Genl Mgr Trevor Harmon

D-U-N-S 24-848-4250 (BR)
VANCOUVER ISLAND HEALTH AUTHORITY
SAANICH PENINSULA HOSPITAL
2166 Mount Newton Cross Rd, Saanichton, BC, V8M 2B2
(250) 652-7531
Emp Here 50
SIC 8011 Offices and clinics of medical doctors

D-U-N-S 24-336-2154 (BR)
WASTE CONNECTIONS OF CANADA INC
2240 Keating Cross Rd, Saanichton, BC, V8M 2A6
(250) 652-4414
Emp Here 30
SIC 4953 Refuse systems

D-U-N-S 24-620-1065 (BR)
WASTE MANAGEMENT OF CANADA COR-

PORATION
(*Suby of* Waste Management, Inc.)
6808 Kirkpatrick Cres, Saanichton, BC, V8M 1Z9
(250) 544-2330
Emp Here 30
SIC 4953 Refuse systems

Salmo, BC V0G
Central Kootenay County

D-U-N-S 25-676-7831 (BR)
SCHOOL DISTRICT NO. 8 (KOOTENAY LAKE)
SALMO SECONDARY HIGH SCHOOL
(*Suby of* School District No. 8 (Kootenay Lake))
715 Davies Ave, Salmo, BC, V0G 1Z0
(250) 357-2226
Emp Here 20
SIC 8211 Elementary and secondary schools

D-U-N-S 25-451-3740 (BR)
SCHOOL DISTRICT NO. 8 (KOOTENAY LAKE)
SALMO ELEMENTARY SCHOOL
(*Suby of* School District No. 8 (Kootenay Lake))
650 Glendale Ave, Salmo, BC, V0G 1Z0
(250) 357-2214
Emp Here 22
SIC 8211 Elementary and secondary schools

Salmon Arm, BC V1E
Columbia - Shuswap County

D-U-N-S 20-424-4263 (HQ)
ASKEW'S FOOD SERVICE LTD
ASKEW'S FOODS
111 Lakeshore Dr Ne, Salmon Arm, BC, V1E 4N3
(250) 832-2064
Emp Here 55   *Emp Total* 105
Sales 14,154,376
SIC 5411 Grocery stores
Pr Pr David Askew
  Colleen Davis

D-U-N-S 25-262-9167 (BR)
BDO CANADA LLP
SALMON ARM ACCOUNTING
571 6 St Ne Unit 201, Salmon Arm, BC, V1E 1R6
(250) 832-7171
Emp Here 20
SIC 8721 Accounting, auditing, and bookkeeping

D-U-N-S 24-491-6383 (BR)
BDO CANADA LIMITED
BDO DUNWOODY
571 6 St Ne Suite 201, Salmon Arm, BC, V1E 1R6
(250) 832-7171
Emp Here 28
SIC 8721 Accounting, auditing, and bookkeeping

D-U-N-S 24-152-7282 (BR)
BANK OF NOVA SCOTIA, THE
SCOTIABANK
391 Hudson St Nw, Salmon Arm, BC, V1E 2S1
(250) 833-3500
Emp Here 20
SIC 6021 National commercial banks

D-U-N-S 25-316-5658 (BR)
BLACK PRESS GROUP LTD
SALMON ARM OBSERVER
171 Shuswap St Sw, Salmon Arm, BC, V1E 4H8

---

(250) 832-2131
Emp Here 30
SIC 2711 Newspapers

D-U-N-S 25-288-8672   (BR)
CANADA POST CORPORATION
SALMON ARM POSTAL OUTLET
370 Hudson St Nw, Salmon Arm, BC, V1E 1A0
(250) 832-3093
Emp Here 30
SIC 4311 U.s. postal service

D-U-N-S 25-300-1879   (BR)
CANADIAN IMPERIAL BANK OF COMMERCE
CIBC
310 Alexander St Ne, Salmon Arm, BC, V1E 1E7
(250) 833-3334
Emp Here 20
SIC 6021 National commercial banks

D-U-N-S 20-334-9050   (SL)
CANADIAN TIRE ASSOCIATE STORE LTD
2090 10 Ave Sw, Salmon Arm, BC, V1E 1T4
(250) 832-5474
Emp Here 49   *Sales* 5,982,777
SIC 5531 Auto and home supply stores
Owner Justin Mondor

D-U-N-S 24-858-9769   (BR)
CENTRAL HARDWARE LTD
HOME BUILDING CENTRE
151 5 St Sw, Salmon Arm, BC, V1E 1S9
(250) 832-7722
Emp Here 25
SIC 5211 Lumber and other building materials

D-U-N-S 25-694-5254   (BR)
CITY OF SALMON ARM
SALMON ARM COMMUNITY CENTRE/ SWIMMING POOL
2600 10 Ave Ne, Salmon Arm, BC, V1E 2S4
(250) 832-4044
Emp Here 40
SIC 7999 Amusement and recreation, nec

D-U-N-S 20-137-2112   (BR)
CITY OF SALMON ARM
CITY OF SALMON ARM FIRE DEPARTMENT, THE
141 Ross St Ne, Salmon Arm, BC, V1E 4N2
(250) 803-4060
Emp Here 84
SIC 7389 Business services, nec

D-U-N-S 24-174-1953   (BR)
DOEPKER INDUSTRIES LTD
5301 40 Ave Se, Salmon Arm, BC, V1E 1X1

Emp Here 100
SIC 3715 Truck trailers

D-U-N-S 25-735-1908   (BR)
FEDERATED CO-OPERATIVES LIMITED
(*Suby of* Federated Co-Operatives Limited)
8160 Trans Can Hwy Ne, Salmon Arm, BC, V1E 2S6
(250) 833-1200
Emp Here 200
SIC 2436 Softwood veneer and plywood

D-U-N-S 25-272-3705   (BR)
GREAT PACIFIC INDUSTRIES INC
OVERWAITEA FOOD GROUP
1151 10 Ave Sw Suite 100, Salmon Arm, BC, V1E 1T3
(250) 832-2278
Emp Here 120
SIC 5411 Grocery stores

D-U-N-S 20-692-9619   (BR)
INTERIOR HEALTH AUTHORITY
BASTION PLACE
700 11 St Ne, Salmon Arm, BC, V1E 2S5
(250) 833-3616
Emp Here 80
SIC 8062 General medical and surgical hospitals

D-U-N-S 25-176-1953   (BR)
INTERIOR HEALTH AUTHORITY
SALMON ARM HEALTH CENTRE
851 16 St Se, Salmon Arm, BC, V1E 1P7
(250) 833-4100
Emp Here 60
SIC 8062 General medical and surgical hospitals

D-U-N-S 25-146-3436   (BR)
JUUSOLA, JACK SALES LTD
CANADIAN TIRE NO 482
2090 10 Ave Sw, Salmon Arm, BC, V1E 0E1
(250) 832-9600
Emp Here 45
SIC 5531 Auto and home supply stores

D-U-N-S 25-658-9581   (BR)
JUUSOLA, JACK SALES LTD
CANADIAN TIRE STORE 482
2090 10 Ave Sw, Salmon Arm, BC, V1E 0E1
(250) 832-5030
Emp Here 50
SIC 5251 Hardware stores

D-U-N-S 20-731-8168   (BR)
LOBLAWS INC
BRAD'S NOFRILLS
360 Trans Canada Hwy Sw Suite 2, Salmon Arm, BC, V1E 1B4
(250) 804-0285
Emp Here 68
SIC 5411 Grocery stores

D-U-N-S 20-224-9590   (BR)
LORDCO PARTS LTD
LORDCO AUTO PARTS
51 Lakeshore Dr Ne, Salmon Arm, BC, V1E 4N3
(250) 832-7030
Emp Here 27
SIC 5531 Auto and home supply stores

D-U-N-S 20-923-8117   (SL)
MCDONALD'S RESTAURANTS
3010 11 Ave Ne, Salmon Arm, BC, V1E 2S8
(250) 832-3919
Emp Here 60   *Sales* 1,824,018
SIC 5812 Eating places

D-U-N-S 20-166-6927   (SL)
NORTH OKANAGAN SHUSWAP SCHOOL DISTRICT 8
CUSTODIAL HEALTH & SAFETY
5911 Auto Rd Se, Salmon Arm, BC, V1E 2X2
(250) 832-9415
Emp Here 50   *Sales* 73,181,219
SIC 7349 Building maintenance services, nec
Mgr Dan Horochuk

D-U-N-S 20-038-0504   (BR)
NORTH OKANAGAN SHUSWAP SCHOOL DISTRICT 83
SHUSWAP MIDDLE SCHOOL
171 30 St Se, Salmon Arm, BC, V1E 1J5
(250) 832-6031
Emp Here 30
SIC 8211 Elementary and secondary schools

D-U-N-S 20-590-9794   (BR)
NORTH OKANAGAN SHUSWAP SCHOOL DISTRICT 83
BASTION ELEMENTARY SCHOOL
2251 12 Ave Ne, Salmon Arm, BC, V1E 2V5
(250) 832-3741
Emp Here 25
SIC 8211 Elementary and secondary schools

D-U-N-S 20-590-9851   (BR)
NORTH OKANAGAN SHUSWAP SCHOOL DISTRICT 83
SUMMON ARM WEST ELEMENTARY
4750 10 Ave Sw, Salmon Arm, BC, V1E 3B5
(250) 832-3862
Emp Here 25
SIC 8211 Elementary and secondary schools

D-U-N-S 20-299-7511   (BR)

NORTH OKANAGAN SHUSWAP SCHOOL DISTRICT 83
SALMON ARM SECONDARY SCHOOL
1641 30 St Ne, Salmon Arm, BC, V1E 2Z5
(250) 832-2188
Emp Here 60
SIC 8211 Elementary and secondary schools

D-U-N-S 20-034-4625   (BR)
NORTH OKANAGAN SHUSWAP SCHOOL DISTRICT 83
JACKSON CAMPUS SEMINAR SECONDARY
551 14 St Ne, Salmon Arm, BC, V1E 2S5
(250) 832-2188
Emp Here 50
SIC 8211 Elementary and secondary schools

D-U-N-S 20-590-9877   (BR)
NORTH OKANAGAN SHUSWAP SCHOOL DISTRICT 83
RANCHERO ELEMENTARY SCHOOL
6285 Ranchero Dr, Salmon Arm, BC, V1E 2R1
(250) 832-7018
Emp Here 25
SIC 8211 Elementary and secondary schools

D-U-N-S 20-590-9786   (BR)
NORTH OKANAGAN SHUSWAP SCHOOL DISTRICT 83
HILLCREST ELEMENTARY
1180 20 St Se, Salmon Arm, BC, V1E 2J4
(250) 832-7195
Emp Here 40
SIC 8211 Elementary and secondary schools

D-U-N-S 20-003-9910   (BR)
NORTH OKANAGAN SHUSWAP SCHOOL DISTRICT 83
SOUTH BROADVIEW ELEMENTARY SCHOOL
3200 6 Ave Ne, Salmon Arm, BC, V1E 1J2
(250) 832-2167
Emp Here 27
SIC 8211 Elementary and secondary schools

D-U-N-S 20-860-9409   (BR)
NORTH OKANAGAN SHUSWAP SCHOOL DISTRICT 83
2960 Okanagan Ave Se Suite 150, Salmon Arm, BC, V1E 1E6

Emp Here 21
SIC 8299 Schools and educational services, nec

D-U-N-S 25-316-6318   (BR)
OKANAGAN COLLEGE
2552 Trans Canada Hwy Ne, Salmon Arm, BC, V1E 2S4
(250) 832-2126
Emp Here 45
SIC 8221 Colleges and universities

D-U-N-S 20-523-4748   (BR)
OKANAGAN COLLEGE
2552 Trans Canada Hwy Ne, Salmon Arm, BC, V1E 2S4
(250) 804-8888
Emp Here 40
SIC 8221 Colleges and universities

D-U-N-S 25-705-0419   (BR)
ROYAL BANK OF CANADA
RBC
(*Suby of* Royal Bank Of Canada)
340 Alexander St Ne, Salmon Arm, BC, V1E 4N8
(250) 832-8071
Emp Here 30
SIC 6021 National commercial banks

D-U-N-S 24-247-5960   (BR)
SOBEYS WEST INC
CANADA SAFEWAY NO. 171
360 Trans Canada Hwy Sw Unit 1, Salmon Arm, BC, V1E 1B4

(250) 832-8086
Emp Here 85
SIC 5411 Grocery stores

Salt Spring Island, BC V8K
Capital County

D-U-N-S 25-164-1841   (BR)
CREDENTIAL SECURITIES INC
124 Mcphillips Ave, Salt Spring Island, BC, V8K 2T5
(250) 537-8868
Emp Here 40
SIC 6211 Security brokers and dealers

D-U-N-S 25-965-7534   (BR)
ISLAND SAVINGS CREDIT UNION
(*Suby of* Island Savings Credit Union)
124 Mcphillips Ave, Salt Spring Island, BC, V8K 2T5
(250) 537-5587
Emp Here 30
SIC 6062 State credit unions

D-U-N-S 20-512-1742   (SL)
MOUAT'S TRADING CO. LTD
MOUAT'S HOME HARDWARE
106 Fulford-Ganges Rd, Salt Spring Island, BC, V8K 2S3
(250) 537-5551
Emp Here 54   *Sales* 4,450,603
SIC 5399 Miscellaneous general merchandise

D-U-N-S 20-192-5935   (BR)
SCHOOL DISTRICT NO. 64 (GULF ISLANDS)
GULF ISLANDS SECONDARY SCHOOL
232 Rainbow Rd, Salt Spring Island, BC, V8K 2K3
(250) 537-9944
Emp Here 50
SIC 8211 Elementary and secondary schools

D-U-N-S 20-590-7376   (BR)
SCHOOL DISTRICT NO. 64 (GULF ISLANDS)
PHOENIX ELEMENTARY
163 Drake Rd, Salt Spring Island, BC, V8K 2K8
(250) 537-1156
Emp Here 25
SIC 8211 Elementary and secondary schools

Sandspit, BC V0T
Skeena-Qn-Charlotte County

D-U-N-S 20-104-8878   (BR)
TEAL CEDAR PRODUCTS LTD
TEAL JONES GROUP
453 Beach Rd, Sandspit, BC, V0T 1T0
(250) 637-5730
Emp Here 25
SIC 2411 Logging

Sechelt, BC V0N
Sunshine Coast County

D-U-N-S 20-572-9507   (BR)
CANADA POST CORPORATION
5557 Inlet Ave, Sechelt, BC, V0N 3A0
(604) 885-2411
Emp Here 20
SIC 4311 U.s. postal service

D-U-N-S 20-268-0562   (BR)
CAPILANO UNIVERSITY
SUNSHINE COAST CAMPUS
5627 Inlet Ave, Sechelt, BC, V0N 3A3
(604) 885-9310
Emp Here 20

SIC 8221 Colleges and universities

D-U-N-S 25-656-8122   (BR)
LEHIGH HANSON MATERIALS LIMITED
LEHIGH NORTHWEST
5784 Sechelt Inlet Rd, Sechelt, BC, V0N 3A3
(604) 885-7595
Emp Here 68
SIC 5032 Brick, stone, and related material

D-U-N-S 25-188-8996   (BR)
OPEN DOOR GROUP, THE
5600 Sunshine Coast Hwy, Sechelt, BC, V0N 3A2
(604) 885-3351
Emp Here 20
SIC 7361 Employment agencies

D-U-N-S 20-978-0902   (BR)
SCHOOL DISTRICT NO. 46 (SUNSHINE COAST)
SUNSHINE COAST ALTERNATIVE SCHOOL
5545 Inlet Ave Rr 3, Sechelt, BC, V0N 3A3
(604) 885-0127
Emp Here 20
SIC 8211 Elementary and secondary schools

D-U-N-S 20-713-4870   (BR)
SCHOOL DISTRICT NO. 46 (SUNSHINE COAST)
KINNIKINNICK ELEMENTARY SCHOOL
6030 Lakehouse Ave, Sechelt, BC, V0N 3A0
(604) 885-6666
Emp Here 50
SIC 8211 Elementary and secondary schools

D-U-N-S 20-591-5767   (BR)
SCHOOL DISTRICT NO. 46 (SUNSHINE COAST)
KINIKINNICK ELEMENTARY SCHOOL
6030 Lighthouse Ave, Sechelt, BC, V0N 3A5
(604) 885-6782
Emp Here 25
SIC 8211 Elementary and secondary schools

D-U-N-S 20-591-5734   (BR)
SCHOOL DISTRICT NO. 46 (SUNSHINE COAST)
WEST SECHELT ELEMENTARY
5609 Mason Rd, Sechelt, BC, V0N 3A8
(604) 885-2825
Emp Here 25
SIC 8211 Elementary and secondary schools

D-U-N-S 20-968-9590   (BR)
SCHOOL DISTRICT NO. 46 (SUNSHINE COAST)
CHATELECH COMMUNITY SECONDARY SCHOOL
5904 Cowrie St, Sechelt, BC, V0N 3A7
(604) 885-3216
Emp Here 68
SIC 8211 Elementary and secondary schools

D-U-N-S 24-228-3559   (BR)
SODEXO CANADA LTD
5544 Sunshine Coast Hwy, Sechelt, BC, V0N 3A0
(604) 885-0244
Emp Here 40
SIC 5812 Eating places

D-U-N-S 25-450-9862   (BR)
SUNSHINE COAST CREDIT UNION
(*Suby of* Sunshine Coast Credit Union)
5655 Teredo St, Sechelt, BC, V0N 3A0
(604) 740-2662
Emp Here 25
SIC 6062 State credit unions

D-U-N-S 25-634-9630   (BR)
SUNSHINE COAST REGIONAL DISTRICT
SUNSHINE COAST TRANSIT SYSTEM
5920 Mason Rd, Sechelt, BC, V0N 3A8
(604) 885-3234
Emp Here 25
SIC 4111 Local and suburban transit

D-U-N-S 25-330-2996   (SL)

SUNSHINE MOTORS (1996) LTD
SUNSHINE GM
1633 Field Rd, Sechelt, BC, V0N 3A1
(604) 885-5131
Emp Here 24   *Sales* 12,174,000
SIC 5511 New and used car dealers
Pr Pr David Meyerink

D-U-N-S 25-290-9239   (SL)
TRAIL BAY HARDWARE LTD
5484 Trail Ave, Sechelt, BC, V0N 3A0
(604) 885-9828
Emp Here 55   *Sales* 2,407,703
SIC 7011 Hotels and motels

Shalalth, BC V0N
Squamish - Lillooet County

D-U-N-S 25-194-2983   (BR)
BRITISH COLUMBIA HYDRO AND POWER AUTHORITY
BRIDGE RIVER GENERATING STATION
3500 Seton Portage Rd, Shalalth, BC, V0N 3C0
(250) 259-8221
Emp Here 35
SIC 4911 Electric services

Shawnigan Lake, BC V0R
Cowichan Valley County

D-U-N-S 20-591-5387   (BR)
SCHOOL DISTRICT NO. 79 (COWICHAN VALLEY)
DISCOVERY ELEMENTARY SCHOOL
2204 Mckean Rd, Shawnigan Lake, BC, V0R 2W1
(250) 743-3291
Emp Here 25
SIC 8211 Elementary and secondary schools

D-U-N-S 20-713-5752   (BR)
SCHOOL DISTRICT NO. 79 (COWICHAN VALLEY)
ELSIE MILE ANNEX ELEMENTARY SCHOOL
1801 Shawnigan Mill Bay Rd, Shawnigan Lake, BC, V0R 2W0

Emp Here 50
SIC 8211 Elementary and secondary schools

D-U-N-S 25-865-8855   (BR)
UNITED CHURCH OF CANADA, THE
GEORGE PRINGLE MEMORIAL CAMP
2520w Shawnigan Lake Rd, Shawnigan Lake, BC, V0R 2W2
(250) 743-2189
Emp Here 25
SIC 8661 Religious organizations

Sicamous, BC V0E
Columbia - Shuswap County

D-U-N-S 20-114-7423   (SL)
572412 B.C. LTD
HYDE MOUNTAIN ON MARA LAKE GOLF COURSE
9851 Old Spallumcheen Rd, Sicamous, BC, V0E 2V3
(250) 836-4689
Emp Here 65   *Sales* 2,772,507
SIC 7992 Public golf courses

D-U-N-S 20-031-6490   (BR)
NORTH OKANAGAN SHUSWAP SCHOOL DISTRICT 83
EAGLE RIVER SECONDARY SCHOOL
518 Finlayson St, Sicamous, BC, V0E 2V2

(250) 836-2831
Emp Here 35
SIC 8211 Elementary and secondary schools

D-U-N-S 25-678-8688   (SL)
SHUSWAP LAKES VACATIONS INC
TWIN ANCHORS HOUSEBOAT VACATION
101 Martin St, Sicamous, BC, V0E 2V1
(250) 804-3485
Emp Here 35   *Sales* 3,502,114
SIC 7999 Amusement and recreation, nec

Sidney, BC V8L
Capital County

D-U-N-S 24-345-2067   (SL)
ADVENTIST HEALTH CARE HOME SOCIETY
REST HAVEN LODGE
2281 Mills Rd Suite 223, Sidney, BC, V8L 2C3
(250) 656-0717
Emp Here 75   *Sales* 3,429,153
SIC 8051 Skilled nursing care facilities

D-U-N-S 20-588-2942   (BR)
BANQUE TORONTO-DOMINION, LA
TD CANADA TRUST
(*Suby of* Toronto-Dominion Bank, The)
2406 Beacon Ave, Sidney, BC, V8L 1X4
(250) 655-5244
Emp Here 20
SIC 6021 National commercial banks

D-U-N-S 20-139-7895   (BR)
BRITISH COLUMBIA FERRY SERVICES INC
BC FERRIES
2070 Henry Ave W, Sidney, BC, V8L 5Y1
(250) 978-1630
Emp Here 40
SIC 4482 Ferries

D-U-N-S 25-363-8183   (BR)
CANADA POST CORPORATION
2065 Mills Rd W, Sidney, BC, V8L 5X2
(250) 953-1372
Emp Here 53
SIC 4311 U.s. postal service

D-U-N-S 20-107-2857   (SL)
FIRST STREET HOLDINGS LTD
SIDNEY SUPER FOODS
(*Suby of* Ko & Shew Ltd)
2531 Beacon Ave Suite 12, Sidney, BC, V8L 1Y1
(250) 656-0727
Emp Here 55   *Sales* 9,637,750
SIC 5411 Grocery stores
Pr Pr Hon Ko
 Dennie Shew

D-U-N-S 24-579-9408   (SL)
G. & E. CONTRACTING LTD
2061 Mills Rd W, Sidney, BC, V8L 5X2
(250) 656-3159
Emp Here 25   *Sales* 1,824,018
SIC 1794 Excavation work

D-U-N-S 24-161-6176   (SL)
HURST MANAGEMENT LTD
SIDNEY CARE HOME
9888 Fifth St, Sidney, BC, V8L 2X3
(250) 656-0121
Emp Here 50   *Sales* 1,824,018
SIC 8361 Residential care

D-U-N-S 24-248-9339   (SL)
KTC TILBY LTD
2042 Mills Rd W Suite 2, Sidney, BC, V8L 5X4
(250) 656-6005
Emp Here 40   *Sales* 5,836,856
SIC 5049 Professional equipment, nec
Pr Richard Tilby

D-U-N-S 24-245-8883   (BR)
LGL LIMITED

ENVIRONMENTAL RESEARCH ASSOCIATES
9768 Second St, Sidney, BC, V8L 3Y8
(250) 656-0127
Emp Here 30
SIC 8748 Business consulting, nec

D-U-N-S 24-624-3609   (BR)
MCDONALD'S RESTAURANTS OF CANADA LIMITED
MCDONALD'S
(*Suby of* McDonald's Corporation)
2220 Beacon Ave, Sidney, BC, V8L 1X1
(250) 655-6040
Emp Here 30
SIC 5812 Eating places

D-U-N-S 20-588-4190   (HQ)
PHILBROOK'S BOATYARD LTD
TOWER MILLWORKS, DIV OF
(*Suby of* We'll See Holding Company Ltd)
2324 Harbour Rd, Sidney, BC, V8L 2P6
(250) 656-1157
Emp Here 65   *Emp Total* 90
Sales 7,806,795
SIC 3732 Boatbuilding and repairing
 Harold Irwin
Pr Pr Andrew Irwin

D-U-N-S 20-591-4877   (BR)
SCHOOL DISTRICT 63 (SAANICH)
NORTH SAANICH MIDDLE SCHOOL
10475 Mcdonald Park Rd, Sidney, BC, V8L 3H9
(250) 656-1129
Emp Here 50
SIC 8211 Elementary and secondary schools

D-U-N-S 20-031-7852   (BR)
SCHOOL DISTRICT 63 (SAANICH)
INDIVIDUAL LEARNING CENTER SIDNEY
9774 Third St, Sidney, BC, V8L 3A4

Emp Here 20
SIC 8211 Elementary and secondary schools

D-U-N-S 20-713-5653   (BR)
SCHOOL DISTRICT 63 (SAANICH)
SIDNEY ELEMENTARY SCHOOL
2281 Henry Ave, Sidney, BC, V8L 2A8
(250) 656-3958
Emp Here 50
SIC 8211 Elementary and secondary schools

D-U-N-S 20-591-4893   (BR)
SCHOOL DISTRICT 63 (SAANICH)
GREENE GATE SCHOOL
2151 Lannon Way, Sidney, BC, V8L 3Z1
(250) 656-1444
Emp Here 25
SIC 8211 Elementary and secondary schools

D-U-N-S 20-993-6749   (HQ)
SLEGG LIMITED PARTNERSHIP
WSB TITAN, DIV OF
2030 Malaview Ave W, Sidney, BC, V8L 5X6
(250) 656-1125
Emp Here 40   *Emp Total* 100
Sales 53,534,312
SIC 5031 Lumber, plywood, and millwork
Pr Timothy Urquhart
 Ronald Slegg
Dir Robert Slegg

D-U-N-S 25-271-0918   (BR)
SOBEYS WEST INC
SAVE ON FOODS
2345 Beacon Ave, Sidney, BC, V8L 1W9
(250) 656-2735
Emp Here 80
SIC 5411 Grocery stores

D-U-N-S 25-262-9449   (BR)
VAN-KAM FREIGHTWAYS LTD
2050 Mills Rd W, Sidney, BC, V8L 5X4
(250) 656-7235
Emp Here 25
SIC 4213 Trucking, except local

▲ Public Company   ■ Public Company Family Member   **HQ** Headquarters   **BR** Branch   **SL** Single Location

Skookumchuck, BC V0B
East Kootenay County

D-U-N-S 24-254-9421 (BR)
DCT CHAMBERS TRUCKING LTD
GLEN TRANSPORT, DIV OF
4631 Farstad Way Rr 1, Skookumchuck, BC,
V0B 2E0
(250) 422-3535
Emp Here 86
SIC 4212 Local trucking, without storage

Smithers, BC V0J
Bulkley - Nechako County

D-U-N-S 25-056-0521 (SL)
206684 BC LTD
MCDONALD'S RESTAURANT
3720 Highway 16 W, Smithers, BC, V0J 2N1
(250) 847-6142
Emp Here 50   *Sales* 1,532,175
SIC 5812 Eating places

D-U-N-S 24-068-6134 (BR)
ASTRAL MEDIA RADIO INC
CJFW RADIO STATION
(*Suby of* Astral Media Radio Inc)
1280 Main St, Smithers, BC, V0J 2N0
(250) 847-5250
Emp Here 30
SIC 4832 Radio broadcasting stations

D-U-N-S 20-348-0280 (BR)
**BANDSTRA TRANSPORTATION SYSTEMS
LTD**
2990 Hwy 16 E, Smithers, BC, V0J 2N0
(250) 847-6451
Emp Here 60
SIC 4213 Trucking, except local

D-U-N-S 25-361-6585 (BR)
BARRICK GOLD CORPORATION
BARRICK GOLD
660 Air Miles North Of Stewart, Smithers, BC,
V0J 2N0
(604) 522-9877
Emp Here 300
SIC 1041 Gold ores

D-U-N-S 24-132-9445 (BR)
**BILLABONG ROAD & BRIDGE MAINTE-
NANCE INC**
2865 Tatlow Rd, Smithers, BC, V0J 2N5
(250) 847-8737
Emp Here 20
SIC 1611 Highway and street construction

D-U-N-S 24-616-5638 (BR)
BLACK PRESS GROUP LTD
SMITHERS INTERIOR NEWS
3764 Broadway Ave, Smithers, BC, V0J 2N0
(250) 847-3266
Emp Here 20
SIC 2711 Newspapers

D-U-N-S 25-216-8646 (HQ)
CENTRAL MOUNTAIN AIR LTD
6431 Airport Rd, Smithers, BC, V0J 2N2
(250) 877-5000
Emp Here 60   *Emp Total* 450
Sales 42,754,970
SIC 4512 Air transportation, scheduled
Pr Pr Douglas Ellwood Mccrea
  Lindsay Clougher

D-U-N-S 24-313-8922 (SL)
F. G. M. HOLDINGS LTD
HUDSON BAY LODGE
3251 16 Hwy E Rr 6, Smithers, BC, V0J 2N6
(250) 847-8827
Emp Here 62   *Sales* 2,699,546
SIC 7011 Hotels and motels

D-U-N-S 24-338-5007 (BR)
GREAT PACIFIC INDUSTRIES INC
BULKLEY VALLEY WHOLESALE
3302 16 Hwy E, Smithers, BC, V0J 2N0
(250) 847-3313
Emp Here 50
SIC 5141 Groceries, general line

D-U-N-S 20-429-1017 (SL)
HOSKINS FORD SALES LTD
3146 16 Hwy E Rr 6, Smithers, BC, V0J 2N6
(250) 847-2241
Emp Here 28   *Sales* 10,214,498
SIC 5511 New and used car dealers
Pr Pr Gordon Williams
  Gordon Williams Jr
  Colin Williams
  Barbara Williams
  Rita Williams

D-U-N-S 24-825-8613 (BR)
NORTHWEST COMMUNITY COLLEGE
SMITHERS CAMPUS
3966 2 Ave, Smithers, BC, V0J 2N0
(250) 847-4461
Emp Here 25
SIC 8249 Vocational schools, nec

D-U-N-S 24-822-1587 (SL)
RAVEN RESCUE
Gd, Smithers, BC, V0J 2N0
(250) 847-2427
Emp Here 55   *Sales* 3,648,035
SIC 8211 Elementary and secondary schools

D-U-N-S 25-964-9242 (BR)
ROYAL BANK OF CANADA
RBC
(*Suby of* Royal Bank Of Canada)
1106 Main St, Smithers, BC, V0J 2N0
(250) 847-4405
Emp Here 25
SIC 6021 National commercial banks

D-U-N-S 20-981-7100 (BR)
**SCHOOL DISTRICT NO. 54 (BULKLEY VAL-
LEY)**
3377 Third Ave, Smithers, BC, V0J 2N3
(250) 847-4846
Emp Here 400
SIC 8211 Elementary and secondary schools

D-U-N-S 20-716-8894 (BR)
**SCHOOL DISTRICT NO. 54 (BULKLEY VAL-
LEY)**
WALNUT PARK ELEMENTARY SCHOOL
4092 Mountainview Dr, Smithers, BC, V0J
2N0
(250) 847-4464
Emp Here 50
SIC 8211 Elementary and secondary schools

D-U-N-S 20-716-8985 (BR)
**SCHOOL DISTRICT NO. 54 (BULKLEY VAL-
LEY)**
BULKLEY VALLEY LEARNING CENTER
3490 Fulton Ave, Smithers, BC, V0J 2N0
(250) 847-2008
Emp Here 50
SIC 8211 Elementary and secondary schools

D-U-N-S 25-165-2855 (BR)
**SMITHERS SCHOOL BOARD DISTRICT #54
(BULKLEY VALLEY)**
CHANDLER PARK MIDDLE SCHOOL
(*Suby of* Smithers School Board District #54
(Bulkley Valley))
1306 Vancouver St, Smithers, BC, V0J 2N0
(250) 847-2211
Emp Here 38
SIC 8211 Elementary and secondary schools

D-U-N-S 20-591-3648 (BR)
**SMITHERS SCHOOL BOARD DISTRICT #54
(BULKLEY VALLEY)**
MUHEIM ELEMENTARY SCHOOL
(*Suby of* Smithers School Board District #54
(Bulkley Valley))
3659 3rd Ave, Smithers, BC, V0J 2N0
(250) 847-2688
Emp Here 40
SIC 8211 Elementary and secondary schools

D-U-N-S 20-591-3663 (BR)
**SMITHERS SCHOOL BOARD DISTRICT #54
(BULKLEY VALLEY)**
SMITHERS SECONDARY SCHOOL
(*Suby of* Smithers School Board District #54
(Bulkley Valley))
4408 Third Ave, Smithers, BC, V0J 2N3
(250) 847-2231
Emp Here 90
SIC 8211 Elementary and secondary schools

D-U-N-S 24-363-3893 (BR)
SOBEYS WEST INC
SMITHERS SAFEWAY
3664 16 Hwy E Rr 6, Smithers, BC, V0J 2N6
(250) 847-4744
Emp Here 130
SIC 5411 Grocery stores

D-U-N-S 24-939-6797 (BR)
SPEEDEE PRINTERS LTD
INTERIOR STATIONERY, DIV OF
(*Suby of* Speedee Printers Ltd)
1156 Main St, Smithers, BC, V0J 2N0
(250) 847-9712
Emp Here 25
SIC 5943 Stationery stores

D-U-N-S 24-368-5377 (BR)
WEST FRASER MILLS LTD
PACIFIC INLAND RESOURCES, DIV OF
2375 Tatlow Rd, Smithers, BC, V0J 2N5
(250) 847-2656
Emp Here 250
SIC 2421 Sawmills and planing mills, general

Sooke, BC V9Z
Capital County

D-U-N-S 25-483-5317 (BR)
CAPITAL REGIONAL DISTRICT
SEAPARC (SOOKE PK + RECREATION)
2168 Phillips Rd, Sooke, BC, V9Z 0Y3
(250) 642-8000
Emp Here 50
SIC 7999 Amusement and recreation, nec

D-U-N-S 20-720-3964 (BR)
**MCDONALD'S RESTAURANTS OF
CANADA LIMITED**
MCDONALD'S #8632
(*Suby of* McDonald's Corporation)
6661 Sooke Rd Unit 107, Sooke, BC, V9Z 0A1
(250) 642-1200
Emp Here 48
SIC 5812 Eating places

D-U-N-S 24-248-8088 (SL)
PHILIP, S & F HOLDINGS LTD
SOOKE HARBOUR HOUSE
1528 Whiffin Spit Rd, Sooke, BC, V9Z 0T4
(250) 642-3421
Emp Here 50   *Sales* 2,188,821
SIC 7011 Hotels and motels

D-U-N-S 20-653-6984 (BR)
SCHOOL DISTRICT NO 62 (SOOKE)
POIRIER ELEMENTARY SCHOOL
6526 Throup Rd, Sooke, BC, V9Z 0W6
(250) 642-0500
Emp Here 30
SIC 8211 Elementary and secondary schools

D-U-N-S 20-653-2728 (BR)
SCHOOL DISTRICT NO 62 (SOOKE)
JOHN MUIR ELEMENTARY SCHOOL
7179 West Coast Rd Suite 790, Sooke, BC,
V9Z 0R9
(250) 642-4421
Emp Here 20

SIC 8211 Elementary and secondary schools

D-U-N-S 20-591-6666 (BR)
SCHOOL DISTRICT NO 62 (SOOKE)
EDWARD MILL COMMUNITY SCHOOL
6218 Sooke Rd, Sooke, BC, V9Z 0G7
(250) 642-5211
Emp Here 25
SIC 8211 Elementary and secondary schools

D-U-N-S 24-150-3010 (SL)
VILLAGE MARKETS LTD
WESTERN FOODS
6660 Sooke Rd Unit 1400, Sooke, BC, V9Z
0A5
(250) 642-4134
Emp Here 90   *Sales* 16,637,800
SIC 5411 Grocery stores
Pr Pr Edward Low

South Slocan, BC V0G
Central Kootenay County

D-U-N-S 20-106-8520 (BR)
**BRITISH COLUMBIA HYDRO AND POWER
AUTHORITY**
KOOTENAY CANAL GENERATING STATION
Gd, South Slocan, BC, V0G 2G0
(250) 359-7287
Emp Here 26
SIC 4911 Electric services

D-U-N-S 24-152-2481 (BR)
FORTISBC INC
3100 West Kootenay Rd, South Slocan, BC,
V0G 2G1
(250) 359-0700
Emp Here 80
SIC 4911 Electric services

D-U-N-S 25-676-7716 (BR)
**SCHOOL DISTRICT NO. 8 (KOOTENAY
LAKE)**
MOUNT SENTINEL SECONDARY SCHOOL
(*Suby of* School District No. 8 (Kootenay
Lake))
1014 Playmor Rd, South Slocan, BC, V0G
2G1
(250) 359-6873
Emp Here 35
SIC 8211 Elementary and secondary schools

Sparwood, BC V0B
East Kootenay County

D-U-N-S 20-306-9237 (BR)
COLUMBIA INDUSTRIES LTD
681 Douglas Fir Rd, Sparwood, BC, V0B 2G0

Emp Here 25
SIC 7699 Repair services, nec

D-U-N-S 20-100-0676 (HQ)
DOLFO TRANSPORT LTD
585 Michel Creek Rd, Sparwood, BC, V0B
2G1
(250) 425-6494
Emp Here 38   *Emp Total* 100
Sales 3,575,074
SIC 4212 Local trucking, without storage

D-U-N-S 24-440-6914 (SL)
ELKFORD INDUSTRIES LTD
200 Industrial Rd 1 Rr 1, Sparwood, BC, V0B
2G1
(250) 425-2519
Emp Here 30   *Sales* 1,992,377
SIC 7389 Business services, nec

D-U-N-S 24-440-6971 (SL)
FERNIE CONTRACTORS LTD
200 Industrial Rd 1 Rr 1 Unit 1, Sparwood, BC,
V0B 2G1

(250) 425-2519
Emp Here 20   *Sales* 3,291,754
SIC 1629 Heavy construction, nec

D-U-N-S 20-645-7376   (BR)
FINNING INTERNATIONAL INC
FINNING (CANADA), DIV. OF
(*Suby of* Finning International Inc)
749 Douglas Fir Rd, Sparwood, BC, V0B 2G0
(250) 425-6282
Emp Here 88
SIC 5084 Industrial machinery and equipment

D-U-N-S 25-267-8982   (BR)
GREAT PACIFIC INDUSTRIES INC
OVERWAITEA FOOD GROUP
113 Red Cedar Dr, Sparwood, BC, V0B 2G0
(250) 425-6489
Emp Here 55
SIC 5411 Grocery stores

D-U-N-S 24-128-2347   (BR)
JOY GLOBAL (CANADA) LTD
621 Douglas Sir Rd, Sparwood, BC, V0B 2G0
(250) 433-4100
Emp Here 80
SIC 3532 Mining machinery

D-U-N-S 20-024-4635   (BR)
SCHOOL DISTRICT NO 5 (SOUTHEAST KOOTENAY)
FRANK J MITCHELL ELEMENTARY SCHOOL
101 Blue Spruce Cres, Sparwood, BC, V0B 2G0
(250) 425-7818
Emp Here 33
SIC 8211 Elementary and secondary schools

D-U-N-S 20-031-1806   (BR)
SCHOOL DISTRICT NO 5 (SOUTHEAST KOOTENAY)
SPARWOOD SECONDARY SCHOOL
101 Pine Spur, Sparwood, BC, V0B 2G0
(250) 425-6666
Emp Here 26
SIC 8211 Elementary and secondary schools

D-U-N-S 25-360-9085   (BR)
TECK COAL LIMITED
LINE CREEK OPERATIONS
Gd, Sparwood, BC, V0B 2G0
(250) 425-2555
Emp Here 530
SIC 1221 Bituminous coal and lignite-surface mining

D-U-N-S 24-367-8856   (BR)
TECK COAL LIMITED
ELKVIEW OPERATIONS
Gd, Sparwood, BC, V0B 2G0
(250) 425-8325
Emp Here 1,060
SIC 1221 Bituminous coal and lignite-surface mining

D-U-N-S 20-552-8180   (BR)
TECK COAL LIMITED
COAL MOUNTAIN OPERATIONS
2261 Corbin Rd, Sparwood, BC, V0B 2G0
(250) 425-6305
Emp Here 320
SIC 1221 Bituminous coal and lignite-surface mining

Squamish, BC V0N
Squamish - Lillooet County

D-U-N-S 25-720-5047   (BR)
GREAT PACIFIC INDUSTRIES INC
SAVE-ON-FOODS
1301 Pemberton Ave, Squamish, BC, V0N 3G0
(604) 892-5976
Emp Here 130

SIC 5411 Grocery stores

D-U-N-S 25-015-0109   (BR)
ROYAL BANK OF CANADA
RBC
(*Suby of* Royal Bank Of Canada)
38100 Second Ave, Squamish, BC, V0N 3G0
(604) 892-3555
Emp Here 25
SIC 6021 National commercial banks

Squamish, BC V8B
Squamish - Lillooet County

D-U-N-S 20-796-2031   (BR)
CAPILANO UNIVERSITY
1150 Carson Pl, Squamish, BC, V8B 0B1
(604) 892-5322
Emp Here 20
SIC 8221 Colleges and universities

D-U-N-S 20-428-2131   (SL)
CARNEY, OWEN G LTD
CARNEY'S WASTE SYSTEMS
38950 Queens Way, Squamish, BC, V8B 0K8
(604) 892-5604
Emp Here 50   *Sales* 3,939,878
SIC 4212 Local trucking, without storage

D-U-N-S 24-749-5633   (BR)
ELAHO LOGGING LTD
WELCH GROUP, THE
Gd, Squamish, BC, V8B 0J2
(604) 892-9891
Emp Here 30
SIC 2411 Logging

D-U-N-S 25-775-5041   (SL)
FRASERWOOD INDUSTRIES LTD
39500 Government Rd, Squamish, BC, V8B 0G3
(604) 898-1385
Emp Here 40   *Sales* 7,760,360
SIC 2421 Sawmills and planing mills, general

D-U-N-S 24-317-1274   (BR)
HOME DEPOT OF CANADA INC
HOME DEPOT
(*Suby of* The Home Depot Inc)
39251 Discovery Way, Squamish, BC, V8B 0M9
(604) 892-8800
Emp Here 20
SIC 5251 Hardware stores

D-U-N-S 24-938-6673   (BR)
ROGERS MEDIA INC
MOUNTAIN FM RADIO
(*Suby of* Rogers Communications Inc)
40147 Glenalder Pl Suite 202, Squamish, BC, V8B 0G2
(604) 892-1021
Emp Here 25
SIC 4832 Radio broadcasting stations

D-U-N-S 20-072-1806   (BR)
SCHOOL DISTRICT NO. 48 (HOWE SOUND)
STAWAMUS ELEMENTARY SCHOOL
38030 Clarke Dr, Squamish, BC, V8B 0A5
(604) 892-5904
Emp Here 20
SIC 8211 Elementary and secondary schools

D-U-N-S 20-591-3614   (BR)
SCHOOL DISTRICT NO. 48 (HOWE SOUND)
VALLEYCLIFFE ELEMENTARY SCHOOL
38430 Westway, Squamish, BC, V8B 0B5
(604) 892-9394
Emp Here 25
SIC 8211 Elementary and secondary schools

D-U-N-S 20-043-7833   (BR)
SCHOOL DISTRICT NO. 48 (HOWE SOUND)
HOWE SOUND SECONDARY
38430 Buckley Ave, Squamish, BC, V8B 0A1

(604) 892-5261
Emp Here 60
SIC 8211 Elementary and secondary schools

D-U-N-S 25-451-4284   (BR)
SCHOOL DISTRICT NO. 48 (HOWE SOUND)
SQUAMISH ELEMENTARY SCHOOL
38370 Buckley Rd, Squamish, BC, V8B 0A7
(604) 892-9307
Emp Here 26
SIC 8211 Elementary and secondary schools

D-U-N-S 25-018-3969   (HQ)
SEA TO SKY COMMUNITY HEALTH COUNCIL
SQUAMISH GENERAL HOSPITAL
(*Suby of* Vancouver Coastal Health Authority)
38140 Behrner Dr, Squamish, BC, V8B 0J3
(604) 892-9337
Emp Here 200   *Emp Total* 24,000
Sales 26,950,609
SIC 8062 General medical and surgical hospitals
 Brian Kines
 Gloria Healy
 Kathryn Kiltatrick

D-U-N-S 25-325-4866   (SL)
SEA TO SKY FORD SALES LTD
SEA TO SKY FORD
1180 Hunter Pl, Squamish, BC, V8B 0B7
(604) 892-3673
Emp Here 24   *Sales* 10,944,105
SIC 5511 New and used car dealers
Pr Donald Carson
Dir Enzo Milia

D-U-N-S 20-913-0405   (BR)
SQUAMISH NATION
TOTEM HALL, THE
1380 Stawamus Rd, Squamish, BC, V8B 0B5
(604) 892-5166
Emp Here 50
SIC 7999 Amusement and recreation, nec

D-U-N-S 20-166-2223   (BR)
SQUAMISH NATION
TOTEM HALL, THE
1380 Stawamus Rd, Squamish, BC, V8B 0B5
(604) 987-1118
Emp Here 40
SIC 8641 Civic and social associations

D-U-N-S 20-623-2159   (SL)
SQUAMISH TERMINALS LTD
37500 Third Ave, Squamish, BC, V8B 0B1
(604) 892-3511
Emp Here 110   *Sales* 16,708,000
SIC 4491 Marine cargo handling
Pr Pr Ronald Anderson
VP Opers Joseph Webber
 Douglas Hackett

D-U-N-S 24-319-5117   (BR)
WAL-MART CANADA CORP
WAL-MART
39210 Discovery Way Suite 1015, Squamish, BC, V8B 0N1
(604) 815-4625
Emp Here 120
SIC 5311 Department stores

D-U-N-S 20-641-9546   (BR)
WHITE SPOT LIMITED
WHITE SPOT RESTAURANT
1200 Hunter Pl Unit 410, Squamish, BC, V8B 0G8
(604) 892-7477
Emp Here 50
SIC 5812 Eating places

Stewart, BC V0T
Kitimat - Stikine County

D-U-N-S 25-216-6327   (BR)

ARROW MINING SERVICES INC
318 Rally St, Stewart, BC, V0T 1W0
(250) 636-2178
Emp Here 35
SIC 4212 Local trucking, without storage

D-U-N-S 25-943-2573   (BR)
ARROW TRANSPORTATION SYSTEMS INC
ARROW TAHLTAN JOINT VENTURE
318 Railway St, Stewart, BC, V0T 1W0
(250) 636-2178
Emp Here 30
SIC 4212 Local trucking, without storage

Summerland, BC V0H
Okanagn-Similkameen County

D-U-N-S 20-027-0945   (BR)
CONSEIL SCOLAIRE FRANCOPHONE DE LA COLOMBIE BRITANNIQUE
SUMMERLAND MIDDLE SCHOOL
13611 Kelly Ave, Summerland, BC, V0H 1Z0
(604) 214-2600
Emp Here 35
SIC 8211 Elementary and secondary schools

D-U-N-S 20-027-0952   (BR)
SCHOOL DISTRICT NO 67 (OKANAGAN SKAHA)
TROUT CREEK ELEMENTARY SCHOOL
5811 Nixon Rd, Summerland, BC, V0H 1Z9
(250) 494-7876
Emp Here 24
SIC 8211 Elementary and secondary schools

D-U-N-S 20-027-0960   (BR)
SCHOOL DISTRICT NO 67 (OKANAGAN SKAHA)
GIANTS HEAD ELEMENTARY
10503 Prairie Valley Rd, Summerland, BC, V0H 1Z4
(250) 770-7671
Emp Here 40
SIC 8211 Elementary and secondary schools

D-U-N-S 20-038-4670   (BR)
SUMMERLAND, CORPORATION OF THE DISTRICT OF
PUBLIC WORKS
9215 Cedar Ave, Summerland, BC, V0H 1Z2
(250) 494-0431
Emp Here 40
SIC 8711 Engineering services

D-U-N-S 24-360-9976   (BR)
SUNOPTA INC
KETTLE VALLEY DRIED FRUITS, DIV OF
14014 Highway 97 N, Summerland, BC, V0H 1Z0
(250) 494-0335
Emp Here 55
SIC 5149 Groceries and related products, nec

Surrey, BC V3R
Greater Vancouver County

D-U-N-S 25-287-9127   (BR)
A & W FOOD SERVICES OF CANADA INC
A & W
10355 152 St, Surrey, BC, V3R 7C3
(604) 498-4370
Emp Here 30
SIC 5812 Eating places

D-U-N-S 20-107-8214   (BR)
AON BENFIELD CANADA ULC
15225 104 Ave Suite 320, Surrey, BC, V3R 6Y8

Emp Here 20
SIC 6211 Security brokers and dealers

D-U-N-S 20-063-6525   (SL)
ACADEMY OF DANCE
15326 103a Ave, Surrey, BC, V3R 7A2
(604) 882-0422
Emp Here 51   Sales 1,039,501
SIC 7911 Dance studios, schools, and halls

D-U-N-S 20-572-2403   (BR)
BANK OF NOVA SCOTIA, THE
SCOTIABANK
15170 104 Ave, Surrey, BC, V3R 1N3
(604) 586-3200
Emp Here 20
SIC 6021 National commercial banks

D-U-N-S 24-695-3681   (SL)
CHERINGTON INTERCARE INC
CHERINGTON PLACE
13453 111a Ave, Surrey, BC, V3R 2C5
(604) 581-2885
Emp Here 65   Sales 2,991,389
SIC 8051 Skilled nursing care facilities

D-U-N-S 25-745-8521   (BR)
CHRISTIAN LABOUR ASSOCIATION OF CANADA
CLAC
15483 104 Ave, Surrey, BC, V3R 1N9
(604) 576-7000
Emp Here 25
SIC 8631 Labor organizations

D-U-N-S 25-745-7119   (BR)
CINEPLEX ODEON CORPORATION
LANDMARK CINEMAS 12 GUILDFORD SURREY
15051 101 Ave, Surrey, BC, V3R 7Z1
(604) 581-1716
Emp Here 20
SIC 7832 Motion picture theaters, except drive-in

D-U-N-S 24-120-7310   (BR)
COMPAGNIE DES CHEMINS DE FER NATIONAUX DU CANADA
13477 116 Ave, Surrey, BC, V3R 6W4
(604) 589-6552
Emp Here 150
SIC 4111 Local and suburban transit

D-U-N-S 20-863-2018   (HQ)
DAMS FORD LINCOLN SALES LTD
14530 104 Ave, Surrey, BC, V3R 1L9
(604) 588-9921
Emp Here 130   Emp Total 1
Sales 100,480,000
SIC 5511 New and used car dealers
Pr Pr Gordon Dams
Gordon Dams Jr

D-U-N-S 20-284-6150   (BR)
DAVIDSTEA INC
DAVIDSTEA
2695 Guildford Town Ctr, Surrey, BC, V3R 7C1
(604) 580-2300
Emp Here 22
SIC 5499 Miscellaneous food stores

D-U-N-S 24-874-8527   (BR)
DAY & ROSS INC
11470 131 St, Surrey, BC, V3R 4S7
(604) 495-8638
Emp Here 20
SIC 4213 Trucking, except local

D-U-N-S 20-641-6559   (SL)
DOLO INVESTIGATIONS LTD
10090 152 St Suite 408, Surrey, BC, V3R 8X8
(604) 951-1600
Emp Here 50   Sales 2,626,585
SIC 7389 Business services, nec

D-U-N-S 20-690-9603   (HQ)
E CARE CONTACT CENTERS LTD
(Suby of E Care Contact Centers Ltd)
15225 104 Ave Suite 400, Surrey, BC, V3R 6Y8

(604) 587-6200
Emp Here 20   Emp Total 500
Sales 33,057,920
SIC 7389 Business services, nec
Pr Pr Kim Dethomas

D-U-N-S 20-153-2202   (SL)
EARLS RESTAURANT GUILDFORD LTD
10160 152 St, Surrey, BC, V3R 9W3
(604) 584-0840
Emp Here 60   Sales 1,824,018
SIC 5812 Eating places

D-U-N-S 25-902-2333   (BR)
FGL SPORTS LTD
ATHLETES WORLD
1214 Guildford Town Ctr, Surrey, BC, V3R 7B7
(604) 585-7293
Emp Here 50
SIC 5699 Miscellaneous apparel and accessory stores

D-U-N-S 24-343-7295   (BR)
FGL SPORTS LTD
SPORT-CHEK
1214 Guildford Town Ctr, Surrey, BC, V3R 7B7
(604) 585-7293
Emp Here 40
SIC 5941 Sporting goods and bicycle shops

D-U-N-S 24-737-1979   (SL)
FLAG AUTOMOTIVE SALES & LEASE LTD
FLAG MITSUBISHI
15250 104 Ave, Surrey, BC, V3R 6N8
(604) 581-8281
Emp Here 49   Sales 24,049,200
SIC 5511 New and used car dealers
Pr Sherrold Haddad

D-U-N-S 24-368-4123   (SL)
FRASER VALLEY CHRISTIAN HIGH SCHOOL ASSOCIATION
FRASER VALLEY CHRISTIAN HIGH SCHOOL
15353 92 Ave, Surrey, BC, V3R 1C3
(604) 581-1033
Emp Here 50   Sales 3,356,192
SIC 8211 Elementary and secondary schools

D-U-N-S 20-349-1076   (BR)
GAP (CANADA) INC
GAP
(Suby of The Gap Inc)
2232 Guildford Town Ctr, Surrey, BC, V3R 7B9
(604) 582-2522
Emp Here 20
SIC 5651 Family clothing stores

D-U-N-S 25-140-7219   (BR)
GIBSON ENERGY ULC
CANWEST PROPANE
13733 116 Ave, Surrey, BC, V3R 0T2
(604) 589-8244
Emp Here 20
SIC 5172 Petroleum products, nec

D-U-N-S 25-267-8610   (BR)
GREAT PACIFIC INDUSTRIES INC
SAVE-ON-FOODS
9014 152 St Suite 2218, Surrey, BC, V3R 4E7
(604) 930-1133
Emp Here 180
SIC 5399 Miscellaneous general merchandise

D-U-N-S 20-921-0876   (SL)
GUILDFORD TOWN CENTRE LIMITED PARTNERSHIP
IVAHOE CAMBRIDGE
2695 Guildford Town Ctr, Surrey, BC, V3R 7C1
(604) 582-7101
Emp Here 23   Sales 2,913,920
SIC 6512 Nonresidential building operators

D-U-N-S 20-871-6980   (BR)
H.Y. LOUIE CO. LIMITED
MARKETPLACE IGA
14865 108 Ave, Surrey, BC, V3R 1W2
(604) 584-2616
Emp Here 30

SIC 5411 Grocery stores

D-U-N-S 25-760-3043   (SL)
HAWTHORNE PARK INC
MCDONALD'S RESTAURANTS
14476 104 Ave, Surrey, BC, V3R 1L9
(604) 587-1040
Emp Here 100   Sales 2,991,389
SIC 5812 Eating places

D-U-N-S 25-128-2000   (BR)
HOMELIFE BENCHMARK REALTY CORP
9128 152 St Suite 102, Surrey, BC, V3R 4E7
(604) 306-3888
Emp Here 55
SIC 6531 Real estate agents and managers

D-U-N-S 20-621-8901   (BR)
HUDSON'S BAY COMPANY
THE BAY
1400 Guildford Town Ctr, Surrey, BC, V3R 7B7
(604) 588-2111
Emp Here 200
SIC 5311 Department stores

D-U-N-S 20-913-9448   (BR)
IGM FINANCIAL INC
INVESTORS GROUP
10428 153 St Suite 100, Surrey, BC, V3R 1E1
(604) 581-8005
Emp Here 20
SIC 6211 Security brokers and dealers

D-U-N-S 24-174-1623   (BR)
INSURANCE CORPORATION OF BRITISH COLUMBIA
ICBC
10470 152 St Suite 405, Surrey, BC, V3R 0Y4
(604) 520-8222
Emp Here 46
SIC 6331 Fire, marine, and casualty insurance

D-U-N-S 25-272-7458   (BR)
INSURANCE CORPORATION OF BRITISH COLUMBIA
I C B C
10262 152a St, Surrey, BC, V3R 6T8
(604) 584-3211
Emp Here 125
SIC 6331 Fire, marine, and casualty insurance

D-U-N-S 24-019-1739   (BR)
KIN'S FARM LTD
2695 Guildford Town Ctr Suite 1285, Surrey, BC, V3R 7C1
(604) 583-6181
Emp Here 26
SIC 5411 Grocery stores

D-U-N-S 24-311-2562   (BR)
LONDON DRUGS LIMITED
2340 Guildford Town Ctr, Surrey, BC, V3R 7B9
(604) 588-7881
Emp Here 115
SIC 5912 Drug stores and proprietary stores

D-U-N-S 25-318-1713   (BR)
MCDONALD'S RESTAURANTS OF CANADA LIMITED
MCDONALD'S #8485
(Suby of McDonald's Corporation)
1000 Guildford Town Ctr, Surrey, BC, V3R 7C3

Emp Here 100
SIC 5812 Eating places

D-U-N-S 25-318-1705   (BR)
MCDONALD'S RESTAURANTS OF CANADA LIMITED
MCDONALD'S #8159
(Suby of McDonald's Corporation)
10250 152 St, Surrey, BC, V3R 6N7
(604) 587-3380
Emp Here 120
SIC 5812 Eating places

D-U-N-S 20-803-5308   (BR)
OPTIONS: SERVICES TO COMMUNITIES

SOCIETY
OPTIONS SERVICES WOMANS TRANSITION
(Suby of OPTIONS: Services to Communities Society)
14668 106 Ave, Surrey, BC, V3R 5Y1
(604) 584-3301
Emp Here 28
SIC 8322 Individual and family services

D-U-N-S 24-367-5790   (BR)
PATTISON, JIM INDUSTRIES LTD
JIM PATTISON TOYOTA SURREY
15389 Guildford Dr, Surrey, BC, V3R 0H9
(604) 583-8886
Emp Here 80
SIC 5511 New and used car dealers

D-U-N-S 25-653-2995   (BR)
PROSPERA CREDIT UNION
15288 Fraser Hwy Suite 100, Surrey, BC, V3R 3P4

Emp Here 20
SIC 6062 State credit unions

D-U-N-S 25-369-3659   (BR)
PWC MANAGEMENT SERVICES LP
10190 152a St 3 Fl, Surrey, BC, V3R 1J7
(604) 806-7000
Emp Here 900
SIC 8721 Accounting, auditing, and bookkeeping

D-U-N-S 20-153-2210   (BR)
SCHOOL DISTRICT NO 36 (SURREY)
BONACCORD ELEMENTARY SCHOOL
14986 98 Ave, Surrey, BC, V3R 1J1
(604) 584-3533
Emp Here 55
SIC 8211 Elementary and secondary schools

D-U-N-S 20-713-3492   (BR)
SCHOOL DISTRICT NO 36 (SURREY)
ECOLE RIVERDALE
14835 108a Ave, Surrey, BC, V3R 1W9
(604) 588-5978
Emp Here 45
SIC 8211 Elementary and secondary schools

D-U-N-S 20-590-9083   (BR)
SCHOOL DISTRICT NO 36 (SURREY)
JAMES ARDIEL ELEMENTARY SCHOOL
13751 112 Ave, Surrey, BC, V3R 2G4
(604) 588-3021
Emp Here 40
SIC 8211 Elementary and secondary schools

D-U-N-S 20-590-9109   (BR)
SCHOOL DISTRICT NO 36 (SURREY)
SURREY TRADITIONAL SCHOOL
13875 113 Ave, Surrey, BC, V3R 2J6
(604) 588-1248
Emp Here 30
SIC 8211 Elementary and secondary schools

D-U-N-S 20-590-9216   (BR)
SCHOOL DISTRICT NO 36 (SURREY)
WILLIAM F DAVIDSON ELEMENTARY SCHOOL
15550 99a Ave, Surrey, BC, V3R 9H5
(604) 584-7688
Emp Here 40
SIC 8211 Elementary and secondary schools

D-U-N-S 20-048-2318   (BR)
SCHOOL DISTRICT NO 36 (SURREY)
ELLENDALE ELEMENTARY SCHOOL
14525 110a Ave, Surrey, BC, V3R 2B4
(604) 584-4754
Emp Here 20
SIC 8211 Elementary and secondary schools

D-U-N-S 20-713-3641   (BR)
SCHOOL DISTRICT NO 36 (SURREY)
GUILDFORD LEARNING CENTRES
10215 152a St, Surrey, BC, V3R 4H6

(604) 951-9553
Emp Here 20
SIC 8211 Elementary and secondary schools

D-U-N-S 20-026-9111   (BR)
SCHOOL DISTRICT NO 36 (SURREY)
JOHNSON HEIGHTS SECONDARY SCHOOL
15350 99 Ave, Surrey, BC, V3R 0R9
(604) 581-5500
Emp Here 90
SIC 8211 Elementary and secondary schools

D-U-N-S 20-590-7566   (BR)
SCHOOL DISTRICT NO 36 (SURREY)
HOLLY ELEMENTARY SCHOOL
10719 150 St, Surrey, BC, V3R 4C8
(604) 585-2566
Emp Here 100
SIC 8211 Elementary and secondary schools

D-U-N-S 20-590-9133   (BR)
SCHOOL DISTRICT NO 36 (SURREY)
HJORTH RD ELEMENTARY SCHOOL
14781 104 Ave, Surrey, BC, V3R 5X4
(604) 581-2327
Emp Here 30
SIC 8211 Elementary and secondary schools

D-U-N-S 20-033-3768   (BR)
SCHOOL DISTRICT NO 36 (SURREY)
BRIDGEVIEW ELEMENTARY SCHOOL
12834 115a Ave, Surrey, BC, V3R 2X4
(604) 580-1047
Emp Here 25
SIC 8211 Elementary and secondary schools

D-U-N-S 20-713-3567   (BR)
SCHOOL DISTRICT NO 36 (SURREY)
BERKSHIRE PARK ELEMENTARY SCHOOL
15372 94 Ave, Surrey, BC, V3R 1E3
(604) 583-7305
Emp Here 50
SIC 8211 Elementary and secondary schools

D-U-N-S 20-713-3518   (BR)
SCHOOL DISTRICT NO 36 (SURREY)
MOUNTAINVIEW MONTESSORI
15225 98 Ave, Surrey, BC, V3R 1J2
(604) 589-1193
Emp Here 50
SIC 8211 Elementary and secondary schools

D-U-N-S 25-095-1456   (BR)
SEARS CANADA INC
1730 Guildford Town Ctr, Surrey, BC, V3R 7B8
(604) 584-4149
Emp Here 150
SIC 5311 Department stores

D-U-N-S 20-747-6932   (BR)
ST JOHN SOCIETY (BRITISH COLUMBIA AND YUKON)
ST JOHN AMBULANCE
8911 152 St, Surrey, BC, V3R 4E5
(604) 953-1603
Emp Here 68
SIC 8322 Individual and family services

D-U-N-S 25-499-1607   (BR)
STARBUCKS COFFEE CANADA, INC
(*Suby of* Starbucks Corporation)
8898 152 St, Surrey, BC, V3R 4E4
(604) 951-9373
Emp Here 25
SIC 5812 Eating places

D-U-N-S 20-806-5099   (BR)
STARBUCKS COFFEE CANADA, INC
STARBUCKS GUILDFORD DRIVE-THRU
(*Suby of* Starbucks Corporation)
10174 152 St, Surrey, BC, V3R 6N7
(604) 951-6633
Emp Here 30
SIC 5812 Eating places

D-U-N-S 24-797-0015   (BR)
SUN LIFE ASSURANCE COMPANY OF CANADA

SUN LIFE FINANCIAL
10470 152 St Suite 170, Surrey, BC, V3R 0Y3
(604) 588-5232
Emp Here 40
SIC 6311 Life insurance

D-U-N-S 24-313-2693   (BR)
SURREY PUBLIC LIBRARY
GUILDFORD LIBRARY
15105 105 Ave Suite 15, Surrey, BC, V3R 7G8
(604) 598-7360
Emp Here 25
SIC 8231 Libraries

D-U-N-S 25-714-6472   (SL)
SUTTON PREMIER REALTY
15357 104 Ave Suite 200, Surrey, BC, V3R 1N5
(604) 580-0495
Emp Here 49   *Sales* 6,184,080
SIC 6531 Real estate agents and managers
Owner Larry Anderson

D-U-N-S 20-589-5746   (BR)
VANCOUVER CITY SAVINGS CREDIT UNION
VANCITY CREDIT UNION
15175 101 Ave Unit 108, Surrey, BC, V3R 7Z1
(604) 877-7302
Emp Here 20
SIC 6062 State credit unions

D-U-N-S 25-130-0125   (SL)
VANCOUVER WAITER RESOURCES LTD
10090 152 St Suite 607, Surrey, BC, V3R 8X8
(778) 571-2425
Emp Here 60   *Sales* 4,377,642
SIC 7363 Help supply services

D-U-N-S 20-632-7207   (BR)
WAKEFIELD CANADA INC
10824 152 St Suite 55, Surrey, BC, V3R 4H2
(604) 585-1030
Emp Here 29
SIC 5172 Petroleum products, nec

D-U-N-S 25-294-8666   (BR)
WAL-MART CANADA CORP
WALMART
1000 Guildford Town Ctr, Surrey, BC, V3R 7C3
(604) 581-1932
Emp Here 350
SIC 5311 Department stores

D-U-N-S 25-949-8731   (BR)
WENDY'S RESTAURANTS OF CANADA INC
WENDY'S
(*Suby of* The Wendy's Company)
10125 152 St, Surrey, BC, V3R 4G6
(604) 581-8832
Emp Here 40
SIC 5812 Eating places

D-U-N-S 25-663-9741   (BR)
WESTERN INVENTORY SERVICE LTD
WIS INTERNATIONAL
14815 108 Ave Unit 230, Surrey, BC, V3R 1W2

Emp Here 30
SIC 7389 Business services, nec

Surrey, BC V3S
Greater Vancouver County

D-U-N-S 20-316-2433   (SL)
8TH AVENUE ELITE REALTY LTD
15252 32 Ave Unit 210, Surrey, BC, V3S 0R7

Emp Here 60   *Sales* 7,255,933
SIC 6531 Real estate agents and managers
Mgr Ashwin Dawodharry

D-U-N-S 24-683-9430   (BR)
ARMTEC LP

ARMTEC
19060 54 Ave, Surrey, BC, V3S 8E5
(604) 576-1808
Emp Here 50
SIC 3312 Blast furnaces and steel mills

D-U-N-S 25-692-0943   (BR)
BANQUE DE DEVELOPPEMENT DU CANADA
BDC
5577 153a St Unit 301, Surrey, BC, V3S 5K7
(604) 586-2410
Emp Here 30
SIC 6141 Personal credit institutions

D-U-N-S 25-082-9645   (BR)
BOYD GROUP INC, THE
BOYD AUTOBODY & GLASS
5726 Landmark Way, Surrey, BC, V3S 7H1
(604) 530-9818
Emp Here 25
SIC 7532 Top and body repair and paint shops

D-U-N-S 24-736-1574   (BR)
CP DISTRIBUTORS LTD
CP DISTRIBUTORS LTD.
15050 54a Ave Suite 5, Surrey, BC, V3S 5X7
(604) 599-0900
Emp Here 30
SIC 5039 Construction materials, nec

D-U-N-S 20-539-5796   (BR)
CANADA POST CORPORATION
SHOPPERS DRUG MART
17790 56 Ave Suite 104, Surrey, BC, V3S 1C7
(604) 574-7436
Emp Here 30
SIC 4311 U.s. postal service

D-U-N-S 25-360-0290   (BR)
CANADIAN UTILITY CONSTRUCTION CORP
(*Suby of* Quanta Services, Inc.)
6739 176 St Unit 1, Surrey, BC, V3S 4G6
(604) 576-9358
Emp Here 100
SIC 1623 Water, sewer, and utility lines

D-U-N-S 24-939-0196   (HQ)
CANADIAN UTILITY CONSTRUCTION CORP
NORTHERN TRAFFIC SERVICE
(*Suby of* Quanta Services, Inc.)
14928 56 Ave Suite 305, Surrey, BC, V3S 2N5
(604) 574-6640
Emp Here 100   *Emp Total* 28,100
Sales 35,896,664
SIC 1623 Water, sewer, and utility lines
 Lorne Kramer
Pr Pr Leigh Ann Shoji-Le
Dir Alan Leschyshyn
Dir Noel Coon
Dir Michael Kemper

D-U-N-S 20-888-7575   (BR)
CITY OF SURREY, THE
CLOVERDALE YOUTH CENTER
6228 184 St, Surrey, BC, V3S 8E6

Emp Here 20
SIC 8322 Individual and family services

D-U-N-S 20-336-7479   (BR)
CITY OF SURREY, THE
ENGINNERING OPERATIONS
6651 148 St Fl 3, Surrey, BC, V3S 3C7
(604) 591-4152
Emp Here 200
SIC 8711 Engineering services

D-U-N-S 25-646-0064   (BR)
COAST CAPITAL SAVINGS CREDIT UNION
17730 56 Ave, Surrey, BC, V3S 1C7
(604) 517-7017
Emp Here 20
SIC 6062 State credit unions

D-U-N-S 25-026-9180   (BR)

ARMTEC
19060 54 Ave, Surrey, BC, V3S 8E5

COMMANDER WAREHOUSE EQUIPMENT LTD
5225 192 St, Surrey, BC, V3S 8E5
(604) 574-5797
Emp Here 20
SIC 5084 Industrial machinery and equipment

D-U-N-S 20-013-5015   (BR)
COTT CORPORATION
COTT BEVERAGES CANADA
15050 54a Ave, Surrey, BC, V3S 5X7
(604) 574-1970
Emp Here 70
SIC 2086 Bottled and canned soft drinks

D-U-N-S 24-289-4574   (SL)
DIXON HEATING & SHEET METAL LTD
17741 65a Ave Unit 101, Surrey, BC, V3S 1Z8
(604) 576-0585
Emp Here 43   *Sales* 3,793,956
SIC 1711 Plumbing, heating, air-conditioning

D-U-N-S 25-671-5863   (BR)
EAGLE QUEST GOLF CENTERS INC
EAGLE QUEST COYOTE CREEK
7778 152 St, Surrey, BC, V3S 3M4
(604) 597-4653
Emp Here 20
SIC 7997 Membership sports and recreation clubs

D-U-N-S 25-714-8031   (BR)
ENTERPRISE RENT-A-CAR CANADA COMPANY
ENTERPRISE RENT A CAR
(*Suby of* The Crawford Group Inc)
19335 Langley Bypass Suite 7, Surrey, BC, V3S 6K1
(604) 532-8969
Emp Here 28
SIC 7514 Passenger car rental

D-U-N-S 20-349-9012   (BR)
EXOVA CANADA INC
BODYCOTE TESTING GROUP
(*Suby of* Exova, Inc.)
19575 55a Ave Suite 104, Surrey, BC, V3S 8P8
(604) 514-3322
Emp Here 20
SIC 6141 Personal credit institutions

D-U-N-S 24-368-2239   (SL)
G4S JUSTICE SERVICES (CANADA) INC
6592 176 St Suite 103, Surrey, BC, V3S 4G5

Emp Here 22   *Sales* 3,210,271
SIC 3825 Instruments to measure electricity

D-U-N-S 20-688-1604   (BR)
GOVERNMENT OF THE PROVINCE OF BRITISH COLUMBIA
BC AMBULANCE SERVICE
5833 176 St, Surrey, BC, V3S 4E3
(604) 576-8843
Emp Here 40
SIC 4119 Local passenger transportation, nec

D-U-N-S 24-887-4661   (HQ)
GROUPHEALTH GLOBAL PARTNERS INC
GROUPHEALTH GLOBAL PARTNER
(*Suby of* GroupHEALTH Global Partners Inc)
2626 Croydon Dr Suite 200, Surrey, BC, V3S 0S8
(604) 542-4100
Emp Here 90   *Emp Total* 120
Sales 22,235,112
SIC 8741 Management services
Pr Pr Matthew Houghton

D-U-N-S 24-314-3539   (BR)
HALTON RECYCLING LTD
EMTERRA ENVIRONMENTAL
6362 148 St, Surrey, BC, V3S 3C4

Emp Here 400
SIC 4953 Refuse systems

D-U-N-S 24-309-1605   (SL)
HARPO ENTERPRISES
MCDONALD'S
17960 56 Ave, Surrey, BC, V3S 1C7
(604) 575-1690
Emp Here 75   *Sales* 2,261,782
SIC 5812 Eating places

D-U-N-S 24-310-4981   (SL)
INTERNATIONAL TENTNOLOGY CORP
TENTNOLOGY CO
15427 66 Ave, Surrey, BC, V3S 2A1
(604) 597-3368
Emp Here 75   *Sales* 3,283,232
SIC 2394 Canvas and related products

D-U-N-S 25-622-7612   (BR)
INTERWEST RESTAURANTS PARTNER-SHIP
WENDY'S RESTAURANTS OF CANADA
(*Suby of* Interwest Restaurants Partnership)
17911 56 Ave, Surrey, BC, V3S 1E2
(604) 574-4494
Emp Here 20
SIC 5812 Eating places

D-U-N-S 20-867-8656   (HQ)
LANGFAB FABRICATORS LTD
(*Suby of* A G & J M Enterprises Ltd)
19405 Enterprise Way, Surrey, BC, V3S 6J8
(604) 530-7227
Emp Here 45   *Emp Total* 2
Sales 7,189,883
SIC 3713 Truck and bus bodies
Pr Pr Adrian Goyer
  Joseph Mckee

D-U-N-S 24-417-4319   (BR)
LOBLAWS INC
EXTRA FOODS
18699 Fraser Hwy, Surrey, BC, V3S 7Y3
(604) 576-3125
Emp Here 50
SIC 5411 Grocery stores

D-U-N-S 25-679-8299   (HQ)
LOWER MAINLAND STEEL (1998) LTD
6320 148 St, Surrey, BC, V3S 3C4
(604) 598-9930
Emp Here 70   *Emp Total* 70
Sales 10,648,318
SIC 1791 Structural steel erection
Pr Pr Ronald Mcneil
  Ivan Harmatny
  Darryl Hebert

D-U-N-S 24-331-8164   (BR)
MNP LLP
5455 152 St Suite 316, Surrey, BC, V3S 5A5
(604) 574-7211
Emp Here 70
SIC 8721 Accounting, auditing, and book-keeping

D-U-N-S 24-818-1179   (BR)
MAGNATE ENGINEERING & ASSOCIATES INC
19425 Langley Bypass Suite 107, Surrey, BC, V3S 6K1
(604) 539-1411
Emp Here 25
SIC 8711 Engineering services

D-U-N-S 25-108-7185   (HQ)
MAINROAD EAST KOOTENAY CONTRACTING LTD
17474 56 Ave, Surrey, BC, V3S 1C3
(604) 575-7020
Emp Here 40   *Emp Total* 400
Sales 16,076,800
SIC 1611 Highway and street construction
Pr David A. Zerr
  Doug Bjornson
Fin Ex Dale Routley

D-U-N-S 25-302-1471   (BR)
MAPLE LEAF FOODS INC
5523 176 St, Surrey, BC, V3S 4C2

Emp Here 250
SIC 2013 Sausages and other prepared meats

D-U-N-S 20-106-8967   (BR)
MCDONALD'S RESTAURANTS OF CANADA LIMITED
MCDONALDS RESTAURANT 8616
(*Suby of* McDonald's Corporation)
17635 64 Ave, Surrey, BC, V3S 1Z2
(604) 575-1670
Emp Here 70
SIC 5812 Eating places

D-U-N-S 25-310-9441   (BR)
MCDONALD'S RESTAURANTS OF CANADA LIMITED
MCDONALD'S
(*Suby of* McDonald's Corporation)
15574 Fraser Hwy, Surrey, BC, V3S 2V9
(604) 507-7900
Emp Here 130
SIC 5812 Eating places

D-U-N-S 24-511-7601   (BR)
MEMORIAL GARDENS CANADA LIMITED
VALLEY VIEW MEMORIAL GARDENS
14644 72 Ave, Surrey, BC, V3S 2E7
(604) 596-7196
Emp Here 30
SIC 6553 Cemetery subdividers and developers

D-U-N-S 25-696-7514   (SL)
NUEST SERVICES LTD
SERVICEMASTER
17858 66 Ave, Surrey, BC, V3S 7X1
(604) 888-1588
Emp Here 100   *Sales* 2,918,428
SIC 7349 Building maintenance services, nec

D-U-N-S 25-912-6472   (SL)
ORANGEVILLE RACEWAY LIMITED
ELEMENTS CASINO
(*Suby of* Great Canadian Gaming Corporation)
17755 60 Ave, Surrey, BC, V3S 1V3
(604) 576-9141
Emp Here 350
SIC 7948 Racing, including track operation

D-U-N-S 20-284-9956   (BR)
ORGILL CANADA HARDLINES ULC
(*Suby of* Orgill, Inc.)
15055 54a Ave, Surrey, BC, V3S 5X7
(604) 576-6939
Emp Here 50
SIC 5039 Construction materials, nec

D-U-N-S 25-598-5566   (BR)
POSTMEDIA NETWORK INC
NOW NEWSPAPER, THE
5460 152 St Unit 102, Surrey, BC, V3S 5J9
(604) 572-0064
Emp Here 50
SIC 2711 Newspapers

D-U-N-S 24-504-1868   (HQ)
QUALITY CRAFT LTD
17750 65a Ave Unit 301, Surrey, BC, V3S 5N4
(604) 575-5550
Emp Here 35   *Emp Total* 190
Sales 6,566,463
SIC 5023 Homefurnishings
  John Brice
Pr Pr Joanne Devost
VP Fin Lynda Finnerty
  Robert Deline

D-U-N-S 25-099-3680   (SL)
QUANTITATIVE IMAGING CORP
QIMAGING
(*Suby of* Roper Technologies, Inc.)
19535 56 Ave Suite 101, Surrey, BC, V3S 6K3
(604) 530-5800
Emp Here 70   *Sales* 3,720,996
SIC 3861 Photographic equipment and sup-

plies

D-U-N-S 24-939-7498   (SL)
RAINTREE LUMBER SPECIALTIES LTD
5390 192 St, Surrey, BC, V3S 8E5
(604) 574-0444
Emp Here 100   *Sales* 9,484,891
SIC 2421 Sawmills and planing mills, general
  Vince Carnovale
  Eric Van Wagbinigin
  Edward Probyn

D-U-N-S 25-625-4806   (BR)
ROYAL BANK OF CANADA
CLOVERDALE BRANCH
(*Suby of* Royal Bank Of Canada)
17931 56 Ave, Surrey, BC, V3S 1E2
(604) 576-5550
Emp Here 22
SIC 6021 National commercial banks

D-U-N-S 20-590-9307   (BR)
SCHOOL DISTRICT NO 36 (SURREY)
GEORGE GREENAWAY ELEMENTARY SCHOOL
17285 61a Ave, Surrey, BC, V3S 1W3
(604) 576-1136
Emp Here 45
SIC 8211 Elementary and secondary schools

D-U-N-S 20-590-9448   (BR)
SCHOOL DISTRICT NO 36 (SURREY)
CLOVERDALE LEARNING CENTER
5741 176 St, Surrey, BC, V3S 4C9
(604) 574-3615
Emp Here 20
SIC 8211 Elementary and secondary schools

D-U-N-S 20-128-0083   (BR)
SCHOOL DISTRICT NO 36 (SURREY)
DON CHRISTIAN ELEMENTARY SCHOOL
6256 184 St, Surrey, BC, V3S 8E6
(604) 576-1381
Emp Here 40
SIC 8211 Elementary and secondary schools

D-U-N-S 20-292-8417   (BR)
SCHOOL DISTRICT NO 36 (SURREY)
ENVER CREEK SECONDARY SCHOOL
14505 84 Ave, Surrey, BC, V3S 8X2
(604) 543-8149
Emp Here 20
SIC 8211 Elementary and secondary schools

D-U-N-S 20-274-2255   (BR)
SCHOOL DISTRICT NO 36 (SURREY)
SCOTT, T.E. ELEMENTARY SCHOOL
7079 148 St, Surrey, BC, V3S 3E5
(604) 596-0357
Emp Here 40
SIC 8211 Elementary and secondary schools

D-U-N-S 20-966-5517   (BR)
SCHOOL DISTRICT NO 36 (SURREY)
LORD TWEEDSMUIR SECONDARY SCHOOL
6151 180 St, Surrey, BC, V3S 4L5
(604) 574-7407
Emp Here 90
SIC 8211 Elementary and secondary schools

D-U-N-S 20-713-3740   (BR)
SCHOOL DISTRICT NO 36 (SURREY)
CHIMNEY HILL ELEMENTARY SCHOOL
14755 74 Ave, Surrey, BC, V3S 8Y8
(604) 592-2913
Emp Here 60
SIC 8211 Elementary and secondary schools

D-U-N-S 20-590-9596   (BR)
SCHOOL DISTRICT NO 36 (SURREY)
COYOTE CREEK ELEMENTARY SCHOOL
8131 156 St, Surrey, BC, V3S 3R4
(604) 597-0858
Emp Here 50
SIC 8211 Elementary and secondary schools

D-U-N-S 24-345-0868   (BR)

SCHOOL DISTRICT NO 36 (SURREY)
MARTHA CURRIE ELEMENTARY SCHOOL
5811 184 St, Surrey, BC, V3S 4N2
(604) 576-8551
Emp Here 55
SIC 8211 Elementary and secondary schools

D-U-N-S 20-590-9588   (BR)
SCHOOL DISTRICT NO 36 (SURREY)
FLEETWOOD PARK SECONDARY SCHOOL
7940 156 St, Surrey, BC, V3S 3R3
(604) 597-2301
Emp Here 100
SIC 8211 Elementary and secondary schools

D-U-N-S 20-047-0628   (BR)
SCHOOL DISTRICT NO 36 (SURREY)
SURREY CENTRE ELEMENTARY SCHOOL
16670 Old Mclellan Rd, Surrey, BC, V3S 1K3
(604) 576-9191
Emp Here 35
SIC 8211 Elementary and secondary schools

D-U-N-S 20-713-3682   (BR)
SCHOOL DISTRICT NO 36 (SURREY)
SUNRISE RIDGE ELEMENTARY
18690 60 Ave, Surrey, BC, V3S 8L8
(604) 576-3000
Emp Here 50
SIC 8211 Elementary and secondary schools

D-U-N-S 20-590-9190   (BR)
SCHOOL DISTRICT NO 36 (SURREY)
FLEET WOOD ELEMENTARY
15289 88 Ave, Surrey, BC, V3S 2S8
(604) 581-9323
Emp Here 25
SIC 8211 Elementary and secondary schools

D-U-N-S 20-590-9398   (BR)
SCHOOL DISTRICT NO 36 (SURREY)
LATIMER ROAD ELEMENTARY SCHOOL
19233 60 Ave, Surrey, BC, V3S 2T5
(604) 576-9184
Emp Here 35
SIC 8211 Elementary and secondary schools

D-U-N-S 20-590-9612   (BR)
SCHOOL DISTRICT NO 36 (SURREY)
JANICE CHURCH HILL ELEMENTARY
8226 146 St, Surrey, BC, V3S 3A5
(604) 543-7187
Emp Here 30
SIC 8211 Elementary and secondary schools

D-U-N-S 20-713-3526   (BR)
SCHOOL DISTRICT NO 36 (SURREY)
SULLIVAN SCHOOL
6016 152 St, Surrey, BC, V3S 3K6
(604) 597-1977
Emp Here 20
SIC 8211 Elementary and secondary schools

D-U-N-S 20-913-6675   (BR)
SCHOOL DISTRICT NO 36 (SURREY)
A J MCLELLAN ELEMENTRY SCHOOL
16545 61 Ave, Surrey, BC, V3S 5V4
(604) 574-7296
Emp Here 50
SIC 8211 Elementary and secondary schools

D-U-N-S 20-590-9323   (BR)
SCHOOL DISTRICT NO 36 (SURREY)
CLOVERDALE TRADITIONAL SCHOOL
17857 56 Ave, Surrey, BC, V3S 1E2
(604) 576-8295
Emp Here 25
SIC 8211 Elementary and secondary schools

D-U-N-S 25-271-7004   (BR)
SOBEYS WEST INC
5710 175 St, Surrey, BC, V3S 4T7

Emp Here 100
SIC 5411 Grocery stores

D-U-N-S 20-959-7632   (SL)
UNITRAN MANUFACTURERS LTD

5225 192 St, Surrey, BC, V3S 8E5
(604) 574-3465
Emp Here 24   *Sales* 2,772,507
SIC 3537 Industrial trucks and tractors

D-U-N-S 24-445-5242   (HQ)
WESTOWER COMMUNICATIONS LTD
17886 55 Ave, Surrey, BC, V3S 6C8
(604) 576-4755
Emp Here 29   *Emp Total* 15,400
Sales 63,038,045
SIC 1623 Water, sewer, and utility lines
Pr Peter Jeffrey
VP Calvin Payne
Dir S Roy Jeffrey

D-U-N-S 25-058-6641   (BR)
YOUNG MEN'S CHRISTIAN ASSOCIATION OF GREATER VANCOUVER
SURREY FAMILY YMCA
14988 57 Ave, Surrey, BC, V3S 7S6
(604) 575-9622
Emp Here 40
SIC 8641 Civic and social associations

D-U-N-S 24-799-0203   (SL)
ZINETTI FOOD PRODUCTS LTD
17760 66 Ave, Surrey, BC, V3S 7X1
(604) 574-2028
Emp Here 60   *Sales* 4,377,642
SIC 2038 Frozen specialties, nec

Surrey, BC V3T
Greater Vancouver County

D-U-N-S 24-349-5749   (SL)
577830 B.C. LTD
13237 King George Blvd, Surrey, BC, V3T 2T3
(604) 585-9955
Emp Here 20   *Sales* 5,371,275
SIC 5033 Roofing, siding, and insulation
Pr Ken Lillejord

D-U-N-S 24-777-6958   (HQ)
APEX COMMUNICATIONS INC
APEX WIRELESS
(Suby of Apex Communications Inc)
13734 104 Ave Suite 201, Surrey, BC, V3T 1W5
(604) 583-3300
Emp Here 20   *Emp Total* 80
Sales 10,208,640
SIC 5999 Miscellaneous retail stores, nec
Pr Pr Andrew Westlund

D-U-N-S 20-571-9094   (BR)
BANK OF MONTREAL
BMO
10155 King George Blvd, Surrey, BC, V3T 5H9
(604) 668-1180
Emp Here 20
SIC 6021 National commercial banks

D-U-N-S 24-363-3828   (BR)
BEST BUY CANADA LTD
(Suby of Best Buy Co., Inc.)
10145 King George Blvd Unit 3200, Surrey, BC, V3T 5H9
(604) 588-5666
Emp Here 50
SIC 5731 Radio, television, and electronic stores

D-U-N-S 25-021-7916   (BR)
BEST BUY CANADA LTD
FUTURE SHOP
(Suby of Best Buy Co., Inc.)
10232c Whalley Blvd Suite 10232, Surrey, BC, V3T 4H2
Emp Here 70
SIC 5734 Computer and software stores

D-U-N-S 24-363-3810   (BR)
BEST BUY CANADA LTD

BEST BUY
(Suby of Best Buy Co., Inc.)
10025 King George Blvd Unit 2153, Surrey, BC, V3T 5H9
(604) 580-7788
Emp Here 50
SIC 5731 Radio, television, and electronic stores

D-U-N-S 24-163-8969   (BR)
BLACKWOOD PARTNERS CORPORATION
CENTRAL CITY SHOPPING CENTRE
10153 King George Blvd Suite 2153, Surrey, BC, V3T 2W1
(604) 587-7778
Emp Here 40
SIC 6512 Nonresidential building operators

D-U-N-S 25-231-7599   (BR)
BRICK WAREHOUSE LP, THE
BRICK, THE
10153 King George Blvd Suite 2151, Surrey, BC, V3T 2W3
(604) 588-0808
Emp Here 25
SIC 5712 Furniture stores

D-U-N-S 25-172-9968   (BR)
BUY-LOW FOODS LTD
10636 King George Blvd, Surrey, BC, V3T 2X3

Emp Here 25
SIC 5411 Grocery stores

D-U-N-S 20-358-9361   (SL)
CDI EDUCATION (ALBERTA) LIMITED PARTNERSHIP
13401 108 Ave Suite 360, Surrey, BC, V3T 5T3
(604) 915-7288
Emp Here 300   *Sales* 20,064,193
SIC 8211 Elementary and secondary schools
 David Kwong

D-U-N-S 20-572-5190   (BR)
CANADA POST CORPORATION
10688 King George Blvd, Surrey, BC, V3T 2X3
(604) 589-3445
Emp Here 20
SIC 4311 U.s. postal service

D-U-N-S 25-663-0765   (BR)
CARA OPERATIONS LIMITED
CHALET ROTISSERIE & GRILL
(Suby of Cara Holdings Limited)
9666 King George Hwy, Surrey, BC, V3T 2V4

Emp Here 45
SIC 5812 Eating places

D-U-N-S 20-279-6900   (BR)
CHARTWELL MASTER CARE LP
CHARTWELL IMPERIAL PLACE RETIREMENT RESIDENCE
13853 102 Ave, Surrey, BC, V3T 5P6
(604) 581-1555
Emp Here 40
SIC 8322 Individual and family services

D-U-N-S 25-949-5810   (BR)
COMMUNITY LIVING SOCIETY
SURREY ACCESS CENTER
13811 103 Ave, Surrey, BC, V3T 5B5
(604) 589-7393
Emp Here 20
SIC 8322 Individual and family services

D-U-N-S 20-797-9410   (HQ)
COMMUNITY SAVINGS CREDIT UNION
(Suby of Community Savings Credit Union)
13450 102 Ave Suite 1600, Surrey, BC, V3T 5X3
(604) 654-2000
Emp Here 25   *Emp Total* 75
Sales 14,569,600
SIC 6062 State credit unions
Pr Doug Eveneshen
Opers Mgr Ken Hodge

Colleen Jordan
Ken Isomura
David Tones
VP Fin Robin Medeko
VP Eric Doomberg

D-U-N-S 20-153-2871   (HQ)
FRASER HEALTH AUTHORITY
13450 102 Ave Suite 400, Surrey, BC, V3T 0H1
(604) 587-4600
Emp Here 12,000   *Emp Total* 60,000
Sales 2,365,677,737
SIC 8062 General medical and surgical hospitals
Pr Nigel Murray
VP Andrew Webb
 Brian Woods
VP Marc Pelletier

D-U-N-S 24-121-0140   (BR)
FRASER HEALTH AUTHORITY
GATEWAY HOME HOUSE
13401 108 Ave Suite 1500, Surrey, BC, V3T 5T3
(604) 953-4950
Emp Here 100
SIC 8059 Nursing and personal care, nec

D-U-N-S 24-327-6115   (BR)
FRASER HEALTH AUTHORITY
NORTH SURREY PUBLIC HEALTH
10362 King George Blvd Suite 220, Surrey, BC, V3T 2W5
(604) 587-7900
Emp Here 40
SIC 8093 Specialty outpatient clinics, nec

D-U-N-S 20-705-8111   (BR)
GREAT-WEST LIFE ASSURANCE COMPANY, THE
13401 108 Ave Suite 1260, Surrey, BC, V3T 5T3

Emp Here 21
SIC 6311 Life insurance

D-U-N-S 24-151-8174   (HQ)
H. & C. MANAGEMENT CONSULTANTS LTD
FITNESS WORLD
(Suby of H. & C. Management Consultants Ltd)
13777 103 Ave, Surrey, BC, V3T 5B5
(604) 581-4447
Emp Here 32   *Emp Total* 600
Sales 27,431,040
SIC 7991 Physical fitness facilities
Pr Pr Henry Polessky

D-U-N-S 25-128-1879   (BR)
H. & C. MANAGEMENT CONSULTANTS LTD
FITNESS WORLD GYM
(Suby of H. & C. Management Consultants Ltd)
13821 103 Ave, Surrey, BC, V3T 5B5
(604) 588-1517
Emp Here 20
SIC 7991 Physical fitness facilities

D-U-N-S 20-982-1672   (BR)
HSBC BANK CANADA
HSBC
10012 King George Blvd, Surrey, BC, V3T 2W4
(604) 581-5281
Emp Here 42
SIC 8742 Management consulting services

D-U-N-S 24-681-4073   (BR)
HSBC BANK CANADA
10388 City Pky, Surrey, BC, V3T 4Y8
(604) 584-1371
Emp Here 22
SIC 6021 National commercial banks

D-U-N-S 24-619-4315   (BR)
LA CAPITALE FINANCIAL SECURITY INSURANCE COMPANY

13889 104 Ave Suite 300, Surrey, BC, V3T 1W8
(604) 589-1381
Emp Here 38
SIC 6321 Accident and health insurance

D-U-N-S 24-311-2620   (BR)
LONDON DRUGS LIMITED
LONDON DRUGS PHARMACY
10348 King George Blvd, Surrey, BC, V3T 2W5
(604) 448-4808
Emp Here 20
SIC 5912 Drug stores and proprietary stores

D-U-N-S 25-718-8243   (BR)
LONDON LIFE INSURANCE COMPANY
FREEDOM 55 FINANCIAL, DIV OF
13401 108 Ave Suite 400, Surrey, BC, V3T 5T3
(604) 585-2424
Emp Here 40
SIC 6311 Life insurance

D-U-N-S 24-856-4502   (BR)
LORDCO PARTS LTD
LORDCO AUTO PARTS
10352 University Dr, Surrey, BC, V3T 4B8
(604) 581-1177
Emp Here 34
SIC 5013 Motor vehicle supplies and new parts

D-U-N-S 25-318-1879   (BR)
MCDONALD'S RESTAURANTS OF CANADA LIMITED
MCDONALD'S #8003
(Suby of McDonald's Corporation)
10240 King George Blvd, Surrey, BC, V3T 2W5
(604) 587-7015
Emp Here 65
SIC 5812 Eating places

D-U-N-S 20-563-4137   (BR)
MCELHANNEY CONSULTING SERVICES LTD
13450 102 Ave Suite 2300, Surrey, BC, V3T 5X3
(604) 596-0391
Emp Here 100
SIC 8748 Business consulting, nec

D-U-N-S 20-806-3578   (SL)
OAKWAY HOLDINGS LTD
COMPASS POINT INN
9850 King George Blvd, Surrey, BC, V3T 4Y3

Emp Here 65   *Sales* 3,378,379
SIC 7011 Hotels and motels

D-U-N-S 25-293-8931   (BR)
PRICEWATERHOUSECOOPERS LLP
13450 102 Ave Suite 1400, Surrey, BC, V3T 5X3
(604) 806-7000
Emp Here 30
SIC 8721 Accounting, auditing, and bookkeeping

D-U-N-S 24-974-8534   (BR)
PROSPERA CREDIT UNION
13747 104 Ave, Surrey, BC, V3T 1W6
(604) 588-0111
Emp Here 28
SIC 6062 State credit unions

D-U-N-S 24-837-4170   (BR)
PWC MANAGEMENT SERVICES LP
13450 102 Ave Suite 1400, Surrey, BC, V3T 5X3
(604) 806-7000
Emp Here 50
SIC 8741 Management services

D-U-N-S 25-950-3696   (BR)
RFGOP RESTAURANT HOLDINGS LTD
BURGER KING
(Suby of RFGOP Restaurant Holdings Ltd)

10344 King George Blvd, Surrey, BC, V3T
2W5
(604) 584-3371
Emp Here 33
SIC 5812 Eating places

D-U-N-S 24-214-6186   (BR)
RESIDENCES ALLEGRO, S.E.C., LES
IMPERIAL PLACE
(*Suby of* Residences Allegro, S.E.C., Les)
13853 102 Ave Suite 213, Surrey, BC, V3T
5P6
(604) 581-1555
Emp Here 38
SIC 6513 Apartment building operators

D-U-N-S 20-590-9075   (BR)
SCHOOL DISTRICT NO 36 (SURREY)
FORSYTH ROAD ELEM SCHOOL
10730 13S St, Surrey, BC, V3T 4L9
(604) 588-8394
Emp Here 30
SIC 8211 Elementary and secondary schools

D-U-N-S 20-713-3450   (BR)
SCHOOL DISTRICT NO 36 (SURREY)
LENA SHAW ELEMENTARY SCHOOL
14250 100a Ave, Surrey, BC, V3T 1K8
(604) 581-1363
Emp Here 60
SIC 8211 Elementary and secondary schools

D-U-N-S 20-138-2186   (BR)
SCHOOL DISTRICT NO 36 (SURREY)
*MARY JANE SHANNON ELEMENTARY
SCHOOL*
10682 144 St, Surrey, BC, V3T 4W1
(604) 588-5991
Emp Here 50
SIC 8211 Elementary and secondary schools

D-U-N-S 20-007-1798   (BR)
SCHOOL DISTRICT NO 36 (SURREY)
OLD YALE ROAD ELEMENTARY SCHOOL
10135 132 St, Surrey, BC, V3T 3T6
(604) 588-5468
Emp Here 40
SIC 8211 Elementary and secondary schools

D-U-N-S 24-974-8542   (BR)
SCHOOL DISTRICT NO 36 (SURREY)
A H P MATTHEW ELEMENTARY SCHOOL
13367 97 Ave, Surrey, BC, V3T 1A4
(604) 588-3415
Emp Here 50
SIC 8211 Elementary and secondary schools

D-U-N-S 24-134-4808   (BR)
SCHOOL DISTRICT NO 36 (SURREY)
KWANTLEN PARK
10441 132 St, Surrey, BC, V3T 3V3
(604) 588-6934
Emp Here 100
SIC 8211 Elementary and secondary schools

D-U-N-S 20-590-9018   (BR)
SCHOOL DISTRICT NO 36 (SURREY)
KB WOODWARD ELEMENTARY
13130 106 Ave, Surrey, BC, V3T 2C3
(604) 588-5918
Emp Here 50
SIC 8211 Elementary and secondary schools

D-U-N-S 24-313-6210   (BR)
SIMON FRASER UNIVERSITY
13450 102 Ave Suite 250, Surrey, BC, V3T
0A3
(778) 782-3111
Emp Here 30
SIC 8221 Colleges and universities

D-U-N-S 24-661-5855   (BR)
STANTEC CONSULTING LTD
13401 108 Ave 10th Floor, Surrey, BC, V3T
5T3
(604) 587-8400
Emp Here 52
SIC 8711 Engineering services

D-U-N-S 25-370-1486   (BR)
STAPLES CANADA INC
STAPLES BUSINESS DEPOT
(*Suby of* Staples, Inc.)
10136 King George Blvd, Surrey, BC, V3T
2W4
(604) 582-6789
Emp Here 40
SIC 5943 Stationery stores

D-U-N-S 20-559-4950   (SL)
SUN FITNESS PRODUCTIONS INC
FITNESS WORLD
13777 103 Ave, Surrey, BC, V3T 5B5
(604) 581-4447
Emp Here 50   *Sales* 1,678,096
SIC 7991 Physical fitness facilities

D-U-N-S 25-003-2885   (SL)
SURREY COMMUNITY SERVICE SOCIETY
9815 140 St, Surrey, BC, V3T 4M4
(604) 951-7342
Emp Here 75   *Sales* 13,153,440
SIC 8399 Social services, nec
  Ivan Menendez
Pr Pr Joan Kloss
VP VP Doug Neale
  Peter Whaites
  Kevin Kilgour
  Clela Beaton
  Lowell Leifso
  John Madsen
  Michael Nowak
  Langton Simbabure

D-U-N-S 24-685-8828   (SL)
UNIKE WEST CONSTRUCTION INC
UNIKE WEST GROUP
10237 133 St Suite 111, Surrey, BC, V3T 0C6

Emp Here 33   *Sales* 8,521,800
SIC 1542 Nonresidential construction, nec
Pr Geovani Rizo

D-U-N-S 24-345-8432   (BR)
**VANCOUVER CAREER COLLEGE (BURN-
ABY) INC**
SURREY CAMPUS
(*Suby of* Chung Family Holdings Inc)
13450 102 Ave Suite 295, Surrey, BC, V3T
5X3
(604) 580-2133
Emp Here 20
SIC 8221 Colleges and universities

D-U-N-S 20-153-2095   (BR)
WESTMINSTER SAVINGS CREDIT UNION
(*Suby of* Westminster Savings Credit Union)
13450 102 Ave Suite 1900, Surrey, BC, V3T
5Y1
(604) 517-0100
Emp Here 55
SIC 6062 State credit unions

D-U-N-S 25-725-7105   (BR)
WHITE SPOT LIMITED
WHITE SPOT RESTAURANT
13580 102 Ave, Surrey, BC, V3T 5C5
(604) 581-2511
Emp Here 55
SIC 5812 Eating places

D-U-N-S 20-331-8998   (BR)
YM INC. (SALES)
URBAN PLANET
10153 King George Unit 204/206, Surrey, BC,
V3T 2W1
(604) 580-1348
Emp Here 20
SIC 5621 Women's clothing stores

Surrey, BC V3V
Greater Vancouver County

D-U-N-S 25-174-1146   (BR)

ASPEN PLANERS LTD
MILL AND TIMBER
12770 116 Ave, Surrey, BC, V3V 7H9
(604) 580-2240
Emp Here 30
SIC 5031 Lumber, plywood, and millwork

D-U-N-S 20-584-1703   (SL)
BEL-PAR INDUSTRIES LTD
12160 103a Ave, Surrey, BC, V3V 3G8
(604) 581-5291
Emp Here 60   *Sales* 4,012,839
SIC 2541 Wood partitions and fixtures

D-U-N-S 24-389-3372   (BR)
BEREZAN MANAGEMENT (B.C.) LTD
WHEELHOUSE PUB
(*Suby of* Berezan Management (B.C.) Ltd)
12867 96 Ave, Surrey, BC, V3V 6V9

Emp Here 40
SIC 5813 Drinking places

D-U-N-S 25-653-5576   (BR)
**BRITISH COLUMBIA CANCER AGENCY
BRANCH**
FRASER VALLEY CANCER CENTRE
13750 96 Ave, Surrey, BC, V3V 1Z2
(604) 930-2098
Emp Here 240
SIC 8069 Specialty hospitals, except psychi-
atric

D-U-N-S 24-104-1628   (BR)
**BRITISH COLUMBIA CANCER FOUNDA-
TION**
13750 96 Ave, Surrey, BC, V3V 1Z2
(604) 930-2098
Emp Here 250
SIC 8621 Professional organizations

D-U-N-S 20-285-0251   (BR)
CANWEL BUILDING MATERIALS LTD
CANWEL BUILDING MATERIALS LTD
9815 Robson Rd, Surrey, BC, V3V 2R9
(604) 585-2511
Emp Here 40
SIC 5039 Construction materials, nec

D-U-N-S 24-335-5505   (BR)
CATALYST PAPER CORPORATION
SURREY DISTRIBUTION CENTRE
10555 Timberland Rd, Surrey, BC, V3V 3T3
(604) 953-0373
Emp Here 88
SIC 2621 Paper mills

D-U-N-S 25-932-6643   (BR)
FIRSTCANADA ULC
FIRST STUDENT
12079 103a Ave, Surrey, BC, V3V 3G7
(604) 583-7060
Emp Here 127
SIC 4151 School buses

D-U-N-S 20-586-5678   (SL)
FRASER, D.H. LTD
PHARMASAVE #167
9558 120 St Suite 167, Surrey, BC, V3V 4C1

Emp Here 26   *Sales* 5,072,500
SIC 5912 Drug stores and proprietary stores
Pr Pr Douglas Fraser

D-U-N-S 25-539-4025   (BR)
GEORGIA-PACIFIC CANADA LP
(*Suby of* Koch Industries, Inc.)
12509 116 Ave, Surrey, BC, V3V 3S6

Emp Here 90
SIC 3275 Gypsum products

D-U-N-S 25-234-3876   (BR)
HOME DEPOT OF CANADA INC
HOME DEPOT
(*Suby of* The Home Depot Inc)
12701 110 Ave, Surrey, BC, V3V 3J7

(604) 580-2159
Emp Here 170
SIC 5251 Hardware stores

D-U-N-S 25-964-0357   (BR)
**MCDONALD'S   RESTAURANTS   OF
CANADA LIMITED**
MCDONALD'S #8550
(*Suby of* McDonald's Corporation)
11011 Scott Rd, Surrey, BC, V3V 8B9
(604) 580-4040
Emp Here 50
SIC 5812 Eating places

D-U-N-S 25-318-1556   (BR)
**MCDONALD'S   RESTAURANTS   OF
CANADA LIMITED**
MCDONALD'S #8249
(*Suby of* McDonald's Corporation)
12930 96 Ave, Surrey, BC, V3V 6A8
(604) 587-3390
Emp Here 100
SIC 5812 Eating places

D-U-N-S 25-215-9793   (HQ)
PACIFIC COAST EXPRESS LIMITED
(*Suby of* Kluskus Holdings Ltd)
10299 Grace Rd, Surrey, BC, V3V 3V7
(604) 582-3230
Emp Here 50   *Emp Total* 603
Sales 11,381,869
SIC 4213 Trucking, except local
Pr Pr John Assman

D-U-N-S 24-802-8438   (BR)
PEPSICO CANADA ULC
FRITO LAY CANADA
(*Suby of* Pepsico, Inc.)
11811 103a Ave, Surrey, BC, V3V 0B5
(604) 587-8300
Emp Here 300
SIC 5145 Confectionery

D-U-N-S 25-760-3688   (BR)
RALPH'S AUTO SUPPLY (B.C.) LTD
A-SCOTT DISCOUNT USED AUTO PARTS
10731 120 St, Surrey, BC, V3V 4G5

Emp Here 20
SIC 5531 Auto and home supply stores

D-U-N-S 20-073-5202   (BR)
REMTEC INC
WWW.MESEARCHER.COM/DEVONA_PUTLAND
(*Suby of* 128707 Canada Inc)
12343 104 Ave Suite A, Surrey, BC, V3V 3H2
(604) 930-3550
Emp Here 30
SIC 3715 Truck trailers

D-U-N-S 25-760-3746   (BR)
ROYAL BANK OF CANADA
RBC
(*Suby of* Royal Bank Of Canada)
9490 120 St, Surrey, BC, V3V 4B9
(604) 665-8992
Emp Here 25
SIC 6021 National commercial banks

D-U-N-S 20-590-9646   (BR)
SCHOOL DISTRICT NO 36 (SURREY)
GREEN TIMBERS ELEMENTARY
8824 144 St, Surrey, BC, V3V 5Z7
(604) 588-5961
Emp Here 50
SIC 8211 Elementary and secondary schools

D-U-N-S 20-590-8994   (BR)
SCHOOL DISTRICT NO 36 (SURREY)
BETTY HUFF ELEMENTARY SCHOOL
13055 Huntley Ave, Surrey, BC, V3V 1V1
(604) 585-3104
Emp Here 50
SIC 8211 Elementary and secondary schools

D-U-N-S 20-590-7608   (BR)
SCHOOL DISTRICT NO 36 (SURREY)
PRINCE CHARLES ELEMENTARY SCHOOL

12405 100 Ave, Surrey, BC, V3V 2X2
(604) 588-5481
Emp Here 30
SIC 8211 Elementary and secondary schools

D-U-N-S 20-713-3344   (BR)
SCHOOL DISTRICT NO 36 (SURREY)
CEDAR HILLS ELEMENTARY SCHOOL
12370 98 Ave, Surrey, BC, V3V 2K3
(604) 581-0407
Emp Here 35
SIC 8211 Elementary and secondary schools

D-U-N-S 20-038-3086   (BR)
SCHOOL DISTRICT NO 36 (SURREY)
KIRKBRIDE ELEMENTARY SCHOOL
12150 92 Ave, Surrey, BC, V3V 1G2
(604) 588-5711
Emp Here 70
SIC 8211 Elementary and secondary schools

D-U-N-S 20-043-9193   (BR)
SCHOOL DISTRICT NO 36 (SURREY)
IVERGARRY ADULT LEARNING CENTRE
9260 140 St Suite 400, Surrey, BC, V3V 5Z4
(604) 583-9554
Emp Here 40
SIC 7389 Business services, nec

D-U-N-S 25-068-3406   (BR)
SCHOOL DISTRICT NO 36 (SURREY)
QUEEN ELIZABETH ADULT EDUCATION
9457 King George Blvd, Surrey, BC, V3V 5W4
(604) 588-1258
Emp Here 50
SIC 8211 Elementary and secondary schools

D-U-N-S 20-713-3674   (BR)
SCHOOL DISTRICT NO 36 (SURREY)
CINDRICH ELEMENTARY SCHOOL
13455 90 Ave, Surrey, BC, V3V 8A2
(604) 590-3211
Emp Here 50
SIC 8211 Elementary and secondary schools

D-U-N-S 20-713-3708   (BR)
SCHOOL DISTRICT NO 36 (SURREY)
CREEKSIDE ELEMENTARY SCHOOL
13838 91 Ave, Surrey, BC, V3V 7K4
(604) 543-9132
Emp Here 65
SIC 8211 Elementary and secondary schools

D-U-N-S 20-590-9695   (BR)
SCHOOL DISTRICT NO 36 (SURREY)
SENATOR REID ELEMENTERY SCHOOL
9341 126 St, Surrey, BC, V3V 5C4
(604) 584-7441
Emp Here 50
SIC 8211 Elementary and secondary schools

D-U-N-S 20-713-3377   (BR)
SCHOOL DISTRICT NO 36 (SURREY)
DAVID BRANKEN ELEMENTARY SCHOOL
9160 128 St, Surrey, BC, V3V 5M8
(604) 585-9547
Emp Here 50
SIC 8211 Elementary and secondary schools

D-U-N-S 20-590-9729   (BR)
SCHOOL DISTRICT NO 36 (SURREY)
L A MATHESON JR SECONDARY SCHOOL
9484 122 St, Surrey, BC, V3V 4M1
(604) 588-3418
Emp Here 25
SIC 8211 Elementary and secondary schools

D-U-N-S 20-713-3500   (BR)
SCHOOL DISTRICT NO 36 (SURREY)
ROYAL HEIGHTS ELEMENTARY SCHOOL
11665 97 Ave, Surrey, BC, V3V 2B9
(604) 581-7622
Emp Here 35
SIC 8211 Elementary and secondary schools

D-U-N-S 20-590-9703   (BR)
SCHOOL DISTRICT NO 36 (SURREY)
SIMON CUNNINGHAM ELEMENTARY

9380 140 St, Surrey, BC, V3V 5Z4
(604) 588-4435
Emp Here 60
SIC 8211 Elementary and secondary schools

D-U-N-S 20-706-3350   (BR)
SERVICES FINANCIERS NCO, INC
AGENCE DE RECOUVREMENT
(*Suby of* Egs Shell Company, Inc.)
11125 124 St, Surrey, BC, V3V 4V2
(604) 953-2801
Emp Here 1,000
SIC 7322 Adjustment and collection services

D-U-N-S 24-394-7566   (SL)
TRIPLE CROWN TRUCKING LTD
12742 King George Blvd, Surrey, BC, V3V 3K5

Emp Here 50   *Sales* 6,874,880
SIC 4213 Trucking, except local
Pr Jack Gill

D-U-N-S 24-805-6905   (SL)
TWO SMALL MEN WITH BIG HEARTS MOVING (BC) CORPORATION
11180 Scott Rd, Surrey, BC, V3V 8B8
(604) 581-1616
Emp Here 250   *Sales* 19,782,750
SIC 4214 Local trucking with storage
Pr Pr Glen Buckler

D-U-N-S 24-882-1472   (BR)
VANCOUVER CAREER COLLEGE (BURNABY) INC
CDI COLLEGE
(*Suby of* Chung Family Holdings Inc)
11125 124 St Suite 100, Surrey, BC, V3V 4V2
(604) 585-8585
Emp Here 30
SIC 8211 Elementary and secondary schools

D-U-N-S 20-589-5720   (BR)
VANCOUVER CITY SAVINGS CREDIT UNION
VANCITY CREDIT UNION
12820 96 Ave, Surrey, BC, V3V 6A8
(604) 877-7440
Emp Here 20
SIC 6062 State credit unions

D-U-N-S 20-979-0257   (BR)
VITRAN EXPRESS CANADA INC
10077 Grace Rd, Surrey, BC, V3V 3V7
(604) 582-4500
Emp Here 300
SIC 4213 Trucking, except local

D-U-N-S 25-746-2457   (BR)
WENDY'S RESTAURANTS OF CANADA INC
WENDY'S
(*Suby of* The Wendy's Company)
9412 120 St, Surrey, BC, V3V 4B9
(604) 581-7744
Emp Here 30
SIC 5812 Eating places

D-U-N-S 25-388-6709   (SL)
WESTERN CLEANWOOD PRESERVERS LP
9815 Robson Rd, Surrey, BC, V3V 2R9
(604) 585-2511
Emp Here 35   *Sales* 6,087,000
SIC 2491 Wood preserving
Pr Pr Amar Doman

Surrey, BC V3W
Greater Vancouver County

D-U-N-S 20-013-4158   (HQ)
428675 BC LTD
NEWTON SQUARE BINGO COUNTRY
(*Suby of* 428675 BC Ltd)
7093 King George Blvd Suite 401a, Surrey, BC, V3W 5A2

(604) 590-3230
Emp Here 50   *Emp Total* 80
Sales 4,377,642
SIC 7999 Amusement and recreation, nec

D-U-N-S 25-287-9168   (BR)
A & W FOOD SERVICES OF CANADA INC
A & W
12133 72 Ave, Surrey, BC, V3W 2M1
(604) 596-2224
Emp Here 30
SIC 5812 Eating places

D-U-N-S 25-287-9242   (BR)
A & W FOOD SERVICES OF CANADA INC
A & W
7330 King George Blvd, Surrey, BC, V3W 5A5
(604) 590-2226
Emp Here 20
SIC 5812 Eating places

D-U-N-S 20-428-5712   (HQ)
APLIN & MARTIN CONSULTANTS LTD
MURRAY & ASSOCIATES
12448 82 Ave Suite 201, Surrey, BC, V3W 3E9
(604) 597-9189
Emp Here 100   *Emp Total* 65
Sales 10,871,144
SIC 8711 Engineering services
Pr Pr Edward Fujii
Dir William Lee
Dir Raymond Janzen
Andrew Baker

D-U-N-S 25-978-4858   (SL)
B.C. FASTENERS & TOOLS (2000) LTD
12824 Anvil Way Unit 101, Surrey, BC, V3W 8E7
(604) 599-5455
Emp Here 25   *Sales* 6,695,700
SIC 5085 Industrial supplies
Pr Pr Thomas Allison
Gerry Miller

D-U-N-S 25-736-0420   (BR)
BANK OF NOVA SCOTIA, THE
SCOTIABANK
7378 120 St, Surrey, BC, V3W 3M9
(604) 501-3325
Emp Here 24
SIC 6021 National commercial banks

D-U-N-S 25-993-4974   (BR)
BANK OF NOVA SCOTIA, THE
SCOTIABANK
13790 72 Ave Suite 101, Surrey, BC, V3W 2P4
(604) 501-5353
Emp Here 25
SIC 6021 National commercial banks

D-U-N-S 20-797-1685   (BR)
BANK OF MONTREAL
BMO
7140 120 St, Surrey, BC, V3W 3M8
(604) 668-1560
Emp Here 20
SIC 6021 National commercial banks

D-U-N-S 24-121-2153   (BR)
BELFOR (CANADA) INC
BELFOR PROPERTY & RESTORATION
7677d 132 St, Surrey, BC, V3W 4M8
(604) 599-9980
Emp Here 200
SIC 1799 Special trade contractors, nec

D-U-N-S 25-185-5995   (BR)
BEST BUY CANADA LTD
FUTURE SHOP #600
(*Suby of* Best Buy Co., Inc.)
7538 120 St, Surrey, BC, V3W 3N1
(778) 578-5746
Emp Here 50
SIC 5731 Radio, television, and electronic stores

D-U-N-S 20-580-1090   (BR)
BRITISH COLUMBIA HYDRO AND POWER

AUTHORITY
BC AGRO
12345 88 Ave, Surrey, BC, V3W 5Z9
(604) 590-7565
Emp Here 20
SIC 4911 Electric services

D-U-N-S 24-341-0631   (BR)
BRITISH COLUMBIA HYDRO AND POWER AUTHORITY
BC HYDRO
12430 88 Ave, Surrey, BC, V3W 3Y1
(604) 590-7662
Emp Here 25
SIC 4911 Electric services

D-U-N-S 20-315-9181   (BR)
BROCK WHITE CANADA COMPANY, LLC
STEELS
7678 132 St, Surrey, BC, V3W 4M9
(604) 576-9131
Emp Here 60
SIC 5039 Construction materials, nec

D-U-N-S 20-575-8597   (BR)
CANADIAN WESTERN BANK
7548 120 St Suite 1, Surrey, BC, V3W 3N1
(604) 591-1898
Emp Here 22
SIC 6021 National commercial banks

D-U-N-S 24-418-5018   (BR)
CINEPLEX ODEON CORPORATION
CINEPLEX CINEMAS STRAWBERRY HILL
12161 72 Ave, Surrey, BC, V3W 2M1
(604) 501-9420
Emp Here 40
SIC 7832 Motion picture theaters, except drive-in

D-U-N-S 25-855-2116   (BR)
CITY OF SURREY, THE
SURREY ART CENTRE
13750 88 Ave, Surrey, BC, V3W 3L1
(604) 501-5566
Emp Here 30
SIC 8412 Museums and art galleries

D-U-N-S 25-287-5331   (BR)
COSTCO WHOLESALE CANADA LTD
COSTCO
(*Suby of* Costco Wholesale Corporation)
7423 King George Blvd Suite 55, Surrey, BC, V3W 5A8
(604) 635-3340
Emp Here 265
SIC 5099 Durable goods, nec

D-U-N-S 24-150-4190   (SL)
CUSTOM PROTECT EAR INC
7789 134 St Unit 681, Surrey, BC, V3W 9E9
(604) 599-1311
Emp Here 50   *Sales* 4,864,998
SIC 3842 Surgical appliances and supplies

D-U-N-S 24-877-4031   (SL)
CYPRESS SECURITY (2013) INC
7028 120 St Suite 203, Surrey, BC, V3W 3M8
(778) 564-4088
Emp Here 100   *Sales* 3,724,879
SIC 7381 Detective and armored car services

D-U-N-S 25-722-9898   (SL)
DELTA SUNSHINE TAXI (1972) LTD
12837 76 Ave Unit 203, Surrey, BC, V3W 2V3
(604) 594-5444
Emp Here 150   *Sales* 4,523,563
SIC 4121 Taxicabs

D-U-N-S 20-880-6377   (BR)
DOLPHIN DELIVERY LTD
DOLPHIN TRANSPORT
(*Suby of* Dolphin Delivery (1985) Ltd)
12091 88 Ave, Surrey, BC, V3W 3J5
(604) 502-7256
Emp Here 20
SIC 4212 Local trucking, without storage

D-U-N-S 25-399-1004   (BR)
E. B. HORSMAN & SON
13055 80 Ave Suite 1, Surrey, BC, V3W 3B1
(604) 596-7111
Emp Here 20
SIC 5063 Electrical apparatus and equipment

D-U-N-S 24-578-7668   (SL)
EAGLEPICHER ENERGY PRODUCTS ULC
EAGLEPICHER MEDICAL POWER
13136 82a Ave, Surrey, BC, V3W 9Y6
(604) 543-4350
Emp Here 125   *Sales* 31,098,411
SIC 2819 Industrial inorganic chemicals, nec
Manager James Hong

D-U-N-S 25-825-4267   (BR)
EARL'S RESTAURANTS LTD
EARL'S STRAWBERRY HILL
(*Suby of* Earl's Restaurants Ltd)
7236 120 St, Surrey, BC, V3W 3M9

Emp Here 85
SIC 5812 Eating places

D-U-N-S 25-625-4111   (BR)
EDENVALE RESTORATION SPECIALISTS LTD
EDENVALE RESTORATION SPECIALISTS
13260 78 Ave Unit 24, Surrey, BC, V3W 0H6
(604) 590-1440
Emp Here 100
SIC 1521 Single-family housing construction

D-U-N-S 24-340-2612   (BR)
FGL SPORTS LTD
SPORT-CHEK
12101 72 Ave Unit 120, Surrey, BC, V3W 2M1
(604) 572-7008
Emp Here 40
SIC 5941 Sporting goods and bicycle shops

D-U-N-S 20-703-8873   (BR)
GREAT PACIFIC INDUSTRIES INC
SAVE-ON-FOODS
12130 Nordel Way Suite 939, Surrey, BC, V3W 1P6
(604) 501-9354
Emp Here 140
SIC 5411 Grocery stores

D-U-N-S 25-754-0963   (SL)
GUILDFORD CAB (1993) LTD
SURREY METRO TAXI
8299 129 St Unit 101, Surrey, BC, V3W 0A6
(604) 585-8888
Emp Here 120   *Sales* 4,711,645
SIC 4121 Taxicabs

D-U-N-S 25-754-2951   (BR)
HOME DEPOT OF CANADA INC
HOME DEPOT
(*Suby of* The Home Depot Inc)
7350 120 St, Surrey, BC, V3W 3M9
(604) 590-2796
Emp Here 200
SIC 5999 Miscellaneous retail stores, nec

D-U-N-S 20-536-2325   (BR)
INDIGO BOOKS & MUSIC INC
CHAPTERS
(*Suby of* Indigo Books & Music Inc)
12101 72 Ave Suite 100, Surrey, BC, V3W 2M1
(604) 501-2877
Emp Here 20
SIC 5942 Book stores

D-U-N-S 24-467-4995   (BR)
INSURANCE CORPORATION OF BRITISH COLUMBIA
ICBC
13072 88 Ave Suite 100, Surrey, BC, V3W 3K3
(604) 507-3640
Emp Here 49
SIC 6331 Fire, marine, and casualty insurance

D-U-N-S 25-272-7375   (BR)

INSURANCE CORPORATION OF BRITISH COLUMBIA
ICBC
13665 68 Ave, Surrey, BC, V3W 0Y6
(604) 597-7600
Emp Here 130
SIC 6331 Fire, marine, and casualty insurance

D-U-N-S 20-277-8283   (BR)
INSURANCE CORPORATION OF BRITISH COLUMBIA
ICBC
7565 132 St Suite 207, Surrey, BC, V3W 1K5

Emp Here 30
SIC 6331 Fire, marine, and casualty insurance

D-U-N-S 20-981-8819   (BR)
INSURANCE CORPORATION OF BRITISH COLUMBIA
ICBC
13426 78 Ave, Surrey, BC, V3W 8J6
(604) 596-8573
Emp Here 43
SIC 6331 Fire, marine, and casualty insurance

D-U-N-S 24-787-2922   (BR)
KEG RESTAURANTS LTD
KEG STEAKHOUSE & BAR, THE
7948 120 St, Surrey, BC, V3W 3N2
(604) 591-6161
Emp Here 120
SIC 5812 Eating places

D-U-N-S 20-113-0564   (SL)
KOBELT MANUFACTURING CO. LTD
8238 129 St, Surrey, BC, V3W 0A6
(604) 572-3935
Emp Here 62   *Sales* 4,504,505
SIC 3732 Boatbuilding and repairing

D-U-N-S 20-049-2192   (BR)
LAFARGE CANADA INC
7455 132 St Suite 200, Surrey, BC, V3W 1J8
(604) 502-7660
Emp Here 40
SIC 5039 Construction materials, nec

D-U-N-S 25-270-1339   (BR)
LOBLAWS INC
REAL CANADIAN SUPERSTORE 1521
7550 King George Blvd Suite 1, Surrey, BC, V3W 2T2
(604) 599-3722
Emp Here 400
SIC 5141 Groceries, general line

D-U-N-S 25-273-1179   (BR)
LORDCO PARTS LTD
LORDCO AUTO PARTS
13537 72 Ave, Surrey, BC, V3W 2N9
(604) 543-7513
Emp Here 20
SIC 5531 Auto and home supply stores

D-U-N-S 20-102-0179   (HQ)
M.A. STEWART & SONS LTD
(*Suby of* M.A. Stewart Holdings Ltd)
12900 87 Ave, Surrey, BC, V3W 3H9
(604) 594-8431
Emp Here 37   *Emp Total* 70
Sales 16,112,269
SIC 5085 Industrial supplies
Pr Pr Dan Hardy
  John Makarchuk
  Peter Pedersen
  Roy Hardy

D-U-N-S 24-380-0047   (BR)
MOUNTAIN EQUIPMENT CO-OPERATIVE
MOUNTAIN EQUIPMENT CO-OPERATIVE
13340 76 Ave, Surrey, BC, V3W 2W1
(604) 598-0515
Emp Here 55
SIC 5941 Sporting goods and bicycle shops

D-U-N-S 20-115-1065   (SL)
MURRAY LATTA PROGRESSIVE MACHINE

INC
8717 132 St, Surrey, BC, V3W 4P1
(604) 599-9598
Emp Here 145   *Sales* 18,277,896
SIC 3569 General industrial machinery, nec
Pr Pr Dan Reader
  Al Dickens
Dir Fin Fatima Sa
Mgr Bob Barnard
Mgr Leo Birkenheuer
Mgr Jon Harbrink

D-U-N-S 24-333-2793   (BR)
NAV CANADA
7421 135 St, Surrey, BC, V3W 0M8
(604) 598-4805
Emp Here 600
SIC 4899 Communication services, nec

D-U-N-S 24-153-1375   (SL)
NORTH STAR PATROL (1996) LTD
12981 80 Ave, Surrey, BC, V3W 3B1

Emp Here 100   *Sales* 3,137,310
SIC 7381 Detective and armored car services

D-U-N-S 24-369-3926   (SL)
NORWOOD PACKAGING LTD
8519 132 St, Surrey, BC, V3W 4N8
(604) 590-0370
Emp Here 25   *Sales* 2,261,590
SIC 2844 Toilet preparations

D-U-N-S 20-064-2630   (BR)
ON SIDE RESTORATION SERVICES LTD
12950 80 Ave Suite 8, Surrey, BC, V3W 3B2
(604) 501-0828
Emp Here 24
SIC 7699 Repair services, nec

D-U-N-S 24-798-0154   (SL)
PARAGON ELECTRICAL INSTALLATIONS LTD
12960 84 Ave Suite 310, Surrey, BC, V3W 1K7
(604) 599-5100
Emp Here 50   *Sales* 4,377,642
SIC 1731 Electrical work

D-U-N-S 24-938-6277   (BR)
POLYBOTTLE GROUP LIMITED
(*Suby of* Cerberus Capital Management, L.P.)
7464 132 St, Surrey, BC, V3W 4M7
(604) 594-4999
Emp Here 40
SIC 3089 Plastics products, nec

D-U-N-S 20-337-8732   (BR)
POMERLEAU INC
8241 129 St, Surrey, BC, V3W 0A6
(604) 592-9767
Emp Here 50
SIC 1542 Nonresidential construction, nec

D-U-N-S 20-517-8614   (BR)
PRISZM LP
KFC
12121 72 Ave, Surrey, BC, V3W 2M1
(604) 543-7879
Emp Here 25
SIC 5812 Eating places

D-U-N-S 24-065-0064   (BR)
PROGRESSIVE INTERCULTURAL COMMUNITY SERVICES SOCIETY
7566 120a St Suite 230, Surrey, BC, V3W 1N3
(604) 596-4242
Emp Here 50
SIC 8631 Labor organizations

D-U-N-S 20-972-3423   (HQ)
R. DIAMOND GROUP OF COMPANIES LTD, THE
DIAMOND DELIVERY SERVICES
(*Suby of* R. Diamond Group Of Companies Ltd, The)
13350 Comber Way, Surrey, BC, V3W 5V9

(604) 591-8641
Emp Here 20   *Emp Total* 35
Sales 10,347,900
SIC 4731 Freight transportation arrangement
  Richard Diamond

D-U-N-S 25-818-3649   (SL)
REGENCY INTERMEDIATE CARE FACILITIES INC
NEWTON REGENCY CARE HOME
13855 68 Ave, Surrey, BC, V3W 2G9
(604) 597-9333
Emp Here 80   *Sales* 2,918,428
SIC 8361 Residential care

D-U-N-S 20-102-5764   (SL)
ROBAR INDUSTRIES LTD
12945 78 Ave, Surrey, BC, V3W 2X8
(604) 591-8811
Emp Here 100
SIC 3321 Gray and ductile iron foundries

D-U-N-S 25-068-2259   (BR)
SCHOOL DISTRICT NO 36 (SURREY)
BEAR CREEK ELEMENTARY SCHOOL
13780 80 Ave, Surrey, BC, V3W 7X6
(604) 594-7501
Emp Here 55
SIC 8211 Elementary and secondary schools

D-U-N-S 20-590-9117   (BR)
SCHOOL DISTRICT NO 36 (SURREY)
FRANK HURT SECONDARY SCHOOL
13940 77 Ave, Surrey, BC, V3W 5Z4
(604) 590-1311
Emp Here 25
SIC 8211 Elementary and secondary schools

D-U-N-S 20-590-9513   (BR)
SCHOOL DISTRICT NO 36 (SURREY)
HIGHLAND ELEMENTARY
6677 140 St, Surrey, BC, V3W 5J3
(604) 543-9347
Emp Here 25
SIC 8211 Elementary and secondary schools

D-U-N-S 20-301-3169   (BR)
SCHOOL DISTRICT NO 36 (SURREY)
TAMANAWIS SECONDARY SCHOOL
12600 66 Ave, Surrey, BC, V3W 2A8
(604) 597-5234
Emp Here 100
SIC 8211 Elementary and secondary schools

D-U-N-S 20-034-7545   (BR)
SCHOOL DISTRICT NO 36 (SURREY)
CURRICULUM AND INSTRUCTIONAL SERVICES CENTRE
7532 134a St, Surrey, BC, V3W 7J1

Emp Here 55
SIC 7361 Employment agencies

D-U-N-S 20-655-2130   (BR)
SCHOOL DISTRICT NO 36 (SURREY)
WESTERMAN ELEMENTARY SCHOOL
7626 122 St, Surrey, BC, V3W 1H4
(604) 572-4054
Emp Here 40
SIC 8211 Elementary and secondary schools

D-U-N-S 24-218-7339   (BR)
SCHOOL DISTRICT NO 36 (SURREY)
BUSINESS MANAGEMENT SERVICES
7565 132 St Suite 119, Surrey, BC, V3W 1K5
(604) 501-8555
Emp Here 25
SIC 1542 Nonresidential construction, nec

D-U-N-S 20-590-9620   (BR)
SCHOOL DISTRICT NO 36 (SURREY)
BROOKSIDE ELEMENTARY SCHOOL
8555 142a St, Surrey, BC, V3W 0S6
(604) 596-8561
Emp Here 25
SIC 8211 Elementary and secondary schools

D-U-N-S 20-266-9441   (BR)
SCHOOL DISTRICT NO 36 (SURREY)

COUGAR CREEK ELEMENTARY SCHOOL
12236 70a Ave, Surrey, BC, V3W 4Z8
(604) 591-9098
Emp Here 65
SIC 8211 Elementary and secondary schools

D-U-N-S 20-033-3206 (BR)
SCHOOL DISTRICT NO 36 (SURREY)
ELLIS, THOMAS G. CENTRE
6700 144 St, Surrey, BC, V3W 5R5
(604) 572-0500
Emp Here 200
SIC 4173 Bus terminal and service facilities

D-U-N-S 20-590-9489 (BR)
SCHOOL DISTRICT NO 36 (SURREY)
BEAVER CREEK ELEMENTARY SCHOOL
6505 123a St, Surrey, BC, V3W 5Y5
(604) 572-6911
Emp Here 25
SIC 8211 Elementary and secondary schools

D-U-N-S 20-590-9034 (BR)
SCHOOL DISTRICT NO 36 (SURREY)
NEWTON ELEMENTARY SCHOOL
13359 81 Ave, Surrey, BC, V3W 3C5
(604) 596-8621
Emp Here 50
SIC 8211 Elementary and secondary schools

D-U-N-S 25-288-4770 (BR)
SCHOOL DISTRICT NO 36 (SURREY)
MARTHA JANE NORRIS SCHOOL
12928 66a Ave, Surrey, BC, V3W 8Z7
(604) 594-7150
Emp Here 40
SIC 8211 Elementary and secondary schools

D-U-N-S 24-974-8609 (BR)
SCHOOL DISTRICT NO 36 (SURREY)
PRINCESS MARGARET SECONDARY
12870 72 Ave, Surrey, BC, V3W 2M9
(604) 594-5458
Emp Here 100
SIC 8211 Elementary and secondary schools

D-U-N-S 20-697-8780 (BR)
SCHOOL DISTRICT NO 36 (SURREY)
INFORMATION MANAGEMENT SERVICES
13018 80 Ave Suite 101, Surrey, BC, V3W 3B2
(604) 590-9422
Emp Here 60
SIC 8999 Services, nec

D-U-N-S 24-450-7468 (BR)
SCHOOL DISTRICT NO 36 (SURREY)
GEORGE VANIER ELEMENTARY SCHL
6985 142 St, Surrey, BC, V3W 5N1
(604) 595-8067
Emp Here 60
SIC 8211 Elementary and secondary schools

D-U-N-S 20-590-9505 (BR)
SCHOOL DISTRICT NO 36 (SURREY)
HENRY BOSE ELEMENTARY SCHOOL
6550 134 St, Surrey, BC, V3W 4S3
(604) 596-6324
Emp Here 55
SIC 8211 Elementary and secondary schools

D-U-N-S 20-590-9539 (BR)
SCHOOL DISTRICT NO 36 (SURREY)
MB SANFORD ELEMENTARY SCHOOL
7318 143 St, Surrey, BC, V3W 7T6
(604) 596-7517
Emp Here 40
SIC 8211 Elementary and secondary schools

D-U-N-S 20-590-9547 (BR)
SCHOOL DISTRICT NO 36 (SURREY)
DR F D SINCLAIR ELEMENTARY SCHOOL
7480 128 St, Surrey, BC, V3W 4E5
(604) 596-1537
Emp Here 60
SIC 8211 Elementary and secondary schools

D-U-N-S 20-590-9570 (BR)
SCHOOL DISTRICT NO 36 (SURREY)

STRAWBERRY HILL ELEMENTARY
SCHOOL
7633 124 St, Surrey, BC, V3W 8N2
(604) 596-5533
Emp Here 48
SIC 8211 Elementary and secondary schools

D-U-N-S 20-139-6491 (BR)
SCHOOL DISTRICT NO 36 (SURREY)
STUDENT SUPPORT CENTRE
12772 88 Ave, Surrey, BC, V3W 3J9
(604) 502-5710
Emp Here 100
SIC 8211 Elementary and secondary schools

D-U-N-S 20-713-3534 (BR)
SCHOOL DISTRICT NO 36 (SURREY)
W E KINVIG ELEMENTARY SCHOOL
13266 70b Ave, Surrey, BC, V3W 8N1
(604) 594-1135
Emp Here 50
SIC 8211 Elementary and secondary schools

D-U-N-S 20-278-1972 (BR)
SCHOOL DISTRICT NO 36 (SURREY)
KENNEDY TRAIL ELEMENTARY SCHOOL
8305 122a St, Surrey, BC, V3W 9P8
(604) 590-1198
Emp Here 45
SIC 8211 Elementary and secondary schools

D-U-N-S 25-482-9328 (BR)
SOBEYS WEST INC
SAFEWAY, DIV
7165 138 St, Surrey, BC, V3W 7T9
(604) 594-4515
Emp Here 100
SIC 5411 Grocery stores

D-U-N-S 25-723-9822 (BR)
SOBEYS WEST INC
SAFEWAY
7450 120 St, Surrey, BC, V3W 3M9
(604) 594-7341
Emp Here 180
SIC 5411 Grocery stores

D-U-N-S 25-948-7825 (BR)
VALUE VILLAGE STORES, INC
VALUE VILLAGE
(*Suby of* Savers, Inc.)
6925 King George Blvd, Surrey, BC, V3W 5A1
(604) 635-1341
Emp Here 40
SIC 5399 Miscellaneous general merchandise

D-U-N-S 20-589-5811 (BR)
VANCOUVER CITY SAVINGS CREDIT UNION
VANCITY CREDIT UNION
7555 King George Blvd, Surrey, BC, V3W 5A8
(604) 877-7271
Emp Here 20
SIC 6062 State credit unions

D-U-N-S 24-330-0527 (BR)
WAL-MART CANADA CORP
12451 88 Ave, Surrey, BC, V3W 1P8
(604) 597-7117
Emp Here 200
SIC 5311 Department stores

D-U-N-S 20-199-3057 (BR)
WINNERS MERCHANTS INTERNATIONAL L.P.
WINNERS
(*Suby of* The TJX Companies Inc)
12101 72 Ave Suite 105, Surrey, BC, V3W 2M1
(604) 501-0153
Emp Here 35
SIC 5651 Family clothing stores

Surrey, BC V3X
Greater Vancouver County

D-U-N-S 20-590-9463 (BR)
SCHOOL DISTRICT NO 36 (SURREY)
SULLIVAN HEIGHTS SECONDARY
6248 144 St, Surrey, BC, V3X 1A1
(604) 543-8749
Emp Here 100
SIC 8211 Elementary and secondary schools

D-U-N-S 20-153-2160 (BR)
SCHOOL DISTRICT NO 36 (SURREY)
BOUNDARY PARK ELEMENTARY SCHOOL
12332 Boundary Dr N, Surrey, BC, V3X 1Z6
(604) 543-8158
Emp Here 30
SIC 8211 Elementary and secondary schools

D-U-N-S 20-590-9430 (BR)
SCHOOL DISTRICT NO 36 (SURREY)
COLEBROOK ELEMENTARY SCHOOL
5404 125a St, Surrey, BC, V3X 1W6
(604) 596-3221
Emp Here 25
SIC 8211 Elementary and secondary schools

D-U-N-S 20-590-7616 (BR)
SCHOOL DISTRICT NO 36 (SURREY)
J T BROWN SCHOOL
12530 60 Ave, Surrey, BC, V3X 2K8
(604) 596-3445
Emp Here 30
SIC 8211 Elementary and secondary schools

D-U-N-S 20-653-3296 (BR)
SCHOOL DISTRICT NO 36 (SURREY)
MCLEOD ROAD ELEMENTARY
6325 142 St, Surrey, BC, V3X 1B9
(604) 595-1060
Emp Here 30
SIC 8211 Elementary and secondary schools

D-U-N-S 20-590-9067 (BR)
SCHOOL DISTRICT NO 36 (SURREY)
NORTH RIDGE ELEMENTARY SCHOOL
13460 62 Ave, Surrey, BC, V3X 2J2
(604) 599-3900
Emp Here 34
SIC 8211 Elementary and secondary schools

D-U-N-S 20-713-3575 (BR)
SCHOOL DISTRICT NO 36 (SURREY)
PANORAMA PARK ELEMENTARY SCHOOL
12878 62 Ave, Surrey, BC, V3X 2E8
(604) 596-0963
Emp Here 30
SIC 8211 Elementary and secondary schools

D-U-N-S 20-653-3601 (BR)
SCHOOL DISTRICT NO 36 (SURREY)
NEWTON LEARNING CENTRE
6329 King George Blvd Suite 102, Surrey, BC, V3X 1G1
(604) 587-2312
Emp Here 20
SIC 8211 Elementary and secondary schools

D-U-N-S 20-887-3807 (SL)
TRADITIONAL LEARNING SOCIETY OF BC
TRADITIONAL LEARNING ACADEMY
6225c 136 St Suite C, Surrey, BC, V3X 1H3
(604) 575-8596
Emp Here 55 *Sales* 3,648,035
SIC 8211 Elementary and secondary schools

Surrey, BC V3Z
Greater Vancouver County

D-U-N-S 24-681-2163 (HQ)
4499034 CANADA INC
TRYDOR INDUSTRIES
19275 25 Ave, Surrey, BC, V3Z 3X1
(604) 542-4773
Emp Here 23 *Emp Total* 33
Sales 6,639,424
SIC 5063 Electrical apparatus and equipment

Pr Pr Murray Leimert

D-U-N-S 25-281-7721 (BR)
4513380 CANADA INC
LIVINGSTON INTERNATIONAL
17735 1 Ave Suite 165, Surrey, BC, V3Z 9S1
(604) 538-1144
Emp Here 20
SIC 4731 Freight transportation arrangement

D-U-N-S 20-108-5404 (SL)
ADVANCE WIRE PRODUCTS LTD
AWP
19095 24 Ave Suite 19095, Surrey, BC, V3Z 3S9
(604) 541-4666
Emp Here 70 *Sales* 3,793,956
SIC 2599 Furniture and fixtures, nec

D-U-N-S 24-124-6029 (BR)
BLACK PRESS GROUP LTD
PEACE ARCH PUBLICATIONS
2411 160 St Unit 200, Surrey, BC, V3Z 0C8
(604) 531-1711
Emp Here 25
SIC 2711 Newspapers

D-U-N-S 20-386-0981 (BR)
CARA OPERATIONS LIMITED
MONTANA'S COOKHOUSE
(*Suby of* Cara Holdings Limited)
16071 24 Ave Suite 3097, Surrey, BC, V3Z 9H7
(604) 542-5230
Emp Here 60
SIC 5812 Eating places

D-U-N-S 20-918-5821 (BR)
CARSON CUSTOM BROKERS LIMITED
CARSON INTERNATIONAL
17735 1 Ave Suite 260, Surrey, BC, V3Z 9S1
(780) 496-9627
Emp Here 40
SIC 4731 Freight transportation arrangement

D-U-N-S 25-218-8750 (BR)
CARSON CUSTOM BROKERS LIMITED
CARSON INTERNATIONAL
17735 1 Ave Unit 206, Surrey, BC, V3Z 9S1
(604) 538-4966
Emp Here 40
SIC 4731 Freight transportation arrangement

D-U-N-S 24-939-3117 (BR)
COLE INTERNATIONAL INC
17637 1 Ave Suite 201, Surrey, BC, V3Z 9S1
(604) 538-1512
Emp Here 20
SIC 4731 Freight transportation arrangement

D-U-N-S 24-384-1181 (BR)
CONVERGINT TECHNOLOGIES LTD
(*Suby of* Convergint Technologies LLC)
2677 192 St Unit 101, Surrey, BC, V3Z 3X1
(604) 536-8979
Emp Here 20
SIC 8711 Engineering services

D-U-N-S 24-342-2016 (BR)
FINANCIERE BANQUE NATIONALE INC
2121 160 St, Surrey, BC, V3Z 9N6
(604) 541-4925
Emp Here 25
SIC 6211 Security brokers and dealers

D-U-N-S 25-972-7191 (SL)
GROUPHEALTH BENEFIT SOLUTIONS
2626 Croydon Dr Suite 200, Surrey, BC, V3Z 0S8
(604) 542-4100
Emp Here 411 *Sales* 36,991,075
SIC 6411 Insurance agents, brokers, and service
Pt Matt Houghton

D-U-N-S 24-361-7292 (BR)
HOME DEPOT OF CANADA INC
HOME DEPOT
(*Suby of* The Home Depot Inc)

2525 160 St, Surrey, BC, V3Z 0C8
(604) 542-3520
Emp Here 150
SIC 5251 Hardware stores

D-U-N-S 24-037-0127   (BR)
KEG RESTAURANTS LTD
MORGAN CREEK KEG
15180 32 Ave Divers, Surrey, BC, V3Z 3M1
(604) 542-9733
Emp Here 120
SIC 5812 Eating places

D-U-N-S 25-417-6738   (SL)
MORGAN CREEK GOLF COURSE
3500 Morgan Creek Way, Surrey, BC, V3Z 0J7
(604) 531-4262
Emp Here 70   *Sales* 2,845,467
SIC 7997 Membership sports and recreation clubs

D-U-N-S 25-662-9635   (BR)
RBC DOMINION SECURITIES INC
RBC WEALTH MANAGEMENT
(*Suby of* Royal Bank Of Canada)
2626 Croydon Dr Unit 400, Surrey, BC, V3Z 0S8
(604) 535-3800
Emp Here 40
SIC 6211 Security brokers and dealers

D-U-N-S 20-713-3757   (BR)
SCHOOL DISTRICT NO 36 (SURREY)
MORGAN ELEMENTARY SCHOOL
3366 156a St, Surrey, BC, V3Z 9Y7
(604) 531-8426
Emp Here 50
SIC 8211 Elementary and secondary schools

D-U-N-S 24-356-8420   (BR)
SLEEP COUNTRY CANADA INC
2365 192 St Unit 101, Surrey, BC, V3Z 3X2
(604) 535-5077
Emp Here 20
SIC 4225 General warehousing and storage

D-U-N-S 24-848-8160   (SL)
VERSACOLD THIRD PARTY LOGISTICS SURREY ULC
VERSACOLD LOGISTIC SERVICES
2755 190 St, Surrey, BC, V3Z 3W6
(778) 545-5700
Emp Here 200   *Sales* 18,969,782
SIC 4225 General warehousing and storage
Pr Pr Georges Jenkins
Fin Ex David Stone

D-U-N-S 24-599-1992   (BR)
WAL-MART CANADA CORP
WALMART
2355 160 St, Surrey, BC, V3Z 9N6
(604) 541-9015
Emp Here 420
SIC 5311 Department stores

D-U-N-S 25-949-2155   (HQ)
WESTLAND INSURANCE LIMITED PART-NERSHIP
(*Suby of* Westland Insurance Limited Partnership)
2121 160 St Unit 200, Surrey, BC, V3Z 9N6
(604) 543-7788
Emp Here 35   *Emp Total* 140
Sales 16,302,292
SIC 6411 Insurance agents, brokers, and service
Ch Bd Jeff Webbs
Pr Pr Colin Thompson
Dir Matt Wubs
VP VP Andy Luiten

D-U-N-S 20-184-3054   (BR)
WINNERS MERCHANTS INTERNATIONAL L.P.
WINNERS
(*Suby of* The TJX Companies Inc)
15715 Croydon Dr, Surrey, BC, V3Z 2L5

(604) 535-0115
Emp Here 40
SIC 5651 Family clothing stores

Surrey, BC V4A
Greater Vancouver County

D-U-N-S 20-563-2958   (BR)
ALLDRITT DEVELOPMENT LIMITED
NORDIC RESORT
2055 152 St Suite 300, Surrey, BC, V4A 4N7
(604) 536-5525
Emp Here 100
SIC 6552 Subdividers and developers, nec

D-U-N-S 25-126-8215   (BR)
BMO NESBITT BURNS INC
1959 152 St Suite 270, Surrey, BC, V4A 9E3
(604) 535-4300
Emp Here 25
SIC 6211 Security brokers and dealers

D-U-N-S 25-314-4752   (BR)
BANK OF MONTREAL
BANK OF MONTREAL
1626 Martin Dr Suite 2, Surrey, BC, V4A 6E7
(604) 531-5581
Emp Here 24
SIC 6021 National commercial banks

D-U-N-S 25-293-9103   (BR)
CIBC WORLD MARKETS INC
CIBC WOOD GUNDY
1688 152 St Unit 408, Surrey, BC, V4A 4N2
(604) 535-3700
Emp Here 30
SIC 6211 Security brokers and dealers

D-U-N-S 20-027-1141   (BR)
CATHOLIC INDEPENDENT SCHOOLS OF VANCOUVER ARCHDIOCESE, THE
STAR OF THE SEA ELEMENTARY SCHOOL
15024 24 Ave, Surrey, BC, V4A 2H8
(604) 531-6316
Emp Here 29
SIC 8211 Elementary and secondary schools

D-U-N-S 24-426-3286   (SL)
CHARTWELL SELECT CRESCENT GARDENS RETIREMENT COMMUNITY
1222 King George Blvd, Surrey, BC, V4A 9W6
(604) 541-8861
Emp Here 20   *Sales* 729,607
SIC 8361 Residential care

D-U-N-S 25-193-1408   (SL)
EARL'S RESTAURANT (WHITE ROCK) LTD
1767 152 St Suite 7, Surrey, BC, V4A 4N3

Emp Here 80   *Sales* 2,407,703
SIC 5812 Eating places

D-U-N-S 24-377-9183   (SL)
FIBRWRAP INSTALLATIONS LIMITED
(*Suby of* Aegion Corporation)
15531 24 Ave Unit 31, Surrey, BC, V4A 2J4
(604) 535-9512
Emp Here 25   *Sales* 1,824,018
SIC 2891 Adhesives and sealants

D-U-N-S 20-933-8875   (BR)
FLYING WEDGE PIZZA CO. LTD
(*Suby of* Flying Wedge Pizza Co. Ltd)
15355 24 Ave Suite 810, Surrey, BC, V4A 2H9

Emp Here 20
SIC 5812 Eating places

D-U-N-S 24-641-7067   (BR)
GREAT PACIFIC INDUSTRIES INC
PRICESMART FOODS
1641 152 St, Surrey, BC, V4A 4N3
(604) 536-4522
Emp Here 250
SIC 5411 Grocery stores

D-U-N-S 25-513-2516   (SL)
GUNGNIR RESOURCES INC
1688 152 St Suite 404, Surrey, BC, V4A 4N2
(604) 683-0484
Emp Here 833   *Sales* 90,544,229
SIC 1041 Gold ores
Jari Paaki
Christopher Robbins
Todd Keast
Garett Macdonald

D-U-N-S 20-697-0076   (SL)
HRC CARE SOCIETY
WESTMINSTER HOUSE
1653 140 St, Surrey, BC, V4A 4H1
(604) 538-5291
Emp Here 85   *Sales* 4,622,080
SIC 8322 Individual and family services

D-U-N-S 25-310-9342   (BR)
MCDONALD'S RESTAURANTS OF CANADA LIMITED
MCDONALD'S 8240
(*Suby of* McDonald's Corporation)
1789 152 St, Surrey, BC, V4A 4N3
(604) 541-7010
Emp Here 70
SIC 5812 Eating places

D-U-N-S 20-867-6143   (BR)
NORDSTRONG EQUIPMENT LIMITED
NORDSTRONG EQUIPMENT LIMITED
(*Suby of* Canerector Inc)
15475 Madrona Dr, Surrey, BC, V4A 5N2

Emp Here 500
SIC 3535 Conveyors and conveying equipment

D-U-N-S 24-107-4439   (SL)
PACIFIC INN CATERING
1160 King George Blvd, Surrey, BC, V4A 4Z2
(604) 535-1432
Emp Here 50   *Sales* 1,532,175
SIC 5812 Eating places

D-U-N-S 20-590-9315   (BR)
SCHOOL DISTRICT NO 36 (SURREY)
H T THRIFT ELEMENTARY SCHOOL
1739 148 St, Surrey, BC, V4A 4M6
(604) 536-8712
Emp Here 30
SIC 8211 Elementary and secondary schools

D-U-N-S 20-034-8592   (BR)
SCHOOL DISTRICT NO 36 (SURREY)
BAYRIDGE ELEMENTARY SCHOOL
1730 142 St, Surrey, BC, V4A 6G7
(604) 531-8082
Emp Here 30
SIC 8211 Elementary and secondary schools

D-U-N-S 24-974-8336   (BR)
SCHOOL DISTRICT NO 36 (SURREY)
SEMIAHMOO SECONDARY SCHOOL
1785 148 St, Surrey, BC, V4A 4M6
(604) 536-2131
Emp Here 150
SIC 8211 Elementary and secondary schools

D-U-N-S 20-590-9364   (BR)
SCHOOL DISTRICT NO 36 (SURREY)
LARONDE ELEMENTARY SCHOOL
1880 Laronde Dr, Surrey, BC, V4A 9S4
(604) 536-1626
Emp Here 35
SIC 8211 Elementary and secondary schools

D-U-N-S 20-033-7454   (BR)
SCHOOL DISTRICT NO 36 (SURREY)
ELGIN PARK SECONDARY SCHOOL
13484 24 Ave, Surrey, BC, V4A 2G5
(604) 538-6678
Emp Here 85
SIC 8211 Elementary and secondary schools

D-U-N-S 20-590-9265   (BR)
SCHOOL DISTRICT NO 36 (SURREY)

SOUTH MERIDIAN ELEMENTARY SCHOOL
16244 13 Ave, Surrey, BC, V4A 8E6
(604) 538-7114
Emp Here 25
SIC 8211 Elementary and secondary schools

D-U-N-S 20-202-7202   (BR)
SCHOOL DISTRICT NO 36 (SURREY)
RAY SHEPHERD ELEMENTARY SCHOOL
1650 136 St, Surrey, BC, V4A 4E4
(604) 531-1471
Emp Here 25
SIC 8211 Elementary and secondary schools

D-U-N-S 20-590-9414   (BR)
SCHOOL DISTRICT NO 36 (SURREY)
SOUTH SURREY WHITE ROCK WORK
2320 King George Blvd Unit 13, Surrey, BC, V4A 5A5
(604) 536-0550
Emp Here 20
SIC 8211 Elementary and secondary schools

D-U-N-S 20-033-3701   (BR)
SCHOOL DISTRICT NO 36 (SURREY)
EARL MARRIOTT SECONDARY SCHOOL
15751 16 Ave, Surrey, BC, V4A 1S1
(604) 531-8354
Emp Here 95
SIC 8211 Elementary and secondary schools

D-U-N-S 20-713-3591   (BR)
SCHOOL DISTRICT NO 36 (SURREY)
OCEANV CLIFF ELEMENTARY
12550 20 Ave, Surrey, BC, V4A 1Y6
(604) 538-1770
Emp Here 50
SIC 8211 Elementary and secondary schools

D-U-N-S 20-713-3724   (BR)
SCHOOL DISTRICT NO 36 (SURREY)
CRESCENT PARK ANNEX
2378 124 St, Surrey, BC, V4A 3M8
(604) 538-1282
Emp Here 50
SIC 8211 Elementary and secondary schools

D-U-N-S 20-590-9406   (BR)
SCHOOL DISTRICT NO 36 (SURREY)
JESSE LEE ELEMENTARY
2064 154 St, Surrey, BC, V4A 4S3
(604) 531-8833
Emp Here 34
SIC 8211 Elementary and secondary schools

D-U-N-S 20-170-4256   (BR)
SCOTIA CAPITAL INC
SCOTIA MCLEOD
1676 Martin Dr Suite 100, Surrey, BC, V4A 6E7
(604) 535-4743
Emp Here 32
SIC 6211 Security brokers and dealers

D-U-N-S 25-271-7269   (BR)
SOBEYS WEST INC
FRIENDLY OCEAN PARK SAFEWAY
12825 16 Ave, Surrey, BC, V4A 1N5
(604) 531-3422
Emp Here 130
SIC 5411 Grocery stores

D-U-N-S 20-860-3980   (BR)
SOURCE (BELL) ELECTRONICS INC, THE
SOURCE, THE
1711 152 St Suite 122, Surrey, BC, V4A 4N3
(604) 531-9323
Emp Here 25
SIC 5999 Miscellaneous retail stores, nec

D-U-N-S 20-506-0275   (BR)
STARBUCKS COFFEE CANADA, INC
(*Suby of* Starbucks Corporation)
15355 24 Ave Suite 900, Surrey, BC, V4A 2H9

Emp Here 20
SIC 5812 Eating places

D-U-N-S 25-658-3006   (BR)
WENDY'S RESTAURANTS OF CANADA INC
WENDY'S
(*Suby of* The Wendy's Company)
1750 152 St, Surrey, BC, V4A 7Z7

Emp Here 47
SIC 5812 Eating places

Surrey, BC V4N
Greater Vancouver County

D-U-N-S 20-639-5241   (BR)
ARCTIC GLACIER INC
9679 186 St, Surrey, BC, V4N 3N8
(604) 888-4311
Emp Here 20
SIC 2097 Manufactured ice

D-U-N-S 25-163-4044   (HQ)
ARCTIC POWER SYSTEMS BC LTD
(*Suby of* Arctic Power Systems BC Ltd)
18509 96 Ave, Surrey, BC V4N 3P7
(877) 551-8588
Emp Here 30   *Emp Total* 30
Sales 6,784,769
SIC 1623 Water, sewer, and utility lines
Pr Pr James Dooley
 Patricia Lynn Dooley
Dir Patricia Briner

D-U-N-S 25-100-5914   (SL)
BI PURE WATER (CANADA) INC
9790 190 St Unit 2, Surrey, BC, V4N 3M9
(604) 882-6650
Emp Here 32   *Sales* 6,178,080
SIC 1629 Heavy construction, nec

D-U-N-S 25-893-2946   (BR)
BELRON CANADA INCORPOREE
VANFAX
18800 96 Ave, Surrey, BC, V4N 3R1
(604) 513-2298
Emp Here 25
SIC 5013 Motor vehicle supplies and new parts

D-U-N-S 20-112-1634   (BR)
BRANDT TRACTOR LTD
9500 190 St, Surrey, BC, V4N 3S2
(604) 882-8888
Emp Here 30
SIC 5084 Industrial machinery and equipment

D-U-N-S 25-328-8344   (SL)
BREETA SALES & MARKETING LTD
BREETA PACKAGING
9775 188 St Suite 104, Surrey, BC, V4N 3N2
(604) 888-2334
Emp Here 35   *Sales* 5,884,100
SIC 5199 Nondurable goods, nec
Pr Pr Paul Godin

D-U-N-S 20-271-0575   (BR)
BRINK'S CANADA LIMITED
(*Suby of* The Brink's Company)
18758 96 Ave Suite 103, Surrey, BC, V4N 3P9
(604) 513-9916
Emp Here 25
SIC 7381 Detective and armored car services

D-U-N-S 20-702-1705   (SL)
CWS VENTURES INC
19490 92 Ave, Surrey, BC, V4N 4G7
(604) 888-9008
Emp Here 150   *Sales* 46,135,200
SIC 3531 Construction machinery
 Earl Hirtz

D-U-N-S 24-417-0861   (BR)
CANADIAN DEWATERING L.P.
19577 94 Ave, Surrey, BC, V4N 4E6
(604) 888-0042
Emp Here 40
SIC 5084 Industrial machinery and equipment

D-U-N-S 25-800-3474   (BR)
CATHOLIC INDEPENDENT SCHOOLS OF VANCOUVER ARCHDIOCESE, THE
HOLY CROSS REGIONAL HIGH SCHOOL
16193 88 Ave, Surrey, BC, V4N 1G3
(604) 581-3023
Emp Here 65
SIC 8211 Elementary and secondary schools

D-U-N-S 25-648-1813   (HQ)
CHECKWELL SOLUTIONS CORPORATION
BACKCHECK DIV OF
19433 96 Ave Suite 200, Surrey, BC, V4N 4C4
(604) 506-4663
Emp Here 154   *Emp Total* 432
Sales 62,759,111
SIC 8748 Business consulting, nec
 Dean Drysdale
Pr Pr Dave Dinesen
Sls Dir Brian Ward-Hall
 Henk Berends

D-U-N-S 24-899-0376   (SL)
CHEETAH TRANSPORT LTD
9785 192 St Suite 103, Surrey, BC, V4N 4C7
(604) 882-7579
Emp Here 60   *Sales* 4,742,446
SIC 4212 Local trucking, without storage

D-U-N-S 25-745-3415   (SL)
CHRISTIAN SCHOOL ASSOCIATION OF SURREY
SURREY CHRISTIAN SCHOOL
8930 162 St, Surrey, BC, V4N 3G1
(604) 581-2474
Emp Here 60   *Sales* 3,939,878
SIC 8561 Religious organizations

D-U-N-S 24-957-0409   (BR)
CLARA INDUSTRIAL SERVICES LIMITED
(*Suby of* Clara Industrial Services Limited)
9800 190 St Suite 3, Surrey, BC, V4N 3M9

Emp Here 50
SIC 1721 Painting and paper hanging

D-U-N-S 24-457-3945   (SL)
COBRA ELECTRIC LTD
9688 190 St, Surrey, BC, V4N 3M9
(604) 594-1633
Emp Here 100   *Sales* 8,755,284
SIC 1731 Electrical work
Pr Pr Murray Berry

D-U-N-S 25-287-5059   (BR)
COMMERCIAL EQUIPMENT CORP
CORPORATION TRUCK EQUIPMENT
9475 192 St, Surrey, BC, V4N 3R7
(604) 888-0513
Emp Here 26
SIC 5084 Industrial machinery and equipment

D-U-N-S 25-384-9566   (BR)
COMPAGNIE DES CHEMINS DE FER NATIONAUX DU CANADA
CN INTERMODAL SERVICES
17569 104 Ave, Surrey, BC, V4N 3M4

Emp Here 56
SIC 4011 Railroads, line-haul operating

D-U-N-S 24-672-6103   (HQ)
FALCON EQUIPMENT LTD
18412 96 Ave, Surrey, BC, V4N 3P8
(604) 888-5066
Emp Here 55   *Emp Total* 62
Sales 10,944,105
SIC 5084 Industrial machinery and equipment
Pr Pr Rick Kielan
VP VP Howard Hartin

D-U-N-S 20-027-1463   (BR)
FINNING INTERNATIONAL INC
FINNING CANADA
(*Suby of* Finning International Inc)
19498 92 Ave, Surrey, BC, V4N 4G7
(604) 888-3406
Emp Here 50

SIC 7538 General automotive repair shops

D-U-N-S 24-367-4178   (BR)
FINNING INTERNATIONAL INC
FINNING
(*Suby of* Finning International Inc)
19100 94 Ave, Surrey, BC, V4N 5C3
(604) 881-2600
Emp Here 150
SIC 5082 Construction and mining machinery

D-U-N-S 20-116-3610   (SL)
GM NAMEPLATE CANADA CORP
SUPERGRAPHICS
(*Suby of* GM Nameplate, Inc.)
9344 192 St, Surrey, BC, V4N 3R8
(604) 888-6333
Emp Here 25   *Sales* 1,532,175
SIC 3993 Signs and advertising specialties

D-U-N-S 25-506-3810   (SL)
GUILDFORD HOTEL LTD
FOUR POINTS BY SHERATON
10410 158 St, Surrey, BC, V4N 5C2
(604) 930-4700
Emp Here 50   *Sales* 2,188,821
SIC 7011 Hotels and motels

D-U-N-S 20-584-6215   (SL)
HIGHLAND FOUNDRY LTD
(*Suby of* Canerector Inc)
9670 187 St, Surrey, BC, V4N 3N6
(604) 888-8444
Emp Here 130   *Sales* 17,583,529
SIC 3325 Steel foundries, nec
Pr Garth Mckay

D-U-N-S 20-076-4348   (HQ)
IMASCO MINERALS INC
IMASCO
(*Suby of* Imasco Minerals Inc)
19287 98a Ave, Surrey, BC, V4N 4C8
(604) 251-3959
Emp Here 38   *Emp Total* 70
Sales 6,596,303
SIC 3299 NonMetallic mineral products,
Pr Pr David Sacks
 A.J. (Abe) Sacks
Dir Ian Adam

D-U-N-S 24-888-3324   (BR)
MASONITE INTERNATIONAL CORPORATION
(*Suby of* Masonite International Corporation)
9255 194 St, Surrey, BC, V4N 4G1
(604) 882-9356
Emp Here 80
SIC 3312 Blast furnaces and steel mills

D-U-N-S 25-973-7377   (BR)
METRIE CANADA LTD
PREFINISHED FOOD PRODUCTS DIVISION
9255 194 St Suite 15, Surrey, BC, V4N 4G1
(604) 882-4982
Emp Here 50
SIC 2431 Millwork

D-U-N-S 20-795-7283   (HQ)
NEW-LINE PRODUCTS LTD
NEW-LINE HOSE & FITTINGS
(*Suby of* New-Line Products Ltd)
9415 189 St Unit 1, Surrey, BC, V4N 5L8
(604) 455-5400
Emp Here 56   *Emp Total* 80
Sales 15,540,629
SIC 5085 Industrial supplies
Pr Pr Kenneth Goller
 Jason Goller
VP VP Justin Goller

D-U-N-S 25-500-9136   (BR)
OAKCREEK GOLF & TURF INC
18785 96 Ave, Surrey, BC, V4N 3P5
(604) 882-8399
Emp Here 20
SIC 5941 Sporting goods and bicycle shops

D-U-N-S 20-051-5935   (SL)
PARAGON REMEDIATION GROUP LTD
ENVIRO-VAC
8815 Harvie Rd, Surrey, BC, V4N 4B9
(604) 513-1324
Emp Here 99   *Sales* 18,386,096
SIC 1542 Nonresidential construction, nec
Ch Bd James Klassen
Pr Steven Parks
VP Michael Baker
 Greg Peterson
 Raymond Zonbag

D-U-N-S 20-513-3531   (HQ)
PETERBILT PACIFIC INC
(*Suby of* Timberline Investments (2005) Inc)
19470 96 Ave, Surrey, BC, V4N 4C2
(604) 888-1411
Emp Here 60   *Emp Total* 4
Sales 102,489,600
SIC 5511 New and used car dealers
Pr Pr Donald Pasiuk
 Terry Pasiuk
Dir Leanne Schroeder

D-U-N-S 24-221-7425   (BR)
REVERA INC
FLEETWOOD VILLA
16028 83 Ave Suite 332, Surrey, BC, V4N 0N2
(604) 590-2889
Emp Here 30
SIC 6513 Apartment building operators

D-U-N-S 20-733-1781   (BR)
SMS EQUIPMENT INC
CONECO
19520 Telegraph Trail, Surrey, BC, V4N 4H1
(604) 888-9700
Emp Here 40
SIC 5084 Industrial machinery and equipment

D-U-N-S 20-026-9228   (BR)
SCHOOL DISTRICT NO 36 (SURREY)
FROST ROAD ELEMENTARY SCHOOL
8606 162 St, Surrey, BC, V4N 1B5
(604) 572-4050
Emp Here 50
SIC 8211 Elementary and secondary schools

D-U-N-S 20-590-9224   (BR)
SCHOOL DISTRICT NO 36 (SURREY)
HAROLD BISHOP ELEMENTARY
15670 104 Ave, Surrey, BC, V4N 2J3
(604) 581-6016
Emp Here 57
SIC 8211 Elementary and secondary schools

D-U-N-S 20-297-2555   (BR)
SCHOOL DISTRICT NO 36 (SURREY)
FRASER HEIGHTS SECONDARY SCHOOL
16060 108 Ave, Surrey, BC, V4N 1M1
(604) 582-9231
Emp Here 130
SIC 8211 Elementary and secondary schools

D-U-N-S 20-590-9281   (BR)
SCHOOL DISTRICT NO 36 (SURREY)
WILLIAM WATSON ELEMENTARY SCHOOL
16450 80 Ave, Surrey, BC, V4N 0H3
(604) 574-4141
Emp Here 30
SIC 8211 Elementary and secondary schools

D-U-N-S 20-590-7558   (BR)
SCHOOL DISTRICT NO 36 (SURREY)
FRASER WOOD ELEMENTARY SCHOOL
10650 164 St, Surrey, BC, V4N 1W8
(604) 589-6442
Emp Here 45
SIC 8211 Elementary and secondary schools

D-U-N-S 20-645-6183   (BR)
SCHOOL DISTRICT NO 36 (SURREY)
BOTHWELL ELEMENTARY SCHOOL
17070 102 Ave, Surrey, BC, V4N 4N6
(604) 589-0369
Emp Here 20

SIC 8211 Elementary and secondary schools

D-U-N-S 20-713-3732　　(BR)
SCHOOL DISTRICT NO 36 (SURREY)
COAST MERIDIAN ELEMENTARY SCHOOL
8222 168a St, Surrey, BC, V4N 4T8
(604) 574-6036
Emp Here 30
SIC 8211 Elementary and secondary schools

D-U-N-S 20-713-3609　　(BR)
SCHOOL DISTRICT NO 36 (SURREY)
SERPENTINE HEIGHTS ELEMENTARY
16126 93a Ave, Surrey, BC, V4N 3A2
(604) 589-6322
Emp Here 50
SIC 8211 Elementary and secondary schools

D-U-N-S 20-590-9737　　(BR)
SCHOOL DISTRICT NO 36 (SURREY)
ANNIEDALE ELEMENTARY SCHOOL
9744 176 St, Surrey, BC, V4N 3V3
(604) 581-5515
Emp Here 25
SIC 8211 Elementary and secondary schools

D-U-N-S 20-034-7552　　(BR)
SCHOOL DISTRICT NO 36 (SURREY)
DOGWOOD ELEMENTARY SCHOOL
10752 157 St, Surrey, BC, V4N 1K6
(604) 581-8111
Emp Here 40
SIC 8211 Elementary and secondary schools

D-U-N-S 20-713-3393　　(BR)
SCHOOL DISTRICT NO 36 (SURREY)
ERNEST STEVENSON ELEMENTARY
10929 160 St, Surrey, BC, V4N 1P3
(604) 583-5419
Emp Here 50
SIC 8211 Elementary and secondary schools

D-U-N-S 20-590-9257　　(BR)
SCHOOL DISTRICT NO 36 (SURREY)
WALNUT ROAD ELEMENTARY SCHOOL
16152 82 Ave, Surrey, BC, V4N 0N5
(604) 572-6617
Emp Here 45
SIC 8211 Elementary and secondary schools

D-U-N-S 20-713-3583　　(BR)
SCHOOL DISTRICT NO 36 (SURREY)
WOODLAND PARK ELEMENTARY SCHOOL
9025 158 St, Surrey, BC, V4N 2Y6
(604) 589-5957
Emp Here 50
SIC 8211 Elementary and secondary schools

D-U-N-S 20-047-8357　　(BR)
SCHOOL DISTRICT NO 36 (SURREY)
NORTH SURREY SECONDARY SCHOOL
15945 96 Ave, Surrey, BC, V4N 2R8
(604) 581-4433
Emp Here 100
SIC 8211 Elementary and secondary schools

D-U-N-S 25-505-9834　　(BR)
SECURITAS CANADA LIMITED
8431 160 St Suite 200, Surrey, BC, V4N 0V6
(778) 578-6063
Emp Here 30
SIC 7381 Detective and armored car services

D-U-N-S 24-343-7543　　(BR)
SUPERIOR PLUS LP
WINROC GAS STI
9698 192 St, Surrey, BC, V4N 4C6
(604) 513-2211
Emp Here 30
SIC 5039 Construction materials, nec

D-U-N-S 25-263-0298　　(HQ)
TENOLD TRANSPORTATION LIMITED PARTNERSHIP
19470 94 Ave, Surrey, BC, V4N 4E5
(604) 888-7822
Emp Here 30　　　Emp Total 5,515
Sales 15,072,767

SIC 4213 Trucking, except local
VP Fin Perry Simpson
Genl Mgr Keith Deblaere
Prs Mgr Lynn Kearney
Off Mgr Cindy Decoste

D-U-N-S 25-326-1358　　(BR)
THYSSENKRUPP MATERIALS CA, LTD
COPPER AND BRASS SALES
19044 95a Ave Suite 38, Surrey, BC, V4N 4P2
(604) 882-3493
Emp Here 25
SIC 5031 Lumber, plywood, and millwork

D-U-N-S 20-315-9934　　(BR)
VARSTEEL LTD
MAKIN METALS
1933 96 Ave Unit 104, Surrey, BC, V4N 4C4
(604) 882-9344
Emp Here 20
SIC 5051 Metals service centers and offices

D-U-N-S 20-045-1990　　(BR)
VICEROY RUBBER & PLASTICS LIMITED
19352 94 Ave, Surrey, BC, V4N 4E4

Emp Here 40
SIC 3089 Plastics products, nec

D-U-N-S 20-919-1543　　(HQ)
WELLONS CANADA CORP
19087 96 Ave, Surrey, BC, V4N 3P2
(604) 888-0122
Emp Here 100　　　Emp Total 350
Sales 15,540,629
SIC 3567 Industrial furnaces and ovens
Pr Patrick Thornton
　Martin Nye

D-U-N-S 20-005-1477　　(BR)
WENDY'S RESTAURANTS OF CANADA INC
(Suby of The Wendy's Company)
15959 Fraser Hwy, Surrey, BC, V4N 0Y3
(604) 599-0219
Emp Here 30
SIC 5812 Eating places

D-U-N-S 25-215-7888　　(SL)
WINDSOR SECURITY LIMITED
10833 160 St Suite 626, Surrey, BC, V4N 1P3

Emp Here 150　　　Sales 4,669,485
SIC 7381 Detective and armored car services

Surrey, BC V4P
Greater Vancouver County

D-U-N-S 24-204-5925　　(SL)
3248 KING GEORGE HWY HOLDINGS LTD
CHOICES MARKET SOUTH SURREY
3248 King George Blvd, Surrey, BC, V4P 1A5
(604) 541-3902
Emp Here 100　　　Sales 4,888,367
SIC 5499 Miscellaneous food stores

D-U-N-S 20-589-5183　　(BR)
BANQUE TORONTO-DOMINION, LA
TD CANADA TRUST
(Suby of Toronto-Dominion Bank, The)
2429 152 St Unit 100, Surrey, BC, V4P 1N4
(604) 541-2052
Emp Here 20
SIC 6021 National commercial banks

D-U-N-S 25-485-6511　　(BR)
CHRISTIAN AND MISSIONARY ALLIANCE IN CANADA, THE
15128 27b Ave, Surrey, BC, V4P 1P2
(604) 531-4733
Emp Here 22
SIC 8661 Religious organizations

D-U-N-S 25-262-8920　　(HQ)
EXPRESS COMPUTER SERVICE CENTER INC

EXPRESS COMPUTERS
(Suby of Express Computer Service Center Inc)
3033 King George Blvd Suite 28, Surrey, BC, V4P 1B8

Emp Here 22　　　Emp Total 52
Sales 3,793,956
SIC 7378 Computer maintenance and repair

D-U-N-S 20-003-9126　　(BR)
GREAT PACIFIC INDUSTRIES INC
SAVE-ON-FOODS
3033 152 St Suite 903, Surrey, BC, V4P 3K1
(604) 538-5467
Emp Here 300
SIC 5411 Grocery stores

D-U-N-S 24-080-1840　　(BR)
KIN'S FARM LTD
KIN'S FARM MARKET
2990 152 St Unit 101, Surrey, BC, V4P 3N7
(604) 538-6872
Emp Here 20
SIC 5431 Fruit and vegetable markets

D-U-N-S 24-773-1867　　(SL)
PACIFICA RESORT LIVING RETIREMENT, THE
THE PACIFICA
2525 King George Blvd, Surrey, BC, V4P 0C8
(604) 535-9194
Emp Here 50　　　Sales 4,377,642
SIC 6513 Apartment building operators

D-U-N-S 24-700-6631　　(BR)
REITMANS (CANADA) LIMITEE
3091 152 St Suite 330, Surrey, BC, V4P 3K1
(604) 538-8828
Emp Here 25
SIC 5621 Women's clothing stores

D-U-N-S 20-713-3633　　(BR)
SCHOOL DISTRICT NO 36 (SURREY)
CHANTRELL CREEK ELEMENTARY SCHOOL
2575 137 St, Surrey, BC, V4P 2K5
(604) 535-6708
Emp Here 38
SIC 8211 Elementary and secondary schools

D-U-N-S 24-171-2723　　(BR)
SCHOOL DISTRICT NO 36 (SURREY)
SUNNYSIDE ELEMENTARY SCHOOL
15250 28 Ave, Surrey, BC, V4P 1B9
(604) 531-4826
Emp Here 45
SIC 8211 Elementary and secondary schools

D-U-N-S 20-001-4756　　(BR)
STAPLES CANADA INC
STAPLES THE BUSINESS DEPOT
(Suby of Staples, Inc.)
3037 152 St, Surrey, BC, V4P 3K1
(604) 541-3850
Emp Here 30
SIC 5943 Stationery stores

D-U-N-S 20-700-4818　　(BR)
TOMMY HILFIGER CANADA INC
TOMMY HILFIGER OUTLET
3091 152 St Suite 300, Surrey, BC, V4P 3K1

Emp Here 30
SIC 5651 Family clothing stores

Tappen, BC V0E
Columbia - Shuswap County

D-U-N-S 20-028-4086　　(BR)
NORTH OKANAGAN SHUSWAP SCHOOL DISTRICT 83
CARLIN ELEMENTARY MIDDLE SCHOOL
4005 Myers Frontage Rd, Tappen, BC, V0E 2X3

(250) 835-4520
Emp Here 31
SIC 8211 Elementary and secondary schools

Taylor, BC V0C
Peace River - Laird County

D-U-N-S 25-191-0741　　(BR)
CANADIAN FOREST PRODUCTS LTD
8300 Cherry Ave E, Taylor, BC, V0C 2K0
(250) 789-9300
Emp Here 110
SIC 2421 Sawmills and planing mills, general

D-U-N-S 24-089-4951　　(BR)
SCHOOL DISTRICT NO. 60 (PEACE RIVER NORTH)
TAYLOR ELEMENTARY SCHOOL
9808 Birch Ave E, Taylor, BC, V0C 2K0
(250) 789-3323
Emp Here 60
SIC 8211 Elementary and secondary schools

Terrace, BC V8G
Kitimat - Stikine County

D-U-N-S 24-330-3257　　(BR)
ALS CANADA LTD
ALS CHEMEX
2912 Molitor St, Terrace, BC, V8G 3A4
(250) 635-3309
Emp Here 35
SIC 8734 Testing laboratories

D-U-N-S 24-806-1012　　(BR)
BANK OF NOVA SCOTIA, THE
SCOTIABANK
4602 Lakelse Ave, Terrace, BC, V8G 1R1
(250) 635-8500
Emp Here 25
SIC 6021 National commercial banks

D-U-N-S 24-024-4124　　(HQ)
BILLABONG ROAD & BRIDGE MAINTENANCE INC
5630 16 Hwy W, Terrace, BC, V8G 0C6
(250) 638-7918
Emp Here 75　　　Emp Total 120
Sales 11,090,026
SIC 1611 Highway and street construction
Pr John Ryan

D-U-N-S 24-750-7692　　(BR)
BLACK PRESS GROUP LTD
TERRACE STANDARD, THE
3210 Clinton St, Terrace, BC, V8G 5R2
(250) 638-7283
Emp Here 25
SIC 2711 Newspapers

D-U-N-S 25-288-8839　　(BR)
CANADA POST CORPORATION
3232 Emerson St, Terrace, BC, V8G 2R8
(250) 638-1862
Emp Here 35
SIC 4311 U.s. postal service

D-U-N-S 20-655-2023　　(BR)
CATHOLIC INDEPENDENT SCHOOLS, DIOCESE OF VICTORIA
VERITAS CATHOLIC SCHOOL
4836 Straume Ave, Terrace, BC, V8G 4G3
(250) 635-3035
Emp Here 22
SIC 8211 Elementary and secondary schools

D-U-N-S 24-310-3855　　(SL)
CLIFTON ENTERPRISES INC
COAST INN OF THE WEST
4620 Lakelse Ave, Terrace, BC, V8G 1R1
(250) 635-6300
Emp Here 50　　　Sales 2,188,821

SIC 7011 Hotels and motels

D-U-N-S 20-713-6362   (BR)
**COAST MOUNTAINS BOARD OF EDUCA-
TION SCHOOL DISTRICT NO. 82**
*CALEDONIA   SENIOR   SECONDARY
SCHOOL*
3605 Munroe St, Terrace, BC, V8G 3C4
(250) 635-6531
Emp Here 60
SIC 8211 Elementary and secondary schools

D-U-N-S 25-937-2894   (BR)
DENCAN RESTAURANTS INC
DENNY'S RESTAURANT
(*Suby of* Northland Properties Corporation)
4828 16 Hwy W, Terrace, BC, V8G 1L6
(250) 635-2295
Emp Here 35
SIC 5812 Eating places

D-U-N-S 25-963-4863   (BR)
DEVERY D. INVESTMENTS INC
TIM HORTONS
4603 Keith Ave, Terrace, BC, V8G 1K2
(250) 635-8128
Emp Here 30
SIC 5812 Eating places

D-U-N-S 20-010-1876   (BR)
ENBRIDGE PIPELINES INC
TERRACEVIEW LODGE
4707 Kerby Ave, Terrace, BC, V8G 2W2
(250) 638-0223
Emp Here 50
SIC 4612 Crude petroleum pipelines

D-U-N-S 25-970-9111   (BR)
FIRSTCANADA ULC
FARWEST FUELS
4904 16 Hwy W, Terrace, BC, V8G 1L8
(250) 635-6617
Emp Here 30
SIC 4111 Local and suburban transit

D-U-N-S 25-267-8974   (BR)
GREAT PACIFIC INDUSTRIES INC
SAVE-ON-FOODS
4741 Lakelse Ave Suite 280, Terrace, BC, V8G
4R9
(250) 635-5950
Emp Here 120
SIC 5411 Grocery stores

D-U-N-S 25-893-5501   (BR)
LOBLAWS INC
REAL CANADIAN WHOLESALE CLUB
4524 Feeney Ave, Terrace, BC, V8G 1J2
(250) 638-1460
Emp Here 26
SIC 5141 Groceries, general line

D-U-N-S 24-724-6283   (SL)
**MOUNT LAYTON HOT SPRING RESORT
LTD**
Gd Lcd Main, Terrace, BC, V8G 4A1
(250) 798-2214
Emp Here 55   *Sales* 2,407,703
SIC 7011 Hotels and motels

D-U-N-S 20-917-0638   (BR)
PACIFIC NORTHERN GAS LTD
2900 Kerr St, Terrace, BC V8G 4L9
(250) 635-7291
Emp Here 30
SIC 4923 Gas transmission and distribution

D-U-N-S 25-059-1724   (BR)
PRISZM LP
KFC
4750 Lakelse Ave, Terrace, BC, V8G 1R6
(250) 635-3663
Emp Here 21
SIC 5812 Eating places

D-U-N-S 24-857-0145   (SL)
SHAMES MOUNTAIN SKI CORPORATION
4544 Lakelse Ave, Terrace, BC, V8G 1P8

(250) 635-3773
Emp Here 55   *Sales* 2,991,389
SIC 7999 Amusement and recreation, nec

D-U-N-S 24-101-0193   (BR)
STAPLES CANADA INC
STAPLES THE BUSINESS DEPOT
(*Suby of* Staples, Inc.)
4645 Greig Ave, Terrace, BC, V8G 5P9
(250) 635-7797
Emp Here 30
SIC 5943 Stationery stores

D-U-N-S 24-504-3104   (SL)
TERRACE & AREA HEALTH COUNCIL
MILLS MEMORIAL HOSPITAL
4720 Haugland Ave, Terrace, BC, V8G 2W7
(250) 635-2211
Emp Here 225   *Sales* 21,811,750
SIC 8062 General medical and surgical hospi-
tals
  Larisa Tarwick
  Bob Kelly
  Nirmal Parmar
Dir Russell Seltenrich
Dir Lani Almas
Dir Les Watmough

D-U-N-S 24-931-0277   (SL)
TERRACE TOTEM HOLDINGS LTD
4631 Keith Ave, Terrace, BC, V8G 1K3
(250) 635-4984
Emp Here 65   *Sales* 9,976,960
SIC 6712 Bank holding companies
Pr Kevin Kennedy
VP Mitchell (Mitch) Shinde
Sec Shane Dejong

D-U-N-S 20-590-5198   (BR)
**THE BOARD OF EDUCATION OF SCHOOL
DISTRICT #82 (COAST MOUNTAIN)**
KITI K' SHAN PRIMARY SCHOOL
4730 Graham Ave, Terrace, BC, V8G 1A8
(250) 635-3115
Emp Here 20
SIC 8211 Elementary and secondary schools

D-U-N-S 20-713-6370   (BR)
**THE BOARD OF EDUCATION OF SCHOOL
DISTRICT #82 (COAST MOUNTAIN)**
SKEENA MIDDLE SCHOOL
3411 Munroe St, Terrace, BC, V8G 3C1
(250) 635-9136
Emp Here 50
SIC 8211 Elementary and secondary schools

D-U-N-S 25-128-6100   (BR)
**THE BOARD OF EDUCATION OF SCHOOL
DISTRICT #82 (COAST MOUNTAIN)**
UPLANDS ELEMENTARY SCHOOL
(*Suby of* The Board of Education of School
District #82 (Coast Mountain))
4110 Thomas St, Terrace, BC, V8G 4L7
(250) 635-2721
Emp Here 40
SIC 8211 Elementary and secondary schools

D-U-N-S 25-241-1215   (BR)
UNIVERSAL RESTORATION SYSTEMS LTD
4535 Greig Ave, Terrace, BC, V8G 1M7
(250) 635-4355
Emp Here 30
SIC 1521 Single-family housing construction

D-U-N-S 24-813-5431   (BR)
VALARD CONSTRUCTION LTD
(*Suby of* Quanta Services, Inc.)
3120 Braun St, Terrace, BC, V8G 5N9

Emp Here 100
SIC 1623 Water, sewer, and utility lines

D-U-N-S 24-080-1642   (BR)
WAL-MART CANADA CORP
4427 16 Hwy W, Terrace, BC, V8G 5L5
(250) 615-4728
Emp Here 150
SIC 5311 Department stores

D-U-N-S 20-199-2422   (BR)
WESTON BAKERIES LIMITED
3111 Blakeburn St, Terrace, BC, V8G 3J1
(250) 635-3808
Emp Here 50
SIC 2051 Bread, cake, and related products

D-U-N-S 25-898-1398   (BR)
**WORKERS' COMPENSATION BOARD OF
BRITISH COLUMBIA**
WORKSAFE BC
4450 Lakelse Ave, Terrace, BC, V8G 1P2
(250) 615-6600
Emp Here 30
SIC 7389 Business services, nec

Thornhill, BC V8G
Kitimat - Stikine County

D-U-N-S 25-133-3233   (BR)
**COAST MOUNTAINS BOARD OF EDUCA-
TION SCHOOL DISTRICT NO. 82**
*THORNHILL   JUNIOR   SECONDARY
SCHOOL*
3120 16 Hwy E, Thornhill, BC, V8G 4N8
(250) 638-4423
Emp Here 26
SIC 8211 Elementary and secondary schools

D-U-N-S 25-128-6134   (BR)
**COAST MOUNTAINS BOARD OF EDUCA-
TION SCHOOL DISTRICT NO. 82**
THORNHILL ELEMENTARY SCHOOL
2906 Clark St, Thornhill, BC, V8G 3S1

Emp Here 25
SIC 8211 Elementary and secondary schools

D-U-N-S 24-070-4841   (SL)
NORTHERN MOTOR INN LTD
3086 16 Hwy E, Thornhill, BC, V8G 3N5
(250) 635-6375
Emp Here 70   *Sales* 3,064,349
SIC 7011 Hotels and motels

D-U-N-S 25-871-5119   (BR)
THOMPSON COMMUNITY SERVICES INC
2228 Spruce St, Thornhill, BC, V8G 5B7

Emp Here 40
SIC 8361 Residential care

Tofino, BC V0R
Alberni - Clayoquot County

D-U-N-S 20-084-0218   (BR)
CERMAQ CANADA LTD
MAIN STREAM
(*Suby of* Cermaq Canada Ltd)
61 4th St, Tofino, BC, V0R 2Z0
(250) 725-1255
Emp Here 200
SIC 2048 Prepared feeds, nec

D-U-N-S 25-965-7567   (BR)
LIONS GATE FISHERIES LTD
612 Campbell St, Tofino, BC, V0R 2Z0
(250) 725-3731
Emp Here 25
SIC 5421 Meat and fish markets

D-U-N-S 20-713-6024   (BR)
**SCHOOL   DISTRICT   #70   (ALBERNI)
SCHOOL BOARD**
WICKANINNICH ELEMENTARY SCHOOL
431 Gibson St, Tofino, BC, V0R 2Z0
(250) 725-3254
Emp Here 50
SIC 8211 Elementary and secondary schools

D-U-N-S 25-980-8137   (SL)
TIN WIS RESORT LTD

BEST WESTERN
1119 Pacific Rim Hwy, Tofino, BC, V0R 2Z0
(250) 725-4445
Emp Here 55   *Sales* 2,407,703
SIC 7011 Hotels and motels

Topley, BC V0J
Bulkley - Nechako County

D-U-N-S 20-590-5024   (BR)
**BOARD OF EDUCATION OF SCHOOL DIS-
TRICT NO. 91 (NECHAKO LAKE), THE**
TOPLEY ELEMENTARY SCHOOL
Gd, Topley, BC, V0J 2Y0

Emp Here 25
SIC 8211 Elementary and secondary schools

Trail, BC V1R
Kootenay Boundary County

D-U-N-S 20-048-0627   (BR)
**AMEC FOSTER WHEELER AMERICAS LIM-
ITED**
1385 Cedar Ave, Trail, BC, V1R 4C3
(250) 368-2400
Emp Here 110
SIC 8711 Engineering services

D-U-N-S 25-288-8870   (BR)
CANADA POST CORPORATION
805 Spokane St, Trail, BC, V1R 3W4
(250) 364-2585
Emp Here 25
SIC 4311 U.s. postal service

D-U-N-S 25-677-7384   (BR)
CANADIAN PACIFIC RAILWAY COMPANY
KOOTENAY VALLEY RAILWAY
101 Ritchie Ave, Trail, BC, V1R 1G8
(250) 364-2021
Emp Here 22
SIC 4011 Railroads, line-haul operating

D-U-N-S 20-739-1702   (BR)
FORTISBC ENERGY INC
FORTISBC
2945 Highway Dr, Trail, BC, V1R 2T2
(250) 368-4013
Emp Here 20
SIC 5541 Gasoline service stations

D-U-N-S 20-918-3177   (SL)
**GREATER TRAIL COMMUNITY HEALTH
COUNCIL**
ALPHA HOUSE
1200 Hospital Bench, Trail, BC, V1R 4M1
(250) 368-3311
Emp Here 1,000   *Sales* 89,898,187
SIC 8062 General medical and surgical hospi-
tals
  Marylynn Rakuson
  Charles Riley

D-U-N-S 25-272-7334   (BR)
**INSURANCE CORPORATION OF BRITISH
COLUMBIA**
ICBC
2985 Highway Dr, Trail, BC, V1R 2T2
(250) 368-5261
Emp Here 20
SIC 6331 Fire, marine, and casualty insurance

D-U-N-S 24-309-1126   (BR)
INTERIOR HEALTH AUTHORITY
*KOOTENAY BOUNDARY REGIONAL HOSPI-
TAL*
1200 Hospital Bench, Trail, BC, V1R 4M1
(250) 368-3311
Emp Here 315
SIC 8062 General medical and surgical hospi-

tals

D-U-N-S 20-875-3454   (BR)
KOOTENAY SAVINGS CREDIT UNION
1199 Cedar Ave Suite 300, Trail, BC, V1R 4B8
(250) 368-2647
Emp Here 25
SIC 6062 State credit unions

D-U-N-S 25-815-1208   (BR)
SCHOOL DISTRICT # 20 (KOOTENAY-COLUMBIA)
WEBSTER, JAMES L ELEMENTARY SCHOOL
(*Suby of* School District # 20 (Kootenay-Columbia))
395 Schofield Hwy, Trail, BC, V1R 2G5
(250) 368-3242
Emp Here 30
SIC 8211 Elementary and secondary schools

D-U-N-S 25-820-5723   (BR)
SCHOOL DISTRICT # 20 (KOOTENAY-COLUMBIA)
GLENMERRY ELEMENTARY SCHOOL
(*Suby of* School District # 20 (Kootenay-Columbia))
3660 Carnation Dr, Trail, BC, V1R 2W6
(250) 364-1353
Emp Here 28
SIC 8211 Elementary and secondary schools

D-U-N-S 20-024-4684   (BR)
SCHOOL DISTRICT # 20 (KOOTENAY-COLUMBIA)
J LLOYD CROWE SECONDARY SCHOOL
1300 Frances Moran Rd, Trail, BC, V1R 4L9
(250) 368-5591
Emp Here 70
SIC 8211 Elementary and secondary schools

D-U-N-S 25-839-3099   (BR)
SELKIRK COLLEGE
SELKIRK COLLEGE TRAIL CAMPUS
900 Helena St, Trail, BC, V1R 4S6
(250) 368-5236
Emp Here 35
SIC 8221 Colleges and universities

D-U-N-S 24-314-2572   (BR)
TECK METALS LTD
600 Bingay Rd, Trail, BC, V1R 4L8
(250) 364-4713
Emp Here 40
SIC 1081 Metal mining services

D-U-N-S 20-108-1627   (BR)
TECK METALS LTD
25 Aldridge Ave, Trail, BC, V1R 4L8
(250) 364-4222
Emp Here 1,500
SIC 1081 Metal mining services

D-U-N-S 25-262-5074   (SL)
TOXCO WASTE MANAGEMENT LTD
RETRIEVE TECHNOLOGIES
9384 22a Hwy, Trail, BC, V1R 4W6
(250) 367-9882
Emp Here 30   *Sales* 3,939,878
SIC 4953 Refuse systems

D-U-N-S 24-026-1433   (BR)
WAL-MART CANADA CORP
WALMART
1601 Marcolin Dr Suite 1011, Trail, BC, V1R 4Y1
(250) 364-1802
Emp Here 100
SIC 5311 Department stores

D-U-N-S 24-319-1108   (BR)
WAL-MART CANADA CORP
WAL-MART
1601 Marcolin Dr Suite 1011, Trail, BC, V1R 4Y1
(250) 364-2688
Emp Here 120
SIC 5311 Department stores

Tumbler Ridge, BC V0C
Peace River - Laird County

D-U-N-S 20-801-5623   (SL)
J8 HOLDINGS LTD
220 Main St Unit 3, Tumbler Ridge, BC, V0C 2W0

Emp Here 20   *Sales* 6,898,600
SIC 4731 Freight transportation arrangement
Dir Raelynn Johnson

D-U-N-S 24-332-5966   (HQ)
LAPRAIRIE CRANE LTD
(*Suby of* LaPrairie Crane Ltd)
Gd, Tumbler Ridge, BC, V0C 2W0
(250) 242-5561
Emp Here 30   *Emp Total* 50
Sales 2,626,585
SIC 7389 Business services, nec

D-U-N-S 20-861-0084   (BR)
LAPRAIRIE CRANE LTD
(*Suby of* LaPrairie Crane Ltd)
235 Front St Suite 209, Tumbler Ridge, BC, V0C 2W0
(250) 242-5561
Emp Here 40
SIC 7353 Heavy construction equipment rental

D-U-N-S 20-297-4023   (BR)
SCHOOL DISTRICT #59 PEACE RIVER SOUTH
TUMBLER RIDGE SECONDARY SCHOOL
180 Southgate, Tumbler Ridge, BC, V0C 2W0
(250) 242-4227
Emp Here 20
SIC 8211 Elementary and secondary schools

D-U-N-S 24-425-8807   (BR)
WESTERN COAL ULC
235 Front St, Tumbler Ridge, BC, V0C 2W0
(250) 242-6000
Emp Here 50
SIC 1221 Bituminous coal and lignite-surface mining

Ucluelet, BC V0R
Alberni - Clayoquot County

D-U-N-S 24-641-2191   (BR)
OAK BAY MARINA LTD
CANADIAN PRINCESS RESORT
1943 Peninsula Rd, Ucluelet, BC, V0R 3A0
(250) 726-7771
Emp Here 150
SIC 7011 Hotels and motels

D-U-N-S 20-035-2578   (BR)
SCHOOL DISTRICT #70 (ALBERNI) SCHOOL BOARD
UCLUELET SECONDARY SCHOOL
1450 Peninsula Rd, Ucluelet, BC, V0R 3A0
(250) 726-7796
Emp Here 20
SIC 8211 Elementary and secondary schools

D-U-N-S 20-653-8642   (BR)
SCHOOL DISTRICT #70 (ALBERNI) SCHOOL BOARD
UCLUELET ELEMENTARY SCHOOL
1350 Peninsula, Ucluelet, BC, V0R 3A0
(250) 726-7793
Emp Here 23
SIC 8211 Elementary and secondary schools

Valemount, BC V0E
Fraser-Fort George County

D-U-N-S 20-591-4323   (BR)
BOARD OF EDUCATION OF SCHOOL DISTRICT NO. 57 (PRINCE GEORGE), THE
VALEMOUNT SECONDARY SCHOOL
(*Suby of* Board of Education of School District No. 57 (Prince George), The)
201 Ash, Valemount, BC, V0E 2Z0
(250) 566-4431
Emp Here 25
SIC 8211 Elementary and secondary schools

D-U-N-S 20-573-3269   (BR)
COMPAGNIE DES CHEMINS DE FER NATIONAUX DU CANADA
870 Beven Cres, Valemount, BC, V0E 2Z0
(250) 566-4759
Emp Here 20
SIC 4011 Railroads, line-haul operating

D-U-N-S 24-773-2550   (BR)
LAKES DISTRICT MAINTENANCE LTD
(*Suby of* Lakes District Maintenance Ltd)
13410 Blackman Rd, Valemount, BC, V0E 2Z0
(250) 566-4474
Emp Here 49
SIC 1611 Highway and street construction

Van Anda, BC V0N
Powell River County

D-U-N-S 25-216-8281   (SL)
TEXADA QUARRYING LTD
2 Airport Rd, Van Anda, BC, V0N 3K0
(604) 486-7627
Emp Here 80
SIC 1422 Crushed and broken limestone

Vancouver, BC D6B
Greater Vancouver County

D-U-N-S 25-326-3321   (BR)
HEWITT ASSOCIATES CORP
401 W Toronto Suite 1200, Vancouver, BC, D6B 5A1
(604) 683-7311
Emp Here 50
SIC 6282 Investment advice

Vancouver, BC V5H
Greater Vancouver County

D-U-N-S 25-533-9061   (HQ)
SCOTT CONSTRUCTION LTD
SCOTT CONSTRUCTION GROUP
(*Suby of* 4215 Investments Ltd)
3777 Kingsway Suite 1750, Vancouver, BC, V5H 3Z7
(604) 874-8228
Emp Here 60   *Emp Total* 60
Sales 24,149,992
SIC 1542 Nonresidential construction, nec
Pr Pr John Scott
Treas Laura Suhner
    Don Nishimura

Vancouver, BC V5K
Greater Vancouver County

D-U-N-S 20-591-0446   (BR)
BOARD OF EDUCATION OF SCHOOL DISTRICT NO. 39 (VANCOUVER), THE
TILLICUM ANNEX ELEMENTARY SCHOOL
2450 Cambridge St, Vancouver, BC, V5K 1L2
(604) 713-4716
Emp Here 25

SIC 8211 Elementary and secondary schools

D-U-N-S 20-591-0453   (BR)
BOARD OF EDUCATION OF SCHOOL DISTRICT NO. 39 (VANCOUVER), THE
SIR JOHN FRANKLIN ELEMENTARY SCHOOL
250 Skeena St, Vancouver, BC, V5K 4N8
(604) 713-4709
Emp Here 25
SIC 8211 Elementary and secondary schools

D-U-N-S 20-033-7546   (BR)
BOARD OF EDUCATION OF SCHOOL DISTRICT NO. 39 (VANCOUVER), THE
DR A R LORD ELEMENTARY SCHOOL
555 Lillooet St, Vancouver, BC, V5K 4G4
(604) 713-4620
Emp Here 30
SIC 8211 Elementary and secondary schools

D-U-N-S 20-713-4052   (BR)
BOARD OF EDUCATION OF SCHOOL DISTRICT NO. 39 (VANCOUVER), THE
HASTINGS ELEMENTARY SCHOOL
2625 Franklin St, Vancouver, BC, V5K 3W7
(604) 713-5507
Emp Here 50
SIC 8211 Elementary and secondary schools

D-U-N-S 20-713-4128   (BR)
BOARD OF EDUCATION OF SCHOOL DISTRICT NO. 39 (VANCOUVER), THE
SIR MATTHEW BEGBIE ELEMENTARY SCHOOL
1430 Lillooet St, Vancouver, BC, V5K 4H6
(604) 713-4686
Emp Here 50
SIC 8211 Elementary and secondary schools

D-U-N-S 25-023-6486   (BR)
CATHOLIC INDEPENDENT SCHOOLS OF VANCOUVER ARCHDIOCESE, THE
NOTRE DAME REGIONAL SECONDARY SCHOOL
2880 Venables St, Vancouver, BC, V5K 4Z6
(604) 255-5454
Emp Here 50
SIC 8211 Elementary and secondary schools

D-U-N-S 20-653-3841   (BR)
CATHOLIC INDEPENDENT SCHOOLS OF VANCOUVER ARCHDIOCESE, THE
OUR LADY OF SORROWS SCHOOL
575 Slocan St, Vancouver, BC, V5K 3X5
(604) 253-2434
Emp Here 20
SIC 8211 Elementary and secondary schools

D-U-N-S 20-068-3428   (SL)
HASTINGS ENTERTAINMENT INC
HASTINGS RACECOURSE & CASINO
188 Renfrew St N, Vancouver, BC, V5K 3N8
(604) 254-1631
Emp Here 300
SIC 7948 Racing, including track operation

D-U-N-S 24-163-0821   (HQ)
INTERCITY PACKERS LTD
ALBION FARMS AND FISHERIES
(*Suby of* Intercity Packers Ltd)
1575 Kootenay St, Vancouver, BC, V5K 4Y3
(604) 291-7796
Emp Here 90   *Emp Total* 120
Sales 30,789,415
SIC 5147 Meats and meat products
Pr Pr Gary Mathies
    Jim Sarangi
    David Gray
    Daniel Gordon
    Dean Noble
    Frank Geier

D-U-N-S 20-006-4157   (BR)
LITTLE MOUNTAIN RESIDENTIAL CARE & HOUSING SOCIETY
ADANAC PARK LODGE
851 Boundary Rd, Vancouver, BC, V5K 4T2

(604) 299-7567
Emp Here 110
SIC 8051 Skilled nursing care facilities

D-U-N-S 25-951-9080   (BR)
MCDONALD'S RESTAURANTS OF CANADA LIMITED
MCDONALD'S #8512
(*Suby of* McDonald's Corporation)
2599 Hastings St E, Vancouver, BC, V5K 1Z2

Emp Here 50
SIC 5812 Eating places

D-U-N-S 20-806-4407   (BR)
STARBUCKS COFFEE CANADA, INC
(*Suby of* Starbucks Corporation)
2795 Hastings St E, Vancouver, BC, V5K 1Z8
(604) 215-2424
Emp Here 32
SIC 5812 Eating places

D-U-N-S 20-810-2850   (SL)
VANCOUVER JUNIOR HOCKEY MANAGEMENT LTD
VANCOUVER GIANTS
100 Renfrew St N, Vancouver, BC, V5K 3N7
(604) 444-2687
Emp Here 20   *Sales* 6,380,400
SIC 7941 Sports clubs, managers, and promoters
Pr Pr Ronald Toigo

Vancouver, BC V5L
Greater Vancouver County

D-U-N-S 24-681-6664   (SL)
ALLSTAR HOLDINGS INCORPORATED
ALLSTAR WATERPROOFING & RESTORATION
1420 Adanac St, Vancouver, BC, V5L 2C3
(604) 255-1135
Emp Here 50   *Sales* 948,489
SIC 7349 Building maintenance services, nec

D-U-N-S 20-109-1147   (HQ)
BEATTY FLOORS LTD
BURRITT BROS. CARPET
(*Suby of* 508348 B.C. Ltd.)
1840 Pandora St, Vancouver, BC, V5L 1M7
(604) 254-9571
Emp Here 20   *Emp Total* 75
Sales 9,788,636
SIC 1752 Floor laying and floor work, nec
Pr Pr Howard Obrand
VP Sls Vance Mcarthy
Prd Mgr Ron Paulger

D-U-N-S 20-650-3117   (BR)
BLACK & MCDONALD LIMITED
1331 Clark Dr, Vancouver, BC, V5L 3K9
(604) 301-1070
Emp Here 25
SIC 1731 Electrical work

D-U-N-S 20-591-0396   (BR)
BOARD OF EDUCATION OF SCHOOL DISTRICT NO. 39 (VANCOUVER), THE
ABORIGINAL FOCUS SCHOOL
1950 Hastings St E, Vancouver, BC, V5L 1T7
(604) 713-4696
Emp Here 25
SIC 8211 Elementary and secondary schools

D-U-N-S 25-484-7361   (BR)
BOARD OF EDUCATION OF SCHOOL DISTRICT NO. 39 (VANCOUVER), THE
TEMPLETON SECONDARY SCHOOL
727 Templeton Dr, Vancouver, BC, V5L 4N8
(604) 713-8984
Emp Here 70
SIC 8211 Elementary and secondary schools

D-U-N-S 20-713-4235   (BR)
BOARD OF EDUCATION OF SCHOOL DIS-

TRICT NO. 39 (VANCOUVER), THE
HASTINGS EDUCATION CENTRE
1661 Napier St, Vancouver, BC, V5L 4X4
(604) 713-5735
Emp Here 20
SIC 8211 Elementary and secondary schools

D-U-N-S 20-153-2541   (BR)
BOARD OF EDUCATION OF SCHOOL DISTRICT NO. 39 (VANCOUVER), THE
LORD NELSON ELEMENTARY SCHOOL
2235 Kitchener St, Vancouver, BC, V5L 2W9
(604) 713-5889
Emp Here 40
SIC 8211 Elementary and secondary schools

D-U-N-S 20-803-2763   (SL)
BROADWAY REFRIGERATION AND AIR CONDITIONING CO. LTD
1490 Venables St, Vancouver, BC, V5L 4X6
(604) 255-2461
Emp Here 50   *Sales* 4,377,642
SIC 1711 Plumbing, heating, air-conditioning

D-U-N-S 20-259-8843   (BR)
CANADA POST CORPORATION
333 Woodland Dr, Vancouver, BC, V5L 0B6
(604) 258-0201
Emp Here 200
SIC 4311 U.s. postal service

D-U-N-S 20-050-7718   (SL)
CANADIAN ROCKPORT HOMES INTERNATIONAL INC
CANADIAN ROCKPORT HOMES
2317 Wall St, Vancouver, BC, V5L 1B8

Emp Here 34   *Sales* 7,033,600
SIC 1521 Single-family housing construction
Pr Pr William R. Malone
Harry Gordon
Ryan Malone
Edward M. Wilby

D-U-N-S 20-321-4325   (BR)
CATHOLIC INDEPENDENT SCHOOLS OF VANCOUVER ARCHDIOCESE, THE
ST. FRANCIS OF ASSISI SCHOOL
870 Victoria Dr, Vancouver, BC, V5L 4E7
(604) 253-7311
Emp Here 20
SIC 8661 Religious organizations

D-U-N-S 20-748-5293   (SL)
COLUMBIA CONTAINERS LTD
2319 Commissioner St, Vancouver, BC, V5L 1A4
(604) 254-9461
Emp Here 24   *Sales* 5,197,506
SIC 5084 Industrial machinery and equipment

D-U-N-S 24-162-7710   (SL)
DRAKE TOWING LTD
1553 Powell St, Vancouver, BC, V5L 5C3
(604) 251-3344
Emp Here 50   *Sales* 2,991,389
SIC 7549 Automotive services, nec

D-U-N-S 24-569-3135   (SL)
FORMAGGIO, PANE E. OPERATIONS LTD
1529 Pender St E, Vancouver, BC, V5L 1V9
(604) 215-8836
Emp Here 23   *Sales* 5,982,777
SIC 5141 Groceries, general line
Pr Mehdi Mohammed

D-U-N-S 20-312-5356   (SL)
FUSION CINE SALES & RENTALS INC
FUSION CINE
(*Suby of* 965591 Alberta Ltd)
1469 Venables St, Vancouver, BC, V5L 2G1
(604) 879-0003
Emp Here 25   *Sales* 3,811,504
SIC 5065 Electronic parts and equipment, nec

D-U-N-S 25-386-9234   (HQ)
JJ BEAN INC
(*Suby of* JJ Bean Inc)

1904 Powell St, Vancouver, BC, V5L 1J3
(604) 254-0169
Emp Here 20   *Emp Total* 100
Sales 2,991,389
SIC 5812 Eating places

D-U-N-S 20-283-1434   (BR)
LOBLAWS INC
NO FRILLS
1460 Hastings St E, Vancouver, BC, V5L 1S3
(604) 253-3349
Emp Here 60
SIC 5411 Grocery stores

D-U-N-S 25-664-1812   (BR)
MCDONALD'S RESTAURANTS OF CANADA LIMITED
MCDONALD'S
(*Suby of* McDonald's Corporation)
1965 Powell St, Vancouver, BC, V5L 1J2
(604) 254-7504
Emp Here 30
SIC 5812 Eating places

D-U-N-S 20-297-4528   (BR)
SHIGS ENTERPRISES LTD
SHIG'S ENTERPRISES LIMITED
912 Clark Dr, Vancouver, BC, V5L 3J8
(604) 251-3711
Emp Here 65
SIC 5812 Eating places

D-U-N-S 24-358-2223   (SL)
SILVERBIRCH NO. 41 OPERATIONS LIMITED PARTNERSHIP
CANNERY SEAFOOD RESTAURANT
2205 Commissioner St, Vancouver, BC, V5L 1A4

Emp Here 80   *Sales* 2,407,703
SIC 5812 Eating places

D-U-N-S 20-773-0784   (SL)
SMIT HARBOUR TOWAGE WESTMINSTER INC
2285 Commissioner St, Vancouver, BC, V5L 1A8
(604) 251-0230
Emp Here 25   *Sales* 2,921,220
SIC 4492 Towing and tugboat service

D-U-N-S 24-887-5452   (SL)
ULTRA-TECH CLEANING SYSTEMS LTD
1420 Adanac St Suite 201, Vancouver, BC, V5L 2C3
(604) 253-4698
Emp Here 115   *Sales* 4,334,713
SIC 7349 Building maintenance services, nec

D-U-N-S 25-138-6827   (BR)
VALUE VILLAGE STORES, INC
(*Suby of* Savers, Inc.)
1820 Hastings St E, Vancouver, BC, V5L 1T2
(604) 254-4282
Emp Here 38
SIC 5399 Miscellaneous general merchandise

D-U-N-S 20-992-0078   (BR)
VALUE VILLAGE STORES, INC
(*Suby of* Savers, Inc.)
1820 Venables St, Vancouver, BC, V5L 2H7
(604) 252-9509
Emp Here 25
SIC 5399 Miscellaneous general merchandise

D-U-N-S 24-167-1866   (SL)
VANCOUVER ABORIGINAL FRIENDSHIP CENTRE SOCIETY
NATIVE FRIENDSHIP CENTRE
1607 Hastings St E, Vancouver, BC, V5L 1S7
(604) 251-4844
Emp Here 50   *Sales* 1,969,939
SIC 8322 Individual and family services

D-U-N-S 20-116-9315   (HQ)
VANCOUVER QUILTING MANUFACTURING LTD
188 Victoria Dr, Vancouver, BC, V5L 4C3

(604) 253-7744
Emp Here 40   *Emp Total* 38
Sales 9,630,812
SIC 5131 Piece goods and notions
Pr Pr Larry Garaway
Darlene Ames

D-U-N-S 25-533-8246   (HQ)
VERSACOLD GROUP LIMITED PARTNERSHIP
2115 Commissioner St Suite 1, Vancouver, BC, V5L 1A6
(604) 255-4656
Emp Here 100   *Emp Total* 1
Sales 503,465,081
SIC 4222 Refrigerated warehousing and storage
H. Brent Sudgen
CEO Joel E. Smith
VP Opers Robert Lewarne
Sec Bruce Mckay
Dir Peter R.B. Armstrong
Dir Samuel Gudewill
Dir Joseph Houssian
Dir Thomas J. Longworth
Dir Eric L. Schwitzer

Vancouver, BC V5M
Greater Vancouver County

D-U-N-S 24-037-3436   (BR)
ACCEO SOLUTIONS INC
BELL CANADA
2985 Virtual Way Suite 260, Vancouver, BC, V5M 4X7

Emp Here 20
SIC 5045 Computers, peripherals, and software

D-U-N-S 24-509-2486   (BR)
AMER SPORTS CANADA INC
ARC'TERYX EQUIPMENT DIV.
2770 Bentall St, Vancouver, BC, V5M 4H4
(604) 960-3001
Emp Here 100
SIC 3949 Sporting and athletic goods, nec

D-U-N-S 20-646-0656   (HQ)
ART INSTITUTE OF VANCOUVER INC, THE
ART INSTITUTE OF VANCOUVER, THE
2665 Renfrew St, Vancouver, BC, V5M 0A7
(604) 683-9200
Emp Here 100   *Emp Total* 20,800
Sales 20,793,800
SIC 8221 Colleges and universities
Pr Brian Parker

D-U-N-S 24-578-7171   (BR)
ASSOCIATION OF NEIGHBOURHOOD HOUSES OF BRITISH COLUMBIA
FROG HOLLOW NEIGHBOURHOOD HOUSE
2131 Renfrew St, Vancouver, BC, V5M 4M5
(604) 251-1225
Emp Here 30
SIC 8322 Individual and family services

D-U-N-S 24-918-7873   (BR)
BANK OF NOVA SCOTIA, THE
SCOTIABANK
2800 1st Ave E Unit 244, Vancouver, BC, V5M 4P1
(604) 668-2075
Emp Here 21
SIC 6021 National commercial banks

D-U-N-S 20-053-7939   (BR)
BANK OF MONTREAL
BMO
3290 Grandview Hwy, Vancouver, BC, V5M 2G2
(604) 665-2514
Emp Here 20
SIC 6021 National commercial banks

D-U-N-S 24-227-9987   (BR)
BELL MOBILITE INC
BELL MOBILITY INC
2925 Virtual Way Suite 400, Vancouver, BC,
V5M 4X5
(604) 678-4160
Emp Here 500
SIC 4899 Communication services, nec

D-U-N-S 20-591-0503   (BR)
**BOARD OF EDUCATION OF SCHOOL DIS-
TRICT NO. 39 (VANCOUVER), THE**
CHIEF MAQUINNA ELEMENTARY
2684 2nd Ave E, Vancouver, BC, V5M 1C9
(604) 713-4705
Emp Here 25
SIC 8211 Elementary and secondary schools

D-U-N-S 25-453-6584   (BR)
**BOARD OF EDUCATION OF SCHOOL DIS-
TRICT NO. 39 (VANCOUVER), THE**
THUNDERBIRD ELEMENTARY SCHOOL
2325 Cassiar St Suite 39, Vancouver, BC,
V5M 3X3
(604) 713-4611
Emp Here 60
SIC 8211 Elementary and secondary schools

D-U-N-S 25-485-7147   (BR)
**BOARD OF EDUCATION OF SCHOOL DIS-
TRICT NO. 39 (VANCOUVER), THE**
*VANCOUVER TECHNICAL SECONDARY
SCHOOL*
2600 Broadway E, Vancouver, BC, V5M 1Y5
(604) 713-8215
Emp Here 150
SIC 8211 Elementary and secondary schools

D-U-N-S 25-023-6452   (BR)
**BOARD OF EDUCATION OF SCHOOL DIS-
TRICT NO. 39 (VANCOUVER), THE**
NOOTKA ELEMENTARY SCHOOL
3375 Nootka St, Vancouver, BC, V5M 3N2
(604) 713-4767
Emp Here 30
SIC 8211 Elementary and secondary schools

D-U-N-S 25-415-0287   (BR)
**BOARD OF EDUCATION OF SCHOOL DIS-
TRICT NO. 39 (VANCOUVER), THE**
*LORD BEACONSFIELD ELEMENTARY
SCHOOL*
3663 Penticton St, Vancouver, BC, V5M 3C9
(604) 713-4605
Emp Here 20
SIC 8211 Elementary and secondary schools

D-U-N-S 20-591-0545   (BR)
**BOARD OF EDUCATION OF SCHOOL DIS-
TRICT NO. 39 (VANCOUVER), THE**
RENFREW ELEMENTARY SCHOOL
3315 22nd Ave E, Vancouver, BC, V5M 2Z2
(604) 713-4851
Emp Here 50
SIC 8211 Elementary and secondary schools

D-U-N-S 25-231-7623   (BR)
BRICK WAREHOUSE LP, THE
BRICK, THE
2999 Grandview Hwy, Vancouver, BC, V5M
2E4
(604) 433-2000
Emp Here 25
SIC 5712 Furniture stores

D-U-N-S 24-270-3556   (BR)
**BRITISH COLUMBIA LOTTERY CORPORA-
TION**
BCLC
2940 Virtual Way, Vancouver, BC, V5M 0A6
(604) 215-0649
Emp Here 20
SIC 7999 Amusement and recreation, nec

D-U-N-S 25-937-2357   (HQ)
CWA ENGINEERS INC
2925 Virtual Way Suite 380, Vancouver, BC,
V5M 4X5

(604) 526-2275
Emp Here 44   *Emp Total* 400
Sales 917,966,185
SIC 8711 Engineering services
Pr Pr Raymond Chu

D-U-N-S 20-125-7727   (BR)
CANADIAN CANCER SOCIETY
3689 1st Ave E Suite 230, Vancouver, BC,
V5M 1C2

Emp Here 30
SIC 8399 Social services, nec

D-U-N-S 24-824-5300   (HQ)
CHEMETICS INC
(*Suby of* Jacobs Engineering Group Inc.)
2930 Virtual Way Suite 200, Vancouver, BC,
V5M 0A5
(604) 734-1200
Emp Here 170   *Emp Total* 64,000
Sales 31,008,298
SIC 8711 Engineering services
Sr VP Andrew Berryman
VP VP Andrew Barr
  Nicole Von Keutz

D-U-N-S 20-644-1342   (BR)
**COMPAGNIE DE TELEPHONE BELL DU
CANADA OU BELL CANADA, LA**
BELL MOBILITY
2980 Virtual Way, Vancouver, BC, V5M 4X3
(604) 678-3101
Emp Here 400
SIC 5963 Direct selling establishments

D-U-N-S 25-311-1983   (BR)
CRAWFORD & COMPANY (CANADA) INC
CRAWFORD CANADA ISRN
(*Suby of* Crawford & Company)
2985 Virtual Way Suite 280, Vancouver, BC,
V5M 4X7
(604) 739-3816
Emp Here 20
SIC 6411 Insurance agents, brokers, and ser-
vice

D-U-N-S 20-049-2291   (SL)
DEELEY, TREV MOTORCYCLES (1991) LTD
(*Suby of* Fred Deeley Limited)
1875 Boundary Rd, Vancouver, BC, V5M 3Y7
(604) 291-1875
Emp Here 50   *Sales* 12,057,600
SIC 5571 Motorcycle dealers
Pr Pr Malcolm Hunter
Dir Donald James

D-U-N-S 24-766-8981   (SL)
DOMINION COMPANY INC, THE
2985 Virtual Way Suite 130, Vancouver, BC,
V5M 4X7

Emp Here 60   *Sales* 39,187,200
SIC 1542 Nonresidential construction, nec
Pr Pr Dennis Burnham
  Philip A. George
VP Fin Vance Hackett

D-U-N-S 25-107-2187   (BR)
G4S CASH SOLUTIONS (CANADA) LTD
GROUP FOR SUCURICOR
2743 Skeena St, Vancouver, BC, V5M 4T1
(604) 787-0277
Emp Here 250
SIC 7381 Detective and armored car services

D-U-N-S 25-635-0851   (BR)
G4S CASH SOLUTIONS (CANADA) LTD
GROUP 4 SECURICOR
2743 Skeena St Suite 200, Vancouver, BC,
V5M 4T1
(604) 665-4651
Emp Here 300
SIC 7381 Detective and armored car services

D-U-N-S 20-111-7652   (SL)
GIZELLA PASTRY ULC
3436 Lougheed Hwy, Vancouver, BC, V5M
2A4

(604) 253-5220
Emp Here 70   *Sales* 4,711,645
SIC 2051 Bread, cake, and related products

D-U-N-S 24-750-8377   (BR)
INTACT INSURANCE COMPANY
ING INSURANCE
2955 Virtual Way Suite 400, Vancouver, BC,
V5M 4X6
(604) 683-5566
Emp Here 130
SIC 6411 Insurance agents, brokers, and ser-
vice

D-U-N-S 25-360-4391   (BR)
INTERWEST RESTAURANTS INC
WENDY'S RESTAURANTS OF CANADA
(*Suby of* Interwest Restaurants Inc)
3698 Grandview Hwy, Vancouver, BC, V5M
2G9
(604) 433-3431
Emp Here 40
SIC 5812 Eating places

D-U-N-S 24-384-2742   (BR)
JOHNSON CONTROLS L.P.
3680 2nd Ave E, Vancouver, BC, V5M 0A4
(604) 707-5200
Emp Here 50
SIC 1731 Electrical work

D-U-N-S 20-112-7719   (BR)
**JOHNSON CONTROLS NOVA SCOTIA
U.L.C.**
(*Suby of* Johnson Controls, Inc.)
3061 Grandview Hwy, Vancouver, BC, V5M
2E4

Emp Here 30
SIC 3822 Environmental controls

D-U-N-S 24-101-1316   (HQ)
KLOHN CRIPPEN BERGER LTD
(*Suby of* Klohn Crippen Berger Holdings Ltd)
2955 Virtual Way Suite 500, Vancouver, BC,
V5M 4X6
(604) 669-3800
Emp Here 214   *Emp Total* 300
Sales 69,906,456
SIC 8711 Engineering services
Ch Bd Bryan Watts
Pr Len Murray
VP Alex Sy
VP Shane Johnson
VP Howard Plewes
VP Brian Rogers
VP Chris Dickinson
VP Fin Stuart Forbes

D-U-N-S 25-270-1388   (BR)
LOBLAWS INC
REAL CANADIAN SUPERSTORE
3185 Grandview Hwy, Vancouver, BC, V5M
2E9
(604) 436-6407
Emp Here 460
SIC 5141 Groceries, general line

D-U-N-S 24-940-4377   (BR)
LOBLAWS INC
3189 Grandview Hwy, Vancouver, BC, V5M
2E9
(604) 439-5400
Emp Here 65
SIC 6712 Bank holding companies

D-U-N-S 20-515-0654   (BR)
MERCEDES-BENZ CANADA INC
3550 Lougheed Hwy, Vancouver, BC, V5M
2A3
(604) 676-3778
Emp Here 40
SIC 5511 New and used car dealers

D-U-N-S 24-389-2705   (BR)
MORNEAU SHEPELL INC
MORNEAU SOBECO BUSINESS DIVISION
(*Suby of* Morneau Shepell Inc)
2925 Virtual Way Suite 10, Vancouver, BC,

V5M 4X5
(604) 688-9839
Emp Here 87
SIC 6411 Insurance agents, brokers, and service

D-U-N-S 24-798-4131   (HQ)
NINTENDO OF CANADA LTD
2925 Virtual Way Suite 150, Vancouver, BC,
V5M 4X5
(604) 279-1600
Emp Here 96   *Emp Total* 5,166
Sales 8,755,284
SIC 5092 Toys and hobby goods and supplies
Dir Ronald Bertram

D-U-N-S 24-881-6647   (BR)
NUCELL-COMM INC
TAC MOBILITY
2748 Rupert St, Vancouver, BC, V5M 3T7
(604) 291-6636
Emp Here 20
SIC 4812 Radiotelephone communication

D-U-N-S 24-682-0252   (BR)
OTIS CANADA, INC
(*Suby of* United Technologies Corporation)
2788 Rupert St, Vancouver, BC, V5M 3T7
(604) 412-3400
Emp Here 100
SIC 3534 Elevators and moving stairways

D-U-N-S 24-268-0275   (SL)
PARAGON TESTING ENTERPRISES INC
2925 Virtual Way Suite 110, Vancouver, BC,
V5M 4X5
(778) 327-6854
Emp Here 60   *Sales* 3,283,232
SIC 8299 Schools and educational services,
nec

D-U-N-S 20-562-7107   (BR)
RBC LIFE INSURANCE COMPANY
(*Suby of* Royal Bank Of Canada)
2985 Virtual Way Suite 300, Vancouver, BC,
V5M 4X7
(604) 718-4300
Emp Here 50
SIC 6311 Life insurance

D-U-N-S 25-912-2117   (SL)
**RENFREW PARK COMMUNITY ASSOCIA-
TION**
RENFREW PARK COMMUNITY CENTRE
2929 22nd Ave E, Vancouver, BC, V5M 2Y3
(604) 257-8388
Emp Here 80   *Sales* 3,137,310
SIC 8322 Individual and family services

D-U-N-S 25-716-0556   (BR)
ROYAL BANK OF CANADA
ROYAL BANK FINANCIAL GROUP
(*Suby of* Royal Bank Of Canada)
1716 Renfrew St, Vancouver, BC, V5M 3H8
(604) 665-8040
Emp Here 20
SIC 6021 National commercial banks

D-U-N-S 25-129-0995   (SL)
THREE LINKS HOUSING SOCIETY
*ODD FELLOWS LOW RENTAL HOUSING
SOCIETY*
2934 22nd Ave E, Vancouver, BC, V5M 2Y4
(778) 452-6501
Emp Here 50   *Sales* 2,685,378
SIC 8052 Intermediate care facilities

D-U-N-S 20-116-8093   (HQ)
UNIVERSAL SUPPLY CO. INC
(*Suby of* Universal Supply Co. Inc)
2835 12th Ave E, Vancouver, BC, V5M 4P9
(604) 253-4000
Emp Here 40   *Emp Total* 75
Sales 17,715,785
SIC 5074 Plumbing and heating equipment
and supplies (hydronics)
Pr Pr Bernard Reed
  Jeff Reed

David Reed

D-U-N-S 24-599-2016   (BR)
WAL-MART CANADA CORP
WALMART
3585 Grandview Hwy, Vancouver, BC, V5M 2G7
(604) 435-6905
Emp Here 50
SIC 5311 Department stores

Vancouver, BC V5N
Greater Vancouver County

D-U-N-S 25-615-8403   (BR)
541907 ONTARIO LIMITED
DAYS INN
2075 Kingsway, Vancouver, BC, V5N 2T2
(604) 876-5531
Emp Here 25
SIC 7011 Hotels and motels

D-U-N-S 20-790-5352   (SL)
551382 BC LTD
SUPERVALUE
1645 1st Ave E Suite 98, Vancouver, BC, V5N 1A8
(604) 254-1214
Emp Here 40   *Sales* 6,594,250
SIC 5411 Grocery stores
Pr Darcey Howser

D-U-N-S 25-663-4205   (BR)
ASSOCIATION OF NEIGHBOURHOOD HOUSES OF BRITISH COLUMBIA
CEDAR COTTAGE NEIGHBOURHOOD HOUSE
4065 Victoria Dr, Vancouver, BC, V5N 4M9
(604) 874-4231
Emp Here 70
SIC 8399 Social services, nec

D-U-N-S 20-026-9475   (BR)
BOARD OF EDUCATION OF SCHOOL DISTRICT NO. 39 (VANCOUVER), THE
TYEE ELEMENTARY SCHOOL
3525 Dumfries St, Vancouver, BC, V5N 3S5
(604) 713-4723
Emp Here 20
SIC 8211 Elementary and secondary schools

D-U-N-S 20-911-3724   (BR)
BOARD OF EDUCATION OF SCHOOL DISTRICT NO. 39 (VANCOUVER), THE
EAST SIDE ALTERNATIVE SCHOOL
3433 Commercial St, Vancouver, BC, V5N 4E8
(604) 713-5858
Emp Here 20
SIC 8211 Elementary and secondary schools

D-U-N-S 20-024-4569   (BR)
BOARD OF EDUCATION OF SCHOOL DISTRICT NO. 39 (VANCOUVER), THE
LORD SELKIRK ELEMENTARY SCHOOL
1750 22nd Ave E, Vancouver, BC, V5N 2P7
(604) 713-4650
Emp Here 65
SIC 8211 Elementary and secondary schools

D-U-N-S 20-027-0639   (BR)
BOARD OF EDUCATION OF SCHOOL DISTRICT NO. 39 (VANCOUVER), THE
LORD SELKIRK ANNEX
4444 Dumfries St, Vancouver, BC, V5N 3T2
(604) 713-4735
Emp Here 20
SIC 8211 Elementary and secondary schools

D-U-N-S 20-026-9467   (BR)
BOARD OF EDUCATION OF SCHOOL DISTRICT NO. 39 (VANCOUVER), THE
GRANDVIEW ELEMENTARY SCHOOL
2055 Woodland Dr, Vancouver, BC, V5N 3N9
(604) 713-4663
Emp Here 35

SIC 8211 Elementary and secondary schools

D-U-N-S 20-591-0289   (BR)
BOARD OF EDUCATION OF SCHOOL DISTRICT NO. 39 (VANCOUVER), THE
QUEEN ALEXANDRA ELEMENTARY SCHOOL
1300 Broadway E Suite 39, Vancouver, BC, V5N 1V6
(604) 713-4599
Emp Here 25
SIC 8211 Elementary and secondary schools

D-U-N-S 20-609-9504   (BR)
CANADA POST CORPORATION
1755 Broadway E, Vancouver, BC, V5N 1W2
(604) 872-8451
Emp Here 50
SIC 4311 U.s. postal service

D-U-N-S 20-587-1861   (BR)
CANADIAN IMPERIAL BANK OF COMMERCE
CIBC
1427 Kingsway, Vancouver, BC, V5N 2R6
(604) 665-1039
Emp Here 20
SIC 6021 National commercial banks

D-U-N-S 24-887-5668   (HQ)
FAMILY SERVICES OF GREATER VANCOUVER
(*Suby of* Family Services of Greater Vancouver)
1638 Broadway E Suite 201, Vancouver, BC, V5N 1W1
(604) 731-4951
Emp Here 30   *Emp Total* 580
Sales 29,400,665
SIC 8322 Individual and family services
Ex Dir Terri Nicholas
Ch Bd Anthony Ostler

D-U-N-S 24-154-4345   (SL)
GRANDVIEW COMMUNITY CENTER ASSOCIATION
THE TROUT LAKE COMMUNITY CENTRE
3350 Victoria Dr, Vancouver, BC, V5N 4M4

Emp Here 50   *Sales* 2,699,546
SIC 7999 Amusement and recreation, nec

D-U-N-S 20-870-7609   (BR)
HUDSON'S BAY COMPANY
FIELDS STORES
1409 Kingsway, Vancouver, BC, V5N 2R6
(604) 874-4811
Emp Here 25
SIC 5311 Department stores

D-U-N-S 20-084-8815   (BR)
JJ BEAN INC
2206 Commercial Dr, Vancouver, BC, V5N 4B5
(604) 254-3723
Emp Here 25
SIC 5149 Groceries and related products, nec

D-U-N-S 20-302-4380   (BR)
LABOUR READY TEMPORARY SERVICES LTD
1688 Broadway E, Vancouver, BC, V5N 1W1
(604) 874-5567
Emp Here 50
SIC 7361 Employment agencies

D-U-N-S 25-318-1911   (BR)
MCDONALD'S RESTAURANTS OF CANADA LIMITED
MCDONALD'S 8067
(*Suby of* McDonald's Corporation)
2021 Kingsway, Vancouver, BC, V5N 2T2
(604) 718-1060
Emp Here 80
SIC 5812 Eating places

D-U-N-S 24-026-7026   (BR)
MULTI LINGUAL ORIENTATION SERVICE

FOR IMMIGRANT COMMUNITIES
2555 Commercial Dr Suite 312, Vancouver, BC, V5N 4C1
(604) 708-3905
Emp Here 100
SIC 8322 Individual and family services

D-U-N-S 25-664-2547   (BR)
REVERA LONG TERM CARE INC
LAKEVIEW CARE CENTRE
3490 Porter St, Vancouver, BC, V5N 5W4
(604) 874-2803
Emp Here 100
SIC 8051 Skilled nursing care facilities

D-U-N-S 25-662-0139   (BR)
ROYAL BANK OF CANADA
RBC
(*Suby of* Royal Bank Of Canada)
1715 Commercial Dr, Vancouver, BC, V5N 4A4
(604) 665-8050
Emp Here 30
SIC 6021 National commercial banks

D-U-N-S 25-271-7285   (BR)
SOBEYS WEST INC
1780 Broadway E, Vancouver, BC, V5N 1W3
(604) 873-0225
Emp Here 110
SIC 5411 Grocery stores

D-U-N-S 20-806-4936   (BR)
STARBUCKS COFFEE CANADA, INC
(*Suby of* Starbucks Corporation)
2517 Commercial Dr, Vancouver, BC, V5N 4C1
(604) 875-6065
Emp Here 20
SIC 5812 Eating places

D-U-N-S 20-506-1109   (BR)
STARBUCKS COFFEE CANADA, INC
(*Suby of* Starbucks Corporation)
1752 Commercial Dr, Vancouver, BC, V5N 4A3
(604) 251-5397
Emp Here 20
SIC 5812 Eating places

D-U-N-S 24-355-3265   (BR)
STRATFORD HALL SCHOOL SOCIETY
STRATFORD HALL
(*Suby of* Stratford Hall School Society)
3000 Commercial Dr, Vancouver, BC, V5N 4E2
(604) 436-0608
Emp Here 50
SIC 8211 Elementary and secondary schools

D-U-N-S 20-074-7405   (HQ)
STRATFORD HALL SCHOOL SOCIETY
(*Suby of* Stratford Hall School Society)
3000 Commercial Dr, Vancouver, BC, V5N 4E2
(604) 436-0608
Emp Here 30   *Emp Total* 55
Sales 3,648,035
SIC 8211 Elementary and secondary schools

D-U-N-S 24-078-0564   (BR)
VANCOUVER COASTAL HEALTH AUTHORITY
GRANDVIEW WOODLANDS
2250 Commercial Dr Unit 300, Vancouver, BC, V5N 5P9

Emp Here 30
SIC 8093 Specialty outpatient clinics, nec

D-U-N-S 24-887-8035   (SL)
WORLD JOURNAL LTD
2288 Clark Dr, Vancouver, BC, V5N 3G8
(604) 876-1338
Emp Here 50   *Sales* 4,158,760
SIC 2711 Newspapers

Vancouver, BC V5P
Greater Vancouver County

D-U-N-S 25-662-3893   (SL)
ASSOCIATION OF NEIGHBOURHOOD HOUSES OF BRITISH COLUMBIA
SOUTH VANCOUVER NEIGHBOURHOOD HOUSE
6470 Victoria Dr, Vancouver, BC, V5P 3X7
(604) 324-6212
Emp Here 65   *Sales* 2,553,625
SIC 8322 Individual and family services

D-U-N-S 24-897-2887   (SL)
BEST COLOR PRESS LTD
1728 E Kent Ave South, Vancouver, BC, V5P 2S7
(604) 327-7382
Emp Here 56   *Sales* 2,772,507
SIC 2759 Commercial printing, nec

D-U-N-S 20-591-0297   (BR)
BOARD OF EDUCATION OF SCHOOL DISTRICT NO. 39 (VANCOUVER), THE
SIR SANDFORD FLEMING ELEMENTARY SCHOOL
1401 49th Ave E, Vancouver, BC, V5P 1S2
(604) 713-4793
Emp Here 25
SIC 8211 Elementary and secondary schools

D-U-N-S 25-266-8777   (BR)
BOARD OF EDUCATION OF SCHOOL DISTRICT NO. 39 (VANCOUVER), THE
DAVID THOMPSON SECONDARY SCHOOL
1755 55th Ave E, Vancouver, BC, V5P 1Z7
(604) 713-8278
Emp Here 135
SIC 8211 Elementary and secondary schools

D-U-N-S 25-676-7617   (BR)
BOARD OF EDUCATION OF SCHOOL DISTRICT NO. 39 (VANCOUVER), THE
DAVID OPPENHEIMER ELEMENTARY SCHOOL
2421 Scarboro Ave, Vancouver, BC, V5P 2L5
(604) 713-4570
Emp Here 30
SIC 8211 Elementary and secondary schools

D-U-N-S 20-591-0321   (BR)
BOARD OF EDUCATION OF SCHOOL DISTRICT NO. 39 (VANCOUVER), THE
TECUMSEH ELEMENTARY SCHOOL
1551 37th Ave E, Vancouver, BC, V5P 1E4
(604) 713-4890
Emp Here 25
SIC 8211 Elementary and secondary schools

D-U-N-S 20-591-0784   (BR)
BOARD OF EDUCATION OF SCHOOL DISTRICT NO. 39 (VANCOUVER), THE
SIR JAMES DOUGLAS ELEMENTARY SCHOOL
7550 Victoria Dr, Vancouver, BC, V5P 3Z7
(604) 713-4817
Emp Here 50
SIC 8211 Elementary and secondary schools

D-U-N-S 20-713-4151   (BR)
BOARD OF EDUCATION OF SCHOOL DISTRICT NO. 39 (VANCOUVER), THE
TACUMSEH ELEMENTARY SCHOOL
1850 41st Ave E, Vancouver, BC, V5P 1K9
(604) 713-5390
Emp Here 50
SIC 8211 Elementary and secondary schools

D-U-N-S 20-800-2816   (HQ)
FINNISH CANADIAN REST HOME ASSOCIATION
FINNISH HOME
(*Suby of* Finnish Canadian Rest Home Association)
2288 Harrison Dr, Vancouver, BC, V5P 2P6

(604) 325-8241
Emp Here 60   *Emp Total* 120
Sales 4,377,642
SIC 8361 Residential care

D-U-N-S 20-911-5757   (SL)
ICELANDIC CARE HOME HOFN SOCIETY, THE
ICELANDIC RESIDENCE
2020 Harrison Dr, Vancouver, BC, V5P 0A1
(604) 321-3812
Emp Here 60   *Sales* 2,845,467
SIC 8051 Skilled nursing care facilities

D-U-N-S 24-504-6180   (BR)
PROVIDENCE HEALTH CARE SOCIETY
HOLY FAMILY HOSPITAL
7801 Argyle St, Vancouver, BC, V5P 3L6
(604) 321-2661
Emp Here 400
SIC 8062 General medical and surgical hospitals

D-U-N-S 25-662-0402   (BR)
VALUE VILLAGE STORES, INC
SAVERS
(*Suby of* Savers, Inc.)
6415 Victoria Dr, Vancouver, BC, V5P 3X5
(604) 327-4434
Emp Here 40
SIC 5399 Miscellaneous general merchandise

Vancouver, BC V5R
Greater Vancouver County

D-U-N-S 20-591-0537   (BR)
BOARD OF EDUCATION OF SCHOOL DISTRICT NO. 39 (VANCOUVER), THE
WINDMERE SECONDARY SCHOOL
3155 27th Ave E, Vancouver, BC, V5R 1P3
(604) 713-8180
Emp Here 25
SIC 8211 Elementary and secondary schools

D-U-N-S 20-153-2558   (BR)
BOARD OF EDUCATION OF SCHOOL DISTRICT NO. 39 (VANCOUVER), THE
DR GEORGE M WEIR ELEMENTARY SCHOOL
2900 44th Ave E, Vancouver, BC, V5R 3A8
(604) 713-4771
Emp Here 35
SIC 8211 Elementary and secondary schools

D-U-N-S 20-153-2566   (BR)
BOARD OF EDUCATION OF SCHOOL DISTRICT NO. 39 (VANCOUVER), THE
SIR WILFRED GRENFELL ELEMENTARY SCHOOL
3323 Wellington Ave, Vancouver, BC, V5R 4Y3
(604) 713-4844
Emp Here 70
SIC 8211 Elementary and secondary schools

D-U-N-S 20-026-9509   (BR)
BOARD OF EDUCATION OF SCHOOL DISTRICT NO. 39 (VANCOUVER), THE
GRAHAM D BRUCE ELEMENTARY SCHOOL
3633 Tanner St, Vancouver, BC, V5R 5P7
(604) 713-4778
Emp Here 40
SIC 8211 Elementary and secondary schools

D-U-N-S 20-591-0651   (BR)
BOARD OF EDUCATION OF SCHOOL DISTRICT NO. 39 (VANCOUVER), THE
JOHN NORQUAY ELEMENTARY SCHOOL
4710 Slocan St, Vancouver, BC, V5R 2A1
(604) 713-4666
Emp Here 50
SIC 8211 Elementary and secondary schools

D-U-N-S 20-008-1631   (BR)
BOARD OF EDUCATION OF SCHOOL DISTRICT NO. 39 (VANCOUVER), THE

CARLETON SIR GUY ELEMENTARY SCHOOL
3250 Kingsway, Vancouver, BC, V5R 5K5
(604) 713-4810
Emp Here 60
SIC 8211 Elementary and secondary schools

D-U-N-S 20-713-4268   (BR)
BOARD OF EDUCATION OF SCHOOL DISTRICT NO. 39 (VANCOUVER), THE
COLLINGWOOD NEIGHBOURHOOD SCHOOL
3417 Euclid Ave, Vancouver, BC, V5R 6H2
(604) 713-5340
Emp Here 50
SIC 8211 Elementary and secondary schools

D-U-N-S 20-802-0255   (BR)
CANADIAN NATIONAL INSTITUTE FOR THE BLIND, THE
CNIB
(*Suby of* Canadian National Institute For The Blind, The)
5055 Joyce St Suite 100, Vancouver, BC, V5R 6B2
(604) 431-2121
Emp Here 40
SIC 8322 Individual and family services

D-U-N-S 20-114-3724   (SL)
ELDORADO KINGSWAY HOTEL LTD
ELDORADO MOTOR HOTEL
2330 Kingsway, Vancouver, BC, V5R 5G9

Emp Here 50   *Sales* 2,188,821
SIC 7011 Hotels and motels

D-U-N-S 20-913-9000   (BR)
HSBC BANK CANADA
3366 Kingsway, Vancouver, BC, V5R 5L2
(604) 430-3261
Emp Here 25
SIC 6082 Foreign trade and international banks

D-U-N-S 20-113-6611   (SL)
MR. SPORT HOTEL HOLDINGS LTD
RAMADA HOTEL & SUITES
3484 Kingsway Suite 101, Vancouver, BC, V5R 5L6
(604) 433-8255
Emp Here 100   *Sales* 4,377,642
SIC 7011 Hotels and motels

D-U-N-S 25-314-8555   (BR)
ROTHESAY HOLDINGS LTD
CHURCH'S CHICKEN
(*Suby of* Rothesay Holdings Ltd)
2504 Kingsway, Vancouver, BC, V5R 5G9
(604) 438-5518
Emp Here 25
SIC 5812 Eating places

D-U-N-S 25-271-7186   (BR)
SOBEYS WEST INC
COLLINGWOOD SAFEWAY
3410 Kingsway, Vancouver, BC, V5R 5L4
(604) 439-0090
Emp Here 50
SIC 5411 Grocery stores

D-U-N-S 20-587-0350   (BR)
VANCOUVER CITY SAVINGS CREDIT UNION
VANCITY CREDIT UNION
3305 Kingsway, Vancouver, BC, V5R 5K6
(604) 877-7134
Emp Here 20
SIC 6062 State credit unions

D-U-N-S 24-345-0405   (BR)
VANCOUVER COASTAL HEALTH AUTHORITY
EVERGREEN COMMUNITY HEALTH CENTRE
3425 Crowley Dr, Vancouver, BC, V5R 6G3
(604) 872-2511
Emp Here 150

SIC 8322 Individual and family services

Vancouver, BC V5S
Greater Vancouver County

D-U-N-S 24-974-7668   (BR)
BOARD OF EDUCATION OF SCHOOL DISTRICT NO. 39 (VANCOUVER), THE
DR H N MACCORKINDALE ELEMENTARY SCHOOL
6100 Battison St, Vancouver, BC, V5S 3M8
(604) 713-4775
Emp Here 37
SIC 8211 Elementary and secondary schools

D-U-N-S 20-591-0743   (BR)
BOARD OF EDUCATION OF SCHOOL DISTRICT NO. 39 (VANCOUVER), THE
CHAMPLAIN HEIGHTS COMMUNITY SCHOOL
6955 Frontenac St, Vancouver, BC, V5S 3T4
(604) 713-4760
Emp Here 25
SIC 8211 Elementary and secondary schools

D-U-N-S 20-591-0552   (BR)
BOARD OF EDUCATION OF SCHOOL DISTRICT NO. 39 (VANCOUVER), THE
CAPTAIN JAMES COOK ELEMENTARY SCHOOL
3340 54th Ave E, Vancouver, BC, V5S 1Z3
(604) 713-4828
Emp Here 40
SIC 8211 Elementary and secondary schools

D-U-N-S 20-591-0735   (BR)
BOARD OF EDUCATION OF SCHOOL DISTRICT NO. 39 (VANCOUVER), THE
SIR CHARLES KINGSFORD SMITH
6901 Elliott St, Vancouver, BC, V5S 2N1
(604) 713-4746
Emp Here 25
SIC 8211 Elementary and secondary schools

D-U-N-S 20-265-3911   (BR)
BOARD OF EDUCATION OF SCHOOL DISTRICT NO. 39 (VANCOUVER), THE
KILLARNEY SECONDARY
6454 Killarney St, Vancouver, BC, V5S 2X7
(604) 713-8950
Emp Here 170
SIC 8211 Elementary and secondary schools

D-U-N-S 20-140-0962   (BR)
BOARD OF EDUCATION OF SCHOOL DISTRICT NO. 39 (VANCOUVER), THE
WAVERLEY ELEMENTARY SCHOOL
6111 Elliott St, Vancouver, BC, V5S 2M1
(604) 713-4752
Emp Here 40
SIC 8211 Elementary and secondary schools

D-U-N-S 20-034-9269   (BR)
CONSEIL SCOLAIRE FRANCOPHONE DE LA COLOMBIE BRITANNIQUE
ECOLE ANNE HEBERT ELEMENTARY SCHOOL
7051 Killarney St, Vancouver, BC, V5S 2Y5
(604) 437-4849
Emp Here 31
SIC 8211 Elementary and secondary schools

D-U-N-S 25-116-9207   (BR)
GOVERNING COUNCIL OF THE SALVATION ARMY IN CANADA, THE
SALVATION ARMY SOUTHVIEW HEIGHTS AND TERRACE
7252 Kerr St, Vancouver, BC, V5S 3V2
(604) 438-3367
Emp Here 50
SIC 8361 Residential care

D-U-N-S 20-991-8296   (BR)
KIN'S FARM LTD
KIN'S FARM MARKET

7060 Kerr St, Vancouver, BC, V5S 4W2
(604) 451-1329
Emp Here 25
SIC 5411 Grocery stores

D-U-N-S 25-754-8792   (SL)
M. KOPERNIK (NICOLAUS COPERNICUS) FOUNDATION
THE KOPERNIK LODGE
3150 Rosemont Dr, Vancouver, BC, V5S 2C9
(604) 438-2474
Emp Here 95   *Sales* 3,502,114
SIC 8361 Residential care

D-U-N-S 20-806-4530   (BR)
STARBUCKS COFFEE CANADA, INC
(*Suby of* Starbucks Corporation)
7010 Kerr St, Vancouver, BC, V5S 4W2
(604) 439-9555
Emp Here 25
SIC 5812 Eating places

D-U-N-S 25-892-8175   (BR)
WEYERHAEUSER COMPANY LIMITED
K3 SPECIALTIES
(*Suby of* Weyerhaeuser Company)
3650 E Kent Ave S, Vancouver, BC, V5S 2J2

Emp Here 80
SIC 2421 Sawmills and planing mills, general

Vancouver, BC V5T
Greater Vancouver County

D-U-N-S 25-215-8423   (HQ)
ANN-LOUISE JEWELLERS LTD
TIME BOUTIQUE
18 2nd Ave E, Vancouver, BC, V5T 1B1
(604) 873-6341
Emp Here 30   *Emp Total* 250
Sales 9,849,695
SIC 5944 Jewelry stores
Pr Pr Jimmy Chen
    Marie Chen
VP Opers Colin Chen

D-U-N-S 25-723-1191   (BR)
ASSOCIATION OF NEIGHBOURHOOD HOUSES OF BRITISH COLUMBIA
MOUNT PLEASANT NEIGBOURHOOD HOUSE
800 Broadway E, Vancouver, BC, V5T 1Y1
(604) 879-8208
Emp Here 40
SIC 8399 Social services, nec

D-U-N-S 25-073-6936   (SL)
AWESPIRING PRODUCTIONS INC
A FOR AWESOME
1256 6th Ave E, Vancouver, BC, V5T 1E7
(604) 484-0266
Emp Here 49   *Sales* 4,244,630
SIC 7336 Commercial art and graphic design

D-U-N-S 20-418-2971   (SL)
BANDAI NAMCO STUDIOS VANCOUVER INC
577 Great Northern Way Suite 210, Vancouver, BC, V5T 1E1
(604) 876-1346
Emp Here 25   *Sales* 1,896,978
SIC 7372 Prepackaged software

D-U-N-S 20-591-0420   (BR)
BOARD OF EDUCATION OF SCHOOL DISTRICT NO. 39 (VANCOUVER), THE
MOUNT PLEASANT ELEMENTARY SCHOOL
2300 Guelph St, Vancouver, BC, V5T 3P1
(604) 713-4617
Emp Here 25
SIC 8211 Elementary and secondary schools

D-U-N-S 25-450-9342   (BR)
BOARD OF EDUCATION OF SCHOOL DIS-

TRICT NO. 39 (VANCOUVER), THE
FLORENCE NIGHTINGALE ELEMENTARY SCHOOL
2740 Guelph St, Vancouver, BC, V5T 3P7
(604) 713-5290
Emp Here 50
SIC 8211 Elementary and secondary schools

D-U-N-S 20-957-7568   (BR)
BRINK'S CANADA LIMITED
(*Suby of* The Brink's Company)
247 1st Ave E, Vancouver, BC, V5T 1A7
(604) 875-6221
Emp Here 100
SIC 7381 Detective and armored car services

D-U-N-S 20-913-0694   (BR)
BUY-LOW FOODS LTD
370 Broadway E, Vancouver, BC, V5T 4G5
(604) 872-5776
Emp Here 50
SIC 5411 Grocery stores

D-U-N-S 20-021-2541   (BR)
CATHOLIC INDEPENDENT SCHOOLS OF VANCOUVER ARCHDIOCESE, THE
ST PATRICK'S ELEMENTARY SCHOOL
2850 Quebec St, Vancouver, BC, V5T 3A9
(604) 879-4411
Emp Here 25
SIC 8211 Elementary and secondary schools

D-U-N-S 20-034-6240   (BR)
CATHOLIC INDEPENDENT SCHOOLS OF VANCOUVER ARCHDIOCESE, THE
ST FRANCIS XAVIER SCHOOL
428 Great Northern Way, Vancouver, BC, V5T 4S5
(604) 254-2727
Emp Here 50
SIC 8211 Elementary and secondary schools

D-U-N-S 24-761-6659   (SL)
DOUGLAS MANUFACTURED HOMES LTD
DOUGLAS HOMES
141 7th Ave E, Vancouver, BC, V5T 1M5
(604) 872-2213
Emp Here 50   *Sales* 9,130,500
SIC 2452 Prefabricated wood buildings
Pr Pr Mark Ando

D-U-N-S 20-321-5900   (SL)
GENER8 MEDIA CORP
138 7th Ave E, Vancouver, BC, V5T 1M6
(604) 669-8885
Emp Here 200   *Sales* 15,521,850
SIC 7819 Services allied to motion pictures
Dir Rory Armes
VP Danielle Michael
Pr Ken Scott

D-U-N-S 20-799-7367   (BR)
H.Y. LOUIE CO. LIMITED
IGA STORES
2949 Main St Suite 10, Vancouver, BC, V5T 3G4
(604) 873-8377
Emp Here 70
SIC 5411 Grocery stores

D-U-N-S 24-383-0937   (BR)
LIVE NATION CANADA, INC
LIVE NATION CANADA INC
56 2nd Ave E Suite 500, Vancouver, BC, V5T 1B1
(604) 683-4233
Emp Here 50
SIC 8743 Public relations services

D-U-N-S 25-654-3950   (BR)
LORDCO PARTS LTD
LORDCO AUTO PARTS
338 2nd Ave E, Vancouver, BC, V5T 1C1
(604) 879-9391
Emp Here 35
SIC 5531 Auto and home supply stores

D-U-N-S 24-939-4065   (HQ)
MARK ANTHONY GROUP INC

MISSION HILL FAMILY ESTATE
887 Great Northern Way Suite 500, Vancouver, BC, V5T 4T5
(888) 394-1122
Emp Here 125   *Emp Total* 100
Sales 14,592,140
SIC 2084 Wines, brandy, and brandy spirits
Pr Pr Anthony Von Mandl
Timothy Howley
Victor Giacomin

D-U-N-S 24-329-9633   (HQ)
MARK ANTHONY PROPERTIES LTD
887 Great Northern Way Suite 101, Vancouver, BC, V5T 4T5
(604) 263-9994
Emp Here 100   *Emp Total* 100
Sales 52,239,861
SIC 6719 Holding companies, nec
Pr Pr Anthony Von Mandl
VP Fin Victor Giacomin

D-U-N-S 24-311-0475   (HQ)
MAYNARDS INDUSTRIES LTD
(*Suby of* Maynards Industries Ltd)
1837 Main St, Vancouver, BC, V5T 3B8
(604) 876-6787
Emp Here 25   *Emp Total* 50
Sales 2,626,585
SIC 7389 Business services, nec

D-U-N-S 25-370-2930   (BR)
MOORE CANADA CORPORATION
R.R. DONNELLEY
(*Suby of* R. R. Donnelley & Sons Company)
901 Great Northern Way, Vancouver, BC, V5T 1E1
(604) 872-2326
Emp Here 60
SIC 2752 Commercial printing, lithographic

D-U-N-S 25-159-4750   (SL)
PROTEC DENTAL LABORATORIES LTD
38 1st Ave E, Vancouver, BC, V5T 1A1
(604) 873-8000
Emp Here 53   *Sales* 9,800,222
SIC 8072 Dental laboratories
Pr Pr Neal Russell

D-U-N-S 25-362-4795   (BR)
PROVIDENCE HEALTH CARE SOCIETY
MOUNT SAINT JOSEPH HOSPITAL
3080 Prince Edward St, Vancouver, BC, V5T 3N4
(604) 877-8302
Emp Here 1,000
SIC 8062 General medical and surgical hospitals

D-U-N-S 20-115-2675   (SL)
REGENCY CATERERS LTD
68 2nd Ave E Suite 300, Vancouver, BC, V5T 1B1
(604) 708-2550
Emp Here 50   *Sales* 1,978,891
SIC 5812 Eating places

D-U-N-S 20-115-8755   (BR)
SHERET, ANDREW LIMITED
SPLASHES BATH & KITCHEN CENTRE
(*Suby of* Sheret, Andrew Holdings Limited)
425 Broadway E, Vancouver, BC, V5T 1W9
(604) 874-8101
Emp Here 20
SIC 5074 Plumbing and heating equipment and supplies (hydronics)

D-U-N-S 20-802-6278   (SL)
SILVER CHEF RENTALS INC
887 Great Northern Way Suite 160, Vancouver, BC, V5T 4T5
(866) 311-3805
Emp Here 25   *Sales* 4,944,378
SIC 6159 Miscellaneous business credit institutions

D-U-N-S 20-506-0796   (BR)
STARBUCKS COFFEE CANADA, INC

(*Suby of* Starbucks Corporation)
2980 Main St, Vancouver, BC, V5T 3G3
(604) 873-5176
Emp Here 20
SIC 5499 Miscellaneous food stores

D-U-N-S 25-271-8085   (BR)
TCG INTERNATIONAL INC
SPEEDY GLASS
392 Kingsway, Vancouver, BC, V5T 3J8
(604) 876-3331
Emp Here 20
SIC 7536 Automotive glass replacement shops

D-U-N-S 20-789-0158   (BR)
TICKETMASTER CANADA LP
58e 2nd Ave E, Vancouver, BC, V5T 1B1
(604) 682-8455
Emp Here 60
SIC 7999 Amusement and recreation, nec

D-U-N-S 20-295-4756   (HQ)
TUNDRA WINDOWS, DOORS & HARDWARE INC
(*Suby of* Radec Group Inc.)
625 16th Ave E, Vancouver, BC, V5T 2V3
(604) 676-0008
Emp Here 25   *Emp Total* 1
Sales 5,884,100
SIC 5211 Lumber and other building materials
CEO Joe Walters

D-U-N-S 20-294-6679   (SL)
UNITED NATURALS INC
2416 Main St Unit 132, Vancouver, BC, V5T 3E2
(604) 999-9999
Emp Here 90   *Sales* 4,012,839
SIC 2833 Medicinals and botanicals

D-U-N-S 24-334-2743   (BR)
UNIVERSITY OF BRITISH COLUMBIA, THE
UNIVERSITY OF BRITISH COLUMBIA FACULTY OF MEDICINE DEPARTMENT OF RADIOLOGY
950 10th Ave E Rm 3350, Vancouver, BC, V5T 2B2
(604) 875-4165
Emp Here 83
SIC 8221 Colleges and universities

D-U-N-S 20-199-7306   (BR)
UNIVERSITY OF BRITISH COLUMBIA, THE
CENTER FOR ADVANCED WOOD PROCESSING
2424 Main St Suite 2900, Vancouver, BC, V5T 3E2
(604) 822-6448
Emp Here 20
SIC 8221 Colleges and universities

D-U-N-S 24-326-1232   (BR)
VANCOUVER COASTAL HEALTH AUTHORITY
VANCOUVER DETOX CENTRE
377 2nd Ave E, Vancouver, BC, V5T 1B9
(604) 658-1253
Emp Here 75
SIC 8062 General medical and surgical hospitals

D-U-N-S 25-364-3902   (BR)
VANCOUVER, CITY OF
MOUNT PLEASANT COMMUNITY CENTRE
(*Suby of* Vancouver, City of)
1 Kingsway, Vancouver, BC, V5T 3H7
(604) 257-3080
Emp Here 20
SIC 8322 Individual and family services

Vancouver, BC V5V
Greater Vancouver County

D-U-N-S 20-161-1329   (SL)

ATLANTIS PROGRAMS INC
ATLANTIS PROGRAMS AND PEDALHEADS
101 4894 Fraser St, Vancouver, BC, V5V 4H5
(604) 874-6464
Emp Here 57   *Sales* 3,064,349
SIC 7999 Amusement and recreation, nec

D-U-N-S 20-265-3945   (BR)
BOARD OF EDUCATION OF SCHOOL DISTRICT NO. 39 (VANCOUVER), THE
SIR CHARLES TUPPER SECONDARY
419 24th Ave E, Vancouver, BC, V5V 2A2
(604) 713-8233
Emp Here 40
SIC 8211 Elementary and secondary schools

D-U-N-S 20-652-2513   (BR)
BOARD OF EDUCATION OF SCHOOL DISTRICT NO. 39 (VANCOUVER), THE
GENERAL BROCK ELEMENTARY SCHOOL
4860 Main St, Vancouver, BC, V5V 3R8
(604) 713-5245
Emp Here 60
SIC 8211 Elementary and secondary schools

D-U-N-S 25-450-7569   (BR)
BOARD OF EDUCATION OF SCHOOL DISTRICT NO. 39 (VANCOUVER), THE
CHARLES DICKENS ELEMENTARY SCHOOL
1010 17th Ave E Suite 39, Vancouver, BC, V5V 0A6
(604) 713-4978
Emp Here 45
SIC 8211 Elementary and secondary schools

D-U-N-S 25-450-9599   (BR)
BOARD OF EDUCATION OF SCHOOL DISTRICT NO. 39 (VANCOUVER), THE
GENERAL WOLFE ELEMENTARY SCHOOL
4251 Ontario St Suite 39, Vancouver, BC, V5V 3G8
(604) 713-4912
Emp Here 50
SIC 8211 Elementary and secondary schools

D-U-N-S 20-652-2984   (BR)
BOARD OF EDUCATION OF SCHOOL DISTRICT NO. 39 (VANCOUVER), THE
DAVID LIVINGSTONE ELEMENTARY SCHOOL
315 23rd Ave E, Vancouver, BC, V5V 1X6
(604) 713-4985
Emp Here 20
SIC 8211 Elementary and secondary schools

D-U-N-S 20-022-1716   (BR)
BOARD OF EDUCATION OF SCHOOL DISTRICT NO. 39 (VANCOUVER), THE
SIR RICHARD MCBRIDE ELEMENTARY SCHOOL
1300 29th Ave E, Vancouver, BC, V5V 2T3
(604) 713-4971
Emp Here 45
SIC 8211 Elementary and secondary schools

D-U-N-S 25-216-2425   (BR)
COASTAL FORD SALES LIMITED
3333 Main St, Vancouver, BC, V5V 3M8
(604) 873-2363
Emp Here 50
SIC 5511 New and used car dealers

D-U-N-S 20-991-6902   (BR)
FAMILY SERVICES OF GREATER VANCOUVER
SAFE HOUSE
(*Suby of* Family Services of Greater Vancouver)
4675 Walden St, Vancouver, BC, V5V 3S8
(604) 877-1234
Emp Here 28
SIC 8322 Individual and family services

D-U-N-S 24-773-2352   (BR)
PROVIDENCE HEALTH CARE SOCIETY
PROVIDENCE HEALTH CARE
749 33rd Ave E, Vancouver, BC, V5V 3A1

(604) 876-7171
Emp Here 20
SIC 8069 Specialty hospitals, except psychiatric

D-U-N-S 25-663-4585   (BR)
ROYAL BANK OF CANADA
RBC
(*Suby of* Royal Bank Of Canada)
4095 Main St, Vancouver, BC, V5V 3P5
(604) 665-3111
Emp Here 20
SIC 6021 National commercial banks

D-U-N-S 24-760-5223   (SL)
SUN SUI WAH SEAFOOD RESTAURANT LTD
3888 Main St, Vancouver, BC, V5V 3N9
(604) 872-8822
Emp Here 153   *Sales* 6,391,350
SIC 5812 Eating places
Pr Pr Tang Chan
   Chiu (Simon) Chan
   Siuman Lui

D-U-N-S 20-587-0525   (BR)
VANCOUVER CITY SAVINGS CREDIT UNION
VANCITY CREDIT UNION
4205 Main St, Vancouver, BC, V5V 3P8
(604) 877-7092
Emp Here 20
SIC 6062 State credit unions

Vancouver, BC V5W
Greater Vancouver County

D-U-N-S 20-153-2574   (BR)
BOARD OF EDUCATION OF SCHOOL DISTRICT NO. 39 (VANCOUVER), THE
SIR WILLIAM VAN HORNE ELEMENTARY SCHOOL
5855 Ontario St, Vancouver, BC, V5W 2L8
(604) 713-4965
Emp Here 30
SIC 8211 Elementary and secondary schools

D-U-N-S 20-034-1068   (BR)
BOARD OF EDUCATION OF SCHOOL DISTRICT NO. 39 (VANCOUVER), THE
SIR ALEXANDER MACKENZIE ELEMENTARY SCHOOL
960 39th Ave E, Vancouver, BC, V5W 1K8
(604) 713-4799
Emp Here 60
SIC 8211 Elementary and secondary schools

D-U-N-S 25-912-6845   (BR)
BOARD OF EDUCATION OF SCHOOL DISTRICT NO. 39 (VANCOUVER), THE
SOUTH HILL EDUCATION CENTRE
6010 Fraser St, Vancouver, BC, V5W 2Z7
(604) 713-5770
Emp Here 50
SIC 8211 Elementary and secondary schools

D-U-N-S 20-651-6226   (BR)
BOARD OF EDUCATION OF SCHOOL DISTRICT NO. 39 (VANCOUVER), THE
JOHN OLIVER SECONDARY SCHOOL
530 41st Ave E, Vancouver, BC, V5W 1P3
(604) 324-1317
Emp Here 40
SIC 8211 Elementary and secondary schools

D-U-N-S 25-485-5489   (BR)
BUY-LOW FOODS LTD
6095 Fraser St, Vancouver, BC, V5W 2Z8
(604) 321-9828
Emp Here 40
SIC 5411 Grocery stores

D-U-N-S 25-148-2162   (BR)
CATHOLIC INDEPENDENT SCHOOLS OF VANCOUVER ARCHDIOCESE, THE
SAINT ANDREW'S CATHOLIC SCHOOL

450 47th Ave E, Vancouver, BC, V5W 2B4
(604) 325-6317
Emp Here 22
SIC 8211 Elementary and secondary schools

D-U-N-S 25-270-0851   (BR)
HSBC BANK CANADA
HSBC
6373 Fraser St, Vancouver, BC, V5W 3A3
(604) 324-2481
Emp Here 29
SIC 6021 National commercial banks

D-U-N-S 25-068-5310   (BR)
KNOWLEDGE NETWORK CORPORATION
GREATER VANCOUVER DISTANCE EDUCATION SCHOOL
530 41st Ave E Suite 123, Vancouver, BC, V5W 1P3
(604) 713-5520
Emp Here 50
SIC 4833 Television broadcasting stations

D-U-N-S 24-322-0451   (BR)
TORONTO-DOMINION BANK, THE
TD CANADA TRUST
(*Suby of* Toronto-Dominion Bank, The)
6499 Fraser St, Vancouver, BC, V5W 3A6
(604) 327-4366
Emp Here 30
SIC 6021 National commercial banks

D-U-N-S 20-587-0483   (BR)
VANCOUVER CITY SAVINGS CREDIT UNION
VANCITY CREDIT UNION
6288 Fraser St, Vancouver, BC, V5W 3A1
(604) 877-7072
Emp Here 30
SIC 6062 State credit unions

Vancouver, BC V5X
Greater Vancouver County

D-U-N-S 25-236-6711   (SL)
B. & C. LIST (1982) LTD
ALBERTA LEGAL & SERVICES DIRECTORY
8278 Manitoba St, Vancouver, BC, V5X 3A2
(604) 482-3100
Emp Here 76   *Sales* 7,852,800
SIC 2721 Periodicals
Pr Pr Shirley Hyman
   Barry Hyman
   Jack Hyman

D-U-N-S 20-572-1686   (BR)
BANK OF MONTREAL
BMO
8156 Main St, Vancouver, BC, V5X 3L6
(604) 668-1404
Emp Here 20
SIC 6021 National commercial banks

D-U-N-S 20-109-2988   (SL)
BLUE BOY MOTOR HOTEL LTD
QUALITY INN AIRPORT
725 Marine Dr Se, Vancouver, BC, V5X 2T9
(604) 321-6611
Emp Here 75   *Sales* 4,521,600
SIC 7011 Hotels and motels

D-U-N-S 20-005-9710   (BR)
BOARD OF EDUCATION OF SCHOOL DISTRICT NO. 39 (VANCOUVER), THE
WALTER MOBERLY ELEMENTARY SCHOOL
1000 59th Ave E, Vancouver, BC, V5X 1Y7
(604) 713-4784
Emp Here 50
SIC 8211 Elementary and secondary schools

D-U-N-S 20-591-0776   (BR)
BOARD OF EDUCATION OF SCHOOL DISTRICT NO. 39 (VANCOUVER), THE
J W SEXSMITH ELEMENTARY SCHOOL
7410 Columbia St, Vancouver, BC, V5X 3C1

(604) 713-4901
Emp Here 25
SIC 8211 Elementary and secondary schools

D-U-N-S 20-286-9322   (BR)
CASCADES CANADA ULC
CASCADES RECOVERY+
8325 Main St, Vancouver, BC, V5X 3M3
(604) 327-5272
Emp Here 20
SIC 4953 Refuse systems

D-U-N-S 20-799-6083   (SL)
CEDARHURST PRIVATE HOSPITAL LTD
AMHERST HOSPITAL & NURSING HOM
375 59th Ave W, Vancouver, BC, V5X 1X3
(604) 321-6777
Emp Here 70   *Sales* 3,283,232
SIC 8051 Skilled nursing care facilities

D-U-N-S 25-723-4716   (BR)
DEVELOPMENTAL DISABILITIES ASSOCIATION OF VANCOUVER-RICHMOND
STAR WORKS PACKAGING AND ASSEMBLY
276 Marine Dr Sw, Vancouver, BC, V5X 2R5
(604) 879-8457
Emp Here 45
SIC 7389 Business services, nec

D-U-N-S 25-618-7147   (BR)
DUECK CHEVROLET BUICK CADILLAC GMC LIMITED
DUECK AUTO GROUP TIRE STORE
400 Marine Dr Se, Vancouver, BC, V5X 4X2
(604) 324-7222
Emp Here 200
SIC 5012 Automobiles and other motor vehicles

D-U-N-S 25-485-5281   (BR)
ENVIROTEST SYSTEMS (B.C.) LTD
VANCOUVER AIR CARE
(*Suby of* Envirotest Systems (B.C.) Ltd)
520 E Kent Ave South, Vancouver, BC, V5X 4V6

Emp Here 20
SIC 7389 Business services, nec

D-U-N-S 25-261-8004   (SL)
GOLDEN GLOBE CONSTRUCTION LTD
8380 St. George St Unit 103b, Vancouver, BC, V5X 3S7

Emp Here 40   *Sales* 8,239,360
SIC 1521 Single-family housing construction
Pr Pr Amin Imani
Off Mgr Payam Imani

D-U-N-S 24-725-0004   (BR)
LAFARGE CANADA INC
LAFARGE CONSTRUCTION MATERIAL
268 E Kent Ave South, Vancouver, BC, V5X 4N6
(604) 322-3851
Emp Here 50
SIC 5032 Brick, stone, and related material

D-U-N-S 24-594-1323   (BR)
LEE VALLEY TOOLS LTD
1180 Marine Dr Se, Vancouver, BC, V5X 2V6
(604) 261-2262
Emp Here 20
SIC 5251 Hardware stores

D-U-N-S 20-955-5833   (HQ)
LUSH MANUFACTURING LTD
8365 Ontario St Suite 120, Vancouver, BC, V5X 3E8
(604) 266-0612
Emp Here 20   *Emp Total* 4,581
Sales 3,502,114
SIC 2844 Toilet preparations

D-U-N-S 25-195-4905   (BR)
PATTISON, JIM INDUSTRIES LTD
CANADIAN FISHING COMPANY
455 E Kent Ave North Suite 22, Vancouver,

BC, V5X 4M2
(604) 324-7141
Emp Here 20
SIC 5146 Fish and seafoods

D-U-N-S 20-115-1255   (HQ)
PURDY, R.C. CHOCOLATES LTD
PURDY'S CHOCOLATES
8330 Chester St, Vancouver, BC, V5X 3Y7
(604) 454-2777
Emp Here 150   *Emp Total* 600
Sales 2,338,878
SIC 2066 Chocolate and cocoa products

D-U-N-S 24-290-7186   (SL)
RATANA INTERNATIONAL LTD
RATANA HOME & FLORAL
8310 Manitoba St, Vancouver, BC, V5X 3A5
(604) 321-6776
Emp Here 65   *Sales* 3,429,153
SIC 5992 Florists

D-U-N-S 25-806-9426   (BR)
ROYAL BANK OF CANADA
RBC
(*Suby of* Royal Bank Of Canada)
6505 Fraser St, Vancouver, BC, V5X 3T4
(604) 665-0882
Emp Here 30
SIC 6021 National commercial banks

D-U-N-S 20-027-0705   (BR)
SCHOOL DISTRICT NO. 44 (NORTH VANCOUVER)
PIERRE ELLIOT TRUDEAU ELEMENTARY SCHOOL
(*Suby of* School District No. 44 (North Vancouver))
449 62nd Ave E, Vancouver, BC, V5X 2G2
(604) 713-4865
Emp Here 30
SIC 8211 Elementary and secondary schools

D-U-N-S 24-312-0339   (BR)
SOFINA FOODS INC
FLETCHER'S FINE FOODS DIV OF
8385 Fraser St, Vancouver, BC, V5X 3X8
(604) 668-5800
Emp Here 300
SIC 2011 Meat packing plants

D-U-N-S 20-623-7927   (SL)
SOUTHSIDE NISSAN LTD
290 Marine Dr Sw, Vancouver, BC, V5X 2R5
(604) 324-4644
Emp Here 40   *Sales* 14,592,140
SIC 5511 New and used car dealers
Pr Pr Frank Affettuso

D-U-N-S 24-762-1576   (BR)
TERMINAL FOREST PRODUCTS LTD
MAINLAND SAWMILL
8708 Yukon St, Vancouver, BC, V5X 2Y9
(604) 327-6344
Emp Here 110
SIC 2421 Sawmills and planing mills, general

D-U-N-S 25-663-9857   (BR)
WENDY'S RESTAURANTS OF CANADA INC
WENDY'S
(*Suby of* The Wendy's Company)
10 Marine Dr Se, Vancouver, BC, V5X 2S3
(604) 327-2912
Emp Here 35
SIC 5812 Eating places

D-U-N-S 20-117-4000   (HQ)
WHITE SPOT LIMITED
WHITE SPOT RESTAURANT
1126 Marine Dr Se, Vancouver, BC, V5X 2V7
(604) 325-8911
Emp Here 45   *Emp Total* 6,000
Sales 92,218,050
SIC 5812 Eating places
Pr Warren Erhart
Dir Larry Bell
Dir Frank Price
   Peter Toigo

Dir Fin Kelvin Lum

Vancouver, BC V5Y
Greater Vancouver County

D-U-N-S 20-812-4987   (SL)
0781337 B.C. LTD
BEAT 94.5 FM
380 2nd Ave W Suite 300, Vancouver, BC,
V5Y 1C8
(604) 699-2328
Emp Here 60   *Sales* 3,793,956
SIC 4832 Radio broadcasting stations

D-U-N-S 24-725-3297   (BR)
3627730 CANADA INC
FREEMAN AUDIO VISUAL
395 8th Ave W, Vancouver, BC, V5Y 1N7
(604) 255-1151
Emp Here 35
SIC 7359 Equipment rental and leasing, nec

D-U-N-S 24-324-7413   (BR)
ALSCO CANADA CORPORATION
ALSCO UNIFORM & LINEN SERVICE
5 4th Ave W, Vancouver, BC, V5Y 1G2
(604) 876-3272
Emp Here 160
SIC 7213 Linen supply

D-U-N-S 20-713-4086   (BR)
**BOARD OF EDUCATION OF SCHOOL DIS-
TRICT NO. 39 (VANCOUVER), THE**
SIMON FRASER ELEMENTARY SCHOOL
100 15th Ave W, Vancouver, BC, V5Y 3B7
(604) 713-4946
Emp Here 20
SIC 8211 Elementary and secondary schools

D-U-N-S 25-680-9492   (SL)
**CANADIAN OVERSEAS MARKETING COR-
PORATION**
2020 Yukon St, Vancouver, BC, V5Y 3N8

Emp Here 300   *Sales* 18,748,560
SIC 7331 Direct mail advertising services
Pr Pr Randy Thiemer

D-U-N-S 20-860-8062   (BR)
CANADIAN RED CROSS SOCIETY, THE
209 6th Ave W, Vancouver, BC, V5Y 1K7
(604) 301-2566
Emp Here 30
SIC 8621 Professional organizations

D-U-N-S 25-369-8211   (BR)
**CHRISTIAN AND MISSIONARY ALLIANCE
IN CANADA, THE**
TENTH AVENUE ALLIANCE CHURCH
11 10th Ave W, Vancouver, BC, V5Y 1R5
(604) 876-2181
Emp Here 24
SIC 8661 Religious organizations

D-U-N-S 24-343-7485   (BR)
FGL SPORTS LTD
SPORT-CHEK BROADWAY
18 Broadway W, Vancouver, BC, V5Y 1P2
(604) 874-6530
Emp Here 20
SIC 5941 Sporting goods and bicycle shops

D-U-N-S 25-918-1514   (SL)
GF EVENTS LTD
GLUTEN FREE EXPO
169 Walter Hardwick Ave Unit 403, Vancouver,
BC, V5Y 0B9
(604) 430-2090
Emp Here 50   *Sales* 1,678,096
SIC 7299 Miscellaneous personal service

D-U-N-S 24-327-7279   (HQ)
INSIGHT FILM STUDIOS LTD
(*Suby of* Insight Film Studios Ltd)
112 6th Ave W, Vancouver, BC, V5Y 1K6

(604) 623-3369
Emp Here 100   *Emp Total* 2,500
Sales 252,073,008
SIC 7812 Motion picture and video production
Pr Pr Kirk Shaw
Sec Wendy Mckernan

D-U-N-S 20-011-6213   (HQ)
LANGARA COLLEGE
(*Suby of* Langara College)
100 49th Ave W, Vancouver, BC, V5Y 2Z6
(604) 323-5511
Emp Here 500   *Emp Total* 1,100
Sales 96,211,755
SIC 8221 Colleges and universities
Pr Pr David Ross
 Anne Lippert
 David Bowra
 Deanna Douglas
 Barry Coulson

D-U-N-S 20-746-3548   (HQ)
LEADING BRANDS OF CANADA, INC
NORTH AMERICAN BOTTLING
(*Suby of* Leading Brands, Inc)
33 8th Ave W Unit 101, Vancouver, BC, V5Y
1M8
(604) 685-5200
Emp Here 20   *Emp Total* 73
Sales 15,159,393
SIC 2086 Bottled and canned soft drinks
Dir Ralph Douglas Mcrae

D-U-N-S 24-897-7100   (HQ)
LEADING BRANDS, INC
(*Suby of* Leading Brands, Inc)
33 8th Ave W Unit 101, Vancouver, BC, V5Y
1M8
(604) 685-5200
Emp Here 50   *Emp Total* 73
Sales 7,715,253
SIC 2033 Canned fruits and specialties
 Ralph Mcrae
VP Thor Matson
 James Corbett
 Darryl Eddy
 Stephen Kane
 Thomas Gaglardi

D-U-N-S 24-069-4505   (HQ)
MARGARETA ORIGINALS LTD
(*Suby of* Margareta Originals Ltd)
196 3rd Ave W Suite 102, Vancouver, BC, V5Y
1E9

Emp Here 23   *Emp Total* 38
Sales 5,693,280
SIC 2335 Women's, junior's, and misses'
dresses
Pr Pr Margareta Termansen

D-U-N-S 24-391-6819   (SL)
MARQUIS OF LONDON MFG. (1979) LTD
33 8th Ave W, Vancouver, BC, V5Y 1M8

Emp Here 50   *Sales* 2,772,003
SIC 2386 Leather and sheep-lined clothing

D-U-N-S 20-030-0494   (SL)
PHOENIX GYMNASTICS CLUB
VANCOUVER PHOENIX GYMNASTICS
4588 Clancy Loranger Way, Vancouver, BC,
V5Y 4B6
(604) 737-7693
Emp Here 50   *Sales* 2,042,900
SIC 7991 Physical fitness facilities

D-U-N-S 24-640-6750   (BR)
ROGERS MEDIA INC
CITYTV VANCOUVER
(*Suby of* Rogers Communications Inc)
180 2nd Ave W, Vancouver, BC, V5Y 3T9
(604) 876-1344
Emp Here 50
SIC 4833 Television broadcasting stations

D-U-N-S 24-881-3776   (BR)
STARBUCKS COFFEE CANADA, INC

(*Suby of* Starbucks Corporation)
128 6th Ave W Suite 200, Vancouver, BC, V5Y
1K6
(604) 871-1192
Emp Here 25
SIC 5812 Eating places

D-U-N-S 25-974-8606   (SL)
VIRTUAL360 SYSTEMS LTD
128 6th Ave W Suite, Vancouver, BC, V5Y 1K6
(604) 253-0360
Emp Here 25   *Sales* 6,965,700
SIC 7379 Computer related services, nec
 Brett Katon
Pr Pr Dan Funaro

D-U-N-S 25-709-9994   (BR)
WENDY'S RESTAURANTS OF CANADA INC
WENDY'S 6516
(*Suby of* The Wendy's Company)
480 8th Ave W, Vancouver, BC, V5Y 1N9
(604) 875-8933
Emp Here 60
SIC 5812 Eating places

Vancouver, BC V5Z
Greater Vancouver County

D-U-N-S 20-352-4186   (SL)
1127770 B.C. LTD
777 Broadway W, Vancouver, BC, V5Z 4J7

Emp Here 1,398   *Sales* 203,998,117
SIC 5047 Medical and hospital equipment
Pr Ralph Vasquez

D-U-N-S 24-798-3869   (SL)
360641 BC LTD
KIRIN SEAFOOD RESTAURANT
555 12th Ave W Unit 201, Vancouver, BC, V5Z
3X7
(604) 879-8038
Emp Here 100   *Sales* 2,991,389
SIC 5812 Eating places

D-U-N-S 25-714-8288   (BR)
**AURUM CERAMIC DENTAL LABORATO-
RIES LTD**
AURUM CERAMIC DENTAL LAB (BC)
936 8th Ave W Suite 305, Vancouver, BC, V5Z
1E5
(604) 737-2010
Emp Here 50
SIC 8072 Dental laboratories

D-U-N-S 20-571-9144   (BR)
BANK OF MONTREAL
BMO
777 Broadway W Suite 105, Vancouver, BC,
V5Z 4J7
(604) 665-7179
Emp Here 20
SIC 6021 National commercial banks

D-U-N-S 25-002-6275   (BR)
BANQUE TORONTO-DOMINION, LA
TD CANADA TRUST
(*Suby of* Toronto-Dominion Bank, The)
511 41st Ave W, Vancouver, BC, V5Z 2M7
(604) 261-7266
Emp Here 50
SIC 6021 National commercial banks

D-U-N-S 25-452-2816   (BR)
BAYSHORE HEALTHCARE LTD.
BAYSHORE HOME HEALTH
555 12th Ave W Unit 410, Vancouver, BC, V5Z
3X7
(604) 873-2545
Emp Here 250
SIC 8082 Home health care services

D-U-N-S 24-011-8682   (BR)
BEST BUY CANADA LTD
BEST BUY
(*Suby of* Best Buy Co., Inc.)

2220 Cambie St, Vancouver, BC, V5Z 2T7
(604) 638-4966
Emp Here 50
SIC 5731 Radio, television, and electronic
stores

D-U-N-S 25-912-6852   (BR)
**BOARD OF EDUCATION OF SCHOOL DIS-
TRICT NO. 39 (VANCOUVER), THE**
ERIC HAMBER SECONDARY SCHOOL
5025 Willow St Suite 39, Vancouver, BC, V5Z
3S1
(604) 713-8927
Emp Here 120
SIC 8211 Elementary and secondary schools

D-U-N-S 20-136-5934   (BR)
**BOARD OF EDUCATION OF SCHOOL DIS-
TRICT NO. 39 (VANCOUVER), THE**
*DR ANNIE B JAMIESON ELEMENTARY
SCHOOL*
6350 Tisdall St, Vancouver, BC, V5Z 3N4
(604) 713-5367
Emp Here 40
SIC 8211 Elementary and secondary schools

D-U-N-S 25-450-7395   (BR)
**BOARD OF EDUCATION OF SCHOOL DIS-
TRICT NO. 39 (VANCOUVER), THE**
EDITH CAVELL ELEMENTARY SCHOOL
500 20th Ave W, Vancouver, BC, V5Z 1X7
(604) 713-4932
Emp Here 35
SIC 8211 Elementary and secondary schools

D-U-N-S 25-718-4325   (BR)
BOUTIQUE JACOB INC
(*Suby of* Boutique Jacob Inc)
650 41st Ave W Unit 179, Vancouver, BC, V5Z
2M9

Emp Here 20
SIC 5621 Women's clothing stores

D-U-N-S 25-316-5310   (BR)
**BRITISH COLUMBIA AUTOMOBILE ASSO-
CIATION**
999 Broadway W Suite 720, Vancouver, BC,
V5Z 1K5
(604) 268-5600
Emp Here 35
SIC 8699 Membership organizations, nec

D-U-N-S 20-913-7736   (HQ)
**BRITISH COLUMBIA CANCER AGENCY
BRANCH**
BC CANCER AGENCY
600 10th Ave W, Vancouver, BC, V5Z 4E6
(604) 877-6000
Emp Here 1,010   *Emp Total* 10,000
Sales 159,117,360
SIC 8069 Specialty hospitals, except psychi-
atric
Pr Simon B Sutcliffe
VP Opers Karim Karmali
Dir Lynda Cranston

D-U-N-S 24-207-0444   (BR)
**BRITISH COLUMBIA CANCER AGENCY
BRANCH**
GENOME SCIENCES CENTRE
570 7th Ave W Suite 100, Vancouver, BC, V5Z
4S6
(604) 707-5800
Emp Here 180
SIC 8731 Commercial physical research

D-U-N-S 20-304-4727   (SL)
**BRITISH COLUMBIA'S CHILDREN'S HOS-
PITAL FOUNDATION**
*BC CHILDREN'S HOSPITAL FOUNDATION
(BCCHF)*
938 28th Ave W, Vancouver, BC, V5Z 4H4
(604) 875-2444
Emp Here 75   *Sales* 69,324,657
SIC 8699 Membership organizations, nec
Pr Teri Nicholas
Ch Bd David Podmore

VP Debora Sweeney
Dir Leslie Arnold
Dir Kevin Bent
Dir David Boig
Dir Doug Gordon
Dir Lisa Hudson
Dir Tammi Kerzner
Dir Michael Lam

D-U-N-S 25-018-4553   (BR)
CANADIAN CANCER SOCIETY
BC AND YUKON DIVISION, THE
565 10th Ave W Suite 44, Vancouver, BC, V5Z 4J4
(604) 872-4400
Emp Here 77
SIC 7389 Business services, nec

D-U-N-S 25-716-4160   (HQ)
COLLEGE EDUCACENTRE COLLEGE
(*Suby of* College Educacentre College)
896 8th Ave W, Vancouver, BC, V5Z 1E2
(604) 708-5100
Emp Here 30   *Emp Total* 60
Sales 2,845,467
SIC 8331 Job training and related services

D-U-N-S 25-976-8943   (BR)
COLLIERS PROJECT LEADERS INC
555 12th Ave W Suite 550, Vancouver, BC, V5Z 3X7
(604) 714-0988
Emp Here 30
SIC 8741 Management services

D-U-N-S 24-855-8900   (BR)
EARL'S RESTAURANTS LTD
EARL'S
(*Suby of* Earl's Restaurants Ltd)
901 Broadway W, Vancouver, BC, V5Z 1K3
(604) 734-0098
Emp Here 50
SIC 5812 Eating places

D-U-N-S 25-127-3892   (BR)
EDDIE BAUER OF CANADA INC
(*Suby of* Golden Gate Capital LP)
650 41st Ave W Suite 279, Vancouver, BC, V5Z 2M9

Emp Here 20
SIC 5699 Miscellaneous apparel and accessory stores

D-U-N-S 25-719-0561   (BR)
GAP (CANADA) INC
BANANA REPUBLIC
(*Suby of* The Gap Inc)
650 41st Ave W Suite 109, Vancouver, BC, V5Z 2M9
(604) 267-3741
Emp Here 30
SIC 5651 Family clothing stores

D-U-N-S 24-866-4047   (SL)
GLOBESPAN TRAVEL LTD
FLY GLOBESPAN
(*Suby of* THE GLOBESPAN GROUP PLC)
660 Leg In Boot Sq Unit C, Vancouver, BC, V5Z 4B3
(604) 879-6466
Emp Here 20   *Sales* 4,742,446
SIC 4724 Travel agencies

D-U-N-S 25-485-6008   (BR)
H. & C. MANAGEMENT CONSULTANTS LTD
FITNESS WORLD
(*Suby of* H. & C. Management Consultants Ltd)
555 12th Ave W Suite 299, Vancouver, BC, V5Z 3X7
(604) 876-1009
Emp Here 30
SIC 7991 Physical fitness facilities

D-U-N-S 25-270-0778   (BR)
HSBC BANK CANADA
5812 Cambie St, Vancouver, BC, V5Z 3A8

(604) 325-1868
Emp Here 29
SIC 6021 National commercial banks

D-U-N-S 24-361-7318   (BR)
HOME DEPOT OF CANADA INC
HOME DEPOT
(*Suby of* The Home Depot Inc)
2388 Cambie St, Vancouver, BC, V5Z 2T8
(604) 675-1260
Emp Here 100
SIC 5251 Hardware stores

D-U-N-S 25-301-2546   (BR)
HUDSON'S BAY COMPANY
BAY, THE
650 41st Ave W, Vancouver, BC, V5Z 2M9
(604) 261-3311
Emp Here 200
SIC 5311 Department stores

D-U-N-S 25-450-1646   (BR)
IVANHOE CAMBRIDGE INC
650 41st Ave W Suite 700, Vancouver, BC, V5Z 2M9
(604) 263-2672
Emp Here 20
SIC 6512 Nonresidential building operators

D-U-N-S 25-453-0033   (SL)
JEWISH COMMUNITY CENTRE OF GREATER VANCOUVER
950 41st Ave W, Vancouver, BC, V5Z 2N7
(604) 257-5111
Emp Here 100   *Sales* 3,939,878
SIC 8322 Individual and family services

D-U-N-S 20-985-0911   (SL)
KAMAKURA JAPANESE CUISINE
601 Broadway W Unit 3, Vancouver, BC, V5Z 4C2

Emp Here 50   *Sales* 1,819,127
SIC 5812 Eating places

D-U-N-S 24-620-3756   (SL)
LIFESTYLE RESTAURANT LTD
RUGBY BEACH CLUB GRILL, THE
950 Broadway W Suite 201, Vancouver, BC, V5Z 1K7
(604) 231-0055
Emp Here 50   *Sales* 1,819,127
SIC 5812 Eating places

D-U-N-S 24-457-6716   (BR)
LONDON DRUGS LIMITED
525 Broadway W, Vancouver, BC, V5Z 1E6
(604) 872-5177
Emp Here 200
SIC 5912 Drug stores and proprietary stores

D-U-N-S 20-648-9093   (BR)
MD MANAGEMENT LIMITED
MD FINANCIAL
(*Suby of* Canadian Medical Association)
575 8th Ave W Suite 200, Vancouver, BC, V5Z 0B2
(604) 736-7778
Emp Here 25
SIC 8742 Management consulting services

D-U-N-S 24-613-3359   (SL)
MONK MCQUEENS FRESH SEAFOOD & OYSTER BARS INC
601 Stamp'S Landng, Vancouver, BC, V5Z 3Z1

Emp Here 60   *Sales* 1,824,018
SIC 5812 Eating places

D-U-N-S 24-169-0200   (SL)
ON4 COMMUNICATIONS INC
628 12th Ave W, Vancouver, BC, V5Z 1M8
(888) 583-7158
Emp Here 50   *Sales* 14,000,100
SIC 5065 Electronic parts and equipment, nec
Pr Pr Clayton Moore
Ryan Madson
Dir Steven Allmen

D-U-N-S 25-452-9530   (SL)
PENRITH INVESTMENTS LTD
HOLIDAY INN
711 Broadway W, Vancouver, BC, V5Z 3Y2
(778) 330-2400
Emp Here 120   *Sales* 7,067,520
SIC 7011 Hotels and motels
Pr Pr Anthony Cheng
Richard J. Jackson
Dir John Paton
Genl Mgr Simon Lam

D-U-N-S 25-195-7833   (SL)
PLAZA 500 HOTELS LTD
500 12th Ave W, Vancouver, BC, V5Z 1M2
(604) 873-1811
Emp Here 100   *Sales* 4,377,642
SIC 7011 Hotels and motels

D-U-N-S 24-551-9830   (SL)
PRECISION SOFTWARE LTD
958 8th Ave W Suite 401, Vancouver, BC, V5Z 1E5

Emp Here 220   *Sales* 21,595,200
SIC 7379 Computer related services, nec
Ch Bd Christopher Hermanson

D-U-N-S 20-917-0174   (BR)
PROVIDENCE HEALTH CARE SOCIETY
YOUVILLE RESIDENCE
4950 Heather St Suite 321, Vancouver, BC, V5Z 3L9
(604) 261-9371
Emp Here 100
SIC 8059 Nursing and personal care, nec

D-U-N-S 25-736-4745   (BR)
PURDY, R.C. CHOCOLATES LTD
PURDY'S CHOCOLATES
(*Suby of* Flavelle, Charles Investments Ltd)
650 41st Ave W Suite 183, Vancouver, BC, V5Z 2M9

Emp Here 20
SIC 5441 Candy, nut, and confectionery stores

D-U-N-S 25-287-9309   (BR)
RAYMOND SALONS LTD
HENNESSEY SALON AND SPA
(*Suby of* Raymond Salons Ltd)
650 41st Ave W Suite 137, Vancouver, BC, V5Z 2M9

Emp Here 40
SIC 7991 Physical fitness facilities

D-U-N-S 24-578-4723   (HQ)
REDPATH FOODS INC
MAX'S BAKERY & DELICATESSEN
(*Suby of* Redpath Foods Inc)
521 8th Ave W, Vancouver, BC, V5Z 1C6
(604) 873-1393
Emp Here 60   *Emp Total* 75
Sales 2,553,625
SIC 5461 Retail bakeries

D-U-N-S 24-369-3558   (SL)
RICK HANSEN INSTITUTE
818 10th Ave W Unit 6400, Vancouver, BC, V5Z 1M9
(604) 827-2421
Emp Here 40   *Sales* 7,348,782
SIC 8733 Noncommercial research organizations
Pr Bill Barrable
Dir Erin Cherban
Dir Rob Hickling
Dir Vanessa K Noonan
Prs Dir Marianne Lowe
Phalgun Joshi
Catherine Ruby
Bernie Bressler
Dir Maria Barrados
Dir Ryan Barrington

D-U-N-S 20-063-3175   (BR)

ROBINSON, B.A. CO. LTD
BCP EXPRESS
2285 Cambie St, Vancouver, BC, V5Z 2T5
(604) 879-6847
Emp Here 35
SIC 5074 Plumbing and heating equipment and supplies (hydronics)

D-U-N-S 24-448-6320   (BR)
ROBINSON, B.A. CO. LTD
ROBINSON LIGHTING & BATH CENTRE
2285 Cambie St, Vancouver, BC, V5Z 2T5
(604) 879-2494
Emp Here 28
SIC 5719 Miscellaneous homefurnishings

D-U-N-S 20-108-6212   (BR)
ROGERS MEDIA INC
JACK- FM 96.9
(*Suby of* Rogers Communications Inc)
2440 Ash St, Vancouver, BC, V5Z 4J6
(604) 872-2557
Emp Here 100
SIC 4832 Radio broadcasting stations

D-U-N-S 20-803-3365   (HQ)
ROMAN CATHOLIC ARCHDIOCESE OF VANCOUVER, THE
(*Suby of* Roman Catholic Archdiocese of Vancouver, The)
4885 Saint John Paul Ii Way, Vancouver, BC, V5Z 0G3
(604) 683-0281
Emp Here 986   *Emp Total* 1,000
Sales 84,903,843
SIC 8661 Religious organizations
Pedro Gallo

D-U-N-S 25-723-2157   (BR)
ROYAL BANK OF CANADA
ROYAL BANK TRANSIT # 5600
(*Suby of* Royal Bank Of Canada)
505 Broadway W, Vancouver, BC, V5Z 1E7
(604) 665-8650
Emp Here 30
SIC 6021 National commercial banks

D-U-N-S 25-125-2748   (BR)
ROYAL BANK OF CANADA
RBC
(*Suby of* Royal Bank Of Canada)
650 41st Ave W Suite 611, Vancouver, BC, V5Z 2M9
(604) 665-0100
Emp Here 44
SIC 6021 National commercial banks

D-U-N-S 24-839-5576   (SL)
SILKWAY TRAVEL & DESTINATION MANAGEMENT INC
SILKWAY TRAVEL & CRUISE
4018 Cambie St Suite 4012, Vancouver, BC, V5Z 2X8

Emp Here 45   *Sales* 10,725,223
SIC 4725 Tour operators
Pr Pr Paulus Ng
Dir Kathy Ng

D-U-N-S 20-556-1785   (BR)
SOBEYS WEST INC
OAKRIDGE SAFEWAY
650 41st Ave W, Vancouver, BC, V5Z 2M9
(604) 263-5502
Emp Here 100
SIC 5411 Grocery stores

D-U-N-S 25-003-6381   (BR)
SOBEYS WEST INC
SAFEWAY
990 King Edward Ave W, Vancouver, BC, V5Z 2E2
(604) 733-0073
Emp Here 135
SIC 5411 Grocery stores

D-U-N-S 25-723-9566   (BR)
SOBEYS WEST INC

555 12th Ave W Unit 40, Vancouver, BC, V5Z 3X7
(604) 872-5077
Emp Here 100
SIC 5411 Grocery stores

D-U-N-S 25-271-7103   (BR)
SOBEYS WEST INC
CITY SQUARE MALL SAFEWAY
555 12th Ave W, Vancouver, BC, V5Z 3X7
(604) 872-8762
Emp Here 100
SIC 5411 Grocery stores

D-U-N-S 24-249-7667   (HQ)
SPENCE DIAMONDS LTD
(*Suby of* Spence Diamonds Ltd)
550 6th Ave W Suite 410, Vancouver, BC, V5Z 1A1
(604) 739-9928
Emp Here 35   *Emp Total* 75
Sales 4,851,006
SIC 5944 Jewelry stores

D-U-N-S 20-918-8747   (SL)
ST JUDE'S ANGLICAN HOME SOCIETY
810 27th Ave W, Vancouver, BC, V5Z 2G7
(604) 874-3200
Emp Here 90   *Sales* 4,085,799
SIC 8051 Skilled nursing care facilities

D-U-N-S 20-506-0481   (BR)
STARBUCKS COFFEE CANADA, INC
(*Suby of* Starbucks Corporation)
682 Broadway W, Vancouver, BC, V5Z 1G1
(604) 708-0030
Emp Here 20
SIC 5812 Eating places

D-U-N-S 20-114-5781   (BR)
STEMCELL TECHNOLOGIES CANADA INC
STEMCELL TECHNOLOGIES INC
570 7th Ave W Suite 400, Vancouver, BC, V5Z 1B3
(604) 877-0713
Emp Here 200
SIC 8733 Noncommercial research organizations

D-U-N-S 24-336-7716   (BR)
UNIVERSITY OF BRITISH COLUMBIA, THE
DIVISION OF ENDOCRINOLOGY
2775 Laurel St App 4116, Vancouver, BC, V5Z 1M9
(604) 875-5929
Emp Here 40
SIC 8011 Offices and clinics of medical doctors

D-U-N-S 20-978-9978   (BR)
UNIVERSITY OF BRITISH COLUMBIA, THE
DEAN'S UNDERGRADUATE OFFICE
2775 Laurel St Suite 5153, Vancouver, BC, V5Z 1M9
(604) 875-4500
Emp Here 35
SIC 8221 Colleges and universities

D-U-N-S 20-587-0566   (BR)
VANCOUVER CITY SAVINGS CREDIT UNION
VANCITY CREDIT UNION
5594 Cambie St, Vancouver, BC, V5Z 3Y5
(604) 683-1956
Emp Here 20
SIC 6062 State credit unions

D-U-N-S 25-450-6439   (BR)
VANCOUVER COASTAL HEALTH AUTHOR-ITY
G F STRONG REHABILITATION CENTRE
(*Suby of* Vancouver Coastal Health Authority)
4255 Laurel St, Vancouver, BC, V5Z 2G9
(604) 734-1313
Emp Here 500
SIC 8093 Specialty outpatient clinics, nec

D-U-N-S 25-933-1270   (BR)
VANCOUVER COASTAL HEALTH AUTHOR-

ITY
RESPIRATORY CLINIC
(*Suby of* Vancouver Coastal Health Authority)
2775 Heather St Suite 111, Vancouver, BC, V5Z 3J5
(604) 875-4122
Emp Here 25
SIC 8011 Offices and clinics of medical doctors

D-U-N-S 25-531-3454   (HQ)
VANCOUVER COASTAL HEALTH AUTHOR-ITY
(*Suby of* Vancouver Coastal Health Authority)
601 Broadway W Suite 750, Vancouver, BC, V5Z 4C2
(604) 875-4111
Emp Here 500   *Emp Total* 24,000
Sales 2,198,032
SIC 8062 General medical and surgical hospitals

D-U-N-S 20-914-9371   (BR)
VANCOUVER COASTAL HEALTH AUTHOR-ITY
RESEARCH INSTITUTE
2647 Willow St Rm 100, Vancouver, BC, V5Z 1M9
(604) 875-4372
Emp Here 500
SIC 8733 Noncommercial research organizations

D-U-N-S 24-336-6403   (BR)
VANCOUVER COASTAL HEALTH AUTHOR-ITY
PURCHASING DEPARTMENT
601 Broadway W Suite 900, Vancouver, BC, V5Z 4C2
(604) 297-9267
Emp Here 100
SIC 8741 Management services

D-U-N-S 24-761-9518   (BR)
VANCOUVER COASTAL HEALTH AUTHOR-ITY
VANCOUVER GENERAL HOSPITAL
855 12th Ave W Suite 101, Vancouver, BC, V5Z 1M9
(604) 875-4111
Emp Here 230
SIC 8062 General medical and surgical hospitals

D-U-N-S 24-364-4569   (BR)
VANCOUVER COASTAL HEALTH AUTHOR-ITY
CENTRE FOR HIP HEALTH AND MOBILITY
2635 Laurel St Level 7, Vancouver, BC, V5Z 1M9
(604) 675-2575
Emp Here 100
SIC 8733 Noncommercial research organizations

D-U-N-S 24-316-2331   (BR)
VANCOUVER COASTAL HEALTH AUTHOR-ITY
VANCOUVER COMMUNITY MENTAL HEALTH SERVICES
520 6th Ave W Suite 200, Vancouver, BC, V5Z 4H5
(604) 874-7626
Emp Here 24
SIC 8741 Management services

D-U-N-S 25-124-8993   (BR)
WHITE SPOT LIMITED
WHITE SPOT RESTAURANT
2850 Cambie St, Vancouver, BC, V5Z 2V5

Emp Here 51
SIC 5812 Eating places

D-U-N-S 25-664-9807   (BR)
WHITE SPOT LIMITED
WHITE SPOT RESTAURANT
650 41st Ave W Suite 613a, Vancouver, BC,

V5Z 2M9
(604) 261-2820
Emp Here 80
SIC 5812 Eating places

Vancouver, BC V6A
Greater Vancouver County

D-U-N-S 25-613-2382   (HQ)
AL-BARAKA INVESTMENTS INC
A & W RESTAURANTS
(*Suby of* Al-Baraka Investments Inc)
1520 Main St, Vancouver, BC, V6A 2W8
(604) 986-5778
Emp Here 45   *Emp Total* 120
Sales 3,648,035
SIC 5812 Eating places

D-U-N-S 25-716-3121   (HQ)
ARITZIA LP
(*Suby of* Aritzia LP)
611 Alexander St Suite 118, Vancouver, BC, V6A 1E1
(604) 251-3132
Emp Here 300   *Emp Total* 800
Sales 48,664,787
SIC 5621 Women's clothing stores
Dir Brian James Hill
Dir Jennifer Wong

D-U-N-S 20-563-8666   (BR)
ASSANTE FINANCIAL MANAGEMENT LTD
ASSANTE WEALTH MANAGEMENT
650 Georgia St W Suite 800, Vancouver, BC, V6A 2A1
(604) 687-7526
Emp Here 60
SIC 8741 Management services

D-U-N-S 20-052-0596   (SL)
AURORA BIOMED INC
1001 Pender St E, Vancouver, BC, V6A 1W2
(604) 215-8700
Emp Here 50   *Sales* 2,699,546
SIC 8731 Commercial physical research

D-U-N-S 20-551-1996   (HQ)
BD CANADA LTD
COBS BREAD
369 Terminal Ave Suite 210, Vancouver, BC, V6A 4C4
(604) 296-3500
Emp Here 30   *Emp Total* 15,000
Sales 20,183,648
SIC 5461 Retail bakeries
Dir Braeden Lord
Dir Roger Gillespie

D-U-N-S 25-297-1114   (BR)
BANK OF NOVA SCOTIA, THE
SCOTIABANK
268 Keefer St Suite 101, Vancouver, BC, V6A 1X5
(604) 668-2163
Emp Here 20
SIC 6021 National commercial banks

D-U-N-S 20-567-1543   (BR)
BANK OF MONTREAL
BMO
168 Pender St E, Vancouver, BC, V6A 1T5
(604) 665-7225
Emp Here 55
SIC 6021 National commercial banks

D-U-N-S 25-185-6597   (BR)
BEAM CANADA INC
611 Alexander St Suite 301, Vancouver, BC, V6A 1E1
(604) 251-3366
Emp Here 25
SIC 8742 Management consulting services

D-U-N-S 25-716-0846   (SL)
BENSEN MANUFACTURING INC
405 Railway St Suite 203, Vancouver, BC, V6A

1A7
(604) 684-4919
Emp Here 60   *Sales* 1,969,939
SIC 2519 Household furniture, nec

D-U-N-S 20-713-4243   (BR)
BOARD OF EDUCATION OF SCHOOL DISTRICT NO. 39 (VANCOUVER), THE
MAIN STREET ADULT EDUCATION CENTRE
333 Terminal Ave Suite 400, Vancouver, BC, V6A 4C1
(604) 713-5731
Emp Here 50
SIC 8211 Elementary and secondary schools

D-U-N-S 20-591-0255   (BR)
BOARD OF EDUCATION OF SCHOOL DISTRICT NO. 39 (VANCOUVER), THE
SEYMOUR ELEMENTARY SCHOOL
1130 Keefer St, Vancouver, BC, V6A 1Z3
(604) 713-4641
Emp Here 30
SIC 8211 Elementary and secondary schools

D-U-N-S 20-591-0727   (BR)
BOARD OF EDUCATION OF SCHOOL DISTRICT NO. 39 (VANCOUVER), THE
LORD STRATHCONA ELEMENTARY SCHOOL
592 Pender St E, Vancouver, BC, V6A 1V5
(604) 713-4630
Emp Here 55
SIC 8211 Elementary and secondary schools

D-U-N-S 25-450-6850   (HQ)
BOSS BAKERY & RESTAURANT LTD, THE
BOSS BAKERY & RESTAURANT
(*Suby of* Boss Bakery & Restaurant Ltd, The)
532 Main St, Vancouver, BC, V6A 2T9
(604) 683-3860
Emp Here 30   *Emp Total* 55
Sales 1,896,978
SIC 5461 Retail bakeries

D-U-N-S 24-658-3389   (BR)
CANADIAN IMPERIAL BANK OF COMMERCE
CIBC
501 Main St Suite 1, Vancouver, BC, V6A 2V2
(604) 665-2071
Emp Here 100
SIC 6021 National commercial banks

D-U-N-S 24-640-1202   (SL)
CANTRAIL COACH LINES LTD
1375 Vernon Dr, Vancouver, BC, V6A 3V4
(604) 294-5541
Emp Here 25   *Sales* 875,528
SIC 4111 Local and suburban transit

D-U-N-S 25-103-7917   (BR)
CITY CENTRE CARE SOCIETY
COOPER PLACE
306 Cordova St E Suite 408, Vancouver, BC, V6A 1L5
(604) 684-2545
Emp Here 37
SIC 8059 Nursing and personal care, nec

D-U-N-S 20-806-0632   (BR)
FETHERSTONHAUGH & CO.
SMART N BIGGER
650 Georgia St E Suite 2200, Vancouver, BC, V6A 2A1

Emp Here 43
SIC 8111 Legal services

D-U-N-S 24-798-5914   (SL)
FLASH COURIER SERVICES INC
1213 Frances St, Vancouver, BC, V6A 1Z4
(604) 689-0826
Emp Here 87   *Sales* 4,377,642
SIC 7389 Business services, nec

D-U-N-S 25-736-1303   (SL)
FLOATA SEAFOOD RESTAURANT (CHINATOWN) LTD

180 Keefer St Suite 400, Vancouver, BC, V6A 4E9
(604) 602-0368
Emp Here 55   *Sales* 1,678,096
SIC 5812 Eating places

D-U-N-S 25-388-2773   (HQ)
FRESHPOINT VANCOUVER, LTD
(*Suby of* Sysco Corporation)
1020 Malkin Ave, Vancouver, BC, V6A 3S9
(604) 253-1551
Emp Here 150   *Emp Total* 51,900
Sales 76,243,932
SIC 5148 Fresh fruits and vegetables
Ex VP Kent Shoemaker
VP Sls Larry Brown
VP Opers Wayne Walling
Dir Bryan Uyesugi
Dir Michael Nichols
Mgr Mark Sanders
Fin Mgr Drew Yurko
Fin Ex Phillip Wong
Pr Pr Brian Sturgeon

D-U-N-S 25-192-6028   (BR)
GCP CANADA INC
GRACE CANADA, INC
(*Suby of* W. R. Grace & Co.)
476 Industrial Ave, Vancouver, BC, V6A 2P3
(604) 669-4642
Emp Here 20
SIC 2819 Industrial inorganic chemicals, nec

D-U-N-S 20-261-4780   (SL)
GCT CANADA LIMITED PARTNERSHIP
(*Suby of* GCT Global Container Terminals Inc)
1285 Franklin St, Vancouver, BC, V6A 1J9
(604) 267-5200
Emp Here 114   *Sales* 291,233,586
SIC 4491 Marine cargo handling
Pr Stephen Edwards

D-U-N-S 20-298-8676   (BR)
GWL REALTY ADVISORS INC
650 Georgia St E Suite 1600, Vancouver, BC, V6A 2A1
(604) 713-6450
Emp Here 35
SIC 6531 Real estate agents and managers

D-U-N-S 20-218-6545   (BR)
GENERAL PAINT CORP
(*Suby of* The Sherwin-Williams Company)
900 Parker, Vancouver, BC, V6A 3L5
(604) 253-3131
Emp Here 35
SIC 2851 Paints and allied products

D-U-N-S 24-695-8326   (HQ)
GENERAL PAINT CORP
(*Suby of* The Sherwin-Williams Company)
950 Raymur Ave, Vancouver, BC, V6A 3L5
(604) 253-3131
Emp Here 150   *Emp Total* 42,550
Sales 78,797,556
SIC 2851 Paints and allied products
Pr Rolph Alcen
VP VP Marcos Levy
VP Shari Co tart
Kent Chester
Pers/VP Dick Glassford
Alfredo Tussie
Marcos Meyohas
Jose Flores

D-U-N-S 24-867-0432   (HQ)
GREAT CANADIAN RAIL TOUR COMPANY LTD
ROCKY MOUNTAINEER VACATIONS
(*Suby of* Armstrong Hospitality Group Ltd)
369 Terminal Ave Suite 101, Vancouver, BC, V6A 4C4
(604) 606-7200
Emp Here 100   *Emp Total* 275
Sales 84,715,377
SIC 4725 Tour operators
Pr Pr Peter R B Armstrong

Laura Lee Armstrong
Mike Phillips
Dir Mackenzie Norris
Dir Sam Gudewill
Dir Jeffrey Lipman
Dir Nick Hafner
Dir Al Duerr
Dir Jim Dinning

D-U-N-S 20-798-0066   (BR)
GREYHOUND CANADA TRANSPORTA-TION ULC
1465 Thornton St, Vancouver, BC, V6A 3V9
(604) 681-1644
Emp Here 54
SIC 4173 Bus terminal and service facilities

D-U-N-S 25-662-0550   (BR)
GREYHOUND CANADA TRANSPORTA-TION ULC
1150 Station St Unit 200, Vancouver, BC, V6A 4C7
(604) 683-8133
Emp Here 100
SIC 4131 Intercity and rural bus transportation

D-U-N-S 24-857-0624   (BR)
GREYHOUND CANADA TRANSPORTA-TION ULC
GREYHOUND COURIER EXPRESS
295 Terminal Ave, Vancouver, BC, V6A 2L7
(604) 681-3526
Emp Here 40
SIC 7389 Business services, nec

D-U-N-S 25-107-0223   (SL)
GRIFFIN TRANSPORTATION SERVICES INC
873 Hastings St E, Vancouver, BC, V6A 1R8
(604) 628-4474
Emp Here 75   *Sales* 3,866,917
SIC 4119 Local passenger transportation, nec

D-U-N-S 24-121-2559   (BR)
HSBC BANK CANADA
1295 Napier St, Vancouver, BC, V6A 2H7

Emp Here 25
SIC 6021 National commercial banks

D-U-N-S 25-822-9723   (BR)
HSBC BANK CANADA
601 Main St, Vancouver, BC, V6A 2V4
(604) 668-4682
Emp Here 40
SIC 6011 Federal reserve banks

D-U-N-S 25-514-3174   (BR)
HOME DEPOT OF CANADA INC
HOME DEPOT
(*Suby of* The Home Depot Inc)
900 Terminal Ave, Vancouver, BC, V6A 4G4
(604) 608-0569
Emp Here 300
SIC 5251 Hardware stores

D-U-N-S 20-622-7852   (HQ)
HON'S WUN-TUN HOUSE LTD
(*Suby of* Hon's Wun-Tun House Ltd)
280 Keefer St, Vancouver, BC, V6A 1X5
(604) 688-0871
Emp Here 30   *Emp Total* 105
Sales 3,724,879
SIC 5812 Eating places

D-U-N-S 25-956-0043   (BR)
LANTIC INC
123 Rogers St, Vancouver, BC, V6A 3N2
(604) 253-1131
Emp Here 185
SIC 2062 Cane sugar refining

D-U-N-S 24-445-8477   (SL)
LARRIVEE, JEAN GUITARS LTD
LARRIVEE GUITARS
780 Cordova St E, Vancouver, BC, V6A 1M3
(604) 253-4553
Emp Here 65   *Sales* 1,969,939

SIC 3931 Musical instruments

D-U-N-S 20-749-1531   (BR)
LONG & MCQUADE LIMITED
LONG & MCQUADE MUSICAL INSTRU-MENTS
368 Terminal Ave, Vancouver, BC, V6A 3W9
(604) 734-4886
Emp Here 100
SIC 5736 Musical instrument stores

D-U-N-S 25-452-2915   (BR)
MCDONALD'S RESTAURANTS OF CANADA LIMITED
MCDONALD'S
(*Suby of* McDonald's Corporation)
1527 Main St, Vancouver, BC, V6A 2W5
(604) 718-1075
Emp Here 100
SIC 5812 Eating places

D-U-N-S 25-311-2874   (BR)
MCDONALD'S RESTAURANTS OF CANADA LIMITED
MCDONALD'S #8437
(*Suby of* McDonald's Corporation)
1150 Station St Suite 1, Vancouver, BC, V6A 4C7

Emp Here 80
SIC 5812 Eating places

D-U-N-S 25-372-1666   (SL)
METALOGIX SOFTWARE CORP
55 E Cordova St Suite 604, Vancouver, BC, V6A 0A5
(604) 677-4636
Emp Here 60   *Sales* 7,709,634
SIC 7372 Prepackaged software
Dir Rasool Rayani

D-U-N-S 24-030-1452   (SL)
NITROGEN STUDIOS CANADA INC
708 Powell St, Vancouver, BC, V6A 1H6
(604) 216-2615
Emp Here 70   *Sales* 3,866,917
SIC 7819 Services allied to motion pictures

D-U-N-S 25-642-7816   (SL)
OUT TO LUNCH CUISINE INC
OTL CATERING
1175 Union St, Vancouver, BC, V6A 2C7
(604) 681-7177
Emp Here 60   *Sales* 1,824,018
SIC 5812 Eating places

D-U-N-S 24-838-7375   (BR)
PATTISON, JIM INDUSTRIES LTD
CANADIAN FISHING COMPANY
1 Gore Ave, Vancouver, BC, V6A 2Y7
(604) 681-0211
Emp Here 60
SIC 2091 Canned and cured fish and seafoods

D-U-N-S 25-662-7803   (BR)
RAINCITY HOUSING AND SUPPORT SOCI-ETY
TRIAGE EMERGENCY SERVICES & CARE SOCIETY, THE
707 Powell St, Vancouver, BC, V6A 1H5
(604) 254-3700
Emp Here 50
SIC 8322 Individual and family services

D-U-N-S 24-383-8315   (BR)
SGS CANADA INC
950 Powell St Unit 203, Vancouver, BC, V6A 1H9
(604) 629-1890
Emp Here 25
SIC 8731 Commercial physical research

D-U-N-S 24-762-0602   (BR)
SCHINDLER ELEVATOR CORPORATION
1206 William St, Vancouver, BC, V6A 2J2
(604) 253-2323
Emp Here 30
SIC 5084 Industrial machinery and equipment

D-U-N-S 24-345-2489   (SL)
ST. JAMES COMMUNITY SERVICE SOCI-ETY
329 Powell St, Vancouver, BC, V6A 1G5
(604) 606-0300
Emp Here 288   *Sales* 18,658,114
SIC 8399 Social services, nec
Pr Pr Brian Moore
Ex Dir Jonathan Oldman

D-U-N-S 24-031-7800   (SL)
STRATHCONA COMMUNITY CENTRE AS-SOCIATION (1972)
STRATHCONA COMMUNITY CENTRE
601 Keefer St, Vancouver, BC, V6A 3V8
(604) 713-1838
Emp Here 100   *Sales* 3,939,878
SIC 8322 Individual and family services

D-U-N-S 24-750-9284   (SL)
STUDIO B PRODUCTIONS INC
190 Alexander St Suite 600, Vancouver, BC, V6A 1B5
(604) 684-2366
Emp Here 70   *Sales* 8,842,240
SIC 7812 Motion picture and video production
Pr Pr Christopher Bartleman
Sec Blair Peters

D-U-N-S 25-974-7772   (SL)
T.N.T. GARMENT MANUFACTURING LTD
BOARDROOM ECO APPAREL
1201 Franklin St, Vancouver, BC, V6A 1L2
(604) 718-7808
Emp Here 50   *Sales* 1,969,939
SIC 2329 Men's and boy's clothing, nec

D-U-N-S 25-618-7493   (BR)
UNITED RENTALS OF CANADA, INC
303 Vernon Dr, Vancouver, BC, V6A 3N3
(604) 708-5506
Emp Here 20
SIC 7359 Equipment rental and leasing, nec

D-U-N-S 20-992-7318   (SL)
UNITOW SERVICES (1978) LTD
1717 Vernon Dr, Vancouver, BC, V6A 3P8
(604) 659-1225
Emp Here 65   *Sales* 3,939,878
SIC 7549 Automotive services, nec

D-U-N-S 20-587-0434   (BR)
VANCOUVER CITY SAVINGS CREDIT UNION
VANCITY CREDIT UNION
183 Terminal Ave, Vancouver, BC, V6A 4G2
(604) 683-1956
Emp Here 20
SIC 6062 State credit unions

D-U-N-S 20-587-0376   (BR)
VANCOUVER CITY SAVINGS CREDIT UNION
VANCITY CREDIT UNION
1285 Main St, Vancouver, BC, V6A 4B6
(604) 877-7640
Emp Here 20
SIC 6062 State credit unions

D-U-N-S 20-117-7248   (BR)
VANCOUVER COASTAL HEALTH AUTHOR-ITY
DOWNTOWN COMMUNITY HEALTH CLINIC
569 Powell St, Vancouver, BC, V6A 1G8
(604) 255-3151
Emp Here 100
SIC 8011 Offices and clinics of medical doc-tors

D-U-N-S 25-429-0018   (BR)
VANCOUVER COASTAL HEALTH AUTHOR-ITY
STRATHCONA MENTAL HEALTH
(*Suby of* Vancouver Coastal Health Authority)
330 Heatley Ave Suite 201, Vancouver, BC, V6A 3G3
(604) 253-4401
Emp Here 52

SIC 8011 Offices and clinics of medical doctors

D-U-N-S 20-981-6870   (BR)
VANCOUVER COASTAL HEALTH AUTHORITY
HEALTH CONTACT CENTER
166 Hastings St E, Vancouver, BC, V6A 1N4

Emp Here 40
SIC 8621 Professional organizations

D-U-N-S 24-330-0006   (BR)
VIA RAIL CANADA INC
1150 Station St Unit 100, Vancouver, BC, V6A 4C7
(604) 640-3771
Emp Here 20
SIC 4111 Local and suburban transit

D-U-N-S 20-958-7872   (SL)
WATERFRONT EMPLOYERS OF B.C.
349 Railway St Suite 400, Vancouver, BC, V6A 1A4
(604) 689-7184
Emp Here 80   Sales 4,377,642
SIC 7374 Data processing and preparation

D-U-N-S 25-068-5989   (BR)
WHITE SPOT LIMITED
WHITE SPOT RESTAURANT
1455 Quebec St Unit 55, Vancouver, BC, V6A 3Z7
(604) 647-0003
Emp Here 25
SIC 5812 Eating places

Vancouver, BC V6B
Greater Vancouver County

D-U-N-S 20-194-1643   (BR)
AMEC FOSTER WHEELER AMERICAS LIMITED
AMEC EARTH & EVIRONMENTAL DIVISION
111 Dunsmuir St Suite 400, Vancouver, BC, V6B 5W3
(604) 664-4315
Emp Here 600
SIC 8711 Engineering services

D-U-N-S 24-750-5324   (BR)
AON CONSULTING INC
AON HEWITT, DIV OF
401 West Georgia, Vancouver, BC, V6B 5A1
(604) 683-7311
Emp Here 30
SIC 8999 Services, nec

D-U-N-S 20-865-7254   (BR)
AON REED STENHOUSE INC
401 W Georgia St Suite 1200, Vancouver, BC, V6B 5A1
(604) 688-4442
Emp Here 180
SIC 6411 Insurance agents, brokers, and service

D-U-N-S 20-515-0944   (BR)
AIR TRANSAT A. T. INC
AIR TRANSAT
Gd Stn Terminal, Vancouver, BC, V6B 3P7
(604) 303-3801
Emp Here 200
SIC 4581 Airports, flying fields, and services

D-U-N-S 20-104-7920   (SL)
APPARENT NETWORKS CANADA INC
321 Water St Suite 400, Vancouver, BC, V6B 1B8
(604) 433-2333
Emp Here 40   Sales 3,575,074
SIC 7371 Custom computer programming services

D-U-N-S 24-677-5287   (BR)
ARAMARK ENTERTAINMENT SERVICES

(CANADA) INC
ARAMARK ENTERTAINMENT SERVICES
800 Griffiths Way, Vancouver, BC, V6B 6G1
(604) 780-7623
Emp Here 100
SIC 8742 Management consulting services

D-U-N-S 20-188-2904   (BR)
ARCADIS CANADA INC
FRANZ ENVIRONMENTAL
1080 Mainland St Unit 308, Vancouver, BC, V6B 2T4
(604) 632-9941
Emp Here 20
SIC 8748 Business consulting, nec

D-U-N-S 20-108-8309   (BR)
ARMY & NAVY DEPT. STORE LIMITED
27 Hastings St W Suite 25, Vancouver, BC, V6B 1G5
(604) 682-6644
Emp Here 150
SIC 5311 Department stores

D-U-N-S 20-689-9333   (SL)
ASENTUS CONSULTING GROUP LTD
(*Suby* of GP Strategies Corporation)
1286 Homer St Suite 200, Vancouver, BC, V6B 2Y5
(604) 609-9993
Emp Here 45   Sales 4,669,485
SIC 8741 Management services

D-U-N-S 20-272-5479   (BR)
ASSANTE FINANCIAL MANAGEMENT LTD
650 Georgia St W Suite 800, Vancouver, BC, V6B 4N8
(604) 678-3444
Emp Here 50
SIC 8741 Management services

D-U-N-S 20-116-7132   (SL)
ATLANTIC HOTELS PARTNERSHIP
510 Hastings St W, Vancouver, BC, V6B 1L8
(604) 687-8813
Emp Here 500   Sales 30,144,000
SIC 7011 Hotels and motels
Dir Roberto Aquilini
Dir Paolo Aquilini
Dir Francesco Aquilini

D-U-N-S 20-960-7618   (BR)
AVIAWEST RESORTS INC
(*Suby* of Aviawest Resorts Inc)
868 Hamilton St, Vancouver, BC, V6B 6A2

Emp Here 20
SIC 7011 Hotels and motels

D-U-N-S 24-316-6662   (HQ)
AVIGILON CORPORATION
AVIGILON
(*Suby* of Avigilon Corporation)
555 Robson St 3rd Fl, Vancouver, BC, V6B 3K9
(604) 629-5182
Emp Here 90   Emp Total 1,159
Sales 353,622,000
SIC 3651 Household audio and video equipment
Alexander Fernandes
Sr VP Sr VP Joel Schuster
VP Sls James Henderson
Sr VP Mahesh Saptharishi
Ric Leong
Murray Teylin
Mike Mcknight
Fred Withers
Murray Tevlin
Wan Jung

D-U-N-S 24-377-4358   (BR)
BRITISH COLUMBIA HYDRO AND POWER AUTHORITY
BC HYDRO
401 Georgia St W, Vancouver, BC, V6B 5A1
(604) 694-8559
Emp Here 50

SIC 4911 Electric services

D-U-N-S 25-951-4321   (BR)
BRITISH COLUMBIA INSTITUTE OF TECHNOLOGY, THE
BCIT
555 Seymour St Suite 750, Vancouver, BC, V6B 3H6

Emp Here 35
SIC 8222 Junior colleges

D-U-N-S 24-080-1279   (BR)
BUY-LOW FOODS LTD
NESTERS MARKET
990 Seymour St, Vancouver, BC, V6B 3L9
(604) 682-3071
Emp Here 110
SIC 5411 Grocery stores

D-U-N-S 24-372-2480   (SL)
BUYATAB ONLINE INC
B1 788 Beatty St, Vancouver, BC, V6B 2M1
(604) 678-3275
Emp Here 56   Sales 4,888,367
SIC 5961 Catalog and mail-order houses

D-U-N-S 20-798-3748   (BR)
CACTUS RESTAURANTS LTD
357 Davie St, Vancouver, BC, V6B 1R2
(604) 685-8070
Emp Here 70
SIC 5812 Eating places

D-U-N-S 20-537-2498   (BR)
CANADA POST CORPORATION
COMMUNICATIONS, PACIFIC DIVISION
Gd Stn Terminal, Vancouver, BC, V6B 3P7

Emp Here 800
SIC 4311 U.s. postal service

D-U-N-S 20-584-8869   (BR)
CANADA POST CORPORATION
349 Georgia St W Unit 100, Vancouver, BC, V6B 0N2
(604) 662-1606
Emp Here 20
SIC 4311 U.s. postal service

D-U-N-S 20-109-8993   (BR)
CANADIAN BROADCASTING CORPORATION
CBC
700 Hamilton St, Vancouver, BC, V6B 2R5
(604) 662-6000
Emp Here 500
SIC 4832 Radio broadcasting stations

D-U-N-S 25-186-2348   (BR)
CANADIAN CHOICE WHOLESALERS LTD
CHOICES MARKET YALETOWN
1202 Richards St, Vancouver, BC, V6B 3G2
(604) 633-2392
Emp Here 60
SIC 5411 Grocery stores

D-U-N-S 24-535-0566   (HQ)
CANADIAN NORTHERN SHIELD INSURANCE COMPANY
CNS
555 Hastings St W Suite 1900, Vancouver, BC, V6B 4N5
(604) 662-2900
Emp Here 89   Emp Total 22,078
Sales 14,986,142
SIC 6411 Insurance agents, brokers, and service
Pr Ken Keenan
VP Fin Alexander Patton
VP Opers Beckie Scarrow

D-U-N-S 25-314-0800   (HQ)
CANADIAN WESTERN TRUST COMPANY
750 Cambie St Suite 300, Vancouver, BC, V6B 0A2
(604) 685-2081
Emp Here 40   Emp Total 2,100
Sales 44,068,263

SIC 6091 Nondeposit trust facilities
Jack Donald
Pr Pr Larry Pollack
VP Rod Sorbo

D-U-N-S 20-792-5673   (SL)
CARA FOODS INC
MILESTONE'S YALETOWN
1109 Hamilton St, Vancouver, BC, V6B 5P6

Emp Here 75   Sales 2,261,782
SIC 5812 Eating places

D-U-N-S 20-351-9111   (SL)
CHARTERED PROFESSIONAL ACCOUNTANTS OF BRITISH COLUMBIA
CPABC
555 Hastings St W Unit 800, Vancouver, BC, V6B 4N5
(604) 872-7222
Emp Here 115   Sales 12,549,240
SIC 8621 Professional organizations
Pr Lori Mathison
Amy Lam
Sabine Rouques

D-U-N-S 20-112-2947   (SL)
CHINA EDUCATION RESOURCES INC
515 Pender St W Suite 300, Vancouver, BC, V6B 6H5
(604) 331-2388
Emp Here 53   Sales 13,420,347
SIC 5999 Miscellaneous retail stores, nec
Chengfeng Zhou
CFO Danny Hon
Li Wang
Yan Tian

D-U-N-S 25-662-3620   (BR)
CHINTZ & COMPANY DECORATIVE FURNISHINGS INC
950 Homer St, Vancouver, BC, V6B 2W7

Emp Here 30
SIC 7389 Business services, nec

D-U-N-S 20-059-6919   (SL)
CINEMARK THEATRES CANADA, INC
CINEMARK TINSELTOWN THEATRES
88 Pender St W Suite 3000, Vancouver, BC, V6B 6N9
(604) 806-0797
Emp Here 65   Sales 2,945,253
SIC 7832 Motion picture theaters, except drive-in

D-U-N-S 25-715-3197   (BR)
CITIZENS BANK OF CANADA
401 Hastings St W Suite 401, Vancouver, BC, V6B 1L5
(604) 708-7800
Emp Here 40
SIC 6021 National commercial banks

D-U-N-S 24-354-8935   (BR)
COSTCO WHOLESALE CANADA LTD
COSTCO
(*Suby* of Costco Wholesale Corporation)
605 Expo Blvd, Vancouver, BC, V6B 1V4
(604) 622-5050
Emp Here 150
SIC 5099 Durable goods, nec

D-U-N-S 20-298-8577   (BR)
CYGNUS SIGN MANAGEMENT INC
1228 Hamilton St Unit 302, Vancouver, BC, V6B 6L2
(604) 261-3330
Emp Here 50
SIC 8712 Architectural services

D-U-N-S 20-813-3723   (SL)
DAVIE STREET MANAGEMENT SERVICES LTD
OPUS HOTEL
322 Davie St, Vancouver, BC, V6B 5Z6
(604) 642-6787
Emp Here 100   Sales 4,377,642

SIC 7011 Hotels and motels

D-U-N-S 25-979-7975   (BR)
DELTA HOTELS LIMITED
DELTA VANCOUVER SUITE HOTEL
550 Hastings St W, Vancouver, BC, V6B 1L6
(604) 689-8188
Emp Here 120
SIC 7011 Hotels and motels

D-U-N-S 24-620-0984   (HQ)
ELAHO LOGGING LTD
WELCH GROUP, THE
555 Hastings St W Suite 2400, Vancouver, BC, V6B 4N6
(604) 892-9891
Emp Here 22   *Emp Total* 100
Sales 4,085,799
SIC 2411 Logging

D-U-N-S 24-339-5691   (SL)
FAIRLEIGH DICKINSON UNIVERSITY OF BRITISH COLUMBIA FOUNDATION
842 Cambie St, Vancouver, BC, V6B 2P6
(604) 682-8112
Emp Here 32   *Sales* 3,356,192
SIC 8221 Colleges and universities

D-U-N-S 25-713-1797   (BR)
FIRST NATIONAL FINANCIAL CORPORATION
1090 Homer St Suite 200, Vancouver, BC, V6B 2W9
(604) 681-5300
Emp Here 55
SIC 6162 Mortgage bankers and loan correspondents

D-U-N-S 24-373-4399   (SL)
GEORGIAN COURT HOTEL INC
773 Beatty St, Vancouver, BC, V6B 2M4
(604) 682-5555
Emp Here 70   *Sales* 3,064,349
SIC 7011 Hotels and motels

D-U-N-S 25-068-6250   (SL)
GOTHAM STEAKHOUSE & COCKTAIL BAR LIMITED PARTNERSHIP
HYS STEAKHOUSE
615 Seymour St, Vancouver, BC, V6B 3K3
(604) 605-8282
Emp Here 80   *Sales* 2,918,428
SIC 5813 Drinking places

D-U-N-S 25-662-0410   (BR)
GOVERNING COUNCIL OF THE SALVATION ARMY IN CANADA, THE
GOVERNING COUNCIL OF THE SALVATION ARMY IN CANADA, THE
555 Homer St Suite 703, Vancouver, BC, V6B 1K8
(604) 681-3405
Emp Here 100
SIC 8322 Individual and family services

D-U-N-S 24-899-0848   (BR)
GRANT THORNTON LLP
CAPSERVCO
333 Seymour St Suite 1600, Vancouver, BC, V6B 0A4
(604) 687-2711
Emp Here 109
SIC 8721 Accounting, auditing, and bookkeeping

D-U-N-S 24-641-1045   (SL)
GRAPHICALLY SPEAKING SERVICES INC
602 West Hastings St Unit 300, Vancouver, BC, V6B 1P2
(604) 682-5500
Emp Here 50   *Sales* 2,772,507
SIC 7374 Data processing and preparation

D-U-N-S 20-107-8867   (BR)
HSBC BANK CANADA
401 W Georgia St Suite 1300, Vancouver, BC, V6B 5A1
(604) 668-4682
Emp Here 90

SIC 8742 Management consulting services

D-U-N-S 24-244-7936   (SL)
HARPER GREY LLP
650 Georgia St W Suite 3200, Vancouver, BC, V6B 4P7
(604) 687-0411
Emp Here 162   *Sales* 13,862,533
SIC 8111 Legal services
Pt Steven Abramson
Pt Kimberly Jakeman
Pt Maureen Lundell
Pt William Macrae
Pt Jonathan Meadows
Pt Barbara Norell
Pt David Pilley
Pt Christopher Rusnak
Pt Raj Samtani
Pt John Sullivan

D-U-N-S 25-500-9177   (BR)
HOTEL SASKATCHEWAN (1990) LTD
SCC GROUP
1118 Homer St Suite 425, Vancouver, BC, V6B 6L5
(604) 688-8291
Emp Here 80
SIC 7011 Hotels and motels

D-U-N-S 25-713-1714   (SL)
I-CORP SECURITY SERVICES LTD
1040 Hamilton St Suite 303, Vancouver, BC, V6B 2R9
(604) 687-8645
Emp Here 150   *Sales* 6,492,800
SIC 7381 Detective and armored car services
Pr Pr Gordon Baker
 Reynold Comeault

D-U-N-S 25-663-4262   (BR)
IMMIGRANT SERVICES SOCIETY OF BRITISH COLUMBIA, THE
530 Drake St, Vancouver, BC, V6B 2H3
(604) 684-7498
Emp Here 35
SIC 7363 Help supply services

D-U-N-S 20-120-3668   (HQ)
IMPERIAL PARKING CANADA CORPORATION
IMPARK
(*Suby of* Gates Group Capital Partners, LLC)
515 Hastings St W Suite 600, Vancouver, BC, V6B 0B2
(604) 681-7311
Emp Here 500   *Emp Total* 5
Sales 46,621,887
SIC 7521 Automobile parking
 Herbert W Anderson Jr
 Walter G Stuelpe
 Bryan L Wallner
VP Fin Allan C Copping
Sr VP Stephen M.G. Richards
Dir Andrew E Saxton
Dir Daniel J Brickman
Dir Anthony Mosse
Dir Paul Clough
Dir Leonard Shavel

D-U-N-S 24-957-7347   (SL)
INCOGNITO SOFTWARE SYSTEMS INC
375 Water St Suite 500, Vancouver, BC, V6B 5C6
(604) 688-4332
Emp Here 103   *Sales* 12,841,083
SIC 7372 Prepackaged software
Pr Pr Stephane Bourque

D-U-N-S 25-676-5413   (SL)
INTRAWEST RESORT OWNERSHIP CORPORATION
CLUB INTRAWEST
(*Suby of* Hawk Holding Company, LLC)
375 Water St Suite 326, Vancouver, BC, V6B 5C6
(604) 689-8816
Emp Here 500   *Sales* 89,483,728
SIC 6531 Real estate agents and managers

 Joe S Houssian
Pr Pr James J Gibbons
VP VP Daniel O Jarvis
VP John E Currie
VP Fin Ron Zimmer
Sec Ross J Meacher

D-U-N-S 24-031-9426   (HQ)
INTRAWEST ULC
BLUE MOUNTAIN RESORT
(*Suby of* Hawk Holding Company, LLC)
375 Water St Suite 710, Vancouver, BC, V6B 5C6
(604) 695-8200
Emp Here 75   *Emp Total* 5,350
Sales 431,392,998
SIC 7011 Hotels and motels
Pr Brian Collins
Dir Trevor Bruno
Dir Sky Foules
Dir Travis Mayer
Dir David Blaiklock
Dir Randal A. Nardone
Dir Hugh Smythe
Dir Andrew Stotesbury
Dir Fin Michael Forsayeth

D-U-N-S 20-647-1489   (BR)
INVESTISSEMENTS HARTCO INC
595 Georgia St W, Vancouver, BC, V6B 1Z5
(604) 688-2662
Emp Here 30
SIC 5734 Computer and software stores

D-U-N-S 20-584-7903   (SL)
KIWI COLLECTION INC
375 Water St Suite 645, Vancouver, BC, V6B 5C6
(604) 737-7397
Emp Here 50   *Sales* 2,845,467
SIC 2731 Book publishing

D-U-N-S 24-750-6686   (SL)
LSC LANGUAGE STUDIES CANADA VANCOUVER LTD
LANGUAGE STUDIES CANADA
570 Dunsmuir St Unit 200, Vancouver, BC, V6B 1Y1
(604) 683-1199
Emp Here 50   *Sales* 2,699,546
SIC 8299 Schools and educational services, nec

D-U-N-S 20-202-0918   (BR)
LABATT BREWING COMPANY LIMITED
1148 Homer St Suite 406, Vancouver, BC, V6B 2X6
(604) 642-6722
Emp Here 42
SIC 8743 Public relations services

D-U-N-S 24-229-8516   (BR)
LEHIGH HANSON MATERIALS LIMITED
OCEAN MARINE TOWING SERVICES
Gd, Vancouver, BC, V6B 3W6
(604) 269-6440
Emp Here 20
SIC 5032 Brick, stone, and related material

D-U-N-S 25-089-7964   (BR)
MATERIAUX DE CONSTRUCTION OLDCASTLE CANADA INC, LES
COAST MASONRY SUPPLIES
Gd Stn Terminal, Vancouver, BC, V6B 3P7
(604) 270-8411
Emp Here 50
SIC 3271 Concrete block and brick

D-U-N-S 24-061-4958   (BR)
MCCANN WORLDGROUP CANADA INC
MACLAREN MCCANN WEST
(*Suby of* The Interpublic Group of Companies Inc)
100 W Pender St 8th Fl, Vancouver, BC, V6B 1R8
(604) 689-1131
Emp Here 26
SIC 7311 Advertising agencies

 Joe S Houssian

D-U-N-S 20-029-2394   (BR)
MCDONALD'S RESTAURANTS OF CANADA LIMITED
MCDONALD'S
(*Suby of* McDonald's Corporation)
275 Robson St Suite 211, Vancouver, BC, V6B 0E7
(604) 689-0804
Emp Here 70
SIC 5812 Eating places

D-U-N-S 20-642-4389   (BR)
MCDONALD'S RESTAURANTS OF CANADA LIMITED
MCDONALD'S #8646
(*Suby of* McDonald's Corporation)
86 Pender St W Unit 1001, Vancouver, BC, V6B 6N8
(604) 718-1165
Emp Here 80
SIC 5812 Eating places

D-U-N-S 24-851-2837   (BR)
MEDIA EXPERTS M.H.S. INC
(*Suby of* 157341 Canada Inc)
134 Abbott St Suite 503, Vancouver, BC, V6B 2K4
(604) 647-4481
Emp Here 30
SIC 7319 Advertising, nec

D-U-N-S 25-721-8420   (BR)
METROPOLITAN CREDIT ADJUSTERS LTD
475 Georgia St W Suite 430, Vancouver, BC, V6B 4M9
(604) 684-0558
Emp Here 20
SIC 7322 Adjustment and collection services

D-U-N-S 24-856-4994   (SL)
MOBIFY RESEARCH AND DEVELOPMENT INC
948 Homer St Fl 3, Vancouver, BC, V6B 2W7
(866) 502-5880
Emp Here 85   *Sales* 10,141,537
SIC 7371 Custom computer programming services
 Igor Faletski
VP Sls Kirk Hasley
VP James Sherrett
 Peter Mclachlan
 John Boxall
Opers Mgr Candace Meagher

D-U-N-S 24-034-4721   (BR)
MORGUARD INVESTMENTS LIMITED
333 Seymour St Suite 400, Vancouver, BC, V6B 5A6
(604) 681-9474
Emp Here 50
SIC 6531 Real estate agents and managers

D-U-N-S 24-325-5432   (SL)
NDG FINANCIAL CORP
Gd Stn Terminal, Vancouver, BC, V6B 3P7

Emp Here 500   *Sales* 96,661,760
SIC 8742 Management consulting services
Pr Pr Peter Ash
 Paul Ash
 Paul Grehan

D-U-N-S 24-373-0822   (BR)
NEWAD MEDIA INC
NEWAD
1120 Hamilton St Suite 209, Vancouver, BC, V6B 2S2
(604) 646-1370
Emp Here 20
SIC 7311 Advertising agencies

D-U-N-S 20-129-0589   (SL)
NEXUS GLOBAL HOLDINGS CORPORATION
NEXUS GLOBAL DIGITAL MARKETING COMPANY
422 Richards St Suite 170, Vancouver, BC, V6B 2Z4

(604) 800-8860
Emp Here 120   *Sales* 17,065,145
SIC 7311 Advertising agencies

D-U-N-S 20-205-1848   (SL)
NORMAN Q CHOW LAW CORPORATION
401 Georgia St W Suite 700, Vancouver, BC, V6B 5A1

Emp Here 50   *Sales* 4,304,681
SIC 8111 Legal services

D-U-N-S 25-316-4883   (BR)
NORTHLAND PROPERTIES CORPORATION
SANDMAN HOTEL VANCOUVER CITY CENTRE
(*Suby of* Northland Properties Corporation)
180 Georgia St W, Vancouver, BC, V6B 4P4
(604) 681-2211
Emp Here 44
SIC 7011 Hotels and motels

D-U-N-S 24-618-7129   (SL)
OUEST BUSINESS SOLUTIONS INC
311 Water St Suite 300, Vancouver, BC, V6B 1B8
(604) 731-9886
Emp Here 40   *Sales* 5,579,750
SIC 8748 Business consulting, nec
Pr Nelson Lai

D-U-N-S 24-566-7241   (SL)
OYEN WIGGS GREEN & MUTALA LLP
601 Cordova St W Suite 480, Vancouver, BC, V6B 1G1
(604) 669-3432
Emp Here 50   *Sales* 4,304,681
SIC 8111 Legal services

D-U-N-S 25-149-6204   (HQ)
PEER 1 NETWORK INC
555 Hastings St W Suite 1000, Vancouver, BC, V6B 4N5
(604) 683-7747
Emp Here 60   *Emp Total* 3,500
Sales 61,936,947
SIC 4813 Telephone communication, except radio
Lance Tracey
Pr Pr Fabio Band
Scott Shaw
Gary Sherlock

D-U-N-S 24-668-2111   (SL)
PLENTYOFFISH MEDIA INC
555 Hastings St W Unit 2525, Vancouver, BC, V6B 1M1
(604) 692-2542
Emp Here 66   *Sales* 2,598,753
SIC 7299 Miscellaneous personal service

D-U-N-S 24-655-8043   (BR)
POLARIS REALTY (CANADA) LIMITED
(*Suby of* Polaris Realty (Canada) Limited)
555 Hastings St W Suite 2000, Vancouver, BC, V6B 4N6
(604) 689-7304
Emp Here 25
SIC 6531 Real estate agents and managers

D-U-N-S 20-922-8811   (SL)
POSITIVE LIVING SOCIETY OF BRITISH COLUMBIA
1101 Seymour St, Vancouver, BC, V6B 5S8
(604) 893-2200
Emp Here 30   *Sales* 7,369,031
SIC 8399 Social services, nec
Ch Bd Neil Self
V Ch Bd Tom Mcaulay
Sec Joel Leung
Treas Walter Petram
Dir Ross Harvey
Dir Elgin Lim

D-U-N-S 24-980-8270   (SL)
PRIME STRATEGIES INC
425 Carrall St Suite 420, Vancouver, BC, V6B 6E3

(604) 689-3446
Emp Here 52   *Sales* 3,205,129
SIC 7389 Business services, nec

D-U-N-S 25-988-2934   (SL)
QUARTERDECK BREWING CO LTD
STEAMWORKS BREWING CO
601 Cordova St W, Vancouver, BC, V6B 1G1
(604) 689-9151
Emp Here 80   *Sales* 2,407,703
SIC 5812 Eating places

D-U-N-S 24-370-5407   (BR)
RAYMOND JAMES (USA) LTD
(*Suby of* Raymond James Financial, Inc.)
333 Seymour St Suite 1450, Vancouver, BC, V6B 5A6
(604) 639-8600
Emp Here 20
SIC 6211 Security brokers and dealers

D-U-N-S 24-685-1286   (SL)
RECON INSTRUMENTS INC
1050 Homer St Suite 220, Vancouver, BC, V6B 2W9
(604) 638-1608
Emp Here 35   *Sales* 3,378,379
SIC 7371 Custom computer programming services

D-U-N-S 25-974-8507   (SL)
RELIC ENTERTAINMENT, INC
THQ CANADA
1040 Hamilton St Suite 400, Vancouver, BC, V6B 2R9
(604) 801-6577
Emp Here 47   *Sales* 4,596,524
SIC 7372 Prepackaged software

D-U-N-S 20-011-8466   (SL)
ROCKSTAR VANCOUVER INC
858 Beatty St Suite 800, Vancouver, BC, V6B 1C1

Emp Here 65   *Sales* 7,223,109
SIC 7372 Prepackaged software
Pr Brian Thalken
Fin Ex Kelly Gibson

D-U-N-S 25-811-7431   (BR)
ROYAL BANK OF CANADA
RBC
(*Suby of* Royal Bank Of Canada)
685 Hastings St W, Vancouver, BC, V6B 1N9
(604) 665-6766
Emp Here 40
SIC 6021 National commercial banks

D-U-N-S 20-551-8447   (BR)
SAVVIS COMMUNICATIONS CANADA, INC
(*Suby of* Centurylink, Inc.)
555 Hastings St W Suite 2600, Vancouver, BC, V6B 4N6
(604) 687-7757
Emp Here 24
SIC 4813 Telephone communication, except radio

D-U-N-S 24-898-5145   (BR)
SCOTIA CAPITAL INC
SCOTIA MCLEOD
650 Georgia St W Unit 1100, Vancouver, BC, V6B 4N9
(604) 668-2094
Emp Here 70
SIC 6211 Security brokers and dealers

D-U-N-S 24-383-9474   (SL)
SEA BREEZE PACIFIC REGIONAL TRANSMISSION SYSTEM, INC
333 Seymour St Suite 1400, Vancouver, BC, V6B 5A6
(604) 689-2991
Emp Here 20   *Sales* 12,858,960
SIC 4911 Electric services
Pr Brian Chernack
Jan Campfens
Sec Paul Manson

D-U-N-S 24-798-2093   (HQ)
SELECT WINE MERCHANTS LTD
SELECT WINE AND SPIRITS
(*Suby of* Select Wine Merchants Ltd)
1122 Mainland St Suite 470, Vancouver, BC, V6B 5L1
(604) 687-8199
Emp Here 30   *Emp Total* 95
Sales 9,557,852
SIC 5182 Wine and distilled beverages
Pr Pr Pierre Doise
Dir Werner Schonberger
Alan Langley

D-U-N-S 25-893-2532   (BR)
SIMON FRASER UNIVERSITY
SFU CENTRE FOR DIALOGUE
515 Hastings St W Suite 3300, Vancouver, BC, V6B 5K3
(778) 782-5000
Emp Here 20
SIC 8221 Colleges and universities

D-U-N-S 24-346-4075   (BR)
SIMON FRASER UNIVERSITY
SIMON FRASER UNIVERSITY BOOKSTORE
555 Hastings St W Suite 17u, Vancouver, BC, V6B 4N5
(778) 782-5235
Emp Here 100
SIC 5942 Book stores

D-U-N-S 20-557-6478   (BR)
SLAVE LAKE PULP CORPORATION
858 Beatty St Suite 501, Vancouver, BC, V6B 1C1
(604) 895-2700
Emp Here 100
SIC 2611 Pulp mills

D-U-N-S 20-191-9979   (BR)
STANTEC ARCHITECTURE LTD
111 Dunsmuir St Suite 1100, Vancouver, BC, V6B 6A3
(604) 696-8000
Emp Here 374
SIC 8712 Architectural services

D-U-N-S 25-361-8714   (BR)
STANTEC CONSULTING LTD
111 Dunsmuir St Suite 1100, Vancouver, BC, V6B 6A3
(604) 696-8000
Emp Here 374
SIC 8711 Engineering services

D-U-N-S 25-705-6804   (BR)
STAPLES CANADA INC
STAPLES THE BUSINESS DEPOT
(*Suby of* Staples, Inc.)
901 Seymour St, Vancouver, BC, V6B 3M1
(604) 602-5959
Emp Here 30
SIC 5943 Stationery stores

D-U-N-S 20-506-0945   (BR)
STARBUCKS COFFEE CANADA, INC
(*Suby of* Starbucks Corporation)
601 Cordova St W Suite 54, Vancouver, BC, V6B 1G1
(604) 685-3758
Emp Here 20
SIC 5812 Eating places

D-U-N-S 25-496-6831   (HQ)
STOCKGROUP MEDIA INC
(*Suby of* Stockgroup Media Inc)
425 Carrall St Suite 190, Vancouver, BC, V6B 6E3
(604) 331-0995
Emp Here 38   *Emp Total* 44
Sales 5,693,280
SIC 4899 Communication services, nec
Pr Pr Leslie Landes
Craig Faulkner
Lindsay Moyle

D-U-N-S 25-850-0115   (BR)

SUKI'S BEAUTY BAZAAR LTD
SUKI'S INTERNATIONAL HAIR DESIGN
(*Suby of* Suki's Beauty Bazaar Ltd)
650 Georgia St W Suite 11506, Vancouver, BC, V6B 4N7

Emp Here 20
SIC 7231 Beauty shops

D-U-N-S 24-384-2973   (SL)
SWIFT POWER CORP
55 Water St Suite 608, Vancouver, BC, V6B 1A1
(604) 637-6393
Emp Here 20   *Sales* 12,858,960
SIC 4911 Electric services
Pr Alexi Zawadzki
Ross Maclachlan
David Turner

D-U-N-S 25-691-7980   (BR)
T & T SUPERMARKET INC
179 Keefer Pl, Vancouver, BC, V6B 6L4
(604) 899-8836
Emp Here 100
SIC 5411 Grocery stores

D-U-N-S 20-552-9337   (BR)
TELUS CORPORATION
TELUS COMMUNICATIONS
555 Robson St Unit 8, Vancouver, BC, V6B 1A6
(604) 697-8044
Emp Here 50
SIC 4813 Telephone communication, except radio

D-U-N-S 20-177-4580   (BR)
TSX INC
650 Georgia St W Unit 2700, Vancouver, BC, V6B 4N9
(604) 689-3334
Emp Here 44
SIC 6231 Security and commodity exchanges

D-U-N-S 20-056-2283   (BR)
TELEFILM CANADA
210 West Georgia St, Vancouver, BC, V6B 0L9
(604) 666-1566
Emp Here 20
SIC 7929 Entertainers and entertainment groups

D-U-N-S 24-163-9194   (SL)
THOMAS DOWNIE HOLDINGS LTD
814 Richards St Suite 100, Vancouver, BC, V6B 3A7
(604) 687-4559
Emp Here 425   *Sales* 103,795,840
SIC 6712 Bank holding companies
Pr Pr Kenneth Downie
VP VP Audrey Williams
John Downie

D-U-N-S 20-801-2138   (HQ)
TOM LEE MUSIC CO. LTD
(*Suby of* Tom Lee Music Co. Ltd)
650 Georgia St W Suite 310, Vancouver, BC, V6B 4N7
(604) 685-8471
Emp Here 20   *Emp Total* 180
Sales 13,132,926
SIC 5736 Musical instrument stores
Pr Pr Henry Lee

D-U-N-S 24-956-9500   (SL)
TOP OF VANCOUVER REVOLVING RESTAURANT (1993) LTD
555 Hastings St W Suite 3400, Vancouver, BC, V6B 4N6
(604) 683-9391
Emp Here 60   *Sales* 1,824,018
SIC 5812 Eating places

D-U-N-S 24-336-2188   (BR)
TORONTO-DOMINION BANK, THE
TD CANADA TRUST
(*Suby of* Toronto-Dominion Bank, The)

1001 Hamilton St, Vancouver, BC, V6B 5T4
(604) 482-2780
Emp Here 150
SIC 6021 National commercial banks

D-U-N-S 25-850-7961   (BR)
TRANSAT TOURS CANADA INC
TRANSAT HOLIDAYS
555 Hastings St W Suite 950, Vancouver, BC, V6B 4N6
(604) 688-3339
Emp Here 60
SIC 4724 Travel agencies

D-U-N-S 24-682-9022   (BR)
TRAVELBRANDS INC
TRAVELBRANDS INC
475 Georgia St W Unit 220, Vancouver, BC, V6B 4M9
(604) 687-0380
Emp Here 60
SIC 4725 Tour operators

D-U-N-S 20-050-0564   (BR)
TRAVELERS INSURANCE COMPANY OF CANADA
ST PAUL TRAVELERS
650 Georgia St W Suite 2500, Vancouver, BC, V6B 4N7
(604) 682-2663
Emp Here 65
SIC 6411 Insurance agents, brokers, and service

D-U-N-S 20-324-9560   (BR)
URBAN SYSTEMS LTD
1090 Homer St Suite 550, Vancouver, BC, V6B 2W9
(604) 235-1701
Emp Here 70
SIC 8711 Engineering services

D-U-N-S 25-103-7123   (SL)
VRX STUDIOS INC
375 Water St Suite 415, Vancouver, BC, V6B 5C6
(604) 605-0050
Emp Here 26   *Sales* 1,896,978
SIC 7379 Computer related services, nec

D-U-N-S 20-733-7820   (BR)
VANCOUVER COASTAL HEALTH AUTHORITY
PENDER CLINIC
59 Pender St W, Vancouver, BC, V6B 1R3
(604) 669-9181
Emp Here 50
SIC 8093 Specialty outpatient clinics, nec

D-U-N-S 25-681-9830   (BR)
VANCOUVER COMMUNITY COLLEGE
CITY CENTRE CAMPUS
250 Pender St W Suite 358, Vancouver, BC, V6B 1S9
(604) 443-8300
Emp Here 1,050
SIC 8221 Colleges and universities

D-U-N-S 25-734-0471   (SL)
VANCOUVER ENGLISH CENTRE INC
250 Smithe St, Vancouver, BC, V6B 1E7
(604) 687-1600
Emp Here 75   *Sales* 5,277,042
SIC 8299 Schools and educational services, nec
Pr Pr Kenneth D Gardner

D-U-N-S 24-824-5391   (HQ)
VANCOUVER FILM SCHOOL LIMITED
(*Suby of* Vancouver Film School Limited)
198 Hastings St W Suite 200, Vancouver, BC, V6B 1H2
(604) 685-5808
Emp Here 30   *Emp Total* 420
Sales 31,550,720
SIC 8299 Schools and educational services, nec
Pr Pr James Griffin
Richard Appleby

Marty Hasselbach

D-U-N-S 25-314-4646   (HQ)
WEST COAST TIMESHARE LTD
(*Suby of* West Coast Timeshare Ltd)
877 Hamilton St, Vancouver, BC, V6B 2R7
(604) 646-0090
Emp Here 35   *Emp Total* 65
Sales 8,507,093
SIC 7389 Business services, nec
Pr Pr John Miller Saldat
Thomas Edward Walker

D-U-N-S 25-928-0907   (BR)
WESTCOAST ENGLISH LANGUAGE CENTER LIMITED
GLOBAL VILLAGE ENGLISH CENTRE
(*Suby of* Westcoast English Language Center Limited)
220 Cambie St Suite 550, Vancouver, BC, V6B 2M9
(604) 684-2354
Emp Here 30
SIC 8299 Schools and educational services, nec

D-U-N-S 20-278-2876   (BR)
WHITE SPOT LIMITED
WHITE SPOT RESTAURANT
405 Dunsmuir St, Vancouver, BC, V6B 1X4
(604) 899-6072
Emp Here 50
SIC 5812 Eating places

D-U-N-S 25-483-9954   (BR)
YOUNG WOMEN'S CHRISTIAN ASSOCIATION
YWCA
733 Beatty St, Vancouver, BC, V6B 2M4
(604) 895-5830
Emp Here 20
SIC 7011 Hotels and motels

Vancouver, BC V6C
Greater Vancouver County

D-U-N-S 20-131-9619   (SL)
10SHEET SERVICES INC
BENCH
(*Suby of* Bench Accounting, Inc.)
717 Pender W Unit 200, Vancouver, BC, V6C 1G9
(888) 760-1940
Emp Here 250   *Sales* 12,993,765
SIC 8721 Accounting, auditing, and bookkeeping
Ian Crosby
VP Adam Saint
VP Sls Felicia Bochicchio
Dir Opers Emily Key
Dir Gibson Turley

D-U-N-S 25-716-3816   (BR)
4211596 CANADA INC
PPI FINANCIAL GROUP
(*Suby of* 4211596 Canada Inc)
666 Burrard St Suite 200, Vancouver, BC, V6C 2X8
(604) 688-8909
Emp Here 35
SIC 6411 Insurance agents, brokers, and service

D-U-N-S 24-760-6887   (SL)
801 WEST GEORGIA LTD
ROSEWOOD GEORGIA HOTEL
801 Georgia St W, Vancouver, BC, V6C 1P7
(604) 682-5566
Emp Here 100   *Sales* 4,377,642
SIC 7011 Hotels and motels

D-U-N-S 24-882-1001   (SL)
ARCHER PETROLEUM CORP
1052 409 Granville St, Vancouver, BC, V6C 1T2

(604) 200-1022
Emp Here 380   *Sales* 103,750,115
SIC 1381 Drilling oil and gas wells
Claude V. Perrier Iii
Pr Pr Colin Bowkett
Robert G. Mcmorran
VP Jeffrey Wilson
Sec James Harris
Victor Barcot

D-U-N-S 25-216-6285   (HQ)
ARROW MINING SERVICES INC
999 Hastings St W Suite 1300, Vancouver, BC, V6C 2W2
(604) 324-1333
Emp Here 35   *Emp Total* 500
Sales 3,137,310
SIC 4212 Local trucking, without storage

D-U-N-S 24-325-0540   (SL)
ASIAN DRAGON GROUP INC
475 Howe St Suite 1100, Vancouver, BC, V6C 2B3
(604) 801-5939
Emp Here 50   *Sales* 5,884,100
SIC 1081 Metal mining services
Pr Pr John Karlsson
Dir Jacques Trottier

D-U-N-S 24-881-3164   (SL)
ATLATSA RESOURCES CORPORATION
666 Burrard St Suite 1700, Vancouver, BC, V6C 2X8
(604) 631-1300
Emp Here 1,500   *Sales* 120,339,846
SIC 1081 Metal mining services
Harold Motaung
Boipelo Lekubo
Joel Kesler
Bava Reddy
Tumelo Motsisi

D-U-N-S 24-672-4645   (BR)
BDO CANADA LLP
VANCOUVER ACCOUNTING
925 Georgia St W Suite 600, Vancouver, BC, V6C 3L2
(604) 688-5421
Emp Here 200
SIC 8721 Accounting, auditing, and bookkeeping

D-U-N-S 24-672-5287   (BR)
BDO CANADA LIMITED
BDO DUNWOODY
925 Georgia St W Suite 600, Vancouver, BC, V6C 3L2
(604) 688-5421
Emp Here 150
SIC 8721 Accounting, auditing, and bookkeeping

D-U-N-S 25-714-2596   (BR)
BMO NESBITT BURNS INC
885 Georgia St W Suite 1800, Vancouver, BC, V6C 3E8
(604) 608-2201
Emp Here 50
SIC 6211 Security brokers and dealers

D-U-N-S 25-295-9481   (BR)
BANK OF NOVA SCOTIA, THE
SCOTIABANK
510 Burrard St Suite 408, Vancouver, BC, V6C 3A8
(604) 718-1500
Emp Here 25
SIC 6021 National commercial banks

D-U-N-S 25-297-0918   (BR)
BANK OF NOVA SCOTIA, THE
SCOTIABANK
815 Hastings St W Suite 300, Vancouver, BC, V6C 1B4
(604) 668-3032
Emp Here 100
SIC 6021 National commercial banks

D-U-N-S 24-206-8182   (BR)

BANK OF NOVA SCOTIA, THE
SCOTIA BANK
409 Granville St Unit 700, Vancouver, BC, V6C 1T2
(604) 630-4000
Emp Here 80
SIC 6021 National commercial banks

D-U-N-S 24-595-2411   (BR)
BANK OF TOKYO-MITSUBISHI UFJ (CANADA)
666 Burrard St Unit 950, Vancouver, BC, V6C 3L1
(604) 691-7300
Emp Here 20
SIC 6021 National commercial banks

D-U-N-S 25-529-7004   (SL)
BELVEDERE RESOURCES LTD
999 Canada Pl Suite 404, Vancouver, BC, V6C 3E2
(604) 513-0007
Emp Here 50   *Sales* 5,472,053
SIC 1041 Gold ores
Pr Pr David Pym
Toby Straus
John Thomson
David Dobson
Charles Donald

D-U-N-S 25-106-8060   (BR)
BORDEN LADNER GERVAIS LLP
BLG
(*Suby of* Borden Ladner Gervais LLP)
200 Burrard St Suite 1200, Vancouver, BC, V6C 3L6
(604) 687-5744
Emp Here 350
SIC 8111 Legal services

D-U-N-S 25-731-1472   (SL)
BOSA CONSTRUCTION INC
838 West Hastings St Unit 1001, Vancouver, BC, V6C 0A6
(604) 299-1363
Emp Here 200   *Sales* 39,836,542
SIC 1522 Residential construction, nec
Pr Pr Robert Bosa
Sec Colin Bosa

D-U-N-S 24-958-1398   (HQ)
BROADRIDGE SOFTWARE LIMITED
BROADRIDGE FINANCIAL SOLUTION
510 Burrard St Suite 600, Vancouver, BC, V6C 3A8
(604) 687-2133
Emp Here 65   *Emp Total* 7,400
Sales 4,851,006
SIC 7374 Data processing and preparation

D-U-N-S 20-957-2304   (SL)
BRYANT FULTON & SHEE ADVERTISING INC
TBWA/VANCOUVER
455 Granville St Suite 300, Vancouver, BC, V6C 1T1

Emp Here 52   *Sales* 8,441,760
SIC 7311 Advertising agencies
Pr Pr Andrea Southcott

D-U-N-S 20-188-1559   (HQ)
CANACCORD GENUITY GROUP INC
(*Suby of* Canaccord Genuity Group Inc)
609 Granville St Suite 2200, Vancouver, BC, V6C 1X6
(604) 643-7300
Emp Here 345   *Emp Total* 749
Sales 669,518,331
SIC 6211 Security brokers and dealers
Pr Pr Dan Daviau
Sr VP Alexis De Rosnay
Don Macfayden
Ex VP Ex VP Adrian Pelosi
Ex VP Stuart Raftus
David Kassie
Charles Bralver
Massimo Carello

Kalpana Desai
Michael Harris

D-U-N-S 24-750-5282　　(BR)
CANADIAN WESTERN BANK
666 Burrard St 22nd Fl, Vancouver, BC, V6C
2X8
(604) 669-0081
Emp Here 500
SIC 6021 National commercial banks

D-U-N-S 20-299-4450　　(BR)
CANON CANADA INC
BUSINESS SOLUTIONS DIVISION
999 Hastings St W Suite 1900, Vancouver,
BC, V6C 2W2
(604) 296-8000
Emp Here 50
SIC 5044 Office equipment

D-U-N-S 20-575-2181　　(BR)
CARLSON WAGONLIT CANADA
CARLSON WAGONLIT TRAVEL
409 Granville St Suite 150, Vancouver, BC,
V6C 1T2
(604) 601-3956
Emp Here 40
SIC 4724 Travel agencies

D-U-N-S 24-838-9751　　(SL)
**CHILLIWACK SALISH PLACE ENTER-
PRISES INC**
*RHOMBUS HOTELS & RESORTS DOWN-
TOWN CHILLIWACK*
409 Granville St Unit 1207, Vancouver, BC,
V6C 1T2

Emp Here 60　　*Sales* 3,118,504
SIC 7011 Hotels and motels

D-U-N-S 20-306-2166　　(SL)
CHOI, GRACE G Y
666 Burrard St Suite 2800, Vancouver, BC,
V6C 2Z7

Emp Here 450　　*Sales* 51,828,480
SIC 8111 Legal services
Owner Grace Choi

D-U-N-S 24-292-5931　　(HQ)
CITIZENS BANK OF CANADA
815 Hastings St W Suite 401, Vancouver, BC,
V6C 1B4
(604) 682-7171
Emp Here 350　　*Emp Total* 2,000
Sales 135,506,910
SIC 6021 National commercial banks
Pr Pr Jason Farris
Ch Bd Tamara Vrooman
V Ch Bd Virginia Weiler
William Knight
Doug Brownridge
Chris Dobrzanski
Alexandra Wilson

D-U-N-S 25-262-4341　　(SL)
DEANS KNIGHT INCOME CORPORATION
999 Hastings St W Suite 1500, Vancouver,
BC, V6C 2W2
(604) 669-0212
Emp Here 27　　*Sales* 11,543,125
SIC 6211 Security brokers and dealers
Craig Langdon
D. Alan Ross
John Brussa
Denyse Chicoyne
Wayne Deans
Philip Hampson
Mark Myles

D-U-N-S 24-327-8798　　(BR)
DENISON MINES INC
885 Georgia St W Suite 2000, Vancouver, BC,
V6C 3E8
(604) 689-7842
Emp Here 30
SIC 1081 Metal mining services

D-U-N-S 24-837-5164　　(BR)

DENTONS CANADA LLP
(*Suby of* Dentons Canada LLP)
250 Howe St Suite 2000, Vancouver, BC, V6C
3R8
(604) 687-4460
Emp Here 125
SIC 8111 Legal services

D-U-N-S 24-824-6563　　(SL)
EASTFIELD RESOURCES LTD
325 Howe St Suite 110, Vancouver, BC, V6C
1Z7
(604) 681-7913
Emp Here 50　　*Sales* 4,231,721
SIC 1081 Metal mining services

D-U-N-S 24-938-4421　　(HQ)
ELDORADO GOLD CORPORATION
ELD
(*Suby of* Eldorado Gold Corporation)
550 Burrard St Suite 1188, Vancouver, BC,
V6C 2B5
(604) 687-4018
Emp Here 35　　*Emp Total* 2,729
Sales 432,727,000
SIC 1041 Gold ores
Pr Pr Paul Wright
Dawn Moss
Fabiana Chubbs
Paul Skayman
Robert Gilmore
K. Ross Cory
Geoffrey A. Handley
Pamela Gibson
Michael Price
Steven Reid

D-U-N-S 24-995-1229　　(SL)
EXETER RESOURCE CORPORATION
999 Hastings St W Suite 1660, Vancouver,
BC, V6C 2W2
(604) 688-9592
Emp Here 45　　*Sales* 150,888
SIC 1041 Gold ores

D-U-N-S 24-866-7701　　(BR)
FAIRMONT HOTELS & RESORTS INC
FAIRMONT HOTEL VANCOUVER, THE
900 Georgia St W, Vancouver, BC, V6C 2W6
(604) 684-3131
Emp Here 500
SIC 7011 Hotels and motels

D-U-N-S 24-930-3686　　(BR)
FAIRMONT HOTELS & RESORTS INC
900 Canada Pl, Vancouver, BC, V6C 3L5
(604) 691-1991
Emp Here 412
SIC 7011 Hotels and motels

D-U-N-S 20-248-8037　　(BR)
FAIRMONT HOTELS INC
FAIRMONT WATERFRONT
900 Canada Pl, Vancouver, BC, V6C 3L5
(604) 691-1832
Emp Here 20
SIC 7011 Hotels and motels

D-U-N-S 24-030-5185　　(BR)
FASKEN MARTINEAU DUMOULIN LLP
550 Burrard St Suite 2900, Vancouver, BC,
V6C 0A3
(604) 631-3131
Emp Here 140
SIC 8111 Legal services

D-U-N-S 20-040-1524　　(BR)
FEDEX OFFICE CANADA LIMITED
FEDEX OFFICE PRINT & SHIP CENTRE
(*Suby of* Fedex Corporation)
779 Pender St W, Vancouver, BC, V6C 1H2
(604) 685-3338
Emp Here 25
SIC 7334 Photocopying and duplicating ser-
vices

D-U-N-S 20-917-9076　　(BR)
FINANCIERE BANQUE NATIONALE INC

NATIONAL BANK FINANCIAL
666 Burrard St Suite 3300, Vancouver, BC,
V6C 2X8
(604) 623-6777
Emp Here 110
SIC 6211 Security brokers and dealers

D-U-N-S 20-111-3784　　(HQ)
FINNING INTERNATIONAL INC
*UNIVERSAL MACHINERY SERVICES, DIV
OF*
(*Suby of* Finning International Inc)
666 Burrard St Suite 1000, Vancouver, BC,
V6C 2X8
(604) 691-6444
Emp Here 897　　*Emp Total* 11,900
Sales 4,162,722,060
SIC 5084 Industrial machinery and equipment
Pr Pr L. Scott Thomson
Ex VP David Cummings
Pers/VP Chad Hiley
Sr VP Sr VP Anna Marks
Steven Nielsen
Juan Carlos Villegas
Sec Jane Murdoch
Douglas W.G. Whitehead
Vicki Avril
Marcelo Awad

D-U-N-S 24-348-6946　　(SL)
GARSON GOLD CORP
470 Granville St Suite 322, Vancouver, BC,
V6C 1V5
(604) 484-2161
Emp Here 20　　*Sales* 2,598,753
SIC 1041 Gold ores

D-U-N-S 24-851-6648　　(BR)
GOODMANS LLP
355 Burrard St Suite 1900, Vancouver, BC,
V6C 2G8
(604) 682-7737
Emp Here 30
SIC 8111 Legal services

D-U-N-S 25-388-7491　　(BR)
GOWLING WLG (CANADA) LLP
GOWLINGS
550 Burrard St Suite 2300, Vancouver, BC,
V6C 2B5
(604) 683-6498
Emp Here 100
SIC 8111 Legal services

D-U-N-S 24-101-7412　　(SL)
GREAT PACIFIC CAPITAL CORPORATION
1067 Cordova St W Suite 1800, Vancouver,
BC, V6C 1C7
(604) 688-6764
Emp Here 25　　*Sales* 2,407,703
SIC 6712 Bank holding companies

D-U-N-S 24-616-4490　　(SL)
HIS INTERNATIONAL TOURS BC INC
636 Hornby St, Vancouver, BC, V6C 2G2
(604) 685-3524
Emp Here 30　　*Sales* 9,234,824
SIC 4724 Travel agencies
Genl Mgr Hiroshi Jiesumasac

D-U-N-S 20-800-5330　　(HQ)
HSBC BANK CANADA
885 Georgia St W, Vancouver, BC, V6C 3G1
(604) 685-1000
Emp Here 300　　*Emp Total* 284,186
Sales 1,289,940,880
SIC 6021 National commercial banks
Pr Pr Sandra Stuart
Samuel Minzberg
Sr VP Kimberly Flood
Jason Henderson
Ex VP Linda Seymour
Sr VP Georgia Stavridis
Ex VP Kim Toews
Ex VP Larry Tomei
Sr VP Sophia Tsui
Sr VP Josee Turcotte

D-U-N-S 24-313-5139　　(BR)
HSBC BANK CANADA
888 Dunsmuir St Suite 900, Vancouver, BC,
V6C 3K4
(604) 641-1893
Emp Here 20
SIC 6021 National commercial banks

D-U-N-S 24-168-4211　　(BR)
HSBC BANK CANADA
885 Georgia St W Suite 620, Vancouver, BC,
V6C 3E8
(604) 641-1122
Emp Here 30
SIC 6021 National commercial banks

D-U-N-S 24-931-1077　　(SL)
HSBC CAPITAL (CANADA) INC
885 Georgia St W Suite 1100, Vancouver, BC,
V6C 3E8
(604) 631-8088
Emp Here 22　　*Sales* 3,551,629
SIC 6211 Security brokers and dealers

D-U-N-S 24-329-2443　　(SL)
HANWEI ENERGY SERVICES CORP
595 Howe St Suite 902, Vancouver, BC, V6C
2T5
(604) 685-2239
Emp Here 123　　*Sales* 5,690,037
SIC 3084 Plastics pipe
Fulai Lang
Yucai Huang
Graham Kwan
Joanne Yan
William Paine
S. Randall Smallbone
Malcolm Clay

D-U-N-S 24-128-8997　　(BR)
HARBOUR AIR LTD
1055 Canada Pl Unit 1, Vancouver, BC, V6C
0C3
(604) 233-3501
Emp Here 350
SIC 4512 Air transportation, scheduled

D-U-N-S 25-687-7861　　(SL)
HATHOR EXPLORATION LIMITED
925 Georgia St W Suite 1810, Vancouver, BC,
V6C 3L2

Emp Here 50　　*Sales* 47,200,320
SIC 1094 Uranium-radium-vanadium ores
Pr Pr Stephen Stanley
Andriyko Herchak
Dir Matthew J. Mason
Dir Benjamin Ainsworth
Dir John Currie
Dir Martin Glynn

D-U-N-S 20-780-5768　　(BR)
HOLT, RENFREW & CIE, LIMITEE
HOLT RENFREW
737 Dunsmuir St, Vancouver, BC, V6C 1N5
(604) 681-3121
Emp Here 660
SIC 5621 Women's clothing stores

D-U-N-S 20-912-2209　　(BR)
HOLT, RENFREW & CIE, LIMITEE
HOLT RENFREW
737 Dunsmuir St, Vancouver, BC, V6C 1N5
(604) 681-3121
Emp Here 400
SIC 5311 Department stores

D-U-N-S 24-620-3749　　(SL)
**HORNBY STREET (VANCOUVER) RESTAU-
RANTS LTD**
KEG CAESARS
595 Hornby St Suite 600, Vancouver, BC, V6C
2E8
(604) 687-4044
Emp Here 150　　*Sales* 4,523,563
SIC 5812 Eating places

D-U-N-S 20-112-4302　　(BR)
HUDSON'S BAY COMPANY

BAY, THE
674 Granville St Suite 9999, Vancouver, BC,
V6C 1Z6
(604) 681-6211
Emp Here 1,300
SIC 5311 Department stores

        D-U-N-S 25-613-6771   (BR)
HY'S OF CANADA LTD
HY'S ENCORE
637 Hornby St, Vancouver, BC, V6C 2G3
(604) 684-3311
Emp Here 50
SIC 5812 Eating places

        D-U-N-S 20-298-4415   (BR)
INNERGEX RENEWABLE ENERGY INC
*INNERGEX RENEWABLE ENERGY SUS-
TAINABLE DEVELOPMENT*
666 Burrard St Suite 200, Vancouver, BC, V6C
2X8
(604) 633-9990
Emp Here 20
SIC 4931 Electric and other services com-
bined

        D-U-N-S 20-315-5668   (BR)
INTACT INSURANCE COMPANY
999 Hastings St W Suite 1100, Vancouver,
BC, V6C 2W2
(604) 891-5400
Emp Here 360
SIC 6331 Fire, marine, and casualty insurance

        D-U-N-S 20-513-7974   (BR)
INTRAWEST ULC
(*Suby of* Intrawest Resorts Holdings, Inc.)
900 Hastings St W Suite 900, Vancouver, BC,
V6C 1E5
(604) 647-0750
Emp Here 64
SIC 4725 Tour operators

        D-U-N-S 24-855-9270   (SL)
IVANHOE CAPITAL CORPORATION
999 Canada Pl Suite 654, Vancouver, BC,
V6C 3E1
(604) 688-7166
Emp Here 45   *Sales* 6,407,837
SIC 6712 Bank holding companies
  Robert Friedland
  Greg Shenton

        D-U-N-S 24-850-9130   (BR)
**JONES LANG LASALLE REAL ESTATE
SERVICES, INC**
(*Suby of* Jones Lang Lasalle Incorporated)
355 Burrard St 14th Flr, Vancouver, BC, V6C
2G6
(604) 998-6001
Emp Here 20
SIC 6531 Real estate agents and managers

        D-U-N-S 20-557-5561   (SL)
KAMINAK GOLD CORPORATION
800 Pender St W Suite 1020, Vancouver, BC,
V6C 2V6
(604) 646-4527
Emp Here 20   *Sales* 1,992,377
SIC 1081 Metal mining services

        D-U-N-S 20-272-2893   (SL)
LAYER 7 TECHNOLOGIES INC
(*Suby of* Ca, Inc.)
885 Georgia St W Suite 500, Vancouver, BC,
V6C 3E8
(604) 681-9377
Emp Here 90   *Sales* 19,923,773
SIC 7371 Custom computer programming ser-
vices
Pr Pr Paul Rochester
  Praveen Gupta
  Dimitri Sirota

        D-U-N-S 20-105-5691   (HQ)
LEDCOR CONSTRUCTION LIMITED
1067 Cordova St W Suite 1200, Vancouver,
BC, V6C 1C7

(604) 681-7500
Emp Here 150   *Emp Total* 7
Sales 46,403,005
SIC 1542 Nonresidential construction, nec
Ch Bd David Lede
Pr Peter Hrdlitschka
VP Jim Logan

        D-U-N-S 20-117-7651   (HQ)
LEDCOR INDUSTRIES INC
LEDCOR GROUP
1067 Cordova St W Suite 1200, Vancouver,
BC, V6C 1C7
(604) 681-7500
Emp Here 800   *Emp Total* 7
Sales 110,793,503
SIC 1611 Highway and street construction
Pr Pr David Lede
  Clifford Lede
  Leroy Sonnenberg

        D-U-N-S 24-164-9008   (HQ)
LEGAL SERVICES SOCIETY
510 Burrard St Suite 400, Vancouver, BC, V6C
3A8
(604) 601-6200
Emp Here 20   *Emp Total* 60,000
Sales 10,135,137
SIC 8111 Legal services
  D. Mayland Mckimm
  Janice Comeau
  David Crossin
  Larry Goble
  Bruce Hardy
  Richard Schwartz
  Geoffrey Cowpower
  Deanna Ludowicz
  Todd Ormiston

        D-U-N-S 24-131-4025   (SL)
LEITH WHEELER FIXED INCOME FUND
400 Burrard St Suite 1500, Vancouver, BC,
V6C 3A6
(604) 683-3391
Emp Here 49   *Sales* 14,592,140
SIC 6722 Management investment, open-end
Owner Kim Gilliland

        D-U-N-S 24-493-4204   (SL)
**LEITH WHEELER INVESTMENT COUNSEL
LTD**
LEITH WHEELER
400 Burrard St Suite 1500, Vancouver, BC,
V6C 3A6
(604) 683-3391
Emp Here 45   *Sales* 14,527,680
SIC 6282 Investment advice
  William Wheeler
Pr Pr David Schaffner
  Gordon Gibbons
  Cecilia Wong
  William (Bill) Dye

        D-U-N-S 25-736-1766   (BR)
LEONE INTERNATIONAL MARKETING INC
L2 LEONE
(*Suby of* Leone International Marketing Inc)
757 Hastings St W Unit R112, Vancouver, BC,
V6C 1A1
(604) 685-9327
Emp Here 50
SIC 5699 Miscellaneous apparel and acces-
sory stores

        D-U-N-S 20-647-3279   (BR)
**MBM INTELLECTUAL PROPERTY LAW
LLP**
200 Granville St Suite 2200, Vancouver, BC,
V6C 1S4
(604) 669-4350
Emp Here 20
SIC 8111 Legal services

        D-U-N-S 20-076-2891   (BR)
**MBM INTELLECTUAL PROPERTY LAW
LLP**
700 Pender St W Suite 700, Vancouver, BC,
V6C 1G8

(604) 669-4350
Emp Here 20
SIC 8111 Legal services

        D-U-N-S 25-100-1558   (BR)
MACKENZIE FINANCIAL CORPORATION
MACKENZIE INVESTMENTS
200 Burrard St Suite 400, Vancouver, BC, V6C
3L6
(604) 685-4231
Emp Here 70
SIC 6282 Investment advice

        D-U-N-S 24-163-2025   (BR)
**MACQUARIE CAPITAL MARKETS CANADA
LTD**
BLACKMONT CAPITAL
550 Burrard St Suite 500, Vancouver, BC, V6C
2B5
(604) 605-3944
Emp Here 160
SIC 6211 Security brokers and dealers

        D-U-N-S 25-368-4518   (BR)
MACQUARIE NORTH AMERICA LTD
MACQUARIE CAPITAL MARKETS CANADA
550 Burrard St Suite 2400, Vancouver, BC,
V6C 2B5
(604) 605-3944
Emp Here 25
SIC 6159 Miscellaneous business credit insti-
tutions

        D-U-N-S 25-301-6349   (BR)
**MANUFACTURERS LIFE INSURANCE
COMPANY, THE**
MANULIFE FINANCIAL
510 Burrard St Suite 1000, Vancouver, BC,
V6C 3A8
(604) 681-6136
Emp Here 30
SIC 6311 Life insurance

        D-U-N-S 24-797-6665   (BR)
MARSH CANADA LIMITED
(*Suby of* Marsh & McLennan Companies, Inc.)
550 Burrard St Suite 800, Vancouver, BC, V6C
2K1
(604) 443-3554
Emp Here 180
SIC 6411 Insurance agents, brokers, and service

        D-U-N-S 24-087-7667   (SL)
MAXHIRE SOLUTIONS INC
(*Suby of* Bullhorn, Inc.)
625 Howe St Suite 650, Vancouver, BC, V6C
2T6
(800) 206-7934
Emp Here 24   *Sales* 1,751,057
SIC 7371 Custom computer programming services

        D-U-N-S 20-995-5640   (BR)
MERCER (CANADA) LIMITED
MMC
(*Suby of* Marsh & McLennan Companies, Inc.)
550 Burrard St Suite 900, Vancouver, BC, V6C
3S8
(604) 683-6761
Emp Here 100
SIC 8999 Services, nec

        D-U-N-S 20-296-1439   (SL)
NEVADA ENERGY METALS INC
789 Pender St W Suite 1220, Vancouver, BC,
V6C 1H2
(604) 428-5690
Emp Here 197   *Sales* 2,188,821
SIC 1081 Metal mining services

        D-U-N-S 24-312-9934   (SL)
NORTH GROUP FINANCE LIMITED
925 West Georgia St Suite 1000, Vancouver,
BC, V6C 3L2
(604) 689-7565
Emp Here 271   *Sales* 1,547
SIC 6282 Investment advice

        D-U-N-S 20-646-3759   (BR)

        D-U-N-S 20-509-6670   (HQ)
NORTHERN SECURITIES INC
400 Burrard St Suite 1110, Vancouver, BC,
V6C 3A6

Emp Here 20
SIC 6211 Security brokers and dealers

        D-U-N-S 20-509-6670   (HQ)
ODLUM BROWN LIMITED
(*Suby of* Odlum Brown Limited)
250 Howe St Suite 1100, Vancouver, BC, V6C
3S9
(604) 669-1600
Emp Here 130   *Emp Total* 200
Sales 37,693,160
SIC 6211 Security brokers and dealers
Pr Pr Stuart Ross Sherwood
Dir Peter Robson
Dir Richard Sales
Dir William Edmonds
Dir Graham Cumpston
Dir Peter Pacholko
  Robert Sutherland
  Nancy Mckinstry
  Debbie Hewson
  William Mcfarlane

        D-U-N-S 24-034-4627   (SL)
ORCA GOLD INC
885 Georgia St W Suite 2000, Vancouver, BC,
V6C 3E8
(604) 689-7842
Emp Here 60   *Sales* 6,493,502
SIC 1041 Gold ores
  Richard Clark
Pr Pr Hugh Stuart
  Kevin Ross
  Jeff Yip
  Simon Jackson
  Alex Davidson
  Robert Chase
  David Field
  Derek White

        D-U-N-S 24-360-6204   (SL)
PPC CANADA ENTERPRISES CORP
625 Howe St Suite 410, Vancouver, BC, V6C
2T6
(604) 687-0407
Emp Here 50   *Sales* 7,632,865
SIC 6719 Holding companies, nec
Dir Keiichi Goto
Dir Toru Higuchi
Dir Eiji Kato
Dir Trevor Scott
  Sandra Lim

        D-U-N-S 24-225-6555   (BR)
PRT GROWING SERVICES LTD
355 Burrard St Suite 410, Vancouver, BC, V6C
2G8
(604) 687-1404
Emp Here 505
SIC 7389 Business services, nec

        D-U-N-S 20-863-0467   (HQ)
**PHILLIPS, HAGER & NORTH INVESTMENT
MANAGEMENT LTD**
(*Suby of* Royal Bank Of Canada)
200 Burrard St Suite 2000, Vancouver, BC,
V6C 3L6
(604) 408-6000
Emp Here 197   *Emp Total* 79,000
Sales 48,529,944
SIC 6371 Pension, health, and welfare funds
Pr Pr Tom Bradley
Dir Dick Bradshaw
  John Montaotano
VP Rick Brooks-Hill
VP Don Panchuk
VP Stewart Marshall
VP VP Scott Lamont
VP VP John Montalbano
VP VP Hanif Mamdani
VP VP Dale Harrison

        D-U-N-S 25-441-9674   (SL)

PLUTONIC POWER CORPORATION
888 Dunsmuir St Suite 600, Vancouver, BC, V6C 3K4
(604) 669-4999
Emp Here 51   *Sales* 32,785,440
SIC 4911 Electric services
Donald A. Mcinnes
Pr Pr Paul Sweeney
Peter G. Wong
Walter T. Segsworth
R. Stuart Angus
William F. Lindqvist
David O'brien
Larry P. Fontaine
Bruce D. Ripley
Grigor Cook

D-U-N-S 24-000-9287   (BR)
POSTMEDIA NETWORK INC
200 Granville St Suite 1, Vancouver, BC, V6C 3N3
(604) 605-2000
Emp Here 500
SIC 2711 Newspapers

D-U-N-S 20-347-9316   (BR)
POSTMEDIA NETWORK INC
PACIFIC NEWSPAPER GROUP DIV OF
200 Granville St Suite 1, Vancouver, BC, V6C 3N3
(604) 605-2000
Emp Here 100
SIC 2711 Newspapers

D-U-N-S 25-330-1949   (HQ)
POWEREX CORP
666 Burrard St Suite 1300, Vancouver, BC, V6C 2X8
(604) 891-5000
Emp Here 124   *Emp Total* 60,000
Sales 70,945,957
SIC 4911 Electric services
Pr Pr Teresa Conway
Ch Bd Larry Blain
CFO Janette Lyons
Dir James Brown
Dir Stephen Bellringer
Dir Amit Budhwar
Dir Mike Macdougall
Prs Dir Julie Mantle

D-U-N-S 24-347-2128   (HQ)
PREMIER MARINE INSURANCE MANAGERS GROUP (WEST) INC
625 Howe St Suite 625, Vancouver, BC, V6C 2T6
(604) 697-5730
Emp Here 45   *Emp Total* 4,567
Sales 40,708,613
SIC 6331 Fire, marine, and casualty insurance
Ch Bd Nat Moreira
Pr Troy Moreira
Sr VP Henry John

D-U-N-S 25-995-4592   (BR)
PRICEWATERHOUSECOOPERS LLP
250 Howe St Suite 700, Vancouver, BC, V6C 3S7
(604) 806-7000
Emp Here 600
SIC 8721 Accounting, auditing, and bookkeeping

D-U-N-S 20-520-8668   (BR)
RBC DOMINION SECURITIES INC
RBC INVESTMENTS
(*Suby of* Royal Bank Of Canada)
666 Burrard St Unit 2500, Vancouver, BC, V6C 2X8
(604) 257-7200
Emp Here 150
SIC 6282 Investment advice

D-U-N-S 24-798-7373   (HQ)
RAYMOND JAMES (USA) LTD
(*Suby of* Raymond James Financial, Inc.)
925 Georgia St W Suite 2100, Vancouver, BC, V6C 3L2

(604) 654-7258
Emp Here 150   *Emp Total* 11,000
Sales 10,900,264
SIC 6211 Security brokers and dealers
Pr Lj Eiben
Ian Brown
Sr VP Trish Campbell
VP Darren Martin
Ex VP Lloyd Costley
Sr VP Mario Addeo

D-U-N-S 20-234-9200   (SL)
ROCKPORT HOMES INTERNATIONAL INC
700 Pender St W Suite 507, Vancouver, BC, V6C 1G8

Emp Here 49   *Sales* 10,145,000
SIC 1521 Single-family housing construction
Pr William Malone

D-U-N-S 20-990-1144   (BR)
ROYAL BANK OF CANADA
RBC ROYAL BANK
(*Suby of* Royal Bank Of Canada)
666 Burrard St Suite 2100, Vancouver, BC, V6C 2X8
(604) 257-7110
Emp Here 20
SIC 6211 Security brokers and dealers

D-U-N-S 24-374-4450   (SL)
SAFEMAP INTERNATIONAL INC
SAFEMAP
666 Burrard St Suite 500, Vancouver, BC, V6C 3P6
(604) 642-6110
Emp Here 45   *Sales* 6,492,800
SIC 8748 Business consulting, nec
Dir Cornelius Pitzer

D-U-N-S 25-716-5555   (BR)
SAP CANADA INC
666 Burrard St Unit 1550, Vancouver, BC, V6C 2X8
(604) 684-1514
Emp Here 32
SIC 7372 Prepackaged software

D-U-N-S 25-299-2680   (BR)
SCDA (2015) INC
625 Howe St Suite 1400, Vancouver, BC, V6C 2T6
(604) 664-8040
Emp Here 24
SIC 6162 Mortgage bankers and loan correspondents

D-U-N-S 20-136-5462   (BR)
SCDA (2015) INC
625 Howe St Suite 900, Vancouver, BC, V6C 2T6
(604) 664-8030
Emp Here 40
SIC 6311 Life insurance

D-U-N-S 24-682-0117   (SL)
SECURED SECURITY GROUP (INTERNATIONAL) LIMITED
3555 Burrard St Suite 1400, Vancouver, BC, V6C 2G8
(604) 385-1555
Emp Here 60   *Sales* 1,896,978
SIC 7381 Detective and armored car services

D-U-N-S 20-191-1398   (BR)
SERVICES FINANCIERS NCO, INC
AGENCE DE RECOUVREMENT
(*Suby of* Egs Shell Company, Inc.)
800 Pender St W Suite 1400, Vancouver, BC, V6C 2V6
(604) 643-7800
Emp Here 65
SIC 7322 Adjustment and collection services

D-U-N-S 20-294-4385   (BR)
SIMON FRASER UNIVERSITY
BEEDIE SCHOOL OF BUSINESS
500 Granville St, Vancouver, BC, V6C 1W6
(778) 782-5013
Emp Here 100

SIC 8244 Business and secretarial schools

D-U-N-S 24-373-7590   (HQ)
SMYTHE RATCLIFFE LLP
(*Suby of* Smythe Ratcliffe LLP)
355 Burrard St Suite 700, Vancouver, BC, V6C 2G8
(604) 687-1231
Emp Here 68   *Emp Total* 80
Sales 3,502,114
SIC 8721 Accounting, auditing, and bookkeeping

D-U-N-S 25-408-9089   (SL)
SOPHOS INC
(*Suby of* SOPHOS GROUP PLC)
580 Granville St Suite 400, Vancouver, BC, V6C 1W6
(604) 484-6400
Emp Here 190   *Sales* 25,609,206
SIC 7371 Custom computer programming services
Pr Steve Munford
Jim Zadra

D-U-N-S 25-326-3990   (BR)
STIKEMAN ELLIOTT LLP
666 Burrard St Suite 1700, Vancouver, BC, V6C 2X8
(604) 631-1300
Emp Here 40
SIC 8111 Legal services

D-U-N-S 25-533-1092   (HQ)
TIO NETWORKS CORP
(*Suby of* TIO Networks Corp)
250 Howe St Suite 1500, Vancouver, BC, V6C 3R8
(604) 298-4636
Emp Here 27   *Emp Total* 30
Sales 58,083,869
SIC 6211 Security brokers and dealers

D-U-N-S 24-961-1757   (SL)
TECK-BULLMOOSE COAL INC
550 Burrard St Suite 3300, Vancouver, BC, V6C 0B3
(604) 699-4000
Emp Here 505   *Sales* 300,762,240
SIC 1221 Bituminous coal and lignite-surface mining
Pr Pr Kieth Steeves
VP VP John Taylor
Treas Larry Mackwood
Sec Karen Dunfee
Norman Keevil
Michael Lipkewich
Richard Mundie
Asst Cont Ron Millos
Fin Ex Howard Chu

D-U-N-S 24-426-2031   (SL)
TEEMA SOLUTIONS GROUP INC
666 Burrard St Suite 500, Vancouver, BC, V6C 3P6
(604) 639-3118
Emp Here 122   *Sales* 15,759,511
SIC 8748 Business consulting, nec
Pr Brian Antenbring

D-U-N-S 25-507-6424   (BR)
TETRA TECH CANADA INC
TETRA TECH CANADA
(*Suby of* Tetra Tech, Inc.)
885 Dunsmuir St Unit 1000, Vancouver, BC, V6C 1N5
(604) 685-0275
Emp Here 42
SIC 8711 Engineering services

D-U-N-S 20-349-4997   (SL)
TONKO REALTY ADVISORS (B.C.) LTD
789 Pender St W Suite 600, Vancouver, BC, V6C 1H2
(604) 684-1198
Emp Here 130   *Sales* 17,043,600
SIC 6531 Real estate agents and managers
VP VP Edith Hewitt

Sr VP Sandy Cruickshank

D-U-N-S 24-120-5306   (BR)
TORONTO-DOMINION BANK, THE
TD CANADA TRUST
(*Suby of* Toronto-Dominion Bank, The)
717 Pender St W Suite 400, Vancouver, BC, V6C 1G9

Emp Here 60
SIC 6021 National commercial banks

D-U-N-S 24-334-9599   (SL)
VANCOUVER BAY CLUBS LTD
STEVE NASH SPORTS CLUB
610 Granville St Suite 201, Vancouver, BC, V6C 3T3
(604) 682-5213
Emp Here 75   *Sales* 4,851,006
SIC 7999 Amusement and recreation, nec

D-U-N-S 20-647-0309   (BR)
VANCOUVER CITY SAVINGS CREDIT UNION
CREDENTIAL SECURITY
900 Hastings St W Suite 310, Vancouver, BC, V6C 1E5
(604) 709-5838
Emp Here 30
SIC 6211 Security brokers and dealers

D-U-N-S 24-312-2785   (HQ)
WESBILD HOLDINGS LTD
WESBILD SHOPPING CENTRES
(*Suby of* Inwest Investments Ltd)
666 Burrard St Suite 2650, Vancouver, BC, V6C 2X8
(604) 694-8800
Emp Here 20   *Emp Total* 200
Sales 6,420,542
SIC 6512 Nonresidential building operators
Pr Kevin Layden
Hassan Khosrowshahi
Maryam Khosrowshahi
Dir Nezhat Khosrowshahi
Dir Golnar Khosrowshahi
Dir Behzad Khosrowshahi

D-U-N-S 25-262-0562   (SL)
WESTBANK PROJECTS CORP
1067 Cordova St W Suite 501, Vancouver, BC, V6C 1C7
(604) 685-8986
Emp Here 22   *Sales* 7,004,227
SIC 6553 Cemetery subdividers and developers
Pr Pr Ian Gillespie
Theodore Ong

D-U-N-S 25-314-0511   (SL)
WILLIAMS OPERATING CORPORATION
550 Burrard St Suite 3300, Vancouver, BC, V6C 0B3
(604) 699-4000
Emp Here 400   *Sales* 238,234,320
SIC 1221 Bituminous coal and lignite-surface mining
VP Fin Ron Millos

D-U-N-S 20-991-6134   (BR)
YOUNG WOMEN'S CHRISTIAN ASSOCIATION
535 Hornby St Suite 100, Vancouver, BC, V6C 2E8
(604) 895-5777
Emp Here 100
SIC 8641 Civic and social associations

D-U-N-S 24-593-8766   (HQ)
ZLC FINANCIAL GROUP LTD
(*Suby of* ZLC Financial Group Ltd)
666 Burrard St Suite 1200, Vancouver, BC, V6C 2X8
(604) 684-3863
Emp Here 40   *Emp Total* 50
Sales 4,523,563
SIC 6411 Insurance agents, brokers, and service

▲ Public Company   ■ Public Company Family Member   **HQ** Headquarters   **BR** Branch   **SL** Single Location

D-U-N-S 24-957-2264 (BR)
ZURICH CANADIAN HOLDINGS LIMITED
ZURICH CANADA
510 Burrard St Suite 709, Vancouver, BC, V6C 3A8
(604) 685-9241
Emp Here 49
SIC 6351 Surety insurance

Vancouver, BC V6E
Greater Vancouver County

D-U-N-S 24-786-9597 (SL)
327647 BRITISH COLUMBIA LTD
1095 Pender St W Suite 900, Vancouver, BC, V6E 2M6
(604) 662-3838
Emp Here 25 *Sales* 10,699,440
SIC 6553 Cemetery subdividers and developers
Pr Pr Terrence Hui
Dir Brian Hansen
Dir Kau-Mo Hui
 Peter Wong
VP VP Peter Yeh

D-U-N-S 24-367-9214 (BR)
4513380 CANADA INC
LIVINGSTON INTERNATIONAL
1140 Pender St W Suite 500, Vancouver, BC, V6E 4H5
(604) 685-3555
Emp Here 40
SIC 4731 Freight transportation arrangement

D-U-N-S 20-959-7236 (BR)
AXA ASSURANCES INC
AXA PACIFIC INSURANCE
1090 Georgia St W Suite 1350, Vancouver, BC, V6E 3V7

Emp Here 160
SIC 6311 Life insurance

D-U-N-S 24-855-9663 (BR)
ALLNORTH CONSULTANTS LIMITED
1100 Melvil e St Unit 1200, Vancouver, BC, V6E 4A6
(604) 602-1175
Emp Here 60
SIC 8742 Management consulting services

D-U-N-S 20-591-0263 (BR)
BOARD OF EDUCATION OF SCHOOL DISTRICT NO. 39 (VANCOUVER), THE
LORD ROBERT ANNEX
1150 Nelson St, Vancouver, BC, V6E 1J2
(604) 713-5495
Emp Here 20
SIC 8211 Elementary and secondary schools

D-U-N-S 25-991-0883 (BR)
CBRE LIMITED
1021 Hastings St W Suite 2500, Vancouver, BC, V6E 0C3
(604) 662-3000
Emp Here 80
SIC 6531 Real estate agents and managers

D-U-N-S 24-011-4830 (BR)
CIBC WORLD MARKETS INC
1285 Pender St W Suite 400, Vancouver, BC, V6E 4B1
(604) 685-3434
Emp Here 55
SIC 6211 Security brokers and dealers

D-U-N-S 25-832-0217 (SL)
CSAV AGENCY LTD
CSAV AGENCY NORTH AMERICA
1166 Alberni St Suite 503, Vancouver, BC, V6E 3Z3
(604) 646-0120
Emp Here 40 *Sales* 12,815,674
SIC 4731 Freight transportation arrangement

Fin Ex Mathew Pulakkavil
Pr Andres Kulka Kuperman

D-U-N-S 25-613-6110 (BR)
CACTUS RESTAURANTS LTD
CACTUS CLUB CAFE
1136 Robson St, Vancouver, BC, V6E 1B2
(604) 687-3278
Emp Here 70
SIC 5812 Eating places

D-U-N-S 24-797-6244 (HQ)
CANWEL BUILDING MATERIALS LTD
SUREWOOD FOREST PRODUCTS, DIV OF
1055 West Georgia St Suite 1100, Vancouver, BC, V6E 3P3
(604) 432-1400
Emp Here 50 *Emp Total* 252
Sales 173,250,200
SIC 5039 Construction materials, nec
 Amar Doman
Pr Pr Marc Seguin
Sec R.S. (Rob) Doman
Prs Dir Julie Wong
 James Code

D-U-N-S 25-359-7140 (BR)
CANADIAN BREAST CANCER FOUNDATION
(*Suby of* Canadian Breast Cancer Foundation)
1090 Pender St W Suite 300, Vancouver, BC, V6E 2N7
(604) 683-2873
Emp Here 26
SIC 8733 Noncommercial research organizations

D-U-N-S 24-207-5674 (BR)
CANADIAN CO CO TOURS, INC
(*Suby of* Canadian Co Co Tours, Inc)
1281 Georgia St W Suite 505, Vancouver, BC, V6E 3J7
(604) 685-6388
Emp Here 20
SIC 4725 Tour operators

D-U-N-S 24-724-6093 (BR)
CANADIAN IMPERIAL BANK OF COMMERCE
CIBC
1036 Georgia St W, Vancouver, BC, V6E 3C7
(604) 665-1478
Emp Here 40
SIC 6021 National commercial banks

D-U-N-S 20-700-6920 (BR)
CANADIAN IMPERIAL BANK OF COMMERCE
CIBC
1066 Hastings St W Suite 1600, Vancouver, BC, V6E 3X1
(604) 688-4330
Emp Here 25
SIC 6021 National commercial banks

D-U-N-S 24-342-2073 (BR)
CARA OPERATIONS LIMITED
MILESTONE'S
(*Suby of* Cara Holdings Limited)
1145 Robson St, Vancouver, BC, V6E 1B5
(604) 682-4477
Emp Here 60
SIC 5812 Eating places

D-U-N-S 24-181-1970 (HQ)
CENGEA SOLUTIONS INC
(*Suby of* Trimble Inc.)
1188 Georgia St W Suite 560, Vancouver, BC, V6E 4A2
(604) 697-6400
Emp Here 23 *Emp Total* 8,388
Sales 6,785,345
SIC 7372 Prepackaged software
Pr Pr K. Garry Rasmussen
VP Fin Darcy Bennett
VP Opers Kenneth Moen

D-U-N-S 20-110-1730 (HQ)
CHEVRON CANADA LIMITED
CHEVRON CANADA RESOURCES
(*Suby of* Chevron Corporation)
1050 Pender St W Suite 1200, Vancouver, BC, V6E 3T4
(604) 668-5300
Emp Here 350 *Emp Total* 61,500
Sales 1,039,501,200
SIC 2911 Petroleum refining
Pr Pr Jeff Gustavos
 Alan Dunlop
Dir Steven Parker

D-U-N-S 25-716-3535 (BR)
COMPAGNIE D'ASSURANCE SONNET
FEDERATION INSURANCE COMPANY OF CANADA
1055 Georgia St W Suite 1900, Vancouver, BC, V6E 0B6

Emp Here 38
SIC 6311 Life insurance

D-U-N-S 24-491-7514 (HQ)
CONNOR, CLARK & LUNN INVESTMENT MANAGEMENT LTD
(*Suby of* Connor, Clark & Lunn Investment Management Ltd)
1111 Georgia St W Suite 2200, Vancouver, BC, V6E 4M3
(604) 685-2020
Emp Here 100 *Emp Total* 174
Sales 41,660,560
SIC 6282 Investment advice
 Larry R. Lunn
Sec Patrick Robitaille
CFO Steve Affleck
 Andrew Lefevre
Dir Gordon H. Macdougall
Dir Warren Stoddart
Dir Martin Gerber
Dir Phillip Cotterill
Dir Brian Eby
Dir Gary Baker

D-U-N-S 25-497-8786 (HQ)
CREDENTIAL SECURITIES INC
CSI
1111 Georgia St W Suite 800, Vancouver, BC, V6E 4T6
(604) 714-3900
Emp Here 20 *Emp Total* 325
Sales 50,885,766
SIC 6211 Security brokers and dealers
Dir Don Rolfe
Dir John G M Fries
Dir Lothar Fabian
Dir Helen Elizabeth Blackburn

D-U-N-S 20-191-1000 (HQ)
CRUISESHIPCENTERS INTERNATIONAL INC
(*Suby of* Cruiseshipcenters International Inc)
1055 Hastings St W Suite 400, Vancouver, BC, V6E 2E9
(604) 685-1221
Emp Here 78 *Emp Total* 103
Sales 23,558,400
SIC 6794 Patent owners and lessors
Pr Pr Michael Drever
VP Fin Rob Jacoby
Fin Ex Julie Wong

D-U-N-S 24-957-4591 (SL)
DALE MATHESON CARR-HILTON LABONTE LLP
1140 Pender St W Suite 1500, Vancouver, BC, V6E 4G1
(604) 687-4747
Emp Here 60 *Sales* 2,626,585
SIC 8721 Accounting, auditing, and bookkeeping

D-U-N-S 24-980-7934 (SL)
DANBIE SYSTEMS GROUP INC
VANTAGEPOINT GROUP

1188 Georgia St W Unit 1050, Vancouver, BC, V6E 4A2
(604) 685-4209
Emp Here 30 *Sales* 5,626,880
SIC 5045 Computers, peripherals, and software
Pr Pr James Hennings
VP VP Daniel Sanderson
CFO Michael Rusch

D-U-N-S 24-641-8263 (HQ)
DASSAULT SYSTEMES CANADA SOFTWARE INC
GEMCOM SOFTWARE INTERNATIONAL
1066 Hastings St W Suite 1100, Vancouver, BC, V6E 3X1
(604) 684-6550
Emp Here 75 *Emp Total* 3,030
Sales 72,936,265
SIC 7371 Custom computer programming services
Pr Pr Richard M. Moignard
 Eric Palmer

D-U-N-S 25-483-5861 (BR)
DENCAN RESTAURANTS INC
DENNY'S RESTAURANT
(*Suby of* Northland Properties Corporation)
1098 Davie St, Vancouver, BC, V6E 1M3
(604) 689-0509
Emp Here 50
SIC 5812 Eating places

D-U-N-S 20-514-0882 (BR)
DOMINION OF CANADA GENERAL INSURANCE COMPANY, THE
(*Suby of* The Travelers Companies Inc)
1055 Georgia St W Suite 2400, Vancouver, BC, V6E 0B6
(604) 684-8127
Emp Here 40
SIC 6411 Insurance agents, brokers, and service

D-U-N-S 25-319-5176 (BR)
DON MICHAEL HOLDINGS INC
ROOTS CANADA LIMITED
1001 Robson St, Vancouver, BC, V6E 1A9
(604) 683-4305
Emp Here 20
SIC 5651 Family clothing stores

D-U-N-S 25-536-2071 (SL)
DYLAN RYAN TELESERVICES
1177 Hastings St W Suite 411, Vancouver, BC, V6E 2K3

Emp Here 100 *Sales* 4,961,328
SIC 7389 Business services, nec

D-U-N-S 25-710-0073 (BR)
EARL'S RESTAURANTS LTD
EARL'S ON TOP
(*Suby of* Earl's Restaurants Ltd)
1185 Robson St, Vancouver, BC, V6E 1B5
(604) 669-0020
Emp Here 50
SIC 5812 Eating places

D-U-N-S 25-413-5049 (SL)
ECO ORO MINERALS CORP
1055 Hastings St W Suite 300, Vancouver, BC, V6E 2E9
(604) 682-8212
Emp Here 46 *Sales* 5,034,288
SIC 1041 Gold ores
Pr Pr Mark Moseley-Williams
 Anna Stylianides
 Paul Robertson
 Hubert R. Marleau
 Derrick H. Weyrauch
 David Kay
 Kevin O'halloran

D-U-N-S 25-321-9786 (BR)
ECONOMICAL MUTUAL INSURANCE COMPANY
1055 Georgia St W Suite 1900, Vancouver,

BC, V6E 0B6
(604) 684-1194
Emp Here 97
SIC 6331 Fire, marine, and casualty insurance

D-U-N-S 24-806-6185   (BR)
ESRI CANADA LIMITED
ESRI CANADA LIMITED
1130 Pender St W Suite 610, Vancouver, BC,
V6E 4A4
(604) 683-9151
Emp Here 22
SIC 7371 Custom computer programming services

D-U-N-S 24-798-9940   (SL)
FAIRMONT SHIPPING (CANADA) LIMITED
1112 Pender St W Suite 300, Vancouver, BC,
V6E 2S1
(604) 685-3318
Emp Here 50   *Sales* 12,403,319
SIC 4731 Freight transportation arrangement
Pr Steven Ho

D-U-N-S 25-052-1184   (HQ)
**FLIGHT CENTRE TRAVEL GROUP
(CANADA) INC**
FLIGHT CENTRE CANADA
1133 Melville St Suite 600s, Vancouver, BC,
V6E 4E5
(604) 682-5202
Emp Here 300   *Emp Total* 19,267
Sales 389,756,059
SIC 4724 Travel agencies
Pr John Beauvais
Pers/VP Kim Knapp
 Mark Wilkie

D-U-N-S 25-360-8566   (BR)
FLUOR CANADA LTD
FLUOR DANIEL
(*Suby of* Fluor Corporation)
1075 Georgia St W Suite 700, Vancouver, BC,
V6E 4M7
(604) 488-2000
Emp Here 400
SIC 8711 Engineering services

D-U-N-S 25-128-0798   (BR)
FOOT LOCKER CANADA CO.
FOOT LOCKER
1124 Robson St, Vancouver, BC, V6E 1B2
(604) 608-1804
Emp Here 20
SIC 5661 Shoe stores

D-U-N-S 25-612-4488   (SL)
**FORTES, JOE SEAFOOD & CHOP HOUSE
LTD**
777 Thurlow St, Vancouver, BC, V6E 3V5
(604) 669-1940
Emp Here 115   *Sales* 3,502,114
SIC 5812 Eating places

D-U-N-S 24-995-3860   (HQ)
FORTISBC ENERGY INC
1111 Georgia St W Suite 1000, Vancouver,
BC, V6E 4M3
(604) 443-6525
Emp Here 300   *Emp Total* 8,000
Sales 1,017,293,640
SIC 4923 Gas transmission and distribution
Pr Pr Michael Mulcahy
VP Opers Doyle Sam
 Ian Lorimer
 Roger Dall'antonia
VP Cynthia Des Brisay
Pers/VP Jody Drope
VP Diane Roy
VP Douglas Stout
VP Dennis Swanson
 Brenda Eaton

D-U-N-S 25-691-8632   (BR)
GAP (CANADA) INC
BANANA REPUBLIC
(*Suby of* The Gap Inc)
1098 Robson St, Vancouver, BC, V6E 1A7

(604) 331-8285
Emp Here 70
SIC 5651 Family clothing stores

D-U-N-S 25-689-6259   (BR)
GAP (CANADA) INC
GAP
(*Suby of* The Gap Inc)
1125 Robson St Suite 9, Vancouver, BC, V6E
1B5
(604) 683-0906
Emp Here 60
SIC 5651 Family clothing stores

D-U-N-S 20-327-4543   (BR)
GENERAL CREDIT SERVICES INC
(*Suby of* General Credit Services Inc)
1190 Melville St Suite 600, Vancouver, BC,
V6E 3W1
(604) 688-6097
Emp Here 26
SIC 7322 Adjustment and collection services

D-U-N-S 20-279-1240   (HQ)
GIBRALTAR MINES LTD
1040 Georgia St W, Vancouver, BC, V6E 4H1
(778) 373-4533
Emp Here 600   *Emp Total* 350
Sales 7,296,070
SIC 1081 Metal mining services
Pr Pr Russell Hallbauer
 Ronald Thiessen
 Trevor Thomas
Dir Robert Dickinson
Dir John Mcmanus

D-U-N-S 25-367-7660   (BR)
GLOBAL PAYMENTS CANADA INC
(*Suby of* Global Payments Inc.)
1130 Pender St W Suite 620, Vancouver, BC,
V6E 4A4
(604) 665-2999
Emp Here 35
SIC 7389 Business services, nec

D-U-N-S 24-447-8616   (SL)
GRANVILLE WEST GROUP LTD
1075 Georgia St W Suite 1425, Vancouver,
BC, V6E 3C9
(604) 687-5570
Emp Here 24   *Sales* 8,239,360
SIC 6282 Investment advice
Pr Pr John Humphries
 Lorne Wilson
 Ian Dixon
 Paul B Shaw

D-U-N-S 24-391-2131   (SL)
GREAT LAKES BASIN ENERGY L.P.
1055 Georgia St W Suite 1100, Vancouver,
BC, V6E 3R5
(604) 488-8000
Emp Here 2,200   *Sales* 941,397,120
SIC 4924 Natural gas distribution
Genl Mgr Dougals P Bloom

D-U-N-S 20-229-5361   (BR)
**GREAT-WEST LIFE ASSURANCE COM-
PANY, THE**
1075 Georgia St W Suite 900, Vancouver, BC,
V6E 4N4
(604) 646-1200
Emp Here 160
SIC 6321 Accident and health insurance

D-U-N-S 24-786-9571   (BR)
**GREAT-WEST LIFE ASSURANCE COM-
PANY, THE**
1177 Hastings St W Suite 1500, Vancouver,
BC V6E 3Y9
(604) 331-2430
Emp Here 30
SIC 6311 Life insurance

D-U-N-S 20-116-1882   (HQ)
GRIEG STAR SHIPPING (CANADA) LTD
1111 Hastings St W Suite 900, Vancouver,
BC, V6E 2J3

(604) 661-2020
Emp Here 35   *Emp Total* 43
Sales 10,360,419
SIC 4731 Freight transportation arrangement
Pr Pr Tom Rasmussen
 Terry Koke
 Tricia D. Pederson
Dir Terje H. Michelsen

D-U-N-S 25-664-7538   (BR)
GROUPE ALDO INC, LE
ALDO
1025 Robson St Unit 128, Vancouver, BC,
V6E 1A9
(604) 683-2443
Emp Here 30
SIC 5661 Shoe stores

D-U-N-S 25-329-3666   (BR)
GROUPE SANTE MEDISYS INC
MEDISYS HEALTH GROUP
1111 Hastings St W Suite 1500, Vancouver,
BC, V6E 2J3

Emp Here 20
SIC 8093 Specialty outpatient clinics, nec

D-U-N-S 24-392-9804   (SL)
GROWTH WORKS LTD
1055 Georgia St W Suite 2600, Vancouver,
BC, V6E 3R5
(604) 895-7279
Emp Here 20   *Sales* 4,019,200
SIC 6211 Security brokers and dealers

D-U-N-S 25-672-0426   (HQ)
GROWTHWORKS CAPITAL LTD
1055 Georgia St W Suite 2600, Vancouver,
BC, V6E 0B6
(604) 633-1418
Emp Here 50   *Emp Total* 50
Sales 9,557,852
SIC 6799 Investors, nec
Pr Pr David Levi

D-U-N-S 25-716-2701   (HQ)
H I S CANADA INC
1090 Georgia St W Suite 488, Vancouver, BC,
V6E 3V7
(604) 685-3524
Emp Here 23   *Emp Total* 10,845
Sales 7,150,149
SIC 4724 Travel agencies
Pr Masuaki Kitaya

D-U-N-S 25-691-9036   (BR)
HSBC BANK CANADA
1188 Georgia St W Suite 108, Vancouver, BC,
V6E 4A2
(604) 687-7441
Emp Here 25
SIC 6021 National commercial banks

D-U-N-S 24-367-1336   (HQ)
**HSBC GLOBAL ASSET MANGEMENT
(CANADA) LIMITED**
1066 Hastings St W, Vancouver, BC, V6E 3X1
(604) 257-1000
Emp Here 65   *Emp Total* 284,186
Sales 28,413,033
SIC 6282 Investment advice
 Brian Bealle

D-U-N-S 25-497-0809   (SL)
**HSBC INVESTMENT FUNDS (CANADA)
INC.**
1066 Hastings St W Suite 1900, Vancouver,
BC, V6E 3X1
(604) 257-1090
Emp Here 83   *Sales* 14,379,767
SIC 6282 Investment advice
VP VP Steve Eccles

D-U-N-S 25-360-4557   (BR)
HATCH CORPORATION
1066 Hastings St W Suite 1010, Vancouver,
BC, V6E 3X2
(604) 629-1736
Emp Here 70

SIC 8711 Engineering services

D-U-N-S 20-273-1779   (BR)
HATCH LTD
1066 Hastings St W Suite 400, Vancouver,
BC, V6E 3X1
(604) 683-9141
Emp Here 135
SIC 8711 Engineering services

D-U-N-S 25-931-8822   (BR)
HEENAN BLAIKIE S.E.N.C.R.L.
1055 Hastings St W Unit 2200, Vancouver,
BC, V6E 2E9
(604) 891-1180
Emp Here 55
SIC 8111 Legal services

D-U-N-S 25-855-7248   (BR)
HERMAN MILLER CANADA, INC
*HERMAN MILLER WORK PLACE RE-
SOURCE*
(*Suby of* Herman Miller, Inc.)
1035 Pender St W Suite 100, Vancouver, BC,
V6E 2M6
(604) 683-8300
Emp Here 20
SIC 5021 Furniture

D-U-N-S 24-640-8629   (SL)
HEWITT MANAGEMENT LTD
(*Suby of* Tempo Acquisition, LLC)
1111 Georgia St W Suite 2010, Vancouver,
BC, V6E 4M3
(604) 683-7311
Emp Here 60   *Sales* 6,858,306
SIC 8741 Management services
 John Allan Brown
Pr Pr Donald M Simkin
 Naveen Kapahi
 John Gordon Argue
 Shelley Ann Wooding
 Peter Michael Muirhead
 Neil Morris Crawford
 Rob J.W. Vandersanden
 Robert J. Beneteau

D-U-N-S 24-469-6431   (SL)
HILLSBOROUGH RESOURCES LIMITED
CANADIAN MINE DEVELOPMENT
1090 Georgia St W Suite 950, Vancouver, BC,
V6E 3V7
(604) 684-9288
Emp Here 50   *Sales* 30,445,440
SIC 1221 Bituminous coal and lignite-surface
mining
Pr David J Slater
Sr VP David Fawcett
 Ian Kirk
Dir Michael Fitch
Dir Barry Irvine
Dir George W Stuart
Dir Herbert G Stephenson
Dir John P Collenette

D-U-N-S 25-261-4284   (BR)
HOGG ROBINSON CANADA INC
BTI CANADA
(*Suby of* HOGG ROBINSON GROUP PLC)
1090 Georgia St W Suite 310, Vancouver, BC,
V6E 3V7
(604) 681-0300
Emp Here 50
SIC 8741 Management services

D-U-N-S 20-361-0217   (BR)
HOMEWOOD HEALTH INC
1050 Pender St W Suite 500, Vancouver, BC,
V6E 3S7
(604) 689-8604
Emp Here 30
SIC 8093 Specialty outpatient clinics, nec

D-U-N-S 20-997-1980   (BR)
HON'S WUN-TUN HOUSE LTD
(*Suby of* Hon's Wun-Tun House Ltd)
1339 Robson St, Vancouver, BC, V6E 1C6

(604) 685-0871
Emp Here 50
SIC 5812 Eating places

D-U-N-S 24-685-6038   (SL)
HUAXING MACHINERY CORP
1066 Hastings St W Suite 2300, Vancouver,
BC, V6E 3X1
(604) 601-8218
Emp Here 50   *Sales* 34,291,138
SIC 3531 Construction machinery
Dir Xiuxue Chai
  Xianhua Sun
CFO Xinlin Huang
Sec Betty Anne Loy
Fin Ex Longfei Xu
Dir Siu (Kendra) Yeung
Dir Thea Koshman
Dir George Dorin

D-U-N-S 24-787-1163   (BR)
IBI GROUP
1285 Pender St W Suite 700, Vancouver, BC,
V6E 4B1
(604) 683-8797
Emp Here 130
SIC 8712 Architectural services

D-U-N-S 24-995-1005   (SL)
INLAND PACIFIC RESOURCES INC
1188 Georgia St W Suite 1160, Vancouver,
BC, V6E 4A2
(604) 697-6700
Emp Here 2,000   *Sales* 471,168,000
SIC 1623 Water, sewer, and utility lines
Pr Brett Hodson

D-U-N-S 24-657-1483   (BR)
**INVESTMENT INDUSTRY REGULATORY
ORGANIZATION OF CANADA**
IIROC
650 Georgia St W Suite 1325, Vancouver, BC,
V6E 2R5
(604) 683-6222
Emp Here 60
SIC 8611 Business associations

D-U-N-S 20-562-7636   (HQ)
IPSOS LIMITED PARTNERSHIP
1285 Pender St W Suite 200, Vancouver, BC,
V6E 4B1
(778) 373-5000
Emp Here 100   *Emp Total* 2
Sales 214,066,694
SIC 8732 Commercial nonphysical research
  Gary Bennewies

D-U-N-S 20-797-8719   (HQ)
**JARDINE LLOYD THOMPSON CANADA
INC**
1111 Georgia St W Suite 1600, Vancouver,
BC, V6E 4G2
(604) 682-4211
Emp Here 85   *Emp Total* 6,212
Sales 21,596,367
SIC 6411 Insurance agents, brokers, and ser-
vice
Pr Pr Paul Murphy
Dir Guido Amantea

D-U-N-S 20-065-9550   (SL)
KBK NO 51 VENTURES LTD
CARMANA PLAZA
1128 Alberni St, Vancouver, BC, V6E 4R6
(604) 683-1399
Emp Here 50   *Sales* 4,377,642
SIC 6513 Apartment building operators

D-U-N-S 25-272-9561   (BR)
KEG RESTAURANTS LTD
KEG STEAKHOUSE & BAR, THE
1121 Alberni St Ste 310, Vancouver, BC, V6E
4T9
(604) 685-4388
Emp Here 70
SIC 5812 Eating places

D-U-N-S 24-536-1563   (SL)
KERAN HOLDINGS LTD

CELEBRITIES NIGHT CLUB
1022 Davie St, Vancouver, BC, V6E 1M3
(604) 685-1300
Emp Here 50   *Sales* 1,824,018
SIC 5813 Drinking places

D-U-N-S 24-897-7134   (HQ)
**KINTETSU INTERNATIONAL EXPRESS
(CANADA) INC**
1140 Pender St W Suite 910, Vancouver, BC,
V6E 4G1
(778) 328-9754
Emp Here 40   *Emp Total* 30,719
Sales 12,403,319
SIC 4724 Travel agencies
Pr Hiaeo Adachi

D-U-N-S 20-573-4361   (SL)
KOBE JAPANESE STEAK HOUSES LTD
1042 Alberni St, Vancouver, BC, V6E 1A3
(604) 684-2451
Emp Here 50   *Sales* 1,532,175
SIC 5812 Eating places

D-U-N-S 20-573-8883   (BR)
KUEHNE + NAGEL LTD
535 Thurlow St Suite 700, Vancouver, BC,
V6E 3L2
(604) 684-4531
Emp Here 60
SIC 4731 Freight transportation arrangement

D-U-N-S 24-593-5044   (BR)
LONDON DRUGS LIMITED
1187 Robson St Suite 19, Vancouver, BC, V6E
1B5
(604) 448-4819
Emp Here 50
SIC 5912 Drug stores and proprietary stores

D-U-N-S 24-445-6133   (BR)
LONDON LIFE INSURANCE COMPANY
FREEDOM 55 FINANCIAL
1111 Georgia St W Suite 1200, Vancouver,
BC, V6E 4M3
(604) 685-6521
Emp Here 85
SIC 6311 Life insurance

D-U-N-S 24-228-4946   (SL)
LUFTHANSA GERMAN AIRLINES
1030 Georgia St W Suite 1401, Vancouver,
BC, V6E 2Y3
(604) 303-3080
Emp Here 30   *Sales* 6,798,400
SIC 4512 Air transportation, scheduled
Brnch Mgr Alexander Von Steun

D-U-N-S 20-152-6469   (BR)
MCW CONSULTANTS LTD
1185 Georgia St W Suite 1400, Vancouver,
BC, V6E 4E6
(604) 687-1821
Emp Here 64
SIC 8711 Engineering services

D-U-N-S 24-136-0445   (HQ)
MACKAY & PARTNERS
(*Suby of* MacKay & Partners)
1177 Hastings St W Suite 1100, Vancouver,
BC, V6E 4T5
(604) 687-4511
Emp Here 60   *Emp Total* 160
Sales 9,046,358
SIC 8721 Accounting, auditing, and book-
keeping
Pt Iain Mackay
Pt Hugh Livingstone
Pt York Wong
Pt Jack Arnold
Pt Peter Busch
Pt Mathew So
Pt Don Henfrey

D-U-N-S 25-105-7394   (HQ)
MAN DIESEL & TURBO CANADA LTD
1177 Hastings St W Suite 1930, Vancouver,
BC, V6E 2K3

(604) 235-2254
Emp Here 29   *Emp Total* 546,406
Sales 8,244,559
SIC 5084 Industrial machinery and equipment
  Klaus Bader
  Risely D'souza
  Dave Samson

D-U-N-S 25-617-3071   (BR)
**MANUFACTURERS LIFE INSURANCE
COMPANY, THE**
MANULIFE FINANCIAL
1095 Pender St W Suite 700, Vancouver, BC,
V6E 2M6
(604) 681-4660
Emp Here 60
SIC 6311 Life insurance

D-U-N-S 24-773-1875   (SL)
MAVRIX FUND MANAGEMENT
1055 Georgia St W Suite 2600, Vancouver,
BC, V6E 3R5
(604) 647-5614
Emp Here 49   *Sales* 9,517,760
SIC 6211 Security brokers and dealers
Pr David Levi

D-U-N-S 20-180-1292   (SL)
MAXIMIZER SOFTWARE INC
1090 Pender St W Suite 10, Vancouver, BC,
V6E 2N7
(604) 331-0284
Emp Here 87   *Sales* 13,985,280
SIC 7372 Prepackaged software
  Terence Hui
Pr John Caputo
Ex VP William Anderson
VP Joseph Hui
VP Fin Kam Sandhu
VP Sls Enzo Dimichele
Dir Mark Skapinker
Dir Tom Bennett
Dir Richard Whittall
Dir Kevin Armitage

D-U-N-S 20-703-9731   (BR)
MCMILLAN LLP
1055 Georgia St W Suite 1500, Vancouver,
BC, V6E 4N7
(604) 689-9111
Emp Here 250
SIC 8111 Legal services

D-U-N-S 24-504-4466   (BR)
MICROSOFT CANADA INC
(*Suby of* Microsoft Corporation)
1111 Georgia St W Suite 1100, Vancouver,
BC, V6E 4M3
(604) 688-9811
Emp Here 50
SIC 5045 Computers, peripherals, and soft-
ware

D-U-N-S 20-088-4224   (BR)
MONTSHIP INC
MITSUI O.S.K. LINES
(*Suby of* Trealmont Transport Inc)
1111 Hastings St W Suite 800, Vancouver,
BC, V6E 2J3
(604) 640-7400
Emp Here 20
SIC 4731 Freight transportation arrangement

D-U-N-S 20-924-0964   (BR)
**MOXIE'S RESTAURANTS, LIMITED PART-
NERSHIP**
808 Bute St, Vancouver, BC, V6E 1Y4

Emp Here 30
SIC 5812 Eating places

D-U-N-S 24-171-0917   (SL)
NAI COMMERCIAL B.C. LTD
535 Thurlow St Suite 100, Vancouver, BC,
V6E 3L2
(604) 683-7535
Emp Here 100   *Sales* 20,290,000
SIC 6211 Security brokers and dealers

Pr Greg Mcphie

D-U-N-S 24-075-2498   (BR)
**NORTHLAND PROPERTIES CORPORA-
TION**
*SANDMAN SUITES VANCOUVER - DAVIE
STREET*
(*Suby of* Northland Properties Corporation)
1160 Davie St, Vancouver, BC, V6E 1N1
(604) 681-7263
Emp Here 20
SIC 7011 Hotels and motels

D-U-N-S 20-241-6736   (BR)
OXFORD PROPERTIES GROUP INC
1055 Hastings St W Suite 1850, Vancouver,
BC, V6E 2E9
(604) 893-3200
Emp Here 35
SIC 6512 Nonresidential building operators

D-U-N-S 20-707-4779   (BR)
PVH CANADA, INC
1088 Robson St, Vancouver, BC, V6E 1A7

Emp Here 27
SIC 5136 Men's and boy's clothing

D-U-N-S 20-187-1600   (SL)
PACIFIC LINK MINING CORP
1055 Georgia St W Suite 2772, Vancouver,
BC, V6E 3P3

Emp Here 50   *Sales* 7,727,098
SIC 6799 Investors, nec
Pr Pr Stephen Oakley
  Ken Z. Cai
Dir Erick Chai
Dir Michael Doggett

D-U-N-S 25-704-0402   (BR)
PANALPINA INC
1100 Melville St Unit 1400, Vancouver, BC,
V6E 4A6
(604) 659-2666
Emp Here 40
SIC 4731 Freight transportation arrangement

D-U-N-S 20-939-9034   (SL)
PANGAEA SYSTEMS INC
1066 Hastings St W Unit 2300, Vancouver,
BC, V6E 3X1
(604) 692-4700
Emp Here 49   *Sales* 7,067,520
SIC 8748 Business consulting, nec
Dir Graham Acres

D-U-N-S 24-321-4496   (HQ)
PEACE RIVER COAL INC
1055 Hastings St W Suite 1900, Vancouver,
BC, V6E 2E9

Emp Here 20   *Emp Total* 91,000
Sales 22,107,092
SIC 1221 Bituminous coal and lignite-surface
mining
Genl Mgr Trevor Hulme
Dir Pat C Devlin

D-U-N-S 24-126-9864   (BR)
RBC DOMINION SECURITIES INC
(*Suby of* Royal Bank Of Canada)
1055 West Georgia St, Vancouver, BC, V6E
3S5
(604) 257-7120
Emp Here 28
SIC 6282 Investment advice

D-U-N-S 24-312-9066   (SL)
ROCHESTER RESOURCES LTD
1090 Georgia St W Suite 1305, Vancouver,
BC, V6E 3V7
(604) 685-9316
Emp Here 200   *Sales* 12,109,342
SIC 1081 Metal mining services
Pr Pr Eduardo Luna
  Nicholas Demare
  Alfredo Parra

Dir Joseph Keane
Dir Marc Cernovitch
Dir Michael Magrum
Dir Simon Tam

D-U-N-S 25-723-1670   (BR)
ROYAL BANK OF CANADA
RBC PRIVATE CLIENT GROUP
(Suby of Royal Bank Of Canada)
1055 Georgia St W Suite 500, Vancouver, BC,
V6E 3N9
(604) 665-5281
Emp Here 40
SIC 6021 National commercial banks

D-U-N-S 20-536-4800   (BR)
ROYAL BANK OF CANADA
RBC
(Suby of Royal Bank Of Canada)
1025 Georgia St W Suite 1000, Vancouver,
BC, V6E 3N9
(604) 665-8376
Emp Here 160
SIC 6021 National commercial banks

D-U-N-S 20-536-6888   (BR)
ROYAL TRUST CORPORATION OF CANADA
(Suby of Royal Bank Of Canada)
1055 Georgia St W Suite 600, Vancouver, BC,
V6E 4P3
(604) 665-9817
Emp Here 20
SIC 6021 National commercial banks

D-U-N-S 20-263-3462   (BR)
SAP CANADA INC
SAP
1095 Pender St W Suite 400, Vancouver, BC,
V6E 2M6
(604) 647-8888
Emp Here 100
SIC 7371 Custom computer programming services

D-U-N-S 25-680-6795   (BR)
SNC-LAVALIN INC
745 Thurlow St Suite 500, Vancouver, BC,
V6E 0C5
(604) 662-3555
Emp Here 300
SIC 8711 Engineering services

D-U-N-S 20-293-3432   (SL)
SAMBA BRAZILIAN STEAK HOUSE (CHURRASCARIA) LTD
1122 Alberni St, Vancouver, BC, V6E 1A5

Emp Here 60   Sales 1,824,018
SIC 5812 Eating places

D-U-N-S 24-364-7729   (HQ)
SEACLIFF CONSTRUCTION CORP
1066 Hastings St W, Vancouver, BC, V6E 3X2
(604) 601-8206
Emp Here 100   Emp Total 586
Sales 237,092,899
SIC 8742 Management consulting services
Dir William Crarer
Brian Bentz
Vance Hackett
Dir Phillip George
Dir Jeff Irivig
Dir Larry Berg
Dir Gary Patterson
Dir Michael Riley

D-U-N-S 20-114-2445   (SL)
SHEARER'S FOODS CANADA, INC
1030 Georgia St W Suite 1900, Vancouver,
BC, V6E 2Y3
(604) 654-8300
Emp Here 30   Sales 5,985,550
SIC 5149 Groceries and related products, nec
Pr Pr John P Frostad
Patrick D Lindenbach
Robert Armstrong
Fin Ex Elaine Price

D-U-N-S 25-054-7544   (BR)
SMART & BIGGAR
FETHERSTONHAYGH SMART & BIGGAR
1055 Georgia St W Suite 2300, Vancouver,
BC, V6E 0B6
(604) 682-7780
Emp Here 60
SIC 8111 Legal services

D-U-N-S 24-033-3856   (BR)
SOCIETY OF COMPOSERS, AUTHORS AND MUSIC PUBLISHERS OF CANADA
SOCAN
1166 Alberni St Suite 504, Vancouver, BC,
V6E 3Z3
(604) 689-8872
Emp Here 20
SIC 6794 Patent owners and lessors

D-U-N-S 24-343-1900   (BR)
SOVEREIGN GENERAL INSURANCE COMPANY, THE
1095 Pender St W Unit 1400, Vancouver, BC,
V6E 2M6
(604) 602-8300
Emp Here 40
SIC 6411 Insurance agents, brokers, and service

D-U-N-S 20-796-7238   (BR)
STAPLES CANADA INC
STAPLES THE BUSINESS DEPOT
(Suby of Staples, Inc.)
1055 Georgia St W Unit 220, Vancouver, BC,
V6E 0B6
(604) 678-4873
Emp Here 30
SIC 5943 Stationery stores

D-U-N-S 20-806-4845   (BR)
STARBUCKS COFFEE CANADA, INC
STARBUCKS COFFEE
(Suby of Starbucks Corporation)
1301 Robson St, Vancouver, BC, V6E 1C6
(604) 801-5820
Emp Here 20
SIC 5812 Eating places

D-U-N-S 20-506-0176   (BR)
STARBUCKS COFFEE CANADA, INC
(Suby of Starbucks Corporation)
1100 Robson St Suite 100, Vancouver, BC,
V6E 1B2

Emp Here 30
SIC 5812 Eating places

D-U-N-S 25-723-9525   (BR)
SUN LIFE ASSURANCE COMPANY OF CANADA
SUN LIFE FINANCIAL
1140 Pender St W Suite 1160, Vancouver, BC,
V6E 4N8
(604) 681-9231
Emp Here 30
SIC 6324 Hospital and medical service plans

D-U-N-S 20-563-1810   (BR)
THOMSON REUTERS CANADA LIMITED
1055 Hastings St W, Vancouver, BC, V6E 2E9

Emp Here 70
SIC 8742 Management consulting services

D-U-N-S 24-856-4627   (SL)
TOTO ENTERPRISES LTD
CINCIN RISTORANTE
1154 Robson St, Vancouver, BC, V6E 1B2
(604) 688-7338
Emp Here 55   Sales 1,678,096
SIC 5812 Eating places

D-U-N-S 25-068-6144   (SL)
UNIGLOBE SPECIALTY TRAVEL LTD
1111 Melville St Suite 820, Vancouver, BC,
V6E 3V6
(604) 688-8816
Emp Here 20   Sales 6,380,400

SIC 4725 Tour operators
Pr Pr Douglas Revell
VP VP Dianne Revell

D-U-N-S 25-148-6924   (SL)
VIVONET ACQUISITION LTD
(Suby of Vivonet Incorporated)
1188 Georgia St W Unit 1790, Vancouver, BC,
V6E 4A2
(866) 512-2033
Emp Here 50   Sales 5,977,132
SIC 7371 Custom computer programming services
Ryan Volberg

D-U-N-S 20-927-4096   (BR)
WENDY'S RESTAURANTS OF CANADA INC
WENDY'S
(Suby of The Wendy's Company)
1150 Alberni St, Vancouver, BC, V6E 1A5
(604) 408-5885
Emp Here 20
SIC 5812 Eating places

D-U-N-S 25-687-2631   (HQ)
WEYERHAEUSER COMPANY LIMITED
WEYERHAEUSER AVIATION
(Suby of Weyerhaeuser Company)
1140 Pender St W Suite 440, Vancouver, BC,
V6E 4G1
(604) 661-8000
Emp Here 200   Emp Total 10,400
Sales 569,093,460
SIC 2421 Sawmills and planing mills, general
Alfred Dzida
Devin Stockfish

D-U-N-S 20-510-6313   (BR)
XEROX CANADA LTD
XEROX
(Suby of Xerox Corporation)
1055 Georgia St W, Vancouver, BC, V6E 0B6
(604) 668-2300
Emp Here 250
SIC 5044 Office equipment

D-U-N-S 24-209-1820   (BR)
YOUNG MEN'S CHRISTIAN ASSOCIATION OF GREATER VANCOUVER
YMCA
1166 Alberni St Suite 200, Vancouver, BC,
V6E 3Z3
(604) 681-9622
Emp Here 20
SIC 8331 Job training and related services

D-U-N-S 25-148-6692   (BR)
ZIM CIE DE SERVICES DE NAVIGATION INTEGREE (CANADA) LTEE
1130 Pender St W, Vancouver, BC, V6E 4A4
(604) 693-2335
Emp Here 20
SIC 4499 Water transportation services,

Vancouver, BC V6G
Greater Vancouver County

D-U-N-S 20-621-9487   (SL)
0319637 B.C. LTD
FISH HOUSE IN STANLEY PARK, THE
8901 Stanley Park Dr, Vancouver, BC, V6G
3E2
(604) 681-7275
Emp Here 80   Sales 3,109,686
SIC 5812 Eating places

D-U-N-S 25-719-2013   (SL)
A POWER INTERNATIONAL TRADING COMPANY
JANG MO JIB KOREAN RESTAURANT
1575 Robson St, Vancouver, BC, V6G 1C3
(604) 872-0712
Emp Here 90   Sales 2,699,546
SIC 5812 Eating places

D-U-N-S 25-371-0495   (SL)
A&M REALTY PARTNERS INC
1500 Georgia St W Suite 1750, Vancouver,
BC, V6G 2Z6
(604) 909-2111
Emp Here 50   Sales 6,380,400
SIC 6531 Real estate agents and managers
Dir Peter Dupuis
Pr Pr Sid Landolt

D-U-N-S 20-703-5648   (BR)
ASSOCIATION OF NEIGHBOURHOOD HOUSES OF BRITISH COLUMBIA
GORDON NEIGHBOURHOOD HOUSE
1019 Broughton St, Vancouver, BC, V6G 2A7
(604) 683-2554
Emp Here 30
SIC 8399 Social services, nec

D-U-N-S 25-928-1418   (HQ)
AXIS INSURANCE MANAGERS INC
WINRAM INSURANCE SERVICES
(Suby of Axis Insurance Managers Inc)
1455 Georgia St W Suite 600, Vancouver,
V6G 2T3
(604) 731-5328
Emp Here 31   Emp Total 52
Sales 4,669,485
SIC 6411 Insurance agents, brokers, and service

D-U-N-S 24-339-5964   (BR)
AXIS INSURANCE MANAGERS INC
1455 W Georgia St Unit 600, Vancouver, BC,
V6G 2T3
(604) 685-4288
Emp Here 46
SIC 6411 Insurance agents, brokers, and service

D-U-N-S 20-589-5126   (BR)
BANQUE TORONTO-DOMINION, LA
TD CANADA TRUST
(Suby of Toronto-Dominion Bank, The)
1690 Davie St, Vancouver, BC, V6G 1V9
(604) 683-5644
Emp Here 20
SIC 6021 National commercial banks

D-U-N-S 20-265-3929   (BR)
BOARD OF EDUCATION OF SCHOOL DISTRICT NO. 39 (VANCOUVER), THE
KING GEORGE SECONDARY
1755 Barclay St, Vancouver, BC, V6G 1K6
(604) 713-8999
Emp Here 40
SIC 8211 Elementary and secondary schools

D-U-N-S 20-591-0222   (BR)
BOARD OF EDUCATION OF SCHOOL DISTRICT NO. 39 (VANCOUVER), THE
LORD ROBERTS SCHOOL
1100 Bidwell St, Vancouver, BC, V6G 2K4
(604) 713-5055
Emp Here 40
SIC 8211 Elementary and secondary schools

D-U-N-S 20-109-8241   (HQ)
CALKINS & BURKE LIMITED
ARROW PACKING COMPANY
1500 Georgia St W Suite 800, Vancouver, BC,
V6G 2Z6
(604) 669-3741
Emp Here 58   Emp Total 60
Sales 21,888,210
SIC 5146 Fish and seafoods
David Calkins
Pr Pr Blair Calkins
Michael Calkins

D-U-N-S 20-798-1767   (BR)
CANNON DESIGN ARCHITECTURE INC
1500 Georgia St W Suite 710, Vancouver, BC,
V6G 2Z6
(604) 688-5710
Emp Here 45
SIC 8712 Architectural services

D-U-N-S 24-996-7464   (BR)
COAST HOTELS LIMITED
COAST PLAZA AT STANLEY PARK
1763 Comox St, Vancouver, BC, V6G 1P6
(604) 688-7711
Emp Here 80
SIC 7011 Hotels and motels

D-U-N-S 25-678-1873   (HQ)
DIAMOND PARKING LTD
DIAMOND PARKING SERVICES
(*Suby of* Diamond Parking Services, LLC)
817 Denman St, Vancouver, BC, V6G 2L7
(604) 681-8797
Emp Here 37   *Emp Total* 1,100
Sales 1,507,726
SIC 7521 Automobile parking

D-U-N-S 25-270-0810   (BR)
HSBC BANK CANADA
HSBC
1010 Denman St, Vancouver, BC, V6G 2M5
(604) 683-8189
Emp Here 20
SIC 6021 National commercial banks

D-U-N-S 24-335-4698   (SL)
HOTHEAD GAMES INC
1555 Pender St W, Vancouver, BC, V6G 2T1
(604) 605-0018
Emp Here 50   *Sales* 5,034,288
SIC 7371 Custom computer programming services
Pr Ian Wilkinson
Dir James Paul Ceraldi
Dir Joel Deyoung
Dir Kenneth Fahlman
  Reinhold Wiesendahl

D-U-N-S 25-709-9663   (BR)
LONDON DRUGS LIMITED
1650 Davie St, Vancouver, BC, V6G 1V9
(604) 669-2884
Emp Here 100
SIC 5912 Drug stores and proprietary stores

D-U-N-S 20-575-8568   (BR)
MCDONALD'S RESTAURANTS OF CANADA LIMITED
MCDONALD'S #8578
(*Suby of* McDonald's Corporation)
1701 Robson St, Vancouver, BC, V6G 1C9
(604) 718-1020
Emp Here 80
SIC 5812 Eating places

D-U-N-S 20-564-4904   (HQ)
NAVIGATA COMMUNICATIONS LTD
1550 Alberni St Suite 300, Vancouver, BC, V6G 1A5
(604) 990-2000
Emp Here 96   *Emp Total* 198
Sales 21,916,150
SIC 4899 Communication services, nec
Pr Pr Peter Legault
  John Warta
VP Don Potts
  Owen J. Gilbert
VP Glen Gregory
VP Fin Tim Sansom

D-U-N-S 24-570-4882   (SL)
POYRY (VANCOUVER) INC.
1550 Alberni St Suite 200, Vancouver, BC, V6G 1A5
(604) 689-0344
Emp Here 36   *Sales* 3,356,192
SIC 8711 Engineering services

D-U-N-S 24-492-3413   (SL)
PROSPECT POINT CAFE LTD
5601 Stanley Park Dr, Vancouver, BC, V6G 3E2
(604) 669-2737
Emp Here 40   *Sales* 1,240,332
SIC 5812 Eating places

D-U-N-S 20-564-4359   (SL)

QUICK INC
1500 Georgia St W Suite 1800, Vancouver, BC, V6G 2Z6
(604) 685-5200
Emp Here 50   *Sales* 7,950,960
SIC 6712 Bank holding companies
Pr Pr Ralph Douglas Mcrae

D-U-N-S 20-915-8732   (HQ)
R P B HOLDINGS LTD
BEST WESTERN SANDS HOTEL
(*Suby of* Rosen Foundation Ltd)
1755 Davie St, Vancouver, BC, V6G 1W5
(604) 682-1831
Emp Here 88   *Emp Total* 25
Sales 33,158,400
SIC 7011 Hotels and motels
Sec Lory Wainberg

D-U-N-S 25-146-8716   (BR)
SEQUOIA COMPANY OF RESTAURANTS INC
SAND BAR, THE
1583 Coal Harbour Quay, Vancouver, BC, V6G 3E7
(604) 687-5684
Emp Here 50
SIC 5812 Eating places

D-U-N-S 25-271-6998   (BR)
SOBEYS WEST INC
1766 Robson St, Vancouver, BC, V6G 1E2
(604) 683-0202
Emp Here 75
SIC 5411 Grocery stores

D-U-N-S 20-702-7603   (BR)
SOBEYS WEST INC
1641 Davie St, Vancouver, BC, V6G 1W1
(604) 669-8131
Emp Here 100
SIC 5411 Grocery stores

D-U-N-S 24-363-3372   (BR)
SONOMA MANAGEMENT LTD
DELANY'S ON DENMAN ST
1105 Denman St, Vancouver, BC, V6G 2M7
(604) 662-3344
Emp Here 25
SIC 5812 Eating places

D-U-N-S 20-806-4985   (BR)
STARBUCKS COFFEE CANADA, INC
(*Suby of* Starbucks Corporation)
1795 Davie St, Vancouver, BC, V6G 1W5
(604) 899-4322
Emp Here 20
SIC 5812 Eating places

D-U-N-S 20-116-4019   (SL)
SYLVIA HOTEL LIMITED
1154 Gilford St, Vancouver, BC, V6G 2P6
(604) 681-9321
Emp Here 50   *Sales* 2,188,821
SIC 7011 Hotels and motels

D-U-N-S 24-979-6132   (SL)
TASKTOP TECHNOLOGIES INCORPORATED
1500 Georgia St W Suite 1100, Vancouver, BC, V6G 2Z6
(778) 588-6896
Emp Here 70   *Sales* 9,557,852
SIC 5045 Computers, peripherals, and software
Ch Bd Gail Murphy
Dir Mik Kersten
Pr Pr Neelan Choksi

D-U-N-S 25-982-4089   (SL)
TRIMARK HEALTHCARE SERVICES LTD
1500 Georgia St W Suite 1300, Vancouver, BC, V6G 2Z6
(604) 425-2208
Emp Here 60   *Sales* 6,858,306
SIC 8741 Management services
  Ted Chu

D-U-N-S 25-088-3535   (SL)
U-PARK ENTERPRISES LTD
(*Suby of* Sp Plus Corporation)
1425 Pender St W, Vancouver, BC, V6G 2S3
(604) 331-1111
Emp Here 40   *Sales* 632,363
SIC 7521 Automobile parking

D-U-N-S 24-081-3761   (SL)
UNIGLOBE ONE TRAVEL INC
1444 Alberni St Suite 300, Vancouver, BC, V6G 2Z4
(604) 688-3551
Emp Here 49   *Sales* 16,232,000
SIC 4724 Travel agencies
Genl Mgr Samantha Howl

D-U-N-S 25-988-2777   (BR)
WHITE SPOT LIMITED
WHITE SPOT RESTAURANT
1616 Georgia St W, Vancouver, BC, V6G 2V5
(604) 681-8034
Emp Here 50
SIC 5812 Eating places

Vancouver, BC V6H
Greater Vancouver County

D-U-N-S 20-591-0594   (BR)
BOARD OF EDUCATION OF SCHOOL DISTRICT NO. 39 (VANCOUVER), THE
EMILY CARR ELEMENTARY SCHOOL
4070 Oak St, Vancouver, BC, V6H 2M8
(604) 713-4941
Emp Here 35
SIC 8211 Elementary and secondary schools

D-U-N-S 20-591-0826   (BR)
BOARD OF EDUCATION OF SCHOOL DISTRICT NO. 39 (VANCOUVER), THE
FALSE CREEK ELEMENTARY SCHOOL
900 School Green, Vancouver, BC, V6H 3N7
(604) 713-4959
Emp Here 25
SIC 8211 Elementary and secondary schools

D-U-N-S 20-591-0271   (BR)
BOARD OF EDUCATION OF SCHOOL DISTRICT NO. 39 (VANCOUVER), THE
L'ECOLE BILINGUE
1166 14th Ave W, Vancouver, BC, V6H 1P6
(604) 713-4585
Emp Here 25
SIC 8211 Elementary and secondary schools

D-U-N-S 25-507-5822   (HQ)
CHILDREN'S & WOMEN'S HEALTH CENTRE OF BRITISH COLUMBIA BRANCH
4500 Oak St, Vancouver, BC, V6H 3N1
(604) 875-2424
Emp Here 2,000   *Emp Total* 10,000
Sales 437,553,850
SIC 8069 Specialty hospitals, except psychiatric
Pr Lynda Cranston

D-U-N-S 20-004-0793   (BR)
CLUB MONACO CORP
CABAN
(*Suby of* Ralph Lauren Corporation)
2912 Granville St, Vancouver, BC, V6H 3J7

Emp Here 30
SIC 5712 Furniture stores

D-U-N-S 24-249-6339   (SL)
D & H GROUP CHARTERED ACCOUNTANTS
1333 Broadway W, Vancouver, BC, V6H 4C1
(604) 731-5881
Emp Here 54   *Sales* 2,334,742
SIC 8721 Accounting, auditing, and bookkeeping

D-U-N-S 20-035-3618   (SL)

DOCKSIDE BREWING COMPANY LTD
1253 Johnston St, Vancouver, BC, V6H 3R9
(604) 685-7070
Emp Here 60   *Sales* 1,824,018
SIC 5812 Eating places

D-U-N-S 20-110-1441   (HQ)
EDWARD CHAPMAN LADIES' SHOP LIMITED
EDWARD CHAPMAN LADIES SHOPS
(*Suby of* Edward Chapman Ladies' Shop Limited)
2596 Granville St, Vancouver, BC, V6H 3G8
(604) 732-1958
Emp Here 20   *Emp Total* 50
Sales 3,064,349
SIC 5621 Women's clothing stores

D-U-N-S 20-812-5174   (HQ)
EVYSIO MEDICAL DEVICES ULC
EVASC MEDICAL SYSTEMS
(*Suby of* Evysio Medical Devices ULC)
1099 8th Ave W Unit 107, Vancouver, BC, V6H 1C3
(604) 742-0600
Emp Here 20   *Emp Total* 50
Sales 8,540,800
SIC 8733 Noncommercial research organizations
Pr Pr Donald Ricci
  Kristine Elliott
Dir George Shukov
  Ian Penn

D-U-N-S 24-127-9178   (SL)
FELDMAN S.L. & ASSOCIATES LTD
1505 2nd Ave W Suite 200, Vancouver, BC, V6H 3Y4
(604) 734-5945
Emp Here 70   *Sales* 10,797,600
SIC 7922 Theatrical producers and services
Dir Samuel Feldman
Pr Pr Vinny Cinquemani
  Shaw Saltzerg
  Jeff Craib
Dir Doug Cucheron
Fin Ex Linda Mccann

D-U-N-S 24-881-0798   (SL)
GRANVILLE ISLAND BREWING CO. LTD
(*Suby of* Molson Coors Brewing Company)
1441 Cartwright St, Vancouver, BC, V6H 3R7
(604) 685-0504
Emp Here 30   *Sales* 5,088,577
SIC 2082 Malt beverages
Ch Bd Ian Freedman
  Carylon Roussy

D-U-N-S 20-919-1977   (BR)
HEART AND STROKE FOUNDATION OF BC & YUKON
1212 Broadway W Suite 200, Vancouver, BC, V6H 3V2
(604) 736-4404
Emp Here 20
SIC 7389 Business services, nec

D-U-N-S 20-297-2324   (BR)
INDIGO BOOKS & MUSIC INC
CHAPTERS
(*Suby of* Indigo Books & Music Inc)
2505 Granville St, Vancouver, BC, V6H 3G7
(604) 731-7822
Emp Here 45
SIC 5942 Book stores

D-U-N-S 20-191-5266   (BR)
INTEL OF CANADA, LTD
INTEL
1333 Broadway W Suite 688, Vancouver, BC, V6H 4C1
(604) 639-1188
Emp Here 40
SIC 8731 Commercial physical research

D-U-N-S 25-611-6534   (BR)
JALM HOLDINGS LTD
BRIDGES RESTAURANT

(Suby of Jalm Holdings Ltd)
1696 Duranleau St Suite 200, Vancouver, BC,
V6H 3S4
(604) 687-4400
Emp Here 40
SIC 5812 Eating places

D-U-N-S 20-008-1664 (BR)
JIM PATTISON BROADCAST GROUP LIMITED PARTNERSHIP
CJJR RADIO CKBD
(Suby of Jim Pattison Broadcast Group Limited Partnership)
1401 8th Ave W Suite 300, Vancouver, BC,
V6H 1C9
(604) 731-7772
Emp Here 40
SIC 4832 Radio broadcasting stations

D-U-N-S 20-112-8014 (HQ)
JORDANS INTERIORS LTD
JORDANS
1470 Broadway W, Vancouver, BC, V6H 1H4
(604) 733-1174
Emp Here 20   Emp Total 240
Sales 13,426,891
SIC 5712 Furniture stores
Pr Pr David Jordan-Knox
 Keith Bradbury

D-U-N-S 24-837-9034 (BR)
KEG RESTAURANTS LTD
KEG STEAKHOUSE & BAR, THE
1499 Anderson St, Vancouver, BC, V6H 3R5
(604) 685-4735
Emp Here 90
SIC 5812 Eating places

D-U-N-S 24-639-8742 (BR)
LEHIGH HANSON MATERIALS LIMITED
LEHIGH CEMENT
1415 Johnston St, Vancouver, BC, V6H 3R9
(604) 684-1833
Emp Here 49
SIC 3273 Ready-mixed concrete

D-U-N-S 25-571-0758 (BR)
OPUS FRAMING LTD
1360 Johnston St, Vancouver, BC, V6H 3S1
(604) 736-7028
Emp Here 40
SIC 5719 Miscellaneous homefurnishings

D-U-N-S 25-996-4422 (BR)
PATTISON, JIM INDUSTRIES LTD
JIM PATTISON SCION SERVICE CENTRE
1395 Broadway W, Vancouver, BC, V6H 1G9
(604) 681-8829
Emp Here 40
SIC 5511 New and used car dealers

D-U-N-S 25-127-9360 (SL)
RED ROBIN RESTAURANT (BROADWAY) LTD
1001 Broadway W Suite 200, Vancouver, BC,
V6H 4B1

Emp Here 65   Sales 2,544,288
SIC 5812 Eating places

D-U-N-S 20-101-9911 (BR)
REDPATH FOODS INC
MAX'S BAKERY & DELICATESSEN
(Suby of Redpath Foods Inc)
3105 Oak St, Vancouver, BC, V6H 2L2
(604) 733-4838
Emp Here 20
SIC 5812 Eating places

D-U-N-S 20-919-3288 (BR)
ROYAL BANK OF CANADA
RBC
(Suby of Royal Bank Cf Canada)
1489 Broadway W, Vancouver, BC, V6H 1H6
(604) 717-2262
Emp Here 200
SIC 6021 National commercial banks

D-U-N-S 24-760-9605 (BR)
ROYAL BANK OF CANADA
RBC
(Suby of Royal Bank Of Canada)
1497 Broadway W, Vancouver, BC, V6H 1H7
(604) 665-5700
Emp Here 65
SIC 6021 National commercial banks

D-U-N-S 25-754-1557 (BR)
SCIPIO HOLDINGS LTD
HAMPTON COURT
(Suby of Scipio Holdings Ltd)
1215 16th Ave W, Vancouver, BC, V6H 1S8

Emp Here 20
SIC 8051 Skilled nursing care facilities

D-U-N-S 20-924-7696 (SL)
SPECTRA HOSPITALITY GROUP INC
RED DOOR PAN ASIAN GRILL
2996 Granville St, Vancouver, BC, V6H 3J7
(604) 733-5699
Emp Here 50   Sales 1,532,175
SIC 5812 Eating places

D-U-N-S 25-370-2237 (BR)
STAPLES CANADA INC
STAPLES THE BUSINESS DEPOT
(Suby of Staples, Inc.)
1322 Broadway W, Vancouver, BC, V6H 1H2
(604) 678-9449
Emp Here 40
SIC 5943 Stationery stores

D-U-N-S 24-014-0876 (BR)
STARBUCKS COFFEE CANADA, INC
(Suby of Starbucks Corporation)
2288 Granville St, Vancouver, BC, V6H 4H7
(604) 732-8961
Emp Here 22
SIC 5499 Miscellaneous food stores

D-U-N-S 24-152-1368 (HQ)
SUKI'S BEAUTY BAZAAR LTD
SUKI'S INTERNATIONAL HAIR DESIGN
(Suby of Suki's Beauty Bazaar Ltd)
3157 Granville St, Vancouver, BC, V6H 3K1
(604) 738-2127
Emp Here 54   Emp Total 110
Sales 2,188,821
SIC 7231 Beauty shops

D-U-N-S 25-662-0246 (BR)
TORONTO-DOMINION BANK, THE
TD BANK
(Suby of Toronto-Dominion Bank, The)
2801 Granville St, Vancouver, BC, V6H 3J2
(604) 654-3775
Emp Here 20
SIC 6021 National commercial banks

D-U-N-S 25-370-0926 (BR)
TRANSCONTINENTAL PRINTING INC
TRANSCONTINENTAL MEDIA GROUP
2608 Granville St Suite 560, Vancouver, BC,
V6H 3V3
(604) 877-7732
Emp Here 40
SIC 2721 Periodicals

D-U-N-S 25-216-8380 (BR)
UCC GROUP INC
1275 6th Ave W Suite 300, Vancouver, BC,
V6H 1A6
(604) 730-4833
Emp Here 25
SIC 1771 Concrete work

D-U-N-S 20-523-6859 (BR)
UNIVERSITY OF BRITISH COLUMBIA, THE
PHYSICIAN RECRUITMENT & COMPENSATION
4480 Oak St Suite B321, Vancouver, BC, V6H
3V4
(604) 875-2318
Emp Here 20
SIC 8221 Colleges and universities

D-U-N-S 25-414-3597 (SL)
VALUE INDUSTRIES WESTERN LTD
1245 Broadway W Suite 400, Vancouver, BC,
V6H 1G7
(604) 606-7017
Emp Here 60   Sales 11,846,340
SIC 6712 Bank holding companies
Pr Pr Arnold Silber

D-U-N-S 24-341-0946 (BR)
VANCOUVER COASTAL HEALTH AUTHORITY
1001 Broadway W Suite 504, Vancouver, BC,
V6H 4B1
(604) 875-5074
Emp Here 20
SIC 8062 General medical and surgical hospitals

D-U-N-S 25-485-6917 (BR)
VANCOUVER COASTAL HEALTH AUTHORITY
KITSILANO FAIRVIEW MENTAL TEAM
(Suby of Vancouver Coastal Health Authority)
1212 Broadway W Suite 400, Vancouver, BC,
V6H 3V1
(604) 736-2881
Emp Here 42
SIC 8093 Specialty outpatient clinics, nec

D-U-N-S 20-646-8568 (BR)
WILLIAMS-SONOMA CANADA, INC
POTTERY BARN
2600 Granville St, Vancouver, BC, V6H 3H8
(604) 678-9897
Emp Here 50
SIC 5719 Miscellaneous homefurnishings

Vancouver, BC V6J
Greater Vancouver County

D-U-N-S 20-714-4247 (SL)
ACME PROTECTIVE SYSTEMS LIMITED
1632 6th Ave W, Vancouver, BC, V6J 1R3
(604) 534-8088
Emp Here 50   Sales 4,377,642
SIC 1731 Electrical work

D-U-N-S 25-419-1984 (SL)
AIRLINER MOTOR HOTEL (1972) LTD
HOWARD JOHNSON HOTEL
2233 Burrard St Suite 309, Vancouver, BC,
V6J 3H9

Emp Here 126   Sales 4,596,524
SIC 5813 Drinking places

D-U-N-S 20-563-1851 (BR)
BMW CANADA INC
2040 Burrard St, Vancouver, BC, V6J 3H5
(604) 736-7381
Emp Here 40
SIC 5511 New and used car dealers

D-U-N-S 20-005-4943 (SL)
BERRIS MANGAN CHARTERED ACCOUNTANTS
1827 5th Ave W, Vancouver, BC, V6J 1P5
(604) 682-8492
Emp Here 54   Sales 2,334,742
SIC 8721 Accounting, auditing, and bookkeeping

D-U-N-S 20-912-6080 (BR)
BOARD OF EDUCATION OF SCHOOL DISTRICT NO. 39 (VANCOUVER), THE
SHAUGHNESSY ELEMENTARY SCHOOL
4250 Marguerite St, Vancouver, BC, V6J 4G3
(604) 713-5500
Emp Here 50
SIC 8211 Elementary and secondary schools

D-U-N-S 20-591-0388 (BR)
BOARD OF EDUCATION OF SCHOOL DISTRICT NO. 39 (VANCOUVER), THE

LORD TENNYSON SCHOOL
1936 10th Ave W, Vancouver, BC, V6J 2B2
(604) 713-5426
Emp Here 25
SIC 8211 Elementary and secondary schools

D-U-N-S 20-713-4227 (BR)
BOARD OF EDUCATION OF SCHOOL DISTRICT NO. 39 (VANCOUVER), THE
ROBERT'S EDUCATION CENTER
1580 Broadway W, Vancouver, BC, V6J 5K8
(604) 713-5495
Emp Here 50
SIC 8211 Elementary and secondary schools

D-U-N-S 25-687-9024 (SL)
BRITISH COLUMBIA COLLEGE OF TEACHERS
BC COLLEGE OF TEACHERS
2025 Broadway W Suite 400, Vancouver, BC,
V6J 1Z6

Emp Here 47   Sales 6,021,606
SIC 8621 Professional organizations
Ch Bd Richard Walker

D-U-N-S 20-789-8888 (BR)
CACTUS RESTAURANTS LTD
CACTUS CLUB CAFE
1530 Broadway W, Vancouver, BC, V6J 5K9
(604) 733-0434
Emp Here 100
SIC 5812 Eating places

D-U-N-S 20-584-4868 (BR)
CANADA POST CORPORATION
2405 Pine St, Vancouver, BC, V6J 3E9
(604) 482-4214
Emp Here 55
SIC 4311 U.s. postal service

D-U-N-S 25-640-0581 (BR)
CARTER MOTOR CARS LTD
CARTER HONDA, DIV OF
1502 3rd Ave W Suite 604, Vancouver, BC,
V6J 1J7
(604) 736-8708
Emp Here 37
SIC 5571 Motorcycle dealers

D-U-N-S 20-806-7686 (HQ)
CENTRAL 1 CREDIT UNION
(Suby of Central 1 Credit Union)
1441 Creekside Dr, Vancouver, BC, V6J 4S7
(604) 734-2511
Emp Here 400   Emp Total 500
Sales 304,060
SIC 6062 State credit unions

D-U-N-S 20-515-1637 (BR)
CHILDREN'S & WOMEN'S HEALTH CENTRE OF BRITISH COLUMBIA BRANCH
1770 7th Ave W Suite 260, Vancouver, BC,
V6J 4Y6

Emp Here 150
SIC 8721 Accounting, auditing, and bookkeeping

D-U-N-S 20-868-0256 (SL)
COLLEGE OF PHARMACISTS OF BRITISH COLUMBIA
1765 8th Ave W Suite 200, Vancouver, BC,
V6J 5C6
(604) 733-2440
Emp Here 25   Sales 7,478,183
SIC 8621 Professional organizations
Pr Bob Nakagawa
 Mike Stonefield
Dir Suzanne Solven
Dir Doreen Leong
Dir Cam Egli
Dir Ashifa Keshavji
Dir Mykle Ludvigsen
Ch Bd Doug Kipp
V Ch Bd Bev Harris

D-U-N-S 24-615-5704 (BR)

COMOR SPORTS CENTRE LTD
COMOR-GO PLAY OUTSIDE
(*Suby of* Comor Sports Centre Ltd)
1980 Burrard St, Vancouver, BC, V6J 3H2
(604) 736-7547
Emp Here 40
SIC 5941 Sporting goods and bicycle shops

D-U-N-S 25-691-9143   (SL)
CULINARY CAPERS CATERING INC
1545 3rd Ave W, Vancouver, BC, V6J 1J8
(604) 875-0123
Emp Here 150   *Sales* 4,523,563
SIC 5812 Eating places

D-U-N-S 24-957-6604   (HQ)
DENCAN RESTAURANTS INC
DENNY'S RESTAURANT
(*Suby of* Northland Properties Corporation)
1755 Broadway W Suite 310, Vancouver, BC,
V6J 4S5
(604) 730-6620
Emp Here 35   *Emp Total* 9,000
Sales 58,424,398
SIC 5812 Eating places
Ch Bd R.Thomas Gaglardi
Pr Bobby Naicker
 Bob Gaglardi

D-U-N-S 24-855-7258   (BR)
EARL'S RESTAURANTS LTD
EARL'S
(*Suby of* Earl's Restaurants Ltd)
1601 Broadway W, Vancouver, BC, V6J 1W9
(604) 736-5663
Emp Here 120
SIC 5812 Eating places

D-U-N-S 24-340-0905   (BR)
FGL SPORTS LTD
1625 Chestnut St, Vancouver, BC, V6J 4M6
(604) 731-6181
Emp Here 21
SIC 5941 Sporting goods and bicycle shops

D-U-N-S 24-938-3431   (BR)
FEDEX OFFICE CANADA LIMITED
FEDEX OFFICE PRINT & SHIP CENTRE
(*Suby of* Fedex Corporation)
1900 Broadway W, Vancouver, BC, V6J 1Z2
(604) 734-2679
Emp Here 29
SIC 7334 Photocopying and duplicating services

D-U-N-S 20-992-0458   (BR)
FRANTIC FILMS CORPORATION
FRANTIC FILMS
1928 Broadway W, Vancouver, BC, V6J 1Z2
(604) 733-7030
Emp Here 20
SIC 7812 Motion picture and video production

D-U-N-S 20-866-4300   (HQ)
FRASER INSTITUTE, THE
(*Suby of* Fraser Institute, The)
1770 Burrard St, Vancouver, BC, V6J 3G7
(604) 688-0221
Emp Here 50   *Emp Total* 50
Sales 8,446,022
SIC 8733 Noncommercial research organizations
Pr Bratt Skinner
VP VP Jason Clemens

D-U-N-S 20-991-7389   (BR)
GENESIS SECURITY INC
(*Suby of* Genesis Security Inc)
1770 Burrard St Unit 310, Vancouver, BC, V6J
3G7
(604) 669-0822
Emp Here 20
SIC 5065 Electronic parts and equipment, nec

D-U-N-S 24-493-1085   (SL)
GOLDILOCKS BAKE SHOP (CANADA) INC
1606 Broadway W, Vancouver, BC, V6J 1X6

(604) 736-2464
Emp Here 50   *Sales* 1,992,377
SIC 5461 Retail bakeries

D-U-N-S 20-688-1380   (BR)
GOVERNMENT OF THE PROVINCE OF BRITISH COLUMBIA
B C AMBULANCE SERVICE
2940 Arbutus St, Vancouver, BC, V6J 3Y9
(604) 731-8745
Emp Here 30
SIC 4119 Local passenger transportation, nec

D-U-N-S 25-499-5590   (SL)
H.R. MACMILLAN SPACE CENTRE SOCIETY
H R MACMILLAN SPACE CENTRE
1100 Chestnut St, Vancouver, BC, V6J 3J9
(604) 738-7827
Emp Here 50   *Sales* 2,699,546
SIC 7999 Amusement and recreation, nec

D-U-N-S 25-054-6736   (BR)
HIGH OUTPUT SPORTS CANADA INC
BOARDROOM SNOWBOARD SHOP
1745 4th Ave W, Vancouver, BC, V6J 1M2
(604) 734-7547
Emp Here 20
SIC 5941 Sporting goods and bicycle shops

D-U-N-S 20-521-9954   (BR)
INTRIA ITEMS INC
CIBC
1745 8th Ave W Suite 1, Vancouver, BC, V6J
4T3
(604) 739-2310
Emp Here 20
SIC 7374 Data processing and preparation

D-U-N-S 25-093-7013   (BR)
INSURANCE CORPORATION OF BRITISH COLUMBIA
ALLWEST INSURANCE SERVICES
1855 Burrard St Unit 2, Vancouver, BC, V6J
3G9
(604) 736-1969
Emp Here 20
SIC 6331 Fire, marine, and casualty insurance

D-U-N-S 24-164-7122   (SL)
LAZY GOURMET INC, THE
1605 5th Ave W, Vancouver, BC, V6J 1N5
(604) 734-2507
Emp Here 60   *Sales* 1,824,018
SIC 5812 Eating places

D-U-N-S 25-031-8305   (SL)
LUVO CANADA INC
1580 Broadway W Suite 410, Vancouver, BC,
V6J 5K8
(604) 730-0054
Emp Here 40   *Sales* 8,761,170
SIC 5142 Packaged frozen goods
Dir Christine Day
Pr Pr David Negus
Treas Jenna Beveridge

D-U-N-S 20-241-5688   (SL)
MACDONALD COMMECIAL REAL ESTATE SERVICES LTD
SOUTH GRANVILLE BUSINESS CENTRE
1827 5th Ave W, Vancouver, BC, V6J 1P5

Emp Here 40   *Sales* 3,793,956
SIC 6531 Real estate agents and managers

D-U-N-S 20-866-7881   (SL)
MAJOR DEVELOPMENT LTD FAIRWAY PROPERTIES LTD
SOUTH GRANVILLE PARK LODGE
1645 14th Ave W, Vancouver, BC, V6J 2J4
(604) 732-8633
Emp Here 55   *Sales* 2,480,664
SIC 8051 Skilled nursing care facilities

D-U-N-S 24-311-1460   (BR)
MOLSON BREWERIES OF CANADA LIMITED
MOLSON COORS BREWING COMPANY

(*Suby of* Molson Coors Brewing Company)
1550 Burrard St, Vancouver, BC, V6J 3G5
(604) 664-1759
Emp Here 300
SIC 2082 Malt beverages

D-U-N-S 24-839-1716   (BR)
MOLSON CANADA 2005
MOLSON BREWERIES
(*Suby of* Molson Coors Brewing Company)
1550 Burrard St, Vancouver, BC, V6J 3G5
(604) 664-1786
Emp Here 325
SIC 2082 Malt beverages

D-U-N-S 25-095-2157   (SL)
NETTWERK MANAGEMENT COMPANY LTD
NETTWERK PRODUCTION
1650 2nd Ave W, Vancouver, BC, V6J 4R3
(604) 654-2929
Emp Here 50   *Sales* 7,913,100
SIC 7922 Theatrical producers and services
Dir Terry Mcbride
Pr Pr Dan Fraser

D-U-N-S 24-672-3589   (HQ)
NETTWERK PRODUCTIONS LTD
(*Suby of* Nettwerk Productions Ltd)
1650 2nd Ave W, Vancouver, BC, V6J 4R3
(604) 654-2929
Emp Here 63   *Emp Total* 120
Sales 9,234,824
SIC 2782 Blankbooks and looseleaf binders
 Terry Mcbride
Pr Pr Ric Arboit
 Mark Jowett

D-U-N-S 20-911-7670   (HQ)
NORTHLAND PROPERTIES CORPORATION
SANDMAN INNS
(*Suby of* Northland Properties Corporation)
1755 Broadway W Suite 310, Vancouver, BC,
V6J 4S5
(604) 730-6610
Emp Here 60   *Emp Total* 9,000
Sales 393,987,780
SIC 7011 Hotels and motels
 Robert Gaglardi
Pr Pr Thomas Gaglardi
VP Fin Shamlin Pillay

D-U-N-S 24-445-9301   (SL)
OPEN SOLUTIONS DTS INC
(*Suby of* Fiserv, Inc.)
1441 Creekside Dr Suite 300, Vancouver, BC,
V6J 4S7
(604) 714-1848
Emp Here 20   *Sales* 33,258,880
SIC 7372 Prepackaged software
Fin Ex Colin Brown
Pr Michael Kelso

D-U-N-S 20-514-1034   (SL)
OPEN SOLUTIONS DATAWEST INC
(*Suby of* Fiserv, Inc.)
1770 Burrard St Suite 300, Vancouver, BC,
V6J 3G7
(604) 734-7494
Emp Here 80   *Sales* 13,055,280
SIC 8742 Management consulting services
Dir Barry Cleaver
Dir Kenneth Saunders
Dir Andrew S. Saunders

D-U-N-S 25-718-4606   (BR)
QUINTERRA PROPERTY MAINTENANCE INC
1681 Chestnut St Suite 400, Vancouver, BC,
V6J 4M6
(604) 689-1800
Emp Here 2,700
SIC 7349 Building maintenance services, nec

D-U-N-S 25-723-9194   (BR)
S.U.C.C.E.S.S. (ALSO KNOWN AS UNITED CHINESE COMMUNITY ENRICHMENT

SERVICES SOCIETY)
S.U.C.C.E.S.S.
1755 Broadway W Suite 200, Vancouver, BC,
V6J 4S5

Emp Here 20
SIC 8741 Management services

D-U-N-S 24-881-8239   (HQ)
SLR CONSULTING (CANADA) LTD
1620 8th Ave W Suite 200, Vancouver, BC,
V6J 1V4
(604) 738-2500
Emp Here 65   *Emp Total* 14
Sales 16,718,644
SIC 8748 Business consulting, nec
Pr Pr Faramarz Bogzaran
Sec Steven Numata
Dir Ruth Ann Pierce
 James Malick
 Richard Johnson

D-U-N-S 24-167-0918   (HQ)
SAWARNE LUMBER CO LTD
(*Suby of* Sawarne Lumber Co Ltd)
1770 Burrard St Suite 280, Vancouver, BC,
V6J 3G7
(604) 324-4666
Emp Here 75   *Emp Total* 90
Sales 8,536,402
SIC 2421 Sawmills and planing mills, general
Pr Pr Sawarne Sangara
 Terry Sangara
Dir Davy Sangara
Dir Kerry Sangara
 Kirpy Sangara

D-U-N-S 25-539-7481   (SL)
SCOTT INDUSTRIES (1995) INC
1818 Cornwall Ave Suite 100, Vancouver, BC,
V6J 1C7
(604) 874-8228
Emp Here 60   *Sales* 9,536,300
SIC 8741 Management services
Pr John C Scott

D-U-N-S 20-801-6303   (SL)
SEYMOUR MEDICAL CLINIC, THE
1530 7th Ave W Suite 200, Vancouver, BC,
V6J 1S3
(604) 738-2151
Emp Here 70   *Sales* 4,231,721
SIC 8011 Offices and clinics of medical doctors

D-U-N-S 24-292-8448   (HQ)
SNOW COVERS SPORTS INC
SNOW COVERS
1701 3rd Ave W, Vancouver, BC, V6J 1K7
(604) 738-3715
Emp Here 22   *Emp Total* 260
Sales 4,377,642
SIC 5941 Sporting goods and bicycle shops

D-U-N-S 24-995-1658   (HQ)
SPECTRA GROUP OF GREAT RESTAURANTS INC, THE
BREAD GARDEN BAKERY CAFE
1880 1st Ave W, Vancouver, BC, V6J 1G5

Emp Here 20   *Emp Total* 9
Sales 38,918,188
SIC 5812 Eating places
 Peter J. Bonner
 Hugh R. Smythe
 Sam Grippo
 Ronald C. Shon

D-U-N-S 24-318-6520   (BR)
SPIN PRODUCTIONS CORPORATION
SPIN WEST VFX
1965 4th Ave W Suite 207, Vancouver, BC,
V6J 1M8
(604) 708-8846
Emp Here 25
SIC 7812 Motion picture and video production

D-U-N-S 20-506-0408   (BR)

STARBUCKS COFFEE CANADA, INC
(*Suby of* Starbucks Corporation)
1500 2nd Ave W, Vancouver, BC, V6J 1H2
(604) 736-5477
Emp Here 20
SIC 5812 Eating places

D-U-N-S 25-974-0975   (BR)
STRATEGIC COMMUNICATIONS INC
1770 7th Ave W Suite 305, Vancouver, BC,
V6J 4Y6
(604) 681-3030
Emp Here 50
SIC 8748 Business consulting, nec

D-U-N-S 20-793-7520   (BR)
SUKI'S BEAUTY BAZAAR LTD
SUKI'S ON 1ST
(*Suby of* Suki's Beauty Bazaar Ltd)
1805 1st Ave W, Vancouver, BC, V6J 5B8
(604) 732-9101
Emp Here 30
SIC 7231 Beauty shops

D-U-N-S 24-676-8134   (BR)
SUN DAWN INTEGRATED SERVICES INC
1606 5th Ave W, Vancouver, BC, V6J 1N8
(604) 739-3801
Emp Here 20
SIC 8711 Engineering services

D-U-N-S 20-099-6911   (BR)
SUN LIFE ASSURANCE COMPANY OF CANADA
SUN LIFE FINANCIAL
1508 Broadway W Suite 701, Vancouver, BC,
V6J 1W8
(604) 683-6905
Emp Here 50
SIC 6311 Life insurance

D-U-N-S 20-586-0919   (SL)
VANCOUVER FREE PRESS PUBLISHING CORP
GEORGIA STRAIGHT
1701 Broadway W, Vancouver, BC, V6J 1Y3
(604) 730-7000
Emp Here 60   *Sales* 4,377,642
SIC 2721 Periodicals

D-U-N-S 20-804-2499   (SL)
VANCOUVER LAWN TENNIS AND BAD-MINTON CLUB
1630 15th Ave W, Vancouver, BC, V6J 2K7
(604) 731-9411
Emp Here 80   *Sales* 3,210,271
SIC 7997 Membership sports and recreation clubs

D-U-N-S 20-868-4951   (BR)
WAWANESA MUTUAL INSURANCE COMPANY, THE
(*Suby of* Wawanesa Mutual Insurance Company, The)
1985 Broadway W Suite 400, Vancouver, BC,
V6J 4Y3
(604) 739-5400
Emp Here 115
SIC 6331 Fire, marine, and casualty insurance

Vancouver, BC V6K
Greater Vancouver County

D-U-N-S 20-978-2858   (BR)
2627 W 16TH AVENUE HOLDINGS LTD
CHOICES MARKET LTD
2627 16th Ave W, Vancouver, BC, V6K 3C2
(604) 736-0009
Emp Here 20
SIC 5411 Grocery stores

D-U-N-S 25-329-0852   (SL)
498224 BC INC
BRADDAN PRIVATE HOSPITAL
2450 2nd Ave W, Vancouver, BC, V6K 1J6

(604) 731-2127
Emp Here 50   *Sales* 2,261,782
SIC 8051 Skilled nursing care facilities

D-U-N-S 25-365-5310   (BR)
BOARD OF EDUCATION OF SCHOOL DISTRICT NO. 39 (VANCOUVER), THE
KITSILANO SECONDARY SCHOOL
2550 10th Ave W, Vancouver, BC, V6K 2J6
(604) 713-8961
Emp Here 70
SIC 8211 Elementary and secondary schools

D-U-N-S 20-713-4037   (BR)
BOARD OF EDUCATION OF SCHOOL DISTRICT NO. 39 (VANCOUVER), THE
GENERAL GORDON ELEMENTARY SCHOOL
2896 6th Ave W, Vancouver, BC, V6K 1X1
(604) 713-5403
Emp Here 50
SIC 8211 Elementary and secondary schools

D-U-N-S 24-343-1397   (BR)
CARA OPERATIONS LIMITED
SWISS CHALET
(*Suby of* Cara Holdings Limited)
3204 Broadway W, Vancouver, BC, V6K 2H4
(604) 732-8100
Emp Here 50
SIC 5812 Eating places

D-U-N-S 24-639-4928   (SL)
FRASER ACADEMY ASSOCIATION
FRASER ACADEMY
2294 West 10th Ave, Vancouver, BC, V6K 2H8
(604) 736-5575
Emp Here 65   *Sales* 4,377,642
SIC 8211 Elementary and secondary schools

D-U-N-S 20-364-5986   (SL)
IDEA PARTNER MARKETING INC, THE
TAPESTRY AT THE O'KEEFE - ARBUTUS WALK
2799 Yew St, Vancouver, BC, V6K 4W2
(604) 736-1640
Emp Here 50   *Sales* 4,377,642
SIC 6513 Apartment building operators

D-U-N-S 20-969-0291   (BR)
LULULEMON ATHLETICA CANADA INC
LULULEMON
2113 4th Ave W, Vancouver, BC, V6K 1N7
(604) 732-6111
Emp Here 25
SIC 2339 Women's and misses' outerwear, nec

D-U-N-S 25-949-9275   (BR)
MCDONALD'S RESTAURANTS OF CANADA LIMITED
MCDONALD'S #8574
(*Suby of* McDonald's Corporation)
2391 4th Ave W, Vancouver, BC, V6K 1P2
(604) 718-1185
Emp Here 20
SIC 5812 Eating places

D-U-N-S 20-749-6597   (SL)
NAAM NATURAL FOODS LTD
NAAM RESTAURANT
2724 4th Ave W, Vancouver, BC, V6K 1R1
(604) 738-7151
Emo Here 55   *Sales* 1,678,096
SIC 5812 Eating places

D-U-N-S 25-271-7111   (BR)
SOBEYS WEST INC
CANADA SAFEWAY
2733 Broadway W, Vancouver, BC, V6K 2G5
(604) 732-5030
Emp Here 100
SIC 5411 Grocery stores

D-U-N-S 25-271-7236   (BR)
SOBEYS WEST INC
SAFEWAY
2315 4th Ave W, Vancouver, BC, V6K 1P2

(604) 737-9803
Emp Here 160
SIC 5411 Grocery stores

D-U-N-S 20-806-4829   (BR)
STARBUCKS COFFEE CANADA, INC
(*Suby of* Starbucks Corporation)
2902 Broadway W Suite 166, Vancouver, BC,
V6K 2G8
(604) 736-7876
Emp Here 20
SIC 5812 Eating places

D-U-N-S 20-272-4246   (HQ)
TRAVEL MASTERS INC
TRAVEL MASTERS PRINCE ALBERT
2678 Broadway W Suite 200, Vancouver, BC,
V6K 2G3
(604) 659-4150
Emp Here 24   *Emp Total* 35
Sales 8,317,520
SIC 4724 Travel agencies
Pr Pr Neil Mcmahon

D-U-N-S 25-664-4014   (BR)
WHITE SPOT LIMITED
WHITE SPOT RESTAURANT
2518 Broadway W, Vancouver, BC, V6K 2G1
(604) 731-2434
Emp Here 70
SIC 5812 Eating places

Vancouver, BC V6L
Greater Vancouver County

D-U-N-S 20-651-7604   (BR)
AMICA MATURE LIFESTYLES INC
AMICA AT ARBUTUS MANOR
2125 Eddington Dr Suite 204, Vancouver, BC,
V6L 3A9
(604) 736-8936
Emp Here 65
SIC 8361 Residential care

D-U-N-S 20-591-0560   (BR)
BOARD OF EDUCATION OF SCHOOL DISTRICT NO. 39 (VANCOUVER), THE
CARNARVON ELEMENTARY SCHOOL
3400 Balaclava St, Vancouver, BC, V6L 2S6
(604) 713-5396
Emp Here 30
SIC 8211 Elementary and secondary schools

D-U-N-S 25-113-8392   (BR)
BOARD OF EDUCATION OF SCHOOL DISTRICT NO. 39 (VANCOUVER), THE
LORD KITCHENER ELEMENTARY SCHOOL
4055 Blenheim St, Vancouver, BC, V6L 2Z1
(604) 713-5454
Emp Here 35
SIC 8211 Elementary and secondary schools

D-U-N-S 20-591-0610   (BR)
BOARD OF EDUCATION OF SCHOOL DISTRICT NO. 39 (VANCOUVER), THE
TRAFALGAR SCHOOL
4170 Trafalgar St, Vancouver, BC, V6L 2M5
(604) 713-5475
Emp Here 35
SIC 8211 Elementary and secondary schools

D-U-N-S 20-031-6698   (BR)
BOARD OF EDUCATION OF SCHOOL DISTRICT NO. 39 (VANCOUVER), THE
BOARD OF SCHOOL TRUSTEES DISTRICT NO. 39 VANCOUVER
2250 Eddington Dr, Vancouver, BC, V6L 2E7
(604) 713-8974
Emp Here 80
SIC 8211 Elementary and secondary schools

D-U-N-S 20-864-4591   (SL)
CALLING FOUNDATION, THE
PARKDALE MANOR
2740 King Edward Ave W Suite 233, Vancouver, BC, V6L 3H5

(604) 737-1125
Emp Here 100   *Sales* 17,043,600
SIC 6513 Apartment building operators
Pr Duncan Hay
Dir Kenneth Smith
Dir John Reid
Dir John Rosborough
Dir Bill Gilmartin
Dir Lawrence Reimer
Dir Richard Reid
Dir James Pasman
Dir Dale Carter
Dir Jonathan Soon

D-U-N-S 24-345-9489   (BR)
REVERA INC
ARBUTUS CARE CENTRE
4505 Valley Dr, Vancouver, BC, V6L 2L1
(604) 261-4292
Emp Here 200
SIC 8051 Skilled nursing care facilities

Vancouver, BC V6M
Greater Vancouver County

D-U-N-S 24-595-2036   (BR)
BLACK & LEE FORMAL WEAR RENTALS LTD
(*Suby of* Black & Lee Formal Wear Rentals Ltd)
2082 41st Ave W, Vancouver, BC, V6M 1Y8

Emp Here 22
SIC 5699 Miscellaneous apparel and accessory stores

D-U-N-S 20-591-0669   (BR)
BOARD OF EDUCATION OF SCHOOL DISTRICT NO. 39 (VANCOUVER), THE
QUILCHENA SCHOOL
5300 Maple St, Vancouver, BC, V6M 3T6
(604) 713-5420
Emp Here 25
SIC 8211 Elementary and secondary schools

D-U-N-S 20-202-7806   (BR)
BOARD OF EDUCATION OF SCHOOL DISTRICT NO. 39 (VANCOUVER), THE
MAGEE SECONDARY SCHOOL
6360 Maple St, Vancouver, BC, V6M 4M2
(604) 713-8200
Emp Here 100
SIC 8211 Elementary and secondary schools

D-U-N-S 25-482-6365   (BR)
BOARD OF EDUCATION OF SCHOOL DISTRICT NO. 39 (VANCOUVER), THE
POINT GREY SECONDARY SCHOOL
5350 East Boulevard, Vancouver, BC, V6M 3V2
(604) 713-8220
Emp Here 110
SIC 8211 Elementary and secondary schools

D-U-N-S 20-034-6059   (BR)
BOARD OF EDUCATION OF SCHOOL DISTRICT NO. 39 (VANCOUVER), THE
MAPLE GROVE ELEMENTARY SCHOOL
6199 Cypress St, Vancouver, BC, V6M 3S3
(604) 713-5356
Emp Here 35
SIC 8211 Elementary and secondary schools

D-U-N-S 24-058-0279   (BR)
BOARD OF EDUCATION OF SCHOOL DISTRICT NO. 39 (VANCOUVER), THE
SIR WILLIAM OSLER EEMENTARY SCHOOL
5970 Selkirk St, Vancouver, BC, V6M 2Y8
(604) 713-4920
Emp Here 25
SIC 8211 Elementary and secondary schools

D-U-N-S 25-316-5278   (BR)
BRITISH COLUMBIA AUTOMOBILE ASSO-

CIATION
BCAA
2347 41st Ave W, Vancouver, BC, V6M 2A3
(604) 268-5800
Emp Here 20
SIC 8699 Membership organizations, nec

D-U-N-S 20-573-4718   (BR)
CIBC WORLD MARKETS INC
CIBC WOOD GUNDY
2052 West 41st Avenue Suite 401, Vancouver,
BC, V6M 1Y8
(604) 267-7110
Emp Here 150
SIC 6722 Management investment, open-end

D-U-N-S 25-453-2062   (BR)
CANADA TRUST COMPANY, THE
TD CANADA TRUST
(*Suby of* Toronto-Dominion Bank, The)
2198 41st Ave W, Vancouver, BC, V6M 1Z1
(604) 261-1301
Emp Here 40
SIC 6021 National commercial banks

D-U-N-S 25-270-1057   (BR)
HSBC BANK CANADA
HSBC
2164 41st Ave W, Vancouver, BC, V6M 1Z1
(604) 261-4251
Emp Here 30
SIC 6021 National commercial banks

D-U-N-S 20-519-6574   (BR)
INVESTORS GROUP FINANCIAL SER-
VICES INC
2052 41st Ave W Suite 200, Vancouver, BC,
V6M 1Y8
(604) 228-7777
Emp Here 35
SIC 8741 Management services

D-U-N-S 24-311-2141   (BR)
LONDON DRUGS LIMITED
2091 42nd Ave W Suite 10, Vancouver, BC,
V6M 2B4
(604) 448-4810
Emp Here 100
SIC 5912 Drug stores and proprietary stores

D-U-N-S 25-686-1717   (SL)
PROVIDENT SECURITY CORP
2309 41st Ave W Suite 400, Vancouver, BC,
V6M 2A3
(604) 664-1087
Emp Here 150   *Sales* 4,669,485
SIC 7381 Detective and armored car services

D-U-N-S 20-299-2595   (BR)
RBC DOMINION SECURITIES INC
(*Suby of* Royal Bank Of Canada)
2052 41st Ave W Suite 200, Vancouver, BC,
V6M 1Y8
(604) 665-0688
Emp Here 40
SIC 6282 Investment advice

D-U-N-S 25-723-1654   (BR)
ROYAL BANK OF CANADA
RBC
(*Suby of* Royal Bank Of Canada)
2208 41st Ave W, Vancouver, BC, V6M 1Z8
(604) 665-0550
Emp Here 50
SIC 6021 National commercial banks

D-U-N-S 25-219-4915   (SL)
STERN REALTY (1994) LTD
COLDWELL BANKER PREMIER REALTY
6272 East Boulevard, Vancouver, BC, V6M
3V7
(604) 266-1364
Emp Here 50   *Sales* 4,742,446
SIC 6531 Real estate agents and managers

D-U-N-S 24-996-6433   (SL)
TOP EDGE HOLDINGS LTD
WHITE SPOT
5367 West Boulevard Unit 607, Vancouver,

BC, V6M 3W4
(604) 266-1288
Emp Here 50   *Sales* 1,532,175
SIC 5812 Eating places

D-U-N-S 25-712-9163   (BR)
TORONTO-DOMINION BANK, THE
TD BANK
(*Suby of* Toronto-Dominion Bank, The)
2105 41st Ave W, Vancouver, BC, V6M 1Z6

Emp Here 35
SIC 6021 National commercial banks

Vancouver, BC V6N
Greater Vancouver County

D-U-N-S 20-591-0677   (BR)
BOARD OF EDUCATION OF SCHOOL DIS-
TRICT NO. 39 (VANCOUVER), THE
SOUTH LAND ELEMENTARY SCHOOL
5351 Camosun St, Vancouver, BC, V6N 2C4
(604) 713-5414
Emp Here 30
SIC 8211 Elementary and secondary schools

D-U-N-S 20-801-5867   (SL)
CROFTON HOUSE SCHOOL
3200 41st Ave W, Vancouver, BC, V6N 3E1
(604) 263-3255
Emp Here 70   *Sales* 4,669,485
SIC 8211 Elementary and secondary schools

D-U-N-S 24-336-6593   (SL)
EURASIA GOLD FIELDS INC
3540 41st Ave W Suite 204, Vancouver, BC,
V6N 3E6

Emp Here 68   *Sales* 6,623,360
SIC 1081 Metal mining services
Pr Pr Agustin Gomez De Segura

D-U-N-S 25-712-9312   (BR)
REVERA INC
CROFTON MANOR
2803 41st Ave W Suite 110, Vancouver, BC,
V6N 4B4
(604) 263-0921
Emp Here 110
SIC 8361 Residential care

D-U-N-S 20-573-1755   (SL)
SHAUGHNESSY GOLF AND COUNTRY
CLUB
4300 Marine Dr Sw, Vancouver, BC, V6N 4A6
(604) 266-4141
Emp Here 80   *Sales* 3,210,271
SIC 7997 Membership sports and recreation
clubs

D-U-N-S 24-668-3408   (SL)
SUPRA PROPERTY SERVICES LTD
3389 41st Ave W, Vancouver, BC, V6N 3E5
(604) 761-6631
Emp Here 60   *Sales* 2,079,002
SIC 7349 Building maintenance services, nec

Vancouver, BC V6P
Greater Vancouver County

D-U-N-S 24-342-3881   (BR)
ANDREW PELLER LIMITED
GRADY WINE MARKETING
1200 73rd Ave W Suite 1000, Vancouver, BC,
V6P 6G5
(604) 264-0554
Emp Here 50
SIC 2084 Wines, brandy, and brandy spirits

D-U-N-S 24-797-7960   (HQ)
AUTHENTIC T-SHIRT COMPANY ULC, THE
SANMAR CANADA
(*Suby of* Authentic T-Shirt Company ULC,

The)
850 Kent Ave South W, Vancouver, BC, V6P
3G1
(778) 732-0258
Emp Here 40   *Emp Total* 95
Sales 20,616,774
SIC 5136 Men's and boy's clothing
Pr Pr Steven Findstein
 Martin Lott
 Bruce Allen

D-U-N-S 24-437-9652   (BR)
BANQUE TORONTO-DOMINION, LA
TD BANK FINANCIAL GROUP
(*Suby of* Toronto-Dominion Bank, The)
8005 Granville St, Vancouver, BC, V6P 4Z5
(604) 257-7830
Emp Here 22
SIC 6021 National commercial banks

D-U-N-S 24-974-6322   (BR)
BOARD OF EDUCATION OF SCHOOL DIS-
TRICT NO. 39 (VANCOUVER), THE
SIR WINSTON CHURCHILL SECONDARY
SCHOOL
7055 Heather St, Vancouver, BC, V6P 3P7
(604) 713-8189
Emp Here 100
SIC 8211 Elementary and secondary schools

D-U-N-S 20-591-0768   (BR)
BOARD OF EDUCATION OF SCHOOL DIS-
TRICT NO. 39 (VANCOUVER), THE
DR. R. E. MCKECHNIE ELEMENTARY
7455 Maple St Suite 39, Vancouver, BC, V6P
5P8
(604) 713-4952
Emp Here 27
SIC 8211 Elementary and secondary schools

D-U-N-S 20-591-0818   (BR)
BOARD OF EDUCATION OF SCHOOL DIS-
TRICT NO. 39 (VANCOUVER), THE
DAVID LLOYD GEORGE ELEMENTARY
SCHOOL
8370 Cartier St, Vancouver, BC, V6P 4T8
(604) 713-4895
Emp Here 40
SIC 8211 Elementary and secondary schools

D-U-N-S 20-713-4144   (BR)
BOARD OF EDUCATION OF SCHOOL DIS-
TRICT NO. 39 (VANCOUVER), THE
SIR WILFRED LAURIER ANNEX SCHOOL
590 65th Ave W, Vancouver, BC, V6P 2P8
(604) 713-5380
Emp Here 20
SIC 8211 Elementary and secondary schools

D-U-N-S 20-591-0750   (BR)
BOARD OF EDUCATION OF SCHOOL DIS-
TRICT NO. 39 (VANCOUVER), THE
SIR WILFRED LAURIER ELEMENTARY
SCHOOL
7350 Laurel St, Vancouver, BC, V6P 3T9
(604) 713-4925
Emp Here 25
SIC 8211 Elementary and secondary schools

D-U-N-S 25-932-7526   (BR)
CESL LIMITED
CESL ENGINEERING
8898 Heather St Unit 107, Vancouver, BC,
V6P 3S8

Emp Here 120
SIC 8731 Commercial physical research

D-U-N-S 24-135-6125   (SL)
CAMBIE ST. CONSTRUCTORS INC
8807 Laurel St, Vancouver, BC, V6P 3V9

Emp Here 75   *Sales* 18,748,560
SIC 1542 Nonresidential construction, nec
 Patrick Rise

D-U-N-S 20-109-9199   (HQ)
CANADIAN FOREST PRODUCTS LTD

CANFOR RESEARCH & DEVELOPMENT
CENTRE
1700 75th Ave W Unit 100, Vancouver, BC,
V6P 6G2
(604) 661-5241
Emp Here 120   *Emp Total* 6,000
Sales 237,122,275
SIC 2421 Sawmills and planing mills, general
Pr Don Kayne
VP Fin Alan Nicholl
VP VP Patrick Elliott
Pers/VP Onkar Athwal
S&M/VP Wayne Guthrie

D-U-N-S 25-539-6996   (BR)
CERIDIAN CANADA LTD
1200 73rd Ave W Suite 1400, Vancouver, BC,
V6P 6G5
(604) 267-6200
Emp Here 80
SIC 8721 Accounting, auditing, and book-
keeping

D-U-N-S 25-327-4203   (HQ)
CLASSIC LIFECARE LTD
(*Suby of* Classic Lifecare Ltd)
1200 73rd Ave W Suite 1500, Vancouver, BC,
V6P 6G5
(604) 263-3621
Emp Here 298   *Emp Total* 300
Sales 19,493,120
SIC 8059 Nursing and personal care, nec
Pr Pr John Sherwood

D-U-N-S 25-713-1367   (BR)
DENCAN RESTAURANTS INC
DENNY'S RESTAURANT
(*Suby of* Northland Properties Corporation)
622 Marine Dr Sw, Vancouver, BC, V6P 5Y1
(604) 325-3712
Emp Here 52
SIC 5812 Eating places

D-U-N-S 20-804-1004   (SL)
DOGWOOD LODGE SOCIETY
DOGWOOD LODGE INTERMEDIATE CARE
500 57th Ave W, Vancouver, BC, V6P 6E8
(604) 324-6882
Emp Here 240   *Sales* 15,724,750
SIC 8051 Skilled nursing care facilities
Treas Burton Holmes
 Ramsey Shankie
 Elizabeth Weese
 Robert Weese

D-U-N-S 20-136-5785   (BR)
GOVERNING COUNCIL OF THE SALVA-
TION ARMY IN CANADA, THE
SALVATION ARMY HOMESTEAD, THE
975 57th Ave W, Vancouver, BC, V6P 1S4

Emp Here 34
SIC 8399 Social services, nec

D-U-N-S 24-777-1637   (BR)
GOWAY TRAVEL LIMITED
1200 73rd Ave W Suite 1050, Vancouver, BC,
V6P 6G5
(604) 264-8088
Emp Here 27
SIC 4724 Travel agencies

D-U-N-S 25-270-0935   (BR)
HSBC BANK CANADA
8118 Granville St, Vancouver, BC, V6P 4Z4
(604) 266-8087
Emp Here 20
SIC 6021 National commercial banks

D-U-N-S 24-311-1213   (BR)
HERITAGE OFFICE FURNISHINGS LTD
1584 Rand Ave, Vancouver, BC, V6P 3G2
(604) 263-2739
Emp Here 20
SIC 4225 General warehousing and storage

D-U-N-S 25-362-3870   (SL)
I.V.M. INVESTMENTS INC

▲ Public Company   ■ Public Company Family Member   **HQ** Headquarters   **BR** Branch   **SL** Single Location

1200 73rd Ave W Suite 550, Vancouver, BC, V6P 6G5
(604) 717-1800
Emp Here 47   *Sales* 7,736,960
SIC 7311 Advertising agencies
Pr Pr Gerry Bruno

D-U-N-S 20-643-3539   (BR)
JAMIESON LABORATORIES LTD
QUEST VITAMINS
1781 75th Ave W, Vancouver, BC, V6P 6P2
(604) 261-0611
Emp Here 55
SIC 2833 Medicinals and botanicals

D-U-N-S 24-321-2011   (BR)
LEHIGH HANSON MATERIALS LIMITED
LEHIGH NORTHWEST MATERIALS
1280 77th Ave W, Vancouver, BC, V6P 3G8
(604) 269-6501
Emp Here 20
SIC 5032 Brick, stone, and related material

D-U-N-S 20-773-7946   (BR)
LEHIGH HANSON MATERIALS LIMITED
OCEAN PIPE DIV OF
9265 Oak St, Vancouver, BC, V6P 4B8
(604) 269-6700
Emp Here 45
SIC 5032 Brick, stone, and related material

D-U-N-S 20-339-0815   (BR)
LUSH MANUFACTURING LTD
8739 Heather St, Vancouver, BC, V6P 3T1

Emp Here 45
SIC 2844 Toilet preparations

D-U-N-S 20-813-3681   (SL)
MARPOLE HOUSE RESTAURANT LTD
WHITE SPOT RESTAURANT
1041 Marine Dr Sw Unit 635, Vancouver, BC, V6P 6L6
(604) 263-6675
Emp Here 50   *Sales* 1,532,175
SIC 5812 Eating places

D-U-N-S 25-908-5801   (SL)
OPTIMAL GEOMATICS INC
625 Kent Ave North W Suite 100, Vancouver, BC, V6P 6T7

Emp Here 55   *Sales* 22,105,600
SIC 7371 Custom computer programming services
Pr Pr Colum Caldwell
    Roger Bannon
Sec Michael Varabioff
    Nizar Somji
Dir Opers Mark Brooks
Dir Fin Vienna Lin
    Verne Pecho

D-U-N-S 24-162-6555   (SL)
PACIFIC BINDERY SERVICES LTD
870 Kent Ave South W, Vancouver, BC, V6P 6Y6
(604) 873-4291
Emp Here 75   *Sales* 3,291,754
SIC 2789 Bookbinding and related work

D-U-N-S 25-003-6365   (BR)
SOBEYS WEST INC
MARPOLE SAFEWAY
8555 Granville St, Vancouver, BC, V6P 0C3
(604) 263-7267
Emp Here 150
SIC 5411 Grocery stores

D-U-N-S 24-166-2480   (BR)
SODEXO CANADA LTD
700 57th Ave W, Vancouver, BC, V6P 1S1
(604) 322-8342
Emp Here 30
SIC 5812 Eating places

D-U-N-S 24-389-5641   (BR)
SPICERS CANADA ULC
SPICERS

(*Suby of* CNG Canada Holding Inc.)
850 Kent Ave South W, Vancouver, BC, V6P 3G1

Emp Here 200
SIC 5111 Printing and writing paper

D-U-N-S 20-506-0119   (BR)
STARBUCKS COFFEE CANADA, INC
STARBUCKS GRANVILLE
(*Suby of* Starbucks Corporation)
8002 Granville St, Vancouver, BC, V6P 4Z4
(604) 266-9222
Emp Here 20
SIC 5812 Eating places

D-U-N-S 20-521-1266   (BR)
SUNRISE NORTH SENIOR LIVING LTD
SUNRISE ASSISTED LIVING & SUNRISE OF VANCOUVER
(*Suby of* Welltower Inc.)
999 57th Ave W, Vancouver, BC, V6P 6Y9
(604) 261-5799
Emp Here 100
SIC 8361 Residential care

D-U-N-S 25-729-8539   (SL)
ULTRATEC FIBER OPTIC CORPORATION
8838 Heather St Suite 111, Vancouver, BC, V6P 3S8

Emp Here 45   *Sales* 6,407,837
SIC 3679 Electronic components, nec
Pr Pr Vito Palmieri
    Victor Elias

D-U-N-S 24-855-6912   (SL)
VANCOUVER AIRPORT HOTEL LIMITED
COAST VANCOUVER AIRPORT HOTEL
1041 Marine Dr Sw, Vancouver, BC, V6P 6L6
(604) 263-1555
Emp Here 50   *Sales* 2,188,821
SIC 7011 Hotels and motels

D-U-N-S 24-637-0923   (BR)
VANCOUVER COASTAL HEALTH AUTHORITY
PEARSON, GEORGE CENTRE
700 57th Ave W Suite 909, Vancouver, BC, V6P 1S1
(604) 321-3231
Emp Here 200
SIC 8331 Job training and related services

D-U-N-S 25-289-2955   (HQ)
WESTPORT FUEL SYSTEMS INC
(*Suby of* Westport Fuel Systems Inc)
1750 75th Ave W Suite 101, Vancouver, BC, V6P 6G2
(604) 718-2000
Emp Here 150   *Emp Total* 1,751
Sales 224,895,000
SIC 3519 Internal combustion engines, nec
    Nancy Gougarty
    Ashoka Achuthan
Ex VP James Arthurs
Ex VP Thomas Rippon
    Andrea Alghisi
Ex VP Jack Keaton
    Brenda Eprile
    Warren Baker
    Anthony Harris
    Colin Johnston

D-U-N-S 20-117-3655   (HQ)
WESTPORT MANUFACTURING CO LTD
(*Suby of* Westport Manufacturing Co Ltd)
1122 Marine Dr Sw, Vancouver, BC, V6P 5Z3
(604) 261-9326
Emp Here 20   *Emp Total* 110
Sales 3,811,504
SIC 2391 Curtains and draperies

D-U-N-S 24-124-9619   (SL)
ZABER TECHNOLOGIES INC
605 Kent Ave North W Unit 2, Vancouver, BC, V6P 6T7

(604) 569-3780
Emp Here 60   *Sales* 4,596,524
SIC 3625 Relays and industrial controls

Vancouver, BC V6R
Greater Vancouver County

D-U-N-S 20-572-0936   (BR)
BANK OF MONTREAL
BMO
4502 10th Ave W, Vancouver, BC, V6R 2J1
(604) 665-7097
Emp Here 20
SIC 6021 National commercial banks

D-U-N-S 20-589-5217   (BR)
BANQUE TORONTO-DOMINION, LA
TD CANADA TRUST
(*Suby of* Toronto-Dominion Bank, The)
3396 Broadway W, Vancouver, BC, V6R 2B2

Emp Here 20
SIC 6021 National commercial banks

D-U-N-S 20-591-0404   (BR)
BOARD OF EDUCATION OF SCHOOL DISTRICT NO. 39 (VANCOUVER), THE
QUEEN MARY ELEMENTARY SCHOOL
2000 Trimble St Suite 39, Vancouver, BC, V6R 3Z4
(604) 713-5464
Emp Here 40
SIC 8211 Elementary and secondary schools

D-U-N-S 20-713-4219   (BR)
BOARD OF EDUCATION OF SCHOOL DISTRICT NO. 39 (VANCOUVER), THE
JULES QUESNEL ELEMENTARY SCHOOL
3050 Crown St, Vancouver, BC, V6R 4K9
(604) 713-4577
Emp Here 50
SIC 8211 Elementary and secondary schools

D-U-N-S 20-591-0602   (BR)
BOARD OF EDUCATION OF SCHOOL DISTRICT NO. 39 (VANCOUVER), THE
QUEEN ELIZABETH ELEMENTARY SCHOOL
4102 16th Ave W, Vancouver, BC, V6R 3E3
(604) 713-5408
Emp Here 40
SIC 8211 Elementary and secondary schools

D-U-N-S 20-007-5559   (BR)
BOARD OF EDUCATION OF SCHOOL DISTRICT NO. 39 (VANCOUVER), THE
LORD BYNG SECONDARY SCHOOL
3939 16th Ave W, Vancouver, BC, V6R 3C9
(604) 713-8171
Emp Here 100
SIC 8211 Elementary and secondary schools

D-U-N-S 25-800-3565   (BR)
CATHOLIC INDEPENDENT SCHOOLS OF VANCOUVER ARCHDIOCESE, THE
OUR LADY OF PERPETUAL HELP SCHOOL
2550 Camosun St, Vancouver, BC, V6R 3W6
(604) 228-8811
Emp Here 40
SIC 8661 Religious organizations

D-U-N-S 25-093-5108   (SL)
GREAT4FILM.COM
3591 11th Ave W, Vancouver, BC, V6R 2K3
(604) 727-2757
Emp Here 20   *Sales* 6,028,800
SIC 7822 Motion picture and tape distribution
Pr Joseph Mackennon

D-U-N-S 25-026-4892   (BR)
HSBC BANK CANADA
4480 10th Ave W, Vancouver, BC, V6R 2H9
(604) 228-1421
Emp Here 20
SIC 6021 National commercial banks

D-U-N-S 20-958-1172   (SL)
JERICHO TENNIS CLUB
3837 Point Grey Rd, Vancouver, BC, V6R 1B3
(604) 224-2348
Emp Here 70   *Sales* 2,845,467
SIC 7997 Membership sports and recreation clubs

D-U-N-S 24-363-3901   (BR)
SOBEYS WEST INC
POINTGRAY SAFEWAY
4575 10th Ave W, Vancouver, BC, V6R 2J2
(604) 228-0891
Emp Here 65
SIC 5411 Grocery stores

Vancouver, BC V6S
Greater Vancouver County

D-U-N-S 25-539-0353   (SL)
49 NORTH MECHANICAL LTD
3641 29th Ave W Suite 201, Vancouver, BC, V6S 1T5
(604) 224-7604
Emp Here 50   *Sales* 4,377,642
SIC 1711 Plumbing, heating, air-conditioning

D-U-N-S 20-567-3770   (BR)
BANK OF MONTREAL
BANK OF MONTREAL
4395 Dunbar St, Vancouver, BC, V6S 2G2
(604) 665-7093
Emp Here 24
SIC 6021 National commercial banks

D-U-N-S 20-299-8196   (BR)
CATHOLIC INDEPENDENT SCHOOLS OF VANCOUVER ARCHDIOCESE, THE
IMMACULATE CONCEPTION SCHOOL
3745 28th Ave W, Vancouver, BC, V6S 1S5
(604) 224-5012
Emp Here 20
SIC 8211 Elementary and secondary schools

D-U-N-S 25-485-5927   (BR)
ST GEORGE'S SCHOOL SOCIETY
ST GEORGE'S SENIOR SCHOOL
(*Suby of* St George's School Society)
3851 29th Ave W, Vancouver, BC, V6S 1T6
(604) 224-4361
Emp Here 50
SIC 8211 Elementary and secondary schools

Vancouver, BC V6T
Greater Vancouver County

D-U-N-S 20-934-8767   (BR)
ALMA MATER SOCIETY OF THE UNIVERSITY OF BRITISH COLUMBIA VANCOUVER
PIE R SQUARED
6138 Sub Blvd Suite 101a, Vancouver, BC, V6T 2A5
(604) 822-4396
Emp Here 35
SIC 5812 Eating places

D-U-N-S 20-713-4177   (BR)
BOARD OF EDUCATION OF SCHOOL DISTRICT NO. 39 (VANCOUVER), THE
UNIVERSITY HILL SECONDARY SCHOOL
2896 Acadia Rd, Vancouver, BC, V6T 1S2
(604) 713-8258
Emp Here 50
SIC 8211 Elementary and secondary schools

D-U-N-S 20-591-0693   (BR)
BOARD OF EDUCATION OF SCHOOL DISTRICT NO. 39 (VANCOUVER), THE
UNIVERSITY HILL ELEMENTARY SCHOOL
5395 Chancellor Blvd, Vancouver, BC, V6T 1E2

---

(604) 713-5350
Emp Here 25
SIC 8211 Elementary and secondary schools

D-U-N-S 20-591-0347   (BR)
BOARD OF EDUCATION OF SCHOOL DISTRICT NO. 39 (VANCOUVER), THE
QUEEN VICTORIA ELEMENTARY SCHOOL
1850 East Mall, Vancouver, BC, V6T 1Z1
(604) 713-4694
Emp Here 25
SIC 8211 Elementary and secondary schools

D-U-N-S 20-707-1486   (BR)
CANADIAN BLOOD SERVICES
2211 Wesbrook Mall, Vancouver, BC, V6T 2B5
(604) 822-7587
Emp Here 25
SIC 8099 Health and allied services, nec

D-U-N-S 24-321-9594   (SL)
DELTA FOODS INTERNATIONAL INC
5630 Montgomery Pl, Vancouver, BC, V6T 2C7
(778) 370-0576
Emp Here 1,003   *Sales* 508,771,750
SIC 5146 Fish and seafoods
Pr Henry Han

D-U-N-S 20-995-5400   (BR)
FPINNOVATIONS
FERIC DIVISIONS
2601 East Mall, Vancouver, BC, V6T 1Z4
(604) 228-4804
Emp Here 40
SIC 8733 Noncommercial research organizations

D-U-N-S 24-391-0705   (BR)
FPINNOVATIONS
FORINTEK, DIV OF
2665 East Mall, Vancouver, BC, V6T 1Z4
(604) 224-3221
Emp Here 150
SIC 8731 Commercial physical research

D-U-N-S 25-664-5334   (BR)
MCDONALD'S RESTAURANTS OF CANADA LIMITED
MCDONALD'S #8523
(*Suby of* McDonald's Corporation)
5728 University Blvd Suite 101, Vancouver, BC, V6T 1K6
(604) 221-2570
Emp Here 50
SIC 5812 Eating places

D-U-N-S 20-730-4580   (SL)
MOTION METRICS INTERNATIONAL CORP
2389 Health Sciences Mall Unit 101, Vancouver, BC, V6T 1Z3
(604) 822-5848
Emp Here 50   *Sales* 4,231,721
SIC 1081 Metal mining services

D-U-N-S 25-664-8270   (BR)
NORDION (CANADA) INC
NORDION
4004 Wesbrook Mall, Vancouver, BC, V6T 2A3
(604) 228-8952
Emp Here 50
SIC 8071 Medical laboratories

D-U-N-S 20-796-7220   (BR)
STAPLES CANADA INC
STAPLES THE BUSINESS DEPOT
(*Suby of* Staples, Inc.)
2135 Allison Rd Unit 101, Vancouver, BC, V6T 1T5
(604) 221-4780
Emp Here 20
SIC 5943 Stationery stores

D-U-N-S 20-944-5316   (BR)
STARBUCKS COFFEE CANADA, INC
STARBUCKS
(*Suby of* Starbucks Corporation)
6190 Agronomy Rd, Vancouver, BC, V6T 1Z3

(604) 221-6434
Emp Here 21
SIC 5812 Eating places

D-U-N-S 20-806-4423   (BR)
STARBUCKS COFFEE CANADA, INC
STARBUCKS
(*Suby of* Starbucks Corporation)
5761 Dalhousie Rd, Vancouver, BC, V6T 2H9
(604) 221-0200
Emp Here 22
SIC 5812 Eating places

D-U-N-S 24-367-8802   (HQ)
TRIUMF
CANADA'S NATIONAL LABORATORY FOR PARTICLE AND NUCLEAR PHYSICS
(*Suby of* TRIUMF)
4004 Wesbrook Mall, Vancouver, BC, V6T 2A3
(604) 222-1047
Emp Here 300   *Emp Total* 500
Sales 55,324,347
SIC 8733 Noncommercial research organizations
   Jonathan Bagger
   Henry Chen
Dir Reiner Kruecken
Dir Robert Laxdal
Dir Remy Dawson
Dir Paul Schaffer
Dir Jens Dilling

D-U-N-S 24-245-8578   (SL)
U B C ALUMNI ASSOCIATION
ALUMI UBC
6163 University Blvd, Vancouver, BC, V6T 1Z1
(604) 822-3313
Emp Here 50   *Sales* 3,575,074
SIC 8641 Civic and social associations

D-U-N-S 25-068-8090   (SL)
U B C TRAFFIC OFFICE
PARKING AND ACCESS CONTROL SERVICES
2075 Wesbrook Mall Suite 204, Vancouver, BC, V6T 1Z1
(604) 822-6786
Emp Here 95   *Sales* 1,240,332
SIC 7521 Automobile parking

D-U-N-S 24-558-2911   (SL)
U.G.C.C. HOLDINGS INC
UNIVERSITY GOLF CLUB
5185 University Blvd, Vancouver, BC, V6T 1X5
(604) 224-1018
Emp Here 75   *Sales* 2,991,389
SIC 7997 Membership sports and recreation clubs

D-U-N-S 20-979-1800   (BR)
UNIVERSITY OF BRITISH COLUMBIA, THE
BLUE CHIP COOKIES
6138 Sub Blvd, Vancouver, BC, V6T 2A5
(604) 822-6999
Emp Here 20
SIC 8221 Colleges and universities

D-U-N-S 20-153-2707   (BR)
UNIVERSITY OF BRITISH COLUMBIA, THE
INSTITUTE FOR COMPUTING, INFORMATION & COGNITIVE SYSTEMS
2366 Main Mall Ste 289, Vancouver, BC, V6T 1Z4
(604) 822-6894
Emp Here 120
SIC 8221 Colleges and universities

D-U-N-S 24-337-3763   (BR)
UNIVERSITY OF BRITISH COLUMBIA, THE
CENTRE FOR INTER CULTURAL COMMUNICATION-CONTINUED STUDIES
5950 University Blvd Suite 410, Vancouver, BC, V6T 1Z3
(604) 822-1436
Emp Here 20
SIC 8221 Colleges and universities

D-U-N-S 20-789-3806   (BR)

UNIVERSITY OF BRITISH COLUMBIA, THE
FACULTY OF DENTISTRY, THE
2199 Wesbrook Mall Suite 350, Vancouver, BC, V6T 1Z3
(604) 822-5773
Emp Here 100
SIC 8221 Colleges and universities

D-U-N-S 20-775-2093   (BR)
UNIVERSITY OF BRITISH COLUMBIA, THE
DEPARTMENT OF MECHANICAL ENGINEERING
6250 Applied Science Lane Rm 2054, Vancouver, BC, V6T 1Z4
(604) 822-2781
Emp Here 60
SIC 8221 Colleges and universities

D-U-N-S 20-536-9874   (BR)
UNIVERSITY OF BRITISH COLUMBIA, THE
UBC HUMAN RESOURCES
2150 Western Pky Unit 209, Vancouver, BC, V6T 1V6
(604) 822-2211
Emp Here 25
SIC 8221 Colleges and universities

D-U-N-S 20-790-4819   (BR)
UNIVERSITY OF BRITISH COLUMBIA, THE
IT DEPARTMENT
6356 Agricultural Rd Suite 420, Vancouver, BC, V6T 1Z2
(604) 822-6611
Emp Here 20
SIC 8221 Colleges and universities

D-U-N-S 24-684-4869   (BR)
UNIVERSITY OF BRITISH COLUMBIA, THE
FACULTY OF DENTISTRY
2194 Health Sciences Mall Unit 3, Vancouver, BC, V6T 1Z6
(604) 822-0738
Emp Here 50
SIC 8221 Colleges and universities

D-U-N-S 20-789-3798   (BR)
UNIVERSITY OF BRITISH COLUMBIA, THE
ANIMAL CARE CENTRE
6199 South Campus Rd, Vancouver, BC, V6T 1W5
(604) 822-6283
Emp Here 20
SIC 8732 Commercial nonphysical research

D-U-N-S 25-080-6759   (BR)
UNIVERSITY OF BRITISH COLUMBIA, THE
TOTEM PARK RESIDENCE
2525 West Mall, Vancouver, BC, V6T 1W9
(604) 822-3304
Emp Here 76
SIC 8221 Colleges and universities

D-U-N-S 20-733-8448   (BR)
UNIVERSITY OF BRITISH COLUMBIA, THE
WOODWARD LIBRARY
2198 Health Sciences Mall Suite 3, Vancouver, BC, V6T 1Z3
(604) 822-4970
Emp Here 28
SIC 8231 Libraries

D-U-N-S 20-179-6138   (BR)
UNIVERSITY OF BRITISH COLUMBIA, THE
EXECUTIVE EDUCATION
2053 Main Mall Suite 160, Vancouver, BC, V6T 1Z2
(604) 822-8400
Emp Here 20
SIC 8221 Colleges and universities

D-U-N-S 20-188-2748   (BR)
UNIVERSITY OF BRITISH COLUMBIA, THE
SAGE BISTRO
6331 Crescent Rd, Vancouver, BC, V6T 1Z2
(604) 822-1500
Emp Here 30
SIC 8221 Colleges and universities

D-U-N-S 20-360-1224   (BR)

UNIVERSITY OF BRITISH COLUMBIA, THE
UNIVERSITY OF BRITISH COLUMBIA
2366 Main Mall Suite 201, Vancouver, BC, V6T 1Z4
(604) 822-3061
Emp Here 100
SIC 8221 Colleges and universities

D-U-N-S 20-981-6656   (BR)
UNIVERSITY OF BRITISH COLUMBIA, THE
UBC MATHEMATICS DEPARTMENT
1984 Mathematics Rd Rm 121, Vancouver, BC, V6T 1Z2
(604) 822-2666
Emp Here 267
SIC 8221 Colleges and universities

D-U-N-S 25-671-6036   (BR)
UNIVERSITY OF BRITISH COLUMBIA, THE
UNIVERSITY INDUSTRY LIASON OFFICE
6190 Agronomy Rd Rm 103, Vancouver, BC, V6T 1Z3
(604) 822-8580
Emp Here 40
SIC 8221 Colleges and universities

D-U-N-S 24-381-8064   (BR)
UNIVERSITY OF BRITISH COLUMBIA, THE
DEPARTMENT OF LANGUAGE AND LITERACY EDUCATION
2125 Main Mall Suite 1100, Vancouver, BC, V6T 1Z4
(604) 822-5235
Emp Here 20
SIC 8221 Colleges and universities

D-U-N-S 24-337-3771   (BR)
UNIVERSITY OF BRITISH COLUMBIA, THE
BIOMEDICAL RESEARCH CENTRE, THE
2222 Health Sciences Mall, Vancouver, BC, V6T 1Z3
(604) 822-7810
Emp Here 90
SIC 8221 Colleges and universities

D-U-N-S 25-325-7356   (BR)
UNIVERSITY OF BRITISH COLUMBIA, THE
PLANT OPERATIONS
2329 West Mall, Vancouver, BC, V6T 1Z4
(604) 822-2172
Emp Here 900
SIC 8221 Colleges and universities

D-U-N-S 24-370-3761   (BR)
UNIVERSITY OF BRITISH COLUMBIA, THE
UBC FINANCIAL SERVICES
2075 Wesbrook Mall Unit 305, Vancouver, BC, V6T 1Z1
(604) 822-2454
Emp Here 65
SIC 8221 Colleges and universities

D-U-N-S 20-301-1411   (BR)
UNIVERSITY OF BRITISH COLUMBIA, THE
DEPARTMENT OF HISTORY, THE
1873 East Mall Rm 1297, Vancouver, BC, V6T 1Z1
(604) 822-2561
Emp Here 54
SIC 8221 Colleges and universities

D-U-N-S 25-735-9604   (BR)
UNIVERSITY OF BRITISH COLUMBIA, THE
UBC CONFERENCE CENTRE
5961 Student Union Blvd, Vancouver, BC, V6T 2C9
(604) 822-1010
Emp Here 60
SIC 7021 Rooming and boarding houses

D-U-N-S 24-341-9111   (BR)
UNIVERSITY OF BRITISH COLUMBIA, THE
CAMPUS SECURITY
2133 The East Mall, Vancouver, BC, V6T 1Z4
(604) 822-2211
Emp Here 20
SIC 8221 Colleges and universities

D-U-N-S 20-979-0125   (BR)

UNIVERSITY OF BRITISH COLUMBIA, THE
UBC FISHERIES CENTRE
2202 Main Mall Rm 230, Vancouver, BC, V6T
1Z4
(604) 822-4329
Emp Here 30
SIC 8733 Noncommercial research organizations

D-U-N-S 24-318-0531   (BR)
UNIVERSITY OF BRITISH COLUMBIA, THE
UBC PSYCHOLOGY DEPARTMENT
2136 West Mall, Vancouver, BC, V6T 1Z4
(604) 822-2755
Emp Here 50
SIC 8221 Colleges and universities

D-U-N-S 20-030-3852   (BR)
UNIVERSITY OF BRITISH COLUMBIA, THE
UBC CAMPUS FAMILY PRACTICE
5804 Fairview Cres, Vancouver, BC, V6T 1Z3
(604) 822-5431
Emp Here 24
SIC 8221 Colleges and universities

D-U-N-S 24-336-7609   (BR)
UNIVERSITY OF BRITISH COLUMBIA, THE
*FACULTY OF PHARMACEUTICAL SCI-
ENCES, THE*
2146 East Mall, Vancouver, BC, V6T 1Z3
(604) 822-2343
Emp Here 50
SIC 8221 Colleges and universities

D-U-N-S 24-337-3789   (BR)
UNIVERSITY OF BRITISH COLUMBIA, THE
UBC CATERING
2071 West Mall, Vancouver, BC, V6T 1Z2
(604) 822-2018
Emp Here 20
SIC 5812 Eating places

D-U-N-S 25-070-5795   (BR)
UNIVERSITY OF BRITISH COLUMBIA, THE
UBC HOUSING & CONFERENCES
2205 Lower Mall, Vancouver, BC, V6T 1Z4
(604) 822-9296
Emp Here 420
SIC 8221 Colleges and universities

D-U-N-S 20-153-2673   (BR)
UNIVERSITY OF BRITISH COLUMBIA, THE
PENSION ADMINSTRATION OFFICE
2389 Health Sciences Mall Unit 201, Vancou-
ver, BC, V6T 1Z3
(604) 822-8100
Emp Here 24
SIC 6371 Pension, health, and welfare funds

D-U-N-S 24-345-0363   (BR)
UNIVERSITY OF BRITISH COLUMBIA, THE
*SCHOOL OF SOCIAL WORK AND FAMILY
STUDIES*
2080 West Mall Suite 300, Vancouver, BC,
V6T 1Z2
(604) 822-2277
Emp Here 20
SIC 8221 Colleges and universities

D-U-N-S 25-325-7646   (BR)
UNIVERSITY OF BRITISH COLUMBIA, THE
DEPT OF PHYSICS & ASTRONOMY
6224 Agricultural Rd Rm 325, Vancouver, BC,
V6T 1Z1
(604) 822-3853
Emp Here 50
SIC 8221 Colleges and universities

D-U-N-S 25-751-0149   (BR)
UNIVERSITY OF BRITISH COLUMBIA, THE
MUSEUM OF ANTHROPOLOGY
6393 Marine Dr Nw, Vancouver, BC, V6T 1Z2
(604) 822-5087
Emp Here 40
SIC 8412 Museums and art galleries

D-U-N-S 20-104-5981   (BR)
UNIVERSITY OF BRITISH COLUMBIA, THE
SAUDER SCHOOL OF BUSINESS

2053 Main Mall Suite 247, Vancouver, BC,
V6T 1Z2
(604) 822-8500
Emp Here 250
SIC 8221 Colleges and universities

D-U-N-S 20-172-3991   (BR)
UNIVERSITY OF BRITISH COLUMBIA, THE
UBC BOOKSTORE
6200 University Blvd, Vancouver, BC, V6T 1Z4
(604) 822-2665
Emp Here 112
SIC 8221 Colleges and universities

D-U-N-S 20-979-0323   (BR)
UNIVERSITY OF BRITISH COLUMBIA, THE
WALTER H GAGE RESIDENCE
5959 Student Union Blvd, Vancouver, BC, V6T
1K2
(604) 822-1020
Emp Here 300
SIC 8221 Colleges and universities

D-U-N-S 24-337-3797   (BR)
UNIVERSITY OF BRITISH COLUMBIA, THE
*DEPARTMENT OF CHEMICAL AND BIO-
LOGICAL ENGINEERING*
2360 East Mall Rm 218, Vancouver, BC, V6T
1Z3
(604) 822-6029
Emp Here 20
SIC 8221 Colleges and universities

D-U-N-S 24-341-0953   (BR)
UNIVERSITY OF BRITISH COLUMBIA, THE
SCIENCE FACULTY
6270 University Blvd Suite 1505, Vancouver,
BC, V6T 1Z4
(604) 822-0220
Emp Here 30
SIC 8221 Colleges and universities

D-U-N-S 24-336-7666   (BR)
UNIVERSITY OF BRITISH COLUMBIA, THE
FACULTY OF MEDECINE
5950 University Blvd Suite 320, Vancouver,
BC, V6T 1Z3
(604) 827-4168
Emp Here 50
SIC 8221 Colleges and universities

D-U-N-S 24-171-7243   (BR)
UNIVERSITY OF BRITISH COLUMBIA, THE
UBC CHILD CARE SERVICES
2881 Acadia Rd, Vancouver, BC, V6T 1S1
(604) 822-5343
Emp Here 120
SIC 8221 Colleges and universities

D-U-N-S 20-300-7476   (BR)
UNIVERSITY OF BRITISH COLUMBIA, THE
ENGLISH LANGUAGE INSTITUTE
2121 West Mall, Vancouver, BC, V6T 1Z4

Emp Here 75
SIC 8221 Colleges and universities

D-U-N-S 24-337-3839   (BR)
UNIVERSITY OF BRITISH COLUMBIA, THE
UBC DEPARTMENT OF GEOGRAPHY
1984 West Mall Suite 217, Vancouver, BC,
V6T 1Z2
(604) 822-3539
Emp Here 75
SIC 8221 Colleges and universities

D-U-N-S 24-334-6405   (BR)
**VANCOUVER COASTAL HEALTH AUTHOR-
ITY**
2211 Wesbrook Mall, Vancouver, BC, V6T 2B5
(604) 822-7121
Emp Here 500
SIC 8062 General medical and surgical hospi-
tals

D-U-N-S 25-098-5785   (SL)
ZALICUS PHARMACEUTICALS LTD
2389 Health Sciences Mall Suite 301, Vancouver, BC, V6T 1Z3

(604) 909-2530
Emp Here 89   *Sales* 6,695,700
SIC 8731 Commercial physical research
Pr Pr Christopher C Gallen
VP VP Terrance P Snutch
Bruce S Colwill
William L Hunter
Mark H N Corrigan
James J Miller
Hartley T Richardson
Kurt C Wheeler
Todd Foley

Vancouver, BC V6X
Greater Vancouver County

D-U-N-S 25-450-1752   (BR)
**FAMILY SERVICES OF GREATER VANCOU-
VER**
VISAC
(*Suby of* Family Services of Greater Vancou-
ver)
5726 Minoru Blvd Suite 201, Vancouver, BC,
V6X 2A9
(604) 874-2938
Emp Here 40
SIC 8399 Social services, nec

Vancouver, BC V6Z
Greater Vancouver County

D-U-N-S 20-575-8803   (SL)
1110 HOWE HOLDINGS INCORPORATED
*HOLIDAY INN VANCOUVER DOWNTOWN
HOTEL*
1110 Howe St, Vancouver, BC, V6Z 1R2
(604) 684-2151
Emp Here 80   *Sales* 3,502,114
SIC 7011 Hotels and motels

D-U-N-S 25-679-1856   (BR)
AON CANADA INC
AON INSURANCE MANAGERS
900 Howe St, Vancouver, BC, V6Z 2M4
(604) 688-4442
Emp Here 200
SIC 6411 Insurance agents, brokers, and ser-
vice

D-U-N-S 20-911-3443   (BR)
ARAMARK CANADA LTD.
ARAMARK HEALTH CARE SERVICES
808 Nelson St Suite 710, Vancouver, BC, V6Z
2H2
(604) 694-6303
Emp Here 20
SIC 7349 Building maintenance services, nec

D-U-N-S 20-571-8997   (BR)
AVIVA CANADA INC
1125 Howe St Suite 1100, Vancouver, BC,
V6Z 2Y6
(604) 699-2040
Emp Here 20
SIC 8741 Management services

D-U-N-S 20-867-2576   (BR)
**AVIVA INSURANCE COMPANY OF
CANADA**
1125 Howe St Suite 1100, Vancouver, BC,
V6Z 2Y6
(604) 669-2626
Emp Here 150
SIC 6331 Fire, marine, and casualty insurance

D-U-N-S 24-383-4723   (BR)
BELL MEDIA INC
CKST AM
969 Robson St Unit 500, Vancouver, BC, V6Z
1X5
(604) 871-9000
Emp Here 160

SIC 4832 Radio broadcasting stations

D-U-N-S 25-681-0748   (BR)
BELL MEDIA INC
C I V T
750 Burrard St Suite 300, Vancouver, BC, V6Z
2V6
(604) 608-2868
Emp Here 200
SIC 4833 Television broadcasting stations

D-U-N-S 24-193-3592   (BR)
BEST BUY CANADA LTD
FUTURE SHOP
(*Suby of* Best Buy Co., Inc.)
798 Granville St Suite 200, Vancouver, BC,
V6Z 3C3
(604) 683-2502
Emp Here 20
SIC 5731 Radio, television, and electronic
stores

D-U-N-S 20-911-3948   (BR)
**BOARD OF EDUCATION OF SCHOOL DIS-
TRICT NO. 39 (VANCOUVER), THE**
ELSIE ROY SCHOOL
150 Drake St, Vancouver, BC, V6Z 2X1
(604) 713-5890
Emp Here 40
SIC 8211 Elementary and secondary schools

D-U-N-S 20-806-0913   (BR)
CANADIAN PRESS, THE
840 Howe St Suite 250, Vancouver, BC, V6Z
2L2
(604) 687-1662
Emp Here 20
SIC 7383 News syndicates

D-U-N-S 24-696-8069   (SL)
CHATEAU GRANVILLE INC
*BEST WESTERN PLUS CHATEAU
GRANVILLE HOTEL*
1100 Granville St, Vancouver, BC, V6Z 2B6
(604) 669-7070
Emp Here 100   *Sales* 4,377,642
SIC 7011 Hotels and motels

D-U-N-S 24-418-5174   (BR)
CINEPLEX ODEON CORPORATION
SCOTIABANK THEATRE VANCOUVER
900 Burrard St, Vancouver, BC, V6Z 3G5
(604) 630-1407
Emp Here 130
SIC 7832 Motion picture theaters, except
drive-in

D-U-N-S 25-663-4494   (BR)
DENCAN RESTAURANTS INC
SUTTON PLACE HOTEL VANCOUVER, THE
(*Suby of* Northland Properties Corporation)
845 Burrard St, Vancouver, BC, V6Z 2K6
(604) 682-5511
Emp Here 45
SIC 5812 Eating places

D-U-N-S 20-690-8563   (HQ)
ECO OUTDOOR SPORTS LTD
(*Suby of* Eco Outdoor Sports Ltd)
792 Granville St, Vancouver, BC, V6Z 1E4
(604) 677-4770
Emp Here 22   *Emp Total* 55
Sales 4,669,485
SIC 5941 Sporting goods and bicycle shops

D-U-N-S 24-979-3373   (BR)
ELITE INSURANCE COMPANY
CTU ELITE
1125 Howe St Suite 1100, Vancouver, BC,
V6Z 2Y6
(604) 669-2626
Emp Here 150
SIC 6411 Insurance agents, brokers, and ser-
vice

D-U-N-S 24-116-4628   (BR)
EMPIRE THEATRES LIMITED
855 Granville St, Vancouver, BC, V6Z 1K7

Emp Here 35
SIC 7832 Motion picture theaters, except drive-in

D-U-N-S 25-386-1926   (BR)
EXECUTIVE HOTELS GENERAL PARTNERSHIP
EXECUTIVE HOTELS & RESORT
1379 Howe St, Vancouver, BC, V6Z 1R7
(604) 688-7678
Emp Here 45
SIC 7011 Hotels and motels

D-U-N-S 25-295-2106   (BR)
FEDERAL EXPRESS CANADA CORPORATION
FEDERAL EXPRESS CANADA LTD
(*Suby of* Fedex Corporation)
941 Hornby St, Vancouver, BC, V6Z 1V3
(800) 463-3339
Emp Here 30
SIC 7389 Business services, nec

D-U-N-S 25-080-9985   (BR)
GREAT PACIFIC INDUSTRIES INC
URBAN FARE
177 Davie St, Vancouver, BC, V6Z 2Y1
(604) 975-7544
Emp Here 190
SIC 5912 Drug stores and proprietary stores

D-U-N-S 20-868-0785   (SL)
GREY ADVERTISING (VANCOUVER) ULC
736 Granville St Suite 1220, Vancouver, BC, V6Z 1G3
(604) 687-1001
Emp Here 20   *Sales* 2,407,703
SIC 7311 Advertising agencies

D-U-N-S 20-347-1615   (BR)
GROUPE ALDO INC, LE
ALDO
972 Granville St, Vancouver, BC, V6Z 1L2
(604) 605-8939
Emp Here 50
SIC 5661 Shoe stores

D-U-N-S 24-728-5153   (BR)
H.Y. LOUIE CO. LIMITED
909 Burrard St Suite 110, Vancouver, BC, V6Z 2N2
(604) 605-0612
Emp Here 70
SIC 5411 Grocery stores

D-U-N-S 24-593-5390   (SL)
HARBOUR DANCE CENTRE
927 Granville St, Vancouver, BC, V6Z 1L3
(604) 684-9542
Emp Here 50   *Sales* 875,528
SIC 7911 Dance studios, schools, and halls

D-U-N-S 20-300-3715   (BR)
INDIGO BOOKS & MUSIC INC
CHAPTERS
(*Suby of* Indigo Books & Music Inc)
788 Robson St, Vancouver, BC, V6Z 1A1

Emp Here 60
SIC 5942 Book stores

D-U-N-S 24-967-4768   (SL)
KNIGHT FACILITIES MANAGEMENT ULC
840 Howe St Suite 1000, Vancouver, BC, V6Z 2M1

Emp Here 100   *Sales* 8,339,840
SIC 8741 Management services
Pr Thomas J Trezek
   Dennis Argyle

D-U-N-S 25-691-8392   (BR)
LENS & SHUTTER CAMERAS LTD
LENS AND SHUTTERS
910 Beatty St, Vancouver, BC, V6Z 3G6
(604) 681-4680
Emp Here 20
SIC 5946 Camera and photographic supply

stores

D-U-N-S 24-725-7306   (BR)
LONDON DRUGS LIMITED
710 Granville St, Vancouver, BC, V6Z 1E4
(604) 685-5292
Emp Here 140
SIC 5912 Drug stores and proprietary stores

D-U-N-S 20-347-0935   (BR)
LULULEMON ATHLETICA CANADA INC
GUEST EDUCATION CENTER
1380 Burrard St Unit 300, Vancouver, BC, V6Z 2H3
(604) 215-9300
Emp Here 100
SIC 2339 Women's and misses' outerwear, nec

D-U-N-S 20-179-0909   (BR)
MILLER THOMSON LLP
840 Howe St Suite 1000, Vancouver, BC, V6Z 2M1
(604) 687-2242
Emp Here 160
SIC 8111 Legal services

D-U-N-S 25-435-0437   (SL)
OCEANAGOLD CORPORATION
777 Hornby Street Suite 1910, Vancouver, BC, V6Z 1S4
(604) 235-3360
Emp Here 950   *Sales* 628,634,000
SIC 1081 Metal mining services
Pr Pr Michael Wilkes
   Scott Mcqueen
Ex VP Mark Cadzow
   Michael Holmes
Ex VP Mark Chamberlain
Ex VP Craig Feebrey
Pers/VP Yuwen Ma
   Liang Tang
   James Askew
   Diane Garrett

D-U-N-S 20-555-7866   (BR)
OMNICOM CANADA CORP
DDB CANADA
(*Suby of* Omnicom Group Inc.)
777 Hornby St Suite 1600, Vancouver, BC, V6Z 2T3
(604) 687-7911
Emp Here 120
SIC 7311 Advertising agencies

D-U-N-S 25-979-2042   (BR)
OMNICOM CANADA CORP
KARACTERS DESIGN GROUP
(*Suby of* Omnicom Group Inc.)
777 Hornby St Suite 1600, Vancouver, BC, V6Z 2T3
(604) 640-4327
Emp Here 22
SIC 7336 Commercial art and graphic design

D-U-N-S 20-845-3493   (BR)
ONE WEST HOLDINGS LTD
88 Pacific Blvd, Vancouver, BC, V6Z 2Z4
(604) 899-8800
Emp Here 20
SIC 6531 Real estate agents and managers

D-U-N-S 24-227-7718   (BR)
PACIFIC LANGUAGE INSTITUTE INC
VANCOUVER SCHOOL ALBERNI
(*Suby of* Graham Holdings Company)
755 Burrard St Suite 300, Vancouver, BC, V6Z 1X6
(604) 688-7350
Emp Here 30
SIC 8299 Schools and educational services, nec

D-U-N-S 24-569-3234   (BR)
PATTISON, JIM INDUSTRIES LTD
JIM PATTISON TOYOTA DOWNTOWN
1290 Burrard St, Vancouver, BC, V6Z 1Z4
(604) 682-0377
Emp Here 45

SIC 5511 New and used car dealers

D-U-N-S 24-444-2005   (SL)
PROMPTON REAL ESTATE SERVICES INC
179 Davie St Suite 201, Vancouver, BC, V6Z 2Y1
(604) 899-2333
Emp Here 40   *Sales* 5,224,960
SIC 6531 Real estate agents and managers
Mgr Richard Collins

D-U-N-S 24-227-5605   (BR)
PROVIDENCE HEALTH CARE SOCIETY
ICAPTURE CENTRE
1081 Burrard St Suite 166, Vancouver, BC, V6Z 1Y6
(604) 806-8007
Emp Here 20
SIC 8733 Noncommercial research organizations

D-U-N-S 24-966-4496   (SL)
SILVERBIRCH NO 1 LIMITED PARTNERSHIP
1234 Hornby St, Vancouver, BC, V6Z 1W2
(604) 601-5254
Emp Here 50   *Sales* 2,598,753
SIC 7011 Hotels and motels

D-U-N-S 20-641-7326   (BR)
STARBUCKS COFFEE CANADA, INC
(*Suby of* Starbucks Corporation)
720 Granville St, Vancouver, BC, V6Z 1E4
(604) 633-9801
Emp Here 30
SIC 5812 Eating places

D-U-N-S 25-499-4502   (BR)
STARBUCKS COFFEE CANADA, INC
(*Suby of* Starbucks Corporation)
788 Robson St, Vancouver, BC, V6Z 1A1
(604) 681-1901
Emp Here 30
SIC 5812 Eating places

D-U-N-S 24-213-0610   (BR)
TIFFANY & CO. CANADA
(*Suby of* Tiffany & Co.)
723 Burrard St, Vancouver, BC, V6Z 2P1
(604) 630-1300
Emp Here 25
SIC 5944 Jewelry stores

D-U-N-S 24-336-7625   (BR)
UNIVERSITY OF BRITISH COLUMBIA, THE
UBC ROBSON SQUARE
800 Robson St Suite 100, Vancouver, BC, V6Z 3B7
(604) 822-0035
Emp Here 120
SIC 8221 Colleges and universities

D-U-N-S 20-981-6698   (BR)
UNIVERSITY OF BRITISH COLUMBIA, THE
SAUDER BUSINESS SCHOOL
1900-800 Robson St, Vancouver, BC, V6Z 3B7
(604) 822-3333
Emp Here 20
SIC 8221 Colleges and universities

D-U-N-S 24-375-7155   (BR)
WSP CANADA GROUP LIMITED
1045 Howe St Suite 700, Vancouver, BC, V6Z 2A9
(604) 685-9381
Emp Here 120
SIC 8711 Engineering services

D-U-N-S 24-456-1577   (SL)
WEDGEWOOD VILLAGE ESTATES LTD
WEDGEWOOD HOTEL, THE
845 Hornby St, Vancouver, BC, V6Z 1V1
(604) 689-7777
Emp Here 110   *Sales* 4,815,406
SIC 7011 Hotels and motels

D-U-N-S 25-361-7674   (BR)
WEST 49 GROUP INC

OFF THE WALL
748 Burrard St, Vancouver, BC, V6Z 2V6

Emp Here 20
SIC 5651 Family clothing stores

D-U-N-S 25-723-4732   (BR)
WEST COAST TITLE SEARCH LTD
WEST COAST PROCESS SERVING
840 Howe St Suite 100, Vancouver, BC, V6Z 2L2
(604) 659-8700
Emp Here 20
SIC 6541 Title abstract offices

D-U-N-S 25-976-2276   (SL)
WESTBERG HOLDINGS INC
HOWARD JOHNSON
1176 Granville St, Vancouver, BC, V6Z 1L8
(604) 688-8701
Emp Here 100   *Sales* 4,377,642
SIC 7011 Hotels and motels

D-U-N-S 25-372-8935   (BR)
WINNERS MERCHANTS INTERNATIONAL L.P.
WINNERS
(*Suby of* The TJX Companies Inc)
798 Granville St Suite 300, Vancouver, BC, V6Z 3C3
(604) 683-1058
Emp Here 80
SIC 5651 Family clothing stores

D-U-N-S 20-064-2739   (BR)
YOUNG MEN'S CHRISTIAN ASSOCIATION OF GREATER VANCOUVER
YMCA INTERNATIONAL COLLEGE
955 Burrard St, Vancouver, BC, V6Z 1Y2
(604) 689-9622
Emp Here 25
SIC 8221 Colleges and universities

Vancouver, BC V7B
Greater Vancouver County

D-U-N-S 20-589-9094   (BR)
NAV CANADA
3511 Mcconnachie Way, Vancouver, BC, V7B 1Y2
(604) 775-9536
Emp Here 20
SIC 4899 Communication services, nec

Vancouver, BC V7L
Greater Vancouver County

D-U-N-S 20-688-1091   (BR)
GOVERNMENT OF THE PROVINCE OF BRITISH COLUMBIA
BC AMBULANCE SERVICE
1410 St. Georges Ave, Vancouver, BC, V7L 4P7
(604) 988-7422
Emp Here 25
SIC 4119 Local passenger transportation, nec

Vancouver, BC V7S
Greater Vancouver County

D-U-N-S 20-780-0421   (BR)
CLUB MONACO CORP
CLUB MONACO
(*Suby of* Ralph Lauren Corporation)
701 Georgia St W, Vancouver, BC, V7S 1S2
(604) 687-5550
Emp Here 26
SIC 5621 Women's clothing stores

Vancouver, BC V7X
Greater Vancouver County

D-U-N-S 20-574-8010 (BR)
AIG INSURANCE COMPANY OF CANADA
(*Suby of* American International Group, Inc.)
595 Burrard St Suite 2073, Vancouver, BC,
V7X 1G4
(604) 684-1514
Emp Here 24
SIC 6411 Insurance agents, brokers, and service

D-U-N-S 25-219-7835 (HQ)
ABSOLUTE SOFTWARE CORPORATION
(*Suby of* Absolute Software Corporation)
1055 Dunsmuir St Suite 1400, Vancouver, BC,
V7X 1K8
(604) 730-9851
Emp Here 207   *Emp Total* 445
Sales 88,798,508
SIC 7371 Custom computer programming services
 Daniel Ryan
CEO Geoff Haydon
 Errol Olsen
 Phil Gardner
Ex VP Thomas Kenny
Dir Ian Giffen
Dir Terry Libin
Dir Gregory Monahan
Dir Ian Reid
Dir Eric Rosenfield

D-U-N-S 24-365-7595 (HQ)
ACCIONA INFRASTRUCTURE CANADA INC
595 Burrard St Suite 2000, Vancouver, BC,
V7X 1J1
(604) 622-6550
Emp Here 20   *Emp Total* 289
Sales 47,037,429
SIC 1541 Industrial buildings and warehouses
Pr Darren Sokoloski
Sec Jeffrey Merrick
 Vincent Blasa
 Francisco Adalberto Claudio-Vazquez

D-U-N-S 20-572-1199 (BR)
BANK OF MONTREAL
BMO
595 Burrard St, Vancouver, BC, V7X 1L7
(604) 668-1218
Emp Here 20
SIC 6021 National commercial banks

D-U-N-S 20-536-6128 (BR)
BANQUE TORONTO-DOMINION, LA
TORONTO-DOMINION BANK, THE
(*Suby of* Toronto-Dominion Bank, The)
1055 Dunsmuir St, Vancouver, BC, V7X 1L4
(604) 659-7452
Emp Here 20
SIC 6021 National commercial banks

D-U-N-S 20-698-0885 (BR)
BANQUE DE DEVELOPPEMENT DU CANADA
BDC
505 Burrard St Suite 2100, Vancouver, BC,
V7X 1M6
(604) 676-0021
Emp Here 45
SIC 6141 Personal credit institutions

D-U-N-S 24-313-2987 (BR)
BENTALL KENNEDY (CANADA) LIMITED PARTNERSHIP
505 Burrard St Suite 770, Vancouver, BC, V7X
1M4
(604) 646-2800
Emp Here 300
SIC 6531 Real estate agents and managers

D-U-N-S 24-824-6852 (BR)
BLAKE, CASSELS & GRAYDON LLP

595 Burrard St Suite 2600, Vancouver, BC,
V7X 1L3
(604) 631-3300
Emp Here 140
SIC 8111 Legal services

D-U-N-S 24-133-8495 (BR)
BOUGHTON LAW CORPORATION
595 Burrard St Suite 1000, Vancouver, BC,
V7X 1S8
(604) 647-4102
Emp Here 120
SIC 8111 Legal services

D-U-N-S 20-916-8801 (BR)
BRITISH COLUMBIA HYDRO AND POWER AUTHORITY
BC HYDRO TRANSMISSION AND DISTRIBUTION, DIV OF
1055 Dunsmuir St Suite 1100, Vancouver, BC,
V7X 1V5
(403) 717-4639
Emp Here 25
SIC 4911 Electric services

D-U-N-S 25-293-9467 (BR)
CIBC WORLD MARKETS INC
1055 Dunsmuir Unit 2434, Vancouver, BC,
V7X 1K8
(604) 661-2300
Emp Here 38
SIC 6211 Security brokers and dealers

D-U-N-S 20-589-7403 (BR)
CANADIAN IMPERIAL BANK OF COMMERCE
CIBC WOODGUNDY
Gd, Vancouver, BC, V7X 1K8
(604) 661-2307
Emp Here 150
SIC 6021 National commercial banks

D-U-N-S 24-861-1766 (SL)
CENTRAL SUN MINING INC
595 Burrard St Suite 3100, Vancouver, BC,
V7X 1L7
(604) 681-8371
Emp Here 350   *Sales* 39,951,120
SIC 1081 Metal mining services
 Roger Richer
 Clive Johnson
 Mark Corra

D-U-N-S 25-853-2605 (BR)
CISCO SYSTEMS CANADA CO
CISCO SYSTEMS
(*Suby of* Cisco Systems, Inc.)
595 Burrard St, Vancouver, BC, V7X 1J1
(604) 647-2300
Emp Here 25
SIC 5065 Electronic parts and equipment, nec

D-U-N-S 25-999-9191 (HQ)
COSCO SHIPPING LINES (CANADA) INC
COSCO
1055 Dunsmuir St Suite 2288, Vancouver, BC,
V7X 1K8
(604) 689-8989
Emp Here 30   *Emp Total* 479
Sales 10,481,637
SIC 4491 Marine cargo handling
Pr Qimin Liu

D-U-N-S 24-167-9591 (BR)
DELOITTE LLP
DELOITTE MANAGEMENT SERVICES
1055 Dunsmuir St Suite 2800, Vancouver, BC,
V7X 1P4
(604) 669-4466
Emp Here 400
SIC 8721 Accounting, auditing, and book-keeping

D-U-N-S 20-202-7392 (BR)
DUNDEE SECURITIES CORPORATION
1055 Dunsmuir Suite 3424, Vancouver, BC,
V7X 1K8
(604) 647-2888
Emp Here 40

SIC 6211 Security brokers and dealers

D-U-N-S 24-681-5955 (BR)
FUJITSU CONSEIL (CANADA) INC
D M R CONSULTING
595 Burrard St Suite 423, Vancouver, BC, V7X
1M4
(604) 669-9077
Emp Here 65
SIC 7379 Computer related services, nec

D-U-N-S 24-866-9087 (HQ)
GLOBAL SECURITIES CORPORATION
3 Bentall Ctr Suite 1100, Vancouver, BC, V7X
1C4
(604) 689-5400
Emp Here 80   *Emp Total* 5
Sales 26,377,000
SIC 6211 Security brokers and dealers
Pr Pr Douglas Garrod
 Arthur Smolensky
Dir Aline Smolensky
 Duncan Boggs

D-U-N-S 20-889-8759 (BR)
GORE MUTUAL INSURANCE COMPANY
(*Suby of* Gore Mutual Insurance Company)
505 Burrard St Unit 1780, Vancouver, BC, V7X
1M6
(604) 682-0998
Emp Here 210
SIC 6331 Fire, marine, and casualty insurance

D-U-N-S 20-868-4886 (BR)
GORE MUTUAL INSURANCE COMPANY
(*Suby of* Gore Mutual Insurance Company)
505 Burrard St Suite 1780, Vancouver, BC,
V7X 1M6
(604) 682-0998
Emp Here 31
SIC 6311 Life insurance

D-U-N-S 24-504-6305 (BR)
GROUPE CONSEIL RES PUBLICA INC
NATIONAL PUBLIC RELATIONS
(*Suby of* Groupe Conseil RES Publica Inc)
505 Burrard St Suite 620, Vancouver, BC, V7X
1M4
(604) 684-6655
Emp Here 20
SIC 8743 Public relations services

D-U-N-S 20-132-1028 (BR)
HALF, ROBERT CANADA INC
HALF, ROBERT FINANCE AND ACCOUNTING
(*Suby of* Robert Half International Inc.)
1055 Dunmere St Suite 724, Vancouver, BC,
V7X 1L4
(604) 688-7572
Emp Here 20
SIC 7361 Employment agencies

D-U-N-S 25-686-9470 (BR)
HALF, ROBERT CANADA INC
ACCOUNTEMPS
(*Suby of* Robert Half International Inc.)
1055 Dunsmuir St Suite 724, Vancouver, BC,
V7X 1L4
(604) 685-4253
Emp Here 30
SIC 7361 Employment agencies

D-U-N-S 25-677-2161 (HQ)
JOEY TOMATO'S
(*Suby of* Joey Tomato's)
505 Burrard St Suite 950, Vancouver, BC, V7X
1M4
(604) 699-5639
Emp Here 513   *Emp Total* 513
Sales 21,301,760
SIC 5812 Eating places
Pr Pr Jeffrey Fuller
 Kent Fowler
 Stan Fuller
 Stewart Fuller

D-U-N-S 24-796-7479 (BR)
MNP LLP

1055 Dunsmuir Suite 2300, Vancouver, BC,
V7X 1J1
(604) 639-0001
Emp Here 100
SIC 8721 Accounting, auditing, and book-keeping

D-U-N-S 24-672-4686 (BR)
MITSUI & CO. (CANADA) LTD
1055 Dunsmuir St Suite 3200, Vancouver, BC,
V7X 1E6
(604) 331-3100
Emp Here 35
SIC 5099 Durable goods, nec

D-U-N-S 25-538-3572 (BR)
MORNEAU SHEPELL LTD
SHEPPELL FGI DIV OF
(*Suby of* Morneau Shepell Inc)
505 Burrard St, Vancouver, BC, V7X 1M6
(604) 642-5200
Emp Here 100
SIC 8999 Services, nec

D-U-N-S 20-863-6068 (SL)
MUSSON CATTELL MACKEY PARTNERSHIP ARCHITECTS DESIGNERS PLANNERS
MUSSON CATTELL MACKEY PARTNERSHIP
555 Burrard St Suite 1600, Vancouver, BC,
V7X 1M9
(604) 687-2990
Emp Here 50   *Sales* 4,961,328
SIC 8712 Architectural services

D-U-N-S 24-761-5628 (BR)
NEXIENT LEARNING CANADA INC
PBSC COMPUTER TRAINING CENTRES
555 Burrard St Suite 400, Vancouver, BC, V7X
1M9
(604) 689-7272
Emp Here 21
SIC 8243 Data processing schools

D-U-N-S 20-758-8955 (HQ)
NORTHBRIDGE INDEMNITY INSURANCE CORPORATION
595 Burrard St Suite 1500, Vancouver, BC,
V7X 1G4
(604) 683-5511
Emp Here 178   *Emp Total* 23,576
Sales 21,396,400
SIC 6411 Insurance agents, brokers, and service
 Ronald Schwab
Pr Pr Timothy R. Ius
 Stewart Woo

D-U-N-S 20-913-8572 (BR)
NORTHBRIDGE PERSONAL INSURANCE CORPORATION
555 Burrard St Suite 600, Vancouver, BC, V7X
1M8
(604) 683-0255
Emp Here 70
SIC 6331 Fire, marine, and casualty insurance

D-U-N-S 20-994-2254 (HQ)
OMICRON ARCHITECTURE ENGINEERING CONSTRUCTION LTD
595 Burrard St, Vancouver, BC, V7X 1M7
(604) 632-3350
Emp Here 160   *Emp Total* 200
Sales 31,550,950
SIC 8712 Architectural services
Dir William Tucker

D-U-N-S 24-373-5594 (SL)
PARKLANE VENTURES LTD
PARKLANE HOMES
1055 Dunsmuir St Suite 2000, Vancouver, BC,
V7X 1L5
(604) 648-1800
Emp Here 54   *Sales* 17,218,725
SIC 6553 Cemetery subdividers and developers
Pr Pr Peter Wesik

Dir Vincent Cheung

D-U-N-S 25-990-9760   (SL)
QTRADE SECURITIES INC
505 Burrard St Suite 1920, Vancouver, BC,
V7X 1M6
(604) 605-4199
Emp Here 35   *Sales* 2,552,160
SIC 7389 Business services, nec

D-U-N-S 24-351-5496   (SL)
RHYOLITE RESOURCES LTD
595 Burrard St Suite 1703, Vancouver, BC,
V7X 1J1
(604) 689-1428
Emp Here 60   *Sales* 4,080
SIC 1481 NonMetallic mineral services

D-U-N-S 20-292-6353   (SL)
**WESGROUP PROPERTIES LIMITED PART-
NERSHIP**
WESGROUP PROPERTIES
1055 Dunsmuir St Suite 2000, Vancouver, BC,
V7X 1J1
(604) 632-1727
Emp Here 50   *Sales* 5,936,673
SIC 6512 Nonresidential building operators
  Peeter Wesik
Fin Ex Cameron Tullis

D-U-N-S 20-703-8956   (BR)
WESTERN FOREST PRODUCTS INC
505 Burrard St Suite 1500, Vancouver, BC,
V7X 1M5
(604) 665-6200
Emp Here 70
SIC 2611 Pulp mills

D-U-N-S 25-361-5819   (SL)
WESTERN PULP LIMITED
505 Burrard St Suite 1500, Vancouver, BC,
V7X 1M5

Emp Here 360   *Sales* 20,809,920
SIC 2611 Pulp mills
Genl Mgr Dave Ingram
Pr Reynold Hert

D-U-N-S 25-692-2071   (BR)
WOLTERS KLUWER CANADA LIMITED
505 Burrard St Suite 1760, Vancouver, BC,
V7X 1M6
(800) 268-4522
Emp Here 450
SIC 2721 Feriodicals

D-U-N-S 24-099-1708   (BR)
ZURICH INSURANCE COMPANY LTD
505 Burrard St Suite 2050, Vancouver, BC,
V7X 1M6
(604) 844-3407
Emp Here 20
SIC 6411 Insurance agents, brokers, and ser-
vice

Vancouver, BC V7Y
Greater Vancouver County

D-U-N-S 20-993-7494   (BR)
ARITZIA LP
701 Georgia St W Suite 53d, Vancouver, BC,
V7Y 1K8
(604) 681-9301
Emp Here 120
SIC 5621 Women's clothing stores

D-U-N-S 24-202-9291   (BR)
BANQUE TORONTO-DOMINION, LA
TORONTO-DOMINION BANK, THE
(*Suby of* Toronto-Dominion Bank, The)
700 Georgia St W, Vancouver, BC, V7Y 1K8
(604) 654-3665
Emp Here 60
SIC 6021 National commercial banks

D-U-N-S 20-867-5608   (BR)

BANQUE TORONTO-DOMINION, LA
TORONTO-DOMINION BANK, THE
(*Suby of* Toronto-Dominion Bank, The)
700 Georgia St W Suite 1000, Vancouver, BC,
V7Y 1K8
(604) 482-8400
Emp Here 49
SIC 6021 National commercial banks

D-U-N-S 20-955-9814   (BR)
**CADILLAC FAIRVIEW CORPORATION LIM-
ITED, THE**
PACIFIC CENTRE
609 Granville St Suite 910, Vancouver, BC,
V7Y 1H4
(604) 688-7236
Emp Here 70
SIC 6512 Nonresidential building operators

D-U-N-S 20-799-3759   (HQ)
CANACCORD GENUITY CORP
(*Suby of* Canaccord Genuity Group Inc)
609 Granville St Suite 2200, Vancouver, BC,
V7Y 1H2
(604) 684-5992
Emp Here 500   *Emp Total* 749
Sales 226,158,960
SIC 6211 Security brokers and dealers
  Peter M Brown
  Michael W Murphy
Pr Pr Michael G Greenwood
  Paul Chalmers
  Douglas Dorion
  Robert M Larose
  Dennis N Burdett
  Kenneth G Macpherson
Dir Alfred E Turton

D-U-N-S 24-174-7554   (BR)
CANACCORD GENUITY CORP
(*Suby of* Canaccord Genuity Group Inc)
609 Granville St Suite 2100, Vancouver, BC,
V7Y 1H2
(604) 331-1444
Emp Here 200
SIC 6211 Security brokers and dealers

D-U-N-S 25-615-4683   (BR)
CORUS ENTERTAINMENT INC
CKNY-FM
700 Georgia St W Suite 2000, Vancouver, BC,
V7Y 1K8
(604) 684-7221
Emp Here 130
SIC 7922 Theatrical producers and services

D-U-N-S 25-014-1736   (BR)
CORUS ENTERTAINMENT INC
AM730
700 Georgia St W Suite 2000, Vancouver, BC,
V7Y 1K8
(604) 331-2711
Emp Here 120
SIC 7922 Theatrical producers and services

D-U-N-S 25-715-2694   (BR)
CORUS ENTERTAINMENT INC
CFMI-FM
700 Georgia St W Suite 2000, Vancouver, BC,
V7Y 1K8
(604) 280-1011
Emp Here 168
SIC 7922 Theatrical producers and services

D-U-N-S 20-795-9081   (BR)
CUSHMAN & WAKEFIELD LTD
CUSHMAN & WAKEFEILD LAPAGE
(*Suby of* Cushman & Wakefield Holdings, Inc.)
700 Georgia St W, Vancouver, BC, V7Y 1K8
(604) 683-3111
Emp Here 100
SIC 6531 Real estate agents and managers

D-U-N-S 24-681-6433   (SL)
**DAVIDSON & COMPANY CHARTERED AC-
COUNTANTS LLP**
609 Grandville St Suite 1200, Vancouver, BC,
V7Y 1G6

---

(604) 687-0947
Emp Here 60   *Sales* 3,118,504
SIC 8721 Accounting, auditing, and book-
keeping

D-U-N-S 20-919-1621   (BR)
ERNST & YOUNG LLP
(*Suby of* Ernst & Young LLP)
700 Georgia St W Suite 2200, Vancouver, BC,
V7Y 1K8
(604) 891-8200
Emp Here 400
SIC 8721 Accounting, auditing, and book-
keeping

D-U-N-S 24-337-3409   (BR)
FGL SPORTS LTD
ATMOSPHERE
777 Dunsmuir St, Vancouver, BC, V7Y 1A1
(604) 687-7668
Emp Here 50
SIC 5941 Sporting goods and bicycle shops

D-U-N-S 20-775-2408   (HQ)
FARRIS, VAUGHAN, WILLS & MURPHY LLP
(*Suby of* Farris, Vaughan, Wills & Murphy
LLP)
700 Georgia St W Suite 25, Vancouver, BC,
V7Y 1K8
(604) 661-1702
Emp Here 80   *Emp Total* 130
Sales 15,521,850
SIC 8111 Legal services
  A. Keith Mitchell
Pt Alan J. Hamilton
Pt Dominic A. Petraroia
COO Jay R. Cathcart

D-U-N-S 20-597-0200   (BR)
GAP (CANADA) INC
BANANA REPUBLIC
(*Suby of* The Gap Inc)
701 Georgia St W, Vancouver, BC, V7Y 1K8
(604) 688-1630
Emp Here 40
SIC 5651 Family clothing stores

D-U-N-S 20-780-0736   (BR)
GAP (CANADA) INC
GAP
(*Suby of* The Gap Inc)
701 Georgia St W, Vancouver, BC, V7Y 1K8
(604) 682-5503
Emp Here 20
SIC 5651 Family clothing stores

D-U-N-S 20-984-8568   (BR)
HOLLISWEALTH INC
DUNDEE SECURITY
609 Granville St Suite 700, Vancouver, BC,
V7Y 1G5
(604) 669-1143
Emp Here 60
SIC 6282 Investment advice

D-U-N-S 20-780-1247   (BR)
HUGO BOSS CANADA INC
HUGO BOSS
701 Georgia St W, Vancouver, BC, V7Y 1K8
(604) 683-6861
Emp Here 60
SIC 5136 Men's and boy's clothing

D-U-N-S 24-856-7604   (BR)
KPMG LLP
(*Suby of* KPMG LLP)
777 Dunsmuir St Suite 900, Vancouver, BC,
V7Y 1K3
(604) 691-3000
Emp Here 800
SIC 8721 Accounting, auditing, and book-
keeping

D-U-N-S 24-323-0765   (SL)
TD TIMBERLANE INVESTMENTS LIMITED
(*Suby of* Toronto-Dominion Bank, The)
700 Georgia St W Suite 1700, Vancouver, BC,
V7Y 1K8

---

(604) 654-3332
Emp Here 50   *Sales* 7,296,070
SIC 6211 Security brokers and dealers
Pr Edmund Clark

Vanderhoof, BC V0J
Bulkley - Nechako County

D-U-N-S 24-867-0101   (SL)
391605 BRITISH COLUMBIA LTD
*VANDERHOOF SPECIALTY WOOD PROD-
UCTS*
3300 Redmond Pit Rd, Vanderhoof, BC, V0J
3A0
(250) 567-3136
Emp Here 75   *Sales* 7,150,149
SIC 2421 Sawmills and planing mills, general
Pr Pr Keith Spencer
  Paul Height
Dir Julius Komlos

D-U-N-S 20-590-4951   (BR)
**BOARD OF EDUCATION OF SCHOOL DIS-
TRICT NO. 91 (NECHAKO LAKE), THE**
EBUS ACADEMY
187 Victoria St, Vanderhoof, BC, V0J 3A0
(250) 567-4413
Emp Here 40
SIC 8211 Elementary and secondary schools

D-U-N-S 24-648-7974   (BR)
**BOARD OF EDUCATION OF SCHOOL DIS-
TRICT NO. 91 (NECHAKO LAKE), THE**
NECHAKO VALLEY HIGH SCHOOL
2608 Bute St, Vanderhoof, BC, V0J 3A1
(250) 567-2291
Emp Here 70
SIC 8211 Elementary and secondary schools

D-U-N-S 20-127-3484   (BR)
**BOARD OF EDUCATION OF SCHOOL DIS-
TRICT NO. 91 (NECHAKO LAKE), THE**
W L MCLEOD ELEMENTARY SCHOOL
187 Victoria St, Vanderhoof, BC, V0J 3A0
(250) 567-2267
Emp Here 25
SIC 8211 Elementary and secondary schools

D-U-N-S 20-590-4944   (BR)
**BOARD OF EDUCATION OF SCHOOL DIS-
TRICT NO. 91 (NECHAKO LAKE), THE**
EVELYN DICKSON ELEMENTARY SCHOOL
1850 Riley, Vanderhoof, BC, V0J 3A0
(250) 567-2258
Emp Here 25
SIC 8211 Elementary and secondary schools

D-U-N-S 20-713-5075   (BR)
**BOARD OF EDUCATION OF SCHOOL DIS-
TRICT NO. 91 (NECHAKO LAKE), THE**
STONEY CREEK JUNIOR ALTERNATE
310 Cashmere Rd, Vanderhoof, BC, V0J 3A0

Emp Here 50
SIC 8211 Elementary and secondary schools

D-U-N-S 20-735-2738   (BR)
CANADIAN FOREST PRODUCTS LTD
CANFOR - PLATEAU
1399 Bearhead Rd, Vanderhoof, BC, V0J 3A2
(250) 567-4725
Emp Here 283
SIC 2421 Sawmills and planing mills, general

D-U-N-S 20-296-1418   (BR)
**CARRIER SEKANI FAMILY SERVICES SO-
CIETY**
(*Suby of* Carrier Sekani Family Services Soci-
ety)
240 Stewart St W, Vanderhoof, BC, V0J 3A0
(250) 567-2900
Emp Here 30
SIC 8322 Individual and family services

D-U-N-S 25-855-3056   (BR)
COLLEGE OF NEW CALEDONIA, THE

(*Suby of* College Of New Caledonia, The)
3231 Hospital Rd, Vanderhoof, BC, V0J 3A2
(250) 567-3200
Emp Here 25
SIC 8221 Colleges and universities

D-U-N-S 25-364-3969   (BR)
LOBLAWS INC
EXTRA FOODS
2110 Ryley Ave, Vanderhoof, BC, V0J 3A0
(250) 567-6000
Emp Here 70
SIC 5411 Grocery stores

D-U-N-S 25-808-7071   (BR)
ROYAL BANK OF CANADA
RBC
(*Suby of* Royal Bank Of Canada)
2517 Burrard Ave, Vanderhoof, BC, V0J 3A0
(250) 567-4776
Emp Here 20
SIC 6021 National commercial banks

Vavenby, BC V0E
Thompson - Nicola County

D-U-N-S 24-957-4864   (BR)
CANADIAN FOREST PRODUCTS LTD
2996 Mccorvie Rd, Vavenby, BC, V0E 3A0
(250) 676-9518
Emp Here 20
SIC 5031 Lumber, plywood, and millwork

Vernon, BC V1B

D-U-N-S 25-677-2328   (BR)
IRL INTERNATIONAL TRUCK CENTRES LTD
7156 Meadowlark Rd, Vernon, BC, V1B 3R6
(250) 545-2381
Emp Here 75
SIC 5511 New and used car dealers

D-U-N-S 20-041-6456   (BR)
INLAND KENWORTH LTD
INLAND KENWORTH
1051 Middleton Way, Vernon, BC, V1B 2N3
(250) 545-4424
Emp Here 26
SIC 5511 New and used car dealers

D-U-N-S 25-503-4522   (BR)
NORTH OKANAGAN REGIONAL HEALTH BOARD
VERNON INTERIOR HEALTH
(*Suby of* North Okanagan Regional Health Board)
1440 14 Ave, Vernon, BC, V1B 2T1
(250) 549-5700
Emp Here 100
SIC 8011 Offices and clinics of medical doctors

D-U-N-S 24-166-3426   (BR)
REGIONAL DISTRICT OF NORTH OKANAGAN
B X-SWAN LAKE FIRE DEPT
5764 Silver Star Rd, Vernon, BC, V1B 3P6
(250) 545-7432
Emp Here 30
SIC 7389 Business services, nec

D-U-N-S 24-897-1277   (SL)
ROSMAN, MIKE AUTO & R.V. SALES
ROSMAN, MIKE R.V. SALES
6395 Hwy 97, Vernon, BC, V1B 3R4
(250) 545-1611
Emp Here 20   *Sales* 5,376,850
SIC 5571 Motorcycle dealers
Genl Mgr Mike Rosman

D-U-N-S 25-820-5822   (BR)

SCHOOL DISTRICT NO 22 (VERNON)
BX ELEMENTARY SCHOOL
5849 Silver Star Rd, Vernon, BC, V1B 3P6
(250) 542-4013
Emp Here 40
SIC 8211 Elementary and secondary schools

Vernon, BC V1H

D-U-N-S 24-067-3905   (SL)
LAWDAN INVESTMENTS LTD
A & W
683 Commonage Rd, Vernon, BC, V1H 1G3
(250) 542-1707
Emp Here 50   *Sales* 9,333,400
SIC 5541 Gasoline service stations
Pr Pr Lawrence Brown
 Dana Brown

D-U-N-S 20-086-5546   (BR)
SCHOOL DISTRICT NO 22 (VERNON)
ELLISON ELEMENTARY SCHOOL
2400 Fulton Rd, Vernon, BC, V1H 1S3
(250) 260-4176
Emp Here 47
SIC 8211 Elementary and secondary schools

D-U-N-S 25-806-7768   (BR)
SCHOOL DISTRICT NO 22 (VERNON)
OKANAGAN LANDING ELEMENTARY SCHOOL
7322 Okanagan Landing Rd, Vernon, BC, V1H 1G6
(250) 542-1181
Emp Here 30
SIC 8211 Elementary and secondary schools

D-U-N-S 25-811-9767   (BR)
SCHOOL DISTRICT NO 22 (VERNON)
CLARENCE FULTON SECONDARY SCHOOL
2301 Fulton Rd, Vernon, BC, V1H 1Y1
(250) 545-1348
Emp Here 80
SIC 8211 Elementary and secondary schools

Vernon, BC V1T

D-U-N-S 25-267-6705   (HQ)
ACUTRUSS INDUSTRIES (1996) LTD
(*Suby of* Maeva Holdings Inc)
2003 43 St, Vernon, BC, V1T 6K7
(250) 545-3215
Emp Here 41   *Emp Total* 2
Sales 6,858,306
SIC 2439 Structural wood members, nec
Pr Pr David Marcoux
 Barry Schick

D-U-N-S 25-268-3818   (BR)
ALL-CAN EXPRESS LTD
A C E COURIER SERVICES
711 Waddington Dr, Vernon, BC, V1T 8T5
(250) 545-3669
Emp Here 22
SIC 7389 Business services, nec

D-U-N-S 25-023-6692   (HQ)
ASSOCIATED ENVIRONMENTAL CONSULTANTS INC
(*Suby of* Ashco Shareholders Inc)
2800 29 St Suite 200, Vernon, BC, V1T 9P9
(250) 545-3672
Emp Here 60   *Emp Total* 255
Sales 8,142,759
SIC 8748 Business consulting, nec
Pr Kerry Rudd
 Brian Guy
Dir Hugh Hamilton

D-U-N-S 20-356-3171   (BR)
BDO CANADA LLP

VERNON ACCOUNTING
2706 30 Ave Suite 202, Vernon, BC, V1T 2B6
(250) 545-2136
Emp Here 20
SIC 8721 Accounting, auditing, and bookkeeping

D-U-N-S 25-297-0934   (BR)
BANK OF NOVA SCOTIA, THE
SCOTIABANK
3213 30 Ave, Vernon, BC, V1T 2C6
(250) 260-5500
Emp Here 25
SIC 6021 National commercial banks

D-U-N-S 25-414-6038   (SL)
BANNGATE HOLDINGS LTD
BANNER RECREATIONAL PRODUCTS
3001 43 Ave Unit 3, Vernon, BC, V1T 3L4
(250) 542-0058
Emp Here 20   *Sales* 5,202,480
SIC 5571 Motorcycle dealers
Pr Pr Derek Bannister
VP VP Brent Bannister
 Georgia Bannister

D-U-N-S 20-698-6312   (BR)
BEST BUY CANADA LTD
FUTURE SHOP
(*Suby of* Best Buy Co., Inc.)
5600 24 St, Vernon, BC, V1T 9T3
(250) 542-0701
Emp Here 50
SIC 5731 Radio, television, and electronic stores

D-U-N-S 24-824-2604   (BR)
BLACK PRESS GROUP LTD
VERNON MORNING STAR
4407 25 Ave, Vernon, BC, V1T 1P5
(250) 542-3558
Emp Here 55
SIC 2711 Newspapers

D-U-N-S 20-786-6422   (BR)
BRANDT TRACTOR LTD
3104v 48 Ave, Vernon, BC, V1T 3R6
(250) 545-2188
Emp Here 25
SIC 5084 Industrial machinery and equipment

D-U-N-S 20-208-4831   (BR)
BUY-LOW FOODS LTD
5301 25 Ave Suite 108, Vernon, BC, V1T 9R1
(250) 503-1110
Emp Here 24
SIC 5411 Grocery stores

D-U-N-S 24-426-1942   (SL)
CSH CARRINGTON PLACE INC
CARRINGTON PLACE RETIREMENT RESIDENCE
4751 23 St, Vernon, BC, V1T 9J4
(250) 545-5704
Emp Here 30   *Sales* 1,094,411
SIC 8361 Residential care

D-U-N-S 25-288-8912   (BR)
CANADA POST CORPORATION
3101 32 Ave, Vernon, BC, V1T 2M2
(250) 545-8239
Emp Here 80
SIC 4311 U.s. postal service

D-U-N-S 25-817-5504   (BR)
CANADIAN CANCER SOCIETY
3402 27 Ave Suite 104, Vernon, BC, V1T 1S1
(250) 542-0770
Emp Here 20
SIC 8399 Social services, nec

D-U-N-S 25-311-6958   (BR)
CANADIAN IMPERIAL BANK OF COMMERCE
CIBC
3201 30 Ave, Vernon, BC, V1T 2C6
(250) 260-6300
Emp Here 30

SIC 6021 National commercial banks

D-U-N-S 25-314-8308   (BR)
CAPRI INSURANCE SERVICES LTD
2702 48 Ave, Vernon, BC, V1T 3R4
(250) 542-0291
Emp Here 27
SIC 6411 Insurance agents, brokers, and service

D-U-N-S 20-699-7756   (BR)
CHARTWELL SENIORS HOUSING REAL ESTATE INVESTMENT TRUST
CARRINGTON PLACE RETIREMENT RESIDENCE
4751 23 St, Vernon, BC, V1T 4K7
(250) 545-5704
Emp Here 50
SIC 6513 Apartment building operators

D-U-N-S 24-761-4878   (BR)
COOPER MARKET LTD
2707 43 Ave, Vernon, BC, V1T 3L2

Emp Here 40
SIC 5411 Grocery stores

D-U-N-S 25-670-4362   (BR)
DENCAN RESTAURANTS INC
DENNY'S RESTAURANT
(*Suby of* Northland Properties Corporation)
4201 32 St Suite 6501, Vernon, BC, V1T 5P3
(250) 542-0079
Emp Here 75
SIC 5812 Eating places

D-U-N-S 25-652-8662   (SL)
EARL'S RESTAURANT VERNON LTD
3101 Highway 6, Vernon, BC, V1T 9H6
(250) 542-3370
Emp Here 60   *Sales* 1,824,018
SIC 5812 Eating places

D-U-N-S 24-343-7386   (BR)
FGL SPORTS LTD
SPORT-CHEK
4900 27 St Unit 0340, Vernon, BC, V1T 7G7
(250) 260-2860
Emp Here 25
SIC 5941 Sporting goods and bicycle shops

D-U-N-S 24-683-2729   (BR)
FINNING INTERNATIONAL INC
(*Suby of* Finning International Inc)
1714 Kalamalka Lake Rd, Vernon, BC, V1T 6V2
(250) 545-2321
Emp Here 30
SIC 5082 Construction and mining machinery

D-U-N-S 24-422-9352   (BR)
FIRSTCANADA ULC
VERNON REGIONAL TRANSIT SYSTEM
4210 24 Ave, Vernon, BC, V1T 1M2
(250) 545-7286
Emp Here 25
SIC 4131 Intercity and rural bus transportation

D-U-N-S 20-609-6666   (SL)
FISHER, DEBBIE & LOCHHEAD, DAN
RE/MAX VERNON
5603 27 St, Vernon, BC, V1T 8Z5
(250) 549-4161
Emp Here 45   *Sales* 5,632,960
SIC 6531 Real estate agents and managers
Pt Debbie Fisher

D-U-N-S 24-417-2594   (BR)
GATEWAY CASINOS & ENTERTAINMENT INC
LAKE CITY CASINO VERNON
4900 Anderson Way, Vernon, BC, V1T 9V2
(250) 545-5428
Emp Here 50
SIC 7011 Hotels and motels

D-U-N-S 24-014-6790   (BR)
GOODLIFE FITNESS CENTRES INC
5001 Anderson Way, Vernon, BC, V1T 9V1

(250) 545-7230
Emp Here 22
SIC 7999 Amusement and recreation, nec

D-U-N-S 25-155-3095   (BR)
GOVERNING COUNCIL OF THE SALVA-TION ARMY IN CANADA, THE
GOVERNING COUNCIL OF THE SALVATION ARMY IN CANADA, THE
3303 32 Ave, Vernon, BC, V1T 2M7
(250) 549-4111
Emp Here 30
SIC 8399 Social services, nec

D-U-N-S 20-911-9424   (BR)
GOVERNMENT OF THE PROVINCE OF BRITISH COLUMBIA
MINISTRY OF CHILDREN AND FAMILY DE-VELOPMENT
3007 35 Ave, Vernon, BC, V1T 2S9
(250) 558-2775
Emp Here 20
SIC 8093 Specialty outpatient clinics, nec

D-U-N-S 20-301-4170   (BR)
GREAT PACIFIC ENTERPRISES INC
NEWGROUP VERNON
1110 Waddington Dr, Vernon, BC, V1T 8T3
(250) 503-3880
Emp Here 26
SIC 5192 Books, periodicals, and newspapers

D-U-N-S 25-267-8818   (BR)
GREAT PACIFIC INDUSTRIES INC
SAVE-ON-FOODS
4900 27 St Unit 425, Vernon, BC, V1T 7G7
(250) 542-8825
Emp Here 120
SIC 5411 Grocery stores

D-U-N-S 25-270-0760   (BR)
HSBC BANK CANADA
3321 30 Ave, Vernon, BC, V1T 2C9
(250) 503-5888
Emp Here 30
SIC 6021 National commercial banks

D-U-N-S 24-344-7708   (BR)
HOME DEPOT OF CANADA INC
(*Suby of* The Home Depot Inc)
5501 Anderson Way, Vernon, BC, V1T 9V1
(250) 550-1600
Emp Here 100
SIC 5251 Hardware stores

D-U-N-S 20-117-8472   (BR)
HUDSON'S BAY COMPANY
THE BAY
4900 27 St Suite 10, Vernon, BC, V1T 2C7
(250) 545-5331
Emp Here 130
SIC 5311 Department stores

D-U-N-S 20-927-3445   (BR)
INLAND RESTAURANTS (KELOWNA) LTD
WENDY'S INLAND RESTAURANT
(*Suby of* Inland Restaurants (Kelowna) Ltd)
5101 26 St, Vernon, BC, V1T 8G4
(250) 542-9832
Emp Here 45
SIC 5812 Eating places

D-U-N-S 25-272-7177   (BR)
INSURANCE CORPORATION OF BRITISH COLUMBIA
ICBC
2302 48 Ave, Vernon, BC, V1T 8K8
(250) 542-2301
Emp Here 30
SIC 6331 Fire, marine, and casualty insurance

D-U-N-S 20-651-8271   (BR)
INTERIOR HEALTH AUTHORITY
VERNON JUBILEE HOSPITAL
2101 32 St, Vernon, BC, V1T 5L2
(250) 545-2211
Emp Here 1,200
SIC 8062 General medical and surgical hospitals

D-U-N-S 24-309-3734   (BR)
INTERIOR HEALTH AUTHORITY
VERNON DOWNTOWN LAB
3100 35 St, Vernon, BC, V1T 9H4
(250) 558-1242
Emp Here 20
SIC 8062 General medical and surgical hospitals

D-U-N-S 20-705-0886   (BR)
INTERIOR HEALTH AUTHORITY
NORIC HOUSE EXTENDED CARE
1400 Mission Rd, Vernon, BC, V1T 9C3
(250) 545-9167
Emp Here 100
SIC 8051 Skilled nursing care facilities

D-U-N-S 24-309-1696   (BR)
INTERIOR HEALTH AUTHORITY
VERNON COMMUNITY CARE HEALTH SERVICES
4505 25 St, Vernon, BC, V1T 4S8
(250) 541-2200
Emp Here 75
SIC 8062 General medical and surgical hospitals

D-U-N-S 25-315-8125   (BR)
INVESTORS GROUP FINANCIAL SER-VICES INC
2899 30 Ave Suite 200, Vernon, BC, V1T 8G1
(250) 545-9188
Emp Here 40
SIC 8742 Management consulting services

D-U-N-S 20-787-8013   (BR)
KPMG LLP
(*Suby of* KPMG LLP)
3205 32 St Unit 300, Vernon, BC, V1T 9A2
(250) 503-5300
Emp Here 30
SIC 8721 Accounting, auditing, and book-keeping

D-U-N-S 20-698-1180   (BR)
LOBLAWS INC
REAL CANADIAN SUPERSTORE
5001 Anderson Way, Vernon, BC, V1T 9V1
(250) 550-2319
Emp Here 300
SIC 5411 Grocery stores

D-U-N-S 24-318-0887   (BR)
LOBLAWS INC
REAL CANADIAN SUPERSTORE
2501 34 St, Vernon, BC, V1T 9S3
(250) 260-4550
Emp Here 70
SIC 5411 Grocery stores

D-U-N-S 20-005-2319   (BR)
LOBLAWS INC
POLSON SUPER A FOODS
2306 Highway 6 Unit 100, Vernon, BC, V1T 7E3
(250) 558-1199
Emp Here 25
SIC 5411 Grocery stores

D-U-N-S 25-273-1419   (BR)
LONDON DRUGS LIMITED
4400 32 St Suite 700, Vernon, BC, V1T 9H2
(250) 549-1551
Emp Here 110
SIC 5912 Drug stores and proprietary stores

D-U-N-S 25-670-4297   (HQ)
NORTH OKANAGAN YOUTH & FAMILY SERVICES
(*Suby of* North Okanagan Youth & Family Services)
2900 32 Ave, Vernon, BC, V1T 2L5
(250) 545-3262
Emp Here 20   *Emp Total* 52
Sales 2,042,900
SIC 8322 Individual and family services

D-U-N-S 20-035-8658   (BR)

OKANAGAN REGIONAL LIBRARY DIS-TRICT
3001 32 Ave, Vernon, BC, V1T 2L8
(250) 542-7610
Emp Here 25
SIC 8231 Libraries

D-U-N-S 25-227-2930   (BR)
PHARMASAVE DRUGS (NATIONAL) LTD
NOLAN'S PHARMACY
(*Suby of* Pharmasave Drugs (National) Ltd)
3101 30 Ave, Vernon, BC, V1T 2C4
(250) 542-4181
Emp Here 30
SIC 5912 Drug stores and proprietary stores

D-U-N-S 20-735-2407   (SL)
PLAZA VENTURES LTD
A & W RESTAURANT
3101 Highway 6 Suite 119, Vernon, BC, V1T 9H6
(250) 549-4317
Emp Here 50   *Sales* 1,532,175
SIC 5812 Eating places

D-U-N-S 20-911-3393   (BR)
RBC DOMINION SECURITIES INC
(*Suby of* Royal Bank Of Canada)
Gd Lcd Main, Vernon, BC, V1T 6L9
(250) 549-4050
Emp Here 20
SIC 6211 Security brokers and dealers

D-U-N-S 24-898-2167   (BR)
ROGERS MEDIA INC
CKIZ-107.5 FM
(*Suby of* Rogers Communications Inc)
3313 32 Ave Suite 1, Vernon, BC, V1T 2E1
(250) 545-2141
Emp Here 26
SIC 4832 Radio broadcasting stations

D-U-N-S 25-696-2788   (BR)
ROYAL BANK OF CANADA
RBC
(*Suby of* Royal Bank Of Canada)
3131 30 Ave, Vernon, BC, V1T 2C4
(250) 558-4300
Emp Here 42
SIC 6021 National commercial banks

D-U-N-S 25-820-5798   (BR)
SCHOOL DISTRICT NO 22 (VERNON)
WEST VERNON ELEMENTARY SCHOOL
2711 38 St, Vernon, BC, V1T 6H5
(250) 542-0249
Emp Here 40
SIC 8211 Elementary and secondary schools

D-U-N-S 25-833-0166   (BR)
SCHOOL DISTRICT NO 22 (VERNON)
W L SEATON SECONDARY SCHOOL
2701 41 Ave, Vernon, BC, V1T 6X3
(250) 542-3361
Emp Here 75
SIC 8211 Elementary and secondary schools

D-U-N-S 25-825-7252   (BR)
SCHOOL DISTRICT NO 22 (VERNON)
SILVER STAR ELEMENTARY SCHOOL
1404 35 Ave, Vernon, BC, V1T 2R6
(250) 545-4409
Emp Here 33
SIC 8211 Elementary and secondary schools

D-U-N-S 25-807-1240   (BR)
SCHOOL DISTRICT NO 22 (VERNON)
MISSION HILL ELEMENTARY
1510 36 St, Vernon, BC, V1T 6C8
(250) 545-0639
Emp Here 45
SIC 8211 Elementary and secondary schools

D-U-N-S 25-161-6306   (BR)
SCHOOL DISTRICT NO 22 (VERNON)
ALEXIS PARK SCHOOL
4205 35 Ave, Vernon, BC, V1T 6C4
(250) 545-7289
Emp Here 40

SIC 8211 Elementary and secondary schools

D-U-N-S 25-483-1266   (BR)
SCHOOL DISTRICT NO 22 (VERNON)
VERNON SECONDARY SCHOOL
2303 18 St, Vernon, BC, V1T 3Z9
(250) 545-0701
Emp Here 100
SIC 8211 Elementary and secondary schools

D-U-N-S 20-591-4778   (BR)
SCHOOL DISTRICT NO 22 (VERNON)
ECO BEAIRSTO ELEMENTARY SCHOOL
3302 27 St, Vernon, BC, V1T 4W7
(250) 542-1388
Emp Here 50
SIC 8211 Elementary and secondary schools

D-U-N-S 20-035-0622   (BR)
SCHOOL DISTRICT NO 22 (VERNON)
HARWOOD ELEMENTARY SCHOOL
4320 20 St, Vernon, BC, V1T 4E3
(250) 542-5385
Emp Here 35
SIC 8211 Elementary and secondary schools

D-U-N-S 25-215-3796   (BR)
SLEEMAN BREWERIES LTD
OKANAGAN SPRING BREWERY
2808 27 Ave, Vernon, BC, V1T 9K4
(250) 542-2337
Emp Here 120
SIC 2082 Malt beverages

D-U-N-S 24-593-8683   (BR)
SOBEYS WEST INC
SAFEWAY LOCAL
4300 32 St, Vernon, BC, V1T 9H1
(250) 542-2627
Emp Here 125
SIC 5411 Grocery stores

D-U-N-S 20-004-0785   (BR)
STAPLES CANADA INC
STAPLES THE BUSINESS DEPOT
(*Suby of* Staples, Inc.)
3202 32 St, Vernon, BC, V1T 5M8
(250) 503-3300
Emp Here 40
SIC 5943 Stationery stores

D-U-N-S 20-058-7827   (BR)
TELUS COMMUNICATIONS INC
4701 25 Ave, Vernon, BC, V1T 1P5
(250) 558-6332
Emp Here 50
SIC 4899 Communication services, nec

D-U-N-S 25-659-1686   (SL)
TIM HORTONS
2601 Highway 6 Unit 14, Vernon, BC, V1T 5G4
(250) 260-7740
Emp Here 50   *Sales* 1,532,175
SIC 5812 Eating places

D-U-N-S 24-679-8784   (BR)
TORONTO-DOMINION BANK, THE
TD BANK
(*Suby of* Toronto-Dominion Bank, The)
5000 Anderson Way, Vernon, BC, V1T 9V2
(250) 550-1250
Emp Here 20
SIC 6021 National commercial banks

D-U-N-S 25-653-9149   (BR)
VALLEY FIRST CREDIT UNION
3101 Highway 6 Unit 110, Vernon, BC, V1T 9H6
(250) 558-5266
Emp Here 30
SIC 6062 State credit unions

D-U-N-S 20-642-5964   (BR)
VALLEY KING FOODS INC
BURGER KING
(*Suby of* Valley King Foods Inc)
2505 53 Ave, Vernon, BC, V1T 8G6
(250) 545-1312
Emp Here 30

SIC 5812 Eating places

D-U-N-S 24-026-9790   (BR)
VALUE VILLAGE STORES, INC
(*Suby of* Savers, Inc.)
5608 24 St, Vernon, BC, V1T 9T3
(250) 558-2900
Emp Here 50
SIC 5399 Miscellaneous general merchandise

D-U-N-S 24-558-632ᵀ   (SL)
VANTAGEONE CREDIT UNION
VANTAGEONE FINANCIAL SERVICES
3108 33 Ave, Vernon, BC, V1T 2N7
(250) 545-9251
Emp Here 49   *Sales* 9,329,057
SIC 6062 State credit unions
Pr Glenn Benischek
Dir Don Main

D-U-N-S 20-914-5630   (SL)
VERNON GOLF AND COUNTRY CLUB
800 Kalamalka Lake Rd, Vernon, BC, V1T 6V2
(250) 542-0110
Emp Here 70   *Sales* 2,845,467
SIC 7997 Membership sports and recreation clubs

D-U-N-S 20-719-9592   (BR)
WAL-MART CANADA CORP
WALMART
2200 58 Ave Suite 3169, Vernon, BC, V1T 9T2
(250) 558-0425
Emp Here 100
SIC 5311 Department stores

D-U-N-S 24-996-6623   (BR)
WHITE SPOT LIMITED
WHITE SPOT RESTAURANT
4400 32 St Suite 800, Vernon, BC, V1T 9H2
(250) 545-7119
Emp Here 45
SIC 5812 Eating places

D-U-N-S 25-372-8976   (BR)
WINNERS MERCHANTS INTERNATIONAL L.P.
WINNERS
(*Suby of* The TJX Companies Inc)
4900 27 St Suite 600, Vernon, BC, V1T 7G7
(250) 545-5954
Emp Here 32
SIC 5651 Family clothing stores

Victoria, BC V8N
Capital County

D-U-N-S 20-654-9888   (BR)
BOARD OF EDUCATION OF SCHOOL DISTRICT NO. 61 (GREATER VICTORIA)
GORDON HEAD ELEMENTARY SCHOOL
1671 Kenmore Rd, Victoria, BC, V8N 4M8
(250) 477-1855
Emp Here 35
SIC 8211 Elementary and secondary schools

D-U-N-S 20-032-3702   (BR)
BOARD OF EDUCATION OF SCHOOL DISTRICT NO. 61 (GREATER VICTORIA)
FRANK HOBBS ELEMENTARY SCHOOL
3875 Haro Rd, Victoria, BC, V8N 4A6
(250) 477-1804
Emp Here 40
SIC 8211 Elementary and secondary schools

D-U-N-S 20-032-0948   (BR)
BOARD OF EDUCATION OF SCHOOL DISTRICT NO. 61 (GREATER VICTORIA)
TORQUAY SCHOOL
4413 Torquay Dr, Victoria, BC, V8N 3L3
(250) 477-9511
Emp Here 20
SIC 8211 Elementary and secondary schools

D-U-N-S 20-653-2348   (BR)

BOARD OF EDUCATION OF SCHOOL DISTRICT NO. 61 (GREATER VICTORIA)
ARBUTUS GLOBAL MIDDLE SCHOOL
2306 Edgelow St, Victoria, BC, V8N 1R5
(250) 477-1878
Emp Here 40
SIC 8211 Elementary and secondary schools

D-U-N-S 20-653-7255   (BR)
BOARD OF EDUCATION OF SCHOOL DISTRICT NO. 61 (GREATER VICTORIA)
HILLCREST ELEMENTARY SCHOOL
4421 Greentree Terr, Victoria, BC, V8N 3S9
(250) 472-1530
Emp Here 25
SIC 8211 Elementary and secondary schools

D-U-N-S 20-041-9005   (BR)
BOARD OF EDUCATION OF SCHOOL DISTRICT NO. 61 (GREATER VICTORIA)
MOUNT DOUGLAS SECONDARY SCHOOL
3970 Gordon Head Rd, Victoria, BC, V8N 3X3
(250) 477-6977
Emp Here 100
SIC 8211 Elementary and secondary schools

D-U-N-S 20-041-8999   (SL)
BOARD OF TRUSTEES OF SCHOOL DISTRICT 61 (GREATER VICTORIA)
LAMBRICK PARK SECONDARY SCHOOL
4139 Torquay Dr, Victoria, BC, V8N 3L1
(250) 477-0181
Emp Here 50   *Sales* 3,356,192
SIC 8211 Elementary and secondary schools

D-U-N-S 24-079-4136   (BR)
CANADIAN IMPERIAL BANK OF COMMERCE
CIBC
3970 Shelbourne St, Victoria, BC, V8N 3E2
(250) 356-4467
Emp Here 30
SIC 8742 Management consulting services

D-U-N-S 25-078-3883   (BR)
CINEPLEX ODEON CORPORATION
LANDMARK CINEMAS UNIVERSITY HEIGHTS
3980 Shelbourne St, Victoria, BC, V8N 6J1
(250) 721-1171
Emp Here 20
SIC 7832 Motion picture theaters, except drive-in

D-U-N-S 20-586-9253   (BR)
EMPIRE THEATRES LIMITED
EMPIRE UNIVERSITY 4 CINEMAS
3980 Shelbourne St Suite 100, Victoria, BC, V8N 6J1
(250) 721-5684
Emp Here 25
SIC 7832 Motion picture theaters, except drive-in

D-U-N-S 20-697-7667   (BR)
HOME DEPOT OF CANADA INC
HOME DEPOT
(*Suby of* The Home Depot Inc)
3986 Shelbourne St, Victoria, BC, V8N 3E3
(250) 853-5350
Emp Here 80
SIC 5251 Hardware stores

D-U-N-S 20-718-4354   (SL)
J E M & RESTAURANTS LTD
TIM HORTONS
3990 Shelbourne St, Victoria, BC, V8N 3E2
(250) 477-9922
Emp Here 65   *Sales* 1,969,939
SIC 5812 Eating places

D-U-N-S 20-082-9047   (BR)
REVERA INC
KENSINGTON, THE
3965 Shelbourne St Suite 437, Victoria, BC, V8N 6J4
(250) 477-1232
Emp Here 51

SIC 8322 Individual and family services

D-U-N-S 25-957-0604   (BR)
ROYAL BANK OF CANADA
RBC
(*Suby of* Royal Bank Of Canada)
3970 Shelbourne St, Victoria, BC, V8N 3E2
(250) 356-4626
Emp Here 50
SIC 6021 National commercial banks

D-U-N-S 24-369-2472   (BR)
SOEURS DE SAINTE-ANNE DU QUEBEC, LES
ST ANN'S RESIDENCE
2474 Arbutus Rd, Victoria, BC, V8N 1V8

Emp Here 33
SIC 8361 Residential care

D-U-N-S 25-069-7224   (BR)
UNIVERSITY OF VICTORIA
DEVELOPMENT OFFICE
3964 Gordon Head Rd, Victoria, BC, V8N 3X3
(250) 721-7624
Emp Here 30
SIC 7389 Business services, nec

D-U-N-S 20-073-9642   (BR)
VANCOUVER ISLAND HEALTH AUTHORITY
QUEEN ALEXANDRA CENTRE FOR CHILDREN
2400 Arbutus Rd, Victoria, BC, V8N 1V7
(250) 519-5390
Emp Here 400
SIC 7389 Business services, nec

D-U-N-S 24-345-0181   (BR)
VANCOUVER ISLAND HEALTH AUTHORITY
QUEEN ALEXANDRA CENTRE FOR CHILDREN'S HEALTH
3970 Haro Rd, Victoria, BC, V8N 4A9
(250) 519-6778
Emp Here 30
SIC 8011 Offices and clinics of medical doctors

Victoria, BC V8P
Capital County

D-U-N-S 25-933-3300   (BR)
BANK OF MONTREAL
BMO
3616 Shelbourne St, Victoria, BC, V8P 5J5
(250) 389-2460
Emp Here 34
SIC 6021 National commercial banks

D-U-N-S 20-589-5522   (BR)
BANQUE TORONTO-DOMINION, LA
TD CANADA TRUST
(*Suby of* Toronto-Dominion Bank, The)
3675 Shelbourne St, Victoria, BC, V8P 4H1
(250) 405-5260
Emp Here 20
SIC 6021 National commercial banks

D-U-N-S 25-481-5731   (BR)
BOARD OF EDUCATION OF SCHOOL DISTRICT NO. 61 (GREATER VICTORIA)
LANSDOWNE JUNIOR SECONDARY SCHOOL
1765 Lansdowne Rd, Victoria, BC, V8P 1A7
(250) 598-3336
Emp Here 50
SIC 8211 Elementary and secondary schools

D-U-N-S 20-033-7116   (BR)
BOARD OF EDUCATION OF SCHOOL DISTRICT NO. 61 (GREATER VICTORIA)
REYNOLDS SECONDARY
3963 Borden St, Victoria, BC, V8P 3H9

(250) 479-1696
Emp Here 100
SIC 8211 Elementary and secondary schools

D-U-N-S 20-713-5406   (BR)
BOARD OF EDUCATION OF SCHOOL DISTRICT NO. 61 (GREATER VICTORIA)
DONCASTER ELEMENTARY SCHOOL
1525 Rowan St, Victoria, BC, V8P 1X4
(250) 370-9110
Emp Here 50
SIC 8211 Elementary and secondary schools

D-U-N-S 24-974-7882   (BR)
BOARD OF EDUCATION OF SCHOOL DISTRICT NO. 61 (GREATER VICTORIA)
CEDAR HILL MIDDLE SCHOOL
3910 Cedar Hill Rd, Victoria, BC, V8P 3Z9
(250) 477-6945
Emp Here 50
SIC 8211 Elementary and secondary schools

D-U-N-S 20-913-5909   (BR)
BOARD OF EDUCATION OF SCHOOL DISTRICT NO. 61 (GREATER VICTORIA)
BRAEFOOT ELEMENTARY SCHOOL
1440 Harrop Rd, Victoria, BC, V8P 2S6
(250) 477-6948
Emp Here 25
SIC 8211 Elementary and secondary schools

D-U-N-S 24-023-7904   (BR)
GOVERNING COUNCIL OF THE SALVATION ARMY IN CANADA, THE
SALVATION ARMY
1551 Cedar Hill Cross Rd, Victoria, BC, V8P 2P3
(250) 382-3714
Emp Here 24
SIC 8399 Social services, nec

D-U-N-S 20-655-3948   (BR)
GREATER VICTORIA PUBLIC LIBRARY BOARD
NELLIE MCCLUNG BRANCH
3950 Cedar Hill Rd, Victoria, BC, V8P 3Z9
(250) 477-7111
Emp Here 26
SIC 8231 Libraries

D-U-N-S 24-245-2266   (SL)
LUTHER COURT SOCIETY
1525 Cedar Hill Cross Rd, Victoria, BC, V8P 5M1
(250) 477-7241
Emp Here 80   *Sales* 3,648,035
SIC 8051 Skilled nursing care facilities

D-U-N-S 25-965-7518   (BR)
RECREATION OAK BAY
HENDERSON CENTRE
(*Suby of* Recreation Oak Bay)
2291 Cedar Hill Cross Rd, Victoria, BC, V8P 5H9
(250) 370-7200
Emp Here 100
SIC 7999 Amusement and recreation, nec

D-U-N-S 25-316-8298   (BR)
SUN LIFE ASSURANCE COMPANY OF CANADA
3962 Borden St Suite 101, Victoria, BC, V8P 3H8
(250) 385-1471
Emp Here 30
SIC 6311 Life insurance

D-U-N-S 25-907-9671   (BR)
SUN LIFE FINANCIAL INVESTMENT SERVICES (CANADA) INC
3962 Borden St Suite 101, Victoria, BC, V8P 3H8
(250) 385-1471
Emp Here 36
SIC 6282 Investment advice

D-U-N-S 20-914-7185   (BR)
UNIVERSITY OF VICTORIA
THE SCHOOL OF EARTH AND OCEAN SCI-

ENCES
3800 Finnerty Rd Right Centre A405, Victoria,
BC, V8P 5P2
(250) 721-6120
Emp Here 25
SIC 8221 Colleges and universities

D-U-N-S 20-703-0789   (BR)
UNIVERSITY OF VICTORIA
NEPTUNE CANADA PROJECT
3800 Finnerty Rd Suite 168, Victoria, BC, V8P
5C2
(250) 472-5400
Emp Here 70
SIC 8731 Commercial physical research

D-U-N-S 25-986-0823   (BR)
UNIVERSITY OF VICTORIA
UNIVERSITY VICTORIA BOOKSTORE
3800a Finnerty Rd Suite 168, Victoria, BC,
V8P 5C2
(250) 721-8311
Emp Here 30
SIC 5942 Book stores

D-U-N-S 20-554-2868   (BR)
UNIVERSITY OF VICTORIA
DEPARTMENT OF ELECTRICAL & COM-
PUTER ENGINEERING
3800 Finnerty Rd, Victoria, BC, V8P 5C2
(250) 721-8686
Emp Here 30
SIC 8221 Colleges and universities

D-U-N-S 20-655-1900   (BR)
UNIVERSITY OF VICTORIA
UVIC CHILDCARE SERVICES
3800 Finnerty Rd Suite 168, Victoria, BC, V8P
5C2
(250) 721-8500
Emp Here 30
SIC 8351 Child day care services

D-U-N-S 20-296-0790   (BR)
UNIVERSITY OF VICTORIA
DIVISION OF CONTINUING STUDIES
3800a Finnerty Rd Suite 168, Victoria, BC,
V8P 5C2
(250) 472-4747
Emp Here 130
SIC 8221 Colleges and universities

Victoria, BC V8R
Capital County

D-U-N-S 20-554-4948   (SL)
1082267 ALBERTA LTD
1640 Oak Bay Ave Unit 201, Victoria, BC, V8R
1B2
(250) 920-9750
Emp Here 22   Sales 10,797,600
SIC 6099 Functions related to deposit banking
Pr Pr Stephen Clark
Dir Mark Macdonald
Fin Ex Rachel Franchuk

D-U-N-S 20-589-5134   (BR)
BANQUE TORONTO-DOMINION, LA
TD CANADA TRUST
(Suby of Toronto-Dominion Bank, The)
2000 Cadboro Bay Rd, Victoria, BC, V8R 5G5
(250) 592-8111
Emp Here 20
SIC 6021 National commercial banks

D-U-N-S 20-653-3742   (BR)
**BOARD OF EDUCATION OF SCHOOL DIS-
TRICT NO. 61 (GREATER VICTORIA)**
OAKLAND ELEMENTARY
2827 Belmont Ave, Victoria, BC, V8R 4B2
(250) 595-2444
Emp Here 60
SIC 8211 Elementary and secondary schools

D-U-N-S 20-655-2189   (BR)

D-U-N-S 20-703-0789

**BOARD OF EDUCATION OF SCHOOL DIS-
TRICT NO. 61 (GREATER VICTORIA)**
WILLOWS ELEMENTARY SCHOOL
2290 Musgrave St, Victoria, BC, V8R 5Y2
(250) 592-2486
Emp Here 40
SIC 8211 Elementary and secondary schools

D-U-N-S 25-362-4035   (BR)
**BRITISH COLUMBIA CANCER AGENCY
BRANCH**
2410 Lee Ave, Victoria, BC, V8R 6V5
(250) 519-5500
Emp Here 100
SIC 8399 Social services, nec

D-U-N-S 20-537-8701   (BR)
CANADA POST CORPORATION
VICTORIA LCD 9
1625 Fort St, Victoria, BC, V8R 1H8
(250) 595-3548
Emp Here 50
SIC 4311 U.s. postal service

D-U-N-S 20-076-8278   (BR)
**CATHOLIC INDEPENDENT SCHOOLS, DIO-
CESE OF VICTORIA**
ST. PATRICKS SCHOOL
2368 Trent St, Victoria, BC, V8R 4Z3
(250) 592-6713
Emp Here 30
SIC 8211 Elementary and secondary schools

D-U-N-S 20-310-3531   (BR)
**CORPORATION OF THE DISTRICT OF OAK
BAY, THE**
PUBLIC WORKS DEPARTMENT
1771 Elgin Rd, Victoria, BC, V8R 5L7
(250) 598-4501
Emp Here 45
SIC 7699 Repair services, nec

D-U-N-S 25-855-3411   (BR)
LASERNETWORKS INC
(Suby of Fcs Industries, Inc.)
2487 Beach Dr, Victoria, BC, V8R 6K2

Emp Here 60
SIC 3577 Computer peripheral equipment,
nec

D-U-N-S 20-988-1486   (SL)
OAKLANDS COMMUNITY CENTRE
OAKLAND COMMUNITY ASSOCIATION
2827 Belmont Ave Suite 1, Victoria, BC, V8R
4B2
(250) 370-9101
Emp Here 25   Sales 6,791,040
SIC 8399 Social services, nec
This Gal

D-U-N-S 20-692-7563   (SL)
PARETOLOGIC INC
1827 Fort St, Victoria, BC, V8R 1J6
(250) 370-9229
Emp Here 90   Sales 14,134,935
SIC 7371 Custom computer programming services

D-U-N-S 25-807-0812   (BR)
REVERA INC
PARKWOOD COURT
3000 Shelbourne St Suite 216, Victoria, BC,
V8R 4M8
(250) 598-1575
Emp Here 70
SIC 8051 Skilled nursing care facilities

D-U-N-S 25-806-7883   (BR)
REVERA INC
PARKWOOD PLACE
3051 Shelbourne St Suite 233, Victoria, BC,
V8R 6T2
(250) 598-1565
Emp Here 52
SIC 8051 Skilled nursing care facilities

D-U-N-S 25-271-0959   (BR)
SOBEYS WEST INC

1950 Foul Bay Rd, Victoria, BC, V8R 5A7
(250) 370-1669
Emp Here 20
SIC 5411 Grocery stores

D-U-N-S 25-931-7758   (SL)
STAYNE PRODUCTIONS
STANDUP COMEDY FEAST
1830b Carnarvon St, Victoria, BC, V8R 2T8

Emp Here 60   Sales 3,866,917
SIC 7929 Entertainers and entertainment
groups

D-U-N-S 25-072-6585   (SL)
VICTORIA HOSPICE SOCIETY
1952 Bay St, Victoria, BC, V8R 1J8
(250) 370-8715
Emp Here 80   Sales 3,648,035
SIC 8051 Skilled nursing care facilities

Victoria, BC V8S
Capital County

D-U-N-S 24-989-3186   (BR)
BAYSHORE HEALTHCARE LTD.
BAYSHORE HOME HEALTH
1512 Fort St, Victoria, BC, V8S 5J2
(250) 370-2253
Emp Here 75
SIC 8082 Home health care services

D-U-N-S 20-655-0233   (BR)
**BOARD OF EDUCATION OF SCHOOL DIS-
TRICT NO. 61 (GREATER VICTORIA)**
MARGARET JENKINS SCHOOL
1824 Fairfield Rd, Victoria, BC, V8S 1G8
(250) 598-5191
Emp Here 35
SIC 8211 Elementary and secondary schools

D-U-N-S 20-119-4180   (HQ)
OAK BAY MARINA LTD
APRIL POINT LODGE
1327 Beach Dr, Victoria, BC, V8S 2N4
(250) 360-6509
Emp Here 80   Emp Total 250
Sales 16,635,040
SIC 4493 Marinas
Pr Pr Robert Wright
VP Fin Graeme Bryson
S&M/VP Lana Denoni

D-U-N-S 25-757-3188   (SL)
ROCKLAND CARE SERVICES LTD
ST. CHARLES MANOR CARE HOME
1006 St. Charles St, Victoria, BC, V8S 3P6
(250) 595-4255
Emp Here 50   Sales 2,261,782
SIC 8051 Skilled nursing care facilities

D-U-N-S 20-866-3229   (SL)
VICTORIA GOLF CLUB
1110 Beach Dr, Victoria, BC, V8S 2M9
(250) 598-4224
Emp Here 50   Sales 2,042,900
SIC 7997 Membership sports and recreation
clubs

Victoria, BC V8T
Capital County

D-U-N-S 24-798-1681   (BR)
AON REED STENHOUSE INC
1803 Douglas St, Victoria, BC, V8T 5C3
(250) 388-7577
Emp Here 30
SIC 6411 Insurance agents, brokers, and service

D-U-N-S 20-118-0866   (SL)
ACME SUPPLIES LTD

2311 Government St, Victoria, BC, V8T 4P4
(250) 383-8822
Emp Here 38   Sales 4,523,563
SIC 5087 Service establishment equipment

D-U-N-S 25-682-0044   (BR)
AECOM CANADA LTD
415 Gorge Rd E Suite 200, Victoria, BC, V8T
2W1
(250) 475-6355
Emp Here 20
SIC 8711 Engineering services

D-U-N-S 24-326-3964   (BR)
AGROPUR COOPERATIVE
ISLAND FARMS
2220 Dowler Pl, Victoria, BC, V8T 4H3
(250) 360-5200
Emp Here 300
SIC 5143 Dairy products, except dried or
canned

D-U-N-S 25-912-0517   (SL)
ANGEL ACCESSIBILITY INC
2508 Bridge St, Victoria, BC, V8T 5H3
(250) 383-0405
Emp Here 21   Sales 2,598,753
SIC 1796 Installing building equipment

D-U-N-S 24-824-8353   (BR)
**AUDIO VISUAL SYSTEMS INTEGRATION
INC**
SHARP'S AUDIO VISUAL
1950 Government St Unit 12, Victoria, BC,
V8T 4N8
(250) 385-3458
Emp Here 20
SIC 5999 Miscellaneous retail stores, nec

D-U-N-S 24-787-1648   (SL)
B C MINERAL STATISTICS
1810 Blanshard St, Victoria, BC, V8T 4J1
(250) 952-0521
Emp Here 30   Sales 13,278,847
SIC 1241 Coal mining services
Genl Mgr Anne Currie

D-U-N-S 25-297-1130   (BR)
BANK OF NOVA SCOTIA, THE
SCOTIABANK
2669 Douglas St, Victoria, BC, V8T 4M2
(250) 953-2500
Emp Here 27
SIC 6021 National commercial banks

D-U-N-S 25-297-0264   (BR)
BANK OF NOVA SCOTIA, THE
SCOTIABANK
1644 Hillside Ave Suite 77, Victoria, BC, V8T
2C5
(250) 953-5560
Emp Here 25
SIC 6021 National commercial banks

D-U-N-S 25-482-6134   (BR)
**BOARD OF EDUCATION OF SCHOOL DIS-
TRICT NO. 61 (GREATER VICTORIA)**
GEORGE JAY ELEMENTARY SCHOOL
1118 Princess Ave, Victoria, BC, V8T 1L3
(250) 385-3381
Emp Here 30
SIC 8211 Elementary and secondary schools

D-U-N-S 25-486-2360   (BR)
**BOARD OF EDUCATION OF SCHOOL DIS-
TRICT NO. 61 (GREATER VICTORIA)**
VICTORIA HIGH SCHOOL
1260 Grant St, Victoria, BC, V8T 1C2
(250) 388-5456
Emp Here 75
SIC 8211 Elementary and secondary schools

D-U-N-S 25-273-4801   (BR)
BRICK WAREHOUSE LP, THE
BRICK CLEARANCE CENTER
2835 Douglas St, Victoria, BC, V8T 4M6
(250) 360-2300
Emp Here 27

SIC 5712 Furniture stores

D-U-N-S 25-851-3654   (BR)
BROWN BROS. AGENCIES LIMITED
(*Suby* of Brown Bros. Agencies Limited)
565 Manchester Rd Suite 204, Victoria, BC,
V8T 2N7
(250) 385-8771
Emp Here 50
SIC 6411 Insurance agents, brokers, and service

D-U-N-S 20-119-7860   (BR)
CANADIAN LINEN AND UNIFORM SERVICE CO
(*Suby* of Ameripride Services, Inc.)
947 North Park St, Victoria, BC, V8T 1C5
(250) 384-8166
Emp Here 50
SIC 7213 Linen supply

D-U-N-S 20-546-6035   (BR)
COAST CAPITAL SAVINGS CREDIT UNION
415 Gorge Rd E Suite 102, Victoria, BC, V8T
2W1
(250) 483-7000
Emp Here 20
SIC 6411 Insurance agents, brokers, and service

D-U-N-S 20-722-3491   (SL)
CORNELL HOLDINGS LTD
COMFORT INN & SUITES
3020 Blanshard St, Victoria, BC, V8T 5C7
(250) 382-4400
Emp Here 64   *Sales* 2,188,821
SIC 7011 Hotels and motels

D-U-N-S 24-153-5269   (BR)
CORPORATION OF THE CITY OF VICTORIA, THE
CRYSTAL POOL & FITNESS CENTER
2275 Quadra St, Victoria, BC, V8T 4C4
(250) 361-0732
Emp Here 50
SIC 7999 Amusement and recreation, nec

D-U-N-S 20-653-4260   (HQ)
CRIDGE CENTRE FOR THE FAMILY, THE
(*Suby* of Cridge Centre For The Family, The)
1307 Hillside Ave Suite 414, Victoria, BC, V8T
0A2
(250) 384-8058
Emp Here 75   *Emp Total* 125
Sales 6,732,160
SIC 8322 Individual and family services
Dir David Rand
Dir Mary-Ethel Audrey
Treas Mike Kridge
CEO Shelley Morris
Pr Rosemary Smith

D-U-N-S 24-070-6838   (SL)
DOMINION DRUG STORES LIMITED
1644 Hillside Ave Suite 83, Victoria, BC, V8T
2C5
(250) 595-5111
Emp Here 50   *Sales* 8,402,635
SIC 5912 Drug stores and proprietary stores

D-U-N-S 20-194-5263   (BR)
ESIT CANADA ENTERPRISE SERVICES CO
ESIT CANADA ENTERPRISE SERVICES CO
(*Suby* of Dxc Technology Company)
710 Redbrick St Suite 200, Victoria, BC, V8T
5J3
(250) 405-2500
Emp Here 65
SIC 7371 Custom computer programming services

D-U-N-S 24-340-1325   (BR)
GLACIER MEDIA INC
TIMES COLONIST
2621 Douglas St, Victoria, BC, V8T 4M2
(250) 380-5211
Emp Here 300
SIC 2711 Newspapers

D-U-N-S 24-824-9062   (BR)
HORTON TRADING LTD
ELAN DATA MAKERS
755 Hillside Ave Suite 100, Victoria, BC, V8T
5B3
(250) 383-2226
Emp Here 25
SIC 7374 Data processing and preparation

D-U-N-S 25-315-5303   (BR)
INSURANCE CORPORATION OF BRITISH COLUMBIA
ICBC
425 Dunedin St, Victoria, BC, V8T 5H7
(250) 480-5600
Emp Here 80
SIC 6331 Fire, marine, and casualty insurance

D-U-N-S 25-969-4420   (SL)
INTER-CULTURAL ASSOCIATION OF GREATER VICTORIA
930 Balmoral Rd, Victoria, BC, V8T 1A8
(250) 388-4728
Emp Here 56   *Sales* 4,815,406
SIC 8111 Legal services

D-U-N-S 25-962-6919   (BR)
JIM PATTISON BROADCAST GROUP LIMITED PARTNERSHIP
100.3 THE Q
(*Suby* of Jim Pattison Broadcast Group Limited Partnership)
2750 Quadra St 3rd Fl, Victoria, BC, V8T 4E8
(250) 475-0100
Emp Here 50
SIC 4832 Radio broadcasting stations

D-U-N-S 24-369-9980   (BR)
JORDANS RUGS LTD
STYLE SOLUTIONS, A DIV OF
2680 Blanshard St, Victoria, BC, V8T 5E1
(250) 385-6746
Emp Here 20
SIC 5713 Floor covering stores

D-U-N-S 20-296-1905   (BR)
KONICA MINOLTA BUSINESS SOLUTIONS (CANADA) LTD
KONICA MINOLTA
2326 Government St, Victoria, BC, V8T 5G5

Emp Here 20
SIC 7334 Photocopying and duplicating services

D-U-N-S 20-119-4313   (BR)
LEHIGH HANSON MATERIALS LIMITED
OCEAN CONCRETE
611 Bay St, Victoria, BC, V8T 1P5
(250) 382-8121
Emp Here 29
SIC 5032 Brick, stone, and related material

D-U-N-S 25-887-9840   (BR)
LORDCO PARTS LTD
LORDCO AUTO PARTS
483 Burnside Rd E, Victoria, BC, V8T 2X4
(250) 380-9956
Emp Here 20
SIC 5015 Motor vehicle parts, used

D-U-N-S 24-418-4201   (BR)
MARK'S WORK WEARHOUSE LTD
WORK WORLD
530 Chatham St Unit 1, Victoria, BC, V8T 5K1
(250) 382-1166
Emp Here 20
SIC 5699 Miscellaneous apparel and accessory stores

D-U-N-S 25-969-5153   (SL)
MCDONALD'S RESTAURANTS LTD
1644 Hillside Ave, Victoria, BC, V8T 2C5

Emp Here 100   *Sales* 2,991,389
SIC 5812 Eating places

D-U-N-S 24-777-2726   (HQ)

MYRA SYSTEMS CORP
(*Suby* of Myra Systems Corp)
488a Bay St, Victoria, BC, V8T 5H2
(250) 381-1335
Emp Here 35   *Emp Total* 50
Sales 4,331,255
SIC 7379 Computer related services, nec

D-U-N-S 24-594-8328   (HQ)
NATIONAL MONEY MART COMPANY
MONEY MART
401 Garbally Rd, Victoria, BC, V8T 5M3
(250) 595-5211
Emp Here 300   *Emp Total* 6,600
Sales 524,081,855
SIC 6099 Functions related to deposit banking
VP Fin Melanie Latoski

D-U-N-S 20-644-7752   (BR)
NORTHLAND PROPERTIES CORPORATION
SANDMAN INN VICTORIA
(*Suby* of Northland Properties Corporation)
2852 Douglas St, Victoria, BC, V8T 4M5
(250) 388-0788
Emp Here 20
SIC 7011 Hotels and motels

D-U-N-S 20-970-9398   (BR)
PARKLAND INDUSTRIES LIMITED PARTNERSHIP
COLUMBIA FUELS
2659 Douglas St Suite 200, Victoria, BC, V8T
4M3
(250) 478-0331
Emp Here 30
SIC 5541 Gasoline service stations

D-U-N-S 20-005-3283   (BR)
PATTISON, JIM INDUSTRIES LTD
JIM PATTISON VOLVO OF VICTORIA
2735 Douglas St, Victoria, BC, V8T 4M4
(250) 382-8131
Emp Here 20
SIC 5511 New and used car dealers

D-U-N-S 24-362-5022   (HQ)
PHOENIX HUMAN SERVICES ASSOCIATION
(*Suby* of Phoenix Human Services Association)
1824 Store St, Victoria, BC, V8T 4R4
(250) 383-4821
Emp Here 100   *Emp Total* 106
Sales 3,866,917
SIC 8361 Residential care

D-U-N-S 24-000-9170   (BR)
POSTMEDIA NETWORK INC
VICTORIA TIMES COLONIST, THE
2621 Douglas St, Victoria, BC, V8T 4M2
(250) 995-4417
Emp Here 50
SIC 2711 Newspapers

D-U-N-S 24-134-1700   (BR)
POSTMEDIA NETWORK INC
CH TELEVISION
780 Kings Rd, Victoria, BC, V8T 5A2
(250) 383-2435
Emp Here 110
SIC 4833 Television broadcasting stations

D-U-N-S 24-777-4805   (SL)
REDD'S ROADHOUSE RESTAURANTS LTD
REDD'S PUB
3020 Blanshard St, Victoria, BC, V8T 5C7
(250) 382-7262
Emp Here 50   *Sales* 1,532,175
SIC 5812 Eating places

D-U-N-S 24-455-2139   (SL)
STM SPORTS TRADE MALL LTD
SPORTS TRADERS - VICTORIA
508 Discovery St, Victoria, BC, V8T 1G8
(250) 383-6443
Emp Here 50   *Sales* 4,231,721
SIC 5941 Sporting goods and bicycle shops

D-U-N-S 20-281-5445   (BR)
SCHNITZER STEEL CANADA LTD
SCHNITZER VICTORIA
307 David St, Victoria, BC, V8T 5C1
(250) 381-5865
Emp Here 25
SIC 7389 Business services, nec

D-U-N-S 25-957-5751   (BR)
SCOTIA CAPITAL INC
SCOTIA MCLEOD
1803 Douglas St Suite 400, Victoria, BC, V8T
5C3
(250) 389-2110
Emp Here 30
SIC 6211 Security brokers and dealers

D-U-N-S 20-619-3674   (BR)
SEARS CANADA INC
3190 Shelbourne St, Victoria, BC, V8T 3A8
(250) 595-9111
Emp Here 50
SIC 5311 Department stores

D-U-N-S 25-855-3973   (BR)
SECURIGUARD SERVICES LIMITED
SECURIGUARD
2750 Quadra St Suite 218, Victoria, BC, V8T
4E8
(250) 388-3118
Emp Here 70
SIC 7381 Detective and armored car services

D-U-N-S 20-192-7907   (HQ)
SHERET, ANDREW HOLDINGS LIMITED
(*Suby* of Sheret, Andrew Holdings Limited)
721 Kings Rd, Victoria, BC, V8T 1W4
(250) 386-7744
Emp Here 20   *Emp Total* 210
Sales 53,261,250
SIC 5074 Plumbing and heating equipment and supplies (hydronics)
Pr Pr Brian Findlay
VP Ed Pratt
VP Eric Findlay

D-U-N-S 20-119-7209   (HQ)
SHERET, ANDREW LIMITED
SPLASHES BATH & KITCHEN CENTRE, A DIV OF
(*Suby* of Sheret, Andrew Holdings Limited)
721 Kings Rd, Victoria, BC, V8T 1W4
(250) 386-7744
Emp Here 25   *Emp Total* 210
Sales 58,895,563
SIC 5074 Plumbing and heating equipment and supplies (hydronics)
Pr Pr Brian Findlay
  David R. Broad
  George Hill

D-U-N-S 24-850-7605   (BR)
SIMPLY COMPUTING INC
2639 Quadra St, Victoria, BC, V8T 4E3
(250) 412-6899
Emp Here 20
SIC 5734 Computer and software stores

D-U-N-S 20-860-4046   (BR)
SOURCE (BELL) ELECTRONICS INC, THE
SOURCE, THE
1644 Hillside Ave Unit 6, Victoria, BC, V8T
2C5

Emp Here 25
SIC 5999 Miscellaneous retail stores, nec

D-U-N-S 20-194-8341   (SL)
TRANSITION HOUSE COMMUNITY OFFICE
3060 Cedar Hill Rd Suite 100, Victoria, BC,
V8T 3J5
(250) 592-2927
Emp Here 45   *Sales* 9,047,127
SIC 8399 Social services, nec

D-U-N-S 24-824-0582   (BR)
VALUE VILLAGE STORES, INC
(*Suby* of Savers, Inc.)

▲ Public Company   ■ Public Company Family Member   **HQ** Headquarters   **BR** Branch   **SL** Single Location

1810 Store St, Victoria, BC, V8T 4R4
(250) 380-9422
Emp Here 35
SIC 5399 Miscellaneous general merchandise

D-U-N-S 20-910-9136   (BR)
VANCOUVER CITY SAVINGS CREDIT UNION
VANCITY CREDIT UNION
3075 Douglas St, Victoria, BC, V8T 4N3
(250) 519-7423
Emp Here 25
SIC 6062 State credit unions

D-U-N-S 25-500-4335   (HQ)
VANCOUVER ISLAND AUTISTIC HOMES SOCIETY
(*Suby of* Vancouver Island Autistic Homes Society)
2750 Quadra St Suite 215, Victoria, BC, V8T 4E8
(250) 475-2566
Emp Here 36   *Emp Total* 65
Sales 2,407,703
SIC 8361 Residential care

D-U-N-S 20-182-0177   (BR)
VICTORIA FORD ALLIANCE LTD
GLENOAK FORD SALES
2829 Douglas St, Victoria, BC, V8T 4M6
(250) 384-1144
Emp Here 60
SIC 5511 New and used car dealers

D-U-N-S 24-421-1954   (BR)
WSP CANADA INC
GENIVAR
401 Garbally Rd Suite 400, Victoria, BC, V8T 5M3
(250) 384-5510
Emp Here 50
SIC 8711 Engineering services

Victoria, BC V8V
Capital County

D-U-N-S 20-798-1978   (SL)
AMICA AT DOUGLAS HOUSE
50 Douglas St, Victoria, BC, V8V 2N8
(250) 383-6258
Emp Here 33   *Sales* 1,992,377
SIC 8361 Residential care

D-U-N-S 25-924-5660   (BR)
AMICA MATURE LIFESTYLES INC
AMICA AT SOMERSET HOUSE
540 Dallas Rd Suite 423, Victoria, BC, V8V 4X9
(250) 380-9121
Emp Here 44
SIC 8361 Residential care

D-U-N-S 20-651-5392   (SL)
BECKLEY FARM LODGE FOUNDATION
BECKLEY FARM LODGE SOCIETY
530 Simcoe St, Victoria, BC, V8V 4W4
(250) 381-4421
Emp Here 85   *Sales* 3,866,917
SIC 8051 Skilled nursing care facilities

D-U-N-S 24-658-8099   (SL)
BLACK BALL TRANSPORT INC
BLACK BALL FERRY LINE
430 Belleville St, Victoria, BC, V8V 1W9
(250) 386-2202
Emp Here 110   *Sales* 18,086,400
SIC 4482 Ferries
Pr Ryan Burles
Treas David Booth

D-U-N-S 20-041-8981   (BR)
BOARD OF EDUCATION OF SCHOOL DISTRICT NO. 61 (GREATER VICTORIA)
CENTRAL MIDDLE SECONDARY SCHOOL
1280 Fort St, Victoria, BC, V8V 3L2

---

(250) 386-3591
Emp Here 45
SIC 8211 Elementary and secondary schools

D-U-N-S 20-655-1314   (BR)
BOARD OF EDUCATION OF SCHOOL DISTRICT NO. 61 (GREATER VICTORIA)
SOUTH PARK FAMILY SCHOOL
508 Douglas St, Victoria, BC, V8V 2P7
(250) 382-5234
Emp Here 40
SIC 8211 Elementary and secondary schools

D-U-N-S 25-747-8941   (BR)
BOARD OF EDUCATION OF SCHOOL DISTRICT NO. 61 (GREATER VICTORIA)
JAMES BAY COMMUNITY SCHOOL
140 Oswego St, Victoria, BC, V8V 2B1
(250) 384-7184
Emp Here 20
SIC 8211 Elementary and secondary schools

D-U-N-S 25-316-5716   (BR)
BRITISH COLUMBIA AUTOMOBILE ASSOCIATION
B C A A
1075 Pandora Ave, Victoria, BC, V8V 3P6

Emp Here 30
SIC 8699 Membership organizations, nec

D-U-N-S 20-041-7264   (BR)
CATHOLIC INDEPENDENT SCHOOLS, DIOCESE OF VICTORIA
ST ANDREWS ELEMENTARY
1002 Pandora Ave, Victoria, BC, V8V 3P5
(250) 382-3815
Emp Here 24
SIC 8211 Elementary and secondary schools

D-U-N-S 24-930-5905   (BR)
COAST HOTELS LIMITED
COAST HARBOURSIDE HOTEL & MARINA, THE
146 Kingston St, Victoria, BC, V8V 1V4
(250) 360-1211
Emp Here 70
SIC 7011 Hotels and motels

D-U-N-S 20-041-7009   (BR)
COAST HOTELS LIMITED
BLUE CRAB BAR & GRILL
146 Kingston St, Victoria, BC, V8V 1V4
(250) 480-1999
Emp Here 28
SIC 5812 Eating places

D-U-N-S 20-352-0676   (SL)
CONGDON CONSTRUCTION (1986) LTD
ROYAL SCOT SUITE HOTEL, THE
425 Quebec St Suite 124, Victoria, BC, V8V 1W7
(250) 388-5463
Emp Here 60   *Sales* 2,626,585
SIC 7011 Hotels and motels

D-U-N-S 25-532-2760   (HQ)
DEVELUS SYSTEMS INC
PROCURA
(*Suby of* Develus Systems Inc)
1112 Fort St Suite 600, Victoria, BC, V8V 3K8
(250) 388-0880
Emp Here 45   *Emp Total* 90
Sales 10,944,105
SIC 7371 Custom computer programming services
Warren Brown

D-U-N-S 20-845-2925   (BR)
FINANCIAL MANAGEMENT (BC) INC
1009 Cook St, Victoria, BC, V8V 3Z6

Emp Here 20
SIC 8741 Management services

D-U-N-S 24-292-8273   (SL)
FRIENDSHIP DEVELOPMENTS LTD
HUNTINGDON HOTEL & SUITES
330 Quebec St, Victoria, BC, V8V 1W3

---

(250) 381-3456
Emp Here 75   *Sales* 3,283,232
SIC 7011 Hotels and motels

D-U-N-S 25-091-9297   (BR)
GOVERNMENT OF THE PROVINCE OF BRITISH COLUMBIA
JAMES BAY COMMUNITY PROJECT
547 Michigan St, Victoria, BC, V8V 1S5
(250) 388-7844
Emp Here 35
SIC 8621 Professional organizations

D-U-N-S 25-235-3586   (BR)
HARBOUR TOWERS LIMITED PARTNERSHIP
HARBOUR TOWERS HOTEL AND SUITES
345 Quebec St, Victoria, BC, V8V 1W4
(250) 385-2405
Emp Here 100
SIC 7011 Hotels and motels

D-U-N-S 25-318-1259   (BR)
MCDONALD'S RESTAURANTS OF CANADA LIMITED
MCDONALD'S
(*Suby of* McDonald's Corporation)
980 Pandora Ave, Victoria, BC, V8V 3P3
(250) 953-8190
Emp Here 60
SIC 5812 Eating places

D-U-N-S 20-994-2163   (SL)
MOXIE'S LTD
FULL MOON FOODS
1010 Yates St Suite 1, Victoria, BC, V8V 3M6
(250) 360-1660
Emp Here 65   *Sales* 1,969,939
SIC 5812 Eating places

D-U-N-S 20-011-7369   (BR)
P SUN'S ENTERPRISES (VANCOUVER) LTD
HOTEL GRAND PACIFIC
463 Belleville St, Victoria, BC, V8V 1X3
(250) 386-0450
Emp Here 180
SIC 7011 Hotels and motels

D-U-N-S 25-907-7220   (BR)
PAUL'S RESTAURANTS LTD
LAUREL POINT INN
680 Montreal St, Victoria, BC, V8V 1Z8
(250) 412-3194
Emp Here 200
SIC 7011 Hotels and motels

D-U-N-S 25-963-9268   (BR)
ROYAL BANK OF CANADA
RBC
(*Suby of* Royal Bank Of Canada)
304 Cook St, Victoria, BC, V8V 3X6

Emp Here 20
SIC 6021 National commercial banks

D-U-N-S 20-506-0457   (BR)
STARBUCKS COFFEE CANADA, INC
STARBUCKS COFFEE SHOP
(*Suby of* Starbucks Corporation)
320 Cook St, Victoria, BC, V8V 3X6
(250) 380-7606
Emp Here 20
SIC 5812 Eating places

D-U-N-S 20-577-7019   (BR)
SUNRISE NORTH SENIOR LIVING LTD
SUNRISE ASSISTED LIVING OF VICTORIA
(*Suby of* Welltower Inc.)
920 Humboldt St Suite 222, Victoria, BC, V8V 4W7
(250) 383-1366
Emp Here 50
SIC 8361 Residential care

D-U-N-S 25-903-5061   (HQ)
WCG INTERNATIONAL CONSULTANTS LTD
(*Suby of* Providence Service Corporation)

---

915 Fort St, Victoria, BC, V8V 3K3
(250) 389-0699
Emp Here 20   *Emp Total* 9,072
Sales 12,403,319
SIC 7361 Employment agencies
Pr Darlene Bailey
VP VP Elizabeth Ferguson
Sr VP Bob Skene
John Parker

Victoria, BC V8W
Capital County

D-U-N-S 24-764-2168   (SL)
ANGEL STAR HOLDINGS LTD
CHATEAU VICTORIA HOTEL & SUITES
740 Burdett Ave Suite 1901, Victoria, BC, V8W 1B2
(250) 382-4221
Emp Here 110   *Sales* 4,815,406
SIC 7011 Hotels and motels

D-U-N-S 24-882-0222   (SL)
AQUACULTURE DEVELOPMENT BRANCH
3rd Fl, Victoria, BC, V8W 2Z7
(250) 356-2238
Emp Here 49   *Sales* 5,253,170
SIC 8748 Business consulting, nec
Dir Al Casteldine

D-U-N-S 24-106-4612   (BR)
ATLIFIC INC
VICTORIA MARRIOTT INNER HARBOUR, THE
(*Suby of* 3376290 Canada Inc)
728 Humboldt St, Victoria, BC, V8W 3Z5
(250) 480-3800
Emp Here 150
SIC 7011 Hotels and motels

D-U-N-S 24-372-8784   (BR)
AVOCETTE TECHNOLOGIES INC
(*Suby of* Avocette Technologies Inc)
1022 Government St Unit Main, Victoria, BC, V8W 1X7
(250) 389-2993
Emp Here 40
SIC 7371 Custom computer programming services

D-U-N-S 20-059-0532   (BR)
BMO NESBITT BURNS INC
730 View St Suite 1000, Victoria, BC, V8W 3Y7
(250) 361-2412
Emp Here 20
SIC 6211 Security brokers and dealers

D-U-N-S 20-556-9833   (BR)
BANK OF NOVA SCOTIA, THE
SCOTIABANK
702 Yates St, Victoria, BC, V8W 1L4
(250) 953-5400
Emp Here 30
SIC 6021 National commercial banks

D-U-N-S 20-175-2495   (BR)
BELL MEDIA INC
CTV VANCOUVER ISLAND
1420 Broad St, Victoria, BC, V8W 2B1
(250) 381-2484
Emp Here 49
SIC 4833 Television broadcasting stations

D-U-N-S 20-807-1670   (HQ)
BROWN BROS. AGENCIES LIMITED
(*Suby of* Brown Bros. Agencies Limited)
1125 Blanshard St, Victoria, BC, V8W 2H7
(250) 385-8771
Emp Here 49   *Emp Total* 55
Sales 4,961,328
SIC 6411 Insurance agents, brokers, and service

D-U-N-S 25-293-9020   (BR)

CIBC WORLD MARKETS INC
CIBC WOOD GUNDY
730 View St Suite 900, Victoria, BC, V8W 3Y7
(250) 388-5131
Emp Here 80
SIC 6211 Security brokers and dealers

   D-U-N-S 20-580-4433   (BR)
CANADA POST CORPORATION
714 Yates St, Victoria, BC, V8W 1L4
(250) 953-1352
Emp Here 20
SIC 4311 U.s. postal service

   D-U-N-S 20-959-7228   (BR)
CANADIAN IMPERIAL BANK OF COMMERCE
CIBC
1175 Douglas St Suite 210, Victoria, BC, V8W 2E1
(800) 465-2422
Emp Here 110
SIC 6021 National commercial banks

   D-U-N-S 25-860-3448   (BR)
CANADIAN NORTHERN SHIELD INSURANCE COMPANY
1675 Douglas St Suite 510, Victoria, BC, V8W 2G5
(250) 388-5454
Emp Here 22
SIC 6211 Security brokers and dealers

   D-U-N-S 20-697-3302   (BR)
CAPSERVCO LIMITED PARTNERSHIP
GRANT THORNTON
(*Suby of* CapServCo Limited Partnership)
888 Fort St Suite 300, Victoria, BC, V8W 1H8
(250) 383-4191
Emp Here 26
SIC 8721 Accounting, auditing, and bookkeeping

   D-U-N-S 24-695-2659   (SL)
CAUSEWAY RESTAURANTS LTD
MILESTONES RESTAURANT
812 Wharf St, Victoria, BC, V8W 1T3
(250) 381-2244
Emp Here 80   *Sales* 2,407,703
SIC 5812 Eating places

   D-U-N-S 25-456-8090   (BR)
CINEPLEX ODEON CORPORATION
CINEPLEX CINEMAS VICTORIA
805 Yates St, Victoria, BC, V8W 1M1
(250) 383-0513
Emp Here 20
SIC 7832 Motion picture theaters, except drive-in

   D-U-N-S 24-694-9390   (BR)
COLLIERS MACAULAY NICOLLS INC
COLLIERS INTERNATIONAL
1175 Douglas St Suite 1110, Victoria, BC, V8W 2E1
(250) 388-6454
Emp Here 43
SIC 6531 Real estate agents and managers

   D-U-N-S 24-336-9613   (BR)
CORPORATION OF THE CITY OF VICTORIA, THE
720 Douglas St, Victoria, BC, V8W 3M7
(250) 361-1000
Emp Here 25
SIC 6512 Nonresidential building operators

   D-U-N-S 20-910-9722   (SL)
DND HMCS HURON
Gd Stn Csc, Victoria, BC, V8W 2L9
(250) 363-5482
Emp Here 50   *Sales* 3,356,192
SIC 4499 Water transportation services,

   D-U-N-S 24-525-7246   (BR)
DELOITTE LLP
737 Yates St Suite 300, Victoria, BC, V8W 1L6
(250) 978-4403
Emp Here 50

SIC 8721 Accounting, auditing, and bookkeeping

   D-U-N-S 25-957-6361   (BR)
EARL'S RESTAURANTS LTD
EARL'S RESTAURANTS
(*Suby of* Earl's Restaurants Ltd)
1703 Blanshard St, Victoria, BC, V8W 2J8

Emp Here 80
SIC 5812 Eating places

   D-U-N-S 20-916-8215   (BR)
EMPIRE THEATRES LIMITED
MARIPLEX CONFECTIONS
805 Yates St, Victoria, BC, V8W 1M1
(250) 384-6811
Emp Here 30
SIC 7832 Motion picture theaters, except drive-in

   D-U-N-S 20-867-4622   (SL)
EXECUTIVE HOUSE LTD
BARTHOLOMEWS BAR & GRILL
777 Douglas St, Victoria, BC, V8W 2B5
(250) 388-5111
Emp Here 80   *Sales* 3,502,114
SIC 7011 Hotels and motels

   D-U-N-S 24-337-3375   (BR)
FGL SPORTS LTD
SPORT CHEK VICTORIA BAY CENTRE
1150 Douglas St Unit 311a, Victoria, BC, V8W 3M9
(250) 388-5103
Emp Here 30
SIC 5941 Sporting goods and bicycle shops

   D-U-N-S 25-026-6269   (BR)
FAIRMONT HOTELS & RESORTS INC
FAIRMONT EMPRESS, THE
721 Government St, Victoria, BC, V8W 1W5
(250) 384-8111
Emp Here 450
SIC 7011 Hotels and motels

   D-U-N-S 25-959-3341   (BR)
FINANCIERE BANQUE NATIONALE INC
737 Yates St Suite 700, Victoria, BC, V8W 1L6
(250) 953-8400
Emp Here 51
SIC 6211 Security brokers and dealers

   D-U-N-S 25-293-3221   (BR)
FUJITSU CONSEIL (CANADA) INC
880 Douglas St Suite 300, Victoria, BC, V8W 2B7
(250) 479-2772
Emp Here 65
SIC 7379 Computer related services, nec

   D-U-N-S 25-962-6810   (SL)
FX CONNECTORS LTD
1203 Wharf St Suite 106, Victoria, BC, V8W 3B9
(250) 380-7888
Emp Here 25   *Sales* 39,252,857
SIC 6099 Functions related to deposit banking
Pr Pr Michael J. O'Neill

   D-U-N-S 25-958-6105   (BR)
GAP (CANADA) INC
GAP
(*Suby of* The Gap Inc)
1319 Government St, Victoria, BC, V8W 1Y9
(250) 920-9925
Emp Here 25
SIC 5651 Family clothing stores

   D-U-N-S 25-933-7285   (BR)
GRANT THORNTON LLP
888 Fort St, Victoria, BC, V8W 1H8
(250) 383-4191
Emp Here 30
SIC 8721 Accounting, auditing, and bookkeeping

   D-U-N-S 25-737-9966   (SL)
GREAT PACIFIC ADVENTURES INC

(*Suby of* Orca Spirit Adventures Ltd)
950 Wharf St, Victoria, BC, V8W 1T3
(250) 386-2277
Emp Here 20   *Sales* 6,594,250
SIC 4725 Tour operators
Pr Pr Andrew Skinner

   D-U-N-S 25-965-8037   (BR)
GREAT PACIFIC ENTERPRISES INC
THE NEWS GROUP DIV
818 Broughton St, Victoria, BC, V8W 1E4
(250) 388-3535
Emp Here 75
SIC 7313 Radio, television, publisher representatives

   D-U-N-S 24-445-7594   (HQ)
GREATER VICTORIA VISITORS & CONVENTION BUREAU
TOURISM VICTORIA
(*Suby of* Greater Victoria Visitors & Convention Bureau)
31 Bastion Sq, Victoria, BC, V8W 1J1
(250) 414-6999
Emp Here 22   *Emp Total* 42
Sales 5,791,440
SIC 8611 Business associations
 Lorinda Staples

   D-U-N-S 24-939-3729   (BR)
HSBC BANK CANADA
752 Fort St, Victoria, BC, V8W 1H2
(250) 388-5511
Emp Here 26
SIC 6021 National commercial banks

   D-U-N-S 20-118-9800   (BR)
HUDSON'S BAY COMPANY
1150 Douglas St Suite 1, Victoria, BC, V8W 2C8
(250) 385-1311
Emp Here 300
SIC 5311 Department stores

   D-U-N-S 20-536-0865   (BR)
INDIGO BOOKS & MUSIC INC
CHAPTERS
(*Suby of* Indigo Books & Music Inc)
1212 Douglas St, Victoria, BC, V8W 2E5
(250) 380-9009
Emp Here 40
SIC 5942 Book stores

   D-U-N-S 25-315-7838   (BR)
INVESTORS GROUP FINANCIAL SERVICES INC
INVESTORS FINANCIAL PLANNING CENTRE, DIV OF
737 Yates St Suite 600, Victoria, BC, V8W 1L6
(250) 388-4234
Emp Here 50
SIC 8741 Management services

   D-U-N-S 24-761-6972   (BR)
INVESTORS GROUP FINANCIAL SERVICES INC
INVESTORS GROUP
737 Yates St Suite 600, Victoria, BC, V8W 1L6
(250) 388-4234
Emp Here 50
SIC 6282 Investment advice

   D-U-N-S 20-866-6649   (SL)
IRISH TIMES PUB CO LTD
IRISH TIMES PUB
1200 Government St, Victoria, BC, V8W 1Y3
(250) 383-5531
Emp Here 80   *Sales* 2,918,428
SIC 5813 Drinking places

   D-U-N-S 25-994-1433   (BR)
ISLAND PUBLISHERS LTD
BLACK PRESS
818 Broughton St, Victoria, BC, V8W 1E4
(250) 480-0755
Emp Here 150
SIC 2711 Newspapers

   D-U-N-S 24-824-1481   (BR)
KPMG LLP
KPMG MSLP
(*Suby of* KPMG LLP)
730 View St Suite 800, Victoria, BC, V8W 3Y7
(250) 480-3500
Emp Here 90
SIC 8721 Accounting, auditing, and bookkeeping

   D-U-N-S 24-121-4816   (BR)
LONDON LIFE INSURANCE COMPANY
FREEDOM 55 FINANCIAL AND QUADRUS INVESTMENTS
1675 Douglas St Suite 620, Victoria, BC, V8W 2G5
(250) 475-1100
Emp Here 30
SIC 6311 Life insurance

   D-U-N-S 24-228-1504   (BR)
MAX WRIGHT REAL ESTATE CORPORATION
SOTHEBY'S INTERNATIONAL REALTY CANADA
752 Douglas St, Victoria, BC, V8W 3M6
(250) 380-3933
Emp Here 25
SIC 6531 Real estate agents and managers

   D-U-N-S 20-839-7120   (SL)
MAXIMILIAN HUXLEY BUILDING & RENOVATIONS LTD
Gd Stn Csc, Victoria, BC, V8W 2L9
(250) 598-2152
Emp Here 30   *Sales* 6,129,280
SIC 1521 Single-family housing construction
Prin Kelly Grinyer

   D-U-N-S 25-691-9689   (BR)
MAYFAIR PROPERTIES LTD
BEST WESTERN CARLTON PLAZA HOTEL
642 Johnson St, Victoria, BC, V8W 1M6
(250) 388-5513
Emp Here 28
SIC 7011 Hotels and motels

   D-U-N-S 25-229-8500   (SL)
MONTREUX COUNSELLING CENTRE LTD
MONTREAU CLINIC
Gd Stn Csc, Victoria, BC, V8W 2L9

Emp Here 100   *Sales* 5,478,300
SIC 8322 Individual and family services
 David Harris
Pr Pr Peggy Claude-Pierre

   D-U-N-S 24-148-4810   (BR)
MOUNTAIN EQUIPMENT CO-OPERATIVE
MOUNTAIN EQUIPMENT CO-OPERATIVE
1450 Government St, Victoria, BC, V8W 1Z2
(250) 386-2667
Emp Here 70
SIC 5651 Family clothing stores

   D-U-N-S 24-369-1487   (HQ)
NATIONAL HEARING SERVICES INC
ISLAND HEARING SERVICES
645 Fort St Suite 312, Victoria, BC, V8W 1G2
(250) 413-2100
Emp Here 50   *Emp Total* 14,089
Sales 36,750,831
SIC 5999 Miscellaneous retail stores, nec
 Craig Cameron
VP Bob Liew

   D-U-N-S 25-537-6808   (SL)
NEWHEIGHTS SOFTWARE CORPORATION
1006 Government St, Victoria, BC, V8W 1X7
(250) 380-0584
Emp Here 45   *Sales* 10,699,440
SIC 7371 Custom computer programming services
 Owen Matthews
 Andrew Fisher

   D-U-N-S 20-183-0861   (SL)
OA HOLDINGS INC

702 Fort St Suite 200, Victoria, BC, V8W 1H2
(250) 385-4333
Emp Here 60　　　*Sales* 14,724,000
SIC 7371 Custom computer programming services
Pr Pr Decro Wong
VP VP Scott Petersen
VP VP Shaun Caldwell

D-U-N-S 25-048-7655　　　(BR)
PACIFIC COACH LINES LTD
700 Douglas St, Victoria, BC, V8W 2B3
(250) 385-6553
Emp Here 30
SIC 4142 Bus charter service, except local

D-U-N-S 25-994-1151　　　(BR)
PRISZM LP
PIZZA HUT
533 Yates St, Victoria, BC, V8W 1K7

Emp Here 20
SIC 5812 Eating places

D-U-N-S 20-108-9492　　　(BR)
RBC DOMINION SECURITIES INC
(*Suby of* Royal Bank Of Canada)
730 View St Suite 500, Victoria, BC, V8W 3Y7
(250) 356-4800
Emp Here 50
SIC 6211 Security brokers and dealers

D-U-N-S 20-048-7325　　　(BR)
RAYMOND JAMES (USA) LTD
(*Suby of* Raymond James Financial, Inc.)
1175 Douglas St Suite 1000, Victoria, BC, V8W 2E1
(250) 405-2400
Emp Here 26
SIC 6211 Security brokers and dealers

D-U-N-S 20-149-2258　　　(BR)
REXALL PHARMACY GROUP LTD
MCGILL & ORME REXALL PHARMACY
(*Suby of* McKesson Corporation)
649 Fort St, Victoria, BC, V8W 1G1
(250) 384-1195
Emp Here 20
SIC 5912 Drug stores and proprietary stores

D-U-N-S 20-119-0196　　　(BR)
ROGERS MEDIA INC
OCEAN AND JACK FM, THE
(*Suby of* Rogers Communications Inc)
817 Fort St, Victoria, BC, V8W 1H6
(250) 382-0900
Emp Here 40
SIC 4832 Radio broadcasting stations

D-U-N-S 24-359-2636　　　(BR)
ROGERS' CHOCOLATES LTD
913 Government St, Victoria, BC, V8W 1X5
(250) 384-1885
Emp Here 50
SIC 2066 Chocolate and cocoa products

D-U-N-S 24-838-7110　　　(BR)
SIERRA SYSTEMS GROUP INC
737 Courtney St, Victoria, BC, V8W 1C3
(250) 385-1535
Emp Here 150
SIC 7379 Computer related services, nec

D-U-N-S 20-860-4079　　　(BR)
SOURCE (BELL) ELECTRONICS INC, THE
SOURCE, THE
1150 Douglas St Suite 119, Victoria, BC, V8W 3M9
(250) 385-1149
Emp Here 25
SIC 5999 Miscellaneous retail stores, nec

D-U-N-S 24-370-1547　　　(BR)
ST VINCENT DE PAUL SOCIETY
833 Yates St, Victoria, BC, V8W 1M1
(250) 382-3213
Emp Here 22
SIC 5932 Used merchandise stores

D-U-N-S 24-806-7050　　　(SL)
SWANS ENTERPRISES LTD
SWANS SUITE HOTELS
506 Pandora Ave Suite 203, Victoria, BC, V8W 1N6
(250) 361-3310
Emp Here 85　　　*Sales* 3,137,310
SIC 5813 Drinking places

D-U-N-S 20-882-4917　　　(BR)
TELUS CORPORATION
826 Yates St Suite 1, Victoria, BC, V8W 2H9
(250) 388-8759
Emp Here 60
SIC 4813 Telephone communication, except radio

D-U-N-S 20-915-6129　　　(BR)
UNIVERSITY OF VICTORIA
ENGLISH LANGUAGE CENTRE
Gd, Victoria, BC, V8W 2Y2
(250) 721-6115
Emp Here 50
SIC 8733 Noncommercial research organizations

D-U-N-S 20-914-7193　　　(BR)
UNIVERSITY OF VICTORIA
ADVANCEMENT SERVICES
Gd, Victoria, BC, V8W 3R4
(250) 721-6270
Emp Here 60
SIC 8221 Colleges and universities

D-U-N-S 20-891-5699　　　(BR)
UNIVERSITY OF VICTORIA
1700 Finnerty Rd Rm 102, Victoria, BC, V8W 2Y2
(250) 721-6243
Emp Here 70
SIC 8221 Colleges and universities

D-U-N-S 20-536-3430　　　(BR)
UNIVERSITY OF VICTORIA
MCPHERSON LIBRARY
Gd, Victoria, BC, V8W 3H5
(250) 721-6488
Emp Here 25
SIC 8221 Colleges and universities

D-U-N-S 20-914-7144　　　(BR)
UNIVERSITY OF VICTORIA
CHILD & YOUTH CARE
Gd, Victoria, BC, V8W 2Y2
(250) 721-7980
Emp Here 50
SIC 8221 Colleges and universities

D-U-N-S 24-351-4036　　　(BR)
UNIVERSITY OF VICTORIA
SCHOOL OF SOCIAL WORK
Gd, Victoria, BC, V8W 2Y2
(250) 721-8036
Emp Here 30
SIC 8399 Social services, nec

D-U-N-S 25-919-6129　　　(BR)
VICTORIA COOL AID SOCIETY, THE
STREET LINK
1634 Store St, Victoria, BC, V8W 1V3
(250) 383-1951
Emp Here 30
SIC 8322 Individual and family services

D-U-N-S 25-084-8728　　　(BR)
WATER　　STREET　　(VANCOUVER) SPAGHETTI CORP
OLD SPAGHETTI FACTORY, THE
(*Suby of* Water Street (Vancouver) Spaghetti Corp)
703 Douglas St, Victoria, BC, V8W 2B4
(250) 381-8444
Emp Here 130
SIC 5812 Eating places

D-U-N-S 25-862-7496　　　(BR)
WEST COAST AIR LTD
1000 Wharf St, Victoria, BC, V8W 1T4

(250) 384-2215
Emp Here 35
SIC 4512 Air transportation, scheduled

D-U-N-S 25-136-0608　　　(BR)
WESTCOAST ENGLISH LANGUAGE CENTER LIMITED
GLOBAL VILLAGE VICTORIA
(*Suby of* Westcoast English Language Center Limited)
1290 Broad St Suite 200, Victoria, BC, V8W 2A5
(250) 384-2199
Emp Here 20
SIC 8299 Schools and educational services, nec

D-U-N-S 24-374-0297　　　(HQ)
YMCA-YWCA OF GREATER VICTORIA
(*Suby of* YMCA-YWCA of Greater Victoria)
851 Broughton St, Victoria, BC, V8W 1E5
(250) 386-7511
Emp Here 150　　　*Emp Total* 150
Sales 5,448,298
SIC 8011 Offices and clinics of medical doctors
CEO Jennifer (Jennie) Edgecombe

Victoria, BC V8X
Capital County

D-U-N-S 25-287-6248　　　(SL)
471540 B.C. LTD
WHITE SPOT FAMILY RESTAURANT
3965 Quadra St, Victoria, BC, V8X 1J8
(250) 727-3931
Emp Here 70　　　*Sales* 2,115,860
SIC 5812 Eating places

D-U-N-S 25-871-5036　　　(BR)
ACCENT INNS INC
3233 Maple St, Victoria, BC, V8X 4Y9
(250) 475-7500
Emp Here 22
SIC 7011 Hotels and motels

D-U-N-S 25-806-6687　　　(BR)
BANQUE TORONTO-DOMINION, LA
TORONTO-DOMINION BANK, THE
(*Suby of* Toronto-Dominion Bank, The)
3530 Blanshard St, Victoria, BC, V8X 1W3
(250) 356-4121
Emp Here 26
SIC 6021 National commercial banks

D-U-N-S 20-655-6560　　　(BR)
BOARD OF EDUCATION OF SCHOOL DISTRICT NO. 61 (GREATER VICTORIA)
CLOVERDALE ELEMENTARY SCHOOL
3427 Quadra St, Victoria, BC, V8X 1G8
(250) 382-7231
Emp Here 40
SIC 8211 Elementary and secondary schools

D-U-N-S 20-027-0234　　　(BR)
BOARD OF EDUCATION OF SCHOOL DISTRICT NO. 61 (GREATER VICTORIA)
LAKE HILL ELEMENTARY SCHOOL
1031 Lucas Ave, Victoria, BC, V8X 5L2
(250) 479-2896
Emp Here 25
SIC 8211 Elementary and secondary schools

D-U-N-S 20-713-5497　　　(BR)
BOARD OF EDUCATION OF SCHOOL DISTRICT NO. 61 (GREATER VICTORIA)
ROGER ELEMENTARY SCHOOL
765 Rogers Ave, Victoria, BC, V8X 5K6
(250) 744-2343
Emp Here 50
SIC 8211 Elementary and secondary schools

D-U-N-S 25-014-9150　　　(BR)
CANADIAN TIRE CORPORATION, LIMITED
CANADIAN TIRE

801 Royal Oak Dr, Victoria, BC, V8X 4V1
(250) 727-6561
Emp Here 65
SIC 5531 Auto and home supply stores

D-U-N-S 24-866-7644　　　(BR)
CANEM SYSTEMS LTD
3311 Oak St Suite B, Victoria, BC, V8X 1P9
(250) 475-1955
Emp Here 30
SIC 1731 Electrical work

D-U-N-S 25-069-7364　　　(BR)
CATHOLIC INDEPENDENT SCHOOLS, DIOCESE OF VICTORIA
ST ANDREW'S REGIONAL HIGH SCHOOL
880 Mckenzie Ave, Victoria, BC, V8X 3G5
(250) 479-1414
Emp Here 45
SIC 8211 Elementary and secondary schools

D-U-N-S 25-189-5608　　　(BR)
CORPORATION OF THE DISTRICT OF SAANICH, THE
SAANICH FIRE DEPARTMENT
780 Vernon Ave, Victoria, BC, V8X 2W6
(250) 475-5500
Emp Here 100
SIC 7389 Business services, nec

D-U-N-S 24-793-4339　　　(SL)
DESJARDINS FINANCIAL SECURITY INDEPENDENT NETWORK
3939 Quadra St Suite 101, Victoria, BC, V8X 1J5
(250) 708-3376
Emp Here 49　　　*Sales* 6,992,640
SIC 8741 Management services

D-U-N-S 24-337-3003　　　(BR)
FGL SPORTS LTD
SPORT CHEK
805 Cloverdale Ave Suite 104, Victoria, BC, V8X 2S9
(250) 475-6851
Emp Here 40
SIC 5941 Sporting goods and bicycle shops

D-U-N-S 24-938-9446　　　(SL)
FULL MOON FOODS LTD
MOXIE'S
3442 Saanich Rd Suite 34, Victoria, BC, V8X 1W7
(250) 360-1660
Emp Here 75　　　*Sales* 2,685,378
SIC 5812 Eating places

D-U-N-S 20-911-9747　　　(BR)
GOVERNMENT OF THE PROVINCE OF BRITISH COLUMBIA
MOUNT VIEW DISABILITY EMPLOYMENT & ASSISTANCE CENTRE
771 Vernon Ave, Victoria, BC, V8X 5A7
(250) 952-4111
Emp Here 25
SIC 8399 Social services, nec

D-U-N-S 25-267-8933　　　(BR)
GREAT PACIFIC INDUSTRIES INC
SAVE-ON-FOODS
3510 Blanshard St Suite 977, Victoria, BC, V8X 1W3
(250) 475-3300
Emp Here 250
SIC 5411 Grocery stores

D-U-N-S 25-270-0802　　　(BR)
HSBC BANK CANADA
771 Vernon Ave Suite 100, Victoria, BC, V8X 5A7
(250) 388-6465
Emp Here 42
SIC 6021 National commercial banks

D-U-N-S 20-039-1600　　　(SL)
HIRSCHFIELD WILLIAMS TIMMINS LTD
4400 Chatterton Way Suite 302, Victoria, BC, V8X 5J2

Emp Here 20   *Sales* 1.751,057
SIC 8711 Engineering services

D-U-N-S 20-316-9677   (BR)
ISM INFORMATION SYSTEM MANAGE-MENT CANADA CORPORATION
ISM CANADA
(*Suby* of International Business Machines Corporation)
3960 Quadra St Suite 200, Victoria, BC, V8X 4A3
(250) 704-1800
Emp Here 150
SIC 7374 Data processing and preparation

D-U-N-S 25-315-7960   (BR)
INVESTORS GROUP FINANCIAL SER-VICES INC
4400 Chatterton Way Suite 101, Victoria, BC, V8X 5J2
(250) 727-9191
Emp Here 60
SIC 8741 Management services

D-U-N-S 20-933-6416   (SL)
JRKB HOLDINS LTD
BOSTON PIZZA
3510 Blanshard St Suite 102, Victoria, BC, V8X 1W3
(250) 477-5561
Emp Here 50   *Sales* 1,532,175
SIC 5812 Eating places

D-U-N-S 20-703-145€   (BR)
JACE HOLDINGS LTD
THRIFTY FOODS
3475 Quadra St Suite 13, Victoria, BC, V8X 1G8
(250) 382-2751
Emp Here 200
SIC 5141 Groceries, general line

D-U-N-S 24-881-285¹   (BR)
KEG RESTAURANTS LTD
KEG STEAKHOUSE & EAR, THE
3940 Quadra St, Victoria, BC, V8X 1J6
(250) 479-1651
Emp Here 55
SIC 5812 Eating places

D-U-N-S 24-577-9970   (HQ)
KINETIC CONSTRUCTION LTD
(*Suby* of Gyles Investments Ltd)
862 Cloverdale Ave Suite 201, Victoria, BC, V8X 2S8
(250) 381-6331
Emp Here 20   *Emp Total* 3
Sales 22,253,014
SIC 1542 Nonresidential construction, nec
Pr Pr William Gyles
   Chris Chalecki
VP VP Mark A. Liudzius
VP VP Thomas W. Plumb
VP VP Mike D. Walz

D-U-N-S 20-352-6108   (SL)
ROGERS ELEMENTARY OUT OF SCHOOL CARE SOCIETY
ROGERS CHILD CARE CENTRE
765 Rogers Ave, Victoria, BC, V8X 5K6
(250) 744-2343
Emp Here 50   *Sales* 1,969,939
SIC 8322 Individual and family services

D-U-N-S 20-030-5865   (BR)
SCHOOL DISTRICT 63 (SAANICH)
LOCHSIDE ELEMENTARY SCHOOL
1145 Royal Oak Dr, Victoria, BC, V8X 3T7
(250) 658-5238
Emp Here 50
SIC 8211 Elementary and secondary schools

D-U-N-S 24-856-9055   (BR)
SHAW CABLESYSTEMS LIMITED
35 Queens Rd, Victoria, BC, V8X 4S7
(250) 748-9113
Emp Here 40
SIC 4841 Cable and other pay television ser-

vices

D-U-N-S 25-271-5503   (BR)
SHAW COMMUNICATIONS INC
SHAW CABLE
861 Cloverdale Ave, Victoria, BC, V8X 4S7
(250) 475-5655
Emp Here 100
SIC 4841 Cable and other pay television services

D-U-N-S 25-314-1956   (BR)
STAPLES CANADA INC
STAPLES THE BUSINESS DEPOT
(*Suby* of Staples, Inc.)
780 Tolmie Ave Suite 3, Victoria, BC, V8X 3W4
(250) 383-8178
Emp Here 45
SIC 5943 Stationery stores

D-U-N-S 20-506-0382   (BR)
STARBUCKS COFFEE CANADA, INC
STARBUCKS COFFEE COMPANY
(*Suby* of Starbucks Corporation)
777 Royal Oak Dr Suite 550, Victoria, BC, V8X 4V1
(250) 744-4225
Emp Here 26
SIC 5812 Eating places

D-U-N-S 20-912-3327   (BR)
VANCOUVER ISLAND HEALTH AUTHOR-ITY
SEVEN OAKS TERTIARY MENTAL HEALTH FACILITY
4575 Blenkinsop Rd, Victoria, BC, V8X 2C7
(250) 479-7373
Emp Here 54
SIC 8093 Specialty outpatient clinics, nec

D-U-N-S 25-361-0356   (BR)
VANCOUVER ISLAND HEALTH AUTHOR-ITY
SAANICH HEALTH PROTECTION OFFICE
771 Vernon Ave Unit 201, Victoria, BC, V8X 5A7
(250) 519-3401
Emp Here 30
SIC 8011 Offices and clinics of medical doctors

D-U-N-S 20-063-3795   (BR)
VANCOUVER ISLAND HEALTH AUTHOR-ITY
SAANICH HEALTH UNIT
3995 Quadra St Suite 314, Victoria, BC, V8X 1J8
(250) 519-5100
Emp Here 50
SIC 8011 Offices and clinics of medical doctors

D-U-N-S 20-063-3787   (BR)
WOLSELEY CANADA INC
KITCHEN & BATH CLASSICS
(*Suby* of WOLSELEY PLC)
840 Cloverdale Ave, Victoria, BC, V8X 2S8
(250) 475-1120
Emp Here 20
SIC 5999 Miscellaneous retail stores, nec

D-U-N-S 25-898-4798   (BR)
WORKERS' COMPENSATION BOARD OF BRITISH COLUMBIA
WORKSAFE BC
4514 Chatterton Way, Victoria, BC, V8X 5H2
(250) 881-3400
Emp Here 70
SIC 6331 Fire, marine, and casualty insurance

Victoria, BC V8Y
Capital County

D-U-N-S 25-902-6763   (SL)
CORDOVA BAY GOLF COURSE LTD

BILL MATTICK'S RESTAURANT & LOUNGE
5333 Cordova Bay Rd, Victoria, BC, V8Y 2L3
(250) 658-4445
Emp Here 75   *Sales* 3,210,271
SIC 7992 Public golf courses

D-U-N-S 24-104-0117   (BR)
RED BARN COUNTRY MARKET LTD
5325 Cordova Bay Rd Suite 129, Victoria, BC, V8Y 2L3
(250) 658-2998
Emp Here 25
SIC 5411 Grocery stores

D-U-N-S 25-984-8042   (BR)
SCHOOL DISTRICT 63 (SAANICH)
CLAREMONT SECONDARY SCHOOL
4980 Wesley Rd, Victoria, BC, V8Y 1Y9
(250) 686-5221
Emp Here 100
SIC 8211 Elementary and secondary schools

D-U-N-S 20-713-5620   (BR)
SCHOOL DISTRICT 63 (SAANICH)
CORDOVA BAY ELEMENTARY SCHOOL
5238 Cordova Bay Rd, Victoria, BC, V8Y 2L2
(250) 658-5315
Emp Here 25
SIC 8211 Elementary and secondary schools

D-U-N-S 20-713-5661   (BR)
SCHOOL DISTRICT 63 (SAANICH)
CHILDREN'S DEVELOPMENT CENTRE & ALTERNATE LEARNING PROGRAM
735 Cordova Bay Rd, Victoria, BC, V8Y 1P7
(250) 658-5412
Emp Here 20
SIC 8211 Elementary and secondary schools

D-U-N-S 20-823-9819   (SL)
TASK ENGINEERING LTD
5141 Cordova Bay Rd, Victoria, BC, V8Y 2K1
(250) 590-2440
Emp Here 50   *Sales* 14,236,238
SIC 7363 Help supply services
Pr Pr Andy Kyfiuk

Victoria, BC V8Z
Capital County

D-U-N-S 20-955-7743   (HQ)
ANDERSON, J E AND ASSOCIATES
(*Suby* of Anderson, J E and Associates)
4212 Glanford Ave, Victoria, BC, V8Z 4B7
(250) 727-2214
Emp Here 31   *Emp Total* 50
Sales 4,961,328
SIC 8713 Surveying services

D-U-N-S 25-181-8048   (BR)
ARITZIA LP
(*Suby* of Aritzia LP)
3147 Douglas St Unit 165, Victoria, BC, V8Z 6E3
(250) 220-6963
Emp Here 20
SIC 5621 Women's clothing stores

D-U-N-S 24-354-7861   (HQ)
ASPREVA INTERNATIONAL LTD
VIFOUR PHARMA ASPREVA
4464 Markham St Unit 1203, Victoria, BC, V8Z 7X8
(250) 744-2488
Emp Here 48   *Emp Total* 45
Sales 7,852,800
SIC 2834 Pharmaceutical preparations
Dir Philippe Weigerstorfer
Dir Fritz Hirsbrunner
Dir Jorg Kneubuhler

D-U-N-S 25-902-2028   (BR)
BC HOUSING MANAGEMENT COMMIS-SION
3440 Douglas St Unit 201, Victoria, BC, V8Z

3L5
(250) 475-7550
Emp Here 20
SIC 6531 Real estate agents and managers

D-U-N-S 20-106-9015   (BR)
BELFOR (CANADA) INC
BELFOR RESTORATION SERVICES
4216 Glanford Ave, Victoria, BC, V8Z 4B7
(250) 978-5556
Emp Here 20
SIC 1799 Special trade contractors, nec

D-U-N-S 25-289-2070   (BR)
BLACK PRESS GROUP LTD
GOLDSTREAM PRESS
770 Enterprise Cres Suite 200, Victoria, BC, V8Z 6R4
(250) 727-2460
Emp Here 50
SIC 2759 Commercial printing, nec

D-U-N-S 20-713-5430   (BR)
BOARD OF EDUCATION OF SCHOOL DIS-TRICT NO. 61 (GREATER VICTORIA)
MARIGOLD ELEMENTARY SCHOOL
3751 Grange Rd, Victoria, BC, V8Z 4T2
(250) 479-8256
Emp Here 50
SIC 8211 Elementary and secondary schools

D-U-N-S 20-810-9665   (BR)
BOARD OF EDUCATION OF SCHOOL DIS-TRICT NO. 61 (GREATER VICTORIA)
COLQUITZ MIDDLE SCHOOL
505 Dumeresq St, Victoria, BC, V8Z 1X3
(250) 479-1678
Emp Here 50
SIC 8211 Elementary and secondary schools

D-U-N-S 25-482-4337   (BR)
BOARD OF EDUCATION OF SCHOOL DIS-TRICT NO. 61 (GREATER VICTORIA)
MCKENZIE ELEMENTARY SCHOOL
4005 Raymond St N, Victoria, BC, V8Z 4K9
(250) 479-1691
Emp Here 22
SIC 8211 Elementary and secondary schools

D-U-N-S 20-027-0275   (BR)
BOARD OF EDUCATION OF SCHOOL DIS-TRICT NO. 61 (GREATER VICTORIA)
NORTHRIDGE ELEMENTARY SCHOOL
4190 Carey Rd, Victoria, BC, V8Z 4G8
(250) 479-8293
Emp Here 30
SIC 8211 Elementary and secondary schools

D-U-N-S 25-026-7499   (BR)
BOARD OF EDUCATION OF SCHOOL DIS-TRICT NO. 61 (GREATER VICTORIA)
SPECTRUM COMMUNITY SCHOOL
957 Burnside Rd W, Victoria, BC, V8Z 6E9
(250) 479-8271
Emp Here 100
SIC 8211 Elementary and secondary schools

D-U-N-S 20-034-7057   (BR)
BOARD OF EDUCATION OF SCHOOL DIS-TRICT NO. 61 (GREATER VICTORIA)
STRAWBERRY VALE ELEMENTARY SCHOOL
4109 Rosedale Ave, Victoria, BC, V8Z 5J5
(250) 479-4014
Emp Here 25
SIC 8211 Elementary and secondary schools

D-U-N-S 25-678-1436   (SL)
CSP INTERNET LTD
PACIFIC INTERCONNECT
4252 Commerce Cir, Victoria, BC, V8Z 4M2

Emp Here 50   *Sales* 7,507,300
SIC 4899 Communication services, nec
  Steven Dean
Pr Pr William Godfrey

D-U-N-S 20-580-3674   (BR)

CANADA POST CORPORATION
4181 Glanford Ave Suite 400, Victoria, BC,
V8Z 7X4

Emp Here 20
SIC 4311 U.s. postal service

D-U-N-S 20-572-8376 (BR)
CANADA POST CORPORATION
3575 Douglas St, Victoria, BC, V8Z 3L6
(250) 475-7572
Emp Here 20
SIC 4311 U.s. postal service

D-U-N-S 20-591-9694 (BR)
CATHOLIC INDEPENDENT SCHOOLS, DIO-CESE OF VICTORIA
ST JOSEPH'S VICTORIA ELEMENTARY SCHOOL
757 Burnside Rd W, Victoria, BC, V8Z 1M9
(250) 479-1232
Emp Here 38
SIC 8211 Elementary and secondary schools

D-U-N-S 24-050-7181 (BR)
CLARK REEFER LINES LTD
4254 Commerce Cir Unit 103, Victoria, BC,
V8Z 4M2
(250) 708-2004
Emp Here 48
SIC 4212 Local trucking, without storage

D-U-N-S 24-946-8224 (BR)
COCA-COLA REFRESHMENTS CANADA COMPANY
(*Suby of* The Coca-Cola Company)
765 Vanalman Ave Suite 105, Victoria, BC,
V8Z 3B8
(250) 727-2222
Emp Here 50
SIC 5149 Groceries and related products, nec

D-U-N-S 25-887-9006 (BR)
CRIDGE CENTRE FOR THE FAMILY, THE
MACDONALD HOUSE RESIDENCE
(*Suby of* Cridge Centre For The Family, The)
1251 Santa Rosa Ave, Victoria, BC, V8Z 2V5
(250) 479-5299
Emp Here 25
SIC 8322 Individual and family services

D-U-N-S 24-980-0624 (HQ)
CUSTOM HOUSE ULC
WESTERN UNION BUSINESS SOLUTIONS
3680 Uptown Blvd Suite 300, Victoria, BC,
V8Z 0B9
(888) 987-7612
Emp Here 100   *Emp Total* 10,000
Sales 1,029,037,713
SIC 6099 Functions related to deposit banking
Pr Pr Kerry Agiasotis
Sr VP Ian Taylor
VP Brian Harris
VP Jacqueline Keogh
VP Adam Tiberi
Crdt Mgr Cecilia Watts
Tony Crivelli
Kenneth Timbers
Scott Smith
Tristan Van Der Vijver

D-U-N-S 20-624-0277 (BR)
DENCAN RESTAURANTS INC
DENNY'S RESTAURANT
(*Suby of* Northland Properties Corporation)
3100 Douglas St Unit 7767, Victoria, BC, V8Z
3K2
(250) 382-3844
Emp Here 40
SIC 5812 Eating places

D-U-N-S 24-824-8841 (BR)
DYNAMEX CANADA LIMITED
DYNAMEX
450 Banga Pl Suite B, Victoria, BC, V8Z 6X5
(250) 383-4121
Emp Here 29
SIC 7389 Business services, nec

D-U-N-S 20-648-1223 (BR)
EDDIE BAUER OF CANADA INC
(*Suby of* Golden Gate Capital LP)
3147 Douglas St Suite 638, Victoria, BC, V8Z
6E3
(250) 383-1322
Emp Here 50
SIC 5699 Miscellaneous apparel and acces-sory stores

D-U-N-S 24-077-8717 (BR)
EUROLINE WINDOWS INC
3352 Tennyson Ave, Victoria, BC, V8Z 3P6
(250) 383-8465
Emp Here 100
SIC 5031 Lumber, plywood, and millwork

D-U-N-S 20-048-4694 (BR)
GOLDER ASSOCIATES LTD
3795 Carey Rd Fl 2, Victoria, BC, V8Z 6T8
(250) 881-7372
Emp Here 75
SIC 8711 Engineering services

D-U-N-S 24-765-1768 (BR)
GOVERNMENT OF THE PROVINCE OF BRITISH COLUMBIA
DISTRIBUTION CENTRE VICTORIA
742 Vanalman Ave, Victoria, BC, V8Z 3B5
(250) 952-4460
Emp Here 25
SIC 5044 Office equipment

D-U-N-S 20-917-3140 (BR)
GOVERNMENT OF THE PROVINCE OF BRITISH COLUMBIA
BC PURCHASING COMMISSION WARE-HOUSE
4234 Glanford Ave, Victoria, BC, V8Z 4B8
(250) 356-8326
Emp Here 25
SIC 7389 Business services, nec

D-U-N-S 20-226-4227 (SL)
HOWARD JOHNSON HOTELS & SUITES
4670 Elk Lake Dr, Victoria, BC, V8Z 5M1
(250) 658-8989
Emp Here 70   *Sales* 3,064,349
SIC 7011 Hotels and motels

D-U-N-S 24-958-0309 (BR)
HUDSON'S BAY COMPANY
THE BAY MAYFAIR
3125 Douglas St, Victoria, BC, V8Z 3K3
(250) 386-3322
Emp Here 250
SIC 5311 Department stores

D-U-N-S 25-883-7186 (SL)
ISLAND BUILDERS LTD
601 Alpha St, Victoria, BC, V8Z 1B5
(250) 475-3569
Emp Here 46   *Sales* 12,368,160
SIC 1522 Residential construction, nec
Pr Allan Novak

D-U-N-S 24-777-8897 (BR)
ISLAND SAVINGS CREDIT UNION
(*Suby of* Island Savings Credit Union)
3195 Douglas St, Victoria, BC, V8Z 3K3
(250) 385-4476
Emp Here 30
SIC 6062 State credit unions

D-U-N-S 20-119-3323 (BR)
KONE INC
4223 Commerce Cir Suite 30, Victoria, BC,
V8Z 6N6
(250) 384-0613
Emp Here 20
SIC 3534 Elevators and moving stairways

D-U-N-S 25-898-8435 (SL)
MED GRILL RESTAURANTS LTD
4512 West Saanich Rd, Victoria, BC, V8Z 3G4
(250) 727-3444
Emp Here 65   *Sales* 1,969,939
SIC 5812 Eating places

D-U-N-S 25-101-0278 (SL)
MONTANA'S COOKHOUSE
315 Burnside Rd W, Victoria, BC, V8Z 7L6
(250) 978-9333
Emp Here 77   *Sales* 2,334,742
SIC 5812 Eating places

D-U-N-S 25-818-3102 (BR)
MORGUARD INVESTMENTS LIMITED
PROPERTIES DIVISION
3531 Uptown Blvd Unit 221, Victoria, BC, V8Z
0B9
(250) 383-8093
Emp Here 20
SIC 6531 Real estate agents and managers

D-U-N-S 25-483-8451 (BR)
OAK LANE ENTERPRISES LTD
COUNTRY GROCER
4420 West Saanich Rd, Victoria, BC, V8Z 3E9
(250) 708-3900
Emp Here 56
SIC 5411 Grocery stores

D-U-N-S 24-838-7086 (BR)
PATTISON, JIM INDUSTRIES LTD
METRO LEXUS TOYOTA VICTORIA
625 Frances Ave, Victoria, BC, V8Z 1A2
(250) 386-3516
Emp Here 117
SIC 5511 New and used car dealers

D-U-N-S 25-320-9308 (BR)
PUROLATOR INC.
PUROLATOR INC
3330 Tennyson Ave, Victoria, BC, V8Z 3P3
(250) 475-9562
Emp Here 50
SIC 7389 Business services, nec

D-U-N-S 25-069-7380 (HQ)
RED BARN COUNTRY MARKET LTD
RED BARN MARKET
751 Vanalman Ave, Victoria, BC, V8Z 3B8
(250) 479-6817
Emp Here 50   *Emp Total* 150
Sales 18,459,057
SIC 5411 Grocery stores
Pr Pr Peter Hansen
Samuel R Schwabe
Dir Ashley Bourque
Dir Russ Benwell

D-U-N-S 20-146-7805 (BR)
REITMANS (CANADA) LIMITEE
RW & CO.
3147 Douglas St Unit 213, Victoria, BC, V8Z
6E3
(250) 381-2214
Emp Here 20
SIC 5621 Women's clothing stores

D-U-N-S 25-814-9392 (BR)
ROYAL BANK OF CANADA
RBC
(*Suby of* Royal Bank Of Canada)
306 Burnside Rd W, Victoria, BC, V8Z 1M1
(250) 356-4675
Emp Here 33
SIC 6021 National commercial banks

D-U-N-S 20-794-9975 (SL)
RYAN COMPANY LIMITED
RYAN VENDING
723a Vanalman Ave, Victoria, BC, V8Z 3B6
(250) 388-4254
Emp Here 50   *Sales* 3,811,504
SIC 5962 Merchandising machine operators

D-U-N-S 20-713-5646 (BR)
SCHOOL DISTRICT 63 (SAANICH)
ROYAL OAKS MIDDLE SCHOOL
4564 West Saanich Rd, Victoria, BC, V8Z 3G4
(250) 479-7128
Emp Here 50
SIC 8211 Elementary and secondary schools

D-U-N-S 25-486-2246 (BR)

SCHOOL DISTRICT 63 (SAANICH)
KEATING ELEMENTARY SCHOOL
6843 Central Saanich Rd, Victoria, BC, V8Z
5V4
(250) 652-9261
Emp Here 40
SIC 8211 Elementary and secondary schools

D-U-N-S 20-528-6805 (BR)
SEARS CANADA INC
SEARS PARTS & SERVICE
765 Vanalman Ave Suite 101, Victoria, BC,
V8Z 3B8

Emp Here 22
SIC 5399 Miscellaneous general merchandise

D-U-N-S 20-575-5077 (SL)
THURBER MANAGEMENT LTD
4396 West Saanich Rd Suite 100, Victoria,
BC, V8Z 3E9
(250) 727-2201
Emp Here 110   *Sales* 19,579,850
SIC 8741 Management services
Pr Pr Richard Izard

D-U-N-S 25-272-9363 (BR)
UAP INC
NAPA
(*Suby of* Genuine Parts Company)
555 Ardersier Rd, Victoria, BC, V8Z 1C8
(250) 382-5184
Emp Here 20
SIC 5013 Motor vehicle supplies and new parts

D-U-N-S 25-988-7578 (BR)
UNITED PARCEL SERVICE CANADA LTD
UPS
4254 Commerce Cir Suite D, Victoria, BC, V8Z
4M2
(250) 744-1534
Emp Here 35
SIC 7389 Business services, nec

D-U-N-S 25-829-5963 (BR)
VANCOUVER ISLAND HEALTH AUTHOR-ITY
VICTORIA GENERAL HOSPITAL
1 Hospital Way, Victoria, BC, V8Z 6R5
(250) 727-4212
Emp Here 500
SIC 8011 Offices and clinics of medical doc-tors

D-U-N-S 20-513-2975 (SL)
VIGIL HEALTH SOLUTIONS INC
4464 Markham St Unit 2102, Victoria, BC, V8Z
7X8
(250) 383-6900
Emp Here 20   *Sales* 5,155,889
SIC 5047 Medical and hospital equipment
Pr Pr Troy I. Griffiths
Nicola Chalmers
Greg J Peet
Harry A Jaako
Stephen R Martin

D-U-N-S 20-049-8272 (BR)
WSP CANADA INC
FOCUS INTEC
57 Cadillac Ave, Victoria, BC, V8Z 1T3
(250) 474-1151
Emp Here 50
SIC 7363 Help supply services

D-U-N-S 24-662-1663 (BR)
WAL-MART CANADA CORP
WALMART
3460 Saanich Rd Suite 3109, Victoria, BC,
V8Z 0B9
(250) 475-3356
Emp Here 485
SIC 5311 Department stores

D-U-N-S 25-944-6987 (BR)
WEIGHT WATCHERS CANADA, LTD
(*Suby of* Weight Watchers International, Inc.)

▲ Public Company ■ Public Company Family Member **HQ** Headquarters **BR** Branch **SL** Single Location

4489 Viewmont Ave Unit 102, Victoria, BC, V8Z 5K8
(250) 472-6291
Emp Here 20
SIC 7991 Physical fitness facilities

D-U-N-S 20-976-7040   (SL)
WESCOR CONTRACTING LTD
3368 Tennyson Ave, Victoria, BC, V8Z 3P6
(250) 475-8882
Emp Here 49   *Sales* 11,779,113
SIC 1542 Nonresidential construction, nec
Pr Richard Green

D-U-N-S 24-389-4917   (BR)
WILSON'S TRANSPORTATION LTD
31 Regina Ave, Victoria, BC, V8Z 1H8
(250) 475-3226
Emp Here 40
SIC 4173 Bus terminal and service facilities

Victoria, BC V9A
Capital County

D-U-N-S 24-620-0534   (BR)
A & W FOOD SERVICES OF CANADA INC
A & W
860 Esquimalt Rd, Victoria, BC, V9A 3M4
(250) 388-5221
Emp Here 20
SIC 5812 Eating places

D-U-N-S 25-216-7473   (BR)
ALBION FISHERIES LTD
ALBION FISHERIES VICTORIA, DIV OF
740 Tyee Rd, Victoria, BC, V9A 6X3
(250) 382-8286
Emp Here 53
SIC 5146 Fish and seafoods

D-U-N-S 20-588-2611   (BR)
BANQUE TORONTO-DOMINION, LA
TD CANADA TRUST
(*Suby of* Toronto-Dominion Bank, The)
184 Wilson St Suite 100, Victoria, BC, V9A 7N6
(250) 405-6100
Emp Here 20
SIC 6021 National commercial banks

D-U-N-S 20-653-3205   (BR)
BOARD OF EDUCATION OF SCHOOL DISTRICT NO. 61 (GREATER VICTORIA)
MCAULAY ELEMENTARY SCHOOL
1010 Wychbury Ave, Victoria, BC, V9A 5K6
(250) 385-3441
Emp Here 50
SIC 8211 Elementary and secondary schools

D-U-N-S 20-027-0291   (BR)
BOARD OF EDUCATION OF SCHOOL DISTRICT NO. 61 (GREATER VICTORIA)
ROCKHEIGHTS MIDDLE SCHOOL
1250 Highrock Ave, Victoria, BC, V9A 4V7
(250) 384-7125
Emp Here 50
SIC 8211 Elementary and secondary schools

D-U-N-S 20-655-2064   (BR)
BOARD OF EDUCATION OF SCHOOL DISTRICT NO. 61 (GREATER VICTORIA)
VICTORIA WEST ELEMENTARY SCHOOL
750 Front St, Victoria, BC, V9A 3Y4
(250) 382-9131
Emp Here 40
SIC 8211 Elementary and secondary schools

D-U-N-S 20-713-5414   (BR)
BOARD OF EDUCATION OF SCHOOL DISTRICT NO. 61 (GREATER VICTORIA)
ESQUIMALT HIGH SCHOOL
847 Colville Rd, Victoria, BC, V9A 4N9
(250) 382-9226
Emp Here 75
SIC 8211 Elementary and secondary schools

D-U-N-S 20-027-0283   (BR)
BOARD OF EDUCATION OF SCHOOL DISTRICT NO. 61 (GREATER VICTORIA)
TILLICUM ELEMENTARY SCHOOL
3155 Albina St, Victoria, BC, V9A 1Z6
(250) 386-1408
Emp Here 40
SIC 8211 Elementary and secondary schools

D-U-N-S 20-165-3990   (SL)
CFB ESQUIMALT MILITARY FAMILY RESOURCE CENTRE
ESQUIMALT MFRC
1505 Esquimalt Rd, Victoria, BC, V9A 7N2
(250) 363-8628
Emp Here 45   *Sales* 9,047,127
SIC 8399 Social services, nec
Ex Dir Gaynor Jackson

D-U-N-S 20-578-5954   (BR)
CANADA POST CORPORATION
COUNTRY GROCER
1153 Esquimalt Rd, Victoria, BC, V9A 3N7
(250) 382-4399
Emp Here 45
SIC 5411 Grocery stores

D-U-N-S 24-317-4070   (BR)
CARMANAH TECHNOLOGIES CORPORATION
203 Harbour Rd Suite 4, Victoria, BC, V9A 3S2
(250) 380-0052
Emp Here 100
SIC 5074 Plumbing and heating equipment and supplies (hydronics)

D-U-N-S 24-359-0549   (SL)
CHIP REIT NO. 40 OPERATIONS LIMITED PARTERSHIP
45 Songhees Rd, Victoria, BC, V9A 6T3
(250) 360-2999
Emp Here 200   *Sales* 11,307,948
SIC 7011 Hotels and motels
Genl Mgr Peter Gillis
Fin Ex Joanne Irving

D-U-N-S 24-418-2783   (BR)
CINEPLEX ODEON CORPORATION
SILVERCITY VICTORIA TILLICUM CENTRE
3130 Tillicum Rd, Victoria, BC, V9A 0B9
(250) 381-9300
Emp Here 49
SIC 7832 Motion picture theaters, except drive-in

D-U-N-S 25-267-5723   (SL)
CLARK & PATTISON (ALBERTA) LTD
929 Ellery St Suite 6, Victoria, BC, V9A 4R9
(250) 386-5232
Emp Here 30   *Sales* 5,727,360
SIC 3441 Fabricated structural Metal
Pr John Clark

D-U-N-S 25-969-6433   (BR)
COAST CAPITAL SAVINGS CREDIT UNION
3170 Tillicum Rd Unit 169, Victoria, BC, V9A 7C9
(250) 483-7000
Emp Here 25
SIC 6062 State credit unions

D-U-N-S 20-699-9091   (BR)
DELTA HOTELS LIMITED
45 Songhees Rd, Victoria, BC, V9A 6T3
(250) 360-2999
Emp Here 214
SIC 7011 Hotels and motels

D-U-N-S 25-415-9650   (SL)
EMPRESS PAINTING LTD
863 Viewfield Rd, Victoria, BC, V9A 4V2
(250) 383-5224
Emp Here 69   *Sales* 4,450,603
SIC 1721 Painting and paper hanging

D-U-N-S 24-824-9989   (SL)
ESQUIMALT ENTERPRISES LTD

ESQUIMALT'S COUNTRY GROCER
1153 Esquimalt Rd Suite 3, Victoria, BC, V9A 3N7
(250) 708-3900
Emp Here 80   *Sales* 14,710,250
SIC 5411 Grocery stores
Pr Pr Peter Cavin
Genl Mgr Mark Wilson

D-U-N-S 25-301-1449   (BR)
FABRICLAND PACIFIC/MIDWEST LIMITED
FABRICLAND
3170 Tillicum Rd Suite 31, Victoria, BC, V9A 7C5
(250) 475-7501
Emp Here 20
SIC 5949 Sewing, needlework, and piece goods

D-U-N-S 24-995-1633   (BR)
G4S CASH SOLUTIONS (CANADA) LTD
SECURICOR CASH SERVICES
744 Fairview Rd Suite 12, Victoria, BC, V9A 5T9
(250) 384-1549
Emp Here 50
SIC 7381 Detective and armored car services

D-U-N-S 25-149-3680   (BR)
GOVERNING COUNCIL OF THE SALVATION ARMY IN CANADA, THE
GOVERNING COUNCIL OF THE SALVATION ARMY IN CANADA, THE
952 Arm St, Victoria, BC, V9A 4G7
(250) 385-3422
Emp Here 132
SIC 8051 Skilled nursing care facilities

D-U-N-S 20-138-9439   (BR)
GREAT PACIFIC INDUSTRIES INC
SAVE-ON-FOODS
172 Wilson St Unit 100, Victoria, BC, V9A 7N6
(250) 389-6115
Emp Here 110
SIC 5411 Grocery stores

D-U-N-S 24-339-6111   (HQ)
ISLAND COMMUNITY MENTAL HEALTH ASSOCIATION
(*Suby of* Island Community Mental Health Association)
125 Skinner St, Victoria, BC, V9A 6X4
(250) 389-1211
Emp Here 50   *Emp Total* 50
Sales 3,283,232
SIC 8093 Specialty outpatient clinics, nec

D-U-N-S 20-703-0219   (BR)
JACE HOLDINGS LTD
THRIFTY FOODS FLOWERS & MORE
1495 Admirals Rd, Victoria, BC, V9A 2P8
(250) 361-3637
Emp Here 180
SIC 5411 Grocery stores

D-U-N-S 20-139-9693   (SL)
KARDEL CONSULTING SERVICE INC
2951 Tillicum Rd Unit 209, Victoria, BC, V9A 2A6
(250) 382-5959
Emp Here 220   *Sales* 14,233,200
SIC 8049 Offices of health practitioner
 Karl Egner

D-U-N-S 20-949-8281   (BR)
LOBLAWS INC
REAL CANADIAN WHOLESALE CLUB
846 Viewfield Rd, Victoria, BC, V9A 4V1
(250) 381-4078
Emp Here 50
SIC 5912 Drug stores and proprietary stores

D-U-N-S 20-923-8083   (SL)
MCDONALD'S RESTAURANTS
KEN CAR ENTERPRISE
1149 Esquimalt Rd, Victoria, BC, V9A 3N6
(250) 405-7294
Emp Here 65   *Sales* 1,969,939

SIC 5812 Eating places

D-U-N-S 25-063-3567   (BR)
OAK LANE ENTERPRISES LTD
COUNTRY GROCER
1153 Esquimalt Rd, Victoria, BC, V9A 3N7
(250) 382-8001
Emp Here 60
SIC 5411 Grocery stores

D-U-N-S 24-087-6461   (BR)
OLD NAVY (CANADA) INC
OLD NAVY
(*Suby of* The Gap Inc)
3170 Tillicum Rd Suite 150, Victoria, BC, V9A 7C5
(250) 386-8797
Emp Here 45
SIC 5651 Family clothing stores

D-U-N-S 20-691-9107   (SL)
POINT HOPE MARITIME LTD
(*Suby of* Ralmax Group Holdings Ltd)
345 Harbour Rd, Victoria, BC, V9A 3S2
(250) 385-3623
Emp Here 21   *Sales* 1,824,018
SIC 3731 Shipbuilding and repairing

D-U-N-S 20-194-5172   (BR)
READ JONES CHRISTOFFERSEN LTD
645 Tyee Rd Suite 220, Victoria, BC, V9A 6X5
(250) 386-7794
Emp Here 30
SIC 8711 Engineering services

D-U-N-S 24-957-6950   (BR)
SLEGG DEVELOPMENTS LTD
SLEGG LUMBER
1496 Admirals Rd, Victoria, BC, V9A 2R1
(250) 388-5443
Emp Here 55
SIC 5039 Construction materials, nec

D-U-N-S 25-970-9681   (BR)
SOBEYS WEST INC
TILLICUM SAFEWAY
3170 Tillicum Rd Unit 108, Victoria, BC, V9A 7C7
(250) 384-7714
Emp Here 50
SIC 5411 Grocery stores

D-U-N-S 24-448-2782   (SL)
SPINNAKERS BREWPUB & GUESTHOUSES INC
SPINNAKERS GASTRO BREWPUB
308 Catherine St, Victoria, BC, V9A 3S8
(250) 386-2739
Emp Here 65   *Sales* 1,969,939
SIC 5812 Eating places

D-U-N-S 20-300-7067   (BR)
STANTEC ARCHITECTURE LTD
655 Tyee Rd Suite 400, Victoria, BC, V9A 6X5
(250) 388-9161
Emp Here 70
SIC 8712 Architectural services

D-U-N-S 24-310-5850   (BR)
STANTEC CONSULTING LTD
655 Tyee Rd Suite 400, Victoria, BC, V9A 6X5
(250) 388-9161
Emp Here 70
SIC 8711 Engineering services

D-U-N-S 20-506-0580   (BR)
STARBUCKS COFFEE CANADA, INC
(*Suby of* Starbucks Corporation)
3170 Tillicum Rd Suite 101a, Victoria, BC, V9A 7C5
(250) 414-0442
Emp Here 20
SIC 5812 Eating places

D-U-N-S 20-032-3199   (SL)
VICTORIA HARBOUR FERRY CO LTD
922 Old Esquimalt Rd, Victoria, BC, V9A 4X3
(250) 708-0201
Emp Here 30   *Sales* 9,942,100

SIC 4725 Tour operators
Pr Paul Miller

D-U-N-S 25-054-5647　　(BR)
WINNERS MERCHANTS INTERNATIONAL L.P.
WINNERS
(*Suby of* The TJX Companies Inc)
3170 Tillicum Rd, Victoria, BC, V9A 7C5
(250) 361-4511
Emp Here 40
SIC 5651 Family clothing stores

Victoria, BC V9B
Capital County

D-U-N-S 24-979-9750　　(BR)
112792 CANADA INC
A M J CAMPBELL VAN LINES
2924f Jacklin Rd Unit 137, Victoria, BC, V9B 3Y5
(250) 474-2225
Emp Here 20
SIC 4214 Local trucking with storage

D-U-N-S 20-021-3585　　(SL)
ALLTERRA CONSTRUCTION LTD
2158 Millstream Rd, Victoria, BC, V9B 6H4
(250) 658-3772
Emp Here 50　　*Sales* 3,648,035
SIC 1794 Excavation work

D-U-N-S 20-917-1453　　(SL)
ALPHA HOME HEALTH CARE LTD
1701 Island Hwy, Victoria, BC, V9B 1J1
(250) 383-4423
Emp Here 60　　*Sales* 2,845,467
SIC 8059 Nursing and personal care, nec

D-U-N-S 20-100-3662　　(HQ)
BALMORAL INVESTMENTS LTD
COMFORT INN & SUITES
(*Suby of* Balmoral Investments Ltd)
101 Island Hwy, Victoria, BC, V9B 1E8
(250) 388-7307
Emp Here 30　　*Emp Total* 300
Sales 18,086,400
SIC 7011 Hotels and motels
　Maria Petraroia
VP VP Dominic Petraroia
Dir Anita Simo

D-U-N-S 20-845-3071　　(BR)
BOARD OF EDUCATION OF SCHOOL DISTRICT NO. 61 (GREATER VICTORIA)
EAGLE VIEW ELEMENTARY SCHOOL
97 Talcott Rd, Victoria, BC, V9B 6L9
(250) 744-2701
Emp Here 25
SIC 8211 Elementary and secondary schools

D-U-N-S 24-345-0959　　(BR)
BOARD OF EDUCATION OF SCHOOL DISTRICT NO. 61 (GREATER VICTORIA)
SHORELINE COMMUNITY SCHOOL
2750 Shoreline Dr, Victoria, BC, V9B 1M6
(250) 386-8367
Emp Here 60
SIC 8299 Schools and educational services, nec

D-U-N-S 20-981-6284　　(BR)
BOARD OF EDUCATION OF SCHOOL DISTRICT NO. 61 (GREATER VICTORIA)
VIEW ROYAL ELEMENTARY SCHOOL
218 Helmcken Rd, Victoria, BC, V9B 1S6
(250) 479-1671
Emp Here 35
SIC 8211 Elementary and secondary schools

D-U-N-S 25-231-7631　　(BR)
BRICK WAREHOUSE LP, THE
2945 Jacklin Rd Suite 500, Victoria, BC, V9B 5E3
(250) 380-1133
Emp Here 25

SIC 5712 Furniture stores

D-U-N-S 20-276-3777　　(SL)
CDG COAST DYNAMICS GROUP LTD
SHOXS
2932 Ed Nixon Ter Unit 102, Victoria, BC, V9B 0B2
(250) 652-6003
Emp Here 26　　*Sales* 5,484,462
SIC 3429 Hardware, nec
Pr Pr Ray Cao

D-U-N-S 25-831-9458　　(BR)
COSTCO WHOLESALE CANADA LTD
(*Suby of* Costco Wholesale Corporation)
799 Mccallum Rd, Victoria, BC, V9B 6A2
(250) 391-1151
Emp Here 200
SIC 5099 Durable goods, nec

D-U-N-S 24-132-4511　　(BR)
DFH REAL ESTATE LTD
650 Goldstream Ave, Victoria, BC, V9B 2W8
(250) 474-6003
Emp Here 32
SIC 6531 Real estate agents and managers

D-U-N-S 24-390-5861　　(BR)
GOLF TOWN LIMITED
GOLF TOWN
2401a Millstream Rd Unit 141, Victoria, BC, V9B 3R5
(250) 391-4500
Emp Here 25
SIC 5941 Sporting goods and bicycle shops

D-U-N-S 25-994-1482　　(BR)
GOVERNING COUNCIL OF THE SALVATION ARMY IN CANADA, THE
GOVERNING COUNCIL OF THE SALVATION ARMY IN CANADA, THE
1746 Island Hwy, Victoria, BC, V9B 1H8
(250) 727-3853
Emp Here 20
SIC 8399 Social services, nec

D-U-N-S 25-684-7443　　(BR)
HOME DEPOT OF CANADA INC
HOME DEPOT
(*Suby of* The Home Depot Inc)
2400 Millstream Rd, Victoria, BC, V9B 3R3
(250) 391-6001
Emp Here 200
SIC 5251 Hardware stores

D-U-N-S 20-106-3935　　(BR)
HUDSON'S BAY COMPANY
HOME OUTFITTERS
759 Mccallum Rd, Victoria, BC, V9B 6A2

Emp Here 45
SIC 5719 Miscellaneous homefurnishings

D-U-N-S 25-958-5487　　(BR)
INTACT INSURANCE COMPANY
2401 Millstream Rd Suite 246, Victoria, BC, V9B 3R5
(250) 385-0866
Emp Here 48
SIC 6331 Fire, marine, and casualty insurance

D-U-N-S 20-958-7989　　(SL)
JENNER CHEVROLET BUICK GMC LTD
1730 Island Hwy, Victoria, BC, V9B 1H8
(250) 474-1255
Emp Here 50　　*Sales* 3,648,035
SIC 7538 General automotive repair shops

D-U-N-S 24-309-0917　　(BR)
KENNAMETAL LTD
(*Suby of* Kennametal Inc.)
873 Station Ave, Victoria, BC, V9B 2S2
(250) 474-1225
Emp Here 55
SIC 3541 Machine tools, Metal cutting type

D-U-N-S 20-949-8240　　(BR)
LOBLAWS INC
DRUGSTORE PHARMACY

---

835 Langford Pky, Victoria, BC, V9B 4V5
(250) 391-3135
Emp Here 20
SIC 5912 Drug stores and proprietary stores

D-U-N-S 25-273-1534　　(BR)
LONDON DRUGS LIMITED
1907 Sooke Rd, Victoria, BC, V9B 1V8
(250) 474-0900
Emp Here 100
SIC 5912 Drug stores and proprietary stores

D-U-N-S 20-570-8238　　(BR)
LORDCO PARTS LTD
LORDCO AUTO PARTS
2901 Jacklin Rd, Victoria, BC, V9B 3Y6
(250) 391-1438
Emp Here 20
SIC 5531 Auto and home supply stores

D-U-N-S 24-890-3747　　(BR)
PRINCESS AUTO LTD
1037 Jacklin Pky, Victoria, BC, V9B 0A5
(250) 391-5652
Emp Here 25
SIC 5511 New and used car dealers

D-U-N-S 20-591-6575　　(BR)
SCHOOL DISTRICT NO 62 (SOOKE)
RUTH KING ELEMENTARY
2764 Jacklin Rd, Victoria, BC, V9B 3X6
(250) 478-8368
Emp Here 40
SIC 8211 Elementary and secondary schools

D-U-N-S 20-032-3678　　(BR)
SCHOOL DISTRICT NO 62 (SOOKE)
LAKEWOOD ELEMENTARY SCHOOL
2363 Setchfield Ave, Victoria, BC, V9B 5W1
(250) 474-3449
Emp Here 23
SIC 8211 Elementary and secondary schools

D-U-N-S 20-591-6583　　(BR)
SCHOOL DISTRICT NO 62 (SOOKE)
WILLWAY ELEMENTARY
2939 Mt. Wells Dr, Victoria, BC, V9B 4T4
(250) 478-1213
Emp Here 25
SIC 8211 Elementary and secondary schools

D-U-N-S 20-713-5596　　(BR)
SCHOOL DISTRICT NO 62 (SOOKE)
SPENCER MIDDLE SCHOOL
1026 Goldstream Ave, Victoria, BC, V9B 2Y5
(250) 474-1291
Emp Here 50
SIC 8211 Elementary and secondary schools

D-U-N-S 20-713-5521　　(BR)
SCHOOL DISTRICT NO 62 (SOOKE)
GLEN LAKE ELEMENTARY SCHOOL
3060 Glen Lake Rd, Victoria, BC, V9B 4B4

Emp Here 50
SIC 8211 Elementary and secondary schools

D-U-N-S 20-713-5604　　(BR)
SCHOOL DISTRICT NO 62 (SOOKE)
CRYSTAL VIEW ELEMENTARY SCHOOL
2662 Silverstone Way, Victoria, BC, V9B 6A6
(250) 478-0576
Emp Here 25
SIC 8211 Elementary and secondary schools

D-U-N-S 20-713-5513　　(BR)
SCHOOL DISTRICT NO 62 (SOOKE)
BELMONT SECONDARY SCHOOL
3067 Jacklin Rd, Victoria, BC, V9B 3Y7
(250) 478-5501
Emp Here 120
SIC 8211 Elementary and secondary schools

D-U-N-S 20-591-6674　　(BR)
SCHOOL DISTRICT NO 62 (SOOKE)
MILL STREAM ELEMENTARY SCHOOL
626 Hoylake Ave, Victoria, BC, V9B 3P7
(250) 478-8348
Emp Here 25

SIC 8211 Elementary and secondary schools

D-U-N-S 20-591-6567　　(BR)
SCHOOL DISTRICT NO 62 (SOOKE)
SAVORY ELEMENTARY SCHOOL
2721 Grainger Rd, Victoria, BC, V9B 3K7
(250) 478-9586
Emp Here 20
SIC 8211 Elementary and secondary schools

D-U-N-S 20-027-0325　　(BR)
SCHOOL DISTRICT NO 62 (SOOKE)
DAVID CAMERON ELEMENTARY SCHOOL
675 Meaford Ave, Victoria, BC, V9B 5Y1
(250) 478-7621
Emp Here 48
SIC 8211 Elementary and secondary schools

D-U-N-S 20-591-6559　　(BR)
SCHOOL DISTRICT NO 62 (SOOKE)
WESTSHORE COLWOOD CAMPUS
1830 Island Hwy Suite 109, Victoria, BC, V9B 1J2
(250) 474-2505
Emp Here 20
SIC 8249 Vocational schools, nec

D-U-N-S 25-086-0756　　(BR)
SLEEP COUNTRY CANADA INC
1045 Henry Eng Pl, Victoria, BC, V9B 6B2
(250) 475-2755
Emp Here 20
SIC 5712 Furniture stores

D-U-N-S 20-569-9395　　(BR)
STAPLES CANADA INC
STAPLES THE BUSINESS DEPOT
(*Suby of* Staples, Inc.)
789 Mccallum Rd, Victoria, BC, V9B 6A2
(250) 391-3070
Emp Here 30
SIC 5943 Stationery stores

D-U-N-S 24-629-6839　　(BR)
STARBUCKS COFFEE CANADA, INC
STARBUCKS
(*Suby of* Starbucks Corporation)
782 Goldstream Ave, Victoria, BC, V9B 2X3
(250) 474-3937
Emp Here 20
SIC 5812 Eating places

D-U-N-S 20-321-6754　　(BR)
SYSCO CANADA, INC
NORTH DOUGLAS SYSCO
(*Suby of* Sysco Corporation)
2881 Amy Rd, Victoria, BC, V9B 0B2
(250) 475-3311
Emp Here 250
SIC 5141 Groceries, general line

D-U-N-S 25-932-6544　　(BR)
VANCOUVER ISLAND HEALTH AUTHORITY
WEST SHORE HEALTH UNIT
345 Wale Rd, Victoria, BC, V9B 6X2
(250) 519-3490
Emp Here 25
SIC 8011 Offices and clinics of medical doctors

D-U-N-S 20-915-2946　　(BR)
VANCOUVER ISLAND HEALTH AUTHORITY
PRIORY, THE
567 Goldstream Ave, Victoria, BC, V9B 2W4
(250) 370-5790
Emp Here 150
SIC 8051 Skilled nursing care facilities

D-U-N-S 20-927-3908　　(BR)
WENDY'S RESTAURANTS OF CANADA INC
WENDY'S
(*Suby of* The Wendy's Company)
1800 Island Hwy, Victoria, BC, V9B 1J2
(250) 478-7511
Emp Here 30
SIC 5812 Eating places

D-U-N-S 20-707-9331 (SL)
WEST SHORE PARKS AND RECREATION SOCIETY
JUAN DE FUCA RECREATION CENTRE
1767 Island Hwy, Victoria, BC, V9B 1J1
(250) 478-8384
Emp Here 170 *Sales* 12,884,150
SIC 7999 Amusement and recreation, nec
Fin Mgr Sue Dickson

D-U-N-S 20-359-5863 (SL)
WESTERN GATEWAY HOTEL HOLDINGS LTD
FOUR POINTS BY SHERATON VICTORIA GATEWAY
829 Mccallum Rd Suite 101, Victoria, BC, V9B 6W6
(250) 474-6063
Emp Here 50 *Sales* 2,188,821
SIC 7011 Hotels and motels

D-U-N-S 25-255-7223 (BR)
WHITE SPOT LIMITED
941 Langford Pky, Victoria, BC, V9B 0A5
(778) 433-8800
Emp Here 60
SIC 5812 Eating places

D-U-N-S 20-860-4186 (BR)
WINNERS MERCHANTS INTERNATIONAL L.P.
WINNERS
(*Suby of* The TJX Companies Inc)
2945 Jacklin Rd Suite 400, Victoria, BC, V9B 5E3
(250) 391-1829
Emp Here 25
SIC 5651 Family clothing stores

D-U-N-S 20-032-0765 (BR)
WORLEYPARSONS CANADA SERVICES LTD
2780 Veterans Memorial Pky Suite 106, Victoria, BC, V9B 3S6

Emp Here 24
SIC 8621 Professional organizations

Victoria, BC V9C
Capital County

D-U-N-S 24-337-1809 (BR)
COLWOOD, CITY OF
COLWOOD FIRE DEPARTMENT
3215 Metchosin Rd, Victoria, BC, V9C 2A4
(250) 478-8321
Emp Here 50
SIC 7389 Business services, nec

D-U-N-S 20-654-1372 (BR)
SCHOOL DISTRICT NO 62 (SOOKE)
HANS HELGESEN ELEMENTARY SCHOOL
4983 Rocky Point Rd, Victoria, BC, V9C 4G4
(250) 478-3410
Emp Here 30
SIC 8211 Elementary and secondary schools

D-U-N-S 20-027-0929 (BR)
SCHOOL DISTRICT NO 62 (SOOKE)
DUNSMUIR MIDDLE SCHOOL
3341 Painter Rd, Victoria, BC, V9C 2J1
(250) 478-5548
Emp Here 75
SIC 8211 Elementary and secondary schools

D-U-N-S 20-713-5539 (BR)
SCHOOL DISTRICT NO 62 (SOOKE)
JOHN STUBBS MEMORIAL SCHOOL
301 Zealous Cres, Victoria, BC, V9C 1H6
(250) 478-5571
Emp Here 60
SIC 8211 Elementary and secondary schools

D-U-N-S 20-713-5570 (BR)
SCHOOL DISTRICT NO 62 (SOOKE)

WISHART ELEMENTARY SCHOOL
3310 Wishart Rd, Victoria, BC, V9C 1R1
(250) 478-9528
Emp Here 35
SIC 8211 Elementary and secondary schools

D-U-N-S 20-591-6625 (BR)
SCHOOL DISTRICT NO 62 (SOOKE)
HAPPY VALLEY ELEMENTARY SCHOOL
3291 Happy Valley Rd, Victoria, BC, V9C 2W3
(250) 478-3232
Emp Here 40
SIC 8211 Elementary and secondary schools

D-U-N-S 20-653-4302 (BR)
SCHOOL DISTRICT NO 62 (SOOKE)
SANGSTER ELEMENTARY SCHOOL
3325 Metchosin Rd, Victoria, BC, V9C 2A4
(250) 478-4441
Emp Here 25
SIC 8211 Elementary and secondary schools

D-U-N-S 25-359-9310 (BR)
SLEGG DEVELOPMENTS LTD
2901 Sooke Rd, Victoria, BC, V9C 3W7
(250) 386-3667
Emp Here 150
SIC 5031 Lumber, plywood, and millwork

Victoria, BC V9E
Capital County

D-U-N-S 20-705-8160 (SL)
INTEGRITY WALL SYSTEMS INC
1371 Courtland Ave, Victoria, BC, V9E 2C5
(250) 480-5500
Emp Here 80 *Sales* 2,918,428
SIC 5714 Drapery and upholstery stores

D-U-N-S 24-685-4157 (BR)
RED BARN COUNTRY MARKET LTD
5550 West Saanich Rd, Victoria, BC, V9E 2G1
(250) 479-8349
Emp Here 50
SIC 5411 Grocery stores

Wasa, BC V0B
East Kootenay County

D-U-N-S 20-590-5131 (BR)
BOARD OF EDUCATION OF SCHOOL DISTRICT NO. 06 (ROCKY MOUNTAIN), THE
WASA ELEMENTARY SCHOOL
6171 Wasa School, Wasa, BC, V0B 2K0
(250) 422-3494
Emp Here 25
SIC 8211 Elementary and secondary schools

West Kelowna, BC V1Z

D-U-N-S 25-679-4959 (BR)
AIR LIQUIDE CANADA INC
SUPERIOR WELDING SUPPLIES
1405 Stevens Rd Unit 360, West Kelowna, BC, V1Z 3Y2
(250) 769-4280
Emp Here 45
SIC 2813 Industrial gases

D-U-N-S 25-014-8145 (BR)
BOARD OF EDUCATION OF SCHOOL DISTRICT NO. 23 (CENTRAL OKANAGAN), THE
ROSE VALLEY ELEMENTARY SCHOOL
1680 Westlake Rd, West Kelowna, BC, V1Z 3G6
(250) 870-5146
Emp Here 40
SIC 8211 Elementary and secondary schools

D-U-N-S 25-015-3236 (BR)
BOARD OF EDUCATION OF SCHOOL DISTRICT NO. 23 (CENTRAL OKANAGAN), THE
HUDSON ROAD ELEMENTARY SCHOOL
1221 Hudson Rd, West Kelowna, BC, V1Z 1J5

Emp Here 26
SIC 8211 Elementary and secondary schools

D-U-N-S 20-713-2551 (BR)
BOARD OF EDUCATION OF SCHOOL DISTRICT NO. 23 (CENTRAL OKANAGAN), THE
CONSTABLE NEIL BRUCE MIDDLE SCHOOL
2010 Daimler Dr, West Kelowna, BC, V1Z 3Y4

Emp Here 50
SIC 8211 Elementary and secondary schools

D-U-N-S 25-841-6502 (BR)
BUY-LOW FOODS LTD
G & H MARKETING ENTERPRISE
891 Anders Rd, West Kelowna, BC, V1Z 1K2
(250) 769-6502
Emp Here 20
SIC 5411 Grocery stores

D-U-N-S 25-648-3322 (BR)
REGIONAL DISTRICT OF CENTRAL OKANAGAN
MOUNT BOUCHERIE COMMUNITY CENTRE
2760 Cameron Rd, West Kelowna, BC, V1Z 2T6
(250) 469-6160
Emp Here 40
SIC 7999 Amusement and recreation, nec

D-U-N-S 25-631-0160 (BR)
VIC VAN ISLE CONSTRUCTION LTD
LORTAP ENTERPRISES
1240 Industrial Rd, West Kelowna, BC, V1Z 1G5
(250) 769-9460
Emp Here 20
SIC 1542 Nonresidential construction, nec

West Kelowna, BC V4T

D-U-N-S 20-713-2536 (BR)
BOARD OF EDUCATION OF SCHOOL DISTRICT NO. 23 (CENTRAL OKANAGAN), THE
HELEN GORMAN ELEMENTARY SCHOOL
3230 Salmon Rd, West Kelowna, BC, V4T 1A7

Emp Here 50
SIC 8211 Elementary and secondary schools

D-U-N-S 20-024-4734 (BR)
BOARD OF EDUCATION OF SCHOOL DISTRICT NO. 23 (CENTRAL OKANAGAN), THE
GLENROSA ELEMENTARY SCHOOL
3430 Webber Rd, West Kelowna, BC, V4T 1G8
(250) 870-5142
Emp Here 30
SIC 8211 Elementary and secondary schools

D-U-N-S 25-150-3926 (BR)
BOARD OF EDUCATION OF SCHOOL DISTRICT NO. 23 (CENTRAL OKANAGAN), THE
GLENROSA MIDDLE SCHOOL
3565 Mciver Rd, West Kelowna, BC, V4T 1H8
(250) 768-1889
Emp Here 60
SIC 8211 Elementary and secondary schools

D-U-N-S 20-591-5544 (BR)
BOARD OF EDUCATION OF SCHOOL DISTRICT NO. 23 (CENTRAL OKANAGAN),

THE
SHANNON LAKE ELEMENTARY SCHOOL
3044 Sandstone Dr, West Kelowna, BC, V4T 1T2
(250) 870-5132
Emp Here 25
SIC 8211 Elementary and secondary schools

D-U-N-S 25-846-7521 (BR)
COOPER MARKET LTD
COOPER'S FOODS
2484 Main St Unit 32, West Kelowna, BC, V4T 2G2
(250) 768-2272
Emp Here 25
SIC 5411 Grocery stores

D-U-N-S 24-682-3207 (BR)
GREAT PACIFIC INDUSTRIES INC
SAVE-ON-FOODS
2475 Dobbin Rd Suite 1, West Kelowna, BC, V4T 2E9
(250) 768-2323
Emp Here 130
SIC 5411 Grocery stores

D-U-N-S 20-734-4099 (BR)
INTERIOR HEALTH AUTHORITY
BROOK HAVEN CARE CENTRE
1775 Shannon Lake Rd, West Kelowna, BC, V4T 2N7
(250) 862-4040
Emp Here 50
SIC 8062 General medical and surgical hospitals

D-U-N-S 25-605-0105 (BR)
INTERIOR SAVINGS CREDIT UNION
3718 Elliott Rd, West Kelowna, BC, V4T 2H7
(250) 469-6550
Emp Here 22
SIC 6062 State credit unions

D-U-N-S 20-733-3290 (SL)
LANG'S VENTURES INC
LVI DIGITAL GROUP & LVI TECHNOLOGY GROUP
3099 Shannon Lake Rd Suite 105, West Kelowna, BC, V4T 2M2
(250) 768-7055
Emp Here 80 *Sales* 3,724,879
SIC 7629 Electrical repair shops

D-U-N-S 24-035-3222 (SL)
MCDONALDS
3605 Gellatly Rd, West Kelowna, BC, V4T 2E6
(250) 768-3806
Emp Here 65 *Sales* 1,969,939
SIC 5812 Eating places

D-U-N-S 25-174-0189 (BR)
PRISZM LP
KFC
3620 Gellatly Rd, West Kelowna, BC, V4T 2E6

Emp Here 20
SIC 5812 Eating places

D-U-N-S 20-348-9633 (BR)
RLK REALTY LTD
ROYAL LEPAGE
2475 Dobbin Rd Suite 11, West Kelowna, BC, V4T 2E9
(250) 768-2161
Emp Here 50
SIC 6531 Real estate agents and managers

D-U-N-S 25-124-9587 (BR)
WILPAT INDUSTRIES LTD
DAIRY QUEEN
(*Suby of* Wilpat Industries Ltd)
2557 Dobbin Rd, West Kelowna, BC, V4T 2J6
(250) 768-4331
Emp Here 25
SIC 5812 Eating places

West Vancouver, BC V7P
Greater Vancouver County

D-U-N-S 25-613-3034   (BR)
EARL'S RESTAURANTS LTD
EARL'S TIN PALACE
(*Suby of* Earl's Restaurants Ltd)
303 Marine Dr, West Vancouver, BC, V7P 3J8
(604) 984-4341
Emp Here 150
SIC 5812 Eating places

West Vancouver, BC V7S
Greater Vancouver County

D-U-N-S 24-995-3761   (SL)
CAPILANO GOLF AND COUNTRY CLUB LIMITED
420 Southborough Dr, West Vancouver, BC, V7S 1M2
(604) 922-9331
Emp Here 67   *Sales* 2,699,546
SIC 7997 Membership sports and recreation clubs

D-U-N-S 20-288-5471   (BR)
COLLINGWOOD SCHOOL SOCIETY
COLLINGWOOD SCHOOL WENTWORTH.
2605 Wentworth Ave, West Vancouver, BC, V7S 3H4
(604) 925-8375
Emp Here 150
SIC 8211 Elementary and secondary schools

D-U-N-S 25-506-8793   (SL)
CYPRESS BOWL ULC
(*Suby of* Boyne Usa, Inc.)
3755 Cypress Bowl Rd, West Vancouver, BC, V7S 3E7
(604) 926-5612
Emp Here 30   *Sales* 1,313,293
SIC 7011 Hotels and motels

D-U-N-S 20-591-0099   (BR)
SCHOOL DISTRICT NO. 45 (WEST VANCOUVER)
CHARTWELL ELEMENTARY SCHOOL
1300 Chartwell Dr, West Vancouver, BC, V7S 2R3
(604) 981-1210
Emp Here 25
SIC 8211 Elementary and secondary schools

D-U-N-S 20-009-7116   (BR)
THE BOARD OF SCHOOL TRUSTEES OF SCHOOL DISTRICT NO. 45 (WEST VANCOUVER)
SENTINEL SECONDARY SCHOOL
(*Suby of* The Board of School Trustees of School District No. 45 (West Vancouver))
1250 Chartwell Dr, West Vancouver, BC, V7S 2R2
(604) 981-1130
Emp Here 85
SIC 8211 Elementary and secondary schools

D-U-N-S 20-009-6498   (BR)
THE BOARD OF SCHOOL TRUSTEES OF SCHOOL DISTRICT NO. 45 (WEST VANCOUVER)
WESTCOT ELEMENTARY SCHOOL
(*Suby of* The Board of School Trustees of School District No. 45 (West Vancouver))
760 Westcot Rd, West Vancouver, BC, V7S 1N7
(604) 981-1270
Emp Here 35
SIC 8211 Elementary and secondary schools

West Vancouver, BC V7T
Greater Vancouver County

D-U-N-S 20-610-5079   (SL)

AMICA AT WEST VANCOUVER
659 Clyde Ave, West Vancouver, BC, V7T 1C8
(604) 921-9181
Emp Here 52   *Sales* 2,480,664
SIC 8059 Nursing and personal care, nec

D-U-N-S 20-191-1638   (BR)
BEST BUY CANADA LTD
FUTURE SHOP
(*Suby of* Best Buy Co., Inc.)
2100 Park Royal S, West Vancouver, BC, V7T 2W4
(604) 913-3336
Emp Here 120
SIC 5731 Radio, television, and electronic stores

D-U-N-S 20-198-8396   (BR)
BRICK WAREHOUSE LP, THE
2205 Park Royal S, West Vancouver, BC, V7T 2W5
(604) 921-4600
Emp Here 26
SIC 5712 Furniture stores

D-U-N-S 25-316-5518   (BR)
BRITISH COLUMBIA AUTOMOBILE ASSOCIATION
BCAA
608 Park Royal N, West Vancouver, BC, V7T 1H9
(604) 268-5650
Emp Here 30
SIC 8699 Membership organizations, nec

D-U-N-S 24-337-3425   (BR)
FGL SPORTS LTD
COAST MOUNTAIN SPORTS
1000 Park Royal S, West Vancouver, BC, V7T 1A1
(604) 922-3336
Emp Here 50
SIC 5941 Sporting goods and bicycle shops

D-U-N-S 25-612-4199   (BR)
GAP (CANADA) INC
GAP
(*Suby of* The Gap Inc)
640 Park Royal N, West Vancouver, BC, V7T 1H9
(604) 925-3639
Emp Here 40
SIC 5651 Family clothing stores

D-U-N-S 20-331-7909   (BR)
GAP (CANADA) INC
BANANA REPUBLIC
(*Suby of* The Gap Inc)
640 Park Royal N, West Vancouver, BC, V7T 1H9
(604) 913-2461
Emp Here 20
SIC 5651 Family clothing stores

D-U-N-S 24-133-5004   (BR)
GIRL GUIDES OF CANADA/GUIDES DU CANADA
1124 Inglewood Ave, West Vancouver, BC, V7T 1Y5
(604) 922-1124
Emp Here 20
SIC 8641 Civic and social associations

D-U-N-S 20-553-6209   (BR)
HOME DEPOT OF CANADA INC
(*Suby of* The Home Depot Inc)
840 Main St Suite E1, West Vancouver, BC, V7T 2Z3
(604) 913-2630
Emp Here 100
SIC 5251 Hardware stores

D-U-N-S 24-957-9327   (BR)
HUDSON'S BAY COMPANY
BAY, THE
725 Park Royal N, West Vancouver, BC, V7T 1H9
(604) 925-1411
Emp Here 225

SIC 5311 Department stores

D-U-N-S 24-224-3496   (BR)
KUMON CANADA INC
1410 Clyde Ave, West Vancouver, BC, V7T 1G1
(604) 926-0169
Emp Here 30
SIC 8299 Schools and educational services, nec

D-U-N-S 24-030-2778   (HQ)
LARCO INVESTMENTS LTD
MAPLE LEAF SELF STORAGE
(*Suby of* Larco Investments Ltd)
100 Park Royal S Suite 300, West Vancouver, BC, V7T 1A2
(604) 925-2700
Emp Here 35   *Emp Total* 50
Sales 7,016,633
SIC 6719 Holding companies, nec
Pr Pr Aminmohamed J. Lalji
  Vazir Kara
Sr VP Mansoor Lalji

D-U-N-S 25-513-7028   (BR)
LARCO INVESTMENTS LTD
PARK ROYAL SHOPPING CENTRE
(*Suby of* Larco Investments Ltd)
2002 Park Royal S, West Vancouver, BC, V7T 2W4
(604) 925-9547
Emp Here 50
SIC 6512 Nonresidential building operators

D-U-N-S 24-027-5433   (BR)
OLD NAVY (CANADA) INC
OLD NAVY
(*Suby of* The Gap Inc)
860 Main St Suite 1d, West Vancouver, BC, V7T 2Z3
(604) 921-8808
Emp Here 50
SIC 5651 Family clothing stores

D-U-N-S 24-882-1621   (SL)
PARK ROYAL SHOPPING CENTRE HOLDINGS LTD
(*Suby of* Larco Investments Ltd)
100 Park Royal S Suite 100, West Vancouver, BC, V7T 1A2
(604) 925-2700
Emp Here 20   *Sales* 2,454,000
SIC 6512 Nonresidential building operators

D-U-N-S 25-717-3328   (BR)
RBC DOMINION SECURITIES INC
(*Suby of* Royal Bank Of Canada)
250 15th St Suite 201, West Vancouver, BC, V7T 2X4
(604) 981-6600
Emp Here 40
SIC 6282 Investment advice

D-U-N-S 25-287-9101   (BR)
RAYMOND SALONS LTD
HENNESSEY RAYMOND SALON
(*Suby of* Raymond Salons Ltd)
988 Park Royal S Suit 2034, West Vancouver, BC, V7T 1A1
(604) 981-3300
Emp Here 27
SIC 7231 Beauty shops

D-U-N-S 25-287-9903   (BR)
RAYMOND SALONS LTD
(*Suby of* Raymond Salons Ltd)
782 Park Royal N, West Vancouver, BC, V7T 1H9

Emp Here 25
SIC 7231 Beauty shops

D-U-N-S 25-613-4834   (BR)
ROYAL BANK OF CANADA
ROYAL BANK FINANCIAL GROUP
(*Suby of* Royal Bank Of Canada)
672 Park Royal N, West Vancouver, BC, V7T

1H9
(604) 981-6500
Emp Here 40
SIC 6021 National commercial banks

D-U-N-S 20-591-0081   (BR)
SCHOOL DISTRICT NO. 45 (WEST VANCOUVER)
RIDGEVIEW ELEMENTARY SCHOOL
1250 Mathers Ave, West Vancouver, BC, V7T 2G3
(604) 981-1250
Emp Here 25
SIC 8211 Elementary and secondary schools

D-U-N-S 25-367-4295   (BR)
STAPLES CANADA INC
STAPLES THE BUSINESS DEPOT
(*Suby of* Staples, Inc.)
2105 Park Royal S, West Vancouver, BC, V7T 2W5
(604) 913-4270
Emp Here 25
SIC 5943 Stationery stores

D-U-N-S 20-009-7553   (BR)
THE BOARD OF SCHOOL TRUSTEES OF SCHOOL DISTRICT NO. 45 (WEST VANCOUVER)
HOLLYBURN ELEMENTARY SCHOOL
(*Suby of* The Board of School Trustees of School District No. 45 (West Vancouver))
1329 Duchess Ave, West Vancouver, BC, V7T 1H5
(604) 981-1220
Emp Here 40
SIC 8211 Elementary and secondary schools

D-U-N-S 25-613-5377   (BR)
TORONTO-DOMINION BANK, THE
TD CANADA TRUST
(*Suby of* Toronto-Dominion Bank, The)
632 Park Royal N, West Vancouver, BC, V7T 1H9
(604) 926-5484
Emp Here 20
SIC 6021 National commercial banks

D-U-N-S 20-860-5167   (BR)
TOWN SHOES LIMITED
SHOE COMPANY, THE
2002 Park Royal S Unit 2021, West Vancouver, BC, V7T 2W4
(604) 922-2253
Emp Here 25
SIC 5661 Shoe stores

D-U-N-S 24-567-0229   (HQ)
WGI MANUFACTURING INC
DIAMOND-KOTE
1455 Bellevue Ave Suite 300, West Vancouver, BC, V7T 1C3
(604) 922-6563
Emp Here 30   *Emp Total* 50
Sales 4,729,099
SIC 2842 Polishes and sanitation goods

D-U-N-S 20-512-9190   (BR)
WHITE SPOT LIMITED
WHITE SPOT RESTAURANT
752 Marine Dr Unit 1108, West Vancouver, BC, V7T 1A6
(604) 922-4520
Emp Here 79
SIC 5812 Eating places

D-U-N-S 20-554-3981   (HQ)
WHOLE FOODS MARKET CANADA INC
925 Main St, West Vancouver, BC, V7T 2Z3
(604) 678-0500
Emp Here 50   *Emp Total* 90,900
Sales 17,338,854
SIC 5411 Grocery stores
Mgr Jorge Sosa

D-U-N-S 20-860-4202   (BR)
WINNERS MERCHANTS INTERNATIONAL L.P.

HOMESENSE
(*Suby of* The TJX Companies Inc)
782 Park Royal N, West Vancouver, BC, V7T
1H9
(604) 913-2990
Emp Here 25
SIC 5651 Family clothing stores

D-U-N-S 20-184-3013   (BR)
**WINNERS MERCHANTS INTERNATIONAL
L.P.**
WINNERS
(*Suby of* The TJX Companies Inc)
2002 Park Royal S Unit 1120, West Vancouver, BC, V7T 2W4
(604) 926-0944
Emp Here 40
SIC 5651 Family clothing stores

West Vancouver, BC V7V
Greater Vancouver County

D-U-N-S 24-337-2104   (BR)
GOLD RUSH PIZZA INC
DOMINO'S PIZZA
(*Suby of* Gold Rush Pizza Inc)
1826 Marine Dr, West Vancouver, BC, V7V
1J6
(604) 922-3013
Emp Here 20
SIC 5812 Eating places

D-U-N-S 25-719-0066   (BR)
MACDONALD REALTY (1974) LTD
1575 Marine Dr, West Vancouver, BC, V7V
1H9
(604) 926-6718
Emp Here 72
SIC 6531 Real estate agents and managers

D-U-N-S 24-382-1019   (BR)
REVERA INC
HOLLYBURN HOUSE
2095 Marine Dr Suite 126, West Vancouver,
BC, V7V 4V5
(604) 922-7616
Emp Here 40
SIC 6513 Apartment building operators

D-U-N-S 25-613-4826   (BR)
ROYAL BANK OF CANADA
ROYAL BANK FINANCIAL GROUP
(*Suby of* Royal Bank Of Canada)
1705 Marine Dr, West Vancouver, BC, V7V
1J5
(604) 981-6550
Emp Here 35
SIC 6021 National commercial banks

D-U-N-S 24-975-0423   (BR)
ROYAL LEPAGE LIMITED
ROYAL LEPAGE NORTH SHORE
2407 Marine Dr, West Vancouver, BC, V7V
1L3
(604) 926-6011
Emp Here 70
SIC 6531 Real estate agents and managers

D-U-N-S 20-021-6682   (BR)
**SCHOOL DISTRICT NO. 45 (WEST VAN-
COUVER)**
WEST BAY ELEMENTARY SCHOOL
3175 Thompson Pl, West Vancouver, BC, V7V
3E3
(604) 981-1260
Emp Here 30
SIC 8211 Elementary and secondary schools

D-U-N-S 24-345-6360   (BR)
**SCHOOL DISTRICT NO. 45 (WEST VAN-
COUVER)**
WEST VANCOUVER SECONDARY SCHOOL
1750 Mathers Ave, West Vancouver, BC, V7V
2G7
(604) 981-1100
Emp Here 150

SIC 8211 Elementary and secondary schools

D-U-N-S 20-939-4522   (BR)
**SCHOOL DISTRICT NO. 45 (WEST VAN-
COUVER)**
*PAULINE JOHNSON FRENCH IMMERSION
SCHOOL*
1150 22nd St, West Vancouver, BC, V7V 4C4
(604) 922-4214
Emp Here 35
SIC 8211 Elementary and secondary schools

D-U-N-S 20-591-0107   (BR)
**SCHOOL DISTRICT NO. 45 (WEST VAN-
COUVER)**
IRWIN PARK ELEMENTARY
2455 Haywood Ave, West Vancouver, BC, V7V
1Y2
(604) 981-1240
Emp Here 35
SIC 8211 Elementary and secondary schools

D-U-N-S 24-341-0839   (BR)
SCOTIA CAPITAL INC
SCOTIA MCLEOD
1555 Marine Dr, West Vancouver, BC, V7V
1H9
(604) 913-7013
Emp Here 30
SIC 6211 Security brokers and dealers

D-U-N-S 20-591-0115   (BR)
**THE BOARD OF SCHOOL TRUSTEES OF
SCHOOL DISTRICT NO. 45 (WEST VAN-
COUVER)**
CYPRESS PARK PRIMARY SCHOOL
(*Suby of* The Board of School Trustees of
School District No. 45 (West Vancouver))
4355 Marine Dr, West Vancouver, BC, V7V
1P2
(604) 922-4211
Emp Here 25
SIC 8211 Elementary and secondary schools

D-U-N-S 24-980-2968   (HQ)
**THE BOARD OF SCHOOL TRUSTEES OF
SCHOOL DISTRICT NO. 45 (WEST VAN-
COUVER)**
SCHOOL DISTRICT #45
(*Suby of* The Board of School Trustees of
School District No. 45 (West Vancouver))
1075 21st St, West Vancouver, BC, V7V 4A9
(604) 981-1000
Emp Here 100   *Emp Total* 550
Sales 49,472,640
SIC 8211 Elementary and secondary schools
Ch Bd Mary-Anne Booth
V Ch Bd Cindy Decker
Trst Cindy Dekker
Superintnt Geoff Jopson
Trst Barry Lindahl

West Vancouver, BC V7W
Greater Vancouver County

D-U-N-S 20-567-8134   (BR)
BANK OF MONTREAL
BMO
5377 Headland Dr, West Vancouver, BC, V7W
3C7
(604) 668-1213
Emp Here 20
SIC 6021 National commercial banks

D-U-N-S 20-591-0156   (BR)
**SCHOOL DISTRICT NO. 45 (WEST VAN-
COUVER)**
GLENEAGLES ELEMENTARY
6350 Marine Dr, West Vancouver, BC, V7W
2S5
(604) 981-1360
Emp Here 31
SIC 8211 Elementary and secondary schools

D-U-N-S 20-115-8177   (HQ)

SERVICE DRUG LTD
PHARMASAVE #214
(*Suby of* Service Drug Ltd)
5331 Headland Dr, West Vancouver, BC, V7W
3C6
(604) 926-5331
Emp Here 40   *Emp Total* 50
Sales 7,077,188
SIC 5912 Drug stores and proprietary stores
Robert Williamson
Patricia Williamson
Pr Pr Alan Williamson

D-U-N-S 25-271-6956   (BR)
SOBEYS WEST INC
SOMEPLACE SPECIAL
5385 Headland Dr, West Vancouver, BC, V7W
3C7
(604) 926-2034
Emp Here 110
SIC 5411 Grocery stores

D-U-N-S 20-027-0713   (BR)
**THE BOARD OF SCHOOL TRUSTEES OF
SCHOOL DISTRICT NO. 45 (WEST VAN-
COUVER)**
CAULFIELD ELEMENTARY SCHOOL
(*Suby of* The Board of School Trustees of
School District No. 45 (West Vancouver))
4685 Keith Rd, West Vancouver, BC, V7W
2M8
(604) 981-1200
Emp Here 40
SIC 8211 Elementary and secondary schools

Westbank, BC V4T
Central Okanagan County

D-U-N-S 20-980-1690   (BR)
**BOARD OF EDUCATION OF SCHOOL DIS-
TRICT NO. 23 (CENTRAL OKANAGAN),
THE**
GEORGE PRINGLE ELEMENTARY SCHOOL
3770 Elliott Rd, Westbank, BC, V4T 1W9
(250) 870-5103
Emp Here 40
SIC 8211 Elementary and secondary schools

D-U-N-S 25-278-7713   (BR)
CARA OPERATIONS LIMITED
SWISS CHALET ROTISSERIE & GRILL
(*Suby of* Cara Holdings Limited)
2115 Louie Dr, Westbank, BC, V4T 1Y2
(250) 707-1900
Emp Here 20
SIC 5812 Eating places

D-U-N-S 20-271-9407   (BR)
DISTRICT OF WEST KELOWNA
*DISTRICT OF WEST KELOWNA FIRE DE-
PARTMENT*
3651 Old Okanagan Hwy, Westbank, BC, V4T
1P6
(250) 769-1640
Emp Here 90
SIC 7389 Business services, nec

D-U-N-S 24-313-6236   (BR)
HOME DEPOT OF CANADA INC
HOME DEPOT
(*Suby of* The Home Depot Inc)
3550 Carrington Rd Unit 401, Westbank, BC,
V4T 2Z1
(250) 707-2300
Emp Here 30
SIC 5251 Hardware stores

D-U-N-S 25-068-3794   (BR)
LOBLAWS INC
EXTRA FOODS
2341 Bering Rd, Westbank, BC, V4T 2P4

Emp Here 100
SIC 5411 Grocery stores

D-U-N-S 24-593-7321   (SL)
**WESTBANK FIRST NATION PINE ACRES
HOME**
PINE ACRES HOME
1902 Pheasant Lane, Westbank, BC, V4T 2H4
(250) 768-7676
Emp Here 85   *Sales* 3,137,310
SIC 8361 Residential care

Whistler, BC V0N
Squamish - Lillooet County

D-U-N-S 24-311-3362   (SL)
ALIK ENTERPRISES LTD
ARAXI RESTAURANT & BAR
4222 Village Sq, Whistler, BC, V0N 1B4
(604) 932-4540
Emp Here 80   *Sales* 2,407,703
SIC 5812 Eating places

D-U-N-S 25-293-2546   (BR)
ATLIFIC INC
WHISTLER VILLAGE INN & SUITES
(*Suby of* 3376290 Canada Inc)
4429 Sundial Pl, Whistler, BC, V0N 1B4
(604) 932-4004
Emp Here 40
SIC 7011 Hotels and motels

D-U-N-S 25-978-7000   (SL)
AVELLO SPA LTD
AVELLO SPA & HEALTH CLUB
4090 Whistler Way Suite 400, Whistler, BC,
V0N 1B4
(604) 935-3444
Emp Here 50   *Sales* 1,678,096
SIC 7991 Physical fitness facilities

D-U-N-S 20-922-4521   (BR)
BLUESHORE FINANCIAL CREDIT UNION
4321 Village Gate Blvd, Whistler, BC, V0N
1B4
(604) 905-4310
Emp Here 20
SIC 6062 State credit unions

D-U-N-S 20-123-0468   (BR)
CANADIAN PACIFIC RAILWAY COMPANY
FAIRMONT CHATEAU WHISTLER
4599 Chateau Blvd, Whistler, BC, V0N 1B4
(604) 938-2086
Emp Here 650
SIC 7011 Hotels and motels

D-U-N-S 20-007-7717   (BR)
CARA OPERATIONS LIMITED
MILESTONE'S GRILL & BAR
(*Suby of* Cara Holdings Limited)
4555 Blackcomb Way, Whistler, BC, V0N 1B4
(604) 905-5422
Emp Here 30
SIC 5812 Eating places

D-U-N-S 24-126-0228   (BR)
COAST HOTELS LIMITED
*COAST   BLACKCOMB   SUITES   AT
WHISTLER*
4899 Painted Cliff Rd, Whistler, BC, V0N 1B4
(604) 905-3400
Emp Here 50
SIC 7011 Hotels and motels

D-U-N-S 25-734-0778   (BR)
EDDIE BAUER OF CANADA INC
EDDIE BAUER OUTDOOR OUTFITTER
(*Suby of* Golden Gate Capital LP)
4295 Blackcomb Way Suite 116, Whistler, BC,
V0N 1B4

Emp Here 20
SIC 5611 Men's and boys' clothing stores

D-U-N-S 25-361-2402   (BR)
FS WHISTLER HOLDINGS LIMITED
FOUR SEASONS RESIDENCES

4591 Blackcomb Way, Whistler, BC, V0N 1B4
(604) 935-3400
Emp Here 300
SIC 7011 Hotels and motels

　D-U-N-S 20-084-8492　　(SL)
FAIRMONT CHATEAU WHISTLER, THE
4612 Blackcomb Way, Whistler, BC, V0N 1B4
(604) 938-2092
Emp Here 50　　　*Sales* 2,188,821
SIC 7992 Public golf courses

　D-U-N-S 24-806-0204　　(BR)
FAIRMONT HOTELS & RESORTS INC
4599 Chateau Blvd, Whistler, BC, V0N 1B4
(604) 938-8000
Emp Here 600
SIC 7011 Hotels and motels

　D-U-N-S 20-002-9135　　(BR)
GAP (CANADA) INC
GAP
(*Suby of* The Gap Inc)
4308 Main St Suite 5, Whistler, BC, V0N 1B4
(604) 938-6364
Emp Here 26
SIC 5651 Family clothing stores

　D-U-N-S 25-827-0610　　(BR)
GOLFBC HOLDINGS INC
DEN AT NICKLAUS NORTH
8080 Nicklaus North Blvd, Whistler, BC, V0N 1B8
(604) 938-9898
Emp Here 100
SIC 5812 Eating places

　D-U-N-S 25-325-9386　　(BR)
H.Y. LOUIE CO. LIMITED
IGA 77
4330 Northlands Blvd, Whistler, BC, V0N 1B4
(604) 938-2850
Emp Here 70
SIC 5411 Grocery stores

　D-U-N-S 25-184-8701　　(SL)
HY'S STEAK HOUSE LTD
4308 Main St, Whistler, BC, V0N 1B4
(604) 905-5555
Emp Here 65　　　*Sales* 1,969,939
SIC 5812 Eating places

　D-U-N-S 25-116-2640　　(BR)
INTRAWEST RESORT CLUB GROUP
EMBARC WHISTLER
(*Suby of* Intrawest Resorts Holdings, Inc.)
4580 Chateau Blvd, Whistler, BC, V0N 1B4
(604) 938-3030
Emp Here 115
SIC 7011 Hotels and motels

　D-U-N-S 25-733-1280　　(BR)
INTRAWEST ULC
MERLIN'S BAR & GRILL
(*Suby of* Intrawest Resorts Holdings, Inc.)
4553 Blackcomb Way, Whistler, BC, V0N 1B4
(604) 938-7700
Emp Here 45
SIC 7011 Hotels and motels

　D-U-N-S 24-325-0953　　(BR)
LODGING OVATIONS CORP
LEGENDS
(*Suby of* Intrawest Resorts Holdings, Inc.)
2036 London Lane, Whistler, BC, V0N 1B2
(604) 938-9999
Emp Here 52
SIC 7011 Hotels and motels

　D-U-N-S 25-909-9356　　(SL)
LONGHORN PUB LTD, THE
LONGHORN SALOON & GRILL
4284 Mountain Sq, Whistler, BC, V0N 1B4
(604) 932-5999
Emp Here 70　　　*Sales* 2,553,625
SIC 5813 Drinking places

　D-U-N-S 25-092-7279　　(BR)
LULULEMON ATHLETICA CANADA INC

LULULEMON
4154 Village Green Suite 118, Whistler, BC, V0N 1B4
(604) 938-9642
Emp Here 35
SIC 2339 Women's and misses' outerwear, nec

　D-U-N-S 24-313-8661　　(BR)
LULULEMON ATHLETICA CANADA INC
LULULEMON
4293 Mountain Sq, Whistler, BC, V0N 1B4
(604) 962-9968
Emp Here 35
SIC 2339 Women's and misses' outerwear, nec

　D-U-N-S 24-851-1532　　(SL)
OHR SPRING MANAGEMENT LTD
THE COAST BLACCOMB SUITES AT WHISTLER
4899 Painted Cliff Rd, Whistler, BC, V0N 1B4
(604) 905-3400
Emp Here 80　　　*Sales* 3,502,114
SIC 7011 Hotels and motels

　D-U-N-S 20-653-6919　　(SL)
OLD SPAGHETTI FACTORY (WHISTLER) LTD
4154 Village Green, Whistler, BC, V0N 1B4
(604) 938-1081
Emp Here 75　　　*Sales* 2,261,782
SIC 5812 Eating places

　D-U-N-S 24-658-8750　　(SL)
PANZEX VANCOUVER INC
THE ORIGINAL RISTORANTE
4270 Mountain Sq, Whistler, BC, V0N 1B4
(604) 932-6945
Emp Here 75　　　*Sales* 2,261,782
SIC 5812 Eating places

　D-U-N-S 25-745-8000　　(BR)
PRINCE GEORGE TRANSIT LTD
WHISTLER TRANSIT
8011 Hwy 99, Whistler, BC, V0N 1B8
(604) 938-0388
Emp Here 70
SIC 4111 Local and suburban transit

　D-U-N-S 20-043-7627　　(BR)
SCHOOL DISTRICT NO. 48 (HOWE SOUND)
WHISTLER SECONDARY - A COMMUNITY SCHOOL
8000 Alpine Way, Whistler, BC, V0N 1B8
(604) 905-2581
Emp Here 30
SIC 8211 Elementary and secondary schools

　D-U-N-S 20-591-8480　　(BR)
SCHOOL DISTRICT NO. 48 (HOWE SOUND)
MYRTLE PHILIP ELEMENTARY SCHOOL
6195 Lorimer Rd, Whistler, BC, V0N 1B6
(604) 932-5321
Emp Here 20
SIC 8211 Elementary and secondary schools

　D-U-N-S 25-023-6890　　(SL)
SHONAN ENTERPRISES INC
SUSHI VILLAGE
4272 Mountain Sq, Whistler, BC, V0N 1B4
(604) 932-3330
Emp Here 50　　　*Sales* 1,532,175
SIC 5812 Eating places

　D-U-N-S 24-837-9075　　(SL)
SNOWLINE RESTAURANTS INC
KEG AT THE MOUNTAIN
4429 Sundial Pl, Whistler, BC, V0N 1B4
(604) 932-5151
Emp Here 80　　　*Sales* 2,407,703
SIC 5812 Eating places

　D-U-N-S 24-420-0486　　(SL)
T & V HOSPITALITY INC
NITA LAKE LODGE
2131 Lake Placid Rd, Whistler, BC, V0N 1B2

(604) 966-5711
Emp Here 67　　　*Sales* 2,918,428
SIC 7011 Hotels and motels

　D-U-N-S 24-248-7411　　(HQ)
WHISKI JACK RESORTS LTD
WHISTLER RENTALS ACCOMADATION CENTRE
4319 Main St Suite 104, Whistler, BC, V0N 1B4

Emp Here 25　　　*Emp Total* 75
Sales 8,834,400
SIC 6513 Apartment building operators
Dir Andrea Siemens
Dir Kent Bubbs
Dir Patricia Bubbs

　D-U-N-S 25-258-2903　　(BR)
WHISTLER & BLACKCOMB MOUNTAIN RESORTS LIMITED
WIZARD GRILL
4545 Blackcomb Way, Whistler, BC, V0N 1B4
(604) 938-7707
Emp Here 20
SIC 5812 Eating places

　D-U-N-S 25-928-6003　　(SL)
WHISTLER TAXI LTD
SEA TO SKY
1080 Millar Creek Rd Suite 201, Whistler, BC, V0N 1B1
(604) 932-4430
Emp Here 80　　　*Sales* 2,858,628
SIC 4121 Taxicabs

　D-U-N-S 25-261-1405　　(SL)
WHISTLER VILLAGE CENTRE HOTEL MANAGEMENT LTD
HOLIDAY INN SUNSPREE
(*Suby of* Larco Investments Ltd)
4295 Blackcomb Way Suite 116, Whistler, BC, V0N 1B4
(604) 938-0878
Emp Here 35　　　*Sales* 1,532,175
SIC 7011 Hotels and motels

White Rock, BC V4B
Greater Vancouver County

　D-U-N-S 25-295-8939　　(BR)
BANK OF NOVA SCOTIA, THE
SCOTIABANK
15190 North Bluff Rd, White Rock, BC, V4B 3E5
(604) 541-3400
Emp Here 30
SIC 6021 National commercial banks

　D-U-N-S 20-334-7518　　(SL)
BOATHOUSE RESTAURANTS OF CANADA
14935 Marine Dr, White Rock, BC, V4B 1C3
(604) 536-7320
Emp Here 120　　　*Sales* 3,648,035
SIC 5812 Eating places

　D-U-N-S 25-002-6309　　(BR)
CANADA TRUST COMPANY, THE
CANADA TRUST
(*Suby of* Toronto-Dominion Bank, The)
1584 Johnston Rd, White Rock, BC, V4B 3Z7

Emp Here 30
SIC 6021 National commercial banks

　D-U-N-S 20-086-6551　　(BR)
CANADIAN CANCER SOCIETY
15240 Thrift Ave Suite 104, White Rock, BC, V4B 2L1
(604) 538-0011
Emp Here 50
SIC 8699 Membership organizations, nec

　D-U-N-S 25-940-7336　　(BR)
COAST CAPITAL SAVINGS CREDIT UNION
15241 Thrift Ave, White Rock, BC, V4B 2K9

(604) 517-7020
Emp Here 30
SIC 6062 State credit unions

　D-U-N-S 24-248-7411　　(HQ)
FRASER HEALTH AUTHORITY
15521 Russell Ave, White Rock, BC, V4B 2R4
(604) 538-4213
Emp Here 25
SIC 8062 General medical and surgical hospitals

　D-U-N-S 24-863-2387　　(BR)
PEACE ARCH COMMUNITY SERVICES SOCIETY
(*Suby of* Peace Arch Community Services Society)
882 Maple St, White Rock, BC, V4B 4M2
(604) 531-6226
Emp Here 25
SIC 8399 Social services, nec

　D-U-N-S 25-018-8497　　(BR)
ROYAL BANK OF CANADA
ROYAL BANK FINANCIAL GROUP
(*Suby of* Royal Bank Of Canada)
1588 Johnston Rd, White Rock, BC, V4B 3Z7
(604) 665-8125
Emp Here 54
SIC 6021 National commercial banks

　D-U-N-S 20-590-7640　　(BR)
SCHOOL DISTRICT NO 36 (SURREY)
WHITE ROCK ELEMENTARY SCHOOL
1273 Fir St, White Rock, BC, V4B 5A6
(604) 531-5731
Emp Here 40
SIC 8211 Elementary and secondary schools

　D-U-N-S 20-713-3468　　(BR)
SCHOOL DISTRICT NO 36 (SURREY)
EASTHEART ELEMENTARY
15877 Roper Ave, White Rock, BC, V4B 2H5
(604) 536-8711
Emp Here 50
SIC 8211 Elementary and secondary schools

Williams Lake, BC V2G
Cariboo County

　D-U-N-S 24-069-6567　　(BR)
ALLIED BLOWER & SHEET METAL LTD
1105 Boundary St, Williams Lake, BC, V2G 4K3
(250) 398-7154
Emp Here 30
SIC 1761 Roofing, siding, and sheetMetal work

　D-U-N-S 20-922-4612　　(BR)
BLACK PRESS GROUP LTD
CARIBOO ADVISOR
188 First Ave N, Williams Lake, BC, V2G 1Y8
(250) 392-2331
Emp Here 50
SIC 2711 Newspapers

　D-U-N-S 20-792-1938　　(BR)
BOSTON PIZZA INTERNATIONAL INC
BOSTON PIZZA
285 Donald Rd, Williams Lake, BC, V2G 4K4
(250) 398-7600
Emp Here 60
SIC 5812 Eating places

　D-U-N-S 25-288-9118　　(BR)
CANADA POST CORPORATION
48 Second Ave S, Williams Lake, BC, V2G 1H6
(250) 392-3647
Emp Here 50
SIC 4311 U.s. postal service

　D-U-N-S 20-585-0006　　(BR)
CANADA POST CORPORATION
711

370 Proctor St, Williams Lake, BC, V2G 4P6
(250) 392-2711
Emp Here 20
SIC 4311 U.s. postal service

D-U-N-S 25-852-7910   (BR)
CANADIAN CANCER SOCIETY
176 Fourth Ave N, Williams Lake, BC, V2G 2C7
(250) 392-3442
Emp Here 68
SIC 8399 Social services, nec

D-U-N-S 25-311-7105   (BR)
CANADIAN IMPERIAL BANK OF COMMERCE
CIBC
220 Oliver St, Williams Lake, BC, V2G 1M1
(250) 392-2351
Emp Here 25
SIC 6021 National commercial banks

D-U-N-S 20-812-4607   (BR)
CANADIAN MENTAL HEALTH ASSOCIATION, THE
CANADIAN MENTAL HEALTH ASSOCIATION-CARIBOO CHILCOTIN BRANCH
(*Suby of* Canadian Mental Health Association, The)
51 Fourth Ave S, Williams Lake, BC, V2G 1J6
(250) 398-8220
Emp Here 25
SIC 8621 Professional organizations

D-U-N-S 24-346-6815   (BR)
CANADIAN TIRE CORPORATION, LIMITED
1050 South Lakeside Dr, Williams Lake, BC, V2G 3A6
(250) 392-3303
Emp Here 50
SIC 5531 Auto and home supply stores

D-U-N-S 24-938-9974   (SL)
CARIBOO CHILCOTIN CHILD DEVELOPMENT CENTRE ASSOCIATION
690 Second Ave N, Williams Lake, BC, V2G 4C4
(250) 392-4481
Emp Here 53   *Sales* 1,605,135
SIC 8351 Child day care services

D-U-N-S 25-778-4231   (SL)
CARIBOO FRIENDSHIP SOCIETY
99 Third Ave S, Williams Lake, BC, V2G 1J1
(250) 398-6831
Emp Here 65   *Sales* 2,553,625
SIC 8322 Individual and family services

D-U-N-S 25-774-6370   (BR)
DENCAN RESTAURANTS INC
DENNY'S RESTAURANT
(*Suby of* Northland Properties Corporation)
664 Oliver St, Williams Lake, BC, V2G 1M6
(250) 398-5343
Emp Here 35
SIC 5812 Eating places

D-U-N-S 24-683-2653   (BR)
FINNING INTERNATIONAL INC
(*Suby of* Finning International Inc)
450 Mackenzie Ave S, Williams Lake, BC, V2G 1C9
(250) 392-3381
Emp Here 32
SIC 5082 Construction and mining machinery

D-U-N-S 20-697-9085   (BR)
GREAT PACIFIC INDUSTRIES INC
SAVE-ON-FOODS
730 Oliver St, Williams Lake, BC, V2G 1N1
(250) 392-7225
Emp Here 155
SIC 5411 Grocery stores

D-U-N-S 24-826-8950   (BR)
IRL INTERNATIONAL TRUCK CENTRES LTD
4775 Cattle Dr, Williams Lake, BC, V2G 5E8

(250) 392-1446
Emp Here 20
SIC 5511 New and used car dealers

D-U-N-S 25-079-6562   (BR)
INLAND DIESEL LTD
FREIGHTLINER WILLIAMS LAKE
(*Suby of* Inland Diesel Ltd)
1100 South Lakeside Dr, Williams Lake, BC, V2G 3A6
(250) 398-7411
Emp Here 20
SIC 7699 Repair services, nec

D-U-N-S 25-133-1989   (BR)
INLAND KENWORTH LTD
INLAND KENWORTH
1560 Broadway Ave S, Williams Lake, BC, V2G 2X3
(250) 392-7101
Emp Here 30
SIC 5511 New and used car dealers

D-U-N-S 20-731-9174   (BR)
INTERIOR HEALTH AUTHORITY
WILLIAMS LAKE MENTAL HEALTH CENTRE
487 Borland St, Williams Lake, BC, V2G 1R9
(250) 392-1483
Emp Here 20
SIC 8062 General medical and surgical hospitals

D-U-N-S 24-777-8418   (BR)
JAMES WESTERN STAR TRUCK & TRAILER LTD
50 Rose St, Williams Lake, BC, V2G 4G5
(250) 392-5050
Emp Here 41
SIC 5084 Industrial machinery and equipment

D-U-N-S 25-088-3543   (BR)
LOBLAWS INC
WHOLESALE CLUB
1000 South Lakeside Dr, Williams Lake, BC, V2G 3A6
(250) 305-2150
Emp Here 80
SIC 5141 Groceries, general line

D-U-N-S 20-569-2259   (BR)
ROYAL BANK OF CANADA
RBC
(*Suby of* Royal Bank Of Canada)
51 Fourth Ave N, Williams Lake, BC, V2G 4S1
(250) 398-2500
Emp Here 20
SIC 6021 National commercial banks

D-U-N-S 24-812-8915   (BR)
SMS EQUIPMENT INC
CONECO EQUIPMENT
1115 Boundary St, Williams Lake, BC, V2G 4K3
(250) 305-1060
Emp Here 40
SIC 5082 Construction and mining machinery

D-U-N-S 25-833-0182   (BR)
SCHOOL DISTRICT NO 27 (CARIBOO-CHILCOTIN)
COLUMNEETZA SECONDARY SCHOOL
1045 Western Ave, Williams Lake, BC, V2G 2J8
(250) 392-4158
Emp Here 60
SIC 8211 Elementary and secondary schools

D-U-N-S 20-590-8614   (BR)
SCHOOL DISTRICT NO 27 (CARIBOO-CHILCOTIN)
350 Second Ave N, Williams Lake, BC, V2G 1Z9
(250) 398-3800
Emp Here 25
SIC 8211 Elementary and secondary schools

D-U-N-S 20-713-2650   (BR)
SCHOOL DISTRICT NO 27 (CARIBOO-CHILCOTIN)

CHILCOTIN ROAD ELEMENTARY SCHOOL
709 Lyne Rd, Williams Lake, BC, V2G 3Z3
(250) 392-5455
Emp Here 50
SIC 8211 Elementary and secondary schools

D-U-N-S 24-450-7328   (BR)
SCHOOL DISTRICT NO 27 (CARIBOO-CHILCOTIN)
NESIKA ELEMENTARY SCHOOL
1180 Moon Ave, Williams Lake, BC, V2G 4A6
(250) 398-7192
Emp Here 30
SIC 8211 Elementary and secondary schools

D-U-N-S 20-713-2700   (BR)
SCHOOL DISTRICT NO 27 (CARIBOO-CHILCOTIN)
MOUNTVIEW SCHOOL
1222 Dog Creek Rd, Williams Lake, BC, V2G 3G9
(250) 392-7344
Emp Here 20
SIC 8211 Elementary and secondary schools

D-U-N-S 20-981-7050   (BR)
SCHOOL DISTRICT NO 27 (CARIBOO-CHILCOTIN)
MAINTENANCE OFFICE
765 Second Ave N, Williams Lake, BC, V2G 4C3
(250) 398-3875
Emp Here 40
SIC 7349 Building maintenance services, nec

D-U-N-S 20-713-2684   (BR)
SCHOOL DISTRICT NO 27 (CARIBOO-CHILCOTIN)
MARIE SHARPE SCHOOL
260 Cameron St, Williams Lake, BC, V2G 1S8
(250) 392-4104
Emp Here 25
SIC 8211 Elementary and secondary schools

D-U-N-S 20-590-8648   (BR)
SCHOOL DISTRICT NO 27 (CARIBOO-CHILCOTIN)
GROW CENTRE, THE
320 Second Ave N, Williams Lake, BC, V2G 1Z9
(250) 398-5800
Emp Here 20
SIC 8211 Elementary and secondary schools

D-U-N-S 25-271-7368   (BR)
SOBEYS WEST INC
WILLIAMS LAKE SAFEWAY
451 Oliver St, Williams Lake, BC, V2G 1M5
(250) 398-8380
Emp Here 50
SIC 5411 Grocery stores

D-U-N-S 20-553-3677   (BR)
STAPLES CANADA INC
STAPLES THE BUSINESS DEPOT
(*Suby of* Staples, Inc.)
850 Oliver St Suite 105, Williams Lake, BC, V2G 3W1
(250) 305-2500
Emp Here 30
SIC 5943 Stationery stores

D-U-N-S 20-639-8062   (BR)
THOMPSON RIVERS UNIVERSITY
1250 Western Ave, Williams Lake, BC, V2G 1H7
(250) 392-8000
Emp Here 40
SIC 8221 Colleges and universities

D-U-N-S 20-878-7791   (BR)
TOLKO INDUSTRIES LTD
925 Second Ave N, Williams Lake, BC, V2G 4P7
(250) 305-3600
Emp Here 35
SIC 2421 Sawmills and planing mills, general

D-U-N-S 20-732-1535   (BR)

TOLKO INDUSTRIES LTD
CREEKSIDE DIVISION
180 Hodgson Rd, Williams Lake, BC, V2G 3P6
(250) 392-3371
Emp Here 50
SIC 2421 Sawmills and planing mills, general

D-U-N-S 25-195-4483   (BR)
TOLKO INDUSTRIES LTD
SODA CREEK DIVISION
5000 Soda Creek Rd, Williams Lake, BC, V2G 5H5
(250) 398-3600
Emp Here 250
SIC 2421 Sawmills and planing mills, general

D-U-N-S 24-329-5479   (BR)
VISTA RADIO LTD
CKWL RADIO
83 First Ave S, Williams Lake, BC, V2G 1H4
(250) 392-6551
Emp Here 25
SIC 4832 Radio broadcasting stations

D-U-N-S 20-120-8006   (BR)
WEST FRASER MILLS LTD
WILLIAMS LAKE PLYWOOD
4200 Mackenzie Ave N, Williams Lake, BC, V2G 1N4
(250) 392-7731
Emp Here 350
SIC 2421 Sawmills and planing mills, general

D-U-N-S 20-795-7564   (BR)
WEST FRASER MILLS LTD
4255 Rottacker Rd, Williams Lake, BC, V2G 5E4
(250) 392-7784
Emp Here 200
SIC 2421 Sawmills and planing mills, general

D-U-N-S 25-774-9960   (BR)
WILLIAMS LAKE, CITY OF
CARIBOO MEMORIAL COMPLEX
525 Proctor St, Williams Lake, BC, V2G 4J1
(250) 398-7665
Emp Here 30
SIC 7999 Amusement and recreation, nec

Winfield, BC V4V
Central Okanagan County

D-U-N-S 25-151-0442   (BR)
BOARD OF EDUCATION OF SCHOOL DISTRICT NO. 23 (CENTRAL OKANAGAN), THE
GEORGE ELLIOT SECONDARY SCHOOL
10241 Bottom Wood Lake Rd, Winfield, BC, V4V 1Y7
(250) 870-5102
Emp Here 65
SIC 8211 Elementary and secondary schools

D-U-N-S 20-034-8022   (BR)
BOARD OF EDUCATION OF SCHOOL DISTRICT NO. 23 (CENTRAL OKANAGAN), THE
DAVIDSON ROAD ELEMENTARY SCHOOL
2115 Davidson Rd, Winfield, BC, V4V 1R3
(250) 870-5117
Emp Here 40
SIC 8211 Elementary and secondary schools

D-U-N-S 25-854-6191   (BR)
OKANAGAN REGIONAL LIBRARY DISTRICT
LAKE COUNTRY LIBRARY BRANCH
10150 Bottom Wood Lake Rd Suite 2, Winfield, BC, V4V 2M1
(250) 766-3141
Emp Here 25
SIC 8231 Libraries

Woss, BC V0N
Mount Waddington County

D-U-N-S 24-372-8300   (BR)
CANADIAN FOREST PRODUCTS LTD
ENGLEWOOD LOGGING, DIV OF
Gd, Woss, BC, V0N 3P0
(250) 281-2300
Emp Here 250
SIC 2421 Sawmills and planing mills, general

D-U-N-S 20-591-2244   (BR)
SCHOOL DISTRICT NO 85 (VANCOUVER ISLAND NORTH)
WOSS LAKE ELEMENTARY SCHOOL
4500 Mac Rae, Woss, BC, V0N 3P0
(250) 281-2233
Emp Here 25
SIC 8211 Elementary and secondary schools

Zeballos, BC V0P
Comox - Strathcona County

D-U-N-S 20-713-6297   (BR)
SCHOOL DISTRICT #84 (VANCOUVER IS-LAND WEST)
ZEBALLOS SCHOOL
675 Keno Cres, Zeballos, BC, V0P 2A0
(250) 761-4227
Emp Here 30
SIC 8211 Elementary and secondary schools

Alonsa, MB R0H

D-U-N-S 20-709-9172   (BR)
TURTLE RIVER SCHOOL DIVISION
ALONSA SCHOOL
Hwy 50, Alonsa, MB, R0H 0A0
(204) 767-2168
Emp Here 20
SIC 8211 Elementary and secondary schools

Altona, MB R0G

D-U-N-S 24-359-2107   (BR)
A & I PRODUCTS CANADA INC
LOEWEN MANUFACTURING, DIV OF
(*Suby of* Deere & Company)
432 Railway St W, Altona, MB, R0G 0B0
(204) 324-8621
Emp Here 66
SIC 5083 Farm and garden machinery

D-U-N-S 24-419-9712   (BR)
ACCESS CREDIT UNION LIMITED
(*Suby of* Access Credit Union Limited)
129 Third Ave Ne, Altona, MB, R0G 0B0
(204) 324-6437
Emp Here 30
SIC 6062 State credit unions

D-U-N-S 20-127-3518   (BR)
BORDER LAND SCHOOL DIVISION
W C MILLAR COLLEGIATE
181 6th St Se Ss 3, Altona, MB, R0G 0B3
(204) 324-6416
Emp Here 56
SIC 8211 Elementary and secondary schools

D-U-N-S 20-709-8273   (BR)
BORDER LAND SCHOOL DIVISION
ECOLE WEST PARK SCHOOL
83 3rd St Nw, Altona, MB, R0G 0B1
(204) 324-5319
Emp Here 27
SIC 8211 Elementary and secondary schools

D-U-N-S 20-723-6493   (BR)
BORDER LAND SCHOOL DIVISION
PARKSIDE JUNIOR HIGH SCHOOL
155 5th St Nw, Altona, MB, R0G 0B1
(204) 324-8206
Emp Here 25
SIC 8211 Elementary and secondary schools

D-U-N-S 20-709-8281   (BR)
BORDER LAND SCHOOL DIVISION
ECOLE ELMWOOD SCHOOL
27 4th St Sw, Altona, MB, R0G 0B2
(204) 324-8611
Emp Here 50
SIC 8211 Elementary and secondary schools

D-U-N-S 24-913-8892   (BR)
BUNGE CANADA
35 10th Ave Nw, Altona, MB, R0G 0B0
(204) 324-6481
Emp Here 70
SIC 2076 Vegetable oil mills, nec

D-U-N-S 25-538-2574   (BR)
GREENVALLEY EQUIPMENT INC
549 Industrial Dr, Altona, MB, R0G 0B0
(204) 324-6456
Emp Here 22
SIC 5083 Farm and garden machinery

D-U-N-S 20-176-5976   (BR)
REGIONAL HEALTH AUTHORITY - CENTRAL MANITOBA INC
ALTONA COMMUNITY MEMORIAL HEALTH CENTRE
240 5th Ave Sw, Altona, MB, R0G 0B2
(204) 324-6411
Emp Here 210

SIC 8059 Nursing and personal care, nec

D-U-N-S 20-641-8472   (BR)
SUPREME OFFICE PRODUCTS LIMITED
SUPREME DISTRIBUTORS
(*Suby of* Placements Denis Latulippe Inc, Les)
120 6th St Ne, Altona, MB, R0G 0B0
(204) 324-5018
Emp Here 50
SIC 5112 Stationery and office supplies

Amaranth, MB R0H

D-U-N-S 24-330-9130   (BR)
CERTAINTEED GYPSUM CANADA, INC
WESTROC INDUSTRIES
Gd, Amaranth, MB, R0H 0B0
(204) 843-2231
Emp Here 50
SIC 3275 Gypsum products

Anola, MB R0E

D-U-N-S 20-709-8158   (BR)
SUNRISE SCHOOL DIVISION
ANOLA ELEMENTARY SCHOOL
736 Academy St, Anola, MB, R0E 0A0
(204) 866-2962
Emp Here 50
SIC 8211 Elementary and secondary schools

Arborg, MB R0C

D-U-N-S 24-171-9384   (SL)
ARBORG & DISTRICT HEALTH CENTER
(*Suby of* Interlake Regional Health Authority Inc)
Gd, Arborg, MB, R0C 0A0
(204) 376-5247
Emp Here 100   *Sales* 6,931,267
SIC 8062 General medical and surgical hospitals
  Ruby Tretiak

D-U-N-S 25-838-6606   (BR)
EVERGREEN SCHOOL DIVISION
ARBORG EARLY MIDDLE SCHOOL
251 David St, Arborg, MB, R0C 0A0
(204) 376-5054
Emp Here 30
SIC 8211 Elementary and secondary schools

D-U-N-S 20-000-2418   (HQ)
INTERLAKE CONSUMERS CO-OPERATIVE LIMITED
(*Suby of* Interlake Consumers Co-operative Limited)
253 Main St, Arborg, MB, R0C 0A0
(204) 376-5245
Emp Here 37   *Emp Total* 90
Sales 21,962,170
SIC 5171 Petroleum bulk stations and terminals
Pr Pr Kris Gudmundson
VP VP Reg Perry
Dir Janet Larkin
Dir Bob Hoffman
Dir Brian Fjeldsted
Dir Lorette Kirby
Dir Robin Kirby
Dir Ted Watson

D-U-N-S 25-289-0934   (BR)
INTERLAKE REGIONAL HEALTH AUTHORITY INC
ARBORG PERSONAL CARE HOME
(*Suby of* Interlake Regional Health Authority Inc)

---

233 St Phillips Dr, Arborg, MB, R0C 0A0
(204) 376-5226
Emp Here 75
SIC 8051 Skilled nursing care facilities

Ashern, MB R0C

D-U-N-S 20-647-6280   (BR)
INTERLAKE REGIONAL HEALTH AUTHORITY INC
LAKESHORE HEALTH CENTER
(*Suby of* Interlake Regional Health Authority Inc)
1 Steenson Dr, Ashern, MB, R0C 0E0
(204) 768-2461
Emp Here 100
SIC 8062 General medical and surgical hospitals

D-U-N-S 25-272-3598   (BR)
LAKESHORE SCHOOL DIVISION
ASHERN CENTRAL SCHOOL
7 Provincial Rd Suite 325, Ashern, MB, R0C 0E0
(204) 768-2571
Emp Here 30
SIC 8211 Elementary and secondary schools

D-U-N-S 25-706-0715   (BR)
NORTH WEST COMPANY LP, THE
Gd, Ashern, MB, R0C 0E0
(204) 768-3864
Emp Here 32
SIC 5411 Grocery stores

Austin, MB R0H

D-U-N-S 25-891-8994   (BR)
PINE CREEK SCHOOL DIVISION
AUSTIN ELEMENTARY SCHOOL
7 Fraser St N, Austin, MB, R0H 0C0
(204) 637-2240
Emp Here 30
SIC 8211 Elementary and secondary schools

Baldur, MB R0K

D-U-N-S 24-916-7982   (BR)
PRAIRIE MOUNTAIN HEALTH
BALDUR HEALTH DISTRICT
(*Suby of* Prairie Mountain Health)
531 Elizabeth Ave E, Baldur, MB, R0K 0B0
(204) 535-2373
Emp Here 60
SIC 8051 Skilled nursing care facilities

D-U-N-S 25-176-7653   (BR)
PRAIRIE SPIRIT SCHOOL DIVISION
BALDUR SCHOOL
627 Elizabeth Ave E, Baldur, MB, R0K 0B0
(204) 535-2314
Emp Here 20
SIC 8211 Elementary and secondary schools

Beausejour, MB R0E

D-U-N-S 20-835-3326   (BR)
GILLIS QUARRIES LIMITED
(*Suby of* Gillis Quarries Limited)
203 Gillis St, Beausejour, MB, R0E 0C0
(204) 268-2934
Emp Here 30
SIC 1411 Dimension stone

D-U-N-S 25-269-0938   (BR)
MANITOBA HYDRO-ELECTRIC BOARD,

THE
MANITOBA HYDRO
Gd, Beausejour, MB, R0E 0C0
(204) 268-1343
Emp Here 35
SIC 4911 Electric services

D-U-N-S 20-836-9413   (BR)
NORTH EASTMAN HEALTH ASSOCIATION INC
BEAUSEJOUR HEALTH CENTRE
151 1 St S, Beausejour, MB, R0E 0C0
(204) 268-1076
Emp Here 175
SIC 8062 General medical and surgical hospitals

D-U-N-S 25-610-7277   (BR)
ROYAL BANK OF CANADA
RBC
(*Suby of* Royal Bank Of Canada)
602 Park Ave, Beausejour, MB, R0E 0C0
(204) 268-1766
Emp Here 22
SIC 6021 National commercial banks

D-U-N-S 20-709-8075   (BR)
SUNRISE SCHOOL DIVISION
BEAUSEJOUR EARLY YEARS SCHOOL
900 James Ave, Beausejour, MB, R0E 0C0
(204) 268-2664
Emp Here 50
SIC 8211 Elementary and secondary schools

D-U-N-S 25-176-8024   (BR)
SUNRISE SCHOOL DIVISION
EDWARD SCHREYER SCHOOL
85 5th St S, Beausejour, MB, R0E 0C0
(204) 268-2423
Emp Here 92
SIC 8211 Elementary and secondary schools

Benito, MB R0L

D-U-N-S 20-047-0966   (BR)
SWAN VALLEY SCHOOL DIVISION
BENITO SCHOOL
(*Suby of* Swan Valley School Division)
Gd, Benito, MB, R0L 0C0
(204) 539-2466
Emp Here 20
SIC 8211 Elementary and secondary schools

Berens River, MB R0B

D-U-N-S 20-845-4186   (BR)
FRONTIER SCHOOL DIVISION
BERENS RIVER SCHOOL
Gd, Berens River, MB, R0B 0A0
(204) 382-2153
Emp Here 57
SIC 8211 Elementary and secondary schools

Binscarth, MB R0J

D-U-N-S 20-716-8662   (BR)
PARK WEST SCHOOL DIVISION
BINSCARTH SCHOOL
242 Russel St, Binscarth, MB, R0J 0G0
(204) 842-2802
Emp Here 20
SIC 8211 Elementary and secondary schools

Birch River, MB R0L

▲ Public Company   ■ Public Company Family Member   **HQ** Headquarters   **BR** Branch   **SL** Single Location

D-U-N-S 20-588-2850   (BR)
BANQUE TORONTO-DOMINION, LA
TD CANADA TRUST
(*Suby of* Toronto-Dominion Bank, The)
137 3rd St, Birch River, MB, R0L 0E0

Emp Here 20
SIC 6021 National commercial banks

Birtle, MB R0M

D-U-N-S 25-204-9051   (SL)
BIRTLE HEALTH SERVICES DISTRICT
BRITLE HEALTH CENTRE
843 Gurethud St, Birtle, MB, R0M 0C0
(204) 842-3317
Emp Here 70   *Sales* 4,888,367
SIC 8062 General medical and surgical hospitals

D-U-N-S 25-097-4839   (BR)
PARK WEST SCHOOL DIVISION
BIRTLE COLLEGIATE INSTITUTE
73 11th St, Birtle, MB, R0M 0C0
(204) 842-3315
Emp Here 30
SIC 8211 Elementary and secondary schools

Blumenort, MB R0A

D-U-N-S 20-710-2757   (BR)
GRANNY'S POULTRY COOPERATIVE (MANITOBA) LTD
4 Penner, Blumenort, MB, R0A 0C0
(204) 452-6315
Emp Here 350
SIC 2015 Poultry slaughtering and processing

D-U-N-S 24-691-4691   (SL)
IMPERIAL METAL INDUSTRIES INC
34009 42 N, Blumenort, MB, R0A 0C0
(204) 326-6683
Emp Here 45   *Sales* 5,803,882
SIC 3441 Fabricated structural Metal
Pr Pr Kelly Friesen
  Karen Friesen

D-U-N-S 24-418-8376   (SL)
SPOOKY LURKER NETWORKS
Gd, Blumenort, MB, R0A 0C0
(204) 381-1230
Emp Here 546   *Sales* 130,723,520
SIC 4813 Telephone communication, except radio
Owner Richard Penner

Boissevain, MB R0K

D-U-N-S 20-835-5979   (BR)
PRAIRIE MOUNTAIN HEALTH
BOISSEVAIN HEALTH CENTRE
(*Suby of* Prairie Mountain Health)
305 Mill Rd, Boissevain, MB, R0K 0E0
(204) 534-2451
Emp Here 60
SIC 8062 General medical and surgical hospitals

D-U-N-S 20-027-1018   (BR)
TURTLE MOUNTAIN SCHOOL DIVISION
BOISSEVAIN SCHOOL
885 Mill Rd N, Boissevain, MB, R0K 0E0
(204) 534-2494
Emp Here 65
SIC 8211 Elementary and secondary schools

Brandon, MB R7A

D-U-N-S 24-967-0290   (SL)
3008754 MANITOBA LTD
GULLIVER'S GRILL
1630 Park Ave, Brandon, MB, R7A 1J5
(204) 728-5930
Emp Here 60   *Sales* 1,824,018
SIC 5812 Eating places

D-U-N-S 25-219-7116   (SL)
3229211 MANITOBA LTD
CANADIAN INN
150 5th St, Brandon, MB, R7A 3K4
(204) 727-6404
Emp Here 62   *Sales* 2,699,546
SIC 7011 Hotels and motels

D-U-N-S 20-741-5816   (BR)
ALIMENTS SAPUTO LIMITEE
SAPUTO
365 Park Ave E, Brandon, MB, R7A 7A5
(204) 725-8600
Emp Here 42
SIC 5451 Dairy products stores

D-U-N-S 25-361-5173   (BR)
ALLSTREAM BUSINESS INC
MTS INC
517 18th St, Brandon, MB, R7A 5Y9
(204) 225-5687
Emp Here 150
SIC 4899 Communication services, nec

D-U-N-S 24-236-8124   (HQ)
ASSINIBOINE COMMUNITY COLLEGE
ACC
1430 Victoria Ave E, Brandon, MB, R7A 2A9
(204) 725-8700
Emp Here 300   *Emp Total* 20,000
Sales 62,196,822
SIC 8222 Junior colleges
Pr Mark Frison
  Harvey Armstrong

D-U-N-S 20-700-3943   (BR)
BDO CANADA LLP
BRANDON ACCOUNTING
148 10th St, Brandon, MB, R7A 4E6
(204) 727-0671
Emp Here 30
SIC 8721 Accounting, auditing, and bookkeeping

D-U-N-S 25-295-8913   (BR)
BANK OF NOVA SCOTIA, THE
SCOTIABANK
1003 Rosser Ave, Brandon, MB, R7A 0L5
(204) 729-3360
Emp Here 23
SIC 6021 National commercial banks

D-U-N-S 25-295-9317   (BR)
BANK OF NOVA SCOTIA, THE
SCOTIABANK
1570 18th St Suite 49, Brandon, MB, R7A 5C5
(204) 729-3870
Emp Here 21
SIC 6021 National commercial banks

D-U-N-S 20-700-0311   (BR)
BANQUE DE DEVELOPPEMENT DU CANADA
BDC
940 Princess Ave Unit 10, Brandon, MB, R7A 0P6
(877) 232-2269
Emp Here 40
SIC 6141 Personal credit institutions

D-U-N-S 25-901-2995   (BR)
BEAUSEJOUR CONSUMERS CO-OPERATIVE LIMITED
822 Park Ave, Brandon, MB, R7A 0A1
(204) 268-1824
Emp Here 22
SIC 5541 Gasoline service stations

D-U-N-S 20-710-4720   (SL)
BEE CLEAN CO (BRANDON) LTD
1515 Parker Blvd, Brandon, MB, R7A 7P7
(204) 727-8322
Emp Here 50   *Sales* 1,884,658
SIC 7349 Building maintenance services, nec

D-U-N-S 24-311-0744   (BR)
BEST BUY CANADA LTD
FUTURE SHOP
(*Suby of* Best Buy Co., Inc.)
901 18th St N Suite A, Brandon, MB, R7A 7S1
(204) 727-6826
Emp Here 40
SIC 5731 Radio, television, and electronic stores

D-U-N-S 20-003-5280   (BR)
BRANDON SCHOOL DIVISION, THE
EARL OXFORD SCHOOL
540 18th St, Brandon, MB, R7A 5B2
(204) 729-3270
Emp Here 42
SIC 8211 Elementary and secondary schools

D-U-N-S 20-709-9438   (BR)
BRANDON SCHOOL DIVISION, THE
GEORGE FITTON SCHOOL
1129 3rd St, Brandon, MB, R7A 3E7
(204) 729-3220
Emp Here 55
SIC 8211 Elementary and secondary schools

D-U-N-S 20-709-9495   (BR)
BRANDON SCHOOL DIVISION, THE
BETTY GIBSON SCHOOL
701 12th St, Brandon, MB, R7A 6H7
(204) 729-3965
Emp Here 35
SIC 8211 Elementary and secondary schools

D-U-N-S 20-071-1567   (BR)
BRANDON SCHOOL DIVISION, THE
GREEN ACRES ELEMENTARY SCHOOL
335 Queens Ave E, Brandon, MB, R7A 2B9
(204) 729-3265
Emp Here 22
SIC 8211 Elementary and secondary schools

D-U-N-S 20-079-3623   (BR)
BRANDON SCHOOL DIVISION, THE
KIRKCALDY HEIGHTS SCHOOL
10 Knowlton Dr, Brandon, MB, R7A 6N7
(204) 729-3290
Emp Here 40
SIC 8211 Elementary and secondary schools

D-U-N-S 20-709-9479   (BR)
BRANDON SCHOOL DIVISION, THE
ST AUGUSTINE SCHOOL
330 3rd St, Brandon, MB, R7A 3C3
(204) 729-3285
Emp Here 25
SIC 8211 Elementary and secondary schools

D-U-N-S 20-709-9453   (BR)
BRANDON SCHOOL DIVISION, THE
RIVERVIEW SCHOOL
1105 Louise Ave E, Brandon, MB, R7A 1Y2
(204) 725-0333
Emp Here 32
SIC 8211 Elementary and secondary schools

D-U-N-S 25-159-0071   (BR)
BRANDON SCHOOL DIVISION, THE
KING GEORGE ELEMENTARY SCHOOL
535 Park St, Brandon, MB, R7A 6M6
(204) 729-3990
Emp Here 25
SIC 8211 Elementary and secondary schools

D-U-N-S 20-038-2484   (BR)
BRANDON SCHOOL DIVISION, THE
ECOLE NEW ERA
527 Louise Ave, Brandon, MB, R7A 0X1
(204) 729-3161
Emp Here 50
SIC 8211 Elementary and secondary schools

D-U-N-S 20-709-9446   (BR)
BRANDON SCHOOL DIVISION, THE
ECOLE HARRISON MIDDLE SCHOOL
415 Queens Ave, Brandon, MB, R7A 1K9
(204) 729-3200
Emp Here 30
SIC 8211 Elementary and secondary schools

D-U-N-S 25-162-7394   (BR)
BRANDON SCHOOL DIVISION, THE
CROCUS PLAINS REGIONAL SECONDARY SCHOOL
1930 1st St, Brandon, MB, R7A 6Y6
(204) 729-3900
Emp Here 80
SIC 8211 Elementary and secondary schools

D-U-N-S 20-835-0322   (HQ)
BRANDON UNIVERSITY
270 18th St, Brandon, MB, R7A 6A9
(204) 728-9520
Emp Here 429   *Emp Total* 20,000
Sales 54,062,475
SIC 8221 Colleges and universities
Pr Pr Deborah Poff
  Scott Lamont

D-U-N-S 20-554-0052   (BR)
BRANDON, CITY OF
BRANDON POLICE SERVICE
1020 Victoria Ave, Brandon, MB, R7A 1A9
(204) 729-2345
Emp Here 120
SIC 7381 Detective and armored car services

D-U-N-S 25-288-9571   (BR)
CANADA POST CORPORATION
914 Douglas St, Brandon, MB, R7A 7B2
(204) 729-3585
Emp Here 80
SIC 4311 U.s. postal service

D-U-N-S 20-510-9635   (BR)
CANADIAN BLOOD SERVICES
800 Rosser Ave, Brandon, MB, R7A 6N5
(204) 571-3100
Emp Here 20
SIC 8099 Health and allied services, nec

D-U-N-S 25-311-6859   (BR)
CANADIAN IMPERIAL BANK OF COMMERCE
CIBC
803 Rosser Ave, Brandon, MB, R7A 0L1
(204) 726-3000
Emp Here 25
SIC 6021 National commercial banks

D-U-N-S 20-702-4352   (BR)
CANDO RAIL SERVICES LTD
830 Douglas St, Brandon, MB, R7A 7B2
(204) 726-4545
Emp Here 25
SIC 1629 Heavy construction, nec

D-U-N-S 24-113-8718   (BR)
CARGILL LIMITED
CARGILL NUTRENA FEEDS
1200 Pacific Ave, Brandon, MB, R7A 0J3

Emp Here 20
SIC 2048 Prepared feeds, nec

D-U-N-S 24-000-5830   (BR)
CHEMTRADE ELECTROCHEM INC
CANEXUS CORPORATION
8080 Richmond Ave E, Brandon, MB, R7A 7R3
(204) 728-3777
Emp Here 20
SIC 2899 Chemical preparations, nec

D-U-N-S 20-946-6937   (HQ)
CHILD & FAMILY SERVICES OF WESTERN MANITOBA
800 Mctavish Ave, Brandon, MB, R7A 7L4
(204) 726-6030
Emp Here 75   *Emp Total* 20,000
Sales 13,333,212

SIC 8322 Individual and family services
 David Mcgregor
Dir Tracy Baker
Dir James Burkart

D-U-N-S 24-818-6207 (BR)
COCA-COLA REFRESHMENTS CANADA COMPANY
(*Suby of* The Coca-Cola Company)
1228 Victoria Ave E, Brandon, MB, R7A 2A8
(204) 728-1525
Emp Here 31
SIC 5149 Groceries and related products, nec

D-U-N-S 20-573-2600 (BR)
COMPAGNIE DES CHEMINS DE FER NATIONAUX DU CANADA
CN
211 Van Horne Ave, Brandon, MB, R7A 7L3
(204) 727-1140
Emp Here 20
SIC 4011 Railroads, line-haul operating

D-U-N-S 25-189-8565 (BR)
DAY & ROSS INC
DAY & ROSS DEDICATED LOGISTICS
6355 Richmond Ave E, Brandon, MB, R7A 7M5
(204) 725-0291
Emp Here 20
SIC 4213 Trucking, except local

D-U-N-S 24-417-2651 (BR)
EMPIRE THEATRES LIMITED
LANDMARK
1570 18th St Unit 100, Brandon, MB, R7A 5C5
(204) 571-0900
Emp Here 40
SIC 7832 Motion picture theaters, except drive-in

D-U-N-S 20-711-0016 (BR)
FEDERATED CO-OPERATIVES LIMITED
CO-OP FEED
(*Suby of* Federated Co-Operatives Limited)
320 6th St N, Brandon, MB, R7A 7N7
(204) 727-0571
Emp Here 20
SIC 2048 Prepared feeds, nec

D-U-N-S 25-125-0528 (BR)
GARDEWINE GROUP INC
GARDEWINE NORTH
1108 Mctavish Ave E, Brandon, MB, R7A 7B9
(204) 726-4441
Emp Here 46
SIC 4731 Freight transportation arrangement

D-U-N-S 24-376-3976 (BR)
GOVERNING COUNCIL OF THE SALVATION ARMY IN CANADA, THE
DINSDALE PERSONAL CARE HOME
510 6th St, Brandon, MB, R7A 3N9
(204) 727-3636
Emp Here 100
SIC 8051 Skilled nursing care facilities

D-U-N-S 25-372-4611 (BR)
HOME DEPOT OF CANADA INC
HOME DEPOT
(*Suby of* The Home Depot Inc)
801 18th St N, Brandon, MB, R7A 7S1
(204) 571-3300
Emp Here 112
SIC 5251 Hardware stores

D-U-N-S 20-276-8669 (SL)
INVENTRONICS LIMITED
1420 Van Horne Ave E, Brandon, MB, R7A 7B6
(204) 728-2001
Emp Here 70   *Sales* 9,095,636
SIC 3499 Fabricated Metal products, nec

D-U-N-S 25-315-7952 (BR)
INVESTORS GROUP FINANCIAL SERVICES INC
857 18th St Suite A, Brandon, MB, R7A 5B8

(204) 729-2000
Emp Here 45
SIC 6211 Security brokers and dealers

D-U-N-S 24-321-9651 (SL)
JIFFY CANADA INC
MCKENZIE SEEDS
30 9th St, Brandon, MB, R7A 7T7

Emp Here 90   *Sales* 43,105,920
SIC 5191 Farm supplies
Genl Mgr Scott Hildebrandt
Dir Aarstein Knutson
Dir John Braun
Pr Pr Daniel Schordt

D-U-N-S 24-546-6131 (SL)
KISUMAR PIZZA LTD
PIZZA HUT
860 18th St, Brandon, MB, R7A 5B7
(204) 726-0600
Emp Here 65   *Sales* 1,969,939
SIC 5812 Eating places

D-U-N-S 24-372-9014 (SL)
KOCH FERTILIZER CANADA, ULC
(*Suby of* Koch Industries, Inc.)
1400 17th St E, Brandon, MB, R7A 7C4
(204) 729-2900
Emp Here 220   *Sales* 176,888,454
SIC 2873 Nitrogenous fertilizers
VP VP Lindsay Kaspik

D-U-N-S 24-329-4639 (BR)
LOBLAWS INC
REAL CANADIAN SUPERSTORE
920 Victoria Ave, Brandon, MB, R7A 1A7
(204) 729-4646
Emp Here 200
SIC 5411 Grocery stores

D-U-N-S 20-082-8692 (BR)
MNP LLP
1401 Princess Ave, Brandon, MB, R7A 7L7
(204) 727-0661
Emp Here 100
SIC 8721 Accounting, auditing, and bookkeeping

D-U-N-S 24-966-5316 (HQ)
MANITOBA AGRICULTURAL SERVICES CORPORATION
1525 1st St Unit 100, Brandon, MB, R7A 7A1
(204) 726-6850
Emp Here 35   *Emp Total* 20,000
Sales 559,196,817
SIC 6159 Miscellaneous business credit institutions
Pr Neil Hamilton
Ch Bd John Plohman
 Jim Lewis

D-U-N-S 25-096-4376 (BR)
MANITOBA PUBLIC INSURANCE CORPORATION, THE
731 1st St, Brandon, MB, R7A 6C3
(204) 729-9400
Emp Here 25
SIC 6331 Fire, marine, and casualty insurance

D-U-N-S 20-190-5275 (BR)
MANITOBA TELECOM SERVICES INC
517 18th St, Brandon, MB, R7A 5Y9
(204) 727-4500
Emp Here 480
SIC 4899 Communication services, nec

D-U-N-S 25-685-0249 (BR)
MAPLE LEAF FOODS INC
MAPLE LEAF PORK
6355 Richmond Ave E, Brandon, MB, R7A 7M5
(204) 571-2500
Emp Here 2,186
SIC 2011 Meat packing plants

D-U-N-S 25-290-8033 (BR)
MARK'S WORK WEARHOUSE LTD
MARK'S WORK WEARHOUSE #300

911 18th St N, Brandon, MB, R7A 7S1
(204) 725-1508
Emp Here 20
SIC 5651 Family clothing stores

D-U-N-S 24-327-2296 (BR)
MARSH, GLENDA PHARMACY LTD
SHOPPERS DRUG MART
1350 18th St Suite 3, Brandon, MB, R7A 5C4
(204) 729-8100
Emp Here 35
SIC 5912 Drug stores and proprietary stores

D-U-N-S 25-909-6647 (BR)
MASTERFEEDS LP
1202 17th St E, Brandon, MB, R7A 7C3
(204) 728-0231
Emp Here 25
SIC 2048 Prepared feeds, nec

D-U-N-S 25-517-8824 (BR)
MENNONITE CENTRAL COMMITTEE CANADA
BRANDON MCC TRIFTH SHOP
414 Pacific Ave, Brandon, MB, R7A 0H5

Emp Here 200
SIC 5932 Used merchandise stores

D-U-N-S 24-376-7089 (BR)
MILLER FARM EQUIPMENT 2005 INC
10 Campbell'S Trailer Crt, Brandon, MB, R7A 5Y5
(204) 725-2273
Emp Here 40
SIC 5999 Miscellaneous retail stores, nec

D-U-N-S 20-918-5573 (BR)
MORGUARD INVESTMENTS LIMITED
1570 18th St Suite 61, Brandon, MB, R7A 5C5
(204) 728-3255
Emp Here 20
SIC 6512 Nonresidential building operators

D-U-N-S 24-655-7763 (BR)
PAUL'S HAULING LTD
1515 Richmond Ave E, Brandon, MB, R7A 7A3
(204) 728-5785
Emp Here 150
SIC 4213 Trucking, except local

D-U-N-S 25-288-2931 (BR)
PERTH SERVICES LTD
PERTH'S
(*Suby of* Perth Services Ltd)
1215 Rosser Ave, Brandon, MB, R7A 0M1

Emp Here 90
SIC 7211 Power laundries, family and commercial

D-U-N-S 20-338-2973 (BR)
PFIZER CANADA INC
PFIZER GLOBAL SUPPLY-BRANDON
(*Suby of* Pfizer Inc.)
720 17th St E, Brandon, MB, R7A 7H2

Emp Here 150
SIC 2834 Pharmaceutical preparations

D-U-N-S 20-835-3198 (BR)
PRAIRIE MOUNTAIN HEALTH
ASSINIBOINE RHA MENTAL HEALTH
(*Suby of* Prairie Mountain Health)
340 9th St Suite 800, Brandon, MB, R7A 6C2

Emp Here 55
SIC 8621 Professional organizations

D-U-N-S 25-518-0507 (BR)
PRAIRIE MOUNTAIN HEALTH
RIDEAU PARK PERSONAL CARE HOME
(*Suby of* Prairie Mountain Health)
525 Victoria Ave E, Brandon, MB, R7A 6S9
(204) 578-2670
Emp Here 115
SIC 8059 Nursing and personal care, nec

D-U-N-S 25-517-7917 (BR)
PRISZM LP
KFC TACO BELL
1350 18th St Unit 2, Brandon, MB, R7A 5C4
(204) 725-0425
Emp Here 20
SIC 5812 Eating places

D-U-N-S 24-324-5144 (BR)
PUROLATOR INC.
PUROLATOR INC
939 Douglas St, Brandon, MB, R7A 7B3
(204) 727-5334
Emp Here 30
SIC 7389 Business services, nec

D-U-N-S 25-300-5524 (BR)
REDBERRY FRANCHISING CORP
BURGER KING
1605 18th St, Brandon, MB, R7A 5C6
(204) 727-2329
Emp Here 26
SIC 5812 Eating places

D-U-N-S 25-517-9863 (BR)
RIDLEY INC
1202 17th St E, Brandon, MB, R7A 7C3
(204) 728-0231
Emp Here 25
SIC 5999 Miscellaneous retail stores, nec

D-U-N-S 20-709-9388 (BR)
ROLLING RIVER SCHOOL DIVISION 39
HUTTERITE HILLSIDE COLONY SCHOOL
(*Suby of* Rolling River School Division 39)
Gd, Brandon, MB, R7A 6Y9

Emp Here 50
SIC 8211 Elementary and secondary schools

D-U-N-S 24-852-4126 (BR)
ROYAL BANK OF CANADA
RBC
(*Suby of* Royal Bank Of Canada)
661 18th St, Brandon, MB, R7A 5B3
(204) 726-3116
Emp Here 24
SIC 6021 National commercial banks

D-U-N-S 25-956-8145 (BR)
ROYAL BANK OF CANADA
ROYAL BANK FINANCIAL GROUP
(*Suby of* Royal Bank Of Canada)
740 Rosser Ave, Brandon, MB, R7A 0K9
(204) 726-3100
Emp Here 34
SIC 6021 National commercial banks

D-U-N-S 20-717-6152 (BR)
SOBEYS CAPITAL INCORPORATED
SOBEY'S BRANDON SOUTH
1645 18th St Suite B, Brandon, MB, R7A 5C6
(204) 726-5255
Emp Here 50
SIC 5411 Grocery stores

D-U-N-S 24-206-5949 (BR)
SOBEYS WEST INC
921 18th St N Suite 921, Brandon, MB, R7A 7S1
(204) 726-8014
Emp Here 150
SIC 5411 Grocery stores

D-U-N-S 24-231-9374 (BR)
SOBEYS WEST INC
SAFEWAY
1020 Victoria Ave, Brandon, MB, R7A 1A9
(204) 728-4124
Emp Here 62
SIC 5411 Grocery stores

D-U-N-S 20-273-7144 (BR)
STAPLES CANADA INC
(*Suby of* Staples, Inc.)
1645 18th St Unit A, Brandon, MB, R7A 5C6
(204) 571-5640
Emp Here 35

SIC 5943 Stationery stores

D-U-N-S 24-427-0401   (SL)
THE OTHER PLACE HOTEL LTD
TRAILS WEST MOTOR INN
210 18th St N, Brandon, MB, R7A 6P3
(204) 727-3800
Emp Here 50   *Sales* 2,188,821
SIC 7011 Hotels and motels

D-U-N-S 24-890-1618   (BR)
TRICAN WELL SERVICE LTD
59 Limestone Rd, Brandon, MB, R7A 7L5

Emp Here 80
SIC 1389 Oil and gas field services, nec

D-U-N-S 25-297-6980   (BR)
WAL-MART CANADA CORP
903 18th St N, Brandon, MB, R7A 7S1
(204) 726-5821
Emp Here 300
SIC 5311 Department stores

D-U-N-S 20-191-3618   (BR)
WESTMAN STEEL INDUSTRIES
CANADA CULVERT
927 Douglas St, Brandon, MB, R7A 7B3
(204) 726-5929
Emp Here 20
SIC 3312 Blast furnaces and steel mills

D-U-N-S 24-313-6145   (BR)
**WINNERS MERCHANTS INTERNATIONAL
L.P.**
WINNERS
(*Suby of* The TJX Companies Inc)
901 18th St, Brandon, MB, R7A 7S1
(204) 729-9029
Emp Here 30
SIC 5651 Family clothing stores

D-U-N-S 20-035-6843   (BR)
IMARKETING SOLUTIONS GROUP INC
800 Rosser Ave Suite D7, Brandon, MB, R7A
6N5
(204) 727-4242
Emp Here 150
SIC 8399 Social services, nec

Brandon, MB R7B

D-U-N-S 24-113-4717   (SL)
35790 MANITOBA LTD
KEG, THE
1836 Brandon Ave, Brandon, MB, R7B 3G8
(204) 725-4223
Emp Here 80   *Sales* 2,407,703
SIC 5812 Eating places

D-U-N-S 24-126-9500   (BR)
BELL MEDIA INC
CKX, DIV OF
2940 Victoria Ave, Brandon, MB, R7B 3Y3
(204) 728-1150
Emp Here 30
SIC 4833 Television broadcasting stations

D-U-N-S 20-023-4313   (BR)
BRANDON SCHOOL DIVISION, THE
WAVERLY PARK SCHOOL
3800 Park Ave, Brandon, MB, R7B 3X2
(204) 729-3250
Emp Here 35
SIC 8211 Elementary and secondary schools

D-U-N-S 20-024-1151   (BR)
BRANDON SCHOOL DIVISION, THE
RIVERHEIGHTS SCHOOL
32 E.Fotheringham Dr, Brandon, MB, R7B
3G3
(204) 729-3210
Emp Here 40
SIC 8211 Elementary and secondary schools

D-U-N-S 20-023-2747   (BR)

BRANDON SCHOOL DIVISION, THE
VALLEYVIEW CENTENNIAL SCHOOL
65 Whillier Dr, Brandon, MB, R7B 0X8
(204) 729-3950
Emp Here 26
SIC 8211 Elementary and secondary schools

D-U-N-S 25-060-5326   (BR)
BRANDON SCHOOL DIVISION, THE
MEADOWS ELEMENTARY SCHOOL
1220 22nd St, Brandon, MB, R7B 1T4
(204) 729-3988
Emp Here 40
SIC 8211 Elementary and secondary schools

D-U-N-S 20-047-0982   (BR)
BRANDON SCHOOL DIVISION, THE
REID, J R SCHOOL
813 26th St, Brandon, MB, R7B 2B6
(204) 729-3955
Emp Here 26
SIC 8211 Elementary and secondary schools

D-U-N-S 20-027-2735   (BR)
BRANDON SCHOOL DIVISION, THE
LINDEN LANES SCHOOL
49 Silver Birch Dr, Brandon, MB, R7B 1A8
(204) 729-3260
Emp Here 30
SIC 8211 Elementary and secondary schools

D-U-N-S 20-517-1866   (BR)
BRANDON SCHOOL DIVISION, THE
VINCENT MASSEY HIGH SCHOOL
715 Mcdiarmid Dr, Brandon, MB, R7B 2H7
(204) 729-3170
Emp Here 85
SIC 8211 Elementary and secondary schools

D-U-N-S 20-948-8352   (HQ)
K.A.S.A. HOLDINGS LTD
MCDONALDS RESTAURANT
(*Suby of* K.A.S.A. Holdings Ltd)
1907 Richmond Ave, Brandon, MB, R7B 0T4
(204) 725-2244
Emp Here 80   *Emp Total* 210
Sales 8,539,920
SIC 5812 Eating places
Pr Pr George Sheard

D-U-N-S 25-321-4456   (BR)
REVERA INC
VALLEYVIEW CARE CENTRE
3015 Victoria Ave Suite 219, Brandon, MB,
R7B 2K2
(204) 728-2030
Emp Here 140
SIC 8051 Skilled nursing care facilities

D-U-N-S 25-522-2788   (BR)
SOBEYS CAPITAL INCORPORATED
SOBEYS WESTEND
3409 Victoria Ave, Brandon, MB, R7B 2L8
(204) 727-3431
Emp Here 95
SIC 5411 Grocery stores

D-U-N-S 20-806-2427   (BR)
SOBEYS CAPITAL INCORPORATED
SOBEYS STORE# 5138
3409 Victoria Ave, Brandon, MB, R7B 2L8
(204) 727-3443
Emp Here 100
SIC 5411 Grocery stores

Brandon, MB R7C

D-U-N-S 24-329-2542   (BR)
FREIGHTLINER MANITOBA LTD
1731 Middleton Ave, Brandon, MB, R7C 1A7
(204) 726-0000
Emp Here 20
SIC 5511 New and used car dealers

D-U-N-S 25-305-3185   (BR)

INNVEST PROPERTIES CORP
COMFORT INN
(*Suby of* Innvest Properties Corp)
925 Middleton Ave, Brandon, MB, R7C 1A8
(204) 727-6232
Emp Here 20
SIC 7011 Hotels and motels

D-U-N-S 24-852-4571   (SL)
J.W. VENTURES INC
SMITTY'S RESTAURANT
1790 Highland Ave, Brandon, MB, R7C 1A7
(204) 571-3152
Emp Here 75   *Sales* 2,261,782
SIC 5812 Eating places

D-U-N-S 25-118-2580   (BR)
LAKEVIEW MANAGEMENT INC
LAKEVIEW INN & SUITES
(*Suby of* Lakeview Management Inc)
1880 18th St N, Brandon, MB, R7C 1A5
(204) 728-1880
Emp Here 20
SIC 7011 Hotels and motels

D-U-N-S 25-517-8923   (BR)
LEECH PRINTING LTD
(*Suby of* Leech Printing Ltd)
601 Braecrest Dr, Brandon, MB, R7C 1B1
(204) 727-3278
Emp Here 40
SIC 7334 Photocopying and duplicating services

D-U-N-S 20-197-2382   (BR)
LEMIQUE ENTERPRISES LTD
MCDONALD'S RESTAURANTS
(*Suby of* K.A.S.A. Holdings Ltd)
1021 Middleton Ave, Brandon, MB, R7C 1A8
(204) 725-0547
Emp Here 53
SIC 5812 Eating places

D-U-N-S 25-808-8301   (BR)
PETERBILT MANITOBA LTD
1809 18th St N, Brandon, MB, R7C 1A6
(204) 725-1991
Emp Here 23
SIC 5531 Auto and home supply stores

D-U-N-S 25-267-4478   (BR)
PRINCESS AUTO LTD
1855 18th St N, Brandon, MB, R7C 1A6
(204) 726-0601
Emp Here 20
SIC 5251 Hardware stores

D-U-N-S 20-191-9003   (BR)
REIMER EXPRESS LINES LTD
(*Suby of* Yrc Worldwide Inc.)
1604 Moreland Ave, Brandon, MB, R7C 1A6
(204) 727-2224
Emp Here 40
SIC 4212 Local trucking, without storage

D-U-N-S 24-231-9135   (BR)
SOBEYS WEST INC
1610 18th St N, Brandon, MB, R7C 1A5

Emp Here 150
SIC 5411 Grocery stores

D-U-N-S 24-319-8376   (BR)
VALUE VILLAGE STORES, INC
(*Suby of* Savers, Inc.)
1408 1st St N, Brandon, MB, R7C 1A4
(204) 727-8050
Emp Here 40
SIC 5399 Miscellaneous general merchandise

Camperville, MB R0L

D-U-N-S 20-835-5995   (BR)
FRONTIER SCHOOL DIVISION
CAMPERVILLE SCHOOL

179 Park Trunk Hwy Suite 20, Camperville,
MB, R0L 0J0
(204) 524-2343
Emp Here 23
SIC 8211 Elementary and secondary schools

Carberry, MB R0K

D-U-N-S 20-709-9099   (BR)
BEAUTIFUL PLAINS SCHOOL DIVISION
RJ WALSH ELEM SCHOOL
309 1st St, Carberry, MB, R0K 0H0
(204) 834-2828
Emp Here 50
SIC 8211 Elementary and secondary schools

D-U-N-S 20-709-9073   (BR)
BEAUTIFUL PLAINS SCHOOL DIVISION
CARBERRY COLLEGIATE
230 Main St, Carberry, MB, R0K 0H0
(204) 834-2172
Emp Here 25
SIC 8211 Elementary and secondary schools

D-U-N-S 20-177-5785   (SL)
KELLER & SONS FARMING LTD
KELLER FARMS
Gd, Carberry, MB, R0K 0H0
(204) 763-4402
Emp Here 40   *Sales* 12,532,976
SIC 5148 Fresh fruits and vegetables

Carman, MB R0G

D-U-N-S 24-851-7690   (SL)
**BOYNE VALLEY HOSTEL CORPORATION,
THE**
BOYNE LODGE PERSONAL CARE HOME
120 4th Ave Sw Rr 3, Carman, MB, R0G 0J0
(204) 745-6715
Emp Here 110   *Sales* 4,012,839
SIC 8361 Residential care

D-U-N-S 20-001-1898   (HQ)
CARMAN CO-OP (1959) LTD
(*Suby of* Carman Co-op (1959) Ltd)
61 Main St, Carman, MB, R0G 0J0
(204) 745-2073
Emp Here 87   *Emp Total* 95
Sales 29,480,071
SIC 5411 Grocery stores
Pr Pr Bill Mceachern
VP Wayne Taylor
Sec Jocelyn Van Koughnet
Sec Dan Depauw
Sec Liza Penner
Sec Doug Penner
Sec Ron Vanderzwaag

D-U-N-S 25-484-7569   (SL)
CARMAN MEMORIAL HOSPITAL
350 4th St Sw, Carman, MB, R0G 0J0
(204) 745-2021
Emp Here 60   *Sales* 4,158,760
SIC 8062 General medical and surgical hospitals

D-U-N-S 25-231-2178   (BR)
WALINGA INC
70 3rd Ave Ne, Carman, MB, R0G 0J0
(204) 745-2951
Emp Here 34
SIC 3713 Truck and bus bodies

Cartwright, MB R0K

D-U-N-S 24-915-8569   (SL)
RAINBOW TRAILERS INC

335 Broadway St, Cartwright, MB, R0K 0L0
(204) 529-2581
Emp Here 30   *Sales* 6,125,139
SIC 3715 Truck trailers
Pr Pr John Rickert
  Dickson Gould
  David Rickert
  Cathrine Rickert

Churchill, MB R0B

D-U-N-S 24-266-5818   (BR)
CALM AIR INTERNATIONAL LP
Gd, Churchill, MB, R0B 0E0
(204) 675-8858
Emp Here 25
SIC 4512 Air transportation, scheduled

D-U-N-S 20-790-7390   (BR)
FRONTIER SCHOOL DIVISION
DUKE OF MARLBOROUGH ELEMENTARY
180 Laverandrye Ave, Churchill, MB, R0B 0E0
(204) 675-2262
Emp Here 25
SIC 8211 Elementary and secondary schools

Cormorant, MB R0B

D-U-N-S 24-266-2765   (BR)
FRONTIER SCHOOL DIVISION
CORMORANT LAKE SCHOOL
5 School Rd, Cormorant, MB, R0B 0G0
(204) 357-2225
Emp Here 27
SIC 8211 Elementary and secondary schools

Cranberry Portage, MB R0B

D-U-N-S 20-709-9859   (BR)
FRONTIER SCHOOL DIVISION
CRANBERRY PORTAGE ELEMENTARY SCHOOL
109 Second Av S, Cranberry Portage, MB, R0B 0H0
(204) 472-3250
Emp Here 50
SIC 8211 Elementary and secondary schools

D-U-N-S 20-027-9110   (BR)
FRONTIER SCHOOL DIVISION
FRONTIER COLLEGIATE INSTITUTE
10 Hwy, Cranberry Portage, MB, R0B 0H0
(204) 472-3431
Emp Here 30
SIC 8211 Elementary and secondary schools

Crane River, MB R0L

D-U-N-S 20-709-9925   (BR)
FRONTIER SCHOOL DIVISION
LAKEFRONT SCHOOL
Gd, Crane River, MB, R0L 0M0
(204) 732-2750
Emp Here 50
SIC 8211 Elementary and secondary schools

Cromer, MB R0M

D-U-N-S 25-696-4826   (BR)
ENBRIDGE PIPELINES INC
Gd, Cromer, MB, R0M 0J0

---

(204) 556-2254
Emp Here 30
SIC 4612 Crude petroleum pipelines

D-U-N-S 24-248-1385   (BR)
ENBRIDGE PIPELINES INC
Gd, Cromer, MB, R0M 0J0
(204) 556-2258
Emp Here 30
SIC 4612 Crude petroleum pipelines

Cross Lake, MB R0B

D-U-N-S 20-064-3141   (BR)
AWASIS AGENCY OF NORTHERN MANI-TOBA
Gd, Cross Lake, MB, R0B 0J0
(204) 676-3902
Emp Here 20
SIC 8699 Membership organizations, nec

D-U-N-S 24-346-4729   (BR)
CROSS LAKE EDUCATION AUTHORITY
MIKISEW MIDDLE SCHOOL
Gd, Cross Lake, MB, R0B 0J0
(204) 676-3030
Emp Here 100
SIC 8211 Elementary and secondary schools

D-U-N-S 24-851-4531   (BR)
NORTH WEST COMPANY LP, THE
NORTHERN STORES
Gd, Cross Lake, MB, R0B 0J0
(204) 676-2371
Emp Here 50
SIC 5411 Grocery stores

Dauphin, MB R7N

D-U-N-S 20-292-9654   (SL)
COOLEY, DEAN MOTORS LTD
COOLEY, DEAN GM
1600 Main St S, Dauphin, MB, R7N 3B3
(204) 638-4026
Emp Here 55   *Sales* 4,012,839
SIC 7538 General automotive repair shops

D-U-N-S 20-001-4496   (HQ)
DAUPHIN CONSUMERS COOPERATIVE LTD
DAUPHIN CO-OP
(*Suby of* Dauphin Consumers Cooperative Ltd)
18 3rd Ave Ne, Dauphin, MB, R7N 0Y6
(204) 638-6003
Emp Here 64   *Emp Total* 133
Sales 53,306,890
SIC 5411 Grocery stores
Genl Mgr Drake Mcmurphy
Pr Pr Eric Irwin

D-U-N-S 20-945-2267   (SL)
DAUPHIN REGIONAL HEALTH CENTRE
625 3rd St Sw, Dauphin, MB, R7N 1R7
(204) 638-3010
Emp Here 300   *Sales* 29,014,700
SIC 8062 General medical and surgical hospitals
  Nell Vrolyk

D-U-N-S 25-055-4649   (BR)
LOBLAWS INC
EXTRA FOODS
15 1st Ave Ne, Dauphin, MB, R7N 3M3
(204) 622-2930
Emp Here 50
SIC 5411 Grocery stores

D-U-N-S 25-268-8213   (BR)
MANITOBA HYDRO-ELECTRIC BOARD, THE
MANITOBA HYDRO

---

101 2nd St Nw, Dauphin, MB, R7N 1G6

Emp Here 35
SIC 4911 Electric services

D-U-N-S 20-709-7119   (BR)
MOUNTAIN VIEW SCHOOL DIVISION
SMITH JACKSON SCHOOL
(*Suby of* Mountain View School Division)
701 1st St Se, Dauphin, MB, R7N 3L4
(204) 638-3134
Emp Here 50
SIC 8211 Elementary and secondary schools

D-U-N-S 20-945-5971   (HQ)
MOUNTAIN VIEW SCHOOL DIVISION
(*Suby of* Mountain View School Division)
182519 Sw, Dauphin, MB, R7N 3B3
(204) 638-3001
Emp Here 25   *Emp Total* 550
Sales 39,237,021
SIC 8211 Elementary and secondary schools
  Floyd Martin
Treas Bart Michaleski

D-U-N-S 25-011-2661   (BR)
MOUNTAIN VIEW SCHOOL DIVISION
MACKENZIE MIDDLE SCHOOL
(*Suby of* Mountain View School Division)
212 1st St Ne, Dauphin, MB, R7N 1B7
(204) 638-3323
Emp Here 40
SIC 8211 Elementary and secondary schools

D-U-N-S 20-709-7135   (BR)
MOUNTAIN VIEW SCHOOL DIVISION
DAUPHIN REGIONAL COMPREHENSIVE SECONDARY SCHOOL
(*Suby of* Mountain View School Division)
330 Mountain Rd, Dauphin, MB, R7N 2V6
(204) 638-4629
Emp Here 100
SIC 8211 Elementary and secondary schools

D-U-N-S 20-709-7127   (BR)
MOUNTAIN VIEW SCHOOL DIVISION
LT COLONEL BARKER SCHOOL
(*Suby of* Mountain View School Division)
1516 Bond St, Dauphin, MB, R7N 0K4
(204) 638-4588
Emp Here 50
SIC 8211 Elementary and secondary schools

D-U-N-S 20-709-7085   (BR)
MOUNTAIN VIEW SCHOOL DIVISION
MACNEILL SCHOOL
(*Suby of* Mountain View School Division)
312 Sandy St, Dauphin, MB, R7N 0K9
(204) 638-3942
Emp Here 20
SIC 8211 Elementary and secondary schools

D-U-N-S 20-709-7077   (BR)
MOUNTAIN VIEW SCHOOL DIVISION
HENDERSON ELEMENTARY SCHOOL
(*Suby of* Mountain View School Division)
911 Bond St, Dauphin, MB, R7N 3J7
(204) 638-4653
Emp Here 50
SIC 8211 Elementary and secondary schools

D-U-N-S 20-709-7101   (BR)
MOUNTAIN VIEW SCHOOL DIVISION
WITHMORE ELEMENTARY SCHOOL
(*Suby of* Mountain View School Division)
28 6th Ave Sw, Dauphin, MB, R7N 1V9
(204) 638-4782
Emp Here 50
SIC 8211 Elementary and secondary schools

D-U-N-S 20-292-4846   (HQ)
PARKLAND REGIONAL HEALTH AUTHOR-ITY INC
(*Suby of* Parkland Regional Health Authority Inc)
625 3rd St Sw, Dauphin, MB, R7N 1R7

---

(204) 638-2118
Emp Here 50   *Emp Total* 2,800
Sales 268,281,600
SIC 8062 General medical and surgical hospitals
  Kevin Mcnight
  Mary Hudyma

D-U-N-S 24-344-9092   (BR)
PARKLAND REGIONAL HEALTH AUTHOR-ITY INC
COMMUNITY HEALTH SERVICES
(*Suby of* Parkland Regional Health Authority Inc)
625 3rd St Sw, Dauphin, MB, R7N 1R7
(204) 638-2118
Emp Here 50
SIC 8099 Health and allied services, nec

D-U-N-S 24-342-7247   (BR)
RICHARDSON PIONEER LIMITED
PIONEER GRAIN
Gd, Dauphin, MB, R7N 2T3
(204) 622-7665
Emp Here 20
SIC 5153 Grain and field beans

D-U-N-S 25-518-2164   (BR)
ROYAL BANK OF CANADA
RBC
(*Suby of* Royal Bank Of Canada)
202 Main St N, Dauphin, MB, R7N 1C4
(204) 638-4920
Emp Here 20
SIC 6021 National commercial banks

D-U-N-S 20-760-3965   (SL)
SANDHU, DR S
Gd Lcd Main, Dauphin, MB, R7N 2T3
(204) 638-2103
Emp Here 56   *Sales* 3,356,192
SIC 8011 Offices and clinics of medical doctors

D-U-N-S 25-297-7509   (BR)
WAL-MART CANADA CORP
1450 Main St S Unit A, Dauphin, MB, R7N 3H4
(204) 638-4808
Emp Here 80
SIC 5311 Department stores

D-U-N-S 20-293-0124   (BR)
WEST REGION CHILD AND FAMILY SER-VICES COMMITTEE INCORPORATED
(*Suby of* West Region Child And Family Services Committee Incorporated)
431 Buchanon Ave, Dauphin, MB, R7N 2J1
(204) 622-5200
Emp Here 30
SIC 8322 Individual and family services

Deloraine, MB R0M

D-U-N-S 20-835-4563   (BR)
PRAIRIE MOUNTAIN HEALTH
DELORAINE HEALTH CENTRE
(*Suby of* Prairie Mountain Health)
109 Kellett St, Deloraine, MB, R0M 0M0
(204) 747-2243
Emp Here 70
SIC 8062 General medical and surgical hospitals

Douglas, MB R0K

D-U-N-S 25-678-1196   (SL)
FAIRWAY COLONY FARMS LTD
Po Box 330, Douglas, MB, R0K 0R0
(204) 763-8707
Emp Here 50   *Sales* 10,554,085
SIC 5261 Retail nurseries and garden stores
Pr Pr Joseph Hofer

Andy Wollman

D-U-N-S 25-127-9311   (BR)
ROLLING RIVER SCHOOL DIVISION 39
DOUGLAS ELEMENTARY SCHOOL
(*Suby of* Rolling River School Division 39)
207 East St, Douglas, MB, R0K 0R0
(204) 763-4480
Emp Here 20
SIC 8211 Elementary and secondary schools

Duck Bay, MB R0L

D-U-N-S 25-127-9337   (BR)
FRONTIER SCHOOL DIVISION
DUCK BAY SCHOOL
65 Government Rd, Duck Bay, MB, R0L 0N0
(204) 524-2355
Emp Here 24
SIC 8211 Elementary and secondary schools

Dugald, MB R0E

D-U-N-S 25-071-6255   (BR)
SUNRISE SCHOOL DIVISION
ECOLE DUGALD SCHOOL
543 Holland St, Dugald, MB, R0E 0K0
(204) 853-7929
Emp Here 42
SIC 8211 Elementary and secondary schools

East St Paul, MB R2E

D-U-N-S 24-776-0259   (HQ)
CANADIAN GUIDE RAIL CORPORATION
MONTEFERRO AMERICA
(*Suby of* Canadian Guide Rail Corporation)
2840 Wenzel St, East St Paul, MB, R2E 1E7
(204) 222-2142
Emp Here 75   *Emp Total* 120
Sales 21,390,868
SIC 3441 Fabricated structural Metal
Dir Jon Olson
Dir Scott Meaney
Dir Bruce Irvine
Giancarlo Besana
Granata Tiziano

D-U-N-S 20-760-1436   (SL)
LUDWICK CATERING LTD
3184 Birds Hill Rd, East St Paul, MB, R2E 1H1
(204) 668-8091
Emp Here 100   *Sales* 2,991,389
SIC 5812 Eating places

D-U-N-S 20-023-9122   (BR)
RIVER EAST TRANSCONA SCHOOL DIVISION
DR F.W.L. HAMILTON SCHOOL
3225 Henderson Hwy, East St Paul, MB, R2E 0J2
(204) 661-2500
Emp Here 29
SIC 8211 Elementary and secondary schools

D-U-N-S 20-709-7929   (BR)
RIVER EAST TRANSCONA SCHOOL DIVISION
BIRD'S HILL SCHOOL
3950 Raleigh St, East St Paul, MB, R2E 0G9
(204) 663-7669
Emp Here 50
SIC 8211 Elementary and secondary schools

Ebb And Flow, MB R0L

D-U-N-S 20-651-7935   (BR)
EBB AND FLOW FIRST NATION EDUCATION AUTHORITY
EBB AND FLOW SCHOOL
Gd, Ebb And Flow, MB, R0L 0R0
(204) 448-2012
Emp Here 80
SIC 8211 Elementary and secondary schools

Elgin, MB R0K

D-U-N-S 24-115-5498   (SL)
SOURIS RIVER COLONY FARMS LTD
Gd, Elgin, MB, R0K 0T0

Emp Here 91   *Sales* 4,523,563
SIC 7389 Business services, nec

Elie, MB R0H

D-U-N-S 20-358-1152   (SL)
AGWEST LTD
Highway 1 W, Elie, MB, R0H 0H0
(204) 353-3850
Emp Here 46   *Sales* 3,720,996
SIC 7359 Equipment rental and leasing, nec

D-U-N-S 24-098-8647   (BR)
TOROMONT INDUSTRIES LTD
Hwy 1 W, Elie, MB, R0H 0H0
(204) 353-3850
Emp Here 22
SIC 5999 Miscellaneous retail stores, nec

Elkhorn, MB R0M

D-U-N-S 20-709-9503   (BR)
FORT LA BOSSE SCHOOL DIVISION
ELKHORN SCHOOL
(*Suby of* Fort La Bosse School Division)
112 Tralee St, Elkhorn, MB, R0M 0N0
(204) 845-2118
Emp Here 30
SIC 8211 Elementary and secondary schools

D-U-N-S 20-709-9552   (BR)
FORT LA BOSSE SCHOOL DIVISION
BOUNDARY LANE COLONY SCHOOL
(*Suby of* Fort La Bosse School Division)
171096 Road 69n, Elkhorn, MB, R0M 0N0
(204) 845-2662
Emp Here 50
SIC 8211 Elementary and secondary schools

Elm Creek, MB R0G

D-U-N-S 20-048-0106   (BR)
PRAIRIE ROSE SCHOOL DIVISION NO 8
ELM CREEK SCHOOL
194 Gordon Ave, Elm Creek, MB, R0G 0N0
(204) 436-3332
Emp Here 29
SIC 8211 Elementary and secondary schools

Elma, MB R0E

D-U-N-S 20-743-1326   (SL)
SUN GRO HORTICULTURE CANADA LTD
SUN GRO HORTICULTURE PROCESSING
Gd, Elma, MB, R0E 0Z0

(204) 426-2121
Emp Here 750   *Sales* 61,292,800
SIC 1499 Miscellaneous nonMetallic minerals, except fuels
Pr Pr Mitch Weaver
Dir Jon Dawson
Dir Douglas Allen
Dir Rodrick Senft
Dir John T Goldsmith

Emerson, MB R0A

D-U-N-S 25-316-1350   (BR)
COLE INTERNATIONAL INC
COLE GROUP
389 Goschen St Suite 5, Emerson, MB, R0A 0L0
(204) 373-2549
Emp Here 20
SIC 4731 Freight transportation arrangement

D-U-N-S 25-706-5193   (BR)
R H A CENTRAL MANITOBA INC.
EMERSON HEALTH CENTRE
26 Main St, Emerson, MB, R0A 0L0
(204) 373-2616
Emp Here 35
SIC 8062 General medical and surgical hospitals

Erickson, MB R0J

D-U-N-S 24-427-7836   (SL)
ROLLING RIVER FIRST NATION TRUCKING LIMITED PARTNERSHIP
Gd, Erickson, MB, R0J 0P0
(204) 636-2211
Emp Here 50   *Sales* 4,677,755
SIC 4212 Local trucking, without storage

D-U-N-S 25-480-8843   (BR)
ROLLING RIVER SCHOOL DIVISION 39
ERICKSON ELEMENTARY SCHOOL
(*Suby of* Rolling River School Division 39)
62 Main St, Erickson, MB, R0J 0P0
(204) 636-2266
Emp Here 20
SIC 8211 Elementary and secondary schools

D-U-N-S 20-709-9347   (BR)
ROLLING RIVER SCHOOL DIVISION 39
ERICKSON COLLEGIATE
(*Suby of* Rolling River School Division 39)
39 Queen Elizabeth Rd, Erickson, MB, R0J 0P0
(204) 636-2605
Emp Here 25
SIC 8211 Elementary and secondary schools

Eriksdale, MB R0C

D-U-N-S 20-034-3809   (BR)
LAKESHORE SCHOOL DIVISION
ERIKSDALE SCHOOL
1 School Rd, Eriksdale, MB, R0C 0W0
(204) 739-2635
Emp Here 29
SIC 8211 Elementary and secondary schools

Ethelbert, MB R0L

D-U-N-S 20-709-7143   (BR)
MOUNTAIN VIEW SCHOOL DIVISION
ETHELBERT SCHOOL
(*Suby of* Mountain View School Division)
15 Collegiate Dr, Ethelbert, MB, R0L 0T0

(204) 742-3265
Emp Here 25
SIC 8211 Elementary and secondary schools

Faulkner, MB R0C

D-U-N-S 25-679-8257   (BR)
GRAYMONT WESTERN CANADA INC
Po Box 1, Faulkner, MB, R0C 0Y0
(204) 449-2078
Emp Here 39
SIC 3274 Lime

Fisher Branch, MB R0C

D-U-N-S 20-709-8448   (BR)
LAKESHORE SCHOOL DIVISION
FISHER BRANCH EARLY YEARS SCHOOL
Gd, Fisher Branch, MB, R0C 0Z0
(204) 372-6615
Emp Here 50
SIC 8211 Elementary and secondary schools

D-U-N-S 20-656-0430   (BR)
LAKESHORE SCHOOL DIVISION
FISHER BRANCH COLLEGIETE
Gd, Fisher Branch, MB, R0C 0Z0
(204) 372-6459
Emp Here 25
SIC 8211 Elementary and secondary schools

Flin Flon, MB R8A

D-U-N-S 25-189-5132   (BR)
FLIN FLON, CITY OF
FIRE DEPARTMENT
96 Hapnot St, Flin Flon, MB, R8A 1L6
(204) 681-7535
Emp Here 30
SIC 7389 Business services, nec

D-U-N-S 25-720-6698   (BR)
GARDEWINE GROUP INC
111 Thimberlane Gd Lcd Main Gd Lcd Main, Flin Flon, MB, R8A 1M5
(204) 687-5132
Emp Here 20
SIC 4731 Freight transportation arrangement

D-U-N-S 20-001-9289   (BR)
HUDSON BAY MINING AND SMELTING CO., LIMITED
HBMS
Gd, Flin Flon, MB, R8A 1N9
(204) 687-2385
Emp Here 1,500
SIC 1021 Copper ores

D-U-N-S 20-001-9578   (SL)
NORTH OF 53 CONSUMERS COOPERATIVE LIMITED
31 Main St Unit 29, Flin Flon, MB, R8A 1J5
(204) 687-7548
Emp Here 42   *Sales* 15,341,359
SIC 5411 Grocery stores
Genl Mgr Tom Therien
Pr Pr David Kendall
VP VP Rob Schiefele
Linda Clark
Dir Erhart Dzuibak
Dir George Rideout
Dir Dennis Whitbread

D-U-N-S 20-523-4532   (BR)
NORTHERN REGIONAL HEALTH AUTHORITY
FLIN FLON GENERAL HOSPITAL
50 Church St, Flin Flon, MB, R8A 1K5

---

(204) 687-7591
Emp Here 150
SIC 8062 General medical and surgical hospitals

D-U-N-S 25-522-8900   (BR)
ROYAL BANK OF CANADA
RBC
(*Suby of* Royal Bank Of Canada)
94 Main St, Flin Flon, MB, R8A 1K1
(204) 687-7551
Emp Here 25
SIC 6021 National commercial banks

Forrest Station, MB R0K

D-U-N-S 25-920-4725   (BR)
ROLLING RIVER SCHOOL DIVISION 39
FORREST ELEMENTARY SCHOOL
(*Suby of* Rolling River School Division 39)
205 Hillman Ave, Forrest Station, MB, R0K 0W0
(204) 728-7674
Emp Here 25
SIC 8211 Elementary and secondary schools

D-U-N-S 25-154-5810   (BR)
ROLLING RIVER SCHOOL DIVISION 39
ELTON COLLEGIATE
(*Suby of* Rolling River School Division 39)
205 Hillman Ave, Forrest Station, MB, R0K 0W0
(204) 728-7676
Emp Here 23
SIC 8211 Elementary and secondary schools

D-U-N-S 25-951-8579   (BR)
VITERRA INC
AGPRO GRAIN
Gd, Forrest Station, MB, R0K 0W0
(204) 727-6669
Emp Here 21
SIC 4221 Farm product warehousing and storage

Gilbert Plains, MB R0L

D-U-N-S 20-048-0650   (BR)
MOUNTAIN VIEW SCHOOL DIVISION
GILBERT PLAINS ELEMENTARY SCHOOL
(*Suby of* Mountain View School Division)
106 Burrows Ave, Gilbert Plains, MB, R0L 0X0
(204) 548-2822
Emp Here 25
SIC 8211 Elementary and secondary schools

Gillam, MB R0B

D-U-N-S 24-227-2040   (BR)
MANITOBA HYDRO-ELECTRIC BOARD, THE
MANITOBA HYDRO
Gd, Gillam, MB, R0B 0L0
(204) 486-1122
Emp Here 30
SIC 4911 Electric services

Gimli, MB R0C

D-U-N-S 25-681-2009   (BR)
BETEL HOME FOUNDATION
(*Suby of* Betel Home Foundation)
96 1st Ave, Gimli, MB, R0C 1B1
(204) 642-5556
Emp Here 90
SIC 8051 Skilled nursing care facilities

D-U-N-S 20-731-4332   (BR)
DIAGEO CANADA INC
(*Suby of* DIAGEO PLC)
19107 Seagram Rd 112 N, Gimli, MB, R0C 1B1
(204) 642-5123
Emp Here 72
SIC 2085 Distilled and blended liquors

D-U-N-S 25-289-4530   (BR)
EVERGREEN SCHOOL DIVISION
DR GEORGE JOHNSON MIDDLE SCHOOL
55 3rd Ave, Gimli, MB, R0C 1B1
(204) 642-8581
Emp Here 30
SIC 8211 Elementary and secondary schools

D-U-N-S 25-288-4937   (BR)
EVERGREEN SCHOOL DIVISION
GIMLI HIGH SCHOOL
52 7th Ave, Gimli, MB, R0C 1B1
(204) 642-8546
Emp Here 30
SIC 8211 Elementary and secondary schools

D-U-N-S 24-230-0473   (SL)
FAROEX LTD
FAROEX COMPOSITE TECHNOLOGIES
123 Anson St, Gimli, MB, R0C 1B1
(204) 642-6400
Emp Here 50   *Sales* 3,648,035
SIC 3299 NonMetallic mineral products,

D-U-N-S 25-073-9869   (BR)
FEDERATED CO-OPERATIVES LIMITED
TGP
(*Suby of* Federated Co-Operatives Limited)
55 Centre St, Gimli, MB, R0C 1B1
(204) 642-7447
Emp Here 25
SIC 5411 Grocery stores

D-U-N-S 24-117-6283   (BR)
INTERLAKE REGIONAL HEALTH AUTHORITY INC
JOHNSON MEMORIAL HOSPITAL, THE
(*Suby of* Interlake Regional Health Authority Inc)
120 6th Ave, Gimli, MB, R0C 1B1
(204) 642-6051
Emp Here 50
SIC 8322 Individual and family services

D-U-N-S 25-098-9621   (HQ)
NOVENTIS CREDIT UNION LIMITED
(*Suby of* Noventis Credit Union Limited)
34 Centre St, Gimli, MB, R0C 1B0
(204) 642-6450
Emp Here 23   *Emp Total* 140
Sales 4,992,094
SIC 6062 State credit unions

Gladstone, MB R0J

D-U-N-S 20-709-8976   (BR)
PINE CREEK SCHOOL DIVISION
GLADSTONE ELEMENTARY SCHOOL
116 Morris Ave S, Gladstone, MB, R0J 0T0
(204) 385-2613
Emp Here 23
SIC 8211 Elementary and secondary schools

D-U-N-S 20-709-8992   (BR)
PINE CREEK SCHOOL DIVISION
WILLIAM MORTOM COLLEGIATE
141 Morris Ave, Gladstone, MB, R0J 0T0
(204) 385-2845
Emp Here 50
SIC 8211 Elementary and secondary schools

D-U-N-S 24-392-6032   (BR)
REGIONAL HEALTH AUTHORITY - CENTRAL MANITOBA INC
SEVEN REGIONS HEALTH CENTRE
24 Mill St, Gladstone, MB, R0J 0T0

(204) 385-2968
Emp Here 160
SIC 8062 General medical and surgical hospitals

D-U-N-S 20-023-8751   (BR)
REGIONAL HEALTH AUTHORITY - CENTRAL MANITOBA INC
THIRD CROSSING MANOR
175 Dennis St W, Gladstone, MB, R0J 0T0
(204) 385-2474
Emp Here 50
SIC 7991 Physical fitness facilities

Glenboro, MB R0K

D-U-N-S 20-709-8752   (BR)
PRAIRIE SPIRIT SCHOOL DIVISION
GLENBORO SCHOOL
221 Cochrane St, Glenboro, MB, R0K 0X0
(204) 827-2593
Emp Here 40
SIC 8211 Elementary and secondary schools

Gods Lake Narrows, MB R0B

D-U-N-S 24-915-2901   (BR)
NORTH WEST COMPANY LP, THE
NORTHERN STORES
Gd, Gods Lake Narrows, MB, R0B 0M0
(204) 335-2323
Emp Here 20
SIC 5411 Grocery stores

Grand Marais, MB R0E

D-U-N-S 20-047-0891   (BR)
LORD SELKIRK SCHOOL DIVISION, THE
WALTER WHYTE SCHOOL
(*Suby of* Lord Selkirk School Division, The)
40005 Jackfish Lake Rd N, Grand Marais, MB, R0E 0T0
(204) 754-2240
Emp Here 20
SIC 8211 Elementary and secondary schools

Grand Rapids, MB R0C

D-U-N-S 24-354-8323   (BR)
FRONTIER SCHOOL DIVISION
GRAND RAPIDS SCHOOL
11 Grand Rapids Dr, Grand Rapids, MB, R0C 1E0
(204) 639-2451
Emp Here 40
SIC 8211 Elementary and secondary schools

D-U-N-S 24-495-4942   (SL)
POWER SUPPLY GRAND RAPIDS GS
Gd, Grand Rapids, MB, R0C 1E0
(204) 639-4138
Emp Here 40   *Sales* 19,115,703
SIC 4911 Electric services
Genl Mgr Brian Fox

Grandview, MB R0L

D-U-N-S 20-839-3587   (SL)
GRANDVIEW PERSONEL CARE HOME INC
PARKLAND REGIONAL HEALTH AUTHORITY
308 Jackson St, Grandview, MB, R0L 0Y0

(204) 546-2769
Emp Here 50   *Sales* 2,334,742
SIC 8059 Nursing and personal care, nec

D-U-N-S 20-709-7184   (BR)
MOUNTAIN VIEW SCHOOL DIVISION
GRANDVIEW SCHOOL
(*Suby of* Mountain View School Division)
117 Rose Ave, Grandview, MB, R0L 0Y0
(204) 546-2882
Emp Here 50
SIC 8211 Elementary and secondary schools

D-U-N-S 25-826-6451   (BR)
PARKLAND REGIONAL HEALTH AUTHORITY INC
GRANDVIEW PERSONAL CARE HOME
(*Suby of* Parkland Regional Health Authority Inc)
308 Jackson St, Grandview, MB, R0L 0Y0
(204) 546-2769
Emp Here 60
SIC 8322 Individual and family services

Gretna, MB R0G

D-U-N-S 20-023-2655   (BR)
BORDER LAND SCHOOL DIVISION
GRETNA ELEMENTARY SCHOOL
622 9th St, Gretna, MB, R0G 0V0
(204) 327-5344
Emp Here 30
SIC 8211 Elementary and secondary schools

Griswold, MB R0M

D-U-N-S 24-547-1982   (SL)
SIOUX VALLEY EDUCATIONAL AUTHORITY INC
SIOUX VALLEY SCHOOL
Gd, Griswold, MB, R0M 0S0
(204) 855-2663
Emp Here 65   *Sales* 4,377,642
SIC 8211 Elementary and secondary schools

Grunthal, MB R0A

D-U-N-S 24-037-3290   (BR)
HANOVER SCHOOL DIVISION
GREEN VALLEY HIGH SCHOOL
(*Suby of* Hanover School Division)
212 Oak Ave, Grunthal, MB, R0A 0R0
(204) 434-6415
Emp Here 60
SIC 8211 Elementary and secondary schools

D-U-N-S 25-920-9971   (BR)
HANOVER SCHOOL DIVISION
SOUTH OAKS ELEMENTARY SCHOOL
(*Suby of* Hanover School Division)
20 Southwood St, Grunthal, MB, R0A 0R0
(204) 434-6165
Emp Here 28
SIC 8211 Elementary and secondary schools

D-U-N-S 25-950-9636   (SL)
MENNO HOME FOR THE AGED
235 Park St, Grunthal, MB, R0A 0R0
(204) 434-6496
Emp Here 80   *Sales* 2,918,428
SIC 8361 Residential care

Hadashville, MB R0E

D-U-N-S 24-255-1260   (SL)
GRIZZLY TRANSPORT LTD

---

8 12 Suite 52, Hadashville, MB, R0E 0X0
(204) 426-5266
Emp Here 52   *Sales* 6,274,620
SIC 4213 Trucking, except local
Pr Shaun Bjorklund
VP VP Shelly Pizzey

D-U-N-S 24-826-9610   (BR)
TOURBIERES BERGER LTEE, LES
43037 Provincial Rd Suite 503, Hadashville, MB, R0E 0X0
(204) 426-2342
Emp Here 32
SIC 1499 Miscellaneous nonMetallic minerals, except fuels

Hamiota, MB R0M

D-U-N-S 25-826-5404   (SL)
CATTLEX LTD
Gd, Hamiota, MB, R0M 0T0
(204) 764-2471
Emp Here 20   *Sales* 16,780,961
SIC 5154 Livestock
Pr Pr Kenneth (Ken) Drake
  Doug Jackson
  Doug Mowat

D-U-N-S 25-011-2984   (BR)
PARK WEST SCHOOL DIVISION
HAMIOTA COLLEGIATE INSTITUTE
91 1st St N, Hamiota, MB, R0M 0T0
(204) 842-2803
Emp Here 24
SIC 8211 Elementary and secondary schools

D-U-N-S 20-555-1349   (BR)
VANGUARD CREDIT UNION LIMITED
(*Suby of* Vanguard Credit Union Limited)
50 Maple Ave E, Hamiota, MB, R0M 0T0
(204) 764-6230
Emp Here 20
SIC 6062 State credit unions

Hartney, MB R0M

D-U-N-S 20-321-3376   (BR)
MAZERGROUP LTD
Po Box 21, Hartney, MB, R0M 0X0
(204) 858-2000
Emp Here 200
SIC 5999 Miscellaneous retail stores, nec

Headingley, MB R4H

D-U-N-S 20-013-0153   (SL)
AMC FORM TECHNOLOGIES
35 Headingley St, Headingley, MB, R4H 0A8
(204) 633-8600
Emp Here 45   *Sales* 6,639,424
SIC 5211 Lumber and other building materials

Ile Des Chenes, MB R0A

D-U-N-S 20-710-0095   (BR)
DIVISION SCOLAIRE FRANCO-MANITOBAINE
ECOLE COLLEGE REGIONAL GABRIELLE ROY
(*Suby of* Division Scolaire Franco-Manitobaine)
310 Lamoureux Rd Ss 1, Ile Des Chenes, MB, R0A 0T1
(204) 878-2147
Emp Here 40

SIC 8211 Elementary and secondary schools

D-U-N-S 25-289-4845   (BR)
SEINE RIVER SCHOOL DIVISION
ILE DES CHENES SCHOOL
(*Suby of* Seine River School Division)
455 D'Auteuil, Ile Des Chenes, MB, R0A 0T0
(204) 878-2898
Emp Here 25
SIC 8211 Elementary and secondary schools

Island Lake, MB R0B

D-U-N-S 20-025-9559   (BR)
GARDEN HILL FIRST NATION
KISTIGANWACHEENG ELEMENTARY SCHOOL
Gd, Island Lake, MB, R0B 0T0
(204) 456-2391
Emp Here 60
SIC 8211 Elementary and secondary schools

Killarney, MB R0K

D-U-N-S 20-002-6839   (SL)
KILLARNEY-CARTWRIGHT CONSUMERS CO-OP LTD
414 Broadway Ave, Killarney, MB, R0K 1G0
(204) 523-4653
Emp Here 79   *Sales* 9,029,050
SIC 5399 Miscellaneous general merchandise
Pr Pr Ken Anderson

D-U-N-S 24-547-1214   (SL)
MAYFAIR COLONY FARMS LTD
MAYFAIR COLONY OF HUTTERIAN BRETHREN-TRUST
Gd, Killarney, MB, R0K 1G0
(204) 523-7317
Emp Here 50   *Sales* 2,626,585
SIC 7389 Business services, nec

D-U-N-S 24-617-6973   (BR)
PATERSON GLOBALFOODS INC
PATERSON GRAIN
544 Broadway Ave, Killarney, MB, R0K 1G0
(204) 523-8936
Emp Here 20
SIC 5153 Grain and field beans

D-U-N-S 24-387-3127   (BR)
PRAIRIE MOUNTAIN HEALTH
TRI-LAKE HEALTH CENTRE
(*Suby of* Prairie Mountain Health)
86 Ellice Dr, Killarney, MB, R0K 1G0
(204) 523-4661
Emp Here 140
SIC 8062 General medical and surgical hospitals

D-U-N-S 20-709-9669   (BR)
TURTLE MOUNTAIN SCHOOL DIVISION
KILLARNEY COLLEGIATE
417 King St, Killarney, MB, R0K 1G0
(204) 523-4696
Emp Here 80
SIC 8211 Elementary and secondary schools

Kleefeld, MB R0A

D-U-N-S 20-709-8208   (BR)
HANOVER SCHOOL DIVISION
KLEEFELD SCHOOL
(*Suby of* Hanover School Division)
101 Friesen Ave, Kleefeld, MB, R0A 0V0
(204) 377-4751
Emp Here 40
SIC 8211 Elementary and secondary schools

Koostatak, MB R0C

D-U-N-S 20-778-4542   (BR)
FISHER RIVER CREE NATION
FISHER RIVER NADAP FIRST NATIONS HEALTH CENTRE
Gd, Koostatak, MB, R0C 1S0
(204) 645-2689
Emp Here 40
SIC 8099 Health and allied services, nec

La Broquerie, MB R0A

D-U-N-S 25-083-6681   (BR)
DIVISION SCOLAIRE FRANCO-MANITOBAINE
ECOLE SAINT-JOACHIM
(*Suby of* Division Scolaire Franco-Manitobaine)
29 Normandeau Bay, La Broquerie, MB, R0A 0W0
(204) 424-5287
Emp Here 50
SIC 8211 Elementary and secondary schools

D-U-N-S 25-835-8738   (BR)
SEINE RIVER SCHOOL DIVISION
ARBORGATE SCHOOL
(*Suby of* Seine River School Division)
139 Principale St, La Broquerie, MB, R0A 0W0
(204) 424-5607
Emp Here 35
SIC 8211 Elementary and secondary schools

La Salle, MB R0G

D-U-N-S 24-128-8781   (BR)
FINMAC LUMBER LIMITED
PERIMETER LUMBER
Gd, La Salle, MB, R0G 1B0
(204) 261-4646
Emp Here 30
SIC 2421 Sawmills and planing mills, general

D-U-N-S 25-844-1963   (BR)
SEINE RIVER SCHOOL DIVISION
LA SALLE SCHOOL
(*Suby of* Seine River School Division)
43 Rue Beaudry, La Salle, MB, R0G 0A1
(204) 736-4366
Emp Here 25
SIC 8211 Elementary and secondary schools

Lac Du Bonnet, MB R0E

D-U-N-S 20-002-7977   (SL)
COLD SPRING GRANITE (CANADA) LTD
(*Suby of* Cold Spring Granite Company Inc)
50 Bruchanski Rd, Lac Du Bonnet, MB, R0E 1A0
(204) 345-2765
Emp Here 28
SIC 1411 Dimension stone

D-U-N-S 25-270-4200   (BR)
MANITOBA HYDRO-ELECTRIC BOARD, THE
MANITOBA HYDRO
120 Minnewawa St, Lac Du Bonnet, MB, R0E 1A0
(204) 345-2392
Emp Here 25
SIC 4911 Electric services

D-U-N-S 20-922-5833   (BR)
NORTH EASTMAN HEALTH ASSOCIATION

INC
LAC DU BONNET DISTRICT HEALTH CENTER
89 Mcintash St, Lac Du Bonnet, MB, R0E 1A0
(204) 345-8647
Emp Here 25
SIC 8051 Skilled nursing care facilities

D-U-N-S 20-709-8109   (BR)
SUNRISE SCHOOL DIVISION
CENTENNIAL SCHOOL
285 Mcarthur Ave, Lac Du Bonnet, MB, R0E 1A0
(204) 345-2462
Emp Here 31
SIC 8211 Elementary and secondary schools

D-U-N-S 20-023-2622   (BR)
SUNRISE SCHOOL DIVISION
LAC DU BONNET SENIOR SCHOOL
125 Mcarthur Rd, Lac Du Bonnet, MB, R0E 1A0
(204) 345-2585
Emp Here 34
SIC 8211 Elementary and secondary schools

Landmark, MB R0A

D-U-N-S 20-709-8216   (BR)
HANOVER SCHOOL DIVISION
LANDMARK COLLEGIATE
(*Suby of* Hanover School Division)
165 Main St, Landmark, MB, R0A 0X0
(204) 355-4020
Emp Here 30
SIC 8211 Elementary and secondary schools

D-U-N-S 25-137-2983   (BR)
HANOVER SCHOOL DIVISION
LANDMARK ELEMENTARY SCHOOL
(*Suby of* Hanover School Division)
177 2nd St E, Landmark, MB, R0A 0X0
(204) 355-4663
Emp Here 26
SIC 8211 Elementary and secondary schools

D-U-N-S 20-059-6125   (BR)
MAPLE LEAF FOODS INC
188 Main St, Landmark, MB, R0A 0X0

Emp Here 30
SIC 2048 Prepared feeds, nec

Leaf Rapids, MB R0B

D-U-N-S 20-710-0004   (BR)
FRONTIER SCHOOL DIVISION
LEAF RAPIDS EDUCATION CENTER
Gd, Leaf Rapids, MB, R0B 1W0
(204) 473-2403
Emp Here 30
SIC 8211 Elementary and secondary schools

Little Bullhead, MB R0C

D-U-N-S 20-709-9875   (BR)
FRONTIER SCHOOL DIVISION
PINE DOCK SCHOOL
Gd, Little Bullhead, MB, R0C 1V0
(204) 276-2177
Emp Here 50
SIC 8211 Elementary and secondary schools

Lockport, MB R1A

D-U-N-S 20-292-9266   (BR)

LORD SELKIRK SCHOOL DIVISION, THE
LOCKPORT SCHOOL
(*Suby* of Lord Selkirk School Division, The)
129 Lockport Rd, Lockport, MB, R1A 3H6
(204) 757-9881
Emp Here 45
SIC 8211 Elementary and secondary schools

Lorette, MB R0A

D-U-N-S 24-968-3962   (HQ)
DIVISION SCOLAIRE FRANCO-MANITOBAINE
(*Suby* of Division Scolaire Franco-Manitobaine)
1263 Dawson Rd, Lorette, MB, R0A 0Y0
(204) 878-9399
Emp Here 50   *Emp Total* 1,000
Sales 89,914,560
SIC 8211 Elementary and secondary schools
Dennis Ferre
Treas Annette Grenier Tetrault

D-U-N-S 25-676-9522   (BR)
DIVISION SCOLAIRE FRANCO-MANITOBAINE
ECOLE LAGIMODIERE
(*Suby* of Division Scolaire Franco-Manitobaine)
361 Senez St, Lorette, MB, R0A 0Y0
(204) 878-3621
Emp Here 25
SIC 8211 Elementary and secondary schools

D-U-N-S 20-709-8174   (BR)
SEINE RIVER SCHOOL DIVISION
LORETTE IMMERSION
475 Senez St Suite 14, Lorette, MB, R0A 0Y0
(204) 878-4713
Emp Here 22
SIC 8211 Elementary and secondary schools

D-U-N-S 25-289-2880   (BR)
SEINE RIVER SCHOOL DIVISION
COLLEGE LORETTE COLLEGIATE
(*Suby* of Seine River School Division)
1082 Dawson Rd Ss 1, Lorette, MB, R0A 0Y0
(204) 878-2887
Emp Here 53
SIC 8211 Elementary and secondary schools

D-U-N-S 25-289-2989   (BR)
SEINE RIVER SCHOOL DIVISION
DAWSON TRAIL SCHOOL
(*Suby* of Seine River School Division)
425 Senez St, Lorette, MB, R0A 0Y0
(204) 878-2929
Emp Here 60
SIC 8211 Elementary and secondary schools

Lundar, MB R0C

D-U-N-S 20-651-5608   (BR)
INTERLAKE REGIONAL HEALTH AUTHORITY INC
LUNDAR PERSONAL CARE HOME
(*Suby* of Interlake Regional Health Authority Inc)
97 1st St S, Lundar, MB, R0C 1Y0
(204) 762-5663
Emp Here 20
SIC 8059 Nursing and personal care, nec

D-U-N-S 20-709-8463   (BR)
LAKESHORE SCHOOL DIVISION
LUNDAR SCHOOL
36 1st St, Lundar, MB, R0C 1Y0
(204) 762-5610
Emp Here 35
SIC 8211 Elementary and secondary schools

Lynn Lake, MB R0B

D-U-N-S 24-365-8684   (BR)
NORTHERN REGIONAL HEALTH AUTHORITY
LYNN LAKE HOSPITAL
640 Camp Street, Lynn Lake, MB, R0B 0W0
(204) 356-2474
Emp Here 37
SIC 8062 General medical and surgical hospitals

Macgregor, MB R0H

D-U-N-S 20-039-3432   (BR)
PINE CREEK SCHOOL DIVISION
MACGREGOR ELEMENTARY SCHOOL
151 Fox St N, Macgregor, MB, R0H 0R0
(204) 685-2249
Emp Here 28
SIC 8211 Elementary and secondary schools

D-U-N-S 20-709-9008   (BR)
PINE CREEK SCHOOL DIVISION
MACGREGROR COLLEGIATE
150 Fox St N, Macgregor, MB, R0H 0R0

Emp Here 50
SIC 8211 Elementary and secondary schools

Manitou, MB R0G

D-U-N-S 20-709-8836   (BR)
PRAIRIE SPIRIT SCHOOL DIVISION
NELLIE MCCLUNG COLLEGIATE
322 Carrie St, Manitou, MB, R0G 1G0
(204) 242-2640
Emp Here 50
SIC 8211 Elementary and secondary schools

D-U-N-S 25-841-7260   (BR)
PRAIRIE SPIRIT SCHOOL DIVISION
MANITOU ELEMENTARY SCHOOL
508 Souris Ave, Manitou, MB, R0G 1G0
(204) 242-2844
Emp Here 30
SIC 8211 Elementary and secondary schools

D-U-N-S 20-023-3406   (BR)
REGIONAL HEALTH AUTHORITY - CENTRAL MANITOBA INC
PEMBINA MANITOU HEALTH CENTRE
232 Carrie St, Manitou, MB, R0G 1G0
(204) 242-2744
Emp Here 60
SIC 8059 Nursing and personal care, nec

Medora, MB R0M

D-U-N-S 20-922-5122   (SL)
VANDAELE SEEDS LTD
Gd, Medora, MB, R0M 1K0
(204) 665-2384
Emp Here 50   *Sales* 10,433,380
SIC 5191 Farm supplies
Pr Calvin Vandaele
Sec Mark Vandaele
Treas Robert Vandaele

Melita, MB R0M

D-U-N-S 24-345-6113   (BR)
PRAIRIE MOUNTAIN HEALTH

MELITA HEALTH CENTER
(*Suby* of Prairie Mountain Health)
147 Summit St, Melita, MB, R0M 1L0
(204) 522-8197
Emp Here 100
SIC 8062 General medical and surgical hospitals

Minitonas, MB R0L

D-U-N-S 25-654-2499   (SL)
VALLEY LIVESTOCK SALES
Hwy 10 E, Minitonas, MB, R0L 1G0

Emp Here 20   *Sales* 23,333,500
SIC 5154 Livestock
Pt Randy Hart

Minnedosa, MB R0J

D-U-N-S 25-676-5264   (BR)
HUSKY OIL OPERATIONS LIMITED
HUSKY OIL MARKETING CO
359 5th Ave Nw, Minnedosa, MB, R0J 1E0
(204) 867-8100
Emp Here 48
SIC 2869 Industrial organic chemicals, nec

D-U-N-S 20-644-4494   (SL)
MINNEDOSA PERSONAL CARE HOME
138 3rd Ave Sw, Minnedosa, MB, R0J 1E0
(204) 867-2569
Emp Here 50   *Sales* 2,772,003
SIC 8059 Nursing and personal care, nec

D-U-N-S 24-171-8360   (BR)
MORRIS INDUSTRIES LTD
284 6th Ave Nw, Minnedosa, MB, R0J 1E0
(204) 867-2713
Emp Here 75
SIC 3523 Farm machinery and equipment

D-U-N-S 20-797-1644   (BR)
PRAIRIE MOUNTAIN HEALTH
(*Suby* of Prairie Mountain Health)
334 1st Sw, Minnedosa, MB, R0J 1E0
(204) 867-2701
Emp Here 150
SIC 8062 General medical and surgical hospitals

D-U-N-S 20-709-9297   (BR)
ROLLING RIVER SCHOOL DIVISION 39
TANNERS CROSSING SCHOOL
(*Suby* of Rolling River School Division 39)
90 Armatage Ave, Minnedosa, MB, R0J 1E0
(204) 867-2591
Emp Here 48
SIC 8211 Elementary and secondary schools

Mitchell, MB R5G

D-U-N-S 20-709-8265   (BR)
HANOVER SCHOOL DIVISION
MITCHELL MIDDLE SCHOOL
(*Suby* of Hanover School Division)
203 Third St, Mitchell, MB, R5G 1H7
(204) 320-9488
Emp Here 30
SIC 8211 Elementary and secondary schools

D-U-N-S 20-709-8257   (BR)
HANOVER SCHOOL DIVISION
MITCHELL ELEMENTARY SCHOOL
(*Suby* of Hanover School Division)
99 Stanway Bay, Mitchell, MB, R5G 1J4
(204) 326-6622
Emp Here 32

SIC 8211 Elementary and secondary schools

Morden, MB R6M

D-U-N-S 24-967-2858   (BR)
3M CANADA COMPANY
(*Suby* of 3M Company)
400 Route 100, Morden, MB, R6M 1Z9
(204) 822-6284
Emp Here 200
SIC 2821 Plastics materials and resins

D-U-N-S 24-419-9738   (BR)
ACCESS CREDIT UNION LIMITED
(*Suby* of Access Credit Union Limited)
430 Stephen St, Morden, MB, R6M 1T6
(204) 822-4485
Emp Here 25
SIC 6062 State credit unions

D-U-N-S 25-145-4096   (BR)
BUHLER INDUSTRIES INC.
MORDEN DIVISION
301 Mountain St S, Morden, MB, R6M 1X7
(204) 822-4467
Emp Here 250
SIC 3523 Farm machinery and equipment

D-U-N-S 25-011-3362   (BR)
JOHN BUHLER INC
BUHLER, JOHN INC
301 Mountain St S, Morden, MB, R6M 1X7
(204) 822-4467
Emp Here 200
SIC 3523 Farm machinery and equipment

D-U-N-S 24-851-1867   (HQ)
RIMER ALCO NORTH AMERICA INC
RANA MEDICAL
(*Suby* of Rimer Alco North America Inc)
205 Stephen St, Morden, MB, R6M 1V2
(204) 822-6595
Emp Here 22   *Emp Total* 50
Sales 4,742,446
SIC 5999 Miscellaneous retail stores, nec

D-U-N-S 20-758-6280   (SL)
TABOR HOME INC
230 9th St S, Morden, MB, R6M 1Y3
(204) 822-4848
Emp Here 100   *Sales* 4,523,563
SIC 8051 Skilled nursing care facilities

D-U-N-S 20-570-6351   (SL)
TERRA CAB LTD
TERRACAB INDUSTRIES
(*Suby* of Satellite Industries Ltd)
300 Route 100, Morden, MB, R6M 1Y4
(204) 822-9100
Emp Here 30   *Sales* 4,331,255
SIC 3523 Farm machinery and equipment

D-U-N-S 25-890-1693   (BR)
WESTERN SCHOOL DIVISION
MINNEWASTA SCHOOL
(*Suby* of Western School Division)
1 Academy Rd, Morden, MB, R6M 1Z4
(204) 822-4580
Emp Here 33
SIC 8211 Elementary and secondary schools

D-U-N-S 25-272-3721   (BR)
WESTERN SCHOOL DIVISION
MORDEN COLLEGIATE INSTITUTE
(*Suby* of Western School Division)
345 5th St, Morden, MB, R6M 1Z1
(204) 822-4425
Emp Here 50
SIC 8211 Elementary and secondary schools

D-U-N-S 25-071-6560   (BR)
WESTERN SCHOOL DIVISION
ECOLE MORDEN MIDDLE SCHOOL
(*Suby* of Western School Division)
150 Wardrop St Suite 150, Morden, MB, R6M

1Z2
(204) 822-6225
Emp Here 65
SIC 8211 Elementary and secondary schools

D-U-N-S 20-027-2685   (BR)
WESTERN SCHOOL DIVISION
MAPLE LEAF ELEMENTARY SCHOOL
(*Suby of* Western School Division)
225 12th St, Morden, MB, R6M 1Z3
(204) 822-4458
Emp Here 40
SIC 8211 Elementary and secondary schools

D-U-N-S 25-362-9513   (BR)
WINKLER CONSUMERS COOPERATIVE LTD
MORDEN COOP
945 Thornhill St, Morden, MB, R6M 1J9
(204) 822-5868
Emp Here 50
SIC 8699 Membership organizations, nec

Morris, MB R0G

D-U-N-S 25-268-8361   (BR)
PATERSON GLOBALFOODS INC
PATERSON GRAIN
8 Stampede Dr, Morris, MB, R0G 1K0
(204) 746-2347
Emp Here 20
SIC 5153 Grain and field beans

D-U-N-S 25-719-9570   (BR)
R H A CENTRAL MANITOBA INC.
RED RIVER VALLEY LODGE
136 Ottawa St W, Morris, MB, R0G 1K0
(204) 746-2394
Emp Here 55
SIC 8059 Nursing and personal care, nec

Neepawa, MB R0J

D-U-N-S 25-892-3416   (BR)
BEAUTIFUL PLAINS SCHOOL DIVISION
NEEPAWA AREA COLLEGIATE
440 Hospital St, Neepawa, MB, R0J 1H0
(204) 476-3305
Emp Here 50
SIC 8211 Elementary and secondary schools

D-U-N-S 20-709-9115   (BR)
BEAUTIFUL PLAINS SCHOOL DIVISION
KELLINGTON, HAZEL M SCHOOL
361 3rd Ave, Neepawa, MB, R0J 1H0
(204) 476-2323
Emp Here 40
SIC 8211 Elementary and secondary schools

D-U-N-S 24-335-7915   (BR)
ENNS BROTHERS LTD
187 Pth 16 W, Neepawa, MB, R0J 1H0
(204) 476-3413
Emp Here 20
SIC 5083 Farm and garden machinery

D-U-N-S 24-362-8851   (BR)
HYLIFE LTD
SPRINGHILL FARMS
623 Main St E, Neepawa, MB, R0J 1H0
(204) 476-3624
Emp Here 350
SIC 2011 Meat packing plants

D-U-N-S 20-788-9184   (BR)
MANITOBA LIQUOR AND LOTTERIES CORPORATION
LIQUOR MART
393 Mountain Ave, Neepawa, MB, R0J 1H0
(204) 476-5769
Emp Here 20
SIC 5921 Licuor stores

D-U-N-S 24-422-5541   (BR)
MAZERGROUP LTD
MAZERGROUP - NEEPAWA
Gd, Neepawa, MB, R0J 1H0
(204) 476-2364
Emp Here 24
SIC 5999 Miscellaneous retail stores, nec

D-U-N-S 20-613-7085   (BR)
PRAIRIE FOREST PRODUCTS LTD
205 Hwy 16, Neepawa, MB, R0J 1H0
(204) 476-7700
Emp Here 55
SIC 2491 Wood preserving

D-U-N-S 24-363-2028   (BR)
SOBEYS WEST INC
NEEPAWA SAFEWAY
Gd, Neepawa, MB, R0J 1H0
(204) 476-5423
Emp Here 50
SIC 5411 Grocery stores

D-U-N-S 20-358-9346   (SL)
T.I.C. PARTS AND SERVICE
BUMPER TO BUMPER
220 Hwy 5 N, Neepawa, MB, R0J 1H0
(204) 476-3809
Emp Here 50   *Sales* 3,648,035
SIC 7538 General automotive repair shops

Nelson House, MB R0B

D-U-N-S 20-035-5720   (BR)
NELSON HOUSE EDUCATION AUTHORITY, INC
OTETISKEWIN KISKINWAMAHTOWEK SCHOOL
1 Roland Lauze Dr, Nelson House, MB, R0B 1A0
(204) 484-2242
Emp Here 70
SIC 8211 Elementary and secondary schools

New Bothwell, MB R0A

D-U-N-S 20-003-5533   (SL)
BOTHWELL CHEESE INC
61 Main St, New Bothwell, MB, R0A 1C0
(204) 388-4666
Emp Here 60   *Sales* 7,538,632
SIC 2022 Cheese; natural and processed
Pr Pr Ivan Balenovic

Newton Siding, MB R0H

D-U-N-S 24-654-5685   (SL)
ELM RIVER COLONY FARMS LTD
Gd, Newton Siding, MB, R0H 0X0
(204) 267-2084
Emp Here 85   *Sales* 4,231,721
SIC 7389 Business services, nec

Ninette, MB R0K

D-U-N-S 20-760-5630   (SL)
SOUTHWEST COMMUNITY OPTIONS INC
210 Queen St, Ninette, MB, R0K 1R0
(204) 528-5060
Emp Here 49   *Sales* 12,368,160
SIC 8399 Social services, nec
Ex Dir Eleanor Struth

D-U-N-S 20-834-6130   (SL)
WELLWOOD COLONY OF HUTTERIAN

BRETHREN TRUST
WELLWOOD COLONY FARMS
23517 Wellwood Rd, Ninette, MB, R0K 1R0
(204) 776-2130
Emp Here 56   *Sales* 6,274,620
SIC 8748 Business consulting, nec
Pr Pr Lawrence Waldner
   Robert Hofer

Niverville, MB R0A

D-U-N-S 20-709-8224   (BR)
HANOVER SCHOOL DIVISION
NIVERVILLE ELEMENTARY SCHOOL
(*Suby of* Hanover School Division)
181 Main St, Niverville, MB, R0A 1E0
(204) 388-4861
Emp Here 42
SIC 8211 Elementary and secondary schools

D-U-N-S 25-272-3648   (BR)
HANOVER SCHOOL DIVISION
NIVERVILLE COLLEGIATE
(*Suby of* Hanover School Division)
161 5th Ave, Niverville, MB, R0A 1E0
(204) 388-4731
Emp Here 28
SIC 8211 Elementary and secondary schools

D-U-N-S 20-760-0156   (HQ)
PURATONE CORPORATION, THE
(*Suby of* Puratone Corporation, The)
295 Main St, Niverville, MB, R0A 1E0
(204) 388-4741
Emp Here 50   *Emp Total* 370
Sales 103,755,120
SIC 5191 Farm supplies
Pr Pr Ab Freig
VP VP Ray Hilderbrand
Dir Patrick Matthews

Norway House, MB R0B

D-U-N-S 20-709-9974   (BR)
FRONTIER SCHOOL DIVISION
HELEN BETTY OSBORNE ININIW EDUCA-TION RESOURCE CENTRE
1 Rossville Rd, Norway House, MB, R0B 1B0
(204) 359-4100
Emp Here 1,005
SIC 8211 Elementary and secondary schools

D-U-N-S 24-915-3131   (BR)
NORTH WEST COMPANY LP, THE
NORTHERN STORES
Gd, Norway House, MB, R0B 1B0
(204) 359-6258
Emp Here 80
SIC 5411 Grocery stores

D-U-N-S 20-837-6285   (SL)
PINAOW WACHI INC
Gd, Norway House, MB, R0B 1B0
(204) 359-6606
Emp Here 52   *Sales* 1,896,978
SIC 8361 Residential care

Notre Dame De Lourdes, MB R0G

D-U-N-S 24-354-6020   (HQ)
CAISSE POPULAIRE PEMBINA LTEE
(*Suby of* Caisse Populaire Pembina Ltee)
151 Notre Dame Ave W, Notre Dame De Lour-des, MB, R0G 1M0
(204) 248-2332
Emp Here 27   *Emp Total* 35
Sales 8,897,700
SIC 6062 State credit unions

Fin Mgr Rene Hebert

D-U-N-S 25-676-9688   (BR)
DIVISION SCOLAIRE FRANCO-MANITOBAINE
ECOLE ELEMENTAIRE NOTRE-DAME-DE-LOURDES
(*Suby of* Division Scolaire Franco-Manitobaine)
70 Notre-Dame Ave, Notre Dame De Lourdes, MB, R0G 1M0
(204) 248-2147
Emp Here 23
SIC 8211 Elementary and secondary schools

D-U-N-S 25-886-0675   (BR)
DIVISION SCOLAIRE FRANCO-MANITOBAINE
COLLEGE REGIONAL NOTRE-DAME
(*Suby of* Division Scolaire Franco-Manitobaine)
45 Notre Dame Ave, Notre Dame De Lourdes, MB, R0G 1M0
(204) 248-2167
Emp Here 26
SIC 8211 Elementary and secondary schools

Oak Bluff, MB R0G

D-U-N-S 25-370-1312   (BR)
MCDIARMID LUMBER LTD
MCDIARMID LUMBER HOME CENTRES
Gd, Oak Bluff, MB, R0G 1N0
(204) 895-7938
Emp Here 75
SIC 5211 Lumber and other building materials

D-U-N-S 20-716-7706   (BR)
RED RIVER VALLEY SCHOOL DIVISION
OAK BLUFF COMMUNITY SCHOOL
(*Suby of* Red River Valley School Division)
155 Egri-Park Rd, Oak Bluff, MB, R0G 1N0
(204) 895-0004
Emp Here 50
SIC 8211 Elementary and secondary schools

D-U-N-S 24-852-7848   (SL)
SAWYER WOOD PRODUCTS INC
BURROWS LUMBER
Gd, Oak Bluff, MB, R0G 1N0

Emp Here 20   *Sales* 7,727,098
SIC 5031 Lumber, plywood, and millwork
Pr Pr Bryan Antoshko

Oak Bluff, MB R4G

D-U-N-S 24-882-4989   (HQ)
AMBASSADOR MECHANICAL L.P.
400 Fort Whyte Way Unit 110, Oak Bluff, MB, R4G 0B1
(204) 231-1094
Emp Here 135   *Emp Total* 1,100
Sales 33,284,025
SIC 1711 Plumbing, heating, air-conditioning
Pr Claude Cloutier
VP Colin Cloutier
   Harold Kunich
   Alan Fowler

D-U-N-S 20-002-0709   (HQ)
KLEYSEN GROUP LTD
2800 Mcgillivray Blvd, Oak Bluff, MB, R4G 0B4
(204) 488-5550
Emp Here 225   *Emp Total* 5,515
Sales 39,544,699
SIC 4213 Trucking, except local
Pr Jeff Kleysen

D-U-N-S 25-106-5009   (SL)
SUPERIOR TRUSS CO LTD

165 Industrial Rd, Oak Bluff, MB, R4G 0A5
(204) 888-7663
Emp Here 690   *Sales* 106,307,280
SIC 2439 Structural wood members, nec
Pr Pr Vince Ryz

Oakbank, MB R0E

D-U-N-S 24-267-5585   (SL)
GEE TEE HOLDINGS INC
Gd, Oakbank, MB, R0E 1J0
(204) 444-3069
Emp Here 60   *Sales* 4,742,446
SIC 4212 Local trucking, without storage

D-U-N-S 20-875-4064   (BR)
NORTH EASTMAN HEALTH ASSOCIATION INC
KIN PLACE HEALTH COMPLEX
689 Main St, Oakbank, MB, R0E 1J2
(204) 444-2227
Emp Here 150
SIC 8011 Offices and clinics of medical doctors

D-U-N-S 20-023-2580   (BR)
SUNRISE SCHOOL DIVISION
SPRINGFIELD COLLEGIATE INSTITUTE
841 Cedar Ave, Oakbank, MB, R0E 1J1
(204) 444-2404
Emp Here 65
SIC 8211 Elementary and secondary schools

D-U-N-S 20-553-1366   (BR)
SUNRISE SCHOOL DIVISION
SPRINGFIELD MIDDLE SCHOOL
760 Cedar Ave, Oakbank, MB, R0E 1J0
(204) 444-2995
Emp Here 40
SIC 8211 Elementary and secondary schools

D-U-N-S 20-553-1515   (BR)
SUNRISE SCHOOL DIVISION
OAKBANK ELEMENTARY SCHOOL
826 Cedar Ave, Oakbank, MB, R0E 1J0
(204) 444-2473
Emp Here 57
SIC 8211 Elementary and secondary schools

Oakville, MB R0H

D-U-N-S 20-709-8497   (BR)
PORTAGE LA PRAIRIE SCHOOL DIVISION
OAKVILLE SCHOOL
(*Suby of* Portage La Prairie School Division)
20125 Road 57n, Oakville, MB, R0H 0Y0
(204) 267-2733
Emp Here 25
SIC 8211 Elementary and secondary schools

Onanole, MB R0J

D-U-N-S 20-838-4941   (SL)
ELKHORN RANCH & RESORT LTD
ELKHORN RESORT SPA & CONFERENCE CENTRE
3 Mooswa Dr E, Onanole, MB, R0J 1N0
(204) 848-2802
Emp Here 80   *Sales* 3,502,114
SIC 7011 Hotels and motels

Otterburne, MB R0A

D-U-N-S 24-121-6501   (BR)
PROVIDENCE UNIVERSITY COLLEGE AND THEOLOGICAL SEMINARY

FOOD SERVICES
11 College Dr Unit 82835001, Otterburne, MB, R0A 1G0
(204) 433-7732
Emp Here 40
SIC 5812 Eating places

Oxford House, MB R0B

D-U-N-S 24-883-3238   (SL)
COLON, GEORGE MEMORIAL HOME INC
Gd, Oxford House, MB, R0B 1C0
(204) 538-2560
Emp Here 55   *Sales* 2,042,900
SIC 8361 Residential care

D-U-N-S 24-915-3222   (BR)
NORTH WEST COMPANY LP, THE
NORTHERN STORES
General Store, Oxford House, MB, R0B 1C0
(204) 538-2359
Emp Here 45
SIC 5411 Grocery stores

D-U-N-S 20-835-2760   (BR)
OXFORD HOUSE FIRST NATION BOARD OF EDUCATION INC
1972 MEMORIAL HIGH SCHOOL
Gd, Oxford House, MB, R0B 1C0
(204) 538-2020
Emp Here 20
SIC 8211 Elementary and secondary schools

D-U-N-S 20-570-3221   (BR)
OXFORD HOUSE FIRST NATION BOARD OF EDUCATION INC
OXFORD HOUSE ELEMENTARY SCHOOL
Gd, Oxford House, MB, R0B 1C0

Emp Here 65
SIC 8211 Elementary and secondary schools

Peguis, MB R0C

D-U-N-S 24-040-4103   (SL)
PEGUIS SCHOOL BOARD
Gd, Peguis, MB, R0C 3J0
(204) 645-2648
Emp Here 250   *Sales* 23,232,050
SIC 8211 Elementary and secondary schools
Superintnt Edwin Mccorrister
Ex Dir Eugene Stevenson
Dir Sharon Stevenson

Pilot Mound, MB R0G

D-U-N-S 25-764-7289   (BR)
ROCK LAKE HEALTH DISTRICT FOUNDATION INC
ROCK LAKE PERSONAL CARE HOME
(*Suby of* Rock Lake Health District Foundation Inc)
115 Brown St Apt 27, Pilot Mound, MB, R0G 1P0
(204) 825-2246
Emp Here 110
SIC 8361 Residential care

Pinawa, MB R0E

D-U-N-S 20-834-8961   (BR)
ATOMIC ENERGY OF CANADA LIMITED
AECL WHITE SHELL LABORATORY
Gd, Pinawa, MB, R0E 1L0
(204) 753-2311
Emp Here 250

SIC 2819 Industrial inorganic chemicals, nec

D-U-N-S 25-720-6979   (HQ)
NORTH EASTMAN HEALTH ASSOCIATION INC
BEAUSEJOUR DISTRICT HOSPITAL
(*Suby of* North Eastman Health Association Inc)
24 Aberdeen Ave, Pinawa, MB, R0E 1L0
(204) 753-2012
Emp Here 20   *Emp Total* 1,100
Sales 215,529,600
SIC 8741 Management services
 Jim Hayes
VP Fin Donna Demarco
Dir Fin Kathy Hanna
 Margaret Mills
 Therese Conroy
 Virginia Mathews
 Fran Thompson
 Robert Carmichael
 Steve Day
 Daniel Franklin

D-U-N-S 25-951-7910   (BR)
NORTH EASTMAN HEALTH ASSOCIATION INC
PINAWA HOSPITAL
(*Suby of* North Eastman Health Association Inc)
3 Vanier Rd, Pinawa, MB, R0E 1L0
(204) 753-2334
Emp Here 35
SIC 8062 General medical and surgical hospitals

Pine Falls, MB R0E

D-U-N-S 25-092-6771   (BR)
SAGKEENG EDUCATION AUTHORITY
ANICINABE COMMUNITY SCHOOL
(*Suby of* Sagkeeng Education Authority)
Gd, Pine Falls, MB, R0E 1M0
(204) 367-2285
Emp Here 37
SIC 8211 Elementary and secondary schools

D-U-N-S 20-035-5886   (BR)
SAGKEENG EDUCATION AUTHORITY
SAGKEENG ANICINABE HIGH SCHOOL
(*Suby of* Sagkeeng Education Authority)
1 Nika Cres, Pine Falls, MB, R0E 1M0
(204) 367-2243
Emp Here 35
SIC 8211 Elementary and secondary schools

Plum Coulee, MB R0G

D-U-N-S 25-288-5769   (BR)
GARDEN VALLEY SCHOOL DIVISION
PLUM COULEE ELEMENTARY SCHOOL
(*Suby of* Garden Valley School Division)
155 Government Rd, Plum Coulee, MB, R0G 1R0
(204) 325-9852
Emp Here 23
SIC 8211 Elementary and secondary schools

Poplar Point, MB R0H

D-U-N-S 24-427-3546   (SL)
WOODLANDS COLONY FARMS LTD
WOODLANDS COLONY OF HUTTERIAN BRETHREN
Gd, Poplar Point, MB, R0H 0Z0
(204) 243-2642
Emp Here 50   *Sales* 2,626,585
SIC 7389 Business services, nec

Portage La Prairie, MB R1N

D-U-N-S 20-721-8897   (SL)
4115155 MANITOBA LIMITED
BOSTON PIZZA
2180 Saskatchewan Ave W, Portage La Prairie, MB, R1N 0P3
(204) 239-8200
Emp Here 65   *Sales* 1,969,939
SIC 5812 Eating places

D-U-N-S 25-959-0198   (BR)
BDO CANADA LLP
PORTAGE LA PRAIRIE ACCOUNTING
480 Saskatchewan Ave W, Portage La Prairie, MB, R1N 0M4
(204) 857-2856
Emp Here 20
SIC 8721 Accounting, auditing, and bookkeeping

D-U-N-S 25-289-0017   (BR)
CANADA POST CORPORATION
9 Saskatchewan Ave W, Portage La Prairie, MB, R1N 0P4
(204) 857-5890
Emp Here 29
SIC 4311 U.s. postal service

D-U-N-S 20-786-5655   (BR)
CANADIAN TIRE CORPORATION, LIMITED
2445 Saskatchewan Ave W, Portage La Prairie, MB, R1N 4A6
(204) 857-3591
Emp Here 55
SIC 5399 Miscellaneous general merchandise

D-U-N-S 25-061-4807   (BR)
ENNS BROTHERS LTD
ENNS BROTHERS PORTAGE
65154 Rd 41 W, Portage La Prairie, MB, R1N 3J9
(204) 857-3451
Emp Here 60
SIC 5083 Farm and garden machinery

D-U-N-S 20-844-9525   (BR)
GOLDEN WEST BROADCASTING LTD
MIX 96
2390 Sissons Dr, Portage La Prairie, MB, R1N 0G5
(204) 239-5111
Emp Here 23
SIC 4832 Radio broadcasting stations

D-U-N-S 25-266-6508   (BR)
MNP LLP
780 Saskatchewan Ave W, Portage La Prairie, MB, R1N 0M7
(204) 239-6117
Emp Here 27
SIC 8721 Accounting, auditing, and bookkeeping

D-U-N-S 25-268-8858   (BR)
MANITOBA HYDRO-ELECTRIC BOARD, THE
50 14th St Nw, Portage La Prairie, MB, R1N 2V3
(204) 857-7868
Emp Here 40
SIC 4911 Electric services

D-U-N-S 20-304-1835   (BR)
MAZERGROUP LTD
Hwy 1a W, Portage La Prairie, MB, R1N 3C3
(204) 857-8711
Emp Here 20
SIC 5999 Miscellaneous retail stores, nec

D-U-N-S 20-283-4834   (BR)
MCMUNN & YATES BUILDING SUPPLIES LTD
2712 Saskatchewan Ave W Hwy 1a W, Portage La Prairie, MB, R1N 3C2

---

(204) 239-8750
Emp Here 23
SIC 5211 Lumber and other building materials

D-U-N-S 20-651-4395   (SL)
PORTAGE CONSUMERS CO OP LTD
2275 Saskatchewan Ave W, Portage La Prairie, MB, R1N 3B3
(204) 856-2127
Emp Here 120   *Sales* 22,420,450
SIC 5541 Gasoline service stations
Genl Mgr Kevin Dales

D-U-N-S 20-003-9936   (BR)
PORTAGE LA PRAIRIE SCHOOL DIVISION
NORTH MEMORIAL SCHOOL
(*Suby of* Portage La Prairie School Division)
410 6th Ave Ne, Portage La Prairie, MB, R1N 0B4
(204) 857-4564
Emp Here 20
SIC 8211 Elementary and secondary schools

D-U-N-S 20-709-8471   (BR)
PORTAGE LA PRAIRIE SCHOOL DIVISION
ECOLE CRESCENTVIEW SCHOOL
(*Suby of* Portage La Prairie School Division)
751 Crescent Rd E, Portage La Prairie, MB, R1N 0Y2
(204) 857-8508
Emp Here 50
SIC 8211 Elementary and secondary schools

D-U-N-S 20-709-8489   (BR)
PORTAGE LA PRAIRIE SCHOOL DIVISION
LABERENDRYE SCHOOL
(*Suby of* Portage La Prairie School Division)
500 7th Ave Nw, Portage La Prairie, MB, R1N 0A5
(204) 857-3478
Emp Here 52
SIC 8211 Elementary and secondary schools

D-U-N-S 20-709-8547   (BR)
PORTAGE LA PRAIRIE SCHOOL DIVISION
GOOD HOPE SCHOOL
(*Suby of* Portage La Prairie School Division)
65 3rd St Sw, Portage La Prairie, MB, R1N 2B6
(204) 252-2568
Emp Here 50
SIC 8211 Elementary and secondary schools

D-U-N-S 25-057-0009   (BR)
PORTAGE LA PRAIRIE SCHOOL DIVISION
PORTAGE COLLEGIATE INSTITUTE
(*Suby of* Portage La Prairie School Division)
65 3rd St Sw, Portage La Prairie, MB, R1N 2B6
(204) 857-6843
Emp Here 60
SIC 8211 Elementary and secondary schools

D-U-N-S 20-709-8505   (BR)
PORTAGE LA PRAIRIE SCHOOL DIVISION
FORT LA REINE SCHOOL
(*Suby of* Portage La Prairie School Division)
36 13th St Nw, Portage La Prairie, MB, R1N 2T5
(204) 857-7687
Emp Here 30
SIC 8211 Elementary and secondary schools

D-U-N-S 25-000-5873   (BR)
PORTAGE LA PRAIRIE SCHOOL DIVISION
YELLOWQUILL SCHOOL
(*Suby of* Portage La Prairie School Division)
3000 Crescent Rd W, Portage La Prairie, MB, R1N 3C4
(204) 857-8714
Emp Here 45
SIC 8211 Elementary and secondary schools

D-U-N-S 24-429-2736   (HQ)
PORTAGE LA PRAIRIE SCHOOL DIVISION
(*Suby of* Portage La Prairie School Division)
535 3rd St Nw, Portage La Prairie, MB, R1N 2C4

(204) 857-8756
Emp Here 500   *Emp Total* 588
Sales 52,908,240
SIC 8211 Elementary and secondary schools
Superintnt Hazen Barrett
    Judy Smith
    Murray Mclenenan
    Charles Morrison
    Carol Chandler
    Yvette Cuthbert
    Allen Dell
    John Harrison
    Shauna-Lei Leslie
    Joan Mccallister

D-U-N-S 24-662-3909   (SL)
PORTAGE REGIONAL RECREATION AUTHORITY INC
245 Royal Rd S, Portage La Prairie, MB, R1N 1T8
(204) 857-7772
Emp Here 50   *Sales* 2,699,546
SIC 7999 Amusement and recreation, nec

D-U-N-S 25-325-3165   (BR)
PRISZM LP
PIZZA HUT
2390 Sissons Dr, Portage La Prairie, MB, R1N 0G5

Emp Here 30
SIC 5812 Eating places

D-U-N-S 24-172-0333   (SL)
RC FOODS LTD
MCDONALD'S RESTAURANT
25 26th St Nw, Portage La Prairie, MB, R1N 3C5
(204) 857-6893
Emp Here 50   *Sales* 1,532,175
SIC 5812 Eating places

D-U-N-S 24-520-0399   (BR)
REGIONAL HEALTH AUTHORITY - CENTRAL MANITOBA INC
PORTAGE DISTRICT GENERAL HOSPITAL
524 5th St Se, Portage La Prairie, MB, R1N 3A8
(204) 239-2211
Emp Here 275
SIC 8062 General medical and surgical hospitals

D-U-N-S 20-291-7142   (SL)
RICHARDSON MILLING LIMITED
1 Can-Oat Dr, Portage La Prairie, MB, R1N 3W1
(204) 857-9700
Emp Here 500   *Sales* 238,873,332
SIC 5153 Grain and field beans
Ch Bd Hartley Richardson

D-U-N-S 25-498-2515   (BR)
WAL-MART CANADA CORP
WALMART #3069
2348 Sissons Dr, Portage La Prairie, MB, R1N 0G5
(204) 857-5011
Emp Here 125
SIC 5311 Department stores

D-U-N-S 24-747-9348   (SL)
WESTWARD FORD SALES LTD
Gd Lcd Main, Portage La Prairie, MB, R1N 3A7
(204) 857-3912
Emp Here 41   *Sales* 18,054,150
SIC 5511 New and used car dealers
Pr Pr Kevin Love
    Michael Ford

Powerview, MB R0E

D-U-N-S 20-709-8059   (BR)
SUNRISE SCHOOL DIVISION
ECOLE POWER VIEW SCHOOL

23 Vincent Ave, Powerview, MB, R0E 1P0
(204) 367-2296
Emp Here 50
SIC 8211 Elementary and secondary schools

Princess Harbour, MB R0C

D-U-N-S 20-076-9060   (BR)
LORD SELKIRK SCHOOL DIVISION, THE
WILLIAM S. PATTERSON SCHOOL
(*Suby of* Lord Selkirk School Division, The)
8461 9 Hwy, Princess Harbour, MB, R0C 2P0
(204) 738-4700
Emp Here 28
SIC 8211 Elementary and secondary schools

Rapid City, MB R0K

D-U-N-S 20-709-9313   (BR)
ROLLING RIVER SCHOOL DIVISION 39
RAPID CITY ELEMENTARY
(*Suby of* Rolling River School Division 39)
640 5 Ave, Rapid City, MB, R0K 1W0
(204) 826-2824
Emp Here 50
SIC 8211 Elementary and secondary schools

Reston, MB R0M

D-U-N-S 20-023-9007   (BR)
FORT LA BOSSE SCHOOL DIVISION
RESTON COLLEGIATE SCHOOL
(*Suby of* Fort La Bosse School Division)
516 1st St, Reston, MB, R0M 1X0
(204) 877-3994
Emp Here 25
SIC 8211 Elementary and secondary schools

D-U-N-S 25-671-3223   (SL)
RESTON DISTRICT HEALTH CENTRE
523 1st St, Reston, MB, R0M 1X0
(204) 877-3925
Emp Here 50   *Sales* 3,502,114
SIC 8062 General medical and surgical hospitals

Richer, MB R0E

D-U-N-S 25-370-2856   (BR)
PREMIER HORTICULTURE LTEE
Gd, Richer, MB, R0E 1S0

Emp Here 70
SIC 5159 Farm-product raw materials, nec

Rivers, MB R0K

D-U-N-S 25-671-2092   (BR)
REDFERN FARM SERVICES LTD
(*Suby of* Redfern Enterprises Inc)
101 2nd Ave, Rivers, MB, R0K 1X0
(204) 328-5325
Emp Here 25
SIC 5191 Farm supplies

D-U-N-S 25-959-0586   (BR)
RIVERDALE HEALTH SERVICES DISTRICT FOUNDATION INC
RIVERDALE HEALTH CENTRE
(*Suby of* Riverdale Health Services District Foundation Inc)
512 Quebec St, Rivers, MB, R0K 1X0

(204) 328-5321
Emp Here 75
SIC 8062 General medical and surgical hospitals

D-U-N-S 20-709-9321   (BR)
ROLLING RIVER SCHOOL DIVISION 39
RIVER ELEMENTARY SCHOOL
(*Suby of* Rolling River School Division 39)
530 Main St, Rivers, MB, R0K 1X0
(204) 328-7416
Emp Here 20
SIC 8211 Elementary and secondary schools

D-U-N-S 20-709-9370   (BR)
ROLLING RIVER SCHOOL DIVISION 39
RIVERS COLLEGIATE
(*Suby of* Rolling River School Division 39)
350 Dominion St, Rivers, MB, R0K 1X0
(204) 328-5364
Emp Here 25
SIC 8211 Elementary and secondary schools

Riverton, MB R0C

D-U-N-S 20-709-8406   (BR)
EVERGREEN SCHOOL DIVISION
RIVERTON COLLEGIATE INSTITUTE
Thompson Dr, Riverton, MB, R0C 2R0
(204) 378-5135
Emp Here 50
SIC 8211 Elementary and secondary schools

D-U-N-S 25-920-9583   (BR)
EVERGREEN SCHOOL DIVISION
RIVERTON EARLY MIDDLE SCHOOL
Gd, Riverton, MB, R0C 2R0
(204) 378-5145
Emp Here 22
SIC 8211 Elementary and secondary schools

Roblin, MB R0L

D-U-N-S 20-709-7192   (BR)
MOUNTAIN VIEW SCHOOL DIVISION
ROBLIN ELEMENTARY SCHOOL
(*Suby of* Mountain View School Division)
330 King St, Roblin, MB, R0L 1P0
(204) 937-2585
Emp Here 32
SIC 8211 Elementary and secondary schools

D-U-N-S 24-343-2924   (BR)
PARKLAND REGIONAL HEALTH AUTHORITY INC
ROBLIN DISTRICT HEALTH CENTRE
(*Suby of* Parkland Regional Health Authority Inc)
Gd, Roblin, MB, R0L 1P0
(204) 937-2142
Emp Here 135
SIC 8062 General medical and surgical hospitals

Rosenort, MB R0G

D-U-N-S 20-360-2727   (BR)
AG GROWTH INTERNATIONAL INC
74 Hwy 205 E, Rosenort, MB, R0G 1W0
(204) 746-2396
Emp Here 300
SIC 3532 Mining machinery

D-U-N-S 20-023-5658   (BR)
MAPLE LEAF FOODS INC
205 W, Rosenort, MB, R0G 1W0
(204) 746-2338
Emp Here 38
SIC 2041 Flour and other grain mill products

D-U-N-S 25-289-2542   (BR)
RED RIVER VALLEY SCHOOL DIVISION
ROSENORT SCHOOL
(*Suby of* Red River Valley School Division)
343 River Rd S, Rosenort, MB, R0G 1W0
(204) 746-8355
Emp Here 30
SIC 8211 Elementary and secondary schools

Rosser, MB R0H

D-U-N-S 24-235-9677   (HQ)
ARCTIC BEVERAGES LP
107 Mountain View Rd Unit 2, Rosser, MB,
R0H 1E0
(204) 633-8686
Emp Here 35   *Emp Total* 70
Sales 11,235,948
SIC 5149 Groceries and related products, nec
Pr Allan Mcleod

Russell, MB R0J

D-U-N-S 24-329-3623   (BR)
BUNGE CANADA
1 Main St, Russell, MB, R0J 1W0
(204) 773-3422
Emp Here 65
SIC 2079 Edible fats and oils

D-U-N-S 25-890-3566   (BR)
PRAIRIE MOUNTAIN HEALTH
PERSONAL CARE HOME
(*Suby of* Prairie Mountain Health)
113 Arsini St E, Russell, MB, R0J 1W0
(204) 773-3117
Emp Here 50
SIC 8051 Skilled nursing care facilities

D-U-N-S 24-394-9844   (BR)
PRAIRIE MOUNTAIN HEALTH
(*Suby of* Prairie Mountain Health)
426 Alexandria Ave, Russell, MB, R0J 1W0
(204) 773-2125
Emp Here 60
SIC 8011 Offices and clinics of medical doctors

Sandy Lake, MB R0J

D-U-N-S 25-484-3410   (BR)
PRAIRIE MOUNTAIN HEALTH
SANDY LAKE PERSONAL CARE HOME
(*Suby of* Prairie Mountain Health)
106 1st W, Sandy Lake, MB, R0J 1X0
(204) 585-2107
Emp Here 40
SIC 8051 Skilled nursing care facilities

Sanford, MB R0G

D-U-N-S 20-716-7508   (BR)
RED RIVER VALLEY SCHOOL DIVISION
J A CUDDY ELEMENTARY SCHOOL
(*Suby of* Red River Valley School Division)
5 Main St, Sanford, MB R0G 2J0

Emp Here 50
SIC 8211 Elementary and secondary schools

Sarto, MB R0A

D-U-N-S 24-819-6099   (SL)
CATERING, PHYLLIS
Gd, Sarto, MB, R0A 1X0
(204) 434-6475
Emp Here 70   *Sales* 2,732,754
SIC 5812 Eating places

Scanterbury, MB R0E

D-U-N-S 24-113-6501   (SL)
SOUTH BEACH CASINO INC
1 Ocean Dr, Scanterbury, MB, R0E 1W0
(204) 766-2100
Emp Here 50   *Sales* 2,188,821
SIC 7011 Hotels and motels

Schanzenfeld, MB R6W

D-U-N-S 25-815-3121   (BR)
GARDEN VALLEY SCHOOL DIVISION
SOUTHWOOD SCHOOL
(*Suby of* Garden Valley School Division)
224 Hespeler Ave E, Schanzenfeld, MB, R6W
1K3
(204) 325-8592
Emp Here 27
SIC 8211 Elementary and secondary schools

Selkirk, MB R1A

D-U-N-S 24-223-1541   (BR)
3177743 MANITOBA LTD
BOSTON PIZZA
(*Suby of* 3177743 Manitoba Ltd)
1018 Manitoba Ave, Selkirk, MB, R1A 4M2
(204) 785-7777
Emp Here 80
SIC 5812 Eating places

D-U-N-S 25-951-9528   (BR)
**BEHAVIOURAL   HEALTH   FOUNDATION
INC, THE**
*BEHAVIOURAL   HEALTH   FOUNDATION
MALE YOUTH SERVICES, THE*
1147 Brezzy Point Rd, Selkirk, MB, R1A 2A7
(204) 482-9711
Emp Here 35
SIC 8361 Residential care

D-U-N-S 25-288-9738   (BR)
CANADA POST CORPORATION
SELKIRK POST OFFICE
356 Main St, Selkirk, MB, R1A 1T6

Emp Here 23
SIC 4311 U.s. postal service

D-U-N-S 20-919-2314   (BR)
FEDERATED CO-OPERATIVES LIMITED
SELKIRK MARKET PLACE
(*Suby of* Federated Co-Operatives Limited)
335 Main St, Selkirk, MB, R1A 1T2
(204) 482-8147
Emp Here 20
SIC 5411 Grocery stores

D-U-N-S 24-428-6407   (BR)
**INTERLAKE REGIONAL HEALTH AUTHOR-
ITY INC**
SELKIRK & DISTRICT GENERAL HOSPITAL
(*Suby of* Interlake Regional Health Authority
Inc)
100 Easton Dr, Selkirk, MB, R1A 2M2
(204) 482-5800
Emp Here 100
SIC 8062 General medical and surgical hospitals

D-U-N-S 25-100-3059   (BR)

LORD SELKIRK SCHOOL DIVISION, THE
DAERWOOD ELEMENTARY SCHOOL
(*Suby of* Lord Selkirk School Division, The)
211 Main St, Selkirk, MB, R1A 1R7
(204) 482-4326
Emp Here 30
SIC 8211 Elementary and secondary schools

D-U-N-S 20-024-2100   (BR)
LORD SELKIRK SCHOOL DIVISION, THE
ECOLE BONAVENTURE IMMERSION
(*Suby of* Lord Selkirk School Division, The)
516 Stanley Ave Suite A, Selkirk, MB, R1A
0S1
(204) 785-8284
Emp Here 30
SIC 8211 Elementary and secondary schools

D-U-N-S 20-834-6460   (HQ)
LORD SELKIRK SCHOOL DIVISION, THE
(*Suby of* Lord Selkirk School Division, The)
205 Mercy St, Selkirk, MB, R1A 2C8
(204) 482-5942
Emp Here 25   *Emp Total* 1,200
Sales 110,427,520
SIC 8211 Elementary and secondary schools
Treas Bruce Cairns

D-U-N-S 20-709-8026   (BR)
LORD SELKIRK SCHOOL DIVISION, THE
*LORD SELKIRK REGIONAL COMPREHEN-
SIVE SECONDARY SCHOOL*
(*Suby of* Lord Selkirk School Division, The)
221 Mercy St, Selkirk, MB, R1A 2C8
(204) 482-6926
Emp Here 250
SIC 8211 Elementary and secondary schools

D-U-N-S 25-066-2236   (BR)
LORD SELKIRK SCHOOL DIVISION, THE
SELKIRK JUNIOR HIGH SCHOOL
(*Suby of* Lord Selkirk School Division, The)
516 Stanley Ave, Selkirk, MB, R1A 0S1
(204) 785-8514
Emp Here 50
SIC 8211 Elementary and secondary schools

D-U-N-S 20-709-8000   (BR)
LORD SELKIRK SCHOOL DIVISION, THE
ROBERT SMITH SCHOOL
(*Suby of* Lord Selkirk School Division, The)
300 Sophia St, Selkirk, MB, R1A 2E2
(204) 482-3677
Emp Here 40
SIC 8211 Elementary and secondary schools

D-U-N-S 25-755-2497   (BR)
LORD SELKIRK SCHOOL DIVISION, THE
CENTENNIAL SCHOOL
(*Suby of* Lord Selkirk School Division, The)
19 Centennial Ave, Selkirk, MB, R1A 0C8
(204) 482-3265
Emp Here 25
SIC 8211 Elementary and secondary schools

D-U-N-S 25-268-8890   (BR)
**MANITOBA   HYDRO-ELECTRIC   BOARD,
THE**
MANITOBA HYDRO SELKIRK LAB
9567 Henderson Hwy, Selkirk, MB, R1A 2B3
(204) 785-7142
Emp Here 20
SIC 4911 Electric services

D-U-N-S 24-802-6705   (BR)
**MANITOBA   HYDRO-ELECTRIC   BOARD,
THE**
SELKIRK GENERATING STATION
9527 Henderson Hwy, Selkirk, MB, R1A 2B3
(204) 785-7140
Emp Here 20
SIC 4911 Electric services

D-U-N-S 20-853-2932   (BR)
**MANITOBA   LIQUOR   AND   LOTTERIES
CORPORATION**
LIQUOR MART
446 Main St, Selkirk, MB, R1A 1V7

---

(204) 482-2360
Emp Here 20
SIC 5921 Liquor stores

D-U-N-S 25-325-3363   (BR)
PRISZM LP
PIZZA HUT
58 Main St, Selkirk, MB, R1A 1R1
(204) 785-2211
Emp Here 25
SIC 5812 Eating places

D-U-N-S 20-788-8830   (BR)
RED RIVER COOPERATIVE LTD
CO-OP GAS BAR
275 Main St, Selkirk, MB, R1A 1S5
(204) 785-2909
Emp Here 21
SIC 5541 Gasoline service stations

D-U-N-S 20-836-3119   (SL)
SELKIRK GOLF & COUNTRY CLUB
100 Sutherland Ave, Selkirk, MB, R1A 0L8
(204) 482-2050
Emp Here 55   *Sales* 2,826,987
SIC 7997 Membership sports and recreation
clubs

D-U-N-S 25-272-0099   (BR)
SOBEYS WEST INC
318 Manitoba Ave, Selkirk, MB, R1A 0Y7
(204) 482-5775
Emp Here 100
SIC 5411 Grocery stores

D-U-N-S 20-210-6717   (BR)
TC INDUSTRIES OF CANADA COMPANY
*TC INDUSTRIES OF CANADA COMPANY
WEST*
480 Pittsburg Ave, Selkirk, MB, R1A 0A9
(204) 482-6900
Emp Here 55
SIC 3462 Iron and steel forgings

D-U-N-S 24-630-1121   (SL)
TUDOR HOUSE LTD
800 Manitoba Ave, Selkirk, MB, R1A 2C9
(204) 482-6601
Emp Here 80   *Sales* 3,648,035
SIC 8051 Skilled nursing care facilities

Sherridon, MB R0B

D-U-N-S 20-709-9842   (BR)
FRONTIER SCHOOL DIVISION
COLD LAKE SCHOOL
63 Eldon Ave, Sherridon, MB, R0B 1L0
(204) 468-2021
Emp Here 50
SIC 8211 Elementary and secondary schools

Shilo, MB R0K

D-U-N-S 20-031-5914   (BR)
BRANDON SCHOOL DIVISION, THE
ECOLE O'KELLY SCHOOL
101 St Barbara St, Shilo, MB, R0K 2A0
(204) 765-7900
Emp Here 35
SIC 8211 Elementary and secondary schools

Shoal Lake, MB R0J

D-U-N-S 25-500-6025   (HQ)
**MARQUETTE   REGIONAL   HEALTH   AU-
THORITY**
NEEPAWA DIST MEMORIAL HOSPITAL
(*Suby of* Marquette Regional Health Authority)
344 Elm St, Shoal Lake, MB, R0J 1Z0

(204) 759-3441
Emp Here 100   *Emp Total* 1,500
Sales 119,891,200
SIC 8062 General medical and surgical hospitals
Ex Dir James E. Bartlett
Ch Bd Robert Buternowsky

D-U-N-S 20-321-3517   (BR)
MAZERGROUP LTD
Po Box 508, Shoal Lake, MB, R0J 1Z0
(204) 759-2126
Emp Here 35
SIC 5999 Miscellaneous retail stores, nec

D-U-N-S 20-003-5608   (SL)
S. H. DAYTON LTD
144 Industrial Rd, Shoal Lake, MB, R0J 1Z0
(204) 759-2065
Emp Here 24   *Sales* 14,672,940
SIC 5083 Farm and garden machinery
Pr Pr Keith Martin
VP VP Peter Baydak
   Calvin Harrison

Shortdale, MB R0L

D-U-N-S 25-362-5123   (BR)
TOOTINAOWAZIIBEENG TREATY RESERVE
TOOTINAOWAZIIBEENG HEALTH
Gd, Shortdale, MB, R0L 1W0
(204) 546-3267
Emp Here 25
SIC 8621 Professional organizations

Skownan, MB R0L

D-U-N-S 20-709-9941   (BR)
FRONTIER SCHOOL DIVISION
SKOWMAN SCHOOL
Gd, Skownan, MB, R0L 1Y0
(204) 628-3315
Emp Here 50
SIC 8211 Elementary and secondary schools

Snow Lake, MB R0B

D-U-N-S 25-121-8426   (BR)
FRONTIER SCHOOL DIVISION
JOSEPH H KERR SCHOOL
201 Cherry Ave, Snow Lake, MB, R0B 1M0
(204) 358-2281
Emp Here 30
SIC 8211 Elementary and secondary schools

Somerset, MB R0G

D-U-N-S 20-709-8893   (BR)
PRAIRIE SPIRIT SCHOOL DIVISION
PRAIRIE MOUNTAIN HIGH SCHOOL
Po Box 250, Somerset, MB, R0G 2L0
(204) 744-2751
Emp Here 50
SIC 8211 Elementary and secondary schools

Souris, MB R0K

D-U-N-S 24-376-4391   (BR)
MAPLE LEAF FOODS INC
MAPLE LEAF AGRI-FARMS DIV OF
Gd, Souris, MB, R0K 2C0

(204) 483-3130
Emp Here 27
SIC 2011 Meat packing plants

D-U-N-S 20-285-2018   (HQ)
PRAIRIE MOUNTAIN HEALTH
(*Suby of* Prairie Mountain Health)
192 1st Ave W, Souris, MB, R0K 2C0
(204) 483-5000
Emp Here 20   *Emp Total* 8,500
Sales 436,111,201
SIC 8011 Offices and clinics of medical doctors
  Penny Gilson

South Indian Lake, MB R0B

D-U-N-S 20-003-5314   (BR)
FRONTIER SCHOOL DIVISION
OSCER BLACKBURN SCHOOL
2 Wasagam Rd, South Indian Lake, MB, R0B 1N0
(204) 374-2056
Emp Here 43
SIC 8211 Elementary and secondary schools

Southport, MB R0H

D-U-N-S 24-097-6600   (BR)
ADDICTIONS FOUNDATION OF MANITOBA, THE
COMPASS RESIDENTIAL YOUTH PROGRAM
175 Nomad St, Southport, MB, R0H 1N1
(204) 428-6600
Emp Here 20
SIC 8361 Residential care

Split Lake, MB R0B

D-U-N-S 20-026-0722   (SL)
CHIEF SAM COOK MAHMUWEE EDUCATION CENTRE
Gd, Split Lake, MB, R0B 1P0
(204) 342-2134
Emp Here 60   *Sales* 4,012,839
SIC 8211 Elementary and secondary schools

D-U-N-S 25-271-4167   (BR)
NORTH WEST COMPANY LP, THE
Gd, Split Lake, MB, R0B 1P0
(204) 342-2260
Emp Here 25
SIC 5411 Grocery stores

Sprague, MB R0A

D-U-N-S 25-121-1413   (BR)
BORDER LAND SCHOOL DIVISION
ROSS L GRAY SCHOOL
21 Canham St, Sprague, MB, R0A 1Z0
(204) 437-2175
Emp Here 25
SIC 8211 Elementary and secondary schools

Springfield, MB R2C

D-U-N-S 24-266-7764   (SL)
ACTION RECYCLED AUTO PARTS (1997) LTD
LKQ
2955 Day St, Springfield, MB, R2C 2Z2

(204) 224-5678
Emp Here 52   *Sales* 8,539,920
SIC 5013 Motor vehicle supplies and new parts
  Willis Thys

D-U-N-S 25-975-6203   (BR)
POLYONE DSS CANADA INC
SPARTECH PROFILE
2954 Day St, Springfield, MB, R2C 2Z2
(204) 224-2791
Emp Here 60
SIC 3089 Plastics products, nec

D-U-N-S 20-299-1584   (SL)
WESTMAN STEEL INC
CANADA CULVERT
2976 Day St, Springfield, MB, R2C 2Z2
(204) 777-5345
Emp Here 200   *Sales* 95,301,600
SIC 3444 Sheet Metalwork
Pr Pr Paul Cunningham
VP Fin Michael Froese

Springfield, MB R2J

D-U-N-S 25-528-2386   (BR)
CARCANADA CORPORATION
136 Lakeside Rd, Springfield, MB, R2J 4G8

Emp Here 55
SIC 5521 Used car dealers

St Adolphe, MB R5A

D-U-N-S 25-127-9519   (BR)
SEINE RIVER SCHOOL DIVISION
ECOLE ST ADOLPHE SCHOOL
(*Suby of* Seine River School Division)
444 La Seine St, St Adolphe, MB, R5A 1C2
(204) 883-2182
Emp Here 30
SIC 8211 Elementary and secondary schools

St Andrews, MB R1A

D-U-N-S 24-852-0124   (SL)
2451379 MANITOBA LTD
LARTERS AT ST ANDREWS GOLF & COUNTRY CLUB
30 River Rd, St Andrews, MB, R1A 2V1
(204) 334-2107
Emp Here 70   *Sales* 2,845,467
SIC 7997 Membership sports and recreation clubs

D-U-N-S 24-034-8862   (HQ)
CUSTOM HELICOPTERS LTD
401 Helicopter Dr, St Andrews, MB, R1A 3P7
(204) 338-7953
Emp Here 35   *Emp Total* 3,951
Sales 4,742,446
SIC 4522 Air transportation, nonscheduled

D-U-N-S 20-709-8034   (BR)
LORD SELKIRK SCHOOL DIVISION, THE
MAPLETON SCHOOL
(*Suby of* Lord Selkirk School Division, The)
112 Calder Rd, St Andrews, MB, R1A 4B5
(204) 482-4409
Emp Here 24
SIC 8211 Elementary and secondary schools

D-U-N-S 20-049-2648   (BR)
LORD SELKIRK SCHOOL DIVISION, THE
ST ANDREWS SCHOOL
(*Suby of* Lord Selkirk School Division, The)
8 St Andrews Rd, St Andrews, MB, R1A 2Y1

(204) 338-7510
Emp Here 45
SIC 8211 Elementary and secondary schools

St Claude, MB R0G

D-U-N-S 20-709-8901   (BR)
PRAIRIE SPIRIT SCHOOL DIVISION
ST CLAUDE SCHOOL COMPLEX
83 Provincial Rd, St Claude, MB, R0G 1Z0
(204) 379-2441
Emp Here 20
SIC 8211 Elementary and secondary schools

D-U-N-S 24-172-0978   (BR)
REGIONAL HEALTH AUTHORITY - CENTRAL MANITOBA INC
ST CLAUDE HEATLH CENTRE
33 Ray St, St Claude, MB, R0G 1Z0
(204) 379-2585
Emp Here 70
SIC 8062 General medical and surgical hospitals

St Jean Baptiste, MB R0G

D-U-N-S 20-710-0103   (BR)
DIVISION SCOLAIRE FRANCO-MANITOBAINE
ECOLE REGIONALE SAINTE JOHN BAPTISTE
(*Suby of* Division Scolaire Franco-Manitobaine)
113 2nd Ave, St Jean Baptiste, MB, R0G 2B0
(204) 758-3501
Emp Here 35
SIC 8211 Elementary and secondary schools

St Laurent, MB R0C

D-U-N-S 25-676-8003   (BR)
DIVISION SCOLAIRE FRANCO-MANITOBAINE
ECOLE COMMUNAUTAIRE AURELE-LEMOINE
(*Suby of* Division Scolaire Franco-Manitobaine)
81, St Laurent, MB, R0C 2S0
(204) 646-2392
Emp Here 21
SIC 8211 Elementary and secondary schools

St Lazare, MB R0M

D-U-N-S 25-676-9696   (BR)
DIVISION SCOLAIRE FRANCO-MANITOBAINE
SAINT LAZARE SCHOOL
(*Suby of* Division Scolaire Franco-Manitobaine)
Gd, St Lazare, MB, R0M 1Y0
(204) 683-2251
Emp Here 23
SIC 8211 Elementary and secondary schools

St Pierre Jolys, MB R0A

D-U-N-S 20-710-0111   (BR)
DIVISION SCOLAIRE FRANCO-MANITOBAINE
ECOLE COMMUNAUTAIRE REAL BERARD
(*Suby of* Division Scolaire Franco-

Manitobaine)
377 Rue Sabourin, St Pierre Jolys, MB, R0A
1V0
(204) 433-7706
Emp Here 30
SIC 8211 Elementary and secondary schools

D-U-N-S 25-919-8299   (BR)
SOUTHERN HEALTH-SANTE SUD
*DESALABERRY DISTRICT HEALTH CEN-
TRE*
354 Prefontaine Ave, St Pierre Jolys, MB, R0A
1V0
(204) 433-7611
Emp Here 80
SIC 8062 General medical and surgical hospi-
tals

St Theresa Point, MB R0B

D-U-N-S 25-271-4407   (BR)
NORTH WEST COMPANY LP, THE
NORTHERN STORES
Po Box 230, St Theresa Point, MB, R0B 1J0
(204) 462-2012
Emp Here 40
SIC 5411 Grocery stores

Starbuck, MB R0G

D-U-N-S 20-327-4915   (BR)
NOVENTIS CREDIT UNION LIMITED
21 Main St, Starbuck, MB, R0G 2P0
(204) 735-2394
Emp Here 20
SIC 6062 State credit unions

D-U-N-S 20-716-7888   (BR)
RED RIVER VALLEY SCHOOL DIVISION
STARBUCK SCHOOL
(*Suby of* Red River Valley School Division)
40 Arena Blvd, Starbuck, MB, R0G 2P0
(204) 735-2779
Emp Here 22
SIC 8211 Elementary and secondary schools

Ste Anne, MB R5H

D-U-N-S 25-676-9761   (BR)
**DIVISION   SCOLAIRE   FRANCO-
MANITOBAINE**
ECOLE POINTE-DES-CHENES
(*Suby of* Division Scolaire Franco-
Manitobaine)
90 Arena Rd, Ste Anne, MB, R5H 1G6
(204) 422-5505
Emp Here 50
SIC 8211 Elementary and secondary schools

D-U-N-S 25-124-1717   (BR)
PREMIER HORTICULTURE LTEE
Gd, Ste Anne, MB, R5H 1C1
(204) 422-9777
Emp Here 70
SIC 5159 Farm-product raw materials, nec

D-U-N-S 24-345-0884   (BR)
SEINE RIVER SCHOOL DIVISION
STE ANNE ELEMENTARY SCHOOL
177 St Alphonse Ave, Ste Anne, MB, R5H 1G3
(204) 422-8776
Emp Here 25
SIC 8211 Elementary and secondary schools

D-U-N-S 25-289-4407   (BR)
SEINE RIVER SCHOOL DIVISION
STE ANNE COLLEGIATE
(*Suby of* Seine River School Division)
197 St Alphonse Ave, Ste Anne, MB, R5H 1G3

(204) 422-5417
Emp Here 24
SIC 8211 Elementary and secondary schools

D-U-N-S 25-289-5271   (BR)
SEINE RIVER SCHOOL DIVISION
ECOLE STE ANNE IMMERSION
(*Suby of* Seine River School Division)
167 St Alphonse Ave, Ste Anne, MB, R5H 1G3
(204) 422-8762
Emp Here 25
SIC 8211 Elementary and secondary schools

Ste Rose Du Lac, MB R0L

D-U-N-S 20-294-4521   (BR)
**ADDICTIONS   FOUNDATION   OF   MANI-
TOBA, THE**
WILLARD MONSON HOUSE
540 Central Ave, Ste Rose Du Lac, MB, R0L
1S0
(204) 447-4040
Emp Here 25
SIC 8093 Specialty outpatient clinics, nec

D-U-N-S 24-851-1748   (SL)
BODNAR DRILLING LTD
23 Delaurier Dr, Ste Rose Du Lac, MB, R0L
1S0
(204) 447-2755
Emp Here 50   *Sales* 2,772,507
SIC 1481 NonMetallic mineral services

D-U-N-S 20-023-8918   (BR)
TURTLE RIVER SCHOOL DIVISION
STE. ROSE SCHOOL
480 Central Ave, Ste Rose Du Lac, MB, R0L
1S0
(204) 447-2088
Emp Here 36
SIC 8211 Elementary and secondary schools

Steinbach, MB R5G

D-U-N-S 20-113-8661   (SL)
4498411 MANITOBA LTD
*LINKS AT QUARRY OAK GOLF & COUNTRY
CLUB (2002), THE*
Gd Stn Main, Steinbach, MB, R5G 1L8
(204) 326-4653
Emp Here 75   *Sales* 3,210,271
SIC 7992 Public golf courses

D-U-N-S 20-700-8710   (SL)
BUCYRUS BLADES OF CANADA LIMITED
ESCO
(*Suby of* Esco Corporation)
62 Life Sciences Pky, Steinbach, MB, R5G
2G6
(204) 326-3461
Emp Here 38   *Sales* 8,682,323
SIC 3531 Construction machinery
Genl Mgr Mark Wowchuk

D-U-N-S 20-613-7200   (HQ)
C.P. LOEWEN ENTERPRISES LTD
LOEWEN WINDOWS
77 Fth 52 W, Steinbach, MB, R5G 1B2
(204) 326-6446
Emp Here 540   *Emp Total* 3
Sales 58,212,067
SIC 2431 Millwork
Pr Al Babiuk
  Charles Loewen
  Clyde Loewen
  Steven Kreitz

D-U-N-S 20-336-6745   (BR)
ENNS BROTHERS LTD
340 Pth 12 N, Steinbach, MB, R5G 1T6
(204) 326-1305
Emp Here 45

SIC 5261 Retail nurseries and garden stores

D-U-N-S 25-961-5391   (BR)
GOLDEN WEST BROADCASTING LTD
MIX 96
32 Brandt St Suite 105, Steinbach, MB, R5G
2J7
(204) 346-0000
Emp Here 90
SIC 4832 Radio broadcasting stations

D-U-N-S 20-709-8240   (BR)
HANOVER SCHOOL DIVISION
WOODLAWN ELEMENTARY SCHOOL
(*Suby of* Hanover School Division)
411 Henry St, Steinbach, MB, R5G 0R1
(204) 326-6110
Emp Here 50
SIC 8211 Elementary and secondary schools

D-U-N-S 20-709-8232   (BR)
HANOVER SCHOOL DIVISION
SOUTHWOOD SCHOOL
(*Suby of* Hanover School Division)
155 Barkman Ave, Steinbach, MB, R5G 0P2
(204) 326-3518
Emp Here 50
SIC 8211 Elementary and secondary schools

D-U-N-S 25-272-4463   (BR)
HANOVER SCHOOL DIVISION
*STEINBACH   REGIONAL   SECONDARY
SCHOOL*
(*Suby of* Hanover School Division)
190 Mckenzie Ave, Steinbach, MB, R5G 0P1
(204) 326-6426
Emp Here 100
SIC 8211 Elementary and secondary schools

D-U-N-S 20-834-1362   (HQ)
HANOVER SCHOOL DIVISION
(*Suby of* Hanover School Division)
5 Chrysler Gate, Steinbach, MB, R5G 0E2
(204) 326-6471
Emp Here 30   *Emp Total* 710
Sales 61,251,385
SIC 8211 Elementary and secondary schools
Superintnt Ken Klassen
  Randy Hildebrand
  Ed Durksen
  Karen Peters
  Marilyn Plett
Treas Kevin Heide
  Ron Falk
  Ruby Wiens
  Lynn Barkman
  Gerry Klassen

D-U-N-S 24-314-1822   (BR)
LOBLAWS INC
EXTRA FOODS
276 Main St, Steinbach, MB, R5G 1Y8
(204) 346-6304
Emp Here 80
SIC 5411 Grocery stores

D-U-N-S 24-325-8964   (BR)
LOBLAWS INC
REAL CANADIAN SUPERSTORES
130 Pth 12 N, Steinbach, MB, R5G 1T4
(204) 320-4101
Emp Here 250
SIC 5411 Grocery stores

D-U-N-S 25-021-3634   (BR)
**MANITOBA   HYDRO-ELECTRIC   BOARD,
THE**
175 North Front Dr, Steinbach, MB, R5G 1X3
(204) 326-9824
Emp Here 50
SIC 4911 Electric services

D-U-N-S 25-325-3124   (BR)
PRISZM LP
PIZZA HUT
105 Pth 12 N, Steinbach, MB, R5G 1T5
(204) 326-5555
Emp Here 30

SIC 5812 Eating places

D-U-N-S 24-207-5369   (BR)
SOBEYS CAPITAL INCORPORATED
STEINBACH GARDEN MARKET
178 Pth 12 N Unit 1, Steinbach, MB, R5G 1T7
(204) 326-1316
Emp Here 150
SIC 5411 Grocery stores

D-U-N-S 20-739-7907   (BR)
SOBEYS WEST INC
SAFEWAY FOOD & DRUG
143 Pth 12 N, Steinbach, MB, R5G 1T5
(204) 346-1555
Emp Here 90
SIC 5411 Grocery stores

D-U-N-S 25-707-3882   (BR)
SOUTHERN HEALTH-SANTE SUD
SOUTHERN HEALTH
365 Reimer Ave, Steinbach, MB, R5G 0R9
(204) 346-6123
Emp Here 60
SIC 8322 Individual and family services

D-U-N-S 20-781-1188   (BR)
SOUTHERN HEALTH-SANTE SUD
BETHESDA HOSPITAL
316 Henry St, Steinbach, MB, R5G 0P9
(204) 326-6411
Emp Here 300
SIC 8062 General medical and surgical hospi-
tals

D-U-N-S 24-330-6276   (BR)
STAPLES CANADA INC
STAPLES THE BUSINESS DEPOT
(*Suby of* Staples, Inc.)
190 Pth 12 N, Steinbach, MB, R5G 1T6
(204) 320-4670
Emp Here 20
SIC 5943 Stationery stores

D-U-N-S 24-669-0841   (BR)
STE ANNE CO-OPERATIVE OIL LTD
CO-OP GAS BAR
110 Brandt St, Steinbach, MB, R5G 0P7

Emp Here 25
SIC 4932 Gas and other services combined

D-U-N-S 25-256-8030   (BR)
STEINBACH, CITY OF
STEINBACH TAX INQUIRIES
225 Reimer Ave, Steinbach, MB, R5G 2J1
(204) 346-6531
Emp Here 49
SIC 7389 Business services, nec

D-U-N-S 25-384-7362   (SL)
STEVE'S LIVESTOCK TRANSPORT INC
122 Pth 52 W, Steinbach, MB, R5G 1Y1
(204) 326-6969
Emp Here 85   *Sales* 9,333,400
SIC 4212 Local trucking, without storage
Pr Pr Lorne Funk
Dir Edna Funk

D-U-N-S 25-365-2291   (SL)
VALART INC
TIM HORTONS
141 Pth 12 N, Steinbach, MB, R5G 1T5
(204) 346-0700
Emp Here 50   *Sales* 1,532,175
SIC 5812 Eating places

Stevenson Island, MB R0B

D-U-N-S 25-271-4373   (BR)
NORTH WEST COMPANY LP, THE
NORTHERN STORE, THE
Gd, Stevenson Island, MB, R0B 2H0
(204) 456-2333
Emp Here 38

SIC 5411 Grocery stores

Stonewall, MB R0C

D-U-N-S 25-217-7233   (SL)
3200221 MANITOBA LTD
TERRACO
Po Box 779, Stonewall, MB, R0C 2Z0
(204) 467-8282
Emp Here 50   *Sales* 18,869,700
SIC 5171 Petroleum bulk stations and terminals
Pr Pr Norbert Desilets
 Conrad Starkell
 Steve Miele

D-U-N-S 25-835-8365   (BR)
BEARSKIN LAKE AIR SERVICE LP
BEARSKIN AIRLINES
585 6th Ave S, Stonewall, MB, R0C 2Z0

Emp Here 300
SIC 8299 Schools and educational services, nec

D-U-N-S 20-107-6218   (BR)
DUCKS UNLIMITED CANADA
INSTITUTE FOR WETLAND & WATERFOWL RESEARCH DEPARTMENT
1 Mallard Bay, Stonewall, MB, R0C 2Z0
(204) 467-3265
Emp Here 24
SIC 8999 Services, nec

D-U-N-S 25-061-1373   (BR)
FEDERATED CO-OPERATIVES LIMITED
MARKETPLACE AT STONEWALL
(*Suby of* Federated Co-Operatives Limited)
420 Main St Suite 4, Stonewall, MB, R0C 2Z0
(204) 467-8469
Emp Here 33
SIC 5411 Grocery stores

D-U-N-S 25-679-3563   (BR)
INTERLAKE REGIONAL HEALTH AUTHORITY INC
RIVERTON COMMUNITY HEALTH OFFICE
(*Suby of* Interlake Regional Health Authority Inc)
68 Main St, Stonewall, MB, R0C 2Z0
(204) 378-2460
Emp Here 100
SIC 8062 General medical and surgical hospitals

D-U-N-S 20-518-9470   (BR)
INTERLAKE REGIONAL HEALTH AUTHORITY INC
ROSEWOOD LODGE
(*Suby of* Interlake Regional Health Authority Inc)
513 1 Ave N, Stonewall, MB, R0C 2Z0
(204) 467-3373
Emp Here 70
SIC 8051 Skilled nursing care facilities

D-U-N-S 25-289-4365   (BR)
INTERLAKE SCHOOL DIVISION
ECOLE STONEWALL CENTENNIAL SCHOOL
(*Suby of* Interlake School Division)
573 Second Ave N, Stonewall, MB, R0C 2Z0
(204) 467-5502
Emp Here 40
SIC 8211 Elementary and secondary schools

D-U-N-S 25-288-5462   (BR)
INTERLAKE SCHOOL DIVISION
STONEWALL COLLEGIATE
(*Suby of* Interlake School Division)
297 5 St W, Stonewall, MB, R0C 2Z0
(204) 467-5539
Emp Here 50
SIC 8211 Elementary and secondary schools

D-U-N-S 20-835-3123   (BR)
JENNINGS CAPITAL INC
BOBBYBEND SCHOOL
377 2 Ave N, Stonewall, MB, R0C 2Z0
(204) 467-5537
Emp Here 20
SIC 8211 Elementary and secondary schools

D-U-N-S 24-087-8178   (SL)
RETAIL ADVANTAGE INC
76134 8e Rd, Stonewall, MB, R0C 2Z0

Emp Here 100   *Sales* 6,604,160
SIC 7389 Business services, nec
VP Karen Elliot

D-U-N-S 24-844-8107   (BR)
SUNOVA CREDIT UNION LIMITED
410 Centre Ave, Stonewall, MB, R0C 2Z0
(204) 467-5574
Emp Here 150
SIC 6062 State credit unions

Stony Mountain, MB R0C

D-U-N-S 20-716-8514   (BR)
INTERLAKE SCHOOL DIVISION
STONY MOUNTAIN SCHOOL
(*Suby of* Interlake School Division)
139 School Rd, Stony Mountain, MB, R0C 3A0
(204) 344-5459
Emp Here 30
SIC 8211 Elementary and secondary schools

Strathclair, MB R0J

D-U-N-S 20-035-5977   (BR)
PARK WEST SCHOOL DIVISION
STRATHCLAIR COMMUNITY SCHOOL
16 Main St, Strathclair, MB, R0J 2C0
(204) 842-2801
Emp Here 25
SIC 8211 Elementary and secondary schools

Swan Lake, MB R0G

D-U-N-S 20-709-8943   (BR)
PRAIRIE SPIRIT SCHOOL DIVISION
PRAIRIE MOUNTAIN ELEMENTARY SCHOOL
4 4th St N, Swan Lake, MB, R0G 2S0
(204) 836-2855
Emp Here 25
SIC 8211 Elementary and secondary schools

D-U-N-S 25-329-3591   (BR)
REGIONAL HEALTH AUTHORITY - CENTRAL MANITOBA INC
LORNE MEMORIAL HOSPITAL
9 Second St N, Swan Lake, MB, R0G 2S0
(204) 836-2132
Emp Here 60
SIC 8062 General medical and surgical hospitals

Swan River, MB R0L

D-U-N-S 24-971-5434   (BR)
BANQUE TORONTO-DOMINION, LA
TORONTO-DOMINION BANK, THE
(*Suby of* Toronto-Dominion Bank, The)
501 Main St E, Swan River, MB, R0L 1Z0
(204) 734-4544
Emp Here 20
SIC 6021 National commercial banks

D-U-N-S 25-387-7237   (BR)
NYKOLAISHEN FARM EQUIPMENT LTD
1930 Hwy 10, Swan River, MB, R0L 1Z0
(204) 734-3466
Emp Here 30
SIC 5083 Farm and garden machinery

D-U-N-S 24-338-5502   (BR)
PARKLAND REGIONAL HEALTH AUTHORITY INC
SWAN RIVER HEALTH CENTRE
(*Suby of* Parkland Regional Health Authority Inc)
1011 Main St E, Swan River, MB, R0L 1Z0
(204) 734-3441
Emp Here 200
SIC 8062 General medical and surgical hospitals

D-U-N-S 25-500-4608   (HQ)
SWAN VALLEY CREDIT UNION LIMITED
SWAN VALLEY CREDIT UNION
(*Suby of* Swan Valley Credit Union Limited)
913 Main St, Swan River, MB, R0L 1Z0
(204) 734-7828
Emp Here 47   *Emp Total* 50
Sales 8,620,604
SIC 6062 State credit unions
CEO Donald Pratt
Pr Pr Brian Cotton

D-U-N-S 20-023-3265   (BR)
SWAN VALLEY SCHOOL DIVISION
ECOLE SWAN RIVER SOUTH SCHOOL
(*Suby of* Swan Valley School Division)
1015 2nd St S, Swan River, MB, R0L 1Z0
(204) 734-4518
Emp Here 40
SIC 8211 Elementary and secondary schools

D-U-N-S 20-709-9271   (BR)
SWAN VALLEY SCHOOL DIVISION
HEYES ELEMENTARY SCHOOL
(*Suby of* Swan Valley School Division)
128 2nd Ave W, Swan River, MB, R0L 1Z0
(204) 734-3385
Emp Here 20
SIC 8211 Elementary and secondary schools

D-U-N-S 25-094-5800   (BR)
SWAN VALLEY SCHOOL DIVISION
SWAN VALLEY REGIONAL SECONDARY SCHOOL
(*Suby of* Swan Valley School Division)
1483 3rd St N, Swan River, MB, R0L 1Z0
(204) 734-4511
Emp Here 90
SIC 8211 Elementary and secondary schools

D-U-N-S 24-372-9915   (BR)
SWAN VALLEY SCHOOL DIVISION
TRANSPORTATION DEPARTMENT
(*Suby of* Swan Valley School Division)
225 Kelsey Trail, Swan River, MB, R0L 1Z0
(204) 734-3415
Emp Here 54
SIC 4151 School buses

D-U-N-S 24-376-4933   (SL)
WESTWOOD INN (SWAN RIVER) INC
473 Westwood Rd, Swan River, MB, R0L 1Z0
(204) 734-4548
Emp Here 50   *Sales* 2,188,821
SIC 7011 Hotels and motels

Teulon, MB R0C

D-U-N-S 20-274-1687   (BR)
INTERLAKE REGIONAL HEALTH AUTHORITY INC
TEULON HUNTER MEMORIAL HOSPITAL
(*Suby of* Interlake Regional Health Authority Inc)
162 3 Ave Se, Teulon, MB, R0C 3B0

(204) 886-2433
Emp Here 80
SIC 8062 General medical and surgical hospitals

D-U-N-S 20-023-2663   (BR)
INTERLAKE SCHOOL DIVISION
TEULON COLLEGIATE
(*Suby of* Interlake School Division)
59 1st St Ne, Teulon, MB, R0C 3B0
(204) 886-2593
Emp Here 30
SIC 8211 Elementary and secondary schools

D-U-N-S 25-111-2298   (BR)
INTERLAKE SCHOOL DIVISION
TEULON ELEMENTARY SCHOOL
(*Suby of* Interlake School Division)
Gd, Teulon, MB, R0C 3B0
(204) 886-2620
Emp Here 23
SIC 8211 Elementary and secondary schools

D-U-N-S 20-725-6103   (SL)
TEULON GOLF & COUNTRY CLUB INC
94089 Pth 7, Teulon, MB, R0C 3B0
(204) 886-2991
Emp Here 50   *Sales* 2,188,821
SIC 7992 Public golf courses

The Pas, MB R9A

D-U-N-S 25-486-2543   (SL)
3327770 MANITOBA LTD
KIKIWAK INN
Hwy 10 North, The Pas, MB, R9A 1K8
(204) 623-1800
Emp Here 67   *Sales* 2,918,428
SIC 7011 Hotels and motels

D-U-N-S 20-588-2488   (BR)
BANQUE TORONTO-DOMINION, LA
TD CANADA TRUST
(*Suby of* Toronto-Dominion Bank, The)
302 Edwards Ave, The Pas, MB, R9A 1K6
(204) 627-4501
Emp Here 20
SIC 6021 National commercial banks

D-U-N-S 24-037-9503   (SL)
CHEEMA SYSTEMS LTD
WESCANA INN
439 Fischer Ave, The Pas, MB, R9A 1M3
(204) 623-5446
Emp Here 60   *Sales* 2,626,585
SIC 7011 Hotels and motels

D-U-N-S 25-417-6068   (SL)
HUDSON BAY RAILWAY COMPANY
OMNITRACK
728 Bignel Ave, The Pas, MB, R9A 1L8
(204) 627-2007
Emp Here 92   *Sales* 4,319,040
SIC 4111 Local and suburban transit

D-U-N-S 20-517-7632   (BR)
KELSEY SCHOOL DIVISION
KELSEY COMMUNITY SCHOOL
120 Stewart St, The Pas, MB, R9A 1R2
(204) 623-7421
Emp Here 40
SIC 8211 Elementary and secondary schools

D-U-N-S 20-709-9776   (BR)
KELSEY SCHOOL DIVISION
MARY DUNCAN SCHOOL
60 3rd St W, The Pas, MB, R9A 1R4
(204) 623-1420
Emp Here 20
SIC 8211 Elementary and secondary schools

D-U-N-S 20-024-1250   (BR)
KELSEY SCHOOL DIVISION
OPASQUIA SCHOOL
27 8th St, The Pas, MB, R9A 1R2

---

(204) 623-3459
Emp Here 39
SIC 8211 Elementary and secondary schools

D-U-N-S 20-709-9768 (BR)
KELSEY SCHOOL DIVISION
*MARGARET BARBOUR COLLEGIATE IN-
STITUTE*
429 Smith St, The Pas, MB, R9A 1P9
(204) 623-3485
Emp Here 55
SIC 8211 Elementary and secondary schools

D-U-N-S 20-023-4867 (BR)
KELSEY SCHOOL DIVISION
SCOTT BATEMAN MIDDLE SCHOOL
272 Grace Lake Rd, The Pas, MB, R9A 1R2
(204) 623-3411
Emp Here 50
SIC 8211 Elementary and secondary schools

D-U-N-S 24-916-6828 (HQ)
KENNEDY ENERGY
(*Suby of* Kennedy Energy)
861 Gordon Ave, The Pas, MB, R9A 1K9
(204) 623-5435
Emp Here 39   *Emp Total* 50
Sales 18,689,280
SIC 5171 Petroleum bulk stations and termi-
nals
Pt Don Kennedy
Pt John Kennedy

D-U-N-S 24-417-5530 (BR)
LOBLAWS INC
EXTRA FOODS
Hwy 10 Po Box 12 Stn Main, The Pas, MB,
R9A 1K3
(204) 623-4799
Emp Here 50
SIC 5411 Grocery stores

D-U-N-S 24-344-9027 (BR)
**MANITOBA HYDRO-ELECTRIC BOARD,
THE**
MANITOBA HYDRO
420 3 St E, The Pas, MB, R9A 1L4
(204) 623-9506
Emp Here 20
SIC 4911 Electric services

D-U-N-S 24-631-1906 (SL)
MCGILLIVARY CARE HOME
Gd Stn Main, The Pas, MB, R9A 1K2
(204) 623-5421
Emp Here 65   *Sales* 2,991,389
SIC 8051 Skilled nursing care facilities

D-U-N-S 20-833-0118 (SL)
NESO CORPORATION LTD
THE PAS I G A
(*Suby of* Opaskwayak Cree Nation)
Gd Stn Main, The Pas, MB, R9A 1K2
(204) 627-7200
Emp Here 50   *Sales* 8,623,250
SIC 5411 Grocery stores
Ch Bd Glen Ross
Genl Mgr Walter Dutkiewicz
Genl Mgr Wanda Mccorrister

D-U-N-S 25-022-0860 (SL)
**PAS SUPER THRIFTY DRUG MART 1984
LTD, THE**
Hwy 10, The Pas, MB, R9A 1P8
(204) 623-5150
Emp Here 20   *Sales* 3,378,379
SIC 5912 Drug stores and proprietary stores

D-U-N-S 25-116-8159 (BR)
TOLKO INDUSTRIES LTD
TOLKO MANITOBA KRAFT PAPERS, DIV OF
Hwy 10 N, The Pas, MB, R9A 1L4
(204) 623-7411
Emp Here 360
SIC 2674 Bags: uncoated paper and multiwall

D-U-N-S 24-174-8164 (BR)
TOLKO INDUSTRIES LTD
TOLKO MANITOBA SOLID WOOD DIVISION

Hwy 10 N, The Pas, MB, R9A 1S1
(204) 623-7411
Emp Here 300
SIC 2499 Wood products, nec

D-U-N-S 20-545-9261 (HQ)
UNIVERSITY COLLEGE OF THE NORTH
436 7th St E, The Pas, MB, R9A 1M7
(204) 627-8500
Emp Here 110   *Emp Total* 20,000
Sales 42,359,810
SIC 8221 Colleges and universities
Pr Pr Konrad Jonasson
 Dwight Botting
 William Schaffer

Thompson, MB R8N

D-U-N-S 25-329-4516 (SL)
3269001 MANITOBA LTD
RAMADA INN BURNTWOOD
146 Selkirk Ave, Thompson, MB, R8N 0N1
(204) 677-4551
Emp Here 70   *Sales* 3,064,349
SIC 7011 Hotels and motels

D-U-N-S 24-222-4009 (SL)
5055091 MANITOBA INC
BOSTON PIZZA
4 Moak Cres, Thompson, MB, R8N 2B7
(204) 677-0111
Emp Here 50   *Sales* 1,532,175
SIC 5812 Eating places

D-U-N-S 20-515-0860 (BR)
**ADDICTIONS FOUNDATION OF MANI-
TOBA, THE**
90 Princeton Dr, Thompson, MB, R8N 0L3
(204) 677-7303
Emp Here 32
SIC 8069 Specialty hospitals, except psychi-
atric

D-U-N-S 20-590-0520 (BR)
BANQUE TORONTO-DOMINION, LA
TORONTO-DOMINION BANK, THE
(*Suby of* Toronto-Dominion Bank, The)
300 Mystery Lake Rd, Thompson, MB, R8N
0M2
(204) 677-6083
Emp Here 20
SIC 6021 National commercial banks

D-U-N-S 25-288-9936 (BR)
CANADA POST CORPORATION
103 Selkirk Ave, Thompson, MB, R8N 0M5
(204) 677-9502
Emp Here 20
SIC 4311 U.s. postal service

D-U-N-S 20-947-5045 (BR)
CEMENTATION CANADA INC
(*Suby of* Cementation Canada Inc)
169 Hayes Rd, Thompson, MB, R8N 1M5

Emp Here 20
SIC 1241 Coal mining services

D-U-N-S 20-569-3831 (BR)
GARDEWINE GROUP INC
GARDEWINE NORTH
136 Hayes Rd, Thompson, MB, R8N 1M4
(204) 778-8311
Emp Here 50
SIC 4731 Freight transportation arrangement

D-U-N-S 20-078-2303 (BR)
**MACDONALD, SR JOHN HUGH MEMORIAL
HOSTEL**
MACDONALD YOUTH SERVICES
(*Suby of* MacDonald, Sr John Hugh Memorial
Hostel)
83 Churchill Dr Suite 204, Thompson, MB,
R8N 0L6

(204) 677-7870
Emp Here 80
SIC 8399 Social services, nec

D-U-N-S 20-078-2311 (BR)
MARYMOUND INC
(*Suby of* Marymound Inc)
116 Hemlock Cres, Thompson, MB, R8N 0R6
(204) 778-5116
Emp Here 20
SIC 8322 Individual and family services

D-U-N-S 20-647-8807 (SL)
**MCMUNN & YATES BUILDING SUPPLIES
(THOMPSON) LTD**
44 Station Rd, Thompson, MB, R8N 0N7
(204) 778-8363
Emp Here 20   *Sales* 2,918,428
SIC 5211 Lumber and other building materials

D-U-N-S 20-845-3873 (BR)
**NORTHERN REGIONAL HEALTH AUTHOR-
ITY**
*BURNTWOOD COMMUNITY HEALTH RE-
SOURCE CENTER*
50 Selkirk Ave, Thompson, MB, R8N 0M7
(204) 677-1777
Emp Here 60
SIC 8093 Specialty outpatient clinics, nec

D-U-N-S 20-613-1955 (BR)
PRENDIVILLE INDUSTRIES LTD
NORWEST MANUFACTURING
68 Crane St, Thompson, MB, R8N 1N1
(204) 677-5060
Emp Here 20
SIC 5211 Lumber and other building materials

D-U-N-S 20-023-2770 (BR)
SCHOOL DISTRICT OF MYSTERY LAKE
EASTWOOD SCHOOL
408 Thompson Dr Suite 2355, Thompson,
MB, R8N 0C5
(204) 677-6140
Emp Here 60
SIC 8211 Elementary and secondary schools

D-U-N-S 20-025-9542 (BR)
SCHOOL DISTRICT OF MYSTERY LAKE
BURNTWOOD SCHOOL
103 Arctic Dr, Thompson, MB, R8N 1G8
(204) 677-6100
Emp Here 40
SIC 8211 Elementary and secondary schools

D-U-N-S 20-710-0020 (BR)
SCHOOL DISTRICT OF MYSTERY LAKE
JUNIPER SCHOOL
306 Juniper Dr, Thompson, MB, R8N 0S9
(204) 677-6242
Emp Here 50
SIC 8211 Elementary and secondary schools

D-U-N-S 20-349-1642 (BR)
SCHOOL DISTRICT OF MYSTERY LAKE
R.D. PARKER COLLEGIATE
272 Thompson Dr N, Thompson, MB, R8N
0C4
(204) 677-6200
Emp Here 70
SIC 8211 Elementary and secondary schools

D-U-N-S 20-710-0038 (BR)
SCHOOL DISTRICT OF MYSTERY LAKE
*RIVERSIDE PUBLIC ELEMENTARY
SCHOOL*
119 Riverside Dr, Thompson, MB, R8N 0X1
(204) 677-6115
Emp Here 50
SIC 8211 Elementary and secondary schools

D-U-N-S 20-027-8666 (BR)
SCHOOL DISTRICT OF MYSTERY LAKE
DEERWOOD SCHOOL
408 Thompson Dr Suite 2355, Thompson,
MB, R8N 0C5
(204) 677-6125
Emp Here 20
SIC 8211 Elementary and secondary schools

(204) 677-7870
Emp Here 80
SIC 8399 Social services, nec

D-U-N-S 20-860-4137 (BR)
SOURCE (BELL) ELECTRONICS INC, THE
SOURCE, THE
300 Mystery Lake Rd, Thompson, MB, R8N
0M2
(204) 677-3709
Emp Here 25
SIC 5999 Miscellaneous retail stores, nec

D-U-N-S 25-316-8090 (BR)
**SUN LIFE ASSURANCE COMPANY OF
CANADA**
CLARICA LIFE FINANCIAL
90 Thompson Dr Unit 7, Thompson, MB, R8N
1Y9
(204) 778-7071
Emp Here 20
SIC 6311 Life insurance

D-U-N-S 20-614-1624 (BR)
WAL-MART CANADA CORP
300 Mystery Lake Rd Suite 3102, Thompson,
MB, R8N 0M2
(204) 778-4669
Emp Here 200
SIC 5311 Department stores

Treherne, MB R0G

D-U-N-S 20-835-2794 (BR)
PRAIRIE MOUNTAIN HEALTH
TIGER HILLS HEALTH CENTRE
(*Suby of* Prairie Mountain Health)
64 Clark St, Treherne, MB, R0G 2V0
(204) 723-2133
Emp Here 70
SIC 8011 Offices and clinics of medical doc-
tors

D-U-N-S 24-373-0988 (BR)
SUNRISE CREDIT UNION LIMITED
(*Suby of* SunRise Credit Union Limited)
197 Broadway, Treherne, MB, R0G 2V0
(204) 723-3250
Emp Here 70
SIC 6062 State credit unions

Tyndall, MB R0E

D-U-N-S 20-079-9273 (BR)
SUNRISE SCHOOL DIVISION
GILLIS SCHOOL
3 Pierson Dr, Tyndall, MB, R0E 2B0
(204) 268-4353
Emp Here 32
SIC 8211 Elementary and secondary schools

Virden, MB R0M

D-U-N-S 20-760-0578 (BR)
324007 ALBERTA LTD
HEARTLAND LIVESTOCK SERVICES
153158 Rd 58 N, Virden, MB, R0M 2C0
(204) 748-2809
Emp Here 35
SIC 5154 Livestock

D-U-N-S 24-205-5796 (BR)
AECOM CANADA LTD
Gd, Virden, MB, R0M 2C0
(204) 748-2796
Emp Here 49
SIC 1389 Oil and gas field services, nec

D-U-N-S 20-709-9537 (BR)
FORT LA BOSSE SCHOOL DIVISION
GOULTER SCHOOL
(*Suby of* Fort La Bosse School Division)
200 Queen St E, Virden, MB, R0M 2C0

(204) 748-2294
Emp Here 25
SIC 8211 Elementary and secondary schools

D-U-N-S 25-132-2707 (BR)
FORT LA BOSSE SCHOOL DIVISION
VIRDEN JR HIGH SCHOOL
(*Suby of* Fort La Bosse School Division)
447 Princess St W, Virden, MB, R0M 2C0
(204) 748-1932
Emp Here 40
SIC 8211 Elementary and secondary schools

D-U-N-S 20-642-9123 (BR)
FORT LA BOSSE SCHOOL DIVISION
MARY MONTGOMERY SCHOOL
(*Suby of* Fort La Bosse School Division)
445 Lyons St W, Virden, MB, R0M 2C0
(204) 748-2575
Emp Here 20
SIC 8211 Elementary and secondary schools

D-U-N-S 20-709-9529 (BR)
FORT LA BOSSE SCHOOL DIVISION
VIRDEN COLLEGIATE
(*Suby of* Fort La Bosse School Division)
251 Kent St, Virden, MB, R0M 2C0
(204) 748-2205
Emp Here 37
SIC 8211 Elementary and secondary schools

D-U-N-S 20-920-0299 (BR)
MANITOBA HYDRO-ELECTRIC BOARD, THE
Gd, Virden, MB, R0M 2C0
(204) 748-2534
Emp Here 20
SIC 4931 Electric and other services combined

D-U-N-S 25-103-4542 (BR)
PRAIRIE MOUNTAIN HEALTH
VIRDEN HEALTH CENTRE
(*Suby of* Prairie Mountain Health)
480 King St E, Virden, MB, R0M 2C0
(204) 748-1230
Emp Here 150
SIC 8062 General medical and surgical hospitals

D-U-N-S 25-363-7441 (BR)
PRAIRIE MOUNTAIN HEALTH
SHERWOOD NURSING HOME
(*Suby of* Prairie Mountain Health)
223 Hargrave St E, Virden, MB, R0M 2C0
(204) 748-1546
Emp Here 20
SIC 8051 Skilled nursing care facilities

D-U-N-S 24-372-2852 (HQ)
SUNRISE CREDIT UNION LIMITED
(*Suby of* SunRise Credit Union Limited)
220 7th Ave S, Virden, MB, R0M 2C0
(204) 748-2907
Emp Here 32 *Emp Total* 160
Sales 30,429,600
SIC 6062 State credit unions
Dir Harry Bowler
Tayona Johnas
Tony Keown

D-U-N-S 24-344-0091 (BR)
SUPERIOR PLUS LP
Gd, Virden, MB, R0M 2C0
(204) 748-6129
Emp Here 21
SIC 2819 Industrial inorganic chemicals, nec

D-U-N-S 24-236-7191 (BR)
TUNDRA OIL & GAS LIMITED
TUNDRA OIL & GAS PARTNERSHIP
295 3rd Ave, Virden, MB, R0M 2C0
(204) 748-3095
Emp Here 200
SIC 1382 Oil and gas exploration services

D-U-N-S 20-006-6603 (HQ)
VALLEYVIEW CONSUMERS CO-OP LTD
(*Suby of* Valleyview Consumers Co-Op Ltd)
250 Princess St W, Virden, MB, R0M 2C0
(204) 748-2520
Emp Here 50 *Emp Total* 75
Sales 11,694,389
SIC 5411 Grocery stores
Off Mgr Maureen Taylor-Miller
Pr Pr Kent Mathieson
VP VP Robert Grieve
Arnold Bailey
Dir Greg Alexander
Dir Steven Soulsby
Dir Peter Mcconnell
Dir Paul Eilers
Dir Sherald Joynt
Dir Bonnie Girardin

D-U-N-S 25-145-6323 (SL)
WESTMAN NURSING HOME INC
427 Frame St E, Virden, MB, R0M 2C0
(204) 748-4335
Emp Here 70 *Sales* 3,210,271
SIC 8051 Skilled nursing care facilities

D-U-N-S 20-436-6181 (BR)
WHEAT CITY CONCRETE PRODUCTS LTD
MID WESTERN REDI-MIX CONCRETE
Gd, Virden, MB, R0M 2C0
(204) 748-1592
Emp Here 25
SIC 3273 Ready-mixed concrete

Vita, MB R0A

D-U-N-S 20-652-3156 (BR)
BORDER LAND SCHOOL DIVISION
SHEVCHENKO SCHOOL
100 School Ave, Vita, MB, R0A 2K0
(204) 425-3535
Emp Here 45
SIC 8211 Elementary and secondary schools

D-U-N-S 20-833-6396 (BR)
SOUTHERN HEALTH-SANTE SUD
VITA AND DISTRICT HEALTH CENTRE
217 1st Ave, Vita, MB, R0A 2K0
(204) 425-3325
Emp Here 80
SIC 8062 General medical and surgical hospitals

Wabowden, MB R0B

D-U-N-S 24-335-9242 (BR)
CANICKEL MINING LIMITED
Gd, Wabowden, MB, R0B 1S0
(204) 689-2972
Emp Here 150
SIC 1081 Metal mining services

D-U-N-S 20-035-5761 (BR)
FRONTIER SCHOOL DIVISION
MEL JOHNSON SCHOOL
269 Fleming Dr, Wabowden, MB, R0B 1S0
(204) 689-2620
Emp Here 25
SIC 8211 Elementary and secondary schools

Wanipigow, MB R0E

D-U-N-S 20-709-9883 (BR)
FRONTIER SCHOOL DIVISION
WANIPIGOW SCHOOL
Gd, Wanipigow, MB, R0E 2E0
(204) 363-7253
Emp Here 50
SIC 8211 Elementary and secondary schools

D-U-N-S 20-731-2906 (BR)
FRONTIER SCHOOL DIVISION
WANIPIGOW ELEMENTARY SCHOOL
Gd, Wanipigow, MB, R0E 2E0
(204) 363-7253
Emp Here 55
SIC 8211 Elementary and secondary schools

Warren, MB R0C

D-U-N-S 25-272-3689 (BR)
INTERLAKE SCHOOL DIVISION
WARREN COLLEGIATE
(*Suby of* Interlake School Division)
119 Macdonald Ave, Warren, MB, R0C 3E0
(204) 322-5586
Emp Here 25
SIC 8211 Elementary and secondary schools

D-U-N-S 20-716-8522 (BR)
INTERLAKE SCHOOL DIVISION
WARREN ELEMENTARY
(*Suby of* Interlake School Division)
300 Hanlan St, Warren, MB, R0C 3E0
(204) 322-5576
Emp Here 33
SIC 8211 Elementary and secondary schools

Wasagamack, MB R0B

D-U-N-S 24-967-7667 (SL)
WASAGAMACK EDUCATION AUTHORITY
GEORGE KNOTT SCHOOL
Gd, Wasagamack, MB, R0B 1Z0

Emp Here 72 *Sales* 4,815,406
SIC 8211 Elementary and secondary schools

Waskada, MB R0M

D-U-N-S 25-898-2529 (BR)
EOG RESOURCES CANADA INC
105 4th St, Waskada, MB, R0M 2E0

Emp Here 45
SIC 1311 Crude petroleum and natural gas

Waterhen, MB R0L

D-U-N-S 20-980-1773 (BR)
FRONTIER SCHOOL DIVISION
WATERHEN SCHOOL
Gd, Waterhen, MB, R0L 2C0
(204) 628-3443
Emp Here 20
SIC 8211 Elementary and secondary schools

Wawanesa, MB R0K

D-U-N-S 24-429-0276 (BR)
WAWANESA MUTUAL INSURANCE COMPANY, THE
(*Suby of* Wawanesa Mutual Insurance Company, The)
107 4th St, Wawanesa, MB, R0K 2G0
(204) 824-2132
Emp Here 50
SIC 6331 Fire, marine, and casualty insurance

West St Paul, MB R2P

D-U-N-S 25-949-0266 (SL)
B & B LANDSCAPE & CARTAGE INC
66 Second St, West St Paul, MB, R2P 0G5
(204) 339-4643
Emp Here 55 *Sales* 4,377,642
SIC 4212 Local trucking, without storage

D-U-N-S 24-228-2775 (BR)
CON-WAY FREIGHT-CANADA INC
85 St Paul Blvd, West St Paul, MB, R2P 2W5
(204) 336-9487
Emp Here 25
SIC 4213 Trucking, except local

D-U-N-S 20-945-1947 (SL)
GKW CONSTRUCTION INC
54 St Paul Blvd, West St Paul, MB, R2P 2W5
(204) 633-7000
Emp Here 60 *Sales* 4,377,642
SIC 1741 Masonry and other stonework

West St Paul, MB R4A

D-U-N-S 24-630-5569 (SL)
MIDDLECHURCH HOME OF WINNIPEG INC
280 Balderstone Rd, West St Paul, MB, R4A 4A6
(204) 339-1947
Emp Here 300 *Sales* 18,355,920
SIC 8051 Skilled nursing care facilities
Laurie Kuivenhoven
Ch Bd Laurie Holgate

Whitemouth, MB R0E

D-U-N-S 25-332-1806 (BR)
NORTH EASTMAN HEALTH ASSOCIATION INC
WHITEMOUTH DISTRICT HEALTH CENTRE
(*Suby of* North Eastman Health Association Inc)
75 Hospital St, Whitemouth, MB, R0E 2G0
(204) 348-7191
Emp Here 70
SIC 8059 Nursing and personal care, nec

D-U-N-S 20-709-8067 (BR)
SUNRISE SCHOOL DIVISION
WHITEMOUTH SCHOOL
55 2nd St, Whitemouth, MB, R0E 2G0
(204) 348-2595
Emp Here 33
SIC 8211 Elementary and secondary schools

Winkler, MB R6W

D-U-N-S 24-114-5841 (BR)
ALIMENTS SAPUTO LIMITEE
SAPUTO
235 Manitoba Rd, Winkler, MB, R6W 0J8
(204) 325-4321
Emp Here 42
SIC 2022 Cheese; natural and processed

D-U-N-S 20-293-0199 (BR)
BDO CANADA LLP
23111 Hwy 14 Unit 3, Winkler, MB, R6W 4B3
(204) 325-4787
Emp Here 29
SIC 8721 Accounting, auditing, and bookkeeping

D-U-N-S 20-341-5757 (BR)
BEHLEN INDUSTRIES INC
U-BUILD STEEL BUILDINGS
355 Pembina Ave E, Winkler, MB, R6W 3N4
(204) 325-4368
Emp Here 20

SIC 3441 Fabricated structural Metal

D-U-N-S 20-569-9101   (SL)
BERDICK MFG. MANITOBA LTD
BERDICK WINDOWS & DOORS
404 Roblin Blvd E, Winkler, MB, R6W 0H2
(204) 325-8053
Emp Here 40   *Sales* 4,304,681
SIC 3089 Plastics products, nec

D-U-N-S 20-518-2756   (BR)
BOARD OF GOVERNOR'S OF RED RIVER COLLEGE, THE
RED RIVER COLLEGE OF APPLIED ARTS, SCIENCE AND TECHNOLOGY
561 Main St Suite 101, Winkler, MB, R6W 1E8
(204) 325-9672
Emp Here 20
SIC 8222 Junior colleges

D-U-N-S 20-295-1823   (SL)
BOUNDARY TRAILS HEALTH CENTRE FOUNDATION INC
Gd, Winkler, MB, R6W 1H8
(204) 331-8808
Emp Here 405   *Sales* 59,583,120
SIC 8621 Professional organizations
Ex Dir Linda Buhr
 Eugene Wiebe
 June Letkeman

D-U-N-S 25-372-0569   (SL)
DELANEY HOLDINGS INC
200 Pacific St, Winkler, MB, R6W 0K2
(204) 325-7376
Emp Here 150
SIC 3321 Gray and ductile iron foundries

D-U-N-S 25-840-2952   (BR)
DOLLARAMA S.E.C.
DOLLARAMA
955 Main St Unit 1, Winkler, MB, R6W 0L7
(204) 331-4723
Emp Here 26
SIC 5311 Department stores

D-U-N-S 25-289-4647   (BR)
GARDEN VALLEY SCHOOL DIVISION
PARKLAND SCHOOL
(*Suby of* Garden Valley School Division)
1100 Roblin Blvd, Winkler, MB, R6W 1G2
(204) 325-6373
Emp Here 50
SIC 8211 Elementary and secondary schools

D-U-N-S 20-709-8729   (BR)
GARDEN VALLEY SCHOOL DIVISION
BORDER VALLEY SCHOOL
296 Border St, Winkler, MB, R6W 4B4
(204) 325-8674
Emp Here 23
SIC 8211 Elementary and secondary schools

D-U-N-S 25-272-4505   (BR)
GARDEN VALLEY SCHOOL DIVISION
GARDEN VALLEY COLLEGIATE
(*Suby of* Garden Valley School Division)
Garden Valley Collegiate, Winkler, MB, R6W 4C8
(204) 325-8008
Emp Here 100
SIC 8211 Elementary and secondary schools

D-U-N-S 24-521-9527   (BR)
GARDEN VALLEY SCHOOL DIVISION
EMERADO CENTENNIAL SCHOOL
675 Prairie View Dr, Winkler, MB, R6W 1M5
(204) 331-4533
Emp Here 42
SIC 8211 Elementary and secondary schools

D-U-N-S 24-937-1527   (BR)
GOLDEN WEST BROADCASTING LTD
CKMW
277 1st St Suite A, Winkler, MB, R6W 3P1
(204) 325-9506
Emp Here 30
SIC 4832 Radio broadcasting stations

D-U-N-S 24-819-5513   (SL)
INTEGRA CASTINGS INC
200 Pacific St, Winkler, MB, R6W 0K2
(204) 325-7376
Emp Here 150
SIC 3321 Gray and ductile iron foundries

D-U-N-S 20-613-0981   (HQ)
JANZEN CHEVROLET BUICK GMC LTD
(*Suby of* Janzen Chevrolet Buick GMC Ltd)
145 Boundary Trail, Winkler, MB, R6W 4B5
(204) 325-9511
Emp Here 40   *Emp Total* 60
Sales 29,448,000
SIC 5511 New and used car dealers
Pr Pr Jake Janzen
Genl Mgr Paul Janzen
 Margaret Janzen

D-U-N-S 25-368-2264   (BR)
LOBLAWS INC
REAL CANADIAN SUPERSTORE
175 Cargill Rd, Winkler, MB, R6W 0K4
(204) 331-2501
Emp Here 280
SIC 5141 Groceries, general line

D-U-N-S 24-678-9205   (BR)
MERIDIAN MANUFACTURING INC
275 Hespler Ave, Winkler, MB, R6W 0J7
(204) 325-7883
Emp Here 25
SIC 3545 Machine tool accessories

D-U-N-S 20-948-5739   (BR)
MONARCH INDUSTRIES LIMITED
280 Monarch Dr, Winkler, MB, R6W 0J6
(204) 325-4393
Emp Here 250
SIC 3321 Gray and ductile iron foundries

D-U-N-S 20-006-8732   (BR)
PURATONE CORPORATION, THE
(*Suby of* Puratone Corporation, The)
550 Centennial St, Winkler, MB, R6W 1J4
(204) 325-8371
Emp Here 30
SIC 5999 Miscellaneous retail stores, nec

D-U-N-S 25-831-7767   (BR)
TRIPLE E CANADA LTD
LODE KING INDUSTRIES, DIV. OF
135 Canada St, Winkler, MB, R6W 0J3
(204) 325-4345
Emp Here 250
SIC 3792 Travel trailers and campers

D-U-N-S 20-759-6883   (HQ)
TRIPLE E CANADA LTD
TRIPLE E RV, DIV OF
301 Roblin Blvd, Winkler, MB, R6W 4C4
(204) 325-4361
Emp Here 150   *Emp Total* 350
Sales 94,295,160
SIC 3711 Motor vehicles and car bodies
Pr Pr Terry Elias
 Philipp R Ens
Dir Lloyd Elias
Sec Robert Hucal
VP Fin Andy Schmidt

D-U-N-S 24-316-9070   (BR)
WAL-MART CANADA CORP
WINKLER WALMART
1000 Navigator Rd, Winkler, MB, R6W 0L8
(204) 325-4160
Emp Here 130
SIC 5311 Department stores

D-U-N-S 24-546-2635   (SL)
WIEBE, DR. C.W. MEDICAL CORPORATION
385 Main St, Winkler, MB, R6W 1J2
(204) 325-4312
Emp Here 55   *Sales* 3,283,232
SIC 8011 Offices and clinics of medical doctors

D-U-N-S 20-944-6608   (SL)

WINKLER CANVAS LTD
WINKLER STRUCTURES
Hwy 14 Greenfarm Rd, Winkler, MB, R6W 4B3
(204) 325-9548
Emp Here 64   *Sales* 2,845,467
SIC 2394 Canvas and related products

D-U-N-S 25-794-9594   (BR)
WINKLER CONSUMERS COOPERATIVE LTD
WINKLER CO-OP GAS BAR
411 Main St, Winkler, MB, R6W 4B2
(204) 325-8021
Emp Here 20
SIC 5541 Gasoline service stations

D-U-N-S 25-517-7768   (BR)
WOODHAVEN CAPITAL CORP
275 Hespler Ave, Winkler, MB, R6W 0J7
(204) 325-7883
Emp Here 80
SIC 3443 Fabricated plate work (boiler shop)

Winnipeg, MB R0H

D-U-N-S 20-082-7801   (BR)
UNITED RENTALS OF CANADA, INC
160 Mountainview, Winnipeg, MB, R0H 1E0
(204) 775-7171
Emp Here 40
SIC 7353 Heavy construction equipment rental

Winnipeg, MB R2C

D-U-N-S 20-010-4453   (SL)
0427802 MANITOBA LTD
PARK CITY MAZDA
1459 Regent Ave W, Winnipeg, MB, R2C 3B2
(204) 661-8181
Emp Here 80   *Sales* 37,693,160
SIC 5511 New and used car dealers
Dir David Dveris
Dir Claire Dveris
Pr Pr Jeff Dveris

D-U-N-S 20-039-8548   (BR)
2814048 MANITOBA LTD
MCDONALD'S
1576 Regent Ave W, Winnipeg, MB, R2C 3B4
(204) 949-6004
Emp Here 30
SIC 5812 Eating places

D-U-N-S 25-288-0612   (BR)
A & W FOOD SERVICES OF CANADA INC
A & W
1639 Regent Ave W, Winnipeg, MB, R2C 4H9
(204) 668-8303
Emp Here 30
SIC 5812 Eating places

D-U-N-S 20-833-0357   (HQ)
ACRYLON PLASTICS INC
2954 Day St, Winnipeg, MB, R2C 2Z2
(204) 669-2224
Emp Here 80   *Emp Total* 2
Sales 14,665,101
SIC 3089 Plastics products, nec
Pr Pr Craig Mcintosh

D-U-N-S 24-309-9913   (BR)
AMSTED CANADA INC
GRIFFIN CANADA
(*Suby of* Amsted Industries Incorporated)
104 Regent Ave E, Winnipeg, MB, R2C 0C1
(204) 222-4252
Emp Here 200
SIC 3462 Iron and steel forgings

D-U-N-S 25-122-5264   (BR)

BANK OF MONTREAL
BMO
1565 Regent Ave W Suite 4, Winnipeg, MB, R2C 3B3
(204) 985-2459
Emp Here 20
SIC 6021 National commercial banks

D-U-N-S 20-104-3150   (BR)
BANQUE TORONTO-DOMINION, LA
TORONTO-DOMINION BANK, THE
(*Suby of* Toronto-Dominion Bank, The)
1615 Regent Ave W Suite 800, Winnipeg, MB, R2C 5C6
(204) 988-2700
Emp Here 25
SIC 6021 National commercial banks

D-U-N-S 24-363-2093   (BR)
BEST BUY CANADA LTD
BEST BUY
(*Suby of* Best Buy Co., Inc.)
1580 Regent Ave W Unit 10, Winnipeg, MB, R2C 2Y9
(204) 661-8157
Emp Here 20
SIC 5731 Radio, television, and electronic stores

D-U-N-S 24-033-7464   (BR)
BEST BUY CANADA LTD
FUTURE SHOP
(*Suby of* Best Buy Co., Inc.)
1570 Regent Ave W, Winnipeg, MB, R2C 3B4
(204) 667-9140
Emp Here 40
SIC 5731 Radio, television, and electronic stores

D-U-N-S 25-289-3045   (BR)
CANAD CORPORATION OF MANITOBA LTD
CANAD TRANSCONA INN
(*Suby of* Canad Corporation Of Canada Inc)
826 Regent Ave W, Winnipeg, MB, R2C 3A8
(204) 224-1681
Emp Here 50
SIC 7011 Hotels and motels

D-U-N-S 20-539-4609   (BR)
CANADA POST CORPORATION
TRANSCONA P.O.
104 Regent Ave E, Winnipeg, MB, R2C 0C1
(204) 985-0189
Emp Here 20
SIC 4311 U.s. postal service

D-U-N-S 25-311-6560   (BR)
CANADIAN IMPERIAL BANK OF COMMERCE
CIBC
1586 Regent Ave W, Winnipeg, MB, R2C 3B4
(204) 944-5900
Emp Here 25
SIC 6021 National commercial banks

D-U-N-S 20-717-3050   (BR)
CARA OPERATIONS LIMITED
MONTANA'S COOKHOUSE
(*Suby of* Cara Holdings Limited)
1574 Regent Ave W, Winnipeg, MB, R2C 3B4
(204) 668-2723
Emp Here 20
SIC 5812 Eating places

D-U-N-S 25-831-7437   (BR)
COMPAGNIE DES CHEMINS DE FER NATIONAUX DU CANADA
SYSTEM ENGINEERING YARD
738 Pandora Ave E, Winnipeg, MB, R2C 3A6
(204) 235-2650
Emp Here 60
SIC 3531 Construction machinery

D-U-N-S 25-152-3148   (BR)
COMPAGNIE DES CHEMINS DE FER NATIONAUX DU CANADA
CN EQUIPMENT

150 Pandora Ave W, Winnipeg, MB, R2C 4H5
(204) 235-2626
Emp Here 550
SIC 4789 Transportation services, nec

D-U-N-S 25-288-9639   (BR)
COSTCO WHOLESALE CANADA LTD
COSTCO
(*Suby of* Costco Wholesale Corporation)
1499 Regent Ave W, Winnipeg, MB, R2C 4M4
(204) 654-4214
Emp Here 178
SIC 5099 Durable goods, nec

D-U-N-S 24-968-3046   (BR)
CREATIVE DOOR SERVICES LTD
64 Hoka St, Winnipeg, MB, R2C 3N2
(204) 224-1224
Emp Here 26
SIC 5031 Lumber, plywood, and millwork

D-U-N-S 20-106-1277   (BR)
DEFEHR FURNITURE (2009) LTD
DEFEHR FURNITURE (2009) LTD
770 Pandora Ave E, Winnipeg, MB, R2C 3N1
(204) 988-5630
Emp Here 350
SIC 2679 Converted paper products, nec

D-U-N-S 25-143-8701   (SL)
ELMHURST GOLF & COUNTRY CLUB
Garven Rd, Winnipeg, MB, R2C 2Z2
(204) 224-2244
Emp Here 60   *Sales* 2,407,703
SIC 7997 Membership sports and recreation clubs

D-U-N-S 20-757-9723   (SL)
EQUINOX INDUSTRIES LTD
401 Chrislind St, Winnipeg, MB, R2C 5G4
(204) 633-7564
Emp Here 92   *Sales* 8,669,427
SIC 3299 NonMetallic mineral products,
Pr Pr Daniel Putter
  David Putter

D-U-N-S 25-660-5643   (BR)
FGL SPORTS LTD
SPORT TECH
1570 Regent Ave W, Winnipeg, MB, R2C 3B4
(204) 669-0808
Emp Here 35
SIC 5699 Miscellaneous apparel and accessory stores

D-U-N-S 24-818-4848   (BR)
FABRICLAND PACIFIC/MIDWEST LIMITED
FABRICLAND
1532 Regent Ave W Suite 7, Winnipeg, MB, R2C 3B4
(204) 661-6426
Emp Here 21
SIC 5949 Sewing, needlework, and piece goods

D-U-N-S 20-518-5705   (HQ)
FRESHWATER FISH MARKETING CORPORATION
1199 Plessis Rd, Winnipeg, MB, R2C 3L4
(204) 983-6500
Emp Here 46   *Emp Total* 570,000
Sales 42,619,549
SIC 2092 Fresh or frozen packaged fish
Pr Pr John Wood
Ch Bd David Tomasson
Pers/VP Wendy Matheson
VP Opers Durga Liske
S&M/VP Paul Cater
CFO Stan Lazar
Dir Ron Ballantyne
Dir Bert Buckley
Dir Ken Campbell
Dir Terry Bennett

D-U-N-S 20-555-2818   (BR)
GENERAL SCRAP PARTNERSHIP
135 Bismarck St, Winnipeg, MB, R2C 4S1

(204) 222-4221
Emp Here 50
SIC 5093 Scrap and waste materials

D-U-N-S 20-008-8680   (SL)
GREENSTEEL INDUSTRIES LTD
770 Pandora Ave E, Winnipeg, MB, R2C 3N1
(204) 774-4533
Emp Here 60   *Sales* 11,555,200
SIC 3442 Metal doors, sash, and trim
Pr Pr Richard Hutchings
Opers Mgr Max Sandilands
Dir Edwin Redekopp
Dir Arthur Redekopp

D-U-N-S 25-095-5606   (BR)
HOME DEPOT OF CANADA INC
HOME DEPOT
(*Suby of* The Home Depot Inc)
1590 Regent Ave W, Winnipeg, MB, R2C 3B4
(204) 654-5400
Emp Here 200
SIC 5251 Hardware stores

D-U-N-S 25-301-2512   (BR)
HUDSON'S BAY COMPANY
HUDSON'S BAY HOME
1580 Regent Ave W Unit 20, Winnipeg, MB, R2C 2Y9
(204) 667-8407
Emp Here 55
SIC 5311 Department stores

D-U-N-S 24-385-7591   (BR)
KARLO TRADE CENTRE LTD
BIRCHWOOD HONDA
1401 Regent Ave W, Winnipeg, MB, R2C 3B2
(204) 661-6644
Emp Here 30
SIC 5511 New and used car dealers

D-U-N-S 20-835-2232   (SL)
KELSEY'S
KELSEY'S REGENT
1582 Regent Ave W, Winnipeg, MB, R2C 3B4

Emp Here 50   *Sales* 1,532,175
SIC 5812 Eating places

D-U-N-S 20-008-1792   (HQ)
KEYSTONE FORD SALES LTD
(*Suby of* Keystone Ford Sales Ltd)
1300 Regent Ave W, Winnipeg, MB, R2C 3A8
(204) 661-9555
Emp Here 58   *Emp Total* 85
Sales 42,704,000
SIC 5511 New and used car dealers
Pr Pr Robert. M Kozminski
  R. Matthew Kozminski
  Deidre Kozminski

D-U-N-S 20-918-9682   (BR)
KITCHEN CRAFT OF CANADA
1500 Regent Ave W Suite 1, Winnipeg, MB, R2C 3A8
(204) 661-6977
Emp Here 50
SIC 5211 Lumber and other building materials

D-U-N-S 20-515-4631   (BR)
LOBLAW COMPANIES LIMITED
EXTRA FOODS
701 Regent Ave W Suite 110, Winnipeg, MB, R2C 1S3
(204) 987-7330
Emp Here 35
SIC 5141 Groceries, general line

D-U-N-S 20-923-8299   (BR)
MCDONALD'S RESTAURANTS OF CANADA LIMITED
MCDONALD'S
(*Suby of* McDonald's Corporation)
15 Reenders Dr, Winnipeg, MB, R2C 5K5
(204) 949-3221
Emp Here 83
SIC 5812 Eating places

D-U-N-S 25-301-7966   (BR)

MCDONALD'S RESTAURANTS OF CANADA LIMITED
MCDONALD'S 8441
(*Suby of* McDonald's Corporation)
1425 Regent Ave W, Winnipeg, MB, R2C 3B2
(204) 949-6061
Emp Here 42
SIC 5812 Eating places

D-U-N-S 25-172-9117   (SL)
MINIC DRYWALL LTD
377 Gunn Rd, Winnipeg, MB, R2C 2Z2
(204) 667-6669
Emp Here 60   *Sales* 4,231,721
SIC 1742 Plastering, drywall, and insulation

D-U-N-S 20-827-6118   (SL)
MONGOS GRILL LIMITED LIABILITY CORP
1570 Regent Ave W Unit 4, Winnipeg, MB, R2C 3B4
(204) 786-6646
Emp Here 53   *Sales* 1,605,135
SIC 5812 Eating places

D-U-N-S 25-809-3533   (BR)
MOXIE'S RESTAURANTS, LIMITED PARTNERSHIP
MOXIE'S BAR AND GRILL
1615 Regent Ave W Suite 200, Winnipeg, MB, R2C 5C6
(204) 654-3345
Emp Here 140
SIC 5812 Eating places

D-U-N-S 24-426-5450   (SL)
NORTHERN BLOWER INC
(*Suby of* Canerector Inc)
901 Regent Ave W, Winnipeg, MB, R2C 2Z8
(204) 222-4216
Emp Here 65   *Sales* 11,892,594
SIC 5084 Industrial machinery and equipment
Genl Mgr Neal Boyd

D-U-N-S 24-232-1826   (BR)
PLASTI-FAB LTD
PLASTI-FAB, DIV OF
2485 Day St, Winnipeg, MB, R2C 2X5
(204) 222-3261
Emp Here 25
SIC 3086 Plastics foam products

D-U-N-S 20-555-4400   (SL)
PRAIRIE INTERNATIONAL CONTAINER & DRAY SERVICES INC
(*Suby of* Trealmont Transport Inc)
135 Saunders St, Winnipeg, MB, R2C 2Z2
(204) 783-3801
Emp Here 20   *Sales* 2,231,900
SIC 7359 Equipment rental and leasing, nec

D-U-N-S 20-010-6581   (HQ)
PRINCESS AUTO LTD
475 Panet Rd, Winnipeg, MB, R2C 2Z1
(204) 667-4630
Emp Here 300   *Emp Total* 1,614
Sales 230,555,812
SIC 5251 Hardware stores
Pr Pr Robert Tallman
  Harold Romanychyn
  Mark Breslauer
VP Rescrh Ken Kumar
  Robert Hucal

D-U-N-S 25-999-0547   (BR)
PROCRANE INC
STERLING CRANE DIV.
(*Suby of* Berkshire Hathaway Inc.)
66 Matheson Parkway, Winnipeg, MB, R2C 2Z2
(204) 233-5542
Emp Here 20
SIC 7353 Heavy construction equipment rental

D-U-N-S 25-660-5007   (BR)
RTM OPERATING COMPANY OF CANADA INC
ARBY'S OF CANADA

(*Suby of* Roark Capital Group Inc.)
1573 Regent Ave W, Winnipeg, MB, R2C 3B3
(204) 954-7481
Emp Here 20
SIC 5812 Eating places

D-U-N-S 25-713-3082   (BR)
RED LOBSTER HOSPITALITY LLC
OLIVE GARDEN
(*Suby of* Red Lobster Seafood Co., LLC)
51 Reenders Dr, Winnipeg, MB, R2C 5E8
(204) 661-8129
Emp Here 80
SIC 5812 Eating places

D-U-N-S 25-300-5243   (BR)
REDBERRY FRANCHISING CORP
BURGER KING
1571 Regent Ave W, Winnipeg, MB, R2C 3B3
(204) 987-8426
Emp Here 50
SIC 5812 Eating places

D-U-N-S 25-890-5025   (SL)
REENDERS CAR WASH LTD
CHAMOIS, THE
(*Suby of* Chamois Car Wash Corp, The)
85 Reenders Dr, Winnipeg, MB, R2C 5E8
(204) 669-9700
Emp Here 100   *Sales* 3,283,232
SIC 7542 Carwashes

D-U-N-S 20-931-3647   (BR)
REGIS HAIRSTYLISTS LTD
REGIS SALON
1555 Regent Ave W, Winnipeg, MB, R2C 4J2
(204) 663-7688
Emp Here 20
SIC 7231 Beauty shops

D-U-N-S 20-122-7845   (BR)
REITMANS (CANADA) LIMITEE
REITMANS
1592 Regent Ave W Unit 3, Winnipeg, MB, R2C 3B4
(204) 668-5683
Emp Here 40
SIC 5621 Women's clothing stores

D-U-N-S 25-268-0897   (BR)
RIVER EAST TRANSCONA SCHOOL DIVISION
MURDOCH MACKAY COLLEGIATE
260 Redonda St, Winnipeg, MB, R2C 1L6
(204) 958-6460
Emp Here 85
SIC 8211 Elementary and secondary schools

D-U-N-S 20-555-3584   (BR)
RIVER EAST TRANSCONA SCHOOL DIVISION
GUNN, JOHN W MIDDLE SCHOOL
351 Harold Ave W, Winnipeg, MB, R2C 2C9
(204) 958-6500
Emp Here 30
SIC 8211 Elementary and secondary schools

D-U-N-S 25-900-8837   (BR)
RIVER EAST TRANSCONA SCHOOL DIVISION
WESTVIEW ELEMENTARY SCHOOL
600 Hoka St, Winnipeg, MB, R2C 2V1
(204) 777-5139
Emp Here 25
SIC 8211 Elementary and secondary schools

D-U-N-S 20-047-0917   (BR)
RIVER EAST TRANSCONA SCHOOL DIVISION
ECOLE REGENT PARK
411 Moroz St, Winnipeg, MB, R2C 2X4
(204) 958-6830
Emp Here 25
SIC 8211 Elementary and secondary schools

D-U-N-S 20-047-0909   (BR)
RIVER EAST TRANSCONA SCHOOL DIVISION

ARTHUR DAY MIDDLE SCHOOL
43 Whitehall Blvd, Winnipeg, MB, R2C 0Y3
(204) 958-6522
Emp Here 50
SIC 8211 Elementary and secondary schools

D-U-N-S 20-023-2598   (BR)
RIVER EAST TRANSCONA SCHOOL DIVISION
ECOLE MARGARET-UNDERHILL
25 Regina Pl, Winnipeg, MB, R2C 0S5
(204) 958-6832
Emp Here 25
SIC 8211 Elementary and secondary schools

D-U-N-S 20-024-0021   (BR)
RIVER EAST TRANSCONA SCHOOL DIVISION
COLLEGE PIERRE ELLIOTT TRUDEAU
216 Redonda St, Winnipeg, MB, R2C 1L6
(204) 958-6888
Emp Here 27
SIC 8211 Elementary and secondary schools

D-U-N-S 20-555-3337   (BR)
RIVER EAST TRANSCONA SCHOOL DIVISION
RADISSON ELEMENTARY SCHOOL
1105 Winona St, Winnipeg, MB, R2C 2P9
(204) 777-0440
Emp Here 20
SIC 8211 Elementary and secondary schools

D-U-N-S 20-081-2654   (BR)
RIVER EAST TRANSCONA SCHOOL DIVISION
TRANSCONA COLLEGIATE
1305 Winona St, Winnipeg, MB, R2C 2P9
(204) 958-6440
Emp Here 56
SIC 8211 Elementary and secondary schools

D-U-N-S 25-193-4816   (BR)
RIVER EAST TRANSCONA SCHOOL DIVISION
BERNIE WOLFE COMMUNITY SCHOOL
95 Bournais Dr, Winnipeg, MB, R2C 3Z2
(204) 669-9412
Emp Here 60
SIC 8211 Elementary and secondary schools

D-U-N-S 20-709-7960   (BR)
RIVER EAST TRANSCONA SCHOOL DIVISION
TERES, JOSEPH ELEMENTARY SCHOOL
131 Sanford Fleming Rd, Winnipeg, MB, R2C 5B8
(204) 958-6860
Emp Here 50
SIC 8211 Elementary and secondary schools

D-U-N-S 20-555-2859   (BR)
RIVER EAST TRANSCONA SCHOOL DIVISION
ECOLE CENTRALE
604 Day St, Winnipeg, MB, R2C 1B6
(204) 224-3877
Emp Here 25
SIC 8211 Elementary and secondary schools

D-U-N-S 20-023-2606   (BR)
RIVER EAST TRANSCONA SCHOOL DIVISION
WAYOATA ELEMENTARY SCHOOL
605 Wayoata St, Winnipeg, MB, R2C 1J8
(204) 958-6840
Emp Here 35
SIC 8211 Elementary and secondary schools

D-U-N-S 20-555-3345   (BR)
RIVER EAST TRANSCONA SCHOOL DIVISION
HAROLD   HATCHER   ELEMENTARY SCHOOL
500 Redonda St, Winnipeg, MB, R2C 3T7
(204) 958-6880
Emp Here 47

SIC 8211 Elementary and secondary schools

D-U-N-S 24-234-9645   (BR)
SEARS CANADA INC
1555 Regent Ave W Suite 14, Winnipeg, MB, R2C 4J2
(204) 661-8470
Emp Here 150
SIC 5311 Department stores

D-U-N-S 20-196-6863   (BR)
SOBEYS CAPITAL INCORPORATED
SOBEY'S STORE
7 Reenders Dr, Winnipeg, MB, R2C 5K5
(204) 669-9966
Emp Here 49
SIC 5411 Grocery stores

D-U-N-S 24-363-2036   (BR)
SOBEYS WEST INC
KILDARE SAFEWAY
654 Kildare Ave E, Winnipeg, MB, R2C 0P8
(204) 222-6902
Emp Here 50
SIC 5411 Grocery stores

D-U-N-S 25-786-6145   (BR)
SOBEYS WEST INC
105 Pandora Ave E, Winnipeg, MB, R2C 0A1
(204) 222-6878
Emp Here 75
SIC 5411 Grocery stores

D-U-N-S 25-271-9927   (BR)
SOBEYS WEST INC
KILDONAN CROSSING SAFEWAY
1615 Regent Ave W Unit 500, Winnipeg, MB, R2C 5C6
(204) 663-6862
Emp Here 100
SIC 5411 Grocery stores

D-U-N-S 20-574-5255   (BR)
STAPLES CANADA INC
(*Suby of* Staples, Inc.)
1540 Regent Ave W, Winnipeg, MB, R2C 3B4
(204) 661-1563
Emp Here 30
SIC 5943 Stationery stores

D-U-N-S 24-114-7016   (SL)
T.W.Y. ENTERPRISES LTD
CATHAY HOUSE
1631 Regent Ave W, Winnipeg, MB, R2C 4H9
(204) 669-1029
Emp Here 70   *Sales* 2,942,050
SIC 5812 Eating places

D-U-N-S 20-698-1776   (BR)
TANDET LOGISTICS INC
640 Plessis Rd Unit B, Winnipeg, MB, R2C 2Z4
(204) 988-6960
Emp Here 24
SIC 4213 Trucking, except local

D-U-N-S 25-293-9335   (BR)
TOYS 'R' US (CANADA) LTD
TOYS 'R' US
(*Suby of* Toys "r" Us, Inc.)
1560 Regent Ave W, Winnipeg, MB, R2C 3B4
(204) 982-8690
Emp Here 30
SIC 5945 Hobby, toy, and game shops

D-U-N-S 24-690-9501   (BR)
U-HAUL CO. (CANADA) LTD
(*Suby of* Amerco)
1341 Regent Ave W, Winnipeg, MB, R2C 3B2
(204) 987-9506
Emp Here 25
SIC 7519 Utility trailer rental

D-U-N-S 20-015-1004   (BR)
VARSTEEL LTD
2475 Day St, Winnipeg, MB, R2C 2X5
(204) 237-6533
Emp Here 21
SIC 5051 Metals service centers and offices

SIC 8211 Elementary and secondary schools

D-U-N-S 20-063-1625   (BR)
VOESTALPINE NORTRAK LTD
NORTRAK
400 Pandora Ave W, Winnipeg, MB, R2C 3A5

Emp Here 25
SIC 3531 Construction machinery

D-U-N-S 24-038-9911   (BR)
WAL-MART CANADA CORP
1576 Regent Ave W, Winnipeg, MB, R2C 3B4
(204) 669-3575
Emp Here 20
SIC 5311 Department stores

D-U-N-S 24-967-9960   (BR)
WINNERS MERCHANTS INTERNATIONAL L.P.
WINNERS
(*Suby of* The TJX Companies Inc)
1520 Regent Ave W, Winnipeg, MB, R2C 3B4
(204) 654-0945
Emp Here 40
SIC 5651 Family clothing stores

D-U-N-S 25-532-7918   (SL)
WINNIPEG (TRANSCONA LIONS CLUB) INC
TRANSCONA COUNTRY CLUB
2070 Dugald Rd, Winnipeg, MB, R2C 3G7
(204) 222-1640
Emp Here 60   *Sales* 1,824,018
SIC 5812 Eating places

D-U-N-S 25-413-5163   (SL)
WINNIPEG FOREST PRODUCTS INC
640 Plessis Rd Unit C, Winnipeg, MB, R2C 2Z4

Emp Here 50   *Sales* 6,576,720
SIC 2448 Wood pallets and skids
Pr Pr Thomas L Fox
   William (Bill) Maskell
   Roxann Conkin

Winnipeg, MB R2G

D-U-N-S 24-653-8052   (SL)
0735290 MANITOBA LTD
SMITTY'S RESTAURANT & LOUNGE
1919 Henderson Hwy Unit 9, Winnipeg, MB, R2G 1P4
(204) 334-1162
Emp Here 60   *Sales* 1,824,018
SIC 5812 Eating places

D-U-N-S 25-311-6479   (BR)
CANADIAN IMPERIAL BANK OF COMMERCE
CIBC
1433 Henderson Hwy, Winnipeg, MB, R2G 1N3
(204) 944-6415
Emp Here 25
SIC 6021 National commercial banks

D-U-N-S 25-948-5332   (BR)
DALE & DALE PIZZA INC
DOMINO'S PIZZA
(*Suby of* Dale & Dale Pizza Inc)
686 Springfield Rd Unit 7, Winnipeg, MB, R2G 4G3
(204) 987-5554
Emp Here 23
SIC 5812 Eating places

D-U-N-S 20-650-7928   (SL)
GREATER   WINNIPEG   SOCIETY   FOR CHRISTIAN EDUCATION I
CALVIN CHRISTIAN SCHOOL
245 Sutton Ave, Winnipeg, MB, R2G 0T1
(204) 338-7981
Emp Here 70   *Sales* 4,669,485
SIC 8211 Elementary and secondary schools

D-U-N-S 24-616-4193   (BR)
HEALTHCARE INSURANCE RECIPROCAL OF CANADA
HIROC
1200 Rothesay St, Winnipeg, MB, R2G 1T7
(204) 943-4125
Emp Here 100
SIC 6411 Insurance agents, brokers, and service

D-U-N-S 24-264-6016   (SL)
JANZ TEAM MINISTRIES INC
TEACHBEYOND
2121a Henderson Hwy, Winnipeg, MB, R2G 1P8
(204) 334-0055
Emp Here 100   *Sales* 9,130,500
SIC 8661 Religious organizations
   Jack Stenekes

D-U-N-S 24-236-3893   (SL)
KNOWLES CENTRE INC
2065 Henderson Hwy, Winnipeg, MB, R2G 1P7
(204) 339-1951
Emp Here 60   *Sales* 2,188,821
SIC 8361 Residential care

D-U-N-S 25-311-2825   (BR)
MCDONALD'S   RESTAURANTS   OF CANADA LIMITED
MCDONALD'S
(*Suby of* McDonald's Corporation)
1460 Henderson Hwy, Winnipeg, MB, R2G 1N4
(204) 949-6074
Emp Here 110
SIC 5812 Eating places

D-U-N-S 24-377-8391   (HQ)
PALLISER FURNITURE UPHOLSTERY LTD
70 Lexington Pk, Winnipeg, MB, R2G 4H2
(204) 988-5600
Emp Here 30   *Emp Total* 1,730
Sales 49,248,473
SIC 2512 Upholstered household furniture
Dir Arthur Defehr
Pr Cary Benson
   Reginald Kliewer
VP Fin Cathy Gillespie
VP Sls Lorri Kelley
VP Heather Goertzen
VP Bryan Andrew
VP Opers Andrew Willms

D-U-N-S 25-261-5604   (HQ)
RIVER CITY SPORTS INC
RIVER CITY SPORTS
(*Suby of* River City Sports Inc)
1074 Henderson Hwy, Winnipeg, MB, R2G 1L1
(204) 654-5085
Emp Here 42   *Emp Total* 50
Sales 2,845,467
SIC 5699 Miscellaneous apparel and accessory stores

D-U-N-S 20-028-7857   (BR)
RIVER EAST TRANSCONA SCHOOL DIVISION
MAPLE LEAF SCHOOL
251 Mcivor Ave, Winnipeg, MB, R2G 0Z7
(204) 661-9509
Emp Here 45
SIC 8211 Elementary and secondary schools

D-U-N-S 20-709-7937   (BR)
RIVER EAST TRANSCONA SCHOOL DIVISION
DONWOOD ELEMENTARY SCHOOL
400 Donwood Dr, Winnipeg, MB, R2G 0X4
(204) 668-9438
Emp Here 50
SIC 8211 Elementary and secondary schools

D-U-N-S 20-555-3246   (BR)
RIVER EAST TRANSCONA SCHOOL DIVISION

CHIEF PEGUIS JUNIOR HIGH SCHOOL
1400 Rothesay St, Winnipeg, MB, R2G 1V2
(204) 668-9442
Emp Here 65
SIC 8211 Elementary and secondary schools

D-U-N-S 20-555-3378   (BR)
RIVER EAST TRANSCONA SCHOOL DIVISION
RIVER EAST COLLEGIATE
295 Sutton Ave, Winnipeg, MB, R2G 0T1
(204) 338-4611
Emp Here 100
SIC 8211 Elementary and secondary schools

D-U-N-S 20-023-2549   (BR)
RIVER EAST TRANSCONA SCHOOL DIVISION
JOHN PRITCHARD SCHOOL
1490 Henderson Hwy, Winnipeg, MB, R2G 1N5
(204) 339-1984
Emp Here 60
SIC 8211 Elementary and secondary schools

D-U-N-S 20-555-3667   (BR)
RIVER EAST TRANSCONA SCHOOL DIVISION
STEWART JOHN G SCHOOL
2069 Henderson Hwy, Winnipeg, MB, R2G 1P7
(204) 338-3670
Emp Here 20
SIC 8211 Elementary and secondary schools

D-U-N-S 25-127-9501   (BR)
RIVER EAST TRANSCONA SCHOOL DIVISION
SUN VALLEY SCHOOL
125 Sun Valley Dr, Winnipeg, MB, R2G 2W4
(204) 663-7664
Emp Here 53
SIC 8211 Elementary and secondary schools

D-U-N-S 25-127-9493   (BR)
RIVER EAST TRANSCONA SCHOOL DIVISION
SPRINGFIELD HEIGHTS ELEMENTARY SCHOOL
505 Sharron Bay, Winnipeg, MB, R2G 0H8
(204) 663-5078
Emp Here 50
SIC 8211 Elementary and secondary schools

D-U-N-S 20-063-0726   (BR)
RIVER EAST TRANSCONA SCHOOL DIVISION
TRANSCONA SCHOOL MAINTENANCE DIVISION
1455 Molson St, Winnipeg, MB, R2G 3S6
(204) 669-5660
Emp Here 20
SIC 1542 Nonresidential construction, nec

D-U-N-S 25-060-5227   (BR)
RIVER EAST TRANSCONA SCHOOL DIVISION
EMERSON ELEMENTARY SCHOOL
323 Emerson Ave, Winnipeg, MB, R2G 1G3
(204) 669-4430
Emp Here 23
SIC 8211 Elementary and secondary schools

D-U-N-S 24-076-2109   (SL)
ROCKY MOUNTAIN INC
1795 Henderson Hwy, Winnipeg, MB, R2G 1P3
(204) 344-5501
Emp Here 37   Sales 11,779,113
SIC 4731 Freight transportation arrangement
Pr Richard Petrosky

D-U-N-S 20-292-9324   (SL)
ROYAL LEPAGE PRIME REAL ESTATE
1877 Henderson Hwy, Winnipeg, MB, R2G 1P4
(204) 989-7900
Emp Here 80   Sales 7,514,952

SIC 6531 Real estate agents and managers
Owner John Froese

D-U-N-S 20-746-1315   (SL)
S.P.I.K.E. INCORPORATED
1940 Henderson Hwy, Winnipeg, MB, R2G 1P2
(204) 339-2990
Emp Here 70   Sales 2,553,625
SIC 8361 Residential care

D-U-N-S 20-513-4302   (SL)
SPRINGFIELD INDUSTRIES LTD
125 Furniture Park, Winnipeg, MB, R2G 1B9

Emp Here 50   Sales 7,362,000
SIC 2821 Plastics materials and resins
Pr Richard De Fehr
VP Shannon Loewenn
Andrew De Fehr
Treas David Loewenn
Dir Daniel Loewenn

Winnipeg, MB R2H

D-U-N-S 20-700-7522   (BR)
AG GROWTH INTERNATIONAL INC
WESTEEL DIVISION
450 Rue Desautels, Winnipeg, MB, R2H 3E6
(204) 233-7133
Emp Here 340
SIC 3443 Fabricated plate work (boiler shop)

D-U-N-S 25-676-9803   (BR)
DIVISION SCOLAIRE FRANCO-MANITOBAINE
ECOLE PRECIEUX-SANG
(Suby of Division Scolaire Franco-Manitobaine)
209 Kenny St, Winnipeg, MB, R2H 2E5
(204) 233-4327
Emp Here 50
SIC 8211 Elementary and secondary schools

D-U-N-S 25-289-2781   (BR)
DIVISION SCOLAIRE FRANCO-MANITOBAINE
COLLEGE LOUIS RIEL
(Suby of Division Scolaire Franco-Manitobaine)
585 Rue St Jean Baptiste, Winnipeg, MB, R2H 2Y2
(204) 237-8927
Emp Here 86
SIC 8221 Colleges and universities

D-U-N-S 25-676-9779   (BR)
DIVISION SCOLAIRE FRANCO-MANITOBAINE
ECOLE TACHE
(Suby of Division Scolaire Franco-Manitobaine)
744 Langevin St, Winnipeg, MB, R2H 2W7
(204) 233-8735
Emp Here 45
SIC 8211 Elementary and secondary schools

D-U-N-S 20-321-4143   (BR)
FIRST NATIONS OF NORTHERN MANITOBA CHILD & FAMILY SERVICES AUTHORITY
383 Provencher Blvd Suite 200, Winnipeg, MB, R2H 0G9
(204) 942-1842
Emp Here 20
SIC 8322 Individual and family services

D-U-N-S 24-771-1922   (SL)
HEALTHWARE TECHNOLOGIES INC
131 Provencher Blvd Suite 308, Winnipeg, MB, R2H 0G2
(204) 272-6476
Emp Here 20   Sales 1,459,214
SIC 7371 Custom computer programming services

D-U-N-S 20-023-9189   (BR)
LOUIS RIEL SCHOOL DIVISION
ECOLE PROVENCHER
320 De La Cathedrale Ave, Winnipeg, MB, R2H 0J4
(204) 233-0222
Emp Here 33
SIC 8211 Elementary and secondary schools

D-U-N-S 25-747-4155   (BR)
LOUIS RIEL SCHOOL DIVISION
HOLY CROSS RC SCHOOL
300 Dubuc St, Winnipeg, MB, R2H 1E4
(204) 237-4936
Emp Here 22
SIC 8211 Elementary and secondary schools

D-U-N-S 25-138-3741   (BR)
LOUIS RIEL SCHOOL DIVISION
HENRI-BURGERON SCHOOL
363 Enfield Cres, Winnipeg, MB, R2H 1C6
(204) 233-7079
Emp Here 30
SIC 8211 Elementary and secondary schools

D-U-N-S 25-272-4257   (BR)
LOUIS RIEL SCHOOL DIVISION
MARION SCHOOL
619 Rue Des Meurons, Winnipeg, MB, R2H 2R1
(204) 237-5176
Emp Here 30
SIC 8211 Elementary and secondary schools

D-U-N-S 20-709-7895   (BR)
LOUIS RIEL SCHOOL DIVISION
NORDALE SCHOOL
99 Birchdale Ave, Winnipeg, MB, R2H 1S2
(204) 237-0202
Emp Here 30
SIC 8211 Elementary and secondary schools

D-U-N-S 25-141-5733   (BR)
LOUIS RIEL SCHOOL DIVISION
NELSON MCINTYRE COLLEGIATE
188 St Mary'S Rd, Winnipeg, MB, R2H 1H9
(204) 237-0219
Emp Here 65
SIC 8211 Elementary and secondary schools

D-U-N-S 25-310-9102   (BR)
MCDONALD'S RESTAURANTS OF CANADA LIMITED
MCDONALD'S
(Suby of McDonald's Corporation)
77 Goulet St, Winnipeg, MB, R2H 0R5
(204) 949-6018
Emp Here 80
SIC 5812 Eating places

D-U-N-S 20-570-7391   (SL)
NORWOOD HOTEL CO LTD
112 Marion St, Winnipeg, MB, R2H 0T1
(204) 233-4475
Emp Here 110   Sales 4,815,406
SIC 7011 Hotels and motels

D-U-N-S 24-363-0857   (BR)
RGIS CANADA ULC
196 Tache Ave Unit 5, Winnipeg, MB, R2H 1Z6
(204) 774-0013
Emp Here 250
SIC 7389 Business services, nec

D-U-N-S 20-757-9772   (SL)
TACHE NURSING CENTRE-HOSPITALIER TACHE INC
CENTRE TACHE CENTRE
185 Rue Despins, Winnipeg, MB, R2H 2B3
(204) 233-3692
Emp Here 430   Sales 26,306,880
SIC 8051 Skilled nursing care facilities
Dir Patrick Dacquay

D-U-N-S 20-947-1341   (BR)
WESTERN INVENTORY SERVICE LTD
WIS INTERNATIONAL
73 Goulet St, Winnipeg, MB, R2H 0R5

(204) 669-6505
Emp Here 120
SIC 7389 Business services, nec

D-U-N-S 20-657-0488   (BR)
WINNIPEG REGIONAL HEALTH AUTHORITY, THE
W R H A COMMUNITY CARE
614 Rue Des Meurons Suite 240, Winnipeg, MB, R2H 2P9
(204) 940-2035
Emp Here 20
SIC 8099 Health and allied services, nec

Winnipeg, MB R2J

D-U-N-S 25-123-2294   (BR)
A & W FOOD SERVICES OF CANADA INC
A & W RESTAURANTS
107 Vermillion Rd Suite 10, Winnipeg, MB, R2J 4A9
(204) 255-2176
Emp Here 39
SIC 5812 Eating places

D-U-N-S 24-207-9825   (BR)
AMJ CAMPBELL INC
1333 Niakwa Rd E Unit 12, Winnipeg, MB, R2J 3T5
(204) 669-9900
Emp Here 35
SIC 4214 Local trucking with storage

D-U-N-S 25-598-0450   (BR)
ACUITY HOLDINGS, INC
ZEP MANUFACTURING
(Suby of NM Z Parent Inc.)
450 Provencher Blvd, Winnipeg, MB, R2J 0B9
(204) 233-3342
Emp Here 25
SIC 2842 Polishes and sanitation goods

D-U-N-S 24-496-6461   (BR)
ALL WEATHER WINDOWS LTD
124 Terracon Pl, Winnipeg, MB, R2J 4G7
(204) 947-2433
Emp Here 28
SIC 5031 Lumber, plywood, and millwork

D-U-N-S 24-717-6522   (BR)
ALLIED SYSTEMS (CANADA) COMPANY
736 Marion St, Winnipeg, MB, R2J 0K4
(204) 233-4924
Emp Here 50
SIC 4213 Trucking, except local

D-U-N-S 24-716-9634   (BR)
ALTEC INDUSTRIES LTD
(Suby of Altec, Inc.)
57 Durand Rd, Winnipeg, MB, R2J 3T1
(204) 663-8362
Emp Here 23
SIC 1799 Special trade contractors, nec

D-U-N-S 20-711-6195   (HQ)
BEAVER BUS LINES LIMITED
(Suby of Beaver Bus Lines Limited)
339 Archibald St, Winnipeg, MB, R2J 0W6
(204) 989-7007
Emp Here 77   Emp Total 85
Sales 4,012,839
SIC 4142 Bus charter service, except local

D-U-N-S 24-883-6280   (BR)
BRENNTAG CANADA INC
681 Plinguet St, Winnipeg, MB, R2J 2X2
(204) 233-3416
Emp Here 28
SIC 5169 Chemicals and allied products, nec

D-U-N-S 24-967-5661   (SL)
BRIDGES, DAVID INC
CHAMP INDUSTRIES
(Suby of Canerector Inc)
360 Dawson Rd N, Winnipeg, MB, R2J 0S7

(204) 233-0500
Emp Here 65 *Sales* 7,879,756
SIC 3399 Primary Metal products
Pr Pr Claudia Bridges
Lise Baker

D-U-N-S 20-855-2112 (HQ)
CABELA'S RETAIL CANADA INC
CABELA'S CANADA
(*Suby of* Cabela's Incorporated)
25 De Baets St, Winnipeg, MB, R2J 4G5
(204) 788-4867
Emp Here 200 *Emp Total* 19,100
Sales 16,999,843
SIC 5941 Sporting goods and bicycle shops
Pr Pr Dennis Highby
VP Patrick Snyder
Sr VP Brian Linneman

D-U-N-S 20-434-3966 (BR)
CANWEL BUILDING MATERIALS LTD
CANWEL
350 De Baets St, Winnipeg, MB, R2J 0H4
(204) 633-4890
Emp Here 20
SIC 5039 Construction materials, nec

D-U-N-S 25-671-2340 (BR)
CANAD CORPORATION OF MANITOBA LTD
CANADA INNS WINDSORS PARK
(*Suby of* Canad Corporation Of Canada Inc)
1034 Elizabeth Rd, Winnipeg, MB, R2J 1B3
(204) 253-2641
Emp Here 200
SIC 7011 Hotels and motels

D-U-N-S 20-700-7555 (SL)
CANADADRUGS.COM LP
24 Terracon Pl, Winnipeg, MB, R2J 4G7

Emp Here 220 *Sales* 42,904,960
SIC 5912 Drug stores and proprietary stores
Dir Kris Thorkelson
Ron Sigurdson

D-U-N-S 25-341-7877 (BR)
CARGILL LIMITED
CARGILL ANIMAL NUTRITION
627 Plinguet St, Winnipeg, MB, R2J 2W9

Emp Here 20
SIC 5191 Farm supplies

D-U-N-S 24-914-8701 (SL)
CARLSON COMMERCIAL & INDUSTRIAL SERVICES LTD
1035 Mission St, Winnipeg, MB, R2J 0A4
(204) 233-0671
Emp Here 25 *Sales* 2,826,987
SIC 1799 Special trade contractors, nec

D-U-N-S 20-107-7844 (BR)
COCA-COLA REFRESHMENTS CANADA COMPANY
(*Suby of* The Coca-Cola Company)
164 Terracon Pl, Winnipeg, MB, R2J 4G7

Emp Here 30
SIC 7699 Repair services, nec

D-U-N-S 20-580-5091 (BR)
COMPAGNIE DES CHEMINS DE FER NA-TIONAUX DU CANADA
CN RAILWAY
821 Lagimodiere Blvd Suite 5, Winnipeg, MB, R2J 0T8
(204) 231-7550
Emp Here 20
SIC 4011 Railroads, line-haul operating

D-U-N-S 24-371-0436 (BR)
DARLING INTERNATIONAL CANADA INC
ROTHSAY
(*Suby of* Darling Ingredients Inc.)
607 Dawson Rd N, Winnipeg, MB, R2J 0T2
(204) 233-7347
Emp Here 50

SIC 4953 Refuse systems

D-U-N-S 24-971-3934 (BR)
DIVISION SCOLAIRE FRANCO-MANITOBAINE
ECOLE LACERTE SCHOOL
(*Suby of* Division Scolaire Franco-Manitobaine)
1101 Autumnwood Dr, Winnipeg, MB, R2J 1C8
(204) 256-4384
Emp Here 50
SIC 8211 Elementary and secondary schools

D-U-N-S 20-004-6126 (SL)
FAIRWAY COACHLINES INC
339 Archibald St, Winnipeg, MB, R2J 0W6
(204) 989-7007
Emp Here 100 *Sales* 7,067,520
SIC 4131 Intercity and rural bus transportation
Pr Pr John Fehr Jr

D-U-N-S 25-106-6148 (SL)
FOXRIDGE HOMES (MANITOBA) LTD
30 Speers Rd, Winnipeg, MB, R2J 1L9
(204) 488-7578
Emp Here 70 *Sales* 13,935,494
SIC 1522 Residential construction, nec
Pr David Freisen

D-U-N-S 20-023-8645 (BR)
FRONTIER SCHOOL DIVISION
MOSAKAHIKAN SCHOOL
30 Speers Rd, Winnipeg, MB, R2J 1L9
(204) 775-9741
Emp Here 87
SIC 8211 Elementary and secondary schools

D-U-N-S 24-882-6968 (BR)
HUSSMANN CANADA INC
50 Terracon Pl, Winnipeg, MB, R2J 4G7

Emp Here 25
SIC 1711 Plumbing, heating, air-conditioning

D-U-N-S 20-517-9146 (SL)
INTERGRAPHICS DECAL LIMITED
180 De Baets St, Winnipeg, MB, R2J 3W6
(204) 958-9570
Emp Here 80 *Sales* 4,012,839
SIC 2759 Commercial printing, nec

D-U-N-S 20-210-5412 (SL)
J & S HOLDINGS INC
TIM HORTONS
1040 Beaverhill Blvd Suite 1, Winnipeg, MB, R2J 4B1
(204) 255-8431
Emp Here 60 *Sales* 2,042,900
SIC 5461 Retail bakeries

D-U-N-S 20-283-2002 (SL)
JACK COOPER TRANSPORT CANADA INC
736 Marion St, Winnipeg, MB, R2J 0K4
(204) 233-4924
Emp Here 30 *Sales* 3,283,232
SIC 4213 Trucking, except local

D-U-N-S 25-691-4524 (BR)
KITCHEN CRAFT OF CANADA
CRAFT LINE COUNTERTOPS
495 Archibald St, Winnipeg, MB, R2J 0X2
(204) 233-3097
Emp Here 47
SIC 2541 Wood partitions and fixtures

D-U-N-S 24-370-4744 (BR)
LAFARGE CANADA INC
LAFARGE NORTH AMERICA
185 Dawson Rd N, Winnipeg, MB, R2J 0S6
(204) 958-6333
Emp Here 150
SIC 1791 Structural steel erection

D-U-N-S 20-064-3398 (BR)
LOUIS RIEL SCHOOL DIVISION
SHAMROCK ELEMENTARY SCHOOL
831 Beaverhill Blvd, Winnipeg, MB, R2J 3K1

(204) 257-0637
Emp Here 80
SIC 8211 Elementary and secondary schools

D-U-N-S 20-913-6527 (BR)
LOUIS RIEL SCHOOL DIVISION
COLLEGE BELIVEAU
296 Speers Rd, Winnipeg, MB, R2J 1M7
(204) 255-3205
Emp Here 50
SIC 8211 Elementary and secondary schools

D-U-N-S 20-046-8119 (BR)
LOUIS RIEL SCHOOL DIVISION
ECOLE HOWDEN
150 Howden Rd, Winnipeg, MB, R2J 1L3
(204) 255-0014
Emp Here 30
SIC 8211 Elementary and secondary schools

D-U-N-S 20-709-7846 (BR)
LOUIS RIEL SCHOOL DIVISION
ARCHWOOD SCHOOL
800 Archibald St, Winnipeg, MB, R2J 0Y4
(204) 233-7983
Emp Here 30
SIC 8211 Elementary and secondary schools

D-U-N-S 20-099-8982 (BR)
LOUIS RIEL SCHOOL DIVISION
NIAKWA PLACE SCHOOL
200 Pebble Beach Rd, Winnipeg, MB, R2J 3K3
(204) 257-0640
Emp Here 38
SIC 8211 Elementary and secondary schools

D-U-N-S 20-709-7879 (BR)
LOUIS RIEL SCHOOL DIVISION
GENERAL VANIER SCHOOL
18 Lomond Blvd, Winnipeg, MB, R2J 1Y2
(204) 255-3576
Emp Here 50
SIC 8211 Elementary and secondary schools

D-U-N-S 25-082-2962 (BR)
LOUIS RIEL SCHOOL DIVISION
FRONTENAC SCHOOL
866 Autumnwood Dr, Winnipeg, MB, R2J 1C1
(204) 257-0609
Emp Here 60
SIC 8211 Elementary and secondary schools

D-U-N-S 25-063-5075 (BR)
LOUIS RIEL SCHOOL DIVISION
J H BRUNS COLLEGIATE
250 Lakewood Blvd, Winnipeg, MB, R2J 3A2
(204) 257-2928
Emp Here 60
SIC 8211 Elementary and secondary schools

D-U-N-S 20-913-6535 (BR)
LOUIS RIEL SCHOOL DIVISION
WINDSOR PARK COLLEGIATE
1015 Cottonwood Rd, Winnipeg, MB, R2J 1G3
(204) 256-7316
Emp Here 70
SIC 8211 Elementary and secondary schools

D-U-N-S 24-971-3959 (BR)
LOUIS RIEL SCHOOL DIVISION
ECOLE GUYOT
400 Willowlake Cres, Winnipeg, MB, R2J 3K2
(204) 257-2540
Emp Here 30
SIC 8211 Elementary and secondary schools

D-U-N-S 20-042-5408 (BR)
LOUIS RIEL SCHOOL DIVISION
ECOLE VAN BELLEGHEM SCHOOL
10 Vermillion Rd Suite 14, Winnipeg, MB, R2J 2T1
(204) 255-1134
Emp Here 23
SIC 8299 Schools and educational services, nec

D-U-N-S 25-235-5474 (SL)
MAPM ENTERPRISES

MARION MOHAWK
1011 Marion St, Winnipeg, MB, R2J 0K9
(204) 231-5997
Emp Here 35 *Sales* 6,594,250
SIC 5541 Gasoline service stations
Pt Marvin Miller
Pt Peggy Miller

D-U-N-S 25-126-9650 (BR)
MANITOBA LIQUOR AND LOTTERIES CORPORATION
LIQUOR MART
67 Vermillion Rd Unit 21, Winnipeg, MB, R2J 3W7
(204) 987-4043
Emp Here 20
SIC 5921 Liquor stores

D-U-N-S 25-302-1117 (BR)
MAPLE LEAF FOODS INC
SCHNEIDER FOODS
140 Panet Rd, Winnipeg, MB, R2J 0S3

Emp Here 50
SIC 2013 Sausages and other prepared meats

D-U-N-S 24-630-6567 (BR)
MAPLE LEAF FOODS INC
MAPLE LEAF CONSUMER FOODS
870 Lagimodiere Blvd Suite 23, Winnipeg, MB, R2J 0T9
(204) 233-2421
Emp Here 400
SIC 2011 Meat packing plants

D-U-N-S 24-852-0975 (BR)
MAPLE LEAF FOODS INC
ROTHSAY RENDERING, DIV OF
607 Dawson Rd N Suite 555, Winnipeg, MB, R2J 0T2
(204) 233-7347
Emp Here 80
SIC 2048 Prepared feeds, nec

D-U-N-S 25-318-1226 (BR)
MCDONALD'S RESTAURANTS OF CANADA LIMITED
MCDONALD'S #8394
(*Suby of* McDonald's Corporation)
65 Vermillion Rd, Winnipeg, MB, R2J 3W7
(204) 949-6015
Emp Here 80
SIC 5812 Eating places

D-U-N-S 24-428-7280 (SL)
MID WEST PACKAGING LIMITED
70 Beghin Ave, Winnipeg, MB, R2J 3R4
(204) 661-6731
Emp Here 27 *Sales* 5,284,131
SIC 2653 Corrugated and solid fiber boxes

D-U-N-S 20-010-1087 (HQ)
MONARCH INDUSTRIES LIMITED
LION HYDRAULICS
51 Burmac Rd, Winnipeg, MB, R2J 4J3
(204) 786-7921
Emp Here 350 *Emp Total* 540
Sales 41,146,923
SIC 3593 Fluid power cylinders and actuators
Dir Gene Dunn
Roy Cook
Daniel O'rourke
VP Mfg Vic Bhayana
Don Streuber
Peter Falk

D-U-N-S 25-388-4415 (BR)
NEW FLYER INDUSTRIES CANADA ULC
NEW FLYER PARTS & PUBLICATIONS
25 De Baets St, Winnipeg, MB, R2J 4G5
(204) 982-8400
Emp Here 200
SIC 3711 Motor vehicles and car bodies

D-U-N-S 20-180-7083 (BR)
NEW FLYER INDUSTRIES CANADA ULC
NEW PRODUCT DEVELOPMENT

45 Beghin Ave Unit 7, Winnipeg, MB, R2J 4B9
(204) 982-8413
Emp Here 30
SIC 3711 Motor vehicles and car bodies

D-U-N-S 25-388-0405   (BR)
NORTH WEST COMPANY LP, THE
CRESCENT MULTI FOODS
2049 Dugald Rd, Winnipeg, MB, R2J 0H3
(204) 943-7461
Emp Here 40
SIC 5411 Grocery stores

D-U-N-S 20-434-7041   (BR)
PPG CANADA INC
PPG PHILLIPS IND COATINGS DIV
(*Suby of* PPG Industries, Inc.)
95 Paquin Rd, Winnipeg, MB, R2J 3V9
(204) 661-6781
Emp Here 40
SIC 2851 Paints and allied products

D-U-N-S 20-855-3383   (BR)
PHARMA PLUS DRUGMARTS LTD
35 Lakewood Blvd, Winnipeg, MB, R2J 2M8
(204) 982-4120
Emp Here 20
SIC 5912 Drug stores and proprietary stores

D-U-N-S 25-012-1084   (BR)
PINCHIN LTD
(*Suby of* 2010282 Ontario Inc)
54 Terracon Pl, Winnipeg, MB, R2J 4G7
(204) 452-0983
Emp Here 30
SIC 8748 Business consulting, nec

D-U-N-S 24-929-4455   (SL)
QUALICO PARTNERSHIP , THE
STERLING HOMES
30 Speers Rd, Winnipeg, MB, R2J 1L9
(204) 233-2451
Emp Here 35   *Sales* 7,304,400
SIC 1521 Single-family housing construction
VP Fin Ronald Reimer
VP Opers Brian Hastings
Pt Ruth Hastings

D-U-N-S 24-314-6979   (SL)
QUALITY EDGE CONVERTING LTD
94 Durand Rd, Winnipeg, MB, R2J 3T2
(204) 256-4115
Emp Here 30   *Sales* 5,197,506
SIC 5049 Professional equipment, nec

D-U-N-S 25-300-6233   (BR)
REDBERRY FRANCHISING CORP
BURGER KING
71 Vermillion Rd, Winnipeg, MB, R2J 3W7
(204) 987-8429
Emp Here 34
SIC 5812 Eating places

D-U-N-S 24-747-8811   (SL)
REGENT CONSTRUCTION (2000) LTD
919 Dugald Rd, Winnipeg, MB, R2J 0G7
(204) 231-3456
Emp Here 20   *Sales* 5,006,160
SIC 1542 Nonresidential construction, nec
Pr Pr Steven Wasiuta
Christina Strass
Dir Robert Jaques
Dir James Kondratuk

D-U-N-S 24-309-3197   (BR)
RIDLEY INC
FEED RITE, DIVISION OF
17 Speers Rd, Winnipeg, MB, R2J 1M1
(204) 233-8418
Emp Here 50
SIC 5999 Miscellaneous retail stores, nec

D-U-N-S 24-377-6601   (BR)
RIDLEY MF INC
EMF NUTRITION
196 Paquin Rd, Winnipeg, MB, R2J 3V4
(204) 667-8959
Emp Here 40

SIC 2048 Prepared feeds, nec

D-U-N-S 20-614-3224   (BR)
ROTHMANS, BENSON & HEDGES INC
(*Suby of* Philip Morris International Inc.)
19 Terracon Pl, Winnipeg, MB, R2J 4B3
(204) 235-0056
Emp Here 20
SIC 5194 Tobacco and tobacco products

D-U-N-S 20-913-7467   (BR)
ROYAL BANK OF CANADA
RBC
(*Suby of* Royal Bank Of Canada)
111 Vermillion Rd, Winnipeg, MB, R2J 4A9
(204) 988-6590
Emp Here 26
SIC 6021 National commercial banks

D-U-N-S 24-333-1548   (BR)
ROYAL CANADIAN MINT
520 Lagimodiere Blvd, Winnipeg, MB, R2J 3E7
(204) 983-6400
Emp Here 450
SIC 5094 Jewelry and precious stones

D-U-N-S 20-040-1754   (BR)
SHOEMAKER DRYWALL SUPPLIES LTD
235 De Baets St, Winnipeg, MB, R2J 4A8
(204) 633-8747
Emp Here 20
SIC 5032 Brick, stone, and related material

D-U-N-S 24-967-8749   (HQ)
STAR BUILDING MATERIALS LTD
STAR TRUSS, DIV OF
16 Speers Rd Suite 118, Winnipeg, MB, R2J 1L8
(204) 233-8687
Emp Here 80   *Emp Total* 27
Sales 22,034,131
SIC 5211 Lumber and other building materials
Pr Pr Ruth Hastings
VP VP Brian Hastings

D-U-N-S 24-310-7070   (BR)
TDG FURNITURE INC
DUFRESNE DISTRIBUTION CENTRE
230 Panet Rd, Winnipeg, MB, R2J 0S3
(204) 989-9888
Emp Here 40
SIC 5712 Furniture stores

D-U-N-S 20-813-0729   (SL)
TRANSCONA SPRINGFIELD EMPLOY-MENT NETWORK INC
232 Reigon Ave W, Winnipeg, MB, R2J 0H3
(204) 777-0302
Emp Here 23   *Sales* 6,784,769
SIC 8399 Social services, nec
Ex Dir Darryl Kippen

D-U-N-S 20-514-3196   (BR)
VANTAGE FOODS INC
41 Paquin Rd, Winnipeg, MB, R2J 3V9
(204) 667-9903
Emp Here 150
SIC 2011 Meat packing plants

D-U-N-S 24-607-9859   (HQ)
VITA HEALTH PRODUCTS INC
150 Beghin Ave, Winnipeg, MB, R2J 3W2
(204) 661-8386
Emp Here 485   *Emp Total* 1,600
Sales 22,107,092
SIC 2833 Medicinals and botanicals
Rachel Cahill
Stephanie Haverstick
Pr Steven J. Conboy
Joseph Looney
Harvey Kamil

D-U-N-S 24-374-1043   (BR)
WSP CANADA INC
G NIVAR
10 Prairie Way, Winnipeg, MB, R2J 3J8

(204) 477-6650
Emp Here 65
SIC 8711 Engineering services

D-U-N-S 24-916-8766   (SL)
WESTERN INDUSTRIAL SERVICES LTD
WISL
300 Dawson Rd N, Winnipeg, MB, R2J 0S7
(204) 956-9475
Emp Here 50   *Sales* 3,210,271
SIC 1721 Painting and paper hanging

D-U-N-S 20-165-3313   (BR)
WINNIPEG REGIONAL HEALTH AUTHOR-ITY, THE
NUTRITION & FOOD SERVICES
345 De Baets St, Winnipeg, MB, R2J 3V6
(204) 654-5100
Emp Here 205
SIC 8099 Health and allied services, nec

D-U-N-S 20-922-6112   (BR)
XPLORNET COMMUNICATIONS INC
275 De Baets St Suite 4, Winnipeg, MB, R2J 4A8
(204) 669-7007
Emp Here 300
SIC 4813 Telephone communication, except radio

Winnipeg, MB R2K

D-U-N-S 25-684-3558   (BR)
7-ELEVEN CANADA, INC
7-ELEVEN STORE #23281
554 Keenleyside St, Winnipeg, MB, R2K 3H2
(204) 985-0135
Emp Here 20
SIC 5411 Grocery stores

D-U-N-S 20-007-2494   (BR)
BARKMAN CONCRETE LTD
909 Gateway Rd, Winnipeg, MB, R2K 3L1
(204) 667-3310
Emp Here 20
SIC 5032 Brick, stone, and related material

D-U-N-S 20-836-0198   (SL)
BETHANIA MENNONITE PERSONAL CARE HOME INC
1045 Concordia Ave, Winnipeg, MB, R2K 3S7
(204) 667-0795
Emp Here 350   *Sales* 17,178,000
SIC 8361 Residential care
Anita Kampen
Ch Bd Tony Driedger

D-U-N-S 20-569-7428   (SL)
BUILDERS FURNITURE LTD
695 Washington Ave, Winnipeg, MB, R2K 1M4
(204) 668-0783
Emp Here 65   *Sales* 4,377,642
SIC 2541 Wood partitions and fixtures

D-U-N-S 20-013-1980   (BR)
CASCADES CANADA ULC
CASCADES BOXBOARD GROUP, DIV OF
531 Golspie St, Winnipeg, MB, R2K 2T9
(204) 667-6600
Emp Here 240
SIC 2657 Folding paperboard boxes

D-U-N-S 20-570-0078   (BR)
CITY OF WINNIPEG, THE
COMMUNITY SERVICES
(*Suby of* City of Winnipeg, The)
909 Concordia Ave, Winnipeg, MB, R2K 2M6
(204) 986-6980
Emp Here 40
SIC 7999 Amusement and recreation, nec

D-U-N-S 20-758-9649   (SL)
CONCORDIA HOSPITAL
1095 Concordia Ave, Winnipeg, MB, R2K 3S8
(204) 667-1560
Emp Here 1,100   *Sales* 98,850,312

SIC 8062 General medical and surgical hospitals
Pr Henry Tessmann
Les Janzen
Ch Bd Elizabeth Wall

D-U-N-S 24-175-7553   (SL)
CONCORDIA WELLNESS PROJECTS
CONCORDIA VILLAGE
1125 Molson St Suite 100, Winnipeg, MB, R2K 0A7
(204) 667-6479
Emp Here 20   *Sales* 6,028,800
SIC 8399 Social services, nec
Prin Les Janzen

D-U-N-S 25-369-3642   (HQ)
JELD-WEN OF CANADA, LTD
JELD-WEN WINDOWS & DOORS
485 Watt St, Winnipeg, MB, R2K 2R9
(204) 694-6012
Emp Here 100   *Emp Total* 192,000
Sales 122,573,976
SIC 2431 Millwork
Pr Barry J Homrighaus
VP Bill Donaldson

D-U-N-S 25-386-1389   (BR)
LOBLAWS INC
REAL-CANADIAN SUPERSTORES
1035 Gateway Rd Suite 1512, Winnipeg, MB, R2K 4C1
(204) 987-7534
Emp Here 200
SIC 5141 Groceries, general line

D-U-N-S 25-756-7529   (BR)
RIVER EAST TRANSCONA SCHOOL DIVISION
PRINCE EDWARD SCHOOL
649 Brazier St, Winnipeg, MB, R2K 2N4
(204) 667-5727
Emp Here 30
SIC 8211 Elementary and secondary schools

D-U-N-S 25-756-7552   (BR)
RIVER EAST TRANSCONA SCHOOL DIVISION
HAMPSTEAD SCHOOL
920 Hampstead Ave, Winnipeg, MB, R2K 2A3
(204) 654-1818
Emp Here 30
SIC 8211 Elementary and secondary schools

D-U-N-S 25-272-3762   (BR)
RIVER EAST TRANSCONA SCHOOL DIVISION
KILDONAN-EAST COLLEGIATE
845 Concordia Ave, Winnipeg, MB, R2K 2M6
(204) 667-2960
Emp Here 125
SIC 8211 Elementary and secondary schools

D-U-N-S 20-555-3709   (BR)
RIVER EAST TRANSCONA SCHOOL DIVISION
MUNROE JUNIOR HIGH SCHOOL
405 Munroe Ave, Winnipeg, MB, R2K 1H5
(204) 661-4451
Emp Here 35
SIC 8211 Elementary and secondary schools

D-U-N-S 25-289-3086   (BR)
RIVER EAST TRANSCONA SCHOOL DIVISION
JOHN HENDERSON JR HIGH SCHOOL
930 Brazier St, Winnipeg, MB, R2K 2P3
(204) 661-2503
Emp Here 50
SIC 8211 Elementary and secondary schools

D-U-N-S 20-074-8429   (BR)
RIVER EAST TRANSCONA SCHOOL DIVISION
JOHN DE GRAFF ELEMENTARY SCHOOL
1020 Louelda St, Winnipeg, MB, R2K 3Z4
(204) 669-1280
Emp Here 50

SIC 8211 Elementary and secondary schools

D-U-N-S 20-555-3386   (BR)
RIVER EAST TRANSCONA SCHOOL DIVISION
MILES MACDONELL COLLEGIATE
757 Roch St, Winnipeg, MB, R2K 2R1
(204) 667-1103
Emp Here 85
SIC 8211 Elementary and secondary schools

D-U-N-S 25-756-7511   (BR)
RIVER EAST TRANSCONA SCHOOL DIVISION
BERTRUN E GLAVIN ELEMENTARY SCHOOL
166 Antrim Rd, Winnipeg, MB, R2K 3L2
(204) 669-1277
Emp Here 45
SIC 8211 Elementary and secondary schools

D-U-N-S 25-756-7560   (BR)
RIVER EAST TRANSCONA SCHOOL DIVISION
LORD WOLSELEY SCHOOL
939 Henderson Hwy, Winnipeg, MB, R2K 2M2
(204) 661-2384
Emp Here 24
SIC 8211 Elementary and secondary schools

D-U-N-S 25-369-8914   (BR)
RIVER EAST TRANSCONA SCHOOL DIVISION
SALISBURY MORSE PLACE SCHOOL
795 Prince Rupert Ave, Winnipeg, MB, R2K 1W6
(204) 668-9304
Emp Here 90
SIC 8211 Elementary and secondary schools

D-U-N-S 25-289-4795   (BR)
RIVER EAST TRANSCONA SCHOOL DIVISION
VALLEY GARDENS MIDDLE SCHOOL
220 Antrim Rd, Winnipeg, MB, R2K 3L2
(204) 668-6249
Emp Here 54
SIC 8211 Elementary and secondary schools

D-U-N-S 25-900-8217   (BR)
RIVER EAST TRANSCONA SCHOOL DIVISION
ANGUS MCKAY SCHOOL
850 Woodvale St, Winnipeg, MB, R2K 2G8
(204) 667-1701
Emp Here 20
SIC 8211 Elementary and secondary schools

D-U-N-S 20-709-7952   (BR)
RIVER EAST TRANSCONA SCHOOL DIVISION
MCLEOD EDUCATION CENTRE
530 Mcleod Ave, Winnipeg, MB, R2K 0B5
(204) 667-6193
Emp Here 30
SIC 8211 Elementary and secondary schools

D-U-N-S 20-023-2556   (BR)
RIVER EAST TRANSCONA SCHOOL DIVISION
POLSON SCHOOL
491 Munroe Ave, Winnipeg, MB, R2K 1H5
(204) 669-5643
Emp Here 35
SIC 8211 Elementary and secondary schools

D-U-N-S 20-555-3626   (BR)
RIVER EAST TRANSCONA SCHOOL DIVISION
NEIL CAMPBELL SCHOOL
845 Golspie St, Winnipeg, MB, R2K 2V5
(204) 661-2848
Emp Here 30
SIC 8211 Elementary and secondary schools

D-U-N-S 24-028-1415   (BR)
SOBEYS CAPITAL INCORPORATED
SOBEYS

965 Henderson Hwy, Winnipeg, MB, R2K 2M2
(204) 338-0349
Emp Here 150
SIC 5411 Grocery stores

D-U-N-S 24-336-6445   (BR)
WINNIPEG REGIONAL HEALTH AUTHORITY, THE
ACCESS RIVER EAST
975 Henderson Hwy, Winnipeg, MB, R2K 4L7
(204) 938-5000
Emp Here 200
SIC 8093 Specialty outpatient clinics, nec

D-U-N-S 25-668-7690   (BR)
YOUNG MEN'S AND YOUNG WOMEN'S CHRISTIAN ASSOCIATION OF WINNIPEG INCORPORATED, THE
EK YUM-YMCA OF WINNIPEG
454 Kimberly Ave, Winnipeg, MB, R2K 0X8
(204) 668-8140
Emp Here 50
SIC 8641 Civic and social associations

Winnipeg, MB R2L

D-U-N-S 24-968-1016   (SL)
3108392 MANITOBA LTD
PONY CORRAL, THE
1050 Nairn Ave, Winnipeg, MB, R2L 0Y4
(204) 668-4414
Emp Here 150   *Sales* 6,289,900
SIC 5812 Eating places
Pr Pr Peter Ginakes

D-U-N-S 25-684-3590   (BR)
7-ELEVEN CANADA, INC
7-ELEVEN STORE #20594
456 Talbot Ave, Winnipeg, MB, R2L 0R5
(204) 985-0142
Emp Here 22
SIC 5411 Grocery stores

D-U-N-S 20-007-0266   (HQ)
ALSIP'S INDUSTRIAL PRODUCTS LTD
(*Suby of* Alliance Securities Corporation Limited)
1 Cole Ave, Winnipeg, MB, R2L 1J3
(204) 667-3330
Emp Here 27   *Emp Total* 30
Sales 6,274,620
SIC 5039 Construction materials, nec
 Frank Wayne Alsip
Pr Bradley Alsip
VP VP Jason Alsip

D-U-N-S 25-295-9200   (BR)
BANK OF NOVA SCOTIA, THE
SCOTIABANK
1150 Nairn Ave, Winnipeg, MB, R2L 0Y5
(204) 985-3700
Emp Here 30
SIC 6021 National commercial banks

D-U-N-S 20-833-6917   (SL)
CORREIA ENTERPRISES LTD
BEE CLEAN CENTRAL
375 Nairn Ave, Winnipeg, MB, R2L 0W8
(204) 668-4420
Emp Here 7,000   *Sales* 281,344,000
SIC 7349 Building maintenance services, nec
Pr Pr Jose Correia

D-U-N-S 25-520-4331   (BR)
MCDIARMID LUMBER LTD
MCDIARMID LUMBER HOME CENTRES
1150 Nairn Ave Unit 12, Winnipeg, MB, R2L 0Y5
(204) 661-4949
Emp Here 35
SIC 5211 Lumber and other building materials

D-U-N-S 25-182-5139   (SL)
MENNONITE BRETHREN COLLEGIATE INSTITUTE

MBCI
180 Riverton Ave, Winnipeg, MB, R2L 2E8
(204) 667-8210
Emp Here 50   *Sales* 3,356,192
SIC 8211 Elementary and secondary schools

D-U-N-S 24-571-5289   (SL)
NAIRN VACUUM & APPLIANCE
929 Nairn Ave, Winnipeg, MB, R2L 0X9
(204) 668-4901
Emp Here 58   *Sales* 4,231,721
SIC 5722 Household appliance stores

D-U-N-S 20-011-0096   (HQ)
NORDSTRONG EQUIPMENT LIMITED
(*Suby of* Canerector Inc)
5 Chester St, Winnipeg, MB, R2L 1W5
(204) 667-1553
Emp Here 85   *Emp Total* 3,000
Sales 19,553,468
SIC 5083 Farm and garden machinery
Pr Terry Milnes
 Cecil Hawkins
 Maynard Young

D-U-N-S 20-552-7950   (SL)
ORTYNSKY AUTOMOTIVE COMPANY LTD
ORTYNSKY, TERRY KIA
980 Nairn Ave, Winnipeg, MB, R2L 0Y2
(204) 654-0440
Emp Here 27   *Sales* 9,849,695
SIC 5511 New and used car dealers
Pr Terry Ortynsky

D-U-N-S 25-678-1063   (SL)
ORTYNSKY NISSAN LTD
980 Nairn Ave, Winnipeg, MB, R2L 0Y2
(204) 669-0791
Emp Here 26   *Sales* 13,062,400
SIC 5511 New and used car dealers
Pr Pr Terry Ortynsky

D-U-N-S 24-820-0537   (SL)
POLAR BUILDING CLEANING LTD
360 Johnson Ave W, Winnipeg, MB, R2L 0J1
(204) 334-3000
Emp Here 50   *Sales* 1,459,214
SIC 7349 Building maintenance services, nec

D-U-N-S 25-375-2422   (BR)
PRAXAIR CANADA INC
PRAXAIR DISTRIBUTION DIV OF
(*Suby of* Praxair, Inc.)
650 Nairn Ave, Winnipeg, MB, R2L 0X5
(204) 663-4393
Emp Here 20
SIC 5169 Chemicals and allied products, nec

D-U-N-S 24-333-8956   (BR)
QSI INTERIORS LTD
975 Thomas Ave Unit 1, Winnipeg, MB, R2L 1P7
(204) 953-1200
Emp Here 75
SIC 1742 Plastering, drywall, and insulation

D-U-N-S 25-538-9611   (BR)
THERMO DESIGN INSULATION LTD
949 Thomas Ave, Winnipeg, MB, R2L 2C6
(204) 953-1630
Emp Here 40
SIC 1711 Plumbing, heating, air-conditioning

D-U-N-S 25-127-4056   (BR)
VALUE VILLAGE STORES, INC
(*Suby of* Savers, Inc.)
970 Nairn Ave, Winnipeg, MB, R2L 0Y2
(204) 661-9045
Emp Here 70
SIC 5399 Miscellaneous general merchandise

D-U-N-S 25-139-1355   (BR)
WINNIPEG SCHOOL DIVISION
RIVER ELM SCHOOL
500 Riverton Ave, Winnipeg, MB, R2L 0N9
(204) 667-9006
Emp Here 50
SIC 8211 Elementary and secondary schools

D-U-N-S 20-709-7374   (BR)
WINNIPEG SCHOOL DIVISION
KENT ROAD SCHOOL
361 Kent Rd, Winnipeg, MB, R2L 1X9
(204) 669-1228
Emp Here 50
SIC 8211 Elementary and secondary schools

D-U-N-S 25-127-9725   (BR)
WINNIPEG SCHOOL DIVISION
LORD SELKIRK SCHOOL
170 Poplar Ave, Winnipeg, MB, R2L 2B6
(204) 667-8495
Emp Here 46
SIC 8211 Elementary and secondary schools

D-U-N-S 20-709-7291   (BR)
WINNIPEG SCHOOL DIVISION
ECOLE GEORGE V SCHOOL
265 Grey St, Winnipeg, MB, R2L 1V6
(204) 669-4482
Emp Here 50
SIC 8211 Elementary and secondary schools

D-U-N-S 25-063-9556   (BR)
WINNIPEG SCHOOL DIVISION
ELMWOOD HIGH SCHOOL
505 Chalmers Ave, Winnipeg, MB, R2L 0G4
(204) 667-8823
Emp Here 60
SIC 8211 Elementary and secondary schools

D-U-N-S 20-709-7325   (BR)
WINNIPEG SCHOOL DIVISION
GLENELM SCHOOL
96 Carmen Ave, Winnipeg, MB, R2L 0E6
(204) 667-8534
Emp Here 50
SIC 8211 Elementary and secondary schools

Winnipeg, MB R2M

D-U-N-S 20-057-4254   (BR)
20 VIC MANAGEMENT INC
ST VITAL CENTRE
1225 St Mary'S Rd Suite 86, Winnipeg, MB, R2M 5E5
(204) 257-4449
Emp Here 40
SIC 6512 Nonresidential building operators

D-U-N-S 25-288-0737   (BR)
A & W FOOD SERVICES OF CANADA INC
A & W
1225 St Mary'S Rd, Winnipeg, MB, R2M 5E5
(204) 255-9338
Emp Here 25
SIC 5812 Eating places

D-U-N-S 20-348-0574   (BR)
BANQUE TORONTO-DOMINION, LA
TORONTO-DOMINION BANK, THE
(*Suby of* Toronto-Dominion Bank, The)
270 St Anne'S Rd, Winnipeg, MB, R2M 3A4

Emp Here 21
SIC 6021 National commercial banks

D-U-N-S 25-903-7724   (BR)
BATH & BODY WORKS INC
(*Suby of* Bath & Body Works Inc)
1225 St Mary'S Rd Suite 95, Winnipeg, MB, R2M 5E5
(204) 256-3636
Emp Here 40
SIC 5719 Miscellaneous homefurnishings

D-U-N-S 25-311-6396   (BR)
CANADIAN IMPERIAL BANK OF COMMERCE
CIBC
1545 St Mary'S Rd, Winnipeg, MB, R2M 3V8
(204) 944-6803
Emp Here 32
SIC 6021 National commercial banks

D-U-N-S 20-643-7373 (SL)
CARA FOODS
MONTANA'S COOKHOUSE SALOON
1221 St Mary's Rd, Winnipeg, MB, R2M 5L5
(204) 254-2128
Emp Here 80   *Sales* 2,407,703
SIC 5812 Eating places

D-U-N-S 24-128-2545 (BR)
CINEPLEX ODEON CORPORATION
SILVERCITY ST. VITAL & XSCAPE
1225 St Mary's Rd Suite 160, Winnipeg, MB,
R2M 5E5
(204) 256-3901
Emp Here 20
SIC 7832 Motion picture theaters, except
drive-in

D-U-N-S 24-776-5084 (SL)
DION HOLDINGS LTD
MAXIME'S RESTAURANT & LOUNGE
1131 St Mary's Rd, Winnipeg, MB, R2M 3T9
(204) 257-1521
Emp Here 69   *Sales* 2,115,860
SIC 5812 Eating places

D-U-N-S 25-120-8310 (SL)
ELK ISLAND LODGE INC
54 Golden Willow Cres, Winnipeg, MB, R2M
4E2
(204) 253-0878
Emp Here 50   *Sales* 2,598,753
SIC 7011 Hotels and motels

D-U-N-S 25-689-6176 (BR)
GAP (CANADA) INC
GAP
(*Suby of* The Gap Inc)
1225 St Mary's Rd Suite 4, Winnipeg, MB,
R2M 5E5
(204) 254-0077
Emp Here 40
SIC 5651 Family clothing stores

D-U-N-S 20-860-5480 (BR)
GLENTEL INC
WIRELESS WAVES
1225 St Mary's Rd, Winnipeg, MB, R2M 5E5
(204) 772-9283
Emp Here 25
SIC 4812 Radiotelephone communication

D-U-N-S 25-514-2812 (BR)
HOME DEPOT OF CANADA INC
HOME DEPOT
(*Suby of* The Home Depot Inc)
1999 Bishop Grandin Blvd, Winnipeg, MB,
R2M 5S1
(204) 253-7649
Emp Here 200
SIC 5251 Hardware stores

D-U-N-S 24-968-5652 (SL)
HOUGHTAM ENTERPRISES
MOXIE'S RESTAURANT
1225 St Mary's Rd Suite 49, Winnipeg, MB,
R2M 5E5
(204) 257-1132
Emp Here 90   *Sales* 2,699,546
SIC 5812 Eating places

D-U-N-S 20-300-4150 (BR)
INDIGO BOOKS & MUSIC INC
CHAPTERS INDIGO
(*Suby of* Indigo Books & Music Inc)
1225 St Mary's Rd Suite 85, Winnipeg, MB,
R2M 5E5
(204) 256-0777
Emp Here 50
SIC 5942 Book stores

D-U-N-S 20-709-7804 (BR)
LOUIS RIEL SCHOOL DIVISION
DARWIN SCHOOL
175 Darwin St, Winnipeg, MB, R2M 4A9
(204) 257-2904
Emp Here 50
SIC 8211 Elementary and secondary schools

D-U-N-S 25-144-2463 (BR)
LOUIS RIEL SCHOOL DIVISION
GLENLAWN COLLEGIATE INSTITUTE
770 St Mary's Rd, Winnipeg, MB, R2M 3N7
(204) 233-3263
Emp Here 100
SIC 8211 Elementary and secondary schools

D-U-N-S 20-035-6322 (BR)
LOUIS RIEL SCHOOL DIVISION
DR D. W. PENNER SCHOOL
121 Hazelwood Cres, Winnipeg, MB, R2M
4E4
(204) 256-1135
Emp Here 20
SIC 8211 Elementary and secondary schools

D-U-N-S 20-046-8366 (BR)
LOUIS RIEL SCHOOL DIVISION
ECOLE VARENNES SCHOOL
22 Varennes Ave, Winnipeg, MB, R2M 0N1
(204) 253-1375
Emp Here 40
SIC 8211 Elementary and secondary schools

D-U-N-S 24-851-6346 (BR)
LOUIS RIEL SCHOOL DIVISION
HASTINGS SCHOOL
95 Pulberry St, Winnipeg, MB, R2M 3X5
(204) 253-1371
Emp Here 50
SIC 8211 Elementary and secondary schools

D-U-N-S 20-023-2523 (BR)
LOUIS RIEL SCHOOL DIVISION
ECOLE MARIE-ANNE-GABOURY
50 Hastings Blvd, Winnipeg, MB, R2M 2E3
(204) 253-9704
Emp Here 30
SIC 8211 Elementary and secondary schools

D-U-N-S 20-709-7812 (BR)
LOUIS RIEL SCHOOL DIVISION
MINNETONKA SCHOOL
200 Minnetonka St, Winnipeg, MB, R2M 3Y6
(204) 257-8114
Emp Here 50
SIC 8211 Elementary and secondary schools

D-U-N-S 20-709-7820 (BR)
LOUIS RIEL SCHOOL DIVISION
ST GEORGE SCHOOL
151 St George Rd, Winnipeg, MB, R2M 3J2
(204) 253-2646
Emp Here 50
SIC 8211 Elementary and secondary schools

D-U-N-S 20-709-7838 (BR)
LOUIS RIEL SCHOOL DIVISION
WINDSOR SCHOOL
80 Cunnington Ave, Winnipeg, MB, R2M 0W7
(204) 237-4057
Emp Here 30
SIC 8211 Elementary and secondary schools

D-U-N-S 20-517-3086 (BR)
LOUIS RIEL SCHOOL DIVISION
DAKOTA COLLEGIATE INSTITUTE
661 Dakota St, Winnipeg, MB, R2M 3K3
(204) 256-4366
Emp Here 100
SIC 8211 Elementary and secondary schools

D-U-N-S 20-047-7110 (BR)
LOUIS RIEL SCHOOL DIVISION
GLENWOOD SCHOOL
51 Blenheim Ave, Winnipeg, MB, R2M 0H9
(204) 233-3619
Emp Here 35
SIC 8211 Elementary and secondary schools

D-U-N-S 20-023-2531 (BR)
LOUIS RIEL SCHOOL DIVISION
LAVALLEE SCHOOL
505 St Anne's Rd, Winnipeg, MB, R2M 3E5
(204) 253-1388
Emp Here 45
SIC 8211 Elementary and secondary schools

D-U-N-S 24-040-4434 (SL)
MANITOBA BAPTIST HOME SOCIETY INC
MEADOWOOD MANOR
577 St Anne's Rd, Winnipeg, MB, R2M 3G5
(204) 257-2394
Emp Here 100   *Sales* 4,742,446
SIC 8051 Skilled nursing care facilities

D-U-N-S 25-127-8602 (BR)
**MANITOBA LIQUOR AND LOTTERIES
CORPORATION**
LIQUOR MART
827 Dakota St Suite 5, Winnipeg, MB, R2M
5M2
(204) 987-4020
Emp Here 20
SIC 5921 Liquor stores

D-U-N-S 25-090-4679 (BR)
MANITOBA MOTOR LEAGUE, THE
CAA MANITOBA
501 St Anne's Rd, Winnipeg, MB, R2M 3E5
(204) 262-6200
Emp Here 21
SIC 4724 Travel agencies

D-U-N-S 20-035-6355 (BR)
**MCDONALD'S RESTAURANTS OF
CANADA LIMITED**
MCDONALD'S
(*Suby of* McDonald's Corporation)
1501 St Mary's Rd, Winnipeg, MB, R2M 5L5
(204) 949-6042
Emp Here 20
SIC 5812 Eating places

D-U-N-S 20-354-0989 (BR)
**MCDONALD'S RESTAURANTS OF
CANADA LIMITED**
MCDONALD'S
(*Suby of* McDonald's Corporation)
1225 St Mary's Rd Suite 54, Winnipeg, MB,
R2M 5E6
(204) 949-5419
Emp Here 50
SIC 5812 Eating places

D-U-N-S 24-882-8378 (SL)
**MEADOWOOD INVESTMENTS LIMITED
PARTNERSHIP**
SMITTY'S RESTAURANT
150 Meadowood Dr Unit 7, Winnipeg, MB,
R2M 5L7
(204) 256-1242
Emp Here 50   *Sales* 1,532,175
SIC 5812 Eating places

D-U-N-S 20-914-2913 (BR)
NORTHERN REFLECTIONS LTD
1225 St Mary's Rd Suite 32, Winnipeg, MB,
R2M 5E5
(204) 255-5025
Emp Here 35
SIC 5621 Women's clothing stores

D-U-N-S 24-915-8650 (SL)
NORVAN ENTERPRISES (1982) LTD
246 Dunkirk Dr, Winnipeg, MB, R2M 3W9
(204) 257-0373
Emp Here 75   *Sales* 2,685,378
SIC 5812 Eating places

D-U-N-S 25-236-6992 (BR)
REITMANS (CANADA) LIMITEE
REITMANS
1225 St Mary's Rd, Winnipeg, MB, R2M 5E5
(204) 255-2224
Emp Here 25
SIC 5621 Women's clothing stores

D-U-N-S 20-050-3089 (BR)
SOBEYS CAPITAL INCORPORATED
ST ANNES SOBEYS
1939 Bishop Grandin Blvd, Winnipeg, MB,
R2M 5S1
(204) 255-5064
Emp Here 192
SIC 5411 Grocery stores

D-U-N-S 25-271-7707 (BR)
SOBEYS WEST INC
SAFEWAY
850 Dakota St, Winnipeg, MB, R2M 5R9
(204) 254-6516
Emp Here 200
SIC 5411 Grocery stores

D-U-N-S 20-836-9215 (SL)
ST AMANT INC
440 River Rd, Winnipeg, MB, R2M 3Z9
(204) 256-4301
Emp Here 1,500   *Sales* 91,405,913
SIC 8059 Nursing and personal care, nec
Pr Pr Carl Stevens
Off Mgr Paulette Perrault
Off Mgr Harry Casey

D-U-N-S 25-668-2675 (SL)
TRAVELODGE WINNIPEG EAST
20 Alpine Ave, Winnipeg, MB, R2M 0Y5
(204) 255-6000
Emp Here 70   *Sales* 3,064,349
SIC 7011 Hotels and motels

D-U-N-S 25-289-0975 (BR)
WAL-MART CANADA CORP
1225 St Mary's Rd Suite 54, Winnipeg, MB,
R2M 5E6
(204) 256-7027
Emp Here 300
SIC 5311 Department stores

D-U-N-S 20-806-2914 (BR)
YM INC. (SALES)
BLUENOTES
1225 St Mary's Rd, Winnipeg, MB, R2M 5E5

Emp Here 25
SIC 5621 Women's clothing stores

Winnipeg, MB R2N

D-U-N-S 20-710-0079 (BR)
**DIVISION SCOLAIRE FRANCO-
MANITOBAINE**
ECOLE CHRISTINE LESPERNACE
(*Suby of* Division Scolaire Franco-
Manitobaine)
425 John Forsyth Rd, Winnipeg, MB, R2N 4J3
(204) 255-2081
Emp Here 50
SIC 8211 Elementary and secondary schools

D-U-N-S 20-047-1295 (BR)
LOUIS RIEL SCHOOL DIVISION
COLLEGE JEANNE-SAUVE
1128 Dakota St, Winnipeg, MB, R2N 3T8
(204) 257-0124
Emp Here 50
SIC 8211 Elementary and secondary schools

D-U-N-S 20-046-2195 (BR)
LOUIS RIEL SCHOOL DIVISION
HIGHBURY SCHOOL
99 Highbury Rd, Winnipeg, MB, R2N 2N5
(204) 254-5078
Emp Here 63
SIC 8211 Elementary and secondary schools

D-U-N-S 20-048-2391 (BR)
LOUIS RIEL SCHOOL DIVISION
ECOLE JULIE-RIEL
316 Ashworth St, Winnipeg, MB, R2N 2L7
(204) 253-2363
Emp Here 45
SIC 8211 Elementary and secondary schools

D-U-N-S 25-289-2450 (BR)
LOUIS RIEL SCHOOL DIVISION
H.S. PAUL SCHOOL
160 Southglen Blvd, Winnipeg, MB, R2N 3J3
(204) 254-7477
Emp Here 60

SIC 8211 Elementary anc secondary schools

D-U-N-S 20-023-2861 (BR)
LOUIS RIEL SCHOOL DIVISION
GEORGE MCDOWELL SCHOOL
366 Paddington Rd, Winnipeg, MB, R2N 1R1
(204) 253-1492
Emp Here 40
SIC 8211 Elementary and secondary schools

D-U-N-S 20-165-3008 (BR)
SOBEYS CAPITAL INCORPORATED
ST VITAL GARDEN MARKET IGA
1500 Dakota St Suite 1, Winnipeg, MB, R2N 3Y7
(204) 253-3663
Emp Here 100
SIC 5411 Grocery stores

D-U-N-S 25-195-1245 (BR)
STARBUCKS COFFEE CANADA, INC
(*Suby of* Starbucks Corporation)
726 St Anne'S Rd Suite A, Winnipeg, MB, R2N 0A2
(204) 253-0401
Emp Here 20
SIC 5812 Eating places

D-U-N-S 24-349-7034 (BR)
WINNIPEG REGIONAL HEALTH AUTHOR-ITY, THE
RIVER PARK GARDENS
735 St Anne'S Rd, Winn peg, MB, R2N 0C4
(204) 255-9073
Emp Here 100
SIC 8361 Residential care

Winnipeg, MB R2P

D-U-N-S 25-890-1750 (BR)
CANAD CORPORATION OF MANITOBA LTD
DYNAMIC ENTERTAINMENT PRODUCTION, DIV OF
(*Suby of* Canad Corporation Of Canada Inc)
930 Jefferson Ave Suite 302, Winnipeg, MB, R2P 1W1
(204) 697-1495
Emp Here 50
SIC 7929 Entertainers and entertainment groups

D-U-N-S 20-072-7873 (HQ)
CANAD CORPORATION OF MANITOBA LTD
CANAD INNS EXPRESS FORT GARRY (CELEBRATIONS, ALLEY CATZ, THE BEACH NIGHT CLUB)
930 Jefferson Ave Suite 3, Winnipeg, MB, R2P 1W1
(204) 697-1495
Emp Here 35   *Emp Total* 1,100
Sales 106,012,800
SIC 7011 Hotels and motels
Pr Pr Leon Norman Ledohowski

D-U-N-S 25-012-3288 (BR)
SEVEN OAKS SCHOOL DIVISION
O.V. JEWITT COMMUNITY SCHOOL
(*Suby of* Seven Oaks School Division)
66 Neville St, Winnipeg, MB, R2P 1W3
(204) 632-9669
Emp Here 50
SIC 8211 Elementary and secondary schools

D-U-N-S 20-568-6905 (BR)
SEVEN OAKS SCHOOL DIVISION
LEILA NORTH COMMUNITY SCHOOL
(*Suby of* Seven Oaks School Division)
20 Allan Blye Dr, Winnipeg, MB, R2P 2S5
(204) 694-8071
Emp Here 70
SIC 8211 Elementary and secondary schools

D-U-N-S 20-914-4307 (BR)

SEVEN OAKS SCHOOL DIVISION
ARTHUR E. WRIGHT SCHOOL
(*Suby of* Seven Oaks School Division)
1520 Jefferson Ave, Winnipeg, MB, R2P 1K1
(204) 632-6314
Emp Here 55
SIC 8211 Elementary and secondary schools

D-U-N-S 25-289-2534 (BR)
SEVEN OAKS SCHOOL DIVISION
CONSTABLE EDWARD FINNEY SCHOOL
(*Suby of* Seven Oaks School Division)
25 Anglia Ave, Winnipeg, MB, R2P 2R1
(204) 694-8688
Emp Here 30
SIC 8211 Elementary and secondary schools

D-U-N-S 25-127-9626 (BR)
SEVEN OAKS SCHOOL DIVISION
MAPLES COLLEGIATE
(*Suby of* Seven Oaks School Division)
1330 Jefferson Ave, Winnipeg, MB, R2P 1L3
(204) 632-6641
Emp Here 133
SIC 8211 Elementary and secondary schools

D-U-N-S 25-484-7643 (BR)
SEVEN OAKS SCHOOL DIVISION
ELWICK COMMUNITY SCHOOL
(*Suby of* Seven Oaks School Division)
30 Maberley Rd, Winnipeg, MB, R2P 0E2
(204) 633-5641
Emp Here 48
SIC 8211 Elementary and secondary schools

D-U-N-S 20-362-3033 (BR)
SOBEYS CAPITAL INCORPORATED
1303 Jefferson Ave, Winnipeg, MB, R2P 1S7

Emp Here 70
SIC 5411 Grocery stores

D-U-N-S 20-063-1401 (SL)
TOTAL CARE HEALTH CARE SERVICES
11 Oakstone Pl, Winnipeg, MB, R2P 2L5

Emp Here 400   *Sales* 25,423,440
SIC 8059 Nursing and personal care, nec
Pt Sandra Mediano

D-U-N-S 25-668-4598 (BR)
VALUE VILLAGE STORES, INC
(*Suby of* Savers, Inc.)
942 Jefferson Ave, Winnipeg, MB, R2P 1W1
(204) 694-6844
Emp Here 65
SIC 5399 Miscellaneous general merchandise

D-U-N-S 24-829-3693 (BR)
WINNIPEG REGIONAL HEALTH AUTHOR-ITY, THE
1050 Leila Ave Suite 3, Winnipeg, MB, R2P 1W6
(204) 938-5600
Emp Here 49
SIC 8062 General medical and surgical hospitals

Winnipeg, MB R2R

D-U-N-S 24-519-5847 (BR)
CANADIAN LINEN AND UNIFORM SER-VICE CO
(*Suby of* Ameripride Services, Inc.)
1860 King Edward St, Winnipeg, MB, R2R 0N2
(204) 633-7261
Emp Here 150
SIC 7213 Linen supply

D-U-N-S 25-137-1134 (HQ)
CARTE INTERNATIONAL INC
1995 Logan Ave, Winnipeg, MB, R2R 0H8

---

(204) 633-7220
Emp Here 305   *Emp Total* 10
Sales 80,214,843
SIC 3612 Transformers, except electric
Pr Pr Brian Klaponski
   Gary Mowat

D-U-N-S 20-007-6032 (BR)
COMSTOCK CANADA LTD
COMSTOCK AN ENCOR
2116 Logan Ave, Winnipeg, MB, R2R 0J2
(204) 633-3830
Emp Here 25
SIC 1711 Plumbing, heating, air-conditioning

D-U-N-S 25-360-0480 (BR)
CUMMINS WESTERN CANADA LIMITED PARTNERSHIP
489 Oak Point Hwy, Winnipeg, MB, R2R 1V2
(204) 632-5470
Emp Here 42
SIC 7629 Electrical repair shops

D-U-N-S 20-794-2595 (BR)
DAY & ROSS INC
255 Haggart Ave, Winnipeg, MB, R2R 2V8
(204) 697-6066
Emp Here 25
SIC 4213 Trucking, except local

D-U-N-S 20-716-6013 (BR)
DAY & ROSS INC
SAMEDAY WORLDWIDE
225 Haggart Ave, Winnipeg, MB, R2R 2V8
(204) 697-6069
Emp Here 50
SIC 4213 Trucking, except local

D-U-N-S 20-137-0546 (SL)
FRESH HEMP FOODS LTD
MANITOBA HARVEST
69 Eagle Dr, Winnipeg, MB, R2R 1V4
(204) 953-0233
Emp Here 150   *Sales* 12,914,044
SIC 2032 Canned specialties
Pr Pr Michael Fata
VP Sls John Durkin
VP Opers Barry Tomiski

D-U-N-S 24-426-8483 (HQ)
GARDEWINE GROUP INC
GARDEWINE NORTH
60 Eagle Dr, Winnipeg, MB, R2R 1V5
(204) 633-5795
Emp Here 50   *Emp Total* 5,515
Sales 247,409,734
SIC 4731 Freight transportation arrangement
Pr Dennis Clarke
   Randy Mcknight

D-U-N-S 24-335-8566 (BR)
INTEGRATED DISTRIBUTION SYSTEMS LIMITED PARTNERSHIP
WAJAX POWER SYSTEMS
2529 Inkster Blvd, Winnipeg, MB, R2R 2Y4
(204) 452-8244
Emp Here 30
SIC 5084 Industrial machinery and equipment

D-U-N-S 25-055-1165 (BR)
KAL TIRE LTD
1777 Brookside Blvd, Winnipeg, MB, R2R 2Y1
(204) 694-8560
Emp Here 20
SIC 5531 Auto and home supply stores

D-U-N-S 24-376-3844 (BR)
KINDERSLEY TRANSPORT LTD
1991 Brookside Blvd, Winnipeg, MB, R2R 2Y3
(204) 633-1707
Emp Here 50
SIC 4212 Local trucking, without storage

D-U-N-S 25-663-7208 (BR)
KROWN PRODUCE INC
(*Suby of* Concorde Group Corp)
75 Meridian Dr Unit 5, Winnipeg, MB, R2R 2V9

---

(204) 697-3300
Emp Here 26
SIC 5141 Groceries, general line

D-U-N-S 20-009-5131 (BR)
LAKEHEAD FREIGHTWAYS INC
2165 Brookside Blvd, Winnipeg, MB, R2R 2Y3
(204) 633-4448
Emp Here 21
SIC 4213 Trucking, except local

D-U-N-S 24-351-2972 (BR)
LAKESIDE PROCESS CONTROLS LTD
7 Sylvan Way, Winnipeg, MB, R2R 2B9
(204) 633-9197
Emp Here 21
SIC 5084 Industrial machinery and equipment

D-U-N-S 25-416-1672 (BR)
MANITOULIN TRANSPORT INC
2165 Brookside Blvd Suite 200, Winnipeg, MB, R2R 2Y3
(204) 633-4448
Emp Here 21
SIC 4213 Trucking, except local

D-U-N-S 25-011-0855 (BR)
MCDONALD'S RESTAURANTS OF CANADA LIMITED
MCDONALD'S
(*Suby of* McDonald's Corporation)
994 Keewatin St, Winnipeg, MB, R2R 2V1
(204) 949-6079
Emp Here 78
SIC 5812 Eating places

D-U-N-S 20-699-7228 (BR)
NORDION INC
MDS LABORATORIES, DIV OF
130 Omands Creek Blvd Unit 6, Winnipeg, MB, R2R 1V7
(204) 694-1632
Emp Here 25
SIC 8071 Medical laboratories

D-U-N-S 25-228-8022 (BR)
PENNER INTERNATIONAL INC
2091 Brookside Blvd, Winnipeg, MB, R2R 2Y3
(204) 633-7550
Emp Here 30
SIC 4213 Trucking, except local

D-U-N-S 20-710-5644 (HQ)
PRAIRIE FOREST PRODUCTS LTD
165 Ryan St, Winnipeg, MB, R2R 0N9
(204) 989-9600
Emp Here 100   *Emp Total* 50
Sales 21,815,249
SIC 2411 Logging
Pr Pr Maureen Patricia Prendiville
VP VP James Ailbe Prendiville
   Michael Lawrence Prendiville

D-U-N-S 25-191-7274 (BR)
PRICE INDUSTRIES LIMITED
PMI MANUFACTURING, DIV OF
404 Egesz St, Winnipeg, MB, R2R 1X5
(204) 633-4808
Emp Here 20
SIC 3732 Boatbuilding and repairing

D-U-N-S 20-010-8686 (BR)
RINGBALL CORPORATION
190 Omands Creek Blvd, Winnipeg, MB, R2R 1V7
(204) 694-1455
Emp Here 20
SIC 5085 Industrial supplies

D-U-N-S 24-171-0300 (BR)
RYDER TRUCK RENTAL CANADA LTD
(*Suby of* Ryder System, Inc.)
200 Lucas Ave, Winnipeg, MB, R2R 2S9
(204) 633-4843
Emp Here 20
SIC 7513 Truck rental and leasing, no drivers

D-U-N-S 20-139-5790 (BR)
S.L.H. TRANSPORT INC

---

255 Haggart Ave, Winnipeg, MB, R2R 2V8
(204) 452-0193
Emp Here 28
SIC 4213 Trucking, except local

D-U-N-S 24-747-9280   (BR)
SHANAHAN'S BUILDING SPECIALTIES LIMITED
SHANAHAN'S INDUSTRIES
90 Park Lane Ave, Winnipeg, MB, R2R 0K2
(204) 694-3301
Emp Here 30
SIC 5039 Construction materials, nec

D-U-N-S 24-354-9024   (BR)
SLEEP COUNTRY CANADA INC
111 Inksbrook Dr Unit 8, Winnipeg, MB, R2R 2V7
(204) 632-9458
Emp Here 20
SIC 5712 Furniture stores

D-U-N-S 25-271-7822   (BR)
SOBEYS WEST INC
BURROWS & KEEWATIN SAFEWAY
850 Keewatin St Suite 12, Winnipeg, MB, R2R 0Z5
(204) 632-6763
Emp Here 100
SIC 5411 Grocery stores

D-U-N-S 20-709-7598   (BR)
ST. JAMES-ASSINIBOIA SCHOOL DIVISION
BROOKLANDS SCHOOL
1950 Pacific Ave W, Winnipeg, MB, R2R 0G4
(204) 633-9630
Emp Here 20
SIC 8211 Elementary and secondary schools

D-U-N-S 24-335-3740   (BR)
TST SOLUTIONS L.P.
1987 Brookside Blvd, Winnipeg, MB, R2R 2Y3
(204) 633-5734
Emp Here 20
SIC 4213 Trucking, except local

D-U-N-S 24-330-9544   (BR)
TST SOLUTIONS L.P.
TST PORTER, DIV OF
1987 Brookside Blvd, Winnipeg, MB, R2R 2Y3
(204) 697-5795
Emp Here 500
SIC 4231 Trucking terminal facilities

D-U-N-S 20-718-2523   (BR)
TOROMONT INDUSTRIES LTD
CATERPILLAR
140 Inksbrook Dr, Winnipeg, MB, R2R 2W3
(204) 453-4343
Emp Here 120
SIC 7699 Repair services, nec

D-U-N-S 24-173-1314   (SL)
VITAL TRANSIT SERVICES LTD
1850 Selkirk Ave, Winnipeg, MB, R2R 0N6
(204) 633-2022
Emp Here 50   *Sales* 1,507,726
SIC 4141 Local bus charter service

D-U-N-S 25-128-3164   (BR)
WINNIPEG SCHOOL DIVISION
PRAIRIE ROSE ELEMENTARY SCHOOL
105 Lucas Ave, Winnipeg, MB, R2R 2S8
(204) 633-4092
Emp Here 42
SIC 8211 Elementary and secondary schools

D-U-N-S 25-022-4094   (BR)
WINNIPEG SCHOOL DIVISION
STANLEY KNOWLES SCHOOL
2424 King Edward St, Winnipeg, MB, R2R 2R2
(204) 694-0483
Emp Here 96
SIC 8211 Elementary and secondary schools

D-U-N-S 25-127-9741   (BR)
WINNIPEG SCHOOL DIVISION

GARDEN GROVE SCHOOL
2340 Burrows Ave, Winnipeg, MB, R2R 1W1
(204) 633-6477
Emp Here 45
SIC 8211 Elementary and secondary schools

D-U-N-S 20-025-9716   (BR)
WINNIPEG SCHOOL DIVISION
MEADOWS WEST SCHOOL
150 Inkster Garden Dr, Winnipeg, MB, R2R 2R8
(204) 633-7656
Emp Here 54
SIC 8211 Elementary and secondary schools

D-U-N-S 24-030-3060   (BR)
WINNSERV INC
(*Suby of* Winnserv Inc)
131 Greenhoven Cres, Winnipeg, MB, R2R 1B5
(204) 633-9004
Emp Here 50
SIC 8361 Residential care

Winnipeg, MB R2V

D-U-N-S 20-571-7994   (BR)
ARMTEC LP
ARMTEC
2500 Ferrier St, Winnipeg, MB, R2V 4P6
(204) 338-9311
Emp Here 80
SIC 3312 Blast furnaces and steel mills

D-U-N-S 24-119-1464   (BR)
BANK OF NOVA SCOTIA, THE
SCOTIABANK
1970 Main St, Winnipeg, MB, R2V 2B6

Emp Here 25
SIC 6021 National commercial banks

D-U-N-S 25-295-9556   (BR)
BANK OF NOVA SCOTIA, THE
SCOTIA BANK
843 Leila Ave Suite 2, Winnipeg, MB, R2V 3J7
(204) 985-3250
Emp Here 30
SIC 6021 National commercial banks

D-U-N-S 25-815-5795   (BR)
BANQUE TORONTO-DOMINION, LA
TORONTO-DOMINION BANK, THE
(*Suby of* Toronto-Dominion Bank, The)
2305 Mcphillips St Suite 400, Winnipeg, MB, R2V 3E1
(204) 988-2457
Emp Here 20
SIC 6021 National commercial banks

D-U-N-S 20-589-5431   (BR)
BANQUE TORONTO-DOMINION, LA
TD CANADA TRUST
(*Suby of* Toronto-Dominion Bank, The)
1375 Mcphillips St Suite 7, Winnipeg, MB, R2V 3V1
(204) 985-4560
Emp Here 20
SIC 6021 National commercial banks

D-U-N-S 24-968-3426   (BR)
CANAD CORPORATION OF CANADA INC
CANAD INNS GARDEN CITY
2100 Mcphillips St, Winnipeg, MB, R2V 3T9
(204) 633-0024
Emp Here 200
SIC 7011 Hotels and motels

D-U-N-S 25-671-5293   (BR)
CITY OF WINNIPEG, THE
NORTHEND WATER POLLUTION CONTROL CENTER
(*Suby of* City of Winnipeg, The)
2230 Main St, Winnipeg, MB, R2V 4T8

(204) 986-4684
Emp Here 80
SIC 1629 Heavy construction, nec

D-U-N-S 25-668-4119   (SL)
COMPLETE CARE INC
1801 Main St, Winnipeg, MB, R2V 2A2
(204) 949-5090
Emp Here 100   *Sales* 4,742,446
SIC 8051 Skilled nursing care facilities

D-U-N-S 24-340-0400   (BR)
FGL SPORTS LTD
SPORT CHECK NORTHGATE CENTRE
1375 Mcphillips St Unit 1, Winnipeg, MB, R2V 3V1
(204) 334-2190
Emp Here 35
SIC 5941 Sporting goods and bicycle shops

D-U-N-S 20-556-0647   (BR)
HOME DEPOT OF CANADA INC
HOME DEPOT
(*Suby of* The Home Depot Inc)
845 Leila Ave, Winnipeg, MB, R2V 3J7
(204) 336-5530
Emp Here 75
SIC 5251 Hardware stores

D-U-N-S 24-115-5522   (BR)
LEHIGH HANSON MATERIALS LIMITED
2494 Ferrier St, Winnipeg, MB, R2V 4P6
(204) 334-6002
Emp Here 50
SIC 5032 Brick, stone, and related material

D-U-N-S 24-851-5827   (BR)
LEHIGH HANSON MATERIALS LIMITED
2494 Ferrier St, Winnipeg, MB, R2V 4P6
(204) 339-9213
Emp Here 30
SIC 5032 Brick, stone, and related material

D-U-N-S 25-270-1149   (BR)
LOBLAWS INC
REAL CANADIAN SUPERSTORE #1505
2132 Mcphillips St, Winnipeg, MB, R2V 3C8
(204) 631-6250
Emp Here 300
SIC 5411 Grocery stores

D-U-N-S 24-607-3241   (SL)
LUTHER HOMES INC
1081 Andrews St, Winnipeg, MB, R2V 2G9
(204) 338-4641
Emp Here 145   *Sales* 26,325,760
SIC 8741 Management services
Dir Keith Bytheway
Ch Bd R Hilderman
  Dale Salk

D-U-N-S 25-126-9486   (BR)
MANITOBA LIQUOR AND LOTTERIES CORPORATION
MLCC LIQUOR MART
915 Leila Ave Suite 2, Winnipeg, MB, R2V 3J7
(204) 987-4005
Emp Here 25
SIC 5921 Liquor stores

D-U-N-S 24-388-8836   (BR)
MANITOBA MOTOR LEAGUE, THE
CAA MANITOBA
2211 Mcphillips St Unit C, Winnipeg, MB, R2V 3M5
(204) 262-6234
Emp Here 21
SIC 8699 Membership organizations, nec

D-U-N-S 20-923-8331   (SL)
MCDONALD'S RESTAURANTS
1887 Main St, Winnipeg, MB, R2V 2A7
(204) 949-6029
Emp Here 50   *Sales* 1,532,175
SIC 5812 Eating places

D-U-N-S 25-311-2908   (BR)
MCDONALD'S RESTAURANTS OF CANADA LIMITED

MCDONALD'S
(*Suby of* McDonald's Corporation)
847 Leila Ave, Winnipeg, MB, R2V 3J7
(204) 949-6066
Emp Here 98
SIC 5812 Eating places

D-U-N-S 25-691-4060   (BR)
MCMUNN & YATES BUILDING SUPPLIES LTD
MCDIARMID LUMBER HOME CENTRES
2366 Mcphillips St, Winnipeg, MB, R2V 4J6
(204) 940-4043
Emp Here 39
SIC 5211 Lumber and other building materials

D-U-N-S 25-300-4675   (BR)
REDBERRY FRANCHISING CORP
BURGER KING
1430 Mcphillips St, Winnipeg, MB, R2V 3C5
(204) 987-8423
Emp Here 30
SIC 5812 Eating places

D-U-N-S 25-961-9500   (BR)
REGIS HAIRSTYLISTS LTD
REGIS SALONS
2305 Mcphillips St, Winnipeg, MB, R2V 3E1
(204) 334-1004
Emp Here 40
SIC 7231 Beauty shops

D-U-N-S 25-126-0519   (BR)
ROYAL BANK OF CANADA
RBC
(*Suby of* Royal Bank Of Canada)
1846 Main St, Winnipeg, MB, R2V 3H2
(204) 988-5830
Emp Here 25
SIC 6021 National commercial banks

D-U-N-S 25-126-0527   (BR)
ROYAL BANK OF CANADA
RBC
(*Suby of* Royal Bank Of Canada)
2350 Mcphillips St, Winnipeg, MB, R2V 4J6
(204) 988-6035
Emp Here 35
SIC 6021 National commercial banks

D-U-N-S 20-011-0393   (HQ)
SALISBURY HOUSE OF CANADA LTD
787 Leila Ave, Winnipeg, MB, R2V 3J7
(204) 594-7257
Emp Here 100   *Emp Total* 2
Sales 25,034,654
SIC 5812 Eating places
Pr Costas Ataliotis
Genl Mgr Patrick Panchuk
  Earl Barish
  Lorne Saifer
  Hersh Wolch
  Harris Liontas

D-U-N-S 24-446-7697   (BR)
SEARS CANADA INC
2311 Mcphillips St, Winnipeg, MB, R2V 3C9
(204) 338-4621
Emp Here 50
SIC 5311 Department stores

D-U-N-S 20-709-7994   (BR)
SEVEN OAKS SCHOOL DIVISION
WEST KILDONAN & COLLEGIATE
(*Suby of* Seven Oaks School Division)
1874 Main St, Winnipeg, MB, R2V 2A6
(204) 339-6959
Emp Here 50
SIC 8211 Elementary and secondary schools

D-U-N-S 25-127-9527   (BR)
SEVEN OAKS SCHOOL DIVISION
H.C. AVERY MIDDLE SCHOOL
(*Suby of* Seven Oaks School Division)
10 Marigold Bay, Winnipeg, MB, R2V 2M1
(204) 334-4391
Emp Here 35

▲ Public Company   ■ Public Company Family Member   **HQ** Headquarters   **BR** Branch   **SL** Single Location

SIC 8211 Elementary and secondary schools

D-U-N-S 25-127-9550   (BR)
SEVEN OAKS SCHOOL DIVISION
ECOLE BELMONT SCHOOL
(*Suby of* Seven Oaks School Division)
525 Belmont Ave, Winnipeg, MB, R2V 0Z6
(204) 338-7893
Emp Here 20
SIC 8211 Elementary and secondary schools

D-U-N-S 25-127-9592   (BR)
SEVEN OAKS SCHOOL DIVISION
FOREST PARK SCHOOL
(*Suby of* Seven Oaks School Division)
130 Forest Park Dr, Winnipeg, MB, R2V 2R8
(204) 338-9341
Emp Here 25
SIC 8211 Elementary and secondary schools

D-U-N-S 25-127-9600   (BR)
SEVEN OAKS SCHOOL DIVISION
GOVERNOR SEMPLE SCHOOL
(*Suby of* Seven Oaks School Division)
150 Hartford Ave, Winnipeg, MB, R2V 0V7
(204) 339-7112
Emp Here 25
SIC 8211 Elementary and secondary schools

D-U-N-S 25-127-9568   (BR)
SEVEN OAKS SCHOOL DIVISION
COLLICUTT SCHOOL
(*Suby of* Seven Oaks School Division)
75 Cottingham St, Winnipeg, MB, R2V 3B5
(204) 338-7937
Emp Here 20
SIC 8211 Elementary and secondary schools

D-U-N-S 20-838-8363   (HQ)
SEVEN OAKS SCHOOL DIVISION
(*Suby of* Seven Oaks School Division)
830 Powers St, Winnipeg, MB, R2V 4E7

Emp Here 20   *Emp Total* 1,000
Sales 112,327,004
SIC 8211 Elementary and secondary schools
Evelyn Mysaiw
Wayne Shimizu
Edward Ploszay

D-U-N-S 25-096-7676   (BR)
SEVEN OAKS SCHOOL DIVISION
SEVEN OAKS SCHOOL DIVISION MET SCHOOL
(*Suby of* Seven Oaks School Division)
711 Jefferson Ave, Winnipeg, MB, R2V 0P7
(204) 336-5050
Emp Here 80
SIC 8211 Elementary and secondary schools

D-U-N-S 20-023-4669   (BR)
SEVEN OAKS SCHOOL DIVISION
ECOLE RIVERBEND COMMUNITY SCHOOL
(*Suby of* Seven Oaks School Division)
123 Red River Blvd W, Winnipeg, MB, R2V 3X9
(204) 334-8417
Emp Here 63
SIC 8211 Elementary and secondary schools

D-U-N-S 25-137-2447   (BR)
SEVEN OAKS SCHOOL DIVISION
ECOLE SEVEN OAKS MIDDLE SCHOOL
(*Suby of* Seven Oaks School Division)
800 Salter St, Winnipeg, MB, R2V 2E6
(204) 586-0327
Emp Here 45
SIC 8211 Elementary and secondary schools

D-U-N-S 25-906-3949   (BR)
SEVEN OAKS SCHOOL DIVISION
MARGARET PARK ELEMENTARY SCHOOL
(*Suby of* Seven Oaks School Division)
385 Cork Ave, Winnipeg, MB, R2V 1R6
(204) 338-9384
Emp Here 40
SIC 8211 Elementary and secondary schools

D-U-N-S 25-127-9642   (BR)
SEVEN OAKS SCHOOL DIVISION
VICTORY SCHOOL
(*Suby of* Seven Oaks School Division)
395 Jefferson Ave, Winnipeg, MB, R2V 0N3
(204) 586-9716
Emp Here 50
SIC 8211 Elementary and secondary schools

D-U-N-S 20-268-1131   (BR)
SEVEN OAKS SCHOOL DIVISION
SEVEN OAKS MAINTENANCE DEPARTMENT
(*Suby of* Seven Oaks School Division)
2536 Mcphillips St Suite 10, Winnipeg, MB, R2V 4J8
(204) 338-7991
Emp Here 70
SIC 7349 Building maintenance services, nec

D-U-N-S 20-709-7986   (BR)
SEVEN OAKS SCHOOL DIVISION
R F MORRISON SCHOOL
(*Suby of* Seven Oaks School Division)
25 Morrison St, Winnipeg, MB, R2V 3B3
(204) 338-7804
Emp Here 30
SIC 8211 Elementary and secondary schools

D-U-N-S 25-271-7863   (BR)
SOBEYS WEST INC
SAFEWAY
841 Leila Ave, Winnipeg, MB, R2V 3J7
(204) 339-4113
Emp Here 75
SIC 5411 Grocery stores

D-U-N-S 20-860-4152   (BR)
SOURCE (BELL) ELECTRONICS INC, THE
SOURCE, THE
2305 Mcphillips St Unit 133, Winnipeg, MB, R2V 3E1
(204) 338-1301
Emp Here 25
SIC 5999 Miscellaneous retail stores, nec

D-U-N-S 25-498-9486   (BR)
STAPLES CANADA INC
STAPLES/BUSINESS DEPOT
(*Suby of* Staples, Inc.)
843 Leila Ave Suite 4, Winnipeg, MB, R2V 3J7
(204) 925-4510
Emp Here 50
SIC 5943 Stationery stores

D-U-N-S 25-294-8419   (BR)
WAL-MART CANADA CORP
2370 Mcphillips St Suite 3118, Winnipeg, MB, R2V 4J6
(204) 334-2273
Emp Here 300
SIC 5311 Department stores

D-U-N-S 25-659-8897   (BR)
WENDY'S RESTAURANTS OF CANADA INC
WENDY'S
(*Suby of* The Wendy's Company)
1420 Mcphillips St, Winnipeg, MB, R2V 3C5
(204) 632-8322
Emp Here 50
SIC 5812 Eating places

D-U-N-S 20-199-3008   (BR)
WINNERS MERCHANTS INTERNATIONAL L.P.
WINNERS
(*Suby of* The TJX Companies Inc)
2305 Mcphillips St Suite 214, Winnipeg, MB, R2V 3E1
(204) 334-4834
Emp Here 35
SIC 5651 Family clothing stores

Winnipeg, MB R2W

D-U-N-S 24-380-5335   (SL)
B.U.I.L.D. BUILDING URBAN INDUSTRIES FOR LOCAL DEVELOPMENT INC
WARM UP WINNIPEG
765 Main St Unit 200, Winnipeg, MB, R2W 3N5
(204) 943-5981
Emp Here 100   *Sales* 14,956,944
SIC 1521 Single-family housing construction
Shaun Loney

D-U-N-S 20-007-1983   (SL)
BROWN & RUTHERFORD CO LTD
5 Sutherland Ave, Winnipeg, MB, R2W 3B6
(204) 942-0701
Emp Here 20   *Sales* 7,103,258
SIC 5031 Lumber, plywood, and millwork
Pr Pr Allan Kaufman
Sec Nora Kaufman
Sylvia Silverberg
Ernest Rady

D-U-N-S 25-369-8302   (BR)
CITY BREAD CO. LTD, THE
238 Dufferin Ave, Winnipeg, MB, R2W 2X6
(204) 586-8409
Emp Here 100
SIC 2051 Bread, cake, and related products

D-U-N-S 20-578-6424   (BR)
CITY OF WINNIPEG, THE
WINNIPEG GARAGE
(*Suby of* City of Winnipeg, The)
1520 Main St, Winnipeg, MB, R2W 3W4
(204) 986-5832
Emp Here 20
SIC 7538 General automotive repair shops

D-U-N-S 20-008-3780   (HQ)
EMPIRE IRON WORKS LTD
717 Jarvis Ave Suite 1, Winnipeg, MB, R2W 3B4
(204) 589-9300
Emp Here 200   *Emp Total* 800
Sales 27,652,105
SIC 3441 Fabricated structural Metal
Pr Pr Campbell Mcintyre
Steve Lockwood

D-U-N-S 25-094-5656   (HQ)
FAITH ACADEMY INC
(*Suby of* Faith Academy Inc)
437 Matheson Ave, Winnipeg, MB, R2W 0E1
(204) 582-3400
Emp Here 40   *Emp Total* 50
Sales 3,356,192
SIC 8211 Elementary and secondary schools

D-U-N-S 20-860-9532   (BR)
GREYHOUND CANADA TRANSPORTATION ULC
110 Sutherland Ave, Winnipeg, MB, R2W 3C7
(204) 949-7348
Emp Here 40
SIC 4111 Local and suburban transit

D-U-N-S 25-753-7043   (SL)
INDIAN AND METIS FRIENDSHIP CENTRE OF WINNIPEG INC
IMFC
45 Robinson St, Winnipeg, MB, R2W 5H5
(204) 582-1296
Emp Here 70   *Sales* 2,772,507
SIC 8322 Individual and family services

D-U-N-S 25-173-6898   (BR)
LOBLAWS INC
EXTRA FOODS
1200 Main St, Winnipeg, MB, R2W 3S8
(204) 734-5190
Emp Here 60
SIC 5141 Groceries, general line

D-U-N-S 25-270-1412   (BR)
LOBLAWS INC
EXTRA FOODS
1445 Main St, Winnipeg, MB, R2W 3V8

Emp Here 60
SIC 5141 Groceries, general line

D-U-N-S 20-554-9665   (BR)
LOBLAWS INC
DISPLAY FIXTURES
494 Jarvis Ave Suite 898, Winnipeg, MB, R2W 3A9
(204) 589-9219
Emp Here 50
SIC 7623 Refrigeration service and repair

D-U-N-S 25-668-4929   (BR)
MCDONALD'S RESTAURANTS OF CANADA LIMITED
MCDONALD'S
(*Suby of* McDonald's Corporation)
1186 Main St, Winnipeg, MB, R2W 3S7
(204) 949-5244
Emp Here 63
SIC 5812 Eating places

D-U-N-S 25-678-1303   (BR)
MEYER'S SHEET METAL LTD
432 Dufferin Ave, Winnipeg, MB, R2W 2Y5
(204) 426-1100
Emp Here 20
SIC 3444 Sheet Metalwork

D-U-N-S 24-749-1921   (SL)
SEVEN OAKS JANITORIAL SERVICES LTD
636 Dufferin Ave, Winnipeg, MB, R2W 2Z2
(204) 586-5660
Emp Here 60   *Sales* 1,751,057
SIC 7349 Building maintenance services, nec

D-U-N-S 20-836-7029   (SL)
SISTER SERVANTS OF MARY IMMACULATE
HOLY FAMILY NURSING HOME
165 Aberdeen Ave, Winnipeg, MB, R2W 1T9
(204) 589-7381
Emp Here 350   *Sales* 20,637,005
SIC 8051 Skilled nursing care facilities
Dir Jean Piche
Ch Bd Joanne Huzel

D-U-N-S 25-271-7434   (BR)
SOBEYS WEST INC
SAFEWAY
1441 Main St, Winnipeg, MB, R2W 3V6
(204) 589-7135
Emp Here 55
SIC 5411 Grocery stores

D-U-N-S 20-709-7358   (BR)
WINNIPEG SCHOOL DIVISION
INKSTER SCHOOL
633 Inkster Blvd, Winnipeg, MB, R2W 0L3
(204) 589-4383
Emp Here 50
SIC 8211 Elementary and secondary schools

D-U-N-S 20-035-6421   (BR)
WINNIPEG SCHOOL DIVISION
NIJI MAHKWA SCHOOL
450 Flora Ave, Winnipeg, MB, R2W 2R8
(204) 589-6742
Emp Here 30
SIC 8211 Elementary and secondary schools

D-U-N-S 25-288-5389   (BR)
WINNIPEG SCHOOL DIVISION
R.B. RUSSELL VOCATIONAL HIGH SCHOOL
364 Dufferin Ave, Winnipeg, MB, R2W 2Y3
(204) 589-5301
Emp Here 42
SIC 8211 Elementary and secondary schools

D-U-N-S 20-035-6454   (BR)
WINNIPEG SCHOOL DIVISION
CHILDREN OF THE EARTH HIGH SCHOOL
100 Salter St, Winnipeg, MB, R2W 5M1
(204) 589-6383
Emp Here 35
SIC 8211 Elementary and secondary schools

D-U-N-S 20-709-7234   (BR)
WINNIPEG SCHOOL DIVISION
CHAMPLAIN SCHOOL
275 Church Ave, Winnipeg, MB, R2W 1B9
(204) 586-5139
Emp Here 30
SIC 8211 Elementary and secondary schools

D-U-N-S 25-453-4076   (BR)
WINNIPEG SCHOOL DIVISION
STRATHCONA SCHOOL
233 Mckenzie St, Winnipeg, MB, R2W 4Z2
(204) 586-8493
Emp Here 35
SIC 8211 Elementary and secondary schools

D-U-N-S 25-900-9231   (BR)
WINNIPEG SCHOOL DIVISION
MACHRAY SCHOOL
320 Mountain Ave, Winnipeg, MB, R2W 1K1
(204) 586-8085
Emp Here 33
SIC 8211 Elementary and secondary schools

D-U-N-S 20-709-7499   (BR)
WINNIPEG SCHOOL DIVISION
ST. JOHN HIGH SCHOOL
401 Church Ave, Winnipeg, MB, R2W 1C4
(204) 589-4374
Emp Here 150
SIC 8211 Elementary and secondary schools

D-U-N-S 20-913-6519   (BR)
WINNIPEG SCHOOL DIVISION
NORQUAY ELEMENTARY SCHOOL
132 Lusted Ave, Winnipeg, MB, R2W 2P2
(204) 943-9541
Emp Here 50
SIC 8211 Elementary and secondary schools

D-U-N-S 25-131-7574   (BR)
WINNIPEG SCHOOL DIVISION
DAVID LIVINGSTONE COMMUNITY SCHOOL
270 Flora Ave, Winnipeg, MB, R2W 2P9
(204) 586-8346
Emp Here 50
SIC 8211 Elementary and secondary schools

D-U-N-S 20-709-7549   (BR)
WINNIPEG SCHOOL DIVISION
WILLIAM WHYTE COMMUNITY SCHOOL
200 Powers St, Winnipeg, MB, R2W 4P3
(204) 589-4313
Emp Here 45
SIC 8211 Elementary and secondary schools

D-U-N-S 20-709-7267   (BR)
WINNIPEG SCHOOL DIVISION
FARADAY SCHOOL
405 Parr St, Winnipeg, MB, R2W 5G1
(204) 586-8583
Emp Here 50
SIC 8211 Elementary and secondary schools

Winnipeg, MB R2X

D-U-N-S 24-390-8782   (HQ)
3225537 NOVA SCOTIA LIMITED
WILSON AUTO ELECTRIC
90 Hutchings St Unit B, Winnipeg, MB, R2X 2X1
(204) 272-2880
Emp Here 50   *Emp Total* 5,000
Sales 12,184,437
SIC 5013 Motor vehicle supplies and new parts
Genl Mgr Mike Silva

D-U-N-S 25-287-9994   (BR)
A & W FOOD SERVICES OF CANADA INC
A & W
817 Keewatin St, Winnipeg, MB, R2X 3B9
(204) 697-2033
Emp Here 28

SIC 5812 Eating places

D-U-N-S 24-040-4848   (BR)
ALUMICOR LIMITED
(*Suby of* Apogee Enterprises, Inc.)
205 Hutchings St, Winnipeg, MB, R2X 2R4
(204) 633-8316
Emp Here 35
SIC 3442 Metal doors, sash, and trim

D-U-N-S 25-205-1826   (SL)
BENTLEYS OF LONDON SLACKS LTD
1309 Mountain Ave, Winnipeg, MB, R2X 2Y1
(204) 786-6081
Emp Here 1,500   *Sales* 129,247,300
SIC 2339 Women's and misses' outerwear, nec
Ch Bd Stephen Freed

D-U-N-S 20-006-0184   (HQ)
BIG FREIGHT SYSTEMS INC
BIG FREIGHT WAREHOUSING
10 Hutchings St, Winnipeg, MB, R2X 2X1
(204) 772-3434
Emp Here 25   *Emp Total* 2
Sales 34,218,568
SIC 4213 Trucking, except local
Pr Pr Gary Coleman
VP VP David Tardi
VP Fin Glen Gursky

D-U-N-S 25-219-5961   (HQ)
BROCK WHITE CANADA COMPANY, LLC
AGES, DIV OF
879 Keewatin St, Winnipeg, MB, R2X 2S7
(204) 772-3991
Emp Here 110   *Emp Total* 429
Sales 76,749,839
SIC 5039 Construction materials, nec
VP VP Neil Fast
Pr Pr Richard D Garland

D-U-N-S 20-919-2686   (BR)
BUCKWOLD WESTERN LTD
70 Plymouth St, Winnipeg, MB, R2X 2V7
(204) 633-7572
Emp Here 20
SIC 5023 Homefurnishings

D-U-N-S 24-340-7454   (BR)
CANWEL BUILDING MATERIALS LTD
BROADLEAF LOGISTICS
1330 Inkster Blvd, Winnipeg, MB, R2X 1P7
(204) 633-7003
Emp Here 20
SIC 5039 Construction materials, nec

D-U-N-S 20-572-6131   (BR)
CANADA POST CORPORATION
1462 Church Ave, Winnipeg, MB, R2X 1T1
(204) 987-5704
Emp Here 110
SIC 4311 U.s. postal service

D-U-N-S 24-038-3950   (SL)
CANADA WEST SHOE MANUFACTURING INC
CANADA WEST BOOT FACTORY OUTLET
1250 Fife St, Winnipeg, MB, R2X 2N6
(204) 632-4110
Emp Here 66   *Sales* 4,012,839
SIC 5661 Shoe stores

D-U-N-S 20-342-8701   (BR)
CANADIAN PACIFIC RAILWAY COMPANY
NETWORK SERVICE CENTER
478 Mcphillips St Bldg 7, Winnipeg, MB, R2X 2G8
(204) 947-8102
Emp Here 200
SIC 4011 Railroads, line-haul operating

D-U-N-S 24-113-2695   (HQ)
CELCO CONTROLS LTD
78 Hutchings St, Winnipeg, MB, R2X 3B1
(204) 788-1677
Emp Here 50   *Sales* 8,922,385
SIC 3613 Switchgear and switchboard apparatus
Dir Clay Derrett
Pr Pr Jeffrey Goodrich
   Murray Burkett
Dir Jerry Anderson

D-U-N-S 24-914-5392   (BR)
COCA-COLA REFRESHMENTS CANADA COMPANY
(*Suby of* The Coca-Cola Company)
1331 Inkster Blvd, Winnipeg, MB, R2X 1P6
(204) 633-2590
Emp Here 250
SIC 2086 Bottled and canned soft drinks

D-U-N-S 24-467-0980   (BR)
COINAMATIC CANADA INC
1496 Church Ave, Winnipeg, MB, R2X 1G4
(204) 633-8974
Emp Here 20
SIC 7215 Coin-operated laundries and cleaning

D-U-N-S 24-774-9906   (BR)
COMARK INC
RICKI'S, DIV OF
(*Suby of* Comark Inc)
1670 Inkster Blvd, Winnipeg, MB, R2X 2W8
(204) 633-5500
Emp Here 100
SIC 5621 Women's clothing stores

D-U-N-S 20-569-9135   (BR)
CONSOLIDATED FASTFRATE INC
477 Keewatin St, Winnipeg, MB, R2X 2S1
(204) 633-8730
Emp Here 50
SIC 4731 Freight transportation arrangement

D-U-N-S 25-360-4177   (BR)
COURTESY FREIGHT SYSTEMS LTD
75 Milner St, Winnipeg, MB, R2X 2P7
(204) 927-1555
Emp Here 25
SIC 4231 Trucking terminal facilities

D-U-N-S 25-959-1139   (HQ)
DALE & DALE PIZZA INC
DOMINO'S PIZZA
(*Suby of* Dale & Dale Pizza Inc)
1353 Mcphillips St Unit B, Winnipeg, MB, R2X 3A6
(204) 987-5552
Emp Here 20   *Emp Total* 65
Sales 1,969,939
SIC 5812 Eating places

D-U-N-S 20-106-0444   (BR)
DYNAMEX CANADA LIMITED
DYNAMEX
300 Keewatin St, Winnipeg, MB, R2X 2R9
(204) 832-7171
Emp Here 30
SIC 7389 Business services, nec

D-U-N-S 24-359-5787   (BR)
ESIT CANADA ENTERPRISE SERVICES CO
ESIT CANADA ENTERPRISE SERVICES CO
(*Suby of* Dxc Technology Company)
1455 Mountain Ave, Winnipeg, MB, R2X 2Y9

Emp Here 275
SIC 7379 Computer related services, nec

D-U-N-S 24-966-6165   (HQ)
ENDURAPAK INC
(*Suby of* Endurapak Inc)
55 Plymouth St, Winnipeg, MB, R2X 2V5
(204) 947-1383
Emp Here 105   *Emp Total* 120
Sales 22,615,896
SIC 2673 Bags: plastic, laminated, and coated
Pr Jay Cumbers
   Bruce Macdonald
VP VP Wayne M Pestaluky
   Clayton Matthes

D-U-N-S 24-572-2892   (BR)
FP CANADIAN NEWSPAPERS LIMITED PARTNERSHIP
WINNIPEG FREE PRESSESS
(*Suby of* FP Canadian Newspapers Limited Partnership)
1355 Mountain Ave, Winnipeg, MB, R2X 3B6
(204) 697-7000
Emp Here 600
SIC 2711 Newspapers

D-U-N-S 24-495-5782   (BR)
FORMER RESTORATION L.P.
925 Keewatin St, Winnipeg, MB, R2X 2X4
(204) 783-9086
Emp Here 30
SIC 1521 Single-family housing construction

D-U-N-S 24-390-1811   (SL)
GASPARD LP
1266 Fife St, Winnipeg, MB, R2X 2N6
(204) 949-5700
Emp Here 350   *Sales* 35,168,000
SIC 2389 Apparel and accessories, nec
Fin Mgr Roddy Premsukh
Off Mgr Valerie Morgan
CEO David Blatt

D-U-N-S 24-098-8423   (BR)
GREAT-WEST LIFE ASSURANCE COMPANY, THE
1658 Church Ave, Winnipeg, MB, R2X 2W9
(204) 946-7760
Emp Here 31
SIC 4225 General warehousing and storage

D-U-N-S 24-852-1135   (BR)
GROUPE EMBALLAGE SPECIALISE S.E.C.
INDUSPAC/SUR-SEAL/PROPAK
1310 Mountain Ave, Winnipeg, MB, R2X 3A3
(204) 832-8001
Emp Here 22
SIC 5199 Nondurable goods, nec

D-U-N-S 20-012-0509   (HQ)
LIFETOUCH CANADA INC
(*Suby of* Lifetouch Inc.)
1410 Mountain Ave Unit 1, Winnipeg, MB, R2X 0A4
(204) 977-3475
Emp Here 218   *Emp Total* 26,175
Sales 14,592,140
SIC 7384 Photofinish laboratories
   Paul Harmel
Fin Ex Andy Vanderzalm
Dir Randolph Pladson
Dir Ted Koenecke
Dir James Campbell
Dir John Anderson
Dir Richard Erickson
Dir Donald Goldfus
Dir P. Robert Larson
Dir Bruce Nicholson

D-U-N-S 20-009-6022   (SL)
LINCOLN MOTOR HOTEL CO LTD
1030 Mcphillips St, Winnipeg, MB, R2X 2K7
(204) 589-7314
Emp Here 60   *Sales* 2,626,585
SIC 7011 Hotels and motels

D-U-N-S 20-316-9875   (BR)
MATADOR CONVERTISSEURS CIE LTEE
(*Suby of* Zumatador Holdings Inc)
1465 Inkster Blvd, Winnipeg, MB, R2X 1P6
(204) 632-6663
Emp Here 26
SIC 2221 Broadwoven fabric mills, manmade

D-U-N-S 25-011-0830   (BR)
MCDONALD'S RESTAURANTS OF CANADA LIMITED
MCDONALD'S
(*Suby of* McDonald's Corporation)
1301 Mcphillips St, Winnipeg, MB, R2X 2L9
(204) 949-6073
Emp Here 70

SIC 5812 Eating places

D-U-N-S 25-318-1424　(BR)
MCDONALD'S RESTAURANTS OF CANADA LIMITED
MCDONALD'S 8440
(Suby of McDonald's Corporation)
484 Mcphillips St, Winnipeg, MB, R2X 2H2
(204) 949-6060
Emp Here 44
SIC 5812 Eating places

D-U-N-S 24-520-0936　(SL)
NOR-TEC ELECTRIC LTD
1615 Inkster Blvd, Winnipeg, MB, R2X 1R2
(204) 694-0330
Emp Here 50　Sales 4,377,642
SIC 1731 Electrical work

D-U-N-S 25-817-0575　(SL)
NOR-TEC GROUP LTD
1615 Inkster Blvd, Winnipeg, MB, R2X 1R2
(204) 694-0330
Emp Here 50　Sales 4,377,642
SIC 1731 Electrical work

D-U-N-S 20-005-1639　(HQ)
OLD DUTCH FOODS LTD
(Suby of Old Dutch Foods Ltd)
100 Bentall St, Winnipeg, MB, R2X 2Y5
(204) 632-0249
Emp Here 100　Emp Total 1,000
SIC 2096 Potato chips and similar snacks

D-U-N-S 24-774-8544　(HQ)
PARAMOUNT STORAGE LTD
10 Hutchings St, Winnipeg, MB, R2X 2X1
(204) 632-0025
Emp Here 32　Emp Total 3
Sales 5,526,400
SIC 4225 General warehousing and storage
Pr Pr Bradley Thiessen

D-U-N-S 20-179-7730　(BR)
PORTAGE CARTAGE & STORAGE LTD
959 Keewatin St Unit A, Winnipeg, MB, R2X 2X4
(204) 633-8059
Emp Here 70
SIC 4214 Local trucking with storage

D-U-N-S 20-009-6089　(BR)
PRAXAIR CANADA INC
PRAXAIR DISTRIBUTION
(Suby of Praxair, Inc.)
635 Mcphillips St, Winnipeg, MB, R2X 2H1
(204) 589-7363
Emp Here 22
SIC 5169 Chemicals and allied products, nec

D-U-N-S 20-435-2736　(SL)
PROTELEC LTD
1450 Mountain Ave Unit 200, Winnipeg, MB, R2X 3C4
(204) 949-1417
Emp Here 60　Sales 1,896,978
SIC 7382 Security systems services

D-U-N-S 25-415-5047　(HQ)
REIMER EXPRESS LINES LTD
(Suby of Yrc Worldwide Inc.)
1400 Inkster Blvd, Winnipeg, MB, R2X 1R1
(204) 958-5000
Emp Here 300　Emp Total 32,000
Sales 120,093,312
SIC 4213 Trucking, except local
Pr Pr Jeffrey A. Rogers
VP VP Richard J. Bronk
Leah K. Dawson
VP Fin Terry Gerrond
Thomas S. Palmer

D-U-N-S 25-415-5005　(BR)
REIMER EXPRESS LINES LTD
(Suby of Yrc Worldwide Inc.)
100 Milner St, Winnipeg, MB, R2X 2X3

Emp Here 40

SIC 4213 Trucking, except local

D-U-N-S 25-867-4753　(BR)
SOBEYS CAPITAL INCORPORATED
SOBEYS WINNIPEG CASH & CARRY
840 Dufferin Ave, Winnipeg, MB, R2X 0A3
(204) 586-7819
Emp Here 28
SIC 5141 Groceries, general line

D-U-N-S 24-034-8235　(BR)
SOBEYS CAPITAL INCORPORATED
SOBEYS WEST
1800 Inkster Blvd, Winnipeg, MB, R2X 2Z5
(204) 632-7100
Emp Here 250
SIC 5141 Groceries, general line

D-U-N-S 24-346-5353　(BR)
SOBEYS CAPITAL INCORPORATED
1870 Burrows Ave, Winnipeg, MB, R2X 3C3
(204) 697-1997
Emp Here 160
SIC 5411 Grocery stores

D-U-N-S 25-387-6981　(SL)
SUPERIOR HEATING & AIR CONDITION-ING/ST. JAMES SHEET METAL LTD
1600 Church Ave, Winnipeg, MB, R2X 1G8
(204) 697-5666
Emp Here 51　Sales 4,450,603
SIC 1731 Electrical work

D-U-N-S 24-314-4396　(BR)
SUPREMEX INC
(Suby of Supremex Inc)
33 Plymouth St, Winnipeg, MB, R2X 2V5
(204) 633-2416
Emp Here 40
SIC 2677 Envelopes

D-U-N-S 20-272-6555　(BR)
THYSSENKRUPP ELEVATOR (CANADA) LIMITED
THYSSENKRUPP ELEVATORS
1635 Burrows Ave Suite 20, Winnipeg, MB, R2X 3B5
(204) 775-8671
Emp Here 35
SIC 1796 Installing building equipment

D-U-N-S 25-328-8542　(BR)
TRANSCONTINENTAL PRINTING INC
SPOT GRAPHICS
1615 Inkster Blvd, Winnipeg, MB, R2X 1R2
(204) 988-9476
Emp Here 100
SIC 2752 Commercial printing, lithographic

D-U-N-S 24-227-1372　(BR)
UPS SCS, INC
350 Keewatin St Unit 4, Winnipeg, MB, R2X 2R9
(204) 633-6510
Emp Here 20
SIC 4731 Freight transportation arrangement

D-U-N-S 25-660-0016　(BR)
UTC FIRE & SECURITY CANADA
(Suby of United Technologies Corporation)
1127 Keewatin St, Winnipeg, MB, R2X 2Z3
(204) 633-5242
Emp Here 50
SIC 5999 Miscellaneous retail stores, nec

D-U-N-S 24-096-9647　(BR)
WESTCON EQUIPMENT & RENTALS LTD
380 Keewatin St, Winnipeg, MB, R2X 2R9
(204) 633-5800
Emp Here 40
SIC 7353 Heavy construction equipment rental

D-U-N-S 24-426-8959　(BR)
WESTROCK COMPANY OF CANADA INC
(Suby of Westrock Company)
1360 Inkster Blvd, Winnipeg, MB, R2X 3C5
(204) 697-5300
Emp Here 210

SIC 2653 Corrugated and solid fiber boxes

D-U-N-S 20-709-7382　(BR)
WINNIPEG SCHOOL DIVISION
LANSDOWNE SCHOOL
715 Wiginton St, Winnipeg, MB, R2X 2G2
(204) 338-7039
Emp Here 50
SIC 8211 Elementary and secondary schools

D-U-N-S 20-709-7218　(BR)
WINNIPEG SCHOOL DIVISION
ANDREW MYNARSKI V.C. SCHOOL
1111 Machray Ave, Winnipeg, MB, R2X 1H6
(204) 586-8497
Emp Here 50
SIC 8211 Elementary and secondary schools

D-U-N-S 20-709-7481　(BR)
WINNIPEG SCHOOL DIVISION
ROBERTSON ELEMENTARY SCHOOL
550 Robertson St, Winnipeg, MB, R2X 2C4
(204) 589-4745
Emp Here 70
SIC 8211 Elementary and secondary schools

D-U-N-S 25-011-5623　(BR)
WINNIPEG SCHOOL DIVISION
KING EDWARD COMMUNITY SCHOOL
825 Selkirk Ave, Winnipeg, MB, R2X 2Y6
(204) 586-8381
Emp Here 50
SIC 8211 Elementary and secondary schools

D-U-N-S 25-289-4449　(BR)
WINNIPEG SCHOOL DIVISION
SHAUGHNESSY PARK SCHOOL
1641 Manitoba Ave, Winnipeg, MB, R2X 0M3
(204) 586-8376
Emp Here 50
SIC 8211 Elementary and secondary schools

D-U-N-S 25-892-6146　(BR)
WINNIPEG SCHOOL DIVISION
SISLER HIGH SCHOOL
1360 Redwood Ave, Winnipeg, MB, R2X 0Z1
(204) 589-8321
Emp Here 135
SIC 8211 Elementary and secondary schools

D-U-N-S 20-709-7416　(BR)
WINNIPEG SCHOOL DIVISION
LORD NELSON SCHOOL
820 Mcphillips St, Winnipeg, MB, R2X 2J7
(204) 586-9625
Emp Here 50
SIC 8211 Elementary and secondary schools

Winnipeg, MB R2Y

D-U-N-S 20-690-6773　(BR)
ALL SENIORS CARE LIVING CENTRES LTD
STURGEON CREEK RETIREMENT RESI-DENCE
(Suby of All Seniors Care Holdings Inc)
10 Hallonquist Dr Suite 318, Winnipeg, MB, R2Y 2M5
(204) 885-1415
Emp Here 75
SIC 8361 Residential care

D-U-N-S 20-710-0137　(BR)
DIVISION SCOLAIRE FRANCO-MANITOBAINE
ECOLE ROMERO DALLAIRE
(Suby of Division Scolaire Franco-Manitobaine)
81 Quail Ridge Rd, Winnipeg, MB, R2Y 2A9
(204) 885-8000
Emp Here 35
SIC 8211 Elementary and secondary schools

D-U-N-S 20-573-6445　(BR)
ESIT CANADA ENTERPRISE SERVICES CO

ESIT CANADA ENTERPRISE SERVICES CO
(Suby of Dxc Technology Company)
99 Corbett Dr, Winnipeg, MB, R2Y 1V4
(204) 837-5507
Emp Here 20
SIC 5734 Computer and software stores

D-U-N-S 25-484-7668　(BR)
GOVERNING COUNCIL OF THE SALVA-TION ARMY IN CANADA, THE
GOVERNING COUNCIL OF THE SALVATION ARMY IN CANADA, THE
811 School Rd, Winnipeg, MB, R2Y 0S8
(204) 888-3311
Emp Here 185
SIC 8322 Individual and family services

D-U-N-S 25-272-0008　(BR)
SOBEYS WEST INC
SAFEWAY
3059 Ness Ave, Winnipeg, MB, R2Y 0G1

Emp Here 85
SIC 5411 Grocery stores

D-U-N-S 20-709-7614　(BR)
ST. JAMES-ASSINIBOIA SCHOOL DIVI-SION
HERITAGE SCHOOL
47 Heritage Blvd, Winnipeg, MB, R2Y 0N9
(204) 837-1394
Emp Here 50
SIC 8211 Elementary and secondary schools

D-U-N-S 25-268-0657　(BR)
ST. JAMES-ASSINIBOIA SCHOOL DIVI-SION
HEDGES MIDDLE SCHOOL
369 Fairlane Ave, Winnipeg, MB, R2Y 0B6
(204) 837-5843
Emp Here 40
SIC 8211 Elementary and secondary schools

D-U-N-S 20-035-6488　(BR)
ST. JAMES-ASSINIBOIA SCHOOL DIVI-SION
JOHN TAYLOR COLLEGIATE
470 Hamilton Ave, Winnipeg, MB, R2Y 0H4
(204) 888-8930
Emp Here 58
SIC 8211 Elementary and secondary schools

D-U-N-S 25-011-5813　(BR)
ST. JAMES-ASSINIBOIA SCHOOL DIVI-SION
LAKEWOOD ELEMENTARY SCHOOL
55 Kay Cres, Winnipeg, MB, R2Y 1L1
(204) 889-9360
Emp Here 30
SIC 8211 Elementary and secondary schools

D-U-N-S 25-484-7551　(BR)
ST. JAMES-ASSINIBOIA SCHOOL DIVI-SION
BUCHANAN ELEMENTARY SCHOOL
815 Buchanan Blvd, Winnipeg, MB, R2Y 1N1
(204) 888-0680
Emp Here 40
SIC 8211 Elementary and secondary schools

D-U-N-S 25-288-5637　(BR)
ST. JAMES-ASSINIBOIA SCHOOL DIVI-SION
NESS MIDDLE SCHOOL
3300 Ness Ave, Winnipeg, MB, R2Y 0G6
(204) 837-1361
Emp Here 35
SIC 8211 Elementary and secondary schools

D-U-N-S 20-023-9932　(BR)
ST. JAMES-ASSINIBOIA SCHOOL DIVI-SION
VOYAGEUR ELEMENTARY SCHOOL
37 Voyageur Ave Suite 12, Winnipeg, MB, R2Y 0H7
(204) 832-4707
Emp Here 30

SIC 8211 Elementary and secondary schools

Winnipeg, MB R3A

D-U-N-S 25-365-7910　　　(BR)
BORDER CHEMICAL COMPANY LIMITED
595 Gunn Rd, Winnipeg, MB, R3A 1L1
(204) 222-3276
Emp Here 70
SIC 2873 Nitrogenous fertilizers

D-U-N-S 20-007-6123　　　(HQ)
CANADIAN FOOTWEAR (1982) LTD
(*Suby of* Canadian Footwear (1982) Ltd)
128 Adelaide St, Winnipeg, MB, R3A 0W5
(204) 944-7460
Emp Here 25　　　*Emp Total* 65
Sales 3,939,878
SIC 5661 Shoe stores

D-U-N-S 20-578-6200　　　(BR)
CITY OF WINNIPEG, THE
FIRE PARAMEDIC SERVICE
(*Suby of* City of Winnipeg, The)
65 Ellen St, Winnipeg, MB, R3A 0Z8
(204) 986-6308
Emp Here 1,200
SIC 4119 Local passenger transportation, nec

D-U-N-S 24-036-2376　　　(SL)
I.D. FASHION LTD
332 Bannatyne Ave, Winnipeg, MB, R3A 0E2
(204) 944-1954
Emp Here 65　　　*Sales* 4,012,839
SIC 2339 Women's and misses' outerwear, nec

D-U-N-S 25-011-6209　　　(SL)
MANITOBA INTERFAITH IMMIGRATION COUNCIL INC
WELCOME PLACE
521 Bannatyne Ave, Winnipeg, MB, R3A 0E4

Emp Here 70　　　*Sales* 2,772,507
SIC 8322 Individual and family services

D-U-N-S 20-613-9271　　　(SL)
RABER GLOVE MFG. CO. LTD
560 Mcdermot Ave, Winnipeg, MB, R3A 0C1
(204) 786-2469
Emp Here 57　　　*Sales* 3,137,310
SIC 3111 Leather tanning and finishing

D-U-N-S 24-245-5447　　　(SL)
SMD FOUNDATION
825 Sherbrook St Suite 401, Winnipeg, MB, R3A 1M5
(204) 975-3108
Emp Here 50　　　*Sales* 2,334,742
SIC 8052 Intermediate care facilities

D-U-N-S 24-916-7370　　　(SL)
SAXON LEATHER LTD
310 Ross Ave, Winnipeg, MB, R3A 0L4
(204) 956-4011
Emp Here 50　　　*Sales* 2,261,782
SIC 5948 Luggage and leather goods stores

D-U-N-S 24-171-3106　　　(HQ)
WINNIPEG PANTS & SPORTSWEAR MFG. LTD
RICHLU MANUFACTURING
85 Adelaide St, Winnipeg, MB, R3A 0V9
(204) 942-3494
Emp Here 150　　　*Emp Total* 200
Sales 35,689,541
SIC 2326 Men's and boy's work clothing
　David Rich
Pr Gavin Rich
　Reva Lerner
　Barry Rich
　Dorothy Kotler
　Beverly Rosove

D-U-N-S 20-875-4122　　　(BR)

WINNIPEG REGIONAL HEALTH AUTHOR-ITY, THE
490 Hargrave St, Winnipeg, MB, R3A 0X7
(204) 940-2665
Emp Here 130
SIC 8093 Specialty outpatient clinics, nec

D-U-N-S 20-052-4812　　　(BR)
WINNIPEG REGIONAL HEALTH AUTHOR-ITY, THE
HEALTH SCIENCES CENTRE (DIV OF)
820 Sherbrook St Suite 543, Winnipeg, MB, R3A 1R9
(204) 774-6511
Emp Here 1,500
SIC 8062 General medical and surgical hospitals

D-U-N-S 25-099-8408　　　(BR)
WINNIPEG REGIONAL HEALTH AUTHOR-ITY, THE
CHILDREN'S HOSPITAL
840 Sherbrook St Suite 709, Winnipeg, MB, R3A 1S1
(204) 787-3038
Emp Here 70
SIC 8069 Specialty hospitals, except psychiatric

D-U-N-S 20-035-6496　　　(BR)
WINNIPEG SCHOOL DIVISION
SACRE-COEUR SCHOOL
809 Furby St, Winnipeg, MB, R3A 1T2
(204) 775-2574
Emp Here 50
SIC 8211 Elementary and secondary schools

D-U-N-S 20-709-7259　　　(BR)
WINNIPEG SCHOOL DIVISION
DUFFERIN SCHOOL
545 Alexander Ave, Winnipeg, MB, R3A 0P1
(204) 774-3409
Emp Here 50
SIC 8211 Elementary and secondary schools

D-U-N-S 20-709-7515　　　(BR)
WINNIPEG SCHOOL DIVISION
VICTORIA ALBERT SCHOOL
110 Ellen St, Winnipeg, MB, R3A 1A1
(204) 943-3459
Emp Here 50
SIC 8211 Elementary and secondary schools

D-U-N-S 25-900-9249　　　(BR)
WINNIPEG SCHOOL DIVISION
HUGH JOHN MACDONALD SCHOOL
567 Bannatyne Ave, Winnipeg, MB, R3A 0G8
(204) 786-5631
Emp Here 44
SIC 8211 Elementary and secondary schools

Winnipeg, MB R3B

D-U-N-S 25-668-1719　　　(SL)
4659555 MANITOBA LTD
PERFECT PLACEMENT SYSTEMS, DIV OF
330a King St, Winnipeg, MB, R3B 3H4
(204) 989-5820
Emp Here 900　　　*Sales* 84,809,610
SIC 7361 Employment agencies
Pr Norman William Kyliuk

D-U-N-S 24-913-6839　　　(BR)
ADM AGRI-INDUSTRIES COMPANY
ADM MILLING, DIV OF
(*Suby of* Archer-Daniels-Midland Company)
7 Higgins Ave, Winnipeg, MB, R3B 0A1
(204) 925-2100
Emp Here 25
SIC 2041 Flour and other grain mill products

D-U-N-S 25-305-0215　　　(BR)
AON CANADA INC
AON REED STENHOUSE
1 Lombard Pl Suite 1800, Winnipeg, MB, R3B

2A3
(204) 956-1070
Emp Here 50
SIC 6411 Insurance agents, brokers, and service

D-U-N-S 20-514-5506　　　(BR)
ADECCO EMPLOYMENT SERVICES LIM-ITED
ADECCO
228 Notre Dame Ave, Winnipeg, MB, R3B 1N7
(204) 956-5454
Emp Here 105
SIC 7361 Employment agencies

D-U-N-S 20-571-8299　　　(BR)
AIR CANADA
355 Portage Ave Suite 3850, Winnipeg, MB, R3B 0J6
(204) 941-2684
Emp Here 600
SIC 4512 Air transportation, scheduled

D-U-N-S 20-023-5526　　　(SL)
ASTRAL MEDIA RADIO
177 Lombard Ave Suite 3, Winnipeg, MB, R3B 0W5
(204) 944-1031
Emp Here 50　　　*Sales* 3,724,879
SIC 4832 Radio broadcasting stations

D-U-N-S 20-040-3462　　　(BR)
AVIVA INSURANCE COMPANY OF CANADA
201 Portage Ave Suite 900, Winnipeg, MB, R3B 3K6
(204) 942-0424
Emp Here 45
SIC 6331 Fire, marine, and casualty insurance

D-U-N-S 24-737-9022　　　(SL)
AXON SOLUTIONS (CANADA) INC
201 Portage Ave Suite 15, Winnipeg, MB, R3B 3K6
(204) 934-2493
Emp Here 50　　　*Sales* 6,502,070
SIC 7371 Custom computer programming services
Dir Michael Sinclair
Dir Prahlad Rai Bansal
Dir Sandip Gupta

D-U-N-S 20-046-2328　　　(BR)
BANQUE TORONTO-DOMINION, LA
TORONTO-DOMINION BANK, THE
(*Suby of* Toronto-Dominion Bank, The)
201 Portage Ave Suite 300, Winnipeg, MB, R3B 3K6
(204) 988-2811
Emp Here 40
SIC 6021 National commercial banks

D-U-N-S 20-650-3869　　　(BR)
BELL MEDIA INC
HOT 103
177 Lombard Ave Suite 3, Winnipeg, MB, R3B 0W5
(204) 944-1031
Emp Here 50
SIC 4832 Radio broadcasting stations

D-U-N-S 24-819-9473　　　(BR)
BELL MOBILITE INC
395 Notre Dame Ave, Winnipeg, MB, R3B 1R2
(204) 943-5544
Emp Here 70
SIC 5065 Electronic parts and equipment, nec

D-U-N-S 20-010-1384　　　(HQ)
BEN MOSS JEWELLERS WESTERN CANADA LTD
BEN MOSS JEWELLERS
201 Portage Ave Suite 300, Winnipeg, MB, R3B 3K6
(204) 947-6682
Emp Here 50　　　*Emp Total* 500
Sales 29,279,284
SIC 5944 Jewelry stores
Pr Pr Brent Trepel

D-U-N-S 20-519-0726　　　(BR)
CIBC WORLD MARKETS INC
CIBC WOOD GUNDY
1 Lombard Pl Suite 1000, Winnipeg, MB, R3B 3N9
(204) 942-0311
Emp Here 85
SIC 6211 Security brokers and dealers

D-U-N-S 20-032-8669　　　(SL)
CANTALK (CANADA) INC
CANTALK USA
70 Arthur St Suite 250, Winnipeg, MB, R3B 1G7
(204) 982-1245
Emp Here 56　　　*Sales* 2,184,358
SIC 4899 Communication services, nec

D-U-N-S 20-814-7780　　　(BR)
CANADIAN BROADCASTING CORPORA-TION
CBC MANITOBA
541 Portage Ave, Winnipeg, MB, R3B 2G1
(204) 788-3222
Emp Here 20
SIC 4833 Television broadcasting stations

D-U-N-S 20-570-8423　　　(HQ)
CANADIAN GOODWILL INDUSTRIES CORP
GOODWILL
(*Suby of* Canadian Goodwill Industries Corp)
70 Princess St, Winnipeg, MB, R3B 1K2
(204) 943-6435
Emp Here 32　　　*Emp Total* 71
Sales 11,856,640
SIC 8699 Membership organizations, nec
Pr Pr Douglas Mckechnie
VP VP Jack Watts
　Bruce Down
Dir Allan Graham
Dir Donald Haddock

D-U-N-S 20-010-4185　　　(BR)
CANADIAN PACIFIC RAILWAY COMPANY
CPR
1 Lombard Pl Suite 1300, Winnipeg, MB, R3B 0X3

Emp Here 20
SIC 4011 Railroads, line-haul operating

D-U-N-S 20-552-9618　　　(BR)
CITY OF WINNIPEG, THE
WATER & WASTE DEPARTMENT CUS-TOMER SERVICE
(*Suby of* City of Winnipeg, The)
510 Main St Suite 102, Winnipeg, MB, R3B 3M1
(204) 986-2455
Emp Here 25
SIC 4941 Water supply

D-U-N-S 24-336-9159　　　(BR)
CITY OF WINNIPEG, THE
WINNIPEG COMMUNITY SERVICE
(*Suby of* City of Winnipeg, The)
395 Main St Suite 7, Winnipeg, MB, R3B 3N8
(204) 986-8023
Emp Here 21
SIC 8611 Business associations

D-U-N-S 24-099-2078　　　(BR)
COLE INTERNATIONAL INC
177 Lombard Ave Suite 400, Winnipeg, MB, R3B 0W5
(204) 944-9200
Emp Here 25
SIC 4731 Freight transportation arrangement

D-U-N-S 25-867-5073　　　(BR)
DIRECT LIMITED PARTNERSHIP
DIRECT MOVING SYSTEMS
47 Gomez St, Winnipeg, MB, R3B 0G4
(204) 632-8448
Emp Here 50
SIC 4214 Local trucking with storage

D-U-N-S 25-417-9831   (BR)
DIRECT LIMITED PARTNERSHIP
DIRECT FLEET MANAGEMENT
100 Higgins Ave, Winnipeg, MB, R3B 0B2
(204) 947-0889
Emp Here 30
SIC 4212 Local trucking, without storage

D-U-N-S 24-423-5862   (BR)
E CARE CONTACT CENTERS LTD
(*Suby of* E Care Contact Centers Ltd)
433 Main St Suite 300, Winnipeg, MB, R3B
1B3
(204) 940-3544
Emp Here 20
SIC 7389 Business services, nec

D-U-N-S 20-844-9608   (BR)
FAIRMONT HOTELS & RESORTS INC
FAIRMONT WINNIPEG
2 Lombard Pl, Winnipeg, MB, R3B 0Y3
(204) 985-6213
Emp Here 250
SIC 7011 Hotels and motels

D-U-N-S 25-993-1785   (BR)
FINANCIERE BANQUE NATIONALE INC
200 Waterfront Dr Suite 400, Winnipeg, MB,
R3B 3P1
(204) 925-2250
Emp Here 100
SIC 6021 National commercial banks

D-U-N-S 25-722-1291   (BR)
**GREYHOUND CANADA TRANSPORTA-
TION ULC**
487 Portage Ave, Winnipeg, MB, R3B 2E3
(204) 783-8857
Emp Here 80
SIC 4131 Intercity and rural bus transportation

D-U-N-S 24-319-2213   (BR)
GROUPE PAGES JAUNES CORP
201 Portage Ave Suite 1750, Winnipeg, MB,
R3B 3K6
(204) 941-8190
Emp Here 50
SIC 4899 Communication services, nec

D-U-N-S 20-009-0744   (BR)
HOLT, RENFREW & CIE, LIMITEE
RENFREW HOLT
393 Portage Ave Suite 200, Winnipeg, MB,
R3B 3H6
(204) 942-7321
Emp Here 25
SIC 5311 Department stores

D-U-N-S 20-570-7318   (BR)
HY'S OF CANADA LTD
HY'S STEAKHOUSE & COCKTAIL BAR
1 Lombard Pl, Winnipeg, MB, R3B 0X3
(204) 942-1000
Emp Here 60
SIC 5812 Eating places

D-U-N-S 20-004-3086   (BR)
IBM CANADA LIMITED
IBM
(*Suby of* International Business Machines
Corporation)
400 Ellice Ave, Winnipeg, MB, R3B 3M3
(204) 946-4900
Emp Here 300
SIC 3571 Electronic computers

D-U-N-S 24-424-8550   (SL)
**INTERNATIONAL   FEDERATION   OF
BIOSAFETY ASSOCIATIONS INC**
445 Ellice Ave, Winnipeg, MB, R3B 3P5
(204) 946-0908
Emp Here 45   *Sales* 6,507,040
SIC 8621 Professional organizations
Dir Maureen Ellis

D-U-N-S 24-852-1775   (HQ)
**INTERNATIONAL INSTITUTE FOR SUS-
TAINABLE DEVELOPMENT**

IISD
(*Suby of* International Institute For Sustain-
able Development)
111 Lombard Ave Suite 325, Winnipeg, MB,
R3B 0T4
(204) 958-7700
Emp Here 54   *Emp Total* 70
Sales 11,213,715
SIC 8733 Noncommercial research organiza-
tions
Pr Thomas Scott Vaughan
 Grace Mota

D-U-N-S 20-758-2172   (HQ)
INVESTORS GROUP TRUST CO. LTD
INVESTORS GROUP
447 Portage Ave, Winnipeg, MB, R3B 3H5
(204) 943-0361
Emp Here 28   *Emp Total* 31,126
Sales 24,952,559
SIC 6021 National commercial banks
Pr Pr Asman Todd
 Sonya Reiss
Dir Jeffrey Carney
Dir Allan Warren
Dir William J. Assini
Dir Rob Macdonald
Dir Bernd Christmas
Dir Martin Cauchon
Dir Jean-Claude Bachand

D-U-N-S 24-519-8791   (SL)
J & J PENNER CONSTRUCTION LTD
93 Lombard Ave Suite 100, Winnipeg, MB,
R3B 3B1
(204) 943-6200
Emp Here 25   *Sales* 6,087,000
SIC 1542 Nonresidential construction, nec
Pr Pr John Penner
 Joanna Penner
Genl Mgr Terry Mckellar
Fin Ex Melanie Penner

D-U-N-S 25-399-4982   (HQ)
JAMES RICHARDSON & SONS, LIMITED
(*Suby of* James Richardson & Sons, Limited)
1 Lombard Pl Suite 3000, Winnipeg, MB, R3B
0Y1
(204) 953-7970
Emp Here 20   *Emp Total* 1,500
Sales 716,619,995
SIC 5153 Grain and field beans
Pr Pr Hartley T. Richardson
 Carolyn A. Hursh

D-U-N-S 24-863-1686   (BR)
JELD-WEN OF CANADA, LTD.
230 Princess St, Winnipeg, MB, R3B 1L6
(204) 594-5820
Emp Here 20
SIC 2431 Millwork

D-U-N-S 25-301-5473   (BR)
KPMG LLP
(*Suby of* KPMG LLP)
1 Lombard Pl Unit 2000, Winnipeg, MB, R3B
0X3
(204) 957-1770
Emp Here 100
SIC 8721 Accounting, auditing, and book-
keeping

D-U-N-S 24-231-1066   (SL)
KAYJET PROMOTIONS LTD
66 King St Suite 700, Winnipeg, MB, R3B 1H6
(204) 942-0778
Emp Here 51   *Sales* 2,626,585
SIC 7389 Business services, nec

D-U-N-S 20-569-7824   (HQ)
KELSEY SPORTSWEAR LTD
KELSEY TRAIL
(*Suby of* Kelsey Trail Holdings Ltd)
563 Notre Dame Ave, Winnipeg, MB, R3B 1S5
(204) 786-1503
Emp Here 40   *Emp Total* 55
Sales 3,064,349

SIC 2321 Men's and boy's furnishings

D-U-N-S 20-517-5628   (BR)
LEGER MARKETING INC
(*Suby of* Leger Marketing Inc)
35 King St Suite 5, Winnipeg, MB, R3B 1H4
(204) 885-7570
Emp Here 105
SIC 8732 Commercial nonphysical research

D-U-N-S 20-930-2777   (HQ)
LEVY'S LEATHERS LIMITED
(*Suby of* Levy's Leathers Limited)
190 Disraeli Fwy, Winnipeg, MB, R3B 2Z4
(204) 957-5139
Emp Here 66   *Emp Total* 94
Sales 4,304,681
SIC 5948 Luggage and leather goods stores

D-U-N-S 20-758-4475   (SL)
**LIONS CLUB OF WINNIPEG SENIOR CITI-
ZENS HOME**
LIONS MANOR
320 Sherbrook St, Winnipeg, MB, R3B 2W6
(204) 784-1240
Emp Here 280   *Sales* 13,742,400
SIC 8361 Residential care
VP John Sinclair
Dir Dan Burton

D-U-N-S 25-270-1545   (BR)
LOBLAWS INC
EXTRA FOODS 9063
600 Notre Dame Ave, Winnipeg, MB, R3B 1S4

Emp Here 52
SIC 5141 Groceries, general line

D-U-N-S 20-651-4924   (BR)
MA MAWI-WI-CHI-ITATA CENTRE INC
443 Spence St, Winnipeg, MB, R3B 2R8
(204) 925-0348
Emp Here 230
SIC 8699 Membership organizations, nec

D-U-N-S 20-041-4840   (SL)
**MANITOBA CONSERVATORY OF MUSIC &
ARTS INCORPORATED, THE**
211 Bannatyne Ave Suite 105, Winnipeg, MB,
R3B 3P2
(204) 943-6090
Emp Here 50   *Sales* 3,205,129
SIC 8299 Schools and educational services,
nec

D-U-N-S 20-651-4965   (BR)
MARSH CANADA LIMITED
(*Suby of* Marsh & McLennan Companies, Inc.)
1 Lombard Pl Suite 1420, Winnipeg, MB, R3B
0X3
(204) 982-6526
Emp Here 23
SIC 8748 Business consulting, nec

D-U-N-S 24-235-3035   (BR)
MERCER (CANADA) LIMITED
(*Suby of* Marsh & McLennan Companies, Inc.)
1 Lombard Pl Suite 1410, Winnipeg, MB, R3B
0X5
(204) 947-0055
Emp Here 30
SIC 8999 Services, nec

D-U-N-S 20-026-5841   (SL)
**MOSAIC-NEWCOMER FAMILY RESOURCE
NETWORK INCORPORATED**
397 Carlton St, Winnipeg, MB, R3B 2K9
(204) 774-7311
Emp Here 48   *Sales* 11,779,113
SIC 8399 Social services, nec
 Briar Jamieson
 Karla Ulloa
Dir Ariana Yaftali
Dir Catherine Moss
Ex Dir Val Cavers

D-U-N-S 25-360-1884   (BR)
MOUNTAIN EQUIPMENT CO-OPERATIVE

MOUNTAIN EQUIPMENT CO-OPERATIVE
303 Portage Ave, Winnipeg, MB, R3B 2B4
(204) 943-4202
Emp Here 40
SIC 5941 Sporting goods and bicycle shops

D-U-N-S 24-818-1851   (HQ)
ONLINE ENTERPRISES INC
ONLINE BUSINESS SYSTEMS
(*Suby of* Online Enterprises Inc)
115 Bannatyne Ave Suite 200, Winnipeg, MB,
R3B 0R3
(204) 982-0200
Emp Here 121   *Emp Total* 234
Sales 32,935,320
SIC 7371 Custom computer programming ser-
vices
 Charles K Loewen
VP Scott Sanders
 Lynne Black
 Tim Siemens
Dir Derek Johannson
Dir Paul Damp
Dir Graham Kemp

D-U-N-S 20-010-4594   (HQ)
PARRISH & HEIMBECKER, LIMITED
MINOTERIES P&H, LES
(*Suby of* Parrish & Heimbecker, Limited)
201 Portage Ave Suite 1400, Winnipeg, MB,
R3B 3K6
(204) 956-2030
Emp Here 25   *Emp Total* 1,224
Sales 223,259,742
SIC 6712 Bank holding companies
Ex VP William S. Parrish
Pr Alan R. Heimbecker
VP Robert J. Heimbecker
Sec James W. Astwood
 Kevin L. Klippenstein
Dir Phillip L. Heimbecker
Dir William B. Parrish

D-U-N-S 20-293-4688   (SL)
PHARMACY NORTH INC
CANADAUSPHARMACY
393 Portage Ave Unit 400, Winnipeg, MB, R3B
3H6

Emp Here 29   *Sales* 5,277,042
SIC 5912 Drug stores and proprietary stores
Pr David Chan

D-U-N-S 20-106-7720   (BR)
POSTMEDIA NETWORK INC
POSTMEDIA BUSINESS TECHNOLOGY
300 Carlton St 6th Fl, Winnipeg, MB, R3B 2K6
(204) 926-4600
Emp Here 200
SIC 7299 Miscellaneous personal service

D-U-N-S 25-961-7975   (BR)
PRICEWATERHOUSECOOPERS LLP
1 Lombard Pl Suite 2300, Winnipeg, MB, R3B
0X6
(204) 926-2400
Emp Here 180
SIC 8721 Accounting, auditing, and book-
keeping

D-U-N-S 25-297-3193   (BR)
RBC DOMINION SECURITIES INC
(*Suby of* Royal Bank Of Canada)
1 Lombard Pl Suite 800, Winnipeg, MB, R3B
0Y2
(204) 982-3450
Emp Here 40
SIC 6211 Security brokers and dealers

D-U-N-S 20-165-3545   (BR)
REVERA INC
*PARKVIEW   PLACE-CENTRAL   PARK
LODGES*
440 Edmonton St, Winnipeg, MB, R3B 2M4
(204) 942-5291
Emp Here 300
SIC 8059 Nursing and personal care, nec

D-U-N-S 24-323-0807   (SL)
RICHARDSON CAPITAL LIMITED
1 Lombard Pl Suite 3000, Winnipeg, MB, R3B
0Y1
(204) 953-7969
Emp Here 100   *Sales* 14,592,140
SIC 6211 Security brokers and dealers
Pr Pr Dave Brown

D-U-N-S 20-010-8488   (HQ)
RICHARDSON INTERNATIONAL LIMITED
RICHARDSON PIONEER GRAIN
1 Lombard Pl Suite 2800, Winnipeg, MB, R3B
0X3
(204) 934-5961
Emp Here 400   *Emp Total* 1,500
Sales 812,125,552
SIC 5153 Grain and field beans
Pr Pr Curt Vossen
Hartley T Richardson
Don Solman
Robert G Puchniak
Sandi J. Mielitz
G. David Richardson
Serge Darkazanli
W. James Benidickson
David A. Dyck
Michael D. Walter

D-U-N-S 20-088-3379   (HQ)
RICHARDSON OILSEED LIMITED
1 Lombard Pl Suite 2800, Winnipeg, MB, R3B
0X3
(204) 934-5961
Emp Here 20   *Emp Total* 1,500
Sales 102,509,784
SIC 2079 Edible fats and oils
Pr Pr Curt R. Vossen
Patrick Van Osch

D-U-N-S 20-010-5575   (HQ)
RICHARDSON PIONEER LIMITED
1 Lombard Pl Suite 2700, Winnipeg, MB, R3B
0X8
(204) 934-5961
Emp Here 100   *Emp Total* 1,500
Sales 238,873,332
SIC 5153 Grain and field beans
Hartley T Richardson
Pr Pr Curtis R Vossen
Robert J Miles
James A Fichardson
Nick W Fox
David G Brown
Bruce Sobkow
Robert G Puchniak
Wallace Mccain

D-U-N-S 25-832-2502   (BR)
SGS CANADA INC
153 Lombard Ave Suite 111, Winnipeg, MB,
R3B 0T4
(204) 942-8557
Emp Here 27
SIC 8734 Testing laboratories

D-U-N-S 20-699-7947   (BR)
STANTEC ARCHITECTURE LTD
STANTEC CONSULTING
500 / 311 Portage Ave, Winnipeg, MB, R3B
2B9
(204) 489-5900
Emp Here 300
SIC 8712 Architectural services

D-U-N-S 25-731-1894   (BR)
TD WATERHOUSE CANADA INC
TD WATERHOUSE
(*Suby of* Toronto-Dominion Bank, The)
201 Portage Ave Suite 1670, Winnipeg, MB,
R3B 3K6
(204) 988-2748
Emp Here 20
SIC 6211 Security brokers and dealers

D-U-N-S 20-048-9487   (SL)
TELL US ABOUT US INC
90 Market Ave Unit 4, Winnipeg, MB, R3B 0P3

(204) 453-4757
Emp Here 32   *Sales* 2,480,664
SIC 7372 Prepackaged software

D-U-N-S 24-235-6251   (SL)
TRI-STAR ELECTRIC CO LTD
356 Furby St Unit 203, Winnipeg, MB, R3B
2V5
(204) 788-4006
Emp Here 50   *Sales* 4,377,642
SIC 1731 Electrical work

D-U-N-S 24-171-0045   (HQ)
TUNDRA OIL & GAS LIMITED
1 Lombard Pl Suite 1700, Winnipeg, MB, R3B
0X3
(204) 934-5850
Emp Here 35   *Emp Total* 1,500
Sales 106,011,897
SIC 1382 Oil and gas exploration services
VP Ken Neufeld
Sr VP Jane Mactaggart
Murray Hanstead
James A Richardson
Hartley T. Richardson
Michael E. Guttormson
Graeme G. Phipps
Daniel Maclean
David J. Boone

D-U-N-S 20-833-7535   (SL)
UNITED WAY OF WINNIPEG
580 Main St, Winnipeg, MB, R3B 1C7
(204) 477-5360
Emp Here 50   *Sales* 26,288,375
SIC 8399 Social services, nec
Pr Susan Lewis
Dir Beverly Passey

D-U-N-S 20-059-1332   (BR)
UNIVERSITY OF MANITOBA
11 The Promenade, Winnipeg, MB, R3B 3J1
(204) 474-6614
Emp Here 25
SIC 8221 Colleges and universities

D-U-N-S 20-064-3455   (BR)
UNIVERSITY OF WINNIPEG, THE
*COLLEGIATE AT THE UNIVERSITY OF WIN-
NIPEG, THE*
515 Portage Ave Rm 4w18, Winnipeg, MB,
R3B 2E9
(204) 786-9221
Emp Here 30
SIC 8211 Elementary and secondary schools

D-U-N-S 20-759-1835   (SL)
W. H. ESCOTT COMPANY LIMITED
BROKERAGE SERVICES, DIV OF
95 Alexander Ave, Winnipeg, MB, R3B 2Y8
(204) 942-5127
Emp Here 25   *Sales* 1,732,502
SIC 7389 Business services, nec

D-U-N-S 24-390-8139   (BR)
WSP CANADA GROUP LIMITED
93 Lombard Ave Suite 111, Winnipeg, MB,
R3B 3B1
(204) 943-3178
Emp Here 56
SIC 8711 Engineering services

D-U-N-S 25-070-0481   (SL)
WESTERN OPINION RESEARCH INC
213 Notre Dame Ave Suite 806, Winnipeg,
MB, R3B 1N3
(204) 989-8999
Emp Here 350   *Sales* 66,919,680
SIC 8732 Commercial nonphysical research
Pr Brian Edward Owen

D-U-N-S 24-309-3593   (SL)
**WINNIPEG CIVICS EMPLOYEES' BENE-
FITS PROGRAM, THE**
185 King St, Winnipeg, MB, R3B 1J1
(204) 986-2522
Emp Here 32   *Sales* 5,526,400
SIC 6371 Pension, health, and welfare funds
Pr Glenda Willis

D-U-N-S 25-327-1142   (SL)
**WINNIPEG GOLDEYES BASEBALL CLUB
INC**
1 Portage Ave E, Winnipeg, MB, R3B 3N3
(204) 982-2273
Emp Here 20   *Sales* 6,380,400
SIC 7941 Sports clubs, managers, and pro-
moters
Pr Pr Sam Katz

D-U-N-S 20-179-7953   (BR)
**WINNIPEG PANTS & SPORTSWEAR MFG.
LTD**
RICHLU MANUFACTURING
90 Annabella St, Winnipeg, MB, R3B 3K7
(204) 975-5011
Emp Here 20
SIC 4225 General warehousing and storage

D-U-N-S 24-883-4269   (BR)
WINNIPEG SCHOOL DIVISION
ARGYLE ALTERNATIVE HIGH SCHOOL
30 Argyle St, Winnipeg, MB, R3B 0H4
(204) 942-4326
Emp Here 25
SIC 8211 Elementary and secondary schools

D-U-N-S 24-038-0324   (BR)
WINNIPEG SCHOOL DIVISION
*SISTER MACNAMARA ELEMENTARY
SCHOOL*
460 Sargent Ave, Winnipeg, MB, R3B 1V5
(204) 942-6965
Emp Here 60
SIC 8211 Elementary and secondary schools

D-U-N-S 20-280-6824   (BR)
**IQMETRIX SOFTWARE DEVELOPMENT
CORP**
IQMETRIX
(*Suby of* iQmetrix Software Development
Corp)
311 Portage Ave Suite 200, Winnipeg, MB,
R3B 2B9
(204) 452-5648
Emp Here 55
SIC 7371 Custom computer programming ser-
vices

Winnipeg, MB R3C

D-U-N-S 20-613-5527   (SL)
1379025 ONTARIO LIMITED
*BEST WESTERN CHARTERHOUSE HO-
TELS*
330 York Ave Suite 508, Winnipeg, MB, R3C
0N9
(204) 942-0101
Emp Here 75   *Sales* 3,283,232
SIC 7011 Hotels and motels

D-U-N-S 20-809-3109   (SL)
2533481 MANITOBA LTD
LEVENE TADMAN GUTKIN & GOLUB
330 St Mary Ave Suite 700, Winnipeg, MB,
R3C 3Z5
(204) 957-0520
Emp Here 50   *Sales* 4,304,681
SIC 8111 Legal services

D-U-N-S 20-081-3322   (BR)
3627730 CANADA INC
FREEMAN AUDIO VISUAL
375 York Av Suite 210, Winnipeg, MB, R3C
3J3
(204) 775-6198
Emp Here 20
SIC 7812 Motion picture and video production

D-U-N-S 24-312-5908   (SL)
4372752 MANITOBA LTD
AMICI RESTAURANT
326 Broadway Suite 400, Winnipeg, MB, R3C
0S5

(204) 943-4997
Emp Here 60   *Sales* 1,824,018
SIC 5812 Eating places

D-U-N-S 25-097-3849   (BR)
**ADESA AUCTIONS CANADA CORPORA-
TION**
ADESA WINNIPEG
Hwy 7 N, Winnipeg, MB, R3C 2E6
(204) 697-4400
Emp Here 200
SIC 5012 Automobiles and other motor vehi-
cles

D-U-N-S 24-511-8245   (BR)
ACKLANDS - GRAINGER INC
AGI
(*Suby of* W.W. Grainger, Inc.)
10 Fort St Suite 300, Winnipeg, MB, R3C 1C4
(204) 956-0880
Emp Here 60
SIC 5085 Industrial supplies

D-U-N-S 25-127-0542   (BR)
**ADDICTIONS FOUNDATION OF MANI-
TOBA, THE**
YOUTH COMMUNITY-BASED SERVICES
200 Osborne St N, Winnipeg, MB, R3C 1V4
(204) 944-6235
Emp Here 31
SIC 8093 Specialty outpatient clinics, nec

D-U-N-S 24-715-8947   (SL)
AGRICULTURE AND AGRIFOOD CANADA
AAFC
Po Box 6100 Stn Main, Winnipeg, MB, R3C
4N3

Emp Here 450   *Sales* 107,976,000
SIC 4899 Communication services, nec
Derek Belinksy

D-U-N-S 20-364-4716   (SL)
ARTIS US HOLDINGS II GP, INC
ARTIS REIT
360 Main St Suite 300, Winnipeg, MB, R3C
3Z3
(204) 947-1250
Emp Here 120   *Sales* 4,815,406
SIC 6519 Real property lessors, nec

D-U-N-S 20-364-4729   (SL)
ARTIS US HOLDINGS II, LLC
ARTIS REIT
360 Main Street Suite 300, Winnipeg, MB,
R3C 3Z3
(204) 494-1250
Emp Here 180   *Sales* 5,253,170
SIC 6519 Real property lessors, nec

D-U-N-S 25-318-1093   (BR)
AVISCAR INC
AVIS
(*Suby of* Avis Budget Group, Inc.)
234 York Ave, Winnipeg, MB, R3C 0N5
(204) 989-7521
Emp Here 20
SIC 7514 Passenger car rental

D-U-N-S 20-648-7691   (BR)
BDO CANADA LLP
WINNIPEG ACCOUNTING
200 Graham Ave Suite 700, Winnipeg, MB,
R3C 4L5
(204) 956-7200
Emp Here 100
SIC 8721 Accounting, auditing, and book-
keeping

D-U-N-S 25-230-2047   (BR)
BMO NESBITT BURNS INC
360 Main St Suite 1400, Winnipeg, MB, R3C
3Z3
(204) 949-2500
Emp Here 140
SIC 6211 Security brokers and dealers

D-U-N-S 25-295-8681   (BR)
BANK OF NOVA SCOTIA, THE

SCOTIABANK
200 Portage Ave, Winnipeg, MB, R3C 2R7
(204) 985-3011
Emp Here 150
SIC 6021 National commercial banks

D-U-N-S 20-700-0352 (BR)
BANQUE DE DEVELOPPEMENT DU CANADA
BDC
155 Carlton St Suite 1100, Winnipeg, MB, R3C 3H8
(204) 983-7900
Emp Here 40
SIC 6141 Personal credit institutions

D-U-N-S 25-678-4091 (BR)
BELL MEDIA INC
CTV WINNIPEG
345 Graham Ave Suite 400, Winnipeg, MB, R3C 5S6
(204) 788-3300
Emp Here 95
SIC 4833 Television broadcasting stations

D-U-N-S 20-023-5468 (BR)
BOARD OF GOVERNOR'S OF RED RIVER COLLEGE, THE
LANGUAGE TRAINING CENTRE
123 Main St Suite 300, Winnipeg, MB, R3C 1A3
(204) 945-6151
Emp Here 45
SIC 8299 Schools and educational services, nec

D-U-N-S 24-571-2971 (BR)
BRINK'S CANADA LIMITED
(Suby of The Brink's Company)
222 York Ave, Winnipeg, MB, R3C 0N5
(204) 985-9400
Emp Here 25
SIC 7381 Detective and armored car services

D-U-N-S 20-177-3269 (BR)
CBRE LIMITED
CHARTIER AND ASSOCIATES
570 Portage Ave Fl 2, Winnipeg, MB, R3C 0G4
(204) 943-5700
Emp Here 20
SIC 6531 Real estate agents and managers

D-U-N-S 24-235-3837 (BR)
CANADIAN CANCER SOCIETY
CANADIAN CANCER SOCIETY MANITOBA DIVISION
193 Sherbrook St Suite 1, Winnipeg, MB, R3C 2B7
(204) 774-7483
Emp Here 30
SIC 8399 Social services, nec

D-U-N-S 25-305-9968 (BR)
CANADIAN DIABETES ASSOCIATION
CDA-MANITOBA
310 Broadway Unit 200, Winnipeg, MB, R3C 0S6
(204) 925-3800
Emp Here 40
SIC 8699 Membership organizations, nec

D-U-N-S 25-951-0782 (BR)
CANADIAN IMPERIAL BANK OF COMMERCE
CIBC
333 St Mary Ave Suite 87, Winnipeg, MB, R3C 4A5
(204) 944-5057
Emp Here 20
SIC 6021 National commercial banks

D-U-N-S 20-778-8741 (BR)
CANADIAN IMPERIAL BANK OF COMMERCE
CIBC
375 Main St, Winnipeg, MB, R3C 2P3
(204) 944-6963
Emp Here 30

SIC 6021 National commercial banks

D-U-N-S 24-381-1630 (SL)
CANADIAN MUSEUM FOR HUMAN RIGHTS
85 Israel Asper Way, Winnipeg, MB, R3C 0L5
(204) 289-2000
Emp Here 50 Sales 1,531,148
SIC 8412 Museums and art galleries

D-U-N-S 20-194-4779 (BR)
CANADIAN UNION OF PUBLIC EMPLOYEES
CUPE MANITOBA REGIONAL OFFICE
275 Broadway Suite 703, Winnipeg, MB, R3C 4M6
(204) 942-0343
Emp Here 30
SIC 8631 Labor organizations

D-U-N-S 25-961-8510 (BR)
CANADIAN UNION OF PUBLIC EMPLOYEES
CUPE LOCAL 2153
275 Broadway Suite 403b, Winnipeg, MB, R3C 4M6
(204) 942-6524
Emp Here 400
SIC 8631 Labor organizations

D-U-N-S 25-316-0212 (BR)
CANADIAN WESTERN BANK
230 Portage Ave, Winnipeg, MB, R3C 0B1
(204) 956-4669
Emp Here 20
SIC 6021 National commercial banks

D-U-N-S 24-338-8357 (BR)
CANCERCARE MANITOBA
MANITOBA BREAST SCREENING PROGRAM
25 Sherbrook St Unit 5, Winnipeg, MB, R3C 2B1
(204) 788-8000
Emp Here 20
SIC 8099 Health and allied services, nec

D-U-N-S 24-326-3741 (BR)
CENGEA SOLUTIONS INC
(Suby of Trimble Inc.)
330 St Mary Ave Suite 1120, Winnipeg, MB, R3C 3Z5
(204) 957-7566
Emp Here 30
SIC 7372 Prepackaged software

D-U-N-S 25-532-9369 (HQ)
CERIDIAN CANADA LTD
125 Garry St, Winnipeg, MB, R3C 3P2
(204) 947-9400
Emp Here 350 Emp Total 9,587
Sales 109,441,050
SIC 7361 Employment agencies
Pr David Mackay
COO Paul Elliott
Ex VP John Cardella
Ex VP Cande Dandele
Ex VP Scott Kitching
Ex VP Sandy Lovell
CFO Suzy Hester

D-U-N-S 25-368-9475 (BR)
CITY OF WINNIPEG, THE
WINNIPEG CENTENNIAL LIBRARY
(Suby of City of Winnipeg, The)
251 Donald St, Winnipeg, MB, R3C 3P5
(204) 986-6450
Emp Here 50
SIC 8231 Libraries

D-U-N-S 20-580-5075 (BR)
COMPAGNIE DES CHEMINS DE FER NATIONAUX DU CANADA
234 Donald St Suite 601, Winnipeg, MB, R3C 1M8
(204) 934-7312
Emp Here 20
SIC 4011 Railroads, line-haul operating

D-U-N-S 20-613-8554 (HQ)

CONTINENTAL TRAVEL BUREAU LTD
(Suby of Continental Travel Bureau Ltd)
222 Osborne St N, Winnipeg, MB, R3C 1V4
(204) 989-8575
Emp Here 26 Emp Total 33
Sales 10,601,280
SIC 4724 Travel agencies
Pr Pr Daryl Silver
Treas Jocelyn Silver

D-U-N-S 20-833-7493 (SL)
CONVENTION CENTRE CORPORATION, THE
WINNIPEG CONVENTION CENTRE
375 York Ave Suite 243, Winnipeg, MB, R3C 3J3
(204) 956-1720
Emp Here 120 Sales 7,632,865
SIC 7389 Business services, nec
Pr Klaus Lahr
Ch Bd Zivan Saper

D-U-N-S 25-329-2577 (BR)
COUGHLIN & ASSOCIATES LTD
175 Hargrave St Suite 100, Winnipeg, MB, R3C 3R8
(204) 942-4438
Emp Here 27
SIC 6411 Insurance agents, brokers, and service

D-U-N-S 24-233-1940 (BR)
DLF PICKSEED CANADA INC
1884 Brookside Blvd, Winnipeg, MB, R3C 2E6
(204) 633-0088
Emp Here 25
SIC 5191 Farm supplies

D-U-N-S 25-386-1306 (SL)
DARCOL INTERNATIONAL INC
1916 Brookside Blvd, Winnipeg, MB, R3C 2E6
(204) 989-5050
Emp Here 44 Sales 7,202,950
SIC 4213 Trucking, except local
Pr Pr Paul Geiger

D-U-N-S 20-936-5944 (BR)
DELTA HOTELS LIMITED
BLAZE BISTRO & LOUNGE
350 St Mary Ave, Winnipeg, MB, R3C 3J2
(204) 944-7259
Emp Here 20
SIC 8741 Management services

D-U-N-S 20-188-2383 (BR)
DELTA HOTELS LIMITED
DELTA WINNIPEG
350 St Mary Ave, Winnipeg, MB, R3C 3J2
(204) 944-7278
Emp Here 250
SIC 7011 Hotels and motels

D-U-N-S 20-570-1881 (HQ)
DOMO GASOLINE CORPORATION LTD
270 Fort St, Winnipeg, MB, R3C 1E5
(204) 943-5920
Emp Here 25 Emp Total 500
Sales 84,338,446
SIC 5541 Gasoline service stations
Douglas C. Everette
Pr Bruce Chwartacki
Dir Richard Bracken
Dir Sarah Everette
Ashleigh Everette

D-U-N-S 24-520-6888 (SL)
DOWNTOWN WATCH
DOWNTOWN WINNIPEG BIZ
426 Portage Ave Suite 101, Winnipeg, MB, R3C 0C9
(204) 958-4620
Emp Here 49 Sales 5,034,288
SIC 8611 Business associations
Dir Stefano Grande

D-U-N-S 24-098-4562 (SL)
DUNHILL MANAGEMENT GROUP LTD, THE
240 Graham Ave Suite 724, Winnipeg, MB,

R3C 0J7
(204) 942-0500
Emp Here 50 Sales 4,304,681
SIC 8111 Legal services

D-U-N-S 24-126-4535 (BR)
ESIT CANADA ENTERPRISE SERVICES CO
ESIT CANADA ENTERPRISE SERVICES CO
(Suby of Dxc Technology Company)
200 Graham Ave Suite 810, Winnipeg, MB, R3C 4L5
(204) 942-4725
Emp Here 30
SIC 5734 Computer and software stores

D-U-N-S 25-168-5830 (BR)
EARL'S RESTAURANTS LTD
EARL'S
(Suby of Earl's Restaurants Ltd)
191 Main St, Winnipeg, MB, R3C 1A7
(204) 989-0103
Emp Here 175
SIC 5812 Eating places

D-U-N-S 25-098-9944 (HQ)
EPIC INFORMATION SOLUTIONS INC
(Suby of Epic Information Solutions Inc)
167 Sherbrook St, Winnipeg, MB, R3C 2B7
(204) 453-2300
Emp Here 49 Emp Total 50
Sales 8,857,893
SIC 5045 Computers, peripherals, and software
Pr Pr David Reid
VP Opers Rob Zacharias
VP VP Arnie Fedorchuk

D-U-N-S 25-297-1551 (BR)
ERNST & YOUNG INC
360 Main St Suite 2700, Winnipeg, MB, R3C 4G9
(204) 947-6519
Emp Here 50
SIC 8721 Accounting, auditing, and bookkeeping

D-U-N-S 24-113-6845 (HQ)
FEDERATED INSURANCE COMPANY OF CANADA
255 Commerce Drive, Winnipeg, MB, R3C 3C9
(204) 786-6431
Emp Here 130 Emp Total 23,576
Sales 146,916,170
SIC 6331 Fire, marine, and casualty insurance
Pr Wayne Connely
Acct Mgr Kenneth Tresoor
VP Fin Rick Hurlin

D-U-N-S 20-122-6896 (BR)
G. J. BELL ENTERPISES LTD
BELL TRAILER SALES
1940 Brookside Blvd, Winnipeg, MB, R3C 2E6
(204) 987-8890
Emp Here 30
SIC 5012 Automobiles and other motor vehicles

D-U-N-S 20-845-3931 (BR)
GLACIER MEDIA INC
FARM BUSINESS COMMUNICATION
Gd, Winnipeg, MB, R3C 3K7
(204) 944-5767
Emp Here 50
SIC 2711 Newspapers

D-U-N-S 20-844-9343 (BR)
GREAT-WEST LIFE ASSURANCE COMPANY, THE
60 Osborne St N, Winnipeg, MB, R3C 1V3
(204) 926-5394
Emp Here 3,000
SIC 6311 Life insurance

D-U-N-S 20-570-0313 (HQ)
GREAT-WEST LIFE ASSURANCE COMPANY, THE
100 Osborne St N Suite 4c, Winnipeg, MB,

R3C 1V3
(204) 946-1190
Emp Here 2,775   *Emp Total* 31,126
Sales 20,289,481,800
SIC 6324 Hospital and medical service plans
R. Jeffrey Orr
Pr Pr Paul A. Mahon
  Laurie E. Speers
Dir Rima Qureshi
Dir Gary A. Doer
Dir James M. Singh
Dir Claude Genereux
Dir Susan J. Mcarthur
Dir Siim Vanaselja
Dir Paul Desmarais Iii

D-U-N-S 24-819-2577   (BR)
HSBC BANK CANADA
330 St Mary Ave Suite 110, Winnipeg, MB,
R3C 3Z5
(204) 956-1632
Emp Here 20
SIC 6021 National commercial banks

D-U-N-S 20-944-9859   (BR)
HATCH LTD
ACRES MANITOBA
500 Portage Ave Suite 600, Winnipeg, MB,
R3C 3Y8
(204) 786-8751
Emp Here 90
SIC 8711 Engineering services

D-U-N-S 25-319-6257   (BR)
HOGG ROBINSON CANADA INC
BTI CANADA
(*Suby of* HOGG ROBINSON GROUP PLC)
155 Carlton St Suite 1405, Winnipeg, MB,
R3C 3H8
(204) 989-0044
Emp Here 56
SIC 4724 Travel agencies

D-U-N-S 24-572-6278   (BR)
HUDSON'S BAY COMPANY
BAY, THE
450 Portage Ave, Winnipeg, MB, R3C 0E7
(204) 783-2112
Emp Here 400
SIC 5311 Department stores

D-U-N-S 20-757-3262   (HQ)
INLAND AUDIO VISUAL LIMITED
INLAND AV
(*Suby of* Inland Audio Visual Limited)
422 Lucas Ave, Winnipeg, MB, R3C 2E6
(204) 786-6521
Emp Here 33   *Emp Total* 100
Sales 8,755,284
SIC 1731 Electrical work
Pr Pr Kim Edward Werbowski
  James Alexander Werbowski

D-U-N-S 20-758-7825   (BR)
INTACT INSURANCE COMPANY
INTACT INSURANCE
386 Broadway Suite 805, Winnipeg, MB, R3C
3R6
(204) 942-8402
Emp Here 20
SIC 6331 Fire, marine, and casualty insurance

D-U-N-S 24-130-6088   (SL)
INVESTORS PREMIUM MONEY MARKET FUND
447 Portage Ave, Winnipeg, MB, R3C 3B6
(204) 957-7383
Emp Here 800   *Sales* 327,966,720
SIC 6722 Management investment, open-end
Pr Murray Taylor

D-U-N-S 20-613-7267   (SL)
JUNIOR'S DRIVE-IN LTD.
558 Portage Ave, Winnipeg, MB, R3C 0G3
(204) 774-6370
Emp Here 50   *Sales* 1,819,127
SIC 5812 Eating places

D-U-N-S 25-116-0289   (HQ)
KEE WEST AUTO CARRIERS INC
(*Suby of* Kee West Auto Carriers Inc)
12-15-2 Epm, Winnipeg, MB, R3C 2E6
(204) 774-2937
Emp Here 105   *Emp Total* 105
Sales 13,351,808
SIC 4213 Trucking, except local
Ken Konrad
Pr Pr Melanie Dickin

D-U-N-S 25-219-3941   (BR)
KEG RESTAURANTS LTD
KEG STEAKHOUSE & BAR, THE
115 Garry St, Winnipeg, MB, R3C 1G5
(204) 942-7619
Emp Here 140
SIC 5812 Eating places

D-U-N-S 25-095-2462   (SL)
KENMAR FOOD SERVICES LTD
PONY CORRAL RESTAURANT & BAR
444 St Mary Ave Suite 135, Winnipeg, MB,
R3C 3T1
(204) 942-4414
Emp Here 250   *Sales* 10,449,350
SIC 5812 Eating places
Pr Pr Peter Ginakes

D-U-N-S 25-329-9713   (HQ)
LAKEVIEW MANAGEMENT INC
FOUR POINTS SHERATON INTERNATIONAL
(*Suby of* Lakeview Management Inc)
185 Carlton St Suite 600, Winnipeg, MB, R3C
3J1
(204) 947-1161
Emp Here 40   *Emp Total* 300
Sales 16,961,922
SIC 7011 Hotels and motels
Pr Pr Keith Levit
  Yetta Levit

D-U-N-S 24-966-5357   (HQ)
LEGAL AID SERVICES SOCIETY OF MANITOBA
LEGALI AID MANITOBA
294 Portage Ave Unit 402, Winnipeg, MB, R3C
0B9
(204) 985-8500
Emp Here 30   *Emp Total* 20,000
Sales 28,206,965
SIC 8111 Legal services
Ch Bd Mario Santos
Dir Gil Clifford
  Robin Dwarka

D-U-N-S 20-024-0427   (BR)
LEGAL AID SERVICES SOCIETY OF MANITOBA
CRIMINAL LAW OFFICE
514 St Mary Ave, Winnipeg, MB, R3C 0N6
(204) 985-8570
Emp Here 28
SIC 8111 Legal services

D-U-N-S 25-659-9077   (BR)
LIONS CLUB OF WINNIPEG PLACE FOR SENIOR CITIZENS INC
LIONS PLACE
610 Portage Ave Suite 1214, Winnipeg, MB,
R3C 0G5
(204) 784-1210
Emp Here 360
SIC 8361 Residential care

D-U-N-S 20-853-2924   (BR)
MANITOBA LIQUOR AND LOTTERIES CORPORATION
LIQUOR MART
333 St Mary Ave, Winnipeg, MB, R3C 4A5
(204) 987-4003
Emp Here 20
SIC 5921 Liquor stores

D-U-N-S 20-838-1103   (HQ)
MANITOBA PUBLIC INSURANCE CORPORATION, THE

234 Donald St Suite 912, Winnipeg, MB, R3C
4A4
(204) 985-7000
Emp Here 700   *Emp Total* 20,000
Sales 337,727,050
SIC 8743 Public relations services
Pr Marilyn Mclaren
  Jake Janzen
  Kerry Bittner
Sec Kathy Kalinowsky
  Heather Reichert

D-U-N-S 25-318-1549   (BR)
MCDONALD'S RESTAURANTS OF CANADA LIMITED
MCDONALD'S #8372
(*Suby of* McDonald's Corporation)
333 St Mary Ave Suite 102, Winnipeg, MB,
R3C 4A5
(204) 949-6038
Emp Here 60
SIC 5812 Eating places

D-U-N-S 25-011-0939   (BR)
MORGUARD INVESTMENTS LIMITED
363 Broadway Suite 1400, Winnipeg, MB,
R3C 3N9
(204) 632-9500
Emp Here 24
SIC 6531 Real estate agents and managers

D-U-N-S 24-345-1965   (BR)
NRG RESEARCH GROUP INC
360 Main St Suite 1910, Winnipeg, MB, R3C
3Z3
(204) 429-8999
Emp Here 200
SIC 8732 Commercial nonphysical research

D-U-N-S 24-336-6643   (HQ)
PAYNE TRANSPORTATION LP
435 Lucas Ave, Winnipeg, MB, R3C 2E6
(204) 953-1400
Emp Here 50   *Emp Total* 5,515
Sales 7,103,258
SIC 4213 Trucking, except local
Pr Tom Payne Jr

D-U-N-S 24-126-3479   (SL)
PEOPLE FIRST HR SERVICES LTD
360 Main St Unit 1800, Winnipeg, MB, R3C
3Z3
(204) 940-3900
Emp Here 50   *Sales* 5,024,000
SIC 7361 Employment agencies
Pr Pr John Mcferran

D-U-N-S 24-538-9379   (SL)
PLACE LOUIS RIEL ALL-SUITE HOTEL
190 Smith St Suite 119, Winnipeg, MB, R3C
1J8
(204) 947-6961
Emp Here 74   *Sales* 3,210,271
SIC 7011 Hotels and motels

D-U-N-S 25-967-6849   (SL)
PLAYERS COURSE LTD, THE
2695 Inkster Blvd, Winnipeg, MB, R3C 2E6
(204) 697-4976
Emp Here 35   *Sales* 1,532,175
SIC 7992 Public golf courses

D-U-N-S 20-650-7860   (BR)
PRISZM LP
PIZZA HUT
141 Donald St, Winnipeg, MB, R3C 1M1

Emp Here 20
SIC 5812 Eating places

D-U-N-S 20-838-4537   (SL)
RIX LTD
TRAINOR LABORATORY
233 Kennedy St Suite 306, Winnipeg, MB,
R3C 0L7
(204) 944-9707
Emp Here 50   *Sales* 4,085,799
SIC 8071 Medical laboratories

D-U-N-S 24-654-1275   (BR)
ROGERS MEDIA INC
CITYTV
(*Suby of* Rogers Communications Inc)
8 Forks Market Rd, Winnipeg, MB, R3C 4Y3
(204) 947-9613
Emp Here 50
SIC 4833 Television broadcasting stations

D-U-N-S 24-915-2679   (BR)
ROMA RIBS LTD
TONY ROMA'S A PLACE FOR RIBS
(*Suby of* Roma Ribs Ltd)
330 St Mary Ave Suite 620, Winnipeg, MB,
R3C 3Z5
(204) 944-0792
Emp Here 50
SIC 5812 Eating places

D-U-N-S 20-946-8685   (BR)
ROYAL BANK OF CANADA
ROYAL BANK FINANCIAL GROUP
(*Suby of* Royal Bank Of Canada)
220 Portage Ave Unit 900, Winnipeg, MB, R3C
0A5
(204) 988-4000
Emp Here 60
SIC 6021 National commercial banks

D-U-N-S 25-414-0494   (BR)
SCOTIA CAPITAL INC
SCOTIA MCLEOD
200 Portage Ave Suite 501, Winnipeg, MB,
R3C 3X2
(204) 944-0025
Emp Here 40
SIC 6211 Security brokers and dealers

D-U-N-S 20-011-1748   (SL)
SHAW LABORATORIES LTD
(*Suby of* Western Dental Industries Ltd)
388 Portage Ave Suite 606, Winnipeg, MB,
R3C 0C8
(204) 943-8883
Emp Here 40   *Sales* 2,334,742
SIC 8072 Dental laboratories

D-U-N-S 25-191-0758   (BR)
SIERRA SYSTEMS GROUP INC
444 St Mary Ave Suite 1050, Winnipeg, MB,
R3C 3T1
(204) 942-2575
Emp Here 60
SIC 8741 Management services

D-U-N-S 24-848-9267   (BR)
STANTEC CONSULTING LTD
386 Broadway Suite 603, Winnipeg, MB, R3C
3R6

Emp Here 45
SIC 8711 Engineering services

D-U-N-S 24-522-0665   (BR)
STANTEC INC
386 Broadway Suite 603, Winnipeg, MB, R3C
3R6

Emp Here 28
SIC 8711 Engineering services

D-U-N-S 20-913-3417   (BR)
SYMCOR INC
195 Fort St, Winnipeg, MB, R3C 3V1
(204) 924-5819
Emp Here 100
SIC 7374 Data processing and preparation

D-U-N-S 20-048-5659   (BR)
T & T TRUCKING LTD
(*Suby of* 601861 Saskatchewan Ltd)
40 Bryan Bay, Winnipeg, MB, R3C 2E6
(204) 987-1200
Emp Here 30
SIC 4213 Trucking, except local

D-U-N-S 24-655-5502   (SL)
TAPPER CUDDY LLP
330 St Mary Ave Suite 1000, Winnipeg, MB,

R3C 3Z5
(204) 944-8777
Emp Here 50   *Sales* 4,304,681
SIC 8111 Legal services

D-U-N-S 24-038-9846   (BR)
TEN TEN SINCLAIR HOUSING INC
FOKUS HOUSING
90 Garry St Suite 806, Winnipeg, MB, R3C
4J4
(204) 943-1073
Emp Here 35
SIC 8361 Residential care

D-U-N-S 25-364-7747   (HQ)
THERMO KING OF MID CANADA CORP
450 Lucas Ave, Winnipeg, MB, R3C 2E6
(204) 694-1368
Emp Here 23   *Emp Total* 28
Sales 12,265,638
SIC 4213 Trucking, except local
Pr Pr Richard Springer
 William Springer

D-U-N-S 20-008-1693   (BR)
**TYCO INTEGRATED FIRE & SECURITY
CANADA, INC**
A D T SECURITY SERVICES
(*Suby of* Johnson Controls, Inc.)
303 Balmoral St, Winnipeg, MB, R3C 4A8
(204) 949-1404
Emp Here 30
SIC 5065 Electronic parts and equipment, nec

D-U-N-S 24-029-6975   (BR)
UNION SECURITIES LTD
360 Main St Suite 1520, Winnipeg, R3C
3Z3
(204) 982-0012
Emp Here 22
SIC 6211 Security brokers and dealers

D-U-N-S 20-035-6546   (BR)
UNIVERSITY OF WINNIPEG, THE
MENNO SIMONS COLLEGE
520 Portage Ave Suite 210, Winnipeg, MB,
R3C 0G2
(204) 953-3855
Emp Here 20
SIC 8221 Colleges and universities

D-U-N-S 25-115-1981   (BR)
UNIVERSITY OF WINNIPEG, THE
CONTINUING EDUCATION, DIVISION OF
460 Portage Ave, Winnipeg, MB, R3C 0E8
(204) 982-6633
Emp Here 23
SIC 8221 Colleges and universities

D-U-N-S 25-668-1537   (BR)
**VANCOUVER CAREER COLLEGE (BURN-
ABY) INC**
CDI COLLEGE
(*Suby of* Chung Family Holdings Inc)
280 Main St, Winnipeg, MB, R3C 1A9
(204) 942-1773
Emp Here 40
SIC 8211 Elementary and secondary schools

D-U-N-S 20-981-7407   (BR)
**VICTORIAN ORDER OF NURSES FOR
CANADA**
VON MANITOBA DISTRICT
425 St Mary Ave, Winnipeg, MB, R3C 0N2
(204) 775-1693
Emp Here 65
SIC 8082 Home health care services

D-U-N-S 25-892-3333   (BR)
W.O.W. HOSPITALITY CONCEPTS INC
MUDDY WATER SMOKE HOUSE
(*Suby of* W.O.W. Hospitality Concepts Inc)
15 Forks Market Rd, Winnipeg, MB, R3C 0A2
(204) 947-6653
Emp Here 45
SIC 5812 Eating places

D-U-N-S 24-655-4786   (HQ)

**WAWANESA LIFE INSURANCE COMPANY,
THE**
(*Suby of* Wawanesa Mutual Insurance Com-
pany, The)
200 Main St Suite 400, Winnipeg, MB, R3C
1A8
(204) 985-3940
Emp Here 78   *Emp Total* 1,688
Sales 163,022,917
SIC 6311 Life insurance
Pr Jeff Goy
Fin Ex Patricia Horncastle

D-U-N-S 24-098-4653   (BR)
**WAWANESA MUTUAL INSURANCE COM-
PANY, THE**
(*Suby of* Wawanesa Mutual Insurance Com-
pany, The)
200 Main St Suite 700, Winnipeg, MB, R3C
1A8
(204) 985-3811
Emp Here 44
SIC 6331 Fire, marine, and casualty insurance

D-U-N-S 20-760-1832   (HQ)
**WAWANESA MUTUAL INSURANCE COM-
PANY, THE**
(*Suby of* Wawanesa Mutual Insurance Com-
pany, The)
191 Broadway Suite 100, Winnipeg, MB, R3C
3P1
(204) 985-3811
Emp Here 217   *Emp Total* 1,688
Sales 806,653,499
SIC 6331 Fire, marine, and casualty insurance

D-U-N-S 20-832-3980   (SL)
WEIGHT WATCHERS OF MANITOBA LTD
274 Smith St Suite 101, Winnipeg, MB, R3C
1K1
(204) 987-7546
Emp Here 100   *Sales* 5,579,750
SIC 7991 Physical fitness facilities
Pr Pr Sheldon Reich
 Joseph J Wilder

D-U-N-S 24-616-6867   (BR)
WESTCORP PROPERTIES INC
PLACE LOUIS RIEL ALL SUITE HOTEL
(*Suby of* Westcorp Properties Inc)
190 Smith St, Winnipeg, MB, R3C 1J8
(204) 947-6961
Emp Here 49
SIC 7011 Hotels and motels

D-U-N-S 24-803-1809   (HQ)
WINNIPEG PUBLIC LIBRARY INC
WINNIPEG MILLENNIUM LIBRARY
(*Suby of* Winnipeg Public Library Inc)
251 Donald St, Winnipeg, MB, R3C 3P5
(204) 986-6462
Emp Here 100   *Emp Total* 400
Sales 23,840,924
SIC 8231 Libraries
Mgr Rick Walker

D-U-N-S 24-228-0316   (BR)
**WINNIPEG REGIONAL HEALTH AUTHOR-
ITY, THE**
WRHA PROJECT MANAGEMENT OFFICE
155 Carlton St Suite 1800, Winnipeg, MB,
R3C 3H8
(204) 926-7179
Emp Here 30
SIC 8741 Management services

Winnipeg, MB R3E

D-U-N-S 20-165-3404   (BR)
ARAMARK CANADA LTD.
727 Mcdermot Ave, Winnipeg, MB, R3E 3P5
(204) 779-1365
Emp Here 20
SIC 5431 Fruit and vegetable markets

D-U-N-S 20-007-6263   (BR)
AIR LIQUIDE CANADA INC
58 Weston St, Winnipeg, MB, R3E 3H7
(204) 989-9353
Emp Here 40
SIC 2813 Industrial gases

D-U-N-S 20-838-8470   (BR)
BLACK & MCDONALD LIMITED
401 Weston St Suite A, Winnipeg, MB, R3E
3H4
(204) 786-5776
Emp Here 90
SIC 1711 Plumbing, heating, air-conditioning

D-U-N-S 24-851-2733   (SL)
BRESARA GROUP LTD
1049 Pacific Ave, Winnipeg, MB, R3E 1G5
(204) 786-8853
Emp Here 60   *Sales* 1,094,411
SIC 7349 Building maintenance services, nec

D-U-N-S 20-587-2646   (BR)
CANADIAN PACIFIC RAILWAY COMPANY
CPR
901 Logan Ave, Winnipeg, MB, R3E 1N7
(204) 946-3401
Emp Here 20
SIC 4011 Railroads, line-haul operating

D-U-N-S 20-758-0960   (HQ)
CANCERCARE MANITOBA
675 Mcdermot Ave Suite 1160, Winnipeg, MB,
R3E 0V9
(204) 787-4143
Emp Here 647   *Emp Total* 20,000
Sales 133,315,996
SIC 8069 Specialty hospitals, except psychi-
atric
Pr Dhali Dhaliwal
Ch Bd Arnold Naimark
V Ch Bd Greg Tallon
Sec Alyson Kennedy
Treas Barb Lillie

D-U-N-S 20-011-9147   (BR)
CERTAINTEED GYPSUM CANADA, INC
1200 Empress St, Winnipeg, MB, R3E 3B4
(204) 786-3424
Emp Here 50
SIC 3275 Gypsum products

D-U-N-S 24-883-2883   (BR)
CITY OF WINNIPEG, THE
WATER & SOLID WASTE
(*Suby of* City of Winnipeg, The)
1199 Pacific Ave Suite 109, Winnipeg, MB,
R3E 3S8
(204) 986-3623
Emp Here 170
SIC 4953 Refuse systems

D-U-N-S 20-023-3216   (BR)
CITY OF WINNIPEG, THE
PUBLIC WORKS
(*Suby of* City of Winnipeg, The)
1155 Pacific Ave Suite 102, Winnipeg, MB,
R3E 3P1
(204) 986-5263
Emp Here 100
SIC 7389 Business services, nec

D-U-N-S 20-517-6212   (BR)
CITY OF WINNIPEG, THE
*WINNEPEG FLEET MANAGEMENT
AGENCY*
(*Suby of* City of Winnipeg, The)
215 Tecumseh St, Winnipeg, MB, R3E 3S4

Emp Here 24
SIC 7699 Repair services, nec

D-U-N-S 20-570-0003   (BR)
CITY OF WINNIPEG, THE
ANIMAL SERVICES
(*Suby of* City of Winnipeg, The)
1057 Logan Ave, Winnipeg, MB, R3E 3N8

(204) 986-2155
Emp Here 20
SIC 8699 Membership organizations, nec

D-U-N-S 20-570-0235   (BR)
CITY OF WINNIPEG, THE
*WINNIPEG SLEET MANAGEMENT
AGENCY*
(*Suby of* City of Winnipeg, The)
195 Tecumseh St, Winnipeg, MB, R3E 3S3
(204) 986-3010
Emp Here 30
SIC 7538 General automotive repair shops

D-U-N-S 24-818-5019   (BR)
DHL EXPRESS (CANADA) LTD
130 Midland St Unit 2, Winnipeg, MB, R3E
3R3

Emp Here 80
SIC 7389 Business services, nec

D-U-N-S 24-417-4343   (BR)
DONG-PHUONG ORIENTAL MARKET LTD
LUCKY SUPERMARKET
1051 Winnipeg Ave, Winnipeg, MB, R3E 0S2
(204) 272-8011
Emp Here 20
SIC 5411 Grocery stores

D-U-N-S 20-050-4186   (SL)
DUFFY'S TAXI (1996) LTD
1100 Notre Dame Ave, Winnipeg, MB, R3E
0N8
(204) 925-0101
Emp Here 154   *Sales* 4,669,485
SIC 4121 Taxicabs

D-U-N-S 24-818-7973   (BR)
EMCO CORPORATION
WESTERN EMCO SUPPLIES, DIV OF
1336 Sargent Ave, Winnipeg, MB, R3E 0G4
(204) 925-8711
Emp Here 25
SIC 5074 Plumbing and heating equipment
and supplies (hydronics)

D-U-N-S 25-300-6340   (BR)
GARDEWINE GROUP INC
1033 Notre Dame Ave, Winnipeg, MB, R3E
0N4
(204) 987-8427
Emp Here 35
SIC 4731 Freight transportation arrangement

D-U-N-S 25-314-4315   (HQ)
GLOBE MOVING & STORAGE LTD
MOVEX MOVING & STORAGE
(*Suby of* Globe Moving & Storage Ltd)
1373 Spruce St, Winnipeg, MB, R3E 2V8
(204) 925-7799
Emp Here 30   *Emp Total* 50
Sales 2,845,467
SIC 4214 Local trucking with storage

D-U-N-S 20-880-1717   (BR)
HALTON RECYCLING LTD
DISTRIBUTION OF HOLTON RECYCLING
1029 Henry Ave, Winnipeg, MB, R3E 1V6
(204) 772-0770
Emp Here 100
SIC 2611 Pulp mills

D-U-N-S 20-759-8327   (SL)
LITZ EQUIPMENT LTD
R LITZ AND SONS
277 Mcphillips St, Winnipeg, MB, R3E 2K7
(204) 783-7979
Emp Here 20   *Sales* 1,824,018
SIC 8741 Management services

D-U-N-S 25-369-5175   (BR)
LOBLAWS INC
REAL CANADIAN SUPERSTORE
1385 Sargent Ave, Winnipeg, MB, R3E 3P8
(204) 784-7901
Emp Here 300
SIC 5141 Groceries, general line

D-U-N-S 24-468-9188 (SL)
LOEWEN DRYWALL LTD
1352 Spruce St, Winnipeg, MB, R3E 2V7
(204) 487-6460
Emp Here 50   *Sales* 4,231,721
SIC 1742 Plastering, drywall, and insulation

D-U-N-S 24-545-8955 (SL)
**MANITOBA ADOLESCENT TREATMENT
CENTRE INC**
MATC
120 Tecumseh St, Winnipeg, MB, R3E 2A9
(204) 477-6391
Emp Here 120   *Sales* 11,971,100
SIC 8063 Psychiatric hospitals
Ch Bd Lesia Szwaluk

D-U-N-S 24-037-3787 (HQ)
NEMCO RESOURCES LTD
25 Midland St, Winnipeg, MB, R3E 3J6
(204) 788-1030
Emp Here 34   *Emp Total* 250
Sales 43,776,420
SIC 2911 Petroleum refining
 Gary Yamada
 Nils Bodtker

D-U-N-S 20-612-6799 (SL)
PACE SETTER SPORTSWEAR INC
655 Logan Ave, Winnipeg, MB, R3E 1M3

Emp Here 65   *Sales* 2,553,625
SIC 2329 Men's and boy's clothing, nec

D-U-N-S 20-010-5252 (HQ)
PERTH SERVICES LTD
PERTH'S
(*Suby of* Perth Services Ltd)
765 Wellington Ave Suite 1, Winnipeg, MB,
R3E 0J1
(204) 697-6100
Emp Here 32   *Emp Total* 300
Sales 12,459,520
SIC 7211 Power laundries, family and com-
mercial
Pr Pr Stewart Leibl

D-U-N-S 20-065-3926 (BR)
PITTSBURGH GLASS WORKS, ULC
1060 Arlington St, Winnipeg, MB, R3E 2G3
(204) 774-1611
Emp Here 43
SIC 3211 Flat glass

D-U-N-S 24-914-1839 (BR)
PRO AUTO LTD
PRO BODY PARTS
1400 Saskatchewan Ave Suite A, Winnipeg,
MB, R3E 0L3
(204) 982-3005
Emp Here 40
SIC 5531 Auto and home supply stores

D-U-N-S 25-450-3162 (SL)
SLEVA, K. CONTRACTING LTD
1147 Sanford St, Winnipeg, MB, R3E 3A1
(204) 897-0442
Emp Here 50   *Sales* 4,231,721
SIC 1742 Plastering, drywall, and insulation

D-U-N-S 20-278-2454 (BR)
SNELLING PAPER & SANITATION LTD
SUR-SEAL PACKAGING, DIV OF
1425 Whyte Ave Suite 200, Winnipeg, MB,
R3E 1V7
(204) 832-8001
Emp Here 25
SIC 5113 Industrial and personal service pa-
per

D-U-N-S 25-831-9227 (BR)
SOBEYS WEST INC
1265 Empress St, Winnipeg, MB, R3E 3N9
(204) 786-8494
Emp Here 22
SIC 5411 Grocery stores

D-U-N-S 20-651-7760 (BR)

SOBEYS WEST INC
LUCERNE FOODS BREAD PLANT
1525 Erin St, Winnipeg, MB, R3E 2T2
(204) 775-0344
Emp Here 90
SIC 2051 Bread, cake, and related products

D-U-N-S 25-686-8589 (BR)
**SOCIETY FOR MANITOBANS WITH DIS-
ABILITIES INC**
SMD WHEELCHAIR SERVICES
1111 Winnipeg Ave, Winnipeg, MB, R3E 0S2
(204) 975-3250
Emp Here 20
SIC 7363 Help supply services

D-U-N-S 20-520-3649 (SL)
STAR TAXI (1989) LTD
SPRING TAXI
880 Logan Ave, Winnipeg, MB, R3E 1N8
(204) 783-0538
Emp Here 60   *Sales* 1,824,018
SIC 4121 Taxicabs

D-U-N-S 25-161-0569 (SL)
STEPHEN GROUP INC., THE
765 Wellington Ave, Winnipeg, MB, R3E 0J1
(204) 697-6100
Emp Here 118   *Sales* 4,523,563
SIC 7215 Coin-operated laundries and cleaning

D-U-N-S 20-800-4254 (BR)
UNIVERSITY OF MANITOBA
MANITOBA INSTITUTE OF CELL BIOLOGY
675 Mcdermot Ave Suite 5008, Winnipeg, MB,
R3E 0V9
(204) 787-2137
Emp Here 135
SIC 8221 Colleges and universities

D-U-N-S 20-647-7742 (BR)
UNIVERSITY OF MANITOBA
JA HILDES NORTHERN MEDICAL UNIT
770 Bannatyne Ave Suite T162, Winnipeg,
MB, R3E 0W3
(204) 789-3711
Emp Here 20
SIC 8221 Colleges and universities

D-U-N-S 24-098-5387 (BR)
VALMONT WC ENGINEERING GROUP LTD
1450 Saskatchewan Ave, Winnipeg, MB, R3E
0L3

Emp Here 25
SIC 2499 Wood products, nec

D-U-N-S 20-011-8545 (HQ)
WELDERS SUPPLIES LIMITED
(*Suby of* Welders Supplies Limited)
150 Mcphillips St, Winnipeg, MB, R3E 2J9
(204) 772-9476
Emp Here 30   *Emp Total* 40
Sales 9,423,290
SIC 5084 Industrial machinery and equipment
Ch Bd Arthur B Cockshott
Pr Pr Grant Cockshott
 Gary Cockshott
Dir Joan Cockshott

D-U-N-S 25-361-1727 (BR)
**WINNIPEG REGIONAL HEALTH AUTHOR-
ITY, THE**
WRHA- HEALTH SCIENCES CENTRE
791 Notre Dame Ave Suite 1, Winnipeg, MB,
R3E 0M1

Emp Here 42
SIC 8062 General medical and surgical hospitals

D-U-N-S 24-336-6742 (BR)
**WINNIPEG REGIONAL HEALTH AUTHOR-
ITY, THE**
*WINNIPEG REGIONAL HEALTH AUTHOR-
ITY*
720 Mcdermot Ave Rm Ad301, Winnipeg, MB,

R3E 0T3
(204) 787-1165
Emp Here 245
SIC 8062 General medical and surgical hospitals

D-U-N-S 25-055-1231 (BR)
WINNIPEG SCHOOL DIVISION
*DANIEL MCINTYRE COLLEGIATE INSTI-
TUTE*
720 Alverstone St, Winnipeg, MB, R3E 2H1
(204) 783-7131
Emp Here 91
SIC 8211 Elementary and secondary schools

D-U-N-S 25-127-9709 (BR)
WINNIPEG SCHOOL DIVISION
WESTON SCHOOL
1410 Logan Ave, Winnipeg, MB, R3E 1R9
(204) 775-2591
Emp Here 30
SIC 8211 Elementary and secondary schools

D-U-N-S 20-709-7564 (BR)
WINNIPEG SCHOOL DIVISION
CECIL RHODES SCHOOL
1570 Elgin Ave W, Winnipeg, MB, R3E 1C2
(204) 783-9012
Emp Here 50
SIC 8211 Elementary and secondary schools

D-U-N-S 25-920-8320 (BR)
WINNIPEG SCHOOL DIVISION
ADOLESCENT PARENT CENTRE
136 Cecil St, Winnipeg, MB, R3E 2Y9
(204) 775-5440
Emp Here 20
SIC 8211 Elementary and secondary schools

D-U-N-S 25-892-6179 (BR)
WINNIPEG SCHOOL DIVISION
SARGENT PARK SCHOOL
2 Sargent Park Pl, Winnipeg, MB, R3E 0V8
(204) 775-8985
Emp Here 80
SIC 8211 Elementary and secondary schools

D-U-N-S 20-709-7440 (BR)
WINNIPEG SCHOOL DIVISION
PINKHAM ELEMENTARY SCHOOL
765 Pacific Ave, Winnipeg, MB, R3E 1G1
(204) 786-5749
Emp Here 35
SIC 8211 Elementary and secondary schools

D-U-N-S 20-709-7242 (BR)
WINNIPEG SCHOOL DIVISION
CLIFTON SCHOOL
1070 Clifton St, Winnipeg, MB, R3E 2T7
(204) 783-7792
Emp Here 30
SIC 8211 Elementary and secondary schools

D-U-N-S 20-709-7507 (BR)
WINNIPEG SCHOOL DIVISION
TECHNICAL VOCATIONAL HIGH SCHOOL
1555 Wall St, Winnipeg, MB, R3E 2S2
(204) 786-1401
Emp Here 100
SIC 8211 Elementary and secondary schools

D-U-N-S 20-706-6460 (BR)
WINNIPEG SCHOOL DIVISION
PRINCIPAL SPARLING
1150 Sherburn St, Winnipeg, MB, R3E 2N4
(204) 783-6195
Emp Here 33
SIC 8211 Elementary and secondary schools

D-U-N-S 24-329-9463 (BR)
WINNIPEG SCHOOL DIVISION
BUILDING DEPARTMENT
1395 Spruce St Suite 1, Winnipeg, MB, R3E
2V8
(204) 786-0344
Emp Here 120
SIC 8211 Elementary and secondary schools

D-U-N-S 20-648-8012 (BR)
WINNIPEG SCHOOL DIVISION
*TRANSPORTATION AND PERMITS DEPART-
MENT*
1180 Notre Dame Ave Suite 109, Winnipeg,
MB, R3E 0P2
(204) 789-0409
Emp Here 35
SIC 8211 Elementary and secondary schools

Winnipeg, MB R3G

D-U-N-S 25-288-0158 (BR)
A & W FOOD SERVICES OF CANADA INC
A & W
1520 Portage Ave, Winnipeg, MB, R3G 0W8
(204) 774-3275
Emp Here 35
SIC 5812 Eating places

D-U-N-S 20-006-9607 (HQ)
ADVANCE ELECTRONICS LTD
ADVANCED AUDIO & VIDEO
1300 Portage Ave, Winnipeg, MB, R3G 0V1
(204) 786-6541
Emp Here 100   *Emp Total* 170
Sales 16,124,315
SIC 5999 Miscellaneous retail stores, nec
Pr Pr Arnold Frieman
 Myra Frieman

D-U-N-S 20-032-3330 (BR)
**CADILLAC FAIRVIEW CORPORATION LIM-
ITED, THE**
POLO PARK SHOPPING CENTER
1485 Portage Ave Suite 66q, Winnipeg, MB,
R3G 0W4
(204) 784-2501
Emp Here 70
SIC 6531 Real estate agents and managers

D-U-N-S 24-572-3028 (SL)
**CANADIAN CORPS OF COMMISSION-
AIRES (MANITOBA AND NORTHWESTERN
ONTARIO DIVISION)**
290 Burnell St, Winnipeg, MB, R3G 2A7
(204) 942-5993
Emp Here 400   *Sales* 16,785,360
SIC 7381 Detective and armored car services
Dir Opers Robert Chmara
Dir Fin Robert Dowe
CEO Thomas W. Reimer
 George Elliott

D-U-N-S 25-311-6792 (BR)
**CANADIAN IMPERIAL BANK OF COM-
MERCE**
CIBC
1485 Portage Ave, Winnipeg, MB, R3G 0W4
(204) 944-5868
Emp Here 55
SIC 6021 National commercial banks

D-U-N-S 25-293-5275 (BR)
**CANADIAN NATIONAL INSTITUTE FOR
THE BLIND, THE**
C N I B
(*Suby of* Canadian National Institute For The
Blind, The)
1080 Portage Ave, Winnipeg, MB, R3G 3M3
(204) 774-5421
Emp Here 40
SIC 8322 Individual and family services

D-U-N-S 20-651-6051 (BR)
CARA OPERATIONS LIMITED
MONTANA'S COOKHOUSE
(*Suby of* Cara Holdings Limited)
665 Empress St, Winnipeg, MB, R3G 3P7
(204) 789-9939
Emp Here 30
SIC 5812 Eating places

D-U-N-S 20-008-1925 (BR)

CASCADES CANADA ULC
NORAMPAC, DIV OF
680 Wall St, Winnipeg, MB, R3G 2T8
(204) 786-5761
Emp Here 120
SIC 2653 Corrugated and solid fiber boxes

D-U-N-S 24-418-2874   (BR)
CINEPLEX ODEON CORPORATION
SILVERCITY POLO PARK
817 St James St, Winnipeg, MB, R3G 3L9
(204) 774-1001
Emp Here 140
SIC 7832 Motion picture theaters, except
drive-in

D-U-N-S 24-882-4047   (BR)
CLUB MONACO CORP
(*Suby of* Ralph Lauren Corporation)
1485 Portage Ave Suite 257, Winnipeg, MB,
R3G 0W4
(204) 788-4391
Emp Here 20
SIC 5632 Women's accessory and specialty
stores

D-U-N-S 20-010-7233   (BR)
CORUS ENTERTAINMENT INC
CJOB-AM
1440 Jack Blick Ave Unit 200, Winnipeg, MB,
R3G 0L4
(204) 786-2471
Emp Here 75
SIC 7922 Theatrical producers and services

D-U-N-S 24-852-1064   (BR)
EMA PROPERTIES (MANITOBA) LTD
WENDY'S
650 St James St, Winnipeg, MB, R3G 3J5
(204) 772-4002
Emp Here 40
SIC 5812 Eating places

D-U-N-S 24-348-6722   (SL)
FABRIS-MILANO GROUP LTD, THE
1035 Erin St, Winnipeg, MB, R3G 2X1
(204) 783-7179
Emp Here 50   *Sales* 4,815,406
SIC 1752 Floor laying and floor work, nec

D-U-N-S 25-170-0951   (BR)
FOOT LOCKER CANADA CO
FOOT LOCKER CANADA CO.
1485 Portage Ave Suite 307, Winnipeg, MB,
R3G 0W4
(204) 943-4639
Emp Here 30
SIC 5699 Miscellaneous apparel and acces-
sory stores

D-U-N-S 20-913-7780   (BR)
G4S CASH SOLUTIONS (CANADA) LTD
994 Wall St, Winnipeg, MB, R3G 2V3
(204) 774-6883
Emp Here 100
SIC 7381 Detective and armored car services

D-U-N-S 25-133-3209   (BR)
GAP (CANADA) INC
GAPKIDS
(*Suby of* The Gap Inc)
1485 Portage Ave, Winnipeg, MB, R3G 0W4
(204) 775-5216
Emp Here 20
SIC 5651 Family clothing stores

D-U-N-S 25-713-0146   (BR)
GAP (CANADA) INC
GAP
(*Suby of* The Gap Inc)
1485 Portage Ave Suite L115, Winnipeg, MB,
R3G 0W4
(204) 775-5330
Emp Here 40
SIC 5651 Family clothing stores

D-U-N-S 20-743-1649   (BR)
GOLF TOWN LIMITED

GOLF TOWN
915 Empress St Unit 600, Winnipeg, MB, R3G
3P8
(204) 775-5534
Emp Here 20
SIC 5941 Sporting goods and bicycle shops

D-U-N-S 24-236-6177   (BR)
HERZING INSTITUTES OF CANADA INC
HERZING COLLEGE
723 Portage Ave, Winnipeg, MB, R3G 0M8
(204) 775-8175
Emp Here 25
SIC 8249 Vocational schools, nec

D-U-N-S 25-514-2853   (BR)
HOME DEPOT OF CANADA INC
HOME DEPOT
(*Suby of* The Home Depot Inc)
727 Empress St, Winnipeg, MB, R3G 3P5
(204) 779-0703
Emp Here 250
SIC 5251 Hardware stores

D-U-N-S 20-698-6627   (BR)
HUDSON'S BAY COMPANY
BAY, THE
1485 Portage Ave, Winnipeg, MB, R3G 0W4
(204) 975-3228
Emp Here 200
SIC 5311 Department stores

D-U-N-S 24-683-8697   (BR)
HUDSON'S BAY COMPANY
HOME OUTFITTERS
710 St James St, Winnipeg, MB, R3G 3J7
(204) 779-4663
Emp Here 20
SIC 5719 Miscellaneous homefurnishings

D-U-N-S 20-300-3855   (BR)
INDIGO BOOKS & MUSIC INC
CHAPTERS
(*Suby of* Indigo Books & Music Inc)
695 Empress St, Winnipeg, MB, R3G 3P6
(204) 775-5999
Emp Here 50
SIC 5942 Book stores

D-U-N-S 20-797-5561   (BR)
INNVEST PROPERTIES CORP
CLARION HOTEL & SUITES
(*Suby of* Innvest Properties Corp)
1445 Portage Ave, Winnipeg, MB, R3G 3P4
(204) 774-5110
Emp Here 50
SIC 7011 Hotels and motels

D-U-N-S 20-837-1062   (SL)
KLINIC INC
KLINIC COMMUNITY HEALTH CENTRE
870 Portage Ave, Winnipeg, MB, R3G 0P1
(204) 784-4090
Emp Here 102   *Sales* 5,579,750
SIC 8322 Individual and family services
Ex Dir Lorie Johnson
Ch Bd Jan Schubert
Dir Fin Holly Banner

D-U-N-S 24-376-2457   (BR)
LE CHATEAU INC
CHATEAU, LE
(*Suby of* Le Chateau Inc)
1395 Ellice Ave Suite 170, Winnipeg, MB, R3G
0G3
(204) 788-1388
Emp Here 30
SIC 5651 Family clothing stores

D-U-N-S 20-340-3428   (BR)
LE CHATEAU INC
(*Suby of* Le Chateau Inc)
1485 Portage Ave Unit 200, Winnipeg, MB,
R3G 0W4
(204) 774-5012
Emp Here 60
SIC 5611 Men's and boys' clothing stores

D-U-N-S 24-202-9895   (BR)
MIG MANITOBA INSURANCE GROUP
1401 Portage Ave, Winnipeg, MB, R3G 0W1
(204) 944-8400
Emp Here 50
SIC 6411 Insurance agents, brokers, and service

D-U-N-S 20-853-2890   (BR)
MANITOBA LIQUOR AND LOTTERIES
CORPORATION
LIQUOR MART
923 Portage Ave, Winnipeg, MB, R3G 0P6
(204) 987-4025
Emp Here 20
SIC 5921 Liquor stores

D-U-N-S 25-384-2330   (SL)
MANITOBA MOOSE TWO LIMITED
MANITOBA MOOSE HOCKEY CLUB
1430 Maroons Rd, Winnipeg, MB, R3G 0L5
(204) 987-7825
Emp Here 55   *Sales* 2,991,389
SIC 7999 Amusement and recreation, nec

D-U-N-S 20-798-4852   (BR)
MCDONALD'S   RESTAURANTS   OF
CANADA LIMITED
MCDONALD'S
(*Suby of* McDonald's Corporation)
1001 Empress St, Winnipeg, MB, R3G 3P8
(204) 949-5121
Emp Here 50
SIC 5812 Eating places

D-U-N-S 25-318-1341   (BR)
MCDONALD'S   RESTAURANTS   OF
CANADA LIMITED
MCDONALD'S 8455
(*Suby of* McDonald's Corporation)
1251 Portage Ave, Winnipeg, MB, R3G 0T7
(204) 949-6058
Emp Here 50
SIC 5812 Eating places

D-U-N-S 25-318-1382   (BR)
MCDONALD'S   RESTAURANTS   OF
CANADA LIMITED
MCDONALD'S
(*Suby of* McDonald's Corporation)
664 Portage Ave, Winnipeg, MB, R3G 0M4
(204) 949-6035
Emp Here 70
SIC 5812 Eating places

D-U-N-S 20-049-9593   (BR)
MCDONALD'S   RESTAURANTS   OF
CANADA LIMITED
MCDONALD'S RESTAURANTS
(*Suby of* McDonald's Corporation)
1440 Ellice Ave, Winnipeg, MB, R3G 0G4
(204) 949-5123
Emp Here 100
SIC 5812 Eating places

D-U-N-S 20-924-0907   (SL)
MOXIE'S CLASSIC GRILL
1485 Portage Ave Suite 234, Winnipeg, MB,
R3G 0W4
(204) 783-1840
Emp Here 100   *Sales* 2,991,389
SIC 5812 Eating places

D-U-N-S 24-883-4657   (SL)
NINE CIRCLES COMMUNITY HEALTH CEN-
TRE INC
705 Broadway, Winnipeg, MB, R3G 0X2
(204) 940-6000
Emp Here 50   *Sales* 2,991,389
SIC 8011 Offices and clinics of medical doc-
tors

D-U-N-S 20-704-9847   (BR)
OLD NAVY (CANADA) INC
OLD NAVY
(*Suby of* The Gap Inc)
830 St James St, Winnipeg, MB, R3G 3J7

(204) 786-3868
Emp Here 50
SIC 5651 Family clothing stores

D-U-N-S 20-364-4344   (SL)
OLIVE GARDEN
1544 Portage Ave, Winnipeg, MB, R3G 0W9
(204) 774-9725
Emp Here 120   *Sales* 3,648,035
SIC 5812 Eating places

D-U-N-S 25-663-6333   (BR)
RED LOBSTER HOSPITALITY LLC
OLIVE GARDEN
(*Suby of* Red Lobster Seafood Co., LLC)
1544 Portage Ave, Winnipeg, MB, R3G 0W9
(204) 774-9725
Emp Here 120
SIC 5812 Eating places

D-U-N-S 24-440-3825   (BR)
RED LOBSTER HOSPITALITY LLC
(*Suby of* Red Lobster Seafood Co., LLC)
1540 Portage Ave, Winnipeg, MB, R3G 0W9
(204) 783-9434
Emp Here 100
SIC 5812 Eating places

D-U-N-S 25-300-6381   (BR)
REDBERRY FRANCHISING CORP
BURGER KING
333 Home St, Winnipeg, MB, R3G 1X5
(204) 987-8428
Emp Here 22
SIC 5812 Eating places

D-U-N-S 25-960-5335   (BR)
ROBINSON, B.A. CO. LTD
ROBINSON LIGHTING, DIV OF
(*Suby of* Ross Group Inc)
995 Milt Stegall Dr, Winnipeg, MB, R3G 3H7

Emp Here 20
SIC 5719 Miscellaneous homefurnishings

D-U-N-S 25-667-8780   (BR)
RUSSELL FOOD EQUIPMENT LIMITED
RUSSELL FOOD SERVICE
941 Erin St, Winnipeg, MB, R3G 2W8
(204) 774-3591
Emp Here 30
SIC 7699 Repair services, nec

D-U-N-S 20-570-8613   (BR)
SEARS CANADA INC
1515 Portage Ave, Winnipeg, MB, R3G 0W7
(204) 775-7011
Emp Here 400
SIC 5311 Department stores

D-U-N-S 25-271-7798   (BR)
SOBEYS WEST INC
POLO PARK SAFEWAY
1485 Portage Ave Suite 160e, Winnipeg, MB,
R3G 0W4
(204) 775-6348
Emp Here 200
SIC 5411 Grocery stores

D-U-N-S 20-859-9816   (BR)
SOURCE (BELL) ELECTRONICS INC, THE
SOURCE, THE
393 Portage Ave, Winnipeg, MB, R3G 3H6

Emp Here 25
SIC 5999 Miscellaneous retail stores, nec

D-U-N-S 25-813-3362   (BR)
ST JOHN'S MUSIC LTD
YAMAHA MUSIC CENTRE
1330 Portage Ave, Winnipeg, MB, R3G 0V6
(204) 783-8899
Emp Here 20
SIC 5736 Musical instrument stores

D-U-N-S 20-806-3524   (BR)
STARBUCKS COFFEE CANADA, INC
STARBUCKS POLO PARK
(*Suby of* Starbucks Corporation)

1485 Portage Ave Suite 153, Winnipeg, MB, R3G 0W4
(204) 772-3659
Emp Here 25
SIC 5812 Eating places

D-U-N-S 24-618-0512 (BR)
STARBUCKS COFFEE CANADA, INC
(*Suby of* Starbucks Corporation)
1430 Ellice Ave Suite 1, Winnipeg, MB, R3G 0G4
(204) 774-1084
Emp Here 25
SIC 5812 Eating places

D-U-N-S 20-010-7282 (SL)
STEER HOLDINGS LTD
RAE & JERRY'S STEAK HOUSE
1405 Portage Ave, Winnipeg, MB, R3G 0W1
(204) 783-1612
Emp Here 65 *Sales* 1,969,939
SIC 5812 Eating places

D-U-N-S 24-041-0733 (BR)
TOMMY HILFIGER CANADA INC
1485 Portage Ave, Winnipeg, MB, R3G 0W4
(204) 784-1340
Emp Here 24
SIC 5651 Family clothing stores

D-U-N-S 20-009-0447 (SL)
UNIGRAPHICS MANITOBA LTD
HIGNELL PRINTING
(*Suby of* Unigraphics Limited)
488 Burnell St, Winnipeg, MB, R3G 2B4
(204) 784-1030
Emp Here 47 *Sales* 2,480,664
SIC 2732 Book printing

D-U-N-S 20-011-7190 (SL)
VALOUR DECORATING (1988) LTD
889 Wall St Winnipeg, MB, R3G 2T9
(204) 786-5875
Emp Here 60 *Sales* 3,866,917
SIC 1721 Painting and paper hanging

D-U-N-S 25-451-1322 (BR)
WAL-MART CANADA CORP
1001 Empress St, Winnipeg, MB, R3G 3P8
(204) 284-6900
Emp Here 200
SIC 5311 Department stores

D-U-N-S 24-845-0769 (SL)
WESTERN LIFE ASSURANCE COMPANY
WESTERN LIFE
717 Portage Ave 4th Floor, Winnipeg, MB, R3G 0M8
(204) 786-6431
Emp Here 40 *Sales* 55,290,250
SIC 6311 Life insurance
Pr John Paisley
VP Bruce Ratzlaff
Ray Novog
VP Fin Dave Derksen
Dir Eric Salsberg
Dir John Varnell
Dir Winslow W Bennett
Dir Paul Fink

D-U-N-S 20-612-8597 (SL)
WESTERN MESSENGER & TRANSFER LIMITED
839 Ellice Ave, Winnipeg, MB, R3G 0C3
(204) 987-7020
Emp Here 60 *Sales* 3,638,254
SIC 7389 Business services, nec

D-U-N-S 25-294-0796 (BR)
WINNERS MERCHANTS INTERNATIONAL L.P.
WINNERS
(*Suby of* The TJX Companies Inc)
1320 Ellice Ave, Winnipeg, MB, R3G 0E9
(204) 774-9070
Emp Here 45
SIC 5651 Family clothing stores

D-U-N-S 25-892-6187 (BR)
WINNIPEG SCHOOL DIVISION
JOHN M. KING SCHOOL
525 Agnes St, Winnipeg, MB, R3G 1N7
(204) 775-4404
Emp Here 50
SIC 8211 Elementary and secondary schools

D-U-N-S 20-027-2503 (BR)
WINNIPEG SCHOOL DIVISION
GREENWAY SCHOOL
390 Burnell St, Winnipeg, MB, R3G 2A8
(204) 775-2455
Emp Here 70
SIC 8211 Elementary and secondary schools

D-U-N-S 25-892-6153 (BR)
WINNIPEG SCHOOL DIVISION
GORDON BELL HIGH SCHOOL
3 Borrowman Pl, Winnipeg, MB, R3G 1M6
(204) 774-5401
Emp Here 140
SIC 8211 Elementary and secondary schools

D-U-N-S 20-709-7556 (BR)
WINNIPEG SCHOOL DIVISION
WOLSELEY SCHOOL
511 Clifton St, Winnipeg, MB, R3G 2X3
(204) 783-3237
Emp Here 32
SIC 8211 Elementary and secondary schools

D-U-N-S 20-517-1262 (BR)
WINNIPEG SCHOOL DIVISION
MULVEY SCHOOL
750 Wolseley Ave, Winnipeg, MB, R3G 1C6
(204) 786-3469
Emp Here 55
SIC 8211 Elementary and secondary schools

D-U-N-S 20-709-7390 (BR)
WINNIPEG SCHOOL DIVISION
LAURA SECORD SCHOOL
960 Wolseley Ave, Winnipeg, MB, R3G 1E7
(204) 786-4796
Emp Here 50
SIC 8211 Elementary and secondary schools

D-U-N-S 20-709-7366 (BR)
WINNIPEG SCHOOL DIVISION
ISAAC BROCK SCHOOL
1265 Barratt Ave, Winnipeg, MB, R3G 0L9
(204) 772-9527
Emp Here 50
SIC 8211 Elementary and secondary schools

D-U-N-S 24-467-5088 (HQ)
WINNSERV INC
(*Suby of* Winnserv Inc)
960 Portage Ave Suite 101, Winnipeg, MB, R3G 0R4
(204) 783-8654
Emp Here 30 *Emp Total* 90
Sales 3,283,232
SIC 8361 Residential care

D-U-N-S 20-175-1570 (BR)
WOLSELEY CANADA INC
WOLSELEY MECHANICAL GROUP
(*Suby of* WOLSELEY PLC)
1300 St Matthews Ave, Winnipeg, MB, R3G 3K4
(204) 786-7861
Emp Here 65
SIC 5074 Plumbing and heating equipment and supplies (hydronics)

Winnipeg, MB R3H

D-U-N-S 24-916-0466 (HQ)
2653193 MANITOBA LTD
DYNA-PRO ENVIRONMENTAL
(*Suby of* 2653193 Manitoba Ltd)
565 Roseberry St, Winnipeg, MB, R3H 0T3

(204) 774-5370
Emp Here 35 *Emp Total* 50
Sales 8,441,760
SIC 3589 Service industry machinery, nec
Dir David Robinson
Dir Paul Robinson

D-U-N-S 20-049-8611 (BR)
668824 ALBERTA LTD
VISIONS ELECTRONICS
1130 St James St, Winnipeg, MB, R3H 0K7
(204) 775-7082
Emp Here 25
SIC 7389 Business services, nec

D-U-N-S 20-346-4136 (SL)
7169311 MANITOBA LTD
FLOWER FACTORY, THE
(*Suby of* 4698658 Manitoba Ltd)
975 Sherwin Rd Unit 1, Winnipeg, MB, R3H 0T8
(855) 838-7852
Emp Here 30 *Sales* 7,056,698
SIC 5193 Flowers and florists supplies
Pr Pr Kim Hannam
Maxine Hannam
Tyler Specula
Fin Ex Aaron Paintner

D-U-N-S 25-107-8275 (BR)
765865 ONTARIO INC
DRYDEN AIR SERVICES
2019 Sargent Ave Unit 18, Winnipeg, MB, R3H 0Z7
(204) 779-0132
Emp Here 20
SIC 4581 Airports, flying fields, and services

D-U-N-S 24-098-8746 (BR)
AIR CANADA
2000 Wellington Ave Rm 222, Winnipeg, MB, R3H 1C1
(204) 788-6953
Emp Here 150
SIC 4581 Airports, flying fields, and services

D-U-N-S 24-381-6555 (BR)
AIR CANADA
AIR CANADA CARGO
2020 Sargent Ave Suite 210, Winnipeg, MB, R3H 0E1
(204) 788-7801
Emp Here 21
SIC 4512 Air transportation, scheduled

D-U-N-S 24-103-8715 (BR)
AIR CANADA
2020 Sargent Ave, Winnipeg, MB, R3H 0E1
(204) 788-7871
Emp Here 100
SIC 4581 Airports, flying fields, and services

D-U-N-S 20-260-1985 (BR)
AIRPORT TERMINAL SERVICES CANADIAN COMPANY
2000 Wellington Ave Unit 249, Winnipeg, MB, R3H 1C2
(204) 774-0665
Emp Here 20
SIC 4581 Airports, flying fields, and services

D-U-N-S 20-526-9579 (BR)
ASSINIBOINE COMMUNITY COLLEGE
ACC
1313 Border St Suite 87, Winnipeg, MB, R3H 0X4
(204) 694-7111
Emp Here 23
SIC 8222 Junior colleges

D-U-N-S 20-106-7316 (SL)
AVION SERVICES CORP
2000 Wellington Ave Suite 503, Winnipeg, MB, R3H 1C1
(204) 784-5800
Emp Here 150 *Sales* 4,669,485
SIC 7381 Detective and armored car services

D-U-N-S 24-678-9379 (BR)

BELFOR (CANADA) INC
BELFOR PROPERTY RESTORATION SERVICES
801 Berry St, Winnipeg, MB, R3H 0S7
(204) 774-8186
Emp Here 20
SIC 1799 Special trade contractors, nec

D-U-N-S 20-835-4068 (HQ)
BOARD OF GOVERNOR'S OF RED RIVER COLLEGE, THE
RRC
2055 Notre Dame Ave, Winnipeg, MB, R3H 0J9
(204) 632-3960
Emp Here 750 *Emp Total* 20,000
Sales 161,988,937
SIC 8222 Junior colleges
Pr Stephanie Forsyth
Ch Bd Richard Lennon
V Ch Bd Cathy Woods
Catherine Rushton

D-U-N-S 20-307-1584 (BR)
CALM AIR INTERNATIONAL LP
930 Ferry Rd, Winnipeg, MB, R3H 0Y8
(204) 956-6101
Emp Here 25
SIC 4581 Airports, flying fields, and services

D-U-N-S 25-961-8072 (BR)
CALM AIR INTERNATIONAL LP
CALM AIR
50 Morberg Way, Winnipeg, MB, R3H 0A4
(204) 956-6196
Emp Here 25
SIC 4512 Air transportation, scheduled

D-U-N-S 20-588-8709 (BR)
CANADIAN IMPERIAL BANK OF COMMERCE
CIBC
37 Stevenson Rd, Winnipeg, MB, R3H 0H9
(204) 944-5129
Emp Here 20
SIC 6021 National commercial banks

D-U-N-S 25-668-6650 (BR)
CANLAN ICE SPORTS CORP
1871 Ellice Ave, Winnipeg, MB, R3H 0C1
(204) 784-8888
Emp Here 47
SIC 7999 Amusement and recreation, nec

D-U-N-S 24-519-3008 (BR)
CANPAR TRANSPORT L.P.
(*Suby of* Canpar Transport L.P.)
750 Berry St Suite A, Winnipeg, MB, R3H 0S6

Emp Here 40
SIC 4213 Trucking, except local

D-U-N-S 20-799-3333 (BR)
CARA OPERATIONS LIMITED
(*Suby of* Cara Holdings Limited)
2000 Wellington Ave Suite 249, Winnipeg, MB, R3H 1C2

Emp Here 29
SIC 5812 Eating places

D-U-N-S 20-570-0029 (BR)
CITY OF WINNIPEG, THE
PLANNING PROPERTY AND DEVELOPMENT
(*Suby of* City of Winnipeg, The)
3001 Notre Dame Ave, Winnipeg, MB, R3H 1B8
(204) 986-4299
Emp Here 20
SIC 6553 Cemetery subdividers and developers

D-U-N-S 25-839-1044 (BR)
CONCORD TRANSPORTATION INC
N AND LAUER TRANSPORTATION
1725 St James St Unit 13, Winnipeg, MB, R3H 1H3

(204) 633-1663
Emp Here 30
SIC 4213 Trucking, except local

D-U-N-S 25-287-5414 (BR)
COSTCO WHOLESALE CANADA LTD
(*Suby of* Costco Wholesale Corporation)
1315 St James St Suite 57, Winnipeg, MB,
R3H 0K9
(204) 788-4754
Emp Here 175
SIC 5099 Durable goods, nec

D-U-N-S 24-968-1438 (HQ)
ELITE COMMUNICATIONS INC
(*Suby of* Elite Communications Inc)
585 Century St, Winnipeg, MB, R3H 0W1
(204) 989-2995
Emp Here 40 *Emp Total* 55
Sales 8,539,920
SIC 4899 Communication services, nec
Dir Scott Greer

D-U-N-S 25-520-3010 (BR)
EMCO CORPORATION
WHOLESALES HEAT SUPPLIES
669 Century St, Winnipeg, MB, R3H 0L9
(204) 925-9630
Emp Here 20
SIC 5064 Electrical appliances, television and
radio

D-U-N-S 20-008-3657 (BR)
EMCO CORPORATION
2030 Notre Dame Ave, Winnipeg, MB, R3H
0J8
(204) 925-8444
Emp Here 49
SIC 5074 Plumbing and heating equipment
and supplies (hydronics)

D-U-N-S 24-170-6209 (BR)
**ENTERPRISE RENT-A-CAR CANADA COM-
PANY**
(*Suby of* The Crawford Group Inc)
2000 Wellington Ave Suite 100, Winnipeg, MB,
R3H 1C1
(204) 925-3529
Emp Here 20
SIC 7514 Passenger car rental

D-U-N-S 24-717-6845 (BR)
**FEDERAL EXPRESS CANADA CORPORA-
TION**
FEDERAL EXPRESS CANADA LTD
(*Suby of* Fedex Corporation)
1950 Sargent Ave, Winnipeg, MB, R3H 1C8
(800) 463-3339
Emp Here 70
SIC 7389 Business services, nec

D-U-N-S 20-008-4895 (BR)
FEDERATED CO-OPERATIVES LIMITED
(*Suby of* Federated Co-Operatives Limited)
1615 King Edward St, Winnipeg, MB, R3H
0R7
(204) 633-8950
Emp Here 206
SIC 5141 Groceries, general line

D-U-N-S 24-367-8146 (BR)
FLOCOR INC
(*Suby of* Entreprises Mirca Inc, Les)
777 Century St, Winnipeg, MB, R3H 0M2
(204) 774-3461
Emp Here 20
SIC 5085 Industrial supplies

D-U-N-S 20-008-5355 (HQ)
FLORISTS SUPPLY LTD
(*Suby of* Floraco Holdings Inc)
35 Airport Rd, Winnipeg, MB, R3H 0V5
(204) 632-1210
Emp Here 40 *Emp Total* 100
Sales 12,038,516
SIC 5193 Flowers and florists supplies
Pr Pr Laurie Nesbitt
VP VP John Forsyth
Jack Cahill

D-U-N-S 20-327-5136 (BR)
FORBES BROS. LTD
INTERLAKE POWER LINE
1780 Wellington Ave Unit 301, Winnipeg, MB,
R3H 1B3
(204) 888-6174
Emp Here 20
SIC 1623 Water, sewer, and utility lines

D-U-N-S 20-048-9503 (BR)
FORTIS INC
GREENWOOD INN, THE
1715 Wellington Ave, Winnipeg, MB, R3H 0G1
(204) 775-9889
Emp Here 30
SIC 4911 Electric services

D-U-N-S 20-139-8653 (SL)
**FOUR POINTS HOTEL SHERATON WIN-
NIPEG INTERNATIONAL AIRPORT**
1999 Wellington Ave, Winnipeg, MB, R3H 1H5
(204) 775-5222
Emp Here 76 *Sales* 3,356,192
SIC 7011 Hotels and motels

D-U-N-S 25-668-0216 (BR)
G.N. JOHNSTON EQUIPMENT CO. LTD
85 Keith Rd, Winnipeg, MB, R3H 0H7
(204) 633-4364
Emp Here 21
SIC 5084 Industrial machinery and equipment

D-U-N-S 24-348-6409 (BR)
G4S SECURE SOLUTIONS (CANADA) LTD
530 Century St Suite 231, Winnipeg, MB, R3H
0Y4
(204) 774-0005
Emp Here 200
SIC 7381 Detective and armored car services

D-U-N-S 20-009-0900 (BR)
HONEYWELL LIMITED
(*Suby of* Honeywell International Inc.)
1391 St James St Unit 2, Winnipeg, MB, R3H
0Z1
(204) 987-8111
Emp Here 41
SIC 3822 Environmental controls

D-U-N-S 20-179-6518 (BR)
INTRIA ITEMS INC
37 Stevenson Rd, Winnipeg, MB, R3H 0H9
(204) 944-6154
Emp Here 25
SIC 7374 Data processing and preparation

D-U-N-S 24-717-9872 (BR)
INNVEST PROPERTIES CORP
COMFORT INN
(*Suby of* Innvest Properties Corp)
1770 Sargent Ave, Winnipeg, MB, R3H 0C8
(204) 783-5627
Emp Here 20
SIC 7011 Hotels and motels

D-U-N-S 24-533-9549 (SL)
JCA INDUSTRIES INC
JCA ELECTRONICS
118 King Edward St E, Winnipeg, MB, R3H
0N8
(204) 415-1104
Emp Here 60 *Sales* 4,511,280
SIC 3625 Relays and industrial controls

D-U-N-S 25-385-9094 (SL)
JOSEPH & COMPANY LTD
ATLAS GRAHAM
1725 Sargent Ave, Winnipeg, MB, R3H 0C5
(204) 775-4451
Emp Here 65
SIC 3991 Brooms and brushes

D-U-N-S 20-434-6985 (HQ)
JOSTENS CANADA LTD
(*Suby of* Newell Brands Inc.)
1643 Dublin Ave, Winnipeg, MB, R3H 0G9
(204) 783-1310
Emp Here 40 *Emp Total* 53,400
Sales 35,949,417

SIC 3961 Costume jewelry
Robert K Sigurdson
Fin Mgr Janice Marsch

D-U-N-S 25-664-4857 (SL)
KMCA ACQUISITION CORPORATION
GOLD BUSINESS SOLUTIONS
791 Bradford St, Winnipeg, MB, R3H 0N2
(204) 633-9264
Emp Here 40 *Sales* 3,429,153
SIC 5943 Stationery stores

D-U-N-S 20-703-1696 (BR)
LAKEVIEW MANAGEMENT INC
*FOUR POINTS SHERATON INTERNA-
TIONAL*
1999 Wellington Ave, Winnipeg, MB, R3H 1H5
(204) 775-5222
Emp Here 50
SIC 7011 Hotels and motels

D-U-N-S 25-295-5687 (BR)
LEON'S FURNITURE LIMITED
LEON'S FURNITURE
1755 Ellice Ave, Winnipeg, MB, R3H 1A6
(204) 783-0533
Emp Here 40
SIC 5712 Furniture stores

D-U-N-S 25-538-9827 (BR)
LOBLAWS INC
REAL CANADIAN WHOLESALE CLUB
1725 Ellice Ave, Winnipeg, MB, R3H 1A6
(204) 775-8280
Emp Here 100
SIC 5141 Groceries, general line

D-U-N-S 24-172-0176 (BR)
MCW CONSULTANTS LTD
M C W / AGE
1821 Wellington Ave Suite 210, Winnipeg, MB,
R3H 0G4
(204) 779-7900
Emp Here 60
SIC 7363 Help supply services

D-U-N-S 20-015-4677 (BR)
MAGELLAN AEROSPACE LIMITED
*MAGELLAN AEROSPACE, WINNIPEG, A DIV
OF*
660 Berry St, Winnipeg, MB, R3H 0S5
(204) 775-8331
Emp Here 700
SIC 3728 Aircraft parts and equipment, nec

D-U-N-S 25-207-3838 (BR)
**MANITOBA PUBLIC INSURANCE CORPO-
RATION, THE**
MPI
125 King Edward St E, Winnipeg, MB, R3H
0V9
(204) 985-7111
Emp Here 40
SIC 6331 Fire, marine, and casualty insurance

D-U-N-S 24-914-7935 (BR)
MANITOBA TELECOM SERVICES INC
1700 Ellice Ave, Winnipeg, MB, R3H 0B1
(204) 941-4111
Emp Here 40
SIC 4899 Communication services, nec

D-U-N-S 20-058-7744 (BR)
NAV CANADA
2000 Wellington Ave Suite 706, Winnipeg, MB,
R3H 1C1
(204) 983-8408
Emp Here 24
SIC 4899 Communication services, nec

D-U-N-S 24-967-9218 (BR)
PLH AVIATION SERVICES INC
1860 Saskatchewan Ave, Winnipeg, MB, R3H
0G8
(204) 958-7670
Emp Here 25
SIC 5172 Petroleum products, nec

D-U-N-S 20-042-5085 (BR)

PITNEY BOWES OF CANADA LTD
PITNEY BOWES DANKA
(*Suby of* Pitney Bowes Inc.)
550 Century St Suite 350, Winnipeg, MB, R3H
0Y1
(204) 489-2220
Emp Here 30
SIC 5712 Furniture stores

D-U-N-S 20-519-2891 (SL)
POWER VAC SERVICES LTD
1355 Border St, Winnipeg, MB, R3H 0N1
(204) 632-4433
Emp Here 50 *Sales* 1,459,214
SIC 7349 Building maintenance services, nec

D-U-N-S 20-350-4923 (SL)
R1 GP INC
EXCHANGE TECHNOLOGY SERVICES
1067 Sherwin Rd, Winnipeg, MB, R3H 0T8
(204) 982-1857
Emp Here 20 *Sales* 1,459,214
SIC 7379 Computer related services, nec

D-U-N-S 24-354-9313 (BR)
ROBINSON, B.A. CO. LTD
B.A. EXPRESS
1760 Ellice Ave, Winnipeg, MB, R3H 0B6
(204) 789-0006
Emp Here 45
SIC 5999 Miscellaneous retail stores, nec

D-U-N-S 20-010-8942 (HQ)
ROBINSON, B.A. CO. LTD
BCP PLUMBING SUPPLIES, DIV OF
619 Berry St, Winnipeg, MB, R3H 0S2
(204) 784-0150
Emp Here 25 *Emp Total* 350
Sales 94,232,900
SIC 5074 Plumbing and heating equipment
and supplies (hydronics)
Pr Pr J Ross Robinson

D-U-N-S 24-851-6023 (BR)
RUSSEL METALS INC
RUSSEL METALS NORTH WINNIPEG
1359 St James St, Winnipeg, MB, R3H 0K9
(204) 772-0321
Emp Here 90
SIC 5051 Metals service centers and offices

D-U-N-S 24-774-5029 (SL)
SCE LIFEWORKS INC
530 Century St Suite 227, Winnipeg, MB, R3H
0Y4
(204) 775-9402
Emp Here 67 *Sales* 3,137,310
SIC 8331 Job training and related services

D-U-N-S 20-519-1562 (SL)
SMS ENGINEERING LTD
770 Bradford St, Winnipeg, MB, R3H 0N3
(204) 775-0291
Emp Here 50 *Sales* 4,961,328
SIC 8711 Engineering services

D-U-N-S 20-732-8084 (BR)
SIEMENS CANADA LIMITED
BUILDING AUTOMATION
675 Berry St, Winnipeg, MB, R3H 1A7
(204) 774-3411
Emp Here 20
SIC 1731 Electrical work

D-U-N-S 25-671-4411 (BR)
SOBEYS WEST INC
LUCERNE FOODS, DIV OF
940 Century St, Winnipeg, MB, R3H 0V7

Emp Here 52
SIC 5143 Dairy products, except dried or
canned

D-U-N-S 20-836-9863 (HQ)
STANDARD AERO LIMITED
33 Allen Dyne Rd, Winnipeg, MB, R3H 1A1

(204) 775-9711
Emp Here 1,200   *Emp Total* 4,000
Sales 116,943,885
SIC 7538 General automotive repair shops
Pr Russell Ford
VP Fin Brent Fawkes
Dir Fin Thomas Brayton
 Mike Scott

D-U-N-S 24-233-1184   (BR)
STAPLES CANADA INC
STAPLES BUSINESS DEPOT
(*Suby of* Staples, Inc.)
947 St James St, Winnipeg, MB, R3H 0X2
(204) 783-7874
Emp Here 60
SIC 5943 Stationery stores

D-U-N-S 25-517-7750   (BR)
TDG FURNITURE INC
DUFRESNE FURNITURE & APPLIANCE
1750 Ellice Ave, Winnipeg, MB, R3H 0B3
(204) 989-9900
Emp Here 30
SIC 5712 Furniture stores

D-U-N-S 20-702-4410   (BR)
TDG FURNITURE INC
ASHLEY FURNITURE
1000 St James St, Winnipeg, MB, R3H 0K3
(204) 783-6400
Emp Here 30
SIC 5712 Furniture stores

D-U-N-S 25-153-7437   (BR)
TERVITA CORPORATION
HAZCO ENVIRONMENTAL SERVICES
(*Suby of* Tervita Corporation)
1199 St James St Suite 1, Winnipeg, MB, R3H 0K8
(204) 832-4561
Emp Here 50
SIC 8748 Business consulting, nec

D-U-N-S 20-316-2912   (SL)
THE GRAND WINNIPEG AIRPORT HOTEL BY LAKEVIEW
1979 Wellington Ave, Winnipeg, MB, R3H 1H5
(204) 479-2493
Emp Here 60   *Sales* 3,118,504
SIC 7011 Hotels and motels

D-U-N-S 24-316-1903   (BR)
TOROMONT INDUSTRIES LTD
TOROMONT LIFT
1214 Border St, Winnipeg, MB, R3H 0M6
(204) 633-4646
Emp Here 24
SIC 7699 Repair services, nec

D-U-N-S 24-427-8958   (BR)
TOROMONT INDUSTRIES LTD
CIMCO REFRIGERATION
1680 Notre Dame Ave Unit 8, Winnipeg, MB, R3H 1H6
(204) 783-1178
Emp Here 35
SIC 1711 Plumbing, heating, air-conditioning

D-U-N-S 24-819-4532   (BR)
TRADER CORPORATION
AUTO TRADER
1749 Ellice Ave Suite G, Winnipeg, MB, R3H 1H9
(204) 949-6444
Emp Here 25
SIC 2721 Periodicals

D-U-N-S 24-852-2187   (BR)
TRADER CORPORATION
HOME BASE
1749 Ellice Ave Suite G, Winnipeg, MB, R3H 1H9
(204) 949-6444
Emp Here 40
SIC 2721 Periodicals

D-U-N-S 24-375-8976   (BR)
TYCO INTEGRATED FIRE & SECURITY

CANADA, INC
SIMPLEXGRINNELL
(*Suby of* Johnson Controls, Inc.)
989 Century St, Winnipeg, MB, R3H 0W4
(204) 694-0140
Emp Here 50
SIC 7389 Business services, nec

D-U-N-S 24-917-1612   (BR)
UAP INC
NAPA AUTO PARTS
(*Suby of* Genuine Parts Company)
1777 Ellice Ave, Winnipeg, MB, R3H 0B4
(204) 779-6200
Emp Here 60
SIC 5013 Motor vehicle supplies and new parts

D-U-N-S 24-099-1385   (BR)
UNITED PARCEL SERVICE CANADA LTD
UPS
1099 King Edward St, Winnipeg, MB, R3H 0R3
(204) 631-0379
Emp Here 30
SIC 7389 Business services, nec

D-U-N-S 25-999-4374   (BR)
VALUE VILLAGE STORES, INC
(*Suby of* Savers, Inc.)
1695 Ellice Ave Unit 2053, Winnipeg, MB, R3H 0A9
(204) 774-1315
Emp Here 30
SIC 5399 Miscellaneous general merchandise

D-U-N-S 20-568-8617   (BR)
VIPOND INC
571 Ferry Rd, Winnipeg, MB, R3H 0T5
(204) 783-2420
Emp Here 30
SIC 1711 Plumbing, heating, air-conditioning

D-U-N-S 20-007-3411   (SL)
VOLTAGE POWER LTD
1313 Border St Unit 21, Winnipeg, MB, R3H 0X4
(204) 594-1140
Emp Here 210   *Sales* 36,772,193
SIC 1623 Water, sewer, and utility lines
Pr Jody Rideout
Dir Opers Grant Petersen
Dir A. Wayne Stewart

D-U-N-S 20-732-9512   (BR)
WHOLESALE SPORTS CANADA LTD
WHOLESALE SPORTS
1225 St James St, Winnipeg, MB, R3H 0K9
(204) 663-1094
Emp Here 40
SIC 5941 Sporting goods and bicycle shops

Winnipeg, MB R3J

D-U-N-S 25-891-9802   (BR)
3177743 MANITOBA LTD
BOSTON PIZZA
(*Suby of* 3177743 Manitoba Ltd)
2517 Portage Ave, Winnipeg, MB, R3J 0P1
(204) 925-4101
Emp Here 50
SIC 5812 Eating places

D-U-N-S 25-660-5502   (BR)
BAYSHORE HEALTHCARE LTD.
BAYSHORE HOMEHEALTH
1700 Ness Ave, Winnipeg, MB, R3J 3Y1
(204) 943-7124
Emp Here 150
SIC 8049 Offices of health practitioner

D-U-N-S 25-747-7596   (BR)
CARTER, DWAYNE ENTERPRISES LTD
MCDONALD'S
2359 Ness Ave Suite 2, Winnipeg, MB, R3J

1A5
(204) 949-3227
Emp Here 20
SIC 5812 Eating places

D-U-N-S 24-336-9142   (BR)
CITY OF WINNIPEG, THE
ST JAMES CIVIC CENTRE
(*Suby of* City of Winnipeg, The)
2055 Ness Ave, Winnipeg, MB, R3J 0Z2
(204) 986-3394
Emp Here 70
SIC 8322 Individual and family services

D-U-N-S 24-775-0029   (BR)
EXTENDICARE INC
EXTENDICARE OAKVIEW PLACE
2395 Ness Ave, Winnipeg, MB, R3J 1A5
(204) 888-3005
Emp Here 300
SIC 8051 Skilled nursing care facilities

D-U-N-S 24-669-2552   (BR)
FORD CREDIT CANADA LIMITED
(*Suby of* Ford Motor Company)
1612 Ness Ave Suite 300, Winnipeg, MB, R3J 0H7
(204) 786-5865
Emp Here 35
SIC 6141 Personal credit institutions

D-U-N-S 25-506-7555   (SL)
G.R.R. HOLDINGS LTD
KEG STEAKHOUSE & BAR
2553 Portage Ave, Winnipeg, MB, R3J 0P3
(204) 885-5275
Emp Here 140   *Sales* 4,231,721
SIC 5812 Eating places

D-U-N-S 25-652-0974   (BR)
GORDON HOTELS & MOTOR INNS LTD
ASSINIBOINE GORDON INN ON THE PARK
1975 Portage Ave, Winnipeg, MB, R3J 0J9
(204) 888-4806
Emp Here 75
SIC 7011 Hotels and motels

D-U-N-S 24-040-5506   (SL)
GOVERNING COUNCIL OF THE SALVATION ARMY IN CANADA, THE
SALVATION ARMY TORONTO GRACE HEALTH CENTRE
300 Booth Dr, Winnipeg, MB, R3J 3M7
(204) 837-8311
Emp Here 1,300   *Sales* 116,848,796
SIC 8062 General medical and surgical hospitals
Ex Dir Major Larry Jenning

D-U-N-S 25-315-7382   (BR)
INVESTORS GROUP FINANCIAL SERVICES INC
1661 Portage Ave Suite 702, Winnipeg, MB, R3J 3T7
(204) 786-2708
Emp Here 80
SIC 8741 Management services

D-U-N-S 24-953-1815   (BR)
LADCO COMPANY LIMITED
HOLIDAY INN AIRPORT WEST
2520 Portage Ave, Winnipeg, MB, R3J 3T6
(204) 885-4478
Emp Here 200
SIC 7011 Hotels and motels

D-U-N-S 25-281-5287   (BR)
MD MANAGEMENT LIMITED
MD FINANCIAL
(*Suby of* Canadian Medical Association)
1661 Portage Ave Suite 606, Winnipeg, MB, R3J 3T7
(204) 783-2463
Emp Here 22
SIC 6722 Management investment, open-end

D-U-N-S 20-610-5970   (BR)
MD PRIVATE TRUST COMPANY

(*Suby of* Canadian Medical Association)
1661 Portage Ave Suite 606, Winnipeg, MB, R3J 3T7
(204) 783-1824
Emp Here 25
SIC 8742 Management consulting services

D-U-N-S 20-078-1230   (BR)
MAJOR DRILLING GROUP INTERNATIONAL INC
(*Suby of* Major Drilling Group International Inc)
180 Cree Cres, Winnipeg, MB, R3J 3W1
(204) 885-7532
Emp Here 26
SIC 1481 NonMetallic mineral services

D-U-N-S 24-618-4027   (BR)
MANITOBA TEACHERS' SOCIETY, THE
EDUCATRICES & EDUATEURS
191 Harcourt St, Winnipeg, MB, R3J 3H2
(204) 837-6953
Emp Here 30
SIC 8631 Labor organizations

D-U-N-S 25-318-1309   (BR)
MCDONALD'S RESTAURANTS OF CANADA LIMITED
MCDONALD'S 8491
(*Suby of* McDonald's Corporation)
2475 Portage Ave, Winnipeg, MB, R3J 0N6
(204) 949-6053
Emp Here 60
SIC 5812 Eating places

D-U-N-S 20-721-0589   (BR)
MOORES THE SUIT PEOPLE INC
MOORES CLOTHING FOR MEN
(*Suby of* Tailored Brands, Inc.)
1600 Ness Ave Suite 310, Winnipeg, MB, R3J 3W7
(204) 783-2857
Emp Here 20
SIC 5611 Men's and boys' clothing stores

D-U-N-S 25-974-9331   (BR)
NAV CANADA
CANADA WINNIPEG AREA CONTROL
777 Moray St, Winnipeg, MB, R3J 3W8
(204) 983-8565
Emp Here 300
SIC 3812 Search and navigation equipment

D-U-N-S 25-684-2691   (BR)
NAV CANADA
4 Hangar Line Rd, Winnipeg, MB, R3J 3Y7
(204) 983-8407
Emp Here 50
SIC 8999 Services, nec

D-U-N-S 24-682-4262   (HQ)
NAYLOR (CANADA), INC
(*Suby of* Naylor (Canada), Inc)
1630 Ness Ave Unit 300, Winnipeg, MB, R3J 3X1
(204) 975-0415
Emp Here 194   *Emp Total* 200
Sales 14,592,140
SIC 2721 Periodicals
Pr Pr Michael Moss
VP Opers Bob Hitesman
VP Sls Chris Coldwell
Fin Ex Craig Gansky
 Brent Naylor

D-U-N-S 25-012-1001   (BR)
NORTH WEST COMPANY LP, THE
100 Murray Park Rd, Winnipeg, MB, R3J 3Y6
(204) 832-3700
Emp Here 65
SIC 5411 Grocery stores

D-U-N-S 24-037-2524   (HQ)
SATELLITE INDUSTRIES LTD
ARGUS INDUSTRIES
(*Suby of* Satellite Industries Ltd)
20 Murray Park Rd, Winnipeg, MB, R3J 3T9

---

(204) 837-4660
Emp Here 55   *Emp Total* 60
Sales 9,120,088
SIC 3069 Fabricated rubber products, nec
Pr Pr D William Easton
 Kristine E Easton

D-U-N-S 20-316-1245   (BR)
SHOCK TRAUMA AIR RESCUE SOCIETY
STARS
155 West Hangar Rd, Winnipeg, MB, R3J 3Z1
(204) 786-4647
Emp Here 46
SIC 4522 Air transportation, nonscheduled

D-U-N-S 25-271-9893   (BR)
SOBEYS WEST INC
1612 Ness Ave, Winnipeg, MB, R3J 0H7
(204) 775-2414
Emp Here 65
SIC 5411 Grocery stores

D-U-N-S 25-154-0167   (BR)
ST. JAMES-ASSINIBOIA SCHOOL DIVISION
ECOLE ASSINIBOINE SCHOOL
175 Winston Rd, Winnipeg, MB, R3J 1N1
(204) 885-2216
Emp Here 25
SIC 8211 Elementary and secondary schools

D-U-N-S 25-484-7817   (BR)
ST. JAMES-ASSINIBOIA SCHOOL DIVISION
ST. JAMES COLLEGIATE
1900 Portage Ave, Winnipeg, MB, R3J 0J1
(204) 888-4867
Emp Here 55
SIC 8211 Elementary and secondary schools

D-U-N-S 20-844-9970   (BR)
ST. JAMES-ASSINIBOIA SCHOOL DIVISION
PROFESSIONAL STAFF DEVELOPMENT CENTRE
150 Moray St, Winnipeg, MB, R3J 3A2
(204) 837-5886
Emp Here 20
SIC 8331 Job training and related services

D-U-N-S 25-450-3055   (BR)
ST. JAMES-ASSINIBOIA SCHOOL DIVISION
SILVER HEIGHTS COLLEGIATE
350 Lodge Ave, Winnipeg, MB, R3J 0S4

Emp Here 65
SIC 8211 Elementary and secondary schools

D-U-N-S 25-288-5660   (BR)
ST. JAMES-ASSINIBOIA SCHOOL DIVISION
BRUCE MIDDLE SCHOOL
333 Booth Dr, Winnipeg, MB, R3J 3M8
(204) 888-1990
Emp Here 45
SIC 8211 Elementary and secondary schools

D-U-N-S 20-709-7606   (BR)
ST. JAMES-ASSINIBOIA SCHOOL DIVISION
ECOLE GOLDEN GATE MIDDLE SCHOOL
330 Bruce Ave, Winnipeg, MB, R3J 0V8
(204) 837-5808
Emp Here 50
SIC 8211 Elementary and secondary schools

D-U-N-S 20-552-4122   (BR)
ST. JAMES-ASSINIBOIA SCHOOL DIVISION
LINWOOD SCHOOL
266 Linwood St, Winnipeg, MB, R3J 2C6
(204) 889-9356
Emp Here 31
SIC 8211 Elementary and secondary schools

D-U-N-S 20-081-6119   (BR)
ST. JAMES-ASSINIBOIA SCHOOL DIVI-

SION
STEVENSON BRITANNIA SCHOOL
1777 Silver Ave, Winnipeg, MB, R3J 1B1
(204) 832-1359
Emp Here 35
SIC 8211 Elementary and secondary schools

D-U-N-S 20-709-7580   (BR)
ST. JAMES-ASSINIBOIA SCHOOL DIVISION
ECOLE BANNATYNE SCHOOL
363 Thompson Dr, Winnipeg, MB, R3J 3E5
(204) 888-1101
Emp Here 30
SIC 8211 Elementary and secondary schools

D-U-N-S 25-073-4282   (BR)
ST. JAMES-ASSINIBOIA SCHOOL DIVISION
ATHLONE SCHOOL
110 Athlone Dr, Winnipeg, MB, R3J 3L4
(204) 832-1373
Emp Here 25
SIC 8211 Elementary and secondary schools

D-U-N-S 25-484-7841   (BR)
ST. JAMES-ASSINIBOIA SCHOOL DIVISION
STRATHMILLAN SCHOOL
339 Strathmillan Rd, Winnipeg, MB, R3J 2V6
(204) 888-0148
Emp Here 60
SIC 8211 Elementary and secondary schools

D-U-N-S 24-029-0432   (BR)
TEN TEN SINCLAIR HOUSING INC
FOKUS 3
299 Queen St Suite 208, Winnipeg, MB, R3J 3V5
(204) 385-7519
Emp Here 20
SIC 6513 Apartment building operators

D-U-N-S 24-360-1403   (BR)
WE CARE HEALTH SERVICES INC
1661 Portage Ave Suite 209, Winnipeg, MB, R3J 3T7
(204) 987-3044
Emp Here 175
SIC 8051 Skilled nursing care facilities

Winnipeg, MB R3K

D-U-N-S 20-569-0469   (BR)
75040 MANITOBA LTD
DESTINATION MAZDA
3690 Portage Ave, Winnipeg, MB, R3K 0Z8
(888) 219-5989
Emp Here 20
SIC 5511 New and used car dealers

D-U-N-S 25-288-0190   (BR)
A & W FOOD SERVICES OF CANADA INC
A & W
3095 Portage Ave, Winnipeg, MB, R3K 0W4
(204) 885-7633
Emp Here 40
SIC 5812 Eating places

D-U-N-S 20-571-8575   (BR)
ARBOR MEMORIAL SERVICES INC
4000 Portage Ave, Winnipeg, MB, R3K 1W3
(204) 982-8100
Emp Here 20
SIC 7261 Funeral service and crematories

D-U-N-S 20-836-5031   (SL)
ASSINIBOINE DENTAL GROUP
3278 Portage Ave, Winnipeg, MB, R3K 0Z1
(204) 958-4444
Emp Here 50   *Sales* 2,845,467
SIC 8021 Offices and clinics of dentists

D-U-N-S 25-786-5139   (BR)
BIRCHWOOD AUTOMOTIVE GROUP LIM-

ITED
POINTE WEST COLLISION CENTRE
3965 Portage Ave Unit 60, Winnipeg, MB, R3K 2H2
(204) 885-1999
Emp Here 30
SIC 7532 Top and body repair and paint shops

D-U-N-S 24-818-2008   (SL)
BIRCHWOOD PONTIAC BUICK LIMITED
BIRCHWOOD CHEVROLET BUICK GMC
3965 Portage Ave Unit 40, Winnipeg, MB, R3K 2H1
(204) 837-5811
Emp Here 72   *Sales* 36,172,800
SIC 5511 New and used car dealers
Pr Mark Chipman
 Stephen Chipman
 Dennis R Tole

D-U-N-S 25-311-6636   (BR)
CANADIAN IMPERIAL BANK OF COMMERCE
CIBC
3369 Portage Ave, Winnipeg, MB, R3K 0W9
(204) 944-6029
Emp Here 35
SIC 6021 National commercial banks

D-U-N-S 25-301-8006   (BR)
CARTER, DWAYNE ENTERPRISES LTD
MCDONALD'S
3401 Portage Ave, Winnipeg, MB, R3K 0W9
(204) 949-6022
Emp Here 100
SIC 5812 Eating places

D-U-N-S 25-318-1267   (BR)
CARTER, DWAYNE ENTERPRISES LTD
MCDONALD'S
3655 Portage Ave Unit 64, Winnipeg, MB, R3K 2G6
(204) 949-6014
Emp Here 50
SIC 5812 Eating places

D-U-N-S 20-799-1683   (BR)
DALE & DALE PIZZA INC
DOMINO'S PIZZA
3059 Portage Ave Unit C, Winnipeg, MB, R3K 0W4
(204) 987-5555
Emp Here 20
SIC 5812 Eating places

D-U-N-S 20-961-4606   (BR)
DOLLARAMA S.E.C.
DOLLARAMA
3421 Portage Ave Suite 15, Winnipeg, MB, R3K 2C9
(204) 832-5440
Emp Here 20
SIC 5399 Miscellaneous general merchandise

D-U-N-S 25-719-2351   (BR)
LOBLAWS INC
REAL CANADIAN SUPERSTORE
3193 Portage Ave, Winnipeg, MB, R3K 0W4
(204) 831-3528
Emp Here 270
SIC 5399 Miscellaneous general merchandise

D-U-N-S 24-126-6738   (SL)
LODGE MANAGEMENT LTD
3278 Portage Ave, Winnipeg, MB, R3K 0Z1
(204) 958-4444
Emp Here 50   *Sales* 3,378,379
SIC 8021 Offices and clinics of dentists

D-U-N-S 24-967-4482   (SL)
MANITOBA JOCKEY CLUB INC
ASSINIBOIA DOWNS
3975 Portage Ave, Winnipeg, MB, R3K 2E9
(204) 885-3330
Emp Here 150
SIC 7948 Racing, including track operation

D-U-N-S 20-835-3920   (SL)
MEDI-VAN TRANSPORTATION SPECIAL-

ISTS INC
MEDI-VAN
284 Rouge Rd, Winnipeg, MB, R3K 1K2
(204) 982-0790
Emp Here 90   *Sales* 3,137,310
SIC 4111 Local and suburban transit

D-U-N-S 24-169-8810   (BR)
MEMORIAL GARDENS CANADA LIMITED
CHAPEL LAWN MEMORIAL GARDEN
4000 Portage Ave, Winnipeg, MB, R3K 1W3
(204) 982-8100
Emp Here 25
SIC 6553 Cemetery subdividers and developers

D-U-N-S 20-557-9886   (BR)
REVERA INC
HERITAGE LODGE PERSONAL CARE
3555 Portage Ave, Winnipeg, MB, R3K 0X2
(204) 888-7940
Emp Here 110
SIC 8051 Skilled nursing care facilities

D-U-N-S 20-536-4594   (BR)
ROYAL BANK OF CANADA
RBC
(*Suby of* Royal Bank Of Canada)
3297 Portage Ave, Winnipeg, MB, R3K 0W7

Emp Here 20
SIC 6021 National commercial banks

D-U-N-S 20-806-2443   (BR)
SOBEYS CAPITAL INCORPORATED
SOBEYS STORE 5104
3635 Portage Ave, Winnipeg, MB, R3K 2G6
(204) 832-8605
Emp Here 100
SIC 5411 Grocery stores

D-U-N-S 20-859-9840   (BR)
SOURCE (BELL) ELECTRONICS INC, THE
SOURCE, THE
3653 Portage Ave Suite 3, Winnipeg, MB, R3K 2G6
(204) 832-9163
Emp Here 25
SIC 5999 Miscellaneous retail stores, nec

D-U-N-S 20-838-7415   (SL)
ST. CHARLES COUNTRY CLUB
100 Country Club Blvd, Winnipeg, MB, R3K 1Z3
(204) 889-4444
Emp Here 90   *Sales* 3,648,035
SIC 7997 Membership sports and recreation clubs

D-U-N-S 25-289-0736   (BR)
ST. JAMES-ASSINIBOIA SCHOOL DIVISION
SANSOME SCHOOL
181 Sansome Ave, Winnipeg, MB, R3K 0N8
(204) 889-6000
Emp Here 40
SIC 8211 Elementary and secondary schools

D-U-N-S 20-709-7630   (BR)
ST. JAMES-ASSINIBOIA SCHOOL DIVISION
BROWNING, ROBERT SCHOOL
130 Browning Blvd, Winnipeg, MB, R3K 0L8
(204) 837-8381
Emp Here 40
SIC 8211 Elementary and secondary schools

D-U-N-S 25-452-4739   (BR)
ST. JAMES-ASSINIBOIA SCHOOL DIVISION
LINCOLN MIDDLE SCHOOL
3180 Mcbey Ave, Winnipeg, MB, R3K 0T7
(204) 837-8397
Emp Here 38
SIC 8211 Elementary and secondary schools

D-U-N-S 20-273-7177   (BR)
STAPLES CANADA INC

(Suby of Staples, Inc.)
3669 Portage Ave, Winnipeg, MB, R3K 2G6
(204) 925-4518
Emp Here 22
SIC 5943 Stationery stores

D-U-N-S 24-736-0428   (SL)
TN ICEPLEX LIMITED PARTNERSHIP
MTS ICEPLEX
3969 Portage Ave, Winnipeg, MB, R3K 1W4
(204) 837-7539
Emp Here 75   Sales 4,085,799
SIC 7999 Amusement and recreation, nec

D-U-N-S 20-561-0681   (SL)
VBALLS TARGET SYSTEMS INC
COMBATBALL
51 Allard Ave, Winnipeg, MB, R3K 0S8
(204) 888-6768
Emp Here 60   Sales 4,961,328
SIC 3949 Sporting and athletic goods, nec

D-U-N-S 25-058-2400   (BR)
WAL-MART CANADA CORP
3655 Portage Ave, Winnipeg, MB, R3K 2G6
(204) 897-3410
Emp Here 115
SIC 5311 Department stores

D-U-N-S 20-555-9607   (BR)
WINNERS MERCHANTS INTERNATIONAL L.P.
WINNERS
(Suby of The TJX Companies Inc)
3625 Portage Ave, Winnipeg, MB, R3K 2G6
(204) 889-8733
Emp Here 50
SIC 5651 Family clothing stores

D-U-N-S 20-913-8168   (BR)
YOUNG MEN'S AND YOUNG WOMEN'S CHRISTIAN ASSOCIATION OF WINNIPEG INCORPORATED, THE
3550 Portage Ave, Winnipeg, MB, R3K 0Z8
(204) 889-8052
Emp Here 75
SIC 8641 Civic and social associations

Winnipeg, MB R3L

D-U-N-S 20-518-1022   (SL)
285 PEMBINA INC
285 Pembina Hwy, Winnipeg, MB, R3L 2E1
(204) 284-0802
Emp Here 100   Sales 9,411,930
SIC 6531 Real estate agents and managers
Dir Henry Neudorf

D-U-N-S 24-967-5844   (SL)
GREEN, E. HOLDINGS LTD
OSBORNE VILLAGE INN
160 Osborne St, Winnipeg, MB, R3L 1Y6
(204) 452-9824
Emp Here 60   Sales 2,626,585
SIC 7011 Hotels and motels

D-U-N-S 20-552-4387   (BR)
LABOUR READY TEMPORARY SERVICES LTD
28 Queen Elizabeth Way, Winnipeg, MB, R3L 2R1
(204) 989-7590
Emp Here 45
SIC 7363 Help supply services

D-U-N-S 20-797-6650   (BR)
MCDONALD'S RESTAURANTS OF CANADA LIMITED
MCDONALD'S
(Suby of McDonald's Corporation)
375 Osborne St, Winnipeg, MB, R3L 2A2
(204) 949-6044
Emp Here 20
SIC 5812 Eating places

D-U-N-S 20-210-6931   (BR)
REDBERRY FRANCHISING CORP
BURGER KING
244 Osborne St, Winnipeg, MB, R3L 1Z5
(204) 987-8433
Emp Here 35
SIC 5812 Eating places

D-U-N-S 24-265-3533   (SL)
RIVERVIEW HEALTH CENTRE INC
1 Morley Ave, Winnipeg, MB, R3L 2P4
(204) 478-6203
Emp Here 850   Sales 47,734,066
SIC 8051 Skilled nursing care facilities
Pr Pr Norman R Kasian
  Romeo Daley
Ch Bd Dal Mccloy
V Ch Bd Marilyn Kapitany
  Shawna Pachal
Dir Rob Stephenson
Dir Ian Smith

D-U-N-S 24-915-3578   (BR)
ROGERS MEDIA INC
92 CITI FM
(Suby of Rogers Communications Inc)
166 Osborne St Suite 4, Winnipeg, MB, R3L 1Y8
(204) 788-3400
Emp Here 35
SIC 4832 Radio broadcasting stations

D-U-N-S 24-914-2647   (HQ)
SHELTER CANADIAN PROPERTIES LIMITED
7 Evergreen Pl Suite 2600, Winnipeg, MB, R3L 2T3
(204) 474-5975
Emp Here 75   Emp Total 300
Sales 36,172,800
SIC 6513 Apartment building operators
Pr Pr Arni Thorsteinson
VP Richard Blair
Acct Mgr Kenneth Dando

D-U-N-S 24-206-5923   (BR)
SOBEYS WEST INC
OSBORNE & KYLEMORE SAFEWAY
655 Osborne St, Winnipeg, MB, R3L 2B7
(204) 475-0793
Emp Here 150
SIC 5411 Grocery stores

D-U-N-S 24-355-9593   (BR)
VIA RAIL CANADA INC
569 Brandon Ave, Winnipeg, MB, R3L 2V7
(204) 924-4716
Emp Here 35
SIC 4111 Local and suburban transit

D-U-N-S 20-709-7473   (BR)
WINNIPEG SCHOOL DIVISION
RIVERVIEW SCHOOL
253 Maplewood Ave, Winnipeg, MB, R3L 2L4
(204) 284-5983
Emp Here 50
SIC 8211 Elementary and secondary schools

D-U-N-S 25-011-6027   (BR)
WINNIPEG SCHOOL DIVISION
LORD ROBERTS COMMUNITY SCHOOL
665 Beresford Ave, Winnipeg, MB, R3L 1J9
(204) 453-6639
Emp Here 70
SIC 8211 Elementary and secondary schools

D-U-N-S 20-709-7309   (BR)
WINNIPEG SCHOOL DIVISION
GLADSTONE SCHOOL
500 Gertrude Ave, Winnipeg, MB, R3L 0M8
(204) 475-4767
Emp Here 30
SIC 8211 Elementary and secondary schools

D-U-N-S 25-138-5456   (BR)
WINNIPEG SCHOOL DIVISION
CHURCHILL HIGH SCHOOL
510 Hay St, Winnipeg, MB, R3L 2L6

(204) 474-1301
Emp Here 90
SIC 8211 Elementary and secondary schools

D-U-N-S 20-709-7275   (BR)
WINNIPEG SCHOOL DIVISION
FORT ROUGE SCHOOL
115 River Ave, Winnipeg, MB, R3L 0A8
(204) 475-5057
Emp Here 30
SIC 8211 Elementary and secondary schools

Winnipeg, MB R3M

D-U-N-S 20-518-1055   (BR)
CANADA TRUST COMPANY, THE
TD CANADA TRUST
(Suby of Toronto-Dominion Bank, The)
1114 Corydon Ave, Winnipeg, MB, R3M 0Y9
(204) 985-4400
Emp Here 20
SIC 6021 National commercial banks

D-U-N-S 25-311-6362   (BR)
CANADIAN IMPERIAL BANK OF COMMERCE
CIBC
1120 Grant Ave Suite 17, Winnipeg, MB, R3M 2A6
(204) 944-5063
Emp Here 25
SIC 6021 National commercial banks

D-U-N-S 20-835-6170   (SL)
CONVALESCENT HOME OF WINNIPEG, THE
276 Hugo St N, Winnipeg, MB, R3M 2N6
(204) 453-4663
Emp Here 98   Sales 4,596,524
SIC 8051 Skilled nursing care facilities

D-U-N-S 20-712-0528   (BR)
LONG & MCQUADE LIMITED
LONG & MCQUADE MUSICAL INSTRUMENTS
651 Stafford St, Winnipeg, MB, R3M 2X7
(204) 284-8992
Emp Here 25
SIC 5736 Musical instrument stores

D-U-N-S 24-116-4367   (SL)
MANITOBA CARDIAC INSTITUTE (REH-FIT) INC
REH-FIT CENTRE
1390 Taylor Ave, Winnipeg, MB, R3M 3V8
(204) 488-8023
Emp Here 50   Sales 3,283,232
SIC 8011 Offices and clinics of medical doctors

D-U-N-S 20-845-4608   (BR)
MANITOBA LIQUOR AND LOTTERIES CORPORATION
MLCC
1120 Grant Ave, Winnipeg, MB, R3M 2A6
(204) 987-4045
Emp Here 20
SIC 5921 Liquor stores

D-U-N-S 25-305-4902   (BR)
MCDONALD'S RESTAURANTS OF CANADA LIMITED
MCDONALD'S 8031
(Suby of McDonald's Corporation)
425 Nathaniel St Suite 1187, Winnipeg, MB, R3M 3X1
(204) 949-6031
Emp Here 80
SIC 5812 Eating places

D-U-N-S 25-011-0863   (BR)
MCDONALD'S RESTAURANTS OF CANADA LIMITED
MCDONALD'S
(Suby of McDonald's Corporation)

630 Pembina Hwy, Winnipeg, MB, R3M 2M5
(204) 949-6091
Emp Here 56
SIC 5812 Eating places

D-U-N-S 25-831-9318   (BR)
MCMUNN & YATES BUILDING SUPPLIES LTD
MCDIARMID LUMBER HOME CENTRES
600 Pembina Hwy, Winnipeg, MB, R3M 2M5
(204) 940-4040
Emp Here 88
SIC 5211 Lumber and other building materials

D-U-N-S 20-758-5548   (SL)
REHABILITATION CENTRE FOR CHILDREN INC
633 Wellington Cres, Winnipeg, MB, R3M 0A8
(204) 452-4311
Emp Here 100   Sales 3,648,035
SIC 8361 Residential care

D-U-N-S 24-915-8494   (BR)
REVERA INC
POSEIDON CARE CENTRE
70 Poseidon Bay Suite 504, Winnipeg, MB, R3M 3E5
(204) 452-6204
Emp Here 300
SIC 8051 Skilled nursing care facilities

D-U-N-S 25-094-5391   (BR)
ROYAL BANK OF CANADA
ROYAL DIRECT
(Suby of Royal Bank Of Canada)
1260 Taylor Ave, Winnipeg, MB, R3M 3Y8
(204) 499-7000
Emp Here 900
SIC 7299 Miscellaneous personal service

D-U-N-S 24-206-5931   (BR)
SOBEYS WEST INC
GRANT PARK PLAZA SAFEWAY
1120 Grant Ave, Winnipeg, MB, R3M 2A6
(204) 452-7197
Emp Here 150
SIC 5411 Grocery stores

D-U-N-S 25-272-3804   (SL)
ST MARY'S ACADEMY INC
550 Wellington Cres, Winnipeg, MB, R3M 0C1
(204) 477-0244
Emp Here 70   Sales 4,669,485
SIC 8211 Elementary and secondary schools

D-U-N-S 20-709-7341   (BR)
WINNIPEG SCHOOL DIVISION
HARROW SCHOOL
550 Harrow St Suite 13, Winnipeg, MB, R3M 3A2
(204) 453-3347
Emp Here 27
SIC 8211 Elementary and secondary schools

D-U-N-S 25-026-4637   (BR)
WINNIPEG SCHOOL DIVISION
GRANT PARK HIGH SCHOOL
450 Nathaniel St, Winnipeg, MB, R3M 3E3
(204) 452-3112
Emp Here 170
SIC 8211 Elementary and secondary schools

D-U-N-S 20-709-7408   (BR)
WINNIPEG SCHOOL DIVISION
ECOLE LA VERENDRYE SCHOOL
290 Lilac St, Winnipeg, MB, R3M 2T5
(204) 452-5015
Emp Here 20
SIC 8211 Elementary and secondary schools

D-U-N-S 20-709-7333   (BR)
WINNIPEG SCHOOL DIVISION
GROSVENOR SCHOOL
1045 Grosvenor Ave, Winnipeg, MB, R3M 0M8
(204) 475-5242
Emp Here 40
SIC 8211 Elementary and secondary schools

D-U-N-S 25-011-6514   (BR)
WINNIPEG SCHOOL DIVISION
MONTROSE SCHOOL
691 Montrose St Suite 1, Winnipeg, MB, R3M 3M4
(204) 488-8112
Emp Here 35
SIC 8211 Elementary and secondary schools

D-U-N-S 25-289-2849   (BR)
WINNIPEG SCHOOL DIVISION
RIVER HEIGHTS SCHOOL
1350 Grosvenor Ave, Winnipeg, MB, R3M 0P2
(204) 488-7090
Emp Here 46
SIC 8211 Elementary and secondary schools

D-U-N-S 24-971-4668   (BR)
WINNIPEG SCHOOL DIVISION
EARL GREY SCHOOL
340 Cockburn St N, Winnipeg, MB, R3M 2P5
(204) 474-1441
Emp Here 32
SIC 8211 Elementary and secondary schools

D-U-N-S 25-450-2396   (BR)
WINNIPEG SCHOOL DIVISION
ROCKWOOD SCHOOL
350 Rockwood St, Winnipeg, MB, R3M 3C5
(204) 452-4210
Emp Here 30
SIC 8211 Elementary and secondary schools

D-U-N-S 25-892-6120   (BR)
WINNIPEG SCHOOL DIVISION
ECOLE ROBERT H. SMITH SCHOOL
315 Oak St, Winnipeg, MB, R3M 3P8
(204) 488-1137
Emp Here 50
SIC 8211 Elementary and secondary schools

D-U-N-S 25-011-5532   (BR)
WINNIPEG SCHOOL DIVISION
KELVIN HIGH SCHOOL
155 Kingsway, Winnipeg, MB, R3M 0G3
(204) 474-1492
Emp Here 110
SIC 8211 Elementary and secondary schools

Winnipeg, MB R3N

D-U-N-S 24-125-5715   (SL)
4395612 MANITOBA LTD
ROYAL LEPAGE DYNAMIC
1450 Corydon Ave Suite 2, Winnipeg, MB, R3N 0J3
(204) 989-5000
Emp Here 70   *Sales* 6,566,463
SIC 6531 Real estate agents and managers
Pr Pr Rick Preston

D-U-N-S 25-659-9069   (BR)
GISELLE'S PROFESSIONAL SKIN CARE LTD
(*Suby of* Giselle's Professional Skin Care Ltd)
1851 Grant Ave, Winnipeg, MB, R3N 1Z2

Emp Here 30
SIC 7231 Beauty shops

D-U-N-S 24-630-3069   (HQ)
GISELLE'S PROFESSIONAL SKIN CARE LTD
(*Suby of* Giselle's Professional Skin Care Ltd)
1700 Corydon Ave Unit 13, Winnipeg, MB, R3N 0K1

Emp Here 22   *Emp Total* 125
Sales 2,480,664
SIC 7231 Beauty shops

D-U-N-S 25-831-0291   (BR)
ROYAL BANK OF CANADA
RBC
(*Suby of* Royal Bank Of Canada)

1700 Corydon Ave Suite 100, Winnipeg, MB, R3N 0K1
(204) 988-5750
Emp Here 250
SIC 6021 National commercial banks

D-U-N-S 20-713-9283   (SL)
SHORE ELEMENTARY SCHOOL
GRAY ACADEMY OF JEWISH EDUCATION
123 Doncaster St Suite A200, Winnipeg, MB, R3N 2B4
(204) 477-7410
Emp Here 50   *Sales* 3,356,192
SIC 8211 Elementary and secondary schools

D-U-N-S 24-242-6067   (BR)
UNIVERSITY OF MANITOBA
BISON SPORTS
124 Frank St, Winnipeg, MB, R3N 1W1
(204) 474-7846
Emp Here 30
SIC 8221 Colleges and universities

D-U-N-S 20-844-9475   (SL)
WINNIPEG BOARD OF JEWISH EDUCA-TION, THE
GREY ACADEMY
123 Doncaster St Suite C300, Winnipeg, MB, R3N 2B2
(204) 477-7402
Emp Here 100   *Sales* 9,244,160
SIC 8211 Elementary and secondary schools
Genl Mgr Paul Rory

D-U-N-S 20-709-7465   (BR)
WINNIPEG SCHOOL DIVISION
QUEENSTON SCHOOL
245 Queenston St, Winnipeg, MB, R3N 0W6
(204) 489-3423
Emp Here 20
SIC 8211 Elementary and secondary schools

D-U-N-S 25-124-9934   (BR)
WINNIPEG SCHOOL DIVISION
CARPATHIA ELEMENTARY SCHOOL
300 Carpathia Rd, Winnipeg, MB, R3N 1T3
(204) 488-4514
Emp Here 40
SIC 8211 Elementary and secondary schools

D-U-N-S 20-709-7226   (BR)
WINNIPEG SCHOOL DIVISION
BROCK CORYDON SCHOOL
1510 Corydon Ave, Winnipeg, MB, R3N 0J6
(204) 488-4422
Emp Here 50
SIC 8211 Elementary and secondary schools

D-U-N-S 20-709-7572   (BR)
WINNIPEG SCHOOL DIVISION
J.B. MITCHELL SCHOOL
1720 John Brebeuf Pl, Winnipeg, MB, R3N 0M1
(204) 488-4517
Emp Here 50
SIC 8211 Elementary and secondary schools

Winnipeg, MB R3P

D-U-N-S 24-027-4550   (BR)
ADIDAS CANADA LIMITED
ADIDAS OUTLET SHOP
1599 Kenaston Blvd Suite 300, Winnipeg, MB, R3P 2N3
(204) 928-4810
Emp Here 20
SIC 5699 Miscellaneous apparel and acces-sory stores

D-U-N-S 20-570-8902   (BR)
AECOM CANADA LTD
SWAN HILLS TREATMENT CENTER
99 Commerce Dr, Winnipeg, MB, R3P 0Y7
(204) 477-5381
Emp Here 146

SIC 8711 Engineering services

D-U-N-S 24-360-1981   (BR)
ANIXTER POWER SOLUTIONS CANADA INC
BRAFASCO
1099 Wilkes Avenue Unit 7, Winnipeg, MB, R3P 2S2
(204) 284-3834
Emp Here 20
SIC 5085 Industrial supplies

D-U-N-S 20-572-3518   (BR)
BASF CANADA INC
7 Ossington Crt, Winnipeg, MB, R3P 2B3
(204) 985-1884
Emp Here 20
SIC 2821 Plastics materials and resins

D-U-N-S 20-918-4667   (BR)
BANQUE DE DEVELOPPEMENT DU CANADA
BDC
1655 Kenaston Blvd Suite 200, Winnipeg, MB, R3P 2M4
(204) 984-7442
Emp Here 20
SIC 6141 Personal credit institutions

D-U-N-S 20-294-0920   (BR)
CABELA'S RETAIL CANADA INC
CABELA'S CANADA
(*Suby of* Cabela's Incorporated)
580 Sterling Lyon Pky, Winnipeg, MB, R3P 1E9
(204) 786-8966
Emp Here 150
SIC 5941 Sporting goods and bicycle shops

D-U-N-S 20-518-1063   (BR)
CANADA TRUST COMPANY, THE
(*Suby of* Toronto-Dominion Bank, The)
2030 Corydon Ave, Winnipeg, MB, R3P 0N2
(204) 985-4620
Emp Here 20
SIC 6021 National commercial banks

D-U-N-S 24-775-2082   (BR)
CARLSTAR GROUP ULC, THE
CARLISLE TIRE & WHEEL
115 Lowson Cres, Winnipeg, MB, R3P 1A6
(204) 488-4974
Emp Here 20
SIC 5531 Auto and home supply stores

D-U-N-S 24-775-0482   (BR)
DIRECT LIMITED PARTNERSHIP
25 Rothwell Rd, Winnipeg, MB, R3P 2M5
(204) 453-8019
Emp Here 70
SIC 4225 General warehousing and storage

D-U-N-S 24-375-0189   (BR)
EXTENDICARE (CANADA) INC
EXTENDICARE TUXEDO VILLA
2060 Corydon Ave, Winnipeg, MB, R3P 0N3
(204) 889-2650
Emp Here 253
SIC 8051 Skilled nursing care facilities

D-U-N-S 20-004-8064   (HQ)
FWS CONSTRUCTION LTD
275 Commerce Dr, Winnipeg, MB, R3P 1B3
(204) 487-2500
Emp Here 63   *Emp Total* 300
Sales 14,883,983
SIC 1541 Industrial buildings and warehouses
Pr Pr Richard Chale
  Michael Evans
  Douglas Patrick
VP VP Troy Valgardson

D-U-N-S 24-248-7663   (BR)
GORDON FOOD SERVICE CANADA LTD
310 Sterling Lyon Pky, Winnipeg, MB, R3P 0Y2
(204) 224-0134
Emp Here 250

SIC 5141 Groceries, general line

D-U-N-S 24-851-9308   (BR)
GRANT THORNTON LLP
CAPSERVCO
94 Commerce Dr, Winnipeg, MB, R3P 0Z3
(204) 944-0100
Emp Here 45
SIC 8721 Accounting, auditing, and book-keeping

D-U-N-S 24-000-3009   (BR)
HOME DEPOT OF CANADA INC
(*Suby of* The Home Depot Inc)
1645 Kenaston Blvd, Winnipeg, MB, R3P 2M4
(204) 928-7110
Emp Here 50
SIC 5072 Hardware

D-U-N-S 20-104-0586   (BR)
HUDSON'S BAY COMPANY
HOME OUTFITTERS
1585 Kenaston Blvd Suite 10, Winnipeg, MB, R3P 2N3
(204) 488-3631
Emp Here 31
SIC 5719 Miscellaneous homefurnishings

D-U-N-S 24-979-5126   (BR)
INDIGO BOOKS & MUSIC INC
INDIGO
(*Suby of* Indigo Books & Music Inc)
1590 Kenaston Blvd Suite 100, Winnipeg, MB, R3P 0Y4
(204) 488-6621
Emp Here 20
SIC 5942 Book stores

D-U-N-S 25-294-6504   (BR)
LONDON LIFE INSURANCE COMPANY
FREEDOM 55 FINANCIAL , DIV OF
124 Nature Park Way, Winnipeg, MB, R3P 0X7
(204) 489-1012
Emp Here 60
SIC 6311 Life insurance

D-U-N-S 25-085-4668   (BR)
MAXIM TRANSPORTATION SERVICES INC
MAXIM TRUCK & TRAILER SERVICE
45 Lowson Cres, Winnipeg, MB, R3P 0T3
(204) 925-7080
Emp Here 20
SIC 7539 Automotive repair shops, nec

D-U-N-S 20-709-7739   (BR)
PEMBINA TRAILS SCHOOL DIVISION, THE
ECOLE TUXEDO PARK SCHOOL
2300 Corydon Ave, Winnipeg, MB, R3P 0N6
(204) 889-3602
Emp Here 22
SIC 8211 Elementary and secondary schools

D-U-N-S 20-709-7788   (BR)
PEMBINA TRAILS SCHOOL DIVISION, THE
VAN WALLEGHEM SCHOOL
1 Princemere Rd, Winnipeg, MB, R3P 1K9
(204) 489-0995
Emp Here 50
SIC 8211 Elementary and secondary schools

D-U-N-S 20-918-5607   (BR)
PEMBINA TRAILS SCHOOL DIVISION, THE
SHAFTESBURY HIGH SCHOOL
2240 Grant Ave, Winnipeg, MB, R3P 0P7
(204) 888-5898
Emp Here 80
SIC 8211 Elementary and secondary schools

D-U-N-S 20-025-9740   (BR)
PEMBINA TRAILS SCHOOL DIVISION, THE
LINDEN MEADOWS SCHOOL
335 Lindenwood Dr E, Winnipeg, MB, R3P 2H1
(204) 489-0799
Emp Here 60
SIC 8211 Elementary and secondary schools

D-U-N-S 25-952-3694   (BR)
PEPSICO CANADA ULC

▲ Public Company   ■ Public Company Family Member   **HQ** Headquarters   **BR** Branch   **SL** Single Location

HOSTESS FRITO-LAY
(*Suby of* Pepsico, Inc.)
1099 Wilkes Ave Unit 11, Winnipeg, MB, R3P 2S2
(204) 925-6040
Emp Here 50
SIC 2096 Potato chips and similar snacks

D-U-N-S 20-562-7446   (BR)
PHOENIX ENTERPRISES LTD
BROADWAY CONSTRUCTION
(*Suby of* Phoenix Enterprises Ltd)
100 Lowson Cres, Winnipeg, MB, R3P 2H8
(204) 261-1524
Emp Here 25
SIC 7349 Building maintenance services, nec

D-U-N-S 20-835-3008   (BR)
REVERA INC
PORTSMOUTH RETIREMENT RESIDENCE
125 Portsmouth Blvd, Winnipeg, MB, R3P 2M3
(204) 284-5432
Emp Here 60
SIC 6513 Apartment building operators

D-U-N-S 20-136-9761   (BR)
SNC-LAVALIN (S.A.) INC
148 Nature Park Way, Winnipeg, MB, R3P 0X7
(204) 786-8080
Emp Here 30
SIC 8711 Engineering services

D-U-N-S 24-342-7544   (BR)
SNC-LAVALIN INC
148 Nature Park Way, Winnipeg, MB, R3P 0X7
(204) 786-8080
Emp Here 60
SIC 8711 Engineering services

D-U-N-S 20-350-6873   (BR)
SOBEYS CAPITAL INCORPORATED
KENASTON SOBEYS
1660 Kenaston Blvd, Winnipeg, MB, R3P 2M6
(204) 489-7007
Emp Here 170
SIC 5411 Grocery stores

D-U-N-S 25-134-3166   (BR)
SOBEYS WEST INC
LINDENRIDGE SAFEWAY
1625 Kenaston Blvd, Winnipeg, MB, R3P 2M4
(204) 488-9404
Emp Here 130
SIC 5411 Grocery stores

D-U-N-S 25-271-7830   (BR)
SOBEYS WEST INC
TUXEDO SAFEWAY
2025 Corydon Ave Suite 150, Winnipeg, MB, R3P 0N5
(204) 489-6498
Emp Here 100
SIC 5411 Grocery stores

D-U-N-S 20-859-9790   (BR)
SOURCE (BELL) ELECTRONICS INC, THE
SOURCE, THE
1659 Kenaston Blvd Suite 4, Winnipeg, MB, R3P 2M4

Emp Here 25
SIC 5999 Miscellaneous retail stores, nec

D-U-N-S 25-272-3887   (SL)
ST. PAUL'S HIGH SCHOOL INC
2200 Grant Ave, Winnipeg, MB, R3P 0P8
(204) 831-2300
Emp Here 55   *Sales* 3,648,035
SIC 8211 Elementary and secondary schools

D-U-N-S 24-344-0216   (BR)
SUPERIOR PLUS LP
WINROC
1122 Kenaston Blvd, Winnipeg, MB, R3P 0R7
(204) 488-4477
Emp Here 20
SIC 5039 Construction materials, nec

D-U-N-S 25-254-9878   (BR)
TFI INTERNATIONAL INC
TRANSFORCE INC
991 Kenaston Blvd, Winnipeg, MB, R3P 1J9
(204) 453-6042
Emp Here 40
SIC 4213 Trucking, except local

D-U-N-S 20-706-0505   (BR)
TOMMY HILFIGER CANADA INC
1585 Kenaston Blvd Suite 14, Winnipeg, MB, R3P 2N3
(204) 487-7240
Emp Here 30
SIC 5651 Family clothing stores

D-U-N-S 20-860-5175   (BR)
TOWN SHOES LIMITED
SHOE COMPANY, THE
1559 Kenaston Blvd Suite 1, Winnipeg, MB, R3P 2N3
(204) 489-6992
Emp Here 20
SIC 5661 Shoe stores

D-U-N-S 24-233-7079   (BR)
UNIVAR CANADA LTD
99 Lowson Cres, Winnipeg, MB, R3P 0T3
(204) 489-0102
Emp Here 60
SIC 2911 Petroleum refining

D-U-N-S 24-025-3463   (BR)
UNIVERSITY OF MANITOBA
857 Wilkes Ave Suite 500, Winnipeg, MB, R3P 2M2
(204) 474-6100
Emp Here 50
SIC 8221 Colleges and universities

D-U-N-S 20-179-8183   (BR)
WAL-MART CANADA CORP
1665 Kenaston Blvd, Winnipeg, MB, R3P 2M4
(204) 488-2052
Emp Here 300
SIC 5311 Department stores

D-U-N-S 20-860-4210   (BR)
WINNERS MERCHANTS INTERNATIONAL L.P.
HOMESENSE
(*Suby of* The TJX Companies Inc)
1585 Kenaston Blvd Unit K6, Winnipeg, MB, R3P 2N3
(204) 487-7512
Emp Here 25
SIC 5651 Family clothing stores

Winnipeg, MB R3R

D-U-N-S 24-243-4160   (BR)
CANADA POST CORPORATION
CHARLESWOOD DEPOT
4910 Roblin Blvd Unit 150, Winnipeg, MB, R3R 0G7

Emp Here 40
SIC 4311 U.s. postal service

D-U-N-S 24-339-8471   (BR)
MCMUNN & YATES BUILDING SUPPLIES LTD
CHARLESWOOD LUMBER
940 Elmhurst Rd, Winnipeg, MB, R3R 3X7
(204) 837-1347
Emp Here 28
SIC 5251 Hardware stores

D-U-N-S 20-709-7770   (BR)
PEMBINA TRAILS SCHOOL DIVISION, THE
450 Laxdal Rd Suite 7, Winnipeg, MB, R3R 0W4
(204) 889-6650
Emp Here 50
SIC 8211 Elementary and secondary schools

D-U-N-S 20-709-7705   (BR)
PEMBINA TRAILS SCHOOL DIVISION, THE
BEAUMONT SCHOOL
5880 Betsworth Ave, Winnipeg, MB, R3R 0J7
(204) 895-2820
Emp Here 50
SIC 8211 Elementary and secondary schools

D-U-N-S 24-227-8344   (BR)
PEMBINA TRAILS SCHOOL DIVISION, THE
MEDIA CENTRE
6691 Rannock Ave, Winnipeg, MB, R3R 1Z3
(204) 895-8213
Emp Here 20
SIC 8211 Elementary and secondary schools

D-U-N-S 20-709-7762   (BR)
PEMBINA TRAILS SCHOOL DIVISION, THE
RIVER WEST PARK SCHOOL
30 Stack St, Winnipeg, MB, R3R 2H3
(204) 895-7225
Emp Here 50
SIC 8211 Elementary and secondary schools

D-U-N-S 20-709-7796   (BR)
PEMBINA TRAILS SCHOOL DIVISION, THE
WESTDALE JUNIOR HIGH SCHOOL
6720 Betsworth Ave Suite 105, Winnipeg, MB, R3R 1W3
(204) 895-8205
Emp Here 50
SIC 8211 Elementary and secondary schools

D-U-N-S 20-027-2586   (BR)
PEMBINA TRAILS SCHOOL DIVISION, THE
WESTGROVE ELEMENTARY SCHOOL
50 Westgrove Way, Winnipeg, MB, R3R 1R7
(204) 895-8208
Emp Here 40
SIC 8211 Elementary and secondary schools

D-U-N-S 20-709-7713   (BR)
PEMBINA TRAILS SCHOOL DIVISION, THE
CHAPMAN ELEMENTARY SCHOOL
3707 Roblin Blvd, Winnipeg, MB, R3R 0E2
(204) 888-3192
Emp Here 30
SIC 8211 Elementary and secondary schools

D-U-N-S 20-709-7721   (BR)
PEMBINA TRAILS SCHOOL DIVISION, THE
DIEPPE SCHOOL
530 Dieppe Rd, Winnipeg, MB, R3R 1C4
(204) 889-1034
Emp Here 50
SIC 8211 Elementary and secondary schools

D-U-N-S 20-023-2507   (BR)
PEMBINA TRAILS SCHOOL DIVISION, THE
ECOLE CHARLESWOOD SCHOOL
505 Oakdale Dr, Winnipeg, MB, R3R 0Z9
(204) 889-9332
Emp Here 55
SIC 8211 Elementary and secondary schools

D-U-N-S 20-855-3607   (BR)
PHARMA PLUS DRUGMARTS LTD
6650 Roblin Blvd, Winnipeg, MB, R3R 2P9

Emp Here 20
SIC 5912 Drug stores and proprietary stores

D-U-N-S 25-271-7715   (BR)
SOBEYS WEST INC
3900 Grant Ave Suite 20, Winnipeg, MB, R3R 3C2
(204) 837-5339
Emp Here 144
SIC 5411 Grocery stores

D-U-N-S 24-967-4581   (SL)
T.E.C.M. LIMITED
103 Kinkora Dr, Winnipeg, MB, R3R 2P5
(204) 227-8556
Emp Here 890   *Sales* 92,172,240
SIC 3625 Relays and industrial controls
Pr Pr Therese Cecille Van Humbeck
Edouard Arthur Van Humbeck

Winnipeg, MB R3T

D-U-N-S 25-533-0243   (HQ)
66295 MANITOBA LTD
(*Suby of* 66295 Manitoba Ltd)
1280 Pembina Hwy, Winnipeg, MB, R3T 2B2
(204) 452-8100
Emp Here 32   *Emp Total* 82
Sales 13,055,280
SIC 5713 Floor covering stores
Pr Pr Wayne Curtis
Jerry Sherby

D-U-N-S 25-287-9952   (BR)
A & W FOOD SERVICES OF CANADA INC
A & W
867 Waverley St, Winnipeg, MB, R3T 5P4
(204) 487-0381
Emp Here 25
SIC 5812 Eating places

D-U-N-S 25-316-2580   (BR)
AECOM CANADA LTD
1479 Buffalo Pl, Winnipeg, MB, R3T 1L7

Emp Here 130
SIC 8711 Engineering services

D-U-N-S 24-376-6037   (BR)
ATLIFIC INC
HOLIDAY INN WINNIPEG SOUTH
(*Suby of* 3376290 Canada Inc)
1330 Pembina Hwy, Winnipeg, MB, R3T 2B4
(204) 452-4747
Emp Here 125
SIC 7011 Hotels and motels

D-U-N-S 24-519-3891   (BR)
BELL MEDIA INC
1445 Pembina Hwy, Winnipeg, MB, R3T 5C2
(204) 477-5120
Emp Here 50
SIC 4832 Radio broadcasting stations

D-U-N-S 20-651-6242   (BR)
BEST BUY CANADA LTD
FUTURE SHOP
(*Suby of* Best Buy Co., Inc.)
1910 Pembina Hwy Unit 6, Winnipeg, MB, R3T 4S5
(204) 982-0551
Emp Here 70
SIC 5731 Radio, television, and electronic stores

D-U-N-S 20-648-3807   (BR)
BOYD GROUP INC, THE
BOYD AUTOBODY & GLASS
2405 Pembina Hwy, Winnipeg, MB, R3T 2H4
(204) 269-5520
Emp Here 22
SIC 7539 Automotive repair shops, nec

D-U-N-S 25-314-2798   (BR)
BRANDT TRACTOR LTD
3700 Mcgillivray Blvd, Winnipeg, MB, R3T 5S3
(204) 231-2333
Emp Here 50
SIC 5084 Industrial machinery and equipment

D-U-N-S 25-417-5078   (BR)
BREWERS' DISTRIBUTOR LTD
B D L
(*Suby of* Brewers' Distributor Ltd)
1370 Sony Pl Unit 300, Winnipeg, MB, R3T 1N5
(204) 958-7930
Emp Here 70
SIC 5181 Beer and ale

D-U-N-S 20-648-3757   (BR)
BUHLER INDUSTRIES INC
BUHLER INDUSTRIES INC.
1260 Clarence Ave Suite 112, Winnipeg, MB, R3T 1T2

Emp Here 200
SIC 3523 Farm machinery and equipment

D-U-N-S 24-628-3147   (SL)
BUHLER VERSATILE INC
1260 Clarence Ave, Winnipeg, MB, R3T 1T2
(204) 284-6100
Emp Here 300   *Sales* 43,052,675
SIC 3523 Farm machinery and equipment
  Yury Ryazanov
  Dmitry Lyubimov

D-U-N-S 25-205-4051   (SL)
CG POWER SYSTEMS CANADA INC
101 Rockman St, Winnipeg, MB, R3T 0L7
(204) 452-7446
Emp Here 265   *Sales* 68,607,079
SIC 3612 Transformers, except electric
VP Sls Ian Harrison
Dir Marc Schillebeeckx
Dir Martin Kelly

D-U-N-S 20-697-8434   (BR)
CWS LOGISTICS LTD
1500 Clarence Ave Suite C, Winnipeg, MB, R3T 1T6
(204) 453-2261
Emp Here 20
SIC 4225 General warehousing and storage

D-U-N-S 25-415-5286   (HQ)
CWS LOGISTICS LTD
(*Suby of* CWS Logistics Ltd)
1664 Seel Ave, Winnipeg, MB, R3T 4X5
(204) 474-2278
Emp Here 100   *Emp Total* 120
Sales 11,381,869
SIC 4225 General warehousing and storage
Pr Pr Lee Stange

D-U-N-S 20-072-2523   (BR)
CANAD CORPORATION OF MANITOBA LTD
CANADA INN EXPRESS FORT GARY
1792 Pembina Hwy, Winnipeg, MB, R3T 2G2
(204) 269-6955
Emp Here 85
SIC 7011 Hotels and motels

D-U-N-S 25-961-9872   (BR)
CANADIAN IMPERIAL BANK OF COMMERCE
CIBC
2866 Pembina Hwy Suite 10, Winnipeg, MB, R3T 2J1
(204) 944-5119
Emp Here 20
SIC 6021 National commercial banks

D-U-N-S 20-307-2137   (BR)
CITY OF WINNIPEG, THE
SOLID WASTE SERVICES
(*Suby of* City of Winnipeg, The)
1120 Waverley St, Winnipeg, MB, R3T 0P4
(204) 986-5311
Emp Here 50
SIC 4953 Refuse systems

D-U-N-S 20-152-6162   (BR)
CITY OF WINNIPEG, THE
PUBLIC WORKS STREET MAINTENANCE
(*Suby of* City of Winnipeg, The)
1539 Waverley St, Winnipeg, MB, R3T 4V7
(204) 986-2224
Emp Here 60
SIC 1611 Highway and street construction

D-U-N-S 25-728-7730   (BR)
CITY OF WINNIPEG, THE
MARGARET GRANT SWIMMING POOL
(*Suby of* City of Winnipeg, The)
685 Dalhousie Dr, Winnipeg, MB, R3T 3Y2
(204) 986-6880
Emp Here 35
SIC 7999 Amusement and recreation, nec

D-U-N-S 20-276-1003   (BR)
CONGEBEC LOGISTIQUE INC

WESTCO
1555 Chevrier Blvd Unit A, Winnipeg, MB, R3T 1Y7
(204) 475-5570
Emp Here 100
SIC 4222 Refrigerated warehousing and storage

D-U-N-S 20-519-8401   (BR)
DILLON CONSULTING LIMITED
(*Suby of* Dillon Consulting Inc)
1558 Willson Pl, Winnipeg, MB, R3T 0Y4
(204) 453-2301
Emp Here 80
SIC 8711 Engineering services

D-U-N-S 25-132-9801   (BR)
DOLLARAMA S.E.C.
1910 Pembina Hwy Suite 2, Winnipeg, MB, R3T 4S5
(204) 275-6468
Emp Here 26
SIC 5331 Variety stores

D-U-N-S 24-025-9619   (BR)
DUNN-RITE FOOD PRODUCTS LTD
15 Trottier Bay, Winnipeg, MB, R3T 3R3
(204) 452-8300
Emp Here 35
SIC 5144 Poultry and poultry products

D-U-N-S 25-341-7760   (BR)
EARL'S RESTAURANTS LTD
(*Suby of* Earl's Restaurants Ltd)
2005 Pembina Hwy, Winnipeg, MB, R3T 5W7

Emp Here 120
SIC 5812 Eating places

D-U-N-S 20-350-8049   (HQ)
EMERGENT BIOSOLUTIONS CANADA INC
155 Innovation Dr, Winnipeg, MB, R3T 5Y3
(204) 275-4200
Emp Here 330   *Emp Total* 1,292
Sales 43,119,774
SIC 5122 Drugs, proprietaries, and sundries
Pr Adam Havey
VP Sean Kirk
VP VP Christopher Sinclair
VP Barbara Solow
Treas Steven Rambo
Sec Eric Burt
  Daniel Abdun-Nabi

D-U-N-S 24-336-1693   (BR)
ENTERPRISE RENT-A-CAR CANADA COMPANY
(*Suby of* The Crawford Group Inc)
1380 Waverley St, Winnipeg, MB, R3T 0P5
(204) 478-5699
Emp Here 40
SIC 7514 Passenger car rental

D-U-N-S 24-343-7287   (BR)
FGL SPORTS LTD
SPORT-CHEK
1910 Pembina Hwy Unit 3, Winnipeg, MB, R3T 4S5
(204) 275-2775
Emp Here 50
SIC 5941 Sporting goods and bicycle shops

D-U-N-S 20-192-5992   (BR)
GENERAL MILLS CANADA CORPORATION
(*Suby of* General Mills, Inc.)
1555 Chevrier Blvd Suite B, Winnipeg, MB, R3T 1Y7
(204) 477-8338
Emp Here 90
SIC 2099 Food preparations, nec

D-U-N-S 20-294-6955   (BR)
IRON MOUNTAIN CANADA OPERATIONS ULC
ARCHIVES IRON MOUNTAIN
1500 Clarence Ave, Winnipeg, MB, R3T 1T6
(204) 949-5401
Emp Here 28

SIC 4226 Special warehousing and storage, nec

D-U-N-S 24-322-2986   (SL)
JENSEN CUSTOMS BROKERS CANADA INC
1146 Waverley St Unit 1, Winnipeg, MB, R3T 0P4
(204) 487-6628
Emp Here 40   *Sales* 13,797,200
SIC 4731 Freight transportation arrangement
Rgnl Mgr Chad Pasosky
Mgr Bruno Biondi

D-U-N-S 25-236-7750   (HQ)
JOHN BUHLER INC
1260 Clarence Ave, Winnipeg, MB, R3T 1T2
(204) 661-8711
Emp Here 300   *Emp Total* 50
Sales 143,537,791
SIC 3523 Farm machinery and equipment
  John Buhler
VP Larry Schroeder
Treas Osama Abouzeid

D-U-N-S 20-177-9811   (BR)
JYSK LINEN'N FURNITURE INC
JYSK LINEN'N FURNITURE INC
2089 Pembina Hwy, Winnipeg, MB, R3T 5L1
(204) 261-9333
Emp Here 20
SIC 5712 Furniture stores

D-U-N-S 20-175-9276   (SL)
KANE BIOTECH INC
196 Innovation Dr Suite 162, Winnipeg, MB, R3T 2N2
(204) 453-1301
Emp Here 70   *Sales* 181,033
SIC 8731 Commercial physical research

D-U-N-S 25-058-2616   (BR)
LOBLAWS INC
REAL CANADIAN SUPERSTORE
80 Bison Dr Suite 1509, Winnipeg, MB, R3T 4Z7
(204) 275-4118
Emp Here 300
SIC 5411 Grocery stores

D-U-N-S 25-126-9510   (BR)
MANITOBA LIQUOR AND LOTTERIES CORPORATION
LIQUOR MART
2855 Pembina Hwy, Winnipeg, MB, R3T 2H5
(204) 987-4040
Emp Here 20
SIC 5921 Liquor stores

D-U-N-S 25-011-6381   (BR)
MCDONALD'S RESTAURANTS OF CANADA LIMITED
MCDONALD'S RESTAURANTS
(*Suby of* McDonald's Corporation)
2027 Pembina Hwy, Winnipeg, MB, R3T 5W7
(204) 949-6019
Emp Here 50
SIC 5812 Eating places

D-U-N-S 25-011-0871   (BR)
MCDONALD'S RESTAURANTS OF CANADA LIMITED
MCDONALDS #8283
(*Suby of* McDonald's Corporation)
3045 Pembina Hwy, Winnipeg, MB, R3T 4R6
(204) 949-6083
Emp Here 70
SIC 5812 Eating places

D-U-N-S 24-775-8022   (HQ)
NATIONAL LEASING GROUP INC
NATIONAL LEASING
1525 Buffalo Pl, Winnipeg, MB, R3T 1L9
(204) 954-9000
Emp Here 230   *Emp Total* 2,100
Sales 44,698,552
SIC 6159 Miscellaneous business credit institutions

Pr Pr Thomas Pundyk
VP Fin Alan Kowalec
Sr VP Michael Dubowec
VP Opers Chris Noonan
Pers/VP Grant Shaw
Crdt Mgr Janice Boulet
Sr VP Jackie Lowe

D-U-N-S 25-678-1725   (SL)
PM CANADA INC
PROFITMASTER CANADA
135 Innovation Dr Unit 300, Winnipeg, MB, R3T 6A8
(204) 889-5320
Emp Here 43   *Sales* 8,138,880
SIC 5045 Computers, peripherals, and software
Genl Mgr Don Kroeker

D-U-N-S 24-805-7049   (BR)
PARKER HANNIFIN CANADA
ELECTRONIC CONTROLS, DIV OF
1305 Clarence Ave, Winnipeg, MB, R3T 1T4
(204) 452-6776
Emp Here 600
SIC 3625 Relays and industrial controls

D-U-N-S 24-352-6238   (BR)
PATENE BUILDING SUPPLIES LTD
102 De Vos Rd, Winnipeg, MB, R3T 5Y1
(204) 275-3000
Emp Here 50
SIC 5039 Construction materials, nec

D-U-N-S 20-833-2213   (SL)
PEMBINA CARE SERVICES LTD
GOLDEN DOOR GERIATRIC CENTRE
1679 Pembina Hwy, Winnipeg, MB, R3T 2G6
(204) 269-6308
Emp Here 80   *Sales* 2,918,428
SIC 8361 Residential care

D-U-N-S 20-709-7689   (BR)
PEMBINA TRAILS SCHOOL DIVISION, THE
CHANCELLOR ELEMENTARY SCHOOL
1520 Chancellor Dr, Winnipeg, MB, R3T 4P8
(204) 261-9535
Emp Here 50
SIC 8211 Elementary and secondary schools

D-U-N-S 25-450-3220   (BR)
PEMBINA TRAILS SCHOOL DIVISION, THE
ST. AVILA ELEMENTARY SCHOOL
633 Patricia Ave, Winnipeg, MB, R3T 3A8
(204) 269-5677
Emp Here 25
SIC 8211 Elementary and secondary schools

D-U-N-S 20-709-7671   (BR)
PEMBINA TRAILS SCHOOL DIVISION, THE
RALPH MAYBANK SCHOOL
20 Donnelly St, Winnipeg, MB, R3T 0S4
(204) 453-4631
Emp Here 50
SIC 8211 Elementary and secondary schools

D-U-N-S 20-292-7435   (BR)
PEMBINA TRAILS SCHOOL DIVISION, THE
VISCOUNT ALEXANDER SCHOOL
810 Waterford Ave, Winnipeg, MB, R3T 1G7
(204) 452-8945
Emp Here 25
SIC 8211 Elementary and secondary schools

D-U-N-S 20-023-2846   (BR)
PEMBINA TRAILS SCHOOL DIVISION, THE
R.H.G. BONNYCASTLE ELEMENTARY SCHOOL
1100 Chancellor Dr, Winnipeg, MB, R3T 4W8
(204) 261-9400
Emp Here 45
SIC 8211 Elementary and secondary schools

D-U-N-S 25-126-1517   (BR)
PEMBINA TRAILS SCHOOL DIVISION, THE
DALHOUSIE ELEMENTARY SCHOOL
262 Dalhousie Dr, Winnipeg, MB, R3T 2Z1

(204) 269-4101
Emp Here 60
SIC 8211 Elementary and secondary schools

D-U-N-S 20-027-2636   (BR)
PEMBINA TRAILS SCHOOL DIVISION, THE
ARTHUR A LEACH JR HIGH SCHOOL
1827 Chancellor Dr, Winnipeg, MB, R3T 4C4
(204) 269-1674
Emp Here 60
SIC 8211 Elementary and secondary schools

D-U-N-S 20-519-5956   (BR)
PEMBINA TRAILS SCHOOL DIVISION, THE
RYERSON ELEMENTARY SCHOOL
10 Ryerson Ave, Winnipeg, MB, R3T 3P9
(204) 269-1400
Emp Here 35
SIC 8211 Elementary and secondary schools

D-U-N-S 20-047-0867   (BR)
PEMBINA TRAILS SCHOOL DIVISION, THE
ACADIA JUNIOR HIGH SCHOOL
175 Killarney Ave, Winnipeg, MB, R3T 3B3
(204) 269-6210
Emp Here 78
SIC 8211 Elementary and secondary schools

D-U-N-S 20-081-2647   (BR)
PEMBINA TRAILS SCHOOL DIVISION, THE
ECOLE CRANE
888 Crane Ave, Winnipeg, MB, R3T 1T9
(204) 453-0539
Emp Here 32
SIC 8211 Elementary and secondary schools

D-U-N-S 20-709-7697   (BR)
PEMBINA TRAILS SCHOOL DIVISION, THE
BAIRDMORE ELEMENTARY SCHOOL
700 Bairdmore Blvd, Winnipeg, MB, R3T 5R3
(204) 261-3350
Emp Here 50
SIC 8211 Elementary and secondary schools

D-U-N-S 25-289-2682   (BR)
PEMBINA TRAILS SCHOOL DIVISION, THE
GENERAL BYNG SCHOOL
1250 Beaumont St, Winnipeg, MB, R3T 0L8
(204) 452-3040
Emp Here 60
SIC 8211 Elementary and secondary schools

D-U-N-S 20-945-4487   (SL)
PHLYN HOLDINGS LTD
(*Suby of* Carleton Hatcheries Ltd)
199 Hamelin St, Winnipeg, MB, R3T 0P2
(204) 452-8379
Emp Here 210   *Sales* 69,290,350
SIC 5144 Poultry and poultry products
Pr Pr Enrico Emil Bertschinger
 Frank Doerksen Funk
VP VP Mario Marcel Bertschinger
Dir Ursula Bertschinger
Dir Frank Lavitt

D-U-N-S 25-900-6138   (BR)
POWER TO CHANGE MINISTRIES
ATHLETES IN ACTION SPORT CAMPS
1345 Pembina Hwy Suite 206, Winnipeg, MB,
R3T 2B6
(204) 943-9924
Emp Here 20
SIC 8661 Religious organizations

D-U-N-S 24-232-9803   (SL)
PRIORITY ELECTRONICS LTD
55 Trottier Bay, Winnipeg, MB, R3T 3R3
(204) 284-0164
Emp Here 79   *Sales* 10,068,577
SIC 5065 Electronic parts and equipment, nec
Pr Pr Blaine Henderson

D-U-N-S 24-324-6035   (SL)
RAZIR TRANSPORT SERVICES LTD
1460 Clarence Ave Suite 204, Winnipeg, MB,
R3T 1T6
(204) 489-2258
Emp Here 45   *Sales* 18,241,472

SIC 4213 Trucking, except local
Pr Pr Karandeep Grewal
VP VP Amandeep Grewal

D-U-N-S 25-664-0921   (BR)
ROMA RIBS LTD
TONY ROMA'S A PLACE FOR RIBS
(*Suby of* Roma Ribs Ltd)
1500 Pembina Hwy, Winnipeg, MB, R3T 2E3
(204) 477-5195
Emp Here 55
SIC 5812 Eating places

D-U-N-S 24-206-8208   (BR)
ROYAL BANK OF CANADA
RBC
(*Suby of* Royal Bank Of Canada)
1525 Buffalo Pl, Winnipeg, MB, R3T 1L9
(204) 954-9054
Emp Here 20
SIC 6021 National commercial banks

D-U-N-S 20-721-2932   (BR)
ROYAL BANK OF CANADA
RBC
(*Suby of* Royal Bank Of Canada)
1300 Pembina Hwy, Winnipeg, MB, R3T 2B4
(204) 988-6410
Emp Here 20
SIC 6021 National commercial banks

D-U-N-S 25-018-8471   (BR)
ROYAL BANK OF CANADA
RBC
(*Suby of* Royal Bank Of Canada)
2855 Pembina Hwy Suite 26, Winnipeg, MB,
R3T 2H5
(204) 988-6062
Emp Here 35
SIC 6021 National commercial banks

D-U-N-S 20-212-7267   (BR)
RUSSEL METALS INC
1510 Clarence Ave, Winnipeg, MB, R3T 1T6
(204) 475-8584
Emp Here 100
SIC 1791 Structural steel erection

D-U-N-S 20-010-8710   (BR)
RYERSON CANADA, INC
1424 Willson Pl, Winnipeg, MB, R3T 0Y3
(204) 284-4480
Emp Here 47
SIC 5051 Metals service centers and offices

D-U-N-S 24-439-6144   (BR)
SCM INSURANCE SERVICES INC
SHUMKA CRAIG AND MOORE ADJUSTERS
1479 Buffalo Pl Suite 200, Winnipeg, MB, R3T
1L7
(204) 985-1777
Emp Here 49
SIC 6411 Insurance agents, brokers, and service

D-U-N-S 25-716-3329   (BR)
**SERVICE CORPORATION INTERNATIONAL
(CANADA) LIMITED**
*THOMPSON IN THE PARK FUNERAL HOME
AND CEMETERY*
1291 Mcgillivray Blvd, Winnipeg, MB, R3T 5Y4
(204) 925-1120
Emp Here 30
SIC 6531 Real estate agents and managers

D-U-N-S 25-451-8434   (BR)
SHAREVENTURES PORTAGE INC
TIM HORTONS
(*Suby of* Shareventures Portage Inc)
1510 Pembina Hwy, Winnipeg, MB, R3T 2E3
(204) 452-3079
Emp Here 40
SIC 5812 Eating places

D-U-N-S 24-718-3403   (BR)
SOBEYS WEST INC
1345 Waverley St Suite 300, Winnipeg, MB,
R3T 5Y7

(204) 487-5797
Emp Here 40
SIC 5411 Grocery stores

D-U-N-S 25-271-9935   (BR)
SOBEYS WEST INC
SAFEWAY
1319 Pembina Hwy, Winnipeg, MB, R3T 2B6
(204) 284-0973
Emp Here 100
SIC 5411 Grocery stores

D-U-N-S 25-271-7541   (BR)
SOBEYS WEST INC
FORT RICHMOND SAFEWAY
2860 Pembina Hwy, Winnipeg, MB, R3T 3L9

Emp Here 50
SIC 5411 Grocery stores

D-U-N-S 20-192-7741   (BR)
**SONOCO FLEXIBLE PACKAGING CANADA
CORPORATION**
(*Suby of* Sonoco Products Company)
1664 Seel Ave, Winnipeg, MB, R3T 4X5

Emp Here 160
SIC 2759 Commercial printing, nec

D-U-N-S 25-728-8233   (SL)
SORRENTO'S LTD
NICOLINO'S
2077 Pembina Hwy Suite 4, Winnipeg, MB,
R3T 5J9
(204) 269-5934
Emp Here 50   *Sales* 1,532,175
SIC 5812 Eating places

D-U-N-S 20-136-7575   (SL)
SOUTHEAST COLLEGE INC
SOUTHEAST EDUCATION CENTRE
1301 Lee Blvd Suite 1, Winnipeg, MB, R3T
5W8
(204) 261-3551
Emp Here 50   *Sales* 3,356,192
SIC 8211 Elementary and secondary schools

D-U-N-S 20-325-8223   (SL)
SOUTHEAST PERSONAL CARE HOME INC
SOUTHEAST PERSONAL CARE HOME
1265 Lee Blvd, Winnipeg, MB, R3T 2M3
(204) 269-7111
Emp Here 80   *Sales* 3,648,035
SIC 8052 Intermediate care facilities

D-U-N-S 25-887-1185   (BR)
STAPLES CANADA INC
STAPLES THE BUSINESS DEPOT
(*Suby of* Staples, Inc.)
1910 Pembina Hwy Unit 9, Winnipeg, MB,
R3T 4S5
(204) 269-5928
Emp Here 40
SIC 5943 Stationery stores

D-U-N-S 24-717-2422   (BR)
SYSCO CANADA, INC
SYSCO FOOD SERVICES OF WINNIPEG
(*Suby of* Sysco Corporation)
1570 Clarence Ave, Winnipeg, MB, R3T 1T6
(204) 478-4000
Emp Here 200
SIC 5411 Grocery stores

D-U-N-S 25-173-1188   (BR)
TELECOMMUNICATIONS RESEARCH LABORATORIES
TR LABS
(*Suby of* Telecommunications Research Laboratories)
135 Innovation Dr Suite 100, Winnipeg, MB,
R3T 6A8
(204) 489-6060
Emp Here 35
SIC 8732 Commercial nonphysical research

D-U-N-S 20-316-0007   (SL)
TESHMONT CONSULTANTS LP
(*Suby of* Teshmont Consultants Inc)

1190 Waverley St, Winnipeg, MB, R3T 0P4
(204) 284-8100
Emp Here 75   *Sales* 9,585,565
SIC 8711 Engineering services
Pr R.D (Ralp) Kurth
 B.K (Brian) Benediktson

D-U-N-S 25-538-7128   (BR)
TOROMONT INDUSTRIES LTD
BATTLEFIELD EQUIPMENT RENTALS
10 Irene St, Winnipeg, MB, R3T 0P1
(204) 474-2411
Emp Here 42
SIC 7353 Heavy construction equipment
rental

D-U-N-S 20-758-4707   (HQ)
UNIVERSITY OF MANITOBA THE
66 Chancellors Cir Rm 406, Winnipeg, MB,
R3T 2N2
(204) 474-8167
Emp Here 300   *Emp Total* 20,000
Sales 998,394,219
SIC 8221 Colleges and universities
Ch Bd Jeffrey Lieberman
V Ch Bd Rafi Mohammed
Pr Pr David Barnard
 Jeffrey Leclerc

D-U-N-S 20-647-7759   (BR)
UNIVERSITY OF MANITOBA
ST PAUL'S COLLEGE
70 Dysart Rd Suite 209, Winnipeg, MB, R3T
2M6
(204) 474-8575
Emp Here 20
SIC 8221 Colleges and universities

D-U-N-S 20-914-4968   (BR)
UNIVERSITY OF MANITOBA
UNIVERSITY OF MANITOBA
Frank Kennedy Bldg 66 Chancellors Cir Rm
124, Winnipeg, MB, R3T 2N2
(204) 474-8234
Emp Here 20
SIC 7389 Business services, nec

D-U-N-S 20-084-1067   (BR)
UNIVERSITY OF MANITOBA
I Q'S CAFE & BILLIARDS
545 University Cres, Winnipeg, MB, R3T 5S6
(204) 474-9449
Emp Here 20
SIC 5812 Eating places

D-U-N-S 24-382-9889   (BR)
UNIVERSITY OF MANITOBA
MARY SPEECHLY HALL
120 Dafoe Rd, Winnipeg, MB, R3T 6B3
(204) 474-9922
Emp Here 20
SIC 7041 Membership-basis organization hotels

D-U-N-S 24-345-0462   (BR)
UNIVERSITY OF MANITOBA
I.H. ASPER SCHOOL OF BUSINESS
181 Freedman Cres Suite 121, Winnipeg, MB,
R3T 5V4
(204) 474-6388
Emp Here 100
SIC 8221 Colleges and universities

D-U-N-S 25-482-5011   (BR)
UNIVERSITY OF MANITOBA
ARCHIVES USED BOOKSTORE
66 Chancellors Cir Suite 107, Winnipeg, MB,
R3T 2N2
(204) 474-6511
Emp Here 50
SIC 5942 Book stores

D-U-N-S 25-137-5101   (BR)
UNIVERSITY OF MANITOBA
TACHE HALL
26 Maclean Cres, Winnipeg, MB, R3T 2N1
(204) 474-9464
Emp Here 20

SIC 7041 Membership-basis organization hotels

D-U-N-S 25-058-5148   (BR)
UNIVERSITY OF MANITOBA
DEPARTMENT OF ADVANCEMENT AND DEVELOPMENT SERVICES
137 Innovation Dr Unit 200, Winnipeg, MB, R3T 6B6
(204) 474-9195
Emp Here 50
SIC 8732 Commercial nonphysical research

D-U-N-S 24-310-6452   (BR)
UNIVERSITY OF MANITOBA
PURCHASING SERVICES
66 Chancellors Cir Rm 410, Winnipeg, MB, R3T 2N2
(204) 474-8348
Emp Here 20
SIC 8221 Colleges and universities

D-U-N-S 20-643-7647   (BR)
UNIVERSITY OF MANITOBA
BIOSYSTEMS ENGINEERING
E2 -376 Eitc 75 A Chancellor Cir, Winnipeg, MB, R3T 2N2
(204) 474-6033
Emp Here 20
SIC 8221 Colleges and universities

D-U-N-S 25-453-3979   (BR)
UNIVERSITY OF MANITOBA
ST JOHN'S COLLEGE
92 Dysart Rd, Winnipeg, MB, R3T 2M5
(204) 474-8531
Emp Here 30
SIC 8221 Colleges and universities

D-U-N-S 20-787-0739   (BR)
UNIVERSITY OF MANITOBA
HISTORY DEPARTMENT
15 Chancellors Cir, Winnipeg, MB, R3T 5V5
(204) 474-8401
Emp Here 30
SIC 8221 Colleges and universities

D-U-N-S 25-659-6834   (BR)
VALUE VILLAGE STORES, INC
(*Suby of* Savers, Inc.)
1729 Pembina Hwy, Winnipeg, MB, R3T 2G6
(204) 261-8719
Emp Here 30
SIC 5399 Miscellaneous general merchandise

D-U-N-S 25-659-9028   (BR)
WENDY'S RESTAURANTS OF CANADA INC
WENDY'S
(*Suby of* The Wendy's Company)
1710 Pembina Hwy, Winnipeg, MB, R3T 2G2
(204) 261-1845
Emp Here 30
SIC 5812 Eating places

D-U-N-S 20-011-9493   (BR)
WESTON BAKERIES LIMITED
WESTON READY BAKE
1485 Chevrier Blvd, Winnipeg, MB, R3T 1Y7
(204) 774-7431
Emp Here 150
SIC 2051 Bread, cake, and related products

D-U-N-S 24-967-9929   (BR)
WINNERS MERCHANTS INTERNATIONAL L.P.
WINNERS
(*Suby of* The TJX Companies Inc)
2127 Pembina Hwy, Winnipeg, MB, R3T 5L1
(204) 261-1804
Emp Here 50
SIC 5651 Family clothing stores

D-U-N-S 24-227-3063   (BR)
WINNIPEG REGIONAL HEALTH AUTHORITY, THE
2735 Pembina Hwy, Winnipeg, MB, R3T 2H5
(204) 940-2320
Emp Here 40

SIC 8062 General medical and surgical hospitals

D-U-N-S 20-011-8987   (BR)
WINNIPEG TECHNICAL COLLEGE
(*Suby of* Winnipeg Technical College)
1551 Pembina Hwy, Winnipeg, MB, R3T 2E5
(204) 989-6566
Emp Here 50
SIC 8222 Junior colleges

D-U-N-S 20-758-2750   (BR)
XEROX CANADA LTD
DOCUMENT COMPANY, THE
(*Suby of* Xerox Corporation)
895 Waverley St, Winnipeg, MB, R3T 5P4
(204) 488-5100
Emp Here 100
SIC 5044 Office equipment

Winnipeg, MB R3V

D-U-N-S 20-647-7267   (HQ)
BRETT-YOUNG SEEDS LIMITED
BRETTYOUNG
(*Suby of* JALO Management Inc)
Hwy 330 And Hwy 100 Sw Corner, Winnipeg, MB, R3V 1L5
(204) 261-7932
Emp Here 100   *Emp Total* 1
Sales 99,247,662
SIC 5191 Farm supplies
CEO Calvin Sonntag
 Andrew Steiman
Fin Ex Peter Smith
 Lloyd Dyck

D-U-N-S 24-802-1235   (BR)
CITY OF WINNIPEG, THE
BRADY ROAD LANDFILL
(*Suby of* City of Winnipeg, The)
1901 Brady Rd, Winnipeg, MB, R3V 0B5
(204) 986-4779
Emp Here 35
SIC 4953 Refuse systems

D-U-N-S 25-267-4486   (BR)
DIVISION SCOLAIRE FRANCO-MANITOBAINE
ECOLE NOEL-RITCHOT
(*Suby of* Division Scolaire Franco-Manitobaine)
45 De La Digue Ave, Winnipeg, MB, R3V 1M7
(204) 261-0380
Emp Here 36
SIC 8211 Elementary and secondary schools

D-U-N-S 20-922-5718   (BR)
FEDERATED CO-OPERATIVES LIMITED
FOOD LAND
(*Suby of* Federated Co-Operatives Limited)
3477 Pembina Hwy, Winnipeg, MB, R3V 1A4
(204) 275-2391
Emp Here 50
SIC 5411 Grocery stores

D-U-N-S 20-047-1568   (BR)
SEINE RIVER SCHOOL DIVISION
ST. NORBERT IMMERSION SCHOOL
900 Ste Therese Ave, Winnipeg, MB, R3V 1H8
(204) 261-4430
Emp Here 25
SIC 8211 Elementary and secondary schools

D-U-N-S 25-892-4489   (BR)
SEINE RIVER SCHOOL DIVISION
PARC LA SALLE SCHOOL
(*Suby of* Seine River School Division)
190 Houde Dr, Winnipeg, MB, R3V 1C5
(204) 275-1521
Emp Here 30
SIC 8211 Elementary and secondary schools

D-U-N-S 20-023-5062   (BR)

SEINE RIVER SCHOOL DIVISION
LA BARRIERE CROSSINGS SCHOOL
245 Le Maire St, Winnipeg, MB, R3V 1M2
(204) 275-5048
Emp Here 28
SIC 8211 Elementary and secondary schools

D-U-N-S 25-022-3773   (BR)
SEINE RIVER SCHOOL DIVISION
COLLEGE ST NORBERT COLLEGIATE
(*Suby of* Seine River School Division)
870 Ste Therese Ave, Winnipeg, MB, R3V 1H8
(204) 269-4920
Emp Here 50
SIC 8211 Elementary and secondary schools

D-U-N-S 20-948-0102   (SL)
SOUTHWOOD GOLF AND COUNTRY CLUB
80 Rue Des Ruines Du Monastere, Winnipeg, MB, R3V 0B1
(204) 269-7867
Emp Here 70   *Sales* 2,845,467
SIC 7997 Membership sports and recreation clubs

Winnipeg, MB R3W

D-U-N-S 25-680-0905   (SL)
3264760 MANITOBA LTD
WESTLAND FASTENERS, DIV OF
165 Cordite Rd, Winnipeg, MB, R3W 1S1
(204) 224-1654
Emp Here 24   *Sales* 8,339,840
SIC 3452 Bolts, nuts, rivets, and washers
Pr Pr Ben Urbanietz
 Lionel J Gervais
 Brian Tkachyk
 David Jaques

Winnipeg, MB R3X

D-U-N-S 20-647-7762   (BR)
INTEGRATED DISTRIBUTION SYSTEMS LIMITED PARTNERSHIP
WAJAX EQUIPMENT
75 Aimes Rd, Winnipeg, MB, R3X 1V4
(204) 255-2214
Emp Here 20
SIC 5084 Industrial machinery and equipment

D-U-N-S 20-228-8085   (BR)
LOUIS RIEL SCHOOL DIVISION
ISLAND LAKES COMMUNITY SCHOOL
445 Island Shore Blvd, Winnipeg, MB, R3X 2B4
(204) 254-6247
Emp Here 40
SIC 8211 Elementary and secondary schools

D-U-N-S 20-721-4896   (SL)
RAINBOW DAY NURSERY INC
445 Island Shore Blvd Unit 11, Winnipeg, MB, R3X 2B4
(204) 256-0672
Emp Here 100   *Sales* 2,991,389
SIC 8351 Child day care services

Winnipeg, MB R3Y

D-U-N-S 25-271-2955   (BR)
7-ELEVEN CANADA, INC
7-ELEVEN FOOD CENTER
5 Scurfield Blvd Unit 30, Winnipeg, MB, R3Y 1G3
(204) 487-3663
Emp Here 30
SIC 5411 Grocery stores

D-U-N-S 24-818-7031   (BR)

AMEC FOSTER WHEELER AMERICAS LIMITED
AMEC EARTH & ENVIRONMENTAL
440 Dovercourt Dr, Winnipeg, MB, R3Y 1G4
(204) 488-2997
Emp Here 49
SIC 8711 Engineering services

D-U-N-S 25-539-0676   (BR)
ASSANTE FINANCIAL MANAGEMENT LTD
ASSANTE WEALTH MANAGEMENT
5 Scurfield Blvd Unit 10, Winnipeg, MB, R3Y 1G3
(204) 982-1860
Emp Here 20
SIC 8741 Management services

D-U-N-S 20-003-3558   (BR)
CANADIAN PACIFIC RAILWAY COMPANY
CPR
14 Fultz Blvd, Winnipeg, MB, R3Y 0L6
(204) 947-8101
Emp Here 300
SIC 4011 Railroads, line-haul operating

D-U-N-S 25-729-2375   (SL)
CINEMA CITY INC
CINEMA CITY MCGILLIVRAY
2190 Mcgillivray Blvd, Winnipeg, MB, R3Y 1S6
(204) 269-9978
Emp Here 50   *Sales* 1,896,978
SIC 7832 Motion picture theaters, except drive-in

D-U-N-S 24-807-8289   (HQ)
CONFIDENCE MANAGEMENT LTD
475 Dovercourt Dr, Winnipeg, MB, R3Y 1G4
(204) 487-2500
Emp Here 50   *Emp Total* 300
Sales 27,330,560
SIC 8741 Management services
Pr Pr Rick Chale
 Michael Evans
 Douglas Patrick
VP Fin Carl Doerksen

D-U-N-S 24-344-7674   (BR)
COSTCO WHOLESALE CANADA LTD
COSTCO
(*Suby of* Costco Wholesale Corporation)
2365 Mcgillivray Blvd Suite 1, Winnipeg, MB, R3Y 0A1
(204) 487-5100
Emp Here 225
SIC 5399 Miscellaneous general merchandise

D-U-N-S 20-702-3925   (BR)
EMERGENT BIOSOLUTIONS CANADA INC
EMERGENT BIOSOLUTIONS CADANA INC
26 Henlow Bay, Winnipeg, MB, R3Y 1G4
(204) 275-4200
Emp Here 200
SIC 8731 Commercial physical research

D-U-N-S 24-391-5696   (BR)
GOLF TOWN LIMITED
GOLF TOWN
2355 Mcgillivray Blvd Unit 150, Winnipeg, MB, R3Y 0A1
(204) 488-7480
Emp Here 30
SIC 5941 Sporting goods and bicycle shops

D-U-N-S 24-571-2609   (BR)
GRAND & TOY LIMITED
(*Suby of* Office Depot, Inc.)
15 Scurfield Blvd, Winnipeg, MB, R3Y 1V4
(204) 284-5100
Emp Here 85
SIC 5943 Stationery stores

D-U-N-S 24-852-2245   (BR)
KEG RESTAURANTS LTD
KEG STEAKHOUSE & BAR, THE
2034 Mcgillivray Blvd, Winnipeg, MB, R3Y 1V5
(204) 477-5300
Emp Here 200

SIC 5812 Eating places

D-U-N-S 20-229-3168   (BR)
**MCDONALD'S   RESTAURANTS   OF
CANADA LIMITED**
MCDONALD'S
(*Suby of* McDonald's Corporation)
1725 Kenaston Blvd, Winnipeg, MB, R3Y 1V5
(204) 949-5128
Emp Here 100
SIC 5812 Eating places

D-U-N-S 20-023-5211   (BR)
PEMBINA TRAILS SCHOOL DIVISION, THE
IZATT, HENRY G MIDDLE SCHOOL
960 Scurfield Blvd, Winnipeg, MB, R3Y 1N6
(204) 489-1239
Emp Here 55
SIC 8211 Elementary and secondary schools

D-U-N-S 20-048-2417   (BR)
PEMBINA TRAILS SCHOOL DIVISION, THE
WHITE RIDGE ELEMENTARY SCHOOL
400 Scurfield Blvd, Winnipeg, MB, R3Y 1L3
(204) 488-4245
Emp Here 60
SIC 8211 Elementary and secondary schools

D-U-N-S 20-613-8257   (BR)
PITNEY BOWES OF CANADA LTD
(*Suby of* Pitney Bowes Inc.)
62 Scurfield Blvd Suite 2, Winnipeg, MB, R3Y
1M5
(204) 489-2220
Emp Here 30
SIC 5044 Office equipment

D-U-N-S 24-141-0476   (BR)
STUART OLSON CONSTRUCTION LTD
BUILDINGS DIVISION
50 Fultz Blvd, Winnipeg, MB, R3Y 0L6
(204) 487-1222
Emp Here 40
SIC 1522 Residential construction, nec

D-U-N-S 24-264-6891   (HQ)
VECTOR CONSTRUCTION LTD
(*Suby of* Vector Management Ltd)
474 Dovercourt Dr, Winnipeg, MB, R3Y 1G4
(204) 489-6300
Emp Here 30   *Emp Total* 400
Sales 19,230,772
SIC 1771 Concrete work
Pr Pr Donald Whitmore
VP VP Robert Spriggs
 Florence Whitmore

D-U-N-S 20-008-6387   (HQ)
VECTOR ENTERPRISES LTD
(*Suby of* Vector Management Ltd)
474 Dovercourt Dr, Winnipeg, MB, R3Y 1G4
(204) 489-6300
Emp Here 30   *Emp Total* 400
Sales 17,510,568
SIC 1611 Highway and street construction
Pr Pr Donald Whitmore
 Florence Whitmore
VP VP Robert Spriggs

Winnipeg Beach, MB R0C

D-U-N-S 25-000-5865   (BR)
EVERGREEN SCHOOL DIVISION
WINNIPEG BEACH SCHOOL
185 Churchill Dr, Winnipeg Beach, MB, R0C
3G0
(204) 389-2176
Emp Here 20
SIC 8211 Elementary and secondary schools

Winnipegosis, MB R0L

D-U-N-S 20-709-7150   (BR)
MOUNTAIN VIEW SCHOOL DIVISION
WINNIPEGOSIS COLLEGIATE
(*Suby of* Mountain View School Division)
310 3rd St, Winnipegosis, MB, R0L 2G0
(204) 656-4792
Emp Here 50
SIC 8211 Elementary and secondary schools

D-U-N-S 20-709-7168   (BR)
MOUNTAIN VIEW SCHOOL DIVISION
WINNIPEGOSIS ELEMENTARY SCHOOL
(*Suby of* Mountain View School Division)
Gd, Winnipegosis, MB, R0L 2G0
(204) 656-4550
Emp Here 50
SIC 8211 Elementary and secondary schools

D-U-N-S 24-115-4178   (SL)
WINNIPEGOSIS GENERAL HOSPITAL INC
230 Bridge St, Winnipegosis, MB, R0L 2G0
(204) 656-4881
Emp Here 70   *Sales* 6,576,720
SIC 8062 General medical and surgical hospi-
tals
 Anthony Fraser

York Landing, MB R0B

D-U-N-S 25-816-2072   (BR)
YORK FACTORY FIRST NATION
GEORGE SAUNDERS MEMORIAL SCHOOL
Gd, York Landing, MB, R0B 2B0
(204) 341-2118
Emp Here 25
SIC 8211 Elementary and secondary schools

Acadie Siding, NB E4Y
Kent County

D-U-N-S 25-173-3556   (BR)
PREMIER HORTICULTURE LTEE
10816 Route 126, Acadie Siding, NB, E4Y 2L4
(506) 775-9182
Emp Here 35
SIC 1499 Miscellaneous nonMetallic minerals, except fuels

Allardville, NB E8L
Gloucester County

D-U-N-S 20-543-1856   (BR)
CONSEIL SCOLAIRE DISTRICT NO 5
FRANCOIS XAVIER DAIGLE
4572 Route 134, Allardville, NB, E8L 1E4
(506) 725-2407
Emp Here 30
SIC 8211 Elementary and secondary schools

Anse-Bleue, NB E8N
Gloucester County

D-U-N-S 25-092-0696   (BR)
BARRY GROUP INC
BARRY GROUP
12 Allee Frigault, Anse-Bleue, NB, E8N 2J2

Emp Here 125
SIC 5421 Meat and fish markets

Aroostook, NB E7H

D-U-N-S 25-296-2972   (BR)
BANK OF NOVA SCOTIA, THE
SCOTIABANK
325 Main St, Aroostook, NB, E7H 2Z4
(506) 392-8020
Emp Here 26
SIC 6021 National commercial banks

Atholville, NB E3N
Restigouche County

D-U-N-S 20-529-9758   (BR)
CANADA POST CORPORATION
255 Rue Notre Dame, Atholville, NB, E3N 4T1
(506) 789-0500
Emp Here 20
SIC 4311 U.s. postal service

D-U-N-S 24-000-2266   (BR)
CIRCLE HOLDINGS INC
TIM HORTONS
(*Suby of* Circle Holdings Inc)
2 Rue Jagoe, Atholville, NB, E3N 5C3
(506) 753-1881
Emp Here 30
SIC 5812 Eating places

D-U-N-S 20-917-8560   (BR)
CONSEIL SCOLAIRE DISTRICT NO 5
ECOLE DERSANT NORD
248 Rue Notre Dame, Atholville, NB, E3N 3Z9
(506) 789-2265
Emp Here 42
SIC 8211 Elementary and secondary schools

D-U-N-S 20-790-2599   (BR)
J. D. IRVING, LIMITED
KENT BUILDING SUPPLLIES

(*Suby of* J. D. Irving, Limited)
15 Av Savoie, Atholville, NB, E3N 4A8
(506) 753-7662
Emp Here 36
SIC 5251 Hardware stores

D-U-N-S 24-318-0796   (BR)
WAL-MART CANADA CORP
WALMART
4 Rue Jagoe, Atholville, NB, E3N 5C3
(506) 753-7105
Emp Here 150
SIC 5311 Department stores

Baie-Sainte-Anne, NB E9A
Northumberland County

D-U-N-S 20-018-5890   (SL)
BAIE STE-ANNE CO-OPERATIVE LTD
5575 Route 117, Baie-Sainte-Anne, NB, E9A 1H2
(506) 228-4211
Emp Here 31   *Sales* 5,072,500
SIC 5411 Grocery stores
Genl Mgr Pierre Turbide
Pr Pr Robert Martin

D-U-N-S 25-241-8173   (BR)
DISTRICT SCOLAIRE 11
ECOLE REGIONALE DE BAIE STE ANNE
(*Suby of* District Scolaire 11)
5362 Route 117, Baie-Sainte-Anne, NB, E9A 1C9
(506) 228-2010
Emp Here 45
SIC 8211 Elementary and secondary schools

D-U-N-S 24-931-9310   (BR)
TOURBIERES BERGER LTEE, LES
BERGER PEATMOSS
4188 Route 117, Baie-Sainte-Anne, NB, E9A 1R7
(506) 228-4978
Emp Here 100
SIC 1499 Miscellaneous nonMetallic minerals, except fuels

Baker Brook, NB E7A
Madawaska County

D-U-N-S 24-312-3036   (BR)
J. D. IRVING, LIMITED
BAKER BROOK SAWMILL
(*Suby of* J. D. Irving, Limited)
3300 Rue Principale, Baker Brook, NB, E7A 1Z7
(506) 258-1150
Emp Here 100
SIC 2421 Sawmills and planing mills, general

Balmoral, NB E8E
Restigouche County

D-U-N-S 25-241-9825   (BR)
CONSEIL SCOLAIRE DISTRICT NO 5
ECOLE DOMAINE DES COPAINS
1821 Des Pionniers Ave, Balmoral, NB, E8E 1C2

Emp Here 30
SIC 8211 Elementary and secondary schools

Bathurst, NB E2A
Gloucester County

D-U-N-S 24-098-3564   (BR)

ARAMARK CANADA LTD.
1750 Sunset Dr, Bathurst, NB, E2A 4L7
(506) 544-3449
Emp Here 60
SIC 5812 Eating places

D-U-N-S 25-878-4339   (BR)
ARMOUR TRANSPORT INC
ARMOUR TRANSPORTATION SYSTEMS
1957 Miramichi Ave, Bathurst, NB, E2A 1Y7
(506) 548-2633
Emp Here 25
SIC 4213 Trucking, except local

D-U-N-S 25-946-4303   (BR)
ATLANTIC WHOLESALERS LTD
REAL ATLANTIC SUPERSTORE, THE
700 St. Peter Ave, Bathurst, NB, E2A 2Y7
(506) 547-3180
Emp Here 178
SIC 5411 Grocery stores

D-U-N-S 25-296-2618   (BR)
BANK OF NOVA SCOTIA, THE
SCOTIABANK
1300 St. Peter Ave Suite 202, Bathurst, NB, E2A 3A6
(506) 548-9921
Emp Here 25
SIC 6021 National commercial banks

D-U-N-S 25-828-8083   (BR)
BATHURST, CITY OF
K C IRVING REGIONAL CENTRE
850 St. Anne St, Bathurst, NB, E2A 6X2
(506) 549-3300
Emp Here 100
SIC 7999 Amusement and recreation, nec

D-U-N-S 25-116-8639   (BR)
BELL ALIANT REGIONAL COMMUNICATIONS INC
275 King Ave, Bathurst, NB, E2A 1N9
(506) 547-3768
Emp Here 20
SIC 4899 Communication services, nec

D-U-N-S 24-912-5246   (BR)
COCA-COLA REFRESHMENTS CANADA COMPANY
(*Suby of* The Coca-Cola Company)
2200 Vanier Blvd, Bathurst, NB, E2A 7B7
(506) 546-8764
Emp Here 30
SIC 5149 Groceries and related products, nec

D-U-N-S 25-241-9221   (BR)
CONSEIL SCOLAIRE DISTRICT NO 5
ACADEMIE ASSOMPTION
1255 Rough Waters Dr, Bathurst, NB, E2A 1Z2
(506) 547-2780
Emp Here 20
SIC 8211 Elementary and secondary schools

D-U-N-S 25-241-7175   (BR)
CONSEIL SCOLAIRE DISTRICT NO 5
ECOLE CITE DE L'AMITIE
1300 St. Joseph Ave, Bathurst, NB, E2A 3R5
(506) 547-2775
Emp Here 50
SIC 8211 Elementary and secondary schools

D-U-N-S 25-241-7092   (BR)
CONSEIL SCOLAIRE DISTRICT NO 5
ECOLE PLACE DES JEUNES
975 St. Anne St, Bathurst, NB, E2A 6X1
(506) 547-2765
Emp Here 30
SIC 8211 Elementary and secondary schools

D-U-N-S 25-241-9502   (BR)
CONSEIL SCOLAIRE DISTRICT NO 5
ECOLE SECONDAIRE NEPISIGUIT
915 St. Anne St, Bathurst, NB, E2A 6X1
(506) 547-2785
Emp Here 115
SIC 8211 Elementary and secondary schools

D-U-N-S 25-887-9527   (BR)
DAY & ROSS INC
11930 Hall Crt Suite 2, Bathurst, NB, E2A 4W7
(506) 546-7400
Emp Here 30
SIC 4213 Trucking, except local

D-U-N-S 25-395-6452   (BR)
GUILLEVIN INTERNATIONAL CIE
1850 Vanier Blvd, Bathurst, NB, E2A 7B7
(506) 546-8220
Emp Here 28
SIC 5063 Electrical apparatus and equipment

D-U-N-S 20-517-1023   (BR)
I.M.P. GROUP INTERNATIONAL INCORPORATED
1850 Vanier Blvd Suite 200, Bathurst, NB, E2A 7B7
(506) 547-7000
Emp Here 85
SIC 4581 Airports, flying fields, and services

D-U-N-S 25-305-1916   (BR)
INNVEST PROPERTIES CORP
COMFORT INN
(*Suby of* Innvest Properties Corp)
1170 St. Peter Ave, Bathurst, NB, E2A 2Z9
(506) 547-8000
Emp Here 25
SIC 7011 Hotels and motels

D-U-N-S 24-248-9255   (BR)
J. D. IRVING, LIMITED
KENT BUILDING SUPPLIES
(*Suby of* J. D. Irving, Limited)
950 St. Anne St, Bathurst, NB, E2A 6X2
(506) 548-2000
Emp Here 45
SIC 5211 Lumber and other building materials

D-U-N-S 24-346-5023   (BR)
LANDIER ENTERPRISES LTD
TIM HORTONS
575 Bridge St, Bathurst, NB, E2A 1W7
(506) 546-3040
Emp Here 20
SIC 5812 Eating places

D-U-N-S 25-955-6066   (HQ)
LANDIER ENTERPRISES LTD
TIM HORTONS
(*Suby of* Landier Enterprises Ltd)
390 Main St, Bathurst, NB, E2A 1B2
(506) 546-8093
Emp Here 25   *Emp Total* 75
Sales 2,261,782
SIC 5812 Eating places

D-U-N-S 24-000-2100   (BR)
LANDIER ENTERPRISES LTD
TIM HORTONS
1420 Vanier Blvd, Bathurst, NB, E2A 7B7
(506) 546-8093
Emp Here 30
SIC 5812 Eating places

D-U-N-S 20-018-7664   (BR)
LOUNSBURY COMPANY LIMITED
LOUNSBURY AUTOMOTIVE
1870 St. Peter Ave, Bathurst, NB, E2A 7J4
(506) 547-0707
Emp Here 35
SIC 5511 New and used car dealers

D-U-N-S 25-299-2151   (BR)
NEW BRUNSWICK POWER CORPORATION
2090 Vanier Blvd, Bathurst, NB, E2A 7B7
(506) 458-4444
Emp Here 45
SIC 4911 Electric services

D-U-N-S 25-320-9167   (BR)
PUROLATOR INC.
PUROLATOR INC
840 Weirden Dr, Bathurst, NB, E2A 3Z1

(506) 548-4452
Emp Here 25
SIC 7389 Business services, nec

D-U-N-S 24-341-0172   (SL)
R. DEGRACE HOLDINGS LTD
ATLANTIC HOST
1450 Vanier Blvd, Bathurst, NB, E2A 7B7
(506) 548-3335
Emp Here 55   *Sales* 2,407,703
SIC 7011 Hotels and motels

D-U-N-S 24-472-1049   (SL)
R. G. MC. GROUP LIMITED
MCDONALDS FAMILY RESTAURANT
620 St. Peter Ave, Bathurst, NB, E2A 2Y7
(506) 548-9555
Emp Here 110   *Sales* 3,283,232
SIC 5812 Eating places

D-U-N-S 24-318-5340   (BR)
REGIONAL HEALTH AUTHORITY A
CHALEUR REGIONAL HOSPITAL
1750 Sunset Dr, Bathurst, NB, E2A 4L7
(506) 544-3000
Emp Here 900
SIC 8062 General medical and surgical hospitals

D-U-N-S 25-953-5078   (BR)
RELIGIEUSES HOSPITALIERES DE SAINT-JOSEPH
RELIGIEUSES HOSPITALIERES DE ST JOSEPH
(*Suby of* Religieuses Hospitalieres de Saint-Joseph)
2144 Vallee Lourdes Dr, Bathurst, NB, E2A 4R9
(506) 547-8320
Emp Here 20
SIC 8661 Religious organizations

D-U-N-S 24-628-8328   (HQ)
ROY CONSULTANTS GROUP LTD
ROY CONSULTANTS
548 King Ave, Bathurst, NB, E2A 1P7
(506) 546-4484
Emp Here 50   *Emp Total* 60
Sales 7,276,508
SIC 8711 Engineering services
Pr Pr Rejean Boudreau
  Paul Arseneau
Dir Wilfred David
Dir Jean-Claude Arsenault
Pr Pr Jacques Roy
  Michel Dusresne

D-U-N-S 20-965-3372   (BR)
ROYAL BANK OF CANADA
RBC
(*Suby of* Royal Bank Of Canada)
230 Main St, Bathurst, NB, E2A 1A8
(506) 547-1020
Emp Here 33
SIC 6021 National commercial banks

D-U-N-S 20-710-0764   (BR)
SCHOOL DISTRICT 15
SUPERIOR MIDDLE SCHOOL
(*Suby of* School District 15)
560 Duke St, Bathurst, NB, E2A 2X5
(506) 547-2750
Emp Here 50
SIC 8211 Elementary and secondary schools

D-U-N-S 20-710-0756   (BR)
SCHOOL DISTRICT 15
(*Suby of* School District 15)
1394 King Ave, Bathurst, NB, E2A 1S8

Emp Here 50
SIC 8211 Elementary and secondary schools

D-U-N-S 24-318-2719   (SL)
SCHOOL DISTRICT NO 15
TERRY FOX ELEMENTARY SCHOOL
155 Basin St, Bathurst, NB, E2A 6N1
(506) 547-2215
Emp Here 50   *Sales* 3,356,192

SIC 8211 Elementary and secondary schools

D-U-N-S 20-657-9844   (BR)
SEARS CANADA INC
1300 St. Peter Ave, Bathurst, NB, E2A 3A6
(506) 546-7800
Emp Here 40
SIC 5311 Department stores

D-U-N-S 25-960-8438   (BR)
SOBEYS CAPITAL INCORPORATED
SOBEYS #490
850 St. Peter Ave, Bathurst, NB, E2A 4K4
(506) 548-3577
Emp Here 60
SIC 5411 Grocery stores

D-U-N-S 25-962-2538   (BR)
ST. ISIDORE ASPHALT LTD
2000 Sunset Dr, Bathurst, NB, E2A 7K8
(506) 548-9841
Emp Here 38
SIC 2951 Asphalt paving mixtures and blocks

D-U-N-S 25-498-9478   (BR)
STAPLES CANADA INC
STAPLES/BUSINESS DEPOT
(*Suby of* Staples, Inc.)
1300 St. Peter Ave Suite 109, Bathurst, NB, E2A 3A6
(506) 545-9060
Emp Here 40
SIC 5943 Stationery stores

D-U-N-S 24-913-2176   (SL)
VILLA CHALEUR INC
795 Champlain St Suite 221, Bathurst, NB, E2A 4M8
(506) 549-5588
Emp Here 40   *Sales* 1,459,214
SIC 8361 Residential care

D-U-N-S 24-097-9042   (BR)
WAL-MART CANADA CORP
WALMART
900 St. Anne St, Bathurst, NB, E2A 6X2
(506) 546-0500
Emp Here 130
SIC 5311 Department stores

Beardsley, NB E7M

D-U-N-S 24-000-2308   (HQ)
MITTON HILL ENTERPRISES LIMITED
TIM HORTONS
(*Suby of* Mitton Hill Enterprises Limited)
194 Beardsley Rd, Beardsley, NB, E7M 3Z7
(506) 325-9321
Emp Here 25   *Emp Total* 75
Sales 2,261,782
SIC 5812 Eating places

Bedell, NB E7M

D-U-N-S 20-006-0890   (BR)
SCHOOL DISTRICT 14
SOUTHERN CARLETON ELEMENTARY SCHOOL
(*Suby of* School District 14)
282 Route 555, Bedell, NB, E7M 4P1
(506) 325-4434
Emp Here 50
SIC 8211 Elementary and secondary schools

Belledune, NB E8G
Gloucester County

D-U-N-S 20-287-1752   (BR)
NEW BRUNSWICK POWER CORPORA-
TION
1558 Main St, Belledune, NB, E8G 2M3

Emp Here 110
SIC 4911 Electric services

D-U-N-S 24-362-8869   (BR)
SHAW GROUP LIMITED, THE
SHAW RESOURCES
52 Hodgins Rd, Belledune, NB, E8G 2E3
(506) 522-2839
Emp Here 20
SIC 2499 Wood products, nec

Beresford, NB E8K
Gloucester County

D-U-N-S 20-047-4968   (BR)
CONSEIL SCOLAIRE DISTRICT NO 5
CARREFOUR ETUDIANT
795 Rue Ecole, Beresford, NB, E8K 1V4
(506) 542-2602
Emp Here 40
SIC 8211 Elementary and secondary schools

D-U-N-S 25-241-9270   (BR)
DISTRICT SCOLAIRE FRANCOPHONE NORD-EST
CARREFOUR ETUDIANT-BERESFORD
795 Rue Ecole, Beresford, NB, E8K 1V4
(506) 542-2602
Emp Here 40
SIC 8211 Elementary and secondary schools

D-U-N-S 25-131-5974   (BR)
LANDIER ENTERPRISES LTD
TIM HORTONS
(*Suby of* Landier Enterprises Ltd)
794 Rue Principale, Beresford, NB, E8K 2G1
(506) 542-1397
Emp Here 25
SIC 5812 Eating places

Berry Mills, NB E1G
Westmoreland County

D-U-N-S 20-016-0815   (BR)
MILLER PAVING LIMITED
INDUSTRIAL COLD MILLING, DIV OF
2276 Route 128, Berry Mills, NB, E1G 4K4
(506) 857-0112
Emp Here 130
SIC 1611 Highway and street construction

Berwick, NB E5P

D-U-N-S 24-000-5947   (SL)
615317 NB INC
BTN ATLANTIC
891 Route 880, Berwick, NB, E5P 3H5
(506) 433-6168
Emp Here 25   *Sales* 2,991,389
SIC 5193 Flowers and florists supplies

Black River, NB E2S

D-U-N-S 24-338-1746   (BR)
LAFARGE CANADA INC
50 Old Black River Rd, Black River, NB, E2S 1Z2
(506) 633-1890
Emp Here 20
SIC 1611 Highway and street construction

Blacks Harbour, NB E5H
Charlotte County

D-U-N-S 25-361-6825   (BR)
CONNORS   BROS.   CLOVER   LEAF SEAFOODS COMPANY
CONNOR BROS., DIV OF
180 Brunswick St, Blacks Harbour, NB, E5H 1G6
(506) 456-1610
Emp Here 700
SIC 5146 Fish and seafoods

D-U-N-S 24-955-5731   (BR)
REGIONAL HEALTH AUTHORITY B
FUNDY HEALTH CENTRE
34 Hospital St, Blacks Harbour, NB, E5H 1K2
(506) 456-4200
Emp Here 70
SIC 8093 Specialty outpatient clinics, nec

D-U-N-S 20-710-0848   (BR)
SCHOOL DISTRICT NO 10
BLACKS HARBOUR SCHOOL
800 Main St, Blacks Harbour, NB, E5H 1E6
(506) 456-4850
Emp Here 20
SIC 8211 Elementary and secondary schools

D-U-N-S 24-314-4420   (HQ)
TRUE NORTH SALMON CO. LTD
HERITAGE SALMON
669 Main St, Blacks Harbour, NB, E5H 1K1
(506) 456-6610
Emp Here 20   *Emp Total* 1,300
Sales 69,040,205
SIC 2092 Fresh or frozen packaged fish
VP VP Glenn Cooke
Pr Pr Gifford Cooke
  Michael Cooke

Blackville, NB E9B
Northumberland County

D-U-N-S 20-710-0541   (BR)
DISTRICT EDUCATION COUNCIL-SCHOOL DISTRICT 16
BLACVILLE SCHOOL
(*Suby of* District Education Council-School District 16)
12 Maclaggan Dr, Blackville, NB, E9B 1Y4
(506) 843-2900
Emp Here 50
SIC 8211 Elementary and secondary schools

Boiestown, NB E6A
Northumberland County

D-U-N-S 24-187-6093   (BR)
ANGLOPHONE WEST SCHOOL DISTRICT (ASD-W)
UPPER MIRAMICHI HIGH SCHOOL
3466 Route 625, Boiestown, NB, E6A 1C8

Emp Here 35
SIC 8211 Elementary and secondary schools

Bouctouche, NB E4S
Kent County

D-U-N-S 20-549-5351   (SL)
BOUCTOUCHE PHARMACY LTD
PHARMASAVE
30 Irving Blvd Suite 200, Bouctouche, NB, E4S 3L2
(506) 743-2434
Emp Here 49   *Sales* 6,931,267

SIC 5912 Drug stores and proprietary stores
Pr Pr Arthur J Mcdonough
Laura Mcdonough

D-U-N-S 20-023-3570   (BR)
DISTRICT SCOLAIRE 11
ECOLE CLEMENT CORMIER
(Suby of District Scolaire 11)
37 Av Richard, Bouctouche, NB, E4S 3T5
(506) 743-7200
Emp Here 75
SIC 8211 Elementary and secondary schools

D-U-N-S 25-722-5359   (BR)
IMVESCOR RESTAURANT GROUP INC
PIZZA DELIGHT
78 Irving Blvd, Bouctouche, NB, E4S 3L4
(506) 743-8010
Emp Here 25
SIC 5812 Eating places

D-U-N-S 24-333-2603   (BR)
J. D. IRVING, LIMITED
KENT HOMES
(Suby of J. D. Irving, Limited)
28 Ch Du Couvent, Bouctouche, NB, E4S 3B9
(506) 743-2481
Emp Here 200
SIC 2452 Prefabricated wood buildings

D-U-N-S 20-018-9546   (BR)
J. D. IRVING, LIMITED
KENT BUILDING SUPPLIES
(Suby of J. D. Irving, Limited)
183 Irving Blvd, Bouctouche, NB, E4S 3K3
(506) 743-2438
Emp Here 20
SIC 5399 Miscellaneous general merchandise

D-U-N-S 20-932-3955   (SL)
MANOIR SAINT-JEAN BAPTISTE INC
5 Av Richard, Bouctouche, NB, E4S 3T2
(506) 743-7344
Emp Here 85   Sales 3,724,879
SIC 8361 Residential care

D-U-N-S 20-282-4009   (SL)
MARITIME DOOR & WINDOW LTD
28 Rue Acadie, Bouctouche, NB, E4S 2T2
(506) 743-2469
Emp Here 65   Sales 12,344,510
SIC 5211 Lumber and other building materials

D-U-N-S 24-383-2966   (BR)
MCCARTHY'S ROOFING LIMITED
26 Rue Industrielle, Bouctouche, NB, E4S 3H9

Emp Here 35
SIC 1761 Roofing, siding, and sheetMetal
work

D-U-N-S 25-358-6341   (HQ)
SYSTEMAIR INC
50 Kanalflakt Way Route, Bouctouche, NB,
E4S 3M5
(506) 743-9500
Emp Here 125   Emp Total 20
Sales 17,583,529
SIC 3564 Blowers and fans
Gerald Engstrom
Pr Pr Roland Mazerolle
Dir Alan Graham

Burtts Corner, NB E6L

D-U-N-S 24-326-5126   (BR)
MAPLE LEAF FOODS INC
425 Route 104, Burtts Corner, NB, E6L 2A9
(506) 363-3052
Emp Here 50
SIC 7389 Business services, nec

D-U-N-S 25-242-1144   (BR)
SCHOOL DISTRICT 14
KESWICK VALLEY MEMORIAL SCHOOL

(Suby of School District 14)
20 Route 617, Burtts Corner, NB, E6L 2X3
(506) 363-4717
Emp Here 33
SIC 8211 Elementary and secondary schools

Campbellton, NB E3N
Restigouche County

D-U-N-S 20-527-4421   (BR)
CANADA POST CORPORATION
CAMPBELLTON POST OFFICE
35 Roseberry St, Campbellton, NB, E3N 2G5
(506) 753-0200
Emp Here 20
SIC 4311 U.s. postal service

D-U-N-S 24-994-6062   (HQ)
CIRCLE HOLDINGS INC
TIM HORTONS
(Suby of Circle Holdings Inc)
75 Roseberry St Suite 550, Campbellton, NB,
E3N 2G6
(506) 789-9148
Emp Here 36   Emp Total 108
Sales 3,283,232
SIC 5812 Eating places

D-U-N-S 25-241-6698   (BR)
CONSEIL SCOLAIRE DISTRICT NO 5
ECOLE APOLLO XI
61 Dover St, Campbellton, NB, E3N 1P7
(506) 789-2260
Emp Here 33
SIC 8211 Elementary and secondary schools

D-U-N-S 25-241-6730   (BR)
CONSEIL SCOLAIRE DISTRICT NO 5
*POLYVALENTE   ROLAND-PEPIN   HIGH
SCHOOL*
45a Rue Du Village, Campbellton, NB, E3N
3G4
(506) 789-2250
Emp Here 75
SIC 8211 Elementary and secondary schools

D-U-N-S 24-912-3688   (HQ)
LEALIN LTD
MCDONALD'S RESTAURANT
(Suby of Lealin Ltd)
185 Roseberry St, Campbellton, NB, E3N 2H4
(506) 759-8888
Emp Here 65   Emp Total 65
Sales 1,969,939
SIC 5812 Eating places

D-U-N-S 20-932-3070   (HQ)
RESTIGOUCHE HEALTH AUTHORITY
CAMPBELLTON REGIONAL HOSPITAL
(Suby of Restigouche Health Authority)
189 Lily Lake Rd, Campbellton, NB, E3N 3H3
(506) 789-5000
Emp Here 800   Emp Total 1,222
Sales 109,781,329
SIC 8062 General medical and surgical hospitals
Pr Dan Arsenault
Jean Boulay

D-U-N-S 24-118-0566   (BR)
SNC-LAVALIN INC
SLP CUSTOMER SUPPORT
88 Sr Green Rd Suite 101, Campbellton, NB,
E3N 3Y6
(506) 759-6350
Emp Here 100
SIC 6798 Real estate investment trusts

D-U-N-S 24-000-9154   (BR)
**SNC-LAVALIN OPERATIONS & MAINTE-
NANCE INC**
88 Sr Green Rd Suite 101, Campbellton, NB,
E3N 3Y6
(866) 440-8144
Emp Here 50

SIC 8741 Management services

D-U-N-S 25-241-6532   (BR)
SCHOOL DISTRICT 15
CAMPBELLTON MIDDLE SCHOOL
(Suby of School District 15)
80 Arran St, Campbellton, NB, E3N 1L7
(506) 789-2120
Emp Here 35
SIC 8211 Elementary and secondary schools

D-U-N-S 25-241-6490   (BR)
SCHOOL DISTRICT 15
LORD BEAVERBROOK SCHOOL
(Suby of School District 15)
113 Arran St, Campbellton, NB, E3N 1M1
(506) 789-2130
Emp Here 25
SIC 8211 Elementary and secondary schools

D-U-N-S 25-309-1797   (BR)
SOBEYS CAPITAL INCORPORATED
SOBEYS
140 Roseberry St, Campbellton, NB, E3N 2G9

Emp Here 100
SIC 5411 Grocery stores

Canterbury, NB E6H

D-U-N-S 25-241-8082   (BR)
SCHOOL DISTRICT 14
CANTERBURY HIGH SCHOOL
(Suby of School District 14)
80 Main St, Canterbury, NB, E6H 1L3
(506) 279-6000
Emp Here 25
SIC 8211 Elementary and secondary schools

Cap-Pele, NB E4N
Westmoreland County

D-U-N-S 25-242-0195   (BR)
DISTRICT SCOLAIRE 11
COLE DONAT ROBICHAUD
(Suby of District Scolaire 11)
2632 Ch Acadie, Cap-Pele, NB, E4N 1E3
(506) 577-2000
Emp Here 48
SIC 8211 Elementary and secondary schools

Caraquet, NB E1W
Gloucester County

D-U-N-S 24-341-8316   (SL)
CARAPRO LTD
60 Boul St-Pierre E, Caraquet, NB, E1W 1B6

Emp Here 25   Sales 5,727,360
SIC 2092 Fresh or frozen packaged fish
Pr Pr Valmond Chiasson
VP VP Alie Lebouthillier
Anatole Godin

D-U-N-S 20-710-0434   (BR)
**DISTRICT   SCOLAIRE   FRANCOPHONE
NORD-EST**
POLYVALENTE LOUIS MAILLOUX SCHOOL
30 Rue Cormier, Caraquet, NB, E1W 1A5
(506) 727-7039
Emp Here 65
SIC 8211 Elementary and secondary schools

D-U-N-S 25-241-9239   (BR)
**DISTRICT   SCOLAIRE   FRANCOPHONE
NORD-EST**
*ECOLE COMMUNAUTAIRE L'ESCALE DES
JEUNES*

Gd, Caraquet, NB, E1W 1B7
(506) 727-7044
Emp Here 30
SIC 8211 Elementary and secondary schools

D-U-N-S 20-710-0442   (BR)
**DISTRICT   SCOLAIRE   FRANCOPHONE
NORD-EST**
*DE LA PENINSULE ACADIENNE ECOLE
MARGUERITE BOURGEOYS*
238 Rue Marguerite Bourgeoys, Caraquet,
NB, E1W 1A4
(506) 727-7040
Emp Here 50
SIC 8211 Elementary and secondary schools

D-U-N-S 20-788-4417   (BR)
PREMIER TECH TECHNOLOGIES LIMITEE
SYSTEMS ERIN
35 Industriel Blvd, Caraquet, NB, E1W 1A9
(506) 727-2703
Emp Here 40
SIC 3559 Special industry machinery, nec

D-U-N-S 24-955-6705   (BR)
REGIONAL HEALTH AUTHORITY A
COMMUNITY HEALTH CENTER
1 Boul St-Pierre O, Caraquet, NB, E1W 1B6
(506) 726-2100
Emp Here 175
SIC 8062 General medical and surgical hospitals

D-U-N-S 25-109-0957   (SL)
VILLA BEAUSEJOUR INC
253 Boul St-Pierre O, Caraquet, NB, E1W 1A4
(506) 726-2744
Emp Here 75   Sales 2,772,507
SIC 8361 Residential care

Cassidy Lake, NB E4E

D-U-N-S 20-029-5363   (BR)
PROGRAM DE PORTAGE INC, LE
PORTAGE NEW BRUNSWICK
1275 Route 865, Cassidy Lake, NB, E4E 5Y6
(506) 839-1200
Emp Here 28
SIC 8059 Nursing and personal care, nec

Chipman, NB E4A
Queens County

D-U-N-S 25-241-7878   (BR)
**ANGLOPHONE WEST SCHOOL DISTRICT
(ASD-W)**
CHIPMAN FOREST AVENUE SCHOOL
33 Forest Ave, Chipman, NB, E4A 1Z8
(506) 339-7015
Emp Here 30
SIC 8211 Elementary and secondary schools

D-U-N-S 20-271-9456   (BR)
J. D. IRVING, LIMITED
(Suby of J. D. Irving, Limited)
290 Main St, Chipman, NB, E4A 2M7
(506) 339-7910
Emp Here 49
SIC 5211 Lumber and other building materials

Clair, NB E7A

D-U-N-S 20-619-0266   (SL)
**CLAIR INDUSTRIAL DEVELOPMENT COR-
PORATION LTD**
LATHS WASKA
(Suby of Clair Industrial Development Corp
Ltd)

14 Av 2 Ieme Industriel, Clair, NB, E7A 2B1
(506) 992-2152
Emp Here 88   *Sales* 12,532,976
SIC 2429 Special product sawmills, nec
Pr Pr Daniel Levasseur
 Jean-Louis Levasseur
 Paul Levasseur
 Jacques Levasseur
Dir Pierre Levasseur
Dir Guy Levasseur

D-U-N-S 20-085-7691   (BR)
DISTRICT SCOLAIRE 3
*CENTRE D'APPRENTISSAGE HAUT
MADAWASKA*
323 Long Blvd, Clair, NB, E7A 2C5
(506) 992-6006
Emp Here 25
SIC 8211 Elementary and secondary schools

D-U-N-S 25-666-9896   (BR)
**FEDERATION DES CAISSES POPULAIRE
ACADIENNES INC, LA**
CAISSE POPULAIRE HAUT MADAWASKA
(*Suby of* Federation Des Caisses Populaire
Acadiennes Inc, La)
821 Rue Principale, Clair, NB, E7A 2H7
(506) 992-2158
Emp Here 28
SIC 6062 State credit unions

D-U-N-S 20-938-9969   (BR)
J. D. IRVING, LIMITED
(*Suby of* J. D. Irving, Limited)
632 Rue Principale, Clair, NB, E7A 2H2
(506) 992-9020
Emp Here 150
SIC 2426 Hardwood dimension and flooring
mills

Cocagne, NB E4R
Kent County

D-U-N-S 25-241-8140   (BR)
DISTRICT SCOLAIRE 11
ECOLE BLANCHE-BOURGEOIS
(*Suby of* District Scolaire 11)
29 Ch Cocagne Cross, Cocagne, NB, E4R 2J1
(506) 576-5006
Emp Here 22
SIC 8211 Elementary and secondary schools

Coteau Road, NB E8T
Gloucester County

D-U-N-S 20-020-6522   (HQ)
SCOTT CANADA LTD
(*Suby of* Scott Canada Ltd)
1571 Route 310, Coteau Road, NB, E8T 3K7
(506) 344-2225
Emp Here 50   *Emp Total* 70
Sales 4,937,631
SIC 1499 Miscellaneous nonMetallic minerals,
except fuels

Cumberland Bay, NB E4A
Queens County

D-U-N-S 25-871-0276   (BR)
**NORTHERN CANADA EVANGELICAL MIS-
SION, INC**
ARROWHEAD NATIVE BIBLE CENTRE
(*Suby of* Northern Canada Evangelical Mis-
sion, Inc)
622 Cox Point Rd, Cumberland Bay, NB, E4A
2Y4
(506) 479-5811
Emp Here 22

SIC 8661 Religious organizations

Dalhousie, NB E8C
Restigouche County

D-U-N-S 20-778-6737   (BR)
CIRCLE HOLDINGS INC
TIM HORTONS
(*Suby of* Circle Holdings Inc)
414 William St, Dalhousie, NB, E8C 2X2
(506) 684-5569
Emp Here 30
SIC 5812 Eating places

D-U-N-S 20-004-9307   (BR)
CONSEIL SCOLAIRE DISTRICT NO 5
ECOLE AUX QUATRE VENTS
499 Prom Jeux Du Canada, Dalhousie, NB,
E8C 1V6
(506) 684-7610
Emp Here 40
SIC 8211 Elementary and secondary schools

D-U-N-S 20-019-4751   (BR)
LOUNSBURY COMPANY LIMITED
LOUNSBURY'S CHEV OLDS
456 William St, Dalhousie, NB, E8C 2X7
(506) 684-3341
Emp Here 24
SIC 5511 New and used car dealers

Deersdale, NB E7L

D-U-N-S 24-101-2025   (BR)
J. D. IRVING, LIMITED
J D IRVING MILL
(*Suby of* J. D. Irving, Limited)
5120 Route 107, Deersdale, NB, E7L 1W5
(506) 246-5528
Emp Here 140
SIC 2611 Pulp mills

Derby, NB E1V
Northumberland County

D-U-N-S 20-023-8348   (BR)
**DISTRICT EDUCATION COUNCIL-SCHOOL
DISTRICT 16**
MILLERTON ELEMENTARY JUNIOR HIGH
(*Suby of* District Education Council-School
District 16)
4711 Route 108, Derby, NB, E1V 5C3
(506) 627-4090
Emp Here 20
SIC 8211 Elementary and secondary schools

Dieppe, NB E1A
Westmoreland County

D-U-N-S 24-955-7083   (SL)
041216 NB LTD
SPRUCE GROVE BUILDING CLEANERS
376 Rue Champlain, Dieppe, NB, E1A 1P3
(506) 858-5085
Emp Here 100   *Sales* 2,918,428
SIC 7349 Building maintenance services, nec

D-U-N-S 20-261-4541   (BR)
**ARTHUR J. GALLAGHER CANADA LIM-
ITED**
GOGUEN CHAMPLAIN INSURANCE
(*Suby of* Arthur J. Gallagher & Co.)
1040 Rue Champlain Suite 200, Dieppe, NB,
E1A 8L8
(506) 862-2070
Emp Here 27

SIC 6411 Insurance agents, brokers, and service

D-U-N-S 25-878-6136   (BR)
**ASSUMPTION MUTUAL LIFE INSURANCE
COMPANY**
ASSUMPTION LIFE
411 Rue Champlain, Dieppe, NB, E1A 1P2
(506) 857-9400
Emp Here 20
SIC 6311 Life insurance

D-U-N-S 20-448-3705   (BR)
BELFOR (CANADA) INC
57 Rue Sylvio, Dieppe, NB, E1A 7X1
(506) 853-0006
Emp Here 20
SIC 1799 Special trade contractors, nec

D-U-N-S 25-081-9133   (SL)
BULMER AIRCRAFT SERVICES LTD
1579 Rue Champlain Suite 2, Dieppe, NB,
E1A 7P5
(506) 858-5472
Emp Here 31   *Sales* 20,188,550
SIC 4581 Airports, flying fields, and services
Pr Pr Bryan Macdonald
 Kevin Barley

D-U-N-S 24-123-3878   (BR)
CANADA POST CORPORATION
680 Boul Malenfant, Dieppe, NB, E1A 5V8

Emp Here 200
SIC 4311 U.s. postal service

D-U-N-S 25-884-4489   (BR)
CARA OPERATIONS LIMITED
SWISS CHALET ROTISSERIE & GRILL
(*Suby of* Cara Holdings Limited)
9 Champlain St, Dieppe, NB, E1A 1N4
(506) 859-8608
Emp Here 40
SIC 5812 Eating places

D-U-N-S 20-562-7669   (HQ)
CAVENDISH FARMS CORPORATION
CAVENDISH PRODUCE, DIV OF
(*Suby of* J. D. Irving, Limited)
100 Prom Midland, Dieppe, NB, E1A 6X4
(506) 858-7777
Emp Here 100   *Emp Total* 15,000
Sales 310,082,975
SIC 5142 Packaged frozen goods
Pr Robert Irving
VP Fin Paul Landry
Genl Mgr Ron Clow

D-U-N-S 24-386-5644   (HQ)
CLS-LEXI TECH LTD.
CLS LEXI-TECH
(*Suby of* LBT Acquisition, Inc.)
10 Rue Dawson, Dieppe, NB, E1A 6C8
(506) 859-5200
Emp Here 78   *Emp Total* 6,000
Sales 12,300,764
SIC 7389 Business services, nec
CEO Lawrence Rogers

D-U-N-S 24-123-3746   (SL)
**CLUB DE GOLF FOX CREEK GOLF CLUB
INC**
200 Rue Du Golf, Dieppe, NB, E1A 8J6
(506) 859-4653
Emp Here 60   *Sales* 2,553,625
SIC 7992 Public golf courses

D-U-N-S 25-658-6827   (BR)
COREY CRAIG LTD
TIM HORTONS
477 Rue Paul, Dieppe, NB, E1A 4X5
(506) 862-7637
Emp Here 35
SIC 5812 Eating places

D-U-N-S 25-881-2585   (BR)
DELUXE FRENCH FRIES LTD
450 Rue Paul, Dieppe, NB, E1A 5T5

---

(506) 388-1920
Emp Here 28
SIC 5812 Eating places

D-U-N-S 25-875-7814   (HQ)
DITECH PAINT CO. LTD
DITECH TESTING
(*Suby of* Ditech Paint Co. Ltd)
561 Boul Ferdinand, Dieppe, NB, E1A 7G1
(506) 384-8197
Emp Here 20   *Emp Total* 55
Sales 4,334,713
SIC 7699 Repair services, nec

D-U-N-S 25-171-0455   (BR)
EDDIE BAUER OF CANADA INC
EDDIE BAUER
(*Suby of* Golden Gate Capital LP)
477 Rue Paul, Dieppe, NB, E1A 4X5
(506) 854-8444
Emp Here 30
SIC 5699 Miscellaneous apparel and acces-
sory stores

D-U-N-S 20-790-1476   (BR)
ELMWOOD HARDWARE LTD
*DIEPPE HOME HARDWARE BUILDING
CENTRE*
205 Av Acadie, Dieppe, NB, E1A 1G6
(506) 382-8100
Emp Here 20
SIC 5211 Lumber and other building materials

D-U-N-S 25-373-5237   (BR)
EMPIRE THEATRES LIMITED
499 Rue Paul, Dieppe, NB, E1A 6S5
(506) 853-8397
Emp Here 30
SIC 7832 Motion picture theaters, except
drive-in

D-U-N-S 25-297-5917   (BR)
**FEDERAL EXPRESS CANADA CORPORA-
TION**
FEDERAL EXPRESS CANADA LTD
(*Suby of* Fedex Corporation)
1785 Rue Champlain, Dieppe, NB, E1A 7P5
(800) 463-3339
Emp Here 30
SIC 7389 Business services, nec

D-U-N-S 25-361-0364   (BR)
FLYNN CANADA LTD
691 Rue Babin, Dieppe, NB, E1A 5M7
(506) 855-3340
Emp Here 40
SIC 1761 Roofing, siding, and sheetMetal
work

D-U-N-S 20-196-2318   (BR)
GAP (CANADA) INC
(*Suby of* The Gap Inc)
477 Rue Paul, Dieppe, NB, E1A 4X5
(506) 382-9005
Emp Here 34
SIC 5651 Family clothing stores

D-U-N-S 24-335-8293   (BR)
GRAND & TOY LIMITED
(*Suby of* Office Depot, Inc.)
146 Boul Dieppe, Dieppe, NB, E1A 6P8
(506) 862-2400
Emp Here 20
SIC 5112 Stationery and office supplies

D-U-N-S 25-833-1362   (BR)
HARVARD RESTAURANTS LTD
WENDY'S RESTAURANT
473 Rue Paul, Dieppe, NB, E1A 5R4
(506) 862-7656
Emp Here 30
SIC 5812 Eating places

D-U-N-S 20-278-9041   (BR)
IMPERIAL BUILDING PRODUCTS INC
500 Boul Ferdinand, Dieppe, NB, E1A 6V9
(506) 859-9908
Emp Here 30

SIC 3564 Blowers and fans

D-U-N-S 25-295-8590   (BR)
INDIGO BOOKS & MUSIC INC
CHAPTERS
(*Suby of* Indigo Books & Music Inc)
1 Bass Pro Drive, Dieppe, NB, E1A 6S5
(506) 855-8075
Emp Here 50
SIC 5942 Book stores

D-U-N-S 20-235-7096   (SL)
INFIKNOWLEDGE, ULC
A TRAFFIX COMPANY
654 Malenfant Blvd, Dieppe, NB, E1A 5V8
(506) 855-2991
Emp Here 74   *Sales* 8,536,402
SIC 7371 Custom computer programming services
Pr Pr Andrew Sturgeon
VP VP George Donovan

D-U-N-S 25-369-6066   (HQ)
IRVING PERSONAL CARE LIMITED
(*Suby of* J. D. Irving, Limited)
100 Prom Midland, Dieppe, NB, E1A 6X4
(506) 857-7713
Emp Here 125   *Emp Total* 15,000
Sales 43,484,577
SIC 5137 Women's and children's clothing
Pr Robert K Irving
James K Irving
Arthur L Irving
John E Irving
James D Irving
John F Irving
Kenneth Irving

D-U-N-S 25-184-7000   (BR)
J. D. IRVING, LIMITED
IRVING TISSUE
(*Suby of* J. D. Irving, Limited)
100 Prom Midland, Dieppe, NB, E1A 6X4
(506) 859-5757
Emp Here 200
SIC 2679 Converted paper products, nec

D-U-N-S 24-574-7639   (BR)
J. D. IRVING, LIMITED
KENT BUILDING SUPPLIES
(*Suby of* J. D. Irving, Limited)
40 Rue Champlain, Dieppe, NB, E1A 1N3
(506) 859-5900
Emp Here 32
SIC 5211 Lumber and other building materials

D-U-N-S 25-952-5769   (BR)
J. D. IRVING, LIMITED
IRVING CONSUMER PRODUCTS
(*Suby of* J. D. Irving, Limited)
102 Rue Dawson, Dieppe, NB, E1A 0C1
(506) 859-5018
Emp Here 195
SIC 2621 Paper mills

D-U-N-S 24-831-7281   (HQ)
LANTECH DRILLING SERVICES INC
398 Dover Ch, Dieppe, NB, E1A 7L6
(506) 853-9131
Emp Here 30   *Emp Total* 900
Sales 2,991,389
SIC 1499 Miscellaneous nonMetallic minerals, except fuels

D-U-N-S 25-687-0361   (BR)
MASTER PACKAGING INC
333 Boul Adelard-Savoie, Dieppe, NB, E1A 7G9
(506) 389-3737
Emp Here 140
SIC 2653 Corrugated and solid fiber boxes

D-U-N-S 24-346-8688   (BR)
MCDONALD'S   RESTAURANTS   OF CANADA LIMITED
MCDONALD'S RESTAURANT
(*Suby of* McDonald's Corporation)
420 Rue Paul, Dieppe, NB, E1A 1Y1

(506) 862-1604
Emp Here 20
SIC 5812 Eating places

D-U-N-S 25-170-4730   (BR)
MIDLAND TRANSPORT LIMITED
MIDLAND COURIER
(*Suby of* J. D. Irving, Limited)
42 Rue Dawson, Dieppe, NB, E1A 6C8
(506) 858-7780
Emp Here 40
SIC 7389 Business services, nec

D-U-N-S 20-195-7425   (BR)
MITTON'S FOOD SERVICE INC
DAIRY QUEEN BRAZIER
(*Suby of* Mitton's Food Service Inc)
533 Rue Champlain, Dieppe, NB, E1A 1P2
(506) 855-5533
Emp Here 20
SIC 5812 Eating places

D-U-N-S 25-980-7758   (BR)
NEW BRUNSWICK LIQUOR CORPORA-TION
NB LIQUOR STORE
513 Rue Regis, Dieppe, NB, E1A 1Y2
(506) 852-2373
Emp Here 30
SIC 5921 Liquor stores

D-U-N-S 25-611-3911   (BR)
PRISZM LP
KFC
477 Rue Paul, Dieppe, NB, E1A 4X5
(905) 677-3813
Emp Here 24
SIC 5812 Eating places

D-U-N-S 20-798-6600   (BR)
ROGERS COMMUNICATIONS INC
(*Suby of* Rogers Communications Inc)
9 Rue Champlain, Dieppe, NB, E1A 1N4
(506) 854-3453
Emp Here 20
SIC 4899 Communication services, nec

D-U-N-S 24-317-8162   (BR)
SCHOOL BOARD DISTRICT 01
ECOLE CARREFOUR DE L'ACADIE
515 Rue Champlain, Dieppe, NB, E1A 1P2
(506) 869-5130
Emp Here 50
SIC 8211 Elementary and secondary schools

D-U-N-S 25-241-7704   (BR)
SCHOOL BOARD DISTRICT 01
ECOLE AMIRAULT
1070 Rue Amirault, Dieppe, NB, E1A 1E2
(506) 856-2590
Emp Here 45
SIC 8211 Elementary and secondary schools

D-U-N-S 24-227-6306   (BR)
SCHOOL BOARD DISTRICT 01
ECCLE MATHIEU MARTIN
511 Rue Champlain, Dieppe, NB, E1A 1P2
(506) 856-2770
Emp Here 110
SIC 8211 Elementary and secondary schools

D-U-N-S 20-069-7543   (BR)
SEARS CANADA INC
SEARS
43 Fue Champlain, Dieppe, NB, E1A 4T2
(506) 853-4002
Emp Here 300
SIC 5311 Department stores

D-U-N-S 24-114-4877   (BR)
SHANNAHAN'S   INVESTIGATION   SECU-RITY LIMITED
(*Suby of* Shannahan's Investigation Security Limited)
777 Av Aviation Suite 10, Dieppe, NB, E1A 7Z5
(506) 855-6615
Emp Here 58

SIC 6289 Security and commodity service

D-U-N-S 20-059-4005   (SL)
SHOPPERS DRUG MART
477 Rue Paul Suite 181, Dieppe, NB, E1A 4X5
(506) 857-0820
Emp Here 70   *Sales* 9,922,655
SIC 5912 Drug stores and proprietary stores
Pr Deirdre O'briain

D-U-N-S 20-278-9454   (BR)
SYSCO CANADA, INC
(*Suby of* Sysco Corporation)
611 Boul Ferdinand, Dieppe, NB, E1A 7G1
(506) 857-6040
Emp Here 107
SIC 5141 Groceries, general line

D-U-N-S 25-297-8481   (BR)
TOYS 'R' US (CANADA) LTD
TOYS 'R' US
(*Suby of* Toys "r" Us, Inc.)
477 Rue Paul, Dieppe, NB, E1A 4X5
(506) 859-8697
Emp Here 35
SIC 5945 Hobby, toy, and game shops

D-U-N-S 20-641-7870   (BR)
WEST 49 (2015) INC
477 Rue Paul, Dieppe, NB, E1A 4X5
(506) 855-6295
Emp Here 22
SIC 5699 Miscellaneous apparel and accessory stores

D-U-N-S 20-867-8057   (BR)
WESTJET AIRLINES LTD
WESTJET ENCORE
777 Av Aviation Unit 15, Dieppe, NB, E1A 7Z5
(506) 388-8930
Emp Here 21
SIC 4512 Air transportation, scheduled

Doaktown, NB E9C
Northumberland County

D-U-N-S 25-241-7506   (BR)
ANGLOPHONE   WEST   SCHOOL   DISTRICT (ASD-W)
DOAKTOWN   CONSOLIDATED   HIGH SCHOOL
430 Main St, Doaktown, NB, E9C 1E8

Emp Here 20
SIC 8211 Elementary and secondary schools

D-U-N-S 24-932-9806   (BR)
J. D. IRVING, LIMITED
(*Suby of* J. D. Irving, Limited)
120 South Rd, Doaktown, NB, E9C 1H2
(506) 365-1020
Emp Here 150
SIC 2421 Sawmills and planing mills, general

D-U-N-S 20-212-2243   (BR)
J. D. IRVING, LIMITED
(*Suby of* J. D. Irving, Limited)
200 South Rd, Doaktown, NB, E9C 1H4
(506) 365-1021
Emp Here 130
SIC 2421 Sawmills and planing mills, general

Drummond, NB E3Y
Victoria County

D-U-N-S 20-710-0806   (BR)
DISTRICT SCOLAIRE 3
ACADEMIE NOTRE DAME
1360 Ch Tobique, Drummond, NB, E3Y 2N8
(506) 473-7760
Emp Here 30
SIC 8211 Elementary and secondary schools

Dsl De Drummond, NB E3Y
Charlotte County

D-U-N-S 25-244-3114   (SL)
TOBIQUE FARMS OPERATING LIMITED
2424 Route 108, Dsl De Drummond, NB, E3Y 2K7
(506) 553-9913
Emp Here 24   *Sales* 7,852,800
SIC 5148 Fresh fruits and vegetables
Pr Pr Henk Tepper
VP VP Berend Tepper

Durham Bridge, NB E6C

D-U-N-S 20-913-6774   (BR)
ANGLOPHONE   WEST   SCHOOL   DISTRICT (ASD-W)
NASHWAK VALLEY SCHOOL
747 Route 628, Durham Bridge, NB, E6C 1N6
(506) 453-3238
Emp Here 20
SIC 8211 Elementary and secondary schools

Edmundston, NB E3V
Madawaska County

D-U-N-S 20-515-3880   (BR)
BRUNSWICK NEWS INC
JOURNAL LE MADAWASKA
(*Suby of* J. D. Irving, Limited)
20 Rue St-Francois, Edmundston, NB, E3V 1E3
(506) 735-5575
Emp Here 20
SIC 2711 Newspapers

D-U-N-S 25-881-0852   (SL)
CERCUEILS ALLIANCE CASKETS INC
ST LAWRENCE CASKET
(*Suby of* Cercueils du Bas St-Laurent Inc)
355 Du Pouvoir Ch, Edmundston, NB, E3V 4K1
(506) 739-6226
Emp Here 125   *Sales* 5,371,275
SIC 3995 Burial caskets
Pr Pr Paul Michaud
Rino Caissey

D-U-N-S 20-573-2543   (BR)
COMPAGNIE DES CHEMINS DE FER NA-TIONAUX DU CANADA
194 Rue St-Francois, Edmundston, NB, E3V 1E9
(506) 735-1201
Emp Here 100
SIC 4011 Railroads, line-haul operating

D-U-N-S 24-120-7401   (BR)
DISTRICT SCOLAIRE 3
CARREFOUR DE LA JEUNESSE
54 21 Ieme Ave, Edmundston, NB, E3V 2B9
(506) 737-4620
Emp Here 45
SIC 8211 Elementary and secondary schools

D-U-N-S 25-241-3497   (BR)
DISTRICT SCOLAIRE 3
ECOLE NOTRE-DAME
(*Suby of* District Scolaire 3)
99 Rue Martin, Edmundston, NB, E3V 2M7
(506) 735-2073
Emp Here 59
SIC 8211 Elementary and secondary schools

D-U-N-S 25-241-8207   (BR)
DISTRICT SCOLAIRE 3
CITE   DES   JEUNES   A.-M.   SORMANY D'EDMUNDSTON
(*Suby of* District Scolaire 3)

300 Martin St, Edmundston, NB, E3V 2N5
(506) 735-2008
Emp Here 150
SIC 8211 Elementary and secondary schools

D-U-N-S 25-241-4297   (HQ)
DISTRICT SCOLAIRE 3
(*Suby of* District Scolaire 3)
298 Rue Martin Suite 3, Edmundston, NB,
E3V 5E5
(506) 737-4567
Emp Here 29   *Emp Total* 897
Sales 77,365,211
SIC 8211 Elementary and secondary schools
Dir Yvan Guerette
Dir Denise Querry

D-U-N-S 20-019-6418   (SL)
G & M CHEVROLET-CADILLAC LTD
605 Rue Victoria, Edmundston, NB, E3V 3M8
(506) 735-3331
Emp Here 32   *Sales* 15,705,600
SIC 5511 New and used car dealers
Pr Pr Gerald Toner
Mgr Maurice Lafrance

D-U-N-S 25-305-1874   (BR)
INNVEST PROPERTIES CORP
COMFORT INN
(*Suby of* Innvest Properties Corp)
5 Bateman Ave, Edmundston, NB, E3V 3L1
(506) 739-8361
Emp Here 30
SIC 7011 Hotels and motels

D-U-N-S 20-797-6056   (BR)
J. D. IRVING, LIMITED
KENT BUILDING SUPPLIES
(*Suby of* J. D. Irving, Limited)
772 Rue Victoria, Edmundston, NB, E3V 3S9
(506) 735-1500
Emp Here 50
SIC 5211 Lumber and other building materials

D-U-N-S 25-366-1201   (BR)
**MCDONALD'S   RESTAURANTS   OF
CANADA LIMITED**
MCDONALD'S 40146
(*Suby of* McDonald's Corporation)
805 Rue Victoria, Edmundston, NB, E3V 3T3
(506) 736-6336
Emp Here 25
SIC 5812 Eating places

D-U-N-S 20-112-8159   (BR)
PATTISON, JIM INDUSTRIES LTD
ENSEIGNES PATTISON SIGN GROUP
8 Av Miller, Edmundston, NB, E3V 4H4
(506) 735-5506
Emp Here 325
SIC 5099 Durable goods, nec

D-U-N-S 25-666-5159   (BR)
REGIONAL HEALTH AUTHORITY NB
REGIONAL HEALTH AUTHORITY B
275h Bert Blvd, Edmundston, NB, E3V 4E4
(506) 739-2160
Emp Here 50
SIC 8051 Skilled nursing care facilities

D-U-N-S 24-347-5410   (BR)
SCHOOL DISTRICT 14
SAINT MARY'S ACADEMY
(*Suby of* School District 14)
52 Av Marmen, Edmundston, NB, E3V 2H2

Emp Here 25
SIC 8211 Elementary and secondary schools

D-U-N-S 20-005-9512   (BR)
**SERVICE D'AIDE A LA FAMILLE EDMUND-
STON GRAND SAULT INC**
13 Rue Dugal, Edmundston, NB, E3V 1X4
(506) 737-8000
Emp Here 250
SIC 8741 Management services

D-U-N-S 25-309-1680   (BR)

SOBEYS CAPITAL INCORPORATED
FRESHCO
26 Rue Michaud, Edmundston, NB, E3V 1X3
(506) 739-8871
Emp Here 24
SIC 5411 Grocery stores

D-U-N-S 25-309-1391   (BR)
SOBEYS CAPITAL INCORPORATED
SOBEYS #745
580 Rue Victoria, Edmundston, NB, E3V 3N1

Emp Here 75
SIC 5411 Grocery stores

D-U-N-S 25-856-6918   (BR)
VITALITE HEALTH NETWORK
PROGRAMME EXTRA-MURAL DU NB
275 Boul Hebert, Edmundston, NB, E3V 4E4
(506) 739-2160
Emp Here 50
SIC 8082 Home health care services

D-U-N-S 20-025-9369   (BR)
VITALITE HEALTH NETWORK
GAMBLING ADDICTION
62 Rue Queen, Edmundston, NB, E3V 1A1
(506) 739-2323
Emp Here 35
SIC 8331 Job training and related services

D-U-N-S 20-364-9483   (BR)
VITALITE HEALTH NETWORK
*SERVICE DE TRAITEMENT DES DEPEN-
DANCES*
345 Boul Hebert, Edmundston, NB, E3V 0E7
(506) 735-2092
Emp Here 35
SIC 8093 Specialty outpatient clinics, nec

D-U-N-S 24-120-3806   (BR)
WAL-MART CANADA CORP
805 Rue Victoria Suite 1033, Edmundston,
NB, E3V 3T3
(506) 735-8412
Emp Here 75
SIC 5311 Department stores

Eel Ground, NB E1V
Northumberland County

D-U-N-S 20-311-4181   (SL)
EEL GROUND FIRST NATION INC
*EEL GROUND COMMUNITY DEVELOP-
MENT CENTER*
40 Micmac Rd, Eel Ground, NB, E1V 4B1
(506) 627-4604
Emp Here 50   *Sales* 1,969,939
SIC 8322 Individual and family services

Florenceville-Bristol, NB E7L

D-U-N-S 24-347-5428   (BR)
**ANGLOPHONE WEST SCHOOL DISTRICT
(ASD-W)**
CARLETON NORTH HIGH SCHOOL
30 School St, Florenceville-Bristol, NB, E7L
2G2
(506) 392-5120
Emp Here 55
SIC 8211 Elementary and secondary schools

D-U-N-S 20-276-8107   (BR)
DAY & ROSS INC
DAY & ROSS TRADE NETWORKS
8734 Main St Unit 3, Florenceville-Bristol, NB,
E7L 3G6
(506) 392-2887
Emp Here 26
SIC 4731 Freight transportation arrangement

D-U-N-S 24-831-4783   (HQ)

MCCAIN PRODUCE INC
8734 Main St Unit 1, Florenceville-Bristol, NB,
E7L 3G6
(506) 392-3036
Emp Here 30   *Emp Total* 40,000
Sales 28,600,594
SIC 5148 Fresh fruits and vegetables
  Stephen Mccain
  Vernon Thomas

D-U-N-S 24-122-2236   (BR)
MITTON HILL ENTERPRISES LIMITED
TIM HORTONS
(*Suby of* Mitton Hill Enterprises Limited)
8826 Main St, Florenceville-Bristol, NB, E7L
2A1
(506) 392-9009
Emp Here 25
SIC 5812 Eating places

D-U-N-S 24-312-0669   (BR)
SCHOOL DISTRICT 14
FLORENCEVILLE ELEMENTARY SCHOOL
(*Suby of* School District 14)
8470 Rte 105, Florenceville-Bristol, NB, E7L
1Y9
(506) 392-5109
Emp Here 25
SIC 8211 Elementary and secondary schools

Fredericton, NB E3A

D-U-N-S 20-787-4855   (SL)
500408 N.B. INC
WENDY'S RESTAURANT
370 Main St, Fredericton, NB, E3A 1E5
(506) 462-9950
Emp Here 55   *Sales* 1,678,096
SIC 5812 Eating places

D-U-N-S 25-241-5591   (BR)
**ANGLOPHONE WEST SCHOOL DISTRICT
(ASD-W)**
NASHWAAKSIS MIDDLE SCHOOL
324 Fulton Ave, Fredericton, NB, E3A 5J4
(506) 453-5436
Emp Here 60
SIC 8211 Elementary and secondary schools

D-U-N-S 20-752-7149   (BR)
**ANGLOPHONE WEST SCHOOL DISTRICT
(ASD-W)**
PARK STREET SCHOOL
111 Park St, Fredericton, NB, E3A 2J6
(506) 453-5423
Emp Here 20
SIC 8211 Elementary and secondary schools

D-U-N-S 20-287-2862   (BR)
**ANGLOPHONE WEST SCHOOL DISTRICT
(ASD-W)**
LEO HAYES HIGH SCHOOL
499 Cliffe St, Fredericton, NB, E3A 9P5
(506) 457-6898
Emp Here 160
SIC 8211 Elementary and secondary schools

D-U-N-S 20-710-0723   (BR)
**ANGLOPHONE WEST SCHOOL DISTRICT
(ASD-W)**
SOUTH DEVON ELEMENTARY SCHOOL
778 Maclaren Ave, Fredericton, NB, E3A 3L7
(506) 453-5429
Emp Here 50
SIC 8211 Elementary and secondary schools

D-U-N-S 25-241-5799   (BR)
**ANGLOPHONE WEST SCHOOL DISTRICT
(ASD-W)**
NASHWAAKSIS MEMORIAL SCHOOL
80 Main St, Fredericton, NB, E3A 1C4
(506) 453-5421
Emp Here 35
SIC 8211 Elementary and secondary schools

D-U-N-S 20-710-0715   (BR)
**ANGLOPHONE WEST SCHOOL DISTRICT
(ASD-W)**
MCADAM AVENUE ELEMENTARY SCHOOL
129 Mcadam Ave, Fredericton, NB, E3A 1G7
(506) 453-5422
Emp Here 21
SIC 8211 Elementary and secondary schools

D-U-N-S 25-241-7514   (BR)
**ANGLOPHONE WEST SCHOOL DISTRICT
(ASD-W)**
BARKERS POINT ELEMENTARY SCHOOL
39 Carman St, Fredericton, NB, E3A 3W9
(506) 453-5402
Emp Here 40
SIC 8211 Elementary and secondary schools

D-U-N-S 25-242-1714   (BR)
**ANGLOPHONE WEST SCHOOL DISTRICT
(ASD-W)**
DEVON MIDDLE SCHOOL
681 Dobie St, Fredericton, NB, E3A 2Z2
(506) 453-5405
Emp Here 45
SIC 8211 Elementary and secondary schools

D-U-N-S 20-294-5619   (BR)
**ANGLOPHONE WEST SCHOOL DISTRICT
(ASD-W)**
ALEXANDER GIBSON MEMORIAL SCHOOL
241 Canada St, Fredericton, NB, E3A 4A1
(506) 453-5431
Emp Here 35
SIC 8211 Elementary and secondary schools

D-U-N-S 25-987-5110   (BR)
ATLANTIC WHOLESALERS LTD
NASHWAAKSIS SUPERSTORE
116 Main St, Fredericton, NB, E3A 9N6
(506) 474-1270
Emp Here 150
SIC 5411 Grocery stores

D-U-N-S 25-296-3053   (BR)
BANK OF NOVA SCOTIA, THE
SCOTIABANK
490 King St, Fredericton, NB, E3A 0A1
(506) 452-9800
Emp Here 40
SIC 6021 National commercial banks

D-U-N-S 25-496-9934   (BR)
**BELL ALIANT REGIONAL COMMUNICA-
TIONS INC**
IBM CANADA LTD
20 Mcgloin St, Fredericton, NB, E3A 5T8
(506) 444-9600
Emp Here 30
SIC 4899 Communication services, nec

D-U-N-S 24-605-7665   (SL)
CAPABLE BUILDING CLEANING LTD
158 Clark St, Fredericton, NB, E3A 2W7
(506) 458-9343
Emp Here 80   *Sales* 2,334,742
SIC 7349 Building maintenance services, nec

D-U-N-S 20-302-2319   (SL)
COLMAR INVESTMENTS INC
480 Riverside Dr, Fredericton, NB, E3A 8C2
(506) 460-5500
Emp Here 50   *Sales* 2,188,821
SIC 7011 Hotels and motels

D-U-N-S 25-779-8108   (BR)
**CORPORATION OF THE CITY OF FREDER-
ICTON**
FREDERICTON TRANSIT
(*Suby of* Corporation of the City of Frederic-
ton)
470 Saint Marys St, Fredericton, NB, E3A 8H5
(506) 460-2210
Emp Here 40
SIC 4111 Local and suburban transit

D-U-N-S 24-532-4041   (SL)
DOBBELSTEYN SERVICE AND MAINTE-

▲ Public Company   ■ Public Company Family Member   **HQ** Headquarters   **BR** Branch   **SL** Single Location

NANCE LTD
891 Riverside Dr, Fredericton, NB, E3A 8P9
(506) 458-9357
Emp Here 50   *Sales* 4,377,642
SIC 1731 Electrical work

D-U-N-S 25-481-5434   (SL)
K. K. FOODS LTD
DAIRY QUEEN
540 Union St, Fredericton, NB, E3A 3N2
(506) 453-1229
Emp Here 60   *Sales* 1,824,018
SIC 5812 Eating places

D-U-N-S 25-059-8497   (BR)
LAWTON'S DRUG STORES LIMITED
LAWTON'S DRUGS
435 Brookside Dr Suite 5, Fredericton, NB,
E3A 8V4
(506) 450-4161
Emp Here 25
SIC 5912 Drug stores and proprietary stores

D-U-N-S 25-363-3499   (BR)
**LUXURY HOTELS INTERNATIONAL OF
CANADA, ULC**
*MARRIOTT REGIONAL WORLD WIDE
RESERVATIONS CANADA ADMINISTRA-
TION OFFICES*
(*Suby of* Marriott International, Inc.)
102 Main St Unit 16, Fredericton, NB, E3A
9N6
(506) 443-7500
Emp Here 300
SIC 7389 Business services, nec

D-U-N-S 24-341-8019   (SL)
MCDONALD RESTAURANT OF CANADA
94 Main St, Fredericton, NB, E3A 9N6
(506) 450-0470
Emp Here 350   *Sales* 14,569,600
SIC 5812 Eating places
Dir Scott Elliott

D-U-N-S 20-779-0705   (BR)
MOORE ENTERPRISES INC
WENDY'S RESTAURANT
(*Suby of* Moore Enterprises Inc)
370 Main St, Fredericton, NB, E3A 1E5
(506) 462-9950
Emp Here 40
SIC 5812 Eating places

D-U-N-S 20-515-7733   (BR)
**NEW BRUNSWICK POWER CORPORA-
TION**
261 Gilbert St, Fredericton, NB, E3A 4B2
(506) 458-4308
Emp Here 50
SIC 4911 Electric services

D-U-N-S 20-512-2570   (BR)
**NEW BRUNSWICK SOUTHERN RAILWAY
COMPANY LIMITED**
IRVING TRANSPORTATION SERVICES
71 Sunset Dr, Fredericton, NB, E3A 1A2
(506) 632-4654
Emp Here 40
SIC 8721 Accounting, auditing, and book-
keeping

D-U-N-S 20-259-4461   (BR)
PROVINCE OF NEW BRUNSWICK
*NEW BRUNSWICK INTERNAL SERVICES
AGENCY*
435 Brookside Dr Suite 30, Fredericton, NB,
E3A 8V4
(888) 487-5050
Emp Here 300
SIC 7372 Prepackaged software

D-U-N-S 20-283-3083   (BR)
PROVINCE OF NEW BRUNSWICK
*NEW BRUNSWICK INTERNAL SERVICES
AGENCY*
435 Brookside Dr Suite 30, Fredericton, NB, E3A 5T8
(506) 453-3742
Emp Here 177

SIC 7389 Business services, nec

D-U-N-S 20-078-2105   (BR)
SENIOR WATCH INC
195 Main St, Fredericton, NB, E3A 1E1
(506) 452-9903
Emp Here 20
SIC 8011 Offices and clinics of medical doctors

D-U-N-S 25-309-1201   (BR)
SOBEYS CAPITAL INCORPORATED
SOBEYS
463 Brookside Dr Suite 349, Fredericton, NB,
E3A 8V4
(506) 450-7109
Emp Here 115
SIC 5411 Grocery stores

D-U-N-S 25-309-1524   (BR)
SOBEYS CAPITAL INCORPORATED
PRICE CHOPPERS
180 Main St, Fredericton, NB, E3A 1C8
(506) 472-7431
Emp Here 30
SIC 5411 Grocery stores

D-U-N-S 25-359-3008   (SL)
**ST MARY'S ECONOMIC DEVELOPMENT
CORPORATION**
ST MARY'S ENTERTAINMENT CENTRE
185 Gabriel Dr, Fredericton, NB, E3A 5V9
(506) 462-9300
Emp Here 80   *Sales* 4,377,642
SIC 7999 Amusement and recreation, nec

D-U-N-S 20-313-2852   (SL)
STANDARD TAXI LTD
Gd, Fredericton, NB, E3A 5G7
(506) 450-4444
Emp Here 50   *Sales* 1,532,175
SIC 4121 Taxicabs

D-U-N-S 25-743-1957   (BR)
**VICTORIAN ORDER OF NURSES FOR
CANADA**
VON FREDERICTON
435 Brookside Dr Unit 8, Fredericton, NB, E3A
8V4
(506) 458-8365
Emp Here 25
SIC 8082 Home health care services

D-U-N-S 24-329-8622   (BR)
WAL-MART CANADA CORP
WALMART
125 Two Nations Xg Suite 1067, Fredericton,
NB, E3A 0T3
(506) 444-8817
Emp Here 200
SIC 5311 Department stores

D-U-N-S 25-078-5839   (SL)
WHEELS & DEALS LTD
402 Saint Marys St, Fredericton, NB, E3A 8H5
(506) 459-6832
Emp Here 30   *Sales* 8,116,000
SIC 5521 Used car dealers
Pr Pr James Gilbert
Dawna Gilbert

D-U-N-S 20-298-3875   (BR)
WYNDHAM WORLDWIDE CANADA INC
AVIS BUDGET CONTACT CENTER
435 Brookside Dr Suite 23, Fredericton, NB,
E3A 8V4

Emp Here 300
SIC 4899 Communication services, nec

Fredericton, NB E3B

D-U-N-S 20-548-9818   (HQ)
ADI LIMITED
1133 Regent St Suite 300, Fredericton, NB,
E3B 3Z2

(506) 452-9000
Emp Here 160   *Emp Total* 200
Sales 28,600,594
SIC 8711 Engineering services
Hollis B. Cole
Paul D. Morrisson
G. A. Robinson

D-U-N-S 20-188-5063   (BR)
**AMEC FOSTER WHEELER AMERICAS LIM-
ITED**
AMEC EARTH & ENVIRONMENTAL
495 Prospect St Suite 1, Fredericton, NB, E3B
9M4
(506) 458-1000
Emp Here 40
SIC 8711 Engineering services

D-U-N-S 24-677-4389   (BR)
ARAMARK CANADA LTD.
ST. THOMAS UNIVERSITY
59 Dineen Dr, Fredericton, NB, E3B 9V7
(506) 460-0310
Emp Here 50
SIC 5812 Eating places

D-U-N-S 20-300-3897   (SL)
ADDICTIONS AND MENTAL HEALTH
65 Brunswick St, Fredericton, NB, E3B 1G5
(506) 453-2132
Emp Here 55   *Sales* 3,575,074
SIC 8093 Specialty outpatient clinics, nec

D-U-N-S 20-019-8265   (BR)
ALIMENTS SAPUTO LIMITEE
SAPUTO
75 Whiting Rd, Fredericton, NB, E3B 5Y5
(506) 451-2400
Emp Here 30
SIC 5143 Dairy products, except dried or
canned

D-U-N-S 25-350-5218   (BR)
**ANGLOPHONE WEST SCHOOL DISTRICT
(ASD-W)**
FREDERICTON HIGH SCHOOL
300 Priestman St, Fredericton, NB, E3B 6J8
(506) 453-5279
Emp Here 200
SIC 8211 Elementary and secondary schools

D-U-N-S 25-241-7399   (BR)
**ANGLOPHONE WEST SCHOOL DISTRICT
(ASD-W)**
MONTGOMERY STREET SCHOOL
692 Montgomery St, Fredericton, NB, E3B
2X8
(506) 453-5433
Emp Here 20
SIC 8211 Elementary and secondary schools

D-U-N-S 25-241-5674   (BR)
**ANGLOPHONE WEST SCHOOL DISTRICT
(ASD-W)**
PRIESTMAN STREET SCHOOL
363 Priestman St, Fredericton, NB, E3B 3B5
(506) 453-5424
Emp Here 60
SIC 8211 Elementary and secondary schools

D-U-N-S 20-710-0707   (BR)
**ANGLOPHONE WEST SCHOOL DISTRICT
(ASD-W)**
ST GEORGE MIDDLE SCHOOL
575 George St, Fredericton, NB, E3B 1K2
(506) 453-5419
Emp Here 50
SIC 8211 Elementary and secondary schools

D-U-N-S 20-287-3399   (BR)
**ANGLOPHONE WEST SCHOOL DISTRICT
(ASD-W)**
CONNAUGHT STREET SCHOOL
184 Connaught St, Fredericton, NB, E3B 2A9
(506) 453-5404
Emp Here 34
SIC 8211 Elementary and secondary schools

D-U-N-S 25-242-2191   (BR)

**ANGLOPHONE WEST SCHOOL DISTRICT
(ASD-W)**
GARDEN CREEK SCHOOL
1360 Woodstock Rd, Fredericton, NB, E3B
9G7
(506) 453-5409
Emp Here 28
SIC 8211 Elementary and secondary schools

D-U-N-S 24-705-5007   (SL)
ATLANTIC NUCLEAR SERVICES INC
125 Hanwell Rd, Fredericton, NB, E3B 2P9
(506) 459-9552
Emp Here 25   *Sales* 9,738,696
SIC 8999 Services, nec
Pr Pr Keith Scott
Barbara Scott

D-U-N-S 24-309-1555   (BR)
ATLANTIC TOWING LIMITED
(*Suby of* J. D. Irving, Limited)
71 Alison Blvd, Fredericton, NB, E3B 5B4

Emp Here 40
SIC 4492 Towing and tugboat service

D-U-N-S 24-101-2678   (BR)
**ATLANTIC TRACTORS & EQUIPMENT LIM-
ITED**
CATERPILLAR
165 Urquhart Cres, Fredericton, NB, E3B 8K4
(506) 452-6651
Emp Here 75
SIC 5082 Construction and mining machinery

D-U-N-S 20-572-4060   (BR)
BMO NESBITT BURNS INC
65 Regent St Suite 200, Fredericton, NB, E3B
7H8
(506) 458-8570
Emp Here 20
SIC 6211 Security brokers and dealers

D-U-N-S 20-267-5062   (BR)
BANK OF MONTREAL
BMO
505 King St, Fredericton, NB, E3B 1E7
(506) 453-0280
Emp Here 30
SIC 6021 National commercial banks

D-U-N-S 20-812-8280   (BR)
BANQUE TORONTO-DOMINION, LA
TORONTO-DOMINION BANK, THE
(*Suby of* Toronto-Dominion Bank, The)
77 Westmorland St Suite 100, Fredericton,
NB, E3B 6Z3
(506) 458-8228
Emp Here 25
SIC 6021 National commercial banks

D-U-N-S 25-881-5422   (BR)
**BELL ALIANT REGIONAL COMMUNICA-
TIONS INC**
XWAVE
64 Elson Blvd, Fredericton, NB, E3B 6G3
(506) 444-6484
Emp Here 60
SIC 4899 Communication services, nec

D-U-N-S 25-371-6872   (BR)
BEST BUY CANADA LTD
FUTURE SHOP
(*Suby of* Best Buy Co., Inc.)
1220 Prospect St, Fredericton, NB, E3B 3C1
(506) 452-1600
Emp Here 50
SIC 5731 Radio, television, and electronic
stores

D-U-N-S 20-618-9623   (HQ)
BIRD, J.W. AND COMPANY LIMITED
BIRD STAIRS
670 Wilsey Rd, Fredericton, NB, E3B 7K4
(506) 453-9915
Emp Here 45   *Emp Total* 100
Sales 19,772,350
SIC 5039 Construction materials, nec

Pr Pr Geoffrey Munn
Brian Moore

D-U-N-S 24-186-5526 (BR)
CANADIAN BROADCASTING CORPORATION
CBC
1160 Regent St, Fredericton, NB, E3B 3Z1
(506) 451-4000
Emp Here 62
SIC 4833 Television broadcasting stations

D-U-N-S 20-815-5531 (BR)
CANADIAN IMPERIAL BANK OF COMMERCE
CANADIAN IMPERIAL BANK OF COMMERCE
448 Queer St, Fredericton, NB, E3B 1B6
(506) 452-9100
Emp Here 20
SIC 6021 National commercial banks

D-U-N-S 25-311-5950 (BR)
CANADIAN IMPERIAL BANK OF COMMERCE
CIBC
1142 Smythe St, Fredericton, NB, E3B 3H5
(506) 458-8774
Emp Here 20
SIC 6021 National commercial banks

D-U-N-S 25-814-6653 (SL)
CENTER FOR ARTS AND TECHNOLOGY ATLANTIC CANADA INC
130 Carleton St, Fredericton, NB, E3B 3T4
(506) 460-1280
Emp Here 50 Sales 3,137,310
SIC 8249 Vocational schools, nec

D-U-N-S 25-085-9543 (BR)
CLEVE'S SPORTING GOODS LIMITED
CLEVE'S SOURCE FOR SPORTS
1055 Prospect St, Fredericton, NB, E3B 3B9

Emp Here 20
SIC 5941 Sporting goods and bicycle shops

D-U-N-S 20-090-6761 (BR)
CONTROLS & EQUIPMENT LTD
245 Hilton Rd Unit 21, Fredericton, NB, E3B 7B5
(506) 457-0707
Emp Here 27
SIC 7629 Electrical repair shops

D-U-N-S 20-800-4494 (BR)
CORPORATION OF THE CITY OF FREDERICTON
FIRE DEPARTMENT
(Suby of Corporation of the City of Fredericton)
520 York St, Fredericton, NB, E3B 3R2
(506) 460-2510
Emp Here 113
SIC 1389 Oil and gas field services, nec

D-U-N-S 20-195-6526 (BR)
COVEY OFFICE GROUP INC
COVEY BASICS
(Suby of Covey Office Group Inc)
896 Prospect St, Fredericton, NB, E3B 2T8
(506) 458-8333
Emp Here 20
SIC 5712 Furniture stores

D-U-N-S 20-510-9932 (BR)
COX & PALMER
371 Queen St Suite 400, Fredericton, NB, E3B 1B1
(506) 444-9284
Emp Here 60
SIC 8111 Legal services

D-U-N-S 25-298-0206 (BR)
CROMBIE DEVELOPMENTS LIMITED
FREDERICTON MALL
1150 Prospect St Suite 535, Fredericton, NB, E3B 3C1

Emp Here 20
SIC 6512 Nonresidential building operators

D-U-N-S 20-005-1907 (BR)
DAY & ROSS INC
SAMEDAY WORLDWIDE
65 Mackenzie Rd, Fredericton, NB, E3B 6B6

Emp Here 20
SIC 4213 Trucking, except local

D-U-N-S 25-095-4948 (BR)
DELTA HOTELS LIMITED
1133 Regent St, Fredericton, NB, E3B 3Z2

Emp Here 280
SIC 8741 Management services

D-U-N-S 20-071-2342 (BR)
DILLON CONSULTING LIMITED
(Suby of Dillon Consulting Inc)
1149 Smythe St Suite 200, Fredericton, NB, E3B 3H4
(506) 444-8820
Emp Here 22
SIC 8711 Engineering services

D-U-N-S 24-348-5856 (BR)
EII LIMITED
OVAL INTERNATIONAL
(Suby of Enterprises International Inc)
115 Whiting Rd, Fredericton, NB, E3B 5Y5
(506) 459-3004
Emp Here 20
SIC 5084 Industrial machinery and equipment

D-U-N-S 24-858-2343 (BR)
EXP SERVICES INC
1133 Regent St Suite 300, Fredericton, NB, E3B 3Z2
(506) 452-9000
Emp Here 110
SIC 8711 Engineering services

D-U-N-S 25-150-8271 (SL)
ENBRIDGE GAS NEW BRUNSWICK LIMITED PARTNERSHIP
440 Wilsey Rd Suite 101, Fredericton, NB, E3B 7G5
(506) 444-7773
Emp Here 80 Sales 22,871,280
SIC 4922 Natural gas transmission
Pr Arunas Pleckaitis
Genl Mgr Andrew Harrington
Mark Butler
Sec Mark Boyce
James Schultz
Ch Bd Stephen Letwin

D-U-N-S 24-574-5633 (SL)
FREDERICTON SOUTH NURSING HOME INC
PINE GROVE NURSING HOME
521 Woodstock Rd, Fredericton, NB, E3B 2J2
(506) 444-3400
Emp Here 100 Sales 4,523,563
SIC 8051 Skilled nursing care facilities

D-U-N-S 20-178-3482 (BR)
GDI SERVICES (CANADA) LP
475 Wilsey Rd, Fredericton, NB, E3B 7K1
(506) 453-1404
Emp Here 400
SIC 7349 Building maintenance services, nec

D-U-N-S 25-297-1478 (BR)
GRANT THORNTON LLP
570 Queen St 4th Fl, Fredericton, NB, E3B 6Z6
(506) 458-8200
Emp Here 30
SIC 8721 Accounting, auditing, and bookkeeping

D-U-N-S 25-305-1833 (BR)
INNVEST PROPERTIES CORP
COMFORT INN
(Suby of Innvest Properties Corp)

797 Prospect St, Fredericton, NB, E3B 5Y4
(506) 453-0800
Emp Here 25
SIC 7011 Hotels and motels

D-U-N-S 25-315-8042 (BR)
INVESTORS GROUP FINANCIAL SERVICES INC
1133 Regent St Suite 405, Fredericton, NB, E3B 3Z2
(506) 458-9930
Emp Here 30
SIC 6211 Security brokers and dealers

D-U-N-S 25-499-3090 (SL)
IRVING TRANSPORTATION SERVICES LIMITED
71 Alison Blvd, Fredericton, NB, E3B 1A1

Emp Here 50 Sales 2,188,821
SIC 8721 Accounting, auditing, and bookkeeping

D-U-N-S 20-005-0438 (SL)
JOBS UNLIMITED INC
YORK STREET COURIER
1079 York St, Fredericton, NB, E3B 3S4
(506) 458-9380
Emp Here 55 Sales 2,845,467
SIC 7389 Business services, nec

D-U-N-S 24-187-4767 (BR)
KPMG LLP
(Suby of KPMG LLP)
77 Westmorland St Suite 700, Fredericton, NB, E3B 6Z3
(506) 452-8000
Emp Here 20
SIC 8721 Accounting, auditing, and bookkeeping

D-U-N-S 25-181-6930 (SL)
KIL INVESTMENTS LTD
DIPLOMAT RESTAURANT, THE
251 Woodstock Rd, Fredericton, NB, E3B 2H8
(506) 454-2400
Emp Here 75 Sales 2,261,782
SIC 5812 Eating places

D-U-N-S 25-743-9083 (BR)
MCG. RESTAURANTS (WONDERLAND) INC
MCGINNIS LANDING
280 King St, Fredericton, NB, E3B 1E2
(506) 458-1212
Emp Here 50
SIC 5812 Eating places

D-U-N-S 24-533-4875 (SL)
MAPLE LEAF HOMES INC
655 Wilsey Rd, Fredericton, NB, E3B 7K3
(506) 459-1335
Emp Here 350 Sales 52,531,704
SIC 2452 Prefabricated wood buildings
Dir Jacques Roy

D-U-N-S 20-618-4897 (SL)
MARITIME LAW BOOK LTD
NATIONAL REPORTER SYSTEM
30 Mackenzie Rd, Fredericton, NB, E3B 6B7
(506) 453-9921
Emp Here 50 Sales 2,845,467
SIC 2731 Book publishing

D-U-N-S 20-094-7286 (SL)
MCDONALD'S RESTAURANTS
MCDONALD'S
1177 Prospect St, Fredericton, NB, E3B 3B9
(506) 444-6231
Emp Here 70 Sales 2,115,860
SIC 5812 Eating places

D-U-N-S 20-005-7656 (BR)
MCINNES COOPER
570 Queen St Suite 600, Fredericton, NB, E3B 6Z6
(506) 458-8572
Emp Here 60

SIC 8111 Legal services

D-U-N-S 24-322-4685 (SL)
MOORE ENTERPRISES INC
WENDY'S
1050 Woodstock Rd, Fredericton, NB, E3B 7R8
(506) 450-3778
Emp Here 100 Sales 2,991,389
SIC 5812 Eating places

D-U-N-S 24-955-8982 (HQ)
MOORE ENTERPRISES INC
WENDY'S RESTAURANT
(Suby of Moore Enterprises Inc)
973 Prospect St, Fredericton, NB, E3B 2T7
(506) 462-9946
Emp Here 45 Emp Total 80
Sales 2,407,703
SIC 5812 Eating places

D-U-N-S 20-295-5720 (BR)
MURPHY, D.P. INC
HOLIDAY INN EXPRESS & SUITE
665 Prospect St, Fredericton, NB, E3B 6B8
(506) 459-0035
Emp Here 40
SIC 7011 Hotels and motels

D-U-N-S 20-337-6124 (HQ)
NEW BRUNSWICK COMMUNITY COLLEGE (NBCC)
284 Smythe St, Fredericton, NB, E3B 3C9
(888) 796-6222
Emp Here 100 Emp Total 45,138
Sales 42,604,049
SIC 8221 Colleges and universities
Pr Marilyn Luscombe

D-U-N-S 20-815-7826 (HQ)
NEW BRUNSWICK LIQUOR CORPORATION
ALCOOL NB LIQUOR
170 Wilsey Rd, Fredericton, NB, E3B 5J1
(506) 452-6826
Emp Here 100 Emp Total 45,138
Sales 348,026,700
SIC 5921 Liquor stores
Pr Brian Harriman
Ch Bd Ron Lindala
Chris Evans

D-U-N-S 20-809-5328 (BR)
NEWFOUNDLAND CAPITAL CORPORATION LIMITED
92.3 FRED FM
77 Westmorland St Suite 400, Fredericton, NB, E3B 6Z3
(506) 455-0923
Emp Here 20
SIC 4832 Radio broadcasting stations

D-U-N-S 24-317-3866 (BR)
OCEAN STEEL & CONSTRUCTION LTD
YORK STEEL
(Suby of Ocean Holdings Inc)
550 Wilsey Rd, Fredericton, NB, E3B 7K2
(506) 444-7989
Emp Here 20
SIC 3441 Fabricated structural Metal

D-U-N-S 25-413-2228 (SL)
PLAZA ATLANTIC LTD
527 Queen St Suite 110, Fredericton, NB, E3B 1B8
(506) 451-1826
Emp Here 80 Sales 10,449,350
SIC 6531 Real estate agents and managers
Pr Pr Earl Brewer
Michael Zakuta
J. Paul Leger

D-U-N-S 25-350-9715 (SL)
PRIORITY PERSONNEL INC
120 Carleton St, Fredericton, NB, E3B 3T4
(506) 459-6668
Emp Here 60 Sales 4,377,642
SIC 7361 Employment agencies

D-U-N-S 24-343-0634   (SL)
PROSPECT INVESTMENTS LTD
HILLTOP GRILL & BEVERAGE CO
1034 Prospect St, Fredericton, NB, E3B 3C1
(506) 458-9057
Emp Here 70   *Sales* 2,115,860
SIC 5812 Eating places

D-U-N-S 20-510-5161   (BR)
PROVINCE OF NEW BRUNSWICK
PNB CHIEF PUBLIC HEALTH OFFICE, CMOH
520 King St, Fredericton, NB, E3B 6G3
(506) 453-2280
Emp Here 20
SIC 7363 Help supply services

D-U-N-S 24-346-9488   (BR)
PROVINCE OF NEW BRUNSWICK
NBCC FREDERICTON CENTRE
284 Smythe St, Fredericton, NB, E3B 3C9
(506) 462-5012
Emp Here 25
SIC 8222 Junior colleges

D-U-N-S 25-320-8474   (BR)
PUROLATOR INC.
PUROLATOR INC
727 Wilsey Rd, Fredericton, NB, E3B 7K3
(506) 450-2776
Emp Here 25
SIC 4731 Freight transportation arrangement

D-U-N-S 25-023-7195   (BR)
REDBERRY FRANCHISING CORP
BURGER KING
1140 Smythe St, Fredericton, NB, E3B 3H5
(506) 453-1462
Emp Here 40
SIC 5812 Eating places

D-U-N-S 25-308-6656   (BR)
REGIONAL HEALTH AUTHORITY NB
REGIONAL HEALTH AUTHORITY B
700 Priestman St, Fredericton, NB, E3B 3B7
(506) 452-5800
Emp Here 92
SIC 8051 Skilled nursing care facilities

D-U-N-S 20-535-7903   (BR)
ROYAL BANK OF CANADA
RBC
(*Suby of* Royal Bank Of Canada)
1206 Prospect St Suite 3, Fredericton, NB, E3B 3C1
(506) 458-0817
Emp Here 20
SIC 6021 National commercial banks

D-U-N-S 25-742-9365   (BR)
ROYAL BANK OF CANADA
ROYAL BANK FINANCIAL GROUP
(*Suby of* Royal Bank Of Canada)
504 Queen St, Fredericton, NB, E3B 1B9
(506) 453-1710
Emp Here 30
SIC 6021 National commercial banks

D-U-N-S 24-347-6004   (BR)
SCHOOL BOARD DISTRICT 01
ECOLE DES BATISSEURS
715 Priestman St, Fredericton, NB, E3B 5W7
(506) 444-3252
Emp Here 50
SIC 8211 Elementary and secondary schools

D-U-N-S 25-241-7274   (BR)
SCHOOL BOARD DISTRICT 01
ECOLE STE ANNE
715 Priestman St, Fredericton, NB, E3B 5W7
(506) 453-3991
Emp Here 80
SIC 8211 Elementary and secondary schools

D-U-N-S 24-943-6452   (BR)
SOBEYS CAPITAL INCORPORATED
SOBEYS
1150 Prospect St, Fredericton, NB, E3B 3C1

(506) 458-8891
Emp Here 125
SIC 5411 Grocery stores

D-U-N-S 24-227-7031   (BR)
SODEXO CANADA LTD
21 Pacey Dr, Fredericton, NB, E3B 5A3
(506) 474-8030
Emp Here 49
SIC 5812 Eating places

D-U-N-S 25-499-0005   (BR)
STAPLES CANADA INC
STAPLES THE BUSINESS DEPOT
(*Suby of* Staples, Inc.)
1150 Prospect St, Fredericton, NB, E3B 3C1
(506) 462-4060
Emp Here 30
SIC 5943 Stationery stores

D-U-N-S 20-287-7655   (BR)
STEWART MCKELVEY STIRLING SCALES
(*Suby of* Stewart McKelvey Stirling Scales)
77 Westmorland St Suite 600, Fredericton, NB, E3B 6Z3
(506) 458-1970
Emp Here 25
SIC 8111 Legal services

D-U-N-S 25-316-8454   (BR)
SUN LIFE FINANCIAL INVESTMENT SERVICES (CANADA) INC
570 Queen St Suite 200, Fredericton, NB, E3B 6Z6
(506) 458-8074
Emp Here 28
SIC 6311 Life insurance

D-U-N-S 24-263-9672   (BR)
TRUEFOAM LIMITED
120 Doak Rd, Fredericton, NB, E3B 7J9
(506) 452-7868
Emp Here 30
SIC 3086 Plastics foam products

D-U-N-S 25-742-4739   (BR)
UNISYS CANADA INC
535 Beaverbrook Crt Suite 150, Fredericton, NB, E3B 1X6
(506) 458-8751
Emp Here 40
SIC 7379 Computer related services, nec

D-U-N-S 24-124-6367   (BR)
UNITED PARCEL SERVICE CANADA LTD
UPS
900 Hanwell Rd, Fredericton, NB, E3B 6A2
(506) 447-3601
Emp Here 500
SIC 4513 Air courier services

D-U-N-S 25-366-3652   (BR)
UNIVERSITY OF NEW BRUNSWICK
UNB FACILITIES MANAGEMENT
767 Kings College, Fredericton, NB, E3B 5A3
(506) 453-4889
Emp Here 100
SIC 8221 Colleges and universities

D-U-N-S 20-837-1224   (BR)
UNIVERSITY OF NEW BRUNSWICK
SECURITY & TRAFFIC
6 Duffie Dr, Fredericton, NB, E3B 5A3
(506) 453-4830
Emp Here 24
SIC 8748 Business consulting, nec

D-U-N-S 20-736-8080   (BR)
UNIVERSITY OF NEW BRUNSWICK
LAW FACILITY
41 Dineen Dr Unit 105a, Fredericton, NB, E3B 5A3
(506) 453-4669
Emp Here 40
SIC 8221 Colleges and universities

D-U-N-S 20-861-4037   (BR)
UNIVERSITY OF NEW BRUNSWICK
DEPARTMENT OF ENGLISH

Gd, Fredericton, NB, E3B 5A3
(506) 453-4676
Emp Here 25
SIC 8221 Colleges and universities

D-U-N-S 24-245-9142   (BR)
UNIVERSITY OF NEW BRUNSWICK
COLLEGE OF EXTENDED LEARNING
6 Duffie Dr Fl 2, Fredericton, NB, E3B 5A3
(506) 453-4646
Emp Here 50
SIC 8221 Colleges and universities

D-U-N-S 24-344-8847   (BR)
UNIVERSITY OF NEW BRUNSWICK
FACULTY OF COMPUTER SCIENCE
540 Windsor St Unit 126, Fredericton, NB, E3B 5A3
(506) 453-4566
Emp Here 50
SIC 8221 Colleges and universities

D-U-N-S 24-122-4836   (BR)
UNIVERSITY OF NEW BRUNSWICK
Gd, Fredericton, NB, E3B 5A3
(506) 453-4524
Emp Here 20
SIC 8221 Colleges and universities

D-U-N-S 25-673-3189   (BR)
UNIVERSITY OF NEW BRUNSWICK
ITS
11 Dineen Dr, Fredericton, NB, E3B 5A3
(506) 453-4666
Emp Here 70
SIC 8221 Colleges and universities

D-U-N-S 20-346-6391   (BR)
WE CARE HEALTH SERVICES INC
1149 Smythe St Suite 102, Fredericton, NB, E3B 3H4
(506) 454-2273
Emp Here 55
SIC 7361 Employment agencies

D-U-N-S 20-742-1983   (SL)
WOOD MOTORS (1972) LIMITED
WOOD MOTORS FORD
880 Prospect St, Fredericton, NB, E3B 2T8
(506) 452-6611
Emp Here 62   *Sales* 22,617,817
SIC 5511 New and used car dealers
Pr Pr Edward Seymour
VP VP Garrett Seymour

Fredericton, NB E3C

D-U-N-S 20-288-5377   (BR)
ANGLOPHONE WEST SCHOOL DISTRICT (ASD-W)
KINGSCLEAR CONSOLIDATED SCHOOL
3188 Woodstock Rd, Fredericton, NB, E3C 1K9
(506) 453-5414
Emp Here 20
SIC 8211 Elementary and secondary schools

D-U-N-S 20-338-2234   (HQ)
BELLBOY DRYCLEANING & LAUNDRY LTD
BELLBOY DRYCLEANING SERVICE
(*Suby of* Bellboy Drycleaning & Laundry Ltd)
426 Hodgson Rd, Fredericton, NB, E3C 2G5
(506) 451-7732
Emp Here 22   *Emp Total* 50
Sales 1,386,253
SIC 7216 Drycleaning plants, except rugs

D-U-N-S 24-827-8249   (BR)
BLUEDROP PERFORMANCE LEARNING INC
BLUEDROP PERFORMANCE LEARNING
50 Crowther Lane Suite 100, Fredericton, NB, E3C 0J1

Emp Here 45

SIC 8299 Schools and educational services, nec

D-U-N-S 24-609-5900   (BR)
CARA OPERATIONS LIMITED
MONTANA'S COOKHOUSE
(*Suby of* Cara Holdings Limited)
6 Av Trinity, Fredericton, NB, E3C 0B8
(506) 457-1483
Emp Here 40
SIC 5812 Eating places

D-U-N-S 20-534-5270   (BR)
COCA-COLA REFRESHMENTS CANADA COMPANY
(*Suby of* The Coca-Cola Company)
64 Alison Blvd, Fredericton, NB, E3C 1N2
(506) 458-0881
Emp Here 20
SIC 4225 General warehousing and storage

D-U-N-S 25-010-2852   (BR)
CONSEILLERS EN GESTION ET INFORMATIQUE CGI INC
CGI
30 Knowledge Park Dr Suite 300, Fredericton, NB, E3C 2R2
(506) 458-5020
Emp Here 60
SIC 7371 Custom computer programming services

D-U-N-S 20-019-9057   (HQ)
COVEY OFFICE GROUP INC
COVEY BASICS
(*Suby of* Covey Office Group Inc)
250 Alison Blvd, Fredericton, NB, E3C 0A9
(506) 458-8333
Emp Here 30   *Emp Total* 50
Sales 3,648,035
SIC 5112 Stationery and office supplies

D-U-N-S 20-618-4178   (BR)
CUMMINS EST DU CANADA SEC
CUMMINS EST DU CANADA SEC
321 Doak Rd, Fredericton, NB, E3C 2E7
(506) 451-1929
Emp Here 20
SIC 5084 Industrial machinery and equipment

D-U-N-S 25-846-2097   (BR)
DOLLARAMA S.E.C.
5 Trinity Ave, Fredericton, NB, E3C 0B7
(506) 472-9744
Emp Here 25
SIC 5311 Department stores

D-U-N-S 25-760-6400   (BR)
EMPIRE THEATRES LIMITED
1381 Regent St, Fredericton, NB, E3C 1A2
(506) 458-9704
Emp Here 50
SIC 7832 Motion picture theaters, except drive-in

D-U-N-S 24-340-0285   (BR)
FGL SPORTS LTD
SPORT-CHEK
1381 Regent St Unit Y200a, Fredericton, NB, E3C 1A2
(506) 474-0625
Emp Here 40
SIC 5941 Sporting goods and bicycle shops

D-U-N-S 20-815-5218   (SL)
FREDERICTON MOTOR INN LTD
FREDERICTON INN
1315 Regent St, Fredericton, NB, E3C 1A1
(506) 455-1430
Emp Here 75   *Sales* 3,283,232
SIC 7011 Hotels and motels

D-U-N-S 24-361-7243   (BR)
HOME DEPOT OF CANADA INC
HOME DEPOT
(*Suby of* The Home Depot Inc)
1450 Regent St, Fredericton, NB, E3C 0A4

(506) 462-9460
Emp Here 100
SIC 5251 Hardware stores

D-U-N-S 20-300-3996　　(BR)
INDIGO BOOKS & MUSIC INC
CHAPTERS
(*Suby of* Indigo Books & Music Inc)
1381 Regent St, Fredericton, NB, E3C 1A2
(506) 459-2616
Emp Here 30
SIC 5942 Book stores

D-U-N-S 25-742-5066　　(BR)
J. D. IRVING, LIMITED
KENT BUILDING SUPPLIES, DIV OF
(*Suby of* J. D. Irving, Limited)
809 Bishop Dr Suite 16, Fredericton, NB, E3C 2M6
(506) 451-3000
Emp Here 149
SIC 5211 Lumber and other building materials

D-U-N-S 20-801-0939　　(BR)
MCDONALD'S RESTAURANTS OF CANADA LIMITED
MCDONALD'S
(*Suby of* McDonald's Corporation)
1381 Regent St, Fredericton, NB, E3C 1A2
(506) 444-6234
Emp Here 30
SIC 5812 Eating places

D-U-N-S 24-393-0612　　(BR)
MIDLAND TRANSPORT LIMITED
MIDLAND COURIER
(*Suby of* J. D. Irving, Limited)
1200 Alison Blvd, Fredericton, NB, E3C 2M2
(506) 458-6330
Emp Here 30
SIC 7389 Business services, nec

D-U-N-S 20-002-7881　　(BR)
MORNEAU SHEPELL LTD
(*Suby of* Morneau Shepell Inc)
40 Crowther Lane Suite 300, Fredericton, NB, E3C 0J1
(506) 458-9081
Emp Here 40
SIC 8999 Services, nec

D-U-N-S 24-350-8699　　(SL)
RADIAN6 TECHNOLOGIES INC
(*Suby of* Salesforce.com, Inc.)
30 Knowledge Park Dr, Fredericton, NB, E3C 2R2
(506) 452-9039
Emp Here 140　　*Sales* 47,426,560
SIC 7371 Custom computer programming services
　Marcel Lebrun
Off Mgr Janet Webb

D-U-N-S 24-187-8776　　(BR)
SEARS CANADA INC
1325 Regent St, Fredericton, NB, E3C 1A2
(506) 452-1591
Emp Here 250
SIC 5311 Department stores

D-U-N-S 25-923-5364　　(BR)
TOYS 'R' US (CANADA) LTD
TOYS 'R' US
(*Suby of* Toys "r" Us, Inc.)
1381 Regent St, Fredericton, NB, E3C 1A2
(506) 457-9206
Emp Here 30
SIC 5945 Hobby, toy, and game shops

D-U-N-S 24-417-1414　　(BR)
VALUE VILLAGE STORES, INC
(*Suby of* Savers, Inc.)
317 Bishop Dr, Fredericton, NB, E3C 2M6
(506) 455-7676
Emp Here 24
SIC 5399 Miscellaneous general merchandise

D-U-N-S 25-297-7749　　(BR)
WAL-MART CANADA CORP

1399 Regent St, Fredericton, NB, E3C 1A3
(506) 452-1511
Emp Here 200
SIC 5311 Department stores

D-U-N-S 20-088-7375　　(BR)
WINNERS MERCHANTS INTERNATIONAL L.P.
WINNERS
(*Suby of* The TJX Companies Inc)
9 Av Riocan Suite 1, Fredericton, NB, E3C 0B9
(506) 457-6264
Emp Here 30
SIC 5651 Family clothing stores

Fredericton, NB E3G

D-U-N-S 20-710-0731　　(BR)
ANGLOPHONE WEST SCHOOL DISTRICT (ASD-W)
ROYAL ROAD ELEMENTARY
340 Royal Rd, Fredericton, NB, E3G 6J9
(506) 453-5438
Emp Here 50
SIC 8211 Elementary and secondary schools

D-U-N-S 24-573-9370　　(SL)
AQUA-POWER CLEANERS (1979) LTD
SERVICEMASTER CLEAN
65 Royal Parkway, Fredericton, NB, E3G 0J9
(506) 458-1113
Emp Here 140　　*Sales* 4,851,006
SIC 7349 Building maintenance services, nec

Fredericton Junction, NB E5L
Sundbury County

D-U-N-S 20-311-3498　　(SL)
WHITE RAPIDS MANOR INC
233 Sunbury Dr, Fredericton Junction, NB, E5L 1S1
(506) 368-6508
Emp Here 60　　*Sales* 2,699,546
SIC 8051 Skilled nursing care facilities

Gagetown, NB E5M
Queens County

D-U-N-S 24-181-9650　　(SL)
WOOLASTOOK LONG TERM CARE FACILITY INC
ORCHARD VIEW LONG TERM CARE FACILITY
2230 Route 102, Gagetown, NB, E5M 1J6
(506) 488-3544
Emp Here 56　　*Sales* 2,553,625
SIC 8051 Skilled nursing care facilities

Grand Bay-Westfield, NB E5K

D-U-N-S 20-710-0350　　(BR)
SCHOOL DISTRICT 8
GRAND BAY PRIMARY
(*Suby of* School District 8)
92 Woolastook Dr, Grand Bay-Westfield, NB, E5K 1S4
(506) 738-6504
Emp Here 50
SIC 8211 Elementary and secondary schools

D-U-N-S 20-005-0479　　(BR)
SCHOOL DISTRICT 8
WESTFIELD SCHOOL
(*Suby of* School District 8)

147 Nerepis Rd, Grand Bay-Westfield, NB, E5K 2Z5
(506) 757-2020
Emp Here 25
SIC 8211 Elementary and secondary schools

D-U-N-S 20-710-0392　　(BR)
SCHOOL DISTRICT 8
RIVER VALLEY MIDDLE SCHOOL
(*Suby of* School District 8)
33 Epworth Park Rd, Grand Bay-Westfield, NB, E5K 1W1
(506) 738-6500
Emp Here 25
SIC 8211 Elementary and secondary schools

Grand Manan, NB E5G
Charlotte County

D-U-N-S 20-196-3787　　(BR)
LOBLAWS SUPERMARKETS LIMITED
GRAND MANAN SAVE EASY
791 Route 776, Grand Manan, NB, E5G 3C4
(506) 662-8152
Emp Here 25
SIC 5411 Grocery stores

D-U-N-S 25-242-1326　　(BR)
SCHOOL DISTRICT NO 10
GRAND MANAN COMMUNITY SCHOOL
(*Suby of* School District No 10)
1144 Route 776, Grand Manan, NB, E5G 4E8
(506) 662-7000
Emp Here 45
SIC 8211 Elementary and secondary schools

Grand-Barachois, NB E4P
Kent County

D-U-N-S 24-344-1362　　(SL)
GAGNON HOLDINGS LTD
9 Quai Des Robichaud Rd, Grand-Barachois, NB, E4P 8A4
(506) 532-2445
Emp Here 150　　*Sales* 33,660,800
SIC 6712 Bank holding companies
Dir Kevin Mckee

D-U-N-S 25-242-0278　　(BR)
SCHOOL BOARD DISTRICT 01
ECOLE PERE EDGAR T LEBLANC
1351 Route 133, Grand-Barachois, NB, E4P 8C8
(506) 533-3370
Emp Here 47
SIC 8211 Elementary and secondary schools

Grand-Sault/Grand Falls, NB E3Y

D-U-N-S 20-544-3141　　(BR)
ATLANTIC WHOLESALERS LTD
REAL ATLANTIC SUPERSTORE, THE
240 Ch Madawaska, Grand-Sault/Grand Falls, NB, E3Y 1A5
(506) 473-4619
Emp Here 20
SIC 5411 Grocery stores

D-U-N-S 25-363-2475　　(BR)
DISTRICT SCOLAIRE 3
POLYVALENTE THOMAS ALBERT
(*Suby of* District Scolaire 3)
215 Rue Guimont, Grand-Sault/Grand Falls, NB, E3Y 1C7
(506) 473-7372
Emp Here 70
SIC 8211 Elementary and secondary schools

D-U-N-S 25-172-9505　　(BR)

J'MIRALCO INC
MCDONALD'S RESTAURANTS
(*Suby of* J'miralco Inc)
230 Ch Madawaska, Grand-Sault/Grand Falls, NB, E3Y 1A7
(506) 473-4473
Emp Here 40
SIC 5812 Eating places

D-U-N-S 25-821-0764　　(BR)
VITALITE HEALTH NETWORK
NEW BRUNSWICK EXTRA-MURAL PROGRAM
532 Ch Madawaska, Grand-Sault/Grand Falls, NB, E3Y 1A3
(506) 473-7492
Emp Here 40
SIC 8082 Home health care services

D-U-N-S 24-123-3860　　(BR)
WAL-MART CANADA CORP
494 Ch Madawaska, Grand-Sault/Grand Falls, NB, E3Y 1A3
(506) 473-6837
Emp Here 50
SIC 5311 Department stores

Grand-Sault/Grand Falls, NB E3Z

D-U-N-S 24-755-9206　　(BR)
BREAU, RAYMOND LTD
PHARMACY JEAN COUTU #95
276 Boul Broadway, Grand-Sault/Grand Falls, NB, E3Z 2K2
(506) 473-3300
Emp Here 35
SIC 5912 Drug stores and proprietary stores

D-U-N-S 20-169-4879　　(BR)
BRUNSWICK NEWS INC
CATARACTE, LA
(*Suby of* J. D. Irving, Limited)
229 Boul Broadway, Grand-Sault/Grand Falls, NB, E3Z 2K1
(506) 473-3083
Emp Here 20
SIC 2711 Newspapers

D-U-N-S 25-001-7878　　(BR)
DISTRICT SCOLAIRE 3
SACRE COEUR SCHOOL
(*Suby of* District Scolaire 3)
689 Boul Everard H Daigle, Grand-Sault/Grand Falls, NB, E3Z 3C5
(506) 473-7385
Emp Here 40
SIC 8211 Elementary and secondary schools

D-U-N-S 24-345-3003　　(BR)
HEALTH CANADA
CANADIAN FOOD INSPECTION AGENCY
377 Boul Broadway, Grand-Sault/Grand Falls, NB, E3Z 2K3
(506) 473-8710
Emp Here 22
SIC 8734 Testing laboratories

D-U-N-S 20-100-3956　　(BR)
PROVINCE OF NEW BRUNSWICK
MENTAL HEALTH CLINIC
131 Pleasant St, Grand-Sault/Grand Falls, NB, E3Z 1G6
(506) 475-2440
Emp Here 20
SIC 8093 Specialty outpatient clinics, nec

D-U-N-S 25-364-3225　　(BR)
SCHOOL DISTRICT 14
JOHN CALDWELL SCHOOL
(*Suby of* School District 14)
130 Rue Victoria, Grand-Sault/Grand Falls, NB, E3Z 3B7
(506) 473-7374
Emp Here 65
SIC 8211 Elementary and secondary schools

D-U-N-S 25-118-9932 (BR)
SOBEYS CAPITAL INCORPORATED
FRESHCO
535 Boul Everard H Daigle, Grand-Sault/Grand Falls, NB, E3Z 2R7
(506) 473-5604
Emp Here 22
SIC 5411 Grocery stores

D-U-N-S 25-331-0197 (BR)
VITALITE HEALTH NETWORK
GRAND FALLS GENERAL HOSPITAL
625 Boul Everard H Daigle, Grand-Sault/Grand Falls, NB, E3Z 2R9
(506) 473-7555
Emp Here 200
SIC 8062 General medical and surgical hospitals

D-U-N-S 20-277-9992 (BR)
WORKPLACE HEALTH, SAFETY & COMPENSATION COMMISSION OF NEW BRUNSWICK
WHSCC
166 Boul Broadway Suite 300, Grand-Sault/Grand Falls, NB, E3Z 2J9
(506) 475-2550
Emp Here 27
SIC 6331 Fire, marine, and casualty insurance

Grande-Digue, NB E4R

D-U-N-S 25-242-0351 (BR)
SCHOOL BOARD DISTRICT 01
ECOLE DE GRANDE DIGUE
365 Route 530, Grande-Digue, NB, E4R 5C8
(506) 533-3399
Emp Here 26
SIC 8211 Elementary and secondary schools

Hampton, NB E5N

D-U-N-S 25-242-3090 (BR)
ANGLOPHONE SOUTH SCHOOL DISTRICT (ASD-S)
HAMPTON MIDDLE SCHOOL
(*Suby of* Anglophone South School District (ASD-S))
11 School St, Hampton, NB, E5N 6B1
(506) 832-6020
Emp Here 40
SIC 8211 Elementary and secondary schools

D-U-N-S 20-710-0210 (BR)
ANGLOPHONE SOUTH SCHOOL DISTRICT (ASD-S)
DR. A. T. LEATHERBARROW PRIMARY SCHOOL
122 School St, Hampton, NB, E5N 6B2
(506) 832-6022
Emp Here 30
SIC 8211 Elementary and secondary schools

D-U-N-S 20-179-6765 (BR)
CHAPMAN'S, DAVID ICE CREAM LIMITED
368 William Bell Dr, Hampton, NB, E5N 2C2
(506) 832-2070
Emp Here 20
SIC 2024 Ice cream and frozen deserts

D-U-N-S 20-321-8982 (BR)
SCHOOL DISTRICT 8
HAMPTON ELEMENTARY SCHOOL
(*Suby of* School District 8)
82 School St, Hampton, NB, E5N 6B2
(506) 832-6021
Emp Here 34
SIC 8211 Elementary and secondary schools

D-U-N-S 24-606-5452 (SL)
SNOW, DR. V. A. CENTRE INC

54 Dernille Crt Suite 14, Hampton, NB, E5N 5S7
(506) 832-6210
Emp Here 80   *Sales* 3,648,035
SIC 8051 Skilled nursing care facilities

Hanwell, NB E3C

D-U-N-S 25-859-7855 (BR)
ARMOUR TRANSPORT INC
ARMOUR TRANSPORTATION SYSTEMS
1746 Route 640, Hanwell, NB, E3C 2B2
(506) 459-5151
Emp Here 43
SIC 4212 Local trucking, without storage

D-U-N-S 25-793-0446 (BR)
MCFADZEN HOLDINGS LIMITED
KINGSWOOD PIZZA HUT EXPRESS
31 Kingswood Way, Hanwell, NB, E3C 2L4
(506) 444-9500
Emp Here 30
SIC 5812 Eating places

Hartland, NB E7P

D-U-N-S 24-723-5609 (SL)
BRENNAN FARMS LTD
40 Industrial Dr, Hartland, NB, E7P 2G6
(506) 375-8602
Emp Here 50   *Sales* 3,939,878
SIC 4212 Local trucking, without storage

D-U-N-S 20-020-4758 (HQ)
DAY & ROSS INC
DAY & ROSS TRANSPORTATION GROUP
398 Main St, Hartland, NB, E7P 1C6
(506) 375-4401
Emp Here 100   *Emp Total* 40,000
Sales 334,889,613
SIC 4213 Trucking, except local
Pr Bill Doherty
 Kevin Chase
VP Patrick Potter
Prs Dir Mark Osborne
 Luc Marcoux

D-U-N-S 20-643-0246 (BR)
MITTON HILL ENTERPRISES LIMITED
TIM HORTONS
(*Suby of* Mitton Hill Enterprises Limited)
542 Main St, Hartland, NB, E7P 2N5
(506) 375-6658
Emp Here 25
SIC 5812 Eating places

D-U-N-S 25-401-8971 (BR)
OLD DUTCH FOODS LTD
HUMPTY DUMPTY OLD DUTCH FOODS
(*Suby of* Old Dutch Foods Ltd)
179 Mclean Ave, Hartland, NB, E7P 2K6
(506) 375-4474
Emp Here 125
SIC 2096 Potato chips and similar snacks

D-U-N-S 25-241-4214 (BR)
SCHOOL DISTRICT 14
HARTLAND COMMUNITY SCHOOL
(*Suby of* School District 14)
217 Rockland Rd, Hartland, NB, E7P 0A2
(506) 375-3000
Emp Here 80
SIC 8211 Elementary and secondary schools

Harvey Station, NB E6K

D-U-N-S 25-242-1797 (BR)
ANGLOPHONE WEST SCHOOL DISTRICT (ASD-W)

HARVEY ELEMENTARY SCHOOL
1908 Route 3, Harvey Station, NB, E6K 2P4
(506) 366-2201
Emp Here 25
SIC 8211 Elementary and secondary schools

D-U-N-S 20-814-1739 (BR)
REGIONAL HEALTH AUTHORITY B
HARVEY COMMUNITY HOSPITAL
2019 Route 3, Harvey Station, NB, E6K 3E9
(506) 366-6400
Emp Here 28
SIC 8011 Offices and clinics of medical doctors

Harvey York Co, NB E6K

D-U-N-S 25-242-1839 (BR)
ANGLOPHONE WEST SCHOOL DISTRICT (ASD-W)
HARVEY HIGH SCHOOL
2055 Route 3, Harvey York Co, NB, E6K 1L1
(506) 366-2200
Emp Here 30
SIC 8211 Elementary and secondary schools

Havelock, NB E4Z

D-U-N-S 25-115-0819 (SL)
GRAYMONT (NB) INC
4634 Route 880, Havelock, NB, E4Z 5K8
(506) 534-2311
Emp Here 45
SIC 1422 Crushed and broken limestone

Hillsborough, NB E4H
Albert County

D-U-N-S 25-242-0054 (BR)
SCHOOL DISTRICT 2
CALEDONIA REGIONAL HIGH SCHOOL
35 School Lane, Hillsborough, NB, E4H 3B8
(506) 734-3710
Emp Here 30
SIC 8211 Elementary and secondary schools

Inkerman, NB E8P
Gloucester County

D-U-N-S 25-095-5408 (SL)
RESIDENCES INKERMAN INC, LES
1171 Ch Pallot, Inkerman, NB, E8P 1C2
(506) 336-3909
Emp Here 55   *Sales* 2,042,900
SIC 8361 Residential care

Island View, NB E3E

D-U-N-S 20-510-3331 (BR)
PROVINCE OF NEW BRUNSWICK
DEPARTMENT OF NATURAL RESOURCES REGION 3
3732 Route 102, Island View, NB, E3E 1G3
(506) 444-4888
Emp Here 33
SIC 7032 Sporting and recreational camps

Jacksonville, NB E7M

D-U-N-S 20-931-6538 (HQ)
BMG HOLDINGS LTD
32 Sawyer Rd, Jacksonville, NB, E7M 3B7
(506) 328-8853
Emp Here 25   *Emp Total* 800
Sales 10,214,498
SIC 5091 Sporting and recreation goods
 Malcolm Barrett
 William Barrett
Pr Pr Edward Barrett

D-U-N-S 20-649-4614 (BR)
XPLORNET COMMUNICATIONS INC
300 Lockhart Mill Rd, Jacksonville, NB, E7M 5C3
(506) 328-1386
Emp Here 25
SIC 4813 Telephone communication, except radio

Juniper, NB E7L

D-U-N-S 24-204-9869 (BR)
NORBORD INDUSTRIES INC
137 Juniper Rd, Juniper, NB, E7L 1G8
(506) 246-1125
Emp Here 120
SIC 2431 Millwork

Kedgwick, NB E8B
Restigouche County

D-U-N-S 20-023-3307 (BR)
DISTRICT SCOLAIRE 3
ECOLE MARIE-GAETANE
16 Rue Fraser, Kedgwick, NB, E8B 1E6
(506) 284-3441
Emp Here 30
SIC 8211 Elementary and secondary schools

Kedgwick Nord, NB E8B

D-U-N-S 25-136-8809 (BR)
J. D. IRVING, LIMITED
(*Suby of* J. D. Irving, Limited)
8050 Route 17, Kedgwick Nord, NB, E8B 1X2

Emp Here 60
SIC 2421 Sawmills and planing mills, general

Keswick Ridge, NB E6L

D-U-N-S 20-005-4281 (BR)
ANGLOPHONE WEST SCHOOL DISTRICT (ASD-W)
KESWICK RIDGE SCHOOL
166 Mckeen Dr, Keswick Ridge, NB, E6L 1N9
(506) 363-4703
Emp Here 25
SIC 8211 Elementary and secondary schools

D-U-N-S 24-629-0290 (BR)
NEW BRUNSWICK POWER CORPORATION
MACTAQUAC GENERATING STATION
451 Route 105, Keswick Ridge, NB, E6L 1B2
(506) 462-3800
Emp Here 75
SIC 4911 Electric services

Kingsclear First Nation, NB E3E

D-U-N-S 25-897-4237   (BR)
KINGSCLEAR FIRST NATION
WULASTUKW ELEMENTARY SCHOOL
712 Church St, Kingsclear First Nation, NB,
E3E 1K8
(506) 363-3019
Emp Here 39
SIC 8211 Elementary and secondary schools

Lagaceville, NB E9G
Northumberland County

D-U-N-S 25-865-9614   (BR)
DISTRICT SCOLAIRE FRANCOPHONE NORD-EST
ECOLE RENE CHOUINARD LAGACEVILLE
3 Ch Drisdelle Settlement, Lagaceville, NB,
E9G 2N3
(506) 776-3866
Emp Here 30
SIC 8211 Elementary and secondary schools

Lameque, NB E8T
Gloucester County

D-U-N-S 20-710-0475   (BR)
DISTRICT SCOLAIRE FRANCOPHONE NORD-EST
ECOLE SOEUR ST-ALEXANDRE
65 Rue De L'Ecole, Lameque, NB, E8T 1B7
(506) 344-3064
Emp Here 50
SIC 8211 Elementary and secondary schools

D-U-N-S 25-391-2414   (BR)
FEDERATION DES CAISSES POPULAIRE ACADIENNES INC, LA
CAISSE POPULAIRE DES ILES
(*Suby of* Federation Des Caisses Populaire
Acadiennes Inc, La)
71 Rue Principale, Lameque, NB, E8T 1N2
(506) 344-1500
Emp Here 21
SIC 6062 State credit unions

D-U-N-S 24-955-6861   (BR)
REGIONAL HEALTH AUTHORITY A
HOPITAL DE LAMEQUE
29 Rue De L'Hopital, Lameque, NB, E8T 1C5
(506) 344-2261
Emp Here 100
SIC 8062 General medical and surgical hospitals

D-U-N-S 20-986-7258   (SL)
RESIDENCES LUCIEN SAINDON INC, LES
26 Rue De L'Hopital, Lameque, NB, E8T 1C3
(506) 344-3232
Emp Here 70   *Sales* 3,210,271
SIC 8051 Skilled nursing care facilities

Lansdowne, NB E7L

D-U-N-S 20-313-3314   (BR)
MCCAIN PRODUCE INC
225 Lansdowne Rd, Lansdowne, NB, E7L 4A8
(506) 375-5019
Emp Here 27
SIC 5148 Fresh fruits and vegetables

Lower Kintore, NB E7H
Victoria County

D-U-N-S 20-814-4642   (SL)
VICTORIA GLEN MANOR INC
30 Beech Glen Rd, Lower Kintore, NB, E7H

1J9
(506) 273-4885
Emp Here 75   *Sales* 3,429,153
SIC 8051 Skilled nursing care facilities

Lutes Mountain, NB E1G
Westmoreland County

D-U-N-S 25-241-8629   (BR)
SCHOOL DISTRICT 2
MAGNETIC HILL SCHOOL
3346 Route 126, Lutes Mountain, NB, E1G 2X4
(506) 856-3428
Emp Here 40
SIC 8211 Elementary and secondary schools

Maces Bay, NB E5J
Charlotte County

D-U-N-S 24-227-3709   (BR)
NEW BRUNSWICK POWER CORPORATION
122 Countyline Rd, Maces Bay, NB, E5J 1W1

Emp Here 750
SIC 4911 Electric services

Mcadam, NB E6J

D-U-N-S 25-242-1870   (BR)
ANGLOPHONE WEST SCHOOL DISTRICT (ASD-W)
MCADAM HIGH SCHOOL
29 Lake Ave, Mcadam, NB, E6J 1N7
(506) 784-6828
Emp Here 25
SIC 8211 Elementary and secondary schools

D-U-N-S 20-792-6739   (BR)
ATLANTIC WHOLESALERS LTD
MCADAMS SAVE EASY
153 Harvey Rd Unit 1, Mcadam, NB, E6J 1A1
(506) 784-2536
Emp Here 25
SIC 5411 Grocery stores

D-U-N-S 20-703-7420   (BR)
CERTAINTEED GYPSUM CANADA, INC
57 Quality Way, Mcadam, NB, E6J 1B1
(506) 784-2215
Emp Here 25
SIC 3275 Gypsum products

D-U-N-S 25-999-9241   (BR)
SOLENO INC
64 North Lane, Mcadam, NB, E6J 1K6
(506) 784-1888
Emp Here 50
SIC 3498 Fabricated pipe and fittings

Meductic, NB E6H

D-U-N-S 20-445-2783   (SL)
SABIAN LTD
219 Main St, Meductic, NB, E6H 2L5
(506) 272-2019
Emp Here 120   *Sales* 4,331,255
SIC 3931 Musical instruments

Memramcook, NB E4K
Westmoreland County

D-U-N-S 20-003-6874   (SL)
BSM SERVICES (1998) LTD
948 Ch Royal, Memramcook, NB, E4K 1Y8
(506) 862-0810
Emp Here 50   *Sales* 4,377,642
SIC 1711 Plumbing, heating, air-conditioning

D-U-N-S 25-951-6060   (BR)
FEDERATION DES CAISSES POPULAIRE ACADIENNES INC, LA
CAISSE POPULAIRE DE MEMRAMCOOK
(*Suby of* Federation Des Caisses Populaire
Acadiennes Inc, La)
587 Rue Centrale, Memramcook, NB, E4K 3R5
(506) 758-9329
Emp Here 20
SIC 6062 State credit unions

D-U-N-S 20-914-4844   (BR)
SCHOOL BOARD DISTRICT 01
ECOLE ABBEY-LANDRY
432 Rue Centrale, Memramcook, NB, E4K 3S5
(506) 758-4004
Emp Here 50
SIC 8211 Elementary and secondary schools

D-U-N-S 20-303-3899   (BR)
VICWEST INC
(*Suby of* Vicwest Inc)
671 Ch Royal, Memramcook, NB, E4K 1X1
(506) 758-8181
Emp Here 50
SIC 3444 Sheet Metalwork

Minto, NB E4B
Queens County

D-U-N-S 25-241-8033   (BR)
ANGLOPHONE WEST SCHOOL DISTRICT (ASD-W)
MINTO MEMORIAL HIGH SCHOOL
126 Park St, Minto, NB, E4B 3K9
(506) 327-3388
Emp Here 26
SIC 8211 Elementary and secondary schools

D-U-N-S 25-242-1953   (BR)
ANGLOPHONE WEST SCHOOL DISTRICT (ASD-W)
MINTO ELEMENTARY & MIDDLE SCHOOL
42 Cedar St, Minto, NB, E4B 2Z9
(506) 327-3365
Emp Here 50
SIC 8211 Elementary and secondary schools

D-U-N-S 20-617-5150   (SL)
EASTLAND INDUSTRIES LIMITED
77 Industrial Park Rd, Minto, NB, E4B 3A6
(506) 327-3321
Emp Here 65   *Sales* 4,504,505
SIC 2434 Wood kitchen cabinets

D-U-N-S 25-758-9416   (SL)
QUEENS NORTH HEALTH COMPLEX INC
W. G. BISHOP NURSING HOME
1100 Pleasant Dr, Minto, NB, E4B 2V7
(506) 327-7853
Emp Here 51   *Sales* 2,334,742
SIC 8051 Skilled nursing care facilities

D-U-N-S 25-528-1552   (BR)
RPS COMPOSITES INC
MARITIME FIBERGLASS , DIV OF
99 Industrial Park Rd, Minto, NB, E4B 3A6
(506) 327-6505
Emp Here 20
SIC 3299 NonMetallic mineral products,

Miramichi, NB E1N
Northumberland County

D-U-N-S 25-881-1017   (BR)
ATLANTIC WHOLESALERS LTD
CHATHAM SUPERVALUE
2 Johnson Ave, Miramichi, NB, E1N 3B7
(506) 773-9792
Emp Here 60
SIC 5411 Grocery stores

D-U-N-S 25-897-3866   (SL)
CANADIAN CORRECTIONAL MANAGEMENT INC
4 Airport Dr, Miramichi, NB, E1N 3W4
(506) 624-2160
Emp Here 150   *Sales* 4,669,485
SIC 7381 Detective and armored car services

D-U-N-S 20-282-1344   (BR)
DEW ENGINEERING AND DEVELOPMENT ULC
(*Suby of* Keystone Holdings, LLC)
99 General Manson Way, Miramichi, NB, E1N 6K6
(506) 778-8000
Emp Here 100
SIC 3795 Tanks and tank components

D-U-N-S 20-930-2496   (HQ)
DISTRICT EDUCATION COUNCIL-SCHOOL DISTRICT 16
SCHOOL DISTRICT 16
(*Suby of* District Education Council-School
District 16)
78 Henderson St, Miramichi, NB, E1N 2R7
(506) 778-6076
Emp Here 50   *Emp Total* 800
Sales 73,651,840
SIC 8211 Elementary and secondary schools
Superintnt Nancy Poucher

D-U-N-S 25-137-3148   (BR)
DISTRICT EDUCATION COUNCIL-SCHOOL DISTRICT 16
SAINT ANDREWS ELEMENTARY SCHOOL
(*Suby of* District Education Council-School
District 16)
77 Chatham Ave, Miramichi, NB, E1N 1G7
(506) 778-6081
Emp Here 30
SIC 8211 Elementary and secondary schools

D-U-N-S 25-241-7381   (BR)
DISTRICT EDUCATION COUNCIL-SCHOOL DISTRICT 16
JAMES M HILL MEMORIAL HIGH SCHOOL
(*Suby of* District Education Council-School
District 16)
128 Henderson St, Miramichi, NB, E1N 2S2
(506) 778-6078
Emp Here 70
SIC 8211 Elementary and secondary schools

D-U-N-S 25-242-0591   (BR)
DISTRICT EDUCATION COUNCIL-SCHOOL DISTRICT 16
DR. LOSIER MIDDLE SCHOOL
(*Suby of* District Education Council-School
District 16)
124 Henderson St, Miramichi, NB, E1N 2S2
(506) 778-6077
Emp Here 30
SIC 8211 Elementary and secondary schools

D-U-N-S 20-023-8314   (BR)
DISTRICT EDUCATION COUNCIL-SCHOOL DISTRICT 16
NELSON RURAL SCHOOL
(*Suby of* District Education Council-School
District 16)
26 St. Patrick'S Dr, Miramichi, NB, E1N 5T9
(506) 627-4074
Emp Here 30
SIC 8211 Elementary and secondary schools

D-U-N-S 25-155-2428   (BR)
M.O.R.E. SERVICES INC
MORE
(*Suby of* M.O.R.E. Services Inc)

---

16 Stanley St, Miramichi, NB, E1N 2S8
(506) 624-5407
Emp Here 65
SIC 8399 Social services, nec

D-U-N-S 20-019-2847   (SL)
R. HOLMES PHARMACY LTD
JEAN COUTU PHARMACY
4 Johnson Ave Suite 12, Miramichi, NB, E1N 3B7
(506) 773-4412
Emp Here 30   *Sales* 5,024,256
SIC 5912 Drug stores and proprietary stores

D-U-N-S 25-264-5994   (BR)
REGIONAL HEALTH AUTHORITY NB
REGIONAL HEALTH AUTHORITY B
1780 Water St Suite 300, Miramichi, NB, E1N 1B6
(506) 778-6877
Emp Here 20
SIC 8099 Health and allied services, nec

D-U-N-S 24-348-1376   (BR)
REGIONAL HEALTH AUTHORITY NB
REGIONAL HEALTH AUTHORITY B
1780 Water St Suite 300, Miramichi, NB, E1N 1B6
(506) 778-6102
Emp Here 30
SIC 8621 Professional organizations

D-U-N-S 25-167-3869   (BR)
SCOTT CANADA LTD
TOURBIERE MIRAMICHI
(*Suby of* Scott Canada Ltd)
1416 Bay Du Vin River Rd, Miramichi, NB, E1N 3A3
(506) 778-2519
Emp Here 70
SIC 1499 Miscellaneous nonMetallic minerals, except fuels

Miramichi, NB E1V
Northumberland County

D-U-N-S 20-822-4378   (BR)
AGROPUR COOPERATIVE
NARTEL
256 Lawlor Lane, Miramichi, NB, E1V 3Z9
(506) 627-7720
Emp Here 250
SIC 5143 Dairy products, except dried or canned

D-U-N-S 20-731-9117   (SL)
AUTO LAC INC
CANADIAN TIRE MIRAMICHI
2491 King George Hwy, Miramichi, NB, E1V 6W3
(506) 773-9448
Emp Here 60   *Sales* 4,888,367
SIC 5399 Miscellaneous general merchandise

D-U-N-S 25-296-2667   (BR)
BANK OF NOVA SCOTIA, THE
SCOTIABANK
139 Henry St, Miramichi, NB, E1V 2N5
(506) 622-1461
Emp Here 24
SIC 6021 National commercial banks

D-U-N-S 24-222-9842   (BR)
BOSTON PIZZA INTERNATIONAL INC
BOSTON PIZZA
98 Douglastown Blvd, Miramichi, NB, E1V 0A3
(506) 778-9940
Emp Here 30
SIC 5812 Eating places

D-U-N-S 24-343-2726   (BR)
BRUNSWICK NEWS INC
MIRAMICHI LEADER
(*Suby of* J. D. Irving, Limited)
2428 King George Hwy, Miramichi, NB, E1V

6V9
(506) 622-2600
Emp Here 22
SIC 2711 Newspapers

D-U-N-S 24-675-6329   (BR)
CANADA POST CORPORATION
305 Pleasant St, Miramichi, NB, E1V 1Y8
(506) 622-4615
Emp Here 60
SIC 4311 U.s. postal service

D-U-N-S 20-195-5601   (BR)
COCA-COLA REFRESHMENTS CANADA COMPANY
(*Suby of* The Coca-Cola Company)
570 Old King George Hwy, Miramichi, NB, E1V 1K1
(506) 622-3101
Emp Here 22
SIC 2086 Bottled and canned soft drinks

D-U-N-S 20-023-3844   (BR)
DISTRICT EDUCATION COUNCIL-SCHOOL DISTRICT 16
CROFT ELEMENTARY SCHOOL
(*Suby of* District Education Council-School District 16)
31 Elizabeth St, Miramichi, NB, E1V 1V8
(506) 627-4086
Emp Here 30
SIC 8211 Elementary and secondary schools

D-U-N-S 25-242-0765   (BR)
DISTRICT EDUCATION COUNCIL-SCHOOL DISTRICT 16
GRETNA GREEN ELEMENTARY SCHOOL
(*Suby of* District Education Council-School District 16)
15 Gretna Green Dr, Miramichi, NB, E1V 5V6
(506) 778-6099
Emp Here 25
SIC 8211 Elementary and secondary schools

D-U-N-S 25-884-6674   (BR)
DISTRICT EDUCATION COUNCIL-SCHOOL DISTRICT 16
HARKINS MIDDLE SCHOOL
(*Suby of* District Education Council-School District 16)
301 Campbell St, Miramichi, NB, E1V 1R4
(506) 627-4088
Emp Here 42
SIC 8211 Elementary and secondary schools

D-U-N-S 25-137-3130   (BR)
DISTRICT EDUCATION COUNCIL-SCHOOL DISTRICT 16
HARKINS ELEMENTARY SCHOOL
(*Suby of* District Education Council-School District 16)
305 Campbell St, Miramichi, NB, E1V 1R4
(506) 627-4087
Emp Here 30
SIC 8211 Elementary and secondary schools

D-U-N-S 24-210-7840   (BR)
DISTRICT SCOLAIRE 11
ECOLE PARREFOUR BAUSOLEIL
(*Suby of* District Scolaire 11)
300 Beaverbrook Rd, Miramichi, NB, E1V 1A1
(506) 627-4135
Emp Here 30
SIC 8211 Elementary and secondary schools

D-U-N-S 20-749-0645   (BR)
EMPIRE THEATRES LIMITED
2480 King George Hwy, Miramichi, NB, E1V 6W4
(506) 778-3441
Emp Here 25
SIC 7832 Motion picture theaters, except drive-in

D-U-N-S 20-575-9314   (BR)
ICT CANADA MARKETING INC
SYKES
(*Suby of* Sykes Enterprises Incorporated)

408 King George Hwy, Miramichi, NB, E1V 0G6
(506) 836-9050
Emp Here 300
SIC 7389 Business services, nec

D-U-N-S 25-143-9915   (BR)
J. D. IRVING, LIMITED
KENT BUILDING SUPPLIES, DIV OF
(*Suby of* J. D. Irving, Limited)
2417 King George Hwy, Miramichi, NB, E1V 6W1
(506) 778-2600
Emp Here 25
SIC 5211 Lumber and other building materials

D-U-N-S 24-993-8093   (SL)
JARDINE SECURITY LTD
107 Tardy Ave, Miramichi, NB, E1V 3Y8
(506) 622-2787
Emp Here 80   *Sales* 2,480,664
SIC 7381 Detective and armored car services

D-U-N-S 20-749-3904   (SL)
K.R.T. & ASSOCIATES INCORPORATED
60 Pleasant St, Miramichi, NB, E1V 1X7
(506) 622-5400
Emp Here 160   *Sales* 29,239,680
SIC 8741 Management services
Pr Pr Kimberley Tompkins

D-U-N-S 24-131-7387   (BR)
LOUNSBURY COMPANY LIMITED
LOUNSBURY AUTOMOTIVE
855 King George Hwy Suite 356, Miramichi, NB, E1V 1P9
(506) 622-2311
Emp Here 36
SIC 5511 New and used car dealers

D-U-N-S 20-932-7337   (SL)
MIRAMICHI CHRYSLER DODGE JEEP INC
1155 King George Hwy, Miramichi, NB, E1V 5J7
(506) 622-3900
Emp Here 23   *Sales* 8,390,481
SIC 5511 New and used car dealers
Pt Bert Mcintyre

D-U-N-S 24-387-8613   (HQ)
REGIONAL HEALTH AUTHORITY NB
HORIZON HEALTH NETWORK
155 Pleasant St, Miramichi, NB, E1V 1Y3
(506) 623-5500
Emp Here 1,000   *Emp Total* 45,138
Sales 822,036,011
SIC 8062 General medical and surgical hospitals
Pr Karen Mcgrath
VP Jean Daigle
VP Gary Foley
VP Geri Geldart
VP Edouard Hendriks
VP Margaret Melanson
Dir Janet Hogan
 Andrea Seymour
 Grace Losier
Dir J. Douglas Baker

D-U-N-S 24-629-7816   (SL)
SKYCO INC
SKY-TEC SATELLITE
734 King George Hwy, Miramichi, NB, E1V 1P8
(506) 622-8890
Emp Here 70   *Sales* 4,231,721
SIC 7699 Repair services, nec

D-U-N-S 20-548-7374   (BR)
SOBEYS CAPITAL INCORPORATED
273 Pleasant St, Miramichi, NB, E1V 1Y7
(506) 622-2098
Emp Here 70
SIC 5411 Grocery stores

D-U-N-S 24-943-5660   (BR)
SOBEYS CAPITAL INCORPORATED
SOBEYS #680

2485 King George Hwy Suite 1, Miramichi, NB, E1V 6W3
(506) 778-2404
Emp Here 150
SIC 5411 Grocery stores

D-U-N-S 24-101-3593   (BR)
STAPLES CANADA INC
STAPLES THE BUSINESS DEPOT
(*Suby of* Staples, Inc.)
99 Douglastown Blvd Suite 275, Miramichi, NB, E1V 0A4
(506) 622-6050
Emp Here 25
SIC 5943 Stationery stores

D-U-N-S 20-813-6069   (HQ)
SUNNY CORNER ENTERPRISES INC
259 Dalton Ave, Miramichi, NB, E1V 3C4
(506) 622-5600
Emp Here 50   *Emp Total* 4
Sales 104,891,360
SIC 1711 Plumbing, heating, air-conditioning
 Gordon Lavoie
VP VP Eugene Nowlan
VP VP William Schenkels
 Jolyon Hunter

D-U-N-S 24-375-7460   (SL)
UMOE SOLAR NEW BRUNSWICK INC
345 Curtis Rd, Miramichi, NB, E1V 3R7

Emp Here 100   *Sales* 48,851,360
SIC 2621 Paper mills
Dir David Wright
Dir Joerk Rimmasch
Dir Oystein Oyehaug

D-U-N-S 24-120-3517   (BR)
WAL-MART CANADA CORP
200 Douglastown Blvd, Miramichi, NB, E1V 7T9
(506) 778-8224
Emp Here 200
SIC 5311 Department stores

Moncton, NB E1A

D-U-N-S 20-075-4658   (BR)
CONSBEC INC
10 Dove Lane, Moncton, NB, E1A 7E1
(506) 857-9466
Emp Here 25
SIC 1442 Construction sand and gravel

D-U-N-S 25-881-3559   (BR)
ICT CANADA MARKETING INC
(*Suby of* Sykes Enterprises Incorporated)
459 Elmwood Dr, Moncton, NB, E1A 2X2

Emp Here 220
SIC 8732 Commercial nonphysical research

D-U-N-S 24-605-3482   (BR)
LAWTON'S DRUG STORES LIMITED
355 Elmwood Dr, Moncton, NB, E1A 1X6
(506) 857-2212
Emp Here 20
SIC 5912 Drug stores and proprietary stores

D-U-N-S 25-878-9544   (SL)
MANOIR NOTRE-DAME MANOR INC
110 Murphy Ave, Moncton, NB, E1A 6Y2
(506) 857-9011
Emp Here 57   *Sales* 2,115,860
SIC 8361 Residential care

D-U-N-S 24-125-8284   (SL)
RIVENWOOD FURNITURE LTD
323 Highland View Rd, Moncton, NB, E1A 2L4
(506) 857-3900
Emp Here 59   *Sales* 3,502,114
SIC 2511 Wood household furniture

D-U-N-S 24-025-0279   (BR)

▲ Public Company   ■ Public Company Family Member   **HQ** Headquarters   **BR** Branch   **SL** Single Location

SCHOOL BOARD DISTRICT 01
ECOLE MASCARET
50 Leopold F. Belliveau Dr, Moncton, NB, E1A 8V3
(506) 869-6299
Emp Here 30
SIC 8211 Elementary and secondary schools

D-U-N-S 24-023-4794   (BR)
SCHOOL BOARD DISTRICT 01
ECOLE L'ODYSSEE
60 Leopold F. Belliveau Dr Suite 60, Moncton, NB, E1A 8V4
(506) 869-6800
Emp Here 100
SIC 8211 Elementary and secondary schools

D-U-N-S 20-934-8189   (BR)
SCHOOL DISTRICT 2
FOREST GLEN SCHOOL
43 Keenan Dr, Moncton, NB, E1A 3P8
(506) 856-3414
Emp Here 50
SIC 8211 Elementary and secondary schools

D-U-N-S 25-080-2642   (BR)
SCHOOL DISTRICT 2
ARNOLD H MCLEOD ELEMENTARY SCHOOL
280 Storey Rd E, Moncton, NB, E1A 5Z3
(506) 856-3475
Emp Here 40
SIC 8211 Elementary and secondary schools

D-U-N-S 25-080-2691   (BR)
SCHOOL DISTRICT 2
LEWISVILLE MIDDLE SCHOOL
45 Mcauley Dr, Moncton, NB, E1A 5R8
(506) 856-3474
Emp Here 30
SIC 8211 Elementary and secondary schools

D-U-N-S 20-733-2334   (BR)
SODEXO QUEBEC LIMITEE
18 Av Antonine-Maillet, Moncton, NB, E1A 3E9
(506) 858-4142
Emp Here 27
SIC 5812 Eating places

D-U-N-S 24-189-0409   (SL)
TAYLOR FORD SALES LTD
TAYLOR FORD LINCOLN
10 Lewisville Rd, Moncton, NB, E1A 2K2
(506) 857-2300
Emp Here 106   *Sales* 53,254,400
SIC 5511 New and used car dealers
Pr Pr Terry Taylor
VP VP Maureen Taylor
 Paul Leblanc

D-U-N-S 24-247-7763   (BR)
UNIVERSITE DE MONCTON
DEAN'S OFFICE
(*Suby of* Universite de Moncton)
65 Massey Ave, Moncton, NB, E1A 3C9
(506) 858-4205
Emp Here 20
SIC 8221 Colleges and universities

D-U-N-S 20-813-6846   (HQ)
UNIVERSITE DE MONCTON
(*Suby of* Universite de Moncton)
18 Av Antonine-Maillet, Moncton, NB, E1A 3E9
(506) 858-4000
Emp Here 636   *Emp Total* 807
Sales 83,904,805
SIC 8221 Colleges and universities
Pr Yvon Fontaine
VP Fin Richard Saillant
VP Neil Boucher
Dir Fin Daniel Godbout
Fin Ex Guy Richard

D-U-N-S 20-861-3930   (BR)
UNIVERSITE DE MONCTON
PAVILLON ADRIEN J CORMIER

(*Suby of* Universite de Moncton)
18 Av Antonine-Maillet, Moncton, NB, E1A 3E9
(506) 863-2132
Emp Here 30
SIC 8221 Colleges and universities

D-U-N-S 20-743-1917   (SL)
VILLA DU REPOS INC
125 Murphy Ave, Moncton, NB, E1A 8V2
(506) 857-3560
Emp Here 125   *Sales* 4,596,524
SIC 8361 Residential care

Moncton, NB E1C

D-U-N-S 25-182-2482   (BR)
3499481 CANADA INC
PETS UNLIMITED
1380 Mountain Rd, Moncton, NB, E1C 2T8
(506) 854-7387
Emp Here 22
SIC 5999 Miscellaneous retail stores, nec

D-U-N-S 25-362-7798   (SL)
515331 N.B. INC
PARAMOUNT LOUNGE
125 Westmorland St, Moncton, NB, E1C 0S3
(506) 850-1060
Emp Here 57   *Sales* 2,115,860
SIC 5813 Drinking places

D-U-N-S 20-555-2727   (HQ)
ACADIAN COACH LINES LP
(*Suby of* Acadian Coach Lines LP)
300 Main St Unit B2-2, Moncton, NB, E1C 1B9

Emp Here 82   *Emp Total* 100
Sales 4,742,446
SIC 4142 Bus charter service, except local

D-U-N-S 20-021-0110   (BR)
AIR LIQUIDE CANADA INC
280 John St, Moncton, NB, E1C 9W3
(506) 857-8390
Emp Here 25
SIC 4932 Gas and other services combined

D-U-N-S 20-017-4279   (BR)
ALLSTATE INSURANCE COMPANY OF CANADA
ALLSTATE CLAIMS SERVICES
60 Queen St, Moncton, NB, E1C 0J1
(506) 859-7820
Emp Here 20
SIC 6411 Insurance agents, brokers, and service

D-U-N-S 24-350-4334   (HQ)
AMBULANCE NEW BRUNSWICK INC
NEW BRUNSWICK EMS FLEET CENTRE
210 John St Suite 101, Moncton, NB, E1C 0B8
(506) 872-6500
Emp Here 100   *Emp Total* 45,138
Sales 82,639,837
SIC 4119 Local passenger transportation, nec
Pr Alan Stephen
Dir Opers Shirley Neville

D-U-N-S 25-370-0942   (BR)
AMERICA ONLINE CANADA INC
AOL CANADA
(*Suby of* Verizon Communications Inc.)
11 Ocean Limited Way, Moncton, NB, E1C 0H1

Emp Here 350
SIC 4899 Communication services, nec

D-U-N-S 20-177-1776   (BR)
AQUILINI INVESTMENT GROUP INC
CROWNE PLAZA MONCTON DOWNTOWN
1005 Main St, Moncton, NB, E1C 1G9
(506) 854-6340
Emp Here 100

SIC 7011 Hotels and motels

D-U-N-S 25-402-6313   (SL)
ASURION CANADA, INC
(*Suby of* New Asurion Corporation)
11 Ocean Limited Way, Moncton, NB, E1C 0H1
(506) 386-9200
Emp Here 500   *Sales* 115,718,001
SIC 4899 Communication services, nec
 Rick Taweel
Mgr Donna Cooke

D-U-N-S 24-956-5623   (BR)
ATLANTIC RETAIL CO-OPERATIVES FEDERATION
CO-OP ATLANTIC
80 Mapleton Rd, Moncton, NB, E1C 7W8
(506) 858-6173
Emp Here 60
SIC 5411 Grocery stores

D-U-N-S 20-945-2957   (BR)
ATLANTIC RETAIL CO-OPERATIVES FEDERATION
CO-OP ATLANTIC
20 Record St, Moncton, NB, E1C 1A6
(506) 858-6173
Emp Here 40
SIC 5411 Grocery stores

D-U-N-S 24-263-5340   (BR)
AVISCAR INC
AVIS RENT A CAR
(*Suby of* Avis Budget Group, Inc.)
515 Main St, Moncton, NB, E1C 1C4
(506) 857-0162
Emp Here 22
SIC 7514 Passenger car rental

D-U-N-S 24-479-2651   (BR)
BANK OF NOVA SCOTIA, THE
SCOTIABANK
780 Main St, Moncton, NB, E1C 1E6
(506) 857-3636
Emp Here 40
SIC 6021 National commercial banks

D-U-N-S 25-296-2782   (BR)
BANK OF NOVA SCOTIA, THE
SCOTIABANK
796 Mountain Rd, Moncton, NB, E1C 2R4
(506) 857-3646
Emp Here 22
SIC 6021 National commercial banks

D-U-N-S 20-267-5260   (BR)
BANK OF MONTREAL
BMO
633 Main St Suite 250, Moncton, NB, E1C 9X9
(506) 853-5724
Emp Here 22
SIC 6021 National commercial banks

D-U-N-S 20-580-1926   (BR)
BANQUE TORONTO-DOMINION, LA
TD BANK
(*Suby of* Toronto-Dominion Bank, The)
860 Main St Suite 500, Moncton, NB, E1C 1G2
(506) 853-4370
Emp Here 29
SIC 6021 National commercial banks

D-U-N-S 24-334-4749   (BR)
BELL ALIANT REGIONAL COMMUNICATIONS INC
27 Alma St, Moncton, NB, E1C 4Y2
(506) 860-8655
Emp Here 80
SIC 4899 Communication services, nec

D-U-N-S 24-832-6175   (BR)
BELL MEDIA INC
ATV ASN NEW BRUNSWICK DIV OF
191 Halifax St, Moncton, NB, E1C 9R6
(506) 857-2600
Emp Here 50

SIC 4833 Television broadcasting stations

D-U-N-S 20-699-1361   (BR)
BEST BUY CANADA LTD
FUTURE SHOP
(*Suby of* Best Buy Co., Inc.)
50 Plaza Blvd, Moncton, NB, E1C 0G4
(506) 853-5188
Emp Here 60
SIC 5731 Radio, television, and electronic stores

D-U-N-S 25-526-9706   (HQ)
BRUNSWICK NEWS INC
TIMES & TRANSCRIPT
(*Suby of* J. D. Irving, Limited)
939 Main St, Moncton, NB, E1C 8P3
(506) 859-4900
Emp Here 400   *Emp Total* 15,000
Sales 45,600,438
SIC 2711 Newspapers
 A L Irving
 J E Irving
 J K Irving

D-U-N-S 20-021-1159   (BR)
CANADA BREAD COMPANY, LIMITED
MAPLE LEAF
235 Botsford St, Moncton, NB, E1C 4X9
(506) 857-9158
Emp Here 130
SIC 2051 Bread, cake, and related products

D-U-N-S 20-573-1925   (BR)
CANADIAN BROADCASTING CORPORATION
250 Archibald St, Moncton, NB, E1C 8N8
(506) 853-6894
Emp Here 260
SIC 4832 Radio broadcasting stations

D-U-N-S 25-615-6985   (BR)
CANADIAN IMPERIAL BANK OF COMMERCE
CIBC
759 Main St, Moncton, NB, E1C 1E5
(506) 859-3717
Emp Here 35
SIC 6021 National commercial banks

D-U-N-S 24-126-8952   (BR)
CAPSERVCO LIMITED PARTNERSHIP
GRANT THORNTON
(*Suby of* CapServCo Limited Partnership)
633 Main St Suite 500, Moncton, NB, E1C 9X9
(506) 857-0100
Emp Here 60
SIC 8721 Accounting, auditing, and bookkeeping

D-U-N-S 20-748-9308   (BR)
CO-OPERATORS GENERAL INSURANCE COMPANY
10 Record St, Moncton, NB, E1C 0B2
(506) 853-1336
Emp Here 250
SIC 6311 Life insurance

D-U-N-S 25-849-3816   (BR)
COMCARE (CANADA) LIMITED
COMCARE HEALTH SERVICES
(*Suby of* Comcare (Canada) Limited)
30 Gordon St Suite 105, Moncton, NB, E1C 1L8
(506) 853-9112
Emp Here 80
SIC 7363 Help supply services

D-U-N-S 24-346-4620   (BR)
COREY CRAIG LTD
TIM HORTONS
1166 Mountain Rd, Moncton, NB, E1C 2T5
(506) 862-7631
Emp Here 40
SIC 5812 Eating places

D-U-N-S 25-366-3553   (BR)
COREY CRAIG LTD

TIM HORTONS
10 Plaza Blvd, Moncton, NB, E1C 0G4
(506) 389-7366
Emp Here 20
SIC 5812 Eating places

D-U-N-S 25-611-4224   (BR)
COREY CRAIG LTD
TIM HORTONS
7 St George St, Moncton, NB, E1C 1S8
(506) 862-7638
Emp Here 35
SIC 5812 Eating places

D-U-N-S 20-287-1799   (BR)
CORPORATION KATIMAVIK-OPCAN
(Suby of Corporation Katimavik-Opcan)
35 Highfield St, Moncton, NB, E1C 5N1

Emp Here 20
SIC 8399 Social services, nec

D-U-N-S 20-554-3239   (BR)
COX & PALMER
644 Main St Suite 502, Moncton, NB, E1C 1E2
(506) 856-9800
Emp Here 22
SIC 8111 Legal services

D-U-N-S 20-609-1550   (SL)
CROWNE PLAZA MONCTON DOWNTOWN HOTEL
1005 Main St, Moncton, NB, E1C 1G9
(506) 854-6340
Emp Here 90   Sales 3,939,878
SIC 7011 Hotels and motels

D-U-N-S 20-191-2123   (BR)
DELUXE FRENCH FRIES LTD
DELUXE FRENCH FRIES
857 Mountain Rd, Moncton, NB, E1C 2R9
(506) 858-8310
Emp Here 25
SIC 5812 Eating places

D-U-N-S 20-607-3665   (BR)
DOLLARAMA S.E.C.
80 Mapleton Rd, Moncton, NB, E1C 7W8
(506) 859-9211
Emp Here 25
SIC 5399 Miscellaneous general merchandise

D-U-N-S 20-310-8527   (BR)
FOURNITURES DE BUREAU DENIS INC
DENIS OFFICE SUPPLIES & FURNITURE
(Suby of Placements Denis Latulippe Inc, Les)
123 Lutz St, Moncton, NB, E1C 5E8
(506) 853-8920
Emp Here 30
SIC 5112 Stationery and office supplies

D-U-N-S 25-580-3827   (BR)
GROUPE CANAM INC
CANAM
95 Foundry St Suite 417, Moncton, NB, E1C 5H7
(506) 857-3164
Emp Here 25
SIC 5082 Construction and mining machinery

D-U-N-S 20-575-1998   (BR)
GUILDFORDS (2005) INC
151 Halifax St, Moncton, NB, E1C 9R6
(506) 859-0818
Emp Here 30
SIC 8711 Engineering services

D-U-N-S 25-829-7001   (BR)
HARVARD RESTAURANTS LTD
WENDY'S RESTAURANT
1100 Mountain Rd, Moncton, NB, E1C 2T2
(506) 862-7647
Emp Here 35
SIC 5812 Eating places

D-U-N-S 20-025-7108   (BR)
HATCH CORPORATION
860 Main St Suite 700, Moncton, NB, E1C 1G2

(506) 857-8708
Emp Here 20
SIC 6099 Functions related to deposit banking

D-U-N-S 20-177-0695   (BR)
HOME DEPOT OF CANADA INC
HOME DEPOT
(Suby of The Home Depot Inc)
235 Mapleton Rd, Moncton, NB, E1C 0G9
(506) 853-8150
Emp Here 100
SIC 5251 Hardware stores

D-U-N-S 25-685-2112   (BR)
HUDSON'S BAY COMPANY
BAY, THE
1100 Main St, Moncton, NB, E1C 1H4

Emp Here 200
SIC 5311 Department stores

D-U-N-S 20-021-2157   (SL)
HYNES RESTAURANT LTD
495 Mountain Rd, Moncton, NB, E1C 2N4
(506) 382-3432
Emp Here 50   Sales 1,532,175
SIC 5812 Eating places

D-U-N-S 20-918-8999   (BR)
INNVEST REAL ESTATE INVESTMENT TRUST
DELTA BEAUSEJOUR
750 Main St, Moncton, NB, E1C 1E6
(506) 854-4344
Emp Here 100
SIC 7011 Hotels and motels

D-U-N-S 20-178-6154   (BR)
INTACT INSURANCE COMPANY
869 Main St, Moncton, NB, E1C 1G5
(506) 854-7281
Emp Here 30
SIC 6331 Fire, marine, and casualty insurance

D-U-N-S 25-315-7507   (BR)
INVESTORS GROUP FINANCIAL SERVICES INC
INVESTORS GROUP
1255 Main St, Moncton, NB, E1C 1H9
(506) 857-8055
Emp Here 45
SIC 8741 Management services

D-U-N-S 24-126-9133   (BR)
KPMG LLP
(Suby of KPMG LLP)
1 Factory Lane Suite 300, Moncton, NB, E1C 9M3
(506) 856-4400
Emp Here 40
SIC 8721 Accounting, auditing, and book-keeping

D-U-N-S 25-360-9481   (BR)
KILLAM PROPERTIES INC
MONCTON OFFICE
1111 Main St Suite 207, Moncton, NB, E1C 1H3
(506) 857-0066
Emp Here 30
SIC 6513 Apartment building operators

D-U-N-S 25-303-9598   (BR)
LONDON LIFE INSURANCE COMPANY
FREEDOM 55 FINANCIAL & QUADRUS INVESTMENTS
777 Main St Suite 900, Moncton, NB, E1C 1E9
(506) 853-6111
Emp Here 25
SIC 6311 Life insurance

D-U-N-S 20-287-6293   (BR)
LONG & MCQUADE LIMITED
LONG & MCQUADE MUSICAL INSTRUMENTS
245 Carson Dr, Moncton, NB, E1C 0M5
(506) 857-1987
Emp Here 20
SIC 5736 Musical instrument stores

D-U-N-S 25-293-2397   (BR)
LOUNSBURY COMPANY LIMITED
LOUNSBURY CHEV OLDS
2155 Main St W, Moncton, NB, E1C 9P2
(506) 857-4300
Emp Here 100
SIC 5511 New and used car dealers

D-U-N-S 24-382-7222   (BR)
LUXURY HOTELS INTERNATIONAL OF CANADA, ULC
RESIDENCE INN, MONCTON
(Suby of Marriott International, Inc.)
600 Main St, Moncton, NB, E1C 0M6
(506) 854-7100
Emp Here 100
SIC 7011 Hotels and motels

D-U-N-S 20-827-7017   (BR)
MCW CONSULTANTS LTD
MCW MARICOR
77 Vaughan Harvey Blvd Suite 200, Moncton, NB, E1C 0K2
(506) 857-8880
Emp Here 42
SIC 8711 Engineering services

D-U-N-S 20-743-4549   (HQ)
MAJOR DRILLING GROUP INTERNATIONAL INC
(Suby of Major Drilling Group International Inc)
111 St George St Suite 100, Moncton, NB, E1C 1T7
(506) 857-8636
Emp Here 27   Emp Total 5,442
Sales 225,683,575
SIC 1481 NonMetallic mineral services
Pr Pr Denis Larocque
VP Kelly Johnson
VP Larry Pisto
Pers/VP Ben Graham
VP Marc Landry
Sec Andrew Mclaughlin
David Balser
David B. Tennant
David Fennell
Edward Breiner

D-U-N-S 20-742-0910   (SL)
MARITIME DOOR & WINDOW LTD
118 Albert St, Moncton, NB, E1C 1B2
(506) 388-3000
Emp Here 60   Sales 4,377,642
SIC 1751 Carpentry work

D-U-N-S 25-881-5661   (BR)
MCINNES COOPER
644 Main St Suite 400, Moncton, NB, E1C 1E2
(506) 857-8970
Emp Here 30
SIC 8111 Legal services

D-U-N-S 24-120-1438   (BR)
MEDAVIE INC
644 Main St, Moncton, NB, E1C 1E2
(506) 853-1811
Emp Here 20
SIC 6321 Accident and health insurance

D-U-N-S 24-629-1371   (HQ)
MONCTON GRECO RESTAURANTS (1983) LTD
GRECO PIZZA & DONAIR
(Suby of Moncton Greco Restaurants (1983) Ltd)
120 Killam Dr, Moncton, NB, E1C 3R7
(506) 853-1051
Emp Here 40   Emp Total 85
Sales 2,553,625
SIC 5812 Eating places

D-U-N-S 20-748-9159   (SL)
MONCTON WILDCATS HOCKEY CLUB LTD
377 Killam Dr, Moncton, NB, E1C 3T1
(506) 858-2252
Emp Here 50   Sales 2,042,900
SIC 7997 Membership sports and recreation

clubs

D-U-N-S 24-353-8571   (BR)
MONCTON, CITY OF
MONCTON COLISEUM COMPLEX
377 Killam Dr Unit 100, Moncton, NB, E1C 3T1
(506) 389-5989
Emp Here 20
SIC 7999 Amusement and recreation, nec

D-U-N-S 25-985-8314   (BR)
NEW BRUNSWICK LIQUOR CORPORATION
ALCOOL NB LIQUOR
936 Mountain Rd, Moncton, NB, E1C 2S2
(506) 852-2380
Emp Here 22
SIC 5921 Liquor stores

D-U-N-S 20-116-5672   (BR)
NORTHFIELD GLASS GROUP LTD
WINDOW MANUFACTURER
230 High St, Moncton, NB, E1C 6C2

Emp Here 40
SIC 3231 Products of purchased glass

D-U-N-S 25-610-6055   (BR)
NORTHUMBERLAND COOPERATIVE LIMITED
1 Foundry St, Moncton, NB, E1C 0L1
(506) 858-8900
Emp Here 40
SIC 5143 Dairy products, except dried or canned

D-U-N-S 25-880-8591   (BR)
NUMERIS
1234 Main St Suite 600, Moncton, NB, E1C 1H7
(506) 859-7700
Emp Here 170
SIC 8732 Commercial nonphysical research

D-U-N-S 24-833-3916   (SL)
PERSONNEL SEARCH LTD
883 Main St, Moncton, NB, E1C 1G5
(506) 857-2156
Emp Here 300   Sales 28,269,870
SIC 7361 Employment agencies
Pr Pr Lynn Breau

D-U-N-S 20-536-7761   (BR)
PROVINCE OF NEW BRUNSWICK
PNB MONCTON DETENTION CENTRE
125 Assomption Blvd, Moncton, NB, E1C 1A2
(506) 386-2155
Emp Here 20
SIC 8361 Residential care

D-U-N-S 25-293-7420   (BR)
RBC DOMINION SECURITIES INC
(Suby of Royal Bank Of Canada)
633 Main St Suite 650, Moncton, NB, E1C 9X9
(506) 869-5444
Emp Here 30
SIC 6211 Security brokers and dealers

D-U-N-S 24-363-0659   (BR)
RGIS CANADA ULC
236 St George St, Moncton, NB, E1C 1W1
(506) 382-9146
Emp Here 106
SIC 7389 Business services, nec

D-U-N-S 20-731-8663   (BR)
RE/MAX REALTY SPECIALISTS LTD
11 Ocean Limited Way Suite 101, Moncton, NB, E1C 0H1
(506) 384-3300
Emp Here 25
SIC 6531 Real estate agents and managers

D-U-N-S 20-801-2273   (BR)
REGIONAL HEALTH AUTHORITY NB
REGIONAL HEALTH AUTHORITY B
81 Albert St, Moncton, NB, E1C 1B3

(506) 856-2444
Emp Here 70
SIC 8093 Specialty outpatient clinics, nec

D-U-N-S 25-850-9561   (BR)
REGIONAL HEALTH AUTHORITY NB
REGIONAL HEALTH AUTHORITY B
125 Mapleton Rd, Moncton, NB, E1C 9G6
(506) 856-2333
Emp Here 33
SIC 8093 Specialty outpatient clinics, nec

D-U-N-S 25-525-7677   (BR)
SCHOOL BOARD DISTRICT 01
SAINT HENRI
101 Gross Ave, Moncton, NB, E1C 7H3
(506) 856-2727
Emp Here 50
SIC 8211 Elementary and secondary schools

D-U-N-S 25-241-7746   (BR)
SCHOOL BOARD DISTRICT 01
ECOLE BEAUSEJOUR
131 Connaught Ave, Moncton, NB, E1C 3P4
(506) 856-2733
Emp Here 30
SIC 8211 Elementary and secondary schools

D-U-N-S 25-241-8348   (BR)
SCHOOL DISTRICT 2
BIRCHMOUNT SCHOOL
256 Ayer Ave, Moncton, NB, E1C 8G8
(506) 856-3405
Emp Here 60
SIC 8211 Elementary and secondary schools

D-U-N-S 25-241-8306   (BR)
SCHOOL DISTRICT 2
QUEEN ELIZABETH SCHOOL
31 Lynch St, Moncton, NB, E1C 3L5
(506) 856-3447
Emp Here 50
SIC 8211 Elementary and secondary schools

D-U-N-S 25-241-8504   (BR)
SCHOOL DISTRICT 2
HARRISSON TRIMBLE
80 Echo Dr, Moncton, NB, E1C 3H8
(506) 856-3417
Emp Here 50
SIC 8211 Elementary and secondary schools

D-U-N-S 25-241-8660   (BR)
SCHOOL DISTRICT 2
MONCTON HIGH SCHOOL
207 Church St, Moncton, NB, E1C 5A3
(506) 856-3439
Emp Here 110
SIC 8211 Elementary and secondary schools

D-U-N-S 25-080-2709   (BR)
SCHOOL DISTRICT 2
EDITH CAVELL
125 Park St, Moncton, NB, E1C 2B4
(506) 856-3473
Emp Here 30
SIC 8211 Elementary and secondary schools

D-U-N-S 25-241-9817   (BR)
SCHOOL DISTRICT 2
BEAVERBROOK SCHOOL
1085 Mountain Rd, Moncton, NB, E1C 2S9
(506) 856-3403
Emp Here 40
SIC 8211 Elementary and secondary schools

D-U-N-S 25-310-1448   (BR)
SCOTSBURN CO-OPERATIVE SERVICES LIMITED
SCOTSBURN DAIRY GROUP
88 Albert St, Moncton, NB, E1C 1B1

Emp Here 25
SIC 2026 Fluid milk

D-U-N-S 24-943-6262   (BR)
SOBEYS CAPITAL INCORPORATED
SOBEYS
1380 Mountain Rd, Moncton, NB, E1C 2T8

(506) 858-8283
Emp Here 180
SIC 5411 Grocery stores

D-U-N-S 20-932-2007   (BR)
SOBEYS CAPITAL INCORPORATED
SOBEYS 756
55 Vaughan Harvey Blvd, Moncton, NB, E1C 0N3
(506) 855-0546
Emp Here 42
SIC 5411 Grocery stores

D-U-N-S 20-859-9956   (BR)
SOURCE (BELL) ELECTRONICS INC, THE
SOURCE, THE
1100 Main St, Moncton, NB, E1C 1H4
(506) 389-3694
Emp Here 25
SIC 5999 Miscellaneous retail stores, nec

D-U-N-S 20-753-6504   (SL)
ST. JAMES GATE LTD
14 Church St, Moncton, NB, E1C 4Y9
(506) 388-4283
Emp Here 50   Sales 1,532,175
SIC 5812 Eating places

D-U-N-S 20-930-9541   (SL)
ST. PATRICK'S FAMILY CENTRE INC
ST PAT'S
34 Providence St, Moncton, NB, E1C 2Z4
(506) 857-2024
Emp Here 50   Sales 1,969,939
SIC 8322 Individual and family services

D-U-N-S 25-880-8831   (BR)
STEWART MCKELVEY STIRLING SCALES
(Suby of Stewart McKelvey Stirling Scales)
644 Main St Suite 601, Moncton, NB, E1C 1E2
(506) 853-1970
Emp Here 34
SIC 8111 Legal services

D-U-N-S 20-115-1714   (BR)
SYKES ASSISTANCE SERVICES CORPORATION
SYKES TELEHEALTH
(Suby of Sykes Enterprises Incorporated)
774 Main St Suite 600, Moncton, NB, E1C 9Y3
(506) 867-3202
Emp Here 50
SIC 8099 Health and allied services, nec

D-U-N-S 24-119-1811   (BR)
TORONTO-DOMINION BANK, THE
TD CANADA TRUST
(Suby of Toronto-Dominion Bank, The)
860 Main St, Moncton, NB, E1C 1G2
(506) 853-4370
Emp Here 25
SIC 6021 National commercial banks

D-U-N-S 25-418-0334   (BR)
UNITED PARCEL SERVICE CANADA LTD
UPS
1 Factory Lane Suite 200, Moncton, NB, E1C 9M3
(506) 877-4929
Emp Here 250
SIC 7389 Business services, nec

D-U-N-S 25-134-0295   (BR)
UNITED PARCEL SERVICE CANADA LTD
UPS
77 Foundry St, Moncton, NB, E1C 5H7
(506) 877-6657
Emp Here 200
SIC 4212 Local trucking, without storage

D-U-N-S 24-174-1136   (BR)
VALUE VILLAGE STORES, INC
(Suby of Savers, Inc.)
15 Plaza Blvd, Moncton, NB, E1C 0E8
(506) 382-3003
Emp Here 43
SIC 5399 Miscellaneous general merchandise

D-U-N-S 20-025-7454   (BR)

VICTORIAN ORDER OF NURSES FOR CANADA
VON MONCTON DISTRICT
1224 Mountain Rd Suite 6, Moncton, NB, E1C 2T6
(506) 857-9115
Emp Here 20
SIC 8082 Home health care services

D-U-N-S 20-618-2339   (SL)
VITO'S PIZZERIA FOOD PRODUCTION LTD
VITO'S
726 Mountain Rd, Moncton, NB, E1C 2P9
(506) 858-5000
Emp Here 150   Sales 6,289,900
SIC 5812 Eating places
 George Georgoudis
Pr Pr Constantin Georgoudis
Fin Ex Peter Georgoudis

D-U-N-S 24-103-2171   (BR)
WAL-MART CANADA CORP
25 Plaza Blvd Suite 3659, Moncton, NB, E1C 0G3
(506) 853-7394
Emp Here 215
SIC 5311 Department stores

D-U-N-S 24-122-1311   (BR)
WE CARE HEALTH SERVICES INC
WE CARE HOME HEALTH SERVICES
236 St George St Suite 110, Moncton, NB, E1C 1W1
(506) 384-2273
Emp Here 84
SIC 8093 Specialty outpatient clinics, nec

D-U-N-S 25-963-1737   (BR)
WESTERN INVENTORY SERVICE LTD
WIS
640 Mountain Rd Suite 6, Moncton, NB, E1C 2P3
(506) 857-2800
Emp Here 20
SIC 7389 Business services, nec

D-U-N-S 25-985-8454   (BR)
WINNERS MERCHANTS INTERNATIONAL L.P.
WINNERS
(Suby of The TJX Companies Inc)
35 Plaza Blvd, Moncton, NB, E1C 0E8
(506) 859-8981
Emp Here 40
SIC 5651 Family clothing stores

Moncton, NB E1E

D-U-N-S 20-524-2402   (BR)
4513380 CANADA INC
LIVINGSTON INTERNATIONAL
1010 St George Blvd, Moncton, NB, E1E 4R5
(506) 857-3026
Emp Here 24
SIC 4731 Freight transportation arrangement

D-U-N-S 20-288-1590   (BR)
501420 NB INC
ROYAL LEPAGE ATLANTIC
320b Edinburgh Dr, Moncton, NB, E1E 2L1
(506) 383-3305
Emp Here 60
SIC 6531 Real estate agents and managers

D-U-N-S 24-371-0428   (BR)
ADI LIMITED
40 Henri Dunant St, Moncton, NB, E1E 1E5
(506) 857-8889
Emp Here 40
SIC 8711 Engineering services

D-U-N-S 20-741-8096   (SL)
ACADIA CONSULTANTS AND INSPECTORS LIMITED
ACI

40 Henri Dunant St, Moncton, NB, E1E 1E5
(506) 857-8313
Emp Here 20   Sales 1,751,057
SIC 8711 Engineering services

D-U-N-S 24-338-5742   (BR)
ACTION CAR AND TRUCK ACCESSORIES INC
ACTION FIBERGLASS & MANUFACTURING LTD
200 Horsman Rd, Moncton, NB, E1E 0E8
(506) 877-1237
Emp Here 30
SIC 5531 Auto and home supply stores

D-U-N-S 24-754-7359   (BR)
ALLIED SYSTEMS (CANADA) COMPANY
699 St George Blvd, Moncton, NB, E1E 2C2

Emp Here 40
SIC 4213 Trucking, except local

D-U-N-S 20-813-4445   (HQ)
ALLSCO BUILDING PRODUCTS LTD
(Suby of Groupe Atis Inc)
70 Rideout St, Moncton, NB, E1E 1E2
(506) 853-8080
Emp Here 90   Emp Total 340
Sales 18,167,214
SIC 3089 Plastics products, nec
 Donald Lahanky
Pr Pr Gordon Lahanky
 Terry Lahanky
 Danica Lahanky
VP Fin Karim Bhibah

D-U-N-S 20-020-9294   (HQ)
APEX INDUSTRIES INC
APEX DARTMOUTH DIV OF
(Suby of Apex Inc)
100 Millennium Blvd, Moncton, NB, E1E 2G8
(506) 857-1677
Emp Here 180   Emp Total 2
Sales 29,257,241
SIC 3442 Metal doors, sash, and trim
 Stephen Stultz
Pr Pr H Jack Stultz

D-U-N-S 20-580-0472   (BR)
ARBOR MEMORIAL SERVICES INC
FAIR HAVEN MEMORIAL GARDENS
1167 Salisbury Rd, Moncton, NB, E1E 3V9
(506) 858-9470
Emp Here 20
SIC 6531 Real estate agents and managers

D-U-N-S 25-357-5112   (BR)
ARMOUR TRANSPORT INC
ARMOUR TRANSPORTATION SYSTEMS
350 English Dr Suite 905, Moncton, NB, E1E 3Y9
(506) 861-0270
Emp Here 47
SIC 4225 General warehousing and storage

D-U-N-S 20-445-7709   (HQ)
ARMOUR TRANSPORT INC
ARMOUR TRANSPORTATION SYSTEMS
689 Edinburgh Dr, Moncton, NB, E1E 2L4
(506) 857-0205
Emp Here 800   Emp Total 2,000
Sales 214,066,694
SIC 4213 Trucking, except local
Pr Pr Wesley Armour
VP Alban Gaudet
VP Mike Gaudet
VP David Miller
VP Don Rawle
VP Wayne Wood
Dir Victoria Armour
 Norm Bourque
 Ken Mutter

D-U-N-S 24-422-4205   (BR)
ARMOUR TRANSPORT INC
ARMOUR TRANSPORTATION SYSTEMS
244 Edinburgh Dr, Moncton, NB, E1E 4C7

Emp Here 20
SIC 4213 Trucking, except local

D-U-N-S 20-813-2522   (HQ)
ATLANTIC COMPRESSED AIR LTD
(*Suby of* Atlantic Compressed Air Ltd)
484 Edinburgh Dr, Moncton, NB, E1E 2L1
(506) 858-9500
Emp Here 20   Emp Total 25
Sales 5,936,673
SIC 5084 Industrial machinery and equipment
Pr Pr Richard Eusanio
Dir Carole Landry
Dir Tom Bourgeois

D-U-N-S 25-495-5552   (BR)
ATLANTIC WHOLESALERS LTD
REAL ATLANTIC SUPERSTORE, THE
100 Baig Blvd, Moncton, NB, E1E 1C8
(506) 852-2000
Emp Here 150
SIC 5141 Groceries, general line

D-U-N-S 25-483-6174   (BR)
ATLANTIC WHOLESALERS LTD
ATLANTIC CASH & CARRY
520 St George Blvd, Moncton, NB, E1E 2B5
(506) 852-2139
Emp Here 25
SIC 5141 Groceries, general line

D-U-N-S 20-287-2847   (BR)
BAYSHORE HEALTHCARE LTD.
BAYSHORE HOME HEALTH
50 Driscoll Cres Suite 201, Moncton, NB, E1E 3R8
(506) 857-9992
Emp Here 79
SIC 8082 Home health care services

D-U-N-S 25-742-4390   (BR)
CHEP CANADA INC
CHEP
145 English Dr, Moncton, NB, E1E 3X3
(506) 858-8393
Emp Here 30
SIC 7359 Equipment rental and leasing, nec

D-U-N-S 24-356-5707   (BR)
CASCADES CANADA ULC
NORAMPAC, DIV OF
232 Baig Blvd, Moncton, NB, E1E 1C8
(506) 869-2200
Emp Here 150
SIC 2653 Corrugated and solid fiber boxes

D-U-N-S 20-580-6271   (BR)
CLARICA MEEL HOLDINGS LIMITED
SUN LIFE FINANCIAL
1133 St George Blvd Suite 400, Moncton, NB, E1E 4E1
(506) 857-3663
Emp Here 20
SIC 6311 Life insurance

D-U-N-S 20-548-7218   (BR)
COAST TIRE & AUTO SERVICE LTD
(*Suby of* Coast Tire & Auto Service Ltd)
258 Baig Blvd, Moncton, NB, E1E 1C8

Emp Here 20
SIC 3011 Tires and inner tubes

D-U-N-S 24-804-5460   (BR)
COCA-COLA REFRESHMENTS CANADA COMPANY
(*Suby of* The Coca-Cola Company)
66 Arsenault Crt, Moncton, NB, E1E 3X8
(506) 855-6525
Emp Here 60
SIC 4225 General warehousing and storage

D-U-N-S 24-262-4088   (BR)
COMPAGNIE DES CHEMINS DE FER NATIONAUX DU CANADA
CN ATLANTIC ZONE
255 Hump Yard Rd, Moncton, NB, E1E 4S3

(506) 853-2866
Emp Here 150
SIC 4231 Trucking terminal facilities

D-U-N-S 25-610-7228   (BR)
COREY CRAIG LTD
TIM HORTONS
750 St George Blvd, Moncton, NB, E1E 2C6
(506) 862-7636
Emp Here 21
SIC 5812 Eating places

D-U-N-S 20-356-3411   (BR)
COREY CRAIG LTD
TIM HORTONS
1840 Main St, Moncton, NB, E1E 4S7
(506) 862-7658
Emp Here 30
SIC 5812 Eating places

D-U-N-S 20-290-0176   (BR)
COUNTERFORCE CORPORATION
(*Suby of* United Technologies Corporation)
1077 St George Blvd, Moncton, NB, E1E 4C9
(506) 862-5500
Emp Here 200
SIC 7382 Security systems services

D-U-N-S 24-473-5411   (BR)
ECONOMICAL MUTUAL INSURANCE COMPANY
ECONOMICAL MUTUAL INSURANCE GROUP
1600 Main St Suite 200, Moncton, NB, E1E 1G5
(506) 857-2211
Emp Here 36
SIC 6331 Fire, marine, and casualty insurance

D-U-N-S 25-223-5353   (BR)
EMCO CORPORATION
SUMNER PLUMBING SUPPLY, DIV OF
1180 St George Blvd Suite 22, Moncton, NB, E1E 4K7
(506) 853-1440
Emp Here 40
SIC 5074 Plumbing and heating equipment and supplies (hydronics)

D-U-N-S 20-913-4035   (BR)
FAIRMONT HOTELS & RESORTS INC
2081 Main St, Moncton, NB, E1E 1J2
(506) 877-3025
Emp Here 300
SIC 7389 Business services, nec

D-U-N-S 24-132-1439   (BR)
FARM CREDIT CANADA
FCC
1133 St George Blvd Suite 200, Moncton, NB, E1E 4E1
(506) 851-6595
Emp Here 60
SIC 6159 Miscellaneous business credit institutions

D-U-N-S 25-400-3775   (BR)
GEMTEC LIMITED
GEMTEC
77 Rooney Cres, Moncton, NB, E1E 4M4
(506) 858-7180
Emp Here 50
SIC 8711 Engineering services

D-U-N-S 25-999-5488   (BR)
GOODFELLOW INC
660 Edinburgh Dr, Moncton, NB, E1E 4C6
(506) 857-2134
Emp Here 22
SIC 5031 Lumber, plywood, and millwork

D-U-N-S 24-628-7049   (SL)
GREYSTONE ENERGY SYSTEMS INC
(*Suby of* Greystone Industries Ltd)
150 English Dr, Moncton, NB, E1E 4G7
(506) 853-3057
Emp Here 78   Sales 4,888,367
SIC 3822 Environmental controls

D-U-N-S 25-308-4958   (BR)
HOYT'S MOVING & STORAGE LIMITED
RONCO TRANSPORTATION
227 Henri Dunant St, Moncton, NB, E1E 1E4
(506) 383-4698
Emp Here 22
SIC 4213 Trucking, except local

D-U-N-S 20-287-5915   (BR)
LABATT BREWING COMPANY LIMITED
INBEV
180 Henri Dunant St, Moncton, NB, E1E 1E6
(506) 852-2583
Emp Here 21
SIC 2082 Malt beverages

D-U-N-S 25-293-2355   (BR)
LOUNSBURY COMPANY LIMITED
LOUNSBURY TRUCK CENTRE
725 St George Blvd, Moncton, NB, E1E 2C2
(506) 857-4345
Emp Here 51
SIC 5511 New and used car dealers

D-U-N-S 20-554-4906   (BR)
MAPLE LEAF FOODS INC
144 Edinburgh Dr, Moncton, NB, E1E 2K7
(506) 387-4734
Emp Here 50
SIC 2011 Meat packing plants

D-U-N-S 24-348-0790   (BR)
MEDIAS TRANSCONTINENTAL S.E.N.C.
425 Edinburgh Dr, Moncton, NB, E1E 2L2

Emp Here 45
SIC 2711 Newspapers

D-U-N-S 20-268-6791   (BR)
MONCTON, CITY OF
MONCTON FIRE DEPT ADMINISTRATION OFFICE
800 St George Blvd, Moncton, NB, E1E 2C7
(506) 857-8800
Emp Here 120
SIC 7389 Business services, nec

D-U-N-S 25-483-2538   (BR)
MONCTON, CITY OF
CODIAC TRANSIT
140 Millennium Blvd, Moncton, NB, E1E 2G8
(506) 857-2008
Emp Here 86
SIC 4131 Intercity and rural bus transportation

D-U-N-S 25-309-1276   (BR)
NEWCAP INC
C103
27 Arsenault Crt, Moncton, NB, E1E 4J8
(506) 858-5525
Emp Here 36
SIC 4832 Radio broadcasting stations

D-U-N-S 20-272-0590   (BR)
ORKIN CANADA CORPORATION
ORKIN PCO SERVICES
(*Suby of* Rollins, Inc.)
305 Baig Blvd, Moncton, NB, E1E 1E1
(506) 857-0870
Emp Here 27
SIC 7342 Disinfecting and pest control services

D-U-N-S 24-628-7148   (BR)
POLE STAR TRANSPORT INCORPORATED
POLE STAR LONG HAUL
689 Edinburgh Dr, Moncton, NB, E1E 2L4
(506) 859-7025
Emp Here 100
SIC 4213 Trucking, except local

D-U-N-S 25-501-0720   (BR)
QUALITY CONCRETE LIMITED
QUALITY CONCRETE
648 Edinburgh Dr, Moncton, NB, E1E 4C6
(506) 857-8093
Emp Here 20
SIC 3273 Ready-mixed concrete

D-U-N-S 25-097-2239   (SL)
R.G. MACLEOD ENTERPRISES LTD
1667 Berry Mills Rd, Moncton, NB, E1E 4R7

Emp Here 45   Sales 7,165,680
SIC 4213 Trucking, except local
Pr Pr Robert Macleod

D-U-N-S 20-020-9997   (HQ)
ROBERT K. BUZZELL LIMITED
ATLANTIC AIR-COOLED ENGINES DIV
254 Horsman Rd, Moncton, NB, E1E 0E8
(506) 853-0936
Emp Here 45   Emp Total 110
Sales 6,712,384
SIC 7699 Repair services, nec
Pr Pr Robert Buzzell
 Jennifer Buzzell

D-U-N-S 24-129-7238   (BR)
ROYAL MUTUAL FUNDS INC
(*Suby of* Royal Bank Of Canada)
1199 St George Blvd, Moncton, NB, E1E 4N4
(506) 864-7000
Emp Here 60
SIC 6211 Security brokers and dealers

D-U-N-S 25-242-9691   (BR)
SCHOOL BOARD DISTRICT 01
SAINTE BERNADETTE SCHOOL
46 Upton St, Moncton, NB, E1E 3Z1
(506) 856-2731
Emp Here 40
SIC 8211 Elementary and secondary schools

D-U-N-S 20-710-0616   (BR)
SCHOOL DISTRICT 2
HILLCREST SCHOOL
60 Parlee Dr, Moncton, NB, E1E 3B3
(506) 856-3419
Emp Here 50
SIC 8211 Elementary and secondary schools

D-U-N-S 25-241-8744   (BR)
SCHOOL DISTRICT 2
BESSBOROUGH SCHOOL
93 Bessborough Ave, Moncton, NB, E1E 1P6
(506) 856-3404
Emp Here 40
SIC 8211 Elementary and secondary schools

D-U-N-S 25-241-8900   (BR)
SCHOOL DISTRICT 2
BERNICE MACNAUGHTON HIGH SCHOOL
999 St George Blvd, Moncton, NB, E1E 2C9
(506) 856-3469
Emp Here 72
SIC 8211 Elementary and secondary schools

D-U-N-S 25-354-3367   (SL)
SOLOMON HOLDINGS INC
SERVICEMASTER CONTRACT SERVICES OF MONCTON
209 Edinburgh Dr, Moncton, NB, E1E 2K9
(506) 388-4884
Emp Here 65   Sales 1,896,978
SIC 7349 Building maintenance services, nec

D-U-N-S 20-769-3883   (BR)
UAP INC
NAPA AUTO PARTS
(*Suby of* Genuine Parts Company)
325 Edinburgh Dr, Moncton, NB, E1E 4A6
(506) 857-0575
Emp Here 65
SIC 5013 Motor vehicle supplies and new parts

D-U-N-S 24-116-4263   (BR)
UTC FIRE & SECURITY CANADA
(*Suby of* United Technologies Corporation)
173 Henri Dunant St, Moncton, NB, E1E 1E4
(506) 857-9224
Emp Here 20
SIC 1711 Plumbing, heating, air-conditioning

D-U-N-S 24-628-8419   (BR)
UNI-SELECT INC

80 Rooney Cres, Moncton, NB, E1E 4M3
(506) 857-8150
Emp Here 40
SIC 5013 Motor vehicle supplies and new parts

D-U-N-S 25-207-5247   (BR)
WAWANESA MUTUAL INSURANCE COMPANY, THE
(*Suby* of Wawanesa Mutual Insurance Company, The)
1010 St George Blvd, Moncton, NB, E1E 4R5
(506) 853-1010
Emp Here 76
SIC 6331 Fire, marine, and casualty insurance

D-U-N-S 24-556-3692   (BR)
WESTERN INVENTORY SERVICE LTD
WIS INTERNATIONAL
607 St George Blvd Unit 110, Moncton, NB, E1E 2C2
(506) 857-2800
Emp Here 20
SIC 7389 Business services, nec

Moncton, NB E1G

D-U-N-S 20-492-6203   (BR)
446987 ONTARIO INC
BOMBAY COMPANY, THE
(*Suby* of Benix & Co. Inc)
78 Wyse St, Moncton, NB, E1G 0Z5
(506) 383-3358
Emp Here 20
SIC 5712 Furniture stores

D-U-N-S 24-243-8971   (BR)
AMSTEL INVESTMENTS INC
AMSTERDAM INN & SUITES
2550 Mountain Rd, Moncton, NB, E1G 1B4
(506) 383-5050
Emp Here 20
SIC 7011 Hotels and motels

D-U-N-S 25-483-6489   (BR)
ATLANTIC WHOLESALERS LTD
REAL ATLANTIC SUPERSTORE
89 Trinity Dr, Moncton, NB, E1G 2J7
(506) 383-4919
Emp Here 160
SIC 5411 Grocery stores

D-U-N-S 25-373-3844   (BR)
CLEVE'S SPORTING GOODS LIMITED
CLEVE'S SOURCE FOR SPORTS
125 Trinity Dr, Moncton, NB, E1G 2J7
(506) 855-2040
Emp Here 20
SIC 5941 Sporting goods and bicycle shops

D-U-N-S 20-349-3395   (BR)
COREY CRAIG LTD
TIM HORTONS
1810 Mountain Rd, Moncton, NB, E1G 1A9
(506) 862-7651
Emp Here 40
SIC 5461 Retail bakeries

D-U-N-S 25-097-2106   (BR)
COSTCO WHOLESALE CANADA LTD
(*Suby* of Costco Wholesale Corporation)
25 Trinity Dr Suite 217, Moncton, NB, E1G 2J7
(506) 858-7959
Emp Here 130
SIC 5399 Miscellaneous general merchandise

D-U-N-S 20-753-6314   (BR)
DAY & ROSS INC
623 Mapleton Rd, Moncton, NB, E1G 2K5
(506) 856-6537
Emp Here 100
SIC 4213 Trucking, except local

D-U-N-S 20-752-4096   (BR)
EMPIRE THEATRES LIMITED

125 Trinity Dr, Moncton, NB, E1G 2J7
(506) 857-8903
Emp Here 20
SIC 7832 Motion picture theaters, except drive-in

D-U-N-S 20-294-5119   (SL)
EXXONMOBIL BUSINESS SUPPORT CENTRE CANADA ULC
95 Boundary Dr, Moncton, NB, E1G 5C6
(800) 567-3776
Emp Here 1,100   *Sales* 217,610,250
SIC 8742 Management consulting services
Pr Brian Cormier

D-U-N-S 20-790-2425   (BR)
GROUPE JEAN COUTU (PJC) INC, LE
(*Suby* of 3958230 Canada Inc)
1789 Mountain Rd, Moncton, NB, E1G 5C4
(506) 387-9001
Emp Here 35
SIC 5912 Drug stores and proprietary stores

D-U-N-S 25-373-4693   (BR)
J. D. IRVING, LIMITED
KENT BUILDING SUPPLIES, DIV OF
(*Suby* of J. D. Irving, Limited)
55 Trinity Dr, Moncton, NB, E1G 2J7
(506) 862-3400
Emp Here 130
SIC 5211 Lumber and other building materials

D-U-N-S 25-881-5463   (BR)
MARITIME-ONTARIO FREIGHT LINES LIMITED
M.O. FREIGHT WORKS
11 Bill Slater Dr, Moncton, NB, E1G 5X5
(506) 857-2297
Emp Here 20
SIC 4731 Freight transportation arrangement

D-U-N-S 20-732-0578   (BR)
MCDONALD'S   RESTAURANTS   OF CANADA LIMITED
MCDONALD'S
(*Suby* of McDonald's Corporation)
10 Ensley Dr, Moncton, NB, E1G 2W6
(506) 862-1620
Emp Here 20
SIC 5812 Eating places

D-U-N-S 24-311-4019   (BR)
MCDONALD'S   RESTAURANTS   OF CANADA LIMITED
MCDONALD'S
(*Suby* of McDonald's Corporation)
10 Ensley Dr, Moncton, NB, E1G 2W6
(506) 862-1616
Emp Here 74
SIC 5812 Eating places

D-U-N-S 20-298-3495   (BR)
PRINCESS AUTO LTD
PRINCESS AUTO
50 Cabela'S Crt, Moncton, NB, E1G 5V7
(506) 388-4400
Emp Here 50
SIC 5251 Hardware stores

D-U-N-S 25-080-2675   (BR)
SCHOOL DISTRICT 2
EVERGREEN PARK SCHOOL
333 Evergreen Dr, Moncton, NB, E1G 2J2
(506) 856-3476
Emp Here 70
SIC 8211 Elementary and secondary schools

D-U-N-S 24-523-0938   (SL)
SONCO GAMING NEW BRUNSWICK LIMITED PARTNERSHIP
CASINO NEW NOUVEAU-BRUNSWICK
21 Casino Dr, Moncton, NB, E1G 0R7
(506) 859-7770
Emp Here 350   *Sales* 18,191,271
SIC 7011 Hotels and motels
Genl Mgr Dan Wilson

D-U-N-S 25-498-9213   (BR)

STAPLES CANADA INC
STAPLES THE BUSINESS DEPOT
(*Suby* of Staples, Inc.)
125 Trinity Dr, Moncton, NB, E1G 2J7
(506) 863-1400
Emp Here 50
SIC 5943 Stationery stores

D-U-N-S 20-860-4228   (BR)
WINNERS MERCHANTS INTERNATIONAL L.P.
HOME SENSE
(*Suby* of The TJX Companies Inc)
107 Trinity Dr, Moncton, NB, E1G 2J7
(506) 860-6700
Emp Here 25
SIC 5651 Family clothing stores

Moncton, NB E1H

D-U-N-S 24-994-0826   (HQ)
AL-PACK ENTERPRISES LTD
60 Commerce St, Moncton, NB, E1H 0A5
(506) 852-4262
Emp Here 58   *Emp Total* 60
Sales 11,781,014
SIC 2653 Corrugated and solid fiber boxes
Pr Pr Louis Leblanc

D-U-N-S 24-000-4023   (BR)
ATLANTIC TRACTORS & EQUIPMENT LIMITED
CATERPILLAR
11 Lynds Ave, Moncton, NB, E1H 1X6
(506) 852-4545
Emp Here 33
SIC 5082 Construction and mining machinery

D-U-N-S 24-319-9804   (HQ)
EAST COAST INTERNATIONAL TRUCKS INC
100 Urquhart Ave, Moncton, NB, E1H 2R5
(506) 857-2857
Emp Here 55   *Emp Total* 12,400
Sales 37,647,721
SIC 5012 Automobiles and other motor vehicles
  Daniel Tkachuk
  Michael Green
  Paul Grzemski

D-U-N-S 20-287-7713   (BR)
HAWKINS TRUCK MART LTD
PETERBILT ATLANTIC
565 Venture Dr, Moncton, NB, E1H 2P4
(506) 854-7383
Emp Here 30
SIC 5511 New and used car dealers

D-U-N-S 24-323-6101   (HQ)
IGT CANADA SOLUTIONS ULC
328 Urquhart Ave, Moncton, NB, E1H 2R6
(506) 878-6000
Emp Here 417   *Emp Total* 1
Sales 36,188,507
SIC 3999 Manufacturing industries, nec
Pr Victor Duarte
  A. Lavaz Watson

D-U-N-S 24-418-6255   (BR)
IRVING PERSONAL CARE LIMITED
(*Suby* of J. D. Irving, Limited)
200 Harrisville Blvd, Moncton, NB, E1H 3N5
(506) 857-7777
Emp Here 105
SIC 2399 Fabricated textile products, nec

D-U-N-S 25-866-8029   (BR)
J. D. IRVING, LIMITED
CHANDLER, DIV. OF
(*Suby* of J. D. Irving, Limited)
365 Frenette Ave, Moncton, NB, E1H 3S5
(506) 859-5970
Emp Here 20

SIC 5112 Stationery and office supplies

D-U-N-S 20-025-7967   (BR)
KOHL & FRISCH LIMITED
(*Suby* of Kohl & Frisch Limited)
255 Urquhart Ave, Moncton, NB, E1H 2R4
(506) 382-8222
Emp Here 20
SIC 5122 Drugs, proprietaries, and sundries

D-U-N-S 24-804-1501   (SL)
MARITIME HYDRAULIC REPAIR CENTRE (1997) LTD
355 Macnaughton Ave, Moncton, NB, E1H 2J9
(506) 858-0393
Emp Here 68   *Sales* 4,158,760
SIC 7699 Repair services, nec

D-U-N-S 25-485-4508   (BR)
MARITIME-ONTARIO FREIGHT LINES LIMITED
FREIGHTWORKS
95 Urquhart Ave, Moncton, NB, E1H 2R4
(506) 857-2297
Emp Here 20
SIC 4731 Freight transportation arrangement

D-U-N-S 20-017-1895   (BR)
MATRIX LOGISTICS SERVICES LIMITED
MATRIX
10 Deware Dr Suite 1, Moncton, NB, E1H 2S6
(506) 863-1300
Emp Here 100
SIC 4225 General warehousing and storage

D-U-N-S 20-107-2605   (BR)
MIDLAND TRANSPORT LIMITED
MIDLAND REFRIGERATED DISTRIBUTION CENTRE
(*Suby* of J. D. Irving, Limited)
435 Macnaughton Ave, Moncton, NB, E1H 2J9
(506) 862-3119
Emp Here 25
SIC 4222 Refrigerated warehousing and storage

D-U-N-S 24-341-0672   (BR)
MOLSON CANADA 2005
MOLSON CANADA
(*Suby* of Molson Coors Brewing Company)
170 Macnaughton Ave, Moncton, NB, E1H 3L9
(506) 389-4355
Emp Here 35
SIC 5181 Beer and ale

D-U-N-S 25-299-2193   (BR)
NEW BRUNSWICK POWER CORPORATION
160 Urquhart Ave, Moncton, NB, E1H 2R5
(506) 857-4515
Emp Here 100
SIC 4911 Electric services

D-U-N-S 20-298-4535   (BR)
PRIME MATERIAL HANDLING EQUIPMENT LIMITED
180 Commerce St, Moncton, NB, E1H 2G2
(506) 388-8811
Emp Here 23
SIC 5084 Industrial machinery and equipment

D-U-N-S 24-122-6815   (BR)
RYDER TRUCK RENTAL CANADA LTD
RYDER INTEGRATED LOGISTICS, DIV OF
(*Suby* of Ryder System, Inc.)
525 Venture Dr, Moncton, NB, E1H 2P4

Emp Here 30
SIC 7513 Truck rental and leasing, no drivers

D-U-N-S 20-267-3500   (BR)
S.L.H. TRANSPORT INC
275 Macnaughton Ave, Moncton, NB, E1H 2S7

Emp Here 100
SIC 4213 Trucking, except local

D-U-N-S 25-322-2905   (BR)
SHOPPERS DRUG MART INC
10 Deware Dr, Moncton, NB, E1H 2S6
(506) 857-3360
Emp Here 30
SIC 8741 Management services

D-U-N-S 25-077-0971   (BR)
STANTEC CONSULTING LTD
115 Harrisville Blvd, Moncton, NB, E1H 3T3
(506) 857-8607
Emp Here 26
SIC 8711 Engineering services

D-U-N-S 24-174-1391   (BR)
SUPERIOR PLUS LP
480 Macnaughton Ave, Moncton, NB, E1H 2K1
(506) 388-4304
Emp Here 40
SIC 5984 Liquefied petroleum gas dealers

D-U-N-S 20-555-5472   (BR)
SYSCO CANADA, INC
SYSCO FOOD SERVICES OF ATLANTIC CANADA
(*Suby of* Sysco Corporation)
460 Macnaughton Ave, Moncton, NB, E1H 2K1
(506) 857-8115
Emp Here 100
SIC 5141 Groceries, general line

Moncton, NB E1Z

D-U-N-S 20-177-3285   (BR)
ATLANTIC RETAIL CO-OPERATIVES FEDERATION
CO-OP ATLANTIC
92 Halifax St, Moncton, NB, E1Z 9E2
(506) 858-6334
Emp Here 32
SIC 2048 Prepared feeds, nec

Nackawic, NB E6G

D-U-N-S 24-126-4105   (BR)
SCHOOL DISTRICT 14
NACKAWIC SENIOR HIGH SCHOOL
(*Suby of* School District 14)
30 Landegger Dr, Nackawic, NB, E6G 1E9
(506) 575-6020
Emp Here 30
SIC 8211 Elementary and secondary schools

D-U-N-S 25-241-7910   (BR)
SCHOOL DISTRICT 14
NACKAWIC ELEMENTARY SCHOOL
(*Suby of* School District 14)
110 Mcnair Dr, Nackawic, NB, E6G 1A8
(506) 575-6000
Emp Here 30
SIC 8211 Elementary and secondary schools

Neguac, NB E9G
Northumberland County

D-U-N-S 24-114-5569   (BR)
DISTRICT SCOLAIRE FRANCOPHONE NORD-EST
CSC LA FONTAINE
700 Rue Principale, Neguac, NB, E9G 1N4
(506) 776-3808
Emp Here 80
SIC 8299 Schools and educational services, nec

New Maryland, NB E3C

D-U-N-S 25-241-7431   (BR)
ANGLOPHONE WEST SCHOOL DISTRICT (ASD-W)
NEW MARYLAND ELEMENTARY SCHOOL
75 Clover St, New Maryland, NB, E3C 1C5
(506) 453-5420
Emp Here 60
SIC 8211 Elementary and secondary schools

Northampton, NB E7N

D-U-N-S 20-698-6171   (SL)
JOLLY FARMER TRANSPORT INC
56 Crabbe Rd, Northampton, NB, E7N 1R6
(506) 325-3850
Emp Here 20   *Sales* 2,858,628
SIC 4213 Trucking, except local

Notre-Dame, NB E4V
Kent County

D-U-N-S 24-261-3990   (SL)
ALLAIN EQUIPMENT MANUFACTURING LTD
(*Suby of* 056623 N.B. Ltd)
577 Route 535, Notre-Dame, NB, E4V 2K4
(506) 576-6436
Emp Here 60   *Sales* 6,028,800
SIC 3599 Industrial machinery, nec
Pr Pr Jacques Goguen
VP VP Bruno Lagace
Off Mgr Lisa Cormier

D-U-N-S 25-241-7944   (BR)
DISTRICT SCOLAIRE 11
ECOLE NOTRE DAME
(*Suby of* District Scolaire 11)
3860 Route 115, Notre-Dame, NB, E4V 2J2
(506) 576-5001
Emp Here 25
SIC 8211 Elementary and secondary schools

D-U-N-S 24-834-1190   (SL)
FUTURE DOORS LTD
4009 Route 115, Notre-Dame, NB, E4V 2G2
(506) 576-9769
Emp Here 60   *Sales* 4,377,642
SIC 1751 Carpentry work

Old Ridge, NB E3L
Charlotte County

D-U-N-S 25-173-2855   (BR)
SCHOOL DISTRICT NO 10
ST STEPHEN HIGH SCHOOL
(*Suby of* School District No 10)
9372 Route 3, Old Ridge, NB, E3L 4X6
(506) 466-7312
Emp Here 60
SIC 8211 Elementary and secondary schools

Oromocto, NB E2V
Sundbury County

D-U-N-S 25-986-2795   (BR)
ATLANTIC WHOLESALERS LTD
REAL ATLANTIC SUPERSTORE, THE
1198 Onondaga St, Oromocto, NB, E2V 1B8
(506) 357-5982
Emp Here 140
SIC 5411 Grocery stores

D-U-N-S 25-296-2865   (BR)
BANK OF NOVA SCOTIA, THE
SCOTIABANK
1024 Onondaga St Suite 80044, Oromocto, NB, E2V 1B8
(506) 357-8441
Emp Here 20
SIC 6021 National commercial banks

D-U-N-S 20-529-0823   (BR)
DEFENCE CONSTRUCTION (1951) LIMITED
DEFENCE CONSTRUCTION CANADA
Building B-71, Oromocto, NB, E2V 4J5
(506) 357-6291
Emp Here 28
SIC 8741 Management services

D-U-N-S 20-082-6571   (BR)
MCDONALD'S RESTAURANTS OF CANADA LIMITED
MCDONALD'S
(*Suby of* McDonald's Corporation)
100 Macdonald Ave, Oromocto, NB, E2V 2R2
(506) 357-9841
Emp Here 60
SIC 5812 Eating places

D-U-N-S 20-570-1167   (BR)
PUBLIC SAFETY CANADA
CANADIAN FORCES HOUSING AGENCY
66 Broad Rd Suite 204, Oromocto, NB, E2V 1C2
(506) 422-2000
Emp Here 20
SIC 6531 Real estate agents and managers

D-U-N-S 20-288-7183   (BR)
SCHOOL BOARD DISTRICT 01
ECOLE ARC-EN-CIEL
95 Drummond Dr, Oromocto, NB, E2V 2A6
(506) 357-4080
Emp Here 40
SIC 8211 Elementary and secondary schools

D-U-N-S 24-532-5964   (BR)
SOBEYS CAPITAL INCORPORATED
SOBEYS DISTRIBUTION CENTRE
1 Lewis St, Oromocto, NB, E2V 4K5
(506) 357-9831
Emp Here 165
SIC 5411 Grocery stores

D-U-N-S 20-806-2450   (BR)
SOBEYS CAPITAL INCORPORATED
SOBEYS STORE 860
375 Miramichi Rd Suite 860, Oromocto, NB, E2V 4T4
(506) 446-5030
Emp Here 25
SIC 5411 Grocery stores

D-U-N-S 24-122-7730   (BR)
VALCOM CONSULTING GROUP INC
281 Restigouche Rd Suite 204, Oromocto, NB, E2V 2H2
(506) 357-5835
Emp Here 110
SIC 8748 Business consulting, nec

Paquetville, NB E8R
Gloucester County

D-U-N-S 25-841-8797   (SL)
MANOIR EDITH B. PINET INC
1189 Rue Des Fondateurs, Paquetville, NB, E8R 1A9
(506) 764-2444
Emp Here 53   *Sales* 2,480,664
SIC 8059 Nursing and personal care, nec

Perth-Andover, NB E7H
Victoria County

D-U-N-S 25-597-7209   (BR)
REGIONAL HEALTH AUTHORITY B
NEW BRUNSWICK EXTRA-MURAL PROGRAM
35 F. Tribe Rd, Perth-Andover, NB, E7H 0A8
(506) 273-7222
Emp Here 20
SIC 8011 Offices and clinics of medical doctors

D-U-N-S 20-733-1096   (BR)
REGIONAL HEALTH AUTHORITY NB
REGIONAL HEALTH AUTHORITY B
10 Woodland Hill, Perth-Andover, NB, E7H 5H5
(506) 273-7100
Emp Here 180
SIC 8062 General medical and surgical hospitals

D-U-N-S 25-503-7756   (BR)
SCHOOL DISTRICT 14
PERTH-ANDOVER MIDDLE SCHOOL
(*Suby of* School District 14)
20 Nissen St, Perth-Andover, NB, E7H 3G1
(506) 273-4760
Emp Here 30
SIC 8211 Elementary and secondary schools

Petit-Cap, NB E4N
Westmoreland County

D-U-N-S 20-812-7423   (SL)
LEBLANC, EMILE C. & FILS LTEE
41 Ch Du Quai, Petit-Cap, NB, E4N 2E8

Emp Here 50   *Sales* 7,460,160
SIC 2091 Canned and cured fish and seafoods
Pr Pr Yvon Leblanc
Leo Leblanc

Petit-Rocher, NB E8J

D-U-N-S 25-223-7177   (BR)
CONSEIL SCOLAIRE DISTRICT NO 5
SCOLAIRE LE TOURNESOL
63 Rue Laplante E, Petit-Rocher, NB, E8J 1H4
(506) 542-2609
Emp Here 34
SIC 8211 Elementary and secondary schools

D-U-N-S 20-710-0160   (BR)
CONSEIL SCOLAIRE DISTRICT NO 5
LE DOMAINE ETUDIANT-PETIT-ROCHER
636 Rue Principale, Petit-Rocher, NB, E8J 1T7
(506) 542-2607
Emp Here 40
SIC 8211 Elementary and secondary schools

D-U-N-S 20-815-2231   (SL)
PECHERIES ALFO LTEE, LES
Gd, Petit-Rocher, NB, E8J 3E7

Emp Here 250   *Sales* 38,551,000
SIC 2091 Canned and cured fish and seafoods
Pr Pr Peter Samson

Petitcodiac, NB E4Z

D-U-N-S 20-294-1535   (BR)
IRVING OIL LIMITED
CIRCLE K
16 Smith St, Petitcodiac, NB, E4Z 4W1

---

(506) 756-2567
Emp Here 20
SIC 5411 Grocery stores

D-U-N-S 25-242-0013   (BR)
SCHOOL DISTRICT 2
PETITCODIAC REGIONAL SCHOOL
1 Corey Ave, Petitcodiac, NB, E4Z 4G3
(506) 756-3104
Emp Here 70
SIC 8211 Elementary and secondary schools

Plaster Rock, NB E7G
Victoria County

D-U-N-S 20-713-9721   (SL)
APOSTOLIC PENTICOSTAL CHURCH
APOSTOLIC CHRISTIAN SCHOOL
123 Main St, Plaster Rock, NB, E7G 2H2
(506) 356-8690
Emp Here 50   *Sales* 3,356,192
SIC 8211 Elementary and secondary schools

D-U-N-S 24-127-2608   (BR)
REGIONAL HEALTH AUTHORITY B
TOBIQUE VALLEY HOSPITAL
120 Main St, Plaster Rock, NB, E7G 2E5
(506) 356-6600
Emp Here 50
SIC 8062 General medical and surgical hospitals

D-U-N-S 24-123-1294   (BR)
SEARS CANADA INC
200 Main St, Plaster Rock, NB, E7G 2E2

Emp Here 50
SIC 5311 Department stores

D-U-N-S 24-736-1723   (BR)
TWIN RIVERS PAPER COMPANY INC
31 Renous Rd Suite 36, Plaster Rock, NB, E7G 4B5
(506) 356-4132
Emp Here 200
SIC 2421 Sawmills and planing mills, general

Pointe-Sapin, NB E9A
Kent County

D-U-N-S 24-303-3446   (BR)
A S B GREENWORLD LTD
200 Daigle Ch, Pointe-Sapin, NB, E9A 1T6
(506) 876-3937
Emp Here 20
SIC 2879 Agricultural chemicals, nec

Pont-Landry, NB E1X
Charlotte County

D-U-N-S 20-710-0491   (BR)
DISTRICT SCOLAIRE FRANCOPHONE NORD-EST
LAPASSERELLE
5067 Route 160, Pont-Landry, NB, E1X 2V5
(506) 394-3600
Emp Here 50
SIC 8211 Elementary and secondary schools

Port Elgin, NB E4M
Westmoreland County

D-U-N-S 20-651-8727   (BR)
SCHOOL DISTRICT 2
PORT ELGIN REGIONAL SCHOOL
33 Moore Rd, Port Elgin, NB, E4M 2E6

---

(506) 538-2121
Emp Here 20
SIC 8211 Elementary and secondary schools

Quispamsis, NB E2E

D-U-N-S 24-470-3471   (BR)
AMSTEL INVESTMENTS INC
QUALITY INN & SUITES AMSTERDAM
114 Millennium Dr, Quispamsis, NB, E2E 0C6
(506) 849-8050
Emp Here 20
SIC 7011 Hotels and motels

D-U-N-S 20-710-0228   (BR)
ANGLOPHONE SOUTH SCHOOL DISTRICT (ASD-S)
LAKEFIELD ELEMENTARY SCHOOL
9 Kensington Ave, Quispamsis, NB, E2E 2T8
(506) 847-6212
Emp Here 55
SIC 8211 Elementary and secondary schools

D-U-N-S 20-298-0780   (BR)
ANGLOPHONE SOUTH SCHOOL DISTRICT (ASD-S)
KENNEBECASIS VALLEY HIGH SCHOOL
398 Hampton Rd, Quispamsis, NB, E2E 4V5
(506) 847-6200
Emp Here 110
SIC 8211 Elementary and secondary schools

D-U-N-S 20-288-7142   (BR)
ANGLOPHONE SOUTH SCHOOL DISTRICT (ASD-S)
QUISPAMSIS MIDDLE SCHOOL
189 Pettingill Rd, Quispamsis, NB, E2E 3S8
(506) 847-6210
Emp Here 40
SIC 8211 Elementary and secondary schools

D-U-N-S 25-242-3256   (BR)
ANGLOPHONE SOUTH SCHOOL DISTRICT (ASD-S)
QUISPAMSIS ELEMENTARY SCHOOL
(*Suby of* Anglophone South School District (ASD-S))
290 Hampton Rd, Quispamsis, NB, E2E 4N1
(506) 847-6207
Emp Here 40
SIC 8211 Elementary and secondary schools

D-U-N-S 25-986-5855   (BR)
ATLANTIC RETAIL CO-OPERATIVES FEDERATION
CO-OP ATLANTIC
1 Market St, Quispamsis, NB, E2E 4B1
(506) 847-6520
Emp Here 20
SIC 5411 Grocery stores

D-U-N-S 24-761-2125   (BR)
BELFOR (CANADA) INC
BELFOR PROPERTY RESTORATION SERVICES
11 William Crt, Quispamsis, NB, E2E 4B1
(506) 847-4169
Emp Here 30
SIC 1799 Special trade contractors, nec

D-U-N-S 24-376-7097   (BR)
BIRD CONSTRUCTION COMPANY LIMITED
BIRD CONSTRUCTION
120 Millennium Dr Suite 200, Quispamsis, NB, E2E 0C6
(506) 849-2473
Emp Here 30
SIC 1541 Industrial buildings and warehouses

D-U-N-S 20-792-4833   (BR)
MCPORT CITY FOOD SERVICES LIMITED
MCDONALD'S
175 Hampton Rd, Quispamsis, NB, E2E 4J8
(506) 847-9003
Emp Here 56

SIC 5812 Eating places

D-U-N-S 24-248-9115   (SL)
SECURITY ELECTRICAL LTD
17 William Crt, Quispamsis, NB, E2E 4B1
(506) 848-0837
Emp Here 50   *Sales* 4,377,642
SIC 1731 Electrical work

Rexton, NB E4W
Kent County

D-U-N-S 20-024-4098   (BR)
DISTRICT EDUCATION COUNCIL-SCHOOL DISTRICT 16
REXTON ELEMENTARY SCHOOL
(*Suby of* District Education Council-School District 16)
19 School St, Rexton, NB, E4W 2E4
(506) 523-7152
Emp Here 35
SIC 8211 Elementary and secondary schools

D-U-N-S 25-924-5728   (BR)
DISTRICT EDUCATION COUNCIL-SCHOOL DISTRICT 16
BONAR LAW MEMORIAL SCHOOL
(*Suby of* District Education Council-School District 16)
197 Main St, Rexton, NB, E4W 2A9
(506) 523-7160
Emp Here 35
SIC 8211 Elementary and secondary schools

Richibucto, NB E4W
Kent County

D-U-N-S 25-611-4489   (BR)
COREY CRAIG LTD
TIM HORTONS
4 Park Dr, Richibucto, NB, E4W 4G5
(506) 524-9087
Emp Here 30
SIC 5812 Eating places

D-U-N-S 20-710-0558   (BR)
DISTRICT EDUCATION COUNCIL-SCHOOL DISTRICT 16
ELEANOR W GRAHAM MIDDLE SCHOOL
(*Suby of* District Education Council-School District 16)
149 Rue Acadie, Richibucto, NB, E4W 3V5
(506) 523-7970
Emp Here 25
SIC 8211 Elementary and secondary schools

D-U-N-S 20-005-0610   (BR)
DISTRICT SCOLAIRE 11
SOLEIL LEVANT
(*Suby of* District Scolaire 11)
45 Rue Morgan, Richibucto, NB, E4W 4E8
(506) 523-7660
Emp Here 50
SIC 8211 Elementary and secondary schools

D-U-N-S 24-624-0944   (BR)
FERO WASTE & RECYCLING INC
Gd, Richibucto, NB, E4W 5P2
(506) 523-8135
Emp Here 20
SIC 4953 Refuse systems

Richibucto Road, NB E3A

D-U-N-S 20-019-9461   (BR)
CANADA BREAD COMPANY, LIMITED
MAPLE LEAF
135 Melissa St Suite B, Richibucto Road, NB, E3A 6V9

---

(506) 452-8808
Emp Here 20
SIC 5149 Groceries and related products, nec

D-U-N-S 24-261-1242   (SL)
JARDINE TRANSPORT LTD
(*Suby of* A.W. Leil Holdings Limited)
60 Melissa St Unit 1, Richibucto Road, NB, E3A 6W1
(506) 453-1811
Emp Here 35   *Sales* 7,518,800
SIC 4213 Trucking, except local
Pr Dion Cull

D-U-N-S 24-123-1344   (BR)
PARKER KAEFER INC
115 Melissa St Unit 2, Richibucto Road, NB, E3A 6V9
(506) 459-7551
Emp Here 30
SIC 5033 Roofing, siding, and insulation

Riverside-Albert, NB E4H
Albert County

D-U-N-S 25-172-9927   (SL)
FOREST DALE HOME INC
5836 King St, Riverside-Albert, NB, E4H 4B9
(506) 882-3015
Emp Here 60   *Sales* 2,188,821
SIC 8361 Residential care

D-U-N-S 20-654-6397   (BR)
REGIONAL HEALTH AUTHORITY B
ALBERT COUNTY HEALTH & WELLNESS CENTRE
8 Forestdale Rd, Riverside-Albert, NB, E4H 3Y7
(506) 882-3100
Emp Here 20
SIC 8011 Offices and clinics of medical doctors

Riverview, NB E1B

D-U-N-S 24-679-3090   (SL)
AJ HOLDINGS LTD
CANADIAN TIRE
525 Pinewood Rd, Riverview, NB, E1B 0K3
(506) 386-3400
Emp Here 45   *Sales* 7,536,000
SIC 5531 Auto and home supply stores
Pr Alex Joannides

D-U-N-S 24-386-7988   (BR)
ADVANCE SAVINGS CREDIT UNION LIMITED
620 Coverdale Rd Unit 6, Riverview, NB, E1B 3K6
(506) 386-2830
Emp Here 20
SIC 6062 State credit unions

D-U-N-S 20-313-1821   (BR)
ATLANTIC WHOLESALERS LTD
RIVERVIEW SUPERSTORE
425 Coverdale Rd, Riverview, NB, E1B 3K3
(506) 387-5992
Emp Here 200
SIC 5411 Grocery stores

D-U-N-S 20-191-7171   (BR)
CONCENTRIX TECHNOLOGIES SERVICES (CANADA) LIMITED
MINACS GROUP INC, THE
720 Coverdale Rd, Riverview, NB, E1B 3L8
(506) 860-5900
Emp Here 700
SIC 4899 Communication services, nec

D-U-N-S 24-667-0975   (BR)
COREY CRAIG LTD
TIM HORTON'S

---

748 Coverdale Rd Suite 2111, Riverview, NB, E1B 3L2

Emp Here 26
SIC 5461 Retail bakeries

D-U-N-S 25-098-9076 (BR)
GOVERNING COUNCIL OF THE SALVATION ARMY IN CANADA, THE
GOVERNING COUNCIL OF THE SALVATION ARMY IN CANADA, THE
50 Suffolk St, Riverview, NB, E1B 4K6

Emp Here 72
SIC 8051 Skilled nursing care facilities

D-U-N-S 20-349-3379 (BR)
HARVARD RESTAURANTS LTD
WENDY'S
430 Coverdale Rd, Riverview, NB, E1B 3K1
(506) 862-7634
Emp Here 40
SIC 5461 Retail bakeries

D-U-N-S 20-191-3162 (BR)
ICT CANADA MARKETING INC
(*Suby of* Sykes Enterprises Incorporated)
720 Coverdale Rd Unit 9, Riverview, NB, E1B 3L8
(506) 387-9050
Emp Here 600
SIC 7389 Business services, nec

D-U-N-S 20-279-7457 (SL)
M R MARTIN CONSTRUCTION INC
612 Pine Glen Rd, Riverview, NB, E1B 4X2
(506) 387-4070
Emp Here 30   *Sales* 7,234,560
SIC 1623 Water, sewer, and utility lines
Pr James Martin

D-U-N-S 20-311-5378 (SL)
MAID EXEC LTD
10 Dale St, Riverview, NB, E1B 4A9
(506) 387-4146
Emp Here 50   *Sales* 1,459,214
SIC 7349 Building maintenance services, nec

D-U-N-S 24-723-1160 (HQ)
MITTON'S FOOD SERVICE INC
DAIRY QUEEN
(*Suby of* Mitton's Food Service Inc)
264 Coverdale Rd, Riverview, NB, E1B 3J2
(506) 386-5229
Emp Here 25   *Emp Total* 60
Sales 1,824,018
SIC 5812 Eating places

D-U-N-S 25-401-7908 (BR)
NAV CANADA
222 Old Coach Rd, Riverview, NB, E1B 4G2
(506) 867-7151
Emp Here 250
SIC 7389 Business services, nec

D-U-N-S 25-241-9858 (BR)
SCHOOL DISTRICT 2
CLAUDE D TAYLOR ELEMENTARY SCHOOL
200 Whitepine Rd, Riverview, NB, E1B 3L7
(506) 856-3467
Emp Here 41
SIC 8211 Elementary and secondary schools

D-U-N-S 25-241-8702 (BR)
SCHOOL DISTRICT 2
RIVERVIEW MIDDLE SCHOOL
45 Devere Rd, Riverview, NB, E1B 2M4
(506) 856-3449
Emp Here 62
SIC 8211 Elementary and secondary schools

D-U-N-S 25-080-2717 (BR)
SCHOOL DISTRICT 2
RIVERVIEW HIGH SCHOOL
Riverview High School, Riverview, NB, E1B 4H8
(506) 856-3470
Emp Here 70
SIC 8211 Elementary and secondary schools

D-U-N-S 25-241-8462 (BR)
SCHOOL DISTRICT 2
RIVERVIEW EAST SCHOOL
49 Chambers Rd, Riverview, NB, E1B 0P5
(506) 856-3416
Emp Here 60
SIC 8211 Elementary and secondary schools

D-U-N-S 20-025-5573 (BR)
SCHOOL DISTRICT 2
WEST RIVERVIEW ELEMENTARY SCHOOL
684 Coverdale Rd, Riverview, NB, E1B 3K6
(506) 856-3451
Emp Here 38
SIC 8211 Elementary and secondary schools

D-U-N-S 20-710-0640 (BR)
SCHOOL DISTRICT 2
FRANK L. BOWSER
424 Cleveland Ave, Riverview, NB, E1B 1Y2
(506) 856-3450
Emp Here 50
SIC 8211 Elementary and secondary schools

D-U-N-S 24-994-8225 (BR)
SHANNEX INCORPORATED
ROYAL COURT RETIREMENT RESIDENCE
822 Coverdale Rd, Riverview, NB, E1B 4V5
(506) 387-7770
Emp Here 60
SIC 8361 Residential care

D-U-N-S 24-943-6387 (BR)
SOBEYS CAPITAL INCORPORATED
SOBEYS #736
1160 Findlay Blvd, Riverview, NB, E1B 0J6
(506) 386-4616
Emp Here 100
SIC 5411 Grocery stores

D-U-N-S 20-867-8040 (BR)
TOWN OF RIVERVIEW
RIVERVIEW FIRE RESCUE
650 Pinewood Rd, Riverview, NB, E1B 5M7
(506) 387-2020
Emp Here 48
SIC 7389 Business services, nec

Riviere-Verte, NB E7C
Madawaska County

D-U-N-S 20-710-0830 (BR)
DISTRICT SCOLAIRE 3
MGR MATTHIEU MAZEROLLE SCHOOL
4 Rue De L'Ecole, Riviere-Verte, NB, E7C 2R5
(506) 263-3500
Emp Here 30
SIC 8211 Elementary and secondary schools

Robertville, NB E8K
Gloucester County

D-U-N-S 25-485-4409 (SL)
VILLA SORMANY INC, LA
1289 Ch Robertville, Robertville, NB, E8K 2V9
(506) 542-2731
Emp Here 62   *Sales* 2,845,467
SIC 8051 Skilled nursing care facilities

Rogersville, NB E4Y
Northumberland County

D-U-N-S 20-287-2540 (BR)
DISTRICT SCOLAIRE 11
WF BOISVERT ECOLE
(*Suby of* District Scolaire 11)
65 Rue De L'Ecole, Rogersville, NB, E4Y 1V4
(506) 775-2010
Emp Here 27

SIC 8211 Elementary and secondary schools

D-U-N-S 25-485-3955 (SL)
SOCIETE D'HABITATION INC (LA)
FOYER ASSOMPTION
62 Rue Assomption, Rogersville, NB, E4Y 1S5
(506) 775-2040
Emp Here 64   *Sales* 3,465,004
SIC 8051 Skilled nursing care facilities

Rothesay, NB E2E

D-U-N-S 20-312-4669 (BR)
501420 NB INC
ROYAL LEPAGE ATLANTIC
103 Hampton Rd, Rothesay, NB, E2E 3L3
(506) 847-2020
Emp Here 30
SIC 6531 Real estate agents and managers

D-U-N-S 20-536-6946 (BR)
ANGLOPHONE SOUTH SCHOOL DISTRICT (ASD-S)
ROTHESAY ELEMENTARY SCHOOL
230 Eriskay Dr, Rothesay, NB, E2E 5G7
(506) 847-6203
Emp Here 50
SIC 8211 Elementary and secondary schools

D-U-N-S 20-710-0236 (BR)
ANGLOPHONE SOUTH SCHOOL DISTRICT (ASD-S)
ROTHESAY PARK SCHOOL
7 Hampton Rd, Rothesay, NB, E2E 5K8
(506) 847-6201
Emp Here 30
SIC 8211 Elementary and secondary schools

D-U-N-S 20-710-0202 (BR)
ANGLOPHONE SOUTH SCHOOL DISTRICT (ASD-S)
HARRY MILLER MIDDLE SCHOOL
63 Hampton Rd, Rothesay, NB, E2E 5L6
(506) 849-5515
Emp Here 50
SIC 8211 Elementary and secondary schools

D-U-N-S 20-710-0186 (BR)
ANGLOPHONE SOUTH SCHOOL DISTRICT (ASD-S)
ROTHESAY HIGH SCHOOL
61 Hampton Rd, Rothesay, NB, E2E 5L6
(506) 847-6204
Emp Here 50
SIC 8211 Elementary and secondary schools

D-U-N-S 24-956-8007 (SL)
KINGS COUNTY HOMECARE SERVICES LTD
103a Hampton Rd, Rothesay, NB, E2E 3L3
(506) 847-5295
Emp Here 100   *Sales* 5,478,300
SIC 8322 Individual and family services
Pr Pr William Thorne

D-U-N-S 25-299-2110 (BR)
NEW BRUNSWICK POWER CORPORATION
88 Marr Rd Suite 2, Rothesay, NB, E2E 3J9
(506) 847-6006
Emp Here 60
SIC 4911 Electric services

D-U-N-S 24-205-1428 (SL)
R & L CONVENIENCE ENTERPRISES INC
1 Ellis Dr, Rothesay, NB, E2E 1A1
(506) 847-2600
Emp Here 75   *Sales* 13,695,750
SIC 5411 Grocery stores
Pr Pr Raymond Campbell
 Louise Campbell

D-U-N-S 24-943-6015 (BR)
SOBEYS CAPITAL INCORPORATED
SOBEYS 495

140a Hampton Rd, Rothesay, NB, E2E 2R1
(506) 847-5697
Emp Here 140
SIC 5411 Grocery stores

Rothesay, NB E2H

D-U-N-S 25-242-3215 (BR)
ANGLOPHONE SOUTH SCHOOL DISTRICT (ASD-S)
KENNEBECASIS PARK ELEMENTARY SCHOOL
(*Suby of* Anglophone South School District (ASD-S))
10 Broadway St, Rothesay, NB, E2H 1B2
(506) 847-6213
Emp Here 22
SIC 8211 Elementary and secondary schools

Sackville, NB E4L
Westmoreland County

D-U-N-S 20-022-1869 (HQ)
ATLANTIC INDUSTRIES LIMITED
(*Suby of* Border Enterprises Limited)
32 York Street, Sackville, NB, E4L 1G6
(506) 364-4600
Emp Here 60   *Emp Total* 2
Sales 18,191,271
SIC 3499 Fabricated Metal products, nec
Pr Pr Michael Wilson
 Brian Muir

D-U-N-S 25-881-7691 (BR)
ATLANTIC RETAIL CO-OPERATIVES FEDERATION
CO-OP ATLANTIC
11 Wright St, Sackville, NB, E4L 4P8
(506) 536-0679
Emp Here 30
SIC 5411 Grocery stores

D-U-N-S 20-349-3403 (BR)
COREY CRAIG LTD
TIM HORTONS
217 Main St, Sackville, NB, E4L 4B9
(506) 536-1076
Emp Here 37
SIC 5461 Retail bakeries

D-U-N-S 20-588-6406 (BR)
MONERIS SOLUTIONS CORPORATION
2 Charlotte St, Sackville, NB, E4L 3S8
(506) 364-1920
Emp Here 225
SIC 8231 Libraries

D-U-N-S 25-873-4011 (BR)
MORMAC LTD
MCDONALD'S RESTAURANT
(*Suby of* Mormac Ltd)
222 Main St, Sackville, NB, E4L 4C1
(506) 364-1997
Emp Here 54
SIC 5812 Eating places

D-U-N-S 20-005-4299 (BR)
REGIONAL HEALTH AUTHORITY B
TANTRAMAR EXTRA-MURAL PROGRAM
8 Main St Unit 111, Sackville, NB, E4L 4A3
(506) 364-4400
Emp Here 20
SIC 8059 Nursing and personal care, nec

D-U-N-S 20-108-8932 (BR)
REGIONAL HEALTH AUTHORITY NB
REGIONAL HEALTH AUTHORITY B
8 Main St, Sackville, NB, E4L 4A3
(506) 364-4100
Emp Here 155
SIC 8062 General medical and surgical hospitals

D-U-N-S 25-362-3268 (BR)
RUSSEL METALS INC
RUSSELL METALS
141 Crescent St, Sackville, NB, E4L 3V2
(506) 364-1234
Emp Here 45
SIC 5051 Metals service centers and offices

D-U-N-S 20-577-7449 (BR)
SCHOOL DISTRICT 2
TANTRAMAR REGIONAL HIGH SCHOOL
223 Main St Suite A, Sackville, NB, E4L 3A7
(506) 364-4060
Emp Here 60
SIC 8211 Elementary and secondary schools

D-U-N-S 25-241-8942 (BR)
SCHOOL DISTRICT 2
MARSHVIEW MIDDLE SCHOOL
19 Queens Rd, Sackville, NB, E4L 4G4
(506) 364-4086
Emp Here 34
SIC 8211 Elementary and secondary schools

D-U-N-S 25-241-9023 (BR)
SCHOOL DISTRICT 2
SALEM ELEMENTARY SCHOOL
70 Queens Rd, Sackville, NB, E4L 4G9
(506) 364-4072
Emp Here 36
SIC 8211 Elementary and secondary schools

Saint John, NB E2H
Saint John County

D-U-N-S 25-381-2689 (SL)
059884 N.B. INC
BROOKVILLE MANUFACTURING COMPANY
1360 Rothesay Rd, Saint John, NB, E2H 2J1
(506) 633-1200
Emp Here 30   *Sales* 6,274,620
SIC 5032 Brick, stone, and related material
Pr Pr Louis Blanchard
Dir Janet Rupert

D-U-N-S 20-022-7601 (BR)
HALIFAX SEED COMPANY INCORPORATED
664 Rothesay Ave, Saint John, NB, E2H 2H4
(506) 632-9347
Emp Here 22
SIC 5191 Farm supplies

D-U-N-S 25-242-1235 (BR)
SCHOOL DISTRICT 8
GLEN FALLS SCHOOL
(*Suby of* School District 8)
10 Princess Crt, Saint John, NB, E2H 1X9
(506) 658-5340
Emp Here 40
SIC 8211 Elementary and secondary schools

Saint John, NB E2J
Saint John County

D-U-N-S 24-322-9353 (BR)
ATLANTIC WHOLESALERS LTD
REAL ATLANTIC SUPERSTORE, THE
168 Rothesay Ave, Saint John, NB, E2J 2B5
(506) 648-1325
Emp Here 40
SIC 5411 Grocery stores

D-U-N-S 24-912-9800 (BR)
ATLANTIC WHOLESALERS LTD
ATLANTIC SUPERSTORE, THE
168 Rothesay Ave, Saint John, NB, E2J 2B5
(506) 648-1320
Emp Here 130
SIC 5411 Grocery stores

D-U-N-S 24-248-8950 (BR)
ATOMIC ENERGY OF CANADA LIMITED
AECL
430 Bayside Dr, Saint John, NB, E2J 1A8
(506) 633-2325
Emp Here 25
SIC 2819 Industrial inorganic chemicals, nec

D-U-N-S 24-533-5625 (SL)
BLT FOODS LTD
DAIRY QUEEN BRAZIER
499 Rothesay Ave, Saint John, NB, E2J 2C6
(506) 633-1098
Emp Here 125   *Sales* 5,275,400
SIC 5812 Eating places
  Robert Dewar
Pr Pr Timothy Dewar
  Lester Dewar

D-U-N-S 20-104-3515 (BR)
BANK OF NOVA SCOTIA, THE
SCOTIABANK
533 Westmorland Rd, Saint John, NB, E2J 2G5
(506) 658-3200
Emp Here 25
SIC 6021 National commercial banks

D-U-N-S 25-880-7965 (BR)
BELL MEDIA INC
251 Bayside Dr, Saint John, NB, E2J 1A7
(506) 658-1010
Emp Here 49
SIC 4833 Television broadcasting stations

D-U-N-S 20-003-8904 (BR)
BEST BUY CANADA LTD
FUTURE SHOP
(*Suby of* Best Buy Co., Inc.)
80 Consumers Dr, Saint John, NB, E2J 4Z3
(506) 657-3680
Emp Here 50
SIC 5731 Radio, television, and electronic stores

D-U-N-S 24-832-6316 (SL)
BRETECH ENGINEERING LTD
49 Mcilveen Dr, Saint John, NB, E2J 4Y6
(506) 633-1774
Emp Here 45   *Sales* 6,087,000
SIC 8711 Engineering services
Pr Pr Michael J Robichaud

D-U-N-S 24-187-7695 (BR)
BRINK'S CANADA LIMITED
(*Suby of* The Brink's Company)
40 Whitebone Way, Saint John, NB, E2J 4W2
(506) 633-0205
Emp Here 25
SIC 7381 Detective and armored car services

D-U-N-S 20-554-8964 (BR)
CANADA BREAD COMPANY, LIMITED
BEN'S
30 Whitebone Way, Saint John, NB, E2J 4W2
(506) 633-1185
Emp Here 21
SIC 5461 Retail bakeries

D-U-N-S 25-305-9596 (BR)
CANADIAN DIABETES ASSOCIATION
CLOTHESLINE
362 Rothesay Ave, Saint John, NB, E2J 2C4
(506) 693-4232
Emp Here 20
SIC 8699 Membership organizations, nec

D-U-N-S 25-311-6545 (BR)
CANADIAN IMPERIAL BANK OF COMMERCE
CIBC
70 Consumers Dr, Saint John, NB, E2J 4Z3
(506) 633-7750
Emp Here 20
SIC 6021 National commercial banks

D-U-N-S 25-673-7107 (BR)
CARQUEST CANADA LTD

CARQUEST #1652
(*Suby of* Advance Auto Parts, Inc.)
550 Mcallister Dr, Saint John, NB, E2J 4N9
(506) 631-3888
Emp Here 40
SIC 5013 Motor vehicle supplies and new parts

D-U-N-S 24-606-2736 (BR)
COSTCO WHOLESALE CANADA LTD
(*Suby of* Costco Wholesale Corporation)
300 Retail Dr, Saint John, NB, E2J 2R2
(506) 635-5300
Emp Here 50
SIC 5099 Durable goods, nec

D-U-N-S 24-804-3093 (BR)
EMPIRE THEATRES LIMITED
EXHIBITION CINEMAS
175 Mcallister Dr, Saint John, NB, E2J 2S6
(506) 632-4200
Emp Here 40
SIC 7832 Motion picture theaters, except drive-in

D-U-N-S 24-340-0947 (BR)
FGL SPORTS LTD
SPORT-CHEK
519 Westmorland Rd, Saint John, NB, E2J 3W9
(506) 696-6228
Emp Here 40
SIC 5941 Sporting goods and bicycle shops

D-U-N-S 20-790-0411 (BR)
GOODLIFE FITNESS CENTRES INC
168 Rothesay Ave, Saint John, NB, E2J 2B5
(506) 693-2240
Emp Here 24
SIC 7991 Physical fitness facilities

D-U-N-S 24-101-5176 (BR)
HOME DEPOT OF CANADA INC
HOME DEPOT
(*Suby of* The Home Depot Inc)
55 Lcd Crt, Saint John, NB, E2J 5E5
(506) 632-9440
Emp Here 100
SIC 5251 Hardware stores

D-U-N-S 20-812-4263 (SL)
INDUSTRIAL SECURITY LIMITED
(*Suby of* J. D. Irving, Limited)
635 Bayside Dr, Saint John, NB, E2J 1B4
(506) 648-3060
Emp Here 120   *Sales* 5,124,480
SIC 7381 Detective and armored car services
Pr Pr James K Irving
Crdt Mgr Rose Cummings-Brown

D-U-N-S 20-698-0547 (BR)
IRON MOUNTAIN CANADA OPERATIONS ULC
ARCHIVES IRON MOUNTAIN
120 Mcdonald St Suite C, Saint John, NB, E2J 1M5

Emp Here 200
SIC 4226 Special warehousing and storage, nec

D-U-N-S 20-311-6236 (BR)
J. D. IRVING, LIMITED
KENT BUILDING SUPPLIES, DIV OF
(*Suby of* J. D. Irving, Limited)
85 Consumers Dr, Saint John, NB, E2J 4Z6
(506) 648-1000
Emp Here 100
SIC 1521 Single-family housing construction

D-U-N-S 20-136-4127 (BR)
J. D. IRVING, LIMITED
CHANDLER SALES
(*Suby of* J. D. Irving, Limited)
225 Thorne Ave, Saint John, NB, E2J 1W8
(506) 658-8000
Emp Here 97
SIC 5021 Furniture

D-U-N-S 25-299-4512 (BR)
LAWTON'S DRUG STORES LIMITED
LAWTON DRUGS 130
519 Westmorland Rd, Saint John, NB, E2J 3W9
(506) 633-8984
Emp Here 20
SIC 5912 Drug stores and proprietary stores

D-U-N-S 20-742-0688 (SL)
LOCH LOMOND VILLA INC
185 Loch Lomond Rd, Saint John, NB, E2J 3S3
(506) 643-7175
Emp Here 350   *Sales* 21,497,040
SIC 8051 Skilled nursing care facilities
Dir Fin Gordon Burnett
Ch Bd Cindy Donovan

D-U-N-S 25-257-1526 (SL)
MASTER MECHANICAL CONTRACTORS INC
(*Suby of* M M C I Holdings Inc)
11 Whitebone Way, Saint John, NB, E2J 4Y3
(506) 633-8001
Emp Here 185   *Sales* 22,521,900
SIC 1711 Plumbing, heating, air-conditioning
Pr Robert Macclean
CEO Styve Dumouchel
  Tod Bethune

D-U-N-S 24-311-3953 (BR)
MCPORT CITY FOOD SERVICES LIMITED
MCDONALD'S
111 Mcallister Dr, Saint John, NB, E2J 2S6
(506) 634-2704
Emp Here 70
SIC 5812 Eating places

D-U-N-S 24-330-3315 (BR)
MELOCHE MONNEX INC
(*Suby of* Toronto-Dominion Bank, The)
420 Rothesay Ave, Saint John, NB, E2J 2C4
(506) 643-5823
Emp Here 20
SIC 6411 Insurance agents, brokers, and service

D-U-N-S 20-619-1009 (BR)
MIDLAND TRANSPORT LIMITED
(*Suby of* J. D. Irving, Limited)
114 Bayside Dr, Saint John, NB, E2J 1A2
(506) 634-1200
Emp Here 40
SIC 4213 Trucking, except local

D-U-N-S 25-363-7847 (BR)
OLD NAVY (CANADA) INC
(*Suby of* The Gap Inc)
90 Consumers Dr, Saint John, NB, E2J 4Z3
(506) 634-7597
Emp Here 40
SIC 5651 Family clothing stores

D-U-N-S 20-918-6795 (HQ)
RST INDUSTRIES LIMITED
(*Suby of* J. D. Irving, Limited)
485 Mcallister Dr, Saint John, NB, E2J 2S8
(506) 634-8800
Emp Here 96   *Emp Total* 15,000
Sales 16,396,525
SIC 4213 Trucking, except local
Genl Mgr Scott Gillis

D-U-N-S 24-966-8273 (BR)
SAFWAY SERVICES CANADA, ULC
(*Suby of* Safway Group Holding LLC)
1143 Bayside Dr, Saint John, NB, E2J 4Y2
(506) 646-8820
Emp Here 25
SIC 1799 Special trade contractors, nec

D-U-N-S 20-022-5555 (SL)
SAINT JOHN TRANSIT COMMISSION
55 Mcdonald St, Saint John, NB, E2J 0C7
(506) 658-4710
Emp Here 90   *Sales* 3,137,310
SIC 4111 Local and suburban transit

D-U-N-S 25-242-1169   (BR)
SCHOOL DISTRICT 8
SIMONDS MIDDLE SCHOOL
(*Suby of* School District 8)
184 Loch Lomond Rd, Saint John, NB, E2J
1Y1

Emp Here 20
SIC 8211 Elementary and secondary schools

D-U-N-S 25-242-1201   (BR)
SCHOOL DISTRICT 8
SIMONDS HIGH SCHOOL
(*Suby of* School District 8)
1490 Hickey Rd, Saint John, NB, E2J 4E7
(506) 658-5367
Emp Here 80
SIC 8211 Elementary and secondary schools

D-U-N-S 25-242-1318   (BR)
SCHOOL DISTRICT 8
CHAMPLAIN HEIGHTS SCHOOL
(*Suby of* School District 8)
111 Champlain Dr, Saint John, NB, E2J 3E4
(506) 658-5335
Emp Here 35
SIC 8211 Elementary and secondary schools

D-U-N-S 25-242-1433   (BR)
SCHOOL DISTRICT 8
BAYSIDE MIDDLE SCHOOL
(*Suby of* School District 8)
75 Bayside Dr, Saint John, NB, E2J 1A1
(506) 658-5331
Emp Here 50
SIC 8211 Elementary and secondary schools

D-U-N-S 20-710-0277   (BR)
SCHOOL DISTRICT 8
LAKE WOOD HEIGHTS ELEMENTARY SCHOOL
(*Suby of* School District 8)
56 Lensdale Cres, Saint John, NB, E2J 3P3
(506) 658-5348
Emp Here 25
SIC 8211 Elementary and secondary schools

D-U-N-S 25-242-1276   (BR)
SCHOOL DISTRICT 8
FOREST HILLS ELEMENTARY SCHOOL
(*Suby of* School District 8)
15 Glengarry Dr, Saint John, NB, E2J 2X9
(506) 658-5338
Emp Here 60
SIC 8211 Elementary and secondary schools

D-U-N-S 25-294-5498   (BR)
SEARS CANADA INC
441 Westmorland Rd, Saint John, NB, E2J
4K2
(506) 632-3630
Emp Here 200
SIC 5311 Department stores

D-U-N-S 24-766-8028   (SL)
SOBEY'S EXTRA 548
44 East Point, Saint John, NB, E2J 0H5
(506) 658-1329
Emp Here 49   *Sales* 6,055,738
SIC 5411 Grocery stores
Genl Mgr Paul Barter

D-U-N-S 24-187-8834   (BR)
SOBEYS CAPITAL INCORPORATED
SOBEYS #692
519 Westmorland Rd, Saint John, NB, E2J
3W9
(506) 633-1187
Emp Here 200
SIC 5411 Grocery stores

D-U-N-S 25-299-3092   (BR)
SOBEYS CAPITAL INCORPORATED
SOBEYS #275
120 Mcdonald St, Saint John, NB, E2J 1M5

Emp Here 50
SIC 5411 Grocery stores

D-U-N-S 20-860-0010   (BR)
SOURCE (BELL) ELECTRONICS INC, THE
SOURCE, THE
519 Westmorland Rd, Saint John, NB, E2J
3W9
(506) 633-1945
Emp Here 25
SIC 5999 Miscellaneous retail stores, nec

D-U-N-S 25-664-7363   (HQ)
SPRINGER INVESTMENTS LTD
TIM HORTONS
(*Suby of* Springer Investments Ltd)
97 Loch Lomond Rd, Saint John, NB, E2J 1X6
(506) 847-9168
Emp Here 25   *Emp Total* 120
Sales 4,085,799
SIC 5461 Retail bakeries

D-U-N-S 20-198-9071   (BR)
SPRINGER INVESTMENTS LTD
TIM HORTONS
447 Rothesay Ave, Saint John, NB, E2J 2C3
(506) 633-8450
Emp Here 25
SIC 5812 Eating places

D-U-N-S 25-871-5580   (BR)
STAPLES CANADA INC
STAPLES THE BUSINESS DEPOT
(*Suby of* Staples, Inc.)
176 Rothesay Ave, Saint John, NB, E2J 2B5
(506) 646-7530
Emp Here 40
SIC 5943 Stationery stores

D-U-N-S 20-548-7739   (HQ)
SUNBURY TRANSPORT LIMITED
(*Suby of* J. D. Irving, Limited)
485 Mcallister Dr, Saint John, NB, E2J 2S8
(800) 786-2878
Emp Here 80   *Emp Total* 15,000
Sales 18,277,896
SIC 4213 Trucking, except local
Pr Pr James Irving
Dir Fin Neil Hossack
Genl Mgr Scott Gillis
VP Wayne Power

D-U-N-S 25-408-4031   (BR)
TIDAN INC
212 Mcallister Dr Suite 102, Saint John, NB,
E2J 2S7
(506) 649-4444
Emp Here 20
SIC 6512 Nonresidential building operators

D-U-N-S 25-194-6240   (BR)
TOYS 'R' US (CANADA) LTD
TOYS 'R' US
(*Suby of* Toys "r" Us, Inc.)
519 Westmorland Rd, Saint John, NB, E2J
3W9
(506) 635-8697
Emp Here 20
SIC 5945 Hobby, toy, and game shops

D-U-N-S 24-000-2589   (BR)
UNILEVER CANADA INC
UNILEVER BEST FOODS
120 Mcdonald St Suite D, Saint John, NB, E2J
1M5
(506) 631-6400
Emp Here 50
SIC 4813 Telephone communication, except radio

D-U-N-S 20-107-2522   (BR)
UPONOR LTD
UPONOR WIRSBO MANUFACTURING
79 Mcilveen Dr, Saint John, NB, E2J 4Y6

Emp Here 130
SIC 3567 Industrial furnaces and ovens

D-U-N-S 20-023-4834   (BR)
VALUE VILLAGE STORES, INC
VALUE VILLAGE

(*Suby of* Savers, Inc.)
212 Mcallister Dr, Saint John, NB, E2J 2S7
(506) 696-5301
Emp Here 42
SIC 5399 Miscellaneous general merchandise

D-U-N-S 25-294-8468   (BR)
WAL-MART CANADA CORP
450 Westmorland Rd Suite 3091, Saint John,
NB, E2J 4Z2
(506) 634-6600
Emp Here 250
SIC 5311 Department stores

D-U-N-S 20-860-4236   (BR)
WINNERS MERCHANTS INTERNATIONAL L.P.
WINNERS
(*Suby of* The TJX Companies Inc)
88 Consumers Dr, Saint John, NB, E2J 4Z3
(506) 634-7921
Emp Here 25
SIC 5651 Family clothing stores

Saint John, NB E2K
Saint John County

D-U-N-S 20-175-6280   (BR)
AIR CANADA
1 Air Canada Way, Saint John, NB, E2K 0B1
(506) 637-2444
Emp Here 250
SIC 7389 Business services, nec

D-U-N-S 25-680-1247   (HQ)
ANGLOPHONE SOUTH SCHOOL DISTRICT (ASD-S)
(*Suby of* Anglophone South School District
(ASD-S))
490 Woodward Ave, Saint John, NB, E2K 5N3
(506) 658-5300
Emp Here 120   *Emp Total* 1,100
Sales 94,892,530
SIC 8211 Elementary and secondary schools
Superintnt Zoe Watson
  John Macdonald

D-U-N-S 25-985-8983   (BR)
ATLANTIC WHOLESALERS LTD
MILLEDGEVILLE SUPERSTORE
650 Somerset St, Saint John, NB, E2K 2Y7
(506) 658-6054
Emp Here 120
SIC 5411 Grocery stores

D-U-N-S 20-311-3423   (BR)
BAYSHORE HEALTHCARE LTD.
BAYSHORE HOME HEALTH
600 Main St Suite C150, Saint John, NB, E2K
1J5
(506) 633-9588
Emp Here 140
SIC 8082 Home health care services

D-U-N-S 24-522-0194   (BR)
BELL ALIANT REGIONAL COMMUNICA-TIONS INC
BELL CANADA
151 Woodward Ave, Saint John, NB, E2K 1Z9
(506) 632-6484
Emp Here 60
SIC 4899 Communication services, nec

D-U-N-S 20-510-9874   (BR)
CANADIAN BLOOD SERVICES
405 University Ave, Saint John, NB, E2K 0H6
(506) 648-5012
Emp Here 50
SIC 8099 Health and allied services, nec

D-U-N-S 24-338-1688   (BR)
CANADIAN BROADCASTING CORPORA-TION
CBC
560 Main St, Saint John, NB, E2K 1J5

(506) 632-7710
Emp Here 20
SIC 4832 Radio broadcasting stations

D-U-N-S 20-052-5488   (BR)
CANADIAN RED CROSS SOCIETY, THE
70 Lansdowne Ave, Saint John, NB, E2K 2Z8
(506) 674-6200
Emp Here 80
SIC 8322 Individual and family services

D-U-N-S 20-022-8328   (HQ)
COAST TIRE & AUTO SERVICE LTD
(*Suby of* Coast Tire & Auto Service Ltd)
130 Somerset St Suite 150, Saint John, NB,
E2K 2X4
(506) 674-9620
Emp Here 30   *Emp Total* 300
Sales 47,116,450
SIC 5531 Auto and home supply stores
Pr Pr Ronald Outerbridge
Dir Robin Hunter
Dir Michael Cosentino
VP Opers Jack Jacobs
VP Fin Peter Coleman
VP Sls John Correia
Dir Arch Cook
Dir Gerald Mcmackin
Dir James Coulter

D-U-N-S 25-849-3113   (BR)
COMCARE (CANADA) LIMITED
COMCARE HEALTH SERVICES
(*Suby of* Comcare (Canada) Limited)
580 Main St Suite B120, Saint John, NB, E2K
1J5
(506) 634-1505
Emp Here 45
SIC 7363 Help supply services

D-U-N-S 20-554-3668   (BR)
COX & PALMER
1 Brunswick Pl Suite 1500, Saint John, NB,
E2K 1B5
(506) 632-8900
Emp Here 100
SIC 8111 Legal services

D-U-N-S 24-241-1650   (SL)
D. P. MURPHY (NB) INC
HOLIDAY INN EXPRESS & SUITES
400 Main St, Saint John, NB, E2K 4N5
(506) 642-2622
Emp Here 25   *Sales* 2,261,782
SIC 6512 Nonresidential building operators

D-U-N-S 20-105-4926   (BR)
EMERA UTILITY SERVICES INCORPO-RATED
895 Ashburn Rd, Saint John, NB, E2K 5J9

Emp Here 30
SIC 1731 Electrical work

D-U-N-S 20-549-1673   (BR)
IBM CANADA LIMITED
(*Suby of* International Business Machines
Corporation)
400 Main St Suite 1000, Saint John, NB, E2K
4N5
(506) 646-4000
Emp Here 100
SIC 7389 Business services, nec

D-U-N-S 20-311-4780   (SL)
INMAR PROMOTIONS - CANADA INC.
MILLENNIUM1 PROMOTIONAL SERVICES
661 Millidge Ave, Saint John, NB, E2K 2N7
(506) 632-1400
Emp Here 150   *Sales* 9,517,523
SIC 7389 Business services, nec
Dir Don Moffatt
Pr Tom Band
VP Opers Jennie Bradley
VP Sls Michael Morrison

D-U-N-S 20-202-0967   (BR)
INNOVATIA INC
1 Brunswick Pl, Saint John, NB, E2K 1B5

(506) 640-4000
Emp Here 300
SIC 4813 Telephone communication, except radio

D-U-N-S 24-342-9792   (SL)
KENNEBEC MANOR INC
475 Woodward Ave, Saint John, NB, E2K 4N1
(506) 632-9628
Emp Here 97   *Sales* 4,450,603
SIC 8051 Skilled nursing care facilities

D-U-N-S 24-122-7755   (BR)
KILLAM PROPERTIES INC
SAINT JOHN OFFICE
55 Magazine St Suite 101, Saint John, NB, E2K 2S5
(506) 652-7368
Emp Here 35
SIC 6513 Apartment building operators

D-U-N-S 25-483-2561   (BR)
MAC'S FOODS LTD
DELUXE FRENCH FRIES
(*Suby of* Mac's Foods Ltd)
5 Wellesley Ave, Saint John, NB, E2K 2V1
(506) 642-2424
Emp Here 100
SIC 5812 Eating places

D-U-N-S 20-792-4791   (BR)
MCDONALD'S   RESTAURANTS   OF CANADA LIMITED
MCDONALD'S
(*Suby of* McDonald's Corporation)
91 Millidge Ave, Saint John, NB, E2K 2M3

Emp Here 70
SIC 5812 Eating places

D-U-N-S 20-797-6585   (BR)
MCPORT CITY FOOD SERVICES LIMITED
MCDONALD'S RESTAURANT
399 Main St, Saint John, NB, E2K 1J3
(506) 634-0256
Emp Here 65
SIC 5812 Eating places

D-U-N-S 20-313-3009   (BR)
NEW BRUNSWICK MUSEUM, THE
277 Douglas Ave, Saint John, NB, E2K 1E5
(506) 643-2322
Emp Here 30
SIC 8412 Museums and art galleries

D-U-N-S 25-672-7793   (SL)
NIGHT SHIFT ANSWERING SERVICE LTD, THE
DIRECTOR'S CHOICE
600 Main St Suite 201, Saint John, NB, E2K 1J5
(506) 637-7010
Emp Here 70   *Sales* 3,575,074
SIC 7389 Business services, nec

D-U-N-S 20-003-7161   (SL)
ROYAL TAXI
CENTURY TAXI
26 Taylor Ave, Saint John, NB, E2K 3E6
(506) 652-5050
Emp Here 60   *Sales* 1,824,018
SIC 4121 Taxicabs

D-U-N-S 20-023-8447   (BR)
SCHOOL BOARD DISTRICT 01
CENTRE SCOLAIRE SAMUEL DE CHAMPLAIN
67 Ragged Point Rd, Saint John, NB, E2K 5C3
(506) 658-4613
Emp Here 40
SIC 8211 Elementary and secondary schools

D-U-N-S 20-710-0301   (BR)
SCHOOL DISTRICT 8
MILLIDGEDILLE NORTH SCHOOL
(*Suby of* School District 8)
500 Woodward Ave, Saint John, NB, E2K 4G7
(506) 658-5353
Emp Here 40

SIC 8211 Elementary and secondary schools

D-U-N-S 20-710-0327   (BR)
SCHOOL DISTRICT 8
PRINCESS ELIZABETH SCHOOL
(*Suby of* School District 8)
20 Sixth St, Saint John, NB, E2K 3M1
(506) 658-5356
Emp Here 50
SIC 8211 Elementary and secondary schools

D-U-N-S 25-242-3454   (BR)
SCHOOL DISTRICT 8
99 Burpee Ave, Saint John, NB, E2K 3V9
(506) 634-1979
Emp Here 20
SIC 8211 Elementary and secondary schools

D-U-N-S 25-242-3413   (BR)
SCHOOL DISTRICT 8
HAZEN WHITE ST. FRANCIS SCHOOL
(*Suby of* School District 8)
540 Sandy Point Rd, Saint John, NB, E2K 3S2
(506) 658-5343
Emp Here 31
SIC 8211 Elementary and secondary schools

D-U-N-S 20-811-5779   (BR)
SCHOOL DISTRICT 8
NEW BRUNSWICK SCHOOL DISTRICT LORNE MIDDLE SCHOOL
(*Suby of* School District 8)
90 Newman St, Saint John, NB, E2K 1M1
(506) 453-5454
Emp Here 22
SIC 8211 Elementary and secondary schools

D-U-N-S 25-242-3777   (BR)
SCHOOL DISTRICT 8
M. GERALD TEED MEMORIAL SCHOOL
(*Suby of* School District 8)
151 Black St, Saint John, NB, E2K 2L6
(506) 658-5352
Emp Here 25
SIC 8211 Elementary and secondary schools

D-U-N-S 25-242-1474   (BR)
SCHOOL DISTRICT 8
HARBOUR VIEW HIGH SCHOOL
(*Suby of* School District 8)
305 Douglas Ave, Saint John, NB, E2K 1E5
(506) 658-5359
Emp Here 80
SIC 8211 Elementary and secondary schools

D-U-N-S 25-359-7058   (BR)
SEABOARD LIQUID CARRIERS LIMITED
SEABOARD TRANSPORT GROUP
120 Ashburn Rd, Saint John, NB, E2K 5J5
(506) 652-7070
Emp Here 110
SIC 4213 Trucking, except local

D-U-N-S 24-187-8891   (BR)
SOBEYS CAPITAL INCORPORATED
149 Lansdowne Ave Suite 233, Saint John, NB, E2K 2Z9
(506) 652-4470
Emp Here 120
SIC 5411 Grocery stores

D-U-N-S 20-605-8906   (HQ)
SOURCE ATLANTIC LIMITED
INDUSTRIAL SUPPLIES
331 Chesley Dr, Saint John, NB, E2K 5P2
(506) 635-7711
Emp Here 100   *Emp Total* 300
Sales 54,720,525
SIC 5084 Industrial machinery and equipment
  John K. F. Irving
Pr Steve Drummond

D-U-N-S 20-279-1984   (BR)
SOURCE ATLANTIC LIMITED
THORNES
331 Chesley Dr, Saint John, NB, E2K 5P2

(506) 635-7711
Emp Here 106
SIC 5084 Industrial machinery and equipment

D-U-N-S 20-986-9452   (BR)
STANTEC CONSULTING LTD
130 Somerset St, Saint John, NB, E2K 2X4
(506) 634-2185
Emp Here 49
SIC 8711 Engineering services

D-U-N-S 20-082-9732   (BR)
WENDY'S RESTAURANTS OF CANADA INC
(*Suby of* The Wendy's Company)
40 University Ave, Saint John, NB, E2K 5B4
(506) 633-7415
Emp Here 40
SIC 5812 Eating places

D-U-N-S 24-319-2809   (BR)
XEROX CANADA LTD
(*Suby of* Xerox Corporation)
400 Main St Suite 2040, Saint John, NB, E2K 4N5
(506) 634-7998
Emp Here 50
SIC 5112 Stationery and office supplies

Saint John, NB E2L
Saint John County

D-U-N-S 20-023-0001   (HQ)
ACADIA BROADCASTING LIMITED
CHSJ 94.1 FM
58 King St Suite 300, Saint John, NB, E2L 1G4
(506) 633-3323
Emp Here 27   *Emp Total* 100
Sales 4,052,015
SIC 4832 Radio broadcasting stations

D-U-N-S 20-571-8922   (BR)
AVIVA CANADA INC
85 Charlotte St Suite 201506, Saint John, NB, E2L 2J2
(506) 634-1111
Emp Here 29
SIC 8741 Management services

D-U-N-S 24-129-0261   (BR)
AVIVA   INSURANCE   COMPANY   OF CANADA
1 Germain St Suite 902, Saint John, NB, E2L 4V1
(506) 634-1111
Emp Here 38
SIC 6411 Insurance agents, brokers, and service

D-U-N-S 24-129-2861   (BR)
BANK OF NOVA SCOTIA, THE
SCOTIABANK
39 King St, Saint John, NB, E2L 4W3
(506) 658-3365
Emp Here 55
SIC 6021 National commercial banks

D-U-N-S 25-296-3061   (BR)
BANK OF NOVA SCOTIA, THE
SCOTIABANK
40 Charlotte St Suite 420, Saint John, NB, E2L 2H6

Emp Here 20
SIC 6021 National commercial banks

D-U-N-S 24-317-5325   (BR)
BANK OF MONTREAL
BMO
15 Market Sq, Saint John, NB, E2L 1E8
(506) 632-0202
Emp Here 24
SIC 6021 National commercial banks

D-U-N-S 20-814-1424   (BR)
BANQUE TORONTO-DOMINION, LA
TORONTO-DOMINION BANK, THE

(*Suby of* Toronto-Dominion Bank, The)
44 Chipman Hill Suite 200, Saint John, NB, E2L 2A9
(506) 634-1870
Emp Here 22
SIC 6021 National commercial banks

D-U-N-S 20-073-8974   (BR)
BELL ALIANT REGIONAL COMMUNICATIONS INC
Gd, Saint John, NB, E2L 4K2
(506) 658-7169
Emp Here 800
SIC 4899 Communication services, nec

D-U-N-S 20-311-6814   (SL)
BIG BROTHERS-BIG SISTERS OF SAINT JOHN INC
(*Suby of* Big Brothers Big Sisters Of Canada)
39 King St, Saint John, NB, E2L 4W3
(506) 635-1145
Emp Here 200   *Sales* 10,601,280
SIC 8322 Individual and family services
VP VP Norm Michaelson
VP VP Cindy Millett
Pr Pr Rhea Bowen
  Betty Hitchcock
  Jennifer Uhryniw
  Fraser Walsh
  Derek Riedle
  Kate Murray
  Shannon Mcgrillvray
  Deborah Fisher

D-U-N-S 25-293-8568   (BR)
CIBC WORLD MARKETS INC
CIBC WOOD GUNDY
44 Chipman Hill Suite 500, Saint John, NB, E2L 2A9
(506) 634-1220
Emp Here 32
SIC 6211 Security brokers and dealers

D-U-N-S 20-509-8796   (BR)
CANADA REVENUE AGENCY
CANADA REVENUE AGENCY SAINT JOHN PSO
126 Prince William St, Saint John, NB, E2L 2B6
(506) 636-4623
Emp Here 300
SIC 8721 Accounting, auditing, and bookkeeping

D-U-N-S 24-248-9180   (BR)
CONRAD, PAUL R HVAC LIMITED
TRANE ATLANTIC
(*Suby of* Kingfisher Developments Limited)
70 Crown St Unit 220, Saint John, NB, E2L 2X6
(506) 633-2300
Emp Here 23
SIC 1711 Plumbing, heating, air-conditioning

D-U-N-S 24-994-4877   (BR)
CORUS MEDIA HOLDINGS INC
SHAW MEDIA INC
1 Germain St Suite A500, Saint John, NB, E2L 4V1

Emp Here 25
SIC 4833 Television broadcasting stations

D-U-N-S 24-407-4881   (BR)
COX & PALMER
1 Germain St Unit 1500, Saint John, NB, E2L 4V1
(506) 632-8900
Emp Here 50
SIC 8111 Legal services

D-U-N-S 20-362-8628   (BR)
COX & PALMER
TEED, WILLIAM H
1 Germain St Suite 1500, Saint John, NB, E2L 4V1
(506) 633-2718
Emp Here 50

SIC 8111 Legal services

D-U-N-S 20-005-4810 (BR)
DELOITTE LLP
44 Chipman Hill Suite 700, Saint John, NB, E2L 2A9
(506) 632-1080
Emp Here 35
SIC 8721 Accounting, auditing, and bookkeeping

D-U-N-S 24-187-0955 (BR)
DELTA HOTELS LIMITED
39 King St, Saint John, NB, E2L 4W3
(506) 648-1981
Emp Here 175
SIC 8741 Management services

D-U-N-S 24-314-9148 (BR)
DILLON CONSULTING LIMITED
(*Suby of* Dillon Consulting Inc)
274 Sydney St Suite 200, Saint John, NB, E2L 0A8
(506) 633-5000
Emp Here 30
SIC 7363 Help supply services

D-U-N-S 24-120-5025 (SL)
ENERGY EFFICIENCY AND CONSERVATION AGENCY OF NEW BRUNSWICK
EFFICIENCY NB
35 Charlotte St Suite 101, Saint John, NB, E2L 2H3
(506) 643-7826
Emp Here 30 *Sales* 19,394,118
SIC 8748 Business consulting, nec
Pr Margaret Ann Blaney

D-U-N-S 25-297-1833 (BR)
ERNST & YOUNG LLP
ERNST & YOUNG
(*Suby of* Ernst & Young LLP)
12 Smythe St Suite 565, Saint John, NB, E2L 5G5
(506) 634-7000
Emp Here 35
SIC 8721 Accounting, auditing, and bookkeeping

D-U-N-S 20-933-2386 (SL)
FUNDY MOTORS (1995) LTD
FUNDY HONDA
160 Rothesay Ave, Saint John, NB, E2L 3V5
(506) 633-1333
Emp Here 34 *Sales* 16,019,593
SIC 5511 New and used car dealers
Pr Pr Richard Buckley
VP VP Ruth Buckley

D-U-N-S 24-956-0806 (BR)
G4S CASH SOLUTIONS (CANADA) LTD
SECURICOR CASH SERVICES
40 Saint Andrews St, Saint John, NB, E2L 1T3
(506) 632-8040
Emp Here 25
SIC 7381 Detective and armored car services

D-U-N-S 20-023-8454 (BR)
GDI SERVICES (CANADA) LP
OMNI FACILITY SERVICES
66 Waterloo St Suite 230, Saint John, NB, E2L 3P4
(506) 632-1882
Emp Here 70
SIC 7349 Building maintenance services, nec

D-U-N-S 20-165-2703 (BR)
GOVERNING COUNCIL OF THE SALVATION ARMY IN CANADA, THE
GOVERNING COUNCIL OF THE SALVATION ARMY IN CANADA, THE
36 St. James St, Saint John, NB, E2L 1V3

Emp Here 33
SIC 8361 Residential care

D-U-N-S 24-338-1860 (BR)
GRANT THORNTON LLP
1 Germain St Suite 1100, Saint John, NB, E2L

4V1
(506) 634-2900
Emp Here 36
SIC 8721 Accounting, auditing, and bookkeeping

D-U-N-S 20-607-2246 (BR)
GRANT THORNTON LLP
87 Canterbury St, Saint John, NB, E2L 2C7
(506) 382-2655
Emp Here 40
SIC 8721 Accounting, auditing, and bookkeeping

D-U-N-S 25-058-6492 (BR)
GRAYBAR CANADA LIMITED
HARRIS & ROOME SUPPLY
(*Suby of* Graybar Electric Company, Inc.)
300 Charlotte St, Saint John, NB, E2L 5A4
(506) 634-2094
Emp Here 20
SIC 5063 Electrical apparatus and equipment

D-U-N-S 20-082-9740 (BR)
HARDMAN GROUP LIMITED, THE
(*Suby of* Hardman Group Limited, The)
1 Market Sq Suite 102, Saint John, NB, E2L 4Z6
(506) 658-3600
Emp Here 25
SIC 8742 Management consulting services

D-U-N-S 20-269-9435 (BR)
HIGHLANDS FUEL DELIVERY G.P.
IRVING ENERGY
10 Sydney St, Saint John, NB, E2L 5E6
(506) 202-2000
Emp Here 300
SIC 4924 Natural gas distribution

D-U-N-S 25-412-4332 (BR)
HILTON CANADA CO.
HILTON
1 Market Sq, Saint John, NB, E2L 4Z6
(506) 693-8484
Emp Here 120
SIC 7011 Hotels and motels

D-U-N-S 25-315-7234 (BR)
INVESTORS GROUP FINANCIAL SERVICES INC
55 Union St Unit 101, Saint John, NB, E2L 5B7
(506) 632-8930
Emp Here 64
SIC 8741 Management services

D-U-N-S 25-195-1935 (SL)
IRVING ENERGY SERVICES LIMITED
10 Sydney St, Saint John, NB, E2L 5E6
(506) 202-2000
Emp Here 30 *Sales* 12,985,600
SIC 4924 Natural gas distribution
Dir Michael Wennberg

D-U-N-S 24-965-2152 (BR)
IRVING SHIPBUILDING INC
HALIFAX SHIPYARD, DIV OF
300 Union St, Saint John, NB, E2L 4Z2
(506) 632-7777
Emp Here 20
SIC 3731 Shipbuilding and repairing

D-U-N-S 20-022-8138 (HQ)
J. D. IRVING, LIMITED
KENT BUILDING SUPPLIES, DIV OF
(*Suby of* J. D. Irving, Limited)
300 Union St Suite 5, Saint John, NB, E2L 4Z2
(506) 632-7777
Emp Here 1,200 *Emp Total* 15,000
Sales 1,422,733,650
SIC 2421 Sawmills and planing mills, general
James Kenneth Irving
Dir Arthur L. Irving

D-U-N-S 25-361-2451 (BR)
J. D. IRVING, LIMITED
SUPPLIERS TO BUSINESS & INDUSTRY
(*Suby of* J. D. Irving, Limited)

225 Thorne Ave, Saint John, NB, E2L 4L9
(506) 633-4095
Emp Here 90
SIC 5169 Chemicals and allied products, nec

D-U-N-S 20-562-7628 (SL)
JARDINE BROOK HOLDINGS LIMITED
300 Union St, Saint John, NB, E2L 4Z2
(506) 632-5110
Emp Here 100 *Sales* 19,600,443
SIC 6712 Bank holding companies
Bruce Drost

D-U-N-S 20-288-0790 (BR)
LAWTON'S DRUG STORES LIMITED
39 King St Suite 115, Saint John, NB, E2L 4W3
(506) 634-1422
Emp Here 20
SIC 5912 Drug stores and proprietary stores

D-U-N-S 25-303-9903 (BR)
LONDON LIFE INSURANCE COMPANY
FREEDOM 55 FINANCIAL
55 Union St Suite 650, Saint John, NB, E2L 5B7
(506) 634-7300
Emp Here 25
SIC 6311 Life insurance

D-U-N-S 24-311-4076 (BR)
MCPORT CITY FOOD SERVICES LIMITED
MCDONALD'S
39 King St, Saint John, NB, E2L 4W3
(506) 634-2700
Emp Here 25
SIC 5812 Eating places

D-U-N-S 20-348-8721 (SL)
NBM RAIL SERVICES INC
(*Suby of* J. D. Irving, Limited)
300 Union St, Saint John, NB, E2L 4Z2
(506) 632-6314
Emp Here 25 *Sales* 875,528
SIC 4111 Local and suburban transit

D-U-N-S 25-285-7461 (BR)
PRICEWATERHOUSECOOPERS LLP
44 Chipman Hill Suite 300, Saint John, NB, E2L 2A9
(506) 632-1810
Emp Here 30
SIC 8721 Accounting, auditing, and bookkeeping

D-U-N-S 25-993-0993 (BR)
PWC MANAGEMENT SERVICES LP
44 Chipman Hill Unit 300, Saint John, NB, E2L 4B9
(506) 653-9499
Emp Here 20
SIC 8721 Accounting, auditing, and bookkeeping

D-U-N-S 25-293-7024 (BR)
RBC DOMINION SECURITIES INC
(*Suby of* Royal Bank Of Canada)
44 Chipman Hill Suite 800, Saint John, NB, E2L 2A9
(506) 637-7500
Emp Here 20
SIC 6211 Security brokers and dealers

D-U-N-S 20-706-6288 (BR)
ROGERS COMMUNICATIONS INC
(*Suby of* Rogers Communications Inc)
55 Waterloo St, Saint John, NB, E2L 4V9
(506) 646-5105
Emp Here 20
SIC 1731 Electrical work

D-U-N-S 20-813-1805 (BR)
ROYAL TRUST CORPORATION OF CANADA
(*Suby of* Royal Bank Of Canada)
100 King St, Saint John, NB, E2L 1G4
(506) 632-8080
Emp Here 53
SIC 6099 Functions related to deposit banking

D-U-N-S 20-006-1252 (BR)
SAINT JOHN, CITY OF
PUBLIC SAFETY COMMUNICATIONS CENTRE
Gd, Saint John, NB, E2L 4L1
(506) 649-6030
Emp Here 25
SIC 7389 Business services, nec

D-U-N-S 25-291-3439 (BR)
SAINT JOHN, CITY OF
HARBOUR STATION
99 Station St, Saint John, NB, E2L 4X4
(506) 657-1234
Emp Here 20
SIC 7922 Theatrical producers and services

D-U-N-S 20-536-1533 (BR)
SAINT JOHN, CITY OF
175 Rothesay Ave, Saint John, NB, E2L 4L1
(506) 658-4455
Emp Here 20
SIC 8111 Legal services

D-U-N-S 25-242-1110 (BR)
SCHOOL DISTRICT 8
ST MALACHY'S MEMORIAL HIGH SCHOOL
(*Suby of* School District 8)
20 Leinster St Suite 2, Saint John, NB, E2L 1H8
(506) 658-5361
Emp Here 75
SIC 8211 Elementary and secondary schools

D-U-N-S 25-242-3389 (BR)
SCHOOL DISTRICT 8
ST JOHN THE BAPTIST-KING EDWARD SCHOOL
(*Suby of* School District 8)
223 St. James St Suite 8, Saint John, NB, E2L 1W3
(506) 658-5357
Emp Here 27
SIC 8211 Elementary and secondary schools

D-U-N-S 20-710-0319 (BR)
SCHOOL DISTRICT 8
PRINCE CHARLES SCHOOL
(*Suby of* School District 8)
319 Union St Suite 317, Saint John, NB, E2L 1B3
(506) 658-5355
Emp Here 50
SIC 8211 Elementary and secondary schools

D-U-N-S 24-390-0565 (BR)
SCHOOL DISTRICT 8
SAINT JOHN HIGH SCHOOL
(*Suby of* School District 8)
200 Prince William St Suite 170, Saint John, NB, E2L 2B7
(506) 658-5358
Emp Here 70
SIC 8211 Elementary and secondary schools

D-U-N-S 24-993-6915 (BR)
SCOTIA CAPITAL INC
SCOTIA MCLEOD
1 Market Sq Suite 402, Saint John, NB, E2L 4Z6
(506) 634-8021
Emp Here 23
SIC 6211 Security brokers and dealers

D-U-N-S 20-692-1194 (SL)
SISTERS OF CHARITY OF THE IMMACULATE CONCEPTION
31 Cliff St, Saint John, NB, E2L 3A9
(506) 847-2065
Emp Here 60 *Sales* 3,939,878
SIC 8661 Religious organizations

D-U-N-S 25-400-4690 (BR)
STEWART MCKELVEY STIRLING SCALES
(*Suby of* Stewart McKelvey Stirling Scales)
44 Chipman Hill Suite 1000, Saint John, NB, E2L 2A9
(506) 632-1970
Emp Here 80

SIC 8111 Legal services

D-U-N-S 20-314-1411   (BR)
TIDAN INC
PRINCE EDWARD SQUARE
100 Prince Edward St, Saint John, NB, E2L 4M5
(506) 649-4445
Emp Here 20
SIC 6513 Apartment building operators

D-U-N-S 24-321-4744   (BR)
UNIVERSAL SALES, LIMITED
UNIVERSAL TRUCK & TRAILER
397 City Rd, Saint John, NB, E2L 5B9
(506) 634-1250
Emp Here 25
SIC 7699 Repair services, nec

D-U-N-S 20-813-0146   (BR)
UNIVERSITY OF NEW BRUNSWICK
UNIVERSITY OF NEW BRUNSWICK SAINT JOHN
100 Tucker Park Rd, Saint John, NB, E2L 4L5
(506) 648-5670
Emp Here 300
SIC 8221 Colleges and universities

D-U-N-S 20-618-1604   (SL)
VETS TAXI LTD
VETS AIRPORT SERVICE
17 North Market St Suite 14, Saint John, NB, E2L 4Z8
(506) 658-2020
Emp Here 70   *Sales* 2,115,860
SIC 4121 Taxicabs

D-U-N-S 25-095-5366   (HQ)
WORKPLACE HEALTH, SAFETY & COMPENSATION COMMISSION OF NEW BRUNSWICK
WHSCC
(*Suby of* Workplace Health, Safety & Compensation Commission of New Brunswick)
1 Portland St, Saint John, NB, E2L 3X9
(506) 632-2200
Emp Here 100   *Emp Total* 493
Sales 326,314,584
SIC 6331 Fire, marine, and casualty insurance
Pr Douglas Stanley
    Roberta Dugas
    Conrad Pitre

Saint John, NB E2M
Saint John County

D-U-N-S 25-296-3343   (BR)
BANK OF NOVA SCOTIA, THE
SCOTIA BANK
35 Main St W, Saint John, NB, E2M 3M9
(506) 658-3360
Emp Here 30
SIC 6021 National commercial banks

D-U-N-S 24-994-7797   (SL)
CARLETON KIRK LODGE NURSING HOME
2 Carleton Kirk Pl, Saint John, NB, E2M 5B8
(506) 643-7040
Emp Here 105   *Sales* 4,815,406
SIC 8051 Skilled nursing care facilities

D-U-N-S 24-803-8366   (HQ)
COX RADIO & TV LTD
COX ELECTRONICS & COMMUNICATIONS
(*Suby of* Brewers Enterprises Limited)
843 Fairville Blvd, Saint John, NB, E2M 5T9
(506) 635-8207
Emp Here 44   *Emp Total* 103
Sales 12,156,044
SIC 5731 Radio, television, and electronic stores
Philip Brewer

D-U-N-S 24-472-0884   (BR)
DAY & ROSS INC

141 Alloy Dr Unit 084, Saint John, NB, E2M 7S9
(506) 635-1212
Emp Here 40
SIC 4731 Freight transportation arrangement

D-U-N-S 25-879-0419   (BR)
DUMVILLE RESTAURANTS LTD
BURGER KING RESTAURANT
(*Suby of* Dumville Restaurants Ltd)
777 Fairville Blvd, Saint John, NB, E2M 5T8
(506) 635-8335
Emp Here 25
SIC 5812 Eating places

D-U-N-S 20-291-4321   (BR)
FER & METAUX AMERICAINS S.E.C.
Pier 10 West Side, Saint John, NB, E2M 5S8
(506) 672-4000
Emp Here 25
SIC 4953 Refuse systems

D-U-N-S 20-814-0959   (BR)
FLEETWAY INC
45 Gifford Rd, Saint John, NB, E2M 5K7
(506) 635-7733
Emp Here 200
SIC 7363 Help supply services

D-U-N-S 25-222-7574   (SL)
I C R GENERAL CONTRACTORS LIMITED
1150 Fairville Blvd, Saint John, NB, E2M 5T6
(506) 672-1482
Emp Here 20   *Sales* 5,006,160
SIC 1542 Nonresidential construction, nec
Dir John Hickey
Dir Patrick Hickey

D-U-N-S 24-363-8421   (BR)
IRVING PULP & PAPER, LIMITED
(*Suby of* J. D. Irving, Limited)
408 Mill St, Saint John, NB, E2M 3H1
(506) 635-6666
Emp Here 100
SIC 2611 Pulp mills

D-U-N-S 25-361-0448   (BR)
J. D. IRVING, LIMITED
SHAMROCK TRUSS & COMPONENTS
(*Suby of* J. D. Irving, Limited)
10 Galbraith Pl, Saint John, NB, E2M 7L1
(506) 634-7474
Emp Here 40
SIC 2439 Structural wood members, nec

D-U-N-S 24-363-8439   (BR)
LAIDLAW CARRIERS VAN LP
BROOKVILLE CARRIERS VAN, DIV OF
65 Alloy Dr, Saint John, NB, E2M 7S9
(506) 633-7555
Emp Here 75
SIC 4213 Trucking, except local

D-U-N-S 25-866-0828   (BR)
LOBLAWS SUPERMARKETS LIMITED
LOBLAWS
621 Fairville Blvd, Saint John, NB, E2M 4X5
(506) 633-2420
Emp Here 20
SIC 5411 Grocery stores

D-U-N-S 20-022-9805   (HQ)
MOOSEHEAD BREWERIES LIMITED
HOP CITY BREWING CO
89 Main St W, Saint John, NB, E2M 3H2
(506) 635-7000
Emp Here 250   *Emp Total* 250
Sales 35,823,704
SIC 2082 Malt beverages
Dir Bruce Mccubbin
    Derek Oland
Pr Andrew Oland
VP Fin Patrick Oland
S&M/VP Jim Eagles
S&M/VP Matthew Johnston
VP Opers Wayne Arsenult
Sec Paul Mcgraw

D-U-N-S 25-018-5279   (BR)
NEW BRUNSWICK POWER CORPORATION
COLESON COVE
4077 King William Rd, Saint John, NB, E2M 7T7
(506) 635-8225
Emp Here 113
SIC 4911 Electric services

D-U-N-S 24-678-9437   (BR)
PARTS FOR TRUCKS, INC
PARTS FOR TRUCKS, INC
1100 Fairville Blvd, Saint John, NB, E2M 5T6
(506) 672-4040
Emp Here 20
SIC 5013 Motor vehicle supplies and new parts

D-U-N-S 25-877-7572   (BR)
PEPSICO CANADA ULC
HOSTESS FRITO LAY CANADA
(*Suby of* Pepsico, Inc.)
35 Stinson Dr, Saint John, NB, E2M 7E3
(506) 674-0923
Emp Here 20
SIC 5145 Confectionery

D-U-N-S 25-320-8599   (BR)
PUROLATOR INC.
PUROLATOR INC
48 Hatheway Cres, Saint John, NB, E2M 5V3
(506) 635-8205
Emp Here 28
SIC 4731 Freight transportation arrangement

D-U-N-S 20-023-8496   (BR)
REGIONAL HEALTH AUTHORITY B
RIDGEWOOD ADDICTION SERVICES
416 Bay St, Saint John, NB, E2M 7L4
(506) 674-4300
Emp Here 70
SIC 8069 Specialty hospitals, except psychiatric

D-U-N-S 20-710-0384   (BR)
SCHOOL DISTRICT 8
ST ROSE ELEMENTARY SCHOOL
(*Suby of* School District 8)
700 Manawagonish Rd, Saint John, NB, E2M 3W5
(506) 658-5364
Emp Here 25
SIC 8211 Elementary and secondary schools

D-U-N-S 20-710-0335   (BR)
SCHOOL DISTRICT 8
ST PATRICK'S
(*Suby of* School District 8)
172 City Line, Saint John, NB, E2M 1L3
(506) 658-5362
Emp Here 30
SIC 8211 Elementary and secondary schools

D-U-N-S 20-650-0105   (BR)
SCHOOL DISTRICT 8
BARNHILL MEMORIAL SCHOOL
(*Suby of* School District 8)
750 Manawagonish Rd, Saint John, NB, E2M 3W5
(506) 658-5393
Emp Here 43
SIC 8211 Elementary and secondary schools

D-U-N-S 25-242-3504   (BR)
SCHOOL DISTRICT 8
HAVELOCK SCHOOL
(*Suby of* School District 8)
520 Young St, Saint John, NB, E2M 2V4
(506) 658-5342
Emp Here 20
SIC 8211 Elementary and secondary schools

D-U-N-S 25-309-1128   (BR)
SOBEYS CAPITAL INCORPORATED
SOBEYS 576
1 Plaza Ave, Saint John, NB, E2M 0C2

(506) 674-1460
Emp Here 125
SIC 5411 Grocery stores

D-U-N-S 25-309-1045   (BR)
SOBEYS CAPITAL INCORPORATED
SOBEYS 562
3701 Westfield Road Suite 562, Saint John, NB, E2M 7T4
(506) 738-2353
Emp Here 38
SIC 5411 Grocery stores

D-U-N-S 24-031-7185   (BR)
T4G LIMITED
384 Lancaster Ave, Saint John, NB, E2M 2L5
(506) 632-2520
Emp Here 50
SIC 7379 Computer related services, nec

D-U-N-S 20-165-5367   (BR)
VICTORIAN ORDER OF NURSES FOR CANADA
VON SAINT JOHN DISTRICT
30 Plaza Ave Suite 6b, Saint John, NB, E2M 0C3
(506) 635-1530
Emp Here 20
SIC 8082 Home health care services

D-U-N-S 25-697-3801   (BR)
VICTORIAN ORDER OF NURSES FOR CANADA
VON SAINT JOHN DISTRICT
30 Plaza Ave Suite 6, Saint John, NB, E2M 0C3

Emp Here 40
SIC 8082 Home health care services

D-U-N-S 20-108-9534   (BR)
WORKPLACE HEALTH, SAFETY & COMPENSATION COMMISSION OF NEW BRUNSWICK
WORKERS REHABILITATION CENTER
3700 Westfield Rd, Saint John, NB, E2M 5Z4
(506) 738-8411
Emp Here 100
SIC 8011 Offices and clinics of medical doctors

Saint John, NB E2N
Saint John County

D-U-N-S 20-338-2135   (BR)
AIR CANADA
AIR CANADA CARGO
4180 Loch Lomond Rd, Saint John, NB, E2N 1L7
(506) 632-1526
Emp Here 300
SIC 4512 Air transportation, scheduled

D-U-N-S 20-710-0285   (BR)
SCHOOL DISTRICT 8
LOCHLAMOND SCHOOL
(*Suby of* School District 8)
25 Evergreen Ave, Saint John, NB, E2N 1H3
(506) 658-5350
Emp Here 32
SIC 8211 Elementary and secondary schools

Saint John, NB E2R
Saint John County

D-U-N-S 24-673-9242   (BR)
ALUMA SYSTEMS INC
ALUMA SYSTEMS (CANADA)
(*Suby of* Clayton, Dubilier & Rice, Inc.)
250 Industrial Dr, Saint John, NB, E2R 1A5
(506) 633-9820
Emp Here 50
SIC 7353 Heavy construction equipment

rental

D-U-N-S 20-814-0918   (BR)
CANADA PIPE COMPANY ULC
CLOW CANADA
245 Industrial Dr, Saint John, NB, E2R 1A4
(506) 633-2541
Emp Here 62
SIC 3491 Industrial valves

D-U-N-S 25-881-3062   (BR)
DRURY'S TRANSFER LTD
11 Expansion Ave, Saint John, NB, E2R 1A6
(506) 634-1380
Emp Here 35
SIC 4212 Local trucking, without storage

D-U-N-S 24-377-3137   (BR)
INTEPLAST BAGS AND FILMS CORPORA-TION
291 Industrial Dr, Saint John, NB, E2R 1A4
(506) 633-8101
Emp Here 55
SIC 2673 Bags: plastic, laminated, and coated

D-U-N-S 25-687-2151   (SL)
SAEPLAST AMERICAS INC
100 Industrial Dr, Saint John, NB, E2R 1A5
(506) 633-0101
Emp Here 56   *Sales* 8,229,385
SIC 3089 Plastics products, nec
Brian Gooding
Dir Fin David Burnham

Saint-Andre, NB E3Y

D-U-N-S 20-710-0822   (BR)
DISTRICT SCOLAIRE 3
REGIONAL SEINGGNGRE SCHOOL
477 Ch De L'Eglise, Saint-Andre, NB, E3Y 2Y2
(506) 473-7762
Emp Here 30
SIC 8211 Elementary and secondary schools

D-U-N-S 20-446-1024   (SL)
PRES DU LAC LTD
AUBERGE PRES DU LAC INN
10039 Route 144, Saint-Andre, NB, E3Y 3H5
(506) 473-1300
Emp Here 50   *Sales* 2,188,821
SIC 7011 Hotels and motels

Saint-Antoine, NB E4V
Kent County

D-U-N-S 20-710-0905   (BR)
DISTRICT SCOLAIRE 11
ECOLE CAMILLE-VAUTOUR
(*Suby of* District Scolaire 11)
7 Clement Ave, Saint-Antoine, NB, E4V 1E2
(506) 525-4000
Emp Here 30
SIC 8211 Elementary and secondary schools

Saint-Basile, NB E7C
Madawaska County

D-U-N-S 25-241-3570   (BR)
DISTRICT SCOLAIRE 3
ECOLE REGIONALE DE ST BASILE
(*Suby of* District Scolaire 3)
247 Rue Principale, Saint-Basile, NB, E7C 1H7
(506) 263-3407
Emp Here 40
SIC 8211 Elementary and secondary schools

D-U-N-S 25-241-3737   (BR)

DISTRICT SCOLAIRE 3
ECOLE ELEMENTARY MAILLET
(*Suby of* District Scolaire 3)
12 Rue Martin, Saint-Basile, NB, E7C 1E4

Emp Here 28
SIC 8211 Elementary and secondary schools

D-U-N-S 24-188-9682   (SL)
OEUVRES DE L'HOTEL-DIEU SAINT-JOSEPH INC, LES
429 Rue Principale, Saint-Basile, NB, E7C 1J2
(506) 263-5546
Emp Here 50   *Sales* 1,824,018
SIC 8361 Residential care

D-U-N-S 20-004-0645   (BR)
STAPLES CANADA INC
STAPLES THE BUSINESS DEPOT
(*Suby of* Staples, Inc.)
11 Boul Centre Madawaska Suite 9, Saint-Basile, NB, E7C 1R7
(506) 736-6956
Emp Here 35
SIC 5943 Stationery stores

Saint-Francois-De-Madawaska, NB E7A

D-U-N-S 20-009-5904   (SL)
GROUPE WESTCO INC
9 Rue Westco, Saint-Francois-De-Madawaska, NB, E7A 1A5
(506) 992-3112
Emp Here 100   *Sales* 6,313,604
SIC 5499 Miscellaneous food stores
Pr Pr Bertin Cyr
Dir Rino Levasseur
Dir Albert Bouchard
Dir Tom Soucy
Dir Rodrigue Nadeau
Dir Yvon Cyr

D-U-N-S 25-065-8341   (BR)
MAPLE LODGE FARMS LTD
NADEAU FERME AVICOLE
2222 Commerciale St, Saint-Francois-De-Madawaska, NB, E7A 1B6
(506) 992-2192
Emp Here 300
SIC 2015 Poultry slaughtering and processing

Saint-Jacques, NB E7B

D-U-N-S 25-241-3653   (BR)
DISTRICT SCOLAIRE 3
ECOLE ST JACQUES
(*Suby of* District Scolaire 3)
10 Rue Ecole, Saint-Jacques, NB, E7B 1E7
(506) 735-2067
Emp Here 44
SIC 8211 Elementary and secondary schools

Saint-Leonard, NB E7E

D-U-N-S 24-334-6884   (BR)
DISTRICT SCOLAIRE 3
ECOLE GRANDE RIVIERE
40 Rue De L'Ecole, Saint-Leonard, NB, E7E 1Y6
(506) 423-3003
Emp Here 51
SIC 8211 Elementary and secondary schools

D-U-N-S 24-573-3423   (SL)
FOYER NOTRE-DAME DE SAINT-LEONARD INC
604 Rue Principale, Saint-Leonard, NB, E7E 2H5

Emp Here 75   *Sales* 2,772,507
SIC 8361 Residential care

D-U-N-S 20-338-1921   (BR)
J. D. IRVING, LIMITED
SAINT-LEONARD SAWMILL DIVISION
(*Suby of* J. D. Irving, Limited)
48 Ch De La Grande-Riviere, Saint-Leonard, NB, E7E 2M7
(506) 423-3333
Emp Here 250
SIC 2421 Sawmills and planing mills, general

Saint-Louis-De-Kent, NB E4X

D-U-N-S 20-023-3054   (SL)
COOPERATIVE DE ST LOUIS, LIMITEE, LA
SEARS CATALOGUE
10547 Rue Principale Unite 1, Saint-Louis-De-Kent, NB, E4X 1E8
(506) 876-2431
Emp Here 56   *Sales* 4,012,839
SIC 5311 Department stores

D-U-N-S 20-710-0897   (BR)
DISTRICT SCOLAIRE 11
NGER, MARCEL FRANCOIS RICHARD
(*Suby of* District Scolaire 11)
49 Rue Du College Suite 1, Saint-Louis-De-Kent, NB, E4X 1C2
(506) 876-3400
Emp Here 50
SIC 8211 Elementary and secondary schools

D-U-N-S 25-290-8884   (SL)
VILLA MARIA INC
19 Rue Du College, Saint-Louis-De-Kent, NB, E4X 1C2
(506) 876-3488
Emp Here 100   *Sales* 4,523,563
SIC 8051 Skilled nursing care facilities

Saint-Quentin, NB E8A

D-U-N-S 24-129-1582   (SL)
RESIDENCE MGR MELANSON INC
11 Rue Levesque, Saint-Quentin, NB, E8A 1T1
(506) 235-6030
Emp Here 50   *Sales* 2,261,782
SIC 8051 Skilled nursing care facilities

D-U-N-S 24-312-0677   (BR)
VITALITE HEALTH NETWORK
HOSPITAL HOTEL DIEU ST JOJEPH DE SAINT QUENTIN
21 Rue Canada, Saint-Quentin, NB, E8A 2P6
(506) 235-2300
Emp Here 50
SIC 8062 General medical and surgical hospitals

Saint-Simon, NB E8P
Gloucester County

D-U-N-S 24-605-4209   (SL)
G.E.M. FISHERIES LTD
1324 Route 335, Saint-Simon, NB, E8P 2B2
(506) 727-5217
Emp Here 150   *Sales* 23,130,600
SIC 2091 Canned and cured fish and seafoods
Pr Pr Roger Foulem

Sainte-Anne-De-Kent, NB E4S
Kent County

Emp Here 75   *Sales* 2,772,507
SIC 8361 Residential care

D-U-N-S 25-412-9992   (SL)
RICHARD, B. A. LTEE
374 Ch Cote Sainte-Anne, Sainte-Anne-De-Kent, NB, E4S 1M6
(506) 743-6198
Emp Here 300   *Sales* 33,270,079
SIC 2091 Canned and cured fish and seafoods
Pr Pr Marcel Richard
Bernard Richard
Emilia Richard

Sainte-Anne-De-Madawaska, NB E7E
Madawaska County

D-U-N-S 20-024-4114   (BR)
DISTRICT SCOLAIRE 3
ECOLE SAINTE-ANNE
39 Rue Saint-Joseph, Sainte-Anne-De-Madawaska, NB, E7E 1K8
(506) 445-6202
Emp Here 25
SIC 8211 Elementary and secondary schools

Sainte-Marie-De-Kent, NB E4S
Kent County

D-U-N-S 20-015-5062   (BR)
DISTRICT SCOLAIRE 11
ECOLE MOUNT CARMEL
(*Suby of* District Scolaire 11)
1545 Route 525, Sainte-Marie-De-Kent, NB, E4S 2H2
(506) 955-6000
Emp Here 20
SIC 8211 Elementary and secondary schools

Sainte-Marie-Saint-Raphael, NB E8T
Gloucester County

D-U-N-S 25-241-8132   (BR)
DISTRICT SCOLAIRE FRANCOPHONE NORD-EST
ECOLE ELEMENTAIRE L'ETINCELLE
70 Rue De L'Eglise, Sainte-Marie-Saint-Raphael, NB, E8T 1N8
(506) 344-3022
Emp Here 24
SIC 8211 Elementary and secondary schools

Salisbury, NB E4J

D-U-N-S 24-422-9436   (SL)
6172245 CANADA INC
CABLEWORKS COMMUNICATIONS
3112 Main St Unit 3, Salisbury, NB, E4J 2L6
(506) 372-9542
Emp Here 50   *Sales* 4,377,642
SIC 1731 Electrical work

D-U-N-S 24-000-2068   (BR)
COREY CRAIG LTD
TIM HORTONS
2980 Fredericton Rd Suite 112, Salisbury, NB, E4J 2G1
(506) 372-4522
Emp Here 50
SIC 5812 Eating places

D-U-N-S 24-607-0791   (SL)
LAVOIE, J. P. & SONS LTD
SALISBURY IRVING BIG STOP
2986 Fredericton Rd, Salisbury, NB, E4J 2G1
(506) 372-3333
Emp Here 95   *Sales* 2,845,467

SIC 5812 Eating places

D-U-N-S 20-710-0657   (BR)
SCHOOL DISTRICT 2
J.M.A. APMSTRONG HIGH SCHOOL AND SALISBURY MIDDLE SCHOOL
55 Douglas St, Salisbury, NB, E4J 2B4
(506) 372-3210
Emp Here 70
SIC 8211 Elementary and secondary schools

D-U-N-S 25-242-8826   (BR)
SCHOOL DISTRICT 2
SALISBURY ELEMENTARY SCHOOL
2646 River Rd, Salisbury, NB, E4J 2R2
(506) 372-3207
Emp Here 35
SIC 8211 Elementary and secondary schools

Scoudouc, NB E4P
Madawaska County

D-U-N-S 24-190-0208   (BR)
ARTERRA WINES CANADA, INC
(*Suby of* Arterra Wines Canada, Inc)
10 Levesque St, Scoudouc, NB, E4P 3P3
(506) 532-4426
Emp Here 20
SIC 2084 Wines, brandy, and brandy spirits

D-U-N-S 20-114-5963   (SL)
CLAYCO CONSTRUCTION (2001) LIMITED
5 Pattison St, Scoudouc, NB, E4P 8Y7
(506) 532-8813
Emp Here 42   *Sales* 20,908,080
SIC 1622 Bridge, tunnel, and elevated highway construction
Pr Pr Douglas Tucker

D-U-N-S 25-672-2794   (BR)
COTT CORPORATION
4 Addison Ave, Scoudouc, NB, E4P 3N4

Emp Here 65
SIC 2086 Bottled and canned soft drinks

D-U-N-S 20-037-6593   (HQ)
ENCLOS CORP
CUPPLES CANADA
31 Addison Ave, Scoudouc, NB, E4P 3N3

Emp Here 49   *Emp Total* 550
Sales 8,763,660
SIC 3449 Miscellaneous Metalwork
Pr Gregg Sage
Fin Ex Doug French

Shediac, NB E4P

D-U-N-S 25-615-7389   (BR)
COREY CRAIG LTD
TIM HORTONS
534 Main St, Shediac, NB, E4P 2H1
(506) 533-3990
Emp Here 38
SIC 5812 Eating places

D-U-N-S 25-241-8066   (BR)
DISTRICT SCOLAIRE 11
POLYVALENTE LOUIS J ROBICHAUD
(*Suby of* District Scolaire 11)
435 Main St, Shediac, NB, E4P 2C1
(506) 856-3333
Emp Here 70
SIC 8211 Elementary and secondary schools

D-U-N-S 25-241-8025   (BR)
SCHOOL BOARD DISTRICT 01
ECOLE MGR FRANCOIS BOURGEOIS
294 Av Belliveau, Shediac, NB, E4P 1H6
(506) 533-3303
Emp Here 50

SIC 8211 Elementary and secondary schools

D-U-N-S 24-556-7487   (BR)
SOBEYS CAPITAL INCORPORATED
SOBEYS
183 Main St Suite 738, Shediac, NB, E4P 2A5
(506) 532-0842
Emp Here 150
SIC 5411 Grocery stores

Shippagan, NB E8S

D-U-N-S 20-209-7809   (BR)
ATLANTIC WHOLESALERS LTD
YOUR INDEPENDENT GROCERY
229j Boul J D Gauthier Suite 2, Shippagan, NB, E8S 1N2
(506) 336-0820
Emp Here 32
SIC 5411 Grocery stores

D-U-N-S 25-241-9635   (BR)
DISTRICT SCOLAIRE FRANCOPHONE NORD-EST
ECOLE L'ENVOLLE
135 Rue De L'Ecole, Shippagan, NB, E8S 1V5
(506) 336-3002
Emp Here 50
SIC 8211 Elementary and secondary schools

D-U-N-S 24-532-8182   (BR)
UNIVERSITE DE MONCTON
UNIVERSITY MONCTON CAMPUS SHIPPAGAN
(*Suby of* Universite de Moncton)
218j Boul J D Gauthier, Shippagan, NB, E8S 1P6
(506) 336-3400
Emp Here 60
SIC 8221 Colleges and universities

Springfield Kings Co, NB E5T

D-U-N-S 25-880-8807   (BR)
ANGLOPHONE SOUTH SCHOOL DISTRICT (ASD-S)
BELLEISLE REGIONAL HIGH SCHOOL
(*Suby of* Anglophone South School District (ASD-S))
1800 Route 124, Springfield Kings Co, NB, E5T 2K2
(506) 485-3030
Emp Here 35
SIC 8211 Elementary and secondary schools

St Andrews, NB E5B
Charlotte County

D-U-N-S 20-815-3577   (SL)
ALGONQUIN PROPERTIES LIMITED
184 Adolphus St, St Andrews, NB, E5B 1T7
(506) 529-8823
Emp Here 23   *Sales* 1,212,751
SIC 7011 Hotels and motels

D-U-N-S 24-000-2027   (BR)
C & P BAKERY LTD
TIM HORTONS
(*Suby of* C & P Bakery Ltd)
203 Mowat Dr, St Andrews, NB, E5B 2N9
(506) 529-4080
Emp Here 25
SIC 5812 Eating places

D-U-N-S 20-665-7160   (BR)
FAIRMONT HOTELS & RESORTS INC
184 Adolphus St, St Andrews, NB, E5B 1T7
(506) 529-7195
Emp Here 200

SIC 7231 Beauty shops

D-U-N-S 25-292-4915   (BR)
FAIRMONT HOTELS & RESORTS INC
184 Adolphus St, St Andrews, NB, E5B 1T7
(506) 529-8823
Emp Here 250
SIC 7011 Hotels and motels

D-U-N-S 20-704-2982   (BR)
FAIRMONT HOTELS INC
465 Brandy Cove Rd, St Andrews, NB, E5B 2L6
(506) 529-7142
Emp Here 30
SIC 7992 Public golf courses

D-U-N-S 25-848-7941   (SL)
HEATHER CURLING CLUB INCORPORATED
24 Reed Ave Suite 1, St Andrews, NB, E5B 1A1
(506) 529-1096
Emp Here 60   *Sales* 2,407,703
SIC 7997 Membership sports and recreation clubs

D-U-N-S 25-242-1441   (BR)
SCHOOL DISTRICT NO 10
SIR JAMES DUNN ACADEMY
(*Suby of* School District No 10)
180 King St, St Andrews, NB, E5B 1Y7
(506) 529-5010
Emp Here 20
SIC 8211 Elementary and secondary schools

St George, NB E5C
Charlotte County

D-U-N-S 20-165-5433   (BR)
SCHOOL DISTRICT NO 10
SAINT GEORGE ELEMENTARY
118 Brunswick St, St George, NB, E5C 1A9
(506) 755-4020
Emp Here 32
SIC 8211 Elementary and secondary schools

D-U-N-S 25-528-2188   (BR)
SCHOOL DISTRICT NO 10
FUNDY HIGH SCHOOL
(*Suby of* School District No 10)
44 Mount Pleasant Rd, St George, NB, E5C 3K4
(506) 755-4005
Emp Here 57
SIC 8211 Elementary and secondary schools

St Stephen, NB E3L
Charlotte County

D-U-N-S 20-752-3114   (HQ)
C & P BAKERY LTD
TIM HORTONS
(*Suby of* C & P Bakery Ltd)
131 King St Suite 638, St Stephen, NB, E3L 2C7
(506) 465-0180
Emp Here 50   *Emp Total* 75
Sales 2,261,782
SIC 5812 Eating places

D-U-N-S 24-000-2456   (BR)
C & P BAKERY LTD
TIM HORTONS
(*Suby of* C & P Bakery Ltd)
78 Milltown Blvd Suite 76, St Stephen, NB, E3L 1G6

Emp Here 25
SIC 5812 Eating places

D-U-N-S 20-023-4094   (HQ)

GANONG BROS., LIMITED
(*Suby of* DAG Holdings Inc)
1 Chocolate Dr, St Stephen, NB, E3L 2X5
(506) 465-5600
Emp Here 300   *Emp Total* 325
Sales 30,625,693
SIC 2064 Candy and other confectionery products
Pr Pr David Ganong
VP Sls J. Terry Arthurs
VP Jean-Marc Lefebvre
VP Sls Dana Branscombe
S&M/VP Greg Fash
Fin Ex Cathy Hastey
Pr Douglas Ettinger

D-U-N-S 24-343-9895   (HQ)
GANONG CHOCOLATIER INC
(*Suby of* DAG Holdings Inc)
1 Chocolate Dr, St Stephen, NB, E3L 2X5
(506) 465-5600
Emp Here 20   *Emp Total* 325
Sales 32,656,000
SIC 2064 Candy and other confectionery products
Pr Pr David Ganong
  Purdy Crawford
Dir Diane Ganong
Dir Doug Ettinger
Dir Krystyna Hoeg
Dir Bruce Mccubbin
Dir William Mcmackin
Dir Richard Oland
Dir Hubert Saint-Onge

D-U-N-S 24-472-9604   (BR)
J. D. IRVING, LIMITED
KENT BUILDING SUPPLIES
(*Suby of* J. D. Irving, Limited)
188 King St, St Stephen, NB, E3L 2E2
(506) 466-1250
Emp Here 40
SIC 5211 Lumber and other building materials

D-U-N-S 20-651-7380   (SL)
LINCOURT MANOR INC
1 Chipman St, St Stephen, NB, E3L 2W9
(506) 466-7855
Emp Here 89   *Sales* 4,085,799
SIC 8051 Skilled nursing care facilities

D-U-N-S 25-984-8737   (BR)
LOBLAWS INC
REAL CANADIAN SUPERSTORE
195 King St, St Stephen, NB, E3L 2E4
(506) 465-1457
Emp Here 130
SIC 5411 Grocery stores

D-U-N-S 25-195-9417   (BR)
REGIONAL HEALTH AUTHORITY NB
REGIONAL HEALTH AUTHORITY B
4 Garden St Suite 219, St Stephen, NB, E3L 2L9
(506) 465-4444
Emp Here 200
SIC 8062 General medical and surgical hospitals

D-U-N-S 25-097-1314   (BR)
SCHOOL DISTRICT NO 10
ST. STEPHEN ELEMENTARY SCHOOL
(*Suby of* School District No 10)
16 Kings Crt, St Stephen, NB, E3L 3B2
(506) 466-7303
Emp Here 50
SIC 8211 Elementary and secondary schools

D-U-N-S 20-710-0863   (BR)
SCHOOL DISTRICT NO 10
ST STEPHEN MIDDLE SCHOOL
11 School St, St Stephen, NB, E3L 2N4
(506) 466-7311
Emp Here 45
SIC 8211 Elementary and secondary schools

St-Joseph-De-Madawaska, NB E7B
Madawaska County

D-U-N-S 25-241-3612   (BR)
DISTRICT SCOLAIRE 3
ECOLE ST JOSEPH
(*Suby of* District Scolaire 3)
562 Ch Toussaint, St-Joseph-De-Madawaska,
NB, E7B 2T8
(506) 735-2956
Emp Here 20
SIC 8211 Elementary and secondary schools

Stanley, NB E6B

D-U-N-S 20-710-0681   (BR)
ANGLOPHONE WEST SCHOOL DISTRICT (ASD-W)
STANLEY REGIONAL SCHOOL
28 Bridge St, Stanley, NB, E6B 1B2
(506) 367-7690
Emp Here 50
SIC 8211 Elementary and secondary schools

D-U-N-S 24-190-1339   (SL)
NASHWAAK VILLA INC
32 Limekiln Rd, Stanley, NB, E6B 1E6
(506) 367-7731
Emp Here 50   *Sales* 2,261,782
SIC 8051 Skilled nursing care facilities

Sunny Corner, NB E9E
Northumberland County

D-U-N-S 20-710-0533   (BR)
DISTRICT EDUCATION COUNCIL-SCHOOL DISTRICT 16
NORTH AND SOUTH ESK REGIONAL HIGH-SCHOOL
(*Suby of* District Education Council-School District 16)
40 Northwest Rd, Sunny Corner, NB, E9E 1J4
(506) 836-7000
Emp Here 30
SIC 8211 Elementary and secondary schools

D-U-N-S 20-037-7237   (BR)
DISTRICT EDUCATION COUNCIL-SCHOOL DISTRICT 16
NORTH & SOUTH ESK ELEMENTARY
(*Suby of* District Education Council-School District 16)
36 Northwest Rd, Sunny Corner, NB, E9E 1J4
(506) 836-7010
Emp Here 40
SIC 8211 Elementary and secondary schools

Sussex, NB E4E

D-U-N-S 25-242-3736   (BR)
ANGLOPHONE SOUTH SCHOOL DISTRICT (ASD-S)
SUSSEX MIDDLE SCHOOL
(*Suby of* Anglophone South School District (ASD-S))
49 Bryant Dr, Sussex, NB, E4E 2P2
(506) 432-2022
Emp Here 62
SIC 8211 Elementary and secondary schools

D-U-N-S 20-297-1714   (BR)
ANGLOPHONE SOUTH SCHOOL DISTRICT (ASD-S)
SUSSEX REGIONAL HIGH SCHOOL
55 Leonard Dr, Sussex, NB, E4E 2P8

(506) 432-2017
Emp Here 92
SIC 8211 Elementary and secondary schools

D-U-N-S 20-086-6031   (BR)
ATLANTIC WHOLESALERS LTD
SUSSEX SUPER VALUE
10 Lower Cove Rd, Sussex, NB, E4E 0B7
(506) 433-9820
Emp Here 90
SIC 5411 Grocery stores

D-U-N-S 20-023-7030   (BR)
CLARK, J & SON LIMITED
NATIONAL CAR RENTAL
50 Leonard Dr, Sussex, NB, E4E 2R4
(506) 433-1160
Emp Here 22
SIC 5511 New and used car dealers

D-U-N-S 25-690-5175   (SL)
DRURY'S TRANSFER REG'D
160 Stewart Ave, Sussex, NB, E4E 2G2

Emp Here 100   *Sales* 10,851,840
SIC 4212 Local trucking, without storage
Pr Pr Westley Armour

D-U-N-S 20-814-2398   (BR)
J. D. IRVING, LIMITED
KENT BUILDING SUPPLIES
(*Suby of* J. D. Irving, Limited)
66 Lower Cove Rd, Sussex, NB, E4E 0B7
(506) 432-2930
Emp Here 40
SIC 5211 Lumber and other building materials

D-U-N-S 24-130-4526   (SL)
KINGSWOOD UNIVERSITY
26 Western St, Sussex, NB, E4E 1E6
(506) 432-4400
Emp Here 56   *Sales* 3,064,349
SIC 8299 Schools and educational services, nec

D-U-N-S 24-532-4603   (SL)
KIWANIS NURSING HOME INC
11 Bryant Dr, Sussex, NB, E4E 2P3
(506) 432-3118
Emp Here 90   *Sales* 4,085,799
SIC 8051 Skilled nursing care facilities

D-U-N-S 20-307-2301   (BR)
POTASH   CORPORATION   OF SASKATCHEWAN INC
Ggd, Sussex, NB, E4E 5L2
(506) 432-8400
Emp Here 20
SIC 1474 Potash, soda, and borate minerals

D-U-N-S 24-955-5970   (BR)
REGIONAL HEALTH AUTHORITY NB
REGIONAL HEALTH AUTHORITY B
75 Leonard Dr, Sussex, NB, E4E 2P7
(506) 432-3100
Emp Here 160
SIC 8062 General medical and surgical hospitals

D-U-N-S 20-810-5705   (BR)
REGIONAL HEALTH AUTHORITY NB
REGIONAL HEALTH AUTHORITY B
20 Kennedy Dr Suite 4, Sussex, NB, E4E 2P1
(506) 432-3280
Emp Here 27
SIC 8082 Home health care services

D-U-N-S 20-700-6565   (BR)
REITMANS (CANADA) LIMITEE
138 Main St, Sussex, NB, E4E 3E1
(506) 432-6244
Emp Here 25
SIC 5621 Women's clothing stores

D-U-N-S 24-329-9257   (BR)
WAL-MART CANADA CORP
80 Main St, Sussex, NB, E4E 1Y6
(506) 432-9333
Emp Here 200

SIC 5311 Department stores

Sussex Corner, NB E4E

D-U-N-S 25-242-3173   (BR)
ANGLOPHONE SOUTH SCHOOL DISTRICT (ASD-S)
SUSSEX CORNER ELEMENTARY SCHOOL
(*Suby of* Anglophone South School District (ASD-S))
12 Dutch Valley Rd, Sussex Corner, NB, E4E 2Y1
(506) 432-2018
Emp Here 36
SIC 8211 Elementary and secondary schools

Tabusintac, NB E9H
Northumberland County

D-U-N-S 20-023-7931   (SL)
HEVECO LTD
4534 Route 11, Tabusintac, NB, E9H 1J4
(506) 779-9277
Emp Here 55   *Sales* 3,283,232
SIC 1499 Miscellaneous nonMetallic minerals, except fuels

The Glades, NB E4J
Westmoreland County

D-U-N-S 24-671-0024   (SL)
JORDAN LIFECARE CENTRE INC
747 Sanatorium Rd, The Glades, NB, E4J 1W6
(506) 756-3355
Emp Here 50   *Sales* 2,261,782
SIC 8051 Skilled nursing care facilities

Tracadie, NB E1X
Gloucester County

D-U-N-S 20-063-2151   (BR)
DISTRICT   SCOLAIRE   FRANCOPHONE NORD-EST
ECOLE LA VILLA DES AMIS
6830 Route 11, Tracadie, NB, E1X 4P4
(506) 394-3560
Emp Here 24
SIC 8211 Elementary and secondary schools

Tracadie-Sheila, NB E1X
Gloucester County

D-U-N-S 25-897-3395   (BR)
ATLANTIC WHOLESALERS LTD
TRACADIE FOOD WAREHOUSE
3409 Rue Principale Suite 31, Tracadie-Sheila, NB, E1X 1C7
(506) 393-1155
Emp Here 120
SIC 5411 Grocery stores

D-U-N-S 20-710-0517   (BR)
DISTRICT   SCOLAIRE   FRANCOPHONE NORD-EST
ECOLE POLYVALENTE
585 Church St, Tracadie-Sheila, NB, E1X 1G5
(506) 394-3500
Emp Here 90
SIC 8211 Elementary and secondary schools

D-U-N-S 25-241-7548   (BR)
DISTRICT   SCOLAIRE   FRANCOPHONE

NORD-EST
COLE PRIMAIRE LA SOURCE
Gd, Tracadie-Sheila, NB, E1X 1G4
(506) 394-3555
Emp Here 52
SIC 8211 Elementary and secondary schools

D-U-N-S 20-852-0929   (BR)
DISTRICT   SCOLAIRE   FRANCOPHONE NORD-EST
ECOLE LE TREMPLIN
520 Rue De L'Eglise, Tracadie-Sheila, NB, E1X 1B1
(506) 394-3494
Emp Here 32
SIC 8211 Elementary and secondary schools

D-U-N-S 20-814-0504   (BR)
DISTRICT   SCOLAIRE   FRANCOPHONE NORD-EST
POLY BALENPE WA LOSOER
585 Rue De L'Eglise, Tracadie-Sheila, NB, E1X 1B1
(506) 394-3508
Emp Here 100
SIC 8211 Elementary and secondary schools

D-U-N-S 20-749-7236   (SL)
GLOUCESTER CONSTRUCTION LTD
4260 Rue Principale, Tracadie-Sheila, NB, E1X 1B9

Emp Here 30   *Sales* 5,545,013
SIC 1542 Nonresidential construction, nec
Pr Pr Stephane Mcgraw

D-U-N-S 20-691-9263   (SL)
MANDATE STEEL ERECTORS LTD
2676 Rue Commerce, Tracadie-Sheila, NB, E1X 1G5
(506) 395-7777
Emp Here 75   *Sales* 11,463,850
SIC 1791 Structural steel erection
Leopold Theriault
Dir Kenneth Pitre

D-U-N-S 20-084-0747   (SL)
MCCRAM INC
MCDONALD'S RESTAURANT
3458 Rue Principale, Tracadie-Sheila, NB, E1X 1C8
(506) 394-1111
Emp Here 140   *Sales* 4,231,721
SIC 5812 Eating places

D-U-N-S 25-090-9959   (BR)
REGIONAL HEALTH AUTHORITY A
CENTRE HOSPITALIER DE TRACADIE
400 Rue Des Hospitalieres, Tracadie-Sheila, NB, E1X 1G5
(506) 394-3000
Emp Here 280
SIC 8062 General medical and surgical hospitals

D-U-N-S 25-878-4784   (BR)
SOBEYS CAPITAL INCORPORATED
FRESHCO
426 Rue Du Moulin, Tracadie-Sheila, NB, E1X 1A4

Emp Here 30
SIC 5411 Grocery stores

D-U-N-S 20-815-2280   (SL)
VILLA ST JOSEPH INC
3400 Rue Albert, Tracadie-Sheila, NB, E1X 1C8
(506) 394-4800
Emp Here 89   *Sales* 4,085,799
SIC 8051 Skilled nursing care facilities

Upper Rexton, NB E4W
Kent County

D-U-N-S 20-337-0143   (BR)

PREMIER HORTICULTURE LTEE
PREMIER TECH HORTICULTURE LTD
9789 Route 116, Upper Rexton, NB, E4W 3C1
(506) 523-9161
Emp Here 40
SIC 5159 Farm-product raw materials, nec

Utopia, NB E5C
Charlotte County

D-U-N-S 24-831-5350   (BR)
J. D. IRVING, LIMITED
LAKE UTOPIA PAPER
(*Suby of* J. D. Irving, Limited)
600 Route 785, Utopia, NB, E5C 2K4
(506) 755-3384
Emp Here 200
SIC 2679 Converted paper products, nec

Val-D'Amour, NB E3N
Restigouche County

D-U-N-S 20-710-0152   (BR)
CONSEIL SCOLAIRE DISTRICT NO 5
M G R NELENSON
3 Rue Ecole, Val-D'Amour, NB, E3N 5E2
(506) 789-2257
Emp Here 20
SIC 8211 Elementary and secondary schools

Welshpool, NB E5E
Charlotte County

D-U-N-S 20-287-2672   (BR)
PROVINCE OF NEW BRUNSWICK
TOURISM COMMUNICATION CENTER
136 Herring Cove Rd, Welshpool, NB, E5E
1B8
(506) 752-7010
Emp Here 20
SIC 7992 Public golf courses

Wilsons Beach, NB E5E
Charlotte County

D-U-N-S 20-710-0855   (BR)
SCHOOL DISTRICT NO 10
CAMPOBELLO SCHOOL
1722 Route 774, Wilsons Beach, NB, E5E 1K7
(506) 752-7000
Emp Here 28
SIC 8211 Elementary and secondary schools

Woodstock, NB E7M

D-U-N-S 20-345-9540   (SL)
659725 NEW BRUNSWICK INC
HAMPTON INN & SUITES
215 Beardsley Rd, Woodstock, NB, E7M 4E1
(506) 328-9848
Emp Here 53   *Sales* 2,772,003
SIC 7011 Hotels and motels

D-U-N-S 25-086-2471   (BR)
ATLANTIC WHOLESALERS LTD
REAL ATLANTIC SUPERSTORE, THE
350 Connell St, Woodstock, NB, E7M 5G8
(506) 328-1100
Emp Here 120
SIC 5411 Grocery stores

D-U-N-S 25-295-8673   (BR)
BANK OF NOVA SCOTIA, THE

SCOTIABANK
570 Main St, Woodstock, NB, E7M 2C3
(506) 328-3341
Emp Here 30
SIC 6021 National commercial banks

D-U-N-S 20-189-2168   (BR)
BANK OF MONTREAL
BMO
656 Main St, Woodstock, NB, E7M 2G9
(506) 328-6631
Emp Here 20
SIC 6021 National commercial banks

D-U-N-S 25-298-0834   (BR)
CANADA BREAD COMPANY, LIMITED
MAPLE LEAF
220 Houlton Rd, Woodstock, NB, E7M 4L9
(506) 325-1600
Emp Here 65
SIC 2051 Bread, cake, and related products

D-U-N-S 20-748-9795   (BR)
MITTON HILL ENTERPRISES LIMITED
TIM HORTONS
(*Suby of* Mitton Hill Enterprises Limited)
360 Connell St, Woodstock, NB, E7M 5G9
(506) 328-0106
Emp Here 25
SIC 5812 Eating places

D-U-N-S 24-097-9323   (BR)
**NEW BRUNSWICK COMMUNITY COLLEGE
(NBCC)**
WOODSTOCK CAMPUS
100 Broadway St, Woodstock, NB, E7M 5C5
(506) 325-4400
Emp Here 20
SIC 8221 Colleges and universities

D-U-N-S 25-241-7407   (BR)
SCHOOL DISTRICT 14
WOODSTOCK HIGH SCHOOL
(*Suby of* School District 14)
144 Connell Park Rd, Woodstock, NB, E7M
1M4
(506) 325-4437
Emp Here 60
SIC 8211 Elementary and secondary schools

D-U-N-S 25-241-4131   (BR)
SCHOOL DISTRICT 14
*WOODSTOCK CENTENNIAL ELEMENTARY
SCHOOL*
(*Suby of* School District 14)
101 Helen St, Woodstock, NB, E7M 1W6
(506) 325-4435
Emp Here 48
SIC 8211 Elementary and secondary schools

D-U-N-S 25-241-7480   (BR)
SCHOOL DISTRICT 14
WOODSTOCK MIDDLE SCHOOL
(*Suby of* School District 14)
135 Green St, Woodstock, NB, E7M 1T9

Emp Here 40
SIC 8211 Elementary and secondary schools

D-U-N-S 24-629-5166   (HQ)
SCHOOL DISTRICT 14
(*Suby of* School District 14)
138 Chapel St, Woodstock, NB, E7M 1H3

Emp Here 45   *Emp Total* 800
Sales 73,651,840
SIC 8211 Elementary and secondary schools
Superintnt Lisa Gallagher

D-U-N-S 24-943-6379   (BR)
SOBEYS CAPITAL INCORPORATED
SOBEYS 846
370 Connell St Unit 11, Woodstock, NB, E7M
5G9
(506) 328-6819
Emp Here 150
SIC 5411 Grocery stores

D-U-N-S 24-756-0816   (SL)
VAN NELLE CANADA LIMITED
147 Heller Rd, Woodstock, NB, E7M 1X4
(506) 325-1930
Emp Here 50   *Sales* 2,626,585
SIC 2655 Fiber cans, drums, and similar products

D-U-N-S 24-319-5182   (BR)
WAL-MART CANADA CORP
WALMART
430 Connell St, Woodstock, NB, E7M 5R5
(506) 324-8099
Emp Here 120
SIC 5311 Department stores

Badgers Quay, NL A0G

D-U-N-S 20-988-1317 (BR)
CENTRAL REGIONAL HEALTH AUTHOR-ITY
BONNEWS LODGE
57262 Main St, Badgers Quay, NL, A0G 1B0
(709) 536-2405
Emp Here 150
SIC 8062 General medical and surgical hospitals

Baie Verte, NL A0K

D-U-N-S 24-351-8862 (BR)
ANACONDA MINING INC
310 Highway 410, Baie Verte, NL, A0K 1B0

Emp Here 42
SIC 1041 Gold ores

D-U-N-S 20-580-2908 (BR)
CANADA POST CORPORATION
29 Main St, Baie Verte, NL, A0K 1B0
(709) 532-4626
Emp Here 20
SIC 4311 U.s. postal service

D-U-N-S 20-968-4419 (BR)
CENTRAL REGIONAL HEALTH AUTHOR-ITY
Gd, Baie Verte, NL, A0K 1B0
(709) 532-4281
Emp Here 50
SIC 8062 General medical and surgical hospitals

D-U-N-S 20-735-8495 (BR)
COLLEGE OF THE NORTH ATLANTIC
BAIE VERTE CAMPUS
1 Terra Nova Rd, Baie Verte, NL, A0K 1B0
(709) 532-8066
Emp Here 25
SIC 8221 Colleges and universities

D-U-N-S 25-241-5609 (BR)
NOVA CENTRAL SCHOOL DISTRICT
BAIE VERTE ACADEMY
4 Hwy 410, Baie Verte, NL, A0K 1B0

Emp Here 50
SIC 8211 Elementary and secondary schools

D-U-N-S 25-241-2721 (BR)
NOVA CENTRAL SCHOOL DISTRICT
BAIE VERTE HIGH SCHOOL
48 High St Unit 42, Baie Verte, NL, A0K 1B0
(709) 532-4288
Emp Here 22
SIC 8211 Elementary and secondary schools

D-U-N-S 24-320-4190 (SL)
RAMBLER METALS AND MINING CANADA LIMITED
RAMBLER MINES
309 410 William Chipp Bldg Hwy, Baie Verte, NL, A0K 1B0
(709) 800-1929
Emp Here 23   *Sales* 2,338,878
SIC 1081 Metal mining services

Bay Roberts, NL A0A

D-U-N-S 24-449-7905 (HQ)
ATLANTIC GROCERY DISTRIBUTORS LIM-ITED
1 Hope Ave, Bay Roberts, NL, A0A 1G0
(709) 786-9720
Emp Here 100   *Emp Total* 85
Sales 34,130,289

SIC 5141 Groceries, general line
Pr Pr David Powell
Treas Isabel Powell

D-U-N-S 25-703-1088 (BR)
COMPASSION HOME CARE INC
COMPASSION HOME HEALTH SERVICES
(*Suby of* Compassion Home Care Inc)
Gd, Bay Roberts, NL, A0A 1G0
(709) 786-8677
Emp Here 100
SIC 8322 Individual and family services

D-U-N-S 25-058-6567 (BR)
LOBLAW COMPANIES LIMITED
DOMINION STORES #906
Gd, Bay Roberts, NL, A0A 1G0
(709) 786-6001
Emp Here 85
SIC 5411 Grocery stores

D-U-N-S 24-317-4807 (BR)
SOBEYS CAPITAL INCORPORATED
FRESHCO
Gd, Bay Roberts, NL, A0A 1G0
(709) 786-7194
Emp Here 29
SIC 5411 Grocery stores

Bell Island, NL A0A

D-U-N-S 20-796-3161 (BR)
EASTERN REGIONAL INTEGRATED HEALTH AUTHORITY
Gd, Bell Island, NL, A0A 4H0
(709) 488-2821
Emp Here 50
SIC 8069 Specialty hospitals, except psychiatric

Benoits Cove, NL A0L

D-U-N-S 25-001-7944 (BR)
WESTERN SCHOOL DISTRICT
ST PETER'S ACADEMY
441 Main Rd, Benoits Cove, NL, A0L 1A0
(709) 789-2761
Emp Here 22
SIC 8211 Elementary and secondary schools

Bishops Falls, NL A0H

D-U-N-S 25-241-9510 (BR)
LABRADOR SCHOOL BOARD
NEW FOUNDLAND AND LABRADOR EN-GLISH SCHOOL DISTRICT
1 First Ave, Bishops Falls, NL, A0H 1C0
(709) 258-6472
Emp Here 26
SIC 8211 Elementary and secondary schools

D-U-N-S 24-766-8085 (BR)
NOVA CENTRAL SCHOOL DISTRICT
HELEN TULK ELEMENTARY
1 First Ave, Bishops Falls, NL, A0H 1C0
(709) 258-6472
Emp Here 25
SIC 8211 Elementary and secondary schools

D-U-N-S 20-023-3984 (BR)
NOVA CENTRAL SCHOOL DISTRICT
LEO BURK ACADEMY
166 Main St, Bishops Falls, NL, A0H 1C0
(709) 258-6337
Emp Here 22
SIC 8211 Elementary and secondary schools

D-U-N-S 20-710-1192 (BR)
NOVA CENTRAL SCHOOL DISTRICT

1 First Ave, Bishops Falls, NL, A0H 1C0

Emp Here 50
SIC 8211 Elementary and secondary schools

D-U-N-S 20-787-1315 (BR)
UNITED CHURCH OF CANADA, THE
BISHOPS FALLS UNITED CHURCH
615 Main St, Bishops Falls, NL, A0H 1C0
(709) 258-5556
Emp Here 27
SIC 8661 Religious organizations

Bloomfield, NL A0C

D-U-N-S 20-547-4286 (SL)
SEXTON LUMBER CO LIMITED
Rte 233 Main Rd, Bloomfield, NL, A0C 1A0
(709) 467-5616
Emp Here 50   *Sales* 4,742,446
SIC 2421 Sawmills and planing mills, general

Bonavista, NL A0C

D-U-N-S 25-074-1568 (BR)
COLLEGE OF THE NORTH ATLANTIC
301 Confederation Dr, Bonavista, NL, A0C 1B0
(709) 468-2610
Emp Here 20
SIC 8221 Colleges and universities

D-U-N-S 24-326-4962 (BR)
EASTERN REGIONAL INTEGRATED HEALTH AUTHORITY
GOLDEN HEIGHTS MANOR
2743 Campbell St, Bonavista, NL, A0C 1B0
(709) 468-7881
Emp Here 20
SIC 8051 Skilled nursing care facilities

D-U-N-S 24-827-5542 (BR)
OCEAN CHOICE INTERNATIONAL L.P.
28 Campbell St Suite 10, Bonavista, NL, A0C 1B0
(709) 468-7840
Emp Here 100
SIC 5421 Meat and fish markets

Botwood, NL A0H

D-U-N-S 20-020-8499 (BR)
ATLANTIC WHOLESALERS LTD
SAVE EASY
4 Fernwood Crt, Botwood, NL, A0H 1E0
(709) 257-4230
Emp Here 23
SIC 5411 Grocery stores

D-U-N-S 20-020-7491 (BR)
CENTRAL REGIONAL HEALTH AUTHOR-ITY
TWOMEY, DR HUGH HEALTH CARE CEN-TRE
25 Pleasantview Rd, Botwood, NL, A0H 1E0
(709) 257-2874
Emp Here 170
SIC 8051 Skilled nursing care facilities

D-U-N-S 20-027-1497 (BR)
NOVA CENTRAL SCHOOL DISTRICT
BOTWOOD COLLEGIATE
Gd, Botwood, NL, A0H 1E0
(709) 257-2497
Emp Here 28
SIC 8211 Elementary and secondary schools

D-U-N-S 20-710-1283 (BR)
PROVINCE OF NEWFOUNDLAND &

LABRADOR

NEWFOUNDLAND AND LABRADOR EN-GLISH SCHOOL DISTRICT
35 Pleasantview Rd, Botwood, NL, A0H 1E0
(709) 257-2346
Emp Here 37
SIC 8211 Elementary and secondary schools

Burgeo, NL A0N

D-U-N-S 24-405-9973 (BR)
BARRY GROUP INC
SEAFREEZ FOODS
3 Fish Plant Rd, Burgeo, NL, A0N 2H0
(709) 886-2325
Emp Here 20
SIC 5146 Fish and seafoods

D-U-N-S 20-553-3016 (BR)
WESTERN SCHOOL DISTRICT
BURGEO ACADEMY
1 School Rd, Burgeo, NL, A0N 2H0
(709) 866-2590
Emp Here 23
SIC 8211 Elementary and secondary schools

Burin, NL A0E

D-U-N-S 25-105-5455 (BR)
EASTERN REGIONAL INTEGRATED HEALTH AUTHORITY
BURIN PENINSULA HEALTH CARE CEN-TRE
85 Main St Suite 51, Burin, NL, A0E 1E0
(709) 891-1040
Emp Here 250
SIC 8062 General medical and surgical hospitals

Burin Bay Arm, NL A0E

D-U-N-S 20-583-3689 (BR)
COLLEGE OF THE NORTH ATLANTIC
105 Main St, Burin Bay Arm, NL, A0E 1G0
(709) 891-5600
Emp Here 56
SIC 8221 Colleges and universities

Carbonear, NL A1Y

D-U-N-S 25-296-5983 (BR)
BANK OF NOVA SCOTIA, THE
SCOTIABANK
92 Powell Dr, Carbonear, NL, A1Y 1A5
(709) 596-4680
Emp Here 25
SIC 6021 National commercial banks

D-U-N-S 24-113-7046 (BR)
CANADIAN TIRE CORPORATION, LIMITED
95 Columbus Dr, Carbonear, NL, A1Y 1A6
(709) 596-5103
Emp Here 20
SIC 5399 Miscellaneous general merchandise

D-U-N-S 24-258-7991 (BR)
DOLLARAMA S.E.C.
99 Powell Dr, Carbonear, NL, A1Y 1A5
(709) 596-8625
Emp Here 20
SIC 5331 Variety stores

D-U-N-S 20-178-8788 (BR)
HICKMAN MOTORS LIMITED
121 Columbus Dr, Carbonear, NL, A1Y 1A6

(709) 596-5005
Emp Here 35
SIC 5511 New and used car dealers

D-U-N-S 25-366-5178   (BR)
ICT CANADA MARKETING INC
(*Suby of* Sykes Enterprises Incorporated)
80 Powell Dr, Carbonear, NL, A1Y 1A5

Emp Here 260
SIC 7389 Business services, nec

D-U-N-S 20-987-5475   (SL)
INTERFAITH SENIOR CITIZENS HOME
45 Water St, Carbonear, NL, A1Y 1B1
(709) 945-5300
Emp Here 106   *Sales* 4,591,130
SIC 8361 Residential care

D-U-N-S 20-797-6619   (BR)
MCDONALD'S RESTAURANTS OF CANADA LIMITED
MCDONALD'S RESTAURANT
(*Suby of* McDonald's Corporation)
229 Columbus Dr, Carbonear, NL, A1Y 1A3

Emp Here 40
SIC 5812 Eating places

D-U-N-S 25-324-7829   (BR)
NEWFOUNDLAND POWER INC
30 Goff Ave, Carbonear, NL, A1Y 1A6
(800) 663-2802
Emp Here 47
SIC 4911 Electric services

D-U-N-S 20-756-6667   (BR)
SOBEYS CAPITAL INCORPORATED
FRESHCO
8 Goff Ave, Carbonear, NL, A1Y 1A6
(709) 596-0659
Emp Here 100
SIC 5411 Grocery stores

D-U-N-S 25-717-9879   (BR)
WAL-MART CANADA CORP
120 Columbus Dr, Carbonear, NL, A1Y 1B3
(709) 596-5009
Emp Here 100
SIC 5311 Department stores

Carmanville, NL A0G

D-U-N-S 25-241-9437   (BR)
NOVA CENTRAL SCHOOL DISTRICT
PHOENIX ACADEMY
200 Main St, Carmanville, NL, A0G 1N0
(709) 534-2840
Emp Here 27
SIC 8211 Elementary and secondary schools

Channel-Port-Aux-Basques, NL A0M

D-U-N-S 24-227-2891   (BR)
CANADIAN TIRE CORPORATION, LIMITED
CANADIAN TIRE ASSOCIATE STORE
1 High St, Channel-Port-Aux-Basques, NL, A0M 1C0
(709) 695-2158
Emp Here 20
SIC 5531 Auto and home supply stores

D-U-N-S 20-192-0472   (BR)
COLLEGE OF THE NORTH ATLANTIC
59 Grandbay Rd, Channel-Port-Aux-Basques, NL, A0M 1C0
(709) 695-3582
Emp Here 30
SIC 8222 Junior colleges

D-U-N-S 20-710-1481   (BR)
CORMACK TRAIL SCHOOL BOARD
SR JAMES ELEMENTARY

(*Suby of* Cormack Trail School Board)
2 Hardy Arterial, Channel-Port-Aux-Basques, NL, A0M 1C0
(709) 695-3186
Emp Here 50
SIC 8211 Elementary and secondary schools

D-U-N-S 25-697-5830   (BR)
LOBLAW COMPANIES LIMITED
SAVE EASY
27 Grand Bay Rd, Channel-Port-Aux-Basques, NL, A0M 1C0

Emp Here 27
SIC 5411 Grocery stores

D-U-N-S 25-725-3815   (BR)
MARINE ATLANTIC INC
Gd, Channel-Port-Aux-Basques, NL, A0M 1C0
(709) 695-4200
Emp Here 150
SIC 4482 Ferries

D-U-N-S 20-809-6474   (BR)
SOBEYS CAPITAL INCORPORATED
27 Grand Bay Rd, Channel-Port-Aux-Basques, NL, A0M 1C0
(709) 695-7689
Emp Here 23
SIC 5411 Grocery stores

D-U-N-S 25-334-2497   (BR)
WESTERN REGIONAL INTEGRATED HEALTH AUTHORITY, THE
LEGROW, DR CHARLES L. HEALTH CENTRE
1 Grand Bay Rd, Channel-Port-Aux-Basques, NL, A0M 1C0
(709) 695-2175
Emp Here 140
SIC 8062 General medical and surgical hospitals

D-U-N-S 20-256-6311   (BR)
WESTERN SCHOOL DISTRICT
ST. JAMES REGIONAL HIGH
Gd, Channel-Port-Aux-Basques, NL, A0M 1C0
(709) 695-3551
Emp Here 24
SIC 8211 Elementary and secondary schools

Clarenville, NL A5A

D-U-N-S 25-296-6064   (BR)
BANK OF NOVA SCOTIA, THE
SCOTIABANK
236a Memorial Dr, Clarenville, NL, A5A 1N9
(709) 466-4601
Emp Here 50
SIC 6021 National commercial banks

D-U-N-S 24-205-0131   (BR)
BARRY GROUP INC
ATLANTIC SHELLFISH
1 Masonic Terrace, Clarenville, NL, A5A 1N2
(709) 466-7186
Emp Here 700
SIC 2092 Fresh or frozen packaged fish

D-U-N-S 20-021-3838   (BR)
BELL ALIANT REGIONAL COMMUNICATIONS INC
244 Memorial Dr, Clarenville, NL, A5A 1N9
(709) 466-6130
Emp Here 23
SIC 4899 Communication services, nec

D-U-N-S 20-449-3324   (SL)
CLARENVILLE AREA CONSUMERS CO-OPERATIVE SOCIETY LTD
238 Memorial Dr, Clarenville, NL, A5A 1N9
(709) 466-2622
Emp Here 90   *Sales* 11,965,555

SIC 5411 Grocery stores
Pr Pr Craig Pardy
Treas Wendy Brinstone

D-U-N-S 24-113-7418   (SL)
CLARENVILLE RETIREMENT CENTRE INC
13 Legion Rd, Clarenville, NL, A5A 1J7
(709) 466-6459
Emp Here 50   *Sales* 1,969,939
SIC 8322 Individual and family services

D-U-N-S 25-082-4174   (BR)
COLLEGE OF THE NORTH ATLANTIC
CLARENVILLE
Gd Lcd Main, Clarenville, NL, A5A 4R1
(709) 466-2250
Emp Here 25
SIC 8221 Colleges and universities

D-U-N-S 24-804-3366   (SL)
CROSS, DR G B MEMORIAL HOSPITAL
67 Manitoba Dr, Clarenville, NL, A5A 1K3
(709) 466-3411
Emp Here 900   *Sales* 86,211,840
SIC 8062 General medical and surgical hospitals
Dir Roy Manuel
Ch Bd Frank Crews

D-U-N-S 20-013-0763   (BR)
HICKMAN MOTORS LIMITED
16 Shoal Harbour Dr, Clarenville, NL, A5A 2C4
(709) 466-2661
Emp Here 38
SIC 5511 New and used car dealers

D-U-N-S 20-277-6550   (BR)
NEWFOUNDLAND POWER INC
112 Manitoba Dr, Clarenville, NL, A5A 1K7
(709) 466-8316
Emp Here 30
SIC 4911 Electric services

D-U-N-S 20-700-6581   (BR)
REITMANS (CANADA) LIMITEE
69 Manitoba Dr, Clarenville, NL, A5A 1K3
(709) 466-7096
Emp Here 25
SIC 5621 Women's clothing stores

Clarkes Beach, NL A0A

D-U-N-S 24-345-6063   (BR)
EASTERN REGIONAL INTEGRATED HEALTH AUTHORITY
PENTECOSTAL SENIOR CITIZENS HOME
Gd, Clarkes Beach, NL, A0A 1W0

Emp Here 110
SIC 8062 General medical and surgical hospitals

Come By Chance, NL A0B

D-U-N-S 24-604-8292   (HQ)
NORTH ATLANTIC REFINING LIMITED
NORTH ATLANTIC PETROLEUM
(*Suby of* Peak Strategic Silver Partners)
1 Refining Rd, Come By Chance, NL, A0B 1N0
(709) 463-8811
Emp Here 600   *Emp Total* 1
Sales 766,087,350
SIC 2911 Petroleum refining
Brent Jones
Changkoo Kang
Kiyuong Kim
Kanghyun Shin

Conception Bay South, NL A0A

D-U-N-S 25-979-9500   (BR)
WDI COFFEE INC
TIM HORTONS
(*Suby of* WDI Coffee Inc)
153 Main Hwy, Conception Bay South, NL, A0A 2Y0
(709) 834-6333
Emp Here 20
SIC 5812 Eating places

Conception Bay South, NL A1W

D-U-N-S 25-198-9120   (BR)
A & W FOOD SERVICES OF CANADA INC
A & W
96 Conception Bay Hwy, Conception Bay South, NL, A1W 3A5
(709) 834-1987
Emp Here 25
SIC 5812 Eating places

D-U-N-S 20-717-5311   (SL)
HURLEY SLATE WORKS COMPANY INC
250 Minerals Rd, Conception Bay South, NL, A1W 5A2
(709) 834-2320
Emp Here 50   *Sales* 4,146,248
SIC 3281 Cut stone and stone products

D-U-N-S 24-098-2996   (BR)
LOBLAW COMPANIES LIMITED
DOMINION
166 Conception Bay Hwy, Conception Bay South, NL, A1W 3A6
(709) 834-2053
Emp Here 120
SIC 2051 Bread, cake, and related products

D-U-N-S 20-779-1500   (BR)
RE/MAX REALTY SPECIALISTS LTD
RE/MAX INFINITY REALTY
54 Conception Bay Hwy, Conception Bay South, NL, A1W 3A1
(709) 834-2066
Emp Here 24
SIC 6531 Real estate agents and managers

Conception Bay South, NL A1X

D-U-N-S 20-100-1836   (BR)
COLLEGE OF THE NORTH ATLANTIC
1670 Conception Bay Hwy, Conception Bay South, NL, A1X 6N1
(709) 744-2047
Emp Here 40
SIC 8221 Colleges and universities

D-U-N-S 25-996-0417   (SL)
GLOBAL TEXTILES EXPORT AND IMPORT INC
SANDY'S INDUSTRIAL SUPPLIES
657 Conception Bay Hwy, Conception Bay South, NL, A1X 3C5
(709) 834-9696
Emp Here 23   *Sales* 7,811,650
SIC 5093 Scrap and waste materials
Pr Pr Wayne Newman
Sandra Newman

D-U-N-S 25-870-9799   (BR)
GRANITE DEPARTMENT STORES INC
PIPERS DEPARTMENT STORES
956 Conception Bay Hwy Unit 2, Conception Bay South, NL, A1X 6Z6
(709) 834-3411
Emp Here 25
SIC 5311 Department stores

D-U-N-S 25-299-3779   (BR)
SOBEYS CAPITAL INCORPORATED

SOBEYS #590
350 Conception Bay Hwy, Conception Bay South, NL, A1X 7A3
(709) 834-9052
Emp Here 150
SIC 5411 Grocery stores

D-U-N-S 20-526-9207   (BR)
SOBEYS CAPITAL INCORPORATED
PRICE CHOPPER
631 Conception Bay Hwy, Conception Bay South, NL, A1X 7L4

Emp Here 29
SIC 5411 Grocery stores

D-U-N-S 24-000-9808   (BR)
WDI COFFEE INC
TIM HORTONS
(*Suby of* WDI Coffee Inc)
911 Conception Bay Hwy Suite 907, Conception Bay South, NL, A1X 7R8
(709) 834-2422
Emp Here 30
SIC 5812 Eating places

Corner Brook, NL A2H

D-U-N-S 25-618-6362   (BR)
10464 NEWFOUNDLAND LTD
JUNGLE JIM'S
(*Suby of* 10464 Newfoundland Ltd)
41 Maple Valley Rd, Corner Brook, NL, A2H 6T2
(709) 639-2222
Emp Here 20
SIC 5812 Eating places

D-U-N-S 25-296-6346   (BR)
BANK OF NOVA SCOTIA, THE
SCOTIABANK
62 Broadway, Corner Brook, NL, A2H 4C8
(709) 637-4720
Emp Here 22
SIC 6021 National commercial banks

D-U-N-S 25-656-8510   (BR)
BELL ALIANT REGIONAL COMMUNICATIONS INC
BELL ALIANT STORE
19 Main St, Corner Brook, NL, A2H 1C2
(709) 637-8219
Emp Here 50
SIC 4899 Communication services, nec

D-U-N-S 20-279-5261   (BR)
BELL ALIANT REGIONAL COMMUNICATIONS INC
332 O'Connell Dr, Corner Brook, NL, A2H 7V1
(709) 637-8395
Emp Here 40
SIC 4899 Communication services, nec

D-U-N-S 20-537-5707   (BR)
CANADA POST CORPORATION
CORNER BROOK STATION MAIN
14 Main St, Corner Brook, NL, A2H 1B8
(709) 637-8807
Emp Here 32
SIC 4311 U.s. postal service

D-U-N-S 20-013-2231   (HQ)
CORNER BROOK PULP AND PAPER LIMITED
DEER LAKE POWER COMPANY DIV OF
1 Mills Rd, Corner Brook, NL, A2H 6B9
(709) 637-3104
Emp Here 264   *Emp Total* 3,369
Sales 146,532,160
SIC 2621 Paper mills
  Joseph Kruger Ii
  George J Bunze
  Walter Mlynaryk
  Dir Donald Cayouette
  Dir Pierre Duhamel

D-U-N-S 24-450-3488   (BR)
DAY & ROSS INC
FASTRAX TRANSPORTATION
Gd Lcd Main, Corner Brook, NL, A2H 6C2
(709) 639-7523
Emp Here 40
SIC 4213 Trucking, except local

D-U-N-S 25-864-1026   (BR)
DAY & ROSS INC
Gd Lcd Main, Corner Brook, NL, A2H 6C2
(709) 635-4228
Emp Here 30
SIC 4213 Trucking, except local

D-U-N-S 25-999-8578   (BR)
DOLLARAMA S.E.C.
1 Mount Bernard Ave, Corner Brook, NL, A2H 6Y5
(709) 634-0364
Emp Here 35
SIC 5311 Department stores

D-U-N-S 24-337-3557   (BR)
FGL SPORTS LTD
SPORT-CHEK
54 Maple Valley Rd Unit M-02a, Corner Brook, NL, A2H 3C5
(709) 634-4700
Emp Here 40
SIC 5941 Sporting goods and bicycle shops

D-U-N-S 20-289-2514   (BR)
ICT CANADA MARKETING INC
(*Suby of* Sykes Enterprises Incorporated)
1 Mount Bernard Ave, Corner Brook, NL, A2H 6Y5

Emp Here 50
SIC 7389 Business services, nec

D-U-N-S 25-362-6444   (BR)
INDUSTRIELLE ALLIANCE, ASSURANCE ET SERVICES FINANCIERS INC
ALLIANCE FINANCIAL GROUP
4 Herald Ave Suite 401, Corner Brook, NL, A2H 4B4
(709) 634-0071
Emp Here 20
SIC 6311 Life insurance

D-U-N-S 24-335-5885   (BR)
LOBLAWS INC
DOMINION CORNER BROOK
5 Murphy Sq Suite 926, Corner Brook, NL, A2H 1R4
(709) 634-9450
Emp Here 100
SIC 5411 Grocery stores

D-U-N-S 24-832-0491   (SL)
MARBLE MOUNTAIN DEVELOPMENT CORPORATION
MARBLE MOUNTAIN RESORT
Trans Canada Hwy, Corner Brook, NL, A2H 2N2
(709) 637-7601
Emp Here 50   *Sales* 2,598,753
SIC 7011 Hotels and motels

D-U-N-S 25-542-6389   (BR)
MEDIAS TRANSCONTINENTAL INC
MEDIAS TRANSCONTINENTAL INC
106 West St, Corner Brook, NL, A2H 2Z3
(709) 634-4348
Emp Here 60
SIC 2711 Newspapers

D-U-N-S 20-797-6676   (BR)
MEMORIAL UNIVERSITY OF NEWFOUNDLAND
CONFERENCE OFFICE
1 University Dr, Corner Brook, NL, A2H 6P9
(709) 637-6255
Emp Here 20
SIC 8221 Colleges and universities

D-U-N-S 24-913-3976   (BR)
MIDLAND TRANSPORT LIMITED

(*Suby of* J. D. Irving, Limited)
22 White Lakes Rd, Corner Brook, NL, A2H 6G1
(709) 634-8080
Emp Here 20
SIC 4213 Trucking, except local

D-U-N-S 25-618-6313   (BR)
NOTRE DAME AGENCIES LIMITED
NOTRE DAME CASTLE BUILDING CENTRE
408 O'Connell Dr, Corner Brook, NL, A2H 6G7
(709) 639-8700
Emp Here 25
SIC 5211 Lumber and other building materials

D-U-N-S 20-984-3192   (BR)
SEARS CANADA INC
54 Maple Valley Rd, Corner Brook, NL, A2H 3C5
(709) 634-6934
Emp Here 40
SIC 5311 Department stores

D-U-N-S 25-299-3811   (BR)
SOBEYS CAPITAL INCORPORATED
SOBEY'S 861
1 Mount Bernard Ave Suite 861, Corner Brook, NL, A2H 6Y5
(709) 639-7193
Emp Here 79
SIC 5411 Grocery stores

D-U-N-S 25-622-0880   (BR)
SPINAL CORD INJURY CANADA
C P A
20 Reids Rd, Corner Brook, NL, A2H 5Y7
(709) 634-9901
Emp Here 20
SIC 8699 Membership organizations, nec

D-U-N-S 20-104-9967   (BR)
STAPLES CANADA INC
STAPLES THE BUSINESS DEPOT
(*Suby of* Staples, Inc.)
14 Murphy Sq, Corner Brook, NL, A2H 1R4
(709) 634-9500
Emp Here 35
SIC 5943 Stationery stores

D-U-N-S 20-573-8607   (BR)
SUN LIFE ASSURANCE COMPANY OF CANADA
8 Murphy Sq Unit C1, Corner Brook, NL, A2H 1R4
(709) 634-3105
Emp Here 20
SIC 6311 Life insurance

D-U-N-S 20-013-3999   (BR)
TOROMONT INDUSTRIES LTD
TOROMONT CAT
22 Confederation Dr, Corner Brook, NL, A2H 6E3
(709) 634-8258
Emp Here 20
SIC 5082 Construction and mining machinery

D-U-N-S 24-317-1845   (BR)
WAL-MART CANADA CORP
WALMART
16 Murphy Sq, Corner Brook, NL, A2H 1R4
(709) 634-2310
Emp Here 130
SIC 5311 Department stores

D-U-N-S 24-932-7933   (SL)
WESTERN BUILDING LTD
25 Poplar Rd, Corner Brook, NL, A2H 4T6
(709) 634-3163
Emp Here 40   *Sales* 7,538,632
SIC 5211 Lumber and other building materials
Pr Pr Lloyd Piercey

D-U-N-S 25-241-0048   (BR)
WESTERN INTERGRATED SCHOOL BOARD
HERDMAN COLLEGIATE SCHOOL
(*Suby of* Western Intergrated School Board)
Po Box 338 Stn Main, Corner Brook, NL, A2H

6E3

Emp Here 45
SIC 8211 Elementary and secondary schools

D-U-N-S 25-518-3154   (BR)
WESTERN REGIONAL INTEGRATED HEALTH AUTHORITY, THE
MENTAL HEALTH SERVICES AND ADDICTION SERVICES
35 Boones Rd, Corner Brook, NL, A2H 6J7
(709) 634-4506
Emp Here 22
SIC 8093 Specialty outpatient clinics, nec

D-U-N-S 25-849-4335   (BR)
WESTERN REGIONAL INTEGRATED HEALTH AUTHORITY, THE
CORNER BROOK INTER-FAITH HOME
1 Elizabeth Dr, Corner Brook, NL, A2H 2N2
(709) 639-9247
Emp Here 20
SIC 8051 Skilled nursing care facilities

D-U-N-S 25-241-2622   (BR)
WESTERN SCHOOL DISTRICT
ST. GERARD'S ELEMENTARY SCHOOL
15 Montgomerie St, Corner Brook, NL, A2H 2P8
(709) 639-8945
Emp Here 20
SIC 8211 Elementary and secondary schools

D-U-N-S 20-020-7194   (BR)
WESTERN SCHOOL DISTRICT
HUMBER ELEMENTARY SCHOOL
10 St. Johns Ave, Corner Brook, NL, A2H 2E5
(709) 634-6333
Emp Here 34
SIC 8211 Elementary and secondary schools

D-U-N-S 25-240-9925   (BR)
WESTERN SCHOOL DISTRICT
J. J. CURLING ELEMENTARY SCHOOL
26 Woodbine Ave, Corner Brook, NL, A2H 3P2
(709) 785-2814
Emp Here 20
SIC 8211 Elementary and secondary schools

D-U-N-S 20-710-1374   (BR)
WESTERN SCHOOL DISTRICT
CORNER BROOK REGIONAL HIGH SCHOOL
12 University Dr, Corner Brook, NL, A2H 5G4
(709) 634-5258
Emp Here 58
SIC 8211 Elementary and secondary schools

D-U-N-S 25-241-2747   (BR)
WESTERN SCHOOL DISTRICT
SACRED HEART ELEMENTARY SCHOOL
473 Curling St, Corner Brook, NL, A2H 3K8
(709) 785-5119
Emp Here 25
SIC 8211 Elementary and secondary schools

D-U-N-S 25-241-0006   (BR)
WESTERN SCHOOL DISTRICT
C. C. LOUGHLIN ELEMENTARY SCHOOL
1 Citadel Dr, Corner Brook, NL, A2H 5M4
(709) 639-8988
Emp Here 38
SIC 8211 Elementary and secondary schools

D-U-N-S 20-514-0200   (BR)
WORKPLACE HEALTH SAFETY & COMPENSATION COMMISSION OF NEWFOUNDLAND AND LABRADOR
2 Herald Ave, Corner Brook, NL, A2H 4B5
(709) 637-2700
Emp Here 25
SIC 6331 Fire, marine, and casualty insurance

Cottlesville, NL A0G

D-U-N-S 25-676-1537   (BR)
BREAKWATER FISHERIES LIMITED
23 Hill View Dr, Cottlesville, NL, A0G 1S0

Emp Here 200
SIC 2092 Fresh or frozen packaged fish

Cow Head, NL A0K

D-U-N-S 25-241-6128   (BR)
WESTERN SCHOOL DISTRICT
LONG RANGE ACADEMY
9 Grades Rd, Cow Head, NL, A0K 2A0
(709) 243-2252
Emp Here 20
SIC 8211 Elementary and secondary schools

Deer Lake, NL A8A

D-U-N-S 25-689-2894   (BR)
CORNER BROOK PULP AND PAPER LIMITED
DEER LAKE POWER
2 Trans Canada Hwy, Deer Lake, NL, A8A 2E4

Emp Here 45
SIC 4911 Electric services

D-U-N-S 20-590-1296   (BR)
NAV CANADA
Gd Stn Main, Deer Lake, NL, A8A 3M4
(709) 635-5251
Emp Here 20
SIC 4899 Communication services, nec

D-U-N-S 25-241-2846   (BR)
WESTERN SCHOOL DISTRICT
ELWOOD ELEMENTARY SCHOOL
22a Farm Rd, Deer Lake, NL, A8A 1J3
(709) 635-2337
Emp Here 35
SIC 8211 Elementary and secondary schools

D-U-N-S 25-241-2887   (BR)
WESTERN SCHOOL DISTRICT
ELWOOD REGIONAL HIGH SCHOOL
22 Farm Rd, Deer Lake, NL, A8A 1J3
(709) 635-2895
Emp Here 22
SIC 8211 Elementary and secondary schools

Dover, NL A0G

D-U-N-S 25-897-5879   (BR)
BARRY GROUP INC
CRIMSON TIDE FISHERIES
Gd, Dover, NL, A0G 1X0
(709) 537-5888
Emp Here 150
SIC 2091 Canned and cured fish and seafoods

D-U-N-S 25-241-2994   (BR)
NOVA CENTRAL SCHOOL DISTRICT
WILLIAM MERCER ACADEMY
97 Wellington Rd, Dover, NL, A0G 1X0
(709) 537-2184
Emp Here 21
SIC 8211 Elementary and secondary schools

Doyles, NL A0N

D-U-N-S 20-710-1473   (BR)
WESTERN SCHOOL DISTRICT
BELANGER MEMORIAL HIGH SCHOOL

Gd, Doyles, NL, A0N 1J0
(709) 955-2940
Emp Here 26
SIC 8211 Elementary and secondary schools

Eastport, NL A0G

D-U-N-S 20-200-7204   (BR)
NOVA CENTRAL SCHOOL DISTRICT
HOLY CROSS SCHOOL COMPLEX
110 Church St, Eastport, NL, A0G 1Z0
(709) 677-3121
Emp Here 24
SIC 8211 Elementary and secondary schools

English Harbour West, NL A0H

D-U-N-S 20-025-8957   (BR)
NOVA CENTRAL SCHOOL DISTRICT
FITZGERALD ACADEMY
Gd, English Harbour West, NL, A0H 1M0
(709) 888-3426
Emp Here 24
SIC 8211 Elementary and secondary schools

D-U-N-S 24-258-1643   (SL)
YARN POINT KNITTERS CORPORATION
Gd, English Harbour West, NL, A0H 1M0
(709) 888-5371
Emp Here 50   Sales 2,425,503
SIC 2241 Narrow fabric mills

Flowers Cove, NL A0K

D-U-N-S 25-241-3208   (BR)
WESTERN SCHOOL DISTRICT
CANON RICHARDS MEMORIAL ACADEMY
99 Main St, Flowers Cove, NL, A0K 2N0
(709) 456-2010
Emp Here 30
SIC 8211 Elementary and secondary schools

Fogo, NL A0G

D-U-N-S 24-257-8797   (BR)
CENTRAL REGIONAL HEALTH AUTHORITY
FOGO ISLAND HOSPITAL
9 Central Island Rd N, Fogo, NL, A0G 2B0
(709) 266-2221
Emp Here 50
SIC 8062 General medical and surgical hospitals

D-U-N-S 25-241-5807   (BR)
NOVA CENTRAL SCHOOL DISTRICT
FOGO ISLAND CENTRAL ACADEMY
Gd, Fogo, NL, A0G 2B0
(709) 266-2560
Emp Here 50
SIC 8211 Elementary and secondary schools

Freshwater Pb, NL A0B

D-U-N-S 25-393-7684   (SL)
ARGENTIA FREEZERS & TERMINALS LIMITED
(Suby of Harvela Investments Ltd)
Gd, Freshwater Pb, NL, A0B 1W0
(709) 227-5603
Emp Here 60   Sales 7,558,320
SIC 4222 Refrigerated warehousing and stor-

age
VP Jerone Mcgrath

Gambo, NL A0G

D-U-N-S 25-241-3232   (BR)
NOVA CENTRAL SCHOOL DISTRICT
SMALLWOOD ACADEMY
39 Victoria Dr, Gambo, NL, A0G 1T0
(709) 674-5336
Emp Here 25
SIC 8211 Elementary and secondary schools

Gander, NL A1V

D-U-N-S 24-258-3227   (BR)
ATLANTIC RETAIL CO-OPERATIVES FEDERATION
CO-OP ATLANTIC
24 Carr Cres, Gander, NL, A1V 2E3
(709) 651-3751
Emp Here 20
SIC 7359 Equipment rental and leasing, nec

D-U-N-S 25-296-2717   (BR)
BANK OF NOVA SCOTIA, THE
SCOTIABANK
68 Elizabeth Dr, Gander, NL, A1V 1J8
(709) 256-1500
Emp Here 25
SIC 6021 National commercial banks

D-U-N-S 24-790-0541   (BR)
BELL ALIANT REGIONAL COMMUNICATIONS INC
185 Airport Blvd, Gander, NL, A1V 1K6
(709) 256-5181
Emp Here 20
SIC 4899 Communication services, nec

D-U-N-S 24-804-2363   (BR)
D-J COMPOSITES INC
1 C. L. Dobbin Dr, Gander, NL, A1V 2V3
(709) 256-6111
Emp Here 49
SIC 5088 Transportation equipment and supplies

D-U-N-S 20-013-8600   (BR)
HICKMAN MOTORS LIMITED
201 Airport Blvd, Gander, NL, A1V 1L5
(709) 256-3906
Emp Here 50
SIC 5012 Automobiles and other motor vehicles

D-U-N-S 20-796-2122   (BR)
INVESTORS GROUP FINANCIAL SERVICES INC
71 Elizabeth Dr, Gander, NL, A1V 1J9
(709) 651-3565
Emp Here 25
SIC 6282 Investment advice

D-U-N-S 20-179-6708   (BR)
NAV CANADA
Gd Lcd Main, Gander, NL, A1V 1W4

Emp Here 24
SIC 4581 Airports, flying fields, and services

D-U-N-S 20-287-7887   (BR)
NOVA CENTRAL SCHOOL DISTRICT
GANDER COLLEGIATE
3 Magee Rd, Gander, NL, A1V 1W1
(709) 256-2581
Emp Here 25
SIC 8211 Elementary and secondary schools

D-U-N-S 20-984-2145   (HQ)
NOVA CENTRAL SCHOOL DISTRICT
203 Elizabeth Dr, Gander, NL, A1V 1H6

(709) 256-2547
Emp Here 1,000   Emp Total 7,000
Sales 175,084,728
SIC 8211 Elementary and secondary schools
Ch Bd Charlie Mccornack
Dir Fin Shawn Brace
   Thomas Kendell
   John George
   Hubert Langdon
   Kerry Noble
   Peter Budgell
   Kim Cheeks
   Peter Gibbons
   Newman Harris

D-U-N-S 25-241-5484   (BR)
NOVA CENTRAL SCHOOL DISTRICT
ST. PAUL'S INTERMEDIATE SCHOOL
5 Magee Rd, Gander, NL, A1V 1W1
(709) 256-8404
Emp Here 40
SIC 8211 Elementary and secondary schools

D-U-N-S 24-118-7512   (BR)
NOVA CENTRAL SCHOOL DISTRICT
GANDER BUS PEOPLE
17 Mccurdy Dr, Gander, NL, A1V 1A1
(709) 256-3571
Emp Here 20
SIC 4151 School buses

D-U-N-S 20-787-5613   (BR)
PROVINCE OF NEWFOUNDLAND & LABRADOR
ARTS & CULTURE CENTRE
155 Airport Blvd, Gander, NL, A1V 1K6
(709) 256-1078
Emp Here 20
SIC 7922 Theatrical producers and services

D-U-N-S 20-756-7517   (BR)
SOBEYS CAPITAL INCORPORATED
FRESHCO
230 Airport Blvd, Gander, NL, A1V 1L7
(709) 256-4860
Emp Here 26
SIC 5411 Grocery stores

D-U-N-S 20-555-7718   (BR)
WAL-MART CANADA CORP
55 Av Roe, Gander, NL, A1V 0H6
(709) 256-7581
Emp Here 200
SIC 5311 Department stores

Glenwood, NL A0G

D-U-N-S 24-324-6696   (SL)
BEAVER BROOK ANTIMONY MINE INC
Gd, Glenwood, NL, A0G 2K0
(709) 679-5866
Emp Here 85   Sales 948,489
SIC 1099 Metal ores, nec

D-U-N-S 25-242-3140   (BR)
NOVA CENTRAL SCHOOL DISTRICT
NOVA CONSOLIDATED SCHOOL DISTRICT
11 Spruce Ave, Glenwood, NL, A0G 2K0
(709) 679-2162
Emp Here 20
SIC 8211 Elementary and secondary schools

Glovertown, NL A0G

D-U-N-S 20-710-1044   (BR)
NOVA CENTRAL SCHOOL DISTRICT
GLOVERTOWN ACADEMY
10 Penny'S Brook Rd, Glovertown, NL, A0G 2L0
(709) 533-2443
Emp Here 50
SIC 8211 Elementary and secondary schools

Grand Bank, NL A0E

D-U-N-S 25-298-7813 (BR)
CLEARWATER SEAFOODS LIMITED PARTNERSHIP
CLEARWATER SEAFOOD
1 Plant Rd, Grand Bank, NL, A0E 1W0
(709) 832-1550
Emp Here 200
SIC 5146 Fish and seafoods

D-U-N-S 24-326-1240 (BR)
DYNAMIC AIR SHELTERS LTD
(*Suby of* Dynamic Shelters Inc)
2a Hickman St, Grand Bank, NL, A0E 1W0
(709) 832-1211
Emp Here 70
SIC 3448 Prefabricated Metal buildings and components

D-U-N-S 20-020-7301 (BR)
EASTERN REGIONAL INTEGRATED HEALTH AUTHORITY
BLUE CREST INTERFAITH HOME
1 Seniors Pl, Grand Bank, NL, A0E 1W0
(709) 832-1660
Emp Here 100
SIC 8051 Skilled nursing care facilities

D-U-N-S 25-299-3738 (BR)
SOBEYS CAPITAL INCORPORATED
SOBEYS 654
Highway Route #210, Grand Bank, NL, A0E 1W0
(709) 832-0091
Emp Here 48
SIC 5411 Grocery stores

Grand Falls-Windsor, NL A2A

D-U-N-S 25-878-6862 (BR)
ARMOUR TRANSPORT INC
ARMOUR TRANSPORTATION SYSTEMS
Gd Lcd Main, Grand Falls-Windsor, NL, A2A 2J1
(709) 489-8487
Emp Here 27
SIC 4213 Trucking, except local

D-U-N-S 25-296-3350 (BR)
BANK OF NOVA SCOTIA, THE
SCOTIABANK
26 Cromer Ave, Grand Falls-Windsor, NL, A2A 1X2
(709) 489-1700
Emp Here 27
SIC 6021 National commercial banks

D-U-N-S 25-696-6540 (BR)
BELL ALIANT REGIONAL COMMUNICATIONS INC
7 Hardy Ave, Grand Falls-Windsor, NL, A2A 2P8
(709) 489-5669
Emp Here 27
SIC 4899 Communication services, nec

D-U-N-S 20-537-8214 (BR)
CANADA POST CORPORATION
GRAND FALLS-WINDSOR STN MAIN
16 High St, Grand Falls-Windsor, NL, A2A 1C6
(709) 489-9533
Emp Here 20
SIC 4311 U.s. postal service

D-U-N-S 20-787-4939 (HQ)
CENTRAL REGIONAL HEALTH AUTHORITY
A.M. GUY MEMORIAL HEALTH CENTRE
50 Union St, Grand Falls-Windsor, NL, A2A 2E1
(709) 292-2500
Emp Here 500   *Emp Total* 7,000
Sales 286,390,985
SIC 8062 General medical and surgical hospitals
CEO Rosemarie Goodyear
Pers/VP Terry Ings
VP Fin John Kattenbusch
Dir Stephanie Power
  Sean Tulk
VP Jef² Cole

D-U-N-S 25-700-2279 (BR)
DAY & ROSS INC
SAMEDAY WORLDWIDE
52 Hardy Ave, Grand Falls-Windsor, NL, A2A 2J3
(709) 489-4104
Emp Here 40
SIC 4213 Trucking, except local

D-U-N-S 25-872-6553 (BR)
DAY & ROSS INC
Gd, Grand Falls-Windsor, NL, A2A 2J3
(709) 489-8860
Emp Here 35
SIC 4213 Trucking, except local

D-U-N-S 25-698-8205 (BR)
ENVIRONMENT RESOURCES MANAGEMENT ASSOCIATION
SALMONID INTERPRETATION CENTRE
(*Suby of* Environment Resources Management Association)
Gd, Grand Falls-Windsor, NL, A2A 2P7
(709) 489-7350
Emp Here 50
SIC 8748 Business consulting, nec

D-U-N-S 24-320-5510 (BR)
ISLANDER R.V. SALES & RENTALS LTD
1 Grenfell Hts, Grand Falls-Windsor, NL, A2A 1W3
(709) 489-9489
Emp Here 20
SIC 7519 Utility trailer rental

D-U-N-S 20-242-1322 (BR)
NEWFOUNDLAND AND LABRADOR HOUSING CORPORATION
5 Hardy Ave, Grand Falls-Windsor, NL, A2A 2P8
(709) 292-1000
Emp Here 22
SIC 6531 Real estate agents and managers

D-U-N-S 20-287-3704 (BR)
NOTRE DAME AGENCIES LIMITED
28 Duggan St, Grand Falls-Windsor, NL, A2A 2K6
(709) 489-7655
Emp Here 24
SIC 5211 Lumber and other building materials

D-U-N-S 20-023-2804 (BR)
NOVA CENTRAL SCHOOL DISTRICT
MILLCREST ACADEMY
1 St. Catherine St, Grand Falls-Windsor, NL, A2A 1V7
(709) 489-3805
Emp Here 30
SIC 8211 Elementary and secondary schools

D-U-N-S 20-608-2567 (BR)
NOVA CENTRAL SCHOOL DISTRICT
EXPLOITS VALLEY HIGH SCHOOL
392 Grenfell Hts, Grand Falls-Windsor, NL, A2A 2J2
(709) 489-4374
Emp Here 32
SIC 8211 Elementary and secondary schools

D-U-N-S 20-020-7988 (BR)
NOVA CENTRAL SCHOOL DISTRICT
GRENFELL INTERMEDIATE SCHOOL
392 Grenfell Hts, Grand Falls-Windsor, NL, A2A 2J2
(709) 489-5701
Emp Here 31

SIC 8211 Elementary and secondary schools

D-U-N-S 25-241-2523 (BR)
NOVA CENTRAL SCHOOL DISTRICT
WOODLAND PRIMARY SCHOOL
Gd Lcd Main, Grand Falls-Windsor, NL, A2A 2J1
(709) 489-4373
Emp Here 33
SIC 8351 Child day care services

D-U-N-S 24-259-8530 (BR)
PF RESOLU CANADA INC
7 Mill Rd, Grand Falls-Windsor, NL, A2A 1B8
(709) 292-3000
Emp Here 500
SIC 2621 Paper mills

D-U-N-S 24-367-8245 (BR)
SOBEYS CAPITAL INCORPORATED
TRA NEWFOUNDLAND
66 Hardy Ave, Grand Falls-Windsor, NL, A2A 2V4
(709) 489-3846
Emp Here 65
SIC 5411 Grocery stores

D-U-N-S 20-547-7524 (BR)
SOBEYS CAPITAL INCORPORATED
21 Cromer Ave, Grand Falls-Windsor, NL, A2A 1X3
(709) 489-8054
Emp Here 60
SIC 5411 Grocery stores

D-U-N-S 25-297-5958 (BR)
WAL-MART CANADA CORP
19 Cromer Ave, Grand Falls-Windsor, NL, A2A 2K5
(709) 489-5739
Emp Here 185
SIC 5311 Department stores

Grand Falls-Windsor, NL A2B

D-U-N-S 24-343-5695 (BR)
CENTRAL REGIONAL HEALTH AUTHORITY
CARMELITE HOUSE
36 Queensway, Grand Falls-Windsor, NL, A2B 1J3

Emp Here 35
SIC 8062 General medical and surgical hospitals

Happy Valley-Goose Bay, NL A0P

D-U-N-S 25-058-7532 (SL)
10663 NEWFOUNDLAND LTD
COASTAL LABRADOR MARINE SERVICES
Gd Happy Valley-Goose Bay Stn C, Happy Valley-Goose Bay, NL, A0P 1C0
(709) 896-2421
Emp Here 120   *Sales* 292,176,000
SIC 4424 Deep sea domestic transportation of freight
Pr Pr Melvin Woodward

D-U-N-S 20-337-8807 (SL)
AIR BOREALIS LIMITED PARTNERSHIP
1 Centralia Dr, Happy Valley-Goose Bay, NL, A0P 1C0
(709) 576-1800
Emp Here 122   *Sales* 20,866,760
SIC 4512 Air transportation, scheduled
  Tom Randell

D-U-N-S 24-385-2311 (BR)
AIR LABRADOR LIMITED
AIR LABRADOR
62 Dakota Dr, Happy Valley-Goose Bay, NL,
A0P 1C0
(709) 896-6747
Emp Here 60
SIC 4512 Air transportation, scheduled

D-U-N-S 20-315-9199 (HQ)
AIR LABRADOR LIMITED
85 Dakota Dr, Happy Valley-Goose Bay, NL, A0P 1C0
(709) 896-6730
Emp Here 50   *Emp Total* 79
Sales 34,145,608
SIC 4512 Air transportation, scheduled
Pr Pr Philip Earle

D-U-N-S 25-860-9841 (BR)
COLLEGE OF THE NORTH ATLANTIC
219 Hamilton Rd, Happy Valley-Goose Bay, NL, A0P 1E0
(709) 896-6300
Emp Here 60
SIC 8221 Colleges and universities

D-U-N-S 20-934-5441 (BR)
HELICOPTERES CANADIENS LIMITEE
CHL HELICOPTERS
30 Toronto Ave, Happy Valley-Goose Bay, NL, A0P 1C0
(709) 896-5259
Emp Here 30
SIC 7359 Equipment rental and leasing, nec

D-U-N-S 24-524-1596 (SL)
INNU MIKUN INC
Gd Stn, Happy Valley-Goose Bay, NL, A0P 1C0
(709) 896-5521
Emp Here 80   *Sales* 13,643,651
SIC 4512 Air transportation, scheduled
Pr Brain Chafe
  Robert Halliday
  Tom Randell
  Kelvin Ash
Dir Virginia Collins
Dir David Hart Jr

D-U-N-S 20-014-1968 (HQ)
LABRADOR MOTORS LIMITED
(*Suby of* Peterco Limited)
12 Loring Dr, Happy Valley-Goose Bay, NL, A0P 1C0
(709) 896-2452
Emp Here 34   *Emp Total* 67
Sales 24,441,835
SIC 5511 New and used car dealers
Pr Pr Peter Woodward
Dir Melvin Woodward
Dir Sybil Woodward

D-U-N-S 20-710-1325 (BR)
LABRADOR SCHOOL BOARD
PEACOCK PRIMARY SCHOOL
9 Cadot Cres, Happy Valley-Goose Bay, NL, A0P 1E0
(709) 896-3896
Emp Here 35
SIC 8211 Elementary and secondary schools

D-U-N-S 25-001-7969 (BR)
LABRADOR SCHOOL BOARD
QUEEN OF PEACE MIDDLE SCHOOL
6 Green St, Happy Valley-Goose Bay, NL, A0P 1E0
(709) 896-5315
Emp Here 35
SIC 8211 Elementary and secondary schools

D-U-N-S 25-242-3850 (BR)
LABRADOR SCHOOL BOARD
MEALY MOUNTAIN COLLEGIATE
1 Voisey Dr, Happy Valley-Goose Bay, NL, A0P 1C0
(709) 896-3366
Emp Here 45
SIC 8211 Elementary and secondary schools

D-U-N-S 25-503-7517 (BR)
SERCO CANADA INC
SERCO FACILITIES MANAGEMENT

271 Canadian Forces, Happy Valley-Goose Bay, NL, A0P 1C0
(709) 896-6946
Emp Here 350
SIC 8741 Management services

D-U-N-S 20-987-5541   (SL)
WOODWARD'S LIMITED
16 Loring Dr, Happy Valley-Goose Bay, NL, A0P 1C0
(709) 896-2421
Emp Here 35   *Sales* 22,086,000
SIC 4581 Airports, flying fields, and services
Pr Pr Melvin Woodward
VP VP Peter Woodward
Sybil Woodward

Harbour Breton, NL A0H

D-U-N-S 24-258-4555   (BR)
CENTRAL REGIONAL HEALTH AUTHORITY
CONNAIGRE PENINSULA HEALTH CENTRE
1 Alexander Ave, Harbour Breton, NL, A0H 1P0
(709) 885-2359
Emp Here 50
SIC 8062 General medical and surgical hospitals

D-U-N-S 25-241-5914   (BR)
NOVA CENTRAL SCHOOL DISTRICT
KING ACADEMY SCHOOL
43 Main Rd N, Harbour Breton, NL, A0H 1P0
(709) 885-2319
Emp Here 21
SIC 8211 Elementary and secondary schools

Holyrood, NL A0A

D-U-N-S 25-308-4719   (BR)
NEWFOUNDLAND & LABRADOR HYDRO
1 Thermal Plant Rd, Holyrood, NL, A0A 2R0
(709) 229-7441
Emp Here 120
SIC 4911 Electric services

Hopedale, NL A0P

D-U-N-S 25-241-4040   (BR)
LABRADOR SCHOOL BOARD
MEMORIAL SCHOOL
Gd, Hopedale, NL, A0P 1G0

Emp Here 25
SIC 8211 Elementary and secondary schools

D-U-N-S 20-023-1285   (BR)
NUNATSIAVUT GOVERNMENT, THE
DEPARTMENT OF HEALTH
3 American Rd, Hopedale, NL, A0P 1G0
(709) 933-3894
Emp Here 33
SIC 8399 Social services, nec

Jacksons Arm, NL A0K

D-U-N-S 20-189-7530   (SL)
NORTHERN SHRIMP COMPANY LTD
Gd, Jacksons Arm, NL, A0K 3H0

Emp Here 120   *Sales* 27,431,040
SIC 2092 Fresh or frozen packaged fish
Pr Pr Martin Sullivan

La Poile, NL A0M

D-U-N-S 25-240-9768   (BR)
WESTERN SCHOOL DISTRICT
DOUGLAS ACADEMY
Gd, La Poile, NL, A0M 1K0
(709) 496-4116
Emp Here 20
SIC 8211 Elementary and secondary schools

La Scie, NL A0K

D-U-N-S 24-524-1703   (BR)
COLD NORTH SEAFOODS LIMITED
2 Water St, La Scie, NL, A0K 3M0

Emp Here 80
SIC 2092 Fresh or frozen packaged fish

D-U-N-S 25-977-8702   (SL)
O/L ENTERPRISES INC
Gd, La Scie, NL, A0K 3M0
(709) 675-2085
Emp Here 80   *Sales* 5,034,288
SIC 4832 Radio broadcasting stations
Pr Pr Larry Butt
Rhoda Butt

D-U-N-S 25-393-7569   (SL)
UNIVERSAL MARINE LTD
14 Slipway Rd, La Scie, NL, A0K 3M0

Emp Here 40   *Sales* 7,608,750
SIC 1629 Heavy construction, nec
Pr Pr Robert Starkes

Labrador City, NL A2V

D-U-N-S 24-426-9291   (SL)
BUYNFLY FOOD LIMITED
IGA BUY N' FLY
208 Humber Ave, Labrador City, NL, A2V 1K9
(709) 944-4003
Emp Here 75   *Sales* 9,849,695
SIC 5411 Grocery stores
Pr Pr Pete Cornick
Dir Alec Snow
Genl Mgr Bill Gidge

D-U-N-S 20-584-8661   (BR)
CANADA POST CORPORATION
500 Vanier Ave Suite 2, Labrador City, NL, A2V 2W7
(709) 944-3979
Emp Here 20
SIC 4311 U.s. postal service

D-U-N-S 25-849-5266   (BR)
COLLEGE OF THE NORTH ATLANTIC
1 Av Campbell, Labrador City, NL, A2V 2Y1
(709) 944-7210
Emp Here 35
SIC 8221 Colleges and universities

D-U-N-S 24-373-7025   (BR)
COMPAGNIE MINIERE IOC INC
Gd, Labrador City, NL, A2V 2L8
(709) 944-8400
Emp Here 1,500
SIC 1011 Iron ores

D-U-N-S 25-718-2741   (BR)
ENERGIE VALERO INC
ALLARD DISTRIBUTING
208 Humphrey Rd, Labrador City, NL, A2V 2K2
(709) 944-5144
Emp Here 20
SIC 5172 Petroleum products, nec

D-U-N-S 24-994-8621   (BR)
LABRADOR MOTORS LIMITED
GENERAL MOTORS DEALER
(Suby of Peterco Limited)
80 Avalon Dr, Labrador City, NL, A2V 2Y2
(709) 944-3633
Emp Here 30
SIC 5511 New and used car dealers

D-U-N-S 25-241-4123   (BR)
LABRADOR SCHOOL BOARD
A P LOW PRIMARY SCHOOL
600 Bartlett Dr, Labrador City, NL, A2V 1G6
(709) 944-5231
Emp Here 31
SIC 8211 Elementary and secondary schools

D-U-N-S 25-000-4785   (BR)
LABRADOR SCHOOL BOARD
MENIHEK HIGH SCHOOL
613 Lakeside Dr, Labrador City, NL, A2V 2W9
(709) 944-7731
Emp Here 50
SIC 8211 Elementary and secondary schools

D-U-N-S 25-173-1865   (SL)
LYNK AUTO PRODUCTS INC
NAPA AUTO PARTS
110 Airport Rd, Labrador City, NL, A2V 2J7

Emp Here 32   *Sales* 5,376,850
SIC 5013 Motor vehicle supplies and new parts
Pr Pr Kevin Lelievre
Dir Nadia Lelievre
Dir Yvonne Lelievre

D-U-N-S 24-450-7620   (SL)
MARSHALL INDUSTRIES LIMITED
(Suby of Marshall-Barwick Holdings Inc)
Airport Rd, Labrador City, NL, A2V 2K6
(709) 944-5515
Emp Here 34   *Sales* 5,006,160
SIC 1791 Structural steel erection
Prs Mgr Paul Moss
Dir Cecil S. Hawkins
Dir Maynard H. Young

D-U-N-S 25-122-9865   (BR)
TETRA TECH INDUSTRIES INC
(Suby of Tetra Tech, Inc.)
109b Drake Ave, Labrador City, NL, A2V 2L8
(709) 944-3650
Emp Here 24
SIC 8711 Engineering services

D-U-N-S 24-319-5109   (BR)
WAL-MART CANADA CORP
WALMART
500 Vanier Ave Suite 1035, Labrador City, NL, A2V 2W7
(709) 944-3378
Emp Here 120
SIC 5311 Department stores

Lark Harbour, NL A0L

D-U-N-S 25-241-5765   (BR)
WESTERN SCHOOL DISTRICT
ST. JAMES ALL GRADE SCHOOL
1 Main Rd, Lark Harbour, NL, A0L 1H0
(709) 681-2620
Emp Here 22
SIC 8211 Elementary and secondary schools

Lewisporte, NL A0G

D-U-N-S 20-150-4987   (SL)
LEWISPORTE CO-OP LTD
465 Main St, Lewisporte, NL, A0G 3A0
(709) 535-6728
Emp Here 44   *Sales* 5,326,131

SIC 5411 Grocery stores
Owen Brinson

D-U-N-S 20-746-2933   (BR)
LOBLAWS INC
252 Main St, Lewisporte, NL, A0G 3A0
(709) 535-6381
Emp Here 26
SIC 5411 Grocery stores

D-U-N-S 20-020-7228   (BR)
NOVA CENTRAL SCHOOL DISTRICT
LEWISPORTE MIDDLE SCHOOL
359 Main St, Lewisporte, NL, A0G 3A0
(709) 535-8282
Emp Here 30
SIC 8211 Elementary and secondary schools

D-U-N-S 25-241-3398   (BR)
NOVA CENTRAL SCHOOL DISTRICT
LEWISPORTE COLLEGIATE
83 Primier Dr, Lewisporte, NL, A0G 3A0
(709) 535-6929
Emp Here 25
SIC 8211 Elementary and secondary schools

D-U-N-S 20-710-1101   (BR)
NOVA CENTRAL SCHOOL DISTRICT
LEWISPORTE ACADEMY
43 Spruce Ave, Lewisporte, NL, A0G 3A0
(709) 535-2115
Emp Here 32
SIC 8211 Elementary and secondary schools

D-U-N-S 20-543-2615   (BR)
SOBEYS CAPITAL INCORPORATED
FRESHCO
465 Main St, Lewisporte, NL, A0G 3A0
(709) 535-8535
Emp Here 22
SIC 5411 Grocery stores

D-U-N-S 24-000-9766   (BR)
SUTHERLAND INVESTMENTS INC
TIM HORTONS
465 Main St, Lewisporte, NL, A0G 3A0
(709) 535-0588
Emp Here 33
SIC 5812 Eating places

Little Bay Islands, NL A0J

D-U-N-S 20-710-1226   (BR)
NOVA CENTRAL SCHOOL DISTRICT
H L STRONG ACADEMY
35 Main St, Little Bay Islands, NL, A0J 1K0

Emp Here 50
SIC 8211 Elementary and secondary schools

Lodge Bay, NL A0K

D-U-N-S 24-347-4157   (BR)
WESTERN SCHOOL DISTRICT
ST. JAMES ELEMENTARY SCHOOL
Gd, Lodge Bay, NL, A0K 1T0
(709) 695-3001
Emp Here 50
SIC 8211 Elementary and secondary schools

Lourdes, NL A0N

D-U-N-S 20-023-7142   (BR)
WESTERN SCHOOL DISTRICT
LOURDES ELEMENTARY SCHOOL
82 Main St, Lourdes, NL, A0N 1R0
(709) 642-5822
Emp Here 20

SIC 8211 Elementary and secondary schools

Marystown, NL A0E

D-U-N-S 20-175-5704   (BR)
CITY HOTELS LIMITED
HOTEL MARYSTOWN
76 Atlantic St, Marystown, NL, A0E 2M0
(709) 279-1600
Emp Here 57
SIC 7011 Hotels and motels

D-U-N-S 24-605-1239   (SL)
NEWFOUNDLAND AND LABRADOR EN-GLISH SCHOOL DISTRICT
Gd, Marystown, NL, A0E 2M0
(709) 891-7101
Emp Here 75   *Sales* 2,115,860
SIC 4151 School buses

D-U-N-S 20-115-6093   (BR)
PETER KIEWIT INFRASTRUCTURE CO.
KIEWIT OFFSHORE SERVICES
(*Suby of* Peter Kiewit Sons', Inc.)
277 Atlantic St Suite 267, Marystown, NL, A0E 2M0

Emp Here 100
SIC 3731 Shipbuilding and repairing

D-U-N-S 20-449-9404   (BR)
SOBEYS CAPITAL INCORPORATED
SOBEYS
23 Columbia Dr, Marystown, NL, A0E 2M0
(709) 279-2471
Emp Here 60
SIC 5411 Grocery stores

D-U-N-S 20-554-8691   (BR)
WAL-MART CANADA CORP
272 Atlantic St, Marystown, NL, A0E 2M0
(709) 279-3022
Emp Here 135
SIC 5311 Department stores

Middle Arm Gb, NL A0K

D-U-N-S 25-154-7709   (BR)
NOVA CENTRAL SCHOOL DISTRICT
MSB REGIONAL ACADEMY
15 John Thomas Rd, Middle Arm Gb, NL, A0K 3R0
(709) 252-2905
Emp Here 22
SIC 8211 Elementary and secondary schools

Millertown, NL A0H

D-U-N-S 20-739-6123   (BR)
TECK RESOURCES LIMITED
DUCK POND OPERATIONS
32 Rte 370, Millertown, NL, A0H 1V0
(709) 852-2195
Emp Here 250
SIC 1081 Metal mining services

Milltown, NL A0H

D-U-N-S 25-686-7185   (BR)
NEWFOUNDLAND & LABRADOR HYDRO
1 Kemp Boggy Road, Milltown, NL, A0H 1W0
(709) 882-2551
Emp Here 100
SIC 4911 Electric services

D-U-N-S 20-649-6494   (BR)

NOVA CENTRAL SCHOOL DISTRICT
BAY D'ESPOIR ACADEMY
78 Main St, Milltown, NL, A0H 1W0
(709) 882-2500
Emp Here 26
SIC 8211 Elementary and secondary schools

Mount Pearl, NL A1N

D-U-N-S 20-113-7705   (SL)
ATLANTIC TRAILER & EQUIPMENT LTD
8 Lintros Pl, Mount Pearl, NL, A1N 5K2
(709) 745-3260
Emp Here 20   *Sales* 5,197,506
SIC 5083 Farm and garden machinery

D-U-N-S 20-064-8736   (BR)
BAKER HUGHES CANADA COMPANY
BAKER PETROLITE
(*Suby of* Baker Hughes, A GE Company)
16 Kyle Ave, Mount Pearl, NL, A1N 4R5
(709) 748-4900
Emp Here 35
SIC 1381 Drilling oil and gas wells

D-U-N-S 25-296-3111   (BR)
BANK OF NOVA SCOTIA, THE
SCOTIABANK
Po Box 70 Rpo Centennial Sq, Mount Pearl, NL, A1N 2C1
(709) 576-7796
Emp Here 20
SIC 6021 National commercial banks

D-U-N-S 24-228-4318   (BR)
BELL ALIANT REGIONAL COMMUNICA-TIONS INC
760 Topsail Rd Suite 2110, Mount Pearl, NL, A1N 3J5
(709) 739-2122
Emp Here 450
SIC 4899 Communication services, nec

D-U-N-S 25-310-8187   (BR)
BRINK'S CANADA LIMITED
(*Suby of* The Brink's Company)
88 Glencoe Dr, Mount Pearl, NL, A1N 4S9
(709) 747-0288
Emp Here 35
SIC 7381 Detective and armored car services

D-U-N-S 20-987-8313   (SL)
BROWNINGS HOLDINGS LTD
HOTEL MOUNT PEARL
7 Park Ave, Mount Pearl, NL, A1N 1J1
(709) 364-7725
Emp Here 50   *Sales* 2,188,821
SIC 7011 Hotels and motels

D-U-N-S 24-878-9596   (SL)
CANADIAN FOLDING CARTONS INC
HUTTON INTERNATIONAL PRESS, A DIV OF
14 Clyde Ave, Mount Pearl, NL, A1N 4S1
(709) 368-2133
Emp Here 37   *Sales* 5,545,013
SIC 2657 Folding paperboard boxes
Dir Noel Hutton
 Christopher Hutton

D-U-N-S 24-329-0249   (BR)
CASCADES CANADA ULC
NEWFOUNDLAND CONTAINERS DIV OF
110 Clyde Ave, Mount Pearl, NL, A1N 4S2
(709) 747-1200
Emp Here 65
SIC 2653 Corrugated and solid fiber boxes

D-U-N-S 20-039-4893   (BR)
CHELSEA FOOD SERVICES LIMITED
KFC
(*Suby of* Chelsea Food Services Limited)
26 Commonwealth Ave, Mount Pearl, NL, A1N 1W6

---

(709) 364-9360
Emp Here 21
SIC 5812 Eating places

D-U-N-S 20-922-4851   (BR)
COCA-COLA REFRESHMENTS CANADA COMPANY
(*Suby of* The Coca-Cola Company)
51 Sagona Ave Unit 3, Mount Pearl, NL, A1N 4P9
(709) 576-1670
Emp Here 20
SIC 5149 Groceries and related products, nec

D-U-N-S 24-722-8414   (HQ)
COMPUSULT LIMITED
COMPUSULT
(*Suby of* Compusult Limited)
40 Bannister St, Mount Pearl, NL, A1N 1W1
(709) 745-7914
Emp Here 45   *Emp Total* 60
Sales 8,736,240
SIC 7371 Custom computer programming services
Pr Pr Barry O'rourke
 Paul Mitten

D-U-N-S 25-716-7932   (BR)
COUNTRY RIBBON INC
1273 Topsail Rd, Mount Pearl, NL, A1N 5G3
(709) 368-3193
Emp Here 25
SIC 2048 Prepared feeds, nec

D-U-N-S 25-411-3251   (BR)
DAY & ROSS INC
SAMEDAY WORLDWIDE
79 Glencoe Dr, Mount Pearl, NL, A1N 4S6
(709) 747-4104
Emp Here 40
SIC 4213 Trucking, except local

D-U-N-S 24-352-6881   (BR)
EASTERN REGIONAL INTEGRATED HEALTH AUTHORITY
EASTERN HEALTH
760 Topsail Rd, Mount Pearl, NL, A1N 3J5
(709) 752-4534
Emp Here 400
SIC 8062 General medical and surgical hospitals

D-U-N-S 20-988-3743   (BR)
EMCO CORPORATION
EMCO SUPPLY
18 Bruce St, Mount Pearl, NL, A1N 4T4
(709) 747-0382
Emp Here 25
SIC 5074 Plumbing and heating equipment and supplies (hydronics)

D-U-N-S 24-260-2811   (BR)
FARMERS CO-OPERATIVE DAIRY LIMITED
CENTRAL DAIRIES
12 Bruce St, Mount Pearl, NL, A1N 4T4
(709) 364-7531
Emp Here 50
SIC 2026 Fluid milk

D-U-N-S 24-228-3567   (BR)
GOODLIFE FITNESS CENTRES INC
12 Merchant Dr, Mount Pearl, NL, A1N 5J5
(709) 368-8347
Emp Here 30
SIC 7991 Physical fitness facilities

D-U-N-S 24-450-2647   (BR)
GRANITE DEPARTMENT STORES INC
PIPERS DEPARTMENT STORES
7 Commonwealth Ave, Mount Pearl, NL, A1N 1W3
(709) 368-8192
Emp Here 20
SIC 5311 Department stores

D-U-N-S 20-295-2214   (SL)
HEDDLE MARINE SERVICE (NL) INC
30 Dundee Ave, Mount Pearl, NL, A1N 4R7

---

(709) 747-9116
Emp Here 46   *Sales* 5,182,810
SIC 3731 Shipbuilding and repairing
Pr Pr Dennis Thorne
 Rick Heddle
 Blair Mckeil

D-U-N-S 20-015-9382   (HQ)
HOUSEHOLD MOVERS AND SHIPPERS LIMITED
NORTH AMERICAN VAN LINES
(*Suby of* Household Movers And Shippers Limited)
19 Clyde Ave, Mount Pearl, NL, A1N 4R8
(709) 747-4222
Emp Here 25   *Emp Total* 50
Sales 3,939,878
SIC 4212 Local trucking, without storage

D-U-N-S 25-308-4990   (BR)
HOYT'S MOVING & STORAGE LIMITED
LE DREW'S EXPRESS
129 Clyde Ave, Mount Pearl, NL, A1N 4R9
(709) 368-2145
Emp Here 30
SIC 4213 Trucking, except local

D-U-N-S 24-347-7457   (BR)
INMARSAT SOLUTIONS (CANADA) INC
34 Glencoe Dr, Mount Pearl, NL, A1N 4S8

Emp Here 125
SIC 5065 Electronic parts and equipment, nec

D-U-N-S 24-913-2838   (HQ)
INMARSAT SOLUTIONS (CANADA) INC
34 Glencoe Dr, Mount Pearl, NL, A1N 4P6
(709) 724-5400
Emp Here 272   *Emp Total* 1,762
Sales 47,497,416
SIC 4899 Communication services, nec
Pr Alison Horrocks
 Sharon Forsey
Dir David Thornhill
Dir Roger Butt

D-U-N-S 20-268-3954   (BR)
J. D. IRVING, LIMITED
KENT HOME IMPROVEMENT WARE-HOUSE
(*Suby of* J. D. Irving, Limited)
60 Old Placentia Rd, Mount Pearl, NL, A1N 4Y1
(709) 748-3500
Emp Here 130
SIC 5211 Lumber and other building materials

D-U-N-S 20-985-3035   (HQ)
K&D PRATT GROUP INC
INDUSTRIAL SALES AND SERVICES
(*Suby of* Jenniker Holdings Inc)
126 Glencoe Dr, Mount Pearl, NL, A1N 4S9
(709) 722-5690
Emp Here 45   *Emp Total* 63
Sales 28,130,974
SIC 5085 Industrial supplies
Pr Pr Andrew Bell
 Jeffrey Macpherson
 Shawn Tobin

D-U-N-S 25-299-4058   (BR)
LAWTON'S DRUG STORES LIMITED
LAWTON'S WHOLESALE
1 Home St, Mount Pearl, NL, A1N 4T5
(709) 738-0251
Emp Here 24
SIC 5122 Drugs, proprietaries, and sundries

D-U-N-S 20-543-1765   (BR)
LAWTON'S DRUG STORES LIMITED
LAWTONS CENTENNIAL SQARE
8 Centennial St, Mount Pearl, NL, A1N 1G5
(709) 368-2663
Emp Here 30
SIC 5912 Drug stores and proprietary stores

D-U-N-S 25-713-8495   (BR)
LOCATION HEWITT INC

---

24 Third St, Mount Pearl, NL, A1N 2A5
(709) 282-5537
Emp Here 80
SIC 5082 Construction and mining machinery

D-U-N-S 25-612-5139   (SL)
MASONIC PARK INC
100 Masonic Dr, Mount Pearl, NL, A1N 3K5

Emp Here 80   *Sales* 3,724,879
SIC 8322 Individual and family services

D-U-N-S 24-913-3893   (BR)
MIDLAND TRANSPORT LIMITED
(*Suby of* J. D. Irving, Limited)
200 Glencoe Dr, Mount Pearl, NL, A1N 4P7
(709) 747-9119
Emp Here 50
SIC 4212 Local trucking, without storage

D-U-N-S 24-428-9687   (BR)
NORTRAX CANADA INC
(*Suby of* Deere & Company)
15 Allston St, Mount Pearl, NL, A1N 0A3
(709) 368-9660
Emp Here 24
SIC 5082 Construction and mining machinery

D-U-N-S 20-200-7469   (BR)
PEPSICO CANADA ULC
FRITO LAY CANADA
(*Suby of* Pepsico, Inc.)
5 Glencoe Dr, Mount Pearl, NL, A1N 4S4
(709) 748-2075
Emp Here 35
SIC 5145 Confectionery

D-U-N-S 20-010-4151   (BR)
ROLLS-ROYCE CANADA LIMITEE
142 Glencoe Dr, Mount Pearl, NL, A1N 4S9
(709) 364-3053
Emp Here 22
SIC 5541 Gasoline service stations

D-U-N-S 25-124-5494   (BR)
SNC-LAVALIN INC
BAE NEWPLAN
1133 Topsail Rd, Mount Pearl, NL, A1N 5G2
(709) 368-0118
Emp Here 80
SIC 8711 Engineering services

D-U-N-S 25-137-3049   (SL)
SAN-I-KLEEN MAINTENANCE LTD
835 Topsail Rd, Mount Pearl, NL, A1N 3J6

Emp Here 65   *Sales* 2,450,055
SIC 7349 Building maintenance services, nec

D-U-N-S 20-304-4305   (BR)
SEARS CANADA INC
9 Glencoe Dr Unit 5740, Mount Pearl, NL, A1N 4S4

Emp Here 40
SIC 5199 Nondurable goods, nec

D-U-N-S 20-520-0012   (BR)
SOBEYS CAPITAL INCORPORATED
SOBEYS
50 Old Placentia Rd, Mount Pearl, NL, A1N 4Y1
(709) 745-8501
Emp Here 100
SIC 5411 Grocery stores

D-U-N-S 24-259-2970   (BR)
SOBEYS CAPITAL INCORPORATED
SYSCO FOOD SERVICES ATLANTIC
10 Old Placentia Rd, Mount Pearl, NL, A1N 4P5
(709) 748-1200
Emp Here 120
SIC 5148 Fresh fruits and vegetables

D-U-N-S 20-182-6257   (BR)
SYSCO CANADA, INC
SYSCO FOOD SERVICES OF ATLANTIC CANADA

(*Suby of* Sysco Corporation)
10 Old Placentia Rd, Mount Pearl, NL, A1N 4P5
(709) 748-1200
Emp Here 100
SIC 5142 Packaged frozen goods

D-U-N-S 24-257-6353   (BR)
WAL-MART CANADA CORP
16 Merchant Dr, Mount Pearl, NL, A1N 5J5
(709) 364-4214
Emp Here 200
SIC 5311 Department stores

D-U-N-S 20-246-0825   (BR)
WESTON BAKERIES LIMITED
17 Bruce St, Mount Pearl, NL, A1N 4T2
(709) 576-1941
Emp Here 60
SIC 2051 Bread, cake, and related products

Musgrave Harbour, NL A0G

D-U-N-S 24-248-3852   (BR)
NOVA CENTRAL SCHOOL DISTRICT
GILL MEMORIAL ACADEMY
17 Lady Peace Ave, Musgrave Harbour, NL, A0G 3J0
(709) 655-2121
Emp Here 21
SIC 8211 Elementary and secondary schools

D-U-N-S 20-710-1051   (BR)
NOVA CENTRAL SCHOOL DISTRICT
GILL MEMORIAL ACADEMY
Gd, Musgrave Harbour, NL, A0G 3J0
(709) 655-2022
Emp Here 50
SIC 8211 Elementary and secondary schools

Nain, NL A0P

D-U-N-S 25-241-4248   (BR)
LABRADOR SCHOOL BOARD
JENS HAVEN MEMORIAL SCHOOL
3 School St, Nain, NL, A0P 1L0
(709) 922-1270
Emp Here 38
SIC 8211 Elementary and secondary schools

Natuashish, NL A0P

D-U-N-S 25-242-3074   (BR)
LABRADOR SCHOOL BOARD
MUSHUAU INNU NATUASHISH SCHOOL
189 Rich St, Natuashish, NL, A0P 1A0
(709) 478-8971
Emp Here 52
SIC 8211 Elementary and secondary schools

Normans Cove, NL A0B

D-U-N-S 24-710-6136   (BR)
DORSET FISHERIES LIMITED
1 Wharf Rd, Normans Cove, NL, A0B 2T0

Emp Here 50
SIC 2092 Fresh or frozen packaged fish

Norris Arm, NL A0G

D-U-N-S 20-710-1150   (BR)
NOVA CENTRAL SCHOOL DISTRICT

HILLVIEW ACADEMY
245 Gillingham Ave, Norris Arm, NL, A0G 3M0
(709) 653-2529
Emp Here 20
SIC 8211 Elementary and secondary schools

Norris Point, NL A0K

D-U-N-S 25-331-0676   (BR)
WESTERN REGIONAL INTEGRATED HEALTH AUTHORITY, THE
Gd, Norris Point, NL, A0K 3V0
(709) 458-2211
Emp Here 100
SIC 8062 General medical and surgical hospitals

North West River, NL A0P

D-U-N-S 25-001-7977   (BR)
LABRADOR SCHOOL BOARD
PEENAMIN MCKENZIE ALL GRADE SCHOOL
Gd, North West River, NL, A0P 1M0

Emp Here 50
SIC 8211 Elementary and secondary schools

Paradise, NL A1L

D-U-N-S 24-826-2941   (SL)
ACAN WINDOWS INC
ACAN WINDOWS AND DOORS
1641 Topsail Rd, Paradise, NL, A1L 1V1

Emp Here 100   *Sales* 14,665,101
SIC 3089 Plastics products, nec
Pr Pr Tae (Ted) Kwon

D-U-N-S 20-965-4875   (BR)
ADESA AUCTIONS CANADA CORPORATION
ADESA ST JOHN'S
192 Mcnamara Dr, Paradise, NL, A1L 0A6
(709) 364-3250
Emp Here 35
SIC 5012 Automobiles and other motor vehicles

D-U-N-S 25-960-5905   (BR)
ARMOUR TRANSPORT INC
ARMOUR TRANSPORTATION SYSTEMS
14 St. Anne'S Cres, Paradise, NL, A1L 1K1
(709) 782-7410
Emp Here 40
SIC 4213 Trucking, except local

D-U-N-S 25-701-9828   (SL)
ENVIRO CLEAN (NFLD.) LIMITED
POWER VAC DISASTER KLEENUP
155 Mcnamara Dr, Paradise, NL, A1L 0A7
(709) 781-3264
Emp Here 50   *Sales* 2,334,742
SIC 7349 Building maintenance services, nec

D-U-N-S 20-208-4997   (BR)
F I OILFIELD SERVICES CANADA ULC
F I CANADA
63 Bremigen'S Blvd, Paradise, NL, A1L 4A2
(709) 745-3330
Emp Here 45
SIC 1389 Oil and gas field services, nec

D-U-N-S 25-794-9875   (BR)
FUTURITY LIMITED
TIM HORTONS 1237
(*Suby of* Futurity Limited)
1316 Topsail Rd, Paradise, NL, A1L 1N9

(709) 782-8467
Emp Here 40
SIC 5812 Eating places

D-U-N-S 24-260-4064   (SL)
NU-WAY KITCHENS (2008) LIMITED
1328 Topsail Rd, Paradise, NL, A1L 1P2
(709) 782-1711
Emp Here 50   *Sales* 3,356,192
SIC 2541 Wood partitions and fixtures

D-U-N-S 24-126-9893   (HQ)
PENNECON ENERGY HYDRAULIC SYSTEMS LIMITED
2 Maverick Pl, Paradise, NL, A1L 0H6
(709) 726-3490
Emp Here 26   *Emp Total* 60
Sales 14,968,940
SIC 7699 Repair services, nec

D-U-N-S 24-679-6622   (SL)
WEATHERFORD SURFACE LOGGING SYSTEMS (CANADA) LTD
8 St. Anne'S Cres, Paradise, NL, A1L 1K1
(709) 782-8683
Emp Here 31   *Sales* 5,202,480
SIC 1389 Oil and gas field services, nec
Dir Geoff Inose

Pasadena, NL A0L

D-U-N-S 24-326-7023   (SL)
RAINBOW ENTERPRISES LTD
SHOPPERS DRUG MART
5 First Ave, Pasadena, NL, A0L 1K0
(709) 686-2063
Emp Here 26   *Sales* 5,072,500
SIC 5912 Drug stores and proprietary stores
Pr Karen Colbourne

D-U-N-S 20-710-1408   (BR)
WESTERN SCHOOL DISTRICT
WESTERN SCHOOL DISTRICT SCHOOLS PASADENA ACADEMY
Gd, Pasadena, NL, A0L 1K0
(709) 686-5091
Emp Here 25
SIC 8211 Elementary and secondary schools

D-U-N-S 25-241-2861   (BR)
WESTERN SCHOOL DISTRICT
PASADENA ELEMENTARY SCHOOL
59 Forest Street, Pasadena, NL, A0L 1K0
(709) 686-2621
Emp Here 23
SIC 8211 Elementary and secondary schools

Placentia, NL A0B

D-U-N-S 24-345-6030   (BR)
EASTERN REGIONAL INTEGRATED HEALTH AUTHORITY
PLACENTIA HEALTH CENTRE
1 Corrigan Pl, Placentia, NL, A0B 2Y0
(709) 227-2061
Emp Here 187
SIC 8051 Skilled nursing care facilities

D-U-N-S 25-299-3571   (BR)
SOBEYS CAPITAL INCORPORATED
SOBEYS 674
Gd, Placentia, NL, A0B 2Y0
(709) 227-5172
Emp Here 50
SIC 5411 Grocery stores

Plum Point, NL A0K

D-U-N-S 24-347-9842   (BR)

WESTERN SCHOOL DISTRICT
VIKING TRAIL ACADEMY
Gd, Plum Point, NL, A0K 4A0
(709) 247-2008
Emp Here 42
SIC 8211 Elementary and secondary schools

Point Leamington, NL A0H

D-U-N-S 25-707-9350   (BR)
SUPERIOR GLOVE WORKS LIMITED
268 Main St, Point Leamington, NL, A0H 1Z0
(709) 484-3596
Emp Here 35
SIC 2381 Fabric dress and work gloves

Port Au Port, NL A0N

D-U-N-S 20-938-4077   (BR)
WESTERN SCHOOL DISTRICT
PICCADILLY CENTRAL HIGH SCHOOL
Gd, Port Au Port, NL, A0N 1T0
(709) 642-5752
Emp Here 23
SIC 8211 Elementary and secondary schools

Port Saunders, NL A0K

D-U-N-S 20-294-7680   (BR)
NEWFOUNDLAND & LABRADOR HYDRO
Gd, Port Saunders, NL, A0K 4H0
(709) 861-3780
Emp Here 40
SIC 4911 Electric services

D-U-N-S 20-256-6261   (BR)
WESTERN SCHOOL DISTRICT
FRENCH SHORE ACADEMY
10 Roncalli Rd, Port Saunders, NL, A0K 4H0
(709) 861-2592
Emp Here 20
SIC 8211 Elementary and secondary schools

Port Union, NL A0C

D-U-N-S 24-345-6048   (BR)
OCEAN CHOICE INTERNATIONAL L.P.
Gd, Port Union, NL, A0C 2J0
(709) 469-2211
Emp Here 150
SIC 2092 Fresh or frozen packaged fish

Portugal Cove-St Philips, NL A1M

D-U-N-S 24-994-9660   (SL)
KELLOWAY CONSTRUCTION LIMITED
1388 Portugal Cove Rd, Portugal Cove-St Philips, NL, A1M 3J9
(709) 895-6532
Emp Here 100   *Sales* 2,918,428
SIC 7349 Building maintenance services, nec

Postville, NL A0P

D-U-N-S 20-801-0954   (BR)
NUNATSIAVUT GOVERNMENT, THE
Gd, Postville, NL, A0P 1N0
(709) 479-9842
Emp Here 20

SIC 8621 Professional organizations

Ramea, NL A0N

D-U-N-S 20-710-1515   (BR)
WESTERN SCHOOL DISTRICT
ST. BONIFACE ALL GRADE
10 School Rd, Ramea, NL, A0N 2J0
(709) 625-2283
Emp Here 50
SIC 8211 Elementary and secondary schools

Robinsons, NL A0N

D-U-N-S 20-023-7134   (BR)
WESTERN SCHOOL DISTRICT
E. A. BUTLER SCHOOL
Gd, Robinsons, NL, A0N 1V0
(709) 645-2330
Emp Here 25
SIC 8211 Elementary and secondary schools

Rocky Harbour, NL A0K

D-U-N-S 20-256-6329   (BR)
WESTERN SCHOOL DISTRICT
GROS MORNE ACADEMY
Gd, Rocky Harbour, NL, A0K 4N0
(709) 458-2457
Emp Here 29
SIC 8211 Elementary and secondary schools

Roddickton, NL A0K

D-U-N-S 24-114-1329   (BR)
LABRADOR-GRENFELL   REGIONAL HEALTH AUTHORITY
Gd, Roddickton, NL, A0K 4P0
(709) 457-2215
Emp Here 36
SIC 8062 General medical and surgical hospitals

D-U-N-S 24-347-7358   (BR)
WESTERN SCHOOL DISTRICT
CLOUD RIVER ACADEMY
23 Cloud Dr, Roddickton, NL, A0K 4P0
(709) 457-2430
Emp Here 24
SIC 8211 Elementary and secondary schools

Sandy Cove, NL A0K

D-U-N-S 20-037-2790   (SL)
STRAITS RURAL DEVELOPMENT ASSOCIATION
SDA
Gd, Sandy Cove, NL, A0K 5C0
(709) 456-2122
Emp Here 50   *Sales* 4,617,412
SIC 8641 Civic and social associations

South Brook Gb, NL A0J

D-U-N-S 20-710-1291   (BR)
NOVA CENTRAL SCHOOL DISTRICT
SOUTH BROOK ACADEMY
Gd, South Brook Gb, NL, A0J 1S0

(709) 868-3001
Emp Here 50
SIC 8211 Elementary and secondary schools

Springdale, NL A0J

D-U-N-S 20-710-1234   (BR)
NOVA CENTRAL SCHOOL DISTRICT
DORSET COLLEGIATE
142 Little Bay Rd, Springdale, NL, A0J 1T0
(709) 673-3715
Emp Here 50
SIC 8211 Elementary and secondary schools

D-U-N-S 20-023-4107   (BR)
NOVA CENTRAL SCHOOL DISTRICT
INDIAN RIVER ACADEMY
140 Little Bay Rd, Springdale, NL, A0J 1T0
(709) 673-3714
Emp Here 23
SIC 8211 Elementary and secondary schools

St Anthony East, NL A0K

D-U-N-S 25-498-1905   (SL)
ST ANTHONY'S SEAFOOD LIMITED PARTNERSHIP
240 East St Suite B, St Anthony East, NL, A0K 4T0
(709) 454-2642
Emp Here 85   *Sales* 19,681,300
SIC 2092 Fresh or frozen packaged fish
Ex Dir Sam Elliott

St Georges, NL A0N

D-U-N-S 25-001-7910   (BR)
WESTERN SCHOOL DISTRICT
APPALACHIA HIGH SCHOOL
10 Flatbay Junction Rd, St Georges, NL, A0N 1Z0
(709) 647-3381
Emp Here 20
SIC 8211 Elementary and secondary schools

D-U-N-S 25-240-9685   (BR)
WESTERN SCHOOL DISTRICT
OUR LADY MERCY ELEMENTARY SCHOOL
Gd, St Georges, NL, A0N 1Z0
(709) 647-3752
Emp Here 24
SIC 8211 Elementary and secondary schools

St Lawrence, NL A0E

D-U-N-S 20-023-7035   (BR)
EASTERN   REGIONAL   INTEGRATED HEALTH AUTHORITY
US MEMORIAL HEALTH CENTRE
Gd, St Lawrence, NL, A0E 2V0
(709) 873-2330
Emp Here 55
SIC 8011 Offices and clinics of medical doctors

St Marys, NL A0B

D-U-N-S 25-888-6449   (SL)
BEST OF CARE LTD, THE
Gd, St Marys, NL, A0B 3B0
(709) 525-2425
Emp Here 50   *Sales* 2,261,782
SIC 8051 Skilled nursing care facilities

St. Anthony, NL A0K

D-U-N-S 20-756-5164   (BR)
COLLEGE OF THE NORTH ATLANTIC
93 E St Suite 83, St. Anthony, NL, A0K 4S0
(709) 454-3559
Emp Here 20
SIC 8222 Junior colleges

D-U-N-S 24-356-3801   (BR)
LABRADOR-GRENFELL   REGIONAL HEALTH AUTHORITY
CHARLES S. CURTIS MEMORIAL HOSPITAL, THE
200 West St Suite 178, St. Anthony, NL, A0K 4S0
(709) 454-3333
Emp Here 20
SIC 8062 General medical and surgical hospitals

D-U-N-S 25-308-4677   (BR)
NEWFOUNDLAND & LABRADOR HYDRO
129 North St, St. Anthony, NL, A0K 4S0
(709) 454-3030
Emp Here 20
SIC 4911 Electric services

D-U-N-S 24-347-4140   (BR)
WESTERN SCHOOL DISTRICT
HARRIOT CURTIS COLLEGIATE
Gd, St. Anthony, NL, A0K 4S0

Emp Here 28
SIC 8211 Elementary and secondary schools

D-U-N-S 24-347-4132   (BR)
WESTERN SCHOOL DISTRICT
WHITE HILLS ACADEMY
Gd, St. Anthony, NL, A0K 4S0
(709) 454-2202
Emp Here 30
SIC 8211 Elementary and secondary schools

St. John'S, NL A1A

D-U-N-S 24-965-0321   (BR)
ACUREN GROUP INC
(*Suby of* Rockwood Service Corporation)
112 Forest Rd, St. John'S, NL, A1A 1E6
(709) 753-2100
Emp Here 50
SIC 8734 Testing laboratories

D-U-N-S 24-955-6341   (SL)
BATTERY MANAGEMENT INC
BATTERY HOTEL & SUITES
100 Signal Hill Rd, St. John'S, NL, A1A 1B3

Emp Here 80   *Sales* 3,502,114
SIC 7011 Hotels and motels

D-U-N-S 20-100-7684   (BR)
BLACK & MCDONALD LIMITED
29 Ottawa St, St. John'S, NL, A1A 2R9
(709) 896-2639
Emp Here 100
SIC 1711 Plumbing, heating, air-conditioning

D-U-N-S 20-984-9256   (BR)
CANADIAN NATIONAL INSTITUTE FOR THE BLIND, THE
C N I B
(*Suby of* Canadian National Institute For The Blind, The)
70 The Boulevard, St. John'S, NL, A1A 1K2
(709) 754-1180
Emp Here 22
SIC 8011 Offices and clinics of medical doctors

D-U-N-S 20-510-9494   (BR)
CANADIAN RED CROSS SOCIETY, THE

▲ Public Company   ■ Public Company Family Member   **HQ** Headquarters   **BR** Branch   **SL** Single Location

17 Major'S Path, St. John'S, NL, A1A 4Z9
(709) 758-8400
Emp Here 22
SIC 8699 Membership organizations, nec

D-U-N-S 25-304-8409   (BR)
CARLSON WAGONLIT CANADA
CARLSON WAGONLIT
92 Elizabeth Ave, St. John'S, NL, A1A 1W7
(709) 726-2900
Emp Here 80
SIC 4724 Travel agencies

D-U-N-S 24-773-3202   (BR)
CHELSEA FOOD SERVICES LIMITED
KENTUCKY FRIED CHICKEN
(*Suby of* Chelsea Food Services Limited)
571 Torbay Rd, St. John'S, NL, A1A 5G9
(709) 753-4941
Emp Here 49
SIC 5812 Eating places

D-U-N-S 24-994-6377   (BR)
CITY HOTELS LIMITED
AIRPORT PLAZA
106 Airport Rd, St. John'S, NL, A1A 4Y3
(709) 753-3500
Emp Here 25
SIC 7011 Hotels and motels

D-U-N-S 24-393-0620   (BR)
COLLINS, P F CUSTOMS BROKER LIMITED
275 E White Hills Rd, St. John'S, NL, A1A 5X7
(709) 726-2121
Emp Here 30
SIC 4225 General warehousing and storage

D-U-N-S 20-287-7986   (BR)
COSTCO WHOLESALE CANADA LTD
(*Suby of* Costco Wholesale Corporation)
28 Stavanger Dr, St. John'S, NL, A1A 5E8
(709) 738-8610
Emp Here 145
SIC 5141 Groceries, general line

D-U-N-S 24-337-3581   (BR)
FGL SPORTS LTD
SPORT-CHEK
75 Aberdeen Dr, St. John'S, NL, A1A 5N6
(709) 739-7708
Emp Here 45
SIC 5941 Sporting goods and bicycle shops

D-U-N-S 25-715-6869   (BR)
GRANITE DEPARTMENT STORES INC
PIPERS DEPARTMENT STORES
Fall River Plaza 272 Torbay Rd, St. John'S, NL, A1A 4E1
(709) 579-1401
Emp Here 22
SIC 5311 Department stores

D-U-N-S 20-779-8000   (BR)
GRANT THORNTON LLP
15 International Pl Suite 300, St. John'S, NL, A1A 0L4
(709) 778-8800
Emp Here 60
SIC 8721 Accounting, auditing, and book-keeping

D-U-N-S 25-923-3054   (BR)
HARMONIE FOODS LIMITED
TIM HORTONS
551 Torbay Rd, St. John'S, NL, A1A 5G9
(709) 726-4050
Emp Here 45
SIC 5812 Eating places

D-U-N-S 24-449-4480   (HQ)
HUNT'S TRANSPORT LIMITED
(*Suby of* Hunt's Transport Limited)
168 Major'S Path, St. John'S, NL, A1A 5A1
(709) 747-4868
Emp Here 38   *Emp Total* 80
Sales 9,995,616
SIC 4213 Trucking, except local
Pr Pr Greer Hunt

D-U-N-S 25-703-0999   (BR)
J. D. IRVING, LIMITED
KENT BUILDING SUPPLIES
(*Suby of* J. D. Irving, Limited)
10 Stavanger Dr, St. John'S, NL, A1A 5E8
(709) 758-2500
Emp Here 150
SIC 5211 Lumber and other building materials

D-U-N-S 24-804-1659   (BR)
LAWTON'S DRUG STORES LIMITED
12 Gleneyre St Suite 173, St. John'S, NL, A1A 2M7
(709) 753-3111
Emp Here 22
SIC 5912 Drug stores and proprietary stores

D-U-N-S 25-697-2712   (BR)
LOBLAWS INC
DOMINION
370 Newfoundland Dr, St. John'S, NL, A1A 4A2
(709) 576-1160
Emp Here 80
SIC 5411 Grocery stores

D-U-N-S 20-566-7434   (BR)
MARK'S WORK WEARHOUSE LTD
WORK WORLD
95 Aberdeen Ave, St. John'S, NL, A1A 5P6
(709) 722-9870
Emp Here 25
SIC 5611 Men's and boys' clothing stores

D-U-N-S 20-735-7398   (SL)
MASK SECURITY INC
38 Pearson St Suite 306, St. John'S, NL, A1A 3R1
(709) 368-4709
Emp Here 50   *Sales* 1,532,175
SIC 7381 Detective and armored car services

D-U-N-S 20-195-8613   (BR)
METRO ONTARIO INC
METRO
55 Stavanger Dr, St. John'S, NL, A1A 5E8
(709) 576-3576
Emp Here 100
SIC 5411 Grocery stores

D-U-N-S 20-016-1537   (SL)
NEWFOUNDLAND BROADCASTING COMPANY LIMITED
NTV
446 Logy Bay Rd, St. John'S, NL, A1A 5C6
(709) 722-5015
Emp Here 70   *Sales* 4,085,799
SIC 4833 Television broadcasting stations

D-U-N-S 20-449-1310   (HQ)
P.F. COLLINS CUSTOMS BROKER LIMITED
P.F. COLLINS INTERNATIONAL SOLUTIONS
251 E White Hills Rd, St. John'S, NL, A1A 5W4
(709) 726-7596
Emp Here 60   *Emp Total* 84
Sales 19,772,350
SIC 4731 Freight transportation arrangement
Pr Pr Bernard Collins
VP VP Brian Collins
    William Collins
    Kathleen Collins

D-U-N-S 20-345-8781   (BR)
PAL AEROSPACE LTD
Hangar 6 St. Johns International Airport, St. John'S, NL, A1A 5B5
(709) 576-1284
Emp Here 30
SIC 4522 Air transportation, nonscheduled

D-U-N-S 20-267-4102   (SL)
PENNECON ENERGY INDUSTRIAL SERVICES LTD
456 Logy Bay Rd, St. John'S, NL, A1A 5C6
(709) 782-4269
Emp Here 20   *Sales* 4,012,839
SIC 1522 Residential construction, nec

D-U-N-S 24-098-4794   (BR)
PROVINCE OF NEWFOUNDLAND & LABRADOR
WORKPLACE HEALTH SAFETY & COMPENSATION SERVICES
148 Forest Rd Suite 148, St. John'S, NL, A1A 1E6
(709) 778-1000
Emp Here 300
SIC 6331 Fire, marine, and casualty insurance

D-U-N-S 25-768-1866   (SL)
PROVINCIAL AVIATION MAINTENANCE SERVICES INC
Hanger No 1 & 6 St, St. John'S, NL, A1A 5B5
(709) 576-1284
Emp Here 40   *Sales* 8,420,350
SIC 4581 Airports, flying fields, and services
VP VP Bill Madore

D-U-N-S 25-284-3966   (SL)
SALVATION ARMY GLENBROOK LODGE
105 Torbay Rd, St. John'S, NL, A1A 2G9
(709) 726-1575
Emp Here 135   *Sales* 6,898,600
SIC 8361 Residential care
    Rex Colbourne

D-U-N-S 25-703-5089   (BR)
SOBEYS CAPITAL INCORPORATED
10 Elizabeth Ave Suite 744, St. John'S, NL, A1A 5L4
(709) 753-3426
Emp Here 150
SIC 5411 Grocery stores

D-U-N-S 20-100-8013   (BR)
SOBEYS CAPITAL INCORPORATED
SOBEYS
360 Torbay Rd, St. John'S, NL, A1A 4E1
(709) 726-0522
Emp Here 70
SIC 5411 Grocery stores

D-U-N-S 20-309-7167   (BR)
STANTEC CONSULTING LTD
99 Airport Rd, St. John'S, NL, A1A 4Y3
(709) 576-8612
Emp Here 35
SIC 8711 Engineering services

D-U-N-S 20-582-9760   (BR)
STAPLES CANADA INC
STAPLES THE BUSINESS DEPOT
(*Suby of* Staples, Inc.)
34 Stavanger Dr, St. John'S, NL, A1A 5E8
(709) 753-4920
Emp Here 40
SIC 5943 Stationery stores

D-U-N-S 25-715-6588   (BR)
SWISSPORT CANADA INC
SERVISAIR
Gd, St. John'S, NL, A1A 5B2
(709) 576-4951
Emp Here 50
SIC 4581 Airports, flying fields, and services

D-U-N-S 24-450-7018   (BR)
SWISSPORT CANADA INC
PENAUILLE SERVISAIR
80 Craig Dobbin'S Way Suite 5, St. John'S, NL, A1A 5T2
(709) 722-7947
Emp Here 40
SIC 4581 Airports, flying fields, and services

D-U-N-S 20-860-5183   (BR)
TOWN SHOES LIMITED
SHOE COMPANY, THE
85 Aberdeen Ave Unit 2, St. John'S, NL, A1A 5P6

Emp Here 25
SIC 5661 Shoe stores

D-U-N-S 25-259-7703   (SL)
VIKING CORPORATION LIMITED

178 Major'S Path, St. John'S, NL, A1A 5A1
(709) 576-4335
Emp Here 20   *Sales* 5,425,920
SIC 1541 Industrial buildings and warehouses
Pr Carl Mallam

D-U-N-S 20-649-8805   (BR)
WAL-MART CANADA CORP
90 Aberdeen Ave, St. John'S, NL, A1A 5N6
(709) 738-4350
Emp Here 30
SIC 5311 Department stores

D-U-N-S 20-184-3245   (BR)
WINNERS MERCHANTS INTERNATIONAL L.P.
WINNERS
(*Suby of* The TJX Companies Inc)
60 Aberdeen Ave, St. John'S, NL, A1A 5T3
(709) 738-7500
Emp Here 40
SIC 5651 Family clothing stores

D-U-N-S 20-779-6517   (HQ)
WORKPLACE HEALTH SAFETY & COMPENSATION COMMISSION OF NEWFOUNDLAND AND LABRADOR
148 Forest Rd Unit 146, St. John'S, NL, A1A 1E6
(709) 778-1000
Emp Here 190   *Emp Total* 7,000
Sales 261,701,405
SIC 6331 Fire, marine, and casualty insurance
Ex Dir Tom Mahoney
Ex Dir Brenda Greenslade
Ex Dir Eric Bartlett
Sec Ann Martin
    Paul Kavanagh
CEO Leslie Galway

St. John'S, NL A1B

D-U-N-S 24-341-3221   (BR)
AMEC FOSTER WHEELER AMERICAS LIMITED
EARTH & ENVIRONMENTAL DIVISION
133 Crosbie Rd Suite 202, St. John'S, NL, A1B 1H3
(709) 722-7023
Emp Here 35
SIC 8741 Management services

D-U-N-S 25-737-1260   (BR)
AMEC FOSTER WHEELER INC
133 Crosbie Rd, St. John'S, NL, A1B 1H3
(709) 724-1900
Emp Here 150
SIC 7373 Computer integrated systems design

D-U-N-S 24-677-4256   (BR)
AON REED STENHOUSE INC
125 Kelsey Dr Suite 100, St. John'S, NL, A1B 0L2
(709) 739-1000
Emp Here 30
SIC 6411 Insurance agents, brokers, and service

D-U-N-S 20-965-6870   (BR)
ACADEMY CANADA INC
169 Kenmount Rd Suite 167, St. John'S, NL, A1B 3P9
(709) 739-6767
Emp Here 40
SIC 8221 Colleges and universities

D-U-N-S 20-304-2759   (BR)
ALLNORTH CONSULTANTS LIMITED
HAWCO KING RENOUF
2 Hunt'S Lane, St. John'S, NL, A1B 2L3
(709) 579-1492
Emp Here 25
SIC 8713 Surveying services

D-U-N-S 20-914-1741   (BR)
ATLANTIC LOTTERY CORPORATION INC,
THE
30 Hallett Cres, St. John'S, NL, A1B 4C5
(709) 724-1700
Emp Here 28
SIC 7999 Amusement and recreation, nec

D-U-N-S 25-296-2600   (BR)
BANK OF NOVA SCOTIA, THE
SCOTIABANK
37 Rowan St, St. John'S, NL, A1B 2X2
(709) 576-1199
Emp Here 25
SIC 6021 National commercial banks

D-U-N-S 25-296-2766   (BR)
BANK OF NOVA SCOTIA, THE
SCOTIABANK
48 Kenmount Rd, St. John'S, NL, A1B 1W3
(709) 576-1300
Emp Here 50
SIC 6021 National commercial banks

D-U-N-S 20-694-2489   (BR)
BELL ALIANT REGIONAL COMMUNICA-
TIONS INC
34 Pippy Pl, St. John'S, NL, A1B 3X4
(709) 722-3748
Emp Here 25
SIC 7359 Equipment rental and leasing, nec

D-U-N-S 25-715-6729   (BR)
BENNETT RESTAURANT
MCDONALD'S RESTAURANTS
75 Kelsey Dr, St. John'S, NL, A1B 0C7
(709) 726-5190
Emp Here 30
SIC 5812 Eating places

D-U-N-S 25-697-0617   (SL)
BENNETT RESTAURANT LTD
MCDONALD'S RESTAURANT
54 Kenmount Rd, St. John'S, NL, A1B 1W2
(709) 754-1254
Emp Here 95   *Sales* 2,845,467
SIC 5812 Eating places

D-U-N-S 20-378-1778   (BR)
BIRD GENERAL CONTRACTORS LTD
H.J. O'CONNELL CONSTRUCTION LIMITED
90 O'Leary Ave Suite 101, St. John'S, NL,
A1B 2C7
(709) 726-9095
Emp Here 20
SIC 1622 Bridge, tunnel, and elevated high-
way construction

D-U-N-S 20-015-5380   (HQ)
BRITISH CONFECTIONERY COMPANY
LIMITED
187 Kenmount Rd Suite 2, St. John'S, NL,
A1B 3P9
(709) 747-2377
Emp Here 50   *Emp Total* 71
Sales 8,489,260
SIC 2679 Converted paper products, nec
Pr Pr David Connolly
  Gerald Connolly Jr

D-U-N-S 20-985-3688   (SL)
BURSEY SERVICES LIMITED
303 Thorburn Rd, St. John'S, NL, A1B 4J9
(709) 722-9576
Emp Here 120   *Sales* 3,502,114
SIC 7349 Building maintenance services, nec

D-U-N-S 24-426-1975   (BR)
CSH ELIZABETH TOWERS INC
CHARTWELL SELECT ELIZABETH TOW-
ERS
100 Elizabeth Ave, St. John'S, NL, A1B 1S1

Emp Here 20   *Sales* 729,607
SIC 8361 Residential care

D-U-N-S 24-242-3684   (SL)
CABOT CALL CENTRE

66 Kenmount Rd Suite 203, St. John'S, NL,
A1B 3V7

Emp Here 100   *Sales* 16,981,680
SIC 8748 Business consulting, nec
Brnch Mgr Mary Denie

D-U-N-S 20-547-1043   (BR)
CANADA BREAD COMPANY, LIMITED
MAPLE LEAF
67 O'Leary Ave, St. John'S, NL, A1B 2C9
(709) 722-5410
Emp Here 60
SIC 2051 Bread, cake, and related products

D-U-N-S 24-309-8709   (BR)
CANADIAN BROADCASTING CORPORA-
TION
CBC TV
95 University Ave, St. John'S, NL, A1B 1Z4
(709) 576-5000
Emp Here 100
SIC 4833 Television broadcasting stations

D-U-N-S 25-499-0195   (BR)
CANADIAN RED CROSS SOCIETY, THE
7 Wicklow St, St. John'S, NL, A1B 3Z9

Emp Here 95
SIC 8099 Health and allied services, nec

D-U-N-S 25-715-6661   (BR)
CHELSEA FOOD SERVICES LIMITED
KFC
(*Suby of* Chelsea Food Services Limited)
336 Freshwater Rd, St. John'S, NL, A1B 1C2

Emp Here 20
SIC 5812 Eating places

D-U-N-S 25-537-5644   (BR)
CITY HOTELS LIMITED
HOTEL ST. JOHN'S
102 Kenmount Rd Suite 102, St. John'S, NL,
A1B 3R2
(709) 722-9330
Emp Here 50
SIC 7011 Hotels and motels

D-U-N-S 24-450-7778   (BR)
CO-OPERATORS FINANCIAL SERVICES
LIMITED
CO OPERATORS, THE
19 Crosbie Pl Suite 1, St. John'S, NL, A1B
3Y8
(709) 758-1178
Emp Here 30
SIC 6331 Fire, marine, and casualty insurance

D-U-N-S 25-960-6218   (BR)
COLLEGE OF THE NORTH ATLANTIC
PRINCE PHILLIP DRIVE CAMPUS
1 Prince Philip Dr, St. John'S, NL, A1B 3R3
(709) 758-7200
Emp Here 30
SIC 8222 Junior colleges

D-U-N-S 24-258-4282   (BR)
CROMBIE DEVELOPMENTS LIMITED
AVELON MALL REGIONAL SHOPPING
CENTRE
48 Kenmount Rd, St. John'S, NL, A1B 1W3
(709) 753-7144
Emp Here 35
SIC 6512 Nonresidential building operators

D-U-N-S 25-722-7850   (BR)
EXP SERVICES INC
60 Pippy Pl Suite 200, St. John'S, NL, A1B
4H7
(709) 579-2027
Emp Here 20
SIC 8711 Engineering services

D-U-N-S 24-804-0628   (BR)
EMPIRE THEATRES LIMITED
MARIPLEX CONFECTIONS
48 Kenmount Rd, St. John'S, NL, A1B 1W3

(709) 722-5775
Emp Here 100
SIC 7832 Motion picture theaters, except
drive-in

D-U-N-S 20-986-5989   (BR)
ENERGIE VALERO INC
39 Pippy Pl, St. John'S, NL, A1B 3X2
(709) 754-1880
Emp Here 35
SIC 5172 Petroleum products, nec

D-U-N-S 25-702-3242   (BR)
FGL SPORTS LTD
INTERSPORT
48 Kenmount Rd, St. John'S, NL, A1B 1W3
(709) 739-0155
Emp Here 20
SIC 5699 Miscellaneous apparel and acces-
sory stores

D-U-N-S 25-504-1444   (SL)
FOG CITY BREWING COMPANY LIMITED
FOG CITY BREWING PUB & RESTAURANT
48 Kenmount Rd Suite 200, St. John'S, NL,
A1B 1W3
(709) 726-4848
Emp Here 50   *Sales* 1,532,175
SIC 5812 Eating places

D-U-N-S 25-387-1172   (HQ)
FUGRO JACQUES GEOSURVEYS INC
25 Pippy Pl, St. John'S, NL, A1B 3X2
(709) 726-4252
Emp Here 34   *Emp Total* 11,245
Sales 30,205,730
SIC 1382 Oil and gas exploration services
Pr Michael Cole

D-U-N-S 25-703-2805   (BR)
GAP (CANADA) INC
GAP
(*Suby of* The Gap Inc)
48 Kenmount Rd, St. John'S, NL, A1B 1W3
(709) 753-3007
Emp Here 30
SIC 5651 Family clothing stores

D-U-N-S 20-015-5869   (BR)
GRAYBAR CANADA LIMITED
GRAYBAR HARRIS & ROOME
(*Suby of* Graybar Electric Company, Inc.)
47 Pippy Pl, St. John'S, NL, A1B 4H8
(709) 722-6161
Emp Here 25
SIC 5063 Electrical apparatus and equipment

D-U-N-S 25-173-5841   (BR)
GUILLEVIN INTERNATIONAL CIE
87 O'Leary Ave, St. John'S, NL, A1B 2C9
(709) 722-1420
Emp Here 20
SIC 5063 Electrical apparatus and equipment

D-U-N-S 20-729-5999   (BR)
HERCULES SLR INC
SPARTAN INDUSTRIAL MARINE
7 Pippy Pl Suite 5, St. John'S, NL, A1B 3X2
(709) 722-4221
Emp Here 30
SIC 5088 Transportation equipment and sup-
plies

D-U-N-S 24-420-0288   (BR)
HICKMAN MOTORS LIMITED
HICKMAN CHRYSLER DODGE & JEEP
20 Peet St, St. John'S, NL, A1B 4S6
(709) 757-4364
Emp Here 30
SIC 5511 New and used car dealers

D-U-N-S 25-697-5970   (BR)
HICKMAN MOTORS LIMITED
BODY WORKS
38 O'Leary Ave, St. John'S, NL, A1B 2C7
(709) 754-4508
Emp Here 26
SIC 7532 Top and body repair and paint shops

D-U-N-S 25-365-8702   (BR)
HOME DEPOT OF CANADA INC
HOME DEPOT
(*Suby of* The Home Depot Inc)
70 Kelsey Dr, St. John'S, NL, A1B 5C7
(709) 570-2400
Emp Here 100
SIC 5251 Hardware stores

D-U-N-S 25-867-5024   (BR)
HONEYWELL LIMITED
(*Suby of* Honeywell International Inc.)
1 Duffy Pl, St. John'S, NL, A1B 4M6
(709) 758-6000
Emp Here 26
SIC 3822 Environmental controls

D-U-N-S 25-136-2406   (BR)
INDIGO BOOKS & MUSIC INC
CHAPTERS
(*Suby of* Indigo Books & Music Inc)
70 Kenmount Rd, St. John'S, NL, A1B 1W2
(709) 726-0375
Emp Here 30
SIC 5942 Book stores

D-U-N-S 25-298-5031   (BR)
JOHNSON INC
95 Elizabeth Ave, St. John'S, NL, A1B 1R6
(709) 737-1500
Emp Here 600
SIC 6411 Insurance agents, brokers, and service

D-U-N-S 25-764-7784   (BR)
KEYCORP INC
KEYIN COLLEGE
44 Austin St, St. John'S, NL, A1B 4C2
(709) 579-1061
Emp Here 30
SIC 8221 Colleges and universities

D-U-N-S 25-134-6540   (BR)
KIA CANADA INC
PENNEY KIA
497 Kenmount Rd, St. John'S, NL, A1B 3P9
(709) 726-4542
Emp Here 20
SIC 5511 New and used car dealers

D-U-N-S 25-703-3548   (BR)
LAWTON'S DRUG STORES LIMITED
LAWTON'S DRUG STORES
48 Kenmount Rd Suite 142, St. John'S, NL,
A1B 1W3
(709) 722-5460
Emp Here 29
SIC 5912 Drug stores and proprietary stores

D-U-N-S 20-003-9035   (BR)
LE CHATEAU INC
LE CHATEAU 245
(*Suby of* Le Chateau Inc)
48 Kenmount Rd, St. John'S, NL, A1B 1W3
(709) 726-1899
Emp Here 20
SIC 5651 Family clothing stores

D-U-N-S 20-449-1500   (SL)
LEGROWS TRAVEL LIMITED
(*Suby of* Maritime Travel Inc)
20 Crosbie Pl, St. John'S, NL, A1B 3Y8
(709) 758-6760
Emp Here 56   *Sales* 18,565,350
SIC 4724 Travel agencies
Pr Pr Mike Donovan
Dir Sandra Harvey

D-U-N-S 25-303-9473   (BR)
LONDON LIFE INSURANCE COMPANY
FREEDOM 55 FINANCIAL
10 Rowan St, St. John'S, NL, A1B 2X1
(709) 722-7861
Emp Here 45
SIC 6311 Life insurance

D-U-N-S 24-878-5537   (BR)
LYNDA AND ALBERT ENTERPRISES INC

DAIRY QUEEN
(*Suby of* Lynda and Albert Enterprises Inc)
273 Portugal Cove Rd, St. John'S, NL, A1B 2N8
(709) 738-1171
Emp Here 40
SIC 5812 Eating places

D-U-N-S 20-803-0648   (BR)
MEMORIAL UNIVERSITY OF NEWFOUND-LAND
MEMORIAL UNIVERSITY OF NEWFOUND-LAND FACULTY ASSOCIATION/MUNFA
300 Prince Philip Dr Suite 4019, St. John'S, NL, A1B 3X5
(709) 637-6200
Emp Here 20
SIC 8699 Membership organizations, nec

D-U-N-S 20-357-7234   (BR)
MEMORIAL UNIVERSITY OF NEWFOUND-LAND
DEPARTMENT OF EARTH SCIENCES
300 Prince Philip Dr, St. John'S, NL, A1B 3X5
(709) 864-8142
Emp Here 47
SIC 8221 Colleges and universities

D-U-N-S 20-272-6191   (BR)
MEMORIAL UNIVERSITY OF NEWFOUND-LAND
QUEEN ELIZABETH LL LIBRARY
234 Elizabeth Ave, St. John'S, NL, A1B 3Y1
(709) 864-7517
Emp Here 100
SIC 8231 Libraries

D-U-N-S 25-172-6550   (BR)
MEMORIAL UNIVERSITY OF NEWFOUND-LAND
RESEARCH GRANT AND CONTRACT SER-VICES
230 Elizabeth Ave, St. John'S, NL, A1B 1T5
(709) 864-4791
Emp Here 20
SIC 8732 Commercial nonphysical research

D-U-N-S 20-288-6623   (BR)
MEMORIAL UNIVERSITY OF NEWFOUND-LAND
ALUMNI AFFAIRS AND DEVELOPMENT
20 Lambe'S Lane, St. John'S, NL, A1B 4E9

Emp Here 22
SIC 8399 Social services, nec

D-U-N-S 24-309-0326   (BR)
MEMORIAL UNIVERSITY OF NEWFOUND-LAND
MARKETING AND COMMUNICATION
230 Elizabeth Ave Room 1024, St. John'S, NL, A1B 1T5
(709) 864-8663
Emp Here 60
SIC 8221 Colleges and universities

D-U-N-S 24-382-7255   (BR)
MEMORIAL UNIVERSITY OF NEWFOUND-LAND
SCHOOL OF PHARMACY
300 Prince Philip Dr Suite 2701, St. John'S, NL, A1B 3V6
(709) 777-8300
Emp Here 40
SIC 8221 Colleges and universities

D-U-N-S 25-703-3829   (BR)
MOORES THE SUIT PEOPLE INC
MOORES CLOTHING FOR MEN
(*Suby of* Tailored Brands, Inc.)
41 Kelsey Dr, St. John'S, NL, A1B 5C8
(709) 579-7951
Emp Here 20
SIC 5611 Men's and boys' clothing stores

D-U-N-S 24-450-3116   (BR)
NEWCAP INC
CJYQ-CKIX

391 Kenmount Rd, St. John'S, NL, A1B 3P9
(709) 726-5590
Emp Here 21
SIC 4832 Radio broadcasting stations

D-U-N-S 20-794-2421   (BR)
NEWFOUNDLAND CAPITAL CORPORA-TION LIMITED
STEEL COMMUNICATION
391 Kenmount Rd, St. John'S, NL, A1B 3P9
(709) 726-5590
Emp Here 100
SIC 4832 Radio broadcasting stations

D-U-N-S 24-260-5699   (HQ)
NEWFOUNDLAND LABRADOR LIQUOR CORPORATION
90 Kenmount Rd, St. John'S, NL, A1B 3R1
(709) 724-1100
Emp Here 105   *Emp Total* 7,000
Sales 197,691,048
SIC 5921 Liquor stores
Pr Pr Steve Winter
Ch Bd Glenn Tobin
V Ch Bd Andrea Marshall
Dir Dick Mccrate
Dir Marjorie Gaulton
Dir Brian Mccormack
Dir Craig Martin

D-U-N-S 20-016-1628   (HQ)
NEWFOUNDLAND POWER INC
55 Kenmount Rd, St. John'S, NL, A1B 3P8
(709) 737-5600
Emp Here 200   *Emp Total* 8,000
Sales 497,138,333
SIC 4911 Electric services
Pr Pr Gary Smith
Jocelyn Perry
VP Peter Alteen
Gary Murray
VP Fin Paige London
Ken Bennett
Fred Cahill
John Gaudet
Susan Hollett
Earl Ludlow

D-U-N-S 25-499-7018   (BR)
ORKIN CANADA CORPORATION
(*Suby of* Rollins, Inc.)
18 Duffy Pl, St. John'S, NL, A1B 4M5
(709) 466-8000
Emp Here 30
SIC 7342 Disinfecting and pest control ser-vices

D-U-N-S 20-970-7004   (BR)
PITNEY BOWES OF CANADA LTD
(*Suby of* Pitney Bowes Inc.)
31 Pippy Pl, St. John'S, NL, A1B 3X2

Emp Here 100
SIC 5044 Office equipment

D-U-N-S 25-750-8960   (BR)
PRICEWATERHOUSECOOPERS LLP
125 Kelsey Drive Suite 200, St. John'S, NL, A1B 0L2
(709) 722-3883
Emp Here 50
SIC 8721 Accounting, auditing, and book-keeping

D-U-N-S 24-933-1976   (SL)
PROGRESS HOMES INC
270 Portugal Cove Rd, St. John'S, NL, A1B 4N6
(709) 754-1165
Emp Here 150   *Sales* 30,847,360
SIC 1521 Single-family housing construction
Pr Pr Gloria Parsons

D-U-N-S 20-135-8764   (BR)
PROVINCIAL INFORMATION & LIBRARY RESOURCES BOARD
ST JOHNS PUBLIC LIBRARIES
125 Allandale Rd, St. John'S, NL, A1B 3A3

(709) 737-3946
Emp Here 30
SIC 8231 Libraries

D-U-N-S 20-985-1666   (BR)
PROVINCIAL INFORMATION & LIBRARY RESOURCES BOARD
A.C. HUNTER LIBRARY
125 Allandale Rd, St. John'S, NL, A1B 3A3
(709) 737-3952
Emp Here 35
SIC 8231 Libraries

D-U-N-S 25-320-8557   (BR)
PUROLATOR INC.
PUROLATOR INC
16 Duffy Pl, St. John'S, NL, A1B 4M5
(709) 579-5671
Emp Here 75
SIC 4731 Freight transportation arrangement

D-U-N-S 24-363-0808   (BR)
RGIS CANADA ULC
66 Kenmount Rd, St. John'S, NL, A1B 3V7

Emp Here 40
SIC 7389 Business services, nec

D-U-N-S 25-989-6256   (BR)
ROGERS COMMUNICATIONS INC
(*Suby of* Rogers Communications Inc)
22 Austin St, St. John'S, NL, A1B 4C2
(709) 753-7583
Emp Here 175
SIC 4841 Cable and other pay television ser-vices

D-U-N-S 20-988-0541   (BR)
SEARS CANADA INC
48 Kenmount Rd, St. John'S, NL, A1B 1W3
(709) 726-3770
Emp Here 200
SIC 7231 Beauty shops

D-U-N-S 25-127-7471   (BR)
SIEMENS CANADA LIMITED
SIEMENS CANADA
89 O'Leary Ave, St. John'S, NL, A1B 2C9
(709) 364-5131
Emp Here 20
SIC 3679 Electronic components, nec

D-U-N-S 25-299-5030   (BR)
SOBEYS CAPITAL INCORPORATED
48 Kenmount Rd, St. John'S, NL, A1B 1W3
(709) 753-9298
Emp Here 125
SIC 5411 Grocery stores

D-U-N-S 24-257-9431   (SL)
ST. PATRICK'S MERCY HOME
146 Elizabeth Ave Suite 202, St. John'S, NL, A1B 1S5
(709) 726-2687
Emp Here 300   *Sales* 18,355,920
SIC 8051 Skilled nursing care facilities
Ch Bd Alice Prim Furlong
  Glenda Reid

D-U-N-S 20-300-7083   (BR)
STANTEC ARCHITECTURE LTD
141 Kelsey Dr, St. John'S, NL, A1B 0L2
(709) 576-8612
Emp Here 25
SIC 8712 Architectural services

D-U-N-S 20-295-8187   (BR)
STANTEC CONSULTING LTD
141 Kelsey Dr, St. John'S, NL, A1B 0L2
(709) 738-0122
Emp Here 85
SIC 8711 Engineering services

D-U-N-S 20-310-8444   (BR)
STAPLES CANADA INC
(*Suby of* Staples, Inc.)
65 Kelsey Dr, St. John'S, NL, A1B 5C8
(709) 722-4350
Emp Here 25

SIC 5943 Stationery stores

D-U-N-S 24-346-7045   (SL)
STUDENT LOAN CORPORATION OF NEW-FOUNDLAND AND LABRADOR, THE
Gd, St. John'S, NL, A1B 4J6
(709) 729-2729
Emp Here 25   *Sales* 31,372,581
SIC 6036 Savings institutions, except federal
Fin Mgr Scott Maloney

D-U-N-S 24-754-9272   (HQ)
SUPERCARS INC
PENNEY MAZDA
(*Suby of* Supercars Inc)
220 Kenmount Rd, St. John'S, NL, A1B 3T2
(709) 726-8555
Emp Here 57   *Emp Total* 62
Sales 22,617,817
SIC 5511 New and used car dealers
Dir Chesley Penney
Pr Pr Daniel Penney

D-U-N-S 24-344-0158   (BR)
SUPERIOR PLUS LP
287 Kenmount Rd, St. John'S, NL, A1B 3P9
(709) 726-1780
Emp Here 24
SIC 5984 Liquefied petroleum gas dealers

D-U-N-S 25-703-5352   (SL)
SUTTON GROUP-CAPITAL REALTY LTD
451 Kenmount Rd, St. John'S, NL, A1B 3P9
(709) 726-6262
Emp Here 50   *Sales* 4,742,446
SIC 6531 Real estate agents and managers

D-U-N-S 25-782-4441   (BR)
SUZUKI CANADA INC.
FRESHWATER SUZUKI
324 Freshwater Rd, St. John'S, NL, A1B 1C2
(709) 754-4676
Emp Here 30
SIC 5511 New and used car dealers

D-U-N-S 20-310-9780   (BR)
TRA ATLANTIC
(*Suby of* TRA Atlantic)
63 Glencoe Dr, St. John'S, NL, A1B 4A5
(709) 364-7771
Emp Here 99
SIC 4213 Trucking, except local

D-U-N-S 25-738-0972   (SL)
THE CALL CENTRE INC
TELELINK CALL CENTRE
5 Pippy Pl Suite 7, St. John'S, NL, A1B 3X2
(709) 722-3730
Emp Here 90   *Sales* 4,523,563
SIC 7389 Business services, nec

D-U-N-S 25-297-8200   (BR)
TOYS 'R' US (CANADA) LTD
TOYS 'R' US
(*Suby of* Toys "r" Us, Inc.)
58 Kenmount Rd, St. John'S, NL, A1B 1W2
(709) 722-8697
Emp Here 40
SIC 5945 Hobby, toy, and game shops

D-U-N-S 20-120-0289   (BR)
TRANSCONTINENTAL INC
TC TRANSCONTINENTAL PRINTING
36 Austin St, St. John'S, NL, A1B 4C2
(709) 722-8500
Emp Here 40
SIC 2711 Newspapers

D-U-N-S 24-383-6645   (SL)
TRANSOCEAN OFFSHORE CANADA SER-VICES LTD
66 Kenmount Rd Suite 302, St. John'S, NL, A1B 3V7
(709) 724-6600
Emp Here 25   *Sales* 6,858,306
SIC 1381 Drilling oil and gas wells
Pr Pr David Matlock
  Michelle Hynes

VP *VP* Steve Mcfadin
VP *VP* Carmel Finlay
VP *VP* Chipman Earl
VP Deepak Munganahalli
VP Ricardo Rosa
VP Paul King
Asst Tr Judith Ellis
Dir Walter Barker

D-U-N-S 25-698-3461   (BR)
VALUE VILLAGE STORES, INC
(*Suby of* Savers, Inc.)
161 Kenmount Rd, St. John'S, NL, A1B 3P9
(709) 726-5200
Emp Here 30
SIC 5399 Miscellaneous general merchandise

D-U-N-S 20-786-1175   (BR)
WAL-MART CANADA CORP
75 Kelsey Dr, St. John'S, NL, A1B 0C7
(709) 722-6707
Emp Here 100
SIC 5311 Department stores

D-U-N-S 20-023-1129   (BR)
WINNERS MERCHANTS INTERNATIONAL L.P.
HOMESENSE
(*Suby of* The TJX Companies Inc)
48 Kenmount Rd, St. John'S, NL, A1B 1W3
(709) 745-7000
Emp Here 30
SIC 5651 Family clothing stores

St. John'S, NL A1C

D-U-N-S 20-524-7554   (BR)
BANK OF MONTREAL
BMO
238 Water St, St. John'S, NL, A1C 1A9
(709) 758-2055
Emp Here 35
SIC 6021 National commercial banks

D-U-N-S 24-098-7938   (BR)
BANQUE DE DEVELOPPEMENT DU CANADA
BUSINESS DEVELOPMENT BANK OF CANADA
215 Water St Suite 800, St. John'S, NL, A1C 6C9
(709) 772-5505
Emp Here 33
SIC 6141 Personal credit institutions

D-U-N-S 24-258-6204   (SL)
BULGIN HOLDINGS LIMITED
354 Water St, St. John'S, NL, A1C 1C4
(709) 722-0311
Emp Here 40   *Sales* 25,120,000
SIC 5621 Women's clothing stores
Pr Pr Cyril Bulgin
 Pamela Bulgin

D-U-N-S 24-258-7681   (BR)
CIBC WORLD MARKETS INC
CIBC WOOD GUNDY
215 Water St Suite 77, St. John'S, NL, A1C 6C9
(709) 576-2700
Emp Here 23
SIC 6211 Security brokers and dealers

D-U-N-S 25-762-3744   (BR)
CANADIAN IMPERIAL BANK OF COMMERCE
CIBC
215 Water St Suite 800, St. John'S, NL, A1C 6C9
(709) 576-8800
Emp Here 30
SIC 6021 National commercial banks

D-U-N-S 20-104-0230   (SL)
CANEX DEVELOPMENT CORPORATION

LIMITED
187 Gower St Suite 300, St. John'S, NL, A1C 1R2
(709) 754-0666
Emp Here 200   *Sales* 11,971,100
SIC 7992 Public golf courses
Pr Brian Dobbin
Dir Rex Philpott
Fin Ex Keith Smith

D-U-N-S 20-449-0544   (HQ)
CHES'S SNACKS LIMITED
CHES'S FISH & CHIPS
(*Suby of* Ches's Snacks Limited)
9 Freshwater Rd, St. John'S, NL, A1C 2N1
(709) 722-4083
Emp Here 35   *Emp Total* 65
Sales 1,969,939
SIC 5812 Eating places

D-U-N-S 24-374-4682   (BR)
CHEVRON CANADA LIMITED
CHEVRON CANADA RESOURCES
(*Suby of* Chevron Corporation)
215 Water St Suite 700, St. John'S, NL, A1C 6C9
(709) 757-6100
Emp Here 25
SIC 2911 Petroleum refining

D-U-N-S 25-768-1874   (BR)
CITY OF ST. JOHN'S
CITY OF ST. JOHN'S
50 New Gower St, St. John'S, NL, A1C 1J3
(709) 758-0997
Emp Here 20
SIC 7941 Sports clubs, managers, and promoters

D-U-N-S 20-988-0699   (BR)
DELOITTE & TOUCHE INC
DELIOTTE LLP
(*Suby of* Deloitte LLP)
10 Factory Lane, St. John'S, NL, A1C 6H5
(709) 576-8480
Emp Here 50
SIC 8721 Accounting, auditing, and bookkeeping

D-U-N-S 20-845-5019   (BR)
EASTERN REGIONAL INTEGRATED HEALTH AUTHORITY
ST CLAIRE MERCY HOSPITAL
154 Lemarchant Rd, St. John'S, NL, A1C 5B8
(709) 777-6300
Emp Here 5,000
SIC 8062 General medical and surgical hospitals

D-U-N-S 20-779-3241   (HQ)
ECLIPSE STORES INC
ECLIPSE
(*Suby of* Eclipse Stores Inc)
354 Water St Suite 401, St. John'S, NL, A1C 1C4
(709) 722-0311
Emp Here 20   *Emp Total* 300
Sales 18,240,175
SIC 5621 Women's clothing stores
Pr Pr Cyril Bulgin
 Pamela Bulgin

D-U-N-S 20-988-0228   (BR)
ERNST & YOUNG LLP
(*Suby of* Ernst & Young LLP)
139 Water St, St. John'S, NL, A1C 1B2
(709) 726-2840
Emp Here 50
SIC 8721 Accounting, auditing, and bookkeeping

D-U-N-S 25-897-6570   (BR)
G4S CASH SOLUTIONS (CANADA) LTD
147 Duckworth St Unit 145, St. John'S, NL, A1C 1E9
(709) 753-2627
Emp Here 60
SIC 7381 Detective and armored car services

D-U-N-S 24-257-9936   (SL)
HOTEL NEWFOUNDLAND (1982)
FAIRMONT NEWFOUNDLAND, THE
Cavendish Sq, St. John'S, NL, A1C 5W8
(709) 726-4980
Emp Here 220   *Sales* 12,438,743
SIC 7011 Hotels and motels
Genl Mgr Armand A Agabab

D-U-N-S 25-673-6372   (BR)
HUSKY ENERGY INC
235 Water St Suite 901, St. John'S, NL, A1C 1B6
(709) 724-3900
Emp Here 50
SIC 1382 Oil and gas exploration services

D-U-N-S 25-675-7097   (BR)
HUSKY OIL OPERATIONS LIMITED
HUSKY ENERGY
351 Water St, St. John'S, NL, A1C 1B6
(709) 724-3900
Emp Here 150
SIC 1311 Crude petroleum and natural gas

D-U-N-S 25-363-6153   (BR)
KEG RESTAURANTS LTD
KEG STEAKHOUSE & BAR, THE
135 Harbour Dr, St. John'S, NL, A1C 6N6
(709) 726-4534
Emp Here 100
SIC 5812 Eating places

D-U-N-S 20-756-6303   (BR)
MCINNES COOPER
10 Fort William Pl, St. John'S, NL, A1C 1K4
(709) 722-8735
Emp Here 47
SIC 8111 Legal services

D-U-N-S 25-365-2929   (BR)
MEMORIAL UNIVERSITY OF NEWFOUNDLAND
SCHOOL OF SOCIAL WORK
208 Elizabeth Ave, St. John'S, NL, A1C 5S7
(709) 864-8399
Emp Here 80
SIC 8221 Colleges and universities

D-U-N-S 25-846-7794   (BR)
MEMORIAL UNIVERSITY OF NEWFOUNDLAND
FISHERIES AND MARINE INSTITUTE
155 Ridge Road, St. John'S, NL, A1C 5R3
(709) 778-0483
Emp Here 600
SIC 8222 Junior colleges

D-U-N-S 20-845-0820   (BR)
MEMORIAL UNIVERSITY OF NEWFOUNDLAND
UNIVERSITY BOOKSTORE
234 Arctic Ave, St. John'S, NL, A1C 5S7
(709) 737-7440
Emp Here 20
SIC 8221 Colleges and universities

D-U-N-S 20-100-1299   (BR)
MOLSON CANADA 2005
(*Suby of* Molson Coors Brewing Company)
131 Circular Rd, St. John'S, NL, A1C 2Z9
(709) 726-1786
Emp Here 110
SIC 2082 Malt beverages

D-U-N-S 20-010-9481   (SL)
NEWFOUNDLAND TRANSSHIPMENT LIMITED
10 Fort William Pl, St. John'S, NL, A1C 1K4
(709) 570-3200
Emp Here 28   *Sales* 7,660,874
SIC 1381 Drilling oil and gas wells
Pr Paul Adams
Dir Ronald Bigsby
Dir Richard Courtney
Dir Robert Hand
Dir William Swett

D-U-N-S 24-259-2392   (BR)
OCEANEX INC
701 Kent Fort William Place, St. John'S, NL, A1C 1K4
(709) 722-6280
Emp Here 350
SIC 4424 Deep sea domestic transportation of freight

D-U-N-S 24-394-3672   (BR)
OCEANEX INC
10 Fort William Pl Suite 701, St. John'S, NL, A1C 1K4
(709) 758-0382
Emp Here 23
SIC 4424 Deep sea domestic transportation of freight

D-U-N-S 25-286-9474   (HQ)
PARAGON OFFSHORE (CANADA) LTD
(*Suby of* PARAGON OFFSHORE PLC)
10 Fort William Pl Suite 102, St. John'S, NL, A1C 1K4
(709) 758-4400
Emp Here 157   *Emp Total* 2,219
Sales 56,445,507
SIC 1381 Drilling oil and gas wells
Pr Pr Kevin Roche

D-U-N-S 20-287-2300   (SL)
PRESENTATION GENERALATE
180 Military Rd, St. John'S, NL, A1C 2E8
(709) 753-8340
Emp Here 55   *Sales* 3,648,035
SIC 8661 Religious organizations

D-U-N-S 24-023-4976   (BR)
SNC-LAVALIN OPERATIONS & MAINTENANCE INC
354 Water St Suite 300, St. John'S, NL, A1C 1C4

Emp Here 20
SIC 8741 Management services

D-U-N-S 24-319-8434   (BR)
SCOTIA CAPITAL INC
SCOTIA MCLEOD
235 Water St Suite 802, St. John'S, NL, A1C 1B6
(709) 576-1305
Emp Here 21
SIC 6211 Security brokers and dealers

D-U-N-S 24-259-2483   (BR)
SECURITAS CANADA LIMITED
215 Water St Suite 611, St. John'S, NL, A1C 6C9
(709) 754-0160
Emp Here 65
SIC 7381 Detective and armored car services

D-U-N-S 20-520-3693   (BR)
SOBEYS CAPITAL INCORPORATED
SOBEYS
8 Merrymeeting Rd, St. John'S, NL, A1C 2V5
(709) 726-2387
Emp Here 100
SIC 5411 Grocery stores

D-U-N-S 24-449-1205   (BR)
STEWART MCKELVEY STIRLING SCALES
(*Suby of* Stewart McKelvey Stirling Scales)
100 New Gower St Suite 1100, St. John'S, NL, A1C 6K3
(709) 722-4270
Emp Here 72
SIC 8111 Legal services

D-U-N-S 25-094-8312   (BR)
SUNCOR ENERGY INC
PETRO-CANADA
235 Water St Suite 201, St. John'S, NL, A1C 1B6
(709) 778-3500
Emp Here 150
SIC 1389 Oil and gas field services, nec

D-U-N-S 24-450-2860   (SL)

SUNDANCE LTD
CLUB ONE
33a George St, St. John'S, NL, A1C 5X3
(709) 753-7822
Emp Here 70   *Sales* 2,115,860
SIC 5812 Eating places

D-U-N-S 20-058-5920   (BR)
WESTMONT HOSPITALITY MANAGEMENT LIMITED
QUALITY HOTEL
2 Hill O' Chips, St. John'S, NL, A1C 6B1
(709) 754-7788
Emp Here 50
SIC 7011 Hotels and motels

D-U-N-S 20-705-0555   (SL)
WILDS AT SALMONIER RIVER INC, THE
THE WILDS
299 Salmonier Line, St. John'S, NL, A1C 5L7
(709) 229-5444
Emp Here 75   *Sales* 3,210,271
SIC 7992 Public golf courses

D-U-N-S 24-850-6540   (BR)
WORLEYPARSONS CANADA SERVICES LTD
215 Water St Suite 604, St. John'S, NL, A1C 6C9

Emp Here 30
SIC 8711 Engineering services

St. John'S, NL A1E

D-U-N-S 20-781-0420   (BR)
AXA ASSURANCES INC
35 Blackmarsh Rd, St. John'S, NL, A1E 1S4
(709) 726-8974
Emp Here 80
SIC 6311 Life insurance

D-U-N-S 20-015-5448   (HQ)
BROWNING HARVEY LIMITED
BEAVER LODGE
(*Suby of* Browning Harvey Limited)
15 Ropewalk Lane, St. John'S, NL, A1E 4P1
(709) 579-4116
Emp Here 95   *Emp Total* 129
Sales 21,296,635
SIC 2086 Bottled and canned soft drinks
  Susan Patten
Pr Pr John Patten

D-U-N-S 25-703-2862   (BR)
CANADIAN IMPERIAL BANK OF COMMERCE
CIBC
470 Topsail Rd, St. John'S, NL, A1E 2C3
(709) 576-8877
Emp Here 20
SIC 6021 National commercial banks

D-U-N-S 25-703-2854   (BR)
CANADIAN IMPERIAL BANK OF COMMERCE
CIBC
15 Hamlyn Rd, St. John'S, NL, A1E 6E2
(709) 576-8909
Emp Here 20
SIC 6021 National commercial banks

D-U-N-S 20-021-6021   (BR)
CITY OF ST. JOHN'S
H. G. R. MEWS COMMUNITY CENTRE
40 Mundy Pond Rd, St. John'S, NL, A1E 1V1
(709) 576-8499
Emp Here 40
SIC 7999 Amusement and recreation, nec

D-U-N-S 24-683-4647   (HQ)
D.F. BARNES SERVICES LIMITED
(*Suby of* D.F. Barnes Services Limited)
22 Sudbury St, St. John'S, NL, A1E 2V1

(709) 579-5041
Emp Here 100   *Emp Total* 150
Sales 22,608,000
SIC 3312 Blast furnaces and steel mills
Pr Glenn Byrnes
Dir Charles Mervin Sanders
Dir Jason Fudge
Dir William Elkington

D-U-N-S 20-015-7238   (HQ)
DICKS AND COMPANY LIMITED
385 Empire Ave, St. John'S, NL, A1E 1W6
(709) 579-5111
Emp Here 68   *Emp Total* 80
Sales 9,047,127
SIC 5712 Furniture stores
  James Austin
Pr Pr Barry Tilley

D-U-N-S 24-620-9055   (BR)
DOLLARAMA S.E.C.
430 Topsail Rd Suite 200, St. John'S, NL, A1E 4N1
(709) 747-4300
Emp Here 20
SIC 5331 Variety stores

D-U-N-S 24-337-3607   (BR)
FGL SPORTS LTD
SPORT CHEK THE VILLAGE SHOPPING CENTRE
430 Topsail Rd Unit 102, St. John'S, NL, A1E 4N1
(709) 364-7068
Emp Here 30
SIC 5941 Sporting goods and bicycle shops

D-U-N-S 24-340-0301   (BR)
FGL SPORTS LTD
SPORT-CHEK
430 Topsail Rd Unit 102, St. John'S, NL, A1E 4N1
(709) 364-7068
Emp Here 30
SIC 5941 Sporting goods and bicycle shops

D-U-N-S 25-982-8515   (BR)
FGL SPORTS LTD
SPORT-CHEK
430 Topsail Rd Unit 3, St. John'S, NL, A1E 4N1
(709) 364-7068
Emp Here 30
SIC 5941 Sporting goods and bicycle shops

D-U-N-S 24-655-9004   (BR)
IDQ CANADA INC
GAIRY QUEEN
672 Topsail Rd, St. John'S, NL, A1E 2E2
(709) 368-2671
Emp Here 33
SIC 5812 Eating places

D-U-N-S 25-622-3751   (BR)
LABATT BREWING COMPANY LIMITED
60 Leslie St, St. John'S, NL, A1E 2V8
(709) 579-0121
Emp Here 100
SIC 2082 Malt beverages

D-U-N-S 20-288-0824   (BR)
LAWTON'S DRUG STORES LIMITED
466 Topsail Rd, St. John'S, NL, A1E 2C2
(709) 364-0188
Emp Here 20
SIC 5912 Drug stores and proprietary stores

D-U-N-S 24-247-7680   (BR)
MEDIAS TRANSCONTINENTAL INC
MEDIAS TRANSCONTINENTAL INC
430 Topsail Rd Suite 86, St. John'S, NL, A1E 4N1
(709) 364-6300
Emp Here 100
SIC 2711 Newspapers

D-U-N-S 20-778-9140   (HQ)
NEWFOUNDLAND AND LABRADOR HOUSING CORPORATION

NEWFOUNDLAND LABRADOR HOUSING
2 Canada Dr, St. John'S, NL, A1E 0A1
(709) 724-3000
Emp Here 197   *Emp Total* 7,000
Sales 115,109,558
SIC 6531 Real estate agents and managers
  Len Simms
  Tom Lawrence
Sec Janette Loveless
  Thomas Baker
  Olive Blake
  Barbara Cull
  Daniel Mccann
  Rhonda Neary
  Verna Northcott
  Kimberley Anne Stroud

D-U-N-S 20-773-1899   (SL)
OZARK ELECTRICAL MARINE LIMITED
OZARK SERVICES
650 Water St, St. John'S, NL, A1E 1B9
(709) 726-4554
Emp Here 45   *Sales* 5,478,300
SIC 1731 Electrical work
  Jeffrey Stanley

D-U-N-S 20-765-0545   (BR)
PATRICK STREET HOLDINGS LIMITED
SPA AT THE MONASTERY AND SUITES
63 Patrick St, St. John'S, NL, A1E 2S5
(709) 754-5800
Emp Here 69   *Sales* 2,261,782
SIC 7991 Physical fitness facilities

D-U-N-S 20-642-9516   (HQ)
PENNECON ENERGY TECHNICAL SERVICES LTD
650 Water St, St. John'S, NL, A1E 1B9
(709) 726-4554
Emp Here 50   *Emp Total* 200
Sales 5,457,381
SIC 7694 Armature rewinding shops
  Chesley Penney
Pr Pr Paul Stanley
VP Don Noseworthy
Dir Jeffrey Stanley
Dir Jerry White

D-U-N-S 20-037-2758   (SL)
RED OAK CATERING INC
50 Hamlyn Rd Suite 466, St. John'S, NL, A1E 5X7
(709) 368-6808
Emp Here 85   *Sales* 2,553,625
SIC 5812 Eating places

D-U-N-S 24-260-2951   (SL)
ROEBOTHAN MCKAY & MARSHALL
70 Brookfield Rd, St. John'S, NL, A1E 3T9
(709) 753-5805
Emp Here 56   *Sales* 4,815,406
SIC 8111 Legal services

D-U-N-S 20-115-5087   (SL)
SANI PRO INC
99 Blackmarsh Rd, St. John'S, NL, A1E 1S6
(709) 579-2151
Emp Here 30   *Sales* 4,085,799
SIC 5046 Commercial equipment, nec

D-U-N-S 20-022-6905   (BR)
SOBEYS CAPITAL INCORPORATED
470 Topsail Rd Suite 340, St. John'S, NL, A1E 2C3
(709) 748-1250
Emp Here 128
SIC 5411 Grocery stores

D-U-N-S 25-299-3654   (BR)
SOBEYS CAPITAL INCORPORATED
SOBEYS
45 Ropewalk Lane, St. John'S, NL, A1E 4P1
(709) 739-8663
Emp Here 200
SIC 5411 Grocery stores

D-U-N-S 25-713-5806   (SL)
TIM HORTONS

30 Ropewalk Lane, St. John'S, NL, A1E 5T2
(709) 739-6325
Emp Here 50   *Sales* 1,532,175
SIC 5812 Eating places

D-U-N-S 25-709-5828   (BR)
VERA PERLIN SOCIETY
WORK ORIENTED REHABILITATION CENTRE
(*Suby of* Vera Perlin Society)
Gd, St. John'S, NL, A1E 3Y3
(709) 739-8701
Emp Here 40
SIC 8331 Job training and related services

D-U-N-S 25-703-1237   (BR)
WESTERN INVENTORY SERVICE LTD
WIS INTERNATIONAL
14 Forbes St Suite 206, St. John'S, NL, A1E 3L5
(709) 364-2010
Emp Here 20
SIC 7389 Business services, nec

D-U-N-S 24-259-6740   (BR)
WESTOWER COMMUNICATIONS LTD
47 Harding Rd, St. John'S, NL, A1E 3Y4
(709) 579-6378
Emp Here 40
SIC 1731 Electrical work

St. John'S, NL A1N

D-U-N-S 20-987-6366   (HQ)
ANGLICAN HOMES INC
SAINT LUKE'S HOME
(*Suby of* Anglican Homes Inc)
Gd Stn Main, St. John'S, NL, A1N 2B9

Emp Here 149   *Emp Total* 150
Sales 9,445,120
SIC 8051 Skilled nursing care facilities
Ch Bd Frank Lee

Stephenville, NL A2N

D-U-N-S 25-293-2181   (BR)
ATLIFIC INC
HOLIDAY INN STEPHENVILLE
(*Suby of* 3376290 Canada Inc)
44 Queen St, Stephenville, NL, A2N 2M5
(709) 643-6666
Emp Here 40
SIC 7011 Hotels and motels

D-U-N-S 20-572-6099   (BR)
CANADA POST CORPORATION
STEPHENVILLE POSTAL OUTLET
144 Main St, Stephenville, NL, A2N 0B5
(709) 643-8350
Emp Here 25
SIC 4311 U.s. postal service

D-U-N-S 20-987-8990   (HQ)
COLLEGE OF THE NORTH ATLANTIC
CNA
432 Massachusetts Dr, Stephenville, NL, A2N 3C1
(709) 643-7868
Emp Here 50   *Emp Total* 7,000
Sales 103,875,642
SIC 8222 Junior colleges
  Cheryl Stagg
Pr Pr Anne Marie Vaughan
VP Cyril Organ
VP Greg Chaytor
Div VP Brian Tobin
Sec Colette Goodyear
  John Hutchings
Dir Fin Richard Vivian
Div/Sub He Corinne Dunne

Prs Dir Garry Pinto

D-U-N-S 20-710-1499   (BR)
CORMACK TRAIL SCHOOL BOARD
WESTERN SCHOOL DISTRICT
(*Suby of* Cormack Trail School Board)
76a West St, Stephenville, NL, A2N 1E4
(709) 643-9525
Emp Here 20
SIC 8211 Elementary and secondary schools

D-U-N-S 20-523-7154   (HQ)
CORMACK TRAIL SCHOOL BOARD
DISTRICT 4
(*Suby of* Cormack Trail School Board)
Gd Lcd Main, Stephenville, NL, A2N 2Y6
(709) 643-9525
Emp Here 40   *Emp Total* 700
Sales 64,407,680
SIC 8211 Elementary and secondary schools
Dir Dennis Parsons

D-U-N-S 20-987-7489   (HQ)
FIRST CHOICE VISION CENTRE LTD
WHEELER, DR WAYNE
(*Suby of* First Choice Vision Centre Ltd)
5 Maine Dr, Stephenville, NL, A2N 2Y2
(709) 643-3496
Emp Here 20   *Emp Total* 64
Sales 3,720,996
SIC 8042 Offices and clinics of optometrists

D-U-N-S 20-984-2731   (HQ)
FOCENCO LIMITED
WESTERN WHOLESALERS, DIV OF
(*Suby of* Coleman Management Services Limited)
383 Connecticut Dr, Stephenville, NL, A2N 2Y6
(709) 637-6600
Emp Here 30   *Emp Total* 30
Sales 63,913,573
SIC 5411 Grocery stores
Pr Pr Frank Coleman
VP Mike Coleman
VP Bob Coleman
Dir Bill Coleman
Darrell Oram

D-U-N-S 25-169-1143   (BR)
LOBLAW FINANCIAL HOLDINGS INC
DOMINION 925
62 Prince Rupert Dr, Stephenville, NL, A2N 3W7
(709) 643-0862
Emp Here 100
SIC 5411 Grocery stores

D-U-N-S 25-618-5968   (BR)
PROVINCE OF NEWFOUNDLAND & LABRADOR
PROVINCE OF NEWFOUNDLAND & LABRADOR
380 Massachusetts Dr, Stephenville, NL, A2N 3A5
(709) 643-4553
Emp Here 20
SIC 7922 Theatrical producers and services

D-U-N-S 24-994-3226   (HQ)
PROVINCIAL INFORMATION & LIBRARY RESOURCES BOARD
48 St. George'S Ave, Stephenville, NL, A2N 1L1
(709) 643-0900
Emp Here 50   *Emp Total* 7,000
Sales 8,557,537
SIC 8231 Libraries
Ex Dir Andrew Hunt

D-U-N-S 25-299-3258   (BR)
SOBEYS CAPITAL INCORPORATED
FRESHCO
42 Queen St, Stephenville, NL, A2N 3A7

Emp Here 35
SIC 5411 Grocery stores

D-U-N-S 20-582-9695   (BR)
WAL-MART CANADA CORP
42 Queen St, Stephenville, NL, A2N 3A7
(709) 643-5018
Emp Here 125
SIC 5311 Department stores

D-U-N-S 20-985-6319   (BR)
WESTERN REGIONAL INTEGRATED HEALTH AUTHORITY, THE
SIR THOMAS RODDICK HOSPITAL
142 Minnesota Dr, Stephenville, NL, A2N 3X9
(709) 643-5111
Emp Here 300
SIC 8062 General medical and surgical hospitals

D-U-N-S 20-710-1531   (BR)
WESTERN SCHOOL DISTRICT
STEPHENVILLE MIDDLE SCHOOL
40 Queen St, Stephenville, NL, A2N 2M5
(709) 643-5101
Emp Here 38
SIC 8211 Elementary and secondary schools

D-U-N-S 25-241-2549   (BR)
WESTERN SCHOOL DISTRICT
STEPHENVILLE PRIMARY SCHOOL
72 West St, Stephenville, NL, A2N 1E3
(709) 643-2331
Emp Here 40
SIC 8211 Elementary and secondary schools

D-U-N-S 20-797-8037   (BR)
WESTERN SCHOOL DISTRICT
STEPHENVILLE HIGH
76a West St, Stephenville, NL, A2N 1E4
(709) 643-9672
Emp Here 22
SIC 8211 Elementary and secondary schools

D-U-N-S 24-124-9163   (BR)
WESTERN SCHOOL DISTRICT
76a West St, Stephenville, NL, A2N 1E4
(709) 643-9525
Emp Here 22
SIC 8211 Elementary and secondary schools

Summerford, NL A0G

D-U-N-S 20-710-1085   (BR)
NOVA CENTRAL SCHOOL DISTRICT
NEWDOWN ACADEMY
150 Rd To The Isles, Summerford, NL, A0G 4E0
(709) 629-3241
Emp Here 40
SIC 8211 Elementary and secondary schools

Torbay, NL A1K

D-U-N-S 20-543-3621   (BR)
SOBEYS CAPITAL INCORPORATED
BRIGHT SHOPPER
1588 Torbay Rd, Torbay, NL, A1K 1H1
(709) 437-1389
Emp Here 23
SIC 5411 Grocery stores

Twillingate, NL A0G

D-U-N-S 20-787-0853   (BR)
WEDGEWOOD INSURANCE LIMITED
15 Toulinquet St, Twillingate, NL, A0G 4M0

Emp Here 60
SIC 6411 Insurance agents, brokers, and service

Wabush, NL A0R

D-U-N-S 25-241-6037   (BR)
LABRADOR SCHOOL BOARD
J R SMALLWOOD MIDDLE SCHOOL
Gd, Wabush, NL, A0R 1B0
(709) 282-3251
Emp Here 35
SIC 8211 Elementary and secondary schools

D-U-N-S 25-090-8316   (BR)
SMS EQUIPMENT INC
10 2nd Ave, Wabush, NL, A0R 1B0
(709) 282-3777
Emp Here 33
SIC 5082 Construction and mining machinery

Wesleyville, NL A0G

D-U-N-S 20-023-3315   (BR)
NOVA CENTRAL SCHOOL DISTRICT
LESTER PEARSON MEMORIAL HIGH
139 143 Main St, Wesleyville, NL, A0G 4R0
(709) 536-2270
Emp Here 20
SIC 8211 Elementary and secondary schools

D-U-N-S 20-164-5210   (BR)
NOVA CENTRAL SCHOOL DISTRICT
PEARSON ACADEMY
139 Main St, Wesleyville, NL, A0G 4R0
(709) 536-2254
Emp Here 30
SIC 8211 Elementary and secondary schools

Whitbourne, NL A0B

D-U-N-S 24-339-4058   (BR)
EASTERN REGIONAL INTEGRATED HEALTH AUTHORITY
NEWHOOK, DR WILLIAM H COMMUNITY HEALTH CENTRE
5 Whitbourne Ave, Whitbourne, NL, A0B 3K0
(709) 759-2300
Emp Here 35
SIC 8093 Specialty outpatient clinics, nec

D-U-N-S 25-308-4834   (BR)
NEWFOUNDLAND & LABRADOR HYDRO
Gd, Whitbourne, NL, A0B 3K0
(709) 759-2700
Emp Here 23
SIC 4911 Electric services

D-U-N-S 20-705-6321   (BR)
PROVINCE OF NEWFOUNDLAND & LABRADOR
NEWFOUNDLAND & LABRADOR YOUTH CENTRE
Bond Rd, Whitbourne, NL, A0B 3K0
(709) 759-2471
Emp Here 150
SIC 8322 Individual and family services

Wings Point, NL A0G

D-U-N-S 20-023-4271   (BR)
NOVA CENTRAL SCHOOL DISTRICT
RIVERWOOD ACADEMY
Gd, Wings Point, NL, A0G 4T0
(709) 676-2009
Emp Here 30
SIC 8211 Elementary and secondary schools

Winterton, NL A0B

D-U-N-S 20-017-2047   (SL)
GREEN, E J & COMPANY LTD
287 Main St, Winterton, NL, A0B 3M0
(709) 583-2670
Emp Here 45   *Sales* 10,347,900
SIC 2092 Fresh or frozen packaged fish
Pr Pr Derek Green
Dir Doris Harnum

SIC 5411 Grocery stores

Behchoko, NT X0E

D-U-N-S 20-255-5194 (BR)
DOGRIB DIVISIONAL BOARD
CHIEF JIMMY BRUNEAU SCHOOL
Gd, Behchoko, NT, X0E 0Y0
(867) 371-4511
Emp Here 35
SIC 8211 Elementary and secondary schools

D-U-N-S 20-802-7354 (BR)
DOGRIB DIVISIONAL BOARD
ELIZABETH MACKENZIE ELEMENTARY SCHOOL
Gd, Behchoko, NT, X0E 0Y0
(867) 392-6078
Emp Here 25
SIC 8211 Elementary and secondary schools

Fort Providence, NT X0E

D-U-N-S 20-070-9397 (BR)
DEHCHO DIVISIONAL EDUCATION COUNCIL
DEH GAH ELEMENTARY & SECONDARY SCHOOL
(*Suby of* Dehcho Divisional Education Council)
Gd, Fort Providence, NT, X0E 0L0
(867) 699-3131
Emp Here 22
SIC 8211 Elementary and secondary schools

Fort Simpson, NT X0E

D-U-N-S 25-482-4998 (BR)
NORTH WEST COMPANY LP, THE
NORTHERN STORE
Gd, Fort Simpson, NT, X0E 0N0
(867) 695-2391
Emp Here 30
SIC 5411 Grocery stores

Fort Smith, NT X0E

D-U-N-S 24-939-7837 (HQ)
AURORA COLLEGE
50 Conibear Cres, Fort Smith, NT, X0E 0P0
(867) 872-7000
Emp Here 100   *Emp Total* 4,501
Sales 25,974,009
SIC 8221 Colleges and universities
Pr Maurice Evans

D-U-N-S 25-016-6642 (BR)
AURORA COLLEGE
THEBACHA CAMPUS
50 Conibear Cres, Fort Smith, NT, X0E 0P0
(867) 872-7500
Emp Here 75
SIC 8222 Junior colleges

D-U-N-S 20-076-6330 (BR)
AURORA COLLEGE
THEBACHA CAMPUS
50 Conibear Cres, Fort Smith, NT, X0E 0P0
(867) 266-4966
Emp Here 58
SIC 8222 Junior colleges

D-U-N-S 24-915-3206 (BR)
NORTH WEST COMPANY LP, THE
NORTHERN STORES
Gd, Fort Smith, NT, X0E 0P0
(867) 897-8811
Emp Here 25

Hay River, NT X0E

D-U-N-S 25-070-8054 (BR)
HUDSON'S BAY COMPANY
FIELDS STORES
77b Woodland Dr, Hay River, NT, X0E 1G1
(867) 874-6881
Emp Here 25
SIC 5311 Department stores

D-U-N-S 25-907-6370 (BR)
KINGLAND FORD SALES LTD
KINGLAND FREIGHTLINER
9 Aspen Rd, Hay River, NT, X0E 0R6

Emp Here 30
SIC 5511 New and used car dealers

D-U-N-S 25-271-4571 (BR)
NORTH WEST COMPANY INC, THE
81 Woodland Dr, Hay River, NT, X0E 1G1
(867) 874-6545
Emp Here 45
SIC 5411 Grocery stores

D-U-N-S 20-506-6475 (HQ)
NORTHWEST TERRITORIES POWER CORPORATION
4 Capital Dr Ss 98 Suite 98, Hay River, NT, X0E 1G2
(867) 874-5200
Emp Here 55   *Emp Total* 4,501
Sales 96,500,361
SIC 4911 Electric services
Pr Leon Courneya
Ch Bd Lew Voytilla

Inuvik, NT X0E

D-U-N-S 24-340-7538 (BR)
AURORA COLLEGE
AURORA CAMPUS
87 Gwich'In Rd, Inuvik, NT, X0E 0T0
(867) 777-7800
Emp Here 50
SIC 8221 Colleges and universities

D-U-N-S 20-003-7195 (BR)
BEAUFORT-DELTA EDUCATION COUNCIL
SAMUEL HEARNE SECONDARY SCHOOL
(*Suby of* Beaufort-Delta Education Council)
Gd, Inuvik, NT, X0E 0T0
(867) 777-7170
Emp Here 30
SIC 8211 Elementary and secondary schools

D-U-N-S 24-866-4054 (HQ)
BEAUFORT-DELTA HEALTH & SOCIAL SERVICES AUTHORITY
(*Suby of* Beaufort-Delta Health & Social Services Authority)
285 Mackenzie Rd, Inuvik, NT, X0E 0T0
(867) 777-8000
Emp Here 125   *Emp Total* 310
Sales 29,742,080
SIC 8062 General medical and surgical hospitals
Dir Fin Grant Sullivan

D-U-N-S 20-914-6005 (BR)
CANADIAN BROADCASTING CORPORATION
CBC
155 Mackenzie Rd Bay, Inuvik, NT, X0E 0T0
(867) 777-7600
Emp Here 20
SIC 4832 Radio broadcasting stations

D-U-N-S 24-367-3654 (HQ)
DOWLAND CONTRACTING LTD

(*Suby of* Inuvialuit Regional Corporation)
29 Industrial Rd, Inuvik, NT, X0E 0T0
(867) 369-5263
Emp Here 30   *Emp Total* 1
Sales 16,637,800
SIC 1522 Residential construction, nec
 Patrick Mcguinness
Pr Pr Guy Pemberton

D-U-N-S 20-700-6987 (BR)
FINNING INTERNATIONAL INC
(*Suby of* Finning International Inc)
Airport Rd, Inuvik, NT, X0E 0T0
(867) 777-2551
Emp Here 20
SIC 5082 Construction and mining machinery

D-U-N-S 20-084-7924 (BR)
NORTH WEST COMPANY LP, THE
NORTH MART
160 Mackenzie Rd, Inuvik, NT, X0E 0T0
(867) 777-2582
Emp Here 30
SIC 5411 Grocery stores

D-U-N-S 20-532-5637 (BR)
SEARS CANADA INC
119 Mackenzie Rd, Inuvik, NT, X0E 0T0
(867) 777-4849
Emp Here 30
SIC 5311 Department stores

Norman Wells, NT X0E

D-U-N-S 24-312-0644 (BR)
IMPERIAL OIL RESOURCES LIMITED
(*Suby of* Exxon Mobil Corporation)
Gd, Norman Wells, NT, X0E 0V0
(867) 587-3100
Emp Here 50
SIC 1382 Oil and gas exploration services

D-U-N-S 20-052-5181 (HQ)
NORTH-WRIGHT AIRWAYS LTD
2200, Norman Wells, NT, X0E 0V0
(867) 587-2288
Emp Here 35   *Emp Total* 60
Sales 9,557,852
SIC 4724 Travel agencies
Pr Pr Warren Wright
 Carolyn Wright

Tuktoyaktuk, NT X0E

D-U-N-S 20-710-1762 (BR)
BEAUFORT-DELTA EDUCATION COUNCIL
MANGILALUK SCHOOL
(*Suby of* Beaufort-Delta Education Council)
477 Mangilaluk Loop, Tuktoyaktuk, NT, X0E 1C0
(867) 977-2255
Emp Here 28
SIC 8211 Elementary and secondary schools

D-U-N-S 24-915-2992 (BR)
NORTH WEST COMPANY LP, THE
NORTHERN STORES
Gd, Tuktoyaktuk, NT, X0E 1C0
(867) 977-2211
Emp Here 20
SIC 5411 Grocery stores

Ulukhaktok, NT X0E

D-U-N-S 20-070-9413 (BR)
BEAUFORT-DELTA EDUCATION COUNCIL
HELEN KALVAK SCHOOL
(*Suby of* Beaufort-Delta Education Council)
Gd, Ulukhaktok, NT, X0E 0S0

(867) 396-3804
Emp Here 20
SIC 8211 Elementary and secondary schools

Whati, NT X0E

D-U-N-S 24-348-1624 (BR)
GOVERNMENT OF THE NORTHWEST TERRITORIES
TILCHO COMMUNITY SERVICE BOARD
Gd, Whati, NT, X0E 1P0
(867) 573-3131
Emp Here 20
SIC 8211 Elementary and secondary schools

Yellowknife, NT X1A

D-U-N-S 20-068-3808 (BR)
A & W FOOD SERVICES OF CANADA INC
MBBC HOLDINGS
22 Otto Dr, Yellowknife, NT, X1A 2T8
(867) 669-7071
Emp Here 20
SIC 5812 Eating places

D-U-N-S 25-015-1149 (BR)
ATCO STRUCTURES & LOGISTICS SERVICES LTD
5109 48 St Suite 203, Yellowknife, NT, X1A 1N5
(867) 669-7370
Emp Here 69
SIC 4581 Airports, flying fields, and services

D-U-N-S 20-512-3362 (SL)
ARSLANIAN CUTTING WORKS NWT LTD
106 Archibald St, Yellowknife, NT, X1A 2P4
(867) 873-0138
Emp Here 48   *Sales* 148,025,280
SIC 3915 Jewelers' materials and lapidary work
Pr Chahe Arslanian
Dir Opers Robert Bies
 Ronen Basal
 Shlomo Drazin

D-U-N-S 25-680-0749 (BR)
BUFFALO AIRWAYS LTD
108 Berry St, Yellowknife, NT, X1A 2R3
(867) 873-6112
Emp Here 60
SIC 4729 Passenger transportation arrangement

D-U-N-S 20-084-2925 (BR)
CB PARTNERS CORPORATION
CLARK BUILDERS
349 Old Airport Rd Suite 206, Yellowknife, NT, X1A 3X6
(867) 873-6337
Emp Here 35
SIC 1542 Nonresidential construction, nec

D-U-N-S 25-015-1073 (BR)
CANADIAN BROADCASTING CORPORATION
CBC NORTH
5002 Forrest Dr, Yellowknife, NT, X1A 2A9
(867) 669-5400
Emp Here 60
SIC 4833 Television broadcasting stations

D-U-N-S 20-012-9521 (HQ)
CANADIAN NORTH INC
5109 48 St 202 Nunasi Bldg., Yellowknife, NT, X1A 1N5
(867) 669-4000
Emp Here 76   *Emp Total* 1,200
Sales 263,852,120
SIC 4729 Passenger transportation arrangement
Pr Steve Hankirk

VP Lorraine Bonner
VP Fin Don Maclellan
VP Opers John Hankirk
Dir Gerry Roy
Dir Wayne Gordon
Dir Patrick Gruben
Dir Cathy Munro
Dir Wilf Wilcox
Dir James Kinney

D-U-N-S 20-720-2003   (SL)
CANARCTIC GRAPHICS LTD
5102 50 St, Yellowknife, NT, X1A 1S2
(867) 873-5924
Emp Here 26   *Sales* 1,896,978
SIC 7335 Commercial photography

D-U-N-S 25-507-5202   (HQ)
DIAVIK DIAMOND MINES (2012) INC
(*Suby of* RIO TINTO PLC)
5201 50 Ave Suite 300, Yellowknife, NT, X1A
3S9
(867) 669-6500
Emp Here 31   *Emp Total* 51,487
Sales 41,149,835
SIC 1499 Miscellaneous nonMetallic minerals,
except fuels
 Denton Henkelman
 Sandeep Thenua
 Nigel Steward

D-U-N-S 25-955-9180   (BR)
DISCOVERY AIR INC
126 Crystal Ave, Yellowknife, NT, X1A 2P3
(867) 873-5350
Emp Here 200
SIC 4522 Air transportation, nonscheduled

D-U-N-S 25-326-5359   (HQ)
**DOMINION DIAMOND EKATI CORPORA-
TION**
EKATI
4920 52 St Suite 1102, Yellowknife, NT, X1A
3T1
(867) 669-9292
Emp Here 50   *Emp Total* 1,631
Sales 118,634,098
SIC 1499 Miscellaneous nonMetallic minerals,
except fuels
 Chantal Lavoie

D-U-N-S 20-272-9120   (BR)
FIRSTCANADA ULC
107 Kam Lake Rd, Yellowknife, NT, X1A 2P8
(867) 873-4693
Emp Here 20
SIC 4151 School buses

D-U-N-S 20-271-3835   (BR)
GOLDER ASSOCIATES LTD
4905 48 St Suite 9, Yellowknife, NT, X1A 3S3
(867) 873-6319
Emp Here 20
SIC 8748 Business consulting, nec

D-U-N-S 20-267-6495   (BR)
**GOVERNING COUNCIL OF THE SALVA-
TION ARMY IN CANADA, THE**
*GOVERNING COUNCIL OF THE SALVATION
ARMY IN CANADA, THE*
4925 45 St, Yellowknife, NT, X1A 1K6
(867) 920-4673
Emp Here 40
SIC 8661 Religious organizations

D-U-N-S 25-601-6023   (BR)
**GOVERNMENT OF THE NORTHWEST TER-
RITORIES**
AIRPORT MANAGERS OFFICE
1 Yellowknife Airport, Yellowknife, NT, X1A 3T2
(867) 873-4680
Emp Here 25
SIC 4581 Airports, flying fields, and services

D-U-N-S 20-510-2382   (BR)
**GOVERNMENT OF THE NORTHWEST TER-
RITORIES**
LEGAL AID

Gd, Yellowknife, NT, X1A 2L9
(867) 920-8024
Emp Here 20
SIC 8111 Legal services

D-U-N-S 24-523-0701   (HQ)
GREAT SLAVE HELICOPTERS LTD
GSH
106 Dickens St, Yellowknife, NT, X1A 2R3
(867) 873-2081
Emp Here 25   *Emp Total* 319
Sales 11,174,638
SIC 4522 Air transportation, nonscheduled
Pr Mark Mcgowan
VP Corey Taylor
 Brian Merker

D-U-N-S 24-948-3194   (SL)
KBL ENVIRONMENTAL LTD
17 Cameron Rd, Yellowknife, NT, X1A 2N8
(867) 873-5263
Emp Here 46   *Sales* 6,055,738
SIC 4953 Refuse systems
Genl Mgr John Oakfield

D-U-N-S 24-313-5162   (BR)
KINGLAND FORD SALES LTD
KINGLAND FORD YELLOWKNIFE
20 Yellowknife Airport, Yellowknife, NT, X1A
3T2
(867) 920-9200
Emp Here 40
SIC 5511 New and used car dealers

D-U-N-S 25-270-1552   (BR)
LOBLAWS INC
EXTRA FOODS
4910 50 Ave Suite 14, Yellowknife, NT, X1A
3S5
(867) 669-9100
Emp Here 26
SIC 5141 Groceries, general line

D-U-N-S 25-059-1740   (SL)
M BOTLAXO LTD
BOSTON PIZZA
(*Suby of* T.C. Enterprises Ltd)
5102 48 St, Yellowknife, NT, X1A 1N6
(867) 920-2000
Emp Here 50   *Sales* 1,532,175
SIC 5812 Eating places

D-U-N-S 24-671-2590   (BR)
MACKAY & PARTNERS
(*Suby of* MacKay & Partners)
5103 51st Streetx1a 2n5, Yellowknife, NT, X1A
2N5
(867) 920-4404
Emp Here 30
SIC 8721 Accounting, auditing, and book-
keeping

D-U-N-S 25-152-3528   (BR)
MACLAB ENTERPRISES CORPORATION
FRASER TOWER SUITES HOTEL
(*Suby of* Maclab Enterprises Corporation)
5303 52 St Suite 100, Yellowknife, NT, X1A
1V1
(867) 873-8700
Emp Here 20
SIC 7011 Hotels and motels

D-U-N-S 20-807-6331   (HQ)
**NORTHWEST TERRITORIES NON-PROFIT
HOUSING CORPORATION**
SOCIAL HOUSING PROGRAMS
Gd Lcd Main, Yellowknife, NT, X1A 2L8
(867) 873-7873
Emp Here 49   *Emp Total* 4,501
Sales 94,098,102
SIC 6531 Real estate agents and managers
Pr Pr David Stewart

D-U-N-S 20-637-4878   (BR)
**NORTHWEST TERRITORIES POWER COR-
PORATION**
Gd Lcd Main, Yellowknife, NT, X1A 2L8
(867) 669-3300
Emp Here 55

SIC 4911 Electric services

D-U-N-S 24-098-4414   (BR)
NORTHWESTEL INC
5201 50 Ave Suite 300, Yellowknife, NT, X1A
3S9
(867) 920-3500
SIC 4899 Communication services, nec

D-U-N-S 24-361-3267   (BR)
NUNASTAR PROPERTIES INC
EXPLORER HOTEL, THE
(*Suby of* Touchstone Holdings Ltd)
4825 49th Ave, Yellowknife, NT, X1A 2R3
(867) 873-3531
Emp Here 90
SIC 7011 Hotels and motels

D-U-N-S 25-399-5542   (SL)
POLAR EXPLOSIVES LTD
349 Old Airport Rd Suite 104, Yellowknife, NT,
X1A 3X6
(867) 880-4613
Emp Here 540   *Sales* 167,451,863
SIC 5169 Chemicals and allied products, nec
Genl Mgr Brad Rhude
Pr Yves Tremblay

D-U-N-S 25-833-0067   (BR)
ROYAL BANK OF CANADA
ROYAL BANK FINANCIAL GROUP
(*Suby of* Royal Bank Of Canada)
4920 52 St Suite 1, Yellowknife, NT, X1A 3T1
(867) 873-5961
Emp Here 20
SIC 6021 National commercial banks

D-U-N-S 25-329-1033   (SL)
RYFAN ELECTRIC LTD
9 Nahanni Dr, Yellowknife, NT, X1A 2P4
(867) 765-6100
Emp Here 125   *Sales* 15,217,500
SIC 1731 Electrical work
Pr Pr Richard Bolivar
 Darren Fraser
 David Tucker

D-U-N-S 20-300-7109   (BR)
STANTEC ARCHITECTURE LTD
4910 53 St 2nd Floor, Yellowknife, NT, X1A
1V2
(867) 920-2882
Emp Here 38
SIC 8712 Architectural services

D-U-N-S 20-300-6929   (BR)
STANTEC CONSULTING LTD
4910 53 St, Yellowknife, NT, X1A 1V2
(867) 920-2882
Emp Here 38
SIC 8711 Engineering services

D-U-N-S 20-897-7108   (HQ)
**STANTON TERRITORIAL HEALTH AU-
THORITY**
STANTON TERRITORIAL HOSPITAL
550 Byrne Rd, Yellowknife, NT, X1A 2N1
(867) 669-4111
Emp Here 475   *Emp Total* 4,501
Sales 49,609,050
SIC 8062 General medical and surgical hospi-
tals
CEO Brenda Fitzgerald
Pr Kay Lewis

D-U-N-S 24-397-9457   (SL)
TWILITE SECURITY LIMITED
4916 49th St, Yellowknife, NT, X1A 2N5
(867) 873-3202
Emp Here 90   *Sales* 3,291,754
SIC 7381 Detective and armored car services

D-U-N-S 24-234-8279   (BR)
**UNLIMITED POTENTIAL COMMUNITY SER-
VICES SOCIETY**
TERRITORIAL TREATMENT CENTRE
5218 52 St, Yellowknife, NT, X1A 1T9

(867) 920-4626
Emp Here 20
SIC 8361 Residential care

D-U-N-S 20-088-5452   (BR)
WAL-MART CANADA CORP
WALMART
313 Old Airport Rd, Yellowknife, NT, X1A 3T3
(867) 873-4545
Emp Here 100
SIC 5311 Department stores

D-U-N-S 25-417-5938   (SL)
**WORKER'S SAFETY AND COMPENSA-
TION COMMISSION**
W S C C
5022 49 St, Yellowknife, NT, X1A 3R8
(867) 920-3888
Emp Here 130   *Sales* 86,333,950
SIC 6331 Fire, marine, and casualty insurance
Ch Bd William Aho
Pr Dave Grundy

D-U-N-S 25-745-2714   (SL)
Y. K. EDUCATION DISTRICT NO 1
FRANKLIN, SIR JOHN HIGH SCHOOL
5402 50 Ave, Yellowknife, NT, X1A 1E5
(867) 766-5050
Emp Here 60   *Sales* 4,764,381
SIC 8211 Elementary and secondary schools

D-U-N-S 24-997-9824   (SL)
**YELLOWKNIFE ASSOCIATION FOR COM-
MUNITY LIVING**
4912 53 St, Yellowknife, NT, X1A 1V2
(867) 920-2644
Emp Here 60   *Sales* 2,188,821
SIC 8361 Residential care

D-U-N-S 25-165-4562   (BR)
**YELLOWKNIFE DISTRICT NO. 1 EDUCA-
TION AUTHORITY**
*MACPHERSON, N J ELEMENTARY
SCHOOL*
525 Range Lake Rd, Yellowknife, NT, X1A 3X1
(867) 873-4372
Emp Here 30
SIC 8211 Elementary and secondary schools

D-U-N-S 20-710-1655   (BR)
**YELLOWKNIFE DISTRICT NO. 1 EDUCA-
TION AUTHORITY**
WILLIAM MACDONALD MIDDLE SCHOOL
50 Taylor Rd, Yellowknife, NT, X1A 3X2
(867) 873-5814
Emp Here 27
SIC 8211 Elementary and secondary schools

D-U-N-S 20-068-3774   (BR)
**YELLOWKNIFE DISTRICT NO. 1 EDUCA-
TION AUTHORITY**
ECOLE J. H. SISSONS SCHOOL
5700 51a Ave, Yellowknife, NT, X1A 1G7
(867) 873-3477
Emp Here 32
SIC 8211 Elementary and secondary schools

D-U-N-S 25-160-6406   (BR)
**YELLOWKNIFE DISTRICT NO. 1 EDUCA-
TION AUTHORITY**
RANGE LAKE NORTH SCHOOL
170 Borden Dr, Yellowknife, NT, X1A 3R1
(867) 920-7567
Emp Here 30
SIC 8211 Elementary and secondary schools

D-U-N-S 25-842-6576   (SL)
YELLOWKNIFE INN LTD
ATITUDES RESTAURANT & BISTRO, L'
5010 49th St, Yellowknife, NT, X1A 2N4
(867) 873-2601
Emp Here 75   *Sales* 2,685,378
SIC 5812 Eating places

D-U-N-S 20-068-3832   (BR)
**YELLOWKNIFE PUBLIC DENOMINA-
TIONAL DISTRICT EDUCATION AUTHOR-
ITY**
SAINT PATRICK HIGH SCHOOL

5010 44 St, Yellowknife, NT, X1A 2S4
(867) 873-4888
Emp Here 45
SIC 8211 Elementary and secondary schools

D-U-N-S 20-278-7045   (BR)
**YELLOWKNIFE   PUBLIC   DENOMINA-
TIONAL DISTRICT EDUCATION AUTHOR-
ITY**
ECOLE SAINT JOSEPH SCHOOL
489 Range Lake Rd, Yellowknife, NT, X1A 2N5
(867) 920-2112
Emp Here 60
SIC 8211 Elementary and secondary schools

D-U-N-S 20-569-7670   (BR)
**YELLOWKNIFE   PUBLIC   DENOMINA-
TIONAL DISTRICT EDUCATION AUTHOR-
ITY**
WELEDEH CATHOLIC SCHOOL
5023 46th St, Yellowknife, NT, X1A 1L3
(867) 873-5591
Emp Here 43
SIC 8211 Elementary and secondary schools

Amherst, NS B4H
Cumberland County

D-U-N-S 20-571-8286   (BR)
AIR LIQUIDE CANADA INC
38 Station St, Amherst, NS, B4H 3E3
(902) 667-0000
Emp Here 20
SIC 2813 Industrial gases

D-U-N-S 25-265-2458   (BR)
AMHERST, TOWN OF
98 East Victoria St, Amherst, NS, B4H 1X6
(902) 667-7743
Emp Here 100
SIC 4953 Refuse systems

D-U-N-S 25-181-8738   (BR)
ATLANTIC WHOLESALERS LTD
REAL ATLANTIC SUPERSTORE
126 Albion St S, Amherst, NS, B4H 2X3
(902) 661-0703
Emp Here 150
SIC 5411 Grocery stores

D-U-N-S 20-537-5384   (BR)
CANADA POST CORPORATION
AMHERST P.O.
126 Albion St S, Amherst, NS, B4H 2X3
(902) 661-0703
Emp Here 190
SIC 4311 U.s. postal service

D-U-N-S 20-537-2282   (BR)
CANADA POST CORPORATION
AMHERST STN MAIN PO
38 Havelock St, Amherst, NS, B4H 4C3
(902) 667-7734
Emp Here 30
SIC 4311 U.s. postal service

D-U-N-S 20-114-8983   (SL)
CHEVERIE PHARMACY SERVICES INC
PHARMASAVE
158 Robert Angus Dr, Amherst, NS, B4H 4R7
(902) 667-3784
Emp Here 36   *Sales* 5,107,249
SIC 5912 Drug stores and proprietary stores
Pr Pr Sean K Cheverie
 Bartley D Butler
 Kelli L Cheverie

D-U-N-S 25-241-4420   (BR)
**CHIGNECTO CENTRAL REGIONAL
SCHOOL BOARD**
WEST HIGHLANDS ELEMENTARY SCHOOL
(*Suby of* Chignecto Central Regional School
Board)
36 Hickman St, Amherst, NS, B4H 2M4

Emp Here 30
SIC 8211 Elementary and secondary schools

D-U-N-S 20-710-2133   (BR)
**CHIGNECTO CENTRAL REGIONAL
SCHOOL BOARD**
*CHIGNECTO CENTRAL ADULT HIGH
SCHOOL, AMHERST*
(*Suby of* Chignecto Central Regional School
Board)
21 Acadia St Suite 2, Amherst, NS, B4H 4W3

Emp Here 50
SIC 8211 Elementary and secondary schools

D-U-N-S 20-710-1945   (BR)
**CHIGNECTO CENTRAL REGIONAL
SCHOOL BOARD**
AMHERST REGIONAL HIGH SCHOOL
(*Suby of* Chignecto Central Regional School
Board)
190 Willow St, Amherst, NS, B4H 3W5
(902) 661-2540
Emp Here 50
SIC 8211 Elementary and secondary schools

D-U-N-S 24-174-6275   (BR)
**CHIGNECTO CENTRAL REGIONAL
SCHOOL BOARD**
CUMBERLAND NORTH ACADEMY
(*Suby of* Chignecto Central Regional School
Board)
879 204 Hwy, Amherst, NS, B4H 3Y1
(902) 661-2464
Emp Here 32
SIC 8211 Elementary and secondary schools

D-U-N-S 20-024-4809   (BR)
**CHIGNECTO CENTRAL REGIONAL
SCHOOL BOARD**
E. B. CHANDLER JUNIOR HIGH SCHOOL
(*Suby of* Chignecto Central Regional School
Board)
28 Dickey St, Amherst, NS, B4H 4R4
(902) 661-2450
Emp Here 40
SIC 8211 Elementary and secondary schools

D-U-N-S 24-931-8122   (BR)
COMPASS MINERALS CANADA CORP
(*Suby of* Compass Minerals International,
Inc.)
327 Smith Rd, Amherst, NS, B4H 3Y4
(902) 667-3388
Emp Here 45
SIC 5169 Chemicals and allied products, nec

D-U-N-S 20-543-3209   (HQ)
CUMBERLAND HEALTH AUTHORITY
*CUMBERLAND REGIONAL HEALTH CARE
CENTRE*
34 Prince Arthur St, Amherst, NS, B4H 1V6
(902) 661-1090
Emp Here 50   *Emp Total* 11,000
Sales 57,865,567
SIC 8062 General medical and surgical hospitals
Ch Bd Bruce Saunders
V Ch Bd Doug Marshall
Sec Nancy Mclelan
Treas Ron Scott
 Jacqueline Beal
 Mary Ellen Clark
 Rick Douglas
 Dora Fuller
 Creighton Mccarthy

D-U-N-S 25-653-6186   (BR)
FIRSTCANADA ULC
LAIDLAW EDUCATION SERVICES
7 Industrial Park Dr, Amherst, NS, B4H 4H7

Emp Here 50
SIC 4151 School buses

D-U-N-S 25-991-4380   (BR)
GEM HEALTH CARE GROUP LIMITED
GABLES LODGE
260 Church St, Amherst, NS, B4H 3C9
(902) 667-3501
Emp Here 115
SIC 8051 Skilled nursing care facilities

D-U-N-S 24-832-8098   (BR)
I.M.P. GROUP LIMITED
AEROSPACE COMPONENTS, DIV OF
13 Tantramar Cres, Amherst, NS, B4H 4J6
(902) 667-3315
Emp Here 250
SIC 4581 Airports, flying fields, and services

D-U-N-S 20-073-2886   (BR)
**MUNICIPALITY OF THE COUNTY OF CUM-
BERLAND, THE**
*CUMBERLAND PSYCHIATRIC & MENTAL
HEALTH DEPARTMENT*
33 Havelock St, Amherst, NS, B4H 4W1
(902) 667-3879
Emp Here 24
SIC 8093 Specialty outpatient clinics, nec

D-U-N-S 20-913-3946   (BR)
NOVA SCOTIA HEALTH AUTHORITY

18 Albion St S, Amherst, NS, B4H 2W3
(902) 661-1090
Emp Here 100
SIC 8062 General medical and surgical hospitals

D-U-N-S 24-556-2256   (SL)
SCOTIA HYUNDAI
108 Robert Angus Dr, Amherst, NS, B4H 4R7
(902) 661-5000
Emp Here 20   *Sales* 10,145,000
SIC 5511 New and used car dealers
Owner Bruce Casey

D-U-N-S 20-806-2476   (BR)
SOBEYS CAPITAL INCORPORATED
SOBEYS STORE
142 Albion St S Suite 729, Amherst, NS, B4H
4H4
(902) 667-2251
Emp Here 25
SIC 5411 Grocery stores

D-U-N-S 25-635-1552   (BR)
THOMPSON, D.W. AGENCIES LIMITED
THOMPSON, D W AGENCIES LTD
(*Suby of* Exxon Mobil Corporation)
34 Clinton St, Amherst, NS, B4H 1K3
(902) 447-2210
Emp Here 23
SIC 5983 Fuel oil dealers

D-U-N-S 25-635-1966   (BR)
UNITED STEELWORKERS OF AMERICA
(*Suby of* United Steelworkers)
10 Tantramar Pl, Amherst, NS, B4H 2A1
(902) 667-0727
Emp Here 182
SIC 8631 Labor organizations

D-U-N-S 24-346-7359   (BR)
**VICTORIAN ORDER OF NURSES FOR
CANADA**
VON CUMBERLAND DISTRICT
43 Prince Arthur St, Amherst, NS, B4H 1V8
(902) 667-8796
Emp Here 160
SIC 8082 Home health care services

D-U-N-S 24-121-2492   (BR)
WAL-MART CANADA CORP
46 Robert Angus Dr, Amherst, NS, B4H 4R7
(902) 661-3476
Emp Here 100
SIC 5311 Department stores

D-U-N-S 20-567-1964   (BR)
WESTON BAKERIES LIMITED
MOISSON DOREE
35 Tantramar Cres, Amherst, NS, B4H 4J6
(902) 661-2253
Emp Here 50
SIC 5461 Retail bakeries

Annapolis Royal, NS B0S
Annapolis County

D-U-N-S 24-187-3843   (SL)
ANNAPOLIS ROYAL NURSING HOME LTD
Gd, Annapolis Royal, NS, B0S 1A0
(902) 532-2240
Emp Here 59   *Sales* 2,699,546
SIC 8051 Skilled nursing care facilities

D-U-N-S 25-504-0354   (BR)
**ANNAPOLIS VALLEY REGIONAL SCHOOL
BOARD**
ANNAPOLIS WEST EDUCATION CENTRE
100 Champlain Dr, Annapolis Royal, NS, B0S
1A0
(902) 532-3150
Emp Here 33
SIC 8211 Elementary and secondary schools

D-U-N-S 25-133-9107   (BR)

ATLANTIC WHOLESALERS LTD
SAVE EASY
21 St Anthony St, Annapolis Royal, NS, B0S
1A0
(902) 532-7791
Emp Here 25
SIC 5411 Grocery stores

D-U-N-S 25-593-3327   (BR)
LAFARGE CANADA INC
209 Kearney Lake Rd, Annapolis Royal, NS,
B0S 1A0
(902) 532-5124
Emp Here 50
SIC 5032 Brick, stone, and related material

D-U-N-S 25-018-9750   (BR)
ROYAL BANK OF CANADA
ROYAL BANK FINANCIAL GROUP
(*Suby of* Royal Bank Of Canada)
248 St. George St, Annapolis Royal, NS, B0S
1A0
(902) 532-2371
Emp Here 20
SIC 6021 National commercial banks

Antigonish, NS B2G
Antigonish County

D-U-N-S 20-955-4331   (BR)
ATLANTIC WHOLESALERS LTD
I G A
100 Post Rd, Antigonish, NS, B2G 2K4
(902) 863-4046
Emp Here 50
SIC 5411 Grocery stores

D-U-N-S 24-321-8158   (BR)
ATLANTIC WHOLESALERS LTD
REAL ATLANTIC SUPERSTORE, THE
26 Market St, Antigonish, NS, B2G 3B4
(902) 863-6711
Emp Here 50
SIC 5411 Grocery stores

D-U-N-S 25-296-6031   (BR)
BANK OF NOVA SCOTIA, THE
SCOTIABANK
255 Main St, Antigonish, NS, B2G 2C1
(902) 863-4800
Emp Here 26
SIC 6021 National commercial banks

D-U-N-S 24-884-7852   (BR)
BOSTON PIZZA INTERNATIONAL INC
135 Church St, Antigonish, NS, B2G 2E2
(902) 867-3444
Emp Here 50
SIC 5812 Eating places

D-U-N-S 20-539-2017   (BR)
CANADA POST CORPORATION
325 Main St, Antigonish, NS, B2G 2C3
(902) 863-3464
Emp Here 25
SIC 4311 U.s. postal service

D-U-N-S 25-411-3137   (BR)
CANADA POST CORPORATION
NATIONAL PHILATELIC CENTRE
75 St Ninian St Suite 1, Antigonish, NS, B2G
2R8
(902) 863-6550
Emp Here 71
SIC 4311 U.s. postal service

D-U-N-S 25-182-0655   (BR)
DOLLARAMA S.E.C.
133 Church St, Antigonish, NS, B2G 2E3
(902) 863-5237
Emp Here 20
SIC 5331 Variety stores

D-U-N-S 25-413-2426   (HQ)
GUYSBOROUGH ANTIGONISH STRAIT

HEALTH AUTHORITY
ST. MARTHA'S REGIONAL HOSPITAL
25 Bay St, Antigonish, NS, B2G 2G5
(902) 867-4500
Emp Here 45   *Emp Total* 11,000
Sales 80,883,346
SIC 8062 General medical and surgical hospitals
Ch Bd David Samson
Dir Lee Mccarron
Dir Charlene Long
Dir Lionel Aucoin
Dir Ed Pencer
Dir Barb Langille
Dir Ted Martins
Dir Barry Lumsden

D-U-N-S 20-299-2082   (BR)
HIGH-CREST ENTERPRISES LIMITED
HIGHLAND CREST HOME
(*Suby of* High-Crest Enterprises Limited)
44 Hillcres St Suite 32, Antigonish, NS, B2G 1Z3
(902) 863-3855
Emp Here 30
SIC 8059 Nursing and personal care, nec

D-U-N-S 24-343-2705   (SL)
HIGHLAND BUILDING SUPPLIES (2008) LTD
HIGHLAND HOME BUILDING CENTRE
1639 Brierly Brook Rd, Antigonish, NS, B2G 2K9
(902) 863-6242
Emp Here 31   *Sales* 6,289,900
SIC 5211 Lumber and other building materials
Pr Pr Andrew Allen
  Cindy Doiron

D-U-N-S 20-024-3384   (SL)
KELTIC MOTORS 1978 LIMITED
KELTIC FORD
100 Main St, Antigonish, NS, B2G 2N8
(902) 863-2771
Emp Here 20   *Sales* 10,048,000
SIC 5511 New and used car dealers
Pr Pr John Chisholm

D-U-N-S 20-199-5565   (BR)
LEVY'S LEATHERS LIMITED
(*Suby of* Levy's Leathers Limited)
1 Angus Macquarrie Dr Suite 1, Antigonish, NS, B2G 2L4
(902) 863-2314
Emp Here 50
SIC 3199 Leather goods, nec

D-U-N-S 20-729-9421   (SL)
MACLELLAN, C.J. & ASSOCIATES INCORPORATED
65 Beech Hill Rd Suite 2, Antigonish, NS, B2G 2P9
(902) 863-1220
Emp Here 24   *Sales* 2,115,860
SIC 8711 Engineering services

D-U-N-S 24-131-6132   (BR)
MARITIME INNS & RESORTS INCORPORATED
MARITIME INN ANTIGONISH
(*Suby of* Mingo Family Trust)
158 Main St, Antigonish, NS, B2G 2B7
(902) 863-4001
Emp Here 36
SIC 7011 Hotels and motels

D-U-N-S 20-640-4472   (BR)
NOVA CAPITAL INCORPORATED
S. & D. SMITH CENTRAL SUPPLIES LIMITED
(*Suby of* Nova Capital Incorporated)
35 Market St, Antigonish, NS, B2G 3B5
(902) 863-6882
Emp Here 200
SIC 5211 Lumber and other building materials

D-U-N-S 20-933-3129   (HQ)
NOVA CAPITAL INCORPORATED

CENTRAL SUPPLIES
(*Suby of* Nova Capital Incorporated)
17 Central Ave, Antigonish, NS, B2G 2L4
(902) 863-6534
Emp Here 60   *Emp Total* 480
Sales 85,509,940
SIC 6712 Bank holding companies
  Stephen Smith
  Linda Macpherson
VP VP Robert Miller

D-U-N-S 20-024-2915   (SL)
RON MACGILLIVRAY CHEVROLET LTD
75 St Andrews St, Antigonish, NS, B2G 2G9
(902) 863-2803
Emp Here 34   *Sales* 17,246,500
SIC 5511 New and used car dealers
Pr Pr Ron Macgillivray

D-U-N-S 24-705-4208   (BR)
SCOTSBURN CO-OPERATIVE SERVICES LIMITED
200 College St, Antigonish, NS, B2G 1Y2

Emp Here 50
SIC 5143 Dairy products, except dried or canned

D-U-N-S 25-299-3175   (BR)
SOBEYS CAPITAL INCORPORATED
SOBEYS # 596
151 Church St, Antigonish, NS, B2G 2E2
(902) 863-6022
Emp Here 100
SIC 5411 Grocery stores

D-U-N-S 24-705-8720   (BR)
SODEXO CANADA LTD
Gd, Antigonish, NS, B2G 2W5
(902) 867-2491
Emp Here 90
SIC 5812 Eating places

D-U-N-S 20-852-7684   (BR)
STAPLES CANADA INC
STAPLES THE BUSINESS DEPOT
(*Suby of* Staples, Inc.)
36 Market St, Antigonish, NS, B2G 3B4
(902) 863-6787
Emp Here 50
SIC 5943 Stationery stores

D-U-N-S 25-240-9933   (BR)
STRAIT REGIONAL SCHOOL BOARD
ST ANDREW JUNIOR SCHOOL
2 Appleseed Dr, Antigonish, NS, B2G 3B6
(902) 863-3046
Emp Here 60
SIC 8211 Elementary and secondary schools

D-U-N-S 25-241-0055   (BR)
STRAIT REGIONAL SCHOOL BOARD
DR JOHN HUGH GILLIS REGIONAL HIGH SCHOOL
105 Braemore Ave, Antigonish, NS, B2G 1L3
(902) 863-1620
Emp Here 75
SIC 8211 Elementary and secondary schools

D-U-N-S 24-317-1860   (BR)
WAL-MART CANADA CORP
WALMART
50 Market St, Antigonish, NS, B2G 3B4
(902) 867-1279
Emp Here 150
SIC 5311 Department stores

Arcadia, NS B0W
Yarmouth County

D-U-N-S 25-240-8687   (BR)
TRI-COUNTY REGIONAL SCHOOL BOARD
ARCADIA CONSOLIDATED SCHOOL
849 Highway 334, Arcadia, NS, B0W 1B0

(902) 749-2870
Emp Here 33
SIC 8211 Elementary and secondary schools

Arichat, NS B0E
Richmond County

D-U-N-S 25-964-2650   (BR)
CLEARWATER FINE FOODS INCORPORATED
441 Cape Auget Rd, Arichat, NS, B0E 1A0
(902) 226-3510
Emp Here 75
SIC 4222 Refrigerated warehousing and storage

D-U-N-S 25-241-0279   (BR)
CONSEIL SCOLAIRE ACADIEN PROVINCIAL
ECOLE BEAU-PORT
2359 Rte 206, Arichat, NS, B0E 1A0
(902) 226-5200
Emp Here 30
SIC 8211 Elementary and secondary schools

Auburn, NS B0P

D-U-N-S 20-921-0207   (BR)
ANNAPOLIS VALLEY REGIONAL SCHOOL BOARD
WEST KINGS DISTRICT HIGH SCHOOL
1941 Hwy 1, Auburn, NS, B0P 1A0
(902) 847-4440
Emp Here 75
SIC 8211 Elementary and secondary schools

Avonport, NS B0P

D-U-N-S 20-754-2528   (BR)
ANNAPOLIS VALLEY REGIONAL SCHOOL BOARD
L E SHAW ELEMENTARY SCHOOL
486 Oak Island Rd, Avonport, NS, B0P 1B0
(902) 542-6900
Emp Here 20
SIC 8211 Elementary and secondary schools

Aylesford, NS B0P

D-U-N-S 20-710-2208   (BR)
ANNAPOLIS VALLEY REGIONAL SCHOOL BOARD
ST MARY'S ELEMENTARY SCHOOL
1276 Victoria Rd, Aylesford, NS, B0P 1C0
(902) 847-4400
Emp Here 25
SIC 8211 Elementary and secondary schools

Baddeck, NS B0E

D-U-N-S 20-906-1654   (SL)
ALDERWOOD CORPORATION
ALDERWOOD REST HOME
42 Jones St, Baddeck, NS, B0E 1B0
(902) 295-2644
Emp Here 110   *Sales* 4,012,839
SIC 8361 Residential care

D-U-N-S 25-241-3661   (BR)
CAPE BRETON-VICTORIA REGIONAL SCHOOL BOARD
BADDECK ACADEMY
320 Shore Rd, Baddeck, NS, B0E 1B0

(902) 295-2359
Emp Here 40
SIC 8211 Elementary and secondary schools

D-U-N-S 20-288-7001   (BR)
EMC EMERGENCY MEDICAL CARE INCORPORATED
EMC BADDECK
27 Big Baddeck Rd, Baddeck, NS, B0E 1B0
(902) 295-3102
Emp Here 22
SIC 4119 Local passenger transportation, nec

D-U-N-S 24-344-5389   (SL)
MACAULAY RESORTS LIMITED
THISTLEDOWN PUB
368 Shore Rd, Baddeck, NS, B0E 1B0
(902) 295-3500
Emp Here 50   *Sales* 2,188,821
SIC 7011 Hotels and motels

Barrington, NS B0W
Shelburne County

D-U-N-S 25-994-0620   (BR)
MURRAY MOTORS YARMOUTH LIMITED PARTNERSHIP
MURRAY G M
349 Oak Park Rd, Barrington, NS, B0W 1E0
(902) 637-4045
Emp Here 80
SIC 5511 New and used car dealers

D-U-N-S 20-298-6258   (BR)
NOVA SCOTIA, PROVINCE OF
COMMUNITY SERVICES
2447 Main Hwy 3, Barrington, NS, B0W 1E0
(902) 637-2335
Emp Here 20
SIC 8611 Business associations

D-U-N-S 20-290-3121   (BR)
TRI-COUNTY REGIONAL SCHOOL BOARD
FOREST RIDGE ACADEMY
59 Forest View Dr, Barrington, NS, B0W 1E0
(902) 637-4340
Emp Here 40
SIC 8211 Elementary and secondary schools

Barrington Passage, NS B0W
Shelburne County

D-U-N-S 20-573-5397   (BR)
EMC EMERGENCY MEDICAL CARE INCORPORATED
EMC BARRINGTON
3874 Highway 3, Barrington Passage, NS, B0W 1G0
(902) 637-3345
Emp Here 20
SIC 4119 Local passenger transportation, nec

D-U-N-S 24-943-5942   (BR)
SOBEYS CAPITAL INCORPORATED
SOBEYS 323
3552 Hwy 3, Barrington Passage, NS, B0W 1G0
(902) 637-3063
Emp Here 99
SIC 5411 Grocery stores

D-U-N-S 24-914-8722   (BR)
VICTORIAN ORDER OF NURSES FOR CANADA
VON CANADA
Highway 3 Unit 5, Barrington Passage, NS, B0W 1G0
(902) 637-2961
Emp Here 55
SIC 8082 Home health care services

D-U-N-S 24-626-1163   (BR)
VICTORIAN ORDER OF NURSES FOR

CANADA
3640 Main St Suite 5, Barrington Passage,
NS, B0W 1G0
(902) 637-2943
Emp Here 60
SIC 8082 Home health care services

Bass River, NS B0M
Colchester County

D-U-N-S 20-710-2117   (BR)
**CHIGNECTO   CENTRAL   REGIONAL
SCHOOL BOARD**
BASS RIVER ELEMENTARY
(*Suby of* Chignecto Central Regional School
Board)
139 Maple Av, Bass River, NS, B0M 1B0
(902) 647-3510
Emp Here 50
SIC 8211 Elementary and secondary schools

Beaver Bank, NS B4E
Halifax County

D-U-N-S 25-361-4978   (BR)
HALIFAX REGIONAL SCHOOL BOARD
BEAVERBANK MONARCH DRIVE
(*Suby of* Halifax Regional School Board)
38 Monarch Dr, Beaver Bank, NS, B4E 3A5
(902) 864-7540
Emp Here 35
SIC 8211 Elementary and secondary schools

Beaver Bank, NS B4G
Halifax County

D-U-N-S 20-710-2729   (BR)
HALIFAX REGIONAL SCHOOL BOARD
*BEAVER BANK KINSAC'S ELEMENTARY
SCHOOL*
28 Kinsac Rd, Beaver Bank, NS, B4G 1C5
(902) 864-6805
Emp Here 50
SIC 8211 Elementary and secondary schools

D-U-N-S 20-023-7894   (BR)
HALIFAX REGIONAL SCHOOL BOARD
*BARRETT, HAROLD T JUNIOR HIGH
SCHOOL*
862 Beaver Bank Rd, Beaver Bank, NS, B4G
1A9
(902) 864-7500
Emp Here 20
SIC 8211 Elementary and secondary schools

D-U-N-S 20-781-0839   (SL)
SCOTIA NURSING HOMES LIMITED
125 Knowles Cres, Beaver Bank, NS, B4G
1E7
(902) 865-6364
Emp Here 56   *Sales* 12,270,000
SIC 8051 Skilled nursing care facilities
Pr Pr Thane Stevens
  Ted Sceles
  R Mishra
  Murray W Knowles
  Stephen Pace

Bedford, NS B4A
Halifax County

D-U-N-S 24-338-8238   (BR)
98599 CANADA LTD
COMMERCIAL CARPET CENTRE
961 Bedford Hwy, Bedford, NS, B4A 1A9

(902) 425-2411
Emp Here 25
SIC 5713 Floor covering stores

D-U-N-S 25-173-6385   (BR)
ATLANTIC WHOLESALERS LTD
1650 Bedford Hwy, Bedford, NS, B4A 4J7
(902) 832-3117
Emp Here 200
SIC 5411 Grocery stores

D-U-N-S 20-563-3464   (BR)
BDO CANADA LLP
BEDFORD ACCOUNTING
1496 Bedford Highway Suite 101, Bedford,
NS, B4A 1E5
(902) 444-5540
Emp Here 20
SIC 8721 Accounting, auditing, and book-
keeping

D-U-N-S 25-018-0106   (BR)
BANQUE TORONTO-DOMINION, LA
TD CANADA TRUST
(*Suby of* Toronto-Dominion Bank, The)
1475 Bedford Hwy, Bedford, NS, B4A 3Z5
(902) 835-7400
Emp Here 32
SIC 6021 National commercial banks

D-U-N-S 25-360-0092   (BR)
BEDFORD INVESTMENTS LTD
ESQUIRE RESTAURANT
(*Suby of* Bedford Investments Ltd)
772 Bedford Hwy, Bedford, NS, B4A 1A2
(902) 835-9033
Emp Here 33
SIC 5812 Eating places

D-U-N-S 24-956-0384   (SL)
**CHADWICK FOOD SERVICE MANAGE-
MENT INCORPORATED**
200 Waterfront Dr Suite 225, Bedford, NS,
B4A 4J4
(902) 832-9489
Emp Here 85   *Sales* 2,553,625
SIC 5812 Eating places

D-U-N-S 24-357-6290   (BR)
CHARLTOM RESTAURANTS LIMITED
WENDY'S
1511 Bedford Hwy, Bedford, NS, B4A 1E3
(902) 832-1050
Emp Here 25
SIC 5812 Eating places

D-U-N-S 24-804-0586   (BR)
EMPIRE THEATRES LIMITED
EMPIRE 6 CINEMAS
961 Bedford Hwy, Bedford, NS, B4A 1A9
(902) 835-9500
Emp Here 20
SIC 7832 Motion picture theaters, except
drive-in

D-U-N-S 24-190-7351   (BR)
**FORD MOTOR COMPANY OF CANADA,
LIMITED**
(*Suby of* Ford Motor Company)
1595 Bedford Hwy Suite 306, Bedford, NS,
B4A 3Y4

Emp Here 22
SIC 5012 Automobiles and other motor vehicles

D-U-N-S 25-241-5062   (BR)
HALIFAX REGIONAL SCHOOL BOARD
BEDFORD JUNIOR HIGH SCHOOL
(*Suby of* Halifax Regional School Board)
426 Rocky Lake Dr, Bedford, NS, B4A 2T5
(902) 832-8952
Emp Here 40
SIC 8211 Elementary and secondary schools

D-U-N-S 25-241-5104   (BR)
HALIFAX REGIONAL SCHOOL BOARD
SUNNYSIDE ELEMENTARY SCHOOL
(*Suby of* Halifax Regional School Board)

210 Eaglewood Dr, Bedford, NS, B4A 3E3
(902) 832-8983
Emp Here 39
SIC 8211 Elementary and secondary schools

D-U-N-S 25-871-6612   (BR)
HALIFAX REGIONAL SCHOOL BOARD
CHARLES P ALLEN HIGH SCHOOL
(*Suby of* Halifax Regional School Board)
670 Rocky Lake Dr, Bedford, NS, B4A 2T6
(902) 832-8964
Emp Here 101
SIC 8211 Elementary and secondary schools

D-U-N-S 20-535-5865   (BR)
HALIFAX REGIONAL SCHOOL BOARD
BASINVIEW DRIVE COMMUNITY SCHOOL
273 Basinview Dr, Bedford, NS, B4A 3X8
(902) 832-8450
Emp Here 45
SIC 8211 Elementary and secondary schools

D-U-N-S 20-710-3032   (BR)
HALIFAX REGIONAL SCHOOL BOARD
ADULT HIGH SCHOOL ADMINISTRATION
1326 Bedford Hwy, Bedford, NS, B4A 1C9
(902) 421-7779
Emp Here 50
SIC 8211 Elementary and secondary schools

D-U-N-S 24-833-1787   (BR)
LAWTON'S DRUG STORES LIMITED
LAWTON'S 158
967 Bedford Hwy, Bedford, NS, B4A 1A9
(902) 832-4388
Emp Here 25
SIC 5912 Drug stores and proprietary stores

D-U-N-S 24-386-8119   (SL)
LUCKETT RETAIL MANAGEMENT INC
PETE'S
1595 Bedford Hwy Suite 122, Bedford, NS,
B4A 3Y4
(902) 835-4997
Emp Here 275   *Sales* 49,943,437
SIC 5411 Grocery stores
Dir Fin Diane Hamilton

D-U-N-S 24-755-5543   (BR)
MARK'S WORK WEARHOUSE LTD
WORK WORLD
1595 Bedford Hwy Suite 199, Bedford, NS,
B4A 3Y4
(902) 832-0119
Emp Here 25
SIC 5651 Family clothing stores

D-U-N-S 24-349-2142   (BR)
**MCDONALD'S   RESTAURANTS   OF
CANADA LIMITED**
MCDONALD'S RESTAURANT
(*Suby of* McDonald's Corporation)
1493 Bedford Hwy, Bedford, NS, B4A 1E3
(902) 835-8851
Emp Here 30
SIC 5812 Eating places

D-U-N-S 24-802-8966   (SL)
**NEWNET COMMUNICATION TECHNOLO-
GIES (CANADA), INC**
26 Union St Suite 305, Bedford, NS, B4A 2B5
(902) 406-8375
Emp Here 28   *Sales* 2,512,128
SIC 7371 Custom computer programming ser-
vices

D-U-N-S 20-206-3199   (SL)
OUR NEIGHBOURHOOD LIVING SOCIETY
15 Dartmouth Rd Suite 210, Bedford, NS, B4A
3X6
(902) 835-8826
Emp Here 90   *Sales* 3,283,232
SIC 8361 Residential care

D-U-N-S 20-852-7494   (SL)
PACRIM HOSPITALITY SERVICES INC
*INTERGY RESERVATION & E-MARKETING
SOLUTIONS, DIV OF*

30 Damascus Rd Suite 201, Bedford, NS, B4A
0C1
(902) 404-7474
Emp Here 75   *Sales* 4,523,563
SIC 8741 Management services

D-U-N-S 24-348-6888   (HQ)
PARKER KAEFER INC
200 Waterfront Dr Suite 100, Bedford, NS,
B4A 4J4
(902) 860-3344
Emp Here 100   *Emp Total* 27,874
Sales 45,478,178
SIC 1742 Plastering, drywall, and insulation
Genl Mgr Thomas I Fitzpatrick
Fin Ex Todd Maceachern

D-U-N-S 20-287-4413   (BR)
POMERLEAU INC
1496 Bedford Hwy Suite 500, Bedford, NS,
B4A 1E5
(902) 468-3669
Emp Here 25
SIC 1521 Single-family housing construction

D-U-N-S 25-562-2375   (BR)
**PORTAGE LA PRAIRIE MUTUAL INSUR-
ANCE CO, THE**
PORTAGE MUTUAL INSURANCE
1595 Bedford Hwy Suite 502, Bedford, NS,
B4A 3Y4
(902) 835-1054
Emp Here 54
SIC 6331 Fire, marine, and casualty insurance

D-U-N-S 20-793-8072   (BR)
SMITTY'S CANADA LIMITED
1552 Bedford Hwy, Bedford, NS, B4A 1E4
(902) 835-7204
Emp Here 60
SIC 5812 Eating places

D-U-N-S 20-921-0033   (BR)
SOBEYS CAPITAL INCORPORATED
SOBEYS
961 Bedford Hwy, Bedford, NS, B4A 1A9
(902) 835-3335
Emp Here 49
SIC 5411 Grocery stores

D-U-N-S 24-262-9434   (BR)
STRESCON LIMITED
131 Duke St, Bedford, NS, B4A 3C3
(902) 494-7400
Emp Here 70
SIC 3272 Concrete products, nec

D-U-N-S 24-329-9265   (BR)
WAL-MART CANADA CORP
141 Damascus Rd, Bedford, NS, B4A 0C2
(902) 865-4000
Emp Here 200
SIC 5311 Department stores

D-U-N-S 20-303-4772   (BR)
**WINNERS MERCHANTS INTERNATIONAL
L.P.**
WINNERS
(*Suby of* The TJX Companies Inc)
181 Damascus Rd, Bedford, NS, B4A 0C2
(902) 835-1662
Emp Here 50
SIC 5651 Family clothing stores

Bedford, NS B4B
Halifax County

D-U-N-S 24-339-0457   (BR)
ALUMICOR LIMITED
(*Suby of* Apogee Enterprises, Inc.)
155 Bluewater Rd, Bedford, NS, B4B 1H1
(902) 835-4545
Emp Here 50
SIC 3444 Sheet Metalwork

D-U-N-S 24-913-1160   (SL)

EISENER'S TRANSPORT LIMITED
61 Bluewater Rd, Bedford, NS, B4B 1G8

Emp Here 110   *Sales* 12,072,550
SIC 4212 Local trucking, without storage
Dir Uwe Petroschke
Pr Pr Rodi Saarloos

D-U-N-S 20-279-6801   (BR)
HALIFAX HERALD LIMITED, THE
THE CHRONICLE HERALD
311 Bluewater Rd, Bedford, NS, B4B 1Z9
(902) 426-2811
Emp Here 80
SIC 2711 Newspapers

D-U-N-S 20-913-4878   (BR)
HENRY SCHEIN CANADA, INC
2 Bluewater Rd Suite 110, Bedford, NS, B4B 1G7
(902) 835-1103
Emp Here 45
SIC 5047 Medical and hospital equipment

D-U-N-S 25-527-4136   (BR)
I.M.P. GROUP LIMITED
CAN-MED HEALTH CARE
200 Bluewater Rd Suite 201, Bedford, NS, B4B 1G9
(902) 455-4649
Emp Here 30
SIC 4581 Airports, flying fields, and services

D-U-N-S 20-025-9104   (BR)
IRON MOUNTAIN CANADA OPERATIONS ULC
RECORDS MANAGEMENT SERVICES
1 Command Crt, Bedford, NS, B4B 1H5
(902) 835-7427
Emp Here 25
SIC 4226 Special warehousing and storage, nec

D-U-N-S 24-994-8068   (BR)
KONE INC
205 Bluewater Rd Suite 1, Bedford, NS, B4B 1H1
(902) 450-1102
Emp Here 25
SIC 1796 Installing building equipment

D-U-N-S 24-872-9329   (HQ)
MAMMOET CANADA EASTERN LTD
2 Bluewater Rd Suite 246, Bedford, NS, B4B 1G7
(902) 450-0550
Emp Here 280   *Emp Total* 60,800
Sales 109,147,626
SIC 4212 Local trucking, without storage
Pr Keith Triginer
VP Fin Kent Lee
VP Sls Jeremy Asher

D-U-N-S 20-555-7650   (BR)
MAXXAM ANALYTICS INTERNATIONAL CORPORATION
MAXXAM ANALYTICS
200 Bluewater Rd Suite 201, Bedford, NS, B4B 1G9
(902) 420-0203
Emp Here 85
SIC 8731 Commercial physical research

D-U-N-S 20-026-5874   (BR)
PPG CANADA INC
GLASS GROUP
(*Suby of* PPG Industries, Inc.)
81 Bluewater Rd, Bedford, NS, B4B 1H4
(902) 835-7281
Emp Here 40
SIC 5039 Construction materials, nec

D-U-N-S 24-803-6964   (BR)
S.L.H. TRANSPORT INC
347 Bluewater Rd, Bedford, NS, B4B 1Y3
(902) 832-4900
Emp Here 176
SIC 4213 Trucking, except local

D-U-N-S 24-912-6749   (BR)
WALLACE EQUIPMENT LTD
60 Symonds Rd, Bedford, NS, B4B 1H3
(902) 835-7474
Emp Here 40
SIC 5084 Industrial machinery and equipment

Belnan, NS B2S
Hants County

D-U-N-S 24-342-6491   (BR)
ATLANTIC ROOFERS LIMITED
674 Highway 214 Unit 1, Belnan, NS, B2S 2N2
(902) 445-5044
Emp Here 20
SIC 1761 Roofing, siding, and sheetMetal work

Berwick, NS B0P

D-U-N-S 25-412-3649   (BR)
ANNAPOLIS VALLEY DISTRICT HEALTH AUTHORITY
WESTERN KINGS MEMORIAL HEALTH CENTRE
121 Orchard St Rr 3 Suite 131, Berwick, NS, B0P 1E0
(902) 538-0096
Emp Here 20
SIC 8062 General medical and surgical hospitals

D-U-N-S 25-504-0867   (BR)
ANNAPOLIS VALLEY REGIONAL SCHOOL BOARD
SOMERSET & DISTRICT ELEMENTARY SCHOOL
4339 Brooklyn St, Berwick, NS, B0P 1E0
(902) 538-4670
Emp Here 28
SIC 8211 Elementary and secondary schools

D-U-N-S 25-504-0396   (BR)
ANNAPOLIS VALLEY REGIONAL SCHOOL BOARD
BERWICK & DISTRICT SCHOOL
220 Veterans Dr, Berwick, NS, B0P 1E0
(902) 538-4720
Emp Here 40
SIC 8211 Elementary and secondary schools

D-U-N-S 25-410-6057   (HQ)
ANNAPOLIS VALLEY REGIONAL SCHOOL BOARD
ANNAPOLIS EAST ELEMENTARY SCHOOL
121 Orchard St Rr 3, Berwick, NS, B0P 1E0
(902) 538-4600
Emp Here 60   *Emp Total* 11,000
Sales 134,361,474
SIC 8211 Elementary and secondary schools
Superintnt Margo Tait

D-U-N-S 25-792-9018   (BR)
ATLANTIC WHOLESALERS LTD
SAVE EASY
197 Commercial St, Berwick, NS, B0P 1E0
(902) 538-8818
Emp Here 25
SIC 5411 Grocery stores

D-U-N-S 24-804-6674   (SL)
LARSEN PACKERS LIMITED
326 Main St Rr 3, Berwick, NS, B0P 1E0

Emp Here 500   *Sales* 83,699,840
SIC 2011 Meat packing plants
Pr Pr Richard Young
Treas Rocco Cappucitti

D-U-N-S 25-821-6068   (BR)
NOVA SCOTIA, PROVINCE OF
ANNAPOLIS VALLEY REGIONAL LIBRARY

236 Commercial St, Berwick, NS, B0P 1E0
(902) 665-2995
Emp Here 60
SIC 8231 Libraries

D-U-N-S 20-184-5984   (BR)
SOBEYS CAPITAL INCORPORATED
PRICE CHOPPERS
223 Commercial St, Berwick, NS, B0P 1E0
(902) 538-3686
Emp Here 30
SIC 5411 Grocery stores

Bible Hill, NS B6L

D-U-N-S 20-100-0895   (SL)
AGRITECH PARK INCORPORATED
90 Research Dr, Bible Hill, NS, B6L 2R2

Emp Here 20   *Sales* 402,066
SIC 8731 Commercial physical research

Blockhouse, NS B0J
Lunenburg County

D-U-N-S 25-804-6143   (BR)
VICTORIAN ORDER OF NURSES FOR CANADA
VON LUNENBURG DISTRICT
1924 Northfield Rd, Blockhouse, NS, B0J 1E0
(902) 624-1897
Emp Here 30
SIC 8082 Home health care services

Bras D'Or, NS B1Y
Cape Breton County

D-U-N-S 25-241-3752   (BR)
CAPE BRETON-VICTORIA REGIONAL SCHOOL BOARD
BRAS D'OR ELEMENTARY SCHOOL
10 Alder Point Rd, Bras D'Or, NS, B1Y 2K1
(902) 736-4000
Emp Here 34
SIC 8211 Elementary and secondary schools

Bridgetown, NS B0S
Annapolis County

D-U-N-S 20-206-2845   (HQ)
ANNAPOLIS COUNTY ADULT RESIDENTIAL CENTRE
(*Suby of* Annapolis County Adult Residential Centre)
200 Church St, Bridgetown, NS, B0S 1C0
(902) 665-4566
Emp Here 48   *Emp Total* 50
Sales 1,824,018
SIC 8361 Residential care

D-U-N-S 25-504-0479   (BR)
ANNAPOLIS VALLEY REGIONAL SCHOOL BOARD
BRIDGETOWN REGIONAL HIGH SCHOOL
456 Granville St, Bridgetown, NS, B0S 1C0
(902) 665-5400
Emp Here 40
SIC 8211 Elementary and secondary schools

D-U-N-S 25-504-0438   (BR)
ANNAPOLIS VALLEY REGIONAL SCHOOL BOARD
BRIDGETOWN REGIONAL ELEMENTARY SCHOOL
7 Park St, Bridgetown, NS, B0S 1C0

(902) 665-5430
Emp Here 23
SIC 8211 Elementary and secondary schools

D-U-N-S 24-000-2076   (BR)
DAKOTA HOLDINGS LIMITED
TIM HORTONS
(*Suby of* Dakota Holdings Limited)
640 Granville St E, Bridgetown, NS, B0S 1C0
(902) 665-4555
Emp Here 21
SIC 5812 Eating places

Bridgewater, NS B4V
Lunenburg County

D-U-N-S 24-353-1170   (BR)
ACADIA BROADCASTING LIMITED
CKBW-FM
215 Dominion St Suite 2, Bridgewater, NS, B4V 2G8
(902) 543-2401
Emp Here 20
SIC 4832 Radio broadcasting stations

D-U-N-S 25-791-2030   (BR)
ATLANTIC WHOLESALERS LTD
REAL ATLANTIC SUPERSTORE, THE
21 Davison Dr, Bridgewater, NS, B4V 3K8
(902) 543-1809
Emp Here 200
SIC 5411 Grocery stores

D-U-N-S 25-789-9872   (BR)
ATLANTIC WHOLESALERS LTD
SAMS NOFRILLLS
240 Dufferin St, Bridgewater, NS, B4V 2G7
(902) 543-4661
Emp Here 60
SIC 5411 Grocery stores

D-U-N-S 25-296-5876   (BR)
BANK OF NOVA SCOTIA, THE
SCOTIABANK
Gd Lcd Main, Bridgewater, NS, B4V 2V8

Emp Here 23
SIC 6021 National commercial banks

D-U-N-S 25-079-4146   (SL)
BRIDGEWATER PHARMACY LIMITED
BRIDGEWATER PHARMASAVE
215 Dominion St Suite 511, Bridgewater, NS, B4V 2K7
(902) 543-3418
Emp Here 50   *Sales* 7,077,188
SIC 5912 Drug stores and proprietary stores
Pr Pr Susan Cochrane
Cameron Cochrane

D-U-N-S 20-540-5116   (BR)
CANADA POST CORPORATION
BRIDGEWATER STN MAIN PO
135 North St, Bridgewater, NS, B4V 8Z8
(902) 543-1960
Emp Here 35
SIC 4311 U.s. postal service

D-U-N-S 20-287-5840   (BR)
EMC EMERGENCY MEDICAL CARE INCORPORATED
EMC BRIDGEWATER
109 North St, Bridgewater, NS, B4V 2V7
(902) 527-2554
Emp Here 28
SIC 4119 Local passenger transportation, nec

D-U-N-S 20-704-4970   (BR)
EMPIRE THEATRES LIMITED
EMPIRE STUDIO 7
349 Lahave St, Bridgewater, NS, B4V 2T6
(902) 527-4021
Emp Here 40
SIC 7832 Motion picture theaters, except drive-in

D-U-N-S 24-573-9271   (SL)
HILLSIDE PINES HOME FOR SPECIAL CARE SOCIETY
77 Exhibition Dr, Bridgewater, NS, B4V 3K6
(902) 543-1525
Emp Here 78   *Sales* 3,575,074
SIC 8051 Skilled nursing care facilities

D-U-N-S 24-573-4017   (SL)
L. & B. ELECTRIC LIMITED
94 Wentzell Dr, Bridgewater, NS, B4V 3V4
(902) 543-9966
Emp Here 21   *Sales* 5,465,508
SIC 5063 Electrical apparatus and equipment
 Ross Bunnell

D-U-N-S 25-790-0837   (BR)
LAHAVE MANOR CORP
SUPPORTED COMMUNITY LIVING OPTIONS
(*Suby of* Lahave Manor Corp)
152 Pleasant St, Bridgewater, NS, B4V 1N5
(902) 543-1147
Emp Here 25
SIC 8322 Individual and family services

D-U-N-S 20-247-1418   (BR)
LEBLANC, GUY ENTERPRISES LIMITED
GUY'S FRENCHYS
(*Suby of* LeBlanc, Guy Enterprises Limited)
61 North St, Bridgewater, NS, B4V 2V7
(902) 245-2458
Emp Here 26
SIC 5932 Used merchandise stores

D-U-N-S 24-932-4732   (SL)
LIGHTHOUSE PUBLISHING LIMITED
LIGHTHOUSE MEDIA GROUP
353 York St, Bridgewater, NS, B4V 3K2
(902) 543-2457
Emp Here 48   *Sales* 5,579,750
SIC 2711 Newspapers
Pr Pr Lynn Margaret Hennigar
 Ralph E Hennigar

D-U-N-S 20-021-1295   (BR)
MUNICIPALITY OF THE DISTRICT OF LUNENBURG
LUNENBURG REGIONAL RECYCLING AND COMPOSTING FACILITY
908 Mullock Rd, Bridgewater, NS, B4V 3J5
(902) 543-2991
Emp Here 35
SIC 4953 Refuse systems

D-U-N-S 25-299-0007   (BR)
NOVA SCOTIA, PROVINCE OF
LUNENBURG CAMPUS
75 High St, Bridgewater, NS, B4V 1V8
(902) 543-4608
Emp Here 75
SIC 8221 Colleges and universities

D-U-N-S 20-025-9112   (BR)
PEPSICO CANADA ULC
PEPSI BOTTLING GROUP
(*Suby of* Pepsico, Inc.)
Gd Lcd Main, Bridgewater, NS, B4V 2V8
(902) 527-1364
Emp Here 50
SIC 2086 Bottled and canned soft drinks

D-U-N-S 20-706-6320   (BR)
RESOLVE CORPORATION
(*Suby of* 2206997 Ontario Inc)
197 Dufferin St Suite 100, Bridgewater, NS, B4V 2G9
(902) 541-3600
Emp Here 600
SIC 8742 Management consulting services

D-U-N-S 25-308-0774   (BR)
ROYAL BANK OF CANADA
RBC
(*Suby of* Royal Bank Of Canada)
565 King St, Bridgewater, NS, B4V 1B3
(902) 543-7161
Emp Here 21

SIC 6021 National commercial banks

D-U-N-S 25-826-6337   (BR)
SOBEYS CAPITAL INCORPORATED
349 Lahave St Suite 322, Bridgewater, NS, B4V 2T6
(902) 543-9244
Emp Here 130
SIC 5411 Grocery stores

D-U-N-S 20-268-9928   (SL)
SOUTH SHORE CHEVROLET
3302775 NOVA SCOTIA LTD
15133 Hebbville Rd, Bridgewater, NS, B4V 2W4
(902) 543-2493
Emp Here 40   *Sales* 14,592,140
SIC 5511 New and used car dealers
Pr Robert Steele

D-U-N-S 20-277-8572   (HQ)
SOUTH SHORE DISTRICT HEALTH AUTHORITY
QUEEN'S GENERAL HOSPITAL
90 Glen Allan Dr, Bridgewater, NS, B4V 3S6
(902) 527-2266
Emp Here 700   *Emp Total* 11,000
Sales 95,621,669
SIC 8062 General medical and surgical hospitals
 Kevin Mcnamara

D-U-N-S 24-877-9316   (BR)
SOUTH SHORE READY MIX LIMITED
1896 King St, Bridgewater, NS, B4V 2W9
(902) 543-4639
Emp Here 49
SIC 3272 Concrete products, nec

D-U-N-S 20-700-5252   (HQ)
SOUTH SHORE REGIONAL SCHOOL BOARD
ASPOTOGAN CONSOLIDATED ELEMENTARY SCHOOL
130 North Park St, Bridgewater, NS, B4V 4G9
(902) 543-2468
Emp Here 50   *Emp Total* 11,000
Sales 73,458,085
SIC 8211 Elementary and secondary schools
Superintnt Nancy Pynch-Worthylake
Dir Fin Wade Tattrie
Prs Dir Tina Munro
Dir Opers Barry Butler
 Steve Prest

D-U-N-S 25-240-9362   (BR)
SOUTH SHORE REGIONAL SCHOOL BOARD
BRIDGEWATER JUNIOR SENIOR HIGH SCHOOL
100 York St, Bridgewater, NS, B4V 1R3
(902) 543-9185
Emp Here 50
SIC 8211 Elementary and secondary schools

D-U-N-S 25-790-0928   (BR)
UNITED CHURCH OF CANADA, THE
BRIDGEWATER UNITED CHURCH
87 Hillcrest St, Bridgewater, NS, B4V 1T2
(902) 543-4833
Emp Here 23
SIC 8661 Religious organizations

D-U-N-S 24-121-7103   (BR)
WAL-MART CANADA CORP
60 New Pine Grove Rd, Bridgewater, NS, B4V 4H2
(902) 543-8680
Emp Here 160
SIC 5311 Department stores

Brookfield, NS B0N
Colchester County

D-U-N-S 25-241-5773   (BR)

CHIGNECTO CENTRAL REGIONAL SCHOOL BOARD
BROOKFIELD JUNIOR HIGH SCHOOL
(*Suby of* Chignecto Central Regional School Board)
233 289 Hwy, Brookfield, NS, B0N 1C0
(902) 673-5050
Emp Here 32
SIC 8211 Elementary and secondary schools

D-U-N-S 20-710-1853   (BR)
CHIGNECTO CENTRAL REGIONAL SCHOOL BOARD
SOUTH COLCHESTER ACADEMY
(*Suby of* Chignecto Central Regional School Board)
207 Highway 289, Brookfield, NS, B0N 1C0
(902) 673-5000
Emp Here 50
SIC 8211 Elementary and secondary schools

D-U-N-S 20-443-8956   (BR)
LAFARGE CANADA INC
87 Cement Plant Rd, Brookfield, NS, B0N 1C0
(902) 673-2281
Emp Here 100
SIC 2891 Adhesives and sealants

D-U-N-S 25-989-6082   (BR)
MARWOOD LTD
66 Pleasant Valley Rd, Brookfield, NS, B0N 1C0
(902) 673-2508
Emp Here 30
SIC 2499 Wood products, nec

Caledonia, NS B0T

D-U-N-S 20-781-1407   (SL)
NORTH QUEENS NURSING HOME INC
9565 Highway 8, Caledonia, NS, B0T 1B0
(902) 682-2553
Emp Here 75   *Sales* 2,772,507
SIC 8361 Residential care

D-U-N-S 20-716-8829   (BR)
SOUTH SHORE REGIONAL SCHOOL BOARD
NORTH QUEEN ELEMENTARY SCHOOL
40 Caledonia Rd W, Caledonia, NS, B0T 1B0
(902) 682-3500
Emp Here 50
SIC 8211 Elementary and secondary schools

Cambridge, NS B0P

D-U-N-S 25-360-0654   (BR)
ANNAPOLIS VALLEY REGIONAL SCHOOL BOARD
CENTRAL KINGS RURAL HIGH SCHOOL
6125 Highway 1 Rr 1, Cambridge, NS, B0P 1G0
(902) 538-4700
Emp Here 65
SIC 8211 Elementary and secondary schools

D-U-N-S 25-504-0552   (BR)
ANNAPOLIS VALLEY REGIONAL SCHOOL BOARD
CAMBRIDGE & DISTRICT COMMUNITY ELEMENTARY SCHOOL
6113 Highway 1, Cambridge, NS, B0P 1G0
(902) 538-4680
Emp Here 32
SIC 8211 Elementary and secondary schools

Canning, NS B0P

D-U-N-S 25-504-0958   (BR)
ANNAPOLIS VALLEY REGIONAL SCHOOL BOARD
GLOOSCAP ELEMENTARY SCHOOL
1017 J Jordan Rd, Canning, NS, B0P 1H0
(902) 582-2010
Emp Here 41
SIC 8211 Elementary and secondary schools

Canso, NS B0H

D-U-N-S 25-413-2657   (BR)
GUYSBOROUGH ANTIGONISH STRAIT HEALTH AUTHORITY
EASTERN MEMORIAL HOSPITAL
1746 Union St, Canso, NS, B0H 1H0
(902) 366-2794
Emp Here 40
SIC 8062 General medical and surgical hospitals

D-U-N-S 25-867-1163   (BR)
STRAIT REGIONAL SCHOOL BOARD
FANNING EDUCATION CENTRE
129 Tickle Rd, Canso, NS, B0H 1H0
(902) 366-2225
Emp Here 20
SIC 8211 Elementary and secondary schools

Central Onslow, NS B6L

D-U-N-S 20-710-1812   (BR)
CHIGNECTO CENTRAL REGIONAL SCHOOL BOARD
CENTRAL COLCHESTER JUNIOR HIGH SCHOOL
(*Suby of* Chignecto Central Regional School Board)
61 Onslow Rd, Central Onslow, NS, B6L 5K4
(902) 896-5570
Emp Here 50
SIC 8211 Elementary and secondary schools

Cherry Brook, NS B2Z
Halifax County

D-U-N-S 20-027-7429   (BR)
HALIFAX REGIONAL SCHOOL BOARD
GRAHAM CREIGHTON JUNIOR HIGH
72 Cherry Brook Rd, Cherry Brook, NS, B2Z 1A8
(902) 464-5164
Emp Here 29
SIC 8211 Elementary and secondary schools

Chester, NS B0J
Lunenburg County

D-U-N-S 20-573-5330   (BR)
EMC EMERGENCY MEDICAL CARE INCORPORATED
EMC CHESTER
149 Central St, Chester, NS, B0J 1J0
(902) 275-2452
Emp Here 20
SIC 4119 Local passenger transportation, nec

D-U-N-S 24-186-0238   (SL)
G.N. PLASTICS COMPANY LIMITED
GN THERMOFORMING EQUIPMENT
345 Old Trunk 3, Chester, NS, B0J 1J0
(902) 275-3571
Emp Here 80   *Sales* 9,484,891
SIC 3559 Special industry machinery, nec
Pr E. Bruce Kelly

Georg Nemeskeri
Monica Nemeskeri

D-U-N-S 20-025-1601   (SL)
HAWBOLDT INDUSTRIES (1989) LTD
HAWBOLDT INDUSTRIES
220 Highway 14, Chester, NS, B0J 1J0
(902) 275-3591
Emp Here 41   *Sales* 4,158,760
SIC 3429 Hardware, nec

D-U-N-S 25-365-1251   (BR)
LOUISIANA-PACIFIC CANADA LTD
(*Suby of* Louisiana-Pacific Corporation)
2005 Highway 14, Chester, NS, B0J 1J0
(902) 275-3556
Emp Here 350
SIC 2493 Reconstituted wood products

D-U-N-S 20-341-0337   (SL)
MDINA ENTERPRISES LTD
SALES BEACON PRODUCTIVITY SOLU-TIONS
121 Duke St Suite 49, Chester, NS, B0J 1J0
(855) 855-3180
Emp Here 85   *Sales* 10,433,380
SIC 8742 Management consulting services
Pr Cynthia Spraggs

D-U-N-S 20-652-0624   (BR)
SOUTH SHORE REGIONAL SCHOOL BOARD
CHESTER AREA MIDDLE SCHOOL
204 Duke St, Chester, NS, B0J 1J0
(902) 275-2720
Emp Here 46
SIC 8211 Elementary and secondary schools

D-U-N-S 25-836-1518   (HQ)
TRADEWINDS REALTY INCORPORATED
(*Suby of* Tradewinds Realty Incorporated)
5 Pleasant St, Chester, NS, B0J 1J0
(902) 275-5613
Emp Here 20   *Emp Total* 50
Sales 6,380,400
SIC 6531 Real estate agents and managers
Pr Pr Timothy Harris

D-U-N-S 25-240-7432   (BR)
TRI-COUNTY REGIONAL SCHOOL BOARD
CHESTER DISTRICT SCHOOL
202 Duke St, Chester, NS, B0J 1J0
(902) 275-2750
Emp Here 35
SIC 8211 Elementary and secondary schools

Chester Basin, NS B0J
Lunenburg County

D-U-N-S 20-716-8753   (BR)
SOUTH SHORE REGIONAL SCHOOL BOARD
FOREST HEIGHTS COMMUNITY SCHOOL
847 Highway 12, Chester Basin, NS, B0J 1K0
(902) 275-2700
Emp Here 35
SIC 8211 Elementary and secondary schools

Cheticamp, NS B0E
Inverness County

D-U-N-S 20-175-0903   (HQ)
ACADIAN CREDIT UNION LIMITED
LA CAISSE POPULAIRE ACADIENNE
(*Suby of* Acadian Credit Union Limited)
15089 Cabot Trail, Cheticamp, NS, B0E 1H0
(902) 224-2055
Emp Here 36   *Emp Total* 41
Sales 7,937,920
SIC 6062 State credit unions
Genl Mgr Denis Larad
Pr Leonard Lefort

D-U-N-S 20-023-5112   (BR)
CONSEIL SCOLAIRE ACADIEN PROVIN-CIAL
ECOLE NDA
15118 Cabot Trail, Cheticamp, NS, B0E 1H0
(902) 224-5300
Emp Here 40
SIC 8211 Elementary and secondary schools

D-U-N-S 24-913-1194   (BR)
INVERNESS MUNICIPAL HOUSING COR-PORATION
FOYER PERE FISET
(*Suby of* Inverness Municipal Housing Corpo-ration)
15092 Cabot Trail Rd, Cheticamp, NS, B0E 1H0
(902) 224-2087
Emp Here 100
SIC 8051 Skilled nursing care facilities

Church Point, NS B0W
Digby County

D-U-N-S 25-241-4982   (BR)
CONSEIL SCOLAIRE ACADIEN PROVIN-CIAL
ECOLE JOSEPH DUGAS
450 Patrice Rd Rr 1, Church Point, NS, B0W 1M0
(902) 769-5430
Emp Here 23
SIC 8211 Elementary and secondary schools

Cleveland, NS B0E
Richmond County

D-U-N-S 25-413-2491   (BR)
GUYSBOROUGH ANTIGONISH STRAIT HEALTH AUTHORITY
STRAIT RICHMOND HOSPITAL
138 Hospital Rd, Cleveland, NS, B0E 1J0
(902) 625-3230
Emp Here 110
SIC 8062 General medical and surgical hospi-tals

D-U-N-S 24-576-8614   (BR)
GUYSBOROUGH ANTIGONISH STRAIT HEALTH AUTHORITY
ADDICTION SERVICES
138 Hospital Rd, Cleveland, NS, B0E 1J0
(902) 625-3100
Emp Here 20
SIC 8069 Specialty hospitals, except psychi-atric

D-U-N-S 20-023-4214   (BR)
STRAIT REGIONAL SCHOOL BOARD
WEST RICHMOND EDUCATION CENTRE
19 School Rd, Cleveland, NS, B0E 1J0

Emp Here 20
SIC 8211 Elementary and secondary schools

Coldbrook, NS B4R

D-U-N-S 25-504-0677   (BR)
ANNAPOLIS VALLEY REGIONAL SCHOOL BOARD
COLDBROOK & DISTRICT SCHOOL
2305 English Mountain Rd, Coldbrook, NS, B4R 1B4
(902) 690-3830
Emp Here 65
SIC 8211 Elementary and secondary schools

Cole Harbour, NS B2V

D-U-N-S 24-379-8415   (BR)
GENERAL DYNAMICS LAND SYSTEMS - CANADA CORPORATION
(*Suby of* General Dynamics Corporation)
31 Av Millbrook, Cole Harbour, NS, B2V 0A2
(902) 406-3701
Emp Here 27
SIC 7371 Custom computer programming ser-vices

Cornwallis, NS B0S
Annapolis County

D-U-N-S 20-514-9409   (BR)
ACADIAN SEAPLANTS LIMITED
698 Conestoga St, Cornwallis, NS, B0S 1H0
(902) 638-8302
Emp Here 40
SIC 2875 Fertilizers, mixing only

Coxheath, NS B1R
Cape Breton County

D-U-N-S 25-241-5427   (BR)
CAPE BRETON-VICTORIA REGIONAL SCHOOL BOARD
COXHEATH ELEMENTARY SCHOOL
30 Mt Florence St, Coxheath, NS, B1R 1T8
(902) 562-4961
Emp Here 25
SIC 8211 Elementary and secondary schools

Currys Corner, NS B0N
Hants County

D-U-N-S 25-503-7285   (BR)
ANNAPOLIS VALLEY REGIONAL SCHOOL BOARD
WINDSOR FORKS DISTRICT SCHOOL
120 Sandster Bridge Rd, Currys Corner, NS, B0N 1H0
(902) 792-6700
Emp Here 21
SIC 8211 Elementary and secondary schools

D-U-N-S 25-593-4473   (BR)
J.M.P. SAYLES HOLDINGS INC
TIM HORTONS
(*Suby of* J.M.P. Sayles Holdings Inc)
7 Cole Dr, Currys Corner, NS, B0N 2T0
(902) 798-0767
Emp Here 40
SIC 5812 Eating places

D-U-N-S 24-532-3530   (SL)
KING'S-EDGEHILL SCHOOL
33 King Edgehill Lane, Currys Corner, NS, B0N 2T0
(902) 798-2278
Emp Here 70   *Sales* 4,669,485
SIC 8211 Elementary and secondary schools

D-U-N-S 25-592-6743   (BR)
NOVA CAPITAL INCORPORATED
S. & D. SMITH CENTRAL SUPPLIES LIM-ITED
(*Suby of* Nova Capital Incorporated)
50 Empire Lane, Currys Corner, NS, B0N 2T0
(902) 798-4488
Emp Here 40
SIC 5211 Lumber and other building materials

D-U-N-S 25-401-8377   (BR)
NOVA SCOTIA HEALTH AUTHORITY
HANTS COMMUNITY HOSPITAL
89 Payzant, Currys Corner, NS, B0N 2T0

(902) 798-8351
Emp Here 200
SIC 8062 General medical and surgical hospi-tals

D-U-N-S 20-905-8635   (SL)
PHILIP BURGESS LTD
ESSO HOME COMFORT
88 Sanford Dr, Currys Corner, NS, B0N 2T0
(902) 798-2204
Emp Here 68   *Sales* 20,024,640
SIC 5983 Fuel oil dealers
Pr Pr Philip Burgess
Patricia Burgess

D-U-N-S 24-606-3069   (BR)
ROYAL BANK OF CANADA
RBC
(*Suby of* Royal Bank Of Canada)
111 Water St, Currys Corner, NS, B0N 2T0
(902) 798-5721
Emp Here 25
SIC 6021 National commercial banks

Dartmouth, NS B2V
Halifax County

D-U-N-S 25-134-0733   (BR)
ATLANTIC WHOLESALERS LTD
REAL ATLANTIC SUPERSTORE, THE
920 Cole Harbour Rd, Dartmouth, NS, B2V 2J5
(902) 462-4500
Emp Here 100
SIC 5411 Grocery stores

D-U-N-S 20-608-2575   (BR)
HALIFAX REGIONAL SCHOOL BOARD
ASTRAL DRIVE JUNIOR HIGH SCHOOL
238 Astral Dr, Dartmouth, NS, B2V 1B8
(902) 462-8700
Emp Here 40
SIC 8211 Elementary and secondary schools

D-U-N-S 25-241-7852   (BR)
HALIFAX REGIONAL SCHOOL BOARD
CALDWELL ROAD ELEMENTARY SCHOOL
(*Suby of* Halifax Regional School Board)
280 Caldwell Rd, Dartmouth, NS, B2V 1A3
(902) 462-6010
Emp Here 30
SIC 8211 Elementary and secondary schools

D-U-N-S 20-852-7312   (BR)
HALIFAX REGIONAL SCHOOL BOARD
ASTRAL DRIVE ELEMENTARY SCHOOL
236 Astral Dr, Dartmouth, NS, B2V 1B8
(902) 462-8500
Emp Here 38
SIC 8211 Elementary and secondary schools

D-U-N-S 20-922-5080   (BR)
LAWTON'S DRUG STORES LIMITED
950 Cole Harbour Rd, Dartmouth, NS, B2V 1E6
(902) 435-5600
Emp Here 29
SIC 5912 Drug stores and proprietary stores

D-U-N-S 20-638-6596   (BR)
PRISZM LP
KFC - DARTMOUTH
960 Cole Harbour Rd, Dartmouth, NS, B2V 1E6

Emp Here 28
SIC 5812 Eating places

Dartmouth, NS B2W
Halifax County

D-U-N-S 24-911-3820   (SL)
2572567 CANADA INC

102 Penhorn Dr, Dartmouth, NS, B2W 1K9
(902) 469-9050
Emp Here 69 *Sales* 35,000,250
SIC 5511 New and used car dealers
Genl Mgr Doug Wilson
Pr Pr Patrick J Priestner
 Charles Milroy
 Daniel E Gibbons

D-U-N-S 20-915-3746 (SL)
ANGUS G FOODS INC
MCDONALD'S RESTAURANT
588 Portland St, Dartmouth, NS, B2W 2M3
(902) 435-3181
Emp Here 85 *Sales* 3,031,879
SIC 5812 Eating places

D-U-N-S 24-473-0438 (HQ)
ATLANTIC FABRICS LIMITED
(*Suby of* Atlantic Fabrics Limited)
114 Woodlawn Rd, Dartmouth, NS, B2W 2S7
(902) 434-1440
Emp Here 20 *Emp Total* 70
Sales 3,031,879
SIC 5949 Sewing, needlework, and piece
goods

D-U-N-S 25-542-6140 (BR)
CHARLTOM RESTAURANTS LIMITED
WENDY'S
(*Suby of* Charltom Restaurants Limited)
4 Forest Hills Pky, Dartmouth, NS, B2W 5G7

Emp Here 32
SIC 5812 Eating places

D-U-N-S 25-982-9430 (BR)
CONSOLIDATED RESTAURANTS LIMITED
STEAK & STEIN RESTAURANT
620 Portland St, Dartmouth, NS, B2W 2M3

Emp Here 75
SIC 5812 Eating places

D-U-N-S 20-349-3270 (BR)
DOWN EAST HOSPITALITY INCORPO-RATED
TIM HORTONS
(*Suby of* Breed, S Holdings Ltd)
577 Main St, Dartmouth, NS, B2W 4K1
(902) 434-8282
Emp Here 30
SIC 5461 Retail bakeries

D-U-N-S 25-241-2614 (BR)
HALIFAX REGIONAL SCHOOL BOARD
BROOKHOUSE ELEMENTARY SCHOOL
(*Suby of* Halifax Regional School Board)
15 Christopher Ave, Dartmouth, NS, B2W 3G2
(902) 435-8318
Emp Here 50
SIC 8211 Elementary and secondary schools

D-U-N-S 20-710-3073 (BR)
HALIFAX REGIONAL SCHOOL BOARD
PORTLAND ELEMENTARY SCHOOL
45 Portland Hills Dr, Dartmouth, NS, B2W 6L5
(902) 433-7100
Emp Here 35
SIC 8211 Elementary and secondary schools

D-U-N-S 20-710-2877 (BR)
HALIFAX REGIONAL SCHOOL BOARD
ERIC GRAVES MEMORIAL JUNIOR HIGH SCHOOL
70 Dorothea Dr, Dartmouth, NS, B2W 4M3
(902) 435-8325
Emp Here 25
SIC 8211 Elementary and secondary schools

D-U-N-S 25-241-4735 (BR)
HALIFAX REGIONAL SCHOOL BOARD
SOUTH WOODSIDE SCHOOL
(*Suby of* Halifax Regional School Board)
5 Everette St, Dartmouth, NS, B2W 1G2
(902) 464-2090
Emp Here 24
SIC 8211 Elementary and secondary schools

D-U-N-S 20-835-3297 (BR)
HALIFAX REGIONAL SCHOOL BOARD
BEL AYR ELEMENTARY SCHOOL
4 Bell St, Dartmouth, NS, B2W 2P3
(902) 435-8353
Emp Here 25
SIC 8211 Elementary and secondary schools

D-U-N-S 20-608-2724 (BR)
HALIFAX REGIONAL SCHOOL BOARD
ROBERT KEMP TURNER ELEMENTARY SCHOOL
141 Circassion Dr, Dartmouth, NS, B2W 4N7
(902) 464-5205
Emp Here 50
SIC 8211 Elementary and secondary schools

D-U-N-S 20-304-0840 (BR)
HALIFAX REGIONAL SCHOOL BOARD
SIR ROBERT BORDEN JUNIOR HIGH
16 Evergreen Dr, Dartmouth, NS, B2W 4A7
(902) 464-5140
Emp Here 25
SIC 8211 Elementary and secondary schools

D-U-N-S 25-240-7192 (BR)
HALIFAX REGIONAL SCHOOL BOARD
MOUNT EDWARD ELEMENTARY SCHOOL
(*Suby of* Halifax Regional School Board)
3 Windward Ave, Dartmouth, NS, B2W 2G9
(902) 435-8459
Emp Here 26
SIC 8211 Elementary and secondary schools

D-U-N-S 20-918-5292 (BR)
HALIFAX REGIONAL SCHOOL BOARD
COLE HARBOUR DISTRICT HIGH SCHOOL
2 Chameau Cres, Dartmouth, NS, B2W 4X4
(902) 464-5220
Emp Here 65
SIC 8211 Elementary and secondary schools

D-U-N-S 25-241-2655 (BR)
HALIFAX REGIONAL SCHOOL BOARD
DARTMOUTH REGIONAL SCHOOL
(*Suby of* Halifax Regional School Board)
2 Bell St, Dartmouth, NS, B2W 2P3
(902) 435-8417
Emp Here 32
SIC 8211 Elementary and secondary schools

D-U-N-S 20-710-2844 (BR)
HALIFAX REGIONAL SCHOOL BOARD
AUBURN DRIVE HIGH SCHOOL
300 Auburn Dr, Dartmouth, NS, B2W 6E9
(902) 462-6900
Emp Here 80
SIC 8211 Elementary and secondary schools

D-U-N-S 20-608-2674 (BR)
HALIFAX REGIONAL SCHOOL BOARD
JOSEPH GILES ELEMENTARY SCHOOL
54 Gregory St, Dartmouth, NS, B2W 3M6
(902) 464-5192
Emp Here 40
SIC 8211 Elementary and secondary schools

D-U-N-S 20-710-2919 (BR)
HALIFAX REGIONAL SCHOOL BOARD
PRINCE ANDREW HIGH SCHOOL
31 Woodlawn Rd, Dartmouth, NS, B2W 2R7
(902) 435-8452
Emp Here 70
SIC 8211 Elementary and secondary schools

D-U-N-S 25-241-5096 (BR)
HALIFAX REGIONAL SCHOOL BOARD
ELLENVALE JUNIOR HIGH SCHOOL
(*Suby of* Halifax Regional School Board)
88 Belle Vista Dr, Dartmouth, NS, B2W 2X7
(902) 435-8420
Emp Here 30
SIC 8211 Elementary and secondary schools

D-U-N-S 20-608-2617 (BR)
HALIFAX REGIONAL SCHOOL BOARD
GEORGE BISSETT ELEMENTARY SCHOOL
170 Arklow Dr, Dartmouth, NS, B2W 4R6

(902) 464-5184
Emp Here 25
SIC 8211 Elementary and secondary schools

D-U-N-S 20-234-7527 (HQ)
MAJA HOLDINGS LTD
TIM HORTONS
(*Suby of* Maja Holdings Ltd)
4 Forest Hills Pky Suite 317, Dartmouth, NS,
B2W 5G7
(902) 462-2032
Emp Here 40 *Emp Total* 75
Sales 2,553,625
SIC 5461 Retail bakeries

D-U-N-S 24-677-7788 (BR)
O'REGAN MOTORS LIMITED
O'REGAN'S GREEN LIGHT USED CAR CENTRE
60 Baker Dr Unit B, Dartmouth, NS, B2W 6L4
(902) 466-5775
Emp Here 20
SIC 5521 Used car dealers

D-U-N-S 20-759-3539 (SL)
RENEX INC
RENOVATIONEXPERTS.COM
73 Tacoma Dr Suite 703, Dartmouth, NS, B2W
3Y6

Emp Here 100 *Sales* 3,283,232
SIC 7299 Miscellaneous personal service

D-U-N-S 25-173-6153 (BR)
SOBEYS CAPITAL INCORPORATED
SOBEYS
612 Main St Suite 622, Dartmouth, NS, B2W
5M5
(902) 433-0140
Emp Here 190
SIC 5411 Grocery stores

D-U-N-S 25-362-2492 (BR)
SOBEYS CAPITAL INCORPORATED
4 Forest Hills Pky, Dartmouth, NS, B2W 5G7
(902) 435-3909
Emp Here 80
SIC 5411 Grocery stores

D-U-N-S 25-370-1650 (BR)
STAPLES CANADA INC
STAPLES THE BUSINESS DEPOT
(*Suby of* Staples, Inc.)
114 Woodlawn Rd Suite 257, Dartmouth, NS,
B2W 2S7
(902) 466-1487
Emp Here 35
SIC 5943 Stationery stores

D-U-N-S 24-946-6348 (SL)
STEELE MAZDA
15 Lansing Crt, Dartmouth, NS, B2W 0K3
(902) 462-6600
Emp Here 41 *Sales* 19,317,745
SIC 5511 New and used car dealers
Genl Mgr Keith Mcneil

D-U-N-S 25-294-0671 (BR)
WINNERS MERCHANTS INTERNATIONAL L.P.
WINNERS
(*Suby of* The TJX Companies Inc)
650 Portland St, Dartmouth, NS, B2W 6A3
(902) 434-2121
Emp Here 30
SIC 5651 Family clothing stores

Dartmouth, NS B2X
Halifax County

D-U-N-S 20-572-2379 (BR)
BANK OF NOVA SCOTIA, THE
SCOTIA BANK
21 Micmac Dr, Dartmouth, NS, B2X 2H4
(902) 420-4921
Emp Here 20

SIC 6021 National commercial banks

D-U-N-S 20-654-8427 (BR)
CONSEIL SCOLAIRE ACADIEN PROVINCIAL
ECOLE BOIS-JOLI
211 Avenue Du Portage, Dartmouth, NS, B2X
3T4
(902) 433-7045
Emp Here 40
SIC 8211 Elementary and secondary schools

D-U-N-S 20-710-3222 (BR)
CONSEIL SCOLAIRE ACADIEN PROVINCIAL
ECOLE DU CARREFOUR
201 Avenue Du Portage, Dartmouth, NS, B2X
3T4
(902) 433-7000
Emp Here 50
SIC 8211 Elementary and secondary schools

D-U-N-S 25-240-7150 (BR)
HALIFAX REGIONAL SCHOOL BOARD
MICHAEL WALLACE ELEMENTARY SCHOOL
(*Suby of* Halifax Regional School Board)
24 Andover St, Dartmouth, NS, B2X 2L9
(902) 435-8357
Emp Here 35
SIC 8211 Elementary and secondary schools

D-U-N-S 20-710-2901 (BR)
HALIFAX REGIONAL SCHOOL BOARD
IAN FORSYTH ELEMENTARY SCHOOL
22 Glencoe Dr, Dartmouth, NS, B2X 1J1
(902) 435-8435
Emp Here 40
SIC 8211 Elementary and secondary schools

D-U-N-S 25-241-5138 (BR)
HALIFAX REGIONAL SCHOOL BOARD
CALEDONIA JUNIOR HIGH SCHOOL
(*Suby of* Halifax Regional School Board)
38 Caledonia Rd, Dartmouth, NS, B2X 1K8
(902) 435-8413
Emp Here 25
SIC 8211 Elementary and secondary schools

D-U-N-S 20-605-8807 (BR)
PERRY RAND TRANSPORTATION GROUP LIMITED
BUS BOYS COMPANY
198 Waverley Rd, Dartmouth, NS, B2X 2C1
(902) 375-3222
Emp Here 30
SIC 4142 Bus charter service, except local

D-U-N-S 25-606-6754 (BR)
PERRY RAND TRANSPORTATION GROUP LIMITED
ZINCK BUS COMPANY
198 Waverley Rd, Dartmouth, NS, B2X 2C1

Emp Here 50
SIC 4173 Bus terminal and service facilities

D-U-N-S 25-010-5285 (BR)
SECURITAS CANADA LIMITED
175 Main St Suite 201, Dartmouth, NS, B2X
1S1
(902) 434-2442
Emp Here 300
SIC 5999 Miscellaneous retail stores, nec

D-U-N-S 25-298-1121 (BR)
SOBEYS CAPITAL INCORPORATED
SOBEYS #772
100 Main St Suite 250, Dartmouth, NS, B2X
1R5
(902) 434-6696
Emp Here 170
SIC 5411 Grocery stores

D-U-N-S 20-860-4244 (BR)
WINNERS MERCHANTS INTERNATIONAL L.P.
WINNERS
(*Suby of* The TJX Companies Inc)

---

21 Micmac Dr, Dartmouth, NS, B2X 2H4
(902) 461-9177
Emp Here 25
SIC 5651 Family clothing stores

D-U-N-S 20-606-4227   (BR)
YM INC. (SALES)
WEST 49
21 Micmac Dr, Dartmouth, NS, B2X 2H4
(902) 463-2215
Emp Here 30
SIC 5621 Women's clothing stores

Dartmouth, NS B2Y
Halifax County

D-U-N-S 24-365-2927   (SL)
3086011 NOVA SCOTIA LIMITED
GREAT CANADIAN DOLLAR STORE, THE
313 Prince Albert Rd, Dartmouth, NS, B2Y
1N3
(902) 469-5850
Emp Here 50   *Sales* 6,594,250
SIC 5999 Miscellaneous retail stores, nec
Michael Melenchuk

D-U-N-S 24-337-2310   (BR)
3094176 NOVA SCOTIA LIMITED
PIZZA HUT
510 Portland St, Dartmouth, NS, B2Y 4W7
(902) 462-3344
Emp Here 40
SIC 5812 Eating places

D-U-N-S 25-151-9831   (SL)
BANC METAL INDUSTRIES LIMITED
BMI
277 Pleasant St Unit 508, Dartmouth, NS, B2Y
4B7
(902) 461-6450
Emp Here 220   *Sales* 39,200,886
SIC 3441 Fabricated structural Metal
Pr Besim Halef

D-U-N-S 24-117-0252   (BR)
BANK OF NOVA SCOTIA, THE
SCOTIABANK
93 Portland St Suite 91, Dartmouth, NS, B2Y
1H5
(902) 420-4940
Emp Here 20
SIC 6021 National commercial banks

D-U-N-S 20-727-2444   (HQ)
CHARM JEWELRY LIMITED
CHARM DIAMOND CENTRES
(*Suby of* Charm Jewelry Limited)
140 Portland St, Dartmouth, NS, B2Y 1J1
(902) 463-7177
Emp Here 50   *Emp Total* 700
Sales 38,304,368
SIC 5944 Jewelry stores
Dir Richard Calder
Pr Pr Troy Calder
Sharon Calder

D-U-N-S 20-573-2345   (BR)
COMPAGNIE DES CHEMINS DE FER NATIONAUX DU CANADA
COMPAGNIE DES CHEMINS DE FER NATIONAUX DU CANADA
12 Alderney Dr, Dartmouth, NS, B2Y 2N3
(902) 428-5475
Emp Here 20
SIC 4011 Railroads, line-haul operating

D-U-N-S 24-129-0543   (SL)
CONRAD'S TRANSPORT LIMITED
4 Connor St, Dartmouth, NS, B2Y 1V6
(902) 434-5040
Emp Here 50   *Sales* 3,939,878
SIC 4212 Local trucking, without storage

D-U-N-S 25-590-5960   (BR)
CROTHALL SERVICES CANADA INC

CENTRAL LAUNDRY & LINEN SERVICES
(*Suby of* Crothall Services Canada Inc)
300 Pleasant St Suite 10, Dartmouth, NS, B2Y
3S3
(902) 464-3115
Emp Here 120
SIC 7219 Laundry and garment services, nec

D-U-N-S 25-730-5763   (SL)
DIGITAL IMAGE F/X INCORPORATED
DIFX
1 Research Dr, Dartmouth, NS, B2Y 4M9
(902) 461-4883
Emp Here 43   *Sales* 5,579,750
SIC 7371 Custom computer programming services
Pr Pr Wayne Bell

D-U-N-S 24-994-9033   (HQ)
DOWN EAST HOSPITALITY INCORPORATED
TIM HORTONS
(*Suby of* Breed, S Holdings Ltd)
335 Prince Albert Rd Suite 1, Dartmouth, NS,
B2Y 1N7
(902) 434-7500
Emp Here 100   *Emp Total* 121
Sales 3,648,035
SIC 5812 Eating places

D-U-N-S 20-205-6441   (BR)
FLYNN CANADA LTD
25 Neptune Cres, Dartmouth, NS, B2Y 4P9
(902) 468-8313
Emp Here 30
SIC 1761 Roofing, siding, and sheetMetal
work

D-U-N-S 25-867-4357   (BR)
HALIFAX REGIONAL MUNICIPALITY
ALDERNEY GATE PUBLIC LIBRARY
60 Alderney Dr, Dartmouth, NS, B2Y 4P8
(902) 490-5745
Emp Here 20
SIC 8231 Libraries

D-U-N-S 25-241-2697   (BR)
HALIFAX REGIONAL SCHOOL BOARD
ALDERNEY SCHOOL
(*Suby of* Halifax Regional School Board)
2 Penhorn Dr, Dartmouth, NS, B2Y 3K1
(902) 464-2040
Emp Here 22
SIC 8211 Elementary and secondary schools

D-U-N-S 25-241-5054   (BR)
HALIFAX REGIONAL SCHOOL BOARD
HAWTHORN ELEMENTARY SCHOOL
(*Suby of* Halifax Regional School Board)
10 Hawthorne St, Dartmouth, NS, B2Y 2Y3
(902) 464-2048
Emp Here 40
SIC 8211 Elementary and secondary schools

D-U-N-S 25-241-4776   (BR)
HALIFAX REGIONAL SCHOOL BOARD
SOUTHDALE NORTH WOODSIDE SCHOOL
(*Suby of* Halifax Regional School Board)
36 Hastings Dr, Dartmouth, NS, B2Y 2C5
(902) 464-2081
Emp Here 37
SIC 8211 Elementary and secondary schools

D-U-N-S 25-241-4859   (BR)
HALIFAX REGIONAL SCHOOL BOARD
PRINCE ARTHUR JUNIOR HIGH SCHOOL
(*Suby of* Halifax Regional School Board)
85 Prince Arthur Ave, Dartmouth, NS, B2Y
0B3
(902) 464-2435
Emp Here 45
SIC 8211 Elementary and secondary schools

D-U-N-S 20-852-7353   (BR)
HALIFAX REGIONAL WATER COMMISSION
HALIFAX WATER
35 Neptune Cres, Dartmouth, NS, B2Y 4W4

---

(902) 490-4965
Emp Here 20
SIC 4941 Water supply

D-U-N-S 20-907-3725   (HQ)
HERITAGE CREDIT UNION LIMITED
(*Suby of* Heritage Credit Union Limited)
155 Ochterloney St Suite 1, Dartmouth, NS,
B2Y 1C9
(902) 463-4220
Emp Here 35   *Emp Total* 40
Sales 7,350,166
SIC 6062 State credit unions
Pr Pr Dave Gray
Dir John Macinnes
Dir Bill Malcolm
Dir Bill Mills
Dir Cathy Mills
Bob Kimball
Terry Adams
Dir Larry Connolly
Dir Weldon Dignan
Dir Errol Hughson

D-U-N-S 24-789-6574   (BR)
HERSHEY CANADA INC
MOIRS DIV OF
(*Suby of* Hershey Company)
375 Pleasant St, Dartmouth, NS, B2Y 4N4

Emp Here 700
SIC 2064 Candy and other confectionery
products

D-U-N-S 20-207-3651   (BR)
J. D. IRVING, LIMITED
IRVING EQUIPMENT
(*Suby of* J. D. Irving, Limited)
43 Atlantic St, Dartmouth, NS, B2Y 4P4
(902) 429-7000
Emp Here 25
SIC 7353 Heavy construction equipment
rental

D-U-N-S 20-543-2367   (HQ)
KARLENE DEVELOPMENTS LIMITED
QUALITY INN SYDNEY
(*Suby of* Karlene Developments Limited)
313 Prince Albert Rd, Dartmouth, NS, B2Y
1N3
(902) 469-5850
Emp Here 30   *Emp Total* 75
Sales 3,283,232
SIC 7011 Hotels and motels

D-U-N-S 25-537-0710   (HQ)
MARITIME PRESSUREWORKS LIMITED
(*Suby of* Maritime Pressureworks Limited)
41 Estates Rd, Dartmouth, NS, B2Y 4K3
(902) 468-8461
Emp Here 30   *Emp Total* 60
Sales 4,711,645
SIC 7699 Repair services, nec

D-U-N-S 20-794-3148   (BR)
SAFWAY SERVICES CANADA, ULC
(*Suby of* Safway Group Holding LLC)
15 Neptune Cres, Dartmouth, NS, B2Y 4P9
(902) 468-9235
Emp Here 30
SIC 1799 Special trade contractors, nec

D-U-N-S 20-208-6323   (SL)
SAGITTARIUS INVESTIGATIONS & SECURITY CONSULTANTS INCORPORATED
12 Queen St Suite 101, Dartmouth, NS, B2Y
1E7

Emp Here 50   *Sales* 1,532,175
SIC 7381 Detective and armored car services

D-U-N-S 24-473-3317   (BR)
SEARS CANADA INC
535 Portland St, Dartmouth, NS, B2Y 4B1
(902) 463-8660
Emp Here 160
SIC 7991 Physical fitness facilities

D-U-N-S 24-341-3002   (SL)

SMITHERS MARINE SERVICES LIMITED
(*Suby of* Smithers International Limited)
1 Canal St, Dartmouth, NS, B2Y 2W1
(902) 465-3400
Emp Here 20   *Sales* 1,313,293
SIC 4499 Water transportation services,

D-U-N-S 25-298-0966   (BR)
SOBEYS CAPITAL INCORPORATED
SOBEYS #120
211 Pleasant St, Dartmouth, NS, B2Y 3R5
(902) 466-2776
Emp Here 40
SIC 5411 Grocery stores

D-U-N-S 20-905-7926   (BR)
SOBEYS CAPITAL INCORPORATED
SOBEYS #776
551 Portland St, Dartmouth, NS, B2Y 4B1
(902) 469-8396
Emp Here 195
SIC 5411 Grocery stores

D-U-N-S 20-298-4600   (BR)
STERICYCLE COMMUNICATION SOLUTIONS, ULC
(*Suby of* Stericycle Communication Solutions,
ULC)
33 Alderney Dr Suite 240, Dartmouth, NS,
B2Y 2N4
(902) 464-6666
Emp Here 70
SIC 4899 Communication services, nec

D-U-N-S 20-002-8111   (SL)
SYDAX DEVELOPMENTS LIMITED
SMITTY'S
300 Prince Albert Rd, Dartmouth, NS, B2Y
4J2
(902) 468-8817
Emp Here 117   *Sales* 3,502,114
SIC 5812 Eating places

D-U-N-S 24-804-0297   (BR)
TOROMONT INDUSTRIES LTD
CIMCO REFRIGERATION
19 Acadia St, Dartmouth, NS, B2Y 2N1
(902) 465-4836
Emp Here 25
SIC 5078 Refrigeration equipment and supplies

D-U-N-S 20-552-1482   (BR)
ULTRA ELECTRONICS MARITIME SYSTEMS INC
40 Atlantic St, Dartmouth, NS, B2Y 4N2
(902) 466-7491
Emp Here 125
SIC 3679 Electronic components, nec

D-U-N-S 25-627-3780   (BR)
VALUE VILLAGE STORES, INC
SAVERS
(*Suby of* Savers, Inc.)
275 Pleasant St, Dartmouth, NS, B2Y 3S2
(902) 463-4054
Emp Here 30
SIC 5399 Miscellaneous general merchandise

Dartmouth, NS B3A
Halifax County

D-U-N-S 20-030-7221   (SL)
ANDRES WINES ATLANTIC LTD
99 Wyse Rd Suite 350, Dartmouth, NS, B3A
4S5
(902) 461-8173
Emp Here 40   *Sales* 1,167,371
SIC 2084 Wines, brandy, and brandy spirits

D-U-N-S 20-021-1196   (BR)
AVIVA CANADA INC
99 Wyse Rd Suite 1600, Dartmouth, NS, B3A
4S5
(902) 460-3100
Emp Here 146

SIC 6411 Insurance agents, brokers, and service

D-U-N-S 24-419-6098   (BR)
CANADIAN TIRE CORPORATION, LIMITED
PARTSOURCE
201 Wyse Rd, Dartmouth, NS, B3A 1N1
(902) 463-0460
Emp Here 20
SIC 5531 Auto and home supply stores

D-U-N-S 25-627-1735   (BR)
DAA GROUP LIMITED
TIM HORTONS
(*Suby of* DAA Group Limited)
180 Wyse Rd, Dartmouth, NS, B3A 1M6
(902) 466-4400
Emp Here 24
SIC 5812 Eating places

D-U-N-S 20-780-4324   (BR)
FOOT LOCKER CANADA CO
FOOT LOCKER CANADA CO.
2nd Fl, Dartmouth, NS, B3A 4K7
(902) 461-1652
Emp Here 20
SIC 5661 Shoe stores

D-U-N-S 25-673-8246   (BR)
FRIENDSHIP INNS LIMITED
COASTAL INN CONCORDE
(*Suby of* Friendship Inns Limited)
379 Windmill Rd, Dartmouth, NS, B3A 1J6
(902) 465-7777
Emp Here 20
SIC 7011 Hotels and motels

D-U-N-S 25-689-7208   (BR)
GAP (CANADA) INC
GAP
(*Suby of* The Gap Inc)
21 Micmac Blvd Suite 300, Dartmouth, NS, B3A 4K7

Emp Here 45
SIC 5651 Family clothing stores

D-U-N-S 20-713-9986   (SL)
HALIFAX DARTMOUTH ISLAMIC SCHOOL
42 Leaman Dr, Dartmouth, NS, B3A 2K9
(902) 469-9490
Emp Here 50   *Sales* 3,356,192
SIC 8211 Elementary and secondary schools

D-U-N-S 25-241-2531   (BR)
HALIFAX REGIONAL SCHOOL BOARD
DARTMOUTH HIGH SCHOOL
(*Suby of* Halifax Regional School Board)
95 Victoria Rd, Dartmouth, NS, B3A 1V2
(902) 464-2457
Emp Here 70
SIC 8211 Elementary and secondary schools

D-U-N-S 25-240-7358   (BR)
HALIFAX REGIONAL SCHOOL BOARD
SHANNON PARK ELEMENTARY SCHOOL
(*Suby of* Halifax Regional School Board)
75 Iroquois Dr, Dartmouth, NS, B3A 4M5
(902) 464-2084
Emp Here 62
SIC 8211 Elementary and secondary schools

D-U-N-S 20-710-2893   (BR)
HALIFAX REGIONAL SCHOOL BOARD
HARBOR VIEW ELEMENTARY
25 Alfred St, Dartmouth, NS, B3A 4E8
(902) 464-2051
Emp Here 50
SIC 8211 Elementary and secondary schools

D-U-N-S 25-241-2572   (BR)
HALIFAX REGIONAL SCHOOL BOARD
CRICHTON PARK ELEMENTARY SCHOOL
(*Suby of* Halifax Regional School Board)
49 Lyngby Ave, Dartmouth, NS, B3A 3V1
(902) 464-2503
Emp Here 30
SIC 8211 Elementary and secondary schools

D-U-N-S 25-241-5013   (BR)
HALIFAX REGIONAL SCHOOL BOARD
JOHN MACNEIL ELEMENTARY SCHOOL
(*Suby of* Halifax Regional School Board)
62 Leaman Dr, Dartmouth, NS, B3A 2K9
(902) 464-2488
Emp Here 30
SIC 8211 Elementary and secondary schools

D-U-N-S 25-241-5179   (BR)
HALIFAX REGIONAL SCHOOL BOARD
BICENTENNIAL SCHOOL
(*Suby of* Halifax Regional School Board)
85 Victoria Rd, Dartmouth, NS, B3A 1T9
(902) 464-3640
Emp Here 50
SIC 8211 Elementary and secondary schools

D-U-N-S 25-241-2457   (BR)
HALIFAX REGIONAL SCHOOL BOARD
JOHN MARTIN JUNIOR HIGH SCHOOL
(*Suby of* Halifax Regional School Board)
7 Brule St, Dartmouth, NS, B3A 4G2
(902) 464-2408
Emp Here 24
SIC 8211 Elementary and secondary schools

D-U-N-S 25-588-3308   (BR)
HERSHEY CANADA INC
(*Suby of* Hershey Company)
99 Wyse Rd, Dartmouth, NS, B3A 0C1

Emp Here 26
SIC 5441 Candy, nut, and confectionery stores

D-U-N-S 25-301-2439   (BR)
HUDSON'S BAY COMPANY
BAY, THE
21 Micmac Blvd, Dartmouth, NS, B3A 4K7
(902) 469-6680
Emp Here 70
SIC 5311 Department stores

D-U-N-S 25-571-9205   (BR)
INNVEST PROPERTIES CORP
COMFORT INN
(*Suby of* Innvest Properties Corp)
456 Windmill Rd, Dartmouth, NS, B3A 1J7
(902) 463-9900
Emp Here 25
SIC 7011 Hotels and motels

D-U-N-S 25-984-8919   (BR)
J. D. IRVING, LIMITED
KENT BUILDING SUPPLIES
(*Suby of* J. D. Irving, Limited)
35 Micmac Blvd, Dartmouth, NS, B3A 4Y8
(902) 469-2000
Emp Here 120
SIC 5211 Lumber and other building materials

D-U-N-S 25-580-5475   (BR)
KILLAM PROPERTIES INC
171 Victoria Rd Unit 6, Dartmouth, NS, B3A 1W1
(902) 464-3786
Emp Here 27
SIC 6513 Apartment building operators

D-U-N-S 25-299-4082   (BR)
LAWTON'S DRUG STORES LIMITED
LAWTON'S DRUGS 123
6 Primrose St Suite 123, Dartmouth, NS, B3A 4C5
(902) 463-2030
Emp Here 20
SIC 5912 Drug stores and proprietary stores

D-U-N-S 25-358-3777   (SL)
MANGA HOTELS (DARTMOUTH) INC
HOLIDAY INN HARBOURVIEW
(*Suby of* Manga Hotels Inc)
101 Wyse Rd, Dartmouth, NS, B3A 1L9
(902) 463-1100
Emp Here 100   *Sales* 4,377,642
SIC 7011 Hotels and motels

D-U-N-S 24-116-3356   (BR)
METROPOLITAIN REGIONAL HOUSING AUTHORITY
15 Green Rd, Dartmouth, NS, B3A 4Y6
(902) 420-2163
Emp Here 20
SIC 6531 Real estate agents and managers

D-U-N-S 25-298-9322   (BR)
NOVA SCOTIA LIQUOR CORPORATION
NSLC
210 Wyse Rd, Dartmouth, NS, B3A 1M9
(902) 466-2240
Emp Here 20
SIC 5921 Liquor stores

D-U-N-S 24-679-3017   (BR)
ROLLS-ROYCE CANADA LIMITEE
461 Windmill Rd, Dartmouth, NS, B3A 1J9
(902) 468-2928
Emp Here 50
SIC 8711 Engineering services

D-U-N-S 25-298-1048   (BR)
SOBEYS CAPITAL INCORPORATED
6 Primrose St, Dartmouth, NS, B3A 4C5
(902) 463-2910
Emp Here 100
SIC 5411 Grocery stores

D-U-N-S 20-914-6146   (BR)
TECSULT EDUPLUS INC
99 Wyse Rd Suite 1100, Dartmouth, NS, B3A 4S5
(902) 461-6600
Emp Here 50
SIC 8299 Schools and educational services, nec

D-U-N-S 24-338-9889   (BR)
U-HAUL CO. (CANADA) LTD
(*Suby of* Amerco)
460 Windmill Rd, Dartmouth, NS, B3A 1J7
(902) 469-4487
Emp Here 30
SIC 7519 Utility trailer rental

D-U-N-S 24-223-2325   (BR)
WENDY'S RESTAURANTS OF CANADA INC
(*Suby of* The Wendy's Company)
118 Wyse Rd, Dartmouth, NS, B3A 1N7
(902) 463-4013
Emp Here 30
SIC 5812 Eating places

D-U-N-S 25-105-4847   (BR)
WESTMONT HOSPITALITY MANAGEMENT LIMITED
HOLIDAY INN
(*Suby of* Westmont Hospitality Management Limited)
101 Wyse Rd, Dartmouth, NS, B3A 1L9
(902) 463-1100
Emp Here 100
SIC 7011 Hotels and motels

Dartmouth, NS B3B
Halifax County

D-U-N-S 20-011-0117   (SL)
3043177 NOVA SCOTIA LIMITED
FRONTIER TECHNOLOGIES
61 Raddall Ave, Dartmouth, NS, B3B 1T4
(902) 446-3940
Emp Here 100   *Sales* 5,472,053
SIC 7374 Data processing and preparation
Pr Pr Raymond Kerr
Rodney Kerr

D-U-N-S 24-795-9534   (BR)
918962 ONTARIO INC
JACK ASTOR'S
(*Suby of* 918962 Ontario Inc)
107 Shubie Dr, Dartmouth, NS, B3B 0C3

(902) 468-6080
Emp Here 70
SIC 5812 Eating places

D-U-N-S 20-108-9989   (BR)
ADP CANADA CO
ADP DEALER SERVICES
(*Suby of* Automatic Data Processing, Inc.)
130 Eileen Stubbs Ave Unit 22, Dartmouth, NS, B3B 2C4
(902) 491-5000
Emp Here 289
SIC 8721 Accounting, auditing, and bookkeeping

D-U-N-S 24-322-4180   (BR)
AGAT LABORATORIES LTD
AGAT
11 Morris Dr Suite 122, Dartmouth, NS, B3B 1M2
(902) 468-8718
Emp Here 25
SIC 8731 Commercial physical research

D-U-N-S 25-362-5719   (BR)
AMEC FOSTER WHEELER AMERICAS LIMITED
130 Eileen Stubbs Ave Suite 201, Dartmouth, NS, B3B 2C4
(902) 420-8900
Emp Here 55
SIC 8711 Engineering services

D-U-N-S 20-605-7007   (BR)
AMEC FOSTER WHEELER AMERICAS LIMITED
AMEC EARTH & ENVIRONMENTAL A DIVISION OF
32 Troop Ave Unit 301, Dartmouth, NS, B3B 1Z1
(902) 468-2848
Emp Here 40
SIC 8711 Engineering services

D-U-N-S 20-731-9612   (BR)
ACOSTA CANADA CORPORATION
ACOSTA CANADA
(*Suby of* Acosta Inc.)
67 Wright Ave, Dartmouth, NS, B3B 1H2
(902) 468-2007
Emp Here 55
SIC 5141 Groceries, general line

D-U-N-S 25-382-5392   (BR)
ADVANTAGE PERSONNEL LTD
75 Akerley Blvd Unit S, Dartmouth, NS, B3B 1R7
(902) 468-5624
Emp Here 125
SIC 7361 Employment agencies

D-U-N-S 20-014-5162   (BR)
AIR LIQUIDE CANADA INC
AIR LIQUIDE
180 Akerley Blvd Suite 100, Dartmouth, NS, B3B 2B7
(902) 468-5152
Emp Here 30
SIC 2813 Industrial gases

D-U-N-S 25-961-5276   (BR)
ALSCOTT AIR SYSTEMS LIMITED
(*Suby of* Alscott Air Systems Limited)
120 Joseph Zatzman Dr, Dartmouth, NS, B3B 1M4
(902) 468-7080
Emp Here 20
SIC 1711 Plumbing, heating, air-conditioning

D-U-N-S 20-009-6431   (SL)
ALTIMAX COURIER (2006) LIMITED
132 Trider Cres, Dartmouth, NS, B3B 1R6
(902) 460-6006
Emp Here 58   *Sales* 2,991,389
SIC 7389 Business services, nec

D-U-N-S 24-831-5228   (BR)
ALUMA SYSTEMS INC
(*Suby of* Clayton, Dubilier & Rice, Inc.)

40 Simmonds Dr, Dartmouth, NS, B3B 1R3
(902) 468-9533
Emp Here 50
SIC 5082 Construction and mining machinery

D-U-N-S 25-562-1765   (BR)
ALWEATHER WINDOWS & DOORS LIMITED
27 Troop Ave, Dartmouth, NS, B3B 2A7
(902) 468-2605
Emp Here 38
SIC 5211 Lumber and other building materials

D-U-N-S 25-993-4730   (BR)
AMITY GOODWILL INDUSTRIES
GOODWILL, THE AMITY GROUP
202 Brownlow Ave Unit 8, Dartmouth, NS, B3B 1T5
(902) 700-9194
Emp Here 20
SIC 8699 Membership organizations, nec

D-U-N-S 25-401-6835   (BR)
ARMOUR TRANSPORT INC
ARMOUR TRANSPORTATION SYSTEMS
80 Guildford Ave, Dartmouth, NS, B3B 0G3
(902) 481-7161
Emp Here 200
SIC 4213 Trucking, except local

D-U-N-S 24-669-6025   (HQ)
ATLANTIC BUSINESS INTERIORS LIMITED
(*Suby of* TAR Investments Limited)
30 Troop Ave, Dartmouth, NS, B3B 1Z1
(902) 468-3200
Emp Here 45   *Emp Total* 45
Sales 17,437,607
SIC 5021 Furniture
Pr Pr Thomas Rose
Goerge Mitchell
Garry Stewart

D-U-N-S 20-297-2084   (BR)
ATLANTIC LOTTERY CORPORATION INC, THE
201 Brownlow Ave Suite 33, Dartmouth, NS, B3B 1W2
(902) 481-8300
Emp Here 25
SIC 7999 Amusement and recreation, nec

D-U-N-S 20-631-6622   (HQ)
ATLANTIC TRACTORS & EQUIPMENT LIMITED
ATLANTIC CAT
175 Akerley Blvd, Dartmouth, NS, B3B 3Z6
(902) 468-0581
Emp Here 170   *Emp Total* 2,075
Sales 56,544,543
SIC 5082 Construction and mining machinery
James W. Hewitt
Pr Pr Andy Hunt

D-U-N-S 25-365-4834   (HQ)
BW FOUNDERS HOLDCO LTD
(*Suby of* BW Founders Holdco Ltd)
30 Oland Crt, Dartmouth, NS, B3B 1V2
(902) 481-0515
Emp Here 35   *Emp Total* 115
Sales 47,627,520
SIC 5172 Petroleum products, nec
Pr Pr William Sanford
Dir Karen Putnam
Ch Bd Allan Bezanson

D-U-N-S 24-317-5002   (BR)
BAKER HUGHES CANADA COMPANY
(*Suby of* Baker Hughes, A GE Company)
141b Joseph Zatzman Dr, Dartmouth, NS, B3B 1M7

Emp Here 20
SIC 5084 Industrial machinery and equipment

D-U-N-S 24-363-5567   (BR)
BEST BUY CANADA LTD
BEST BUY
(*Suby of* Best Buy Co., Inc.)

119 Gale Terr, Dartmouth, NS, B3B 0C4
(902) 468-0075
Emp Here 130
SIC 5731 Radio, television, and electronic stores

D-U-N-S 24-186-1574   (BR)
BLACK & MCDONALD LIMITED
60 Cutler Ave, Dartmouth, NS, B3B 0J6
(902) 468-3101
Emp Here 250
SIC 1711 Plumbing, heating, air-conditioning

D-U-N-S 24-371-1566   (HQ)
BLUE WATER (QUEBEC) LIMITED
BLUE WATER AGENCIES
40 Topple Dr, Dartmouth, NS, B3B 1L6
(902) 468-4900
Emp Here 47   *Emp Total* 140
Sales 18,386,096
SIC 5172 Petroleum products, nec
Pr Pr Patrick Wilson
VP David Babin

D-U-N-S 24-393-5389   (HQ)
BLUEWAVE ENERGY LTD
30 Oland Crt, Dartmouth, NS, B3B 1V2
(902) 481-0515
Emp Here 65   *Emp Total* 2,300
Sales 74,870,100
SIC 5541 Gasoline service stations
Shaun Peesker

D-U-N-S 24-654-7439   (BR)
BLUEWAVE ENERGY LTD
201 Brownlow Ave Unit 15, Dartmouth, NS, B3B 1W2
(902) 468-2244
Emp Here 25
SIC 5541 Gasoline service stations

D-U-N-S 20-026-5379   (BR)
BRINK'S CANADA LIMITED
(*Suby of* The Brink's Company)
19 Ilsley Ave, Dartmouth, NS, B3B 1L5
(902) 468-7124
Emp Here 90
SIC 7381 Detective and armored car services

D-U-N-S 24-738-8747   (BR)
BROOKFIELD FOODS LIMITED
SCOTSBURN DAIRY GROUP
1 Wright Ave, Dartmouth, NS, B3B 1G5
(902) 468-7417
Emp Here 50
SIC 5142 Packaged frozen goods

D-U-N-S 20-333-7605   (SL)
BROOKFIELD NOVA COLD LTD
NOVA COLD STORAGE
635 Av Wilkinson, Dartmouth, NS, B3B 0H4
(902) 468-1328
Emp Here 40   *Sales* 3,793,956
SIC 4222 Refrigerated warehousing and storage

D-U-N-S 24-364-4338   (BR)
C.D.M.V. INC
340 Wright Ave Unit 5, Dartmouth, NS, B3B 0B3

Emp Here 35
SIC 5047 Medical and hospital equipment

D-U-N-S 24-804-0594   (BR)
CANWEL BUILDING MATERIALS LTD
CANWEL
120 Ilsley Ave, Dartmouth, NS, B3B 1S7
(902) 468-8585
Emp Here 30
SIC 5031 Lumber, plywood, and millwork

D-U-N-S 20-538-8684   (BR)
CANADA POST CORPORATION
DARTMOUTH DELIVERY CENTER
28 Topple Dr, Dartmouth, NS, B3B 1L6
(902) 494-4672
Emp Here 200

SIC 4311 U.s. postal service

D-U-N-S 20-547-3692   (BR)
CANADIAN LINEN AND UNIFORM SERVICE CO
QUEBEC LINGE
(*Suby of* Ameripride Services, Inc.)
41 Thornhill Dr Suite 136, Dartmouth, NS, B3B 1R9
(902) 468-2155
Emp Here 95
SIC 7213 Linen supply

D-U-N-S 25-261-6842   (BR)
CANADIAN RED CROSS SOCIETY, THE
HOME PARTNERS
133 Troop Ave, Dartmouth, NS, B3B 2A7
(902) 496-0103
Emp Here 85
SIC 8361 Residential care

D-U-N-S 25-369-4657   (BR)
CANMARC REIT
11 Akerley Blvd Suite 200, Dartmouth, NS, B3B 0H1

Emp Here 20
SIC 6513 Apartment building operators

D-U-N-S 24-805-1349   (BR)
CANSEL SURVEY EQUIPMENT INC
CANSEL
(*Suby of* Cansel Survey Equipment Inc)
100 Ilsley Ave Suite C & D, Dartmouth, NS, B3B 1L3
(902) 429-5002
Emp Here 24
SIC 5049 Professional equipment, nec

D-U-N-S 20-556-2056   (BR)
CERIDIAN CANADA LTD
238 Brownlow Ave Suite 310, Dartmouth, NS, B3B 1Y2
(902) 442-3200
Emp Here 30
SIC 8721 Accounting, auditing, and bookkeeping

D-U-N-S 24-989-7542   (BR)
CO-OPERATORS GENERAL INSURANCE COMPANY
202 Brownlow Ave Suite 302, Dartmouth, NS, B3B 1T5
(902) 468-2789
Emp Here 20
SIC 6411 Insurance agents, brokers, and service

D-U-N-S 20-987-2605   (HQ)
COASTAL DOOR & FRAME INC
DOORTECH, DIV OF
40 Raddall Ave, Dartmouth, NS, B3B 1T2
(902) 468-2333
Emp Here 29   *Emp Total* 300
Sales 7,296,070
SIC 5039 Construction materials, nec
Dir Susan Andrea
Dir Thane Stevens
Scott Stevens
Dir Chris Sangster

D-U-N-S 20-904-4437   (HQ)
COBHAM TRACKING & LOCATING LTD
COBHAM SURVEILLANCE
(*Suby of* COBHAM PLC)
120 Eileen Stubbs Ave Suite 200, Dartmouth, NS, B3B 1Y1
(902) 468-3007
Emp Here 90   *Emp Total* 12,044
Sales 30,838,536
SIC 4899 Communication services, nec
Pr Pr Micheal Morris

D-U-N-S 25-749-4872   (BR)
CORUS MEDIA HOLDINGS INC
SHAW MEDIA INC
14 Akerley Blvd, Dartmouth, NS, B3B 1J3
(902) 481-7400
Emp Here 85

SIC 4833 Television broadcasting stations

D-U-N-S 24-599-1885   (BR)
COSTCO WHOLESALE CANADA LTD
(*Suby of* Costco Wholesale Corporation)
137 Countryview Dr, Dartmouth, NS, B3B 0E7
(902) 481-7635
Emp Here 50
SIC 5099 Durable goods, nec

D-U-N-S 25-138-3084   (BR)
CRANE CANADA CO.
CRANE SUPPLY
(*Suby of* Crane Co.)
58 Wright Ave, Dartmouth, NS, B3B 1H3
(902) 468-1650
Emp Here 25
SIC 4619 Pipelines, nec

D-U-N-S 20-298-9583   (BR)
CRANE CARRIER (CANADA) LIMITED
(*Suby of* Illinois Tool Works Inc.)
656 Windmill Rd, Dartmouth, NS, B3B 1B8
(902) 468-6220
Emp Here 30
SIC 5531 Auto and home supply stores

D-U-N-S 25-999-0505   (SL)
CUMMINS EASTERN MARINE INC
(*Suby of* Cummins Inc.)
50 Simmonds Dr, Dartmouth, NS, B3B 1R3
(902) 468-7938
Emp Here 22   *Sales* 5,024,000
SIC 5088 Transportation equipment and supplies
Div Mgr Steve Macniell
Pr Pr Amy Davis
CFO Leanne Flannery

D-U-N-S 25-358-5897   (BR)
CUMMINS EST DU CANADA SEC
CUMMINS EST DU CANADA SEC
50 Simmonds Dr, Dartmouth, NS, B3B 1R3
(902) 468-7938
Emp Here 25
SIC 5063 Electrical apparatus and equipment

D-U-N-S 20-190-6463   (HQ)
DORA CONSTRUCTION LIMITED
(*Suby of* DORA Construction Limited)
60 Dorey Ave Suite 101, Dartmouth, NS, B3B 0B1
(902) 468-2941
Emp Here 95   *Emp Total* 100
Sales 18,532,018
SIC 1542 Nonresidential construction, nec
Pr Pr John Young
VP VP Donald Macdonald

D-U-N-S 24-877-9548   (BR)
DIRECT ENERGY MARKETING LIMITED
121 Ilsley Ave, Dartmouth, NS, B3B 1S4
(902) 466-6655
Emp Here 20
SIC 1711 Plumbing, heating, air-conditioning

D-U-N-S 20-573-5447   (BR)
EMC EMERGENCY MEDICAL CARE INCORPORATED
EMC WILKINSON FLEET
795 Av Wilkinson, Dartmouth, NS, B3B 0H4
(902) 468-9314
Emp Here 20
SIC 4119 Local passenger transportation, nec

D-U-N-S 24-319-9812   (BR)
EAST COAST INTERNATIONAL TRUCKS INC
1 Morris Dr, Dartmouth, NS, B3B 1K7
(902) 468-7160
Emp Here 26
SIC 5012 Automobiles and other motor vehicles

D-U-N-S 20-023-5377   (BR)
ECONOMICAL MUTUAL INSURANCE COMPANY
238a Brownlow Ave Suite 310, Dartmouth,

NS, B3B 2B4
(902) 835-6214
Emp Here 100
SIC 6331 Fire, marine, and casualty insurance

D-U-N-S 25-628-7947   (BR)
EMCO CORPORATION
SANDALE UTILITY PRODUCTS
111 Wright Ave, Dartmouth, NS, B3B 1K6

Emp Here 101
SIC 5074 Plumbing and heating equipment and supplies (hydronics)

D-U-N-S 24-760-3496   (SL)
ENERCON SERVICES NOVA SCOTIA INC
202 Brownlow Ave Unit D100, Dartmouth, NS, B3B 1T5
(902) 406-4610
Emp Here 40   *Sales* 6,219,371
SIC 3523 Farm machinery and equipment
Genl Mgr Zdena Cerny
  Volker Kendziorra
  Gael Gravenor

D-U-N-S 25-370-0637   (SL)
ENTERPRISE OFFSHORE CREWING LIMITED
11 Morris Dr Suite 206, Dartmouth, NS, B3B 1M2
(902) 468-3116
Emp Here 60   *Sales* 7,134,080
SIC 3731 Shipbuilding and repairing
Pr Pr Shawn Frank
Dir Steinar Engeset

D-U-N-S 24-533-1616   (SL)
ENVIRONCLEAN LIMITED
POWER VAC BELFOR
51 Raddall Ave Unit 15, Dartmouth, NS, B3B 1T6
(902) 860-2425
Emp Here 75   *Sales* 8,559,367
SIC 7349 Building maintenance services, nec
Pr Will Cook
Opers Mgr Ron Rizzo

D-U-N-S 20-184-8418   (BR)
EXCO TECHNOLOGIES LIMITED
NEOCON INT'L A DIVISION OF
35 Akerley Blvd, Dartmouth, NS, B3B 1J7
(902) 468-6663
Emp Here 100
SIC 3089 Plastics products, nec

D-U-N-S 25-007-4093   (BR)
FIDUCIAIRES DU FONDS DE PLACEMENT IMMOBILIER COMINAR, LES
COMINAR REIT
32 Akerley Blvd Suite 103, Dartmouth, NS, B3B 1N1
(902) 469-8151
Emp Here 50
SIC 6799 Investors, nec

D-U-N-S 24-340-3144   (SL)
FOCAL TECHNOLOGIES CORPORATION
MOOG COMPONENTS GROUP
(*Suby of* Moog Inc.)
77 Frazee Ave, Dartmouth, NS, B3B 1Z4
(902) 468-2263
Emp Here 180   *Sales* 14,956,944
SIC 3621 Motors and generators
  John R Scannell
Pr Pr Lawrence J Ball
  Michael Glister
  Timothy P Balkin

D-U-N-S 25-879-2100   (BR)
FUGRO JACQUES GEOSURVEYS INC
131 Ilsley Ave Unit B, Dartmouth, NS, B3B 1T1
(902) 468-1130
Emp Here 25
SIC 4499 Water transportation services,

D-U-N-S 25-627-2329   (BR)
G.N. JOHNSTON EQUIPMENT CO. LTD
15 Garland Ave Suite 3, Dartmouth, NS, B3B

0A6
(902) 468-1457
Emp Here 24
SIC 5084 Industrial machinery and equipment

D-U-N-S 20-955-7490   (SL)
G3 GALVANIZING LIMITED
160 Joseph Zatzman Dr, Dartmouth, NS, B3B 1P1
(902) 468-1040
Emp Here 50   *Sales* 3,502,114
SIC 3479 Metal coating and allied services

D-U-N-S 20-023-3125   (BR)
G4S CASH SOLUTIONS (CANADA) LTD
170 Joseph Zatzman Dr Suite 13, Dartmouth, NS, B3B 1L9
(902) 468-5602
Emp Here 150
SIC 7381 Detective and armored car services

D-U-N-S 20-169-4937   (BR)
GDI SERVICES (CANADA) LP
202 Brownlow Ave, Dartmouth, NS, B3B 1T5
(902) 468-3103
Emp Here 90
SIC 7349 Building maintenance services, nec

D-U-N-S 24-756-0857   (SL)
GATEWAY HOMES INC
1000 Windmill Rd Suite 17, Dartmouth, NS, B3B 1L7
(902) 454-0145
Emp Here 65   *Sales* 8,826,150
SIC 6514 Dwelling operators, except apartments
  Robert Feetham
Treas Barrie Croft
Dir Betty Evens
Dir Diane Trudel
Pr Linda Zambolin

D-U-N-S 24-390-5879   (BR)
GOLF TOWN LIMITED
GOLF TOWN
80 Gale Terr, Dartmouth, NS, B3B 0B7
(902) 481-0479
Emp Here 20
SIC 5941 Sporting goods and bicycle shops

D-U-N-S 24-670-8291   (BR)
GOODFELLOW INC
20 Vidito Dr, Dartmouth, NS, B3B 1P5
(902) 468-2256
Emp Here 28
SIC 5031 Lumber, plywood, and millwork

D-U-N-S 25-513-7903   (BR)
GRAND & TOY LIMITED
(*Suby of* Office Depot, Inc.)
15 Garland Ave Suite 1, Dartmouth, NS, B3B 0A6
(902) 450-1258
Emp Here 22
SIC 5112 Stationery and office supplies

D-U-N-S 25-627-0273   (BR)
GRAYBAR CANADA LIMITED
HARRIS & ROOME SUPPLY
(*Suby of* Graybar Electric Company, Inc.)
260 Brownlow Ave, Dartmouth, NS, B3B 1V9
(902) 468-6665
Emp Here 40
SIC 5063 Electrical apparatus and equipment

D-U-N-S 24-531-0375   (BR)
GRAYBAR ELECTRIC CANADA LIMITED
HARRIS & ROOME SUPPLY
(*Suby of* Graybar Electric Company, Inc.)
260 Brownlow Ave, Dartmouth, NS, B3B 1V9
(902) 468-6665
Emp Here 46
SIC 5063 Electrical apparatus and equipment

D-U-N-S 24-342-2362   (BR)
HGS CANADA INC
OLS
250 Brownlow Ave Suite 11, Dartmouth, NS, B3B 1W9

(902) 481-9475
Emp Here 125
SIC 7389 Business services, nec

D-U-N-S 24-834-0150   (BR)
HALIFAX REGIONAL MUNICIPALITY
METRO TRANSIT
200 Ilsley Ave, Dartmouth, NS, B3B 1V1
(902) 490-6614
Emp Here 576
SIC 4111 Local and suburban transit

D-U-N-S 25-395-3780   (HQ)
HALIFAX REGIONAL SCHOOL BOARD
(*Suby of* Halifax Regional School Board)
33 Spectacle Lake Dr, Dartmouth, NS, B3B 1X7
(902) 464-2000
Emp Here 200   *Emp Total* 9,000
Sales 365,409,362
SIC 8211 Elementary and secondary schools
Ch Bd Dave Wright
V Ch Bd Cindy Littlefair

D-U-N-S 24-625-4085   (BR)
HALIFAX-DARTMOUTH BRIDGE COMMISSION
A MURRAY MACKAY BRIDGE
100 Princess Margaret Blvd, Dartmouth, NS, B3B 1A2
(902) 463-2459
Emp Here 35
SIC 4785 Inspection and fixed facilities

D-U-N-S 24-831-8727   (BR)
HARRIS STEEL ULC
HARRIS REBAR
(*Suby of* Nucor Corporation)
150 Joseph Zatzman Dr, Dartmouth, NS, B3B 1P1
(902) 468-2526
Emp Here 30
SIC 5051 Metals service centers and offices

D-U-N-S 25-628-8036   (BR)
HARVARD RESTAURANTS LTD
WENDY'S RESTAURANT
106 Ilsley Ave Unit 6741, Dartmouth, NS, B3B 1L3

Emp Here 33
SIC 5812 Eating places

D-U-N-S 24-309-3163   (BR)
HERCULES SLR INC
520 Windmill Rd Suite 499, Dartmouth, NS, B3B 1B3
(902) 468-0300
Emp Here 50
SIC 5051 Metals service centers and offices

D-U-N-S 20-004-0694   (BR)
HOME DEPOT OF CANADA INC
HOME DEPOT TOOL RENTAL
(*Suby of* The Home Depot Inc)
40 Finnian Row, Dartmouth, NS, B3B 0B6
(902) 460-4700
Emp Here 100
SIC 5251 Hardware stores

D-U-N-S 20-583-3903   (SL)
IMPERIAL CLEANERS LTD
617 Windmill Rd, Dartmouth, NS, B3B 1B6
(902) 434-9989
Emp Here 50   *Sales* 1,459,214
SIC 7349 Building maintenance services, nec

D-U-N-S 25-503-2138   (BR)
INGENIERIE CARMICHAEL LTEE
CARMICHAEL ENGINEERING
(*Suby of* Gestions Miller Carmichael Inc)
10 Morris Dr Suite 40, Dartmouth, NS, B3B 1K8
(902) 468-9837
Emp Here 26
SIC 1711 Plumbing, heating, air-conditioning

D-U-N-S 25-673-8972   (BR)
INTACT INSURANCE COMPANY

20 Hector Gate Suite 200, Dartmouth, NS, B3B 0K3
(902) 420-1732
Emp Here 170
SIC 6331 Fire, marine, and casualty insurance

D-U-N-S 24-187-9865   (BR)
INTEGRATED DISTRIBUTION SYSTEMS LIMITED PARTNERSHIP
WAJAX EQUIPMENT
151 Thornhill Dr, Dartmouth, NS, B3B 1S2
(902) 468-7352
Emp Here 30
SIC 5084 Industrial machinery and equipment

D-U-N-S 20-321-6536   (BR)
INTEGRATED DISTRIBUTION SYSTEMS LIMITED PARTNERSHIP
WAJAX POWER SYSTEMS
70 Raddall Ave, Dartmouth, NS, B3B 1T2
(902) 468-6200
Emp Here 32
SIC 5084 Industrial machinery and equipment

D-U-N-S 25-315-8034   (BR)
INVESTORS GROUP FINANCIAL SERVICES INC
238 Brownlow Ave Suite 104, Dartmouth, NS, B3B 1Y2
(902) 468-3444
Emp Here 42
SIC 8741 Management services

D-U-N-S 20-027-0171   (HQ)
J.W. LINDSAY ENTERPRISES LIMITED
LINDSAY CONSTRUCTION SERVICES
134 Eileen Stubbs Ave Suite 105, Dartmouth, NS, B3B 0A9
(902) 468-5000
Emp Here 100   *Emp Total* 175
Sales 59,462,971
SIC 1541 Industrial buildings and warehouses
Ch Bd S. Ernest Porter
Pr Pr Cory Bell
  Kirby Putnam
VP VP Benjamin Stokdijk
  Laurence Smith
Dir Devin Hartnell

D-U-N-S 24-449-6725   (HQ)
JAZZ AVIATION LP
AIR CANADA EXPRESS
3 Spectacle Lake Dr Suite 100, Dartmouth, NS, B3B 1W8
(902) 873-5000
Emp Here 650   *Emp Total* 4,442
Sales 837,296,993
SIC 4512 Air transportation, scheduled
Pr Pr Joseph D. Randell
  Gary Osborne
VP Engg Kal Rebin
VP Opers Franco Giampa
  Rick Flynn
  Jolene Mahody

D-U-N-S 24-977-2877   (BR)
K&D PRATT GROUP INC
(*Suby of* Jenniker Holdings Inc)
55 Akerley Blvd, Dartmouth, NS, B3B 1M3
(902) 468-1955
Emp Here 20
SIC 5085 Industrial supplies

D-U-N-S 25-684-1008   (BR)
KONICA MINOLTA BUSINESS SOLUTIONS (CANADA) LTD
KONICA MINOLTA
130 Eileen Stubbs Ave Suite 6, Dartmouth, NS, B3B 2C4
(902) 468-6176
Emp Here 30
SIC 5044 Office equipment

D-U-N-S 20-026-4851   (HQ)
LAWTON'S DRUG STORES LIMITED
236 Brownlow Ave Suite 270, Dartmouth, NS, B3B 1V5

(902) 468-1000
Emp Here 100   *Emp Total* 125,000
Sales 302,581,474
SIC 5912 Drug stores and proprietary stores
Genl Mgr Vivek Sood
Dir Rob Sobey

D-U-N-S 25-674-3188   (BR)
LAWTON'S DRUG STORES LIMITED
LAWTON'S DRUGS WHOLESALE DIV
81 Thornhill Dr, Dartmouth, NS, B3B 1R9
(902) 468-4637
Emp Here 95
SIC 5122 Drugs, proprietaries, and sundries

D-U-N-S 24-831-4098   (BR)
LEON'S FURNITURE LIMITED
LEON'S SUPERSTORE
140 Akerley Blvd, Dartmouth, NS, B3B 2E4
(902) 468-5201
Emp Here 70
SIC 5712 Furniture stores

D-U-N-S 25-701-2992   (BR)
LIFTOW LIMITED
110 Wright Ave, Dartmouth, NS, B3B 1R6
(902) 469-6721
Emp Here 23
SIC 8748 Business consulting, nec

D-U-N-S 24-120-7302   (BR)
LOBLAW COMPANIES LIMITED
800 Windmill Rd, Dartmouth, NS, B3B 1L1
(902) 468-4347
Emp Here 22
SIC 5141 Groceries, general line

D-U-N-S 25-400-9301   (BR)
MACDONALD, DETTWILER AND ASSO-CIATES CORPORATION
1000 Windmill Rd Suite 60, Dartmouth, NS, B3B 1L7
(902) 468-3356
Emp Here 55
SIC 3812 Search and navigation equipment

D-U-N-S 24-419-4333   (BR)
MARK'S WORK WEARHOUSE LTD
WORK WORLD
30 Lamont Terr, Dartmouth, NS, B3B 0B5
(902) 464-1128
Emp Here 24
SIC 5699 Miscellaneous apparel and accessory stores

D-U-N-S 25-285-1118   (BR)
METRIE CANADA LTD
MOULDING & MILLWOR
200 Akerley Blvd, Dartmouth, NS, B3B 1Z9
(902) 468-9292
Emp Here 20
SIC 5031 Lumber, plywood, and millwork

D-U-N-S 25-980-3773   (BR)
MIDLAND TRANSPORT LIMITED
MIDLAND COURIER
(*Suby of* J. D. Irving, Limited)
10 Simmonds Dr, Dartmouth, NS, B3B 1R3
(902) 494-5511
Emp Here 25
SIC 7389 Business services, nec

D-U-N-S 20-727-6718   (BR)
MIDLAND TRANSPORT LIMITED
(*Suby of* J. D. Irving, Limited)
31 Simmonds Dr, Dartmouth, NS, B3B 1R4
(902) 494-5555
Emp Here 150
SIC 4111 Local and suburban transit

D-U-N-S 25-528-1743   (BR)
MONDART HOLDINGS LIMITED
DISCOUNT CAR & TRUCK RENTAL
135 Ilsley Ave Unit A, Dartmouth, NS, B3B 1T1
(902) 468-4650
Emp Here 30
SIC 7514 Passenger car rental

D-U-N-S 20-523-1418   (BR)

MOOSEHEAD BREWERIES LIMITED
656 Windmill Rd, Dartmouth, NS, B3B 1B8
(902) 468-7040
Emp Here 50
SIC 5181 Beer and ale

D-U-N-S 24-955-9113   (HQ)
NORTHEASTERN INVESTIGATIONS IN-CORPORATED
NORTHEASTERN PROTECTION SERVICE
(*Suby of* Northeastern Investigations Incorporated)
202 Brownlow Ave Suite 1, Dartmouth, NS, B3B 1T5
(902) 435-1336
Emp Here 85   *Emp Total* 160
Sales 4,961,328
SIC 7381 Detective and armored car services

D-U-N-S 25-503-8077   (BR)
NORTHFIELD GLASS GROUP LTD
75 Macdonald Ave Unit 2, Dartmouth, NS, B3B 1T8
(902) 468-1977
Emp Here 35
SIC 1751 Carpentry work

D-U-N-S 24-561-3042   (BR)
NOVA SCOTIA HEALTH AUTHORITY
EAST COAST FORENSIC PYSCHIATRIC HOSPITAL
88 Gloria Mccluskey Ave, Dartmouth, NS, B3B 2B8
(902) 460-7300
Emp Here 20
SIC 8063 Psychiatric hospitals

D-U-N-S 25-174-5816   (HQ)
NUBODY'S FITNESS CENTRES INC
(*Suby of* Nubody's Fitness Centres Inc)
51 Raddall Ave, Dartmouth, NS, B3B 1T6
(902) 468-8920
Emp Here 25   *Emp Total* 750
Sales 34,263,680
SIC 7991 Physical fitness facilities
Pr Pr Dean Hartman

D-U-N-S 20-727-4739   (BR)
OTIS CANADA, INC
(*Suby of* United Technologies Corporation)
51 Raddall Ave Suite 7, Dartmouth, NS, B3B 1T6
(902) 481-8200
Emp Here 25
SIC 3534 Elevators and moving stairways

D-U-N-S 20-956-3175   (BR)
PCL CONSTRUCTORS CANADA INC
111 Ilsley Ave Suite 300, Dartmouth, NS, B3B 1S8
(902) 481-8500
Emp Here 50
SIC 1542 Nonresidential construction, nec

D-U-N-S 20-051-9218   (BR)
PENNECON ENERGY HYDRAULIC SYSTEMS LIMITED
41 Ilsley Ave, Dartmouth, NS, B3B 1K9
(902) 468-6640
Emp Here 23
SIC 1799 Special trade contractors, nec

D-U-N-S 24-336-3228   (BR)
PHOENIX PETROLEUM LTD
42 Fielding Ave, Dartmouth, NS, B3B 1E4
(902) 481-0620
Emp Here 21
SIC 8711 Engineering services

D-U-N-S 24-789-7432   (SL)
PINAUD DRYWALL & ACOUSTICAL LIM-ITED
150 Akerley Blvd Suite 1, Dartmouth, NS, B3B 1Z5
(902) 468-9248
Emp Here 50   *Sales* 4,231,721
SIC 1742 Plastering, drywall, and insulation

D-U-N-S 20-031-4524   (HQ)

POLE STAR TRANSPORT INCORPORATED
ARMOUR TRANSPORT
80 Guildford Ave, Dartmouth, NS, B3B 0G3
(902) 468-8855
Emp Here 100   *Emp Total* 2,000
Sales 59,743,659
SIC 4213 Trucking, except local
Pr Pr Wesley Armour
Dir Ruth Leblanc

D-U-N-S 20-037-3210   (BR)
PRAXAIR CANADA INC
PRAXAIR DISTRIBUTION
(*Suby of* Praxair, Inc.)
40 Gurholt Dr, Dartmouth, NS, B3B 1J9
(902) 468-0985
Emp Here 20
SIC 2813 Industrial gases

D-U-N-S 20-287-1922   (BR)
PRINCESS AUTO LTD
81 Wright Ave, Dartmouth, NS, B3B 1H4
(902) 468-8396
Emp Here 34
SIC 5251 Hardware stores

D-U-N-S 24-338-7941   (BR)
PROTECTION INCENDIE VIKING INC
VIKING FIRE PROTECTION
78 Trider Cres, Dartmouth, NS, B3B 1R6
(902) 468-3235
Emp Here 25
SIC 5087 Service establishment equipment

D-U-N-S 20-727-5124   (BR)
PUROLATOR INC.
PUROLATOR INC
220 Joseph Zatzman Dr, Dartmouth, NS, B3B 1P4
(902) 468-1611
Emp Here 100
SIC 7389 Business services, nec

D-U-N-S 25-114-9696   (BR)
PYLON ELECTRONICS INC
PYLON ATLANTIC
31 Trider Cres, Dartmouth, NS, B3B 1V6
(902) 468-3344
Emp Here 25
SIC 7629 Electrical repair shops

D-U-N-S 20-025-4571   (HQ)
QUALITY CONCRETE LIMITED
20 Macdonald Ave, Dartmouth, NS, B3B 1C5
(902) 468-8040
Emp Here 20   *Emp Total* 300
Sales 17,802,411
SIC 3273 Ready-mixed concrete
Pr Pr Daryl Cail
  Scott Stevens
Dir Thane Stevens
  Chris Sangster

D-U-N-S 24-335-4144   (BR)
QUINCAILLERIE RICHELIEU LTEE
RICHELIEU
71 Ilsley Ave Unit 3, Dartmouth, NS, B3B 1L5
(902) 468-2324
Emp Here 20
SIC 5251 Hardware stores

D-U-N-S 25-645-5627   (BR)
ROYAL & SUN ALLIANCE INSURANCE COMPANY OF CANADA
50 Garland Ave Suite 101, Dartmouth, NS, B3B 0A3
(902) 493-1500
Emp Here 150
SIC 6331 Fire, marine, and casualty insurance

D-U-N-S 20-002-8566   (BR)
ROYAL BANK OF CANADA
RBC
(*Suby of* Royal Bank Of Canada)
202 Brownlow Ave Suite 100, Dartmouth, NS, B3B 1T5
(902) 421-8825
Emp Here 25

SIC 6021 National commercial banks

D-U-N-S 24-238-1021   (SL)
SEABOARD BULK TERMINALS LIMITED
721 Wilkinson Avenue, Dartmouth, NS, B3B 0H4
(902) 468-4447
Emp Here 25   *Sales* 2,407,703
SIC 4225 General warehousing and storage

D-U-N-S 20-741-6777   (SL)
SEABOARD TRANSPORT GROUP
RALPH'S TRANSPORT DIV OF
721 Av Wilkinson, Dartmouth, NS, B3B 0H4
(902) 468-4447
Emp Here 45   *Sales* 5,326,131
SIC 4213 Trucking, except local
Pr Pr Mark Shannon
VP Sls Jim Dibbin
VP Opers Bob Macquarrie
VP Opers David Macdonald
Dir Fin Bryant Deveaux

D-U-N-S 25-297-6717   (BR)
SIEMENS CANADA LIMITED
120 Troop Ave Suite 100, Dartmouth, NS, B3B 1Z1
(902) 468-9791
Emp Here 25
SIC 5063 Electrical apparatus and equipment

D-U-N-S 25-891-7012   (BR)
SLEEMAN BREWERIES LTD
SLEEMAN MARITIMES
612 Windmill Rd, Dartmouth, NS, B3B 1B5

Emp Here 40
SIC 5921 Liquor stores

D-U-N-S 25-999-6507   (BR)
SOURCE ATLANTIC LIMITED
HYDRAULICS, RIGGING & RUBBER
14 Akerley Blvd, Dartmouth, NS, B3B 1J3
(902) 494-5054
Emp Here 250
SIC 5999 Miscellaneous retail stores, nec

D-U-N-S 24-851-2514   (BR)
SOURCE ATLANTIC LIMITED
SCHOONER INDUSTRIAL
100 Raddall Ave, Dartmouth, NS, B3B 1T2
(902) 468-8100
Emp Here 30
SIC 5085 Industrial supplies

D-U-N-S 24-340-5094   (BR)
STANLEY BLACK & DECKER CANADA CORPORATION
STANLEY SECURITY SOLUTIONS
36 Frazee Ave, Dartmouth, NS, B3B 1X4
(902) 468-2728
Emp Here 20
SIC 3429 Hardware, nec

D-U-N-S 25-213-7096   (BR)
STAPLES CANADA INC
STAPLES THE BUSINESS DEPOT
(*Suby of* Staples, Inc.)
202 Brownlow Ave, Dartmouth, NS, B3B 1T5
(902) 468-3412
Emp Here 65
SIC 5943 Stationery stores

D-U-N-S 25-727-4154   (BR)
STARBUCKS COFFEE CANADA, INC
DARTMOUTH CROSSING
(*Suby of* Starbucks Corporation)
32 Foulis Row, Dartmouth, NS, B3B 0E1
(902) 481-9006
Emp Here 20
SIC 5812 Eating places

D-U-N-S 25-627-4309   (BR)
STOCK TRANSPORTATION LTD
51 Frazee Ave, Dartmouth, NS, B3B 1Z4
(902) 481-8400
Emp Here 350
SIC 4151 School buses

D-U-N-S 25-244-1829   (BR)
STRONGCO ENGINEERED SYSTEMS INC
STRONGCO EQUIPMENT
55 Isnor Dr, Dartmouth, NS, B3B 1N6
(902) 468-5010
Emp Here 22
SIC 3541 Machine tools, Metal cutting type

D-U-N-S 25-412-4928   (BR)
TRC HYDRAULICS INC
7 Mosher Dr, Dartmouth, NS, B3B 1E5
(902) 468-4605
Emp Here 32
SIC 5084 Industrial machinery and equipment

D-U-N-S 25-196-2023   (HQ)
THOMPSON'S MOVING GROUP LIMITED
THOMPSON'S MOVING & STORAGE
(*Suby of* Thompson's Moving Group Limited)
51 Thornhill Dr, Dartmouth, NS, B3B 1R9
(902) 469-2090
Emp Here 48   *Emp Total* 50
Sales 3,939,878
SIC 4212 Local trucking, without storage

D-U-N-S 20-191-8278   (BR)
THOMPSON'S MOVING GROUP LIMITED
OCEAN MOVING & STORAGE
51 Thornhill Dr, Dartmouth, NS, B3B 1R9
(902) 468-5959
Emp Here 50
SIC 4214 Local trucking with storage

D-U-N-S 20-939-7806   (BR)
THYSSENKRUPP ELEVATOR (CANADA) LIMITED
7 Mellor Ave Unit 4, Dartmouth, NS, B3B 0E8
(902) 454-2456
Emp Here 50
SIC 7699 Repair services, nec

D-U-N-S 25-628-7772   (BR)
TRADER CORPORATION
11 Akerley Blvd Suite 400a, Dartmouth, NS, B3B 1V7
(902) 468-2899
Emp Here 30
SIC 2721 Periodicals

D-U-N-S 20-522-2883   (BR)
TRADER CORPORATION
AUTO TRADER
11 Akerley Blvd Suite 400a, Dartmouth, NS, B3B 1V7
(902) 421-1332
Emp Here 30
SIC 2721 Periodicals

D-U-N-S 20-703-5085   (BR)
TROY LIFE & FIRE SAFETY LTD
EDWARDS SPRINKLER
80 Raddall Ave Suite 5, Dartmouth, NS, B3B 1T7
(902) 468-9500
Emp Here 25
SIC 3669 Communications equipment, nec

D-U-N-S 20-717-3774   (HQ)
TUDHOPE CARTAGE LIMITED
4 Vidito Dr, Dartmouth, NS, B3B 1P9
(902) 468-4447
Emp Here 20   *Emp Total* 750
Sales 16,396,525
SIC 4213 Trucking, except local
Pr Pr Mark Shannon

D-U-N-S 24-738-4399   (BR)
TYCO INTEGRATED FIRE & SECURITY CANADA, INC
ADT
(*Suby of* Johnson Controls, Inc.)
75 Akerley Blvd Unit E, Dartmouth, NS, B3B 1R7
(902) 468-1649
Emp Here 20
SIC 1731 Electrical work

D-U-N-S 20-729-7474   (BR)
TYCO INTEGRATED FIRE & SECURITY

CANADA, INC
SIMPLEXGRINNELL
(*Suby of* Johnson Controls, Inc.)
600 Windmill Rd Unit G, Dartmouth, NS, B3B 1B5
(902) 468-9100
Emp Here 42
SIC 7389 Business services, nec

D-U-N-S 20-321-3277   (BR)
UNITED RENTALS OF CANADA, INC
UNITED RENTALS
37 Payzant Ave, Dartmouth, NS, B3B 2E1
(902) 468-6668
Emp Here 50
SIC 7353 Heavy construction equipment rental

D-U-N-S 20-115-8669   (BR)
UNIVERSAL SALES, LIMITED
THORNES
14 Akerley Blvd, Dartmouth, NS, B3B 1J3
(902) 494-5377
Emp Here 21
SIC 5063 Electrical apparatus and equipment

D-U-N-S 25-297-7467   (BR)
WAL-MART CANADA CORP
90 Lamont Terr, Dartmouth, NS, B3B 0B5
(902) 461-4474
Emp Here 249
SIC 5311 Department stores

D-U-N-S 20-702-7934   (BR)
XEROX CANADA LTD
DOCUMENT COMPANY, THE
(*Suby of* Xerox Corporation)
237 Brownlow Ave Suite 100, Dartmouth, NS, B3B 2C6
(902) 470-3007
Emp Here 146
SIC 5044 Office equipment

Dayspring, NS B4V

D-U-N-S 24-994-7755   (HQ)
LAHAVE MANOR CORP
(*Suby of* Lahave Manor Corp)
171 Leary Fraser Rd, Dayspring, NS, B4V 5S7
(902) 543-7851
Emp Here 60   *Emp Total* 90
Sales 4,231,721
SIC 8052 Intermediate care facilities

Debert, NS B0M
Colchester County

D-U-N-S 25-369-1851   (BR)
ATLANTICA DIVERSIFIED TRANSPORTATION SYSTEMS
31 John Snook Blvd, Debert, NS, B0M 1G0

Emp Here 32
SIC 4213 Trucking, except local

D-U-N-S 20-260-7602   (BR)
CHIGNECTO CENTRAL REGIONAL SCHOOL BOARD
DEBERT ELEMENTARY SCHOOL
(*Suby of* Chignecto Central Regional School Board)
1320 Masstown Rd, Debert, NS, B0M 1G0
(902) 662-4400
Emp Here 22
SIC 8211 Elementary and secondary schools

D-U-N-S 20-023-2838   (BR)
CHIGNECTO CENTRAL REGIONAL SCHOOL BOARD
CHIGANOIS ELEMENTARY SCHOOL
(*Suby of* Chignecto Central Regional School Board)

11145 2 Hwy, Debert, NS, B0M 1G0
(902) 662-4420
Emp Here 20
SIC 8211 Elementary and secondary schools

D-U-N-S 20-272-9666   (BR)
CLEAN HARBORS CANADA, INC
640 Mcelmon Rd, Debert, NS, B0M 1G0
(902) 662-3336
Emp Here 23
SIC 4953 Refuse systems

D-U-N-S 24-671-1618   (BR)
HOME HARDWARE STORES LIMITED
HOME HARDWARE DISTRIBUTION CENTRE
336 Lancaster Cres, Debert, NS, B0M 1G0
(902) 662-2800
Emp Here 200
SIC 5211 Lumber and other building materials

D-U-N-S 20-937-5666   (HQ)
NEWPORT CUSTOM METAL FABRICATIONS INC
114 Lancaster Cres Lot 208, Debert, NS, B0M 1G0
(902) 662-3840
Emp Here 45   *Emp Total* 170
Sales 9,788,636
SIC 3585 Refrigeration and heating equipment
Pr Pr Kenneth Johnson
VP VP Jim Johnson
VP VP Nancy Newport

D-U-N-S 20-298-7686   (BR)
TDL GROUP CORP, THE
TIM HORTON REGIONAL OFFICE
478 Macelmon Rd, Debert, NS, B0M 1G0
(902) 662-2155
Emp Here 20
SIC 5812 Eating places

D-U-N-S 20-340-6244   (BR)
TDL GROUP CORP, THE
TIM HORTONS
476 Macelmon Rd, Debert, NS, B0M 1G0
(902) 662-2522
Emp Here 20
SIC 5812 Eating places

D-U-N-S 25-298-8308   (SL)
WILLIAM NEWPORT HOLDINGS LIMITED
208 Lancaster Cres, Debert, NS, B0M 1G0
(902) 662-3840
Emp Here 75   *Sales* 14,710,250
SIC 6712 Bank holding companies
Pr Pr Kenneth Johnson
Dir Nancy Newport
Sec Gail Johnson
Dir James Johnson

Digby, NS B0V
Digby County

D-U-N-S 25-082-5973   (BR)
ATLANTIC WHOLESALERS LTD
ATLANTIC SUPERSTORE, THE
470 Warwick St, Digby, NS, B0V 1A0
(902) 245-4108
Emp Here 95
SIC 5411 Grocery stores

D-U-N-S 20-571-8427   (BR)
BELL ALIANT REGIONAL COMMUNICATIONS INC
23 Water St, Digby, NS, B0V 1A0
(902) 245-8331
Emp Here 20
SIC 4899 Communication services, nec

D-U-N-S 25-412-3847   (BR)
NOVA SCOTIA HEALTH AUTHORITY
DIGBY GENERAL HOSPITAL
75 Warwick St, Digby, NS, B0V 1A0

---

(902) 245-2501
Emp Here 140
SIC 8062 General medical and surgical hospitals

D-U-N-S 20-205-5674   (BR)
SOBEYS CAPITAL INCORPORATED
SOBEYS
110 Warwick St, Digby, NS, B0V 1A0
(902) 245-6183
Emp Here 90
SIC 5411 Grocery stores

D-U-N-S 20-754-3096   (BR)
TRI-COUNTY REGIONAL SCHOOL BOARD
DIGBY ELEMENTARY SCHOOL
20 Shreve St, Digby, NS, B0V 1A0
(902) 245-7550
Emp Here 20
SIC 8211 Elementary and secondary schools

D-U-N-S 20-205-0584   (BR)
TRI-COUNTY REGIONAL SCHOOL BOARD
DIGBY REGIONAL HIGH SCHOOL
107 King St, Digby, NS, B0V 1A0
(902) 245-7500
Emp Here 50
SIC 8211 Elementary and secondary schools

D-U-N-S 24-120-9902   (BR)
WAL-MART CANADA CORP
492 Hwy 303, Digby, NS, B0V 1A0
(902) 245-6020
Emp Here 60
SIC 5311 Department stores

Dominion, NS B1G
Cape Breton County

D-U-N-S 24-000-2159   (BR)
WILSON'S INVESTMENTS LIMITED
TIM HORTONS
29 Commercial St, Dominion, NS, B1G 1B3
(902) 849-2077
Emp Here 25
SIC 5812 Eating places

Donkin, NS B1A
Cape Breton County

D-U-N-S 20-710-2455   (BR)
CAPE BRETON-VICTORIA REGIONAL SCHOOL BOARD
DONKIN GOWRIE COMPLEX
81 Centre Ave, Donkin, NS, B1A 6N4
(902) 737-2120
Emp Here 25
SIC 8211 Elementary and secondary schools

Dutch Settlement, NS B2S
Halifax County

D-U-N-S 25-241-7779   (BR)
HALIFAX REGIONAL SCHOOL BOARD
DUTCH SETTLEMENT SCHOOL
(*Suby of* Halifax Regional School Board)
990 Highway 277, Dutch Settlement, NS, B2S 2J5
(902) 883-3000
Emp Here 22
SIC 8211 Elementary and secondary schools

East Bay, NS B1J
Cape Breton County

D-U-N-S 25-241-5500   (BR)

CAPE BRETON-VICTORIA REGIONAL SCHOOL BOARD
MOUNTAIN VIEW/ EAST BAY ELEMENTARY
3546 East Bay Hwy, East Bay, NS, B1J 1A3
(902) 828-2010
Emp Here 47
SIC 8211 Elementary and secondary schools

Eastern Passage, NS B3G
Halifax County

D-U-N-S 25-324-0196   (BR)
AECON CONSTRUCTION GROUP INC
AECON ATLANTIC GROUP
1387 Eastern Passage Hwy, Eastern Passage, NS, B3G 1M5

Emp Here 30
SIC 1622 Bridge, tunnel, and elevated highway construction

D-U-N-S 20-286-6195   (BR)
AECON GROUP INC
AECON ATLANTIC GROUP
1387 Main Rd, Eastern Passage, NS, B3G 1M5

Emp Here 30
SIC 1522 Residential construction, nec

D-U-N-S 20-103-2484   (BR)
ENERGIE VALERO INC
ULTAMAR HOMENERGY
1356 Pleasant St, Eastern Passage, NS, B3G 1M4
(902) 468-7979
Emp Here 50
SIC 5085 Industrial supplies

D-U-N-S 20-710-3057   (BR)
HALIFAX REGIONAL SCHOOL BOARD
EASTERN PASSAGE EDUCATION CENTRE
93 Samuel Danial Dr, Eastern Passage, NS, B3G 1S8
(902) 462-8401
Emp Here 50
SIC 8211 Elementary and secondary schools

D-U-N-S 25-935-5972   (BR)
HALIFAX REGIONAL SCHOOL BOARD
TALLAHASSEE COMMUNITY SCHOOL
(*Suby of* Halifax Regional School Board)
168 Redoubt Way, Eastern Passage, NS, B3G 1E4
(902) 465-8650
Emp Here 45
SIC 8211 Elementary and secondary schools

D-U-N-S 25-137-6364   (BR)
HALIFAX REGIONAL SCHOOL BOARD
SEASIDE ELEMENTARY
(*Suby of* Halifax Regional School Board)
1881 Caldwell Rd, Eastern Passage, NS, B3G 1J3
(902) 465-7600
Emp Here 25
SIC 8211 Elementary and secondary schools

D-U-N-S 20-023-2895   (BR)
HALIFAX REGIONAL SCHOOL BOARD
OCEANVIEW ELEMENTARY SCHOOL
51 Oceanview School Rd, Eastern Passage, NS, B3G 1J3
(902) 465-8670
Emp Here 30
SIC 8211 Elementary and secondary schools

Edwardsville, NS B2A
Cape Breton County

D-U-N-S 25-363-2269   (BR)
COCA-COLA REFRESHMENTS CANADA

COMPANY
(*Suby of* The Coca-Cola Company)
418 Portsway Ave, Edwardsville, NS, B2A 4T8
(902) 567-2726
Emp Here 24
SIC 5149 Groceries and related products, nec

Elmsdale, NS B2S
Hants County

D-U-N-S 25-706-4105   (HQ)
ASSOCIATED MARITIME PHARMACIES LIMITED
PHARMASAVE
(*Suby of* Associated Maritime Pharmacies Limited)
269 Highway 214 Unit 2, Elmsdale, NS, B2S 1K1
(902) 883-8018
Emp Here 50   *Emp Total* 80
Sales 11,308,909
SIC 5912 Drug stores and proprietary stores
Pr Pr Arthur Mcdonough Jr
   John Macintyre
Sec Andrew Buffett
   Arthur Mcdonough Sr

D-U-N-S 20-743-4700   (BR)
ATLANTIC WHOLESALERS LTD
REAL ATLANTIC SUPERSTORE, THE
295 Highway 214, Elmsdale, NS, B2S 2L1
(902) 883-1180
Emp Here 80
SIC 5411 Grocery stores

D-U-N-S 25-241-9619   (BR)
CHIGNECTO CENTRAL REGIONAL SCHOOL BOARD
ELMSDALE DISTRICT ELEMENTARY SCHOOL
(*Suby of* Chignecto Central Regional School Board)
75 Macmillan Dr, Elmsdale, NS, B2S 1A5
(902) 883-5350
Emp Here 32
SIC 8211 Elementary and secondary schools

D-U-N-S 24-761-1648   (BR)
EAST HANTS, MUNICIPALITY OF
EAST HANTS RESOURCE CENTRE
230-15 Commerce Crt, Elmsdale, NS, B2S 3K5
(902) 883-2299
Emp Here 65
SIC 7291 Tax return preparation services

D-U-N-S 25-635-2543   (HQ)
GALLANT AGGREGATES LIMITED
(*Suby of* Gallant Aggregates Limited)
100 Bedrock Lane, Elmsdale, NS, B2S 2B1
(902) 883-3020
Emp Here 40   *Emp Total* 46
Sales 12,858,960
SIC 5032 Brick, stone, and related material
Pr Pr Frederick Benere

D-U-N-S 20-208-0805   (BR)
MILLER PAVING LIMITED
MILLER WASTE, DIV OF
3 First St, Elmsdale, NS, B2S 2L5
(902) 883-2574
Emp Here 30
SIC 1611 Highway and street construction

D-U-N-S 24-804-1477   (BR)
SOBEYS CAPITAL INCORPORATED
SOBEYS #660
269 Highway 214 Unit 1, Elmsdale, NS, B2S 1K1
(902) 883-8111
Emp Here 180
SIC 5411 Grocery stores

Enfield, NS B2T
Hants County

D-U-N-S 24-123-1575   (BR)
AIR CANADA
1 Bell Blvd Suite 7, Enfield, NS, B2T 1K2
(902) 873-2350
Emp Here 100
SIC 4581 Airports, flying fields, and services

D-U-N-S 20-523-2700   (BR)
AVISCAR INC
(*Suby of* Avis Budget Group, Inc.)
1 Bell Blvd Suite 7, Enfield, NS, B2T 1K2
(902) 429-0963
Emp Here 30
SIC 7514 Passenger car rental

D-U-N-S 20-710-1903   (BR)
CHIGNECTO CENTRAL REGIONAL SCHOOL BOARD
ENFIELD DISTRICT ELEMENTARY SCHOOL
(*Suby of* Chignecto Central Regional School Board)
29 Catherine St, Enfield, NS, B2T 1L4
(902) 883-5300
Emp Here 50
SIC 8211 Elementary and secondary schools

D-U-N-S 25-588-3969   (BR)
ENTERPRISE RENT-A-CAR CANADA COMPANY
(*Suby of* The Crawford Group Inc)
81 Bell Blvd, Enfield, NS, B2T 1K3
(902) 873-3502
Emp Here 30
SIC 7514 Passenger car rental

D-U-N-S 24-381-3727   (SL)
HUDSON GROUP CANADA, INC
THE HUDSON GROUP
1 Bell Blvd Suite 1621, Enfield, NS, B2T 1K2
(902) 873-3282
Emp Here 60   *Sales* 3,283,232
SIC 5947 Gift, novelty, and souvenir shop

D-U-N-S 25-293-2264   (SL)
INTERNATIONAL HOTEL HALIFAX LTD
60 Sky Blvd, Enfield, NS, B2T 1K3
(902) 873-3000
Emp Here 55   *Sales* 2,407,703
SIC 7011 Hotels and motels

D-U-N-S 20-733-7119   (BR)
PLH AVIATION SERVICES INC
438 Cygnet Dr, Enfield, NS, B2T 1K3
(902) 873-3543
Emp Here 20
SIC 5172 Petroleum products, nec

D-U-N-S 24-386-5065   (SL)
SPRINGFIELD HOTELS (HALIFAX) INCORPORATED
HILTON GARDEN INN HALIFAX AIRPORT
200 Pratt Whitney Dr, Enfield, NS, B2T 0A2
(902) 873-1400
Emp Here 70   *Sales* 3,638,254
SIC 7011 Hotels and motels

D-U-N-S 25-324-4578   (BR)
SWISSPORT CANADA INC
HUDSON GENERAL AVIATION SERVICE
1 Bell Blvd Suite 7, Enfield, NS, B2T 1K2
(902) 873-3947
Emp Here 70
SIC 4581 Airports, flying fields, and services

D-U-N-S 20-529-1698   (BR)
TRANSPORT CANADA
HALIFAX INTERNATIONAL AIRPORT AUTHORITY
1 Bell Blvd Fl 3, Enfield, NS, B2T 1K2
(902) 873-4423
Emp Here 150
SIC 4581 Airports, flying fields, and services

Eskasoni, NS B1W
Cape Breton County

D-U-N-S 25-394-4318   (BR)
ESKASONI SCHOOL BOARD
ESKASONI ELEMENTARY & MIDDLE SCHOOL
4675 Shore Rd, Eskasoni, NS, B1W 1B8
(902) 379-2825
Emp Here 100
SIC 8211 Elementary and secondary schools

Fall River, NS B2T
Halifax County

D-U-N-S 20-573-5421   (BR)
EMC EMERGENCY MEDICAL CARE INCORPORATED
EMC
3064 Highway 2, Fall River, NS, B2T 1J5
(902) 832-8346
Emp Here 20
SIC 4119 Local passenger transportation, nec

D-U-N-S 24-336-1172   (BR)
HALIFAX REGIONAL MUNICIPALITY
GORDON R SNOW COMMUNITY CENTRE, THE
1359 Fall River Rd, Fall River, NS, B2T 1E5
(902) 860-4570
Emp Here 22
SIC 7999 Amusement and recreation, nec

D-U-N-S 20-568-9289   (BR)
HALIFAX REGIONAL SCHOOL BOARD
LOCKVIEW HIGH SCHOOL
148 Lockview Rd, Fall River, NS, B2T 1J1
(902) 860-6000
Emp Here 72
SIC 8211 Elementary and secondary schools

D-U-N-S 25-968-1989   (BR)
HALIFAX REGIONAL SCHOOL BOARD
GEORGES P VANIER JUNIOR HIGH
(*Suby of* Halifax Regional School Board)
1410 Fall River Rd, Fall River, NS, B2T 1J1
(902) 860-4182
Emp Here 30
SIC 8211 Elementary and secondary schools

D-U-N-S 25-241-7456   (BR)
HALIFAX REGIONAL SCHOOL BOARD
ASH LEE JEFFERSON ELEMENTARY SCHOOL
(*Suby of* Halifax Regional School Board)
10 Lockview Rd, Fall River, NS, B2T 1J1
(902) 860-4163
Emp Here 50
SIC 8211 Elementary and secondary schools

D-U-N-S 25-363-8456   (BR)
MCDONALD'S RESTAURANTS OF CANADA LIMITED
MCDONALD'S
(*Suby of* McDonald's Corporation)
3291 Highway 2, Fall River, NS, B2T 1J5
(902) 860-3007
Emp Here 20
SIC 5812 Eating places

D-U-N-S 20-359-3616   (BR)
SOBEYS CAPITAL INCORPORATED
SOBEYS
3286 Hwy 2, Fall River, NS, B2T 1L8
(902) 860-2291
Emp Here 100
SIC 5411 Grocery stores

Falmouth, NS B0P
Hants County

D-U-N-S 20-710-2232   (BR)
ANNAPOLIS VALLEY REGIONAL SCHOOL BOARD
FALMOUTH ELEMENTARY SCHOOL
106 School St, Falmouth, NS, B0P 1L0
(902) 792-6710
Emp Here 30
SIC 8211 Elementary and secondary schools

Fletchers Lake, NS B2T
Halifax County

D-U-N-S 20-023-4909   (BR)
HALIFAX REGIONAL SCHOOL BOARD
HOLLAND ROAD SCHOOL
181 Holland Rd, Fletchers Lake, NS, B2T 1A1
(902) 860-4170
Emp Here 30
SIC 8211 Elementary and secondary schools

Florence, NS B1Y
Cape Breton County

D-U-N-S 25-241-3430   (BR)
CAPE BRETON-VICTORIA REGIONAL SCHOOL BOARD
DR T L SULLIVAN JUNIOR HIGH SCHOOL
256 Park Rd, Florence, NS, B1Y 1N2
(902) 736-6273
Emp Here 45
SIC 8211 Elementary and secondary schools

Fortress Of Louisbourg, NS B1C
Cape Breton County

D-U-N-S 25-503-2864   (SL)
FORTRESS OF LOUISBOURG ASSOCIATION
259 Park Service Rd, Fortress Of Louisbourg, NS, B1C 2L2
(902) 733-2280
Emp Here 50   *Sales* 2,772,507
SIC 5947 Gift, novelty, and souvenir shop

Freeport, NS B0V
Digby County

D-U-N-S 20-710-3156   (BR)
TRI-COUNTY REGIONAL SCHOOL BOARD
ISLANDS CONSOLIDATED SCHOOL
75 Overcove Rd, Freeport, NS, B0V 1B0
(902) 839-6300
Emp Here 50
SIC 8211 Elementary and secondary schools

Glace Bay, NS B1A
Cape Breton County

D-U-N-S 25-614-5509   (BR)
ATLANTIC WHOLESALERS LTD
REAL ATLANTIC SUPERSTORE, THE
155 Reserve St, Glace Bay, NS, B1A 4W3
(902) 842-9609
Emp Here 108
SIC 5411 Grocery stores

D-U-N-S 20-835-3347   (BR)
CAPE BRETON REGIONAL MUNICIPALITY
DEPARTMENT OF PUBLIC WORKS
24 West Ave, Glace Bay, NS, B1A 6E9
(902) 842-1171
Emp Here 53

SIC 7699 Repair services, nec

D-U-N-S 25-241-5047   (BR)
CAPE BRETON-VICTORIA REGIONAL SCHOOL BOARD
JOHN BERNARD CROAK V C MEMORIAL SCHOOL
10 Second St, Glace Bay, NS, B1A 5Z4
(902) 849-2003
Emp Here 23
SIC 8211 Elementary and secondary schools

D-U-N-S 25-241-5088   (BR)
CAPE BRETON-VICTORIA REGIONAL SCHOOL BOARD
BRIDGEPORT SCHOOL
1260 Main St, Glace Bay, NS, B1A 5A4
(902) 842-2285
Emp Here 26
SIC 8211 Elementary and secondary schools

D-U-N-S 24-912-6012   (SL)
GLACE BAY HEALTH CARE FACILITY
GLACE BAY HOSPITAL
300 South St, Glace Bay, NS, B1A 1W5
(902) 849-5511
Emp Here 500   *Sales* 46,822,320
SIC 8062 General medical and surgical hospitals
VP James (Jim) Merkley

D-U-N-S 25-299-4710   (BR)
LAWTON'S DRUG STORES LIMITED
LAWTONS DRUGS
290 Commercial St, Glace Bay, NS, B1A 3C6
(902) 849-7573
Emp Here 20
SIC 5912 Drug stores and proprietary stores

D-U-N-S 20-198-5160   (BR)
SOBEYS CAPITAL INCORPORATED
SOBEYS
144 Reserve St, Glace Bay, NS, B1A 4W5
(902) 842-1033
Emp Here 106
SIC 5411 Grocery stores

D-U-N-S 24-804-4182   (BR)
SOBEYS CAPITAL INCORPORATED
GLACE BAY FOODLAND
25 Brookside St, Glace Bay, NS, B1A 1K2
(902) 849-7205
Emp Here 40
SIC 5411 Grocery stores

D-U-N-S 20-514-2552   (BR)
STREAM INTERNATIONAL CANADA ULC
STREAM
(*Suby of* Convergys Corporation)
95 Union St, Glace Bay, NS, B1A 2P6
(902) 842-3800
Emp Here 909
SIC 7389 Business services, nec

D-U-N-S 24-761-3826   (HQ)
XSTRATA COAL CANADA LIMITED
633 Main St, Glace Bay, NS, B1A 6J3
(902) 849-9235
Emp Here 50   *Emp Total* 5,215
Sales 30,739,350
SIC 1221 Bituminous coal and lignite-surface mining
Dir Stephen Young

Glenwood, NS B0W
Yarmouth County

D-U-N-S 20-020-8309   (SL)
NAKILE HOUSING CORPORATION
NAKILE HOME FOR SPECIAL CARE
35 Nakile Dr, Glenwood, NS, B0W 1W0
(902) 643-2707
Emp Here 74   *Sales* 3,356,192
SIC 8051 Skilled nursing care facilities

D-U-N-S 25-924-2915   (BR)
TRI-COUNTY REGIONAL SCHOOL BOARD
DRUMLIN HEIGHTS CONSOLIDATED SCHOOL
5428 Highway 3, Glenwood, NS, B0W 1W0
(902) 643-6000
Emp Here 60
SIC 8211 Elementary and secondary schools

Goffs, NS B2T
Halifax County

D-U-N-S 20-294-2959   (BR)
ADESA AUCTIONS CANADA CORPORATION
ADESA HALIFAX
300 Sky Blvd, Goffs, NS, B2T 1K3
(902) 873-4400
Emp Here 70
SIC 5012 Automobiles and other motor vehicles

D-U-N-S 25-367-5292   (BR)
ASPLUNDH CANADA ULC
ASPLUNDH TREE SERVICE ULC
(*Suby of* Asplundh Tree Expert Co.)
645 Pratt And Whitney Dr Suite 1, Goffs, NS, B2T 0H4
(902) 468-8733
Emp Here 80
SIC 7299 Miscellaneous personal service

D-U-N-S 20-702-4956   (BR)
AVISCAR INC
(*Suby of* Avis Budget Group, Inc.)
111 Selfridge Way, Goffs, NS, B2T 0C1
(902) 429-8769
Emp Here 150
SIC 7514 Passenger car rental

D-U-N-S 20-700-8934   (BR)
AVISCAR INC
AVIS BUDGET GROUP
(*Suby of* Avis Budget Group, Inc.)
111 Selfridge Way, Goffs, NS, B2T 0C1
(902) 492-7512
Emp Here 45
SIC 7514 Passenger car rental

D-U-N-S 24-803-7624   (BR)
CHC HELICOPTER HOLDING S.A.R.L.
CHC HELICOPTER CORPORATION
799 Barnes Dr Suite 1, Goffs, NS, B2T 1R8

Emp Here 33
SIC 4522 Air transportation, nonscheduled

D-U-N-S 24-244-9903   (BR)
HELICOPTERES CANADIENS LIMITEE
637 Barnes Dr, Goffs, NS, B2T 1K3
(902) 873-3721
Emp Here 20
SIC 4522 Air transportation, nonscheduled

D-U-N-S 25-106-3111   (BR)
I.M.P. GROUP INTERNATIONAL INCORPORATED
CANJET AIRLINES
677 Barnes Dr, Goffs, NS, B2T 1K3
(902) 873-7800
Emp Here 500
SIC 4581 Airports, flying fields, and services

D-U-N-S 24-317-5176   (BR)
L-3 COMMUNICATIONS ELECTRONIC SYSTEMS INC
(*Suby of* L3 Technologies, Inc.)
249 Aerotech Dr, Goffs, NS, B2T 1K3
(902) 873-2000
Emp Here 159
SIC 3812 Search and navigation equipment

D-U-N-S 25-365-0311   (BR)
NAV CANADA
1610 Old Guysborough Rd, Goffs, NS, B2T

1B9
(902) 873-1382
Emp Here 70
SIC 4899 Communication services, nec

D-U-N-S 24-738-5396   (BR)
PROVINCIAL AIRLINES LIMITED
PAL AVIATION SERVICES
647 Barnes Dr, Goffs, NS, B2T 1K3
(902) 873-3575
Emp Here 48
SIC 4581 Airports, flying fields, and services

D-U-N-S 24-879-1568   (SL)
PROVINCIAL POLE SPECIALISTS INCORPORATED
645 Pratt And Whitney Dr Suite 1, Goffs, NS, B2T 0H4
(902) 468-8404
Emp Here 80   *Sales* 19,478,400
SIC 1623 Water, sewer, and utility lines
Pr Pr Steven Christiansen
VP VP Tim Oickle
  Reginald Mackinnon

D-U-N-S 25-524-8874   (SL)
RACAL PELAGOS CANADA LTD
209 Aerotech Dr Suite 3a, Goffs, NS, B2T 1K3

Emp Here 40   *Sales* 5,224,960
SIC 8711 Engineering services
Off Mgr Suzanne Daoust
Pr William C Speidel
VP Stewart Cannon
Treas Randall Ashley

Goldboro, NS B0H

D-U-N-S 24-385-4630   (BR)
EXXONMOBIL CANADA LTD
(*Suby of* Exxon Mobil Corporation)
500 Sable Rd, Goldboro, NS, B0H 1L0
(902) 387-3020
Emp Here 25
SIC 1311 Crude petroleum and natural gas

Goodwood, NS B3T
Halifax County

D-U-N-S 25-408-4528   (SL)
HALIFAX C & D RECYCLING LTD
HALIFAX CONSTRUCTION & DEBRIS
16 Mills Dr, Goodwood, NS, B3T 1P3
(902) 876-8644
Emp Here 28   *Sales* 5,072,500
SIC 4953 Refuse systems
Pr Pr Dan Chassie
Dir Lee-Anne Chassie

Granville Ferry, NS B0S
Annapolis County

D-U-N-S 25-504-0271   (BR)
ANNAPOLIS VALLEY REGIONAL SCHOOL BOARD
CHAMPLAIN ELEMENTARY SCHOOL
109 North St, Granville Ferry, NS, B0S 1K0
(902) 532-3270
Emp Here 30
SIC 8211 Elementary and secondary schools

Greenwood, NS B0P

D-U-N-S 25-504-0792   (BR)
ANNAPOLIS VALLEY REGIONAL SCHOOL BOARD

DWIGHT ROSS ELEMENTARY SCHOOL
Gd, Greenwood, NS, B0P 1N0
(902) 765-7510
Emp Here 20
SIC 8211 Elementary and secondary schools

D-U-N-S 20-710-3230   (BR)
CONSEIL SCOLAIRE ACADIEN PROVIN-CIAL
ECOLE ROSE-DES-VENTS
Gd, Greenwood, NS, B0P 1N0
(902) 765-7100
Emp Here 50
SIC 8211 Elementary and secondary schools

D-U-N-S 25-785-6443   (SL)
PEMAC PHARMACY LIMITED
SHOPPERS DRUG MART
1124 Bridge St, Greenwood, NS, B0P 1N0
(902) 765-3060
Emp Here 44   *Sales* 8,623,250
SIC 5912 Drug stores and proprietary stores
Pr Pr Michael G. Peters

Guysborough, NS B0H

D-U-N-S 24-378-7806   (BR)
ATLANTIC WHOLESALERS LTD
9996 Rte 16, Guysborough, NS, B0H 1N0
(902) 533-4070
Emp Here 20
SIC 5141 Groceries, general line

D-U-N-S 25-413-2574   (BR)
GUYSBOROUGH ANTIGONISH STRAIT HEALTH AUTHORITY
GUYSBOROUGH MEMORIAL HOSPITAL
10560 Hwy 16, Guysborough, NS, B0H 1N0
(902) 533-3702
Emp Here 50
SIC 8062 General medical and surgical hospitals

D-U-N-S 20-905-9872   (SL)
MILFORD HAVEN CORPORATION-HOME FOR SPECIAL CARE
10558 Main St, Guysborough, NS, B0H 1N0
(902) 533-2828
Emp Here 70   *Sales* 3,210,271
SIC 8051 Skilled nursing care facilities

D-U-N-S 25-241-4461   (BR)
STRAIT REGIONAL SCHOOL BOARD
CHEDABUCTO EDUCATION CENTRE
27 Green St, Guysborough, NS, B0H 1N0
(902) 533-2288
Emp Here 50
SIC 8211 Elementary and secondary schools

D-U-N-S 25-241-4586   (BR)
STRAIT REGIONAL SCHOOL BOARD
GUYSBORCUGH ACADEMY
27 Green St, Guysborough, NS, B0H 1N0
(902) 533-4006
Emp Here 50
SIC 8211 Elementary and secondary schools

Halifax, NS B3F
Halifax County

D-U-N-S 24-348-0816   (BR)
MEDIAS TRANSCONTINENTAL S.E.N.C.
211 Horshoe Lake Drive, Halifax, NS, B3F 0B9
(902) 468-8027
Emp Here 20
SIC 2731 Book publishing

Halifax, NS B3H
Halifax County

D-U-N-S 20-793-6589   (BR)
ARAMARK CANADA LTD.
923 Robie St, Halifax, NS, B3H 3C3
(902) 420-5599
Emp Here 150
SIC 5812 Eating places

D-U-N-S 25-891-4605   (BR)
ATLANTIC WHOLESALERS LTD
BARRINGTON MARKET SUPERSTORE
1075 Barrington St, Halifax, NS, B3H 4P1
(902) 492-3240
Emp Here 200
SIC 5411 Grocery stores

D-U-N-S 25-296-6122   (BR)
BANK OF NOVA SCOTIA, THE
SCOTIABANK
6005 Coburg Rd, Halifax, NS, B3H 1Y8
(902) 420-4929
Emp Here 20
SIC 6021 National commercial banks

D-U-N-S 20-788-4995   (BR)
CANADIAN CANCER SOCIETY
5826 South St Suite 1, Halifax, NS, B3H 1S6
(902) 423-6183
Emp Here 30
SIC 8399 Social services, nec

D-U-N-S 20-728-1478   (BR)
COMMONWEALTH HOSPITALITY LTD
HOLIDAY INN
(*Suby of* WXI/WWH Parallel Amalco (Ontario) Ltd)
1980 Robie St, Halifax, NS, B3H 3G5
(902) 423-1161
Emp Here 120
SIC 7011 Hotels and motels

D-U-N-S 25-948-7189   (BR)
DALHOUSIE UNIVERSITY
DEPARTMENT OF FAMILY MEDICINE
5909 Veterans Memorial Lane, Halifax, NS, B3H 2E2
(902) 473-4747
Emp Here 40
SIC 8221 Colleges and universities

D-U-N-S 25-359-7793   (BR)
DALHOUSIE UNIVERSITY
DALHOUSIE HEALTH SERVICES
6230 Coburg Rd, Halifax, NS, B3H 4J5
(902) 494-2171
Emp Here 50
SIC 8221 Colleges and universities

D-U-N-S 20-287-5097   (BR)
DALHOUSIE UNIVERSITY
HUMAN COMMUNICATION DISORDER PROGRAM
5850 College St 2nd Fl Rm 2c01, Halifax, NS, B3H 1X5
(902) 494-7052
Emp Here 20
SIC 8221 Colleges and universities

D-U-N-S 25-334-2257   (BR)
DALHOUSIE UNIVERSITY
OFFICE EXTERNAL RELATIONS, THE
6300 Coburg Rd Rm 100, Halifax, NS, B3H 2A3
(902) 494-2211
Emp Here 45
SIC 8221 Colleges and universities

D-U-N-S 24-424-8865   (BR)
DALHOUSIE UNIVERSITY
DEPARTMENT OF PSYCHIATRY, INTERNATIONAL PSYCHIATRY SECTION
5909 Veterans Memorial Lane Suite 3088, Halifax, NS, B3H 2E2
(902) 473-4252
Emp Here 29
SIC 8221 Colleges and universities

D-U-N-S 20-346-9846   (BR)

DALHOUSIE UNIVERSITY
FACULTY OF ARTS AND SOCIAL SCIENCES
6135 University Ave Rm 3030, Halifax, NS, B3H 4P9
(902) 494-1440
Emp Here 200
SIC 8221 Colleges and universities

D-U-N-S 20-346-6537   (BR)
DALHOUSIE UNIVERSITY
FACULTY OF MEDICINE
1276 South Park St Rm 225, Halifax, NS, B3H 2Y9
(902) 473-7736
Emp Here 300
SIC 8221 Colleges and universities

D-U-N-S 20-514-5993   (BR)
DALHOUSIE UNIVERSITY
DALHOUSIE UNIVERSITY BOOKSTORE
6136 University Ave Suite 314, Halifax, NS, B3H 4J2
(902) 494-2460
Emp Here 25
SIC 5942 Book stores

D-U-N-S 20-346-9861   (BR)
DALHOUSIE UNIVERSITY
DEPARTMENT OF HISTORY
6135 University Ave, Halifax, NS, B3H 4P9
(902) 494-2011
Emp Here 20
SIC 8221 Colleges and universities

D-U-N-S 24-345-5347   (BR)
DALHOUSIE UNIVERSITY
COLLEGE OF CONTINUING EDUCATION
1459 Lemarchant St Suite 2201, Halifax, NS, B3H 3P8
(902) 494-2526
Emp Here 40
SIC 8221 Colleges and universities

D-U-N-S 20-296-3869   (BR)
DALHOUSIE UNIVERSITY
6061 University Ave, Halifax, NS, B3H 4H9
(902) 494-2640
Emp Here 20
SIC 8221 Colleges and universities

D-U-N-S 20-063-8141   (BR)
DALHOUSIE UNIVERSITY
DEPARTMENT OF ANATOMY
5850 College St Unit 13b, Halifax, NS, B3H 1X5
(902) 494-6850
Emp Here 75
SIC 8221 Colleges and universities

D-U-N-S 25-241-3372   (BR)
HALIFAX REGIONAL SCHOOL BOARD
GROSEBROOK JUNIOR HIGH SCHOOL
(*Suby of* Halifax Regional School Board)
5966 South St, Halifax, NS, B3H 1S6
(902) 421-6758
Emp Here 35
SIC 8211 Elementary and secondary schools

D-U-N-S 25-746-6946   (BR)
HALIFAX REGIONAL SCHOOL BOARD
SIR CHARLES TUPPER SCHOOL
(*Suby of* Halifax Regional School Board)
1930 Cambridge St, Halifax, NS, B3H 4S5
(902) 421-6775
Emp Here 30
SIC 8211 Elementary and secondary schools

D-U-N-S 20-048-0320   (BR)
HALIFAX REGIONAL SCHOOL BOARD
LEMARCHANT ST THOMAS
6141 Watt St, Halifax, NS, B3H 2B7
(902) 421-6769
Emp Here 35
SIC 8211 Elementary and secondary schools

D-U-N-S 25-176-5301   (BR)
HALIFAX REGIONAL SCHOOL BOARD
INGLIS STREET ELEMENTARY SCHOOL

(*Suby of* Halifax Regional School Board)
5985 Inglis St, Halifax, NS, B3H 1K7
(902) 421-6767
Emp Here 30
SIC 8211 Elementary and secondary schools

D-U-N-S 20-580-8152   (BR)
HALIFAX REGIONAL SCHOOL BOARD
HALIFAX CENTRAL JUNIOR HIGH
1787 Preston St, Halifax, NS, B3H 3V7
(902) 421-6777
Emp Here 40
SIC 8211 Elementary and secondary schools

D-U-N-S 20-938-2642   (BR)
LAWTON'S DRUG STORES LIMITED
LAWTON'S HALIFAX PROFESSIONAL CENTRE
5991 Spring Garden Rd Suite 132, Halifax, NS, B3H 1Y6
(902) 423-9356
Emp Here 25
SIC 5912 Drug stores and proprietary stores

D-U-N-S 25-783-4614   (BR)
NOVA SCOTIA HEALTH AUTHORITY
HALIFAX INFIRMARY
1278 Tower Rd, Halifax, NS, B3H 2Y9
(902) 473-1787
Emp Here 2,000
SIC 8062 General medical and surgical hospitals

D-U-N-S 25-783-4606   (BR)
NOVA SCOTIA HEALTH AUTHORITY
Q E II
1796 Summer St, Halifax, NS, B3H 3A7
(902) 473-2700
Emp Here 22
SIC 8062 General medical and surgical hospitals

D-U-N-S 20-728-6089   (HQ)
NOVA SCOTIA HEALTH AUTHORITY
QUEEN ELIZABETH II HEALTH SCIENCES CENTRE
1276 South Park St Suite 1278, Halifax, NS, B3H 2Y9
(902) 473-5117
Emp Here 200   *Emp Total* 11,000
Sales 834,962,251
SIC 8062 General medical and surgical hospitals
Ch Bd Steve Parker
V Ch Bd George Unsworth
Pr Janet Knox
VP Allan Horsburgh
VP Lindsay Peach
VP Tricia Cochrane
VP Tim Guest
VP Paula Bond
VP Lynne Harrigan
VP Colin Stevenson

D-U-N-S 20-552-8271   (BR)
NOVA SCOTIA HEALTH AUTHORITY
REGIONAL TISSUE BANK
5788 University Ave Rm 431, Halifax, NS, B3H 1V8
(902) 473-7360
Emp Here 25
SIC 8062 General medical and surgical hospitals

D-U-N-S 24-127-5697   (BR)
NOVA SCOTIA LIQUOR CORPORATION
1075 Barrington St, Halifax, NS, B3H 4P1
(902) 424-3754
Emp Here 20
SIC 5921 Liquor stores

D-U-N-S 24-677-8588   (BR)
PARRISH & HEIMBECKER, LIMITED
P&H MILLING GROUP
(*Suby of* Parrish & Heimbecker, Limited)
730 Marginal Rd, Halifax, NS, B3H 0A1
(902) 429-0622
Emp Here 50

▲ Public Company   ■ Public Company Family Member   **HQ** Headquarters   **BR** Branch   **SL** Single Location

SIC 5153 Grain and field beans

D-U-N-S 20-268-4713   (SL)
SACRED HEART SCHOOL OF HALIFAX
5820 Spring Garden Rd, Halifax, NS, B3H 1X8
(902) 422-4459
Emp Here 70   *Sales* 4,669,485
SIC 8211 Elementary and secondary schools

D-U-N-S 24-387-3168   (BR)
SAINT MARY'S UNIVERSITY
TOWER, THE
920 Tower Rd, Halifax, NS, B3H 2Y4
(902) 420-5555
Emp Here 70
SIC 7991 Physical fitness facilities

D-U-N-S 24-877-7781   (BR)
SOBEYS CAPITAL INCORPORATED
SOBEYS #574
1120 Queen St, Halifax, NS, B3H 2R9
(902) 422-7605
Emp Here 200
SIC 5411 Grocery stores

D-U-N-S 20-194-4241   (BR)
SODEXO CANADA LTD
6350 Coburg Rd, Halifax, NS, B3H 2A1
(902) 423-1756
Emp Here 30
SIC 5812 Eating places

D-U-N-S 25-485-4961   (BR)
SODEXO CANADA LTD
6136 University Ave Suite 322, Halifax, NS, B3H 4J2
(902) 494-2126
Emp Here 20
SIC 5812 Eating places

D-U-N-S 20-799-2111   (SL)
THE HALIFAX GRAMMAR SCHOOL
945 Tower Rd, Halifax, NS, B3H 2Y2
(902) 423-9312
Emp Here 63   *Sales* 4,231,721
SIC 8211 Elementary and secondary schools

D-U-N-S 20-321-4127   (BR)
UNIVERSAL PROPERTY MANAGEMENT LIMITED
SOUTHPOINT APARTMENTS
5415 Victoria Rd Suite 214, Halifax, NS, B3H 4K5
(902) 830-1863
Emp Here 100
SIC 6513 Apartment building operators

D-U-N-S 20-788-5729   (BR)
UNIVERSITE SAINTE-ANNE
UNIVERSITE SAINTE ANNE CAMPUS HALIFAX
1589 Walnut St, Halifax, NS, B3H 3S1
(902) 424-2630
Emp Here 30
SIC 8221 Colleges and universities

D-U-N-S 20-920-9043   (BR)
UNIVERSITE SAINTE-ANNE
RICHMOND COMMUNITY ACCESS SOCIETY
1589 Walnut St, Halifax, NS, B3H 3S1
(902) 424-4462
Emp Here 30
SIC 8221 Colleges and universities

D-U-N-S 20-703-6430   (BR)
VIA RAIL CANADA INC
1161 Hollis St, Halifax, NS, B3H 2P6
(902) 494-7900
Emp Here 300
SIC 4111 Local and suburban transit

Halifax, NS B3J
Halifax County

D-U-N-S 20-571-8211   (BR)

AON REED STENHOUSE INC
1969 Upper Water St Suite 1001, Halifax, NS, B3J 3R7
(902) 429-7310
Emp Here 20
SIC 6411 Insurance agents, brokers, and service

D-U-N-S 25-094-1531   (SL)
ATLANTIC CONTAINER LINE AB
1969 Upper Water St Suite 1608, Halifax, NS, B3J 3R7
(800) 225-1235
Emp Here 34   *Sales* 7,660,874
SIC 4424 Deep sea domestic transportation of freight
Fritz King

D-U-N-S 24-361-2129   (SL)
ATRIUM GROUP INC, THE
PETE'S EUROPEAN DELI
1515 Dresden Row, Halifax, NS, B3J 4B1
(902) 425-5700
Emp Here 50   *Sales* 4,304,681
SIC 5431 Fruit and vegetable markets

D-U-N-S 20-205-6029   (BR)
BMO NESBITT BURNS INC
1969 Upper Water St Suite 1901, Halifax, NS, B3J 3R7
(902) 429-3710
Emp Here 50
SIC 6211 Security brokers and dealers

D-U-N-S 24-376-4524   (BR)
BANK OF NOVA SCOTIA, THE
SCOTIABANK
5201 Duke St Suite Upper, Halifax, NS, B3J 1N9
(902) 420-4971
Emp Here 30
SIC 6021 National commercial banks

D-U-N-S 24-130-2884   (BR)
BANK OF NOVA SCOTIA, THE
SCOTIABANK
1709 Hollis St, Halifax, NS, B3J 1W1
(902) 420-3567
Emp Here 65
SIC 6021 National commercial banks

D-U-N-S 20-754-1975   (BR)
BANK OF NOVA SCOTIA, THE
SCOTIABANK
1465 Brenton St Suite 301, Halifax, NS, B3J 3T3
(902) 420-7100
Emp Here 37
SIC 6021 National commercial banks

D-U-N-S 20-303-3258   (BR)
BANQUE DE DEVELOPPEMENT DU CANADA
BDC
2000 Barrington St Suite 1400, Halifax, NS, B3J 3K1
(902) 426-0341
Emp Here 40
SIC 6141 Personal credit institutions

D-U-N-S 24-621-1259   (SL)
BARRINGTON CONSULTING GROUP INCORPORATED, THE
1326 Barrington St, Halifax, NS, B3J 1Z1
(902) 491-4462
Emp Here 51   *Sales* 5,545,013
SIC 8741 Management services
Dir Andrew Creaser

D-U-N-S 20-194-0041   (BR)
BELL ALIANT REGIONAL COMMUNICATIONS INC
1505 Barrington St Suite 1102, Halifax, NS, B3J 3K5
(902) 487-4609
Emp Here 711
SIC 4899 Communication services, nec

D-U-N-S 20-547-0821   (SL)

BISHOP'S CELLAR LIMITED, THE
1477 Lower Water St, Halifax, NS, B3J 3Z4
(902) 490-2675
Emp Here 21   *Sales* 2,115,860
SIC 5182 Wine and distilled beverages

D-U-N-S 25-167-1897   (SL)
BURCHELLS LLP
1801 Hollis St Suite 1800, Halifax, NS, B3J 3N4
(902) 423-6361
Emp Here 52   *Sales* 4,450,603
SIC 8111 Legal services

D-U-N-S 20-630-9072   (HQ)
CBCL LIMITED
(*Suby of* Canadian-British Consulting Group Limited)
1489 Hollis St, Halifax, NS, B3J 3M5
(902) 421-7241
Emp Here 160   *Emp Total* 224
Sales 35,431,570
SIC 8711 Engineering services
Pr Pr Michael R Macdonald
Ch Bd Walter Strachan

D-U-N-S 20-515-7972   (BR)
CIBC WORLD MARKETS INC
CIBC WOOD GUNDY
1969 Upper Water St Suite 1801, Halifax, NS, B3J 3R7
(902) 425-6900
Emp Here 65
SIC 6211 Security brokers and dealers

D-U-N-S 24-227-7676   (BR)
CITCO (CANADA) INC
5151 George St Suite 700, Halifax, NS, B3J 1M5
(902) 442-4242
Emp Here 150
SIC 8741 Management services

D-U-N-S 24-705-8761   (SL)
CAMBRIDGE SUITES LIMITED, THE
1601 Lower Water St Suite 700, Halifax, NS, B3J 3P6
(902) 421-1601
Emp Here 200   *Sales* 11,779,200
SIC 7011 Hotels and motels
Sec Frank Medjuck
Pr Ralph Medjuck

D-U-N-S 25-688-2762   (BR)
CANADA LANDS COMPANY CLC LIMITED
1505 Barrington St Suite 1205, Halifax, NS, B3J 3K5
(416) 952-6100
Emp Here 30
SIC 6531 Real estate agents and managers

D-U-N-S 20-572-9515   (BR)
CANADA POST CORPORATION
1526 Dresden Row, Halifax, NS, B3J 3K3
(902) 420-1594
Emp Here 20
SIC 4311 U.s. postal service

D-U-N-S 20-716-4893   (BR)
CANADIAN BROADCASTING CORPORATION
CBC
5600 Sackville St, Halifax, NS, B3J 1L2
(902) 420-4483
Emp Here 300
SIC 4832 Radio broadcasting stations

D-U-N-S 25-094-5219   (BR)
CANADIAN IMPERIAL BANK OF COMMERCE
CIBC CUSTOMER CONTACT CENTRE
5367 Cogswell St, Halifax, NS, B3J 3X5
(902) 420-3920
Emp Here 425
SIC 6021 National commercial banks

D-U-N-S 24-132-2262   (BR)
CANADIAN IMPERIAL BANK OF COMMERCE

CIBC
1809 Barrington St Suite 1501, Halifax, NS, B3J 3K8
(902) 428-4750
Emp Here 32
SIC 6021 National commercial banks

D-U-N-S 20-905-1721   (BR)
CANADIAN RED CROSS SOCIETY, THE
1940 Gottingen St, Halifax, NS, B3J 3Y2
(902) 423-3680
Emp Here 80
SIC 8322 Individual and family services

D-U-N-S 20-819-3979   (HQ)
CANADIAN-BRITISH CONSULTING GROUP LIMITED
(*Suby of* Canadian-British Consulting Group Limited)
1489 Hollis St, Halifax, NS, B3J 3M5
(902) 421-7241
Emp Here 29   *Emp Total* 224
Sales 52,551,040
SIC 6712 Bank holding companies
Pr Pr Alan Perry

D-U-N-S 20-321-6353   (BR)
CAPSERVCO LIMITED PARTNERSHIP
(*Suby of* CapServCo Limited Partnership)
2000 Barrington St Suite 1100, Halifax, NS, B3J 3K1
(902) 421-1734
Emp Here 100
SIC 8721 Accounting, auditing, and bookkeeping

D-U-N-S 24-568-2823   (SL)
CENTUM MORTGAGE SPECIALISTS
1649 Brunswick St, Halifax, NS, B3J 2G3
(902) 420-9090
Emp Here 26   *Sales* 6,125,139
SIC 6163 Loan brokers
Owner Stephen Spellman

D-U-N-S 25-092-3547   (SL)
CHRISCO RESTAURANTS LIMITED
ARGYLE BAR & GRILL
1575 Argyle St, Halifax, NS, B3J 2B2
(902) 492-8844
Emp Here 52   *Sales* 1,896,978
SIC 5813 Drinking places

D-U-N-S 25-175-4982   (BR)
CONCENTRIX TECHNOLOGIES SERVICES (CANADA) LIMITED
MINACS GROUP INC, THE
1949 Upper Water St Suite 101, Halifax, NS, B3J 3N3
(902) 428-9999
Emp Here 300
SIC 4899 Communication services, nec

D-U-N-S 25-675-3732   (BR)
CONSEILLERS EN GESTION ET INFORMATIQUE CGI INC
1809 Barrington St, Halifax, NS, B3J 3K8
(902) 423-2862
Emp Here 30
SIC 7379 Computer related services, nec

D-U-N-S 25-370-7624   (BR)
CROMBIE DEVELOPMENTS LIMITED
HALIFAX DEVELOPMENTS
2000 Barrington St Suite 1210, Halifax, NS, B3J 3K1
(902) 429-3660
Emp Here 200
SIC 6512 Nonresidential building operators

D-U-N-S 20-702-4089   (BR)
DALHOUSIE UNIVERSITY
DEPARTMENT OF MECHANICAL ENGINEERING
5269 Morris St Rm C360, Halifax, NS, B3J 1B4
(902) 494-3989
Emp Here 25
SIC 8221 Colleges and universities

D-U-N-S 20-346-9838   (BR)
DALHOUSIE UNIVERSITY
SCHOOL OF ARCHITECTURE
5410 Spring Garden Rd, Halifax, NS, B3J 1G1
(902) 494-3971
Emp Here 45
SIC 8221 Colleges and universities

D-U-N-S 20-346-9754   (BR)
DALHOUSIE UNIVERSITY
FACULTY OF ENGINEERING
5248 Morris St, Halifax, NS, B3J 1B4
(902) 494-8431
Emp Here 150
SIC 8221 Colleges and universities

D-U-N-S 20-346-9820   (BR)
DALHOUSIE UNIVERSITY
DEPARTMENT OF PROCESS ENGINEER-
ING AND APPLIED SCIENCE
1360 Barrington St, Halifax, NS, B3J 1Y9
(902) 494-3953
Emp Here 22
SIC 8221 Colleges and universities

D-U-N-S 20-906-1068   (BR)
DELOITTE & TOUCHE MANAGEMENT
CONSULTANTS
(*Suby of* Deloitte & Touche Management Con-
sultants)
1969 Upper Water St Suite 1500, Halifax, NS,
B3J 3R7
(902) 422-8541
Emp Here 100
SIC 8741 Management services

D-U-N-S 24-188-1325   (BR)
DELOITTE LLP
1969 Upper Water St Suite 1500, Halifax, NS,
B3J 3R7
(902) 422-8541
Emp Here 100
SIC 8721 Accounting, auditing, and book-
keeping

D-U-N-S 24-789-4637   (BR)
DELTA HOTELS LIMITED
DELTA HALIFAX
1990 Barrington St, Halifax, NS, B3J 1P2
(902) 425-6700
Emp Here 50
SIC 8741 Management services

D-U-N-S 20-221-2254   (HQ)
ESIT CANADA ENTERPRISE SERVICES CO
(*Suby of* Dxc Technology Company)
1969 Upper Water St, Halifax, NS, B3J 3R7

Emp Here 885   *Emp Total* 178,750
Sales 357,507,430
SIC 5734 Computer and software stores
Pr Pr Arif Manji
  Sonia Price

D-U-N-S 20-304-8991   (BR)
ESIT CANADA ENTERPRISE SERVICES CO
ESIT CANADA ENTERPRISE SERVICES CO
(*Suby of* Dxc Technology Company)
1718 Argyle St Suite 420, Halifax, NS, B3J
3N6

Emp Here 30
SIC 5734 Computer and software stores

D-U-N-S 25-394-1942   (BR)
ENCANA CORPORATION
1701 Hollis St Unit 700, Halifax, NS, B3J 3M8
(902) 422-4500
Emp Here 30
SIC 1382 Oil and gas exploration services

D-U-N-S 24-343-1442   (SL)
ENERGETIC FOODS INCORPORATED
MCKELVIE'S RESTAURANT
1680 Lower Water St, Halifax, NS, B3J 1S4

Emp Here 60   *Sales* 1,824,018
SIC 5812 Eating places

D-U-N-S 25-297-1718   (BR)
ERNST & YOUNG INC
Rbc Waterside Ctr 1871 Hollis Suite 500, Hal-
ifax, NS, B3J 0C3
(902) 420-1080
Emp Here 90
SIC 8721 Accounting, auditing, and book-
keeping

D-U-N-S 20-032-2159   (BR)
ERNST & YOUNG LLP
(*Suby of* Ernst & Young LLP)
1959 Upper Water St Suite 1301, Halifax, NS,
B3J 3N2
(902) 420-1080
Emp Here 40
SIC 8721 Accounting, auditing, and book-
keeping

D-U-N-S 25-562-6277   (SL)
FEDERATED BUILDING SERVICES LIM-
ITED
1505 Barrington St Suite 1310, Halifax, NS,
B3J 3K5

Emp Here 80   *Sales* 2,334,742
SIC 7349 Building maintenance services, nec

D-U-N-S 24-705-1618   (HQ)
FENCO SHAWINIGAN ENGINEERING LIM-
ITED
FSEL
5657 Spring Garden Rd Suite 200, Halifax,
NS, B3J 3R4
(902) 492-4544
Emp Here 75   *Emp Total* 33,000
Sales 16,589,040
SIC 8711 Engineering services
Pr Pr Albert Williams

D-U-N-S 25-358-4098   (SL)
FIVE FISHERMEN LIMITED, THE
FIVE FISHERMEN RESTAURANT
1740 Argyle St, Halifax, NS, B3J 2B6
(902) 454-9344
Emp Here 60   *Sales* 1,824,018
SIC 5812 Eating places

D-U-N-S 24-309-9764   (BR)
FORTIS PROPERTIES CORPORATION
FOUR POINTS BY SHERATON HALIFAX
1496 Hollis St, Halifax, NS, B3J 3Z1
(902) 423-4444
Emp Here 36
SIC 6512 Nonresidential building operators

D-U-N-S 24-263-7775   (BR)
FUJITSU CONSEIL (CANADA) INC
FUJITSU CONSULTING
1505 Barrington St Suite 1102, Halifax, NS,
B3J 3K5
(902) 420-1119
Emp Here 20
SIC 7379 Computer related services, nec

D-U-N-S 20-861-4516   (BR)
GDI SERVICES (CANADA) LP
2000 Barrington St Suite 1210, Halifax, NS,
B3J 3K1

Emp Here 50
SIC 7349 Building maintenance services, nec

D-U-N-S 25-542-2677   (SL)
GRAFTON CONNOR GROUP INC
(*Suby of* Graftons Connor Property Inc)
1741 Grafton St, Halifax, NS, B3J 2C6
(902) 454-9344
Emp Here 300   *Sales* 20,799,360
SIC 5812 Eating places
Pr Pr Gary Hurst

D-U-N-S 24-671-1030   (HQ)
GRAFTONS CONNOR PROPERTY INC
(*Suby of* Graftons Connor Property Inc)
1741 Grafton St, Halifax, NS, B3J 2C6
(902) 454-9344
Emp Here 100   *Emp Total* 100
Sales 3,648,035

SIC 5813 Drinking places

D-U-N-S 20-646-1126   (BR)
GRANT THORNTON LLP
2000 Barrington St Suite 1100, Halifax, NS,
B3J 3K1
(902) 421-1734
Emp Here 150
SIC 8721 Accounting, auditing, and book-
keeping

D-U-N-S 25-175-4388   (BR)
GREAT-WEST LIFE ASSURANCE COM-
PANY, THE
ATLANTIC PROVINCES GROUP SALES OF-
FICE
1801 Hollis St Suite 1900, Halifax, NS, B3J
3N4
(902) 429-8374
Emp Here 20
SIC 6411 Insurance agents, brokers, and ser-
vice

D-U-N-S 25-094-4196   (SL)
GROWTHWORKS ENTERPRISES LTD
1801 Hollis St Suite 310, Halifax, NS, B3J 3N4
(902) 423-9367
Emp Here 33   *Sales* 6,695,700
SIC 6211 Security brokers and dealers
  Brent W Barrie
  Stephen Rankin
Dir Richard Coles
Dir William Eeuwes
Dir Robert Steele
Dir Diane Macdiarmid
  Anita Fifield

D-U-N-S 20-710-2984   (BR)
HALIFAX REGIONAL SCHOOL BOARD
ST MARY'S SCHOOL
5614 Morris St, Halifax, NS, B3J 1C2
(902) 421-6749
Emp Here 25
SIC 8211 Elementary and secondary schools

D-U-N-S 20-813-4676   (HQ)
HARDMAN GROUP LIMITED, THE
(*Suby of* Hardman Group Limited, The)
1226 Hollis St, Halifax, NS, B3J 1T6
(902) 429-3743
Emp Here 20   *Emp Total* 55
Sales 10,836,784
SIC 6553 Cemetery subdividers and develop-
ers
Pr Pr William N Hardman
  William B Hardman
  Clayton Hardman
Dir Shirley Hardman

D-U-N-S 20-754-6081   (SL)
HIGHWAY 104 WESTERN ALIGNMENT
CORPORATION
COBEQUID PASS
1969 Upper Water St Suite 1905, Halifax, NS,
B3J 3R7
(902) 422-6764
Emp Here 23   *Sales* 18,558,998
SIC 4785 Inspection and fixed facilities
Genl Mgr Paul Richard
Fin Ex Eva Hislop

D-U-N-S 25-573-4584   (BR)
HOGG ROBINSON CANADA INC
BTI CANADA
(*Suby of* HOGG ROBINSON GROUP PLC)
1894 Barrington St Unit 700, Halifax, NS, B3J
2A8
(902) 425-1212
Emp Here 70
SIC 4724 Travel agencies

D-U-N-S 20-352-7320   (SL)
HORIZON MARITIME SERVICES LTD
1459 Hollis St, Halifax, NS, B3J 1V1
(902) 468-2341
Emp Here 50   *Sales* 3,648,035
SIC 7361 Employment agencies

D-U-N-S 20-407-1104   (SL)
HOWATT WAYNE F
1801 Hollis St Unit 1800, Halifax, NS, B3J 3N4
(902) 423-6361
Emp Here 49   *Sales* 5,024,256
SIC 8111 Legal services

D-U-N-S 24-790-0459   (SL)
JACK FRIDAY'S LIMITED
MY APARTMENT
1740 Argyle St, Halifax, NS, B3J 2B6
(902) 454-9344
Emp Here 85   *Sales* 2,553,625
SIC 5812 Eating places

D-U-N-S 20-191-2321   (BR)
KPMG LLP
(*Suby of* KPMG LLP)
1959 Upper Water St Suite 1500, Halifax, NS,
B3J 3N2
(902) 492-6000
Emp Here 70
SIC 8721 Accounting, auditing, and book-
keeping

D-U-N-S 25-580-3207   (BR)
KUEHNE + NAGEL LTD
KN CUSTOMS BROKERS
1969 Upper Water St Suite 1710, Halifax, NS,
B3J 3R7
(902) 420-6500
Emp Here 20
SIC 4731 Freight transportation arrangement

D-U-N-S 25-299-4439   (BR)
LAWTON'S DRUG STORES LIMITED
LAWTONS DRUGS #114
5675 Spring Garden Rd Suite 6a, Halifax, NS,
B3J 1H1
(902) 422-9686
Emp Here 35
SIC 5912 Drug stores and proprietary stores

D-U-N-S 25-299-4876   (BR)
LAWTON'S DRUG STORES LIMITED
LAWTON'S DRUGS 144
5201 Duke St Suite 144, Halifax, NS, B3J 1N9
(902) 429-5436
Emp Here 20
SIC 5912 Drug stores and proprietary stores

D-U-N-S 20-930-4195   (BR)
LONDON LIFE INSURANCE COMPANY
FREEDOM 55 FINANCIAL
1959 Upper Water St, Halifax, NS, B3J 3N2
(902) 422-1631
Emp Here 60
SIC 6311 Life insurance

D-U-N-S 20-315-9843   (BR)
LUXURY HOTELS INTERNATIONAL OF
CANADA, ULC
MARRIOTT HALIFAX HARBOURFRONT HO-
TEL
(*Suby of* Marriott International, Inc.)
1919 Upper Water St, Halifax, NS, B3J 3J5
(902) 421-1700
Emp Here 50
SIC 7011 Hotels and motels

D-U-N-S 20-607-7658   (BR)
MACQUARIE CAPITAL MARKETS CANADA
LTD
1969 Upper Water St Suite 2004, Halifax, NS,
B3J 3R7

Emp Here 20
SIC 6282 Investment advice

D-U-N-S 20-728-8887   (HQ)
MARITIME TRAVEL INC
BAY TRAVEL, THE
(*Suby of* Maritime Travel Inc)
2000 Barrington St Suite 202, Halifax, NS, B3J
3K1
(902) 420-1554
Emp Here 45   *Emp Total* 375
Sales 89,376,858

SIC 4725 Tour operators
Robert Dexter
Pr Pr Gary Gaudry
Sec Erica Allmark
Dir Deanna Skinner
Dir Julie Gaudry

D-U-N-S 25-497-3944   (HQ)
MARITIMES & NORTHEAST PIPELINE MANAGEMENT LTD
MARITIMES & NORTHEAST PIPELINE
1801 Hollis St Suite 1600, Halifax, NS, B3J 3N4
(902) 425-4474
Emp Here 20   *Emp Total* 7,733
Sales 6,493,502
SIC 1623 Water, sewer, and utility lines
Pr Douglas Bloom

D-U-N-S 25-743-9257   (BR)
MARSH CANADA LIMITED
(*Suby of* Marsh & McLennan Companies, Inc.)
1801 Hollis St Suite 1300, Halifax, NS, B3J 3N4
(902) 429-6710
Emp Here 27
SIC 6411 Insurance agents, brokers, and service

D-U-N-S 24-385-3681   (BR)
MARSH CANADA LIMITED
(*Suby of* Marsh & McLennan Companies, Inc.)
5657 Spring Garden Rd Suite 701, Halifax, NS, B3J 3R4
(902) 429-2769
Emp Here 44
SIC 8721 Accounting, auditing, and bookkeeping

D-U-N-S 20-905-9435   (HQ)
MARTEC LIMITED
1888 Brunswick St Suite 400, Halifax, NS, B3J 3J8
(902) 425-5101
Emp Here 40   *Sales* 5,107,249
SIC 8748 Business consulting, nec
Pr Magnus Wollstrum
VP VP Mervyn Earl Norwood
Dir James L Warner
Dir James P Warner

D-U-N-S 20-273-8811   (BR)
MCINNES COOPER
ACCOUNTING DEPARTMENT
5151 George St Suite 900, Halifax, NS, B3J 1M5
(902) 425-6500
Emp Here 35
SIC 8111 Legal services

D-U-N-S 24-342-1880   (BR)
MERCER (CANADA) LIMITED
MERCER
(*Suby of* Marsh & McLennan Companies, Inc.)
1801 Hollis St Suite 1300, Halifax, NS, B3J 3N4
(902) 429-7050
Emp Here 24
SIC 8999 Services, nec

D-U-N-S 20-280-1817   (SL)
MERRILL LYNCH COMMODITIES CANADA, ULC
(*Suby of* Bank of America Corporation)
1969 Upper Water St Suite 1300, Halifax, NS, B3J 3R7
(800) 681-2100
Emp Here 50   *Sales* 50,725,000
SIC 6799 Investors, nec
Pr Pr Rupert Tanna
Mark Elliott
VP VP Dennis Albrecht
VP VP Trent Stout
Todd Hansen

D-U-N-S 25-593-3236   (SL)
METROPOLITAN   ENTERTAINMENT GROUP

CASINO NOVA SCOTIA HALIFAX
(*Suby of* Great Canadian Gaming Corporation)
1983 Upper Water St, Halifax, NS, B3J 3Y5
(902) 425-7777
Emp Here 800   *Sales* 51,628,560
SIC 7999 Amusement and recreation, nec
Patsy Barker

D-U-N-S 24-317-3973   (BR)
MICROSOFT CANADA INC
(*Suby of* Microsoft Corporation)
1969 Upper Water St Suite 2200, Halifax, NS, B3J 3R7
(902) 491-4470
Emp Here 30
SIC 5045 Computers, peripherals, and software

D-U-N-S 25-308-4164   (BR)
MODIS CANADA INC
AJILON CONSULTING
1959 Upper Water St Suite 1700, Halifax, NS, B3J 3N2
(902) 421-2025
Emp Here 20
SIC 8742 Management consulting services

D-U-N-S 25-412-4134   (BR)
MOUNTAIN EQUIPMENT CO-OPERATIVE
MOUNTAIN EQUIPMENT CO-OPERATIVE
1550 Granville St, Halifax, NS, B3J 1X1
(902) 421-2667
Emp Here 34
SIC 5941 Sporting goods and bicycle shops

D-U-N-S 25-306-0750   (BR)
NTT DATA CANADA, INC.
2000 Barrington St Suite 300, Halifax, NS, B3J 3K1
(902) 422-6036
Emp Here 49
SIC 7376 Computer facilities management

D-U-N-S 24-168-2640   (HQ)
NTT DATA CANADA, INC.
2000 Barrington St Suite 300, Halifax, NS, B3J 3K1
(902) 422-6036
Emp Here 700   *Emp Total* 274,850
Sales 94,232,900
SIC 7379 Computer related services, nec
CEO John W. Mcclain
Lawrence Whelan
John Gillis
Sue Churchill

D-U-N-S 25-373-7621   (BR)
NATIONAL BANK FINANCIAL LTD
1969 Upper Water St Unit 1601, Halifax, NS, B3J 3R7
(902) 496-7700
Emp Here 25
SIC 6211 Security brokers and dealers

D-U-N-S 24-756-5229   (SL)
NEW PALACE CABARET LIMITED, THE
1721 Brunswick St, Halifax, NS, B3J 2G4
(902) 420-0015
Emp Here 75   *Sales* 2,772,507
SIC 5813 Drinking places

D-U-N-S 25-395-6353   (SL)
NORTHERN FIBRE TERMINAL INCORPORATED
1869 Upper Water St, Halifax, NS, B3J 1S9
(902) 422-3030
Emp Here 50   *Sales* 2,115,860
SIC 2611 Pulp mills

D-U-N-S 20-443-2637   (HQ)
NOVA SCOTIA POWER INCORPORATED
1223 Lower Water St, Halifax, NS, B3J 3S8
(902) 428-6230
Emp Here 600   *Emp Total* 3,600
Sales 1,002,958,620
SIC 4911 Electric services
Pr Pr Karen Hutt

Mark Sidebottom
Ex VP Judith Ferguson
VP Paul Casey
VP Sasha Irving
VP David Landrigan
VP Fin Claudette Porter
Ch Bd Scott Balfour
Lee Bragg
Sandra Greer

D-U-N-S 20-794-5671   (BR)
NOVA SCOTIA, PROVINCE OF
TRANSPORTATION AND INFRASTRUCTURE RENEWAL
1672 Granville St, Halifax, NS, B3J 3Z8
(902) 424-2297
Emp Here 20
SIC 4212 Local trucking, without storage

D-U-N-S 25-135-6143   (BR)
NUBODY'S FITNESS CENTRES INC
NUBODY'S
(*Suby of* Nubody's Fitness Centres Inc)
2000 Barrington St, Halifax, NS, B3J 3K1
(902) 492-9289
Emp Here 25
SIC 7999 Amusement and recreation, nec

D-U-N-S 20-699-2203   (BR)
PATTERSON LAW
1718 Argyle St Suite 510, Halifax, NS, B3J 3N6
(902) 405-8000
Emp Here 25
SIC 8111 Legal services

D-U-N-S 24-358-9715   (SL)
PINKY SKOOPMORE'S ICE CREAM FUN
1888 Brunswick St, Halifax, NS, B3J 3J8
(902) 431-1700
Emp Here 150   *Sales* 6,289,900
SIC 5812 Eating places
Pt Kevin Riles

D-U-N-S 20-930-4799   (BR)
PRICEWATERHOUSECOOPERS LLP
PWC DEBT SOLUTIONS
1601 Lower Water St Suite 400, Halifax, NS, B3J 3P6
(902) 491-7400
Emp Here 90
SIC 8721 Accounting, auditing, and bookkeeping

D-U-N-S 24-335-9952   (HQ)
PRIMERO GOLD CANADA INC
1969 Upper Water St Suite 2001, Halifax, NS, B3J 3R7
(902) 422-1421
Emp Here 220   *Emp Total* 602
Sales 29,712,409
SIC 1041 Gold ores
Wade Dawe
Ex VP Jennifer Nicholson
VP Howard Bird
VP Fin Jon Legatto
Dana Hatfiled
Sec Daniel Gallivan

D-U-N-S 20-561-9450   (BR)
QUEST SOFTWARE CANADA INC
DELL SOFTWARE CANADA INC
(*Suby of* Francisco Partners Management, L.P.)
5151 George St, Halifax, NS, B3J 1M5
(902) 442-5700
Emp Here 104
SIC 7372 Prepackaged software

D-U-N-S 24-189-0169   (BR)
RBC DOMINION SECURITIES INC
(*Suby of* Royal Bank Of Canada)
1959 Upper Water St Suite 1400, Halifax, NS, B3J 3N2
(902) 424-1000
Emp Here 50
SIC 6211 Security brokers and dealers

D-U-N-S 25-573-4840   (SL)
RADISSON SUITE HOTEL HALIFAX
HOLLOWAY LODGING
1649 Hollis St, Halifax, NS, B3J 1V8
(902) 429-7233
Emp Here 50   *Sales* 2,188,821
SIC 7011 Hotels and motels

D-U-N-S 20-536-7191   (BR)
ROYAL TRUST CORPORATION OF CANADA
(*Suby of* Royal Bank Of Canada)
5161 George St Suite 1103, Halifax, NS, B3J 1M7
(902) 421-7446
Emp Here 20
SIC 6021 National commercial banks

D-U-N-S 25-315-6442   (BR)
SNC-LAVALIN INC
5657 Spring Garden Rd Suite 200, Halifax, NS, B3J 3R4
(902) 492-4544
Emp Here 80
SIC 8711 Engineering services

D-U-N-S 20-797-5074   (BR)
SNC-LAVALIN OPERATIONS & MAINTENANCE INC
SNC LAVALIN
1660 Hollis St Suite 301, Halifax, NS, B3J 1V7

Emp Here 20
SIC 8742 Management consulting services

D-U-N-S 25-590-0037   (BR)
SAINT MARY'S UNIVERSITY
ST MARY'S UNIVERSITY BUSINESS DEVELOPMENT CENTRE
1546 Barrington St, Halifax, NS, B3J 3X7

Emp Here 25
SIC 8741 Management services

D-U-N-S 20-727-6726   (BR)
SCOTIA CAPITAL INC
SCOTIA MCLEOD
1959 Upper Water St, Halifax, NS, B3J 3N2
(902) 420-2220
Emp Here 58
SIC 6211 Security brokers and dealers

D-U-N-S 20-207-6514   (BR)
SIERRA SYSTEMS GROUP INC
1809 Barrington St Suite 1004, Halifax, NS, B3J 3K8
(902) 425-6688
Emp Here 40
SIC 7379 Computer related services, nec

D-U-N-S 25-577-4036   (SL)
SILVERBIRCH NO. 15 OPERATIONS LIMITED PARTNERSHIP
HAMPTON INN AND HOMEWOOD SUITES HALIFAX DOWNTOWN, THE
1960 Brunswick St, Halifax, NS, B3J 2G7
(902) 422-1391
Emp Here 85   *Sales* 2,845,467
SIC 7299 Miscellaneous personal service

D-U-N-S 24-231-8371   (SL)
SNAP TOGETHER PRODUCTIONS
5091 Terminal Rd, Halifax, NS, B3J 3Y1
(902) 422-6287
Emp Here 70   *Sales* 4,085,799
SIC 4833 Television broadcasting stations

D-U-N-S 24-832-5789   (HQ)
STEWART MCKELVEY STIRLING SCALES
SMSS
(*Suby of* Stewart McKelvey Stirling Scales)
1959 Upper Water St Suite 900, Halifax, NS, B3J 3N2
(902) 420-3200
Emp Here 150   *Emp Total* 200
Sales 17,145,765
SIC 8111 Legal services
Pt John M Rogers

Pt James Dickinson

D-U-N-S 20-965-6094   (BR)
SYMCOR INC
5251 Duke St Suite 214, Halifax, NS, B3J 1P3

Emp Here 400
SIC 7374 Data processing and preparation

D-U-N-S 20-920-0620   (BR)
SYMCOR INC
1580 Grafton St, Halifax, NS, B3J 2C2
(902) 404-4606
Emp Here 200
SIC 4226 Special warehousing and storage, nec

D-U-N-S 25-174-7374   (SL)
SYMPHONY NOVA SCOTIA SOCIETY
5657 Spring Garden Rd Suite 301, Halifax, NS, B3J 3R4
(902) 421-1300
Emp Here 50   *Sales* 3,210,271
SIC 7929 Entertainers and entertainment groups

D-U-N-S 20-023-4347   (BR)
TD WATERHOUSE CANADA INC
(*Suby of* Toronto-Dominion Bank, The)
1601 Lower Water St Suite Lower, Halifax, NS, B3J 3P6
(902) 420-3202
Emp Here 30
SIC 6211 Security brokers and dealers

D-U-N-S 20-028-2635   (BR)
TORONTO-DOMINION BANK, THE
TD CANADA TRUST
(*Suby of* Toronto-Dominion Bank, The)
1785 Barrington St, Halifax, NS, B3J 0B2
(902) 420-8040
Emp Here 30
SIC 6021 National commercial banks

D-U-N-S 20-934-5888   (BR)
UNISYS CANADA INC
1809 Barrington St Suite M104, Halifax, NS, B3J 3K8

Emp Here 57
SIC 7371 Custom computer programming services

D-U-N-S 20-929-4404   (HQ)
YMCA OF GREATER HALI-FAX/DARTMOUTH, THE
(*Suby of* YMCA Of Greater Halifax/Dartmouth, The)
5670 Spring Garden Rd Suite 306, Halifax, NS, B3J 1H6
(902) 423-9709
Emp Here 65   *Emp Total* 255
Sales 6,793,432
SIC 8641 Civic and social associations
Pr Pr Bette Watson-Borg
VP Leslie Tinkham
VP Lorrie Turnbull
Benjamin Davis
Barbara Miller
Arlene Seto

Halifax, NS B3K
Halifax County

D-U-N-S 24-804-4117   (SL)
1887780 NOVA SCOTIA LIMITED
(*Suby of* Forbes Group Limited)
3330 Kempt Rd, Halifax, NS, B3K 4X1

Emp Here 32   *Sales* 16,232,000
SIC 5511 New and used car dealers
Pr Pr Patrick W Forbes
Treas Rick Joedicke
Genl Mgr Ivan Forbes

D-U-N-S 20-719-5962   (SL)
3025052 NOVA SCOTIA LIMITED
VOLVO OF HALIFAX
3363 Kempt Rd, Halifax, NS, B3K 4X5
(902) 453-2110
Emp Here 36   *Sales* 16,780,961
SIC 5012 Automobiles and other motor vehicles
Fin Ex Maryjean Denicola

D-U-N-S 20-563-8500   (BR)
ASSANTE CAPITAL MANAGEMENT LTD
ASSANTE WEALTH MANAGEMENT
5548 Kaye St Suite 201, Halifax, NS, B3K 1Y5
(902) 423-1200
Emp Here 48
SIC 6211 Security brokers and dealers

D-U-N-S 20-207-3974   (BR)
BELL MEDIA INC
CTV ATLANTIC
2885 Robie St, Halifax, NS, B3K 5Z4
(902) 453-4000
Emp Here 100
SIC 4833 Television broadcasting stations

D-U-N-S 20-027-2995   (BR)
BELL MEDIA INC
CJCH 920-C 100 FM
2900 Agricola St, Halifax, NS, B3K 6A7
(902) 453-2524
Emp Here 53
SIC 4832 Radio broadcasting stations

D-U-N-S 24-228-1371   (SL)
CALL-US INFO LTD
6009 Quinpool Rd, Halifax, NS, B3K 5J7

Emp Here 90   *Sales* 4,523,563
SIC 7389 Business services, nec

D-U-N-S 20-026-4570   (SL)
CANADIAN ASSOCIATED LABORATORIES LIMITED
2457 Maynard St, Halifax, NS, B3K 3V2
(902) 429-1820
Emp Here 70   *Sales* 4,085,799
SIC 8072 Dental laboratories

D-U-N-S 25-573-0988   (BR)
CARA OPERATIONS LIMITED
HARVEY'S RESTAURANT
(*Suby of* Cara Holdings Limited)
3434 Kempt Rd, Halifax, NS, B3K 4X7
(902) 454-8495
Emp Here 20
SIC 5812 Eating places

D-U-N-S 24-263-2073   (BR)
CERESCORP COMPANY
4755 Barrington St, Halifax, NS, B3K 6A8
(902) 453-4590
Emp Here 20
SIC 4491 Marine cargo handling

D-U-N-S 24-722-6715   (BR)
COCA-COLA REFRESHMENTS CANADA COMPANY
(*Suby of* The Coca-Cola Company)
Gd, Halifax, NS, B3K 5L8
(902) 876-8661
Emp Here 50
SIC 5149 Groceries and related products, nec

D-U-N-S 20-002-6131   (BR)
CREDIT UNION CENTRAL OF CANADA
CREDIT UNION CENTRAL NOVA SCOTIA
6074 Lady Hammond Rd, Halifax, NS, B3K 2R7
(902) 453-0680
Emp Here 150
SIC 6062 State credit unions

D-U-N-S 25-891-5651   (BR)
DALHOUSIE UNIVERSITY
DALHOUSIE LEGAL AID SERVICE
2209 Gottingen St, Halifax, NS, B3K 3B5

(902) 423-8105
Emp Here 25
SIC 8111 Legal services

D-U-N-S 20-814-8432   (BR)
DALHOUSIE UNIVERSITY
DALHOUSIE UNIVERSITY CLINICAL VISION SCIENCE
5850 University Ave, Halifax, NS, B3K 6R8
(902) 470-8019
Emp Here 20
SIC 8069 Specialty hospitals, except psychiatric

D-U-N-S 20-573-5538   (BR)
EMC EMERGENCY MEDICAL CARE IN-CORPORATED
EMC
5830 Duffus St, Halifax, NS, B3K 5L6
(902) 484-0003
Emp Here 20
SIC 4119 Local passenger transportation, nec

D-U-N-S 24-132-0928   (SL)
EDMONDS LANDSCAPE & CONSTRUC-TION SERVICES LIMITED
EDMONDS CONSTRUCTION SERVICES
2675 Clifton St, Halifax, NS, B3K 4V4
(902) 453-5500
Emp Here 50   *Sales* 4,231,721
SIC 4959 Sanitary services, nec

D-U-N-S 25-274-3141   (BR)
EMCO CORPORATION
SUMNER PLUMBING SUPPLIES
6355 Lady Hammond Rd, Halifax, NS, B3K 2S2
(902) 453-4410
Emp Here 20
SIC 5074 Plumbing and heating equipment and supplies (hydronics)

D-U-N-S 25-792-9190   (BR)
FARMERS CO-OPERATIVE DAIRY LIMITED
FARMERS DAIRY
Gd, Halifax, NS, B3K 5Y6

Emp Here 350
SIC 5143 Dairy products, except dried or canned

D-U-N-S 25-241-3299   (BR)
HALIFAX REGIONAL SCHOOL BOARD
JOSEPH HOWE SCHOOL
(*Suby of* Halifax Regional School Board)
2557 Maynard St, Halifax, NS, B3K 3V6
(902) 421-6785
Emp Here 25
SIC 8211 Elementary and secondary schools

D-U-N-S 25-174-7671   (BR)
HALIFAX REGIONAL SCHOOL BOARD
HIGHLAND PARK JUNIOR HIGH SCHOOL
(*Suby of* Halifax Regional School Board)
3479 Robie St, Halifax, NS, B3K 4S4
(902) 493-5124
Emp Here 25
SIC 8211 Elementary and secondary schools

D-U-N-S 25-174-6061   (BR)
HALIFAX REGIONAL SCHOOL BOARD
ST JOSEPH ALEXANDER MCKAY SCHOOL
(*Suby of* Halifax Regional School Board)
5389 Russell St, Halifax, NS, B3K 1W8
(902) 493-5180
Emp Here 25
SIC 8211 Elementary and secondary schools

D-U-N-S 20-710-3016   (BR)
HALIFAX REGIONAL SCHOOL BOARD
ST STEPHEN SCHOOL
3669 Highland Ave, Halifax, NS, B3K 4J9
(902) 493-5155
Emp Here 50
SIC 8211 Elementary and secondary schools

D-U-N-S 25-998-5679   (SL)
HOYT'S SPECIALIZED TRANSPORTATION GROUP OF COMPANIES INC

HOYT'S MOVING AND STORAGE
Gd, Halifax, NS, B3K 5M7
(902) 876-8202
Emp Here 100   *Sales* 5,212,143
SIC 4214 Local trucking with storage
Pr Don Campbell
VP Barry Hoyt

D-U-N-S 24-833-8204   (BR)
HUSSMANN CANADA INC
2631 King St, Halifax, NS, B3K 4T7
(902) 455-2123
Emp Here 60
SIC 1711 Plumbing, heating, air-conditioning

D-U-N-S 24-386-4167   (BR)
I.M.P. GROUP LIMITED
HARDING MEDICAL
3447 Kempt Rd, Halifax, NS, B3K 5T7
(902) 484-2002
Emp Here 25
SIC 4581 Airports, flying fields, and services

D-U-N-S 25-995-9104   (BR)
IRVING SHIPBUILDING INC
HALIFAX SHIPYARD, DIV OF
3099 Barrington St, Halifax, NS, B3K 2X6
(902) 423-9271
Emp Here 300
SIC 3731 Shipbuilding and repairing

D-U-N-S 20-311-3543   (BR)
IZAAK WALTON KILLAM HEALTH CENTRE, THE
RESEARCH SERCVICES, DEPARTMENT OF
Gd, Halifax, NS, B3K 6R8
(902) 470-6682
Emp Here 3,200
SIC 8731 Commercial physical research

D-U-N-S 25-364-5196   (BR)
IZAAK WALTON KILLAM HEALTH CENTRE, THE
OBSTRETICS & GYNECOLOGY, DEPART-MENT OF
5980 University Ave, Halifax, NS, B3K 6R8
(902) 470-6460
Emp Here 30
SIC 8062 General medical and surgical hospitals

D-U-N-S 20-931-6348   (HQ)
IZAAK WALTON KILLAM HEALTH CENTRE, THE
IWK HEALTH CENTRE
585 0/5980 University Ave, Halifax, NS, B3K 6R8
(902) 470-8888
Emp Here 3,500   *Emp Total* 11,000
Sales 223,441,330
SIC 8069 Specialty hospitals, except psychiatric
Pr Tracey Kitch
Ch Bd Bob Hanf
V Ch Bd Karen Kitch
Doug Doucet
Larry Evans
Kimberly Horrelt
Dawn Jutla
Karl Logan
Shannon Macphee
Catherine Macpherson

D-U-N-S 24-189-7479   (BR)
IZAAK WALTON KILLAM HEALTH CENTRE, THE
IWK COMMUNITY MENTAL HEALTH
6080 Young St Suite 1001, Halifax, NS, B3K 5L2
(902) 464-4110
Emp Here 30
SIC 8062 General medical and surgical hospitals

D-U-N-S 20-051-8053   (BR)
LAWTON'S DRUG STORES LIMITED
LAWTON'S DRUGS

5515 Duffus St Suite 172, Halifax, NS, B3K 2M5
(902) 454-7471
Emp Here 20
SIC 5912 Drug stores and proprietary stores

D-U-N-S 20-782-9607   (HQ)
LEAGUE SAVINGS & MORTGAGE COMPANY
6074 Lady Hammond Rd, Halifax, NS, B3K 2R7
(902) 453-4220
Emp Here 32   *Emp Total* 160
Sales 9,849,695
SIC 6162 Mortgage bankers and loan correspondents
Pr Bernie O'neil
 Marion Garlick

D-U-N-S 25-612-8463   (BR)
LEAGUE SAVINGS & MORTGAGE COMPANY
6074 Lady Hammond Rd, Halifax, NS, B3K 2R7
(902) 453-0680
Emp Here 45
SIC 6162 Mortgage bankers and loan correspondents

D-U-N-S 24-533-3943   (HQ)
NATIONAL ART LIMITED
MARITIME FRAME-IT
(*Suby of* R C R Investments Ltd)
5426 Portland Pl, Halifax, NS, B3K 1A1

Emp Here 20   *Emp Total* 125
Sales 4,377,642
SIC 5023 Homefurnishings

D-U-N-S 24-789-4751   (SL)
NORTHWOOD HOMECARE LTD
5355 Russell St, Halifax, NS, B3K 1W8
(902) 425-2273
Emp Here 300   *Sales* 17,621,552
SIC 8051 Skilled nursing care facilities
 Lloyd Brown
 Paul Tracy
Ex Dir Bob St. Laurent
Ch Bd Sheldon Lipkus

D-U-N-S 20-589-2938   (SL)
NORTHWOODCARE INCORPORATED
2615 Northwood Terr, Halifax, NS, B3K 3S5
(902) 454-8311
Emp Here 700   *Sales* 34,356,000
SIC 8361 Residential care
 Rick Kelly
 Paul Tracy
 Kate Neonakis

D-U-N-S 24-662-1762   (BR)
NOVA SCOTIA COMMUNITY COLLEGE
NSCC ONLINE LEARNING
5685 Leeds St, Halifax, NS, B3K 2T3
(902) 491-6774
Emp Here 2,000
SIC 8221 Colleges and universities

D-U-N-S 20-728-9158   (HQ)
NOVA SCOTIA COMMUNITY COLLEGE
INSTITUTE OF TECHNOLOGY
5685 Leeds St, Halifax, NS, B3K 2T3
(902) 491-6722
Emp Here 75   *Emp Total* 11,000
Sales 191,896,779
SIC 8222 Junior colleges
Pr Don Bureaux
VP Pamela Reid
VP Fin Bob Shedden
Dir Fin Monica Foster

D-U-N-S 20-939-6840   (SL)
QUEST - A SOCIETY FOR ADULT SUPPORT AND REHABILITATION
2131 Gottingen St Suite 101, Halifax, NS, B3K 5Z7
(902) 490-7200
Emp Here 75   *Sales* 2,772,507

SIC 8361 Residential care

D-U-N-S 25-580-5301   (BR)
ROBIE & KEMPT SERVICES LIMITED
TIM HORTONS
6034 Lady Hammond Rd, Halifax, NS, B3K 2R6
(902) 455-2894
Emp Here 30
SIC 5812 Eating places

D-U-N-S 20-002-5034   (BR)
ROGERS COMMUNICATIONS INC
ROGERS WIRELESS
(*Suby of* Rogers Communications Inc)
6080 Young St Suite 905, Halifax, NS, B3K 5L2
(902) 453-1400
Emp Here 26
SIC 4899 Communication services, nec

D-U-N-S 24-796-9863   (BR)
ROGERS MEDIA INC
ROGERS RADIO
(*Suby of* Rogers Communications Inc)
6080 Young St Suite 911, Halifax, NS, B3K 5L2
(902) 493-7200
Emp Here 27
SIC 4832 Radio broadcasting stations

D-U-N-S 24-043-6506   (BR)
SERVICE CORPORATION INTERNATIONAL (CANADA) LIMITED
J A SNOW FUNERAL HOME
2666 Windsor St, Halifax, NS, B3K 5C9
(902) 455-0531
Emp Here 20
SIC 7261 Funeral service and crematories

D-U-N-S 24-471-3723   (BR)
SOBEYS CAPITAL INCORPORATED
SOBEYS STORE
2651 Windsor St Suite 554, Halifax, NS, B3K 5C7
(902) 455-8508
Emp Here 80
SIC 5411 Grocery stores

D-U-N-S 25-088-3634   (BR)
STAPLES CANADA INC
STAPLES THE BUSINESS DEPOT
(*Suby of* Staples, Inc.)
2003 Gottingen St, Halifax, NS, B3K 3B1
(902) 474-5100
Emp Here 75
SIC 5943 Stationery stores

D-U-N-S 24-375-4012   (BR)
STEELE AUTO GROUP LIMITED
VOLVO OF HALIFAX
3363 Kempt Rd, Halifax, NS, B3K 4X5
(902) 453-2110
Emp Here 20
SIC 5511 New and used car dealers

D-U-N-S 24-472-2377   (BR)
WENDY'S RESTAURANTS OF CANADA INC
WENDY'S RESTAURANTS
(*Suby of* The Wendy's Company)
3580 Kempt Rd, Halifax, NS, B3K 4X8
(902) 455-6065
Emp Here 35
SIC 5812 Eating places

D-U-N-S 24-189-4187   (BR)
WESTERN INVENTORY SERVICE LTD
WIS INTERNATIONAL
3200 Kempt Rd Suite 210, Halifax, NS, B3K 4X1
(902) 468-3811
Emp Here 25
SIC 7389 Business services, nec

Halifax, NS B3L
Halifax County

D-U-N-S 25-543-0878   (BR)
20 VIC MANAGEMENT INC
HALIFAX SHOPPING CENTRE
7001 Mumford Rd Suite 202, Halifax, NS, B3L 2H8
(902) 454-8666
Emp Here 30
SIC 6512 Nonresidential building operators

D-U-N-S 25-628-7004   (BR)
501420 NB INC
ROYAL LEPAGE ATLANTIC
7075 Bayers Rd Suite 216, Halifax, NS, B3L 2C2
(902) 453-1700
Emp Here 65
SIC 6531 Real estate agents and managers

D-U-N-S 20-336-6062   (SL)
AFFINIO INC
2717 Joseph Howe Dr Suite 300, Halifax, NS, B3L 4T9
(866) 991-3263
Emp Here 50   *Sales* 4,742,446
SIC 5734 Computer and software stores

D-U-N-S 24-666-1982   (BR)
BANQUE TORONTO-DOMINION, LA
TD CANADA TRUST
(*Suby of* Toronto-Dominion Bank, The)
6239 Quinpool Rd, Halifax, NS, B3L 1A4
(902) 422-7471
Emp Here 20
SIC 6021 National commercial banks

D-U-N-S 25-295-3914   (BR)
BAYSHORE HEALTHCARE LTD.
BAYSHORE HOME HEALTH
7071 Bayers Rd Suite 237, Halifax, NS, B3L 2C2
(902) 425-7683
Emp Here 120
SIC 8059 Nursing and personal care, nec

D-U-N-S 20-005-6971   (BR)
CHARLTOM RESTAURANTS LIMITED
WENDY'S
6169 Quinpool Rd, Halifax, NS, B3L 4P8
(902) 429-3824
Emp Here 29
SIC 5812 Eating places

D-U-N-S 25-321-6287   (BR)
CLUB MONACO CORP
(*Suby of* Ralph Lauren Corporation)
7001 Mumford Rd Suite 183, Halifax, NS, B3L 2H8
(902) 453-3520
Emp Here 20
SIC 5651 Family clothing stores

D-U-N-S 25-174-9347   (BR)
COMCARE (CANADA) LIMITED
COMCARE HEALTH SERVICES
(*Suby of* Comcare (Canada) Limited)
7071 Bayers Rd Suite 1151, Halifax, NS, B3L 2C2
(902) 453-0838
Emp Here 250
SIC 8051 Skilled nursing care facilities

D-U-N-S 20-573-3111   (BR)
COMPAGNIE DES CHEMINS DE FER NATIONAUX DU CANADA
CN
6800 Chisholm Ave, Halifax, NS, B3L 2R9
(902) 428-5306
Emp Here 20
SIC 4011 Railroads, line-haul operating

D-U-N-S 25-117-0155   (BR)
FOOT LOCKER CANADA CO
FOOT LOCKER CANADA CO.
7001 Mumford Rd Suite 1800, Halifax, NS, B3L 2H8
(902) 454-0649
Emp Here 22
SIC 5651 Family clothing stores

D-U-N-S 24-794-6457   (BR)
GAP (CANADA) INC
BANANA REPUBLIC
(*Suby of* The Gap Inc)
7001 Mumford Rd, Halifax, NS, B3L 2H8
(902) 454-8071
Emp Here 20
SIC 5651 Family clothing stores

D-U-N-S 24-621-0095   (BR)
GOODLIFE FITNESS CENTRES INC
3601 Joseph Howe Dr, Halifax, NS, B3L 4H8
(902) 453-7724
Emp Here 20
SIC 7999 Amusement and recreation, nec

D-U-N-S 20-295-3738   (BR)
GOVERNING COUNCIL OF THE SALVATION ARMY IN CANADA, THE
GOVERNING COUNCIL OF THE SALVATION ARMY IN CANADA, THE
7071 Bayers Rd Suite 282, Halifax, NS, B3L 2C2
(902) 455-1201
Emp Here 40
SIC 7032 Sporting and recreational camps

D-U-N-S 25-193-0764   (HQ)
GRAYBAR CANADA LIMITED
HARRIS & ROOME SUPPLY
(*Suby of* Graybar Electric Company, Inc.)
3600 Joseph Howe Dr, Halifax, NS, B3L 4H7
(902) 457-8787
Emp Here 80   *Emp Total* 8,500
Sales 137,127,533
SIC 5063 Electrical apparatus and equipment
Pr Robert Lyons
Ex VP Ex VP Peter Horncastle
 Mike E. Williamson
Sr VP Brian D. Thomas
Dir Opers Mike B. Boivin
Prs Dir Mark Kehoe

D-U-N-S 25-612-6384   (BR)
GRAYBAR CANADA LIMITED
HARRIS & ROOME SUPPLY
(*Suby of* Graybar Electric Company, Inc.)
3600 Joseph Howe Dr, Halifax, NS, B3L 4H7
(902) 457-8730
Emp Here 24
SIC 5063 Electrical apparatus and equipment

D-U-N-S 24-129-6011   (SL)
H.R.D.A. ENTERPRISES LIMITED
STONE HEARTH BAKERY, DIV OF
7071 Bayers Rd Suite 5009, Halifax, NS, B3L 2C2
(902) 454-2851
Emp Here 60   *Sales* 10,956,600
SIC 4953 Refuse systems
Ch Bd Ron Singer
Pr Mark Lever
Sec Eric Crowell
Dir Michael White

D-U-N-S 20-906-6422   (SL)
HALIFAX GOLF & COUNTRY CLUB, LIMITED
ASHBURN GOLF CLUB
3250 Joseph Howe Dr, Halifax, NS, B3L 4G1
(902) 443-8260
Emp Here 100   *Sales* 4,012,839
SIC 7997 Membership sports and recreation clubs

D-U-N-S 25-241-3216   (BR)
HALIFAX REGIONAL SCHOOL BOARD
OXFORD SCHOOL
(*Suby of* Halifax Regional School Board)
6364 North St, Halifax, NS, B3L 1P6
(902) 421-6763
Emp Here 45
SIC 8211 Elementary and secondary schools

D-U-N-S 20-710-3008   (BR)
HALIFAX REGIONAL SCHOOL BOARD
ST PATRICK'S HIGH SCHOOL
6067 Quinpool Rd, Halifax, NS, B3L 1A2

▲ Public Company   ■ Public Company Family Member   **HQ** Headquarters   **BR** Branch   **SL** Single Location

(902) 424-0233
Emp Here 50
SIC 8211 Elementary and secondary schools

D-U-N-S 20-710-2976   (BR)
HALIFAX REGIONAL SCHOOL BOARD
ST. CATHERINE'S ELEMENTARY SCHOOL
3299 Connolly St, Halifax, NS, B3L 3P7
(902) 493-5143
Emp Here 50
SIC 8211 Elementary and secondary schools

D-U-N-S 25-241-3133   (BR)
HALIFAX REGIONAL SCHOOL BOARD
ST. AGNES JUNIOR HIGH SCHOOL
(*Suby of* Halifax Regional School Board)
6981 Mumford Rd, Halifax, NS, B3L 2H7
(902) 493-5132
Emp Here 35
SIC 8211 Elementary and secondary schools

D-U-N-S 25-301-2678   (BR)
HUDSON'S BAY COMPANY
BAY, THE
7067 Chebucto Rd Suite 111, Halifax, NS, B3L 4R5

Emp Here 140
SIC 5311 Department stores

D-U-N-S 20-017-2661   (BR)
I.M.P. GROUP LIMITED
IMP SOLUTIONS
2651 Joseph Howe Dr Suite 202, Halifax, NS, B3L 4T1
(902) 482-1600
Emp Here 27
SIC 4581 Airports, flying fields, and services

D-U-N-S 20-929-3943   (BR)
IGM FINANCIAL INC
INVESTORS GROUP
7001 Mumford Rd Suite 207, Halifax, NS, B3L 2H8
(902) 423-8294
Emp Here 45
SIC 6211 Security brokers and dealers

D-U-N-S 24-833-1670   (BR)
LAWTON'S INCORPORATED
LAWTON'S DRUG STORE 112
7071 Bayers Rd Suite 112, Halifax, NS, B3L 2C2
(902) 453-1920
Emp Here 35
SIC 5912 Drug stores and proprietary stores

D-U-N-S 25-359-3206   (BR)
LOBLAW PROPERTIES LIMITED
ATLANTIC WHOLESALERS
3711 Joseph Howe Dr, Halifax, NS, B3L 4H8
(902) 468-8866
Emp Here 80
SIC 5411 Grocery stores

D-U-N-S 25-281-5600   (BR)
MD MANAGEMENT LIMITED
MD FINANCIAL
(*Suby of* Canadian Medical Association)
7051 Bayers Rd Suite 500, Halifax, NS, B3L 2C1
(902) 425-4646
Emp Here 30
SIC 6282 Investment advice

D-U-N-S 20-561-3925   (BR)
MANUFACTURERS LIFE INSURANCE COMPANY, THE
MANULIFE FINANCIAL
2727 Joseph Howe Dr, Halifax, NS, B3L 4G6
(902) 453-4300
Emp Here 800
SIC 6311 Life insurance

D-U-N-S 24-345-6170   (BR)
MELOCHE MONNEX INC
(*Suby of* Toronto-Dominion Bank, The)
7051 Bayers Rd Suite 200, Halifax, NS, B3L 2C1

(902) 420-1112
Emp Here 105
SIC 6331 Fire, marine, and casualty insurance

D-U-N-S 24-533-1541   (BR)
MEMORIAL GARDENS CANADA LIMITED
ATLANTIC FUNERAL HOME
6552 Bayers Rd, Halifax, NS, B3L 2B3
(902) 453-1434
Emp Here 33
SIC 7261 Funeral service and crematories

D-U-N-S 20-932-8954   (BR)
MORNEAU SHEPELL LTD
SHEPPELL FGI DIV OF
(*Suby of* Morneau Shepell Inc)
7071 Bayers Rd Suite 3007, Halifax, NS, B3L 2C2
(902) 429-8013
Emp Here 70
SIC 8999 Services, nec

D-U-N-S 25-298-9033   (BR)
NOVA SCOTIA LIQUOR CORPORATION
6169 Quinpool Rd, Halifax, NS, B3L 4P8
(902) 423-7126
Emp Here 20
SIC 5921 Liquor stores

D-U-N-S 20-922-7201   (BR)
PRISZM LP
KFC
6310 Quinpool Rd, Halifax, NS, B3L 1A5
(902) 492-8587
Emp Here 31
SIC 5812 Eating places

D-U-N-S 25-018-9560   (BR)
ROYAL BANK OF CANADA
RBC
(*Suby of* Royal Bank Of Canada)
6390 Quinpool Rd, Halifax, NS, B3L 4N2
(902) 421-8420
Emp Here 20
SIC 6021 National commercial banks

D-U-N-S 20-356-1758   (SL)
SALTWIRE NETWORK INC
2717 Joseph Howe Dr, Halifax, NS, B3L 4T9
(902) 426-8211
Emp Here 50   *Sales* 3,648,035
SIC 2721 Periodicals

D-U-N-S 20-757-9322   (BR)
SEARS CANADA INC
SEARS OULET STORE, THE
7101 Chebucto Rd, Halifax, NS, B3L 1N3
(902) 454-5009
Emp Here 96
SIC 5311 Department stores

D-U-N-S 20-027-3969   (BR)
SEARS CANADA INC
7001 Mumford Rd, Halifax, NS, B3L 2H8
(902) 454-5111
Emp Here 200
SIC 5311 Department stores

D-U-N-S 20-731-8671   (BR)
WAL-MART CANADA CORP
WALMART
6990 Mumford Rd Suite 3636, Halifax, NS, B3L 4W4
(902) 454-7990
Emp Here 150
SIC 5311 Department stores

D-U-N-S 20-184-3120   (BR)
WINNERS MERCHANTS INTERNATIONAL L.P.
WINNERS
(*Suby of* The TJX Companies Inc)
6970 Mumford Rd, Halifax, NS, B3L 4W6
(902) 454-5500
Emp Here 40
SIC 5651 Family clothing stores

Halifax, NS B3M
Halifax County

D-U-N-S 25-296-5801   (BR)
BANK OF NOVA SCOTIA, THE
SCOTIABANK
255 Lacewood Dr, Halifax, NS, B3M 4G2
(902) 420-3590
Emp Here 25
SIC 6021 National commercial banks

D-U-N-S 24-533-2275   (SL)
CARROLL PONTIAC BUICK GMC LTD
CAROLL PONTIAC BUICK
44 Bedford Hwy, Halifax, NS, B3M 2J2

Emp Here 82   *Sales* 41,196,800
SIC 5511 New and used car dealers
Pr Pr John P. Carroll
  James Maclellan

D-U-N-S 20-727-9233   (SL)
CHINA TOWN & CO LTD
CHINA TOWN RESTAURANT & LOUNGE
381 Bedford Hwy, Halifax, NS, B3M 2L3
(902) 443-2444
Emp Here 50   *Sales* 1,532,175
SIC 5812 Eating places

D-U-N-S 20-710-3289   (BR)
CONSEIL SCOLAIRE ACADIEN PROVINCIAL
BEAUBASSIN
54 Larry Uteck Blvd, Halifax, NS, B3M 4R9
(902) 457-6810
Emp Here 35
SIC 8211 Elementary and secondary schools

D-U-N-S 25-161-7192   (BR)
GOODLIFE FITNESS CENTRES INC
41 Peakview Way, Halifax, NS, B3M 0G2
(902) 835-6696
Emp Here 25
SIC 7991 Physical fitness facilities

D-U-N-S 25-882-4317   (BR)
HALIFAX REGIONAL SCHOOL BOARD
CLAYTON PARK JUNIOR HIGH SCHOOL
(*Suby of* Halifax Regional School Board)
45 Plateau Cres, Halifax, NS, B3M 2V7
(902) 457-8930
Emp Here 30
SIC 8211 Elementary and secondary schools

D-U-N-S 20-608-2666   (BR)
HALIFAX REGIONAL SCHOOL BOARD
DUC D'ANVILLE ELEMENTARY SCHOOL
12 Clayton Park Dr, Halifax, NS, B3M 1L3
(902) 457-8940
Emp Here 40
SIC 8211 Elementary and secondary schools

D-U-N-S 25-834-7392   (BR)
HALIFAX REGIONAL SCHOOL BOARD
ECOLE ROCKINGHAM ELEMENTARY SCHOOL
(*Suby of* Halifax Regional School Board)
31 Tremont Dr, Halifax, NS, B3M 1X8
(902) 457-8986
Emp Here 30
SIC 8211 Elementary and secondary schools

D-U-N-S 25-754-4056   (SL)
INDEPENDENT ARMOURED TRANSPORT ATLANTIC INC
287 Lacewood Dr Unit 103, Halifax, NS, B3M 3Y7
(902) 450-1396
Emp Here 60   *Sales* 1,896,978
SIC 7381 Detective and armored car services

D-U-N-S 20-051-1066   (SL)
INDEPENDENT SECURITY SERVICES ATLANTIC INC
ISS
287 Lacewood Dr Unit 103, Halifax, NS, B3M 3Y7

(902) 450-1396
Emp Here 87   *Sales* 2,699,546
SIC 7381 Detective and armored car services

D-U-N-S 25-299-4314   (BR)
LAWTON'S DRUG STORES LIMITED
LAWTON'S DRUGS 128
287 Lacewood Dr Suite 128, Halifax, NS, B3M 3Y7
(902) 443-4446
Emp Here 20
SIC 5912 Drug stores and proprietary stores

D-U-N-S 20-027-0874   (SL)
MARKLAND ASSOCIATES LIMITED
21 Hamshaw Dr, Halifax, NS, B3M 2G9
(902) 445-8920
Emp Here 50   *Sales* 3,648,035
SIC 1793 Glass and glazing work

D-U-N-S 25-298-9074   (BR)
NOVA SCOTIA LIQUOR CORPORATION
117 Kearney Lake Rd, Halifax, NS, B3M 4N9
(902) 443-9607
Emp Here 20
SIC 5921 Liquor stores

D-U-N-S 25-746-4776   (HQ)
PACRIM DEVELOPMENTS INC
HOLIDAY INN EXPRESS-MONCTON
117 Kearney Lake Rd Suite 11, Halifax, NS, B3M 4N9
(902) 457-0144
Emp Here 30   *Sales* 63,694,691
SIC 6552 Subdividers and developers, nec
  Guy Lam
Pr Pr Edward Good
Sr VP Glenn Squires
Dir Malcom Bell

D-U-N-S 25-175-7183   (BR)
ROYAL BANK OF CANADA
ROYAL BANK FINANCIAL GROUP
(*Suby of* Royal Bank Of Canada)
271 Lacewood Dr, Halifax, NS, B3M 4K3
(902) 421-8435
Emp Here 35
SIC 6021 National commercial banks

D-U-N-S 24-804-8258   (BR)
SHANNEX INCORPORATED
MAPLE STONE
245 Main Ave, Halifax, NS, B3M 1B7
(902) 443-1971
Emp Here 250
SIC 8051 Skilled nursing care facilities

D-U-N-S 24-338-0748   (HQ)
SISTERS OF CHARITY
MOUNT ST VINCENT MOTHER HOUSE
(*Suby of* Sisters Of Charity)
215 Seton Rd, Halifax, NS, B3M 0C9
(902) 406-8100
Emp Here 150   *Emp Total* 700
Sales 59,460,960
SIC 8661 Religious organizations
Dir Donna Geernaert
Dir Joan Butler

D-U-N-S 24-943-6056   (BR)
SOBEYS CAPITAL INCORPORATED
SOBEYS
287 Lacewood Dr Suite 644, Halifax, NS, B3M 3Y7
(902) 457-2102
Emp Here 200
SIC 5411 Grocery stores

Halifax, NS B3N
Halifax County

D-U-N-S 20-572-0050   (BR)
BANK OF MONTREAL
BMO
21 Alma Cres, Halifax, NS, B3N 2C4

---

(902) 421-3400
Emp Here 20
SIC 6021 National commercial banks

D-U-N-S 25-577-3749   (BR)
GEM HEALTH CARE GROUP LIMITED
GLADES LODGE
25 Alton Dr, Halifax, NS, B3N 1M1
(902) 477-1777
Emp Here 140
SIC 8051 Skilled nursing care facilities

D-U-N-S 25-241-4370   (BR)
HALIFAX REGIONAL SCHOOL BOARD
FAIRVIEW JUNIOR HIGH SCHOOL
(*Suby of* Halifax Regional School Board)
155 Rosedale Ave, Halifax, NS, B3N 2K2
(902) 457-8960
Emp Here 35
SIC 8211 Elementary and secondary schools

D-U-N-S 25-893-6566   (BR)
HALIFAX REGIONAL SCHOOL BOARD
FAIRVIEW HEIGHTS ANNEX
(*Suby of* Halifax Regional School Board)
142 Rufus Ave, Halifax, NS, B3N 2M1
(902) 457-8953
Emp Here 30
SIC 8211 Elementary and secondary schools

D-U-N-S 25-240-7390   (BR)
HALIFAX REGIONAL SCHOOL BOARD
SPRINGVALE SCHOOL
(*Suby of* Halifax Regional School Board)
92 Downs Ave, Halifax, NS, B3N 1Y6
(902) 479-4606
Emp Here 25
SIC 8211 Elementary and secondary schools

D-U-N-S 25-139-1488   (BR)
HALIFAX REGIONAL SCHOOL BOARD
FAIRVIEW HEIGHTS ELEMENTARY SCHOOL
(*Suby of* Halifax Regional School Board)
210 Coronation Ave, Halifax, NS, B3N 2Y3
(902) 457-8953
Emp Here 40
SIC 8211 Elementary and secondary schools

D-U-N-S 25-241-4537   (BR)
HALIFAX REGIONAL SCHOOL BOARD
ECOLE BURTON ETTINGER ELEMENTARY
(*Suby of* Halifax Regional School Board)
52 Alex St, Halifax, NS, B3N 2W4
(902) 457-8922
Emp Here 40
SIC 8211 Elementary and secondary schools

D-U-N-S 24-363-0782   (BR)
RGIS CANADA ULC
19 Alma Cres Suite 201, Halifax, NS, B3N 2C4
(902) 468-7866
Emp Here 20
SIC 7389 Business services, nec

Halifax, NS B3P
Halifax County

D-U-N-S 25-991-4620   (BR)
GEM HEALTH CARE GROUP LIMITED
GEM MANAGEMENT HOLDINGS
15 Shoreham Ln Suite 101, Halifax, NS, B3P 2R3
(902) 429-6227
Emp Here 700
SIC 6712 Bank holding companies

D-U-N-S 25-241-2812   (BR)
HALIFAX REGIONAL SCHOOL BOARD
ECOLE CHEBUCTO HEIGHTS ELEMENTARY SCHOOL
(*Suby of* Halifax Regional School Board)
230 Cowie Hill Rd, Halifax, NS, B3P 2M3
(902) 479-4298
Emp Here 50
SIC 8211 Elementary and secondary schools

D-U-N-S 20-710-2927   (BR)
HALIFAX REGIONAL SCHOOL BOARD
CUNARD JUNIOR HIGH SCHOOL
121 Williams Lake Rd, Halifax, NS, B3P 1T6
(902) 479-4418
Emp Here 23
SIC 8211 Elementary and secondary schools

D-U-N-S 20-710-2968   (BR)
HALIFAX REGIONAL SCHOOL BOARD
JOHN W MACLEOD FLEMING TOWER SCHOOL
159 Purcells Cove Rd, Halifax, NS, B3P 1B7
(902) 479-4437
Emp Here 50
SIC 8211 Elementary and secondary schools

D-U-N-S 25-298-9199   (BR)
NOVA SCOTIA LIQUOR CORPORATION
SPRYFIELD STORE
279 Herring Cove Rd, Halifax, NS, B3P 1M2
(902) 477-4615
Emp Here 20
SIC 5921 Liquor stores

D-U-N-S 20-004-0728   (BR)
SOBEYS CAPITAL INCORPORATED
SOBEYS
279 Herring Cove Rd, Halifax, NS, B3P 1M2
(902) 477-2817
Emp Here 130
SIC 5411 Grocery stores

Halifax, NS B3R
Halifax County

D-U-N-S 24-378-2492   (SL)
DAMAD HOLDINGS INC
315 Herring Cove Rd, Halifax, NS, B3R 1V5
(902) 477-1210
Emp Here 75   *Sales* 13,758,003
SIC 5912 Drug stores and proprietary stores
Dominic Gniewek

D-U-N-S 20-710-2935   (BR)
HALIFAX REGIONAL SCHOOL BOARD
ELIZABETH SUTHERLAND SCHOOL
66 Rockingstone Rd, Halifax, NS, B3R 2C9
(902) 479-4427
Emp Here 50
SIC 8211 Elementary and secondary schools

D-U-N-S 20-608-2633   (BR)
HALIFAX REGIONAL SCHOOL BOARD
CENTRAL SPRYFIELD SCHOOL
364 Herring Cove Rd, Halifax, NS, B3R 1V8
(902) 479-4286
Emp Here 40
SIC 8211 Elementary and secondary schools

D-U-N-S 25-175-4578   (BR)
HALIFAX REGIONAL SCHOOL BOARD
J L ILSLEY HIGH
(*Suby of* Halifax Regional School Board)
38 Sylvia Ave, Halifax, NS, B3R 1J9
(902) 479-4612
Emp Here 40
SIC 8211 Elementary and secondary schools

D-U-N-S 25-241-2853   (BR)
HALIFAX REGIONAL SCHOOL BOARD
ROCKINGSTONE HEIGHTS SCHOOL
(*Suby of* Halifax Regional School Board)
1 Regan Dr, Halifax, NS, B3R 2J1
(902) 479-4452
Emp Here 44
SIC 8211 Elementary and secondary schools

D-U-N-S 24-120-0489   (BR)
METROPOLITAIN REGIONAL HOUSING AUTHORITY
2 Indigo Walk, Halifax, NS, B3R 1G2
(902) 420-6049
Emp Here 25
SIC 6513 Apartment building operators

D-U-N-S 25-562-5824   (BR)
ROYAL BANK OF CANADA
RBC
(*Suby of* Royal Bank Of Canada)
339 Herring Cove Rd, Halifax, NS, B3R 1V5
(902) 421-8494
Emp Here 21
SIC 6021 National commercial banks

Halifax, NS B3S
Halifax County

D-U-N-S 25-580-4130   (BR)
3499481 CANADA INC
PETS UNLIMITED
215e Chain Lake Dr, Halifax, NS, B3S 1C9

Emp Here 30
SIC 5999 Miscellaneous retail stores, nec

D-U-N-S 25-094-7652   (BR)
ARROW ELECTRONICS CANADA LTD
ARROW ADVANTAGE
(*Suby of* Arrow Electronics, Inc.)
155 Chain Lake Dr Suite 27, Halifax, NS, B3S 1B3
(902) 450-2600
Emp Here 40
SIC 5065 Electronic parts and equipment, nec

D-U-N-S 25-590-0268   (BR)
ATLANTIC WHOLESALERS LTD
REAL ATLANTIC SUPERSTORE, THE
210 Chain Lake Dr, Halifax, NS, B3S 1C5
(902) 450-5317
Emp Here 200
SIC 5411 Grocery stores

D-U-N-S 24-095-2960   (SL)
BLUEDROP SIMULATION SERVICES INC
36 Solutions Dr Suite 300, Halifax, NS, B3S 1N2
(800) 563-3638
Emp Here 140   *Sales* 35,776,166
SIC 3728 Aircraft parts and equipment, nec
Pr Andrew Day
  Carolyn Goddout
VP Opers Jay Konduros
  Chris Lewis
Dir George Chiarucci

D-U-N-S 24-756-6193   (SL)
C & D CLEANING & SECURITY SERVICES LIMITED
106 Chain Lake Dr Unit 2a, Halifax, NS, B3S 1A8
(902) 450-5654
Emp Here 125   *Sales* 3,648,035
SIC 7349 Building maintenance services, nec

D-U-N-S 25-311-5257   (BR)
CANADIAN IMPERIAL BANK OF COMMERCE
CIBC
18 Parkland Dr, Halifax, NS, B3S 1T5
(902) 428-4701
Emp Here 20
SIC 6021 National commercial banks

D-U-N-S 25-542-6108   (BR)
CHARLTOM RESTAURANTS LIMITED
WENDY'S
(*Suby of* Charltom Restaurants Limited)
11 Lakelands Blvd, Halifax, NS, B3S 1G4
(902) 450-5643
Emp Here 40
SIC 5812 Eating places

D-U-N-S 24-993-5206   (BR)
CLARKE TRANSPORT INC
CLARKE TRANSPORT
68 Chain Lake Dr, Halifax, NS, B3S 1A2
(902) 450-5177
Emp Here 50
SIC 4213 Trucking, except local

D-U-N-S 20-173-7306   (BR)
CLEVE'S SPORTING GOODS LIMITED
204 Chain Lake Dr, Halifax, NS, B3S 1C5
(902) 450-5353
Emp Here 24
SIC 5941 Sporting goods and bicycle shops

D-U-N-S 25-528-2162   (BR)
COSTCO WHOLESALE CANADA LTD
COSTCO WHOLESALE STORE # 519
(*Suby of* Costco Wholesale Corporation)
230 Chain Lake Dr, Halifax, NS, B3S 1C5
(902) 450-1078
Emp Here 180
SIC 5099 Durable goods, nec

D-U-N-S 25-975-7011   (BR)
DILLON CONSULTING LIMITED
(*Suby of* Dillon Consulting Inc)
137 Chain Lake Dr Suite 100, Halifax, NS, B3S 1B3
(902) 450-4000
Emp Here 45
SIC 8711 Engineering services

D-U-N-S 20-835-2273   (SL)
ESM BAYERS INC
EASTSIDE MARIO'S
186 Chain Lake Dr, Halifax, NS, B3S 1C5
(902) 450-1311
Emp Here 50   *Sales* 1,532,175
SIC 5812 Eating places

D-U-N-S 24-343-7279   (BR)
FGL SPORTS LTD
SPORT-CHEK
215 Chain Lake Dr Unit F, Halifax, NS, B3S 1C9
(902) 450-1014
Emp Here 45
SIC 5941 Sporting goods and bicycle shops

D-U-N-S 20-710-2950   (BR)
HALIFAX REGIONAL SCHOOL BOARD
HALIFAX WEST HIGHSCHOOL
283 Thomas Raddall Dr, Halifax, NS, B3S 1R1
(902) 457-8900
Emp Here 100
SIC 8211 Elementary and secondary schools

D-U-N-S 20-085-7162   (BR)
HALIFAX REGIONAL SCHOOL BOARD
HERRING COVE JUNIOR HIGH SCHOOL
7 Lancaster Dr, Halifax, NS, B3S 1E7
(902) 479-4214
Emp Here 28
SIC 8211 Elementary and secondary schools

D-U-N-S 20-710-3065   (BR)
HALIFAX REGIONAL SCHOOL BOARD
PARK WEST SCHOOL
206 Langbrae Dr, Halifax, NS, B3S 1L5
(902) 457-7800
Emp Here 50
SIC 8211 Elementary and secondary schools

D-U-N-S 25-098-8359   (BR)
HOME DEPOT OF CANADA INC
(*Suby of* The Home Depot Inc)
368 Lacewood Dr, Halifax, NS, B3S 1L8
(902) 457-3480
Emp Here 160
SIC 5211 Lumber and other building materials

D-U-N-S 20-698-6742   (BR)
HUDSON'S BAY COMPANY
HOME OUTFITTERS
201 Chain Lake Dr, Halifax, NS, B3S 1C8
(902) 450-0273
Emp Here 60
SIC 5311 Department stores

D-U-N-S 25-891-5289   (BR)
INDIGO BOOKS & MUSIC INC
CHAPTERS
(*Suby of* Indigo Books & Music Inc)
188 Chain Lake Dr, Halifax, NS, B3S 1C5
(902) 450-1023
Emp Here 45

SIC 5942 Book stores

D-U-N-S 24-101-2470 (BR)
J. D. IRVING, LIMITED
KENT BUILDING SUPPLIES
(Suby of J. D. Irving, Limited)
225 Chain Lake Dr, Halifax, NS, B3S 1C9
(902) 450-2000
Emp Here 20
SIC 5211 Lumber and other building materials

D-U-N-S 20-780-6365 (BR)
JOHNSON INC
84 Chain Lake Dr Suite 200, Halifax, NS, B3S 1A2
(902) 453-1010
Emp Here 67
SIC 6411 Insurance agents, brokers, and service

D-U-N-S 20-136-9209 (BR)
MILLER PAVING LIMITED
MILLER WASTE SYSTEMS
20 Horseshoe Lake Dr, Halifax, NS, B3S 0B7
(902) 490-6640
Emp Here 30
SIC 1611 Highway and street construction

D-U-N-S 20-931-1372 (HQ)
NOVA SCOTIA LIQUOR CORPORATION
93 Chain Lake Dr, Halifax, NS, B3S 1A3
(902) 450-6752
Emp Here 150   *Emp Total* 11,000
Sales 438,879,911
SIC 5921 Liquor stores
Pr Bret Mitchell
Sherry Porter
Sr VP Roddy Macdonald
Tim Pellerin
Liz Cody
John Mackinnon
James Wilson
Paul Kent
Kim Brooks
Michele Mckenzie

D-U-N-S 24-000-7828 (BR)
NOVA SCOTIA POWER INCORPORATED
5 Long Lake Dr, Halifax, NS, B3S 1N8
(800) 428-6230
Emp Here 50
SIC 4911 Electric services

D-U-N-S 20-339-8719 (SL)
REDWOOD GRILL INCORPORATED
30 Fairfax Dr, Halifax, NS, B3S 1P1
(902) 446-4243
Emp Here 50   *Sales* 1,532,175
SIC 5812 Eating places

D-U-N-S 20-316-2276 (SL)
RESMED INC
38 Solutions Dr Suite 300, Halifax, NS, B3S 0H1
(877) 242-1703
Emp Here 50   *Sales* 5,034,288
SIC 7371 Custom computer programming services
Pr Pr Raju Sodhi
Mgr Jody Walker

D-U-N-S 25-175-0337 (BR)
SIR CORP
JACK ASTOR'S BAR & GRILL
184 Chain Lake Dr, Halifax, NS, B3S 1C5
(902) 450-1370
Emp Here 82
SIC 5812 Eating places

D-U-N-S 20-608-8952 (SL)
SMITTY'S FAMILY RESTAURANT
SYDAX DEVELOPMENT
362 Lacewood Dr Suite 1, Halifax, NS, B3S 1M7
(902) 457-6032
Emp Here 50   *Sales* 1,532,175
SIC 5812 Eating places

D-U-N-S 25-213-7211 (BR)

STAPLES CANADA INC
STAPLES THE BUSINESS DEPOT
(Suby of Staples, Inc.)
215 Chain Lake Dr Unit A, Halifax, NS, B3S 1C9
(902) 450-5241
Emp Here 45
SIC 5943 Stationery stores

D-U-N-S 24-419-9514 (BR)
TRANSCONTINENTAL INC
11 Ragged Lake Blvd, Halifax, NS, B3S 1R3
(902) 450-5611
Emp Here 100
SIC 2752 Commercial printing, lithographic

D-U-N-S 25-573-6746 (BR)
VALUE VILLAGE STORES, INC
(Suby of Savers, Inc.)
165 Chain Lake Dr, Halifax, NS, B3S 1B3
(902) 450-5134
Emp Here 63
SIC 5399 Miscellaneous general merchandise

D-U-N-S 25-498-3026 (BR)
WAL-MART CANADA CORP
220 Chain Lake Dr, Halifax, NS, B3S 1C5
(902) 450-5570
Emp Here 200
SIC 5311 Department stores

D-U-N-S 20-860-4251 (BR)
WINNERS MERCHANTS INTERNATIONAL L.P.
HOMESENSE
(Suby of The TJX Companies Inc)
9 Washmill Lake Dr, Halifax, NS, B3S 0A2
(902) 450-5007
Emp Here 25
SIC 5651 Family clothing stores

D-U-N-S 25-895-3397 (BR)
WINNERS MERCHANTS INTERNATIONAL L.P.
WINNERS
(Suby of The TJX Companies Inc)
206 Chain Lake Dr, Halifax, NS, B3S 1C5
(902) 450-5114
Emp Here 45
SIC 5651 Family clothing stores

Hammonds Plains, NS B3Z

D-U-N-S 24-262-7768 (BR)
I.M.P. GROUP LIMITED
IMP ELECTRONIC SYSTEMS
3101 Hammonds Plains Rd, Hammonds Plains, NS, B3Z 1H7
(902) 835-4433
Emp Here 110
SIC 4581 Airports, flying fields, and services

Hammonds Plains, NS B4B

D-U-N-S 25-241-7894 (BR)
HALIFAX REGIONAL SCHOOL BOARD
HAMMONDS PLAINS CONSOLIDATED SCHOOL
(Suby of Halifax Regional School Board)
2180 Hammonds Plains Rd, Hammonds Plains, NS, B4B 1M5
(902) 832-8412
Emp Here 47
SIC 8211 Elementary and secondary schools

D-U-N-S 25-361-5900 (BR)
MARWOOD LTD
CAPE COD WOOD SIDINGS DIV OF
1948 Hammonds Plains Rd, Hammonds Plains, NS, B4B 1P4
(902) 835-9629
Emp Here 110

SIC 2421 Sawmills and planing mills, general

Hantsport, NS B0P
Hants County

D-U-N-S 25-504-0347 (BR)
ANNAPOLIS VALLEY REGIONAL SCHOOL BOARD
HANTSPORT SCHOOL
11 School St, Hantsport, NS, B0P 1P0
(902) 684-4005
Emp Here 22
SIC 8211 Elementary and secondary schools

D-U-N-S 20-027-5857 (HQ)
CKF INC
48 Prince St, Hantsport, NS, B0P 1P0
(902) 684-3231
Emp Here 350   *Emp Total* 23
Sales 105,574,133
SIC 3086 Plastics foam products
Dir George Bishop

Harrietsfield, NS B3V
Halifax County

D-U-N-S 25-241-5286 (BR)
HALIFAX REGIONAL SCHOOL BOARD
HARRIETSFIELD ELEMENTARY SCHOOL
(Suby of Halifax Regional School Board)
1150 Old Sambro Rd, Harrietsfield, NS, B3V 1B1
(902) 479-4230
Emp Here 26
SIC 8211 Elementary and secondary schools

Hatchet Lake, NS B3T
Halifax County

D-U-N-S 20-027-5464 (BR)
HALIFAX REGIONAL SCHOOL BOARD
PROSPECT ROAD ELEMENTARY SCHOOL
2199 Prospect Rd, Hatchet Lake, NS, B3T 1R8
(902) 852-2441
Emp Here 20
SIC 8211 Elementary and secondary schools

D-U-N-S 20-710-2695 (BR)
HALIFAX REGIONAL SCHOOL BOARD
BROOKSIDE JUNIOR HIGH SCHOOL
2239 Prospect Rd, Hatchet Lake, NS, B3T 1R8
(902) 852-2062
Emp Here 35
SIC 8211 Elementary and secondary schools

Head Of Chezzetcook, NS B0J
Halifax County

D-U-N-S 20-710-3040 (BR)
HALIFAX REGIONAL SCHOOL BOARD
O'CONNELL DRIVE ELEMENTARY
40 O'Connell Dr, Head Of Chezzetcook, NS, B0J 1N0
(902) 827-4112
Emp Here 50
SIC 8211 Elementary and secondary schools

D-U-N-S 20-023-2911 (BR)
HALIFAX REGIONAL SCHOOL BOARD
GAETZ BROOK JUNIOR HIGH SCHOOL
6856 Highway 207 Rr 2, Head Of Chezzetcook, NS, B0J 1N0
(902) 827-4666
Emp Here 40

SIC 8211 Elementary and secondary schools

Head Of Jeddore, NS B0J
Halifax County

D-U-N-S 25-299-4983 (BR)
SOBEYS CAPITAL INCORPORATED
WESTERN UNION (SOBEYS INC #555)
8990 Highway 7, Head Of Jeddore, NS, B0J 1P0
(902) 889-2794
Emp Here 30
SIC 5411 Grocery stores

Head Of St Margarets Bay, NS B3Z
Halifax County

D-U-N-S 20-710-2687 (BR)
HALIFAX REGIONAL SCHOOL BOARD
ST MARGARET'S BAY ELEMENTARY
24 Ridgewood Dr, Head Of St Margarets Bay, NS, B3Z 2H4
(902) 826-3300
Emp Here 50
SIC 8211 Elementary and secondary schools

Heatherton, NS B0H
Antigonish County

D-U-N-S 24-547-7786 (SL)
EASTERN PAPER PRODUCTS LTD
45 Roderick Ave, Heatherton, NS, B0H 1R0
(902) 386-2467
Emp Here 55
SIC 2621 Paper mills

D-U-N-S 25-241-6052 (BR)
STRAIT REGIONAL SCHOOL BOARD
MACDONALD, REV H.J. SCHOOL
42 Summerside Rd, Heatherton, NS, B0H 1R0
(902) 386-2809
Emp Here 20
SIC 8211 Elementary and secondary schools

Hebbville, NS B4V

D-U-N-S 24-120-7419 (SL)
BOLIVAR, W R TRANSPORT LTD
15813 Highway 3, Hebbville, NS, B4V 6X9
(902) 530-3046
Emp Here 34   *Sales* 5,202,480
SIC 4213 Trucking, except local
Pr Wayne Bolivar

Hebron, NS B0W
Yarmouth County

D-U-N-S 20-710-3115 (BR)
TRI-COUNTY REGIONAL SCHOOL BOARD
MAPLE GROVE EDUCATION CENTRE
52 Grove Memorial Dr, Hebron, NS, B0W 1X0
(902) 749-5160
Emp Here 50
SIC 8211 Elementary and secondary schools

Hebron, NS B5A
Yarmouth County

D-U-N-S 24-123-8497 (SL)
RESIDENTIAL CARE

DEPARTMENT OF CO
Gd Yarmouth Stn Hebron, Hebron, NS, B5A 5Z9

Emp Here 20   *Sales* 6,087,000
SIC 8399 Social services, nec
Dir Chris Maxwell

Herring Cove, NS B3V
Halifax County

D-U-N-S 25-241-5328   (BR)
HALIFAX REGIONAL SCHOOL BOARD
WILLIAM KING ELEMENTARY SCHOOL
(*Suby of* Halifax Regional School Board)
91 St Pauls Ave, Herring Cove, NS, B3V 1H6
(902) 479-4200
Emp Here 30
SIC 8211 Elementary and secondary schools

Hubbards, NS B0J

D-U-N-S 20-716-8738   (BR)
SOUTH SHORE REGIONAL SCHOOL BOARD
ASPOTOGAN CONSOLIDATED ELEMENTARY SCHOOL
105 Parkwood Dr, Hubbards, NS, B0J 1T0
(902) 857-2600
Emp Here 30
SIC 8211 Elementary and secondary schools

Hubley, NS B3Z
Halifax County

D-U-N-S 25-393-1976   (SL)
TRECAN COMBUSTION LIMITED
4049 St. Margaret'S Bay Rd, Hubley, NS, B3Z 1C2
(902) 876-0457
Emp Here 50   *Sales* 5,072,500
SIC 3599 Industrial machinery, nec
Pr Pr David Burnett
VP VP Glen Burnett
Diana Burnett

Inverness, NS B0E
Inverness County

D-U-N-S 24-803-7447   (SL)
CABOT LINKS AT INVERNESS, LIMITED PARTNERSHIP
15933 Central Ave, Inverness, NS, B0E 1N0
(902) 258-4653
Emp Here 50   *Sales* 2,188,821
SIC 7992 Public golf courses

D-U-N-S 25-861-5715   (BR)
CAPE BALD PACKERS, LIMITED
126 Beach Rd, Inverness, NS, B0E 1N0
(902) 258-2272
Emp Here 40
SIC 7389 Business services, nec

D-U-N-S 24-188-4444   (HQ)
INVERNESS MUNICIPAL HOUSING CORPORATION
INVERARY MANOR
(*Suby of* Inverness Municipal Housing Corporation)
72 Maple St, Inverness, NS, B0E 1N0
(902) 258-2842
Emp Here 92   *Emp Total* 188
Sales 9,001,800
SIC 8051 Skilled nursing care facilities

Michael Macdougall

D-U-N-S 25-241-0220   (BR)
STRAIT REGIONAL SCHOOL BOARD
INVERNESS ACADEMY
59 Veterans Memorial Court, Inverness, NS, B0E 1N0
(902) 258-3700
Emp Here 35
SIC 8211 Elementary and secondary schools

D-U-N-S 20-710-2372   (BR)
STRAIT REGIONAL SCHOOL BOARD
INVERNESS EDUCATION CENTER ACADEMY
59 Veterans Memorial Ct, Inverness, NS, B0E 1N0
(902) 258-3700
Emp Here 50
SIC 8211 Elementary and secondary schools

Kennetcook, NS B0N
Hants County

D-U-N-S 20-072-3620   (BR)
CHIGNECTO CENTRAL REGIONAL SCHOOL BOARD
HANTS NORTH RURAL HIGH SCHOOL
(*Suby of* Chignecto Central Regional School Board)
4369 Highway 236, Kennetcook, NS, B0N 1P0
(902) 362-3300
Emp Here 45
SIC 8211 Elementary and secondary schools

Kentville, NS B4N

D-U-N-S 24-765-2972   (SL)
ACA
11 Calkin Dr Suite 1, Kentville, NS, B4N 3V7
(902) 678-1335
Emp Here 49   *Sales* 5,630,632
SIC 2015 Poultry slaughtering and processing
Genl Mgr Syed Asad Masood

D-U-N-S 24-524-3956   (BR)
ANNAPOLIS VALLEY DISTRICT HEALTH AUTHORITY
150 Exhibieln St, Kentville, NS, B4N 5E3
(902) 678-7381
Emp Here 100
SIC 8062 General medical and surgical hospitals

D-U-N-S 25-504-0420   (BR)
ANNAPOLIS VALLEY REGIONAL SCHOOL BOARD
KINGS COUNTY ACADEMY
35 Gary Pearl Dr, Kentville, NS, B4N 0H4
(902) 690-3850
Emp Here 70
SIC 8211 Elementary and secondary schools

D-U-N-S 25-504-0156   (BR)
ANNAPOLIS VALLEY REGIONAL SCHOOL BOARD
ALDERSHOT ELEMENTARY SCHOOL
446 Aldershot Rd, Kentville, NS, B4N 3A1
(902) 690-3820
Emo Here 40
SIC 8211 Elementary and secondary schools

D-U-N-S 24-955-6267   (BR)
ATLANTIC WHOLESALERS LTD
KENTVILLE SAVE-EASY
451 Main St, Kentville, NS, B4N 1K9
(902) 678-3893
Emp Here 31
SIC 5411 Grocery stores

D-U-N-S 25-296-5538   (BR)
BANK OF NOVA SCOTIA, THE

SCOTIABANK
47 Aberdeen St, Kentville, NS, B4N 2M9
(902) 678-2181
Emp Here 20
SIC 6021 National commercial banks

D-U-N-S 20-781-9590   (BR)
BANQUE TORONTO-DOMINION, LA
TORONTO-DOMINION BANK, THE
(*Suby of* Toronto-Dominion Bank, The)
42 Webster St, Kentville, NS, B4N 1H7
(902) 678-2131
Emp Here 25
SIC 6021 National commercial banks

D-U-N-S 20-206-2076   (BR)
BELL ALIANT REGIONAL COMMUNICATIONS INC
363 Main St, Kentville, NS, B4N 1K7
(902) 678-3308
Emp Here 40
SIC 4899 Communication services, nec

D-U-N-S 20-207-5870   (BR)
BELL ALIANT REGIONAL COMMUNICATIONS INC
852 Park St, Kentville, NS, B4N 3V7
(902) 679-2162
Emp Here 40
SIC 4899 Communication services, nec

D-U-N-S 20-537-2647   (BR)
CANADA POST CORPORATION
KENTVILLE STATION MAIN
495 Main St Suite 1, Kentville, NS, B4N 3W5
(902) 678-0773
Emp Here 32
SIC 4311 U.s. postal service

D-U-N-S 20-287-4371   (BR)
EMC EMERGENCY MEDICAL CARE INCORPORATED
EMC KENTVILLE FLEET
90 Aberdeen St, Kentville, NS, B4N 2N3
(902) 678-3686
Emp Here 26
SIC 4119 Local passenger transportation, nec

D-U-N-S 20-287-6095   (BR)
EMC EMERGENCY MEDICAL CARE INCORPORATED
EMC KENTVILLE
181 Cornwallis St, Kentville, NS, B4N 2E7
(902) 678-6993
Emp Here 100
SIC 4119 Local passenger transportation, nec

D-U-N-S 24-131-3972   (HQ)
EASSONS TRANSPORT LIMITED
ETL LOGISTICS, DIV OF
(*Suby of* Easson, William & Sons Limited)
1505 Harrington Rd, Kentville, NS, B4N 3V7
(902) 679-1098
Emp Here 20   *Emp Total* 3
Sales 38,981,295
SIC 4213 Trucking, except local
Pr Pr Paul Easson
Thomas Easson
VP VP Peter Easson

D-U-N-S 24-932-5358   (SL)
FLYER SERVICES (1989) LIMITED
(*Suby of* Hector Publishing Company Limited)
21 Chipman Dr, Kentville, NS, B4N 3V7
(902) 678-9217
Emp Here 35   *Sales* 8,638,080
SIC 7319 Advertising, nec
Pr Sean Murray
Dir Shirley Murray

D-U-N-S 24-975-9036   (BR)
GRANT THORNTON LLP
15 Webster St, Kentville, NS, B4N 1H4
(902) 678-7307
Emp Here 30
SIC 8721 Accounting, auditing, and bookkeeping

D-U-N-S 20-027-7846   (BR)
LAWTON'S DRUG STORES LIMITED
LAWTON'S PHARMACY
363 Main St, Kentville, NS, B4N 1K7
(902) 678-3308
Emp Here 20
SIC 5912 Drug stores and proprietary stores

D-U-N-S 24-579-3471   (BR)
NOVA SCOTIA HEALTH AUTHORITY
AVH CHIPMAN
5 Chipman Dr, Kentville, NS, B4N 3V7
(902) 365-1700
Emp Here 100
SIC 8062 General medical and surgical hospitals

D-U-N-S 24-711-6879   (BR)
NOVA SCOTIA, PROVINCE OF
ADDICTION SERVICES
15 Chipman Dr, Kentville, NS, B4N 3V7
(902) 679-2392
Emp Here 20
SIC 8069 Specialty hospitals, except psychiatric

D-U-N-S 20-102-7575   (BR)
PEPSICO CANADA ULC
FRITO LAY CANADA
(*Suby of* Pepsico, Inc.)
59 Warehouse Rd, Kentville, NS, B4N 3W9
(902) 681-2923
Emp Here 100
SIC 2096 Potato chips and similar snacks

D-U-N-S 20-027-8273   (BR)
PEPSICO CANADA ULC
FRITO LAY CANADA
(*Suby of* Pepsico, Inc.)
Gd, Kentville, NS, B4N 3W9
(902) 681-6183
Emp Here 200
SIC 2096 Potato chips and similar snacks

D-U-N-S 25-331-4488   (SL)
PLANTERS EQUIPMENT LIMITED
JOHN DEERE
Gd, Kentville, NS, B4N 3X1
(902) 678-5555
Emp Here 50   *Sales* 6,594,250
SIC 5999 Miscellaneous retail stores, nec
 Earl Kidston
 Jeffrey Griffin
Genl Mgr Dale Townsend
Dir Robert Atkinson
Ch Bd Ch Bd Raymond Parsons

D-U-N-S 24-606-0529   (BR)
POLE STAR TRANSPORT INCORPORATED
1568 Harrington Rd, Kentville, NS, B4N 3V7
(902) 678-4444
Emp Here 40
SIC 4212 Local trucking, without storage

D-U-N-S 25-320-8912   (BR)
PUROLATOR INC.
PUROLATOR INC
25 Roscoe Dr, Kentville, NS, B4N 3V7
(902) 678-0019
Emp Here 30
SIC 4731 Freight transportation arrangement

D-U-N-S 24-119-2116   (BR)
SCOTIA CAPITAL INC
1 Webster St, Kentville, NS, B4N 1H4
(902) 678-0777
Emp Here 20
SIC 6211 Security brokers and dealers

Kingston, NS B0P

D-U-N-S 20-710-2182   (BR)
ANNAPOLIS VALLEY REGIONAL SCHOOL BOARD
KINGSTON ELEMENTARY SCHOOL

---

625 Pine Ridge Ave, Kingston, NS, B0P 1R0
(902) 765-7530
Emp Here 55
SIC 8211 Elementary and secondary schools

D-U-N-S 24-098-3499   (BR)
ATLANTIC WHOLESALERS LTD
REAL ATLANTIC SUPERSTORE, THE
470 Main St, Kingston, NS, B0P 1R0
(902) 765-3516
Emp Here 20
SIC 5411 Grocery stores

Lake Echo, NS B3E
Halifax County

D-U-N-S 20-023-7803   (BR)
HALIFAX REGIONAL SCHOOL BOARD
BELL PARK ACADEMIC CENTRE
4 Thomas St, Lake Echo, NS, B3E 1M6
(902) 829-2388
Emp Here 30
SIC 8211 Elementary and secondary schools

Lake Loon, NS B2W

D-U-N-S 20-710-2786   (BR)
HALIFAX REGIONAL SCHOOL BOARD
HUMBERPARK SCHOOL
5 Smallwood Ave, Lake Loon, NS, B2W 3R6
(902) 464-5177
Emp Here 30
SIC 8211 Elementary and secondary schools

Lakeside, NS B3T
Halifax County

D-U-N-S 20-026-6294   (BR)
COCA-COLA LTD
COCA-COLA BOTTLING
(*Suby of* The Coca-Cola Company)
20 Lakeside Park Dr, Lakeside, NS, B3T 1L8
(902) 876-8661
Emp Here 100
SIC 5149 Groceries and related products, nec

D-U-N-S 20-706-6353   (BR)
COCA-COLA REFRESHMENTS CANADA COMPANY
(*Suby of* The Coca-Cola Company)
20 Lakeside Park Dr, Lakeside, NS, B3T 1L8
(902) 876-8661
Emp Here 100
SIC 2086 Bottled and canned soft drinks

D-U-N-S 20-014-6590   (HQ)
EMERA UTILITY SERVICES INCORPORATED
CABLECOM DIV.
31 Dominion Cres, Lakeside, NS, B3T 1M3
(902) 832-7999
Emp Here 143   *Emp Total* 3,600
Sales 13,132 926
SIC 1731 Electrical work
Pr Craig Sutherland
  Peter Murray
Dir Fin Scott Lafleur
Dir Opers Phil Stevens

D-U-N-S 24-521-9519   (BR)
EMERA UTILITY SERVICES INCORPORATED
31 Dominion Cres, Lakeside, NS, B3T 1M3
(902) 832-7999
Emp Here 30
SIC 1629 Heavy construction, nec

D-U-N-S 25-356-6079   (BR)
RUSSEL METALS INC

RUSSEL METALS-ATLANTIC
28 Lakeside Park Dr, Lakeside, NS, B3T 1A3
(902) 876-7861
Emp Here 80
SIC 5051 Metals service centers and offices

D-U-N-S 24-877-5389   (BR)
SYSCO CANADA, INC
SYSCO FOOD SERVICES OF ATLANTIC CANADA
(*Suby of* Sysco Corporation)
1 Duck Pond Rd Suite 1, Lakeside, NS, B3T 1M5
(902) 876-2311
Emp Here 250
SIC 5812 Eating places

Lanesville, NS B0N

D-U-N-S 20-931-2172   (SL)
STEWIACKE HARDWARE & BUILDING SUPPLIES LIMITED
STEWIAKE HOME HARDWARE BUILDING CENTRE
275 George St, Lanesville, NS, B0N 2J0

Emp Here 50   *Sales* 6,478,560
SIC 5251 Hardware stores
Pr Pr Joely Isenor-Killen
  Brett Isenor
Dir James Isenor

Lantz, NS B2S
Hants County

D-U-N-S 24-207-9643   (BR)
SHAW GROUP LIMITED, THE
1101 Highway 2, Lantz, NS, B2S 1M9
(902) 883-2201
Emp Here 300
SIC 3251 Brick and structural clay tile

Lawrencetown, NS B0S
Annapolis County

D-U-N-S 24-472-2195   (BR)
NOVA SCOTIA, PROVINCE OF
NOVA SCOTIA COMMUNITY COLLEGE
50 Elliott Rd Suite 1, Lawrencetown, NS, B0S 1M0
(902) 584-2226
Emp Here 91
SIC 8222 Junior colleges

Leitches Creek, NS B2A
Cape Breton County

D-U-N-S 24-343-9937   (BR)
SUPERIOR PLUS LP
SUPERIOR PROPANE
1526 Keltic Dr, Leitches Creek, NS, B2A 4Y1
(902) 539-1060
Emp Here 21
SIC 5984 Liquefied petroleum gas dealers

Liverpool, NS B0T

D-U-N-S 20-739-5893   (BR)
ATLANTIC WHOLESALERS LTD
LIVERPOOL MARKET SUPERSTORE
50 Milton Rd, Liverpool, NS, B0T 1K0
(902) 354-5776
Emp Here 80

SIC 5411 Grocery stores

D-U-N-S 24-123-5915   (BR)
NOVA SCOTIA POWER INCORPORATED
14 River Rd, Liverpool, NS, B0T 1K0
(902) 354-7141
Emp Here 35
SIC 4911 Electric services

D-U-N-S 24-342-7382   (SL)
QUEENS HOME FOR SPECIAL CARE SOCIETY
QUEENS MANOR
20 Hollands Dr, Liverpool, NS, B0T 1K0
(902) 354-3451
Emp Here 80   *Sales* 2,918,428
SIC 8361 Residential care

D-U-N-S 24-943-5868   (BR)
SOBEYS CAPITAL INCORPORATED
SOBEYS 588
180 Bristol Ave, Liverpool, NS, B0T 1K0
(902) 354-4225
Emp Here 100
SIC 5411 Grocery stores

D-U-N-S 24-357-6589   (BR)
SOUTH SHORE DISTRICT HEALTH AUTHORITY
QUEENS GENERAL HOSPITAL
175 School St, Liverpool, NS, B0T 1K0
(902) 354-5785
Emp Here 128
SIC 8069 Specialty hospitals, except psychiatric

D-U-N-S 20-716-8852   (BR)
SOUTH SHORE REGIONAL SCHOOL BOARD
SOUTH QUEENS JR HIGH SCHOOL
178 Waterloo, Liverpool, NS, B0T 1K0
(902) 354-7640
Emp Here 50
SIC 8211 Elementary and secondary schools

D-U-N-S 20-716-8787   (BR)
SOUTH SHORE REGIONAL SCHOOL BOARD
LIVERPOOL REGIONAL HIGH SCHOOL
104 College St, Liverpool, NS, B0T 1K0
(902) 354-7600
Emp Here 35
SIC 8211 Elementary and secondary schools

D-U-N-S 20-716-8746   (BR)
SOUTH SHORE REGIONAL SCHOOL BOARD
DR JOHN C WICKWIRE ACADEMY
311 Old Port Mouton Rd, Liverpool, NS, B0T 1K0
(902) 354-7660
Emp Here 58
SIC 8211 Elementary and secondary schools

Lockeport, NS B0T
Shelburne County

D-U-N-S 24-804-1121   (BR)
CLEARWATER FINE FOODS INCORPORATED
PIERCE FISHERIES
68 Water St, Lockeport, NS, B0T 1L0
(902) 656-2413
Emp Here 225
SIC 2092 Fresh or frozen packaged fish

Louisdale, NS B0E
Richmond County

D-U-N-S 20-710-2448   (BR)
STRAIT REGIONAL SCHOOL BOARD
RICHMOND ACADEMY

3238 White Side Rd, Louisdale, NS, B0E 1V0
(902) 345-4949
Emp Here 50
SIC 8211 Elementary and secondary schools

D-U-N-S 20-027-8898   (BR)
STRAIT REGIONAL SCHOOL BOARD
RICHMOND EDUCATION CENTER AND ACADEMY
3238 Whiteside Rd, Louisdale, NS, B0E 1V0
(902) 345-4949
Emp Here 50
SIC 8211 Elementary and secondary schools

D-U-N-S 20-710-2430   (BR)
STRAIT REGIONAL SCHOOL BOARD
FELIX MARCHAND ELEMENTARY
Gd, Louisdale, NS, B0E 1V0
(902) 345-2560
Emp Here 20
SIC 8211 Elementary and secondary schools

Lower Sackville, NS B4C
Halifax County

D-U-N-S 25-296-6098   (BR)
BANK OF NOVA SCOTIA, THE
SCOTIABANK
518 Sackville Dr, Lower Sackville, NS, B4C 2R8
(902) 864-2228
Emp Here 30
SIC 6021 National commercial banks

D-U-N-S 25-615-0111   (BR)
CARA OPERATIONS LIMITED
SWISS CHALET ROTISSERIE GRILL
(*Suby of* Cara Holdings Limited)
560 Sackville Dr, Lower Sackville, NS, B4C 2S2

Emp Here 44
SIC 5812 Eating places

D-U-N-S 20-573-5439   (BR)
EMC EMERGENCY MEDICAL CARE INCORPORATED
EMC COBEQUID
308 Cobequid Rd, Lower Sackville, NS, B4C 4C5
(902) 864-7648
Emp Here 20
SIC 4119 Local passenger transportation, nec

D-U-N-S 24-340-1049   (BR)
ENTERTAINMENT ONE GP LIMITED
CD PLUS GROUP OF STORES
(*Suby of* 4384768 Canada Inc)
22 Glendale Ave Unit 8, Lower Sackville, NS, B4C 3M1
(902) 864-3773
Emp Here 20
SIC 5099 Durable goods, nec

D-U-N-S 25-241-6888   (BR)
HALIFAX REGIONAL MUNICIPALITY
HALIFAX REGIONAL LIBRARY
636 Sackville Dr, Lower Sackville, NS, B4C 2S3
(902) 865-8653
Emp Here 20
SIC 8231 Libraries

D-U-N-S 25-241-5302   (BR)
HALIFAX REGIONAL SCHOOL BOARD
CAUDLE PARK ELEMENTARY SCHOOL
(*Suby of* Halifax Regional School Board)
35 Mcgee Dr, Lower Sackville, NS, B4C 2J1
(902) 864-6864
Emp Here 30
SIC 8211 Elementary and secondary schools

D-U-N-S 25-241-4479   (BR)
HALIFAX REGIONAL SCHOOL BOARD
HILLSIDE PARK ELEMENTARY SCHOOL
(*Suby of* Halifax Regional School Board)

▲ Public Company   ■ Public Company Family Member   **HQ** Headquarters   **BR** Branch   **SL** Single Location

15 Hillside Ave, Lower Sackville, NS, B4C 1W6
(902) 864-6873
Emp Here 23
SIC 8211 Elementary and secondary schools

D-U-N-S 25-065-6345   (BR)
HALIFAX REGIONAL SCHOOL BOARD
SMOKEY DRIVE ELEMENTARY SCHOOL
(*Suby of* Halifax Regional School Board)
241 Smokey Dr, Lower Sackville, NS, B4C 3G1
(902) 864-6838
Emp Here 20
SIC 8211 Elementary and secondary schools

D-U-N-S 20-350-1536   (BR)
HALIFAX REGIONAL SCHOOL BOARD
CAVALIER DRIVE SCHOOL
116 Cavalier Dr, Lower Sackville, NS, B4C 3L9
(902) 864-7524
Emp Here 51
SIC 8211 Elementary and secondary schools

D-U-N-S 25-241-5229   (BR)
HALIFAX REGIONAL SCHOOL BOARD
SYCAMORE LANE ELEMENTARY SCHOOL
(*Suby of* Halifax Regional School Board)
69 Sycamore Lane, Lower Sackville, NS, B4C 1E8
(902) 864-6730
Emp Here 31
SIC 8211 Elementary and secondary schools

D-U-N-S 25-895-2274   (BR)
HALIFAX REGIONAL SCHOOL BOARD
SACKVILLE HIGH SCHOOL
(*Suby of* Halifax Regional School Board)
1 Kingfisher Way, Lower Sackville, NS, B4C 2Y9
(902) 864-6700
Emp Here 70
SIC 8211 Elementary and secondary schools

D-U-N-S 25-821-3883   (BR)
HALIFAX REGIONAL SCHOOL BOARD
A. J. SMELTZER JUNIOR HIGH SCHOOL
(*Suby of* Halifax Regional School Board)
46 Prince St, Lower Sackville, NS, B4C 1L1
(902) 864-6846
Emp Here 35
SIC 8211 Elementary and secondary schools

D-U-N-S 25-241-0261   (BR)
HALIFAX REGIONAL SCHOOL BOARD
LESLIE THOMAS JUNIOR HIGH SCHOOL
(*Suby of* Halifax Regional School Board)
100 Metropolitan Ave, Lower Sackville, NS, B4C 2Z8
(902) 864-6785
Emp Here 32
SIC 8211 Elementary and secondary schools

D-U-N-S 24-321-8299   (BR)
HALIFAX REGIONAL WATER COMMISSION
HALIFAX WATER
2 Park Ave, Lower Sackville, NS, B4C 4A3
(902) 869-4290
Emp Here 24
SIC 4941 Water supply

D-U-N-S 20-021-2848   (BR)
IZAAK WALTON KILLAM HEALTH CENTRE, THE
IWK COMMUNITY MENTAL HEALTH
40 Freer Lane, Lower Sackville, NS, B4C 0A2
(902) 864-8668
Emp Here 20
SIC 8062 General medical and surgical hospitals

D-U-N-S 25-299-4322   (BR)
LAWTON'S DRUG STORES LIMITED
LAWTON'S DRUGS NO 171
528 Sackville Dr, Lower Sackville, NS, B4C 2R8
(902) 865-9393
Emp Here 25
SIC 5912 Drug stores and proprietary stores

D-U-N-S 20-589-4277   (BR)
NOVA SCOTIA, PROVINCE OF
COBIQUIT COMMUNITY HEALTH CENTER
40 Freer Ln, Lower Sackville, NS, B4C 0A2
(902) 865-6101
Emp Here 23
SIC 8062 General medical and surgical hospitals

D-U-N-S 20-349-3296   (BR)
SCOTT, T ENTERPRISES LIMITED
TIM HORTONS
(*Suby of* Scott, T Enterprises Limited)
629 Sackville Dr, Lower Sackville, NS, B4C 2S4
(902) 865-6618
Emp Here 30
SIC 5812 Eating places

D-U-N-S 24-349-6291   (BR)
WILSON FUEL CO. LIMITED
WILSON HOME HEATING
473 Cobequid Rd, Lower Sackville, NS, B4C 4E9
(902) 444-4246
Emp Here 50
SIC 5983 Fuel oil dealers

Lower Sackville, NS B4E
Halifax County

D-U-N-S 24-670-7665   (BR)
ATLANTIC WHOLESALERS LTD
REAL ATLANTIC SUPERSTORE, THE
745 Sackville Dr, Lower Sackville, NS, B4E 2R2
(902) 864-2299
Emp Here 300
SIC 5411 Grocery stores

D-U-N-S 25-891-6261   (BR)
ICT CANADA MARKETING INC
I C T GROUP
(*Suby of* Sykes Enterprises Incorporated)
800 Sackville Dr, Lower Sackville, NS, B4E 1R8
(902) 869-9050
Emp Here 200
SIC 7389 Business services, nec

D-U-N-S 24-803-4134   (BR)
J. D. IRVING, LIMITED
KENT BUILDING SUPPLIES, DIV OF
(*Suby of* J. D. Irving, Limited)
874 Sackville Dr, Lower Sackville, NS, B4E 1R9
(902) 864-2000
Emp Here 100
SIC 5211 Lumber and other building materials

D-U-N-S 25-298-9116   (BR)
NOVA SCOTIA LIQUOR CORPORATION
720 Sackville Dr, Lower Sackville, NS, B4E 3A4
(902) 864-3883
Emp Here 24
SIC 5921 Liquor stores

D-U-N-S 24-532-4413   (HQ)
SCOTT, T ENTERPRISES LIMITED
TIM HORTONS
(*Suby of* Scott, T Enterprises Limited)
808 Sackville Dr, Lower Sackville, NS, B4E 1R7

Emp Here 20   *Emp Total* 100
Sales 2,991,389
SIC 5812 Eating places

D-U-N-S 25-629-5510   (BR)
SCOTT, T ENTERPRISES LIMITED
TIM HORTONS
(*Suby of* Scott, T Enterprises Limited)
84 Beaver Bank Rd, Lower Sackville, NS, B4E 1J7

(902) 864-7141
Emp Here 45
SIC 5812 Eating places

D-U-N-S 25-298-1162   (BR)
SOBEYS CAPITAL INCORPORATED
SOBEYS #670
752 Sackville Dr Suite 670, Lower Sackville, NS, B4E 1R7
(902) 865-5057
Emp Here 200
SIC 5411 Grocery stores

D-U-N-S 24-224-5350   (BR)
WENDY'S RESTAURANTS OF CANADA INC
WENDY'S OLD FASHION HAMBURGERS
(*Suby of* The Wendy's Company)
750 Sackville Dr, Lower Sackville, NS, B4E 1R7
(902) 864-3745
Emp Here 50
SIC 5812 Eating places

Lower Truro, NS B6L

D-U-N-S 25-095-0321   (BR)
CLASSIC FREIGHT SYSTEMS (2011) LIMITED
34 Lower Truro Rd, Lower Truro, NS, B6L 1L9
(902) 895-1858
Emp Here 60
SIC 4213 Trucking, except local

D-U-N-S 20-523-3166   (SL)
TIDEVIEW ENTERPRISES LIMITED
PALLISER RESTAURANT MOTEL & GIFT SHOP, THE
104 Tidal Bore Rd, Lower Truro, NS, B6L 1T9

Emp Here 50   *Sales* 1,532,175
SIC 5812 Eating places

D-U-N-S 25-769-7797   (HQ)
TREATY ENTERPRISE INC
TREATY ENTERTAINMENT
(*Suby of* Treaty Enterprise Inc)
10 Treaty Trail, Lower Truro, NS, B6L 1V9
(902) 897-2650
Emp Here 50   *Emp Total* 100
Sales 18,488,320
SIC 5411 Grocery stores
Dir Jack Paul

Lower West Pubnico, NS B0W
Yarmouth County

D-U-N-S 20-444-6355   (SL)
INSHORE FISHERIES LIMITED
95 Dennis Point Rd, Lower West Pubnico, NS, B0W 2M0
(902) 762-2522
Emp Here 70   *Sales* 11,600,751
SIC 2092 Fresh or frozen packaged fish
Pr Pr Shawn D'entremont
Sec Connie D'entremont
    Yvon D'entremont

Lower Woods Harbour, NS B0W
Shelburne County

D-U-N-S 20-515-0159   (BR)
ACADIAN SEAPLANTS LIMITED
8421 Hwy 3, Lower Woods Harbour, NS, B0W 2E0
(902) 723-2678
Emp Here 65
SIC 2875 Fertilizers, mixing only

Lunenburg, NS B0J
Lunenburg County

D-U-N-S 24-756-5096   (BR)
CLEARWATER FINE FOODS INCORPORATED
CLEARWATER DEEP SEA TRAWLERS
240 Montague St, Lunenburg, NS, B0J 2C0
(902) 634-8049
Emp Here 300
SIC 2092 Fresh or frozen packaged fish

D-U-N-S 24-363-3539   (BR)
CLEARWATER SEAFOODS LIMITED PARTNERSHIP
CLEARWATER FLEET OPERATIONS
240 Montague St, Lunenburg, NS, B0J 2C0
(902) 634-8049
Emp Here 39
SIC 8741 Management services

D-U-N-S 25-738-1285   (SL)
LUNENBURG INDUSTRIAL FOUNDRY & ENGINEERING LTD
LIFE
53 Falkland St, Lunenburg, NS, B0J 2C0
(902) 634-8827
Emp Here 60   *Sales* 7,202,950
SIC 3731 Shipbuilding and repairing
Pr Pr Peter Kinley
    David Allen
Dir Kevin Feindel

D-U-N-S 24-335-0076   (BR)
NOVA SCOTIA, PROVINCE OF
ADDICTION SERVICES
14 High St, Lunenburg, NS, B0J 2C0
(902) 634-7325
Emp Here 30
SIC 8062 General medical and surgical hospitals

D-U-N-S 24-932-3197   (SL)
NOVA WOOD PRODUCTS LIMITED
145 Schnares Crossing Rd Rr 3, Lunenburg, NS, B0J 2C0
(902) 634-4120
Emp Here 30   *Sales* 1,969,939
SIC 2541 Wood partitions and fixtures

D-U-N-S 25-891-7756   (BR)
SOUTH SHORE REGIONAL SCHOOL BOARD
CENTRE CONSOLIDATED SCHOOL
11788 Highway 3, Lunenburg, NS, B0J 2C0
(902) 634-2200
Emp Here 40
SIC 8211 Elementary and secondary schools

D-U-N-S 24-956-6902   (HQ)
STELIA AEROSPACE NORTH AMERICA INC
STELIA NORTH AMERICA
71 Hall St, Lunenburg, NS, B0J 2C0
(902) 634-8448
Emp Here 416   *Emp Total* 11,080
Sales 94,630,028
SIC 3728 Aircraft parts and equipment, nec
Sec Claude Baril
Dir Jim Eisenhauer
Dir Xavier Flory
Dir Cedric Gautier
Dir Alain Tropis
Dir Guillaume Vuillermoz

Mabou, NS B0E
Inverness County

D-U-N-S 24-576-9463   (BR)
STRAIT REGIONAL SCHOOL BOARD
DALBRAE ACADEMY
11156 Route 19, Mabou, NS, B0E 1X0

(902) 945-5325
Emp Here 35
SIC 8211 Elementary and secondary schools

D-U-N-S 20-710-2406 (BR)
STRAIT REGIONAL SCHOOL BOARD
DALBRAE ACADEMY
Gd, Mabou, NS, B0E 1X0

Emp Here 50
SIC 8211 Elementary and secondary schools

Mahone Bay, NS B0J
Lunenburg County

D-U-N-S 20-781-2975 (SL)
GERA-CARE INVESTMENTS INC
*SURF LODGE COMMUNITY CONTINUING
CARE CENTRE*
640 Main St, Mahone Bay, NS, B0J 2E0
(902) 624-8341
Emp Here 35   *Sales* 5,376,850
SIC 8051 Skilled nursing care facilities
Pr Pr Bruce Stevenson
  Brian Macleod
  William Curry

D-U-N-S 20-648-2387 (BR)
**SOUTH SHORE REGIONAL SCHOOL
BOARD**
BAYVIEW COMMUNITY SCHOOL
110 Clearway St, Mahone Bay, NS, B0J 2E0
(902) 624-2120
Emp Here 46
SIC 8211 Elementary and secondary schools

Malagash, NS B0K
Cumberland County

D-U-N-S 24-533-7704 (SL)
JOST VINEYARDS LIMITED
48 Vintage Lane Suite 1, Malagash, NS, B0K
1E0
(902) 257-2636
Emp Here 50   *Sales* 1,732,502
SIC 2084 Wines, brandy, and brandy spirits

Membertou, NS B1S
Cape Breton County

D-U-N-S 24-765-2964 (BR)
DORA CONSTRUCTION LIMITED
DORA CONSTRUCTION LIMITED
(*Suby of* DORA Construction Limited)
201 Churchill Dr Suite 203, Membertou, NS,
B1S 0H1
(902) 562-3400
Emp Here 20
SIC 1522 Residential construction, nec

D-U-N-S 20-300-6986 (BR)
STANTEC CONSULTING LTD
201 Churchill Dr Suite 207, Membertou, NS,
B1S 0H1
(902) 564-1855
Emp Here 22
SIC 8711 Engineering services

Meteghan, NS B0W
Digby County

D-U-N-S 24-000-2233 (BR)
ARJENAM FOODS LIMITED
TIM HORTONS
8226 Highway 1, Meteghan, NS, B0W 2J0
(902) 645-2919
Emp Here 25

SIC 5812 Eating places

Meteghan Centre, NS B0W
Digby County

D-U-N-S 20-281-1865 (BR)
**RIVERSIDE LOBSTER INTERNATIONAL
INC**
11 John Thibodeau Rd, Meteghan Centre, NS,
B0W 2K0
(902) 645-3455
Emp Here 175
SIC 2092 Fresh or frozen packaged fish

Meteghan River, NS B0W
Digby County

D-U-N-S 25-395-3707 (HQ)
**CONSEIL SCOLAIRE ACADIEN PROVIN-
CIAL**
CENTRE SCOLAIRE ETOILE DE L'ACADIE
9248 Route 1, Meteghan River, NS, B0W 2L0
(902) 769-5458
Emp Here 30   *Emp Total* 11,000
Sales 55,355,181
SIC 8211 Elementary and secondary schools
Genl Mgr Darrell Samson

D-U-N-S 20-024-7299 (BR)
**CONSEIL SCOLAIRE ACADIEN PROVIN-
CIAL**
ECOLE SECONDAIRE DE CLARE
80 Placide Comeau Rd, Meteghan River, NS,
B0W 2L0
(902) 769-5400
Emp Here 33
SIC 8211 Elementary and secondary schools

D-U-N-S 20-696-3394 (SL)
SALMON RIVER SALMON ASSOCIATION
80 Placide Comeau Rd, Meteghan River, NS,
B0W 2L0
(902) 769-5400
Emp Here 50   *Sales* 3,575,074
SIC 8641 Civic and social associations

Middle Musquodoboit, NS B0N
Halifax County

D-U-N-S 20-583-4476 (SL)
ATLANTIC MINING NS CORP
6749 Moose River Rd, Middle Musquodoboit,
NS, B0N 1X0
(902) 384-2772
Emp Here 20   *Sales* 2,598,753
SIC 1041 Gold ores

D-U-N-S 24-366-2272 (SL)
ENLIGNA CANADA INC
9156 Hwy 224, Middle Musquodoboit, NS,
B0N 1X0
(902) 568-2429
Emp Here 48   *Sales* 6,229,760
SIC 2421 Sawmills and planing mills, general
Pr Fraser Gray

D-U-N-S 20-023-2903 (BR)
HALIFAX REGIONAL SCHOOL BOARD
MUSQUODOBOIT RURAL HIGH SCHOOL
11980 Highway 224, Middle Musquodoboit,
NS, B0N 1X0
(902) 384-2320
Emp Here 50
SIC 8211 Elementary and secondary schools

D-U-N-S 20-710-2836 (BR)
HALIFAX REGIONAL SCHOOL BOARD
*MUSQUODOBOIT VALLEY EDUCATION
CENTRE*

12046 Hwy 224, Middle Musquodoboit, NS,
B0N 1X0
(902) 384-2555
Emp Here 50
SIC 8211 Elementary and secondary schools

Middle Sackville, NS B4E
Halifax County

D-U-N-S 25-122-0315 (BR)
HALIFAX REGIONAL SCHOOL BOARD
MILLWOOD ELEMENTARY SCHOOL
(*Suby of* Halifax Regional School Board)
190 Beaver Bank Cross Rd, Middle Sackville,
NS, B4E 1K5
(902) 864-7510
Emp Here 40
SIC 8211 Elementary and secondary schools

D-U-N-S 25-241-4438 (BR)
HALIFAX REGIONAL SCHOOL BOARD
*HARRY R. HAMILTON ELEMENTARY
SCHOOL*
(*Suby of* Halifax Regional School Board)
40 Hamilton Dr, Middle Sackville, NS, B4E
3A9
(902) 864-6815
Emp Here 30
SIC 8211 Elementary and secondary schools

D-U-N-S 25-241-5260 (BR)
HALIFAX REGIONAL SCHOOL BOARD
*SACKVILLE HEIGHTS ELEMENTARY
SCHOOL*
(*Suby of* Halifax Regional School Board)
1225 Old Sackville Rd, Middle Sackville, NS,
B4E 3A6
(902) 869-4700
Emp Here 25
SIC 8211 Elementary and secondary schools

D-U-N-S 20-710-2711 (BR)
HALIFAX REGIONAL SCHOOL BOARD
*SACKVILLE HEIGHTS JUNIOR HIGH
SCHOOL*
956 Sackville Dr, Middle Sackville, NS, B4E
1S4
(902) 869-3800
Emp Here 45
SIC 8211 Elementary and secondary schools

Middle West Pubnico, NS B0W
Yarmouth County

D-U-N-S 20-754-1967 (BR)
**COASTAL FINANCIAL CREDIT UNION LIM-
ITED**
9 Abbotsharbour Rd, Middle West Pubnico,
NS, B0W 2M0
(902) 762-2372
Emp Here 60
SIC 8742 Management consulting services

Middleton, NS B0S

D-U-N-S 20-921-0223 (BR)
**ANNAPOLIS VALLEY REGIONAL SCHOOL
BOARD**
MIDDLETON REGIONAL HIGHSCHOOL
18 Gates Ave, Middleton, NS, B0S 1P0
(902) 825-5350
Emp Here 60
SIC 8211 Elementary and secondary schools

D-U-N-S 20-547-7917 (BR)
BANK OF NOVA SCOTIA, THE
SCOTIABANK
301 Main St Unit 293, Middleton, NS, B0S 1P0

(902) 825-4894
Emp Here 30
SIC 6021 National commercial banks

D-U-N-S 25-516-4501 (BR)
DAKOTA HOLDINGS LIMITED
TIM HORTONS
(*Suby of* Dakota Holdings Limited)
241 Main St, Middleton, NS, B0S 1P0
(902) 825-2145
Emp Here 25
SIC 5812 Eating places

D-U-N-S 24-131-6736 (BR)
HOYT'S MOVING & STORAGE LIMITED
193 Marshall St, Middleton, NS, B0S 1P0
(902) 825-6434
Emp Here 20
SIC 4212 Local trucking, without storage

D-U-N-S 24-975-9333 (BR)
ROYAL BANK OF CANADA
ROYAL BANK FINANCIAL GROUP
(*Suby of* Royal Bank Of Canada)
6 Commercial St, Middleton, NS, B0S 1P0
(902) 825-3417
Emp Here 25
SIC 6021 National commercial banks

D-U-N-S 25-593-4580 (BR)
SOBEYS CAPITAL INCORPORATED
FRESHCO
170 Commercial St, Middleton, NS, B0S 1P0
(902) 825-6444
Emp Here 30
SIC 5411 Grocery stores

D-U-N-S 24-877-5421 (BR)
SOBEYS CAPITAL INCORPORATED
TRA ATLANTIC, DIV OF
12827 Lower Main St, Middleton, NS, B0S
1P0
(902) 825-3404
Emp Here 100
SIC 5141 Groceries, general line

D-U-N-S 24-261-1853 (SL)
**SOLDIERS MEMORIAL HOSPITAL FOUN-
DATION**
462 Main St, Middleton, NS, B0S 1P0
(902) 825-3411
Emp Here 276   *Sales* 26,681,350
SIC 8062 General medical and surgical hospi-
tals
Ch Bd James C Mosher
Dir Jo-Anne Wentzell
  Carrie Schell
  Bill Hines
  Marilyn Wilkins

D-U-N-S 20-523-0105 (HQ)
VALLEY DRUG MART LTD
PHARMASAVE 546
(*Suby of* Valley Drug Mart Ltd)
26 Commercial St, Middleton, NS, B0S 1P0
(902) 825-4822
Emp Here 35   *Emp Total* 55
Sales 7,806,795
SIC 5912 Drug stores and proprietary stores
Pr Pr Sandra Penny
  Kathryn Spurrell
  Robert Perry

Milford, NS B0N
Hants County

D-U-N-S 25-241-5658 (BR)
**CHIGNECTO CENTRAL REGIONAL
SCHOOL BOARD**
HANTS EAST RURAL HIGH SCHOOL
(*Suby of* Chignecto Central Regional School
Board)
2331 Highway 2, Milford, NS, B0N 1Y0
(902) 758-4620
Emp Here 50

SIC 8211 Elementary and secondary schools

Milton, NS B0T

D-U-N-S 25-728-5932   (SL)
QUEEN'S ASSOCIATION FOR SUPPORTED LIVING
PENNY LANE ENTERPRISES
44 Pleasent St, Milton, NS, B0T 1P0
(902) 354-2723
Emp Here 70   *Sales* 3,283,232
SIC 8331 Job training and related services

Monastery, NS B0H
Antigonish County

D-U-N-S 25-240-9693   (BR)
STRAIT REGIONAL SCHOOL BOARD
EAST ANTIGONISH EDUCATION CENTRE & ACADEMY
Gd, Monastery, NS, B0H 1W0
(902) 232-2810
Emp Here 46
SIC 8211 Elementary and secondary schools

Mount Uniacke, NS B0N
Hants County

D-U-N-S 20-260-7594   (BR)
CHIGNECTO CENTRAL REGIONAL SCHOOL BOARD
UNIACKE DISTRICT SCHOOL
(*Suby of* Chignecto Central Regional School Board)
551 Highway 1, Mount Uniacke, NS, B0N 1Z0
(902) 866-5100
Emp Here 50
SIC 8211 Elementary and secondary schools

Mulgrave, NS B0E

D-U-N-S 20-190-8121   (BR)
DSM NUTRITIONAL PRODUCTS CANADA INC
39 England Dr, Mulgrave, NS, B0E 2G0
(902) 747-3500
Emp Here 140
SIC 2077 Animal and marine fats and oils

D-U-N-S 20-852-7536   (BR)
STRAIT REGIONAL SCHOOL BOARD
45 England Ave, Mulgrave, NS, B0E 2G0
(902) 747-3647
Emp Here 250
SIC 4151 School buses

Musquodoboit Harbour, NS B0J
Halifax County

D-U-N-S 20-023-7530   (BR)
HALIFAX REGIONAL SCHOOL BOARD
EASTERN SHORE DISTRICT HIGH SCHOOL
35 West Petpeswick Rd, Musquodoboit Harbour, NS, B0J 2L0
(902) 889-4025
Emp Here 40
SIC 8211 Elementary and secondary schools

D-U-N-S 24-189-8154   (SL)
TWIN OAKS SENIOR CITIZENS ASSOCIATION

BIRCHES NURSING HOME, THE
7702 # 7 Hwy, Musquodoboit Harbour, NS, B0J 2L0
(902) 889-3474
Emp Here 75   *Sales* 2,772,507
SIC 8361 Residential care

Neils Harbour, NS B0C

D-U-N-S 25-060-7611   (SL)
BUCHANAN MEMORIAL HEALTH CARE COMPLEX
32610 Cabot Trail, Neils Harbour, NS, B0C 1N0
(902) 336-2200
Emp Here 50   *Sales* 3,502,114
SIC 8062 General medical and surgical hospitals

D-U-N-S 25-241-4305   (BR)
CAPE BRETON-VICTORIA REGIONAL SCHOOL BOARD
CABOT SECONDARY SCHOOL
32039 Cabot Trail, Neils Harbour, NS, B0C 1N0
(902) 336-2266
Emp Here 27
SIC 8211 Elementary and secondary schools

D-U-N-S 20-573-5496   (BR)
EMC EMERGENCY MEDICAL CARE INCORPORATED
EMC NEILS HARBOUR
32610 Cabot Trail, Neils Harbour, NS, B0C 1N0
(902) 336-2315
Emp Here 20
SIC 4119 Local passenger transportation, nec

D-U-N-S 25-413-2459   (BR)
GUYSBOROUGH ANTIGONISH STRAIT HEALTH AUTHORITY
BUCHANAN MEMORIAL HOSPITAL
Gd, Neils Harbour, NS, B0C 1N0
(902) 336-2200
Emp Here 30
SIC 8062 General medical and surgical hospitals

New Germany, NS B0R
Lunenburg County

D-U-N-S 24-913-4537   (SL)
ROSEDALE HOME FOR SPECIAL CARE
4927 Highway 10, New Germany, NS, B0R 1E0
(902) 644-2008
Emp Here 50   *Sales* 2,261,782
SIC 8051 Skilled nursing care facilities

D-U-N-S 25-365-0949   (BR)
SOUTH SHORE REGIONAL SCHOOL BOARD
NEW GERMANY ELEMENTARY SCHOOL
150 School St, New Germany, NS, B0R 1E0
(902) 644-5020
Emp Here 25
SIC 8211 Elementary and secondary schools

New Glasgow, NS B2H
Pictou County

D-U-N-S 24-932-6802   (SL)
ALLEN, S & SONS FIRE RESTORATION & GENERAL CONTRACTORS LTD
ALLEN, S & SONS DISASTER KLEENUP
49 Riverside St, New Glasgow, NS, B2H 2N2
(902) 755-3473
Emp Here 50   *Sales* 6,087,000

SIC 1799 Special trade contractors, nec
Pr Pr Stephen Allen

D-U-N-S 20-091-0086   (BR)
ATLANTIC WHOLESALERS LTD
REAL ATLANTIC SUPERSTORE, THE
394 Westville Rd, New Glasgow, NS, B2H 2J7
(902) 928-0066
Emp Here 20
SIC 5912 Drug stores and proprietary stores

D-U-N-S 20-571-8070   (BR)
BELL ALIANT REGIONAL COMMUNICATIONS INC
ALIANT TELECOM
4852 Plymouth Rd, New Glasgow, NS, B2H 5C5
(902) 752-5345
Emp Here 40
SIC 4899 Communication services, nec

D-U-N-S 24-216-3413   (BR)
BRICK WAREHOUSE LP, THE
BRICK, THE
280 Stellarton Rd, New Glasgow, NS, B2H 1M5
(902) 752-0309
Emp Here 20
SIC 5722 Household appliance stores

D-U-N-S 20-538-8718   (BR)
CANADA POST CORPORATION
NEW GLASGOW PO
280 Stellarton Rd, New Glasgow, NS, B2H 1M5
(902) 755-9588
Emp Here 50
SIC 4311 U.s. postal service

D-U-N-S 25-822-3254   (BR)
CANADIAN CANCER SOCIETY
Gd Lcd Main, New Glasgow, NS, B2H 5C9

Emp Here 20
SIC 8399 Social services, nec

D-U-N-S 20-108-9393   (BR)
CHIGNECTO CENTRAL REGIONAL SCHOOL BOARD
ACADIA STREET ELEMENTARY SCHOOL
(*Suby of* Chignecto Central Regional School Board)
246 Acadia St, New Glasgow, NS, B2H 4G8
(902) 755-8420
Emp Here 20
SIC 8211 Elementary and secondary schools

D-U-N-S 25-240-9388   (BR)
CHIGNECTO CENTRAL REGIONAL SCHOOL BOARD
NEW GLASGOW JUNIOR HIGH SCHOOL
(*Suby of* Chignecto Central Regional School Board)
93 Albert St, New Glasgow, NS, B2H 5W8
(902) 755-8400
Emp Here 30
SIC 8211 Elementary and secondary schools

D-U-N-S 20-260-7545   (BR)
CHIGNECTO CENTRAL REGIONAL SCHOOL BOARD
A. G. BAILLIE MEMORIAL SCHOOL
(*Suby of* Chignecto Central Regional School Board)
477 Victoria Ave Exten, New Glasgow, NS, B2H 1X1
(902) 755-8240
Emp Here 25
SIC 8211 Elementary and secondary schools

D-U-N-S 20-101-7972   (SL)
CHILDREN'S AID SOCIETY OF PICTOU COUNTY
7 Campbell'S Lane, New Glasgow, NS, B2H 2H9
(902) 755-5950
Emp Here 50   *Sales* 3,118,504
SIC 7389 Business services, nec

D-U-N-S 20-573-5462   (BR)
EMC EMERGENCY MEDICAL CARE INCORPORATED
E H S
372 Stewart St, New Glasgow, NS, B2H 5W9
(902) 755-2355
Emp Here 27
SIC 4119 Local passenger transportation, nec

D-U-N-S 24-471-4515   (HQ)
EMPIRE THEATRES LIMITED
610 East River Rd Suite 205, New Glasgow, NS, B2H 3S2
(902) 755-7620
Emp Here 52   *Emp Total* 125,000
Sales 2,712,960
SIC 7832 Motion picture theaters, except drive-in

D-U-N-S 20-266-7593   (BR)
EMPIRE THEATRES LIMITED
EMPIRE THEATRES
610 East River Rd Suite 205, New Glasgow, NS, B2H 3S2

Emp Here 30
SIC 7832 Motion picture theaters, except drive-in

D-U-N-S 20-781-7156   (SL)
GLEN HAVEN MANOR CORPORATION
739 East River Rd, New Glasgow, NS, B2H 5E9
(902) 752-2588
Emp Here 280   *Sales* 17,178,000
SIC 8051 Skilled nursing care facilities
Ch Bd Donald Hussher

D-U-N-S 20-008-9394   (BR)
HIGH-CREST ENTERPRISES LIMITED
HIGH CREST PLACE
(*Suby of* High-Crest Enterprises Limited)
222 Provost St, New Glasgow, NS, B2H 2R3
(902) 755-9559
Emp Here 20
SIC 8361 Residential care

D-U-N-S 20-287-5519   (BR)
ICT CANADA MARKETING INC
(*Suby of* Sykes Enterprises Incorporated)
690 East River Rd, New Glasgow, NS, B2H 3S1
(902) 755-9050
Emp Here 100
SIC 7389 Business services, nec

D-U-N-S 25-305-1726   (BR)
INNVEST PROPERTIES CORP
COMFORT INN
(*Suby of* Innvest Properties Corp)
740 Westville Rd, New Glasgow, NS, B2H 2J8
(902) 755-6450
Emp Here 20
SIC 7011 Hotels and motels

D-U-N-S 20-631-2589   (BR)
LAWTON'S DRUG STORES LIMITED
LAWTONS DRUGS
810 East River Rd, New Glasgow, NS, B2H 3S3
(902) 752-1860
Emp Here 20
SIC 5912 Drug stores and proprietary stores

D-U-N-S 20-028-7845   (HQ)
MACKAY, J J CANADA LIMITED
MACKAY METERS
(*Suby of* 137954 Canada Ltd)
1342 Abercrombie Rd, New Glasgow, NS, B2H 5C6
(902) 752-5124
Emp Here 75   *Emp Total* 130
Sales 15,359,963
SIC 3824 Fluid meters and counting devices
Pr Pr George Mackay
Tom Curry

D-U-N-S 24-350-1926   (BR)

MARITIME STEEL AND FOUNDRIES LIM-ITED
379 Glasgow St, New Glasgow, NS, B2H 5C3

Emp Here 80
SIC 3325 Steel foundries, nec

D-U-N-S 20-523-4933   (SL)
O'FARRELL, W. A. CHEVROLET LIMITED
O'FARRELLS CHEVROLET
465 Westville Rd, New Glasgow, NS, B2H 2J6

Emp Here 32   Sales 15,705,600
SIC 5511 New and used car dealers
 Debbie Martin
Pr Michael O'farrell

D-U-N-S 25-412-4860   (HQ)
PICTOU COUNTY HEALTH AUTHORITY
ABERDEEN HOSPITAL
835 East River Rd, New Glasgow, NS, B2H 3S6
(902) 752-8311
Emp Here 30   Emp Total 11,000
Sales 72,394,447
SIC 8621 Professional organizations
Dir Patrick Lee
 Brian White

D-U-N-S 25-980-4193   (SL)
PICTOU COUNTY YMCA YWCA
YMCA YWCA
558 South Frederick St, New Glasgow, NS, B2H 3P5
(902) 752-0202
Emp Here 50   Sales 3,575,074
SIC 8641 Civic and social associations

D-U-N-S 20-650-9080   (BR)
SEARS CANADA INC
689 Westville Rd, New Glasgow, NS, B2H 2J6

Emp Here 45
SIC 5311 Department stores

D-U-N-S 20-987-2589   (SL)
SHANNON, BRENDA CONTRACTS LIM-ITED
DAVE'S COMMERCIAL CLEANING
130 George St, New Glasgow, NS, B2H 2K6
(902) 755-5445
Emp Here 100   Sales 2,918,428
SIC 7349 Building maintenance services, nec

D-U-N-S 25-298-0883   (BR)
SOBEYS CAPITAL INCORPORATED
SOBEYS
38 George St Suite 652, New Glasgow, NS, B2H 2K1
(902) 752-6258
Emp Here 140
SIC 5411 Grocery stores

D-U-N-S 25-370-2351   (BR)
STAPLES CANADA INC
STAPLES THE BUSINESS DEPOT
(Suby of Staples, Inc.)
556 Westville Rd, New Glasgow, NS, B2H 2J8
(902) 752-5291
Emp Here 30
SIC 5943 Stationery stores

D-U-N-S 24-789-6889   (BR)
THOMSON REUTERS CANADA LIMITED
THE EVENING NEWS
352 East River Rd, New Glasgow, NS, B2H 3P7
(902) 752-3000
Emp Here 30
SIC 2711 Newspapers

D-U-N-S 25-319-2397   (BR)
TORONTO-DOMINION BANK, THE
TD BANK
(Suby of Toronto-Dominion Bank, The)
156 Riverside Pky, New Glasgow, NS, B2H 5R3
(902) 755-0068
Emp Here 32

SIC 6021 National commercial banks

D-U-N-S 25-758-0639   (BR)
VICTORIAN ORDER OF NURSES FOR CANADA
VON PICTOU DISTRICT
835 East River Rd, New Glasgow, NS, B2H 3S6
(902) 752-3184
Emp Here 70
SIC 8082 Home health care services

D-U-N-S 25-294-7429   (BR)
WAL-MART CANADA CORP
713 Westville Rd Suite 3061, New Glasgow, NS, B2H 2J6
(902) 928-0008
Emp Here 200
SIC 5311 Department stores

New Minas, NS B4N

D-U-N-S 24-657-5372   (BR)
501420 NB INC
8999 Commercial St, New Minas, NS, B4N 3E3
(902) 681-4663
Emp Here 24
SIC 6531 Real estate agents and managers

D-U-N-S 20-757-0784   (BR)
ANNAPOLIS VALLEY REGIONAL SCHOOL BOARD
EVANGELINE MIDDLE SCHOOL
9387 Commercial St, New Minas, NS, B4N 3G3
(709) 922-2003
Emp Here 33
SIC 8211 Elementary and secondary schools

D-U-N-S 20-652-0582   (BR)
ANNAPOLIS VALLEY REGIONAL SCHOOL BOARD
NEW MINAS ELEMENTARY SCHOOL
34 Jones Rd, New Minas, NS, B4N 3N1
(902) 681-4900
Emp Here 36
SIC 8211 Elementary and secondary schools

D-U-N-S 20-524-4155   (BR)
ATLANTIC RETAIL CO-OPERATIVES FED-ERATION
CO-OP ATLANTIC
47 Minas Ware House Rd, New Minas, NS, B4N 5A5
(902) 681-6124
Emp Here 35
SIC 5191 Farm supplies

D-U-N-S 25-658-4616   (BR)
ATLANTIC WHOLESALERS LTD
ATLANTIC SUPERSTORE
9064 Commercial St, New Minas, NS, B4N 3E4
(902) 681-0665
Emp Here 150
SIC 5411 Grocery stores

D-U-N-S 24-343-2788   (SL)
B S D RESTAURANTS LIMITED
BURGER KING
9148 Commercial St, New Minas, NS, B4N 3E5
(902) 681-1203
Emp Here 50   Sales 1,532,175
SIC 5812 Eating places

D-U-N-S 20-754-2106   (BR)
CANADIAN MENTAL HEALTH ASSOCIA-TION, THE
CANADIAN MENTAL HEALTH ASSOCIATION-KINGS COUNTY BRANCH
(Suby of Canadian Mental Health Association, The)
8736 Commercial St, New Minas, NS, B4N 3C5

(902) 690-2422
Emp Here 22
SIC 8621 Professional organizations

D-U-N-S 20-543-2375   (BR)
EMPIRE THEATRES LIMITED
8944 Commercial St, New Minas, NS, B4N 3C9
(902) 681-3456
Emp Here 25
SIC 7832 Motion picture theaters, except drive-in

D-U-N-S 24-343-7444   (BR)
FGL SPORTS LTD
SPORT-CHEK
9107 Commercial St, New Minas, NS, B4N 3E7
(902) 681-1485
Emp Here 20
SIC 5941 Sporting goods and bicycle shops

D-U-N-S 20-929-6029   (SL)
FLOWER CART, THE
BAKERS CHOICE FINE FOODS
9412 Commercial St, New Minas, NS, B4N 3E9
(902) 681-6766
Emp Here 50   Sales 2,334,742
SIC 8331 Job training and related services

D-U-N-S 24-832-8460   (BR)
J. D. IRVING, LIMITED
KENT BUILDING SUPPLIES
(Suby of J. D. Irving, Limited)
9036 Commercial St Suite 2, New Minas, NS, B4N 3E2
(902) 681-5993
Emp Here 45
SIC 5211 Lumber and other building materials

D-U-N-S 25-299-2698   (BR)
NOVA SCOTIA LIQUOR CORPORATION
NEW MINAS LIQUOR STORE
9256 Commercial St Suite 15, New Minas, NS, B4N 4A9
(902) 681-3557
Emp Here 21
SIC 5921 Liquor stores

D-U-N-S 20-588-0987   (BR)
PRISZM LP
KFC
9024 Commercial St, New Minas, NS, B4N 3E2
(902) 681-7900
Emp Here 25
SIC 5812 Eating places

D-U-N-S 25-294-5571   (BR)
SEARS CANADA INC
9256 Commercial St, New Minas, NS, B4N 4A9
(902) 681-1566
Emp Here 60
SIC 5311 Department stores

D-U-N-S 24-943-5900   (BR)
SOBEYS CAPITAL INCORPORATED
SOBEYS #747
9256 Commercial St, New Minas, NS, B4N 4A9
(902) 681-3723
Emp Here 150
SIC 5411 Grocery stores

D-U-N-S 25-082-6252   (BR)
STAPLES CANADA INC
STAPLES THE BUSINESS DEPOT
(Suby of Staples, Inc.)
9081 Commercial St, New Minas, NS, B4N 3E6
(902) 681-3840
Emp Here 30
SIC 5943 Stationery stores

D-U-N-S 20-120-0206   (BR)
TRANSCONTINENTAL INC
KENTVILLE PUBLISHING
9185 Commercial St Suite 2, New Minas, NS,

B4N 3G1
(902) 681-2121
Emp Here 125
SIC 2711 Newspapers

D-U-N-S 24-120-9936   (BR)
WAL-MART CANADA CORP
9097 Commercial St Suite 3738, New Minas, NS, B4N 3E6
(902) 681-4271
Emp Here 200
SIC 5311 Department stores

New Ross, NS B0J
Lunenburg County

D-U-N-S 24-533-0311   (BR)
NOVA SCOTIA, PROVINCE OF
ROSS FARM MUSEUM
4568 Highway 12, New Ross, NS, B0J 2M0
(902) 689-2210
Emp Here 28
SIC 8412 Museums and art galleries

New Waterford, NS B1H
Cape Breton County

D-U-N-S 25-241-7373   (BR)
CAPE BRETON-VICTORIA REGIONAL SCHOOL BOARD
ST AGNES ELEMEMTARY SCHOOL
319 James St, New Waterford, NS, B1H 2X9

Emp Here 36
SIC 8211 Elementary and secondary schools

D-U-N-S 25-241-4834   (BR)
CAPE BRETON-VICTORIA REGIONAL SCHOOL BOARD
MOUNT CARMEL ELEMENTARY SCHOOL
3237 Nicholson Ave, New Waterford, NS, B1H 1N9
(902) 862-7127
Emp Here 35
SIC 8211 Elementary and secondary schools

D-U-N-S 25-299-4355   (BR)
LAWTON'S DRUG STORES LIMITED
LAWTON'S DRUGS #20
3415 Plummer Ave, New Waterford, NS, B1H 1Z2
(902) 862-6409
Emp Here 20
SIC 5912 Drug stores and proprietary stores

D-U-N-S 20-523-4842   (HQ)
PARAMOUNT PHARMACIES LIMITED
MIDTOWN PHARMASAVE
(Suby of Paramount Pharmacies Limited)
3435 Plummer Ave Suite 529, New Waterford, NS, B1H 1Z4
(902) 862-7186
Emp Here 25   Emp Total 75
Sales 10,652,262
SIC 5912 Drug stores and proprietary stores
Pr Pr Donald Morrison

D-U-N-S 25-622-9972   (BR)
WILSON'S INVESTMENTS LIMITED
TIM HORTONS
3400 Plummer Ave, New Waterford, NS, B1H 1Y9
(902) 862-8393
Emp Here 25
SIC 5461 Retail bakeries

Newport, NS B0N
Hants County

D-U-N-S 25-504-0511   (BR)
ANNAPOLIS VALLEY REGIONAL SCHOOL BOARD
BROOKLYN DISTRICT ELEMENTARY SCHOOL
8008 Highway 14, Newport, NS, B0N 2A0
(902) 757-4120
Emp Here 38
SIC 8211 Elementary and secondary schools

North River, NS B6L

D-U-N-S 25-241-5971   (BR)
CHIGNECTO CENTRAL REGIONAL SCHOOL BOARD
NORTH RIVER ELEMENTARY SCHOOL
(*Suby of* Chignecto Central Regional School Board)
80 Mountain Lee Rd, North River, NS, B6L 6M2
(902) 896-5530
Emp Here 25
SIC 8211 Elementary and secondary schools

North Sydney, NS B2A
Cape Breton County

D-U-N-S 20-321-2725   (BR)
ATLANTIC WHOLESALERS LTD
ATLANTIC SUPERSTORE
125 King St Suite 321, North Sydney, NS, B2A 3S1
(902) 794-7111
Emp Here 100
SIC 5411 Grocery stores

D-U-N-S 24-118-1861   (BR)
BANK OF NOVA SCOTIA, THE
SCOTIABANK
302 Commercial St, North Sydney, NS, B2A 1C2
(902) 794-4754
Emp Here 20
SIC 6021 National commercial banks

D-U-N-S 25-241-3745   (BR)
CAPE BRETON-VICTORIA REGIONAL SCHOOL BOARD
THOMPSON JUNIOR HIGH SCHOOL
30 Regent St, North Sydney, NS, B2A 2E6
(902) 794-2492
Emp Here 24
SIC 8211 Elementary and secondary schools

D-U-N-S 25-241-3703   (BR)
CAPE BRETON-VICTORIA REGIONAL SCHOOL BOARD
ST. JOSEPH'S ELEMENTARY SCHOOL
33 Napoleon St, North Sydney, NS, B2A 3G6
(902) 794-7037
Emp Here 30
SIC 8211 Elementary and secondary schools

D-U-N-S 20-710-2596   (BR)
CAPE BRETON-VICTORIA REGIONAL SCHOOL BOARD
SETON ELEMENTARY
25 Wilkie Ave, North Sydney, NS, B2A 1Y5
(902) 794-2419
Emp Here 25
SIC 8211 Elementary and secondary schools

D-U-N-S 20-024-1086   (BR)
JUSTIN RESTAURANTS INC
MCDONALD'S RESTAURANT
101 King St, North Sydney, NS, B2A 3S1
(902) 794-7255
Emp Here 55
SIC 5812 Eating places

D-U-N-S 24-722-7143   (BR)
MAGNA POWERTRAIN INC

PRECISION FINISHED COMPONENTS
65 Memorial Dr, North Sydney, NS, B2A 0B9

Emp Here 300
SIC 3089 Plastics products, nec

D-U-N-S 24-705-1329   (BR)
MARINE ATLANTIC INC
355 Purves St, North Sydney, NS, B2A 3V2
(902) 794-5200
Emp Here 300
SIC 4482 Ferries

D-U-N-S 25-019-0683   (BR)
ROYAL BANK OF CANADA
RBC
(*Suby of* Royal Bank Of Canada)
291 Commercial St, North Sydney, NS, B2A 1B9

Emp Here 21
SIC 6021 National commercial banks

D-U-N-S 24-311-8523   (BR)
SOBEYS CAPITAL INCORPORATED
116 King St, North Sydney, NS, B2A 3R7
(902) 794-7088
Emp Here 70
SIC 5411 Grocery stores

D-U-N-S 20-059-2553   (SL)
UPSOURCE CANADA CORP
(*Suby of* Upsource, Inc.)
116 King St Unit 9a, North Sydney, NS, B2A 3R7
(902) 794-7222
Emp Here 65   *Sales* 8,171,598
SIC 4899 Communication services, nec
Pr Pr Joan Chaput

Old Barns, NS B6L

D-U-N-S 20-260-7552   (BR)
CHIGNECTO CENTRAL REGIONAL SCHOOL BOARD
COBEQUID CONSOLIDATED ELEMENTARY SCHOOL
(*Suby of* Chignecto Central Regional School Board)
2998 Hwy 236, Old Barns, NS, B6L 1K3
(902) 896-5560
Emp Here 25
SIC 8211 Elementary and secondary schools

Oldham, NS B2T
Halifax County

D-U-N-S 20-025-9950   (SL)
LEDWIDGE LUMBER COMPANY LIMITED
195 Old Post Rd, Oldham, NS, B2T 1E2
(902) 883-9889
Emp Here 72   *Sales* 6,858,306
SIC 2421 Sawmills and planing mills, general
James Ledwidge
Dir Douglas Ledwidge

Oxford, NS B0M
Cumberland County

D-U-N-S 25-241-4545   (BR)
CHIGNECTO CENTRAL REGIONAL SCHOOL BOARD
OXFORD REGIONAL HIGH SCHOOL
(*Suby of* Chignecto Central Regional School Board)
249 Lower Main St, Oxford, NS, B0M 1P0
(902) 447-4513
Emp Here 35

SIC 8211 Elementary and secondary schools

D-U-N-S 25-241-4503   (BR)
CHIGNECTO CENTRAL REGIONAL SCHOOL BOARD
OXFORD REGIONAL ELEMENTARY SCHOOL
(*Suby of* Chignecto Central Regional School Board)
41 Jackson St, Oxford, NS, B0M 1P0

Emp Here 20
SIC 8211 Elementary and secondary schools

D-U-N-S 20-212-1310   (BR)
STANFIELD'S LIMITED
(*Suby of* Cobequid Investments Ltd)
466 Foundary St, Oxford, NS, B0M 1P0
(902) 447-2510
Emp Here 35
SIC 2322 Men's and boy's underwear and nightwear

Parrsboro, NS B0M
Cumberland County

D-U-N-S 25-241-4628   (BR)
CHIGNECTO CENTRAL REGIONAL SCHOOL BOARD
PARRSBORO REGIONAL ELEMENTARY SCHOOL
(*Suby of* Chignecto Central Regional School Board)
43 School St, Parrsboro, NS, B0M 1S0
(902) 254-5605
Emp Here 21
SIC 8211 Elementary and secondary schools

D-U-N-S 25-334-4428   (BR)
CUMBERLAND HEALTH AUTHORITY
SOUTH CUMBERLAND COMMUNITY CARE CENTRE
50 Jeanks Ave, Parrsboro, NS, B0M 1S0
(902) 254-2540
Emp Here 20
SIC 8062 General medical and surgical hospitals

Peggys Cove, NS B3Z
Halifax County

D-U-N-S 20-029-2274   (SL)
SOU'WESTER GIFT & RESTAURANT COMPANY LIMITED
178 Peggys Point Rd, Peggys Cove, NS, B3Z 3S2
(902) 823-2349
Emp Here 50   *Sales* 3,007,520
SIC 5947 Gift, novelty, and souvenir shop

Petit De Grat, NS B0E
Richmond County

D-U-N-S 20-287-7515   (BR)
CONSEIL SCOLAIRE ACADIEN PROVINCIAL
3435 Rte 206, Petit De Grat, NS, B0E 2L0
(902) 226-5232
Emp Here 500
SIC 8211 Elementary and secondary schools

Pictou, NS B0K
Pictou County

D-U-N-S 24-956-4873   (HQ)
ADVOCATE MEDIA INCORPORATED

PICTOU ADVOCATE, THE
(*Suby of* Hector Publishing Company Limited)
181 Brown'S Point Rd, Pictou, NS, B0K 1H0
(902) 485-1990
Emp Here 20   *Emp Total* 298
Sales 3,203,919
SIC 2711 Newspapers

D-U-N-S 20-728-0157   (HQ)
ADVOCATE PRINTING AND PUBLISHING COMPANY LIMITED
ADVOCATE SIGNS AND BANNERS
(*Suby of* Hector Publishing Company Limited)
Gd, Pictou, NS, B0K 1H0
(902) 485-1990
Emp Here 150   *Emp Total* 298
Sales 13,513,516
SIC 2731 Book publishing
Pr Pr Sean Murray
Dir Shirley Murray
Jill Murray

D-U-N-S 25-240-9719   (BR)
CHIGNECTO CENTRAL REGIONAL SCHOOL BOARD
PICTOU ACADEMY
(*Suby of* Chignecto Central Regional School Board)
88 Patterson St, Pictou, NS, B0K 1H0
(902) 485-7200
Emp Here 25
SIC 8211 Elementary and secondary schools

D-U-N-S 20-710-2125   (BR)
CHIGNECTO CENTRAL REGIONAL SCHOOL BOARD
DR. THOMAS MCCULLOCH JUNIOR HIGH SCHOOL
(*Suby of* Chignecto Central Regional School Board)
200 Louise St, Pictou, NS, B0K 1H0
(902) 485-7200
Emp Here 50
SIC 8211 Elementary and secondary schools

D-U-N-S 20-300-3640   (BR)
CHIGNECTO CENTRAL REGIONAL SCHOOL BOARD
PICTOU ELEMENTARY SCHOOL
(*Suby of* Chignecto Central Regional School Board)
350 Wellington St, Pictou, NS, B0K 1H0
(902) 485-7991
Emp Here 40
SIC 8211 Elementary and secondary schools

D-U-N-S 20-628-7059   (BR)
CHIGNECTO CENTRAL REGIONAL SCHOOL BOARD
WEST PICTOU CONSOLIDATED SCHOOL
(*Suby of* Chignecto Central Regional School Board)
1999 Highway 376, Pictou, NS, B0K 1H0
(902) 485-7960
Emp Here 40
SIC 8211 Elementary and secondary schools

D-U-N-S 20-287-9230   (BR)
EMC EMERGENCY MEDICAL CARE INCORPORATED
EMC PICTOU
190 Haliburton Rd, Pictou, NS, B0K 1H0
(902) 485-2569
Emp Here 29
SIC 4119 Local passenger transportation, nec

D-U-N-S 24-115-5071   (BR)
NOVA SCOTIA, PROVINCE OF
DEPARTMENT OF ADDICTION SERVICES
199 Elliot St, Pictou, NS, B0K 1H0
(902) 485-4335
Emp Here 40
SIC 8069 Specialty hospitals, except psychiatric

D-U-N-S 24-574-5864   (SL)
P C V INVESTMENTS LIMITED

PICTOU LODGE RESORT
172 Lodge Rd, Pictou, NS, B0K 1H0
(902) 485-4322
Emp Here 50   *Sales* 2,188,821
SIC 7011 Hotels and motels

D-U-N-S 24-671-0818   (HQ)
PARTNERS CONSTRUCTION LIMITED
PARTNERS INDUSTRIAL CRANE RENTAL
(*Suby of* Partners Construction Limited)
Gd, Pictou, NS, B0K 1H0
(902) 485-4576
Emp Here 30   *Emp Total* 60
Sales 4,815,406
SIC 7353 Heavy construction equipment rental

D-U-N-S 25-412-4829   (BR)
PICTOU COUNTY HEALTH AUTHORITY
SUTHERLAND HARRIS MEMORIAL HOSPITAL
222 Haliburton Rd, Pictou, NS, B0K 1H0
(902) 485-4324
Emp Here 60
SIC 8621 Professional organizations

D-U-N-S 20-029-3157   (BR)
SOBEYS CAPITAL INCORPORATED
SOBEYS
239 West River Rd, Pictou, NS, B0K 1H0
(902) 485-5841
Emp Here 106
SIC 5411 Grocery stores

Point Aconi, NS B1Y
Cape Breton County

D-U-N-S 25-364-4744   (BR)
NOVA SCOTIA POWER INCORPORATED
1800 Prince Mine Rd, Point Aconi, NS, B1Y 2A6
(902) 736-1828
Emp Here 68
SIC 4911 Electric services

Port Dufferin, NS B0J
Halifax County

D-U-N-S 20-286-2652   (BR)
RESSOURCES APPALACHES INC
1080 Dufferin Mines Rd, Port Dufferin, NS, B0J 2R0
(902) 297-3667
Emp Here 50
SIC 1081 Metal mining services

Port Hawkesbury, NS B9A
Inverness County

D-U-N-S 25-861-5723   (BR)
CAPE BRETON & CENTRAL NOVA SCOTIA RAILWAY LIMITED
C B N S
(*Suby of* Genesee & Wyoming Inc.)
4 Macsween St, Port Hawkesbury, NS, B9A 2H7
(902) 625-5715
Emp Here 70
SIC 4111 Local and suburban transit

D-U-N-S 20-207-8858   (SL)
MACDONALD, R & G ENTERPRISES LIMITED
TIM HORTONS
603 Reeves St, Port Hawkesbury, NS, B9A 2R8
(902) 625-1199
Emp Here 60   *Sales* 2,042,900
SIC 5461 Retail bakeries

D-U-N-S 25-721-5624   (BR)
NOVA CAPITAL INCORPORATED
S. & D. SMITH CENTRAL SUPPLIES LIMITED
(*Suby of* Nova Capital Incorporated)
16 Paint St Unit 1, Port Hawkesbury, NS, B9A 3J6
(902) 625-5555
Emp Here 55
SIC 5211 Lumber and other building materials

D-U-N-S 20-324-7770   (SL)
PORT HAWKESBURY PAPER LIMITED PARTNERSHIP
(*Suby of* Belgravia Investments Limited)
120 Pulp Mill Rd Point Tupper Industrial Park, Port Hawkesbury, NS, B9A 1A1
(902) 625-2460
Emp Here 320   *Sales* 117,539,688
SIC 2621 Paper mills
Ronald Stern
Pr Wayne Nystrom
Shawn Lewis
Brian Konen
VP Neil De Gelder
Shamsh Kassam

D-U-N-S 25-866-2600   (BR)
SEABOARD LIQUID CARRIERS LIMITED
SEABOARD TRANSPORT GROUP
23 Paint St, Port Hawkesbury, NS, B9A 3J7
(902) 625-3320
Emp Here 30
SIC 4213 Trucking, except local

D-U-N-S 24-804-4224   (BR)
SOBEYS CAPITAL INCORPORATED
SOBEYS #704
622 Reeves St Unit 1, Port Hawkesbury, NS, B9A 2R7
(902) 625-1242
Emp Here 95
SIC 5411 Grocery stores

D-U-N-S 20-706-7799   (BR)
STRAIT REGIONAL SCHOOL BOARD
STRAIT AREA EDUCATION-RECREATION CENTRE
304 Pitt St Unit 1, Port Hawkesbury, NS, B9A 2T9
(902) 625-1929
Emp Here 28
SIC 8211 Elementary and secondary schools

D-U-N-S 20-655-8855   (BR)
STRAIT REGIONAL SCHOOL BOARD
TAMARAC EDUCATION CENTRE
57 Tamarac Dr Unit 1, Port Hawkesbury, NS, B9A 3G2
(902) 625-6650
Emp Here 43
SIC 8211 Elementary and secondary schools

D-U-N-S 25-498-3307   (BR)
WAL-MART CANADA CORP
47 Paint St Unit 17, Port Hawkesbury, NS, B9A 3J9
(902) 625-0954
Emp Here 100
SIC 5311 Department stores

Port Hood, NS B0E
Inverness County

D-U-N-S 25-867-4951   (SL)
HOME SUPPORT CENTRAL SOCIETY
30 Water St, Port Hood, NS, B0E 2W0
(902) 787-3449
Emp Here 90   *Sales* 4,231,721
SIC 8059 Nursing and personal care, nec

D-U-N-S 20-710-2380   (BR)
STRAIT REGIONAL SCHOOL BOARD
BAYVIEW EDUCATION CENTRE
133 Company Rd, Port Hood, NS, B0E 2W0

(902) 787-5220
Emp Here 50
SIC 8211 Elementary and secondary schools

Port Mouton, NS B0T

D-U-N-S 24-755-5949   (SL)
QUARTERDECK COTTAGES & RESTAURANT LIMITED
QUARTERDECK BEACHSIDE VILLAS & GRILL
7499 Rte 3, Port Mouton, NS, B0T 1T0
(902) 683-2998
Emp Here 50   *Sales* 2,188,821
SIC 7011 Hotels and motels

Port Williams, NS B0P

D-U-N-S 24-877-7922   (BR)
A. LASSONDE INC
GREATVALLEY JUICES, DIV OF
(*Suby of* 3346625 Canada Inc)
19 Collins Rd, Port Williams, NS, B0P 1T0
(902) 542-2224
Emp Here 30
SIC 2033 Canned fruits and specialties

D-U-N-S 25-504-0784   (BR)
ANNAPOLIS VALLEY REGIONAL SCHOOL BOARD
PORT WILLIAMS ELEMENTARY SCHOOL
1261 Belcher St, Port Williams, NS, B0P 1T0
(902) 542-6074
Emp Here 30
SIC 8211 Elementary and secondary schools

Porters Lake, NS B3E
Halifax County

D-U-N-S 20-710-2828   (BR)
HALIFAX REGIONAL SCHOOL BOARD
LAKE VIEW CONSOLIDATED
5261 Highway 7, Porters Lake, NS, B3E 1J7
(902) 827-2525
Emp Here 30
SIC 8211 Elementary and secondary schools

Pugwash, NS B0K
Cumberland County

D-U-N-S 20-648-2510   (BR)
CHIGNECTO CENTRAL REGIONAL SCHOOL BOARD
CYRUS EATON ELEMENTARY SCHOOL
(*Suby of* Chignecto Central Regional School Board)
171 Queen St, Pugwash, NS, B0K 1L0
(902) 243-3900
Emp Here 20
SIC 8211 Elementary and secondary schools

D-U-N-S 25-241-4669   (BR)
CHIGNECTO CENTRAL REGIONAL SCHOOL BOARD
PUGWASH DISTRICT HIGH SCHOOL
(*Suby of* Chignecto Central Regional School Board)
192 Church St, Pugwash, NS, B0K 1L0
(902) 243-3930
Emp Here 30
SIC 8211 Elementary and secondary schools

D-U-N-S 24-803-3631   (SL)
CUMBERLAND SENIOR CARE CORPORATION
EAST CUMBERLAND LODGE

262 Church St, Pugwash, NS, B0K 1L0
(902) 243-2504
Emp Here 90   *Sales* 3,283,232
SIC 8361 Residential care

D-U-N-S 20-029-5053   (BR)
K+S SEL WINDSOR LTEE
106 Sheas Island Rd, Pugwash, NS, B0K 1L0
(902) 243-2511
Emp Here 200
SIC 1479 Chemical and fertilizer mining

D-U-N-S 20-185-0430   (BR)
SEAGULL COMPANY INCORPORATED, THE
SEGULL TUTOR
10016 Sunrise Trail, Pugwash, NS, B0K 1L0
(902) 243-2516
Emp Here 20
SIC 3914 Silverware and plated ware

River Hebert, NS B0L
Cumberland County

D-U-N-S 20-710-1978   (BR)
CHIGNECTO CENTRAL REGIONAL SCHOOL BOARD
RIVER HEBERT DISTRICT HIGH SCHOOL
(*Suby of* Chignecto Central Regional School Board)
2843 Barrensfield Rd, River Hebert, NS, B0L 1G0
(902) 251-3200
Emp Here 50
SIC 8211 Elementary and secondary schools

River Ryan, NS B1H
Cape Breton County

D-U-N-S 20-710-2463   (BR)
CAPE BRETON-VICTORIA REGIONAL SCHOOL BOARD
GREENFIELD ELEMENTARY SCHOOL
25 James St, River Ryan, NS, B1H 1B8
(902) 862-4000
Emp Here 50
SIC 8211 Elementary and secondary schools

Salmon River, NS B6L

D-U-N-S 20-914-1469   (BR)
FARMERS CO-OPERATIVE DAIRY LIMITED
1024 Salmon River Rd, Salmon River, NS, B6L 4E1
(902) 895-7906
Emp Here 60
SIC 5143 Dairy products, except dried or canned

Salt Springs, NS B0K
Pictou County

D-U-N-S 20-007-5544   (BR)
CHIGNECTO CENTRAL REGIONAL SCHOOL BOARD
SALT SPRINGS ELEMENTARY SCHOOL
(*Suby of* Chignecto Central Regional School Board)
2080 West River Station Rd, Salt Springs, NS, B0K 1P0
(902) 925-6000
Emp Here 20
SIC 8211 Elementary and secondary schools

Sambro, NS B3V
Halifax County

D-U-N-S 20-710-2851 (BR)
HALIFAX REGIONAL SCHOOL BOARD
SAMBRO-KETCH HARBOUR ELEMENTARY SCHOOL
3725 Old Sambro Rd, Sambro, NS, B3V 1G1
(902) 868-2717
Emp Here 22
SIC 8211 Elementary and secondary schools

Scotchtown, NS B1H
Cape Breton County

D-U-N-S 25-299-3498 (BR)
SOBEYS CAPITAL INCORPORATED
SOBEYS 470
3500 Emerald St, Scotchtown, NS, B1H 1H5
(902) 862-8770
Emp Here 52
SIC 5411 Grocery stores

Sheet Harbour, NS B0J
Halifax County

D-U-N-S 25-241-4594 (BR)
HALIFAX REGIONAL SCHOOL BOARD
SHEET HARBOUR CONSOLIDATED SCHOOL
(*Suby of* Halifax Regional School Board)
479 Church Point Rd, Sheet Harbour, NS, B0J 3B0
(902) 885-2236
Emp Here 25
SIC 8211 Elementary and secondary schools

D-U-N-S 24-364-1904 (HQ)
SHAW & SHAW LIMITED
(*Suby of* Shaw & Shaw Limited)
Gd, Sheet Harbour, NS, B0J 3B0

Emp Here 20   *Emp Total* 102
Sales 9,942,100
SIC 3479 Metal coating and allied services
Pr Bert Frizzell
Dir Jack Marshall

D-U-N-S 24-364-1912 (BR)
SHAW & SHAW LIMITED
(*Suby of* Shaw & Shaw Limited)
629 Marine Gateway, Sheet Harbour, NS, B0J 3B0
(902) 885-3204
Emp Here 82
SIC 2851 Paints and allied products

Shelburne, NS B0T
Shelburne County

D-U-N-S 24-804-7110 (BR)
CLEARWATER FINE FOODS INCORPORATED
CONTINENTAL SEAFOODS
84 Water St, Shelburne, NS, B0T 1W0

Emp Here 55
SIC 5146 Fish and seafoods

D-U-N-S 24-101-2876 (BR)
IRVING SHIPBUILDING INC
SHELBURNE SHIP REPAIR
29 Hero Rd, Shelburne, NS, B0T 1W0
(902) 875-8100
Emp Here 50
SIC 3731 Shipbuilding and repairing

D-U-N-S 25-412-3888 (BR)

NOVA SCOTIA HEALTH AUTHORITY
ROSEWAY HOSPITAL
1606 Lake Rd, Shelburne, NS, B0T 1W0
(902) 875-3011
Emp Here 130
SIC 8062 General medical and surgical hospitals

D-U-N-S 20-589-9789 (BR)
NOVA SCOTIA, PROVINCE OF
NOVA SCOTIA COMMUNITY COLLEGE
1575 Lake Rd, Shelburne, NS, B0T 1W0
(902) 875-8640
Emp Here 20
SIC 8222 Junior colleges

D-U-N-S 20-907-0846 (SL)
ROSEWAY MANOR INCORPORATED
1604 Lake Rd, Shelburne, NS, B0T 1W0
(902) 875-4707
Emp Here 101   *Sales* 3,720,996
SIC 8361 Residential care

D-U-N-S 20-328-3106 (BR)
TDL GROUP CORP, THE
TIM HORTONS
85 Ohio Rd Suite 1772, Shelburne, NS, B0T 1W0
(902) 875-2513
Emp Here 20
SIC 5812 Eating places

D-U-N-S 20-710-3180 (BR)
TRI-COUNTY REGIONAL SCHOOL BOARD
HILLCREST ACADEMY
127 King St, Shelburne, NS, B0T 1W0
(902) 875-5300
Emp Here 30
SIC 8211 Elementary and secondary schools

D-U-N-S 20-652-0632 (BR)
TRI-COUNTY REGIONAL SCHOOL BOARD
SHELBURNE HIGH SCHOOL
415 Woodlawn, Shelburne, NS, B0T 1W0
(902) 875-4900
Emp Here 40
SIC 8211 Elementary and secondary schools

Sherbrooke, NS B0J

D-U-N-S 25-413-2418 (BR)
GUYSBOROUGH ANTIGONISH STRAIT HEALTH AUTHORITY
ST MARY'S MEMORIAL HOSPITAL
91 Hospital Rd, Sherbrooke, NS, B0J 3C0
(902) 522-2882
Emp Here 30
SIC 8062 General medical and surgical hospitals

D-U-N-S 24-098-3051 (BR)
HIGH-CREST ENTERPRISES LIMITED
(*Suby of* High-Crest Enterprises Limited)
53 Court St, Sherbrooke, NS, B0J 3C0
(902) 522-2147
Emp Here 54
SIC 8059 Nursing and personal care, nec

D-U-N-S 25-241-4826 (BR)
STRAIT REGIONAL SCHOOL BOARD
ST MARY'S ACADEMY
121 Old Rd Hill, Sherbrooke, NS, B0J 3C0
(902) 522-2035
Emp Here 27
SIC 8211 Elementary and secondary schools

Shubenacadie, NS B0N
Hants County

D-U-N-S 25-241-9775 (BR)
CHIGNECTO CENTRAL REGIONAL SCHOOL BOARD

SHUBENACADIE DISTRICT ELEMENTARY SCHOOL
(*Suby of* Chignecto Central Regional School Board)
54 Mill Village Rd, Shubenacadie, NS, B0N 2H0
(902) 758-4600
Emp Here 40
SIC 8211 Elementary and secondary schools

South Bar, NS B1N
Cape Breton County

D-U-N-S 25-365-6953 (BR)
CAPE BRETON-VICTORIA REGIONAL SCHOOL BOARD
SOUTH BAR SCHOOL
2185 New Waterford Hwy, South Bar, NS, B1N 3H7
(902) 562-0776
Emp Here 20
SIC 8211 Elementary and secondary schools

Springhill, NS B0M
Cumberland County

D-U-N-S 20-710-2000 (BR)
CHIGNECTO CENTRAL REGIONAL SCHOOL BOARD
SPRINGHILL JUNIOR SENIOR HIGH SCHOOL
(*Suby of* Chignecto Central Regional School Board)
84 Church St, Springhill, NS, B0M 1X0
(902) 597-4250
Emp Here 50
SIC 8211 Elementary and secondary schools

D-U-N-S 24-230-4645 (BR)
CHIGNECTO CENTRAL REGIONAL SCHOOL BOARD
JUNCTION ROAD ELEMENTARY SCHOOL
(*Suby of* Chignecto Central Regional School Board)
19 Junction Rd, Springhill, NS, B0M 1X0
(902) 597-4240
Emp Here 20
SIC 8211 Elementary and secondary schools

D-U-N-S 24-261-3867 (BR)
HIGH-CREST ENTERPRISES LIMITED
HIGH-CREST SPRINGHILL
(*Suby of* High-Crest Enterprises Limited)
11 Sproul St, Springhill, NS, B0M 1X0
(902) 597-2797
Emp Here 90
SIC 8361 Residential care

D-U-N-S 24-489-9535 (BR)
MARITIME PRESSUREWORKS LIMITED
11 Pond Dr, Springhill, NS, B0M 1X0
(902) 597-3500
Emp Here 25
SIC 3634 Electric housewares and fans

D-U-N-S 20-025-6378 (HQ)
NATIONAL GYPSUM (CANADA) LTD
1707 Highway 2 Rr 1, Springhill, NS, B0M 1X0
(902) 758-3256
Emp Here 77   *Emp Total* 2,100
SIC 1499 Miscellaneous nonMetallic minerals, except fuels

D-U-N-S 20-536-0196 (BR)
NOVA SCOTIA COMMUNITY COLLEGE
CUMBERLAND CAMPUS
1 Main St, Springhill, NS, B0M 1X0
(902) 597-3737
Emp Here 50
SIC 8221 Colleges and universities

D-U-N-S 20-589-4215 (BR)

ROPAK CANADA INC
ROPAK PACKAGING - NORTHEAST DIVISION
(*Suby of* Stone Canyon Industries LLC)
29 Memorial Cres, Springhill, NS, B0M 1X0
(902) 597-3787
Emp Here 110
SIC 3089 Plastics products, nec

D-U-N-S 25-647-9585 (BR)
SOBEYS CAPITAL INCORPORATED
FOODLAND
21 Main St, Springhill, NS, B0M 1X0
(902) 597-8777
Emp Here 30
SIC 5411 Grocery stores

D-U-N-S 20-029-6135 (SL)
SURRETTE BATTERY COMPANY LIMITED
1 Station Rd, Springhill, NS, B0M 1X0
(902) 597-3767
Emp Here 55   *Sales* 4,504,505
SIC 3691 Storage batteries

St Andrews, NS B0H
Antigonish County

D-U-N-S 25-240-9859 (BR)
STRAIT REGIONAL SCHOOL BOARD
ST ANDREWS CONSOLIDATED SCHOOL
3892 Rte 316, St Andrews, NS, B0H 1X0
(902) 863-2512
Emp Here 25
SIC 8211 Elementary and secondary schools

St Peters, NS B0E
Richmond County

D-U-N-S 20-710-2422 (BR)
STRAIT REGIONAL SCHOOL BOARD
EAST RICHMOND EDUCATION CENTRE
5081 Argyle St, St Peters, NS, B0E 3B0

Emp Here 22
SIC 8211 Elementary and secondary schools

D-U-N-S 20-814-8630 (BR)
STRAIT REGIONAL SCHOOL BOARD
EAST RICHMOND EDUCATION CENTRE
9359 Pepperell St, St Peters, NS, B0E 3B0
(902) 535-2066
Emp Here 35
SIC 8211 Elementary and secondary schools

Stellarton, NS B0K
Pictou County

D-U-N-S 24-605-4555 (SL)
BIG 8 BEVERAGES LIMITED
120 North Foord St, Stellarton, NS, B0K 0A2
(902) 755-6333
Emp Here 35   *Sales* 4,450,603
SIC 2086 Bottled and canned soft drinks

D-U-N-S 20-108-9435 (BR)
CHIGNECTO CENTRAL REGIONAL SCHOOL BOARD
DR W.A. MACLEOD ELEMENTARY SCHOOL
(*Suby of* Chignecto Central Regional School Board)
6193 Trafalgar Rd, Stellarton, NS, B0K 1S0
(902) 755-8450
Emp Here 29
SIC 8211 Elementary and secondary schools

D-U-N-S 20-710-2034 (BR)
CHIGNECTO CENTRAL REGIONAL SCHOOL BOARD
G. R. SAUNDERS ELEMENTARY SCHOOL

(*Suby of* Chignecto Central Regional School
Board)
71 Bridge Ave, Stellarton, NS, B0K 0A2
(902) 755-8230
Emp Here 35
SIC 8211 Elementary and secondary schools

D-U-N-S 20-780-1705   (BR)
**COCA-COLA REFRESHMENTS CANADA
COMPANY**
(*Suby of* The Coca-Cola Company)
101 Macgregor Ave, Stellarton, NS, B0K 0A2
(902) 752-3505
Emp Here 20
SIC 5149 Groceries and related products, nec

D-U-N-S 24-472-8978   (HQ)
CONNORS TRANSFER LIMITED
(*Suby of* Connors Transfer Limited)
39 Connors Ln, Stellarton, NS, B0K 0A2
(902) 752-1142
Emp Here 35   *Emp Total* 192
Sales 25,025,520
SIC 4213 Trucking, except local
Pr Pr Lauchie Connors
VP VP Glenn Connors
VP Robert Small
Dir Opers Robert Small
  Donald Macgillivray

D-U-N-S 20-782-7767   (HQ)
CROMBIE DEVELOPMENTS LIMITED
HIGHFIELD SQUARE
115 King St, Stellarton, NS, B0K 0A2
(902) 755-4440
Emp Here 30   *Emp Total* 125,000
Sales 56,570,240
SIC 6512 Nonresidential building operators
Pr Donald Clow
  Frank C Sobey

D-U-N-S 25-172-1817   (SL)
E.C.L. INVESTMENTS LIMITED
115 King St, Stellarton, NS, B0K 0A2
(902) 755-4440
Emp Here 50   *Sales* 8,138,880
SIC 6712 Bank holding companies
Pr Paul Sobey

D-U-N-S 25-370-7582   (HQ)
ECL PROPERTIES LIMITED
115 King St, Stellarton, NS, B0K 0A2
(902) 755-4440
Emp Here 29   *Emp Total* 125,000
Sales 7,950,960
SIC 6712 Bank holding companies
Pr Pr Frank Sobey
  Paul Beesley

D-U-N-S 20-444-3345   (SL)
KOUYAS ENTERPRISES LIMITED
SAM'S RESTAURANT & LOUNGE
255 Foord St, Stellarton, NS, B0K 1S0
(902) 752-5655
Emp Here 65   *Sales* 1,969,939
SIC 5812 Eating places

D-U-N-S 24-339-0358   (BR)
NOVA CAPITAL INCORPORATED
*S. & D. SMITH CENTRAL SUPPLIES LIM-
ITED*
(*Suby of* Nova Capital Incorporated)
60 Lawrence Blvd, Stellarton, NS, B0K 1S0
(902) 755-2555
Emp Here 49
SIC 5211 Lumber and other building materials

D-U-N-S 20-347-0737   (BR)
NOVA SCOTIA COMMUNITY COLLEGE
*NOVA SCOTIA COMMUNITY COLLEGE PIC-
TOU CAMPUS*
39 Acadia Ave, Stellarton, NS, B0K 1S0
(902) 752-2002
Emp Here 110
SIC 8222 Junior colleges

D-U-N-S 24-318-7130   (BR)
PROUDFOOTS INCORPORATED

*PROUDFOOTS HOME HARDWARE BUILD-
ING CENTER*
130 Vista Dr, Stellarton, NS, B0K 0A2
(902) 752-1585
Emp Here 75
SIC 5251 Hardware stores

D-U-N-S 25-542-0895   (HQ)
PROUDFOOTS INCORPORATED
PROUDFOOTS HOME HARDWARE
(*Suby of* Proudfoot Holdings Limited)
339 South Foord St, Stellarton, NS, B0K 0A2
(902) 752-4600
Emp Here 25   *Emp Total* 70
Sales 7,449,759
SIC 5251 Hardware stores
Pr Pr James Proudfoot
  Kendell Proudfoot
  James E Proudfoot Sr
  John A Proudfoot

D-U-N-S 20-781-7420   (BR)
**SCOTSBURN CO-OPERATIVE SERVICES
LIMITED**
SCOTSBURN DAIRY
230 Ford St, Stellarton, NS, B0K 0A2
(902) 752-6181
Emp Here 35
SIC 5143 Dairy products, except dried or
canned

D-U-N-S 25-174-2219   (BR)
SOBEYS CAPITAL INCORPORATED
SOBEYS DISTRIBUTION CENTER
123 Foord St, Stellarton, NS, B0K 0A2
(902) 752-8371
Emp Here 70
SIC 4222 Refrigerated warehousing and stor-
age

D-U-N-S 20-172-3236   (HQ)
SOBEYS CAPITAL INCORPORATED
115 King St, Stellarton, NS, B0K 0A2
(902) 752-8371
Emp Here 200   *Emp Total* 125,000
Sales 12,031,219,430
SIC 5141 Groceries, general line
Pr Pr Michael Medline
  Karen Mccaskill
  Michael Vels

D-U-N-S 25-299-3290   (BR)
SOBEYS CAPITAL INCORPORATED
SOBEYS
293 Foord St, Stellarton, NS, B0K 1S0
(902) 755-1830
Emp Here 55
SIC 5411 Grocery stores

D-U-N-S 24-124-6524   (BR)
SOBEYS CAPITAL INCORPORATED
SOBEYS
123 Foord St, Stellarton, NS, B0K 0A2
(902) 662-2132
Emp Here 100
SIC 5411 Grocery stores

D-U-N-S 20-268-9089   (BR)
SOBEYS CAPITAL INCORPORATED
SOBEYS ATLANTIC
123 Foord St, Stellarton, NS, B0K 0A2
(902) 752-8371
Emp Here 70
SIC 5141 Groceries, general line

D-U-N-S 25-543-7774   (HQ)
SOBEYS INC
SOBEYS
115 King St, Stellarton, NS, B0K 0A2
(902) 752-8371
Emp Here 500   *Emp Total* 125,000
Sales 19,163,076,970
SIC 5411 Grocery stores
Pr Pr Michael Medline
  James Dickson
Ex VP Francois Vimard
CFO Clinton Keay

Pers/VP Simon Gagne
  Lyne Castonguay
VP Opers Jason Potter
  Karin Mccaskill

Stillwater Lake, NS B3Z

D-U-N-S 25-363-4877   (BR)
**MCDONALD'S RESTAURANTS OF
CANADA LIMITED**
MCDONALDS
(*Suby of* McDonald's Corporation)
4 Westwood Blvd, Stillwater Lake, NS, B3Z
1H3
(902) 826-1763
Emp Here 45
SIC 5812 Eating places

Sydney, NS B1L
Cape Breton County

D-U-N-S 25-361-9647   (BR)
**ATLANTIC RETAIL CO-OPERATIVES FED-
ERATION**
CO-OP ATLANTIC
440 Keltic Dr, Sydney, NS, B1L 1B8

Emp Here 33
SIC 5141 Groceries, general line

D-U-N-S 25-364-3621   (BR)
**CAPE BRETON-VICTORIA REGIONAL
SCHOOL BOARD**
TRANSPORTATION SCHOOL BUSSING
999 Alexandra St, Sydney, NS, B1L 1E5
(902) 562-4595
Emp Here 100
SIC 8211 Elementary and secondary schools

D-U-N-S 24-124-1848   (SL)
**FIRST STRIKE SECURITY & INVESTIGA-
TION LTD**
2145 Kings Rd, Sydney, NS, B1L 1C2
(902) 539-9991
Emp Here 65   *Sales* 2,042,900
SIC 7381 Detective and armored car services

D-U-N-S 24-676-3945   (BR)
NEWCAP INC
THE GIANT 101.9
5 Detheridge Dr, Sydney, NS, B1L 1B8
(902) 270-1019
Emp Here 30
SIC 4832 Radio broadcasting stations

D-U-N-S 24-587-9606   (BR)
**NEWFOUNDLAND CAPITAL CORPORA-
TION LIMITED**
5 Detheridge Dr, Sydney, NS, B1L 1B8
(902) 270-1019
Emp Here 40
SIC 4832 Radio broadcasting stations

Sydney, NS B1M
Cape Breton County

D-U-N-S 20-118-3162   (SL)
SYDNEY COAL RAILWAY INC
1139 Grand Lake Rd, Sydney, NS, B1M 1A2
(902) 563-8430
Emp Here 21   *Sales* 729,607
SIC 4111 Local and suburban transit

Sydney, NS B1N
Cape Breton County

D-U-N-S 20-934-7314   (BR)
**CAPE BRETON-VICTORIA REGIONAL
SCHOOL BOARD**
WHITNEY PIER MEMORIAL JR HIGH
199 Jameson St, Sydney, NS, B1N 2P7
(902) 562-6130
Emp Here 50
SIC 8211 Elementary and secondary schools

D-U-N-S 20-643-1632   (BR)
LOGISTEC STEVEDORING INC
55 Dominion St, Sydney, NS, B1N 0A1
(902) 563-4463
Emp Here 21
SIC 4491 Marine cargo handling

D-U-N-S 25-717-6719   (BR)
WILSON'S INVESTMENTS LIMITED
TIM HORTONS
915 Victoria Rd, Sydney, NS, B1N 1K5

Emp Here 25
SIC 5812 Eating places

Sydney, NS B1P
Cape Breton County

D-U-N-S 25-962-1506   (BR)
ARMOUR TRANSPORT INC
ARMOUR TRANSPORTATION SYSTEMS
443 Massey Dr, Sydney, NS, B1P 2T8
(902) 539-4185
Emp Here 40
SIC 4213 Trucking, except local

D-U-N-S 25-981-1198   (BR)
ATLANTIC WHOLESALERS LTD
SYDNEY SUPERVALU 333
332 Welton St, Sydney, NS, B1P 5S4
(902) 562-8281
Emp Here 102
SIC 5411 Grocery stores

D-U-N-S 20-571-8088   (BR)
**BELL ALIANT REGIONAL COMMUNICA-
TIONS INC**
56 Pitt St, Sydney, NS, B1P 5X5
(902) 539-9450
Emp Here 20
SIC 4899 Communication services, nec

D-U-N-S 24-363-5773   (BR)
BEST BUY CANADA LTD
FUTURE SHOP
(*Suby of* Best Buy Co., Inc.)
800 Grand Lake Rd Unit E60, Sydney, NS,
B1P 6S9
(902) 539-5877
Emp Here 50
SIC 5731 Radio, television, and electronic
stores

D-U-N-S 20-794-5796   (BR)
CBCL LIMITED
(*Suby of* Canadian-British Consulting Group
Limited)
164 Charlotte St, Sydney, NS, B1P 1C3
(902) 539-1330
Emp Here 25
SIC 8711 Engineering services

D-U-N-S 20-582-5602   (BR)
CANADA POST CORPORATION
SYDNEY PROCESSING PLANT
1230 Upper Prince St, Sydney, NS, B1P 0C5

Emp Here 80
SIC 4311 U.s. postal service

D-U-N-S 20-572-6487   (BR)
CANADA POST CORPORATION
17 Archibald Ave, Sydney, NS, B1P 3L6
(902) 794-5020
Emp Here 23
SIC 4311 U.s. postal service

D-U-N-S 25-400-3296   (HQ)
CAPE BRETON DISTRICT HEALTH AUTHORITY
CAPE BRETON REGIONAL HOSPITAL
1482 George St, Sydney, NS, B1P 1P3
(902) 567-8000
Emp Here 1,000   *Emp Total* 11,000
Sales 269,487,797
SIC 8062 General medical and surgical hospitals
Pr Pr John Malcom
Ch Bd Yvon Leblanc

D-U-N-S 24-914-8441   (BR)
CAPE BRETON REGIONAL MUNICIPALITY
ENGINEERING AND PUBLIC WORKS
320 Esplanade St Suite 300, Sydney, NS, B1P 7B9
(902) 563-5180
Emp Here 49
SIC 8711 Engineering services

D-U-N-S 20-606-0043   (BR)
CAPE BRETON REGIONAL MUNICIPALITY
CENTRE 200
481 George St Suite 200, Sydney, NS, B1P 1K5
(902) 564-2200
Emp Here 60
SIC 7389 Business services, nec

D-U-N-S 20-273-2785   (BR)
CAPE BRETON REGIONAL MUNICIPALITY
WASTE MANAGEMENT
575 Grand Lake Rd, Sydney, NS, B1P 5T3
(902) 563-5593
Emp Here 45
SIC 4953 Refuse systems

D-U-N-S 25-241-6250   (BR)
CAPE BRETON-VICTORIA REGIONAL SCHOOL BOARD
MIRA ROAD ELEMENTARY SCHOOL
1464 George St, Sydney, NS, B1P 1P3
(902) 564-5636
Emp Here 20
SIC 8211 Elementary and secondary schools

D-U-N-S 20-906-6984   (HQ)
CAPE BRETON-VICTORIA REGIONAL SCHOOL BOARD
275 George St, Sydney, NS, B1P 1J7
(902) 564-8293
Emp Here 35   *Emp Total* 11,000
Sales 169,106,655
SIC 8211 Elementary and secondary schools
Dir Fin George Boudreau
Lorne Green
Joan Currie

D-U-N-S 25-244-3122   (BR)
DELTA HOTELS LIMITED
300 Esplanade St, Sydney, NS, B1P 1A7
(902) 562-7500
Emp Here 80
SIC 8741 Management services

D-U-N-S 24-232-1847   (BR)
DEPARTMENT OF COMMUNITY SERVICES
CHILD WELFARE
25 Cossitt Heights Dr, Sydney, NS, B1P 7B4
(902) 563-0561
Emp Here 26
SIC 8699 Membership organizations, nec

D-U-N-S 20-072-0071   (BR)
ESIT CANADA ENTERPRISE SERVICES CO
ESIT CANADA ENTERPRISE SERVICES CO
(*Suby of* Dxc Technology Company)
370 Welton St, Sydney, NS, B1P 5S4
(902) 563-4600
Emp Here 500
SIC 7371 Custom computer programming services

D-U-N-S 24-977-2182   (BR)
FGL SPORTS LTD
SPORT CHEK MAYFLOWER MALL

800 Grand Lake Rd Unit E57, Sydney, NS, B1P 6S9
(902) 539-8597
Emp Here 45
SIC 5941 Sporting goods and bicycle shops

D-U-N-S 25-297-2468   (BR)
GRANT THORNTON LLP
500 George St Suite 200, Sydney, NS, B1P 1K6
(902) 562-5581
Emp Here 22
SIC 8721 Accounting, auditing, and bookkeeping

D-U-N-S 20-780-6670   (SL)
HILLMAN'S TRANSFER LIMITED
1159 Upper Prince St, Sydney, NS, B1P 5P8
(902) 564-8113
Emp Here 60   *Sales* 7,369,031
SIC 4213 Trucking, except local
Pr Pr Edward Hillman
Shauna Ley

D-U-N-S 25-370-8234   (BR)
HOME DEPOT OF CANADA INC
(*Suby of* The Home Depot Inc)
50 Sydney Port Access Rd, Sydney, NS, B1P 7H2
(902) 564-3250
Emp Here 100
SIC 5251 Hardware stores

D-U-N-S 20-072-4149   (BR)
HUDSON'S BAY COMPANY
BAY, THE
800 Grand Lake Rd, Sydney, NS, B1P 6S9
(902) 539-8350
Emp Here 60
SIC 5399 Miscellaneous general merchandise

D-U-N-S 20-287-5485   (BR)
ICT CANADA MARKETING INC
(*Suby of* Sykes Enterprises Incorporated)
325 Vulcan Ave, Sydney, NS, B1P 5X1

Emp Here 363
SIC 7389 Business services, nec

D-U-N-S 20-023-3851   (BR)
JUSTIN RESTAURANTS INC
MCDONALD'S RESTAURANT
417 Welton St, Sydney, NS, B1P 5S6
(902) 539-3636
Emp Here 65
SIC 5812 Eating places

D-U-N-S 25-299-4520   (BR)
LAWTON'S DRUG STORES LIMITED
LAWTONS DRUGS #150
719 George St, Sydney, NS, B1P 1L3
(902) 564-8200
Emp Here 20
SIC 5912 Drug stores and proprietary stores

D-U-N-S 24-187-2449   (SL)
LYNK, R.K. ENTERPRISES LIMITED
BURGER KING
390 Welton St, Sydney, NS, B1P 5S4
(902) 539-2555
Emp Here 50   *Sales* 1,532,175
SIC 5812 Eating places

D-U-N-S 24-324-1176   (BR)
MAXXAM ANALYTICS INTERNATIONAL CORPORATION
MAXXAM ANALYTICS
90 Esplanade St, Sydney, NS, B1P 1A1
(902) 567-1255
Emp Here 21
SIC 8734 Testing laboratories

D-U-N-S 24-348-0865   (BR)
MEDIAS TRANSCONTINENTAL S.E.N.C.
THE CAPE BRETON POST
255 George St, Sydney, NS, B1P 1J7
(902) 564-5451
Emp Here 90

SIC 2711 Newspapers

D-U-N-S 25-483-7529   (SL)
METROPOLITAN ENTERTAINMENT GROUP
CASINO NOVA SCOTIA SYDNEY
(*Suby of* Great Canadian Gaming Corporation)
525 George St, Sydney, NS, B1P 1K5
(902) 563-7777
Emp Here 225   *Sales* 14,553,017
SIC 7999 Amusement and recreation, nec
VP Fin John Macfarland

D-U-N-S 20-524-1367   (BR)
NOVA SCOTIA POWER INCORPORATED
Po Box 610 Stn A, Sydney, NS, B1P 6H8
(902) 564-5457
Emp Here 235
SIC 4911 Electric services

D-U-N-S 25-324-3620   (BR)
PARAMOUNT PHARMACIES LIMITED
PHARMASAVE
(*Suby of* Paramount Pharmacies Limited)
351 Charlotte St, Sydney, NS, B1P 1E1
(902) 564-4141
Emp Here 22
SIC 5912 Drug stores and proprietary stores

D-U-N-S 20-757-0479   (BR)
ROYAL BANK OF CANADA
RBC FINANCIAL GROUP
(*Suby of* Royal Bank Of Canada)
325 Prince St, Sydney, NS, B1P 5K6
(902) 567-7452
Emp Here 30
SIC 6021 National commercial banks

D-U-N-S 24-705-6104   (BR)
S. & D. SMITH CENTRAL SUPPLIES LIMITED
CENTRAL HOME IMPROVEMENT, DIV OF
(*Suby of* Nova Capital Incorporated)
530 Grand Lake Rd, Sydney, NS, B1P 5T4
(902) 562-7000
Emp Here 100
SIC 5211 Lumber and other building materials

D-U-N-S 25-614-5244   (BR)
SCOTSBURN CO-OPERATIVE SERVICES LIMITED
SCOTSBURN DAIRY GROUP
1120 Upper Prince St, Sydney, NS, B1P 5P6

Emp Here 120
SIC 2026 Fluid milk

D-U-N-S 25-298-1006   (BR)
SOBEYS CAPITAL INCORPORATED
SOBEYS 648
800 Grand Lake Rd, Sydney, NS, B1P 6S9

Emp Here 100
SIC 5411 Grocery stores

D-U-N-S 24-263-5514   (BR)
SOBEYS CAPITAL INCORPORATED
272b Prince St, Sydney, NS, B1P 5K6
(902) 562-1762
Emp Here 115
SIC 5411 Grocery stores

D-U-N-S 24-943-5025   (BR)
SOEURS DE LA CONGREGATION DE NOTRE-DAME, LES
HOLY ANGELS CONVENT
170 George St, Sydney, NS, B1P 1J2
(902) 539-6089
Emp Here 23
SIC 8661 Religious organizations

D-U-N-S 25-498-9320   (BR)
STAPLES CANADA INC
STAPLES/BUSINESS DEPOT
(*Suby of* Staples, Inc.)
800 Grand Lake Rd, Sydney, NS, B1P 6S9

(902) 539-4027
Emp Here 35
SIC 5943 Stationery stores

D-U-N-S 24-574-5823   (SL)
SYDNEY CO-OPERATIVE SOCIETY LIMITED
SYDNEY CO-OP FOOD MARKET
512 Prince St, Sydney, NS, B1P 5L9

Emp Here 140   *Sales* 26,681,350
SIC 5411 Grocery stores
Genl Mgr Milton Macdonald

D-U-N-S 20-071-3506   (BR)
VALUE VILLAGE STORES, INC
VALUE VILLAGE STORES
(*Suby of* Savers, Inc.)
370 Welton St, Sydney, NS, B1P 5S4
(902) 562-6205
Emp Here 40
SIC 5399 Miscellaneous general merchandise

D-U-N-S 25-294-8781   (BR)
WAL-MART CANADA CORP
800 Grand Lake Rd, Sydney, NS, B1P 6S9
(902) 562-1110
Emp Here 200
SIC 5311 Department stores

D-U-N-S 24-224-5426   (BR)
WENDY'S RESTAURANTS OF CANADA INC
WENDY'S
(*Suby of* The Wendy's Company)
300 Welton St, Sydney, NS, B1P 5S4
(902) 562-1113
Emp Here 25
SIC 5812 Eating places

D-U-N-S 25-619-0752   (BR)
WILSON'S INVESTMENTS LIMITED
TIM HORTONS
396 Welton St, Sydney, NS, B1P 5S7
(902) 562-5033
Emp Here 30
SIC 5461 Retail bakeries

D-U-N-S 20-806-3433   (BR)
YM INC. (SALES)
BLUENOTES
800 Grand Lake Rd, Sydney, NS, B1P 6S9
(902) 539-5453
Emp Here 25
SIC 5621 Women's clothing stores

Sydney, NS B1R
Cape Breton County

D-U-N-S 20-710-2497   (BR)
CAPE BRETON-VICTORIA REGIONAL SCHOOL BOARD
ROBIN FOOTE ELEMENTARY SCHOOL
125 Sunnydale Dr, Sydney, NS, B1R 1J4
(902) 539-3031
Emp Here 25
SIC 8211 Elementary and secondary schools

Sydney, NS B1S
Cape Breton County

D-U-N-S 20-287-4264   (BR)
ADI LIMITED
301 Alexandra St, Sydney, NS, B1S 2E8
(902) 562-2394
Emp Here 27
SIC 8711 Engineering services

D-U-N-S 25-612-7622   (BR)
ATLANTIC WHOLESALERS LTD
REAL ATLANTIC SUPERSTORE, THE
1225 Kings Rd, Sydney, NS, B1S 1E1

(902) 539-7657
Emp Here 140
SIC 5411 Grocery stores

D-U-N-S 25-613-1376   (BR)
CANADIAN BROADCASTING CORPORA-TION
285 Alexandra St, Sydney, NS, B1S 2E8
(902) 539-5050
Emp Here 25
SIC 4833 Television broadcasting stations

D-U-N-S 20-020-7251   (BR)
CAPE BRETON-VICTORIA REGIONAL SCHOOL BOARD
SYDNEY RIVER ELEMENTARY SCHOOL
35 Phillip St, Sydney, NS, B1S 1M8
(902) 567-2144
Emp Here 50
SIC 8211 Elementary and secondary schools

D-U-N-S 20-710-2539   (BR)
CAPE BRETON-VICTORIA REGIONAL SCHOOL BOARD
SHIPYARD ELEMENTARY SCHOOL
30 Mt Kemmel St, Sydney, NS, B1S 3V6
(902) 562-8878
Emp Here 50
SIC 8211 Elementary and secondary schools

D-U-N-S 20-352-7614   (BR)
CAPE BRETON-VICTORIA REGIONAL SCHOOL BOARD
MALCOLM MUNROE MEMORIAL JUNIOR HIGH SCHOOL
125 Kenwood Dr, Sydney, NS, B1S 1T8
(902) 564-4587
Emp Here 50
SIC 8211 Elementary and secondary schools

D-U-N-S 24-124-1756   (BR)
DOLLARAMA S.E.C.
7 Keltic Dr, Sydney, NS, B1S 1P4
(902) 539-0473
Emp Here 25
SIC 5331 Variety stores

D-U-N-S 20-780-7496   (BR)
HATCH CORPORATION
106-200 Church Hill Dr, Sydney, NS, B1S 0H5
(902) 564-5583
Emp Here 20
SIC 8711 Engineering services

D-U-N-S 25-305-1841   (BR)
INNVEST PROPERTIES CORP
COMFORT 'NN
(*Suby of* Innvest Properties Corp)
368 Kings Rd, Sydney, NS, B1S 1A8
(902) 562-0200
Emp Here 20
SIC 7011 Hotels and motels

D-U-N-S 20-630-1525   (SL)
JONELJIM CONCRETE CONSTRUCTION (1994) LIMITED
90 Riverview Dr, Sydney, NS, B1S 1N5
(902) 562-2400
Emp Here 100   *Sales* 42,612,189
SIC 1542 Nonresidential construction, nec
Pr Pr James Kehoe
Treas Everett Knickle

D-U-N-S 20-905-7355   (SL)
JUSTIN RESTAURANTS INC
MCDONALD'S
1189 Kings Rd, Sydney, NS, B1S 1E1
(902) 539-7706
Emp Here 180   *Sales* 7,507,300
SIC 5812 Eating places
Pr Pr Wayne Kennerkencht

D-U-N-S 20-641-6443   (BR)
JUSTIN RESTAURANTS INC
MCDONALD'S
65 Keltic Dr, Sydney, NS, B1S 1P4

Emp Here 40

SIC 5812 Eating places

D-U-N-S 20-788-8756   (BR)
KARLENE DEVELOPMENTS LIMITED
QUALITY INN
(*Suby of* Karlene Developments Limited)
560 Kings Rd, Sydney, NS, B1S 1B9
(902) 539-8101
Emp Here 35
SIC 7011 Hotels and motels

D-U-N-S 25-018-1351   (BR)
LONDON LIFE INSURANCE COMPANY
FREEDOM 55 FINANCIAL DIVISION OF
380 Kings Rd Suite 200, Sydney, NS, B1S 1A8
(902) 539-1160
Emp Here 27
SIC 8742 Management consulting services

D-U-N-S 25-299-8984   (BR)
NOVA SCOTIA LIQUOR CORPORATION
7 Keltic Dr, Sydney, NS, B1S 1P4
(902) 539-9150
Emp Here 20
SIC 5921 Liquor stores

D-U-N-S 25-616-8568   (BR)
R.K.M. INVESTMENTS LIMITED
SUBWAY SANDWICHES & SALADS
(*Suby of* R.K.M. Investments Limited)
1102 Kings Rd, Sydney, NS, B1S 1C7
(902) 567-1499
Emp Here 21
SIC 5812 Eating places

D-U-N-S 20-861-4607   (SL)
SERVICOM CANADA, LIMITED
1173 Kings Rd, Sydney, NS, B1S 3B3
(902) 562-4193
Emp Here 500   *Sales* 32,294,640
SIC 7389 Business services, nec
Mgr Todd Riley
Pr Pr David Jefferson
Gene Caldwell

D-U-N-S 20-100-1703   (BR)
SOBEYS CAPITAL INCORPORATED
SOBEYS
95 Keltic Dr, Sydney, NS, B1S 1P4
(902) 562-5110
Emp Here 100
SIC 5411 Grocery stores

D-U-N-S 25-299-3415   (BR)
SOBEYS CAPITAL INCORPORATED
SOBEYS BRANCH 630
95 Keltic Dr, Sydney, NS, B1S 1P4
(902) 562-5110
Emp Here 120
SIC 5411 Grocery stores

D-U-N-S 25-294-8740   (BR)
WAL-MART CANADA CORP
WAL-MART
65 Keltic Dr, Sydney, NS, B1S 1P4
(902) 562-3353
Emp Here 200
SIC 5311 Department stores

Sydney Mines, NS B1V
Cape Breton County

D-U-N-S 25-240-9040   (BR)
CAPE BRETON-VICTORIA REGIONAL SCHOOL BOARD
ST JOSEPH ELEMENTARY SCHOOL
2 School St, Sydney Mines, NS, B1V 1R3
(902) 736-8382
Emp Here 40
SIC 8211 Elementary and secondary schools

D-U-N-S 25-240-9206   (BR)
CAPE BRETON-VICTORIA REGIONAL SCHOOL BOARD
SYDNEY MINES MIDDLE SCHOOL

596 Main St, Sydney Mines, NS, B1V 2K8
(902) 736-8549
Emp Here 25
SIC 8211 Elementary and secondary schools

D-U-N-S 25-240-9164   (BR)
CAPE BRETON-VICTORIA REGIONAL SCHOOL BOARD
MEMORIAL HIGH SCHOOL
300 Memorial Dr, Sydney Mines, NS, B1V 2Y5
(902) 736-6233
Emp Here 49
SIC 8211 Elementary and secondary schools

D-U-N-S 20-024-9006   (BR)
CAPE BRETON-VICTORIA REGIONAL SCHOOL BOARD
JUBILEE ELEMENTARY SCHOOL
755 Main St, Sydney Mines, NS, B1V 2L4
(902) 736-8140
Emp Here 28
SIC 8211 Elementary and secondary schools

D-U-N-S 24-833-6463   (SL)
NORTHSIDE HOMEMAKER SERVICE SO-CIETY
735 Main St, Sydney Mines, NS, B1V 2L3
(902) 736-2701
Emp Here 52   *Sales* 2,042,900
SIC 8322 Individual and family services

D-U-N-S 25-082-6286   (BR)
SOBEYS CAPITAL INCORPORATED
FRESHCO
39 Pitt St, Sydney Mines, NS, B1V 1R7
(902) 736-6416
Emp Here 30
SIC 5411 Grocery stores

Tatamagouche, NS B0K
Colchester County

D-U-N-S 20-287-4595   (BR)
CHIGNECTO CENTRAL REGIONAL SCHOOL BOARD
TATAMAGOUCHE ELEMENTARY SCHOOL
(*Suby of* Chignecto Central Regional School Board)
30 Church Rd, Tatamagouche, NS, B0K 1V0
(902) 657-6220
Emp Here 21
SIC 8211 Elementary and secondary schools

D-U-N-S 20-710-1879   (BR)
CHIGNECTO CENTRAL REGIONAL SCHOOL BOARD
NORTH COLCHESTER HIGHSCHOOL
(*Suby of* Chignecto Central Regional School Board)
90 Blair Ave, Tatamagouche, NS, B0K 1V0
(902) 657-6200
Emp Here 23
SIC 8211 Elementary and secondary schools

D-U-N-S 24-605-5016   (SL)
FIRE STOP ENTERPRISES LTD
2034 Balmoral Rd Rr 4, Tatamagouche, NS, B0K 1V0
(902) 657-2290
Emp Here 20   *Sales* 2,407,703
SIC 5087 Service establishment equipment

D-U-N-S 24-804-5593   (BR)
TIM HORTON CHILDREN'S FOUNDATION, INC
Gd, Tatamagouche, NS, B0K 1V0
(902) 657-2359
Emp Here 65
SIC 7032 Sporting and recreational camps

D-U-N-S 24-189-6943   (SL)
WILLOW LODGE ASSOCIATION
100 Blair Ave, Tatamagouche, NS, B0K 1V0
(902) 657-3101
Emp Here 70   *Sales* 3,210,271

SIC 8051 Skilled nursing care facilities

Thorburn, NS B0K
Pictou County

D-U-N-S 25-242-9139   (BR)
CHIGNECTO CENTRAL REGIONAL SCHOOL BOARD
THORBURN CONSOLIDATED SCHOOL
(*Suby of* Chignecto Central Regional School Board)
13 New Row, Thorburn, NS, B0K 1W0
(902) 922-3840
Emp Here 35
SIC 8211 Elementary and secondary schools

D-U-N-S 20-710-2026   (BR)
CHIGNECTO CENTRAL REGIONAL SCHOOL BOARD
EAST PICTEAU MIDDLE SCHOOL
(*Suby of* Chignecto Central Regional School Board)
163 School Rd, Thorburn, NS, B0K 1W0
(902) 922-3800
Emp Here 29
SIC 8211 Elementary and secondary schools

D-U-N-S 20-260-7560   (BR)
CHIGNECTO CENTRAL REGIONAL SCHOOL BOARD
F. H. MACDONALD ELEMENTARY SCHOOL
(*Suby of* Chignecto Central Regional School Board)
123 School Rd, Thorburn, NS, B0K 1W0
(902) 922-3820
Emp Here 30
SIC 8211 Elementary and secondary schools

Timberlea, NS B3T

D-U-N-S 24-838-6083   (BR)
CANADA PIPE COMPANY ULC
156 James St, Timberlea, NS, B3T 1P1
(902) 444-7350
Emp Here 50
SIC 5051 Metals service centers and offices

D-U-N-S 25-241-4727   (BR)
HALIFAX REGIONAL SCHOOL BOARD
BEECHVILLE LAKESIDE TIMBERLEA ELE-MENTARY SCHOOL
(*Suby of* Halifax Regional School Board)
22 James St, Timberlea, NS, B3T 1G9
(902) 876-3230
Emp Here 60
SIC 8211 Elementary and secondary schools

D-U-N-S 25-364-8737   (BR)
ROBIE & KEMPT SERVICES LIMITED
TIM HORTONS
1844 St Margarets Bay Rd, Timberlea, NS, B3T 1B8
(902) 431-2992
Emp Here 36
SIC 5812 Eating places

Trenton, NS B0K
Pictou County

D-U-N-S 20-710-2067   (BR)
CHIGNECTO CENTRAL REGIONAL SCHOOL BOARD
TRENTON MIDDLE SCHOOL
(*Suby of* Chignecto Central Regional School Board)
37 Dickie St, Trenton, NS, B0K 1X0
(902) 755-8440
Emp Here 30
SIC 8211 Elementary and secondary schools

D-U-N-S 24-593-2558   (SL)
DSME TRENTON LTD
DSTN
34 Powerplant Rd, Trenton, NS, B0K 1X0
(902) 753-7777
Emp Here 100   *Sales* 16,372,144
SIC 3441 Fabricated structural Metal
Dir Marvyn C Robar

D-U-N-S 20-695-0193   (SL)
NOVA FORGE CORP
34 Power Plant Rd, Trenton, NS, B0K 1X0
(902) 752-0989
Emp Here 900   *Sales* 236,479,950
SIC 3743 Railroad equipment
Genl Mgr Robert Maceachern
Pr Kevin Crowley
VP VP R. Mark Hamlin Jr
Dir Richard M. Hamlin

D-U-N-S 20-102-5983   (BR)
NOVA SCOTIA POWER INCORPORATED
108 Power Plant Rd, Trenton, NS, B0K 1X0
(902) 755-5811
Emp Here 150
SIC 4911 Electric services

D-U-N-S 20-287-7309   (BR)
UNITED STEELWORKERS OF AMERICA
(*Suby of* United Steelworkers)
1 Diamond St, Trenton, NS, B0K 1X0

Emp Here 1,201
SIC 8631 Labor organizations

Truro, NS B2N
Colchester County

D-U-N-S 20-151-1222   (SL)
3032948 NOVA SCOTIA LIMITED
HOLIDAY INN HOTEL & CONFERENCE CENTRE
437 Prince St, Truro, NS, B2N 1E6
(902) 895-1651
Emp Here 80   *Sales* 3,502,114
SIC 7011 Hotels and motels

D-U-N-S 25-635-2147   (BR)
ARMOUR TRANSPORT INC
ARMOUR TRANSPORTATION SYSTEMS
204 Willow St, Truro, NS, B2N 5A2
(902) 897-9777
Emp Here 20
SIC 4213 Trucking, except local

D-U-N-S 20-030-7775   (BR)
ASTRAL MEDIA RADIO ATLANTIC INC
CKTO BIG DOG
187 Industrial Ave, Truro, NS, B2N 6V3
(902) 893-6060
Emp Here 20
SIC 4832 Radio broadcasting stations

D-U-N-S 20-932-0290   (BR)
ATLANTIC RETAIL CO-OPERATIVES FEDERATION
CO-OP ATLANTIC
349 Willow St, Truro, NS, B2N 5A6
(902) 895-3854
Emp Here 40
SIC 2048 Prepared feeds, nec

D-U-N-S 20-700-0386   (BR)
BANQUE DE DEVELOPPEMENT DU CANADA
BDC
622 Prince St, Truro, NS, B2N 1G4
(902) 895-6377
Emp Here 40
SIC 6141 Personal credit institutions

D-U-N-S 20-571-8112   (BR)
BELL ALIANT REGIONAL COMMUNICATIONS INC
810 Prince St, Truro, NS, B2N 1H1

(902) 486-2620
Emp Here 20
SIC 4899 Communication services, nec

D-U-N-S 20-718-4792   (BR)
BELL MEDIA INC
CAT COUNTRY
187 Industrial Ave, Truro, NS, B2N 6V3
(902) 893-6060
Emp Here 21
SIC 4832 Radio broadcasting stations

D-U-N-S 20-608-9158   (BR)
BOONE FOOD SERVICES LIMITED
A & W RESTAURANT
(*Suby of* Boone Food Services Limited)
245 Robie St, Truro, NS, B2N 5N6
(902) 453-5330
Emp Here 20
SIC 5812 Eating places

D-U-N-S 20-568-9966   (BR)
CANADA POST CORPORATION
366 Industrial Ave, Truro, NS, B2N 6V7
(902) 897-3341
Emp Here 45
SIC 4311 U.s. postal service

D-U-N-S 20-540-6387   (BR)
CANADA POST CORPORATION
TRURO POSTAL OUTLET
664 Prince St, Truro, NS, B2N 1G6
(902) 893-7277
Emp Here 42
SIC 4311 U.s. postal service

D-U-N-S 20-906-5127   (BR)
CANADIAN IMPERIAL BANK OF COMMERCE
CIBC
813 Prince St, Truro, NS, B2N 1G7
(902) 895-5341
Emp Here 25
SIC 6021 National commercial banks

D-U-N-S 20-589-5097   (BR)
CASEY CONCRETE LIMITED
69 Glenwood Dr, Truro, NS, B2N 1E9
(902) 895-1618
Emp Here 125
SIC 3273 Ready-mixed concrete

D-U-N-S 25-241-7084   (BR)
CHIGNECTO CENTRAL REGIONAL SCHOOL BOARD
TRURO JUNIOR HIGH SCHOOL
(*Suby of* Chignecto Central Regional School Board)
445 Young St, Truro, NS, B2N 7H9
(902) 896-5550
Emp Here 50
SIC 8211 Elementary and secondary schools

D-U-N-S 25-241-3521   (BR)
CHIGNECTO CENTRAL REGIONAL SCHOOL BOARD
ST. MARY'S ELEMENTARY SCHOOL
(*Suby of* Chignecto Central Regional School Board)
171 King St, Truro, NS, B2N 3L3
(902) 243-3900
Emp Here 30
SIC 8211 Elementary and secondary schools

D-U-N-S 24-129-7373   (HQ)
CHIGNECTO CENTRAL REGIONAL SCHOOL BOARD
(*Suby of* Chignecto Central Regional School Board)
60 Lorne St, Truro, NS, B2N 3K3
(902) 897-8900
Emp Here 2,717   *Emp Total* 4,837
Sales 156,793,650
SIC 8211 Elementary and secondary schools
Superintnt Gary Adams
Ch Bd Trudy Thompson
V Ch Bd Marilyn Murray
Dir Fin Valerie Gauthier

Dir Opers Herb Steeves
Prs Dir Allison Mcgrath

D-U-N-S 25-242-0690   (BR)
CHIGNECTO CENTRAL REGIONAL SCHOOL BOARD
COBEQUID EDUCATIONAL CENTRE
(*Suby of* Chignecto Central Regional School Board)
34 Lorne St, Truro, NS, B2N 3K3
(902) 896-5700
Emp Here 125
SIC 8211 Elementary and secondary schools

D-U-N-S 20-710-1820   (BR)
CHIGNECTO CENTRAL REGIONAL SCHOOL BOARD
HUMAN RESOURCE SERVICES
(*Suby of* Chignecto Central Regional School Board)
60 Lorne St, Truro, NS, B2N 3K3
(902) 897-8900
Emp Here 50
SIC 8211 Elementary and secondary schools

D-U-N-S 20-045-7955   (BR)
CHIGNECTO CENTRAL REGIONAL SCHOOL BOARD
BIBLE HILL JUNIOR HIGH SCHOOL
(*Suby of* Chignecto Central Regional School Board)
741 College Rd, Truro, NS, B2N 5Y9
(902) 896-5500
Emp Here 25
SIC 8211 Elementary and secondary schools

D-U-N-S 25-650-9076   (SL)
COLCHESTER RESIDENTIAL SERVICES SOCIETY
CRSS
35 Commercial St Suite 201, Truro, NS, B2N 3H9
(902) 893-4273
Emp Here 120   *Sales* 14,913,150
SIC 8322 Individual and family services
Ex Dir Shannon Mclellan
Judy Baird

D-U-N-S 20-573-2196   (BR)
COMPAGNIE DES CHEMINS DE FER NATIONAUX DU CANADA
100 Esplanade St, Truro, NS, B2N 2K3
(902) 893-4689
Emp Here 20
SIC 4011 Railroads, line-haul operating

D-U-N-S 25-702-3726   (BR)
DALHOUSIE UNIVERSITY
FACULTY OF AGRICULTURE
62 Cumming Dr, Truro, NS, B2N 5E3
(902) 893-6600
Emp Here 400
SIC 8221 Colleges and universities

D-U-N-S 20-248-4341   (BR)
DARLING INTERNATIONAL CANADA INC
ROTHSAY
(*Suby of* Darling Ingredients Inc.)
169 Lower Truro Rd, Truro, NS, B2N 5C1
(902) 895-2801
Emp Here 100
SIC 4953 Refuse systems

D-U-N-S 25-720-1343   (BR)
DEXTER CONSTRUCTION COMPANY LIMITED
PAVING BUILDING ROADS
44 Meadow Dr, Truro, NS, B2N 5V4
(902) 895-6952
Emp Here 200
SIC 1611 Highway and street construction

D-U-N-S 20-076-6942   (BR)
DOLLARAMA S.E.C.
DOLLARAMA
245 Robie St, Truro, NS, B2N 5N6
(902) 893-7789
Emp Here 25

SIC 5399 Miscellaneous general merchandise

D-U-N-S 24-977-1895   (BR)
FGL SPORTS LTD
SPORT CHEK
245 Robie St Unit 109, Truro, NS, B2N 5N6
(902) 895-3383
Emp Here 26
SIC 5941 Sporting goods and bicycle shops

D-U-N-S 20-786-2017   (BR)
GEM HEALTH CARE GROUP LIMITED
MIRA, THE
426 Young St, Truro, NS, B2N 7B1
(902) 895-8715
Emp Here 135
SIC 8059 Nursing and personal care, nec

D-U-N-S 20-030-8203   (SL)
GLENGARRY MOTEL & RESTAURANT LIMITED
BEST WESTERN GLENGARRY
150 Willow St, Truro, NS, B2N 4Z6
(902) 893-4311
Emp Here 75   *Sales* 3,283,232
SIC 7011 Hotels and motels

D-U-N-S 25-297-2344   (BR)
GRANT THORNTON LLP
35 Commercial St Suite 400, Truro, NS, B2N 3H9
(902) 893-1150
Emp Here 21
SIC 8721 Accounting, auditing, and bookkeeping

D-U-N-S 20-702-5854   (BR)
GROUPE DES MEDIAS TRANSCONTINENTAL DE LA NOUVELLE-ECOSSE INC
TRURO DAILY NEWS
(*Suby of* Groupe Des Medias Transcontinental de la Nouvelle-Ecosse Inc)
6 Louise St, Truro, NS, B2N 3K2
(902) 895-4404
Emp Here 25
SIC 2711 Newspapers

D-U-N-S 25-481-4072   (BR)
HINSPERGERS POLY INDUSTRIES LTD
80 Blakeney Dr, Truro, NS, B2N 6X1
(902) 893-4458
Emp Here 40
SIC 2394 Canvas and related products

D-U-N-S 25-305-1882   (BR)
INNVEST PROPERTIES CORP
COMFORT INN
(*Suby of* Innvest Properties Corp)
12 Meadow Dr, Truro, NS, B2N 5V4
(902) 893-0330
Emp Here 20
SIC 7011 Hotels and motels

D-U-N-S 24-831-7760   (BR)
INTERTAPE POLYMER INC
ENGINEERED COATED PRODUCTS
50 Abbey Ave, Truro, NS, B2N 6W4
(902) 895-1686
Emp Here 450
SIC 2221 Broadwoven fabric mills, manmade

D-U-N-S 20-196-8992   (BR)
J. D. IRVING, LIMITED
KENT BUILDING SUPPLIES, DIV OF
(*Suby of* J. D. Irving, Limited)
104 Wade Rd, Truro, NS, B2N 6S9
(902) 897-6300
Emp Here 50
SIC 5211 Lumber and other building materials

D-U-N-S 25-640-1670   (BR)
JRM 277 INVESTMENTS LIMITED
TIM HORTONS
(*Suby of* JRM 277 Investments Limited)
184 Pictou Rd, Truro, NS, B2N 2T1
(902) 893-7979
Emp Here 30
SIC 5812 Eating places

D-U-N-S 25-639-9643   (BR)
JRM 277 INVESTMENTS LIMITED
TIM HORTONS
(*Suby of* JRM 277 Investments Limited)
322 Willow St, Truro, NS, B2N 5A5
(902) 897-0404
Emp Here 30
SIC 5812 Eating places

D-U-N-S 20-287-2094   (BR)
LOBLAW PROPERTIES LIMITED
TRURO SUPERSTORE
46 Elm St, Truro, NS, B2N 3H6
(902) 895-4306
Emp Here 200
SIC 5411 Grocery stores

D-U-N-S 24-994-2376   (BR)
MIDLAND TRANSPORT LIMITED
TRURO TERMINAL
(*Suby of* J. D. Irving, Limited)
52 Dunlap Ave, Truro, NS, B2N 5E3
(902) 897-6334
Emp Here 21
SIC 4212 Local trucking, without storage

D-U-N-S 24-189-3031   (SL)
NOVA SCOTIA PROVINCIAL EXHIBITION COMMISSION
TRURO RACEWAY/EXHIBITION
73 Ryland Ave, Truro, NS, B2N 2V5
(902) 893-9222
Emp Here 51
SIC 7948 Racing, including track operation

D-U-N-S 20-537-1565   (BR)
NOVA SCOTIA, PROVINCE OF
DELHOUSIE UNIVERSITY
50 Pictou Rd Suite 258, Truro, NS, B2N 5E3
(902) 893-6700
Emp Here 35
SIC 8221 Colleges and universities

D-U-N-S 24-118-1333   (BR)
PUROLATOR INC.
PUROLATOR INC
1 Bayview Dr, Truro, NS, B2N 5A9
(902) 895-7952
Emp Here 20
SIC 7389 Business services, nec

D-U-N-S 25-366-7893   (HQ)
RESOURCE RECOVERY FUND BOARD, INCORPORATED
RRFB NOVA SCOTIA
35 Commercial St Suite 400, Truro, NS, B2N 3H9
(902) 895-7732
Emp Here 24   *Emp Total* 11,000
Sales 40,304,474
SIC 4953 Refuse systems
 William Ring
Dir Opers Jerome Paris
 Richard Ramsay
 Einar Christensen
 Bill Karsten
 Ray Cote
 Richie Cotton
 Tim Dietrich
 Charles Eastman
 Gary Johnson

D-U-N-S 24-629-5901   (BR)
ROYAL BANK OF CANADA
RBC
(*Suby of* Royal Bank Of Canada)
940 Prince St, Truro, NS, B2N 1H5
(902) 843-3333
Emp Here 25
SIC 6021 National commercial banks

D-U-N-S 20-780-9773   (BR)
SCOTSBURN CO-OPERATIVE SERVICES LIMITED
SCOTSBURN DAIRY GROUP
85 Blakeney Dr, Truro, NS, B2N 6W9

Emp Here 50

SIC 2024 Ice cream and frozen deserts

D-U-N-S 25-294-5613   (BR)
SEARS CANADA INC
245 Robie St, Truro, NS, B2N 5N6
(902) 893-1101
Emp Here 46
SIC 5311 Department stores

D-U-N-S 25-640-3122   (BR)
SHANNEX INCORPORATED
CEDARSTONE ENHANCED CARE
378 Young St, Truro, NS, B2N 7H2
(902) 895-2891
Emp Here 150
SIC 8051 Skilled nursing care facilities

D-U-N-S 20-300-0380   (BR)
SOBEYS CAPITAL INCORPORATED
985 Prince St, Truro, NS, B2N 1H7
(902) 895-9785
Emp Here 100
SIC 5411 Grocery stores

D-U-N-S 24-943-5983   (BR)
SOBEYS CAPITAL INCORPORATED
SOBEYS #594
68 Robie St Suite 594, Truro, NS, B2N 1L2
(902) 893-9388
Emp Here 160
SIC 5411 Grocery stores

D-U-N-S 20-588-3502   (BR)
SOBEYS CAPITAL INCORPORATED
FOODLAND 9334
241 Pictou Rd, Truro, NS, B2N 2S7
(902) 893-7986
Emp Here 31
SIC 5411 Grocery stores

D-U-N-S 25-091-4603   (BR)
STAPLES CANADA INC
STAPLES THE BUSINESS DEPOT
(*Suby of* Staples, Inc.)
68 Robie St, Truro, NS, B2N 1L2
(902) 895-1572
Emp Here 33
SIC 5943 Stationery stores

D-U-N-S 25-650-9100   (BR)
SUBACH LIMITED
HARVEY'S RESTAURANT/SWISS CHALET
79 Robie St, Truro, NS, B2N 1K8
(902) 895-6699
Emp Here 25
SIC 5812 Eating places

D-U-N-S 24-684-6617   (HQ)
TANDUS FLOORING LIMITED
TANDUS GROUP
435 Willow St Suite 30, Truro, NS, B2N 6T2
(902) 895-5491
Emp Here 250   *Emp Total* 3
Sales 102,144,980
SIC 2273 Carpets and rugs
Dir Morgan Palmer
Dir Randy Rawlston

D-U-N-S 24-188-0327   (BR)
TORONTO-DOMINION BANK, THE
TD BANK
(*Suby of* Toronto-Dominion Bank, The)
22 Inglis Pl, Truro, NS, B2N 4B4

Emp Here 21
SIC 6021 National commercial banks

D-U-N-S 25-638-3530   (BR)
VICTORIAN ORDER OF NURSES FOR CANADA
VON COLCHESTER EAST HANTS DISTRICT
30 Duke St Suite 5, Truro, NS, B2N 2A1
(902) 893-3803
Emp Here 200
SIC 8082 Home health care services

D-U-N-S 24-120-9423   (BR)
WAL-MART CANADA CORP

140 Wade Rd, Truro, NS, B2N 7H3
(902) 893-5582
Emp Here 80
SIC 5311 Department stores

Truro Heights, NS B6L

D-U-N-S 20-301-2062   (SL)
MBW COURIER INCORPORATED
142 Parkway Dr, Truro Heights, NS, B6L 1N8
(902) 895-5120
Emp Here 90   *Sales* 4,523,563
SIC 7389 Business services, nec

Tusket, NS B0W
Yarmouth County

D-U-N-S 20-192-6537   (BR)
CONSEIL SCOLAIRE ACADIEN PROVINCIAL
ECOLE BELLEVILLE
84 Belleville Rd Rr 3, Tusket, NS, B0W 3M0
(902) 648-5920
Emp Here 25
SIC 8211 Elementary and secondary schools

D-U-N-S 20-811-6025   (BR)
CONSEIL SCOLAIRE ACADIEN PROVINCIAL
ECOLE SECONDAIRE DE PAREN EN BAS
4258 Rte 308 Ns, Tusket, NS, B0W 3M0
(902) 648-5900
Emp Here 40
SIC 8211 Elementary and secondary schools

D-U-N-S 20-443-7032   (SL)
TUSKET SALES & SERVICE LIMITED
TUSKET FORD
4143 Gavel Rd, Tusket, NS, B0W 3M0
(902) 648-2600
Emp Here 65   *Sales* 4,669,485
SIC 7532 Top and body repair and paint shops

Upper Musquodoboit, NS B0N
Halifax County

D-U-N-S 20-085-8087   (BR)
HALIFAX REGIONAL SCHOOL BOARD
UPPER MUSQUODOBOIT CONSOLIDATED SCHOOL
8416 Hwy 224, Upper Musquodoboit, NS, B0N 2M0
(902) 568-2285
Emp Here 40
SIC 8211 Elementary and secondary schools

Upper Stewiacke, NS B0N
Colchester County

D-U-N-S 20-710-1861   (BR)
CHIGNECTO CENTRAL REGIONAL SCHOOL BOARD
UPPER STEWIACKE ELEMENTARY SCHOOL
(*Suby of* Chignecto Central Regional School Board)
5327 Hwy 289, Upper Stewiacke, NS, B0N 2P0
(902) 671-3000
Emp Here 50
SIC 8211 Elementary and secondary schools

Upper Tantallon, NS B3Z
Halifax County

D-U-N-S 25-296-6296   (BR)
BANK OF NOVA SCOTIA, THE
SCOTIABANK
3650 Hammonds Plains Rd Suite 368, Upper Tantallon, NS, B3Z 4R3
(902) 826-2124
Emp Here 21
SIC 6021 National commercial banks

D-U-N-S 25-241-4677   (BR)
HALIFAX REGIONAL SCHOOL BOARD
TENTALLON JUNIOR HIGH
(*Suby of* Halifax Regional School Board)
31 Scholars Rd, Upper Tantallon, NS, B3Z 0C3
(902) 826-3222
Emp Here 32
SIC 8211 Elementary and secondary schools

D-U-N-S 20-025-9088   (BR)
HALIFAX REGIONAL SCHOOL BOARD
TANTALLON JUNIOR ELEMENTARY SCHOOL
3 French Village Station Rd Suite Upper, Upper Tantallon, NS, B3Z 1E4
(902) 826-1200
Emp Here 35
SIC 8211 Elementary and secondary schools

D-U-N-S 20-024-4072   (BR)
IRVING OIL LIMITED
TANTALLON BLUE CANOE
5210 St Margarets Bay Rd, Upper Tantallon, NS, B3Z 4H3
(902) 826-1924
Emp Here 21
SIC 5541 Gasoline service stations

D-U-N-S 24-573-3725   (BR)
SOBEYS CAPITAL INCORPORATED
SOBEYS
3650 Hammonds Plains Rd Suite 684, Upper Tantallon, NS, B3Z 4R3
(902) 826-1046
Emp Here 25
SIC 5411 Grocery stores

Valley, NS B6L

D-U-N-S 20-024-9014   (BR)
CHIGNECTO CENTRAL REGIONAL SCHOOL BOARD
REDCLIFF MIDDLE SCHOOL
(*Suby of* Chignecto Central Regional School Board)
33 Sunset Lane, Valley, NS, B6L 4K1
(902) 896-5520
Emp Here 50
SIC 8211 Elementary and secondary schools

D-U-N-S 20-337-8757   (BR)
J. D. IRVING, LIMITED
J.D. IRVING SPROULE LUMBER
(*Suby of* J. D. Irving, Limited)
529 Valleydale Rd, Valley, NS, B6L 2Y2
(902) 895-4451
Emp Here 75
SIC 2421 Sawmills and planing mills, general

Wagmacook, NS B0E

D-U-N-S 20-786-1506   (BR)
WAGMATCOOK BAND COUNCIL
WAGMATCOOK SCHOOL
1 Sugarbush Rd, Wagmatcook, NS, B0E 3N0
(902) 295-3491
Emp Here 30
SIC 8211 Elementary and secondary schools

Waverley, NS B2R
Halifax County

D-U-N-S 20-710-2745   (BR)
HALIFAX REGIONAL SCHOOL BOARD
WAVERLEY ELEMENTARY SCHOOL
1279 Rocky Lake Dr, Waverley, NS, B2R 1S1
(902) 860-4150
Emp Here 50
SIC 8211 Elementary and secondary schools

D-U-N-S 25-964-6867   (BR)
MUNICIPAL CONTRACTING LIMITED
927 Rocky Lake Dr, Waverley, NS, B2R 1S1
(902) 835-3381
Emp Here 1,500
SIC 1611 Highway and street construction

D-U-N-S 20-259-4235   (BR)
SHANNAHAN'S INVESTIGATION SECURITY LIMITED
(*Suby of* Shannahan's Investigation Security Limited)
30 Brookfalls Crt, Waverley, NS, B2R 1J2
(902) 873-4536
Emp Here 105
SIC 7381 Detective and armored car services

Wedgeport, NS B0W
Yarmouth County

D-U-N-S 20-710-3255   (BR)
CONSEIL SCOLAIRE ACADIEN PROVINCIAL
ECOLE DE WEDGEPORT
44 Ditcher Rd, Wedgeport, NS, B0W 3P0
(902) 663-5000
Emp Here 20
SIC 8211 Elementary and secondary schools

Wellington, NS B2T
Halifax County

D-U-N-S 24-382-0821   (BR)
WESTOWER COMMUNICATIONS LTD
4671 Highway 2, Wellington, NS, B2T 1B7
(902) 860-2186
Emp Here 35
SIC 1623 Water, sewer, and utility lines

West Pubnico, NS B0W
Yarmouth County

D-U-N-S 20-024-4981   (BR)
CONSEIL SCOLAIRE ACADIEN PROVINCIAL
ECOLE PUBNICO-OUEST
811 Rte 335, West Pubnico, NS, B0W 3S0
(902) 762-4400
Emp Here 24
SIC 8211 Elementary and secondary schools

Western Shore, NS B0J
Lunenburg County

D-U-N-S 20-058-0442   (BR)
I.M.P. GROUP INTERNATIONAL INCORPORATED
OAK ISLAND RESORT
36 Treasure Dr, Western Shore, NS, B0J 3M0
(902) 627-2600
Emp Here 50
SIC 4581 Airports, flying fields, and services

Westphal, NS B2Z
Halifax County

D-U-N-S 25-653-3290   (SL)
2356723 NOVA SCOTIA LIMITED
CLARKE, K B RESTORATION
14 Lake Major Rd, Westphal, NS, B2Z 1B1
(902) 434-7199
Emp Here 30   *Sales* 6,188,450
SIC 1521 Single-family housing construction
Pr Pr Kevin B Clarke

D-U-N-S 20-710-2760   (BR)
HALIFAX REGIONAL SCHOOL BOARD
ROSS ROAD ELEMENTARY AND JUNIOR HIGH SCHOOL
336 Ross Rd, Westphal, NS, B2Z 1H2
(902) 462-8340
Emp Here 40
SIC 8211 Elementary and secondary schools

Westville, NS B0K
Pictou County

D-U-N-S 20-710-2075   (BR)
CHIGNECTO CENTRAL REGIONAL SCHOOL BOARD
WALTER DUGGAN CONSOLIDATED SCHOOL
(*Suby of* Chignecto Central Regional School Board)
2370 Spring Garden Rd, Westville, NS, B0K 2A0
(902) 396-2700
Emp Here 40
SIC 8211 Elementary and secondary schools

D-U-N-S 20-710-2109   (BR)
CHIGNECTO CENTRAL REGIONAL SCHOOL BOARD
HIGHLAND CONSOLIDATED MIDDLE SCHOOL
(*Suby of* Chignecto Central Regional School Board)
2157 Main St S, Westville, NS, B0K 2A0

Emp Here 60
SIC 8211 Elementary and secondary schools

D-U-N-S 20-710-2083   (BR)
CHIGNECTO CENTRAL REGIONAL SCHOOL BOARD
NORTHTHUMBERLAND REGIONAL HIGH SCHOOL
(*Suby of* Chignecto Central Regional School Board)
104 Alma Rd, Westville, NS, B0K 2A0
(902) 396-2750
Emp Here 50
SIC 8211 Elementary and secondary schools

Weymouth, NS B0W
Digby County

D-U-N-S 20-914-8860   (BR)
ROYAL BANK OF CANADA
RBC
(*Suby of* Royal Bank Of Canada)
Gd, Weymouth, NS, B0W 3T0
(902) 837-5136
Emp Here 24
SIC 6021 National commercial banks

D-U-N-S 20-710-3164   (BR)
TRI-COUNTY REGIONAL SCHOOL BOARD
WEYMOUTH CONSOLIDATED SCHOOL
Gd, Weymouth, NS, B0W 3T0
(902) 837-2310
Emp Here 25

SIC 8211 Elementary and secondary schools

D-U-N-S 20-288-3463   (BR)
TRI-COUNTY REGIONAL SCHOOL BOARD
ST MARY'S BAY ACADEMY
4079 1 Hwy, Weymouth, NS, B0W 3T0
(902) 837-2340
Emp Here 45
SIC 8211 Elementary and secondary schools

Whites Lake, NS B3T
Halifax County

D-U-N-S 25-242-4965   (BR)
HALIFAX REGIONAL SCHOOL BOARD
ATLANTIC MEMORIAL ELEMENTARY SCHOOL
(*Suby of* Halifax Regional School Board)
3591 Prospect Rd, Whites Lake, NS, B3T 1Z3
(902) 852-2424
Emp Here 30
SIC 8211 Elementary and secondary schools

Whycocomagh, NS B0E
Inverness County

D-U-N-S 25-241-7043   (BR)
STRAIT REGIONAL SCHOOL BOARD
WHYCOCOMAGH EDUCATION CENTRE
50 Norman Mcleod Rd, Whycocomagh, NS, B0E 3M0
(902) 756-2441
Emp Here 25
SIC 8211 Elementary and secondary schools

Windsor, NS B0N
Hants County

D-U-N-S 20-287-6244   (BR)
ANNAPOLIS VALLEY REGIONAL SCHOOL BOARD
103 Morrison Dr, Windsor, NS, B0N 2T0
(902) 538-4600
Emp Here 36
SIC 8211 Elementary and secondary schools

D-U-N-S 25-503-7327   (BR)
ANNAPOLIS VALLEY REGIONAL SCHOOL BOARD
AVON VIEW HIGH SCHOOL
225 Payzant Dr, Windsor, NS, B0N 2T0
(902) 792-6740
Emp Here 90
SIC 8211 Elementary and secondary schools

D-U-N-S 20-652-4808   (BR)
ANNAPOLIS VALLEY REGIONAL SCHOOL BOARD
THREE MILE PLAINS DISTRICT SCHOOL
4555 Highway 1, Windsor, NS, B0N 2T0
(902) 792-6720
Emp Here 25
SIC 8211 Elementary and secondary schools

D-U-N-S 25-133-9602   (BR)
ATLANTIC WHOLESALERS LTD
ATLANTIC SUPERSTORE
11 Cole Dr, Windsor, NS, B0N 2T0
(902) 798-9537
Emp Here 110
SIC 5411 Grocery stores

D-U-N-S 24-342-0317   (BR)
COBHAM TRACKING & LOCATING LTD
(*Suby of* COBHAM PLC)
90 Sanford Dr, Windsor, NS, B0N 2T0
(902) 798-8999
Emp Here 70
SIC 3663 Radio and t.v. communications

equipment

D-U-N-S 24-350-3732   (HQ)
J.M.P. SAYLES HOLDINGS INC
TIM HORTONS
(*Suby of* J.M.P. Sayles Holdings Inc)
4 King St Exten, Windsor, NS, B0N 2T0
(902) 798-4715
Emp Here 30   *Emp Total* 94
Sales 2,845,467
SIC 5812 Eating places

D-U-N-S 25-299-4959   (BR)
LAWTON'S DRUG STORES LIMITED
LAWTON'S DRUGS #119
625 O'Brien St, Windsor, NS, B0N 2T0
(902) 798-2202
Emp Here 31
SIC 5912 Drug stores and proprietary stores

D-U-N-S 24-993-7863   (SL)
SEPRACOR CANADA (NOVA SCOTIA) LIMITED
(*Suby of* Sepracor Canada, Inc)
24 Irven Dr, Windsor, NS, B0N 2T0
(902) 798-4100
Emp Here 32   *Sales* 1,751,057
SIC 8731 Commercial physical research

D-U-N-S 24-943-6189   (BR)
SOBEYS CAPITAL INCORPORATED
SOBEYS #672
50 Empire Lane Wentworth Rd, Windsor, NS, B0N 2T0
(902) 798-0992
Emp Here 120
SIC 5411 Grocery stores

D-U-N-S 20-765-1485   (SL)
USG CANADIAN MINING LTD
FUNDY GYPSUM COMPANY, A DIV OF
669 Wentworth Rd, Windsor, NS, B0N 2T0
(902) 798-4676
Emp Here 150
SIC 1499 Miscellaneous nonMetallic minerals, except fuels

Windsor Junction, NS B2T
Halifax County

D-U-N-S 24-989-8029   (BR)
MARID INDUSTRIES LIMITED
99 Windsor Junction Rd, Windsor Junction, NS, B2T 1G7
(902) 860-1138
Emp Here 100
SIC 1791 Structural steel erection

Wolfville, NS B4P

D-U-N-S 20-780-7710   (SL)
ACADIA STUDENTS' UNION INC
CAJUN'S CLOTHING STORE
30 Highland Ave, Wolfville, NS, B4P 2R5
(902) 585-2110
Emp Here 80   *Sales* 133,445,120
SIC 6321 Accident and health insurance
Genl Mgr Ian Morrison

D-U-N-S 20-300-5025   (BR)
ANNAPOLIS VALLEY REGIONAL SCHOOL BOARD
HORTON HIGH SCHOOL
75 Greenwich Rd S Suite 2, Wolfville, NS, B4P 2R2
(902) 542-6060
Emp Here 75
SIC 8211 Elementary and secondary schools

D-U-N-S 25-503-7368   (BR)
ANNAPOLIS VALLEY REGIONAL SCHOOL BOARD

WOLFVILLE SCHOOL
19 Acadia St, Wolfville, NS, B4P 1K8
(902) 542-6050
Emp Here 45
SIC 8211 Elementary and secondary schools

D-U-N-S 25-504-0917   (BR)
ANNAPOLIS VALLEY REGIONAL SCHOOL BOARD
GASPEREAU VALLEY ELEMENTARY SCHOOL
2781 Greenfield Rd, Wolfville, NS, B4P 2R1
(902) 542-6090
Emp Here 25
SIC 8211 Elementary and secondary schools

D-U-N-S 20-031-4334   (HQ)
COCHRANE, D. ROSS PHARMACY LIMITED
COCHRANE'S PHARMASAVE
(Suby of Cochrane, D. Ross Pharmacy Limited)
442 Main St, Wolfville, NS, B4P 1E2
(902) 542-3624
Emp Here 30   Emp Total 50
Sales 7,077,188
SIC 5912 Drug stores and proprietary stores
Pr Pr John Mcneil

D-U-N-S 25-559-9805   (SL)
JUST USU COFFEE ROASTERS CO-OPERATIVE LIMITED
JUST USU
11865 Highway 1, Wolfville, NS, B4P 2R3
(902) 542-7474
Emp Here 30   Sales 2,115,860
SIC 5812 Eating places

D-U-N-S 24-262-1688   (SL)
L D PROPERTIES LTD
708 Main St, Wolfville, NS, B4P 1G4
(902) 542-2237
Emp Here 55   Sales 3,648,035
SIC 8211 Elementary and secondary schools

D-U-N-S 20-729-3945   (SL)
OLD ORCHARD INN LIMITED
153 Greenwich Rd S, Wolfville, NS, B4P 2R2
(902) 542-5751
Emp Here 90   Sales 3,939,878
SIC 7011 Hotels and motels

D-U-N-S 20-631-3462   (SL)
RAFUSE BUILDING SUPPLIES (1977) LTD
RAFUSE HOME HARDWARE BUILDING CENTRE
200 Dykeland St, Wolfville, NS, B4P 1A2
(902) 542-2211
Emp Here 84   Sales 17,145,050
SIC 5211 Lumber and other building materials
Pr Pr Donna Bishop
  Raymond B shop

D-U-N-S 20-906-5812   (SL)
WOLFVILLE NURSING HOMES LIMITED
THE ELMS, THE DIV OF
601 Main St Suite 2, Wolfville, NS, B4P 1E9
(902) 542-2429
Emp Here 100   Sales 4,523,563
SIC 8051 Sk lled nursing care facilities

Yarmouth, NS B5A
Yarmouth County

D-U-N-S 24-187-8875   (BR)
ACADIAN SEAPLANTS LIMITED
133 Islandview Rd, Yarmouth, NS, B5A 4A6
(902) 742-9159
Emp Here 40
SIC 8731 Commercial physical research

D-U-N-S 20-090-7298   (BR)
ATLANTIC WHOLESALERS LTD
YARMOUTH ATLANTIC SUPERSTORE, THE
104 Starrs Rd, Yarmouth, NS, B5A 2T5

(902) 742-3392
Emp Here 90
SIC 5992 Florists

D-U-N-S 25-296-5827   (BR)
BANK OF NOVA SCOTIA, THE
SCOTIABANK
389 Main St, Yarmouth, NS, B5A 4B1
(902) 742-7116
Emp Here 20
SIC 6021 National commercial banks

D-U-N-S 20-700-0501   (BR)
BANQUE DE DEVELOPPEMENT DU CANADA
BDC
396 Main St, Yarmouth, NS, B5A 1E9

Emp Here 40
SIC 6141 Personal credit institutions

D-U-N-S 20-529-9659   (BR)
CANADA POST CORPORATION
15 Willow St, Yarmouth, NS, B5A 1T8
(902) 742-4221
Emp Here 30
SIC 4311 U.s. postal service

D-U-N-S 24-120-5983   (BR)
CAPSERVCO LIMITED PARTNERSHIP
(Suby of CapServCo Limited Partnership)
328 Main St, Yarmouth, NS, B5A 1E4
(902) 742-7842
Emp Here 20
SIC 8721 Accounting, auditing, and book-keeping

D-U-N-S 24-747-7875   (BR)
CLEVE'S SPORTING GOODS LIMITED
76 Starrs Rd, Yarmouth, NS, B5A 2T5
(902) 742-8135
Emp Here 75
SIC 5941 Sporting goods and bicycle shops

D-U-N-S 20-022-8117   (BR)
GERMAIN MECHANICAL & ELECTRICAL LIMITED
244 Water St, Yarmouth, NS, B5A 1M1
(902) 742-2452
Emp Here 70
SIC 1731 Electrical work

D-U-N-S 20-443-9582   (SL)
GRAND HOTEL COMPANY LIMITED
RODD'S GRAND HOTEL & CONVENTION
417 Main St, Yarmouth, NS, B5A 1G3
(902) 742-2446
Emp Here 70   Sales 3,064,349
SIC 7011 Hotels and motels

D-U-N-S 20-190-8774   (BR)
J. D. IRVING, LIMITED
KENT BUILDING SUPPLIES
(Suby of J. D. Irving, Limited)
116 Starrs Rd, Yarmouth, NS, B5A 2T5
(902) 749-5000
Emp Here 25
SIC 5211 Lumber and other building materials

D-U-N-S 25-299-4769   (BR)
LAWTON'S DRUG STORES LIMITED
LAWTON'S DRUGS #169
76 Starrs Rd, Yarmouth, NS, B5A 2T5
(902) 742-1900
Emp Here 23
SIC 5912 Drug stores and proprietary stores

D-U-N-S 24-348-0899   (BR)
MEDIAS TRANSCONTINENTAL S.E.N.C.
2 Second St, Yarmouth, NS, B5A 1T2
(902) 742-7111
Emp Here 20
SIC 7319 Advertising, nec

D-U-N-S 20-922-7219   (BR)
PRISZM LP
TACO BELL
536 Main St, Yarmouth, NS, B5A 1H8
(902) 742-4581
Emp Here 21

SIC 5812 Eating places

D-U-N-S 25-082-6278   (BR)
SOBEYS CAPITAL INCORPORATED
FRESHCO
130 Starrs Rd, Yarmouth, NS, B5A 4E5

Emp Here 30
SIC 5411 Grocery stores

D-U-N-S 24-943-6023   (BR)
SOBEYS CAPITAL INCORPORATED
SOBEYS STORE 612
76 Starrs Rd, Yarmouth, NS, B5A 2T5
(902) 742-2882
Emp Here 75
SIC 5411 Grocery stores

D-U-N-S 25-171-2402   (HQ)
SOUTH WEST NOVA DISTRICT HEALTH AUTHORITY
SOUTH WEST HEALTH
60 Vancouver St, Yarmouth, NS, B5A 2P5
(902) 742-3541
Emp Here 25   Emp Total 11,000
Sales 100,745,108
SIC 8062 General medical and surgical hospitals
  Blaise Macneil
  Deborah Nickerspm
VP Opers Anthony Muise
  Gerald Pothier

D-U-N-S 25-753-0972   (BR)
SOUTH WEST NOVA DISTRICT HEALTH AUTHORITY
DISTRICT HEALTH AUTHORITY # 2
60 Vancouver St, Yarmouth, NS, B5A 2P5
(902) 742-2406
Emp Here 30
SIC 8062 General medical and surgical hospitals

D-U-N-S 20-031-6289   (SL)
SPEARS & MACLEOD PHARMACY LIMITED
PHARMASAVE #519
(Suby of MacLeod, J F Holdings Limited)
333 Main St Suite 519, Yarmouth, NS, B5A 1E5
(902) 742-7825
Emp Here 40   Sales 5,690,935
SIC 5912 Drug stores and proprietary stores
Pr Pr James Macleod
Dir David Cogan

D-U-N-S 24-101-2306   (BR)
STAPLES CANADA INC
STAPLES THE BUSINESS DEPOT
(Suby of Staples, Inc.)
110 Starrs Rd, Yarmouth, NS, B5A 2T5
(902) 749-0417
Emp Here 20
SIC 5943 Stationery stores

D-U-N-S 20-079-4464   (BR)
TOULON DEVELOPMENT CORPORATION
YARMOUTH MALL ADMINISTRATION
76 Starrs Rd, Yarmouth, NS, B5A 2T5
(902) 742-9518
Emp Here 500
SIC 7299 Miscellaneous personal service

D-U-N-S 25-240-9487   (BR)
TRI-COUNTY REGIONAL SCHOOL BOARD
YARMOUTH CENTRAL SCHOOL
53 Parade St, Yarmouth, NS, B5A 3B1
(902) 749-2860
Emp Here 43
SIC 8211 Elementary and secondary schools

D-U-N-S 20-710-3107   (BR)
TRI-COUNTY REGIONAL SCHOOL BOARD
MEADOWFIELDS COMMUNITY SCHOOL
106 Prospect St, Yarmouth, NS, B5A 4J2
(902) 749-2880
Emp Here 54
SIC 8211 Elementary and secondary schools

D-U-N-S 20-710-3123   (BR)
TRI-COUNTY REGIONAL SCHOOL BOARD
YARMOUTH CONSOLIDATED MEMORIAL HIGH SCHOOL
52 Parade St, Yarmouth, NS, B5A 3A9
(902) 749-2810
Emp Here 65
SIC 8211 Elementary and secondary schools

D-U-N-S 24-761-0558   (BR)
VICTORIAN ORDER OF NURSES FOR CANADA
VON TRI-COUNTY DISTRICT
55 Starrs Rd Suite 7, Yarmouth, NS, B5A 2T2
(902) 742-4512
Emp Here 20
SIC 8082 Home health care services

D-U-N-S 20-021-6815   (BR)
VICTORIAN ORDER OF NURSES GREATER HALIFAX
V O N
55 Starrs Rd Unit 7, Yarmouth, NS, B5A 2T2
(902) 742-4512
Emp Here 35
SIC 8741 Management services

D-U-N-S 24-348-1350   (BR)
WAL-MART CANADA CORP
WALMART
108 Starrs Rd, Yarmouth, NS, B5A 2T5
(902) 749-2306
Emp Here 120
SIC 5311 Department stores

D-U-N-S 24-892-9176   (HQ)
WESTERN COUNTIES REGIONAL LIBRARY
(Suby of Western Counties Regional Library)
405 Main St, Yarmouth, NS, B5A 1G3
(902) 742-5040
Emp Here 25   Emp Total 55
Sales 2,553,625
SIC 8231 Libraries

D-U-N-S 25-813-4436   (SL)
YARMOUTH INNS LTD
RODD COLONY HARBOUR INN
6 Forest St, Yarmouth, NS, B5A 3K8
(902) 742-9194
Emp Here 65   Sales 2,845,467
SIC 7011 Hotels and motels

Arviat, NU X0C

D-U-N-S 24-436-0736   (BR)
NORTH WEST COMPANY INC, THE
NORTHERN STORE
Gd, Arviat, NU, X0C 0E0
(867) 857-2826
Emp Here 62
SIC 5311 Department stores

D-U-N-S 25-271-4340   (BR)
NORTH WEST COMPANY LP, THE
NORTHERN
Gd, Arviat, NU, X0C 0E0
(867) 857-2826
Emp Here 52
SIC 5411 Grocery stores

D-U-N-S 25-500-5233   (HQ)
NUNAVUT ARCTIC COLLEGE
(*Suby of* Nunavut Arctic College)
Gd, Arviat, NU, X0C 0E0
(867) 857-8600
Emp Here 25   *Emp Total* 100
Sales 14,507,350
SIC 8221 Colleges and universities
Pr Michael Shouldice

Baker Lake, NU X0C

D-U-N-S 25-456-5476   (HQ)
QULLIQ ENERGY CORPORATION
NUNAVUT ENERGY CENTRE
Gd, Baker Lake, NU, X0C 0A0
(866) 710-4200
Emp Here 36   *Emp Total* 1,850
Sales 100,458,740
SIC 4911 Electric services
Pr Bruno Pereira
 Elijah Evaluarjuk

Cambridge Bay, NU X0B

D-U-N-S 20-170-3688   (BR)
NORTH WEST COMPANY LP, THE
Gd, Cambridge Bay, NU, X0B 0C0
(867) 983-2571
Emp Here 30
SIC 5399 Miscellaneous general merchandise

D-U-N-S 25-497-9016   (BR)
NUNAVUT ARCTIC COLLEGE
(*Suby of* Nunavut Arctic College)
13 Migika St, Cambridge Bay, NU, X0B 0C0
(867) 983-4107
Emp Here 20
SIC 8221 Colleges and universities

Cape Dorset, NU X0A

D-U-N-S 20-170-8463   (BR)
NORTH WEST COMPANY LP, THE
NORTHERN STORE
Gd, Cape Dorset, NU, X0A 0C0
(867) 897-8811
Emp Here 20
SIC 5411 Grocery stores

D-U-N-S 24-319-8855   (BR)
NUNAVUT ARCTIC COLLEGE
Gd, Cape Dorset, NU, X0A 0C0
(867) 897-8825
Emp Here 40
SIC 8221 Colleges and universities

Gjoa Haven, NU X0B

D-U-N-S 20-287-6376   (BR)
ARCTIC CO-OPERATIVES LIMITED
QIKIQTAQ CO OP
Gd, Gjoa Haven, NU, X0B 1J0
(867) 360-7271
Emp Here 30
SIC 5411 Grocery stores

D-U-N-S 24-915-2752   (BR)
NORTH WEST COMPANY LP, THE
NORTHERN STORE
Gd, Gjoa Haven, NU, X0B 1J0
(867) 360-7261
Emp Here 20
SIC 5411 Grocery stores

Iqaluit, NU X0A

D-U-N-S 24-107-8406   (BR)
ATCO STRUCTURES & LOGISTICS SER-VICES LTD
ATCO STRUCTURES & LOGISTICS SER-VICES LTD
Gd, Iqaluit, NU, X0A 0H0
(867) 979-2782
Emp Here 20
SIC 4581 Airports, flying fields, and services

D-U-N-S 20-170-8489   (BR)
CANADIAN BROADCASTING CORPORA-TION
CBC NORTH
Gd, Iqaluit, NU, X0A 0H0
(867) 979-6100
Emp Here 25
SIC 4833 Television broadcasting stations

D-U-N-S 24-329-1437   (BR)
NORTHVIEW APARTMENT REAL ESTATE INVESTMENT TRUST
NORTHERN PROPERTY REIT
1089 Airport Rd, Iqaluit, NU, X0A 0H0
(867) 979-3537
Emp Here 22
SIC 6531 Real estate agents and managers

D-U-N-S 25-015-1016   (BR)
NORTHWESTEL INC
Gd, Iqaluit, NU, X0A 0H0
(867) 979-4001
Emp Here 31
SIC 4899 Communication services, nec

D-U-N-S 24-318-8419   (BR)
NUNAVUT ARCTIC COLLEGE
NUNATTA CAMPUS
Gd, Iqaluit, NU, X0A 0H0
(867) 979-7200
Emp Here 100
SIC 8211 Elementary and secondary schools

D-U-N-S 25-541-2058   (HQ)
QIKIQTAALUK ENVIRONMENTAL INC.
QIKIQTAALUK
922 Nianiaqunngusiaq Rd, Iqaluit, NU, X0A 0H0
(867) 979-8400
Emp Here 28   *Emp Total* 55
Sales 25,034,654
SIC 4959 Sanitary services, nec
 George Qulaut
Pr Pr Harry Flaherty
VP Lynn Kilabuk
 John Baker
 Peter Keenainak
 Moses Appaqaq
 Joe Arlooktoo
 Loseosie Paneak
 Ludy Pudluk

D-U-N-S 20-100-4228   (BR)
ROYAL CANADIAN LEGION, THE
BRANCH 168
(*Suby of* Royal Canadian Legion, The)
Building 946, Iqaluit, NU, X0A 0H0
(867) 979-6215
Emp Here 30
SIC 8641 Civic and social associations

Kugluktuk, NU X0B

D-U-N-S 24-915-2844   (BR)
NORTH WEST COMPANY LP, THE
Gd, Kugluktuk, NU, X0B 0E0
(867) 982-4171
Emp Here 25
SIC 5411 Grocery stores

Resolute, NU X0A

D-U-N-S 24-404-5063   (SL)
SOUTH CAMP ENTERPRISES
1 Main St, Resolute, NU, X0A 0V0
(867) 252-3737
Emp Here 30   *Sales* 5,545,013
SIC 1542 Nonresidential construction, nec

Acton, ON L7J
Halton County

D-U-N-S 24-345-2500 (BR)
BEATTY FOODS LTD
MCDONALD'S
374 Queen St E, Acton, ON, L7J 2Y5
(519) 853-9128
Emp Here 80
SIC 5812 Eating places

D-U-N-S 20-540-2170 (BR)
CANADA POST CORPORATION
ACTON STATION MAIN
53 Bower St, Acton, ON, L7J 1E1
(519) 853-0410
Emp Here 20
SIC 4311 U.s. postal service

D-U-N-S 24-850-0873 (SL)
CANADIAN ASSOCIATION OF TOKEN COLLECTORS
273 Mill St E, Acton, ON, L7J 1J7
(519) 853-3812
Emp Here 230   *Sales* 18,846,720
SIC 7699 Repair services, nec
VP Scott Douglas

D-U-N-S 25-606-3066 (BR)
CLUBLINK CORPORATION ULC
BLUE SPRINGS GOLF CLUB
(*Suby of* TWC Enterprises Limited)
13448 Dublin Line Suite 1, Acton, ON, L7J 2L7
(519) 853-0904
Emp Here 80
SIC 7992 Public golf courses

D-U-N-S 20-031-6941 (SL)
DENNY BUS LINES LTD
5414 4th Line & County Rd 124, Acton, ON, L7J 2L8
(519) 833-9117
Emp Here 120   *Sales* 3,356,192
SIC 4151 School buses

D-U-N-S 20-292-1065 (BR)
HALTON CATHOLIC DISTRICT SCHOOL BOARD
MCKENZIE SMITH BENNETT PUBLIC SCHOOL
69 Acton Blvd, Acton, ON, L7J 2H4
(519) 853-3800
Emp Here 50
SIC 8211 Elementary and secondary schools

D-U-N-S 20-711-0730 (BR)
HALTON CATHOLIC DISTRICT SCHOOL BOARD
ST JOSEPH SCHOOL
147 Mill St W, Acton, ON, L7J 1G7
(519) 853-3730
Emp Here 45
SIC 8211 Elementary and secondary schools

D-U-N-S 25-138-6033 (BR)
HALTON DISTRICT SCHOOL BOARD
ROBERT LITTLE PUBLIC SCHOOL
41 School Lane, Acton, ON, L7J 1B9
(519) 853-2540
Emp Here 35
SIC 8211 Elementary and secondary schools

D-U-N-S 25-120-2982 (BR)
HALTON DISTRICT SCHOOL BOARD
ACTON DISTRICT HIGH SCHOOL
21 Cedar Rd, Acton, ON, L7J 2V2
(519) 853-2920
Emp Here 60
SIC 8211 Elementary and secondary schools

D-U-N-S 20-185-1610 (BR)
PARRISH & HEIMBECKER, LIMITED
P&H MILLING GROUP
(*Suby of* Parrish & Heimbecker, Limited)
62 Mill St W, Acton, ON, L7J 1G4
(519) 853-2850
Emp Here 25

SIC 5153 Grain and field beans

D-U-N-S 20-648-4078 (BR)
PHARMA PLUS DRUGMARTS LTD
MEDITRUST
372 Queen St E, Acton, ON, L7J 2Y5
(519) 853-2220
Emp Here 35
SIC 5912 Drug stores and proprietary stores

D-U-N-S 25-971-8039 (BR)
PREMIER EQUIPMENT LTD.
(*Suby of* Premier Equipment Ltd.)
8911 Wellington Rd 124, Acton, ON, L7J 2L9
(519) 833-9332
Emp Here 22
SIC 5083 Farm and garden machinery

D-U-N-S 24-179-8805 (BR)
PUMPCRETE CORPORATION
MODERN CRANE
9 Mansewood Crt, Acton, ON, L7J 0A1
(905) 878-5559
Emp Here 50
SIC 7353 Heavy construction equipment rental

Addison, ON K0E
Leeds County

D-U-N-S 20-711-5333 (BR)
UPPER CANADA DISTRICT SCHOOL BOARD, THE
MEADOWVIEW PUBLIC SCHOOL
7463 County Rd 28, Addison, ON, K0E 1A0
(613) 924-2880
Emp Here 50
SIC 8211 Elementary and secondary schools

Ailsa Craig, ON N0M
Middlesex County

D-U-N-S 24-676-2707 (BR)
THAMES VALLEY DISTRICT SCHOOL BOARD
MCGILLIVRAY CENTRAL PUBLIC SCHOOL
34714 Creamery Rd, Ailsa Craig, ON, N0M 1A0
(519) 293-3342
Emp Here 25
SIC 8211 Elementary and secondary schools

D-U-N-S 20-710-5516 (BR)
THAMES VALLEY DISTRICT SCHOOL BOARD
EAST WILLIAMS MEMORIAL PUBLIC ELEMENTARY SCHOOL
4441 Queens Ave, Ailsa Craig, ON, N0M 1A0
(519) 232-4505
Emp Here 22
SIC 8211 Elementary and secondary schools

Ajax, ON L1S

D-U-N-S 20-773-1360 (SL)
2046223 ONTARIO INC
FIRST IMPRESSIONS GENERAL CONTRACTING
31 Barr Rd Unit 14, Ajax, ON, L1S 3Y1

Emp Here 61   *Sales* 7,636,480
SIC 6512 Nonresidential building operators
Dir Danny Iannucci

D-U-N-S 20-051-8988 (SL)
AJAX TOCCO MAGNETHERMIC CANADA LIMITED
(*Suby of* Park-Ohio Holdings Corp.)
333 Station St, Ajax, ON, L1S 1S3

(905) 683-4980
Emp Here 40   *Sales* 5,763,895
SIC 3567 Industrial furnaces and ovens
Genl Mgr John Caruso
Pr Pr Thomas Illencik

D-U-N-S 20-547-7412 (BR)
ARTIK/OEM INC
(*Suby of* Entreprises Pol R Inc)
560b Finley Ave, Ajax, ON, L1S 2E3
(905) 428-8728
Emp Here 25
SIC 3086 Plastics foam products

D-U-N-S 20-323-0420 (HQ)
AXALTA COATING SYSTEMS CANADA COMPANY
(*Suby of* Axalta Coating Systems Ltd.)
408 Fairall St, Ajax, ON, L1S 1R6
(905) 683-5500
Emp Here 25   *Emp Total* 13,000
Sales 34,909,915
SIC 5013 Motor vehicle supplies and new parts
 Michael Oxley
Sec Paul Klasios
Dir Opers Al Forsyth

D-U-N-S 25-306-7797 (BR)
BINGO COUNTRY HOLDINGS LIMITED
(*Suby of* Bingo Country Holdings Limited)
610 Monarch Ave, Ajax, ON, L1S 6M4
(905) 427-8572
Emp Here 30
SIC 7999 Amusement and recreation, nec

D-U-N-S 20-135-5203 (SL)
BRITMAN INDUSTRIES LIMITED
BRITMAN PACKAGING SERVICES
655 Finley Ave Suite 1, Ajax, ON, L1S 3V3
(905) 619-1477
Emp Here 60   *Sales* 3,064,349
SIC 7389 Business services, nec

D-U-N-S 20-967-7210 (HQ)
COMMUNITY LIVING AJAX–PICKERING & WHITBY
ARC INDUSTRIES, DIV OF
(*Suby of* Community Living Ajax–Pickering & Whitby)
36 Emperor St, Ajax, ON, L1S 1M7
(905) 427-3300
Emp Here 24   *Emp Total* 130
Sales 4,742,446
SIC 8361 Residential care

D-U-N-S 20-517-1270 (BR)
CONSEIL SCOLAIRE DE DISTRICT CATHOLIQUE CENTRE-SUD
ECOLE NOTRE DAME DE LA JEUNESSE
71 Ritchie Ave, Ajax, ON, L1S 6S5
(905) 428-1460
Emp Here 30
SIC 8211 Elementary and secondary schools

D-U-N-S 24-345-5305 (BR)
CORPORATION OF THE TOWN OF AJAX, THE
AJAX FIRE AND EMERGENCY SERVICES
435 Monarch Ave, Ajax, ON, L1S 2G7
(905) 683-3050
Emp Here 99
SIC 7389 Business services, nec

D-U-N-S 25-372-4793 (BR)
DIE-MAX TOOL AND DIE LTD
729 Finley Ave, Ajax, ON, L1S 3T1
(905) 619-9380
Emp Here 20
SIC 3469 Metal stampings, nec

D-U-N-S 24-937-3580 (SL)
DISTICOR DIRECT RETAILER SERVICES INC
(*Suby of* Microvite Investments Limited)
695 Westney Rd S Unit 14, Ajax, ON, L1S 6M9

(905) 619-6565
Emp Here 20   *Sales* 2,407,703
SIC 5192 Books, periodicals, and newspapers

D-U-N-S 25-481-5913 (BR)
DOMINION COLOUR CORPORATION
(*Suby of* H.I.G. Capital, L.L.C.)
445 Finley Ave, Ajax, ON, L1S 2E2
(905) 683-0231
Emp Here 90
SIC 2816 Inorganic pigments

D-U-N-S 24-525-4326 (BR)
DURHAM CATHOLIC DISTRICT SCHOOL BOARD
CARRUTHERS CREEK PUBLIC SCHOOL
1 Greenhall Dr, Ajax, ON, L1S 7N6
(905) 683-0921
Emp Here 25
SIC 8211 Elementary and secondary schools

D-U-N-S 25-265-1807 (BR)
DURHAM CATHOLIC DISTRICT SCHOOL BOARD
ARCHBISHOP DENIS O'CONNOR CATHOLIC HIGH SCHOOL
80 Mandrake St, Ajax, ON, L1S 5H4
(905) 427-6667
Emp Here 90
SIC 8211 Elementary and secondary schools

D-U-N-S 20-025-0228 (BR)
DURHAM CATHOLIC DISTRICT SCHOOL BOARD
ST FRANCIS DE SALES CATHOLIC SCHOOL
72 Church St S, Ajax, ON, L1S 6B3
(905) 683-3320
Emp Here 25
SIC 8211 Elementary and secondary schools

D-U-N-S 25-265-1955 (BR)
DURHAM CATHOLIC DISTRICT SCHOOL BOARD
ST. BERNADETTE CATHOLIC SCHOOL
41 Bayly St E, Ajax, ON, L1S 1P2
(905) 683-0571
Emp Here 45
SIC 8211 Elementary and secondary schools

D-U-N-S 20-711-3700 (BR)
DURHAM CATHOLIC DISTRICT SCHOOL BOARD
ST JAMES CATHOLIC SCHOOL
10 Clover Ridge Dr W, Ajax, ON, L1S 3E5
(905) 427-3327
Emp Here 50
SIC 8211 Elementary and secondary schools

D-U-N-S 25-300-8031 (BR)
DURHAM DISTRICT SCHOOL BOARD
LORD ELGIN PUBLIC SCHOOL
24 Ontario St, Ajax, ON, L1S 1T6
(905) 683-3581
Emp Here 33
SIC 8211 Elementary and secondary schools

D-U-N-S 25-300-7736 (BR)
DURHAM DISTRICT SCHOOL BOARD
DUFFIN'S BAY PUBLIC SCHOOL
66 Pittmann Cres, Ajax, ON, L1S 3G3
(905) 683-6023
Emp Here 33
SIC 8211 Elementary and secondary schools

D-U-N-S 25-300-8189 (BR)
DURHAM DISTRICT SCHOOL BOARD
LAKESIDE PUBLIC SCHOOL
4 Parkes Dr, Ajax, ON, L1S 4X1
(905) 686-3014
Emp Here 40
SIC 8211 Elementary and secondary schools

D-U-N-S 25-300-8072 (BR)
DURHAM DISTRICT SCHOOL BOARD
LINCOLN AVENUE PUBLIC SCHOOL
70 Lincoln St, Ajax, ON, L1S 6C9
(905) 683-4941
Emp Here 50

SIC 8211 Elementary and secondary schools

D-U-N-S 25-301-7305   (BR)
DURHAM DISTRICT SCHOOL BOARD
SOUTHWOOD PARK PUBLIC SCHOOL
28 Lambard Cres, Ajax, ON, L1S 1M5
(905) 683-5230
Emp Here 48
SIC 8211 Elementary and secondary schools

D-U-N-S 25-300-8056   (BR)
DURHAM DISTRICT SCHOOL BOARD
AJAX HIGH SCHOOL
105 Bayly St E, Ajax, ON, L1S 1P2
(905) 683-1610
Emp Here 100
SIC 8211 Elementary and secondary schools

D-U-N-S 25-300-7751   (BR)
DURHAM DISTRICT SCHOOL BOARD
ROLAND MICHENER PUBLIC SCHOOL
95 Ritchie Ave, Ajax, ON, L1S 6S2
(905) 686-5437
Emp Here 40
SIC 8211 Elementary and secondary schools

D-U-N-S 20-032-0331   (SL)
GENERAL MAGNAPLATE CANADA LTD
72 Orchard Rd, Ajax, ON, L1S 6L1

Emp Here 34   *Sales* 2,261,782
SIC 3471 Plating and polishing

D-U-N-S 20-032-1073   (SL)
IDEAL INDUSTRIES (CANADA), CORP
TUFF-TOTE
(*Suby of* Ideal Industries, Inc.)
33 Fuller Rd, Ajax, ON, L1S 2E1
(905) 683-3400
Emp Here 70   *Sales* 24,660,717
SIC 3699 Electrical equipment and supplies, nec
Pr Nick Shkordoff
Dir Robert Ackford
Ch Bd Dave Juday

D-U-N-S 24-154-1726   (BR)
INNOCON INC
57a Notion Rd, Ajax, ON, L1S 6K7
(905) 683-1650
Emp Here 30
SIC 3273 Ready-mixed concrete

D-U-N-S 20-188-2292   (BR)
MALPACK LTD
510 Finley Ave, Ajax, ON, L1S 2E3
(905) 426-4989
Emp Here 75
SIC 2673 Bags: plastic, laminated, and coated

D-U-N-S 24-652-9945   (SL)
MANU FORTI CORPORATION LTD
MCDONALDS RESTAURANT
222 Bayly St W, Ajax, ON, L1S 3V4
(905) 686-2133
Emp Here 100   *Sales* 2,991,389
SIC 5812 Eating places

D-U-N-S 24-357-9302   (BR)
MARTINREA AUTOMOTIVE SYSTEMS CANADA LTD
MARTINREA AUTOMOTIVE SYSTEMS CANADA (AJAX)
650 Finley Ave, Ajax, ON, L1S 6N1
(905) 428-3737
Emp Here 95
SIC 3711 Motor vehicles and car bodies

D-U-N-S 24-335-0522   (BR)
METRO ONTARIO INC
FOOD BASICS
280 Harwood Ave S, Ajax, ON, L1S 2J1
(905) 683-6951
Emp Here 75
SIC 5411 Grocery stores

D-U-N-S 24-508-3589   (BR)

METROLAND MEDIA GROUP LTD
AJAX PICKERING NEWS ADVERTISER
130 Commercial Ave, Ajax, ON, L1S 2H5
(905) 683-5110
Emp Here 50
SIC 2711 Newspapers

D-U-N-S 25-403-8953   (BR)
ONTARIO POWER GENERATION INC
230 Westney Rd S Suite 302, Ajax, ON, L1S 7J5
(905) 428-4000
Emp Here 100
SIC 4911 Electric services

D-U-N-S 20-878-3253   (HQ)
PERFORMANCE ORTHOTICS INC
291 Clements Rd W, Ajax, ON, L1S 3W7
(905) 428-2692
Emp Here 30   *Emp Total* 449
Sales 6,219,371
SIC 3842 Surgical appliances and supplies
Pr Glenn Copelend

D-U-N-S 25-662-8777   (BR)
PHARMA PLUS DRUGMARTS LTD
PHARMA PLUS DRUGMART
955 Westney Rd S Unit 7, Ajax, ON, L1S 3K7
(905) 683-1314
Emp Here 20
SIC 5912 Drug stores and proprietary stores

D-U-N-S 25-695-3050   (BR)
PHARMA PLUS DRUGMARTS LTD
240 Harwood Ave S, Ajax, ON, L1S 2H6
(905) 683-1210
Emp Here 40
SIC 5912 Drug stores and proprietary stores

D-U-N-S 24-347-4496   (BR)
PICKERING AUTOMOBILES INC
ACURA EAST
250 Westney Rd S, Ajax, ON, L1S 7P9
(905) 428-8888
Emp Here 25
SIC 5511 New and used car dealers

D-U-N-S 24-077-3465   (BR)
PITNEY BOWES OF CANADA LTD
(*Suby of* Pitney Bowes Inc.)
314 Harwood Ave S Suite 200, Ajax, ON, L1S 2J1
(905) 427-9772
Emp Here 185
SIC 7389 Business services, nec

D-U-N-S 25-313-6287   (BR)
PLASTI-FAB LTD
PLASTI-FAB AJAX
40 Mills Rd, Ajax, ON, L1S 2H1
(905) 686-7739
Emp Here 27
SIC 3086 Plastics foam products

D-U-N-S 20-032-1560   (SL)
PRECISION VALVE (CANADA) LIMITED
85 Fuller Rd, Ajax, ON, L1S 2E1
(905) 683-0121
Emp Here 60   *Sales* 10,550,800
SIC 3089 Plastics products, nec
Linda Pelkey
Ian Tyler
Fin Mgr Peter Osborne
Pr Pr John P Abplanalp

D-U-N-S 25-363-6344   (BR)
PRIME RESTAURANTS INC
EAST SIDE MARIOS
(*Suby of* Cara Holdings Limited)
100 Westney Rd S Suite 11, Ajax, ON, L1S 7H3
(905) 619-2229
Emp Here 45
SIC 5812 Eating places

D-U-N-S 24-350-7998   (BR)
PRO-BEL ENTERPRISES LIMITED
765 Westney Rd S, Ajax, ON, L1S 6W1

(905) 427-0616
Emp Here 100
SIC 5084 Industrial machinery and equipment

D-U-N-S 25-300-5193   (BR)
REDBERRY FRANCHISING CORP
BURGER KING
345 Mackenzie Ave, Ajax, ON, L1S 2G2
(905) 686-2331
Emp Here 34
SIC 5812 Eating places

D-U-N-S 25-637-8555   (HQ)
ROCKBRUNE BROTHERS LIMITED
ALL STAR MOVING IN NEW MARKET
(*Suby of* Rockbrune Brothers Limited)
725 Finley Ave, Ajax, ON, L1S 3T1
(905) 683-4321
Emp Here 22   *Emp Total* 90
Sales 1,428,572
SIC 4214 Local trucking with storage

D-U-N-S 25-137-8105   (BR)
ROUGE VALLEY HEALTH SYSTEM
NUTRITION & FOOD SERVICES
580 Harwood Ave S Suite 199, Ajax, ON, L1S 2J4
(905) 683-2320
Emp Here 100
SIC 6324 Hospital and medical service plans

D-U-N-S 25-018-9826   (BR)
ROYAL BANK OF CANADA
RBC
(*Suby of* Royal Bank Of Canada)
2 Harwood Ave S, Ajax, ON, L1S 7L8
(905) 683-2291
Emp Here 30
SIC 6021 National commercial banks

D-U-N-S 20-032-0695   (HQ)
SAFRAN LANDING SYSTEMS CANADA INC
574 Monarch Ave, Ajax, ON, L1S 2G8
(905) 683-3100
Emp Here 600   *Emp Total* 1,577
Sales 172,114,291
SIC 3728 Aircraft parts and equipment, nec
Bryan Teed
VP VP John Domen
Sec Gordon Hofkirchner
Helene Seguinotte
Crystian Darveau
Gilles Bouctot

D-U-N-S 24-312-1790   (BR)
SIEMENS CANADA LIMITED
INDUSTRIAL SOLUTIONS & SERVICES
167 Hunt St, Ajax, ON, L1S 1P6
(905) 683-8200
Emp Here 50
SIC 3625 Relays and industrial controls

D-U-N-S 24-423-2760   (BR)
SISLEY MOTORS LIMITED
SISLEY HYUNDAI
170 Westney Rd S, Ajax, ON, L1S 2C8
(905) 427-0111
Emp Here 50
SIC 5511 New and used car dealers

D-U-N-S 25-664-7256   (BR)
STAPLES CANADA INC
STAPLES THE BUSINESS DEPOT
(*Suby of* Staples, Inc.)
16 Harwood Ave S, Ajax, ON, L1S 7L8
(905) 686-1422
Emp Here 50
SIC 5943 Stationery stores

D-U-N-S 25-354-2948   (BR)
TFI FOODS LTD
PIRANHA BAY
335 Frankcom St, Ajax, ON, L1S 1R4

Emp Here 30
SIC 2092 Fresh or frozen packaged fish

D-U-N-S 20-120-6492   (BR)
TWINCORP INC
PIZZA HUT
252 Bayly St W, Ajax, ON, L1S 3V4
(905) 686-3023
Emp Here 20
SIC 5812 Eating places

D-U-N-S 20-344-1860   (BR)
VANCOUVER CAREER COLLEGE (BURNABY) INC
CDI COLLEGE
(*Suby of* Chung Family Holdings Inc)
100 Westney Rd S, Ajax, ON, L1S 7H3
(905) 427-1922
Emp Here 25
SIC 8211 Elementary and secondary schools

D-U-N-S 20-152-4170   (HQ)
VOLKSWAGEN GROUP CANADA INC
VOLKSWAGEN
777 Bayly St W, Ajax, ON, L1S 7G7
(905) 428-6700
Emp Here 140   *Emp Total* 546,406
Sales 93,024,893
SIC 5012 Automobiles and other motor vehicles
John White
Lorie-Ann Roxburgh
Sec Arthur Bode
Dir Axel Strobek
Dir Peter Schwarzenbauer
Dir Christian Klingler
Dir Arno Antlitz

D-U-N-S 20-005-2269   (BR)
WENDY'S RESTAURANTS OF CANADA INC
WENDY'S
(*Suby of* The Wendy's Company)
80 Bayly St W, Ajax, ON, L1S 1N9
(905) 427-2332
Emp Here 30
SIC 5812 Eating places

Ajax, ON L1T

D-U-N-S 24-338-6427   (BR)
446987 ONTARIO INC
BOMBAY COMPANY, THE
(*Suby of* Benix & Co. Inc)
20 Kingston Rd W, Ajax, ON, L1T 4K8
(905) 683-0819
Emp Here 20
SIC 5712 Furniture stores

D-U-N-S 20-346-2775   (SL)
AAILSOFT INC
88 Telford St, Ajax, ON, L1T 4Z5
(416) 452-5687
Emp Here 52   *Sales* 4,504,505
SIC 7379 Computer related services, nec

D-U-N-S 24-247-2442   (BR)
ARBOR MEMORIAL SERVICES INC
PINE RIDGE
1757 Church St N, Ajax, ON, L1T 4R3
(905) 428-2051
Emp Here 20
SIC 6531 Real estate agents and managers

D-U-N-S 20-569-7365   (BR)
ARBOR MEMORIAL SERVICES INC
PINE RIDGE MEMORIAL GARDENS
541 Taunton Rd W, Ajax, ON, L1T 4T2
(289) 275-2047
Emp Here 20
SIC 6531 Real estate agents and managers

D-U-N-S 25-296-9399   (BR)
BANK OF NOVA SCOTIA, THE
SCOTIABANK
15 Westney Rd N Suite 2, Ajax, ON, L1T 1P5
(905) 427-3255
Emp Here 20

SIC 6021 National commercial banks

D-U-N-S 20-810-5846   (BR)
BEST BUY CANADA LTD
BEST BUY
(*Suby of* Best Buy Co., Inc.)
20 Kingston Rd W, Ajax, ON, L1T 4K8
(905) 619-6977
Emp Here 50
SIC 5731 Radio, television, and electronic stores

D-U-N-S 25-303-1728   (BR)
CANADIAN IMPERIAL BANK OF COMMERCE
CIBC
15 Westney Rd N Suite 2, Ajax, ON, L1T 1P4
(905) 683-1412
Emp Here 20
SIC 6021 National commercial banks

D-U-N-S 25-667-6362   (BR)
CORPORATION OF THE TOWN OF AJAX, THE
MCLEAN COMMUNITY CENTRE
95 Magill Dr, Ajax, ON, L1T 4M5
(905) 428-7711
Emp Here 25
SIC 8322 Individual and family services

D-U-N-S 24-525-4334   (BR)
DURHAM CATHOLIC DISTRICT SCHOOL BOARD
VIMY RIDGE PUBLIC SCHOOL
40 Telford St, Ajax, ON, L1T 4Z4
(905) 686-4376
Emp Here 25
SIC 8211 Elementary and secondary schools

D-U-N-S 20-711-3775   (BR)
DURHAM CATHOLIC DISTRICT SCHOOL BOARD
NOTREDAME CATHOLIC SECONDARY SCHOOL
1375 Harwood Ave N, Ajax, ON, L1T 4G8
(905) 686-4300
Emp Here 100
SIC 8211 Elementary and secondary schools

D-U-N-S 20-711-3726   (BR)
DURHAM CATHOLIC DISTRICT SCHOOL BOARD
SAINT JUDE CATHOLIC SCHOOL
68 Coles Ave, Ajax, ON, L1T 3H5
(905) 428-9304
Emp Here 50
SIC 8211 Elementary and secondary schools

D-U-N-S 20-026-1357   (BR)
DURHAM DISTRICT SCHOOL BOARD
DR ROBERTA BONDAR PUBLIC SCHOOL
25 Sullivan Dr, Ajax, ON, L1T 3L3
(905) 665-5500
Emp Here 40
SIC 8211 Elementary and secondary schools

D-U-N-S 20-711-3536   (BR)
DURHAM DISTRICT SCHOOL BOARD
APPLECROP PUBLIC SCHOOL
55 Coles Ave, Ajax, ON, L1T 3H5
(905) 428-2775
Emp Here 35
SIC 8211 Elementary and secondary schools

D-U-N-S 25-301-7065   (BR)
DURHAM DISTRICT SCHOOL BOARD
WESTNEY HEIGHTS PUBLIC SCHOOL
45 Brennan Rd, Ajax, ON, L1T 1X5
(905) 427-7819
Emp Here 55
SIC 8211 Elementary and secondary schools

D-U-N-S 25-300-8106   (BR)
DURHAM DISTRICT SCHOOL BOARD
LINCOLN ALEXANDER PUBLIC SCHOOL
95 Church St N, Ajax, ON, L1T 2W4
(905) 619-0357
Emp Here 43

SIC 8211 Elementary and secondary schools

D-U-N-S 20-592-0866   (BR)
DURHAM DISTRICT SCHOOL BOARD
ALEXANDER GRAHAM BELL PUBLIC SCHOOL
25 Harkins Dr, Ajax, ON, L1T 3T6
(905) 683-7368
Emp Here 60
SIC 8211 Elementary and secondary schools

D-U-N-S 24-194-4722   (BR)
DURHAM DISTRICT SCHOOL BOARD
NOTTINGHAM PUBLIC SCHOOL
50 Seggar Ave, Ajax, ON, L1T 4Y4
(905) 683-0536
Emp Here 40
SIC 8211 Elementary and secondary schools

D-U-N-S 25-300-8114   (BR)
DURHAM DISTRICT SCHOOL BOARD
LESTER B PEARSON PUBLIC SCHOOL
21 Coughlen St, Ajax, ON, L1T 2M9
(905) 427-4658
Emp Here 40
SIC 8211 Elementary and secondary schools

D-U-N-S 24-822-6755   (SL)
DURHAM SCHOOL OF MUSIC LTD
DURHAM MUSIC CENTRE
100 Old Kingston Rd, Ajax, ON, L1T 2Z9
(905) 428-6266
Emp Here 50   *Sales* 2,699,546
SIC 8299 Schools and educational services, nec

D-U-N-S 25-996-0771   (SL)
J D NELSON & SONS LTD
4 Marks Crt, Ajax, ON, L1T 3N3
(647) 223-1245
Emp Here 20   *Sales* 5,579,750
SIC 1522 Residential construction, nec
Pr James Nelson

D-U-N-S 24-329-6832   (BR)
LOBLAWS INC
REAL CANADIAN SUPERSTORE
30 Kingston Rd W Suite 1012, Ajax, ON, L1T 4K8
(905) 683-2272
Emp Here 200
SIC 5411 Grocery stores

D-U-N-S 20-732-1170   (BR)
LOBLAWS SUPERMARKETS LIMITED
REAL CANADIAN SUPERSTORE
30 Kingston Rd W Suite 1012, Ajax, ON, L1T 4K8
(905) 683-5573
Emp Here 75
SIC 5411 Grocery stores

D-U-N-S 20-657-9406   (BR)
OLD NAVY (CANADA) INC
(*Suby of* The Gap Inc)
20 Kingston Rd W, Ajax, ON, L1T 4K8
(905) 426-1221
Emp Here 56
SIC 5651 Family clothing stores

D-U-N-S 25-446-8937   (BR)
PRISZM LP
KFC
15 Westney Rd N Unit 2, Ajax, ON, L1T 1P5
(905) 428-3324
Emp Here 23
SIC 5812 Eating places

D-U-N-S 20-290-7502   (BR)
REVERA LONG TERM CARE INC
WINBOURNE PARK
1020 Westney Rd N, Ajax, ON, L1T 4K6

Emp Here 120
SIC 8059 Nursing and personal care, nec

D-U-N-S 24-080-3171   (BR)
SOBEYS CAPITAL INCORPORATED

1935 Ravenscroft Rd, Ajax, ON, L1T 0K4
(905) 686-7475
Emp Here 50
SIC 5411 Grocery stores

D-U-N-S 20-793-0798   (BR)
SOBEYS CAPITAL INCORPORATED
SOBEYS
260 Kingston Rd W, Ajax, ON, L1T 4E4
(905) 426-7144
Emp Here 100
SIC 5411 Grocery stores

D-U-N-S 25-120-2040   (BR)
TORONTO-DOMINION BANK, THE
TD CANADA TRUST
(*Suby of* Toronto-Dominion Bank, The)
15 Westney Rd N Suite 2, Ajax, ON, L1T 1P4
(905) 686-1218
Emp Here 25
SIC 6021 National commercial banks

D-U-N-S 25-116-8803   (HQ)
VERIDIAN CONNECTIONS INC
(*Suby of* Veridian Corporation)
55 Taunton Rd E, Ajax, ON, L1T 3V3
(905) 427-9870
Emp Here 110   *Emp Total* 152
Sales 91,346,796
SIC 4911 Electric services
Pr Pr Michael Angemeer
Ex VP Axel Starck
  Glenn Rainbird

D-U-N-S 25-686-5676   (HQ)
VERIDIAN CORPORATION
(*Suby of* Veridian Corporation)
55 Taunton Rd E, Ajax, ON, L1T 3V3
(905) 427-9870
Emp Here 35   *Emp Total* 152
Sales 100,078,080
SIC 4911 Electric services
Ch Bd John Wiersma
Pr Michael Angemeer

Ajax, ON L1Z

D-U-N-S 25-981-7120   (BR)
CARA OPERATIONS LIMITED
HARVEY'S
(*Suby of* Cara Holdings Limited)
50 Kingston Rd E, Ajax, ON, L1Z 1G1

Emp Here 20
SIC 5812 Eating places

D-U-N-S 25-287-6016   (BR)
COSTCO WHOLESALE CANADA LTD
COSTCO
(*Suby of* Costco Wholesale Corporation)
150 Kingston Rd E, Ajax, ON, L1Z 1E5
(905) 619-6677
Emp Here 178
SIC 5099 Durable goods, nec

D-U-N-S 24-676-3093   (BR)
DURHAM CATHOLIC DISTRICT SCHOOL BOARD
ROMEO DALLAIRE PUBLIC SCHOOL
300 Williamson Dr E, Ajax, ON, L1Z 0H6
(905) 428-6868
Emp Here 25
SIC 8211 Elementary and secondary schools

D-U-N-S 20-648-0431   (BR)
DURHAM CATHOLIC DISTRICT SCHOOL BOARD
CADARACKQUE PUBLIC SCHOOL
15 Miles Dr, Ajax, ON, L1Z 1C7
(905) 427-6105
Emp Here 30
SIC 8211 Elementary and secondary schools

D-U-N-S 20-711-3759   (BR)

DURHAM CATHOLIC DISTRICT SCHOOL BOARD
MOTHER THERESA CATHOLIC SCHOOL
15 Fishlock St, Ajax, ON, L1Z 1H1
(905) 426-7065
Emp Here 50
SIC 8211 Elementary and secondary schools

D-U-N-S 20-711-3593   (BR)
DURHAM DISTRICT SCHOOL BOARD
TERRY FOX PUBLIC SCHOOL
30 Kerrison Dr W, Ajax, ON, L1Z 1K1
(905) 686-2135
Emp Here 50
SIC 8211 Elementary and secondary schools

D-U-N-S 24-977-1978   (BR)
FGL SPORTS LTD
SPORT CHEK AJAX
135 Harwood Ave N Unit 1, Ajax, ON, L1Z 1E8
(905) 683-3807
Emp Here 40
SIC 5941 Sporting goods and bicycle shops

D-U-N-S 20-597-4509   (SL)
FIONN MACCOOL'S
36 Kingston Rd E, Ajax, ON, L1Z 1G1
(905) 619-9048
Emp Here 50   *Sales* 1,824,018
SIC 5813 Drinking places

D-U-N-S 25-168-9691   (SL)
G.R.B. RESTAURANT INC
MONTANA'S COOKHOUSE SALOON
268 Kingston Rd E, Ajax, ON, L1Z 1G1
(905) 426-9741
Emp Here 80   *Sales* 2,407,703
SIC 5812 Eating places

D-U-N-S 25-273-7820   (HQ)
HAZMASTERS INC
4-651 Harwood Ave N, Ajax, ON, L1Z 0K4
(905) 231-0011
Emp Here 40   *Emp Total* 165
Sales 20,270,273
SIC 5099 Durable goods, nec
  Roger James

D-U-N-S 25-080-7187   (BR)
HOME DEPOT OF CANADA INC
HOME DEPOT
(*Suby of* The Home Depot Inc)
260 Kingston Rd E, Ajax, ON, L1Z 1G1
(905) 428-7939
Emp Here 200
SIC 5211 Lumber and other building materials

D-U-N-S 24-651-9854   (SL)
IMMEDIATE DELIVERY & COURIER SERVICE INC
255 Salem Rd S Unit D2, Ajax, ON, L1Z 0B1
(905) 427-7733
Emp Here 50   *Sales* 2,626,585
SIC 7389 Business services, nec

D-U-N-S 25-916-1453   (BR)
INDIGO BOOKS & MUSIC INC
CHAPTERS
(*Suby of* Indigo Books & Music Inc)
90 Kingston Rd E Suite 8, Ajax, ON, L1Z 1G1
(905) 426-4431
Emp Here 25
SIC 5942 Book stores

D-U-N-S 24-320-9934   (BR)
ONTARIO LOTTERY AND GAMING CORPORATION
OLG SLOTS AT AJAX DOWNS
50 Alexanders Crossing, Ajax, ON, L1Z 2E6
(905) 619-2690
Emp Here 50
SIC 7999 Amusement and recreation, nec

D-U-N-S 24-183-1341   (SL)
PICOV DOWNS INC
AJAX DOWN SIMULCAST
380 Kingston Rd E, Ajax, ON, L1Z 1W4

▲ Public Company   ■ Public Company Family Member   **HQ** Headquarters   **BR** Branch   **SL** Single Location

(905) 686-8001
Emp Here 50
SIC 7948 Racing, including track operation

D-U-N-S 25-092-7956   (BR)
POWER BATTERY SALES LTD
EAST PENN CANADA
165 Harwood Ave N, Ajax, ON, L1Z 1L9
(905) 427-3035
Emp Here 150
SIC 5013 Motor vehicle supplies and new parts

D-U-N-S 24-210-1772   (HQ)
POWER BATTERY SALES LTD
EAST PENN CANADA
165 Harwood Ave N, Ajax, ON, L1Z 1L9
(905) 427-2718
Emp Here 122   *Emp Total* 8,000
Sales 30,424,612
SIC 5013 Motor vehicle supplies and new parts
Pr Pr James Bouchard
VP VP Michael Wells
Delight Breidegam

D-U-N-S 24-038-4458   (SL)
R A F HOLDINGS LTD
TIM HORTONS
989 Harwood Ave N, Ajax, ON, L1Z 1Y7
(905) 426-3186
Emp Here 40   *Sales* 5,277,042
SIC 6712 Bank holding companies
Mgr Annie Man

D-U-N-S 20-506-1059   (BR)
STARBUCKS COFFEE CANADA, INC
STARBUCKS
(*Suby of* Starbucks Corporation)
90 Kingston Rd E Suite 3, Ajax, ON, L1Z 1G1
(905) 426-5885
Emp Here 20
SIC 5812 Eating places

D-U-N-S 20-878-6079   (SL)
TRI-WENT INDUSTRIES LIMITED
75 Chambers Dr Unit 1, Ajax, ON, L1Z 1E1
(905) 831-6964
Emp Here 20   *Sales* 2,407,703
SIC 3498 Fabricated pipe and fittings

D-U-N-S 24-319-8384   (BR)
VALUE VILLAGE STORES, INC
(*Suby of* Savers, Inc.)
155 Harwood Ave N Unit D, Ajax, ON, L1Z 0A1
(905) 427-9338
Emp Here 30
SIC 5399 Miscellaneous general merchandise

D-U-N-S 25-297-7814   (BR)
WAL-MART CANADA CORP
270 Kingston Rd E, Ajax, ON, L1Z 1G1
(905) 426-6160
Emp Here 300
SIC 5311 Department stores

D-U-N-S 24-224-5418   (BR)
WENDY'S RESTAURANTS OF CANADA INC
WENDY'S
(*Suby of* The Wendy's Company)
274 Kingston Rd E, Ajax, ON, L1Z 1G1
(905) 427-4555
Emp Here 25
SIC 5812 Eating places

D-U-N-S 20-646-3668   (SL)
WILLIAM B. RATTRAY HOLDINGS INC
CANADIAN TIRE
250 Kingston Rd E Suite 160, Ajax, ON, L1Z 1G1
(905) 683-2277
Emp Here 50   *Sales* 4,085,799
SIC 5399 Miscellaneous general merchandise

D-U-N-S 20-181-4774   (BR)
WINNERS MERCHANTS INTERNATIONAL L.P.
WINNERS

(*Suby of* The TJX Companies Inc)
40 Kingston Rd E, Ajax, ON, L1Z 1E9
(905) 426-3850
Emp Here 40
SIC 5651 Family clothing stores

D-U-N-S 24-312-4331   (BR)
WINNERS MERCHANTS INTERNATIONAL L.P.
HOMESENSE
(*Suby of* The TJX Companies Inc)
125 Harwood Ave N, Ajax, ON, L1Z 1E6
(905) 426-5659
Emp Here 45
SIC 5651 Family clothing stores

Akwesasne, ON K6H
Stormont County

D-U-N-S 20-031-1657   (BR)
MOHAWK COUNCIL OF AKWESASNE
AHKWESAHSNE MOHAWK SCHOOL
Gd, Akwesasne, ON, K6H 5T7
(613) 932-3366
Emp Here 34
SIC 7389 Business services, nec

D-U-N-S 25-124-4737   (BR)
MOHAWK COUNCIL OF AKWESASNE
AHKWESAHSNE MOHAWK BOARD OF ED-UCATION
169 Akwesasne International Rd, Akwesasne, ON, K6H 0G5
(613) 933-0409
Emp Here 150
SIC 8211 Elementary and secondary schools

D-U-N-S 20-011-8979   (BR)
MOHAWK COUNCIL OF AKWESASNE
TSI ION KWA NONH SO TE ADULT CARE FACILITY
70 Kawenoke Apartment Rd Unit Rd, Akwesasne, ON, K6H 5R7
(613) 932-1409
Emp Here 63
SIC 8052 Intermediate care facilities

Alexandria, ON K0C
Glengarry County

D-U-N-S 20-711-5267   (BR)
CATHOLIC DISTRICT SCHOOL BOARD OF EASTERN ONTARIO
SAINT FINNAN
220 Alexandria Main St S, Alexandria, ON, K0C 1A0
(613) 525-4274
Emp Here 25
SIC 8211 Elementary and secondary schools

D-U-N-S 20-031-1350   (BR)
CONSEIL SCOLAIRE DE DISTRICT CATHOLIQUE DE L'EST ONTARIEN
ECOLE ELEMENTAIRE CATHOLIQUE ELDA-ROULEAU
115 Sandfield Ave, Alexandria, ON, K0C 1A0
(613) 525-1281
Emp Here 40
SIC 8211 Elementary and secondary schools

D-U-N-S 20-031-1343   (BR)
CONSEIL SCOLAIRE DE DISTRICT CATHOLIQUE DE L'EST ONTARIEN
ECOLE SECONDAIRE LE RELAIS
100 Mcnabb St, Alexandria, ON, K0C 1A0
(613) 525-3315
Emp Here 25
SIC 8211 Elementary and secondary schools

D-U-N-S 20-024-2985   (BR)
CONSEIL DES ECOLES PUBLIQUES DE L'EST DE L'ONTARIO

ECOLE TERRE DES JEUNES
33 Lochiel St E, Alexandria, ON, K0C 1A0
(613) 525-1843
Emp Here 20
SIC 8211 Elementary and secondary schools

D-U-N-S 25-902-1293   (BR)
EASTERN ONTARIO HEALTH UNIT
60 Anik St Suite 2, Alexandria, ON, K0C 1A0
(613) 525-1112
Emp Here 20
SIC 8621 Professional organizations

D-U-N-S 24-383-2250   (SL)
GLENGARRY BUS LINE INC
104 Viau St, Alexandria, ON, K0C 1A0
(613) 525-1443
Emp Here 100   *Sales* 2,845,467
SIC 4151 School buses

D-U-N-S 25-959-5221   (BR)
GROUPE JEAN COUTU (PJC) INC, LE
JEAN COUTU
(*Suby of* 3958230 Canada Inc)
Gd, Alexandria, ON, K0C 1A0
(613) 525-3333
Emp Here 20
SIC 5912 Drug stores and proprietary stores

D-U-N-S 24-860-2583   (HQ)
KP BUILDING PRODUCTS LTD
BONNEVILLE SOLUTIONS
(*Suby of* Administration F.L.T. Ltee)
300 Macdonald Blvd, Alexandria, ON, K0C 1A0
(613) 525-3065
Emp Here 330   *Emp Total* 900
Sales 65,748,451
SIC 3089 Plastics products, nec
VP Fin Mitchell Laxer

D-U-N-S 20-032-2501   (HQ)
LANTHIER BAKERY LTD
58 Dominion St, Alexandria, ON, K0C 1A0
(613) 525-2435
Emp Here 40   *Emp Total* 110
Sales 6,125,139
SIC 2051 Bread, cake, and related products
Pr Pr Marc Lanthier
Dir Claude Lanthier
Fin Ex Jean-Marc Longtin

D-U-N-S 24-370-4736   (BR)
MOULURE ALEXANDRIA MOULDING INC
(*Suby of* Moulure Alexandria Moulding Inc)
95 Lochiel St, Alexandria, ON, K0C 1A0
(613) 525-2784
Emp Here 50
SIC 5031 Lumber, plywood, and millwork

D-U-N-S 20-032-2196   (HQ)
MOULURE ALEXANDRIA MOULDING INC
(*Suby of* Moulure Alexandria Moulding Inc)
20352 Power Dam Rd Rr 6, Alexandria, ON, K0C 1A0
(613) 525-2784
Emp Here 450   *Emp Total* 800
Sales 65,372,787
SIC 2431 Millwork
Pr Pr Andre Cholette
 Richard Cholette
 Jacques Cholette
Genl Mgr Martin Savard

D-U-N-S 25-847-1747   (BR)
TOWNSHIP OF NORTH GLENGARRY
ALEXANDRIA FIRE DEPARTMENT
188 Kenyon St W, Alexandria, ON, K0C 1A0
(613) 525-1240
Emp Here 22
SIC 7389 Business services, nec

D-U-N-S 25-126-0956   (BR)
UPPER CANADA DISTRICT SCHOOL BOARD, THE
GLENGARRY DISTRICT HIGH SCHOOL
(*Suby of* Upper Canada District School Board, The)

212 Main St N, Alexandria, ON, K0C 1A0
(613) 525-1066
Emp Here 45
SIC 8211 Elementary and secondary schools

Alfred, ON K0B
Prescott County

D-U-N-S 25-238-6800   (BR)
CONSEIL SCOLAIRE DE DISTRICT CATHOLIQUE DE L'EST ONTARIEN
ECOLE ELEMENTAIRE CATHOLIQUE SAINT-VICTOR
(*Suby of* Conseil Scolaire De District Catholique De L'Est Ontarien)
38 St Paul St, Alfred, ON, K0B 1A0
(613) 679-4373
Emp Here 28
SIC 8211 Elementary and secondary schools

D-U-N-S 25-362-0637   (BR)
UNIVERSITY OF GUELPH
COLLEGE D'ALFRED DE L'UNIVERSITE DE GUELPH
31 St Paul St, Alfred, ON, K0B 1A0

Emp Here 60
SIC 8221 Colleges and universities

Allanburg, ON L0S
Welland County

D-U-N-S 24-886-3789   (BR)
2014767 ONTARIO LIMITED
BROWN PACKAGING
1827 Allanport Rd, Allanburg, ON, L0S 1A0
(905) 227-0521
Emp Here 20
SIC 2653 Corrugated and solid fiber boxes

D-U-N-S 24-597-1379   (BR)
TRIMAC TRANSPORTATION SERVICES LIMITED PARTNERSHIP
MUNICIPAL TANK LINES
2170 Allanport Rd, Allanburg, ON, L0S 1A0

Emp Here 22
SIC 4212 Local trucking, without storage

Alliston, ON L9R
Simcoe County

D-U-N-S 20-279-8500   (SL)
ALP (AUTO LOGISTICS PROVIDERS) CANADA LIMITED
AUTO LOGISTICS PROVIDERS CANADA
(*Suby of* Auto Warehousing Co., Inc.)
4700 Industrial Pky, Alliston, ON, L9R 1V4
(905) 435-0377
Emp Here 120   *Sales* 11,869,650
SIC 4231 Trucking terminal facilities
Pr Stephen Seher

D-U-N-S 25-296-9472   (BR)
BANK OF NOVA SCOTIA, THE
SCOTIABANK
13 Victoria St W, Alliston, ON, L9R 1S9
(705) 435-4344
Emp Here 32
SIC 6021 National commercial banks

D-U-N-S 20-508-7968   (BR)
BAXTER CORPORATION
(*Suby of* Baxter International Inc.)
89 Centre St S, Alliston, ON, L9R 1J4
(705) 435-6261
Emp Here 430
SIC 5122 Drugs, proprietaries, and sundries

D-U-N-S 25-143-8958   (SL)
CDN AUTO RELEASING LTD
4700 Tottenham Rd, Alliston, ON, L9R 1W7

Emp Here 86   Sales 9,128,880
SIC 4226 Special warehousing and storage, nec
Pr Pr Tony Zurba
VP VP Marilyn Zurba
Off Mgr Sandra Sypulski

D-U-N-S 25-084-5914   (BR)
CARA OPERATIONS LIMITED
SWISS CHALET
(Suby of Cara Holdings Limited)
36 Young St, Alliston, ON, L9R 1P8
(705) 434-9990
Emp Here 50
SIC 5812 Eating places

D-U-N-S 20-774-6272   (SL)
GOOD SAMARITAN NURSING HOMES LTD
481 Victoria St E, Alliston, ON, L9R 1J8
(705) 435-5722
Emp Here 60   Sales 2,699,546
SIC 8051 Skilled nursing care facilities

D-U-N-S 24-951-3920   (BR)
HONDA CANADA INC
HONDA OF CANADA MFG DIV
4700 Tottenham Rd, Alliston, ON, L9R 1A2
(705) 435-5561
Emp Here 2,000
SIC 3711 Motor vehicles and car bodies

D-U-N-S 20-175-8278   (BR)
HYDRO ONE INC
7690 89 Hwy W, Alliston, ON, L9R 1V1

Emp Here 20
SIC 4911 Electric services

D-U-N-S 20-357-6517   (SL)
LEADEC (CA) CORP
(Suby of Leadec Corp.)
4700 Tottenham Rd, Alliston, ON, L9R 1A2
(705) 435-5077
Emp Here 80   Sales 2,334,742
SIC 7349 Building maintenance services, nec

D-U-N-S 20-792-4965   (SL)
MACKINNON RESTAURANTS INC
MCDONALD'S RESTAURANT 25004
137 Yonge St W, Alliston, ON, L9R 1V1
(705) 434-0003
Emp Here 100   Sales 2,991,389
SIC 5812 Eating places

D-U-N-S 25-361-6973   (BR)
NISSIN TRANSPORT (CANADA) INC
292 Church St S, Alliston, ON, L9R 2B7
(705) 434-3136
Emp Here 40
SIC 4225 General warehousing and storage

D-U-N-S 24-688-5016   (BR)
PITTSBURGH GLASS WORKS, ULC
222 Church St S, Alliston, ON, L9R 2B7

Emp Here 22
SIC 3231 Products of purchased glass

D-U-N-S 25-292-4949   (BR)
SIMCOE COUNTY DISTRICT SCHOOL BOARD, THE
ALLISTON UNION PUBLIC SCHOOL
(Suby of Simcoe County District School Board, The)
25 Albert St W, Alliston, ON, L9R 1H2
(705) 435-7391
Emp Here 50
SIC 8211 Elementary and secondary schools

D-U-N-S 25-297-6246   (BR)
SIMCOE COUNTY DISTRICT SCHOOL BOARD, THE
CUMBERLAND, ERNEST ELEMENTARY SCHOOL

(Suby of Simcoe County District School Board, The)
160 8th Ave, Alliston, ON, L9R 1A5
(705) 435-0676
Emp Here 38
SIC 8211 Elementary and secondary schools

D-U-N-S 20-711-2066   (BR)
SIMCOE COUNTY DISTRICT SCHOOL BOARD, THE
ALLISTON ADULT LEARNING CENTER
(Suby of Simcoe County District School Board, The)
46 Wellington St W Unit 3, Alliston, ON, L9R 2B8
(705) 435-7778
Emp Here 50
SIC 8211 Elementary and secondary schools

D-U-N-S 20-655-1447   (BR)
SIMCOE COUNTY DISTRICT SCHOOL BOARD, THE
BANTING MEMORIAL HIGH SCHOOL
(Suby of Simcoe County District School Board, The)
203 Victoria St E, Alliston, ON, L9R 1G5
(705) 435-6288
Emp Here 150
SIC 8211 Elementary and secondary schools

D-U-N-S 20-711-2157   (BR)
SIMCOE MUSKOKA CATHOLIC DISTRICT SCHOOL BOARD
SAINT PAUL ELEMENTARY SCHOOL
(Suby of Simcoe Muskoka Catholic District School Board)
100 James A Mccague Ave, Alliston, ON, L9R 0G5
(705) 435-7211
Emp Here 70
SIC 8211 Elementary and secondary schools

D-U-N-S 20-711-2215   (BR)
SIMCOE MUSKOKA CATHOLIC DISTRICT SCHOOL BOARD
HOLY FAMILY SCHOOL
(Suby of Simcoe Muskoka Catholic District School Board)
180 King St S, Alliston, ON, L9R 1B9
(705) 435-3989
Emp Here 50
SIC 8211 Elementary and secondary schools

D-U-N-S 20-806-2484   (BR)
SOBEYS CAPITAL INCORPORATED
FRESHCO
161 Young St, Alliston, ON, L9R 2A9
(705) 434-9512
Emp Here 100
SIC 5411 Grocery stores

D-U-N-S 24-101-3635   (BR)
STAPLES CANADA INC
STAPLES THE BUSINESS DEPOT
(Suby of Staples, Inc.)
92 Young St, Alliston, ON, L9R 1P8
(705) 434-4992
Emp Here 20
SIC 5943 Stationery stores

D-U-N-S 24-992-6890   (BR)
TSC STORES L.P.
TSC STORES
4874 Concession Rd 7, Alliston, ON, L9R 1V1
(705) 435-8845
Emp Here 30
SIC 5251 Hardware stores

D-U-N-S 25-213-8672   (SL)
THOMSON, PETER & SONS INC
256 Victoria St W, Alliston, ON, L9R 1L9
(705) 435-3711
Emp Here 35   Sales 10,506,341
SIC 5031 Lumber, plywood, and millwork
Pr Pr Robert Bewell
John Melnick

D-U-N-S 20-971-4133   (BR)

TORONTO DISTRICT SCHOOL BOARD
SHELDON CENTRE FOR OUTDOOR EDUCATION
995243 Mono-Adjala Tline, Alliston, ON, L9R 1V1
(705) 435-4266
Emp Here 20
SIC 8211 Elementary and secondary schools

D-U-N-S 24-599-1810   (BR)
WAL-MART CANADA CORP
WALMART
30 Dunham Dr, Alliston, ON, L9R 0G1
(705) 435-7100
Emp Here 50
SIC 5311 Department stores

D-U-N-S 24-606-1969   (BR)
WAL-MART CANADA CORP
WALMART SUPERCENTRE
30 Dunham Dr, Alliston, ON, L9R 0G1
(705) 435-5129
Emp Here 40
SIC 5311 Department stores

Alma, ON N0B
Wellington County

D-U-N-S 20-105-7127   (SL)
CONESTOGO AGRI SYSTEMS INC
7506 Wellington Road 11, Alma, ON, N0B 1A0
(519) 638-3022
Emp Here 27   Sales 5,909,817
SIC 5083 Farm and garden machinery
Pr Richard Struyk

Almonte, ON K0A
Lanark County

D-U-N-S 25-237-9714   (BR)
CATHOLIC DISTRICT SCHOOL BOARD OF EASTERN ONTARIO
HOLY NAME MARY ELEMENTARY SCHOOL
(Suby of Catholic District School Board of Eastern Ontario)
110 Paterson St, Almonte, ON, K0A 1A0
(613) 256-2532
Emp Here 25
SIC 8211 Elementary and secondary schools

D-U-N-S 20-977-2701   (BR)
LOBLAW COMPANIES LIMITED
PATRICE'S INDEPENDENT GROCER
401 Ottawa St, Almonte, ON, K0A 1A0
(613) 256-2080
Emp Here 75
SIC 5411 Grocery stores

D-U-N-S 20-328-3114   (BR)
TDL GROUP CORP, THE
TIM HORTONS
105 Sadler Dr, Almonte, ON, K0A 1A0
(613) 256-2157
Emp Here 30
SIC 5812 Eating places

D-U-N-S 20-025-0665   (BR)
UPPER CANADA DISTRICT SCHOOL BOARD, THE
NAISMITH MEMORIAL PUBLIC SCHOOL
126 Martin St N, Almonte, ON, K0A 1A0
(613) 256-3773
Emp Here 30
SIC 8211 Elementary and secondary schools

D-U-N-S 20-591-9058   (BR)
UPPER CANADA DISTRICT SCHOOL BOARD, THE
R TAIT MCKENZIE PUBLIC SCHOOL
175 Paterson St, Almonte, ON, K0A 1A0
(613) 256-8248
Emp Here 28

SIC 8211 Elementary and secondary schools

D-U-N-S 20-074-8817   (BR)
UPPER CANADA DISTRICT SCHOOL BOARD, THE
ALMONTE & DISTRICT HIGH SCHOOL
126 Martin St N, Almonte, ON, K0A 1A0
(613) 256-1470
Emp Here 45
SIC 8211 Elementary and secondary schools

Alton, ON L7K
Peel County

D-U-N-S 24-125-9084   (SL)
MILLCROFT HOSPITALITY SERVICES INC
MILLCROFT INN & SPA, THE
55 John St, Alton, ON, L7K 0C4
(519) 941-8111
Emp Here 50   Sales 2,188,821
SIC 7011 Hotels and motels

Alvinston, ON N0N
Lambton County

D-U-N-S 20-710-4600   (BR)
LAMBTON KENT DISTRICT SCHOOL BOARD
BROOKE CENTRAL PUBLIC SCHOOL
7989 Brooke Line, Alvinston, ON, N0N 1A0
(519) 847-5218
Emp Here 50
SIC 8211 Elementary and secondary schools

Ameliasburg, ON K0K
Prince Edward County

D-U-N-S 25-143-0013   (BR)
HASTINGS AND PRINCE EDWARD DISTRICT SCHOOL BOARD
KENTE PUBLIC SCHOOL
264 County Rd 19 Suite 68, Ameliasburg, ON, K0K 1A0
(613) 962-7533
Emp Here 25
SIC 8211 Elementary and secondary schools

Amherstburg, ON N9V
Essex County

D-U-N-S 24-078-2763   (SL)
BARRON POULTRY LIMITED
7470 County Road 18, Amherstburg, ON, N9V 2Y7
(519) 726-5252
Emp Here 49   Sales 9,266,009
SIC 2015 Poultry slaughtering and processing
Pr Pr Richard Barron
Sharon Barron

D-U-N-S 24-763-0366   (SL)
BELWOOD POULTRY LIMITED
4272 4th Conc N, Amherstburg, ON, N9V 2Y9
(519) 736-2236
Emp Here 40   Sales 9,484,891
SIC 5144 Poultry and poultry products
Pr Dave Maxwell

D-U-N-S 20-537-1854   (BR)
CANADA POST CORPORATION
AMHERSTBURG STN MAIN POST OFFICE
66 Richmond St, Amherstburg, ON, N9V 1E9
(519) 736-3992
Emp Here 23
SIC 4311 U.s. postal service

D-U-N-S 24-184-2702   (BR)
COMMUNITY LIVING ESSEX COUNTY
260 Bathurst St, Amherstburg, ON, N9V 1Y9
(519) 736-5077
Emp Here 30
SIC 8699 Membership organizations, nec

D-U-N-S 20-290-5696   (BR)
CONSEIL SCOLAIRE DE DISTRICT DES ECOLES CATHOLIQUES DU SUD-OUEST
ECOLE SAINT JEAN BAPTISTE
365 Fryer St, Amherstburg, ON, N9V 0C3
(519) 736-6427
Emp Here 40
SIC 8211 Elementary and secondary schools

D-U-N-S 20-515-1363   (BR)
DIAGEO CANADA INC
(*Suby of* DIAGEO PLC)
110 St. Arnaud St, Amherstburg, ON, N9V 2N8
(519) 736-2161
Emp Here 200
SIC 2085 Distilled and blended liquors

D-U-N-S 25-249-1782   (BR)
GREATER ESSEX COUNTY DISTRICT SCHOOL BOARD
WESTERN SECONDARY SCHOOL
5791 North Town Line, Amherstburg, ON, N9V 2Y9
(519) 726-6138
Emp Here 70
SIC 8211 Elementary and secondary schools

D-U-N-S 20-026-0482   (BR)
GREATER ESSEX COUNTY DISTRICT SCHOOL BOARD
GENERAL AMHERST HIGH SCHOOL
130 Sandwich St S, Amherstburg, ON, N9V 1Z8
(519) 736-2149
Emp Here 55
SIC 8211 Elementary and secondary schools

D-U-N-S 25-249-2129   (BR)
GREATER ESSEX COUNTY DISTRICT SCHOOL BOARD
MALDEN CENTRAL ELEMENTARY SCHOOL
5620 County Road 20, Amherstburg, ON, N9V 0C8
(519) 736-4529
Emp Here 25
SIC 8211 Elementary and secondary schools

D-U-N-S 25-249-2087   (BR)
GREATER ESSEX COUNTY DISTRICT SCHOOL BOARD
AMHERSTBURG PUBLIC SCHOOL
252 Hamilton Dr, Amherstburg, ON, N9V 1E1
(519) 736-2189
Emp Here 45
SIC 8211 Elementary and secondary schools

D-U-N-S 25-249-3176   (BR)
GREATER ESSEX COUNTY DISTRICT SCHOOL BOARD
ANDERDON PUBLIC SCHOOL
3170 Middle Side Rd N, Amherstburg, ON, N9V 2Y9
(519) 736-2592
Emp Here 30
SIC 8211 Elementary and secondary schools

D-U-N-S 20-981-2036   (BR)
SOBEYS CAPITAL INCORPORATED
83 Sandwich St S, Amherstburg, ON, N9V 1Z5
(519) 736-4520
Emp Here 170
SIC 5411 Grocery stores

D-U-N-S 24-098-6120   (BR)
UNIFOR
CAW CANADA
110 St. Arnaud St, Amherstburg, ON, N9V 2N8
(519) 730-0099
Emp Here 384

SIC 8631 Labor organizations

D-U-N-S 24-714-2768   (BR)
WAL-MART CANADA CORP
WALMART
400 Sandwich St S Suite 1, Amherstburg, ON, N9V 3L4
(519) 736-5600
Emp Here 50
SIC 5311 Department stores

D-U-N-S 20-710-6092   (BR)
WINDSOR-ESSEX CATHOLIC DISTRICT SCHOOL BOARD, THE
STELLA MARIS ELEMENTARY CATHOLIC SCHOOL
140 Girard St, Amherstburg, ON, N9V 2X3
(519) 736-6408
Emp Here 24
SIC 8211 Elementary and secondary schools

D-U-N-S 20-710-6043   (BR)
WINDSOR-ESSEX CATHOLIC DISTRICT SCHOOL BOARD, THE
ST BERNARD SCHOOL
320 Richmond St, Amherstburg, ON, N9V 1H4
(519) 736-2166
Emp Here 27
SIC 8211 Elementary and secondary schools

Amherstview, ON K7N
Addington County

D-U-N-S 25-263-6790   (BR)
ALGONQUIN & LAKESHORE CATHOLIC DISTRICT SCHOOL BOARD
OUR LADY OF MOUNT CARMEL CATHOLIC SCHOOL
97 Park Cres, Amherstview, ON, K7N 1L7
(613) 389-1122
Emp Here 35
SIC 8211 Elementary and secondary schools

D-U-N-S 25-263-5123   (BR)
LIMESTONE DISTRICT SCHOOL BOARD
AMHERSTVIEW PUBLIC SCHOOL
70 Fairfield Blvd, Amherstview, ON, K7N 1L4
(613) 389-0628
Emp Here 35
SIC 8211 Elementary and secondary schools

Ancaster, ON L9G
Wentworth County

D-U-N-S 24-911-3572   (HQ)
ACTIVATION LABORATORIES LTD
ACTLABS
41 Bittern St, Ancaster, ON, L9G 4V5
(905) 648-9611
Emp Here 150   *Emp Total* 230
Sales 23,514,157
SIC 8731 Commercial physical research
Pr Pr Felyce Hoffman
VP Fin VP Fin Michael Hoffman

D-U-N-S 20-647-2149   (SL)
BAKER, WALTER & CHANTAL SALES LTD
CANADIAN TIRE
1060 Wilson St W, Ancaster, ON, L9G 3K9
(905) 304-0000
Emp Here 85   *Sales* 11,905,280
SIC 5531 Auto and home supply stores
Pr Walter Baker
Off Mgr Chantal Baker

D-U-N-S 20-795-8310   (BR)
BANQUE TORONTO-DOMINION, LA
TORONTO-DOMINION BANK, THE
(*Suby of* Toronto-Dominion Bank, The)
98 Wilson St W, Ancaster, ON, L9G 1N3
(905) 648-1805
Emp Here 20

SIC 6021 National commercial banks

D-U-N-S 25-147-3690   (SL)
BICK FINANCIAL SECURITY CORPORATION
BICK FINANCIAL
241 Wilson St E, Ancaster, ON, L9G 2B8
(905) 648-9559
Emp Here 40   *Sales* 13,162,880
SIC 6282 Investment advice
VP VP Leonard Bick
Pr Pr Clarence Bick

D-U-N-S 24-626-8697   (BR)
CAMBRIDGE PRO FAB INC
1362 Osprey Dr Suite 76, Ancaster, ON, L9G 4V5
Emp Here 60
SIC 3621 Motors and generators

D-U-N-S 24-659-7090   (BR)
CITY OF HAMILTON, THE
SPRING VALLEY ARENA
29 Orchard Dr, Ancaster, ON, L9G 1Z6
(905) 648-4404
Emp Here 25
SIC 8322 Individual and family services

D-U-N-S 24-826-2115   (BR)
FIRSTCANADA ULC
FIRST STUDENT
1185 Smith Rd, Ancaster, ON, L9G 3L1
(905) 648-1386
Emp Here 300
SIC 4151 School buses

D-U-N-S 24-972-4287   (SL)
HAMILTON ASSOCIATION FOR CHRISTIAN EDUCATION INCORPORATED
HAMILTON DISTRICT CHRISTIAN HIGH SCHOOL
92 Glancaster Rd, Ancaster, ON, L9G 3K9
(905) 648-6655
Emp Here 50   *Sales* 3,356,192
SIC 8211 Elementary and secondary schools

D-U-N-S 20-653-8089   (BR)
HAMILTON-WENTWORTH CATHOLIC SCHOOL BOARD
ST ANN'S SCHOOL
24 Fiddler'S Green Rd, Ancaster, ON, L9G 1W1
Emp Here 30
SIC 8211 Elementary and secondary schools

D-U-N-S 20-290-5472   (BR)
HAMILTON-WENTWORTH CATHOLIC SCHOOL BOARD
ROUSSEAU PUBLIC SCHOOL
103 Mcniven Rd, Ancaster, ON, L9G 3T7
(905) 648-6142
Emp Here 20
SIC 8211 Elementary and secondary schools

D-U-N-S 25-292-6936   (BR)
HAMILTON-WENTWORTH CATHOLIC SCHOOL BOARD
ST JOACHIM SCHOOL
75 Concerto Crt, Ancaster, ON, L9G 4V6
(905) 523-2341
Emp Here 25
SIC 8211 Elementary and secondary schools

D-U-N-S 24-039-5504   (BR)
HAMILTON-WENTWORTH CATHOLIC SCHOOL BOARD
BISHOP TONNOS SECONDARY SCHOOL
100 Panabaker Dr, Ancaster, ON, L9G 5E3
(905) 523-2331
Emp Here 20
SIC 8211 Elementary and secondary schools

D-U-N-S 20-290-5068   (BR)
HAMILTON-WENTWORTH DISTRICT SCHOOL BOARD, THE
C H BRAY ELEMENTARY SHOOL
99 Dunham Dr, Ancaster, ON, L9G 1X7

(905) 648-4353
Emp Here 25
SIC 8211 Elementary and secondary schools

D-U-N-S 20-590-5495   (BR)
HAMILTON-WENTWORTH DISTRICT SCHOOL BOARD, THE
ANCASTER SENIOR PUBLIC SCHOOL
292 Nakoma Rd, Ancaster, ON, L9G 1T2
(905) 648-4439
Emp Here 25
SIC 8211 Elementary and secondary schools

D-U-N-S 20-290-6157   (BR)
HAMILTON-WENTWORTH DISTRICT SCHOOL BOARD, THE
FESSENDEN SCHOOL
168 Huron Ave, Ancaster, ON, L9G 1V7
(905) 648-4115
Emp Here 25
SIC 8211 Elementary and secondary schools

D-U-N-S 20-710-8148   (BR)
HAMILTON-WENTWORTH DISTRICT SCHOOL BOARD, THE
ANCASTER HIGH SCHOOL
374 Jerseyville Rd W, Ancaster, ON, L9G 3K8
(905) 648-4468
Emp Here 75
SIC 8211 Elementary and secondary schools

D-U-N-S 24-470-8418   (SL)
KNOLLWOOD GOLF LIMITED
KNOLLWOOD GOLF CLUB
1276 Shaver Rd, Ancaster, ON, L9G 3L1
(905) 648-6687
Emp Here 80   *Sales* 4,722,560
SIC 7992 Public golf courses

D-U-N-S 20-348-3391   (BR)
LOWE'S COMPANIES CANADA, ULC
LOWE'S COMPANIES CANADA ULC
100 Portia Dr, Ancaster, ON, L9G 0G1
(905) 304-7507
Emp Here 60
SIC 5211 Lumber and other building materials

D-U-N-S 25-841-8136   (BR)
PIONEER FOOD SERVICES LIMITED
TIM HORTONS
(*Suby of* Pioneer Food Services Limited)
1180 2 Hwy Suite 2, Ancaster, ON, L9G 3K9
(905) 648-5222
Emp Here 75
SIC 5812 Eating places

D-U-N-S 20-290-3592   (BR)
REVERA INC
MEADOWS LONG TERM CARE CENTRE, THE
12 Tranquility Ave Suite 1, Ancaster, ON, L9G 5C2
(905) 304-1993
Emp Here 150
SIC 8322 Individual and family services

D-U-N-S 25-172-5628   (BR)
SCHINDLER ELEVATOR CORPORATION
1377 Cormorant Rd Suite 103, Ancaster, ON, L9G 4V5
(905) 304-0633
Emp Here 45
SIC 7699 Repair services, nec

D-U-N-S 20-296-0662   (HQ)
STACKPOLE INTERNATIONAL POWDER METAL, LTD.
1325 Cormorant Rd, Ancaster, ON, L9G 4V5
(905) 304-9455
Emp Here 42   *Emp Total* 1,250
Sales 198,161,261
SIC 3714 Motor vehicle parts and accessories
Pr Pr Peter Ballantyne
    Rahim Suleman

D-U-N-S 24-395-3838   (BR)
STATE REALTY LIMITED
ROYAL LEPAGE
1122 Wilson St W, Ancaster, ON, L9G 3K9

(905) 648-4451
Emp Here 103
SIC 6531 Real estate agents and managers

D-U-N-S 24-425-4434   (BR)
TDL GROUP CORP, THE
TIM HORTONS
1290 Cormorant Rd, Ancaster, ON, L9G 4V5
(905) 304-2620
Emp Here 25
SIC 5812 Eating places

D-U-N-S 24-190-8123   (BR)
VANDERWESTEN & RUTHERFORD ASSOCIATES, INC
1349 Sandhill Dr Suite 201, Ancaster, ON, L9G 4V5
(905) 648-0373
Emp Here 22
SIC 8711 Engineering services

D-U-N-S 20-343-0723   (SL)
VULCRAFT CANADA, INC
(*Suby of* Nucor Corporation)
1362 Osprey Dr, Ancaster, ON, L9G 4V5
(289) 443-2000
Emp Here 45   *Sales* 6,496,883
SIC 3312 Blast furnaces and steel mills
Genl Mgr Mike Fernie

D-U-N-S 24-316-9088   (BR)
WAL-MART CANADA CORP
WALMART SUPERCENTRE
1051 Garner Rd W Suite 3127, Ancaster, ON, L9G 3K9
(905) 648-9980
Emp Here 520
SIC 5311 Department stores

Ancaster, ON L9K
Wentworth County

D-U-N-S 20-569-2127   (BR)
BANK OF NOVA SCOTIA, THE
SCOTIABANK
851 Golf Links Rd, Ancaster, ON, L9K 1L5
(905) 304-4100
Emp Here 20
SIC 6021 National commercial banks

D-U-N-S 20-809-7852   (BR)
CARA OPERATIONS LIMITED
MONTANAS
(*Suby of* Cara Holdings Limited)
771 Golf Links Rd, Ancaster, ON, L9K 1L5
(905) 304-4980
Emp Here 50
SIC 5812 Eating places

D-U-N-S 25-836-5840   (BR)
CARA OPERATIONS LIMITED
KELSEY'S
(*Suby of* Cara Holdings Limited)
771 Golf Links Rd, Ancaster, ON, L9K 1L5
(905) 304-5100
Emp Here 50
SIC 5812 Eating places

D-U-N-S 25-543-0167   (BR)
COSTCO WHOLESALE CANADA LTD
(*Suby of* Ccstco Wholesale Corporation)
100 Legend Crt Suite 1105, Ancaster, ON, L9K 1J3
(905) 304-0344
Emp Here 151
SIC 5099 Durable goods, nec

D-U-N-S 24-337-3243   (BR)
FGL SPORTS LTD
SPORT CHEK MEADOWLANDS POWER CENTRE
14 Martindale Cres Unit 2, Ancaster, ON, L9K 1J9
(905) 304-9234
Emp Here 42
SIC 5941 Sporting goods and bicycle shops

D-U-N-S 24-200-4146   (BR)
GOLF TOWN LIMITED
GOLF TOWN
1100 Golf Links Rd Unit 1, Ancaster, ON, L9K 1J8
(905) 304-7405
Emp Here 20
SIC 5941 Sporting goods and bicycle shops

D-U-N-S 24-676-3184   (BR)
HAMILTON-WENTWORTH CATHOLIC SCHOOL BOARD
ANCASTER MEADOW ELEMENTARY PUBLIC SCHOOL
93 Kitty Murray Lane, Ancaster, ON, L9K 1S3
(905) 304-3255
Emp Here 25
SIC 8211 Elementary and secondary schools

D-U-N-S 20-770-5190   (BR)
HOME DEPOT OF CANADA INC
(*Suby of* The Home Depot Inc)
122 Martindale Cres, Ancaster, ON, L9K 1J9
(905) 304-6826
Emp Here 300
SIC 5211 Lumber and other building materials

D-U-N-S 25-079-1167   (BR)
HOME DEPOT OF CANADA INC
HOME DEPOT
(*Suby of* The Home Depot Inc)
122 Martindale Cres, Ancaster, ON, L9K 1J9
(905) 304-5900
Emp Here 250
SIC 5211 Lumber and other building materials

D-U-N-S 20-245-7136   (BR)
INDIGO BOOKS & MUSIC INC
CHAPTERS
(*Suby of* Indigo Books & Music Inc)
737 Golf Links Rd Unit 1, Ancaster, ON, L9K 1L5
(905) 648-7155
Emp Here 30
SIC 5942 Book stores

D-U-N-S 24-388-3790   (SL)
JARVIS, S. M. FOOD SERVICES LTD
MCDONALD'S RESTAURANT
1015 Golf Links Rd, Ancaster, ON, L9K 1L6
(905) 648-7915
Emp Here 70   *Sales* 2,115,860
SIC 5812 Eating places

D-U-N-S 20-511-8933   (SL)
LOYALIST INSURANCE BROKERS LIMITED
911 Golf Links Rd Suite 111, Ancaster, ON, L9K 1H9
(905) 648-6767
Emp Here 25   *Sales* 2,261,782
SIC 6411 Insurance agents, brokers, and service

D-U-N-S 24-363-0832   (BR)
RGIS CANADA ULC
911 Golf Links Rd, Ancaster, ON, L9K 1H9
(905) 304-9700
Emp Here 100
SIC 7389 Business services, nec

D-U-N-S 20-614-4003   (BR)
SIR CORP
JACK ASTOR'S BAR & GRILL
839 Golf Links Rd, Ancaster, ON, L9K 1L5
(905) 304-1721
Emp Here 100
SIC 5812 Eating places

D-U-N-S 20-301-1338   (BR)
SEARS CANADA INC
SEARS CATALOGUE, DIV OF
45 Legend Crt, Ancaster, ON, L9K 1J3

Emp Here 30
SIC 5719 Miscellaneous homefurnishings

D-U-N-S 25-911-7554   (BR)
SOBEYS CAPITAL INCORPORATED

SOBEYS FOOD VILLAGE
977 Golf Links Rd, Ancaster, ON, L9K 1K1
(905) 648-3534
Emp Here 150
SIC 5411 Grocery stores

D-U-N-S 25-486-5611   (BR)
STAPLES CANADA INC
STAPLES THE BUSINESS DEPOT
(*Suby of* Staples, Inc.)
1015 Golf Links Rd Suite 1, Ancaster, ON, L9K 1L6
(905) 648-6047
Emp Here 45
SIC 5943 Stationery stores

D-U-N-S 20-506-0960   (BR)
STARBUCKS COFFEE CANADA, INC
(*Suby of* Starbucks Corporation)
737 Golf Links Rd Suite 1, Ancaster, ON, L9K 1L5
(905) 304-7070
Emp Here 20
SIC 5812 Eating places

D-U-N-S 20-860-5191   (BR)
TOWN SHOES LIMITED
SHOE COMPANY, THE
14 Martindale Cres, Ancaster, ON, L9K 1J9

Emp Here 25
SIC 5661 Shoe stores

D-U-N-S 20-718-5948   (BR)
WENDY'S RESTAURANTS OF CANADA INC
WENDY'S
(*Suby of* The Wendy's Company)
977 Golf Links Rd, Ancaster, ON, L9K 1K1
(905) 648-7963
Emp Here 25
SIC 5812 Eating places

D-U-N-S 20-184-2908   (BR)
WINNERS MERCHANTS INTERNATIONAL L.P.
HOMESENSE
(*Suby of* The TJX Companies Inc)
14 Martindale Cres, Ancaster, ON, L9K 1J9
(905) 304-9612
Emp Here 40
SIC 5651 Family clothing stores

D-U-N-S 20-106-3539   (BR)
WINNERS MERCHANTS INTERNATIONAL L.P.
WINNERS
(*Suby of* The TJX Companies Inc)
44 Legend Crt, Ancaster, ON, L9K 1J3
(905) 304-8277
Emp Here 50
SIC 5651 Family clothing stores

Angus, ON L0M
Simcoe County

D-U-N-S 24-826-7353   (SL)
ANGUS TIGER LIMITED
GIANT TIGER STORE
3 Massey St Unit 4, Angus, ON, L0M 1B0
(705) 424-1890
Emp Here 80   *Sales* 8,740,800
SIC 5399 Miscellaneous general merchandise
Donald Cotter

D-U-N-S 24-121-0447   (BR)
BANK OF NOVA SCOTIA, THE
SCOTIABANK
17 King St Unit 15, Angus, ON, L0M 1B2
(705) 424-5588
Emp Here 20
SIC 6021 National commercial banks

D-U-N-S 25-296-9316   (BR)
BANK OF NOVA SCOTIA, THE
SCOTIABANK

17 King St Unit 5, Angus, ON, L0M 1B2
(705) 424-5761
Emp Here 20
SIC 6021 National commercial banks

D-U-N-S 24-224-5962   (BR)
PIZZA PIZZA LIMITED
193 Mill St Plaza, Angus, ON, L0M 1B0
(705) 424-1111
Emp Here 40
SIC 5812 Eating places

D-U-N-S 20-653-3957   (BR)
SIMCOE COUNTY DISTRICT SCHOOL BOARD, THE
PINE RIVERS ELEMNTARY SCHOOL
(*Suby of* Simcoe County District School Board, The)
45 Brian Ave, Angus, ON, L0M 1B3
(705) 424-3317
Emp Here 40
SIC 8211 Elementary and secondary schools

D-U-N-S 25-238-2361   (BR)
SIMCOE MUSKOKA CATHOLIC DISTRICT SCHOOL BOARD
OUR LADY OF GRACE SCHOOL
(*Suby of* Simcoe Muskoka Catholic District School Board)
24 Roth St, Angus, ON, L0M 1B2
(705) 424-6162
Emp Here 45
SIC 8211 Elementary and secondary schools

D-U-N-S 20-702-4220   (BR)
SOBEYS CAPITAL INCORPORATED
SOBEY'S
247 Mill St, Angus, ON, L0M 1B2
(705) 424-1588
Emp Here 125
SIC 5411 Grocery stores

Ariss, ON N0B
Wellington County

D-U-N-S 24-708-5236   (BR)
LINAMAR CORPORATION
ARISS MANUFACTURING
Gd, Ariss, ON, N0B 1B0
(519) 822-4080
Emp Here 230
SIC 3531 Construction machinery

Armstrong Station, ON P0T
Thunder Bay County

D-U-N-S 25-091-4157   (BR)
LAKEHEAD DISTRICT SCHOOL BOARD
ARMSTRONG PUBLIC SCHOOL
Gd, Armstrong Station, ON, P0T 1A0
(807) 583-2076
Emp Here 22
SIC 8211 Elementary and secondary schools

Arnprior, ON K7S
Renfrew County

D-U-N-S 25-296-9274   (BR)
BANK OF NOVA SCOTIA, THE
SCOTIABANK
169 John St N, Arnprior, ON, K7S 2N8
(613) 623-7314
Emp Here 25
SIC 6021 National commercial banks

D-U-N-S 20-541-1932   (BR)
CANADA POST CORPORATION
90 Madawaska St Suite 1, Arnprior, ON, K7S

1S3
(613) 623-4318
Emp Here 20
SIC 4311 U.s. postal service

D-U-N-S 25-694-2897   (HQ)
CROSSROADS FOODS ONTARIO INC
TIM HORTONS
(*Suby of* Crossroads Foods Ontario Inc)
2 Staye Court Dr, Arnprior, ON, K7S 0E7
(613) 623-1000
Emp Here 67   Emp Total 120
Sales 3,648,035
SIC 5812 Eating places

D-U-N-S 20-081-8164   (BR)
CROSSROADS FOODS ONTARIO INC
TIM HORTONS
201 Madawaska Blvd, Arnprior, ON, K7S 1S6
(613) 622-7525
Emp Here 35
SIC 5812 Eating places

D-U-N-S 20-033-0595   (HQ)
M. SULLIVAN & SON LIMITED
ARNPRIOR BUILDERS SUPPLIES, DIV OF
(*Suby of* M. Sullivan & Son Limited)
236 Madawaska Blvd Suite 100, Arnprior, ON,
K7S 0A3
(613) 623-6584
Emp Here 55   Emp Total 60
Sales 11,892,594
SIC 1541 Industrial buildings and warehouses
  Thomas E Sullivan
Pr Robert Maclaren
  Kerry Hisko
Dir William Holmes

D-U-N-S 24-794-8003   (SL)
MCGONIGAL CONSTRUCTION LTD
MCGONIGAL MASONRY CONSTRUCTION
245 Fifth Ave, Arnprior, ON, K7S 3M3
(613) 623-3613
Emp Here 50   Sales 3,648,035
SIC 1741 Masonry and other stonework

D-U-N-S 24-344-5066   (BR)
METRO ONTARIO INC
METRO
70 Elgin St W, Arnprior, ON, K7S 1N5
(613) 623-2380
Emp Here 50
SIC 5411 Grocery stores

D-U-N-S 20-555-6512   (BR)
METRO ONTARIO INC
METRO
375 Daniel St S, Arnprior, ON, K7S 3K6
(613) 623-6273
Emp Here 100
SIC 5411 Grocery stores

D-U-N-S 24-578-9284   (HQ)
PACIFIC SAFETY PRODUCTS INC
PACIFIC EMERGENCY PRODUCTS
(*Suby of* Maui Acquisition Corp.)
124 Fourth Ave, Arnprior, ON, K7S 0A9
(613) 623-6001
Emp Here 75   Emp Total 2,500
Sales 13,497,730
SIC 3842 Surgical appliances and supplies
  Terry Vaudry
  Sherrie Dontigny
  Derek Mcdorman
Mgr Jen Murch
  Fraser Campbell
  Ken Hight

D-U-N-S 20-844-5788   (BR)
PEPSICO CANADA ULC
FRITO LAY CANADA
(*Suby of* Pepsico, Inc.)
1 Kenwood Pl, Arnprior, ON, K7S 1K9
(613) 623-8140
Emp Here 20
SIC 2096 Potato chips and similar snacks

D-U-N-S 20-094-3079   (BR)

**RENFREW COUNTY CATHOLIC DISTRICT
SCHOOL BOARD**
ST JOHN XXIII CATHOLIC SCHOOL
(*Suby of* Renfrew County Catholic District
School Board)
75 Edey St, Arnprior, ON, K7S 1B9
(613) 623-2828
Emp Here 25
SIC 8211 Elementary and secondary schools

D-U-N-S 20-711-6927   (BR)
**RENFREW COUNTY CATHOLIC DISTRICT
SCHOOL BOARD**
ST JOSEPH'S CATHOLIC SCHOOL
(*Suby of* Renfrew County Catholic District
School Board)
324 John St N, Arnprior, ON, K7S 2P6
(613) 623-2347
Emp Here 27
SIC 8211 Elementary and secondary schools

D-U-N-S 20-655-0845   (BR)
**RENFREW COUNTY DISTRICT SCHOOL
BOARD**
A J CHARBONNEAU PUBLIC SCHOOL
1164 Stewartville Rd, Arnprior, ON, K7S 3G8
(613) 623-6512
Emp Here 25
SIC 8211 Elementary and secondary schools

D-U-N-S 25-925-6071   (BR)
**RENFREW COUNTY DISTRICT SCHOOL
BOARD**
AMPRIOR DISTRICT HIGH SCHOOL
59 Ottawa St, Arnprior, ON, K7S 1X2
(613) 623-3183
Emp Here 70
SIC 8211 Elementary and secondary schools

D-U-N-S 25-238-6537   (BR)
**RENFREW COUNTY DISTRICT SCHOOL
BOARD**
WALTER ZADOW PUBLIC SCHOOL
79 Ottawa St, Arnprior, ON, K7S 1X2
(613) 623-4235
Emp Here 41
SIC 8211 Elementary and secondary schools

D-U-N-S 25-238-6339   (BR)
**RENFREW COUNTY DISTRICT SCHOOL
BOARD**
MCNAB PUBLIC SCHOOL
1164 Stewartville Rd, Arnprior, ON, K7S 3G8
(613) 623-5746
Emp Here 30
SIC 8211 Elementary and secondary schools

D-U-N-S 25-410-8327   (BR)
REVERA INC
*ARNPRIOR VILLA RETIREMENT RESI-
DENCE*
15 Arthur St, Arnprior, ON, K7S 1A1
(613) 623-0414
Emp Here 26
SIC 6513 Apartment building operators

D-U-N-S 25-655-6382   (BR)
REXALL PHARMACY GROUP LTD
REXALL
(*Suby of* McKesson Corporation)
22 Baskin Dr, Arnprior, ON, K7S 3G8
(613) 623-6591
Emp Here 35
SIC 5912 Drug stores and proprietary stores

D-U-N-S 25-627-4226   (SL)
ROXSON ENTERPRISES LIMITED
VALLEY CATERERS
80 Mcgonigal St W, Arnprior, ON, K7S 1M3

Emp Here 75   Sales 2,261,782
SIC 5812 Eating places

D-U-N-S 24-268-2953   (BR)
ROYAL CANADIAN LEGION, THE
ARNPRIOR LEGION BRANCH 174
(*Suby of* Royal Canadian Legion, The)

49 Daniel St N, Arnprior, ON, K7S 2K6
(613) 623-4722
Emp Here 450
SIC 8641 Civic and social associations

D-U-N-S 24-846-5312   (BR)
SANDVIK CANADA, INC
*SANDVIK MATERIALS TECHNOLOGY
CANADA*
425 Mccartney, Arnprior, ON, K7S 3P3
(613) 623-6501
Emp Here 230
SIC 3312 Blast furnaces and steel mills

D-U-N-S 24-686-3583   (SL)
TERRAY CORPORATION
49 Jackson Lane, Arnprior, ON, K7S 3G8
(613) 623-3310
Emp Here 50   Sales 4,815,406
SIC 3842 Surgical appliances and supplies

D-U-N-S 25-653-3753   (BR)
W.O. STINSON & SON LIMITED
7 Van Jumar Dr, Arnprior, ON, K7S 3G8
(613) 623-4207
Emp Here 20
SIC 5541 Gasoline service stations

D-U-N-S 25-652-2129   (BR)
WENDY'S RESTAURANTS OF CANADA INC
WENDY'S
(*Suby of* The Wendy's Company)
2 Staye Court Dr, Arnprior, ON, K7S 0E7
(613) 623-8910
Emp Here 41
SIC 5812 Eating places

Arthur, ON N0G
Wellington County

D-U-N-S 20-707-5149   (BR)
CANARM LTD
7686 Sixteenth Line Rr 4, Arthur, ON, N0G
1A0
(519) 848-3910
Emp Here 40
SIC 5063 Electrical apparatus and equipment

D-U-N-S 24-909-5142   (BR)
COATS CANADA INC
COATS BELL
451 Smith St, Arthur, ON, N0G 1A0

Emp Here 20
SIC 2284 Thread mills

D-U-N-S 25-502-1560   (HQ)
MUSASHI AUTO PARTS CANADA INC
333 Domville St, Arthur, ON, N0G 1A0
(519) 848-2800
Emp Here 230   Emp Total 15,351
Sales 52,312,822
SIC 3714 Motor vehicle parts and accessories
Pr Pr Haru Ohtsuka

D-U-N-S 24-422-8628   (BR)
MUSASHI AUTO PARTS CANADA INC
500 Domville St, Arthur, ON, N0G 1A0
(519) 848-2800
Emp Here 100
SIC 3714 Motor vehicle parts and accessories

D-U-N-S 20-623-2097   (SL)
TIM HORTONS
8008 Wellington Rd Suite 109, Arthur, ON,
N0G 1A0
(519) 848-5333
Emp Here 65   Sales 1,969,939
SIC 5812 Eating places

D-U-N-S 20-653-4724   (BR)
**WELLINGTON CATHOLIC DISTRICT
SCHOOL BOARD**
ST JOHN CATHOLIC SCHOOL
315 Tucker St, Arthur, ON, N0G 1A0

(519) 848-2445
Emp Here 22
SIC 8211 Elementary and secondary schools

Arva, ON N0M
Middlesex County

D-U-N-S 25-249-1055   (BR)
**THAMES VALLEY DISTRICT SCHOOL
BOARD**
MEDWAY HIGH SCHOOL
14405 Medway Rd, Arva, ON, N0M 1C0
(519) 660-8418
Emp Here 90
SIC 8211 Elementary and secondary schools

D-U-N-S 25-249-3424   (BR)
**THAMES VALLEY DISTRICT SCHOOL
BOARD**
CENTENNIAL CENTRAL PUBLIC SCHOOL
14774 Medway Rd, Arva, ON, N0M 1C0
(519) 660-8193
Emp Here 27
SIC 8211 Elementary and secondary schools

Ashburn, ON L0B

D-U-N-S 20-904-2233   (SL)
DAGMAR RESORT LIMITED
1220 Lakeridge Rd Rr 1, Ashburn, ON, L0B
1A0
(905) 649-2002
Emp Here 270   Sales 15,901,920
SIC 7011 Hotels and motels
Pr Alex Nagy

Astorville, ON P0H
Nipissing County

D-U-N-S 25-238-8111   (BR)
**CONSEIL SCOLAIRE CATHOLIQUE DU
DISTRICT FRANCO-NORD**
ECOLE ST THOMAS D'AQUIN
(*Suby of* Conseil Scolaire Catholique Du Dis-
trict Franco-Nord)
1392 Village Rd, Astorville, ON, P0H 1B0
(705) 752-1200
Emp Here 22
SIC 8211 Elementary and secondary schools

D-U-N-S 24-818-0077   (SL)
EAST FERRIS BUS LINES LTD
49 Belecque Rd, Astorville, ON, P0H 1B0
(705) 752-1326
Emp Here 60   Sales 1,678,096
SIC 4151 School buses

Astra, ON K0K
Hastings County

D-U-N-S 25-062-9995   (SL)
RCAF MEMORIAL MUSEUM
Gd Po Stn Forces, Astra, ON, K0K 3W0

Emp Here 100   Sales 10,550,800
SIC 8412 Museums and art galleries
Ex Dir Chris Colton

Athens, ON K0E
Leeds County

D-U-N-S 24-510-5598   (SL)
DONALDSON CANADA INC

---

34 Mill St, Athens, ON, K0E 1B0

Emp Here 21   *Sales* 2,921,220
SIC 3569 General industrial machinery, nec

D-U-N-S 20-577-8087   (SL)
HOWARD, R. A. BUS SERVICE LIMITED
31 Henry St, Athens, ON, K0E 1B0
(613) 924-2720
Emp Here 75   *Sales* 2,115,860
SIC 4151 School buses

D-U-N-S 20-033-1783   (HQ)
TACKABERRY, G & SONS CONSTRUCTION COMPANY LIMITED
SWEET SAND & GRAVEL
(*Suby of* 528561 Ontario Limited)
109 Washburn Rd, Athens, ON, K0E 1B0
(613) 924-2634
Emp Here 20   *Emp Total* 200
Sales 5,836,856
SIC 1611 Highway and street construction
Pr Pr George Tackaberry
Treas June Knapp

D-U-N-S 20-889-8486   (BR)
UNITED COUNTIES OF LEEDS AND GRENVILLE
MAPLE VIEW LODGE
746 County Rd 42, Athens, ON, K0E 1B0
(613) 924-2696
Emp Here 85
SIC 8361 Residential care

D-U-N-S 25-263-5289   (BR)
UPPER CANADA DISTRICT SCHOOL BOARD, THE
PINEVIEW PUBLIC SCHOOL
(*Suby of* Upper Canada District School Board, The)
8 George St, Athens, ON, K0E 1B0
(613) 924-2055
Emp Here 30
SIC 8211 Elementary and secondary schools

D-U-N-S 25-263-5396   (BR)
UPPER CANADA DISTRICT SCHOOL BOARD, THE
ATHENS DISTRICT HIGH SCHOOL
(*Suby of* Upper Canada District School Board, The)
21 Church St, Athens, ON, K0E 1B0
(613) 924-2618
Emp Here 45
SIC 8211 Elementary and secondary schools

Atikokan, ON P0T
Rainy River County

D-U-N-S 24-676-3044   (BR)
NORTHWEST CATHOLIC DISTRICT SCHOOL BOARD, THE
ST PATRICK'S SCHOOL
160 Hemlock Ave, Atikokan, ON, P0T 1C1
(807) 597-2633
Emp Here 25
SIC 8211 Elementary and secondary schools

D-U-N-S 20-106-4388   (BR)
ONTARIO POWER GENERATION INC
Hwy 622, Atikokan, ON, P0T 1C1
(807) 597-1110
Emp Here 96
SIC 4911 Electric services

D-U-N-S 20-133-7115   (BR)
RAINY RIVER DISTRICT SCHOOL BOARD
NORTH STAR COMMUNITY SCHOOL
209 Hawthorne Rd, Atikokan, ON, P0T 1C1
(807) 597-6640
Emp Here 25
SIC 8211 Elementary and secondary schools

D-U-N-S 20-068-3915   (BR)
RAINY RIVER DISTRICT SCHOOL BOARD

ATIKOKAN HIGH SCHOOL
324 Mercury Ave, Atikokan, ON, P0T 1C1
(807) 597-2703
Emp Here 40
SIC 8211 Elementary and secondary schools

Attawapiskat, ON P0L
Kenora County

D-U-N-S 25-901-4058   (SL)
ATTAWAPISKAT FIRST NATION EDUCATION AUTHORITY
J. R. NAKOGEE SCHOOL
91a Reserve, Attawapiskat, ON, P0L 1A0
(705) 997-2114
Emp Here 70   *Sales* 4,669,485
SIC 8211 Elementary and secondary schools

D-U-N-S 20-064-2184   (BR)
JAMES BAY GENERAL HOSPITAL
3 Riverside Dr, Attawapiskat, ON, P0L 1A0
(705) 997-2150
Emp Here 40
SIC 8062 General medical and surgical hospitals

Atwood, ON N0G
Perth County

D-U-N-S 20-647-2438   (BR)
AVON MAITLAND DISTRICT SCHOOL BOARD
ELMA TOWNSHIP PUBLIC SCHOOL
5972 Line 72, Atwood, ON, N0G 1B0
(519) 356-2241
Emp Here 40
SIC 8211 Elementary and secondary schools

Aurora, ON L4G
York County

D-U-N-S 24-360-6097   (SL)
AEROQUEST LIMITED
AEROQUEST SURVEYS
245 Industrial Pky N, Aurora, ON, L4G 4C4
(905) 672-9129
Emp Here 20   *Sales* 3,429,153
SIC 8713 Surveying services

D-U-N-S 20-549-9643   (SL)
ANDREWS MAILING SERVICE LTD
226 Industrial Pky N Unit 7, Aurora, ON, L4G 4C3
(905) 503-1700
Emp Here 50   *Sales* 2,553,625
SIC 7331 Direct mail advertising services

D-U-N-S 24-858-3226   (BR)
ANNEX PUBLISHING & PRINTING INC
222 Edward St, Aurora, ON, L4G 1W6
(905) 727-0077
Emp Here 38
SIC 2721 Periodicals

D-U-N-S 25-296-9357   (BR)
BANK OF NOVA SCOTIA, THE
SCOTIABANK
14720 Yonge St, Aurora, ON, L4G 7H8
(905) 727-1307
Emp Here 30
SIC 6021 National commercial banks

D-U-N-S 25-001-8041   (BR)
BANK OF MONTREAL
BMO
15252 Yonge St, Aurora, ON, L4G 1N4
(905) 727-4228
Emp Here 20
SIC 6021 National commercial banks

D-U-N-S 24-872-8867   (SL)
BARFITT BROS. HARDWARE (AURORA) LTD
AURORA HOME HARDWARE & BUILDING CENTRE
289 Wellington St E, Aurora, ON, L4G 6H6
(905) 727-4751
Emp Here 50   *Sales* 4,815,406
SIC 5251 Hardware stores

D-U-N-S 20-880-3627   (SL)
BLUE HILLS ACADEMY
BLUE HILLS CHILD & FAMILY CENTRE
402 Bloomington Rd, Aurora, ON, L4G 0L9
(905) 773-4323
Emp Here 70   *Sales* 4,596,524
SIC 8093 Specialty outpatient clinics, nec

D-U-N-S 20-537-2233   (BR)
CANADA POST CORPORATION
AURORA STN MAIN PO
20 Wellington St E, Aurora, ON, L4G 1H5

Emp Here 40
SIC 4311 U.s. postal service

D-U-N-S 20-918-9013   (SL)
CANADIAN LAWYER MAGAZINE INC
240 Edward St, Aurora, ON, L4G 3S9
(905) 841-6480
Emp Here 40   *Sales* 5,717,257
SIC 5192 Books, periodicals, and newspapers

D-U-N-S 20-081-3710   (BR)
CANADIAN MENTAL HEALTH ASSOCIATION, YORK REGION BRANCH
CMHA
15150 Yonge St Suite 3a, Aurora, ON, L4G 1M2

Emp Here 32
SIC 8093 Specialty outpatient clinics, nec

D-U-N-S 24-776-6640   (BR)
CHARTWELL MASTER CARE LP
15055 Yonge St, Aurora, ON, L4G 6T4
(905) 727-2952
Emp Here 50
SIC 8322 Individual and family services

D-U-N-S 24-776-6632   (BR)
CHARTWELL MASTER CARE LP
CHARTWELL AURORA LONG TERM CARE RESIDENCE
32 Mill St, Aurora, ON, L4G 2R9
(905) 727-1939
Emp Here 49
SIC 8322 Individual and family services

D-U-N-S 24-345-7152   (BR)
CHARTWELL SENIORS HOUSING REAL ESTATE INVESTMENT TRUST
32 Mill St, Aurora, ON, L4G 2R9
(905) 727-1939
Emp Here 260
SIC 8051 Skilled nursing care facilities

D-U-N-S 25-885-0569   (BR)
CHARTWELL SENIORS HOUSING REAL ESTATE INVESTMENT TRUST
KINGSWAY ARMS AURORA RETIREMENT RESIDENCE
145 Murray Dr, Aurora, ON, L4G 2C7
(905) 841-2777
Emp Here 20
SIC 6513 Apartment building operators

D-U-N-S 20-289-9352   (BR)
CONSEIL SCOLAIRE DE DISTRICT CATHOLIQUE CENTRE-SUD
ECOLE SAINT-JEAN
90 Walton Dr, Aurora, ON, L4G 3K4
(905) 727-0131
Emp Here 34
SIC 8211 Elementary and secondary schools

D-U-N-S 20-711-7420   (BR)
CONSEIL SCOLAIRE DE DISTRICT

CATHOLIQUE CENTRE-SUD
ECOLE ELEMENTAIRE CATHOLIQUE RENAISSANCE
700 Bloomington Rd, Aurora, ON, L4G 0E1
(905) 727-4631
Emp Here 50
SIC 8211 Elementary and secondary schools

D-U-N-S 25-885-2664   (BR)
CORPORATION OF THE TOWN OF AURORA, THE
LEISURE COMPLEX
135 Industrial Pky N, Aurora, ON, L4G 4C4
(905) 841-7529
Emp Here 75
SIC 7999 Amusement and recreation, nec

D-U-N-S 25-280-0636   (BR)
COUTTS, WILLIAM E. COMPANY, LIMITED
HALLMARK CARDS
(*Suby of* Hallmark Cards, Incorporated)
100 Vandorf Sideroad, Aurora, ON, L4G 3G9

Emp Here 100
SIC 5947 Gift, novelty, and souvenir shop

D-U-N-S 24-573-2990   (BR)
DOLLARAMA S.E.C.
DOLLARAMA
15260 Yonge St, Aurora, ON, L4G 1N4
(905) 751-0517
Emp Here 20
SIC 5999 Miscellaneous retail stores, nec

D-U-N-S 24-391-5647   (BR)
GOLF TOWN LIMITED
GOLF TOWN
52 First Commerce Dr Unit 1, Aurora, ON, L4G 0H5
(905) 841-0191
Emp Here 35
SIC 5941 Sporting goods and bicycle shops

D-U-N-S 25-354-3524   (BR)
GREAT PACIFIC ENTERPRISES LIMITED PARTNERSHIP
GENPAK DIV OF
325 Industrial Pky S, Aurora, ON, L4G 3V8
(905) 727-0121
Emp Here 200
SIC 3081 Unsupported plastics film and sheet

D-U-N-S 20-402-0317   (SL)
HOLLISTER LIMITED
(*Suby of* Hollister Incorporated)
95 Mary St, Aurora, ON, L4G 1G3
(905) 727-4344
Emp Here 40   *Sales* 5,836,856
SIC 5047 Medical and hospital equipment
Pr Scott Holloway

D-U-N-S 20-514-3386   (BR)
HOME DEPOT OF CANADA INC
HOME DEPOT
(*Suby of* The Home Depot Inc)
15360 Bayview Ave, Aurora, ON, L4G 7J1
(905) 726-4500
Emp Here 180
SIC 5251 Hardware stores

D-U-N-S 20-707-4365   (BR)
INNOVATION, SCIENCE AND ECONOMIC DEVELOPMENT CANADA
INDUSTRY CANADA SPECTRUM MANAGEMENT
126 Wellington St W Suite 204, Aurora, ON, L4G 2N9
(905) 713-2096
Emp Here 20
SIC 8741 Management services

D-U-N-S 20-526-6414   (HQ)
IRWIN INDUSTRIAL AGENCIES LIMITED
(*Suby of* 899464 Ontario Limited)
205 Industrial Pkwy N Unit 2, Aurora, ON, L4G 4C4

---

(905) 889-9100
Emp Here 25   *Emp Total* 30
Sales 11,094,675
SIC 5065 Electronic parts and equipment, nec
Pr Pr Glenn Irwin

D-U-N-S 24-764-6565   (HQ)
KTI LIMITED
(*Suby* of KTI Limited)
33 Isaacson Cres, Aurora, ON, L4G 0A4
(905) 727-8807
Emp Here 25   *Emp Total* 28
Sales 6,973,235
SIC 5085 Industrial supplies
 Dean Iwai
VP VP Darryl Iwai
Dir Fin Steven Lovitsotto

D-U-N-S 25-033-8597   (HQ)
KERRY'S PLACE AUTISM SERVICES
(*Suby* of Kerry's Place Autism Services)
34 Berczy St Unit 190, Aurora, ON, L4G 1W9
(905) 841-6611
Emp Here 600   *Emp Total* 1,000
Sales 30,278,691
SIC 8399 Social services, nec
Pr Sue Vandevelde-Coke
 Deborah Compton

D-U-N-S 24-336-6676   (BR)
KINARK CHILD AND FAMILY SERVICES
24 Orchard Heights Blvd Suite 101a, Aurora,
ON, L4G 6T5
(905) 713-0700
Emp Here 40
SIC 8093 Specialty outpatient clinics, nec

D-U-N-S 24-197-9223   (BR)
LOBLAWS INC
REAL CANADIAN SUPERSTORE, THE
15900 Bayview Ave Suite 1, Aurora, ON, L4G
7Y3
(905) 726-9532
Emp Here 50
SIC 5411 Grocery stores

D-U-N-S 24-678-5831   (SL)
**MAGNA E-CAR SYSTEMS LIMITED PART-
NERSHIP**
375 Magna Dr, Aurora, ON, L4G 7L6
(905) 726-7300
Emp Here 25   *Sales* 10,365,619
SIC 3692 Primary batteries, dry and wet
 Sean Johns

D-U-N-S 24-550-2927   (BR)
MAGNA EXTERIORS INC
EXTERION
200 Industrial Pky N, Aurora, ON, L4G 4C3

Emp Here 300
SIC 3714 Motor vehicle parts and accessories

D-U-N-S 20-555-4632   (BR)
MAGNA INTERNATIONAL INC
*STRONACH CENTRE FOR INNOVATION,
DIV OF*
375 Magna Dr, Aurora, ON, L4G 7L6
(905) 726-7200
Emp Here 200
SIC 3714 Motor vehicle parts and accessories

D-U-N-S 25-398-7556   (BR)
MAGNA INTERNATIONAL INC
M I DEVELOPMENTS
455 Magna Dr, Aurora, ON, L4G 7A9
(905) 713-6322
Emp Here 30
SIC 6712 Bank holding companies

D-U-N-S 25-357-5757   (BR)
MAGNA POWERTRAIN INC
UNIMOTION GEAR
245 Edward St, Aurora, ON, L4G 3M7
(905) 713-0746
Emp Here 260
SIC 3714 Motor vehicle parts and accessories

D-U-N-S 25-253-1520   (BR)

MAGNA SEATING INC
CAM-SLIDE MANUFACTURING
455 Magna Dr, Aurora, ON, L4G 7A9
(905) 713-6050
Emp Here 500
SIC 3465 Automotive stampings

D-U-N-S 20-016-8115   (HQ)
MAGNA SEATING INC
INTEGRAM-WINDSOR, DIV OF
337 Magna Dr, Aurora, ON, L4G 7K1
(905) 726-2462
Emp Here 100   *Emp Total* 155,450
Sales 3,820,951,859
SIC 3714 Motor vehicle parts and accessories
Pr Patrick Mccann
 Siegfried Wolf

D-U-N-S 24-151-1430   (BR)
MARK'S WORK WEARHOUSE LTD
WORK WORLD
15380 Bayview Ave, Aurora, ON, L4G 7J1
(905) 713-2935
Emp Here 20
SIC 5611 Men's and boys' clothing stores

D-U-N-S 25-731-0581   (BR)
MASTERMIND LP
14872 Yonge St, Aurora, ON, L4G 1N2
(905) 841-9119
Emp Here 24
SIC 5999 Miscellaneous retail stores, nec

D-U-N-S 25-058-4398   (BR)
METRO ONTARIO INC
METRO 767
1 Henderson Dr Unit 1, Aurora, ON, L4G 4J7
(905) 727-0185
Emp Here 140
SIC 5411 Grocery stores

D-U-N-S 24-603-7048   (BR)
METROLAND MEDIA GROUP LTD
ERA BANNER NEWSPAPER, THE
250 Industrial Pky N, Aurora, ON, L4G 4C3

Emp Here 100
SIC 5963 Direct selling establishments

D-U-N-S 24-681-5679   (BR)
MILLER, P.G. ENTERPRISES LIMITED
MCDONALD'S
135 First Commerce Dr, Aurora, ON, L4G 0G2
(905) 841-5584
Emp Here 30
SIC 5812 Eating places

D-U-N-S 24-319-3117   (HQ)
NCI CANADA INC
(*Suby* of NCI Canada Inc)
66 Don Hillock Dr, Aurora, ON, L4G 0H6
(905) 727-5545
Emp Here 21   *Emp Total* 25
Sales 6,219,371
SIC 5085 Industrial supplies

D-U-N-S 20-971-4646   (BR)
NEWMARCO FOOD LIMITED
EASTSIDE MARIOS
15370 Bayview Ave, Aurora, ON, L4G 7J1
(905) 841-4065
Emp Here 40
SIC 5812 Eating places

D-U-N-S 24-242-1092   (BR)
OLAMETER INC
300 Industrial Pky S, Aurora, ON, L4G 3T9
(905) 841-1167
Emp Here 35
SIC 7389 Business services, nec

D-U-N-S 25-033-8761   (BR)
OMNI HEALTH CARE LTD
WILLOWS ESTATE NURSING HOME, THE
13837 Yonge St, Aurora, ON, L4G 0N9
(905) 727-0128
Emp Here 84
SIC 8051 Skilled nursing care facilities

D-U-N-S 24-985-4829   (SL)
**RENAISSANCE LEARNING OF CANADA
CO**
73 Industrial Pky N Suite 3, Aurora, ON, L4G
4C4
(905) 726-8110
Emp Here 37   *Sales* 3,724,879
SIC 7371 Custom computer programming services

D-U-N-S 25-702-7854   (SL)
**RICOH DOCUMENT MANAGEMENT LIM-
ITED PARTNERSHIP**
R. D. M.
205 Industrial Pky N Unit 2, Aurora, ON, L4G
4C4
(905) 841-8433
Emp Here 70   *Sales* 4,012,839
SIC 2731 Book publishing

D-U-N-S 20-875-4317   (HQ)
**SF INSURANCE PLACEMENT CORPORA-
TION OF CANADA**
STATE FARM INSURANCE
333 First Commerce Dr, Aurora, ON, L4G 8A4
(905) 750-4100
Emp Here 30   *Emp Total* 68,000
Sales 573,398,141
SIC 6331 Fire, marine, and casualty insurance
 Robert Cooke
Dir David Hill
Dir Barbara Kirchgasler
Dir Stan Ommen
Dir Dale Egeberg
Dir Russell Schopp

D-U-N-S 25-484-2396   (SL)
SAN MIGUEL FOODS LTD
SWISS CHALET HARVEY'S
1 Henderson Dr Unit 4, Aurora, ON, L4G 4J7
(905) 727-7918
Emp Here 250   *Sales* 10,349,440
SIC 5812 Eating places
Pr Pr Joe Anselmo Sr
 Mario Medeiros
Dir Joe Anselmo Jr

D-U-N-S 25-469-0787   (BR)
**SERVICE CORPORATION INTERNATIONAL
(CANADA) LIMITED**
THOMPSON FUNERAL HOME
530 Industrial Pky S, Aurora, ON, L4G 6W8
(905) 727-5421
Emp Here 20
SIC 7261 Funeral service and crematories

D-U-N-S 20-405-6808   (HQ)
SINCLAIR TECHNOLOGIES INC
85 Mary St, Aurora, ON, L4G 6X5
(905) 727-0165
Emp Here 65   *Emp Total* 6,754
Sales 13,852,236
SIC 3663 Radio and t.v. communications
equipment
Pr Calven Iwata
 Valerie Sinclair
 Andrea Sinclair

D-U-N-S 25-911-8685   (BR)
SOBEYS CAPITAL INCORPORATED
SOBEYS
15500 Bayview Ave, Aurora, ON, L4G 7J1
(905) 726-2530
Emp Here 150
SIC 5411 Grocery stores

D-U-N-S 20-553-3719   (BR)
STAPLES CANADA INC
STAPLES/BUSINESS DEPOT
(*Suby* of Staples, Inc.)
14800 Yonge St Unit 180, Aurora, ON, L4G
1N3
(905) 713-0367
Emp Here 30
SIC 5943 Stationery stores

D-U-N-S 25-253-9663   (SL)
STRATEGIC PACKAGING SOLUTIONS INC

38 Watts Meadow, Aurora, ON, L4G 7L7

Emp Here 25   *Sales* 5,595,120
SIC 2653 Corrugated and solid fiber boxes
Pr Pr Ted Bolak
 Zina Bolak
VP VP Mario Giachini

D-U-N-S 20-808-9073   (BR)
SUNRISE NORTH SENIOR LIVING LTD
SUNRISE OF AURORA
(*Suby* of Welltower Inc.)
3 Golf Links Dr Suite 2, Aurora, ON, L4G 7Y4
(905) 841-0022
Emp Here 100
SIC 8361 Residential care

D-U-N-S 25-120-2032   (BR)
TORONTO-DOMINION BANK, THE
TD BANK
(*Suby* of Toronto-Dominion Bank, The)
14845 Yonge St Suite 11, Aurora, ON, L4G
6H8
(905) 727-4123
Emp Here 25
SIC 6021 National commercial banks

D-U-N-S 25-319-2371   (BR)
TORONTO-DOMINION BANK, THE
TD BANK
(*Suby* of Toronto-Dominion Bank, The)
15255 Yonge St, Aurora, ON, L4G 1N5
(905) 727-2220
Emp Here 20
SIC 6021 National commercial banks

D-U-N-S 20-312-2577   (BR)
TRANSCONTINENTAL PRINTING INC
275 Wellington St E, Aurora, ON, L4G 6J9
(905) 841-4400
Emp Here 600
SIC 2752 Commercial printing, lithographic

D-U-N-S 24-417-8328   (SL)
ULLMAN, KEN ENTERPRISES INC
KUE PERSONAL CARE PRODUCTS
92 Kennedy St W, Aurora, ON, L4G 2L7
(905) 727-5677
Emp Here 100   *Sales* 2,042,900
SIC 2841 Soap and other detergents

D-U-N-S 24-364-4619   (BR)
VAN-ROB INC
95 Dunning Ave, Aurora, ON, L4G 3G8
(905) 727-8585
Emp Here 50
SIC 3465 Automotive stampings

D-U-N-S 24-359-1489   (BR)
WAL-MART CANADA CORP
135 First Commerce Dr, Aurora, ON, L4G 0G2
(905) 841-0300
Emp Here 75
SIC 5311 Department stores

D-U-N-S 20-184-2924   (BR)
**WINNERS MERCHANTS INTERNATIONAL
L.P.**
WINNERS
(*Suby* of The TJX Companies Inc)
14740 Yonge St, Aurora, ON, L4G 7H8
(905) 751-0378
Emp Here 40
SIC 5651 Family clothing stores

D-U-N-S 25-106-9407   (BR)
**YORK CATHOLIC DISTRICT SCHOOL
BOARD**
ST JOSEPH CATHOLIC SCHOOL
2 Glass Dr, Aurora, ON, L4G 2E8
(905) 727-5782
Emp Here 30
SIC 8211 Elementary and secondary schools

D-U-N-S 25-134-0691   (BR)
**YORK CATHOLIC DISTRICT SCHOOL
BOARD**
CARDINAL CARTER CATHOLIC HIGH

SCHOOL
210 Bloomington Rd Suite Side, Aurora, ON,
L4G 0P9
(905) 727-2455
Emp Here 145
SIC 8211 Elementary and secondary schools

D-U-N-S 24-525-4300   (BR)
YORK CATHOLIC DISTRICT SCHOOL BOARD
ST JEROME CATHOLIC ELEMENTARY SCHOOL
20 Bridgenorth Dr, Aurora, ON, L4G 7P3
(905) 727-6593
Emp Here 25
SIC 8211 Elementary and secondary schools

D-U-N-S 20-711-4591   (BR)
YORK CATHOLIC DISTRICT SCHOOL BOARD
HOLY SPIRIT CATHOLIC ELEMENTARY SCHOOL
315 Stone Rd, Aurora, ON, L4G 6Y7
(905) 713-6813
Emp Here 50
SIC 8211 Elementary and secondary schools

D-U-N-S 25-106-9324   (BR)
YORK CATHOLIC DISTRICT SCHOOL BOARD
LIGHT OF CHRIST ELEMENTARY SCHOOL
290 Mcclellan Way, Aurora, ON, L4G 6P3
(905) 841-7742
Emp Here 40
SIC 8211 Elementary and secondary schools

D-U-N-S 20-591-2319   (BR)
YORK REGION DISTRICT SCHOOL BOARD
AURORA SENIOR PUBLIC SCHOOL
(Suby of York Region District School Board)
125 Wellington St W, Aurora, ON, L4G 2P3
(905) 727-9751
Emp Here 25
SIC 8211 Elementary and secondary schools

D-U-N-S 20-711-3940   (BR)
YORK REGION DISTRICT SCHOOL BOARD
REGENCY ACRES PUBLIC SCHOOL
(Suby of York Region District School Board)
123 Murray Dr, Aurora, ON, L4G 2C7
(905) 727-9811
Emp Here 31
SIC 8211 Elementary and secondary schools

D-U-N-S 20-711-4294   (BR)
YORK REGION DISTRICT SCHOOL BOARD
AURORA GROVE PUBLIC SCHOOL
(Suby of York Region District School Board)
415 Stone Rd, Aurora, ON, L4G 6Z5
(905) 727-4435
Emp Here 60
SIC 8211 Elementary and secondary schools

D-U-N-S 20-591-2715   (BR)
YORK REGION DISTRICT SCHOOL BOARD
DEVINS DRIVE PUBLIC SCHOOL
(Suby of York Region District School Board)
70 Devins Dr, Aurora, ON, L4G 2Z4
(905) 727-2022
Emp Here 30
SIC 8211 Elementary and secondary schools

D-U-N-S 24-126-4063   (BR)
YORK REGION DISTRICT SCHOOL BOARD
LESTER B. PEARSON CHILDREN'S ACADEMY & KID'S CLUB
(Suby of York Region District School Board)
15 Odin Cres, Aurora, ON, L4G 3T3
(905) 727-0450
Emp Here 50
SIC 8211 Elementary and secondary schools

D-U-N-S 24-676-5163   (BR)
YORK REGION DISTRICT SCHOOL BOARD
HARTMAN PUBLIC SCHOOL
(Suby of York Region District School Board)
130 River Ridge Blvd, Aurora, ON, L4G 7T7

(905) 727-5938
Emp Here 50
SIC 8211 Elementary and secondary schools

D-U-N-S 20-568-0098   (BR)
YORK REGION DISTRICT SCHOOL BOARD
NORTHERN LIGHTS PUBLIC SCHOOL
(Suby of York Region District School Board)
40 Bridgenorth Dr, Aurora, ON, L4G 7S6
(905) 727-4224
Emp Here 45
SIC 8211 Elementary and secondary schools

D-U-N-S 20-939-9526   (HQ)
YORK REGION DISTRICT SCHOOL BOARD
(Suby of York Region District School Board)
60 Wellington St W, Aurora, ON, L4G 3H2
(905) 727-3141
Emp Here 200   *Emp Total* 15,000
Sales 1,259,112
SIC 8211 Elementary and secondary schools

D-U-N-S 25-293-6505   (BR)
YORK REGION DISTRICT SCHOOL BOARD
AURORA HEIGHTS PUBLIC SCHOOL
(Suby of York Region District School Board)
85 Tecumseh Dr, Aurora, ON, L4G 2X5
(905) 727-6902
Emp Here 40
SIC 8211 Elementary and secondary schools

D-U-N-S 20-711-4229   (BR)
YORK REGION DISTRICT SCHOOL BOARD
HIGHVIEW PUBLIC SCHOOL
(Suby of York Region District School Board)
240 Mcclellan Way, Aurora, ON, L4G 6N9
(905) 727-6642
Emp Here 50
SIC 8211 Elementary and secondary schools

Avonmore, ON K0C
Stormont County

D-U-N-S 20-893-9264   (SL)
DELANEY BUS LINES LTD
16935 County Rd 43, Avonmore, ON, K0C 1C0
(613) 346-2511
Emp Here 60   *Sales* 1,678,096
SIC 4151 School buses

D-U-N-S 20-711-5655   (BR)
UPPER CANADA DISTRICT SCHOOL BOARD, THE
TAGWI SECONDARY SCHOOL
16750 Hwy 43, Avonmore, ON, K0C 1C0
(613) 346-2122
Emp Here 50
SIC 8211 Elementary and secondary schools

Aylmer, ON N5H
Elgin County

D-U-N-S 24-345-4589   (SL)
BADDER GROUP INCORPORATED, THE
(Suby of Badder Bus Service Limited)
50 Progress Dr, Aylmer, ON, N5H 3J1
(519) 765-1100
Emp Here 70   *Sales* 1,969,939
SIC 4151 School buses

D-U-N-S 25-311-9820   (SL)
BROWNSVILLE HOLDINGS INC
Gd Lcd Main, Aylmer, ON, N5H 2R7
(519) 866-3446
Emp Here 50   *Sales* 5,909,817
SIC 6712 Bank holding companies
Pr Pr Patricia Perovich

D-U-N-S 24-426-2965   (SL)
CSH CHATEAU GARDENS AYLMER INC
465 Talbot St W, Aylmer, ON, N5H 1K8

(519) 773-3423
Emp Here 20   *Sales* 729,607
SIC 8361 Residential care

D-U-N-S 24-703-1164   (BR)
CORPORATION OF THE COUNTY OF EL-GIN
TERRACE LODGE HOME FOR THE AGED
475 Talbot St E, Aylmer, ON, N5H 3A5
(519) 773-9205
Emp Here 100
SIC 8361 Residential care

D-U-N-S 24-468-2238   (BR)
IMPERIAL TOBACCO LEAF INC
516 John St N, Aylmer, ON, N5H 0A6

Emp Here 49
SIC 2141 Tobacco stemming and redrying

D-U-N-S 24-317-7339   (BR)
INFORMATION COMMUNICATION SERVICES (ICS) INC
ICS COURIER
300 Talbot St W Suite 6, Aylmer, ON, N5H 1K2
(519) 773-1300
Emp Here 40
SIC 4212 Local trucking, without storage

D-U-N-S 20-697-9358   (BR)
LOBLAWS SUPERMARKETS LIMITED
NO FRILLS
657 John St N, Aylmer, ON, N5H 2R2
(519) 765-2811
Emp Here 100
SIC 5411 Grocery stores

D-U-N-S 25-753-2549   (BR)
LONDON DISTRICT CATHOLIC SCHOOL BOARD
ASSUMPTION CATHOLIC SCHOOL
42 South St E, Aylmer, ON, N5H 1P6
(519) 660-2770
Emp Here 25
SIC 8211 Elementary and secondary schools

D-U-N-S 25-658-2446   (SL)
MCKEEN RESTAURANT, THE
MCDONALD'S RESTAURANT
200 Talbot St W, Aylmer, ON, N5H 1K1
(519) 773-5377
Emp Here 20   *Sales* 1,532,175
SIC 5812 Eating places

D-U-N-S 20-691-5527   (SL)
PRECISION FAB INC
259 Elm St, Aylmer, ON, N5H 3H3
(519) 773-5244
Emp Here 50   *Sales* 5,472,053
SIC 3499 Fabricated Metal products, nec
Pr Pr Isaak Wall
Dir Albert Wiebe

D-U-N-S 20-565-9886   (SL)
REM-TECH INDUSTRIES INC
69 White St, Aylmer, ON, N5H 3G9
(519) 773-3459
Emp Here 50   *Sales* 4,672,543
SIC 3599 Industrial machinery, nec

D-U-N-S 20-128-5780   (SL)
TECUMSEH PRODUCTS OF CANADA, LIMITED
(Suby of Tecumseh Products Holdings LLC)
200 Elm St, Aylmer, ON, N5H 2M8
(519) 765-1556
Emp Here 45   *Sales* 8,244,559
SIC 5084 Industrial machinery and equipment
Pr Pr James Connor

D-U-N-S 20-837-3683   (BR)
THAMES VALLEY DISTRICT SCHOOL BOARD
SUMMERS CORNERS PUBLIC SCHOOL
50576 Talbot St E, Aylmer, ON, N5H 2R1
(519) 773-8106
Emp Here 35
SIC 8211 Elementary and secondary schools

D-U-N-S 20-554-0425   (BR)
THAMES VALLEY DISTRICT SCHOOL BOARD
EAST ELGIN SECONDARY SCHOOL
362 Talbot St W, Aylmer, ON, N5H 1K6
(519) 773-3174
Emp Here 100
SIC 8211 Elementary and secondary schools

D-U-N-S 20-655-1751   (BR)
THAMES VALLEY DISTRICT SCHOOL BOARD
DAVENPORT PUBLIC SCHOOL
80 Rutherford Ave, Aylmer, ON, N5H 2N8
(519) 773-9216
Emp Here 30
SIC 8211 Elementary and secondary schools

D-U-N-S 20-710-5474   (BR)
THAMES VALLEY DISTRICT SCHOOL BOARD
MCGREGOR PUBLIC SCHOOL
204 John St S, Aylmer, ON, N5H 2C8
(519) 773-3362
Emp Here 50
SIC 8211 Elementary and secondary schools

Ayr, ON N0B
Waterloo County

D-U-N-S 25-526-1489   (SL)
3447693 CANADA INC
15 Waydom Dr, Ayr, ON, N0B 1E0
(519) 623-5005
Emp Here 28   *Sales* 3,378,379
SIC 3089 Plastics products, nec

D-U-N-S 25-190-1625   (BR)
ADESA AUCTIONS CANADA CORPORATION
ADESA KITCHENER
55 Waydom Dr Suite 1, Ayr, ON, N0B 1E0
(519) 622-9500
Emp Here 100
SIC 5012 Automobiles and other motor vehicles

D-U-N-S 20-290-4624   (BR)
AGRATURF EQUIPMENT SERVICES INC
(Suby of Agraturf Equipment Services Inc)
3160 Alps Rd, Ayr, ON, N0B 1E0
(519) 632-8998
Emp Here 20
SIC 5999 Miscellaneous retail stores, nec

D-U-N-S 24-305-5936   (SL)
AYR FARMERS' MUTUAL INSURANCE COMPANY
1400 Northumberland St Rr 1, Ayr, ON, N0B 1E0
(519) 632-7413
Emp Here 26   *Sales* 19,723,939
SIC 6331 Fire, marine, and casualty insurance
Genl Mgr Donald Davidson
 David Paterson
Pr Pr Robert Gurney
VP VP Mike Murdoch
Dir Gordon Forth
Dir Les Leck
Dir Gerry Pullin
Dir Brian Sayles

D-U-N-S 25-673-4286   (BR)
BEND ALL AUTOMOTIVE INCORPORATED
PLANT 2
655 Waydom Dr, Ayr, ON, N0B 1E0
(519) 623-2002
Emp Here 300
SIC 2531 Public building and related furniture

D-U-N-S 25-193-8593   (BR)
BEND ALL AUTOMOTIVE INCORPORATED
PLANT # 4
115 Wanless Crt, Ayr, ON, N0B 1E0

(519) 623-2001
Emp Here 100
SIC 3671 Electron tubes

D-U-N-S 24-845-6030   (HQ)
BEND ALL AUTOMOTIVE INCORPORATED
575 Waydom Dr, Ayr, ON, N0B 1E0
(519) 623-2001
Emp Here 350   *Emp Total* 226
Sales 81,860,720
SIC 3499 Fabricated Metal products, nec
Pr Pr Alfred Napolitano
 Udo Petersen

D-U-N-S 24-513-7641   (SL)
CAMBRIDGE RIGGING CENTRAL LIMITED
60 Wanless Crt Suite 3, Ayr, ON, N0B 1E0
(519) 623-4000
Emp Here 50   *Sales* 3,939,878
SIC 4212 Local trucking, without storage

D-U-N-S 25-837-9106   (BR)
CANPAR TRANSPORT L.P.
(*Suby of* Canpar Transport L.P.)
120 Wanless Crt, Ayr, ON, N0B 1E0
(800) 387-9335
Emp Here 50
SIC 7389 Business services, nec

D-U-N-S 24-719-1950   (HQ)
DSM NUTRITIONAL PRODUCTS CANADA INC
395 Waydom Dr Suite 2, Ayr, ON, N0B 1E0
(519) 622-2200
Emp Here 20   *Emp Total* 20,627
Sales 3,638,254
SIC 5122 Drugs, proprietaries, and sundries

D-U-N-S 25-280-7789   (SL)
HERITAGE TRUCK LINES INC
105 Guthrie St, Ayr, ON, N0B 1E0
(519) 632-9052
Emp Here 60   *Sales* 7,369,031
SIC 4213 Trucking, except local
Pr Pr Steven Lowe

D-U-N-S 24-947-2937   (HQ)
J. & R. HALL TRANSPORT INC
552 Piper St, Ayr, ON, N0B 1E0
(519) 632-7429
Emp Here 116   *Emp Total* 122
Sales 23,369,759
SIC 4213 Trucking, except local
Pr Pr Jeffrey Hall
 Andrew Hall
 Lynn D'aguilar
Dir Robert Hall

D-U-N-S 24-370-4975   (BR)
LEHIGH HANSON MATERIALS LIMITED
380 Waydom Dr, Ayr, ON, N0B 1E0
(519) 621-4790
Emp Here 40
SIC 3272 Concrete products, nec

D-U-N-S 24-358-1514   (BR)
MAMMOET CRANE INC
127 Earl Thompson Rd, Ayr, ON, N0B 1E0
(450) 923-9706
Emp Here 20
SIC 7389 Business services, nec

D-U-N-S 25-411-7591   (BR)
MAPLE LEAF FOODS INC
180 Northumberland St, Ayr, ON, N0B 1E0
(519) 632-7416
Emp Here 160
SIC 2013 Sausages and other prepared meats

D-U-N-S 25-409-8528   (BR)
MARTIN SPROCKET & GEAR CANADA INC
(*Suby of* Martin Sprocket & Gear, Inc.)
320 Darrell Dr Suite 1, Ayr, ON, N0B 1E0
(519) 621-0546
Emp Here 40
SIC 5085 Industrial supplies

D-U-N-S 24-953-8877   (BR)

NIAGARA GRAIN & FEED (1984) LIMITED
AYR FEED & SUPPLY
143 Northumberland St, Ayr, ON, N0B 1E0
(519) 632-7425
Emp Here 25
SIC 2048 Prepared feeds, nec

D-U-N-S 24-451-3420   (SL)
PATCO EQUIPMENT INC
PATCO TRANSPORTATION
7 Cochran Dr Suite 1, Ayr, ON, N0B 1E0
(519) 622-2430
Emp Here 45   *Sales* 5,326,131
SIC 4213 Trucking, except local
Pr Pr Brad Lichty

D-U-N-S 24-023-3515   (BR)
PETERBILT OF ONTARIO INC
PETERBILT OF WATERLOO
7 Cochran Dr Suite 97, Ayr, ON, N0B 1E0
(519) 622-7799
Emp Here 25
SIC 5511 New and used car dealers

D-U-N-S 25-369-6272   (SL)
PRIMEMAX ENERGY INC
(*Suby of* Ayrline Holdings Inc)
2558 Cedar Creek Rd Suite 1, Ayr, ON, N0B 1E0
(519) 740-8209
Emp Here 60   *Sales* 10,459,852
SIC 5984 Liquefied petroleum gas dealers
Pr Michael Taylor

D-U-N-S 25-320-4218   (BR)
RUSSELL A. FARROW LIMITED
CANADIAN BROKERS
(*Suby of* Farrow Group Inc)
106 Earl Thompson Rd, Ayr, ON, N0B 1E0
(519) 740-9866
Emp Here 125
SIC 4731 Freight transportation arrangement

D-U-N-S 25-252-3209   (BR)
SEMPLE-GOODER ROOFING CORPORATION
309 Darrell Dr, Ayr, ON, N0B 1E0
(519) 623-3300
Emp Here 200
SIC 1761 Roofing, siding, and sheetMetal work

D-U-N-S 25-194-3106   (BR)
UNILOCK LTD
2977 Cedar Creek Rd, Ayr, ON, N0B 1E0
(519) 632-8660
Emp Here 20
SIC 3272 Concrete products, nec

D-U-N-S 20-710-7504   (BR)
WATERLOO CATHOLIC DISTRICT SCHOOL BOARD
ST BRIGID CATHOLIC ELEMENTARY SCHOOL
50 Broom St, Ayr, ON, N0B 1E0
(519) 632-5101
Emp Here 21
SIC 8211 Elementary and secondary schools

D-U-N-S 20-967-9948   (BR)
WATERLOO CATHOLIC DISTRICT SCHOOL BOARD
ST BRIGID SCHOOL
50 Broom St, Ayr, ON, N0B 1E0
(519) 632-5131
Emp Here 25
SIC 8211 Elementary and secondary schools

D-U-N-S 20-591-4695   (BR)
WATERLOO REGION DISTRICT SCHOOL BOARD
CEDAR CREEK PUBLIC SCHOOL
55 Hilltop Dr, Ayr, ON, N0B 1E0
(519) 632-5255
Emp Here 47
SIC 8211 Elementary and secondary schools

Ayton, ON N0G
Grey County

D-U-N-S 25-238-9010   (BR)
BLUEWATER DISTRICT SCHOOL BOARD
NORMANBY COMMUNITY SCHOOL
574 Louisa St, Ayton, ON, N0G 1C0
(519) 665-7783
Emp Here 20
SIC 8211 Elementary and secondary schools

Azilda, ON P0M
Sudbury County

D-U-N-S 25-239-0828   (BR)
CONSEIL SCOLAIRE DE DISTRICT CATHOLIQUE DU NOUVEL-ONTARIO, LE
ECOLE STE MARIE
25 Marier St, Azilda, ON, P0M 1B0
(705) 983-4254
Emp Here 30
SIC 8211 Elementary and secondary schools

Baden, ON N3A
Waterloo County

D-U-N-S 24-039-4564   (BR)
CORPORATION OF THE TOWN OF GRIMSBY
(*Suby of* Corporation Of The Town Of Grimsby)
162 Livingston Blvd, Baden, ON, N3A 4K9
(905) 945-1288
Emp Here 20
SIC 8322 Individual and family services

D-U-N-S 24-827-0162   (BR)
ERB TRANSPORT LIMITED
ERB TRANSPORT LIMITED
1473 Gingerich Rd, Baden, ON, N3A 3J7
(519) 634-8080
Emp Here 50
SIC 4212 Local trucking, without storage

D-U-N-S 20-033-6998   (BR)
MASTERFEEDS INC
76 Mill St, Baden, ON, N3A 2N6
(519) 634-5474
Emp Here 22
SIC 2048 Prepared feeds, nec

D-U-N-S 24-525-4276   (BR)
WATERLOO REGION DISTRICT SCHOOL BOARD
BADEN PUBLIC SCHOOL
155 Livingston Blvd, Baden, ON, N3A 4M6
(519) 634-9320
Emp Here 25
SIC 8211 Elementary and secondary schools

D-U-N-S 25-228-1647   (BR)
WATERLOO REGION DISTRICT SCHOOL BOARD
WATERLOO OXFORD DISTRICT SECONDARY SCHOOL
1206 Snyder'S Rd W, Baden, ON, N3A 1A4
(519) 634-5441
Emp Here 90
SIC 8211 Elementary and secondary schools

Bailieboro, ON K0L
Peterborough County

D-U-N-S 20-141-0958   (SL)
BUCKHAM TRANSPORT LIMITED

Hwy 28, Bailieboro, ON, K0L 1B0
(705) 939-6311
Emp Here 65   *Sales* 11,052,800
SIC 4213 Trucking, except local
Pr Pr Cathrine Buckham
VP Jason Hedges
 Leanore Buckham

Balmertown, ON P0V
Kenora County

D-U-N-S 24-676-8175   (BR)
GOLDCORP INC
RED LAKE GOLD MINES
17 Mine Rd Bag 2000, Balmertown, ON, P0V 1C0
(807) 735-2077
Emp Here 50
SIC 1041 Gold ores

D-U-N-S 25-265-1278   (BR)
KEEWATIN PATRICIA DISTRICT SCHOOL BOARD
GOLDEN LEARNING CENTRE
Gd, Balmertown, ON, P0V 1C0
(807) 735-2088
Emp Here 30
SIC 8211 Elementary and secondary schools

Baltimore, ON K0K

D-U-N-S 25-237-9912   (BR)
KAWARTHA PINE RIDGE DISTRICT SCHOOL BOARD
BALTIMORE ELEMENTARY SCHOOL
9320 Burwash Rd, Baltimore, ON, K0K 1C0
(905) 372-2431
Emp Here 20
SIC 8211 Elementary and secondary schools

Bancroft, ON K0L
Hastings County

D-U-N-S 20-590-7012   (BR)
ALGONQUIN & LAKESHORE CATHOLIC DISTRICT SCHOOL BOARD
OUR LADY OF MERCY CATHOLIC SCHOOL
192 Bridge St W, Bancroft, ON, K0L 1C0
(613) 332-3300
Emp Here 25
SIC 8211 Elementary and secondary schools

D-U-N-S 25-296-7427   (BR)
BANK OF NOVA SCOTIA, THE
SCOTIABANK
50 Hastings St N, Bancroft, ON, K0L 1C0
(613) 332-2040
Emp Here 21
SIC 6021 National commercial banks

D-U-N-S 25-893-9826   (BR)
CAMPBELL, JAMES INC
MCDONALD'S RESTAURANT
(*Suby of* Campbell, James Inc)
141 Hastings St N, Bancroft, ON, K0L 1C0
(613) 332-2029
Emp Here 35
SIC 5812 Eating places

D-U-N-S 20-629-4535   (SL)
EAGLE'S NEST COFFEE AND BAKED GOODS INC
TIM HORTONS
234 Hastings St N, Bancroft, ON, K0L 1C0
(613) 332-0299
Emp Here 80   *Sales* 2,407,703
SIC 5812 Eating places

D-U-N-S 20-552-0062   (BR)

EXTENDICARE (CANADA) INC
PARAMED HOME HEALTH CARE
5 Fairway Blvd Unit 10, Bancroft, ON, K0L 1C0
(613) 332-0590
Emp Here 40
SIC 8051 Skilled nursing care facilities

D-U-N-S 25-094-5941   (BR)
HALIBURTON BROADCASTING GROUP INC
CHMS
30674 Hwy 28 East, Bancroft, ON, K0L 1C0
(613) 332-1423
Emp Here 20
SIC 4832 Radio broadcasting stations

D-U-N-S 25-265-3399   (BR)
HASTINGS AND PRINCE EDWARD DISTRICT SCHOOL BOARD
YORK RIVER PUBLIC SCHOOL
132 Newkirk Blvd, Bancroft, ON, K0L 1C0
(613) 332-3000
Emp Here 45
SIC 8211 Elementary and secondary schools

D-U-N-S 25-265-3274   (BR)
HASTINGS AND PRINCE EDWARD DISTRICT SCHOOL BOARD
NORTH HASTINGS HIGH SCHOOL
16 Monck St Suite 14, Bancroft, ON, K0L 1C0
(613) 332-1220
Emp Here 75
SIC 8211 Elementary and secondary schools

D-U-N-S 25-265-3837   (BR)
HASTINGS AND PRINCE EDWARD DISTRICT SCHOOL BOARD
BIRDS CREEK PUBLIC SCHOOL
33 Baptist Lake Rd S, Bancroft, ON, K0L 1C0
(613) 332-3721
Emp Here 20
SIC 8211 Elementary and secondary schools

D-U-N-S 20-031-1541   (BR)
HASTINGS AND PRINCE EDWARD DISTRICT SCHOOL BOARD
NORTH HASTINGS SENIOR ELEMENTAY SCHOOL
132 Newkirk Blvd, Bancroft, ON, K0L 1C0
(613) 332-1833
Emp Here 21
SIC 8211 Elementary and secondary schools

D-U-N-S 20-922-1423   (SL)
HASTINGS CENTENNIAL MANOR
1 Manor Lane, Bancroft, ON, K0L 1C0
(613) 332-2070
Emp Here 118   *Sales* 5,928,320
SIC 8361 Residential care
Off Mgr Kathy Plunkett

D-U-N-S 24-345-2468   (BR)
HIGHLAND SHORES CHILDREN'S AID SOCIETY
16 Billa St, Bancroft, ON, K0L 1C0
(613) 332-2425
Emp Here 20
SIC 8322 Individual and family services

D-U-N-S 20-861-3120   (BR)
QUINTE HEALTHCARE CORPORATION
NORTH HASTINGS
1h Manor Lane, Bancroft, ON, K0L 1C0
(613) 332-2825
Emp Here 200
SIC 8069 Specialty hospitals, except psychiatric

D-U-N-S 24-156-0437   (BR)
SOBEYS CAPITAL INCORPORATED
FRESHCO
337 Hastings St N, Bancroft, ON, K0L 1C0
(613) 332-6664
Emp Here 40
SIC 5411 Grocery stores

D-U-N-S 24-201-7122   (BR)
WESTON BAKERIES LIMITED

MOISSON DOREE
Gd, Bancroft, ON, K0L 1C0
(613) 332-1122
Emp Here 50
SIC 2051 Bread, cake, and related products

Barrie, ON L4M
Simcoe County

D-U-N-S 25-359-4105   (SL)
1500451 ONTARIO LIMITED
JOE'S NO FRILLS
165 Wellington St E, Barrie, ON, L4M 2C7
(705) 737-0389
Emp Here 170   *Sales* 27,893,282
SIC 5411 Grocery stores
Pr Pr Joe Corsaro

D-U-N-S 24-689-3184   (BR)
2063414 ONTARIO LIMITED
SIENNA SENIOR LIVING
(*Suby of* 2063414 Ontario Limited)
130 Owen St, Barrie, ON, L4M 3H7
(705) 726-8621
Emp Here 70
SIC 8051 Skilled nursing care facilities

D-U-N-S 25-296-8227   (BR)
BANK OF NOVA SCOTIA, THE
SCOTIABANK
509 Bayfield St, Barrie, ON, L4M 4Z8
(705) 726-3690
Emp Here 23
SIC 6021 National commercial banks

D-U-N-S 20-779-7213   (BR)
BANK OF MONTREAL
BMO
509 Bayfield St Unit J016, Barrie, ON, L4M 4Z8
(705) 734-7930
Emp Here 20
SIC 6021 National commercial banks

D-U-N-S 20-589-4830   (BR)
BANQUE TORONTO-DOMINION, LA
TD CANADA TRUST
(*Suby of* Toronto-Dominion Bank, The)
320 Bayfield St, Barrie, ON, L4M 3C1
(705) 721-6005
Emp Here 20
SIC 6021 National commercial banks

D-U-N-S 24-117-5079   (BR)
BANQUE TORONTO-DOMINION, LA
TORONTO-DOMINION BANK, THE
(*Suby of* Toronto-Dominion Bank, The)
33 Collier St Suite Fl2, Barrie, ON, L4M 1G5
(705) 721-6001
Emp Here 25
SIC 6021 National commercial banks

D-U-N-S 25-255-8119   (SL)
BARRIE COMMUNITY HEALTH CENTRE
56 Bayfield St, Barrie, ON, L4M 3A5
(705) 734-9690
Emp Here 60   *Sales* 4,331,255
SIC 8011 Offices and clinics of medical doctors

D-U-N-S 25-134-7316   (SL)
BARRIE NATIONAL PINES GOLF & COUNTRY CLUB
Gd Stn Main, Barrie, ON, L4M 4S8
(705) 431-7000
Emp Here 75   *Sales* 3,551,629
SIC 7997 Membership sports and recreation clubs

D-U-N-S 20-964-7387   (SL)
BARRIE PUBLIC LIBRARY
60 Worsley St, Barrie, ON, L4M 1L6
(705) 728-1010
Emp Here 50   *Sales* 2,334,742
SIC 8231 Libraries

D-U-N-S 25-066-1543   (BR)
BEST BUY CANADA LTD
FUTURE SHOP
(*Suby of* Best Buy Co., Inc.)
411 Bayfield St Suite 1, Barrie, ON, L4M 6E5
(705) 727-4950
Emp Here 50
SIC 5731 Radio, television, and electronic stores

D-U-N-S 25-158-2631   (BR)
BOOTLEGGER CLOTHING INC
BOOTLEGGER
509 Bayfield St, Barrie, ON, L4M 4Z8
(705) 726-3630
Emp Here 20
SIC 5651 Family clothing stores

D-U-N-S 25-481-4825   (BR)
CADILLAC FAIRVIEW CORPORATION LIMITED, THE
RIOCAN GEORGIAN MALL
509 Bayfield St Suite K003, Barrie, ON, L4M 4Z8
(705) 726-9411
Emp Here 20
SIC 6512 Nonresidential building operators

D-U-N-S 25-303-2114   (BR)
CANADIAN IMPERIAL BANK OF COMMERCE
CIBC
46 Dunlop St E, Barrie, ON, L4M 1A3
(705) 728-2459
Emp Here 40
SIC 6021 National commercial banks

D-U-N-S 20-780-9067   (BR)
CANADIAN UNION OF POSTAL WORKERS
CUPW
109 Bayfield St Suite 303, Barrie, ON, L4M 3A9
(705) 722-3491
Emp Here 230
SIC 8742 Management consulting services

D-U-N-S 24-471-0539   (BR)
CARA OPERATIONS LIMITED
SWISS CHALET
(*Suby of* Cara Holdings Limited)
397 Bayfield St, Barrie, ON, L4M 3C5
(705) 737-5272
Emp Here 80
SIC 5812 Eating places

D-U-N-S 20-811-0366   (BR)
CARA OPERATIONS LIMITED
KELSEY'S RESTAURANT
(*Suby of* Cara Holdings Limited)
458 Bayfield St, Barrie, ON, L4M 5A2
(705) 735-6598
Emp Here 20
SIC 5812 Eating places

D-U-N-S 20-805-0398   (HQ)
CATULPA COMMUNITY SUPPORT SERVICES
CATULPA-COMMUNITY SUPPORT SERVICES
(*Suby of* Catulpa Community Support Services)
165 Ferris Lane, Barrie, ON, L4M 2Y1
(705) 733-3227
Emp Here 22   *Emp Total* 80
Sales 3,137,310
SIC 8322 Individual and family services

D-U-N-S 24-764-1541   (HQ)
CENTURY 21 B J ROTH REALTY LTD
CENTURY 21
(*Suby of* Century 21 B J Roth Realty Ltd)
355 Bayfield St Suite 5, Barrie, ON, L4M 3C3
(705) 721-9111
Emp Here 65   *Emp Total* 100
Sales 9,411,930
SIC 6531 Real estate agents and managers
Pr Pr Bernard Roth

D-U-N-S 25-293-5572   (BR)
CONSEIL SCOLAIRE DE DISTRICT CATHOLIQUE CENTRE-SUD
ECOLE ELEMENTAIRE CATHOLIQUE FRERE-ANDRE
273 Cundles Rd E, Barrie, ON, L4M 6L1
(705) 726-5525
Emp Here 40
SIC 8211 Elementary and secondary schools

D-U-N-S 20-813-9969   (BR)
CORPORATION OF THE CITY OF BARRIE, THE
WATER POLLUTION CONTROL CENTER
249 Bradford St, Barrie, ON, L4M 4T5
(705) 739-4221
Emp Here 42
SIC 8711 Engineering services

D-U-N-S 20-290-9441   (BR)
CORUS ENTERTAINMENT INC
CIQB-AM
1125 Bayfield St N, Barrie, ON, L4M 4Y6
(705) 726-9500
Emp Here 40
SIC 7922 Theatrical producers and services

D-U-N-S 25-915-4755   (BR)
CORUS ENTERTAINMENT INC
CHAY-FM
1125 Bayfield St N, Barrie, ON, L4M 4S5
(705) 737-3511
Emp Here 45
SIC 7922 Theatrical producers and services

D-U-N-S 20-936-2370   (BR)
DYNAPPLE MANAGEMENT CORP
APPLEBEE'S NEIGHBORHOOD GRILL & BAR
(*Suby of* Dynapple Management Corp)
326 Bayfield St, Barrie, ON, L4M 3B9
(705) 739-8597
Emp Here 30
SIC 5812 Eating places

D-U-N-S 24-337-2781   (BR)
FGL SPORTS LTD
NATIONAL SPORTS
353 Bayfield St, Barrie, ON, L4M 3C3
(705) 725-0434
Emp Here 25
SIC 5941 Sporting goods and bicycle shops

D-U-N-S 25-367-0210   (BR)
GOLDEN THEATRES LIMITED
BAYFIELD 7 CINEMAS
320 Bayfield St Suite 83, Barrie, ON, L4M 3C1
(705) 726-3456
Emp Here 26
SIC 7832 Motion picture theaters, except drive-in

D-U-N-S 25-464-5260   (BR)
GOVERNING COUNCIL OF THE SALVATION ARMY IN CANADA, THE
SALVATION ARMY BARRIE BAYSIDE MISSION CENTRE, THE
16 Bayfield St, Barrie, ON, L4M 3A4
(705) 728-3737
Emp Here 32
SIC 8322 Individual and family services

D-U-N-S 24-826-6074   (SL)
HORSESHOE VALLEY LIMITED PARTNERSHIP
1101 Horseshoe Valley Rd, Barrie, ON, L4M 4Y8
(705) 835-2790
Emp Here 280   *Sales* 16,490,880
SIC 7011 Hotels and motels
VP Fin Derek Carmichael
Martin Kimble

D-U-N-S 25-998-3419   (BR)
HUDSON'S BAY COMPANY
BAY, THE
465 Bayfield St, Barrie, ON, L4M 4Z9

(705) 726-2200
Emp Here 50
SIC 5311 Department stores

D-U-N-S 25-300-0558   (BR)
METRO ONTARIO INC
METRO
400 Bayfield St Suite 1, Barrie, ON, L4M 5A1
(705) 722-8284
Emp Here 120
SIC 5411 Grocery stores

D-U-N-S 24-154-0579   (SL)
MOXIE'S CLASSIC GRILL
509 Bayfield St, Barrie, ON, L4M 4Z8
(705) 733-5252
Emp Here 145   *Sales* 4,377,642
SIC 5812 Eating places

D-U-N-S 20-278-6930   (SL)
NAPOLEON HOME COMFORT BARRIE INC
24 Napoleon Rd, Barrie, ON, L4M 0G8
(705) 721-1214
Emp Here 500   *Sales* 49,849,204
SIC 5719 Miscellaneous homefurnishings
Pr Pr Wolfgang Schroeter
 Ingrid Schroeter
 Christopher Schroeter
 Stephen Schroeter

D-U-N-S 24-354-7887   (HQ)
**NEW PATH YOUTH & FAMILY COUN-
SELLING SERVICES OF SIMCOE COUNTY**
(*Suby of* New Path Youth & Family Coun-
selling Services Of Simcoe County)
165 Ferris Lane, Barrie, ON, L4M 2Y1
(705) 733-2654
Emp Here 40   *Emp Total* 100
Sales 3,939,878
SIC 8322 Individual and family services

D-U-N-S 24-197-9025   (BR)
OLD NAVY (CANADA) INC
OLD NAVY
(*Suby of* The Gap Inc)
468 Bayfield St, Barrie, ON, L4M 5A2
(705) 725-0067
Emp Here 50
SIC 5651 Family clothing stores

D-U-N-S 20-521-9699   (SL)
**ONTARIO PROVINCIAL POLICE ASSOCIA-
TION CREDIT UNION LIMITED**
OPPA CREDIT UNION
123 Ferris Lane, Barrie, ON, L4M 2Y1
(705) 726-5656
Emp Here 28   *Sales* 5,236,767
SIC 6062 State credit unions
Dir Bryan Neely
 Andrew Shannon
Mgr Debbie Sokoloskie
Crdt Mgr Karen Zammit
Mgr Laurie Dennis

D-U-N-S 24-120-6205   (BR)
PARTY CITY CANADA INC
(*Suby of* Party City Canada Inc)
400 Bayfield St Suite 53, Barrie, ON, L4M 5A1
(705) 719-7498
Emp Here 20
SIC 5947 Gift, novelty, and souvenir shop

D-U-N-S 25-979-9203   (BR)
PRISZM LP
KFC
315 Bayfield St, Barrie, ON, L4M 3C2
(705) 726-7220
Emp Here 20
SIC 5812 Eating places

D-U-N-S 25-156-3896   (BR)
RED LOBSTER HOSPITALITY LLC
RED LOBSTER RESTAURANTS
(*Suby of* Red Lobster Seafood Co., LLC)
319 Bayfield St, Barrie, ON, L4M 3C2
(705) 728-2401
Emp Here 75
SIC 5812 Eating places

D-U-N-S 20-715-6154   (BR)
ROGERS COMMUNICATIONS INC
(*Suby of* Rogers Communications Inc)
1 Sterling Dr, Barrie, ON, L4M 6B8
(705) 737-4660
Emp Here 50
SIC 1731 Electrical work

D-U-N-S 25-446-9125   (BR)
SECURITAS CANADA LIMITED
SECURITAS CANADA
400 Bayfield St Suite 215, Barrie, ON, L4M 5A1
(705) 728-7777
Emp Here 96
SIC 7381 Detective and armored car services

D-U-N-S 25-297-6360   (BR)
**SIMCOE COUNTY DISTRICT SCHOOL
BOARD, THE**
CUNDLES HEIGHTS PUBLIC SCHOOL
(*Suby of* Simcoe County District School
Board, The)
60 Cundles Rd E, Barrie, ON, L4M 2Z7
(705) 728-9658
Emp Here 48
SIC 8211 Elementary and secondary schools

D-U-N-S 25-297-6428   (BR)
**SIMCOE COUNTY DISTRICT SCHOOL
BOARD, THE**
BARRIE NORTH COLLEGIATE
(*Suby of* Simcoe County District School
Board, The)
110 Grove St E, Barrie, ON, L4M 2P3
(705) 726-6541
Emp Here 130
SIC 8211 Elementary and secondary schools

D-U-N-S 25-297-6386   (BR)
**SIMCOE COUNTY DISTRICT SCHOOL
BOARD, THE**
STEELE STREET PUBLIC SCHOOL
(*Suby of* Simcoe County District School
Board, The)
36 Steel St, Barrie, ON, L4M 2E7
(705) 728-9292
Emp Here 45
SIC 8211 Elementary and secondary schools

D-U-N-S 20-711-2124   (BR)
**SIMCOE COUNTY DISTRICT SCHOOL
BOARD, THE**
FOX, TERRY ELEMENTARY SCHOOL
(*Suby of* Simcoe County District School
Board, The)
100 Livingstone St E, Barrie, ON, L4M 6X9
(705) 727-4267
Emp Here 30
SIC 8211 Elementary and secondary schools

D-U-N-S 25-297-6451   (BR)
**SIMCOE COUNTY DISTRICT SCHOOL
BOARD, THE**
MAPLE GROVE PUBLIC SCHOOL
(*Suby of* Simcoe County District School
Board, The)
242 Grove St E, Barrie, ON, L4M 2P9
(705) 728-5201
Emp Here 35
SIC 8211 Elementary and secondary schools

D-U-N-S 25-294-4392   (BR)
**SIMCOE COUNTY DISTRICT SCHOOL
BOARD, THE**
OAKLEY PARK PUBLIC SCHOOL
(*Suby of* Simcoe County District School
Board, The)
22 Davidson St, Barrie, ON, L4M 3R8
(705) 728-3307
Emp Here 25
SIC 8211 Elementary and secondary schools

D-U-N-S 25-292-4857   (BR)
**SIMCOE COUNTY DISTRICT SCHOOL
BOARD, THE**
CODRINGTON PUBLIC SCHOOL
(*Suby of* Simcoe County District School

Board, The)
217 Codrington St, Barrie, ON, L4M 1S4
(705) 728-3084
Emp Here 25
SIC 8211 Elementary and secondary schools

D-U-N-S 25-294-4277   (BR)
**SIMCOE COUNTY DISTRICT SCHOOL
BOARD, THE**
JOHNSTON STREET PUBLIC SCHOOL
(*Suby of* Simcoe County District School
Board, The)
105 Johnson St, Barrie, ON, L4M 4R4
(705) 728-9251
Emp Here 20
SIC 8211 Elementary and secondary schools

D-U-N-S 24-676-2665   (BR)
**SIMCOE COUNTY DISTRICT SCHOOL
BOARD, THE**
*SAINT GABRIEL THE ARCHANGEL
CATHOLIC SCHOOL*
(*Suby of* Simcoe County District School
Board, The)
130 Prince William Way, Barrie, ON, L4M 7G4
(705) 797-8446
Emp Here 25
SIC 8211 Elementary and secondary schools

D-U-N-S 20-020-6477   (BR)
**SIMCOE COUNTY DISTRICT SCHOOL
BOARD, THE**
EASTVIEW SECONDARY SCHOOL
(*Suby of* Simcoe County District School
Board, The)
421 Grove St E, Barrie, ON, L4M 5S1
(705) 728-1321
Emp Here 150
SIC 8211 Elementary and secondary schools

D-U-N-S 25-293-5416   (BR)
**SIMCOE MUSKOKA CATHOLIC DISTRICT
SCHOOL BOARD**
CAREER CENTRE, THE
(*Suby of* Simcoe Muskoka Catholic District
School Board)
320 Bayfield St Suite 57, Barrie, ON, L4M 3C1
(705) 797-2020
Emp Here 30
SIC 8331 Job training and related services

D-U-N-S 24-918-6743   (HQ)
**SIMCOE MUSKOKA CATHOLIC DISTRICT
SCHOOL BOARD**
(*Suby of* Simcoe Muskoka Catholic District
School Board)
46 Alliance Blvd, Barrie, ON, L4M 5K3
(705) 722-3555
Emp Here 100   *Emp Total* 3,000
Sales 258,857,776
SIC 8211 Elementary and secondary schools
Dir Michael O'keefe
Dir Fin Peter Derochie

D-U-N-S 25-238-2601   (BR)
**SIMCOE MUSKOKA CATHOLIC DISTRICT
SCHOOL BOARD**
MONSIGNOR CLAIR SCHOOL
(*Suby of* Simcoe Muskoka Catholic District
School Board)
345 Livingstone St E, Barrie, ON, L4M 7B5
(705) 737-2812
Emp Here 40
SIC 8211 Elementary and secondary schools

D-U-N-S 25-293-5564   (BR)
**SIMCOE MUSKOKA CATHOLIC DISTRICT
SCHOOL BOARD**
ST JOSEPHS HIGH SCHOOL
(*Suby of* Simcoe Muskoka Catholic District
School Board)
243 Cundles Rd E, Barrie, ON, L4M 6L1
(705) 728-3120
Emp Here 80
SIC 8211 Elementary and secondary schools

D-U-N-S 20-711-2322   (BR)

**SIMCOE MUSKOKA CATHOLIC DISTRICT
SCHOOL BOARD**
SISTER CATHERINE DONNELLY SCHOOL
(*Suby of* Simcoe Muskoka Catholic District
School Board)
123 Hanmer St E, Barrie, ON, L4M 6W2
(705) 726-1221
Emp Here 50
SIC 8211 Elementary and secondary schools

D-U-N-S 20-711-2140   (BR)
**SIMCOE MUSKOKA CATHOLIC DISTRICT
SCHOOL BOARD**
ST MONICA'S CATHOLIC SCHOOL
(*Suby of* Simcoe Muskoka Catholic District
School Board)
90 Steel St, Barrie, ON, L4M 2E9
(705) 726-8221
Emp Here 40
SIC 8211 Elementary and secondary schools

D-U-N-S 25-296-9688   (BR)
SIMSAK CORPORATION
PETRO CANADA
341 Bayfield St, Barrie, ON, L4M 3C3
(705) 737-3488
Emp Here 20
SIC 5541 Gasoline service stations

D-U-N-S 25-309-1284   (BR)
SOBEYS CAPITAL INCORPORATED
SOBEYS 634
409 Bayfield St Suite C1, Barrie, ON, L4M 6E5
(705) 739-1100
Emp Here 120
SIC 5411 Grocery stores

D-U-N-S 20-804-5752   (BR)
SOBEYS CAPITAL INCORPORATED
FRESHCO
320 Bayfield St, Barrie, ON, L4M 3C1
(705) 734-6212
Emp Here 20
SIC 5411 Grocery stores

D-U-N-S 24-383-2826   (HQ)
SOURCE (BELL) ELECTRONICS INC, THE
SOURCE, THE
279 Bayview Dr, Barrie, ON, L4M 4W5
(705) 728-2262
Emp Here 372   *Emp Total* 48,090
Sales 291,842,800
SIC 5731 Radio, television, and electronic
stores
Pr Charles Brown
 Steven Boyack
Dir Wade Oosterman
Dir Siim Vanaselja
Dir Michael Cole
Dir George Cope
Dir Kevin Crull
Dir David Wells

D-U-N-S 25-279-3117   (BR)
TD WATERHOUSE CANADA INC
TD WATERHOUSE DISC BROKER
(*Suby of* Toronto-Dominion Bank, The)
33 Collier St, Barrie, ON, L4M 1G5
(705) 726-3353
Emp Here 20
SIC 6311 Life insurance

D-U-N-S 20-644-2753   (BR)
TORONTO-DOMINION BANK, THE
TD BANK
(*Suby of* Toronto-Dominion Bank, The)
534 Bayfield St, Barrie, ON, L4M 5A2
(705) 728-4878
Emp Here 40
SIC 6021 National commercial banks

D-U-N-S 25-166-6582   (BR)
WAL-MART CANADA CORP
450 Bayfield St, Barrie, ON, L4M 5A2
(705) 728-2833
Emp Here 200
SIC 5311 Department stores

D-U-N-S 20-184-3187   (BR)
WINNERS MERCHANTS INTERNATIONAL L.P.
HOMESENSE
(*Suby of* The TJX Companies Inc)
509 Bayfield St, Barrie, ON, L4M 4Z8
(705) 726-6663
Emp Here 40
SIC 5651 Family clothing stores

D-U-N-S 25-985-5773   (BR)
WINNERS MERCHANTS INTERNATIONAL L.P.
WINNERS
(*Suby of* The TJX Companies Inc)
320 Bayfield St, Barrie, ON, L4M 3C1
(705) 739-1200
Emp Here 30
SIC 5651 Family clothing stores

D-U-N-S 20-552-7497   (BR)
WOLF STEEL LTD
NAPOLECN FIREPLACES
9 Napoleon Rd, Barrie, ON, L4M 0G8
(705) 721-1212
Emp Here 350
SIC 3433 Heating equipment, except electric

Barrie, ON L4N
Simcoe County

D-U-N-S 25-214-7202   (SL)
1073849 ONTARIO LIMITED
TOLLOS
75 Dyment Rd, Barrie, ON, L4N 3H6
(705) 733-C022
Emp Here 55   *Sales* 4,888,367
SIC 3841 Surgical and medical instruments

D-U-N-S 20-178-0561   (SL)
1304003 ONTARIO LTD
PROFESSIONAL REHABILIATION OUT-REACH
80 Bradford St Suite 507, Barrie, ON, L4N 6S7
(705) 727-7888
Emp Here 55   *Sales* 2,626,585
SIC 8049 Offices of health practitioner

D-U-N-S 24-594-1112   (SL)
1381667 ONTARIO INC
AMJ CAMPBELL VAN LINES
64 Saunders Rd, Barrie, ON, L4N 9A8
(705) 721-4501
Emp Here 50   *Sales* 3,939,878
SIC 4212 Local trucking, without storage

D-U-N-S 24-335-7014   (SL)
1399731 ONTARIO INC
181 Big Bay Point Rd, Barrie, ON, L4N 8M5
(705) 722-9809
Emp Here 39   *Sales* 8,420,350
SIC 3443 Fabricated plate work (boiler shop)
Pr Pr Murray Hawman

D-U-N-S 24-863-3245   (SL)
1569243 ONTARIO INC
ROCK SOLID SUPPLY
316 Bayview Dr, Barrie, ON, L4N 8X9
(705) 719-4E70
Emp Here 45   *Sales* 5,107,249
SIC 5712 Furniture stores
Pr Pr Mike Brunelle

D-U-N-S 20-606-9486   (SL)
1894359 ONTARIO INC
455 Welham Rd, Barrie, ON, L4N 8Z6
(705) 726-5841
Emp Here 125   *Sales* 13,278,847
SIC 3569 General industrial machinery, nec
Pr Pr Saprapalli Ravalli
David Crook
Mauro Mozzato

D-U-N-S 25-354-2112   (SL)
2111964 ONTARIO INC

TIM HORTONS
350 Yonge St, Barrie, ON, L4N 4C8
(705) 739-9788
Emp Here 50   *Sales* 1,532,175
SIC 5812 Eating places

D-U-N-S 20-732-4257   (BR)
AMJ CAMPBELL INC
AMJ VAN LINES
20 Mills Rd Unit N, Barrie, ON, L4N 6H4
(705) 721-4501
Emp Here 37
SIC 4214 Local trucking with storage

D-U-N-S 24-986-0255   (SL)
ADVANCE TECH GRAPHICS INC
ADVANCE TECH
190 Nanette'S Point Rd Suite 315, Barrie, ON, L4N 8J8
(416) 315-4579
Emp Here 37   *Sales* 5,123,500
SIC 7336 Commercial art and graphic design
Pr Pr Joseph Santos

D-U-N-S 24-709-4170   (HQ)
ADVANCED MOTION & CONTROLS LTD
(*Suby of* Advanced Motion & Controls Ltd)
26 Saunders Rd, Barrie, ON, L4N 9A8
(705) 726-2260
Emp Here 35   *Emp Total* 41
Sales 6,784,769
SIC 5065 Electronic parts and equipment, nec
Pr Pr Mark Schick
Dir David Lawson

D-U-N-S 24-487-9300   (BR)
AECON CONSTRUCTION GROUP INC
AECON UTILITIES
40 Churchill Dr, Barrie, ON, L4N 8Z5
(705) 733-2543
Emp Here 56
SIC 1623 Water, sewer, and utility lines

D-U-N-S 24-684-6778   (SL)
ALLANDALE SCHOOL TRANSIT LIMITED
SIMCOE COUNTY AIRPORT SERVICES
137 Brock St, Barrie, ON, L4N 2M3
(705) 728-1148
Emp Here 130   *Sales* 3,648,035
SIC 4151 School buses

D-U-N-S 24-181-8244   (SL)
B & I TRUCK PARTS INC
COMPLETE SPRING & TRAILER SERVICE
480 Dunlop St W, Barrie, ON, L4N 9W5
(705) 737-3201
Emp Here 46   *Sales* 7,736,960
SIC 5531 Auto and home supply stores
Pr Pr Gary Inskeep
Heike Inskeep

D-U-N-S 24-184-8118   (BR)
BDO CANADA LLP
BDO CANADA
300 Lakeshore Dr Suite 300, Barrie, ON, L4N 0B4
(705) 726-6331
Emp Here 50
SIC 8721 Accounting, auditing, and book-keeping

D-U-N-S 25-087-6885   (BR)
BAD BOY FURNITURE WAREHOUSE LIMITED
LAST MAN BAD BOY
42 Caplan Ave, Barrie, ON, L4N 0M5
(705) 722-7132
Emp Here 20
SIC 5712 Furniture stores

D-U-N-S 20-004-5594   (BR)
BANK OF NOVA SCOTIA, THE
SCOTIA BANK
19 Mapleview Dr W, Barrie, ON, L4N 9H5
(705) 725-2670
Emp Here 20
SIC 6021 National commercial banks

D-U-N-S 25-296-7468   (BR)
BANK OF NOVA SCOTIA, THE
SCOTIABANK
190 Minet'S Point Rd, Barrie, ON, L4N 8J8
(705) 725-7320
Emp Here 20
SIC 6021 National commercial banks

D-U-N-S 25-296-8268   (BR)
BANK OF NOVA SCOTIA, THE
SCOTIABANK
1 Dunlop St W, Barrie, ON, L4N 1A1
(705) 726-0217
Emp Here 32
SIC 6021 National commercial banks

D-U-N-S 25-878-9619   (BR)
BARDON SUPPLIES LIMITED
(*Suby of* Entreprises Mirca Inc, Les)
500 Dunlop St W, Barrie, ON, L4N 9W5
(705) 722-9909
Emp Here 25
SIC 5074 Plumbing and heating equipment and supplies (hydronics)

D-U-N-S 25-063-9358   (SL)
BARRETT HIDES INC
75 Welham Rd, Barrie, ON, L4N 8Y3
(705) 734-9905
Emp Here 34   *Sales* 7,441,991
SIC 5159 Farm-product raw materials, nec
Pr Pr Jim Barrett

D-U-N-S 20-179-9926   (BR)
BARRIE WELDING & MACHINE (1974) LIMITED
BWM INDUSTRIAL AUTOMATION
136 Victoria St, Barrie, ON, L4N 2J4
(705) 734-1926
Emp Here 20
SIC 3569 General industrial machinery, nec

D-U-N-S 24-466-4194   (BR)
BELL MEDIA INC
CKVR-TV CHANNEL 3
33 Beacon Rd, Barrie, ON, L4N 9J9
(705) 734-3300
Emp Here 55
SIC 4833 Television broadcasting stations

D-U-N-S 25-501-1488   (BR)
BELL TECHNICAL SOLUTIONS INC
777 Bayview Dr Unit 1, Barrie, ON, L4N 9A5
(705) 737-1575
Emp Here 43
SIC 1731 Electrical work

D-U-N-S 25-807-2727   (BR)
BELRON CANADA INCORPOREE
SPEEDY GLASS
1 King St Unit 1, Barrie, ON, L4N 6B5
(705) 726-5711
Emp Here 55
SIC 7536 Automotive glass replacement shops

D-U-N-S 20-657-8820   (BR)
BREWERS RETAIL INC
BEER STORE, THE
30 Anne St S, Barrie, ON, L4N 2C6
(705) 728-4043
Emp Here 30
SIC 5921 Liquor stores

D-U-N-S 25-231-7060   (BR)
BRICK WAREHOUSE LP, THE
BRICK, THE
52 Caplan Ave, Barrie, ON, L4N 9J2
(705) 721-4106
Emp Here 40
SIC 5712 Furniture stores

D-U-N-S 20-864-7136   (BR)
BRIGAR ENTERPRISES INC
TIM HORTONS
3 Sarjeant Dr, Barrie, ON, L4N 4V9
(705) 739-4811
Emp Here 40

SIC 5812 Eating places

D-U-N-S 24-211-5061   (BR)
BRINK'S CANADA LIMITED
(*Suby of* The Brink's Company)
240 Bayview Dr Suite 4, Barrie, ON, L4N 4Y8
(705) 726-6720
Emp Here 73
SIC 7381 Detective and armored car services

D-U-N-S 20-063-2516   (BR)
CIBC WORLD MARKETS INC
CIBC WOOD GUNDY
126 Wellington St W Suite 100, Barrie, ON, L4N 1K9
(705) 728-6215
Emp Here 29
SIC 6211 Security brokers and dealers

D-U-N-S 20-085-3534   (SL)
CAMLANE GROUP INC, THE
10 Patterson Rd, Barrie, ON, L4N 5P4

Emp Here 40   *Sales* 6,492,800
SIC 4213 Trucking, except local
Pr Pr David Maclean
S&M/VP Troy Maclean

D-U-N-S 20-652-2190   (BR)
CANADA POST CORPORATION
BARRIE SORTATION PLANT
73 Morrow Rd, Barrie, ON, L4N 3V7
(705) 728-3592
Emp Here 250
SIC 4311 U.s. postal service

D-U-N-S 25-604-9727   (BR)
CANADIAN LINEN AND UNIFORM SERVICE CO
QUEBEC LINGE
(*Suby of* Ameripride Services, Inc.)
116 Victoria St, Barrie, ON, L4N 2J1
(705) 739-0573
Emp Here 100
SIC 7213 Linen supply

D-U-N-S 24-790-5354   (BR)
CANADIAN MENTAL HEALTH ASSOCIATION, SIMCOE COUNTY BRANCH
CMHA
151 Essa Rd Suite 202, Barrie, ON, L4N 3L2
(705) 725-5491
Emp Here 22
SIC 8093 Specialty outpatient clinics, nec

D-U-N-S 24-388-2040   (BR)
CANPAR TRANSPORT L.P.
CANPAR COURIER
(*Suby of* Canpar Transport L.P.)
168 John St, Barrie, ON, L4N 2L2
(705) 728-3335
Emp Here 25
SIC 7389 Business services, nec

D-U-N-S 20-101-3018   (HQ)
CANPLAS INDUSTRIES LTD
500 Veterans Dr Suite 1800, Barrie, ON, L4N 9J5
(705) 726-3361
Emp Here 200   *Emp Total* 40
Sales 40,453,922
SIC 3088 Plastics plumbing fixtures
Pr Pr Jeffrey D Bayley
Dir Paul Graddon
Dir David Temple
Dir Bruce Clark
VP Mfg Steve Thompson
VP VP Ron Marsden
Fin Ex James Renaud

D-U-N-S 20-788-8228   (BR)
CARA OPERATIONS LIMITED
HARVEY'S SWISS CHALET
(*Suby of* Cara Holdings Limited)
75 Barrie View Dr, Barrie, ON, L4N 8V4
(705) 733-0791
Emp Here 85
SIC 5812 Eating places

D-U-N-S 20-321-8276   (BR)
CARA OPERATIONS LIMITED
MILESTONE'S GRILL & BAR
(*Suby of* Cara Holdings Limited)
150 Park Place Blvd, Barrie, ON, L4N 6P1
(705) 722-7667
Emp Here 50
SIC 5812 Eating places

D-U-N-S 25-835-9041   (BR)
CARA OPERATIONS LIMITED
KELSEY'S RESTAURANT
(*Suby of* Cara Holdings Limited)
27 Mapleview Dr W, Barrie, ON, L4N 9H5
(705) 739-2220
Emp Here 30
SIC 5812 Eating places

D-U-N-S 20-039-3515   (BR)
CASCADES CANADA ULC
NORAMPAC- JELLCO, DIV OF
35 Fraser Crt, Barrie, ON, L4N 5J5
(705) 737-0470
Emp Here 44
SIC 2631 Paperboard mills

D-U-N-S 24-444-0058   (BR)
CENTURY 21 B J ROTH REALTY LTD
(*Suby of* Century 21 B J Roth Realty Ltd)
300 Lakeshore Dr Unit 100, Barrie, ON, L4N
0B4
(705) 737-3664
Emp Here 45
SIC 6531 Real estate agents and managers

D-U-N-S 25-165-5858   (BR)
CINEPLEX ODEON CORPORATION
GALAXY CINEMAS BARRIE
72 Commerce Park Dr, Barrie, ON, L4N 8W8
(705) 728-1171
Emp Here 20
SIC 7832 Motion picture theaters, except
drive-in

D-U-N-S 20-793-1499   (BR)
CO-OPERATORS GROUP LIMITED, THE
14 Cedar Pointe Dr Suite 1502, Barrie, ON,
L4N 5R7
(705) 739-7700
Emp Here 30
SIC 6411 Insurance agents, brokers, and ser-
vice

D-U-N-S 20-288-6073   (BR)
COBER PRINTING LIMITED
COBER EVOLVING SOLUTIONS
84 Saunders Rd, Barrie, ON, L4N 9A8
(705) 722-4437
Emp Here 50
SIC 2752 Commercial printing, lithographic

D-U-N-S 25-093-6080   (BR)
**COMPAGNIE DE TELEPHONE BELL DU
CANADA OU BELL CANADA, LA**
114 John St, Barrie, ON, L4N 2K9
(705) 722-2214
Emp Here 60
SIC 4899 Communication services, nec

D-U-N-S 20-797-8938   (BR)
**COMPAGNIE DE TELEPHONE BELL DU
CANADA OU BELL CANADA, LA**
40 Beacon Rd Suite 1, Barrie, ON, L4N 9J8
(705) 733-4187
Emp Here 50
SIC 4225 General warehousing and storage

D-U-N-S 25-293-5374   (BR)
**CONSEIL SCOLAIRE DE DISTRICT
CATHOLIQUE CENTRE-SUD**
*ECOLE ELEMENTAIRE CATHOLIQUE
NOUVELLE-ALLIANCE*
249 Anne St N, Barrie, ON, L4N 0B5
(705) 737-5260
Emp Here 50
SIC 8211 Elementary and secondary schools

D-U-N-S 25-238-2411   (BR)

D-U-N-S 20-026-7693   (BR)
**CORPORATION OF THE CITY OF BARRIE,
THE**
*BARRIE ALLANDALE RECREATION CEN-
TRE*
190 Bayview Dr, Barrie, ON, L4N 4Y8
(705) 728-5141
Emp Here 20
SIC 7999 Amusement and recreation, nec

D-U-N-S 24-369-9191   (BR)
COSTCO WHOLESALE CANADA LTD
COSTCO
(*Suby of* Costco Wholesale Corporation)
41 Mapleview Dr E, Barrie, ON, L4N 9A9
(705) 728-2350
Emp Here 250
SIC 5099 Durable goods, nec

D-U-N-S 25-852-3463   (BR)
DANA CANADA CORPORATION
120 Welham Rd, Barrie, ON, L4N 8Y4
(705) 737-2300
Emp Here 300
SIC 3714 Motor vehicle parts and accessories

D-U-N-S 20-735-7914   (SL)
DEL PHARMACEUTICS (CANADA) INC
316 Bayview Dr, Barrie, ON, L4N 8X9

Emp Here 68   *Sales* 8,480,961
SIC 2834 Pharmaceutical preparations
 Charlie Hinkaty
Pr Pr Dan Wassong

D-U-N-S 20-976-1217   (BR)
DONEX ENTERPRISES (BARRIE) INC
TIM HORTONS
109 Mapleview Dr W, Barrie, ON, L4N 9H7
(705) 735-3371
Emp Here 50
SIC 5812 Eating places

D-U-N-S 20-811-3006   (BR)
DONEX ENTERPRISES (BARRIE) INC
TIM HORTONS
13 Susan Pl, Barrie, ON, L4N 5P3
(705) 739-1375
Emp Here 20
SIC 5812 Eating places

D-U-N-S 24-193-6376   (BR)
DUCKS UNLIMITED CANADA
NATIVE PLANT SOLUTIONS
740 Huronia Rd Suite 1, Barrie, ON, L4N 6C6
(705) 721-4444
Emp Here 25
SIC 8641 Civic and social associations

D-U-N-S 24-886-4324   (SL)
DUNCOR ENTERPRISES INC
101 Big Bay Point Rd, Barrie, ON, L4N 8M5
(705) 730-1999
Emp Here 40   *Sales* 6,030,906
SIC 1611 Highway and street construction

D-U-N-S 20-958-0245   (BR)
ECL GROUP OF COMPANIES LTD
ECL TRANSPORTATION
400 Huronia Rd Unit 3, Barrie, ON, L4N 8Y9

Emp Here 30
SIC 4213 Trucking, except local

D-U-N-S 25-321-8697   (BR)
ERB TRANSPORT LIMITED
ERB TRANSPORT LIMITED
75 Ellis Dr, Barrie, ON, L4N 8Z3
(888) 875-0558
Emp Here 35
SIC 4212 Local trucking, without storage

D-U-N-S 20-355-1580   (BR)
EXP SERVICES INC
561 Bryne Dr, Barrie, ON, L4N 9Y3
(705) 734-6222
Emp Here 23
SIC 8711 Engineering services

D-U-N-S 20-588-9129   (BR)
**ECONOMICAL MUTUAL INSURANCE COM-
PANY**
ECONOMICAL INSURANCE
204 Pine Dr, Barrie, ON, L4N 4H5
(705) 722-3975
Emp Here 20
SIC 6331 Fire, marine, and casualty insurance

D-U-N-S 20-034-2558   (BR)
G&K SERVICES CANADA INC
(*Suby of* Cintas Corporation)
116 Big Bay Point Rd, Barrie, ON, L4N 9B4
(705) 728-5160
Emp Here 25
SIC 7299 Miscellaneous personal service

D-U-N-S 25-282-1459   (BR)
GARAGA INC
(*Suby of* Gestion 3MEI Inc)
333 Bayview Dr, Barrie, ON, L4N 8X9
(705) 733-1173
Emp Here 30
SIC 3442 Metal doors, sash, and trim

D-U-N-S 20-816-4178   (BR)
GEORGIAN CHEVROLET BUICK GMC INC
SOUTH BARRIE COLLISION CENTRE
72 Caplan Ave, Barrie, ON, L4N 9J2
(705) 733-3447
Emp Here 50
SIC 7532 Top and body repair and paint shops

D-U-N-S 20-644-7521   (BR)
GOLDEN ARCH FOOD SERVICES LTD
MCDONALDS
80 Barrie View Dr, Barrie, ON, L4N 8V4
(705) 735-1700
Emp Here 100
SIC 5812 Eating places

D-U-N-S 20-648-8517   (BR)
GOLDER ASSOCIATES LTD
121 Commerce Park Dr Unit L, Barrie, ON,
L4N 8X1
(705) 722-4492
Emp Here 20
SIC 8711 Engineering services

D-U-N-S 25-164-6451   (BR)
GOODLIFE FITNESS CENTRES INC
42 Commerce Park Dr, Barrie, ON, L4N 8W8
(705) 735-2226
Emp Here 40
SIC 7991 Physical fitness facilities

D-U-N-S 20-101-7873   (BR)
**GREYHOUND CANADA TRANSPORTA-
TION ULC**
PMCL
24 Maple Ave Unit 205, Barrie, ON, L4N 7W4

Emp Here 100
SIC 4131 Intercity and rural bus transportation

D-U-N-S 20-296-0498   (BR)
GROUPHEALTH GLOBAL PARTNERS INC
(*Suby of* GroupHEALTH Global Partners Inc)
556 Bryne Dr Suite 20, Barrie, ON, L4N 9P6
(705) 797-5142
Emp Here 30
SIC 8741 Management services

D-U-N-S 25-079-2314   (BR)
HOME DEPOT OF CANADA INC
HOME DEPOT
(*Suby of* The Home Depot Inc)
10 Barrie View Dr, Barrie, ON, L4N 8V4
(705) 733-2800
Emp Here 300
SIC 5251 Hardware stores

D-U-N-S 20-895-2171   (SL)
HOT BANANA SOFTWARE INC
12 Fairview Rd Suite 201, Barrie, ON, L4N
4P3

Emp Here 26   *Sales* 1,969,939
SIC 7372 Prepackaged software

D-U-N-S 20-698-7054   (BR)
HUDSON'S BAY COMPANY
HOME OUTFITTERS
436 Bryne Dr, Barrie, ON, L4N 9R1
(705) 734-0793
Emp Here 40
SIC 5311 Department stores

D-U-N-S 20-302-3119   (BR)
HYDRO ONE INC
45 Sarjeant Dr, Barrie, ON, L4N 4V9
(705) 728-5017
Emp Here 23
SIC 4911 Electric services

D-U-N-S 24-196-2091   (BR)
IDEAL SUPPLY COMPANY LIMITED
GLOBAL TOOLS
24 Cedar Pointe Dr, Barrie, ON, L4N 5R7
(705) 728-5662
Emp Here 24
SIC 5063 Electrical apparatus and equipment

D-U-N-S 20-303-8174   (BR)
INDIGO BOOKS & MUSIC INC
CHAPTERS
(*Suby of* Indigo Books & Music Inc)
76 Barrie View Dr, Barrie, ON, L4N 8V4
(705) 735-6735
Emp Here 30
SIC 5942 Book stores

D-U-N-S 20-582-1692   (BR)
**INFORMATION COMMUNICATION SER-
VICES (ICS) INC**
369 Huronia Rd, Barrie, ON, L4N 8Z1
(705) 725-1200
Emp Here 22
SIC 7389 Business services, nec

D-U-N-S 24-140-9960   (SL)
INJECTECH INDUSTRIES INC
690 Bayview Dr, Barrie, ON, L4N 9A6

Emp Here 350   *Sales* 75,857,485
SIC 3089 Plastics products, nec
Pr Pr Gert Walter

D-U-N-S 25-315-7424   (BR)
**INVESTORS GROUP FINANCIAL SER-
VICES INC**
128 Wellington St W Suite 103, Barrie, ON,
L4N 8J6
(705) 726-7836
Emp Here 25
SIC 8741 Management services

D-U-N-S 25-818-6873   (BR)
KINARK CHILD AND FAMILY SERVICES
34 Simcoe St Suite 3, Barrie, ON, L4N 6T4
(705) 726-8861
Emp Here 100
SIC 8322 Individual and family services

D-U-N-S 24-466-4210   (BR)
LAFARGE CANADA INC
LAFARGE BARRIE
275 Saunders Rd, Barrie, ON, L4N 9A3
(705) 734-3600
Emp Here 20
SIC 3273 Ready-mixed concrete

D-U-N-S 25-656-9708   (BR)
LAFARGE CANADA INC
701 Dunlop St W, Barrie, ON, L4N 9W9
(705) 726-6424
Emp Here 85
SIC 1611 Highway and street construction

D-U-N-S 25-088-6678   (BR)
LEON'S FURNITURE LIMITED

81 Bryne Dr, Barrie, ON, L4N 8V8
(705) 730-1777
Emp Here 80
SIC 5712 Furniture stores

D-U-N-S 20-819-0525   (BR)
LINK-LINE CONSTRUCTION LTD
10 Churchill Dr, Barrie, ON, L4N 8Z5
(705) 721-9284
Emp Here 100
SIC 1521 Single-family housing construction

D-U-N-S 25-317-9147   (BR)
LIQUOR CONTROL BOARD OF ONTARIO, THE
L.C.B.O.
37 Caplan Ave, Barrie, ON, L4N 6K3
(705) 726-6021
Emp Here 20
SIC 5921 Liquor stores

D-U-N-S 24-858-2186   (BR)
LOWE'S COMPANIES CANADA, ULC
71 Bryne Dr, Barrie, ON, L4N 8V8
(905) 952-2950
Emp Here 150
SIC 5211 Lumber and other building materials

D-U-N-S 25-163-6775   (BR)
M. A. T. ENTERPRISES INC
WENDY'S RESTAURANT
(*Suby of* M. A. T. Enterprises Inc)
411 Dunlop St W, Barrie, ON, L4N 1C3
(705) 735-6470
Emp Here 45
SIC 5812 Eating places

D-U-N-S 24-843-8376   (BR)
MARK'S WORK WEARHOUSE LTD
WORK WORLD
27 Caplan Ave, Barrie, ON, L4N 6K3
(705) 739-3512
Emp Here 20
SIC 5651 Family clothing stores

D-U-N-S 20-976-1282   (SL)
MARKET HOSPITALITY CORP
RETRO PLANET
141 Mapleview Dr W, Barrie, ON, L4N 9H7
(705) 726-9376
Emp Here 65   *Sales* 1,969,939
SIC 5812 Eating places

D-U-N-S 24-826-9102   (BR)
MCDONALD'S   RESTAURANTS   OF CANADA LIMITED
MCDONALD'S
(*Suby of* McDonald's Corporation)
201 Fairview Rd, Barrie, ON, L4N 9B1
(905) 823-8500
Emp Here 100
SIC 5812 Eating places

D-U-N-S 20-792-5301   (BR)
MCDONALD'S   RESTAURANTS   OF CANADA LIMITED
MCDONALD'S
(*Suby of* McDonald's Corporation)
85 Dunlop St W, Barrie, ON, L4N 1A5
(705) 726-6500
Emp Here 80
SIC 5812 Eating places

D-U-N-S 25-686-5635   (BR)
MICHAELS OF CANADA, ULC
(*Suby of* The Michaels Companies Inc)
33 Molson Park Dr E Unit 1, Barrie, ON, L4N 9A9
(705) 726-4474
Emp Here 30
SIC 5945 Hobby, toy, and game shops

D-U-N-S 24-189-9710   (SL)
MONTANA'S COOKHOUSE SALOON
66 Barrie View Dr, Barrie, ON, L4N 8V4
(705) 726-3375
Emp Here 75   *Sales* 2,261,782
SIC 5812 Eating places

D-U-N-S 24-099-5373   (HQ)
MOORE PACKAGING CORPORATION
191 John St, Barrie, ON, L4N 2L4
(705) 737-1023
Emp Here 200   *Emp Total* 2
Sales 44,178,801
SIC 2653 Corrugated and solid fiber boxes
 Peter Moore
Pr Daniel D Faber

D-U-N-S 25-170-8046   (HQ)
MUELLER CANADA LTD
MUELLER FLOW CONTROL, DIV OF
(*Suby of* Mueller Water Products, Inc.)
82 Hooper Rd, Barrie, ON, L4N 8Z9
(705) 719-9965
Emp Here 60   *Emp Total* 3,900
Sales 92,082,481
SIC 5085 Industrial supplies
Pr Greg Rogowski
 Frederick Welsh

D-U-N-S 25-501-7022   (BR)
NESTLE CANADA INC
NESTLE PROFESSIONAL VITALITY
28 Mollard Crt, Barrie, ON, L4N 8Y1
(705) 722-9049
Emp Here 58
SIC 2033 Canned fruits and specialties

D-U-N-S 25-162-9986   (SL)
NORTHERN   COMFORT   WINDOWS   & DOORS LTD
556 Bryne Dr Unit 7, Barrie, ON, L4N 9P6
(705) 733-9600
Emp Here 27   *Sales* 5,300,640
SIC 5211 Lumber and other building materials
Pr Pr Ernest Ebner

D-U-N-S 25-157-2277   (SL)
NORTHERN TAXI SUPPLY
37 Saunders Rd, Barrie, ON, L4N 9A7
(705) 739-7104
Emp Here 50   *Sales* 1,532,175
SIC 4121 Taxicabs

D-U-N-S 20-358-9387   (SL)
NUDURA INC
27 Hooper Rd Unit 10, Barrie, ON, L4N 9S3
(705) 726-9499
Emp Here 32   *Sales* 3,064,349
SIC 5999 Miscellaneous retail stores, nec

D-U-N-S 25-746-7506   (BR)
PETO MACCALLUM LTD
19 Churchill Dr, Barrie, ON, L4N 8Z5
(705) 734-3900
Emp Here 30
SIC 8711 Engineering services

D-U-N-S 20-178-8945   (SL)
POWDER TECH LIMITED
699 Bayview Dr, Barrie, ON, L4N 9A5
(705) 726-4580
Emp Here 50   *Sales* 3,502,114
SIC 3479 Metal coating and allied services

D-U-N-S 25-157-6666   (BR)
PRINCESS AUTO LTD
11 Commerce Park Dr, Barrie, ON, L4N 8X1
(705) 739-0575
Emp Here 25
SIC 5531 Auto and home supply stores

D-U-N-S 20-807-2319   (BR)
R & F CONSTRUCTION INC
112 Commerce Park Dr Unit K&L, Barrie, ON, L4N 8W8
(705) 325-5746
Emp Here 40
SIC 1521 Single-family housing construction

D-U-N-S 20-562-6976   (BR)
RBC DOMINION SECURITIES INC
(*Suby of* Royal Bank Of Canada)
11 Victoria St Suite 100, Barrie, ON, L4N 6T3
(705) 725-7400
Emp Here 28

SIC 6282 Investment advice

D-U-N-S 24-329-9638   (BR)
RJM56 INVESTMENTS INC
RJ MCCARTHY UNIFORMS
134 Anne St S, Barrie, ON, L4N 6A2
(416) 593-6900
Emp Here 20
SIC 5699 Miscellaneous apparel and accessory stores

D-U-N-S 20-887-6057   (BR)
RENFREW   COUNTY   DISTRICT   SCHOOL BOARD
TRILLIUM WOODS ELEMENTARY SCHOOL
20 Elmbrook Dr, Barrie, ON, L4N 0Z1
(705) 792-7766
Emp Here 25
SIC 8211 Elementary and secondary schools

D-U-N-S 24-676-2681   (BR)
RENFREW   COUNTY   DISTRICT   SCHOOL BOARD
HEWITT'S CREEK PUBLIC SCHOOL
41 Sandringham Dr, Barrie, ON, L4N 0J9
(705) 728-2774
Emp Here 25
SIC 8211 Elementary and secondary schools

D-U-N-S 20-003-3053   (BR)
ROYAL BANK OF CANADA
ROYAL BANK FINANCIAL GROUP
(*Suby of* Royal Bank Of Canada)
128 Wellington St W Suite 308, Barrie, ON, L4N 8J6
(705) 725-7800
Emp Here 30
SIC 6021 National commercial banks

D-U-N-S 20-026-7677   (SL)
ROYAL LE PAGE FIRST CONTACT REALTY
ROYAL LE PAGE
299 Lakeshore Dr, Barrie, ON, L4N 7Y9
(705) 727-6111
Emp Here 45   *Sales* 5,693,280
SIC 6531 Real estate agents and managers
Owner Barbara Giles

D-U-N-S 24-861-8795   (BR)
ROYCO HOTELS & RESORTS LTD
TRAVELODGE HOTEL
55 Hart Dr, Barrie, ON, L4N 5M3
(705) 734-9500
Emp Here 25
SIC 7011 Hotels and motels

D-U-N-S 25-542-8278   (HQ)
S.A.E. INVESTMENTS INC
(*Suby of* S.A.E. Investments Inc)
15 Sarjeant Dr, Barrie, ON, L4N 4V9
(705) 728-2460
Emp Here 100   *Emp Total* 150
Sales 80,025,600
SIC 5032 Brick, stone, and related material
Pr Pr Scott Elliott

D-U-N-S 20-614-4011   (BR)
SIR CORP
JACK ASTOR'S BAR AND GRILL
70 Mapleview Dr W, Barrie, ON, L4N 9H6
(705) 722-4737
Emp Here 50
SIC 5812 Eating places

D-U-N-S 20-609-2561   (HQ)
SARJEANT COMPANY LIMITED, THE
CUSTOM CONCRETE NORTHERN, DIV OF
15 Sarjeant Dr, Barrie, ON, L4N 4V9
(705) 728-2460
Emp Here 75   *Emp Total* 150
Sales 25,987,530
SIC 3273 Ready-mixed concrete
Pr Pr Scott Elliott
 John Elliott

D-U-N-S 20-270-0535   (BR)
SEARS CANADA INC
42 Caplan Ave Suite A, Barrie, ON, L4N 0M5

(705) 727-9287
Emp Here 34
SIC 5712 Furniture stores

D-U-N-S 24-822-1665   (SL)
SIMCOE COUNTY CLEANING LIMITED
SERVICE MASTER
49 Morrow Rd Unit 14, Barrie, ON, L4N 3V7
(705) 722-7203
Emp Here 75   *Sales* 2,188,821
SIC 7349 Building maintenance services, nec

D-U-N-S 25-297-6626   (BR)
SIMCOE   COUNTY   DISTRICT   SCHOOL BOARD, THE
ASSIKINACK PUBLIC SCHOOL
(*Suby of* Simcoe County District School Board, The)
226 Little Ave, Barrie, ON, L4N 6L3
(705) 726-4256
Emp Here 50
SIC 8211 Elementary and secondary schools

D-U-N-S 25-297-6055   (BR)
SIMCOE   COUNTY   DISTRICT   SCHOOL BOARD, THE
HILLCREST PUBLIC SCHOOL
(*Suby of* Simcoe County District School Board, The)
184 Toronto St, Barrie, ON, L4N 1V5
(705) 728-5246
Emp Here 45
SIC 8221 Colleges and universities

D-U-N-S 20-655-2080   (BR)
SIMCOE   COUNTY   DISTRICT   SCHOOL BOARD, THE
W C LITTLE ELEMENTARY SCHOOL
(*Suby of* Simcoe County District School Board, The)
11 Bear Creek Dr, Barrie, ON, L4N 9M9
(705) 725-7970
Emp Here 60
SIC 8211 Elementary and secondary schools

D-U-N-S 25-297-6220   (BR)
SIMCOE   COUNTY   DISTRICT   SCHOOL BOARD, THE
PORTAGE VIEW PUBLIC SCHOOL
(*Suby of* Simcoe County District School Board, The)
124 Letitia St, Barrie, ON, L4N 1P5
(705) 728-1302
Emp Here 40
SIC 8211 Elementary and secondary schools

D-U-N-S 20-711-2090   (BR)
SIMCOE   COUNTY   DISTRICT   SCHOOL BOARD, THE
ALGONQUIN   RIDGE   ELEMENTARY SCHOOL
(*Suby of* Simcoe County District School Board, The)
191 Golden Meadow Rd, Barrie, ON, L4N 9R6
(705) 737-4080
Emp Here 60
SIC 8211 Elementary and secondary schools

D-U-N-S 25-292-4543   (BR)
SIMCOE   COUNTY   DISTRICT   SCHOOL BOARD, THE
WEST BAYFIELD ELEMENTARY SCHOOL
(*Suby of* Simcoe County District School Board, The)
49 Ford St, Barrie, ON, L4N 7J4
(705) 725-8229
Emp Here 60
SIC 8211 Elementary and secondary schools

D-U-N-S 25-297-6261   (BR)
SIMCOE   COUNTY   DISTRICT   SCHOOL BOARD, THE
PRINCE OF WALES PUBLIC SCHOOL
(*Suby of* Simcoe County District School Board, The)
50 Bradford St, Barrie, ON, L4N 3A8
(705) 728-3105
Emp Here 25

SIC 8211 Elementary and secondary schools

D-U-N-S 20-591-8191   (BR)
SIMCOE COUNTY DISTRICT SCHOOL BOARD, THE,
MAPLEVIEW HEIGHTS ELEMENTARY
(*Suby of* Simcoe County District School Board, The)
180 Esther Dr, Barrie, ON, L4N 9S9
(705) 725-7980
Emp Here 50
SIC 8211 Elementary and secondary schools

D-U-N-S 25-297-6204   (BR)
SIMCOE COUNTY DISTRICT SCHOOL BOARD, THE,
FERNDALE WOODS ELEMENTARY SCHOOL
(*Suby of* Simcoe County District School Board, The)
170 Ferndale Dr S, Barrie, ON, L4N 8A1
(705) 733-5636
Emp Here 60
SIC 8211 Elementary and secondary schools

D-U-N-S 25-297-6584   (BR)
SIMCOE COUNTY DISTRICT SCHOOL BOARD, THE,
BARRIE CENTRAL COLLEGIATE INSTITUTE
(*Suby of* Simcoe County District School Board, The)
125 Dunlop St W, Barrie, ON, L4N 1A9

Emp Here 100
SIC 8211 Elementary and secondary schools

D-U-N-S 25-297-6741   (BR)
SIMCOE COUNTY DISTRICT SCHOOL BOARD, THE,
ALLANDALE HEIGHTS PUBLIC SCHOOL
(*Suby of* Simcoe County District School Board, The)
124 Bayview Dr, Barrie, ON, L4N 3P4
(705) 728-3601
Emp Here 40
SIC 8211 Elementary and secondary schools

D-U-N-S 20-034-1993   (BR)
SIMCOE COUNTY DISTRICT SCHOOL BOARD, THE,
WILLOW LANDING ELEMENTARY SCHOOL
(*Suby of* Simcoe County District School Board, The)
330 Big Bay Point Rd, Barrie, ON, L4N 8A8
(705) 728-3937
Emp Here 45
SIC 8211 Elementary and secondary schools

D-U-N-S 20-026-2561   (BR)
SIMCOE COUNTY DISTRICT SCHOOL BOARD, THE,
EMMA KING SCHOOL
(*Suby of* Simcoe County District School Board, The)
383 Cundles Rd W, Barrie, ON, L4N 7C7
(705) 728-5401
Emp Here 44
SIC 8211 Elementary and secondary schools

D-U-N-S 25-297-6899   (BR)
SIMCOE COUNTY DISTRICT SCHOOL BOARD, THE,
ANDREW HUNTER ELEMENTARY SCHOOL
(*Suby of* Simcoe County District School Board, The)
59 Lampman Lane, Barrie, ON, L4N 5G4
(705) 728-5420
Emp Here 50
SIC 8211 Elementary and secondary schools

D-U-N-S 20-591-4562   (BR)
SIMCOE MUSKOKA CATHOLIC DISTRICT SCHOOL BOARD
ST CATHERINES OF SIENNA
(*Suby of* Simcoe Muskoka Catholic District School Board)

111 Summerset Dr, Barrie, ON, L4N 0A6
(705) 728-7301
Emp Here 50
SIC 8211 Elementary and secondary schools

D-U-N-S 20-591-4786   (BR)
SIMCOE MUSKOKA CATHOLIC DISTRICT SCHOOL BOARD
ST MICHAEL THE ARCHANGEL SCHOOL
(*Suby of* Simcoe Muskoka Catholic District School Board)
349 Big Bay Point Rd, Barrie, ON, L4N 8A2
(705) 733-9611
Emp Here 25
SIC 8211 Elementary and secondary schools

D-U-N-S 20-026-2694   (BR)
SIMCOE MUSKOKA CATHOLIC DISTRICT SCHOOL BOARD
SAINT BERNADETTE CATHOLIC SCHOOL
(*Suby of* Simcoe Muskoka Catholic District School Board)
101 Marsellus Dr, Barrie, ON, L4N 8R6
(705) 733-0459
Emp Here 54
SIC 8211 Elementary and secondary schools

D-U-N-S 20-026-1209   (BR)
SIMCOE MUSKOKA CATHOLIC DISTRICT SCHOOL BOARD
ST. PETER'S SECONDARY SCHOOL
(*Suby of* Simcoe Muskoka Catholic District School Board)
201 Ashford Dr, Barrie, ON, L4N 6A3
(705) 734-0168
Emp Here 100
SIC 8211 Elementary and secondary schools

D-U-N-S 20-711-2223   (BR)
SIMCOE MUSKOKA CATHOLIC DISTRICT SCHOOL BOARD
ST NICHOLAS SCHOOL
(*Suby of* Simcoe Muskoka Catholic District School Board)
100 Lougheed Rd, Barrie, ON, L4N 8E1
(705) 737-9082
Emp Here 30
SIC 8211 Elementary and secondary schools

D-U-N-S 20-081-2878   (BR)
SIMCOE MUSKOKA CATHOLIC DISTRICT SCHOOL BOARD
GOOD SHEPHERD CATHOLIC SCHOOL, THE
(*Suby of* Simcoe Muskoka Catholic District School Board)
23 Cloughley Dr, Barrie, ON, L4N 7Y3
(705) 728-2302
Emp Here 39
SIC 8211 Elementary and secondary schools

D-U-N-S 25-293-4740   (BR)
SIMCOE MUSKOKA CATHOLIC DISTRICT SCHOOL BOARD
ST MARY'S SCHOOL
(*Suby of* Simcoe Muskoka Catholic District School Board)
340 Leacock Dr, Barrie, ON, L4N 6J8
(705) 726-1843
Emp Here 25
SIC 8211 Elementary and secondary schools

D-U-N-S 25-280-6971   (BR)
SIMCOE MUSKOKA CATHOLIC DISTRICT SCHOOL BOARD
ST MARGUERITE D'YOUVILLE SCHOOL
(*Suby of* Simcoe Muskoka Catholic District School Board)
240 Kozlov St, Barrie, ON, L4N 7H6
(705) 726-5849
Emp Here 35
SIC 8211 Elementary and secondary schools

D-U-N-S 25-293-5499   (BR)
SIMCOE MUSKOKA CATHOLIC DISTRICT SCHOOL BOARD
POPE JOHN PAUL II SCHOOL

(*Suby of* Simcoe Muskoka Catholic District School Board)
211 Ashford Dr, Barrie, ON, L4N 6A3
(705) 722-0212
Emp Here 50
SIC 8211 Elementary and secondary schools

D-U-N-S 20-793-8965   (BR)
SOBEYS CAPITAL INCORPORATED
37 Mapleview Dr W, Barrie, ON, L4N 9H5
(705) 728-9858
Emp Here 150
SIC 5411 Grocery stores

D-U-N-S 20-860-1372   (BR)
SOURCE (BELL) ELECTRONICS INC, THE
SOURCE, THE
21 Commerce Park Dr Suite A, Barrie, ON, L4N 8X1
(705) 726-6965
Emp Here 25
SIC 5999 Miscellaneous retail stores, nec

D-U-N-S 20-496-8189   (BR)
SPECIALTY CARE INC
SIMCOE TERRACE
(*Suby of* Specialty Care Inc)
44 Donald St Suite 229, Barrie, ON, L4N 1E3
(705) 722-5750
Emp Here 40
SIC 6513 Apartment building operators

D-U-N-S 25-486-5660   (BR)
STAPLES CANADA INC
(*Suby of* Staples, Inc.)
36 Barrie View Dr, Barrie, ON, L4N 8V4
(705) 733-3329
Emp Here 50
SIC 5943 Stationery stores

D-U-N-S 24-344-0802   (BR)
SUPERIOR PLUS LP
SUPERIOR PROPANE
789 Bayview Dr, Barrie, ON, L4N 9A5
(705) 726-1861
Emp Here 20
SIC 5984 Liquefied petroleum gas dealers

D-U-N-S 20-755-5228   (HQ)
SUZUKI CANADA INC.
360 Saunders Rd, Barrie, ON, L4N 9Y2
(905) 889-2600
Emp Here 65   *Emp Total* 62,992
Sales 45,600,438
SIC 5012 Automobiles and other motor vehicles
Pr Satoshi Shimizu
VP Fin VP Fin Piero Caleca

D-U-N-S 20-823-3098   (SL)
T.R.Y. JACKSON BROTHERS LIMITED
JACKSONS TOYOTA
181 Mapleview Dr W, Barrie, ON, L4N 9E8
(705) 726-0288
Emp Here 55   *Sales* 20,064,193
SIC 5511 New and used car dealers
Pr Pr Robert B Jackson
Dir Heather Jackson

D-U-N-S 24-324-0764   (SL)
TALK IS FREE THEATRE INC
100 Mapleview Dr W, Barrie, ON, L4N 9H6
(705) 792-1949
Emp Here 49   *Sales* 7,558,320
SIC 7922 Theatrical producers and services
Mgr Arkady Spivak

D-U-N-S 20-517-1395   (BR)
TERRAPROBE LIMITED
(*Suby of* Terraprobe Limited)
220 Bayview Dr Unit 25, Barrie, ON, L4N 4Y8
(705) 739-8355
Emp Here 20
SIC 8748 Business consulting, nec

D-U-N-S 20-703-7164   (BR)
THETA INDUSTRIES LIMITED
THETA TTS

151 Tiffin St, Barrie, ON, L4N 2N3
(705) 733-4150
Emp Here 75
SIC 3544 Special dies, tools, jigs, and fixtures

D-U-N-S 20-128-3509   (BR)
TORBA RESTAURANTS INC
WENDY'S RESTAURANT
6 Fairview Rd, Barrie, ON, L4N 4P3
(705) 727-0233
Emp Here 40
SIC 5812 Eating places

D-U-N-S 25-163-6809   (BR)
TORBA RESTAURANTS INC
WENDY'S RESTAURANT
450 Bryne Dr, Barrie, ON, L4N 9R1
(705) 735-4143
Emp Here 20
SIC 5812 Eating places

D-U-N-S 24-150-3353   (BR)
TOROMONT INDUSTRIES LTD
BATTLEFIELD EQUIPMENT RENTALS
430 Huronia Rd, Barrie, ON, L4N 8Y9
(705) 721-1919
Emp Here 25
SIC 7359 Equipment rental and leasing, nec

D-U-N-S 25-403-8169   (BR)
UNITED PARCEL SERVICE CANADA LTD
UPS
474 Welham Rd, Barrie, ON, L4N 8Z4
(705) 733-1438
Emp Here 42
SIC 4212 Local trucking, without storage

D-U-N-S 25-671-4114   (BR)
UNITED RENTALS OF CANADA, INC
630 Dunlop St W, Barrie, ON, L4N 9W5
(705) 722-8181
Emp Here 20
SIC 7353 Heavy construction equipment rental

D-U-N-S 24-335-4730   (SL)
VALMONT WC ENGINEERING GROUP LTD
POWCO, DIV OF
100 Ellis Dr, Barrie, ON, L4N 9B2
(705) 721-1090
Emp Here 35   *Sales* 3,866,917
SIC 3312 Blast furnaces and steel mills

D-U-N-S 20-958-0054   (BR)
VALUE VILLAGE STORES, INC
(*Suby of* Savers, Inc.)
165 Wellington St W, Barrie, ON, L4N 1L7
(705) 733-9224
Emp Here 60
SIC 5399 Miscellaneous general merchandise

D-U-N-S 24-408-8717   (BR)
WAL-MART CANADA CORP
35 Mapleview Dr W, Barrie, ON, L4N 9H5
(705) 728-8931
Emp Here 50
SIC 5311 Department stores

D-U-N-S 25-294-8575   (BR)
WAL-MART CANADA CORP
35 Mapleview Dr W, Barrie, ON, L4N 9H5
(705) 728-9122
Emp Here 175
SIC 5311 Department stores

D-U-N-S 24-927-6668   (BR)
WASTE MANAGEMENT OF CANADA CORPORATION
(*Suby of* Waste Management, Inc.)
13 Saunders Rd, Barrie, ON, L4N 9A7
(705) 728-9649
Emp Here 25
SIC 4953 Refuse systems

D-U-N-S 24-947-7399   (BR)
WATSON BUILDING SUPPLIES INC
WATSON INSULATORS
733 Bayview Dr, Barrie, ON, L4N 9A5

(705) 734-0557
Emp Here 25
SIC 5039 Construction materials, nec

D-U-N-S 24-369-2550   (BR)
WE CARE HEALTH SERVICES INC
WE CARE HOME HEALTH SERVICES
64 Cedar Pointe Dr Suite 1413, Barrie, ON,
L4N 5R7
(705) 734-2235
Emp Here 50
SIC 8082 Home health care services

D-U-N-S 24-443-3293   (SL)
WEB.COM CANADA, INC
1SHOPPINGCART.COM
128 Wellington St W Suite 304, Barrie, ON,
L4N 8J6
(705) 792-1961
Emp Here 45   *Sales* 2,480,664
SIC 7374 Data processing and preparation

D-U-N-S 20-958-0211   (BR)
WILLIAMS, JIM LEASING LIMITED
BAYCITY KIA
165 Bradford St, Barrie, ON, L4N 3B4
(705) 739-8020
Emp Here 20
SIC 5511 New and used car dealers

D-U-N-S 20-184-3096   (BR)
**WINNERS MERCHANTS INTERNATIONAL
L.P.**
WINNERS
(*Suby of* The TJX Companies Inc)
37 Molson Park Dr E, Barrie, ON, L4N 9A9
(705) 792-1437
Emp Here 40
SIC 5651 Family clothing stores

D-U-N-S 24-377-2402   (SL)
WIRECOMM SYSTEMS (2008), INC
(*Suby of* Unitek Global Services, Inc.)
122 Saunders Rd Suite 10, Barrie, ON, L4N
9A8
(905) 405-8018
Emp Here 167   *Sales* 27,287,302
SIC 4899 Communication services, nec
Pr Christopher Scott Hisey
VP VP Daniel Hopkin
VP VP Peter Brodsky
    Dean Macconald

D-U-N-S 20-809-7894   (BR)
YMCA OF GREATER TORONTO
22 Grove St W, Barrie, ON, L4N 1M7
(705) 726-6421
Emp Here 200
SIC 8699 Membership organizations, nec

D-U-N-S 25-034-0189   (SL)
**YANCH HEATING AND AIR CONDITIONING
(BARRIE) LIMITED**
89 Rawson Ave, Barrie, ON, L4N 6E5
(705) 728-5406
Emp Here 70   *Sales* 6,128,699
SIC 1711 Plumbing, heating, air-conditioning
Pr Pr Christopher Yanch

D-U-N-S 25-911-8651   (BR)
ZEHRMART INC
ZEHRS MARKETS
620 Yonge St, Barrie, ON, L4N 4E6
(705) 735-2390
Emp Here 200
SIC 5411 Grocery stores

Barrys Bay, ON K0J
Renfrew County

D-U-N-S 20-571-9979   (BR)
BANK OF MONTREAL
BMO BANK OF MONTREAL
2 Opeongo Line, Barrys Bay, ON, K0J 1B0
(613) 756-2693
Emp Here 20

SIC 6021 National commercial banks

D-U-N-S 24-344-5017   (BR)
METRO ONTARIO INC
28 Bay'S St, Barrys Bay, ON, K0J 1B0
(613) 756-7098
Emp Here 40
SIC 5411 Grocery stores

D-U-N-S 24-828-9175   (BR)
PLAINTREE SYSTEMS INC
MADAWASKA DOORS
14 Conway St, Barrys Bay, ON, K0J 1B0
(613) 756-7066
Emp Here 120
SIC 2431 Millwork

D-U-N-S 25-238-6362   (BR)
**RENFREW COUNTY DISTRICT SCHOOL
BOARD**
*MADAWASKA VALLEY DISTRICT HIGH
SCHOOL*
341 John St Suite 1, Barrys Bay, ON, K0J 1B0
(613) 756-0526
Emp Here 60
SIC 8211 Elementary and secondary schools

Batawa, ON K0K
Hastings County

D-U-N-S 24-372-1052   (SL)
INVAR MANUFACTURING CORP
1 Parry Dr, Batawa, ON, K0K 1E0

Emp Here 134   *Sales* 29,239,680
SIC 3714 Motor vehicle parts and accessories
Dir Linda Hasenfratz
Mgr Edward Mcgregor
Opers Mgr Bruce Read

Bath, ON K0H
Lennox County

D-U-N-S 25-364-7754   (BR)
INVISTA (CANADA) COMPANY
INVISTA (CANADA) COMPANY
(*Suby of* Koch Industries, Inc.)
Gd, Bath, ON, K0H 1G0
(613) 634-5124
Emp Here 100
SIC 2299 Textile goods, nec

D-U-N-S 20-818-2782   (BR)
LAFARGE CANADA INC
Gd, Bath, ON, K0H 1G0
(613) 352-7711
Emp Here 100
SIC 2891 Adhesives and sealants

D-U-N-S 25-250-7520   (BR)
LIMESTONE DISTRICT SCHOOL BOARD
BATH PUBLIC SCHOOL
247 Church St, Bath, ON, K0H 1G0
(613) 352-7543
Emp Here 25
SIC 8211 Elementary and secondary schools

D-U-N-S 25-999-5124   (BR)
ONTARIO POWER GENERATION INC
7263 Hwy 33, Bath, ON, K0H 1G0
(613) 352-3525
Emp Here 163
SIC 4911 Electric services

Battersea, ON K0H

D-U-N-S 25-305-5255   (BR)
LIMESTONE DISTRICT SCHOOL BOARD
STORRINGTON PUBLIC SCHOOL

4576 Battersea Rd, Battersea, ON, K0H 1H0
(613) 353-2868
Emp Here 24
SIC 8211 Elementary and secondary schools

Bayfield, ON N0M
Huron County

D-U-N-S 20-733-2883   (SL)
LITTLE INN OF BAYFIELD LIMITED, THE
26 Main St N, Bayfield, ON, N0M 1G0
(519) 565-2611
Emp Here 50   *Sales* 2,188,821
SIC 7011 Hotels and motels

Beachburg, ON K0J
Renfrew County

D-U-N-S 24-268-9172   (SL)
**OTTAWA RIVER WHITE WATER RAFTING
LIMITED**
RIVER RUN
1260 Grant Settlement Rd, Beachburg, ON,
K0J 1C0
(613) 646-2501
Emp Here 75   *Sales* 4,085,799
SIC 7999 Amusement and recreation, nec

D-U-N-S 25-238-6131   (BR)
**RENFREW COUNTY DISTRICT SCHOOL
BOARD**
BEACHBURG PUBLIC SCHOOL
20 Cameron St, Beachburg, ON, K0J 1C0
(613) 582-3528
Emp Here 20
SIC 8211 Elementary and secondary schools

Beamsville, ON L0R
Lincoln County

D-U-N-S 20-051-3901   (SL)
308462 ONTARIO INC
M.C. HEALTHCARE PRODUCTS
4658 Ontario St, Beamsville, ON, L0R 1B4
(905) 563-8264
Emp Here 52   *Sales* 2,845,467
SIC 2599 Furniture and fixtures, nec

D-U-N-S 20-802-2025   (BR)
**ALBRIGHT GARDENS HOMES INCORPO-
RATED**
5050 Hillside Dr, Beamsville, ON, L0R 1B2
(905) 563-8252
Emp Here 300
SIC 8322 Individual and family services

D-U-N-S 24-029-9672   (BR)
CRH CANADA GROUP INC
DUFFERIN CONSTRUCTION
4240 Bartlett Rd, Beamsville, ON, L0R 1B1
(905) 563-5412
Emp Here 20
SIC 3273 Ready-mixed concrete

D-U-N-S 25-291-1409   (SL)
CHRI-GYN LTD
TIM HORTONS
5005 South Service Rd Ss 1, Beamsville, ON,
L0R 1B4
(905) 563-1760
Emp Here 300   *Sales* 14,067,200
SIC 5461 Retail bakeries
Pr Pr John Riediger
    Marie Riediger

D-U-N-S 20-803-7635   (BR)
**CORPORATION OF THE TOWN OF LIN-
COLN**
THE FLEMMING CENTRE

(*Suby of* Corporation Of The Town Of Lincoln)
5020 Serena Dr, Beamsville, ON, L0R 1B0
(905) 563-2799
Emp Here 25
SIC 8322 Individual and family services

D-U-N-S 24-060-9982   (BR)
DANA CANADA CORPORATION
SERVICE PARTS DIVISION
5095 South Service Rd, Beamsville, ON, L0R
1B0

Emp Here 96
SIC 5013 Motor vehicle supplies and new
parts

D-U-N-S 20-245-4661   (BR)
DENDRES CORP
MCDONALD'S RESTAURANT
(*Suby of* Dendres Corp)
4748 Ontario St, Beamsville, ON, L0R 1B4
(905) 563-3331
Emp Here 20
SIC 5812 Eating places

D-U-N-S 20-025-2562   (BR)
DISTRICT SCHOOL BOARD OF NIAGARA
*BEAMSVILLE DISTRICT SECONDARY
SCHOOL*
4317 Central Ave, Beamsville, ON, L0R 1B0
(905) 563-8267
Emp Here 72
SIC 8211 Elementary and secondary schools

D-U-N-S 20-710-8445   (BR)
DISTRICT SCHOOL BOARD OF NIAGARA
JACOB BEAM PUBLIC SCHOOL
4300 William St, Beamsville, ON, L0R 1B7
(905) 563-8209
Emp Here 25
SIC 8211 Elementary and secondary schools

D-U-N-S 20-591-3192   (BR)
DISTRICT SCHOOL BOARD OF NIAGARA
SENATOR GIBSON PUBLIC SCHOOL
4944 John St, Beamsville, ON, L0R 1B6
(905) 563-7431
Emp Here 25
SIC 8211 Elementary and secondary schools

D-U-N-S 20-358-9788   (SL)
GUARDIAN INTERNATIONAL
4460 Ontario St Suite 3, Beamsville, ON, L0R
1B5
(905) 563-5080
Emp Here 50   *Sales* 1,532,175
SIC 7381 Detective and armored car services

D-U-N-S 20-971-5361   (BR)
MSC INDUSTRIAL SUPPLY ULC
BARNES DISTRIBUTION
4660 Delta Way, Beamsville, ON, L0R 1B4
(905) 563-4844
Emp Here 42
SIC 5085 Industrial supplies

D-U-N-S 20-710-9237   (BR)
**NIAGARA CATHOLIC DISTRICT SCHOOL
BOARD**
*ST MARK CATHOLIC ELEMENTARY
SCHOOL*
4114 Mountain St, Beamsville, ON, L0R 1B7
(905) 563-9191
Emp Here 50
SIC 8211 Elementary and secondary schools

D-U-N-S 20-710-9153   (BR)
**NIAGARA CATHOLIC DISTRICT SCHOOL
BOARD**
ST JOHN SCHOOL
5684 Regional Rd 81, Beamsville, ON, L0R
1B0
(905) 945-5331
Emp Here 25
SIC 8211 Elementary and secondary schools

D-U-N-S 24-987-6673   (HQ)
NIAGARA PISTON INC
MAPLE MANUFACTURING, DIV OF

(Suby of 33139 Ontario Limited)
4708 Ontario St Suite 1, Beamsville, ON, L0R 1B4
(905) 563-4981
Emp Here 53   Emp Total 60
Sales 25,755,127
SIC 3592 Carburetors, pistons, piston rings and valves
Pr Pr Douglas Major
Michael Court
Suzanne Court
Philip Court

D-U-N-S 24-912-0072   (SL)
OPPLAST INC
4743 Christie Dr, Beamsville, ON, L0R 1B4
(905) 563-4987
Emp Here 55   Sales 7,969,509
SIC 3089 Plastics products, nec
Pr Pr Heiner Ophardt
VP VP Tony Knortleve-Snider
Fin Ex Sylvia Theroux

D-U-N-S 20-552-1110   (BR)
PARKER HANNIFIN CANADA
FLUID CONNECTORS DIV.
4635 Durham Rd Rr 3, Beamsville, ON, L0R 1B3
(905) 945-2274
Emp Here 100
SIC 3714 Motor vehicle parts and accessories

D-U-N-S 25-720-2762   (BR)
PHARMA PLUS DRUGMARTS LTD
PHARMA PLUS DRUGMART
4486 Ontario St, Beamsville, ON, L0R 1B5
(905) 563-7122
Emp Here 20
SIC 5912 Drug stores and proprietary stores

D-U-N-S 20-609-0946   (HQ)
RANNIE PUBLICATIONS LIMITED
(Suby of Rannie Publications Limited)
4309 Central Ave, Beamsville, ON, L0R 1B0

Emp Here 30   Emp Total 90
Sales 10,012,320
SIC 2711 Newspapers
Pr Henry Burgoyne
VP Allan Telher

D-U-N-S 20-793-0806   (BR)
SOBEYS CAPITAL INCORPORATED
4610 Ontario St, Beamsville, ON, L0R 1B3
(905) 563-1088
Emp Here 110
SIC 5411 Grocery stores

D-U-N-S 24-377-5538   (BR)
ST. DAVIDS HYDROPONICS LTD
4860 Martin Rd, Beamsville, ON, L0R 1B1
(905) 562-5636
Emp Here 25
SIC 5148 Fresh fruits and vegetables

D-U-N-S 24-227-6025   (BR)
TROY LIFE & FIRE SAFETY LTD
EDWARD'S SPRINKLER
4697 Christie St, Beamsville, ON, L0R 1B4
(905) 563-4889
Emp Here 30
SIC 1711 Plumbing, heating, air-conditioning

Beaverton, ON L0K
(Simcoe County)

D-U-N-S 25-263-6626   (BR)
DURHAM DISTRICT SCHOOL BOARD
THORAH CENTRAL PUBLIC SCHOOL
Gd, Beaverton, ON, L0K 1A0
(705) 426-5858
Emp Here 20
SIC 8211 Elementary and secondary schools

D-U-N-S 20-034-6773   (BR)
VENTRA GROUP CO

FLEX-N-GATE SEEBURN
530 Park St, Beaverton, ON, L0K 1A0
(705) 426-7311
Emp Here 570
SIC 3423 Hand and edge tools, nec

Beeton, ON L0G
Simcoe County

D-U-N-S 20-034-6930   (SL)
BORDEN METAL PRODUCTS (CANADA) LIMITED
50 Dayfoot St, Beeton, ON, L0G 1A0
(905) 729-2229
Emp Here 55   Sales 4,815,406
SIC 3446 Architectural Metalwork

D-U-N-S 20-535-5048   (BR)
GOVERNMENT OF ONTARIO
D.A.R.E. (DRUG ABUSE RESISTANCE EDUCATION) ONTARIO
29 Main St W, Beeton, ON, L0G 1A0
(905) 729-4004
Emp Here 75
SIC 8069 Specialty hospitals, except psychiatric

D-U-N-S 25-292-4741   (BR)
SIMCOE COUNTY DISTRICT SCHOOL BOARD, THE
TECUMSETH BEETON PUBLIC SCHOOL
(Suby of Simcoe County District School Board, The)
43 Patterson St, Beeton, ON, L0G 1A0
(905) 729-2631
Emp Here 42
SIC 8211 Elementary and secondary schools

D-U-N-S 20-591-4349   (BR)
SIMCOE MUSKOKA CATHOLIC DISTRICT SCHOOL BOARD
MONSENIOR RONAN
(Suby of Simcoe Muskoka Catholic District School Board)
10 Lilly St E, Beeton, ON, L0G 1A0
(905) 729-3473
Emp Here 25
SIC 8211 Elementary and secondary schools

D-U-N-S 20-717-2644   (SL)
W. D. POTATO LIMITED
3644 Side Rd Suite 10, Beeton, ON, L0G 1A0
(905) 729-2263
Emp Here 50   Sales 4,742,446
SIC 4225 General warehousing and storage

Belle River, ON N0R
Essex County

D-U-N-S 24-342-8161   (BR)
CHARTWELL SENIORS HOUSING REAL ESTATE INVESTMENT TRUST
CHARTWELL SELECT OAK PARK LAKE SHORE
1700 County Rd 22, Belle River, ON, N0R 1A0
(519) 727-0034
Emp Here 40
SIC 6513 Apartment building operators

D-U-N-S 25-249-1790   (BR)
CONSEIL SCOLAIRE DE DISTRICT DES ECOLES CATHOLIQUES DU SUD-OUEST
PAVILLON DES JEUNES
326 Rourke Line Rr 3, Belle River, ON, N0R 1A0
(519) 727-6044
Emp Here 32
SIC 8211 Elementary and secondary schools

D-U-N-S 25-249-1832   (BR)
GREATER ESSEX COUNTY DISTRICT SCHOOL BOARD

BELLE RIVER DISTRICT HIGH SCHOOL
333 South St, Belle River, ON, N0R 1A0
(519) 728-1212
Emp Here 80
SIC 8211 Elementary and secondary schools

D-U-N-S 25-249-3135   (BR)
GREATER ESSEX COUNTY DISTRICT SCHOOL BOARD
BELLE RIVER PUBLIC SCHOOL
370 St Peter St, Belle River, ON, N0R 1A0
(519) 728-1310
Emp Here 30
SIC 8211 Elementary and secondary schools

D-U-N-S 25-407-8850   (BR)
ROYAL BANK OF CANADA
RBC ROYAL BANK
(Suby of Royal Bank Of Canada)
549 Notre-Dame St N, Belle River, ON, N0R 1A0
(519) 728-3413
Emp Here 22
SIC 6021 National commercial banks

D-U-N-S 25-249-1709   (BR)
WINDSOR-ESSEX CATHOLIC DISTRICT SCHOOL BOARD, THE
ST JOHN BAPTIST ELEMENTARY SCHOOL
494 St Peter St, Belle River, ON, N0R 1A0
(519) 728-2150
Emp Here 49
SIC 8211 Elementary and secondary schools

Belleville, ON K8N
Hastings County

D-U-N-S 25-914-8666   (BR)
(MADD CANADA) MOTHERS AGAINST DRUNK DRIVING
MADD QUINTE CHAPTER
Gd Stn Main, Belleville, ON, K8N 4Z8

Emp Here 30
SIC 8399 Social services, nec

D-U-N-S 24-128-5696   (BR)
ALGONQUIN & LAKESHORE CATHOLIC DISTRICT SCHOOL BOARD
ST THERESA CATHOLIC SECONDARY SCHOOL
135 Adam St, Belleville, ON, K8N 5K3
(613) 968-6993
Emp Here 50
SIC 8211 Elementary and secondary schools

D-U-N-S 25-237-7965   (BR)
ALGONQUIN & LAKESHORE CATHOLIC DISTRICT SCHOOL BOARD
NICHOLSON CATHOLIC COLLEGE
301 Church St, Belleville, ON, K8N 3C7
(613) 967-0404
Emp Here 80
SIC 8211 Elementary and secondary schools

D-U-N-S 25-486-9621   (BR)
ALGONQUIN & LAKESHORE CATHOLIC DISTRICT SCHOOL BOARD
ST MICHAEL CATHOLIC SCHOOL
273 Church St, Belleville, ON, K8N 3C7
(613) 968-5765
Emp Here 35
SIC 8211 Elementary and secondary schools

D-U-N-S 20-025-0566   (BR)
ALGONQUIN & LAKESHORE CATHOLIC DISTRICT SCHOOL BOARD
ST. JOSEPH CATHOLIC SCHOOL
405 Bridge St E, Belleville, ON, K8N 1P7
(613) 962-3653
Emp Here 30
SIC 8211 Elementary and secondary schools

D-U-N-S 24-176-9913   (BR)
ALUMI-BUNK CORPORATION

FREIGHTLINER OF BELLEVILLE
21 Enterprise Dr, Belleville, ON, K8N 4Z5

Emp Here 25
SIC 7539 Automotive repair shops, nec

D-U-N-S 25-409-9062   (BR)
BANK OF MONTREAL
BMO
201 Front St, Belleville, ON, K8N 5A4
(613) 967-4300
Emp Here 25
SIC 6021 National commercial banks

D-U-N-S 25-319-2652   (BR)
BANQUE TORONTO-DOMINION, LA
TORONTO-DOMINION BANK, THE
(Suby of Toronto-Dominion Bank, The)
202 Front St, Belleville, ON, K8N 2Z2
(613) 967-2222
Emp Here 20
SIC 6021 National commercial banks

D-U-N-S 20-536-1694   (HQ)
BARDON SUPPLIES LIMITED
(Suby of Entreprises Mirca Inc, Les)
405 College St E, Belleville, ON, K8N 4Z6
(613) 966-5643
Emp Here 60   Emp Total 1,342
Sales 46,694,848
SIC 5074 Plumbing and heating equipment and supplies (hydronics)
VP Barry Raycroft
Fin Ex Mark Horwood

D-U-N-S 25-016-9471   (BR)
CANADIAN IMPERIAL BANK OF COMMERCE
CIBC
237 Front St, Belleville, ON, K8N 2Z4
(613) 966-2641
Emp Here 33
SIC 6021 National commercial banks

D-U-N-S 24-372-9873   (BR)
CASCADES CANADA ULC
CASCADES CONTAINERBOARD PACKAGING BELLEVILLE
340 University Ave, Belleville, ON, K8N 5T6
(613) 968-3581
Emp Here 40
SIC 2653 Corrugated and solid fiber boxes

D-U-N-S 20-321-9886   (BR)
COCO PAVING INC
6520 Hwy 62, Belleville, ON, K8N 5A5
(613) 962-3461
Emp Here 90
SIC 1611 Highway and street construction

D-U-N-S 20-976-1464   (BR)
COMCARE (CANADA) LIMITED
COMCARE HEALTH SERVICES
470 Dundas St E Unit 7b, Belleville, ON, K8N 1G1
(613) 968-3477
Emp Here 30
SIC 8049 Offices of health practitioner

D-U-N-S 20-573-2659   (BR)
COMPAGNIE DES CHEMINS DE FER NATIONAUX DU CANADA
257 Airport Pky, Belleville, ON, K8N 4Z6
(613) 969-2247
Emp Here 200
SIC 4011 Railroads, line-haul operating

D-U-N-S 24-151-0465   (BR)
CRUICKSHANK CONSTRUCTION LIMITED
53 Grills Rd, Belleville, ON, K8N 4Z5

Emp Here 40
SIC 1622 Bridge, tunnel, and elevated highway construction

D-U-N-S 20-877-4018   (SL)
DUNDAS VALLEY GOLF AND CURLING CLUB LIMITED

10 Woodley Crt, Belleville, ON, K8N 5W5
(905) 628-6731
Emp Here 70   *Sales* 2,845,467
SIC 7997 Membership sports and recreation clubs

D-U-N-S 20-610-2266   (BR)
EMPIRE THEATRES LIMITED
321 Front St, Belleville, ON, K8N 2Z9
(613) 969-0099
Emp Here 45
SIC 7832 Motion picture theaters, except drive-in

D-U-N-S 25-594-0777   (BR)
ENERGIE VALERO INC
ULTRAMAR HOME ENERGY
406 Maitland Dr Rr 5, Belleville, ON, K8N 4Z5
(613) 962-4504
Emp Here 25
SIC 5172 Petroleum products, nec

D-U-N-S 25-484-2651   (BR)
GREER GALLOWAY GROUP INC, THE
1620 Wallbridge-Loyalist Rd Suite 5, Belleville, ON, K8N 4Z5
(613) 966-3068
Emp Here 30
SIC 8711 Engineering services

D-U-N-S 24-079-0402   (SL)
HANNAFIN, E.J. ENTERPRISES LIMITED
10 ACRE TRUCK STOP
57 Cannifton Rd, Belleville, ON, K8N 4V1
(613) 966-7017
Emp Here 30   *Sales* 15,014,600
SIC 5541 Gasoline service stations
Pr Pr J. Roland Belanger
John Belanger

D-U-N-S 25-413-9595   (HQ)
HANON SYSTEMS CANADA INC
VISTEON
360 University Ave Suite 2, Belleville, ON, K8N 5T6
(613) 969-1460
Emp Here 460   *Emp Total* 2
Sales 76,098,010
SIC 3714 Motor vehicle parts and accessories
Pr Pr Tom Mckay
Rene Veillette

D-U-N-S 25-830-1571   (BR)
HASTINGS AND PRINCE EDWARD DISTRICT SCHOOL BOARD
BAYSIDE SECONDARY SCHOOL
Po Box 6500 Stn Csc, Belleville, ON, K8N 5M6
(613) 966-2922
Emp Here 70
SIC 8211 Elementary and secondary schools

D-U-N-S 25-237-7890   (BR)
HASTINGS AND PRINCE EDWARD DISTRICT SCHOOL BOARD
HILLCREST PUBLIC SCHOOL
88 West St, Belleville, ON, K8N 4X7
(613) 962-1177
Emp Here 20
SIC 8211 Elementary and secondary schools

D-U-N-S 25-237-8013   (BR)
HASTINGS AND PRINCE EDWARD DISTRICT SCHOOL BOARD
QUEEN ELIZABETH PUBLIC SCHOOL
135 Macdonald Ave, Belleville, ON, K8N 3Y4
(613) 968-9173
Emp Here 28
SIC 8211 Elementary and secondary schools

D-U-N-S 25-265-4231   (BR)
HASTINGS AND PRINCE EDWARD DISTRICT SCHOOL BOARD
TYENDINAGA PUBLIC SCHOOL
156 Ann St, Belleville, ON, K8N 3L3
(613) 966-1170
Emp Here 26
SIC 8211 Elementary and secondary schools

D-U-N-S 25-237-8138   (BR)
HASTINGS AND PRINCE EDWARD DISTRICT SCHOOL BOARD
MOIRA SECONDARY SCHOOL
275 Farley Ave, Belleville, ON, K8N 4M2
(613) 962-2149
Emp Here 70
SIC 7389 Business services, nec

D-U-N-S 20-913-6956   (BR)
HASTINGS AND PRINCE EDWARD DISTRICT SCHOOL BOARD
QUEEN VICTORIA ELEM SCHOOL
46 Pine St, Belleville, ON, K8N 2M2
(613) 968-4547
Emp Here 32
SIC 8211 Elementary and secondary schools

D-U-N-S 25-779-0196   (BR)
HASTINGS AND PRINCE EDWARD DISTRICT SCHOOL BOARD
SUSANA MOODY SCHOOL
376 Avonlough Rd, Belleville, ON, K8N 4Z2
(613) 966-8186
Emp Here 25
SIC 8211 Elementary and secondary schools

D-U-N-S 25-237-7809   (BR)
HASTINGS AND PRINCE EDWARD DISTRICT SCHOOL BOARD
HARRY J CLARKE PUBLIC SCHOOL
77 Rollins Dr, Belleville, ON, K8N 4J6
(613) 969-0140
Emp Here 53
SIC 8211 Elementary and secondary schools

D-U-N-S 20-246-0593   (BR)
HYDRO ONE INC
120 Adam St, Belleville, ON, K8N 2X9

Emp Here 75
SIC 4911 Electric services

D-U-N-S 24-117-4460   (BR)
INVESTORS GROUP FINANCIAL SERVICES INC
81 Millennium Pky Suite A, Belleville, ON, K8N 4Z5
(613) 962-7777
Emp Here 23
SIC 8742 Management consulting services

D-U-N-S 25-615-2331   (BR)
INVESTORS GROUP TRUST CO. LTD
81 Millennium Pky Suite A, Belleville, ON, K8N 4Z5
(613) 962-7777
Emp Here 30
SIC 8741 Management services

D-U-N-S 24-345-9125   (BR)
JONES DESLAURIERS INSURANCE MANAGEMENT INC
1 Millennium Pky Suite 103, Belleville, ON, K8N 4Z5
(613) 967-2000
Emp Here 25
SIC 6411 Insurance agents, brokers, and service

D-U-N-S 24-363-1855   (BR)
KELLOGG CANADA INC
(*Suby of* Kellogg Company)
501 College St E, Belleville, ON, K8N 0A3
(613) 210-4002
Emp Here 20
SIC 2043 Cereal breakfast foods

D-U-N-S 25-585-8870   (HQ)
KELLY'S HOME CARE CENTRE
(*Suby of* Kelly's Home Care Centre)
411 Bridge St E, Belleville, ON, K8N 1P7
(613) 962-5387
Emp Here 20   *Emp Total* 65
Sales 3,064,349
SIC 8059 Nursing and personal care, nec

D-U-N-S 24-868-9770   (SL)

KENNAMETAL STELLITE, INC
(*Suby of* Kennametal Inc.)
471 Dundas St E, Belleville, ON, K8N 1G2
(613) 968-3481
Emp Here 230   *Sales* 22,710,129
SIC 3369 Nonferrous foundries, nec
CEO Simone Pratesi
Dir Opers Don Williams
Joe Overton
Ron Betournay

D-U-N-S 25-264-2574   (BR)
KINGSTON GENERAL HOSPITAL
BELLEVILLE DIALYSIS CLINIC
(*Suby of* Kingston General Hospital)
345 College St E, Belleville, ON, K8N 5S7
(613) 966-2300
Emp Here 20
SIC 8011 Offices and clinics of medical doctors

D-U-N-S 25-364-8372   (BR)
LAFARGE PAVING & CONSTRUCTION (EASTERN) LIMITED
6520 Hwy 62 & 401, Belleville, ON, K8N 5A5
(613) 962-3461
Emp Here 25
SIC 1611 Highway and street construction

D-U-N-S 20-015-0147   (BR)
LENNOX CANADA INC
SERVICE EXPERTS D & K HEATING AND AIR CONDITIONING
6833 Hwy 62, Belleville, ON, K8N 4Z5
(613) 210-0887
Emp Here 40
SIC 1711 Plumbing, heating, air-conditioning

D-U-N-S 25-303-9648   (BR)
LONDON LIFE INSURANCE COMPANY
FREEDOM 55 DIV OF
100 1 Millennium Pky, Belleville, ON, K8N 4Z5
(613) 968-6449
Emp Here 20
SIC 6311 Life insurance

D-U-N-S 24-803-7512   (BR)
LOWE'S COMPANIES CANADA, ULC
219 Millennium Pky, Belleville, ON, K8N 4Z5
(416) 730-7300
Emp Here 140
SIC 5211 Lumber and other building materials

D-U-N-S 20-014-2425   (BR)
MAGNA INTERNATIONAL INC
AUTOSYSTEMS
345 University Ave Suite 1, Belleville, ON, K8N 5T7
(613) 969-1122
Emp Here 1,090
SIC 3647 Vehicular lighting equipment

D-U-N-S 20-814-2039   (BR)
MAXWELL PAPER CANADA INC
435 College St E, Belleville, ON, K8N 2Z2
(613) 962-7700
Emp Here 20
SIC 5112 Stationery and office supplies

D-U-N-S 25-300-0327   (BR)
METRO ONTARIO INC
FOOD BASICS
470 Dundas St E Suite 7, Belleville, ON, K8N 1G1

Emp Here 40
SIC 5411 Grocery stores

D-U-N-S 20-823-4963   (HQ)
MEYERS TRANSPORT LIMITED
(*Suby of* Mosaic Logistics Limited)
53 Grills Rd, Belleville, ON, K8N 4Z5
(613) 967-8440
Emp Here 50   *Emp Total* 30
Sales 84,810,240
SIC 4213 Trucking, except local
Larry Meyers
Pr Pr Evan Meyers

VP Fin David Joyce
Mireille Meyers

D-U-N-S 20-968-1381   (BR)
NAVY LEAGUE OF CANADA, THE
ROYAL CANADIAN SEA CADETS
16 South Front St, Belleville, ON, K8N 2Y3
(613) 962-4647
Emp Here 20
SIC 8641 Civic and social associations

D-U-N-S 20-034-9546   (SL)
OMG BELLEVILLE LIMITED
30 Dussek St, Belleville, ON, K8N 5R8
(613) 966-8881
Emp Here 23   *Sales* 3,283,232
SIC 2851 Paints and allied products

D-U-N-S 20-058-7819   (BR)
PLASTIQUES BERRY CANADA INC
323 University Ave, Belleville, ON, K8N 5T7
(613) 391-0180
Emp Here 70
SIC 3081 Unsupported plastics film and sheet

D-U-N-S 25-375-2067   (BR)
PRAXAIR CANADA INC
MEDIGAS
(*Suby of* Praxair, Inc.)
125 Church St S, Belleville, ON, K8N 3B7
(613) 969-4450
Emp Here 22
SIC 8082 Home health care services

D-U-N-S 24-316-1911   (BR)
PROCTER & GAMBLE INC
(*Suby of* The Procter & Gamble Company)
355 University Ave, Belleville, ON, K8N 5T8
(613) 966-5130
Emp Here 400
SIC 2676 Sanitary paper products

D-U-N-S 20-035-1724   (HQ)
QUINTE BROADCASTING COMPANY LIMITED
CJBQ RADIO
(*Suby of* Quinte Broadcasting Company Limited)
10 South Front St, Belleville, ON, K8N 2Y3
(613) 969-5555
Emp Here 55   *Emp Total* 57
Sales 3,575,074
SIC 4832 Radio broadcasting stations

D-U-N-S 24-687-6580   (BR)
REXALL PHARMACY GROUP LTD
PHARMA PLUS DRUG STORE
(*Suby of* McKesson Corporation)
173 Dundas St E, Belleville, ON, K8N 1C9
(613) 966-6297
Emp Here 23
SIC 5912 Drug stores and proprietary stores

D-U-N-S 20-035-1914   (SL)
RICHMOND SCHOOL COACH (BELLEVILLE) (1983) LIMITED
RICHMOND'S SCHOOL COACH
425 Bellevue Dr, Belleville, ON, K8N 4Z5
(613) 962-7744
Emp Here 60   *Sales* 1,678,096
SIC 4151 School buses

D-U-N-S 20-107-2688   (BR)
SEARS CANADA INC
500 College St E, Belleville, ON, K8N 5T2
(613) 391-3106
Emp Here 1,700
SIC 4225 General warehousing and storage

D-U-N-S 24-344-5124   (BR)
SERVICES FINANCIERS NCO, INC
(*Suby of* Egs Shell Company, Inc.)
610 Dundas St E, Belleville, ON, K8N 1G7

Emp Here 500
SIC 7322 Adjustment and collection services

D-U-N-S 25-099-4514   (SL)
SIGMA STRETCH FILM OF CANADA CO

▲ Public Company   ■ Public Company Family Member   **HQ** Headquarters   **BR** Branch   **SL** Single Location

219 Jamieson Bone Rd, Belleville, ON, K8N 5T4
(613) 966-4400
Emp Here 54   *Sales* 6,566,463
SIC 3081 Unsupported plastics film and sheet
Pr Pr Per W Nylen
Alfred S Teo
Harold Van Winssen
Mark Teo
John Reier
Robert S Nocek
William Lenchinsky

D-U-N-S 20-325-0238   (SL)
STREAMLINE FOODS INC.
(*Suby of* American Sugar Refining, Inc.)
315 University Ave, Belleville, ON, K8N 5T7
(613) 961-1265
Emp Here 80
SIC 2061 Raw cane sugar

D-U-N-S 24-343-9952   (BR)
SUPERIOR PLUS LP
686a Dundas St W, Belleville, ON, K8N 4Z2
(613) 962-9151
Emp Here 20
SIC 5984 Liquefied petroleum gas dealers

D-U-N-S 24-708-6549   (HQ)
TEMPLEMAN MENNINGA LLP
(*Suby of* Templeman Menninga LLP)
205 Dundas St E Suite 200, Belleville, ON, K8N 5K6
(613) 966-2620
Emp Here 35   *Emp Total* 57
Sales 4,888,367
SIC 8111 Legal services

D-U-N-S 24-345-7145   (BR)
TRENTWAY-WAGAR INC
COACH CANADA
75 Bridge St E, Belleville, ON, K8N 1L9
(613) 962-2163
Emp Here 265
SIC 5963 Direct selling establishments

D-U-N-S 24-347-4355   (BR)
TUDHOPE CARTAGE LIMITED
239 Casey Rd, Belleville, ON, K8N 4Z6

Emp Here 40
SIC 4213 Trucking, except local

D-U-N-S 25-066-1451   (BR)
UNITED PARCEL SERVICE CANADA LTD
UPS
31 Dussek St, Belleville, ON, K8N 5R9
(613) 967-2500
Emp Here 50
SIC 4212 Local trucking, without storage

D-U-N-S 25-725-3278   (BR)
WAL-MART CANADA CORP
274 Cloverleaf Dr, Belleville, ON, K8N 4Z5
(613) 966-9466
Emp Here 200
SIC 5311 Department stores

D-U-N-S 24-504-7977   (BR)
WATSON BUILDING SUPPLIES INC
130 Adam St, Belleville, ON, K8N 2X9
(613) 969-7070
Emp Here 30
SIC 1761 Roofing, siding, and sheetMetal work

D-U-N-S 20-939-8973   (BR)
WELCH LLP
525 Dundas St E, Belleville, ON, K8N 1G4
(613) 966-2844
Emp Here 30
SIC 8721 Accounting, auditing, and bookkeeping

D-U-N-S 25-813-3735   (BR)
WENDY'S RESTAURANTS OF CANADA INC
WENDY'S
(*Suby of* The Wendy's Company)

350 N Front St, Belleville, ON, K8N 5M5
(613) 967-9636
Emp Here 40
SIC 5812 Eating places

D-U-N-S 25-908-3517   (BR)
WILKINSON & COMPANY LLP
(*Suby of* Wilkinson & Company LLP)
139 Front St Suite 100, Belleville, ON, K8N 2Y6
(613) 966-1871
Emp Here 30
SIC 8721 Accounting, auditing, and bookkeeping

D-U-N-S 20-106-3455   (BR)
WINNERS MERCHANTS INTERNATIONAL L.P.
WINNERS
(*Suby of* The TJX Companies Inc)
390 Front St Unit 292, Belleville, ON, K8N 2Z8
(613) 966-5738
Emp Here 35
SIC 5651 Family clothing stores

D-U-N-S 24-506-4522   (SL)
YMCA OF BELLEVILLE AND QUINTE
433 Victoria Ave, Belleville, ON, K8N 2G1
(613) 962-9245
Emp Here 120   *Sales* 8,942,720
SIC 7999 Amusement and recreation, nec
David Allen
CEO Robert Gallagher

Belleville, ON K8P
Hastings County

D-U-N-S 20-048-5357   (HQ)
AIRBORNE SYSTEMS CANADA LTD
(*Suby of* Transdigm Group Incorporated)
35 Wilson Ave, Belleville, ON, K8P 1R7
(613) 967-8069
Emp Here 50   *Emp Total* 8,200
Sales 9,703,773
SIC 2399 Fabricated textile products, nec
Genl Mgr Charles Matthewson
Dir Fin Lisa Donovan

D-U-N-S 24-249-1632   (SL)
APPLEBEE'S NEIGHBORHOOD GRILL & BAR
265 North Front St, Belleville, ON, K8P 3C3

Emp Here 50   *Sales* 1,532,175
SIC 5812 Eating places

D-U-N-S 25-296-7625   (BR)
BANK OF NOVA SCOTIA, THE
SCOTIABANK
390 North Front St, Belleville, ON, K8P 3E1
(613) 967-6750
Emp Here 30
SIC 6021 National commercial banks

D-U-N-S 25-305-2484   (BR)
BANK OF NOVA SCOTIA, THE
SCOTIABANK
305 North Front St, Belleville, ON, K8P 3C3
(613) 962-3408
Emp Here 20
SIC 6021 National commercial banks

D-U-N-S 20-928-3253   (BR)
BEAUTYROCK HOLDINGS INC
3 Applewood Dr Suite 3, Belleville, ON, K8P 4E3
(613) 932-2525
Emp Here 200
SIC 7389 Business services, nec

D-U-N-S 25-878-7936   (BR)
BENSON GROUP INC
BENSON AUTO PARTS
(*Suby of* Benapac Inc)
35 Harriett St, Belleville, ON, K8P 1V4

(613) 962-9535
Emp Here 20
SIC 5013 Motor vehicle supplies and new parts

D-U-N-S 25-878-9254   (BR)
BRICK WAREHOUSE LP, THE
BRICK, THE
200 Bell Blvd, Belleville, ON, K8P 5L8
(613) 967-1006
Emp Here 27
SIC 5712 Furniture stores

D-U-N-S 20-085-9739   (BR)
CANADIAN RED CROSS SOCIETY, THE
365 North Front St, Belleville, ON, K8P 5A5
(613) 332-2444
Emp Here 225
SIC 8322 Individual and family services

D-U-N-S 25-282-8991   (BR)
CARA OPERATIONS LIMITED
SWISS CHALET
(*Suby of* Cara Holdings Limited)
15 Bell Blvd, Belleville, ON, K8P 4S5
(613) 962-7010
Emp Here 63
SIC 5812 Eating places

D-U-N-S 20-976-1563   (BR)
CARA OPERATIONS LIMITED
MONTANA'S COOKHOUSE
(*Suby of* Cara Holdings Limited)
170 Bell Blvd, Belleville, ON, K8P 5L2
(613) 967-9970
Emp Here 65
SIC 5812 Eating places

D-U-N-S 20-244-9372   (BR)
CINEPLEX ODEON CORPORATION
GALAXY CINEMAS BELLEVILLE
160 Bell Blvd, Belleville, ON, K8P 5L2
(613) 969-8469
Emp Here 20
SIC 7832 Motion picture theaters, except drive-in

D-U-N-S 20-741-6541   (BR)
CORPORATION OF THE CITY OF BELLEVILLE, THE
TRANSIT
400 Coleman St, Belleville, ON, K8P 3J4
(613) 967-3200
Emp Here 30
SIC 4131 Intercity and rural bus transportation

D-U-N-S 20-790-6020   (BR)
CORPORATION OF THE CITY OF BELLEVILLE, THE
BELLEVILLE WATERS
195 College St W, Belleville, ON, K8P 2H1
(613) 966-3657
Emp Here 40
SIC 4941 Water supply

D-U-N-S 25-585-9696   (BR)
CROWN RIDGE HEALTH CARE SERVICES INC
WESTGATE LODGE
37 Wilkie St, Belleville, ON, K8P 4E4
(613) 966-1323
Emp Here 85
SIC 8051 Skilled nursing care facilities

D-U-N-S 24-337-2997   (BR)
FGL SPORTS LTD
SPORT CHECK
390 North Front St Suite 200, Belleville, ON, K8P 3E1
(613) 962-3113
Emp Here 50
SIC 5941 Sporting goods and bicycle shops

D-U-N-S 25-639-2556   (BR)
FRED GUY MOVING & STORAGE LTD
PARKWAY VANLINE
20 Hanna Crt, Belleville, ON, K8P 5J2
(613) 969-7478
Emp Here 20

SIC 4214 Local trucking with storage

D-U-N-S 25-237-8054   (BR)
HASTINGS AND PRINCE EDWARD DISTRICT SCHOOL BOARD
SIR MACKENZIE BOWELL SCHOOL
138 Leland Dr, Belleville, ON, K8P 1G7

Emp Here 21
SIC 8211 Elementary and secondary schools

D-U-N-S 25-237-7882   (BR)
HASTINGS AND PRINCE EDWARD DISTRICT SCHOOL BOARD
WILLIAM R KIRK SCHOOL
224 Palmer Rd, Belleville, ON, K8P 4E1
(613) 962-2516
Emp Here 86
SIC 8211 Elementary and secondary schools

D-U-N-S 25-237-8088   (BR)
HASTINGS AND PRINCE EDWARD DISTRICT SCHOOL BOARD
SIR JOHN A MACDONALD SCHOOL
22 Harder Dr, Belleville, ON, K8P 1H2
(613) 962-6400
Emp Here 23
SIC 8211 Elementary and secondary schools

D-U-N-S 25-237-8096   (BR)
HASTINGS AND PRINCE EDWARD DISTRICT SCHOOL BOARD
CENTENNIAL SECONDARY SCHOOL
160 Palmer Rd, Belleville, ON, K8P 4E1
(613) 962-9233
Emp Here 75
SIC 8211 Elementary and secondary schools

D-U-N-S 25-237-8120   (BR)
HASTINGS AND PRINCE EDWARD DISTRICT SCHOOL BOARD
QUINTE SECONDARY SCHOOL
45 College St W, Belleville, ON, K8P 2G3
(613) 962-9295
Emp Here 90
SIC 8211 Elementary and secondary schools

D-U-N-S 20-025-0541   (BR)
HASTINGS AND PRINCE EDWARD DISTRICT SCHOOL BOARD
PRINCE OF WALES PUBLIC SCHOOL
37 Prince Of Wales Dr, Belleville, ON, K8P 2T6
(613) 968-8321
Emp Here 35
SIC 8211 Elementary and secondary schools

D-U-N-S 25-263-5610   (BR)
HASTINGS AND PRINCE EDWARD DISTRICT SCHOOL BOARD
PARK DALE PUBLIC SCHOOL
73 Poplar St, Belleville, ON, K8P 4J3
(613) 962-1341
Emp Here 38
SIC 8211 Elementary and secondary schools

D-U-N-S 25-174-2011   (BR)
HOME DEPOT OF CANADA INC
(*Suby of* The Home Depot Inc)
210 Bell Blvd, Belleville, ON, K8P 5L8
(613) 961-5340
Emp Here 150
SIC 5251 Hardware stores

D-U-N-S 25-305-3383   (BR)
INNVEST PROPERTIES CORP
FAIRFIELD INN & SUITES BY MARRIOTT
(*Suby of* Innvest Properties Corp)
407 North Front St, Belleville, ON, K8P 3C8
(613) 962-9211
Emp Here 50
SIC 7011 Hotels and motels

D-U-N-S 25-305-3425   (BR)
INNVEST PROPERTIES CORP
COMFORT INN
(*Suby of* Innvest Properties Corp)
200 North Park St, Belleville, ON, K8P 2Y9

(613) 966-7703
Emp Here 20
SIC 7011 Hotels and motels

D-U-N-S 20-276-5244   (BR)
MAGNA INTERNATIONAL INC
AUTOSYSTEMS
345 Bell Blvd, Belleville, ON, K8P 5H9
(613) 969-1122
Emp Here 200
SIC 3647 Vehicular lighting equipment

D-U-N-S 25-409-9427   (BR)
MARK'S WORK WEARHOUSE LTD
WORK WORLD
214 Bell Blvd, Belleville, ON, K8P 5L8
(613) 966-4583
Emp Here 30
SIC 5651 Family clothing stores

D-U-N-S 24-333-1753   (BR)
METRO ONTARIO INC
METRO
150 Sidney St, Belleville, ON, K8P 5E2

Emp Here 100
SIC 5411 Grocery stores

D-U-N-S 20-555-6553   (BR)
METRO ONTARIO INC
METRO
110 North Front St, Belleville, ON, K8P 5J8
(613) 962-0056
Emp Here 110
SIC 5411 Grocery stores

D-U-N-S 25-486-7633   (BR)
NORTEL NETWORKS LIMITED
250 Sidney St, Belleville, ON, K8P 3Z3

Emp Here 1,000
SIC 4899 Communication services, nec

D-U-N-S 20-016-7968   (BR)
OLD NAVY (CANADA) INC
(*Suby of* The Gap Inc)
390 North Front St, Belleville, ON, K8P 3E1
(613) 962-0484
Emp Here 20
SIC 5651 Family clothing stores

D-U-N-S 20-859-8644   (BR)
PACIFIC LINK COMMUNICATIONS INC
BELL WORLD
390 North Front St, Belleville, ON, K8P 3E1
(613) 968-8042
Emp Here 25
SIC 5999 Miscellaneous retail stores, nec

D-U-N-S 20-920-8131   (SL)
PARKHURST, AL TRANSPORTATION LTD
125 College St E, Belleville, ON, K8P 5A2
(613) 968-5109
Emp Here 80   *Sales* 2,921,220
SIC 4151 School buses

D-U-N-S 24-779-6576   (BR)
PEPSICO CANADA ULC
FRITO LAY CANADA
(*Suby of* Pepsico, Inc.)
87 Wallbridge Cres, Belleville, ON, K8P 1Z5
(800) 267-0944
Emp Here 50
SIC 2086 Bottled and canned soft drinks

D-U-N-S 24-354-6525   (SL)
**QUINTE GARDENS RETIREMENT RESI-
DENCE LTD**
30 College St W, Belleville, ON, K8P 0A9
(613) 966-5815
Emp Here 72   *Sales* 2,626,585
SIC 8361 Residential care

D-U-N-S 25-341-8511   (BR)
**RTM OPERATING COMPANY OF CANADA
INC**
HANSON RESTAURANT
(*Suby of* Roark Capital Group Inc.)
281 North Front St, Belleville, ON, K8P 3C3

(613) 966-1844
Emp Here 20
SIC 5812 Eating places

D-U-N-S 25-308-4644   (BR)
ROYAL BANK OF CANADA
RBC
(*Suby of* Royal Bank Of Canada)
246 North Front St, Belleville, ON, K8P 3C2
(613) 969-6101
Emp Here 27
SIC 6021 National commercial banks

D-U-N-S 20-002-8038   (BR)
SEARS CANADA INC
PARKS AND SERVICE
315 Bell Blvd, Belleville, ON, K8P 5H3
(800) 469-4663
Emp Here 20
SIC 7629 Electrical repair shops

D-U-N-S 20-528-1616   (BR)
SEARS CANADA INC
390 North Front St, Belleville, ON, K8P 3E1
(613) 966-3661
Emp Here 30
SIC 5311 Department stores

D-U-N-S 25-319-8469   (BR)
SECURITAS CANADA LIMITED
205 North Front St Suite 10, Belleville, ON,
K8P 3C3
(613) 966-3690
Emp Here 50
SIC 7381 Detective and armored car services

D-U-N-S 20-003-8979   (BR)
STAPLES CANADA INC
STAPLES THE BUSINESS DEPOT
(*Suby of* Staples, Inc.)
190 Bell Blvd, Belleville, ON, K8P 5L2
(613) 961-7399
Emp Here 40
SIC 5943 Stationery stores

D-U-N-S 20-506-7783   (BR)
STARBUCKS COFFEE CANADA, INC
(*Suby of* Starbucks Corporation)
390 North Front St, Belleville, ON, K8P 3E1
(613) 962-0479
Emp Here 30
SIC 5812 Eating places

D-U-N-S 24-326-5951   (BR)
SULLIVAN, EVAN PHARMACY LIMITED
SHOPPERS DRUG MART
390 North Front St, Belleville, ON, K8P 3E1
(613) 966-7298
Emp Here 60
SIC 5912 Drug stores and proprietary stores

D-U-N-S 25-316-8660   (BR)
**SUN LIFE ASSURANCE COMPANY OF
CANADA**
366 North Front St, Belleville, ON, K8P 5E6
(613) 962-8606
Emp Here 25
SIC 6311 Life insurance

D-U-N-S 20-613-9870   (SL)
TIM HORTONS
165 College St W, Belleville, ON, K8P 2G7
(613) 967-2197
Emp Here 50   *Sales* 1,678,096
SIC 5461 Retail bakeries

D-U-N-S 20-641-7383   (BR)
UNIFOR
CAW LOCAL 1839
160 Catharine St, Belleville, ON, K8P 1M8
(613) 962-8122
Emp Here 85
SIC 8631 Labor organizations

D-U-N-S 24-319-8368   (BR)
VALUE VILLAGE STORES, INC
(*Suby of* Savers, Inc.)
151 Bell Blvd, Belleville, ON, K8P 5N8
(613) 968-9188
Emp Here 30

SIC 5399 Miscellaneous general merchandise

Belmont, ON N0L
Elgin County

D-U-N-S 25-633-4467   (SL)
**WESTMINSTER MUTUAL INSURANCE
COMPANY**
14122 Belmont Rd, Belmont, ON, N0L 1B0
(519) 644-1663
Emp Here 22   *Sales* 10,506,341
SIC 6331 Fire, marine, and casualty insurance
  Michael Streib
Pr Pr Christine Van Daele
  Paul Knill
  Lenard Jones
  Tom Grieve
  Tracy Wintermute
  Doug Crockett

Bethany, ON L0A
Durham County

D-U-N-S 20-590-0546   (BR)
TORONTO-DOMINION BANK, THE
TD CANADA TRUST
(*Suby of* Toronto-Dominion Bank, The)
1475 Hwy 7a, Bethany, ON, L0A 1A0
(705) 277-2042
Emp Here 20
SIC 6021 National commercial banks

D-U-N-S 20-002-7311   (BR)
**TRILLIUM LAKELANDS DISTRICT
SCHOOL BOARD**
ROLLING HILLS PUBLIC SCHOOL
694 Hwy 7a, Bethany, ON, L0A 1A0
(705) 277-9515
Emp Here 25
SIC 8211 Elementary and secondary schools

D-U-N-S 25-833-1008   (BR)
**TRILLIUM LAKELANDS DISTRICT
SCHOOL BOARD**
GRANDVIEW PUBLIC SCHOOL
698 7a Hwy, Bethany, ON, L0A 1A0
(705) 277-2322
Emp Here 31
SIC 8211 Elementary and secondary schools

Big Trout Lake, ON P0V
Kenora County

D-U-N-S 24-032-1286   (SL)
**BIG TROUT LAKE BAND PERSONNEL OF-
FICE**
Gd, Big Trout Lake, ON, P0V 1G0

Emp Here 200   *Sales* 33,459,840
SIC 8699 Membership organizations, nec
Chief Donny Morris

Binbrook, ON L0R
Wentworth County

D-U-N-S 24-676-4984   (BR)
**HAMILTON-WENTWORTH CATHOLIC
SCHOOL BOARD**
*ST MATTHEW CATHOLIC ELEMENTARY
SCHOOL*
200 Windwood Dr, Binbrook, ON, L0R 1C0
(905) 523-2316
Emp Here 80
SIC 8211 Elementary and secondary schools

D-U-N-S 25-885-3019   (BR)
**HAMILTON-WENTWORTH CATHOLIC
SCHOOL BOARD**
BELLMOORE PUBLIC SCHOOL
35 Pumpkin Pass, Binbrook, ON, L0R 1C0
(905) 692-5435
Emp Here 70
SIC 8211 Elementary and secondary schools

D-U-N-S 20-702-7236   (SL)
**O'NEIL'S FARM EQUIPMENT (1971) LIM-
ITED**
2461 Hwy 56, Binbrook, ON, L0R 1C0
(905) 572-6714
Emp Here 26   *Sales* 5,690,935
SIC 5083 Farm and garden machinery
Pr Larry Smith
VP Craig Smith
  Carolyn Smith

D-U-N-S 20-035-4678   (SL)
WILLS MOTORS LTD
WILLS BUS LINES
2187 56 Hwy, Binbrook, ON, L0R 1C0
(905) 692-4423
Emp Here 60   *Sales* 2,845,467
SIC 4142 Bus charter service, except local

Blackstock, ON L0B
Durham County

D-U-N-S 25-300-7504   (BR)
DURHAM DISTRICT SCHOOL BOARD
CARTWRIGHT CENTRAL PUBLIC SCHOOL
10 Alexander St, Blackstock, ON, L0B 1B0
(905) 986-4227
Emp Here 37
SIC 8211 Elementary and secondary schools

Blenheim, ON N0P

D-U-N-S 20-004-9489   (BR)
**LAMBTON KENT DISTRICT SCHOOL
BOARD**
BLENHEIM DISTRICT HIGH SCHOOL
163 Chatham St, Blenheim, ON, N0P 1A0
(519) 676-5485
Emp Here 50
SIC 8211 Elementary and secondary schools

D-U-N-S 20-710-4949   (BR)
**LAMBTON KENT DISTRICT SCHOOL
BOARD**
W. J. BAIRD PUBLIC SCHOOL
182 King St, Blenheim, ON, N0P 1A0
(519) 676-5407
Emp Here 25
SIC 8211 Elementary and secondary schools

D-U-N-S 24-487-7734   (BR)
REVERA LONG TERM CARE INC
*BLENHEIM COMMUNITY VILLAGE RETIRE-
MENT RESIDENCE*
10 Marys St, Blenheim, ON, N0P 1A0
(519) 676-8119
Emp Here 100
SIC 8051 Skilled nursing care facilities

D-U-N-S 20-025-3354   (BR)
**ST. CLAIR CATHOLIC DISTRICT SCHOOL
BOARD**
ST ANNE CATHOLIC SCHOOL
Gd, Blenheim, ON, N0P 1A0
(519) 676-7352
Emp Here 30
SIC 8211 Elementary and secondary schools

D-U-N-S 20-087-0314   (BR)
**ST. CLAIR CATHOLIC DISTRICT SCHOOL
BOARD**
ST MARY CATHOLIC SCSHOOL

94 George St, Blenheim, ON, N0P 1A0

Emp Here 20
SIC 8211 Elementary and secondary schools

D-U-N-S 25-092-0639   (BR)
THOMPSONS LIMITED
125 George St, Blenheim, ON, N0P 1A0
(519) 676-5446
Emp Here 40
SIC 5153 Grain and field beans

D-U-N-S 20-192-2122   (BR)
WOODBRIDGE FOAM CORPORATION
WOODBRIDGE GROUP, THE
140 Cathcart St, Blenheim, ON, N0P 1A0
(519) 676-3626
Emp Here 240
SIC 3086 Plastics foam products

Blind River, ON P0R
Algoma County

D-U-N-S 24-195-4957   (BR)
A.J. BUS LINES LIMITED
370 Leacock St, Blind River, ON, P0R 1B0
(705) 356-7889
Emp Here 42
SIC 4151 School buses

D-U-N-S 25-239-0455   (BR)
ALGOMA DISTRICT SCHOOL BOARD
W.C. EAKET SECONDARY SCHOOL
(*Suby of* Algoma District School Board)
147 Woodward Ave, Blind River, ON, P0R 1B0
(705) 356-2221
Emp Here 40
SIC 8211 Elementary and secondary schools

D-U-N-S 24-550-1775   (SL)
BLIND RIVER DISTRICT HEALTH CENTRE AUXILIARY INC
BRDHC
525 Causley, Blind River, ON, P0R 1B0
(705) 356-2265
Emp Here 50   *Sales* 13,137,181
SIC 8062 General medical and surgical hospitals
  Wolf Kirchmeir
  Roger Boyer Ii

D-U-N-S 24-312-1816   (BR)
CARMEUSE LIME (CANADA) LIMITED
CARMEUSE LIME CANADA (BLIND RIVER)
3136b Highway 17 E, Blind River, ON, P0R 1B0
(705) 849-2201
Emp Here 30
SIC 3274 Lime

D-U-N-S 25-126-1194   (BR)
CONSEIL SCOLAIRE DE DISTRICT CATHOLIQUE DU NOUVEL-ONTARIO, LE
ECOLE ST-JOSEPH
44 Lawton St, Blind River, ON, P0R 1B0
(705) 356-2246
Emp Here 24
SIC 8211 Elementary and secondary schools

D-U-N-S 20-710-4139   (BR)
CONSEIL SCOLAIRE DE DISTRICT CATHOLIQUE DU NOUVEL-ONTARIO, LE
ECOLE SECONDAIRE
117 Ch Colonization, Blind River, ON, P0R 1B0
(705) 356-1688
Emp Here 50
SIC 8211 Elementary and secondary schools

D-U-N-S 20-710-3958   (BR)
HURON-SUPERIOR CATHOLIC DISTRICT SCHOOL BOARD
ST MARY CATHOLIC SCHOOL

25 Michigan Ave, Blind River, ON, P0R 1B0
(705) 356-7621
Emp Here 20
SIC 8211 Elementary and secondary schools

D-U-N-S 25-986-8198   (BR)
LOBLAW COMPANIES LIMITED
HUTTON VALU-MART
105 Causley St, Blind River, ON, P0R 1B0
(705) 356-1311
Emp Here 30
SIC 5411 Grocery stores

Bloomfield, ON K0K
Prince Edward County

D-U-N-S 20-589-7411   (BR)
CANADIAN IMPERIAL BANK OF COMMERCE
CIBC
257 Main St, Bloomfield, ON, K0K 1G0
(613) 393-3150
Emp Here 20
SIC 6021 National commercial banks

D-U-N-S 20-711-5127   (BR)
HASTINGS AND PRINCE EDWARD DISTRICT SCHOOL BOARD
PINECREST MEMORIAL ELEMENTARY SCHOOL
27 Corey St, Bloomfield, ON, K0K 1G0
(613) 393-3262
Emp Here 50
SIC 8211 Elementary and secondary schools

Bloomingdale, ON N0B
Waterloo County

D-U-N-S 24-193-2565   (SL)
SIMPSON SCREEN PRINT & LITHOGRAPHY LTD
865 Sawmill Rd, Bloomingdale, ON, N0B 1K0
(519) 744-3745
Emp Here 60   *Sales* 4,523,563
SIC 2752 Commercial printing, lithographic

Blue Mountains, ON L9Y

D-U-N-S 20-343-0301   (SL)
BLUE MOUNTAIN RESORTS LIMITED PARTNERSHIP
108 Jozo Weider Blvd, Blue Mountains, ON, L9Y 3Z2
(705) 445-0231
Emp Here 50   *Sales* 2,188,821
SIC 7011 Hotels and motels

D-U-N-S 20-742-6078   (SL)
COPPER BLUES
156 Jozo Weider Blvd Unit 3, Blue Mountains, ON, L9Y 3Z2
(705) 446-2643
Emp Here 50   *Sales* 1,824,018
SIC 5813 Drinking places

D-U-N-S 24-019-4006   (BR)
INTRAWEST RESORT CLUB GROUP
EMBARC BLUE MOUNTAIN
(*Suby of* Intrawest Resorts Holdings, Inc.)
276 Jozo Weider Blvd, Blue Mountains, ON, L9Y 3Z2
(705) 443-4500
Emp Here 30
SIC 7011 Hotels and motels

D-U-N-S 24-024-9107   (BR)
INTRAWEST ULC
WESTIN TRILLIUM HOUSE BLUE MOUNTAIN, THE

(*Suby of* Intrawest Resorts Holdings, Inc.)
220 Mountain Dr, Blue Mountains, ON, L9Y 0V9
(705) 443-8080
Emp Here 80
SIC 7011 Hotels and motels

D-U-N-S 20-262-5919   (BR)
INTRAWEST ULC
BLUE MOUNTAIN RESORT
(*Suby of* Intrawest Resorts Holdings, Inc.)
108 Jozo Weider Blvd, Blue Mountains, ON, L9Y 3Z2
(705) 445-0231
Emp Here 400
SIC 7011 Hotels and motels

D-U-N-S 24-987-5261   (SL)
SHIRWOOD FOOD SERVICES LTD
164 Craigleith Rd, Blue Mountains, ON, L9Y 0S4

Emp Here 60   *Sales* 1,824,018
SIC 5812 Eating places

D-U-N-S 25-412-7897   (SL)
WINDY O'NEILL'S @ BLUE INC
WINDY O'NEILL'S
108 Jozo Weider Blvd Unit C, Blue Mountains, ON, L9Y 3Z2
(705) 446-9989
Emp Here 50   *Sales* 1,532,175
SIC 5812 Eating places

Blyth, ON N0M
Huron County

D-U-N-S 20-629-8622   (SL)
HOWSON & HOWSON LIMITED
HOWSON MILLS
232 Westmoreland St, Blyth, ON, N0M 1H0
(519) 523-4241
Emp Here 50   *Sales* 4,961,328
SIC 2041 Flour and other grain mill products

D-U-N-S 20-716-5978   (HQ)
SPARLING'S PROPANE CO. LIMITED
82948 London Rd, Blyth, ON, N0M 1H0
(519) 523-4256
Emp Here 30   *Emp Total* 2,300
Sales 5,690,935
SIC 5984 Liquefied petroleum gas dealers
Pr Robert Espey
VP VP Jane Savage
VP VP Donna Strating
VP VP Allan Willms
Sr VP Michael Lambert
VP Fin Andrew Cruickshank
VP VP Mike Mcmillan
VP VP Robert Fink
VP VP Peter Kilty
VP VP William Rouse

Bobcaygeon, ON K0M

D-U-N-S 20-904-0542   (SL)
CASE MANOR
28 Boyd St, Bobcaygeon, ON, K0M 1A0
(705) 738-2374
Emp Here 75   *Sales* 3,429,153
SIC 8051 Skilled nursing care facilities

D-U-N-S 20-035-7903   (HQ)
KAWARTHA DAIRY LIMITED
(*Suby of* Kawartha Dairy Limited)
89 Prince St W, Bobcaygeon, ON, K0M 1A0
(705) 738-5123
Emp Here 60   *Emp Total* 100
Sales 31,651,200
SIC 5143 Dairy products, except dried or canned

Pr Pr Jeff Crowe
  Donald Crowe
VP VP Blake Frazer

D-U-N-S 25-361-1826   (SL)
MEDLAW CORPORATION LIMITED
PINECREST NURSING HOME
3418 County Rd 36 S, Bobcaygeon, ON, K0M 1A0
(705) 738-2366
Emp Here 65   *Sales* 2,991,389
SIC 8051 Skilled nursing care facilities

D-U-N-S 24-036-7347   (SL)
SPECIALTY CARE CASE MANOR INC
18 Boyd St, Bobcaygeon, ON, K0M 1A0
(705) 738-2374
Emp Here 100   *Sales* 4,523,563
SIC 8051 Skilled nursing care facilities

D-U-N-S 20-031-1558   (BR)
TRILLIUM LAKELANDS DISTRICT SCHOOL BOARD
BOBCAYGEON PUBLIC SCHOOL
30 Balaclava St, Bobcaygeon, ON, K0M 1A0
(705) 738-5105
Emp Here 40
SIC 8211 Elementary and secondary schools

Bolton, ON L7C
Peel County

D-U-N-S 25-297-1387   (BR)
PEEL DISTRICT SCHOOL BOARD
MACVILLE PUBLIC SCHOOL
(*Suby of* Peel District School Board)
7280 King St, Bolton, ON, L7C 0S3
(905) 857-3448
Emp Here 24
SIC 8211 Elementary and secondary schools

Bolton, ON L7E
Peel County

D-U-N-S 24-360-1619   (SL)
1421239 ONTARIO INC
124 Commercial Rd, Bolton, ON, L7E 1K4
(905) 951-6800
Emp Here 125   *Sales* 27,492,950
SIC 6712 Bank holding companies
Pr Pr Robert J Murray
  Michael Mccarron

D-U-N-S 20-773-9285   (SL)
ADRIAN STEEL OF CANADA INC
40 Simpson Rd, Bolton, ON, L7E 1Y4
(905) 565-0540
Emp Here 50   *Sales* 4,669,485
SIC 2542 Partitions and fixtures, except wood

D-U-N-S 24-195-8529   (HQ)
ALUMA SYSTEMS INC
(*Suby of* Clayton, Dubilier & Rice, Inc.)
2 Manchester Court, Bolton, ON, L7E 2J3
(905) 669-5282
Emp Here 150   *Emp Total* 33,045
Sales 48,372,944
SIC 7353 Heavy construction equipment rental
Pr Pr Paul Wood
Treas Nikolai Mondi
Dir Stephen Tisdall
Dir Dave Witsken

D-U-N-S 24-826-2631   (BR)
BEST BUY CANADA LTD
BEST BUY
(*Suby of* Best Buy Co., Inc.)
86 Pillsworth Rd, Bolton, ON, L7E 4G8

Emp Here 50
SIC 5731 Radio, television, and electronic

stores

D-U-N-S 25-197-7443   (HQ)
CALEDON COMMUNITY SERVICES
(*Suby of* Caledon Community Services)
18 King St E Suite 2, Bolton, ON, L7E 1E8
(905) 584-9460
Emp Here 55   *Emp Total* 65
Sales 2,553,625
SIC 8322 Individual and family services

D-U-N-S 20-968-2017   (BR)
CALEDON SAND & GRAVEL INC
14442 Regional Road 50 Suite 50, Bolton,
ON, L7E 3E2
(905) 951-2244
Emp Here 500
SIC 5032 Brick, stone, and related material

D-U-N-S 20-321-5223   (BR)
CARA OPERATIONS LIMITED
KELSEY'S RESTAURANT
(*Suby of* Cara Holdings Limited)
20 Mcewan Dr E, Bolton, ON, L7E 2Y3
(905) 857-9913
Emp Here 60
SIC 5812 Eating places

D-U-N-S 24-318-2933   (BR)
CLUBLINK CORPORATION ULC
CALDON WOODS GOLFS CLUB
15608 Regional Road 50, Bolton, L7E
3E5
(905) 880-1400
Emp Here 80
SIC 7992 Public golf courses

D-U-N-S 20-279-7577   (SL)
DAYTONA FREIGHT SYSTEMS INC
124 Commercial Rd, Bolton, ON, L7E 1K4
(416) 744-2020
Emp Here 95   *Sales* 6,010,292
SIC 4213 Trucking, except local
Pr Pr Jasbinder Matharu
Inderpal Kahlon
Tejinder Dhot
Gagan Sidhu
Sukhwinder Singh Gill

D-U-N-S 20-303-9078   (BR)
DIBCO UNDERGROUND LIMITED
135 Commercial Rd, Bolton, ON, L7E 1R6
(905) 857-0458
Emp Here 50
SIC 1623 Water, sewer, and utility lines

D-U-N-S 20-035-8455   (HQ)
DICK, JAMES CONSTRUCTION LIMITED
14442 Regional Rd 50, Bolton, L7E 3E2
(905) 857-3500
Emp Here 100   *Emp Total* 350
Sales 74,237,711
SIC 5032 Brick, stone, and related material
Pr Pr James Dick
Anne Dick

D-U-N-S 25-092-1533   (BR)
DICK, JAMES CONSTRUCTION LIMITED
JAMES DICK CONSTRUCTION LIMITED
14442 Regional Road 50, Bolton, L7E
3E2
(905) 857-3122
Emp Here 49
SIC 4212 Local trucking, without storage

D-U-N-S 20-325-2080   (BR)
DOKA CANADA LTD./LTEE
12673 Coleraine Dr, Bolton, ON, L7E 3B5
(905) 951-0225
Emp Here 20
SIC 5039 Construction materials, nec

D-U-N-S 20-711-0250   (BR)
**DUFFERIN-PEEL CATHOLIC DISTRICT
SCHOOL BOARD**
ST NICHOLAS SCHOOL
120 Harvest Moon Dr, Bolton, ON, L7E 2W1
(905) 857-7582
Emp Here 50

SIC 8211 Elementary and secondary schools

D-U-N-S 20-710-9625   (BR)
**DUFFERIN-PEEL CATHOLIC DISTRICT
SCHOOL BOARD**
HOLY FAMILY SCHOOL
61 Allan Dr, Bolton, ON, L7E 1P7
(905) 857-1300
Emp Here 50
SIC 8211 Elementary and secondary schools

D-U-N-S 25-273-8711   (HQ)
ENERSYS CANADA INC
61 Parr Blvd Unit 3, Bolton, ON, L7E 4E3
(905) 951-2228
Emp Here 40   *Emp Total* 9,400
Sales 61,557,868
SIC 5063 Electrical apparatus and equipment
Pr Jim Arshad
VP Sls Robert Bryan

D-U-N-S 24-876-5831   (BR)
FGL SPORTS LTD
SPORT CHEK BOLTON
12730 50 Hwy Unit 1, Bolton, ON, L7E 4G1
(905) 857-2090
Emp Here 20
SIC 5941 Sporting goods and bicycle shops

D-U-N-S 24-325-1902   (SL)
GENDON POLYMER SERVICES INC
(*Suby of* Berkshire Hathaway Inc.)
38 Nixon Rd, Bolton, ON, L7E 1W2
(905) 951-6118
Emp Here 35   *Sales* 1,896,978
SIC 8731 Commercial physical research

D-U-N-S 20-525-4485   (HQ)
**HUSKY INJECTION MOLDING SYSTEMS
LTD**
500 Queen St S, Bolton, ON, L7E 5S5
(905) 951-5000
Emp Here 500   *Emp Total* 3,036
Sales 540,273,984
SIC 6712 Bank holding companies
Pr Pr John Galt
VP Sls Gerardo Chiaia
VP Fin George Halatsis
VP Steve Lawrynuik
Jeffery Macdonald
VP Su Taylor
Keith Carlton

D-U-N-S 24-377-4333   (BR)
JAN WOODLANDS (2001) INC
641 Hardwick Rd, Bolton, ON, L7E 5R2
(905) 951-4495
Emp Here 40
SIC 2491 Wood preserving

D-U-N-S 24-006-6985   (SL)
KING NURSING HOME LIMITED
49 Sterne St, Bolton, ON, L7E 1B9
(905) 857-4117
Emp Here 75   *Sales* 3,429,153
SIC 8051 Skilled nursing care facilities

D-U-N-S 20-307-0115   (BR)
MARS CANADA INC
(*Suby of* Mars, Incorporated)
12315 Coleraine Dr, Bolton, ON, L7E 3B4
(905) 857-5620
Emp Here 300
SIC 2064 Candy and other confectionery
products

D-U-N-S 20-878-1070   (HQ)
MARS CANADA INC
MASTERFOODS, DIV OF
(*Suby of* Mars, Incorporated)
37 Holland Dr, Bolton, ON, L7E 5S4
(905) 857-5700
Emp Here 300   *Emp Total* 80,000
Sales 51,072,490
SIC 2064 Candy and other confectionery
products
Pr Pr Rena Crumplen
Mary Jane Dowling

VP VP Tami Majer
Ellen Kollar
VP Sls Roy Benin

D-U-N-S 20-691-9818   (BR)
**MATERIAUX DE CONSTRUCTION OLD-
CASTLE CANADA INC, LES**
PERMACON BOLTON (DIV)
3 Betomat Crt, Bolton, ON, L7E 2V9
(905) 857-6773
Emp Here 25
SIC 3272 Concrete products, nec

D-U-N-S 20-130-6792   (SL)
MCGILLION TRANSPORT LTD
141 Healey Rd Suite 4, Bolton, ON, L7E 5B2

Emp Here 50   *Sales* 8,049,120
SIC 4213 Trucking, except local
Pr Pr Charles Mcgillion Sr
Charles Mcgillion Jr

D-U-N-S 20-294-2371   (SL)
METRIE CANADA LTD
13371 Coleraine Dr, Bolton, ON, L7E 3B6
(905) 857-2662
Emp Here 50   *Sales* 4,085,799
SIC 2431 Millwork

D-U-N-S 24-155-2699   (BR)
METRIE CANADA LTD
41 Simpson Rd, Bolton, ON, L7E 2R6
(905) 951-2662
Emp Here 50
SIC 2431 Millwork

D-U-N-S 25-221-4630   (SL)
**NATIONAL   ELECTRONIC   ARTICLE
SURVEILLANCE SYSTEMS LTD**
NATIONAL EAS
13 Holland Dr Suite 10, Bolton, ON, L7E 1G4

Emp Here 70   *Sales* 12,909,907
SIC 3699 Electrical equipment and supplies,
nec
Pr Pr James Grant

D-U-N-S 24-451-0178   (SL)
OLIVER OLIVES INC
SARDO FOODS
99 Pillsworth Rd, Bolton, ON, L7E 4E4
(905) 951-9096
Emp Here 67   *Sales* 3,210,271
SIC 2033 Canned fruits and specialties

D-U-N-S 20-859-9303   (BR)
PACIFIC LINK COMMUNICATIONS INC
BELL WORLD
40 Mcewan Dr E Suite 9, Bolton, ON, L7E 2Y3
(905) 951-1888
Emp Here 25
SIC 5999 Miscellaneous retail stores, nec

D-U-N-S 25-297-1304   (BR)
PEEL DISTRICT SCHOOL BOARD
JAMES BOLTON PUBLIC SCHOOL
(*Suby of* Peel District School Board)
225 Kingsview Dr, Bolton, ON, L7E 3X8
(905) 857-2666
Emp Here 30
SIC 8211 Elementary and secondary schools

D-U-N-S 25-297-1346   (BR)
PEEL DISTRICT SCHOOL BOARD
ELLWOOD MEMORIAL PUBLIC SCHOOL
(*Suby of* Peel District School Board)
35 Ellwood Dr E, Bolton, ON, L7E 2A7
(905) 857-3021
Emp Here 26
SIC 8211 Elementary and secondary schools

D-U-N-S 20-591-3861   (BR)
PEEL DISTRICT SCHOOL BOARD
ALLAN DRIVE MIDDLE SCHOOL
(*Suby of* Peel District School Board)
254 Allan Dr, Bolton, ON, L7E 1R9
(905) 857-9144
Emp Here 25

SIC 8211 Elementary and secondary schools

D-U-N-S 25-998-6644   (HQ)
PERI FORMWORK SYSTEMS INC
45 Nixon Rd, Bolton, ON, L7E 1K1
(905) 951-5400
Emp Here 99   *Emp Total* 5,471
Sales 14,812,892
SIC 7353 Heavy construction equipment
rental
Stephen Jones
Carl Heathcote
Alexander Schwoerer

D-U-N-S 25-091-8299   (BR)
RE/MAX WEST REALTY INC
1 Queensgate Blvd Unit 9, Bolton, ON, L7E
2X7
(905) 857-7653
Emp Here 55
SIC 6531 Real estate agents and managers

D-U-N-S 25-397-3549   (BR)
REXALL PHARMACY GROUP LTD
BOLTON REXALL DRUG STORE
(*Suby of* McKesson Corporation)
405 Queen St S, Bolton, ON, L7E 2B5
(905) 857-3766
Emp Here 40
SIC 5912 Drug stores and proprietary stores

D-U-N-S 25-989-3717   (SL)
SILCOTECH NORTH AMERICA INC
54 Nixon Rd, Bolton, ON, L7E 1W2
(905) 857-9998
Emp Here 75   *Sales* 8,244,559
SIC 2821 Plastics materials and resins
Pr Pr Michael Maloney
VP VP Isolde Boettger
Dir Udo Lange
Dir Holger Lange
Yogesh Chauhan
Virendra Aggarwal

D-U-N-S 24-327-8343   (BR)
STAPLES CANADA INC
STAPLES THE BUSINESS DEPOT
(*Suby of* Staples, Inc.)
471 Queen St S Suite 2, Bolton, ON, L7E 2B5
(905) 951-1640
Emp Here 30
SIC 5943 Stationery stores

D-U-N-S 24-330-6474   (SL)
TITANIUM TRUCKING SERVICES INC
32 Simpson Rd, Bolton, ON, L7E 1G9
(905) 851-1688
Emp Here 200   *Sales* 26,119,931
SIC 4213 Trucking, except local
Pr Pr Ted Daniel
Mgr Marilyn Daniel

D-U-N-S 24-307-8771   (BR)
**UNITED LUMBER AND BUILDING SUP-
PLIES COMPANY LIMITED**
HOME HARDWARE BUILDING CENTRE
12833 Hwy 50, Bolton, L7E 1M5
(905) 857-6970
Emp Here 30
SIC 5211 Lumber and other building materials

D-U-N-S 24-644-0614   (SL)
**VERA M DAVIS COMMUNITY CARE CEN-
TRE**
DAVIS CENTRE, THE
80 Allan Dr, Bolton, ON, L7E 1P7
(905) 857-0975
Emp Here 70   *Sales* 3,210,271
SIC 8051 Skilled nursing care facilities

D-U-N-S 24-795-9711   (SL)
VERSATILE SPRAY PAINTING LTD
102 Healey Rd, Bolton, ON, L7E 5A7
(905) 857-4915
Emp Here 60   *Sales* 4,144,998
SIC 3479 Metal coating and allied services

D-U-N-S 24-207-4099   (BR)

WSI SIGN SYSTEMS LTD
KING ARCHITECTURAL PRODUCTS, DIV OF
31 Simpson Rd Suite 1, Bolton, ON, L7E 2R6
(905) 857-2804
Emp Here 55
SIC 3993 Signs and advertising specialties

D-U-N-S 24-124-1665   (BR)
WAL-MART CANADA CORP
150 Mcewan Dr E, Bolton, ON, L7E 2Y3
(905) 857-7004
Emp Here 40
SIC 5611 Men's and boys' clothing stores

D-U-N-S 24-356-7851   (BR)
WINNERS MERCHANTS INTERNATIONAL L.P.
WINNERS
(*Suby of* The TJX Companies Inc)
471 Queen St S, Bolton, ON, L7E 2B5
(905) 951-7317
Emp Here 40
SIC 5651 Family clothing stores

D-U-N-S 25-362-2013   (SL)
WOOD WASTE SOLUTIONS CANADA INC
12673 Coleraine Dr, Bolton, ON, L7E 3B5
(905) 857-7672
Emp Here 110   *Sales* 14,913,150
SIC 2448 Wood pallets and skids
Pr Pr Tim Mcgillion

D-U-N-S 25-297-8622   (BR)
ZEHRMART INC
ZEHRS MARKETS 58
487 Queen St S, Bolton, ON, L7E 2B4
(905) 951-7505
Emp Here 220
SIC 5411 Grocery stores

Borden, ON L0M

D-U-N-S 20-026-6935   (BR)
SIMCOE COUNTY DISTRICT SCHOOL BOARD, THE
FREDERICK CAMPBELL ELEMENTARY SCHOOL
(*Suby of* Simcoe County District School Board, The)
145 Somme Blvd, Borden, ON, L0M 1C0

Emp Here 25
SIC 8211 Elementary and secondary schools

Bourget, ON K0A
Russell County

D-U-N-S 20-789-0245   (SL)
261911 ONTARIO INC
CARESSANT CARE BOURGET
2279 Laval St, Bourget, ON, K0A 1E0
(613) 487-2331
Emp Here 50   *Sales* 2,261,782
SIC 8051 Skilled nursing care facilities

D-U-N-S 20-747-4768   (SL)
AUTOBUS LALONDE BUS LINES INC, LES
LALONDE BUS LINES
2207 Etchier St, Bourget, ON, K0A 1E0
(613) 487-2230
Emp Here 38   *Sales* 1,413,494
SIC 4151 School buses

Bowmanville, ON L1C
Durham County

D-U-N-S 25-750-6402   (SL)
1214391 ONTARIO INC

EAST SIDE MARIO'S
101 Clarington Blvd, Bowmanville, ON, L1C 4Z3
(905) 697-3702
Emp Here 55   *Sales* 1,678,096
SIC 5812 Eating places

D-U-N-S 20-035-9941   (BR)
127323 CANADA INC
ALLIN CABLE REELS DIV OF
(*Suby of* 127323 Canada Inc)
179 Baseline Rd E, Bowmanville, ON, L1C 3L4
(905) 623-4455
Emp Here 30
SIC 2499 Wood products, nec

D-U-N-S 25-835-8183   (SL)
1429634 ONTARIO LIMITED
PHOENIX TRANSPORTATION
51 Port Darlington Rd Suite 1, Bowmanville, ON, L1C 3K3
(905) 697-0503
Emp Here 89   *Sales* 2,480,664
SIC 4151 School buses

D-U-N-S 25-296-7740   (BR)
BANK OF NOVA SCOTIA, THE
SCOTIABANK
100 Clarington Blvd, Bowmanville, ON, L1C 4Z3
(905) 623-2122
Emp Here 22
SIC 6021 National commercial banks

D-U-N-S 20-588-2033   (BR)
BANQUE TORONTO-DOMINION, LA
TD CANADA TRUST
(*Suby of* Toronto-Dominion Bank, The)
2379 Highway 2, Bowmanville, ON, L1C 5A4
(905) 623-2514
Emp Here 20
SIC 6021 National commercial banks

D-U-N-S 20-084-7395   (BR)
CARA OPERATIONS LIMITED
HARVEY'S SERVING SWISS CHALET
(*Suby of* Cara Holdings Limited)
170 Liberty St S, Bowmanville, ON, L1C 4W4
(905) 623-0650
Emp Here 28
SIC 5812 Eating places

D-U-N-S 20-052-8888   (BR)
CINEPLEX ODEON CORPORATION
CINEPLEX CINEMAS CLARINGTON PLACE
111 Clarington Blvd, Bowmanville, ON, L1C 4Z3
(905) 697-0611
Emp Here 20
SIC 7832 Motion picture theaters, except drive-in

D-U-N-S 25-092-3898   (BR)
COCO PAVING INC
3075 Maple Grove Rd, Bowmanville, ON, L1C 3K4
(905) 697-0400
Emp Here 100
SIC 1611 Highway and street construction

D-U-N-S 24-311-8549   (BR)
CONTITECH CANADA, INC
45 Raynes Ave, Bowmanville, ON, L1C 1J3
(905) 623-2606
Emp Here 20
SIC 5085 Industrial supplies

D-U-N-S 20-026-7057   (BR)
CORPORATION OF THE MUNICIPALITY OF CLARINGTON
RICKARD, GARNET B RECREATION COMPLEX
2440 King St, Bowmanville, ON, L1C 1K5
(905) 623-5728
Emp Here 30
SIC 7389 Business services, nec

D-U-N-S 24-783-9202   (SL)

DETOX ENVIRONMENTAL LTD
322 Bennett Rd, Bowmanville, ON, L1C 3Z2
(905) 623-1367
Emp Here 60   *Sales* 10,851,840
SIC 4953 Refuse systems
Pr Pr Brian Ritchie
  Randall Duffy
  Beate Ritchie

D-U-N-S 20-699-6402   (BR)
EXTENDICARE INC
MARNWOOD LIFECARE CENTRE
26 Elgin St, Bowmanville, ON, L1C 3C8
(905) 623-5731
Emp Here 70
SIC 8051 Skilled nursing care facilities

D-U-N-S 20-699-6683   (BR)
EXTENDICARE INC
STRATHHAVEN LIFECARE CENTRE
264 King St E Suite 306, Bowmanville, ON, L1C 1P9
(905) 623-2553
Emp Here 100
SIC 8051 Skilled nursing care facilities

D-U-N-S 25-321-1197   (BR)
FIRSTCANADA ULC
80 Mearns Crt, Bowmanville, ON, L1C 4A2
(905) 623-3811
Emp Here 140
SIC 4151 School buses

D-U-N-S 25-265-4439   (BR)
KAWARTHA PINE RIDGE DISTRICT SCHOOL BOARD
ONTARIO STREET PUBLIC SCHOOL
116 Ontario St, Bowmanville, ON, L1C 2T4
(905) 623-5437
Emp Here 25
SIC 8211 Elementary and secondary schools

D-U-N-S 20-711-5721   (BR)
KAWARTHA PINE RIDGE DISTRICT SCHOOL BOARD
CENTRAL PUBLIC SCHOOL
120 Wellington St, Bowmanville, ON, L1C 1V9
(905) 623-5614
Emp Here 25
SIC 8211 Elementary and secondary schools

D-U-N-S 20-591-6468   (BR)
KAWARTHA PINE RIDGE DISTRICT SCHOOL BOARD
WAVERLY
168 Waverley Rd, Bowmanville, ON, L1C 3Y8
(905) 623-4323
Emp Here 25
SIC 8211 Elementary and secondary schools

D-U-N-S 20-711-5804   (BR)
KAWARTHA PINE RIDGE DISTRICT SCHOOL BOARD
HAROLD LONGWORTH PUBLIC SCHOOL
350 Longworth Ave, Bowmanville, ON, L1C 5J5
(905) 623-3682
Emp Here 50
SIC 8211 Elementary and secondary schools

D-U-N-S 20-591-6492   (BR)
KAWARTHA PINE RIDGE DISTRICT SCHOOL BOARD
DR ROSS TILLEY PUBLIC SCHOOL
45 West Side Dr, Bowmanville, ON, L1C 4Y8
(905) 623-3841
Emp Here 50
SIC 8211 Elementary and secondary schools

D-U-N-S 24-191-7934   (BR)
KAWARTHA PINE RIDGE DISTRICT SCHOOL BOARD
CLARINGTON CENTRAL SECONDARY SCHOOL
200 Clarington Blvd, Bowmanville, ON, L1C 5N8
(905) 697-9857
Emp Here 150

SIC 8211 Elementary and secondary schools

D-U-N-S 25-265-3670   (BR)
KAWARTHA PINE RIDGE DISTRICT SCHOOL BOARD
VINCENT MASSEY PUBLIC SCHOOL
10 Church St, Bowmanville, ON, L1C 1S3
(905) 623-6279
Emp Here 25
SIC 8211 Elementary and secondary schools

D-U-N-S 20-591-6476   (BR)
KAWARTHA PINE RIDGE DISTRICT SCHOOL BOARD
JOHN M JAMES PUBLIC SCHOOL
175 Mearns Ave, Bowmanville, ON, L1C 5C6
(905) 697-7817
Emp Here 45
SIC 8211 Elementary and secondary schools

D-U-N-S 25-528-8532   (BR)
LAKERIDGE HEALTH
LAKERIDGE HEALTH BOWANVILLE
(*Suby of* Lakeridge Health)
47 Liberty St S, Bowmanville, ON, L1C 2N4
(905) 623-3331
Emp Here 400
SIC 6324 Hospital and medical service plans

D-U-N-S 25-076-3588   (SL)
LANGLEY UTILITIES CONTRACTING LTD
71 Mearns Crt Unit 220, Bowmanville, ON, L1C 4N4
(905) 623-5798
Emp Here 48   *Sales* 31,956,750
SIC 4911 Electric services
Dir D Shane Hastings
  Ken Rerrie
Dir Anthony Rerrie

D-U-N-S 20-644-3496   (BR)
LOBLAWS SUPERMARKETS LIMITED
LOBLAWS
2375 Highway 2 Suite 300, Bowmanville, ON, L1C 5A3
(905) 623-2600
Emp Here 20
SIC 5411 Grocery stores

D-U-N-S 25-504-7375   (SL)
MATTCO SERVICES LIMITED
TIM HORTONS
350 Waverley Rd, Bowmanville, ON, L1C 4Y4
(905) 623-0175
Emp Here 52   *Sales* 1,751,057
SIC 5461 Retail bakeries

D-U-N-S 20-859-9469   (BR)
PACIFIC LINK COMMUNICATIONS INC
BELL WORLD
2377 Hwy 2 Clarington Pl Suite 106, Bowmanville, ON, L1C 5A5
(905) 697-8800
Emp Here 25
SIC 5999 Miscellaneous retail stores, nec

D-U-N-S 20-711-6158   (BR)
PETERBOROUGH VICTORIA NORTHUMBERLAND AND CLARINGTON CATHOLIC DISTRICT SCHOOL BOARD
ST ELIZABETH ELEMENTARY SCHOOL
610 Longworth Ave, Bowmanville, ON, L1C 5B8
(905) 697-9155
Emp Here 50
SIC 8211 Elementary and secondary schools

D-U-N-S 20-349-7045   (BR)
PETERBOROUGH VICTORIA NORTHUMBERLAND AND CLARINGTON CATHOLIC DISTRICT SCHOOL BOARD
ST. STEPHEN CATHOLIC SECONDARY SCHOOL
300 Scugog St, Bowmanville, ON, L1C 3K2
(905) 623-3990
Emp Here 80
SIC 8211 Elementary and secondary schools

▲ Public Company   ■ Public Company Family Member   **HQ** Headquarters   **BR** Branch   **SL** Single Location

D-U-N-S 20-711-6042   (BR)
PETERBOROUGH VICTORIA NORTHUM-
BERLAND AND CLARINGTON CATHOLIC
DISTRICT SCHOOL BOARD
ST JOSEPH'S SCHOOL
90 Parkway Cres, Bowmanville, ON, L1C 1C3
(905) 623-5151
Emp Here 25
SIC 8211 Elementary and secondary schools

D-U-N-S 24-248-0908   (BR)
PETERBOROUGH VICTORIA NORTHUM-
BERLAND AND CLARINGTON CATHOLIC
DISTRICT SCHOOL BOARD
HOLY FAMILY CATHOLIC SCHOOL
125 Aspen Springs Dr, Bowmanville, ON, L1C
0C6
(905) 623-6255
Emp Here 45
SIC 8211 Elementary and secondary schools

D-U-N-S 25-637-9579   (BR)
PIZZA PIZZA LIMITED
200 King St E, Bowmanville, ON, L1C 1P3
(905) 697-1111
Emp Here 38
SIC 5812 Eating places

D-U-N-S 24-354-3134   (BR)
PROMARK-TELECON INC
160 Baseline Rd E Suite D, Bowmanville, ON,
L1C 1A2
(905) 697-0274
Emp Here 20
SIC 1799 Special trade contractors, nec

D-U-N-S 20-010-9093   (SL)
PRYCE AUTOMOTIVE INC
14 Carlson Pl, Bowmanville, ON, L1C 5P6
(905) 260-1994
Emp Here 60   *Sales* 3,648,035
SIC 7549 Automotive services, nec

D-U-N-S 20-981-4388   (BR)
RANDSTAD INTERIM INC
200 Baseline Rd E Suite 6, Bowmanville, ON,
L1C 1A2

Emp Here 60
SIC 7361 Employment agencies

D-U-N-S 25-195-0494   (BR)
VOMAR INDUSTRIES INC
TANK TRADERS, DIV OF
40 Port Darlington Rd, Bowmanville, ON, L1C
3K3
(905) 697-0907
Emp Here 20
SIC 5984 Liquefied petroleum gas dealers

D-U-N-S 24-377-1842   (BR)
WILSON FOODS BOWMANVILLE LTD
MCDONALD'S RESTAURANT
(*Suby of* Wilson Foods Bowmanville Ltd)
2387 Highway 2, Bowmanville, ON, L1C 5A3
(905) 623-4200
Emp Here 50
SIC 5812 Eating places

Bracebridge, ON P1L
Muskoka County

D-U-N-S 20-648-5323   (SL)
876224 ONTARIO LIMITED
HARVEY'S/SWISS CHALET
150 Muskoka Rd 118 W, Bracebridge, ON,
P1L 1T4
(705) 645-7947
Emp Here 50   *Sales* 1,532,175
SIC 5812 Eating places

D-U-N-S 25-296-8060   (BR)
BANK OF NOVA SCOTIA, THE
SCOTIABANK
248 Manitoba St Suite 5, Bracebridge, ON,

P1L 2E1
Emp Here 20
SIC 6021 National commercial banks

D-U-N-S 24-513-5595   (SL)
CHILDREN'S AID SOCIETY OF THE DIS-
TRICT OF MUSKOKA, THE
MUSKOKA FAMILY & CHILDRENS SER-
VICES
49 Pine St, Bracebridge, ON, P1L 1K8
(705) 645-4426
Emp Here 50   *Sales* 2,338,878
SIC 8322 Individual and family services

D-U-N-S 25-187-2016   (HQ)
COMMUNITY LIVING-SOUTH MUSKOKA
(*Suby of* Community Living-South Muskoka)
15 Depot Dr, Bracebridge, ON, P1L 0A1
(705) 645-5494
Emp Here 20   *Emp Total* 130
Sales 10,944,105
SIC 8322 Individual and family services
Ex Dir Ann Kenney
Pr Pr David Morrison

D-U-N-S 20-068-1497   (BR)
DISTRICT MUNICIPALITY OF MUSKOKA,
THE
PINES LONG TERM CARE RESIDENCE
98 Pine St Suite 610, Bracebridge, ON, P1L
1N5
(705) 645-4488
Emp Here 225
SIC 8051 Skilled nursing care facilities

D-U-N-S 24-892-5125   (SL)
DOTY, RONALD T. LIMITED
CANADIAN TIRE
Hwy 118 W, Bracebridge, ON, P1L 1V4
(705) 645-5261
Emp Here 58   *Sales* 4,158,760
SIC 5311 Department stores

D-U-N-S 20-699-6725   (BR)
EXTENDICARE INC
PINES LONG-TERM CARE RESIDENCE
98 Pine St Suite 610, Bracebridge, ON, P1L
1N5
(705) 645-4488
Emp Here 25
SIC 8051 Skilled nursing care facilities

D-U-N-S 25-481-2860   (HQ)
FAMILY, YOUTH & CHILD SERVICES OF
MUSKOKA
(*Suby of* Family, Youth & Child Services of
Muskoka)
49 Pine St, Bracebridge, ON, P1L 1K8
(705) 645-4426
Emp Here 48   *Emp Total* 63
Sales 2,480,664
SIC 8322 Individual and family services

D-U-N-S 25-318-8999   (BR)
FIRSTCANADA ULC
LAIDLAW EDUCATIONAL SERVICES
23 Gray Rd, Bracebridge, ON, P1L 1P8

Emp Here 100
SIC 4151 School buses

D-U-N-S 25-833-2410   (BR)
GEORGIAN COLLEGE OF APPLIED ARTS
AND TECHNOLOGY, THE
GEORGIAN COLLEGE
111 Wellington St, Bracebridge, ON, P1L 1E2
(705) 646-7629
Emp Here 24
SIC 8221 Colleges and universities

D-U-N-S 25-511-7681   (SL)
GREAVETTE CHEVROLET PONTIAC
BUICK CADILLAC GMC LTD
375 Echostone Dr, Bracebridge, ON, P1L 1T6
(705) 645-2241
Emp Here 40   *Sales* 14,592,140
SIC 5511 New and used car dealers

Pr Pr Glen Greavette

D-U-N-S 24-345-9620   (BR)
HANDS THEFAMILYHELPNETWORK.CA
23 Ball'S Dr, Bracebridge, ON, P1L 1T1
(705) 645-3155
Emp Here 30
SIC 8322 Individual and family services

D-U-N-S 20-176-6990   (BR)
HOME DEPOT OF CANADA INC
HOME DEPOT
(*Suby of* The Home Depot Inc)
20 Lcd Dr, Bracebridge, ON, P1L 0A1
(705) 646-5600
Emp Here 150
SIC 5251 Hardware stores

D-U-N-S 24-224-3470   (BR)
KUMON CANADA INC
126 Kimberley Ave, Bracebridge, ON, P1L 1Z9

Emp Here 30
SIC 8299 Schools and educational services,
nec

D-U-N-S 24-885-3777   (SL)
LAKELAND ENERGY LTD
LAKELAND NETWORKS
196 Taylor Rd, Bracebridge, ON, P1L 1J9
(705) 646-1846
Emp Here 30   *Sales* 6,566,463
SIC 3612 Transformers, except electric
Dir Chris Litschko

D-U-N-S 24-333-1704   (BR)
METRO ONTARIO INC
METRO
505 Muskoka Rd Hwy Suite 118, Bracebridge,
ON, P1L 1T3
(705) 645-8751
Emp Here 107
SIC 5411 Grocery stores

D-U-N-S 24-364-5707   (BR)
METROLAND MEDIA GROUP LTD
BRACEBRIDGE EXAMINER
34 E.P. Lee Dr, Bracebridge, ON, P1L 0A1
(705) 645-8771
Emp Here 40
SIC 2711 Newspapers

D-U-N-S 24-316-0889   (BR)
MUSKOKA ALGONQUIN HEALTHCARE
75 Ann St, Bracebridge, ON, P1L 2E4
(705) 645-4404
Emp Here 50
SIC 8062 General medical and surgical hospitals

D-U-N-S 20-966-3355   (HQ)
MUSKOKA FAMILY FOCUS AND CHIL-
DREN'S PLACE
(*Suby of* Muskoka Family Focus And Chil-
dren's Place)
20 Entrance Dr, Bracebridge, ON, P1L 1S4
(705) 645-3027
Emp Here 66   *Emp Total* 75
Sales 2,261,782
SIC 8351 Child day care services

D-U-N-S 20-703-8316   (HQ)
MUSKOKA TRANSPORT LIMITED
456 Ecclestone Dr, Bracebridge, ON, P1L 1R1
(705) 645-4481
Emp Here 125   *Emp Total* 535
Sales 22,763,738
SIC 4213 Trucking, except local
 Paul G Hammond
Pr D'arcy Hammond

D-U-N-S 20-814-2013   (BR)
MUSKOKA TRANSPORT LIMITED
456 Ecclestone Dr, Bracebridge, ON, P1L 1R1
(705) 645-4481
Emp Here 180
SIC 4213 Trucking, except local

D-U-N-S 20-859-9105   (BR)
PACIFIC LINK COMMUNICATIONS INC
BELL WORLD
295 Wellington St Unit 6, Bracebridge, ON,
P1L 1P3
(705) 646-2000
Emp Here 25
SIC 5999 Miscellaneous retail stores, nec

D-U-N-S 20-581-8417   (BR)
PHARMA PLUS DRUGMARTS LTD
125 Muskoka Rd, Bracebridge, ON, P1L 1H6
(705) 645-8738
Emp Here 20
SIC 5912 Drug stores and proprietary stores

D-U-N-S 20-711-2207   (BR)
SIMCOE MUSKOKA CATHOLIC DISTRICT
SCHOOL BOARD
MONSIGNOR MICHAEL O'LEARY SCHOOL
(*Suby of* Simcoe Muskoka Catholic District
School Board)
2 Tamarack Trail, Bracebridge, ON, P1L 1Z2
(705) 645-8759
Emp Here 28
SIC 8211 Elementary and secondary schools

D-U-N-S 25-292-4204   (BR)
SIMCOE MUSKOKA CATHOLIC DISTRICT
SCHOOL BOARD
ST DOMINIC CATHOLIC SECONDARY
SCHOOL
(*Suby of* Simcoe Muskoka Catholic District
School Board)
955 Cedar Lane, Bracebridge, ON, P1L 0A1
(705) 646-8772
Emp Here 30
SIC 8211 Elementary and secondary schools

D-U-N-S 20-310-8451   (BR)
STAPLES CANADA INC
(*Suby of* Staples, Inc.)
500 Muskoka Rd 118 W Unit 102, Brace-
bridge, ON, P1L 1T4
(705) 646-2775
Emp Here 25
SIC 5943 Stationery stores

D-U-N-S 20-021-6690   (BR)
TRILLIUM   LAKELANDS   DISTRICT
SCHOOL BOARD
BRACEBRIDGE PUBLIC SCHOOL
90 Mcmurray St, Bracebridge, ON, P1L 2G1
(705) 645-5209
Emp Here 35
SIC 8211 Elementary and secondary schools

D-U-N-S 20-024-3355   (BR)
TRILLIUM   LAKELANDS   DISTRICT
SCHOOL BOARD
MUSKOKA FALLS PUBLIC SCHOOL
42 Morrow Dr, Bracebridge, ON, P1L 0A1
(705) 645-2463
Emp Here 20
SIC 8211 Elementary and secondary schools

D-U-N-S 20-711-3841   (BR)
TRILLIUM   LAKELANDS   DISTRICT
SCHOOL BOARD
BRACEBRIDGE LEARNING CENTER
57 Armstrong St, Bracebridge, ON, P1L 1C1
(705) 645-2646
Emp Here 50
SIC 8211 Elementary and secondary schools

D-U-N-S 25-238-8145   (BR)
TRILLIUM   LAKELANDS   DISTRICT
SCHOOL BOARD
MACAULAY PUBLIC SCHOOL
1270 Cedar Lane, Bracebridge, ON, P1L 1W9
(705) 645-5410
Emp Here 23
SIC 8211 Elementary and secondary schools

D-U-N-S 24-599-1695   (BR)
WAL-MART CANADA CORP
40 Depot Dr, Bracebridge, ON, P1L 0A1

(705) 646-0550
Emp Here 30
SIC 5311 Department stores

D-U-N-S 20-298-3156   (BR)
WASTE CONNECTIONS OF CANADA INC
BFI CANADA
580 Ecclestone Dr, Bracebridge, ON, P1L 1R2
(705) 645-4453
Emp Here 80
SIC 4953 Refuse systems

Bradford, ON L3Z
Simcoe County

D-U-N-S 24-762-4708   (BR)
ARRAY CANADA INC
35 Reagen'S Industrial Pky, Bradford, ON,
L3Z 0Z9
(905) 775-5630
Emp Here 60
SIC 2542 Partitions and fixtures, except wood

D-U-N-S 25-360-8681   (BR)
ARRAY CANADA INC
35 Reagen'S Industrial Pky, Bradford, ON,
L3Z 0Z9
(416) 213-5740
Emp Here 55
SIC 3993 Signs and advertising specialties

D-U-N-S 24-036-7388   (BR)
BRADFORD GREENHOUSES LIMITED
*BRADFORD GREENHOUSES GARDEN
GALLERY*
2433 12th Conc, Bradford, ON, L3Z 2B2
(905) 775-4769
Emp Here 80
SIC 5191 Farm supplies

D-U-N-S 24-861-8803   (BR)
**CANADIAN IMPERIAL BANK OF COM-
MERCE**
CIBC 1042
549 Holland St W, Bradford, ON, L3Z 0C1
(905) 775-9304
Emp Here 25
SIC 6021 National commercial banks

D-U-N-S 20-423-5527   (BR)
DOLLARAMA S.E.C.
DOLLARAMA
537 Holland Street W, Bradford, ON, L3Z 0C1
(905) 778-0312
Emp Here 25
SIC 5331 Variety stores

D-U-N-S 24-860-9794   (BR)
DOMINION CITRUS LIMITED
DOMINION FARMS PRODUCE
215 Dissette St, Bradford, ON, L3Z 3G9
(905) 775-3388
Emp Here 50
SIC 2051 Bread, cake, and related products

D-U-N-S 20-305-3665   (BR)
FRESHOUSE FOODS LTD
65 Reagen'S Industrial Pky, Bradford, ON,
L3Z 0Z9
(905) 775-8880
Emp Here 100
SIC 5149 Groceries and related products, nec

D-U-N-S 20-337-7734   (SL)
GALATA CHEMICALS (CANADA) INC
10 Reagen'S Industrial Pky, Bradford, ON,
L3Z 2A4
(905) 775-5000
Emp Here 70   *Sales* 19,923,773
SIC 5169 Chemicals and allied products, nec
Pr Pr Steven Mckeown
  Matthew Yopchick
  Joseph Salsbury

D-U-N-S 24-986-9637   (SL)
HKH OPPORTUNITIES INC

TIM HORTONS
118 Holland St W, Bradford, ON, L3Z 2B4
(905) 775-0282
Emp Here 55   *Sales* 1,896,978
SIC 5461 Retail bakeries

D-U-N-S 24-361-7185   (BR)
HOME DEPOT OF CANADA INC
HOME DEPOT
(*Suby of* The Home Depot Inc)
470 Holland St W, Bradford, ON, L3Z 0A2
(905) 778-2100
Emp Here 100
SIC 5251 Hardware stores

D-U-N-S 24-321-7986   (BR)
MAGNA CLOSURES INC
CLOSURE METAL PRODUCTS, DIV OF
3066 8th Line, Bradford, ON, L3Z 2A5
(905) 898-1883
Emp Here 350
SIC 5013 Motor vehicle supplies and new
parts

D-U-N-S 20-772-6308   (HQ)
MITEK CANADA, INC
(*Suby of* Berkshire Hathaway Inc.)
100 Industrial Rd, Bradford, ON, L3Z 3G7
(905) 952-2900
Emp Here 80   *Emp Total* 331,000
Sales 21,377,485
SIC 3448 Prefabricated Metal buildings and
components
  Ronald Blackburn
  Michael Sandbrook
  Tom Manenti

D-U-N-S 25-672-8098   (SL)
RHUCON PIPELINE CONSTRUCTION LTD
Gd Stn Main, Bradford, ON, L3Z 2A3

Emp Here 30   *Sales* 7,304,400
SIC 1623 Water, sewer, and utility lines
Pr Alex Lawson

D-U-N-S 24-360-2559   (BR)
ROYAL GROUP, INC
SOLUCOR, DIV OF
10 Reagen'S Industrial Pky Suite 1, Bradford,
ON, L3Z 0Z8
(905) 775-5000
Emp Here 64
SIC 3089 Plastics products, nec

D-U-N-S 24-123-3782   (SL)
ROYAL WOODWORKING CO. LIMITED
(*Suby of* Moulure Alexandria Moulding Inc)
60 Industrial Rd, Bradford, ON, L3Z 3G7
(905) 727-2755
Emp Here 45   *Sales* 3,648,035
SIC 2431 Millwork

D-U-N-S 25-292-4469   (BR)
**SIMCOE COUNTY DISTRICT SCHOOL
BOARD, THE**
BRADFORD DISTRICT HIGH SCHOOL
(*Suby of* Simcoe County District School
Board, The)
70 Professor Day Dr, Bradford, ON, L3Z 3B9
(905) 775-2262
Emp Here 85
SIC 8211 Elementary and secondary schools

D-U-N-S 25-292-4782   (BR)
**SIMCOE COUNTY DISTRICT SCHOOL
BOARD, THE**
W. H. DAY ELEMENTARY SCHOOL
(*Suby of* Simcoe County District School
Board, The)
410 Maplegrove Ave, Bradford, ON, L3Z 2V4
(905) 775-9691
Emp Here 47
SIC 8211 Elementary and secondary schools

D-U-N-S 20-591-7656   (BR)
**SIMCOE COUNTY DISTRICT SCHOOL
BOARD, THE**
FIELDCREST ELEMENTARY

(*Suby of* Simcoe County District School
Board, The)
100 Professory Day Dr, Bradford, ON, L3Z
2B3
(905) 778-2010
Emp Here 48
SIC 8211 Elementary and secondary schools

D-U-N-S 25-292-4907   (BR)
**SIMCOE COUNTY DISTRICT SCHOOL
BOARD, THE**
BRADFORD ELEMENTARY SCHOOL
(*Suby of* Simcoe County District School
Board, The)
177 Church St, Bradford, ON, L3Z 1R4
(905) 778-4323
Emp Here 25
SIC 8211 Elementary and secondary schools

D-U-N-S 25-238-2288   (BR)
**SIMCOE COUNTY DISTRICT SCHOOL
BOARD, THE**
FRED C COOK PUBLIC SCHOOL
(*Suby of* Simcoe County District School
Board, The)
20 Fletcher St, Bradford, ON, L3Z 1L9
(905) 775-4821
Emp Here 35
SIC 8211 Elementary and secondary schools

D-U-N-S 25-297-6170   (BR)
**SIMCOE COUNTY DISTRICT SCHOOL
BOARD, THE**
*HONORABLE EARL ROWE PUBLIC
SCHOOL*
(*Suby of* Simcoe County District School
Board, The)
2516 12th Line, Bradford, ON, L3Z 2A5
(905) 775-3031
Emp Here 20
SIC 8211 Elementary and secondary schools

D-U-N-S 24-451-2674   (BR)
**SIMCOE COUNTY DISTRICT SCHOOL
BOARD, THE**
MOTHER TERESA CATHOLIC SCHOOL
(*Suby of* Simcoe County District School
Board, The)
110 Northgate Dr, Bradford, ON, L3Z 2Z7
(905) 778-0617
Emp Here 25
SIC 8211 Elementary and secondary schools

D-U-N-S 25-238-2643   (BR)
**SIMCOE MUSKOKA CATHOLIC DISTRICT
SCHOOL BOARD**
MARIE OF THE INCARNATION SCHOOL
(*Suby of* Simcoe Muskoka Catholic District
School Board)
105 Colborne St, Bradford, ON, L3Z 1C4
(905) 775-3492
Emp Here 30
SIC 8211 Elementary and secondary schools

D-U-N-S 25-292-4188   (BR)
**SIMCOE MUSKOKA CATHOLIC DISTRICT
SCHOOL BOARD**
HOLY TRINITY HIGH SCHOOL
(*Suby of* Simcoe Muskoka Catholic District
School Board)
100 Melbourne Dr, Bradford, ON, L3Z 2B3
(905) 775-4841
Emp Here 55
SIC 8211 Elementary and secondary schools

D-U-N-S 25-292-4220   (BR)
**SIMCOE MUSKOKA CATHOLIC DISTRICT
SCHOOL BOARD**
ST JEAN DE BREBEUF
(*Suby of* Simcoe Muskoka Catholic District
School Board)
151 Miller Park Ave, Bradford, ON, L3Z 2K3
(905) 775-8460
Emp Here 30
SIC 8211 Elementary and secondary schools

D-U-N-S 20-628-9493   (BR)
SPECIALTY CARE INC

SPECIALTY CARE BRADFORD VALLEY
(*Suby of* Specialty Care Inc)
2656 Line 6, Bradford, ON, L3Z 2A1
(905) 952-2270
Emp Here 200
SIC 8059 Nursing and personal care, nec

D-U-N-S 20-180-2530   (BR)
VENTRA GROUP CO
FLEX-N-GATE BRADFORD
75 Reagen'S Industrial Pky, Bradford, ON,
L3Z 0Z9
(905) 778-7900
Emp Here 310
SIC 3465 Automotive stampings

D-U-N-S 24-583-7336   (BR)
WAL-MART CANADA CORP
WALMART
545 Holland St W, Bradford, ON, L3Z 0C1
(905) 775-1610
Emp Here 50
SIC 5311 Department stores

Brampton, ON L6P
Peel County

D-U-N-S 20-912-2642   (BR)
2063414 ONTARIO LIMITED
LEISUREWORLD CAREGIVING CENTRE
(*Suby of* 2063414 Ontario Limited)
9257 Goreway Dr, Brampton, ON, L6P 0N5
(905) 799-7502
Emp Here 70
SIC 8051 Skilled nursing care facilities

D-U-N-S 24-676-3077   (BR)
**DUFFERIN-PEEL CATHOLIC DISTRICT
SCHOOL BOARD**
*FATHER FRANCIS MCSPIRITT CATHOLIC
ELEMENTARY SCHOOL*
55 Lexington Rd, Brampton, ON, L6P 2B1
(905) 794-5031
Emp Here 25
SIC 8211 Elementary and secondary schools

D-U-N-S 20-490-3827   (BR)
**ONTARIO PUBLIC SERVICE EMPLOYEES
UNION**
OPSEU
67 Beresford Cres, Brampton, ON, L6P 2M1
(416) 326-2591
Emp Here 500
SIC 8631 Labor organizations

D-U-N-S 24-174-6234   (BR)
PEEL DISTRICT SCHOOL BOARD
MOUNT ROYAL PUBLIC SCHOOL
(*Suby of* Peel District School Board)
65 Mount Royal Cir, Brampton, ON, L6P 2K4
(905) 794-4733
Emp Here 60
SIC 8211 Elementary and secondary schools

D-U-N-S 20-711-1928   (BR)
PEEL DISTRICT SCHOOL BOARD
CLAIREVILLE PUBLIC SCHOOL
(*Suby of* Peel District School Board)
97 Gallucci Cres, Brampton, ON, L6P 1R6
(905) 794-8714
Emp Here 50
SIC 8211 Elementary and secondary schools

D-U-N-S 24-676-3283   (BR)
PEEL DISTRICT SCHOOL BOARD
CALDERSTONE MIDDLE SCHOOL
(*Suby of* Peel District School Board)
160 Calderstone Rd, Brampton, ON, L6P 2L7
(905) 913-1162
Emp Here 50
SIC 8211 Elementary and secondary schools

D-U-N-S 24-555-4253   (BR)
PEEL DISTRICT SCHOOL BOARD
RED WILLOW PUBLIC SCHOOL

(Suby of Peel District School Board)
80 Redwillow Rd, Brampton, ON, L6P 2B1
(905) 794-4728
Emp Here 25
SIC 8211 Elementary and secondary schools

D-U-N-S 24-227-6652   (BR)
PEEL DISTRICT SCHOOL BOARD
THORNDALE PUBLIC SCHOOL
(Suby of Peel District School Board)
133 Thorndale Rd, Brampton, ON, L6P 1K5
(905) 913-1490
Emp Here 60
SIC 8211 Elementary and secondary schools

D-U-N-S 24-535-5198   (BR)
SOBEYS CAPITAL INCORPORATED
FRESHCO
3998 Cottrelle Blvd, Brampton, ON, L6P 2R1
(905) 794-2263
Emp Here 30
SIC 5411 Grocery stores

Brampton, ON L6R
Peel County

D-U-N-S 20-709-2623   (BR)
2063414 ONTARIO LIMITED
LEISUREWORLD CAREGIVING CENTRE
(Suby of 2063414 Ontario Limited)
215 Sunny Meadow Blvd, Brampton, ON, L6R 3B5
(905) 458-7604
Emp Here 100
SIC 8059 Nursing and personal care, nec

D-U-N-S 25-187-7908   (BR)
446987 ONTARIO INC
BOMBAY COMPANY, THE
(Suby of Benix & Co. Inc)
70 Great Lakes Dr Suite 148, Brampton, ON, L6R 2K7
(905) 458-7533
Emp Here 20
SIC 5712 Furniture stores

D-U-N-S 20-805-0950   (BR)
BANQUE TORONTO-DOMINION, LA
TORONTO-DOMINION BANK, THE
(Suby of Toronto-Dominion Bank, The)
90 Great Lakes Dr, Brampton, ON, L6R 2K7
(905) 790-8557
Emp Here 25
SIC 6021 National commercial banks

D-U-N-S 20-797-6346   (BR)
BOUTIQUE LA VIE EN ROSE INC
BOUTIQUE LA VIE EN ROSE INC
40 Great Lakes Dr, Brampton, ON, L6R 2K7
(905) 458-5336
Emp Here 20
SIC 5632 Women's accessory and specialty stores

D-U-N-S 25-373-0139   (BR)
CANADIAN IMPERIAL BANK OF COMMERCE
CIBC # 03032
630 Peter Robertson Blvd Unit 9, Brampton, ON, L6R 1T4
(905) 793-5644
Emp Here 24
SIC 6021 National commercial banks

D-U-N-S 25-092-2291   (BR)
DUFFERIN-PEEL CATHOLIC DISTRICT SCHOOL BOARD
FATHER CLAIR TIPPING SCHOOL
25 Mountainberry Rd, Brampton, ON, L6R 1J3
(905) 840-3121
Emp Here 30
SIC 8211 Elementary and secondary schools

D-U-N-S 20-591-0354   (BR)
DUFFERIN-PEEL CATHOLIC DISTRICT

SCHOOL BOARD
OUR LADY OF PROVIDENCE
35 Black Oak Dr, Brampton, ON, L6R 1B9
(905) 458-7080
Emp Here 25
SIC 8211 Elementary and secondary schools

D-U-N-S 20-711-0193   (BR)
DUFFERIN-PEEL CATHOLIC DISTRICT SCHOOL BOARD
GOOD SHEPPARD CATHOLIC SCHOOL
28 Red River Dr, Brampton, ON, L6R 2H9
(905) 791-1039
Emp Here 40
SIC 8211 Elementary and secondary schools

D-U-N-S 24-676-3051   (BR)
DUFFERIN-PEEL CATHOLIC DISTRICT SCHOOL BOARD
ST ISAAC JOGUES ELEMENTARY SCHOOL
300 Great Lakes Dr, Brampton, ON, L6R 2W7
(905) 799-2558
Emp Here 25
SIC 8211 Elementary and secondary schools

D-U-N-S 20-614-3609   (SL)
EAST SIDE MARIOS
130 Great Lakes Dr Suite 125, Brampton, ON, L6R 2K7
(905) 790-0040
Emp Here 60   Sales 1,824,018
SIC 5812 Eating places

D-U-N-S 24-977-1929   (BR)
FGL SPORTS LTD
SPORT CHEK TRINITY COMMON
30 Great Lakes Dr Unit 112, Brampton, ON, L6R 2K7
(905) 792-1830
Emp Here 20
SIC 5941 Sporting goods and bicycle shops

D-U-N-S 25-080-7237   (BR)
HOME DEPOT OF CANADA INC
HOME DEPOT
(Suby of The Home Depot Inc)
60 Great Lakes Dr, Brampton, ON, L6R 2K7
(905) 792-5430
Emp Here 150
SIC 5251 Hardware stores

D-U-N-S 20-644-2977   (BR)
MARK'S WORK WEARHOUSE LTD
WORK WORLD
30 Great Lakes Dr Suite 111, Brampton, ON, L6R 2K7
(905) 790-1599
Emp Here 20
SIC 5651 Family clothing stores

D-U-N-S 25-091-7606   (BR)
MCDONALD'S RESTAURANTS OF CANADA LIMITED
MCDONALD'S
(Suby of McDonald's Corporation)
45 Mountainash Rd, Brampton, ON, L6R 1W4
(905) 458-7488
Emp Here 100
SIC 5812 Eating places

D-U-N-S 25-087-6687   (BR)
METRO ONTARIO INC
A AND P FOOD STORES 083
20 Great Lakes Dr, Brampton, ON, L6R 2K7
(905) 789-6161
Emp Here 180
SIC 5411 Grocery stores

D-U-N-S 24-521-1698   (BR)
PEEL DISTRICT SCHOOL BOARD
EAGLE PLAINS PUBLIC SCHOOL
(Suby of Peel District School Board)
40 Eagle Plains Dr, Brampton, ON, L6R 2X8
(905) 793-4969
Emp Here 25
SIC 8211 Elementary and secondary schools

D-U-N-S 24-676-3275   (BR)

PEEL DISTRICT SCHOOL BOARD
SHAW PUBLIC SCHOOL
(Suby of Peel District School Board)
10 Father Tobin Rd, Brampton, ON, L6R 3K2
(905) 790-6095
Emp Here 25
SIC 8211 Elementary and secondary schools

D-U-N-S 20-711-1837   (BR)
PEEL DISTRICT SCHOOL BOARD
LARKSPUR PUBLIC SCHOOL
(Suby of Peel District School Board)
111 Larkspur Rd, Brampton, ON, L6R 1X2
(905) 799-2952
Emp Here 50
SIC 8211 Elementary and secondary schools

D-U-N-S 20-591-3895   (BR)
PEEL DISTRICT SCHOOL BOARD
GREAT LAKES PUBLIC SCHOOL
(Suby of Peel District School Board)
285 Great Lakes Dr, Brampton, ON, L6R 2R8
(905) 793-8532
Emp Here 25
SIC 8211 Elementary and secondary schools

D-U-N-S 20-711-1969   (BR)
PEEL DISTRICT SCHOOL BOARD
HAROLD M BRATHWAITE SECONDARY SCHOOL
(Suby of Peel District School Board)
415 Great Lakes Dr, Brampton, ON, L6R 2Z4
(905) 793-2155
Emp Here 50
SIC 8211 Elementary and secondary schools

D-U-N-S 24-347-5204   (BR)
PEEL DISTRICT SCHOOL BOARD
SANDALWOOD HEIGHTS SECONDARY SCHOOL
(Suby of Peel District School Board)
2671 Sandalwood Pky E, Brampton, ON, L6R 0K7
(905) 494-0023
Emp Here 60
SIC 8211 Elementary and secondary schools

D-U-N-S 24-676-5304   (BR)
PEEL DISTRICT SCHOOL BOARD
CARBERRY PUBLIC SCHOOL
(Suby of Peel District School Board)
526 Fernforest Dr, Brampton, ON, L6R 0W1
(905) 458-6771
Emp Here 25
SIC 8211 Elementary and secondary schools

D-U-N-S 20-591-3879   (BR)
PEEL DISTRICT SCHOOL BOARD
FERNFOREST PUBLIC SCHOOL
(Suby of Peel District School Board)
275 Fernforest Dr, Brampton, ON, L6R 1L9
(905) 793-6157
Emp Here 80
SIC 8211 Elementary and secondary schools

D-U-N-S 24-116-9668   (BR)
PEEL DISTRICT SCHOOL BOARD
SUNNY VIEW MIDDLE SCHOOL
(Suby of Peel District School Board)
30 Chapparal Dr, Brampton, ON, L6R 3C4
(905) 789-1707
Emp Here 50
SIC 8211 Elementary and secondary schools

D-U-N-S 24-218-6950   (BR)
PEEL DISTRICT SCHOOL BOARD
STANLEY MILLS PUBLIC SCHOOL
(Suby of Peel District School Board)
286 Sunny Meadow Blvd, Brampton, ON, L6R 3C3
(905) 789-0925
Emp Here 50
SIC 8211 Elementary and secondary schools

D-U-N-S 20-653-7610   (BR)
PEEL DISTRICT SCHOOL BOARD
MOUNTAIN ASH MIDDLE SCHOOL
(Suby of Peel District School Board)

280 Mountainash Rd, Brampton, ON, L6R 3G2
(905) 793-7595
Emp Here 70
SIC 8211 Elementary and secondary schools

D-U-N-S 20-711-1936   (BR)
PEEL DISTRICT SCHOOL BOARD
SPRINGDALE PUBLIC SCHOOL
(Suby of Peel District School Board)
100 Dewside Dr, Brampton, ON, L6R 3B6
(905) 791-5081
Emp Here 50
SIC 8211 Elementary and secondary schools

D-U-N-S 24-525-4235   (BR)
PEEL DISTRICT SCHOOL BOARD
LOUGHEED MIDDLE SCHOOL
(Suby of Peel District School Board)
475 Father Tobin Rd, Brampton, ON, L6R 0J9
(905) 789-8751
Emp Here 25
SIC 8211 Elementary and secondary schools

D-U-N-S 25-092-3109   (BR)
PEEL DISTRICT SCHOOL BOARD
ROBERT J LEE PUBLIC SCHOOL
(Suby of Peel District School Board)
160 Mountainash Rd, Brampton, ON, L6R 1J1
(905) 792-2195
Emp Here 60
SIC 8211 Elementary and secondary schools

D-U-N-S 24-676-3291   (BR)
PEEL DISTRICT SCHOOL BOARD
HEWSON ELEMENTARY PUBLIC SCHOOL
(Suby of Peel District School Board)
235 Father Tobin Rd, Brampton, ON, L6R 0G2
(905) 595-1386
Emp Here 25
SIC 8211 Elementary and secondary schools

D-U-N-S 20-860-1505   (BR)
SOURCE (BELL) ELECTRONICS INC, THE
SOURCE, THE
150 Great Lakes Dr Suite 133, Brampton, ON, L6R 2K7
(905) 793-6452
Emp Here 25
SIC 5999 Miscellaneous retail stores, nec

D-U-N-S 20-338-1322   (BR)
TDG FURNITURE INC
ASHLEY FURNITURE HOME STORE
70 Great Lakes Dr Unit 149, Brampton, ON, L6R 2K7
(905) 799-3284
Emp Here 21
SIC 5712 Furniture stores

D-U-N-S 25-087-7255   (BR)
TOWN SHOES LIMITED
SHOE COMPANY, THE
80 Great Lakes Dr Suite 152, Brampton, ON, L6R 2K7
(905) 789-8181
Emp Here 25
SIC 5661 Shoe stores

D-U-N-S 25-686-9629   (HQ)
WILLIAM OSLER HEALTH SYSTEM
BRAMPTON CIVIC HOSPITAL
(Suby of William Osler Health System)
2100 Bovaird Dr E, Brampton, ON, L6R 3J7
(905) 494-2120
Emp Here 2,500   Emp Total 4,150
Sales 288,778,451
SIC 8062 General medical and surgical hospitals
 Matthew Anderson
Dir Bryan Held
Dir Pushminder Judge
Dir Marlin Morrell
Dir Donna Northeast
Dir Arnold Pundsack
Dir Paul Rosenberg
Dir Ian Smith
Dir Ed Upenieks

▲ Public Company   ■ Public Company Family Member   **HQ** Headquarters   **BR** Branch   **SL** Single Location

Dir Karen Leggett

D-U-N-S 24-352-6220   (BR)
WILLIAM OSLER HEALTH SYSTEM
BRAMPTON CIVIC HOSPITAL
2100 Bovaird Dr E, Brampton, ON, L6R 3J7
(905) 494-2120
Emp Here 100
SIC 8062 General medical and surgical hospitals

D-U-N-S 20-106-3208   (BR)
WINNERS MERCHANTS INTERNATIONAL L.P.
WINNERS
(*Suby of* The TJX Companies Inc)
80 Great Lakes Dr Unit 153, Brampton, ON, L6R 2K7
(905) 789-7132
Emp Here 40
SIC 5651 Family clothing stores

Brampton, ON L6S
Peel County

D-U-N-S 24-919-3657   (SL)
1131170 ONTARIO INC
R.S. COATINGS
2023 Williams Pky Unit 12, Brampton, ON, L6S 5N1
(905) 790-2655
Emp Here 20   *Sales* 4,331,255
SIC 7532 Top and body repair and paint shops

D-U-N-S 24-255-4801   (SL)
2065858 ONTARIO LIMITED
EAST SIDE MARIO'S
9055 Airport Rd, Brampton, ON, L6S 0B8
(905) 793-0443
Emp Here 60   *Sales* 1,824,018
SIC 5812 Eating places

D-U-N-S 24-483-1959   (SL)
575636 ONTARIO LIMITED
GLOBAL DISTRIBUTION AND WAREHOUSING
1 Lascelles Blvd, Brampton, ON, L6S 3T1

Emp Here 43   *Sales* 14,331,360
SIC 4731 Freight transportation arrangement
Pr John Cosgrostove

D-U-N-S 25-321-4688   (BR)
ALLIED SYSTEMS (CANADA) COMPANY
2000 Williams Pky, Brampton, ON, L6S 6B3
(905) 458-0900
Emp Here 100
SIC 4213 Trucking, except local

D-U-N-S 24-304-1175   (SL)
ANDROID INDUSTRIES LLC
14 Precidio Crt, Brampton, ON, L6S 6E3
(905) 458-4774
Emp Here 49   *Sales* 5,748,207
SIC 3694 Engine electrical equipment
Genl Mgr Fabio Nichilo

D-U-N-S 25-504-4760   (HQ)
APEX MOTOR EXPRESS LTD
60 Ward Rd, Brampton, ON, L6S 4L5
(905) 789-5000
Emp Here 100   *Emp Total* 2
Sales 38,981,295
SIC 4213 Trucking, except local
Ch Bd Don Reimer
Pr Elmer Schwarz
VP Tom Santaguida

D-U-N-S 20-027-7718   (BR)
BARRETT CORPORATION
BARRETT SAUNDERS ASSOCIATES
100 Corporation Dr, Brampton, ON, L6S 6B5
(905) 789-7575
Emp Here 50
SIC 5063 Electrical apparatus and equipment

D-U-N-S 24-101-1761   (BR)
BEST BUY CANADA LTD
(*Suby of* Best Buy Co., Inc.)
9250 Airport Rd Suite 1, Brampton, ON, L6S 6K5
(905) 494-7272
Emp Here 700
SIC 5065 Electronic parts and equipment, nec

D-U-N-S 24-514-2216   (BR)
CAMPBELL BROS. MOVERS LIMITED
145 Sun Pac Blvd, Brampton, ON, L6S 5Z6
(905) 853-1322
Emp Here 40
SIC 4214 Local trucking with storage

D-U-N-S 20-573-0992   (BR)
CANADA POST CORPORATION
9780 Bramalea Rd Suite 301, Brampton, ON, L6S 2P1

Emp Here 20
SIC 4311 U.s. postal service

D-U-N-S 24-000-9022   (BR)
CANADIAN TIRE CORPORATION, LIMITED
9263 Airport Rd, Brampton, ON, L6S 0B6
(905) 494-6303
Emp Here 20
SIC 5399 Miscellaneous general merchandise

D-U-N-S 24-796-8345   (BR)
CARA OPERATIONS LIMITED
MONTANA'S COOKHOUSE
(*Suby of* Cara Holdings Limited)
9065 Airport Rd Suite 3034, Brampton, ON, L6S 0B8
(905) 799-6129
Emp Here 50
SIC 5812 Eating places

D-U-N-S 20-181-3925   (BR)
CARA OPERATIONS LIMITED
KELSEY'S RESTAURANTS
(*Suby of* Cara Holdings Limited)
2870 Queen St E, Brampton, ON, L6S 6E8
(905) 791-5655
Emp Here 40
SIC 5812 Eating places

D-U-N-S 20-165-1416   (SL)
CARPE DIEM RESIDENTIAL TREATMENT HOMES FOR CHILDREN INC
CARPE DIEM
29 Crescent Hill Dr N, Brampton, ON, L6S 1C6
(905) 799-2947
Emp Here 100   *Sales* 3,648,035
SIC 8361 Residential care

D-U-N-S 24-337-2757   (BR)
CASCADES CANADA ULC
1925 Williams Pky Unit 123, Brampton, ON, L6S 2M3

Emp Here 48
SIC 2679 Converted paper products, nec

D-U-N-S 24-214-8401   (HQ)
CEVA LOGISTICS CANADA, ULC
CEVA LOGISTICS
2600 North Park Dr, Brampton, ON, L6S 6E2
(905) 789-2904
Emp Here 90   *Emp Total* 2
Sales 7,879,756
SIC 4212 Local trucking, without storage
Dir Jonathan Gardner
Dir Bruce Rodgers
Fin Mgr Michael Todt
Dir Matthew Ryan
Dir David Souza
  David J Siler

D-U-N-S 25-153-0960   (SL)
CHENG SHIN RUBBER CANADA, INC
MAXXIS INTERNATIONAL-CANADA
400 Chrysler Dr Unit C, Brampton, ON, L6S 5Z5
(905) 789-0882
Emp Here 25   *Sales* 4,815,406

SIC 5085 Industrial supplies

D-U-N-S 25-874-2493   (BR)
CONSEIL SCOLAIRE DE DISTRICT CATHOLIQUE CENTRE-SUD
ECOLE ELEMENTAIRE CATHOLIQUE SAINTE-JEANNE-D'ARC
25 Laurelcrest St, Brampton, ON, L6S 4C4
(905) 453-8561
Emp Here 40
SIC 8211 Elementary and secondary schools

D-U-N-S 25-786-9446   (BR)
CORPORATION OF THE CITY OF BRAMPTON, THE
GREENBRIAR RECREATION CENTRE
1100 Central Park Dr, Brampton, ON, L6S 2C9
(905) 791-2240
Emp Here 30
SIC 8322 Individual and family services

D-U-N-S 20-025-3289   (BR)
CORPORATION OF THE CITY OF BRAMPTON, THE
TERRY MILLER RECREATION CENTRE
1295 Williams Pky, Brampton, ON, L6S 3J8
(905) 791-8211
Emp Here 40
SIC 7999 Amusement and recreation, nec

D-U-N-S 25-747-6960   (BR)
CORPORATION OF THE CITY OF BRAMPTON, THE
HOWDEN RECREATION CENTRE
150 Howden Blvd, Brampton, ON, L6S 2G1
(905) 793-4645
Emp Here 50
SIC 8322 Individual and family services

D-U-N-S 25-797-6159   (BR)
CORPORATION OF THE CITY OF BRAMPTON, THE
PROFESSOR'S LAKE RECREATION CENTRE
1660 North Park Dr, Brampton, ON, L6S 4B4
(905) 791-7751
Emp Here 40
SIC 8322 Individual and family services

D-U-N-S 25-226-9014   (BR)
DUFFERIN-PEEL CATHOLIC DISTRICT SCHOOL BOARD
ST JOHN BOSCO ELEMENTARY SCHOOL
1025 North Park Dr, Brampton, ON, L6S 4E1
(905) 792-0890
Emp Here 35
SIC 8211 Elementary and secondary schools

D-U-N-S 20-026-7909   (BR)
DUFFERIN-PEEL CATHOLIC DISTRICT SCHOOL BOARD
ST ANTHONY ELEMENTARY SCHOOL
950 North Park Dr, Brampton, ON, L6S 3L5
(905) 792-2282
Emp Here 500
SIC 8211 Elementary and secondary schools

D-U-N-S 25-117-1799   (BR)
DUFFERIN-PEEL CATHOLIC DISTRICT SCHOOL BOARD
ST THOMAS AQUINAS SECONDARY SCHOOL
25 Corporation Dr, Brampton, ON, L6S 6A2
(905) 791-1195
Emp Here 160
SIC 8211 Elementary and secondary schools

D-U-N-S 25-224-8695   (BR)
DUFFERIN-PEEL CATHOLIC DISTRICT SCHOOL BOARD
ST MARGUERITE BOURGEOYS SCHOOL
550 North Park Dr, Brampton, ON, L6S 4J8
(905) 454-3979
Emp Here 30
SIC 8211 Elementary and secondary schools

D-U-N-S 25-926-3473   (BR)
DUFFERIN-PEEL CATHOLIC DISTRICT

SCHOOL BOARD
LESTER B. PEARSON CATHOLIC SCHOOL
140 Howden Blvd, Brampton, ON, L6S 2G1
(905) 793-4861
Emp Here 40
SIC 8211 Elementary and secondary schools

D-U-N-S 25-265-2912   (BR)
DUFFERIN-PEEL CATHOLIC DISTRICT SCHOOL BOARD
ST. JEAN BREBEUF ELEMENTARY SCHOOL
63 Glenforest Rd, Brampton, ON, L6S 1L8
(905) 791-8529
Emp Here 27
SIC 8211 Elementary and secondary schools

D-U-N-S 25-375-8189   (HQ)
E S G TORBRAM LTD
TIM HORTONS
(*Suby of* E S G Torbram Ltd)
2400 Queen St E, Brampton, ON, L6S 5X9
(905) 458-9470
Emp Here 65   *Emp Total* 125
Sales 3,793,956
SIC 5812 Eating places

D-U-N-S 20-325-2424   (BR)
EXPORT PACKERS COMPANY LIMITED
3 Edvac Dr, Brampton, ON, L6S 5X8
(905) 595-0777
Emp Here 50
SIC 5142 Packaged frozen goods

D-U-N-S 24-369-9423   (BR)
FEDEX SUPPLY CHAIN DISTRIBUTION SYSTEM OF CANADA, INC
GENCO DISTRIBUTION SYSTEM OF CANADA, INC
(*Suby of* Fedex Corporation)
9150 Airport Rd Unit C, Brampton, ON, L6S 6G1
(800) 463-3339
Emp Here 50
SIC 4731 Freight transportation arrangement

D-U-N-S 20-177-7757   (BR)
G&K SERVICES CANADA INC
(*Suby of* Cintas Corporation)
140 Sun Pac Blvd, Brampton, ON, L6S 6E4
(905) 494-0322
Emp Here 23
SIC 7218 Industrial launderers

D-U-N-S 24-390-5846   (BR)
GOLF TOWN LIMITED
GOLF TOWN
9145 Airport Rd Unit 1, Brampton, ON, L6S 0B8

Emp Here 26
SIC 5941 Sporting goods and bicycle shops

D-U-N-S 24-315-7331   (BR)
HOME DEPOT OF CANADA INC
(*Suby of* The Home Depot Inc)
9105 Airport Rd, Brampton, ON, L6S 0B8
(905) 494-2200
Emp Here 50
SIC 5251 Hardware stores

D-U-N-S 24-308-3610   (BR)
HOPEWELL LOGISTICS INC
9050 Airport Rd Suite 201, Brampton, ON, L6S 6G6
(905) 458-1041
Emp Here 50
SIC 4225 General warehousing and storage

D-U-N-S 24-752-2899   (SL)
MBS STEEL LTD
62 Progress Crt, Brampton, ON, L6S 5X2

Emp Here 47   *Sales* 8,736,240
SIC 3441 Fabricated structural Metal
Pr Pr Wolf Mrusek
  Peter Boyle

D-U-N-S 25-372-3142   (SL)
MACDONALD, DETTWILER AND ASSO-CIATES INC
MDA
9445 Airport Rd Suite 100, Brampton, ON, L6S 4J3
(905) 790-2800
Emp Here 480
SIC 3769 Space vehicle equipment, nec

D-U-N-S 24-889-5625   (BR)
MARITIME-ONTARIO FREIGHT LINES LIMITED
MARITIME-ONTARIO PARCEL, DIV OF
1 Maritime Ontario Blvd Suite 100, Brampton, ON, L6S 6G4
(905) 602-0670
Emp Here 80
SIC 4212 Local trucking, without storage

D-U-N-S 20-015-9502   (BR)
MARTINREA INTERNATIONAL INC
HYDROFORM SOLUTIONS, DIV OF
1995 Williams Pky, Brampton, ON, L6S 6E5
(905) 799-2498
Emp Here 216
SIC 3499 Fabricated Metal products, nec

D-U-N-S 25-318-2125   (BR)
MCDONALD'S   RESTAURANTS   OF CANADA LIMITED
DEMRELL
(*Suby of* McDonald's Corporation)
2450 Queen St E, Brampton, ON, L6S 5X9
(905) 793-5295
Emp Here 100
SIC 5812 Eating places

D-U-N-S 24-665-9858   (BR)
METRIE CANADA LTD
MOULDING & MILLWORK
390 Chrysler Dr, Brampton, ON, L6S 5Z5
(905) 792-1144
Emp Here 25
SIC 2431 Millwork

D-U-N-S 24-799-6429   (BR)
MICHAELS OF CANADA, ULC
(*Suby of* The Michaels Companies Inc)
9065 Airport Rd Unit 20, Brampton, ON, L6S 0B8
(905) 595-0874
Emp Here 30
SIC 5945 Hobby, toy, and game shops

D-U-N-S 20-273-7664   (SL)
MODULAR SPACE CORPORATION
MODSPACE
(*Suby of* Modular Space Corporation)
2300 North Park Dr, Brampton, ON, L6S 6C6
(800) 451-3951
Emp Here 35   *Sales* 3,551,629
SIC 7519 Utility trailer rental

D-U-N-S 20-316-8588   (BR)
MOTION INDUSTRIES (CANADA), INC
(*Suby of* Genuine Parts Company)
1925 Williams Pky Unit 1, Brampton, ON, L6S 2M3
(905) 595-2477
Emp Here 20
SIC 5085 Industrial supplies

D-U-N-S 25-404-8481   (BR)
NESTLE CANADA INC
9050 Airport Rd Suite 101, Brampton, ON, L6S 6G9
(905) 458-3600
Emp Here 50
SIC 5143 Dairy products, except dried or canned

D-U-N-S 25-297-1817   (BR)
PEEL DISTRICT SCHOOL BOARD
JEFFERSON PUBLIC SCHOOL
(*Suby of* Peel District School Board)
48 Jefferson Rd, Brampton, ON, L6S 2N9

(905) 791-2818
Emp Here 30
SIC 8211 Elementary and secondary schools

D-U-N-S 20-914-4158   (BR)
PEEL DISTRICT SCHOOL BOARD
GOLDCREST PUBLIC SCHOOL
(*Suby of* Peel District School Board)
24 Goldcrest Rd, Brampton, ON, L6S 1G3
(905) 791-8558
Emp Here 25
SIC 8211 Elementary and secondary schools

D-U-N-S 25-483-5952   (BR)
PEEL DISTRICT SCHOOL BOARD
RUSSELL D. BARBER PUBLIC SCHOOL
(*Suby of* Peel District School Board)
255 North Park Dr, Brampton, ON, L6S 6A5
(905) 455-7177
Emp Here 50
SIC 8211 Elementary and secondary schools

D-U-N-S 24-721-2418   (BR)
PEEL DISTRICT SCHOOL BOARD
CHINGUACOUSY SECONDARY SCHOOL
(*Suby of* Peel District School Board)
1370 Williams Pky, Brampton, ON, L6S 1V3
(905) 791-2400
Emp Here 100
SIC 8211 Elementary and secondary schools

D-U-N-S 20-913-8705   (BR)
PEEL DISTRICT SCHOOL BOARD
HANOVER PUBLIC SCHOOL
(*Suby of* Peel District School Board)
215 Hanover Rd, Brampton, ON, L6S 1B6
(905) 793-4237
Emp Here 20
SIC 8211 Elementary and secondary schools

D-U-N-S 25-297-1866   (BR)
PEEL DISTRICT SCHOOL BOARD
JUDITH NYMAN SECONDARY SCHOOL
(*Suby of* Peel District School Board)
1305 Williams Pky, Brampton, ON, L6S 3J8
(905) 791-6770
Emp Here 90
SIC 8211 Elementary and secondary schools

D-U-N-S 25-263-7806   (BR)
PEEL DISTRICT SCHOOL BOARD
GREENBRIAR SENIOR PUBLIC SCHOOL
(*Suby of* Peel District School Board)
1140 Central Park Dr, Brampton, ON, L6S 2C9
(905) 791-2332
Emp Here 45
SIC 8211 Elementary and secondary schools

D-U-N-S 25-263-7848   (BR)
PEEL DISTRICT SCHOOL BOARD
GRENOBLE PUBLIC SCHOOL
(*Suby of* Peel District School Board)
33 Greenbriar Rd, Brampton, ON, L6S 1V8
(905) 791-2333
Emp Here 25
SIC 8211 Elementary and secondary schools

D-U-N-S 25-297-1577   (BR)
PEEL DISTRICT SCHOOL BOARD
MASSEY STREET PUBLIC SCHOOL
(*Suby of* Peel District School Board)
95 Massey St, Brampton, ON, L6S 3A3
(905) 791-9392
Emp Here 35
SIC 8211 Elementary and secondary schools

D-U-N-S 25-263-7525   (BR)
PEEL DISTRICT SCHOOL BOARD
HILLDALE PUBLIC SCHOOL
(*Suby of* Peel District School Board)
100 Hilldale Cres, Brampton, ON, L6S 2N3
(905) 793-4452
Emp Here 20
SIC 8211 Elementary and secondary schools

D-U-N-S 25-297-1171   (BR)
PEEL DISTRICT SCHOOL BOARD
NORTH PARK SECONDARY SCHOOL

(*Suby of* Peel District School Board)
10 North Park Dr, Brampton, ON, L6S 3M1
(905) 456-1906
Emp Here 120
SIC 8211 Elementary and secondary schools

D-U-N-S 25-263-8127   (BR)
PEEL DISTRICT SCHOOL BOARD
WILLIAMS PARKWAY SENIOR PUBLIC SCHOOL
(*Suby of* Peel District School Board)
1285 Williams Pky, Brampton, ON, L6S 3J8
(905) 791-4324
Emp Here 50
SIC 8211 Elementary and secondary schools

D-U-N-S 25-801-7409   (BR)
PRISZM LP
KFC
9025 Torbram Rd Suite 12, Brampton, ON, L6S 3L2
(905) 791-5540
Emp Here 22
SIC 5812 Eating places

D-U-N-S 24-077-3507   (SL)
R B & W CORPORATION OF CANADA
(*Suby of* Park-Ohio Holdings Corp.)
10 Sun Pac Blvd, Brampton, ON, L6S 4R5
(905) 595-9700
Emp Here 115   *Sales* 28,965,398
SIC 3452 Bolts, nuts, rivets, and washers
  Dennis Bolden
Pr Pr Craig Cowan

D-U-N-S 24-451-5706   (SL)
ROVA PRODUCTS CANADA INC
30 Automatic Rd, Brampton, ON, L6S 5N8
(905) 793-1955
Emp Here 50   *Sales* 10,068,577
SIC 5065 Electronic parts and equipment, nec
Pr Pr Lloyd Hermelyn
VP VP Nicole Hermelyn

D-U-N-S 25-988-2272   (BR)
SOBEYS CAPITAL INCORPORATED
SOBEY'S
930 North Park Dr, Brampton, ON, L6S 3Y5
(905) 458-7673
Emp Here 200
SIC 5411 Grocery stores

D-U-N-S 24-509-2796   (HQ)
SONEPAR CANADA INC
LUMEN
250 Chrysler Dr Unit 4, Brampton, ON, L6S 6B6
(905) 696-2838
Emp Here 50   *Emp Total* 14
Sales 341,456,076
SIC 5063 Electrical apparatus and equipment
  David Gabriel
Pr Pr Francois Anquetil
  Paul Trudel
  Olivier Verley
  Francois Poncet
  Philippe De Moustier
  Franck Bruel

D-U-N-S 24-309-2561   (BR)
STERLING PACKERS LIMITED
CONFEDERATION FREEZERS
14 Precidio Crt, Brampton, ON, L6S 6E3

Emp Here 50
SIC 4222 Refrigerated warehousing and storage

D-U-N-S 24-213-2942   (SL)
SUN PAC FOODS LIMITED
MCDOWELL OVENS, DIV OF
(*Suby of* Liquibrands Inc)
10 Sun Pac Blvd, Brampton, ON, L6S 4R5
(905) 792-2700
Emp Here 100   *Sales* 6,594,250
SIC 2033 Canned fruits and specialties
Pr Pr Jack Riddell

VP Fin Vincent Mcewan
Treas Cathy Knowles

D-U-N-S 20-213-3828   (BR)
SUN RICH FRESH FOODS INC
35 Bramtree Crt Unit 1, Brampton, ON, L6S 6G2
(905) 789-0200
Emp Here 310
SIC 2033 Canned fruits and specialties

D-U-N-S 20-514-4640   (BR)
THOMSON TERMINALS LIMITED
KIMBERLY CLARK WAREHOUSE
2 Bramkay St, Brampton, ON, L6S 6E9
(905) 792-6540
Emp Here 35
SIC 4225 General warehousing and storage

D-U-N-S 20-298-4030   (SL)
TIMBER 188 INC
DENNY'S FAMILY RESTAURANT
2452 Queen St E, Brampton, ON, L6S 5X9
(905) 791-8168
Emp Here 60   *Sales* 1,824,018
SIC 5812 Eating places

Brampton, ON L6T
Peel County

D-U-N-S 20-563-3238   (BR)
115161 CANADA INC
FASHION DISIRIBUTORS, THE
1 Wilkinson Rd Suite 2, Brampton, ON, L6T 4M6
(905) 455-1500
Emp Here 40
SIC 4225 General warehousing and storage

D-U-N-S 25-535-3088   (SL)
3283313 CANADA INC
FEDERAL AUCTION SERVICE
80 Devon Rd Unit 3, Brampton, ON, L6T 5B3

Emp Here 100   *Sales* 6,898,600
SIC 7389 Business services, nec
Pr Pr Amir Durrani

D-U-N-S 24-561-2718   (SL)
376973 ONTARIO LIMITED
A-1 DELIVERY SERVICE LOGISTICS
7 Strathearn Ave Suite A, Brampton, ON, L6T 4P1
(905) 799-3900
Emp Here 50   *Sales* 3,939,878
SIC 4212 Local trucking, without storage

D-U-N-S 24-335-6248   (HQ)
446987 ONTARIO INC
BOMBAY COMPANY, THE
(*Suby of* Benix & Co. Inc)
3389 Steeles Ave E, Brampton, ON, L6T 5W4
(905) 494-1118
Emp Here 200   *Emp Total* 922
Sales 86,798,350
SIC 5712 Furniture stores
Dir David Stewart

D-U-N-S 24-847-3266   (SL)
821373 ONTARIO LTD
MASTER CRAFTSMAN
3 Brewster Rd Suite 5, Brampton, ON, L6T 5G9
(905) 794-2074
Emp Here 40   *Sales* 5,717,257
SIC 5087 Service establishment equipment

D-U-N-S 25-263-3706   (BR)
A. LASSONDE INC
(*Suby of* 3346625 Canada Inc)
390 Orenda Rd, Brampton, ON, L6T 1G8
(905) 791-5300
Emp Here 20
SIC 2033 Canned fruits and specialties

D-U-N-S 25-140-8761   (BR)

ABB INC
201 Westcreek Blvd, Brampton, ON, L6T 5S6
(905) 460-3000
Emp Here 250
SIC 5065 Electronic parts and equipment, nec

D-U-N-S 24-752-4416   (BR)
ABC GROUP INC
ABC GROUP PRODUCT DEVELOPMENT, DIV. OF
(*Suby of* Cerberus Capital Management, L.P.)
303 Orenda Rd Suite B, Brampton, ON, L6T 5C3
(905) 450-3600
Emp Here 300
SIC 3089 Plastics products, nec

D-U-N-S 24-829-4472   (HQ)
ABF FREIGHT SYSTEM CANADA, LTD
(*Suby of* Arcbest Corporation)
15 Strathearn Ave, Brampton, ON, L6T 4P1
(905) 458-5888
Emp Here 60   *Emp Total* 13,000
Sales 17,652,300
SIC 4213 Trucking, except local
Pr Robert Davidson
CEO Judy Mcreynolds

D-U-N-S 25-359-6126   (BR)
ADESA AUCTIONS CANADA CORPORATION
ADESA TORONTO
55 Auction Lane, Brampton, ON, L6T 5P4
(905) 790-7653
Emp Here 200
SIC 5012 Automobiles and other motor vehicles

D-U-N-S 25-173-7615   (HQ)
ADESA AUCTIONS CANADA CORPORATION
ADESA CANADA
55 Auction Lane 2nd Floor, Brampton, ON, L6T 5P4
(905) 790-7653
Emp Here 35   *Emp Total* 14,400
Sales 1,201,469,475
SIC 5012 Automobiles and other motor vehicles
Pr Stephane St-Hilaire
Sec Sheryl Watson
Trevor Henderson
Eric Loughmiller

D-U-N-S 25-137-1811   (BR)
ACCOR CANADA INC
MOTEL 6
160 Steelwell Rd Suite 126, Brampton, ON, L6T 5T3
(905) 451-3313
Emp Here 20
SIC 7011 Hotels and motels

D-U-N-S 25-648-6515   (BR)
AGORA MANUFACTURING INC
(*Suby of* Agora Manufacturing Inc)
104 Hedgedale Rd, Brampton, ON, L6T 5L2
(905) 459-5100
Emp Here 25
SIC 3499 Fabricated Metal products, nec

D-U-N-S 20-347-8990   (BR)
AIR LIQUIDE CANADA INC
1700 Steeles Ave E Suite 387, Brampton, ON, L6T 1A6
(905) 793-2000
Emp Here 50
SIC 2813 Industrial gases

D-U-N-S 24-849-3280   (SL)
ALPHA POLY CORPORATION
296 Walker Dr, Brampton, ON, L6T 4B3
(905) 789-6770
Emp Here 50   *Sales* 7,296,070
SIC 2673 Bags: plastic, laminated, and coated
Patrick Kerrigan
Pr Pr Paul Kerrigan

Matthew Kerrigan
Carole Kerrigan
Fin Ex Martin Boeykens

D-U-N-S 20-719-0174   (HQ)
ALUMINART PRODUCTS LIMITED
(*Suby of* Aluminart Products Limited)
1 Summerlea Rd, Brampton, ON, L6T 4V2
(905) 791-7521
Emp Here 150   *Emp Total* 250
Sales 44,949,093
SIC 3442 Metal doors, sash, and trim
Pr Pr Frank Raponi

D-U-N-S 25-275-1136   (BR)
ANIXTER CANADA INC
7956 Torbram Rd Unit 1, Brampton, ON, L6T 5A2
(905) 790-9100
Emp Here 35
SIC 3644 Noncurrent-carrying wiring devices

D-U-N-S 20-145-2364   (SL)
ANTI-FRICTION ENTERPRISES (1985) LIMITED
150 Summerlea Rd, Brampton, ON, L6T 4X3
(905) 793-4493
Emp Here 40   *Sales* 3,205,129
SIC 3471 Plating and polishing

D-U-N-S 24-662-9158   (HQ)
APPS CARTAGE INC
APPS INTERNATIONAL
275 Orenda Rd, Brampton, ON, L6T 3T7
(905) 451-2720
Emp Here 148   *Emp Total* 300
Sales 31,902,000
SIC 4212 Local trucking, without storage
Pr Pr Robert M. Mcdonald
VP VP Brent T. Byers

D-U-N-S 20-769-1692   (SL)
ARTCRAFT ELECTRIC LIMITED
8050 Torbram Rd, Brampton, ON, L6T 3T2
(905) 791-1551
Emp Here 50   *Sales* 4,596,524
SIC 3645 Residential lighting fixtures

D-U-N-S 20-272-8267   (SL)
BHI INSTALLATION INC
278 Orenda Rd, Brampton, ON, L6T 4X6
(905) 791-2850
Emp Here 50   *Sales* 4,331,255
SIC 1751 Carpentry work

D-U-N-S 24-829-0918   (HQ)
BACARDI CANADA INC
1000 Steeles Ave E, Brampton, ON, L6T 1A1
(905) 451-6100
Emp Here 90   *Emp Total* 100
Sales 70,079,706
SIC 2085 Distilled and blended liquors
Richard Andrews
Lisa Smith
John P Esposito

D-U-N-S 25-027-7803   (BR)
BAGOS BUN BAKERY LTD
SONS BAKERY
8 Atlas Crt, Brampton, ON, L6T 5C1
(905) 458-0388
Emp Here 35
SIC 5461 Retail bakeries

D-U-N-S 25-296-8029   (BR)
BANK OF NOVA SCOTIA, THE
SCOTIABANK
36 Avondale Blvd, Brampton, ON, L6T 1H3

Emp Here 20
SIC 6021 National commercial banks

D-U-N-S 20-589-5480   (BR)
BANQUE TORONTO-DOMINION, LA
TD CANADA TRUST
(*Suby of* Toronto-Dominion Bank, The)
25 Peel Centre Dr, Brampton, ON, L6T 3R5

(905) 793-4880
Emp Here 20
SIC 6021 National commercial banks

D-U-N-S 25-528-0695   (BR)
BARDON SUPPLIES LIMITED
(*Suby of* Entreprises Mirca Inc, Les)
24 Melanie Dr, Brampton, ON, L6T 4K9
(905) 791-4500
Emp Here 35
SIC 5074 Plumbing and heating equipment and supplies (hydronics)

D-U-N-S 24-795-3342   (SL)
BERNEL MASONRY LTD
131 Delta Park Blvd Suite 1, Brampton, ON, L6T 5M8
(905) 791-8818
Emp Here 50   *Sales* 4,331,255
SIC 1741 Masonry and other stonework

D-U-N-S 24-363-5625   (BR)
BEST BUY CANADA LTD
BEST BUY
(*Suby of* Best Buy Co., Inc.)
25 Peel Centre Dr Unit 451, Brampton, ON, L6T 3R5
(905) 494-2179
Emp Here 50
SIC 5731 Radio, television, and electronic stores

D-U-N-S 25-368-5135   (BR)
BRAMBLES CANADA INC
RECALL TOTAL INFORMATION MANAGEMENT
50 Driver Rd, Brampton, ON, L6T 5V2
(905) 458-1521
Emp Here 40
SIC 4226 Special warehousing and storage, nec

D-U-N-S 20-175-3295   (BR)
CHEP CANADA INC
76 Wentworth Crt, Brampton, ON, L6T 5M7
(905) 790-2437
Emp Here 35
SIC 7359 Equipment rental and leasing, nec

D-U-N-S 24-380-0153   (SL)
CWI CLIMATEWORX INTERNATIONAL INC
18 Chelsea Lane, Brampton, ON, L6T 3Y4
(905) 405-0800
Emp Here 25   *Sales* 8,317,520
SIC 5075 Warm air heating and air conditioning
Pr Izabela Bedard
Dir Lori Holjevac

D-U-N-S 24-204-1395   (SL)
CANADIAN ECO RUBBER LTD
EMTERRA TIRE RECYCLING
8 Bramwin Crt Suite 18, Brampton, ON, L6T 5G2
(905) 487-2824
Emp Here 20   *Sales* 2,407,703
SIC 5531 Auto and home supply stores

D-U-N-S 20-588-8634   (BR)
CANADIAN IMPERIAL BANK OF COMMERCE
CIBC
16 Lisa St, Brampton, ON, L6T 5R2
(905) 451-1497
Emp Here 20
SIC 6021 National commercial banks

D-U-N-S 24-953-5568   (HQ)
CANPAR TRANSPORT L.P.
CANPAR COURIER
(*Suby of* Canpar Transport L.P.)
201 Westcreek Blvd Suite 102, Brampton, ON, L6T 0G8
(905) 499-2699
Emp Here 120   *Emp Total* 1,600
Sales 76,389,853
SIC 7389 Business services, nec
Pr Jim Houston

D-U-N-S 25-366-0039   (BR)
CARA OPERATIONS LIMITED
SWISS CHALET
(*Suby of* Cara Holdings Limited)
150 West Dr, Brampton, ON, L6T 4P9
(905) 457-0504
Emp Here 50
SIC 5812 Eating places

D-U-N-S 24-805-1364   (BR)
CARDINAL MEAT SPECIALISTS LIMITED
HEDGEDALE MANUFACTURING PLANT
(*Suby of* Cardinal Meat Specialists Limited)
155 Hedgedale Rd, Brampton, ON, L6T 5P3
(905) 459-4436
Emp Here 20
SIC 2011 Meat packing plants

D-U-N-S 20-754-6110   (BR)
CARGILL LIMITED
SUN VALLEY FOODS
235 Nuggett Crt, Brampton, ON, L6T 5H4
(905) 790-8660
Emp Here 45
SIC 2013 Sausages and other prepared meats

D-U-N-S 25-140-3176   (SL)
CEN-COMM COMMUNICATIONS INC
5 Blair Dr, Brampton, ON, L6T 2H4
(905) 457-7152
Emp Here 50   *Sales* 4,377,642
SIC 1731 Electrical work

D-U-N-S 20-791-4438   (BR)
CHILDREN'S PLACE (CANADA) LP, THE
25 Peel Centre Dr, Brampton, ON, L6T 3R5
(905) 799-8626
Emp Here 35
SIC 5641 Children's and infants' wear stores

D-U-N-S 20-693-1565   (HQ)
CLARKE TRANSPORT INC
201 Westcreek Blvd Suite 200, Brampton, ON, L6T 5S6
(905) 291-3000
Emp Here 75   *Emp Total* 25,438
Sales 63,149,698
SIC 4731 Freight transportation arrangement
Pr Darell Hornby
Josiane Melanie Langlois
VP Chantal Martel
Crdt Mgr Rocco Biase

D-U-N-S 20-178-8846   (BR)
COCA-COLA REFRESHMENTS CANADA COMPANY
(*Suby of* The Coca-Cola Company)
15 Westcreek Blvd Suite 1, Brampton, ON, L6T 5T4
(905) 874-7200
Emp Here 1,200
SIC 2086 Bottled and canned soft drinks

D-U-N-S 24-098-2582   (BR)
COMPAGNIE DES CHEMINS DE FER NATIONAUX DU CANADA
76 Intermodal Dr, Brampton, ON, L6T 5N6
(905) 789-4300
Emp Here 50
SIC 4119 Local passenger transportation, nec

D-U-N-S 20-022-3746   (BR)
CORPORATION OF THE CITY OF BRAMPTON, THE
PARKS & RECREATION
44 Eastbourne Dr, Brampton, ON, L6T 3M2
(905) 792-2224
Emp Here 20
SIC 7999 Amusement and recreation, nec

D-U-N-S 20-276-7596   (BR)
CRAWFORD PACKAGING INC
CRAWFORD PROVINCIAL
115 Walker Dr Unit A, Brampton, ON, L6T 5P5
(905) 670-7904
Emp Here 115
SIC 5084 Industrial machinery and equipment

D-U-N-S 24-132-8400   (HQ)
DHL EXPRESS (CANADA) LTD
18 Parkshore Dr, Brampton, ON, L6T 0G7
(905) 861-3400
Emp Here 150   *Emp Total* 498,459
Sales 276 666,974
SIC 4212 Local trucking, without storage
Pr Gregory Hewitt
   David Duncan
S&M/VP Andrew Paul
   Joshua Frank

D-U-N-S 24-408-8134   (HQ)
DSV AIR & SEA INC
70 Driver Rd Unit 4, Brampton, ON, L6T 5V2
(905) 494-5519
Emp Here 26   *Emp Total* 350
Sales 11,090,026
SIC 4731 Freight transportation arrangement
Pr Pr Carsten Trolle
   Pamla Bronn
Acct Mgr Saeed Dashtban

D-U-N-S 20-053-2641   (HQ)
DAWN FOOD PRODUCTS (CANADA), LTD
(*Suby of* Dawn Foods, Inc.)
275 Steelwell Rd, Brampton, ON, L6T 0C8
(289) 505-4640
Emp Here 70   *Emp Total* 4,000
Sales 71,379,082
SIC 5149 Groceries and related products, nec
   Carrie Barber
   Ronald Jones
VP VP Glenn Anderson
Dir Stuart Smith
CFO David Knowlton

D-U-N-S 24-423-8585   (HQ)
DEALER TIRE CANADA ULC
DEALER TIRE
30 Driver Rd Suite 1, Brampton, ON, L6T 5V2
(905) 458-1752
Emp Here 33   *Emp Total* 800
Sales 17,510,568
SIC 5014 Tires and tubes
Pr Roger Ferguson

D-U-N-S 25-265-2698   (BR)
DUFFERIN-PEEL CATHOLIC DISTRICT SCHOOL BOARD
GEORGES VANIER ELEMENTARY SCHOOL
28 Finchgate Blvd, Brampton, ON, L6T 3H9
(905) 792-2251
Emp Here 26
SIC 8211 Elementary and secondary schools

D-U-N-S 20-711-0060   (BR)
DUFFERIN-PEEL CATHOLIC DISTRICT SCHOOL BOARD
GENESIS II CATHOLIC SCHOOL
150 Central Park Dr, Brampton, ON, L6T 1B4
(905) 458-5976
Emp Here 50
SIC 8211 Elementary and secondary schools

D-U-N-S 20-710-9682   (BR)
DUFFERIN-PEEL CATHOLIC DISTRICT SCHOOL BOARD
ST. PATRICK SCHOOL
Rr 9 Wildfield, Brampton, ON, L6T 3Z8
(905) 794-0411
Emp Here 50
SIC 8211 Elementary and secondary schools

D-U-N-S 25-145-8782   (BR)
DUNDAS JAFINE INC
15 Bramalea Rd Unit 102, Brampton, ON, L6T 2W4
(905) 458-4733
Emp Here 35
SIC 3433 Heating equipment, except electric

D-U-N-S 24-466-9623   (BR)
EM PLASTIC & ELECTRIC PRODUCTS LIMITED
14 Brewster Rd, Brampton, ON, L6T 5B7

Emp Here 45

SIC 5162 Plastics materials and basic shapes

D-U-N-S 20-562-7826   (BR)
EXP SERVICES INC
1595 Clark Blvd, Brampton, ON, L6T 4V1
(905) 793-9800
Emp Here 200
SIC 8711 Engineering services

D-U-N-S 25-220-9762   (HQ)
ELECTRONICS BOUTIQUE CANADA INC
EB GAMES
8995 Airport Rd Suite 512, Brampton, ON, L6T 5T2
(905) 790-9262
Emp Here 100   *Emp Total* 20,000
Sales 189,697,820
SIC 5734 Computer and software stores
VP VP Jim Tyo

D-U-N-S 24-685-1026   (BR)
EMBALLAGES B. & C. LTEE, LES
EMBALLAGES B & C LTEE, LES
125 East Dr, Brampton, ON, L6T 1B5
(905) 791-5249
Emp Here 40
SIC 2673 Bags: plastic, laminated, and coated

D-U-N-S 25-173-2517   (HQ)
ENTERTAINMENT ONE GP LIMITED
CD PLUS GROUP OF STORES
(*Suby of* 4384768 Canada Inc)
70 Driver Rd Unit 1, Brampton, ON, L6T 5V2
(905) 624-7337
Emp Here 300   *Emp Total* 302
Sales 103,385,312
SIC 5099 Durable goods, nec
Pr Darren Throop
   Joseph Sparacio

D-U-N-S 20-807-6328   (SL)
ESSAG CANADA INC
HOLIDAY INN TORONTO BRAMPTON HOTEL & CONFERENCE CENTRE
30 Peel Centre Dr, Brampton, ON, L6T 4G3

Emp Here 80   *Sales* 3,502,114
SIC 7011 Hotels and motels

D-U-N-S 20-164-7948   (HQ)
EXPORT PACKERS COMPANY LIMITED
107 Walker Dr, Brampton, ON, L6T 5K5
(905) 792-9700
Emp Here 160   *Emp Total* 220
Sales 72,377,014
SIC 5142 Packaged frozen goods
   Jeffrey Rubenstein
   Daniel Leblanc
Div VP Ralph Gobbi
Div VP Peter Kwong
Ex VP Werter Mior
   Brian Lampert
   Max Rubenstein

D-U-N-S 24-337-3177   (BR)
FGL SPORTS LTD
SPORT CHEK BRAMALEA CITY CENTRE
25 Peel Centre Dr, Brampton, ON, L6T 3R5
(905) 789-8965
Emp Here 40
SIC 5941 Sporting goods and bicycle shops

D-U-N-S 25-801-5833   (BR)
FAIRWEATHER LTD
25 Peel Centre Dr, Brampton, ON, L6T 3R5
(905) 793-4697
Emp Here 32
SIC 5621 Women's clothing stores

D-U-N-S 20-214-7265   (HQ)
FERRARA CANDY CO. LTD
(*Suby of* Ferrara Candy Company)
10 Colony Crt, Brampton, ON, L6T 4E4
(905) 799-1235
Emp Here 32   *Emp Total* 1,100
Sales 5,072,500
SIC 2064 Candy and other confectionery

---

products
Pr Pr Salvatore Ferrara
   James Buffardi
Genl Mgr Anthony Di Marco

D-U-N-S 25-370-4829   (BR)
FOOT LOCKER CANADA CO.
CHAMPS SPORTS
25 Peel Centre Dr, Brampton, ON, L6T 3R5
(905) 790-1366
Emp Here 20
SIC 5699 Miscellaneous apparel and accessory stores

D-U-N-S 25-406-5089   (BR)
FORD MOTOR COMPANY OF CANADA, LIMITED
JAGUAR CANADA, DIV OF
(*Suby of* Ford Motor Company)
8 Indell Lane, Brampton, ON, L6T 3Y3
(905) 792-9400
Emp Here 30
SIC 5013 Motor vehicle supplies and new parts

D-U-N-S 20-596-0107   (BR)
FORD MOTOR COMPANY OF CANADA, LIMITED
BRAMALEA SALES PARTS DISTRIBUTION CENTRE
(*Suby of* Ford Motor Company)
8000 Dixie Rd, Brampton, ON, L6T 2J7
(905) 459-2210
Emp Here 300
SIC 5013 Motor vehicle supplies and new parts

D-U-N-S 24-411-1019   (SL)
FORMOST DATA PRODUCTS INC
FORMOST MEDIA ONE
6 Kenview Blvd, Brampton, ON, L6T 5E4
(905) 793-7295
Emp Here 55   *Sales* 8,857,893
SIC 2761 Manifold business forms
Pr Pr John Gaudet
VP Fin Sharon Bell
VP Sls Neil Bishop

D-U-N-S 24-966-1849   (SL)
FOUR SEASONS SITE DEVELOPMENT LTD
42 Wentworth Crt Unit 1, Brampton, ON, L6T 5K6
(905) 670-7655
Emp Here 49   *Sales* 5,690,935
SIC 1611 Highway and street construction
   Rohit Bansal

D-U-N-S 25-318-8684   (BR)
GAP (CANADA) INC
GAP
(*Suby of* The Gap Inc)
89 Walker Dr, Brampton, ON, L6T 5K5
(905) 793-8888
Emp Here 150
SIC 5651 Family clothing stores

D-U-N-S 25-162-5027   (SL)
GARDENA CANADA LTD
100 Summerlea Rd, Brampton, ON, L6T 4X3
(905) 792-9330
Emp Here 20   *Sales* 4,377,642
SIC 5083 Farm and garden machinery

D-U-N-S 25-997-1141   (HQ)
GENERAL CABLE COMPANY
156 Parkshore Rd, Brampton, ON, L6T 5M1
(905) 791-6886
Emp Here 35   *Emp Total* 275
Sales 40,800,422
SIC 3315 Steel wire and related products
VP Sls Robert Jamieson
Pr Pr Gregory Kenny
   Christopher Virgulak
   Robert Siverd
VP Jeffrey Whelan

D-U-N-S 24-420-1054   (BR)
GENERAL PAINT CORP

PARA PAINTS
(*Suby of* The Sherwin-Williams Company)
11 Kenview Blvd Suite B, Brampton, ON, L6T 5G5

Emp Here 50
SIC 5198 Paints, varnishes, and supplies

D-U-N-S 20-182-7854   (HQ)
GESCO INDUSTRIES INC
50 Kenview Blvd, Brampton, ON, L6T 5S8
(905) 789-3755
Emp Here 20   *Emp Total* 800
Sales 16,961,922
SIC 5023 Homefurnishings
Pr Edward Du Domaine
Dir Sean Ward
Dir Charles Chaikin
Dir William Lloyd
Dir Neil Sethi

D-U-N-S 25-192-3751   (SL)
GRAY TOOLS CANADA INC
299 Orenda Rd, Brampton, ON, L6T 1E8
(905) 457-3014
Emp Here 62   *Sales* 4,596,524
SIC 3423 Hand and edge tools, nec

D-U-N-S 25-099-0348   (HQ)
GUNNEBO CANADA INC
9 Van Der Graaf Crt, Brampton, ON, L6T 5E5
(905) 595-4140
Emp Here 75   *Emp Total* 20
Sales 19,188,664
SIC 5065 Electronic parts and equipment, nec
Pr Pr John Haining
Dir Eric Schneider

D-U-N-S 24-424-4450   (BR)
HARRIS STEEL ULC
(*Suby of* Nucor Corporation)
980 Intermodal Dr, Brampton, ON, L6T 0B5
(905) 799-1220
Emp Here 60
SIC 3312 Blast furnaces and steel mills

D-U-N-S 24-317-5028   (BR)
HERCULES SLR INC
8026 Torbram Rd Unit 802a, Brampton, ON, L6T 3T2
(905) 564-3387
Emp Here 25
SIC 3496 Miscellaneous fabricated wire products

D-U-N-S 25-831-7403   (BR)
HUDSON'S BAY COMPANY
RSCL
8550 Airport Rd, Brampton, ON, L6T 5A3

Emp Here 160
SIC 5099 Durable goods, nec

D-U-N-S 24-803-2265   (BR)
HUDSON'S BAY COMPANY
SAKS FIFTH AVENUE CANADA
8925 Torbram Rd, Brampton, ON, L6T 4G1
(905) 792-4400
Emp Here 80
SIC 5311 Department stores

D-U-N-S 25-092-7423   (BR)
HUDSON'S BAY COMPANY
BAY, THE
25 Peel Centre Dr Suite 3, Brampton, ON, L6T 3R5
(905) 793-5100
Emp Here 300
SIC 5311 Department stores

D-U-N-S 20-112-6468   (BR)
INDIGO BOOKS & MUSIC INC
DISTRIBUTION & SUPPLY DIVISION
(*Suby of* Indigo Books & Music Inc)
100 Alfred Kuehne Blvd, Brampton, ON, L6T 4K4
(905) 789-1234
Emp Here 200

SIC 5192 Books, periodicals, and newspapers

D-U-N-S 20-626-4749   (SL)
INTERNATIONAL PLAYING CARD COMPANY LIMITED
JARDEN
(*Suby* of Newell Brands Inc.)
845 Intermodal Dr Unit 1, Brampton, ON, L6T 0C6
(905) 488-7102
Emp Here 25   *Sales* 4,331,255
SIC 5092 Toys and hobby goods and supplies

D-U-N-S 20-708-9769   (BR)
IRON MOUNTAIN CANADA OPERATIONS ULC
ARCHIVES IRON MOUNTAIN
10 Tilbury Crt, Brampton, ON, L6T 3T4
(905) 454-2400
Emp Here 20
SIC 8742 Management consulting services

D-U-N-S 25-367-8650   (BR)
ITALPASTA LIMITED
199 Summerlea Rd, Brampton, ON, L6T 4E5
(905) 792-9928
Emp Here 200
SIC 2098 Macaroni and spaghetti

D-U-N-S 25-092-4243   (BR)
ITALPASTA LIMITED
140 Nuggett Crt, Brampton, ON, L6T 5H4
(905) 792-9928
Emp Here 200
SIC 2098 Macaroni and spaghetti

D-U-N-S 25-242-2428   (SL)
J.D. TRANSPORTATION SERVICES 2003 INC
15 Bramalea Rd Unit 6, Brampton, ON, L6T 2W4
(905) 793-2005
Emp Here 50   *Sales* 4,326,914
SIC 4213 Trucking, except local

D-U-N-S 20-267-4177   (SL)
JOINT TRAINING & APPRENTICESHIP COMMITTEE
JTAC
419 Deerhurst Dr, Brampton, ON, L6T 5K3
(905) 790-9662
Emp Here 60   *Sales* 2,845,467
SIC 8331 Job training and related services

D-U-N-S 24-369-7187   (BR)
JONES PACKAGING INC
JONES CONTRACT PACKAGING SERVICES, DIV OF
55 Walker Dr, Brampton, ON, L6T 5K5
(905) 790-0302
Emp Here 150
SIC 7389 Business services, nec

D-U-N-S 25-528-6551   (BR)
KEYSTONE AUTOMOTIVE INDUSTRIES ON INC
3485 Steeles Ave E Suite 2, Brampton, ON, L6T 5W7
(905) 454-5580
Emp Here 50
SIC 7532 Top and body repair and paint shops

D-U-N-S 20-699-1304   (BR)
KONE INC
48 West Dr, Brampton, ON, L6T 3T6
(905) 454-1222
Emp Here 48
SIC 7699 Repair services, nec

D-U-N-S 20-337-8588   (BR)
KONICA MINOLTA BUSINESS SOLUTIONS (CANADA) LTD
IT WEAPONS DIV.
7965 Goreway Dr Unit 1, Brampton, ON, L6T 5T5
(905) 494-1040
Emp Here 100
SIC 7379 Computer related services, nec

D-U-N-S 24-312-5296   (BR)
KRUGER INC
10 Pedigree Crt, Brampton, ON, L6T 5T8
(905) 793-1799
Emp Here 195
SIC 2653 Corrugated and solid fiber boxes

D-U-N-S 24-771-1856   (HQ)
LIBERTE NATURAL FOODS INC
91 Delta Park Blvd Unit 2, Brampton, ON, L6T 5E7
(905) 458-8696
Emp Here 115   *Emp Total* 249
Sales 9,423,290
SIC 5499 Miscellaneous food stores
Pr Paul Roach

D-U-N-S 24-376-5802   (BR)
LINDE CANADA LIMITED
BOC GASES
2090 Steeles Ave E, Brampton, ON, L6T 1A7
(905) 790-3679
Emp Here 50
SIC 5169 Chemicals and allied products, nec

D-U-N-S 25-317-9238   (BR)
LIQUOR CONTROL BOARD OF ONTARIO, THE
L.C.B.O.#416
80 Peel Centre Dr Suite A, Brampton, ON, L6T 4G8
(905) 793-8027
Emp Here 30
SIC 5921 Liquor stores

D-U-N-S 24-139-0061   (SL)
LIV CANADA GIFT GROUP INC
PANHANDLERS DIV
294 Walker Dr Unit 2, Brampton, ON, L6T 4Z2
(905) 790-9023
Emp Here 25   *Sales* 4,231,721
SIC 6794 Patent owners and lessors

D-U-N-S 24-199-0050   (BR)
LOCHER EVERS INTERNATIONAL INC
LOCHER EVERS INTERNATIONAL
30 Midair Crt, Brampton, ON, L6T 5V1
(905) 494-0880
Emp Here 45
SIC 4731 Freight transportation arrangement

D-U-N-S 25-370-7608   (BR)
MAGNA INTERNATIONAL INC
MASSIV AUTOMATED SYSTEMS
2550 Steeles Ave E, Brampton, ON, L6T 5R3
(905) 790-9246
Emp Here 100
SIC 3714 Motor vehicle parts and accessories

D-U-N-S 25-998-6636   (BR)
MAGNA INTERNATIONAL INC
PLASTCOAT, DIV OF
26 Kenview Blvd, Brampton, ON, L6T 5S8
(905) 458-5740
Emp Here 450
SIC 3465 Automotive stampings

D-U-N-S 24-665-5914   (BR)
MAGNA INTERNATIONAL INC
MASSIV DIE-FORM
7655 Bramalea Rd, Brampton, ON, L6T 4Y5
(905) 458-4041
Emp Here 350
SIC 3714 Motor vehicle parts and accessories

D-U-N-S 24-361-7367   (BR)
MAGNA INTERNATIONAL INC
COSMA INTERNATIONAL CANADA, DIV OF
2550 Steeles Ave E, Brampton, ON, L6T 5R3
(905) 799-7654
Emp Here 50
SIC 3465 Automotive stampings

D-U-N-S 20-014-3852   (BR)
MAGNA INTERNATIONAL INC
MTTC
2550 Steeles Ave E, Brampton, ON, L6T 5R3

Emp Here 30
SIC 8741 Management services

D-U-N-S 25-683-6396   (HQ)
MAGNATE ENGINEERING & ASSOCIATES INC
220 Advance Blvd, Brampton, ON, L6T 4J5
(905) 799-8220
Emp Here 40   *Emp Total* 15,000
Sales 7,369,031
SIC 8711 Engineering services
Pr Elizabeth Stanmore
VP VP Debbie Kingston

D-U-N-S 25-531-0104   (BR)
MAPLEHURST BAKERIES INC
READY BAKE FOODS INC
379 Orenda Rd, Brampton, ON, L6T 1G6
(905) 791-7400
Emp Here 200
SIC 2051 Bread, cake, and related products

D-U-N-S 25-685-4258   (BR)
MARTINREA INTERNATIONAL INC
ATLAS FLUID SYSTEMS
(*Suby* of Martinrea International Inc)
10 Atlas Crt, Brampton, ON, L6T 5C1
(905) 791-7119
Emp Here 400
SIC 3499 Fabricated Metal products, nec

D-U-N-S 20-306-2146   (SL)
MASTER PLANT-PROD INC
314 Orenda Rd, Brampton, ON, L6T 1G1
(905) 793-8000
Emp Here 25   *Sales* 4,071,380
SIC 2874 Phosphatic fertilizers

D-U-N-S 20-792-4858   (BR)
MCDONALD'S RESTAURANTS OF CANADA LIMITED
MCDONALD'S 16711
(*Suby* of McDonald's Corporation)
30 Coventry Rd, Brampton, ON, L6T 5P9
(905) 789-0030
Emp Here 46
SIC 5812 Eating places

D-U-N-S 20-641-8118   (BR)
MCDONALD'S RESTAURANTS OF CANADA LIMITED
MCDONALD'S #29148
(*Suby* of McDonald's Corporation)
2439 Steeles Ave E, Brampton, ON, L6T 5J9
(905) 494-1134
Emp Here 50
SIC 5812 Eating places

D-U-N-S 24-348-0840   (BR)
MEDIAS TRANSCONTINENTAL S.E.N.C.
66 Nuggett Crt, Brampton, ON, L6T 5A9

Emp Here 116
SIC 7336 Commercial art and graphic design

D-U-N-S 20-270-1330   (BR)
MIDLAND TRANSPORT LIMITED
MIDLAND LOGISTICS & FREIGHT BROKERAGE, DIV OF
(*Suby* of J. D. Irving, Limited)
102 Glidden Rd, Brampton, ON, L6T 5N4

Emp Here 100
SIC 4212 Local trucking, without storage

D-U-N-S 24-195-8933   (BR)
MIDLAND TRANSPORT LIMITED
MIDLAND
(*Suby* of J. D. Irving, Limited)
102 Glidden Rd, Brampton, ON, L6T 5N4
(905) 456-5555
Emp Here 100
SIC 4213 Trucking, except local

D-U-N-S 25-226-9121   (BR)
MINI-SKOOL A CHILD'S PLACE INC
27 Kings Cross Rd, Brampton, ON, L6T 3V5

(905) 792-2230
Emp Here 30
SIC 8351 Child day care services

D-U-N-S 25-405-5130   (BR)
MORGUARD INVESTMENTS LIMITED
25 Peel Centre Dr Suite 127, Brampton, ON, L6T 3R5
(905) 793-4682
Emp Here 25
SIC 6512 Nonresidential building operators

D-U-N-S 20-036-7472   (HQ)
NCH CANADA INC
LUBEMASTER CONSTRUCTION
247 Orenda Rd, Brampton, ON, L6T 1E6
(905) 457-5220
Emp Here 40   *Emp Total* 8,500
Sales 48,510,056
SIC 5169 Chemicals and allied products, nec
Pr Pr Irvin Levy
  Russ Price
  Lester Levy
Dir Milton Levy
Dir Carlos A. Cerqueira

D-U-N-S 25-398-1922   (BR)
NATIONAL IMPORTERS CANADA LTD
1555 Clark Blvd, Brampton, ON, L6T 4G2
(905) 791-1322
Emp Here 55
SIC 5141 Groceries, general line

D-U-N-S 24-078-1922   (SL)
NATURE'S SUNSHINE PRODUCTS OF CANADA LTD
(*Suby* of Natures Sunshine Products, Inc.)
44 Peel Centre Dr Unit 402, Brampton, ON, L6T 4B5
(905) 458-6100
Emp Here 28   *Sales* 4,012,839
SIC 5149 Groceries and related products, nec

D-U-N-S 24-477-2315   (HQ)
NEXCYCLE PLASTICS INC
NPI
235 Wilkinson Rd, Brampton, ON, L6T 4M2
(905) 454-2666
Emp Here 77   *Emp Total* 175
Sales 22,982,621
SIC 4953 Refuse systems
Pr Laurie Borg
  Christopher Turney

D-U-N-S 25-027-7787   (BR)
NISSAN CANADA INC
60 Steelwell Rd, Brampton, ON, L6T 5L9
(905) 459-6070
Emp Here 50
SIC 5013 Motor vehicle supplies and new parts

D-U-N-S 24-624-5237   (SL)
NORD GEAR LIMITED
41 West Dr, Brampton, ON, L6T 4A1
(905) 796-6796
Emp Here 35   *Sales* 4,523,563
SIC 3566 Speed changers, drives, and gears

D-U-N-S 25-333-1227   (BR)
OLYMEL S.E.C.
318 Orenda Rd, Brampton, ON, L6T 1G1
(905) 793-5757
Emp Here 400
SIC 2015 Poultry slaughtering and processing

D-U-N-S 24-688-4209   (BR)
PACCAR OF CANADA LTD
PACCAR LEASING
(*Suby* of Paccar Inc)
108 Summerlea Rd, Brampton, ON, L6T 4X3
(905) 791-0021
Emp Here 30
SIC 5013 Motor vehicle supplies and new parts

D-U-N-S 20-859-9378   (BR)
PACIFIC LINK COMMUNICATIONS INC
BELL WORLD

25 Peel Centre Dr, Brampton, ON, L6T 3R5
(905) 791-1140
Emp Here 25
SIC 5999 Miscellaneous retail stores, nec

D-U-N-S 24-306-4433   (BR)
PARRISH & HEIMBECKER, LIMITED
DOVER CUP DIVISION
(*Suby of* Parrish & Heimbecker, Limited)
308 Orenda Rd, Brampton, ON, L6T 1G1
(905) 789-8585
Emp Here 77
SIC 5153 Grain and field beans

D-U-N-S 24-771-2870   (SL)
**PECHINEY   PLASTIC   PACKAGING
(CANADA) INC**
ALCAN PACKAGING
(*Suby of* RIO TINTO PLC)
40 Driver Rd, Brampton, ON, L6T 5V2
(905) 494-1111
Emp Here 100   *Sales* 19,730,160
SIC 3082 Unsupported plastics profile shapes
Ch Bd Ch Bd Ilene S Gordon
VP Claudine Marineau
VP Michael S Schmitt
VP Donald Seberger
Eileen Lerum
Treas Robert J Mosesian
Dir Roy Millington
Sec Hugh Berwick

D-U-N-S 25-293-9277   (BR)
PEEL DISTRICT SCHOOL BOARD
EASTBOURNE DRIVE PUBLIC SCHOOL
(*Suby of* Peel District School Board)
702 Balmoral Dr, Brampton, ON, L6T 1X3
(905) 792-2264
Emp Here 30
SIC 8211 Elementary and secondary schools

D-U-N-S 25-283-1409   (BR)
PEEL DISTRICT SCHOOL BOARD
NORTH FIELD OFFICE
(*Suby of* Peel District School Board)
215 Orenda Rd, Brampton, ON, L6T 5L1
(905) 451-2362
Emp Here 140
SIC 8211 Elementary and secondary schools

D-U-N-S 25-293-9319   (BR)
PEEL DISTRICT SCHOOL BOARD
EARNSCLIFFE SENIOR PUBLIC SCHOOL
(*Suby of* Peel District School Board)
50 Earnscliffe Cir, Brampton, ON, L6T 2B2
(905) 793-2903
Emp Here 60
SIC 8211 Elementary and secondary schools

D-U-N-S 25-265-3027   (BR)
PEEL DISTRICT SCHOOL BOARD
BALMORAL DRIVE MIDDLE SCHOOL
(*Suby of* Peel District School Board)
233 Balmoral Dr, Brampton, ON, L6T 1V5
(905) 793-6070
Emp Here 60
SIC 8211 Elementary and secondary schools

D-U-N-S 25-265-2946   (BR)
PEEL DISTRICT SCHOOL BOARD
BIRCHBANK ELEMENTARY SCHOOL
(*Suby of* Peel District School Board)
52 Birchbank Rd, Brampton, ON, L6T 1L7
(905) 793-7984
Emp Here 40
SIC 8211 Elementary and secondary schools

D-U-N-S 25-265-2789   (BR)
PEEL DISTRICT SCHOOL BOARD
CLARK BOULEVARD PUBLIC SCHOOL
(*Suby of* Peel District School Board)
201 Clark Blvd, Brampton, ON, L6T 2C9
(905) 793-6060
Emp Here 50
SIC 8211 Elementary and secondary schools

D-U-N-S 25-293-7628   (BR)

PEEL DISTRICT SCHOOL BOARD
FALLINGDALE PUBLIC SCHOOL
(*Suby of* Peel District School Board)
510 Clark Blvd, Brampton, ON, L6T 2E4
(905) 791-8543
Emp Here 30
SIC 8211 Elementary and secondary schools

D-U-N-S 25-265-3068   (BR)
PEEL DISTRICT SCHOOL BOARD
ALOMA CRESCENT PUBLIC SCHOOL
(*Suby of* Peel District School Board)
57 Aloma Cres, Brampton, ON, L6T 2N8
(905) 793-7070
Emp Here 35
SIC 8211 Elementary and secondary schools

D-U-N-S 25-297-1981   (BR)
PEEL DISTRICT SCHOOL BOARD
MAYFIELD SECONDARY SCHOOL
(*Suby of* Peel District School Board)
5000 Mayfield Rd Rr 4, Brampton, ON, L6T
3S1
(905) 846-6060
Emp Here 130
SIC 8211 Elementary and secondary schools

D-U-N-S 25-293-9194   (BR)
PEEL DISTRICT SCHOOL BOARD
FOLKSTONE PUBLIC SCHOOL
(*Suby of* Peel District School Board)
104 Folkstone Cres, Brampton, ON, L6T 3M5
(905) 792-2266
Emp Here 40
SIC 8211 Elementary and secondary schools

D-U-N-S 25-055-7337   (BR)
PENSKE TRUCK LEASING CANADA INC
(*Suby of* Penske Corporation)
37 West Dr, Brampton, ON, L6T 4A1
(905) 450-7676
Emp Here 20
SIC 7513 Truck rental and leasing, no drivers

D-U-N-S 20-609-9558   (SL)
**POCZO MANUFACTURING COMPANY LIM-
ITED**
215 Wilkinson Rd, Brampton, ON, L6T 4M2
(905) 452-0567
Emp Here 50   *Sales* 4,711,645
SIC 3599 Industrial machinery, nec

D-U-N-S 24-380-8966   (BR)
POLARPAK INC
PAR-PAK
(*Suby of* Newell Brands Inc.)
200 Summerlea Rd, Brampton, ON, L6T 4E6
(905) 792-3000
Emp Here 25
SIC 3089 Plastics products, nec

D-U-N-S 24-207-9791   (BR)
PRAXAIR CANADA INC
(*Suby of* Praxair, Inc.)
80 Westcreek Blvd Unit 1, Brampton, ON, L6T
0B8
(905) 595-3788
Emp Here 100
SIC 2813 Industrial gases

D-U-N-S 24-092-7160   (SL)
QUEST BRANDS INC
1 Van Der Graaf Crt, Brampton, ON, L6T 5E5
(905) 789-6868
Emp Here 45   *Sales* 6,639,424
SIC 5211 Lumber and other building materials
David Webb
Pr Leeanne Murray

D-U-N-S 24-423-5388   (SL)
QUIET HARMONY INC
CALIFORNIA CLEANING
30 Intermodal Dr Unit 43, Brampton, ON, L6T
5K1
(905) 794-0622
Emp Here 125   *Sales* 3,648,035
SIC 7349 Building maintenance services, nec

D-U-N-S 24-205-0008   (BR)
R.J. BURNSIDE & ASSOCIATES LIMITED
170 Steelwell Rd Suite 200, Brampton, ON,
L6T 5T3
(905) 793-9239
Emp Here 35
SIC 8711 Engineering services

D-U-N-S 20-556-9668   (SL)
R.M. FERGUSON & COMPANY INC
*FERGUSON CHEMICAL INNOVATION, DIV
OF*
235 Advance Blvd Suite 1, Brampton, ON, L6T
4J2
(905) 458-5553
Emp Here 25   *Sales* 5,982,777
SIC 5169 Chemicals and allied products, nec
Pr Pr David Jackson

D-U-N-S 25-801-9611   (BR)
REITMANS (CANADA) LIMITEE
REITMANS
25 Peel Centre Dr, Brampton, ON, L6T 3R5
(905) 793-4477
Emp Here 25
SIC 5621 Women's clothing stores

D-U-N-S 20-646-1100   (BR)
ROSS VIDEO LIMITED
46 West Dr, Brampton, ON, L6T 3T6
(905) 453-8833
Emp Here 100
SIC 7336 Commercial art and graphic design

D-U-N-S 24-965-9558   (BR)
ROYAL BANK OF CANADA
RBC
(*Suby of* Royal Bank Of Canada)
25 Peel Centre Dr Suite 792, Brampton, ON,
L6T 3R5
(905) 790-7120
Emp Here 50
SIC 6021 National commercial banks

D-U-N-S 24-244-3831   (BR)
RYDER TRUCK RENTAL CANADA LTD
(*Suby of* Ryder System, Inc.)
30 Pedigree Crt Suite 1, Brampton, ON, L6T
5T8
(905) 759-2000
Emp Here 200
SIC 8721 Accounting, auditing, and book-
keeping

D-U-N-S 25-293-8998   (BR)
RYDER TRUCK RENTAL CANADA LTD
RYDER CANADA
(*Suby of* Ryder System, Inc.)
10a Tilbury Crt, Brampton, ON, L6T 3T4
(905) 457-7262
Emp Here 25
SIC 7513 Truck rental and leasing, no drivers

D-U-N-S 20-220-9388   (BR)
S.P. RICHARDS CO. CANADA INC
(*Suby of* Genuine Parts Company)
1325 Clark Blvd, Brampton, ON, L6T 5R5
(905) 789-6351
Emp Here 40
SIC 2678 Stationery products

D-U-N-S 20-881-5985   (HQ)
**SEW-EURODRIVE COMPANY OF CANADA
LTD**
210 Walker Dr, Brampton, ON, L6T 3W1
(905) 791-1553
Emp Here 100   *Sales* 22,471,896
SIC 3566 Speed changers, drives, and gears
VP VP Anthony Peluso
Fin Ex Audrey Gallop

D-U-N-S 25-796-2431   (BR)
SIR CORP
JACK ASTORS RESTAURANTS
154 West Dr, Brampton, ON, L6T 5P1
(905) 457-5200
Emp Here 100
SIC 5812 Eating places

D-U-N-S 20-280-5040   (SL)
SARATOGA POTATO CHIP COMPANY INC
OLDE YORK POTATO CHIPS
230 Deerhurst Dr, Brampton, ON, L6T 5R8
(905) 458-4100
Emp Here 100
SIC 2096 Potato chips and similar snacks

D-U-N-S 24-544-9095   (HQ)
SAVARIA CONCORD LIFTS INC
2 Walker Dr, Brampton, ON, L6T 5E1
(905) 791-5555
Emp Here 140   *Emp Total* 376
Sales 14,466,392
SIC 3534 Elevators and moving stairways
Pr Marcel Bourassa
Dir Jean-Marie Bourassa

D-U-N-S 25-685-3466   (BR)
SEALED AIR (CANADA) CO./CIE
(*Suby of* Sealed Air Corporation)
95 Glidden Rd, Brampton, ON, L6T 2H8
(905) 456-0701
Emp Here 60
SIC 3081 Unsupported plastics film and sheet

D-U-N-S 24-964-9260   (BR)
SEARS CANADA INC
25 Peel Centre Dr, Brampton, ON, L6T 3R5
(905) 458-1141
Emp Here 500
SIC 5311 Department stores

D-U-N-S 20-104-4398   (BR)
SHERWAY WAREHOUSING INC
11 Finley Rd, Brampton, ON, L6T 1B1

Emp Here 20
SIC 4225 General warehousing and storage

D-U-N-S 20-027-7726   (BR)
SHERWAY WAREHOUSING INC
SHERWAY GROUP
104 Walker Dr, Brampton, ON, L6T 4H6
(905) 789-8119
Emp Here 30
SIC 4225 General warehousing and storage

D-U-N-S 20-403-0563   (HQ)
SIMPSON STRONG-TIE CANADA LIMITED
SST
(*Suby of* Simpson Manufacturing Co., Inc.)
5 Kenview Blvd, Brampton, ON, L6T 5G5
(905) 458-5538
Emp Here 55   *Emp Total* 2,647
Sales 39,012,421
SIC 3452 Bolts, nuts, rivets, and washers
Pr Pr Steve Lamson
Dir Mike Petrovic

D-U-N-S 24-420-1070   (SL)
**SITHE GLOBAL CANADIAN POWER SER-
VICES LTD**
8600 Goreway Dr, Brampton, ON, L6T 0A8
(905) 595-4700
Emp Here 25   *Sales* 15,454,196
SIC 4911 Electric services
Mgr Ron Sigur

D-U-N-S 20-554-7750   (HQ)
SOLUTIONS 2 GO INC
(*Suby of* Solutions 2 GO Inc)
15 Production Dr, Brampton, ON, L6T 4N8
(905) 564-1140
Emp Here 120   *Emp Total* 160
Sales 28,016,909
SIC 5072 Hardware
Oliver Bock
Pr Pr Gabrielle Chevalier
Jason Gonsalves

D-U-N-S 20-257-1303   (SL)
SOLUTIONS 2 GO LATAM INC
15 Production Rd, Brampton, ON, L6T 4N8
(905) 564-1140
Emp Here 50   *Sales* 7,296,070
SIC 5092 Toys and hobby goods and supplies

Grabrielle Chevalier
Oliver Bock
Luis San Martin

D-U-N-S 20-543-6566 (BR)
STAPLES CANADA INC
STAPLES THE BUSINESS DEPOT
(*Suby of* Staples, Inc.)
2937 Queen St E, Brampton, ON, L6T 5J1
(905) 791-4522
Emp Here 35
SIC 5943 Stationery stores

D-U-N-S 24-422-9782 (BR)
STERICYCLE, ULC
95 Deerhurst Dr Suite 1, Brampton, ON, L6T 5R7
(905) 789-6660
Emp Here 100
SIC 4953 Refuse systems

D-U-N-S 25-412-2856 (HQ)
STERICYCLE, ULC
19 Armthorpe Rd, Brampton, ON, L6T 5M4
(905) 595-2651
Emp Here 35 *Emp Total* 25,000
Sales 39,398,778
SIC 4953 Refuse systems
Pr Pr Charles A. Alutto
Daniel V. Ginnetti
Sr VP Paul Saabas
VP VP Ron Waine
Felix Reney
Dir Fin Diane Knight

D-U-N-S 20-175-3246 (BR)
STERLING PACKERS LIMITED
CONFEDERATION FREEZERS
240 Nuggett Crt, Brampton, ON, L6T 5H4
(905) 799-3609
Emp Here 50
SIC 4222 Refrigerated warehousing and storage

D-U-N-S 24-624-9614 (BR)
SWISSPLAS LIMITED
116 Walker Dr, Brampton, ON, L6T 4G9
(905) 791-8825
Emp Here 20
SIC 5085 Industrial supplies

D-U-N-S 20-344-1043 (BR)
TFT GLOBAL INC
(*Suby of* 1596101 Ontario Inc)
115 Walker Dr Unit B, Brampton, ON, L6T 5P5
(519) 842-4540
Emp Here 30
SIC 4225 General warehousing and storage

D-U-N-S 24-350-1009 (HQ)
TI AUTOMOTIVE CANADA INC
316 Orenda Rd, Brampton, ON, L6T 1G3
(905) 793-7100
Emp Here 90 *Emp Total* 2,587
Sales 12,841,083
SIC 3465 Automotive stampings
William Kozyra
Pr Joachim Eurkhardt
Michael Drover
Timothy Guerriero

D-U-N-S 20-191-6835 (BR)
TNT FOODS INTERNATIONAL INC
20 Westwyn Crt, Brampton, ON, L6T 4T5
(905) 672-1787
Emp Here 80
SIC 5144 Poultry and poultry products

D-U-N-S 20-626-3295 (SL)
TARO PHARMACEUTICALS INC
TAROPHARMA
130 East Dr, Brampton, ON, L6T 1C1
(905) 791-8276
Emp Here 500 *Sales* 57,519,066
SIC 2834 Pharmaceutical preparations
VP VP Sunil Mehta
VP Andreas Wegner
Angela Moi

S&M/VP Elizabeth Ivey
VP Jayesh Shah
Sec Stephen Manzano
Harshad Tarekh
Sudhir Valia
James Kedrowski

D-U-N-S 24-424-1386 (HQ)
TENCORR PACKAGING INC
6 Shaftsbury Lane, Brampton, ON, L6T 3X7
(905) 799-9955
Emp Here 85 *Emp Total* 153
Sales 75,080,700
SIC 2679 Converted paper products, nec
Pr Pr Christopher Bartlett

D-U-N-S 25-517-3874 (SL)
THINKPATH INC
201 Westcreek Blvd, Brampton, ON, L6T 5S6
(416) 622-5200
Emp Here 160 *Sales* 24,818,560
SIC 8711 Engineering services
Ch Bd Declan French
Kelly Hankinson
Dir Llcyd Maclean
Dir Patrick Power
Dir David Barnes

D-U-N-S 25-845-1038 (BR)
TOROMONT INDUSTRIES LTD
BATTLEFIELD EQUIPMENT RENTALS
27 Finley Rd, Brampton, ON, L6T 1B2
(905) 457-7977
Emp Here 60
SIC 7353 Heavy construction equipment rental

D-U-N-S 25-319-3064 (BR)
TORONTO-DOMINION BANK, THE
TD BANK
(*Suby of* Toronto-Dominion Bank, The)
8125 Dixie Rd, Brampton, ON, L6T 2J9
(905) 793-6666
Emp Here 30
SIC 6021 National commercial banks

D-U-N-S 25-293-9095 (BR)
TOYS 'R' US (CANADA) LTD
TOYS 'R' US
(*Suby of* Toys "r" Us, Inc.)
150 West Dr, Brampton, ON, L6T 4P9
(905) 454-8697
Emp Here 45
SIC 5945 Hobby, toy, and game shops

D-U-N-S 24-312-4406 (BR)
TRIPLE M METAL LP
NON FERROUS
900 Intermodal Dr, Brampton, ON, L6T 0B5
(905) 494-3999
Emp Here 20
SIC 3341 Secondary nonferrous Metals

D-U-N-S 25-145-6596 (BR)
TRIPLE M METAL LP
331 Intermodal Dr, Brampton, ON, L6T 5G4
(905) 791-7203
Emp Here 30
SIC 7389 Business services, nec

D-U-N-S 25-529-0918 (BR)
TWINCORP INC
PIZZA HUT
3 Gateway Blvd, Brampton, ON, L6T 4X2
(905) 793-5811
Emp Here 25
SIC 5812 Eating places

D-U-N-S 24-665-2895 (HQ)
UTI, CANADA, INC
70 Driver Rd Unit 4, Brampton, ON, L6T 5V2

Emp Here 35 *Emp Total* 350
Sales 42,895,920
SIC 4731 Freight transportation arrangement
Pr Pr Chris Penley
Judy Carvajal

D-U-N-S 20-778-2371 (BR)
UNI-SELECT INC
145 Walker Dr Suite 1, Brampton, ON, L6T 5P5
(905) 789-0115
Emp Here 100
SIC 5013 Motor vehicle supplies and new parts

D-U-N-S 20-981-5450 (BR)
UNIFOR
CAW LOCAL 973
15 Westcreek Blvd Suite 1, Brampton, ON, L6T 5T4
(905) 874-4026
Emp Here 700
SIC 8631 Labor organizations

D-U-N-S 20-007-9304 (BR)
UNILEVER CANADA INC
UNILEVER CANADA
307 Orenda Rd, Brampton, ON, L6T 1G4
(416) 964-1857
Emp Here 295
SIC 2034 Dried and dehydrated fruits, vegetables and soup mixes

D-U-N-S 25-999-5777 (BR)
VALLE FOAM INDUSTRIES (1995) INC
317 Orenda Rd, Brampton, ON, L6T 1G4

Emp Here 30
SIC 3086 Plastics foam products

D-U-N-S 24-610-9128 (HQ)
VALLE FOAM INDUSTRIES (1995) INC
4 West Dr, Brampton, ON, L6T 2H7
(905) 453-8054
Emp Here 140 *Emp Total* 1,000
Sales 80,214,843
SIC 3086 Plastics foam products
Pr Pr Antonio Vallecoccia
VP Mfg Dale Mcneill
S&M/VP Robert Valle

D-U-N-S 25-999-4382 (BR)
VALUE VILLAGE STORES, INC
(*Suby of* Savers, Inc.)
150 West Dr Unit 12, Brampton, ON, L6T 4P9
(905) 451-7975
Emp Here 43
SIC 5399 Miscellaneous general merchandise

D-U-N-S 20-003-8060 (BR)
VARI-FORM INC
TI GROUP AUTOMOTIVE OF CANADA
316 Orenda Rd, Brampton, ON, L6T 1G3
(905) 793-7100
Emp Here 100
SIC 3089 Plastics products, nec

D-U-N-S 25-347-4902 (HQ)
VISION TRANSPORTATION SYSTEMS INC
(*Suby of* Vision Transportation Systems Inc)
7659 Bramalea Rd, Brampton, ON, L6T 5V3
(905) 858-7333
Emp Here 22 *Emp Total* 24
Sales 5,107,249
SIC 4731 Freight transportation arrangement
Pr Pr Tony D'attoma
VP VP Jason Georgie

D-U-N-S 20-337-2763 (SL)
WFS TRANSPORT
10-8550 Torbram Rd Unit 418, Brampton, ON, L6T 0H7

Emp Here 63 *Sales* 4,180,344
SIC 4225 General warehousing and storage

D-U-N-S 25-498-3109 (BR)
WAL-MART CANADA CORP
30 Coventry Rd, Brampton, ON, L6T 5P9
(905) 793-1983
Emp Here 200
SIC 5311 Department stores

D-U-N-S 20-027-5126 (BR)

WASTE MANAGEMENT OF CANADA CORPORATION
WASTE MANAGEMENT OF CANADA CORPORATION
(*Suby of* Waste Management, Inc.)
117 Wentworth Crt, Brampton, ON, L6T 5L4
(905) 595-3360
Emp Here 60
SIC 4953 Refuse systems

D-U-N-S 20-040-2860 (BR)
WATERGROUP COMPANIES INC
CULLIGAN
(*Suby of* Clayton, Dubilier & Rice, Inc.)
8985 Airport Rd, Brampton, ON, L6T 5T2
(416) 590-0225
Emp Here 25
SIC 3589 Service industry machinery, nec

D-U-N-S 24-977-6675 (BR)
WINNERS MERCHANTS INTERNATIONAL L.P.
WINNERS
(*Suby of* The TJX Companies Inc)
55 West Dr, Brampton, ON, L6T 4A1
(905) 451-7200
Emp Here 500
SIC 5651 Family clothing stores

D-U-N-S 20-184-3252 (BR)
WINNERS MERCHANTS INTERNATIONAL L.P.
WINNERS
(*Suby of* The TJX Companies Inc)
10 Coventry Rd, Brampton, ON, L6T 5P9
(905) 458-0218
Emp Here 40
SIC 5651 Family clothing stores

D-U-N-S 24-338-9892 (HQ)
XPEDX CANADA, INC
XPEDX STORE
(*Suby of* International Paper Company)
156 Parkshore Dr, Brampton, ON, L6T 5M1
(905) 595-4351
Emp Here 36 *Emp Total* 55,000
Sales 30,424,612
SIC 5111 Printing and writing paper
Pr Pr Arthur J Douville
Walter R Klein
Michael Kearney

D-U-N-S 24-764-8801 (HQ)
YUSEN LOGISTICS (CANADA) INC
261 Parkhurst Sq, Brampton, ON, L6T 5H5
(905) 458-9622
Emp Here 36 *Emp Total* 34,276
Sales 9,557,852
SIC 4731 Freight transportation arrangement
T. Furusawa
VP VP Kenneth Mitchell
VP Brian Macalpine

D-U-N-S 24-212-5144 (SL)
ZOCHEM INC
1 Tilbury Crt, Brampton, ON, L6T 3T4
(905) 453-4100
Emp Here 40
SIC 3339 Primary nonferrous Metals, nec

Brampton, ON L6V
Peel County

D-U-N-S 24-891-3899 (BR)
ALGOMA UNIVERSITY
(*Suby of* Algoma University)
24 Queen St E Suite 102, Brampton, ON, L6V 1A3
(905) 451-0100
Emp Here 140
SIC 8221 Colleges and universities

D-U-N-S 20-800-9865 (BR)
BEATTY FOODS LTD

MCDONALDS 10731
372 Main St N, Brampton, ON, L6V 1P8
(905) 455-2841
Emp Here 90
SIC 5812 Eating places

D-U-N-S 20-024-4494   (BR)
BEATTY FOODS LTD
MCDONALD'S
50 Quarry Edge Dr, Brampton, ON, L6V 4K2
(905) 451-8371
Emp Here 50
SIC 5812 Eating places

D-U-N-S 24-138-5798   (HQ)
BRAMGATE AUTOMOTIVE INC
BRAMGATE VOLKSWAGEN
268 Queen St E, Brampton, ON, L6V 1B9
(905) 459-6040
Emp Here 20   Emp Total 54
Sales 30,625,693
SIC 5511 New and used car dealers
Pr Pr William Johnston Sr
  William A Johnston
  Bradley Johnston
Treas Gary Turner

D-U-N-S 25-295-1660   (BR)
BREWERS RETAIL INC
BEER STORE , THE
198 Queen St E, Brampton, ON, L6V 1B7
(905) 451-4685
Emp Here 20
SIC 5921 Liquor stores

D-U-N-S 25-796-3991   (BR)
CARA OPERATIONS LIMITED
KELSEY'S RESTAURANT
(Suby of Cara Holdings Limited)
70 Quarry Edge Dr, Brampton, ON, L6V 4K2
(905) 796-1700
Emp Here 60
SIC 5812 Eating places

D-U-N-S 20-514-7148   (BR)
CONSEIL SCOLAIRE VIAMONDE
ECOLE ELEMENTAIRE CARREFOUR DES
JEUNES
375 Centre St N, Brampton, ON, L6V 4N4
(905) 455-7038
Emp Here 40
SIC 8211 Elementary and secondary schools

D-U-N-S 25-796-0617   (BR)
CORPORATION OF THE CITY OF BRAMP-
TON, THE
CENTURY GARDENS RECREATION CEN-
TRE
340 Vodden St E, Brampton, ON, L6V 2N2
(905) 874-2814
Emp Here 100
SIC 7999 Amusement and recreation, nec

D-U-N-S 25-373-0618   (BR)
CORPORATION OF THE CITY OF BRAMP-
TON, THE
HERITAGE THEATRE
86 Main St N, Brampton, ON, L6V 1N7
(905) 874-2844
Emp Here 50
SIC 7922 Theatrical producers and services

D-U-N-S 25-265-3522   (BR)
DUFFERIN-PEEL CATHOLIC DISTRICT
SCHOOL BOARD
ST. ANNE ELEMENTARY SCHOOL
124 Vodden St E, Brampton, ON, L6V 1M5
(905) 459-7621
Emp Here 45
SIC 8211 Elementary and secondary schools

D-U-N-S 25-265-2755   (BR)
DUFFERIN-PEEL CATHOLIC DISTRICT
SCHOOL BOARD
ST. JOCAM SCHOOL
435 Rutherford Rd N, Brampton, ON, L6V 3V9
(905) 453-4472
Emp Here 55

SIC 8211 Elementary and secondary schools

D-U-N-S 25-265-2797   (BR)
DUFFERIN-PEEL CATHOLIC DISTRICT
SCHOOL BOARD
C W SULLIVAN ELEMENTARY SCHOOL
62 Seaborn Rd, Brampton, ON, L6V 2C1
(905) 453-5020
Emp Here 30
SIC 8211 Elementary and secondary schools

D-U-N-S 20-303-9461   (BR)
DUFFERIN-PEEL CATHOLIC DISTRICT
SCHOOL BOARD
ST CECILIA CATHOLIC ELEMENTARY
SCHOOL
10 Brickyard Way, Brampton, ON, L6V 4L5
(905) 459-0575
Emp Here 35
SIC 8211 Elementary and secondary schools

D-U-N-S 25-050-7654   (BR)
FORTINOS SUPERMARKET LTD
60 Quarry Edge Dr, Brampton, ON, L6V 4K2
(905) 453-3600
Emp Here 100
SIC 5411 Grocery stores

D-U-N-S 24-622-7128   (HQ)
GABOUR FOODS LTD
HARVEYS
(Suby of Gabour Foods Ltd)
320 Main St N Suite 14, Brampton, ON, L6V
4A3
(905) 454-3977
Emp Here 30   Emp Total 60
Sales 1,824,018
SIC 5812 Eating places

D-U-N-S 25-424-3645   (SL)
GRAINGER, FREDRIC R. MEDICINE PRO-
FESSIONAL CORPORATION
QUEENS SQUARE DOCTORS
36 Vodden St E Suite 200, Brampton, ON, L6V
4H4
(905) 455-1455
Emp Here 50   Sales 2,991,389
SIC 8011 Offices and clinics of medical doc-
tors

D-U-N-S 20-303-8927   (BR)
INDIGO BOOKS & MUSIC INC
CHAPTERS 927
(Suby of Indigo Books & Music Inc)
52 Quarry Edge Dr, Brampton, ON, L6V 4K2
(905) 456-7177
Emp Here 50
SIC 5942 Book stores

D-U-N-S 24-597-8742   (BR)
INVESTORS GROUP INC
24 Queen St E Suite 200, Brampton, ON, L6V
1A3
(905) 450-2891
Emp Here 50
SIC 6722 Management investment, open-end

D-U-N-S 25-053-7073   (BR)
LONG & MCQUADE LIMITED
LONG & MCQUADE MUSICAL INSTRU-
MENTS
370 Main St N, Brampton, ON, L6V 4A4
(905) 450-4334
Emp Here 20
SIC 5736 Musical instrument stores

D-U-N-S 20-610-7989   (BR)
MCDONALD'S RESTAURANTS OF
CANADA LIMITED
MCDONALD'S
(Suby of McDonald's Corporation)
344 Queen St E, Brampton, ON, L6V 1C3
(905) 459-8800
Emp Here 112
SIC 5812 Eating places

D-U-N-S 25-801-6054   (BR)
METRO ONTARIO INC

FOOD BASICS
227 Vodden St E, Brampton, ON, L6V 1N2
(905) 451-7842
Emp Here 105
SIC 5411 Grocery stores

D-U-N-S 24-963-3801   (BR)
MINI-SKOOL A CHILD'S PLACE INC
178 Church St E, Brampton, ON, L6V 1H1
(905) 457-1248
Emp Here 35
SIC 8351 Child day care services

D-U-N-S 25-413-0453   (SL)
PARKINSON COACH LINES 2000 INC
10 Kennedy Rd N, Brampton, ON, L6V 1X4
(416) 451-4776
Emp Here 90   Sales 2,553,625
SIC 4151 School buses

D-U-N-S 25-237-9763   (BR)
PEEL DISTRICT SCHOOL BOARD
CENTRAL PEEL SECONDARY SCHOOL
(Suby of Peel District School Board)
32 Kennedy Rd N, Brampton, ON, L6V 1X4
(905) 451-0432
Emp Here 112
SIC 8211 Elementary and secondary schools

D-U-N-S 25-293-7743   (BR)
PEEL DISTRICT SCHOOL BOARD
ARNOTT CHARLTON PUBLIC SCHOOL
(Suby of Peel District School Board)
140 Winterfold Dr, Brampton, ON, L6V 3V8
(905) 456-3159
Emp Here 45
SIC 8211 Elementary and secondary schools

D-U-N-S 25-297-1858   (BR)
PEEL DISTRICT SCHOOL BOARD
MADOC DRIVE PUBLIC SCHOOL
(Suby of Peel District School Board)
49 Madoc Dr, Brampton, ON, L6V 2A1
(905) 457-3440
Emp Here 30
SIC 8211 Elementary and secondary schools

D-U-N-S 25-220-8095   (BR)
PEEL DISTRICT SCHOOL BOARD
HAROLD F. LOUGHIN ELEMENTARY PUB-
LIC SCHOOL
(Suby of Peel District School Board)
39 Herkley Dr, Brampton, ON, L6V 2E7
(905) 457-6812
Emp Here 34
SIC 8211 Elementary and secondary schools

D-U-N-S 20-711-1811   (BR)
PEEL DISTRICT SCHOOL BOARD
WESTERVELTS CORNERS PUBLIC
SCHOOL
(Suby of Peel District School Board)
20 Brickyard Way, Brampton, ON, L6V 4L5
(905) 459-3456
Emp Here 50
SIC 8211 Elementary and secondary schools

D-U-N-S 25-237-8690   (BR)
PEEL DISTRICT SCHOOL BOARD
KINGSWOOD DRIVE PUBLIC SCHOOL
(Suby of Peel District School Board)
235 Kingswood Dr, Brampton, ON, L6V 3B3
(905) 457-9971
Emp Here 55
SIC 8211 Elementary and secondary schools

D-U-N-S 25-265-3183   (BR)
PEEL DISTRICT SCHOOL BOARD
AGNES TAYLOR ELEMENTARY SCHOOL
(Suby of Peel District School Board)
80 Beech St, Brampton, ON, L6V 1V6
(905) 451-2531
Emp Here 35
SIC 8211 Elementary and secondary schools

D-U-N-S 25-297-1932   (BR)
PEEL DISTRICT SCHOOL BOARD
GORDON GRAYDON SENIOR PUBLIC

SCHOOL
(Suby of Peel District School Board)
170 Rutherford Rd N, Brampton, ON, L6V 2X9
(905) 453-1775
Emp Here 45
SIC 8211 Elementary and secondary schools

D-U-N-S 25-263-7921   (BR)
PEEL DISTRICT SCHOOL BOARD
SIR JOHN A MACDONALD SENIOR PUBLIC
SCHOOL
(Suby of Peel District School Board)
250 Centre St N, Brampton, ON, L6V 2R4
(905) 457-5535
Emp Here 35
SIC 8211 Elementary and secondary schools

D-U-N-S 25-786-9958   (BR)
PHARMA PLUS DRUGMARTS LTD
227 Vodden St E, Brampton, ON, L6V 1N2
(905) 457-2955
Emp Here 20
SIC 5912 Drug stores and proprietary stores

D-U-N-S 25-010-6945   (BR)
PRISZM LP
KFC
190 Queen St E, Brampton, ON, L6V 1B3
(905) 457-7422
Emp Here 25
SIC 5812 Eating places

D-U-N-S 25-172-4902   (BR)
RED LOBSTER HOSPITALITY LLC
RED LOBSTER RESTAURANTS
(Suby of Red Lobster Seafood Co., LLC)
368 Queen St E Suite 6, Brampton, ON, L6V
1C3
(905) 459-6334
Emp Here 72
SIC 5812 Eating places

D-U-N-S 25-808-3708   (BR)
T & L EAGLES INVESTMENTS INC
TIM HORTONS
(Suby of T & L Eagles Investments Inc)
225 Vodden St E, Brampton, ON, L6V 4M1
(905) 457-6692
Emp Here 40
SIC 5812 Eating places

D-U-N-S 25-120-2289   (BR)
TORONTO-DOMINION BANK, THE
TD CANADA TRUST
(Suby of Toronto-Dominion Bank, The)
130 Brickyard Way, Brampton, ON, L6V 4N1
(905) 451-1355
Emp Here 35
SIC 6021 National commercial banks

D-U-N-S 25-294-8815   (BR)
WAL-MART CANADA CORP
BRAMPTON NORTH SUPERCENTRE
50 Quarry Edge Dr, Brampton, ON, L6V 4K2
(905) 874-0112
Emp Here 350
SIC 5311 Department stores

Brampton, ON L6W
Peel County

D-U-N-S 20-536-6149   (SL)
389259 ONTARIO LIMITED
HANSEN AUTOMOTIVE
236 Rutherford Rd S, Brampton, ON, L6W 3J6
(905) 451-6470
Emp Here 43   Sales 7,067,520
SIC 5013 Motor vehicle supplies and new
parts
Pr Pr Hans Hansen
  Carolyn Hansen

D-U-N-S 20-769-1171   (BR)
AMCOR RIGID PLASTICS ATLANTIC, INC
AMCOR RIGID PLASTICS - BRAMPTON

95 Biscayne Cres, Brampton, ON, L6W 4R2
(905) 450-5579
Emp Here 100
SIC 3089 Plastics products, nec

D-U-N-S 20-168-0808   (HQ)
ASAHI REFINING CANADA LTD
130 Glidden Rd, Brampton, ON, L6W 3M8
(905) 453-6120
Emp Here 56   *Emp Total* 1,961
Sales 51,145,451
SIC 3339 Primary nonferrous Metals, nec
  Keith Neureuther
Dir Keitaro Shigemasa
Dir Kazuo Kawabata

D-U-N-S 20-922-2801   (BR)
BDI CANADA INC
52 Bramsteele Rd Unit 1, Brampton, ON, L6W
3M5
(905) 459-5202
Emp Here 23
SIC 5084 Industrial machinery and equipment

D-U-N-S 20-588-2306   (BR)
BANQUE TORONTO-DOMINION, LA
TD CANADA TRUST
(*Suby of* Toronto-Dominion Bank, The)
295a Queen St E, Brampton, ON, L6W 3R1
(905) 451-4280
Emp Here 20
SIC 6021 National commercial banks

D-U-N-S 20-845-0403   (SL)
BRAMPTON GOLF CLUB LIMITED
7700 Kennedy Rd, Brampton, ON, L6W 0A1
(905) 457-5700
Emp Here 50   *Sales* 2,638,521
SIC 7997 Membership sports and recreation
clubs

D-U-N-S 24-308-1184   (BR)
BREWERS RETAIL INC
BEER STORE DISTRIBUTION CENTRE
69 First Gulf Blvd, Brampton, ON, L6W 4T8
(905) 450-2799
Emp Here 300
SIC 5181 Beer and ale

D-U-N-S 25-231-7078   (BR)
BRICK WAREHOUSE LP, THE
BRICK STORE, THE
188 Clarence St, Brampton, ON, L6W 1T4
(905) 454-3100
Emp Here 40
SIC 5712 Furniture stores

D-U-N-S 24-386-9992   (SL)
BRITA CANADA CORPORATION
(*Suby of* The Clorox Company)
150 Biscayne Cres, Brampton, ON, L6W 4V3
(905) 789-2465
Emp Here 50   *Sales* 9,120,088
SIC 5074 Plumbing and heating equipment
and supplies (hydronics)
Pr Pr Mark S. Malo
VP VP Faroek Hanif
  Lawrence S. Peiros

D-U-N-S 20-036-4693   (BR)
**BUTCHER ENGINEERING ENTERPRISES
LIMITED, THE**
120 Orenda Rd, Brampton, ON, L6W 1W2
(905) 459-3030
Emp Here 200
SIC 7389 Business services, nec

D-U-N-S 20-251-5433   (BR)
**CANADA COLORS AND CHEMICALS LIM-
ITED**
*CANADA COLORS AND CHEMICALS LIM-
ITED*
238 Glidden Rd Suite 3, Brampton, ON, L6W
1H8
(905) 459-1232
Emp Here 50
SIC 5169 Chemicals and allied products, nec

D-U-N-S 20-024-1870   (BR)
CANADA POST CORPORATION
26 Hale Rd, Brampton, ON, L6W 3M1
(905) 453-6806
Emp Here 200
SIC 4311 U.s. postal service

D-U-N-S 24-342-8088   (BR)
CARA OPERATIONS LIMITED
SWISS CHALET
(*Suby of* Cara Holdings Limited)
2 County Court Blvd Suite 170, Brampton, ON,
L6W 3W8
(905) 452-0947
Emp Here 60
SIC 5812 Eating places

D-U-N-S 25-297-3474   (BR)
CARA OPERATIONS LIMITED
KELSEY'S RESTAURANT
(*Suby of* Cara Holdings Limited)
289 Queen St E, Brampton, ON, L6W 2C2

Emp Here 50
SIC 5812 Eating places

D-U-N-S 20-778-7248   (BR)
CINEPLEX ODEON CORPORATION
CINEPLEX CINEMAS ORION GATE
20 Biscayne Cres, Brampton, ON, L6W 4S1
(905) 455-1590
Emp Here 20
SIC 7832 Motion picture theaters, except
drive-in

D-U-N-S 20-733-6728   (HQ)
**CLOROX COMPANY OF CANADA, LTD,
THE**
BRITA
(*Suby of* The Clorox Company)
150 Biscayne Cres, Brampton, ON, L6W 4V3
(905) 595-8200
Emp Here 80   *Emp Total* 7,700
Sales 28,819,477
SIC 5169 Chemicals and allied products, nec
Dir Jerry Johnston
Dir Faroek Hanif
Treas Karen Rose

D-U-N-S 25-863-4406   (BR)
CONTROLE TOTAL LOGISTIQUE INC
(*Suby of* Controle Total Logistique Inc)
297 Rutherford Rd S, Brampton, ON, L6W 3J8
(905) 595-2364
Emp Here 50
SIC 4731 Freight transportation arrangement

D-U-N-S 20-718-3729   (BR)
**CORPORATION OF THE CITY OF BRAMP-
TON, THE**
*BRAMPTON FIRE & EMERGENCY SER-
VICES*
8 Rutherford Rd S, Brampton, ON, L6W 3J1
(905) 874-2700
Emp Here 400
SIC 7389 Business services, nec

D-U-N-S 25-797-5789   (BR)
**CORPORATION OF THE CITY OF BRAMP-
TON, THE**
PEEL VILLAGE GOLF COURSE
29 Hartford Trail Unit A, Brampton, ON, L6W
4K2
(905) 874-2995
Emp Here 20
SIC 7992 Public golf courses

D-U-N-S 25-287-5737   (BR)
COSTCO WHOLESALE CANADA LTD
COSTCO
(*Suby of* Costco Wholesale Corporation)
100 Biscayne Cres, Brampton, ON, L6W 4S1
(905) 450-2092
Emp Here 200
SIC 5099 Durable goods, nec

D-U-N-S 20-154-6934   (HQ)
CROSBY CANADA INC

(*Suby of* The Crosby Group LLC)
145 Heart Lake Rd, Brampton, ON, L6W 3K3
(905) 451-9261
Emp Here 138   *Emp Total* 685
Sales 18,896,821
SIC 3462 Iron and steel forgings
  Paul Jones
Pr Pr James Slattery
  Matthew Nozemack
Dir Garry Elliot Barnes
Dir Geoffrey Peter Martin

D-U-N-S 20-911-4839   (BR)
DSV SOLUTIONS INC
250 First Gulf Blvd, Brampton, ON, L6W 4T5
(905) 763-3365
Emp Here 30
SIC 4225 General warehousing and storage

D-U-N-S 25-796-2324   (BR)
DAIRY QUEEN CANADA INC
DAIRY QUEEN
133 Queen St E, Brampton, ON, L6W 2A9
(905) 453-5591
Emp Here 20
SIC 5812 Eating places

D-U-N-S 25-282-2507   (BR)
**DESJARDINS SECURITE FINANCIERE,
COMPAGNIE D'ASSURANCE VIE**
LAURENTIAN FINANCIAL SERVICES
350a Rutherford Rd S Unit 7, Brampton, ON,
L6W 3P6

Emp Here 20
SIC 6411 Insurance agents, brokers, and service

D-U-N-S 24-803-2430   (BR)
**DICOM   TRANSPORTATION   GROUP
CANADA, INC**
*DICOM   TRANSPORTATION   GROUP
CANADA INC*
300 Biscayne Cres, Brampton, ON, L6W 4S7
(905) 457-7757
Emp Here 25
SIC 4212 Local trucking, without storage

D-U-N-S 24-418-1509   (BR)
**DIVERSICARE CANADA MANAGEMENT
SERVICES CO., INC**
TULLAMORE NURSING HOME
133 Kennedy Rd S, Brampton, ON, L6W 3G3
(905) 459-2324
Emp Here 160
SIC 8051 Skilled nursing care facilities

D-U-N-S 25-265-4447   (BR)
**DUFFERIN-PEEL   CATHOLIC   DISTRICT
SCHOOL BOARD**
ST MARY'S ELEMENTARY SCHOOL
66 Main St S, Brampton, ON, L6W 2C6
(905) 451-1020
Emp Here 25
SIC 8211 Elementary and secondary schools

D-U-N-S 20-590-9901   (BR)
**DUFFERIN-PEEL   CATHOLIC   DISTRICT
SCHOOL BOARD**
ST FRANCIS SCHOOL
111 Bartley Bull Pky, Brampton, ON, L6W 2J8
(905) 459-0646
Emp Here 25
SIC 8211 Elementary and secondary schools

D-U-N-S 24-342-2321   (BR)
EASTON'S GROUP OF HOTELS INC
*COURTYARD BY MARRIOTT TORONTO-
BRAMPTON, THE*
90 Biscayne Cres, Brampton, ON, L6W 4S1
(905) 455-9000
Emp Here 70
SIC 7011 Hotels and motels

D-U-N-S 24-337-2799   (BR)
FGL SPORTS LTD
NATIONAL SPORTS
295 Queen St E, Brampton, ON, L6W 3R1

(905) 454-7880
Emp Here 25
SIC 5941 Sporting goods and bicycle shops

D-U-N-S 24-340-0533   (BR)
FGL SPORTS LTD
SPORT CHEK ORION GATE
547 Steeles Ave E Unit 1b, Brampton, ON,
L6W 4S2
(905) 456-7161
Emp Here 50
SIC 5941 Sporting goods and bicycle shops

D-U-N-S 24-139-5136   (SL)
G M F TRANSPORT LIMITED
110 Orenda Rd, Brampton, ON, L6W 3W6
(905) 459-1693
Emp Here 50   *Sales* 3,939,878
SIC 4212 Local trucking, without storage

D-U-N-S 24-324-0095   (BR)
G. H. MEDICAL INC
8 Bram Crt, Brampton, ON, L6W 3R6
(905) 455-6771
Emp Here 40
SIC 1799 Special trade contractors, nec

D-U-N-S 25-091-9982   (SL)
HANRAHAN YOUTH SERVICES INC
114 Main St S, Brampton, ON, L6W 2C8
(905) 450-4685
Emp Here 55   *Sales* 2,813,440
SIC 8361 Residential care

D-U-N-S 25-213-7815   (BR)
HOME DEPOT OF CANADA INC
HOME DEPOT
(*Suby of* The Home Depot Inc)
49 First Gulf Blvd, Brampton, ON, L6W 4R8
(905) 457-1800
Emp Here 220
SIC 5211 Lumber and other building materials

D-U-N-S 24-849-4544   (HQ)
**HUNTER DOUGLAS CANADA HOLDINGS
INC**
HUNTER DOUGLAS WINDOW FASHIONS
132 First Gulf Blvd, Brampton, ON, L6W 4T7
(905) 796-7883
Emp Here 150   *Emp Total* 300
Sales 32,832,315
SIC 5023 Homefurnishings
  Randy Liken
Fin Ex Christine Mikler

D-U-N-S 20-766-7437   (HQ)
I.G. MACHINE & FIBERS LTD
I.G. MACHINE
87 Orenda Rd, Brampton, ON, L6W 1V8
(905) 457-0745
Emp Here 35   *Emp Total* 100
Sales 12,474,014
SIC 3444 Sheet Metalwork
Dir David Koschitzky
Dir David Laven

D-U-N-S 20-830-0095   (HQ)
IKO INDUSTRIES LTD
ARMOROOF DIV OF
80 Stafford Dr, Brampton, ON, L6W 1L4
(905) 457-2880
Emp Here 200   *Emp Total* 100
Sales 127,681,225
SIC 2952 Asphalt felts and coatings
VP VP Henry Koschitzky
Pr Pr David Koschitzky
VP VP Saul Koschitzky
  Corbet Elder
Dir Shel Laven

D-U-N-S 24-810-4189   (BR)
IKO INDUSTRIES LTD
ARMOROOF DIV OF
80 Stafford Dr, Brampton, ON, L6W 1L4
(905) 457-2880
Emp Here 50
SIC 2952 Asphalt felts and coatings

D-U-N-S 25-315-9024   (BR)
INVESTORS GROUP FINANCIAL SER-VICES INC
208 County Court Blvd, Brampton, ON, L6W 4S9
(905) 450-1500
Emp Here 100
SIC 8741 Management services

D-U-N-S 20-405-4480   (HQ)
LAIRD PLASTICS (CANADA) INC
(*Suby of* Laird Plastics, Inc.)
155 Orenda Rd Unit 4, Brampton, ON, L6W 1W3
(905) 595-4800
Emp Here 25   *Emp Total* 500
Sales 114,085,257
SIC 5162 Plastics materials and basic shapes
Pr Pr Mark Kramer

D-U-N-S 25-840-1165   (BR)
LIQUOR CONTROL BOARD OF ONTARIO, THE
LCBO ORiON GATE
545 Steeles Ave E, Brampton, ON, L6W 4S2
(905) 454-7980
Emp Here 40
SIC 5921 Liquor stores

D-U-N-S 24-352-6287   (BR)
LOWE'S COMPANIES CANADA, ULC
370 Kennedy Rd S, Brampton, ON, L6W 4V2
(905) 874-5000
Emp Here 50
SIC 5211 Lumber and other building materials

D-U-N-S 20-117-6257   (BR)
MSO CONSTRUCTION LIMITED
TJ POUNDER
106 Orenda Rd, Brampton, ON, L6W 3W6
(905) 459-4331
Emp Here 50
SIC 1611 Highway and street construction

D-U-N-S 24-337-6410   (BR)
MAPLE LEAF FOODS INC
MAPLE LEAF POULTRY
32 Kennedy Rd S, Brampton, ON, L6W 3E3
(905) 453-6262
Emp Here 20
SIC 2015 Poultry slaughtering and processing

D-U-N-S 25-895-8081   (BR)
MCDONALD'S RESTAURANTS OF CANADA LIMITED
MCDONALD'S
(*Suby of* McDonald's Corporation)
539 Steeles Ave E Suite 2, Brampton, ON, L6W 4S2
(905) 453-4954
Emp Here 50
SIC 5812 Eating places

D-U-N-S 20-165-6014   (HQ)
MERITOR AFTERMARKET CANADA INC
ARVINMER!TOR CANADA
350 First Gulf Blvd, Brampton, ON, L6W 4T5
(905) 454-7070
Emp Here 40   *Emp Total* 8,000
Sales 84,719,348
SIC 3714 Motor vehicle parts and accessories
Charles Mcclure

D-U-N-S 25-300-0624   (BR)
METRO ONTARIO INC
FOOD BASICS
1 Bartley Bull Pky, Brampton, ON, L6W 3T7
(905) 456-1212
Emp Here 62
SIC 5411 Grocery stores

D-U-N-S 24-896-5238   (BR)
METRO ONTARIO INC
METRO STORES
156 Main St S, Brampton, ON, L6W 2C9
(905) 459-6212
Emp Here 90
SIC 5411 Grocery stores

D-U-N-S 24-395-6260   (BR)
MILLER PAVING LIMITED
MILLER WASTE SYSTEMS
106 Orenda Rd, Brampton, ON, L6W 3W6
(905) 455-6377
Emp Here 20
SIC 1611 Highway and street construction

D-U-N-S 25-486-5603   (BR)
MILLS GROUP INC, THE
BURGER KING
(*Suby of* Mills Group Inc, The)
285 Queen St E, Brampton, ON, L6W 2C2
(905) 453-5818
Emp Here 75
SIC 5812 Eating places

D-U-N-S 24-987-2854   (HQ)
NORBA INVESTMENTS LTD
TIM HORTONS
(*Suby of* Norba Investments Ltd)
200 County Court Blvd, Brampton, ON, L6W 4K7
(905) 450-9433
Emp Here 45   *Emp Total* 76
Sales 2,261,782
SIC 5812 Eating places

D-U-N-S 24-851-0435   (SL)
OZBURN-HESSEY LOGISTICS
300 Kennedy Rd S Unit B, Brampton, ON, L6W 4V2
(905) 450-1151
Emp Here 60   *Sales* 14,811,022
SIC 4731 Freight transportation arrangement
Dir Shahzad Dad

D-U-N-S 24-227-4889   (BR)
PEEL DISTRICT SCHOOL BOARD
PEEL ALTERNATIVE SCHOOL NORTH
(*Suby of* Peel District School Board)
315 Bartley Bull Pky, Brampton, ON, L6W 2L4
(905) 455-1225
Emp Here 20
SIC 8211 Elementary and secondary schools

D-U-N-S 20-711-1761   (BR)
PEEL DISTRICT SCHOOL BOARD
TURNER FENTON SECONDARY SCHOOL
(*Suby of* Peel District School Board)
7935 Kennedy Rd, Brampton, ON, L6W 0A2
(905) 453-9220
Emp Here 150
SIC 8211 Elementary and secondary schools

D-U-N-S 25-297-1700   (BR)
PEEL DISTRICT SCHOOL BOARD
SIR WINSTON CHURCHILL PUBLIC SCHOOL
(*Suby of* Peel District School Board)
89 Ardglen Dr, Brampton, ON, L6W 1V1
(905) 459-2320
Emp Here 35
SIC 8211 Elementary and secondary schools

D-U-N-S 25-000-6665   (BR)
PEEL DISTRICT SCHOOL BOARD
WILLIAM GRENVILLE DAVIS SENIOR PUB-LIC SCHOOL
(*Suby of* Peel District School Board)
491 Bartley Bull Pky, Brampton, ON, L6W 2M7
(905) 459-3661
Emp Here 35
SIC 8211 Elementary and secondary schools

D-U-N-S 25-263-7483   (BR)
PEEL DISTRICT SCHOOL BOARD
SIR WILFRID LAURIER PUBLIC SCHOOL
(*Suby of* Peel District School Board)
364 Bartley Bull Pky, Brampton, ON, L6W 2L8
(905) 451-1415
Emp Here 30
SIC 8211 Elementary and secondary schools

D-U-N-S 25-265-2136   (BR)
PEEL DISTRICT SCHOOL BOARD
PARKWAY PUBLIC SCHOOL
(*Suby of* Peel District School Board)

24 Duncan Bull Dr, Brampton, ON, L6W 1H4
(905) 451-8440
Emp Here 40
SIC 8211 Elementary and secondary schools

D-U-N-S 25-297-1692   (BR)
PEEL DISTRICT SCHOOL BOARD
HELEN WILSON PUBLIC SCHOOL
(*Suby of* Peel District School Board)
9 Abbey Rd, Brampton, ON, L6W 2T7
(905) 451-1165
Emp Here 31
SIC 8211 Elementary and secondary schools

D-U-N-S 24-764-7225   (BR)
PENNER INTERNATIONAL INC
297 Rutherford Rd S, Brampton, ON, L6W 3J8
(905) 624-6411
Emp Here 40
SIC 4213 Trucking, except local

D-U-N-S 20-703-6646   (BR)
PEPSICO CANADA ULC
FRITO-LAY CANADA
(*Suby of* Pepsico, Inc.)
12 Clipper Crt, Brampton, ON, L6W 4T9
(905) 460-2400
Emp Here 500
SIC 5145 Confectionery

D-U-N-S 24-340-8452   (BR)
PRAXAIR CANADA INC
(*Suby of* Praxair, Inc.)
165 Biscayne Cres, Brampton, ON, L6W 4R3
(905) 450-9353
Emp Here 100
SIC 5169 Chemicals and allied products, nec

D-U-N-S 25-542-2743   (BR)
PRE-CON INC
35 Rutherford Rd S, Brampton, ON, L6W 3J4
(905) 457-4140
Emp Here 150
SIC 3272 Concrete products, nec

D-U-N-S 25-010-6952   (BR)
PRISZM LP
KFC
1 Steeles Ave E Unit 1, Brampton, ON, L6W 4J4
(905) 452-9851
Emp Here 20
SIC 5812 Eating places

D-U-N-S 20-921-0132   (BR)
RE/MAX REAL ESTATE CENTRE INC
2 County Court Blvd Suite 150, Brampton, ON, L6W 3W8
(905) 456-1177
Emp Here 80
SIC 6531 Real estate agents and managers

D-U-N-S 25-803-5666   (BR)
REGIONAL MUNICIPALITY OF PEEL, THE
PEEL ART GALLERY, MUSEUM AND ARCHIVES
9 Wellington St E, Brampton, ON, L6W 1Y1
(905) 791-4055
Emp Here 30
SIC 8412 Museums and art galleries

D-U-N-S 20-569-5328   (SL)
RENEW LIFE CANADA INC
(*Suby of* The Clorox Company)
150 Biscayne Cres, Brampton, ON, L6W 4V3
(800) 485-0960
Emp Here 22   *Sales* 2,115,860
SIC 2834 Pharmaceutical preparations

D-U-N-S 20-750-1743   (HQ)
ROOFMART HOLDINGS LIMITED
(*Suby of* Roofmart Holdings Limited)
305 Rutherford Rd S, Brampton, ON, L6W 3R5
(905) 453-7870
Emp Here 50   *Emp Total* 100
Sales 20,866,760
SIC 5033 Roofing, siding, and insulation

Pr Pr Henry Koschitzky
Mira Koschitzky

D-U-N-S 25-409-7553   (BR)
ROTHMANS, BENSON & HEDGES INC
(*Suby of* Philip Morris International Inc.)
174 Kennedy Rd S, Brampton, ON, L6W 3G6
(905) 595-3000
Emp Here 50
SIC 5194 Tobacco and tobacco products

D-U-N-S 24-964-7579   (BR)
SEARS CANADA INC
SEARS LIQUIDATION CENTRE
253 Queen St E, Brampton, ON, L6W 2B8

Emp Here 70
SIC 7389 Business services, nec

D-U-N-S 25-092-3489   (BR)
SEARS CANADA INC
SEARS OUTLET
295 Queen St E, Brampton, ON, L6W 3R1

Emp Here 50
SIC 5311 Department stores

D-U-N-S 25-802-1526   (BR)
SOUTHERN SANITATION INC
WASTECO
150 Orenda Rd, Brampton, ON, L6W 1W2
(905) 459-2716
Emp Here 20
SIC 4953 Refuse systems

D-U-N-S 20-180-9980   (BR)
STORMTECH PERFORMANCE APPAREL LTD
STORMTECH BRAMPTON FACTORY OUT-LET
396 Clarence St Unit 2, Brampton, ON, L6W 1T5
(905) 796-0803
Emp Here 20
SIC 5136 Men's and boy's clothing

D-U-N-S 25-529-8168   (HQ)
T & L EAGLES INVESTMENTS INC
TIM HORTONS
(*Suby of* T & L Eagles Investments Inc)
87 Kennedy Rd S, Brampton, ON, L6W 3G1
(905) 457-4641
Emp Here 45   *Emp Total* 105
Sales 3,137,310
SIC 5812 Eating places

D-U-N-S 24-127-5960   (BR)
TD WATERHOUSE CANADA INC
(*Suby of* Toronto-Dominion Bank, The)
201 County Court Blvd Suite 402, Brampton, ON, L6W 4L2
(905) 456-2070
Emp Here 20
SIC 6211 Security brokers and dealers

D-U-N-S 24-096-2472   (HQ)
TERRAPROBE LIMITED
(*Suby of* Terraprobe Limited)
10 Bram Crt, Brampton, ON, L6W 3R6
(905) 796-2650
Emp Here 40   *Emp Total* 90
Sales 4,085,799
SIC 8999 Services, nec

D-U-N-S 24-346-3242   (BR)
TURTLE JACK'S RESTAURANT INC
200 County Court Blvd, Brampton, ON, L6W 4K7
(905) 457-3733
Emp Here 20
SIC 5812 Eating places

D-U-N-S 24-337-2153   (BR)
TWINCORP INC
PIZZA HUT
295 Queen St E, Brampton, ON, L6W 3R1
(905) 454-8888
Emp Here 25

SIC 5812 Eating places

D-U-N-S 25-978-5020   (BR)
UNITED RENTALS OF CANADA, INC
89 Heart Lake Rd, Brampton, ON, L6W 3K1
(905) 458-4462
Emp Here 40
SIC 7353 Heavy construction equipment rental

D-U-N-S 24-308-4022   (BR)
VALLE FOAM INDUSTRIES (1995) INC
170 Glidden Rd, Brampton, ON, L6W 3L2

Emp Here 100
SIC 3086 Plastics foam products

D-U-N-S 20-526-6765   (BR)
VITALAIRE CANADA INC
VITALAIRE
8 Bram Crt, Brampton, ON, L6W 3R6
(905) 455-2449
Emp Here 35
SIC 5169 Chemicals and allied products, nec

Brampton, ON L6X
Peel County

D-U-N-S 24-310-3624   (BR)
ARCELORMITTAL TUBULAR PRODUCTS CANADA G.P.
(*Suby of* ArcelorMittal Tubular Products Canada G.P.)
14 Holtby Ave, Brampton, ON, L6X 2M3
(905) 451-2400
Emp Here 100
SIC 3714 Motor vehicle parts and accessories

D-U-N-S 20-707-7053   (BR)
CHILDREN'S AID SOCIETY OF THE REGION OF PEEL, THE
PEEL CHILDREN'S AIDE
175 Vodden St W, Brampton, ON, L6X 2W8
(905) 457-5410
Emp Here 20
SIC 8399 Social services, nec

D-U-N-S 25-796-0625   (BR)
CORPORATION OF THE CITY OF BRAMPTON, THE
GIBSON, CHRIS RECREATION CENTRE
125 Mclaughlin Rd N, Brampton, ON, L6X 1Y9
(905) 874-2820
Emp Here 50
SIC 8322 Individual and family services

D-U-N-S 20-711-0201   (BR)
DUFFERIN-PEEL CATHOLIC DISTRICT SCHOOL BOARD
ST URSULA SCHOOL
11 Dwellers Rd, Brampton, ON, L6X 5C1
(905) 454-5213
Emp Here 50
SIC 8211 Elementary and secondary schools

D-U-N-S 25-924-5819   (BR)
DUFFERIN-PEEL CATHOLIC DISTRICT SCHOOL BOARD
OUR LADY OF PEACE
15 Fincham Ave, Brampton, ON, L6X 3V2
(905) 452-7010
Emp Here 45
SIC 8211 Elementary and secondary schools

D-U-N-S 25-265-4488   (BR)
DUFFERIN-PEEL CATHOLIC DISTRICT SCHOOL BOARD
ST JOSEPHS ELEMENTARY SCHOOL
8 Parkway Ave, Brampton, ON, L6X 2G4
(905) 451-8501
Emp Here 20
SIC 8211 Elementary and secondary schools

D-U-N-S 25-224-9206   (BR)
DUFFERIN-PEEL CATHOLIC DISTRICT

SCHOOL BOARD
OUR LADY OF FATIMA
39 Sunset Blvd, Brampton, ON, L6X 1X1
(905) 459-4737
Emp Here 50
SIC 8211 Elementary and secondary schools

D-U-N-S 25-117-1757   (BR)
DUFFERIN-PEEL CATHOLIC DISTRICT SCHOOL BOARD
ST MARIA GORETTI SCHOOL
121 Royal Orchard Dr, Brampton, ON, L6X 4K9
(905) 454-1477
Emp Here 30
SIC 8211 Elementary and secondary schools

D-U-N-S 24-206-9602   (BR)
GAP (CANADA) INC
(*Suby of* The Gap Inc)
9500 Mclaughlin Rd, Brampton, ON, L6X 0B8
(905) 460-2060
Emp Here 100
SIC 5651 Family clothing stores

D-U-N-S 24-330-8777   (BR)
GOVERNING COUNCIL OF THE SALVATION ARMY IN CANADA, THE
GOVERNING COUNCIL OF THE SALVATION ARMY IN CANADA, THE
535 Main St N, Brampton, ON, L6X 3C9
(905) 451-4115
Emp Here 50
SIC 8322 Individual and family services

D-U-N-S 25-422-5147   (BR)
GOVERNING COUNCIL OF THE SALVATION ARMY IN CANADA, THE
GOVERNING COUNCIL OF THE SALVATION ARMY IN CANADA, THE
44 Nelson St W, Brampton, ON, L6X 1C1
(905) 453-0988
Emp Here 23
SIC 8399 Social services, nec

D-U-N-S 20-264-4944   (BR)
HOME DEPOT OF CANADA INC
(*Suby of* The Home Depot Inc)
9515 Mississauga Rd, Brampton, ON, L6X 0Z8
(905) 453-3900
Emp Here 150
SIC 5251 Hardware stores

D-U-N-S 24-452-2561   (BR)
KEG RESTAURANTS LTD
KEG STEAKHOUSE & BAR, THE
70 Gillingham Dr, Brampton, ON, L6X 4X7
(905) 456-3733
Emp Here 75
SIC 5812 Eating places

D-U-N-S 20-310-9343   (BR)
MERITOR AFTERMARKET CANADA INC
MASCOT TRUCK PARTS
60 Gillingham Dr, Brampton, ON, L6X 4X7
(905) 454-7070
Emp Here 50
SIC 3714 Motor vehicle parts and accessories

D-U-N-S 24-346-5510   (BR)
NORBA INVESTMENTS LTD
TIM HORTONS
(*Suby of* Norba Investments Ltd)
400 Queen St W Suite 3, Brampton, ON, L6X 1B3
(905) 874-9929
Emp Here 30
SIC 5812 Eating places

D-U-N-S 25-297-1775   (BR)
PEEL DISTRICT SCHOOL BOARD
HUTTONVILLE PUBLIC SCHOOL
(*Suby of* Peel District School Board)
2322 Embleton Rd, Brampton, ON, L6X 0C9
(905) 455-8480
Emp Here 50
SIC 8211 Elementary and secondary schools

D-U-N-S 25-297-1494   (BR)
PEEL DISTRICT SCHOOL BOARD
NORTHWOOD PUBLIC SCHOOL
(*Suby of* Peel District School Board)
70 Gretna Dr, Brampton, ON, L6X 2E9
(905) 451-6464
Emp Here 45
SIC 8211 Elementary and secondary schools

D-U-N-S 25-293-7909   (BR)
PEEL DISTRICT SCHOOL BOARD
GLENDALE PUBLIC SCHOOL
(*Suby of* Peel District School Board)
35 Sunset Blvd, Brampton, ON, L6X 1X1
(905) 451-2463
Emp Here 30
SIC 8211 Elementary and secondary schools

D-U-N-S 25-265-2987   (BR)
PEEL DISTRICT SCHOOL BOARD
BEATTY FLEMING SENIOR PUBLIC SCHOOL
(*Suby of* Peel District School Board)
21 Campbell Dr, Brampton, ON, L6X 2H6
(905) 457-6107
Emp Here 40
SIC 8211 Elementary and secondary schools

D-U-N-S 24-525-4250   (BR)
PEEL DISTRICT SCHOOL BOARD
JAMES POTTER PUBLIC SCHOOL
(*Suby of* Peel District School Board)
9775 Creditview Rd, Brampton, ON, L6X 0H7
(905) 595-1495
Emp Here 25
SIC 8211 Elementary and secondary schools

D-U-N-S 25-840-1660   (BR)
PHARMA PLUS DRUGMARTS LTD
400 Queen St W, Brampton, ON, L6X 1B3
(905) 459-4570
Emp Here 20
SIC 5912 Drug stores and proprietary stores

D-U-N-S 25-293-6935   (BR)
RBC DOMINION SECURITIES INC
(*Suby of* Royal Bank Of Canada)
50 Queen St W Suite 300, Brampton, ON, L6X 4H3

Emp Here 25
SIC 6211 Security brokers and dealers

D-U-N-S 24-120-0125   (SL)
ROYAL ORCHARD MIDDLE SCHOOL
77 Royal Orchard Dr, Brampton, ON, L6X 4M4
(905) 453-3760
Emp Here 60   *Sales* 4,012,839
SIC 8211 Elementary and secondary schools

D-U-N-S 25-301-3908   (BR)
SCOTIA CAPITAL INC
SCOTIA MCLEOD
1 Nelson St W Unit 6, Brampton, ON, L6X 3E4
(905) 796-2424
Emp Here 20
SIC 6211 Security brokers and dealers

D-U-N-S 24-849-8446   (BR)
TRILLIUM FUNERAL SERVICE CORPORATION
SCOTT FUNERAL HOME
289 Main St N, Brampton, ON, L6X 1N5
(905) 451-1100
Emp Here 20
SIC 7261 Funeral service and crematories

D-U-N-S 20-004-6915   (BR)
WENDY'S RESTAURANTS OF CANADA INC
WENDY'S RESTAURANTS OF CANADA INC
(*Suby of* The Wendy's Company)
353 Main St N, Brampton, ON, L6X 1N6
(905) 452-8915
Emp Here 25
SIC 5812 Eating places

D-U-N-S 24-190-1938   (BR)
YMCA OF GREATER TORONTO

8 Nelson St W, Brampton, ON, L6X 4J2

Emp Here 20
SIC 8699 Membership organizations, nec

Brampton, ON L6Y
Peel County

D-U-N-S 20-517-8200   (SL)
1388688 ONTARIO LIMITED
SHOPPERS WORLD BRAMPTON
499 Main St S Suite 56, Brampton, ON, L6Y 1N7
(905) 459-1337
Emp Here 53   *Sales* 4,815,406
SIC 6512 Nonresidential building operators

D-U-N-S 24-198-3209   (SL)
351658 ONTARIO LIMITED
LIONHEAD GOLF & COUNTRY CLUB
8525 Mississauga Rd, Brampton, ON, L6Y 0C1
(905) 455-8400
Emp Here 100   *Sales* 4,304,681
SIC 7992 Public golf courses

D-U-N-S 20-911-0431   (BR)
BANK OF NOVA SCOTIA, THE
SCOTIABANK
1 Main St S, Brampton, ON, L6Y 1M8
(905) 451-7330
Emp Here 25
SIC 6021 National commercial banks

D-U-N-S 25-296-7708   (BR)
BANK OF NOVA SCOTIA, THE
SCOTIABANK
7700 Hurontario St Unit 301, Brampton, ON, L6Y 4M3
(905) 453-7020
Emp Here 21
SIC 6021 National commercial banks

D-U-N-S 25-796-1599   (BR)
BANK OF MONTREAL
BMO
499 Main St S, Brampton, ON, L6Y 1N7
(905) 459-9330
Emp Here 26
SIC 6021 National commercial banks

D-U-N-S 25-319-3221   (BR)
BANQUE TORONTO-DOMINION, LA
TORONTO-DOMINION BANK, THE
(*Suby of* Toronto-Dominion Bank, The)
545 Steeles Ave W, Brampton, ON, L6Y 4E7
(905) 454-3540
Emp Here 20
SIC 6021 National commercial banks

D-U-N-S 25-374-9410   (BR)
BANQUE TORONTO-DOMINION, LA
TORONTO-DOMINION BANK, THE
(*Suby of* Toronto-Dominion Bank, The)
7686 Hurontario St, Brampton, ON, L6Y 5B5
(905) 457-3201
Emp Here 36
SIC 6021 National commercial banks

D-U-N-S 25-301-6067   (BR)
CANADIAN MENTAL HEALTH ASSOCIATION/PEEL BRANCH
CMHA RESSOURCE CENTRE
7700 Hurontario St Suite 601, Brampton, ON, L6Y 4M3
(905) 451-2123
Emp Here 100
SIC 8621 Professional organizations

D-U-N-S 20-770-1541   (HQ)
CANON CANADA INC
8000 Mississauga Rd, Brampton, ON, L6Y 0C3
(905) 795-1111
Emp Here 300   *Emp Total* 189,571
Sales 194,906,475

▲ Public Company   ■ Public Company Family Member   **HQ** Headquarters   **BR** Branch   **SL** Single Location

SIC 5044 Office equipment
Pr Ted Egawa
Sr VP Tony Valenti
VP VP Maria Tesla
Ch Bd Yoroku Adachi

D-U-N-S 24-525-7360   (BR)
CONSEIL SCOLAIRE VIAMONDE
ECOLE SECONDAIRE JEUNES SANS
FRONTI PES
7585 Financial Dr, Brampton, ON, L6Y 5P4
(905) 450-1106
Emp Here 25
SIC 8211 Elementary and secondary schools

D-U-N-S 24-156-1427   (BR)
**CORPORATION OF THE CITY OF BRAMP-
TON, THE**
MEMORIAL ARENA
69 Elliott St, Brampton, ON, L6Y 1W2
(905) 874-2874
Emp Here 20
SIC 7941 Sports clubs, managers, and pro-
moters

D-U-N-S 24-333-7024   (SL)
D & H CANADA ULC
(Suby of D & H Distributing Company)
7975 Heritage Rd Suite 20, Brampton, ON,
L6Y 5X5
(905) 796-0030
Emp Here 30   Sales 4,591,130
SIC 5065 Electronic parts and equipment, nec

D-U-N-S 25-117-1682   (BR)
DOLLARAMA S.E.C.
DOLLARAMA
499 Main St S Unit 204, Brampton, ON, L6Y
1N7
(905) 866-6948
Emp Here 23
SIC 5331 Variety stores

D-U-N-S 25-117-1732   (BR)
**DUFFERIN-PEEL CATHOLIC DISTRICT
SCHOOL BOARD**
BISHOP FRANCIS ALLEN SCHOOL
325 Mcmurchy Ave S, Brampton, ON, L6Y 1Z4
(905) 457-4677
Emp Here 45
SIC 8211 Elementary and secondary schools

D-U-N-S 25-237-8732   (BR)
**DUFFERIN-PEEL CATHOLIC DISTRICT
SCHOOL BOARD**
ST BRIGID CATHOLIC SCHOOL
81 Torrance Woods, Brampton, ON, L6Y 2X4
(905) 454-0316
Emp Here 32
SIC 8211 Elementary and secondary schools

D-U-N-S 25-926-3465   (BR)
**DUFFERIN-PEEL CATHOLIC DISTRICT
SCHOOL BOARD**
ST. AUGUSTINE SECONDARY SCHOOL
27 Drinkwater Rd, Brampton, ON, L6Y 4T6
(905) 450-9993
Emp Here 50
SIC 8211 Elementary and secondary schools

D-U-N-S 20-710-9955   (BR)
**DUFFERIN-PEEL CATHOLIC DISTRICT
SCHOOL BOARD**
PAULINE VANIER CATHOLIC E S
56 Oaklea Blvd, Brampton, ON, L6Y 4W7
(905) 455-1001
Emp Here 50
SIC 8211 Elementary and secondary schools

D-U-N-S 20-711-0029   (BR)
**DUFFERIN-PEEL CATHOLIC DISTRICT
SCHOOL BOARD**
ST. MONICA SCHOOL
60 Sterritt Dr, Brampton, ON, L6Y 5B6
(905) 454-6346
Emp Here 50
SIC 8211 Elementary and secondary schools

D-U-N-S 20-699-6550   (BR)
EXTENDICARE INC
EXTENDICARE BRAMPTON
7891 Mclaughlin Rd, Brampton, ON, L6Y 5H8
(905) 459-4904
Emp Here 25
SIC 8051 Skilled nursing care facilities

D-U-N-S 20-806-6535   (BR)
HUDSON'S BAY COMPANY
BAY, THE
499 Main St S Suite 60e, Brampton, ON, L6Y
1N7

Emp Here 50
SIC 5311 Department stores

D-U-N-S 20-076-7619   (BR)
KANEFF PROPERTIES LIMITED
KANEFF GROUP OF COMPANIES
8501 Mississauga Rd Ste 200, Brampton, ON,
L6Y 5G8
(905) 454-0221
Emp Here 30
SIC 6553 Cemetery subdividers and develop-
ers

D-U-N-S 20-353-7209   (BR)
KANEFF PROPERTIES LIMITED
KANEFFGOLF
8525 Mississauga Rd, Brampton, ON, L6Y
0C1
(905) 455-8400
Emp Here 50
SIC 7992 Public golf courses

D-U-N-S 20-613-7437   (SL)
LAWRENCE LAWRENCE STEVENSON LLP
43 Queen St W, Brampton, ON, L6Y 1L9
(905) 452-6873
Emp Here 49   Sales 5,884,100
SIC 8111 Legal services
Pt Edwin Upenieks

D-U-N-S 20-413-7475   (HQ)
LOBLAW COMPANIES LIMITED
DOMINION
1 Presidents Choice Cir, Brampton, ON, L6Y
5S5
(905) 459-2500
Emp Here 80   Emp Total 138,000
Sales 34,308,433,325
SIC 5411 Grocery stores
Galen G Weston
Pr Sarah R Davis
Richard Dufresne
Sr VP Robert Chant
Paul M Beeston
Christie J.B. Clark
John S Lacey
Nancy H.O. Lockhart
Thomas C O'neill
Scott Bonham

D-U-N-S 24-538-4359   (HQ)
LOBLAW PROPERTIES LIMITED
1 Presidents Choice Cir, Brampton, ON, L6Y
5S5
(905) 459-2500
Emp Here 22   Emp Total 138,000
Sales 8,662,510
SIC 6512 Nonresidential building operators
Robert Balcom
S. Jane Marshall
Jeremy Roberts
Sarah Davis

D-U-N-S 24-383-8930   (BR)
LOBLAWS INC
REAL CANADIAN SUPERSTORE
85 Steeles Ave W, Brampton, ON, L6Y 0K3
(905) 451-0917
Emp Here 150
SIC 5411 Grocery stores

D-U-N-S 24-719-1679   (HQ)
LOBLAWS SUPERMARKETS LIMITED
ST CLAIR MARKET

1 Presidents Choice Cir, Brampton, ON, L6Y
5S5
(905) 459-2500
Emp Here 300   Emp Total 138,000
Sales 2,307,382,138
SIC 5411 Grocery stores
Pr Allan Leighton

D-U-N-S 25-796-1276   (BR)
LONGO BROTHERS FRUIT MARKETS INC
LONGO'S FRUIT MARKET
7700 Hurontario St Suite 202, Brampton, ON,
L6Y 4M3
(905) 455-3135
Emp Here 300
SIC 5431 Fruit and vegetable markets

D-U-N-S 25-826-4134   (BR)
MAPLE LODGE FARMS LTD
CHICKEN SHOP, THE
8175 Winston Churchill Blvd, Brampton, ON,
L6Y 0A3
(905) 454-5388
Emp Here 20
SIC 5411 Grocery stores

D-U-N-S 20-285-1044   (BR)
MATRIX LOGISTICS SERVICES LIMITED
2675 Steeles Ave W, Brampton, ON, L6Y 5X3
(905) 451-6792
Emp Here 800
SIC 4225 General warehousing and storage

D-U-N-S 20-563-2628   (BR)
**MCDONALD'S RESTAURANTS OF
CANADA LIMITED**
MCDONALD'S 8575
(Suby of McDonald's Corporation)
7690 Hurontario St, Brampton, ON, L6Y 5B5
(905) 456-2233
Emp Here 50
SIC 5812 Eating places

D-U-N-S 20-628-6130   (HQ)
MEDTRONIC OF CANADA LTD
99 Hereford St, Brampton, ON, L6Y 0R3
(905) 460-3800
Emp Here 50   Emp Total 126
Sales 17,498,270
SIC 3845 Electromedical equipment
Pr Pr Neil Fraser
Dir Fin Laura Cameron-Brookbank
George Wilson
William George

D-U-N-S 24-194-4888   (SL)
PEEL FAMILY EDUCATION CENTRE
4 Sir Lou Dr Suite 104, Brampton, ON, L6Y
4J7
(905) 452-0332
Emp Here 35   Sales 8,828,245
SIC 8399 Social services, nec
Ex Dir Lynn Hand

D-U-N-S 25-297-1536   (BR)
PEEL DISTRICT SCHOOL BOARD
MORTON WAY PUBLIC SCHOOL
(Suby of Peel District School Board)
200 Morton Way, Brampton, ON, L6Y 2P8
(905) 452-6116
Emp Here 60
SIC 8211 Elementary and secondary schools

D-U-N-S 25-293-7982   (BR)
PEEL DISTRICT SCHOOL BOARD
CHERRYTREE PUBLIC SCHOOL
(Suby of Peel District School Board)
155 Cherrytree Dr, Brampton, ON, L6Y 3M9
(905) 454-2251
Emp Here 35
SIC 8211 Elementary and secondary schools

D-U-N-S 20-248-9464   (BR)
PEEL DISTRICT SCHOOL BOARD
CHURCHVILLE PUBLIC SCHOOL
(Suby of Peel District School Board)
90 Bonnie Braes Dr, Brampton, ON, L6Y 0Y3

(905) 796-4445
Emp Here 49
SIC 8211 Elementary and secondary schools

D-U-N-S 25-297-1908   (BR)
PEEL DISTRICT SCHOOL BOARD
BRAMPTON CENTENNIAL SECONDARY
SCHOOL
(Suby of Peel District School Board)
251 Mcmurchy Ave S, Brampton, ON, L6Y 1Z4
(905) 451-2860
Emp Here 101
SIC 8211 Elementary and secondary schools

D-U-N-S 25-092-3067   (BR)
PEEL DISTRICT SCHOOL BOARD
HICKORY WOOD PUBLIC SCHOOL
(Suby of Peel District School Board)
630 Ray Lawson Blvd, Brampton, ON, L6Y
4W8
(905) 451-3444
Emp Here 70
SIC 8211 Elementary and secondary schools

D-U-N-S 24-497-6226   (BR)
PEEL DISTRICT SCHOOL BOARD
ROBERTA BONDAR PUBLIC SCHOOL
(Suby of Peel District School Board)
30 Pantomine Blvd, Brampton, ON, L6Y 5N2
(905) 457-1799
Emp Here 25
SIC 8211 Elementary and secondary schools

D-U-N-S 24-676-5064   (BR)
PEEL DISTRICT SCHOOL BOARD
COPELAND PUBLIC SCHOOL
(Suby of Peel District School Board)
5 Young Dr, Brampton, ON, L6Y 0P4
(905) 451-2217
Emp Here 60
SIC 8211 Elementary and secondary schools

D-U-N-S 20-591-3945   (BR)
PEEL DISTRICT SCHOOL BOARD
FLETCHERS CREEK SENIOR PUBLIC
SCHOOL
(Suby of Peel District School Board)
92 Malta Ave, Brampton, ON, L6Y 4C8
(905) 796-8226
Emp Here 25
SIC 8211 Elementary and secondary schools

D-U-N-S 20-913-6899   (BR)
PEEL DISTRICT SCHOOL BOARD
MCHUGH ELEMENTARY SCHOOL
(Suby of Peel District School Board)
31 Craig St, Brampton, ON, L6Y 1J2
(905) 451-2515
Emp Here 23
SIC 8211 Elementary and secondary schools

D-U-N-S 25-153-2271   (BR)
PEEL DISTRICT SCHOOL BOARD
RIDGEWOOD PUBLIC SCHOOL
(Suby of Peel District School Board)
25 Brenda Ave, Brampton, ON, L6Y 2A1
(905) 451-6332
Emp Here 45
SIC 8211 Elementary and secondary schools

D-U-N-S 25-293-7941   (BR)
PEEL DISTRICT SCHOOL BOARD
CENTENNIAL SENIOR PUBLIC SCHOOL
(Suby of Peel District School Board)
50 Ladore Dr, Brampton, ON, L6Y 1V5
(905) 459-5200
Emp Here 60
SIC 8211 Elementary and secondary schools

D-U-N-S 20-688-9144   (BR)
PEEL DISTRICT SCHOOL BOARD
QUEEN STREET PUBLIC SCHOOL
(Suby of Peel District School Board)
20 Academic Dr, Brampton, ON, L6Y 0R7
(905) 455-6144
Emp Here 62
SIC 8211 Elementary and secondary schools

D-U-N-S 24-676-5072   (BR)
PEEL DISTRICT SCHOOL BOARD
SIR WILLIAM GAGE MIDDLE SCHOOL
(*Suby of* Peel District School Board)
625 Queen St W, Brampton, ON, L6Y 5L6
(905) 456-3394
Emp Here 25
SIC 8211 Elementary and secondary schools

D-U-N-S 24-077-2202   (BR)
PHARMA PLUS DRUGMARTS LTD
499 Main St S, Brampton, ON, L6Y 1N7

Emp Here 40
SIC 5912 Drug stores and proprietary stores

D-U-N-S 24-483-9106   (BR)
SHERIDAN COLLEGE INSTITUTE OF TECHNOLOGY AND ADVANCED LEARNING
DAVIS CAMPUS
7899 Mclaughlin Rd, Brampton, ON, L6Y 5H9
(905) 459-7533
Emp Here 257
SIC 8222 Junior colleges

D-U-N-S 20-793-0723   (BR)
SOBEYS CAPITAL INCORPORATED
8975 Chinguacousy Rd, Brampton, ON, L6Y 0J2
(905) 796-1517
Emp Here 200
SIC 5411 Grocery stores

D-U-N-S 25-844-9602   (BR)
SOBEYS CAPITAL INCORPORATED
FRESHCO
499 Main St S, Brampton, ON, L6Y 1N7

Emp Here 70
SIC 5411 Grocery stores

D-U-N-S 25-370-1155   (BR)
STAPLES CANADA INC
STAPLES THE BUSINESS DEPOT
(*Suby of* Staples, Inc.)
499 Main St S, Brampton, ON, L6Y 1N7
(905) 796-2403
Emp Here 40
SIC 5943 Stationery stores

D-U-N-S 20-176-3042   (SL)
SUNBEAM CORPORATION (CANADA) LIMITED
JARDEN CONSUMER SOLUTIONS
(*Suby of* Newell Brands Inc.)
20 Hereford St Suite B, Brampton, ON, L6Y 0M1
(905) 593-6100
Emp Here 109   *Sales* 39,934,171
SIC 5064 Electrical appliances, television and radio
Pr Pr Dave Simmons
 Mike Ricci

D-U-N-S 20-106-3653   (BR)
WINNERS MERCHANTS INTERNATIONAL L.P.
WINNERS
(*Suby of* The TJX Companies Inc)
499 Main St S Suite 183b, Brampton, ON, L6Y 1N7
(905) 457-1552
Emp Here 45
SIC 5651 Family clothing stores

D-U-N-S 20-174-9181   (HQ)
ZEHRMART INC
ZEHRS MARKETS
1 Presidents Choice Cir, Brampton, ON, L6Y 5S5
(905) 459-2500
Emp Here 150   *Emp Total* 138,000
Sales 1,968,728,648
SIC 5411 Grocery stores
 Galen Weston
Pr Pr John A. Lederer
 Carmen Fortino

VP Fin Mila Cruz
VP Opers Ken Code
Ex VP Glen Gonder
 David Bragg

Brampton, ON L6Z
Peel County

D-U-N-S 25-796-0658   (BR)
CORPORATION OF THE CITY OF BRAMPTON, THE
LOAFERS LAKE RECREATION CENTRE
30 Loafer'S Lake Lane, Brampton, ON, L6Z 1X9
(905) 846-2370
Emp Here 50
SIC 7999 Amusement and recreation, nec

D-U-N-S 20-803-2263   (BR)
CORPORATION OF THE CITY OF BRAMPTON, THE
JIM ARCHDEKIN RECREATION CENTRE, THE
292 Conestoga Dr, Brampton, ON, L6Z 3M1
(905) 840-1023
Emp Here 57
SIC 8211 Elementary and secondary schools

D-U-N-S 25-598-0567   (HQ)
DP ENVIRONMENTAL SERVICE INC
(*Suby of* DP Environmental Service Inc)
39 Shadywood Rd, Brampton, ON, L6Z 4M1
(905) 840-4480
Emp Here 26   *Emp Total* 50
Sales 4,231,721
SIC 4959 Sanitary services, nec

D-U-N-S 20-302-5411   (BR)
DUFFERIN-PEEL CATHOLIC DISTRICT SCHOOL BOARD
NOTRE DAME SECONDARY SCHOOL
2 Notre Dame Ave, Brampton, ON, L6Z 4L5
(905) 840-2802
Emp Here 140
SIC 8211 Elementary and secondary schools

D-U-N-S 25-926-3481   (BR)
DUFFERIN-PEEL CATHOLIC DISTRICT SCHOOL BOARD
SACRED HEART ELEMENTARY SCHOOL
24 Kerwood Pl, Brampton, ON, L6Z 1Y1
(905) 846-0802
Emp Here 32
SIC 8211 Elementary and secondary schools

D-U-N-S 20-711-0268   (BR)
DUFFERIN-PEEL CATHOLIC DISTRICT SCHOOL BOARD
ST RITA SCHOOL
30 Summer Valley Dr, Brampton, ON, L6Z 4V6
(905) 595-0911
Emp Here 60
SIC 8211 Elementary and secondary schools

D-U-N-S 20-710-9989   (BR)
DUFFERIN-PEEL CATHOLIC DISTRICT SCHOOL BOARD
ST AGNES ELEMENTARY SCHOOL
103 Richvale Dr S, Brampton, ON, L6Z 4G6
(905) 450-0571
Emp Here 50
SIC 8211 Elementary and secondary schools

D-U-N-S 20-710-9971   (BR)
DUFFERIN-PEEL CATHOLIC DISTRICT SCHOOL BOARD
ST. STEPHEN ELEMENTARY SCHOOL
17 Colonel Bertram Rd, Brampton, ON, L6Z 4N8
(905) 840-3921
Emp Here 50
SIC 8211 Elementary and secondary schools

D-U-N-S 25-317-8537   (BR)
LIQUOR CONTROL BOARD OF ONTARIO,

THE
L.C.B.O. # 171
170 Sandalwood Pky E, Brampton, ON, L6Z 1Y5
(905) 846-4373
Emp Here 20
SIC 5921 Liquor stores

D-U-N-S 24-353-6658   (BR)
LOWE'S COMPANIES CANADA, ULC
LOWE'S OF NORTH BRAMPTON
10111 Heart Lake Rd, Brampton, ON, L6Z 0E4
(905) 840-2351
Emp Here 200
SIC 5211 Lumber and other building materials

D-U-N-S 24-333-1688   (BR)
METRO ONTARIO INC
METRO
180 Sandalwood Pky E, Brampton, ON, L6Z 1Y4
(905) 846-2222
Emp Here 170
SIC 5411 Grocery stores

D-U-N-S 25-224-8851   (BR)
PEEL DISTRICT SCHOOL BOARD
ROBERT H LAGERQUIST SENIOR PUBLIC SCHOOL
(*Suby of* Peel District School Board)
105 Richvale Dr N, Brampton, ON, L6Z 1Y6
(905) 846-0576
Emp Here 40
SIC 8211 Elementary and secondary schools

D-U-N-S 25-092-3042   (BR)
PEEL DISTRICT SCHOOL BOARD
ESKER LAKE PUBLIC SCHOOL
(*Suby of* Peel District School Board)
10420 Heart Lake Rd, Brampton, ON, L6Z 4S2
(905) 840-5442
Emp Here 30
SIC 8211 Elementary and secondary schools

D-U-N-S 25-293-9434   (BR)
PEEL DISTRICT SCHOOL BOARD
CONESTOGA PUBLIC SCHOOL
(*Suby of* Peel District School Board)
300 Conestoga Dr, Brampton, ON, L6Z 3M1
(905) 846-2311
Emp Here 45
SIC 8211 Elementary and secondary schools

D-U-N-S 20-034-2041   (BR)
PEEL DISTRICT SCHOOL BOARD
HEART LAKE SECONDARY SCHOOL
(*Suby of* Peel District School Board)
296 Conestoga Dr, Brampton, ON, L6Z 3M1
(905) 840-2328
Emp Here 95
SIC 8211 Elementary and secondary schools

D-U-N-S 25-297-1940   (BR)
PEEL DISTRICT SCHOOL BOARD
TERRY FOX PUBLIC SCHOOL
(*Suby of* Peel District School Board)
95 Richvale Dr N, Brampton, ON, L6Z 1Y6
(905) 846-1262
Emp Here 35
SIC 8211 Elementary and secondary schools

D-U-N-S 25-224-9966   (BR)
PEEL DISTRICT SCHOOL BOARD
SOMERSET DRIVE PUBLIC SCHOOL
(*Suby of* Peel District School Board)
50 Somerset Dr, Brampton, ON, L6Z 1C7
(905) 846-2500
Emp Here 40
SIC 8211 Elementary and secondary schools

D-U-N-S 25-308-4891   (BR)
ROYAL BANK OF CANADA
RBC
(*Suby of* Royal Bank Of Canada)
164 Sandalwood Pky E, Brampton, ON, L6Z 3S4

(905) 840-1644
Emp Here 20
SIC 6021 National commercial banks

D-U-N-S 20-614-5836   (SL)
SABRITIN HOSPITALITY INC
SWISS CHALET
370 Bovaird Dr E, Brampton, ON, L6Z 2S8
(905) 846-3321
Emp Here 80   *Sales* 2,407,703
SIC 5812 Eating places

D-U-N-S 25-840-0878   (BR)
SOBEYS CAPITAL INCORPORATED
FRESHCO
380 Bovaird Dr E Suite 29, Brampton, ON, L6Z 2S8
(905) 840-0770
Emp Here 110
SIC 5411 Grocery stores

D-U-N-S 20-643-2010   (BR)
SOBEYS CAPITAL INCORPORATED
SOBEYS
11965 Hurontario St, Brampton, ON, L6Z 4P7
(905) 846-5658
Emp Here 100
SIC 5411 Grocery stores

D-U-N-S 24-347-4645   (BR)
SPECIALTY CARE INC
SPECIALTY CARE WOODHALL PARK
(*Suby of* Specialty Care Inc)
10260 Kennedy Rd, Brampton, ON, L6Z 4N7
(905) 495-4695
Emp Here 1,000
SIC 8059 Nursing and personal care, nec

Brampton, ON L7A
Peel County

D-U-N-S 20-571-8492   (BR)
ARBOR MEMORIAL SERVICES INC
BRAMPTON FUNERAL HOME & CEMETERY
10061 Chinguacousy Rd, Brampton, ON, L7A 0H6
(905) 840-3400
Emp Here 20
SIC 7261 Funeral service and crematories

D-U-N-S 25-496-5098   (SL)
AUTOMATED FULFILLMENT SYSTEM INC
AFS
80 Van Kirk Dr Suite 5, Brampton, ON, L7A 1B1
(905) 840-4141
Emp Here 50   *Sales* 2,553,625
SIC 7331 Direct mail advertising services

D-U-N-S 20-802-8907   (BR)
BEATTY FOODS LTD
MCDONALD'S RESTAURANTS
11670 Hurontario St, Brampton, ON, L7A 1R2
(905) 846-3677
Emp Here 70
SIC 5812 Eating places

D-U-N-S 25-203-2743   (BR)
BINGO COUNTRY HOLDINGS LIMITED
(*Suby of* Bingo Country Holdings Limited)
190 Bovaird Dr W Suite 49, Brampton, ON, L7A 1A2
(905) 451-7771
Emp Here 30
SIC 7999 Amusement and recreation, nec

D-U-N-S 24-658-9923   (BR)
BRAMPTON BRICK LIMITED
225 Wanless Dr, Brampton, ON, L7A 1E9

Emp Here 49
SIC 3251 Brick and structural clay tile

D-U-N-S 20-163-2676   (BR)
DAY & ROSS INC

170 Van Kirk Dr, Brampton, ON, L7A 1K9
(905) 846-6300
Emp Here 200
SIC 4213 Trucking, except local

D-U-N-S 20-911-4243   (BR)
DIRECT ENERGY MARKETING LIMITED
180 Bovaird Dr W, Brampton, ON, L7A 0H3
(905) 451-1444
Emp Here 250
SIC 4924 Natural gas distribution

D-U-N-S 20-653-2249   (BR)
DUFFERIN-PEEL CATHOLIC DISTRICT SCHOOL BOARD
GUARDIAN ANGELS CATHOLIC ELEMEN-TARY SCHOOL
62 Heatherdale Dr, Brampton, ON, L7A 2H4
(905) 595-0909
Emp Here 50
SIC 8211 Elementary and secondary schools

D-U-N-S 24-676-3069   (BR)
DUFFERIN-PEEL CATHOLIC DISTRICT SCHOOL BOARD
ST. JOSEPHINE BAKHITA CATHOLIC ELE-MENTARY SCHOOL
430 Van Kirk Dr, Brampton, ON, L7A 0J2
(905) 846-0078
Emp Here 25
SIC 8211 Elementary and secondary schools

D-U-N-S 20-591-2012   (BR)
DUFFERIN-PEEL CATHOLIC DISTRICT SCHOOL BOARD
ST. AIDAN CATHOLIC ELEMENTARY SCHOOL
34 Buick Blvd, Brampton, ON, L7A 3B9
(905) 840-3042
Emp Here 25
SIC 8211 Elementary and secondary schools

D-U-N-S 24-419-3611   (SL)
EXACTA TOOL 2010 ULC
WILSON TOOL CANADA
(*Suby of* Wilson Tool International Inc.)
120 Van Kirk Dr, Brampton, ON, L7A 1B1
(905) 840-2240
Emp Here 25   *Sales* 5,457,381
SIC 5084 Industrial machinery and equipment
Dir Brian E. Robinson

D-U-N-S 24-314-8157   (BR)
EXEL CANADA LTD
100 Sandalwood Pky W, Brampton, ON, L7A 1A8
(905) 970-7200
Emp Here 25
SIC 4225 General warehousing and storage

D-U-N-S 24-394-0298   (SL)
GCCL CONTRACTING LIMITED
12 Canam Cres, Brampton, ON, L7A 1A9
(905) 454-1078
Emp Here 20   *Sales* 2,772,003
SIC 1611 Highway and street construction

D-U-N-S 20-573-6494   (BR)
HSBC BANK CANADA
HSBC FINANCE
11670 Hurontario St Unit 2, Brampton, ON, L7A 1R2

Emp Here 20
SIC 6141 Personal credit institutions

D-U-N-S 25-802-5329   (BR)
HYUNDAI CANADA INC
ATTRELL MOTOR
100 Canam Cres, Brampton, ON, L7A 1A9
(905) 451-1699
Emp Here 40
SIC 5511 New and used car dealers

D-U-N-S 20-911-4680   (BR)
JASWALL INC
70 Van Kirk Dr, Brampton, ON, L7A 1B1

(905) 495-6584
Emp Here 80
SIC 3449 Miscellaneous Metalwork

D-U-N-S 25-991-5791   (SL)
LEVEL-RITE SYSTEMS COMPANY
(*Suby of* Rite-Hite Holding Corporation)
29 Regan Rd, Brampton, ON, L7A 1B2

Emp Here 35   *Sales* 2,991,389
SIC 3999 Manufacturing industries, nec

D-U-N-S 24-189-4737   (BR)
MCDONALD'S RESTAURANTS OF CANADA LIMITED
MCDONALD'S RESTAURANTS
(*Suby of* McDonald's Corporation)
30 Brisdale Dr, Brampton, ON, L7A 3G1
(905) 495-1122
Emp Here 80
SIC 5812 Eating places

D-U-N-S 24-333-1621   (BR)
METRO ONTARIO INC
METRO
10088 Mclaughlin Rd Suite 1, Brampton, ON, L7A 2X6

Emp Here 300
SIC 5411 Grocery stores

D-U-N-S 25-263-7566   (BR)
PEEL DISTRICT SCHOOL BOARD
PARKHOLME SCHOOL
(*Suby of* Peel District School Board)
10750 Chinguacousy Rd, Brampton, ON, L7A 2Z7
(905) 451-1263
Emp Here 150
SIC 8211 Elementary and secondary schools

D-U-N-S 24-525-4227   (BR)
PEEL DISTRICT SCHOOL BOARD
BRISDALE PUBLIC SCHOOL
(*Suby of* Peel District School Board)
370 Brisdale Dr, Brampton, ON, L7A 3K7
(905) 840-2135
Emp Here 85
SIC 8211 Elementary and secondary schools

D-U-N-S 24-497-8982   (BR)
PEEL DISTRICT SCHOOL BOARD
ROWNTREE PUBLIC SCHOOL
(*Suby of* Peel District School Board)
254 Queen Mary Dr, Brampton, ON, L7A 3L6
(905) 840-4601
Emp Here 25
SIC 8211 Elementary and secondary schools

D-U-N-S 24-120-6684   (BR)
PEEL DISTRICT SCHOOL BOARD
EDENBROOK HILL PUBLIC SCHOOL
(*Suby of* Peel District School Board)
61 Edenbrook Hill Dr, Brampton, ON, L7A 1X6
(905) 452-8296
Emp Here 52
SIC 8211 Elementary and secondary schools

D-U-N-S 20-704-0150   (BR)
PEEL DISTRICT SCHOOL BOARD
BURNT ELM PUBLIC SCHOOL
(*Suby of* Peel District School Board)
85 Burnt Elm Dr, Brampton, ON, L7A 1T8
(905) 495-9368
Emp Here 50
SIC 8211 Elementary and secondary schools

D-U-N-S 20-653-8907   (BR)
PEEL DISTRICT SCHOOL BOARD
WORTHINGTON PUBLIC SCHOOL
(*Suby of* Peel District School Board)
71 Worthington Ave, Brampton, ON, L7A 1N9
(905) 495-8336
Emp Here 70
SIC 8211 Elementary and secondary schools

D-U-N-S 24-224-1037   (BR)
PEEL DISTRICT SCHOOL BOARD
CHEYNE MIDDLE SCHOOL

(*Suby of* Peel District School Board)
236 Queen Mary Dr, Brampton, ON, L7A 3L3
(905) 840-0402
Emp Here 25
SIC 8211 Elementary and secondary schools

D-U-N-S 24-120-9639   (BR)
PEEL DISTRICT SCHOOL BOARD
FLETCHER'S MEADOW SECONDARY SCHOOL
(*Suby of* Peel District School Board)
10750 Chinguacousy Rd, Brampton, ON, L7A 2Z7
(905) 495-2675
Emp Here 120
SIC 8211 Elementary and secondary schools

D-U-N-S 24-179-4820   (SL)
SDH INC
CLINTAR LANDSCAPE MANAGEMENT
190 Bovaird Dr W Suite 15, Brampton, ON, L7A 1A2
(905) 796-5849
Emp Here 50   *Sales* 1,884,090
SIC 4212 Local trucking, without storage

D-U-N-S 24-126-2539   (BR)
SAFETY-KLEEN CANADA INC.
25 Regan Rd, Brampton, ON, L7A 1B2
(905) 840-0118
Emp Here 37
SIC 7389 Business services, nec

D-U-N-S 25-508-1127   (SL)
V.S.I. INC
VISTA SECURITY AND INVESTIGATIONS
18 Regan Rd Unit 31, Brampton, ON, L7A 1C2
(905) 840-4085
Emp Here 100   *Sales* 3,137,310
SIC 7381 Detective and armored car services

D-U-N-S 24-991-8293   (BR)
VULSAY INDUSTRIES LTD
35 Regan Rd, Brampton, ON, L7A 1B2
(905) 846-2200
Emp Here 63   *Sales* 3,811,504
SIC 7389 Business services, nec

D-U-N-S 24-224-5624   (BR)
WENDY'S RESTAURANTS OF CANADA INC
(*Suby of* The Wendy's Company)
10041 Mclaughlin Rd, Brampton, ON, L7A 2X5
(905) 840-0476
Emp Here 40
SIC 5812 Eating places

Branchton, ON N0B
Waterloo County

D-U-N-S 24-183-5326   (BR)
CHRISTIAN HORIZONS
(*Suby of* Christian Horizons)
1966 6 Conc W, Branchton, ON, N0B 1L0
(519) 620-2990
Emp Here 27
SIC 8361 Residential care

Brantford, ON N3P
Brant County

D-U-N-S 20-710-6357   (BR)
BRANT HALDIMAND NORFOLK CATHOLIC DISTRICT SCHOOL BOARD
NOTRE DAME ELEMENTARY SCHOOL
238 Brantwood Park Rd, Brantford, ON, N3P 1N9
(519) 756-2288
Emp Here 50
SIC 8211 Elementary and secondary schools

D-U-N-S 20-068-0481   (BR)

GRAND ERIE DISTRICT SCHOOL BOARD
BANBURY HEIGHTS ELEMENTARY SCHOOL
(*Suby of* Grand Erie District School Board)
141 Banbury Rd, Brantford, ON, N3P 1E3
(519) 751-0142
Emp Here 35
SIC 8211 Elementary and secondary schools

D-U-N-S 20-591-3275   (BR)
GRAND ERIE DISTRICT SCHOOL BOARD
BRANLYN COMMUNITY SCHOOL
(*Suby of* Grand Erie District School Board)
238 Brantwood Park Rd, Brantford, ON, N3P 1N9
(519) 759-7240
Emp Here 35
SIC 8211 Elementary and secondary schools

D-U-N-S 24-703-6718   (HQ)
MIURA CANADA CO., LTD
8 Copernicus Blvd, Brantford, ON, N3P 1Y4
(519) 758-8111
Emp Here 30   *Emp Total* 4,409
Sales 6,201,660
SIC 3443 Fabricated plate work (boiler shop)
Pr Pr Masaaki Ishikawa

D-U-N-S 24-704-0991   (SL)
NICHIRIN INC
139 Copernicus Blvd, Brantford, ON, N3P 1N4
(519) 752-2925
Emp Here 22   *Sales* 16,724,600
SIC 3714 Motor vehicle parts and accessories
Pr Jaunai Eakashima
VP Junji Takeshima
Treas Masatoshi Kamatani
Fin Ex Loranda Saoema
Sls Mgr Toshihiro Nakamura

D-U-N-S 20-280-8671   (HQ)
PAN-GLO CANADA PAN COATINGS INC
(*Suby of* Pan-Glo Canada Pan Coatings Inc)
84 Easton Rd, Brantford, ON, N3P 1J5
(519) 756-2800
Emp Here 37   *Emp Total* 65
Sales 3,939,878
SIC 7699 Repair services, nec

Brantford, ON N3R
Brant County

D-U-N-S 25-826-9307   (SL)
1193055 ONTARIO INC
MOOSE WINOOSKI'S
45 King George Rd, Brantford, ON, N3R 5K2
(519) 751-4042
Emp Here 50   *Sales* 1,532,175
SIC 5812 Eating places

D-U-N-S 20-812-3351   (SL)
1565720 ONTARIO LIMITED
MONTANA'S BARBEQUE AND BAR
84 Lynden Rd, Brantford, ON, N3R 6B8
(519) 754-0303
Emp Here 50   *Sales* 1,532,175
SIC 5812 Eating places

D-U-N-S 24-347-1526   (BR)
1690651 ONTARIO INC
FOOD BASICS
(*Suby of* 1690651 Ontario Inc)
265 King George Rd, Brantford, ON, N3R 6Y1
(519) 759-0571
Emp Here 20
SIC 5411 Grocery stores

D-U-N-S 24-625-9006   (BR)
2063414 ONTARIO LIMITED
LEISUREWORLD CAREGIVING CENTER
(*Suby of* 2063414 Ontario Limited)
389 West St, Brantford, ON, N3R 3V9
(519) 759-4666
Emp Here 120

SIC 8051 Skilled nursing care facilities

D-U-N-S 24-188-2229   (BR)
AGG HOLDINGS LTD
300 King George Rd, Brantford, ON, N3R 5L8
(519) 752-8088
Emp Here 20
SIC 5999 Miscellaneous retail stores, nec

D-U-N-S 25-946-4998   (HQ)
AGRIUM ADVANCED TECHNOLOGIES INC
(*Suby of* Agrium Canada Partnership)
10 Craig St, Brantford, ON, N3R 7J1
(519) 757-0077
Emp Here 50   *Emp Total* 15,200
Sales 43,995,302
SIC 2873 Nitrogenous fertilizers
Pr Pr Andrew Mittag

D-U-N-S 25-989-2388   (BR)
ANDRITZ HYDRO CANADA INC
ANDRITZ DRT SERVICE CENTRE
45 Roy Blvd, Brantford, ON, N3R 7K1
(519) 754-4590
Emp Here 35
SIC 3554 Paper industries machinery

D-U-N-S 24-117-6218   (BR)
BANK OF NOVA SCOTIA, THE
SCOTIABANK
61 Lynden Rd, Brantford, ON, N3R 7J9
(519) 751-5030
Emp Here 23
SIC 6021 National commercial banks

D-U-N-S 24-938-2466   (SL)
BEACON INTERNATIONAL WAREHOUS-ING LIMITED
325 West St Suite B110, Brantford, ON, N3R 3V6
(519) 756-6463
Emp Here 30   *Sales* 10,347,900
SIC 4731 Freight transportation arrangement
Pr Pr Rolf Von Fintel

D-U-N-S 20-792-4981   (BR)
BIMAC MANAGEMENT LIMITED
MCDONALD'S
(*Suby of* Bimac Management Limited)
300 King George Rd Suite 1, Brantford, ON, N3R 5L7
(519) 756-2046
Emp Here 25
SIC 5812 Eating places

D-U-N-S 20-704-2417   (SL)
BRANT COUNTY FORD SALES LIMITED
85 Lynden Rd, Brantford, ON, N3R 7J9
(519) 752-7858
Emp Here 50   *Sales* 3,575,074
SIC 7532 Top and body repair and paint shops

D-U-N-S 20-710-6332   (BR)
BRANT HALDIMAND NORFOLK CATHOLIC DISTRICT SCHOOL BOARD
FERRIS ELEMENTARY SCHOOL
65 Sky Acres Dr, Brantford, ON, N3R 5W6
(519) 756-5751
Emp Here 50
SIC 8211 Elementary and secondary schools

D-U-N-S 20-590-7194   (BR)
BRANT HALDIMAND NORFOLK CATHOLIC DISTRICT SCHOOL BOARD
OUR LADY PROVIDENCE SCHOOL
55 Kent Rd, Brantford, ON, N3R 7X8
(519) 758-5056
Emp Here 33
SIC 8211 Elementary and secondary schools

D-U-N-S 20-710-6316   (BR)
BRANT HALDIMAND NORFOLK CATHOLIC DISTRICT SCHOOL BOARD
80 Paris Rd, Brantford, ON, N3R 1H9
(519) 758-0466
Emp Here 50
SIC 8211 Elementary and secondary schools

D-U-N-S 24-397-1470   (BR)

BRANT HALDIMAND NORFOLK CATHOLIC DISTRICT SCHOOL BOARD
ST JOHNS COLLEGE SECONDARY SCHOOL
80 Paris Rd, Brantford, ON, N3R 1H9
(519) 759-2318
Emp Here 93
SIC 8211 Elementary and secondary schools

D-U-N-S 20-200-6891   (BR)
BRANT HALDIMAND NORFOLK CATHOLIC DISTRICT SCHOOL BOARD
ST PATRICK SCHOOL
320 Fairview Dr, Brantford, ON, N3R 2X6
(519) 759-0380
Emp Here 20
SIC 8211 Elementary and secondary schools

D-U-N-S 25-228-0771   (BR)
BRANT HALDIMAND NORFOLK CATHOLIC DISTRICT SCHOOL BOARD
ST LEO ELEMENTARY SCHOOL
233 Memorial Dr, Brantford, ON, N3R 5T2
(519) 759-3314
Emp Here 25
SIC 8211 Elementary and secondary schools

D-U-N-S 20-845-0973   (SL)
BRANTMAC MANAGEMENT LIMITED
MACDONALD'S RESTAURANT
73 King George Rd, Brantford, ON, N3R 5K2
(519) 756-7350
Emp Here 75   *Sales* 2,261,782
SIC 5812 Eating places

D-U-N-S 20-806-5834   (BR)
BRICK WAREHOUSE LP, THE
BRICK, THE
410 Fairview Dr, Brantford, ON, N3R 7V7
(519) 753-3700
Emp Here 30
SIC 5712 Furniture stores

D-U-N-S 24-356-1243   (BR)
BRUCE R. SMITH LIMITED
5 Craig St, Brantford, ON, N3R 7H8
(519) 426-0904
Emp Here 30
SIC 4212 Local trucking, without storage

D-U-N-S 25-303-2064   (BR)
CANADIAN IMPERIAL BANK OF COM-MERCE
CIBC
84 Lynden Rd, Brantford, ON, N3R 6B8
(519) 759-1250
Emp Here 20
SIC 6021 National commercial banks

D-U-N-S 24-342-8096   (BR)
CARA OPERATIONS LIMITED
SWISS CHALET
(*Suby of* Cara Holdings Limited)
84 Lynden Rd Suite 1771, Brantford, ON, N3R 6B8
(519) 759-6990
Emp Here 75
SIC 5812 Eating places

D-U-N-S 24-687-5657   (BR)
CARA OPERATIONS LIMITED
HARVEY'S
(*Suby of* Cara Holdings Limited)
57 King George Rd, Brantford, ON, N3R 5K2
(519) 759-2142
Emp Here 30
SIC 5812 Eating places

D-U-N-S 25-305-0819   (BR)
CINEPLEX ODEON CORPORATION
GALAXY CINEMAS BRANTFORD
300 King George Rd Suite 1, Brantford, ON, N3R 5L7
(519) 759-7011
Emp Here 30
SIC 7832 Motion picture theaters, except drive-in

D-U-N-S 20-923-1211   (BR)
COMCARE (CANADA) LIMITED
REVERA HOME HEALTH
425 Park Rd N Suite 104, Brantford, ON, N3R 7G5
(519) 756-4606
Emp Here 361
SIC 7363 Help supply services

D-U-N-S 20-562-7693   (BR)
CORPORATION OF THE CITY OF BRANT-FORD, THE
NORTH RIDGE MUNICIPAL GOLF COURSE
(*Suby of* Corporation of the City of Brantford, The)
320 Balmoral Dr, Brantford, ON, N3R 7S2
(519) 756-6345
Emp Here 65
SIC 7992 Public golf courses

D-U-N-S 20-935-1019   (BR)
DOLLARAMA S.E.C.
410 Fairview Dr, Brantford, ON, N3R 7V7
(519) 758-8826
Emp Here 23
SIC 5399 Miscellaneous general merchandise

D-U-N-S 20-610-6635   (HQ)
DOMCLEAN LIMITED
DOMINION EQUIPMENT & CHEMICAL, DIV OF
29 Craig St, Brantford, ON, N3R 7H8
(519) 753-8421
Emp Here 20   *Emp Total* 325
Sales 12,250,277
SIC 7349 Building maintenance services, nec
Pr Pr Ross Buzek

D-U-N-S 24-340-0871   (BR)
FGL SPORTS LTD
SPORT CHEK LYNDEN PARK MALL
84 Lynden Rd, Brantford, ON, N3R 6B8
(519) 750-0101
Emp Here 40
SIC 5941 Sporting goods and bicycle shops

D-U-N-S 20-291-6651   (BR)
GOVERNMENT OF ONTARIO
FAIRVIEW ELEMENTARY SCHOOL
34 Norman St, Brantford, ON, N3R 2Y1
(519) 751-2891
Emp Here 25
SIC 8211 Elementary and secondary schools

D-U-N-S 25-238-8640   (BR)
GRAND ERIE DISTRICT SCHOOL BOARD
GRANDVIEW ELEMENTARY SCHOOL
(*Suby of* Grand Erie District School Board)
68 North Park St, Brantford, ON, N3R 4J9
(519) 752-1422
Emp Here 20
SIC 8211 Elementary and secondary schools

D-U-N-S 20-591-3291   (BR)
GRAND ERIE DISTRICT SCHOOL BOARD
PRINCE CHARLES SCHOOL
(*Suby of* Grand Erie District School Board)
40 Morton Ave, Brantford, ON, N3R 2N5
(519) 752-9687
Emp Here 25
SIC 8211 Elementary and secondary schools

D-U-N-S 20-710-6209   (BR)
GRAND ERIE DISTRICT SCHOOL BOARD
TOLLGATE TECHNOLOGICAL SKILLS CEN-TRE
(*Suby of* Grand Erie District School Board)
112 Toll Gate Rd, Brantford, ON, N3R 4Z6
Emp Here 60
SIC 8211 Elementary and secondary schools

D-U-N-S 25-238-8426   (BR)
GRAND ERIE DISTRICT SCHOOL BOARD
CENTENNIAL GRAND WOODLANDS EL-EMETARY SCHOOL
(*Suby of* Grand Erie District School Board)
41 Ellenson Dr, Brantford, ON, N3R 3E7

(519) 759-4570
Emp Here 20
SIC 8211 Elementary and secondary schools

D-U-N-S 20-291-6677   (BR)
GRAND ERIE DISTRICT SCHOOL BOARD
BRANTFORD CORONATION ELEMENTARY SCHOOL
(*Suby of* Grand Erie District School Board)
54 Ewing Dr, Brantford, ON, N3R 5H8
(519) 752-9332
Emp Here 30
SIC 8211 Elementary and secondary schools

D-U-N-S 25-238-9093   (BR)
GRAND ERIE DISTRICT SCHOOL BOARD
CEDARLAND ELEMENTARY SCHOOL
(*Suby of* Grand Erie District School Board)
60 Ashgrove Ave, Brantford, ON, N3R 6E5
(519) 753-2910
Emp Here 24
SIC 8211 Elementary and secondary schools

D-U-N-S 25-238-9135   (BR)
GRAND ERIE DISTRICT SCHOOL BOARD
BRIER PARK PUBLIC SCHOOL
(*Suby of* Grand Erie District School Board)
10 Blackfriar Lane, Brantford, ON, N3R 6C5
(519) 759-8682
Emp Here 35
SIC 8211 Elementary and secondary schools

D-U-N-S 20-710-6183   (BR)
GRAND ERIE DISTRICT SCHOOL BOARD
RUSELL REED SCHOOL
(*Suby of* Grand Erie District School Board)
43 Cambridge Dr, Brantford, ON, N3R 5E3
(519) 753-7727
Emp Here 50
SIC 8211 Elementary and secondary schools

D-U-N-S 25-238-8384   (BR)
GRAND ERIE DISTRICT SCHOOL BOARD
JAMES HILLIER ELEMENTARY SCHOOL
(*Suby of* Grand Erie District School Board)
62 Queensway Dr, Brantford, ON, N3R 4W8
(519) 752-2296
Emp Here 30
SIC 8211 Elementary and secondary schools

D-U-N-S 20-003-8870   (BR)
HOME DEPOT OF CANADA INC
HOME DEPOT
(*Suby of* The Home Depot Inc)
25 Holiday Dr, Brantford, ON, N3R 7J4
(519) 757-3534
Emp Here 150
SIC 5251 Hardware stores

D-U-N-S 20-090-0707   (BR)
INVESTORS GROUP FINANCIAL SER-VICES INC
260 Lynden Rd Unit 1, Brantford, ON, N3R 0B9
(519) 756-5834
Emp Here 20
SIC 8742 Management consulting services

D-U-N-S 25-150-3389   (BR)
JEMPAK GK INC
(*Suby of* JemPak GK Inc)
48 Alice St, Brantford, ON, N3R 1Y2
Emp Here 20
SIC 2841 Soap and other detergents

D-U-N-S 24-896-5329   (BR)
METRO ONTARIO INC
FOOD BASICS
84 Lynden Rd, Brantford, ON, N3R 6B8
(519) 759-5850
Emp Here 50
SIC 5411 Grocery stores

D-U-N-S 24-333-1761   (BR)
METRO ONTARIO INC
METRO
371 St Paul Ave, Brantford, ON, N3R 4N5

(519) 758-0300
Emp Here 150
SIC 5411 Grocery stores

D-U-N-S 24-849-2113   (BR)
MOLD-MASTERS (2007) LIMITED
(*Suby of* Milacron Holdings Corp.)
92 Roy Blvd, Brantford, ON, N3R 7K2
(519) 758-8441
Emp Here 70
SIC 3559 Special industry machinery, nec

D-U-N-S 20-281-5452   (SL)
MOVATI ATHLETIC (BRANTFORD) INC.
595 West St, Brantford, ON, N3R 7C5
(519) 756-0123
Emp Here 75   *Sales* 3,551,629
SIC 7991 Physical fitness facilities

D-U-N-S 20-290-4905   (BR)
MOVATI ATHLETIC (LONDON SOUTH) INC.
MOVATI ATHLETIC
595 West St, Brantford, ON, N3R 7C5
(519) 756-0123
Emp Here 75
SIC 7991 Physical fitness facilities

D-U-N-S 24-351-7880   (HQ)
NEZIOL INSURANCE BROKERS LTD
NEZIOL GROUP, THE
(*Suby of* Neziol Insurance Brokers Ltd)
53 Charing Cross St Suite 1, Brantford, ON, N3R 7K9
(519) 759-2110
Emp Here 22   *Emp Total* 50
Sales 4,523,563
SIC 6411 Insurance agents, brokers, and service

D-U-N-S 20-058-4170   (BR)
NORMERICA INC
46 Morton Ave E, Brantford, ON, N3R 7J7
(519) 756-8414
Emp Here 75
SIC 3999 Manufacturing industries, nec

D-U-N-S 24-752-4259   (HQ)
NU-GRO LTD
AGRIUM ADVANCED TECHNOLOGIES
(*Suby of* Agrium Canada Partnership)
10 Craig St, Brantford, ON, N3R 7J1
(519) 757-0077
Emp Here 40   *Emp Total* 15,200
Sales 63,840,613
SIC 2875 Fertilizers, mixing only
Pr Andrew Mittag
  John Leal
Fin Mgr Chris Brandt

D-U-N-S 24-793-3807   (BR)
PMT INDUSTRIES LIMITED
PURE METAL GALVANIZING, DIV OF
32 Bodine Dr, Brantford, ON, N3R 7M4
(519) 758-5505
Emp Here 85
SIC 3479 Metal coating and allied services

D-U-N-S 20-859-8438   (BR)
PACIFIC LINK COMMUNICATIONS INC
BELL WORLD
84 Lynden Rd, Brantford, ON, N3R 6B8
(519) 756-6742
Emp Here 25
SIC 5999 Miscellaneous retail stores, nec

D-U-N-S 25-034-2904   (SL)
PARTICIPATION HOUSE
422 Powerline Rd, Brantford, ON, N3R 8A1
(519) 756-1430
Emp Here 70   *Sales* 2,553,625
SIC 8361 Residential care

D-U-N-S 24-991-1025   (BR)
PIONEER FOOD SERVICES LIMITED
TIM HORTONS
(*Suby of* Pioneer Food Services Limited)
1290 Colborne St E, Brantford, ON, N3R 0C3
(519) 759-7155
Emp Here 42

SIC 5812 Eating places

D-U-N-S 20-175-3881   (BR)
PRECISION VENEER PRODUCTS LTD
110 Morton Ave E, Brantford, ON, N3R 7J7
(519) 758-0960
Emp Here 30
SIC 2435 Hardwood veneer and plywood

D-U-N-S 20-808-6525   (BR)
RAMKEY COMMUNICATIONS INC
20 Roy Blvd Unit 2, Brantford, ON, N3R 7K2
(519) 759-8884
Emp Here 30
SIC 1731 Electrical work

D-U-N-S 20-005-2194   (BR)
RED LOBSTER HOSPITALITY LLC
RED LOBSTER RESTAURANTS
(*Suby of* Red Lobster Seafood Co., LLC)
67 King George Rd, Brantford, ON, N3R 5K2
(519) 759-7121
Emp Here 75
SIC 5812 Eating places

D-U-N-S 24-466-3675   (BR)
REDBERRY FRANCHISING CORP
BURGER KING
605 West St, Brantford, ON, N3R 7C5

Emp Here 20
SIC 5812 Eating places

D-U-N-S 24-395-2582   (BR)
RELIANCE COMFORT LIMITED PARTNERSHIP
37 Morton Ave E Unit A, Brantford, ON, N3R 7J5
(519) 756-1493
Emp Here 30
SIC 4961 Steam and air-conditioning supply

D-U-N-S 24-077-2756   (BR)
REVERA LONG TERM CARE INC
VERSA-CARE CENTRE OF BRANTFORD
425 Park Rd N, Brantford, ON, N3R 7G5
(519) 759-1040
Emp Here 150
SIC 8051 Skilled nursing care facilities

D-U-N-S 24-847-2300   (BR)
REXALL PHARMACY GROUP LTD
REXALL
(*Suby of* McKesson Corporation)
260 St Paul Ave, Brantford, ON, N3R 4M7
(519) 756-6363
Emp Here 30
SIC 5912 Drug stores and proprietary stores

D-U-N-S 20-070-4935   (BR)
ROYAL BANK OF CANADA
RBC
(*Suby of* Royal Bank Of Canada)
95 Lynden Rd, Brantford, ON, N3R 7J9
(519) 758-2500
Emp Here 46
SIC 6021 National commercial banks

D-U-N-S 25-311-1207   (BR)
SEARS CANADA INC
84 Lynden Rd Suite 1, Brantford, ON, N3R 5V1
(519) 756-7451
Emp Here 200
SIC 5311 Department stores

D-U-N-S 25-459-5671   (BR)
ST. LEONARD'S COMMUNITY SERVICES
ADDICTIONS & MENTAL HEALTH SERVICES
225 Fairview Dr Unit 1, Brantford, ON, N3R 7E3
(519) 754-0253
Emp Here 23
SIC 8069 Specialty hospitals, except psychiatric

D-U-N-S 25-498-9684   (BR)
STAPLES CANADA INC

STAPLES THE BUSINESS DEPOT
(*Suby of* Staples, Inc.)
595 West St, Brantford, ON, N3R 7C5
(519) 752-3367
Emp Here 50
SIC 5943 Stationery stores

D-U-N-S 20-104-5379   (BR)
TIGERCAT INDUSTRIES INC
54 Morton Ave E, Brantford, ON, N3R 7J7
(519) 753-2000
Emp Here 120
SIC 3531 Construction machinery

D-U-N-S 20-285-8817   (BR)
TIGERCAT INDUSTRIES INC
54 Morton Ave E, Brantford, ON, N3R 7J7
(519) 753-2000
Emp Here 150
SIC 3531 Construction machinery

D-U-N-S 20-614-0746   (SL)
TIM HORTONS
226 West St, Brantford, ON, N3R 3V2
(519) 756-4555
Emp Here 55   *Sales* 1,678,096
SIC 5812 Eating places

D-U-N-S 20-413-1833   (BR)
UAP INC
NAPA AUTO PARTS
(*Suby of* Genuine Parts Company)
17 Woodyatt Dr, Brantford, ON, N3R 7K3
(519) 752-5421
Emp Here 20
SIC 5013 Motor vehicle supplies and new parts

D-U-N-S 25-908-6213   (BR)
VALUE VILLAGE STORES, INC
(*Suby of* Savers, Inc.)
595 West St, Brantford, ON, N3R 7C5
(519) 751-4424
Emp Here 30
SIC 5399 Miscellaneous general merchandise

D-U-N-S 20-738-7353   (BR)
WAL-MART CANADA CORP
300 King George Rd Suite 1, Brantford, ON, N3R 5L7
(519) 759-3450
Emp Here 200
SIC 5311 Department stores

D-U-N-S 20-774-5600   (SL)
WAY, G RESTAURANTS SERVICES LTD
BOSTON PIZZA
299 Wayne Gretzky Pky, Brantford, ON, N3R 8A5
(519) 751-2304
Emp Here 75   *Sales* 2,261,782
SIC 5812 Eating places

D-U-N-S 20-641-6310   (SL)
WENDY'S OLD FASHIONED HAMBURGERS
68 King George Rd, Brantford, ON, N3R 5K4

Emp Here 50   *Sales* 1,532,175
SIC 5812 Eating places

D-U-N-S 20-106-2960   (BR)
WINNERS MERCHANTS INTERNATIONAL L.P.
WINNERS
(*Suby of* The TJX Companies Inc)
84 Lynden Rd Suite C15, Brantford, ON, N3R 6B8
(519) 750-0556
Emp Here 26
SIC 5651 Family clothing stores

D-U-N-S 25-297-8093   (BR)
ZEHRMART INC
ZEHRS MARKETS
410 Fairview Dr Suite 1, Brantford, ON, N3R 7V7
(519) 754-4932
Emp Here 150

SIC 5411 Grocery stores

Brantford, ON N3S
Brant County

D-U-N-S 20-360-0098   (SL)
1743088 ONTARIO LTD
46 Adams Blvd, Brantford, ON, N3S 7V2
(519) 752-5900
Emp Here 60   *Sales* 7,879,756
SIC 4953 Refuse systems
Pr Milos Stanisavljevic

D-U-N-S 25-135-4759   (SL)
4460596 CANADA INC
NEO-NUTRITIONALS
87 Sinclair Blvd, Brantford, ON, N3S 7X6
(519) 770-4770
Emp Here 20   *Sales* 2,261,590
SIC 2032 Canned specialties

D-U-N-S 24-805-9565   (BR)
A-LINE ATLANTIC INC
30 Sinclair Blvd, Brantford, ON, N3S 7Y1
(519) 758-1953
Emp Here 45
SIC 5112 Stationery and office supplies

D-U-N-S 24-319-9499   (SL)
ADDISONMCKEE CANADA ULC
ADDITION MANUFACTURING TECHNOLOGIES
333 Henry St Unit B, Brantford, ON, N3S 7R4
(519) 720-6800
Emp Here 22   *Sales* 3,118,504
SIC 3559 Special industry machinery, nec

D-U-N-S 25-882-8250   (BR)
ADIDAS CANADA LIMITED
156 Adams Blvd, Brantford, ON, N3S 7V5
(519) 752-7311
Emp Here 90
SIC 5661 Shoe stores

D-U-N-S 20-360-0093   (BR)
AEVITAS INC
46 Adams Blvd, Brantford, ON, N3S 7V2
(519) 752-5900
Emp Here 60
SIC 4953 Refuse systems

D-U-N-S 24-389-3174   (HQ)
ARYZTA CANADA CO.
115 Sinclair Blvd Suite 1, Brantford, ON, N3S 7X6
(519) 720-2000
Emp Here 300   *Emp Total* 18,733
Sales 106,548,873
SIC 5145 Confectionery
Hilliard Lombard
VP VP Deborah Cochrane
  Culbert Lu
Dir Pat Morrissey
Dir John Yamin
Dir Steve Ricks
Dir Ronan Minahan
  Noel Herterich

D-U-N-S 24-209-4006   (BR)
BELL TECHNICAL SOLUTIONS INC
BELL CANADA
353 Elgin St, Brantford, ON, N3S 7P5
(519) 756-2886
Emp Here 30
SIC 7629 Electrical repair shops

D-U-N-S 25-228-0854   (BR)
BRANT HALDIMAND NORFOLK CATHOLIC DISTRICT SCHOOL BOARD
JEAN VANIER CATHOLIC ELEMENTARY SCHOOL
120 Ninth Ave, Brantford, ON, N3S 1E7
(519) 753-5283
Emp Here 30
SIC 8211 Elementary and secondary schools

D-U-N-S 20-025-0764   (BR)
BRANT HALDIMAND NORFOLK CATHOLIC DISTRICT SCHOOL BOARD
ST MARY'S CATHOLIC LEARNING CENTER
455 Colborne St, Brantford, ON, N3S 3N8
(519) 753-0552
Emp Here 25
SIC 8211 Elementary and secondary schools

D-U-N-S 25-228-0730   (BR)
BRANT HALDIMAND NORFOLK CATHOLIC DISTRICT SCHOOL BOARD
HOLY CROSS ELEMENTARY SCHOOL
358 Marlborough St, Brantford, ON, N3S 4V1
(519) 756-5032
Emp Here 25
SIC 8211 Elementary and secondary schools

D-U-N-S 20-269-0046   (BR)
BRANT INSTORE CORPORATION
BRANT SCREEN CRAFT
254 Henry St, Brantford, ON, N3S 7R5
(519) 759-4361
Emp Here 175
SIC 2759 Commercial printing, nec

D-U-N-S 25-123-8416   (SL)
BRANT WHOLESALE LTD.
112 Grey St, Brantford, ON, N3S 4V9
(519) 756-8010
Emp Here 21   *Sales* 7,101,500
SIC 5148 Fresh fruits and vegetables
Pr Pr Stellio Di Pietro
VP VP Anthony Di Pietro
Dir Brian Eadie
Dir Frank Uvanile

D-U-N-S 20-572-8004   (BR)
CANADA POST CORPORATION
794 Colborne St, Brantford, ON, N3S 3S4
(519) 752-2892
Emp Here 20
SIC 4311 U.s. postal service

D-U-N-S 20-321-8888   (BR)
CARA OPERATIONS LIMITED
HARVEY'S
(*Suby of* Cara Holdings Limited)
218 Henry St Suite 1, Brantford, ON, N3S 0E3
(519) 770-0573
Emp Here 34
SIC 5812 Eating places

D-U-N-S 25-093-2675   (BR)
CASCADES CANADA ULC
CASCADES RECOVERY+
434 Henry St, Brantford, ON, N3S 7W1
(519) 756-5264
Emp Here 100
SIC 4953 Refuse systems

D-U-N-S 25-144-7975   (BR)
COMMUNITY LIVING BRANT
DUNN ENTERPRISES
440 Elgin St, Brantford, ON, N3S 7P7
(519) 753-6303
Emp Here 50
SIC 8322 Individual and family services

D-U-N-S 24-984-9811   (BR)
COONEY TRANSPORT LTD
76 Sinclair Blvd, Brantford, ON, N3S 7Y1
(519) 756-5253
Emp Here 35
SIC 4213 Trucking, except local

D-U-N-S 25-758-2858   (BR)
CORPORATION OF THE CITY OF BRANTFORD, THE
WOODMAN PARK AND RECREATIONAL COMMUNITY CENTRE
(*Suby of* Corporation of the City of Brantford, The)
491 Grey St, Brantford, ON, N3S 7L7
(519) 752-0890
Emp Here 20
SIC 8322 Individual and family services

D-U-N-S 25-991-2202   (BR)
ECONO-RACK GROUP (2015) INC, THE
ENRACK-SYSTEMS DIV OF
132 Adams Blvd, Brantford, ON, N3S 7V2
(519) 753-2227
Emp Here 150
SIC 2542 Partitions and fixtures, except wood

D-U-N-S 25-146-3584   (SL)
EUROTEX NORTH AMERICA INC
122 Middleton St, Brantford, ON, N3S 7V7
(519) 753-5656
Emp Here 50   *Sales* 2,480,664
SIC 2759 Commercial printing, nec

D-U-N-S 24-325-0862   (BR)
EXEL CANADA LTD
225 Henry St Suite 4, Brantford, ON, N3S 7R4
(519) 754-0155
Emp Here 32
SIC 4225 General warehousing and storage

D-U-N-S 20-037-2878   (HQ)
GATES CANADA INC
GATES WINDSOR OPERATIONS, DIV OF
225 Henry St Suite 8, Brantford, ON, N3S 7R4
(519) 759-4141
Emp Here 163   *Sales* 129,140,439
SIC 5085 Industrial supplies
Rahim Suleman

D-U-N-S 24-059-4788   (HQ)
GRAND ERIE DISTRICT SCHOOL BOARD
(*Suby of* Grand Erie District School Board)
349 Erie Ave, Brantford, ON, N3S 2H7
(519) 756-6301
Emp Here 600   *Emp Total* 2,692
Sales 232,284,099
SIC 8211 Elementary and secondary schools
Dir John Forbeck
Treas Jamie Gunn
Rita Collver
Ch Bd Bill Johnston
Don Werden
Jane Angus
V Ch Bd Shari Cann
Carol Ann Sloat
Dir Arlene Everets
Dir Michael Hurley

D-U-N-S 20-784-7927   (BR)
GRAND ERIE DISTRICT SCHOOL BOARD
GRAND ERIE LEARNING ALTERNATIVE
(*Suby of* Grand Erie District School Board)
365 Rawdon St, Brantford, ON, N3S 6J3
(519) 770-1288
Emp Here 20
SIC 8211 Elementary and secondary schools

D-U-N-S 25-238-9218   (BR)
GRAND ERIE DISTRICT SCHOOL BOARD
KING GEORGE ELEMENTARY SCHOOL
(*Suby of* Grand Erie District School Board)
265 Rawdon St, Brantford, ON, N3S 6G7
(519) 752-7486
Emp Here 35
SIC 8211 Elementary and secondary schools

D-U-N-S 25-238-8509   (BR)
GRAND ERIE DISTRICT SCHOOL BOARD
BELLVIEW- JOSEPH BRANT SCHOOL
(*Suby of* Grand Erie District School Board)
97 Tenth Ave, Brantford, ON, N3S 1G5
(519) 752-7414
Emp Here 25
SIC 8211 Elementary and secondary schools

D-U-N-S 25-238-9457   (BR)
GRAND ERIE DISTRICT SCHOOL BOARD
JOHNSON, PAULINE COLLEGIATE VOCATIONAL SCHOOL
(*Suby of* Grand Erie District School Board)
627 Colborne St, Brantford, ON, N3S 3M8
(519) 756-1320
Emp Here 110
SIC 8211 Elementary and secondary schools

D-U-N-S 25-238-9333   (BR)

GRAND ERIE DISTRICT SCHOOL BOARD
MAJOR   BALLACHEY   ELEMENTARY SCHOOL
(*Suby of* Grand Erie District School Board)
105 Rawdon St, Brantford, ON, N3S 6C7
(519) 752-1643
Emp Here 25
SIC 8211 Elementary and secondary schools

D-U-N-S 25-113-5505   (SL)
ITML HOLDINGS INC
75 Plant Farm Blvd, Brantford, ON, N3S 7W2
(519) 753-2666
Emp Here 200   *Sales* 46,869,900
SIC 6712 Bank holding companies
Pr Pr Kees Hensen
VP VP Kleis Hensen

D-U-N-S 20-818-0752   (SL)
LOCKERBIE & HOLE EASTERN INC
451 Elgin St, Brantford, ON, N3S 7P5
(519) 751-8000
Emp Here 30   *Sales* 45,652,500
SIC 3499 Fabricated Metal products, nec
Pr Philip Ward

D-U-N-S 24-352-6261   (BR)
LOWE'S COMPANIES CANADA, ULC
215 Henry St, Brantford, ON, N3S 7R4
(519) 720-2060
Emp Here 50
SIC 5211 Lumber and other building materials

D-U-N-S 24-965-5705   (BR)
MASCO CANADA LIMITED
BRASS CRAFT
(*Suby of* Masco Corporation)
46 Bosworth Crt, Brantford, ON, N3S 7Y3

Emp Here 50
SIC 5074 Plumbing and heating equipment and supplies (hydronics)

D-U-N-S 20-121-0945   (HQ)
MITTEN INC
MITTEN VINYL
(*Suby of* Ply Gem Holdings, Inc.)
225 Henry St Unit 5a, Brantford, ON, N3S 7R4
(519) 805-4701
Emp Here 150   *Emp Total* 8,669
Sales 70,203,511
SIC 3089 Plastics products, nec
Pr Pr Douglas Mitten
VP Opers Gary Ball
Dir Andrew Vann

D-U-N-S 20-259-6631   (BR)
NUTRABLEND FOODS INC
150 Adams Blvd, Brantford, ON, N3S 7V2
(519) 622-2500
Emp Here 100
SIC 3556 Food products machinery

D-U-N-S 25-570-6269   (SL)
O I EMPLOYEE LEASING INC
O I GROUP
188 Mohawk St, Brantford, ON, N3S 2X2
(519) 752-2230
Emp Here 500   *Sales* 29,448,000
SIC 8721 Accounting, auditing, and book-keeping
Dir Ljuba Irwin
Pr Pr Roger Obonsawin

D-U-N-S 25-362-1031   (SL)
R.B.F. HOLDINGS LIMITED
100 Market St S, Brantford, ON, N3S 2E5
(519) 759-8220
Emp Here 45   *Sales* 6,832,640
SIC 6712 Bank holding companies
Dir Robert Forbes

D-U-N-S 25-365-1947   (BR)
REVOLUTION ENVIRONMENTAL SOLUTIONS LP
TERRAPURE ENVIRONMENTAL
(*Suby of* Revolution Environmental Solutions LP)

112 Adams Blvd, Brantford, ON, N3S 7V2
(519) 756-9770
Emp Here 20
SIC 4953 Refuse systems

D-U-N-S 20-965-4305   (HQ)
SCP DISTRIBUTORS CANADA INC
373 Elgin St, Brantford, ON, N3S 7P5
(519) 720-9219
Emp Here 20   *Emp Total* 100
Sales 11,381,869
SIC 5091 Sporting and recreation goods
Genl Mgr Brent Milburn
Rgnl Mgr John Bliszczuk

D-U-N-S 24-845-8085   (BR)
SAFETY-KLEEN CANADA INC.
SAFETY-KLEEN SYSTEMS
60 Bury Crt, Brantford, ON, N3S 0B1
(519) 750-7910
Emp Here 30
SIC 4953 Refuse systems

D-U-N-S 24-027-2047   (BR)
SAMUEL, SON & CO., LIMITED
SAMUEL METAL BLANKING
546 Elgin St, Brantford, ON, N3S 7P8
(519) 758-2710
Emp Here 85
SIC 5051 Metals service centers and offices

D-U-N-S 24-074-8426   (BR)
SERVICES FINANCIERS NCO, INC
NCO GROUP
(*Suby of* Egs Shell Company, Inc.)
33 Sinclair Blvd Unit 4, Brantford, ON, N3S 7X6
(519) 750-6000
Emp Here 700
SIC 7322 Adjustment and collection services

D-U-N-S 24-805-1075   (BR)
SHERWIN-WILLIAMS CANADA INC
BECKER ACROMA
(*Suby of* The Sherwin-Williams Company)
140 Garden Ave, Brantford, ON, N3S 7W4
(519) 758-1508
Emp Here 50
SIC 2851 Paints and allied products

D-U-N-S 20-290-1703   (BR)
SOBEYS CAPITAL INCORPORATED
BRANTFORD PRICE CHOPPER
655 Colborne St, Brantford, ON, N3S 3M8

Emp Here 50
SIC 5411 Grocery stores

D-U-N-S 24-889-6516   (BR)
SOBEYS CAPITAL INCORPORATED
CALBECK'S SUPERMARKET
655 Colborne St, Brantford, ON, N3S 3M8

Emp Here 50
SIC 5411 Grocery stores

D-U-N-S 20-119-7394   (HQ)
SONOCO CANADA CORPORATION
ROLL PACKAGING TECHNOLOGY
(*Suby of* Sonoco Products Company)
33 Park Ave E, Brantford, ON, N3S 7R9
(905) 823-7910
Emp Here 80   *Emp Total* 20,400
Sales 52,677,625
SIC 2655 Fiber cans, drums, and similar products
Dir Fin David Baxter
Pr Jack Sanders

D-U-N-S 25-283-8909   (SL)
STONE STRAW LIMITED
72 Plant Farm Blvd, Brantford, ON, N3S 7W3
(519) 756-1974
Emp Here 60
SIC 2656 Sanitary food containers

D-U-N-S 20-982-6775   (SL)
TEKSIGN INC

(Suby of Teksign Holdings Inc)
86 Plant Farm Blvd, Brantford, ON, N3S 7W3
(519) 756-1089
Emp Here 70   Sales 4,231,721
SIC 3993 Signs and advertising specialties

D-U-N-S 25-140-5015   (BR)
UNITED PARCEL SERVICE CANADA LTD
UPS
20 Ryan Pl, Brantford, ON, N3S 7S1
(519) 751-0981
Emp Here 46
SIC 7389 Business services, nec

D-U-N-S 24-174-2787   (BR)
WENDCORP HOLDINGS INC
WENDYS RESTAURANTS
78 Icomm Dr, Brantford, ON, N3S 2X5
(519) 753-7708
Emp Here 30
SIC 5812 Eating places

D-U-N-S 20-920-1917   (SL)
WENTWORTH MOLD LTD
BLOW MOLD GROUP
156 Adams Blvd, Brantford, ON, N3S 7V5
(519) 754-5400
Emp Here 95   Sales 10,433,380
SIC 2821 Plastics materials and resins
Pr Pr Walter T Kuskowski
Treas Jeffrey Barclay

D-U-N-S 25-367-4824   (BR)
WISMER DEVELOPMENTS INC
PILLERS FINE FOODS
38 Middletcn St, Brantford, ON, N3S 7V7
(519) 757-C663
Emp Here 20
SIC 5147 Meats and meat products

D-U-N-S 24-790-3748   (BR)
**YMCA   OF   HAMIL-
TON/BURLINGTON/BRANTFORD**
BRANTFORD YMCA FAMILY PROGRAM
143 Wellington St, Brantford, ON, N3S 3Y8
(519) 752-6568
Emp Here 25
SIC 8351 Child day care services

Brantford, ON N3T
Brant County

D-U-N-S 20-984-0537   (HQ)
APOTEX PHARMACHEM INC
34 Spalding Dr, Brantford, ON, N3T 6B8
(519) 756-8942
Emp Here 385   Emp Total 5,000
Sales 38,742,132
SIC 2834 Pharmaceutical preparations
Keshava Murthy
James Berhalter
VP Opers Darren Hall
VP Stephen Horne
Pers/VP Peter Morris
S&M/VP Ramandeep Singh Bagga
VP Ed Carey
VP VP Pere Paton

D-U-N-S 24-850-1897   (BR)
APOTEX PHARMACHEM INC
34 Spalding Dr, Brantford, ON, N3T 6B8
(519) 756-8942
Emp Here 440
SIC 2834 Pharmaceutical preparations

D-U-N-S 25-296-7617   (BR)
BANK OF NOVA SCOTIA, THE
SCOTIABANK
170 Colborne St, Brantford, ON, N3T 2G6
(519) 751-5000
Emp Here 25
SIC 6021 National commercial banks

D-U-N-S 25-042-1153   (SL)
BANNESTER, DR LESLIE R

AVENUE MEDICAL CENTRE
221 Brant Ave Suite 1, Brantford, ON, N3T 3J2
(519) 753-8666
Emp Here 80   Sales 4,815,406
SIC 8011 Offices and clinics of medical doctors

D-U-N-S 20-245-7078   (BR)
BANQUE TORONTO-DOMINION, LA
TORONTO-DOMINION BANK, THE
(Suby of Toronto-Dominion Bank, The)
70 Market St, Brantford, ON, N3T 2Z7
(519) 759-5679
Emp Here 40
SIC 6021 National commercial banks

D-U-N-S 24-304-2330   (SL)
BRANT FOOD CENTER LTD
94 Grey St, Brantford, ON, N3T 2T5
(519) 756-8002
Emp Here 50   Sales 4,304,681
SIC 5431 Fruit and vegetable markets

D-U-N-S 25-228-0847   (BR)
**BRANT HALDIMAND NORFOLK CATHOLIC
DISTRICT SCHOOL BOARD**
ST THERESA ELEMENTARY SCHOOL
12 Dalewood Ave, Brantford, ON, N3T 0M5
(519) 753-8953
Emp Here 27
SIC 8211 Elementary and secondary schools

D-U-N-S 24-227-7833   (BR)
**BRANT HALDIMAND NORFOLK CATHOLIC
DISTRICT SCHOOL BOARD**
ASSUMPTION COLLEGE SCHOOL
257 Shellard'S Lane, Brantford, ON, N3T 5L5
(519) 751-2030
Emp Here 135
SIC 8211 Elementary and secondary schools

D-U-N-S 20-291-6610   (BR)
**BRANT HALDIMAND NORFOLK CATHOLIC
DISTRICT SCHOOL BOARD**
ASSUMPTION COLLAGE SCHOOL
257 Shellard'S Lane, Brantford, ON, N3T 5L5
(519) 751-2030
Emp Here 115
SIC 8211 Elementary and secondary schools

D-U-N-S 20-710-6514   (BR)
**BRANT HALDIMAND NORFOLK CATHOLIC
DISTRICT SCHOOL BOARD**
ST GABRIEL SCHOOL
14 Flanders Dr, Brantford, ON, N3T 6M2
(519) 756-4706
Emp Here 31
SIC 8211 Elementary and secondary schools

D-U-N-S 25-228-0722   (BR)
**BRANT HALDIMAND NORFOLK CATHOLIC
DISTRICT SCHOOL BOARD**
CHRIST THE KING ELEMENTARY SCHOOL
165 Dufferin Ave, Brantford, ON, N3T 4R4
(519) 759-4211
Emp Here 20
SIC 8211 Elementary and secondary schools

D-U-N-S 20-816-8310   (SL)
**BRANTFORD GOLF AND COUNTRY CLUB,
LIMITED**
60 Ava Rd, Brantford, ON, N3T 5H2
(519) 752-3731
Emp Here 70   Sales 3,956,550
SIC 7997 Membership sports and recreation clubs

D-U-N-S 20-943-3259   (HQ)
BRANTFORD PUBLIC LIBRARY BOARD
(Suby of Brantford Public Library Board)
173 Colborne St, Brantford, ON, N3T 2G8
(519) 756-2220
Emp Here 69   Emp Total 70
Sales 3,210,271
SIC 8231 Libraries

D-U-N-S 24-615-2768   (BR)
CAMBRIDGE PRO FAB INC

84 Shaver Rd, Brantford, ON, N3T 5M1
(519) 751-4351
Emp Here 40
SIC 4911 Electric services

D-U-N-S 25-369-9649   (BR)
CANADA POST CORPORATION
58 Dalhousie St, Brantford, ON, N3T 2J2
(519) 752-2505
Emp Here 100
SIC 4311 U.s. postal service

D-U-N-S 20-406-2582   (SL)
**CITY   CAB   (BRANTFORD-DARLING
STREET) LIMITED**
CITY TAXI
40 Dalhousie St, Brantford, ON, N3T 2H8
(519) 759-7800
Emp Here 75   Sales 2,261,782
SIC 4121 Taxicabs

D-U-N-S 24-313-4207   (BR)
CONCEPT PLASTICS LIMITED
(Suby of Indus Limited)
27 Catharine Ave, Brantford, ON, N3T 1X5
(519) 759-1900
Emp Here 40
SIC 3089 Plastics products, nec

D-U-N-S 24-888-6566   (HQ)
CONCEPT PLASTICS LIMITED
(Suby of Indus Limited)
27 Catharine Ave, Brantford, ON, N3T 1X5
(905) 670-2124
Emp Here 40   Emp Total 150
Sales 13,253,640
SIC 3089 Plastics products, nec
Pr Pr Kiran Kulkarni

D-U-N-S 25-835-1873   (BR)
**CORPORATION OF THE CITY OF BRANT-
FORD, THE**
*SANDERSON CENTRE FOR THE PER-
FORMING ARTS*
(Suby of Corporation of the City of Brantford,
The)
88 Dalhousie St, Brantford, ON, N3T 2J2
(519) 752-9910
Emp Here 50
SIC 7922 Theatrical producers and services

D-U-N-S 24-787-4204   (BR)
**CORPORATION OF THE CITY OF BRANT-
FORD, THE**
BRANTFORD MUNICIPAL AIRPORT
(Suby of Corporation of the City of Brantford,
The)
110 Aviation Ave, Brantford, ON, N3T 5L7
(519) 753-2521
Emp Here 50
SIC 4581 Airports, flying fields, and services

D-U-N-S 24-779-1163   (BR)
DELHI INDUSTRIES INC
(Suby of Delhi Industries Inc)
83 Shaver Rd, Brantford, ON, N3T 5M1

Emp Here 30
SIC 3564 Blowers and fans

D-U-N-S 24-241-9732   (BR)
**DIVERSICARE CANADA MANAGEMENT
SERVICES CO., INC**
HARDY TERRACE LTC
612 Mount Pleasant Rd, Brantford, ON, N3T
5L5
(519) 484-2500
Emp Here 130
SIC 8051 Skilled nursing care facilities

D-U-N-S 20-272-9513   (BR)
**DIVERSICARE CANADA MANAGEMENT
SERVICES CO., INC**
*HARDY TERRACE LONG-TERM CARE FA-
CILITY*
612 Mount Pleasant Rd, Brantford, ON, N3T
5L5

(519) 484-2431
Emp Here 100
SIC 8051 Skilled nursing care facilities

D-U-N-S 25-255-9000   (SL)
**DOWNIE, THOMPSON MEDICINE PROFES-
SIONAL CORPORATION**
AVENUE MEDICAL CENTRE
221 Brant Ave Suite 1, Brantford, ON, N3T 3J2
(519) 753-8666
Emp Here 50   Sales 2,991,389
SIC 8011 Offices and clinics of medical doctors

D-U-N-S 20-270-0910   (BR)
EMERSON ELECTRIC CANADA LIMITED
ASCO NUMATICS
(Suby of Emerson Electric Co.)
17 Airport Rd, Brantford, ON, N3T 5M8
(519) 758-2700
Emp Here 105
SIC 3492 Fluid power valves and hose fittings

D-U-N-S 24-846-4703   (BR)
EMERSON ELECTRIC CANADA LIMITED
EMERSON CLIMATE TECHNOLOGIES
(Suby of Emerson Electric Co.)
145 Sherwood Dr, Brantford, ON, N3T 1N8
(519) 756-6157
Emp Here 60
SIC 3585 Refrigeration and heating equipment

D-U-N-S 20-107-4114   (BR)
EMERSON ELECTRIC CANADA LIMITED
*ASCO POWER TECHNOLOGIES CANADA,
DIV OF*
(Suby of Emerson Electric Co.)
17 Airport Rd, Brantford, ON, N3T 5L7
(519) 758-8450
Emp Here 22
SIC 3625 Relays and industrial controls

D-U-N-S 20-624-9419   (HQ)
EXTEND COMMUNICATIONS INC
YOUR TELEPHONE SECRETARY
(Suby of Extend Communications Inc)
49 Charlotte St, Brantford, ON, N3T 2W4
(416) 534-0477
Emp Here 24   Emp Total 65
Sales 3,283,232
SIC 7389 Business services, nec

D-U-N-S 25-496-2459   (BR)
GRAND ERIE DISTRICT SCHOOL BOARD
*BRANTFORD COLLEGIATE & VOCATIONAL
INSTITUTE*
(Suby of Grand Erie District School Board)
120 Brant Ave, Brantford, ON, N3T 3H3

Emp Here 100
SIC 8222 Junior colleges

D-U-N-S 20-007-1673   (BR)
GRAND ERIE DISTRICT SCHOOL BOARD
RIVERVIEW SCHOOL
(Suby of Grand Erie District School Board)
10 Wade Ave, Brantford, ON, N3T 1W7

Emp Here 20
SIC 8211 Elementary and secondary schools

D-U-N-S 25-238-8301   (BR)
GRAND ERIE DISTRICT SCHOOL BOARD
LANSDOWNE ELEMENTARY SCHOOL
(Suby of Grand Erie District School Board)
21 Preston Blvd, Brantford, ON, N3T 5B1
(519) 753-0390
Emp Here 25
SIC 8211 Elementary and secondary schools

D-U-N-S 25-238-9416   (BR)
GRAND ERIE DISTRICT SCHOOL BOARD
*ONONDAGA-BRANT   ELEMENTARY
SCHOOL*
(Suby of Grand Erie District School Board)
21 Brant School Rd, Brantford, ON, N3T 5L4
(519) 753-8885
Emp Here 20

SIC 8211 Elementary and secondary schools

D-U-N-S 25-238-8541   (BR)
GRAND ERIE DISTRICT SCHOOL BOARD
ANGES G HODGE ELEMENTARY SCHOOL
(*Suby of* Grand Erie District School Board)
52 Clench Ave, Brantford, ON, N3T 1B6
(519) 756-4950
Emp Here 35
SIC 8211 Elementary and secondary schools

D-U-N-S 24-315-7281   (BR)
HARRIS STEEL GROUP INC
LEC STEEL
(*Suby of* Nucor Corporation)
84 Shaver Rd, Brantford, ON, N3T 5M1

Emp Here 45
SIC 3315 Steel wire and related products

D-U-N-S 20-180-7711   (SL)
HARTMANN DOMINION INC
HARTMANN NORTH AMERICA
58 Frank St, Brantford, ON, N3T 5E2
(519) 756-8500
Emp Here 257   *Sales* 56,932,800
SIC 3086 Plastics foam products
Pr Ash Sahi
Dir Per Vinge Frederiksen
Dir Michael Hedegaard Lyng

D-U-N-S 25-375-2596   (BR)
INGENIA POLYMERS CORP
565 Greenwich St, Brantford, ON, N3T 5M8
(519) 758-8941
Emp Here 100
SIC 2821 Plastics materials and resins

D-U-N-S 24-525-5732   (BR)
KPM INDUSTRIES LTD
KING PACKAGED MATERIALS
541 Oak Park Rd, Brantford, ON, N3T 5L8
(519) 756-6177
Emp Here 25
SIC 3272 Concrete products, nec

D-U-N-S 20-037-1052   (BR)
MAPLE LEAF FOODS INC
10 Canning St, Brantford, ON, N3T 1P1
(519) 759-4751
Emp Here 220
SIC 2033 Canned fruits and specialties

D-U-N-S 20-818-2303   (HQ)
MILLARD, ROUSE & ROSEBRUGH LLP
(*Suby of* Millard, Rouse & Rosebrugh LLP)
96 Nelson St, Brantford, ON, N3T 2N1
(519) 759-3511
Emp Here 65   *Emp Total* 100
Sales 4,377,642
SIC 8721 Accounting, auditing, and book-keeping

D-U-N-S 25-368-5937   (BR)
MITTEN INC
(*Suby of* Ply Gem Holdings, Inc.)
85 Morrell St, Brantford, ON, N3T 4J6
(519) 753-0007
Emp Here 55
SIC 4225 General warehousing and storage

D-U-N-S 20-552-6242   (BR)
OC CANADA HOLDINGS COMPANY
OWENS CORNING SOLUTIONS GROUP
11 Spalding Dr, Brantford, ON, N3T 6B7
(519) 752-5436
Emp Here 75
SIC 3296 Mineral wool

D-U-N-S 25-481-1748   (BR)
PRISZM LP
KFC
27 Dalhousie St, Brantford, ON, N3T 2H6
(519) 753-4623
Emp Here 20
SIC 5812 Eating places

D-U-N-S 25-320-9191   (BR)
PUROLATOR INC.

PUROLATOR INC
769 Powerline Rd, Brantford, ON, N3T 5L8
(519) 754-4463
Emp Here 30
SIC 4731 Freight transportation arrangement

D-U-N-S 25-018-9941   (BR)
ROYAL BANK OF CANADA
RBC
(*Suby of* Royal Bank Of Canada)
22 Colborne St Suite 522, Brantford, ON, N3T 2G2
(519) 758-2056
Emp Here 22
SIC 6021 National commercial banks

D-U-N-S 20-037-4171   (HQ)
S.C. JOHNSON AND SON, LIMITED
1 Webster St, Brantford, ON, N3T 5A3
(519) 756-7900
Emp Here 350   *Sales* 48,510,056
SIC 2842 Polishes and sanitation goods
Pr Chris Moeller
Sec Kristin Hietpas
Dir Stephen L. Rose
Dir Jay E Gueldner

D-U-N-S 20-595-2682   (HQ)
SHARP BUS LINES LIMITED
(*Suby of* 608705 Ontario Limited)
567 Oak Park Rd, Brantford, ON, N3T 5L8
(519) 751-3434
Emp Here 150   *Emp Total* 2
Sales 49,784,038
SIC 4151 School buses
Pr John Sharp
   William Sharp
   Donald Sharp
   Mary Sharp

D-U-N-S 20-113-9578   (BR)
STERLING PACKERS LIMITED
CONFEDERATION FREEZERS
21 York Rd, Brantford, ON, N3T 6H2
(519) 752-1177
Emp Here 40
SIC 4222 Refrigerated warehousing and storage

D-U-N-S 20-304-6263   (BR)
T.F. WARREN GROUP INC
BLASTECH
57 Old Onondaga Rd W, Brantford, ON, N3T 5M1
(519) 756-8222
Emp Here 75
SIC 5169 Chemicals and allied products, nec

D-U-N-S 20-700-0048   (BR)
TRIPLE M METAL LP
BRANTFORD METALS DISPOSAL
144 Mohawk Rd, Brantford, ON, N3T 5L9
(519) 752-4351
Emp Here 20
SIC 5093 Scrap and waste materials

D-U-N-S 20-288-5567   (BR)
WASTE CONNECTIONS OF CANADA INC
BFI CANADA
779 Powerline Rd, Brantford, ON, N3T 5L8
(519) 759-4370
Emp Here 30
SIC 4953 Refuse systems

D-U-N-S 20-049-2978   (BR)
WILFRID LAURIER UNIVERSITY
73 George St, Brantford, ON, N3T 2Y3
(519) 756-8228
Emp Here 25
SIC 8221 Colleges and universities

D-U-N-S 24-348-1202   (BR)
WOODVIEW CHILDREN'S CENTRE
WOODVIEW CHILDREN'S MENTAL HEALTH AND AUTISM SERVICES
233 Colborne St Suite 200, Brantford, ON, N3T 2H4
(519) 752-5308
Emp Here 25

SIC 8069 Specialty hospitals, except psychiatric

Brantford, ON N3V
Brant County

D-U-N-S 20-703-1357   (BR)
FERRERO CANADA LIMITED
1 Ferrero Blvd, Brantford, ON, N3V 1G3
(519) 756-6205
Emp Here 20
SIC 2064 Candy and other confectionery products

D-U-N-S 25-365-8033   (BR)
PROCTER & GAMBLE INC
(*Suby of* The Procter & Gamble Company)
59 Fen Ridge Crt, Brantford, ON, N3V 1G2
(519) 720-1200
Emp Here 20
SIC 2841 Soap and other detergents

D-U-N-S 20-565-8565   (SL)
WESTERN WAFFLES CORP
WESTERN WAFFLES
(*Suby of* Conagra Brands, Inc.)
175 Savannah Oaks Dr, Brantford, ON, N3V 1E8
(519) 759-2025
Emp Here 400   *Sales* 37,693,160
SIC 2038 Frozen specialties, nec
Dir Opers Tom Carle
Mfg Mgr Warren Feerer
Dir Kevin Aksherbabher

Brechin, ON L0K

D-U-N-S 25-364-3647   (BR)
CRH CANADA GROUP INC
DUFFERIN AGGREGATES
2671 Simcoe St, Brechin, ON, L0K 1B0
(705) 484-0073
Emp Here 40
SIC 1422 Crushed and broken limestone

D-U-N-S 24-728-4227   (BR)
LAFARGE CANADA INC
2080 Concession Rd 2, Brechin, ON, L0K 1B0
(705) 484-5881
Emp Here 27
SIC 5032 Brick, stone, and related material

D-U-N-S 20-707-3367   (BR)
MILLER PAVING LIMITED
MILLER AGGREGATE RESOURCES
356 Millers Rd, Brechin, ON, L0K 1B0
(705) 484-0195
Emp Here 20
SIC 1611 Highway and street construction

D-U-N-S 25-297-6600   (BR)
SIMCOE COUNTY DISTRICT SCHOOL BOARD, THE
BRECHIN PUBLIC SCHOOL
(*Suby of* Simcoe County District School Board, The)
3226 County Rd 47 Suite 1, Brechin, ON, L0K 1B0
(705) 484-5711
Emp Here 23
SIC 8211 Elementary and secondary schools

Breslau, ON N0B
Waterloo County

D-U-N-S 24-424-2418   (HQ)
CONESTOGA MEAT PACKERS LTD
CONESTOGA MEATS
313 Menno St, Breslau, ON, N0B 1M0

(519) 648-2506
Emp Here 807   *Emp Total* 250
Sales 225,242,100
SIC 5147 Meats and meat products
Pr Arnold Drung
VP Fin Tony Millington

D-U-N-S 24-770-5486   (SL)
CORPORATION OF ST. JOHN'S-KILMARNOCK SCHOOL
2201 Shantz Station Rd, Breslau, ON, N0B 1M0
(519) 648-2183
Emp Here 60   *Sales* 4,012,839
SIC 8211 Elementary and secondary schools

D-U-N-S 20-037-8925   (HQ)
GEORGE AND ASMUSSEN LIMITED
G A MASONRY
5093 Fountain St N, Breslau, ON, N0B 1M0
(519) 648-2285
Emp Here 75   *Emp Total* 25
Sales 13,663,771
SIC 1741 Masonry and other stonework
Pr Pr Eugene George
   Patrick George
Dir Ian Letford

D-U-N-S 24-285-2895   (HQ)
KITCHENER AERO AVIONICS LIMITED
MID-CANADA MOD CENTER
(*Suby of* Kitchener Aero Avionics Limited)
4881 Fountain St Suite 6, Breslau, ON, N0B 1M0
(519) 648-2921
Emp Here 50   *Emp Total* 80
Sales 3,137,310
SIC 7629 Electrical repair shops

D-U-N-S 20-751-2666   (HQ)
SAFETY-KLEEN CANADA INC.
300 Woolwich St S Rr 2, Breslau, ON, N0B 1M0
(519) 648-2291
Emp Here 100   *Emp Total* 12,400
Sales 291,926,587
SIC 2992 Lubricating oils and greases
   Dale Macintyre
Manager Rainer Malcharek

D-U-N-S 25-228-1290   (BR)
WATERLOO REGION DISTRICT SCHOOL BOARD
BRESLAU ELEMENTARY SCHOOL
58 Joseph St Rr 2, Breslau, ON, N0B 1M0
(519) 648-2242
Emp Here 28
SIC 8211 Elementary and secondary schools

Bridgenorth, ON K0L
Peterborough County

D-U-N-S 25-263-5669   (BR)
KAWARTHA PINE RIDGE DISTRICT SCHOOL BOARD
CHEMONG PUBLIC SCHOOL
1029 Gore St, Bridgenorth, ON, K0L 1H0
(705) 292-9594
Emp Here 40
SIC 8211 Elementary and secondary schools

D-U-N-S 20-711-6067   (BR)
PETERBOROUGH VICTORIA NORTHUMBERLAND AND CLARINGTON CATHOLIC DISTRICT SCHOOL BOARD
ST. JOSEPH CATHOLIC ELEMENTARY SCHOOL
405 4th Line, Bridgenorth, ON, K0L 1H0
(705) 652-3961
Emp Here 20
SIC 8211 Elementary and secondary schools

Brigden, ON N0N
Lambton County

D-U-N-S 24-198-7747   (BR)
CORPORATION OF THE TOWNSHIP OF ST. CLAIR, THE
BRIGDEN VOLUNTEER FIRE HALL
1561 First St Ss 1, Brigden, ON, N0N 1B0
(519) 864-1290
Emp Here 30
SIC 7389 Business services, nec

D-U-N-S 25-238-6719   (BR)
LAMBTON KENT DISTRICT SCHOOL BOARD
BRIGDEN PUBLIC SCHOOL
1540 Duncan St Ss 1 Suite 1, Brigden, ON, N0N 1B0
(519) 864-1125
Emp Here 20
SIC 8211 Elementary and secondary schools

D-U-N-S 24-376-4789   (SL)
ST. CLAIR MECHANICAL INC
2963 Brigden Rd Suite 1, Brigden, ON, N0N 1B0
(519) 864-0927
Emp Here 75   *Sales* 9,120,088
SIC 3498 Fabricated pipe and fittings
Pr Pr John Dawson
VP VP Tracy Dawson

Bright'S Grove, ON N0N
Lambton County

D-U-N-S 20-710-4592   (BR)
LAMBTON KENT DISTRICT SCHOOL BOARD
BRIGHT'S GROVE ELEMENTARY SCHOOL
2612 Hamilton Rd, Bright'S Grove, ON, N0N 1C0
(519) 869-4284
Emp Here 28
SIC 8211 Elementary and secondary schools

D-U-N-S 25-249-3739   (BR)
ST. CLAIR CATHOLIC DISTRICT SCHOOL BOARD
ST MICHAEL SCHOOL
(*Suby of* St. Clair Catholic District School Board)
1930 Wildwood Dr, Bright'S Grove, ON, N0N 1C0
(519) 869-4204
Emp Here 35

Brighton, ON K0K

D-U-N-S 20-264-3219   (BR)
AGRIUM ADVANCED TECHNOLOGIES INC
(*Suby of* Agrium Canada Partnership)
10 Loyalist Dr, Brighton, ON, K0K 1H0
(613) 475-1262
Emp Here 30
SIC 2879 Agricultural chemicals, nec

D-U-N-S 25-360-7287   (BR)
DI CANADA INC
DRESSER WAYNE
(*Suby of* General Electric Company)
40 Sharpe Rd, Brighton, ON, K0K 1H0
(613) 475-3313
Emp Here 26
SIC 3569 General industrial machinery, nec

D-U-N-S 25-237-9367   (BR)
KAWARTHA PINE RIDGE DISTRICT SCHOOL BOARD
SPRING VALLEY PUBLIC SCHOOL
212 County Rd Suite 26, Brighton, ON, K0K 1H0

(613) 475-2578
Emp Here 28
SIC 8211 Elementary and secondary schools

D-U-N-S 25-237-9896   (BR)
KAWARTHA PINE RIDGE DISTRICT SCHOOL BOARD
BRIGHTON PUBLIC SCHOOL
24 Elizabeth St, Brighton, ON, K0K 1H0
(613) 475-2814
Emp Here 30
SIC 8211 Elementary and secondary schools

D-U-N-S 20-711-5853   (BR)
KAWARTHA PINE RIDGE DISTRICT SCHOOL BOARD
SMITHFIELD PUBLIC SCHOOL
2 Drewry St, Brighton, ON, K0K 1H0
(613) 475-2301
Emp Here 50
SIC 8211 Elementary and secondary schools

D-U-N-S 25-237-9516   (BR)
KAWARTHA PINE RIDGE DISTRICT SCHOOL BOARD
EAST NORTHUMBERLAND SECONDARY SCHOOL
71 Dundas St, Brighton, ON, K0K 1H0
(613) 475-0540
Emp Here 120
SIC 8211 Elementary and secondary schools

D-U-N-S 25-001-5492   (BR)
OMNI HEALTH CARE LTD
MAPLEWOOD, DIV OF
12 Applewood Dr, Brighton, ON, K0K 1H0
(613) 475-2442
Emp Here 60
SIC 8051 Skilled nursing care facilities

D-U-N-S 20-251-5698   (BR)
PREMIER TECH BRIGHTON LTD
4 Craig Blvd, Brighton, ON, K0K 1H0
(613) 475-1262
Emp Here 30
SIC 2873 Nitrogenous fertilizers

Brockville, ON K6V
Leeds County

D-U-N-S 25-540-8692   (BR)
3M CANADA COMPANY
(*Suby of* 3M Company)
1360 California Ave, Brockville, ON, K6V 5V8
(613) 345-0111
Emp Here 100
SIC 2891 Adhesives and sealants

D-U-N-S 20-267-9416   (BR)
3M CANADA COMPANY
(*Suby of* 3M Company)
60 California Ave, Brockville, ON, K6V 7N5
(613) 498-5900
Emp Here 180
SIC 2672 Paper; coated and laminated, nec

D-U-N-S 25-305-1932   (BR)
BANK OF NOVA SCOTIA, THE
SCOTIABANK
7 King St W, Brockville, ON, K6V 3P7
(613) 342-0140
Emp Here 25
SIC 6021 National commercial banks

D-U-N-S 25-590-7719   (BR)
BELL MEDIA INC
CFJR-CJPT, DIVISION OF
601 Stuart Blvd, Brockville, ON, K6V 5V9
(613) 345-1666
Emp Here 30
SIC 4832 Radio broadcasting stations

D-U-N-S 24-784-1398   (BR)
BLACK & DECKER CANADA INC
STANLEY BLACK & DECKER CANADA
100 Central Ave W, Brockville, ON, K6V 4N8

(613) 342-6641
Emp Here 21
SIC 5084 Industrial machinery and equipment

D-U-N-S 25-459-5770   (SL)
BROCKVILLE & DISTRICT ASSOCIATION FOR COMMUNITY INVOLVEMENT
2495 Parkedale Ave Unit 4, Brockville, ON, K6V 3H2
(613) 345-4092
Emp Here 60   *Sales* 3,939,878
SIC 8093 Specialty outpatient clinics, nec

D-U-N-S 20-771-3384   (BR)
BROCKVILLE AREA CENTRE FOR DEVELOPMENTALLY HANDICAPPED PERSONS INC
DEVELOPMENTAL SERVICES OF LEEDS AND GRENVILLE
61 King St E, Brockville, ON, K6V 1B2
(613) 345-1290
Emp Here 80
SIC 8322 Individual and family services

D-U-N-S 20-286-2470   (BR)
BROCKVILLE GENERAL HOSPITAL
42 Garden St, Brockville, ON, K6V 2C3
(613) 345-5645
Emp Here 350
SIC 8062 General medical and surgical hospitals

D-U-N-S 25-921-0433   (SL)
BROCKVILLE POLICE ASSOCIATION
2269 Parkedale Ave W, Brockville, ON, K6V 3G9
(613) 342-0127
Emp Here 75   *Sales* 7,952,716
SIC 8631 Labor organizations
Pr Tom Nappo

D-U-N-S 20-572-7360   (BR)
CANADA POST CORPORATION
2399 Parkedale Ave, Brockville, ON, K6V 3G9
(613) 342-6701
Emp Here 20
SIC 4311 U.s. postal service

D-U-N-S 25-303-3583   (BR)
CANADIAN IMPERIAL BANK OF COMMERCE
CIBC
98 King St W, Brockville, ON, K6V 3P9
(613) 342-6651
Emp Here 21
SIC 6021 National commercial banks

D-U-N-S 20-087-1882   (BR)
CANADIAN RED CROSS SOCIETY, THE
80 Charles St, Brockville, ON, K6V 1T3
(613) 342-3523
Emp Here 175
SIC 8322 Individual and family services

D-U-N-S 24-342-7981   (BR)
CARA OPERATIONS LIMITED
HARVEY'S
(*Suby of* Cara Holdings Limited)
358 Stewart Blvd, Brockville, ON, K6V 4X1
(613) 498-1465
Emp Here 30
SIC 5812 Eating places

D-U-N-S 25-402-1058   (BR)
CATHOLIC DISTRICT SCHOOL BOARD OF EASTERN ONTARIO
ST JOHN BOSCO SCHOOL
(*Suby of* Catholic District School Board of Eastern Ontario)
12 Durham St, Brockville, ON, K6V 7A4
(613) 342-1479
Emp Here 38
SIC 8211 Elementary and secondary schools

D-U-N-S 20-026-6562   (BR)
CATHOLIC DISTRICT SCHOOL BOARD OF EASTERN ONTARIO
J.L. JORDAN CATHOLIC SCHOOL
294 First Ave, Brockville, ON, K6V 3B7

(613) 342-7711
Emp Here 20
SIC 8211 Elementary and secondary schools

D-U-N-S 25-237-9631   (BR)
CATHOLIC DISTRICT SCHOOL BOARD OF EASTERN ONTARIO
ST FRANCIS XAVIER SCHOOL
(*Suby of* Catholic District School Board of Eastern Ontario)
74 Church St, Brockville, ON, K6V 3X6
(613) 342-0510
Emp Here 25
SIC 8211 Elementary and secondary schools

D-U-N-S 20-913-5586   (BR)
CATHOLIC DISTRICT SCHOOL BOARD OF EASTERN ONTARIO
ST MARY CATHOLIC HIGH SCHOOL
40 Central Ave W, Brockville, ON, K6V 4N5
(613) 342-4911
Emp Here 90
SIC 8211 Elementary and secondary schools

D-U-N-S 25-572-1813   (BR)
CHARTWELL SENIORS HOUSING REAL ESTATE INVESTMENT TRUST
ROSEDALE RETIREMENT CENTRE
1813 County Rd 2 E, Brockville, ON, K6V 5T1
(613) 342-0200
Emp Here 25
SIC 8322 Individual and family services

D-U-N-S 24-120-5991   (SL)
CHEVRON CONSTRUCTION SERVICES LTD
4475 County 15 Rd, Brockville, ON, K6V 5T2
(613) 926-0690
Emp Here 35   *Sales* 6,931,267
SIC 1541 Industrial buildings and warehouses
Pr Pr David Vaughan
James Annable
Dir Darren Ross

D-U-N-S 24-418-2726   (BR)
CINEPLEX ODEON CORPORATION
GALAXY CINEMAS BROCKVILLE
2399 Parkedale Ave, Brockville, ON, K6V 3G9
(613) 498-2217
Emp Here 20
SIC 7832 Motion picture theaters, except drive-in

D-U-N-S 24-119-3668   (BR)
COMPAGNIE DES CHEMINS DE FER NATIONAUX DU CANADA
135 Perth St, Brockville, ON, K6V 5Y6
(613) 498-3018
Emp Here 50
SIC 4111 Local and suburban transit

D-U-N-S 25-753-1764   (BR)
CONSEIL DES ECOLES CATHOLIQUES DE LANGUE FRANCAISE DU CENTRE-EST
ACADEMIE ANGE GABRIEL
1515 Kensington Pky, Brockville, ON, K6V 6H9
(613) 345-5914
Emp Here 25
SIC 8211 Elementary and secondary schools

D-U-N-S 20-799-0149   (BR)
CORPORATION OF THE CITY OF BROCKVILLE
CITY OF BROCKVILLE FIRE DEPT
61 Perth St, Brockville, ON, K6V 5C6
(613) 498-1363
Emp Here 40
SIC 7389 Business services, nec

D-U-N-S 24-324-1655   (BR)
DATA COMMUNICATIONS MANAGEMENT CORP
DATA GROUP OF COMPANIES
1201 California Ave, Brockville, ON, K6V 5V8

Emp Here 23
SIC 2761 Manifold business forms

D-U-N-S 20-043-9743   (HQ)
DELHI INDUSTRIES INC
(*Suby of* Delhi Industries Inc)
2157 Parkedale Ave, Brockville, ON, K6V 0B4
(613) 342-5424
Emp Here 80   *Emp Total* 95
Sales 12,841,083
SIC 3564 Blowers and fans
 David Beatty
Pr James Cooper

D-U-N-S 20-615-5392   (BR)
DOUGLAS BARWICK INC
(*Suby of* Marshall-Barwick Holdings Inc)
150 California Ave, Brockville, ON, K6V 5W1
(613) 342-8471
Emp Here 65
SIC 3498 Fabricated pipe and fittings

D-U-N-S 20-306-9513   (BR)
G.T. WHOLESALE LIMITED
(*Suby of* Giant Tiger Stores Limited)
240 Laurier Blvd, Brockville, ON, K6V 7J6
(613) 341-8699
Emp Here 34
SIC 4222 Refrigerated warehousing and storage

D-U-N-S 24-150-6877   (BR)
GOODLIFE FITNESS CENTRES INC
1972 Parkedale Ave, Brockville, ON, K6V 5T2
(613) 345-4623
Emp Here 29
SIC 7999 Amusement and recreation, nec

D-U-N-S 20-441-6523   (HQ)
HANSLER SMITH LIMITED
(*Suby of* Hansler Smith Limited)
1385 California Ave, Brockville, ON, K6V 5V5
(613) 342-4408
Emp Here 20   *Emp Total* 70
Sales 13,570,690
SIC 5085 Industrial supplies
 Allan Smith
Pr Pr Brian Boucher
 Steven Smith
 Jon Brinkworth

D-U-N-S 24-393-4796   (HQ)
**HENDRIX HOTEL & RESTAURANT EQUIP-
MENT & SUPPLIES LTD**
HENDRIX RESTAURANT EQUIPMENT
3011 Highway 29 Rr 4, Brockville, ON, K6V
5T4
(613) 342-0616
Emp Here 40   *Emp Total* 1,220
Sales 25,974,009
SIC 5046 Commercial equipment, nec
Pr Mike Kane
VP Mark Morris
 Charley Geiger
 Tom Pitera
 Lawrence Martin Vander Baaren
 Kevin Kerr

D-U-N-S 20-870-2063   (BR)
HOME DEPOT OF CANADA INC
HOME DEPOT
(*Suby of* The Home Depot Inc)
2120 Parkedale Ave, Brockville, ON, K6V 7N6
(613) 498-9600
Emp Here 50
SIC 5251 Hardware stores

D-U-N-S 20-507-8090   (BR)
**INDUSTRIAL   ELECTRICAL   CONTRAC-
TORS LIMITED**
185 North Augusta Rd, Brockville, ON, K6V
2Y2
(613) 342-6252
Emp Here 25
SIC 1731 Electrical work

D-U-N-S 20-086-4168   (BR)
LAFARGE CANADA INC
LAFARGEHOLCIM
1864 2 Hwy E, Brockville, ON, K6V 5V2

(613) 342-0262
Emp Here 25
SIC 3272 Concrete products, nec

D-U-N-S 24-121-0397   (BR)
LOBLAWS INC
REAL CANADIAN SUPERSTORE
1972 Parkedale Ave Suite 1017, Brockville,
ON, K6V 7N4
(613) 498-0994
Emp Here 220
SIC 5411 Grocery stores

D-U-N-S 25-303-9507   (BR)
LONDON LIFE INSURANCE COMPANY
FREEDOM 55 FINANCIAL
7 King St W Suite 200, Brockville, ON, K6V
3P7
(613) 342-4401
Emp Here 25
SIC 6311 Life insurance

D-U-N-S 25-295-5802   (BR)
MARCH OF DIMES CANADA
6 Glenn Wood Pl Unit 6, Brockville, ON, K6V
2T3
(613) 342-1935
Emp Here 50
SIC 8331 Job training and related services

D-U-N-S 25-311-0076   (BR)
**MCDONALD'S   RESTAURANTS   OF
CANADA LIMITED**
MCDONALD'S #8386
(*Suby of* McDonald's Corporation)
2454 Parkedale Ave, Brockville, ON, K6V 3G8
(613) 342-5551
Emp Here 80
SIC 5812 Eating places

D-U-N-S 25-980-8087   (BR)
METRO INC
LOEB
237 King St W, Brockville, ON, K6V 3S2
(613) 345-4260
Emp Here 85
SIC 5411 Grocery stores

D-U-N-S 20-803-7742   (BR)
METRO ONTARIO INC
FOOD BASICS
3049 Jefferson Dr, Brockville, ON, K6V 6N7
(613) 345-0272
Emp Here 45
SIC 5411 Grocery stores

D-U-N-S 25-108-5957   (HQ)
NEWTERRA LTD
1291 California Ave, Brockville, ON, K6V 7N5
(613) 498-1876
Emp Here 50   *Emp Total* 225
Sales 17,151,770
SIC 3589 Service industry machinery, nec
Pr Pr Bruce Lounsbury
 Robert Kennedy
 Ben Fash
 Tom Pokorsky
 David Henderson
 Daniel Weiss
 James Iglesias
 Robert Kulhawy
 Samuel Saintonge

D-U-N-S 24-858-5809   (BR)
NORTHERN CABLES INC
1245 California Ave, Brockville, ON, K6V 7N5
(613) 345-2083
Emp Here 20
SIC 3357 Nonferrous wiredrawing and insulating

D-U-N-S 25-984-3340   (BR)
NORTHERN REFLECTIONS LTD
NORTHERN EXPERIENCE
2399 Parkedale Ave, Brockville, ON, K6V 3G9
(613) 345-0166
Emp Here 20
SIC 5621 Women's clothing stores

D-U-N-S 24-104-4726   (BR)
PROCTER & GAMBLE INC
(*Suby of* The Procter & Gamble Company)
1475 California Ave, Brockville, ON, K6V 6K4
(613) 342-9592
Emp Here 900
SIC 2841 Soap and other detergents

D-U-N-S 20-279-7598   (BR)
**PROCTER & GAMBLE INVESTMENT COR-
PORATION**
(*Suby of* The Procter & Gamble Company)
1475 California Ave, Brockville, ON, K6V 6K4
(613) 342-9592
Emp Here 400
SIC 2841 Soap and other detergents

D-U-N-S 20-650-4800   (BR)
PUROLATOR INC.
PUROLATOR INC
1365 California Ave, Brockville, ON, K6V 5T6
(613) 498-2063
Emp Here 35
SIC 7389 Business services, nec

D-U-N-S 24-827-8632   (BR)
RIO TINTO ALCAN INC
ALCAN SPECIALTY ALUMINOUS
(*Suby of* RIO TINTO PLC)
4000 Development Dr, Brockville, ON, K6V
5V5
(613) 342-7462
Emp Here 55
SIC 3297 Nonclay refractories

D-U-N-S 20-076-4434   (SL)
RIPNET LIMITED
101 Water St W Suite 96, Brockville, ON, K6V
3M1
(613) 342-3946
Emp Here 29   *Sales* 2,638,521
SIC 4813 Telephone communication, except
radio

D-U-N-S 20-656-0398   (BR)
**ROYAL OTTAWA MENTAL HEALTH CEN-
TRE**
BROCKVILLE MENTAL HEALTH CENTRE
1804 Highway 2 E, Brockville, ON, K6V 5T1
(613) 345-1461
Emp Here 400
SIC 8093 Specialty outpatient clinics, nec

D-U-N-S 24-845-8473   (HQ)
SPX FLOW TECHNOLOGY CANADA INC
1415 California Ave, Brockville, ON, K6V 7H7
(613) 345-2280
Emp Here 20   *Emp Total* 7,000
Sales 5,110,881
SIC 3567 Industrial furnaces and ovens
 Kevin L Lilly
 Richard Bays

D-U-N-S 25-311-1249   (BR)
SEARS CANADA INC
SEARS
2399 Parkedale Ave Unit 1047, Brockville, ON,
K6V 3G9
(613) 345-1163
Emp Here 50
SIC 5311 Department stores

D-U-N-S 20-190-5614   (BR)
SELKIRK CANADA CORPORATION
(*Suby of* Selkirk Americas, L.P.)
1400 California Ave, Brockville, ON, K6V 5V3
(888) 693-9563
Emp Here 118
SIC 3259 Structural clay products, nec

D-U-N-S 24-392-0605   (BR)
SHELL CANADA LIMITED
250 Laurier Blvd, Brockville, ON, K6V 5V7
(613) 498-5700
Emp Here 75
SIC 5541 Gasoline service stations

D-U-N-S 20-921-8036   (BR)
STAPLES CANADA INC

STAPLES THE BUSINESS DEPOT
(*Suby of* Staples, Inc.)
2399 Parkedale Ave, Brockville, ON, K6V 3G9
(613) 498-2616
Emp Here 20
SIC 5943 Stationery stores

D-U-N-S 20-353-0761   (BR)
STARBUCKS COFFEE CANADA, INC
STARBUCKS COFFEE CO
(*Suby of* Starbucks Corporation)
1981 Parkedale Ave Suite D, Brockville, ON,
K6V 0B4

Emp Here 20
SIC 5812 Eating places

D-U-N-S 20-746-1901   (BR)
TALLMAN TRUCK CENTRE LIMITED
KEMPTVILLE TRUCK CENTRE
2420 Parkedale Ave, Brockville, ON, K6V 3G8
(613) 345-3668
Emp Here 26
SIC 5511 New and used car dealers

D-U-N-S 25-319-2876   (BR)
TORONTO-DOMINION BANK, THE
TD CANADA TRUST
(*Suby of* Toronto-Dominion Bank, The)
125 Stewart Blvd, Brockville, ON, K6V 4W4
(613) 345-1810
Emp Here 20
SIC 6021 National commercial banks

D-U-N-S 24-975-1439   (BR)
TORONTO-DOMINION BANK, THE
TD CANADA TRUST
(*Suby of* Toronto-Dominion Bank, The)
133 King St W Suite 204, Brockville, ON, K6V
6Z1
(613) 345-1815
Emp Here 23
SIC 6021 National commercial banks

D-U-N-S 20-208-5408   (BR)
**UNITED   COUNTIES   OF   LEEDS   AND
GRENVILLE**
25 Central Ave W Suite 100, Brockville, ON,
K6V 4N6
(613) 341-8937
Emp Here 100
SIC 4119 Local passenger transportation, nec

D-U-N-S 25-486-5132   (BR)
**UPPER   CANADA   DISTRICT   SCHOOL
BOARD, THE**
VANIER SCHOOL, THE
(*Suby of* Upper Canada District School Board,
The)
40 Vanier Dr, Brockville, ON, K6V 3J5
(613) 342-8081
Emp Here 30
SIC 8211 Elementary and secondary schools

D-U-N-S 25-238-0209   (BR)
**UPPER   CANADA   DISTRICT   SCHOOL
BOARD, THE**
WESTMINSTER SCHOOL
(*Suby of* Upper Canada District School Board,
The)
29 Central Ave W, Brockville, ON, K6V 4N6
(613) 345-5552
Emp Here 40
SIC 8211 Elementary and secondary schools

D-U-N-S 25-156-2906   (BR)
**UPPER   CANADA   DISTRICT   SCHOOL
BOARD, THE**
BROCKVILLE COLLEGIATE INSTITUTE
(*Suby of* Upper Canada District School Board,
The)
90 Pearl St E, Brockville, ON, K6V 1P8
(613) 345-5641
Emp Here 20
SIC 8211 Elementary and secondary schools

D-U-N-S 25-486-5074   (BR)
UPPER   CANADA   DISTRICT   SCHOOL

BOARD, THE
THOUSAND ISLANDS SECONDARY SCHOOL
(*Suby of* Upper Canada District School Board, The)
2510 Parkedale Ave, Brockville, ON, K6V 3H1
(613) 342-1100
Emp Here 120
SIC 8211 Elementary and secondary schools

D-U-N-S 25-263-4969   (BR)
UPPER CANADA DISTRICT SCHOOL BOARD, THE
TONIATA PUBLIC SCHOOL
(*Suby of* Upper Canada District School Board, The)
24 Scace Ave, Brockville, ON, K6V 2A4
(613) 342-6310
Emp Here 24
SIC 8211 Elementary and secondary schools

D-U-N-S 25-263-5040   (BR)
UPPER CANADA DISTRICT SCHOOL BOARD, THE
COMMONWEALTH PUBLIC SCHOOL
(*Suby of* Upper Canada District School Board, The)
166 Pearl St E, Brockville, ON, K6V 1R4
(613) 345-5031
Emp Here 35
SIC 8211 Elementary and secondary schools

D-U-N-S 25-542-7957   (HQ)
UPPER CANADA DISTRICT SCHOOL BOARD, THE
(*Suby of* Upper Canada District School Board, The)
225 Central Ave W, Brockville, ON, K6V 5X1
(613) 342-0371
Emp Here 100   *Emp Total* 4,000
Sales 341,747,210
SIC 8211 Elementary and secondary schools
Dir David Thomas
Superintnt Rick Gales
  Greg Pietersma
  Joan Hodge
  Sherri Moore-Arbour
  Art Bucklard
  Mildred Craig
  David Dargie
  Patti Lennox
  William Macpherson

D-U-N-S 24-318-0770   (BR)
WAL-MART CANADA CORP
WALMART
1942 Parkedale Ave Suite 3006, Brockville, ON, K6V 7N4
(613) 342-9293
Emp Here 150
SIC 5311 Department stores

D-U-N-S 20-654-8823   (BR)
WENDY'S RESTAURANTS OF CANADA INC
WENDY'S
(*Suby of* The Wendy's Company)
3040 Parkedale Ave, Brockville, ON, K6V 3G6

Emp Here 30
SIC 5812 Eating places

D-U-N-S 20-209-7080   (BR)
WILLS TRANSFER LIMITED
(*Suby of* Wills Transfer Limited)
2210 Parkedale Ave, Brockville, ON, K6V 6M2
(613) 345-8030
Emp Here 20
SIC 4213 Trucking, except local

Bruce Mines, ON P0R
Algoma County

D-U-N-S 25-238-0845   (BR)
ALGOMA DISTRICT SCHOOL BOARD

HENDERSON, ARTHUR PUBLIC SCHOOL
(*Suby of* Algoma District School Board)
2 Henderson Lane Rr 2, Bruce Mines, ON, P0R 1C0
(705) 785-3483
Emp Here 25
SIC 8211 Elementary and secondary schools

D-U-N-S 20-822-6050   (SL)
FOSTER'S RED & WHITE LTD
FOSTER'S FRESHMART
4 Robinson Dr, Bruce Mines, ON, P0R 1C0
(705) 785-3728
Emp Here 1,614   *Sales* 322,408,100
SIC 5411 Grocery stores
Pr Pr Darren Foster

D-U-N-S 24-361-0537   (BR)
TOMLINSON, R. W. LIMITED
ONTARIO TRAP ROCK
(*Suby of* Tomlinson, R. W. Limited)
9630 17 Hwy, Bruce Mines, ON, P0R 1C0
(705) 785-3833
Emp Here 25
SIC 1411 Dimension stone

Brucefield, ON N0M
Huron County

D-U-N-S 25-249-1618   (BR)
AVON MAITLAND DISTRICT SCHOOL BOARD
HURON CENTENNIAL ELEMENTARY SCHOOL
39978 Centennial Rd, Brucefield, ON, N0M 1J0
(519) 233-3330
Emp Here 35
SIC 8211 Elementary and secondary schools

Burford, ON N0E
Brant County

D-U-N-S 24-525-7329   (BR)
BRANT HALDIMAND NORFOLK CATHOLIC DISTRICT SCHOOL BOARD
BLESSED SACRAMENT ELEMENTARY SCHOOL
185 King St W, Burford, ON, N0E 1A0
(519) 449-2984
Emp Here 25
SIC 8211 Elementary and secondary schools

D-U-N-S 20-037-1813   (HQ)
DAVIS FUEL COMPANY LIMITED
FLYING M TRUCK STOP
22 King St, Burford, ON, N0E 1A0
(519) 449-2417
Emp Here 25   *Emp Total* 100
Sales 22,544,856
SIC 5172 Petroleum products, nec
Pr Pr Roger Davis
  Donald Kersey
  Edith Davis
  Brenda Kersey
  Gerome Davis
  Floyd Davis

D-U-N-S 20-710-6134   (BR)
GRAND ERIE DISTRICT SCHOOL BOARD
BURFORD DISTRICT ELEMENTARY SCHOOL
(*Suby of* Grand Erie District School Board)
35 Alexander St, Burford, ON, N0E 1A0
(519) 449-2457
Emp Here 50
SIC 8211 Elementary and secondary schools

Burks Falls, ON P0A
Parry Sound County

D-U-N-S 25-249-7144   (BR)
MUSKOKA ALGONQUIN HEALTHCARE
BURKE FALLS AND DISTRICT HEALTH CENTER
150 Huston St, Burks Falls, ON, P0A 1C0
(705) 382-2900
Emp Here 40
SIC 8062 General medical and surgical hospitals

D-U-N-S 20-710-4329   (BR)
NEAR NORTH DISTRICT SCHOOL BOARD
LAND OF LAKE SENIOR PUBLIC SCHOOL
92 Ontario St, Burks Falls, ON, P0A 1C0
(705) 382-2924
Emp Here 25
SIC 8211 Elementary and secondary schools

D-U-N-S 25-238-1777   (BR)
NEAR NORTH DISTRICT SCHOOL BOARD
MA WITTICK JR PUBLIC SCHOOL
178 Yonge St, Burks Falls, ON, P0A 1C0
(705) 382-3038
Emp Here 25
SIC 8211 Elementary and secondary schools

Burlington, ON L7L
Halton County

D-U-N-S 24-346-3945   (SL)
1574626 ONTARIO LTD
AUTOSPA EXPRESS
1227 Appleby Line, Burlington, ON, L7L 5H9
(905) 315-7710
Emp Here 50   *Sales* 2,991,389
SIC 7549 Automotive services, nec

D-U-N-S 25-965-5702   (BR)
2014767 ONTARIO LIMITED
BROWN PACKAGING
4331 Mainway, Burlington, ON, L7L 5N9
(905) 335-4225
Emp Here 50
SIC 2653 Corrugated and solid fiber boxes

D-U-N-S 24-484-8248   (SL)
864773 ONTARIO INC
TENDER CHOICE FOODS
4480 Paletta Crt, Burlington, ON, L7L 5R2
(905) 825-1856
Emp Here 250   *Sales* 29,111,319
SIC 2011 Meat packing plants
Pr Pr Pasquale Paletta
  Anita Paletta
  Angelo Paletta

D-U-N-S 20-995-4804   (BR)
ALS CANADA LTD
ALS ENVIRONMENTAL
1435 Norjohn Crt Unit 1, Burlington, ON, L7L 0E6
(905) 331-3111
Emp Here 35
SIC 8734 Testing laboratories

D-U-N-S 20-045-7172   (BR)
ALS CANADA LTD
1435 Norjohn Crt Unit 1, Burlington, ON, L7L 0E6
(905) 331-3111
Emp Here 40
SIC 8731 Commercial physical research

D-U-N-S 25-087-5820   (BR)
AIR LIQUIDE CANADA INC
5315 North Service Rd, Burlington, ON, L7L 6C1
(905) 335-4877
Emp Here 45
SIC 2813 Industrial gases

D-U-N-S 24-101-8501   (BR)
ALSCO CANADA CORPORATION

ALSCO UNIFORM & LINEN SERVICE
5475 North Service Rd Suite 7, Burlington, ON, L7L 5H7
(905) 315-7502
Emp Here 60
SIC 7213 Linen supply

D-U-N-S 24-653-4791   (BR)
AMHIL ENTERPRISES LTD
5330 Mainway, Burlington, ON, L7L 6A4
(905) 332-9765
Emp Here 50
SIC 3089 Plastics products, nec

D-U-N-S 24-779-4290   (HQ)
AMICO CANADA INC
AMICO-ISG
(*Suby of* Gibraltar Industries, Inc.)
1080 Corporate Dr, Burlington, ON, L7L 5R6
(905) 335-4474
Emp Here 56   *Emp Total* 2,311
Sales 8,317,520
SIC 3499 Fabricated Metal products, nec
Pr Henning Kornbrekke
VP Timothy F Murphy
Dir Jamie L. Peritore
Dir Mackay Glenn
  Frank G. Heard

D-U-N-S 20-563-9110   (BR)
ASSANTE FINANCIAL MANAGEMENT LTD
ASSANTE WEALTH MANAGEMENT
4145 North Service Rd Suite 100, Burlington, ON, L7L 6A3
(905) 332-5503
Emp Here 22
SIC 8741 Management services

D-U-N-S 25-240-7853   (HQ)
ASSOCIATED MATERIALS CANADA LIMITED
1001 Corporate Dr, Burlington, ON, L7L 5V5
(905) 319-5561
Emp Here 200   *Emp Total* 600
Sales 63,038,045
SIC 3444 Sheet Metalwork
  Robert Hastings

D-U-N-S 24-923-6142   (SL)
ATOTECH CANADA LTD
1180 Corporate Dr, Burlington, ON, L7L 5R6
(905) 332-0111
Emp Here 35   *Sales* 5,107,249
SIC 2899 Chemical preparations, nec
  Gene Torcoletti

D-U-N-S 24-684-8266   (BR)
AUSENCO ENGINEERING CANADA INC
AUSENCO
1016b Sutton Dr Suite 100, Burlington, ON, L7L 6B8
(905) 319-1698
Emp Here 55
SIC 8711 Engineering services

D-U-N-S 20-677-1557   (BR)
BANQUE TORONTO-DOMINION, LA
TORONTO-DOMINION BANK, THE
(*Suby of* Toronto-Dominion Bank, The)
5515 North Service Rd Unit 400, Burlington, ON, L7L 6G4
(905) 331-7511
Emp Here 30
SIC 8742 Management consulting services

D-U-N-S 20-589-4475   (BR)
BANQUE TORONTO-DOMINION, LA
TD CANADA TRUST
(*Suby of* Toronto-Dominion Bank, The)
2000 Appleby Line Unit G1, Burlington, ON, L7L 6M6
(905) 332-2240
Emp Here 20
SIC 6021 National commercial banks

D-U-N-S 24-125-2415   (BR)
BANQUE DE DEVELOPPEMENT DU CANADA

BUSINESS DEVELOPMENT BANK OF CANADA
4145 North Service Rd Suite 401, Burlington, ON, L7L 6A3
(905) 315-9248
Emp Here 27
SIC 6141 Personal credit institutions

D-U-N-S 20-736-9992   (HQ)
BOEHRINGER INGELHEIM (CANADA) LTD
ANIMAL HEALTH, DIV OF
5180 South Service Rd, Burlington, ON, L7L 5H4
(905) 639-0333
Emp Here 250   *Emp Total* 45,692
Sales 38,669,171
SIC 8731 Commercial physical research
Pr Richard Mole
Dir Sara Mcclelland

D-U-N-S 25-231-7110   (BR)
BRICK WAREHOUSE LP, THE
990 Fraser Dr, Burlington, ON, L7L 5P5
(905) 333-5533
Emp Here 50
SIC 5712 Furniture stores

D-U-N-S 20-755-5707   (HQ)
BUNZL CANADA INC
BUNZL DISTRIBUTION
4240 Harvester Rd Unit 3, Burlington, ON, L7L 0E8
(905) 637-4040
Emp Here 72   *Emp Total* 245
Sales 40,201,346
SIC 5113 Industrial and personal service paper
Pr Pr Patrick Larmon
VP Dan Deambrosio
VP VP John Howlett
Sec Daniel Lett
Treas Jim Mccool
Dir Barry Hentz

D-U-N-S 25-057-9414   (SL)
BURKERT CONTROMATIC INC
BURKERT FLUID CONTROL SYSTEMS
5002 South Service Rd, Burlington, ON, L7L 5Y7
(905) 632-3033
Emp Here 24   *Sales* 4,669,485
SIC 5085 Industrial supplies

D-U-N-S 24-561-7803   (SL)
BURLINGTON AUTOMATION CORP.
5041 Fairview St, Burlington, ON, L7L 4W8
(905) 681-9622
Emp Here 40   *Sales* 5,690,935
SIC 3011 Tires and inner tubes
Pr Rob Tyler

D-U-N-S 24-877-3749   (BR)
CCTF CORPORATION
EMCO
4151 North Service Rd Unit 2, Burlington, ON, L7L 4X6
(905) 335-5320
Emp Here 100
SIC 8721 Accounting, auditing, and bookkeeping

D-U-N-S 24-889-9531   (BR)
CCTF CORPORATION
4151 North Service Rd Suite 2, Burlington, ON, L7L 4X6
(905) 335-5320
Emp Here 22
SIC 5085 Industrial supplies

D-U-N-S 20-104-5494   (BR)
CARGILL LIMITED
WILBUR CARGILL
5305 Harvester Rd, Burlington, ON, L7L 5K9
(905) 333-9301
Emp Here 30
SIC 2066 Chocolate and cocoa products

D-U-N-S 24-986-2780   (SL)

CHILDREN'S AID SOCIETY OF THE REGIONAL MUNICIPALITY OF HALTON
HALTON'S CHILDREN'S AID SOCIETY
1445 Norjohn Crt, Burlington, ON, L7L 0E6
(905) 333-4441
Emp Here 78   *Sales* 3,064,349
SIC 8322 Individual and family services

D-U-N-S 25-404-3730   (HQ)
CLASSIC CARE PHARMACY CORPORATION
1320 Heine Crt, Burlington, ON, L7L 6L9
(905) 631-9027
Emp Here 95   *Emp Total* 449
Sales 11,381,869
SIC 5999 Miscellaneous retail stores, nec
Pr Pr Moe Green
Dir Girish Bansal

D-U-N-S 24-181-7840   (HQ)
CLYDE UNION CANADA LIMITED
SPX CLYDE UNION CANADA
4151 North Service Rd Unit 1, Burlington, ON, L7L 4X6
(905) 315-3800
Emp Here 110   *Emp Total* 7,000
Sales 3,638,254
SIC 3561 Pumps and pumping equipment

D-U-N-S 25-073-7830   (BR)
CONNEX TELECOMMUNICATIONS INC
CONNEX SEE SERVICE INC
940 Gateway, Burlington, ON, L7L 5K7
(905) 632-6894
Emp Here 72
SIC 5065 Electronic parts and equipment, nec

D-U-N-S 24-336-5199   (BR)
CORPORATION OF THE CITY OF BURLINGTON
NELSON POOL/ARENA
4235 New St, Burlington, ON, L7L 1T3
(905) 637-0632
Emp Here 50
SIC 7999 Amusement and recreation, nec

D-U-N-S 20-903-2648   (HQ)
CROWN WORLDWIDE LTD
CROWN RELOCATIONS
1375 Artisans Crt, Burlington, ON, L7L 5Y2
(905) 827-4899
Emp Here 27   *Emp Total* 30
Sales 5,472,053
SIC 4783 Packing and crating
Dir Fin Robert Hannon
Genl Mgr Dean Hefford

D-U-N-S 24-137-8574   (BR)
DELTA HOTELS LIMITED
HOMEWOOD SUITES HOTEL
975 Syscon Rd, Burlington, ON, L7L 5S3
(905) 631-8300
Emp Here 30
SIC 8741 Management services

D-U-N-S 24-802-4379   (SL)
ECS COFFEE INC
1370 Artisans Crt, Burlington, ON, L7L 5Y2
(905) 631-1524
Emp Here 45   *Sales* 2,918,428
SIC 5499 Miscellaneous food stores

D-U-N-S 24-078-4561   (HQ)
EATON INDUSTRIES (CANADA) COMPANY
EATON ELECTRICAL, CANADIAN OPERATIONS DIV OF
5050 Mainway, Burlington, ON, L7L 5Z1
(905) 333-6442
Emp Here 50   *Emp Total* 750
Sales 95,797,399
SIC 5065 Electronic parts and equipment, nec
Pr Pr Sandy Cutler
VP VP Steve Boccadoro
Sls Mgr Rick Hampton

D-U-N-S 24-063-3268   (SL)
EDGE IMAGING TORONTO INC
940 Gateway, Burlington, ON, L7L 5K7

(905) 631-5588
Emp Here 50   *Sales* 1,969,939
SIC 7221 Photographic studios, portrait

D-U-N-S 24-044-6166   (HQ)
EDGEWORTH PROPERTIES INC
(*Suby of* Edgeworth Ventures Inc)
5500 North Service Rd Suite 106, Burlington, ON, L7L 6W6

Emp Here 20   *Emp Total* 300
Sales 17,584,000
SIC 6552 Subdividers and developers, nec
Pr C. Vaughan Minor
Ch Bd Donald G. Hurst
Ex VP Patrick Oliver-Kelley

D-U-N-S 24-049-1100   (BR)
EMPIRE LIFE INSURANCE COMPANY, THE
5500 North Service Rd Suite 402, Burlington, ON, L7L 6W6
(905) 336-1209
Emp Here 25
SIC 6311 Life insurance

D-U-N-S 24-845-4043   (HQ)
ENDRESS + HAUSER CANADA LTD
1075 Sutton Dr, Burlington, ON, L7L 5Z8
(905) 681-9292
Emp Here 90   *Emp Total* 1,664
Sales 29,712,409
SIC 5084 Industrial machinery and equipment
Genl Mgr Anthony Varga

D-U-N-S 20-408-9890   (HQ)
EVERTZ MICROSYSTEMS LTD
(*Suby of* Evertz Technologies Limited)
5292 John Lucas Dr, Burlington, ON, L7L 5Z9
(905) 335-3700
Emp Here 380   *Emp Total* 1,097
Sales 54,428,682
SIC 3663 Radio and t.v. communications equipment
Pr Pr Romolo Magarelli
Ch Bd Douglas Deburin
VP Fin Anthony Gridley

D-U-N-S 24-823-9134   (BR)
FGL SPORTS LTD
SPORT CHEK APPLEBY CROSSING
2445 Appleby Line Unit A03, Burlington, ON, L7L 0B6
(905) 331-2560
Emp Here 20
SIC 5941 Sporting goods and bicycle shops

D-U-N-S 24-602-1836   (SL)
FIKE CANADA, INC
FIKE
(*Suby of* The Fike Corporation)
4400 Mainway, Burlington, ON, L7L 5Y5
(905) 681-3100
Emp Here 24   *Sales* 3,137,310
SIC 3494 Valves and pipe fittings, nec

D-U-N-S 24-339-4124   (SL)
GEMALTO CANADA INC
5347 John Lucas Dr, Burlington, ON, L7L 6A8
(905) 335-9681
Emp Here 100   *Sales* 12,532,976
SIC 7389 Business services, nec
Pr Pr Francois Le Bel
Dir Jack Jania
Dir Anthony Pingelli
Dir Ajay Basavarajaiah

D-U-N-S 24-176-3775   (BR)
GENERAL ELECTRIC CANADA COMPANY
GE HEALTHCARE
(*Suby of* General Electric Company)
5450 Harvester Rd, Burlington, ON, L7L 5N5
(905) 333-1789
Emp Here 30
SIC 3625 Relays and industrial controls

D-U-N-S 24-847-2789   (SL)
GENSTAR CAPITAL, ULC
1001 Corporate Dr, Burlington, ON, L7L 5V5

(905) 319-5645
Emp Here 2,800   *Sales* 716,237,000
SIC 6719 Holding companies, nec
Pr William Macdonald

D-U-N-S 20-134-2623   (HQ)
GERRIE ELECTRIC WHOLESALE LIMITED
GERRIE SUPPLY CHAIN SERVICES
(*Suby of* Gerrie Electric Wholesale Limited)
4104 South Service Rd, Burlington, ON, L7L 4X5
(905) 681-3660
Emp Here 80   *Emp Total* 250
Sales 59,598,069
SIC 5063 Electrical apparatus and equipment
Dir Ken Gerrie
Pr Heather Gerrie-Kwant
S&M/VP Carmen Stewart
Dir Richard Solonenko
Dir Elaine Valentino

D-U-N-S 25-145-9335   (BR)
GOODRICH AEROSPACE CANADA LTD
GOODRICH LANDING GEAR SERVICES
(*Suby of* United Technologies Corporation)
5415 North Service Rd, Burlington, ON, L7L 5H7
(905) 319-3006
Emp Here 150
SIC 7699 Repair services, nec

D-U-N-S 25-409-8775   (HQ)
GRANITE HEALTH SOLUTIONS LP
SIBLEY & ASSOCIATES REHABILITATION, DIV OF
1122 International Blvd Suite 104, Burlington, ON, L7L 6Z8
(800) 363-8900
Emp Here 119   *Emp Total* 550
Sales 15,623,300
SIC 6411 Insurance agents, brokers, and service
Pr Pr Steven Sibley

D-U-N-S 25-686-9512   (BR)
HALF, ROBERT CANADA INC
ACCOUNTEMPS, DIV OF
(*Suby of* Robert Half International Inc.)
11011 International Blvd Suite 104, Burlington, ON, L7L 6W1
(905) 319-9384
Emp Here 20
SIC 7361 Employment agencies

D-U-N-S 24-253-2567   (BR)
HALTON CATHOLIC DISTRICT SCHOOL BOARD
CORPUS CHRISTI CATHOLIC SECONDARY SCHOOL
5150 Upper Middle Rd Suite Upper, Burlington, ON, L7L 0E5
(905) 331-5591
Emp Here 65
SIC 8211 Elementary and secondary schools

D-U-N-S 20-591-2798   (BR)
HALTON CATHOLIC DISTRICT SCHOOL BOARD
ST PATRICK'S SCHOOL
200 Kenwood Ave, Burlington, ON, L7L 4L8
(905) 639-3975
Emp Here 30
SIC 8211 Elementary and secondary schools

D-U-N-S 20-711-0706   (BR)
HALTON CATHOLIC DISTRICT SCHOOL BOARD
ST. RAINFIELD
4056 New St, Burlington, ON, L7L 1S9
(905) 637-3810
Emp Here 30
SIC 8211 Elementary and secondary schools

D-U-N-S 24-676-3127   (BR)
HALTON CATHOLIC DISTRICT SCHOOL BOARD
ST. CHRISTOPHER CATHOLIC ELEMENTARY SCHOOL

2400 Sutton Dr, Burlington, ON, L7L 7N2
(905) 335-7553
Emp Here 25
SIC 8211 Elementary and secondary schools

D-U-N-S 20-711-0599   (BR)
HALTON CATHOLIC DISTRICT SCHOOL BOARD
ASCENSION CATHOLIC ELEMENTARY
5205 New St, Burlington, ON, L7L 1V3
(905) 333-3374
Emp Here 35
SIC 8211 Elementary and secondary schools

D-U-N-S 20-025-2315   (BR)
HALTON DISTRICT SCHOOL BOARD
ROBERT BATEMAN HIGH SCHOOL
5151 New St, Burlington, ON, L7L 1V3
(905) 632-5151
Emp Here 165
SIC 8211 Elementary and secondary schools

D-U-N-S 20-026-8006   (BR)
HALTON DISTRICT SCHOOL BOARD
FRONTENAC PUBLIC SCHOOL
5140 Pinedale Ave, Burlington, ON, L7L 3V4
(905) 632-1690
Emp Here 60
SIC 8211 Elementary and secondary schools

D-U-N-S 20-026-7990   (BR)
HALTON DISTRICT SCHOOL BOARD
PINELAND PUBLIC SCHOOL
5121 Meadowhill Rd, Burlington, ON, L7L 3K7
(905) 634-2311
Emp Here 50
SIC 8211 Elementary and secondary schools

D-U-N-S 20-711-0433   (BR)
HALTON DISTRICT SCHOOL BOARD
PAULINE JOHNSON PUBLIC SCHOOL
4350 Longmoor Dr, Burlington, ON, L7L 1X7
(905) 632-2492
Emp Here 25
SIC 8211 Elementary and secondary schools

D-U-N-S 20-025-1895   (BR)
HALTON DISTRICT SCHOOL BOARD
NELSON SECONDARY SCHOOL
4181 New St, Burlington, ON, L7L 1T3
(905) 637-3325
Emp Here 100
SIC 8211 Elementary and secondary schools

D-U-N-S 20-711-0565   (BR)
HALTON DISTRICT SCHOOL BOARD
ORCHARD PARK
5151 Dryden Ave, Burlington, ON, L7L 7J3
(905) 331-7233
Emp Here 40
SIC 8211 Elementary and secondary schools

D-U-N-S 24-794-3616   (BR)
HARRIS STEEL ULC
FISHER & LUDLOW, DIV OF
(*Suby of* Nucor Corporation)
750 Appleby Line, Burlington, ON, L7L 2Y7
(905) 632-2121
Emp Here 140
SIC 3446 Architectural Metalwork

D-U-N-S 24-719-1547   (BR)
HARRIS STEEL ULC
LAUREL STEEL
(*Suby of* Nucor Corporation)
5400 Harvester Rd, Burlington, ON, L7L 5N5
(905) 681-6811
Emp Here 200
SIC 3312 Blast furnaces and steel mills

D-U-N-S 24-850-2929   (BR)
HATCH CORPORATION
5035 South Service Rd, Burlington, ON, L7L 6M9
(519) 772-1201
Emp Here 80
SIC 8711 Engineering services

D-U-N-S 20-134-5410   (HQ)
HENNIGES AUTOMOTIVE SCHLEGEL CANADA INC
4445 Fairview St, Burlington, ON, L7L 2A4
(289) 636-4461
Emp Here 250   *Emp Total* 450,000
Sales 21,829,525
SIC 3465 Automotive stampings
 Mario Daddio

D-U-N-S 20-875-1198   (BR)
HERCULES SLR INC
UNALLOY-IWRC, DIV OF
737 Oval Crt, Burlington, ON, L7L 6A9
(905) 790-3112
Emp Here 100
SIC 5051 Metals service centers and offices

D-U-N-S 20-317-0022   (SL)
HYGRID LOGISTICS INC
4151 North Service Rd Suite 3, Burlington, ON, L7L 4X6

Emp Here 45   *Sales* 7,165,680
SIC 4213 Trucking, except local
Pr Kevin Guminny

D-U-N-S 24-044-7177   (SL)
INVITROGEN CANADA INC
LIFE TECHNOLOGIES
(*Suby of* Thermo Fisher Scientific Inc.)
5250 Mainway, Burlington, ON, L7L 5Z1
(905) 335-2255
Emp Here 60   *Sales* 9,517,523
SIC 5122 Drugs, proprietaries, and sundries
Fin Mgr Jane Vowles
Dir John Cottingham

D-U-N-S 24-626-9526   (SL)
IRCO AUTOMATION INC
1080 Clay Ave Unit 3, Burlington, ON, L7L 0A1
(905) 336-2862
Emp Here 25   *Sales* 1,905,752
SIC 5962 Merchandising machine operators

D-U-N-S 24-344-7302   (HQ)
KAVERIT CRANES & SERVICE ULC
1040 Sutton Dr, Burlington, ON, L7L 6B8
(905) 631-1611
Emp Here 62   *Emp Total* 11,398
Sales 7,369,031
SIC 7389 Business services, nec
Pr Sadi Arbid
VP VP Scott Gilbey
Treas Francis Kelch
Sec Jennifer Dine

D-U-N-S 25-250-2620   (BR)
KIRBY INTERNATIONAL TRUCKS LTD
ALTRUCK TRANSPORTATION
5280 South Service Rd, Burlington, ON, L7L 5H5
(905) 681-6500
Emp Here 20
SIC 5511 New and used car dealers

D-U-N-S 25-372-9750   (BR)
KONECRANES CANADA INC
5300 Mainway, Burlington, ON, L7L 6A4
(905) 332-9494
Emp Here 90
SIC 7699 Repair services, nec

D-U-N-S 20-418-1978   (HQ)
KONECRANES CANADA INC
KCICRANE PRO SERVICES
5300 Mainway, Burlington, ON, L7L 6A4
(905) 332-9494
Emp Here 60   *Emp Total* 11,398
Sales 10,135,137
SIC 7699 Repair services, nec
Pr Sadi Arbid
 Guy Shumaker
VP Eric Blinkhorn
Sec Todd Robenson
Dir Thomas Sothard

D-U-N-S 20-550-6954   (SL)

LOCAL EATERY & REFUGE INC
4155 Fairview St, Burlington, ON, L7L 2A4
(905) 633-9464
Emp Here 55   *Sales* 1,678,096
SIC 5812 Eating places

D-U-N-S 24-827-1830   (HQ)
MC COMMERCIAL INC.
5420 North Service Rd Suite 300, Burlington, ON, L7L 6C7
(905) 315-2300
Emp Here 75   *Emp Total* 18,817
Sales 91,649,356
SIC 5064 Electrical appliances, television and radio
Pr Mike Mccrea
Dir Fin Jennifer Caldwell
 James Fleck
 Luis Berrondo
 Francisco Berrondo

D-U-N-S 20-995-4739   (BR)
MNP LLP
1122 International Blvd Unit 602, Burlington, ON, L7L 6Z8
(905) 639-3328
Emp Here 40
SIC 8721 Accounting, auditing, and bookkeeping

D-U-N-S 20-895-7543   (BR)
MTE CONSULTANTS INC
1016 Sutton Dr Suite A, Burlington, ON, L7L 6B8
(905) 639-2552
Emp Here 30
SIC 8711 Engineering services

D-U-N-S 25-486-9415   (BR)
MAPLE LEAF FOODS INC
MAPLE LEAF DISTRIBUTION CENTRE
5100 Harvester Rd, Burlington, ON, L7L 4X4
(905) 681-5050
Emp Here 80
SIC 5147 Meats and meat products

D-U-N-S 24-991-9028   (HQ)
MARMON/KEYSTONE CANADA INC
SPECIALTY STEELS
(*Suby of* Berkshire Hathaway Inc.)
1220 Heritage Rd, Burlington, ON, L7L 4X9
(905) 319-4646
Emp Here 50   *Emp Total* 331,000
Sales 621,708,343
SIC 5051 Metals service centers and offices
Pr Lou Germano
Fin Ex Ron Carlucci

D-U-N-S 20-641-1675   (BR)
MCBURL CORP
MCDONALD'S RESTAURANTS
4490 Fairview St, Burlington, ON, L7L 5P9

Emp Here 70
SIC 5812 Eating places

D-U-N-S 20-644-4395   (SL)
MCDONALD'S RESTAURANT
2040 Appleby Line Unit H, Burlington, ON, L7L 6M6
(905) 336-6364
Emp Here 50   *Sales* 1,532,175
SIC 5812 Eating places

D-U-N-S 24-335-0555   (BR)
METRO ONTARIO INC
METRO
2010 Appleby Line, Burlington, ON, L7L 6M6
(905) 331-7900
Emp Here 300
SIC 5411 Grocery stores

D-U-N-S 25-300-0137   (BR)
METRO ONTARIO INC
FOOD BASIC
5353 Lakeshore Rd, Burlington, ON, L7L 1C8
(905) 634-1804
Emp Here 100

SIC 5411 Grocery stores

D-U-N-S 24-986-7763   (BR)
METROLAND MEDIA GROUP LTD
BURLINGTON POST, THE
5046 Mainway Unit 2, Burlington, ON, L7L 5Z1
(905) 632-4444
Emp Here 80
SIC 2711 Newspapers

D-U-N-S 25-495-4969   (HQ)
MOTTLAB INC
5230 South Service Rd, Burlington, ON, L7L 5K2
(905) 331-1877
Emp Here 21   *Emp Total* 250
Sales 3,984,755
SIC 5049 Professional equipment, nec

D-U-N-S 24-353-8761   (HQ)
NATIONAL TIRE DISTRIBUTORS INC
5035 South Service Rd 4th Fl, Burlington, ON, L7L 6M9
(877) 676-0007
Emp Here 40   *Emp Total* 630
Sales 229,826,205
SIC 5014 Tires and tubes
Pr Mike Kustra

D-U-N-S 24-364-9779   (HQ)
O.C. TANNER RECOGNITION COMPANY LIMITED
4200 Fairview St, Burlington, ON, L7L 4Y8
(905) 632-7255
Emp Here 80   *Emp Total* 1,700
Sales 7,296,070
SIC 3911 Jewelry, precious Metal
Pr John Mcveigh

D-U-N-S 20-350-1650   (BR)
O.C. TANNER RECOGNITION COMPANY LIMITED
4200 Fairview St, Burlington, ON, L7L 4Y8
(905) 632-7255
Emp Here 80
SIC 3999 Manufacturing industries, nec

D-U-N-S 20-327-4845   (BR)
PARKLAND FUEL CORPORATION
PIONEER ENERGY DIV.
1122 International Blvd Suite 700, Burlington, ON, L7L 6Z8
(905) 639-2060
Emp Here 25
SIC 5172 Petroleum products, nec

D-U-N-S 25-948-4350   (BR)
PATHEON INC
977 Century Dr, Burlington, ON, L7L 5J8
(905) 639-5254
Emp Here 120
SIC 2834 Pharmaceutical preparations

D-U-N-S 25-839-4063   (BR)
PHARMA PLUS DRUGMARTS LTD
5111 New St, Burlington, ON, L7L 1V2
(905) 637-2331
Emp Here 25
SIC 5912 Drug stores and proprietary stores

D-U-N-S 24-525-4037   (HQ)
RCAP LEASING INC
(*Suby of* Royal Bank Of Canada)
5575 North Service Rd Suite 300, Burlington, ON, L7L 6M1
(905) 639-3995
Emp Here 150   *Emp Total* 79,000
Sales 21,223,150
SIC 6159 Miscellaneous business credit institutions
Pr Eugene Basolini
Crdt Mgr Carl Crechiolo

D-U-N-S 20-173-1841   (HQ)
RHI CANADA INC
4355 Fairview St, Burlington, ON, L7L 2A4
(905) 633-4500
Emp Here 130   *Emp Total* 7,678

SIC 3297 Nonclay refractories

D-U-N-S 24-348-1319   (BR)
REVERA INC
*APPLEBY PLACE RETIREMENT RESI-
DENCE*
500 Appleby Line Suite 119, Burlington, ON,
L7L 5Z6
(905) 333-1611
Emp Here 56
SIC 6513 Apartment building operators

D-U-N-S 20-268-5178   (HQ)
**REVOLUTION ENVIRONMENTAL SOLU-
TIONS LP**
TERRAPURE ENVIRONMENTAL
(*Suby of* Revolution Environmental Solutions
LP)
1100 Burloak Dr Suite 500, Burlington, ON,
L7L 6B2
(800) 263-8602
Emp Here 25   *Emp Total* 950
Sales 80,037,888
SIC 4959 Sanitary services, nec
Pr Todd Moser

D-U-N-S 24-371-6722   (BR)
**REVOLUTION ENVIRONMENTAL SOLU-
TIONS LP**
TERRAPURE ENVIRONMENTAL
(*Suby of* Revolution Environmental Solutions
LP)
1100 Burloak Dr Suite 500, Burlington, ON,
L7L 6B2
(905) 315-6300
Emp Here 75
SIC 4953 Refuse systems

D-U-N-S 20-268-4809   (SL)
REVOLUTION VSC LP
TERRAPURE
1100 Burloak Dr Suite 500, Burlington, ON,
L7L 6B2
(800) 863-8602
Emp Here 60   *Sales* 124,762,797
SIC 4953 Refuse systems
Pt Todd Moser

D-U-N-S 24-524-4306   (HQ)
RYERSON CANADA, INC
1219 Corporate Dr Suite 2, Burlington, ON,
L7L 5V5
(416) 622-3100
Emp Here 40   *Emp Total* 3,200
Sales 185,320,178
SIC 5051 Metals service centers and offices
Pr Pr Edward Lehner
CFO Erich Schnaufer
 Mark Silver
Ex VP Leong Fang

D-U-N-S 24-364-5210   (BR)
SKF CANADA LIMITED
4380 South Service Rd Unit 17, Burlington,
ON, L7L 5Y6
(905) 631-1821
Emp Here 20
SIC 5172 Petroleum products, nec

D-U-N-S 24-817-7904   (BR)
SAMUEL, SON & CO., LIMITED
GO PACKAGING - BURLINGTON
735 Oval Crt Suite 1, Burlington, ON, L7L 6A9
(905) 632-3662
Emp Here 50
SIC 5051 Metals service centers and offices

D-U-N-S 20-354-5793   (BR)
SAMUEL, SON & CO., LIMITED
1250 Appleby Line, Burlington, ON, L7L 5G6
(905) 335-9195
Emp Here 100
SIC 5051 Metals service centers and offices

D-U-N-S 24-310-3749   (BR)
SAMUEL, SON & CO., LIMITED
GERRARD-OVALSTRAPPING
735 Oval Crt, Burlington, ON, L7L 6A9

(905) 632-3662
Emp Here 75
SIC 5051 Metals service centers and offices

D-U-N-S 20-703-1431   (BR)
SANDVIK CANADA, INC
E J C
4445 Fairview St, Burlington, ON, L7L 2A4

Emp Here 175
SIC 3532 Mining machinery

D-U-N-S 20-366-1566   (SL)
SEMTECH CANADA CORPORATION
4281 Harvester Rd, Burlington, ON, L7L 5M4
(905) 632-2996
Emp Here 350   *Sales* 43,849,381
SIC 3679 Electronic components, nec
Pr Pr Emeka Chukwu
 Charles B. Ammann
 Gary Beauchamp
 James Lindstrom
 James Burra

D-U-N-S 20-818-9142   (HQ)
SEMTECH CANADA INC
4281 Harvester Rd, Burlington, ON, L7L 5M4
(905) 632-2996
Emp Here 350   *Emp Total* 1
Sales 578,827,000
SIC 3679 Electronic components, nec
Pr Pr Franz J. Fink
Dir Steven J. Bilodeau
Dir Thomas W. Cryer
Dir Jeffrey S. Mccreary
Dir Alexander Adam
 Roger M. Dickhout
Dir Fred Shlapak
Ch Bd Robert S. Weiss

D-U-N-S 24-165-7829   (BR)
SHEEHAN'S TRUCK CENTRE INC
ONTARIO AUTOCAR
4320 Harvester Rd, Burlington, ON, L7L 5S4
(905) 333-0779
Emp Here 60
SIC 5012 Automobiles and other motor vehi-
cles

D-U-N-S 20-547-4690   (SL)
SHOPLOGIX INC
5100 South Service Rd Suite 39, Burlington,
ON, L7L 6A5
(905) 469-9994
Emp Here 60   *Sales* 6,493,502
SIC 7371 Custom computer programming ser-
vices
Pr Pr Martin Ambrose
VP Fin Mike Fricke
VP VP Sean Clare
 Steve Celestini

D-U-N-S 24-002-8717   (BR)
**SHOPPERS   HOME   HEALTH   CARE
(CANADA) INC**
SHOPPERS HOME HEALTH CARE
4087 Harvester Rd Suite 11, Burlington, ON,
L7L 5M3
(905) 631-8664
Emp Here 20
SIC 5047 Medical and hospital equipment

D-U-N-S 20-117-8618   (BR)
SIEMENS CANADA LIMITED
1550 Appleby Line, Burlington, ON, L7L 6X7
(905) 331-0629
Emp Here 200
SIC 3625 Relays and industrial controls

D-U-N-S 24-686-3294   (HQ)
SODEXO CANADA LTD
SODEXO
1100 Burloak Dr Unit 401, Burlington, ON, L7L
6B2
(905) 632-8592
Emp Here 60   *Emp Total* 337
Sales 331,752,303
SIC 5812 Eating places

 Barry Telford
Pr Pr Dean Johnson
 Jerome Vos

D-U-N-S 25-156-2661   (BR)
STARBUCKS COFFEE CANADA, INC
(*Suby of* Starbucks Corporation)
675 Appleby Line, Burlington, ON, L7L 2Y5
(905) 637-7018
Emp Here 20
SIC 5812 Eating places

D-U-N-S 20-271-7187   (BR)
STATE FARM INSURANCE
5420 North Service Rd Suite 400, Burlington,
ON, L7L 6C7
(905) 315-3900
Emp Here 175
SIC 6411 Insurance agents, brokers, and ser-
vice

D-U-N-S 25-998-6263   (BR)
STRONGCO ENGINEERED SYSTEMS INC
STRONGCO CRANE GROUP
1051 Heritage Rd, Burlington, ON, L7L 4Y1
(905) 335-3863
Emp Here 55
SIC 3541 Machine tools, Metal cutting type

D-U-N-S 20-526-6849   (BR)
SUNRISE NORTH SENIOR LIVING LTD
*SUNRISE SENIOR LIVING OF BURLING-
TON*
(*Suby of* Welltower Inc.)
5401 Lakeshore Rd, Burlington, ON, L7L 6S5
(905) 333-9969
Emp Here 80
SIC 8361 Residential care

D-U-N-S 20-640-6287   (SL)
SURF PARADISE INC
4380 South Service Rd Unit 20, Burlington,
ON, L7L 5Y6
(905) 637-4448
Emp Here 45   *Sales* 5,376,850
SIC 5941 Sporting goods and bicycle shops
Pr George Morrison

D-U-N-S 25-052-6662   (BR)
TD WATERHOUSE CANADA INC
TD WEALTH
(*Suby of* Toronto-Dominion Bank, The)
5515 North Service Rd Suite 400, Burlington,
ON, L7L 6G4
(905) 331-7511
Emp Here 25
SIC 6211 Security brokers and dealers

D-U-N-S 20-343-7058   (SL)
TECH-CON AUTOMATION ULC
(*Suby of* Shape Technologies Group Parent
Holdings Inc)
1219 Corporate Dr, Burlington, ON, L7L 5V5
(905) 639-4989
Emp Here 30   *Sales* 2,598,753
SIC 3599 Industrial machinery, nec

D-U-N-S 25-344-4939   (SL)
TEMPEL CANADA COMPANY
BCL MAGNETICS
(*Suby of* Tempel Steel Company)
5045 North Service Rd, Burlington, ON, L7L
5H6
(905) 335-2530
Emp Here 375   *Sales* 55,503,178
SIC 3469 Metal stampings, nec
 Vincent Buonanno
 Gary Wagner
Fin Ex David Dibono

D-U-N-S 25-080-6168   (BR)
TERVITA CORPORATION
(*Suby of* Tervita Corporation)
5045 North Service Rd 2nd Fl, Burlington, ON,
L7L 5H6

Emp Here 30
SIC 8748 Business consulting, nec

D-U-N-S 24-340-4790   (SL)
THAMES RIVER CHEMICAL CORP
5230 Harvester Rd, Burlington, ON, L7L 4X4
(905) 681-5353
Emp Here 27   *Sales* 6,493,502
SIC 5169 Chemicals and allied products, nec
Pr Pr Daniel Wiggins
 Ann Wiggins

D-U-N-S 25-972-5034   (SL)
TRANSCAT CANADA INC
916 Gateway, Burlington, ON, L7L 5K7
(905) 632-5869
Emp Here 25   *Sales* 2,252,253
SIC 8734 Testing laboratories

D-U-N-S 24-201-4293   (BR)
UPS SCS, INC
UPS SUPPLY CHAIN SOLUTIONS
4156 Mainway, Burlington, ON, L7L 0A7
(905) 315-5500
Emp Here 600
SIC 7389 Business services, nec

D-U-N-S 25-530-4925   (HQ)
UPS SCS, INC
UPS SUPPLY CHAIN SOLUTION
4156 Mainway, Burlington, ON, L7L 0A7
(905) 315-5500
Emp Here 300   *Emp Total* 434,000
Sales 204,202,694
SIC 4212 Local trucking, without storage
Ex VP William Hook
VP Opers Reg Sheen
 Brad Mitchell

D-U-N-S 24-007-6505   (HQ)
UNITED PARCEL SERVICE CANADA LTD
UPS CANADA
1022 Champlain Ave, Burlington, ON, L7L
0C2
(905) 676-1708
Emp Here 100   *Emp Total* 434,000
Sales 1,027,505,538
SIC 4212 Local trucking, without storage
VP VP Alan Gershenhorn
Pr Pr Christoph Atz
VP Paul Winters
VP Craig Podrebarac
 Bill Fahrlender
Dir Edwin Langdon
 Amgad Shehata
Dir Alice Lee
Pers/VP Daniel Shea
 Pat Stanghieri

D-U-N-S 24-384-1306   (SL)
VMWARE CANADA INC
1122 International Blvd Suite 200, Burlington,
ON, L7L 6Z8
(905) 315-6000
Emp Here 20   *Sales* 1,884,658
SIC 7372 Prepackaged software

D-U-N-S 20-703-2736   (BR)
VOESTALPINE ROTEC SUMMO CORP
SUMMO CORP
1200 Burloak Dr, Burlington, ON, L7L 6B4
(905) 336-0014
Emp Here 160
SIC 5051 Metals service centers and offices

D-U-N-S 24-205-0081   (BR)
VOESTALPINE ROTEC SUMMO CORP
SUMMO CORP
1180 Burloak Dr, Burlington, ON, L7L 6B3
(905) 336-3306
Emp Here 60
SIC 5051 Metals service centers and offices

D-U-N-S 20-528-0832   (BR)
**WALDORF SCHOOL ASSOCIATION OF ON-
TARIO INC**
HALTON WALDORF
2193 Orchard Rd, Burlington, ON, L7L 7J8
(905) 331-4387
Emp Here 20

SIC 8211 Elementary and secondary schools

D-U-N-S 20-182-9447   (HQ)
**WATTS   WATER   TECHNOLOGIES
(CANADA) INC**
(*Suby of* Watts Water Technologies, Inc.)
5435 North Service Rd, Burlington, ON, L7L
5H7
(905) 332-4090
Emp Here 130   *Emp Total* 4,800
Sales 34,303,540
SIC 5085 Industrial supplies
VP VP Daniel Bowes
  William C Mccartney

D-U-N-S 20-921-7368   (HQ)
WAXMAN INDUSTRIAL SERVICES CORP
4350 Harvester Rd, Burlington, ON, L7L 5S4
(905) 639-1111
Emp Here 30   *Emp Total* 1,000
Sales 9,703,773
SIC 5093 Scrap and waste materials
Pr Pr Aaron D Waxman
  Jeremy Waxman

D-U-N-S 24-486-8717   (SL)
WHITE RADIO LP
940 Gateway, Burlington, ON, L7L 5K7
(905) 632-6894
Emp Here 30   *Sales* 8,420,350
SIC 5065 Electronic parts and equipment, nec
Pr Pr Jack Van Kessel

D-U-N-S 24-978-0016   (BR)
**WINNERS MERCHANTS INTERNATIONAL
L.P.**
WINNERS
(*Suby of* The TJX Companies Inc)
2445 Appleby Line, Burlington, ON, L7L 0B6
(905) 332-7878
Emp Here 60
SIC 5651 Family clothing stores

D-U-N-S 25-869-3522   (BR)
WOLSELEY CANADA INC
FRONTIER WOLSELEY
(*Suby of* WOLSELEY PLC)
5145 North Service Rd, Burlington, ON, L7L
5H6
(905) 335-4232
Emp Here 20
SIC 5075 Warm air heating and air condition-
ing

D-U-N-S 24-577-2926   (SL)
ZIMMARK INC
4380 South Service Rd Suite 17, Burlington,
ON, L7L 5Y6
(905) 632-5410
Emp Here 40   *Sales* 6,594,250
SIC 3559 Special industry machinery, nec
VP VP Ken Attard
  Paul Bokrossy

D-U-N-S 24-425-2821   (SL)
ZIP SIGNS LTD
5040 North Service Rd, Burlington, ON, L7L
5R5
(905) 332-8332
Emp Here 70   *Sales* 4,888,367
SIC 3993 Signs and advertising specialties

Burlington, ON L7M
Halton County

D-U-N-S 25-102-1127   (SL)
ACCRAPLY CANADA, INC
3070 Mainway Unit 16 19, Burlington, ON,
L7M 3X1
(905) 336-8880
Emp Here 30   *Sales* 3,210,271
SIC 3565 Packaging machinery

D-U-N-S 25-010-9923   (BR)
AECON CONSTRUCTION GROUP INC

AECON UTILITIES
3090 Harrison Crt, Burlington, ON, L7M 0W4
(905) 336-8787
Emp Here 35
SIC 1731 Electrical work

D-U-N-S 24-524-9826   (BR)
BOSCH REXROTH CANADA CORP
3426 Mainway, Burlington, ON, L7M 1A8
(905) 335-5511
Emp Here 65
SIC 5084 Industrial machinery and equipment

D-U-N-S 24-925-2156   (SL)
BUTLER BUILDING CANADA
3070 Mainway Unit 21, Burlington, ON, L7M
3X1
(905) 332-7786
Emp Here 49   *Sales* 5,399,092
SIC 1791 Structural steel erection
Owner Wendy Karens

D-U-N-S 25-988-3916   (BR)
CAMPBELL BROS. MOVERS LIMITED
BURLINGTON MOVERS
1160 Blair Rd Unit 9, Burlington, ON, L7M 1K9
(905) 336-9947
Emp Here 20
SIC 4214 Local trucking with storage

D-U-N-S 20-949-6491   (BR)
CAMPBELL BROS. MOVERS LIMITED
CESAR VAN AND STORAGE
1160 Blair Rd Suite 9, Burlington, ON, L7M
1K9
(905) 332-4262
Emp Here 20
SIC 4214 Local trucking with storage

D-U-N-S 20-303-3329   (BR)
CARA OPERATIONS LIMITED
KELSEY'S RESTAURANT
(*Suby of* Cara Holdings Limited)
4511 Dundas St, Burlington, ON, L7M 5B4
(905) 335-2051
Emp Here 25
SIC 5812 Eating places

D-U-N-S 24-790-6428   (BR)
**CENTRAL WEST SPECIALIZED DEVELOP-
MENTAL SERVICES**
STAR LANE
3782 Star Lane, Burlington, ON, L7M 5A0
(905) 336-4248
Emp Here 250
SIC 8322 Individual and family services

D-U-N-S 20-523-2122   (BR)
DALTON TIMMIS INSURANCE GROUP INC
4125 Upper Middle Rd Suite 1, Burlington,
ON, L7M 4X5
(905) 633-9019
Emp Here 20
SIC 6411 Insurance agents, brokers, and ser-
vice

D-U-N-S 24-721-1527   (BR)
FIRSTCANADA ULC
BURLINGTON LAIDLAW
5401 Dundas St, Burlington, ON, L7M 0Y8
(905) 335-7010
Emp Here 200
SIC 4151 School buses

D-U-N-S 24-751-9812   (BR)
GENERAL ELECTRIC CANADA COMPANY
GE ENERGY SERVICES
(*Suby of* General Electric Company)
1150 Walker'S Line, Burlington, ON, L7M 1V2
(905) 335-6301
Emp Here 75
SIC 3625 Relays and industrial controls

D-U-N-S 20-024-9931   (BR)
**HALTON CATHOLIC DISTRICT SCHOOL
BOARD**
*CANADIAN   MARTYRS   ELEMENTARY
SCHOOL*

3201 Lansdown Dr, Burlington, ON, L7M 1K1
(905) 336-5792
Emp Here 35
SIC 8211 Elementary and secondary schools

D-U-N-S 20-025-2331   (BR)
**HALTON CATHOLIC DISTRICT SCHOOL
BOARD**
*NOTRE DAME ROMAN CATHOLIC SEC-
ONDARY SCHOOL*
2333 Headon Forest Dr, Burlington, ON, L7M
3X6
(905) 335-1544
Emp Here 100
SIC 8211 Elementary and secondary schools

D-U-N-S 20-711-0847   (BR)
**HALTON CATHOLIC DISTRICT SCHOOL
BOARD**
SACRED HEART OF JESUS SCHOOL
2222 Country Club Dr, Burlington, ON, L7M
4S5
(905) 331-4656
Emp Here 50
SIC 8211 Elementary and secondary schools

D-U-N-S 20-591-2905   (BR)
**HALTON CATHOLIC DISTRICT SCHOOL
BOARD**
ST TIMOTHY ELEMENTARY SCHOOL
2141 Deer Run Ave, Burlington, ON, L7M 4C7
(905) 332-5253
Emp Here 40
SIC 8211 Elementary and secondary schools

D-U-N-S 20-026-1423   (BR)
HALTON DISTRICT SCHOOL BOARD
C. H. NORTON PUBLIC SCHOOL
2120 Cleaver Ave, Burlington, ON, L7M 4B6
(905) 332-3897
Emp Here 40
SIC 8211 Elementary and secondary schools

D-U-N-S 20-711-0458   (BR)
HALTON DISTRICT SCHOOL BOARD
CHARLES BEAUDOIN PUBLIC SCHOOL
4313 Clubview Dr, Burlington, ON, L7M 5A1
(905) 637-8297
Emp Here 50
SIC 8211 Elementary and secondary schools

D-U-N-S 20-037-5678   (BR)
HALTON DISTRICT SCHOOL BOARD
DR CHARLES BEST PUBLIC SCHOOL
3110 Parkgate Cres, Burlington, ON, L7M 1C7
(905) 332-2474
Emp Here 20
SIC 8211 Elementary and secondary schools

D-U-N-S 20-229-8753   (BR)
HALTON DISTRICT SCHOOL BOARD
SIR ERNEST MACMILLAN PUBLIC SCHOOL
1350 Headon Rd, Burlington, ON, L7M 1V8
(905) 336-7602
Emp Here 43
SIC 8211 Elementary and secondary schools

D-U-N-S 20-024-9907   (BR)
HALTON DISTRICT SCHOOL BOARD
LESTER B PEARSON HIGH SCHOOL
1433 Headon Rd, Burlington, ON, L7M 1V7
(905) 335-0961
Emp Here 80
SIC 8211 Elementary and secondary schools

D-U-N-S 20-711-0334   (BR)
HALTON DISTRICT SCHOOL BOARD
FLORENCE MEARES PUBLIC SCHOOL
2102 Berwick Dr, Burlington, ON, L7M 4W6
(905) 319-9936
Emp Here 50
SIC 8211 Elementary and secondary schools

D-U-N-S 25-514-2937   (BR)
HOME DEPOT OF CANADA INC
HOME DEPOT
(*Suby of* The Home Depot Inc)
3050 Davidson Crt, Burlington, ON, L7M 4M9

(905) 331-1700
Emp Here 250
SIC 5211 Lumber and other building materials

D-U-N-S 24-420-1047   (BR)
JOHNSON CONTROLS L.P.
3070 Mainway Suite 10, Burlington, ON, L7M
3X1
(905) 335-3325
Emp Here 20
SIC 1731 Electrical work

D-U-N-S 20-567-3697   (BR)
LEE VALLEY TOOLS LTD
3060 Davidson Crt Unit 3, Burlington, ON,
L7M 4X7
(905) 319-9110
Emp Here 20
SIC 5261 Retail nurseries and garden stores

D-U-N-S 20-732-4968   (BR)
LONG & MCQUADE LIMITED
*LONG & MCQUADE MUSICAL INSTRU-
MENTS*
3180 Mainway, Burlington, ON, L7M 1A5
(905) 319-7919
Emp Here 40
SIC 5736 Musical instrument stores

D-U-N-S 25-921-4328   (BR)
LONGO BROTHERS FRUIT MARKETS INC
LONGO'S FRUIT MARKET
2900 Walker'S Line, Burlington, ON, L7M 4M8
(905) 331-1645
Emp Here 150
SIC 5148 Fresh fruits and vegetables

D-U-N-S 24-779-5792   (SL)
MARCOR AUTOMOTIVE INC
1164 Walker'S Line, Burlington, ON, L7M 1V2
(905) 549-6445
Emp Here 50   *Sales* 6,055,738
SIC 5013 Motor vehicle supplies and new
parts
Pr Dan Moscardini

D-U-N-S 20-562-3890   (SL)
MAUSER CANADA LTD
(*Suby of* Clayton, Dubilier & Rice, Inc.)
1121 Pioneer Rd, Burlington, ON, L7M 1K5
(416) 869-1227
Emp Here 60
SIC 3412 Metal barrels, drums, and pails

D-U-N-S 20-923-7838   (BR)
MCBURL CORP
MCDONALD'S RESTAURANT
2991 Walker'S Line, Burlington, ON, L7M 4K5
(905) 336-8761
Emp Here 50
SIC 5812 Eating places

D-U-N-S 24-736-7808   (BR)
**MORGAN   ADVANCED   MATERIALS
CANADA INC**
*MORGAN ADVANCE MATERIALS CANADA
INC*
1185 Walker'S Line, Burlington, ON, L7M 1L1
(905) 335-3414
Emp Here 50
SIC 3443 Fabricated plate work (boiler shop)

D-U-N-S 25-943-3290   (BR)
**PARTICIPATION HOUSE HAMILTON AND
DISTRICT**
(*Suby of* Participation House Hamilton And
District)
3097 Palmer Dr, Burlington, ON, L7M 4G8
(905) 335-3166
Emp Here 20
SIC 8059 Nursing and personal care, nec

D-U-N-S 24-992-3772   (BR)
PIONEER FOOD SERVICES LIMITED
TIM HORTONS
(*Suby of* Pioneer Food Services Limited)
3500 Dundas St Suite 5, Burlington, ON, L7M
4B8

---

(905) 336-8533
Emp Here 42
SIC 5461 Retail bakeries

D-U-N-S 20-788-2734   (BR)
PRIME ENTERPRISES INC
WENDY'S
(*Suby of* Prime Enterprises Inc)
4000 Mainway, Burlington, ON, L7M 4B9
(905) 336-9232
Emp Here 40
SIC 5812 Eating places

D-U-N-S 24-978-1238   (SL)
PRODU-KAKE CANADA INC
3285 Mainway Suite 4, Burlington, ON, L7M 1A6
(905) 335-1136
Emp Here 25   *Sales* 7,067,520
SIC 2819 Industrial inorganic chemicals, nec
Pr Pr W G Neil Smith
Sec Mary Jamieson

D-U-N-S 25-320-9274   (BR)
PUROLATOR INC.
PUROLATOR COURIER
3455 Mainway, Burlington, ON, L7M 1A9
(905) 336-3230
Emp Here 140
SIC 4731 Freight transportation arrangement

D-U-N-S 24-216-4499   (BR)
QUADRA CHIMIE LTEE
1100 Blair Rd, Burlington, ON, L7M 1K9
(905) 336-9133
Emp Here 38
SIC 5169 Chemicals and allied products, nec

D-U-N-S 24-383-8682   (SL)
REVSTONE INDUSTRIES CANADA INC
3267 Mainway, Burlington, ON, L7M 1A6

Emp Here 329   *Sales* 52,166,901
SIC 3714 Motor vehicle parts and accessories
Kelvin Lynch

D-U-N-S 20-039-2348   (HQ)
SIMPSON, S. B. GROUP INC
JACKSON ROBSON INDUSTRIAL SUPPLY
3210 Mainway, Burlington, ON, L7M 1A5
(905) 335-6575
Emp Here 40   *Emp Total* 140
Sales 9,630,812
SIC 5251 Hardware stores
Craig Simpson
Pr Pr Scott Simpson

D-U-N-S 20-796-4409   (BR)
STAPLES CANADA INC
STAPLES THE BUSINESS DEPOT
(*Suby of* Staples, Inc.)
3060 Davidson Crt Unit C2, Burlington, ON, L7M 4X7
(905) 332-1071
Emp Here 40
SIC 5943 Stationery stores

D-U-N-S 24-876-3336   (SL)
THORDON BEARINGS INC
THORFLEX
3225 Mainway, Burlington, ON, L7M 1A6
(905) 335-1440
Emp Here 100   *Sales* 21,304,524
SIC 5085 Industrial supplies
Pr Terry Mcgowan
George Thomson
Anna Galoni

D-U-N-S 24-329-8671   (BR)
WAL-MART CANADA CORP
4515 Dundas St Suite 1, Burlington, ON, L7M 5B4
(905) 331-0027
Emp Here 200
SIC 5311 Department stores

D-U-N-S 24-101-6836   (HQ)
WESTLAKE INDUSTRIES INC
1149 Northside Rd, Burlington, ON, L7M 1H5

(905) 336-5200
Emp Here 30   *Emp Total* 90
Sales 7,796,259
SIC 3499 Fabricated Metal products, nec
Pr Pr Richard Westlake
VP Fin Joan Westlake

D-U-N-S 20-152-4766   (SL)
WHEELABRATOR GROUP (CANADA) LTD
WHEELABRATOR
4900 Palladium Way Suite 200, Burlington, ON, L7M 0W7
(905) 319-7930
Emp Here 125   *Sales* 15,765,768
SIC 3569 General industrial machinery, nec
Pr Pr Robert Joyce

Burlington, ON L7N
Halton County

D-U-N-S 25-998-6156   (SL)
1343929 ONTARIO LIMITED
880 Laurentian Dr Suite 1, Burlington, ON, L7N 3V6
(905) 632-0864
Emp Here 84   *Sales* 13,898,650
SIC 7371 Custom computer programming services
Pr Pr Brian Currie
G Colin Rayner

D-U-N-S 20-151-7641   (BR)
ABB INC
3450 Harvester Rd, Burlington, ON, L7N 3W5
(905) 639-8840
Emp Here 300
SIC 3823 Process control instruments

D-U-N-S 20-301-8239   (BR)
AMEC FOSTER WHEELER AMERICAS LIMITED
AMEC FOSTER WHEELER
3215 North Service Rd, Burlington, ON, L7N 3G2
(905) 335-2353
Emp Here 85
SIC 8711 Engineering services

D-U-N-S 25-145-4336   (BR)
ALSTOM CANADA INC
(*Suby of* General Electric Company)
845 Harrington Crt, Burlington, ON, L7N 3P3
(905) 333-3667
Emp Here 20
SIC 5084 Industrial machinery and equipment

D-U-N-S 25-852-6417   (BR)
ARO INC
ACCOUNTS RECOVERY
3370 South Service Rd Suite 10, Burlington, ON, L7N 3M6

Emp Here 45
SIC 7322 Adjustment and collection services

D-U-N-S 25-922-2214   (BR)
BDO CANADA LLP
BURLINGTON ACCOUNTING
3115 Harvester Rd Suite 400, Burlington, ON, L7N 3N8
(905) 639-9500
Emp Here 120
SIC 8721 Accounting, auditing, and book-keeping

D-U-N-S 24-714-3584   (BR)
BDO CANADA LIMITED
BDO DUNWOODY
3115 Harvester Rd Suite 400, Burlington, ON, L7N 3N8
(905) 637-8554
Emp Here 100
SIC 8111 Legal services

D-U-N-S 25-965-0919   (BR)
BANK OF MONTREAL

BMO
865 Harrington Crt, Burlington, ON, L7N 3P3
(905) 319-4800
Emp Here 77
SIC 6021 National commercial banks

D-U-N-S 20-212-8752   (BR)
BEHLEN INDUSTRIES INC
3390 South Service Rd, Burlington, ON, L7N 3J5
(905) 319-8125
Emp Here 20
SIC 1541 Industrial buildings and warehouses

D-U-N-S 24-314-9549   (HQ)
BIOLAB EQUIPMENT LTD
MAR COR PURIFICATION
(*Suby of* Mar Cor Services, Inc.)
3250 Harvester Rd Unit 6, Burlington, ON, L7N 3W9
(905) 639-7025
Emp Here 20   *Emp Total* 68
Sales 16,112,269
SIC 3821 Laboratory apparatus and furniture
Opers Mgr Darcy Mccabe
VP VP Kathryn Mcisaac
Benjamin Roczniak
Ralph Brown

D-U-N-S 25-488-4794   (BR)
CANADIAN RED CROSS SOCIETY, THE
HALTON HOMEMAKING SERVICES
3210 Harvester Rd, Burlington, ON, L7N 3T1
(905) 632-9420
Emp Here 40
SIC 8322 Individual and family services

D-U-N-S 20-778-2017   (BR)
CANON CANADA INC
BUSINESS SOLUTIONS DIVISION
3375 North Service Rd Suite A 10, Burlington, ON, L7N 3G2

Emp Here 60
SIC 5045 Computers, peripherals, and software

D-U-N-S 20-922-9111   (SL)
CEDAR SPRINGS TENNIS LIMITED
CEDAR SPRINGS HEALTH RACQUET & SPORTS CLUB
960 Cumberland Ave, Burlington, ON, L7N 3J6
(905) 632-9758
Emp Here 125   *Sales* 6,773,040
SIC 7997 Membership sports and recreation clubs
Pr Pr Jack Dennison

D-U-N-S 24-413-0464   (SL)
COGENT POWER INC
845 Laurentian Dr, Burlington, ON, L7N 3W7
(905) 637-3033
Emp Here 310   *Sales* 148,256,142
SIC 4911 Electric services
Pr Pr Ronald Harper
Matthew Stimac

D-U-N-S 25-695-9958   (BR)
COLLIERS PROJECT LEADERS INC
3027 Harvester Rd Suite 101, Burlington, ON, L7N 3G7
(905) 639-2425
Emp Here 30
SIC 8741 Management services

D-U-N-S 24-585-8816   (BR)
COMMONWEALTH HOSPITALITY LTD
HOLIDAY INN
(*Suby of* WXI/WWH Parallel Amalco (Ontario) Ltd)
3063 South Service Rd, Burlington, ON, L7N 3E9
(905) 639-4443
Emp Here 200
SIC 7011 Hotels and motels

D-U-N-S 20-513-3056   (BR)

CORPORATION OF THE CITY OF BURLINGTON
BURLINGTON TRANSIT
3332 Harvester Rd, Burlington, ON, L7N 3M8
(905) 335-7600
Emp Here 50
SIC 4131 Intercity and rural bus transportation

D-U-N-S 20-070-0073   (BR)
CORPORATION OF THE CITY OF BURLINGTON
CITY OF BURLINGTON ROAD & PARK MAINTENANCE
3330 Harvester Rd, Burlington, ON, L7N 3M8
(905) 333-6166
Emp Here 90
SIC 7349 Building maintenance services, nec

D-U-N-S 25-932-4564   (SL)
DUKE MARINE TECHNICAL SERVICES CANADA INC
3425 Harvester Rd Suite 213, Burlington, ON, L7N 3N1
(905) 631-6089
Emp Here 90   *Sales* 5,997,600
SIC 7361 Employment agencies
Pr Pr John Logue
VP VP Sonia Logue

D-U-N-S 24-326-1026   (BR)
EII LIMITED
GO RESILIENT CANADA
(*Suby of* Enterprises International Inc)
3250 Harvester Rd #3, Burlington, ON, L7N 3T1
(905) 635-3113
Emp Here 26
SIC 5084 Industrial machinery and equipment

D-U-N-S 24-744-3039   (SL)
ELSTER SOLUTIONS CANADA, INC
ELSTER METERING
(*Suby of* Honeywell International Inc.)
1100 Walker'S Line Suite 302, Burlington, ON, L7N 2G3
(905) 634-4895
Emp Here 21   *Sales* 3,866,917
SIC 5084 Industrial machinery and equipment

D-U-N-S 20-935-2769   (BR)
EQUIPEMENTS CONTRO VALVE INC, LES
3375 North Service Rd Unit B4 6, Burlington, ON, L7N 3G2
(905) 319-5545
Emp Here 20
SIC 5084 Industrial machinery and equipment

D-U-N-S 25-300-4824   (BR)
FABRICLAND DISTRIBUTORS INC
3515 Fairview St, Burlington, ON, L7N 2R4
(905) 639-2516
Emp Here 20
SIC 5949 Sewing, needlework, and piece goods

D-U-N-S 20-703-7370   (BR)
GREAT PACIFIC ENTERPRISES INC
THE NEWS GROUP DIV
3320 South Service Rd, Burlington, ON, L7N 3M6
(905) 681-1113
Emp Here 20
SIC 5192 Books, periodicals, and newspapers

D-U-N-S 20-034-2074   (BR)
HALTON CATHOLIC DISTRICT SCHOOL BOARD
ASSUMPTION CATHOLIC SECONDARY SCHOOL
3230 Woodward Ave, Burlington, ON, L7N 3P1
(905) 634-1835
Emp Here 20
SIC 8211 Elementary and secondary schools

D-U-N-S 20-711-0698   (BR)
HALTON CATHOLIC DISTRICT SCHOOL BOARD

ST PAUL CATHOLIC SCHOOL
530 Cumberland Ave, Burlington, ON, L7N 2X2
(905) 632-1424
Emp Here 50
SIC 8211 Elementary and secondary schools

D-U-N-S 20-229-9801　　(BR)
HALTON DISTRICT SCHOOL BOARD
JOHN T TUCK PUBLIC SCHOOL
3365 Spruce Ave, Burlington, ON, L7N 1J7
(905) 637-3881
Emp Here 44
SIC 8211 Elementary and secondary schools

D-U-N-S 25-456-8058　　(BR)
HALTON DISTRICT SCHOOL BOARD
TECUMSEH ELEMENTARY SCHOOL
3141 Woodward Ave, Burlington, ON, L7N 2M3
(905) 639-8330
Emp Here 45
SIC 8211 Elementary and secondary schools

D-U-N-S 20-711-0573　　(BR)
HALTON DISTRICT SCHOOL BOARD
BAY AREA LEARNING CENTER
860 Harrington Crt, Burlington, ON, L7N 3N4
(905) 333-3499
Emp Here 50
SIC 8211 Elementary and secondary schools

D-U-N-S 20-229-9314　　(BR)
HALTON DISTRICT SCHOOL BOARD
RYERSON SCHOOL ELEMENTARY
565 Woodview Rd, Burlington, ON, L7N 2Z9
(905) 632-1766
Emp Here 20
SIC 8211 Elementary and secondary schools

D-U-N-S 20-913-6576　　(BR)
HALTON DISTRICT SCHOOL BOARD
GARY ALLAN HIGH SCHOOL
3250 New St, Burlington, ON, L7N 1M8
(905) 631-6120
Emp Here 50
SIC 8211 Elementary and secondary schools

D-U-N-S 20-364-1936　　(SL)
HITACHI CAPITAL CANADA CORP
3390 South Service Rd Suite 301, Burlington, ON, L7N 3J5
(866) 241-9021
Emp Here 50　　Sales 5,399,092
SIC 8741 Management services

D-U-N-S 20-207-1218　　(BR)
INDIGO BOOKS & MUSIC INC
CHAPTERS
(Suby of Indigo Books & Music Inc)
3315 Fairview St Suite 3, Burlington, ON, L7N 3N9
(905) 681-2410
Emp Here 35
SIC 5942 Book stores

D-U-N-S 20-364-0248　　(SL)
INNOMOTIVE SOLUTIONS GROUP INC
3435 South Service Rd, Burlington, ON, L7N 3W6
(877) 845-3816
Emp Here 90　　Sales 12,549,240
SIC 3442 Metal doors, sash, and trim
Pr Bruce Whitehouse

D-U-N-S 20-706-5751　　(BR)
JNE CONSULTING LTD
3370 South Service Rd Suite 107, Burlington, ON, L7N 3M6

Emp Here 30
SIC 8748 Business consulting, nec

D-U-N-S 20-820-5344　　(BR)
LEON'S FURNITURE LIMITED
LEON'S
3167 North Service Rd, Burlington, ON, L7N 3G2

(905) 335-1811
Emp Here 50
SIC 5712 Furniture stores

D-U-N-S 24-896-3886　　(BR)
METRO ONTARIO INC
METRO
3365 Fairview St, Burlington, ON, L7N 3N9
(905) 634-1896
Emp Here 160
SIC 5411 Grocery stores

D-U-N-S 24-305-6645　　(BR)
METRO ONTARIO PHARMACIES LIMITED
3365 Fairview St, Burlington, ON, L7N 3N9
(905) 634-2391
Emp Here 22
SIC 5912 Drug stores and proprietary stores

D-U-N-S 20-945-2270　　(SL)
NATIONAL FITNESS BURLINGTON
3430 Fairview St, Burlington, ON, L7N 2R5

Emp Here 50　　Sales 2,699,546
SIC 7999 Amusement and recreation, nec

D-U-N-S 20-281-5478　　(BR)
NEWTERRA LTD
3310 South Service Rd Suite 307, Burlington, ON, L7N 3M6
(800) 420-4056
Emp Here 20
SIC 5074 Plumbing and heating equipment and supplies (hydronics)

D-U-N-S 20-298-9740　　(BR)
PARSONS BRINCKERHOFF HALSALL INC
3050 Harvester Rd Unit 100, Burlington, ON, L7N 3J1
(905) 681-8481
Emp Here 20
SIC 8621 Professional organizations

D-U-N-S 24-418-7738　　(BR)
RBC DOMINION SECURITIES INC
RBC ROYAL BANK
(Suby of Royal Bank Of Canada)
3405 Harvester Rd Unit 105, Burlington, ON, L7N 3N1

Emp Here 27
SIC 6211 Security brokers and dealers

D-U-N-S 20-771-8909　　(BR)
RYDER TRUCK RENTAL CANADA LTD
(Suby of Ryder System, Inc.)
3407 North Service Rd, Burlington, ON, L7N 3G2
(905) 335-3807
Emp Here 20
SIC 7513 Truck rental and leasing, no drivers

D-U-N-S 24-402-7715　　(BR)
SIR CORP
ASTOR'S, JACK BAR & GRILL
3140 South Service Rd, Burlington, ON, L7N 3J3
(905) 333-0066
Emp Here 73
SIC 5812 Eating places

D-U-N-S 20-053-3144　　(SL)
SATCON POWER SYSTEMS CANADA LTD
835 Harrington Crt, Burlington, ON, L7N 3P3

Emp Here 70　　Sales 7,435,520
SIC 3625 Relays and industrial controls
Pr David B Eisenhaure
Dir Joseph Levagnie

D-U-N-S 20-939-4493　　(HQ)
SHAKLEE CANADA INC
(Suby of Shaklee International, Inc)
3100 Harvester Rd Unit 7, Burlington, ON, L7N 3W8
(905) 681-1422
Emp Here 25　　Emp Total 100
Sales 3,429,153
SIC 5122 Drugs, proprietaries, and sundries

D-U-N-S 24-378-2351　　(BR)
SUPERIOR PLUS LP
WINROC
1121 Walker'S Line Unit 3, Burlington, ON, L7N 2G4
(800) 561-3495
Emp Here 20
SIC 5039 Construction materials, nec

D-U-N-S 25-396-8028　　(HQ)
TECTURA (CANADA), INC
MICROSOFT
3410 South Service Rd Suite 200, Burlington, ON, L7N 3T2
(905) 681-2100
Emp Here 42　　Emp Total 420
Sales 8,292,495
SIC 8748 Business consulting, nec
VP Sls David Savel

D-U-N-S 25-855-7222　　(BR)
THE GOLDEN GRIDDLE CORPORATION
GOLDEN GRIDDLE FAMILY RESTAURANT
3485 Harvester Rd, Burlington, ON, L7N 3T3

Emp Here 30
SIC 5812 Eating places

D-U-N-S 24-680-7767　　(BR)
TRANS UNION OF CANADA, INC
(Suby of Transunion)
3115 Harvester Rd Suite 201, Burlington, ON, L7N 3N8
(905) 340-1000
Emp Here 160
SIC 7323 Credit reporting services

D-U-N-S 25-938-6902　　(BR)
WESTMONT HOSPITALITY MANAGEMENT LIMITED
QUALITY HOTEL BURLINGTON
(Suby of Westmont Hospitality Management Limited)
950 Walker'S Line, Burlington, ON, L7N 2G2
(905) 639-9290
Emp Here 30
SIC 7011 Hotels and motels

D-U-N-S 25-195-3881　　(HQ)
WOLSELEY CANADA INC
CRONKITE, DIV OF
(Suby of WOLSELEY PLC)
880 Laurentian Dr Suite 1, Burlington, ON, L7N 3V6
(905) 335-7373
Emp Here 200　　Emp Total 48,226
Sales 492,484,725
SIC 5074 Plumbing and heating equipment and supplies (hydronics)
CEO Ian Meakins
CFO John Martin

Burlington, ON L7P
Halton County

D-U-N-S 20-055-3725　　(HQ)
ALBERICI CONSTRUCTORS, LTD
(Suby of Alberici Corporation)
1005 Skyview Dr Suite 300, Burlington, ON, L7P 5B1
(905) 315-3000
Emp Here 54　　Emp Total 2,080
Sales 71,899,703
SIC 1542 Nonresidential construction, nec
Pr Pr Dave Gough
　John Alberici
Dir Sherman Ladner

D-U-N-S 20-535-8778　　(BR)
BANK OF MONTREAL
BMO
1505 Guelph Line, Burlington, ON, L7P 3B6
(905) 336-2484
Emp Here 20

SIC 6021 National commercial banks

D-U-N-S 20-588-2264　　(BR)
BANQUE TORONTO-DOMINION, LA
TD CANADA TRUST
(Suby of Toronto-Dominion Bank, The)
1505 Guelph Line, Burlington, ON, L7P 3B6
(905) 335-1990
Emp Here 20
SIC 6021 National commercial banks

D-U-N-S 25-371-6468　　(BR)
BEST BUY CANADA LTD
BEST BUY
(Suby of Best Buy Co., Inc.)
1200 Brant St Unit 1, Burlington, ON, L7P 5C6

Emp Here 100
SIC 5731 Radio, television, and electronic stores

D-U-N-S 25-459-4302　　(SL)
CAMA WOODLANDS NURSING HOME
159 Panin Rd, Burlington, ON, L7P 5A6
(905) 681-6441
Emp Here 80　　Sales 3,648,035
SIC 8051 Skilled nursing care facilities

D-U-N-S 24-566-0394　　(BR)
CANADIAN REFORMED SOCIETY FOR A HOME FOR THE AGED INC
MOUNT NEMO CHRISTIAN NURSING HOME
4486 Guelph Line, Burlington, ON, L7P 0N2
(905) 335-3636
Emp Here 75
SIC 8051 Skilled nursing care facilities

D-U-N-S 25-062-2388　　(BR)
CARA OPERATIONS LIMITED
HARVEY RESTUARANT
(Suby of Cara Holdings Limited)
2025 Guelph Line Suite 1, Burlington, ON, L7P 4M8

Emp Here 35
SIC 5812 Eating places

D-U-N-S 25-657-7156　　(BR)
CINEPLEX ODEON CORPORATION
SILVERCITY BURLINGTON
1250 Brant St, Burlington, ON, L7P 1X8
(905) 319-8677
Emp Here 20
SIC 7832 Motion picture theaters, except drive-in

D-U-N-S 20-031-1673　　(BR)
CORPORATION OF THE CITY OF BURLINGTON
BURLINGTON ANGELA COUGHLAN POOL
2425 Upper Middle Rd, Burlington, ON, L7P 3N9
(905) 335-7000
Emp Here 55
SIC 7999 Amusement and recreation, nec

D-U-N-S 20-519-0270　　(BR)
COSTCO WHOLESALE CANADA LTD
(Suby of Costco Wholesale Corporation)
1225 Brant St, Burlington, ON, L7P 1X7
(905) 336-6714
Emp Here 168
SIC 5099 Durable goods, nec

D-U-N-S 25-301-4021　　(BR)
DELOITTE LLP
1005 Skyview Dr Suite 202, Burlington, ON, L7P 5B1
(905) 315-6770
Emp Here 100
SIC 8721 Accounting, auditing, and bookkeeping

D-U-N-S 20-532-7914　　(BR)
FERN HILL SCHOOL MISSISSAUGA INC
FERN HILL SCHOOL
(Suby of Fern Hill School Mississauga Inc)

---

801 North Service Rd, Burlington, ON, L7P 5B6
(905) 634-8652
Emp Here 20
SIC 8211 Elementary and secondary schools

D-U-N-S 20-025-0731   (BR)
HALTON CATHOLIC DISTRICT SCHOOL BOARD
ST. MARK ELEMENTARY CATHOLIC SCHOOL
2145 Upper Middle Rd, Burlington, ON, L7P 4G1
(905) 336-3911
Emp Here 42
SIC 8211 Elementary and secondary schools

D-U-N-S 20-591-3234   (BR)
HALTON CATHOLIC DISTRICT SCHOOL BOARD
ST GABRIELS ROMAN CATHOLIC
2227 Parkway Dr, Burlington, ON, L7P 1S9
(905) 332-3333
Emp Here 25
SIC 8211 Elementary and secondary schools

D-U-N-S 20-229-8621   (BR)
HALTON DISTRICT SCHOOL BOARD
PAUL A FISHER PUBLIC SCHOOL PUBLIC
2175 Cavendish Dr, Burlington, ON, L7P 3J8
(905) 335-2542
Emp Here 100
SIC 8211 Elementary and secondary schools

D-U-N-S 20-913-6881   (BR)
HALTON DISTRICT SCHOOL BOARD
CLARKDALE PUBLIC SCHOOL
2399 Mountainside Dr, Burlington, ON, L7P 1C6
(905) 335-5605
Emp Here 45
SIC 8211 Elementary and secondary schools

D-U-N-S 20-591-2889   (BR)
HALTON DISTRICT SCHOOL BOARD
KILBRIDE PUBLIC SCHOOL
6611 Panton St, Burlington, ON, L7P 0L8
(905) 335-6394
Emp Here 26
SIC 8211 Elementary and secondary schools

D-U-N-S 20-229-8670   (BR)
HALTON DISTRICT SCHOOL BOARD
MM ROBINSON HIGHSCHOOL
2425 Upper Middle Rd, Burlington, ON, L7P 3N9
(905) 335-5588
Emp Here 80
SIC 8211 Elementary and secondary schools

D-U-N-S 20-027-1042   (BR)
HALTON DISTRICT SCHOOL BOARD
ROLLING MEADOWS PUBLIC SCHOOL
1522 Mountain Grove Ave, Burlington, ON, L7P 2H5
(905) 332-6000
Emp Here 25
SIC 8211 Elementary and secondary schools

D-U-N-S 20-711-0508   (BR)
HALTON DISTRICT SCHOOL BOARD
BRUCE T LINDLEY PUBLIC SCHOOL
2510 Cavendish Dr, Burlington, ON, L7P 4K5
(905) 335-0679
Emp Here 50
SIC 8211 Elementary and secondary schools

D-U-N-S 25-916-0190   (BR)
INDIGO BOOKS & MUSIC INC
INDIGO
(*Suby of* Indigo Books & Music Inc)
1250 Brant St Suite 102, Burlington, ON, L7P 1X8
(905) 331-1860
Emp Here 55
SIC 5942 Book stores

D-U-N-S 20-107-2084   (SL)
JAN KELLEY MARKETING

1005 Skyview Dr Suite 322, Burlington, ON, L7P 5B1
(905) 631-7934
Emp Here 60   *Sales* 7,223,109
SIC 4899 Communication services, nec
Pr Pr Jim Letwin
   Ken Nicholson

D-U-N-S 25-811-1160   (BR)
KPM INDUSTRIES LTD
KING TRUCK CENTRE
1077 Howard Rd, Burlington, ON, L7P 0T7
(905) 639-4401
Emp Here 20
SIC 7538 General automotive repair shops

D-U-N-S 25-282-7811   (BR)
LOBLAW COMPANIES LIMITED
FORTINOS UPPER MIDDLE
2025 Guelph Line, Burlington, ON, L7P 4M8
(905) 336-6566
Emp Here 25
SIC 5411 Grocery stores

D-U-N-S 20-800-5988   (BR)
MCBURL CORP
MCDONALD'S RESTAURANT
1505 Guelph Line, Burlington, ON, L7P 3B6
(905) 336-2331
Emp Here 20
SIC 5812 Eating places

D-U-N-S 20-338-2585   (BR)
MERIDIAN BRICK CANADA LTD
FORTERRA BRICK, LTD
1570 Yorkton Crt, Burlington, ON, L7P 5B7
(905) 633-7384
Emp Here 40
SIC 3251 Brick and structural clay tile

D-U-N-S 20-809-7829   (BR)
METRO ONTARIO INC
FOOD BASICS
1505 Guelph Line, Burlington, ON, L7P 3B6
(905) 336-2525
Emp Here 20
SIC 5411 Grocery stores

D-U-N-S 20-935-2298   (BR)
MORRISON HERSHFIELD LIMITED
1005 Skyview Dr Suite 175, Burlington, ON, L7P 5B1
(905) 319-6668
Emp Here 50
SIC 7363 Help supply services

D-U-N-S 20-077-3930   (BR)
PIONEER FOOD SERVICES LIMITED
TIM HORTONS
(*Suby of* Pioneer Food Services Limited)
2400 Guelph Line Suite 16, Burlington, ON, L7P 4M7
(905) 332-9779
Emp Here 25
SIC 5812 Eating places

D-U-N-S 24-610-4590   (SL)
REISER (CANADA) CO.
REISER
(*Suby of* Robert Reiser & Co, Inc.)
1549 Yorkton Crt Unit 4, Burlington, ON, L7P 5B7
(905) 631-6611
Emp Here 25   *Sales* 4,596,524
SIC 5084 Industrial machinery and equipment

D-U-N-S 25-111-5424   (BR)
SENTREX COMMUNICATIONS INC
BETHLEHEM, WILLIAM TRENCHING
1154 Pettit Rd, Burlington, ON, L7P 2T5
(905) 319-3003
Emp Here 25
SIC 1629 Heavy construction, nec

D-U-N-S 20-555-5068   (BR)
SOBEYS CAPITAL INCORPORATED
SOBEYS
1250 Brant St, Burlington, ON, L7P 1X8

(905) 332-3373
Emp Here 120
SIC 5411 Grocery stores

D-U-N-S 20-935-2819   (BR)
SOBEYS CAPITAL INCORPORATED
2201 Brant St, Burlington, ON, L7P 3N8
(905) 335-2466
Emp Here 40
SIC 5411 Grocery stores

D-U-N-S 20-039-2587   (SL)
SUNSHINE BUILDING MAINTENANCE INC
2500 Industrial St, Burlington, ON, L7P 1A5
(905) 335-2020
Emp Here 100   *Sales* 3,769,316
SIC 7349 Building maintenance services, nec

D-U-N-S 25-319-3072   (BR)
TORONTO-DOMINION BANK, THE
TD FINANCIAL GROUP
(*Suby of* Toronto-Dominion Bank, The)
2025 Guelph Line Suite 36, Burlington, ON, L7P 4M8
(905) 336-1012
Emp Here 20
SIC 6021 National commercial banks

D-U-N-S 24-460-4539   (BR)
VEOLIA ES CANADA SERVICES INDUS-TRIELS INC
2250 Industrial St, Burlington, ON, L7P 1A1

Emp Here 27
SIC 8748 Business consulting, nec

Burlington, ON L7R
Halton County

D-U-N-S 24-917-7221   (SL)
609369 ONTARIO LIMITED
HIDDEN LAKE GOLF & COUNTRY CLUB
Gd Lcd 1, Burlington, ON, L7R 3X7
(905) 336-3660
Emp Here 60   *Sales* 2,407,703
SIC 7997 Membership sports and recreation clubs

D-U-N-S 25-156-9364   (SL)
975445 ONTARIO INC
EMMA'S BACKPORCH
2084 Old Lakeshore Rd, Burlington, ON, L7R 1A3
(905) 634-2084
Emp Here 80   *Sales* 2,407,703
SIC 5812 Eating places

D-U-N-S 25-296-7732   (BR)
BANK OF NOVA SCOTIA, THE
SCOTIABANK
547 Brant St, Burlington, ON, L7R 2G6
(905) 637-5509
Emp Here 28
SIC 6021 National commercial banks

D-U-N-S 24-923-5557   (SL)
BELLM, A. J. HOLDINGS INC
2300 Fairview St, Burlington, ON, L7R 2E4
(905) 632-5371
Emp Here 40   *Sales* 5,626,880
SIC 6712 Bank holding companies
Pr Pr John Bellm
VP Peter Bellm
VP Richard Bellm

D-U-N-S 20-344-8217   (BR)
CIBC WORLD MARKETS INC
CIBC WOOD GUNDY
390 Brant St Suite 500, Burlington, ON, L7R 4J4
(905) 634-2200
Emp Here 20
SIC 6211 Security brokers and dealers

D-U-N-S 24-228-6784   (BR)
CANADIAN IMPERIAL BANK OF COM-

MERCE
CIBC
2400 Fairview St, Burlington, ON, L7R 2E4
(905) 632-5622
Emp Here 45
SIC 6021 National commercial banks

D-U-N-S 25-094-9146   (BR)
CHARTWELL SENIORS HOUSING REAL ESTATE INVESTMENT TRUST
CHARTWELL REIT
2109 Lakeshore Rd, Burlington, ON, L7R 4Z4
(905) 637-7757
Emp Here 32
SIC 8361 Residential care

D-U-N-S 25-301-3056   (BR)
COUTTS, WILLIAM E. COMPANY, LIMITED
HALLMARK CARDS
(*Suby of* Hallmark Cards, Incorporated)
777 Guelph Line Suite E6, Burlington, ON, L7R 3N2
(905) 637-6647
Emp Here 20
SIC 5947 Gift, novelty, and souvenir shop

D-U-N-S 25-169-7652   (SL)
CROSSROADS TELEVISION SYSTEM
CTS TELEVISON
1295 North Service Rd, Burlington, ON, L7R 4X5
(905) 331-7333
Emp Here 50   *Sales* 2,918,428
SIC 4833 Television broadcasting stations

D-U-N-S 24-058-7170   (HQ)
CUMIS LIFE INSURANCE COMPANY
151 North Service Rd, Burlington, ON, L7R 4C2
(905) 632-1221
Emp Here 100   *Emp Total* 500
Sales 192,517,815
SIC 6311 Life insurance
   Gabe Kalmar
VP Fin Kenneth Bolton
Sec Craig Marshall

D-U-N-S 24-815-8297   (SL)
DOUGORD LIMITED
SERVICEMASTER CONTRACT SERVICES
920 Brant St Suite 8, Burlington, ON, L7R 4J1
(905) 637-1411
Emp Here 70   *Sales* 2,042,900
SIC 7349 Building maintenance services, nec

D-U-N-S 24-340-2547   (BR)
FGL SPORTS LTD
SPORT CHEK BURLINGTON MALL
777 Guelph Line, Burlington, ON, L7R 3N2
(905) 637-6868
Emp Here 30
SIC 5941 Sporting goods and bicycle shops

D-U-N-S 20-261-1625   (BR)
GOODLIFE FITNESS CENTRES INC
GOODLIFE FITNESS
777 Guelph Line, Burlington, ON, L7R 3N2
(905) 634-9461
Emp Here 40
SIC 7991 Physical fitness facilities

D-U-N-S 20-300-6734   (BR)
HALTON ALCOHOL DRUG AND GAM-BLING ASSESSMENT PREVENTION AND TREATMENT SERVICES
777 Guelph Line Suite 214, Burlington, ON, L7R 3N2
(905) 639-6537
Emp Here 40
SIC 8699 Membership organizations, nec

D-U-N-S 20-711-0664   (BR)
HALTON CATHOLIC DISTRICT SCHOOL BOARD
ST JOHN'S SCHOOL
653 Brant St, Burlington, ON, L7R 2H1
(905) 632-3541
Emp Here 32

SIC 8211 Elementary and secondary schools

D-U-N-S 20-024-9824　　　(BR)
HALTON DISTRICT SCHOOL BOARD
CENTRAL PUBLIC SCHOOL
638 Brant St, Burlington, ON, L7R 2H2
(905) 634-7739
Emp Here 23
SIC 8211 Elementary and secondary schools

D-U-N-S 20-024-9840　　　(BR)
HALTON DISTRICT SCHOOL BOARD
LAKESHORE PUBLIC SCHOOL
2243 Lakeshore Rd, Burlington, ON, L7R 1B1
(905) 634-3244
Emp Here 30
SIC 8211 Elementary and secondary schools

D-U-N-S 20-711-0441　　　(BR)
HALTON DISTRICT SCHOOL BOARD
TOM THOMSON PUBLIC SCHOOL
2171 Prospect St, Burlington, ON, L7R 1Z6
(905) 639-2010
Emp Here 30
SIC 8211 Elementary and secondary schools

D-U-N-S 20-714-7294　　　(SL)
HAMILTON NIAGARA HALDIMAND BRANT COMMUNITY CARE ACCESS CENTRE
HNHB CCAC
440 Elizabeth St, Burlington, ON, L7R 2M1
(905) 639-5228
Emp Here 100　　　*Sales* 4,742,446
SIC 8059 Nursing and personal care, nec

D-U-N-S 24-302-3223　　　(HQ)
HOOD PACKAGING CORPORATION
(*Suby of* Hood Packaging Corporation)
2380 Mcdowell Rd, Burlington, ON, L7R 4A1
(905) 637-5611
Emp Here 25　　　*Emp Total* 90
Sales 130,803,901
SIC 2674 Bags: uncoated paper and multiwall
Ch Bd Ch Bd Warren A. Hood Jr
V Ch Bd Richard Markell
Pr Robert Morris
VP Fin Todd D.G. Eby
Dir John Joseph Mccabe
Pers/VP Ron J. More
Pur/VP Gary W. Cameron
VP John Johnson
John A. Burnam

D-U-N-S 24-909-5936　　　(BR)
HUDSON'S BAY COMPANY
BAY, THE
777 Guelph Line Unit 8, Burlington, ON, L7R 3N2
(905) 634-8866
Emp Here 180
SIC 5311 Department stores

D-U-N-S 20-299-2637　　　(BR)
IGM FINANCIAL INC
INVESTORS GROUP
390 Brant St Suite 600, Burlington, ON, L7R 4J4
(905) 333-3335
Emp Here 30
SIC 8741 Management services

D-U-N-S 25-903-0443　　　(BR)
MCBURL CORP
MCDONALD'S RESTAURANTS
689 Guelph Line, Burlington, ON, L7R 3M7
(905) 639-1661
Emp Here 75
SIC 5812 Eating places

D-U-N-S 20-175-3360　　　(BR)
MERIDIAN BRICK CANADA LTD
FORTERRA BRICK, LTD
5155 Dundas St Rr 1, Burlington, ON, L7R 3X4
(905) 335-9017
Emp Here 120
SIC 3251 Brick and structural clay tile

D-U-N-S 20-104-0263　　　(BR)
NALCO CANADA CO.
1055 Truman St, Burlington, ON, L7R 3V7
(905) 632-8791
Emp Here 100
SIC 5074 Plumbing and heating equipment and supplies (hydronics)

D-U-N-S 20-718-4334　　　(BR)
R DENNINGER LIMITED
DENNINGER'S FOODS OF THE WORLD
(*Suby of* Denninger, R Limited)
699 Guelph Line, Burlington, ON, L7R 3M7
(905) 639-0510
Emp Here 32
SIC 5421 Meat and fish markets

D-U-N-S 24-963-4122　　　(BR)
RE/MAX GARDEN CITY REALTY INC BROKERAGE
720 Guelph Line, Burlington, ON, L7R 4E2
(905) 333-3500
Emp Here 72
SIC 6531 Real estate agents and managers

D-U-N-S 25-172-4951　　　(BR)
RED LOBSTER HOSPITALITY LLC
RED LOBSTER RESTAURANTS
(*Suby of* Red Lobster Seafood Co., LLC)
2423 Fairview St, Burlington, ON, L7R 2E3
(905) 637-3454
Emp Here 60
SIC 5812 Eating places

D-U-N-S 24-194-3658　　　(BR)
SHOPPERS DRUG MART CORPORATION
3023 New St Suite 739, Burlington, ON, L7R 1K3
(905) 632-2312
Emp Here 20
SIC 5047 Medical and hospital equipment

D-U-N-S 25-944-1947　　　(BR)
SIMPSONWIGLE LAW LLP
(*Suby of* SimpsonWigle Law LLP)
390 Brant St Suite 501, Burlington, ON, L7R 4J4
(905) 639-1052
Emp Here 20
SIC 8111 Legal services

D-U-N-S 20-039-2447　　　(HQ)
SMITH'S FUNERAL SERVICE (BURLINGTON) LIMITED
SMITH'S FUNERAL HOMES
(*Suby of* Smith's Funeral Service (Burlington) Limited)
485 Brant St, Burlington, ON, L7R 2G5
(905) 632-3333
Emp Here 25　　　*Emp Total* 50
Sales 5,072,500
SIC 7261 Funeral service and crematories
Pr Pr Donald Scott Smith

D-U-N-S 25-807-5217　　　(BR)
VALUE VILLAGE STORES, INC
(*Suby of* Savers, Inc.)
2340 Fairview St, Burlington, ON, L7R 2E4
(905) 631-6990
Emp Here 35
SIC 5399 Miscellaneous general merchandise

D-U-N-S 24-374-3973　　　(BR)
WAL-MART CANADA CORP
WALMART SUPERCENTRE
2065 Fairview St, Burlington, ON, L7R 0B4
(905) 637-3100
Emp Here 200
SIC 5999 Miscellaneous retail stores, nec

D-U-N-S 20-004-6923　　　(BR)
WENDY'S RESTAURANTS OF CANADA INC
WENDY'S
(*Suby of* The Wendy's Company)
2387 Fairview St, Burlington, ON, L7R 2E3
(905) 333-1199
Emp Here 35
SIC 5812 Eating places

D-U-N-S 25-802-4504　　　(BR)
WESTERN INVENTORY SERVICE LTD
WIS INTERNATIONAL
720 Guelph Line Suite 720, Burlington, ON, L7R 4E2
(905) 335-4492
Emp Here 50
SIC 7389 Business services, nec

D-U-N-S 20-184-2940　　　(BR)
WINNERS MERCHANTS INTERNATIONAL L.P.
HOMESENSE
(*Suby of* The TJX Companies Inc)
777 Guelph Line Unit G16, Burlington, ON, L7R 3N2
(905) 631-0521
Emp Here 60
SIC 5651 Family clothing stores

D-U-N-S 24-828-0687　　　(BR)
YMCA OF HAMILTON/BURLINGTON/BRANTFORD
RON EDWARDS FAMILY YMCA
500 Drury Lane, Burlington, ON, L7R 2X2
(905) 632-5000
Emp Here 500
SIC 7997 Membership sports and recreation clubs

Burlington, ON L7S
Halton County

D-U-N-S 24-506-7012　　　(SL)
465439 ONTARIO INC
TAYLOR MOVING AND STORAGE
1200 Plains Rd E, Burlington, ON, L7S 1W6
(905) 632-8010
Emp Here 70　　　*Sales* 4,012,839
SIC 4214 Local trucking with storage

D-U-N-S 24-831-0773　　　(SL)
882547 ONTARIO INC
MANDARIN RESTAURANT
1235 Fairview St Suite 1, Burlington, ON, L7S 2H9
(905) 632-6000
Emp Here 80　　　*Sales* 2,407,703
SIC 5812 Eating places

D-U-N-S 24-015-6708　　　(BR)
BOUTIQUE JACOB INC
JACOB
(*Suby of* Boutique Jacob Inc)
900 Maple Ave Unit 110, Burlington, ON, L7S 2J8

Emp Here 20
SIC 5621 Women's clothing stores

D-U-N-S 20-860-4996　　　(BR)
BOUTIQUE LA VIE EN ROSE INC
BOUTIQUE LA VIE EN ROSE INC
900 Maple Ave, Burlington, ON, L7S 2J8
(905) 681-0049
Emp Here 25
SIC 5632 Women's accessory and specialty stores

D-U-N-S 24-139-2927　　　(SL)
BURLINGTON GYMNASTICS CLUB INC
710 Maple Ave, Burlington, ON, L7S 1M6
(905) 637-5774
Emp Here 52　　　*Sales* 2,115,860
SIC 7991 Physical fitness facilities

D-U-N-S 20-568-1153　　　(BR)
CONSEIL SCOLAIRE VIAMONDE
RENAISSANCE
1226 Lockhart Rd, Burlington, ON, L7S 1H1
(905) 637-3852
Emp Here 24
SIC 8211 Elementary and secondary schools

D-U-N-S 24-665-2473　　　(SL)

DALLOV HOLDINGS LIMITED
MAPLE VILLA LONG TERM CARE CENTRE
441 Maple Ave, Burlington, ON, L7S 1L8
(905) 639-2264
Emp Here 105　　　*Sales* 4,815,406
SIC 8051 Skilled nursing care facilities

D-U-N-S 24-737-0315　　　(HQ)
ELLIOTT TURBOMACHINERY CANADA INC
955 Maple Ave, Burlington, ON, L7S 2J4
(905) 333-4101
Emp Here 26　　　*Emp Total* 16,440
Sales 4,331,255
SIC 7699 Repair services, nec

D-U-N-S 20-738-2230　　　(BR)
FOOT LOCKER CANADA CO
FOOT LOCKER CANADA CO.
900 Maple Ave, Burlington, ON, L7S 2J8
(905) 333-4221
Emp Here 20
SIC 5661 Shoe stores

D-U-N-S 24-798-8442　　　(BR)
FOREVER XXI ULC
900 Maple Ave, Burlington, ON, L7S 2J8
(905) 681-6111
Emp Here 60
SIC 5621 Women's clothing stores

D-U-N-S 24-004-7634　　　(BR)
GAP (CANADA) INC
GAPKIDS
(*Suby of* The Gap Inc)
900 Maple Ave Suite 9, Burlington, ON, L7S 2J8
(905) 637-2658
Emp Here 40
SIC 5651 Family clothing stores

D-U-N-S 20-860-5951　　　(BR)
GLENTEL INC
WIRELESS WAVES
900 Maple Ave Ste 14a, Burlington, ON, L7S 2J8
(905) 632-5665
Emp Here 25
SIC 4812 Radiotelephone communication

D-U-N-S 20-920-1552　　　(BR)
HALTON CATHOLIC DISTRICT SCHOOL BOARD
BURLINGTON CENTRAL HIGH SCHOOL
1433 Baldwin St, Burlington, ON, L7S 1K4
(905) 634-7768
Emp Here 30
SIC 8211 Elementary and secondary schools

D-U-N-S 25-301-1936　　　(BR)
HUDSON'S BAY COMPANY
900 Maple Ave, Burlington, ON, L7S 2J8
(416) 681-0030
Emp Here 60
SIC 5311 Department stores

D-U-N-S 20-789-5314　　　(BR)
HUDSON'S BAY COMPANY
900 Maple Ave, Burlington, ON, L7S 2J8
(905) 681-0030
Emp Here 100
SIC 5311 Department stores

D-U-N-S 25-295-2536　　　(SL)
IVANHOE CAMBRIDGE II INC.
IVANHOE CAMBRIDGE
900 Maple Ave, Burlington, ON, L7S 2J8
(905) 681-2900
Emp Here 300　　　*Sales* 35,337,338
SIC 6512 Nonresidential building operators
Dir Lescia Valentini

D-U-N-S 24-720-6352　　　(BR)
LONGO BROTHERS FRUIT MARKETS INC
LONGO'S FRUIT MARKET
1225 Fairview St, Burlington, ON, L7S 1Y3
(905) 637-3804
Emp Here 135

SIC 5431 Fruit and vegetable markets

D-U-N-S 20-075-4971 (BR)
MICHAELS OF CANADA, ULC
(*Suby of* The Michaels Companies Inc)
1881 Fairview St, Burlington, ON, L7S 2K4
(905) 639-8146
Emp Here 50
SIC 5945 Hobby, toy, and game shops

D-U-N-S 20-165-1382 (BR)
PRIME RESTAURANTS INC
EASTSIDE MARIO'S RESTAURANT
(*Suby of* Cara Holdings Limited)
900 Maple Ave, Burlington, ON, L7S 2J8

Emp Here 80
SIC 5812 Eating places

D-U-N-S 25-311-1975 (BR)
SEARS CANADA INC
SEARS
900 Maple Ave, Burlington, ON, L7S 2J8
(905) 632-4111
Emp Here 300
SIC 5311 Department stores

D-U-N-S 24-210-2106 (SL)
SPENCER'S AT THE WATERFRONT
1340 Lakeshore Rd, Burlington, ON, L7S 1Y2
(905) 633-7494
Emp Here 70   *Sales* 2,115,860
SIC 5812 Eating places

D-U-N-S 25-033-6948 (BR)
SUN CHEMICAL LIMITED
GENERAL PRINTING INK
1274 Plains Rd E, Burlington, ON, L7S 1W6
(905) 639-2561
Emp Here 25
SIC 2893 Printing ink

D-U-N-S 20-039-2728 (SL)
TAYLOR MOVING & STORAGE LIMITED
TAYLOR INTERNATIONAL
1200 Plains Rd E, Burlington, ON, L7S 1W6
(905) 632-8010
Emp Here 70   *Sales* 4,012,839
SIC 4214 Local trucking with storage

Burlington, ON L7T
Halton County

D-U-N-S 24-850-7089 (SL)
BENZY HOGAN INVESTMENTS LTD
GARDEN MOTORCAR
181 Plains Rd W, Burlington, ON, L7T 0B1

Emp Here 49   *Sales* 24,855,250
SIC 5511 New and used car dealers
Pr Steven Lewis

D-U-N-S 20-783-2593 (SL)
BURLINGTON GOLF AND COUNTRY CLUB LIMITED
422 North Shore Blvd E, Burlington, ON, L7T 1W9
(905) 634-7726
Emp Here 80   *Sales* 3,210,271
SIC 7997 Membership sports and recreation clubs

D-U-N-S 20-711-7479 (BR)
CONSEIL SCOLAIRE DE DISTRICT CATHOLIQUE CENTRE-SUD
ECOLE ELEMENTAIRE CATHOLIQUE SAINT PHIELEPPE
901 Francis Rd, Burlington, ON, L7T 3Y3
(905) 639-6100
Emp Here 25
SIC 8211 Elementary and secondary schools

D-U-N-S 20-940-4644 (BR)
FORTINOS SUPERMARKET LTD
1059 Plains Rd E, Burlington, ON, L7T 4K1

(905) 634-1591
Emp Here 50
SIC 5411 Grocery stores

D-U-N-S 25-250-3008 (BR)
HALTON DISTRICT SCHOOL BOARD
ALDERSHOT SCHOOL
50 Fairwood Pl W, Burlington, ON, L7T 1E5
(905) 637-2383
Emp Here 60
SIC 8211 Elementary and secondary schools

D-U-N-S 25-348-6310 (BR)
HALTON DISTRICT SCHOOL BOARD
MAPLEHURST PUBLIC SCHOOL
481 Plains Rd E, Burlington, ON, L7T 2E2
(905) 634-2373
Emp Here 35
SIC 8211 Elementary and secondary schools

D-U-N-S 20-711-0391 (BR)
HALTON DISTRICT SCHOOL BOARD
KING'S ROAD PUBLIC SCHOOL
660 Greenwood Dr, Burlington, ON, L7T 3P3
(905) 637-3477
Emp Here 27
SIC 8211 Elementary and secondary schools

D-U-N-S 20-591-2830 (BR)
HALTON DISTRICT SCHOOL BOARD
GLENVIEW PUBLIC SCHOOL
143 Townsend Ave, Burlington, ON, L7T 1Z1
(905) 634-6789
Emp Here 30
SIC 8211 Elementary and secondary schools

D-U-N-S 20-799-6831 (BR)
HYDRO ONE INC
1225 King Rd, Burlington, ON, L7T 0B7
(905) 681-4421
Emp Here 100
SIC 4911 Electric services

D-U-N-S 25-203-6082 (BR)
ONTARIO POWER GENERATION INC
BURLINGTON TRANSFORMER STATION
1225 King Rd, Burlington, ON, L7T 0B7
(905) 681-4400
Emp Here 20
SIC 4911 Electric services

D-U-N-S 25-310-8252 (HQ)
PARTICIPATION HOUSE HAMILTON AND DISTRICT
(*Suby of* Participation House Hamilton And District)
1022 Waterdown Rd, Burlington, ON, L7T 1N3
(905) 333-3553
Emp Here 70   *Emp Total* 250
Sales 12,560,000
SIC 8361 Residential care
Ex Dir Cindy Kinnon
Dir Opers Stan Holko
  Sharon Gallant
  Harry Traini
  Doug Morden
  Vaughan Galbraith

D-U-N-S 20-753-9537 (HQ)
POLLARD WINDOWS INC
(*Suby of* Pollard Windows Inc)
1217 King Rd, Burlington, ON, L7T 0B7
(905) 634-2365
Emp Here 225   *Emp Total* 250
Sales 20,428,996
SIC 2431 Millwork
Pr Karen Pollard-Josling
  Reginald Pollard
  Carol Pollard
Dir Gary Pollard

D-U-N-S 25-355-0792 (BR)
ROMAN CATHOLIC EPISCOPAL CORPORATION OF THE DIOCESE OF HAMILTON IN ONTARIO, THE
CATHOLIC CEMETARY
600 Spring Gardens Rd, Burlington, ON, L7T 1J1

(905) 522-7727
Emp Here 50
SIC 6531 Real estate agents and managers

D-U-N-S 24-851-0203 (SL)
SWITZER-CARTY TRANSPORTATION SERVICES INC
1006 Plains Rd E, Burlington, ON, L7T 4K2
(289) 288-1366
Emp Here 90   *Sales* 3,031,879
SIC 4151 School buses

D-U-N-S 20-229-8969 (HQ)
UNGER NURSING HOMES LIMITED
HAMPTON TERRACE CARE CENTRE
(*Suby of* Unger Nursing Homes Limited)
75 Plains Rd W Suite 214, Burlington, ON, L7T 1E8
(905) 631-0700
Emp Here 100   *Emp Total* 100
Sales 4,523,563
SIC 8051 Skilled nursing care facilities

D-U-N-S 24-652-2353 (BR)
VIA RAIL CANADA INC
1199 Waterdown Rd, Burlington, ON, L7T 4A8

Emp Here 400
SIC 4111 Local and suburban transit

D-U-N-S 20-005-7003 (BR)
WENDY'S RESTAURANTS OF CANADA INC
WENDY'S
(*Suby of* The Wendy's Company)
145 Plains Rd E, Burlington, ON, L7T 2C4
(905) 634-4882
Emp Here 20
SIC 5812 Eating places

Caistor Centre, ON L0R

D-U-N-S 20-292-1180 (BR)
DISTRICT SCHOOL BOARD OF NIAGARA
CAISTOR CENTRAL PUBLIC SCHOOL
1794 Regional Rd 6, Caistor Centre, ON, L0R 1E0
(905) 957-7473
Emp Here 26
SIC 8211 Elementary and secondary schools

Calabogie, ON K0J
Renfrew County

D-U-N-S 20-711-6935 (BR)
RENFREW COUNTY CATHOLIC DISTRICT SCHOOL BOARD
ST JOSEPH'S SEPARATE HIGH SCHOOL
(*Suby of* Renfrew County Catholic District School Board)
12649 Lanark Rd, Calabogie, ON, K0J 1H0
(613) 752-2808
Emp Here 50
SIC 8211 Elementary and secondary schools

Caledon, ON L7C
Peel County

D-U-N-S 24-034-7067 (SL)
CHEEMA CLEANING SERVICES LTD
12366 Airport Rd, Caledon, ON, L7C 2W1
(905) 951-7156
Emp Here 100   *Sales* 2,918,428
SIC 7349 Building maintenance services, nec

D-U-N-S 20-333-5104 (BR)
EXEL CANADA LTD
DHL SUPPLY CHAIN
12333 Airport Rd, Caledon, ON, L7C 2X3

(905) 951-6838
Emp Here 20
SIC 4225 General warehousing and storage

D-U-N-S 24-194-7720 (SL)
FLEX-MOR INDUSTRIES LTD
7072 Mayfield Rd, Caledon, ON, L7C 0Z9
(905) 266-3010
Emp Here 65   *Sales* 11,159,500
SIC 4213 Trucking, except local
Pr Pr Sheldon Black
  Gregory Black
Dir Morley Black

D-U-N-S 24-595-7506 (BR)
GRO-BARK (ONTARIO) LTD
816 Mayfield Rd, Caledon, ON, L7C 0Y6
(905) 846-1515
Emp Here 20
SIC 5261 Retail nurseries and garden stores

D-U-N-S 20-703-0532 (BR)
PIONEER HI-BRED PRODUCTION LTD
(*Suby of* E. I. Du Pont De Nemours and Company)
12111 Mississauga Rd, Caledon, ON, L7C 1X1
(905) 843-9166
Emp Here 50
SIC 8731 Commercial physical research

D-U-N-S 24-222-6165 (HQ)
TORBRAM ELECTRIC SUPPLY CORPORATION
T E S
10 Perdue Crt Unit 6, Caledon, ON, L7C 3M6
(905) 495-0535
Emp Here 44   *Emp Total* 3,124
Sales 17,072,804
SIC 5063 Electrical apparatus and equipment
Dir Thomas Mackie
  Andrew Dawes
  Phil Flaherty

D-U-N-S 20-165-1390 (HQ)
TOTAL ELECTRIC SUPPLY LIMITED
TORBRAM ELECTRIC SUPPLY
10 Perdue Crt Unit 6, Caledon, ON, L7C 3M6
(905) 495-3538
Emp Here 300   *Emp Total* 3,124
Sales 71,552,333
SIC 5063 Electrical apparatus and equipment
Dir Alan Renton
Dir Giancarlo Commisso
Dir Fin Todd Mcnamara

Caledon, ON L7E
Peel County

D-U-N-S 24-101-6125 (BR)
DICK, JAMES CONSTRUCTION LIMITED
JAMES DICK CONSTRUCTION LIMITED
13975 Humber Station Rd, Caledon, ON, L7E 5T4
(905) 857-8709
Emp Here 22
SIC 3273 Ready-mixed concrete

D-U-N-S 25-252-8039 (BR)
TORONTO AND REGION CONSERVATION AUTHORITY
ALBION HILLS
(*Suby of* Toronto and Region Conservation Authority)
16500 Regional Road 50, Caledon, ON, L7E 3E7
(905) 880-0227
Emp Here 21
SIC 7032 Sporting and recreational camps

Caledon East, ON L7C
Peel County

D-U-N-S 20-710-9880   (BR)
DUFFERIN-PEEL CATHOLIC DISTRICT SCHOOL BOARD
ST CORNELIUS SCHOOL
16066 Innis Lake Rd, Caledon East, ON, L7C 2Z2
(905) 584-2245
Emp Here 50
SIC 8211 Elementary and secondary schools

D-U-N-S 20-026-3395   (BR)
DUFFERIN-PEEL CATHOLIC DISTRICT SCHOOL BOARD
ROBERT S FRANK HALL
6500 Old Church Rd, Caledon East, ON, L7C 0H3
(905) 584-1670
Emp Here 120
SIC 8211 Elementary and secondary schools

D-U-N-S 25-297-1262   (BR)
PEEL DISTRICT SCHOOL BOARD
CALEDON EAST PUBLIC SCHOOL
(*Suby of* Peel District School Board)
15738 Airport Rd, Caledon East, ON, L7C 2W8
(905) 584-2701
Emp Here 25
SIC 8211 Elementary and secondary schools

D-U-N-S 25-822-2629   (BR)
SOBEYS CAPITAL INCORPORATED
IGA
15771 Airport Rd, Caledon East, ON, L7C 1K2
(905) 584-9677
Emp Here 60
SIC 5411 Grocery stores

Caledon Village, ON L7K

D-U-N-S 20-039-4153   (BR)
CALEDON SAND & GRAVEL INC
17847 Hurontario St, Caledon Village, ON, L7K 1X2
(519) 927-5224
Emp Here 60
SIC 5032 Brick, stone, and related material

D-U-N-S 24-894-0694   (BR)
PEEL DISTRICT SCHOOL BOARD
CALEDON CENTRAL PUBLIC SCHOOL
(*Suby of* Peel District School Board)
18357 Kennedy Rd, Caledon Village, ON, L7K 1Y7
(519) 927-5231
Emp Here 50
SIC 8211 Elementary and secondary schools

Caledonia, ON N3W
Haldimand County

D-U-N-S 20-710-6498   (BR)
BRANT HALDIMAND NORFOLK CATHOLIC DISTRICT SCHOOL BOARD
NOTRE DAME SCHOOL
35 Braemar Ave, Caledonia, ON, N3W 2M5
(905) 765-0649
Emp Here 20
SIC 8211 Elementary and secondary schools

D-U-N-S 25-467-1316   (BR)
BRANT HALDIMAND NORFOLK CATHOLIC DISTRICT SCHOOL BOARD
ST PATRICK'S SCHOOL
81 Orkney St E, Caledonia, ON, N3W 1L3
(905) 765-4626
Emp Here 30
SIC 8211 Elementary and secondary schools

D-U-N-S 25-373-4834   (BR)
GEORGIA-PACIFIC CANADA LP
(*Suby of* Koch Industries, Inc.)

350 Argyle St N, Caledonia, ON, N3W 1M2

Emp Here 120
SIC 3275 Gypsum products

D-U-N-S 20-009-9419   (BR)
GRAND ERIE DISTRICT SCHOOL BOARD
ONEIDA CENTRAL PUBLIC SCHOOL
(*Suby of* Grand Erie District School Board)
661 4th Line, Caledonia, ON, N3W 2B2
(905) 765-4700
Emp Here 20
SIC 8211 Elementary and secondary schools

D-U-N-S 20-545-2597   (BR)
GRAND ERIE DISTRICT SCHOOL BOARD
CALEDONIA CENTENNIAL PUBLIC SCHOOL
(*Suby of* Grand Erie District School Board)
110 Shetland St, Caledonia, ON, N3W 2H1
(905) 765-4860
Emp Here 25
SIC 8211 Elementary and secondary schools

D-U-N-S 20-591-3283   (BR)
GRAND ERIE DISTRICT SCHOOL BOARD
RIVER HEIGHTS PUBLIC SCHOOL
(*Suby of* Grand Erie District School Board)
37 Forfar St E, Caledonia, ON, N3W 1L6
(905) 765-5437
Emp Here 25
SIC 8211 Elementary and secondary schools

D-U-N-S 20-913-5669   (BR)
GRAND ERIE DISTRICT SCHOOL BOARD
MCKINNON PARK SECONDARY SCHOOL
(*Suby of* Grand Erie District School Board)
91 Haddington St Suite 765, Caledonia, ON, N3W 2H2
(905) 765-4466
Emp Here 25
SIC 8211 Elementary and secondary schools

D-U-N-S 20-923-7846   (SL)
HALDIMAND FAMILY RESTAURANTS LIMITED
MCDONALD'S RESTAURANT
282 Argyle St S, Caledonia, ON, N3W 1K7
(905) 765-9660
Emp Here 64   *Sales* 1,896,978
SIC 5812 Eating places

D-U-N-S 20-801-9344   (BR)
HYDRO ONE INC
411 Baptist Church Rd, Caledonia, ON, N3W 2G9

Emp Here 20
SIC 4911 Electric services

D-U-N-S 24-199-4743   (BR)
NESTLE CANADA INC
NESTLE PURINA PETCARE CANADA
50 Orkney St W, Caledonia, ON, N3W 1B1
(905) 765-3161
Emp Here 65
SIC 3295 Minerals, ground or treated

D-U-N-S 20-107-1144   (BR)
NICHOLSON AND CATES LIMITED
NICHOLSON AND CATES LIMITED
15 Alabastine Ave, Caledonia, ON, N3W 1K9
(905) 765-5513
Emp Here 32
SIC 5031 Lumber, plywood, and millwork

D-U-N-S 20-077-0498   (BR)
SALVERDA ENTERPRISES INC
TIM HORTONS
172 Argyle St N, Caledonia, ON, N3W 2J7
(905) 765-8888
Emp Here 20
SIC 5812 Eating places

Callander, ON P0H
Parry Sound County

D-U-N-S 25-238-1850   (BR)
NEAR NORTH DISTRICT SCHOOL BOARD
M T DAVIDSON PUBLIC SCHOOL
330 Lansdowne St E, Callander, ON, P0H 1H0
(705) 472-5970
Emp Here 32
SIC 8211 Elementary and secondary schools

D-U-N-S 20-591-9918   (BR)
NIPISSING PARRY SOUND CATHOLIC DISTRICT SCHOOL BOARD
ST-THERESA CATHOLIC SCHOOL
1475 Main St N, Callander, ON, P0H 1H0
(705) 752-4407
Emp Here 20
SIC 8211 Elementary and secondary schools

Cambridge, ON N1P
Waterloo County

D-U-N-S 20-590-7749   (BR)
WATERLOO CATHOLIC DISTRICT SCHOOL BOARD
HOLY SPIRIT CATHOLIC ELEMENTARY SCHOOL
15 Gatehouse Dr, Cambridge, ON, N1P 1C7
(519) 621-8973
Emp Here 50
SIC 8211 Elementary and secondary schools

D-U-N-S 25-228-2108   (BR)
WATERLOO CATHOLIC DISTRICT SCHOOL BOARD
ST BENEDICT CATHOLIC SECONDARY SCHOOL
50 Saginaw Pky, Cambridge, ON, N1P 1A1
(519) 621-4050
Emp Here 140
SIC 8211 Elementary and secondary schools

Cambridge, ON N1R
Waterloo County

D-U-N-S 25-366-8750   (SL)
2018429 ONTARIO LTD
48 Cowansview Rd, Cambridge, ON, N1R 7N3
(519) 740-3757
Emp Here 130   *Sales* 27,877,440
SIC 6712 Bank holding companies
 William Nicholls Jr
Pr Pr Bill Nicholls Sr

D-U-N-S 24-360-4597   (SL)
3L FILTERS 2007 INC
427 Elgin St N, Cambridge, ON, N1R 8G4
(519) 621-9949
Emp Here 40   *Sales* 5,465,508
SIC 3569 General industrial machinery, nec
Pr Pr Harold Roozen
Genl Mgr Gene Allevato

D-U-N-S 24-704-9489   (BR)
A.G. SIMPSON AUTOMOTIVE INC
A G S AUTOMOTIVE
560 Conestoga Blvd, Cambridge, ON, N1R 7P7
(519) 621-7953
Emp Here 150
SIC 3465 Automotive stampings

D-U-N-S 25-167-2051   (BR)
AECON CONSTRUCTION GROUP INC
AECON INDUSTRIAL - CENTRAL CANADA
150 Sheldon Dr, Cambridge, ON, N1R 7K9
(519) 653-3200
Emp Here 300
SIC 1541 Industrial buildings and warehouses

D-U-N-S 20-038-9005   (HQ)
BWXT CANADA LTD
581 Coronation Blvd, Cambridge, ON, N1R 3E9
(519) 621-2130
Emp Here 900   *Emp Total* 2,137
Sales 177,367,462
SIC 3621 Motors and generators
Pr Rex Geveden
Ch Bd John Fees
Pr John Macquarrie
 David Black
Sr VP James Canafax
VP Regina Carter
 Jason Kerr
Pers/VP Richard Loving
VP M. Alan Nethery
 William Russell

D-U-N-S 25-295-9572   (BR)
BANK OF NOVA SCOTIA, THE
SCOTIABANK
72 Main St, Cambridge, ON, N1R 1V7
(519) 740-4050
Emp Here 22
SIC 6021 National commercial banks

D-U-N-S 25-296-7898   (BR)
BANK OF NOVA SCOTIA, THE
SCOTIABANK
544 Hespeler Rd, Cambridge, ON, N1R 6J8
(519) 740-4004
Emp Here 30
SIC 6021 National commercial banks

D-U-N-S 25-319-3239   (BR)
BANQUE TORONTO-DOMINION, LA
TORONTO-DOMINION BANK, THE
(*Suby of* Toronto-Dominion Bank, The)
81 Main St, Cambridge, ON, N1R 1W1

Emp Here 21
SIC 6021 National commercial banks

D-U-N-S 20-589-5332   (BR)
BANQUE TORONTO-DOMINION, LA
TD CANADA TRUST
(*Suby of* Toronto-Dominion Bank, The)
200 Franklin Blvd, Cambridge, ON, N1R 8N8
(519) 622-1010
Emp Here 20
SIC 6021 National commercial banks

D-U-N-S 24-384-5844   (HQ)
BONNIE TOGS CHILDREN'S LIMITED
(*Suby of* Bonnie Togs Children's Limited)
65 Struck Crt, Cambridge, ON, N1R 8L2
(519) 624-6574
Emp Here 25   *Emp Total* 500
Sales 30,435,000
SIC 5641 Children's and infants' wear stores
 Paul Rubinstein

D-U-N-S 25-303-4227   (BR)
CANADIAN IMPERIAL BANK OF COMMERCE
CIBC
11 Main St, Cambridge, ON, N1R 1V5
(519) 621-5030
Emp Here 25
SIC 6021 National commercial banks

D-U-N-S 25-309-7323   (BR)
CANADIAN PACIFIC RAILWAY COMPANY
CPR
10 Malcolm St, Cambridge, ON, N1R 1L8
(519) 621-4130
Emp Here 20
SIC 4011 Railroads, line-haul operating

D-U-N-S 20-303-3261   (BR)
CARA OPERATIONS LIMITED
KELSEY'S
(*Suby of* Cara Holdings Limited)
40 Pinebush Rd, Cambridge, ON, N1R 8K5
(519) 620-2411
Emp Here 65

SIC 5812 Eating places

D-U-N-S 20-321-8920 (BR)
CARA OPERATIONS LIMITED
HARVEY'S
(*Suby of* Cara Holdings Limited)
600 Hespeler Rd, Cambridge, ON, N1R 8H2
(519) 620-7887
Emp Here 25
SIC 5812 Eating places

D-U-N-S 25-591-7338 (BR)
CHILDREN'S AID SOCIETY OF THE RE-GIONAL MUNICIPALITY OF WATERLOO, THE
FAMILY AND CHILDREN'S SERVICES OF THE REGIONAL MUNICIPALITY OF WATER-LOO
168 Hespeler Rd, Cambridge, ON, N1R 6V7
(519) 576-0540
Emp Here 55
SIC 8322 Individual and family services

D-U-N-S 20-543-9433 (HQ)
COM DEV LTD
COM DEV SPACE
(*Suby of* Honeywell International Inc.)
155 Sheldon Dr, Cambridge, ON, N1R 7H6
(519) 622-2300
Emp Here 700   *Emp Total* 131,000
Sales 104,479,722
SIC 3669 Communications equipment, nec
 Michael Pley
 Terry Reidel
Pr Mike Williams
Pers/VP Paul Dyck
 Gary Calhoun

D-U-N-S 25-832-6099 (BR)
COMMUNITY LIVING CAMBRIDGE
(*Suby of* Community Living Cambridge)
160 Hespeler Rd, Cambridge, ON, N1R 6V7
(519) 623-7490
Emp Here 400
SIC 8011 Offices and clinics of medical doctors

D-U-N-S 25-312-2188 (HQ)
COMMUNITY LIVING CAMBRIDGE
(*Suby of* Community Living Cambridge)
160 Hespeler Rd, Cambridge, ON, N1R 6V7
(519) 623-7490
Emp Here 80   *Emp Total* 280
Sales 18,469,648
SIC 8322 Individual and family services
Ex Dir Michael Mullen

D-U-N-S 24-345-4670 (BR)
COMMUNITY LIVING CAMBRIDGE
ARC INDUSTRIES
466 Franklin Blvd, Cambridge, ON, N1R 8G6
(519) 621-0680
Emp Here 90
SIC 8331 Job training and related services

D-U-N-S 25-182-6996 (BR)
COMPAGNIE DE TELEPHONE BELL DU CANADA OU BELL CANADA, LA
355 Hespeler Rd, Cambridge, ON, N1R 6B3
(519) 740-8220
Emp Here 20
SIC 4899 Communication services, nec

D-U-N-S 25-800-8358 (HQ)
CORONATION DENTAL SPECIALTY GROUP
(*Suby of* Coronation Dental Specialty Group)
350 Conestoga Blvd Unit B17, Cambridge, ON, N1R 7L7
(519) 623-3810
Emp Here 50   *Emp Total* 56
Sales 3,210,271
SIC 8021 Offices and clinics of dentists

D-U-N-S 25-783-4028 (BR)
CORPORATION OF THE CITY OF CAM-BRIDGE, THE

DOLSON, JOHN CENTRE
212 South St, Cambridge, ON, N1R 2P4
(519) 623-0270
Emp Here 50
SIC 7999 Amusement and recreation, nec

D-U-N-S 24-333-3627 (BR)
CORPORATION OF THE CITY OF CAM-BRIDGE, THE
CAMBRIDGE FIRE DEPARTMENT
1625 Bishop St N, Cambridge, ON, N1R 7J4
(519) 621-6001
Emp Here 138
SIC 7389 Business services, nec

D-U-N-S 24-097-3565 (BR)
CORUS ENTERTAINMENT INC
107.5 DAVE FM
1315 Bishop St N Suite 100, Cambridge, ON, N1R 6Z2

Emp Here 25
SIC 7299 Miscellaneous personal service

D-U-N-S 20-980-3451 (BR)
DANA CANADA CORPORATION
THERMAL PRODUCTS LONG MANUFAC-TURING DIV OF
401 Franklin Blvd, Cambridge, ON, N1R 8G8
(519) 621-1303
Emp Here 200
SIC 3714 Motor vehicle parts and accessories

D-U-N-S 20-644-4833 (BR)
DAUBOIS INC
1501 Whistle Bare Rd, Cambridge, ON, N1R 5S3
(416) 787-4917
Emp Here 25
SIC 5032 Brick, stone, and related material

D-U-N-S 25-560-2385 (BR)
EXOVA CANADA INC
EXOVA
(*Suby of* Exova, Inc.)
15 High Ridge Crt, Cambridge, ON, N1R 7L3
(519) 621-8191
Emp Here 25
SIC 8734 Testing laboratories

D-U-N-S 24-059-6247 (BR)
EXTEND COMMUNICATIONS INC
YOUR TELEPHONE SECRETARY
(*Suby of* Extend Communications Inc)
51 Water St N, Cambridge, ON, N1R 3B3
(519) 621-6730
Emp Here 20
SIC 7389 Business services, nec

D-U-N-S 24-340-0996 (BR)
FGL SPORTS LTD
NATIONAL SPORTS
600 Hespeler Rd Unit 83, Cambridge, ON, N1R 8H2
(519) 620-4499
Emp Here 20
SIC 5941 Sporting goods and bicycle shops

D-U-N-S 25-687-5170 (HQ)
FORTERRA PIPE & PRECAST, LTD
2099 Roseville Rd Suite 2, Cambridge, ON, N1R 5S3
(519) 622-7574
Emp Here 100   *Emp Total* 2
Sales 47,037,429
SIC 3272 Concrete products, nec
Dir Plamen Jordanoff
 Leo Steffler

D-U-N-S 20-810-6166 (BR)
GOVERNMENT OF ONTARIO
FAMILY & CHILDREN SERVICES OF THE WATERLOO REGION
168 Hespeler Rd, Cambridge, ON, N1R 6V7
(519) 576-0540
Emp Here 65
SIC 8322 Individual and family services

D-U-N-S 25-756-4716 (BR)
GRAND VALLEY REAL ESTATE LIMITED
GRAND VALLEY REAL ESTATE
(*Suby of* Grand Valley Real Estate Limited)
471 Hespeler Rd Unit 4, Cambridge, ON, N1R 6J2
(519) 621-2000
Emp Here 50
SIC 6531 Real estate agents and managers

D-U-N-S 25-524-2794 (BR)
HAMILTON REGION CONSERVATION AU-THORITY
VALENS CONSERVATION AREA
1667 Regional Road 97, Cambridge, ON, N1R 5S7
(905) 525-2183
Emp Here 30
SIC 7033 Trailer parks and campsites

D-U-N-S 20-553-6399 (BR)
HOME DEPOT OF CANADA INC
HOME DEPOT
(*Suby of* The Home Depot Inc)
35 Pinebush Rd, Cambridge, ON, N1R 8E2
(519) 624-2700
Emp Here 100
SIC 5211 Lumber and other building materials

D-U-N-S 25-143-2241 (BR)
HUDSON'S BAY COMPANY
BAY, THE
355 Hespeler Rd Unit 1, Cambridge, ON, N1R 8J9
(519) 622-4919
Emp Here 100
SIC 5311 Department stores

D-U-N-S 24-565-6348 (BR)
INVESTORS GROUP FINANCIAL SER-VICES INC
1150 Franklin Blvd Suite 104, Cambridge, ON, N1R 7J2
(519) 624-9348
Emp Here 20
SIC 8741 Management services

D-U-N-S 25-952-6259 (BR)
JMP ENGINEERING INC
1425 Bishop St N Unit 8, Cambridge, ON, N1R 6J9

Emp Here 100
SIC 8711 Engineering services

D-U-N-S 24-189-5767 (BR)
KANE VETERINARY SUPPLIES LTD
30 Struck Crt, Cambridge, ON, N1R 8L2
(519) 740-0733
Emp Here 40
SIC 5999 Miscellaneous retail stores, nec

D-U-N-S 20-772-0470 (SL)
M J L GOODEATS CORP
EAST SIDE MARIO'S
355 Hespeler Rd Suite 262, Cambridge, ON, N1R 6B3
(519) 622-5218
Emp Here 50   *Sales* 1,532,175
SIC 5812 Eating places

D-U-N-S 20-227-7877 (HQ)
MW CANADA LTD
291 Elgin St N, Cambridge, ON, N1R 7H9
(519) 621-5460
Emp Here 60   *Emp Total* 62
Sales 12,532,976
SIC 2591 Drapery hardware and window blinds and shades
Pr Pr Robert Berger
 Howard Bornstein
VP Fin Dwayne Schmidt

D-U-N-S 25-318-1374 (BR)
MCDONALD'S RESTAURANTS OF CANADA LIMITED
MCDONALD'S
(*Suby of* McDonald's Corporation)

Gd Stn Galt, Cambridge, ON, N1R 5S8

Emp Here 100
SIC 5812 Eating places

D-U-N-S 20-290-7481 (BR)
METRO ONTARIO INC
FOOD BASICS
95 Water St N, Cambridge, ON, N1R 3B5
(519) 623-3652
Emp Here 125
SIC 5141 Groceries, general line

D-U-N-S 24-045-4863 (BR)
MICHAELS OF CANADA, ULC
(*Suby of* The Michaels Companies Inc)
18a Pinebush Rd Unit 1, Cambridge, ON, N1R 8K5
(519) 740-1100
Emp Here 50
SIC 5945 Hobby, toy, and game shops

D-U-N-S 24-340-1457 (BR)
MILL CREEK MOTOR FREIGHT L.P.
51 Water St N, Cambridge, ON, N1R 3B3
(519) 623-6632
Emp Here 200
SIC 4213 Trucking, except local

D-U-N-S 20-657-9679 (BR)
OLD NAVY (CANADA) INC
(*Suby of* The Gap Inc)
70 Pinebush Rd, Cambridge, ON, N1R 8K5
(519) 621-4612
Emp Here 50
SIC 5651 Family clothing stores

D-U-N-S 24-125-6325 (BR)
PEPSICO CANADA ULC
FRITO LAY CANADA, DIV OF
(*Suby of* Pepsico, Inc.)
1185 Franklin Blvd Unit 1, Cambridge, ON, N1R 7Y5
(519) 740-5644
Emp Here 60
SIC 5145 Confectionery

D-U-N-S 25-687-6921 (HQ)
PRIDE BODIES LTD
(*Suby of* Pride One Holdings Ltd)
37 Raglin Pl, Cambridge, ON, N1R 7J2
(519) 620-8787
Emp Here 36   *Emp Total* 4
Sales 5,284,131
SIC 3713 Truck and bus bodies
VP VP Ross Williamson
VP VP Russ Lanthier

D-U-N-S 24-469-1176 (BR)
PRISZM LP
KFC
499 Dundas St, Cambridge, ON, N1R 5R8
(519) 621-7000
Emp Here 20
SIC 5812 Eating places

D-U-N-S 24-745-4788 (HQ)
PROCESS GROUP INC
555 Conestoga Blvd, Cambridge, ON, N1R 7P5
(519) 622-5520
Emp Here 75   *Emp Total* 250
Sales 28,480,521
SIC 1796 Installing building equipment
 Cliff Snyder
Pr Pr Jeff Snyder
 Peter Fitton
 Brent Heard

D-U-N-S 24-224-5285 (BR)
QUICKER FOODS INC
WENDY'S
(*Suby of* Quicker Foods Inc)
430 Hespeler Rd, Cambridge, ON, N1R 6J7
(519) 623-4700
Emp Here 20
SIC 5812 Eating places

D-U-N-S 24-424-1738   (SL)
QUIKRETE TORONTO INC
1501 Whistle Bare Rd, Cambridge, ON, N1R 5S3
(519) 621-3093
Emp Here 24   *Sales* 6,313,604
SIC 3272 Concrete products, nec
Pr James Winchester

D-U-N-S 25-137-2020   (BR)
RANDSTAD INTERIM INC
RANDSTAD CANADA
1315 Bishop St N, Cambridge, ON, N1R 6Z2
(519) 740-6944
Emp Here 80
SIC 7361 Employment agencies

D-U-N-S 25-876-2475   (BR)
RE/MAX TWIN CITY REALTY INC
1400 Bishop St N, Cambridge, ON, N1R 6W8
(519) 740-3690
Emp Here 50
SIC 6531 Real estate agents and managers

D-U-N-S 25-300-5151   (BR)
REDBERRY FRANCHISING CORP
BURGER KING RESTAURANTS
561 Hespeler Rd Suite 23, Cambridge, ON, N1R 6J4
(519) 623-2402
Emp Here 28
SIC 5812 Eating places

D-U-N-S 20-703-2025   (BR)
RELIANCE COMFORT LIMITED PARTNERSHIP
RELIANCE HOME COMFORT, DIV
539 Collier Macmillan Dr Suite A, Cambridge, ON, N1R 7P3
(519) 622-2772
Emp Here 20
SIC 1711 Plumbing, heating, air-conditioning

D-U-N-S 25-169-5425   (BR)
REVERA INC
614 Coronation Blvd Suite 200, Cambridge, ON, N1R 3E8
(519) 622-1840
Emp Here 100
SIC 8051 Skilled nursing care facilities

D-U-N-S 25-028-5236   (BR)
REVERA LONG TERM CARE INC
RIVERBEND PLACE CAMBRIDGE
650 Coronation Blvd, Cambridge, ON, N1R 7S6
(519) 740-3820
Emp Here 90
SIC 8051 Skilled nursing care facilities

D-U-N-S 20-139-8588   (HQ)
RINK PARTNERS CORPORATION
CAMBRIDGE ICE PARK
(*Suby of* Rink Partners Corporation)
1001 Franklin Blvd, Cambridge, ON, N1R 8B5
(519) 622-4494
Emp Here 45   *Emp Total* 140
Sales 10,449,920
SIC 7999 Amusement and recreation, nec
Pr Pr Bob Macintosh
Dir Bryan Santarossa

D-U-N-S 20-019-8153   (HQ)
ROCKWELL AUTOMATION CANADA CONTROL SYSTEMS
135 Dundas St, Cambridge, ON, N1R 5N9
(519) 623-1810
Emp Here 650   *Emp Total* 1,200
Sales 124,368,720
SIC 3625 Relays and industrial controls
Prin Charles Cipolla

D-U-N-S 25-556-6440   (BR)
ROYAL BANK OF CANADA
RBC
(*Suby of* Royal Bank Of Canada)
480 Hespeler Rd, Cambridge, ON, N1R 7R9

(519) 623-1012
Emp Here 20
SIC 6021 National commercial banks

D-U-N-S 25-964-3260   (BR)
SEARS CANADA INC
SEARS CAMBRIDGE
355 Hespeler Rd, Cambridge, ON, N1R 6B3
(519) 623-2327
Emp Here 140
SIC 5311 Department stores

D-U-N-S 24-794-3566   (BR)
SECURITAS CANADA LIMITED
1425 Bishop St N Suite 14, Cambridge, ON, N1R 6J9
(519) 620-9864
Emp Here 300
SIC 7381 Detective and armored car services

D-U-N-S 24-823-4239   (BR)
SERVICE CORPORATION INTERNATIONAL (CANADA) LIMITED
LITTLE FUNERAL & CREMATION CENTER
223 Main St, Cambridge, ON, N1R 1X2
(519) 623-1290
Emp Here 20
SIC 7261 Funeral service and crematories

D-U-N-S 25-191-9015   (BR)
SHRED-IT INTERNATIONAL ULC
SHRED-IT CAMBRIDGE/KITCHENER
135 Pinebush Rd, Cambridge, ON, N1R 7H8
(519) 650-4065
Emp Here 20
SIC 7389 Business services, nec

D-U-N-S 25-188-1355   (BR)
SOBEYS CAPITAL INCORPORATED
FRESCHO
75 Dundas St, Cambridge, ON, N1R 6G5
(519) 620-9022
Emp Here 130
SIC 5411 Grocery stores

D-U-N-S 25-949-5281   (SL)
SOFTWARE AG (CANADA) INC
73 Water St N Suite 504, Cambridge, ON, N1R 7L6
(519) 622-0889
Emp Here 39   *Sales* 3,429,153
SIC 7372 Prepackaged software

D-U-N-S 25-486-9324   (BR)
STAPLES CANADA INC
STAPLES THE BUSINESS DEPOT
(*Suby of* Staples, Inc.)
26 Pinebush Rd, Cambridge, ON, N1R 8K5
(519) 622-5280
Emp Here 25
SIC 5943 Stationery stores

D-U-N-S 20-892-7918   (HQ)
TAKHAR COLLECTION SERVICES LTD
202 Beverly St, Cambridge, ON, N1R 3Z8
(519) 622-4141
Emp Here 60   *Emp Total* 80
Sales 27,484,800
SIC 7322 Adjustment and collection services
Pr Nicholas Papeo

D-U-N-S 24-421-6128   (SL)
TENNECO AUTOMOTIVE
(*Suby of* Tenneco Inc.)
500 Conestoga Blvd, Cambridge, ON, N1R 7P6
(519) 621-3360
Emp Here 40   *Sales* 84,719,348
SIC 3714 Motor vehicle parts and accessories

D-U-N-S 24-806-3799   (BR)
TOMMY HILFIGER CANADA INC
34 Pinebush Rd Suite 1, Cambridge, ON, N1R 8K5
(519) 624-9104
Emp Here 30
SIC 5136 Men's and boy's clothing

D-U-N-S 25-083-5840   (BR)

TRUE NORTH RESTAURANTS INC
APPLEBEE'S NEIGHBORHOOD GRILL
(*Suby of* True North Restaurants Inc)
355 Hespeler Rd Suite 276, Cambridge, ON, N1R 6B3
(519) 740-8220
Emp Here 65
SIC 5812 Eating places

D-U-N-S 25-079-3296   (BR)
VALUE VILLAGE STORES, INC
VALUE VILLAGE 2031
(*Suby of* Savers, Inc.)
480 Hespeler Rd, Cambridge, ON, N1R 7R9
(519) 624-1812
Emp Here 60
SIC 5399 Miscellaneous general merchandise

D-U-N-S 25-498-2622   (BR)
WAL-MART CANADA CORP
WAL MART
22 Pinebush Rd, Cambridge, ON, N1R 8K5
(519) 624-7467
Emp Here 300
SIC 5311 Department stores

D-U-N-S 20-710-7462   (BR)
WATERLOO CATHOLIC DISTRICT SCHOOL BOARD
ST LOUIS ADULT LEARNING & CONTINUING EDUCATION CENTRE
82 Beverly St, Cambridge, ON, N1R 3Z7
(519) 745-1201
Emp Here 50
SIC 8211 Elementary and secondary schools

D-U-N-S 25-228-2074   (BR)
WATERLOO CATHOLIC DISTRICT SCHOOL BOARD
ST FRANCIS ELEMENTARY SCHOOL
60 Mcdonald Ave, Cambridge, ON, N1R 4J2
(519) 621-0371
Emp Here 26
SIC 8211 Elementary and secondary schools

D-U-N-S 20-590-7962   (BR)
WATERLOO CATHOLIC DISTRICT SCHOOL BOARD
ST AMBROSE
25 Chalmers St S, Cambridge, ON, N1R 5B3

Emp Here 25
SIC 8211 Elementary and secondary schools

D-U-N-S 20-590-8937   (BR)
WATERLOO CATHOLIC DISTRICT SCHOOL BOARD
ST PETER CATHOLIC SCHOOL
92 Avenue Rd, Cambridge, ON, N1R 1C1
(519) 621-5211
Emp Here 25
SIC 8211 Elementary and secondary schools

D-U-N-S 20-982-8458   (BR)
WATERLOO CATHOLIC DISTRICT SCHOOL BOARD
MONSIGNOR DOYLE
185 Myers Rd, Cambridge, ON, N1R 7H2
(519) 622-1290
Emp Here 80
SIC 8211 Elementary and secondary schools

D-U-N-S 25-137-3940   (BR)
WATERLOO CATHOLIC DISTRICT SCHOOL BOARD
CHRIST THE KING CATHOLIC SCHOOL
70 Acorn Way, Cambridge, ON, N1R 8M5
(519) 621-6680
Emp Here 35
SIC 8211 Elementary and secondary schools

D-U-N-S 20-004-8556   (BR)
WATERLOO CATHOLIC DISTRICT SCHOOL BOARD
ST VINCENT DE PAUL SCHOOL
25 Chalmers St S, Cambridge, ON, N1R 5B3
(519) 740-0678
Emp Here 30

SIC 8211 Elementary and secondary schools

D-U-N-S 20-653-4575   (BR)
WATERLOO CATHOLIC DISTRICT SCHOOL BOARD
ST ANNE SEPARATE SCHOOL
127 Elgin St N, Cambridge, ON, N1R 5H6
(519) 621-8920
Emp Here 20
SIC 8211 Elementary and secondary schools

D-U-N-S 25-237-8922   (BR)
WATERLOO REGION DISTRICT SCHOOL BOARD
MANCHESTER PUBLIC SCHOOL
455 Dundas St, Cambridge, ON, N1R 5R5
(519) 621-8240
Emp Here 40
SIC 8211 Elementary and secondary schools

D-U-N-S 25-228-1555   (BR)
WATERLOO REGION DISTRICT SCHOOL BOARD
GALT COLLEGIATE INST & VOCATIONAL
200 Water St N, Cambridge, ON, N1R 6V2
(519) 623-3600
Emp Here 120
SIC 8211 Elementary and secondary schools

D-U-N-S 25-228-1209   (BR)
WATERLOO REGION DISTRICT SCHOOL BOARD
ALISON PARK ELEMENTARY SCHOOL
455 Myers Rd, Cambridge, ON, N1R 5S2

Emp Here 20
SIC 8211 Elementary and secondary schools

D-U-N-S 20-158-0409   (BR)
WATERLOO REGION DISTRICT SCHOOL BOARD
STEWART AVENUE PUBLIC SCHOOL
145 Stewart Ave, Cambridge, ON, N1R 2V5
(519) 621-4171
Emp Here 40
SIC 8211 Elementary and secondary schools

D-U-N-S 25-228-1407   (BR)
WATERLOO REGION DISTRICT SCHOOL BOARD
CENTRAL PUBLIC SCHOOL
175 Main St, Cambridge, ON, N1R 1W5
(519) 623-0940
Emp Here 28
SIC 8211 Elementary and secondary schools

D-U-N-S 25-228-1423   (BR)
WATERLOO REGION DISTRICT SCHOOL BOARD
CHALMERS STREET PUBLIC SCHOOL
35 Chalmers St S, Cambridge, ON, N1R 5B4
(519) 623-0950
Emp Here 35
SIC 8211 Elementary and secondary schools

D-U-N-S 25-228-1514   (BR)
WATERLOO REGION DISTRICT SCHOOL BOARD
GLENVIEW PARK SECONDARY SCHOOL
55 Mckay St, Cambridge, ON, N1R 4G6
(519) 621-9510
Emp Here 110
SIC 8211 Elementary and secondary schools

D-U-N-S 20-158-0664   (BR)
WATERLOO REGION DISTRICT SCHOOL BOARD
ELGIN STREET PUBLIC SCHOOL
685 Elgin St N, Cambridge, ON, N1R 7W6
(519) 622-0611
Emp Here 30
SIC 8211 Elementary and secondary schools

D-U-N-S 24-224-5665   (BR)
WENDY'S RESTAURANTS OF CANADA INC
WENDY'S
(*Suby of* The Wendy's Company)
225 Franklin Blvd, Cambridge, ON, N1R 8P1

(519) 740-1287
Emp Here 25
SIC 5812 Eating places

D-U-N-S 25-221-2899   (BR)
WINNERS MERCHANTS INTERNATIONAL L.P.
WINNERS
(*Suby of* The TJX Companies Inc)
22 Pinebush Rd, Cambridge, ON, N1R 8K5
(519) 740-9597
Emp Here 30
SIC 5651 Family clothing stores

D-U-N-S 20-184-2833   (BR)
WINNERS MERCHANTS INTERNATIONAL L.P.
HOMESENSE
(*Suby of* The TJX Companies Inc)
600 Hespeler Rd Unit 73b, Cambridge, ON, N1R 8H2
(519) 624-6063
Emp Here 30
SIC 5651 Family clothing stores

D-U-N-S 20-806-2971   (BR)
YM INC. (SALES)
STITCHES
355 Hespeler Rd Unit 348/349, Cambridge, ON, N1R 6B3

Emp Here 25
SIC 5621 Women's clothing stores

D-U-N-S 25-226-7059   (HQ)
YWCA OF CAMBRIDGE
(*Suby of* YWCA Of Cambridge)
55 Dickson St, Cambridge, ON, N1R 7A5
(519) 267-6444
Emp Here 45   *Emp Total* 50
Sales 1,969,939
SIC 8322 Individual and family services

D-U-N-S 25-953-0582   (BR)
YOUR NEIGHBOURHOOD CREDIT UNION LIMITED
GRAND RIVER CREDIT UNION
385 Hespeler Rd, Cambridge, ON, N1R 6J1
(519) 622-3377
Emp Here 20
SIC 6062 State credit unions

D-U-N-S 24-327-4615   (BR)
ZEHRMART INC
ZEHRS MARKETS
400 Conestoga Blvd, Cambridge, ON, N1R 7L7
(519) 620-1376
Emp Here 300
SIC 5411 Grocery stores

Cambridge, ON N1S
Waterloo County

D-U-N-S 20-068-0242   (SL)
QUEEN'S SQUARE TERRACE
201 43-10 Melville St N, Cambridge, ON, N1S 1H5
(519) 621-2777
Emp Here 45   *Sales* 3,939,878
SIC 6513 Apartment building operators

D-U-N-S 20-291-3047   (BR)
REVERA LONG TERM CARE INC
STIRLING HEIGHTS
200 Stirling Macgregor Dr, Cambridge, ON, N1S 5B7
(519) 622-3434
Emp Here 75
SIC 8051 Skilled nursing care facilities

D-U-N-S 25-309-1003   (BR)
SOBEYS CAPITAL INCORPORATED
SOBEYS 678
130 Cedar St, Cambridge, ON, N1S 1W4

(519) 622-8906
Emp Here 115
SIC 5411 Grocery stores

D-U-N-S 25-228-1944   (BR)
WATERLOO CATHOLIC DISTRICT SCHOOL BOARD
ST GREGORY CATHOLIC ELEMENTARY SCHOOL
34 Osborne St, Cambridge, ON, N1S 3H1
(519) 621-6770
Emp Here 28
SIC 8211 Elementary and secondary schools

D-U-N-S 20-710-7439   (BR)
WATERLOO CATHOLIC DISTRICT SCHOOL BOARD
ST AUGUSTINE CATHOLIC SCHOOL
177 Bismark Dr, Cambridge, ON, N1S 4Y2
(519) 740-3530
Emp Here 40
SIC 8211 Elementary and secondary schools

D-U-N-S 25-228-1050   (BR)
WATERLOO REGION DISTRICT SCHOOL BOARD
TAIT STREET PUBLIC SCHOOL
184 Tait St, Cambridge, ON, N1S 3G3
(519) 621-7621
Emp Here 30
SIC 8211 Elementary and secondary schools

D-U-N-S 25-228-1548   (BR)
WATERLOO REGION DISTRICT SCHOOL BOARD
SOUTHWOOD SECONDARY SCHOOL
30 Southwood Dr, Cambridge, ON, N1S 4K3
(519) 621-5920
Emp Here 150
SIC 8211 Elementary and secondary schools

D-U-N-S 25-228-1316   (BR)
WATERLOO REGION DISTRICT SCHOOL BOARD
ST ANDREW'S SENIOR PUBLIC SCHOOL
65 Victoria Ave, Cambridge, ON, N1S 1X2
(519) 621-7170
Emp Here 40
SIC 8211 Elementary and secondary schools

D-U-N-S 25-237-9300   (BR)
WATERLOO REGION DISTRICT SCHOOL BOARD
DICKSON PUBLIC SCHOOL
65 St Andrews St, Cambridge, ON, N1S 1M6
(519) 570-0003
Emp Here 20
SIC 8211 Elementary and secondary schools

D-U-N-S 20-024-9436   (BR)
WATERLOO REGION DISTRICT SCHOOL BOARD
HIGHLAND PUBLIC SCHOOL
125 Salisbury Ave, Cambridge, ON, N1S 1J8
(519) 621-9981
Emp Here 43
SIC 8211 Elementary and secondary schools

Cambridge, ON N1T
Waterloo County

D-U-N-S 24-330-6946   (HQ)
1625443 ONTARIO INC
TVM
75 Lingard Rd, Cambridge, ON, N1T 2A8
(519) 624-9914
Emp Here 65   *Emp Total* 287
Sales 30,036,960
SIC 4731 Freight transportation arrangement
Pr Pr Theodore Vance
Sec Lynn West

D-U-N-S 24-362-0890   (BR)
3033441 NOVA SCOTIA COMPANY
ALLIED FITTING

1700 Bishop St N, Cambridge, ON, N1T 1T2
(519) 624-9451
Emp Here 20
SIC 5085 Industrial supplies

D-U-N-S 24-977-6022   (SL)
742906 ONTARIO INC
ACCUCAM MACHINING
300 Sheldon Dr, Cambridge, ON, N1T 1A8
(519) 740-7797
Emp Here 60   *Sales* 4,377,642
SIC 3599 Industrial machinery, nec

D-U-N-S 20-911-0910   (BR)
ARI FINANCIAL SERVICES INC
(*Suby of* Holman Enterprises Inc.)
95 Raglin Rd, Cambridge, ON, N1T 1X9
(905) 624-8733
Emp Here 250
SIC 7515 Passenger car leasing

D-U-N-S 25-412-0603   (BR)
ANCHOR DANLY INC
311 Pinebush Rd, Cambridge, ON, N1T 1B2
(519) 740-3060
Emp Here 50
SIC 3544 Special dies, tools, jigs, and fixtures

D-U-N-S 24-684-7370   (HQ)
BARRDAY, INC
BARRDAY PROTECTIVE SOLUTIONS
(*Suby of* Barrday, Inc)
75 Moorefield St, Cambridge, ON, N1T 1S2
(519) 621-3620
Emp Here 50   *Emp Total* 100
Sales 11,090,026
SIC 2299 Textile goods, nec
  Michael Buckstein
Pr Tony Siorenzini
VP Mfg Andrew Galbraith

D-U-N-S 24-384-3331   (HQ)
BROLAIN DISTRIBUTORS LTD
1731 Bishop St, Cambridge, ON, N1T 1N5
(519) 740-9311
Emp Here 26   *Emp Total* 2
Sales 6,712,384
SIC 5169 Chemicals and allied products, nec
Pr Pr Bruce Radke
  Terry Chamberlain

D-U-N-S 25-306-4414   (BR)
CO-OPERATORS GENERAL INSURANCE COMPANY
CO-OPERATORS, THE
1720 Bishop St Suite 200, Cambridge, ON, N1T 1T2
(519) 623-8405
Emp Here 40
SIC 6411 Insurance agents, brokers, and service

D-U-N-S 20-051-5971   (SL)
COURT GALVANIZING LIMITED
225 Thompson Dr, Cambridge, ON, N1T 2B9
(519) 624-5544
Emp Here 40   *Sales* 2,845,467
SIC 3479 Metal coating and allied services

D-U-N-S 25-302-4293   (HQ)
DOMINO'S PIZZA NS CO
DOMINO'S PIZZA
(*Suby of* Domino's Pizza, Inc.)
490 Pinebush Rd Unit 2, Cambridge, ON, N1T 0A5
(519) 620-6606
Emp Here 36   *Emp Total* 11,900
Sales 10,068,577
SIC 5149 Groceries and related products, nec
Pr Patrick Doyle

D-U-N-S 20-124-4324   (SL)
DUPAR CONTROLS INC
1751 Bishop St, Cambridge, ON, N1T 1N5
(519) 624-2510
Emp Here 45   *Sales* 4,428,946
SIC 3625 Relays and industrial controls

D-U-N-S 24-369-7989   (BR)
ECLIPSE AUTOMATION INC
JR'S WELDING & CUSTOM FABRICATING
130 Thompson Dr, Cambridge, ON, N1T 2E5
(519) 624-8287
Emp Here 20
SIC 3599 Industrial machinery, nec

D-U-N-S 20-056-4792   (BR)
ELECTRICAL SAFETY AUTHORITY
CUSTOMER SERVICE CENTRE
400 Sheldon Dr Unit 1, Cambridge, ON, N1T 2H9
(519) 622-2506
Emp Here 70
SIC 7389 Business services, nec

D-U-N-S 20-114-5625   (HQ)
ENDRIES INTERNATIONAL CANADA INC
(*Suby of* WOLSELEY PLC)
255 Pinebush Rd Unit A, Cambridge, ON, N1T 1B9
(519) 740-3523
Emp Here 52   *Emp Total* 48,226
Sales 23,042,277
SIC 5085 Industrial supplies
Dir Keith Vandervennet
Dir Frank Wemyss Roach
Dir Gilles Petrin
Fin Ex Sheldon Brewster
VP VP Matthew Vechart

D-U-N-S 24-662-7178   (HQ)
FUCHS LUBRICANTS CANADA LTD
405 Dobbie Dr, Cambridge, ON, N1T 1S8
(519) 622-2040
Emp Here 25   *Emp Total* 4,876
Sales 14,154,376
SIC 5172 Petroleum products, nec
Ch Bd L Frank Kleinman
VP VP Derek Scott
  Daniel Woo
  Ronald Gelens
  John Jedlinski

D-U-N-S 25-403-7666   (BR)
G&K SERVICES CANADA INC
(*Suby of* Cintas Corporation)
205 Turnbull Crt, Cambridge, ON, N1T 1W1
(519) 623-7703
Emp Here 130
SIC 7216 Drycleaning plants, except rugs

D-U-N-S 24-347-6285   (BR)
GOLDER ASSOCIATES LTD
210 Sheldon Dr Suite 201, Cambridge, ON, N1T 1A8

Emp Here 30
SIC 8711 Engineering services

D-U-N-S 24-379-4521   (BR)
GROBER INC
DELFT BLUE, DIV OF
425 Dobbie Dr, Cambridge, ON, N1T 1S9
(519) 740-8327
Emp Here 100
SIC 5147 Meats and meat products

D-U-N-S 20-975-3565   (HQ)
GROBER INC
DELFT BLUE, DIV OF
162 Savage Dr, Cambridge, ON, N1T 1S4
(519) 622-2500
Emp Here 200   *Emp Total* 200
Sales 58,952,246
SIC 2048 Prepared feeds, nec
Pr Pr Jerry Bartelse
  Ari Nuys

D-U-N-S 25-953-1473   (BR)
GROBER INC
DELFT BLUE
425 Dobbie Dr, Cambridge, ON, N1T 1S9
(519) 740-8325
Emp Here 200
SIC 2011 Meat packing plants

D-U-N-S 25-149-9141   (SL)
LOGISENSE CORPORATION
278 Pinebush Rd Suite 102, Cambridge, ON,
N1T 1Z6
(519) 249-0508
Emp Here 50   *Sales* 3,866,259
SIC 7371 Custom computer programming services

D-U-N-S 24-345-9448   (BR)
MATTAMY HOMES LIMITED
605 Sheldon Dr, Cambridge, ON, N1T 2K1

Emp Here 100
SIC 1522 Residential construction, nec

D-U-N-S 24-868-5299   (SL)
MIRION TECHNOLOGIES (IST CANADA) INC
IMAGING AND SENSING TECHNOLOGY
465 Dobbie Dr, Cambridge, ON, N1T 1T1
(519) 623-4880
Emp Here 54   *Sales* 21,314,762
SIC 3829 Measuring and controlling devices, nec
Pr Pr Iain Wilson
  Thomas Logan

D-U-N-S 20-209-4103   (HQ)
NUTRABLEND FOODS INC
162 Savage Dr, Cambridge, ON, N1T 1S4
(519) 622-4178
Emp Here 20   *Emp Total* 200
Sales 3,638,254
SIC 3556 Food products machinery

D-U-N-S 20-809-8025   (BR)
REVERA INC
140 Turnbull Crt, Cambridge, ON, N1T 1J2
(519) 620-8038
Emp Here 50
SIC 8361 Residential care

D-U-N-S 25-367-4097   (SL)
T.V. MINORITY COMPANY, INC
(*Suby of* Fcs Industries, Inc.)
75 Lingard Rd, Cambridge, ON, N1T 2A8
(519) 624-9914
Emp Here 60   *Sales* 9,517,523
SIC 4213 Trucking, except local
Genl Mgr Dave Hicks

D-U-N-S 25-018-4801   (BR)
TRANSPORT TFI 5, S.E.C.
KINGSWAY TRANSPORT (DIV)
130 Werlich Dr, Cambridge, ON, N1T 1N6
(519) 621-2428
Emp Here 37
SIC 4213 Trucking, except local

D-U-N-S 25-256-0719   (HQ)
URBAN MACHINERY CORPORATION
125 Werlich Dr, Cambridge, ON, N1T 1N7
(519) 624-0080
Emp Here 25   *Emp Total* 250
Sales 5,909,817
SIC 3559 Special industry machinery, nec
Pr Pr Martin Urban
Fin Ex Joanne Wheeldon
Dir Thomas Urban

D-U-N-S 20-025-0913   (BR)
WATERLOO CATHOLIC DISTRICT SCHOOL BOARD
ST MARGARET'S OF SCOTLAND
210 Cowan Blvd, Cambridge, ON, N1T 1V4
(519) 622-6100
Emp Here 37
SIC 8211 Elementary and secondary schools

D-U-N-S 20-710-7496   (BR)
WATERLOO CATHOLIC DISTRICT SCHOOL BOARD
BLESSED MOTHER TERESA SCHOOL
520 Saginaw Pky, Cambridge, ON, N1T 1W9
(519) 624-7115
Emp Here 50

SIC 8211 Elementary and secondary schools

D-U-N-S 20-591-4711   (BR)
WATERLOO REGION DISTRICT SCHOOL BOARD
SAGINAW PUBLIC SCHOOL
740 Saginaw Pky, Cambridge, ON, N1T 1V6
(519) 624-7111
Emp Here 40
SIC 8211 Elementary and secondary schools

D-U-N-S 20-591-4638   (BR)
WATERLOO REGION DISTRICT SCHOOL BOARD
CLEMENS MILL PUBLIC SCHOOL
335 Saginaw Pky, Cambridge, ON, N1T 1R6
(519) 740-2364
Emp Here 70
SIC 8211 Elementary and secondary schools

Cambridge, ON N2V
Waterloo County

D-U-N-S 24-344-5850   (SL)
NIKON METROLOGY CANADA INC
55 Fleming Dr Suite 13, Cambridge, ON, N2V 2B8
(519) 831-6924
Emp Here 45   *Sales* 3,203,919
SIC 8731 Commercial physical research

Cambridge, ON N3C
Waterloo County

D-U-N-S 24-335-4433   (BR)
CRH CANADA GROUP INC
DUFFERIN AGGREGATES
7108 Concession 2, Cambridge, ON, N3C 2V4
(519) 763-7337
Emp Here 32
SIC 1442 Construction sand and gravel

D-U-N-S 25-561-8050   (SL)
CAPITAL PAVING INC
6678 Wellington Road 34, Cambridge, ON, N3C 2V4
(519) 220-1753
Emp Here 20
SIC 1442 Construction sand and gravel

D-U-N-S 25-540-7850   (SL)
CELCOR LIMITED
(*Suby of* Illinois Tool Works Inc.)
25 Sheffield St Suite 3, Cambridge, ON, N3C 1C4
(519) 220-0743
Emp Here 24   *Sales* 2,626,585
SIC 2631 Paperboard mills

D-U-N-S 24-485-3818   (SL)
COLLECTRITE ONTARIO (SW86) INC
COLLECTION DIVISION
181 Groh Ave, Cambridge, ON, N3C 1Y8
(519) 654-7350
Emp Here 25   *Sales* 1,826,100
SIC 7322 Adjustment and collection services

D-U-N-S 20-121-0465   (SL)
CROWE FOUNDRY LIMITED
95 Sheffield St, Cambridge, ON, N3C 1C4
(905) 658-9376
Emp Here 150
SIC 3321 Gray and ductile iron foundries

D-U-N-S 25-318-0632   (BR)
LONDON LIFE INSURANCE COMPANY
FREEDOM 55 FINANCIAL
260 Holiday Inn Dr Suite 30, Cambridge, ON, N3C 4E8
(519) 249-0708
Emp Here 80

SIC 6311 Life insurance

D-U-N-S 25-310-9771   (BR)
MCDONALD'S RESTAURANTS OF CANADA LIMITED
MCDONALD'S
(*Suby of* McDonald's Corporation)
401 Westbound Hwy, Cambridge, ON, N3C 4B1

Emp Here 135
SIC 5812 Eating places

D-U-N-S 20-192-4292   (BR)
METRO ONTARIO INC
FOOD BASICS
100 Jamieson Pky, Cambridge, ON, N3C 4B3
(519) 658-1150
Emp Here 80
SIC 5411 Grocery stores

D-U-N-S 24-587-8970   (BR)
NORFOLK KNITTERS LIMITED
LEN'S MILL STORE
215 Queen St W, Cambridge, ON, N3C 1G6
(519) 658-8182
Emp Here 26
SIC 5949 Sewing, needlework, and piece goods

D-U-N-S 24-850-6672   (SL)
RHC DESIGN-BUILD
REID'S HERITAGE CONSTRUCTION
6783 Wellington Road 34, Cambridge, ON, N3C 2V4
(519) 249-0758
Emp Here 24   *Sales* 4,669,485
SIC 1542 Nonresidential construction, nec

D-U-N-S 25-156-3235   (HQ)
REVERA LONG TERM CARE INC
HILLSIDE MANOR
600 Jamieson Pky, Cambridge, ON, N3C 0A6
(519) 622-1840
Emp Here 85   *Emp Total* 570,000
Sales 229,903,015
SIC 8051 Skilled nursing care facilities
Dir Donna Kingelin

D-U-N-S 20-741-6384   (BR)
SAMUEL, SON & CO., LIMITED
BOTHWELL
133 Troh Ave, Cambridge, ON, N3C 4B1
(519) 658-4693
Emp Here 100
SIC 1791 Structural steel erection

D-U-N-S 20-043-1604   (BR)
SAMUEL, SON & CO., LIMITED
BOTHWELL STEEL
133 Groh Ave, Cambridge, ON, N3C 1Y8

Emp Here 50
SIC 5051 Metals service centers and offices

D-U-N-S 24-423-1460   (SL)
SCHIEDEL CONSTRUCTION INCORPORATED
405 Queen St W, Cambridge, ON, N3C 1G6
(519) 658-9317
Emp Here 35   *Sales* 8,952,126
SIC 1541 Industrial buildings and warehouses
Pr Pr Fred Schiedel
  Philip Schiedel

D-U-N-S 25-683-5786   (SL)
SIEMPELKAMP CANADA INC
50 Groh Ave, Cambridge, ON, N3C 1Y9
(519) 500-5888
Emp Here 20   *Sales* 1,532,175
SIC 3625 Relays and industrial controls

D-U-N-S 20-590-0561   (BR)
TORONTO-DOMINION BANK, THE
TD CANADA TRUST
(*Suby of* Toronto-Dominion Bank, The)
180 Holiday Inn Dr, Cambridge, ON, N3C 1Z4

(519) 658-5752
Emp Here 20
SIC 6021 National commercial banks

D-U-N-S 25-228-2066   (BR)
WATERLOO CATHOLIC DISTRICT SCHOOL BOARD
OUR LADY OF FATIMA ELEMENTARY SCHOOL
55 Hammet St, Cambridge, ON, N3C 2H5
(519) 658-4041
Emp Here 37
SIC 8211 Elementary and secondary schools

D-U-N-S 24-450-9480   (BR)
WATERLOO CATHOLIC DISTRICT SCHOOL BOARD
ST ELIZABETH SCHOOL
50 Adler Dr, Cambridge, ON, N3C 4B7
(519) 651-0400
Emp Here 40
SIC 8211 Elementary and secondary schools

D-U-N-S 20-158-2660   (BR)
WATERLOO REGION DISTRICT SCHOOL BOARD
WOODLAND PARK PUBLIC SCHOOL
555 Ellis Rd, Cambridge, ON, N3C 4K2
(519) 654-9402
Emp Here 55
SIC 8211 Elementary and secondary schools

D-U-N-S 25-228-1415   (BR)
WATERLOO REGION DISTRICT SCHOOL BOARD
CENTENNIAL PUBLIC SCHOOL
100 Weaver St, Cambridge, ON, N3C 1W4
(519) 658-5121
Emp Here 20
SIC 8211 Elementary and secondary schools

D-U-N-S 20-710-7140   (BR)
WATERLOO REGION DISTRICT SCHOOL BOARD
SILVERHEIGHTS PUBLIC SCHOOL
390 Scott Rd, Cambridge, ON, N3C 3Z7
(519) 658-9023
Emp Here 70
SIC 8211 Elementary and secondary schools

D-U-N-S 25-237-8963   (BR)
WATERLOO REGION DISTRICT SCHOOL BOARD
HESPELER PUBLIC SCHOOL
300 Winston Blvd, Cambridge, ON, N3C 3J6
(519) 658-4691
Emp Here 40
SIC 8211 Elementary and secondary schools

D-U-N-S 25-237-9235   (BR)
WATERLOO REGION DISTRICT SCHOOL BOARD
HILLCREST ELEMENTARY SCHOOL
31 Renwick Ave, Cambridge, ON, N3C 2T5
(519) 658-5187
Emp Here 35
SIC 8211 Elementary and secondary schools

D-U-N-S 25-137-3874   (BR)
WATERLOO REGION DISTRICT SCHOOL BOARD
JACOB HESPELER SECONDARY SCHOOL
355 Holiday Inn Dr, Cambridge, ON, N3C 1Z2
(519) 658-4910
Emp Here 120
SIC 8211 Elementary and secondary schools

Cambridge, ON N3E
Waterloo County

D-U-N-S 24-425-9813   (BR)
AMEC FOSTER WHEELER AMERICAS LIMITED
AMEC EARTH & ENVIRONMENTAL, DIV OF
405 Maple Grove Rd Suite 6, Cambridge, ON,

N3E 1B6
(519) 653-3570
Emp Here 30
SIC 8741 Management services

D-U-N-S 20-187-1378   (SL)
ALLCARD LIMITED
765 Boxwood Dr Suite 650, Cambridge, ON, N3E 1A4
(519) 650-9515
Emp Here 55   *Sales* 3,551,629
SIC 5947 Gift, novelty, and souvenir shop

D-U-N-S 24-585-6935   (HQ)
CHALLENGER MOTOR FREIGHT INC
300 Maple Grove Rd, Cambridge, ON, N3E 1B7
(519) 653-6226
Emp Here 1,200   *Emp Total* 140
Sales 238,219,025
SIC 4213 Trucking, except local
 Daniel Einwechter
Pr Eugene Moser

D-U-N-S 25-272-2686   (BR)
EXP SERVICES INC
405 Maple Grove Rd Unit 6, Cambridge, ON, N3E 1B6
(519) 650-4918
Emp Here 20
SIC 8711 Engineering services

D-U-N-S 24-325-8469   (BR)
GRAND RIVER FOODS LTD
685 Boxwood Dr, Cambridge, ON, N3E 1B4
(519) 653-3577
Emp Here 300
SIC 2015 Poultry slaughtering and processing

D-U-N-S 20-280-5644   (SL)
TM3 INC
250 Royal Oak Rd, Cambridge, ON, N3E 0A4
(519) 650-7444
Emp Here 40   *Sales* 3,502,114
SIC 1731 Electrical work

D-U-N-S 20-179-0289   (HQ)
TOYOTA TSUSHO CANADA INC
TTCI
1080 Fountain St N Unit 2, Cambridge, ON, N3E 1A3
(519) 653-6600
Emp Here 40   *Emp Total* 58,082
Sales 20,183,648
SIC 5013 Motor vehicle supplies and new parts
 Takashi Hasegawa
 William Weiner
 George A Pierce
 Yasumasa Noguchi
Asst VP Ali Tharia
 Atsushi Shimizu

D-U-N-S 25-542-9938   (HQ)
TRADE-MARK INDUSTRIAL INC
250 Royal Oak Rd, Cambridge, ON, N3E 0A4
(519) 650-7444
Emp Here 20   *Emp Total* 180
Sales 18,532,018
SIC 1796 Installing building equipment
Pr Pr Russ Straus
 Linda Straus
 Mark Depass
 Terry Moore
 David Straus
 Tom Straus
 Dan Straus
 Connie Workman

D-U-N-S 24-892-2630   (BR)
UAP INC
UPA PIECES D'AUTO
(*Suby of* Genuine Parts Company)
525 Boxwood Dr, Cambridge, ON, N3E 1A5
(519) 650-4444
Emp Here 150
SIC 5015 Motor vehicle parts, used

Cambridge, ON N3H
Waterloo County

D-U-N-S 24-188-1502   (BR)
1059936 ONTARIO INC
TEAM RECLAMATION
1574 Eagle St N, Cambridge, ON, N3H 4S5
(519) 653-6565
Emp Here 20
SIC 3471 Plating and polishing

D-U-N-S 24-091-9712   (HQ)
ATS AUTOMATION TOOLING SYSTEMS INC
ATS ADVANCE MANUFACTURING, DIV OF
(*Suby of* ATS Automation Tooling Systems Inc)
730 Fountain St N Suite 2b, Cambridge, ON, N3H 4R7
(519) 653-6500
Emp Here 100   *Emp Total* 3,500
Sales 769,509,223
SIC 3569 General industrial machinery, nec
 Andrew Hider
S&M/VP Tom Kramer
Sr VP Helmut Hock
Sr VP Eric Kiisel
Sr VP Simon Roberts
 Maria Perrella
VP VP Carl Galloway
VP Charles Gyles
VP Stewart Mccuaig
VP Tom Hayes

D-U-N-S 25-017-4174   (BR)
BANQUE TORONTO-DOMINION, LA
TD CANADA TRUST
(*Suby of* Toronto-Dominion Bank, The)
699 King St E, Cambridge, ON, N3H 3N7
(519) 653-2363
Emp Here 26
SIC 6021 National commercial banks

D-U-N-S 24-359-8757   (SL)
BAUMEIER CORPORATION
BAUMEIER ENGINEERED PRODUCTS DIV OF
1050 Fountain St N, Cambridge, ON, N3H 4R7
(519) 650-5553
Emp Here 50   *Sales* 3,648,035
SIC 3599 Industrial machinery, nec

D-U-N-S 20-341-7266   (BR)
BEND ALL AUTOMOTIVE INCORPORATED
498 Eagle St N Units 3 & 4, Cambridge, ON, N3H 1C2
(519) 623-2001
Emp Here 115
SIC 3499 Fabricated Metal products, nec

D-U-N-S 24-205-6864   (SL)
CAMBRIDGE HOTEL AND CONFERENCE CENTRE LIMITED
700 Hespeler Rd, Cambridge, ON, N3H 5L8
(519) 622-1505
Emp Here 55   *Sales* 2,407,703
SIC 7011 Hotels and motels

D-U-N-S 25-144-9872   (BR)
CANADIAN PACIFIC RAILWAY COMPANY
ST LAWRENCE & HUDSON RAILWAY
800 Fountain St N, Cambridge, ON, N3H 4R7
(519) 650-0458
Emp Here 40
SIC 4011 Railroads, line-haul operating

D-U-N-S 25-463-7986   (BR)
CARESSANT-CARE NURSING AND RE-TIREMENT HOMES LIMITED
CAMBRIDGE COUNTRY MANOR
3680 Speedsville Rd Suite 3, Cambridge, ON, N3H 4R6
(519) 650-0100
Emp Here 80

SIC 8051 Skilled nursing care facilities

D-U-N-S 24-323-6036   (BR)
CHALLENGER MOTOR FREIGHT INC
866 Langs Dr, Cambridge, ON, N3H 5P6
(519) 650-3904
Emp Here 20
SIC 4225 General warehousing and storage

D-U-N-S 25-911-2290   (BR)
COMMUNITY LIVING CAMBRIDGE
VALENTINE GROUP HOME
(*Suby of* Community Living Cambridge)
1124 Valentine Dr, Cambridge, ON, N3H 2N8
(519) 650-5091
Emp Here 200
SIC 8361 Residential care

D-U-N-S 25-228-1985   (BR)
CONSEIL SCOLAIRE DE DISTRICT CATHOLIQUE CENTRE-SUD
EEC SAINT-NOEL-CHABANEL
640 Trico Dr, Cambridge, ON, N3H 5P2
(519) 650-3219
Emp Here 30
SIC 8211 Elementary and secondary schools

D-U-N-S 20-711-7438   (BR)
CONSEIL SCOLAIRE DE DISTRICT CATHOLIQUE CENTRE-SUD
ECOLE SECONDAIRE PERE-RENE-DE-GALINEE
450 Maple Grove Rd, Cambridge, ON, N3H 4R7
(519) 650-9444
Emp Here 50
SIC 8211 Elementary and secondary schools

D-U-N-S 20-784-1024   (BR)
DILLON CONSULTING LIMITED
(*Suby of* Dillon Consulting Inc)
5 Cherry Blossom Rd Unit 1, Cambridge, ON, N3H 4R7

Emp Here 30
SIC 8711 Engineering services

D-U-N-S 20-730-0682   (SL)
EAGLE NORTH HOLDINGS INC
CAMBRIDGE TOYOTA
2400 Eagle St N, Cambridge, ON, N3H 4R7
(519) 653-7030
Emp Here 45   *Sales* 16,416,158
SIC 5511 New and used car dealers
Pr Cameron Beaton
VP VP Carol Cullen

D-U-N-S 20-317-0709   (BR)
FRANKLIN EMPIRE INC
28 Cherry Blossom Rd, Cambridge, ON, N3H 4R7
(519) 650-1182
Emp Here 55
SIC 5063 Electrical apparatus and equipment

D-U-N-S 25-297-3201   (BR)
INFORMATION COMMUNICATION SER-VICES (ICS) INC
INSURANCE COURIER SERVICES, DIV OF
655 Industrial Rd, Cambridge, ON, N3H 5C9
(519) 650-9292
Emp Here 24
SIC 7389 Business services, nec

D-U-N-S 25-924-2998   (BR)
KIRBY INTERNATIONAL TRUCKS LTD
ALTRUCK IDEALEASE
120 Mcgovern Dr, Cambridge, ON, N3H 4R7
(519) 650-3670
Emp Here 40
SIC 7513 Truck rental and leasing, no drivers

D-U-N-S 24-927-6270   (BR)
KIRBY INTERNATIONAL TRUCKS LTD
ALTRUCK INTERNATIONAL
120 Mcgovern Dr, Cambridge, ON, N3H 4R7
(519) 651-1184
Emp Here 30

SIC 7538 General automotive repair shops

D-U-N-S 25-138-0903   (BR)
MANITOULIN TRANSPORT INC
790 Industrial Rd, Cambridge, ON, N3H 4W1
(519) 291-4700
Emp Here 20
SIC 4213 Trucking, except local

D-U-N-S 24-802-1081   (BR)
PARRISH & HEIMBECKER, LIMITED
P&H MILLING GROUP
(*Suby of* Parrish & Heimbecker, Limited)
140 King St W, Cambridge, ON, N3H 1B6
(519) 653-6267
Emp Here 20
SIC 5153 Grain and field beans

D-U-N-S 20-299-3080   (BR)
PEPSICO CANADA ULC
FRITO LAY CANADA
(*Suby of* Pepsico, Inc.)
1001 Bishop St N, Cambridge, ON, N3H 4V8
(519) 653-5721
Emp Here 500
SIC 2096 Potato chips and similar snacks

D-U-N-S 24-626-1234   (SL)
PRECISION RESOURCE CANADA LTD
(*Suby of* Precision Resource, Inc.)
4 Cherry Blossom Rd, Cambridge, ON, N3H 4R7
(519) 653-7777
Emp Here 200   *Sales* 22,617,817
SIC 3469 Metal stampings, nec
Pr Pr Peter Wolcott
Dir Kaveh Vafaei
Dir John Weiland

D-U-N-S 24-749-4813   (SL)
PRESTON HOSPITALITY INC
FOUR POINTS SHERATON
210 Preston Pky, Cambridge, ON, N3H 5N1
(519) 653-2690
Emp Here 50   *Sales* 2,188,821
SIC 7011 Hotels and motels

D-U-N-S 20-702-3008   (BR)
RE/MAX REAL ESTATE CENTRE INC
766 Hespeler Rd Suite 202, Cambridge, ON, N3H 5L8
(519) 623-6200
Emp Here 115
SIC 6531 Real estate agents and managers

D-U-N-S 24-345-2849   (BR)
REGIONAL MUNICIPALITY OF WATERLOO, THE
100 Maple Grove Rd, Cambridge, ON, N3H 4R7
(519) 650-8264
Emp Here 26
SIC 8731 Commercial physical research

D-U-N-S 20-188-6459   (BR)
RUSSEL METALS INC
RUSSEL-LEROUX
15 Cherry Blossom Rd, Cambridge, ON, N3H 4R7
(519) 650-1666
Emp Here 50
SIC 5051 Metals service centers and offices

D-U-N-S 24-859-5501   (BR)
SUPERIOR PLUS LP
WINROC BUILDING SUPPLIES
36 Cherry Blossom Rd, Cambridge, ON, N3H 4R7
(519) 653-6111
Emp Here 40
SIC 5039 Construction materials, nec

D-U-N-S 24-350-0977   (BR)
TI AUTOMOTIVE CANADA INC
1090 Fountain St N Unit 9, Cambridge, ON, N3H 4R7
(519) 653-0900
Emp Here 30
SIC 3465 Automotive stampings

D-U-N-S 25-246-6016 (BR)
TOROMONT INDUSTRIES LTD
TOROMONT CAT
290 Industrial Rd, Cambridge, ON, N3H 4R7
(519) 650-1211
Emp Here 55
SIC 5082 Construction and mining machinery

D-U-N-S 20-574-2377 (BR)
TOROMONT INDUSTRIES LTD
BATTLEFIELD EQUIPMENT RENTALS
260 Industrial Rd, Cambridge, ON, N3H 4R7
(519) 650-4040
Emp Here 22
SIC 5082 Construction and mining machinery

D-U-N-S 25-352-6693 (BR)
TRANSFREIGHT INC
1055 Fountain St N, Cambridge, ON, N3H 4R7
(519) 653-0067
Emp Here 20
SIC 4213 Trucking, except local

D-U-N-S 25-251-1613 (BR)
TYCO INTEGRATED FIRE & SECURITY CANADA, INC
SIMPLEXGRINNELL
(*Suby of* Johnson Controls, Inc.)
125 Mcgovern Dr Unit 8, Cambridge, ON, N3H 4R7
(519) 650-5056
Emp Here 25
SIC 5999 Miscellaneous retail stores, nec

D-U-N-S 24-177-6546 (BR)
UAP INC
TRACTION CAMBRIDGE
(*Suby of* Genuine Parts Company)
1090 Fountain St N Unit 12-13, Cambridge, ON, N3H 4R7
(519) 653-3427
Emp Here 20
SIC 5013 Motor vehicle supplies and new parts

D-U-N-S 25-228-1951 (BR)
WATERLOO CATHOLIC DISTRICT SCHOOL BOARD
ST. JOSEPHS CATHOLIC ELEMENTARY SCHOOL
980 Westminster Dr S, Cambridge, ON, N3H 1V2
(519) 653-4482
Emp Here 30
SIC 8211 Elementary and secondary schools

D-U-N-S 25-228-1910 (BR)
WATERLOO CATHOLIC DISTRICT SCHOOL BOARD
ST-MICHAELS ELEMENTARY SCHOOL
1150 Concession Rd, Cambridge, ON, N3H 4L6
(519) 653-3351
Emp Here 24
SIC 8211 Elementary and secondary schools

D-U-N-S 25-228-1308 (BR)
WATERLOO REGION DISTRICT SCHOOL BOARD
RYERSON PUBLIC SCHOOL
749 Grand Valley Dr, Cambridge, ON, N3H 2S3
(519) 653-5532
Emp Here 20
SIC 8211 Elementary and secondary schools

D-U-N-S 20-710-7090 (BR)
WATERLOO REGION DISTRICT SCHOOL BOARD
PRESTON HIGH SCHOOL
550 Rose St, Cambridge, ON, N3H 2E6
(519) 653-2367
Emp Here 100
SIC 8211 Elementary and secondary schools

D-U-N-S 20-591-4729 (BR)
WATERLOO REGION DISTRICT SCHOOL

BOARD
CORONATION PUBLIC SCHOOL
757 Concession Rd, Cambridge, ON, N3H 4L1
(519) 653-1141
Emp Here 40
SIC 8211 Elementary and secondary schools

D-U-N-S 20-591-4612 (BR)
WATERLOO REGION DISTRICT SCHOOL BOARD
PRESTON PUBLIC SCHOOL
210 Westminster Dr N, Cambridge, ON, N3H 5C8
(519) 653-0387
Emp Here 25
SIC 8211 Elementary and secondary schools

D-U-N-S 20-710-7058 (BR)
WATERLOO REGION DISTRICT SCHOOL BOARD
WILLIAM G DAVIS SENIOR PUBLIC SCHOOL
530 Langs Dr, Cambridge, ON, N3H 5G5
(519) 653-2384
Emp Here 50
SIC 8211 Elementary and secondary schools

Cameron, ON K0M

D-U-N-S 25-184-2498 (BR)
TRILLIUM LAKELANDS DISTRICT SCHOOL BOARD
FENELON TOWNSHIP PUBLIC SCHOOL
50 Cameron Rd, Cameron, ON, K0M 1G0
(705) 359-1366
Emp Here 25
SIC 8211 Elementary and secondary schools

Camlachie, ON N0N
Lambton County

D-U-N-S 20-573-1222 (BR)
CANADA POST CORPORATION
CAMLACHIE PO
6705 Camlachie Rd, Camlachie, ON, N0N 1E0

Emp Here 20
SIC 4311 U.s. postal service

Campbellcroft, ON L0A
Durham County

D-U-N-S 20-025-0590 (BR)
KAWARTHA PINE RIDGE DISTRICT SCHOOL BOARD
NORTH HOPE CENTRAL PUBLIC SCHOOL
3278 Ganaraska Rd, Campbellcroft, ON, L0A 1B0
(905) 797-2991
Emp Here 25
SIC 8211 Elementary and secondary schools

Campbellford, ON K0L

D-U-N-S 24-351-5694 (SL)
BLOMMER CHOCOLATE COMPANY OF CANADA INC
(*Suby of* The Blommer Chocolate Company)
103 Second Ave, Campbellford, ON, K0L 1L0
(705) 653-5821
Emp Here 50   *Sales* 259,875
SIC 2066 Chocolate and cocoa products

D-U-N-S 20-267-9044 (SL)

CAMBRO LASERTEK LTD
34 Tanner Ind Pk, Campbellford, ON, K0L 1L0
(905) 355-3224
Emp Here 50   *Sales* 4,961,328
SIC 1761 Roofing, siding, and sheetMetal work

D-U-N-S 25-137-3536 (BR)
KAWARTHA PINE RIDGE DISTRICT SCHOOL BOARD
HILLCREST PUBLIC SCHOOL
55 Elmore St, Campbellford, ON, K0L 1L0
(705) 653-1430
Emp Here 30
SIC 8211 Elementary and secondary schools

D-U-N-S 25-237-9789 (BR)
KAWARTHA PINE RIDGE DISTRICT SCHOOL BOARD
KENT PUBLIC SCHOOL
150 Kent St, Campbellford, ON, K0L 1L0
(705) 653-1540
Emp Here 35
SIC 8211 Elementary and secondary schools

D-U-N-S 25-237-8385 (BR)
KAWARTHA PINE RIDGE DISTRICT SCHOOL BOARD
CAMPBELLFORD DISTRICT HIGH SCHOOL
119 Ranney St N Unit 960, Campbellford, ON, K0L 1L0
(705) 653-3060
Emp Here 105
SIC 8211 Elementary and secondary schools

D-U-N-S 25-906-0556 (SL)
MCCARTHY-ELLIS MERCANTILE LTD
CANADIAN TIRE
130 Grand Rd, Campbellford, ON, K0L 1L0
(705) 653-3250
Emp Here 50   *Sales* 3,575,074
SIC 5311 Department stores

D-U-N-S 25-882-5090 (BR)
OMNI HEALTH CARE LTD
BURNBRAE GARDENS
320 Burnbrae Rd E Rr 3, Campbellford, ON, K0L 1L0
(705) 653-4100
Emp Here 50
SIC 8051 Skilled nursing care facilities

D-U-N-S 25-943-3803 (BR)
PETERBOROUGH VICTORIA NORTHUMBERLAND AND CLARINGTON CATHOLIC DISTRICT SCHOOL BOARD
ST MARY'S SEPARATE SCHOOL
(*Suby of* Peterborough Victoria Northumberland and Clarington Catholic District School Board)
35 Centre St, Campbellford, ON, K0L 1L0
(705) 653-1370
Emp Here 25
SIC 8211 Elementary and secondary schools

D-U-N-S 25-807-5134 (BR)
ROYAL BANK OF CANADA
ROYAL BANK OF CANADA
(*Suby of* Royal Bank Of Canada)
15 Doxsee Ave N, Campbellford, ON, K0L 1L0
(705) 653-2210
Emp Here 20
SIC 6021 National commercial banks

D-U-N-S 24-353-4489 (BR)
SPECIALTY CARE INC
SPECIALTY LIVING ISLAND PARK
(*Suby of* Specialty Care Inc)
18 Trent Dr Rr 1, Campbellford, ON, K0L 1L0
(705) 653-3100
Emp Here 28
SIC 6513 Apartment building operators

Campbellville, ON L0P
Halton County

D-U-N-S 20-191-8237 (HQ)
GENERVATIONS INC
(*Suby of* GenerVations Inc)
44 Crawford Cres, Campbellville, ON, L0P 1B0
(905) 873-8700
Emp Here 30   *Emp Total* 39
Sales 44,073,840
SIC 5154 Livestock
Pr Pr David Eastman

D-U-N-S 24-217-9869 (BR)
GOODFELLOW INC
9184 Twiss Rd, Campbellville, ON, L0P 1B0
(905) 854-5800
Emp Here 170
SIC 5031 Lumber, plywood, and millwork

D-U-N-S 24-676-5296 (BR)
HALTON DISTRICT SCHOOL BOARD
BROOKVILLE PUBLIC SCHOOL
11325 Guelph Line, Campbellville, ON, L0P 1B0
(905) 854-2424
Emp Here 40
SIC 8211 Elementary and secondary schools

D-U-N-S 24-685-7692 (SL)
MERITCO INDUSTRIES LTD
RIDLEY WINDOWS & DOORS
2675 Reid Side Rd, Campbellville, ON, L0P 1B0
(905) 854-2228
Emp Here 23   *Sales* 6,931,267
SIC 5031 Lumber, plywood, and millwork
Pr Pr Paul Merritt

Cannifton, ON K0K
Hastings County

D-U-N-S 25-188-2221 (SL)
KEAY NURSING HOMES INC
MCQUIGGE, E. J. LODGE
38 Black Diamond Rd, Cannifton, ON, K0K 1K0
(613) 966-7717
Emp Here 64   *Sales* 2,918,428
SIC 8051 Skilled nursing care facilities

Cannington, ON L0E

D-U-N-S 20-063-6954 (BR)
CHARTWELL SENIORS HOUSING REAL ESTATE INVESTMENT TRUST
BON AIR RESIDENCE
131 Laidlaw St, Cannington, ON, L0E 1E0
(705) 432-2385
Emp Here 73
SIC 8051 Skilled nursing care facilities

D-U-N-S 25-300-7512 (BR)
DURHAM DISTRICT SCHOOL BOARD
MCCASKILL'S MILLS PUBLIC SCHOOL
Gd, Cannington, ON, L0E 1E0
(705) 432-2461
Emp Here 40
SIC 8211 Elementary and secondary schools

D-U-N-S 20-711-3478 (BR)
DURHAM DISTRICT SCHOOL BOARD
MCCASKILL MILLS
85 Albert St, Cannington, ON, L0E 1E0
(705) 432-2601
Emp Here 50
SIC 8211 Elementary and secondary schools

Capreol, ON P0M
Sudbury County

D-U-N-S 24-335-7394   (BR)
ACROBAT RESEARCH LTD
ACROBAT RESULT MARKETING
Gd, Capreol, ON, P0M 1H0
(705) 858-4343
Emp Here 100
SIC 8732 Commercial nonphysical research

D-U-N-S 20-569-6342   (BR)
COMPAGNIE DES CHEMINS DE FER NA-TIONAUX DU CANADA
10 Front St, Capreol, ON, P0M 1H0
(705) 858-4085
Emp Here 20
SIC 4011 Railroads, line-haul operating

D-U-N-S 20-273-0644   (BR)
FLYNN CANADA LTD
21 Regional Rd 84, Capreol, ON, P0M 1H0
(705) 858-8000
Emp Here 20
SIC 1761 Roofing, siding, and sheetMetal work

D-U-N-S 24-389-3414   (SL)
LAYNE CHRISTENSEN CANADA LIMITED
(*Suby of* Layne Christensen Company)
9 Regional Rd 84 Unit 84, Capreol, ON, P0M 1H0
(705) 858-6460
Emp Here 78   *Sales* 5,936,673
SIC 1499 Miscellaneous nonMetallic minerals, except fuels
  George R Demers
  Eric R Despain
  Andrew B Schmitt

D-U-N-S 20-590-4803   (BR)
RAINBOW DISTRICT SCHOOL BOARD
C R JUDD PUBLIC SCHOOL
8 Lincoln St, Capreol, ON, P0M 1H0

Emp Here 25
SIC 8211 Elementary and secondary schools

Caramat, ON P0T
Thunder Bay County

D-U-N-S 20-068-3931   (BR)
SUPERIOR GREENSTONE DISTRICT SCHOOL BOARD
CARAMAT DISTRICT PUBLIC SCHOOL
1551 Birch Cres, Caramat, ON, P0T 1J0
(807) 872-2648
Emp Here 25
SIC 8211 Elementary and secondary schools

Cardinal, ON K0E
Grenville County

D-U-N-S 24-830-0436   (SL)
730 TRUCK STOP INC
730 GAS BAR
2085 Shanly Rd, Cardinal, ON, K0E 1E0
(613) 657-3155
Emp Here 78   *Sales* 14,135,040
SIC 5541 Gasoline service stations
Pr Pr Robert Lodge

D-U-N-S 25-073-9588   (BR)
INGREDION CANADA CORPORATION
(*Suby of* Ingredion Incorporated)
4040 James St, Cardinal, ON, K0E 1E0

Emp Here 20
SIC 2046 Wet corn milling

Carleton Place, ON K7C
Lanark County

D-U-N-S 20-272-0228   (BR)
ALMONTE GENERAL HOSPITAL
LANARK COUNTY PARAMEDIC SERVICE
37 Neelin St, Carleton Place, ON, K7C 2J6

Emp Here 85
SIC 4119 Local passenger transportation, nec

D-U-N-S 25-296-8011   (BR)
BANK OF NOVA SCOTIA, THE
SCOTIABANK
85 Bridge St, Carleton Place, ON, K7C 2V4
(613) 253-5400
Emp Here 21
SIC 6021 National commercial banks

D-U-N-S 20-539-6992   (BR)
CANADA POST CORPORATION
CARLETON PLACE POST OFFICE
42 Bridge St, Carleton Place, ON, K7C 2V1
(613) 257-3324
Emp Here 27
SIC 4311 U.s. postal service

D-U-N-S 20-321-8925   (BR)
CARA OPERATIONS LIMITED
HARVEY'S
(*Suby of* Cara Holdings Limited)
10455 Hwy #7, Carleton Place, ON, K7C 3P2
(613) 257-5248
Emp Here 30
SIC 5812 Eating places

D-U-N-S 25-237-9557   (BR)
CATHOLIC DISTRICT SCHOOL BOARD OF EASTERN ONTARIO
ST MARY'S CATHOLIC SCHOOL
(*Suby of* Catholic District School Board of Eastern Ontario)
4 Hawthorne Ave, Carleton Place, ON, K7C 3A9
(613) 257-1538
Emp Here 22
SIC 8211 Elementary and secondary schools

D-U-N-S 25-464-1442   (BR)
CATHOLIC DISTRICT SCHOOL BOARD OF EASTERN ONTARIO
NOTRE DAME CATHOLIC HIGH SCHOOL
(*Suby of* Catholic District School Board of Eastern Ontario)
157 Mckenzie St, Carleton Place, ON, K7C 4P2
(613) 253-4700
Emp Here 45
SIC 8211 Elementary and secondary schools

D-U-N-S 24-500-5611   (BR)
CATHOLIC DISTRICT SCHOOL BOARD OF EASTERN ONTARIO
ST. GREGORY CATHOLIC SCHOOL
176 Townline Rd W, Carleton Place, ON, K7C 3P7
(613) 257-8468
Emp Here 36
SIC 8211 Elementary and secondary schools

D-U-N-S 20-037-1636   (BR)
CORPORATION OF THE TOWN OF CAR-LETON PLACE
CARLETON PLACE COMMUNITY CENTRE
75 Neelin St, Carleton Place, ON, K7C 2J6
(613) 257-1690
Emp Here 40
SIC 8322 Individual and family services

D-U-N-S 24-361-7201   (BR)
HOME DEPOT OF CANADA INC
HOME DEPOT
(*Suby of* The Home Depot Inc)
570 Mcneely Ave, Carleton Place, ON, K7C 0A7
(613) 253-3870
Emp Here 100
SIC 5251 Hardware stores

D-U-N-S 25-685-0959   (SL)
KINGSWAY ARMS MANAGEMENT (AT CARLETON PLACE) INC
6 Arthur St, Carleton Place, ON, K7C 4S4
(613) 253-7360
Emp Here 55   *Sales* 4,815,406
SIC 6513 Apartment building operators

D-U-N-S 25-028-5848   (BR)
ONTARIO CLEAN WATER AGENCY
122 Patterson Cres, Carleton Place, ON, K7C 4P3
(613) 257-4990
Emp Here 30
SIC 4941 Water supply

D-U-N-S 25-028-5251   (BR)
REVERA LONG TERM CARE INC
STONERIDGE MANOR
256 High St, Carleton Place, ON, K7C 1X1
(613) 257-4355
Emp Here 75
SIC 8051 Skilled nursing care facilities

D-U-N-S 20-003-4465   (BR)
ROYAL BANK OF CANADA
RBC
(*Suby of* Royal Bank Of Canada)
93 Bridge St, Carleton Place, ON, K7C 2V4
(613) 257-3800
Emp Here 21
SIC 6021 National commercial banks

D-U-N-S 24-101-8837   (SL)
SEAGRAVE FIRE APPARATUS COMPANY
(*Suby of* FWD Seagrave Holdings, LP)
7 Industrial Ave, Carleton Place, ON, K7C 3V7
(613) 257-8197
Emp Here 38   *Sales* 10,797,600
SIC 3711 Motor vehicles and car bodies
Genl Mgr Dwight Mcmillan
Fin Ex Edward (Ed) Holmes
Pr Pr Joseph Neiner

D-U-N-S 20-989-7078   (BR)
SOBEYS CAPITAL INCORPORATED
FRESHCO
110 Lansdowne Ave, Carleton Place, ON, K7C 2T7
(613) 253-6141
Emp Here 50
SIC 5411 Grocery stores

D-U-N-S 25-797-1838   (BR)
SOBEYS CAPITAL INCORPORATED
IGA CARLETON PLACE
26 Industrial Ave, Carleton Place, ON, K7C 3T2
(613) 256-5401
Emp Here 56
SIC 5411 Grocery stores

D-U-N-S 24-252-3137   (BR)
STOCK TRANSPORTATION LTD
11384 Hwy 7, Carleton Place, ON, K7C 3P1
(613) 253-2232
Emp Here 100
SIC 4151 School buses

D-U-N-S 25-962-1910   (BR)
TDL GROUP CORP, THE
TIM HORTONS
10418 Hwy 7, Carleton Place, ON, K7C 3P1
(613) 253-0446
Emp Here 40
SIC 5812 Eating places

D-U-N-S 25-137-9707   (BR)
UPPER CANADA DISTRICT SCHOOL BOARD, THE
CARAMBECK PUBLIC SCHOOL
(*Suby of* Upper Canada District School Board, The)
351 Bridge St, Carleton Place, ON, K7C 3H9

Emp Here 27
SIC 8211 Elementary and secondary schools

D-U-N-S 20-711-5465   (BR)
UPPER CANADA DISTRICT SCHOOL BOARD
ARK LAN SCHOOL
123 Patterson Cres, Carleton Place, ON, K7C 4R2
(613) 257-8113
Emp Here 50
SIC 8211 Elementary and secondary schools

D-U-N-S 20-711-5499   (BR)
UPPER CANADA DISTRICT SCHOOL BOARD, THE
CARLETON PLACE HIGH SCHOOL
215 Lake Ave W, Carleton Place, ON, K7C 1M3
(613) 257-2720
Emp Here 50
SIC 8211 Elementary and secondary schools

D-U-N-S 20-711-5473   (BR)
UPPER CANADA DISTRICT SCHOOL BOARD, THE
CALDWELL STREET ELEMENTARY SCHOOL
70 Caldwell St, Carleton Place, ON, K7C 3A5
(613) 257-1270
Emp Here 50
SIC 8211 Elementary and secondary schools

D-U-N-S 25-255-6980   (BR)
UPPER CANADA DISTRICT SCHOOL BOARD, THE
BECKWITH PUBLIC SCHOOL
(*Suby of* Upper Canada District School Board, The)
1523 9 Line, Carleton Place, ON, K7C 3P2
(613) 253-0427
Emp Here 45
SIC 8211 Elementary and secondary schools

Carlisle, ON L0R
Wentworth County

D-U-N-S 25-928-2903   (BR)
KANEFF PROPERTIES LIMITED
CARLISLE GOLF & COUNTRY CLUB
523 Carlisle Dr, Carlisle, ON, L0R 1H0
(905) 689-8820
Emp Here 60
SIC 7997 Membership sports and recreation clubs

Carp, ON K0A
Carleton County

D-U-N-S 25-719-4639   (SL)
1252336 ONTARIO LTD
GRACE MONUMENTS
106 Reis Rd, Carp, ON, K0A 1L0
(613) 836-1473
Emp Here 95   *Sales* 12,579,800
SIC 5999 Miscellaneous retail stores, nec
Pr Pr Arthur Goveas
  Dora Goveas

D-U-N-S 20-442-5664   (SL)
C&M ELECTRIC LTD
3038 Carp Rd, Carp, ON, K0A 1L0
(613) 839-3232
Emp Here 55   *Sales* 4,815,406
SIC 1731 Electrical work

D-U-N-S 24-100-7780   (SL)
CARR, EARL ELECTRIC LTD
120 Walgreen Rd, Carp, ON, K0A 1L0
(613) 831-9179
Emp Here 35   *Sales* 3,064,349
SIC 1731 Electrical work

D-U-N-S 25-330-6195   (BR)
CASSIDY'S TRANSFER & STORAGE LIM-

ITED
128 Willowlea Rd, Carp, ON, K0A 1L0
(613) 836-4225
Emp Here 30
SIC 4213 Trucking, except local

D-U-N-S 20-117-9210   (SL)
DAC INTERNATIONAL INC
3140 Carp Rd, Carp, ON, K0A 1L0
(613) 839-0888
Emp Here 35   *Sales* 6,391,350
SIC 2452 Prefabricated wood buildings
Pr Pr Jeffrey Armstrong

D-U-N-S 24-525-4862   (SL)
KARSON ASPHALT PAVING INC
3725 Carp Rd, Carp, ON, K0A 1L0
(613) 839-2816
Emp Here 20   *Sales* 2,407,703
SIC 4213 Trucking, except local

D-U-N-S 20-577-0589   (BR)
MODERN NIAGARA DESIGN SERVICES INC
2171 Mcgee Side Rd, Carp, ON, K0A 1L0
(613) 831-9488
Emp Here 60
SIC 1711 Plumbing, heating, air-conditioning

D-U-N-S 25-087-9442   (BR)
NORTRAX CANADA INC
(*Suby of* Deere & Company)
189 Cardevco Rd Suite 2, Carp, ON, K0A 1L0
(613) 831-4044
Emp Here 20
SIC 5082 Construction and mining machinery

D-U-N-S 25-825-5025   (BR)
OTTAWA CATHOLIC DISTRICT SCHOOL BOARD
ST MICHAEL SCHOOL
(*Suby of* Ottawa Catholic District School Board)
1572 Corkery Rd, Carp, ON, K0A 1L0
(613) 256-3672
Emp Here 23
SIC 8211 Elementary and secondary schools

D-U-N-S 25-263-6261   (BR)
OTTAWA-CARLETON DISTRICT SCHOOL BOARD
HUNTLEY CENTENNIAL PUBLIC SCHOOL
118 Langstaff Dr, Carp, ON, K0A 1L0
(613) 839-2020
Emp Here 37
SIC 8211 Elementary and secondary schools

D-U-N-S 24-619-9504   (BR)
TOMLINSON ENVIRONMENTAL SERVICES LTD
(*Suby of* Tomlinson, R. W. Limited)
106 Westhunt Dr, Carp, ON, K0A 1L0
(613) 836-6069
Emp Here 50
SIC 4212 Local trucking, without storage

D-U-N-S 24-764-7647   (BR)
WASTE MANAGEMENT OF CANADA CORPORATION
WASTE MANAGEMENT
(*Suby of* Waste Management, Inc.)
254 Westbrook Rd, Carp, ON, K0A 1L0
(613) 831-1281
Emp Here 150
SIC 4953 Refuse systems

D-U-N-S 25-407-8025   (HQ)
WEST CARLETON SAND & GRAVEL INC
KARSON AGGREGATES
3232 Carp, Carp, ON, K0A 1L0
(613) 839-2816
Emp Here 25   *Emp Total* 12,000
Sales 21,888,210
SIC 1771 Concrete work
Pr Pr William Karson
 Peter Geick
Dir John Adshead

Casselman, ON K0A
Russell County

D-U-N-S 20-711-6620   (BR)
CONSEIL SCOLAIRE DE DISTRICT CATHOLIQUE DE L'EST ONTARIEN
ECOLE ELEMENTAIRES CATHOLIQUE DE CASELMAN
133 Laurier St Rr 4, Casselman, ON, K0A 1M0
(613) 764-2960
Emp Here 50
SIC 8211 Elementary and secondary schools

D-U-N-S 25-955-2453   (BR)
CONSEIL SCOLAIRE DE DISTRICT CATHOLIQUE DE L'EST ONTARIEN
ECOLE ST-EUPHEMIE
(*Suby of* Conseil Scolaire De District Catholique De L'Est Ontarien)
215 Rue Laurier, Casselman, ON, K0A 1M0
(613) 764-2855
Emp Here 30
SIC 8211 Elementary and secondary schools

D-U-N-S 24-155-8266   (BR)
CONSEIL DES ECOLES PUBLIQUES DE L'EST DE L'ONTARIO
ECOLE ELEMENTAIRE L'ACADEMIE DE LA SEIGNEURIE
731 Rue Des Pommiers, Casselman, ON, K0A 1M0
(613) 764-0550
Emp Here 25
SIC 8211 Elementary and secondary schools

D-U-N-S 20-364-5338   (BR)
MATERIAUX PONT MASSON INC
MATERIAUX PONT MASSON INC
8 Racine St, Casselman, ON, K0A 1M0
(613) 764-2876
Emp Here 20
SIC 5211 Lumber and other building materials

D-U-N-S 24-344-5025   (BR)
METRO ONTARIO INC
21 Richer Cir, Casselman, ON, K0A 1M0
(613) 764-3882
Emp Here 70
SIC 5411 Grocery stores

D-U-N-S 24-159-5045   (BR)
VALORIS POUR ENFANTS ET ADULTES DE PRESCOTT-RUSSELL
133 Laurier St, Casselman, ON, K0A 1M0
(613) 764-3642
Emp Here 20
SIC 8322 Individual and family services

D-U-N-S 24-351-0117   (BR)
VALORIS POUR ENFANTS ET ADULTES DE PRESCOTT-RUSSELL
SERVICE AUX ENFANTS ET ADULTES DE PRESCOTT-RUSSELL
Gd, Casselman, ON, K0A 1M0
(613) 673-5148
Emp Here 50
SIC 8399 Social services, nec

Castleton, ON K0K

D-U-N-S 25-237-9888   (BR)
KAWARTHA PINE RIDGE DISTRICT SCHOOL BOARD
CASTLETON ELEMENTARY SCHOOL
2246 Spring St, Castleton, ON, K0K 1M0
(905) 344-7361
Emp Here 50
SIC 8211 Elementary and secondary schools

Cavan Monaghan, ON K9J

D-U-N-S 25-192-8735   (SL)
LEISUREWEAR CANADA LTD
LEISUREWEAR CANADA
2345 Whittington Dr, Cavan Monaghan, ON, K9J 0G5
(705) 742-7461
Emp Here 40   *Sales* 10,048,000
SIC 5136 Men's and boy's clothing
Pr Pr Grant Seabrooke
 Brian Seabrooke
 Glen Seabrooke
 Allan Seabrooke
Dir Janice Killen
Dir Paul Gauvin

Cayuga, ON N0A
Haldimand County

D-U-N-S 25-367-3255   (SL)
1233481 ONTARIO INC
TORONTO MOTORSPORTS PARK
1040 Kohler Rd, Cayuga, ON, N0A 1E0
(905) 772-0303
Emp Here 100
SIC 7948 Racing, including track operation

D-U-N-S 20-710-6480   (BR)
BRANT HALDIMAND NORFOLK CATHOLIC DISTRICT SCHOOL BOARD
ST STEPHEN'S SCHOOL
17 Brant St W, Cayuga, ON, N0A 1E0
(905) 772-3863
Emp Here 50
SIC 8211 Elementary and secondary schools

D-U-N-S 24-514-2476   (SL)
CAYUGA DISPLAYS INC
5585 Hwy 3, Cayuga, ON, N0A 1E0
(905) 772-0183
Emp Here 70   *Sales* 4,669,485
SIC 2541 Wood partitions and fixtures

D-U-N-S 25-823-4715   (BR)
GRAND ERIE DISTRICT SCHOOL BOARD
MITCHENER, J L PUBLIC SCHOOL
(*Suby of* Grand Erie District School Board)
60 Munsee St S, Cayuga, ON, N0A 1E0
(905) 772-5071
Emp Here 40
SIC 8211 Elementary and secondary schools

D-U-N-S 20-789-7294   (BR)
GRAND RIVER CONSERVATION AUTHORITY
TAQUANYAH CONSERVATION AREA
Gd, Cayuga, ON, N0A 1E0
(905) 768-3288
Emp Here 200
SIC 8641 Civic and social associations

Centralia, ON N0M
Huron County

D-U-N-S 24-914-6283   (BR)
PARRISH & HEIMBECKER, LIMITED
CENTRALIA GRAIN ELEVATOR
(*Suby of* Parrish & Heimbecker, Limited)
39648 Mount Carmel Dr, Centralia, ON, N0M 1K0
(519) 228-6661
Emp Here 20
SIC 5153 Grain and field beans

Chalk River, ON K0J
Renfrew County

D-U-N-S 24-875-5498   (SL)

BUBBLE TECHNOLOGY INDUSTRIES INC
BTI
31278 Hwy 17 W, Chalk River, ON, K0J 1J0
(613) 589-2456
Emp Here 50   *Sales* 2,699,546
SIC 8731 Commercial physical research

D-U-N-S 20-711-6893   (BR)
RENFREW COUNTY CATHOLIC DISTRICT SCHOOL BOARD
SAINT ANTHONY SCHOOL
(*Suby of* Renfrew County Catholic District School Board)
2 Mccarthy Dr, Chalk River, ON, K0J 1J0
(613) 589-2775
Emp Here 50
SIC 8211 Elementary and secondary schools

Chapleau, ON P0M
Sudbury County

D-U-N-S 25-238-0472   (BR)
ALGOMA DISTRICT SCHOOL BOARD
CHAPLEAU HIGH SCHOOL
(*Suby of* Algoma District School Board)
20 Teak St, Chapleau, ON, P0M 1K0
(705) 864-1452
Emp Here 22
SIC 8211 Elementary and secondary schools

D-U-N-S 20-710-4147   (BR)
CONSEIL SCOLAIRE DE DISTRICT CATHOLIQUE DU NOUVEL-ONTARIO, LE
ECOLE SECONDAIRE CATHOLIQUE TRILLIUM
9 Rue Broomhead, Chapleau, ON, P0M 1K0
(705) 864-1211
Emp Here 25
SIC 8211 Elementary and secondary schools

D-U-N-S 20-971-6922   (BR)
TEMBEC INC
175 Planer Rd, Chapleau, ON, P0M 1K0
(705) 864-3014
Emp Here 169
SIC 2421 Sawmills and planing mills, general

Charlton, ON P0J
Timiskaming County

D-U-N-S 24-320-0271   (BR)
DISTRICT SCHOOL BOARD ONTARIO NORTH EAST
CHARLTON SAVARD PUBLIC SCHOOL
Rr 1, Charlton, ON, P0J 1B0

Emp Here 20
SIC 8211 Elementary and secondary schools

Chatham, ON N7L

D-U-N-S 20-004-7608   (BR)
AFFINITY FOOD GROUP INC
WENDY'S RESTAURANT
720 Grand Ave W, Chatham, ON, N7L 1C6

Emp Here 20
SIC 5812 Eating places

D-U-N-S 20-572-2809   (BR)
BANK OF NOVA SCOTIA, THE
SCOTIA BANK
635 Grand Ave W, Chatham, ON, N7L 1C5
(519) 354-5110
Emp Here 20
SIC 6021 National commercial banks

D-U-N-S 20-708-7094   (BR)

BAYSHORE HEALTHCARE LTD.
BAYSHORE HOME HEALTH
857 Grand Ave W Suite 206, Chatham, ON,
N7L 4T1
(519) 354-2019
Emp Here 160
SIC 8059 Nursing and personal care, nec

D-U-N-S 24-341-0789   (BR)
BEST BUY CANADA LTD
FUTURE SHOP
(*Suby of* Best Buy Co., Inc.)
802 St Clair St, Chatham, ON, N7L 0E8
(519) 354-5525
Emp Here 50
SIC 5731 Radio, television, and electronic
stores

D-U-N-S 20-572-8921   (BR)
CANADA POST CORPORATION
416 St Clair St, Chatham, ON, N7L 3K5

Emp Here 20
SIC 4311 U.s. postal service

D-U-N-S 20-688-8088   (BR)
CARA OPERATIONS LIMITED
CHATHAM HARVEY STORE
(*Suby of* Cara Holdings Limited)
25 St Clair St, Chatham, ON, N7L 3H6
(519) 352-1262
Emp Here 28
SIC 5812 Eating places

D-U-N-S 20-521-7404   (SL)
CHATHAM-KENT CHILDREN'S SERVICE
495 Grand Ave W, Chatham, ON, N7L 1C5
(519) 352-0440
Emp Here 263   *Sales* 15,265,730
SIC 8322 Individual and family services
Ex Dir Michael Stevens

D-U-N-S 25-280-6591   (SL)
**CHILDREN'S TREATMENT CENTRE OF
CHATHAM KENT**
355 Lark St, Chatham, ON, N7L 5B2
(519) 354-0520
Emp Here 60   *Sales* 3,939,878
SIC 8093 Specialty outpatient clinics, nec

D-U-N-S 25-945-1276   (BR)
COMMUNITY LIVING CHATHAM-KENT
PARKFIELD RESTAURANT & GIFT SHOP
(*Suby of* Community Living Chatham-Kent)
1099 Park Ave W, Chatham, ON, N7L 0A1
(519) 352-5418
Emp Here 23
SIC 5947 Gift, novelty, and souvenir shop

D-U-N-S 24-339-8992   (BR)
COMPUGEN INC
50 Keil Dr N, Chatham, ON, N7L 3V9
(519) 436-4600
Emp Here 20
SIC 7373 Computer integrated systems design

D-U-N-S 20-299-5838   (BR)
**CONSEIL SCOLAIRE DE DISTRICT DES
ECOLES CATHOLIQUES DU SUD-OUEST**
*ECOLE   ELEMENTAIRE   CATHOLIQUE
SAINTE-MARIE*
90 Dale Dr, Chatham, ON, N7L 0B2
(519) 354-1225
Emp Here 25
SIC 8211 Elementary and secondary schools

D-U-N-S 20-515-2577   (BR)
**DIVERSICARE CANADA MANAGEMENT
SERVICES CO., INC**
MAPLE CITY RETIREMENT RESIDENCE
97 Mcfarlane Ave Suite 202, Chatham, ON,
N7L 4V6
(519) 354-7111
Emp Here 25
SIC 8361 Residential care

D-U-N-S 24-337-3078   (BR)
FGL SPORTS LTD

*SPORT CHEK CHATHAM 10THAMES LEA
PLAZA*
653 Grand Ave W, Chatham, ON, N7L 1C5
(519) 354-0123
Emp Here 35
SIC 5941 Sporting goods and bicycle shops

D-U-N-S 20-879-5018   (BR)
**GOODWILL INDUSTRIES-ESSEX KENT
LAMBTON INC**
GOODWILL
255 Grand Ave W, Chatham, ON, N7L 1C3
(519) 351-9486
Emp Here 22
SIC 5932 Used merchandise stores

D-U-N-S 25-862-8643   (BR)
**INVESTORS GROUP FINANCIAL SER-
VICES INC**
245 St Clair St, Chatham, ON, N7L 3J8
(519) 358-1115
Emp Here 26
SIC 8741 Management services

D-U-N-S 20-188-2490   (BR)
JARLETTE LTD
MEADOW PARK CHATHAM
110 Sandys St, Chatham, ON, N7L 4X3
(519) 351-1330
Emp Here 110
SIC 8051 Skilled nursing care facilities

D-U-N-S 25-263-7038   (BR)
**LAMBTON   KENT   DISTRICT   SCHOOL
BOARD**
TECUMSEH PUBLIC SCHOOL
287 Mcnaughton Ave W, Chatham, ON, N7L
1R8
(519) 354-2480
Emp Here 50
SIC 8211 Elementary and secondary schools

D-U-N-S 25-225-1186   (BR)
**LAMBTON   KENT   DISTRICT   SCHOOL
BOARD**
*GREGORY DRIVE ELEMENTARY PUBLIC
SCHOOL*
180 Gregory Dr W, Chatham, ON, N7L 2L4
(519) 352-6856
Emp Here 24
SIC 8211 Elementary and secondary schools

D-U-N-S 25-263-7236   (BR)
**LAMBTON   KENT   DISTRICT   SCHOOL
BOARD**
KING GEORGE VL SCHOOL
227 Delaware Ave, Chatham, ON, N7L 2W5
(519) 354-2440
Emp Here 23
SIC 8211 Elementary and secondary schools

D-U-N-S 20-591-6344   (BR)
**LAMBTON   KENT   DISTRICT   SCHOOL
BOARD**
MCNAUGHTON AVE PUBLIC SCHOOL
476 Mcnaughton Ave W, Chatham, ON, N7L
4J3
(519) 354-3770
Emp Here 25
SIC 8211 Elementary and secondary schools

D-U-N-S 20-650-9932   (BR)
**LAMBTON   KENT   DISTRICT   SCHOOL
BOARD**
CHATHAM-KENT SECONDARY SCHOOL
285 Mcnaughton Ave E, Chatham, ON, N7L
2G7
(519) 352-2870
Emp Here 100
SIC 8211 Elementary and secondary schools

D-U-N-S 20-591-6427   (BR)
**LAMBTON   KENT   DISTRICT   SCHOOL
BOARD**
JOHN AND GIVEN PUBLIC SCHOOL
92 Churchill St, Chatham, ON, N7L 3T5
(519) 354-6100
Emp Here 25

SIC 8211 Elementary and secondary schools

D-U-N-S 25-263-7319   (BR)
**LAMBTON   KENT   DISTRICT   SCHOOL
BOARD**
MCNAUGHTON AVE PUBLIC SCHOOL
480 Mcnaughton Ave E, Chatham, ON, N7L
2G9
(519) 352-8252
Emp Here 74
SIC 8211 Elementary and secondary schools

D-U-N-S 24-793-1256   (BR)
LIFELABS LP
LIFELABS
857 Grand Ave W Unit 106, Chatham, ON,
N7L 4T1

Emp Here 40
SIC 8071 Medical laboratories

D-U-N-S 24-345-7111   (BR)
LOBLAWS INC
REAL CANADIAN SUPERSTORE
791 St Clair St, Chatham, ON, N7L 0E9
(519) 352-4982
Emp Here 150
SIC 5411 Grocery stores

D-U-N-S 20-040-7732   (BR)
N. TEPPERMAN LIMITED
BARGAIN ANNEX
535 Grand Ave E, Chatham, ON, N7L 3Z2
(519) 351-6034
Emp Here 20
SIC 5712 Furniture stores

D-U-N-S 25-263-7079   (BR)
**ST. CLAIR CATHOLIC DISTRICT SCHOOL
BOARD**
URSULINE COLLEGE (THE PINES)
(*Suby of* St.   Clair Catholic District School
Board)
85 Grand Ave W, Chatham, ON, N7L 1B6
(519) 351-2987
Emp Here 160
SIC 8221 Colleges and universities

D-U-N-S 20-710-5045   (BR)
**ST. CLAIR CATHOLIC DISTRICT SCHOOL
BOARD**
OUR LADY OF FATIMA SCHOOL
545 Baldoon Rd, Chatham, ON, N7L 5A9
(519) 351-4040
Emp Here 30
SIC 8211 Elementary and secondary schools

D-U-N-S 25-249-3275   (BR)
**ST. CLAIR CATHOLIC DISTRICT SCHOOL
BOARD**
MONSIGNOR UYEN CATHOLIC SCHOOL
(*Suby of* St.   Clair Catholic District School
Board)
255 Lark St, Chatham, ON, N7L 1G9
(519) 352-1880
Emp Here 30
SIC 8211 Elementary and secondary schools

D-U-N-S 25-010-7653   (BR)
**STEEVES & ROZEMA ENTERPRISES LIM-
ITED**
RESIDENCE ON THE THAMES
850 Grand Ave W Suite 116, Chatham, ON,
N7L 5H5
(519) 351-7220
Emp Here 30
SIC 6513 Apartment building operators

D-U-N-S 25-848-8626   (BR)
TWINCORP INC
TACO BELL
328 St Clair St, Chatham, ON, N7L 3K1

Emp Here 28
SIC 5812 Eating places

D-U-N-S 20-040-8144   (HQ)
UNION GAS LIMITED
50 Keil Dr N Suite 2001, Chatham, ON, N7L

3V9
(519) 352-3100
Emp Here 900   *Emp Total* 7,733
Sales 1,130,917,205
SIC 4923 Gas transmission and distribution
Stephen Baker
CFO Patrick Reddy
VP VP Bruce E. Pydee
VP Bohdan Bodnar

D-U-N-S 24-183-6584   (HQ)
**URSULINE RELIGIOUS OF THE DIOCESE
OF LONDON IN ONTARIO**
(*Suby of* Ursuline Religious Of The Diocese
Of London In Ontario)
20 Merici Way, Chatham, ON, N7L 3L8
(519) 352-5225
Emp Here 50   *Emp Total* 53
Sales 3,502,114
SIC 8661 Religious organizations

D-U-N-S 25-297-7269   (BR)
WAL-MART CANADA CORP
881 St Clair St, Chatham, ON, N7L 0E9
(519) 352-1142
Emp Here 200
SIC 5311 Department stores

D-U-N-S 20-657-1569   (BR)
WENDY'S RESTAURANTS OF CANADA INC
(*Suby of* The Wendy's Company)
450 St Clair St, Chatham, ON, N7L 3K7
(519) 351-6653
Emp Here 35
SIC 5812 Eating places

Chatham, ON N7M

D-U-N-S 25-364-9594   (SL)
1670002 ONTARIO LIMITED
GLOBAL INDUSTRIAL SERVICES
48 Fifth St S Suite 406, Chatham, ON, N7M
4V8
(519) 436-1250
Emp Here 150   *Sales* 15,217,500
SIC 7361 Employment agencies
Pr Pr Robert D Ryan

D-U-N-S 20-703-2439   (BR)
ADVANTAGE ENGINEERING INC
830 Richmond St, Chatham, ON, N7M 5J5

Emp Here 24
SIC 3089 Plastics products, nec

D-U-N-S 24-423-5243   (SL)
ALLMET ROOF PRODUCTS, LTD
650 Riverview Dr Unit 1, Chatham, ON, N7M
0N2
(519) 380-9265
Emp Here 25   *Sales* 4,504,505
SIC 3069 Fabricated rubber products, nec

D-U-N-S 20-555-1620   (BR)
ARCTIC GLACIER INC
745 Park Ave W, Chatham, ON, N7M 1X3
(519) 352-1400
Emp Here 20
SIC 2097 Manufactured ice

D-U-N-S 25-305-2575   (BR)
BANK OF NOVA SCOTIA, THE
SCOTIABANK
213 King St W Suite 518, Chatham, ON, N7M
1E6
(519) 354-5560
Emp Here 25
SIC 6021 National commercial banks

D-U-N-S 20-995-7369   (BR)
BLACKBURN RADIO INC
117 Keil Dr S, Chatham, ON, N7M 3H3
(519) 354-2200
Emp Here 50
SIC 4832 Radio broadcasting stations

▲ Public Company   ■ Public Company Family Member   **HQ** Headquarters   **BR** Branch   **SL** Single Location

D-U-N-S 20-040-2964   (HQ)
BRAD-LEA MEADOWS LIMITED
BEST WESTERN WHEELS INN
(*Suby of* First Chatham Corporation Ltd)
615 Richmond St, Chatham, ON, N7M 1R2
(519) 436-5506
Emp Here 400   *Emp Total* 500
Sales 25,987,530
SIC 7011 Hotels and motels
 John Bradley
Pr Pr Dean Bradley
 Larry Bradley

D-U-N-S 25-835-4166   (BR)
BRUCE R. SMITH LIMITED
370 Colborne St, Chatham, ON, N7M 5J4

Emp Here 40
SIC 4213 Trucking, except local

D-U-N-S 25-224-9289   (SL)
CALVIN CHRISTIAN SCHOOLS SOCIETY OF CHATHAM INC
CHATHAM CHRISTIAN HIGH SCHOOL
475 Keil Dr S, Chatham, ON, N7M 6L8
(519) 352-4980
Emp Here 50   *Sales* 3,356,192
SIC 8211 Elementary and secondary schools

D-U-N-S 20-922-5671   (SL)
CAN-AM TRACTOR LTD
(*Suby of* Kucera Group Inc)
9831 Longwoods Rd Suite 1, Chatham, ON, N7M 5J7
(519) 351-4300
Emp Here 20   *Sales* 4,377,642
SIC 5083 Farm and garden machinery

D-U-N-S 20-543-0494   (BR)
CANADA POST CORPORATION
120 Wellington St W, Chatham, ON, N7M 4V9
(519) 352-1310
Emp Here 50
SIC 4311 U.s. postal service

D-U-N-S 25-016-9422   (BR)
CANADIAN IMPERIAL BANK OF COMMERCE
CIBC
99 King St E, Chatham, ON, N7M 3M9
(519) 352-7150
Emp Here 20
SIC 6021 National commercial banks

D-U-N-S 20-117-5895   (SL)
CANQUEST COMMUNICATIONS (ONLINE) INC
14 William St N, Chatham, ON, N7M 4L1
(519) 351-8647
Emp Here 60   *Sales* 9,947,520
SIC 4813 Telephone communication, except radio
Dir John Smith
Pr Pr Brent Ward

D-U-N-S 20-303-3477   (BR)
CARA OPERATIONS LIMITED
KELSEY'S
(*Suby of* Cara Holdings Limited)
804 Richmond St, Chatham, ON, N7M 5J5
(519) 351-0330
Emp Here 20
SIC 5812 Eating places

D-U-N-S 25-639-3463   (BR)
CENTRELINE EQUIPMENT RENTALS LTD
VOLVO RENTS
401 Richmond St, Chatham, ON, N7M 1P5
(519) 354-2671
Emp Here 20
SIC 7359 Equipment rental and leasing, nec

D-U-N-S 20-628-0609   (BR)
CHRISTIAN HORIZONS
(*Suby of* Christian Horizons)
241 Wellington St E, Chatham, ON, N7M 3P4
(519) 358-1516
Emp Here 20

SIC 8361 Residential care

D-U-N-S 20-040-4465   (BR)
COCA-COLA REFRESHMENTS CANADA COMPANY
(*Suby of* The Coca-Cola Company)
71 Park Ave E, Chatham, ON, N7M 3V5
(519) 352-2632
Emp Here 50
SIC 2086 Bottled and canned soft drinks

D-U-N-S 25-462-6518   (BR)
COMCARE (CANADA) LIMITED
COMCARE HEALTH SERVICES
(*Suby of* Comcare (Canada) Limited)
48 Centre St, Chatham, ON, N7M 4W2

Emp Here 20
SIC 8051 Skilled nursing care facilities

D-U-N-S 20-573-2857   (BR)
COMPAGNIE DES CHEMINS DE FER NATIONAUX DU CANADA
360 Queen St, Chatham, ON, N7M 2H6
(519) 792-1926
Emp Here 20
SIC 4011 Railroads, line-haul operating

D-U-N-S 24-006-3305   (BR)
CORPORATION OF THE MUNICIPALITY OF CHATHAM-KENT, THE
CHATHAM-KENT PUBLIC LIBRARY
120 Queen St, Chatham, ON, N7M 2G6
(519) 354-2940
Emp Here 67
SIC 8231 Libraries

D-U-N-S 20-104-8894   (BR)
DANA CANADA CORPORATION
SEALING PRODUCTS
1010 Richmond St, Chatham, ON, N7M 5J5
(519) 351-1221
Emp Here 100
SIC 2298 Cordage and twine

D-U-N-S 25-145-4856   (SL)
ENTEGRUS SERVICS INC
320 Queen St, Chatham, ON, N7M 2H6
(519) 352-6300
Emp Here 30   *Sales* 3,580,850
SIC 8742 Management consulting services

D-U-N-S 24-788-5879   (BR)
FIRSTCANADA ULC
FIRST STUDENT CANADA
100 Currie St, Chatham, ON, N7M 6L9
(519) 352-1920
Emp Here 100
SIC 4151 School buses

D-U-N-S 20-261-1633   (BR)
GOODLIFE FITNESS CENTRES INC
GOODLIFE FITNESS CLUBS
100 King St W, Chatham, ON, N7M 6A9
(519) 352-6868
Emp Here 20
SIC 7991 Physical fitness facilities

D-U-N-S 25-999-5884   (BR)
GREENFIELD GLOBAL, INC
275 Bloomfield Rd, Chatham, ON, N7M 0N6
(519) 436-1130
Emp Here 50
SIC 2869 Industrial organic chemicals, nec

D-U-N-S 20-040-7781   (SL)
GUSPRO INC
BLADEMASTER
566 Riverview Line Unit 101, Chatham, ON, N7M 0N2
(519) 352-4550
Emp Here 48   *Sales* 6,931,267
SIC 3567 Industrial furnaces and ovens
Pr Pr Paul Sunnen
Dir August Sunnen

D-U-N-S 20-936-2545   (BR)
HANSON RESTAURANTS (TB) INC
ARBY'S RESTAURANT

1070 Richmond St, Chatham, ON, N7M 5J5

Emp Here 25
SIC 5812 Eating places

D-U-N-S 24-086-5340   (BR)
HOME DEPOT OF CANADA INC
(*Suby of* The Home Depot Inc)
8582 Pioneer Line, Chatham, ON, N7M 5J1
(519) 380-2040
Emp Here 100
SIC 5211 Lumber and other building materials

D-U-N-S 24-364-6804   (BR)
KOHL & FRISCH LIMITED
(*Suby of* Kohl & Frisch Limited)
20 Currie St Unit D, Chatham, ON, N7M 6L9
(519) 380-9487
Emp Here 20
SIC 5122 Drugs, proprietaries, and sundries

D-U-N-S 25-263-7434   (BR)
LAMBTON KENT DISTRICT SCHOOL BOARD
WINSTON CHURCHILL PUBLIC SCHOOL
30 Crystal Dr, Chatham, ON, N7M 3C7
(519) 352-8680
Emp Here 25
SIC 8211 Elementary and secondary schools

D-U-N-S 25-263-7350   (BR)
LAMBTON KENT DISTRICT SCHOOL BOARD
VICTOR LAURISTON SCHOOL
44 Alexandra Ave, Chatham, ON, N7M 1Y1
(519) 352-4530
Emp Here 32
SIC 8211 Elementary and secondary schools

D-U-N-S 25-263-7475   (BR)
LAMBTON KENT DISTRICT SCHOOL BOARD
JOHN MCGREGOR SECONDARY SCHOOL
300 Cecile Ave, Chatham, ON, N7M 2C6
(519) 354-1740
Emp Here 75
SIC 8211 Elementary and secondary schools

D-U-N-S 20-591-6419   (BR)
LAMBTON KENT DISTRICT SCHOOL BOARD
QUEEN ELIZABETH II PUBLIC SCHOOL
79 Eugenie St, Chatham, ON, N7M 3Y9
(519) 354-2560
Emp Here 25
SIC 8211 Elementary and secondary schools

D-U-N-S 25-263-7194   (BR)
LAMBTON KENT DISTRICT SCHOOL BOARD
INDIAN CREEK ROAD PUBLIC SCHOOL
511 Indian Creek Rd W, Chatham, ON, N7M 0P5
(519) 352-3137
Emp Here 50
SIC 8211 Elementary and secondary schools

D-U-N-S 24-392-0514   (HQ)
MSSC CANADA INC
201 Park Ave E Suite 312, Chatham, ON, N7M 3V7
(905) 878-2395
Emp Here 50   *Emp Total* 3,655
Sales 14,119,891
SIC 3492 Fluid power valves and hose fittings
Pr John Trapp
Asst VP Tom Marayuma
Treas Charles Weisbaum

D-U-N-S 20-703-2962   (BR)
MSSC CANADA INC
201 Park Ave E, Chatham, ON, N7M 3V7
(519) 354-1100
Emp Here 270
SIC 3493 Steel springs, except wire

D-U-N-S 25-295-6537   (BR)
MARCH OF DIMES CANADA

555 Richmond St, Chatham, ON, N7M 1R2
(519) 351-8464
Emp Here 30
SIC 8331 Job training and related services

D-U-N-S 20-178-5396   (BR)
MONSANTO CANADA INC
(*Suby of* Monsanto Company)
301 Richmond St, Chatham, ON, N7M 1P5
(519) 352-5310
Emp Here 20
SIC 2879 Agricultural chemicals, nec

D-U-N-S 20-406-3515   (BR)
NAVISTAR CANADA, INC
508 Richmond St, Chatham, ON, N7M 1R3

Emp Here 777
SIC 3711 Motor vehicles and car bodies

D-U-N-S 20-706-9217   (SL)
ONE WORLD LOGISTICS OF AMERICA INC
O W L
400 National Rd, Chatham, ON, N7M 5J5
(519) 380-0800
Emp Here 155   *Sales* 27,898,750
SIC 4213 Trucking, except local
Rgnl Mgr Paul Cox

D-U-N-S 20-859-9543   (BR)
PACIFIC LINK COMMUNICATIONS INC
BELL WORLD
100 King St W, Chatham, ON, N7M 6A9
(519) 351-7976
Emp Here 25
SIC 5999 Miscellaneous retail stores, nec

D-U-N-S 25-986-7885   (BR)
PRISZM LP
KFC
541 Queen St, Chatham, ON, N7M 2J4
(519) 354-1030
Emp Here 22
SIC 5812 Eating places

D-U-N-S 25-528-0281   (BR)
ROYAL BANK OF CANADA
RBC
(*Suby of* Royal Bank Of Canada)
171 Keil Dr S, Chatham, ON, N7M 3H3
(519) 354-4340
Emp Here 30
SIC 6021 National commercial banks

D-U-N-S 20-580-5950   (BR)
ROYAL BANK OF CANADA
RBC
(*Suby of* Royal Bank Of Canada)
190 King St E, Chatham, ON, N7M 3N4
(519) 354-1680
Emp Here 20
SIC 6021 National commercial banks

D-U-N-S 20-040-7252   (SL)
RUSSELL TOOL & DIE LIMITED
NARMCO GROUP
381 Park Ave W, Chatham, ON, N7M 1W6
(519) 352-8168
Emp Here 60   *Sales* 4,961,328
SIC 3544 Special dies, tools, jigs, and fixtures

D-U-N-S 24-382-2637   (BR)
SELECTCORE LTD
SELECTCORE COMMUNICATIONS
(*Suby of* SelectCore Ltd)
14 William St N, Chatham, ON, N7M 4L1
(519) 351-8647
Emp Here 30
SIC 4813 Telephone communication, except radio

D-U-N-S 24-288-7370   (SL)
SHILLINGTON ROWLANDS INSURANCE INC
121 Heritage Rd, Chatham, ON, N7M 5W7
(519) 352-2860
Emp Here 70   *Sales* 8,724,700
SIC 6411 Insurance agents, brokers, and ser-

vice
Pr Pr Michael Burke

D-U-N-S 20-517-3797   (BR)
SOBEYS CAPITAL INCORPORATED
SOBEYS 732
215 Park Ave W, Chatham, ON, N7M 1W3
(519) 380-0550
Emp Here 200
SIC 5411 Grocery stores

D-U-N-S 24-125-2055   (BR)
SONOCO CANADA CORPORATION
(*Suby of* Sonoco Products Company)
674 Richmond St, Chatham, ON, N7M 5K4
(519) 352-8201
Emp Here 75
SIC 2655 Fiber cans, drums, and similar products

D-U-N-S 20-860-1620   (BR)
SOURCE (BELL) ELECTRONICS INC, THE
SOURCE, THE
801 St Clair St, Chatham, ON, N7M 5J7

Emp Here 25
SIC 5999 Miscellaneous retail stores, nec

D-U-N-S 20-973-4375   (SL)
ST. ANDREW'S RESIDENCE, CHATHAM
99 Park St, Chatham, ON, N7M 3R5
(519) 354-8103
Emp Here 50   *Sales* 1,824,018
SIC 8361 Residential care

D-U-N-S 25-249-3515   (BR)
ST. CLAIR CATHOLIC DISTRICT SCHOOL BOARD
ST URSULA CATHOLIC SCHOOL
(*Suby of* St. Clair Catholic District School Board)
426 Lacroix St, Chatham, ON, N7M 2W3
(519) 352-3620
Emp Here 35
SIC 8211 Elementary and secondary schools

D-U-N-S 20-590-5636   (BR)
ST. CLAIR CATHOLIC DISTRICT SCHOOL BOARD
ST JOSEPH CATHOLIC SCHOOL
25 Raleigh St Suite 25, Chatham, ON, N7M 2M6
(519) 354-4642
Emp Here 30
SIC 8211 Elementary and secondary schools

D-U-N-S 20-940-8624   (HQ)
TRANSIT TRAILER LIMITED
22217 Bloomfield Rd Suite 3, Chatham, ON, N7M 5J3
(519) 354-9944
Emp Here 20   *Emp Total* 1
Sales 27,044,842
SIC 5012 Automobiles and other motor vehicles
Pr Pr Murray Campbell

D-U-N-S 20-997-9819   (BR)
VALUE VILLAGE STORES, INC
(*Suby of* Savers, Inc.)
80 Keil Dr S, Chatham, ON, N7M 3H1
(519) 354-9325
Emp Here 45
SIC 5399 Miscellaneous general merchandise

D-U-N-S 25-370-3128   (BR)
WASTE CONNECTIONS OF CANADA INC
BFI CANADA
91 Sass Rd, Chatham, ON, N7M 5J4
(519) 360-9435
Emp Here 30
SIC 4953 Refuse systems

D-U-N-S 24-048-1846   (HQ)
WAYCON INTERNATIONAL TRUCKS LTD
WAYCON INTERNATIONAL TRUCKS OF CHATHAM
(*Suby of* 397217 Ontario Limited)

700 Richmond St, Chatham, ON, N7M 5J5
(519) 352-7242
Emp Here 62   *Emp Total* 276
Sales 24,587,756
SIC 5531 Auto and home supply stores
Pr Pr Bradley Connor
Jodie Schepanwoski
Timothy K (Tim) Derrough
Richard (Rick) Holdaway
John Procter
Theodore (Ted) Tar

Chatsworth, ON N0H
Grey County

D-U-N-S 24-824-9604   (BR)
HURON TRACTOR LTD
CAN-EAST EQUIPMENT
802802 Grey Rd 40, Chatsworth, ON, N0H 1G0
(519) 794-2480
Emp Here 20
SIC 5083 Farm and garden machinery

D-U-N-S 25-732-7478   (BR)
REVERA LONG TERM CARE INC
CHATSWORTH HEALTH CARE CENTRE
Gd, Chatsworth, ON, N0H 1G0

Emp Here 40
SIC 8051 Skilled nursing care facilities

Chelmsford, ON P0M
Sudbury County

D-U-N-S 25-239-0307   (BR)
CONSEIL SCOLAIRE DE DISTRICT CATHOLIQUE DU NOUVEL-ONTARIO, LE
ECOLE SECONDAIRE CATHOLIQUE CHAMPLAIN
61 Brookside Rd, Chelmsford, ON, P0M 1L0
(705) 855-9046
Emp Here 45
SIC 8211 Elementary and secondary schools

D-U-N-S 24-213-0404   (BR)
CONSEIL SCOLAIRE DE DISTRICT DU GRAND NORD DE L'ONTARIO
CONSEIL SCOLAIRE DE DISTRICT DU GRAND NORD DE L'ON
370 Cote Ave, Chelmsford, ON, P0M 1L0
(705) 855-8733
Emp Here 25
SIC 8211 Elementary and secondary schools

D-U-N-S 24-344-5082   (BR)
METRO ONTARIO INC
METRO
3442 Errington Ave Suite 1, Chelmsford, ON, P0M 1L0
(705) 855-4328
Emp Here 60
SIC 5411 Grocery stores

D-U-N-S 24-165-8793   (BR)
ONTARIO LOTTERY AND GAMING CORPORATION
400 Bonin, Chelmsford, ON, P0M 1L0
(705) 855-7164
Emp Here 160
SIC 7993 Coin-operated amusement devices

D-U-N-S 25-239-9894   (BR)
RAINBOW DISTRICT SCHOOL BOARD
CHELMSFORD VALLEY DISTRICT SCHOOL
(*Suby of* Rainbow District School Board)
3594 144 Hwy, Chelmsford, ON, P0M 1L0
(705) 675-0225
Emp Here 37
SIC 8211 Elementary and secondary schools

D-U-N-S 25-239-9902   (BR)
RAINBOW DISTRICT SCHOOL BOARD
CHELMSFORD PUBLIC SCHOOL
(*Suby of* Rainbow District School Board)
121 Charlotte Ave, Chelmsford, ON, P0M 1L0
(705) 671-5945
Emp Here 25
SIC 8211 Elementary and secondary schools

D-U-N-S 25-239-0802   (BR)
SUDBURY CATHOLIC DISTRICT SCHOOL BOARD
ST CHARLES SCHOOL
26 Charlotte Ave, Chelmsford, ON, P0M 1L0
(705) 673-5620
Emp Here 25
SIC 8211 Elementary and secondary schools

Cheltenham, ON L7C
Peel County

D-U-N-S 24-966-4111   (SL)
BRAMPTON FLYING CLUB
BRAMPTON CESSNA
13691 Mclaughlin Rd, Cheltenham, ON, L7C 2B2
(416) 798-7928
Emp Here 75   *Sales* 4,085,799
SIC 8299 Schools and educational services, nec

Cherry Valley, ON K0K
Prince Edward County

D-U-N-S 20-025-0624   (BR)
HASTINGS AND PRINCE EDWARD DISTRICT SCHOOL BOARD
ATHOL CENTRAL ELEMENTARY SCHOOL
1764 County Rd 10, Cherry Valley, ON, K0K 1P0
(613) 476-3974
Emp Here 20
SIC 8211 Elementary and secondary schools

Chesley, ON N0G
Bruce County

D-U-N-S 25-238-8814   (BR)
BLUEWATER DISTRICT SCHOOL BOARD
CHESLEY DISTRICT HIGH SCHOOL
231 4th Ave Se, Chesley, ON, N0G 1L0
(519) 363-2344
Emp Here 30
SIC 8211 Elementary and secondary schools

D-U-N-S 20-710-6530   (BR)
BLUEWATER DISTRICT SCHOOL BOARD
KINGHURST COMMUNITY SCHOOL
307 1st Ave N, Chesley, ON, N0G 1L0
(519) 363-3225
Emp Here 20
SIC 8211 Elementary and secondary schools

D-U-N-S 24-347-1567   (BR)
SOUTH BRUCE GREY HEALTH CENTRE
39 2 Conc Rr 3, Chesley, ON, N0G 1L0
(519) 363-2340
Emp Here 50
SIC 8062 General medical and surgical hospitals

Chesterville, ON K0C
Dundas County

D-U-N-S 20-041-0504   (BR)
NESTLE CANADA INC

171 Main St N, Chesterville, ON, K0C 1H0

Emp Here 300
SIC 2095 Roasted coffee

D-U-N-S 25-224-8273   (BR)
UPPER CANADA DISTRICT SCHOOL BOARD, THE
MAPLE RIDGE SENIOR PUBLIC SCHOOL
(*Suby of* Upper Canada District School Board, The)
12820 Highway 43, Chesterville, ON, K0C 1H0

Emp Here 20
SIC 8211 Elementary and secondary schools

D-U-N-S 20-153-3200   (BR)
UPPER CANADA DISTRICT SCHOOL BOARD, THE
NORTH DUNDAS DISTRICT HIGH SCHOOL
12835 Highway 43, Chesterville, ON, K0C 1H0
(613) 448-2328
Emp Here 70
SIC 8211 Elementary and secondary schools

Claremont, ON L1Y

D-U-N-S 25-300-7892   (BR)
DURHAM DISTRICT SCHOOL BOARD
CLAREMONT PUBLIC SCHOOL
1675 Central St, Claremont, ON, L1Y 1A8
(905) 649-2000
Emp Here 21
SIC 8211 Elementary and secondary schools

Clarence Creek, ON K0A
Russell County

D-U-N-S 20-891-1289   (SL)
CENTRE D'ACCEUIL ROGER SEGUIN
435 Lemay St, Clarence Creek, ON, K0A 1N0
(613) 488-2053
Emp Here 135   *Sales* 4,961,328
SIC 8361 Residential care

D-U-N-S 25-987-0327   (BR)
CONSEIL SCOLAIRE DE DISTRICT CATHOLIQUE DE L'EST ONTARIEN
ECOLE ELEMENTAIRE CATHOLIQUE SAINTE-FELICITE
(*Suby of* Conseil Scolaire De District Catholique De L'Est Ontarien)
1647 Landry St, Clarence Creek, ON, K0A 1N0
(613) 488-3030
Emp Here 30
SIC 8211 Elementary and secondary schools

D-U-N-S 20-893-0180   (SL)
LAFLEUR SCHOOL TRANSPORTATION LTD
1546 Baseline Rd, Clarence Creek, ON, K0A 1N0
(613) 488-2337
Emp Here 85   *Sales* 2,407,703
SIC 4151 School buses

Clarksburg, ON N0H
Grey County

D-U-N-S 20-556-2106   (BR)
A. LASSONDE INC
GOLDEN TOWN APPLE PRODUCTS
(*Suby of* 3346625 Canada Inc)
496648 Grey Rd No. 2, Clarksburg, ON, N0H 1J0

---

(519) 599-6300
Emp Here 40
SIC 2033 Canned fruits and specialties

D-U-N-S 20-289-1201   (BR)
HINCKS-DELLCREST TREATMENT CEN-TRE, THE
HINCKS DELLCREST FARM SCHOOL
(*Suby of* Hincks-Dellcrest Treatment Centre, The)
P.O. Box 339, Clarksburg, ON, N0H 1J0
(519) 599-3020
Emp Here 30
SIC 8093 Specialty outpatient clinics, nec

Clinton, ON N0M
Huron County

D-U-N-S 24-984-9357   (BR)
AVON MAITLAND DISTRICT SCHOOL BOARD
CLINTON ELEMENTARY PUBLIC SCHOOL
27 Percival St, Clinton, ON, N0M 1L0
(519) 482-9424
Emp Here 33
SIC 8211 Elementary and secondary schools

D-U-N-S 24-451-1981   (BR)
AVON MAITLAND DISTRICT SCHOOL BOARD
HOLMESVILLE PUBLIC SCHOOL
670 Cut Line Rd, Clinton, ON, N0M 1L0
(519) 482-3471
Emp Here 25
SIC 8211 Elementary and secondary schools

D-U-N-S 20-707-8242   (BR)
AVON MAITLAND DISTRICT SCHOOL BOARD
LEARNING RESOURCES CENTRE
163 Princess St E, Clinton, ON, N0M 1L0
(519) 482-8795
Emp Here 30
SIC 8299 Schools and educational services, nec

D-U-N-S 20-651-0849   (BR)
AVON MAITLAND DISTRICT SCHOOL BOARD
CENTRAL HURON SECONDARY SCHOOL
165 Princess St E, Clinton, ON, N0M 1L0
(519) 482-3471
Emp Here 60
SIC 8211 Elementary and secondary schools

D-U-N-S 20-026-3361   (BR)
HURON PERTH CATHOLIC DISTRICT SCHOOL BOARD
ST ANNE CATHOLIC SECONDARY SCHOOL
353 Ontario St, Clinton, ON, N0M 1L0
(519) 482-5454
Emp Here 73
SIC 8211 Elementary and secondary schools

D-U-N-S 24-683-7079   (BR)
HURON PERTH HEALTHCARE ALLIANCE
CLINTON PUBLIC HOSPITAL, THE
98 Shipley St, Clinton, ON, N0M 1L0
(519) 482-3447
Emp Here 140
SIC 8062 General medical and surgical hospitals

D-U-N-S 20-911-4490   (BR)
HYDRO ONE INC
77144 London Rd Rr 5, Clinton, ON, N0M 1L0
(519) 525-2811
Emp Here 30
SIC 4911 Electric services

D-U-N-S 24-539-3483   (BR)
MURPHY, J & T LIMITED
MURPHY'S BUS LINE
64 Huron St, Clinton, ON, N0M 1L0

---

(519) 482-3493
Emp Here 50
SIC 4151 School buses

Cloyne, ON K0H
Addington County

D-U-N-S 20-022-2094   (BR)
LIMESTONE DISTRICT SCHOOL BOARD
NORTH ADDINGTON EDUCATION CENTRE
14196 Hwy 41, Cloyne, ON, K0H 1K0
(613) 336-8991
Emp Here 45
SIC 8211 Elementary and secondary schools

Cobalt, ON P0J
Timiskaming County

D-U-N-S 20-591-8639   (BR)
NORTHEASTERN CATHOLIC DISTRICT SCHOOL BOARD
ST PATRICK SCHOOL
116 Lang St, Cobalt, ON, P0J 1C0
(705) 679-5575
Emp Here 20
SIC 8211 Elementary and secondary schools

Cobden, ON K0J
Renfrew County

D-U-N-S 20-892-2989   (SL)
CARESSANT CARE NURSING HOME COBDEN
12 Wren Dr, Cobden, ON, K0J 1K0
(613) 646-2109
Emp Here 75   *Sales* 3,429,153
SIC 8051 Skilled nursing care facilities

D-U-N-S 25-238-6099   (BR)
RENFREW COUNTY DISTRICT SCHOOL BOARD
COBDEN DISTRICT ELEMENTARY SCHOOL
16 Cowley St, Cobden, ON, K0J 1K0
(613) 646-2271
Emp Here 30
SIC 8211 Elementary and secondary schools

Coboconk, ON K0M

D-U-N-S 20-025-3388   (BR)
TRILLIUM LAKELANDS DISTRICT SCHOOL BOARD
RIDGEWOOD PUBLIC SCHOOL
6763 35 Hwy, Coboconk, ON, K0M 1K0
(705) 454-3351
Emp Here 35
SIC 8211 Elementary and secondary schools

Cobourg, ON K9A

D-U-N-S 25-296-8128   (BR)
BANK OF NOVA SCOTIA, THE
SCOTIABANK
68 King St W, Cobourg, ON, K9A 2M3
(905) 372-3361
Emp Here 32
SIC 6021 National commercial banks

D-U-N-S 20-344-8183   (BR)
CIBC WORLD MARKETS INC
CIBC WOOD GUNDY
72 King St W Suite 302, Cobourg, ON, K9A

2M3
(905) 372-5330
Emp Here 20
SIC 6211 Security brokers and dealers

D-U-N-S 24-952-6724   (SL)
CANADA PALLET CORP
CPS WOOD PRODUCTS
755 Division St, Cobourg, ON, K9A 3T1
(905) 373-0761
Emp Here 125   *Sales* 12,184,437
SIC 2448 Wood pallets and skids
Pr Pr Thomas Haar
     Daniel Dunkley
     Shawn Hicks

D-U-N-S 25-303-3716   (BR)
CANADIAN IMPERIAL BANK OF COMMERCE
CIBC
51 King St W, Cobourg, ON, K9A 2M1
(905) 372-4381
Emp Here 20
SIC 6021 National commercial banks

D-U-N-S 24-342-2123   (BR)
CARA OPERATIONS QUEBEC LTD
SWISS CHALET
(*Suby of* Cara Holdings Limited)
70 Strathy Rd, Cobourg, ON, K9A 5X4
(905) 377-0533
Emp Here 40
SIC 5812 Eating places

D-U-N-S 25-298-5874   (BR)
CASCADES CANADA ULC
CASCADES BOX BOARD COBOURG
Gd Lcd Main, Cobourg, ON, K9A 4K1
(905) 372-5199
Emp Here 70
SIC 2631 Paperboard mills

D-U-N-S 25-929-3694   (BR)
CHRISTIAN HORIZONS
(*Suby of* Christian Horizons)
5 Maplewood Blvd, Cobourg, ON, K9A 4J4
(905) 372-2603
Emp Here 20
SIC 8361 Residential care

D-U-N-S 24-017-6474   (BR)
CHRISTIAN HORIZONS
(*Suby of* Christian Horizons)
700 Burnham St, Cobourg, ON, K9A 4X4
(905) 377-1701
Emp Here 20
SIC 8361 Residential care

D-U-N-S 24-421-5260   (BR)
CORPORATION OF THE COUNTY OF NORTHUMBERLAND
GOLDEN PLOUGH LODGE
983 Burnham St Suite 1321, Cobourg, ON, K9A 5J6
(905) 372-8759
Emp Here 175
SIC 8361 Residential care

D-U-N-S 20-289-6374   (BR)
EXTENDICARE INC
EXTENDICARE COBOURG
130 New Densmore Rd, Cobourg, ON, K9A 5W2
(905) 372-0377
Emp Here 100
SIC 8051 Skilled nursing care facilities

D-U-N-S 24-977-2059   (BR)
FGL SPORTS LTD
SPORT CHEK NORTHUMBERLAND
1111 Elgin St W Unit M7, Cobourg, ON, K9A 5H7
(905) 372-4199
Emp Here 40
SIC 5941 Sporting goods and bicycle shops

D-U-N-S 24-361-7219   (BR)
HOME DEPOT OF CANADA INC

HOME DEPOT
(*Suby of* The Home Depot Inc)
1050 Depalma Dr, Cobourg, ON, K9A 0A8
(905) 377-7600
Emp Here 100
SIC 5251 Hardware stores

D-U-N-S 24-379-0065   (BR)
ITW CANADA INVESTMENTS LIMITED PARTNERSHIP
STRAPEX CANADA
(*Suby of* Illinois Tool Works Inc.)
5 Northam Industrial Pk, Cobourg, ON, K9A 4L3
(905) 372-6886
Emp Here 23
SIC 3081 Unsupported plastics film and sheet

D-U-N-S 20-914-6112   (BR)
KAPSCH TRAFFICCOM IVHS CORP
Gd, Cobourg, ON, K9A 4K1
(905) 372-7225
Emp Here 90
SIC 3663 Radio and t.v. communications equipment

D-U-N-S 24-676-3192   (BR)
KAWARTHA PINE RIDGE DISTRICT SCHOOL BOARD
TERRY FOX PUBLIC SCHOOL
1065 Riddell Ave, Cobourg, ON, K9A 5N4
(905) 372-8800
Emp Here 25
SIC 8211 Elementary and secondary schools

D-U-N-S 24-676-5015   (BR)
KAWARTHA PINE RIDGE DISTRICT SCHOOL BOARD
CAMBORNE PUBLIC SCHOOL
3546 Kennedy Rd, Cobourg, ON, K9A 4J7
(905) 342-2874
Emp Here 25
SIC 8211 Elementary and secondary schools

D-U-N-S 20-711-5770   (BR)
KAWARTHA PINE RIDGE DISTRICT SCHOOL BOARD
GRANT SINE PUBLIC SCHOOL
780 D'Arcy St, Cobourg, ON, K9A 4B3
(905) 372-9611
Emp Here 20
SIC 8211 Elementary and secondary schools

D-U-N-S 25-238-0282   (BR)
KAWARTHA PINE RIDGE DISTRICT SCHOOL BOARD
COBOURG DISTRICT COLLEGIATE INSTITUTE EAST
335 King St E, Cobourg, ON, K9A 1M2
(905) 372-2271
Emp Here 110
SIC 8211 Elementary and secondary schools

D-U-N-S 25-238-0290   (BR)
KAWARTHA PINE RIDGE DISTRICT SCHOOL BOARD
COBOURG WEST DISTRICT HIGH SCHOOL
135 King St W, Cobourg, ON, K9A 2M7
(905) 372-2191
Emp Here 50
SIC 8211 Elementary and secondary schools

D-U-N-S 20-654-0499   (BR)
KAWARTHA PINE RIDGE DISTRICT SCHOOL BOARD
BROOKSIDE SECONDARY SCHOOL
390 King St W, Cobourg, ON, K9A 2N7
(905) 372-5105
Emp Here 35
SIC 8211 Elementary and secondary schools

D-U-N-S 20-648-2783   (BR)
KAWARTHA PINE RIDGE DISTRICT SCHOOL BOARD
C R GUMMOW SCHOOL
311 Cottesmore Ave, Cobourg, ON, K9A 4E3
(905) 372-9752
Emp Here 45

SIC 8211 Elementary and secondary schools

D-U-N-S 25-507-6879   (SL)
KWENDILL HOLDINGS LIMITED
569 D'Arcy St, Cobourg, ON, K9A 4B1
(905) 373-4100
Emp Here 42   *Sales* 6,330,240
SIC 3499 Fabricated Metal products, nec
Pr Pr William Lee
VP VP Jack Russell
 Joe Mclinden

D-U-N-S 25-311-8509   (SL)
LAKEFRONT UTILITY SERVICES INC
207 Division St, Cobourg, ON, K9A 3P6
(905) 372-2193
Emp Here 28   *Sales* 1,240,332
SIC 8721 Accounting, auditing, and book-keeping

D-U-N-S 25-488-4836   (BR)
METROLAND MEDIA GROUP LTD
NORTHUMBERLAND NEWS
884 Division St Unit 212, Cobourg, ON, K9A 5V6
(905) 373-7355
Emp Here 20
SIC 2711 Newspapers

D-U-N-S 25-638-9537   (BR)
OMNI HEALTH CARE LTD
STREAMWAY VILLA
19 James St W, Cobourg, ON, K9A 2J8
(905) 372-0163
Emp Here 50
SIC 8051 Skilled nursing care facilities

D-U-N-S 20-560-0260   (SL)
PXL CROSS LINKED FOAM CORPORA-TION
840 Division St, Cobourg, ON, K9A 5V2
(905) 373-0000
Emp Here 35   *Sales* 3,720,996
SIC 3081 Unsupported plastics film and sheet

D-U-N-S 20-094-5827   (BR)
PETERBOROUGH VICTORIA NORTHUM-BERLAND AND CLARINGTON CATHOLIC DISTRICT SCHOOL BOARD
NOTREDAME CATHOLIC ELEMENTARY SCHOOL
760 Burnham St, Cobourg, ON, K9A 2X6
(905) 377-9967
Emp Here 23
SIC 8211 Elementary and secondary schools

D-U-N-S 25-137-3684   (BR)
PETERBOROUGH VICTORIA NORTHUM-BERLAND AND CLARINGTON CATHOLIC DISTRICT SCHOOL BOARD
ST MICHAELS SCHOOL IN COBOURG
(*Suby of* Peterborough Victoria Northumber-land and Clarington Catholic District School Board)
23 University Ave W, Cobourg, ON, K9A 2G6
(905) 372-4391
Emp Here 20
SIC 8211 Elementary and secondary schools

D-U-N-S 25-137-3585   (BR)
PETERBOROUGH VICTORIA NORTHUM-BERLAND AND CLARINGTON CATHOLIC DISTRICT SCHOOL BOARD
ST. MARY'S SECONDARY SCHOOL
(*Suby of* Peterborough Victoria Northumber-land and Clarington Catholic District School Board)
1050 Birchwood Trail, Cobourg, ON, K9A 5S9
(905) 372-4339
Emp Here 90
SIC 8211 Elementary and secondary schools

D-U-N-S 20-711-6125   (BR)
PETERBOROUGH VICTORIA NORTHUM-BERLAND AND CLARINGTON CATHOLIC DISTRICT SCHOOL BOARD
SAINT JOSEPH ELEMENTARY SCHOOL
919 D'Arcy St, Cobourg, ON, K9A 4B4

(905) 372-6879
Emp Here 30
SIC 8211 Elementary and secondary schools

D-U-N-S 25-638-7416   (BR)
REDBERRY FRANCHISING CORP
BURGER KING
985 Elgin St W, Cobourg, ON, K9A 5J3

Emp Here 30
SIC 5812 Eating places

D-U-N-S 25-308-4651   (BR)
ROYAL BANK OF CANADA
RBC
(*Suby of* Royal Bank Of Canada)
66 King St W, Cobourg, ON, K9A 2L9
(905) 372-2101
Emp Here 20
SIC 6021 National commercial banks

D-U-N-S 24-379-7763   (SL)
SABIC INNOVATIVE PLASTICS CANADA INC
44 Normar Rd, Cobourg, ON, K9A 4L7
(905) 372-6801
Emp Here 190   *Sales* 45,600,438
SIC 5162 Plastics materials and basic shapes
 Paul Van Laren
Dir Niyazi Demir

D-U-N-S 25-311-1322   (BR)
SEARS CANADA INC
SEARS 1317
1111 Elgin St W, Cobourg, ON, K9A 5H7

Emp Here 40
SIC 5311 Department stores

D-U-N-S 25-319-3544   (BR)
TORONTO-DOMINION BANK, THE
TD BANK
(*Suby of* Toronto-Dominion Bank, The)
1 King St W, Cobourg, ON, K9A 2L8
(905) 372-5471
Emp Here 20
SIC 6021 National commercial banks

D-U-N-S 24-329-8663   (BR)
WAL-MART CANADA CORP
73 Strathy Rd, Cobourg, ON, K9A 5W8
(905) 373-1239
Emp Here 200
SIC 5311 Department stores

D-U-N-S 20-551-1173   (SL)
WEETABIX OF CANADA LIMITED
751 D'Arcy St, Cobourg, ON, K9A 4B1
(905) 372-5441
Emp Here 260   *Sales* 518,020,970
SIC 2043 Cereal breakfast foods
Genl Mgr Jeff Bakker
 David W Burn
Dir A.T. Connell

Cochrane, ON N0H
Cochrane County

D-U-N-S 20-647-0481   (BR)
DISTRICT SCHOOL BOARD ONTARIO NORTH EAST
COCHRANE PUBLIC SCHOOL
453 Chalmers Ave, Cochrane, ON, N0H 2T0
(705) 272-3246
Emp Here 40
SIC 8211 Elementary and secondary schools

Cochrane, ON P0L
Cochrane County

D-U-N-S 20-282-2219   (SL)
1835755 ONTARIO LIMITED

NORTH   ROCK   CONSTRUCTION PROJECTS
227 Hwy 11 S, Cochrane, ON, P0L 1C0
(705) 272-2090
Emp Here 75   *Sales* 8,755,284
SIC 1611 Highway and street construction
 Carl Swanson
Dir David Lanther

D-U-N-S 25-225-1434   (BR)
CONSEIL SCOLAIRE CATHOLIQUE DE DISTRICT DES GRANDES RIVIERES, LE
ECOLE SECONDAIRE JEUNESSE NORD
399 Eight St, Cochrane, ON, P0L 1C0
(705) 272-3080
Emp Here 21
SIC 8211 Elementary and secondary schools

D-U-N-S 20-710-4535   (BR)
DISTRICT SCHOOL BOARD ONTARIO NORTH EAST
COCHRANE HIGH SCHOOL
Gd, Cochrane, ON, P0L 1C0
(705) 272-4372
Emp Here 50
SIC 8211 Elementary and secondary schools

D-U-N-S 25-228-0839   (BR)
DISTRICT SCHOOL BOARD ONTARIO NORTH EAST
ECOLE SECONDAIRE COCHRANE HIGH SCHOOL
453b Chalmers Ave, Cochrane, ON, P0L 1C0
(705) 272-4372
Emp Here 45
SIC 8211 Elementary and secondary schools

D-U-N-S 20-041-7939   (HQ)
FORTIER BEVERAGES LIMITED
AQUA-NOR DIV
158 Second Ave, Cochrane, ON, P0L 1C0
(705) 272-4305
Emp Here 38   *Emp Total* 50
Sales 7,150,149
SIC 5149 Groceries and related products, nec
Pr Pr Raymond Fortier
VP VP Sylvie Gravelle
 Germaine Fortier

D-U-N-S 24-393-2345   (SL)
KEVIN P. SMITH HOLDINGS LTD
CANADIAN TIRE
Po Box 1058, Cochrane, ON, P0L 1C0
(705) 272-4341
Emp Here 50   *Sales* 4,085,799
SIC 5399 Miscellaneous general merchandise

D-U-N-S 20-792-1607   (BR)
LOBLAW COMPANIES LIMITED
CHARTRAND VALUE MART
31 Hwy 11 W Unit 1, Cochrane, ON, P0L 1C0
(705) 272-4238
Emp Here 50
SIC 5411 Grocery stores

D-U-N-S 24-483-9221   (BR)
NORBORD INDUSTRIES INC
ROCKSHIELD ENGINEERED WOOD PROD-UCTS
4 Boisvert Cres, Cochrane, ON, P0L 1C0
(705) 272-4210
Emp Here 250
SIC 2435 Hardwood veneer and plywood

D-U-N-S 25-225-1350   (BR)
NORTHEASTERN CATHOLIC DISTRICT SCHOOL BOARD
AILEEN WRIGHT ENGLISH CATHOLIC SCHOOL
75 6th St, Cochrane, ON, P0L 1C0
(705) 272-4707
Emp Here 20
SIC 8211 Elementary and secondary schools

D-U-N-S 20-707-4225   (BR)
ONTARIO NORTHLAND TRANSPORTA-TION COMMISSION
20 Boisvert Cres, Cochrane, ON, P0L 1C0

(705) 272-4610
Emp Here 50
SIC 4899 Communication services, nec

D-U-N-S 24-075-3236   (BR)
ROYAL CANADIAN LEGION, THE
(*Suby of* Royal Canadian Legion, The)
151 6th Ave, Cochrane, ON, P0L 1C0
(705) 272-3205
Emp Here 48
SIC 8641 Civic and social associations

D-U-N-S 25-407-5831   (BR)
TEMBEC INC
70 17th Ave, Cochrane, ON, P0L 1C0
(705) 272-4321
Emp Here 170
SIC 2421 Sawmills and planing mills, general

Colborne, ON K0K
Norfolk County

D-U-N-S 20-249-8572   (BR)
ANIXTER POWER SOLUTIONS CANADA INC
188 Purdy Rd Rr 2, Colborne, ON, K0K 1S0
(905) 355-2474
Emp Here 45
SIC 1731 Electrical work

D-U-N-S 20-036-4479   (HQ)
ANIXTER POWER SOLUTIONS CANADA INC
188 Purdy Rd, Colborne, ON, K0K 1S0
(905) 355-2474
Emp Here 100   *Emp Total* 8,900
Sales 184,251,588
SIC 5085 Industrial supplies
Pr Pr Vasken Altounian

D-U-N-S 24-315-3103   (BR)
CANADA COLORS AND CHEMICALS LIM-ITED
CANADA COLORS AND CHEMICALS LIM-ITED
263 Purdy Rd, Colborne, ON, K0K 1S0
(905) 355-3226
Emp Here 65
SIC 2821 Plastics materials and resins

D-U-N-S 25-237-9698   (BR)
KAWARTHA PINE RIDGE DISTRICT SCHOOL BOARD
COLBORNE PUBLIC SCHOOL
8 Alfred St, Colborne, ON, K0K 1S0
(905) 355-2532
Emp Here 23
SIC 8211 Elementary and secondary schools

Coldwater, ON L0K
Simcoe County

D-U-N-S 25-297-6527   (BR)
SIMCOE COUNTY DISTRICT SCHOOL BOARD, THE
COLDWATER PUBLIC SCHOOL
(*Suby of* Simcoe County District School Board, The)
33 Gray St, Coldwater, ON, L0K 1E0
(705) 686-7780
Emp Here 30
SIC 8211 Elementary and secondary schools

Collingwood, ON L9Y
Simcoe County

D-U-N-S 20-558-3818   (HQ)
AINLEY & ASSOCIATES LIMITED
280 Pretty River Pky N, Collingwood, ON, L9Y

4J5
(705) 445-3451
Emp Here 55   *Emp Total* 2
Sales 8,536,402
SIC 8711 Engineering services
Pr Pr Joseph Mullan
Ch Bd Simon Ainley
VP VP Mike Ainley
VP VP Mike Neumann
VP VP Tammy Kalimootoo
Dir P. William Ainley

D-U-N-S 20-820-7485   (BR)
ARNOTT CONSTRUCTION LIMITED
46 Stewart Rd, Collingwood, ON, L9Y 4K1
(705) 445-5459
Emp Here 50
SIC 4959 Sanitary services, nec

D-U-N-S 24-975-4011   (BR)
BDO CANADA LLP
186 Hurontario St Suite 202, Collingwood, ON, L9Y 4T4
(705) 445-4421
Emp Here 23
SIC 8721 Accounting, auditing, and book-keeping

D-U-N-S 25-296-7880   (BR)
BANK OF NOVA SCOTIA, THE
SCOTIABANK
247 Hurontario St, Collingwood, ON, L9Y 2M4
(705) 445-0580
Emp Here 30
SIC 6021 National commercial banks

D-U-N-S 20-079-3672   (BR)
BANQUE TORONTO-DOMINION, LA
TORONTO-DOMINION BANK, THE
(*Suby of* Toronto-Dominion Bank, The)
104 Hurontario St, Collingwood, ON, L9Y 2L8
(705) 445-4881
Emp Here 37
SIC 6021 National commercial banks

D-U-N-S 24-437-5718   (BR)
BANQUE TORONTO-DOMINION, LA
TORONTO-DOMINION BANK, THE
(*Suby of* Toronto-Dominion Bank, The)
104 Hurontario St, Collingwood, ON, L9Y 2L9
(705) 445-8243
Emp Here 26
SIC 6021 National commercial banks

D-U-N-S 20-934-6725   (SL)
BAY HAVEN NURSING HOME INC
BAY HAVEN SENIOR CARE COMMUNITY
499 Hume St Suite 18, Collingwood, ON, L9Y 4H8
(705) 445-6501
Emp Here 85   *Sales* 3,866,917
SIC 8051 Skilled nursing care facilities

D-U-N-S 25-353-3996   (SL)
CANADIAN BASE OPERATORS INC
101 Pretty River Pky S Suite 6, Collingwood, ON, L9Y 4M8
(705) 446-9019
Emp Here 50   *Sales* 3,648,035
SIC 7538 General automotive repair shops

D-U-N-S 25-303-3831   (BR)
CANADIAN IMPERIAL BANK OF COMMERCE
CIBC
86 Hurontario St, Collingwood, ON, L9Y 2L8
(705) 445-2780
Emp Here 20
SIC 6021 National commercial banks

D-U-N-S 20-303-2859   (BR)
CARA OPERATIONS LIMITED
KELSEY'S
(*Suby of* Cara Holdings Limited)
371 First St, Collingwood, ON, L9Y 1B3
(705) 444-5711
Emp Here 45
SIC 5812 Eating places

D-U-N-S 24-776-7085   (BR)
CHARTWELL MASTER CARE LP
CHARTWELL GEORGIAN TRADITION
57 Trott Blvd, Collingwood, ON, L9Y 0A3
(705) 444-6431
Emp Here 45
SIC 8322 Individual and family services

D-U-N-S 24-418-2916   (BR)
CINEPLEX ODEON CORPORATION
GALAXY CINEMAS COLLINGWOOD
6 Mountain Rd, Collingwood, ON, L9Y 4S8
(705) 443-4271
Emp Here 20
SIC 7832 Motion picture theaters, except drive-in

D-U-N-S 24-182-8078   (BR)
COMPAGNIE DE TELEPHONE BELL DU CANADA OU BELL CANADA, LA
1 Mountain Rd, Collingwood, ON, L9Y 4C4
(705) 722-2412
Emp Here 20
SIC 4812 Radiotelephone communication

D-U-N-S 24-829-9612   (HQ)
E3 (EDUCATE, ENABLE, EMPOWER) COMMUNITY SERVICES INC
E3 COMMUNITY SERVICES
(*Suby of* E3 (Educate, Enable, Empower) Community Services Inc)
100 Pretty River Pky N, Collingwood, ON, L9Y 4X2
(705) 445-6351
Emp Here 40   *Emp Total* 250
Sales 7,514,952
SIC 8351 Child day care services
Ex Dir Gordon Anton
  Don Mcnally
  Mary Jane Santori
  Judith Traynor
  Peter Roberts
Pr Pr Matthew Wells
  Brian Saunderson
  Derek Munch
  Farel Anderson
  Karen Burland

D-U-N-S 24-193-5738   (SL)
GEORGIAN MANOR RESORT AND COUNTRY CLUB INC
10 Vacation Inn Dr, Collingwood, ON, L9Y 5G4
(705) 445-9422
Emp Here 80   *Sales* 3,210,271
SIC 7997 Membership sports and recreation clubs

D-U-N-S 24-253-2161   (BR)
GOVERNMENT OF ONTARIO
GEORGIAN BAY FAMILY HEALTH TEAM
186 Erie St Suite 100, Collingwood, ON, L9Y 4T3
(705) 444-5885
Emp Here 42
SIC 8011 Offices and clinics of medical doctors

D-U-N-S 24-315-7349   (BR)
HOME DEPOT OF CANADA INC
(*Suby of* The Home Depot Inc)
10 High St, Collingwood, ON, L9Y 3J6
(705) 446-3100
Emp Here 50
SIC 5251 Hardware stores

D-U-N-S 20-335-1598   (SL)
JSI STORE FIXTURES CANADA INC
395 Raglan St, Collingwood, ON, L9Y 3Z1
(705) 445-6190
Emp Here 50   *Sales* 4,331,255
SIC 1751 Carpentry work

D-U-N-S 25-370-0785   (BR)
KGHM INTERNATIONAL LTD
QUADRA MINING
7 Cranberry Shores, Collingwood, ON, L9Y 5C3

(705) 444-1316
Emp Here 480
SIC 1081 Metal mining services

D-U-N-S 25-318-6993   (BR)
LIQUOR CONTROL BOARD OF ONTARIO, THE
L.C.B.O. #31
1 First St Unit 1, Collingwood, ON, L9Y 1A1
(705) 445-3341
Emp Here 25
SIC 5921 Liquor stores

D-U-N-S 25-902-0188   (BR)
LOBLAWS SUPERMARKETS LIMITED
LOBLAWS
12 Hurontario St, Collingwood, ON, L9Y 2L6
(705) 445-0461
Emp Here 170
SIC 5411 Grocery stores

D-U-N-S 24-333-1654   (BR)
METRO ONTARIO INC
METRO
640 First St, Collingwood, ON, L9Y 4Y7
(705) 444-5252
Emp Here 200
SIC 5411 Grocery stores

D-U-N-S 20-924-0535   (SL)
MONTANA'S RESTAURANT
79 Balsam St, Collingwood, ON, L9Y 3Y6
(705) 444-0278
Emp Here 50   *Sales* 1,532,175
SIC 5812 Eating places

D-U-N-S 25-903-2258   (BR)
PARKVIEW TRANSIT INC
PARKVIEW TRANSIT
(*Suby of* Parkview Transit Inc)
37 Campbell St, Collingwood, ON, L9Y 2K9
(705) 526-2847
Emp Here 35
SIC 4151 School buses

D-U-N-S 20-402-8658   (HQ)
PILKINGTON GLASS OF CANADA LTD
1000 Hwy, Collingwood, ON, L9Y 4V8
(705) 445-4780
Emp Here 240   *Emp Total* 27,371
Sales 27,360,263
SIC 3231 Products of purchased glass
Mgr Skip Vermilya

D-U-N-S 20-118-2776   (BR)
R.J. BURNSIDE & ASSOCIATES LIMITED
3 Ronell Cres Suite 2, Collingwood, ON, L9Y 4J6
(705) 446-0515
Emp Here 67
SIC 8711 Engineering services

D-U-N-S 24-022-5602   (BR)
SIMCOE COUNTY ASSOCIATION FOR THE PHYSICALLY DISABLED
12 Erie St, Collingwood, ON, L9Y 1P4
(705) 444-7680
Emp Here 25
SIC 8361 Residential care

D-U-N-S 20-807-3051   (BR)
SIMCOE COUNTY DISTRICT SCHOOL BOARD, THE
NOTTAWA ELEMENTARY SCHOOL
(*Suby of* Simcoe County District School Board, The)
81 Batteaux, Collingwood, ON, L9Y 3Z1
(705) 445-1827
Emp Here 25
SIC 8211 Elementary and secondary schools

D-U-N-S 25-297-6691   (BR)
SIMCOE COUNTY DISTRICT SCHOOL BOARD, THE
MOUNTAIN VIEW ELEMENTARY SCHOOL
(*Suby of* Simcoe County District School Board, The)
300 Spruce St, Collingwood, ON, L9Y 3H1

(705) 445-1501
Emp Here 35
SIC 8211 Elementary and secondary schools

D-U-N-S 25-297-6568   (BR)
SIMCOE COUNTY DISTRICT SCHOOL BOARD, THE
CAMERON STREET PUBLIC SCHOOL
(*Suby of* Simcoe County District School Board, The)
575 Cameron St, Collingwood, ON, L9Y 2J4
(705) 445-2902
Emp Here 40
SIC 8211 Elementary and secondary schools

D-U-N-S 25-292-5029   (BR)
SIMCOE COUNTY DISTRICT SCHOOL BOARD, THE
COLLINGWOOD COLLEGIATE INSTITUTE
(*Suby of* Simcoe County District School Board, The)
6 Cameron St, Collingwood, ON, L9Y 2J2
(705) 445-3161
Emp Here 100
SIC 8211 Elementary and secondary schools

D-U-N-S 25-292-4865   (BR)
SIMCOE COUNTY DISTRICT SCHOOL BOARD, THE
CONNAUGHT PUBLIC SCHOOL
(*Suby of* Simcoe County District School Board, The)
300 Peel St, Collingwood, ON, L9Y 3W2
(705) 445-1241
Emp Here 40
SIC 8211 Elementary and secondary schools

D-U-N-S 25-293-5093   (BR)
SIMCOE MUSKOKA CATHOLIC DISTRICT SCHOOL BOARD
JEAN VANIER CATHOLIC HIGH SCHOOL
(*Suby of* Simcoe Muskoka Catholic District School Board)
160 Collins St, Collingwood, ON, L9Y 4R1
(705) 445-2043
Emp Here 60
SIC 8211 Elementary and secondary schools

D-U-N-S 25-293-5069   (BR)
SIMCOE MUSKOKA CATHOLIC DISTRICT SCHOOL BOARD
ST MARY'S SCHOOL
(*Suby of* Simcoe Muskoka Catholic District School Board)
18 Saunders St, Collingwood, ON, L9Y 0G2
(705) 445-6132
Emp Here 40
SIC 8211 Elementary and secondary schools

D-U-N-S 20-244-8879   (BR)
SKIIS LTD
SKIIS & BIIKES
445 First St, Collingwood, ON, L9Y 1B7
(705) 445-9777
Emp Here 20
SIC 5941 Sporting goods and bicycle shops

D-U-N-S 24-486-0516   (BR)
SOBEYS CAPITAL INCORPORATED
FRESHCO
55 Mountain Rd, Collingwood, ON, L9Y 4M2
(705) 445-7080
Emp Here 21
SIC 5411 Grocery stores

D-U-N-S 24-599-1562   (BR)
STAPLES CANADA INC
(*Suby of* Staples, Inc.)
15 Balsam St Unit 1, Collingwood, ON, L9Y 5H6
(705) 445-0505
Emp Here 20
SIC 5943 Stationery stores

D-U-N-S 24-121-3933   (SL)
TORONTO SKI CLUB INC
796456 Gray Rd Suite 19, Collingwood, ON, L9Y 3Z4

(705) 445-1890
Emp Here 50   *Sales* 2,188,821
SIC 7011 Hotels and motels

D-U-N-S 20-026-8220   (BR)
UNITED STEELWORKERS OF AMERICA
LOCAL 252
(*Suby of* United Steelworkers)
1000 26 Hwy, Collingwood, ON, L9Y 4V8

Emp Here 300
SIC 8631 Labor organizations

D-U-N-S 25-351-7973   (SL)
VOA CANADA INC
(*Suby of* Autoliv, Inc.)
190 Macdonald Rd, Collingwood, ON, L9Y 4N6
(705) 444-2561
Emp Here 120   *Sales* 30,223,320
SIC 2241 Narrow fabric mills
 David Helm
Dir Michael S Anderson
Dir Steve Fredin

D-U-N-S 24-319-5091   (BR)
WAL-MART CANADA CORP
WALMART
10 Cambridge, Collingwood, ON, L9Y 0A1
(705) 445-0139
Emp Here 170
SIC 5311 Department stores

Comber, ON N0P
Essex County

D-U-N-S 25-249-2079   (BR)
GREATER ESSEX COUNTY DISTRICT SCHOOL BOARD
CENTENNIAL CENTRAL PUBLIC SCHOOL
6420 Taylor Ave, Comber, ON, N0P 1J0
(519) 687-2022
Emp Here 25
SIC 8211 Elementary and secondary schools

Concord, ON L4K
York County

D-U-N-S 24-022-7079   (BR)
1353042 ONTARIO LIMITED
NORTHERN CALL SOLUTIONS
177 Creditstone Rd, Concord, ON, L4K 1N5

Emp Here 50
SIC 1731 Electrical work

D-U-N-S 25-099-2393   (SL)
1360548 ONTARIO LIMITED
PRIME PASTRIES
370 North Rivermede Rd Unit 1, Concord, ON, L4K 3N2
(905) 669-5883
Emp Here 50   *Sales* 1,678,096
SIC 5461 Retail bakeries

D-U-N-S 20-955-8290   (SL)
1406284 ONTARIO INC
HILTON GARDEN INN HOTEL AND CONFERENCE CENTRE
3201 Highway 7, Concord, ON, L4K 5Z7
(905) 660-4700
Emp Here 75   *Sales* 3,283,232
SIC 7011 Hotels and motels

D-U-N-S 20-269-1291   (SL)
2400318 ONTARIO INC
PRODIGY GRAPHICS
731 Millway Ave, Concord, ON, L4K 3S8
(905) 677-7776
Emp Here 50   *Sales* 3,793,956
SIC 2752 Commercial printing, lithographic

D-U-N-S 25-367-6506   (SL)

6268595 CANADA INC
DEAD SEA SECRETS
150 Connie Cres Suite 3, Concord, ON, L4K 1L9
(905) 660-3289
Emp Here 110   *Sales* 18,869,700
SIC 5122 Drugs, proprietaries, and sundries
Pr Pr Tomer Rotem

D-U-N-S 25-246-5794   (SL)
679137 ONTARIO LIMITED
CORSTEEL HYDRAULICS
200 Spinnaker Way, Concord, ON, L4K 5E5
(905) 738-3682
Emp Here 40   *Sales* 5,197,506
SIC 3542 Machine tools, Metal forming type

D-U-N-S 20-982-5736   (SL)
838116 ONTARIO INC
DONUT TIME
35 Adesso Dr Suite 18, Concord, ON, L4K 3C7
(905) 760-0850
Emp Here 70   *Sales* 4,331,255
SIC 2051 Bread, cake, and related products

D-U-N-S 20-924-2759   (SL)
A & D PRECISION LIMITED
289 Bradwick Dr, Concord, ON, L4K 1K5
(905) 669-5888
Emp Here 50   *Sales* 3,064,349
SIC 7699 Repair services, nec

D-U-N-S 24-335-8897   (BR)
ABC GROUP INC
SALGA ASSOCIATES
(*Suby of* Cerberus Capital Management, L.P.)
161 Snidercroft Rd Unit A, Concord, ON, L4K 2J8
(905) 669-0999
Emp Here 250
SIC 3089 Plastics products, nec

D-U-N-S 24-693-9185   (HQ)
ACCUBID SYSTEMS LTD
(*Suby of* Accubid Systems Ltd)
7725 Jane St Suite 200, Concord, ON, L4K 1X4
(905) 761-8800
Emp Here 65   *Emp Total* 80
Sales 12,662,640
SIC 7371 Custom computer programming services
Pr Pr Giovanni Marcelli
Dir Fin Justin Emmanuel
 Almiro Ricci
 Mark Mandarelli

D-U-N-S 20-078-1397   (HQ)
ALEXANDER DENNIS (CANADA) INC
130 Pippin Rd Unit B, Concord, ON, L4K 4X9
(905) 660-8400
Emp Here 40   *Emp Total* 2,400
Sales 12,040,889
SIC 3711 Motor vehicles and car bodies
Pr Pr Colin Robertson
 Frank Hunnisett
 Stephen Walsh
 Michael Gavin Stewart

D-U-N-S 25-338-4069   (SL)
ALLIANCE ENVELOPE LIMITED
ROYAL ENVELOPE
111 Jacob Keffer Pky Suite 1, Concord, ON, L4K 4V1
(905) 417-4002
Emp Here 27   *Sales* 3,429,153
SIC 2677 Envelopes

D-U-N-S 25-321-4720   (BR)
ALLIED SYSTEMS (CANADA) COMPANY
8950 Keele St, Concord, ON, L4K 2N2
(905) 669-2930
Emp Here 70
SIC 4213 Trucking, except local

D-U-N-S 25-793-6260   (SL)
ANAX INC

---

173 Adesso Dr Unit 1, Concord, ON, L4K 3C3
(416) 480-2247
Emp Here 50   *Sales* 4,961,328
SIC 1761 Roofing, siding, and sheetMetal work

D-U-N-S 24-779-1320   (SL)
ARCELORMITTAL TAILORED BLANKS AMERICAS LIMITED
ARCELORMITTAL TAILORED BLANKS MERELBEKE
55 Confederation Pky, Concord, ON, L4K 4Y7
(905) 761-1525
Emp Here 40   *Sales* 4,377,642
SIC 3542 Machine tools, Metal forming type

D-U-N-S 24-019-4709   (BR)
ARITZIA LP
1 Bass Pro Mills Dr, Concord, ON, L4K 5W4
(905) 660-8049
Emp Here 25
SIC 5621 Women's clothing stores

D-U-N-S 24-860-8101   (HQ)
ASSA ABLOY OF CANADA LTD
160 Four Valley Dr, Concord, ON, L4K 4T9
(905) 738-2466
Emp Here 35   *Emp Total* 200
Sales 31,185,036
SIC 5072 Hardware
Pr Pr Greg Erwin
 Andre Gougeon

D-U-N-S 24-952-3853   (SL)
AUSTEN FURNITURE (1992) LTD
241 Snidercroft Rd, Concord, ON, L4K 2J8
(905) 761-0911
Emp Here 58   *Sales* 4,231,721
SIC 2514 Metal household furniture

D-U-N-S 20-572-3583   (BR)
BASF CANADA INC
90 Snidercroft Rd, Concord, ON, L4K 2K1
(905) 669-4628
Emp Here 20
SIC 2821 Plastics materials and resins

D-U-N-S 20-159-4959   (HQ)
BAILEY METAL PRODUCTS LIMITED
(*Suby of* Bailey-Hunt Limited)
1 Caldari Rd, Concord, ON, L4K 3Z9
(905) 738-9267
Emp Here 175   *Emp Total* 380
Sales 111,546,799
SIC 3312 Blast furnaces and steel mills
 David Hunt
Pr Pr Angelo Sarracini
VP Stuart Hunt
 Susan Schalburg
Dir Fin Paul Chan

D-U-N-S 24-150-4435   (SL)
BASAD LOGISTICS INC
21 Staffern Dr, Concord, ON, L4K 2X2
(905) 532-0422
Emp Here 20   *Sales* 2,252,253
SIC 4225 General warehousing and storage

D-U-N-S 20-560-5863   (HQ)
BASS PRO SHOPS CANADA INC
1 Bass Pro Mills Dr, Concord, ON, L4K 5W4
(905) 761-4000
Emp Here 25   *Emp Total* 12,000
Sales 29,038,359
SIC 5941 Sporting goods and bicycle shops
Genl Mgr Dave Jessop

D-U-N-S 20-192-7774   (BR)
BEACON ROOFING SUPPLY CANADA COMPANY
MATERIAUX DE TOITURES BEACON DU CANADA
(*Suby of* Beacon Roofing Supply, Inc.)
8400 Keele St Unit 1, Concord, ON, L4K 2A6
(905) 761-1762
Emp Here 25
SIC 5033 Roofing, siding, and insulation

D-U-N-S 24-877-2998   (SL)
BOLTKRETE SERVICES (2004) INC
381 Spinnaker Way, Concord, ON, L4K 4N4
(905) 738-9859
Emp Here 20   *Sales* 2,334,742
SIC 1611 Highway and street construction

D-U-N-S 25-184-4952   (BR)
BONDFIELD CONSTRUCTION COMPANY LIMITED
407 Basaltic Rd, Concord, ON, L4K 4W8
(416) 667-8422
Emp Here 49
SIC 1542 Nonresidential construction, nec

D-U-N-S 24-892-8723   (SL)
BRADLEY AIR-CONDITIONING LIMITED
150 Connie Cres Suite 14, Concord, ON, L4K 1L9
(905) 660-5400
Emp Here 50   *Sales* 6,028,800
SIC 1711 Plumbing, heating, air-conditioning
Off Mgr Teresa Connors

D-U-N-S 24-986-8092   (SL)
BUSHNELL CORPORATION OF CANADA
BUSHNELL PERFORMANCE OPTICS
(*Suby of* Vista Outdoor Inc.)
B-140 Great Gulf Dr, Concord, ON, L4K 5W1
(905) 771-2980
Emp Here 20   *Sales* 1,167,371
SIC 3827 Optical instruments and lenses

D-U-N-S 24-579-5091   (HQ)
BUSY BEE MACHINE TOOLS LTD
(*Suby of* Busy Bee Machine Tools Ltd)
130 Great Gulf Dr, Concord, ON, L4K 5W1
(800) 461-2879
Emp Here 35   *Emp Total* 50
Sales 4,815,406
SIC 5251 Hardware stores

D-U-N-S 24-336-4361   (HQ)
C.R. LAURENCE OF CANADA LIMITED
65 Tigi Crt, Concord, ON, L4K 5E4
(905) 303-7966
Emp Here 45   *Emp Total* 86,778
Sales 6,931,267
SIC 3211 Flat glass
Pr Gavin Brin
 Don Friese

D-U-N-S 24-334-7577   (BR)
CN WORLDWIDE AMERIQUE DU NORD (CANADA) INC
CN WORLDWIDE NORTH AMERICA (CANADA)
1 Administration Rd, Concord, ON, L4K 1B9
(905) 669-3384
Emp Here 100
SIC 4424 Deep sea domestic transportation of freight

D-U-N-S 20-270-1744   (BR)
CN WORLDWIDE DISTRIBUTION SERVICES (CANADA) INC
CN METAL DISTRIBUTION
619 Creditstone Rd Suite 19, Concord, ON, L4K 4N2
(905) 669-3076
Emp Here 20
SIC 4212 Local trucking, without storage

D-U-N-S 25-371-3473   (BR)
CRH CANADA GROUP INC
DUFFERIN CUSTOM-CONCRETE GROUP
2300 Steeles Ave W Suite 300, Concord, ON, L4K 5X6
(905) 761-7000
Emp Here 70
SIC 1771 Concrete work

D-U-N-S 24-423-7942   (SL)
CAESARSTONE CANADA INC
CAESARSTONE
8899 Jane St, Concord, ON, L4K 2M6
(416) 479-8400
Emp Here 20

SIC 3253 Ceramic wall and floor tile

D-U-N-S 25-192-3702   (BR)
CAMFIL CANADA INC
CAMFIL FARR FILTERS
2700 Steeles Ave W, Concord, ON, L4K 3C8
(905) 660-0688
Emp Here 91
SIC 3569 General industrial machinery, nec

D-U-N-S 24-720-0397   (SL)
CAN AM LOGISTICS INC
VITRAN LOGISTICS
1201 Creditstone Rd, Concord, ON, L4K 0C2
(416) 798-4965
Emp Here 25   *Sales* 2,845,467
SIC 4213 Trucking, except local

D-U-N-S 25-995-2216   (BR)
CANADA BREAD COMPANY, LIMITED
CANADA DOUGH DELIGHT
711 Rivermede Rd, Concord, ON, L4K 2G9
(905) 660-3034
Emp Here 300
SIC 2051 Bread, cake, and related products

D-U-N-S 24-451-0525   (SL)
CANADIAN BRASS & COPPER CO
CBC SPECIALTY METALS
225 Doney Cres Suite 1, Concord, ON, L4K 1P6
(416) 736-0797
Emp Here 35   *Sales* 14,081,415
SIC 5051 Metals service centers and offices
Genl Mgr Randy Coupland

D-U-N-S 24-313-8406   (SL)
CANADIAN RAILINGS LIMITED
CONCORD RAILINGS
596 Oster Lane, Concord, ON, L4K 2C1
(905) 669-9221
Emp Here 50   *Sales* 4,851,006
SIC 2431 Millwork

D-U-N-S 20-845-8760   (SL)
CANBERRA CO
50b Caldari Rd, Concord, ON, L4K 4N8
(905) 660-5373
Emp Here 41   *Sales* 5,370,756
SIC 3829 Measuring and controlling devices, nec

D-U-N-S 25-828-5212   (BR)
CANPAR TRANSPORT L.P.
(*Suby of* Canpar Transport L.P.)
473 Basaltic Rd, Concord, ON, L4K 4W8
(905) 303-7725
Emp Here 60
SIC 7389 Business services, nec

D-U-N-S 20-421-9471   (HQ)
CARA OPERATIONS QUEBEC LTD
(*Suby of* Cara Holdings Limited)
199 Four Valley Dr, Concord, ON, L4K 0B8
(905) 760-2244
Emp Here 240   *Emp Total* 14,038
Sales 109,058,750
SIC 5812 Eating places
VP Fin Michael Forsayeth
Sec Ian C Wilkie
Dir Amir Adjani
Dir David Barlow
Dir James B Williams
Dir Fred Cress
Dir Steven Tsambalieros

D-U-N-S 24-423-5235   (HQ)
CARDINAL HEALTH CANADA INC
DISMED
(*Suby of* Cardinal Health, Inc.)
1000 Tesma Way, Concord, ON, L4K 5R8
(905) 417-2900
Emp Here 50   *Emp Total* 26,500
Sales 131,926,060
SIC 5047 Medical and hospital equipment
Ch Bd David H Lees
Pr Martha Huston
Sr VP Sr VP Samer Abdul-Samad

Fernando Pica
Sec Rylan O Rawlins

D-U-N-S 20-010-0886   (BR)
CASCADES CANADA ULC
NORAMPAC- VAUGHAN
655 Creditstone Rd Suite 41, Concord, ON, L4K 5P9
(905) 760-3900
Emp Here 250
SIC 2653 Corrugated and solid fiber boxes

D-U-N-S 24-348-2101   (SL)
CEDARDALE REALTY HOLDINGS INC
7077 Keele St Suite 102, Concord, ON, L4K 0B6
(905) 738-0754
Emp Here 20   *Sales* 6,347,581
SIC 6553 Cemetery subdividers and developers
Neil Brown
Pr Gary Silver

D-U-N-S 20-182-0792   (SL)
CENTENNIAL MATERIAL HANDLING LIMITED
300 Bradwick Dr, Concord, ON, L4K 1K8
(416) 661-4609
Emp Here 55   *Sales* 4,231,721
SIC 2542 Partitions and fixtures, except wood

D-U-N-S 24-846-6237   (SL)
CHERISON ENTERPRISES INC
53 Courtland Ave Suite 1, Concord, ON, L4K 3T2
(905) 882-6168
Emp Here 50   *Sales* 5,982,777
SIC 5199 Nondurable goods, nec
Pr Pr Clement Chan
Dir Rita Chan

D-U-N-S 20-791-4479   (BR)
CHILDREN'S PLACE (CANADA) LP, THE
CHILDREN'S PLACE, THE
1 Bass Pro Mills Dr Suite F4, Concord, ON, L4K 5W4
(905) 738-1435
Emp Here 50
SIC 5641 Children's and infants' wear stores

D-U-N-S 20-320-1504   (BR)
CIRCA ENTERPRISES INC
CIRCA METALS DIV.
206 Great Gulf Dr, Concord, ON, L4K 5W1
(905) 669-5511
Emp Here 50
SIC 3499 Fabricated Metal products, nec

D-U-N-S 20-922-2660   (BR)
CLARKE TRANSPORT INC
CLARKE TRANSPORT
751 Bowes Rd Suite 2, Concord, ON, L4K 5C9
(416) 665-5585
Emp Here 250
SIC 4213 Trucking, except local

D-U-N-S 20-128-7666   (BR)
CLASSIC DENTAL LABORATORIES LTD
SPACE MAINTENERS
40 Pippin Rd Unit 11, Concord, ON, L4K 4M6
(416) 410-1330
Emp Here 20
SIC 8072 Dental laboratories

D-U-N-S 24-452-4302   (SL)
CLEVELAND RANGE LTD
(*Suby of* Welbilt, Inc.)
8251 Keele St, Concord, ON, L4K 1Z1
(905) 660-4747
Emp Here 160   *Sales* 23,908,528
SIC 3589 Service industry machinery, nec
Dir Robert Pirtt

D-U-N-S 24-395-6997   (BR)
COMPAGNIE DES CHEMINS DE FER NATIONAUX DU CANADA
75 Diesel Dr, Concord, ON, L4K 1B9
(905) 669-3159
Emp Here 120

SIC 4789 Transportation services, nec

D-U-N-S 20-581-4903   (BR)
COMPAGNIE DES CHEMINS DE FER NATIONAUX DU CANADA
CN RAIL
73 Diesel Dr Unit 1b, Concord, ON, L4K 1B9

Emp Here 355
SIC 4011 Railroads, line-haul operating

D-U-N-S 25-094-7033   (BR)
COMPAGNIE DES CHEMINS DE FER NATIONAUX DU CANADA
CN METAL DISTRIBUTION
619 Creditstone Rd, Concord, ON, L4K 4N2
(905) 669-3076
Emp Here 20
SIC 4212 Local trucking, without storage

D-U-N-S 25-194-9004   (BR)
COMPAGNIE DES CHEMINS DE FER NATIONAUX DU CANADA
Gd, Concord, ON, L4K 1B9
(905) 669-3009
Emp Here 115
SIC 4789 Transportation services, nec

D-U-N-S 24-123-1617   (BR)
COMPAGNIE DES CHEMINS DE FER NATIONAUX DU CANADA
CN NORTH AMERICA
Gd, Concord, ON, L4K 1B9
(905) 669-3302
Emp Here 600
SIC 4011 Railroads, line-haul operating

D-U-N-S 24-770-7375   (SL)
CONBORA FORMING INC
109 Edilcan Dr, Concord, ON, L4K 3S6
(905) 738-7979
Emp Here 55   *Sales* 6,055,738
SIC 1771 Concrete work
Pr Pr Irving Teper

D-U-N-S 20-191-7692   (BR)
CONCORD METAL MANUFACTURING INC
14 Citron Crt, Concord, ON, L4K 2P5
(905) 738-2127
Emp Here 25
SIC 2542 Partitions and fixtures, except wood

D-U-N-S 24-912-1518   (SL)
CORRADO CARPENTER CONTRACTOR LIMITED
445 Edgeley Blvd Suite 20, Concord, ON, L4K 4G1
(905) 660-4411
Emp Here 50   *Sales* 3,648,035
SIC 1751 Carpentry work

D-U-N-S 20-806-6782   (BR)
COUTTS, WILLIAM E. COMPANY, LIMITED
HALLMARK CARDS & GIFTS
(*Suby of* Hallmark Cards, Incorporated)
1 Bass Pro Mills Dr Unit 300, Concord, ON, L4K 5W4

Emp Here 25
SIC 2771 Greeting cards

D-U-N-S 24-120-1115   (BR)
CROWN METAL PACKAGING CANADA LP
(*Suby of* Crown Holdings Inc.)
7250 Keele St, Concord, ON, L4K 1Z8

Emp Here 100
SIC 3411 Metal cans

D-U-N-S 24-631-2789   (SL)
CRYSTAL FOUNTAINS HOLDINGS INC
DECORATIVE FOUNTAIN CO, DIV OF
60 Snow Blvd Suite 3, Concord, ON, L4K 4B3
(905) 660-6674
Emp Here 60   *Sales* 6,566,463
SIC 3499 Fabricated Metal products, nec
Pr Pr Paul L'heureux
David L'heureux

D-U-N-S 24-796-8043   (SL)
D.J. INDUSTRIAL SALES AND MANUFACTURING INC
25 North Rivermede Rd Unit 1-3, Concord, ON, L4K 5V4
(416) 798-7575
Emp Here 25   *Sales* 8,646,620
SIC 5084 Industrial machinery and equipment
Pr David Brown
VP Christopher Brown

D-U-N-S 20-105-7325   (BR)
DCL INTERNATIONAL INC
140 Cidermill Ave Suite D, Concord, ON, L4K 4T5
(905) 660-6451
Emp Here 30
SIC 3714 Motor vehicle parts and accessories

D-U-N-S 20-273-4778   (SL)
DNS INDUSTRIES LIMITED
77 Courtland Ave Unit 3, Concord, ON, L4K 3S9
(905) 761-9568
Emp Here 50   *Sales* 3,356,192
SIC 2541 Wood partitions and fixtures

D-U-N-S 24-214-8500   (SL)
DSI INDUSTRIES INC
OFGO
115 Cidermill Ave, Concord, ON, L4K 4G5
(905) 669-1357
Emp Here 60   *Sales* 4,012,839
SIC 2521 Wood office furniture

D-U-N-S 25-253-2460   (SL)
DSI UPHOLSTERY INC
DESIGN SOURCE INTERNATIONAL
115 Cidermill Ave, Concord, ON, L4K 4G5
(905) 669-1357
Emp Here 150   *Sales* 14,000,100
SIC 2521 Wood office furniture
Pr Pr David Shamir

D-U-N-S 20-979-6460   (BR)
DAL-TILE OF CANADA ULC
40 Graniteridge Rd Suite 1, Concord, ON, L4K 5M8
(905) 738-2099
Emp Here 30
SIC 5032 Brick, stone, and related material

D-U-N-S 20-183-7283   (HQ)
DE BOER'S FURNITURE LIMITED
(*Suby of* De Boer's Furniture Limited)
275 Drumlin Cir, Concord, ON, L4K 3E4

Emp Here 30   *Emp Total* 110
Sales 17,347,950
SIC 5712 Furniture stores
Pr Pr John De Boer
Genl Mgr Suanne De Boer
Fin Ex Hank Kampen

D-U-N-S 24-333-3051   (HQ)
DIGI CANADA INCORPORATED
87 Moyal Crt, Concord, ON, L4K 4R8
(905) 879-0833
Emp Here 35   *Emp Total* 1,127
Sales 15,925,360
SIC 5046 Commercial equipment, nec
Pr Pr Prashant Parekh

D-U-N-S 24-660-1603   (SL)
DIMAR CANADA LTD
45 Tandem Rd, Concord, ON, L4K 3G1
(905) 738-7919
Emp Here 20   *Sales* 1,459,214
SIC 3423 Hand and edge tools, nec

D-U-N-S 25-418-5515   (SL)
DOCUCOM LIMITED PARTNERSHIP
121 Romina Dr, Concord, ON, L4K 4Z9

Emp Here 28   *Sales* 5,325,440
SIC 5044 Office equipment
VP Martin Mollot
Pr Raymond Patterson

D-U-N-S 20-332-3944   (BR)
DOLLARAMA S.E.C.
DOLLARAMA
3255 Rutherford Rd Unit 37, Concord, ON,
L4K 5Y5
(905) 738-1393
Emp Here 22
SIC 5331 Variety stores

D-U-N-S 25-936-7498   (BR)
DORFIN INC
CONSUMER PRODUCTS
66 Drumlin Cir Suite 5, Concord, ON, L4K 3E9
(905) 761-5522
Emp Here 20
SIC 5113 Industrial and personal service paper

D-U-N-S 24-101-8683   (SL)
ESW CANADA INC
335 Connie Cres, Concord, ON, L4K 5R2
(905) 695-4141
Emp Here 23   *Sales* 3,648,035
SIC 3714 Motor vehicle parts and accessories

D-U-N-S 24-181-3286   (SL)
**EASY PLASTIC CONTAINERS CORPORA-
TION**
101 Jardin Dr Unit 10, Concord, ON, L4K 1X6
(905) 669-4466
Emp Here 125   *Sales* 22,609,151
SIC 3089 Plastics products, nec
Pr Pr George Seretis
Dir Nick Seretis

D-U-N-S 24-708-4778   (SL)
**EMPIRE (THE CONTINENTAL) LIMITED
PARTNERSHIP**
125 Villarboit Cres, Concord, ON, L4K 4K2
(905) 307-8102
Emp Here 100   *Sales* 19,317,745
SIC 1521 Single-family housing construction
Pr Pr Daniel Guizzetti

D-U-N-S 20-773-3234   (SL)
ENERPOWER UTILITIES INC
585 Applewood Cres, Concord, ON, L4K 5V7
(905) 761-9415
Emp Here 150   *Sales* 26,265,852
SIC 1623 Water, sewer, and utility lines
Pr Pr Frank Mongillo
 Simon Degasperis

D-U-N-S 25-882-8391   (BR)
**EXCEL LIGHTING & MANUFACTURING
LTD**
GALAXY LIGHTING
388 Romina Dr, Concord, ON, L4K 5X9
(416) 747-1388
Emp Here 30
SIC 5063 Electrical apparatus and equipment

D-U-N-S 24-214-8625   (HQ)
EXECUTIVE WOODWORK LTD
(*Suby of* Executive Woodwork Ltd)
330 Spinnaker Way, Concord, ON, L4K 4W1
(905) 669-6429
Emp Here 30   *Emp Total* 65
Sales 3,283,232
SIC 7389 Business services, nec

D-U-N-S 20-645-6662   (BR)
EXTREME FITNESS GROUP INC
(*Suby of* Extreme Fitness Group Inc)
90 Interchange Way, Concord, ON, L4K 5C3
(905) 850-4402
Emp Here 20
SIC 7991 Physical fitness facilities

D-U-N-S 24-337-2955   (BR)
FGL SPORTS LTD
NATIONAL SPORTS
2160 Highway 7 Suite 6, Concord, ON, L4K
1W6
(905) 669-2030
Emp Here 20
SIC 5941 Sporting goods and bicycle shops

D-U-N-S 24-664-6541   (SL)
FAVA INVESTMENTS INC
25 Interchange Way, Concord, ON, L4K 5W3
(905) 660-4111
Emp Here 34   *Sales* 8,142,759
SIC 5063 Electrical apparatus and equipment
Pr Pr Frank Vanelli

D-U-N-S 20-695-2637   (SL)
FERNBROOK DEVELOPMENTS LTD
2220 Highway 7 Unit 5, Concord, ON, L4K
1W7
(416) 667-0447
Emp Here 50   *Sales* 2,626,585
SIC 7389 Business services, nec

D-U-N-S 20-695-2595   (SL)
**FERNBROOK HOMES (LAKE OF DREAMS)
LIMITED**
2220 Highway 7 Unit 5, Concord, ON, L4K
1W7
(416) 667-0447
Emp Here 50   *Sales* 13,665,280
SIC 1522 Residential construction, nec
Owner Daniel Salvatore

D-U-N-S 24-351-7955   (BR)
FOOT LOCKER CANADA CO
FOOT LOCKER CANADA CO.
1 Bass Pro Mills Dr, Concord, ON, L4K 5W4
(905) 738-0564
Emp Here 40
SIC 5661 Shoe stores

D-U-N-S 24-645-0506   (SL)
FOSS, G.A. TRANSPORT LTD
FOSS TRANSPORT
220 Doney Cres, Concord, ON, L4K 3A8
(905) 738-6272
Emp Here 24   *Sales* 1,605,135
SIC 4212 Local trucking, without storage

D-U-N-S 25-283-2522   (SL)
FOX RUN CANADA CORP
FOX RUN CRAFTSMEN
(*Suby of* Fox Run Holdings, Inc)
460 Applewood Cres Suite 2, Concord, ON,
L4K 4Z3
(905) 669-4145
Emp Here 20   *Sales* 2,188,821
SIC 5023 Homefurnishings

D-U-N-S 24-221-7685   (HQ)
FRANCOTYP-POSTALIA CANADA INC
FP MAILING SOLUTIONS
82 Corstate Ave Suite 2000, Concord, ON,
L4K 4X2
(905) 761-6554
Emp Here 33   *Emp Total* 1,045
Sales 5,617,974
SIC 5044 Office equipment
Dir Taby Briones
Dir James Lister
Fin Ex James Rogerson

D-U-N-S 24-020-8913   (BR)
**FRENCH CONNECTION (CANADA) LIM-
ITED**
(*Suby of* FRENCH CONNECTION GROUP
PLC)
1 Bass Pro Mills Dr Unit 528, Concord, ON,
L4K 5W4

Emp Here 20
SIC 5651 Family clothing stores

D-U-N-S 24-253-2062   (BR)
GAP (CANADA) INC
GAP OUTLET
(*Suby of* The Gap Inc)
1 Bass Pro Mills Dr, Concord, ON, L4K 5W4
(905) 761-7577
Emp Here 85
SIC 5651 Family clothing stores

D-U-N-S 25-510-3137   (SL)
GLOBAL PHOENIX MANUFACTURING INC
141 Snidercroft Rd Suite 4, Concord, ON, L4K
5B8

2J8
Emp Here 50   *Sales* 3,984,755
SIC 2521 Wood office furniture

D-U-N-S 25-529-8275   (BR)
GLOBAL UPHOLSTERY CO. INC
GLOBAL EXPRESS
177 Snidercroft Rd Suite A, Concord, ON, L4K
2J8
(905) 660-5101
Emp Here 60
SIC 5021 Furniture

D-U-N-S 25-838-1680   (BR)
GLOBE SPRING & CUSHION CO. LTD
25 Doney Cres, Concord, ON, L4K 1P6

Emp Here 50
SIC 2511 Wood household furniture

D-U-N-S 24-652-8962   (SL)
GOLDFARB SHULMAN PATEL & CO LLP
400 Bradwick Dr Suite 100, Concord, ON, L4K
5V9
(416) 226-6800
Emp Here 90   *Sales* 3,939,878
SIC 8721 Accounting, auditing, and book-
keeping

D-U-N-S 20-558-9588   (SL)
**GOTTARDO MASONRY & CONTRACTING
LTD**
277 Pennsylvania Ave, Concord, ON, L4K 5R9
(905) 532-0735
Emp Here 56   *Sales* 4,085,799
SIC 1741 Masonry and other stonework

D-U-N-S 20-151-7815   (BR)
GUILLEVIN INTERNATIONAL CIE
8200 Jane St, Concord, ON, L4K 5A7

Emp Here 25
SIC 5063 Electrical apparatus and equipment

D-U-N-S 24-096-6031   (SL)
H & M HENNES & MAURITZ INC
H & M
1 Bass Pro Mills Dr, Concord, ON, L4K 5W4
(905) 760-1769
Emp Here 60   *Sales* 3,648,035
SIC 5651 Family clothing stores

D-U-N-S 20-629-2849   (SL)
**HAREMAR PLASTIC MANUFACTURING
LIMITED**
200 Great Gulf Dr, Concord, ON, L4K 5W1
(905) 761-7552
Emp Here 100   *Sales* 18,940,813
SIC 3081 Unsupported plastics film and sheet
Pr Pr Fela Lichtblau
 Mark Lichtblau
VP Opers Cheryl Babcock

D-U-N-S 20-918-0715   (BR)
HENRY SCHEIN CANADA, INC
221 Jacob Keffer Pky, Concord, ON, L4K 5T9
(905) 832-9101
Emp Here 50
SIC 5047 Medical and hospital equipment

D-U-N-S 20-013-0248   (HQ)
HEWITT MATERIAL HANDLING INC
HEWITT MATERIAL HANDLING SYSTEMS
425 Millway Ave, Concord, ON, L4K 3V8
(905) 669-6590
Emp Here 80   *Emp Total* 2,075
Sales 31,227,180
SIC 5084 Industrial machinery and equipment
Pr Pr James William Hewitt
 Roni Farah
Dir Suzanne Bergeron
Dir Marie Diamond

D-U-N-S 24-355-8132   (BR)
HIGH LINER FOODS INCORPORATED
8000 Jane St Suite 301, Concord, ON, L4K
5B8

(905) 761-3242
Emp Here 50
SIC 2092 Fresh or frozen packaged fish

D-U-N-S 20-289-1086   (BR)
HOMELIFE/METROPARK REALTY INC
9222 Keele St Unit 11, Concord, ON, L4K 5A3
(416) 798-7777
Emp Here 40
SIC 6531 Real estate agents and managers

D-U-N-S 24-792-0932   (SL)
HOMELIFE METRO PARK REALTY
9222 Keele St Suite 11, Concord, ON, L4K
5A3
(905) 303-9558
Emp Here 49   *Sales* 6,184,080
SIC 6531 Real estate agents and managers
Brnch Mgr Don Ferri

D-U-N-S 24-373-2851   (BR)
HUDSON'S BAY COMPANY
HOME OUTFITTERS
3200 Highway 7, Concord, ON, L4K 5Z5
(905) 760-1759
Emp Here 20
SIC 5311 Department stores

D-U-N-S 24-953-4181   (HQ)
HUGO BOSS CANADA INC
2600 Steeles Ave W Suite 2, Concord, ON,
L4K 3C8
(905) 739-2677
Emp Here 50   *Emp Total* 15,833
Sales 27,360,263
SIC 5136 Men's and boy's clothing
Pr Pr Leslie Minion
Treas Bernard Resnick

D-U-N-S 24-325-8444   (HQ)
**IAC AUTOMOTIVE COMPONENTS AL-
BERTA ULC**
IAC
375 Basaltic Rd, Concord, ON, L4K 4W8
(905) 879-0292
Emp Here 250   *Emp Total* 2
Sales 80,214,843
SIC 3089 Plastics products, nec
Manager Bob Cook
Dir William Mclaughlin
Dir Daniel Ninvaggi

D-U-N-S 24-254-6294   (SL)
IPC CANADA PHOTO SERVICES INC
56 Pennsylvania Ave Unit 2, Concord, ON,
L4K 3V9
(905) 738-6630
Emp Here 50   *Sales* 3,648,035
SIC 7335 Commercial photography

D-U-N-S 20-181-4345   (BR)
**IRON MOUNTAIN CANADA OPERATIONS
ULC**
ARCHIVES IRON MOUNTAIN
70 Talman Crt Suite 415, Concord, ON, L4K
4L5
(905) 760-0769
Emp Here 200
SIC 4226 Special warehousing and storage,
nec

D-U-N-S 24-248-0924   (BR)
IVANHOE CAMBRIDGE II INC.
VAUGHAN MILLS SHOPPING CENTRE
1 Bass Pro Mills Dr Suite A1, Concord, ON,
L4K 5W4
(905) 879-1777
Emp Here 50
SIC 6512 Nonresidential building operators

D-U-N-S 25-938-1739   (BR)
JELD-WEN OF CANADA, LTD.
UNITED WINDOWS & DOORS
8550 Keele St, Concord, ON, L4K 2N2
(416) 798-7166
Emp Here 200
SIC 2431 Millwork

D-U-N-S 25-507-6804   (HQ)

JEMPAK GK INC
(*Suby of* JemPak GK Inc)
80 Doney Cres, Concord, ON, L4K 3P1
(905) 738-5656
Emp Here 53   *Emp Total* 103
Sales 2,425,503
SIC 2841 Soap and other detergents

D-U-N-S 24-602-6447   (SL)
JONES APPAREL GROUP CANADA ULC
(*Suby of* Jasper Parent LLC)
388 Applewood Cres, Concord, ON, L4K 4B4
(905) 760-6000
Emp Here 400   *Sales* 32,039,186
SIC 2339 Women's and misses' outerwear, nec
Pr Mary Ann Curran

D-U-N-S 24-891-6165   (HQ)
K-G SPRAY-PAK INC
ASSURED PACKAGING DIVISION
(*Suby of* Plz Aeroscience Corporation)
8001 Keele St, Concord, ON, L4K 1Y8
(905) 669-9855
Emp Here 50   *Emp Total* 350
Sales 19,991,232
SIC 2813 Industrial gases
VP VP Wayne Houston
   Walter Drozdowsky
Dir Eva Morris
   Kent Horne

D-U-N-S 25-406-2136   (HQ)
KIK HOLDCO COMPANY INC
KIK CUSTOM PRODUCTS
(*Suby of* KIK Custom Products Inc)
101 Macintosh Blvd, Concord, ON, L4K 4R5
(905) 660-0444
Emp Here 850   *Emp Total* 5
Sales 181,818,064
SIC 6719 Holding companies, nec
Dir Jeffrey Nodland
VP Fin Alay Shah
   Ben Kaak

D-U-N-S 20-515-4185   (BR)
KIK OPERATING PARTNERSHIP
33 Macintosh Blvd, Concord, ON, L4K 4L5
(905) 660-0444
Emp Here 25
SIC 4225 General warehousing and storage

D-U-N-S 20-511-6051   (BR)
KPMG INC
100 New Park Pl Suite 1400, Concord, ON, L4K 0J3

Emp Here 490
SIC 8721 Accounting, auditing, and bookkeeping

D-U-N-S 24-373-1093   (BR)
KAR INDUSTRIEL INC
DURAMILL, DIVISION OF
21 Bradwick Dr Unit 2, Concord, ON, L4K 1K6
(905) 738-8665
Emp Here 20
SIC 5085 Industrial supplies

D-U-N-S 20-358-0535   (SL)
KATAND ENTERPRISES INC
TIM HORTON'S
1600 Langstaff Rd, Concord, ON, L4K 3S3
(905) 669-7574
Emp Here 90   *Sales* 2,699,546
SIC 5812 Eating places

D-U-N-S 20-151-4122   (HQ)
KAWNEER COMPANY CANADA LIMITED
(*Suby of* Arconic Inc.)
200 Confederation Pky Unit 2, Concord, ON, L4K 4T8
(289) 982-0200
Emp Here 300   *Emp Total* 41,500
Sales 62,370,072
SIC 3446 Architectural Metalwork
   Rob D Macdonald
   Patrick M Moore

Dir Cleve A Miyashiro
Dir Kulasingam Sivakumar
Dir John P Spadaro
Dir Wards Sellers

D-U-N-S 20-176-4136   (BR)
KEMIRA WATER SOLUTIONS CANADA INC
500 Creditstone Rd, Concord, ON, L4K 3Z3

Emp Here 30
SIC 2899 Chemical preparations, nec

D-U-N-S 24-211-3595   (HQ)
KENWORTH TORONTO LTD
KENWORTH LONDON
500 Creditstone Rd, Concord, ON, L4K 3Z3
(905) 695-0740
Emp Here 75   *Emp Total* 2
Sales 165,713,816
SIC 5012 Automobiles and other motor vehicles
Pr Pr Vince Tarola
   Armida Tarola

D-U-N-S 24-780-0014   (SL)
KING KOATING ROOFING INC
41 Peelar Rd, Concord, ON, L4K 1A3
(905) 669-1771
Emp Here 50   *Sales* 4,961,328
SIC 1761 Roofing, siding, and sheetMetal work

D-U-N-S 20-168-6532   (HQ)
KOHL & FRISCH LIMITED
(*Suby of* Kohl & Frisch Limited)
7622 Keele St, Concord, ON, L4K 2R5
(905) 660-7622
Emp Here 250   *Emp Total* 850
Sales 104,771,565
SIC 5122 Drugs, proprietaries, and sundries
Pr Pr Ronald Frisch
VP VP Lance Fielding
VP Fin Sharon Fligel

D-U-N-S 24-101-4864   (BR)
KRISTOFOAM INDUSTRIES INC
160 Planchet Rd, Concord, ON, L4K 2C7
(905) 669-6616
Emp Here 50
SIC 3086 Plastics foam products

D-U-N-S 25-104-5431   (HQ)
KUMON CANADA INC
640 Applewood Cres, Concord, ON, L4K 4B4
(416) 490-1434
Emp Here 30   *Emp Total* 3,940
Sales 2,188,821
SIC 8299 Schools and educational services, nec

D-U-N-S 24-693-3550   (BR)
LAFARGE CANADA INC
7880 Keele St, Concord, ON, L4K 4G7
(905) 738-7070
Emp Here 150
SIC 3272 Concrete products, nec

D-U-N-S 24-344-7252   (BR)
LAFARGE CANADA INC
LAFARGE PAVING & CONSTRUCTION, DIV OF
7880 Keele St, Concord, ON, L4K 4G7
(905) 738-7070
Emp Here 30
SIC 1611 Highway and street construction

D-U-N-S 20-161-0979   (BR)
LAFARGE CANADA INC
7880 Keele St, Concord, ON, L4K 4G7
(905) 764-5260
Emp Here 150
SIC 5032 Brick, stone, and related material

D-U-N-S 24-644-1596   (BR)
LAFARGE CANADA INC
7880 Keele St, Concord, ON, L4K 4G7
(905) 629-3760
Emp Here 80

SIC 1542 Nonresidential construction, nec

D-U-N-S 25-365-1897   (HQ)
LAFARGE PAVING & CONSTRUCTION (EASTERN) LIMITED
7880 Keele St, Concord, ON, L4K 4G7
(905) 738-7070
Emp Here 250   *Emp Total* 90,903
Sales 78,429,840
SIC 1611 Highway and street construction
Pr Pr Greg Sheardown
Asst Tr Jean Marc Bissonnette
   Alain Fredette
   Kenneth R. Cathcart
Dir David Guptill

D-U-N-S 20-140-2117   (HQ)
LAW DEVELOPMENT GROUP (1989) LIMITED
(*Suby of* Law Development Group (1989) Limited)
8000 Jane St Suite 201, Concord, ON, L4K 5B8
(416) 331-9688
Emp Here 20   *Emp Total* 20
Sales 8,539,920
SIC 6552 Subdividers and developers, nec
Pr Pr Larry Law

D-U-N-S 24-851-1425   (SL)
LEICA MICROSYSTEMS (CANADA) INC
(*Suby of* Fortive Corporation)
71 Four Valley Dr, Concord, ON, L4K 4V8
(905) 762-2000
Emp Here 100   *Sales* 75,386,320
SIC 3827 Optical instruments and lenses
Pr Arnd Kaldowski

D-U-N-S 20-362-1024   (BR)
LEON'S FURNITURE LIMITED
APPLIANCE CANADA, A DIV OF LEON'S FURNITURE LIMITED
8701 Jane St Unit 1, Concord, ON, L4K 2M6
(800) 374-3437
Emp Here 130
SIC 5712 Furniture stores

D-U-N-S 25-530-2564   (BR)
LITENS AUTOMOTIVE PARTNERSHIP
150 Courtland Ave, Concord, ON, L4K 3T6
(905) 760-9177
Emp Here 125
SIC 3429 Hardware, nec

D-U-N-S 24-802-8115   (BR)
LOWE'S COMPANIES CANADA, ULC
100 Edgeley Blvd, Concord, ON, L4K 5W7
(905) 532-5630
Emp Here 100
SIC 5211 Lumber and other building materials

D-U-N-S 24-631-4389   (SL)
M.B. PRODUCT RESEARCH DISTRIBUTING INC
INTER-CANADA FISHERIES, DIV OF
270 Pennsylvania Ave Unit 11-13, Concord, ON, L4K 3Z7
(905) 660-1421
Emp Here 28   *Sales* 10,214,498
SIC 5146 Fish and seafoods
Pr Pr Marc Benhaim

D-U-N-S 20-280-8085   (SL)
MGC SYSTEMS INTERNATIONAL LTD
25 Interchange Way, Concord, ON, L4K 5W3
(905) 660-4655
Emp Here 20   *Sales* 19,334,880
SIC 3669 Communications equipment, nec
Pr Pr Mark Falbo
Dir Tony Falbo
Dir Frank Vanelli

D-U-N-S 20-355-5748   (SL)
MAGICAL PEST CONTROL INC
29 Tandem Rd Unit 3, Concord, ON, L4K 3G1
(416) 665-7378
Emp Here 60   *Sales* 3,648,035
SIC 7342 Disinfecting and pest control services

D-U-N-S 20-699-6873   (HQ)
MAGNA EXTERIORS INC
50 Casmir Crt, Concord, ON, L4K 4J5
(905) 669-2888
Emp Here 1,000   *Emp Total* 155,450
Sales 475,630,803
SIC 3714 Motor vehicle parts and accessories
Pr Pr Joseph Pittel
VP Michael Mccarthy
VP Francis Seguin
VP Jeffrey Palmer
   Vincent Galifi
   Tom Skudutis

D-U-N-S 24-092-9703   (BR)
MAGNA INTERNATIONAL INC
MAPLE STAMPING
401 Caldari Rd Suite B, Concord, ON, L4K 5P1
(905) 738-8033
Emp Here 140
SIC 3714 Motor vehicle parts and accessories

D-U-N-S 25-531-0500   (BR)
MAGNA INTERNATIONAL INC
ROLLSTAMP MANUFACTURING, DIV OF
591 Basaltic Rd, Concord, ON, L4K 4W8
(905) 738-3700
Emp Here 100
SIC 3714 Motor vehicle parts and accessories

D-U-N-S 24-006-1978   (BR)
MAGNA INTERNATIONAL INC
NORMARK MANUFACTURING
120 Spinnaker Way, Concord, ON, L4K 2P6
(905) 738-0452
Emp Here 100
SIC 3714 Motor vehicle parts and accessories

D-U-N-S 24-317-3981   (BR)
MAGNA INTERNATIONAL INC
P&F TOOL & DIE
210 Citation Dr, Concord, ON, L4K 2V2
(905) 738-4108
Emp Here 300
SIC 3714 Motor vehicle parts and accessories

D-U-N-S 24-176-3205   (BR)
MAGNA INTERNATIONAL INC
P&F TOOL & DIE
180 Confederation Pky, Concord, ON, L4K 4T8
(905) 761-1316
Emp Here 200
SIC 8741 Management services

D-U-N-S 20-123-8628   (BR)
MAGNA INTERNATIONAL INC
ROLLSTAMP MANUFACTURING, DIV OF
141 Staffern Dr, Concord, ON, L4K 2R2
(905) 738-3700
Emp Here 200
SIC 3711 Motor vehicles and car bodies

D-U-N-S 24-719-1612   (BR)
MAGNA INTERNATIONAL INC
DECOMA EXTERIOR TRIM, DIV OF
50 Casmir Crt, Concord, ON, L4K 4J5
(905) 669-2888
Emp Here 100
SIC 3465 Automotive stampings

D-U-N-S 20-188-5683   (BR)
MAGNA INTERNATIONAL INC
TYCOS TOOL & DIE
2000 Langstaff Rd, Concord, ON, L4K 3B5
(905) 669-2350
Emp Here 120
SIC 3544 Special dies, tools, jigs, and fixtures

D-U-N-S 20-108-3164   (BR)
MAGNA POWERTRAIN INC
MPT FLUID PRESSURE & CONTROLS GROUP, DIV OF
800 Tesma Way, Concord, ON, L4K 5C2
(905) 303-0960
Emp Here 90

SIC 3714 Motor vehicle parts and accessories

D-U-N-S 20-176-6123　　(BR)
MAGNA POWERTRAIN INC
TESMA ENGINES TECHNOLOGIES, DIV OF
800 Tesma Way, Concord, ON, L4K 5C2
(905) 303-0690
Emp Here 40
SIC 3714 Motor vehicle parts and accessories

D-U-N-S 24-764-5765　　(HQ)
MAGNA POWERTRAIN INC
ROTO FORM, DIV OF
50 Casmir Crt, Concord, ON, L4K 4J5
(905) 532-2100
Emp Here 25　　　　*Emp Total* 155,450
Sales 745,147,629
SIC 3714 Motor vehicle parts and accessories
VP Fin Thomas More
VP Daind Minss

D-U-N-S 20-286-1662　　(BR)
MAGNA POWERTRAIN INC
STT TECHNOLOGIES DIV
600 Tesma Way, Concord, ON, L4K 5C2
(905) 303-3745
Emp Here 250
SIC 3714 Motor vehicle parts and accessories

D-U-N-S 24-079-7746　　(BR)
MAGNA POWERTRAIN INC
ADVANCED PRODUCT TECHNOLOGIES, DIV OF
800 Tesma Way, Concord, ON, L4K 5C2
(905) 303-1689
Emp Here 270
SIC 3714 Motor vehicle parts and accessories

D-U-N-S 20-709-1070　　(SL)
MAPLE LEAF BREAD LTD
MAPLE LEAF BREAD
144 Viceroy Rd, Concord, ON, L4K 2L8
(905) 738-1242
Emp Here 50　　　　*Sales* 4,961,328
SIC 2041 Flour and other grain mill products

D-U-N-S 20-708-8118　　(BR)
MAPLE TERRAZZO MARBLE & TILE INCORPORATED
200 Edgeley Blvd Unit 9, Concord, ON, L4K 3Y8
(905) 760-1776
Emp Here 700
SIC 8631 Labor organizations

D-U-N-S 24-738-2906　　(SL)
MARTINO CONTRACTORS LTD
150 Connie Cres Unit 16, Concord, ON, L4K 1L9
(905) 760-9894
Emp Here 50　　　*Sales* 4,377,642
SIC 1711 Plumbing, heating, air-conditioning

D-U-N-S 24-861-9652　　(BR)
MASONITE INTERNATIONAL CORPORATION
(*Suby of* Masonite International Corporation)
7171 Jane St, Concord, ON, L4K 1A7
(905) 660-3007
Emp Here 70
SIC 2431 Millwork

D-U-N-S 20-525-6746　　(BR)
MASONITE INTERNATIONAL CORPORATION
INDUSTRIES MANUFACTURIERES MEGANTIC, DIV OF
(*Suby of* Masonite International Corporation)
2771 Rutherford Rd, Concord, ON, L4K 2N6
(905) 482-2370
Emp Here 50　　　*Sales* 1,973,964,000
SIC 2431 Millwork

D-U-N-S 20-876-6758　　(HQ)
MASTERS INSURANCE LIMITED
(*Suby of* Masters Insurance Limited)
7501 Keele St Suite 400, Concord, ON, L4K 1Y2

(905) 738-4164
Emp Here 20　　　　*Emp Total* 50
Sales 4,523,563
SIC 6411 Insurance agents, brokers, and service

D-U-N-S 20-119-3385　　(SL)
MATTAMY DEVELOPMENT CORPORATION
500, Concord, ON, L4K 4G7
(905) 907-8888
Emp Here 25　　　*Sales* 7,952,716
SIC 6552 Subdividers and developers, nec
Pr Pr David Stewart

D-U-N-S 20-784-8540　　(HQ)
MCINTOSH PERRY LIMITED
(*Suby of* Signal Hill Equity Partners Inc)
7900 Keele St Suite 200, Concord, ON, L4K 2A3
(905) 856-5200
Emp Here 100　　　*Emp Total* 300
Sales 19,845,310
SIC 8742 Management consulting services
Pr Gus Sarrouh
　Parvaneh (Gina) Baktash-Cody
Sec James Johnson

D-U-N-S 24-660-5323　　(SL)
METCON SALES AND ENGINEERING LIMITED
15 Connie Cres Unit 3, Concord, ON, L4K 1L3
(905) 738-2355
Emp Here 45　　　*Sales* 8,244,559
SIC 5084 Industrial machinery and equipment
Pr Lawrence Rosen

D-U-N-S 24-101-4435　　(BR)
MIDLAND TRANSPORT LIMITED
(*Suby of* J. D. Irving, Limited)
101 Doney Cres, Concord, ON, L4K 1P6
(905) 738-5544
Emp Here 30
SIC 4212 Local trucking, without storage

D-U-N-S 24-816-8700　　(HQ)
MIELE LIMITED
161 Four Valley Dr, Concord, ON, L4K 4V8
(905) 532-2270
Emp Here 100　　　*Emp Total* 10,500
Sales 30,862,376
SIC 5064 Electrical appliances, television and radio
Pr Jan Heck

D-U-N-S 20-408-4313　　(HQ)
MISTER KEYS LIMITED
KEYMAN ENGRAVABLES, THE
(*Suby of* Mister Keys Limited)
161 North Rivermede Rd Unit 5, Concord, ON, L4K 2V3
(905) 738-1811
Emp Here 25　　　*Emp Total* 300
Sales 22,608,000
SIC 5947 Gift, novelty, and souvenir shop
Pr Pr David Bellisario
　Pat Bellisario
Dir Donald Bellisario

D-U-N-S 25-274-8777　　(SL)
MOBILE CLIMATE CONTROL, INC
7540 Jane St, Concord, ON, L4K 0A6
(905) 482-2750
Emp Here 300　　　*Sales* 56,479,565
SIC 3714 Motor vehicle parts and accessories
Pr Pr Robert Kuzminski
VP Fin Maurizio Caranfa

D-U-N-S 25-204-6289　　(HQ)
MOOD MEDIA ENTERTAINMENT LTD
AVALON MUSIC
(*Suby of* Mood Media Corporation)
99 Sante Dr Suite B, Concord, ON, L4K 3C4
(905) 761-4300
Emp Here 50　　　*Emp Total* 850
Sales 4,961,328
SIC 7389 Business services, nec

D-U-N-S 25-407-0022　　(BR)
MOORE, BENJAMIN & CO., LIMITED

(*Suby of* Berkshire Hathaway Inc.)
161 Cidermill Ave, Concord, ON, L4K 4G5
(905) 660-7769
Emp Here 32
SIC 2851 Paints and allied products

D-U-N-S 20-171-1769　　(HQ)
MOORE, BENJAMIN & CO., LIMITED
(*Suby of* Berkshire Hathaway Inc.)
8775 Keele St, Concord, ON, L4K 2N1
(905) 761-4800
Emp Here 100　　　*Emp Total* 331,000
Sales 28,673,555
SIC 2851 Paints and allied products
Pr Pr Brian Palardy

D-U-N-S 20-227-8826　　(HQ)
MORRIS NATIONAL INC
(*Suby of* Morris National Inc)
100 Jacob Keffer Pky, Concord, ON, L4K 4W3
(905) 879-7777
Emp Here 20　　　*Emp Total* 200
Sales 52,020,979
SIC 5145 Confectionery
　Gerry Morris Zubatoff
　Abe Morris Zubatoff
VP Sls Jean-Pierre Lefebvre

D-U-N-S 24-370-8299　　(HQ)
MULTY HOME LP
(*Suby of* Multy Home LP)
100 Pippin Rd, Concord, ON, L4K 4X9
(905) 760-3737
Emp Here 100　　　*Emp Total* 150
Sales 16,416,158
SIC 5023 Homefurnishings
Pr Derek Erdman

D-U-N-S 25-068-2028　　(SL)
NETWORK MECHANICAL INC
73 Corstate Ave Unit 1, Concord, ON, L4K 4Y2
(905) 761-1417
Emp Here 50　　　*Sales* 4,377,642
SIC 1711 Plumbing, heating, air-conditioning

D-U-N-S 25-504-4075　　(SL)
OLDCASTLE BUILDINGENVELOPE CANADA INC
210 Great Gulf Dr, Concord, ON, L4K 5W1
(905) 660-4520
Emp Here 350　　　*Emp Total* 86,778
Sales 84,853,294
SIC 3211 Flat glass
Pr Edwin Hathaway
　Mary Carol Whitry

D-U-N-S 20-811-4046　　(SL)
ONTARIO STEEL HAULERS INC
111 Rayette Rd, Concord, ON, L4K 2E9
(800) 209-2756
Emp Here 25　　　*Sales* 3,378,379
SIC 4213 Trucking, except local

D-U-N-S 20-209-4665　　(BR)
ORKIN CANADA CORPORATION
ORKIN PCO SERVICES
(*Suby of* Rollins, Inc.)
40 Pippin Rd Suite 5, Concord, ON, L4K 4M6
(905) 660-5100
Emp Here 25
SIC 7342 Disinfecting and pest control services

D-U-N-S 20-982-5298　　(SL)
PARADISE BANQUET HALL & RESTAURANT (CONCORD) INC
7601 Jane St, Concord, ON, L4K 1X2
(416) 661-6612
Emp Here 60　　　*Sales* 1,969,939
SIC 7299 Miscellaneous personal service

D-U-N-S 24-385-4445　　(SL)
PARC DINING & BANQUET LTD, LE
20 North Rivermede Rd, Concord, ON, L4K 2H2

Emp Here 50　　*Sales* 1,532,175
SIC 5812 Eating places

D-U-N-S 24-990-9441　　(BR)
PARK AVENUE FURNITURE CORPORATION
POSTURE BEAUTY SLEEP PRODUCTS
61 Rayette Rd, Concord, ON, L4K 2E8

Emp Here 25
SIC 5021 Furniture

D-U-N-S 25-863-8279　　(HQ)
PARSEC INTERMODAL OF CANADA LIMITED
751 Bowes Rd Suite 2, Concord, ON, L4K 5C9
(905) 669-7901
Emp Here 20　　　*Emp Total* 1,506
Sales 37,680,000
SIC 1629 Heavy construction, nec
Pr Pr Otto Pudig
Rgnl Mgr Al Peroddin

D-U-N-S 20-058-1127　　(SL)
PETER & PAUL'S MANOR LTD
8601 Jane St Unit 6, Concord, ON, L4K 5N9
(905) 326-4438
Emp Here 100　　　*Sales* 3,898,130
SIC 7299 Miscellaneous personal service

D-U-N-S 20-295-6033　　(SL)
PETROLEUM ATS DIVISION
400 Applewood Cres, Concord, ON, L4K 0C3
(905) 482-2587
Emp Here 25　　　*Sales* 6,219,371
SIC 3533 Oil and gas field machinery
Owner Alex Tijerina

D-U-N-S 20-550-5048　　(SL)
POLYCOTE INC
8120 Keele St, Concord, ON, L4K 2A3
(905) 660-7552
Emp Here 58　　　*Sales* 4,851,006
SIC 3479 Metal coating and allied services

D-U-N-S 20-047-2087　　(BR)
PRISZM LP
101 Exchange Ave, Concord, ON, L4K 5R6
(416) 739-2900
Emp Here 20
SIC 5812 Eating places

D-U-N-S 24-326-8955　　(BR)
PROTEMP GLASS INC
WOODBRIDGE GLASS
421 Applewood Cres, Concord, ON, L4K 4J3
(905) 738-4246
Emp Here 20
SIC 5039 Construction materials, nec

D-U-N-S 24-816-8163　　(HQ)
PROCESS PRODUCTS LIMITED
(*Suby of* Process Products Limited)
100 Locke St, Concord, ON, L4K 5R4
(416) 781-3399
Emp Here 40　　　*Emp Total* 60
Sales 11,600,751
SIC 5085 Industrial supplies
　Samuel Stupp
Pr Pr Sydney Stupp

D-U-N-S 20-770-0175　　(BR)
PUROLATOR INC.
PUROLATOR INC
1550 Creditstone Rd, Concord, ON, L4K 5N1
(905) 660-6007
Emp Here 100
SIC 7389 Business services, nec

D-U-N-S 24-525-0621　　(SL)
QRX TECHNOLOGY GROUP INC
(*Suby of* 2172004 Ontario Inc)
200 Connie Cres Unit 4, Concord, ON, L4K 1M1
(905) 738-1688
Emp Here 25　　　*Sales* 21,304,500
SIC 5112 Stationery and office supplies
　Grace Martin

D-U-N-S 24-776-4066　　(SL)
QUALITY & COMPANY INC

67 Jacob Keffer Pky, Concord, ON, L4K 5N8
(905) 660-6996
Emp Here 130   *Sales* 7,004,227
SIC 2599 Furniture and fixtures, nec
Pr Frank Caruso
Dir Rinaldo Caruso

D-U-N-S 20-714-8425   (BR)
RBC DOMINION SECURITIES INC
(*Suby of* Royal Bank Of Canada)
3300 Highway 7 Suite 701, Concord, ON, L4K 4M3
(905) 738-4510
Emp Here 22
SIC 8742 Management consulting services

D-U-N-S 24-363-6284   (BR)
RPM CANADA
RUST-OLEUM CONSUMER BRANDS CANADA, DIV OF
(*Suby of* RPM International Inc.)
200 Confederation Pky, Concord, ON, L4K 4T8
(800) 363-0667
Emp Here 20
SIC 2851 Paints and allied products

D-U-N-S 24-525-0928   (BR)
RPM CANADA
RUST-OLEUM CONSUMERS BRANDS CANADA, DIV OF
(*Suby of* RPM International Inc.)
200 Confederation Pky, Concord, ON, L4K 4T8
(800) 363-0667
Emp Here 50
SIC 5231 Paint, glass, and wallpaper stores

D-U-N-S 24-078-3006   (BR)
REDBERRY FRANCHISING CORP
BURGER KING
23 Jacob Keffer Pky, Concord, ON, L4K 5N8
(905) 303-6428
Emp Here 30
SIC 5812 Eating places

D-U-N-S 20-333-7928   (BR)
RIVERSIDE NATURAL FOODS LTD
2700 Steeles Ave W Bldg 5, Concord, ON, L4K 3C8
(416) 360-8200
Emp Here 30
SIC 2032 Canned specialties

D-U-N-S 24-418-0399   (SL)
RIVIERA PARQUE, BANQUET & CONVENTION CENTRE INC
2800 Highway 7 Suite 301, Concord, ON, L4K 1W8
(905) 669-4933
Emp Here 150   *Sales* 4,961,328
SIC 7299 Miscellaneous personal service

D-U-N-S 24-783-9046   (SL)
ROSENBERG SMITH & PARTNERS LLP
2000 Steeles Ave W Unit 200, Concord, ON, L4K 3E9
(905) 660-3800
Emp Here 70   *Sales* 3,638,254
SIC 8721 Accounting, auditing, and bookkeeping

D-U-N-S 20-088-4778   (BR)
ROYAL BANK OF CANADA
RBC
(*Suby of* Royal Bank Of Canada)
3300 Highway 7 Suite 100, Concord, ON, L4K 4M3
(905) 738-3200
Emp Here 42
SIC 6021 National commercial banks

D-U-N-S 24-353-0057   (BR)
ROYAL GROUP, INC
GEORGIA GULF COMPOUND - CONCORD
121 Pippin Rd, Concord, ON, L4K 4J9
(905) 761-8529
Emp Here 50
SIC 3089 Plastics products, nec

D-U-N-S 24-354-7044   (BR)
ROYAL GROUP, INC
RESIDENTIAL BUILDING PRODUCTS
750 Creditstone Rd, Concord, ON, L4K 5A5
(905) 738-4171
Emp Here 50
SIC 5039 Construction materials, nec

D-U-N-S 24-254-6682   (BR)
RYDER TRUCK RENTAL CANADA LTD
RYDER CANADA
(*Suby of* Ryder System, Inc.)
700 Creditstone Rd, Concord, ON, L4K 5A5
(905) 660-7255
Emp Here 23
SIC 7359 Equipment rental and leasing, nec

D-U-N-S 24-197-7631   (BR)
SIR CORP
CANYON CREEK CHOP HOUSE
255 Bass Pro Mills Dr Unit 504, Concord, ON, L4K 0A2
(905) 532-0857
Emp Here 40
SIC 5812 Eating places

D-U-N-S 20-304-1991   (BR)
SAMUEL, SON & CO., LIMITED
SAMUEL STRAPPING SYSTEMS - CONCORD
21 Corrine Crt, Concord, ON, L4K 4W2
(905) 279-9580
Emp Here 30
SIC 5051 Metals service centers and offices

D-U-N-S 25-371-9785   (SL)
SANDRINGHAM PLACE INC
30 Floral Pky Suite 300, Concord, ON, L4K 4R1
(905) 669-5571
Emp Here 30   *Sales* 12,344,510
SIC 6552 Subdividers and developers, nec
Pr Alfredo Degasperis

D-U-N-S 24-752-6692   (SL)
SCHAEFFER & ASSOCIATES LTD
SHAEFFERS CONSULTING ENGINEERS
6 Ronrose Dr Suite 100, Concord, ON, L4K 4R3

Emp Here 110   *Sales* 14,081,415
SIC 8742 Management consulting services
Pr Pr Allan Steedman
     Zaven Sarkissian

D-U-N-S 24-453-7486   (BR)
SECURITE POLYGON INC
VIKING FIRE PROTECTION
130 Citation Dr, Concord, ON, L4K 2W9
(905) 760-8700
Emp Here 70
SIC 1711 Plumbing, heating, air-conditioning

D-U-N-S 24-991-4185   (SL)
SEENERGY FOODS LIMITED
475 North Rivermede Rd, Concord, ON, L4K 3N1
(905) 660-0041
Emp Here 80   *Sales* 2,918,428
SIC 2035 Pickles, sauces, and salad dressings

D-U-N-S 20-280-9745   (BR)
SIEMENS CANADA LIMITED
RUGGEDCOM SIEMENS
300 Applewood Cres Suite 1, Concord, ON, L4K 5C7
(905) 856-5288
Emp Here 100
SIC 3625 Relays and industrial controls

D-U-N-S 25-372-0361   (HQ)
SMARTREIT MANAGEMENT INC
SMARTREIT
(*Suby of* Smartreit Management Inc)
700 Applewood Cres Suite 100, Concord, ON, L4K 5X3

(905) 760-6200
Emp Here 275   *Emp Total* 300
Sales 27,360,263
SIC 6512 Nonresidential building operators
     Mitchell Goldhar
Pr Huw Thomas
     Peter Sweeney

D-U-N-S 20-104-4620   (BR)
SMITH, J.D. & SONS LIMITED
J.D. SMITH & SONS LIMITED
8711 Keele St, Concord, ON, L4K 2N1
(905) 760-8480
Emp Here 20
SIC 4225 General warehousing and storage

D-U-N-S 20-104-4661   (BR)
SMITH, J.D. & SONS LIMITED
J.D. SMITH & SONS LIMITED
539 Bowes Rd, Concord, ON, L4K 1J5
(905) 738-3900
Emp Here 20
SIC 4225 General warehousing and storage

D-U-N-S 20-287-2180   (SL)
SOMERSET GROUP LIMITED
99 Sante Dr, Concord, ON, L4K 3C4
(905) 761-4300
Emp Here 35   *Sales* 5,072,500
SIC 5099 Durable goods, nec
Pr Pr Rico Micallef

D-U-N-S 20-860-3394   (BR)
SOURCE (BELL) ELECTRONICS INC, THE
SOURCE, THE
1 Bass Pro Mills Dr, Concord, ON, L4K 5W4
(905) 761-7453
Emp Here 25
SIC 5999 Miscellaneous retail stores, nec

D-U-N-S 24-462-8061   (HQ)
SPIRAX SARCO CANADA LIMITED
SPIRAX SARCO
(*Suby of* SPIRAX-SARCO ENGINEERING PLC)
383 Applewood Cres, Concord, ON, L4K 4J3
(905) 660-5510
Emp Here 29   *Emp Total* 4,998
Sales 9,484,891
SIC 5075 Warm air heating and air conditioning
Pr Mike Gillick

D-U-N-S 25-360-3104   (BR)
SUNOPTA INC
SUNOPTA FOOD DISTRIBUTION GROUP
8755 Keele St, Concord, ON, L4K 2N1
(905) 738-4304
Emp Here 130
SIC 5149 Groceries and related products, nec

D-U-N-S 24-693-3675   (HQ)
SUNPROJECT OF CANADA INC
(*Suby of* Sunproject Of Canada Inc)
511 Edgeley Blvd, Concord, ON, L4K 4G4
(905) 660-3117
Emp Here 45   *Emp Total* 47
Sales 10,148,480
SIC 2591 Drapery hardware and window blinds and shades
Pr Pr Enrico Nardone
VP VP Luca Giovannoni
Dir Ginni Bermagaschi

D-U-N-S 20-551-6503   (HQ)
SUNRISE MEDICAL CANADA INC
(*Suby of* V.S.M. Investors, LLC)
237 Romina Dr Unit 3, Concord, ON, L4K 4V3
(905) 660-2459
Emp Here 41   *Emp Total* 4,500
Sales 7,441,991
SIC 5047 Medical and hospital equipment
Pr Michel Papillon

D-U-N-S 24-764-3232   (SL)
SUNSWEET FUNDRAISING INC
30 Rayette Rd, Concord, ON, L4K 2G3
(905) 669-6600
Emp Here 100   *Sales* 5,540,856

SIC 5145 Confectionery
Pr Pr Howard Garr
Fin Ex Joanne Marchese

D-U-N-S 24-857-2609   (BR)
SUPERIOR PLUS LP
WINROC
225 Spinnaker Way Suite 2, Concord, ON, L4K 5T8
(905) 660-4456
Emp Here 20
SIC 5039 Construction materials, nec

D-U-N-S 20-291-5724   (HQ)
SUPERIOR SEATING HOSPITALITY INC
SUPERIOR FRAMES
(*Suby of* Superior Seating Hospitality Inc)
212 Millway Ave, Concord, ON, L4K 3W4
(905) 738-7900
Emp Here 70   *Emp Total* 90
Sales 3,808,655
SIC 2599 Furniture and fixtures, nec

D-U-N-S 20-700-7241   (BR)
SYSCO CANADA, INC
SYSCO FINE MEATS OF TORONTO
(*Suby of* Sysco Corporation)
1400 Creditstone Rd Suite B, Concord, ON, L4K 0E2
(905) 760-7200
Emp Here 75
SIC 2011 Meat packing plants

D-U-N-S 20-943-3416   (SL)
TARGET INVESTIGATION & SECURITY LTD
2900 Langstaff Rd Unit 3, Concord, ON, L4K 4R9
(905) 760-9090
Emp Here 85   *Sales* 2,626,585
SIC 7381 Detective and armored car services

D-U-N-S 24-126-5706   (BR)
TEKNION LIMITED
TEKNION FORM
1400 Alness St Unit 12, Concord, ON, L4K 2W6
(905) 669-2035
Emp Here 120
SIC 2522 Office furniture, except wood

D-U-N-S 20-145-4311   (HQ)
THYSSENKRUPP MATERIALS CA, LTD
THYSSENKRUPP MATERIALS NA
2821 Langstaff Rd, Concord, ON, L4K 5C6
(905) 669-0247
Emp Here 300   *Emp Total* 155,584
Sales 100,466,884
SIC 6221 Commodity contracts brokers, dealers
VP James Tatsakos
Dir Norbert Goertz

D-U-N-S 25-086-6241   (SL)
TIAKA FOODS INC
KFC / PIZZA HUT
10 Jacob Keffer Pky Unit 1, Concord, ON, L4K 5E3
(905) 303-7244
Emp Here 50   *Sales* 1,532,175
SIC 5812 Eating places

D-U-N-S 20-983-6352   (HQ)
TOKMAKJIAN INC
CAN-AR COACH, DIV OF
221 Caldari Rd, Concord, ON, L4K 3Z9
(905) 669-2850
Emp Here 100   *Emp Total* 2
Sales 16,562,079
SIC 4142 Bus charter service, except local
Pr Pr Cy Tokmakjian
Fin Ex Robert Duni
     Ajay Mehra

D-U-N-S 24-390-6992   (BR)
TOOTSIE ROLL OF CANADA ULC
CONCORD CONFECTIONS
(*Suby of* Tootsie Roll Industries, Inc.)
519 North Rivermede Rd, Concord, ON, L4K

3N1
(905) 738-9108
Emp Here 300
SIC 2064 Candy and other confectionery products

D-U-N-S 25-989-4004   (HQ)
TOROMONT ENERGY LTD
3131 Highway 7 Suite A, Concord, ON, L4K 5E1
(416) 667-5758
Emp Here 24   *Emp Total* 3,600
Sales 11,965,555
SIC 4911 Electric services
Dir Robert M Ogilvie

D-U-N-S 25-317-4056   (BR)
TOROMONT INDUSTRIES LTD
TOROMONT REMAN
548 Edgeley Blvd, Concord, ON, L4K 4G4
(416) 667-5900
Emp Here 150
SIC 5082 Construction and mining machinery

D-U-N-S 20-860-5381   (BR)
TOWN SHOES LIMITED
SHOE COMPANY, THE
1 Bass Pro Mills Dr Suite 330, Concord, ON, L4K 5W4
(905) 669-2828
Emp Here 25
SIC 5661 Shoe stores

D-U-N-S 24-450-8503   (HQ)
TOYS 'R' US (CANADA) LTD
(*Suby of* Toys "r" Us, Inc.)
2777 Langstaff Rd, Concord, ON, L4K 4M5
(905) 660-2000
Emp Here 250   *Emp Total* 64,000
Sales 176,628,579
SIC 5945 Hobby, toy, and game shops
Pr Pr Kevin J Macnab
VP VP Robert Zara
VP Fin Pasquale Naccarato

D-U-N-S 25-167-4479   (HQ)
TRANSCARE SUPPLY CHAIN MANAGEMENT INC
7491 Jane St Unit 3, Concord, ON, L4K 2M7

Emp Here 23   *Emp Total* 498,459
Sales 4,334,713
SIC 4226 Special warehousing and storage, nec

D-U-N-S 25-116-8761   (BR)
TRIMAC TRANSPORTATION SERVICES LIMITED PARTNERSHIP
CARGO FLOW TERMINAL
8820 Keele St, Concord, ON, L4K 2N2
(905) 669-3330
Emp Here 40
SIC 4213 Trucking, except local

D-U-N-S 20-734-3539   (BR)
UPS SCS, INC
UPS SUPPLY CHAIN SOLUTION
777 Creditstone Rd, Concord, ON, L4K 5R5
(905) 660-6040
Emp Here 100
SIC 7389 Business services, nec

D-U-N-S 24-424-1261   (SL)
UNIQUE STORE FIXTURES LTD
SIGNATURE SHOWCASE DIV
554 Millway Ave, Concord, ON, L4K 3V5
(905) 738-6588
Emp Here 65   *Sales* 4,377,642
SIC 2541 Wood partitions and fixtures

D-U-N-S 24-924-7255   (BR)
UNITED PARCEL SERVICE CANADA LTD
UPS CANADA
2900 Steeles Ave W, Concord, ON, L4K 3S2
(905) 660-8595
Emp Here 120
SIC 4212 Local trucking, without storage

D-U-N-S 24-340-3594   (BR)
VLR FOOD CORPORATION
575 Oster Lane, Concord, ON, L4K 2B9
(905) 669-0700
Emp Here 50
SIC 2038 Frozen specialties, nec

D-U-N-S 24-314-4404   (BR)
VPC GROUP INC
ENGINEERED FOAM PRODUCTS CANADA, DIV OF
(*Suby of* VPC Group Inc)
111 Snidercroft Rd Unit B, Concord, ON, L4K 2J8

Emp Here 46
SIC 5999 Miscellaneous retail stores, nec

D-U-N-S 25-679-5431   (BR)
VALEANT CANADA LP
BAUSCH & LOMB CANADA
(*Suby of* Valeant Canada LP)
520 Applewood Cres Suite 2, Concord, ON, L4K 4B4
(905) 695-7700
Emp Here 30
SIC 5122 Drugs, proprietaries, and sundries

D-U-N-S 25-981-7484   (BR)
VALUE VILLAGE STORES, INC
VALUE VILLAGE
(*Suby of* Savers, Inc.)
1520 Steeles Ave W, Concord, ON, L4K 3B9
(905) 761-7990
Emp Here 50
SIC 5399 Miscellaneous general merchandise

D-U-N-S 20-195-2699   (SL)
VAUGHAN SPORTS VILLAGE INC
SPORTS VILLAGE
2600 Rutherford Rd, Concord, ON, L4K 5R1
(905) 738-7574
Emp Here 50   *Sales* 2,699,546
SIC 7999 Amusement and recreation, nec

D-U-N-S 20-105-0882   (SL)
VEGEWAX CANDLEWORX LTD
SCENTS ALIVE
300 North Rivermede Rd, Concord, ON, L4K 3N6
(905) 760-7942
Emp Here 50   *Sales* 3,502,114
SIC 2844 Toilet preparations

D-U-N-S 25-341-7455   (SL)
VILLA DI MANNO BAKERY LTD
22 Buttermill Ave, Concord, ON, L4K 3X4
(905) 761-9191
Emp Here 67   *Sales* 4,523,179
SIC 2051 Bread, cake, and related products

D-U-N-S 25-498-2507   (BR)
WAL-MART CANADA CORP
101 Edgeley Blvd Suite 3145, Concord, ON, L4K 4Z4
(905) 761-7945
Emp Here 400
SIC 5311 Department stores

D-U-N-S 25-362-8093   (BR)
WASTE MANAGEMENT OF CANADA CORPORATION
(*Suby of* Waste Management, Inc.)
550 Bowes Rd, Concord, ON, L4K 1K2
(905) 669-7196
Emp Here 80
SIC 4953 Refuse systems

D-U-N-S 25-693-5107   (SL)
WELDA WINDOWS INDUSTRIES
1950a Highway 7 Suite 26, Concord, ON, L4K 3P2
(416) 667-1444
Emp Here 50   *Sales* 4,851,006
SIC 2431 Millwork

D-U-N-S 25-193-0327   (BR)
WELDED TUBE OF CANADA CORP
MAKSTEEL SERVICE CENTRE, DIV OF

111 Rayette Rd, Concord, ON, L4K 2E9
(905) 669-1111
Emp Here 300
SIC 5051 Metals service centers and offices

D-U-N-S 20-179-3713   (BR)
WELDED TUBE OF CANADA CORP
541 Bowes Rd, Concord, ON, L4K 1J5
(905) 761-7825
Emp Here 150
SIC 3317 Steel pipe and tubes

D-U-N-S 24-224-5558   (BR)
WENDY'S RESTAURANTS OF CANADA INC
WENDY'S
(*Suby of* The Wendy's Company)
1600 Langstaff Rd, Concord, ON, L4K 3S3
(905) 669-6163
Emp Here 30
SIC 5812 Eating places

D-U-N-S 20-643-0618   (BR)
WENDY'S RESTAURANTS OF CANADA INC
(*Suby of* The Wendy's Company)
9151 Keele St, Concord, ON, L4K 5B4
(905) 832-1257
Emp Here 30
SIC 5812 Eating places

D-U-N-S 20-181-8270   (BR)
WESTON BAKERIES LIMITED
273 Edgeley Blvd, Concord, ON, L4K 3Y7
(905) 660-1440
Emp Here 20
SIC 2051 Bread, cake, and related products

D-U-N-S 20-057-5616   (HQ)
WHITESELL CANADA CORPORATION
(*Suby of* Whitesell Canada Corporation)
590 Basaltic Rd, Concord, ON, L4K 5A2
(905) 879-0433
Emp Here 50   *Emp Total* 58
Sales 11,235,948
SIC 5085 Industrial supplies
  Neil Whitesell
Pr Peter Kapogines

D-U-N-S 20-271-5017   (SL)
WINDSOR GREEN HOMES INC
171 Basaltic Rd Suite 1, Concord, ON, L4K 1G4
(905) 669-5003
Emp Here 25   *Sales* 6,898,600
SIC 1522 Residential construction, nec
Pr Marc Muzzo
  Morris Atamanchuk

D-U-N-S 24-312-4364   (BR)
WINNERS MERCHANTS INTERNATIONAL L.P.
WINNERS
(*Suby of* The TJX Companies Inc)
1 Bass Pro Mill Dr, Concord, ON, L4K 5N4
(905) 660-0595
Emp Here 30
SIC 5651 Family clothing stores

D-U-N-S 25-332-5203   (BR)
WOLSELEY CANADA INC
(*Suby of* WOLSELEY PLC)
1290 Creditstone Unit 1&2, Concord, ON, L4K 5T7
(905) 879-0034
Emp Here 40
SIC 1711 Plumbing, heating, air-conditioning

D-U-N-S 25-117-5113   (SL)
YONGE BAYVIEW HOLDINGS INC
30 Floral Pky, Concord, ON, L4K 4R1
(905) 669-9714
Emp Here 25   *Sales* 7,952,716
SIC 6552 Subdividers and developers, nec
Dir Alfredo Degasperis
Dir Marc A Muzzo

D-U-N-S 25-106-9522   (BR)
YORK CATHOLIC DISTRICT SCHOOL BOARD

OUR LADY OF THE ROSARY ELEMENTARY SCHOOL
206 Glen Shields Ave, Concord, ON, L4K 1T8
(905) 669-6690
Emp Here 40
SIC 8211 Elementary and secondary schools

D-U-N-S 25-297-9067   (BR)
YORK REGION DISTRICT SCHOOL BOARD
GLEN SHIELDS PUBLIC SCHOOL
(*Suby of* York Region District School Board)
158 Glen Shields Ave, Concord, ON, L4K 1T8
(905) 738-0333
Emp Here 46
SIC 8211 Elementary and secondary schools

D-U-N-S 24-020-9366   (BR)
IMARKETING SOLUTIONS GROUP INC
8000 Jane St Suite 401, Concord, ON, L4K 5B8

Emp Here 30
SIC 8399 Social services, nec

D-U-N-S 24-042-8909   (HQ)
MORTGAGEBROKERS.COM INC
(*Suby of* mortgagebrokers.com Inc)
260 Edgeley Blvd Suite 11, Concord, ON, L4K 3Y4
(877) 410-4848
Emp Here 300   *Emp Total* 330
Sales 82,896,000
SIC 6163 Loan brokers
  Alex Haditaghi
VP Opers Dong Lee
VP Sls Gary Laughlin
  Robert Hyde
Fin Ex Davindra (David) Persaud
VP Sls Lindsay Miller

Conestogo, ON N0B
Waterloo County

D-U-N-S 20-025-5060   (BR)
WATERLOO REGION DISTRICT SCHOOL BOARD
CONESTOGO PUBLIC SCHOOL
1948 Sawmill Rd Ss 6, Conestogo, ON, N0B 1N0
(519) 664-3773
Emp Here 26
SIC 8211 Elementary and secondary schools

Coniston, ON P0M
Sudbury County

D-U-N-S 20-157-7819   (BR)
CONSEIL SCOLAIRE DE DISTRICT CATHOLIQUE DU NOUVEL-ONTARIO, LE
ECOLE NOPRE GANE DE LA MERCI
2 Edward Ave, Coniston, ON, P0M 1M0
(705) 694-4402
Emp Here 20
SIC 8211 Elementary and secondary schools

D-U-N-S 25-239-0505   (BR)
SUDBURY CATHOLIC DISTRICT SCHOOL BOARD
ST PAUL THE APOSTLE SCHOOL
1 Edward Ave, Coniston, ON, P0M 1M0
(705) 694-4482
Emp Here 30
SIC 8211 Elementary and secondary schools

Consecon, ON K0K
Prince Edward County

D-U-N-S 20-714-1248   (SL)

BAYFIELD SCHOOL INC
30 County Road 39, Consecon, ON, K0K 1T0
(613) 392-3551
Emp Here 50   *Sales* 3,356,192
SIC 8211 Elementary and secondary schools

Cookstown, ON L0L
Simcoe County

D-U-N-S 24-735-9672   (SL)
COOKSTOWN AUTO CENTRE LTD
5046 5th, Cookstown, ON, L0L 1L0
(416) 364-0743
Emp Here 29   *Sales* 7,077,188
SIC 5093 Scrap and waste materials
Pr Pr John Bucko Sr
 Olive Bucko

D-U-N-S 25-318-1895   (BR)
**MCDONALD'S   RESTAURANTS   OF
CANADA LIMITED**
MCDONALD'S
(*Suby of* McDonald's Corporation)
3464 County Rd 89, Cookstown, ON, L0L 1L0

Emp Here 100
SIC 5812 Eating places

D-U-N-S 25-497-8646   (SL)
ONTARIO STOCKYARDS INC
3807 89 Hwy, Cookstown, ON, L0L 1L0
(705) 458-4000
Emp Here 30   *Sales* 35,000,250
SIC 5154 Livestock
Pr Wayne Small

D-U-N-S 20-711-2082   (BR)
**SIMCOE   COUNTY   DISTRICT   SCHOOL
BOARD, THE**
TECUMSETH NORTH PUBLIC SCHOOL
(*Suby of* Simcoe County District School
Board, The)
4063 10th Side Rd, Cookstown, ON, L0L 1L0

Emp Here 20
SIC 8211 Elementary and secondary schools

D-U-N-S 25-297-6485   (BR)
**SIMCOE   COUNTY   DISTRICT   SCHOOL
BOARD, THE**
COOKSTOWN CENTRAL PUBLIC SCHOOL
(*Suby of* Simcoe County District School
Board, The)
5088 County Road 27, Cookstown, ON, L0L
1L0
(705) 458-4461
Emp Here 45
SIC 8211 Elementary and secondary schools

D-U-N-S 20-700-4610   (BR)
TOMMY HILFIGER CANADA INC
TOMMY HILFIGER OUTLET
3311 County Rd 89 Unit B26, Cookstown, ON,
L0L 1L0
(705) 458-8601
Emp Here 30
SIC 5651 Family clothing stores

Copper Cliff, ON P0M
Sudbury County

D-U-N-S 20-042-9447   (HQ)
**CLARKE   PHILLIPS   SUPPLY   COMPANY
LIMITED**
NORTHWEAR
(*Suby of* Clarke Phillips Supply Company Limited)
7 Temperance St, Copper Cliff, ON, P0M 1N0

Emp Here 21   *Emp Total* 27
Sales 6,407,837

SIC 5136 Men's and boy's clothing
Pr Pr Carl Nurmi
VP VP Joan Nurmi
 Karl Nurmi
 Andrea Miller
Recvr George Medakovic

D-U-N-S 20-913-6790   (BR)
RAINBOW DISTRICT SCHOOL BOARD
COPPER CLIFF PUBLIC SCHOOL
Gd, Copper Cliff, ON, P0M 1N0
(705) 682-4721
Emp Here 20
SIC 8211 Elementary and secondary schools

Corbeil, ON P0H
Nipissing County

D-U-N-S 20-704-5373   (BR)
NEAR NORTH DISTRICT SCHOOL BOARD
FERRIS GLEN PUBLIC SCHOOL
30 Voyer Rd, Corbeil, ON, P0H 1K0
(705) 475-2323
Emp Here 25
SIC 8211 Elementary and secondary schools

Corbyville, ON K0K
Hastings County

D-U-N-S 24-037-7197   (SL)
BLACK BEAR RIDGE INC
BLACK BEAR RIDGE GOLF COURSE
501 Harmony Rd, Corbyville, ON, K0K 1V0
(613) 968-2327
Emp Here 50   *Sales* 2,188,821
SIC 7992 Public golf courses

D-U-N-S 25-265-3910   (BR)
**HASTINGS AND PRINCE EDWARD DIS-
TRICT SCHOOL BOARD**
*HASTINGS AND PRINCE EDWARD DIS-
TRICT SCHOOL BOARD*
626 Harmony Rd, Corbyville, ON, K0K 1V0
(613) 962-7867
Emp Here 28
SIC 8211 Elementary and secondary schools

Cornwall, ON K6H
Stormont County

D-U-N-S 25-221-9183   (SL)
1036274 ONTARIO INC
FIFTH WHEEL CORNWALL
1901 Mcconnell Ave Ss 42, Cornwall, ON,
K6H 0B9
(613) 933-8363
Emp Here 50   *Sales* 1,532,175
SIC 5812 Eating places

D-U-N-S 25-138-5266   (SL)
1808963 ONTARIO INC
1495 Gerald St, Cornwall, ON, K6H 7G8
(613) 932-5326
Emp Here 91   *Sales* 3,118,504
SIC 7349 Building maintenance services, nec

D-U-N-S 24-324-0087   (BR)
AS CANADA, ULC
AMERICAN STANDARD
(*Suby of* AS Canada, ULC)
235 Saunders Dr, Cornwall, ON, K6H 5R6
(613) 933-0408
Emp Here 70
SIC 3431 Metal sanitary ware

D-U-N-S 24-977-2968   (BR)
AEVITAS INC
2425 Industrial Park Dr, Cornwall, ON, K6H
7M4

(613) 938-7575
Emp Here 20
SIC 4953 Refuse systems

D-U-N-S 20-420-8755   (SL)
AMSTERDAM PRODUCTS LTD
(*Suby of* Taylor Corporation)
2 Montreal Rd, Cornwall, ON, K6H 6L4
(613) 933-7393
Emp Here 80   *Sales* 5,182,810
SIC 7389 Business services, nec
Mgr Travis Seward
Pr Kim Broadhead

D-U-N-S 24-633-6507   (SL)
BEAUTYROCK INC
16 Second St E Suite A, Cornwall, ON, K6H
1Y3
(613) 932-2525
Emp Here 160   *Sales* 46,429,680
SIC 7389 Business services, nec
Pr Pr Stan Body

D-U-N-S 24-437-4492   (HQ)
BENAPAC INC
(*Suby of* Benapac Inc)
700 Education Rd, Cornwall, ON, K6H 6B8
(613) 933-1700
Emp Here 150   *Emp Total* 950
Sales 160,595,350
SIC 5013 Motor vehicle supplies and new
parts
Pr Pr Gerald Benson
VP VP Claudette Benson
 James Benson
Dir Marty Benson
Dir Kelly Benson

D-U-N-S 24-100-2245   (HQ)
BENSON GROUP INC
AUTO-PAK
(*Suby of* Benapac Inc)
700 Education Rd, Cornwall, ON, K6H 6B8
(613) 933-1700
Emp Here 50   *Emp Total* 950
Sales 109,441,050
SIC 5013 Motor vehicle supplies and new
parts
Pr Pr Martin Benson
 James Benson
 Gerald Benson
 Denis Mathieu
 Gary O'connor

D-U-N-S 20-936-4814   (BR)
BILLY K'S RESTAURANT INC
1380 Second St E, Cornwall, ON, K6H 2B8

Emp Here 20
SIC 5812 Eating places

D-U-N-S 24-426-1967   (SL)
CSH CHATEAU CORNWALL INC
CHATEAU CORNWALL
41 Amelia St Suite 109, Cornwall, ON, K6H
7E5
(613) 937-4700
Emp Here 20   *Sales* 729,607
SIC 8361 Residential care

D-U-N-S 20-573-0562   (BR)
CANADA POST CORPORATION
805 Boundary Rd Suite 2, Cornwall, ON, K6H
6K8
(613) 938-3911
Emp Here 70
SIC 4311 U.s. postal service

D-U-N-S 25-303-3914   (BR)
**CANADIAN IMPERIAL BANK OF COM-
MERCE**
CIBC
1 Second St W, Cornwall, ON, K6H 5E3
(613) 932-3200
Emp Here 20
SIC 6021 National commercial banks

D-U-N-S 20-557-9951   (BR)
CANADIAN RED CROSS SOCIETY, THE

165 Montreal Rd, Cornwall, ON, K6H 1B2
(613) 932-3412
Emp Here 95
SIC 8059 Nursing and personal care, nec

D-U-N-S 25-225-0386   (BR)
**CATHOLIC DISTRICT SCHOOL BOARD OF
EASTERN ONTARIO**
*BISHOP   MACDONELL   ELEMENTARY
SCHOOL*
(*Suby of* Catholic District School Board of
Eastern Ontario)
300 Adolphus St, Cornwall, ON, K6H 3S6
(613) 933-6739
Emp Here 45
SIC 8211 Elementary and secondary schools

D-U-N-S 25-137-3718   (BR)
**CATHOLIC DISTRICT SCHOOL BOARD OF
EASTERN ONTARIO**
IMMACULATE CONCEPTION SCHOOL
(*Suby of* Catholic District School Board of
Eastern Ontario)
600 Mcconnell Ave, Cornwall, ON, K6H 4M1
(613) 932-3455
Emp Here 25
SIC 8211 Elementary and secondary schools

D-U-N-S 24-676-4950   (BR)
**CATHOLIC DISTRICT SCHOOL BOARD OF
EASTERN ONTARIO**
*HOLY TRINITY CATHOLIC ELEMENTARY
SCHOOL*
18044 Tyotown Rd, Cornwall, ON, K6H 5R5
(613) 936-0319
Emp Here 50
SIC 8211 Elementary and secondary schools

D-U-N-S 20-711-5283   (BR)
**CATHOLIC DISTRICT SCHOOL BOARD OF
EASTERN ONTARIO**
ST PETER CATHOLIC SCHOOL
1811 Second St E, Cornwall, ON, K6H 6P1
(613) 933-1007
Emp Here 25
SIC 8211 Elementary and secondary schools

D-U-N-S 20-590-7277   (BR)
**CATHOLIC DISTRICT SCHOOL BOARD OF
EASTERN ONTARIO**
ST COLUMBUS EAST SCHOOL
300 Adolphus St, Cornwall, ON, K6H 3S6
(613) 932-7768
Emp Here 25
SIC 8211 Elementary and secondary schools

D-U-N-S 24-417-5613   (BR)
CINEPLEX ODEON CORPORATION
GALAXY CINEMAS CORNWALL
1325 Second St E, Cornwall, ON, K6H 7C4
(613) 933-7124
Emp Here 20
SIC 7832 Motion picture theaters, except
drive-in

D-U-N-S 20-573-2279   (BR)
**COMPAGNIE DES CHEMINS DE FER NA-
TIONAUX DU CANADA**
109a Balmoral St, Cornwall, ON, K6H 7E7
(613) 932-6533
Emp Here 20
SIC 4011 Railroads, line-haul operating

D-U-N-S 24-975-3088   (BR)
**CONSEIL   SCOLAIRE   DE   DISTRICT
CATHOLIQUE DE L'EST ONTARIEN**
*ECOLE SECONDAIRE CATHOLIQUE LA
CITADELLE*
510 Mcconnell Ave, Cornwall, ON, K6H 4M1
(613) 933-0172
Emp Here 90
SIC 8211 Elementary and secondary schools

D-U-N-S 25-224-9818   (BR)
**CONSEIL   SCOLAIRE   DE   DISTRICT
CATHOLIQUE DE L'EST ONTARIEN**
*ECOLE   ELEMENTAIRE   CATHOLIQUE
MARIE-TANGUAY*

(Suby of Conseil Scolaire De District Catholique De L'Est Ontarien)
1500 Holy Cross Blvd, Cornwall, ON, K6H 2X1
(613) 938-9337
Emp Here 25
SIC 8211 Elementary and secondary schools

D-U-N-S 20-592-0338   (BR)
CONSEIL DES ECOLES PUBLIQUES DE L'EST DE L'ONTARIO
ECOLE ELEMENTAIRE PUBLIQUE ROSE DES VENTS
1650 Second St E, Cornwall, ON, K6H 2C3
(613) 932-4183
Emp Here 25
SIC 8211 Elementary and secondary schools

D-U-N-S 20-653-1597   (BR)
CONSEIL DES ECOLES PUBLIQUES DE L'EST DE L'ONTARIO
ECOLE SECONDAIRE PUBLIQUE S'HEIRATAGE
1111 Montreal Rd, Cornwall, ON, K6H 1E1
(613) 933-3318
Emp Here 30
SIC 8211 Elementary and secondary schools

D-U-N-S 25-460-4457   (BR)
CORNWALL COMMUNITY HOSPITAL
TRI-COUNTY MENTAL HEALTH SERVICES
132 Second St E Unit 104, Cornwall, ON, K6H 1Y4
(613) 932-9940
Emp Here 20
SIC 8093 Specialty outpatient clinics, nec

D-U-N-S 24-101-3148   (BR)
CORPORATION OF THE CITY OF CORNWALL
MUNICIPAL WORKS AND SERVICES
1225 Ontario St, Cornwall, ON, K6H 4E1
(613) 930-2787
Emp Here 50
SIC 7699 Repair services, nec

D-U-N-S 25-092-2619   (BR)
CORPORATION OF THE CITY OF CORNWALL
PARKS & RECREATION SERVICES
100 Water St E, Cornwall, ON, K6H 6G4
(613) 933-3586
Emp Here 50
SIC 7999 Amusement and recreation, nec

D-U-N-S 24-204-9943   (BR)
CORUS ENTERTAINMENT INC
CJSS-FM
709 Cotton Mill St, Cornwall, ON, K6H 7K7
(613) 932-5180
Emp Here 35
SIC 7922 Theatrical producers and services

D-U-N-S 25-299-6863   (BR)
DOLLARAMA S.E.C.
DOLLARAMA LP
1380 Second St E Unit 20, Cornwall, ON, K6H 2B8
(613) 933-4028
Emp Here 26
SIC 5399 Miscellaneous general merchandise

D-U-N-S 25-357-3539   (BR)
DOREL INDUSTRIES INC
RIDGEWOOD INDUSTRIES
3305 Loyalist St, Cornwall, ON, K6H 6W6
(613) 937-0711
Emp Here 350
SIC 2511 Wood household furniture

D-U-N-S 24-390-4773   (BR)
DYER ROAD LEASING LTD
850 Education Rd, Cornwall, ON, K6H 6B8
(613) 932-1326
Emp Here 30
SIC 4213 Trucking, except local

D-U-N-S 25-767-9514   (BR)
FARM BOY 2012 INC

FARM BOY FRESH MARKETS
814 Sydney St, Cornwall, ON, K6H 3J8
(613) 938-8566
Emp Here 109
SIC 5431 Fruit and vegetable markets

D-U-N-S 25-486-4382   (BR)
GROUPE JEAN COUTU (PJC) INC, LE
JEAN COUTU 64
(Suby of 3958230 Canada Inc)
5 Ninth St E, Cornwall, ON, K6H 6R3
(613) 938-7339
Emp Here 45
SIC 5912 Drug stores and proprietary stores

D-U-N-S 24-314-1160   (BR)
HOME HARDWARE STORES LIMITED
10 Thirteenth St E, Cornwall, ON, K6H 6V9
(613) 932-3225
Emp Here 20
SIC 5072 Hardware

D-U-N-S 20-105-7374   (BR)
JOHNS MANVILLE CANADA INC
(Suby of Berkshire Hathaway Inc.)
3330 Marleau Ave, Cornwall, ON, K6H 6B5
(613) 932-4565
Emp Here 40
SIC 3299 NonMetallic mineral products,

D-U-N-S 24-270-5762   (BR)
MARIMAC INC
(Suby of 3476847 Canada Inc)
3400 Montreal Rd, Cornwall, ON, K6H 5R5
(613) 937-4777
Emp Here 35
SIC 2258 Lace and warp knit fabric mills

D-U-N-S 24-827-8371   (BR)
MATRIX LOGISTICS SERVICES LIMITED
1330 Optimum Dr, Cornwall, ON, K6H 0B1
(613) 361-3860
Emp Here 30
SIC 4225 General warehousing and storage

D-U-N-S 25-672-3248   (BR)
METRO ONTARIO INC
METRO
1315 Second St E Unit 282, Cornwall, ON, K6H 7C4
(613) 932-0514
Emp Here 80
SIC 5411 Grocery stores

D-U-N-S 20-002-9549   (SL)
MISTEREL INC
CANADIAN TIRE ASSOCIATE STORE, DIV OF
201 Ninth St E, Cornwall, ON, K6H 2V1
(613) 933-0592
Emp Here 50   Sales 4,815,406
SIC 5251 Hardware stores

D-U-N-S 20-902-7957   (BR)
MUNICIPAL PROPERTY ASSESSMENT CORPORATION
132 Second St E Suite 201, Cornwall, ON, K6H 1Y4
(613) 933-7249
Emp Here 22
SIC 7389 Business services, nec

D-U-N-S 25-971-6280   (BR)
NAV CANADA
NAV CENTRE
1950 Montreal Rd, Cornwall, ON, K6H 6L2
(613) 936-5050
Emp Here 210
SIC 8249 Vocational schools, nec

D-U-N-S 20-746-6467   (SL)
NORBRO HOLDINGS LTD
BEST WESTERN PARKWAY INN
1515 Vincent Massey Dr, Cornwall, ON, K6H 5R6
(613) 932-0451
Emp Here 95   Sales 4,158,760
SIC 7011 Hotels and motels

D-U-N-S 20-255-6130   (BR)
OLYMEL S.E.C.
2330 Industrial Park Dr, Cornwall, ON, K6H 7N1
(613) 323-3040
Emp Here 200
SIC 2011 Meat packing plants

D-U-N-S 24-852-8007   (BR)
OTTAWA-CARLETON ASSOCIATION FOR PERSONS WITH DEVELOPMENTAL DISABILITIES
OPEN HANDS
1141 Sydney St Unit 1, Cornwall, ON, K6H 7C2
(613) 933-9520
Emp Here 100
SIC 8322 Individual and family services

D-U-N-S 20-859-9493   (BR)
PACIFIC LINK COMMUNICATIONS INC
BELL WORLD
1 Water St E, Cornwall, ON, K6H 6M2
(613) 932-1676
Emp Here 25
SIC 5999 Miscellaneous retail stores, nec

D-U-N-S 20-844-5945   (BR)
PEPSICO CANADA ULC
FRITO LAY CANADA
(Suby of Pepsico, Inc.)
18075 Tyotown Rd, Cornwall, ON, K6H 5R5

Emp Here 20
SIC 2096 Potato chips and similar snacks

D-U-N-S 24-987-2441   (BR)
PHILIPS LIGHTING CANADA LTD
CANADIAN FLUORESCENT INDUSTRIES
525 Education Rd, Cornwall, ON, K6H 6C7

Emp Here 120
SIC 3641 Electric lamps

D-U-N-S 24-977-4993   (BR)
POLYONE DSS CANADA INC
SPARTECH PLASTICS
2950 Marleau Ave, Cornwall, ON, K6H 6B5

Emp Here 37
SIC 3083 Laminated plastics plate and sheet

D-U-N-S 25-320-9118   (BR)
PUROLATOR INC.
PUROLATOR INC
725 Boundary Rd, Cornwall, ON, K6H 6K8
(613) 932-5509
Emp Here 30
SIC 7389 Business services, nec

D-U-N-S 25-963-6900   (BR)
REDBERRY FRANCHISING CORP
BURGER KING
1317 Second St E, Cornwall, ON, K6H 7C4
(613) 937-3877
Emp Here 22
SIC 5812 Eating places

D-U-N-S 25-311-1363   (BR)
SEARS CANADA INC
1 Water St E, Cornwall, ON, K6H 6M2
(613) 938-9305
Emp Here 200
SIC 5311 Department stores

D-U-N-S 25-204-4904   (SL)
SEAWAY EXPRESS INC
605 Boundary Rd, Cornwall, ON, K6H 6K8
(613) 933-8984
Emp Here 50   Sales 3,939,878
SIC 4212 Local trucking, without storage

D-U-N-S 24-860-6543   (SL)
SEAWAY INTERNATIONAL BRIDGE CORPORATION LTD, THE
Gd Stn Main, Cornwall, ON, K6H 5R8
(613) 932-6601
Emp Here 20   Sales 10,568,262

SIC 4785 Inspection and fixed facilities
Genl Mgr Hendrik H Saaltink
Pr Pr Micheline Dube
VP VP Sal Pisani
Sec Norman Willans
Guy Berthiaume

D-U-N-S 25-282-7142   (BR)
SODEXO CANADA LTD
1950 Montreal Rd, Cornwall, ON, K6H 6L2
(613) 936-5800
Emp Here 150
SIC 5812 Eating places

D-U-N-S 25-464-3828   (BR)
ST. LAWRENCE COLLEGE OF APPLIED ARTS AND TECHNOLOGY, THE
ST LAWRENCE COLLEGE/ ONT SKILL
2 St Lawrence Dr, Cornwall, ON, K6H 4Z1
(613) 933-6080
Emp Here 600
SIC 8221 Colleges and universities

D-U-N-S 20-312-0563   (BR)
STAPLES CANADA INC
(Suby of Staples, Inc.)
7 Ninth St E, Cornwall, ON, K6H 6R3
(613) 936-6952
Emp Here 20
SIC 5943 Stationery stores

D-U-N-S 24-201-8997   (BR)
TDL GROUP CORP, THE
TIM HORTONS
360 Balmoral Ave, Cornwall, ON, K6H 6K1
(613) 933-3386
Emp Here 25
SIC 5812 Eating places

D-U-N-S 24-308-9690   (BR)
TALLMAN TRUCK CENTRE LIMITED
1750 Mcconnell Ave, Cornwall, ON, K6H 0C1
(613) 933-4425
Emp Here 30
SIC 7538 General automotive repair shops

D-U-N-S 24-003-8757   (BR)
TRIOVEST REALTY ADVISORS INC
CORNWALL SQUARE
1 Water St E, Cornwall, ON, K6H 6M2
(613) 938-2118
Emp Here 20
SIC 6512 Nonresidential building operators

D-U-N-S 20-733-5147   (BR)
UNION GAS LIMITED
SPECTRA ENERGY COMPANY
2910 Copeland St, Cornwall, ON, K6H 6W2
(613) 933-3534
Emp Here 22
SIC 4923 Gas transmission and distribution

D-U-N-S 25-246-3765   (BR)
UNIVERSITY OF OTTAWA
SCHOOL OF PSYCHOLOGY
610 Mcconnell Ave, Cornwall, ON, K6H 4M1
(613) 938-6989
Emp Here 50
SIC 8221 Colleges and universities

D-U-N-S 20-711-5598   (BR)
UPPER CANADA DISTRICT SCHOOL BOARD, THE
CENTRAL PUBLIC SCHOOL
200 Amelia St Suite 1, Cornwall, ON, K6H 0A5
(613) 932-0857
Emp Here 20
SIC 8211 Elementary and secondary schools

D-U-N-S 20-655-1629   (BR)
UPPER CANADA DISTRICT SCHOOL BOARD, THE
ST LAWRENCE SECONDARY SCHOOL
1450 Second St E, Cornwall, ON, K6H 5Z8
(613) 933-8410
Emp Here 40
SIC 8211 Elementary and secondary schools

D-U-N-S 25-138-2677   (BR)

UPPER CANADA DISTRICT SCHOOL BOARD, THE
CORNWALL COLLEGIATE & VOCATIONAL SCHOOL
(*Suby of* Upper Canada District School Board, The)
437 Sydney St, Cornwall, ON, K6H 3H9
(613) 932-8360
Emp Here 70
SIC 8211 Elementary and secondary schools

D-U-N-S 20-552-0492 (BR)
VALSPAR INC
(*Suby of* The Sherwin-Williams Company)
1915 Second St W, Cornwall, ON, K6H 5R6
(613) 932-8960
Emp Here 130
SIC 2821 Plastics materials and resins

D-U-N-S 24-347-2516 (BR)
WAL-MART CANADA CORP
6227 Boundary Rd, Cornwall, ON, K6H 5R5
(613) 932-7879
Emp Here 75
SIC 4212 Local trucking, without storage

D-U-N-S 20-333-2437 (BR)
WAL-MART CANADA CORP
1501 Industrial Park Dr, Cornwall, ON, K6H 7M4
(613) 933-8665
Emp Here 40
SIC 4225 General warehousing and storage

D-U-N-S 20-106-2929 (BR)
WINNERS MERCHANTS INTERNATIONAL L.P.
WINNERS
(*Suby of* The TJX Companies Inc)
501 Tollgate Rd W, Cornwall, ON, K6H 0B4
(613) 936-8099
Emp Here 35
SIC 5651 Family clothing stores

Cornwall, ON K6J
Stormont County

D-U-N-S 25-278-8583 (SL)
458422 ONTARIO LIMITED
SANDFIELD PLACE
220 Emma Ave, Cornwall, ON, K6J 5V8
(613) 933-6972
Emp Here 70 *Sales* 3,210,271
SIC 8051 Skilled nursing care facilities

D-U-N-S 20-113-1088 (BR)
ARCHITECTURE49 INC
1345 Rosemount Ave, Cornwall, ON, K6J 3E5
(613) 933-5602
Emp Here 55
SIC 8711 Engineering services

D-U-N-S 20-577-7238 (BR)
BASF CANADA INC
501 Wallrich Ave, Cornwall, ON, K6J 2B5
(613) 933-5330
Emp Here 21
SIC 2821 Plastics materials and resins

D-U-N-S 24-745-7088 (BR)
BANK OF MONTREAL
BANK OF MONTREAL
159 Pitt St, Cornwall, ON, K6J 3P5
(613) 938-5617
Emp Here 26
SIC 6021 National commercial banks

D-U-N-S 25-487-3540 (BR)
BAYSHORE HEALTHCARE LTD.
BAYSHORE HOME HEALTH
112 Second St W, Cornwall, ON, K6J 1G5
(613) 938-1691
Emp Here 100
SIC 8082 Home health care services

D-U-N-S 20-513-8402 (BR)
BRENNTAG CANADA INC
BRENNTAG CORNWALL PLANT
730 Seventh St W, Cornwall, ON, K6J 5Y1
(613) 937-4004
Emp Here 25
SIC 7389 Business services, nec

D-U-N-S 25-301-5184 (HQ)
CANADIAN MENTAL HEALTH ASSOCIATION-CHAMPLAIN EST
CMHA
(*Suby of* Canadian Mental Health Association-Champlain Est)
329 Pitt St, Cornwall, ON, K6J 3R1
(613) 933-5845
Emp Here 50 *Emp Total* 50
Sales 1,081,986
SIC 8011 Offices and clinics of medical doctors

D-U-N-S 25-370-3102 (BR)
CAPITAL SECURITY & INVESTIGATIONS
(*Suby of* Capital Security & Investigations)
504 Pitt St, Cornwall, ON, K6J 3R5
(613) 937-4111
Emp Here 120
SIC 7381 Detective and armored car services

D-U-N-S 20-809-7886 (BR)
CARA OPERATIONS LIMITED
KELSEY'S RESTAURANT
(*Suby of* Cara Holdings Limited)
960 Brookdale Ave Suite 18, Cornwall, ON, K6J 4P5
(613) 930-2353
Emp Here 75
SIC 5812 Eating places

D-U-N-S 25-137-3726 (BR)
CATHOLIC DISTRICT SCHOOL BOARD OF EASTERN ONTARIO
ST JOSEPH'S SECONDARY SCHOOL
(*Suby of* Catholic District School Board of Eastern Ontario)
1500a Cumberland St, Cornwall, ON, K6J 5V9
(613) 932-0349
Emp Here 100
SIC 8211 Elementary and secondary schools

D-U-N-S 20-590-7327 (BR)
CATHOLIC DISTRICT SCHOOL BOARD OF EASTERN ONTARIO
ST ANNE SCHOOL
607 Surgenor St, Cornwall, ON, K6J 2H5
(613) 933-4615
Emp Here 25
SIC 8211 Elementary and secondary schools

D-U-N-S 25-224-9628 (BR)
CATHOLIC DISTRICT SCHOOL BOARD OF EASTERN ONTARIO
SACRED HEART SCHOOL
(*Suby of* Catholic District School Board of Eastern Ontario)
1424 Aubin Ave, Cornwall, ON, K6J 4S2
(613) 933-3337
Emp Here 33
SIC 8211 Elementary and secondary schools

D-U-N-S 20-711-5234 (BR)
CATHOLIC DISTRICT SCHOOL BOARD OF EASTERN ONTARIO
ST COLUMBAN'S WEST SCHOOL
323 Augustus St, Cornwall, ON, K6J 3W4
(613) 933-3113
Emp Here 30
SIC 8211 Elementary and secondary schools

D-U-N-S 20-043-5246 (BR)
COMPAGNIE CANADIAN TECHNICAL TAPE LTEE
CANTECH
1400 Rosemount Ave, Cornwall, ON, K6J 3E6
(613) 932-3105
Emp Here 80
SIC 2672 Paper; coated and laminated, nec

D-U-N-S 20-592-0486 (BR)
CONSEIL SCOLAIRE DE DISTRICT CATHOLIQUE DE L'EST ONTARIEN
ECOLE ELEMENTAIRE CATHOLIQUE NOTRE-DAME
420 Fifteenth St W, Cornwall, ON, K6J 3K5
(613) 936-8457
Emp Here 35
SIC 8211 Elementary and secondary schools

D-U-N-S 25-960-7687 (BR)
CORPORATION OF THE CITY OF CORNWALL
CORNWALL TRANSIT
863 Second St W, Cornwall, ON, K6J 1H5
(613) 930-2636
Emp Here 50
SIC 4141 Local bus charter service

D-U-N-S 25-370-3565 (BR)
DOLLARAMA S.E.C.
DOLLARAMA
1400 Vincent Massey Dr, Cornwall, ON, K6J 5N4
(613) 930-2464
Emp Here 23
SIC 5331 Variety stores

D-U-N-S 25-918-2830 (BR)
EXTENDICARE (CANADA) INC
PARAMED HOME HEALTH CARE
812 Pitt St Suite 16, Cornwall, ON, K6J 5R1
(613) 932-4661
Emp Here 265
SIC 8051 Skilled nursing care facilities

D-U-N-S 25-318-9112 (BR)
FIRSTCANADA ULC
FIRST STUDENT CANADA
120 Tollgate Rd W Suite 204, Cornwall, ON, K6J 5M3
(613) 938-8000
Emp Here 55
SIC 4151 School buses

D-U-N-S 20-894-3464 (SL)
GREAT LAKES PILOTAGE AUTHORITY
202 Pitt St 2nd Fl, Cornwall, ON, K6J 3P7
(613) 933-2991
Emp Here 80 *Sales* 6,879,002
SIC 4499 Water transportation services,
Robert Lemire
Rejean Menard
Dir Opers Daniel Trottier

D-U-N-S 20-553-6282 (BR)
HOME DEPOT OF CANADA INC
HOME DEPOT
(*Suby of* The Home Depot Inc)
1825 Brookdale Ave, Cornwall, ON, K6J 5X7
(613) 930-4470
Emp Here 100
SIC 5211 Lumber and other building materials

D-U-N-S 20-005-5965 (SL)
M & K RESTAURANT MANAGEMENT (CORNWALL) INC
WENDY'S RESTAURANT
1397 Brookdale Ave, Cornwall, ON, K6J 5X1
(613) 932-0995
Emp Here 70 *Sales* 2,115,860
SIC 5812 Eating places

D-U-N-S 20-793-1838 (BR)
METRO ONTARIO INC
FOOD BASICS
960 Brookdale Ave Suite 16, Cornwall, ON, K6J 4P5
(613) 933-4341
Emp Here 50
SIC 5411 Grocery stores

D-U-N-S 25-187-5043 (BR)
METRO RICHELIEU INC
METRO STORE
1400 Vincent Massey Dr, Cornwall, ON, K6J 5N4
Emp Here 90

SIC 5411 Grocery stores

D-U-N-S 20-536-2754 (BR)
SAINT ELIZABETH HEALTH CARE
1916 Pitt St Unit 5, Cornwall, ON, K6J 5H3
(613) 936-8668
Emp Here 56
SIC 8082 Home health care services

D-U-N-S 24-103-9247 (BR)
TANK TRUCK TRANSPORT INC
TOLL LEASING
1300 Rosemount Ave, Cornwall, ON, K6J 3E6
(613) 932-5285
Emp Here 20
SIC 4213 Trucking, except local

D-U-N-S 20-043-5287 (BR)
THOMSON REUTERS CANADA LIMITED
STANDARD FREEHOLDER
44 Pitt St, Cornwall, ON, K6J 3P2
(613) 933-3160
Emp Here 50
SIC 2711 Newspapers

D-U-N-S 25-224-7945 (BR)
UPPER CANADA DISTRICT SCHOOL BOARD, THE
GENERAL VANIER INTERMEDIATE SCHOOL
(*Suby of* Upper Canada District School Board, The)
1500 Cumberland St, Cornwall, ON, K6J 4K9
(613) 933-9626
Emp Here 70
SIC 8211 Elementary and secondary schools

D-U-N-S 25-137-3734 (BR)
UPPER CANADA DISTRICT SCHOOL BOARD, THE
T R LEGER ALTERNATIVE SCHOOLS
(*Suby of* Upper Canada District School Board, The)
1500 Cumberland St, Cornwall, ON, K6J 4K9
(613) 937-0120
Emp Here 50
SIC 8211 Elementary and secondary schools

D-U-N-S 25-137-3742 (BR)
UPPER CANADA DISTRICT SCHOOL BOARD, THE
KINSMEN/ VINCENT MASSEY SCHOOL
(*Suby of* Upper Canada District School Board, The)
1520 Cumberland St, Cornwall, ON, K6J 4L1

Emp Here 24
SIC 8211 Elementary and secondary schools

D-U-N-S 25-137-3775 (BR)
UPPER CANADA DISTRICT SCHOOL BOARD, THE
MEMORIAL PARK PUBLIC SCHOOL
(*Suby of* Upper Canada District School Board, The)
235 Third St W, Cornwall, ON, K6J 0B6
(613) 938-8723
Emp Here 27
SIC 8211 Elementary and secondary schools

D-U-N-S 24-417-1455 (BR)
VALUE VILLAGE STORES, INC
VALUE VILLAGE
(*Suby of* Savers, Inc.)
1400 Vincent Massey Dr, Cornwall, ON, K6J 5N4
(613) 938-0226
Emp Here 20
SIC 5399 Miscellaneous general merchandise

D-U-N-S 25-074-6567 (BR)
WAL-MART CANADA CORP
950 Brookdale Ave, Cornwall, ON, K6J 4P5
(613) 933-8366
Emp Here 150
SIC 5311 Department stores

Cornwall, ON K6K
Stormont County

D-U-N-S 25-135-0773   (SL)
LAURENCREST YOUTH SERVICES INC
510 Mercier St, Cornwall, ON, K6K 1K2
(613) 933-6362
Emp Here 30   *Sales* 9,914,160
SIC 8322 Individual and family services
Ex Dir Wayne Kyte

D-U-N-S 25-224-7846   (BR)
UPPER CANADA DISTRICT SCHOOL BOARD, THE
EAMERS CORNERS PUBLIC SCHOOL
(*Suby of* Upper Canada District School Board, The)
2258 Pitt St, Cornwall, ON, K6K 1A3
(613) 933-0644
Emp Here 45
SIC 8211 Elementary and secondary schools

Corunna, ON N0N
Lambton County

D-U-N-S 25-367-0178   (BR)
AFTON CHEMICAL CANADA CORPORATION
(*Suby of* Newmarket Corporation)
220 St Clair Pky Rr 2, Corunna, ON, N0N 1G0

Emp Here 45
SIC 2911 Petroleum refining

D-U-N-S 20-043-5758   (BR)
ETHYL CANADA INC
(*Suby of* Newmarket Corporation)
220 St Clair Pky, Corunna, ON, N0N 1G0

Emp Here 45
SIC 2819 Industrial inorganic chemicals, nec

D-U-N-S 24-608-9812   (SL)
FOODLAND
420 Lyndoch St, Corunna, ON, N0N 1G0
(519) 862-5213
Emp Here 49   *Sales* 6,055,738
SIC 5411 Grocery stores
Ch Bd Jenai Wall

D-U-N-S 20-064-5997   (BR)
GATX RAIL CANADA CORPORATION
CORPORATION GATX RAIL CANADA
403 Lasalle Line Rr 2, Corunna, ON, N0N 1G0
(519) 344-1130
Emp Here 30
SIC 4789 Transportation services, nec

D-U-N-S 25-073-2989   (BR)
LAMBTON KENT DISTRICT SCHOOL BOARD
COLONEL CAMERON ELEMENTARY SCHOOL
338 Cameron St, Corunna, ON, N0N 1G0
(519) 862-1116
Emp Here 25
SIC 8211 Elementary and secondary schools

D-U-N-S 25-249-3796   (BR)
LAMBTON KENT DISTRICT SCHOOL BOARD
SIR JOHN MOORE COMMUNITY SCHOOL
274 St Clair Blvd, Corunna, ON, N0N 1G0
(519) 862-1089
Emp Here 30
SIC 8211 Elementary and secondary schools

D-U-N-S 24-325-9632   (BR)
LAPORTE, MARCEL PHARMACY INC
SHOPPERS DRUG MART
420 Lyndoch St, Corunna, ON, N0N 1G0
(519) 862-1451
Emp Here 22

SIC 5912 Drug stores and proprietary stores

D-U-N-S 25-975-0412   (BR)
PIONEER HI-BRED LIMITED
(*Suby of* E. I. Du Pont De Nemours and Company)
291 Albert St, Corunna, ON, N0N 1G0
(519) 862-5700
Emp Here 80
SIC 2824 Organic fibers, noncellulosic

D-U-N-S 24-125-9790   (BR)
SHELL CANADA LIMITED
339 Lasalle Line Rr 1, Corunna, ON, N0N 1G0

Emp Here 300
SIC 2992 Lubricating oils and greases

D-U-N-S 20-029-8508   (BR)
ST. CLAIR CATHOLIC DISTRICT SCHOOL BOARD
ST JOSEPH'S SCHOOL
535 Birchbank Dr, Corunna, ON, N0N 1G0
(519) 862-1479
Emp Here 30
SIC 8211 Elementary and secondary schools

Cottam, ON N0R
Essex County

D-U-N-S 20-771-9530   (SL)
1560804 ONTARIO INC
DINIRO HOTHOUSE
40 Cameron E, Cottam, ON, N0R 1B0

Emp Here 75   *Sales* 5,104,320
SIC 7389 Business services, nec
Pr Nick Diniro

D-U-N-S 25-249-2020   (BR)
GREATER ESSEX COUNTY DISTRICT SCHOOL BOARD
GOSFIELD NORTH PUBLIC SCHOOL
302 County Rd 27, Cottam, ON, N0R 1B0
(519) 839-4811
Emp Here 40
SIC 8211 Elementary and secondary schools

Courtice, ON L1E
Durham County

D-U-N-S 24-419-3509   (BR)
BLACK & MCDONALD LIMITED
81 Osborne Rd, Courtice, ON, L1E 2R3
(905) 837-1291
Emp Here 35
SIC 1711 Plumbing, heating, air-conditioning

D-U-N-S 24-986-7615   (SL)
COURTICE DONUTS LTD
TIM HORTONS
1403 Highway 2, Courtice, ON, L1E 2J6
(905) 728-0026
Emp Here 210   *Sales* 9,942,100
SIC 5461 Retail bakeries
Pr Pr Marco Rocca

D-U-N-S 20-705-2650   (BR)
DIVERSICARE CANADA MANAGEMENT SERVICES CO., INC
WHITE CLIFFE TERRACE
1460 Highway 2, Courtice, ON, L1E 3C4
(905) 579-0800
Emp Here 50
SIC 6513 Apartment building operators

D-U-N-S 25-106-5447   (BR)
KAWARTHA PINE RIDGE DISTRICT SCHOOL BOARD
CURTICE SECONDARY SCHOOL
1717 Nash Rd, Courtice, ON, L1E 2L8

(905) 436-2074
Emp Here 120
SIC 8211 Elementary and secondary schools

D-U-N-S 20-711-5861   (BR)
KAWARTHA PINE RIDGE DISTRICT SCHOOL BOARD
COURTICE NORTH PUBLIC SCHOOL
1675 Nash Rd, Courtice, ON, L1E 2Y4
(905) 436-2055
Emp Here 50
SIC 8211 Elementary and secondary schools

D-U-N-S 20-688-8617   (BR)
KAWARTHA PINE RIDGE DISTRICT SCHOOL BOARD
DR. G.J. MACGUILLIVRAY PUBLIC SCHOOL
75 Meadowglade Rd Suite 1, Courtice, ON, L1E 3G7
(905) 436-2054
Emp Here 70
SIC 8211 Elementary and secondary schools

D-U-N-S 20-711-5879   (BR)
KAWARTHA PINE RIDGE DISTRICT SCHOOL BOARD
DR EMILY STOWE PUBLIC SCHOOL
71 Sandringham Dr, Courtice, ON, L1E 1W8
(905) 433-8747
Emp Here 50
SIC 8211 Elementary and secondary schools

D-U-N-S 20-591-8134   (BR)
KAWARTHA PINE RIDGE DISTRICT SCHOOL BOARD
LYDIA TRULL PUBLIC SCHOOL
80 Avondale Dr, Courtice, ON, L1E 3C2
(905) 438-9648
Emp Here 20
SIC 8211 Elementary and secondary schools

D-U-N-S 20-711-5747   (BR)
KAWARTHA PINE RIDGE DISTRICT SCHOOL BOARD
S.T.WORDEN PUBLIC SCHOOL
1462 Nash Rd, Courtice, ON, L1E 1S7
(905) 436-0715
Emp Here 25
SIC 8211 Elementary and secondary schools

D-U-N-S 20-711-6133   (BR)
PETERBOROUGH VICTORIA NORTHUMBERLAND AND CLARINGTON CATHOLIC DISTRICT SCHOOL BOARD
MOTHER THERESA SCHOOL
78 Glenabbey Dr, Courtice, ON, L1E 2B5
(905) 433-5512
Emp Here 50
SIC 8211 Elementary and secondary schools

D-U-N-S 25-143-4239   (BR)
PETERBOROUGH VICTORIA NORTHUMBERLAND AND CLARINGTON CATHOLIC DISTRICT SCHOOL BOARD
MONSIGNOR LEO CLEARY CATHOLIC ELEMENTARY SCHOOL
(*Suby of* Peterborough Victoria Northumberland and Clarington Catholic District School Board)
3820 Courtice Rd N, Courtice, ON, L1E 2L5
(905) 433-0331
Emp Here 50
SIC 8211 Elementary and secondary schools

D-U-N-S 20-568-0510   (BR)
PETERBOROUGH VICTORIA NORTHUMBERLAND AND CLARINGTON CATHOLIC DISTRICT SCHOOL BOARD
HOLY TRINITY CATHOLIC SECONDARY SCHOOL
2260 Courtice Rd, Courtice, ON, L1E 2M8
(905) 404-9349
Emp Here 100
SIC 8211 Elementary and secondary schools

D-U-N-S 20-653-2181   (BR)
PETERBOROUGH VICTORIA NORTHUMBERLAND AND CLARINGTON CATHOLIC

DISTRICT SCHOOL BOARD
GOOD SHEPHERD CATHOLIC ELEMENTARY SCHOOL
20 Farmington Dr, Courtice, ON, L1E 3B9
(905) 404-9868
Emp Here 52
SIC 8211 Elementary and secondary schools

Courtland, ON N0J
Norfolk County

D-U-N-S 20-934-7749   (HQ)
AGRATURF EQUIPMENT SERVICES INC
(*Suby of* Agraturf Equipment Services Inc)
170 County Road 13, Courtland, ON, N0J 1E0
(519) 688-1011
Emp Here 30   *Emp Total* 110
Sales 14,036,880
SIC 5999 Miscellaneous retail stores, nec
Pr Pr Joseph Fewer
Keith Murray
Derek Scholten
Ernest Scholten
David Moore

D-U-N-S 20-352-9557   (BR)
CARESSANT-CARE NURSING AND RETIREMENT HOMES LIMITED
4850 Highway 59, Courtland, ON, N0J 1E0
(519) 668-0710
Emp Here 60
SIC 8051 Skilled nursing care facilities

D-U-N-S 20-702-3198   (BR)
CARGILL LIMITED
159 Talbot St Rr 1, Courtland, ON, N0J 1E0
(519) 688-2151
Emp Here 20
SIC 5191 Farm supplies

D-U-N-S 20-025-2984   (BR)
GRAND ERIE DISTRICT SCHOOL BOARD
COURTLAND PUBLIC SCHOOL
(*Suby of* Grand Erie District School Board)
1012 Queen St, Courtland, ON, N0J 1E0
(519) 688-2110
Emp Here 20
SIC 8211 Elementary and secondary schools

Courtright, ON N0N
Lambton County

D-U-N-S 24-078-4095   (BR)
COMSTOCK CANADA LTD
Gd, Courtright, ON, N0N 1H0

Emp Here 35
SIC 1711 Plumbing, heating, air-conditioning

D-U-N-S 24-334-8484   (BR)
GREENFIELD ENERGY CENTRE LP
Gd, Courtright, ON, N0N 1H0
(519) 867-5000
Emp Here 45
SIC 4911 Electric services

D-U-N-S 24-920-0056   (BR)
ONTARIO POWER GENERATION INC
LAMBTON GENERATING STATION
1886 St Clair Pky, Courtright, ON, N0N 1H0
(519) 867-2663
Emp Here 450
SIC 4911 Electric services

Creemore, ON L0M
Simcoe County

D-U-N-S 24-343-2718   (BR)
2063412 INVESTMENT LP

LEISUREWORLD CAREGIVING CENTRE - CREEDAN VALLEY
(*Suby of* 2063412 Investment LP)
143 Mary St, Creemore, ON, L0M 1G0
(705) 466-3437
Emp Here 80
SIC 8051 Skilled nursing care facilities

D-U-N-S 25-860-5435   (BR)
2063414 ONTARIO LIMITED
LEISUREWORLD CAREGIVING CENTRE
(*Suby of* 2063414 Ontario Limited)
143 Mary St, Creemore, ON, L0M 1G0
(705) 466-3437
Emp Here 75
SIC 8051 Skilled nursing care facilities

D-U-N-S 24-664-3480   (HQ)
CREEMORE SPRINGS BREWERY LIMITED
(*Suby of* Molson Coors Brewing Company)
139 Mill St Suite 369, Creemore, ON, L0M 1G0
(705) 466-2240
Emp Here 59   *Emp Total* 17,400
Sales 11,746,673
SIC 2082 Malt beverages
Ian Freedman
VP Prd Gordon Fuller

D-U-N-S 24-876-3856   (SL)
MAD RIVER GOLF CLUB, THE
2008 Airport Rd, Creemore, ON, L0M 1G0
(705) 428-3673
Emp Here 60   *Sales* 2,407,703
SIC 7997 Membership sports and recreation clubs

D-U-N-S 20-711-1993   (BR)
SIMCOE COUNTY DISTRICT SCHOOL BOARD, THE
NOTTAWASAGA & CREEMORE PUBLIC SCHOOL
(*Suby of* Simcoe County District School Board, The)
240 Collingwood St, Creemore, ON, L0M 1G0
(705) 466-2624
Emp Here 25
SIC 8211 Elementary and secondary schools

Crystal Beach, ON L0S
Welland County

D-U-N-S 20-026-7016   (BR)
DISTRICT SCHOOL BOARD OF NIAGARA
CRYSTAL BEACH PUBLIC SCHOOL
145 Derby Rd, Crystal Beach, ON, L0S 1B0
(905) 894-3900
Emp Here 40
SIC 8211 Elementary and secondary schools

D-U-N-S 20-710-8882   (BR)
NIAGARA CATHOLIC DISTRICT SCHOOL BOARD
ST GEORGE CATHOLIC ELEMENTARY SCHOOL
3800 Wellington Rd, Crystal Beach, ON, L0S 1B0
(905) 894-3670
Emp Here 50
SIC 8211 Elementary and secondary schools

Cumberland, ON K4C
Carleton County

D-U-N-S 20-052-6155   (SL)
1329481 ONTARIO INC
C AND C ENTERPRISES
2930 French Hill Rd, Cumberland, ON, K4C 1K7
(613) 833-1917
Emp Here 55   *Sales* 4,377,642

SIC 4212 Local trucking, without storage

D-U-N-S 20-271-9089   (BR)
GODDARD'S SONSHINE FAMILIES INC
SONSHINE FAMILIES
852 Apple Lane, Cumberland, ON, K4C 1C1
(613) 833-0521
Emp Here 25
SIC 8361 Residential care

Curve Lake, ON K0L
Peterborough County

D-U-N-S 20-291-4011   (BR)
UNION OF ONTARIO INDIANS
ANISHINABEK NATION
1024 Mississauga Rd, Curve Lake, ON, K0L 1R0
(705) 657-9383
Emp Here 100
SIC 8399 Social services, nec

Dalkeith, ON K0B
Glengarry County

D-U-N-S 20-732-6302   (BR)
UPPER CANADA DISTRICT SCHOOL BOARD, THE
LAGGAN PUBLIC SCHOOL
20345 County Road 24, Dalkeith, ON, K0B 1E0
(613) 525-3112
Emp Here 20
SIC 8211 Elementary and secondary schools

Dashwood, ON N0M
Huron County

D-U-N-S 24-852-9138   (SL)
HOFFMANS PATIENT TRANSFER LTD
37700 Dashwood Rd, Dashwood, ON, N0M 1N0
(519) 237-3631
Emp Here 50   *Sales* 2,411,520
SIC 4111 Local and suburban transit

Deep River, ON K0J
Renfrew County

D-U-N-S 24-438-2842   (SL)
534592 ONTARIO INC
LAURENTIAN VIEW INVESTMENTS
33373 Hwy 17, Deep River, ON, K0J 1P0

Emp Here 35   *Sales* 7,736,960
SIC 2026 Fluid milk
Pr Pr Daryl Blimke

D-U-N-S 24-103-6425   (BR)
715152 ONTARIO INC
VALLEY TRANSPORTATION
(*Suby of* 715152 Ontario Inc)
33005 Highway 17 East Rr 1, Deep River, ON, K0J 1P0
(613) 584-4776
Emp Here 20
SIC 4151 School buses

D-U-N-S 24-390-8998   (SL)
H.S. PIKE HOLDINGS INC
CANADIAN TIRE
366 Burkes Rd Rr 1, Deep River, ON, K0J 1P0
(613) 584-3337
Emp Here 45   *Sales* 5,472,053
SIC 5531 Auto and home supply stores
Pr Stephen Pike

D-U-N-S 25-457-8123   (SL)
NORTH RENFREW LONG-TERM CARE SERVICES INC
47 Ridge Rd, Deep River, ON, K0J 1P0
(613) 584-1900
Emp Here 65   *Sales* 2,991,389
SIC 8051 Skilled nursing care facilities

D-U-N-S 24-046-2189   (SL)
PEMBROKE OLD TIME FIDDLING ASSOCI-ATION INCORPORATED
Gd, Deep River, ON, K0J 1P0
(613) 635-7200
Emp Here 100   *Sales* 12,111,476
SIC 8699 Membership organizations, nec
Dir Diane Hickey
Dir Laurie Serran
Dir Brian Adams
Dir Romeo Levesseur
Dir Richard Jones
Dir Dan Schyrer
Dir Don Rosien
Dir Ian Hamilton

D-U-N-S 20-702-3271   (BR)
PHARMA PLUS DRUGMARTS LTD
REXALL PHARMA PLUS
11 Champlain St, Deep River, ON, K0J 1P0

Emp Here 21
SIC 5912 Drug stores and proprietary stores

D-U-N-S 20-711-6950   (BR)
RENFREW COUNTY CATHOLIC DISTRICT SCHOOL BOARD
ST. MARY'S CATHOLIC SCHOOL
(*Suby of* Renfrew County Catholic District School Board)
331110d Hwy 17, Deep River, ON, K0J 1P0
(613) 584-3567
Emp Here 50
SIC 8211 Elementary and secondary schools

D-U-N-S 25-238-6248   (BR)
RENFREW COUNTY DISTRICT SCHOOL BOARD
MACKENZIE HIGH SCHOOL
Gd, Deep River, ON, K0J 1P0
(613) 584-3361
Emp Here 60
SIC 8211 Elementary and secondary schools

D-U-N-S 25-238-6255   (BR)
RENFREW COUNTY DISTRICT SCHOOL BOARD
KEYS PUBLIC SCHOOL
87 Brockhouse Way, Deep River, ON, K0J 1P0
(613) 584-3361
Emp Here 24
SIC 8211 Elementary and secondary schools

D-U-N-S 25-238-6321   (BR)
RENFREW COUNTY DISTRICT SCHOOL BOARD
MORISON PUBLIC SCHOOL
12 Avon St, Deep River, ON, K0J 1P0

Emp Here 35
SIC 8211 Elementary and secondary schools

Deer Lake, ON P0V
Kenora County

D-U-N-S 24-094-9169   (BR)
NORTH WEST COMPANY LP, THE
Gd, Deer Lake, ON, P0V 1N0
(807) 775-2351
Emp Here 20
SIC 5411 Grocery stores

Delaware, ON N0L
Middlesex County

D-U-N-S 25-237-8559   (BR)
LONDON DISTRICT CATHOLIC SCHOOL BOARD
OUR LADY OF LOURDES CATHOLIC SCHOOL
2436 Gideon Dr, Delaware, ON, N0L 1E0
(519) 660-2775
Emp Here 30
SIC 8211 Elementary and secondary schools

Delhi, ON N4B
Norfolk County

D-U-N-S 20-000-0326   (BR)
ANNEX PUBLISHING & PRINTING INC
300 Argyle Ave, Delhi, ON, N4B 2Y1

Emp Here 35
SIC 2711 Newspapers

D-U-N-S 20-710-6423   (BR)
BRANT HALDIMAND NORFOLK CATHOLIC DISTRICT SCHOOL BOARD
ST FRANCIS CABRINI SCHOOL
373 Northern Ave, Delhi, ON, N4B 2R4
(519) 582-2470
Emp Here 50
SIC 8211 Elementary and secondary schools

D-U-N-S 24-315-3350   (SL)
DELHI NURSING HOME LIMITED
DELHI LONG TERM CARE CENTER
750 Gibralter St, Delhi, ON, N4B 3B3
(519) 582-3400
Emp Here 80   *Sales* 3,648,035
SIC 8051 Skilled nursing care facilities

D-U-N-S 20-081-7042   (BR)
GRAND ERIE DISTRICT SCHOOL BOARD
DELHI PUBLIC SCHOOL
(*Suby of* Grand Erie District School Board)
227 Queen St, Delhi, ON, N4B 2K6
(519) 582-1890
Emp Here 35
SIC 8211 Elementary and secondary schools

D-U-N-S 20-004-8515   (BR)
GRAND ERIE DISTRICT SCHOOL BOARD
DELHI DISTRICT SECONDARY SCHOOL
(*Suby of* Grand Erie District School Board)
393 James St, Delhi, ON, N4B 2B6
(519) 582-0410
Emp Here 40
SIC 8211 Elementary and secondary schools

Denfield, ON N0M
Middlesex County

D-U-N-S 24-914-6440   (BR)
PARRISH & HEIMBECKER, LIMITED
NEW LIFE MILLS - DENFIELD FEED MILL
(*Suby of* Parrish & Heimbecker, Limited)
24162 Denfield Rd Suite 2, Denfield, ON, N0M 1P0
(519) 666-1400
Emp Here 30
SIC 5153 Grain and field beans

Desbarats, ON P0R
Algoma County

D-U-N-S 25-238-2130   (BR)
ALGOMA DISTRICT SCHOOL BOARD
CENTRAL ALGOMA SECONDARY SCHOOL
(*Suby of* Algoma District School Board)
32 Kensington Rd, Desbarats, ON, P0R 1E0

---

(705) 782-6263
Emp Here 60
SIC 8211 Elementary and secondary schools

Deseronto, ON K0K
Hastings County

D-U-N-S 20-031-1475   (SL)
MANORCARE PARTNERS II
FRIENDLY MANOR NURSING HOME
9756 County Rd 2, Deseronto, ON, K0K 1X0
(613) 396-3438
Emp Here 65   *Sales* 2,407,703
SIC 8361 Residential care

D-U-N-S 20-302-4695   (BR)
MOHAWKS OF THE BAY OF QUINTE
QUINTE MOHAWK SCHOOL
(*Suby of* Mohawks Of The Bay Of Quinte)
1624 York Rd, Deseronto, ON, K0K 1X0
(613) 966-6984
Emp Here 40
SIC 8211 Elementary and secondary schools

Devlin, ON P0W
Rainy River County

D-U-N-S 20-591-7128   (BR)
RAINY RIVER DISTRICT SCHOOL BOARD
CROSSROADS SCHOOL
Gd, Devlin, ON, P0W 1C0
(807) 486-3329
Emp Here 35
SIC 8211 Elementary and secondary schools

Dobie, ON P0K
Timiskaming County

D-U-N-S 20-641-8258   (BR)
CANADIAN MALARTIC GP
(*Suby of* Canadian Malartic GP)
72 Upper Canada Drive, Dobie, ON, P0K 1B0
(705) 567-4377
Emp Here 25
SIC 1481 NonMetallic mineral services

Dorchester, ON N0L
Middlesex County

D-U-N-S 24-373-6241   (SL)
1767168 ONTARIO LTD
TIM HORTONS
2147 Dorchester Rd, Dorchester, ON, N0L 1G2
(519) 268-1100
Emp Here 60   *Sales* 1,824,018
SIC 5812 Eating places

D-U-N-S 20-104-1451   (SL)
ARMATEC SURVIVABILITY CORP
One Newton Ave, Dorchester, ON, N0L 1G4
(519) 268-2999
Emp Here 60
SIC 3795 Tanks and tank components

D-U-N-S 25-204-0662   (BR)
BOW GROUPE DE PLOMBERIE INC
BOW METALLICS
531 Shaw Rd, Dorchester, ON, N0L 1G4

Emp Here 26
SIC 3351 Copper rolling and drawing

D-U-N-S 25-797-2216   (BR)
LONDON DISTRICT CATHOLIC SCHOOL BOARD
ST DAVID SCHOOL

3966 Catherine St, Dorchester, ON, N0L 1G0
(519) 660-2779
Emp Here 30
SIC 8211 Elementary and secondary schools

D-U-N-S 24-683-6907   (SL)
LONDON ECO-METAL MANUFACTURING INC
531 Shaw Rd, Dorchester, ON, N0L 1G4
(519) 451-7663
Emp Here 20   *Sales* 12,804,096
SIC 1761 Roofing, siding, and sheetMetal work

D-U-N-S 25-249-0750   (BR)
THAMES VALLEY DISTRICT SCHOOL BOARD
RIVER HEIGHTS PUBLIC SCHOOL
4269 Hamilton Rd, Dorchester, ON, N0L 1G3
(519) 268-7884
Emp Here 25
SIC 8211 Elementary and secondary schools

D-U-N-S 25-249-3580   (BR)
THAMES VALLEY DISTRICT SCHOOL BOARD
LORD DORCHESTER SECONDARY SCHOOL
61 Queen St, Dorchester, ON, N0L 1G2
(519) 268-7351
Emp Here 50
SIC 8211 Elementary and secondary schools

D-U-N-S 25-249-0552   (BR)
THAMES VALLEY DISTRICT SCHOOL BOARD
NORTH DEL CENTRAL PUBLIC SCHOOL
3860 Catherines St, Dorchester, ON, N0L 1G0
(519) 268-7862
Emp Here 35
SIC 8211 Elementary and secondary schools

D-U-N-S 20-514-8153   (HQ)
UNITED AGRI PRODUCTS CANADA INC
UAP
(*Suby of* Agrium Canada Partnership)
789 Donnybrook Dr Suite 2, Dorchester, ON, N0L 1G5
(519) 268-8001
Emp Here 49   *Emp Total* 15,200
Sales 11,521,138
SIC 2879 Agricultural chemicals, nec
 Murray Pickel

Douglas, ON K0J
Renfrew County

D-U-N-S 25-238-6404   (BR)
RENFREW COUNTY DISTRICT SCHOOL BOARD
OPEONGO HIGH SCHOOL
1990 Cobden Rd, Douglas, ON, K0J 1S0
(613) 735-7587
Emp Here 55
SIC 8211 Elementary and secondary schools

Douro, ON K0L
Peterborough County

D-U-N-S 20-025-5227   (BR)
PETERBOROUGH VICTORIA NORTHUMBERLAND AND CLARINGTON CATHOLIC DISTRICT SCHOOL BOARD
ST JOSEPH'S SCHOOL
405 Forth Line, Douro, ON, K0L 1S0
(705) 652-3961
Emp Here 25
SIC 8211 Elementary and secondary schools

Dowling, ON P0M
Sudbury County

D-U-N-S 25-471-8158   (SL)
982598 ONTARIO LIMITED
DOWLING VALU-MART
65 Main St, Dowling, ON, P0M 1R0
(705) 855-9018
Emp Here 49   *Sales* 7,821,331
SIC 5411 Grocery stores
Pr Leon Berthiaume

D-U-N-S 25-239-0448   (BR)
CONSEIL SCOLAIRE DE DISTRICT CATHOLIQUE DU NOUVEL-ONTARIO, LE
ECOLE ST ETIENNE
79 Houle Ave, Dowling, ON, P0M 1R0
(705) 855-4333
Emp Here 20
SIC 8211 Elementary and secondary schools

Drayton, ON N0G
Wellington County

D-U-N-S 24-478-0284   (HQ)
NIEUWLAND FEED & SUPPLY LIMITED
(*Suby of* 868229 Ontario Limited)
96 Wellington St, Drayton, ON, N0G 1P0
(519) 638-3008
Emp Here 42   *Emp Total* 54
Sales 72,599,621
SIC 5191 Farm supplies
Pr Pr Arthur Nieuwland
 Scott Nieuwland

D-U-N-S 20-688-8849   (BR)
UPPER GRAND DISTRICT SCHOOL BOARD, THE
DRAYTON HEIGHTS PUBLIC SCHOOL
(*Suby of* Upper Grand District School Board, The)
75 Wellington St S, Drayton, ON, N0G 1P0
(519) 638-3067
Emp Here 25
SIC 8211 Elementary and secondary schools

Dresden, ON N0P

D-U-N-S 24-325-8626   (BR)
CONAGRA FOODS CANADA INC
(*Suby of* Lamb Weston Holdings Inc)
759 Wellington St, Dresden, ON, N0P 1M0
(519) 683-4422
Emp Here 150
SIC 2032 Canned specialties

D-U-N-S 25-360-7741   (BR)
CORPORATION OF THE MUNICIPALITY OF CHATHAM-KENT, THE
DRESDEN ARENA, LAMBTON KENT MEMORIAL AGRICULTURAL CENTRE
1212 North St Rr 5, Dresden, ON, N0P 1M0
(519) 683-2572
Emp Here 25
SIC 7941 Sports clubs, managers, and promoters

D-U-N-S 25-092-0555   (BR)
DEL MONTE CANADA INC
(*Suby of* Conagra Brands, Inc.)
Gd, Dresden, ON, N0P 1M0
(519) 683-4422
Emp Here 200
SIC 2032 Canned specialties

D-U-N-S 25-633-2750   (BR)
DIVERSICARE CANADA MANAGEMENT SERVICES CO., INC
PARK STREET PLACE
650 Park St Rr 5, Dresden, ON, N0P 1M0

(519) 683-4474
Emp Here 25
SIC 8361 Residential care

D-U-N-S 25-079-0417   (BR)
LAMBTON KENT DISTRICT SCHOOL BOARD
LAMBTON KENT COMPOSITE SCHOOL
231 St. George St, Dresden, ON, N0P 1M0
(519) 683-4475
Emp Here 40
SIC 8211 Elementary and secondary schools

D-U-N-S 20-710-4857   (BR)
LAMBTON KENT DISTRICT SCHOOL BOARD
DRESDEN AREA CENTRAL SCHOOL
941 North St, Dresden, ON, N0P 1M0
(519) 683-4457
Emp Here 25
SIC 8211 Elementary and secondary schools

D-U-N-S 24-859-2198   (BR)
MARTINREA INTERNATIONAL INC
DRESDEN ASSEMBLY, DIV OF
1130 Wellington St, Dresden, ON, N0P 1M0
(519) 683-6233
Emp Here 100
SIC 3499 Fabricated Metal products, nec

D-U-N-S 25-480-3380   (BR)
UNION GAS LIMITED
DAWN OPERATION CENTER
3332 Bentpath Line, Dresden, ON, N0P 1M0
(519) 683-4468
Emp Here 150
SIC 4923 Gas transmission and distribution

Dryden, ON P8N
Kenora County

D-U-N-S 25-321-5321   (SL)
588990 ONTARIO INC
MCDONALD'S
520 Government St, Dryden, ON, P8N 2P7
(807) 223-4884
Emp Here 70   *Sales* 2,115,860
SIC 5812 Eating places

D-U-N-S 20-541-3086   (BR)
CANADA POST CORPORATION
DRYDEN STN MAIN
97 King St, Dryden, ON, P8N 1B8
(807) 223-2473
Emp Here 22
SIC 4311 U.s. postal service

D-U-N-S 24-191-2224   (BR)
COMCARE (CANADA) LIMITED
COMCARE HEALTH SERVICES
58 Goodall St, Dryden, ON, P8N 1V8
(807) 223-5337
Emp Here 100
SIC 8049 Offices of health practitioner

D-U-N-S 20-984-8303   (BR)
COMMUNITY LIVING DRYDEN
DRYDEN COMMUNITY LIVING
288 Arthur St Suite 4, Dryden, ON, P8N 1K8

Emp Here 20
SIC 8322 Individual and family services

D-U-N-S 25-361-9746   (BR)
CORPORATION OF THE CITY OF DRYDEN, THE
DRYDEN MUNICIPAL TELEPHONE SYSTEM
65 Princess St, Dryden, ON, P8N 1C8
(807) 223-1100
Emp Here 20
SIC 4813 Telephone communication, except radio

D-U-N-S 24-468-3140   (BR)

DINGWALL FORD SALES LTD
246 Grand Trunk Ave, Dryden, ON, P8N 2X2
(807) 223-2235
Emp Here 30
SIC 5511 New and used car dealers

D-U-N-S 25-238-0837   (BR)
DRYDEN BOARD OF EDUCATION
DRYDEN HIGH SCHOOL
79 Casimir Ave, Dryden, ON, P8N 2H4
(807) 223-2316
Emp Here 100
SIC 8211 Elementary and secondary schools

D-U-N-S 25-238-0407   (BR)
KEEWATIN PATRICIA DISTRICT SCHOOL BOARD
PINEWOOD ELEMENTARY SCHOOL
91 Rourke Ave, Dryden, ON, P8N 2N6
(807) 223-5311
Emp Here 25
SIC 8211 Elementary and secondary schools

D-U-N-S 25-238-1926   (BR)
KEEWATIN PATRICIA DISTRICT SCHOOL BOARD
OPEN ROADS PUBLIC SCHOOL
20 Davis St, Dryden, ON, P8N 1R4
(807) 223-4418
Emp Here 31
SIC 8211 Elementary and secondary schools

D-U-N-S 20-767-7746   (BR)
MILLER PAVING LIMITED
MILLER NORTHWEST
351 Kennedy Rd, Dryden, ON, P8N 2Z2
(807) 223-2844
Emp Here 50
SIC 1611 Highway and street construction

D-U-N-S 20-710-3321   (BR)
NORTHWEST CATHOLIC DISTRICT SCHOOL BOARD, THE
ST JOSEPH SCHOOL
185 Parkdale Rd, Dryden, ON, P8N 1S5
(807) 223-5227
Emp Here 45
SIC 8211 Elementary and secondary schools

D-U-N-S 24-337-2393   (BR)
R.A.S. FOOD SERVICES INC
PIZZA HUT
(*Suby of* R.A.S. Food Services Inc)
397 Government St, Dryden, ON, P8N 2P4
(807) 223-6621
Emp Here 35
SIC 5812 Eating places

D-U-N-S 20-046-1416   (SL)
RIVERVIEW LODGE LIMITED, THE
148 Earl Ave, Dryden, ON, P8N 1Y1
(807) 223-2371
Emp Here 50   *Sales* 2,188,821
SIC 7011 Hotels and motels

D-U-N-S 20-657-0926   (BR)
SOBEYS CAPITAL INCORPORATED
DRYDEN IGA
303 Government St, Dryden, ON, P8N 2P4

Emp Here 50
SIC 5411 Grocery stores

D-U-N-S 25-272-0016   (BR)
SOBEYS WEST INC
SAFEWAY
75 Whyte Ave, Dryden, ON, P8N 3E6
(807) 223-3276
Emp Here 120
SIC 5411 Grocery stores

D-U-N-S 20-796-1603   (BR)
UNIFOR
CAW LOCAL 105
34 Queen St, Dryden, ON, P8N 1A3
(807) 223-8146
Emp Here 350
SIC 8631 Labor organizations

D-U-N-S 25-294-7577   (BR)
WAL-MART CANADA CORP
Hwy 17 E, Dryden, ON, P8N 2Y6
(807) 223-7190
Emp Here 250
SIC 5311 Department stores

Dublin, ON N0K
Perth County

D-U-N-S 20-710-6738   (BR)
HURON PERTH CATHOLIC DISTRICT SCHOOL BOARD
ST COLUMBAN SCHOOL
44106 Line 34, Dublin, ON, N0K 1E0
(519) 345-2086
Emp Here 50
SIC 8211 Elementary and secondary schools

D-U-N-S 20-046-1804   (SL)
LOOBY BUILDERS (DUBLIN) LIMITED
10 Matilda St, Dublin, ON, N0K 1E0
(519) 345-2800
Emp Here 25   *Sales* 11,967,578
SIC 1622 Bridge, tunnel, and elevated highway construction
    Stan Connelly
    Louis Looby Jr
    Joseph Looby
Dir Kenneth Devereaux

D-U-N-S 24-476-7828   (SL)
LOOBY, L.J. CONTRACTING LTD
10 Matilda St, Dublin, ON, N0K 1E0
(519) 345-2800
Emp Here 25   *Sales* 12,466,320
SIC 1622 Bridge, tunnel, and elevated highway construction
    Stan Connelly
VP VP Louis Looby Jr
    Joe Looby
    Kenneth Devereaux

D-U-N-S 24-322-1814   (BR)
SOFINA FOODS INC
147 John St, Dublin, ON, N0K 1E0
(519) 345-2270
Emp Here 60
SIC 2015 Poultry slaughtering and processing

Dubreuilville, ON P0S
Algoma County

D-U-N-S 24-021-1339   (BR)
MINES RICHMONT INC
ISLAND GOLD PROJECT
Gd, Dubreuilville, ON, P0S 1B0
(705) 884-2805
Emp Here 20
SIC 1041 Gold ores

Dundalk, ON N0C
Grey County

D-U-N-S 20-710-6589   (BR)
BLUEWATER DISTRICT SCHOOL BOARD
DUNDALK & PROTON COMMUNITY SCHOOL
251 Young St, Dundalk, ON, N0C 1B0
(519) 923-2622
Emp Here 50
SIC 8211 Elementary and secondary schools

D-U-N-S 20-983-0744   (BR)
FIRSTCANADA ULC
FIRST STUDENT CANADA
159061 Hwy 10, Dundalk, ON, N0C 1B0
(519) 923-2513
Emp Here 65

SIC 4151 School buses

D-U-N-S 25-473-3934   (BR)
L & M FOOD MARKET (ONTARIO) LIMITED
L & M FOODLAND
320 Main St E, Dundalk, ON, N0C 1B0
(519) 923-3630
Emp Here 25
SIC 5411 Grocery stores

D-U-N-S 24-000-3975   (SL)
METAL SYSTEMS OF CANADA ULC
(*Suby of* Patriarch Partners, LLC)
280 Victoria St, Dundalk, ON, N0C 1B0
(519) 923-2017
Emp Here 40   *Sales* 3,378,379
SIC 3465 Automotive stampings

Dundas, ON L9H
Wentworth County

D-U-N-S 20-563-3071   (BR)
3618358 CANADA INC
ATS ANDLAUER TRANSPORTATION SERVICES
465 Ofield Rd S, Dundas, ON, L9H 5E2
(905) 628-5277
Emp Here 30
SIC 4731 Freight transportation arrangement

D-U-N-S 25-296-8037   (BR)
BANK OF NOVA SCOTIA, THE
SCOTIABANK
101 Osler Dr Suite 138, Dundas, ON, L9H 4H4
(905) 627-9273
Emp Here 25
SIC 6021 National commercial banks

D-U-N-S 25-002-9725   (BR)
BANQUE TORONTO-DOMINION, LA
TD CANADA TRUST
(*Suby of* Toronto-Dominion Bank, The)
82 King St W, Dundas, ON, L9H 1T9
(905) 627-3559
Emp Here 25
SIC 6021 National commercial banks

D-U-N-S 24-286-1938   (HQ)
BEVERLY GROUP INC, THE
BENSON BEVERLY TIRE
(*Suby of* Beverly Group Inc, The)
525 6 Hwy, Dundas, ON, L9H 7K1
(905) 525-9240
Emp Here 30   *Emp Total* 185
Sales 29,023,733
SIC 5531 Auto and home supply stores
Pr William Streeter
VP Fin Gail Cameron

D-U-N-S 24-021-1537   (SL)
BIBLES FOR MISSIONS THRIFT STORE
33 King St E, Dundas, ON, L9H 5R1
(905) 627-2412
Emp Here 50   *Sales* 4,377,642
SIC 5932 Used merchandise stores

D-U-N-S 20-940-3377   (SL)
BLACKADAR CONTINUING CARE CENTRE LTD
101 Creighton Rd, Dundas, ON, L9H 3B7
(905) 627-5465
Emp Here 65   *Sales* 2,991,389
SIC 8051 Skilled nursing care facilities

D-U-N-S 20-561-4139   (BR)
CARMEUSE LIME (CANADA) LIMITED
600 5 Hwy W, Dundas, ON, L9H 5E2
(905) 628-8800
Emp Here 60
SIC 3274 Lime

D-U-N-S 25-829-9056   (BR)
CHARTWELL RETIREMENT RESIDENCES
CHARTWELL SENIORS HOUSING REAL ESTATE INVESTMENT TRUST

255 Governors Rd Suite 109, Dundas, ON, L9H 3K4
(905) 627-8444
Emp Here 23
SIC 8361 Residential care

D-U-N-S 25-483-6844   (BR)
CITY OF HAMILTON, THE
WENTWORTH LODGE
41 South St W Suite 207, Dundas, ON, L9H 4C4
Emp Here 200
SIC 8051 Skilled nursing care facilities

D-U-N-S 25-116-7342   (BR)
COMPAGNIE DE TELEPHONE BELL DU CANADA OU BELL CANADA, LA
BELL CANADA ENGINEERING
20 Hunter St, Dundas, ON, L9H 1E6
(905) 577-6247
Emp Here 30
SIC 8748 Business consulting, nec

D-U-N-S 24-505-3756   (HQ)
CURLCO INDUSTRIES INC
HAIRCRAFTERS
(*Suby of* Curlco Industries Inc)
85 Little John Rd Suite 1585, Dundas, ON, L9H 4H1
(905) 628-4287
Emp Here 172   *Emp Total* 207
Sales 4,085,799
SIC 7231 Beauty shops

D-U-N-S 24-926-3096   (BR)
DARLING INTERNATIONAL CANADA INC
ROTHSAY
(*Suby of* Darling Ingredients Inc.)
880 5 Hwy W, Dundas, ON, L9H 5E2
(905) 628-2258
Emp Here 120
SIC 4953 Refuse systems

D-U-N-S 20-876-3631   (SL)
FLAMBORO DOWNS HOLDINGS LIMITED
FLAMBORO DOWNS RACEWAY
967 5 Hwy W, Dundas, ON, L9H 5E2
(905) 627-3561
Emp Here 270
SIC 7948 Racing, including track operation

D-U-N-S 24-816-1408   (BR)
HAMILTON PUBLIC LIBRARY BOARD, THE
HAMILTON PUBLIC LIBRARY
18 Ogilvie St, Dundas, ON, L9H 2S2
(905) 627-3507
Emp Here 20
SIC 8231 Libraries

D-U-N-S 24-771-2644   (BR)
HAMILTON REGION CONSERVATION AUTHORITY
CHRISTIE LAKE CONSERVATION AREA
1000 5 Hwy W, Dundas, ON, L9H 5E2
(905) 628-3060
Emp Here 20
SIC 7999 Amusement and recreation, nec

D-U-N-S 20-655-1405   (BR)
HAMILTON-WENTWORTH CATHOLIC SCHOOL BOARD
ST AUGUSTINE CATHOLIC SCHOOL
25 Alma St, Dundas, ON, L9H 2C9
(905) 523-2338
Emp Here 30
SIC 8211 Elementary and secondary schools

D-U-N-S 25-293-9772   (BR)
HAMILTON-WENTWORTH CATHOLIC SCHOOL BOARD
ST AUGUSTINE'S SCHOOL
25 Alma St, Dundas, ON, L9H 2C9
(905) 523-2338
Emp Here 30
SIC 8211 Elementary and secondary schools

D-U-N-S 24-451-0934   (BR)

HAMILTON-WENTWORTH CATHOLIC SCHOOL BOARD
DUNDAS CENTRAL PUBLIC SCHOOL
73 Melville St, Dundas, ON, L9H 2A2
(905) 627-3521
Emp Here 25
SIC 8211 Elementary and secondary schools

D-U-N-S 20-653-4609   (BR)
HAMILTON-WENTWORTH CATHOLIC SCHOOL BOARD
SAINT BERNADETH CATHOLIC SCHOOL
270 Governors Rd, Dundas, ON, L9H 5E3
(905) 523-2336
Emp Here 35
SIC 8211 Elementary and secondary schools

D-U-N-S 20-590-5693   (BR)
HAMILTON-WENTWORTH DISTRICT SCHOOL BOARD, THE
PARKSIDE HIGH SCHOOL
31 Parkside Ave, Dundas, ON, L9H 2S8

Emp Here 60
SIC 8211 Elementary and secondary schools

D-U-N-S 20-139-9818   (BR)
HAMILTON-WENTWORTH DISTRICT SCHOOL BOARD, THE
HIGHLAND SECONDARY SCHOOL
310 Governors Rd, Dundas, ON, L9H 5P8
(905) 628-2203
Emp Here 70
SIC 8211 Elementary and secondary schools

D-U-N-S 20-138-1170   (BR)
HAMILTON-WENTWORTH DISTRICT SCHOOL BOARD, THE
GREENSVILLE PUBLIC SCHOOL
625 Harvest Rd, Dundas, ON, L9H 5K8
(905) 979-0538
Emp Here 20
SIC 8211 Elementary and secondary schools

D-U-N-S 20-590-5552   (BR)
HAMILTON-WENTWORTH DISTRICT SCHOOL BOARD, THE
SPENCER VALLEY PUBLIC SCHOOL
441 Old Brock Rd, Dundas, ON, L9H 6A7
(905) 627-2238
Emp Here 25
SIC 8211 Elementary and secondary schools

D-U-N-S 24-024-1146   (BR)
HAMILTON-WENTWORTH DISTRICT SCHOOL BOARD, THE
CENTRAL PARK PUBLIC SCHOOL
14 Kemp Dr, Dundas, ON, L9H 2M9

Emp Here 21
SIC 8211 Elementary and secondary schools

D-U-N-S 24-896-3571   (BR)
METRO ONTARIO INC
119 Osler Dr, Dundas, ON, L9H 6X4
(905) 628-0177
Emp Here 250
SIC 5411 Grocery stores

D-U-N-S 25-300-0467   (BR)
METRO ONTARIO INC
METRO
15 Governors Rd, Dundas, ON, L9H 6L9
(905) 627-4791
Emp Here 130
SIC 5411 Grocery stores

D-U-N-S 20-294-9202   (BR)
PRICE INDUSTRIES LIMITED
340 Hatt St, Dundas, ON, L9H 2J1
(905) 628-8989
Emp Here 40
SIC 3496 Miscellaneous fabricated wire products

D-U-N-S 24-322-1939   (BR)
REXALL PHARMACY GROUP LTD
REXALL

(*Suby of* McKesson Corporation)
60 Hatt St, Dundas, ON, L9H 7T6
(905) 627-2909
Emp Here 20
SIC 5912 Drug stores and proprietary stores

D-U-N-S 20-877-1829   (SL)
SFS INTEC, INC
40 Innovation Dr, Dundas, ON, L9H 7P3
(905) 847-5400
Emp Here 35   *Sales* 3,957,782
SIC 3429 Hardware, nec

Dunnville, ON N1A
Haldimand County

D-U-N-S 20-710-6464   (BR)
BRANT HALDIMAND NORFOLK CATHOLIC DISTRICT SCHOOL BOARD
ST. MICHAEL SCHOOL
209 Alder St W, Dunnville, ON, N1A 1R3
(905) 774-6052
Emp Here 26
SIC 8211 Elementary and secondary schools

D-U-N-S 20-584-2540   (BR)
CANADA POST CORPORATION
DUNNVILLE STATION MAIN PO
201 Broad St E, Dunnville, ON, N1A 1G1
(905) 774-6545
Emp Here 22
SIC 4311 U.s. postal service

D-U-N-S 24-007-3049   (BR)
CORPORATION OF HALDIMAND COUNTY, THE
GRANDVIEW LODGE
657 Lock St W Suite A, Dunnville, ON, N1A 1V9
(905) 774-7547
Emp Here 140
SIC 8361 Residential care

D-U-N-S 24-350-1298   (SL)
EDGEWATER GARDENS LONG-TERM CARE CENTRE
428 Broad St W, Dunnville, ON, N1A 1T3
(905) 774-2503
Emp Here 100   *Sales* 4,523,563
SIC 8051 Skilled nursing care facilities

D-U-N-S 20-045-9332   (BR)
GRAND ERIE DISTRICT SCHOOL BOARD
THOMPSON CREEK ELEMENTARY SCHOOL
(*Suby of* Grand Erie District School Board)
800 Cross St W, Dunnville, ON, N1A 1N7
(905) 774-5460
Emp Here 28
SIC 8211 Elementary and secondary schools

D-U-N-S 25-778-5816   (BR)
GRAND ERIE DISTRICT SCHOOL BOARD
DUNNVILLE CENTRAL PUBLIC SCHOOL
(*Suby of* Grand Erie District School Board)
121 Alder St W, Dunnville, ON, N1A 1R2
(905) 774-6033
Emp Here 20
SIC 8211 Elementary and secondary schools

D-U-N-S 25-745-2722   (BR)
GRAND ERIE DISTRICT SCHOOL BOARD
FAIRVIEW AVENUE PUBLIC SCHOOL
(*Suby of* Grand Erie District School Board)
223 Fairview Ave W, Dunnville, ON, N1A 1M4
(905) 774-6144
Emp Here 40
SIC 8211 Elementary and secondary schools

D-U-N-S 25-745-2730   (BR)
GRAND ERIE DISTRICT SCHOOL BOARD
DUNNVILLE SECONDARY SCHOOL
(*Suby of* Grand Erie District School Board)
110 Helena St, Dunnville, ON, N1A 2S5
(905) 774-7401
Emp Here 60

SIC 8211 Elementary and secondary schools

D-U-N-S 25-126-1608   (SL)
GRANDERIE FARM & COUNTRY LTD
HOME HARDWARE DIV OF
1051 Broad St E, Dunnville, ON, N1A 2Z1
(905) 774-6115
Emp Here 30   *Sales* 6,274,620
SIC 5191 Farm supplies

D-U-N-S 24-021-1727   (BR)
METRO ONTARIO INC
FOOD BASICS
107 Bridge St, Dunnville, ON, N1A 2G9
(905) 774-6852
Emp Here 50
SIC 5411 Grocery stores

D-U-N-S 20-556-1934   (SL)
ROSA FLORA GROWERS LIMITED
Gd Lcd Main, Dunnville, ON, N1A 2W9
(905) 774-8044
Emp Here 153   *Sales* 9,702,011
SIC 5992 Florists
Pr Otto Bulk

Dunrobin, ON K0A
Carleton County

D-U-N-S 24-372-1458   (BR)
CLUBLINK CORPORATION ULC
EAGLE CREEK GOLF CLUB
109 Royal Troon Lane, Dunrobin, ON, K0A 1T0
(613) 832-3804
Emp Here 100
SIC 7992 Public golf courses

D-U-N-S 20-025-3156   (BR)
OTTAWA-CARLETON DISTRICT SCHOOL BOARD
WEST CARLETON SECONDARY SCHOOL
3088 Dunrobin Rd, Dunrobin, ON, K0A 1T0
(613) 832-2773
Emp Here 75
SIC 8211 Elementary and secondary schools

Dunsford, ON K0M

D-U-N-S 20-541-4639   (BR)
CANADA POST CORPORATION
DUNSFORD GENERAL STORE
92 Dunsford Rd Suite 1, Dunsford, ON, K0M 1L0

Emp Here 54
SIC 4311 U.s. postal service

D-U-N-S 20-711-3833   (BR)
TRILLIUM LAKELANDS DISTRICT SCHOOL BOARD
DUNSFORD DISTRICT ELEMENTARY SCHOOL
33 Dunsford Rd, Dunsford, ON, K0M 1L0
(705) 793-2088
Emp Here 25
SIC 8211 Elementary and secondary schools

Durham, ON N0G
Grey County

D-U-N-S 25-238-9150   (BR)
BLUEWATER DISTRICT SCHOOL BOARD
DURHAM DIST COMMUNITY SCHOOL
426 George St E, Durham, ON, N0G 1R0

Emp Here 23
SIC 8211 Elementary and secondary schools

D-U-N-S 25-238-8632   (BR)
BLUEWATER DISTRICT SCHOOL BOARD
SPRUCE RIDGE COMMUNITY SCHOOL
239 Kincardine St, Durham, ON, N0G 1R0
(519) 369-2217
Emp Here 50
SIC 8211 Elementary and secondary schools

D-U-N-S 25-705-3173   (BR)
CORPORATION OF THE COUNTY OF GREY
ROCKWOOD TERRACE
575 Saddler St, Durham, ON, N0G 1R0
(519) 369-6035
Emp Here 130
SIC 8051 Skilled nursing care facilities

D-U-N-S 25-650-2121   (BR)
L & M FOOD MARKET (ONTARIO) LIMITED
L & M FOOD MARKET
344 Garafraxa St, Durham, ON, N0G 1R0
(519) 369-3130
Emp Here 40
SIC 5411 Grocery stores

D-U-N-S 24-827-3617   (SL)
THURO-WEB LTD
201 Elm St E, Durham, ON, N0G 1R0
(519) 369-6410
Emp Here 65   *Sales* 6,576,720
SIC 2752 Commercial printing, lithographic
Off Mgr Corinne Johnston
Manager Rodney Piercey

D-U-N-S 20-714-1776   (BR)
WALDORF SCHOOL ASSOCIATION OF ONTARIO INC
EDGEHILL COUNTRY SCHOOL
Rr 1, Durham, ON, N0G 1R0
(519) 369-3195
Emp Here 20
SIC 8211 Elementary and secondary schools

Dutton, ON N0L
Elgin County

D-U-N-S 20-939-4352   (BR)
CORPORATION OF THE COUNTY OF ELGIN
BOBIER VILLA
29491 Pioneer Line, Dutton, ON, N0L 1J0
(519) 762-2417
Emp Here 50
SIC 8051 Skilled nursing care facilities

D-U-N-S 25-238-8210   (BR)
THAMES VALLEY DISTRICT SCHOOL BOARD
DUNWICH DUTTON PUBLIC SCHOOL
239 Miller Rd, Dutton, ON, N0L 1J0
(519) 762-2419
Emp Here 28
SIC 8211 Elementary and secondary schools

Earlton, ON P0J
Timiskaming County

D-U-N-S 20-272-0777   (SL)
KOCH GRAIN ELEVATORS (EARLTON) INC
P&H EARLTON
(*Suby of* Parrish & Heimbecker, Limited)
125364 Gravel Rd, Earlton, ON, P0J 1E0
(705) 563-8325
Emp Here 30   *Sales* 90,176,729
SIC 4221 Farm product warehousing and storage
Pr Pr Norman Koch

East Gwillimbury, ON L9N

D-U-N-S 25-371-6302   (BR)
BEST BUY CANADA LTD
BEST BUY
(*Suby of* Best Buy Co., Inc.)
175 Green Lane E, East Gwillimbury, ON, L9N 0C9
(905) 954-1262
Emp Here 100
SIC 5731 Radio, television, and electronic stores

D-U-N-S 20-789-9787   (BR)
COSTCO WHOLESALE CANADA LTD
(*Suby of* Costco Wholesale Corporation)
18182 Yonge St, East Gwillimbury, ON, L9N 0J3
(905) 954-4733
Emp Here 220
SIC 5311 Department stores

D-U-N-S 24-349-1433   (BR)
PRINCESS AUTO LTD
18195 Leslie St, East Gwillimbury, ON, L9N 0M2
(905) 952-2107
Emp Here 20
SIC 5251 Hardware stores

D-U-N-S 20-260-6737   (BR)
YORK REGION DISTRICT SCHOOL BOARD
PHOEBE GILMAN PUBLIC SCHOOL
(*Suby of* York Region District School Board)
145 Harvest Hills Blvd, East Gwillimbury, ON, L9N 0C1
(905) 235-5136
Emp Here 70
SIC 8211 Elementary and secondary schools

Echo Bay, ON P0S
Algoma County

D-U-N-S 25-648-2571   (BR)
A.J. BUS LINES LIMITED
3474 Highway 17, Echo Bay, ON, P0S 1C0
(705) 248-2157
Emp Here 40
SIC 4151 School buses

D-U-N-S 20-708-3143   (BR)
CARILLION CANADA INC
3532 Highway 17, Echo Bay, ON, P0S 1C0

Emp Here 40
SIC 1611 Highway and street construction

D-U-N-S 25-643-8144   (SL)
ECHO BAY ELKS LODGE NO. 535 OF THE BENEVOLENT & PROTECTIVE ORDER OF ELKS OF CANADA, INC
96 Church St, Echo Bay, ON, P0S 1C0
(705) 248-2989
Emp Here 50   *Sales* 3,575,074
SIC 8641 Civic and social associations

Eganville, ON K0J
Renfrew County

D-U-N-S 24-119-4252   (SL)
BRIAN SMITH OUTDOOR EDUCATION CENTRE
CAMP SMITTY
98 Mink Lake Rd, Eganville, ON, K0J 1T0
(613) 628-2403
Emp Here 50   *Sales* 4,231,721
SIC 7032 Sporting and recreational camps

D-U-N-S 20-711-6794   (BR)
RENFREW COUNTY DISTRICT SCHOOL BOARD
EGANVILLE PUBLIC SCHOOL
259 Jane St, Eganville, ON, K0J 1T0

(613) 628-2606
Emp Here 35
SIC 8211 Elementary and secondary schools

Egbert, ON L0L
Simcoe County

D-U-N-S 25-410-7550   (BR)
SIMCOE COUNTY DISTRICT SCHOOL BOARD, THE
BAXTER CENTRAL PUBLIC SCHOOL
(*Suby of* Simcoe County District School Board, The)
62 Denney Dr, Egbert, ON, L0L 1N0
(705) 424-9992
Emp Here 32
SIC 8211 Elementary and secondary schools

Elgin, ON K0G
Leeds County

D-U-N-S 24-102-2656   (HQ)
LEEDS TRANSIT INC
AMERICAN BUS PRODUCTS
(*Suby of* Leeds Holdings Inc)
542 Main St, Elgin, ON, K0G 1E0
(613) 359-5344
Emp Here 32   *Emp Total* 42
Sales 41,406,798
SIC 5012 Automobiles and other motor vehicles
Kelly Backholm
Ronald Stenzl

D-U-N-S 20-655-0928   (BR)
UPPER CANADA DISTRICT SCHOOL BOARD, THE
RIDEAU DISTRICT HIGH SCHOOL
251 Main St Suite 2, Elgin, ON, K0G 1E0
(613) 359-5391
Emp Here 35
SIC 8211 Elementary and secondary schools

D-U-N-S 25-237-9565   (BR)
UPPER CANADA DISTRICT SCHOOL BOARD, THE
SOUTH CROSBY PUBLIC SCHOOL
(*Suby of* Upper Canada District School Board, The)
1 Halladay St, Elgin, ON, K0G 1E0
(613) 359-5933
Emp Here 25
SIC 8211 Elementary and secondary schools

Elginburg, ON K0H

D-U-N-S 25-305-4761   (BR)
LIMESTONE DISTRICT SCHOOL BOARD
ELGINBURG PUBLIC SCHOOL
2100 Unity Rd, Elginburg, ON, K0H 1M0
(613) 542-8387
Emp Here 20
SIC 8211 Elementary and secondary schools

Elliot Lake, ON P5A
Algoma County

D-U-N-S 20-046-9757   (HQ)
A.J. BUS LINES LIMITED
2 Charles Walk, Elliot Lake, ON, P5A 2A3
(705) 848-3013
Emp Here 50   *Emp Total* 125
Sales 12,768,123
SIC 5943 Stationery stores
Pr Pr Tom Shamas

VP VP John Shamas

D-U-N-S 25-239-0539   (BR)
ALGOMA DISTRICT SCHOOL BOARD
CENTRAL AVENUE PUBLIC SCHOOL
(*Suby of* Algoma District School Board)
81 Central Ave, Elliot Lake, ON, P5A 2G4
(705) 848-3951
Emp Here 30
SIC 8211 Elementary and secondary schools

D-U-N-S 25-239-0299   (BR)
ALGOMA DISTRICT SCHOOL BOARD
ELLIOT LAKE SECONDARY SCHOOL
(*Suby of* Algoma District School Board)
303 Mississauga Ave, Elliot Lake, ON, P5A 1E8
(705) 848-7162
Emp Here 70
SIC 8211 Elementary and secondary schools

D-U-N-S 25-238-0480   (BR)
CONSEIL SCOLAIRE DE DISTRICT DU GRAND NORD DE L'ONTARIO
CONSEIL SCOLAIRE DE DISTRICT DU GRAND NORD DE L'ON
11 Edinburgh Rd, Elliot Lake, ON, P5A 2M3
(705) 848-2259
Emp Here 25
SIC 8211 Elementary and secondary schools

D-U-N-S 20-045-3087   (BR)
CORPORATION OF THE CITY OF ELLIOT LAKE, THE
ELLIOT LAKE MUNICIPAL POOL
303 Mississauga Ave, Elliot Lake, ON, P5A 1E8

Emp Here 31
SIC 7999 Amusement and recreation, nec

D-U-N-S 20-592-7762   (BR)
DENISON MINES INC
8 Kilborn Way, Elliot Lake, ON, P5A 2T1
(705) 848-9191
Emp Here 50
SIC 8748 Business consulting, nec

D-U-N-S 20-939-1838   (SL)
HURON LODGE COMMUNITY SERVICE BOARD INC
100 Manitoba Rd, Elliot Lake, ON, P5A 3T1
(705) 848-2019
Emp Here 60   *Sales* 2,188,821
SIC 8361 Residential care

D-U-N-S 25-238-0415   (BR)
HURON-SUPERIOR CATHOLIC DISTRICT SCHOOL BOARD
OUR LADY OF LOURDES SCHOOL
139 Mississauga Ave, Elliot Lake, ON, P5A 1E3
(705) 848-3421
Emp Here 20
SIC 8211 Elementary and secondary schools

D-U-N-S 25-238-0449   (BR)
HURON-SUPERIOR CATHOLIC DISTRICT SCHOOL BOARD
OUR LADY OF FATIMA SCHOOL
140 Hillside Dr N, Elliot Lake, ON, P5A 1X7
(705) 848-4664
Emp Here 24
SIC 8211 Elementary and secondary schools

D-U-N-S 24-215-6586   (BR)
K.J BEAMISH CONSTRUCTION CO. LTD
34 Perini Rd, Elliot Lake, ON, P5A 2T1
(705) 848-5488
Emp Here 30
SIC 1611 Highway and street construction

Elmira, ON N3B
Waterloo County

D-U-N-S 20-533-0983   (BR)

2063414 ONTARIO LIMITED
LEISUREWORLD CAREGIVING CENTRE
(*Suby of* 2063414 Ontario Limited)
120 Barnswallow Dr, Elmira, ON, N3B 2Y9
(519) 669-5777
Emp Here 100
SIC 8051 Skilled nursing care facilities

D-U-N-S 25-171-2014   (SL)
3436080 CANADA INC
HOME BUILDING CENTRE ELMIRA
5 Duke St, Elmira, ON, N3B 2W2

Emp Here 20   *Sales* 5,595,120
SIC 5039 Construction materials, nec
Pr John Geddes

D-U-N-S 25-251-2298   (SL)
AT THE CROSSROADS FAMILY RESTAURANT LTD
384 Arthur St S, Elmira, ON, N3B 2P4
(519) 669-9428
Emp Here 50   *Sales* 1,532,175
SIC 5812 Eating places

D-U-N-S 25-561-8258   (SL)
CSH CHATEAU GARDENS ELMIRA INC
11 Herbert St, Elmira, ON, N3B 2B8
(519) 669-2921
Emp Here 20   *Sales* 729,607
SIC 8361 Residential care

D-U-N-S 24-341-4294   (BR)
CANADA COLORS AND CHEMICALS (EASTERN) LIMITED
SULCO CHEMICALS
60 First St W, Elmira, ON, N3B 1G6
(519) 669-1332
Emp Here 20
SIC 2819 Industrial inorganic chemicals, nec

D-U-N-S 24-891-3246   (SL)
ELMIRA GOLF CLUB LIMITED
40 Eldale Rd, Elmira, ON, N3B 2Z5
(519) 669-1651
Emp Here 50   *Sales* 2,425,503
SIC 7997 Membership sports and recreation clubs

D-U-N-S 25-614-7919   (SL)
EVANGELICAL INTERNATIONAL CRUSADE (CANADA) INC
INTERNATIONAL TEAMS OF CANADA
1 Union St, Elmira, ON, N3B 3J9
(519) 669-8844
Emp Here 49   *Sales* 8,049,120
SIC 8699 Membership organizations, nec
Neil Ostrender
Dir Allen Findlay

D-U-N-S 24-827-3901   (BR)
GLOBAL EGG CORPORATION
115 Bonnie Cres, Elmira, ON, N3B 3G2
(416) 231-2309
Emp Here 50
SIC 2015 Poultry slaughtering and processing

D-U-N-S 25-596-1666   (BR)
KINDRED CREDIT UNION LIMITED
MENNONITE SAVINGS AND CREDIT UNION (ONTARIO) LIMITED
25 Hampton St, Elmira, ON, N3B 1L6
(519) 669-1529
Emp Here 23
SIC 6062 State credit unions

D-U-N-S 20-178-5581   (HQ)
LANXESS CANADA CO./CIE
ANDEROL CANADA
25 Erb St, Elmira, ON, N3B 3A3
(519) 669-1671
Emp Here 218   *Emp Total* 16,643
Sales 215,088,144
SIC 2992 Lubricating oils and greases
VP VP Dalip Puri
Sec Arthur Fullerton
Asst Tr Nancy Bissommette
Dir Billie Flaherty

▲ Public Company   ■ Public Company Family Member   **HQ** Headquarters   **BR** Branch   **SL** Single Location

Noel Blake
Dir Stephen Forsyth
Dimitri Makres

D-U-N-S 20-264-2963   (BR)
MARTIN'S FAMILY FRUIT FARM LTD
MARTIN'S PROCESSING
22 Donway Crt, Elmira, ON, N3B 0B3
(519) 669-9822
Emp Here 21
SIC 2034 Dried and dehydrated fruits, vegetables and soup mixes

D-U-N-S 25-146-0424   (HQ)
PREMIER EQUIPMENT LTD.
(*Suby of* Premier Equipment Ltd.)
275 Church St W, Elmira, ON, N3B 1N3
(519) 669-5453
Emp Here 55   *Emp Total* 260
Sales 29,279,284
SIC 5999 Miscellaneous retail stores, nec
VP VP Ian Verbeek
Treas Allan Dueck
Dir Merle Brubacher

D-U-N-S 24-488-0738   (HQ)
PROGRAMMED INSURANCE BROKERS INC
P I B
(*Suby of* Programmed Insurance Brokers Inc)
49 Industrial Dr, Elmira, ON, N3B 3B1
(519) 669-1631
Emp Here 79   *Emp Total* 92
Sales 8,317,520
SIC 6411 Insurance agents, brokers, and service
Dir Bruce Burnham
VP VP Charles Wood
VP VP Robert Burnham
Pr Pr James A Mcdonough

D-U-N-S 24-375-1059   (BR)
TOYOTA BOSHOKU CANADA, INC
45 South Field Dr Suite 1, Elmira, ON, N3B 3L6
(519) 669-8883
Emp Here 315
SIC 3089 Plastics products, nec

D-U-N-S 25-757-6314   (BR)
TRYLON TSF INC
TRYLON TSF
21 S Field Dr, Elmira, ON, N3B 2Z4
(519) 669-5421
Emp Here 26
SIC 1623 Water, sewer, and utility lines

D-U-N-S 25-228-1894   (BR)
WATERLOO CATHOLIC DISTRICT SCHOOL BOARD
ST TERESA OF AVILA ELEMENTARY SCHOOL
69 First St W, Elmira, ON, N3B 1G5
(519) 669-8843
Emp Here 22
SIC 8211 Elementary and secondary schools

D-U-N-S 25-121-2536   (BR)
WATERLOO REGION DISTRICT SCHOOL BOARD
PARK MANOR SENIOR PUBLIC SCHOOL
18 Mockingbird Dr, Elmira, ON, N3B 1T1
(519) 669-5183
Emp Here 22
SIC 8211 Elementary and secondary schools

D-U-N-S 24-974-4582   (BR)
WATERLOO REGION DISTRICT SCHOOL BOARD
ELMIRA DISTRICT SECONDARY SCHOOL
4 University Ave W, Elmira, ON, N3B 1K2
(519) 669-5414
Emp Here 110
SIC 8211 Elementary and secondary schools

D-U-N-S 25-237-9037   (BR)
WATERLOO REGION DISTRICT SCHOOL BOARD

FLORADALE PUBLIC SCHOOL
35 Florapine Rd, Elmira, ON, N3B 2Z1
(519) 669-5193
Emp Here 24
SIC 8211 Elementary and secondary schools

D-U-N-S 25-228-0979   (BR)
WATERLOO REGION DISTRICT SCHOOL BOARD
RIVERSIDE PUBLIC SCHOOL
14a William St, Elmira, ON, N3B 1N9
(519) 669-5417
Emp Here 25
SIC 8211 Elementary and secondary schools

D-U-N-S 20-200-6321   (BR)
WESTOWER COMMUNICATIONS LTD
60 South Field Dr, Elmira, ON, N3B 2Z2
(519) 669-5908
Emp Here 51
SIC 1623 Water, sewer, and utility lines

Elmvale, ON L0L
Simcoe County

D-U-N-S 24-092-8887   (SL)
HAPAMP LIMITED
100 Yonge St N Unit B, Elmvale, ON, L0L 1P0
(705) 322-1353
Emp Here 35   *Sales* 6,128,699
SIC 1623 Water, sewer, and utility lines
Pr Pr Lorne Ogden

D-U-N-S 20-792-5012   (BR)
MCAMM ENTERPRIZES LTD
MCDONALD'S
(*Suby of* Mcamm Enterprizes Ltd)
24 Yonge St N Unit D, Elmvale, ON, L0L 1P0
(705) 322-4444
Emp Here 50
SIC 5812 Eating places

D-U-N-S 25-350-4419   (BR)
REVERA INC
SARA VISTA LONG TERM CARE FACILITY
27 Simcoe St, Elmvale, ON, L0L 1P0
(705) 322-2182
Emp Here 60
SIC 8051 Skilled nursing care facilities

D-U-N-S 25-297-6212   (BR)
SIMCOE COUNTY DISTRICT SCHOOL BOARD, THE
HURONIA CENTENNIAL ELEMENTARY SCHOOL
(*Suby of* Simcoe County District School Board, The)
28 Simcoe St, Elmvale, ON, L0L 1P0
(705) 322-1101
Emp Here 35
SIC 8211 Elementary and secondary schools

D-U-N-S 25-292-4576   (BR)
SIMCOE COUNTY DISTRICT SCHOOL BOARD, THE
ELMVALE DISTRICT HIGH SCHOOL
(*Suby of* Simcoe County District School Board, The)
25 Lawson St, Elmvale, ON, L0L 1P0
(705) 322-2201
Emp Here 40
SIC 8211 Elementary and secondary schools

D-U-N-S 25-238-2494   (BR)
SIMCOE MUSKOKA CATHOLIC DISTRICT SCHOOL BOARD
OUR LADY OF LOURDES SCHOOL
(*Suby of* Simcoe Muskoka Catholic District School Board)
34 Kerr St, Elmvale, ON, L0L 1P0
(705) 322-1622
Emp Here 25
SIC 8211 Elementary and secondary schools

Elora, ON N0B
Wellington County

D-U-N-S 24-124-9283   (SL)
ELORA MILL LIMITED, THE
ELORA MILL INN
77 Mill St W, Elora, ON, N0B 1S0

Emp Here 70   *Sales* 4,220,160
SIC 7011 Hotels and motels

D-U-N-S 24-423-7496   (BR)
HENDRIX GENETICS LIMITED
HYBRID TURKEYS
Gd, Elora, ON, N0B 1S0
(519) 846-5410
Emp Here 20
SIC 7389 Business services, nec

D-U-N-S 24-023-0065   (BR)
HUNTER AMENITIES INTERNATIONAL LTD
37 York St E, Elora, ON, N0B 1S0
(519) 846-2489
Emp Here 100
SIC 2841 Soap and other detergents

D-U-N-S 20-413-9885   (BR)
L & M FOOD MARKET (ONTARIO) LIMITED
169 Geddes St, Elora, ON, N0B 1S0

Emp Here 20
SIC 5411 Grocery stores

D-U-N-S 24-120-0075   (BR)
ONTARIO LOTTERY AND GAMING CORPORATION
7445 County Rd 21, Elora, ON, N0B 1S0
(519) 846-2022
Emp Here 160
SIC 7999 Amusement and recreation, nec

D-U-N-S 20-508-9779   (BR)
POLYCORP LTD
33 York St W, Elora, ON, N0B 1S0
(519) 846-2075
Emp Here 150
SIC 3069 Fabricated rubber products, nec

D-U-N-S 25-952-5806   (BR)
PROGRAMME DE PORTAGE RELATIF A LA DEPENDENCE DE LA DROGUE INC, LE
PORTAGE ONTARIO
(*Suby of* Programme de Portage Relatif a la Dependence de la Drogue Inc, Le)
Gd, Elora, ON, N0B 1S0
(519) 846-0945
Emp Here 30
SIC 8361 Residential care

D-U-N-S 20-025-4303   (BR)
UPPER GRAND DISTRICT SCHOOL BOARD, THE
ELORA PUBLIC SCHOOL
(*Suby of* Upper Grand District School Board, The)
288 Mill St E, Elora, ON, N0B 1S0
(519) 846-5999
Emp Here 40
SIC 8211 Elementary and secondary schools

D-U-N-S 20-024-9576   (BR)
WELLINGTON CATHOLIC DISTRICT SCHOOL BOARD
ST MARY'S CATHOLIC SCHOOL
251 Irvine St, Elora, ON, N0B 1S0
(519) 846-9921
Emp Here 25
SIC 8211 Elementary and secondary schools

D-U-N-S 20-921-3867   (SL)
WOOLWICH AGRICULTURAL SOCIETY
ELMIRA COUNTRY FAIR, THE
7445 Wellington Rd 21, Elora, ON, N0B 1S0
(519) 846-5455
Emp Here 130
SIC 7948 Racing, including track operation

Embro, ON N0J
Oxford County

D-U-N-S 25-910-6342   (BR)
AECON CONSTRUCTION GROUP INC
AECON UTILITIES
7879 Howard Ave, Embro, ON, N0J 1J0
(519) 726-7361
Emp Here 25
SIC 1623 Water, sewer, and utility lines

D-U-N-S 24-537-7580   (BR)
ELGIE BUS LINES LIMITED
77 Union St, Embro, ON, N0J 1J0
(519) 475-6000
Emp Here 49
SIC 4131 Intercity and rural bus transportation

D-U-N-S 25-249-1394   (BR)
THAMES VALLEY DISTRICT SCHOOL BOARD
ZORRA HIGHLAND PARK ELEMENTARY SCHOOL
376368 37th Line, Embro, ON, N0J 1J0
(519) 475-4121
Emp Here 28
SIC 8211 Elementary and secondary schools

Embrun, ON K0A
Russell County

D-U-N-S 20-891-8185   (SL)
412506 ONTARIO LTD
ST-JACQUES NURSING HOME
915 Notre Dame St, Embrun, ON, K0A 1W0
(613) 443-3442
Emp Here 70   *Sales* 3,210,271
SIC 8051 Skilled nursing care facilities

D-U-N-S 25-320-9571   (BR)
BDO CANADA LLP
EMBRUN ACCOUNTING
991 Limoges Rd, Embrun, ON, K0A 1W0
(613) 443-5201
Emp Here 30
SIC 8721 Accounting, auditing, and bookkeeping

D-U-N-S 25-238-6677   (BR)
CONSEIL SCOLAIRE DE DISTRICT CATHOLIQUE DE L'EST ONTARIEN
ECOLE ST-JEAN
(*Suby of* Conseil Scolaire De District Catholique De L'Est Ontarien)
1045 Rue Notre-Dame, Embrun, ON, K0A 1W0
(613) 443-2850
Emp Here 35
SIC 8211 Elementary and secondary schools

D-U-N-S 20-711-6737   (BR)
CONSEIL SCOLAIRE DE DISTRICT CATHOLIQUE DE L'EST ONTARIEN
PAVILLON LE CROISEE
1215 Rue St-Augustin, Embrun, ON, K0A 1W0
(613) 443-4881
Emp Here 50
SIC 8211 Elementary and secondary schools

D-U-N-S 20-656-2584   (BR)
CONSEIL SCOLAIRE DE DISTRICT CATHOLIQUE DE L'EST ONTARIEN
ECOLE SECONDAIRE CATHOLIQUE EMBRUN
1276 Rue St Jacques, Embrun, ON, K0A 1W0
(613) 443-2186
Emp Here 40
SIC 8211 Elementary and secondary schools

D-U-N-S 20-780-9745   (BR)
COOPERATIVE AGRICOLE D'EMBRUN LIMITED, LA

▲ Public Company   ■ Public Company Family Member   **HQ** Headquarters   **BR** Branch   **SL** Single Location

Gd, Embrun, ON, K0A 1W0
(613) 443-2892
Emp Here 100
SIC 5411 Grocery stores

D-U-N-S 20-009-7041   (BR)
UPPER CANADA DISTRICT SCHOOL BOARD, THE
CAMBRIDGE PUBLIC SCHOOL
2123 Route 500 W, Embrun, ON, K0A 1W0
(613) 443-3024
Emp Here 27
SIC 8211 Elementary and secondary schools

Emeryville, ON N0R
Essex County

D-U-N-S 25-906-4830   (BR)
GREATER ESSEX COUNTY DISTRICT SCHOOL BOARD
PUCE PUBLIC SCHOOL
962 Old Tecumseh Rd, Emeryville, ON, N0R 1C0

Emp Here 40
SIC 8211 Elementary and secondary schools

D-U-N-S 24-525-4359   (BR)
GREATER ESSEX COUNTY DISTRICT SCHOOL BOARD
LAKESHORE DISCOVERY PUBLIC SCHOOL
376 Ic Roy Blvd, Emeryville, ON, N0R 1C0
(519) 727-4207
Emp Here 25
SIC 8211 Elementary and secondary schools

D-U-N-S 20-731-8262   (SL)
STEVENSON, G & L TRANSPORT LIMITED
1244 County Road 22, Emeryville, ON, N0R 1C0
(519) 727-3478
Emp Here 115   *Sales* 3,210,271
SIC 4151 School buses

D-U-N-S 20-710-6084   (BR)
WINDSOR-ESSEX CATHOLIC DISTRICT SCHOOL BOARD, THE
ST. WILLIAMS CATHOLIC SCHOOL
1217 Faith Dr, Emeryville, ON, N0R 1C0
(519) 727-3393
Emp Here 55
SIC 8211 Elementary and secondary schools

D-U-N-S 25-070-0408   (BR)
WINDSOR-ESSEX CATHOLIC DISTRICT SCHOOL BOARD, THE
ST. WILLIAMS SCHOOL
1217 Faith St, Emeryville, ON, N0R 1C0
(519) 727-3393
Emp Here 25
SIC 8211 Elementary and secondary schools

Emo, ON P0W
Rainy River County

D-U-N-S 25-238-0613   (BR)
RAINY RIVER DISTRICT SCHOOL BOARD
DONALD YOUNG ELEMENTARY SCHOOL
57 Colonizat on Rd, Emo, ON, P0W 1E0
(807) 482-2271
Emp Here 26
SIC 8211 Elementary and secondary schools

D-U-N-S 20-273-1378   (BR)
RIVERSIDE HEALTH CARE FACILITIES INC
EMO HEALTH CENTRE
170 Front St, Emo, ON, P0W 1E0
(807) 274-3261
Emp Here 45
SIC 8062 General medical and surgical hospitals

D-U-N-S 25-478-8961   (BR)
RIVERSIDE HEALTH CARE FACILITIES INC
EMO HEALTH CENTRE
72 Front St, Emo, ON, P0W 1E0

Emp Here 38
SIC 8059 Nursing and personal care, nec

Emsdale, ON P0A
Parry Sound County

D-U-N-S 20-710-4311   (BR)
NEAR NORTH DISTRICT SCHOOL BOARD
EVERGREEN HEIGHTS EDUCATION CENTER
2510 592 Hwy, Emsdale, ON, P0A 1J0
(705) 636-5955
Emp Here 24
SIC 8211 Elementary and secondary schools

Englehart, ON P0J
Timiskaming County

D-U-N-S 25-263-7251   (BR)
DISTRICT SCHOOL BOARD ONTARIO NORTH EAST
ENGLEHART PUBLIC SCHOOL
70 8th Ave, Englehart, ON, P0J 1H0
(705) 544-2345
Emp Here 25
SIC 8211 Elementary and secondary schools

D-U-N-S 20-349-8787   (BR)
ONTARIO NORTHLAND TRANSPORTATION COMMISSION
1 Railway St, Englehart, ON, P0J 1H0
(705) 544-2292
Emp Here 80
SIC 4111 Local and suburban transit

D-U-N-S 25-654-2234   (BR)
TIMISKAMING HOME SUPPORT/SOUTIEN A DOMICILE
(*Suby of* Timiskaming Home Support/Soutien A Domicile)
61 Fifth Ave, Englehart, ON, P0J 1H0

Emp Here 60
SIC 8399 Social services, nec

Ennismore, ON K0L
Peterborough County

D-U-N-S 20-025-0616   (BR)
PETERBOROUGH VICTORIA NORTHUMBERLAND AND CLARINGTON CATHOLIC DISTRICT SCHOOL BOARD
ST MARTIN'S ELEMENTARY SCHOOL
531 Ennis Rd, Ennismore, ON, K0L 1T0
(705) 292-8997
Emp Here 28
SIC 8211 Elementary and secondary schools

Erin, ON N0B
Wellington County

D-U-N-S 24-926-6610   (SL)
CALERIN GOLF CLUB INC
9521 10th Side Rd, Erin, ON, N0B 1T0
(519) 833-2168
Emp Here 20   *Sales* 802,568
SIC 7997 Membership sports and recreation clubs

D-U-N-S 25-797-4824   (BR)

CORPORATION OF THE TOWN OF ERIN, THE
ERIN COMMUNITY CENTRE
14 Boland Dr Ss 1 Suite 662, Erin, ON, N0B 1T0
(519) 833-2114
Emp Here 20
SIC 8322 Individual and family services

D-U-N-S 24-926-9713   (SL)
T.S. SIMMS & CO.
300 Main St, Erin, ON, N0B 1T0
(905) 362-1470
Emp Here 60
SIC 3991 Brooms and brushes

D-U-N-S 20-654-0051   (BR)
UPPER GRAND DISTRICT SCHOOL BOARD, THE
BRISBANE PUBLIC SCHOOL
(*Suby of* Upper Grand District School Board, The)
9426 Wellington Rd 124, Erin, ON, N0B 1T0
(519) 833-9621
Emp Here 25
SIC 8211 Elementary and secondary schools

D-U-N-S 20-025-1671   (BR)
UPPER GRAND DISTRICT SCHOOL BOARD, THE
ERIN PUBLIC SCHOOL
(*Suby of* Upper Grand District School Board, The)
185 Daniel St Ss 1, Erin, ON, N0B 1T0
(519) 833-9685
Emp Here 35
SIC 8211 Elementary and secondary schools

D-U-N-S 20-810-5937   (BR)
UPPER GRAND DISTRICT SCHOOL BOARD, THE
ERIN DISTRICT HIGH SCHOOL
(*Suby of* Upper Grand District School Board, The)
14 Boland Dr Ss 1, Erin, ON, N0B 1T0
(519) 833-9665
Emp Here 50
SIC 8211 Elementary and secondary schools

Espanola, ON P5E
Sudbury County

D-U-N-S 25-238-2114   (BR)
CONSEIL SCOLAIRE DE DISTRICT CATHOLIQUE DU NOUVEL-ONTARIO, LE
ST. JOSEPH ELEMENTARY SCHOOL
333 Mead Blvd, Espanola, ON, P5E 1C4
(705) 869-3530
Emp Here 20
SIC 8211 Elementary and secondary schools

D-U-N-S 25-238-2106   (BR)
HURON-SUPERIOR CATHOLIC DISTRICT SCHOOL BOARD
SACRED HEART SCHOOL
273 Mead Blvd, Espanola, ON, P5E 1B3
(705) 869-4070
Emp Here 35
SIC 8211 Elementary and secondary schools

D-U-N-S 25-784-6980   (SL)
MCKECHNIE, ANDY BUILDING MATERIALS LTD
ESPANOLA HOME HARDWARE
830 Centre St, Espanola, ON, P5E 1J1
(705) 869-2130
Emp Here 50   *Sales* 7,369,031
SIC 5211 Lumber and other building materials
Pr Pr Andrew Mckechnie
VP VP Ann Mckechnie

D-U-N-S 24-019-8320   (BR)
OUR CHILDREN, OUR FUTURE
(*Suby of* Our Children, Our Future)

273 Mead Blvd, Espanola, ON, P5E 1B3
(705) 869-5545
Emp Here 100
SIC 8351 Child day care services

D-U-N-S 25-238-0688   (BR)
RAINBOW DISTRICT SCHOOL BOARD
A B ELLIS PUBLIC ELEMENTARY SCHOOL
(*Suby of* Rainbow District School Board)
128 Park St, Espanola, ON, P5E 1S7
(705) 869-1651
Emp Here 50
SIC 8211 Elementary and secondary schools

D-U-N-S 20-155-4677   (BR)
RAINBOW DISTRICT SCHOOL BOARD
ESPANOLA HIGH SCHOOL
147 Spruce Ave Suite 2, Espanola, ON, P5E 1R7
(705) 869-1590
Emp Here 55
SIC 8211 Elementary and secondary schools

D-U-N-S 24-021-3426   (BR)
SOBEYS CAPITAL INCORPORATED
FRESHCO
800 Centre St Suite 500, Espanola, ON, P5E 1J3
(705) 869-6777
Emp Here 50
SIC 5411 Grocery stores

D-U-N-S 24-344-5835   (BR)
T BELL TRANSPORT INC
2242 Lee Valley Rd, Espanola, ON, P5E 1P6
(705) 869-1041
Emp Here 25
SIC 1629 Heavy construction, nec

Essex, ON N8M
Essex County

D-U-N-S 25-016-9752   (BR)
CANADIAN IMPERIAL BANK OF COMMERCE
CIBC
33 Talbot St N, Essex, ON, N8M 1A3
(519) 776-5226
Emp Here 20
SIC 6021 National commercial banks

D-U-N-S 25-249-2103   (BR)
GREATER ESSEX COUNTY DISTRICT SCHOOL BOARD
MAPLEWOOD PUBLIC SCHOOL
72 Brien Ave E, Essex, ON, N8M 2N8
(519) 776-5044
Emp Here 30
SIC 8211 Elementary and secondary schools

D-U-N-S 25-249-2046   (BR)
GREATER ESSEX COUNTY DISTRICT SCHOOL BOARD
COLCHESTER NORTH PUBLIC SCHOOL
2651 County Rd 12, Essex, ON, N8M 2X6
(519) 776-8118
Emp Here 25
SIC 8211 Elementary and secondary schools

D-U-N-S 20-710-5839   (BR)
GREATER ESSEX COUNTY DISTRICT SCHOOL BOARD
SUN PARLOR PUBLIC SCHOOL
125 Maidstone Ave W, Essex, ON, N8M 2W2

Emp Here 50
SIC 8211 Elementary and secondary schools

D-U-N-S 24-609-7161   (SL)
JEFF'S NO FRILLS
53 Arthur Ave, Essex, ON, N8M 2N1
(519) 776-4944
Emp Here 49   *Sales* 6,055,738
SIC 5411 Grocery stores
Owner Jeff Nacthee

D-U-N-S 20-965-3182   (BR)
MAPLEHURST BAKERIES INC
READY BAKE FOODS INC
22 Victor St, Essex, ON, N8M 1J7
(519) 776-1568
Emp Here 115
SIC 2053 Frozen bakery products, except bread

D-U-N-S 25-001-3968   (BR)
REVERA INC
ILER LODGE RETIREMENT HOME
111 Iler Ave Suite 1, Essex, ON, N8M 1T6
(519) 776-5243
Emp Here 85
SIC 8051 Skilled nursing care facilities

D-U-N-S 25-302-5647   (BR)
REVERA LONG TERM CARE INC
ILER LODGE
111 Iler Ave Suite 318, Essex, ON, N8M 1T6
(519) 776-9482
Emp Here 50
SIC 8051 Skilled nursing care facilities

D-U-N-S 25-249-1865   (BR)
WINDSOR-ESSEX CATHOLIC DISTRICT SCHOOL BOARD, THE
HOLY NAME CATHOLIC ELEMENTARY SCHOOL
200 Fairview Ave W, Essex, ON, N8M 1Y1
(519) 776-7351
Emp Here 38
SIC 8211 Elementary and secondary schools

D-U-N-S 25-482-5094   (BR)
YMCA OF GREATER TORONTO
WINDSOR-ESSEX COUNTY FAMILY YMCA
35 Victoria Ave, Essex, ON, N8M 1M4
(519) 776-7305
Emp Here 60
SIC 8641 Civic and social associations

Etobicoke, ON L5B
York County

D-U-N-S 24-511-5196   (BR)
BENEFIT PLAN ADMINISTRATORS LIMITED
(*Suby of* Benefit Plan Administrators Limited)
90 Burnhamthorpe Rd W, Etobicoke, ON, L5B 3C3
(905) 275-6466
Emp Here 180
SIC 8742 Management consulting services

Etobicoke, ON M8V
York County

D-U-N-S 24-793-3872   (SL)
A B C COMPANY LIMITED
CANADIAN STORES
123 Fourth St, Etobicoke, ON, M8V 2Y6
(905) 812-5941
Emp Here 110   *Sales* 35,170,120
SIC 5311 Department stores
Pr Pr Terry Smith
 Bob Henderson
 Trevor Lawrence

D-U-N-S 24-219-6504   (SL)
AMBATOVY JOINT VENTURE
AMBATOVY PROJECT
2200 Lake Shore Blvd W, Etobicoke, ON, M8V 1A4
(416) 924-4551
Emp Here 8,000   *Sales* 1,277,421,192
SIC 1061 Ferroalloy ores, except vanadium
 Jerry Bolton

D-U-N-S 24-815-9949   (HQ)
BPSR CORPORATION

BPSR NOVELTIES
(*Suby of* BPSR Corporation)
123 Fourth St, Etobicoke, ON, M8V 2Y6
(905) 999-9999
Emp Here 100   *Emp Total* 182
Sales 18,045,376
SIC 5311 Department stores
Pr Pr Terry Smith
 Bob Henderson
 Trevor Lawrence
Off Mgr Debbie Potter
Sls Mgr Michele Goulding
Sls Mgr Samatha Pretty

D-U-N-S 20-161-0771   (HQ)
CAMPBELL COMPANY OF CANADA
(*Suby of* Campbell Soup Company)
60 Birmingham St, Etobicoke, ON, M8V 2B8
(416) 251-1131
Emp Here 700   *Emp Total* 18,600
Sales 166,886,466
SIC 2032 Canned specialties
Pr Pr Phillip E Donne
VP VP Greg Smith
VP Fin Earl Ellis

D-U-N-S 25-214-8671   (BR)
CORPORATION OF THE CITY OF TORONTO
JOHN ENGLISH COMMUNITY SCHOOL
95 Mimico Ave Suite 100b, Etobicoke, ON, M8V 1R4
(416) 394-8711
Emp Here 30
SIC 7999 Amusement and recreation, nec

D-U-N-S 24-987-6517   (BR)
DOMINION COLOUR CORPORATION
(*Suby of* H.I.G. Capital, L.L.C.)
199 New Toronto St, Etobicoke, ON, M8V 3X4
(416) 253-4260
Emp Here 80
SIC 2816 Inorganic pigments

D-U-N-S 24-242-8063   (SL)
EDEN TRATTORIA 11
58 Marine Parade Dr Suite Ph10, Etobicoke, ON, M8V 4G1
(416) 255-5588
Emp Here 50   *Sales* 1,532,175
SIC 5812 Eating places

D-U-N-S 24-523-4484   (BR)
GAMBLES ONTARIO PRODUCE INC
(*Suby of* Gambles Ontario Produce Inc)
302 Dwight Ave, Etobicoke, ON, M8V 2W7
(877) 528-0444
Emp Here 50
SIC 5148 Fresh fruits and vegetables

D-U-N-S 24-984-6809   (BR)
HUMBER COLLEGE INSTITUTE OF TECHNOLOGY AND ADVANCE
3199 Lake Shore Blvd W, Etobicoke, ON, M8V 1K8
(416) 675-6622
Emp Here 250
SIC 8221 Colleges and universities

D-U-N-S 24-382-2660   (BR)
HUMBER COLLEGE INSTITUTE OF TECHNOLOGY AND ADVANCE
SAILING AND POWER BOATING CENTRE
100 Humber Bay Park Rd W, Etobicoke, ON, M8V 3X7
(416) 252-7291
Emp Here 20
SIC 8221 Colleges and universities

D-U-N-S 25-318-2059   (BR)
MCDONALD'S RESTAURANTS OF CANADA LIMITED
MCDONALD'S 5772
(*Suby of* McDonald's Corporation)
2736 Lake Shore Blvd W, Etobicoke, ON, M8V 1H1

(416) 259-3201
Emp Here 65
SIC 5812 Eating places

D-U-N-S 25-202-8279   (SL)
Q & I COMPUTER SYSTEMS INC
115 Symons St, Etobicoke, ON, M8V 1V1
(416) 253-5555
Emp Here 500   *Sales* 95,706,000
SIC 7371 Custom computer programming services
Pr Pr Jonathan Schloo
VP VP Ben Schloo

D-U-N-S 25-352-1942   (SL)
SHELTON CORPORATION LIMITED
2200 Lake Shore Blvd W Suite 103, Etobicoke, ON, M8V 1A4
(416) 251-8517
Emp Here 33   *Sales* 13,797,200
SIC 5172 Petroleum products, nec
 Zenon Potoczny
Pr Pr Serhiy Rys
 Serhiy Kryvosheya

D-U-N-S 25-132-1998   (BR)
TORONTO CATHOLIC DISTRICT SCHOOL BOARD
FR. JOHN REDMOND CATHOLIC SECONDARY SCHOOL
28 Colonel Samuel Smith Park Dr, Etobicoke, ON, M8V 4B7
(416) 393-5540
Emp Here 70
SIC 8211 Elementary and secondary schools

D-U-N-S 20-711-1308   (BR)
TORONTO CATHOLIC DISTRICT SCHOOL BOARD
ST. LEO CATHOLIC SCHOOL
165 Stanley Ave, Etobicoke, ON, M8V 1P1
(416) 393-5333
Emp Here 50
SIC 8211 Elementary and secondary schools

D-U-N-S 20-711-2793   (BR)
TORONTO DISTRICT SCHOOL BOARD
20TH ST SCHOOL
3190 Lake Shore Blvd W, Etobicoke, ON, M8V 1L8
(416) 394-7810
Emp Here 37
SIC 8211 Elementary and secondary schools

D-U-N-S 20-698-7161   (BR)
TORONTO DISTRICT SCHOOL BOARD
LAKESHORE COLLEGIATE INSTITUTE
350 Kipling Ave, Etobicoke, ON, M8V 3L1
(416) 394-7650
Emp Here 70
SIC 8211 Elementary and secondary schools

D-U-N-S 20-711-2710   (BR)
TORONTO DISTRICT SCHOOL BOARD
JOHN ENGLISH JUNIOR MIDDLE SCHOOL
95 Mimico Ave, Etobicoke, ON, M8V 1R4
(416) 394-7660
Emp Here 60
SIC 8211 Elementary and secondary schools

D-U-N-S 24-097-4246   (SL)
YORK CONDOMINIUM CORPORATION NO 382
PALACE PIER
2045 Lake Shore Blvd W, Etobicoke, ON, M8V 2Z6
(416) 252-7701
Emp Here 50   *Sales* 4,742,446
SIC 6531 Real estate agents and managers

Etobicoke, ON M8W
York County

D-U-N-S 25-252-8013   (SL)
ALL WOOD FINE INTERIORS LTD
81 Akron Rd Suite 101, Etobicoke, ON, M8W

1T3
(416) 252-2552
Emp Here 50   *Sales* 3,356,192
SIC 2541 Wood partitions and fixtures

D-U-N-S 25-889-3486   (BR)
BANK OF MONTREAL
BMO
863 Browns Line, Etobicoke, ON, M8W 3V7
(416) 259-3236
Emp Here 20
SIC 6021 National commercial banks

D-U-N-S 20-160-5953   (BR)
BRINK'S CANADA LIMITED
BRINKS TORONTO
(*Suby of* The Brink's Company)
95 Browns Line, Etobicoke, ON, M8W 3S2
(416) 461-0261
Emp Here 300
SIC 7381 Detective and armored car services

D-U-N-S 25-419-6983   (BR)
CASCADES CANADA ULC
CASCADES CONTAINERBOARD PACKAGING - ART & DIE
450 Evans Ave, Etobicoke, ON, M8W 2T5
(416) 255-8541
Emp Here 157
SIC 2657 Folding paperboard boxes

D-U-N-S 20-016-9634   (SL)
EVENT SCAPE INC
4 Bestobell Rd, Etobicoke, ON, M8W 4H3
(416) 231-8855
Emp Here 60   *Sales* 3,638,254
SIC 7389 Business services, nec

D-U-N-S 25-093-4911   (BR)
INTEGRATED DISTRIBUTION SYSTEMS LIMITED PARTNERSHIP
WAJAX POWER SYSTEMS
(*Suby of* Integrated Distribution Systems Limited Partnership)
10 Diesel Dr, Etobicoke, ON, M8W 2T8
(416) 259-3281
Emp Here 100
SIC 8711 Engineering services

D-U-N-S 24-422-9568   (BR)
INTERIOR MANUFACTURING GROUP INC
324 Horner Ave Unit B1, Etobicoke, ON, M8W 1Z3
(416) 253-9100
Emp Here 45
SIC 2542 Partitions and fixtures, except wood

D-U-N-S 24-889-4792   (SL)
LISTER, F.G. TRANSPORTATION INC
475 Horner Ave, Etobicoke, ON, M8W 4X7
(416) 259-7621
Emp Here 25   *Sales* 2,845,467
SIC 4213 Trucking, except local

D-U-N-S 24-473-7571   (SL)
LUMENIX CORPORATION
LUMENIX
15 Akron Rd, Etobicoke, ON, M8W 1T3
(855) 586-3649
Emp Here 200   *Sales* 38,888,053
SIC 3674 Semiconductors and related devices
Pr Bryant Tse
Ch Bd Scott Delaney
VP Derek Thomas
VP Sls Liam Ellis
Ex Dir Robert Richards
Dir Joseph Clark
Dir George Brookman
Dir Andrew Wilkes

D-U-N-S 25-991-3957   (SL)
MORTGAGE ALLIANCE
3385 Lake Shore Blvd W, Etobicoke, ON, M8W 1N2

Emp Here 21   *Sales* 5,182,810
SIC 6162 Mortgage bankers and loan correspondents

Owner Michael Beckette

D-U-N-S 20-091-6034   (SL)
NEW HAVEN LEARNING CENTRE FOR CHILDREN
301 Lanor Ave, Etobicoke, ON, M8W 2R1
(416) 259-4445
Emp Here 55   *Sales* 3,648,035
SIC 8211 Elementary and secondary schools

D-U-N-S 24-096-2969   (HQ)
SAM KOTZER LIMITED
SAMKO SALES
(*Suby of* Sam Kotzer Limited)
77 Fima Cres, Etobicoke, ON, M8W 3R1
(416) 532-1114
Emp Here 40   *Emp Total* 50
Sales 4,805,878
SIC 5945 Hobby, toy, and game shops

D-U-N-S 20-711-0904   (BR)
TORONTO CATHOLIC DISTRICT SCHOOL BOARD
CHRIST THE KING CATHOLIC SCHOOL
3672 Lake Shore Blvd W, Etobicoke, ON, M8W 1N6
(416) 393-5257
Emp Here 20
SIC 8211 Elementary and secondary schools

D-U-N-S 20-025-1531   (BR)
TORONTO DISTRICT SCHOOL BOARD
SIR ADAM BECK JUNIOR SCHOOL
544 Horner Ave, Etobicoke, ON, M8W 2C2
(416) 394-7670
Emp Here 40
SIC 8211 Elementary and secondary schools

D-U-N-S 20-711-2728   (BR)
TORONTO DISTRICT SCHOOL BOARD
LANOR JUNIOR MIDDLE SCHOOL
450 Lanor Ave, Etobicoke, ON, M8W 2S1
(416) 394-7800
Emp Here 50
SIC 8211 Elementary and secondary schools

D-U-N-S 24-677-0429   (BR)
VEG-PAK PRODUCE LIMITED
25 Belvia Rd, Etobicoke, ON, M8W 3R2
(416) 255-7400
Emp Here 50
SIC 5148 Fresh fruits and vegetables

D-U-N-S 25-366-4312   (HQ)
WAKEFIELD CANADA INC
(*Suby of* Wakefield Canada Inc)
3620 Lake Shore Blvd W, Etobicoke, ON, M8W 1N6
(416) 252-5511
Emp Here 137   *Emp Total* 192
Sales 57,784,874
SIC 5172 Petroleum products, nec
Pr Pr Rober: Mcdonald
Dir Robert Saurette
S&M/VP Kent Rennie

Etobicoke, ON M8X
York County

D-U-N-S 24-195-0203   (HQ)
ADP CANADA CO
(*Suby of* Automatic Data Processing, Inc.)
3250 Bloor St W Suite 1600, Etobicoke, ON, M8X 2X9
(416) 207-2900
Emp Here 700   *Emp Total* 55,000
Sales 103,950,120
SIC 8721 Accounting, auditing, and bookkeeping
Pr Pr Greg Secord
Liane Lacroix
Russell Wong

D-U-N-S 25-821-8056   (BR)
BANK OF MONTREAL

BMO
3022 Bloor St W, Etobicoke, ON, M8X 1C4
(416) 231-2255
Emp Here 20
SIC 6021 National commercial banks

D-U-N-S 25-374-0047   (BR)
BANQUE LAURENTIENNE DU CANADA
2972 Bloor St W, Etobicoke, ON, M8X 1B9
(416) 236-1761
Emp Here 35
SIC 6021 National commercial banks

D-U-N-S 24-574-8512   (HQ)
BEAM CANADA INC
MAXXIUM CANADA
3300 Bloor St W Ctr Tower 5th Suite 40, Etobicoke, ON, M8X 2X3
(416) 849-7300
Emp Here 63   *Emp Total* 55
Sales 16,051,354
SIC 5182 Wine and distilled beverages
William Newlands
CFO Robert Probst

D-U-N-S 24-463-0604   (HQ)
CBI LIMITED
CBI HEALTH
(*Suby of* CBI Limited)
3300 Bloor St W Suite 900, Etobicoke, ON, M8X 2X2
(800) 463-2225
Emp Here 50   *Emp Total* 4,700
Sales 268,104,685
SIC 8049 Offices of health practitioner
Pr Pr Christopher Szybbo
Dir Timothy J. Patterson
Dir Jonathan Mccarthy

D-U-N-S 20-073-6754   (BR)
CANADIAN RED CROSS SOCIETY, THE
4210 Dundas St W, Etobicoke, ON, M8X 1Y6
(416) 236-1791
Emp Here 20
SIC 8699 Membership organizations, nec

D-U-N-S 25-419-8054   (BR)
CARA OPERATIONS LIMITED
SWISS CHALET CHICKEN & RIBS
(*Suby of* Cara Holdings Limited)
2955 Bloor St W, Etobicoke, ON, M8X 1B8
(416) 233-4573
Emp Here 50
SIC 5812 Eating places

D-U-N-S 24-678-9650   (SL)
CONQUEST VEHICLES INC
3300 Bloor St W Suite 3100, Etobicoke, ON, M8X 2X3
(905) 882-0606
Emp Here 40   *Sales* 11,768,200
SIC 3711 Motor vehicles and car bodies
Pr Pr William Maizlin
VP VP Tim Chapman
Roger Elgner
John Kehl

D-U-N-S 25-301-2298   (BR)
EXTENDICARE (CANADA) INC
PARAMED HOME HEALTH CARE
56 Aberfoyle Cres, Etobicoke, ON, M8X 2W4
(416) 236-1061
Emp Here 300
SIC 8051 Skilled nursing care facilities

D-U-N-S 20-812-8111   (BR)
GUELPH, CITY OF
MEMORIAL POOL AND HEALTHCLUB
44 Montgomery Rd, Etobicoke, ON, M8X 1Z4
(416) 394-8731
Emp Here 40
SIC 7999 Amusement and recreation, nec

D-U-N-S 24-215-6826   (SL)
LARK HOSPITALITY INC
THE OLD MILL INN
21 Old Mill Rd, Etobicoke, ON, M8X 1G5

(416) 232-3700
Emp Here 270   *Sales* 11,590,647
SIC 7299 Miscellaneous personal service
Pr Pr Michael Kalmar
Blaine Parsons

D-U-N-S 25-318-7082   (BR)
LIQUOR CONTROL BOARD OF ONTARIO, THE
L.C.B.O. #149
2946 Bloor St W, Etobicoke, ON, M8X 1B7
(416) 239-3065
Emp Here 30
SIC 5921 Liquor stores

D-U-N-S 25-109-4413   (BR)
MARKET PROBE CANADA COMPANY
1243 Islington Ave Suite 200, Etobicoke, ON, M8X 1Y9
(416) 233-1555
Emp Here 140
SIC 8732 Commercial nonphysical research

D-U-N-S 20-544-0477   (BR)
MOMENTIS CANADA CORP
ONTARIO ENERGY SAVINGS
1243 Islington Ave Suite 1201, Etobicoke, ON, M8X 1Y9

Emp Here 30
SIC 7311 Advertising agencies

D-U-N-S 25-925-5149   (BR)
RBC DOMINION SECURITIES INC
(*Suby of* Royal Bank Of Canada)
3250 Bloor St W Suite 705, Etobicoke, ON, M8X 2X9
(416) 231-6766
Emp Here 35
SIC 6211 Security brokers and dealers

D-U-N-S 20-325-2036   (BR)
ROYAL BANK OF CANADA
RBC AUTOMOTIVE FINANCE
(*Suby of* Royal Bank Of Canada)
3250 Bloor St W Suite 800, Etobicoke, ON, M8X 2X9

Emp Here 100
SIC 6159 Miscellaneous business credit institutions

D-U-N-S 24-829-9836   (BR)
ROYAL LEPAGE LIMITED
3031 Bloor St W, Etobicoke, ON, M8X 1C5
(416) 236-1871
Emp Here 120
SIC 6531 Real estate agents and managers

D-U-N-S 25-977-0394   (HQ)
SITEL CANADA CORPORATION
3250 Bloor St W, Etobicoke, ON, M8X 2X9

Emp Here 700   *Sales* 98,671,360
SIC 7389 Business services, nec
Ch Bd Tom Harbison
Dir Anne Marie Greer

D-U-N-S 20-506-0846   (BR)
STARBUCKS COFFEE CANADA, INC
(*Suby of* Starbucks Corporation)
2940 Bloor St W, Etobicoke, ON, M8X 1B6
(416) 236-9191
Emp Here 21
SIC 5812 Eating places

D-U-N-S 25-191-9395   (BR)
TD WATERHOUSE CANADA INC
(*Suby of* Toronto-Dominion Bank, The)
3250 Bloor St W Suite 126, Etobicoke, ON, M8X 2X9

Emp Here 20
SIC 6211 Security brokers and dealers

D-U-N-S 25-419-5019   (BR)
TORONTO CATHOLIC DISTRICT SCHOOL BOARD
OUR LADY OF SORROWS CATHOLIC

SCHOOL
32 Montgomery Rd, Etobicoke, ON, M8X 1Z4
(416) 393-5246
Emp Here 38
SIC 8211 Elementary and secondary schools

D-U-N-S 20-025-3636   (BR)
TORONTO DISTRICT SCHOOL BOARD
LAMBTON KINGSWAY JUNIOR MIDDLE SCHOOL
525 Prince Edward Dr N, Etobicoke, ON, M8X 2M6
(416) 394-7890
Emp Here 50
SIC 8211 Elementary and secondary schools

D-U-N-S 20-034-2454   (BR)
TORONTO PUBLIC LIBRARY BOARD
BRENTWOOD LIBRARY
36 Brentwood Rd N, Etobicoke, ON, M8X 2B5
(416) 394-5240
Emp Here 20
SIC 8231 Libraries

Etobicoke, ON M8Y
York County

D-U-N-S 20-077-0290   (BR)
CONSEIL SCOLAIRE DE DISTRICT CATHOLIQUE CENTRE-SUD
SAINTE-MARGUERITE-D'YOUVILLE
755 Royal York Rd, Etobicoke, ON, M8Y 2T3
(416) 393-5418
Emp Here 35
SIC 8211 Elementary and secondary schools

D-U-N-S 24-794-5652   (HQ)
GAMBLES ONTARIO PRODUCE INC
165 The Queensway Suite 240, Etobicoke, ON, M8Y 1H8
(416) 259-6391
Emp Here 150   *Emp Total* 200
Sales 48,445,905
SIC 5148 Fresh fruits and vegetables
Pr Pr Jeffrey Hughes
VP VP Robert Giles

D-U-N-S 25-957-4148   (SL)
GET A BETTER MORTGAGE
642 The Queensway, Etobicoke, ON, M8Y 1K5
(416) 252-9000
Emp Here 49   *Sales* 9,630,812
SIC 6162 Mortgage bankers and loan correspondents
Owner Robert Distefano

D-U-N-S 20-168-5096   (SL)
KING & RAPHAEL TORONTO LIMITED
165 The Queensway Suite 226, Etobicoke, ON, M8Y 1H8

Emp Here 20   *Sales* 6,695,700
SIC 5148 Fresh fruits and vegetables
Pr Pr Anthony Badali

D-U-N-S 24-216-7158   (BR)
PROCTER & GAMBLE INC
(*Suby of* The Procter & Gamble Company)
66 Humbervale Blvd, Etobicoke, ON, M8Y 3P4
(416) 730-4200
Emp Here 50
SIC 2844 Toilet preparations

D-U-N-S 25-818-7467   (SL)
RUSSELL, J.E. PRODUCE LTD
165 The Queensway Suite 332, Etobicoke, ON, M8Y 1H8
(416) 252-7838
Emp Here 40   *Sales* 11,521,138
SIC 5148 Fresh fruits and vegetables
Pr Pr John Russell
Diana Russell

D-U-N-S 25-419-9540   (BR)

TORONTO CATHOLIC DISTRICT SCHOOL BOARD
BISHOP ALLEN ACADEMY
721 Royal York Rd, Etobicoke, ON, M8Y 2T3
(416) 393-5549
Emp Here 115
SIC 8211 Elementary and secondary schools

D-U-N-S 20-711-1316   (BR)
TORONTO CATHOLIC DISTRICT SCHOOL BOARD
ST. LOUIS CATHOLIC SCHOOL
11 Morgan Ave, Etobicoke, ON, M8Y 2Z7
(416) 393-5331
Emp Here 50
SIC 8211 Elementary and secondary schools

D-U-N-S 20-697-6305   (BR)
TORONTO CATHOLIC DISTRICT SCHOOL BOARD
ST. MARK CATHOLIC SCHOOL
45 Cloverhill Rd, Etobicoke, ON, M8Y 1T4
(416) 393-5332
Emp Here 40
SIC 8211 Elementary and secondary schools

D-U-N-S 25-991-0263   (BR)
TORONTO DISTRICT SCHOOL BOARD
ETOBICOKE SCHOOL OF THE ARTS
675 Royal York Rd, Etobicoke, ON, M8Y 2T1
(416) 394-6910
Emp Here 100
SIC 8211 Elementary and secondary schools

D-U-N-S 20-026-0250   (BR)
TORONTO DISTRICT SCHOOL BOARD
ETIENNE BRULE JR PUBLIC SCHOOL
50 Cloverhill Rd, Etobicoke, ON, M8Y 1T3
(416) 394-7850
Emp Here 20
SIC 8211 Elementary and secondary schools

D-U-N-S 24-676-5106   (BR)
TORONTO DISTRICT SCHOOL BOARD
KAREN KAIN SCHOOL OF THE ARTS
60 Berl Ave, Etobicoke, ON, M8Y 3C7
(416) 394-7979
Emp Here 20
SIC 8299 Schools and educational services, nec

D-U-N-S 20-003-5066   (BR)
TORONTO DISTRICT SCHOOL BOARD
PARK LAWN JUNIOR MIDDLE SCHOOL
71 Ballacaine Dr, Etobicoke, ON, M8Y 4B6
(416) 394-7120
Emp Here 45
SIC 8211 Elementary and secondary schools

Etobicoke, ON M8Z
York County

D-U-N-S 20-108-8353   (SL)
3831906 CANADA INC
SOLUTIONSOEUFS
283 Horner Ave, Etobicoke, ON, M8Z 4Y4
(416) 231-2309
Emp Here 25   *Sales* 2,407,703
SIC 2015 Poultry slaughtering and processing

D-U-N-S 24-307-2253   (BR)
3M CANADA COMPANY
3M PROMOTIONAL MARKETS
(*Suby of* 3M Company)
14 Plastics Ave, Etobicoke, ON, M8Z 4B7
(416) 503-3911
Emp Here 20
SIC 2678 Stationery products

D-U-N-S 24-335-4214   (SL)
427 AUTO COLLISION LIMITED
395 Evans Ave, Etobicoke, ON, M8Z 1K8
(416) 259-6344
Emp Here 50   *Sales* 3,575,074
SIC 7532 Top and body repair and paint shops

D-U-N-S 24-923-5037   (SL)
621828 ONTARIO LTD
7a Taymall Ave, Etobicoke, ON, M8Z 3Y8
(416) 252-1186
Emp Here 55   *Sales* 8,857,893
SIC 6712 Bank holding companies
Pr Tracy Parzych

D-U-N-S 25-203-4889   (BR)
ARAMARK CANADA LTD.
ARAMARK REFRESHMENT SERVICES
105 The East Mall Unit 1, Etobicoke, ON, M8Z 5X9
(416) 231-3186
Emp Here 40
SIC 5962 Merchandising machine operators

D-U-N-S 20-554-4117   (SL)
ANDORRA BUILDING MAINTENANCE LTD
46 Chauncey Ave, Etobicoke, ON, M8Z 2Z4
(416) 537-7772
Emp Here 160   *Sales* 4,669,485
SIC 7349 Building maintenance services, nec

D-U-N-S 20-893-3924   (SL)
ASBURY BUILDING SERVICES INC
323 Evans Ave, Etobicoke, ON, M8Z 1K2

Emp Here 450   *Sales* 1,499,400
SIC 7349 Building maintenance services, nec

D-U-N-S 20-580-1017   (BR)
BANK OF NOVA SCOTIA, THE
SCOTIABANK
85 The East Mall, Etobicoke, ON, M8Z 5W4
(416) 503-1800
Emp Here 20
SIC 6021 National commercial banks

D-U-N-S 20-580-0548   (BR)
BANK OF NOVA SCOTIA, THE
SCOTIABANK
1037 The Queensway, Etobicoke, ON, M8Z 6C7
(416) 503-1550
Emp Here 20
SIC 6021 National commercial banks

D-U-N-S 25-118-1434   (BR)
BANK OF MONTREAL
BMO
1230 The Queensway, Etobicoke, ON, M8Z 1R8
(416) 259-9691
Emp Here 20
SIC 6021 National commercial banks

D-U-N-S 20-973-7436   (SL)
BATTENFELD GREASE (CANADA) LTD.
(*Suby of* Battenfeld Management, Inc.)
68 Titan Rd, Etobicoke, ON, M8Z 2J8
(416) 239-1548
Emp Here 32   *Sales* 35,021,136
SIC 2911 Petroleum refining
Pr Barbara Bellanti

D-U-N-S 20-703-3932   (BR)
BLANCO CANADA INC
37 Jutland Rd, Etobicoke, ON, M8Z 2G6
(416) 251-4733
Emp Here 50
SIC 3431 Metal sanitary ware

D-U-N-S 24-887-6497   (SL)
BO SERIES INC
124 The East Mall, Etobicoke, ON, M8Z 5V5
(416) 234-5900
Emp Here 50   *Sales* 6,391,350
SIC 7812 Motion picture and video production
Mgr James Crouch

D-U-N-S 24-846-5247   (HQ)
BRENNTAG CANADA INC
43 Jutland Rd, Etobicoke, ON, M8Z 2G6
(413) 259-8231
Emp Here 80   *Emp Total* 14,832
Sales 120,093,312
SIC 5169 Chemicals and allied products, nec
Pr Mike Staley

D-U-N-S 25-936-9890   (SL)
CCFGLM ONTARIO LIMITED
MANDARIN RESTAURANT
1255 The Queensway, Etobicoke, ON, M8Z 1S1
(416) 252-5000
Emp Here 90   *Sales* 2,699,546
SIC 5812 Eating places

D-U-N-S 25-990-8689   (BR)
CANADIAN IMPERIAL BANK OF COMMERCE
CIBC
1582 The Queensway Suite 1508, Etobicoke, ON, M8Z 1V1
(416) 255-4483
Emp Here 22
SIC 6021 National commercial banks

D-U-N-S 25-364-6236   (BR)
CANADIAN PACIFIC RAILWAY COMPANY
CP INTERMODAL SERVICES
36 North Queen St, Etobicoke, ON, M8Z 2C4

Emp Here 75
SIC 4011 Railroads, line-haul operating

D-U-N-S 25-140-7573   (SL)
CANADIAN TELECOMMUNICATION DEVELOPMENT CORPORATION
ONE STOP WIRELESS
55 Chauncey Ave, Etobicoke, ON, M8Z 2Z2

Emp Here 50   *Sales* 7,507,300
SIC 4899 Communication services, nec
Pr Pr Charles Rees
 Bert Barker
 Penny Barker

D-U-N-S 25-420-0504   (BR)
CARA OPERATIONS LIMITED
HARVEY'S RESTAURANTS
(*Suby of* Cara Holdings Limited)
805 The Queensway, Etobicoke, ON, M8Z 1N6
(416) 251-6746
Emp Here 30
SIC 5812 Eating places

D-U-N-S 20-810-5853   (BR)
CARA OPERATIONS QUEBEC LTD
MILESTONE GRILL AND BAR
(*Suby of* Cara Holdings Limited)
1001 The Queensway, Etobicoke, ON, M8Z 6C7
(416) 255-0464
Emp Here 80
SIC 5812 Eating places

D-U-N-S 20-337-8810   (BR)
CASCADES CANADA ULC
CASCADES RECOVERY+ - TORONTO
66 Shorncliffe Rd, Etobicoke, ON, M8Z 5K1
(416) 231-2525
Emp Here 362
SIC 2611 Pulp mills

D-U-N-S 25-528-6353   (BR)
COMMUNITY LIVING TORONTO
288 Judson St Unit 17, Etobicoke, ON, M8Z 5T6
(416) 252-1171
Emp Here 200
SIC 7389 Business services, nec

D-U-N-S 24-023-9652   (BR)
COMPAGNIE DE TELEPHONE BELL DU CANADA OU BELL CANADA, LA
55 North Queen St, Etobicoke, ON, M8Z 2C7

Emp Here 100
SIC 4899 Communication services, nec

D-U-N-S 20-573-3376   (BR)
COMPAGNIE DES CHEMINS DE FER NATIONAUX DU CANADA
123 Judson St, Etobicoke, ON, M8Z 1A4
(416) 253-6395
Emp Here 100

SIC 4011 Railroads, line-haul operating

D-U-N-S 24-220-5318   (SL)
CORPORATION OF QUEENSWAY CATHEDRAL
QUEENSWAY CHRISTIAN SCHOOL, DIV OF
1536 The Queensway, Etobicoke, ON, M8Z 1T5
(416) 255-0141
Emp Here 54   *Sales* 3,575,074
SIC 8661 Religious organizations

D-U-N-S 20-697-8590   (BR)
COSTCO WHOLESALE CANADA LTD
COSTCO
(*Suby of* Costco Wholesale Corporation)
50 Queen Elizabeth Blvd Suite 524, Etobicoke, ON, M8Z 1M1
(416) 251-2832
Emp Here 200
SIC 5399 Miscellaneous general merchandise

D-U-N-S 24-772-0071   (SL)
DEL-BROOK CONTRACTING LTD.
55 Magnificent Rd, Etobicoke, ON, M8Z 4T4

Emp Here 40   *Sales* 5,300,640
SIC 1623 Water, sewer, and utility lines
Pr Pr Emily Tudino

D-U-N-S 24-389-8645   (SL)
EMERY OLEOCHEMICALS CANADA LTD
425 Kipling Ave, Etobicoke, ON, M8Z 5C7

Emp Here 80   *Sales* 25,816,080
SIC 5169 Chemicals and allied products, nec
 Robert Squires
 Allan Chiu

D-U-N-S 24-059-7583   (BR)
ESSILOR GROUPE CANADA INC
ESSILOR
347 Evans Ave, Etobicoke, ON, M8Z 1K2
(416) 252-5458
Emp Here 150
SIC 5049 Professional equipment, nec

D-U-N-S 24-343-7337   (BR)
FGL SPORTS LTD
SPORT CHEK
1255 The Queensway, Etobicoke, ON, M8Z 1S1
(416) 255-2391
Emp Here 30
SIC 5941 Sporting goods and bicycle shops

D-U-N-S 20-165-5735   (HQ)
FUTURE BAKERY LIMITED
(*Suby of* Future Bakery Limited)
106 North Queen St, Etobicoke, ON, M8Z 2E2
(416) 231-1491
Emp Here 65   *Emp Total* 70
Sales 3,648,035
SIC 2051 Bread, cake, and related products

D-U-N-S 24-645-4995   (HQ)
GEORGE HULL CENTRE FOR CHILDREN & FAMILIES, THE
(*Suby of* George Hull Centre For Children & Families, The)
81 The East Mall 3rd Floor, Etobicoke, ON, M8Z 5W3
(416) 622-8833
Emp Here 31   *Emp Total* 100
Sales 7,117,393
SIC 8322 Individual and family services
 Rick Arseneau
Dir Debora Haak
Dir Louise Lore
Dir Akela Peoples
Dir Richard Smith
Dir Alison Irvine
Dir Philip Allmen
Dir Paul Laberge
Dir Gordon Lownds
 Brigid Murphy

D-U-N-S 24-391-5605   (BR)

GOLF TOWN LIMITED
GOLF TOWN
1561 The Queensway, Etobicoke, ON, M8Z
1T8
(416) 503-8330
Emp Here 20
SIC 5941 Sporting goods and bicycle shops

D-U-N-S 20-195-1014   (BR)
GROUPE SANTE MEDISYS INC
INDEPENDENT MEDICAL ASSESSMENT
365 Evans Ave Suite 100, Etobicoke, ON, M8Z
1K2
(416) 251-2611
Emp Here 23
SIC 6321 Accident and health insurance

D-U-N-S 20-047-6802   (SL)
HELMITIN INC
99 Shorncliffe Rd, Etobicoke, ON, M8Z 5K7
(416) 239-3105
Emp Here 35   *Sales* 3,031,879
SIC 2891 Adhesives and sealants

D-U-N-S 24-010-9652   (SL)
HIGHLAND EQUIPMENT INC
136 The East Mall, Etobicoke, ON, M8Z 5V5
(416) 236-9610
Emp Here 74   *Sales* 9,615,386
SIC 3499 Fabricated Metal products, nec
Pr Pr David Smith
  David R Mamon
VP Fin Rodney Allen
  Larry Kelln

D-U-N-S 20-784-5298   (SL)
HYMOPACK LTD
55 Medulla Ave, Etobicoke, ON, M8Z 5L6
(416) 232-1733
Emp Here 175   *Sales* 32,981,515
SIC 2673 Bags: plastic, laminated, and
coated
  Harvey Rosenbloom
Pr Pr Gerry Maldoff
  Nicki Lang
  Raffaele D'alfonso

D-U-N-S 20-181-2109   (BR)
IKEA CANADA LIMITED PARTNERSHIP
IKEA CANADA LIMITED PARTNERSHIP
1475 The Queensway, Etobicoke, ON, M8Z
1T3
(416) 646-4532
Emp Here 150
SIC 5712 Furniture stores

D-U-N-S 25-406-4611   (BR)
**INFORMATION COMMUNICATION SER-
VICES (ICS) INC**
ICS COURIER SERVICES
288 Judson St Suite 1, Etobicoke, ON, M8Z
5T6

Emp Here 200
SIC 7389 Business services, nec

D-U-N-S 20-042-5783   (HQ)
**INTERNATIONAL TIME RECORDER COM-
PANY LIMITED**
ITR
(*Suby of* International Time Recorder Com-
pany Limited)
7 Taymall Ave Suite A, Etobicoke, ON, M8Z
3Y8
(416) 252-1186
Emp Here 30   *Emp Total* 50
Sales 1,459,214
SIC 3579 Office machines, nec

D-U-N-S 20-647-3027   (HQ)
JAN-MAR SALES LIMITED
514 Kipling Ave, Etobicoke, ON, M8Z 5E3
(416) 255-8535
Emp Here 23   *Emp Total* 11,956
Sales 3,210,271
SIC 5087 Service establishment equipment

D-U-N-S 20-168-4305   (HQ)

KERR BROS. LIMITED
KERRS
956 Islington Ave, Etobicoke, ON, M8Z 4P6
(416) 252-7341
Emp Here 97   *Emp Total* 100
Sales 8,662,510
SIC 2064 Candy and other confectionery
products
Pr Pr Fayez Zakaria
VP Fin Laura Lu
Sec Ryan Martic

D-U-N-S 20-261-9227   (SL)
KINECTRICS NORTH AMERICA INC
KINECTRICS
800 Kipling Ave Unit 2, Etobicoke, ON, M8Z
5G5
(416) 207-6000
Emp Here 20   *Sales* 875,528
SIC 8999 Services, nec

D-U-N-S 25-816-4974   (BR)
LOUIS DREYFUS COMPANY CANADA ULC
LOUIS DREYFUS COMMODITIES
55 Torlake Cres, Etobicoke, ON, M8Z 1B4
(416) 259-7851
Emp Here 48
SIC 6221 Commodity contracts brokers, deal-
ers

D-U-N-S 24-805-0663   (BR)
LOWE'S COMPANIES CANADA, ULC
1604 The Queensway, Etobicoke, ON, M8Z
1V1
(416) 253-2570
Emp Here 100
SIC 5211 Lumber and other building materials

D-U-N-S 24-172-6582   (BR)
LUCAS & MARCO INC
MCDONALD'S
1000 Islington Ave, Etobicoke, ON, M8Z 4P8
(416) 255-4152
Emp Here 80
SIC 5812 Eating places

D-U-N-S 25-411-9787   (BR)
LUSH HANDMADE COSMETICS LTD
LUSH MANUFACTURING
63 Advance Rd Unit 826, Etobicoke, ON, M8Z
2S6
(416) 538-7360
Emp Here 20
SIC 5999 Miscellaneous retail stores, nec

D-U-N-S 20-171-5851   (SL)
MMG CANADA LIMITED
10 Vansco Rd, Etobicoke, ON, M8Z 5J4
(416) 251-2831
Emp Here 45   *Sales* 4,304,681
SIC 5995 Optical goods stores

D-U-N-S 20-122-9452   (BR)
MAPLE LEAF FOODS INC
SCHNEIDER FOODS
550 Kipling Ave, Etobicoke, ON, M8Z 5E9

Emp Here 120
SIC 2011 Meat packing plants

D-U-N-S 25-530-4636   (SL)
**MARTIN AIR HEATING & AIR CONDITION-
ING SERVICES LIMITED**
DIRECT ENERGY
30 Fieldway Rd, Etobicoke, ON, M8Z 0E3
(416) 247-1777
Emp Here 50   *Sales* 4,377,642
SIC 1711 Plumbing, heating, air-conditioning

D-U-N-S 20-643-0600   (BR)
MCGREGOR INDUSTRIES INC
MCGREGOR SOCKS
70 The East Mall, Etobicoke, ON, M8Z 5W2
(416) 252-3716
Emp Here 50
SIC 5632 Women's accessory and specialty
stores

D-U-N-S 25-704-7639   (BR)
MERCEDES-BENZ CANADA INC
1156 The Queensway, Etobicoke, ON, M8Z
1R4
(416) 255-1132
Emp Here 25
SIC 5511 New and used car dealers

D-U-N-S 24-752-0885   (SL)
MIFIN FOODS LIMITED
SWISS CHALET NO. 745
1255 The Queensway Suite 1745, Etobicoke,
ON, M8Z 1S1
(416) 251-4100
Emp Here 75   *Sales* 2,261,782
SIC 5812 Eating places

D-U-N-S 25-511-5099   (BR)
MIROLIN INDUSTRIES CORP
(*Suby of* Masco Corporation)
200 Norseman St, Etobicoke, ON, M8Z 2R4
(416) 231-9030
Emp Here 270
SIC 3431 Metal sanitary ware

D-U-N-S 24-138-2415   (HQ)
MIROLIN INDUSTRIES CORP
(*Suby of* Masco Corporation)
60 Shorncliffe Rd, Etobicoke, ON, M8Z 5K1
(416) 231-5790
Emp Here 30   *Emp Total* 26,000
Sales 64,455,304
SIC 3089 Plastics products, nec
Pr Pr Domenic Primucci

D-U-N-S 24-390-3445   (BR)
MYLAN PHARMACEUTICALS ULC
(*Suby of* Mylan Canada, ULC)
214 Norseman St, Etobicoke, ON, M8Z 2R4
(416) 236-2631
Emp Here 50
SIC 2834 Pharmaceutical preparations

D-U-N-S 24-485-5003   (HQ)
MYLAN PHARMACEUTICALS ULC
(*Suby of* Mylan Canada, ULC)
85 Advance Rd, Etobicoke, ON, M8Z 2S6
(416) 236-2631
Emp Here 200   *Emp Total* 600
Sales 69,040,205
SIC 2834 Pharmaceutical preparations
Pr Pr Richard M Guest
VP David Blais

D-U-N-S 24-206-6798   (BR)
MYLEX LIMITED
(*Suby of* Mylex Limited)
1460 The Queensway, Etobicoke, ON, M8Z
1S7
(416) 745-1733
Emp Here 200
SIC 2517 Wood television and radio cabinets

D-U-N-S 24-192-7748   (SL)
**NEKISON ENGINEERING & CONTRAC-
TORS LIMITED**
17 Saint Lawrence Ave, Etobicoke, ON, M8Z
5T8
(416) 259-4631
Emp Here 55   *Sales* 4,815,406
SIC 1711 Plumbing, heating, air-conditioning

D-U-N-S 25-172-4985   (HQ)
NEW HORIZON SYSTEM SOLUTIONS INC
800 Kipling Ave Suite 8, Etobicoke, ON, M8Z
5G5
(416) 207-6800
Emp Here 200   *Emp Total* 3
Sales 107,537,000
SIC 8741 Management services
VP Jane Diercks
  Gert Kollenhoven

D-U-N-S 20-152-9323   (BR)
ONTARIO POWER GENERATION INC
800 Kipling Ave Suite 1, Etobicoke, ON, M8Z
5G5
(416) 231-4111
Emp Here 700

SIC 4911 Electric services

D-U-N-S 25-420-4928   (BR)
**PENTECOSTAL   ASSEMBLIES   OF
CANADA, THE**
CHURCH ON THE QUEENSWAY
1536 The Queensway, Etobicoke, ON, M8Z
1T5
(416) 255-0141
Emp Here 45
SIC 8661 Religious organizations

D-U-N-S 24-350-2676   (BR)
PIZZA PIZZA LIMITED
58 Advance Rd, Etobicoke, ON, M8Z 2T7
(416) 236-1894
Emp Here 250
SIC 5812 Eating places

D-U-N-S 24-387-8712   (BR)
PLASTIC MOULDERS LIMITED
90 The East Mall, Etobicoke, ON, M8Z 5X3
(416) 252-2241
Emp Here 20
SIC 3089 Plastics products, nec

D-U-N-S 24-116-9577   (BR)
PUROLATOR INC.
PUROLATOR INC
800 Kipling Ave Suite 10, Etobicoke, ON, M8Z
5G5
(416) 207-3900
Emp Here 50
SIC 4731 Freight transportation arrangement

D-U-N-S 20-173-6014   (SL)
**QUEENSWAY MACHINE PRODUCTS LIM-
ITED, THE**
8 Rangemore Rd, Etobicoke, ON, M8Z 5H7
(416) 259-4261
Emp Here 52   *Sales* 3,793,956
SIC 3599 Industrial machinery, nec

D-U-N-S 25-362-4977   (BR)
REDBERRY FRANCHISING CORP
BURGER KING
1560 The Queensway, Etobicoke, ON, M8Z
1T5
(416) 201-8239
Emp Here 25
SIC 5812 Eating places

D-U-N-S 25-018-8026   (BR)
ROYAL BANK OF CANADA
ROYAL BANK FINANCIAL GROUP
(*Suby of* Royal Bank Of Canada)
1233 The Queensway, Etobicoke, ON, M8Z
1S1
(416) 253-8465
Emp Here 165
SIC 6021 National commercial banks

D-U-N-S 20-628-5223   (BR)
RUSSELL FOOD EQUIPMENT LIMITED
70 Coronet Rd Suite 1, Etobicoke, ON, M8Z
2M1
(416) 207-9000
Emp Here 23
SIC 5046 Commercial equipment, nec

D-U-N-S 25-293-9111   (BR)
RYDER TRUCK RENTAL CANADA LTD
(*Suby of* Ryder System, Inc.)
672 Kipling Ave, Etobicoke, ON, M8Z 5G3
(416) 255-4427
Emp Here 40
SIC 7513 Truck rental and leasing, no drivers

D-U-N-S 24-873-0400   (HQ)
SEA MERCHANTS INC
55 Vansco Rd, Etobicoke, ON, M8Z 5Z8
(416) 255-2700
Emp Here 22   *Emp Total* 50
Sales 9,120,088
SIC 5146 Fish and seafoods
Pr Pr Harry Gorman
VP Andre Chabot

D-U-N-S 24-993-2534   (HQ)

▲ Public Company   ■ Public Company Family Member   **HQ** Headquarters   **BR** Branch   **SL** Single Location

SOUTHERN GRAPHIC SYSTEMS-CANADA LTD
(*Suby of* Logo Holdings I Corporation)
2 Dorchester Ave, Etobicoke, ON, M8Z 4W3
(416) 252-9331
Emp Here 99   *Emp Total* 2,410
Sales 21,502,720
SIC 3555 Printing trades machinery
Pr David Corsin
Prs Dir Rick Degendorfor

D-U-N-S 25-361-6841   (BR)
SUNRISE MARKETS INC
SUNRISE SOYA FOODS
21 Medulla Ave, Etobicoke, ON, M8Z 5L6
(416) 233-2337
Emp Here 30
SIC 2099 Food preparations, nec

D-U-N-S 25-361-4689   (BR)
SYSCO CANADA, INC
SYSCO CANADA INC
(*Suby of* Sysco Corporation)
61 Torlake Cres, Etobicoke, ON, M8Z 1B4
(416) 259-4201
Emp Here 31
SIC 2013 Sausages and other prepared meats

D-U-N-S 25-364-7879   (BR)
TELUS COMMUNICATIONS INC
TELUS BUSINESS SOLUTIONS
310 Judson St Unit 5, Etobicoke, ON, M8Z 5T6
(416) 251-3355
Emp Here 70
SIC 4899 Communication services, nec

D-U-N-S 25-512-4356   (SL)
TALON CUSTOMIZING HOUSE LIMITED
TALON RETAIL STRATEGIES GROUP
956 Islington Ave, Etobicoke, ON, M8Z 4P6
(416) 644-0506
Emp Here 40   *Sales* 2,918,428
SIC 7336 Commercial art and graphic design

D-U-N-S 20-597-6046   (SL)
TORCAD LIMITED
275 Norseman St, Etobicoke, ON, M8Z 2R5
(416) 239-3928
Emp Here 65   *Sales* 4,377,642
SIC 3471 Plating and polishing

D-U-N-S 20-711-0912   (BR)
TORONTO CATHOLIC DISTRICT SCHOOL BOARD
HOLY ANGELS CATHOLIC SHCOOL
65 Jutland Rd, Etobicoke, ON, M8Z 2G6
(416) 393-5329
Emp Here 50
SIC 8211 Elementary and secondary schools

D-U-N-S 20-799-6633   (BR)
TRAILERMASTER FREIGHT CARRIERS LTD
34 Canmotor Ave, Etobicoke, ON, M8Z 4E5
(416) 252-7721
Emp Here 30
SIC 4215 Courier services, except by air

D-U-N-S 24-581-7890   (SL)
URBAN ENVIRONMENT CENTRE (TORONTO), THE
GREENSAVER
74 Six Point Rd, Etobicoke, ON, M8Z 2X2
(416) 203-3106
Emp Here 60   *Sales* 6,858,306
SIC 8748 Business consulting, nec
Pr Vladan M. Veljovic
Ch Bd Peter D'uva
  Maija Nappi
Sec Tyler Moore
Treas Tim Stoate
Dir Jens Lohmueller
Dir David House
Dir Dusanka Filipovic
Dir Hazel Mccallion

D-U-N-S 20-004-5248   (BR)
WENDY'S RESTAURANTS OF CANADA INC
WENDY'S
(*Suby of* The Wendy's Company)
1569 The Queensway, Etobicoke, ON, M8Z 1T8
(416) 251-7991
Emp Here 45
SIC 5812 Eating places

D-U-N-S 20-645-3586   (BR)
WESTROCK COMPANY OF CANADA INC
ROCKTENN MERCHANDISING DISPLAY, DIV OF
(*Suby of* Westrock Company)
730 Islington Ave, Etobicoke, ON, M8Z 4N8
(416) 259-8421
Emp Here 200
SIC 2653 Corrugated and solid fiber boxes

D-U-N-S 20-550-0176   (HQ)
WILLIAM F. WHITE INTERNATIONAL INC
800 Islington Ave, Etobicoke, ON, M8Z 6A1
(416) 239-5050
Emp Here 100   *Emp Total* 100
Sales 15,246,018
SIC 7819 Services allied to motion pictures
  Paul A. Bronfman
VP Fin Munir Noorbhai

Etobicoke, ON M9A
York County

D-U-N-S 25-296-3756   (BR)
BANK OF NOVA SCOTIA, THE
SCOTIABANK
270 The Kingsway Suite 8, Etobicoke, ON, M9A 3T7
(416) 233-2136
Emp Here 20
SIC 6021 National commercial banks

D-U-N-S 20-823-6638   (SL)
ISLINGTON GOLF CLUB, LIMITED
45 Riverbank Dr, Etobicoke, ON, M9A 5B8
(416) 231-1114
Emp Here 130   *Sales* 5,253,170
SIC 7997 Membership sports and recreation clubs
Genl Mgr David Fox

D-U-N-S 20-355-9039   (SL)
LABDARA LITHUANIAN NURSING HOME
5 Resurrection Rd, Etobicoke, ON, M9A 5G1
(416) 232-2112
Emp Here 100   *Sales* 4,523,563
SIC 8051 Skilled nursing care facilities

D-U-N-S 20-048-1658   (BR)
LOBLAWS SUPERMARKETS LIMITED
LOBLAWS
270 The Kingsway, Etobicoke, ON, M9A 3T7
(416) 231-0931
Emp Here 97
SIC 5411 Grocery stores

D-U-N-S 25-079-2793   (BR)
PHARMA PLUS DRUGMARTS LTD
PHARMA PLUS
4890 Dundas St W, Etobicoke, ON, M9A 1B5
(416) 239-8360
Emp Here 28
SIC 5912 Drug stores and proprietary stores

D-U-N-S 24-991-4896   (BR)
RE/MAX PROFESSIONALS INC
RE MAX PROFESSIONALS
(*Suby of* Re/Max Professionals Inc)
270 The Kingsway Suite 200, Etobicoke, ON, M9A 3T7
(416) 236-1241
Emp Here 80
SIC 6531 Real estate agents and managers

D-U-N-S 25-308-4289   (BR)

ROYAL BANK OF CANADA
RBC
(*Suby of* Royal Bank Of Canada)
4860 Dundas St W, Etobicoke, ON, M9A 1B5
(416) 239-8175
Emp Here 30
SIC 6021 National commercial banks

D-U-N-S 20-860-1703   (BR)
SOURCE (BELL) ELECTRONICS INC, THE
SOURCE, THE
270 The Kingsway Suite 160, Etobicoke, ON, M9A 3T7

Emp Here 25
SIC 5999 Miscellaneous retail stores, nec

D-U-N-S 20-877-9660   (SL)
ST. GEORGE'S GOLF AND COUNTRY CLUB
1668 Islington Ave, Etobicoke, ON, M9A 3M9
(416) 231-3393
Emp Here 80   *Sales* 3,210,271
SIC 7997 Membership sports and recreation clubs

D-U-N-S 20-698-7468   (BR)
TORONTO DISTRICT SCHOOL BOARD
ETOBICOKE COLLEGIATE INSTITUTE
86 Montgomery Rd, Etobicoke, ON, M9A 3N5
(416) 394-7840
Emp Here 120
SIC 8211 Elementary and secondary schools

D-U-N-S 20-025-2174   (BR)
TORONTO DISTRICT SCHOOL BOARD
ISLINGTON JUNIOR MIDDLE SCHOOL
44 Cordova Ave, Etobicoke, ON, M9A 2H5
(416) 394-7870
Emp Here 49
SIC 8211 Elementary and secondary schools

D-U-N-S 20-698-7617   (BR)
TORONTO DISTRICT SCHOOL BOARD
RICHVIEW COLLEGIATE INSTITUTE
1738 Islington Ave, Etobicoke, ON, M9A 3N2
(416) 394-7980
Emp Here 74
SIC 8211 Elementary and secondary schools

Etobicoke, ON M9B
York County

D-U-N-S 25-405-1675   (SL)
1093641 ONTARIO LIMITED
CKDX RADIO
5302 Dundas St W, Etobicoke, ON, M9B 1B2
(416) 213-1035
Emp Here 25   *Sales* 1,605,135
SIC 4832 Radio broadcasting stations

D-U-N-S 20-650-4529   (HQ)
ASSOCIATED ENGINEERING (ONT.) LTD
(*Suby of* Ashco Shareholders Inc)
304 The East Mall Suite 800, Etobicoke, ON, M9B 6E2
(416) 622-9502
Emp Here 35   *Emp Total* 255
Sales 6,785,345
SIC 8711 Engineering services
Pr Kerry Rudd
  Bill Deangelis

D-U-N-S 25-296-9084   (BR)
BANK OF NOVA SCOTIA, THE
SCOTIABANK
250 The East Mall, Etobicoke, ON, M9B 3Y8
(416) 233-5547
Emp Here 45
SIC 6021 National commercial banks

D-U-N-S 20-161-0912   (HQ)
CANADA BREAD COMPANY, LIMITED
DEMPSTER BREAD, DIV OF
10 Four Seasons Pl Suite 1200, Etobicoke,

ON, M9B 6H7
(416) 622-2040
Emp Here 200   *Emp Total* 130,913
Sales 221,362,764
SIC 2051 Bread, cake, and related products
Pr Pr Dan Curtis
VP VP Ian Macpherson
VP VP Glen Sivec
  Darrell Miller

D-U-N-S 25-865-5042   (SL)
DUFFERIN COMMUNICATIONS INC
Z 103.5 FM
5312 Dundas St W, Etobicoke, ON, M9B 1B3
(416) 213-1035
Emp Here 50   *Sales* 3,137,310
SIC 4832 Radio broadcasting stations

D-U-N-S 20-699-6287   (BR)
EXTENDICARE INC
HIGHBOURNE LIFECARE CENTRE
420 The East Mall, Etobicoke, ON, M9B 3Z9
(416) 621-8000
Emp Here 300
SIC 8051 Skilled nursing care facilities

D-U-N-S 20-969-2552   (BR)
K-BRO LINEN SYSTEMS INC
15 Shorncliffe Rd, Etobicoke, ON, M9B 3S4
(416) 233-5555
Emp Here 150
SIC 7219 Laundry and garment services, nec

D-U-N-S 25-088-1612   (BR)
LOBLAWS SUPERMARKETS LIMITED
LOBLAWS 1066
380 The East Mall, Etobicoke, ON, M9B 6L5
(416) 695-8990
Emp Here 300
SIC 5411 Grocery stores

D-U-N-S 20-210-9190   (SL)
MKJ SIMAN INVESTMENTS INC
TIM HORTONS
5250 Dundas St W, Etobicoke, ON, M9B 1A9
(416) 234-8900
Emp Here 65   *Sales* 1,969,939
SIC 5812 Eating places

D-U-N-S 20-320-0170   (BR)
MANION WILKINS & ASSOCIATES LTD
21 Four Seasons Pl Suite 500, Etobicoke, ON, M9B 0A5
(416) 234-5044
Emp Here 49
SIC 8742 Management consulting services

D-U-N-S 25-672-2455   (BR)
METRO ONTARIO INC
METRO
201 Lloyd Manor Rd, Etobicoke, ON, M9B 6H6
(416) 236-3217
Emp Here 300
SIC 5411 Grocery stores

D-U-N-S 25-988-9293   (BR)
METRO ONTARIO INC
250 The East Mall, Etobicoke, ON, M9B 3Y8
(416) 233-4149
Emp Here 200
SIC 5411 Grocery stores

D-U-N-S 24-802-8586   (SL)
NOCO CANADA COMPANY
5468 Dundas St W Suite 401, Etobicoke, ON, M9B 6E3
(416) 232-6626
Emp Here 50   *Sales* 15,029,904
SIC 5172 Petroleum products, nec
  Philippa Sutcliffe
  Michael Bradley
  Michael Newman

D-U-N-S 20-052-1768   (HQ)
NORTHERN REFLECTIONS LTD
21 Four Seasons Pl Suite 200, Etobicoke, ON, M9B 6J8

(416) 626-2500
Emp Here 108   *Emp Total* 2,100
Sales 124,762,797
SIC 5621 Women's clothing stores
Pr Pr Michael Stanek
Lalonnie Biggar
William (Bill) Booth

D-U-N-S 20-122-0050   (BR)
PHARMA PLUS DRUGMARTS LTD
250 The East Mall, Etobicoke, ON, M9B 3Y8
(416) 239-3511
Emp Here 20
SIC 5912 Drug stores and proprietary stores

D-U-N-S 20-327-4860   (HQ)
PRIMUS MANAGEMENT ULC
PRIMUS CANADA
5343 Dundas St W Suite 400, Etobicoke, ON, M9B 6K5
(416) 236-3636
Emp Here 300   *Emp Total* 3,485
Sales 39,414,421
SIC 4813 Telephone communication, except radio
Bradley Fisher
VP Tamara Flemington
Pers/VP Maureen Merkler
VP Jill C. Schatz

D-U-N-S 25-138-4863   (HQ)
PROFILE INVESTIGATION INC
(*Suby of* Profile Investigation Inc)
936 The East Mall Suite 300, Etobicoke, ON, M9B 6J9
(416) 695-1260
Emp Here 80   *Emp Total* 85
Sales 4,231,721
SIC 7389 Business services, nec

D-U-N-S 24-384-0019   (BR)
SNC-LAVALIN OPERATIONS & MAINTE-NANCE INC
304 The East Mall, Etobicoke, ON, M9B 6E2
(416) 207-4700
Emp Here 150
SIC 6531 Real estate agents and managers

D-U-N-S 25-221-4382   (SL)
SANTEK INVESTMENTS (1991) INC
VALHALLA INN TORONTO
1 Valhalla Inn Rd, Etobicoke, ON, M9B 1S9

Emp Here 100   *Sales* 4,377,642
SIC 7011 Hotels and motels

D-U-N-S 20-860-3121   (BR)
SOURCE (BELL) ELECTRONICS INC, THE
SOURCE, THE
250 The East Mall Suite 279, Etobicoke, ON, M9B 3Y8
(416) 239-0290
Emp Here 25
SIC 5999 Miscellaneous retail stores, nec

D-U-N-S 20-033-0376   (SL)
TELEPARTNERS CALL CENTRE INC
ANSWERNET
(*Suby of* Answernet, Inc.)
5429 Dundas St W, Etobicoke, ON, M9B 1B5
(416) 231-0520
Emp Here 60   *Sales* 3,064,349
SIC 7389 Business services, nec

D-U-N-S 25-225-1194   (BR)
TORONTO CATHOLIC DISTRICT SCHOOL BOARD
JOSYF CARDINAL SLIPYJ CATHOLIC SCHOOL
35 West Deane Park Dr, Etobicoke, ON, M9B 2R5
(416) 393-5413
Emp Here 50
SIC 8211 Elementary and secondary schools

D-U-N-S 20-025-0947   (BR)
TORONTO DISTRICT SCHOOL BOARD
WEDGEWOOD JUNIOR SCHOOL
5 Swan Ave, Etobicoke, ON, M9B 1V1

(416) 394-7150
Emp Here 30
SIC 8211 Elementary and secondary schools

D-U-N-S 20-738-4822   (BR)
WENDY'S RESTAURANTS OF CANADA INC
WENDY'S
(*Suby of* The Wendy's Company)
5250 Dundas St W, Etobicoke, ON, M9B 1A9
(416) 234-8666
Emp Here 30
SIC 5812 Eating places

D-U-N-S 24-312-4299   (BR)
WINNERS MERCHANTS INTERNATIONAL L.P.
WINNERS
(*Suby of* The TJX Companies Inc)
250 The East Mall, Etobicoke, ON, M9B 3Y8
(416) 207-0245
Emp Here 30
SIC 5651 Family clothing stores

Etobicoke, ON M9C
York County

D-U-N-S 25-406-5899   (SL)
1148305 ONTARIO INC
VIA ALEGRO RISTORANTE
1750 The Queensway Suite 443, Etobicoke, ON, M9C 5H5
(416) 622-6677
Emp Here 50   *Sales* 1,532,175
SIC 5812 Eating places

D-U-N-S 24-181-2689   (BR)
ARITZIA LP
25 The West Mall, Etobicoke, ON, M9C 1B8
(416) 695-8493
Emp Here 40
SIC 5621 Women's clothing stores

D-U-N-S 20-185-1248   (BR)
ASSOCIATION   D'HOSPITALISATION CANASSURANCE
ONTARIO BLUE CROSS
185 The West Mall Suite 610, Etobicoke, ON, M9C 5L5
(416) 626-1688
Emp Here 30
SIC 6321 Accident and health insurance

D-U-N-S 20-780-6915   (BR)
BCBG MAX AZRIA CANADA INC
BCBG MAX AZRIA
25 The West Mall Suite 1766, Etobicoke, ON, M9C 1B8
(416) 695-0606
Emp Here 21
SIC 5137 Women's and children's clothing

D-U-N-S 20-557-5231   (SL)
BCS GLOBAL NETWORKS INC
PINNACA
5525 Eglinton Ave W Unit 128, Etobicoke, ON, M9C 5K5
(647) 722-8500
Emp Here 70   *Sales* 9,120,088
SIC 4899 Communication services, nec
Clive Sawkins
Catherine Playford

D-U-N-S 24-196-9914   (BR)
CANADA BREAD COMPANY, LIMITED
35 Rakely Crt Suite 1, Etobicoke, ON, M9C 5A5
(416) 622-2040
Emp Here 200
SIC 2051 Bread, cake, and related products

D-U-N-S 20-213-4029   (HQ)
CANADA STARCH OPERATING COMPANY INC
(*Suby of* Ingredion Incorporated)
405 The West Mall Suite 600, Etobicoke, ON, M9C 0A1

Emp Here 45   *Emp Total* 11,000
Sales 27,798,706
SIC 2046 Wet corn milling
Robert D D Kee
Cheryl K Beebe
Jack C Fortnum

D-U-N-S 20-051-1975   (HQ)
CATELLI FOODS CORPORATION
CATELLI
401 The West Mall Suite 11, Etobicoke, ON, M9C 5J5
(416) 626-3500
Emp Here 60   *Emp Total* 355
Sales 36,991,075
SIC 2099 Food preparations, nec
Pr Douglas M Watt
Sec Elizabeth B. Woodard
Dir Gregory Richardson
Dir Antonio Hernandez Callejas

D-U-N-S 24-345-7186   (BR)
CHARTWELL SENIORS HOUSING REAL ESTATE INVESTMENT TRUST
495 The West Mall, Etobicoke, ON, M9C 5S3
(416) 622-7094
Emp Here 210
SIC 8059 Nursing and personal care, nec

D-U-N-S 25-321-5081   (BR)
CLUB MONACO CORP
(*Suby of* Ralph Lauren Corporation)
25 The West Mall Suite D38, Etobicoke, ON, M9C 1B8

Emp Here 34
SIC 5621 Women's clothing stores

D-U-N-S 25-917-7228   (BR)
COMMUNITY LIVING TORONTO
295 The West Mall Suite 204, Etobicoke, ON, M9C 4Z4
(416) 236-7621
Emp Here 30
SIC 8322 Individual and family services

D-U-N-S 25-367-5631   (BR)
CORPORATION OF THE CITY OF TORONTO
WESBURN MANOR
400 The West Mall, Etobicoke, ON, M9C 5S1
(416) 394-3600
Emp Here 200
SIC 8059 Nursing and personal care, nec

D-U-N-S 25-319-7362   (BR)
DON MICHAEL HOLDINGS INC
25 The West Mall Suite 25, Etobicoke, ON, M9C 1B8
(416) 622-8494
Emp Here 20
SIC 5651 Family clothing stores

D-U-N-S 24-953-7861   (SL)
EMERAUD CANADA LIMITED
SAN-O-PHONE HEALTH CARE DIV.
145 The West Mall, Etobicoke, ON, M9C 1C2
(416) 767-4200
Emp Here 72   *Sales* 12,376,900
SIC 5122 Drugs, proprietaries, and sundries
Pr Pr Steven Shah
Charles Bennett
Roy Hill
Sam Richards
D P Shah
Ex VP N D Shah

D-U-N-S 20-708-3580   (BR)
EXTENDICARE INC
MCCALL CENTRE FOR CONTINUING CARE
140 Sherway Dr, Etobicoke, ON, M9C 1A4
(416) 259-2573
Emp Here 190
SIC 8051 Skilled nursing care facilities

D-U-N-S 20-780-0686   (BR)
GAP (CANADA) INC

BANANA REPUBLIC
(*Suby of* The Gap Inc)
25 The West Mall Suite 1127, Etobicoke, ON, M9C 1B8
(416) 622-3797
Emp Here 60
SIC 5651 Family clothing stores

D-U-N-S 24-355-2341   (SL)
GLOBETROTTER LOGISTICS INC
35 Rakely Crt, Etobicoke, ON, M9C 5A5
(416) 742-2232
Emp Here 110   *Sales* 23,420,385
SIC 4731 Freight transportation arrangement
Pr Pr Anca Nediu
Adrian Nediu

D-U-N-S 25-293-7321   (BR)
HARRY ROSEN INC
HARRY ROSEN GENTLEMENS APPAREL
25 The West Mall Suite 114, Etobicoke, ON, M9C 1B8
(416) 620-6967
Emp Here 20
SIC 5611 Men's and boys' clothing stores

D-U-N-S 20-108-5599   (BR)
HOME DEPOT OF CANADA INC
HOME DEPOT
(*Suby of* The Home Depot Inc)
193 North Queen St, Etobicoke, ON, M9C 1A7
(416) 626-9800
Emp Here 350
SIC 5251 Hardware stores

D-U-N-S 24-023-2400   (BR)
HUDSON'S BAY COMPANY
HOME OUTFITTERS
1880 The Queensway, Etobicoke, ON, M9C 5H5
(416) 847-0494
Emp Here 28
SIC 5311 Department stores

D-U-N-S 24-977-3847   (BR)
HUDSON'S BAY COMPANY
THE BAY
25 The West Mall, Etobicoke, ON, M9C 1B8
(416) 626-4711
Emp Here 200
SIC 5311 Department stores

D-U-N-S 24-172-7655   (BR)
HUMBER COLLEGE INSTITUTE OF TECH-NOLOGY AND ADVANCE
HUMBER CORPORATE EDUCATION CEN-TRE
401 The West Mall Suite 630, Etobicoke, ON, M9C 5J5
(416) 675-6622
Emp Here 20
SIC 8221 Colleges and universities

D-U-N-S 25-292-7843   (BR)
INDIGO BOOKS & MUSIC INC
CHAPTERS
(*Suby of* Indigo Books & Music Inc)
1950 The Queensway, Etobicoke, ON, M9C 5H5
(416) 364-4499
Emp Here 50
SIC 5942 Book stores

D-U-N-S 24-010-5080   (BR)
INVESTORS GROUP FINANCIAL SER-VICES INC
INVESTORS GROUP
295 The West Mall Suite 700, Etobicoke, ON, M9C 4Z4
(416) 695-8600
Emp Here 80
SIC 8742 Management consulting services

D-U-N-S 20-643-2069   (SL)
J D C RESTAURANTS LTD
MCDONALDS
195 North Queen St, Etobicoke, ON, M9C 1A7
(416) 621-2952
Emp Here 64   *Sales* 1,896,978

▲ Public Company   ■ Public Company Family Member   **HQ** Headquarters   **BR** Branch   **SL** Single Location

SIC 5812 Eating places

D-U-N-S 24-316-2208   (BR)
J.F. & L. RESTAURANTS LIMITED
PICKLE BARREL, THE
(*Suby of J.F. & L. Restaurants Limited*)
25 The West Mall Suite 1019, Etobicoke, ON, M9C 1B8
(416) 621-4465
Emp Here 120
SIC 5812 Eating places

D-U-N-S 25-400-4492   (HQ)
JONVIEW CANADA INC
VACANCES TOURBEC
191 The West Mall Suite 800, Etobicoke, ON, M9C 5K8
(416) 323-9090
Emp Here 50   *Emp Total* 5,000
Sales 21,450,446
SIC 4725 Tour operators
Pr Lise Gagnon
Sec Bernard Bussieres
Mng Dir David Mounteer
Dir Michel Bellefeuille

D-U-N-S 24-576-5219   (BR)
KEG RESTAURANTS LTD
KEG STEAKHOUSE & BAR, THE
291 The West Mall Suite 512, Etobicoke, ON, M9C 4Z6
(416) 626-3707
Emp Here 70
SIC 5812 Eating places

D-U-N-S 25-531-0153   (HQ)
LENNOX CANADA INC
SERVICE EXPERTS
(*Suby of Lennox Canada Inc*)
400 Norris Glen Rd, Etobicoke, ON, M9C 1H5
(416) 621-9302
Emp Here 20   *Emp Total* 250
Sales 107,802,438
SIC 5075 Warm air heating and air conditioning
Pr Pr John Bergsma
Kenneth Fernandez
VP Anthony Jannetta
VP Dave Nichols
John Vanrijn

D-U-N-S 20-047-7370   (HQ)
LENNOX INDUSTRIES (CANADA) LTD
(*Suby of Lennox International Inc.*)
400 Norris Glen Rd, Etobicoke, ON, M9C 1H5
(416) 621-9302
Emp Here 350   *Emp Total* 10,600
Sales 2,037,062,744
SIC 3634 Electric housewares and fans
Kenneth C. Fernandez
Timothy G. Inch

D-U-N-S 20-096-2129   (BR)
LOCK, R.E. & ASSOCIATES LTD
LOCK SEARCH GROUP
405 The West Mall Suite 910, Etobicoke, ON, M9C 5J1
(416) 626-8383
Emp Here 20
SIC 7361 Employment agencies

D-U-N-S 25-092-7378   (BR)
LULULEMON ATHLETICA CANADA INC
LULULEMON
25 The West Mall Suite 1328a, Etobicoke, ON, M9C 1B8
(416) 620-6518
Emp Here 20
SIC 2339 Women's and misses' outerwear, nec

D-U-N-S 24-122-5572   (SL)
MSCM LLP
701 Evans Ave Suite 800, Etobicoke, ON, M9C 1A3
(416) 626-6000
Emp Here 60   *Sales* 2,626,585
SIC 8721 Accounting, auditing, and book-

keeping

D-U-N-S 20-780-5099   (BR)
MCDONALD'S RESTAURANTS OF CANADA LIMITED
MCDONALD'S
(*Suby of McDonald's Corporation*)
25 The West Mall Suite 416, Etobicoke, ON, M9C 1B8
(416) 626-0559
Emp Here 20
SIC 5812 Eating places

D-U-N-S 25-092-6185   (BR)
METRO ONTARIO INC
170 The West Mall Suite 800, Etobicoke, ON, M9C 5L6
(416) 626-4910
Emp Here 400
SIC 4225 General warehousing and storage

D-U-N-S 20-848-9625   (HQ)
NBS TECHNOLOGIES INC
703 Evans Ave Suite 400, Etobicoke, ON, M9C 5E9
(416) 621-2798
Emp Here 20   *Emp Total* 55,700
Sales 64,738,002
SIC 3699 Electrical equipment and supplies, nec
Pr Bryan Hills
Ex VP Ex VP Drazen Ivanovic

D-U-N-S 24-676-7391   (BR)
NATIONAL MONEY MART COMPANY
MONEY MART
703 Evans Ave Suite 600, Etobicoke, ON, M9C 5E9
(647) 260-3104
Emp Here 25
SIC 6099 Functions related to deposit banking

D-U-N-S 25-409-5375   (SL)
NEXT GENERATION SOLUTIONS INC
401 The West Mall Suite 400, Etobicoke, ON, M9C 5J5

Emp Here 35   *Sales* 6,695,700
SIC 5045 Computers, peripherals, and software
Pr Markus Luft
VP VP Chris Beard

D-U-N-S 20-859-8727   (BR)
PACIFIC LINK COMMUNICATIONS INC
BELL WORLD
25 The West Mall, Etobicoke, ON, M9C 1B8
(416) 622-2252
Emp Here 25
SIC 5999 Miscellaneous retail stores, nec

D-U-N-S 20-594-2167   (HQ)
PARMALAT CANADA INC
ALIMENTS AULT
405 The West Mall 10th Fl, Etobicoke, ON, M9C 5J1
(416) 626-1973
Emp Here 100   *Emp Total* 1
Sales 145,921,400
SIC 2023 Dry, condensed and evaporated dairy products
Fabio Genitrini
Louis Frenette
Pierluigi Bonavita

D-U-N-S 20-047-7412   (SL)
PARTROSE DRUGS LIMITED
PHARMASAVE
666 Burnhamthorpe Rd, Etobicoke, ON, M9C 2Z4
(416) 621-2330
Emp Here 180   *Sales* 30,232,160
SIC 5912 Drug stores and proprietary stores
Pr Pr Marshal Partnoy

D-U-N-S 20-534-4273   (BR)
PERFORMANCE EQUIPMENT LTD
VOLVO TRUCKS
111 The West Mall, Etobicoke, ON, M9C 1C1

(416) 626-3555
Emp Here 20
SIC 7538 General automotive repair shops

D-U-N-S 25-798-8576   (SL)
RJKN GROUP INC
TIM HORTONS
25 The West Mall, Etobicoke, ON, M9C 1B8
(416) 622-0515
Emp Here 70   *Sales* 2,942,050
SIC 5812 Eating places

D-U-N-S 25-122-0877   (BR)
RED LOBSTER HOSPITALITY LLC
RED LOBSTER RESTAURANTS
(*Suby of Red Lobster Seafood Co., LLC*)
1790 The Queensway, Etobicoke, ON, M9C 5H5
(416) 620-9990
Emp Here 80
SIC 5812 Eating places

D-U-N-S 20-977-4074   (HQ)
REDBERRY FRANCHISING CORP
BURGER KING
401 The West Mall Suite 700, Etobicoke, ON, M9C 5J4
(416) 626-6464
Emp Here 55   *Emp Total* 64
Sales 1,143,269,520
SIC 6794 Patent owners and lessors
Grant Sutherland
Barbara Lee
Genl Mgr Francois De L'etoile

D-U-N-S 25-320-3624   (BR)
RUSSELL A. FARROW LIMITED
(*Suby of Farrow Group Inc*)
5397 Eglinton Ave W Suite 220, Etobicoke, ON, M9C 5K6

Emp Here 70
SIC 4731 Freight transportation arrangement

D-U-N-S 25-534-8047   (BR)
SIR CORP
CANYON CREEK CHOPHOUSE
1900 The Queensway, Etobicoke, ON, M9C 5H5
(416) 621-6255
Emp Here 30
SIC 5812 Eating places

D-U-N-S 20-048-8026   (BR)
SNC-LAVALIN INC
195 The West Mall, Etobicoke, ON, M9C 5K1
(416) 252-5311
Emp Here 640
SIC 8711 Engineering services

D-U-N-S 20-301-8879   (BR)
SEARS CANADA INC
25 The West Mall, Etobicoke, ON, M9C 1B8

Emp Here 100
SIC 5961 Catalog and mail-order houses

D-U-N-S 25-738-6417   (SL)
SHAW MANAGEMENT CONSULTANTS INC
145 The West Mall, Etobicoke, ON, M9C 1C2
(416) 767-4200
Emp Here 78   *Sales* 12,760,800
SIC 8741 Management services
Pr Pr Steven Shah
Charles Bennett

D-U-N-S 25-808-7360   (BR)
SINCERE TRADING OF K.B.A. CO-OPERATIVE LTD
169 The West Mall, Etobicoke, ON, M9C 1C2

Emp Here 21
SIC 5141 Groceries, general line

D-U-N-S 25-455-9099   (SL)
SLOVENIAN LINDEN FOUNDATION
DOM LIPA NURSING HOME
52 Neilson Dr, Etobicoke, ON, M9C 1V7

(416) 621-3820
Emp Here 85   *Sales* 3,866,917
SIC 8051 Skilled nursing care facilities

D-U-N-S 20-860-1729   (BR)
SOURCE (BELL) ELECTRONICS INC, THE
SOURCE, THE
25 The West Mall, Etobicoke, ON, M9C 1B8

Emp Here 25
SIC 5999 Miscellaneous retail stores, nec

D-U-N-S 25-905-6372   (BR)
SPORTING LIFE INC
SPORTING LIFE SHERWAY GARDENS
25 The West Mall Suite 7, Etobicoke, ON, M9C 1B8
(416) 620-7002
Emp Here 200
SIC 5941 Sporting goods and bicycle shops

D-U-N-S 25-213-7260   (BR)
STAPLES CANADA INC
STAPLES THE BUSINESS DEPOT
(*Suby of Staples, Inc.*)
1750 The Queensway Suite 1, Etobicoke, ON, M9C 5H5
(416) 620-5674
Emp Here 30
SIC 5943 Stationery stores

D-U-N-S 20-806-4159   (BR)
STARBUCKS COFFEE CANADA, INC
(*Suby of Starbucks Corporation*)
1950 The Queensway, Etobicoke, ON, M9C 5H5
(416) 626-1995
Emp Here 24
SIC 5812 Eating places

D-U-N-S 20-711-1167   (BR)
TORONTO CATHOLIC DISTRICT SCHOOL BOARD
ST. CLEMENT CATHOLIC SCHOOL
4319 Bloor St W, Etobicoke, ON, M9C 2A2
(416) 393-5307
Emp Here 50
SIC 8211 Elementary and secondary schools

D-U-N-S 25-265-4025   (BR)
TORONTO CATHOLIC DISTRICT SCHOOL BOARD
NATIVITY OF OUR LORD SCHOOL
35 Saffron Cres, Etobicoke, ON, M9C 3T8
(416) 393-5288
Emp Here 44
SIC 8211 Elementary and secondary schools

D-U-N-S 20-025-5128   (BR)
TORONTO DISTRICT SCHOOL BOARD
BLOORDALE MIDDLE SCHOOL
10 Toledo Rd, Etobicoke, ON, M9C 2H3
(416) 394-7020
Emp Here 50
SIC 8211 Elementary and secondary schools

D-U-N-S 20-034-2835   (BR)
TORONTO DISTRICT SCHOOL BOARD
HOLLYCREST MIDDLE SCHOOL
630 Renforth Dr, Etobicoke, ON, M9C 2N6
(416) 394-7050
Emp Here 30
SIC 8211 Elementary and secondary schools

D-U-N-S 20-711-2736   (BR)
TORONTO DISTRICT SCHOOL BOARD
MILL VALLEY SCHOOL
411 Mill Rd, Etobicoke, ON, M9C 1Y9
(416) 394-7060
Emp Here 50
SIC 8211 Elementary and secondary schools

D-U-N-S 20-025-5144   (BR)
TORONTO DISTRICT SCHOOL BOARD
WELLESWORTH JUNIOR SCHOOL
225 Wellesworth Dr, Etobicoke, ON, M9C 4S5
(416) 394-7080
Emp Here 35
SIC 8211 Elementary and secondary schools

D-U-N-S 20-592-1286 (BR)
TORONTO DISTRICT SCHOOL BOARD
BRIARCREST JUNIOR SCHOOL
60 Wellesworth Dr, Etobicoke, ON, M9C 4R3
(416) 394-6180
Emp Here 28
SIC 8211 Elementary and secondary schools

D-U-N-S 20-024-9972 (BR)
TORONTO DISTRICT SCHOOL BOARD
SENECA ELEMENTARY SCHOOL
580 Rathburn Rd, Etobicoke, ON, M9C 3T3
(416) 394-4600
Emp Here 60
SIC 8211 Elementary and secondary schools

D-U-N-S 20-024-9295 (BR)
TORONTO DISTRICT SCHOOL BOARD
MILLWOOD JUNIOR SCHOOL
222 Mill Rd, Etobicoke, ON, M9C 1Y2
(416) 394-7070
Emp Here 40
SIC 8211 Elementary and secondary schools

D-U-N-S 25-120-2172 (BR)
TORONTO-DOMINION BANK, THE
TD CANADA TRUST
(*Suby of* Toronto-Dominion Bank, The)
4335 Bloor St W, Etobicoke, ON, M9C 2A5
(416) 621-8320
Emp Here 30
SIC 6021 National commercial banks

D-U-N-S 20-860-5217 (BR)
TOWN SHOES LIMITED
SHOE COMPANY, THE
171 North Queen St Suite 3, Etobicoke, ON, M9C 1A7
(416) 622-3883
Emp Here 20
SIC 5661 Shoe stores

D-U-N-S 20-942-9463 (HQ)
TRADER CORPORATION
AUTO TRADER
405 The West Mall Suite 110, Etobicoke, ON, M9C 5J1
(416) 789-3311
Emp Here 400   *Emp Total* 278
Sales 51,975,060
SIC 2721 Periodicals
Dir Mitch Truitt
Dir Irina Hemmers
Dir Marcelo Gigliani
Dir Sebastien Baldwin
Dir John King
Dir Lawrence S Chernin
Dir Norman Theberge

D-U-N-S 20-804-3153 (BR)
TRANSAT DISTRIBUTION CANADA INC
TRAVELPLUS
191 The West Mall Suite 700, Etobicoke, ON, M9C 5K8
(416) 620-8080
Emp Here 90
SIC 4724 Travel agencies

D-U-N-S 25-297-7707 (BR)
WAL-MART CANADA CORP
165 North Queen St Suite 3031, Etobicoke, ON, M9C 1A7
(416) 239-7090
Emp Here 150
SIC 5311 Department stores

D-U-N-S 20-567-9389 (BR)
WILLIAMS-SONOMA CANADA, INC
25 The West Mall Suite 1394, Etobicoke, ON, M9C 1B8
(416) 621-9005
Emp Here 20
SIC 5719 Miscellaneous homefurnishings

D-U-N-S 20-860-4301 (BR)
WINNERS MERCHANTS INTERNATIONAL L.P.
HOMESENSE

(*Suby of* The TJX Companies Inc)
1840 The Queensway, Etobicoke, ON, M9C 5H5
(416) 621-4275
Emp Here 25
SIC 5651 Family clothing stores

Etobicoke, ON M9P
York County

D-U-N-S 25-302-9656 (BR)
CANADIAN IMPERIAL BANK OF COMMERCE
CIBC
1500 Royal York Rd Suite 1, Etobicoke, ON, M9P 3B6
(416) 249-5013
Emp Here 20
SIC 6021 National commercial banks

D-U-N-S 25-404-2609 (SL)
HOTELS OF ISLINGTON LIMITED
QUALITY HOTELS & SUITES
2180 Islington Ave, Etobicoke, ON, M9P 3P1
(416) 240-9090
Emp Here 64   *Sales* 2,772,507
SIC 7011 Hotels and motels

D-U-N-S 24-953-0403 (BR)
METRO ONTARIO INC
DOMINION
1500 Royal York Rd Suite 1, Etobicoke, ON, M9P 3B6
(416) 244-7169
Emp Here 70
SIC 5411 Grocery stores

D-U-N-S 20-698-6767 (BR)
TORONTO CATHOLIC DISTRICT SCHOOL BOARD
ST. DEMETRIUS CATHOLIC SCHOOL
125 La Rose Ave, Etobicoke, ON, M9P 1A6
(416) 393-5384
Emp Here 35
SIC 8211 Elementary and secondary schools

D-U-N-S 20-112-2574 (BR)
TORONTO DISTRICT SCHOOL BOARD
HILLTOP MIDDLE SCHOOL
35 Trehorne Dr, Etobicoke, ON, M9P 1N8
(416) 394-7730
Emp Here 50
SIC 8211 Elementary and secondary schools

D-U-N-S 20-711-2744 (BR)
TORONTO DISTRICT SCHOOL BOARD
SCARLETT HEIGHTS ENTREPRENEURIAL ACADEMY
15 Trehorne Dr, Etobicoke, ON, M9P 1N8
(416) 394-7750
Emp Here 50
SIC 8211 Elementary and secondary schools

D-U-N-S 20-025-5250 (BR)
TORONTO DISTRICT SCHOOL BOARD
WESTMOUNT JUNIOR SCHOOL
95 Chapman Rd, Etobicoke, ON, M9P 1E9
(416) 394-7720
Emp Here 35
SIC 8211 Elementary and secondary schools

D-U-N-S 24-331-5509 (BR)
TORONTO PUBLIC LIBRARY BOARD
RICHVIEW BRANCH
1806 Islington Ave, Etobicoke, ON, M9P 3N3
(416) 394-5120
Emp Here 40
SIC 8231 Libraries

D-U-N-S 25-909-2328 (BR)
WESTON GOLF AND COUNTRY CLUB LIMITED, THE
PRO SHOP, DIV OF
(*Suby of* Weston Golf and Country Club Limited, The)

50 St Phillips Rd, Etobicoke, ON, M9P 2N6
(416) 241-5254
Emp Here 20
SIC 5941 Sporting goods and bicycle shops

D-U-N-S 20-648-6115 (BR)
YWCA TORONTO
JUMP PROGRAM
222 Dixon Rd Suite 207, Etobicoke, ON, M9P 3S5
(416) 964-3883
Emp Here 20
SIC 8331 Job training and related services

Etobicoke, ON M9R
York County

D-U-N-S 24-224-3520 (BR)
KUMON CANADA INC
ALBION KUMON CENTRE
31 Farley Cres, Etobicoke, ON, M9R 2A5
(416) 621-1632
Emp Here 50
SIC 8299 Schools and educational services, nec

D-U-N-S 25-790-7386 (BR)
PHARMA PLUS DRUGMARTS LTD
REXALL PHARMA PLUS
250 Wincott Dr, Etobicoke, ON, M9R 2R5
(416) 248-9538
Emp Here 30
SIC 5912 Drug stores and proprietary stores

D-U-N-S 20-816-3915 (SL)
STATE BUILDING MAINTENANCE LIMITED
34 Ashmount Cres, Etobicoke, ON, M9R 1C7
(416) 247-1290
Emp Here 90   *Sales* 2,626,585
SIC 7349 Building maintenance services, nec

D-U-N-S 20-700-1889 (BR)
TORONTO CATHOLIC DISTRICT SCHOOL BOARD
TRANSFIGURATION OF OUR LORD CATHOLIC SCHOOL
55 Ludstone Dr, Etobicoke, ON, M9R 2J2
(416) 393-5276
Emp Here 40
SIC 8211 Elementary and secondary schools

D-U-N-S 20-700-2689 (BR)
TORONTO DISTRICT SCHOOL BOARD
CENTRAL ETOBICOKE HIGH SCHOOL
10 Denfield St, Etobicoke, ON, M9R 3H1
(416) 394-7090
Emp Here 70
SIC 8211 Elementary and secondary schools

D-U-N-S 20-913-5685 (BR)
TORONTO DISTRICT SCHOOL BOARD
WESTWAY JUNIOR SCHOOL
25 Poynter Dr, Etobicoke, ON, M9R 1K8
(416) 394-7970
Emp Here 25
SIC 8211 Elementary and secondary schools

D-U-N-S 20-025-0970 (BR)
TORONTO DISTRICT SCHOOL BOARD
KINGSVIEW VILLAGE JUNIOR SCHOOL
1 York Rd, Etobicoke, ON, M9R 3C8
(416) 394-7950
Emp Here 53
SIC 8211 Elementary and secondary schools

D-U-N-S 25-449-2788 (BR)
TORONTO DISTRICT SCHOOL BOARD
KIPLING COLLEGIATE INSTITUTE
380 The Westway, Etobicoke, ON, M9R 1H4
(416) 394-7930
Emp Here 65
SIC 8211 Elementary and secondary schools

D-U-N-S 25-321-2922 (BR)
TORONTO-DOMINION BANK, THE

TD BANK
(*Suby of* Toronto-Dominion Bank, The)
250 Wincott Dr Suite 1, Etobicoke, ON, M9R 2R5
(416) 248-6631
Emp Here 45
SIC 6021 National commercial banks

Etobicoke, ON M9V
York County

D-U-N-S 25-420-6980 (BR)
1327698 ONTARIO LTD
TIM HORTONS
(*Suby of* 1327698 Ontario Ltd)
1751 Albion Rd, Etobicoke, ON, M9V 1C3
(416) 746-6962
Emp Here 34
SIC 5812 Eating places

D-U-N-S 20-571-9680 (BR)
BANK OF MONTREAL
BMO
1530 Albion Rd Suite 215, Etobicoke, ON, M9V 1B4
(416) 740-5705
Emp Here 20
SIC 6021 National commercial banks

D-U-N-S 20-587-1838 (BR)
CANADIAN IMPERIAL BANK OF COMMERCE
CIBC
89 Humber College Blvd, Etobicoke, ON, M9V 4B8
(416) 749-4116
Emp Here 20
SIC 6021 National commercial banks

D-U-N-S 25-303-0779 (BR)
CANADIAN IMPERIAL BANK OF COMMERCE
CIBC
1530 Albion Rd, Etobicoke, ON, M9V 1B4
(416) 741-2102
Emp Here 20
SIC 6021 National commercial banks

D-U-N-S 25-100-1210 (SL)
ETOBICOKE HOSPITAL VOLUNTEER ASSOCIATION GIFT SHOP
101 Humber College Blvd, Etobicoke, ON, M9V 1R8
(416) 747-3400
Emp Here 50   *Sales* 2,772,507
SIC 5947 Gift, novelty, and souvenir shop

D-U-N-S 20-015-1400 (HQ)
FORBO FLOORING SYSTEMS
111 Westmore Dr, Etobicoke, ON, M9V 3Y6
(416) 745-4200
Emp Here 40   *Emp Total* 40
Sales 5,997,600
SIC 5023 Homefurnishings
Pr Pr Dennis Darragh

D-U-N-S 25-988-1894 (BR)
FORTINOS SUPERMARKET LTD
FORTINOS
1530 Albion Rd, Etobicoke, ON, M9V 1B4

Emp Here 225
SIC 5411 Grocery stores

D-U-N-S 20-571-0747 (BR)
GARDEWINE GROUP INC
15 Warrendale Crt, Etobicoke, ON, M9V 1P9
(416) 326-0647
Emp Here 25
SIC 4731 Freight transportation arrangement

D-U-N-S 24-826-1005 (BR)
GOVERNMENT OF ONTARIO
MINISTRY OF HEALTH
101 Humber College Blvd, Etobicoke, ON,

M9V 1R8
(416) 747-3400
Emp Here 100
SIC 8062 General medical and surgical hospitals

D-U-N-S 24-023-1527   (BR)
METRO ONTARIO PHARMACIES LIMITED
DRUG BASICS
900 Albion Rd, Etobicoke, ON, M9V 1A5
(416) 743-4485
Emp Here 50
SIC 5411 Grocery stores

D-U-N-S 20-171-8293   (SL)
NORBEL METAL SERVICE LIMITED
100 Guided Crt, Etobicoke, ON, M9V 4K6
(416) 744-9988
Emp Here 80   Sales 4,012,839
SIC 7389 Business services, nec

D-U-N-S 25-446-8861   (BR)
PRISZM LP
KFC
1743 Albion Rd, Etobicoke, ON, M9V 1C3
(416) 743-7486
Emp Here 22
SIC 5812 Eating places

D-U-N-S 25-420-7988   (BR)
TORONTO CATHOLIC DISTRICT SCHOOL BOARD
MSGR JOHN CORRIGAN CATHOLIC SCHOOL
100 Royalcrest Rd, Etobicoke, ON, M9V 5B4
(416) 393-5399
Emp Here 20
SIC 8211 Elementary and secondary schools

D-U-N-S 20-032-5079   (BR)
TORONTO CATHOLIC DISTRICT SCHOOL BOARD
SPECIAL SERVICES - WEST REGION
155 John Garland Blvd Rm 204, Etobicoke, ON, M9V 1N7
(416) 393-5402
Emp Here 50
SIC 8211 Elementary and secondary schools

D-U-N-S 25-406-3688   (BR)
TORONTO CATHOLIC DISTRICT SCHOOL BOARD
ST. ANDREWS CATHOLIC SCHOOL
2533 Kipling Ave, Etobicoke, ON, M9V 3A8
(416) 393-5295
Emp Here 53
SIC 8211 Elementary and secondary schools

D-U-N-S 20-711-1092   (BR)
TORONTO CATHOLIC DISTRICT SCHOOL BOARD
ST. ANGELA ELEMENTARY SCHOOL
220 Mount Olive Dr, Etobicoke, ON, M9V 3Z5
(416) 393-5361
Emp Here 50
SIC 8211 Elementary and secondary schools

D-U-N-S 20-711-1175   (BR)
TORONTO CATHOLIC DISTRICT SCHOOL BOARD
ST. DOROTHY CATHOLIC SCHOOL
155 John Garland Blvd Suite 204, Etobicoke, ON, M9V 1N7
(416) 393-5341
Emp Here 34
SIC 8211 Elementary and secondary schools

D-U-N-S 20-025-1952   (BR)
TORONTO DISTRICT SCHOOL BOARD
NORTH ALBION COLLEGIATE INSTITUTE
2580 Kipling Ave, Etobicoke, ON, M9V 3B2
(416) 394-7550
Emp Here 75
SIC 8211 Elementary and secondary schools

D-U-N-S 20-700-2754   (BR)
TORONTO DISTRICT SCHOOL BOARD
BEAUMONDE HEIGHTS JUNIOR & MIDDLE

SCHOOL
70 Monterrey Dr, Etobicoke, ON, M9V 1T1
(416) 394-7790
Emp Here 50
SIC 8211 Elementary and secondary schools

D-U-N-S 20-026-0243   (BR)
TORONTO DISTRICT SCHOOL BOARD
MELODY VILLAGE JUNIOR SCHOOL
520 Silverstone Dr, Etobicoke, ON, M9V 3L5
(416) 394-7620
Emp Here 40
SIC 8211 Elementary and secondary schools

D-U-N-S 25-000-6749   (BR)
TORONTO DISTRICT SCHOOL BOARD
WEST HUMBER COLLEGIATE INSTITUTE
1675 Martin Grove Rd, Etobicoke, ON, M9V 3S3
(416) 394-7570
Emp Here 100
SIC 8211 Elementary and secondary schools

D-U-N-S 20-027-1778   (BR)
TORONTO DISTRICT SCHOOL BOARD
JOHN D PARKER JUNIOR SCHOOL
202 Mount Olive Dr, Etobicoke, ON, M9V 3Z5
(416) 394-7530
Emp Here 60
SIC 8211 Elementary and secondary schools

D-U-N-S 20-700-2929   (BR)
TORONTO DISTRICT SCHOOL BOARD
CLAIREVILLE JUNIOR SCHOOL
350 Silverstone Dr, Etobicoke, ON, M9V 3J4
(416) 394-7500
Emp Here 45
SIC 8211 Elementary and secondary schools

D-U-N-S 20-085-5455   (BR)
TORONTO DISTRICT SCHOOL BOARD
SMITHFIELD MIDDLE SCHOOL
175 Mount Olive Dr, Etobicoke, ON, M9V 2E3
(416) 394-7540
Emp Here 55
SIC 8211 Elementary and secondary schools

D-U-N-S 24-331-4924   (BR)
TORONTO PUBLIC LIBRARY BOARD
ALBION BRANCH
1515 Albion Rd, Etobicoke, ON, M9V 1B2
(416) 394-5170
Emp Here 40
SIC 8231 Libraries

D-U-N-S 20-078-0166   (BR)
VENETOR EQUIPMENT RENTAL INC
11 Mars Rd, Etobicoke, ON, M9V 2K2
(416) 679-8480
Emp Here 20
SIC 7353 Heavy construction equipment rental

D-U-N-S 25-687-3019   (BR)
WILLIAM OSLER HEALTH SYSTEM
ETOBICOKE GENERAL HOSPITAL
(Suby of William Osler Health System)
101 Humber College Blvd, Etobicoke, ON, M9V 1R8
(416) 494-2120
Emp Here 1,000
SIC 8062 General medical and surgical hospitals

Etobicoke, ON M9W
York County

D-U-N-S 25-255-8374   (SL)
1060412 ONTARIO LIMITED
COMMANDER TRANSPORT
280 Belfield Rd, Etobicoke, ON, M9W 1H6

Emp Here 60   Sales 4,742,446
SIC 4212 Local trucking, without storage

D-U-N-S 25-974-8655   (SL)

1112308 ONTARIO INC
246 Attwell Dr, Etobicoke, ON, M9W 5B4
(416) 675-1635
Emp Here 210   Sales 12,695,162
SIC 7342 Disinfecting and pest control services
Pr Pr John Abell

D-U-N-S 24-688-9232   (HQ)
1125151 ONTARIO LIMITED
SI VOUS PLAY SPORTS
(Suby of 1125151 Ontario Limited)
6931 Steeles Ave W Suite 1, Etobicoke, ON, M9W 6K7
(416) 675-9235
Emp Here 30   Emp Total 61
Sales 4,158,005
SIC 5699 Miscellaneous apparel and accessory stores

D-U-N-S 24-966-1570   (BR)
1561716 ONTARIO LTD
LONE STAR CAFE
(Suby of 1561716 Ontario Ltd)
930 Dixon Rd, Etobicoke, ON, M9W 1J9
(416) 674-7777
Emp Here 80
SIC 5812 Eating places

D-U-N-S 24-938-1468   (SL)
939927 ONTARIO LIMITED
MANDARIN RESTAURANT
200 Queen'S Plate Dr, Etobicoke, ON, M9W 6Y9
(416) 746-6000
Emp Here 80   Sales 2,407,703
SIC 5812 Eating places

D-U-N-S 20-554-1399   (BR)
A. LASSONDE INC
LASSONDE BEVERAGES CANADA, DIV OF
(Suby of 3346625 Canada Inc)
95 Vulcan St, Etobicoke, ON, M9W 1L4
(416) 244-4224
Emp Here 100
SIC 2086 Bottled and canned soft drinks

D-U-N-S 25-222-0694   (HQ)
ABC AIR MANAGEMENT SYSTEMS INC
(Suby of Cerberus Capital Management, L.P.)
110 Ronson Dr, Etobicoke, ON, M9W 1B6
(416) 744-3113
Emp Here 75   Emp Total 143,502
Sales 14,665,101
SIC 3089 Plastics products, nec
Pr Mike Schmidt

D-U-N-S 20-111-2674   (BR)
ABC AIR MANAGEMENT SYSTEMS INC
(Suby of Cerberus Capital Management, L.P.)
2200 Islington Ave Suite 100, Etobicoke, ON, M9W 3W5

Emp Here 100
SIC 3089 Plastics products, nec

D-U-N-S 25-214-7277   (SL)
ABC CLIMATE CONTROL SYSTEMS INC
(Suby of Cerberus Capital Management, L.P.)
54 Bethridge Rd, Etobicoke, ON, M9W 1N1
(416) 744-3113
Emp Here 320   Sales 53,407,232
SIC 3089 Plastics products, nec
Ch Bd Helga Schmidt

D-U-N-S 24-318-6546   (BR)
ABC GROUP INC
ABC PLASTICS MOULDING, A DIV OF
(Suby of Cerberus Capital Management, L.P.)
20 Brydon Dr, Etobicoke, ON, M9W 5R6
(416) 743-6731
Emp Here 200
SIC 3089 Plastics products, nec

D-U-N-S 20-559-5858   (HQ)
ABC INOAC EXTERIOR SYSTEMS INC.
(Suby of Cerberus Capital Management, L.P.)
220 Brockport Dr, Etobicoke, ON, M9W 5S1

(416) 675-7480
Emp Here 350   Emp Total 143,502
Sales 58,733,364
SIC 3089 Plastics products, nec
Opers Mgr Angelo Cesta
Mgr Alexander Dimoski

D-U-N-S 25-373-7779   (SL)
ABC INTERIOR SYSTEMS INC
(Suby of Cerberus Capital Management, L.P.)
10 Disco Rd, Etobicoke, ON, M9W 1L7
(416) 675-2220
Emp Here 300   Sales 49,905,119
SIC 3089 Plastics products, nec
Pr Mike Schmidt
VP Tim Schmidt

D-U-N-S 20-772-8221   (HQ)
AECON CONSTRUCTION GROUP INC
AECON UTILITIES
20 Carlson Crt Suite 800, Etobicoke, ON, M9W 7K6
(416) 293-7004
Emp Here 250   Emp Total 12,000
Sales 846,635,963
SIC 1541 Industrial buildings and warehouses
John M Beck
Brian Swartz
Paul Koenderman

D-U-N-S 24-977-4464   (HQ)
AECON CONSTRUCTION AND MATERIALS LIMITED
20 Carlson Crt Suite 800, Etobicoke, ON, M9W 7K6
(905) 454-1078
Emp Here 500   Emp Total 12,000
Sales 68,437,137
SIC 1629 Heavy construction, nec
Pr Pr Scott C Balfour

D-U-N-S 25-252-1299   (BR)
AFFILIATED AGENTS EN DOUANES LIMI-TEE
AFFILIATED AGENTS EN DOUANES LIMI-TEE
500 Carlingview Dr, Etobicoke, ON, M9W 5R3

Emp Here 50
SIC 4731 Freight transportation arrangement

D-U-N-S 20-404-2774   (HQ)
AKZO NOBEL COATINGS LTD
110 Woodbine Downs Blvd Unit 4, Etobicoke, ON, M9W 5S6
(416) 674-6633
Emp Here 20   Emp Total 46,100
Sales 14,300,297
SIC 2851 Paints and allied products
Genl Mgr David Smith
Fin Mgr Clara Chin

D-U-N-S 20-213-5315   (HQ)
ALLEGION CANADA INC
SECURITY AND SAFETY, DIV OF
51 Worcester Rd, Etobicoke, ON, M9W 4K2
(416) 213-4500
Emp Here 40   Emp Total 280
Sales 65,963,030
SIC 5084 Industrial machinery and equipment
Dir Mark Wilson
Fin Ex Shawn White
Prs Mgr Janice Telfer

D-U-N-S 24-124-9879   (HQ)
ALTERNA SAVINGS
(Suby of Alterna Savings)
165 Attwell Dr, Etobicoke, ON, M9W 5Y5
(416) 252-5621
Emp Here 100   Emp Total 600
Sales 109,592,863
SIC 6062 State credit unions
Pr Gary Seveny
Dir Donald Altman

D-U-N-S 20-557-6023   (BR)
APOTEX INC

50 Steinway Blvd Suite 3, Etobicoke, ON, M9W 6Y3
(416) 675-0338
Emp Here 900
SIC 2834 Pharmaceutical preparations

D-U-N-S 25-421-0032   (SL)
ARIZONA B BAR & GRILL INC
215 Carlingview Dr, Etobicoke, ON, M9W 5X8
(416) 674-7772
Emp Here 50   *Sales* 1,532,175
SIC 5812 Eating places

D-U-N-S 20-016-6143   (BR)
ATLIFIC INC
COURTYARD BY MARRIOTT - TORONTO-AIRPORT
(*Suby of* 3376290 Canada Inc)
231 Carlingview Dr, Etobicoke, ON, M9W 5E8
(416) 675-0411
Emp Here 100
SIC 7011 Hotels and motels

D-U-N-S 20-210-7801   (HQ)
AVISCAR INC
AVIS
(*Suby of* Avis Budget Group, Inc.)
1 Convair Dr, Etobicoke, ON, M9W 6Z9
(416) 213-8400
Emp Here 400   *Emp Total* 30,000
Sales 321,985,497
SIC 7514 Passenger car rental
Dir Larry De Shon
Pr David B. Wyshner
Sec Jean-Marie Sera
 Jon Zuber

D-U-N-S 20-056-3935   (SL)
BDP CANADA ULC
BDP INTERNATIONAL
(*Suby of* Bdp International, Inc.)
10 Carlson Crt Suite 801, Etobicoke, ON, M9W 6L2
(905) 602-0200
Emp Here 21   *Sales* 5,284,131
SIC 4731 Freight transportation arrangement
Mgr Barry Murphy
 John Bolte
Pr Pr Richard J Bolte, Jr
Dir Robert Bolte

D-U-N-S 25-370-0223   (HQ)
BSM TECHNOLOGIES LTD
(*Suby of* BSM Technologies Inc)
75 International Blvd Suite 100, Etobicoke, ON, M9W 6L9
(416) 675-1201
Emp Here 195   *Emp Total* 242
Sales 103,093,469
SIC 3699 Electrical equipment and supplies, nec
Pr Aly Rahemtulla
 Louis De Jong
 Larry Juba

D-U-N-S 20-572-3856   (BR)
BAYER INC
BAYER HEALTHCARE
77 Belfield Rd Suite 621, Etobicoke, ON, M9W 1G6
(416) 248-0771
Emp Here 20
SIC 5122 Drugs, proprietaries, and sundries

D-U-N-S 24-144-2818   (BR)
BENTALL KENNEDY (CANADA) LIMITED PARTNERSHIP
10 Carlson Crt Suite 500, Etobicoke, ON, M9W 6L2
(416) 674-7707
Emp Here 80
SIC 6531 Real estate agents and managers

D-U-N-S 24-393-1222   (BR)
BODY BLUE 2006 INC
(*Suby of* Corporation Developpement Knowlton Inc)
130 Claireville Dr, Etobicoke, ON, M9W 5Y3

(905) 677-8333
Emp Here 20
SIC 5122 Drugs, proprietaries, and sundries

D-U-N-S 20-116-3099   (HQ)
BRENLO LTD
(*Suby of* LBS Group Limited)
41 Racine Rd, Etobicoke, ON, M9W 2Z4
(416) 749-6857
Emp Here 100   *Emp Total* 1
Sales 11,607,763
SIC 2431 Millwork
Pr Pr John W F Kitchen
 James Maxwell
Sec S Jill Kitchen

D-U-N-S 20-174-7193   (BR)
BRENNTAG CANADA INC
35 Vulcan St, Etobicoke, ON, M9W 1L3
(416) 243-9615
Emp Here 35
SIC 5198 Paints, varnishes, and supplies

D-U-N-S 24-425-6152   (HQ)
BROKERHOUSE DISTRIBUTORS INC
(*Suby of* Brokerhouse Distributors Inc)
108 Woodbine Downs Blvd Unit 4, Etobicoke, ON, M9W 5S6
(416) 798-3537
Emp Here 30   *Emp Total* 50
Sales 3,648,035
SIC 5722 Household appliance stores

D-U-N-S 20-120-4216   (HQ)
BROOK CROMPTON LTD
264 Attwell Dr, Etobicoke, ON, M9W 5B2
(416) 675-3844
Emp Here 50   *Emp Total* 15,153
Sales 10,652,262
SIC 5063 Electrical apparatus and equipment
Dir Wolfgang Kloser
Dir Simon Chung
Dir Giovanni Bindoni
Dir Graham David Harries
Dir Neil Anthony Stewardson
Dir Leo A. Mcguire

D-U-N-S 20-924-0241   (HQ)
BUDGETAUTO INC
A-BUDGET CAR AND TRUCK RENTALS
(*Suby of* Avis Budget Group, Inc.)
1 Convair Dr, Etobicoke, ON, M9W 6Z9
(416) 213-8400
Emp Here 31   *Emp Total* 30,000
Sales 72,765,084
SIC 7514 Passenger car rental
Pr David B. Wyshner
Dir Jon Zuber
Dir Larry De Shon

D-U-N-S 24-391-6355   (SL)
CEFEX - CENTRE FOR FIDUCIARY EXCELLENCE LLC
CEFEX
20 Carlson Crt Suite 100, Etobicoke, ON, M9W 7K6
(416) 401-8702
Emp Here 20   *Sales* 9,423,290
SIC 6099 Functions related to deposit banking
Genl Mgr Carlos Panksep

D-U-N-S 25-420-5693   (BR)
CRH CANADA GROUP INC
DUFFERIN-CUSTOM CONCRETE GROUP
1184 Martin Grove Rd, Etobicoke, ON, M9W 5M9
(416) 744-2206
Emp Here 50
SIC 5999 Miscellaneous retail stores, nec

D-U-N-S 25-119-1714   (BR)
CANADA POST CORPORATION
ETOBICOKE STATION B POST OFFICE
2110 Kipling Ave, Etobicoke, ON, M9W 4K5
(416) 743-8755
Emp Here 50
SIC 4311 U.s. postal service

D-U-N-S 25-362-1072   (BR)

CANADIAN UNION OF PUBLIC EMPLOYEES
AIRLINE DIVISION OF CUPE
25 Belfield Rd, Etobicoke, ON, M9W 1E8
(416) 798-3399
Emp Here 20
SIC 8631 Labor organizations

D-U-N-S 20-844-5098   (BR)
CANAROPA (1954) INC
1866 Kipling Ave, Etobicoke, ON, M9W 4J1
(416) 241-4445
Emp Here 25
SIC 5072 Hardware

D-U-N-S 25-790-3914   (BR)
CARA OPERATIONS LIMITED
HARVEY'S RESTAURANT
(*Suby of* Cara Holdings Limited)
648 Dixon Rd, Etobicoke, ON, M9W 1J1
(416) 244-1841
Emp Here 20
SIC 5812 Eating places

D-U-N-S 24-937-0230   (BR)
CARGILL LIMITED
CARGILL FOODS
71 Rexdale Blvd, Etobicoke, ON, M9W 1P1

Emp Here 800
SIC 2011 Meat packing plants

D-U-N-S 20-791-4370   (BR)
CHILDREN'S PLACE (CANADA) LP, THE
CHILDREN'S PLACE, THE
500 Rexdale Blvd, Etobicoke, ON, M9W 6K5
(416) 798-3683
Emp Here 23
SIC 5641 Children's and infants' wear stores

D-U-N-S 24-334-5159   (SL)
CLUB COFFEE L.P.
55 Carrier Dr Suite 1, Etobicoke, ON, M9W 5V9
(416) 675-1300
Emp Here 150   *Sales* 21,523,407
SIC 5149 Groceries and related products, nec
Ltd Pt John Pigott
Ltd Pt Alan Halter
 Wes Douglas

D-U-N-S 20-206-7125   (SL)
CO-PAK PACKAGING CORP
1231 Martin Grove Rd, Etobicoke, ON, M9W 4X2
(905) 799-0092
Emp Here 80   *Sales* 4,764,381
SIC 7389 Business services, nec

D-U-N-S 20-556-5450   (BR)
COMPAGNIE COMMONWEALTH PLYWOOD LTEE, LA
25 Dansk Crt, Etobicoke, ON, M9W 5N6
(416) 675-3266
Emp Here 24
SIC 5031 Lumber, plywood, and millwork

D-U-N-S 25-093-4366   (BR)
CONGEBEC INC
225 Rexdale Blvd, Etobicoke, ON, M9W 1P7
(416) 743-7038
Emp Here 25
SIC 4222 Refrigerated warehousing and storage

D-U-N-S 20-107-2274   (BR)
CONREX STEEL LTD
GARTH INDUSTRIES
(*Suby of* Marshall-Barwick Holdings Inc)
46 Taber Rd, Etobicoke, ON, M9W 3A8
(416) 747-0511
Emp Here 20
SIC 5085 Industrial supplies

D-U-N-S 20-413-1411   (HQ)
CONREX STEEL LTD
GARTH INDUSTRIES, DIV OF
(*Suby of* Marshall-Barwick Holdings Inc)

50 Taber Rd, Etobicoke, ON, M9W 3A8
(416) 747-4665
Emp Here 45   *Emp Total* 565
Sales 7,189,883
SIC 3312 Blast furnaces and steel mills
Pr Pr Cecil Hawkins
Fin Ex Kent Udit
Sec Maynard Young

D-U-N-S 20-016-6960   (SL)
CORE MANUFACTURING INC
275 Carrier Dr, Etobicoke, ON, M9W 5Y8
(416) 675-1177
Emp Here 50   *Sales* 3,648,035
SIC 3519 Internal combustion engines, nec

D-U-N-S 24-120-7492   (SL)
CORRON INVESTMENTS INC
MACDONALDS
25 Carrier Dr, Etobicoke, ON, M9W 6J1
(416) 674-1207
Emp Here 55   *Sales* 1,678,096
SIC 5812 Eating places

D-U-N-S 24-302-0765   (HQ)
CURTIS INTERNATIONAL LTD
315 Attwell Dr, Etobicoke, ON, M9W 5C1
(416) 674-2123
Emp Here 37   *Emp Total* 40
Sales 321,543,055
SIC 5065 Electronic parts and equipment, nec
Pr Pr Aaron Herzog
 Jacob Herzog

D-U-N-S 25-996-2546   (SL)
DATAWIRE COMMUNICATION NETWORKS INC
10 Carlson Crt Suite 300, Etobicoke, ON, M9W 6L2
(416) 213-2001
Emp Here 41   *Sales* 6,631,680
SIC 4899 Communication services, nec
 Patrick Cummiskey
Ch Bd James Meenan
Pr Mike Geihsler
VP Mark Longo
VP Fin Jack Nichols
 Philip Ladoucheur
 Bryan Kerdman

D-U-N-S 20-292-7950   (HQ)
DECO ADHESIVE PRODUCTS (1985) LIMITED
(*Suby of* Deco Adhesive Products (1985) Limited)
28 Greensboro Dr, Etobicoke, ON, M9W 1E1
(416) 247-7878
Emp Here 32   *Emp Total* 50
Sales 3,648,035
SIC 7336 Commercial art and graphic design

D-U-N-S 24-869-1545   (HQ)
DESCO PLUMBING AND HEATING SUPPLY INC
(*Suby of* Entreprises Mirca Inc, Les)
65 Worcester Rd Suite 416, Etobicoke, ON, M9W 5N7
(416) 213-1580
Emp Here 41   *Emp Total* 1,342
Sales 34,677,707
SIC 5074 Plumbing and heating equipment and supplies (hydronics)
Pr Pr Jacques Deschenes
VP John Leeson
 Martin Deschenes
Dir Joe Senese

D-U-N-S 24-834-1997   (BR)
DOLLARAMA S.E.C.
DOLLARAMA
2257 Islington Ave, Etobicoke, ON, M9W 3W6
(416) 640-1564
Emp Here 31
SIC 5331 Variety stores

D-U-N-S 20-554-1605   (SL)
ECMM SOLUTION CANADA INC
123 Claireville Dr, Etobicoke, ON, M9W 6K9

Emp Here 26   *Sales* 3,575,074
SIC 5045 Computers, peripherals, and software

D-U-N-S 25-116-5288   (BR)
ENBRIDGE GAS DISTRIBUTION INC
40 Kelfield St, Etobicoke, ON, M9W 5A2
(416) 249-0001
Emp Here 30
SIC 4924 Natural gas distribution

D-U-N-S 20-057-6051   (HQ)
ENTIRE IMAGING SOLUTIONS INC
(*Suby of* Entire Imaging Solutions Inc)
31 Constellation Crt, Etobicoke, ON, M9W 1K4
(905) 673-2000
Emp Here 60   *Emp Total* 75
Sales 3,866,917
SIC 7334 Photocopying and duplicating services

D-U-N-S 25-408-3827   (HQ)
EXPERTECH NETWORK INSTALLATION INC
240 Attwell Dr, Etobicoke, ON, M9W 5B2

Emp Here 100   *Emp Total* 48,090
Sales 444,272,160
SIC 1623 Water, sewer, and utility lines
Marylynne Campbell
Bernard Le Duc
Mary Ann Turcke
Sylvie Couture

D-U-N-S 24-358-4138   (BR)
FEDEX SUPPLY CHAIN DISTRIBUTION SYSTEM OF CANADA, INC
GENCO DISTRIBUTION SYSTEM OF CANADA, INC
(*Suby of* Fedex Corporation)
160 Carrier Dr Suite 129, Etobicoke, ON, M9W 0A9
(800) 463-3339
Emp Here 75
SIC 4225 General warehousing and storage

D-U-N-S 24-661-9894   (SL)
FERMAR CRUSHING & RECYCLING LTD
1921 Albion Rd, Etobicoke, ON, M9W 5S8
(416) 675-3550
Emp Here 40   *Sales* 11,565,300
SIC 5032 Brick, stone, and related material
Pr Pr Ashton Armien Martin
Malcolm Martin

D-U-N-S 20-528-1884   (SL)
FLASH REPRODUCTIONS LIMITED
51 Galaxy Blvd Suite 1, Etobicoke, ON, M9W 5P1
(416) 742-1244
Emp Here 50   *Sales* 3,793,956
SIC 2752 Commercial printing, lithographic

D-U-N-S 20-181-0822   (HQ)
GDI SERVICES (CANADA) LP
GDI INTEGRATED FACILITY SERVICES
60 Worcester Rd, Etobicoke, ON, M9W 5X2
(416) 736-1144
Emp Here 30   *Emp Total* 13,000
Sales 210,126,816
SIC 7349 Building maintenance services, nec
Pr Daniel Sklivas
Claude Bigras
Michael Boychuck
David A. Galloway
Murray Leimert
Richard G. Roy
Carl Youngman
David G. Samuel

D-U-N-S 24-353-9728   (SL)
GENESENSE TECHNOLOGIES INC
(*Suby of* Aptose Biosciences Inc)
2 Meridian Rd, Etobicoke, ON, M9W 4Z7
(416) 798-1200
Emp Here 30   *Sales* 5,173,950

SIC 8733 Noncommercial research organizations
Pr Pr Aiping Young
Dir Fin Elizabeth Williams
Dir Jim Wright
Dir Peter Korth

D-U-N-S 20-912-4143   (BR)
GENERAL PAINT CORP
(*Suby of* The Sherwin-Williams Company)
172 Belfield Rd, Etobicoke, ON, M9W 1H1
(416) 243-7578
Emp Here 35
SIC 5231 Paint, glass, and wallpaper stores

D-U-N-S 24-803-3391   (HQ)
GIFFELS CORPORATION
2 International Blvd, Etobicoke, ON, M9W 1A2
(416) 798-5500
Emp Here 125   *Emp Total* 1,000
Sales 32,051,287
SIC 8741 Management services
Dir Victor Smith
Dir Fin Marc Turcotte

D-U-N-S 25-362-8622   (HQ)
GLASSCELL ISOFAB INC
1000 Martin Grove Rd Suite 1, Etobicoke, ON, M9W 4V8
(416) 241-8663
Emp Here 45   *Emp Total* 130
Sales 35,862,791
SIC 5033 Roofing, siding, and insulation
John Rudyk
Pr Pr Ross Wilson
George Gilley

D-U-N-S 25-372-7895   (BR)
GLOBAL PAYMENTS CANADA INC
(*Suby of* Global Payments Inc.)
151 Carlingview Dr Unit 17, Etobicoke, ON, M9W 5S4
(416) 798-2627
Emp Here 35
SIC 7389 Business services, nec

D-U-N-S 20-801-1218   (BR)
GOVERNMENT OF ONTARIO
PARK FORESTRY RECREATION CENTER
45 Golfdown Dr, Etobicoke, ON, M9W 2H8
(416) 394-8722
Emp Here 30
SIC 7999 Amusement and recreation, nec

D-U-N-S 24-614-0552   (HQ)
HAIN-CELESTIAL CANADA, ULC
180 Attwell Dr Suite 410, Etobicoke, ON, M9W 6A9
(416) 849-6210
Emp Here 50   *Emp Total* 7,700
Sales 134,355,530
SIC 2075 Soybean oil mills
Beena Goldenberg
VP Fin Jeff Scott

D-U-N-S 20-699-1395   (BR)
HAWORTH, LTD
110 Carrier Dr, Etobicoke, ON, M9W 5R1

Emp Here 180
SIC 2542 Partitions and fixtures, except wood

D-U-N-S 24-000-0435   (BR)
HENKEL CANADA CORPORATION
165 Rexdale Blvd, Etobicoke, ON, M9W 1P7
(905) 814-6511
Emp Here 163
SIC 2819 Industrial inorganic chemicals, nec

D-U-N-S 20-145-3024   (SL)
HOLIDAY INN TORONTO AIRPORT EAST
600 Dixon Rd, Etobicoke, ON, M9W 1J1
(416) 240-7511
Emp Here 100   *Sales* 4,377,642
SIC 7011 Hotels and motels

D-U-N-S 25-080-7203   (BR)
HOME DEPOT OF CANADA INC
HOME DEPOT

(*Suby of* The Home Depot Inc)
1983 Kipling Ave, Etobicoke, ON, M9W 4J4
(416) 746-1357
Emp Here 167
SIC 5251 Hardware stores

D-U-N-S 24-006-4311   (BR)
HUDSON'S BAY COMPANY
HBC LOGISTICS
145 Carrier Dr, Etobicoke, ON, M9W 5N5
(416) 798-5755
Emp Here 530
SIC 5099 Durable goods, nec

D-U-N-S 25-118-1871   (BR)
HUDSON'S BAY COMPANY
BAY, THE
500 Rexdale Blvd, Etobicoke, ON, M9W 6K5
(416) 674-6000
Emp Here 200
SIC 5311 Department stores

D-U-N-S 24-308-3594   (BR)
HUDSON'S BAY COMPANY
BAY, THE
160 Carrier Dr, Etobicoke, ON, M9W 0A9
(416) 644-2600
Emp Here 70
SIC 4225 General warehousing and storage

D-U-N-S 20-105-3639   (BR)
HUMBER COLLEGE INSTITUTE OF TECHNOLOGY AND ADVANCE
HUMBER COLLEGE CHILD DEVELOPMENT CENTRE
205 Humber College Blvd, Etobicoke, ON, M9W 5L7
(416) 675-5057
Emp Here 30
SIC 8351 Child day care services

D-U-N-S 20-560-5921   (SL)
HUMBERLINE PACKAGING INC
(*Suby of* Cerberus Capital Management, L.P.)
310 Humberline Dr Suite 1, Etobicoke, ON, M9W 5S2
(416) 243-1552
Emp Here 40   *Sales* 2,115,860
SIC 7389 Business services, nec

D-U-N-S 24-319-4776   (SL)
ICRM BUILDING SERVICE CONTRACTORS LTD
5 Mclachlan Dr, Etobicoke, ON, M9W 1E3
(416) 798-9898
Emp Here 50   *Sales* 1,732,502
SIC 7349 Building maintenance services, nec

D-U-N-S 25-203-3188   (SL)
IMPORT CUSTOMS SERVICES INC
190 Attwell Dr Suite 602, Etobicoke, ON, M9W 6H8
(905) 502-7776
Emp Here 20   *Sales* 6,674,880
SIC 4731 Freight transportation arrangement
Pr Pr John D Lamont
Tina Ling
Barbara Frost
Sls Mgr Allan Carey

D-U-N-S 24-380-3769   (SL)
INDEPENDENT MECHANICAL SUPPLY INC
310 Carlingview Dr, Etobicoke, ON, M9W 5G1
(416) 679-1048
Emp Here 68   *Sales* 12,403,319
SIC 5075 Warm air heating and air conditioning
Pr Pr Gregory Tester
VP VP Paul Blaik

D-U-N-S 24-105-8916   (HQ)
INTEL OF CANADA, LTD
200 Ronson Dr Suite 201, Etobicoke, ON, M9W 5Z9
(647) 259-0101
Emp Here 50   *Emp Total* 106,000
Sales 13,716,612
SIC 5045 Computers, peripherals, and soft-

ware
Doug Cooper

D-U-N-S 20-272-2021   (SL)
JM (RETAIL) INC
100 Ronson Dr, Etobicoke, ON, M9W 1B6

Emp Here 150   *Sales* 11,779,113
SIC 5621 Women's clothing stores
Pr Ilaria Varoli
Sec Roger Elgner
Treas Michael Sourial

D-U-N-S 25-361-0042   (BR)
KIK OPERATING PARTNERSHIP
KIK CUSTOM PRODUCTS
2000 Kipling Ave, Etobicoke, ON, M9W 4J6
(416) 743-6255
Emp Here 900
SIC 2842 Polishes and sanitation goods

D-U-N-S 24-631-9701   (SL)
KOP-FLEX CANADA LTD
(*Suby of* Emerson Electric Co.)
19 Meteor Dr, Etobicoke, ON, M9W 1A3
(416) 675-7144
Emp Here 23   *Sales* 1,313,293
SIC 3568 Power transmission equipment, nec

D-U-N-S 20-145-5557   (HQ)
L-3 COMMUNICATIONS ELECTRONIC SYSTEMS INC
L-3 ELECTRONIC SYSTEM SERVICES
(*Suby of* L3 Technologies, Inc.)
25 City View Dr, Etobicoke, ON, M9W 5A7
(416) 249-1231
Emp Here 150   *Emp Total* 38,075
Sales 51,022,184
SIC 3812 Search and navigation equipment
Pr Pr Trevor Ratcliffe

D-U-N-S 20-015-5245   (SL)
LSG LEASE SERVICES GROUP INC
45 Constellation Crt, Etobicoke, ON, M9W 1K4
(416) 675-7950
Emp Here 30   *Sales* 3,638,254
SIC 7515 Passenger car leasing

D-U-N-S 24-385-5108   (SL)
LIBERTY SPRING (TORONTO) INC
25 Worcester Rd, Etobicoke, ON, M9W 1K9
(416) 675-9072
Emp Here 35   *Sales* 1,313,293
SIC 3492 Fluid power valves and hose fittings

D-U-N-S 25-098-2204   (SL)
LOGISTI-SOLVE INC
TRUSTED RETAIL SOLUTIONS
172 Bethridge Rd, Etobicoke, ON, M9W 1N3

Emp Here 300   *Sales* 87,920,000
SIC 4731 Freight transportation arrangement
Pr Pr Peter Reaume
Dir Terry Vukosa

D-U-N-S 20-861-2825   (BR)
LUXURY HOTELS INTERNATIONAL OF CANADA, ULC
(*Suby of* Marriott International, Inc.)
901 Dixon Rd, Etobicoke, ON, M9W 1J5
(416) 674-9400
Emp Here 275
SIC 7011 Hotels and motels

D-U-N-S 20-747-5711   (BR)
LUXURY HOTELS INTERNATIONAL OF CANADA, ULC
RESIDENCE BY MARRIOTT TORONTO
(*Suby of* Marriott International, Inc.)
17 Reading Crt, Etobicoke, ON, M9W 7K7
(416) 798-2900
Emp Here 35
SIC 7011 Hotels and motels

D-U-N-S 24-736-8384   (SL)
M.R.S. COMPANY LIMITED
MANAGEMENT REPORTING SYSTEMS

242 Galaxy Blvd, Etobicoke, ON, M9W 5R8
(416) 620-2720
Emp Here 56   *Sales* 4,851,006
SIC 7379 Computer related services, nec

D-U-N-S 24-242-0578   (SL)
MSB PLASTICS MANUFACTURING LTD
(*Suby of* Cerberus Capital Management, L.P.)
23 Disco Rd, Etobicoke, ON, M9W 1M2
(416) 674-1471
Emp Here 250   *Sales* 41,076,874
SIC 3089 Plastics products, nec
Pr Pr Mike Schmidt

D-U-N-S 24-660-2577   (BR)
MAGNA INTERNATIONAL INC
DECO AUTOMOTIVE, DIV OF
225 Claireville Dr, Etobicoke, ON, M9W 6K9
(416) 674-5598
Emp Here 400
SIC 3465 Automotive stampings

D-U-N-S 20-300-7505   (BR)
MARTINREA AUTOMOTIVE INC
ALFIELD INDUSTRIES
340 Carlingview Dr, Etobicoke, ON, M9W 5G5
(416) 213-1717
Emp Here 40
SIC 3471 Plating and polishing

D-U-N-S 20-044-4529   (BR)
MCCAIN FOODS LIMITED
MCCAIN FOODS CANADA
10 Carlson Crt Unit 200, Etobicoke, ON, M9W 6L2
(416) 679-1700
Emp Here 20
SIC 2037 Frozen fruits and vegetables

D-U-N-S 20-559-6588   (SL)
MCCLUSKEY TRANSPORTATION SERVICES LIMITED
514 Carlingview Dr Unit 200, Etobicoke, ON, M9W 5R3
(416) 246-1422
Emp Here 90   *Sales* 2,553,625
SIC 4151 School buses

D-U-N-S 24-348-0782   (BR)
MEDIAS TRANSCONTINENTAL S.E.N.C.
8 Tidemore Ave, Etobicoke, ON, M9W 5H4
(416) 741-1900
Emp Here 300
SIC 2752 Commercial printing, lithographic

D-U-N-S 25-322-4364   (BR)
MEDICAL PHARMACIES GROUP LIMITED
170 Brockport Dr Unit 102, Etobicoke, ON, M9W 5C8
(416) 213-0844
Emp Here 22
SIC 5912 Drug stores and proprietary stores

D-U-N-S 24-469-7884   (SL)
MERIT METAL INDUSTRIES INC
25 Racine Rd, Etobicoke, ON, M9W 2Z4
(416) 745-2015
Emp Here 50   *Sales* 3,866,917
SIC 2542 Partitions and fixtures, except wood

D-U-N-S 24-364-6023   (HQ)
METRO COMPACTOR SERVICE INC
(*Suby of* Metro Compactor Service Inc)
40 Bethridge Rd, Etobicoke, ON, M9W 1N1
(416) 743-8484
Emp Here 35   *Emp Total* 51
Sales 3,638,254
SIC 7699 Repair services, nec

D-U-N-S 24-885-8409   (BR)
METROLAND MEDIA GROUP LTD
ETOBICOKE GUARDIAN
307 Humberline Dr, Etobicoke, ON, M9W 5V1
(416) 493-4400
Emp Here 55
SIC 2711 Newspapers

D-U-N-S 24-010-9298   (BR)
MOLSON CANADA 2005

(*Suby of* Molson Coors Brewing Company)
1 Carlingview Dr, Etobicoke, ON, M9W 5E5
(416) 675-1786
Emp Here 1,000
SIC 2082 Malt beverages

D-U-N-S 24-212-1416   (HQ)
MOORES THE SUIT PEOPLE INC
MOORES CLOTHING FOR MEN
(*Suby of* Tailored Brands, Inc.)
129 Carlingview Dr, Etobicoke, ON, M9W 5E7
(416) 675-1900
Emp Here 80   *Emp Total* 22,500
Sales 132,277,749
SIC 5611 Men's and boys' clothing stores
Pr Dave Starrett
  Richard Bull
VP Opers Denis Button

D-U-N-S 25-691-5836   (BR)
MUGGS, J J INC
J J MUGGS GOURMET GRILL
(*Suby of* Muggs, J J Inc)
500 Rexdale Blvd, Etobicoke, ON, M9W 6K5

Emp Here 30
SIC 5812 Eating places

D-U-N-S 20-105-0106   (BR)
NFI DOMINION CANADA, ULC
DOMINION WAREHOUSING & DISTRIBUTION SERVICES LTD
225 Carrier Dr, Etobicoke, ON, M9W 5Y8

Emp Here 20
SIC 4731 Freight transportation arrangement

D-U-N-S 24-566-0006   (SL)
NTN INTERACTIVE NETWORK INC
14 Meteor Dr, Etobicoke, ON, M9W 1A4

Emp Here 50   *Sales* 2,918,428
SIC 4841 Cable and other pay television services

D-U-N-S 24-359-5894   (BR)
NESTLE CANADA INC
335 Carlingview Dr Unit 2, Etobicoke, ON, M9W 5G8

Emp Here 25
SIC 4225 General warehousing and storage

D-U-N-S 25-365-1988   (BR)
NEWALTA CORPORATION
55 Vulcan St, Etobicoke, ON, M9W 1L3
(416) 245-8338
Emp Here 20
SIC 4953 Refuse systems

D-U-N-S 25-693-5073   (BR)
NEWGEN RESTAURANT SERVICES INC
TUCKER'S MARKETPLACE
15 Carlson Crt, Etobicoke, ON, M9W 6A2
(416) 675-8818
Emp Here 75
SIC 5812 Eating places

D-U-N-S 24-232-5749   (BR)
NORTHLAND PROPERTIES CORPORATION
SANDMAN SIGNATURE TORONTO AIRPORT HOTEL
(*Suby of* Northland Properties Corporation)
55 Reading Crt, Etobicoke, ON, M9W 7K7
(416) 798-8840
Emp Here 25
SIC 7011 Hotels and motels

D-U-N-S 24-247-3697   (SL)
ONTARIO RACING COMMISSION
10 Carlson Crt Suite 400, Etobicoke, ON, M9W 6L2
(416) 213-0520
Emp Here 80
SIC 7948 Racing, including track operation

D-U-N-S 20-859-8867   (BR)

PACIFIC LINK COMMUNICATIONS INC
BELL WORLD
500 Rexdale Blvd, Etobicoke, ON, M9W 6K5
(416) 798-3178
Emp Here 25
SIC 5999 Miscellaneous retail stores, nec

D-U-N-S 25-320-1263   (SL)
PERKINS FAMILY RESTAURANT, THE
600 Dixon Rd, Etobicoke, ON, M9W 1J1
(416) 240-7511
Emp Here 50   *Sales* 1,532,175
SIC 5812 Eating places

D-U-N-S 20-325-1970   (BR)
PETON DISTRIBUTORS INC
1211 Martin Grove Rd, Etobicoke, ON, M9W 4X2
(416) 742-7138
Emp Here 50
SIC 5999 Miscellaneous retail stores, nec

D-U-N-S 20-647-6918   (BR)
PHILIPS ELECTRONICS LTD
TOR SALES CENTER
91 Skyway Ave Unit 100, Etobicoke, ON, M9W 6R5
(416) 674-6101
Emp Here 22
SIC 3648 Lighting equipment, nec

D-U-N-S 20-772-1861   (BR)
PHILIPS LIGHTING CANADA LTD
LIGHTOLIER-CFI, DIV. OF
91 Skyway Ave Unit 100, Etobicoke, ON, M9W 6R5
(416) 674-6101
Emp Here 22
SIC 3645 Residential lighting fixtures

D-U-N-S 20-912-3756   (BR)
PLASTIPAK INDUSTRIES INC
260 Rexdale Blvd, Etobicoke, ON, M9W 1R2
(416) 744-4220
Emp Here 130
SIC 3089 Plastics products, nec

D-U-N-S 20-081-0609   (BR)
PRISZM LP
TACO BELL
2068 Kipling Ave, Etobicoke, ON, M9W 4J9

Emp Here 22
SIC 5812 Eating places

D-U-N-S 24-850-3559   (HQ)
PRUDENT BENEFITS ADMINISTRATION SERVICES INC
PBAS
(*Suby of* Prudent Benefits Administration Services Inc)
61 International Blvd Suite 110, Etobicoke, ON, M9W 6K4
(416) 674-8581
Emp Here 60   *Emp Total* 130
Sales 16,926,882
SIC 8742 Management consulting services
Pr Pr Joan S Tanaka

D-U-N-S 24-816-9096   (BR)
PUROLATOR INC.
PUROLATOR INC
62 Vulcan St, Etobicoke, ON, M9W 1L2
(416) 241-4496
Emp Here 1,500
SIC 4731 Freight transportation arrangement

D-U-N-S 24-345-5065   (BR)
PUROLATOR INC.
PUROLATOR INC
1151 Martin Grove Rd Suite 7, Etobicoke, ON, M9W 0C1
(416) 614-0300
Emp Here 150
SIC 4731 Freight transportation arrangement

D-U-N-S 25-684-1271   (HQ)
QPS EVALUATION SERVICES INC
QPS

(*Suby of* QPS Evaluation Services Inc)
81 Kelfield St Unit 8, Etobicoke, ON, M9W 5A3
(416) 241-8857
Emp Here 45   *Emp Total* 77
Sales 3,866,917
SIC 7389 Business services, nec

D-U-N-S 25-150-8487   (SL)
RT FRESH PREPARED FOODS INC
315 Humberline Dr, Etobicoke, ON, M9W 5T6
(416) 213-1077
Emp Here 20   *Sales* 2,115,860
SIC 2099 Food preparations, nec

D-U-N-S 24-344-6668   (BR)
REDBERRY FRANCHISING CORP
BURGER KING
500 Rexdale Blvd, Etobicoke, ON, M9W 6K5
(416) 679-8777
Emp Here 23
SIC 5812 Eating places

D-U-N-S 25-322-8951   (SL)
REGIONAL GROUP (TORONTO) INC.
135 Queen'S Plate Dr Suite 300, Etobicoke, ON, M9W 6V1

Emp Here 86   *Sales* 10,459,852
SIC 6531 Real estate agents and managers
Pr Pr John Bassel
  Tasso Eracles

D-U-N-S 25-907-2437   (BR)
RES PRECAST INC
514 Carlingview Dr, Etobicoke, ON, M9W 5R3

Emp Here 20
SIC 5999 Miscellaneous retail stores, nec

D-U-N-S 25-213-4721   (SL)
RICMAR ENTERPRISES LTD
PAT & MARIO'S RESTAURANT
925 Dixon Rd, Etobicoke, ON, M9W 1J8
(416) 674-3031
Emp Here 75   *Sales* 2,261,782
SIC 5812 Eating places

D-U-N-S 24-817-3916   (BR)
ROMA RIBS LTD
TONY ROMA'S 'FAMOUS FOR RIBS'
(*Suby of* Roma Ribs Ltd)
10 Carlson Crt, Etobicoke, ON, M9W 6L2

Emp Here 50
SIC 5812 Eating places

D-U-N-S 20-793-5024   (HQ)
ROYAL ADHESIVES & SEALANTS CANADA LTD
CHEMQUE
266 Humberline Dr, Etobicoke, ON, M9W 5X1
(416) 679-5676
Emp Here 83   *Emp Total* 1,220
Sales 14,592,140
SIC 2899 Chemical preparations, nec
Pr Pr Ted Clark
Dir Sam Ghaly
Dir Gary Stenke

D-U-N-S 25-798-8675   (BR)
ROYAL HOST INC
TRAVELODGE TORONTO AIRPORT
925 Dixon Rd, Etobicoke, ON, M9W 1J8
(416) 674-2222
Emp Here 150
SIC 7011 Hotels and motels

D-U-N-S 24-666-2878   (HQ)
ROYAL LASER MFG INC
(*Suby of* 1836826 Ontario Inc)
25 Claireville Dr, Etobicoke, ON, M9W 5Z7
(416) 679-9474
Emp Here 50   *Emp Total* 2
Sales 12,993,765
SIC 3499 Fabricated Metal products, nec
Pr John Cheung
  William Iannaci
VP Fin Samir Dalal

D-U-N-S 20-211-0255 (BR)
RYDER TRUCK RENTAL CANADA LTD
RYDER INTEGRATED LOGISTICS
(*Suby of* Ryder System, Inc.)
123 Claireville Dr, Etobicoke, ON, M9W 6K9
(416) 679-6700
Emp Here 40
SIC 4225 General warehousing and storage

D-U-N-S 25-397-5254 (HQ)
SCI GROUP INC
(*Suby of* Canada Post Corporation)
180 Attwell Dr Suite 600, Etobicoke, ON, M9W 6A9
(416) 401-3011
Emp Here 300 *Emp Total* 63,000
Sales 103,090,793
SIC 4213 Trucking, except local
Pr John Ferguson
  Roger Rees
VP Opers Paul Ragan

D-U-N-S 24-848-4698 (HQ)
SCI LOGISTICS LTD
AMG LOGISTICS
(*Suby of* Canada Post Corporation)
180 Attwell Dr Suite 600, Etobicoke, ON, M9W 6A9
(866) 773-7735
Emp Here 50 *Emp Total* 63,000
Sales 12,622,201
SIC 8741 Management services
  John Ferguson

D-U-N-S 20-337-4632 (BR)
SAAND INC
355 Attwell Dr, Etobicoke, ON, M9W 5C2
(416) 674-6945
Emp Here 91
SIC 5039 Construction materials, nec

D-U-N-S 25-155-8318 (BR)
SAFWAY SERVICES CANADA, ULC
(*Suby of* Safway Group Holding LLC)
503 Carlingview Dr, Etobicoke, ON, M9W 5H2
(416) 675-2449
Emp Here 100
SIC 1799 Special trade contractors, nec

D-U-N-S 25-311-1850 (BR)
SEARS CANADA INC
SEARS WOODBINE
500 Rexdale Blvd, Etobicoke, ON, M9W 6K5
(416) 798-3800
Emp Here 100
SIC 5311 Department stores

D-U-N-S 25-406-3159 (SL)
SELIENT INC
93 Skyway Ave Suite 201, Etobicoke, ON, M9W 6N6
(416) 234-0098
Emp Here 28 *Sales* 2,512,128
SIC 7371 Custom computer programming services

D-U-N-S 24-318-1682 (BR)
SMUCKER FOODS OF CANADA CORP
ROBIN HOOD MULTIFOODS
(*Suby of* The J M Smucker Company)
191 Attwell Dr Suite 4, Etobicoke, ON, M9W 5Z2
(416) 675-2541
Emp Here 25
SIC 8731 Commercial physical research

D-U-N-S 24-817-4802 (BR)
SOCIETE XYLEM CANADA
XYLEM WATER SOLUTION
93 Claireville Dr, Etobicoke, ON, M9W 6K9
(416) 679-1199
Emp Here 28
SIC 6531 Real estate agents and managers

D-U-N-S 25-831-4780 (BR)
SPRINGWALL SLEEP PRODUCTS INC
1821 Albion Rd Suite 5, Etobicoke, ON, M9W 5W8

(888) 760-2311
Emp Here 50
SIC 2515 Mattresses and bedsprings

D-U-N-S 25-213-7302 (BR)
STAPLES CANADA INC
STAPLES THE BUSINESS DEPOT
(*Suby of* Staples, Inc.)
180 Queen'S Plate Dr Suite 10, Etobicoke, ON, M9W 6Y9
(416) 749-9932
Emp Here 20
SIC 5943 Stationery stores

D-U-N-S 24-453-1562 (HQ)
STARBURST COIN MACHINES INC
(*Suby of* Starburst Coin Machines Inc)
70 Ronson Dr, Etobicoke, ON, M9W 1B6
(416) 251-2122
Emp Here 62 *Emp Total* 90
Sales 4,815,406
SIC 7993 Coin-operated amusement devices

D-U-N-S 25-591-6561 (BR)
STOCK TRANSPORTATION LTD
STOCK ON THE JOURNEY OF LEARNING
60 Mcculloch Ave, Etobicoke, ON, M9W 4M6
(416) 244-5341
Emp Here 280
SIC 4151 School buses

D-U-N-S 20-346-1181 (BR)
STRAUSS, LEVI & CO. (CANADA) INC
90 Claireville Dr, Etobicoke, ON, M9W 5Y1
(416) 679-2049
Emp Here 70
SIC 5632 Women's accessory and specialty stores

D-U-N-S 24-501-1114 (SL)
STRUDELL INDUSTRIES
1911 Albion Rd, Etobicoke, ON, M9W 5S8
(416) 675-2025
Emp Here 35 *Sales* 18,944,880
SIC 5051 Metals service centers and offices
Owner Nick Laird

D-U-N-S 25-320-1404 (BR)
SUPREMEX INC
(*Suby of* Supremex Inc)
400 Humberline Dr, Etobicoke, ON, M9W 5T3
(416) 675-9370
Emp Here 160
SIC 2677 Envelopes

D-U-N-S 20-216-7651 (SL)
SWIFTRANS SERVICES LTD
71 City View Dr, Etobicoke, ON, M9W 5A5
(416) 614-9560
Emp Here 50 *Sales* 2,334,742
SIC 4142 Bus charter service, except local

D-U-N-S 24-947-2853 (SL)
TAC MECHANICAL INC
215 Carlingview Dr Suite 311, Etobicoke, ON, M9W 5X8
(416) 798-8400
Emp Here 50 *Sales* 4,377,642
SIC 1711 Plumbing, heating, air-conditioning

D-U-N-S 25-819-1642 (HQ)
TWI FOODS INC
40 Shaft Rd Suite 1, Etobicoke, ON, M9W 4M2
(647) 775-1400
Emp Here 150 *Emp Total* 105
Sales 19,916,778
SIC 2051 Bread, cake, and related products
Pr Pr Ali Kizilbash
VP Yuhana Kizilbash

D-U-N-S 24-760-3421 (BR)
TECHNOLOGIES METAFORE INC
830 Dixon Rd, Etobicoke, ON, M9W 6Y8
(905) 362-8300
Emp Here 90
SIC 7371 Custom computer programming services

D-U-N-S 25-996-4195 (SL)

TETI BAKERY INC
27 Signal Hill Ave Suite 3, Etobicoke, ON, M9W 6V8
(416) 798-8777
Emp Here 50 *Sales* 2,167,357
SIC 5461 Retail bakeries

D-U-N-S 24-965-3734 (BR)
THOMSON TERMINALS LIMITED
55 City View Dr, Etobicoke, ON, M9W 5A5
(416) 240-0648
Emp Here 100
SIC 4225 General warehousing and storage

D-U-N-S 24-926-5273 (SL)
TORONTO AIRPORT MARRIOTT LTD, THE
(*Suby of* Marriott International, Inc.)
901 Dixon Rd, Etobicoke, ON, M9W 1J5
(416) 674-9400
Emp Here 250 *Sales* 10,944,105
SIC 7011 Hotels and motels
Ch Bd J.W. Marriott Jr
Pr Arne Sorenson
VP VP Carl Berquist

D-U-N-S 20-711-1118 (BR)
TORONTO CATHOLIC DISTRICT SCHOOL BOARD
ST. BENEDICT CATHOLIC SCHOOL
2202 Kipling Ave, Etobicoke, ON, M9W 4K9
(416) 393-5267
Emp Here 50
SIC 8211 Elementary and secondary schools

D-U-N-S 20-711-1472 (BR)
TORONTO CATHOLIC DISTRICT SCHOOL BOARD
ST. STEPHEN ELEMENTARY SCHOOL
55 Goldfawn Dr, Etobicoke, ON, M9W 2H8
(416) 393-5284
Emp Here 50
SIC 8211 Elementary and secondary schools

D-U-N-S 25-420-9364 (BR)
TORONTO CATHOLIC DISTRICT SCHOOL BOARD
MONSIGNOR PERCY JOHNSON CATHOLIC SECONDARY SCHOOL
2170 Kipling Ave, Etobicoke, ON, M9W 4K9
(416) 393-5535
Emp Here 70
SIC 8211 Elementary and secondary schools

D-U-N-S 20-711-2785 (BR)
TORONTO DISTRICT SCHOOL BOARD
THE ELMS JUNIOR MIDDLE SCHOOL
45 Goldfawn Dr, Etobicoke, ON, M9W 2H8
(416) 394-7900
Emp Here 50
SIC 8211 Elementary and secondary schools

D-U-N-S 20-025-5235 (BR)
TORONTO DISTRICT SCHOOL BOARD
BRAEBURN JUNIOR SCHOOL
15 Tandridge Cres, Etobicoke, ON, M9W 2N8
(416) 394-7770
Emp Here 40
SIC 8211 Elementary and secondary schools

D-U-N-S 20-025-5243 (BR)
TORONTO DISTRICT SCHOOL BOARD
ELMLEA JUNIOR SCHOOL
50 Hadrian Dr, Etobicoke, ON, M9W 1V4
(416) 394-7910
Emp Here 40
SIC 8211 Elementary and secondary schools

D-U-N-S 20-026-2090 (BR)
TORONTO DISTRICT SCHOOL BOARD
HUMBERWOOD DOWNS JUNIOR MIDDLE ACAMEDY
850 Humberwood Blvd, Etobicoke, ON, M9W 7A6
(416) 394-4750
Emp Here 64
SIC 8211 Elementary and secondary schools

D-U-N-S 20-019-9243 (SL)

TORONTO HYDRO ENERGY SERVICES INC
10 Belfield Rd, Etobicoke, ON, M9W 1G1

Emp Here 20 *Sales* 1,824,018
SIC 8748 Business consulting, nec

D-U-N-S 25-092-8764 (SL)
TOWER EVENTS & SEATING RENTALS INC
365 Attwell Dr, Etobicoke, ON, M9W 5C2
(416) 213-1666
Emp Here 100 *Sales* 4,961,328
SIC 7389 Business services, nec

D-U-N-S 25-068-0329 (SL)
UNI-TRI MASONRY (1989) LIMITED
23 Haas Rd, Etobicoke, ON, M9W 3A1
(416) 745-2724
Emp Here 55 *Sales* 4,012,839
SIC 1741 Masonry and other stonework

D-U-N-S 25-097-2825 (BR)
UNILEVER CANADA INC
195 Belfield Rd, Etobicoke, ON, M9W 1G8
(416) 246-1650
Emp Here 100
SIC 2099 Food preparations, nec

D-U-N-S 25-802-1369 (BR)
VALUE VILLAGE STORES, INC
(*Suby of* Savers, Inc.)
45 Woodbine Downs Blvd Suite 3a, Etobicoke, ON, M9W 6N5
(416) 675-7450
Emp Here 35
SIC 5399 Miscellaneous general merchandise

D-U-N-S 24-330-0485 (BR)
WAL-MART CANADA CORP
2245 Islington Ave Suite 3740, Etobicoke, ON, M9W 3W7
(416) 747-6499
Emp Here 200
SIC 5311 Department stores

D-U-N-S 24-627-4682 (SL)
WELKE CUSTOMS BROKERS LTD
116 Skyway Ave, Etobicoke, ON, M9W 4Y9
(416) 674-0592
Emp Here 50 *Sales* 3,939,878
SIC 4212 Local trucking, without storage

D-U-N-S 20-004-4860 (BR)
WENDY'S RESTAURANTS OF CANADA INC
(*Suby of* The Wendy's Company)
2136 Kipling Ave, Etobicoke, ON, M9W 4K5
(416) 745-3118
Emp Here 36
SIC 5812 Eating places

D-U-N-S 25-722-6662 (BR)
WESTMONT HOSPITALITY MANAGEMENT LIMITED
HOLIDAY INN
(*Suby of* Westmont Hospitality Management Limited)
600 Dixon Rd, Etobicoke, ON, M9W 1J1
(416) 240-7511
Emp Here 80
SIC 7011 Hotels and motels

D-U-N-S 24-926-3435 (BR)
WHOLESOME HARVEST BAKING LTD
WHOLESOME HARVEST BAKING LTD.
271 Attwell Dr, Etobicoke, ON, M9W 5B9
(416) 674-4555
Emp Here 20
SIC 2051 Bread, cake, and related products

D-U-N-S 25-934-5148 (BR)
WINNERS MERCHANTS INTERNATIONAL L.P.
WINNERS
(*Suby of* The TJX Companies Inc)
160 Queen'S Plate Dr, Etobicoke, ON, M9W 6Y9
(416) 746-7588
Emp Here 40

SIC 5651 Family clothing stores

D-U-N-S 24-745-0216   (HQ)
XTL TRANSPORT INC
(*Suby of* Serga Holding Inc)
75 Rexdale Blvd, Etobicoke, ON, M9W 1P1
(416) 742-0610
Emp Here 80   *Emp Total* 1
Sales 114,070,286
SIC 4213 Trucking, except local
  Serge Gagnon
  Pr Pr Genevieve Gagnon
  Andre Leroux

Everett, ON L0M
Simcoe County

D-U-N-S 25-292-4931   (BR)
SIMCOE COUNTY DISTRICT SCHOOL BOARD, THE
TOSORONTIO CENTRAL PUBLIC SCHOOL
(*Suby of* Simcoe County District School Board, The)
7016 County Rd 13 Suite 13, Everett, ON, L0M 1J0
(705) 435-6023
Emp Here 28
SIC 8211 Elementary and secondary schools

Exeter, ON N0M
Huron County

D-U-N-S 25-800-9067   (BR)
AVON MAITLAND DISTRICT SCHOOL BOARD
SOUTH HURON DISTRICT HIGH SCHOOL
92 Gidley E, Exeter, ON, N0M 1S0
(519) 235-0880
Emp Here 75
SIC 8211 Elementary and secondary schools

D-U-N-S 25-249-1659   (BR)
AVON MAITLAND DISTRICT SCHOOL BOARD
EXETER ELEMENTARY SCHOOL
93 Victoria St E Ss 1, Exeter, ON, N0M 1S1
(519) 235-2630
Emp Here 34
SIC 8211 Elementary and secondary schools

D-U-N-S 20-643-0915   (SL)
HANSEN'S YOUR INDEPENDENT GROCER
62 Thames Rd W Ss 3, Exeter, ON, N0M 1S3
(519) 235-6131
Emp Here 49   *Sales* 8,147,280
SIC 5411 Grocery stores
Owner Mike Hansen

D-U-N-S 25-228-1829   (BR)
HURON PERTH CATHOLIC DISTRICT SCHOOL BOARD
PRECIOUS BLOOD SCHOOL
133 Sanders St W Ss 2 Suite 2, Exeter, ON, N0M 1S2
(519) 235-1691
Emp Here 20
SIC 8211 Elementary and secondary schools

D-U-N-S 25-517-6760   (SL)
JAYARMIKER INVESTMENTS LTD
MCDONALD'S RESTAURANT
261 Main St N Ss 3, Exeter, ON, N0M 1S3
(519) 271-5866
Emp Here 44   *Sales* 1,532,175
SIC 5812 Eating places

D-U-N-S 24-150-4955   (BR)
LONDON BRIDGE CHILD CARE SERVICES INC
RELOUW EARLY CHILDHOOD LEARNING CENTRE
80 Victoria St E Ss 1 Suite 1, Exeter, ON, N0M

1S1
(519) 235-0710
Emp Here 22
SIC 8351 Child day care services

D-U-N-S 24-020-0621   (BR)
MCCANN REDI-MIX INC
140 Thames Rd W Ss 3, Exeter, ON, N0M 1S3
(519) 235-0338
Emp Here 113
SIC 3273 Ready-mixed concrete

D-U-N-S 20-321-4549   (BR)
MOFFATT & POWELL LIMITED
RONA
265 Main St N Ss 3, Exeter, ON, N0M 1S3
(519) 235-2081
Emp Here 30
SIC 5211 Lumber and other building materials

D-U-N-S 20-717-2453   (SL)
SMITH-PEAT ROOFING AND SHEET METAL LTD
152 Thames Rd W Ss 3, Exeter, ON, N0M 1S3
(519) 235-2802
Emp Here 50   *Sales* 4,961,328
SIC 1761 Roofing, siding, and sheetMetal work

Falconbridge, ON P0M

D-U-N-S 24-379-7474   (BR)
GLENCORE CANADA CORPORATION
XPS
6 Edison Rd, Falconbridge, ON, P0M 1S0
(705) 699-3400
Emp Here 40
SIC 1021 Copper ores

Fenelon Falls, ON K0M

D-U-N-S 20-528-5823   (SL)
FENELON COURT LONG TERM CARE CENTRE
44 Wychwood Cres, Fenelon Falls, ON, K0M 1N0
(705) 887-2100
Emp Here 80   *Sales* 3,648,035
SIC 8051 Skilled nursing care facilities

D-U-N-S 20-778-0243   (BR)
LAFARGE CANADA INC
LAFARGE CONSTRUCTION MATERIALS
Gd, Fenelon Falls, ON, K0M 1N0
(705) 887-2820
Emp Here 20
SIC 1611 Highway and street construction

D-U-N-S 20-790-2391   (BR)
SOBEYS CAPITAL INCORPORATED
SOBEYS FENELON FALLS
15 Lindsay St, Fenelon Falls, ON, K0M 1N0
(705) 887-3611
Emp Here 100
SIC 5411 Grocery stores

D-U-N-S 25-850-1246   (BR)
TRILLIUM LAKELANDS DISTRICT SCHOOL BOARD
LANGTON PUBLIC SCHOOL
35 Wychwood Cres, Fenelon Falls, ON, K0M 1N0
(705) 887-2001
Emp Here 50
SIC 8211 Elementary and secondary schools

D-U-N-S 25-061-5010   (BR)
TRILLIUM LAKELANDS DISTRICT SCHOOL BOARD
FENELON FALLS SECONDARY SCHOOL
66 Lindsay St, Fenelon Falls, ON, K0M 1N0

(705) 887-2018
Emp Here 100
SIC 8211 Elementary and secondary schools

Fenwick, ON L0S
Welland County

D-U-N-S 24-386-1895   (SL)
WIERENGA GREENHOUSES LIMITED
1768 Balfour St, Fenwick, ON, L0S 1C0
(905) 892-5962
Emp Here 20   *Sales* 5,371,275
SIC 5191 Farm supplies

Fergus, ON N1M
Wellington County

D-U-N-S 20-321-8797   (BR)
CARA OPERATIONS LIMITED
HARVEY'S
(*Suby of* Cara Holdings Limited)
793 Tower St S, Fergus, ON, N1M 2R2
(519) 843-3527
Emp Here 20
SIC 5812 Eating places

D-U-N-S 25-971-2230   (BR)
COMMUNITY LIVING GUELPH WELLINGTON
280 St Patrick St W, Fergus, ON, N1M 1L7
(519) 787-1539
Emp Here 30
SIC 8399 Social services, nec

D-U-N-S 25-626-6636   (SL)
ELLIOTT COACH LINES (FERGUS) LTD
680 Glen Garry Cres, Fergus, ON, N1M 2W8
(519) 787-5225
Emp Here 85   *Sales* 2,407,703
SIC 4151 School buses

D-U-N-S 25-952-5590   (BR)
GRANDI COMPANY LIMITED
MCDONALDS RESTAURANT
(*Suby of* GranDi Company Limited)
870 Tower St S, Fergus, ON, N1M 3N7
(519) 787-5125
Emp Here 80
SIC 5812 Eating places

D-U-N-S 24-773-0976   (BR)
HOME HARDWARE STORES LIMITED
DIXON HOME HARDWARE BUILDING CENTRE
745 St David St N, Fergus, ON, N1M 2L1
(519) 843-1171
Emp Here 20
SIC 5251 Hardware stores

D-U-N-S 24-126-4048   (BR)
MARCH OF DIMES CANADA
238 St Patrick St E, Fergus, ON, N1M 1M6
(519) 787-3833
Emp Here 25
SIC 8331 Job training and related services

D-U-N-S 20-048-0929   (BR)
MOORE CANADA CORPORATION
R.R. DONNELLEY
(*Suby of* R. R. Donnelley & Sons Company)
650 Victoria Terr, Fergus, ON, N1M 1G7
(519) 843-2510
Emp Here 150
SIC 2761 Manifold business forms

D-U-N-S 24-764-1210   (SL)
ONTARIO NUTRI LAB INC
6589 First Line Suite 3, Fergus, ON, N1M 2W4
(519) 843-5669
Emp Here 50   *Sales* 3,720,996
SIC 8734 Testing laboratories

D-U-N-S 24-858-4315   (BR)

PARKER HANNIFIN CANADA
925 Glengarry Cres, Fergus, ON, N1M 2W7
(519) 787-0001
Emp Here 22
SIC 3052 Rubber and plastics hose and beltings

D-U-N-S 25-019-1103   (BR)
ROYAL BANK OF CANADA
ROYAL BANK FINANCIAL GROUP
(*Suby of* Royal Bank Of Canada)
100 St Andrew St E, Fergus, ON, N1M 1P8
(519) 843-2590
Emp Here 26
SIC 6021 National commercial banks

D-U-N-S 24-852-2570   (BR)
TRAVERSE INDEPENDENCE NOT-FOR-PROFIT
165 Gordon St, Fergus, ON, N1M 0A7
(519) 787-1630
Emp Here 20
SIC 8361 Residential care

D-U-N-S 25-554-7168   (BR)
TRELLIS MENTAL HEALTH AND DEVELOPMENTAL SERVICES
(*Suby of* Trellis Mental Health And Developmental Services)
234 St Patrick St E, Fergus, ON, N1M 1M6
(519) 843-6191
Emp Here 25
SIC 8093 Specialty outpatient clinics, nec

D-U-N-S 20-609-2673   (BR)
UPPER GRAND DISTRICT SCHOOL BOARD, THE
JOHN BLACK PUBLIC SCHOOL
(*Suby of* Upper Grand District School Board, The)
150 Lamond St, Fergus, ON, N1M 2A1
(519) 843-2665
Emp Here 20
SIC 8211 Elementary and secondary schools

D-U-N-S 25-126-1061   (BR)
UPPER GRAND DISTRICT SCHOOL BOARD, THE
J D HOGARTH SCHOOL
(*Suby of* Upper Grand District School Board, The)
360 Belsyde Ave E, Fergus, ON, N1M 1Z5
(519) 787-0151
Emp Here 35
SIC 8211 Elementary and secondary schools

D-U-N-S 20-710-7595   (BR)
UPPER GRAND DISTRICT SCHOOL BOARD, THE
CENTRE WELLINGTON DISTRICT HIGH SCHOOL
(*Suby of* Upper Grand District School Board, The)
905 Scotland St Suite Upper, Fergus, ON, N1M 1Y7
(519) 843-2500
Emp Here 50
SIC 8211 Elementary and secondary schools

D-U-N-S 20-286-9207   (BR)
UPPER GRAND DISTRICT SCHOOL BOARD, THE
JAMES MCQUEEN SCHOOL
(*Suby of* Upper Grand District School Board, The)
365 St George St W, Fergus, ON, N1M 1J4
(519) 843-1700
Emp Here 23
SIC 8211 Elementary and secondary schools

D-U-N-S 25-126-1103   (BR)
UPPER GRAND DISTRICT SCHOOL BOARD, THE
VICTORIA TERRACE PUBLIC SCHOOL
(*Suby of* Upper Grand District School Board, The)
500 Victoria Terr, Fergus, ON, N1M 2G5

---

(519) 843-2720
Emp Here 33
SIC 8211 Elementary and secondary schools

D-U-N-S 20-068-0226   (BR)
WELLINGTON CATHOLIC DISTRICT SCHOOL BOARD
ST JOSEPH SCHOOL
150 Strathallan St, Fergus, ON, N1M 1A1
(519) 843-3810
Emp Here 35
SIC 8211 Elementary and secondary schools

D-U-N-S 25-297-8051   (BR)
ZEHRMART INC
ZEHRS MARKETS
800 Tower St S, Fergus, ON, N1M 2R3
(519) 843-5500
Emp Here 150
SIC 5411 Grocery stores

Fitzroy Harbour, ON K0A
Carleton County

D-U-N-S 20-591-0230   (BR)
OTTAWA CATHOLIC DISTRICT SCHOOL BOARD
ST MICHAEL SCHOOL
(*Suby of* Ottawa Catholic District School Board)
159 Kedey St, Fitzroy Harbour, ON, K0A 1X0
(613) 623-3114
Emp Here 20
SIC 8211 Elementary and secondary schools

Flesherton, ON N0C
Grey County

D-U-N-S 25-238-9051   (BR)
BLUEWATER DISTRICT SCHOOL BOARD
MACPHAIL MEMORIAL ELEMENTARY SCHOOL
29 Campbell St, Flesherton, ON, N0C 1E0
(519) 924-2752
Emp Here 38
SIC 8211 Elementary and secondary schools

D-U-N-S 24-126-2802   (BR)
SPARLING'S PROPANE CO. LIMITED
774304 10 Hwy, Flesherton, ON, N0C 1E0
(519) 924-3331
Emp Here 30
SIC 5984 Liquefied petroleum gas dealers

Florence, ON N0P
Lambton County

D-U-N-S 24-209-3250   (SL)
LAMBTON CONVEYOR LIMITED
1247 Florence Rd Rr 2, Florence, ON, N0P 1R0

Emp Here 140   *Sales* 27,230,080
SIC 3535 Conveyors and conveying equipment
Pr Pr Raymond Moorhouse
VP VP Christopher Moorhouse
Dir Patricia Moorhouse
Dir Dorothea Moorhouse

Fonthill, ON L0S
Welland County

D-U-N-S 24-972-9393   (BR)
DISTRICT SCHOOL BOARD OF NIAGARA
E L CROSSLEY SECONDARY SCHOOL

350 Hwy 20 W, Fonthill, ON, L0S 1E0
(905) 892-2635
Emp Here 85
SIC 8211 Elementary and secondary schools

D-U-N-S 24-676-5288   (BR)
DISTRICT SCHOOL BOARD OF NIAGARA
GLYNN A GREEN PUBLIC SCHOOL
1353 Pelham St, Fonthill, ON, L0S 1E0
(905) 892-3821
Emp Here 30
SIC 8211 Elementary and secondary schools

D-U-N-S 20-291-6701   (BR)
DISTRICT SCHOOL BOARD OF NIAGARA
A K WIGG PUBLIC SCHOOL
1337 Haist St, Fonthill, ON, L0S 1E0
(905) 892-2605
Emp Here 25
SIC 8211 Elementary and secondary schools

D-U-N-S 20-180-3363   (BR)
FERRELL BUILDERS SUPPLY LIMITED
FONTHILL BUILDING SUPPLIES
2560 Hwy 20, Fonthill, ON, L0S 1E6
(905) 892-2694
Emp Here 30
SIC 5211 Lumber and other building materials

D-U-N-S 25-010-4783   (BR)
MERIDIAN CREDIT UNION LIMITED
1401 Pelham St, Fonthill, ON, L0S 1E0
(905) 892-2626
Emp Here 20
SIC 6062 State credit unions

D-U-N-S 20-710-8916   (BR)
NIAGARA CATHOLIC DISTRICT SCHOOL BOARD
ST ALEXANDER SCHOOL
26 Hwy 20 E, Fonthill, ON, L0S 1E0
(905) 892-3841
Emp Here 50
SIC 8211 Elementary and secondary schools

D-U-N-S 20-806-2492   (BR)
SOBEYS CAPITAL INCORPORATED
SOBEYS STORE# 7329
110 20 Hwy E, Fonthill, ON, L0S 1E0
(905) 892-2570
Emp Here 125
SIC 5411 Grocery stores

Forest, ON N0N

D-U-N-S 24-324-1259   (SL)
1147699 ONTARIO LTD
6974 Forest Rd, Forest, ON, N0N 1J0
(519) 786-5335
Emp Here 51   *Sales* 6,631,680
SIC 5999 Miscellaneous retail stores, nec
Genl Mgr Cameron Currie

D-U-N-S 20-547-2090   (BR)
CORPORATION OF THE COUNTY OF LAMBTON
NORTH LAMBTON LODGE
39 Morris St, Forest, ON, N0N 1J0
(519) 786-2151
Emp Here 100
SIC 8059 Nursing and personal care, nec

D-U-N-S 20-075-5077   (HQ)
DELTA POWER EQUIPMENT
(*Suby of* 1476399 Ontario Limited)
6974 Forest Rd, Forest, ON, N0N 1J0
(519) 786-5335
Emp Here 29   *Emp Total* 52
Sales 5,717,257
SIC 5999 Miscellaneous retail stores, nec
Cameron Currie

D-U-N-S 25-249-3713   (BR)
LAMBTON KENT DISTRICT SCHOOL BOARD

NORTH LAMBTON SECONDARY SCHOOL
15 George St, Forest, ON, N0N 1J0
(519) 786-2166
Emp Here 65
SIC 8211 Elementary and secondary schools

D-U-N-S 25-249-3754   (BR)
LAMBTON KENT DISTRICT SCHOOL BOARD
KINNWOOD CENTRAL SCHOOL
63 Macdonald St, Forest, ON, N0N 1J0
(519) 786-5351
Emp Here 25
SIC 8211 Elementary and secondary schools

Formosa, ON N0G
Bruce County

D-U-N-S 24-964-3321   (BR)
BRICK BREWING CO. LIMITED
FORMOSA SPRINGS BREWERY
(*Suby of* Brick Brewing Co. Limited)
1 Old Brewing Lane, Formosa, ON, N0G 1W0
(519) 367-2995
Emp Here 40
SIC 2082 Malt beverages

D-U-N-S 25-238-9721   (BR)
BRUCE-GREY CATHOLIC DISTRICT SCHOOL BOARD
IMMACULATE CONCEPTION SCHOOL
201 Concession 12, Formosa, ON, N0G 1W0
(519) 367-2900
Emp Here 20
SIC 8211 Elementary and secondary schools

Fort Albany, ON P0L
Cochrane County

D-U-N-S 24-286-3280   (BR)
JAMES BAY GENERAL HOSPITAL
FORT ALBANY WING
Gd, Fort Albany, ON, P0L 1H0
(705) 278-3330
Emp Here 75
SIC 8062 General medical and surgical hospitals

Fort Erie, ON L2A
Welland County

D-U-N-S 24-359-0416   (BR)
4513380 CANADA INC
LIVINGSTON CUSTOM BROKERAGE
33 Walnut St, Fort Erie, ON, L2A 1S7
(905) 871-1606
Emp Here 230
SIC 4731 Freight transportation arrangement

D-U-N-S 20-732-2608   (SL)
ABATEMENT TECHNOLOGIES LIMITED
(*Suby of* Abatement Technologies, Inc.)
7 High St, Fort Erie, ON, L2A 3P6
(905) 871-4720
Emp Here 40   *Sales* 155,187,409
SIC 3634 Electric housewares and fans
Pr Norma Harber

D-U-N-S 24-424-8969   (HQ)
AIRBUS HELICOPTERS CANADA LIMITED
AIRBUS HELICOPTERS
1100 Gilmore Rd, Fort Erie, ON, L2A 5M4
(905) 871-7772
Emp Here 161   *Emp Total* 11,080
Sales 26,995,459
SIC 3721 Aircraft
Pr Guy Joannes
Dir Rudy Palladina

Dir Raymond Henault
Dir Mesrob Karalekian
Dir Jerome Rougeot
Dir Veronique Raoul
Dir Serge Panabiere
Dir Philippe Monteux
Dir James Doak
Genl Mgr Arnaud Montalvo

D-U-N-S 25-296-7369   (BR)
BANK OF NOVA SCOTIA, THE
SCOTIABANK
200 Garrison Rd, Fort Erie, ON, L2A 5S6
(905) 871-5824
Emp Here 21
SIC 6021 National commercial banks

D-U-N-S 25-179-3717   (BR)
CANADA POST CORPORATION
CANADA POST FORT ERIE
55 Jarvis St, Fort Erie, ON, L2A 0B2
(905) 871-5510
Emp Here 30
SIC 4311 U.s. postal service

D-U-N-S 25-179-4566   (BR)
DISTRICT SCHOOL BOARD OF NIAGARA
FORT ERIE PUBLIC SCHOOL
474 Central Ave, Fort Erie, ON, L2A 3T7

Emp Here 30
SIC 8211 Elementary and secondary schools

D-U-N-S 25-179-4582   (BR)
DISTRICT SCHOOL BOARD OF NIAGARA
GARRISON ROAD SCHOOL
1110 Garrison Rd, Fort Erie, ON, L2A 1N9
(905) 871-4830
Emp Here 30
SIC 8211 Elementary and secondary schools

D-U-N-S 25-178-6836   (BR)
DISTRICT SCHOOL BOARD OF NIAGARA
FORT ERIE D SECONDERY SCHOOL
7 Tait Ave, Fort Erie, ON, L2A 3P1
(905) 871-4610
Emp Here 40
SIC 8211 Elementary and secondary schools

D-U-N-S 24-318-6561   (SL)
FLEET CANADA INC
1011 Gilmore Rd, Fort Erie, ON, L2A 5M4
(905) 871-2100
Emp Here 160   *Sales* 34,437,450
SIC 3728 Aircraft parts and equipment, nec
Pr Pr Glenn Stansfield
Paul Williams

D-U-N-S 24-560-2248   (SL)
FORT ERIE NATIVE CULTURAL CENTRE INC
FORT ERIE NATIVE FRIENDSHIP CENTRE
796 Buffalo Rd, Fort Erie, ON, L2A 5H2
(905) 871-6592
Emp Here 100   *Sales* 3,939,878
SIC 8322 Individual and family services

D-U-N-S 25-059-0155   (BR)
GRUYICH SERVICES INC
HOLIDAY INN FORT ERIE NIAGRA CONVENION CENTER
1485 Garrison Rd, Fort Erie, ON, L2A 1P8
(905) 871-8333
Emp Here 50
SIC 7011 Hotels and motels

D-U-N-S 20-710-9039   (BR)
NIAGARA CATHOLIC DISTRICT SCHOOL BOARD
ST. PHILOMENA CATHOLIC ELEMENTARY SCHOOL
1332 Phillips St, Fort Erie, ON, L2A 3C2
(905) 871-1842
Emp Here 20
SIC 8211 Elementary and secondary schools

D-U-N-S 20-710-8908   (BR)
NIAGARA CATHOLIC DISTRICT SCHOOL

BOARD
OUR LADY OF VICTORY
300 Central Ave, Fort Erie, ON, L2A 3T3
(905) 871-3092
Emp Here 50
SIC 8211 Elementary and secondary schools

D-U-N-S 24-048-3024   (SL)
NIAGARA CHRISTIAN COLLEGIATE
NIAGARA CHRISTIAN COMMUNITY OF
SCHOOLS
2619 Niagara Pky, Fort Erie, ON, L2A 5M4
(905) 871-6980
Emp Here 65   Sales 5,667,556
SIC 8211 Elementary and secondary schools
Pr Scott Herron

D-U-N-S 24-348-7357   (BR)
**REVOLUTION ENVIRONMENTAL SOLU-
TIONS LP**
TERRAPURE ENVIRONMENTAL
(Suby of Revolution Environmental Solutions
LP)
1731 Pettit Rd, Fort Erie, ON, L2A 5N1
(905) 994-1900
Emp Here 20
SIC 4953 Refuse systems

D-U-N-S 25-541-4138   (BR)
SHERWIN-WILLIAMS CANADA INC
(Suby of The Sherwin-Williams Company)
224 Catherine St, Fort Erie, ON, L2A 0B1
(905) 871-2724
Emp Here 80
SIC 2851 Paints and allied products

D-U-N-S 24-204-2583   (BR)
SOBEYS CAPITAL INCORPORATED
310 Garrison Rd, Fort Erie, ON, L2A 1M7
(905) 994-7467
Emp Here 50
SIC 5411 Grocery stores

D-U-N-S 20-531-0563   (BR)
SOBEYS CAPITAL INCORPORATED
450 Garrison Rd, Fort Erie, ON, L2A 1N2
(905) 871-0463
Emp Here 100
SIC 5411 Grocery stores

D-U-N-S 20-827-1440   (SL)
STEWART, RICK CONSTRUCTION LTD
1071 Benner Ave, Fort Erie, ON, L2A 4N6
(905) 994-7408
Emp Here 23   Sales 5,727,360
SIC 1521 Single-family housing construction
Owner Richard Stewart

D-U-N-S 25-194-9512   (SL)
TRUK-KING LOGISTICS INC
1799 Pettit Rd, Fort Erie, ON, L2A 5M4
(905) 994-1000
Emp Here 50   Sales 3,939,878
SIC 4212 Local trucking, without storage

D-U-N-S 25-644-1841   (BR)
UPS SCS, INC
UPS SUPPLY CHAIN SOLUTION
38 Princess St, Fort Erie, ON, L2A 1V6

Emp Here 30
SIC 4731 Freight transportation arrangement

D-U-N-S 24-329-8655   (BR)
WAL-MART CANADA CORP
750 Garrison Rd, Fort Erie, ON, L2A 1N7
(905) 991-9971
Emp Here 200
SIC 5311 Department stores

D-U-N-S 20-004-5115   (BR)
WENDY'S RESTAURANTS OF CANADA INC
WENDY'S
(Suby of The Wendy's Company)
165 Garrison Rd, Fort Erie, ON, L2A 1M3
(905) 871-5621
Emp Here 27
SIC 5812 Eating places

D-U-N-S 20-651-2241   (BR)
WILLSON INTERNATIONAL LIMITED
10 Queen St Suite 328, Fort Erie, ON, L2A
6M4
(905) 871-1310
Emp Here 20
SIC 4731 Freight transportation arrangement

D-U-N-S 20-508-9316   (BR)
YMCA OF GREATER TORONTO
FORT ERIE YMCA
1555 Garrison Rd, Fort Erie, ON, L2A 1P8
(905) 871-9622
Emp Here 68
SIC 8699 Membership organizations, nec

Fort Frances, ON P9A
Rainy River County

D-U-N-S 20-302-9397   (SL)
387742 ONTARIO LIMITED
MCDONALD'S
831 King'S Hwy, Fort Frances, ON, P9A 2X5
(807) 274-8535
Emp Here 74   Sales 2,261,782
SIC 5812 Eating places

D-U-N-S 24-817-3887   (BR)
BOSTON PIZZA INTERNATIONAL INC
BOSTON PIZZA
840 King'S Hwy, Fort Frances, ON, P9A 2X4
(807) 274-2727
Emp Here 49
SIC 5812 Eating places

D-U-N-S 20-539-0433   (BR)
CANADA POST CORPORATION
FORT FRANCES STN MAIN
301 Scott St, Fort Frances, ON, P9A 1H1
(807) 274-5573
Emp Here 25
SIC 4311 U.s. postal service

D-U-N-S 25-303-4003   (BR)
**CANADIAN IMPERIAL BANK OF COM-
MERCE**
CIBC FINANCIAL CENTRE
203 Scott St, Fort Frances, ON, P9A 1G8
(807) 274-5391
Emp Here 23
SIC 6021 National commercial banks

D-U-N-S 25-472-9304   (BR)
**FORT FRANCES, CORPORATION OF THE
TOWN OF**
MEMORIAL SPORT CENTER
740 Scott St, Fort Frances, ON, P9A 1H8
(807) 274-3494
Emp Here 30
SIC 7941 Sports clubs, managers, and pro-
moters

D-U-N-S 24-466-6145   (SL)
NORFAB BUILDING COMPONENTS LTD
732 Riverview Dr, Fort Frances, ON, P9A 2W2
(807) 274-7401
Emp Here 46   Sales 7,304,400
SIC 2439 Structural wood members, nec
Pr Pr Melvin Degagne

D-U-N-S 20-710-3339   (BR)
**NORTHWEST CATHOLIC DISTRICT
SCHOOL BOARD, THE**
ST MICHAEL SCHOOL
820 Fifth St E, Fort Frances, ON, P9A 1V4
(807) 274-9232
Emp Here 30
SIC 8211 Elementary and secondary schools

D-U-N-S 25-238-1256   (BR)
**NORTHWEST CATHOLIC DISTRICT
SCHOOL BOARD, THE**
ST FRANCIS SCHOOL
675 Flinders Ave, Fort Frances, ON, P9A 3L2

(807) 274-7756
Emp Here 34
SIC 8211 Elementary and secondary schools

D-U-N-S 25-275-2696   (BR)
PF RESOLU CANADA INC
427 Mowat Ave, Fort Frances, ON, P9A 1Y8
(807) 274-5311
Emp Here 427
SIC 2611 Pulp mills

D-U-N-S 24-337-2195   (BR)
R.A.S. FOOD SERVICES INC
PIZZA HUT
(Suby of R.A.S. Food Services Inc)
862 King'S Hwy, Fort Frances, ON, P9A 2X4

Emp Here 35
SIC 5812 Eating places

D-U-N-S 25-238-0308   (BR)
RAINY RIVER DISTRICT SCHOOL BOARD
J.W. WALKER ELEMENTARY SCHOOL
475 Keating Ave, Fort Frances, ON, P9A 3K8
(807) 274-3616
Emp Here 35
SIC 8211 Elementary and secondary schools

D-U-N-S 20-349-2475   (BR)
RAINY RIVER DISTRICT SCHOOL BOARD
ROBERT MOORE ELEMENTARY SCHOOL
528 Second St E, Fort Frances, ON, P9A 1N4
(807) 274-9818
Emp Here 67
SIC 8211 Elementary and secondary schools

D-U-N-S 25-238-2213   (BR)
RAINY RIVER DISTRICT SCHOOL BOARD
EDUCATION CENTRE, THE
522 Second St E, Fort Frances, ON, P9A 1N4
(807) 274-9857
Emp Here 20
SIC 8211 Elementary and secondary schools

D-U-N-S 20-569-5547   (SL)
**RENDEZ-VOUS RESTAURANT FORT
FRANCES LIMITED**
LA PLACE RENDEZ-VOUS
1201 Idlywild Dr, Fort Frances, ON, P9A 3M3
(807) 274-9811
Emp Here 50   Sales 2,188,821
SIC 7011 Hotels and motels

D-U-N-S 20-009-9682   (BR)
SHAW CABLESYSTEMS G.P.
1037 First St E, Fort Frances, ON, P9A 1L8
(807) 274-5522
Emp Here 200
SIC 4841 Cable and other pay television services

D-U-N-S 24-317-1951   (BR)
WAL-MART CANADA CORP
WALMART
1250 King'S Hwy, Fort Frances, ON, P9A 2X6
(807) 274-1373
Emp Here 150
SIC 5311 Department stores

Foxboro, ON K0K
Hastings County

D-U-N-S 25-265-4033   (BR)
**HASTINGS AND PRINCE EDWARD DIS-
TRICT SCHOOL BOARD**
FOXBORO ELEMENTARY SCHOOL
658 Ashley St, Foxboro, ON, K0K 2B0
(613) 962-5151
Emp Here 25
SIC 8211 Elementary and secondary schools

D-U-N-S 20-711-5085   (BR)
**HASTINGS AND PRINCE EDWARD DIS-
TRICT SCHOOL BOARD**
FOXBORO PUBLIC SCHOOL
658 Ashley St, Foxboro, ON, K0K 2B0

(613) 962-5151
Emp Here 35
SIC 8211 Elementary and secondary schools

Frankford, ON K0K
Hastings County

D-U-N-S 24-075-5561   (SL)
ANAMET CANADA INC
36 Wolfe St, Frankford, ON, K0K 2C0
(613) 398-1313
Emp Here 25   Sales 4,450,603
SIC 3644 Noncurrent-carrying wiring devices

D-U-N-S 24-795-5631   (SL)
FRANKFORD FOODLAND
30 Mill St, Frankford, ON, K0K 2C0
(613) 398-7879
Emp Here 35   Sales 5,782,650
SIC 5411 Grocery stores
Owner Gord Smith

D-U-N-S 25-265-4116   (BR)
**HASTINGS AND PRINCE EDWARD DIS-
TRICT SCHOOL BOARD**
FRANKFORD PUBLIC SCHOOL
36 Adelaide St, Frankford, ON, K0K 2C0
(613) 398-6425
Emp Here 32
SIC 8211 Elementary and secondary schools

D-U-N-S 25-238-0142   (BR)
**KAWARTHA PINE RIDGE DISTRICT
SCHOOL BOARD**
STOCKDALE PUBLIC SCHOOL
994 Will Johnson Rd, Frankford, ON, K0K 2C0
(613) 398-7200
Emp Here 20
SIC 8211 Elementary and secondary schools

Frankville, ON K0E
Leeds County

D-U-N-S 25-237-9607   (BR)
**UPPER CANADA DISTRICT SCHOOL
BOARD, THE**
SCHOOL EFFECTIVENESS - SPECIAL ED-
UCATION
(Suby of Upper Canada District School Board,
The)
231 Hwy 29, Frankville, ON, K0E 1H0
(613) 275-2928
Emp Here 25
SIC 8211 Elementary and secondary schools

Fraserville, ON K0L

D-U-N-S 20-648-6289   (BR)
GREAT CANADIAN CASINOS INC
SHORELINES CASINO KAWARTHA
DOWNS
1382 County Road 28, Fraserville, ON, K0L
1V0
(705) 939-2400
Emp Here 200
SIC 7999 Amusement and recreation, nec

D-U-N-S 20-939-3875   (SL)
KAWARTHA DOWNS LTD
KAWARTHA DOWNS & SPEEDWAY
1382 County Road 28, Fraserville, ON, K0L
1V0
(705) 939-6316
Emp Here 200
SIC 7948 Racing, including track operation

Freelton, ON L0R
Wentworth County

D-U-N-S 20-026-6968   (BR)
HAMILTON-WENTWORTH   DISTRICT SCHOOL BOARD, THE
BALACLAVA SCHOOL
280 Tenth Conc E, Freelton, ON, L0R 1K0
(905) 659-3396
Emp Here 35
SIC 8211 Elementary and secondary schools

Gananoque, ON K7G
Leeds County

D-U-N-S 20-788-0261   (SL)
CARVETH NURSING HOME LIMITED
CARVETH CARE CENTRE
375 James St, Gananoque, ON, K7G 2Z1
(613) 382-4752
Emp Here 100   *Sales* 4,523,563
SIC 8051 Skilled nursing care facilities

D-U-N-S 25-238-0217   (BR)
CATHOLIC DISTRICT SCHOOL BOARD OF EASTERN ONTARIO
ST JOSEPH CATHOLIC SCHOOL
(*Suby of* Catholic District School Board of Eastern Ontario)
235 Georgiana St, Gananoque, ON, K7G 1M9
(613) 382-2361
Emp Here 30
SIC 8211 Elementary and secondary schools

D-U-N-S 20-649-8669   (HQ)
GANANOQUE BOAT LINE LIMITED
(*Suby of* Gananoque Boat Line Limited)
280 Main St, Gananoque, ON, K7G 2M2
(613) 382-2144
Emp Here 57   *Emp Total* 60
Sales 2,772,507
SIC 4489 Water passenger transportation

D-U-N-S 20-650-4636   (SL)
GOSTLIN, DAN ENTERPRISES INC
CANADIAN TIRE
705 King St E, Gananoque, ON, K7G 1H4
(613) 382-3900
Emp Here 54   *Sales* 5,284,131
SIC 5399 Miscellaneous general merchandise

D-U-N-S 24-325-5895   (BR)
GREAT CANADIAN CASINOS INC
SHORELINES CASINO THOUSAND IS-LANDS
Hwy 380, Gananoque, ON, K7G 2V4
(705) 946-6450
Emp Here 50
SIC 7993 Coin-operated amusement devices

D-U-N-S 25-300-0368   (BR)
METRO ONTARIO INC
METRO
333 King St E, Gananoque, ON, K7G 1G6
(613) 382-7090
Emp Here 100
SIC 5411 Grocery stores

D-U-N-S 24-337-6535   (BR)
ONTARIO LOTTERY AND GAMING CORPORATION
1000 ISLANDS CHARITY CASINO
380 Second St, Gananoque, ON, K7G 2J9
(866) 266-8422
Emp Here 500
SIC 7999 Amusement and recreation, nec

D-U-N-S 20-923-9024   (BR)
RKJL FOODS LTD
MCDONALD'S   RESTAURANTS   OF GANANOQUE
(*Suby of* RKJL Foods Ltd)
670 King St E, Gananoque, ON, K7G 1H3
(613) 382-4466
Emp Here 40

SIC 5812 Eating places

D-U-N-S 25-263-5677   (BR)
UPPER CANADA DISTRICT SCHOOL BOARD, THE
LINKLATER PUBLIC SCHOOL
(*Suby of* Upper Canada District School Board, The)
300 Stone St N, Gananoque, ON, K7G 1Y8
(613) 382-3689
Emp Here 30
SIC 8211 Elementary and secondary schools

D-U-N-S 20-621-1067   (BR)
UPPER CANADA DISTRICT SCHOOL BOARD, THE
GANANOQUE SECONDARY SCHOOL
175 William St S, Gananoque, ON, K7G 1S8
(613) 382-4741
Emp Here 60
SIC 8211 Elementary and secondary schools

Garden River, ON P6A
Algoma County

D-U-N-S 25-082-1568   (HQ)
ANISHINABEK POLICE SERVICE LTD
(*Suby of* Anishinabek Police Service Ltd)
1436 Highway 17 B, Garden River, ON, P6A 6Z1
(705) 946-2539
Emp Here 25   *Emp Total* 84
Sales 2,626,585
SIC 7381 Detective and armored car services

Garson, ON P3L
Sudbury County

D-U-N-S 25-919-4371   (BR)
CONSEIL   SCOLAIRE   DE   DISTRICT CATHOLIQUE   DU   NOUVEL-ONTARIO, LE
ECOLE ST AUGUSTIN
648 O'Neil Dr W, Garson, ON, P3L 1T6
(705) 693-2424
Emp Here 25
SIC 8211 Elementary and secondary schools

D-U-N-S 20-009-7835   (BR)
RAINBOW DISTRICT SCHOOL BOARD
NORTHEASTERN ELEMENTARY SCHOOL
45 Spruce St, Garson, ON, P3L 1P8
(705) 675-0204
Emp Here 45
SIC 8211 Elementary and secondary schools

D-U-N-S 24-380-1961   (BR)
SGS CANADA INC
1209 O'Neil Dr W, Garson, ON, P3L 1L5
(705) 693-4555
Emp Here 30
SIC 8731 Commercial physical research

D-U-N-S 20-711-7636   (BR)
SUDBURY CATHOLIC DISTRICT SCHOOL BOARD
ST JOHN SCHOOL
181 William St, Garson, ON, P3L 1T7
(705) 693-2213
Emp Here 50
SIC 8211 Elementary and secondary schools

Georgetown, ON L7G
Halton County

D-U-N-S 25-647-4201   (SL)
AERODROME INTERNATIONAL MAINTENANCE INC
A.I.M

---

330 Guelph St Unit 4, Georgetown, ON, L7G 4B5
(905) 873-8777
Emp Here 103   *Sales* 457,039
SIC 4212 Local trucking, without storage

D-U-N-S 24-375-6249   (BR)
ALIMENTS SAPUTO LIMITEE
SAPUTO FOODS
279 Guelph St, Georgetown, ON, L7G 4B3
(905) 702-7200
Emp Here 250
SIC 2026 Fluid milk

D-U-N-S 24-685-1740   (SL)
BFG CANADA LTD
88 Todd Rd, Georgetown, ON, L7G 4R7
(905) 873-8744
Emp Here 50   *Sales* 5,180,210
SIC 2099 Food preparations, nec
Dir Trent Hillbert

D-U-N-S 24-408-9348   (SL)
BRC BUSINESS ENTERPRISES LTD
24 Armstrong Ave, Georgetown, ON, L7G 4R9
(905) 873-8509
Emp Here 50   *Sales* 4,334,713
SIC 2521 Wood office furniture

D-U-N-S 25-016-7335   (BR)
BANQUE TORONTO-DOMINION, LA
TD CANADA TRUST
(*Suby of* Toronto-Dominion Bank, The)
29 Main St S, Georgetown, ON, L7G 3G2
(905) 877-2266
Emp Here 24
SIC 6021 National commercial banks

D-U-N-S 25-295-1736   (BR)
BREWERS RETAIL INC
BEER STORE, THE
236 Guelph St, Georgetown, ON, L7G 4B1
(905) 873-9191
Emp Here 20
SIC 5921 Liquor stores

D-U-N-S 20-022-5121   (BR)
CANADA POST CORPORATION
112 Guelph St, Georgetown, ON, L7G 3Z5
(905) 877-1917
Emp Here 50
SIC 4311 U.s. postal service

D-U-N-S 24-227-2610   (BR)
CARA OPERATIONS LIMITED
KELSEY'S
(*Suby of* Cara Holdings Limited)
256 Guelph St Suite 3, Georgetown, ON, L7G 4B1
(905) 877-7150
Emp Here 55
SIC 5812 Eating places

D-U-N-S 24-986-3556   (BR)
CARA OPERATIONS LIMITED
SWISS CHALET
(*Suby of* Cara Holdings Limited)
320 Guelph St, Georgetown, ON, L7G 4B5
(905) 873-6392
Emp Here 52
SIC 5812 Eating places

D-U-N-S 20-009-9716   (BR)
CLUBLINK CORPORATION ULC
EAGLE RIDGE GOLF CLUB
11742 Tenth Line Suite 4, Georgetown, ON, L7G 4S7
(905) 877-8468
Emp Here 100
SIC 7992 Public golf courses

D-U-N-S 20-288-7311   (BR)
COMMUNICATIONS & POWER INDUSTRIES CANADA INC
SATCOM DIV.
Lower Level 45 River Dr, Georgetown, ON, L7G 2J4
(905) 877-0161
Emp Here 150

SIC 3663 Radio and t.v. communications equipment

D-U-N-S 20-069-5786   (BR)
COMMUNITY LIVING NORTH HALTON
HORIZON PACKAGING
12 Todd Rd, Georgetown, ON, L7G 4R7
(905) 702-8415
Emp Here 30
SIC 7389 Business services, nec

D-U-N-S 20-020-4449   (BR)
CONSEIL   SCOLAIRE   DE   DISTRICT CATHOLIQUE CENTRE-SUD
+COLE SACRE-COEUR
34 Miller Dr, Georgetown, ON, L7G 5P7
(905) 873-0510
Emp Here 25
SIC 8211 Elementary and secondary schools

D-U-N-S 20-287-2032   (BR)
COOPER-STANDARD   AUTOMOTIVE CANADA LIMITED
SEALING SYSTEMS GROUP
346 Guelph St, Georgetown, ON, L7G 4B5
(905) 873-6921
Emp Here 357
SIC 2891 Adhesives and sealants

D-U-N-S 20-939-2265   (BR)
CORPORATION OF THE TOWN OF HALTON HILLS
MOLD-MASTERS SPORTSPLEX, THE
221 Guelph St, Georgetown, ON, L7G 4A8
(905) 877-8488
Emp Here 25
SIC 7999 Amusement and recreation, nec

D-U-N-S 25-818-2740   (BR)
CORPORATION OF THE TOWN OF HALTON HILLS
HALTON HILLS PUBLIC LIBRARIES
9 Church St, Georgetown, ON, L7G 2A3
(905) 873-2681
Emp Here 26
SIC 8231 Libraries

D-U-N-S 24-158-9287   (BR)
DOLLARAMA S.E.C.
DOLLARAMA
235 Guelph St Unit 2, Georgetown, ON, L7G 4A8
(905) 873-0379
Emp Here 23
SIC 5999 Miscellaneous retail stores, nec

D-U-N-S 20-732-2249   (HQ)
EFCO CANADA CO
EFCO
30 Todd Rd, Georgetown, ON, L7G 4R7
(905) 877-6957
Emp Here 73   *Emp Total* 1,100
Sales 11,892,594
SIC 3444 Sheet Metalwork
Dir Steve Eyre

D-U-N-S 20-699-6592   (BR)
EXTENDICARE INC
EXTENDICARE HALTON HILLS
9 Lindsay Crt, Georgetown, ON, L7G 6G9
(905) 702-8760
Emp Here 25
SIC 8051 Skilled nursing care facilities

D-U-N-S 24-406-9035   (HQ)
FLO-DRAULIC CONTROLS LTD
45 Sinclair Ave, Georgetown, ON, L7G 4X4
(905) 702-9456
Emp Here 31   *Emp Total* 65
Sales 8,755,284
SIC 5084 Industrial machinery and equipment
Pr Pr Lou Laskis

D-U-N-S 24-562-4692   (SL)
GEORGETOWN HOSPITAL FOUNDATION, THE
1 Princess Anne Dr, Georgetown, ON, L7G 2B8

---

(905) 873-0111
Emp Here 100   *Sales* 2,448,661
SIC 8062 General medical and surgical hospitals

D-U-N-S 20-711-0623   (BR)
HALTON CATHOLIC DISTRICT SCHOOL BOARD
HOLY CROSS SCHOOL
222 Maple Ave, Georgetown, ON, L7G 1X2
(905) 877-4451
Emp Here 50
SIC 8211 Elementary and secondary schools

D-U-N-S 20-711-0656   (BR)
HALTON CATHOLIC DISTRICT SCHOOL BOARD
ST BRIGID CATHOLIC SCHOOL
73 Miller Dr, Georgetown, ON, L7G 5T2
(905) 877-1779
Emp Here 65
SIC 8211 Elementary and secondary schools

D-U-N-S 20-711-0896   (BR)
HALTON CATHOLIC DISTRICT SCHOOL BOARD
CHRIST THE KING SECONDARY
161 Guelph St, Georgetown, ON, L7G 4A1
(905) 702-8838
Emp Here 130
SIC 8211 Elementary and secondary schools

D-U-N-S 24-391-0911   (BR)
HALTON CATHOLIC DISTRICT SCHOOL BOARD
GEORGETOWN DISTRICT HIGH SCHOOL
70 Guelph St, Georgetown, ON, L7G 3Z5
(905) 877-6966
Emp Here 110
SIC 8211 Elementary and secondary schools

D-U-N-S 20-024-9857   (BR)
HALTON DISTRICT SCHOOL BOARD
PARK PUBLIC SCHOOL
6 Hyde Park Dr, Georgetown, ON, L7G 2B6
(905) 877-9301
Emp Here 25
SIC 8211 Elementary and secondary schools

D-U-N-S 25-119-2571   (BR)
HALTON DISTRICT SCHOOL BOARD
CENTENNIAL SCHOOL
233 Delrex Blvd, Georgetown, ON, L7G 4G1
(905) 877-6976
Emp Here 45
SIC 8211 Elementary and secondary schools

D-U-N-S 20-568-2912   (BR)
HALTON DISTRICT SCHOOL BOARD
SILVER CREEK PUBLIC SCHOOL
170 Eaton St, Georgetown, ON, L7G 5V6
(905) 877-0151
Emp Here 80
SIC 8211 Elementary and secondary schools

D-U-N-S 20-591-2871   (BR)
HALTON DISTRICT SCHOOL BOARD
HARRISON PUBLIC SCHOOL
59 Rexway Dr, Georgetown, ON, L7G 1P9
(905) 877-4421
Emp Here 30
SIC 8211 Elementary and secondary schools

D-U-N-S 20-546-5706   (BR)
HALTON DISTRICT SCHOOL BOARD
STERWARTTOWN MIDDLE SCHOOL
13068 15 Sideroad, Georgetown, ON, L7G 4S5
(905) 873-1637
Emp Here 55
SIC 8211 Elementary and secondary schools

D-U-N-S 24-525-4383   (BR)
HALTON DISTRICT SCHOOL BOARD
GARDINER PUBLIC SCHOOL
14365 Danby Rd, Georgetown, ON, L7G 6L8
(905) 877-3849
Emp Here 25

SIC 8211 Elementary and secondary schools

D-U-N-S 20-711-0342   (BR)
HALTON DISTRICT SCHOOL BOARD
GLEN WILLIAMS PUBLIC SCHOOL
512 Main St, Georgetown, ON, L7G 3S8
(905) 877-9112
Emp Here 25
SIC 8211 Elementary and secondary schools

D-U-N-S 20-045-9670   (BR)
HALTON DISTRICT SCHOOL BOARD
PINEVIEW PUBLIC SCHOOL
13074 Fiveside Rd, Georgetown, ON, L7G 4S5
(905) 877-4363
Emp Here 25
SIC 8211 Elementary and secondary schools

D-U-N-S 24-220-6969   (HQ)
HOWELL PLUMBING SUPPLIES DASCO LIMITED
HOWELL PIPE & SUPPLY, DIV OF
11 Armstrong Ave, Georgetown, ON, L7G 4S1
(905) 877-2293
Emp Here 44   *Emp Total* 58
Sales 9,703,773
SIC 5085 Industrial supplies
Pr Pr Duncan Stacey
    Martin Glaude
VP Fin Lene Fisker
    Wayne Singer

D-U-N-S 24-379-0073   (BR)
ITW CANADA INC
ITW PERMATEX CANADA, DIV OF
(*Suby of* Illinois Tool Works Inc.)
35 Brownridge Rd Unit 1, Georgetown, ON, L7G 0C6
(905) 693-8900
Emp Here 26
SIC 5169 Chemicals and allied products, nec

D-U-N-S 24-154-1510   (BR)
LAFARGE CANADA INC
LAFARGE READY MIX
55 Armstrong Ave, Georgetown, ON, L7G 4S1
(905) 873-0254
Emp Here 20
SIC 1771 Concrete work

D-U-N-S 24-383-7122   (BR)
LOBLAWS INC
REAL CANADIAN SUPERSTORE
171 Guelph St Suite 2811, Georgetown, ON, L7G 4A1
(905) 877-7005
Emp Here 300
SIC 5411 Grocery stores

D-U-N-S 25-797-7637   (BR)
LOBLAWS SUPERMARKETS LIMITED
300 Guelph St, Georgetown, ON, L7G 4B1
(905) 877-4711
Emp Here 275
SIC 5411 Grocery stores

D-U-N-S 20-011-8870   (BR)
MATSU MANUFACTURING INC
MATCOR METAL FABRICATION, DIV OF
71 Todd Rd, Georgetown, ON, L7G 4R8

Emp Here 150
SIC 8711 Engineering services

D-U-N-S 20-793-1960   (BR)
METRO ONTARIO INC
FOOD BASICS
235 Guelph St, Georgetown, ON, L7G 4A8
(905) 877-5648
Emp Here 55
SIC 5411 Grocery stores

D-U-N-S 20-920-9949   (SL)
NORTH HALTON GOLF AND COUNTRY CLUB LIMITED
CLUB AT NORTH HALTON, THE
363 Maple Ave, Georgetown, ON, L7G 4S5

(905) 877-5236
Emp Here 60   *Sales* 2,407,703
SIC 7997 Membership sports and recreation clubs

D-U-N-S 20-768-6887   (SL)
OTEL ENTERPRISES INC
222 Mountainview Rd N, Georgetown, ON, L7G 3R2
(905) 877-1800
Emp Here 42   *Sales* 5,072,500
SIC 6513 Apartment building operators
Pr Christoph Summer

D-U-N-S 25-802-1781   (BR)
PADDON + YORKE INC
360 Guelph St Unit 36b, Georgetown, ON, L7G 4B5
(905) 873-2295
Emp Here 20
SIC 8111 Legal services

D-U-N-S 25-018-9420   (BR)
ROYAL BANK OF CANADA
ROYAL BANK FINANCIAL GROUP
(*Suby of* Royal Bank Of Canada)
232 Guelph St, Georgetown, ON, L7G 4B1
(905) 877-2244
Emp Here 31
SIC 6021 National commercial banks

D-U-N-S 24-189-4919   (BR)
SOBEYS CAPITAL INCORPORATED
PRICE CHOPPER
325 Guelph St, Georgetown, ON, L7G 4B3
(905) 873-0622
Emp Here 60
SIC 5411 Grocery stores

D-U-N-S 20-860-1745   (BR)
SOURCE (BELL) ELECTRONICS INC, THE
SOURCE, THE
262 Guelph St, Georgetown, ON, L7G 4B1
(905) 877-5411
Emp Here 25
SIC 5999 Miscellaneous retail stores, nec

D-U-N-S 25-802-3209   (BR)
UNITED LUMBER AND BUILDING SUPPLIES COMPANY LIMITED
UNITED LUMBER HOME HARDWARE
333 Guelph St, Georgetown, ON, L7G 4B3
(905) 873-8007
Emp Here 40
SIC 5211 Lumber and other building materials

D-U-N-S 25-802-2524   (BR)
VISION TRAVEL
VISION 2000 TRAVEL GROUP
328 Guelph St, Georgetown, ON, L7G 4B5
(905) 873-2002
Emp Here 20
SIC 4724 Travel agencies

D-U-N-S 20-945-7139   (BR)
VISION TRAVEL
328 Guelph St, Georgetown, ON, L7G 4B5
(905) 873-2000
Emp Here 25
SIC 4724 Travel agencies

D-U-N-S 24-607-8559   (BR)
WAL-MART CANADA CORP
WALMART
300 Guelph St Suite 3034, Georgetown, ON, L7G 4B1
(905) 873-0400
Emp Here 50
SIC 5311 Department stores

D-U-N-S 24-356-7869   (BR)
WINNERS MERCHANTS INTERNATIONAL L.P.
WINNERS
(*Suby of* The TJX Companies Inc)
280 Guelph St, Georgetown, ON, L7G 4B1
(905) 702-5705
Emp Here 40
SIC 5651 Family clothing stores

Georgian Bluffs, ON N0H

D-U-N-S 20-642-4660   (SL)
ASHCROFT & ASSOCIATES NATURAL STONE LTD
A & A NATURAL STONE
381297 Concession 17, Georgian Bluffs, ON, N0H 2T0
(519) 534-5966
Emp Here 50
SIC 1411 Dimension stone

Geraldton, ON P0T
Thunder Bay County

D-U-N-S 25-237-9342   (BR)
SUPERIOR GREENSTONE DISTRICT SCHOOL BOARD
GERALDTON COMPOSITE HIGH SCHOOL
500 2nd St W, Geraldton, ON, P0T 1M0
(807) 854-0130
Emp Here 45
SIC 8211 Elementary and secondary schools

D-U-N-S 25-238-1249   (BR)
SUPERIOR GREENSTONE DISTRICT SCHOOL BOARD
B. A. PARKER ELEMENTARY SCHOOL
501 Hogarth Ave W, Geraldton, ON, P0T 1M0
(807) 854-1683
Emp Here 23
SIC 8211 Elementary and secondary schools

Glenburnie, ON K0H

D-U-N-S 20-891-5868   (SL)
FAIRMOUNT HOME FOR THE AGED
2069 Battersea Rd, Glenburnie, ON, K0H 1S0
(613) 548-9400
Emp Here 100   *Sales* 3,648,035
SIC 8361 Residential care

D-U-N-S 20-123-4903   (HQ)
MULROONEY, K TRUCKING LIMITED
(*Suby of* Mulrooney, K Trucking Limited)
1280 Mcadoo'S Lane, Glenburnie, ON, K0H 1S0
(613) 548-4427
Emp Here 50   *Emp Total* 50
Sales 4,677,755
SIC 4212 Local trucking, without storage

D-U-N-S 25-649-7678   (BR)
MULROONEY, K TRUCKING LIMITED
SPEEDWAY AUTO WRECKERS
(*Suby of* Mulrooney, K Trucking Limited)
1280 Mcadoo'S Lane, Glenburnie, ON, K0H 1S0
(613) 548-4427
Emp Here 49
SIC 5531 Auto and home supply stores

Glencoe, ON N0L

D-U-N-S 24-720-2815   (BR)
COOPER-STANDARD AUTOMOTIVE CANADA LIMITED
FLUID HANDLING SYSTEMS DIV
268 Appin Rd Rr 4, Glencoe, ON, N0L 1M0
(519) 287-2450
Emp Here 60
SIC 3714 Motor vehicle parts and accessories

D-U-N-S 20-591-7870   (BR)
THAMES VALLEY DISTRICT SCHOOL BOARD

GLENCOE DISTRICT HIGH SCHOOL
3581 Concession Dr, Glencoe, ON, N0L 1M0
(519) 287-3310
Emp Here 34
SIC 8211 Elementary and secondary schools

D-U-N-S 25-249-0784   (BR)
THAMES VALLEY DISTRICT SCHOOL BOARD
EKCOE CENTRAL PUBLIC SCHOOL
3719 Parkhouse Rd, Glencoe, ON, N0L 1M0
(519) 287-3330
Emp Here 42
SIC 8211 Elementary and secondary schools

Gloucester, ON K1A
Carleton County

D-U-N-S 20-277-7533   (SL)
KNOWLEDGE MANAGEMENT
1200m Montreal Rd Suite 60, Gloucester, ON, K1A 0S2
(613) 993-9251
Emp Here 125   *Sales* 5,763,895
SIC 8231 Libraries
Dir Kathleen O'connell

Gloucester, ON K1B
Carleton County

D-U-N-S 24-365-8890   (BR)
AMICA MATURE LIFESTYLES INC
AMICA AT BEARBROOK
2645 Innes Rd Suite 342, Gloucester, ON, K1B 3J7
(613) 837-8720
Emp Here 75
SIC 8361 Residential care

D-U-N-S 24-726-4922   (HQ)
BOONE PLUMBING AND HEATING SUP-PLY INC
DESROSIERS DISTRIBUTEURS
(*Suby of* Entreprises Mirca Inc, Les)
1282 Algoma Rd Suite 613, Gloucester, ON, K1B 3W8
(613) 746-9960
Emp Here 107   *Emp Total* 1,342
Sales 32,981,515
SIC 5074 Plumbing and heating equipment and supplies (hydronics)
VP VP Jacques Deschenes
Pr Martin Deschenes
VP VP Claude Desrosier
Francois Deschenes
Marc Lapierre

D-U-N-S 25-129-5317   (BR)
BRICK WAREHOUSE LP, THE
BRICK, THE
1960 Cyrville Rd, Gloucester, ON, K1B 1A5
(613) 746-8600
Emp Here 50
SIC 5712 Furniture stores

D-U-N-S 20-538-7728   (BR)
CANADA POST CORPORATION
BLACKBURN HAMLET P.O.
2638 Innes Rd, Gloucester, ON, K1B 4Z5
(613) 824-2257
Emp Here 30
SIC 4311 U.s. postal service

D-U-N-S 25-771-0905   (BR)
CARQUEST CANADA LTD
CARQUEST AUTO PARTS
(*Suby of* Advance Auto Parts, Inc.)
1528 Star Top Rd Suite 7, Gloucester, ON, K1B 3W6
(613) 749-5220
Emp Here 20
SIC 5013 Motor vehicle supplies and new parts

D-U-N-S 24-345-5206   (BR)
CITY OF OTTAWA
GLOUCESTER BIBLIOTHEQUE PUBLIC
(*Suby of* City of Ottawa)
1595 Telesat Crt Suite 800, Gloucester, ON, K1B 5R3

Emp Here 75
SIC 8231 Libraries

D-U-N-S 25-265-3126   (BR)
CONSEIL DES ECOLES CATHOLIQUES DE LANGUE FRANCAISE DU CENTRE-EST
ECOLE DES PINS
1487 Ridgebrook Dr, Gloucester, ON, K1B 4K6
(613) 741-2354
Emp Here 23
SIC 8211 Elementary and secondary schools

D-U-N-S 24-369-9217   (BR)
COSTCO WHOLESALE CANADA LTD
COSTCO
(*Suby of* Costco Wholesale Corporation)
1900 Cyrville Rd, Gloucester, ON, K1B 1A5
(613) 748-9966
Emp Here 280
SIC 5199 Nondurable goods, nec

D-U-N-S 20-137-0053   (BR)
CRANE CANADA CO.
CRANE SUPPLY
(*Suby of* Crane Co.)
1630 Star Top Rd, Gloucester, ON, K1B 3W6
(613) 745-9135
Emp Here 30
SIC 5085 Industrial supplies

D-U-N-S 24-104-6259   (SL)
DILFO MECHANICAL LIMITED
1481 Cyrville Rd, Gloucester, ON, K1B 3L7
(613) 741-7731
Emp Here 50   *Sales* 5,197,506
SIC 1711 Plumbing, heating, air-conditioning

D-U-N-S 24-102-1252   (BR)
G4S CASH SOLUTIONS (CANADA) LTD
1303 Michael St, Gloucester, ON, K1B 3M9

Emp Here 150
SIC 4212 Local trucking, without storage

D-U-N-S 20-973-3224   (SL)
GUARANTEE CO OF NORTH AMERICA, (THE)
36 Parkridge Cres, Gloucester, ON, K1B 3E7

Emp Here 50   *Sales* 4,523,563
SIC 6411 Insurance agents, brokers, and service

D-U-N-S 25-749-2595   (BR)
HOME DEPOT OF CANADA INC
HOME DEPOT
(*Suby of* The Home Depot Inc)
1616 Cyrville Rd, Gloucester, ON, K1B 3L8
(613) 744-1700
Emp Here 250
SIC 5251 Hardware stores

D-U-N-S 24-688-7350   (BR)
LAFARGE CANADA INC
1649 Bearbrook Rd, Gloucester, ON, K1B 1B8
(613) 837-4223
Emp Here 25
SIC 5039 Construction materials, nec

D-U-N-S 25-509-7180   (HQ)
MBNA CANADA BANK
(*Suby of* Toronto-Dominion Bank, The)
1600 James Naismith Dr Suite 800, Gloucester, ON, K1B 5N8
(613) 907-4800
Emp Here 1,250   *Emp Total* 81,233
Sales 330,001,246
SIC 6021 National commercial banks

Pr Joe Desantis

D-U-N-S 25-236-5705   (BR)
MARK'S WORK WEARHOUSE LTD
MARK'S WORK WEARHOUSE #158
1940 Innes Rd, Gloucester, ON, K1B 3K5
(613) 744-2499
Emp Here 26
SIC 5651 Family clothing stores

D-U-N-S 20-342-3801   (BR)
MEDICAL PHARMACIES GROUP LIMITED
ONTARIO MEDICAL SUPPLY
1100 Algoma Rd, Gloucester, ON, K1B 0A3
(613) 244-8620
Emp Here 20
SIC 5912 Drug stores and proprietary stores

D-U-N-S 24-344-5033   (BR)
METRO ONTARIO INC
2636 Innes Rd, Gloucester, ON, K1B 4Z5
(613) 837-1845
Emp Here 50
SIC 5411 Grocery stores

D-U-N-S 25-224-9735   (BR)
OTTAWA CATHOLIC DISTRICT SCHOOL BOARD
JOHN PAUL II CATHOLIC SCHOOL
(*Suby of* Ottawa Catholic District School Board)
1500 Beaverpond Dr, Gloucester, ON, K1B 3R9
(613) 744-3591
Emp Here 25
SIC 8211 Elementary and secondary schools

D-U-N-S 25-131-4407   (BR)
OTTAWA CATHOLIC DISTRICT SCHOOL BOARD
GOOD SHEPHERD SCHOOL
(*Suby of* Ottawa Catholic District School Board)
101 Bearbrook Rd, Gloucester, ON, K1B 3H5
(613) 824-4531
Emp Here 35
SIC 8211 Elementary and secondary schools

D-U-N-S 25-263-5966   (BR)
OTTAWA-CARLETON DISTRICT SCHOOL BOARD
GLEN OGILVIE ELEMENTARY SCHOOL
46 Centrepark Dr, Gloucester, ON, K1B 3C1
(613) 824-4014
Emp Here 42
SIC 8211 Elementary and secondary schools

D-U-N-S 25-263-5768   (BR)
OTTAWA-CARLETON DISTRICT SCHOOL BOARD
EMILY CARR MIDDLE SCHOOL
2681 Innes Rd, Gloucester, ON, K1B 3J7
(613) 824-5455
Emp Here 27
SIC 8211 Elementary and secondary schools

D-U-N-S 20-136-3181   (HQ)
SWISS PASTRIES & DELICATESSEN OF OTTAWA LIMITED
(*Suby of* Swiss Pastries & Delicatessen Of Ottawa Limited)
1423 Star Top Rd, Gloucester, ON, K1B 3W5
(613) 749-2389
Emp Here 26   *Emp Total* 67
Sales 2,261,782
SIC 5461 Retail bakeries

D-U-N-S 20-700-4409   (BR)
TYCO INTEGRATED FIRE & SECURITY CANADA, INC
SIMPLEXGRINNELL
(*Suby of* Johnson Controls, Inc.)
1257 Algoma Rd Unit 4, Gloucester, ON, K1B 3W7
(613) 699-6710
Emp Here 30
SIC 6311 Life insurance

D-U-N-S 25-769-6773   (HQ)
WW CANADA (ONE) NOMINEE CORP
TRAVELODGE OTTAWA EAST
(*Suby of* Westmont Hospitality Management Limited)
1486 Innes Rd, Gloucester, ON, K1B 3V5
(613) 745-1133
Emp Here 30   *Emp Total* 100
Sales 3,502,114
SIC 7011 Hotels and motels

Gloucester, ON K1G
Carleton County

D-U-N-S 20-086-7914   (BR)
1300323 ONTARIO INC
AMJ CAMPBELL VAN LINES
2710 Stevenage Dr, Gloucester, ON, K1G 5N2
(613) 737-0000
Emp Here 60
SIC 4214 Local trucking with storage

D-U-N-S 25-190-0853   (BR)
ARMTEC LP
ARMTEC
5598 Power Rd, Gloucester, ON, K1G 3N4
(613) 822-1488
Emp Here 30
SIC 1791 Structural steel erection

D-U-N-S 25-769-5320   (BR)
DOCDOR INDUSTRIES INC
DOOR DOCTOR
5649 Power Rd, Gloucester, ON, K1G 3N4
(613) 749-3667
Emp Here 20
SIC 5211 Lumber and other building materials

D-U-N-S 20-702-3503   (BR)
FLYNN CANADA LTD
5661 Power Rd, Gloucester, ON, K1G 3N4

Emp Here 100
SIC 1761 Roofing, siding, and sheetMetal work

D-U-N-S 25-290-6383   (BR)
INTEGRATED DISTRIBUTION SYSTEMS LIMITED PARTNERSHIP
WAJAX EQUIPMENT
(*Suby of* Integrated Distribution Systems Limited Partnership)
4139 Belgreen Dr, Gloucester, ON, K1G 3N2
(613) 739-2990
Emp Here 22
SIC 5084 Industrial machinery and equipment

D-U-N-S 24-438-4863   (SL)
MCDONALD, GRANT P. HOLDINGS INC
SCHOONER TRANSPORT
2680 Overton Dr, Gloucester, ON, K1G 6T4
(613) 225-9588
Emp Here 50   *Sales* 3,648,035
SIC 7538 General automotive repair shops

D-U-N-S 24-151-9698   (SL)
TROIA HOMES INC
5669 Power Rd, Gloucester, ON, K1G 3N4
(613) 822-9422
Emp Here 40   *Sales* 10,699,440
SIC 1522 Residential construction, nec
Pr Americo Rego

Gloucester, ON K1J
Carleton County

D-U-N-S 25-083-1443   (SL)
1310281 ONTARIO INC
EAST SIDE MARIO'S GLOUCESTER
1820 Ogilvie Rd, Gloucester, ON, K1J 7P4
(613) 748-6931
Emp Here 65   *Sales* 1,969,939

SIC 5812 Eating places

D-U-N-S 25-349-7036   (SL)
3705391 CANADA LIMITED
PREMIERE VAN LINES
5370 Canotek Rd Unit 1, Gloucester, ON, K1J 9E6
(613) 742-7555
Emp Here 70   *Sales* 4,012,839
SIC 4214 Local trucking with storage

D-U-N-S 25-145-4278   (BR)
ALSTOM CANADA INC
(*Suby of* General Electric Company)
1430 Blair Pl Suite 600, Gloucester, ON, K1J 9N2
(613) 747-5222
Emp Here 96
SIC 7699 Repair services, nec

D-U-N-S 25-296-7526   (BR)
BANK OF NOVA SCOTIA, THE
SCOTIABANK
2339 Ogilvie Rd, Gloucester, ON, K1J 8M6
(613) 741-6265
Emp Here 25
SIC 6021 National commercial banks

D-U-N-S 20-192-3898   (BR)
BANK OF NOVA SCOTIA, THE
SCOTIABANK
2400 City Park Dr, Gloucester, ON, K1J 1H6
(613) 748-6001
Emp Here 33
SIC 6021 National commercial banks

D-U-N-S 20-002-8293   (BR)
BANQUE TORONTO-DOMINION, LA
TORONTO-DOMINION BANK, THE
(*Suby of* Toronto-Dominion Bank, The)
1648 Montreal Rd, Gloucester, ON, K1J 6N5
(613) 745-6533
Emp Here 20
SIC 6021 National commercial banks

D-U-N-S 24-919-6684   (BR)
BELL MOBILITE INC
1420 Blair Pl Suite 700, Gloucester, ON, K1J 9L8

Emp Here 120
SIC 5063 Electrical apparatus and equipment

D-U-N-S 20-793-1754   (BR)
BEST BUY CANADA LTD
FUTURE SHOP
(*Suby of* Best Buy Co., Inc.)
1525 City Prk Dr, Gloucester, ON, K1J 1H3

Emp Here 100
SIC 5731 Radio, television, and electronic stores

D-U-N-S 25-771-0749   (HQ)
CAPITAL SECURITY & INVESTIGATIONS
(*Suby of* Capital Security & Investigations)
1128 Cadboro Rd, Gloucester, ON, K1J 7R1
(613) 744-1194
Emp Here 130   *Emp Total* 300
Sales 12,861,440
SIC 7381 Detective and armored car services
Owner George Lalande

D-U-N-S 20-245-3176   (BR)
CINEPLEX ODEON CORPORATION
SILVERCITY GLOUCESTER
2385 City Park Dr, Gloucester, ON, K1J 1G1
(613) 749-5861
Emp Here 200
SIC 7832 Motion picture theaters, except drive-in

D-U-N-S 25-784-3185   (BR)
CITY OF OTTAWA
VILLE D'OTTAWA
(*Suby of* City of Ottawa)
2040 Ogilvie Rd, Gloucester, ON, K1J 7N8
(613) 748-4222
Emp Here 50

SIC 7999 Amusement and recreation, nec

D-U-N-S 25-265-2763   (BR)
CONSEIL DES ECOLES CATHOLIQUES DE LANGUE FRANCAISE DU CENTRE-EST
CECCE
4000 Labelle St, Gloucester, ON, K1J 1A1
(613) 744-2555
Emp Here 200
SIC 8211 Elementary and secondary schools

D-U-N-S 25-265-2920   (BR)
CONSEIL DES ECOLES CATHOLIQUES DE LANGUE FRANCAISE DU CENTRE-EST
ECOLE LA VIRENDRYE
614 Eastvale Dr, Gloucester, ON, K1J 6Z6
(613) 749-2349
Emp Here 50
SIC 8211 Elementary and secondary schools

D-U-N-S 24-324-2570   (BR)
CONSEILLERS EN GESTION ET INFORMATIQUE CGI INC
CGI
1410 Blair Pl, Gloucester, ON, K1J 9B9
(613) 740-5900
Emp Here 200
SIC 7379 Computer related services, nec

D-U-N-S 25-462-6302   (SL)
COSMIC ADVENTURES INC
1373 Ogilvie Rd, Gloucester, ON, K1J 7P5
(613) 742-8989
Emp Here 50   *Sales* 1,896,978
SIC 7996 Amusement parks

D-U-N-S 24-011-6223   (BR)
DATA COMMUNICATIONS MANAGEMENT CORP
DATA GROUP OF COMPANIES
1400 Blair Pl Suite 202, Gloucester, ON, K1J 9B8
(613) 748-0420
Emp Here 20
SIC 5112 Stationery and office supplies

D-U-N-S 25-318-8304   (BR)
DILLON CONSULTING LIMITED
(*Suby of* Dillon Consulting Inc)
5335 Canotek Rd Suite 200, Gloucester, ON, K1J 9L4
(613) 745-2213
Emp Here 30
SIC 8711 Engineering services

D-U-N-S 20-699-6360   (BR)
EXTENDICARE INC
EXTENDICARE LAURIER MANOR
1715 Montreal Rd, Gloucester, ON, K1J 6N4
(613) 741-5122
Emp Here 250
SIC 8051 Skilled nursing care facilities

D-U-N-S 24-985-6907   (HQ)
GLOBAL CHILD CARE SERVICES
(*Suby of* Global Child Care Services)
1714 Montreal Rd, Gloucester, ON, K1J 6N5
(613) 742-5500
Emp Here 20   *Emp Total* 90
Sales 2,699,546
SIC 8351 Child day care services

D-U-N-S 20-575-7466   (BR)
GROUPE PICHE CONSTRUCTION INC
GROUPE PICHE ONTARIO
5460 Canotek Rd Unit 98, Gloucester, ON, K1J 9G9
(613) 742-4217
Emp Here 20
SIC 1542 Nonresidential construction, nec

D-U-N-S 25-102-5466   (SL)
IMPACT DENTAL LABORATORY LIMITED
(*Suby of* Geodigm Corporation)
5300 Canotek Rd Suite 200, Gloucester, ON, K1J 1A4
(613) 746-0602
Emp Here 45   *Sales* 2,626,585
SIC 8072 Dental laboratories

D-U-N-S 25-297-5610   (BR)
INDIGO BOOKS & MUSIC INC
CHAPTERS
(*Suby of* Indigo Books & Music Inc)
2401 City Park Dr, Gloucester, ON, K1J 1G1
(613) 744-5175
Emp Here 50
SIC 5942 Book stores

D-U-N-S 25-309-7299   (BR)
INDUSTRIELLE ALLIANCE, ASSURANCE ET SERVICES FINANCIERS INC
INDUSTRIELLE-ALLIANCE ASSURANCE ET SERVICES FINANCIER
1900 City Park Dr Suite 510, Gloucester, ON, K1J 1A3
(613) 744-8255
Emp Here 20
SIC 6411 Insurance agents, brokers, and service

D-U-N-S 25-320-8698   (BR)
KONICA MINOLTA BUSINESS SOLUTIONS (CANADA) LTD
KONICA MINOLTA
1900 City Park Dr Suite 100, Gloucester, ON, K1J 1A3
(613) 749-5588
Emp Here 45
SIC 5999 Miscellaneous retail stores, nec

D-U-N-S 24-118-6316   (BR)
LOBLAWS SUPERMARKETS LIMITED
LOBLAWS
1980 Ogilvie Rd, Gloucester, ON, K1J 9L3
(613) 746-5724
Emp Here 250
SIC 5411 Grocery stores

D-U-N-S 25-303-9549   (BR)
LONDON LIFE INSURANCE COMPANY
FREEDOM 55
1223 Michael St Suite 300, Gloucester, ON, K1J 7T2
(613) 748-3455
Emp Here 160
SIC 6311 Life insurance

D-U-N-S 25-285-9483   (SL)
MARCIL LAVALLEE
1420 Blair Pl Suite 400, Gloucester, ON, K1J 9L8
(613) 745-8387
Emp Here 60   *Sales* 2,626,585
SIC 8721 Accounting, auditing, and bookkeeping

D-U-N-S 24-348-0758   (BR)
MEDIAS TRANSCONTINENTAL S.E.N.C.
5300 Canotek Rd Unit 30, Gloucester, ON, K1J 1A4
(613) 744-4800
Emp Here 30
SIC 2711 Newspapers

D-U-N-S 24-344-4994   (BR)
METRO ONTARIO INC
1930 Montreal Rd, Gloucester, ON, K1J 6N2
(613) 744-2961
Emp Here 115
SIC 5411 Grocery stores

D-U-N-S 25-156-2062   (BR)
OTTAWA CATHOLIC DISTRICT SCHOOL BOARD
ST. BROTHER ANDRE CATHOLIC SCHOOL
(*Suby of* Ottawa Catholic District School Board)
1923 Elmridge Dr, Gloucester, ON, K1J 8G7
(613) 741-0100
Emp Here 25
SIC 8211 Elementary and secondary schools

D-U-N-S 25-033-4190   (BR)
OTTAWA CATHOLIC DISTRICT SCHOOL BOARD
PEARSON, LESTER B CATHOLIC HIGH SCHOOL

(*Suby of* Ottawa Catholic District School Board)
2072 Jasmine Cres, Gloucester, ON, K1J 8M5
(613) 741-4525
Emp Here 100
SIC 8211 Elementary and secondary schools

D-U-N-S 20-047-1147   (BR)
OTTAWA CATHOLIC DISTRICT SCHOOL BOARD
THOMAS DARCY MCGEE CATHOLIC SCHOOL
(*Suby of* Ottawa Catholic District School Board)
635 La Verendrye Dr, Gloucester, ON, K1J 7C2
(613) 749-2251
Emp Here 24
SIC 8211 Elementary and secondary schools

D-U-N-S 20-025-0657   (BR)
OTTAWA-CARLETON DISTRICT SCHOOL BOARD
HENRY MUNRO MIDDLE SCHOOL
2105 Kender Ave, Gloucester, ON, K1J 6J7
(613) 748-0060
Emp Here 45
SIC 8211 Elementary and secondary schools

D-U-N-S 25-263-6105   (BR)
OTTAWA-CARLETON DISTRICT SCHOOL BOARD
ROBERT HOPKINS PUBLIC SCHOOL
2011 Glenfern Ave, Gloucester, ON, K1J 6H2
(613) 745-2119
Emp Here 25
SIC 8211 Elementary and secondary schools

D-U-N-S 25-263-5917   (BR)
OTTAWA-CARLETON DISTRICT SCHOOL BOARD
CARSON GROVE ELEMENTARY SCHOOL
1401 Matheson Rd, Gloucester, ON, K1J 8B5
(613) 745-0195
Emp Here 40
SIC 8211 Elementary and secondary schools

D-U-N-S 25-263-6147   (BR)
OTTAWA-CARLETON DISTRICT SCHOOL BOARD
COLONEL BY SECONDARY SCHOOL
2381 Ogilvie Rd, Gloucester, ON, K1J 7N4
(613) 745-9411
Emp Here 70
SIC 8211 Elementary and secondary schools

D-U-N-S 25-318-8890   (BR)
OTTAWA-CARLETON DISTRICT SCHOOL BOARD
GLOUCESTER HIGH SCHOOL
2060 Ogilvie Rd, Gloucester, ON, K1J 7N8
(613) 745-7176
Emp Here 150
SIC 8211 Elementary and secondary schools

D-U-N-S 25-570-8026   (BR)
PMA BRETHOUR REAL ESTATE CORPORATION INC
1010 Polytek St Suite 18, Gloucester, ON, K1J 9J1
(613) 747-6766
Emp Here 25
SIC 8742 Management consulting services

D-U-N-S 20-203-0651   (BR)
PARSONS INC
DELCAN
1223 Michael St Suite 100, Gloucester, ON, K1J 7T2
(613) 738-4160
Emp Here 65
SIC 8711 Engineering services

D-U-N-S 20-921-1122   (BR)
PERFORMANCE REALTY LTD
(*Suby of* Performance Realty Ltd)
5300 Canotek Rd Suite 201, Gloucester, ON, K1J 1A4

(613) 744-2000
Emp Here 32
SIC 6531 Real estate agents and managers

D-U-N-S 25-248-5826　(BR)
PERSONAL INSURANCE COMPANY, THE
PERSONAL INSURANCE COMPANY OF CANADA, THE
1900 City Park Dr Suite 300, Gloucester, ON, K1J 1A3
(613) 742-5000
Emp Here 70
SIC 6331 Fire, marine, and casualty insurance

D-U-N-S 25-779-3208　(BR)
RE/MAX METRO-CITY REALTY LTD
1740 Montreal Rd, Gloucester, ON, K1J 6N3
(613) 748-1223
Emp Here 40
SIC 6531 Real estate agents and managers

D-U-N-S 25-466-7165　(BR)
REVERA INC
ELMSMERE RESIDENCE
889 Elmsmere Rd Suite 217, Gloucester, ON, K1J 9L5
(613) 745-2409
Emp Here 20
SIC 8361 Residential care

D-U-N-S 25-769-6542　(BR)
REVERA INC
OGILVIE VILLA RETIREMENT HOME
1345 Ogilvie Rd, Gloucester, ON, K1J 7P5
(613) 742-6524
Emp Here 30
SIC 8361 Residential care

D-U-N-S 24-588-9688　(BR)
REXALL PHARMACY GROUP LTD
PHARMA PLUS
(*Suby of* McKesson Corporation)
1980 Ogilvie Rd Suite 144, Gloucester, ON, K1J 9L3
(613) 745-9497
Emp Here 20
SIC 5912 Drug stores and proprietary stores

D-U-N-S 20-785-6241　(BR)
STARBUCKS COFFEE CANADA, INC
STARBUCKS
(*Suby of* Starbucks Corporation)
2401 City Park Dr, Gloucester, ON, K1J 1G1
(613) 744-2663
Emp Here 25
SIC 5812 Eating places

D-U-N-S 25-784-6196　(SL)
STUDY BREAK LIMITED
BYTOWN CATERING
5480 Canotek Rd Suite 20, Gloucester, ON, K1J 9H7
(613) 745-6389
Emp Here 90　　*Sales* 2,699,546
SIC 5812 Eating places

D-U-N-S 25-941-2237　(BR)
TELE-MOBILE COMPANY
TELUS MOBILITY
1900 City Park Dr Suite 110, Gloucester, ON, K1J 1A3

Emp Here 40
SIC 4899 Communication services, nec

D-U-N-S 20-139-2503　(BR)
TIPPET-RICHARDSON LIMITED
5499 Canotek Rd, Gloucester, ON, K1J 9J5
(613) 741-3015
Emp Here 120
SIC 4214 Local trucking with storage

D-U-N-S 25-769-4935　(BR)
VALUE VILLAGE STORES, INC
(*Suby of* Savers, Inc.)
1162 Cyrville Rd, Gloucester, ON, K1J 7S9
(613) 749-4977
Emp Here 40
SIC 5399 Miscellaneous general merchandise

Gloucester, ON K1T
Carleton County

D-U-N-S 20-810-5747　(SL)
1364279 ONTARIO INC
BANK STREET KIA
2559 Bank St, Gloucester, ON, K1T 1M8
(613) 736-7022
Emp Here 30　　*Sales* 14,724,000
SIC 5511 New and used car dealers

D-U-N-S 24-444-3040　(SL)
CANADIAN TIRE
4792 Bank Street, Gloucester, ON, K1T 3W7
(613) 822-2163
Emp Here 30　　*Sales* 14,134,935
SIC 5014 Tires and tubes
Owner Michael Medline

D-U-N-S 20-108-8023　(BR)
CHARTWELL RETIREMENT RESIDENCES
CHARTWELL SENIORS HOUSING REAL ESTATE INVESTMENT TRUST
3998 Bridle Path Dr, Gloucester, ON, K1T 4H4
(613) 521-1977
Emp Here 20
SIC 8361 Residential care

D-U-N-S 20-030-0346　(BR)
CITY OF OTTAWA
SAWMILL CREEK POOL
(*Suby of* City of Ottawa)
3380 D'Aoust Ave, Gloucester, ON, K1T 1R5
(613) 521-4092
Emp Here 20
SIC 7999 Amusement and recreation, nec

D-U-N-S 20-711-7057　(BR)
CONSEIL DES ECOLES CATHOLIQUES DE LANGUE FRANCAISE DU CENTRE-EST
ECOLE ELEMENTAIRE CATHOLIQUE SAINTE-BERNADETTE
3781 Sixth St, Gloucester, ON, K1T 1K5
(613) 521-0875
Emp Here 50
SIC 8211 Elementary and secondary schools

D-U-N-S 25-130-8508　(BR)
CONSEIL DES ECOLES PUBLIQUES DE L'EST DE L'ONTARIO
ECCLE GABRIELLE ROY
3395 D'Aoust Ave, Gloucester, ON, K1T 4A8
(613) 733-8301
Emp Here 28
SIC 8211 Elementary and secondary schools

D-U-N-S 25-792-4019　(BR)
FRISBY TIRE CO. (1974) LIMITED
1780 Queensdale Ave, Gloucester, ON, K1T 1J8
(613) 521-4080
Emp Here 25
SIC 5531 Auto and home supply stores

D-U-N-S 25-464-3455　(SL)
HUNT CLUB MOTORS LIMITED
HUNT CLUB VOLKSWAGEN
2655 Bank St, Gloucester, ON, K1T 1N1
(613) 521-2300
Emp Here 40　　*Sales* 14,592,140
SIC 5511 New and used car dealers
Dir Allyson Bell

D-U-N-S 20-052-3335　(SL)
OTTAWA ROTARY HOME, THE
4637 Bank St, Gloucester, ON, K1T 3W6
(613) 236-3200
Emp Here 55　　*Sales* 2,042,900
SIC 8361 Residential care

D-U-N-S 25-263-6360　(BR)
OTTAWA-CARLETON DISTRICT SCHOOL BOARD
SAWMILL CREEK ELEMENTARY SCHOOL
3400 D'Aoust Ave, Gloucester, ON, K1T 1R5
(613) 521-5922
Emp Here 50

SIC 8211 Elementary and secondary schools

D-U-N-S 24-104-1003　(SL)
RLD INDUSTRIES LTD
4210 Albion Rd, Gloucester, ON, K1T 3W2
(613) 822-4000
Emp Here 51　　*Sales* 4,923,520
SIC 3479 Metal coating and allied services

D-U-N-S 25-322-2046　(BR)
TORONTO-DOMINION BANK, THE
TD BANK
(*Suby of* Toronto-Dominion Bank, The)
2544 Bank St, Gloucester, ON, K1T 1M9

Emp Here 25
SIC 6021 National commercial banks

Gloucester, ON K1V
Carleton County

D-U-N-S 25-361-4531　(BR)
CITY OF OTTAWA
RIDEAVIEW COMMUNITY CENTRE
(*Suby of* City of Ottawa)
4310 Shoreline Dr, Gloucester, ON, K1V 1N4
(613) 822-7887
Emp Here 25
SIC 8322 Individual and family services

D-U-N-S 24-228-5372　(BR)
CONSEIL DES ECOLES CATHOLIQUES DE LANGUE FRANCAISE DU CENTRE-EST
ECOLE BERNARD GRANDMAITRE
4170 Spratt Rd, Gloucester, ON, K1V 0Z5
(613) 820-3814
Emp Here 20
SIC 8211 Elementary and secondary schools

D-U-N-S 25-983-5700　(SL)
HYLANDS GOLF CLUB
2101 Alert Rd, Gloucester, ON, K1V 1J9
(613) 521-1842
Emp Here 80　　*Sales* 3,210,271
SIC 7997 Membership sports and recreation clubs

D-U-N-S 24-117-7117　(BR)
LOBLAWS SUPERMARKETS LIMITED
MONCION'S YIG
671 River Rd, Gloucester, ON, K1V 2G2
(613) 822-4749
Emp Here 200
SIC 5411 Grocery stores

D-U-N-S 20-175-0440　(BR)
NAV CANADA
1601 Tom Roberts Ave, Gloucester, ON, K1V 1E6
(613) 248-3863
Emp Here 212
SIC 4899 Communication services, nec

D-U-N-S 24-676-5056　(BR)
OTTAWA CATHOLIC DISTRICT SCHOOL BOARD
ST. FRANCIS XAVIER CATHOLIC SCHOOL
(*Suby of* Ottawa Catholic District School Board)
3740 Spratt Rd, Gloucester, ON, K1V 2M1
(613) 822-7900
Emp Here 25
SIC 8211 Elementary and secondary schools

D-U-N-S 20-711-6554　(BR)
OTTAWA CATHOLIC DISTRICT SCHOOL BOARD
SAINT JEROME CATHOLIC SCHOOL
(*Suby of* Ottawa Catholic District School Board)
4330 Spratt Rd, Gloucester, ON, K1V 2A7
(613) 822-1116
Emp Here 40
SIC 8211 Elementary and secondary schools

SIC 8211 Elementary and secondary schools

D-U-N-S 25-131-4449　(BR)
OTTAWA-CARLETON DISTRICT SCHOOL BOARD
ELIZABETH PARK SCHOOL
15 De Niverville Pvt, Gloucester, ON, K1V 7N9
(613) 523-5406
Emp Here 35
SIC 8211 Elementary and secondary schools

Gloucester, ON K1X
Carleton County

D-U-N-S 25-265-3936　(BR)
OTTAWA CATHOLIC DISTRICT SCHOOL BOARD
ST MARY'S SCHOOL
(*Suby of* Ottawa Catholic District School Board)
5536 Bank St, Gloucester, ON, K1X 1G9
(613) 822-2985
Emp Here 33
SIC 8211 Elementary and secondary schools

Goderich, ON N7A
Huron County

D-U-N-S 25-393-3246　(SL)
1260269 ONTARIO INC
SKY HARBOUR AIRCRAFT
33862 Airport Rd, Goderich, ON, N7A 3Y2

Emp Here 80　　*Sales* 16,392,720
SIC 4581 Airports, flying fields, and services
Pr Pr Sandy Wellman
Recvr Christopher John Mazur

D-U-N-S 20-710-6829　(BR)
AVON MAITLAND DISTRICT SCHOOL BOARD
ST MARY'S CENTRAL PUBLIC SCHOOL
189 Elizabeth St, Goderich, ON, N7A 3T9

Emp Here 25
SIC 8211 Elementary and secondary schools

D-U-N-S 25-033-4588　(BR)
AVON MAITLAND DISTRICT SCHOOL BOARD
ROBERTSON MEMORIAL PUBLIC SCHOOL
125 Blake St W, Goderich, ON, N7A 1Z1
(519) 524-8972
Emp Here 25
SIC 8211 Elementary and secondary schools

D-U-N-S 25-238-6909　(BR)
AVON MAITLAND DISTRICT SCHOOL BOARD
VICTORIA PUBLIC SCHOOL
135 Gibbons St, Goderich, ON, N7A 3J5

Emp Here 35
SIC 8211 Elementary and secondary schools

D-U-N-S 24-286-9592　(BR)
COMPASS MINERALS CANADA CORP
COMPASS MINERAL
(*Suby of* Compass Minerals International, Inc.)
Gd, Goderich, ON, N7A 3Y4
(519) 524-8351
Emp Here 35
SIC 1481 NonMetallic mineral services

D-U-N-S 24-097-2653　(BR)
COMPASS MINERALS CANADA CORP
SIFTO SALT, DIV OF
(*Suby of* Compass Minerals International, Inc.)
245 Regent St, Goderich, ON, N7A 3Y5
(519) 524-8338
Emp Here 100

SIC 2899 Chemical preparations, nec

D-U-N-S 20-859-8214   (BR)
FGL SPORTS LTD
ATHLETES WORLD
397 Bayfield Rd Suite 31/32, Goderich, ON,
N7A 4E9
(519) 524-8300
Emp Here 25
SIC 5661 Shoe stores

D-U-N-S 24-778-6606   (BR)
FIRSTCANADA ULC
FIRSTCANADA
257 Cambridge St, Goderich, ON, N7A 2Y7
(519) 524-5316
Emp Here 45
SIC 4151 School buses

D-U-N-S 20-710-6779   (BR)
**HURON PERTH CATHOLIC DISTRICT
SCHOOL BOARD**
ST MARY'S SCHOOL
70 Bennett St E, Goderich, ON, N7A 1A4
(519) 524-9901
Emp Here 50
SIC 8211 Elementary and secondary schools

D-U-N-S 20-050-7267   (BR)
IDEAL SUPPLY COMPANY LIMITED
GLOBAL TOOLS
208 Suncoast Dr E, Goderich, ON, N7A 4K4
(519) 524-8389
Emp Here 21
SIC 7539 Automotive repair shops, nec

D-U-N-S 20-019-7981   (BR)
MAC'S CONVENIENCE STORES INC
50 Victoria St N, Goderich, ON, N7A 2R6
(519) 524-8992
Emp Here 50
SIC 5411 Grocery stores

D-U-N-S 20-514-5860   (BR)
METRO ONTARIO INC
FOOD BASICS
397 Bayfield Rd, Goderich, ON, N7A 4E9
(519) 524-7818
Emp Here 42
SIC 5411 Grocery stores

D-U-N-S 25-543-1488   (BR)
REVERA INC
MAITLAND MANOR
290 South St, Goderich, ON, N7A 4G6
(519) 524-7324
Emp Here 100
SIC 8361 Residential care

D-U-N-S 25-028-5285   (BR)
REVERA LONG TERM CARE INC
MAITLAND MANOR
290 South St, Goderich, ON, N7A 4G6
(519) 524-7324
Emp Here 25
SIC 8051 Skilled nursing care facilities

D-U-N-S 20-215-1721   (BR)
ROSE CORPORATION, THE
BENMILLER INN & SPA
81175 Benmiller Li, Goderich, ON, N7A 3Y1
(519) 524-2191
Emp Here 50
SIC 7011 Hotels and motels

D-U-N-S 25-294-8690   (BR)
WAL-MART CANADA CORP
35400 Huron Rd, Goderich, ON, N7A 3X8
(519) 524-5060
Emp Here 180
SIC 5311 Department stores

D-U-N-S 20-922-5551   (BR)
WAYCON INTERNATIONAL TRUCKS LTD
*WAYCON INTERNATIONAL TRUCKS OF
GODERICH*
(Suby of 397217 Ontario Limited)
33910 Airport Rd, Goderich, ON, N7A 3Y2

(519) 524-7379
Emp Here 30
SIC 5511 New and used car dealers

D-U-N-S 24-194-9051   (BR)
ZEHRMART INC
ZEHRS MARKETS
Hwy 8 S, Goderich, ON, N7A 4C6
(519) 524-2229
Emp Here 180
SIC 5411 Grocery stores

Gogama, ON P0M
Sudbury County

D-U-N-S 25-238-2080   (BR)
**DISTRICT SCHOOL BOARD ONTARIO
NORTH EAST**
ECOLE NOTRE DAME DU ROSAIRE
51 Harris St, Gogama, ON, P0M 1W0
(705) 894-2775
Emp Here 25
SIC 8211 Elementary and secondary schools

Goodwood, ON L0C

D-U-N-S 25-300-8007   (BR)
DURHAM DISTRICT SCHOOL BOARD
GOODWOOD PUBLIC SCHOOL
4340 Front St, Goodwood, ON, L0C 1A0
(905) 640-3092
Emp Here 20
SIC 8211 Elementary and secondary schools

D-U-N-S 24-659-7066   (HQ)
MINE RADIO SYSTEMS INC
394 Highway 47, Goodwood, ON, L0C 1A0
(905) 640-1839
Emp Here 24   Emp Total 26
Sales 5,006,160
SIC 3669 Communications equipment, nec
Pr Kenneth Morrell
Patrick Waye
VP Fin Paul Cote

D-U-N-S 24-138-2741   (SL)
WSC CORPORATION
COPPINWOOD GOLF CLUB
2320 4th Concession Rd, Goodwood, ON,
L0C 1A0
(905) 649-2800
Emp Here 50   Sales 2,425,503
SIC 7997 Membership sports and recreation
clubs

Gore Bay, ON P0P
Manitoulin County

D-U-N-S 24-565-9198   (SL)
584482 ONTARIO INC
MANITOULIN LODGE NURSING HOME
3 Main St, Gore Bay, ON, P0P 1H0
(705) 282-2007
Emp Here 65   Sales 2,991,389
SIC 8051 Skilled nursing care facilities

D-U-N-S 25-238-2049   (BR)
RAINBOW DISTRICT SCHOOL BOARD
CHARLES C MCLEAN PUBLIC SCHOOL
(Suby of Rainbow District School Board)
43 Hall St, Gore Bay, ON, P0P 1H0
(705) 368-7015
Emp Here 24
SIC 8211 Elementary and secondary schools

D-U-N-S 24-818-1919   (HQ)
SMOOTH FREIGHT LTD
154 540b Hwy Rr 1, Gore Bay, ON, P0P 1H0

(705) 282-2640
Emp Here 22   Emp Total 100
Sales 3,575,074
SIC 4213 Trucking, except local

Gorham, ON P7G

D-U-N-S 25-238-1496   (BR)
LAKEHEAD DISTRICT SCHOOL BOARD
*GORHAM AND WARE COMMUNITY
SCHOOL*
2032 Kam-Current Rd, Gorham, ON, P7G 0K5
(807) 767-4241
Emp Here 30
SIC 8211 Elementary and secondary schools

Gormley, ON L0H
York County

D-U-N-S 25-370-7251   (BR)
ALPA ROOF TRUSSES INC
ALPA ROOF TRUSSES
5532 Slaters Rd, Gormley, ON, L0H 1G0
(905) 713-6616
Emp Here 130
SIC 2439 Structural wood members, nec

D-U-N-S 20-571-8518   (BR)
ARBOR MEMORIAL SERVICES INC
HIGH LAND HILLS
12492 Woodbine Ave S, Gormley, ON, L0H
1G0
(905) 888-0734
Emp Here 20
SIC 6553 Cemetery subdividers and developers

D-U-N-S 24-687-7385   (SL)
B. G. HIGH VOLTAGE SYSTEMS LIMITED
27 Cardico Dr, Gormley, ON, L0H 1G0
(905) 888-6677
Emp Here 30   Sales 7,304,400
SIC 1623 Water, sewer, and utility lines
Pr Pr Bertrand Berneche

D-U-N-S 20-707-8770   (BR)
CLUBLINK CORPORATION ULC
STATION CREEK GOLF CLUB
12657 Woodbine Ave S, Gormley, ON, L0H
1G0
(905) 888-1219
Emp Here 90
SIC 7992 Public golf courses

D-U-N-S 24-078-7945   (SL)
DEEP FOUNDATIONS CONTRACTORS INC
145 Ram Forest Rd, Gormley, ON, L0H 1G0
(905) 750-5900
Emp Here 50   Sales 3,648,035
SIC 1794 Excavation work

D-U-N-S 25-727-5453   (SL)
EHV POWER ULC
(Suby of Quanta Services, Inc.)
21 Cardico Dr, Gormley, ON, L0H 1G0
(905) 888-7266
Emp Here 23   Sales 2,042,900
SIC 8711 Engineering services

D-U-N-S 25-842-4779   (BR)
MILLER PAVING LIMITED
MILLER CONCRETE
287 Ram Forest Rd, Gormley, ON, L0H 1G0
(905) 713-2526
Emp Here 50
SIC 1611 Highway and street construction

D-U-N-S 25-964-7220   (BR)
STOCK TRANSPORTATION LTD
24 Cardico Dr, Gormley, ON, L0H 1G0
(905) 888-1938
Emp Here 275

SIC 4111 Local and suburban transit

D-U-N-S 20-591-6500   (BR)
**YORK CATHOLIC DISTRICT SCHOOL
BOARD**
*ALL SAINTS CATHOLIC ELEMENTARY
SCHOOL*
130 Castlemore, Gormley, ON, L0H 1G0
(905) 887-8780
Emp Here 25
SIC 8211 Elementary and secondary schools

Goulais River, ON P0S
Algoma County

D-U-N-S 20-064-2218   (BR)
ALGOMA DISTRICT SCHOOL BOARD
MOUNTAIN VIEW PUBLIC SCHOOL
(Suby of Algoma District School Board)
Mahler Rd, Goulais River, ON, P0S 1E0
(705) 649-2130
Emp Here 30
SIC 8211 Elementary and secondary schools

Gowanstown, ON N0G
Perth County

D-U-N-S 25-249-1238   (BR)
**AVON MAITLAND DISTRICT SCHOOL
BOARD**
WALLACE PUBLIC SCHOOL
8727 164 Rd, Gowanstown, ON, N0G 1Y0
(519) 291-2380
Emp Here 20
SIC 8211 Elementary and secondary schools

Grafton, ON K0K

D-U-N-S 20-070-0099   (BR)
926715 ONTARIO INC
HALIDIMAND HILLS SPAS VILLAGE, THE
384 Academy Hill Rd Rr 1, Grafton, ON, K0K
2G0
(905) 349-2493
Emp Here 185
SIC 7991 Physical fitness facilities

D-U-N-S 20-291-5943   (BR)
**CORPORATION OF THE COUNTY OF
NORTHUMBERLAND**
MATERIAL RECOVERY FACILITY
280 Edwardson Rd, Grafton, ON, K0K 2G0
(905) 349-3900
Emp Here 55
SIC 4953 Refuse systems

D-U-N-S 25-237-9748   (BR)
**KAWARTHA PINE RIDGE DISTRICT
SCHOOL BOARD**
GRAFTON PUBLIC SCHOOL
654 Station Rd, Grafton, ON, K0K 2G0
(905) 349-2591
Emp Here 23
SIC 8211 Elementary and secondary schools

D-U-N-S 20-711-6109   (BR)
**PETERBOROUGH VICTORIA NORTHUM-
BERLAND AND CLARINGTON CATHOLIC
DISTRICT SCHOOL BOARD**
*ST. MARY CATHOLIC ELEMENTARY
SCHOOL*
103b Lyle St S, Grafton, ON, K0K 2G0
(905) 349-2061
Emp Here 22
SIC 8211 Elementary and secondary schools

Grand Bend, ON N0M

D-U-N-S 20-588-2512   (BR)
BANQUE TORONTO-DOMINION, LA
TD CANADA TRUST
(*Suby of* Toronto-Dominion Bank, The)
81 Crescent St Suite 24, Grand Bend, ON,
N0M 1T0
(519) 238-8435
Emp Here 20
SIC 6021 National commercial banks

D-U-N-S 20-710-4675   (BR)
**LAMBTON KENT DISTRICT SCHOOL
BOARD**
GRAND BEND PUBLIC SCHOOL
15 Gill Rd, Grand Bend, ON, N0M 1T0
(519) 238-2091
Emp Here 20
SIC 8211 Elementary and secondary schools

D-U-N-S 20-556-9486   (SL)
**OAKWOOD INN & GOLF CLUB (GRAND
BEND) INC**
OAKWOOD RESORT GOLF & SPA
70671 Bluewater Hwy, Grand Bend, ON, N0M
1T0
(519) 238-2324
Emp Here 65   *Sales* 2,845,467
SIC 7011 Hotels and motels

D-U-N-S 24-560-2495   (SL)
**OKE WOODSMITH BUILDING SYSTEMS
INC**
LITE FORM ONTARIO, DIVISION OF
70964 Bluewater Hwy Suite 9, Grand Bend,
ON, N0M 1T0
(519) 238-8893
Emp Here 43   *Sales* 8,638,080
SIC 1521 Single-family housing construction
Pr Pr Randall Oke
VP VP Wayne Oke
VP VP Kevin Oke
Bradley Oke

D-U-N-S 20-025-5581   (BR)
RICE DEVELOPMENT COMPANY INC
GRAND COVE ESTATES
21 Hwy, Grand Bend, ON, N0M 1T0
(519) 238-8444
Emp Here 20
SIC 1531 Operative builders

D-U-N-S 20-806-2500   (BR)
SOBEYS CAPITAL INCORPORATED
SOBEYS STORE 6722
55 Main St E, Grand Bend, ON, N0M 1T0
(519) 238-8944
Emp Here 80
SIC 5411 Grocery stores

Grand Valley, ON L9W
Dufferin County

D-U-N-S 20-031-5567   (BR)
**UPPER GRAND DISTRICT SCHOOL
BOARD, THE**
*GRAND VALLEY & DISTRICT PUBLIC
SCHOOL*
(*Suby of* Upper Grand District School Board,
The)
120 Main St N, Grand Valley, ON, L9W 7N4
(519) 928-2172
Emp Here 30
SIC 8211 Elementary and secondary schools

Grande Pointe, ON N0P

D-U-N-S 20-545-2910   (BR)
**CONSEIL SCOLAIRE DE DISTRICT DES
ECOLES CATHOLIQUES DU SUD-OUEST**

*ECOLE ELEMENTAIRE CATHOLIQUE
SAINT-PHILIPPE*
7195 St Philippes Line, Grande Pointe, ON,
N0P 1S0
(519) 352-9579
Emp Here 20
SIC 8211 Elementary and secondary schools

Granton, ON N0M
Middlesex County

D-U-N-S 24-353-1477   (SL)
**PENNER FARM SERVICES (AVONBANK)
LTD**
PENNER FARM SERVICES
15456 Elginfield Rd Rr 3, Granton, ON, N0M
1V0
(519) 225-2507
Emp Here 63   *Sales* 18,890,240
SIC 5083 Farm and garden machinery
Dir Frank Hogervorster
VP Jerry Martens
Darrel Penner
Reg Penner

Gravenhurst, ON P1P
Muskoka County

D-U-N-S 25-604-8729   (BR)
2063414 ONTARIO LIMITED
LEISUREWORLD CAREGIVING CENTRE
(*Suby of* 2063414 Ontario Limited)
200 Kelly Dr, Gravenhurst, ON, P1P 1P3
(705) 687-3444
Emp Here 180
SIC 8051 Skilled nursing care facilities

D-U-N-S 24-342-2057   (BR)
CARA OPERATIONS LIMITED
HARVEY'S
(*Suby of* Cara Holdings Limited)
Hwy 11 S, Gravenhurst, ON, P1P 1R1
(705) 684-8288
Emp Here 24
SIC 5812 Eating places

D-U-N-S 20-288-1764   (BR)
CHARTWELL RETIREMENT RESIDENCES
*CHARTWELL SENIORS HOUSING REAL
ESTATE INVESTMENT TRUST*
300 Muskoka Rd N Suite 308, Gravenhurst,
ON, P1P 1N8
(705) 687-3356
Emp Here 20
SIC 6513 Apartment building operators

D-U-N-S 20-117-3783   (SL)
GREAT GULF (MUSKOKA) LTD
TABOO GOLF
1209 Muskoka Beach Rd, Gravenhurst, ON,
P1P 1R1
(705) 687-2233
Emp Here 50   *Sales* 2,598,753
SIC 7992 Public golf courses

D-U-N-S 25-398-8026   (BR)
LAKES OF MUSKOKA REALTY INC
ROYAL LE PAGE
390 Muskoka Rd S Suite 5, Gravenhurst, ON,
P1P 1J4
(705) 687-3496
Emp Here 24
SIC 6531 Real estate agents and managers

D-U-N-S 20-358-4933   (SL)
MUSKOKA BAY CLUB
MUSKOKA RESORT
1217 North Muldrew Lake Road, Gravenhurst,
ON. P1P 1T9
(705) 687-7900
Emp Here 50   *Sales* 2,042,900
SIC 7997 Membership sports and recreation

clubs

D-U-N-S 20-358-4990   (SL)
MUSKOKA BAY GOLF CORPORATION
1217 North Muldrew Lake Rd, Gravenhurst,
ON, P1P 1T9
(705) 687-4900
Emp Here 75   *Sales* 3,210,271
SIC 7992 Public golf courses

D-U-N-S 24-373-7132   (SL)
MUSKOKA WHARF CORPORATION
275 Steamship Bay Rd, Gravenhurst, ON,
P1P 1Z9
(705) 687-0006
Emp Here 25   *Sales* 10,952,320
SIC 6553 Cemetery subdividers and developers
Pr Pr Gregg Evans
Dir Marie Evans

D-U-N-S 20-095-6162   (BR)
ONTARIO POWER GENERATION INC
EVERGREEN ENERGY
325 Pinedale Rd, Gravenhurst, ON, P1P 1L8
(705) 687-6551
Emp Here 21
SIC 4911 Electric services

D-U-N-S 20-026-2298   (SL)
**RENAISSANCE LEISURE GROUP (2004)
INC**
TABOO MUSKOKA
1209 Muskoka Beach Rd, Gravenhurst, ON,
P1P 1R1
(705) 687-2233
Emp Here 50   *Sales* 2,598,753
SIC 7011 Hotels and motels

D-U-N-S 25-631-8213   (BR)
**SIMCOE MUSKOKA DISTRICT HEALTH
UNIT**
*EARLY WORDS MUSKOKA PARRY SOUND
HEALTH UNIT SERVIN*
5 Pineridge Gate Suite 2, Gravenhurst, ON,
P1P 1Z3
(705) 684-9090
Emp Here 40
SIC 8011 Offices and clinics of medical doctors

D-U-N-S 24-610-1880   (BR)
SOBEYS CAPITAL INCORPORATED
SOBEYS
225 Edward St, Gravenhurst, ON, P1P 1K8
(705) 684-8302
Emp Here 50
SIC 5411 Grocery stores

D-U-N-S 20-788-1108   (BR)
**STELMASCHUK, W. J. AND ASSOCIATES
LTD**
345 Segwun Blvd, Gravenhurst, ON, P1P 1C5
(705) 687-8042
Emp Here 25
SIC 8399 Social services, nec

D-U-N-S 20-711-3866   (BR)
**TRILLIUM LAKELANDS DISTRICT
SCHOOL BOARD**
GRAVENHURST HIGH SCHOOL
325 Mary St S, Gravenhurst, ON, P1P 1X7
(705) 687-2283
Emp Here 45
SIC 8211 Elementary and secondary schools

D-U-N-S 20-711-3882   (BR)
**TRILLIUM LAKELANDS DISTRICT
SCHOOL BOARD**
GRAVENHURST PUBLIC SCHOOL
301 Mary St S, Gravenhurst, ON, P1P 1X6
(705) 687-2011
Emp Here 35
SIC 8211 Elementary and secondary schools

D-U-N-S 20-009-7462   (BR)
**TRILLIUM LAKELANDS DISTRICT
SCHOOL BOARD**

*MUSKOKA BEECHGROVE PUBLIC
SCHOOL*
395 Muskoka Beach Rd, Gravenhurst, ON,
P1P 1M9
(705) 687-2162
Emp Here 30
SIC 8211 Elementary and secondary schools

Greely, ON K4P
Carleton County

D-U-N-S 20-021-2012   (BR)
**OTTAWA-CARLETON DISTRICT SCHOOL
BOARD**
GREELY ELEMENTARY SCHOOL
7066 Parkway Rd, Greely, ON, K4P 1A9
(613) 821-2291
Emp Here 25
SIC 8211 Elementary and secondary schools

D-U-N-S 20-711-6257   (BR)
**OTTAWA-CARLETON DISTRICT SCHOOL
BOARD**
CASTOR VALLEY ELEMENTARY SCHOOL
2630 Grey'S Creek Rd, Greely, ON, K4P 1N2
(613) 821-1272
Emp Here 50
SIC 8211 Elementary and secondary schools

D-U-N-S 25-504-2905   (SL)
TERLIN CONSTRUCTION LTD
6961 Mckeown Dr Suite 1, Greely, ON, K4P
1A2
(613) 821-0768
Emp Here 35   *Sales* 8,942,720
SIC 1542 Nonresidential construction, nec
Pr Pr Terry Mclaughlin

Green Valley, ON K0C
Glengarry County

D-U-N-S 20-711-6703   (BR)
**CONSEIL SCOLAIRE DE DISTRICT
CATHOLIQUE DE L'EST ONTARIEN**
*ECOLE CATHOLIQUE SAINT-MARIE
GREENVALLEY*
4152 Rte 3, Green Valley, ON, K0C 1L0
(613) 525-3660
Emp Here 50
SIC 8211 Elementary and secondary schools

D-U-N-S 24-382-5601   (BR)
CRUICKSHANK CONSTRUCTION LIMITED
CRUICKSHANK-GLENGARRY DIVISION
4139 Hwy 34, Green Valley, ON, K0C 1L0
(613) 525-1750
Emp Here 80
SIC 1611 Highway and street construction

D-U-N-S 25-953-0483   (BR)
CRUICKSHANK CONSTRUCTION LIMITED
*CRUICKSHANK CONSTRUCTION GLEN-
GARRY AGGREGATES & CONCRETE, DIV
OF*
4139 Hwy 34, Green Valley, ON, K0C 1L0
(613) 525-4000
Emp Here 40
SIC 5999 Miscellaneous retail stores, nec

Greenwood, ON L0H
Ontario County

D-U-N-S 25-301-7156   (BR)
DURHAM DISTRICT SCHOOL BOARD
VALLEY VIEW PUBLIC SCHOOL
3530 Westney Rd, Greenwood, ON, L0H 1H0
(905) 683-6208
Emp Here 23

SIC 8211 Elementary and secondary schools

D-U-N-S 24-320-5643   (SL)
KLEENZONE LTD
2489 Sixth Concession Rd, Greenwood, ON,
L0H 1H0
(905) 686-6500
Emp Here 130   *Sales* 3,793,956
SIC 7349 Building maintenance services, nec

Grimsby, ON L3M

D-U-N-S 25-929-0856   (BR)
ANDREW PELLER LIMITED
VINEYARD ESTATE WINES
697 South Service Rd, Grimsby, ON, L3M 4E8
(905) 643-7333
Emp Here 400
SIC 2084 Wines, brandy, and brandy spirits

D-U-N-S 20-918-8247   (BR)
ANDREW PELLER LIMITED
697 South Service Rd, Grimsby, ON, L3M 4E8
(905) 643-4131
Emp Here 50
SIC 5812 Eating places

D-U-N-S 20-572-8988   (BR)
CANADA POST CORPORATION
2 Main St W, Grimsby, ON, L3M 1R4

Emp Here 20
SIC 4311 U.s. postal service

D-U-N-S 24-369-2295   (BR)
**CHRISTIAN LABOUR ASSOCIATION OF
CANADA**
89 South Service Rd, Grimsby, ON, L3M 5K3
(905) 945-1500
Emp Here 40
SIC 8631 Labor organizations

D-U-N-S 24-450-9535   (SL)
CIMCORP AUTOMATION LTD
635 South Service Rd, Grimsby, ON, L3M 4E8
(905) 643-9700
Emp Here 55   *Sales* 6,930,008
SIC 3569 General industrial machinery, nec
Pr Pr Douglas Pickard

D-U-N-S 25-411-4994   (BR)
DENDRES CORP
MCDONALD'S RESTAURANT
(*Suby of* Dendres Corp)
34 Livingston Ave, Grimsby, ON, L3M 1L1
(905) 945-5491
Emp Here 72
SIC 5812 Eating places

D-U-N-S 20-710-8361   (BR)
DISTRICT SCHOOL BOARD OF NIAGARA
CENTRAL PUBLIC SCHOOL
10 Livingston Ave, Grimsby, ON, L3M 1K7
(905) 945-5459
Emp Here 35
SIC 8211 Elementary and secondary schools

D-U-N-S 25-818-2716   (BR)
DISTRICT SCHOOL BOARD OF NIAGARA
LAKEVIEW PUBLIC SCHOOL
33 Olive St, Grimsby, ON, L3M 2B9
(905) 945-5427
Emp Here 30
SIC 8211 Elementary and secondary schools

D-U-N-S 20-025-1903   (BR)
DISTRICT SCHOOL BOARD OF NIAGARA
GRIMSBY HIGH SECONDARY SCHOOL
5 Boulton Ave, Grimsby, ON, L3M 1H6
(905) 945-5416
Emp Here 90
SIC 8211 Elementary and secondary schools

D-U-N-S 25-518-6405   (BR)
DURWARD JONES BARKWELL & COM-

PANY LLP
(*Suby of* Durward Jones Barkwell & Company
LLP)
4 Christie St, Grimsby, ON, L3M 4H4
(905) 945-5439
Emp Here 25
SIC 8721 Accounting, auditing, and book-
keeping

D-U-N-S 24-394-7798   (BR)
FIFTH WHEEL CORPORATION
398 North Service Rd, Grimsby, ON, L3M 4E8

Emp Here 50
SIC 5541 Gasoline service stations

D-U-N-S 20-166-6369   (SL)
**HANDLING SPECIALTY MANUFACTURING
LIMITED**
HANDLING SPECIALTY
219 South Service Rd, Grimsby, ON, L3M 1Y6
(905) 945-9661
Emp Here 57   *Sales* 4,158,760
SIC 3599 Industrial machinery, nec

D-U-N-S 24-373-0574   (SL)
**HEALTH INTEGRATION NETWORK OF
HAMILTON NIAGARA HALDIMAND BRANT**
*HAMILTON NIAGARA HALDIMAND BRANT
LHIN*
264 Main St E, Grimsby, ON, L3M 1P8
(905) 945-4930
Emp Here 35   *Sales* 5,275,400
SIC 8621 Professional organizations
Ch Bd Michael Shey
CEO Donna Cripps

D-U-N-S 25-315-8992   (BR)
**INVESTORS GROUP FINANCIAL SER-
VICES INC**
155 Main St E Suite 207, Grimsby, ON, L3M
1P2
(905) 945-4554
Emp Here 40
SIC 8741 Management services

D-U-N-S 24-383-7130   (BR)
LOBLAWS INC
REAL CANADIAN SUPERSTORE
361 South Service Rd Suite 2806, Grimsby,
ON, L3M 4E8
(905) 309-3911
Emp Here 300
SIC 5411 Grocery stores

D-U-N-S 25-000-3118   (BR)
**NIAGARA CATHOLIC DISTRICT SCHOOL
BOARD**
OUR LADY OF FATIMA CATHOLIC SCHOOL
69 Olive St, Grimsby, ON, L3M 2C3
(905) 945-5500
Emp Here 25
SIC 8211 Elementary and secondary schools

D-U-N-S 20-710-9179   (BR)
**NIAGARA CATHOLIC DISTRICT SCHOOL
BOARD**
ST JOSEPH SCHOOL
5 Robinson St N, Grimsby, ON, L3M 3C8
(905) 945-4955
Emp Here 50
SIC 8211 Elementary and secondary schools

D-U-N-S 25-323-3118   (SL)
PREMIER IMPRESSIONS INC
194 Woolverton Rd, Grimsby, ON, L3M 4E7
(905) 945-1878
Emp Here 25   *Sales* 1,896,978
SIC 2752 Commercial printing, lithographic

D-U-N-S 25-188-7725   (BR)
**RE/MAX GARDEN CITY REALTY INC BRO-
KERAGE**
64 Main St W, Grimsby, ON, L3M 1R6
(905) 945-0660
Emp Here 20
SIC 6531 Real estate agents and managers

D-U-N-S 24-212-6902   (BR)
RED-D-ARC LIMITED
RED-D-ARC WELDER RENTALS
667 S Service Rd, Grimsby, ON, L3M 4G1
(905) 629-2423
Emp Here 50
SIC 7359 Equipment rental and leasing, nec

D-U-N-S 20-652-1093   (BR)
REVERA INC
*MAPLECREST VILLAGE RETIREMENT
RESIDENCE*
85 Main St E, Grimsby, ON, L3M 1N6
(905) 945-7044
Emp Here 75
SIC 6513 Apartment building operators

D-U-N-S 20-652-1085   (BR)
REVERA LONG TERM CARE INC
KILEAN LODGE
83 Main St E, Grimsby, ON, L3M 1N6
(905) 945-9243
Emp Here 50
SIC 8051 Skilled nursing care facilities

D-U-N-S 20-205-9338   (BR)
**ROYAL LEPAGE NIAGARA REAL ESTATE
CENTRE**
22 Main St W, Grimsby, ON, L3M 1R4
(905) 945-1234
Emp Here 50
SIC 6531 Real estate agents and managers

D-U-N-S 20-189-1822   (BR)
SHERWIN-WILLIAMS CANADA INC
*DURACOAT POWDER MANUFACTURING
DIV*
(*Suby of* The Sherwin-Williams Company)
13 Iroquois Trail, Grimsby, ON, L3M 5E6
(905) 945-3802
Emp Here 80
SIC 2851 Paints and allied products

D-U-N-S 25-309-1839   (BR)
SOBEYS CAPITAL INCORPORATED
SOBEYS
44 Livingston Ave, Grimsby, ON, L3M 1L1
(905) 945-9973
Emp Here 75
SIC 5411 Grocery stores

D-U-N-S 20-860-1778   (BR)
SOURCE (BELL) ELECTRONICS INC, THE
SOURCE, THE
44 Livingston Ave Unit 1006a, Grimsby, ON,
L3M 1L1
(905) 945-3871
Emp Here 25
SIC 5999 Miscellaneous retail stores, nec

D-U-N-S 20-207-0970   (SL)
VIBRATORY TOOLING AND REPAIR INC
VTR
623 South Service Rd Unit 6, Grimsby, ON,
L3M 4E8
(905) 643-7300
Emp Here 45   *Sales* 5,326,131
SIC 3559 Special industry machinery, nec
Pr Pr Tom Davies

D-U-N-S 20-706-2675   (BR)
WENDY'S RESTAURANTS OF CANADA INC
(*Suby of* The Wendy's Company)
424 South Service Rd, Grimsby, ON, L3M 4E8
(905) 309-6071
Emp Here 40
SIC 5812 Eating places

D-U-N-S 25-037-3164   (SL)
WEST LINCOLN MEMORIAL HOSPITAL
169 Main St E, Grimsby, ON, L3M 1P3
(905) 945-2253
Emp Here 385   *Sales* 34,583,474
SIC 8062 General medical and surgical hospi-
tals
Pr Rob Macisaac
Brenda Flaherty
Dave Mccaig

Dir Peter Fitzgerald
Dir Rebecca Repa
Dir Teresa Smith
Dir Barry Lumb

Guelph, ON N1C
Wellington County

D-U-N-S 20-590-4845   (BR)
**UPPER GRAND DISTRICT SCHOOL
BOARD, THE**
KORTRIGHT HILLS PUBLIC SCHOOL
(*Suby of* Upper Grand District School Board,
The)
23 Ptarmigan Dr Suite Upper, Guelph, ON,
N1C 1B5
(519) 827-1601
Emp Here 25
SIC 8211 Elementary and secondary schools

D-U-N-S 20-724-9665   (HQ)
WURTH CANADA LIMITED
345 Hanlon Creek Blvd, Guelph, ON, N1C
0A1
(905) 564-6225
Emp Here 100   *Emp Total* 70,553
Sales 78,917,583
SIC 5085 Industrial supplies
Pr Ernest Sweeney

Guelph, ON N1E
Wellington County

D-U-N-S 20-004-7145   (BR)
BANQUE TORONTO-DOMINION, LA
TORONTO-DOMINION BANK, THE
(*Suby of* Toronto-Dominion Bank, The)
350 Eramosa Rd, Guelph, ON, N1E 2M9
(519) 763-2020
Emp Here 20
SIC 6021 National commercial banks

D-U-N-S 25-594-6832   (SL)
BARTLE BROS INC
TIM HORTONS
204 Victoria Rd S, Guelph, ON, N1E 5R1
(519) 766-9751
Emp Here 50   *Sales* 1,532,175
SIC 5812 Eating places

D-U-N-S 24-425-8575   (BR)
CARGILL LIMITED
*BETTER BEEF-CARGILL MEAT SOLU-
TIONS, DIV OF*
781 York Rd, Guelph, ON, N1E 6N1
(519) 823-5200
Emp Here 1,540
SIC 2011 Meat packing plants

D-U-N-S 25-915-0894   (BR)
**CONESTOGA COLLEGE COMMUNICA-
TIONS CORPORATION**
460 Speedvale Ave E, Guelph, ON, N1E 1P1
(519) 824-9390
Emp Here 50
SIC 8222 Junior colleges

D-U-N-S 24-089-8150   (BR)
GOVERNMENT OF ONTARIO
*ONTARIO YOUTH APPRENTICESHIPS
PROGRAM*
500 Victoria Rd N, Guelph, ON, N1E 6K2
(519) 766-9140
Emp Here 20
SIC 8211 Elementary and secondary schools

D-U-N-S 24-214-7072   (SL)
ITALIAN-CANADIAN CLUB OF GUELPH
135 Ferguson St, Guelph, ON, N1E 2Y9
(519) 821-1110
Emp Here 60   *Sales* 4,304,681
SIC 8641 Civic and social associations

D-U-N-S 24-471-1354   (BR)
**LAPOINTE-FISHER NURSING HOME, LIM-
ITED**
271 Metcalfe St, Guelph, ON, N1E 4Y8
(519) 821-9030
Emp Here 100
SIC 8051 Skilled nursing care facilities

D-U-N-S 24-607-8351   (BR)
METRO ONTARIO INC
FOOD BASIC
380 Eramosa Rd, Guelph, ON, N1E 6R2
(519) 824-8700
Emp Here 160
SIC 5411 Grocery stores

D-U-N-S 25-333-1771   (SL)
NGF CANADA LIMITED
255 York Rd, Guelph, ON, N1E 3G4
(519) 836-9228
Emp Here 36
SIC 2296 Tire cord and fabrics

D-U-N-S 24-978-0362   (BR)
OC CANADA HOLDINGS COMPANY
247 York Rd, Guelph, ON, N1E 3G4
(519) 824-0120
Emp Here 300
SIC 3296 Mineral wool

D-U-N-S 20-727-2886   (SL)
**PESTALTO ENVIRONMENTAL HEALTH
SERVICES INC**
400 Elizabeth St Unit I, Guelph, ON, N1E 2Y1

Emp Here 75   *Sales* 8,198,262
SIC 4959 Sanitary services, nec
Pr Pr Barry Tyler

D-U-N-S 25-831-8377   (BR)
POLYMER DISTRIBUTION INC
351 Elizabeth St, Guelph, ON, N1E 2X9
(519) 837-4535
Emp Here 25
SIC 4225 General warehousing and storage

D-U-N-S 25-407-5666   (SL)
RED CAR SERVICE INC
RED CAR AIRPORT SERVICE
530 Elizabeth St, Guelph, ON, N1E 6C3
(519) 824-9344
Emp Here 80   *Sales* 4,158,760
SIC 4131 Intercity and rural bus transportation

D-U-N-S 25-971-2594   (BR)
STEELE FOODS LTD
TIM HORTONS
380 Eramosa Rd Unit 18, Guelph, ON, N1E
6R2
(519) 763-8016
Emp Here 20
SIC 5812 Eating places

D-U-N-S 24-525-4144   (BR)
**UPPER CANADA DISTRICT SCHOOL
BOARD, THE**
DANBY, KEN PUBLIC SCHOOL
525 Grange Rd, Guelph, ON, N1E 7C4
(519) 836-4545
Emp Here 25
SIC 8211 Elementary and secondary schools

D-U-N-S 20-068-0101   (BR)
**UPPER GRAND DISTRICT SCHOOL
BOARD, THE**
WAVERLEY DRIVE PUBLIC SCHOOL
(*Suby of* Upper Grand District School Board,
The)
140 Waverley Dr, Guelph, ON, N1E 1H2
(519) 824-7742
Emp Here 35
SIC 8211 Elementary and secondary schools

D-U-N-S 20-024-9485   (BR)
**UPPER GRAND DISTRICT SCHOOL
BOARD, THE**
TYTLER PUBLIC SCHOOL
(*Suby of* Upper Grand District School Board,

The)
131 Ontario St, Guelph, ON, N1E 3B3
(519) 822-9271
Emp Here 25
SIC 8211 Elementary and secondary schools

D-U-N-S 20-004-8481   (BR)
**UPPER GRAND DISTRICT SCHOOL
BOARD, THE**
LAURINE AVE PUBLIC SCHOOL
(*Suby of* Upper Grand District School Board,
The)
50 Laurine Ave, Guelph, ON, N1E 4M9
(519) 824-4760
Emp Here 20
SIC 8211 Elementary and secondary schools

D-U-N-S 20-710-7603   (BR)
**UPPER GRAND DISTRICT SCHOOL
BOARD, THE**
JOHN F. ROSS CVI
(*Suby of* Upper Grand District School Board,
The)
21 Meyer Dr, Guelph, ON, N1E 4H1
(519) 822-7090
Emp Here 50
SIC 8211 Elementary and secondary schools

D-U-N-S 20-591-9959   (BR)
**UPPER GRAND DISTRICT SCHOOL
BOARD, THE**
KING GEORGE PUBLIC SCHOOL
(*Suby of* Upper Grand District School Board,
The)
72 Lemon St, Guelph, ON, N1E 2H5
(519) 822-1911
Emp Here 40
SIC 8211 Elementary and secondary schools

D-U-N-S 20-025-9583   (BR)
**UPPER GRAND DISTRICT SCHOOL
BOARD, THE**
OTTAWA CRESCENT PUBLIC SCHOOL
(*Suby of* Upper Grand District School Board,
The)
75 Ottawa Cres, Guelph, ON, N1E 2A8
(519) 822-6880
Emp Here 30
SIC 8211 Elementary and secondary schools

D-U-N-S 20-292-0323   (BR)
**UPPER GRAND DISTRICT SCHOOL
BOARD, THE**
ST GEORGE'S CENTER FOR ESL
(*Suby of* Upper Grand District School Board,
The)
21 King St, Guelph, ON, N1E 4P5
(519) 766-9551
Emp Here 25
SIC 8211 Elementary and secondary schools

D-U-N-S 20-286-9181   (BR)
**UPPER GRAND DISTRICT SCHOOL
BOARD, THE**
BRANT AVENUE PUBLIC SCHOOL
(*Suby of* Upper Grand District School Board,
The)
64 Brant Ave, Guelph, ON, N1E 1G2
(519) 824-2671
Emp Here 20
SIC 8211 Elementary and secondary schools

D-U-N-S 20-710-7553   (BR)
**UPPER GRAND DISTRICT SCHOOL
BOARD, THE**
EDWARD JOHNSON PUBLIC SCHOOL
(*Suby of* Upper Grand District School Board,
The)
397 Stevenson St N, Guelph, ON, N1E 5C1
(519) 763-7374
Emp Here 50
SIC 8211 Elementary and secondary schools

D-U-N-S 20-939-3941   (HQ)
**UPPER GRAND DISTRICT SCHOOL
BOARD, THE**
COLLEGE HEIGHTS S.S.

(*Suby of* Upper Grand District School Board,
The)
500 Victoria Rd N, Guelph, ON, N1E 6K2
(519) 766-9140
Emp Here 80   *Emp Total* 3,500
Sales 344,843,254
SIC 8211 Elementary and secondary schools
Ch Bd Bob Borden
   Martha Rogers
   Janice Wright

D-U-N-S 20-655-1546   (BR)
**WELLINGTON CATHOLIC DISTRICT
SCHOOL BOARD**
ST. JOHN CATHOLIC SCHOOL
63 Victoria Rd N, Guelph, ON, N1E 5G9
(519) 824-4710
Emp Here 43
SIC 8211 Elementary and secondary schools

D-U-N-S 20-710-7801   (BR)
**WELLINGTON CATHOLIC DISTRICT
SCHOOL BOARD**
HOLY TRINITY CATHOLIC SCHOOL
487 Grange Rd, Guelph, ON, N1E 7C4
(519) 821-0156
Emp Here 50
SIC 8211 Elementary and secondary schools

D-U-N-S 20-024-9584   (BR)
**WELLINGTON CATHOLIC DISTRICT
SCHOOL BOARD**
ST PATRICK SCHOOL
391 Victoria Rd N, Guelph, ON, N1E 5J9
(519) 822-0200
Emp Here 35
SIC 8211 Elementary and secondary schools

D-U-N-S 20-024-9527   (BR)
**WELLINGTON CATHOLIC DISTRICT
SCHOOL BOARD**
SACRED HEART SCHOOL
125 Huron St, Guelph, ON, N1E 5L5
(519) 824-2751
Emp Here 24
SIC 8211 Elementary and secondary schools

D-U-N-S 20-710-7702   (BR)
**WELLINGTON CATHOLIC DISTRICT
SCHOOL BOARD**
HOLY ROSARY CATHOLIC SCHOOL
365 Stevenson St N, Guelph, ON, N1E 5B7
(519) 824-5620
Emp Here 30
SIC 8211 Elementary and secondary schools

D-U-N-S 20-024-9543   (BR)
**WELLINGTON CATHOLIC DISTRICT
SCHOOL BOARD**
ST. JAMES CATHOLIC HIGH SCHOOL
57 Victoria Rd N, Guelph, ON, N1E 5G9
(519) 822-4290
Emp Here 125
SIC 8211 Elementary and secondary schools

D-U-N-S 25-556-8834   (BR)
**YOUNG MEN'S AND YOUNG WOMEN'S
CHRISTIAN ASSOCIATION OF GUELPH**
KENSINGTON Y CHILD CARE
84 Kensington St, Guelph, ON, N1E 3P9
(519) 821-8173
Emp Here 20
SIC 8351 Child day care services

D-U-N-S 25-297-8010   (BR)
ZEHRMART INC
ZEHRS MARKETS
297 Eramosa Rd, Guelph, ON, N1E 2M7
(519) 763-4550
Emp Here 150
SIC 5411 Grocery stores

Guelph, ON N1G
Wellington County

D-U-N-S 24-985-8820   (HQ)
779414 ONTARIO INC
TIM HORTONS
(*Suby of* 779414 Ontario Inc)
304 Stone Rd W, Guelph, ON, N1G 4W4
(519) 836-4950
Emp Here 50   *Emp Total* 90
Sales 2,699,546
SIC 5812 Eating places

D-U-N-S 20-012-1619   (SL)
ABS ON TIME LOGISTICS INC
525 Southgate Dr Unit 1, Guelph, ON, N1G
3W6
(519) 826-9910
Emp Here 60   *Sales* 10,145,000
SIC 5013 Motor vehicle supplies and new
parts
   Rick Jamieson
Pr John Burns

D-U-N-S 25-531-4015   (HQ)
AGRICORP
1 Stone Rd W, Guelph, ON, N1G 4Y2
(888) 247-4999
Emp Here 420   *Emp Total* 90,000
Sales 133,897
SIC 6331 Fire, marine, and casualty insurance

D-U-N-S 25-293-2348   (BR)
ATLIFIC INC
RAMADA HOTEL
(*Suby of* 3376290 Canada Inc)
716 Gordon St, Guelph, ON, N1G 1Y6
(519) 836-1240
Emp Here 40
SIC 7011 Hotels and motels

D-U-N-S 20-118-5613   (SL)
BARBER GROUP INVESTMENTS INC
485 Southgate Dr, Guelph, ON, N1G 3W6

Emp Here 110   *Sales* 31,855,300
SIC 5039 Construction materials, nec
Pr Pr John Barber

D-U-N-S 24-095-6206   (BR)
BAYER CROPSCIENCE INC
160 Research Lane Suite 5, Guelph, ON, N1G
5B2
(519) 767-3366
Emp Here 20
SIC 5169 Chemicals and allied products, nec

D-U-N-S 24-363-5732   (BR)
BEST BUY CANADA LTD
FUTURE SHOP
(*Suby of* Best Buy Co., Inc.)
151 Stone Rd W, Guelph, ON, N1G 5L4
(519) 766-4660
Emp Here 50
SIC 5731 Radio, television, and electronic
stores

D-U-N-S 20-966-2881   (BR)
BOREALIS CAPITAL CORPORATION
STONE ROAD MALL
435 Stone Rd W Suite 204, Guelph, ON, N1G
2X6
(519) 265-9077
Emp Here 50
SIC 6282 Investment advice

D-U-N-S 25-908-7419   (BR)
BORGES, P J INC
SWISS CHALET ROTISSERIE & GRILL
(*Suby of* Borges, P J Inc)
502 Edinburgh Rd S, Guelph, ON, N1G 4Z1
(519) 823-5787
Emp Here 60
SIC 5812 Eating places

D-U-N-S 25-359-4279   (BR)
COU HOLDING ASSOCIATION INC
*ONTARIO UNIVERSITIES' APPLICATION
CENTRE*
170 Research Lane, Guelph, ON, N1G 5E2

(519) 823-1940
Emp Here 45
SIC 8621 Professional organizations

D-U-N-S 25-113-8491   (HQ)
CAMIS INC
(*Suby of* Camis Inc)
649 Scottsdale Dr Suite 90, Guelph, ON, N1G
4T7
(519) 766-0901
Emp Here 80   *Emp Total* 86
Sales 14,268,160
SIC 7372 Prepackaged software
Pr Pr Doug Hall
Acct Mgr Kathy Layinby

D-U-N-S 20-002-9531   (BR)
CANADA TRUST COMPANY, THE
(*Suby of* Toronto-Dominion Bank, The)
585 Scottsdale Dr, Guelph, ON, N1G 3E7

Emp Here 26
SIC 6021 National commercial banks

D-U-N-S 24-362-1179   (BR)
CANADIAN TIRE CORPORATION, LIMITED
127 Stone Rd W Unit 42, Guelph, ON, N1G
5G4
(519) 822-9521
Emp Here 20
SIC 5531 Auto and home supply stores

D-U-N-S 20-321-8420   (BR)
CARA OPERATIONS LIMITED
MONTANA'S COOKHOUSE
(*Suby of* Cara Holdings Limited)
201 Stone Rd W, Guelph, ON, N1G 5L4
(519) 766-1549
Emp Here 50
SIC 5812 Eating places

D-U-N-S 25-410-7972   (BR)
CINTAS CANADA LIMITED
(*Suby of* Cintas Corporation)
412 Laird Rd, Guelph, ON, N1G 3X7
(519) 836-1772
Emp Here 22
SIC 7213 Linen supply

D-U-N-S 20-267-0308   (SL)
COLDWELL BANKER NEUMANN REAL ES-TATE
824 Gordon St Unit 2, Guelph, ON, N1G 1Y7
(519) 821-3600
Emp Here 50   *Sales* 4,742,446
SIC 6531 Real estate agents and managers

D-U-N-S 20-027-1810   (BR)
CONSEIL SCOLAIRE DE DISTRICT CATHOLIQUE CENTRE-SUD
ECOLE ST RENE GOUPIL
221 Scottsdale Dr, Guelph, ON, N1G 3A1
(519) 821-7542
Emp Here 20
SIC 8211 Elementary and secondary schools

D-U-N-S 20-784-0919   (SL)
D. L. PAGANI LIMITED
RAMADA HOTEL & CONFERENCE CENTRE
716 Gordon St, Guelph, ON, N1G 1Y6
(519) 836-1240
Emp Here 80   *Sales* 3,502,114
SIC 7011 Hotels and motels

D-U-N-S 20-650-7907   (HQ)
DARLING INTERNATIONAL CANADA INC
ROTHSAY
(*Suby of* Darling Ingredients Inc.)
150 Research Lane Suite 307, Guelph, ON,
N1G 4T2
(519) 780-3342
Emp Here 60   *Emp Total* 10,000
Sales 84,809,610
SIC 4953 Refuse systems
VP Alan Rickard

D-U-N-S 24-355-7340   (BR)
DELTA HOTELS LIMITED
DELTA GUELPH HOTEL & CONFERENCE

CENTRE
50 Stone Rd W, Guelph, ON, N1G 0A9
(519) 780-3700
Emp Here 20
SIC 7011 Hotels and motels

D-U-N-S 24-009-4706   (BR)
ELI LILLY CANADA INC
ELANCO
(*Suby of* Eli Lilly and Company)
150 Research Lane Suite 120, Guelph, ON,
N1G 4T2
(519) 821-0277
Emp Here 30
SIC 8732 Commercial nonphysical research

D-U-N-S 24-119-9780   (BR)
FLIGHT SHOPS INC, THE
FLIGHT CENTRE
435 Stone Rd W Suite A6a, Guelph, ON, N1G
2X6
(519) 763-2262
Emp Here 20
SIC 4724 Travel agencies

D-U-N-S 24-616-2791   (BR)
GOODLIFE FITNESS CENTRES INC
435 Stone Rd W, Guelph, ON, N1G 2X6
(519) 826-9228
Emp Here 20
SIC 7991 Physical fitness facilities

D-U-N-S 25-952-1532   (BR)
GRANDI COMPANY LIMITED
MCDONALD'S RESTAURANTS
(*Suby of* GranDi Company Limited)
372 Stone Rd W, Guelph, ON, N1G 4T8
(519) 763-8842
Emp Here 75
SIC 5812 Eating places

D-U-N-S 20-810-6133   (BR)
GUELPH HYDRO INC
395 Southgate Dr, Guelph, ON, N1G 4Y1
(519) 822-3017
Emp Here 50
SIC 4911 Electric services

D-U-N-S 25-149-2658   (HQ)
HAMMOND POWER SOLUTIONS INC
HPS
(*Suby of* Hammond Power Solutions Inc)
595 Southgate Dr, Guelph, ON, N1G 3W6
(519) 822-2441
Emp Here 800   *Emp Total* 1,300
Sales 203,249,268
SIC 3612 Transformers, except electric
William Hammond
Christopher Huether
Douglas Baldwin
David Fitzgibbon
Dahra Granovsky
Frederick Jaques
Donald Macadam
Grant Robinson
Richard Waterman

D-U-N-S 25-147-8608   (BR)
INVESTORS GROUP FINANCIAL SER-VICES INC
649 Scottsdale Dr Suite 401, Guelph, ON,
N1G 4T7
(519) 836-6320
Emp Here 45
SIC 8741 Management services

D-U-N-S 25-318-7272   (BR)
LIQUOR CONTROL BOARD OF ONTARIO, THE
L.C.B.O. #495
615 Scottsdale Dr, Guelph, ON, N1G 3P4

Emp Here 30
SIC 5921 Liquor stores

D-U-N-S 24-624-2903   (HQ)
MACKINNON TRANSPORT INC
405 Laird Rd, Guelph, ON, N1G 4P7

(519) 821-2311
Emp Here 100   *Emp Total* 180
Sales 16,396,525
SIC 4213 Trucking, except local
Pr Pr Evan Mackinnon
VP Fin Alex Mackinnon
VP Richard Sharpe

D-U-N-S 25-302-1034   (BR)
MAPLE LEAF FOODS INC
SCHNEIDER FOODS
362 Laird Rd, Guelph, ON, N1G 3X7
(519) 837-4848
Emp Here 150
SIC 1541 Industrial buildings and warehouses

D-U-N-S 24-155-0891   (BR)
MAXXAM ANALYTICS INTERNATIONAL CORPORATION
MAXXAM ANALYTICS
335 Laird Rd Unit 2, Guelph, ON, N1G 4P7
(519) 836-2400
Emp Here 26
SIC 8734 Testing laboratories

D-U-N-S 24-335-0399   (BR)
METRO ONTARIO INC
METRO
500 Edinburgh Rd S, Guelph, ON, N1G 4Z1
(519) 763-3552
Emp Here 300
SIC 5411 Grocery stores

D-U-N-S 20-837-0705   (BR)
MILLER THOMSON LLP
100 Stone Rd W Suite 301, Guelph, ON, N1G
5L3
(519) 822-4680
Emp Here 50
SIC 8111 Legal services

D-U-N-S 25-494-9688   (SL)
NSF-GFTC
GFTC
125 Chancellors Way, Guelph, ON, N1G 0E7
(519) 821-1246
Emp Here 50   *Sales* 2,699,546
SIC 8731 Commercial physical research

D-U-N-S 24-357-6837   (HQ)
NUTRECO CANADA INC
SHUR-GAIN
150 Research Lane Suite 200, Guelph, ON,
N1G 4T2
(519) 823-7000
Emp Here 35   *Emp Total* 60,800
Sales 218,882,100
SIC 2048 Prepared feeds, nec
Ex VP Jerry Vergeer
VP Fin Eduardo Perugini
  Cees Van Rijn

D-U-N-S 24-333-7271   (BR)
OLD NAVY (CANADA) INC
(*Suby of* The Gap Inc)
435 Stone Rd W, Guelph, ON, N1G 2X6
(519) 763-4158
Emp Here 50
SIC 5651 Family clothing stores

D-U-N-S 25-687-2938   (SL)
ONTARIO ONE CALL LIMITED
335 Laird Rd Unit 8, Guelph, ON, N1G 4P7
(519) 766-4821
Emp Here 60   *Sales* 3,957,782
SIC 7389 Business services, nec

D-U-N-S 20-805-8698   (BR)
ONTARIO REALTY CORPORATION
1 Stone Rd W 4th Fl, Guelph, ON, N1G 4Y2
(519) 826-3182
Emp Here 28
SIC 6531 Real estate agents and managers

D-U-N-S 20-859-8784   (BR)
PACIFIC LINK COMMUNICATIONS INC
BELL WORLD
435 Stone Rd W Suite 204, Guelph, ON, N1G
2X6

(519) 821-3792
Emp Here 25
SIC 5999 Miscellaneous retail stores, nec

D-U-N-S 25-092-3856   (BR)
PARRISH & HEIMBECKER, LIMITED
GRAIN DIVISION - OPERATIONS OFFICE
(*Suby of* Parrish & Heimbecker, Limited)
150 Research Lane Suite 205, Guelph, ON,
N1G 4T2
(519) 821-0505
Emp Here 300
SIC 5153 Grain and field beans

D-U-N-S 24-761-4535   (SL)
POLY-NOVA TECHNOLOGIES LIMITED PARTNERSHIP
125 Southgate Dr, Guelph, ON, N1G 3M5
(519) 822-2109
Emp Here 120   *Sales* 18,240,175
SIC 3069 Fabricated rubber products, nec
Dir John Timmerman

D-U-N-S 25-560-0561   (SL)
PRIME RESTAURANTS
EAST SIDE MARIO'S
370 Stone Rd W Suite Side, Guelph, ON, N1G
4V9
(519) 763-7861
Emp Here 80   *Sales* 2,407,703
SIC 5812 Eating places

D-U-N-S 24-033-3583   (HQ)
PROMINENT FLUID CONTROLS LTD
490 Southgate Dr, Guelph, ON, N1G 4P5
(519) 836-5692
Emp Here 42   *Emp Total* 2,419
Sales 11,779,113
SIC 5074 Plumbing and heating equipment
and supplies (hydronics)
VP Garth Debruyn
Pr Pr Victor Dulger

D-U-N-S 24-951-9984   (BR)
RE/MAX REAL ESTATE CENTRE INC
679 Southgate Dr Suite 101, Guelph, ON,
N1G 4S2
(519) 837-1300
Emp Here 50
SIC 6531 Real estate agents and managers

D-U-N-S 20-175-3493   (HQ)
RWDI AIR INC
600 Southgate Dr, Guelph, ON, N1G 4P6
(519) 823-1311
Emp Here 200   *Emp Total* 300
Sales 40,973,672
SIC 8711 Engineering services
Pr Michael Soligo
Dir Mark Vanderheyden
Dir David Chadder
Dir Anton Davies
  Peter Irwin

D-U-N-S 20-552-3298   (BR)
RE/MAX REALTY SPECIALISTS INC
(*Suby of* Re/Max Realty Specialists Inc)
679 Southgate Dr Suite 101, Guelph, ON,
N1G 4S2
(519) 837-1300
Emp Here 50
SIC 6531 Real estate agents and managers

D-U-N-S 24-343-4193   (BR)
REVERA INC
STONE LODGE
165 Cole Rd, Guelph, ON, N1G 4N9
(519) 767-0880
Emp Here 60
SIC 8051 Skilled nursing care facilities

D-U-N-S 25-965-5504   (BR)
ROYAL BANK OF CANADA
ROYAL BANK FINANCIAL GROUP, DIV. OF
(*Suby of* Royal Bank Of Canada)
987 Gordon St Suite 1, Guelph, ON, N1G 4W3
(519) 821-5610
Emp Here 20
SIC 6021 National commercial banks

D-U-N-S 25-279-4243   (BR)
SEARS CANADA INC
435 Stone Rd W Suite 100, Guelph, ON, N1G
2X6
(519) 822-3280
Emp Here 200
SIC 5311 Department stores

D-U-N-S 20-269-6225   (SL)
SHEARER'S FOODS CANADA, INC
745 Southgate Dr, Guelph, ON, N1G 3R3
(519) 746-0045
Emp Here 225
SIC 2096 Potato chips and similar snacks

D-U-N-S 20-506-1067   (BR)
STARBUCKS COFFEE CANADA, INC
(*Suby of* Starbucks Corporation)
435 Stone Rd W, Guelph, ON, N1G 2X6
(519) 822-5733
Emp Here 25
SIC 5812 Eating places

D-U-N-S 25-996-4930   (HQ)
**SYNGENTA CROP PROTECTION CANADA,
INC**
140 Research Lane, Guelph, ON, N1G 4Z3
(519) 836-5665
Emp Here 50   *Emp Total* 137,478
Sales 29,184,280
SIC 5191 Farm supplies
Pr Pr Jay Bradshaw
Dir Christopher Legge
Dir Valdemar Fischer
Dir Gregory Jowett

D-U-N-S 20-918-4915   (BR)
UNISYNC GROUP LIMITED
1 Rutherford Crt, Guelph, ON, N1G 4N5
(519) 836-2581
Emp Here 50
SIC 2311 Men's and boy's suits and coats

D-U-N-S 20-073-8115   (BR)
UNIVERSITY OF GUELPH
OFFICE OF OPEN LEARNING
50 Stone Rd E Suite 158, Guelph, ON, N1G
2W1
(519) 824-4120
Emp Here 40
SIC 8211 Elementary and secondary schools

D-U-N-S 20-113-7556   (BR)
UNIVERSITY OF GUELPH
LABORATORY SERVICES
95 Stone Rd W, Guelph, ON, N1G 2Z4
(519) 767-6299
Emp Here 250
SIC 8221 Colleges and universities

D-U-N-S 20-068-0143   (BR)
**UPPER GRAND DISTRICT SCHOOL
BOARD, THE**
COLLEGE AVE PUBLIC SCHOOL
(*Suby of* Upper Grand District School Board,
The)
195 College Ave W, Guelph, ON, N1G 1S6
(519) 821-4510
Emp Here 20
SIC 8211 Elementary and secondary schools

D-U-N-S 20-591-7730   (BR)
**UPPER GRAND DISTRICT SCHOOL
BOARD, THE**
HAMILTON, FRED A PUBLIC SCHOOL
(*Suby of* Upper Grand District School Board,
The)
160 Ironwood Rd, Guelph, ON, N1G 3R4
(519) 836-0080
Emp Here 25
SIC 8211 Elementary and secondary schools

D-U-N-S 20-024-9451   (BR)
**UPPER GRAND DISTRICT SCHOOL
BOARD, THE**
JOHN MCCRAE PUBLIC SCHOOL
(*Suby of* Upper Grand District School Board,
The)

189 Water St, Guelph, ON, N1G 1B3
(519) 824-0028
Emp Here 33
SIC 8211 Elementary and secondary schools

D-U-N-S 20-276-9691   (BR)
**UPPER GRAND DISTRICT SCHOOL
BOARD, THE**
JEAN LITTLE PUBLIC SCHOOL
(*Suby of* Upper Grand District School Board,
The)
56 Youngman Dr, Guelph, ON, N1G 4L2
(519) 837-9582
Emp Here 37
SIC 8211 Elementary and secondary schools

D-U-N-S 24-252-8250   (BR)
**UPPER GRAND DISTRICT SCHOOL
BOARD, THE**
RICKSON RIDGE PUBLIC SCHOOL
(*Suby of* Upper Grand District School Board,
The)
177 Rickson Ave Suite 2, Guelph, ON, N1G
4Y6
(519) 766-0862
Emp Here 36
SIC 8211 Elementary and secondary schools

D-U-N-S 20-710-7777   (BR)
**WELLINGTON CATHOLIC DISTRICT
SCHOOL BOARD**
MARY PHELAN CATHOLIC SCHOOL
8 Bishop Crt, Guelph, ON, N1G 2R9
(519) 821-1060
Emp Here 30
SIC 8211 Elementary and secondary schools

D-U-N-S 20-591-9777   (BR)
**WELLINGTON CATHOLIC DISTRICT
SCHOOL BOARD**
ST MICHAEL CATHOLIC SCHOOL
9 Mcelderry Rd, Guelph, ON, N1G 4W7
(519) 823-2455
Emp Here 40
SIC 8211 Elementary and secondary schools

D-U-N-S 24-426-2924   (SL)
WELLINGTON PARK TERRACE
181 Janefield Ave Suite 310, Guelph, ON,
N1G 1V2
(519) 763-7474
Emp Here 20   *Sales* 866,251
SIC 8361 Residential care

D-U-N-S 24-550-7736   (BR)
**WESTMONT HOSPITALITY MANAGEMENT
LIMITED**
HOLIDAY INN GUELPH
601 Scottsdale Dr, Guelph, ON, N1G 3E7
(519) 836-0231
Emp Here 150
SIC 7011 Hotels and motels

Guelph, ON N1H
Wellington County

D-U-N-S 25-594-8309   (SL)
1180207 ONTARIO LIMITED
TIM HORTONS
232 Silvercreek Pky N, Guelph, ON, N1H 7P8
(519) 836-5858
Emp Here 50   *Sales* 1,532,175
SIC 5812 Eating places

D-U-N-S 20-811-1075   (BR)
122164 CANADA LIMITED
NEW YORK FRIES
(*Suby of* 122164 Canada Limited)
10 Fox Run Dr, Guelph, ON, N1H 6H9
(519) 763-7200
Emp Here 40
SIC 5812 Eating places

D-U-N-S 20-578-3405   (SL)
1411337 ONTARIO INC

DOYLE TRANSPORTATION
5072 Whitelaw Rd, Guelph, ON, N1H 6J4
(519) 827-0431
Emp Here 55   *Sales* 2,335,176
SIC 4213 Trucking, except local

D-U-N-S 24-318-5167   (SL)
AOC RESINS AND COATINGS COMPANY
(*Suby of* The Alpha Corporation of Ten-
nessee)
38 Royal Rd, Guelph, ON, N1H 1G3
(519) 821-5180
Emp Here 95   *Sales* 12,387,389
SIC 2821 Plastics materials and resins
Sec Myron Dzulynsky
Fin Ex Stephen Lee
Pr Pr Randall Weghorst
 Frederick Norman
VP Reagan Stephens
Sec James Griffith

D-U-N-S 20-563-2271   (HQ)
ARMTEC HOLDINGS LIMITED
370 Speedvale Ave W Suite 101, Guelph, ON,
N1H 7M7
(519) 822-0210
Emp Here 250   *Emp Total* 1,626
Sales 91,877,078
SIC 3272 Concrete products, nec
Pr Charles Phillips
CFO James Newell

D-U-N-S 24-828-8920   (BR)
ARMTEC LP
ARMTEC
370 Speedvale Ave W, Guelph, ON, N1H 7M7
(519) 822-0210
Emp Here 30
SIC 3312 Blast furnaces and steel mills

D-U-N-S 24-849-5082   (BR)
ARMTEC LP
ARMTEC
41 George St, Guelph, ON, N1H 1S5
(519) 822-0046
Emp Here 25
SIC 3312 Blast furnaces and steel mills

D-U-N-S 20-278-4716   (BR)
ARMTEC LP
ARMTEC ONTARIO CENTRAL SALES
370 Speedvale Ave W Suite 101, Guelph, ON,
N1H 7M7
(519) 822-0210
Emp Here 35
SIC 3312 Blast furnaces and steel mills

D-U-N-S 20-311-3816   (SL)
AXIS SORTING INC
300 Willow Rd Unit 102b, Guelph, ON, N1H
7C6
(519) 212-4990
Emp Here 75   *Sales* 4,523,563
SIC 7549 Automotive services, nec

D-U-N-S 25-967-3093   (BR)
BANK OF MONTREAL
BMO
78 St Georges Sq, Guelph, ON, N1H 6K9
(519) 824-3920
Emp Here 25
SIC 6021 National commercial banks

D-U-N-S 20-589-4814   (BR)
BANQUE TORONTO-DOMINION, LA
TD CANADA TRUST
(*Suby of* Toronto-Dominion Bank, The)
170 Silvercreek Pky N, Guelph, ON, N1H 7P7
(519) 824-8100
Emp Here 20
SIC 6021 National commercial banks

D-U-N-S 20-572-3872   (BR)
BAYER INC
BAYER HEALTHCARE
75 Oxford St, Guelph, ON, N1H 2M5
(905) 282-5541
Emp Here 20

SIC 5122 Drugs, proprietaries, and sundries

D-U-N-S 25-303-4326   (BR)
**CANADIAN IMPERIAL BANK OF COM-
MERCE**
CIBC
59 Wyndham St N, Guelph, ON, N1H 4E7
(519) 766-6400
Emp Here 30
SIC 6021 National commercial banks

D-U-N-S 25-301-5382   (BR)
**CANADIAN MENTAL HEALTH ASSOCIA-
TION GRAND RIVER BRANCH**
CMHA GUELPH
(*Suby of* Canadian Mental Health Association
Grand River Branch)
147 Wyndham St N, Guelph, ON, N1H 4E9
(519) 836-6220
Emp Here 40
SIC 8093 Specialty outpatient clinics, nec

D-U-N-S 20-939-6233   (HQ)
CASCADE (CANADA) LTD
4 Nicholas Beaver Rd, Guelph, ON, N1H 6H9
(519) 763-3675
Emp Here 250   *Emp Total* 52,426
Sales 45,045,052
SIC 3537 Industrial trucks and tractors
Pr Robert Warren
Mgr Vince Burzomato

D-U-N-S 20-852-7507   (HQ)
**CO-OPERATORS GENERAL INSURANCE
COMPANY**
130 Macdonell St, Guelph, ON, N1H 2Z6
(519) 824-4400
Emp Here 500   *Emp Total* 4,567
Sales 272,654,136
SIC 6411 Insurance agents, brokers, and ser-
vice
Pr Katherine Bardswick
 Bruce West

D-U-N-S 24-420-0270   (BR)
COMCARE (CANADA) LIMITED
COMCARE HEALTH SERVICES
255 Woodlawn Rd W Unit 108, Guelph, ON,
N1H 8J1
(519) 341-9367
Emp Here 50
SIC 7363 Help supply services

D-U-N-S 24-704-8796   (BR)
**COMMUNITY LIVING GUELPH WELLING-
TON**
ARC INDUSTRIES
8 Royal Rd, Guelph, ON, N1H 1G3
(519) 824-7147
Emp Here 120
SIC 8322 Individual and family services

D-U-N-S 25-504-3747   (BR)
**CONOCOPHILLIPS CANADA RESOURCES
CORP**
SUPERIOR PROPANE, DIV OF
Gd Stn Main, Guelph, ON, N1H 6J5
(519) 822-7780
Emp Here 23
SIC 1311 Crude petroleum and natural gas

D-U-N-S 24-559-5863   (SL)
CONTRACT EXPRESS LIMITED
34 Mclean Rd, Guelph, ON, N1H 6H9
(519) 767-2772
Emp Here 50   *Sales* 7,727,098
SIC 4213 Trucking, except local
Pr Sean O'brien
 Steve Davenport
 Jennifer O'neil
 Jason O'neil

D-U-N-S 20-051-5922   (HQ)
COOKE & DENISON LIMITED
(*Suby of* Cooke & Denison Limited)
242 Speedvale Ave W, Guelph, ON, N1H 1C4

(519) 824-3710
Emp Here 40   *Emp Total* 50
Sales 4,711,645
SIC 3599 ndustrial machinery, nec

D-U-N-S 20-861-2015   (BR)
CORPORATION OF THE COUNTY OF WELLINGTON
CENTRAL GARAGE
(*Suby of* Corporation Of The County Of Wellington)
Gd Stn Main, Guelph, ON, N1H 6J5
(519) 821-2090
Emp Here 50
SIC 1611 Highway and street construction

D-U-N-S 24-844-2915   (BR)
DELOITTE LLP
98 Macdonell St Suite 400, Guelph, ON, N1H 8K9
(519) 824-5244
Emp Here 40
SIC 8721 Accounting, auditing, and book-keeping

D-U-N-S 24-334-4061   (SL)
ETSM TECHNICAL SERVICES LTD
407 Silvercreek Pky N, Guelph, ON, N1H 8G8
(519) 827-1500
Emp Here 52   *Sales* 3,793,956
SIC 3599 Industrial machinery, nec

D-U-N-S 20-784-7153   (SL)
EDEN HOUSE CARE FACILITY INC
5016 Wellington Road 29, Guelph, ON, N1H 6H8
(519) 856-4622
Emp Here 78   *Sales* 3,575,074
SIC 8051 Skilled nursing care facilities

D-U-N-S 24-951-9398   (HQ)
FLOWSERVE CANADA CORP
FLOWSERVE PUMP, DIV OF
(*Suby of* Flowserve Corporation)
225 Speedvale Ave W, Guelph, ON, N1H 1C5
(519) 824-4600
Emp Here 124   *Emp Total* 18,000
Sales 9,788,636
SIC 3561 Pumps and pumping equipment
Dir Lewis M Kling
Pr Matthew Irwin

D-U-N-S 20-264-6675   (BR)
GE WATER & PROCESS TECHNOLOGIES CANADA
(*Suby of* General Electric Company)
18 Royal Rd, Guelph, ON, N1H 1G3

Emp Here 50
SIC 5169 Chemicals and allied products, nec

D-U-N-S 20-771-2928   (BR)
GAY LEA FOODS CO-OPERATIVE LIMITED
GAY LEA FOODS
21 Speedvale Ave W, Guelph, ON, N1H 1J5
(519) 822-5530
Emp Here 75
SIC 2021 Creamery butter

D-U-N-S 25-626-6750   (BR)
GRANDI COMPANY LIMITED
MCDONALD'S RESTAURANT
(*Suby of* GranDi Company Limited)
243 Woodlawn Rd W, Guelph, ON, N1H 8J1
(519) 826-0507
Emp Here 85
SIC 5812 Eating places

D-U-N-S 20-638-8063   (BR)
GRANDI COMPANY LIMITED
MCDONALD'S RESTAURANT
65 Gordon St, Guelph, ON, N1H 4H5
(519) 836-3070
Emp Here 70
SIC 5812 Eating places

D-U-N-S 20-100-1901   (BR)
GRANDI COMPANY LIMITED
MCDONALD'S

735 Woolwich St, Guelph, ON, N1H 3Z2

Emp Here 60
SIC 5812 Eating places

D-U-N-S 20-769-4621   (SL)
GUELPH CUTTEN CLUB
CUTTEN FIELDS
Gd Stn Main, Guelph, ON, N1H 6J5
(519) 824-2650
Emp Here 60   *Sales* 2,407,703
SIC 7997 Membership sports and recreation clubs

D-U-N-S 20-005-7284   (BR)
GUELPH MANUFACTURING GROUP INC
GUELPH TOOL INC
39 Royal Rd, Guelph, ON, N1H 1G2
(519) 822-5401
Emp Here 150
SIC 3465 Automotive stampings

D-U-N-S 24-336-5306   (BR)
GUELPH, CITY OF
COMMUNITY SERVICES
19 Northumberland St, Guelph, ON, N1H 3A6
(519) 822-3550
Emp Here 200
SIC 8611 Business associations

D-U-N-S 24-336-1321   (BR)
GUELPH, CITY OF
GUELPH FIRE DEPARTMENT
50 Wyndham St S, Guelph, ON, N1H 4E1
(519) 824-6590
Emp Here 149
SIC 7389 Business services, nec

D-U-N-S 24-060-2144   (BR)
GUELPH, CITY OF
GUELPH PUBLIC LIBRARY
100 Norfolk St, Guelph, ON, N1H 4J6
(519) 824-6220
Emp Here 80
SIC 8231 Libraries

D-U-N-S 20-563-1927   (BR)
HAMMOND MANUFACTURING COMPANY LIMITED
7 Nicholas Beaver Rd, Guelph, ON, N1H 6H9
(519) 763-1047
Emp Here 30
SIC 3469 Metal stampings, nec

D-U-N-S 24-011-4020   (BR)
HOLLISWEALTH ADVISORY SERVICES INC.
MIZEN INVESTMENT MANAGEMENT
50 Yarmouth St, Guelph, ON, N1H 4G3
(519) 836-5190
Emp Here 20
SIC 6282 Investment advice

D-U-N-S 24-000-2969   (BR)
HOME DEPOT OF CANADA INC
(*Suby of* The Home Depot Inc)
63 Woodlawn Rd W, Guelph, ON, N1H 1G8
(519) 780-3400
Emp Here 150
SIC 5251 Hardware stores

D-U-N-S 24-057-6553   (BR)
IMPERIAL TOBACCO COMPAGNIE LIMI-TEE
107 Woodlawn Rd W, Guelph, ON, N1H 1B4

Emp Here 600
SIC 2111 Cigarettes

D-U-N-S 25-305-2872   (BR)
INNVEST PROPERTIES CORP
COMFORT INN
(*Suby of* Innvest Properties Corp)
480 Silvercreek Pky N, Guelph, ON, N1H 7R5
(519) 763-1900
Emp Here 20
SIC 7011 Hotels and motels

D-U-N-S 25-136-0637   (BR)
LEON'S FURNITURE LIMITED
LEONS FURNITURE GUELPH
121 Silvercreek Pky N, Guelph, ON, N1H 3T3
(519) 767-5366
Emp Here 30
SIC 5712 Furniture stores

D-U-N-S 25-306-1931   (BR)
LINAMAR CORPORATION
VEHCOM MANUFACTURING
74 Campbell Rd, Guelph, ON, N1H 1C1
(519) 821-1650
Emp Here 482
SIC 3714 Motor vehicle parts and accessories

D-U-N-S 25-116-2343   (BR)
LINAMAR CORPORATION
ESTON MANUFACTURING
351 Silvercreek Pky N, Guelph, ON, N1H 1E6
(519) 763-0063
Emp Here 200
SIC 3714 Motor vehicle parts and accessories

D-U-N-S 20-109-5747   (BR)
LINAMAR CORPORATION
TRAXLE MANUFACTURING
280 Speedvale Ave W, Guelph, ON, N1H 1C4
(519) 824-8899
Emp Here 228
SIC 3714 Motor vehicle parts and accessories

D-U-N-S 25-105-7402   (BR)
LINAMAR CORPORATION
COMTECH MANUFACTURING
355 Silvercreek Pky N, Guelph, ON, N1H 1E6
(519) 821-7576
Emp Here 230
SIC 3714 Motor vehicle parts and accessories

D-U-N-S 24-494-3838   (BR)
LINAMAR CORPORATION
LPP MANUFACTURING
347 Silvercreek Pky N, Guelph, ON, N1H 1E6
(519) 837-3055
Emp Here 100
SIC 3714 Motor vehicle parts and accessories

D-U-N-S 25-690-4939   (HQ)
MAMMOET CANADA HOLDINGS INC
7504 Mclean Rd E, Guelph, ON, N1H 6H9
(519) 740-0550
Emp Here 70   *Emp Total* 60,800
Sales 149,948,048
SIC 6712 Bank holding companies
Dir Tim Sittler
Dir Roderik Van Seumeren

D-U-N-S 20-279-6710   (SL)
MAMMOET CRANE (ASSETS) INC
7504 Mclean Rd E, Guelph, ON, N1H 6H9
(519) 740-0550
Emp Here 100   *Sales* 13,860,016
SIC 3537 Industrial trucks and tractors
Pr Keith Triginer

D-U-N-S 20-251-5748   (BR)
MAPLE LEAF FOODS INC
7474 Mclean Rd, Guelph, ON, N1H 6H9
(519) 780-3560
Emp Here 30
SIC 8731 Commercial physical research

D-U-N-S 25-615-4980   (BR)
METRO ONTARIO INC
FOOD BASICS
222 Silvercreek Pky N, Guelph, ON, N1H 7P8
(519) 766-4666
Emp Here 45
SIC 5411 Grocery stores

D-U-N-S 25-503-1569   (BR)
METROLAND MEDIA GROUP LTD
GUELPH MERCURY, THE
14 Macdonell St Unit 8, Guelph, ON, N1H 2Z3
(519) 822-4310
Emp Here 60
SIC 2711 Newspapers

D-U-N-S 24-367-5274   (BR)
METSO MINERALS CANADA INC
644 Imperial Rd N, Guelph, ON, N1H 7M3
(519) 821-7070
Emp Here 20
SIC 5082 Construction and mining machinery

D-U-N-S 20-179-2681   (BR)
NESTLE CANADA INC
NESTLE WATERS CANADA DIV
101 Brock Rd S, Guelph, ON, N1H 6H9
(519) 763-9462
Emp Here 200
SIC 5149 Groceries and related products, nec

D-U-N-S 24-346-6278   (SL)
ORION FOUNDRY (CANADA), ULC
MOXY MEDIA
503 Imperial Rd N, Guelph, ON, N1H 6T9
(519) 827-1999
Emp Here 70   *Sales* 3,866,917
SIC 7374 Data processing and preparation

D-U-N-S 24-386-3854   (BR)
PNR RAILWORKS INC
65 Massey Rd Unit C, Guelph, ON, N1H 7M6
(519) 837-2018
Emp Here 25
SIC 1629 Heavy construction, nec

D-U-N-S 24-849-9175   (SL)
PANOPTIC SOFTWARE INC
367 Woodlawn Rd W Unit 2, Guelph, ON, N1H 7K9
(519) 504-1232
Emp Here 40   *Sales* 7,350,166
SIC 3663 Radio and t.v. communications equipment
Pr Pr Marc Lacoste

D-U-N-S 25-594-7541   (BR)
PAVACO PLASTICS INC
551 Imperial Rd N, Guelph, ON, N1H 7M2

Emp Here 50
SIC 2821 Plastics materials and resins

D-U-N-S 24-318-5105   (SL)
QUALITY PLATES & PROFILES LIMITED
(*Suby of* Canerector Inc)
20 Nicholas Beaver Rd, Guelph, ON, N1H 6H9
(519) 837-4000
Emp Here 40   *Sales* 5,197,506
SIC 3312 Blast furnaces and steel mills

D-U-N-S 20-288-9759   (BR)
R.J. BURNSIDE & ASSOCIATES LIMITED
292 Speedvale Ave W Unit 7, Guelph, ON, N1H 1C4
(519) 823-4995
Emp Here 20
SIC 8711 Engineering services

D-U-N-S 24-062-1862   (HQ)
RLB LLP
(*Suby of* RLB LLP)
15 Lewis Rd Suite 1, Guelph, ON, N1H 1E9
(519) 822-9933
Emp Here 43   *Emp Total* 55
Sales 2,407,703
SIC 8721 Accounting, auditing, and book-keeping

D-U-N-S 25-300-4998   (BR)
REDBERRY FRANCHISING CORP
BURGER KING
200 Silvercreek Pky N, Guelph, ON, N1H 7P7
(519) 763-8281
Emp Here 25
SIC 5812 Eating places

D-U-N-S 25-965-2170   (BR)
ROYAL BANK OF CANADA
RBC
(*Suby of* Royal Bank Of Canada)
117 Silvercreek Pky N, Guelph, ON, N1H 3T2
(519) 767-4750
Emp Here 25

SIC 6021 National commercial banks

D-U-N-S 24-816-9153   (BR)
RUSSEL METALS INC
COMCO PIPE & SUPPLY COMPANY
14 Curve Cres, Guelph, ON, N1H 6H9
(519) 763-1114
Emp Here 30
SIC 5051 Metals service centers and offices

D-U-N-S 20-320-1483   (BR)
SGS CANADA INC
SGS AGRI-FOOD LABORATORY
503 Imperial Rd N Suite 1, Guelph, ON, N1H 6T9
(519) 837-1600
Emp Here 25
SIC 8731 Commercial physical research

D-U-N-S 24-336-4424   (HQ)
SANIMAX LTD
5068 Whitelaw Rd Suite 6, Guelph, ON, N1H 6J3
(519) 824-2381
Emp Here 56   *Emp Total* 1,120
Sales 8,536,402
SIC 4953 Refuse systems
Pr Martin Couture

D-U-N-S 24-346-5379   (BR)
SCHLEGEL VILLAGES INC
THE VILLAGE OF RIVERSIDE GLEN
60 Woodlawn Rd E, Guelph, ON, N1H 8M8
(519) 822-5272
Emp Here 130
SIC 6513 Apartment building operators

D-U-N-S 24-468-0398   (BR)
SKYJACK INC
PLANT 1
55 Campbell Rd, Guelph, ON, N1H 1B9
(519) 837-0888
Emp Here 100
SIC 3694 Engine electrical equipment

D-U-N-S 20-082-6043   (SL)
SMITH VALERIOTE LAW FIRM LLP
105 Silvercreek Pky N Unit 100, Guelph, ON, N1H 6S4
(519) 837-2100
Emp Here 50   *Sales* 4,304,681
SIC 8111 Legal services

D-U-N-S 20-699-6238   (SL)
SNOWBEAR LIMITED
SNOWBEAR TRAILERS
(*Suby of* Catalyst Capital Group Inc, The)
155 Dawson Rd, Guelph, ON, N1H 1A4
(519) 767-1115
Emp Here 80   *Sales* 12,532,976
SIC 3523 Farm machinery and equipment
Andre Sa Machado
Pr Pr Tim French
Dir George So
Dir Newton Glassman

D-U-N-S 24-429-6778   (BR)
SOCIETE XYLEM CANADA
XYLEM APPLIED WATER SYSTEMS
55 Royal Rd, Guelph, ON, N1H 1T1
(519) 821-1900
Emp Here 90
SIC 5084 Industrial machinery and equipment

D-U-N-S 24-101-2108   (BR)
STAPLES CANADA INC
STAPLES THE BUSINESS DEPOT
(*Suby of* Staples, Inc.)
20 Woodlawn Rd E, Guelph, ON, N1H 1G7
(519) 822-2344
Emp Here 40
SIC 5943 Stationery stores

D-U-N-S 24-344-0760   (BR)
SUPERIOR PLUS LP
SUPERIOR PROPANE
7022 Wellington Rd, Guelph, ON, N1H 6H8
(807) 223-2980
Emp Here 170

SIC 5984 Liquefied petroleum gas dealers

D-U-N-S 24-318-6736   (BR)
SYNNEX CANADA LIMITED
EMJ DATA SYSTEMS DIV OF
107 Woodlawn Rd W, Guelph, ON, N1H 1B4
(519) 837-2444
Emp Here 140
SIC 5045 Computers, peripherals, and software

D-U-N-S 24-211-6143   (HQ)
TEUTECH INDUSTRIES INC
361 Speedvale Ave W Suite 29, Guelph, ON, N1H 1C7
(519) 836-3180
Emp Here 20   *Emp Total* 150
Sales 11,781,014
SIC 3599 Industrial machinery, nec
Pr Pr Antony Steer
Judith Steer

D-U-N-S 25-642-1780   (BR)
TEUTECH INDUSTRIES INC
SPEEDVALE MANUFACTURING LOCATION
361 Speedvale Ave W, Guelph, ON, N1H 1C7
(519) 822-8012
Emp Here 20
SIC 3599 Industrial machinery, nec

D-U-N-S 24-210-1496   (SL)
TIM HORTONS LTD
1 Nicholas Beaver Rd, Guelph, ON, N1H 6H9
(519) 822-4748
Emp Here 50   *Sales* 1,992,377
SIC 5461 Retail bakeries

D-U-N-S 24-849-1938   (SL)
TRASHETERIA INC
52 Macdonell St, Guelph, ON, N1H 2Z3
(519) 767-1694
Emp Here 55   *Sales* 2,042,900
SIC 5813 Drinking places

D-U-N-S 25-302-1778   (BR)
UPI INC
CENTRAL ONTARIO ENERGY ALLIANCE
7060 Wellington Road 124, Guelph, ON, N1H 6J3
(519) 824-7370
Emp Here 25
SIC 5171 Petroleum bulk stations and terminals

D-U-N-S 24-310-7641   (BR)
UNISYNC GROUP LIMITED
72 Farquhar St, Guelph, ON, N1H 3N3

Emp Here 80
SIC 2337 Women's and misses' suits and coats

D-U-N-S 20-025-4139   (BR)
UPPER GRAND DISTRICT SCHOOL BOARD, THE
GUELPH COLLEGIATE & VOCATIONAL INSTITUTE
(*Suby of* Upper Grand District School Board, The)
155 Paisley St Suite Upper, Guelph, ON, N1H 2P3
(519) 824-9800
Emp Here 100
SIC 8211 Elementary and secondary schools

D-U-N-S 20-024-9493   (BR)
UPPER GRAND DISTRICT SCHOOL BOARD, THE
WILLOW ROAD PUBLIC SCHOOL
(*Suby of* Upper Grand District School Board, The)
125 Willow Rd, Guelph, ON, N1H 1W4
(519) 821-1760
Emp Here 50
SIC 8211 Elementary and secondary schools

D-U-N-S 20-025-5078   (BR)
UPPER GRAND DISTRICT SCHOOL

BOARD, THE
PAISLEY ROAD PUBLIC SCHOOL
(*Suby of* Upper Grand District School Board, The)
406 Paisley Rd, Guelph, ON, N1H 2R3
(519) 822-0675
Emp Here 40
SIC 8211 Elementary and secondary schools

D-U-N-S 20-004-8507   (BR)
UPPER GRAND DISTRICT SCHOOL BOARD, THE
WESTWOOD PUBLIC SCHOOL
(*Suby of* Upper Grand District School Board, The)
495 Willow Rd, Guelph, ON, N1H 7C7
(519) 823-5450
Emp Here 40
SIC 8211 Elementary and secondary schools

D-U-N-S 20-291-3096   (BR)
UPPER GRAND DISTRICT SCHOOL BOARD, THE
MITCHELL WOOD PUBLIC SCHOOL
(*Suby of* Upper Grand District School Board, The)
670 Willow Rd, Guelph, ON, N1H 8K2
(519) 829-3123
Emp Here 40
SIC 8211 Elementary and secondary schools

D-U-N-S 20-290-5183   (BR)
UPPER GRAND DISTRICT SCHOOL BOARD, THE
CENTRAL PUBLIC SCHOOL
(*Suby of* Upper Grand District School Board, The)
97 Dublin St N, Guelph, ON, N1H 4N2
(519) 821-7990
Emp Here 20
SIC 8211 Elementary and secondary schools

D-U-N-S 25-625-9367   (BR)
VALUE VILLAGE STORES, INC
(*Suby of* Savers, Inc.)
214 Silvercreek Pky N, Guelph, ON, N1H 7P8
(519) 821-9994
Emp Here 60
SIC 5399 Miscellaneous general merchandise

D-U-N-S 24-329-8515   (BR)
WAL-MART CANADA CORP
11 Woodlawn Rd W, Guelph, ON, N1H 1G8
(519) 767-1600
Emp Here 200
SIC 5311 Department stores

D-U-N-S 24-343-2692   (BR)
WATERLOO WELLINGTON COMMUNITY CARE ACCESS CENTRE
WATERLOO WELLINGTON CCAC
450 Speedvale Ave W Suite 201, Guelph, ON, N1H 7G7
(519) 823-2550
Emp Here 150
SIC 8082 Home health care services

D-U-N-S 20-804-2981   (BR)
WAYCON INTERNATIONAL TRUCKS LTD
(*Suby of* 397217 Ontario Limited)
48 Dawson Rd, Guelph, ON, N1H 5V1
(519) 821-0070
Emp Here 45
SIC 5511 New and used car dealers

D-U-N-S 20-591-9868   (BR)
WELLINGTON CATHOLIC DISTRICT SCHOOL BOARD
ST PETER CATHOLIC SCHOOL
150 Westwood Rd, Guelph, ON, N1H 7G1
(519) 836-3730
Emp Here 50
SIC 8211 Elementary and secondary schools

D-U-N-S 20-710-7728   (BR)
WELLINGTON CATHOLIC DISTRICT SCHOOL BOARD
ST JOSEPH CATHOLIC SCHOOL

10 Guelph St, Guelph, ON, N1H 5Y8
(519) 836-2671
Emp Here 30
SIC 8211 Elementary and secondary schools

D-U-N-S 20-024-9519   (BR)
WELLINGTON CATHOLIC DISTRICT SCHOOL BOARD
OUR LADY OF LOURDES CATHOLIC HIGH SCHOOL
54 Westmount Rd, Guelph, ON, N1H 5H7
(519) 836-2170
Emp Here 75
SIC 8211 Elementary and secondary schools

D-U-N-S 24-306-4391   (BR)
WESTROCK COMPANY OF CANADA INC
(*Suby of* Westrock Company)
390 Woodlawn Rd W, Guelph, ON, N1H 7K3
(519) 821-4930
Emp Here 350
SIC 2653 Corrugated and solid fiber boxes

D-U-N-S 25-594-7640   (BR)
WINNERS MERCHANTS INTERNATIONAL L.P.
WINNERS
(*Suby of* The TJX Companies Inc)
130 Silvercreek Pky N, Guelph, ON, N1H 7Y5
(519) 823-2636
Emp Here 40
SIC 5651 Family clothing stores

Guelph, ON N1K
Wellington County

D-U-N-S 25-251-7388   (SL)
ACC FARMERS' FINANCIAL
ACC
660 Speedvale Ave W Unit 201, Guelph, ON, N1K 1E5
(519) 766-0544
Emp Here 40   *Sales* 54,871,440
SIC 6159 Miscellaneous business credit institutions
Genl Mgr Brian Hughes
Dir Kenneth Smith
Donald Ledrew

D-U-N-S 20-973-5299   (BR)
BDO CANADA LLP
660 Speedvale Ave W Suite 201, Guelph, ON, N1K 1E5
(519) 824-5410
Emp Here 25
SIC 8721 Accounting, auditing, and bookkeeping

D-U-N-S 24-212-8734   (BR)
HOOD PACKAGING CORPORATION
(*Suby of* Hood Packaging Corporation)
364 Massey Rd, Guelph, ON, N1K 1C4
(519) 821-2570
Emp Here 50
SIC 2674 Bags: uncoated paper and multiwall

D-U-N-S 24-623-5746   (BR)
JOHNSON & JOHNSON INC
MCNEIL CONSUMER HEALTH CARE DIV OF
(*Suby of* Johnson & Johnson)
890 Woodlawn Rd W, Guelph, ON, N1K 1A5

Emp Here 350
SIC 2834 Pharmaceutical preparations

D-U-N-S 24-386-8374   (BR)
JOHNSON & JOHNSON INC
MCNEIL CONSUMER HEALTH CARE DIV OF
(*Suby of* Johnson & Johnson)
890 Woodlawn Rd W, Guelph, ON, N1K 1A5
(519) 826-6226
Emp Here 300

SIC 2834 Pharmaceutical preparations

D-U-N-S 25-595-5999   (BR)
JONES PACKAGING INC
271 Massey Rd, Guelph, ON, N1K 1B2

Emp Here 100
SIC 2657 Folding paperboard boxes

D-U-N-S 20-515-2171   (BR)
LINAMAR CORPORATION
TRANSGEAR MANUFACTURING
400 Massey Rd, Guelph, ON, N1K 1C4
(519) 763-5370
Emp Here 50
SIC 3714 Motor vehicle parts and accessories

D-U-N-S 25-687-4405   (BR)
LINAMAR CORPORATION
LINAMAR PERFORMANCE CENTRE
30 Minto Rd, Guelph, ON, N1K 1H5
(519) 821-1429
Emp Here 400
SIC 3714 Motor vehicle parts and accessories

D-U-N-S 24-926-6941   (BR)
LINAMAR CORPORATION
AUTOCOM MANUFACTURING
375 Massey Rd, Guelph, ON, N1K 1B2
(519) 822-9008
Emp Here 380
SIC 3714 Motor vehicle parts and accessories

D-U-N-S 24-390-3643   (BR)
LINAMAR CORPORATION
*THE FRANK HASENFRATZ CENTRE OF EX-
CELLENCE IN MANUFACTURING, DIV OF*
700 Woodlawn Rd W, Guelph, ON, N1K 1G4
(519) 515-0001
Emp Here 50
SIC 3714 Motor vehicle parts and accessories

D-U-N-S 20-109-5663   (BR)
LINAMAR CORPORATION
LINEX MANUFACTURING
355 Massey Rd, Guelph, ON, N1K 1B2
(519) 763-0680
Emp Here 490
SIC 7389 Business services, nec

D-U-N-S 24-844-0059   (BR)
LINAMAR CORPORATION
QUADRAD MANUFACTURING
30 Malcolm Rd, Guelph, ON, N1K 1A9
(519) 767-0219
Emp Here 400
SIC 3714 Motor vehicle parts and accessories

D-U-N-S 24-858-3648   (BR)
LINAMAR CORPORATION
HASTECH MFG. PLANT 2
381 Massey Rd, Guelph, ON, N1K 1B2
(519) 767-9711
Emp Here 100
SIC 3714 Motor vehicle parts and accessories

D-U-N-S 20-104-0677   (BR)
LINAMAR CORPORATION
SPINIC MANUFACTURING
285 Massey Rd, Guelph, ON, N1K 1B2
(519) 763-0704
Emp Here 170
SIC 3714 Motor vehicle parts and accessories

D-U-N-S 24-802-3744   (BR)
LINAMAR CORPORATION
POWERCOR MANUFACTURING
545 Elmira Rd N, Guelph, ON, N1K 1C2
(226) 326-0125
Emp Here 26
SIC 3714 Motor vehicle parts and accessories

D-U-N-S 24-318-5290   (BR)
LINAMAR CORPORATION
CAMCOR MANUFACTURING
150 Arrow Rd, Guelph, ON, N1K 1T4
(519) 837-0100
Emp Here 20

SIC 3531 Construction machinery

D-U-N-S 20-176-3070   (BR)
LINAMAR CORPORATION
CAMTAC MANUFACTURING
148 Arrow Rd, Guelph, ON, N1K 1T4
(519) 780-2270
Emp Here 425
SIC 3714 Motor vehicle parts and accessories

D-U-N-S 25-362-6592   (BR)
LINAMAR CORPORATION
HASTECH MANUFACTURING
301 Massey Rd, Guelph, ON, N1K 1B2
(519) 836-7554
Emp Here 275
SIC 3714 Motor vehicle parts and accessories

D-U-N-S 24-341-0565   (BR)
LINAMAR CORPORATION
CEMTOL MANUFACTURING
150 Arrow Rd, Guelph, ON, N1K 1T4
(519) 822-6627
Emp Here 250
SIC 3714 Motor vehicle parts and accessories

D-U-N-S 25-542-4285   (BR)
LINAMAR CORPORATION
CORVEX MANUFACTURING
12 Independence Pl, Guelph, ON, N1K 1H8
(519) 763-7786
Emp Here 250
SIC 3714 Motor vehicle parts and accessories

D-U-N-S 25-192-2977   (BR)
LINAMAR CORPORATION
ROCTEL MANUFACTURING
415 Elmira Rd N, Guelph, ON, N1K 1H3
(519) 763-5369
Emp Here 250
SIC 3714 Motor vehicle parts and accessories

D-U-N-S 24-000-6077   (BR)
LINAMAR CORPORATION
LINAMAR GEAR
32 Independence Pl, Guelph, ON, N1K 1H8
(519) 827-9423
Emp Here 80
SIC 3714 Motor vehicle parts and accessories

D-U-N-S 25-676-1834   (BR)
MAGNA EXTERIORS INC
POLYCON INDUSTRIES
65 Independence Pl, Guelph, ON, N1K 1H8
(519) 763-6042
Emp Here 35
SIC 3714 Motor vehicle parts and accessories

D-U-N-S 25-627-3061   (SL)
MARBLE ELECTRONICS INC
650 Woodlawn Rd W Suite 16a, Guelph, ON,
N1K 1B8
(519) 767-2863
Emp Here 50
SIC 3647 Vehicular lighting equipment

D-U-N-S 24-359-2412   (SL)
PATENE (1997) LIMITED
641 Speedvale Ave W, Guelph, ON, N1K 1E6
(519) 822-1890
Emp Here 370   *Sales* 84,149,980
SIC 6712 Bank holding companies
Pr Pr Patrick George

D-U-N-S 25-320-9043   (BR)
PUROLATOR INC.
PUROLATOR INC
147 Massey Rd, Guelph, ON, N1K 1B2
(905) 660-6007
Emp Here 200
SIC 4731 Freight transportation arrangement

D-U-N-S 20-051-9668   (SL)
RANGER METAL PRODUCTS LIMITED
31 Malcolm Rd, Guelph, ON, N1K 1A7

Emp Here 250   *Sales* 58,378,880
SIC 3496 Miscellaneous fabricated wire prod-

ucts
Pr Pr Marc A Dube
VP Mfg Peter Valeriote
Dir Gary Paprocki
Recvr Joseph Edward Allan Albert

D-U-N-S 24-075-5298   (SL)
ROSMAR DRYWALL LTD
355 Elmira Rd N Unit 131, Guelph, ON, N1K
1S5
(519) 821-6056
Emp Here 50   *Sales* 4,231,721
SIC 1742 Plastering, drywall, and insulation

D-U-N-S 25-477-9135   (SL)
ROYAL CITY AMBULANCE SERVICE LTD
355 Elmira Rd N Suite 134, Guelph, ON, N1K
1S5
(519) 824-1510
Emp Here 95   *Sales* 4,888,367
SIC 4119 Local passenger transportation, nec

D-U-N-S 24-875-6371   (BR)
SANDVIK CANADA, INC
*SANDVIK PROCESS SYSTEMS OF
CANADA*
510 Governors Rd, Guelph, ON, N1E 1E3
(519) 836-4322
Emp Here 20
SIC 3535 Conveyors and conveying equip-
ment

D-U-N-S 20-592-0031   (BR)
**UPPER GRAND DISTRICT SCHOOL
BOARD, THE**
TAYLOR EVANS PUBLIC SCHOOL
(*Suby of* Upper Grand District School Board,
The)
271 Stephanie Dr, Guelph, ON, N1K 1T1
(519) 766-4544
Emp Here 40
SIC 8211 Elementary and secondary schools

D-U-N-S 20-024-9535   (BR)
**WELLINGTON CATHOLIC DISTRICT
SCHOOL BOARD**
ST FRANCIS OF ASSISI SCHOOL
287 Imperial Rd S, Guelph, ON, N1K 1Z4
(519) 821-9160
Emp Here 45
SIC 8211 Elementary and secondary schools

Guelph, ON N1L
Wellington County

D-U-N-S 20-556-6235   (SL)
ELLIOTT, FRED COACH LINES LIMITED
ELMIRA BUS LINES, A DIV OF
760 Victoria Rd S, Guelph, ON, N1L 1C6
(519) 822-5225
Emp Here 85   *Sales* 3,109,686
SIC 4151 School buses

D-U-N-S 25-595-6252   (BR)
**GOVERNING COUNCIL OF THE SALVA-
TION ARMY IN CANADA, THE**
THE SALVATION ARMY
1320 Gordon St, Guelph, ON, N1L 1H3
(519) 836-9360
Emp Here 20
SIC 8661 Religious organizations

D-U-N-S 24-341-0755   (SL)
SAPPORO CANADA INC
SLEEMAN BREWERY
551 Clair Rd W, Guelph, ON, N1L 1E9
(519) 822-1834
Emp Here 100   *Sales* 15,175,826
SIC 6712 Bank holding companies
Dir John W. Sleeman
Dir Nobuhiro Hashiba
Dir Yoshiyuki Mochida

D-U-N-S 24-737-5322   (HQ)
SLEEMAN BREWERIES LTD

OKANAGAN SPRING BREWERY
551 Clair Rd W, Guelph, ON, N1L 1E9
(519) 822-1834
Emp Here 200   *Emp Total* 7,484
Sales 115,991,009
SIC 2082 Malt beverages
John W Sleeman
Rick Knudson
Sec Dan Rogozynski
Dan Fox
Steve Pelkey
John Bailey

D-U-N-S 24-351-7005   (BR)
**STUDENT TRANSPORTATION OF CANADA
INC**
760 Victoria Rd S, Guelph, ON, N1L 1C6
(519) 822-5225
Emp Here 20
SIC 4151 School buses

D-U-N-S 24-319-8525   (BR)
TDL GROUP CORP, THE
TIM HORTON REGIONAL OFFICE
950 Southgate Dr, Guelph, ON, N1L 1S7
(519) 824-1304
Emp Here 100
SIC 5812 Eating places

D-U-N-S 20-655-1272   (BR)
**UPPER GRAND DISTRICT SCHOOL
BOARD, THE**
SIR ISAAC BROCK PUBLIC SCHOOL
(*Suby of* Upper Grand District School Board,
The)
111 Colonial Dr, Guelph, ON, N1L 1R3
(519) 824-1442
Emp Here 40
SIC 8211 Elementary and secondary schools

D-U-N-S 20-861-1959   (BR)
**UPPER GRAND DISTRICT SCHOOL
BOARD, THE**
*WELLINGTON CENTRE FOR CONTINUING
EDUCATION*
(*Suby of* Upper Grand District School Board,
The)
1428 Gordon St, Guelph, ON, N1L 1C8
(519) 836-7280
Emp Here 250
SIC 8211 Elementary and secondary schools

D-U-N-S 20-524-3335   (BR)
**WELLINGTON CATHOLIC DISTRICT
SCHOOL BOARD**
*BISHOP MACDONELL CATHOLIC HIGH
SCHOOL*
200 Clair Rd W, Guelph, ON, N1L 1G1
(519) 822-8502
Emp Here 700
SIC 8211 Elementary and secondary schools

D-U-N-S 24-095-6164   (BR)
**WELLINGTON CATHOLIC DISTRICT
SCHOOL BOARD**
ST PAUL CATHOLIC SCHOOL
182 Clairfields Dr E, Guelph, ON, N1L 1N4
(519) 824-9470
Emp Here 35
SIC 8211 Elementary and secondary schools

Hagersville, ON N0A
Haldimand County

D-U-N-S 20-410-7908   (SL)
ALMAS, R. F. COMPANY LIMITED
2146 Sandusk Rd, Hagersville, ON, N0A 1H0
(905) 768-3170
Emp Here 50   *Sales* 3,064,349
SIC 5651 Family clothing stores

D-U-N-S 20-710-6449   (BR)
**BRANT HALDIMAND NORFOLK CATHOLIC
DISTRICT SCHOOL BOARD**

ST MARY'S SCHOOL
92 Main St, Hagersville, ON, N0A 1H0
(905) 768-5151
Emp Here 24
SIC 8211 Elementary and secondary schools

D-U-N-S 20-699-6527   (BR)
EXTENDICARE INC
ANSON PLACE CARE CENTRE
85 Main St Rr 6, Hagersville, ON, N0A 1H0
(905) 768-1641
Emp Here 60
SIC 8051 Skilled nursing care facilities

D-U-N-S 20-710-6241   (BR)
GRAND ERIE DISTRICT SCHOOL BOARD
HAGERSVILLE ELEMENTARY SCHOOL
(*Suby of* Grand Erie District School Board)
40 Parkview Rd, Hagersville, ON, N0A 1H0
(905) 768-3012
Emp Here 50
SIC 8211 Elementary and secondary schools

D-U-N-S 20-291-6693   (BR)
GRAND ERIE DISTRICT SCHOOL BOARD
HAGERSVILLE SECONDARY SCHOOL
(*Suby of* Grand Erie District School Board)
70 Parkview Rd, Hagersville, ON, N0A 1H0
(905) 768-3318
Emp Here 80
SIC 8211 Elementary and secondary schools

D-U-N-S 24-095-6479   (BR)
HEWITT'S DAIRY LIMITED
DAIRY BAR
4210 Highway 6 Rr 6, Hagersville, ON, N0A 1H0
(905) 768-5266
Emp Here 20
SIC 5812 Eating places

D-U-N-S 20-052-1771   (HQ)
HEWITT'S DAIRY LIMITED
128 King St E, Hagersville, ON, N0A 1H0
(905) 768-3524
Emp Here 44   *Emp Total* 412
Sales 18,092,717
SIC 5143 Dairy products, except dried or canned
Pr Michael Barrett
Sec Ove Hansen
Dir Steve Dolson
Treas John Rebry
Dir Mark Hamel
Dir Roger Harrop
Dir Paul Vickers

D-U-N-S 25-295-6255   (BR)
MARCH OF DIMES CANADA
24 Main St N, Hagersville, ON, N0A 1H0
(905) 768-0041
Emp Here 30
SIC 8331 Job training and related services

D-U-N-S 20-009-9427   (BR)
PETERBILT OF ONTARIO INC
PETERBILT OF HALDIMAND
4011 Highway 6 S, Hagersville, ON, N0A 1H0
(905) 768-1300
Emp Here 31
SIC 5013 Motor vehicle supplies and new parts

D-U-N-S 24-346-5478   (BR)
SALVERDA ENTERPRISES INC
TIM HORTONS
5 Railway St, Hagersville, ON, N0A 1H0
(905) 768-7777
Emp Here 44
SIC 5812 Eating places

Haileybury, ON P0J
Timiskaming County

D-U-N-S 25-318-8510   (BR)

BOART LONGYEAR CANADA
BOART LONGYEAR
310 Niven St S, Haileybury, ON, P0J 1K0
(705) 672-3800
Emp Here 50
SIC 3532 Mining machinery

D-U-N-S 25-263-6857   (BR)
CONSEIL SCOLAIRE CATHOLIQUE DE DISTRICT DES GRANDES RIVIERES, LE
ECOLE CATHOLIQUE STE CROIX
304 Rorke Ave, Haileybury, ON, P0J 1K0
(705) 672-3661
Emp Here 23
SIC 8211 Elementary and secondary schools

D-U-N-S 25-700-3384   (BR)
EXTENDICARE INC
EXTENDICARE TRI TOWN
143 Bruce St, Haileybury, ON, P0J 1K0
(705) 672-2151
Emp Here 55
SIC 8051 Skilled nursing care facilities

D-U-N-S 25-591-3139   (BR)
JARLETTE LTD
TEMISKAMING LODGE
100 Bruce St, Haileybury, ON, P0J 1K0
(705) 672-2123
Emp Here 80
SIC 8051 Skilled nursing care facilities

D-U-N-S 25-645-7789   (BR)
LOBLAWS INC
VALU-MART
100 Rorke Ave, Haileybury, ON, P0J 1K0

Emp Here 35
SIC 5411 Grocery stores

D-U-N-S 20-980-7445   (BR)
NORTHERN COLLEGE OF APPLIED ARTS & TECHNOLOGY
640 Latford St, Haileybury, ON, P0J 1K0
(705) 672-3376
Emp Here 30
SIC 8221 Colleges and universities

Haley Station, ON K0J
Renfrew County

D-U-N-S 20-193-6494   (BR)
MAGELLAN AEROSPACE LIMITED
HALEY INDUSTRIES
634 Magnesium Rd, Haley Station, ON, K0J 1Y0
(613) 432-8441
Emp Here 500
SIC 3365 Aluminum foundries

D-U-N-S 20-052-2928   (BR)
TIMMINCO LIMITED
TIMMINCO METALS
962 Magnesium Rd Gd, Haley Station, ON, K0J 1Y0

Emp Here 50
SIC 2819 Industrial inorganic chemicals, nec

Haliburton, ON K0M
Haliburton County

D-U-N-S 24-991-8806   (SL)
2114185 ONTARIO CORP
PINESTONE RESORT & CONFERENCE CENTRE
4252 County Rd 21 Rr 3, Haliburton, ON, K0M 1S0
(705) 457-1800
Emp Here 50   *Sales* 2,188,821
SIC 7011 Hotels and motels

D-U-N-S 20-845-0473   (BR)
CENTRAL EAST COMMUNITY CARE ACCESS CENTRE FOUNDATION
13321 Hwy 118, Haliburton, ON, K0M 1S0
(905) 430-3308
Emp Here 40
SIC 8322 Individual and family services

D-U-N-S 24-485-5714   (BR)
COMMUNITY LIVING ONTARIO
COMMUNITY LIVING HALIBURTON
713 Mountain St, Haliburton, ON, K0M 1S0
(705) 457-1452
Emp Here 30
SIC 8699 Membership organizations, nec

D-U-N-S 20-552-0104   (BR)
EXTENDICARE (CANADA) INC
EXTENDICARE HALIBURTON
167 Park St, Haliburton, ON, K0M 1S0
(705) 457-1722
Emp Here 30
SIC 8051 Skilled nursing care facilities

D-U-N-S 25-181-5684   (BR)
FIRSTCANADA ULC
FIRST STUDENT
19 Wallings Rd, Haliburton, ON, K0M 1S0
(705) 457-2567
Emp Here 60
SIC 4151 School buses

D-U-N-S 25-646-2342   (BR)
HALIBURTON HIGHLANDS HEALTH SERVICES CORPORATION
HALIBURTON HOSPITAL
7199 Gelert Rd, Haliburton, ON, K0M 1S0
(705) 457-1392
Emp Here 210
SIC 8062 General medical and surgical hospitals

D-U-N-S 25-069-1888   (SL)
PATIENT NEWS PUBLISHING LTD
5152 County Rd 121, Haliburton, ON, K0M 1S0
(705) 457-4030
Emp Here 70   *Sales* 4,085,799
SIC 2741 Miscellaneous publishing

D-U-N-S 20-288-5948   (BR)
SIR SANDFORD FLEMING COLLEGE OF APPLIED ARTS AND TECHNOLOGY
FLEMING COLLEGE HALIBURTON SCHOOL OF THE ARTS
297 College Dr, Haliburton, ON, K0M 1S0
(705) 457-1680
Emp Here 20
SIC 8222 Junior colleges

D-U-N-S 24-120-2741   (SL)
TODD'S YIG 803 LTD
5121 County Rd 21 Rr 3, Haliburton, ON, K0M 1S0
(705) 455-9775
Emp Here 70   *Sales* 12,681,250
SIC 5411 Grocery stores
Pr Steve Todd

D-U-N-S 20-009-6621   (BR)
TRILLIUM LAKELANDS DISTRICT SCHOOL BOARD
STUART BAKER ELEMENTARY SCHOOL
1080 Grasslake Rd, Haliburton, ON, K0M 1S0
(705) 457-1342
Emp Here 30
SIC 8211 Elementary and secondary schools

D-U-N-S 25-185-2935   (BR)
TRILLIUM LAKELANDS DISTRICT SCHOOL BOARD
HALIBURTON HIGHLANDS SECONDARY SCHOOL
5358 County Rd 21, Haliburton, ON, K0M 1S0
(705) 457-2950
Emp Here 50
SIC 8211 Elementary and secondary schools

D-U-N-S 20-025-2570   (BR)
TRILLIUM LAKELANDS DISTRICT SCHOOL BOARD
J DOUGLAS HODGSON ELEMENTARY SCHOOL
1020 Grasslake Rd, Haliburton, ON, K0M 1S0
(705) 457-2922
Emp Here 45
SIC 8211 Elementary and secondary schools

D-U-N-S 24-124-5476   (BR)
YMCA OF HAMILTON/BURLINGTON/BRANTFORD
YMCA WANAKITA
1883 Koshlong Lake Rd, Haliburton, ON, K0M 1S0
(705) 457-2132
Emp Here 100
SIC 7999 Amusement and recreation, nec

Hallebourg, ON P0L
Cochrane County

D-U-N-S 24-069-6083   (SL)
INDUSTRIES LACWOOD INC
949 Hwy 11 E, Hallebourg, ON, P0L 1L0
(705) 372-1978
Emp Here 50   *Sales* 4,666,700
SIC 2541 Wood partitions and fixtures

Halton Hills, ON L7G
Halton County

D-U-N-S 20-158-4042   (SL)
BRADFORD WHITE - CANADA INC
(*Suby of* Bradford White Corporation)
9 Brigden Gate, Halton Hills, ON, L7G 0A3
(905) 203-0600
Emp Here 30   *Sales* 9,266,009
SIC 5064 Electrical appliances, television and radio
Pr Nicholas Giuffre

Hamilton, ON L8E
Wentworth County

D-U-N-S 25-321-1049   (BR)
ABF FREIGHT SYSTEM CANADA, LTD
ABF TERMINAL #245
(*Suby of* Arcbest Corporation)
400 Grays Rd Suite 218, Hamilton, ON, L8E 3J6
(905) 573-0603
Emp Here 20
SIC 4213 Trucking, except local

D-U-N-S 20-525-8452   (BR)
AECOM CANADA LTD
45 Goderich Rd Suite 201, Hamilton, ON, L8E 4W8
(905) 578-3040
Emp Here 20
SIC 8711 Engineering services

D-U-N-S 24-000-2738   (BR)
CAA SOUTH CENTRAL ONTARIO
CAA STONEY CREEK
163 Centennial Pky N Suite 201, Hamilton, ON, L8E 1H8
(905) 525-1520
Emp Here 20
SIC 4724 Travel agencies

D-U-N-S 20-717-3790   (BR)
CANADIAN LINEN AND UNIFORM SERVICE CO
CANADIAN LINEN AND UNIFORM SERVICE CO
(*Suby of* Ameripride Services, Inc.)
350 Grays Rd, Hamilton, ON, L8E 2Z2

---

(905) 560-2411
Emp Here 20
SIC 7213 Linen supply

D-U-N-S 25-826-8192　　(BR)
CANPAR TRANSPORT L.P.
CANPAR HAMILTON
(*Suby of* Canpar Transport L.P.)
41 Brockley Dr Suite 1, Hamilton, ON, L8E
3C3
(905) 573-3077
Emp Here 35
SIC 7389 Business services, nec

D-U-N-S 20-303-3147　　(BR)
CARA OPERATIONS LIMITED
KELSEY'S
(*Suby of* Cara Holdings Limited)
200 Centennial Pky N, Hamilton, ON, L8E 4A1

Emp Here 90
SIC 5812 Eating places

D-U-N-S 20-095-1874　　(BR)
E.S. FOX LIMITED
35 Goderich Rd Unit 1-3, Hamilton, ON, L8E
4P2
(905) 547-7225
Emp Here 25
SIC 1731 Electrical work

D-U-N-S 25-318-9583　　(BR)
FIRSTCANADA ULC
FIRST STUDENT
50 Covington St, Hamilton, ON, L8E 2Y5
(905) 522-3232
Emp Here 250
SIC 4151 School buses

D-U-N-S 25-943-4769　　(BR)
G&K SERVICES CANADA INC
(*Suby of* Cintas Corporation)
440 Lake Ave N Suite 2, Hamilton, ON, L8E
3C2
(905) 560-4737
Emp Here 31
SIC 7299 Miscellaneous personal service

D-U-N-S 20-301-5339　　(BR)
GRAND & TOY LIMITED
(*Suby of* Office Depot, Inc.)
15 Keefer Crt, Hamilton, ON, L8E 4V4
(905) 561-3413
Emp Here 25
SIC 5112 Stationery and office supplies

D-U-N-S 20-185-0612　　(BR)
HAMILTON REGION CONSERVATION AUTHORITY
WILD WATERWORKS
585 Van Wagners Beach Rd, Hamilton, ON,
L8E 3L8
(905) 561-2292
Emp Here 103
SIC 7996 Amusement parks

D-U-N-S 20-710-7918　　(BR)
**HAMILTON-WENTWORTH　　DISTRICT
SCHOOL BOARD, THE**
LAKE AVENUE ELEMENTARY SCHOOL
157 Lake Ave N, Hamilton, ON, L8E 1L5
(905) 561-0402
Emp Here 65
SIC 8211 Elementary and secondary schools

D-U-N-S 25-514-3133　　(BR)
HOME DEPOT OF CANADA INC
HOME DEPOT
(*Suby of* The Home Depot Inc)
350 Centennial Pky N, Hamilton, ON, L8E 2X4
(905) 561-9755
Emp Here 250
SIC 5251 Hardware stores

D-U-N-S 20-088-6773　　(BR)
KIRBY INTERNATIONAL TRUCKS LTD
2 Arrowsmith Rd, Hamilton, ON, L8E 4H8
(905) 578-2211
Emp Here 40

SIC 5012 Automobiles and other motor vehicles

D-U-N-S 24-324-0004　　(BR)
KROMET INTERNATIONAL INC
ALUMABRITE ANODIZING, DIV
20 Milburn Rd, Hamilton, ON, L8E 3L9
(905) 561-7773
Emp Here 75
SIC 3469 Metal stampings, nec

D-U-N-S 24-686-8447　　(BR)
LE CHATEAU INC
(*Suby of* Le Chateau Inc)
75 Centennial Pky N Suite E1, Hamilton, ON,
L8E 2P2
(905) 573-8890
Emp Here 20
SIC 5621 Women's clothing stores

D-U-N-S 20-572-0683　　(BR)
LIFTOW LIMITED
21 Keefer Crt, Hamilton, ON, L8E 4V4
(905) 561-3351
Emp Here 20
SIC 5084 Industrial machinery and equipment

D-U-N-S 24-151-6934　　(BR)
LOCOCO, A. WHOLESALE LTD
2371 Barton St E, Hamilton, ON, L8E 2W9
(905) 561-3229
Emp Here 30
SIC 5431 Fruit and vegetable markets

D-U-N-S 25-484-2503　　(BR)
MAPLE LEAF FOODS INC
21 Brockley Dr, Hamilton, ON, L8E 3C3

Emp Here 350
SIC 2011 Meat packing plants

D-U-N-S 24-853-4252　　(BR)
METRO ONTARIO INC
FOOD BASICS
2500 Barton St E, Hamilton, ON, L8E 4A2
(905) 578-5454
Emp Here 120
SIC 5411 Grocery stores

D-U-N-S 25-486-6403　　(SL)
**NORTHAMPTON INNS (OAKVILLE EAST)
INC**
QUALITY HOTEL HAMILTON
51 Keefer Crt, Hamilton, ON, L8E 4W8
(905) 578-1212
Emp Here 55　　*Sales* 2,407,703
SIC 7011 Hotels and motels

D-U-N-S 20-859-9576　　(BR)
PACIFIC LINK COMMUNICATIONS INC
BELL WORLD
75 Centennial Pky N, Hamilton, ON, L8E 2P2

Emp Here 25
SIC 5999 Miscellaneous retail stores, nec

D-U-N-S 24-894-1804　　(SL)
PARKWAY NISSAN LTD
191 Centennial Pky N, Hamilton, ON, L8E 1H8
(905) 667-9001
Emp Here 20　　*Sales* 9,423,290
SIC 5511 New and used car dealers
Genl Mgr Ilya Pinassi

D-U-N-S 24-950-5819　　(BR)
PRAXAIR CANADA INC
PRAXAIR
(*Suby of* Praxair, Inc.)
171 Brockley Dr, Hamilton, ON, L8E 3C4
(905) 560-0533
Emp Here 38
SIC 5084 Industrial machinery and equipment

D-U-N-S 20-902-2334　　(BR)
PUROLATOR INC.
PUROLATOR INC
21 Warrington St, Hamilton, ON, L8E 3L1
(888) 744-7123
Emp Here 100

SIC 7389 Business services, nec

D-U-N-S 20-055-6116　　(BR)
SEARS CANADA INC
75 Centennial Pky N, Hamilton, ON, L8E 2P2
(905) 545-4741
Emp Here 20
SIC 5311 Department stores

D-U-N-S 24-919-5264　　(SL)
TAYLOR CHRYSLER DODGE INC
260 Centennial Pky N, Hamilton, ON, L8E 2X4
(905) 561-0333
Emp Here 50　　*Sales* 24,540,000
SIC 5511 New and used car dealers
Pr Pr Micheal W Taylor
　Michael Coughlan
　David Grosvenor

D-U-N-S 20-572-4250　　(BR)
**THYSSENKRUPP ELEVATOR (CANADA)
LIMITED**
505 Kenora Ave Suite 1, Hamilton, ON, L8E
3P2
(905) 526-8181
Emp Here 60
SIC 1796 Installing building equipment

D-U-N-S 20-650-7035　　(BR)
TRIOVEST REALTY ADVISORS INC
EASTGATE SQUARE
75 Centennial Pky N, Hamilton, ON, L8E 2P2
(905) 561-2444
Emp Here 20
SIC 6512 Nonresidential building operators

D-U-N-S 20-847-8834　　(BR)
**TYCO INTEGRATED FIRE & SECURITY
CANADA, INC**
SIMPLEXGRINNELL
(*Suby of* Johnson Controls, Inc.)
45 Goderich Rd Suite 1, Hamilton, ON, L8E
4W8
(905) 297-8795
Emp Here 25
SIC 6211 Security brokers and dealers

D-U-N-S 20-486-0592　　(BR)
UTC FIRE & SECURITY CANADA
CHUBB EDWARDS
(*Suby of* United Technologies Corporation)
7 Keefer Crt, Hamilton, ON, L8E 4V4
(905) 643-6201
Emp Here 25
SIC 3669 Communications equipment, nec

D-U-N-S 25-403-8086　　(BR)
UNITED PARCEL SERVICE CANADA LTD
UPS
456 Grays Rd, Hamilton, ON, L8E 2Z4
(905) 578-2699
Emp Here 100
SIC 7389 Business services, nec

D-U-N-S 25-294-8583　　(BR)
WAL-MART CANADA CORP
510 Centennial Pky N, Hamilton, ON, L8E
0G2
(905) 561-7600
Emp Here 200
SIC 5311 Department stores

D-U-N-S 20-860-4319　　(BR)
**WINNERS MERCHANTS INTERNATIONAL
L.P.**
HOMESENSE
(*Suby of* The TJX Companies Inc)
75 Centennial Pky N, Hamilton, ON, L8E 2P2
(905) 561-2301
Emp Here 25
SIC 5651 Family clothing stores

Hamilton, ON L8G
Wentworth County

D-U-N-S 25-360-0548　　(BR)
1260848 ONTARIO INC
TIM HORTONS
706 Queenston Rd, Hamilton, ON, L8G 1A2
(905) 560-9615
Emp Here 50
SIC 5812 Eating places

D-U-N-S 24-395-3796　　(SL)
AND 07 CONSULTING
674 Queenston Rd, Hamilton, ON, L8G 1A3
(905) 561-8960
Emp Here 45　　*Sales* 5,544,006
SIC 8748 Business consulting, nec

D-U-N-S 25-278-8500　　(BR)
CARA OPERATIONS LIMITED
SWISS CHALET
(*Suby of* Cara Holdings Limited)
735 Queenston Rd, Hamilton, ON, L8G 1A1
(905) 561-8323
Emp Here 70
SIC 5812 Eating places

D-U-N-S 24-213-5320　　(BR)
CARA OPERATIONS LIMITED
HARVEY'S RESTAURANTS
(*Suby of* Cara Holdings Limited)
724 Queenston Rd, Hamilton, ON, L8G 1A2
(905) 561-8284
Emp Here 25
SIC 5812 Eating places

D-U-N-S 20-653-4666　　(BR)
**HAMILTON-WENTWORTH　　CATHOLIC
SCHOOL BOARD**
ST DAVID CATHOLIC SCHOOL
33 Cromwell Cres, Hamilton, ON, L8G 2E9
(905) 560-3533
Emp Here 40
SIC 8211 Elementary and secondary schools

D-U-N-S 20-915-9172　　(BR)
PRIME RESTAURANTS INC
EAST SIDE MARIO'S
(*Suby of* Cara Holdings Limited)
750 Queenston Rd Suite Side, Hamilton, ON,
L8G 1A4
(905) 573-9442
Emp Here 49
SIC 5812 Eating places

D-U-N-S 24-556-7495　　(BR)
SOBEYS CAPITAL INCORPORATED
FRESHCO
700 Queenston Rd Unit A, Hamilton, ON, L8G
1A3
(905) 560-8111
Emp Here 110
SIC 5411 Grocery stores

D-U-N-S 20-703-6042　　(BR)
**ST. JOSEPH'S HEALTHCARE FOUNDA-
TION, HAMILTON**
*ST JOSEPH HEALTHCARE CENTRE FOR
AMBULATORY*
2757 King St E, Hamilton, ON, L8G 5E4
(905) 573-7777
Emp Here 300
SIC 8093 Specialty outpatient clinics, nec

D-U-N-S 25-848-7826　　(BR)
TWINCORP INC
TACO BELL
744 Queenston Rd, Hamilton, ON, L8G 1A4
(905) 573-0733
Emp Here 20
SIC 5812 Eating places

Hamilton, ON L8H
Wentworth County

D-U-N-S 24-403-2764　　(BR)
**AMEC FOSTER WHEELER AMERICAS LIM-
ITED**

AMEC AMERICAS
505 Woodward Ave Suite 1, Hamilton, ON, L8H 6N6
(905) 312-0700
Emp Here 60
SIC 8711 Engineering services

D-U-N-S 25-459-4633   (SL)
AGE LINK PERSONNEL SERVICES INC
SENIORS FOR SENIORS
400 Parkdale Ave N Unit 2a, Hamilton, ON, L8H 5Y2
(905) 572-6162
Emp Here 75   *Sales* 2,918,428
SIC 8322 Individual and family services

D-U-N-S 25-296-7757   (BR)
BANK OF NOVA SCOTIA, THE
SCOTIABANK
1255 Barton St E, Hamilton, ON, L8H 2V4
(905) 549-3521
Emp Here 27
SIC 6021 National commercial banks

D-U-N-S 24-451-9211   (HQ)
C.F.F. STAINLESS STEELS INC
1840 Burlington St E, Hamilton, ON, L8H 3L4
(905) 549-2603
Emp Here 113   *Emp Total* 130
Sales 57,432,441
SIC 5051 Metals service centers and offices
Pr Pr Brian Mccomb
Harriet Thomas

D-U-N-S 20-540-4465   (BR)
CANADA POST CORPORATION
HAMILTON RPO CSC
60 Kenilworth Ave N, Hamilton, ON, L8H 4R5

Emp Here 60
SIC 4311 U.s. postal service

D-U-N-S 20-852-5048   (BR)
CANADIAN NATIONAL INSTITUTE FOR THE BLIND, THE
C N I B
(*Suby of* Canadian National Institute For The Blind, The)
115 Parkdale Ave N, Hamilton, ON, L8H 5X1
(905) 528-8555
Emp Here 55
SIC 8331 Job training and related services

D-U-N-S 25-459-0599   (BR)
CARDINAL COURIERS LTD
CARDINAL COURIERS
1930 Barton St E, Hamilton, ON, L8H 2Y6
(905) 543-0092
Emp Here 20
SIC 7389 Business services, nec

D-U-N-S 20-800-8420   (BR)
CITY OF HAMILTON, THE
CHURCHILL RECREATION CENTRE
1715 Main St E, Hamilton, ON, L8H 1E3
(905) 546-4775
Emp Here 30
SIC 7999 Amusement and recreation, nec

D-U-N-S 20-552-6622   (BR)
COCA-COLA REFRESHMENTS CANADA COMPANY
(*Suby of* The Coca-Cola Company)
1575 Barton St E, Hamilton, ON, L8H 7K6
(905) 548-3206
Emp Here 100
SIC 2086 Bottled and canned soft drinks

D-U-N-S 25-915-9259   (BR)
COMSTOCK CANADA LTD
EMCOR
400 Parkdale Ave N Unit 2a, Hamilton, ON, L8H 5Y2

Emp Here 20
SIC 1711 Plumbing, heating, air-conditioning

D-U-N-S 20-053-1804   (BR)
CRANE CANADA CO.

CRANE SUPPLY
(*Suby of* Crane Co.)
1755 Burlington St E, Hamilton, ON, L8H 3L5
(905) 547-1951
Emp Here 24
SIC 5085 Industrial supplies

D-U-N-S 20-271-9808   (BR)
EASTGATE FORD SALES & SERVICE (1982) COMPANY INC
EASTGATE TRUCK CENTER
1831 Barton St E, Hamilton, ON, L8H 2Y7
(905) 578-2000
Emp Here 60
SIC 5511 New and used car dealers

D-U-N-S 24-374-4054   (BR)
FER & METAUX AMERICAINS S.E.C.
A I M
75 Steel City Crt, Hamilton, ON, L8H 3Y2
(905) 547-5533
Emp Here 80
SIC 4953 Refuse systems

D-U-N-S 20-261-7346   (BR)
FIRSTONTARIO CREDIT UNION LIMITED
1299 Barton St E, Hamilton, ON, L8H 2V4
(800) 616-8878
Emp Here 400
SIC 6062 State credit unions

D-U-N-S 25-684-3392   (BR)
GDI SERVICES (CANADA) LP
GDI INTEGRATED FACILITY SVC
39 Dunbar Ave, Hamilton, ON, L8H 3E3
(905) 561-9990
Emp Here 120
SIC 7349 Building maintenance services, nec

D-U-N-S 20-267-8025   (BR)
GAY LEA FOODS CO-OPERATIVE LIMITED
20 Morley St, Hamilton, ON, L8H 3R7
(905) 544-6281
Emp Here 1,000
SIC 2021 Creamery butter

D-U-N-S 24-010-0255   (SL)
HAMILTON EAST KIWANIS BOYS & GIRLS CLUB INCORPORATED
BOYS & GIRLS CLUBS OF HAMILTON
45 Ellis Ave, Hamilton, ON, L8H 4L8

Emp Here 100   *Sales* 4,012,839
SIC 7997 Membership sports and recreation clubs

D-U-N-S 25-478-9878   (BR)
HAMILTON YOUNG WOMEN'S CHRISTIAN ASSOCIATION, THE
Y W C A HAMILTON
52 Ottawa St N, Hamilton, ON, L8H 3Y7
(905) 522-9922
Emp Here 60
SIC 8641 Civic and social associations

D-U-N-S 25-292-6787   (BR)
HAMILTON-WENTWORTH CATHOLIC SCHOOL BOARD
HOLY FAMILY SEPARATE SCHOOL
190 Britannia Ave, Hamilton, ON, L8H 1X5
(905) 549-3541
Emp Here 24
SIC 8211 Elementary and secondary schools

D-U-N-S 20-290-5399   (BR)
HAMILTON-WENTWORTH DISTRICT SCHOOL BOARD, THE
HILLCREST SCHOOL
40 Eastwood St, Hamilton, ON, L8H 6R7
(905) 545-6558
Emo Here 51
SIC 8211 Elementary and secondary schools

D-U-N-S 24-972-5771   (BR)
HAMILTON-WENTWORTH DISTRICT SCHOOL BOARD, THE
ROXBOROUGH PARK JUNIOR SCHOOL
20 Reid Ave N, Hamilton, ON, L8H 6E1

Emp Here 30
SIC 8211 Elementary and secondary schools

D-U-N-S 20-290-5407   (BR)
HAMILTON-WENTWORTH DISTRICT SCHOOL BOARD, THE
PARKDALE ELEMENTARY
139 Parkdale Ave N, Hamilton, ON, L8H 5X3
(905) 545-6216
Emp Here 20
SIC 8211 Elementary and secondary schools

D-U-N-S 20-024-9691   (BR)
HAMILTON-WENTWORTH DISTRICT SCHOOL BOARD, THE
W. H. BALLARD SCHOOL
801 Dunsmure Rd, Hamilton, ON, L8H 1H9
(905) 547-1689
Emp Here 70
SIC 8211 Elementary and secondary schools

D-U-N-S 20-710-7975   (BR)
HAMILTON-WENTWORTH DISTRICT SCHOOL BOARD, THE
QUEEN MARY ELEMENTARY SCHOOLS
1292 Cannon St E, Hamilton, ON, L8H 1V6
(905) 547-0321
Emp Here 70
SIC 8211 Elementary and secondary schools

D-U-N-S 20-025-5094   (BR)
HAMILTON-WENTWORTH DISTRICT SCHOOL BOARD, THE
WOODWARD AVENUE SCHOOL
575 Woodward Ave, Hamilton, ON, L8H 6P2
(905) 545-8819
Emp Here 20
SIC 8211 Elementary and secondary schools

D-U-N-S 20-590-5560   (BR)
HAMILTON-WENTWORTH DISTRICT SCHOOL BOARD, THE
HILLCREST ELEMENTARY SCHOOL
460 Melvin Ave, Hamilton, ON, L8H 2L7
(905) 549-3076
Emp Here 30
SIC 8211 Elementary and secondary schools

D-U-N-S 24-352-6279   (BR)
LOWE'S COMPANIES CANADA, ULC
LOWE'S
1945 Barton St E, Hamilton, ON, L8H 2Y7
(905) 312-5670
Emp Here 50
SIC 5211 Lumber and other building materials

D-U-N-S 20-054-6885   (HQ)
MCNALLY CONSTRUCTION INC
MCNALLY MARINE, DIV OF
1855 Barton St E Suite 4, Hamilton, ON, L8H 2Y7
(905) 549-6561
Emp Here 50   *Emp Total* 1,500
Sales 8,142,759
SIC 1629 Heavy construction, nec
Pr Murray Malott
VP VP David Stanyar
VP VP Greg Burke
VP VP Corrie Prince
VP VP Arthur Smeding
Dir Matthew Reece

D-U-N-S 24-577-5226   (SL)
NEWFAST LIMITED
NUFAST
503 Woodward Ave Unit A, Hamilton, ON, L8H 6N6
(905) 544-1100
Emp Here 21   *Sales* 5,376,850
SIC 5084 Industrial machinery and equipment
Pr Pr Wendy Kline
Donald Kline

D-U-N-S 25-748-7199   (SL)
OLYMPIA BANQUET CENTRE INC
OLYMPIA CATERING & BANQUET CENTRE
1162 Barton St E, Hamilton, ON, L8H 2V6

(905) 643-4291
Emp Here 55   *Sales* 1,678,096
SIC 5812 Eating places

D-U-N-S 25-812-8438   (BR)
PIONEER FOOD SERVICES LIMITED
TIM HORTONS
(*Suby of* Pioneer Food Services Limited)
1600 Barton St E, Hamilton, ON, L8H 2X9
(905) 549-3385
Emp Here 40
SIC 5812 Eating places

D-U-N-S 24-009-9978   (SL)
POSNER METALS LIMITED
(*Suby of* 537013 Ontario Limited)
610 Beach Rd, Hamilton, ON, L8H 3L1
(905) 544-1881
Emp Here 40   *Sales* 9,703,773
SIC 5093 Scrap and waste materials
Pr Pr Fred Posner
Mgr Michael Kam

D-U-N-S 25-748-6878   (BR)
PRINCESS AUTO LTD
1850 Barton St E, Hamilton, ON, L8H 2Y6
(905) 561-9400
Emp Here 45
SIC 5251 Hardware stores

D-U-N-S 25-318-4261   (BR)
REXALL PHARMACY GROUP LTD
DELL PHARMACY
(*Suby of* McKesson Corporation)
234 Parkdale Ave N, Hamilton, ON, L8H 5X5
(905) 547-2174
Emp Here 20
SIC 5912 Drug stores and proprietary stores

D-U-N-S 25-542-6918   (BR)
SAMUEL, SON & CO., LIMITED
SAMUEL FLAT ROLLED PROCESSING GROUP
410 Nash Rd N, Hamilton, ON, L8H 7R9
(905) 573-9100
Emp Here 135
SIC 5051 Metals service centers and offices

D-U-N-S 24-318-3506   (HQ)
TERRATEC ENVIRONMENTAL LTD
200 Eastport Blvd, Hamilton, ON, L8H 7S4
(905) 544-0444
Emp Here 35   *Emp Total* 140
Sales 17,810,018
SIC 4953 Refuse systems
Dir Dan Goldhawk

D-U-N-S 25-975-2129   (BR)
TRIPLE M METAL LP
1640 Brampton St, Hamilton, ON, L8H 3S1
(905) 545-7083
Emp Here 75
SIC 5093 Scrap and waste materials

D-U-N-S 20-912-2287   (BR)
WEBB, JERVIS B. COMPANY OF CANADA, LTD
1647 Burlington St E, Hamilton, ON, L8H 3L2
(905) 547-0411
Emp Here 100
SIC 3535 Conveyors and conveying equipment

D-U-N-S 20-056-0894   (HQ)
WEBB, JERVIS B. COMPANY OF CANADA, LTD
1647 Burlington St E, Hamilton, ON, L8H 3L2
(905) 547-0411
Emp Here 130   *Emp Total* 8,689
Sales 32,467,512
SIC 3535 Conveyors and conveying equipment
John Doychich
Robert Meijer
Pr Pr Brian Stewart
Sec Tim Veeser

Hamilton, ON L8K
Wentworth County

D-U-N-S 20-588-2736   (BR)
BANQUE TORONTO-DOMINION, LA
TD CANADA TRUST
(*Suby of* Toronto-Dominion Bank, The)
1900 King St E, Hamilton, ON, L8K 1W1
(905) 545-7903
Emp Here 20
SIC 6021 National commercial banks

D-U-N-S 25-895-6663   (BR)
BROCK UNIVERSITY
BROCK UNIVERSITY FACULTY EDUCA
1842 King St E, Hamilton, ON, L8K 1V7
(905) 547-3555
Emp Here 65
SIC 8221 Colleges and universities

D-U-N-S 20-655-8269   (BR)
COGECO COMMUNICATIONS INC
695 Lawrence Rd, Hamilton, ON, L8K 6P1
(905) 548-8002
Emp Here 50
SIC 4841 Cable and other pay television services

D-U-N-S 25-293-9889   (BR)
HAMILTON-WENTWORTH   CATHOLIC SCHOOL BOARD
ST EUGENE SCHOOL
120 Parkdale Ave S, Hamilton, ON, L8K 3P3
(905) 545-9598
Emp Here 36
SIC 8211 Elementary and secondary schools

D-U-N-S 25-292-6795   (BR)
HAMILTON-WENTWORTH   CATHOLIC SCHOOL BOARD
ST LUKE'S SCHOOL
345 Albright Rd, Hamilton, ON, L8K 6N3
(905) 561-3966
Emp Here 48
SIC 8211 Elementary and secondary schools

D-U-N-S 25-292-6902   (BR)
HAMILTON-WENTWORTH   CATHOLIC SCHOOL BOARD
ST JOHN THE BAPTISTE SCHOOL
115 London St S, Hamilton, ON, L8K 2G6
(905) 549-8203
Emp Here 33
SIC 8211 Elementary and secondary schools

D-U-N-S 25-292-6910   (BR)
HAMILTON-WENTWORTH   CATHOLIC SCHOOL BOARD
ST ANTHONY SCHOOL
12 Ambrose Ave, Hamilton, ON, L8K 6E2
(905) 561-1144
Emp Here 20
SIC 8211 Elementary and secondary schools

D-U-N-S 20-295-1963   (BR)
HAMILTON-WENTWORTH   DISTRICT SCHOOL BOARD, THE
GLEN ECHO JUNIOR ELEMENTARY SCHOOL
140 Glen Echo Dr, Hamilton, ON, L8K 4J1
(905) 561-0719
Emp Here 26
SIC 8211 Elementary and secondary schools

D-U-N-S 24-193-0135   (BR)
HAMILTON-WENTWORTH   DISTRICT SCHOOL BOARD, THE
GLENDALE SECONDARY SCHOOL
145 Rainbow Dr, Hamilton, ON, L8K 4G1
(905) 560-7343
Emp Here 25
SIC 8211 Elementary and secondary schools

D-U-N-S 20-030-5576   (BR)
HAMILTON-WENTWORTH   DISTRICT SCHOOL BOARD, THE
ELIZABETH BAGSHAW SCHOOL
350 Albright Rd, Hamilton, ON, L8K 5J4
(905) 561-9520
Emp Here 35
SIC 8211 Elementary and secondary schools

D-U-N-S 24-024-1104   (BR)
HAMILTON-WENTWORTH   DISTRICT SCHOOL BOARD, THE
A M CUNNINGHAM JUNIOR SCHOOL
100 Wexford Ave S, Hamilton, ON, L8K 2N8
(905) 544-7771
Emp Here 35
SIC 8211 Elementary and secondary schools

D-U-N-S 20-648-7642   (BR)
HAMILTON-WENTWORTH   DISTRICT SCHOOL BOARD, THE
DELTA SECONDARY SCHOOL
1284 Main St E, Hamilton, ON, L8K 1B2
(905) 549-3031
Emp Here 20
SIC 8211 Elementary and secondary schools

D-U-N-S 20-024-9683   (BR)
HAMILTON-WENTWORTH   DISTRICT SCHOOL BOARD, THE
ROSEDALE SCHOOL
25 Erindale Ave, Hamilton, ON, L8K 4R2
(905) 549-4233
Emp Here 20
SIC 8211 Elementary and secondary schools

D-U-N-S 20-590-5370   (BR)
HAMILTON-WENTWORTH   DISTRICT SCHOOL BOARD, THE
BISCOUNT MONTGOMERY SCHOOL
1525 Lucerne Ave, Hamilton, ON, L8K 1R3
(905) 544-5670
Emp Here 25
SIC 8211 Elementary and secondary schools

D-U-N-S 20-292-0984   (BR)
HAMILTON-WENTWORTH   DISTRICT SCHOOL BOARD, THE
SIR WILFRID LAURIER SCHOOL
70 Albright Rd, Hamilton, ON, L8K 5J3
(905) 573-7540
Emp Here 40
SIC 8211 Elementary and secondary schools

D-U-N-S 20-161-1659   (BR)
HAMILTON-WENTWORTH   DISTRICT SCHOOL BOARD, THE
GLEN BRAE MIDDLE SCHOOL
50 Secord Dr, Hamilton, ON, L8K 3W7
(905) 560-6732
Emp Here 20
SIC 8211 Elementary and secondary schools

D-U-N-S 24-569-9033   (BR)
METRO ONTARIO INC
METRO SUPERMARKETS
1900 King St E, Hamilton, ON, L8K 1W1
(905) 545-5929
Emp Here 100
SIC 5411 Grocery stores

Hamilton, ON L8L
Wentworth County

D-U-N-S 24-309-7040   (SL)
1650473 ONTARIO INC
SCRAPMEN
10 Hillyard St, Hamilton, ON, L8L 8J9
(905) 522-9222
Emp Here 100   *Sales* 24,295,913
SIC 5093 Scrap and waste materials
Pr Pr Seema Boparai
Dir Randy Boparai

D-U-N-S 25-361-9944   (BR)
AIR LIQUIDE CANADA INC
AIR LIQUIDE CANADA DISTRIBUTION CENTRE
680 Burlington St E, Hamilton, ON, L8L 4J8
(905) 529-0500
Emp Here 45
SIC 5169 Chemicals and allied products, nec

D-U-N-S 25-167-6490   (BR)
AIR LIQUIDE CANADA INC
131 Birmingham St, Hamilton, ON, L8L 6W6
(905) 547-1602
Emp Here 50
SIC 2813 Industrial gases

D-U-N-S 20-716-1258   (BR)
ARBOR MEMORIAL SERVICES INC
DODSWORTH & BROWN FUNERAL HOME ROBINSON CHAPEL
15 West Ave N, Hamilton, ON, L8L 5B9
(905) 522-2496
Emp Here 20
SIC 7261 Funeral service and crematories

D-U-N-S 25-310-7767   (BR)
BRINK'S CANADA LIMITED
BRINK'S HAMILTON
(*Suby of* The Brink's Company)
75 Lansdowne Ave, Hamilton, ON, L8L 8A3
(905) 549-5997
Emp Here 100
SIC 7381 Detective and armored car services

D-U-N-S 24-925-1356   (BR)
BUNGE CANADA
515 Victoria Ave N, Hamilton, ON, L8L 8G7
(905) 527-9121
Emp Here 130
SIC 2076 Vegetable oil mills, nec

D-U-N-S 20-801-7298   (BR)
CITY OF HAMILTON, THE
NORMAN PINKY LEWIS RECREATION COMPLEX
192 Wentworth St N, Hamilton, ON, L8L 5V7
(905) 546-3122
Emp Here 20
SIC 7999 Amusement and recreation, nec

D-U-N-S 24-381-3016   (BR)
HAMILTON HEALTH SCIENCES CORPORATION
POPULATION HEALTH RESEARCH INSTITUTE
(*Suby of* Hamilton Health Sciences Corporation)
237 Barton St E Suite 120, Hamilton, ON, L8L 2X2
(905) 527-4322
Emp Here 20
SIC 8093 Specialty outpatient clinics, nec

D-U-N-S 25-292-6852   (BR)
HAMILTON-WENTWORTH   CATHOLIC SCHOOL BOARD
ST BRIGID'S SCHOOL
24 Smith Ave, Hamilton, ON, L8L 5P1
(905) 529-2848
Emp Here 35
SIC 8211 Elementary and secondary schools

D-U-N-S 25-292-6837   (BR)
HAMILTON-WENTWORTH   CATHOLIC SCHOOL BOARD
ST LAWRENCE SCHOOL
88 Macaulay St E, Hamilton, ON, L8L 3X3
(905) 529-6625
Emp Here 35
SIC 8211 Elementary and secondary schools

D-U-N-S 24-676-3176   (BR)
HAMILTON-WENTWORTH   CATHOLIC SCHOOL BOARD
PRINCE OF WHALES ELEMENTARY SCHOOL
77 Melrose Ave N, Hamilton, ON, L8L 6X4
(905) 544-0522
Emp Here 25
SIC 8211 Elementary and secondary schools

D-U-N-S 25-293-9657   (BR)
HAMILTON-WENTWORTH   CATHOLIC SCHOOL BOARD
ST ANN SCHOOL
120 Sherman Ave N, Hamilton, ON, L8L 6M6
(905) 547-5444
Emp Here 25
SIC 8211 Elementary and secondary schools

D-U-N-S 24-972-5896   (BR)
HAMILTON-WENTWORTH   CATHOLIC SCHOOL BOARD
HOLY NAME OF JESUS SCHOOL
181 Belmont Ave, Hamilton, ON, L8L 7M5
(905) 549-6767
Emp Here 25
SIC 8211 Elementary and secondary schools

D-U-N-S 20-591-6872   (BR)
HAMILTON-WENTWORTH   CATHOLIC SCHOOL BOARD
CATHEDRAL HIGH SCHOOL
30 Wentworth St N, Hamilton, ON, L8L 8H5
(905) 522-3581
Emp Here 20
SIC 8211 Elementary and secondary schools

D-U-N-S 25-000-3092   (BR)
HAMILTON-WENTWORTH   CATHOLIC SCHOOL BOARD
HOLY SPIRIT SCHOOL
115 Barnesdale Ave N, Hamilton, ON, L8L 6S6
(905) 545-1832
Emp Here 22
SIC 8211 Elementary and secondary schools

D-U-N-S 20-590-5545   (BR)
HAMILTON-WENTWORTH   DISTRICT SCHOOL BOARD, THE
PRINCE OF WALES SCHOOL
40 Lottridge St, Hamilton, ON, L8L 6T9
(905) 544-3379
Emp Here 25
SIC 8211 Elementary and secondary schools

D-U-N-S 20-590-5446   (BR)
HAMILTON-WENTWORTH   DISTRICT SCHOOL BOARD, THE
CATHY WEVER ELEMENTARY SCHOOL
160 Wentworth St N, Hamilton, ON, L8L 5V7
(905) 522-9965
Emp Here 50
SIC 8211 Elementary and secondary schools

D-U-N-S 25-000-3068   (BR)
HAMILTON-WENTWORTH   DISTRICT SCHOOL BOARD, THE
SANDFORD AVENUE PUBLIC SCHOOL
149 Sanford Ave N, Hamilton, ON, L8L 5Z4

Emp Here 30
SIC 8211 Elementary and secondary schools

D-U-N-S 20-290-5787   (BR)
HAMILTON-WENTWORTH   DISTRICT SCHOOL BOARD, THE
PARKVIEW SCHOOL
60 Balsam Ave N, Hamilton, ON, L8L 6Y3
(905) 545-5315
Emp Here 45
SIC 8211 Elementary and secondary schools

D-U-N-S 20-590-5610   (BR)
HAMILTON-WENTWORTH   DISTRICT SCHOOL BOARD, THE
KING GEORGE ELEMENTARY SCHOOL
77 Gage Ave N, Hamilton, ON, L8L 6Z8

Emp Here 30
SIC 8211 Elementary and secondary schools

D-U-N-S 20-710-8130   (BR)
HAMILTON-WENTWORTH   DISTRICT SCHOOL BOARD, THE
GLEN BRAE SCHOOL
50 Murray St W, Hamilton, ON, L8L 1B3
(905) 560-6732
Emp Here 50
SIC 8211 Elementary and secondary schools

D-U-N-S 20-911-0852   (BR)
HATCH LTD
500 Sherman Ave N, Hamilton, ON, L8L 8J6
(905) 543-8555
Emp Here 30
SIC 1742 Plastering, drywall, and insulation

D-U-N-S 24-183-5292   (BR)
JNE CONSULTING LTD
121 Shaw St, Hamilton, ON, L8L 3P6
(905) 529-5122
Emp Here 350
SIC 8711 Engineering services

D-U-N-S 24-676-5833   (SL)
MAX AICHER (NORTH AMERICA) REALTY INC
MANA
855 Industrial Dr, Hamilton, ON, L8L 0B2
(289) 426-5670
Emp Here 125   *Sales* 13,716,612
SIC 3312 Blast furnaces and steel mills
Thomas Fetzer
Jim Etzl
Dave Cameron
Ch Bd Max Aicher
Gerhard Weichenhain

D-U-N-S 24-505-3509   (SL)
MIRDEN NURSING HOMES LTD
VICTORIA GARDINS LONG TERM CARE
176 Victoria Ave N, Hamilton, ON, L8L 5G1
(905) 527-9111
Emp Here 70   *Sales* 3,210,271
SIC 8051 Skilled nursing care facilities

D-U-N-S 20-346-3542   (SL)
NATT TOOLS GROUP INC
INGERSOL TILLAGE GROUP
460 Sherman Ave N, Hamilton, ON, L8L 8J6
(905) 549-7433
Emp Here 120   *Sales* 26,994,824
SIC 3523 Farm machinery and equipment
Pr Stephen Garrette

D-U-N-S 24-560-8542   (SL)
PROVMAR FUELS INC
(*Suby of* Upper Lakes Group Inc)
605 James St N Suite 202, Hamilton, ON, L8L 1J9
(905) 549-9402
Emp Here 20   *Sales* 7,727,098
SIC 5172 Petroleum products, nec
Pr Adrian Mitterhuber

D-U-N-S 24-793-4722   (BR)
R DENNINGER LIMITED
DENNINGER
(*Suby of* Denninger, R Limited)
55 Brant St, Hamilton, ON, L8L 4C7
(905) 522-2414
Emp Here 50
SIC 2013 Sausages and other prepared meats

D-U-N-S 20-273-0193   (BR)
SAINT ELIZABETH REHAB
COMMUNITY REHAB
605 James St N Suite 601, Hamilton, ON, L8L 1J9
(905) 529-2020
Emp Here 50
SIC 8049 Offices of health practitioner

D-U-N-S 20-052-9295   (BR)
SIEMENS CANADA LIMITED
SIEMENS POWER GENERATION
30 Milton Ave, Hamilton, ON, L8L 6E6
(905) 528-8811
Emp Here 900
SIC 3511 Turbines and turbine generator sets

D-U-N-S 20-891-5723   (BR)
SOBEYS CAPITAL INCORPORATED
SOBEYS
869 Barton St E, Hamilton, ON, L8L 3B4
(905) 549-3573
Emp Here 65

SIC 5411 Grocery stores

D-U-N-S 25-227-7090   (SL)
ST. MATTHEW'S HOUSE
414 Barton St E, Hamilton, ON, L8L 2Y3
(905) 523-5546
Emp Here 100   *Sales* 14,167,680
SIC 8399 Social services, nec
Ex Dir Wendy Roy

D-U-N-S 20-751-0009   (SL)
THOMAS CARTAGE LTD
THOMAS SOLUTIONS
70 Beach Rd, Hamilton, ON, L8L 8K3
(905) 545-8808
Emp Here 50   *Sales* 3,939,878
SIC 4212 Local trucking, without storage

D-U-N-S 20-911-4250   (BR)
TRIPLE CROWN ENTERPRISES LTD
TCE
(*Suby of* 1438771 Ontario Inc)
170 Shaw St, Hamilton, ON, L8L 3P7
(905) 540-1630
Emp Here 50
SIC 1731 Electrical work

D-U-N-S 20-821-1920   (BR)
VEOLIA ES CANADA SERVICES INDUS-TRIELS INC
VEOLIA ES CANADA SERVICES INDUS-TRIELS INC
80 Birmingham St, Hamilton, ON, L8L 6W5
(905) 547-5661
Emp Here 50
SIC 1721 Painting and paper hanging

D-U-N-S 24-926-2585   (BR)
VICTORIAN ORDER OF NURSES FOR CANADA
VON HAMILTON DISTRICT
414 Victoria Ave N Suite M2, Hamilton, ON, L8L 5G8
(905) 529-0700
Emp Here 200
SIC 8082 Home health care services

D-U-N-S 20-190-3569   (BR)
VOPAK TERMINALS OF CANADA INC
655 Victoria Ave N Suite 11, Hamilton, ON, L8L 8G7
(905) 529-1339
Emp Here 20
SIC 4226 Special warehousing and storage, nec

D-U-N-S 20-047-3580   (SL)
WELLINGTON MEDICAL CENTRE INC
414 Victoria Ave N Suite M1, Hamilton, ON, L8L 5G8
(905) 529-5221
Emp Here 50   *Sales* 2,991,389
SIC 8011 Offices and clinics of medical doctors

Hamilton, ON L8M
Wentworth County

D-U-N-S 20-711-7461   (BR)
CONSEIL SCOLAIRE DE DISTRICT CATHOLIQUE CENTRE-SUD
ELEMENTARY SCHOOL CATHOLIC NOTRE-DAME
400 Cumberland Ave, Hamilton, ON, L8M 2A2
(905) 545-3393
Emp Here 50
SIC 8211 Elementary and secondary schools

D-U-N-S 25-374-6507   (SL)
CROWE INDUSTRIES LTD
116 Burris St, Hamilton, ON, L8M 2J5

Emp Here 54   *Sales* 15,116,640
SIC 5033 Roofing, siding, and insulation
Pr Pr James Crowe

D-U-N-S 24-023-6583   (BR)
GOVERNING COUNCIL OF THE SALVA-TION ARMY IN CANADA, THE
GOVERNING COUNCIL OF THE SALVATION ARMY IN CANADA, THE
533 Main St E, Hamilton, ON, L8M 1H9
(905) 527-6212
Emp Here 168
SIC 8399 Social services, nec

D-U-N-S 25-292-6811   (BR)
HAMILTON-WENTWORTH   CATHOLIC SCHOOL BOARD
ST COLUMBA SCHOOL
770 Main St E, Hamilton, ON, L8M 1L1
(905) 544-9495
Emp Here 20
SIC 8211 Elementary and secondary schools

D-U-N-S 20-159-8732   (BR)
HAMILTON-WENTWORTH   DISTRICT SCHOOL BOARD, THE
ADELAIDE HOODLESS SCHOOL
71 Maplewood Ave, Hamilton, ON, L8M 1W7
(905) 549-1339
Emp Here 45
SIC 8211 Elementary and secondary schools

D-U-N-S 20-290-5571   (BR)
HAMILTON-WENTWORTH   DISTRICT SCHOOL BOARD, THE
RAY LEWIS SCHOOL
1175 Main St E, Hamilton, ON, L8M 1P3
(905) 549-3095
Emp Here 50
SIC 8211 Elementary and secondary schools

D-U-N-S 25-666-8195   (BR)
ROYAL BANK OF CANADA
RBC
(*Suby of* Royal Bank Of Canada)
1405 King St E, Hamilton, ON, L8M 1H7
(905) 576-5521
Emp Here 23
SIC 6021 National commercial banks

D-U-N-S 24-354-4116   (BR)
SERVICE CORPORATION INTERNATIONAL (CANADA) LIMITED
MARLATT FUNERAL & CREMATION CEN-TRE
615 Main St E, Hamilton, ON, L8M 1J4
(905) 528-6303
Emp Here 20
SIC 7261 Funeral service and crematories

D-U-N-S 24-369-2527   (BR)
WE CARE HEALTH SERVICES INC
WE CARE HOME HEALTH SERVICES
848 Main St E, Hamilton, ON, L8M 1L9
(905) 545-2273
Emp Here 50
SIC 8082 Home health care services

Hamilton, ON L8N
Wentworth County

D-U-N-S 24-075-4507   (BR)
BANK OF NOVA SCOTIA, THE
SCOTIABANK
12 King St E, Hamilton, ON, L8N 4G9
(905) 528-7501
Emp Here 50
SIC 6021 National commercial banks

D-U-N-S 24-525-7217   (SL)
BLUE LINE TRANSPORTATION LTD
BLUE LINE TAXI
160 John St S, Hamilton, ON, L8N 2C4
(905) 525-2583
Emp Here 75   *Sales* 2,261,782
SIC 4121 Taxicabs

D-U-N-S 20-510-9676   (BR)
CANADIAN BLOOD SERVICES

BONE MARROW - HAMILTON
397 Ontario St Suite 395, Hamilton, ON, L8N 1H8
(888) 236-6283
Emp Here 50
SIC 8099 Health and allied services, nec

D-U-N-S 20-521-4500   (BR)
COWAN INSURANCE GROUP LTD
105 Main St E Suite 602, Hamilton, ON, L8N 1G6
(905) 523-8507
Emp Here 22
SIC 6411 Insurance agents, brokers, and service

D-U-N-S 25-887-5160   (BR)
CRAWFORD SMITH & SWALLOW CHAR-TERED ACCOUNTANTS LLP
(*Suby of* Crawford Smith & Swallow Chartered Accountants LLP)
75 Young St, Hamilton, ON, L8N 1V4
(905) 528-4600
Emp Here 50
SIC 8111 Legal services

D-U-N-S 20-053-2893   (HQ)
DENNINGER, R LIMITED
DENNINGER'S FOODS OF THE WORLD
(*Suby of* Denninger, R Limited)
284 King St E, Hamilton, ON, L8N 1B7
(905) 528-8468
Emp Here 150   *Emp Total* 300
Sales 13,132,926
SIC 2013 Sausages and other prepared meats
Pr Pr Rudolph Denninger
Herta Murray
Dir Herman Denninger
Dir Gabriella Frank

D-U-N-S 20-848-2638   (HQ)
EFFORT TRUST COMPANY, THE
(*Suby of* Effort Corporation)
242 Main St E Suite 240, Hamilton, ON, L8N 1H5
(905) 528-8956
Emp Here 84   *Emp Total* 100
Sales 82,900,221
SIC 6021 National commercial banks
Pr Pr Thomas J Weisz
Arthur Weisz

D-U-N-S 24-830-7753   (BR)
HSBC BANK CANADA
40 King St E, Hamilton, ON, L8N 1A3
(905) 525-8730
Emp Here 20
SIC 6021 National commercial banks

D-U-N-S 20-645-6324   (BR)
HAMILTON HEALTH SCIENCES CORPO-RATION
HHS VOLUNTEER ASSOCIATION
(*Suby of* Hamilton Health Sciences Corporation)
1200 Main St W Rm 2, Hamilton, ON, L8N 3Z5
(905) 521-2100
Emp Here 100
SIC 8699 Membership organizations, nec

D-U-N-S 20-653-2256   (BR)
HAMILTON-WENTWORTH   CATHOLIC SCHOOL BOARD
GUARDIAN ANGELS SCHOOL
705 Centre Rd, Hamilton, ON, L8N 2Z7
(905) 523-2345
Emp Here 50
SIC 8211 Elementary and secondary schools

D-U-N-S 25-293-9566   (BR)
HAMILTON-WENTWORTH   CATHOLIC SCHOOL BOARD
OUR LADY OF ASSUMPTION SCHOOL
Gd, Hamilton, ON, L8N 3R9
(905) 664-7628
Emp Here 25
SIC 8211 Elementary and secondary schools

D-U-N-S 25-292-6555   (BR)
**HAMILTON-WENTWORTH   CATHOLIC
SCHOOL BOARD**
ST CHARLES MOUNTAIN SCHOOL
150 5th St E, Hamilton, ON, L8N 3R9
(905) 575-5202
Emp Here 40
SIC 8211 Elementary and secondary schools

D-U-N-S 24-676-3168   (BR)
**HAMILTON-WENTWORTH   CATHOLIC
SCHOOL BOARD**
QUEEN ViCTORIA ELEMENTARY SCHOOL
166 Forest Ave, Hamilton, ON, L8N 0A5
(905) 667-5880
Emp Here 25
SIC 8211 Elementary and secondary schools

D-U-N-S 25-295-6453   (BR)
MARCH OF DIMES CANADA
50 King St E, Hamilton, ON, L8N 1A6
(905) 522-2253
Emp Here 25
SIC 8331 Job training and related services

D-U-N-S 25-283-2118   (BR)
MCMASTER UNIVERSITY
(*Suby of* McMaster University)
Po Box 2000 Stn Lcd 1, Hamilton, ON, L8N
3Z5
(905) 521-2100
Emp Here 2,182
SIC 8221 Colleges and universities

D-U-N-S 25-823-3931   (BR)
METCAP LIVING INC
HAMILTON CONTINUING CARE
125 Wentworth St S, Hamilton, ON, L8N 2Z1
(905) 527-1482
Emp Here 71
SIC 8051 Skilled nursing care facilities

D-U-N-S 25-468-8229   (SL)
MORRIS, B. LAW GROUP
ACCIDENT BENEFITS CONSULTANT
125 Main St E, Hamilton, ON, L8N 3Z3
(905) 522-6845
Emp Here 50   *Sales* 5,825,660
SIC 8111 Legal services
Owner William Morris

D-U-N-S 20-974-6734   (SL)
PASWORD COMMUNICATIONS INC
122 Hughson St S, Hamilton, ON, L8N 2B2
(905) 974-1683
Emp Here 75   *Sales* 3,793,956
SIC 7389 Business services, nec

D-U-N-S 24-364-7281   (SL)
PASWORD GROUP INC, THE
ANSWER PLUS
122 Hughson St S, Hamilton, ON, L8N 2B2
(905) 645-1162
Emp Here 100   *Sales* 4,961,328
SIC 7389 Business services, nec

D-U-N-S 25-248-9976   (BR)
REVERA LONG TERM CARE INC
VERSA-CARE CENTRE HAMILTON
330 Main St E, Hamilton, ON, L8N 3T9
(905) 523-1604
Emp Here 260
SIC 8051 Skilled nursing care facilities

D-U-N-S 24-010-1246   (SL)
RIZZUTO BROS. LIMITED
160 John St S, Hamilton, ON, L8N 2C4
(905) 522-2525
Emp Here 90   *Sales* 2,699,546
SIC 4121 Taxicabs

D-U-N-S 24-208-9670   (HQ)
SIMPSONWIGLE LAW LLP
(*Suby of* SimpsonWigle Law LLP)
1 Hunter St E Suite 200, Hamilton, ON, L8N
3W1
(905) 528-8411
Emp Here 60   *Emp Total* 75
Sales 6,420,542

SIC 8111 Legal services
Pt Timothy Bullock
Genl Mgr Linda Jackson

D-U-N-S 24-409-3782   (SL)
TAYLOR LEIBOW INC
105 Main St E Suite 700, Hamilton, ON, L8N
1G6
(905) 523-0000
Emp Here 49   *Sales* 12,466,320
SIC 6733 Trusts, nec
Pr Catherine Allard

D-U-N-S 20-750-8896   (HQ)
TAYLOR, LEIBOW LLP
(*Suby of* Taylor, Leibow LLP)
105 Main St E Suite 700, Hamilton, ON, L8N
1G6
(905) 523-0003
Emp Here 45   *Emp Total* 65
Sales 3,828,240
SIC 8721 Accounting, auditing, and book-
keeping

D-U-N-S 24-138-1495   (SL)
TIM HORTONS
1470 6 Hwy N, Hamilton, ON, L8N 2Z7
(905) 690-2200
Emp Here 60   *Sales* 1,824,018
SIC 5812 Eating places

D-U-N-S 20-875-5363   (BR)
TORONTO STAR NEWSPAPERS LIMITED
HAMILTON SPECTATOR, THE
44 Frid St, Hamilton, ON, L8N 3G3
(905) 526-3333
Emp Here 400
SIC 2711 Newspapers

D-U-N-S 24-422-0596   (BR)
TORONTO-DOMINION BANK, THE
TD CANADA TRUST
(*Suby of* Toronto-Dominion Bank, The)
46 King St E, Hamilton, ON, L8N 1A6
(905) 521-2450
Emp Here 22
SIC 6021 National commercial banks

D-U-N-S 25-173-9884   (BR)
TORSTAR CORPORATION
HAMILTON SPECTATOR
44 Frid St, Hamilton, ON, L8N 3G3
(905) 526-3590
Emp Here 60
SIC 2752 Commercial printing, lithographic

D-U-N-S 25-363-9371   (BR)
TRANS UNION OF CANADA, INC
(*Suby of* Transunion)
170 Jackson St E, Hamilton, ON, L8N 1L4
(905) 572-6004
Emp Here 50
SIC 7323 Credit reporting services

D-U-N-S 25-846-6093   (BR)
IMARKETING SOLUTIONS GROUP INC
(*Suby of* iMarketing Solutions Group Inc)
4 Hughson St S Suite P400, Hamilton, ON,
L8N 3Z1
(905) 529-7896
Emp Here 100
SIC 8399 Social services, nec

Hamilton, ON L8P
Wentworth County

D-U-N-S 25-250-5599   (SL)
AGRO ZAFFIRO LLP
1 James St S Suite 400 4th Fl, Hamilton, ON,
L8P 4R5
(905) 527-6877
Emp Here 50   *Sales* 4,304,681
SIC 8111 Legal services

D-U-N-S 20-002-6685   (BR)
AMEX CANADA INC

AMERICAN EXPRESS
(*Suby of* American Express Company)
100 King St W Suite 600, Hamilton, ON, L8P
1A2

Emp Here 23
SIC 4724 Travel agencies

D-U-N-S 24-421-3989   (BR)
ASSANTE CAPITAL MANAGEMENT LTD
ASSANTE WEALTH MANAGEMENT
175 Longwood Rd S Suite 400, Hamilton, ON,
L8P 0A1
(905) 526-0485
Emp Here 50
SIC 6211 Security brokers and dealers

D-U-N-S 24-425-9078   (BR)
ATRIA NETWORKS LP
120 King St W Suite 950, Hamilton, ON, L8P
4V2

Emp Here 20
SIC 4899 Communication services, nec

D-U-N-S 24-060-3886   (BR)
**AVIVA   INSURANCE   COMPANY   OF
CANADA**
1 King St W Suite 600, Hamilton, ON, L8P 1A4
(905) 523-5936
Emp Here 130
SIC 6331 Fire, marine, and casualty insurance

D-U-N-S 24-179-7344   (BR)
BDO CANADA LIMITED
BDO DUNWOODY
25 Main St W Suite 805, Hamilton, ON, L8P
1H1
(905) 524-1008
Emp Here 20
SIC 8111 Legal services

D-U-N-S 24-117-4486   (BR)
BANQUE TORONTO-DOMINION, LA
TORONTO-DOMINION BANK, THE
(*Suby of* Toronto-Dominion Bank, The)
100 King St W Suite 1500, Hamilton, ON, L8P
1A2
(905) 527-3626
Emp Here 20
SIC 6021 National commercial banks

D-U-N-S 24-025-1207   (BR)
BANQUE TORONTO-DOMINION, LA
TORONTO-DOMINION BANK, THE
(*Suby of* Toronto-Dominion Bank, The)
100 King St W Suite 500, Hamilton, ON, L8P
1A2
(905) 527-3626
Emp Here 45
SIC 6021 National commercial banks

D-U-N-S 25-293-9285   (BR)
CIBC WORLD MARKETS INC
CIBC WOOD GUNDY
21 King St W Suite 600, Hamilton, ON, L8P
4W7
(905) 526-4700
Emp Here 30
SIC 6211 Security brokers and dealers

D-U-N-S 20-583-0404   (BR)
CANADA POST CORPORATION
75 Frid St, Hamilton, ON, L8P 0A9

Emp Here 100
SIC 4311 U.s. postal service

D-U-N-S 20-588-9012   (BR)
CANADIAN PACIFIC RAILWAY COMPANY
CPR
20 Studholme Rd, Hamilton, ON, L8P 4Z1
(905) 523-9412
Emp Here 20
SIC 4011 Railroads, line-haul operating

D-U-N-S 20-573-3822   (BR)
CANADIAN PACIFIC RAILWAY COMPANY
20 Studholme Rd, Hamilton, ON, L8P 4Z1

(905) 523-9433
Emp Here 20
SIC 7011 Hotels and motels

D-U-N-S 24-733-0827   (SL)
CGU INSURANCE CO. OF CANADA
1 King St W Suite 600, Hamilton, ON, L8P 1A4

Emp Here 75   *Sales* 9,128,880
SIC 6411 Insurance agents, brokers, and service

D-U-N-S 20-113-3704   (SL)
CHINMAYA MISSION (HALTON REGION)
CORD
206 Locke St S, Hamilton, ON, L8P 4B4
(905) 570-0159
Emp Here 500   *Sales* 73,620,000
SIC 8621 Professional organizations
Pr Pr Joti Chakraburtty
    Meenakshi Bhaga
Dir Sneh Chakraburtty

D-U-N-S 20-059-9186   (BR)
CITY OF HAMILTON, THE
CITY OF HAMILTON LEGAL DEPARTMENT
21 King St W 12th Fl, Hamilton, ON, L8P 4W7
(905) 546-4520
Emp Here 40
SIC 8111 Legal services

D-U-N-S 20-820-1772   (SL)
CLARKE, A. J. AND ASSOCIATES LTD
25 Main St W Unit 300, Hamilton, ON, L8P
1H1
(905) 528-8761
Emp Here 50   *Sales* 4,961,328
SIC 8713 Surveying services

D-U-N-S 20-981-3096   (BR)
COMPAGNIE TRUST ROYAL, LA
RBC ROYAL BANK
(*Suby of* Royal Bank Of Canada)
100 King St W Suite 900, Hamilton, ON, L8P
1A2

Emp Here 23
SIC 6021 National commercial banks

D-U-N-S 25-311-1504   (BR)
CRAWFORD & COMPANY (CANADA) INC
(*Suby of* Crawford & Company)
38 James St S, Hamilton, ON, L8P 4W6
(905) 529-9600
Emp Here 60
SIC 6411 Insurance agents, brokers, and ser-
vice

D-U-N-S 20-817-5281   (HQ)
CUNNINGHAM LINDSEY CANADA LIMITED
ENVIROMENTAL SOLUTIONS
67 Frid St Unit 5, Hamilton, ON, L8P 4M3
(905) 524-1523
Emp Here 20   *Emp Total* 23,576
Sales 46,950,804
SIC 6411 Insurance agents, brokers, and ser-
vice
Pr Rob Seal
Sr VP Gary Dalton
Sr VP Claudine Davoodi

D-U-N-S 25-294-6447   (BR)
CUNNINGHAM LINDSEY CANADA LIMITED
25 Main St W Suite 1810, Hamilton, ON, L8P
1H1
(905) 528-1481
Emp Here 150
SIC 6411 Insurance agents, brokers, and service

D-U-N-S 20-647-1976   (BR)
**DESJARDINS   SECURITE   FINANCIERE,
COMPAGNIE D'ASSURANCE VIE**
120 King St W Suite 210, Hamilton, ON, L8P
4V2
(905) 570-1200
Emp Here 33
SIC 6311 Life insurance

D-U-N-S 20-981-7261   (BR)
ECONOMICAL MUTUAL INSURANCE COMPANY
ECONOMICAL INSURANCE
120 King St W Suite 750, Hamilton, ON, L8P 4V2

Emp Here 100
SIC 6331 Fire, marine, and casualty insurance

D-U-N-S 20-699-6642   (BR)
EXTENDICARE INC
ST. OLGA'S LIFECARE CENTRE
570 King St W, Hamilton, ON, L8P 1C2
(905) 524-1283
Emp Here 25
SIC 8051 Skilled nursing care facilities

D-U-N-S 24-654-5219   (BR)
FORMER RESTORATION L.P.
FIRSTONSITE
180 Chatham St, Hamilton, ON, L8P 2B6
(905) 545-4703
Emp Here 25
SIC 1799 Special trade contractors, nec

D-U-N-S 20-188-4330   (BR)
G-WLG LP
1 Main St W, Hamilton, ON, L8P 4Z5
(905) 540-8208
Emp Here 140
SIC 8111 Legal services

D-U-N-S 20-207-6852   (BR)
GOVERNING COUNCIL OF THE SALVATION ARMY IN CANADA, THE
GRACE HAVEN
138 Herkimer St, Hamilton, ON, L8P 2H1
(905) 522-7336
Emp Here 28
SIC 8322 Individual and family services

D-U-N-S 25-311-8244   (BR)
GOWLING WLG (CANADA) LLP
1 Main St W, Hamilton, ON, L8P 4Z5
(905) 540-8208
Emp Here 135
SIC 8111 Legal services

D-U-N-S 24-079-0055   (BR)
GREAT-WEST LIFE ASSURANCE COMPANY, THE
HAMILTON OFFICE
1 King St W Suite 825, Hamilton, ON, L8P 1A4
(905) 317-2650
Emp Here 21
SIC 6311 Life insurance

D-U-N-S 25-292-6878   (BR)
HAMILTON-WENTWORTH   CATHOLIC SCHOOL BOARD
ST JOSEPH CATHOLIC ELEMENTARY SCHOOL
270 Locke St S, Hamilton, ON, L8P 4C1
(905) 529-1002
Emp Here 45
SIC 8211 Elementary and secondary schools

D-U-N-S 20-025-0681   (BR)
HAMILTON-WENTWORTH   DISTRICT SCHOOL BOARD, THE
CENTRAL ELEMENTARY SCHOOL
75 Hunter St W, Hamilton, ON, L8P 1P9
(905) 522-9690
Emp Here 20
SIC 8211 Elementary and secondary schools

D-U-N-S 20-590-5701   (BR)
HAMILTON-WENTWORTH   DISTRICT SCHOOL BOARD, THE
100 Main St W, Hamilton, ON, L8P 1H6
(905) 527-5092
Emp Here 25
SIC 8211 Elementary and secondary schools

D-U-N-S 20-965-3745   (BR)
HAMILTON-WENTWORTH   DISTRICT SCHOOL BOARD, THE

EARL KITCHENER JUNIOR SCHOOL
300 Dundurn St S, Hamilton, ON, L8P 4L3
(905) 528-0223
Emp Here 37
SIC 8211 Elementary and secondary schools

D-U-N-S 20-009-6571   (BR)
HAMILTON-WENTWORTH   DISTRICT SCHOOL BOARD, THE
RYERSON MIDDLE SCHOOL
222 Robinson St, Hamilton, ON, L8P 1Z9
(905) 528-7975
Emp Here 34
SIC 8211 Elementary and secondary schools

D-U-N-S 25-928-8322   (BR)
HANBALI, JEFF DRUGS LTD
SHOPPERS DRUG MART
113 Herkimer St, Hamilton, ON, L8P 2G8
(905) 527-2133
Emp Here 20
SIC 5912 Drug stores and proprietary stores

D-U-N-S 25-499-6267   (SL)
HILL PROGRAM INC
366 Queen St S, Hamilton, ON, L8P 3T9
(905) 521-1484
Emp Here 50   *Sales* 3,283,232
SIC 8093 Specialty outpatient clinics, nec

D-U-N-S 20-354-0992   (SL)
INNOCARE LTD
INNOCARE
55 Frid St Unit 1, Hamilton, ON, L8P 4M3
(905) 523-5777
Emp Here 20   *Sales* 1,459,214
SIC 7372 Prepackaged software

D-U-N-S 20-270-8343   (BR)
INSTITUT NATIONAL D'OPTIQUE
INO
175 Longwood Rd S Suite 316 A, Hamilton, ON, L8P 0A1
(905) 529-7016
Emp Here 25
SIC 8731 Commercial physical research

D-U-N-S 25-315-8141   (BR)
INVESTORS GROUP FINANCIAL SERVICES INC
INVESTORS GROUP
21 King St W Unit 400, Hamilton, ON, L8P 4W7
(905) 529-7165
Emp Here 50
SIC 8742 Management consulting services

D-U-N-S 20-943-5510   (BR)
KPMG LLP
(*Suby of* KPMG LLP)
21 King St W Suite 700, Hamilton, ON, L8P 4W7
(905) 523-2259
Emp Here 100
SIC 8721 Accounting, auditing, and bookkeeping

D-U-N-S 25-281-5360   (BR)
MD MANAGEMENT LIMITED
MD FINANCIAL
(*Suby of* Canadian Medical Association)
1 King St W Suite 1200, Hamilton, ON, L8P 1A4
(905) 526-8999
Emp Here 20
SIC 8741 Management services

D-U-N-S 25-251-7537   (BR)
MANULIFE SECURITIES INVESTMENT SERVICES INC
MANULIFE SECURITIES
168 Jackson St W, Hamilton, ON, L8P 1L9
(905) 529-3863
Emp Here 30
SIC 6722 Management investment, open-end

D-U-N-S 20-923-8638   (BR)
MCDONALD'S   RESTAURANTS   OF CANADA LIMITED

MCDONALD'S RESTAURANT
(*Suby of* McDonald's Corporation)
2 King St W, Hamilton, ON, L8P 1A1

Emp Here 30
SIC 5812 Eating places

D-U-N-S 20-300-8073   (BR)
MCMASTER UNIVERSITY
MCMASTER AUTOMOTIVE RESEARCH AND TECHNOLOGY
(*Suby of* McMaster University)
200 Longwood Rd S Suite 20, Hamilton, ON, L8P 0A6
(289) 674-0253
Emp Here 50
SIC 8221 Colleges and universities

D-U-N-S 20-205-9080   (BR)
MEDICAL PHARMACIES GROUP LIMITED
MEDICAL PHARMACY
45 Frid St Suite 5, Hamilton, ON, L8P 4M3
(905) 522-7741
Emp Here 20
SIC 5912 Drug stores and proprietary stores

D-U-N-S 24-182-1644   (SL)
OLD REPUBLIC INSURANCE COMPANY OF CANADA
(*Suby of* Old Republic International Corporation)
100 King St W Suite 1100, Hamilton, ON, L8P 1A2
(905) 523-5936
Emp Here 28   *Sales* 17,963,280
SIC 6331 Fire, marine, and casualty insurance
Dir Paul Field
Ch Bd Al Zucaro
Pr Joe Henderson

D-U-N-S 24-213-5119   (BR)
PRICEWATERHOUSECOOPERS LLP
21 King St W Suite 100, Hamilton, ON, L8P 4W7

Emp Here 76
SIC 8721 Accounting, auditing, and bookkeeping

D-U-N-S 25-293-7412   (BR)
RBC DOMINION SECURITIES INC
RBC INVESTMENTS
(*Suby of* Royal Bank Of Canada)
100 King St W Unit 900, Hamilton, ON, L8P 1A2
(905) 546-5716
Emp Here 40
SIC 6211 Security brokers and dealers

D-U-N-S 20-900-2856   (SL)
RELIABLE LIFE INSURANCE COMPANY
(*Suby of* Old Republic International Corporation)
100 King St W, Hamilton, ON, L8P 1A2
(905) 525-5031
Emp Here 120   *Sales* 119,217,784
SIC 6311 Life insurance
   Paul Field
   Aldo Zucaro
   Brian Reeve
   J W Nevil Thomas
   Thomas A Hickey
   Spencer Leroy
   Gary E Lewis

D-U-N-S 24-058-4904   (BR)
ROYAL BANK OF CANADA
ROYAL BANK FINANCIAL GROUP # 01822
(*Suby of* Royal Bank Of Canada)
100 King St W Suite 900, Hamilton, ON, L8P 1A2
(905) 521-2000
Emp Here 44
SIC 6021 National commercial banks

D-U-N-S 20-846-6834   (BR)
SCM INSURANCE SERVICES INC
CLAIMSPRO

120 King St W Suite 660, Hamilton, ON, L8P 4V2
(905) 529-1387
Emp Here 30
SIC 6411 Insurance agents, brokers, and service

D-U-N-S 24-425-8971   (BR)
SP DATA CAPITAL ULC
110 King St W Suite 500, Hamilton, ON, L8P 4S6
(905) 645-5610
Emp Here 400
SIC 7389 Business services, nec

D-U-N-S 20-177-9613   (BR)
SCOTIA CAPITAL INC
SCOTIA MCLEOD
1 King St W Suite 1402, Hamilton, ON, L8P 1A4
(905) 570-7960
Emp Here 30
SIC 6211 Security brokers and dealers

D-U-N-S 24-976-3533   (HQ)
SECOND REAL PROPERTIES LIMITED
(*Suby of* Immeubles Yale Limitee, Les)
100 King St, Hamilton, ON, L8P 1A2
(905) 522-3501
Emp Here 100   *Emp Total* 40
Sales 13,716,612
SIC 6512 Nonresidential building operators
Pr Pr Emile Mashaal
   Edward Quigg
   Victor Mashaal
   Elise Bourret
   Kevin Powers
   Ingrid Gendreau
   Peter Hill
   Michael Mashaal
   Ronald Mashaal
   Jacques Phaneuf

D-U-N-S 25-849-0283   (BR)
TWINCORP INC
TACO BELL
460 Main St W, Hamilton, ON, L8P 1K7
(905) 525-4890
Emp Here 30
SIC 5812 Eating places

D-U-N-S 24-868-9093   (BR)
WORKPLACE SAFETY & INSURANCE BOARD, THE
WSIB
120 King St W, Hamilton, ON, L8P 4V2

Emp Here 400
SIC 6331 Fire, marine, and casualty insurance

D-U-N-S 25-873-6149   (SL)
WORLDWIDE EVANGELIZATION FOR CHRIST
WEC INTERNATIONAL
37 Aberdeen Ave, Hamilton, ON, L8P 2N6
(905) 529-0166
Emp Here 72   *Sales* 3,648,035
SIC 7389 Business services, nec

Hamilton, ON L8R
Wentworth County

D-U-N-S 20-349-9728   (HQ)
ALECTRA UTILITIES CORPORATION
55 John St N, Hamilton, ON, L8R 3M8
(905) 522-6611
Emp Here 345   *Emp Total* 20
Sales 203,268,510
SIC 4911 Electric services
Pr Pr Max Cananzi
VP VP Peter Gregg
   Brian Bentz
   Robert Hull
   Dennis Nolan
   Lawrence Wilde

John Basilio

D-U-N-S 24-420-0734   (BR)
ARMTEC LP
DURISOL, DIV OF
505 York Blvd Suite 2, Hamilton, ON, L8R 3K4
(905) 521-0999
Emp Here 20
SIC 3312 Blast furnaces and steel mills

D-U-N-S 25-204-0985   (BR)
BMO NESBITT BURNS INC
NESBITT BURNS
77 James St N Suite 301, Hamilton, ON, L8R 2K3
(905) 570-8600
Emp Here 26
SIC 6211 Security brokers and dealers

D-U-N-S 25-833-3723   (BR)
CITY OF HAMILTON, THE
DUNDURN NATIONAL HISTORIC SITE
600 York Blvd, Hamilton, ON, L8R 3H1
(905) 546-2872
Emp Here 30
SIC 8412 Museums and art galleries

D-U-N-S 20-699-6212   (BR)
EXTENDICARE INC
DUNDURN PLACE CARE CENTRE
39 Mary St, Hamilton, ON, L8R 3L8
(905) 523-6427
Emp Here 25
SIC 8051 Skilled nursing care facilities

D-U-N-S 25-359-6241   (BR)
FERCAN DEVELOPMENTS INC
77 James St N, Hamilton, ON, L8R 2K3
(905) 522-7808
Emp Here 20
SIC 6553 Cemetery subdividers and developers

D-U-N-S 20-879-0233   (SL)
GO BEE INDUSTRIES INC
300 York Blvd, Hamilton, ON, L8R 3K6

Emp Here 1,000   *Sales* 235,582,250
SIC 7319 Advertising, nec
Pr Pr Stephen Deighton

D-U-N-S 24-107-7465   (BR)
GOOD SHEPHERD NON-PROFIT HOMES INC
MC GINTY HOUSE
131 Catharine St N Suite 9, Hamilton, ON, L8R 1J5
(905) 525-7884
Emp Here 20
SIC 8361 Residential care

D-U-N-S 25-292-6944   (BR)
HAMILTON-WENTWORTH   CATHOLIC SCHOOL BOARD
ST MARY'S ELEMENTARY SCHOOL
209 Macnab St N, Hamilton, ON, L8R 2M5
(905) 528-8797
Emp Here 25
SIC 8211 Elementary and secondary schools

D-U-N-S 20-590-7426   (BR)
HAMILTON-WENTWORTH   CATHOLIC SCHOOL BOARD
90 Mulberry St, Hamilton, ON, L8R 2C8

Emp Here 100
SIC 8211 Elementary and secondary schools

D-U-N-S 25-823-1398   (BR)
HAMILTON-WENTWORTH   DISTRICT SCHOOL BOARD, THE
SIR JOHN A MACDONALD SECONDARY SCHOOL
130 York Blvd, Hamilton, ON, L8R 1Y5
(905) 528-8363
Emp Here 120
SIC 8211 Elementary and secondary schools

D-U-N-S 20-590-5685   (BR)

HAMILTON-WENTWORTH   DISTRICT SCHOOL BOARD, THE
DR J E DAVEY JUNIOR PUBLIC SCHOOL
99 Ferguson Ave N, Hamilton, ON, L8R 1L6
(905) 667-2612
Emp Here 25
SIC 8211 Elementary and secondary schools

D-U-N-S 20-914-1949   (BR)
HAMILTON-WENTWORTH   DISTRICT SCHOOL BOARD, THE
HESS STREET ELEMENTARY SCHOOL
107 Hess St N, Hamilton, ON, L8R 2T1
(905) 527-1439
Emp Here 36
SIC 8211 Elementary and secondary schools

D-U-N-S 25-093-1748   (BR)
HARSCO CANADA CORPORATION
MULTISERV
(*Suby of* Harsco Corporation)
151 York Blvd, Hamilton, ON, L8R 3M2
(905) 522-8123
Emp Here 215
SIC 3295 Minerals, ground or treated

D-U-N-S 24-909-5175   (BR)
MARCH OF DIMES CANADA
20 Jarvis St, Hamilton, ON, L8R 1M2
(905) 528-4261
Emp Here 30
SIC 8059 Nursing and personal care, nec

D-U-N-S 25-254-2634   (BR)
SERVICE CORPORATION INTERNATIONAL (CANADA) LIMITED
AWARD LIMOUSINE SERVICES
100 Oxford St, Hamilton, ON, L8R 2X1
(905) 308-8314
Emp Here 20
SIC 4119 Local passenger transportation, nec

D-U-N-S 20-324-8885   (SL)
TOUCH COMMUNICATION INC
118 James St N Suite 300, Hamilton, ON, L8R 2K7
(905) 667-5757
Emp Here 50   *Sales* 1,633,733
SIC 4899 Communication services, nec

D-U-N-S 20-522-2107   (HQ)
TRAVEL SUPERSTORE INC
TRIPCENTRAL.CA
77 James St N Suite 230, Hamilton, ON, L8R 2K3
(905) 570-9999
Emp Here 20   *Emp Total* 5,000
Sales 15,248,786
SIC 4724 Travel agencies
Pr Pr Richard Vanderlubbe
Dir Sean Furlong

Hamilton, ON L8S
Wentworth County

D-U-N-S 20-590-2070   (SL)
2014595 ONTARIO INC
PHOENIX FITNESS
1685 Main St W Unit 5, Hamilton, ON, L8S 1G5
(905) 577-0626
Emp Here 55   *Sales* 2,991,389
SIC 7999 Amusement and recreation, nec

D-U-N-S 20-580-0480   (BR)
ARBOR MEMORIAL SERVICES INC
WHITE CHAPEL
1895 Main St W, Hamilton, ON, L8S 1J2
(905) 528-1128
Emp Here 20
SIC 6531 Real estate agents and managers

D-U-N-S 20-308-7973   (BR)
CARA OPERATIONS LIMITED
KELSEY'S

(*Suby of* Cara Holdings Limited)
875 Main St W, Hamilton, ON, L8S 4P9
(905) 524-0995
Emp Here 50
SIC 5812 Eating places

D-U-N-S 20-800-8552   (BR)
CITY OF HAMILTON, THE
1150 Main St W, Hamilton, ON, L8S 1C2
(905) 546-4946
Emp Here 20
SIC 7999 Amusement and recreation, nec

D-U-N-S 24-585-6810   (BR)
CORUS ENTERTAINMENT INC
CHML-AM
875 Main St W Suite 900, Hamilton, ON, L8S 4R1
(905) 521-9900
Emp Here 45
SIC 7922 Theatrical producers and services

D-U-N-S 20-206-5756   (SL)
CORUS RADIO COMPANY
CING FM
875 Main St W Suite 900, Hamilton, ON, L8S 4R1
(905) 521-9900
Emp Here 50   *Sales* 3,137,310
SIC 4832 Radio broadcasting stations

D-U-N-S 20-751-0322   (HQ)
HAMILTON HEALTH SCIENCES CORPORATION
MCMASTER UNIVERSITY MEDICAL CENTER
(*Suby of* Hamilton Health Sciences Corporation)
1200 Main St W, Hamilton, ON, L8S 4J9
(905) 521-2100
Emp Here 4,000   *Emp Total* 10,000
Sales 695,826,196
SIC 8062 General medical and surgical hospitals
  Murray T. Martin
  Kathy Watts
  Craig Laviolette
  Mark Rizzo
  Paul Chapin
Dir Lloyd Ferguson
Dir Glenn Gibson
Dir Anita Isaac
Dir Mila Ray-Daniels
Dir Gary Reynolds

D-U-N-S 25-465-1953   (SL)
HAMILTON JEWISH HOME FOR THE AGED
SHALOM VILLAGE
70 Macklin St N, Hamilton, ON, L8S 3S1
(905) 528-5377
Emp Here 120   *Sales* 4,377,642
SIC 8361 Residential care

D-U-N-S 25-292-6670   (BR)
HAMILTON-WENTWORTH   CATHOLIC SCHOOL BOARD
ST. MARY'S CATHOLIC SECONDARY SCHOOL
200 Whitney Ave, Hamilton, ON, L8S 2G7
(905) 528-0214
Emp Here 100
SIC 8211 Elementary and secondary schools

D-U-N-S 24-676-3143   (BR)
HAMILTON-WENTWORTH   CATHOLIC SCHOOL BOARD
PRINCE PHILIP ELEMENTARY SCHOOL
125 Rifle Range Rd, Hamilton, ON, L8S 3B7
(905) 527-6512
Emp Here 25
SIC 8211 Elementary and secondary schools

D-U-N-S 20-291-5802   (BR)
HAMILTON-WENTWORTH   DISTRICT SCHOOL BOARD, THE
GLENWOOD SPECIAL DAY SCHOOL
150 Lower Horning Rd, Hamilton, ON, L8S 4P2

(905) 525-2140
Emp Here 40
SIC 8211 Elementary and secondary schools

D-U-N-S 20-301-6717   (BR)
HAMILTON-WENTWORTH   DISTRICT SCHOOL BOARD, THE
WESTDALE SECONDARY SCHOOL
700 Main St W, Hamilton, ON, L8S 1A5
(905) 522-1387
Emp Here 150
SIC 8211 Elementary and secondary schools

D-U-N-S 20-290-5340   (BR)
HAMILTON-WENTWORTH   DISTRICT SCHOOL BOARD, THE
DALEWOOD MIDDLE SCHOOL
1150 Main St W, Hamilton, ON, L8S 1C2
(905) 528-8631
Emp Here 30
SIC 8211 Elementary and secondary schools

D-U-N-S 20-590-5677   (BR)
HAMILTON-WENTWORTH   DISTRICT SCHOOL BOARD, THE
GEORGE R ALLAN PUBLIC SCHOOL
900 King St W, Hamilton, ON, L8S 1K6
(905) 522-0601
Emp Here 25
SIC 8211 Elementary and secondary schools

D-U-N-S 24-329-2245   (SL)
MCMASTER STUDENTS UNION INCORPORATED
1280 Main St W Rm 1, Hamilton, ON, L8S 4K1
(905) 525-9140
Emp Here 700   *Sales* 99,632,400
SIC 8631 Labor organizations
Pr Pr John Popham

D-U-N-S 20-357-9214   (BR)
MCMASTER UNIVERSITY
AUTOMOTIVE & VEHICLE TECHNOLOGY PRO
(*Suby of* McMaster University)
1280 Main St W Etb 513, Hamilton, ON, L8S 4L8
(905) 525-9140
Emp Here 32
SIC 8221 Colleges and universities

D-U-N-S 20-732-9061   (BR)
MEMORIAL GARDENS CANADA LIMITED
WHITE CHAPEL MEMORIAL GARDENS
1895 Main St W, Hamilton, ON, L8S 1J2
(905) 522-5790
Emp Here 20
SIC 6553 Cemetery subdividers and developers

D-U-N-S 25-292-3974   (BR)
METRO ONTARIO INC
METRO
845 King St W, Hamilton, ON, L8S 1K4
(905) 523-5044
Emp Here 180
SIC 5411 Grocery stores

D-U-N-S 20-155-3240   (BR)
ONTARIO FEDERATION FOR CEREBRAL PALSY
1100 Main St W Unit 301, Hamilton, ON, L8S 1B3
(905) 522-2928
Emp Here 40
SIC 8699 Membership organizations, nec

D-U-N-S 25-180-1114   (BR)
PINCHIN LTD
(*Suby of* 2010282 Ontario Inc)
875 Main St W Suite 11, Hamilton, ON, L8S 4P9
(905) 577-6206
Emp Here 25
SIC 1799 Special trade contractors, nec

D-U-N-S 20-535-7614   (BR)
ROYAL BANK OF CANADA
RBC

(Suby of Royal Bank Of Canada)
1845 Main St W, Hamilton, ON, L8S 1J2
(905) 521-2021
Emp Here 20
SIC 6021 National commercial banks

D-U-N-S 25-357-8215   (BR)
ST. JOSEPH'S HEALTHCARE FOUNDA-
TION, HAMILTON
WOMANKIND ADDICTION SERVICE
431 Whitney Ave, Hamilton, ON, L8S 2H6
(905) 521-9591
Emp Here 30
SIC 8322 Individual and family services

D-U-N-S 24-252-6940   (BR)
STARBUCKS COFFEE CANADA, INC
STARBUCKS COFFEE COMPANY
(Suby of Starbucks Corporation)
1100 Wilson St E, Hamilton, ON, L8S 4K5
(905) 304-8494
Emp Here 25
SIC 5812 Eating places

D-U-N-S 20-005-2350   (BR)
WENDY'S RESTAURANTS OF CANADA INC
WENDY'S
(Suby of The Wendy's Company)
1585 Main St W, Hamilton, ON, L8S 1E6
(905) 527-1464
Emp Here 25
SIC 5812 Eating places

D-U-N-S 25-226-9428   (BR)
YMCA   OF   HAMIL-
TON/BURLINGTON/BRANTFORD
YMCA SCHOOL AGE CHILD CARE
125 Rifle Range Rd, Hamilton, ON, L8S 3B7
(905) 527-6512
Emp Here 25
SIC 8211 Elementary and secondary schools

Hamilton, ON L8T
Wentworth County

D-U-N-S 25-296-7674   (BR)
BANK OF NOVA SCOTIA, THE
SCOTIABANK
997a Fennell Ave E, Hamilton, ON, L8T 1R1
(905) 574-9010
Emp Here 25
SIC 6021 National commercial banks

D-U-N-S 20-589-5241   (BR)
BANQUE TORONTO-DOMINION, LA
TD CANADA TRUST
(Suby of Toronto-Dominion Bank, The)
1119 Fennell Ave E, Hamilton, ON, L8T 1S2
(905) 387-9500
Emp Here 20
SIC 6021 National commercial banks

D-U-N-S 20-812-8640   (BR)
CITY OF HAMILTON, THE
HUNTINGTON PARK RECREATION CEN-
TRE
87 Brentwood Dr, Hamilton, ON, L8T 3W4
(905) 546-4880
Emp Here 50
SIC 7999 Amusement and recreation, nec

D-U-N-S 20-592-0452   (BR)
CONSEIL   SCOLAIRE   DE   DISTRICT
CATHOLIQUE CENTRE-SUD
ACADEMIE CATHOLIQUE MERE-TERESA
50 Lisgar Crt, Hamilton, ON, L8T 4Y4
(905) 389-4055
Emp Here 35
SIC 8211 Elementary and secondary schools

D-U-N-S 20-973-3927   (BR)
CONSEIL SCOLAIRE VIAMONDE
CONSEIL SCOLAIRE VIAMONDE
105 High St, Hamilton, ON, L8T 3Z4

(905) 318-3816
Emp Here 27
SIC 8211 Elementary and secondary schools

D-U-N-S 25-293-9699   (BR)
HAMILTON-WENTWORTH   CATHOLIC
SCHOOL BOARD
ST MARGARET MARY SCHOOL
25 Brentwood Dr, Hamilton, ON, L8T 3V9
(905) 383-8122
Emp Here 30
SIC 8211 Elementary and secondary schools

D-U-N-S 20-009-6522   (BR)
HAMILTON-WENTWORTH   DISTRICT
SCHOOL BOARD, THE
HIGHVIEW ELEMENTARY SCHOOL
1040 Queensdale Ave E, Hamilton, ON, L8T
1J4
(905) 385-2341
Emp Here 40
SIC 8211 Elementary and secondary schools

D-U-N-S 24-024-1112   (BR)
HAMILTON-WENTWORTH   DISTRICT
SCHOOL BOARD, THE
LISGAR ELEMENTARY SCHOOL
110 Anson Ave, Hamilton, ON, L8T 2X6
(905) 389-1309
Emp Here 28
SIC 8211 Elementary and secondary schools

D-U-N-S 24-391-0986   (BR)
HAMILTON-WENTWORTH   DISTRICT
SCHOOL BOARD, THE
BARTON SECONDARY SCHOOL
75 Palmer Rd, Hamilton, ON, L8T 3G1
(905) 389-2234
Emp Here 85
SIC 8211 Elementary and secondary schools

D-U-N-S 20-590-5644   (BR)
HAMILTON-WENTWORTH   DISTRICT
SCHOOL BOARD, THE
RICHARD BEASLEY SCHOOL
80 Currie St, Hamilton, ON, L8T 3M9
(905) 387-5655
Emp Here 25
SIC 8211 Elementary and secondary schools

D-U-N-S 24-333-1738   (BR)
METRO ONTARIO INC
FOOD BASICS
724 Mohawk Rd E, Hamilton, ON, L8T 2P8
(905) 575-1113
Emp Here 50
SIC 5411 Grocery stores

D-U-N-S 20-812-8582   (BR)
METRO RICHELIEU INC
BARN, THE
967 Fennell Ave E, Hamilton, ON, L8T 1R1
(905) 318-7777
Emp Here 85
SIC 5411 Grocery stores

D-U-N-S 25-318-4824   (BR)
REXALL PHARMACY GROUP LTD
REXALL
(Suby of McKesson Corporation)
1119 Fennell Ave E, Hamilton, ON, L8T 1S2
(905) 383-3386
Emp Here 50
SIC 5912 Drug stores and proprietary stores

D-U-N-S 24-310-5413   (BR)
WESTERN INVENTORY SERVICE LTD
WIS INTERNATIONAL
1119 Fennell Ave E Unit 205, Hamilton, ON,
L8T 1S2

Emp Here 20
SIC 7389 Business services, nec

Hamilton, ON L8V
Wentworth County

D-U-N-S 25-642-2825   (BR)
BAYSHORE HEALTHCARE LTD.
BAYSHORE HOME HEALTH
755 Concession St Suite 100, Hamilton, ON,
L8V 1C4
(905) 523-5999
Emp Here 315
SIC 8082 Home health care services

D-U-N-S 25-282-4552   (BR)
CITY OF HAMILTON, THE
MACASSA LODGE
701 Upper Sherman Ave, Hamilton, ON, L8V
3M7
(905) 546-2800
Emp Here 300
SIC 8051 Skilled nursing care facilities

D-U-N-S 25-319-6190   (BR)
FIRSTONTARIO CREDIT UNION LIMITED
486 Upper Sherman Ave, Hamilton, ON, L8V
3L8
(905) 389-5533
Emp Here 30
SIC 6062 State credit unions

D-U-N-S 25-867-2153   (SL)
FORTINOS (MALL 1994) LTD
FORTINO'S SUPERMARKET
65 Mall Rd, Hamilton, ON, L8V 5B8
(905) 387-7673
Emp Here 260   Sales 49,080,000
SIC 5411 Grocery stores
Pr Pr Carmine Gallo

D-U-N-S 24-365-7616   (BR)
HAMILTON HEALTH SCIENCES CORPO-
RATION
JURAVINSKI CANCER CENTRE GYN ON-
COLOGY CENTRE
(Suby of Hamilton Health Sciences Corpora-
tion)
699 Concession St Suite 3, Hamilton, ON, L8V
5C2
(905) 389-5688
Emp Here 400
SIC 8093 Specialty outpatient clinics, nec

D-U-N-S 20-025-4444   (BR)
HAMILTON HEALTH SCIENCES CORPO-
RATION
HENDERSON HOSPITAL
(Suby of Hamilton Health Sciences Corpora-
tion)
711 Concession St Suite 201, Hamilton, ON,
L8V 1C3
(905) 521-2100
Emp Here 1,345
SIC 8062 General medical and surgical hospi-
tals

D-U-N-S 25-292-6589   (BR)
HAMILTON-WENTWORTH   CATHOLIC
SCHOOL BOARD
OUR LADY OF LOURDES SCHOOL
420 Mohawk Rd E, Hamilton, ON, L8V 2H7
(905) 383-9233
Emp Here 40
SIC 8211 Elementary and secondary schools

D-U-N-S 25-292-6951   (BR)
HAMILTON-WENTWORTH   CATHOLIC
SCHOOL BOARD
SACRED HEART SCHOOL
5 Hamilton Ave, Hamilton, ON, L8V 2S3
(905) 383-6811
Emp Here 25
SIC 8211 Elementary and secondary schools

D-U-N-S 25-292-6563   (BR)
HAMILTON-WENTWORTH   CATHOLIC
SCHOOL BOARD
BLESSED SACRAMENT SCHOOL
315 East 37th St, Hamilton, ON, L8V 4B5
(905) 383-6844
Emp Here 35
SIC 8211 Elementary and secondary schools

D-U-N-S 24-972-4253   (BR)
HAMILTON-WENTWORTH   DISTRICT
SCHOOL BOARD, THE
FRANKLIN JUNIOR ELEMENTARY
500 Franklin Rd, Hamilton, ON, L8V 2A4
(905) 388-4731
Emp Here 35
SIC 8211 Elementary and secondary schools

D-U-N-S 20-590-5412   (BR)
HAMILTON-WENTWORTH   DISTRICT
SCHOOL BOARD, THE
HATTS OFF
155 Macassa Ave, Hamilton, ON, L8V 2B5
(905) 318-1883
Emp Here 25
SIC 8299 Schools and educational services,
nec

D-U-N-S 24-024-1096   (BR)
HAMILTON-WENTWORTH   DISTRICT
SCHOOL BOARD, THE
LAWFIELD ELEMENTARY SCHOOL
45 Berko Ave, Hamilton, ON, L8V 2R3
(905) 387-1087
Emp Here 20
SIC 8211 Elementary and secondary schools

D-U-N-S 20-710-8023   (BR)
HAMILTON-WENTWORTH   DISTRICT
SCHOOL BOARD, THE
VERN AMES SCHOOL
205 Berko Ave, Hamilton, ON, L8V 2R3
(905) 385-3239
Emp Here 30
SIC 8211 Elementary and secondary schools

D-U-N-S 20-590-5388   (BR)
HAMILTON-WENTWORTH   DISTRICT
SCHOOL BOARD, THE
EAST MOUNT PARK SCHOOL
155 East 26th St, Hamilton, ON, L8V 3C5
(905) 387-0172
Emp Here 25
SIC 8211 Elementary and secondary schools

D-U-N-S 20-025-1978   (BR)
HAMILTON-WENTWORTH   DISTRICT
SCHOOL BOARD, THE
BURKHOLDER MIDDLE SCHOOL
430 East 25th St, Hamilton, ON, L8V 3B4
(905) 388-1058
Emp Here 22
SIC 8211 Elementary and secondary schools

D-U-N-S 20-790-2334   (BR)
LOBLAW COMPANIES LIMITED
MARCO AND SANDRA'S NO FRILLS
499 Mohawk Rd E, Hamilton, ON, L8V 4L7
(905) 574-6819
Emp Here 70
SIC 5411 Grocery stores

D-U-N-S 25-202-7297   (BR)
MCMASTER UNIVERSITY
HENDERSON RESEARCH CENTRE, THE
(Suby of McMaster University)
711 Concession St, Hamilton, ON, L8V 1C3
(905) 527-2299
Emp Here 50
SIC 8069 Specialty hospitals, except psychi-
atric

D-U-N-S 20-002-7972   (BR)
ROYAL BANK OF CANADA
RBC
(Suby of Royal Bank Of Canada)
810 Upper Gage Ave, Hamilton, ON, L8V 4K4
(905) 575-4911
Emp Here 27
SIC 6021 National commercial banks

D-U-N-S 25-988-9798   (BR)
VALUE VILLAGE STORES, INC
VALUE VILLAGE #245
(Suby of Savers, Inc.)
530 Fennell Ave E, Hamilton, ON, L8V 1S9

(905) 318-0409
Emp Here 40
SIC 5399 Miscellaneous general merchandise

Hamilton, ON L8W
Wentworth County

D-U-N-S 24-023-5218   (BR)
BANYAN COMMUNITY SERVICES INC
ARRELL YOUTH CENTRE
320 Anchor Rd, Hamilton, ON, L8W 3R2
(905) 574-0610
Emp Here 50
SIC 8322 Individual and family services

D-U-N-S 20-038-2070   (BR)
CANADA BREAD COMPANY, LIMITED
DEMPSTER BREAD, DIV OF
155 Nebo Rd Suite 1, Hamilton, ON, L8W 2E1
(905) 387-3935
Emp Here 100
SIC 5149 Groceries and related products, nec

D-U-N-S 20-321-9258   (BR)
CARA OPERATIONS LIMITED
HARVEY'S
(*Suby of* Cara Holdings Limited)
1575 Upper Ottawa St, Hamilton, ON, L8W 3E2
(905) 574-5555
Emp Here 27
SIC 5812 Eating places

D-U-N-S 24-128-4772   (SL)
CARMENS INC
CARMENS CATERER
1520 Stone Church Rd E, Hamilton, ON, L8W 3P9
(905) 387-9490
Emp Here 50   *Sales* 1,678,096
SIC 7299 Miscellaneous personal service

D-U-N-S 20-402-5498   (SL)
CENTURA (HAMILTON) LIMITED
CENTURA FLOOR & WALL TILE
(*Suby of* Centura Limited)
140 Nebo Rd, Hamilton, ON, L8W 2E4
(905) 383-5100
Emp Here 33   *Sales* 4,331,255
SIC 5023 Homefurnishings

D-U-N-S 25-306-4372   (BR)
CO-OPERATORS GENERAL INSURANCE COMPANY
THE CO-OPERATORS
1575 Upper Ottawa St Unit B4, Hamilton, ON, L8W 3E2
(905) 560-9067
Emp Here 25
SIC 6411 Insurance agents, brokers, and service

D-U-N-S 20-558-9794   (SL)
DIVAL DEVELOPMENTS LTD
NU-WALL
90 Trinity Church Rd, Hamilton, ON, L8W 3S2
(905) 387-8214
Emp Here 50   *Sales* 4,711,645
SIC 1794 Excavation work

D-U-N-S 24-242-9418   (SL)
EVENT MEDICAL STAFF INC
38a Bigwin Rd Unit 5, Hamilton, ON, L8W 3R4

Emp Here 40   *Sales* 12,073,680
SIC 8399 Social services, nec
Pr Kelly Gimblett

D-U-N-S 20-940-1132   (HQ)
FORTINOS SUPERMARKET LTD
1275 Rymal Rd E Suite 2, Hamilton, ON, L8W 3N1
(905) 318-4532
Emp Here 80   *Emp Total* 138,000
Sales 55,873,190
SIC 5141 Groceries, general line

Vince Scornaienchi
Elaine Martin

D-U-N-S 24-549-8261   (SL)
HAMILTON ENERGY CENTRE
1447 Upper Ottawa St Suite 11, Hamilton, ON, L8W 3J6
(905) 385-2999
Emp Here 23   *Sales* 6,797,150
SIC 4961 Steam and air-conditioning supply
Owner Peter Poirier

D-U-N-S 20-590-7525   (BR)
HAMILTON-WENTWORTH   CATHOLIC SCHOOL BOARD
BLESSED TERESA OF CALCUTTA SCHOOL
1 Rexford Dr, Hamilton, ON, L8W 3E8
(905) 318-7933
Emp Here 25
SIC 8211 Elementary and secondary schools

D-U-N-S 20-913-8796   (BR)
HAMILTON-WENTWORTH   CATHOLIC SCHOOL BOARD
ST. KATERI TEKAKWITHA CATHOLIC ELEMENTARY SCHOOL
22 Queensbury Dr, Hamilton, ON, L8W 1Z6
(905) 385-8212
Emp Here 30
SIC 8211 Elementary and secondary schools

D-U-N-S 25-292-6621   (BR)
HAMILTON-WENTWORTH   CATHOLIC SCHOOL BOARD
ST JEAN DE BREBEUF SCHOOL
200 Acadia Dr, Hamilton, ON, L8W 1B8
(905) 388-7020
Emp Here 135
SIC 8211 Elementary and secondary schools

D-U-N-S 20-582-4365   (BR)
HAMILTON-WENTWORTH   DISTRICT SCHOOL BOARD, THE
TEMPLEMEAD SCHOOL
62 Templemead Dr, Hamilton, ON, L8W 3Z7
(905) 383-8348
Emp Here 40
SIC 8211 Elementary and secondary schools

D-U-N-S 20-590-5578   (BR)
HAMILTON-WENTWORTH   DISTRICT SCHOOL BOARD, THE
LINCOLN ALEXANDER ELEMENTARY SCHOOL
50 Ravenbury Dr, Hamilton, ON, L8W 2B5
(905) 574-4323
Emp Here 25
SIC 8211 Elementary and secondary schools

D-U-N-S 20-710-7827   (BR)
HAMILTON-WENTWORTH   DISTRICT SCHOOL BOARD, THE
CECIL B STIRLING SCHOOL
340 Queen Victoria Dr, Hamilton, ON, L8W 1T9
(905) 385-5374
Emp Here 50
SIC 8211 Elementary and secondary schools

D-U-N-S 20-793-1853   (BR)
METRO ONTARIO INC
FOOD BASICS
505 Rymal Rd E Suite 3, Hamilton, ON, L8W 3X1
(905) 574-5298
Emp Here 210
SIC 5411 Grocery stores

D-U-N-S 25-292-3933   (BR)
METRO ONTARIO INC
1070 Stone Church Rd E, Hamilton, ON, L8W 3K8

Emp Here 100
SIC 5411 Grocery stores

D-U-N-S 25-370-9513   (BR)
PATENE BUILDING SUPPLIES LTD
PATENE

255 Nebo Rd, Hamilton, ON, L8W 2E1
(905) 574-1110
Emp Here 30
SIC 5039 Construction materials, nec

D-U-N-S 25-138-3089   (BR)
SOBEYS CAPITAL INCORPORATED
FRESHCO
905 Rymal Rd E, Hamilton, ON, L8W 3M2
(905) 383-9930
Emp Here 150
SIC 5411 Grocery stores

D-U-N-S 20-025-5409   (BR)
STATE REALTY LIMITED
987 Rymal Rd E, Hamilton, ON, L8W 3M2
(905) 574-4600
Emp Here 100
SIC 6531 Real estate agents and managers

D-U-N-S 24-183-7210   (SL)
TARESCO LTD
QSI
175a Nebo Rd, Hamilton, ON, L8W 2E1
(905) 575-8078
Emp Here 50   *Sales* 3,648,035
SIC 1751 Carpentry work

D-U-N-S 25-106-0810   (BR)
TYCO INTEGRATED FIRE & SECURITY CANADA, INC
SIMPLEXGRINNELL
(*Suby of* Johnson Controls, Inc.)
40 Hempstead Dr Suite 1, Hamilton, ON, L8W 2E7
(905) 577-4077
Emp Here 60
SIC 7389 Business services, nec

D-U-N-S 20-927-3965   (BR)
WENDY'S RESTAURANTS OF CANADA INC
WENDYS
(*Suby of* The Wendy's Company)
967 Rymal Rd E, Hamilton, ON, L8W 3M2
(905) 388-8988
Emp Here 40
SIC 5812 Eating places

D-U-N-S 25-283-9261   (BR)
WESTON BAKERIES LIMITED
GOLDEN MILL BAKERY
1275 Rymal Rd E Unit 1, Hamilton, ON, L8W 3N1
(905) 575-5830
Emp Here 50
SIC 2051 Bread, cake, and related products

Hamilton, ON L9A
Wentworth County

D-U-N-S 20-178-0348   (SL)
1555965 ONTARIO INC
TIM HORTONS
473 Concession St, Hamilton, ON, L9A 1C1
(905) 383-7160
Emp Here 70   *Sales* 3,109,686
SIC 5461 Retail bakeries

D-U-N-S 25-118-9593   (BR)
CADILLAC FAIRVIEW CORPORATION LIMITED, THE
LIME RIDGE MALL
999 Upper Wentworth St Suite 145, Hamilton, ON, L9A 4X5
(905) 387-4455
Emp Here 50
SIC 6512 Nonresidential building operators

D-U-N-S 20-580-4581   (BR)
CANADA POST CORPORATION
999 Upper Wentworth St, Hamilton, ON, L9A 4X5
(905) 388-8459
Emp Here 20
SIC 4311 U.s. postal service

D-U-N-S 20-415-1539   (BR)
DOLLARAMA S.E.C.
DOLLARAMA
998 Upper Wentworth, Hamilton, ON, L9A 4V8
(905) 388-9265
Emp Here 35
SIC 5331 Variety stores

D-U-N-S 24-523-3031   (BR)
ENTERPRISE 1000 INC
TIM HORTONS
(*Suby of* Enterprise 1000 Inc)
990 Upper Wentworth St Suite 11, Hamilton, ON, L9A 5E9
(905) 389-4611
Emp Here 20
SIC 5812 Eating places

D-U-N-S 24-523-3056   (BR)
ENTERPRISE 1000 INC
TIM HORTONS
(*Suby of* Enterprise 1000 Inc)
999 Upper Wentworth St, Hamilton, ON, L9A 4X5
(905) 383-1337
Emp Here 20
SIC 5812 Eating places

D-U-N-S 25-301-2405   (BR)
EXTENDICARE (CANADA) INC
PARAMED HOME HEALTH CARE
883 Upper Wentworth St Suite 301, Hamilton, ON, L9A 4Y6
(905) 318-8522
Emp Here 200
SIC 8051 Skilled nursing care facilities

D-U-N-S 24-340-2679   (BR)
FGL SPORTS LTD
FORZANI
999 Upper Wentworth St, Hamilton, ON, L9A 4X5
(905) 383-5012
Emp Here 80
SIC 5941 Sporting goods and bicycle shops

D-U-N-S 24-337-2807   (BR)
FGL SPORTS LTD
NATIONAL SPORTS
970 Upper Wentworth St Suite 2, Hamilton, ON, L9A 4V8
(905) 388-1566
Emp Here 20
SIC 5941 Sporting goods and bicycle shops

D-U-N-S 25-487-5412   (BR)
GAP (CANADA) INC
GAP
(*Suby of* The Gap Inc)
999 Upper Wentworth St, Hamilton, ON, L9A 4X5
(905) 574-3444
Emp Here 50
SIC 5651 Family clothing stores

D-U-N-S 25-292-6639   (BR)
HAMILTON-WENTWORTH   CATHOLIC SCHOOL BOARD
ST. MICHAEL SCHOOL
135 Hester St, Hamilton, ON, L9A 2N9
(905) 383-2986
Emp Here 60
SIC 8211 Elementary and secondary schools

D-U-N-S 25-292-6860   (BR)
HAMILTON-WENTWORTH   CATHOLIC SCHOOL BOARD
STS PETER AND PAUL SCHOOL
49 Fennell Ave E, Hamilton, ON, L9A 1R5
(905) 383-4911
Emp Here 40
SIC 8211 Elementary and secondary schools

D-U-N-S 25-292-6019   (BR)
HAMILTON-WENTWORTH   CATHOLIC SCHOOL BOARD
SAINT CHARLES ADULT EDUCATION CON-

TINUING EDUCATION
150 East 5th St, Hamilton, ON, L9A 2Z8
(905) 575-5202
Emp Here 150
SIC 8211 Elementary and secondary schools

D-U-N-S 24-676-4992   (BR)
HAMILTON-WENTWORTH   CATHOLIC SCHOOL BOARD
ELEMENTARY ALTER-ED PROGRAM
50 Millwood Pl, Hamilton, ON, L9A 2M8
(905) 383-5111
Emp Here 25
SIC 8211 Elementary and secondary schools

D-U-N-S 20-590-5537   (BR)
HAMILTON-WENTWORTH   DISTRICT SCHOOL BOARD, THE
LINDEN PARK PUBLIC SCHOOL
4 Vickers Rd, Hamilton, ON, L9A 1Y1
(905) 385-2336
Emp Here 25
SIC 8211 Elementary and secondary schools

D-U-N-S 20-710-7983   (BR)
HAMILTON-WENTWORTH   DISTRICT SCHOOL BOARD, THE
QUEENSDALE ELEMENTARY SCHOOL
67 Queensdale Ave E, Hamilton, ON, L9A 1K4
(905) 389-9311
Emp Here 25
SIC 8211 Elementary and secondary schools

D-U-N-S 20-024-9667   (BR)
HAMILTON-WENTWORTH   DISTRICT SCHOOL BOARD, THE
PAULINE JOHNSON SCHOOL
25 Hummingbird Lane, Hamilton, ON, L9A 4B1
(905) 388-4447
Emp Here 25
SIC 8211 Elementary and secondary schools

D-U-N-S 20-590-5420   (BR)
HAMILTON-WENTWORTH   DISTRICT SCHOOL BOARD, THE
NORWOOD PARK
165 Terrace Dr, Hamilton, ON, L9A 2Z2

Emp Here 25
SIC 8211 Elementary and secondary schools

D-U-N-S 20-025-5086   (BR)
HAMILTON-WENTWORTH   DISTRICT SCHOOL BOARD, THE
CARDINAL HEIGHTS SCHOOL
70 Bobolink Rd, Hamilton, ON, L9A 2P5
(905) 385-5344
Emp Here 25
SIC 8211 Elementary and secondary schools

D-U-N-S 20-024-9253   (BR)
HAMILTON-WENTWORTH   DISTRICT SCHOOL BOARD, THE
HILL PARK SCHOOL
465 East 16th St, Hamilton, ON, L9A 4K6
(905) 318-1291
Emp Here 125
SIC 8211 Elementary and secondary schools

D-U-N-S 20-590-5651   (BR)
HAMILTON-WENTWORTH   DISTRICT SCHOOL BOARD, THE
HAMILTON SCHOOL
20 Education Ct, Hamilton, ON, L9A 0B9
(905) 527-5092
Emp Here 25
SIC 8211 Elementary and secondary schools

D-U-N-S 25-301-2090   (BR)
HUDSON'S BAY COMPANY
THE BAY LIMERIDGE
999 Upper Wentworth St, Hamilton, ON, L9A 4X5
(905) 318-8008
Emp Here 200
SIC 5311 Department stores

D-U-N-S 25-051-2407   (BR)

LE CHATEAU INC
CHATEAU STORE 038, LE
(*Suby* of Le Chateau Inc)
999 Upper Wentworth St, Hamilton, ON, L9A 4X5
(905) 385-4379
Emp Here 20
SIC 5651 Family clothing stores

D-U-N-S 24-189-2210   (BR)
OLD NAVY (CANADA) INC
OLD NAVY
(*Suby* of The Gap Inc)
999 Upper Wentworth St, Hamilton, ON, L9A 4X5
(905) 318-4506
Emp Here 65
SIC 5651 Family clothing stores

D-U-N-S 20-734-1947   (BR)
PRISZM LP
KFC
999 Upper Wentworth St, Hamilton, ON, L9A 4X5
(905) 318-6565
Emp Here 25
SIC 5812 Eating places

D-U-N-S 25-311-1496   (BR)
SEARS CANADA INC
999 Upper Wentworth St, Hamilton, ON, L9A 4X5
(905) 389-4441
Emp Here 360
SIC 5311 Department stores

D-U-N-S 20-945-2296   (BR)
SERVICE CORPORATION INTERNATIONAL (CANADA) LIMITED
CRESMOUNT FUNERAL HOME
322 Fennell Ave E, Hamilton, ON, L9A 1T2
(905) 387-2111
Emp Here 20
SIC 7261 Funeral service and crematories

D-U-N-S 24-783-9322   (BR)
SHAW CABLESYSTEMS G.P.
141 Hester St Suite 1, Hamilton, ON, L9A 2N9
(705) 223-2120
Emp Here 125
SIC 4841 Cable and other pay television services

D-U-N-S 20-796-4375   (BR)
STAPLES CANADA INC
STAPLES THE BUSINESS DEPOT
(*Suby* of Staples, Inc.)
970 Upper Wentworth St, Hamilton, ON, L9A 4V8
(905) 383-7913
Emp Here 30
SIC 5943 Stationery stores

D-U-N-S 20-700-4867   (BR)
TOMMY HILFIGER CANADA INC
999 Upper Wentworth St, Hamilton, ON, L9A 4X5

Emp Here 25
SIC 5136 Men's and boy's clothing

D-U-N-S 20-559-4125   (HQ)
TURKSTRA INDUSTRIES INC
TURKSTRA MILL
1050 Upper Wellington St, Hamilton, ON, L9A 3S6
(905) 388-8222
Emp Here 100   *Emp Total* 195
Sales 9,776,734
SIC 2431 Millwork
Pr Pr Carl Turkstra

Hamilton, ON L9B
Wentworth County

D-U-N-S 25-088-2735   (SL)

651233 ONTARIO INC
SWEET PARADISE BAKERY
630 Stone Church Rd W, Hamilton, ON, L9B 1A7
(905) 389-3487
Emp Here 55   *Sales* 1,896,978
SIC 5461 Retail bakeries

D-U-N-S 24-219-7569   (BR)
B&B HOSPITALITY INC
BEAVER AND BULLDOG SPORTS PUB & WINGERY
1400 Upper James St Suite 26, Hamilton, ON, L9B 1K3
(905) 385-9998
Emp Here 40
SIC 5812 Eating places

D-U-N-S 25-882-7666   (BR)
BRICK WAREHOUSE LP, THE
BRICK, THE
1441 Upper James St, Hamilton, ON, L9B 1K2
(905) 387-7002
Emp Here 54
SIC 5712 Furniture stores

D-U-N-S 25-487-5438   (BR)
CARA OPERATIONS LIMITED
MONTANA'S COOKHOUSE SALOON
(*Suby* of Cara Holdings Limited)
1508 Upper James St, Hamilton, ON, L9B 1K3
(905) 318-3992
Emp Here 50
SIC 5812 Eating places

D-U-N-S 20-303-3154   (BR)
CARA OPERATIONS LIMITED
KELSEY'S
(*Suby* of Cara Holdings Limited)
1550 Upper James St. Hamilton, ON, L9B 2L6
(905) 575-8696
Emp Here 50
SIC 5812 Eating places

D-U-N-S 24-524-9912   (BR)
HAMILTON HEALTH SCIENCES CORPORATION
CRITICALL ONTARIO
(*Suby* of Hamilton Health Sciences Corporation)
1725 Upper James St Suite 2, Hamilton, ON, L9B 1K7
(289) 396-7000
Emp Here 50
SIC 8399 Social services, nec

D-U-N-S 25-292-6720   (BR)
HAMILTON-WENTWORTH   CATHOLIC SCHOOL BOARD
CORPUS CHRISTI ELEMENTARY SCHOOL
25 Alderson Dr, Hamilton, ON, L9B 1G3
(905) 389-3940
Emp Here 30
SIC 8211 Elementary and secondary schools

D-U-N-S 25-292-6522   (BR)
HAMILTON-WENTWORTH   CATHOLIC SCHOOL BOARD
ST THOMAS MORE CATHOLIC SECONDARY SCHOOL
1045 Upper Paradise Rd, Hamilton, ON, L9B 2N4
(905) 388-3030
Emp Here 180
SIC 8211 Elementary and secondary schools

D-U-N-S 25-292-6753   (BR)
HAMILTON-WENTWORTH   CATHOLIC SCHOOL BOARD
ST. MARGUERITE D'YOUVILLE SCHOOL
20 Bonaparte Way, Hamilton, ON, L9B 2E3
(905) 387-4600
Emp Here 40
SIC 8211 Elementary and secondary schools

D-U-N-S 20-710-8114   (BR)
HAMILTON-WENTWORTH   DISTRICT SCHOOL BOARD, THE

HELEN DETWILER SCHOOL
320 Brigade Dr, Hamilton, ON, L9B 2E3
(905) 574-2662
Emp Here 50
SIC 8211 Elementary and secondary schools

D-U-N-S 24-341-8782   (BR)
IAN MARTIN LIMITED
(*Suby* of Martin, Ian Technology Staffing Limited)
34 Stone Church Rd E Suite 201, Hamilton, ON, L9B 1A9
(905) 304-7383
Emp Here 40
SIC 7361 Employment agencies

D-U-N-S 25-050-0261   (SL)
LSL HOLDINGS INC
ALOTA CARS
55 Rymal Rd E, Hamilton, ON, L9B 1B9

Emp Here 30   *Sales* 15,217,500
SIC 5511 New and used car dealers
Pr Leighan Leggat

D-U-N-S 20-758-3068   (BR)
LICK'S ICE CREAM & BURGER SHOPS INC
(*Suby* of Lick's Ice Cream & Burger Shops Inc)
1441 Upper James St, Hamilton, ON, L9B 1K2

Emp Here 50
SIC 5812 Eating places

D-U-N-S 20-792-3157   (SL)
LITTLE CEASAR
930 Upper Paradise Rd, Hamilton, ON, L9B 2N1
(905) 387-4510
Emp Here 50   *Sales* 1,532,175
SIC 5812 Eating places

D-U-N-S 20-732-9822   (SL)
NETHERCOTT CHEVROLET INC
1591 Upper James St, Hamilton, ON, L9B 1K2

Emp Here 58   *Sales* 27,327,541
SIC 5511 New and used car dealers
Pr Pr William R Nethercott

D-U-N-S 24-224-5574   (BR)
PIONEER FAST FOODS INC
WENDY'S RESTAURANTS
(*Suby* of Pioneer Fast Foods Inc)
1550 Upper James St, Hamilton, ON, L9B 2L6
(905) 389-1787
Emp Here 36
SIC 5812 Eating places

D-U-N-S 20-195-9322   (BR)
PRIME RESTAURANTS INC
EAST SIDE MARIO'S
(*Suby* of Cara Holdings Limited)
1389 Upper James St Suite Side, Hamilton, ON, L9B 1K2
(905) 574-3890
Emp Here 75
SIC 5812 Eating places

D-U-N-S 25-311-9259   (BR)
REXALL PHARMACY GROUP LTD
REXALL
(*Suby* of McKesson Corporation)
930 Upper Paradise Rd Suite 13, Hamilton, ON, L9B 2N1
(905) 318-5383
Emp Here 20
SIC 5912 Drug stores and proprietary stores

D-U-N-S 20-518-0685   (BR)
SCHLEGEL VILLAGES INC
THE VILLAGE OF WENTWORTH HEIGHTS
1620 Upper Wentworth St, Hamilton, ON, L9B 2W3
(905) 575-4735
Emp Here 200
SIC 8051 Skilled nursing care facilities

D-U-N-S 25-623-4352   (HQ)

ST. ELIZABETH HOME SOCIETY (HAMILTON ONTARIO)
ST. ELIZABETH VILLA
(Suby of St. Elizabeth Home Society (Hamilton Ontario))
391 Rymal Rd W Suite 304, Hamilton, ON, L9B 1V2
(905) 388-9691
Emp Here 45   Emp Total 56
Sales 2,188,821
SIC 8322 Individual and family services

D-U-N-S 24-194-9804   (BR)
THRIFT MAGIC LP
TALIZE
1428 Upper James St, Hamilton, ON, L9B 1K3
(905) 318-2376
Emp Here 25
SIC 7389 Business services, nec

D-U-N-S 25-221-3178   (BR)
WINNERS MERCHANTS INTERNATIONAL L.P.
WINNERS
(Suby of The TJX Companies Inc)
1508 Upper James St, Hamilton, ON, L9B 1K3
(905) 318-6555
Emp Here 55
SIC 5651 Family clothing stores

Hamilton, ON L9C
Wentworth County

D-U-N-S 25-145-3981   (SL)
718695 ONTARIO INC
KEG STEAKHOUSE & BAR, THE
1170 Upper James St, Hamilton, ON, L9C 3B1
(905) 574-7380
Emp Here 83   Sales 2,480,664
SIC 5812 Eating places

D-U-N-S 25-296-7997   (BR)
BANK OF NOVA SCOTIA, THE
SCOTIABANK
630 Upper James St, Hamilton, ON, L9C 2Z1
(905) 575-6520
Emp Here 20
SIC 6021 National commercial banks

D-U-N-S 20-639-5253   (SL)
BEAR, JOHN PONTIAC BUICK CADILLAC LTD
1200 Upper James St, Hamilton, ON, L9C 3B1
(905) 575-9400
Emp Here 100   Sales 49,080,000
SIC 5511 New and used car dealers
Pr Pr John Bear
VP VP Jamie Lalande

D-U-N-S 25-303-2825   (BR)
CANADIAN IMPERIAL BANK OF COMMERCE
CIBC
673d Upper James St, Hamilton, ON, L9C 5R9
(905) 387-1382
Emp Here 22
SIC 6021 National commercial banks

D-U-N-S 25-465-0179   (BR)
CANCER CARE ONTARIO
ONTARIO BREAST SCREENING PROGRAM
565 Sanatorium Rd Suite 207, Hamilton, ON, L9C 7N4
(905) 389-0101
Emp Here 20
SIC 8099 Health and allied services, nec

D-U-N-S 20-812-8681   (BR)
CITY OF HAMILTON, THE
WESTMOUNT RECREATION CENTRE
35 Lynbrook Dr, Hamilton, ON, L9C 2K6
(905) 546-4932
Emp Here 25
SIC 7999 Amusement and recreation, nec

D-U-N-S 25-292-6746   (BR)
CONSEIL SCOLAIRE DE DISTRICT CATHOLIQUE CENTRE-SUD
ECOLE ELEMENTAIRE MONSEIGNEUR-DE-LAVAL
135 Bendamere Ave, Hamilton, ON, L9C 1N4
(905) 387-6448
Emp Here 50
SIC 8211 Elementary and secondary schools

D-U-N-S 20-552-0146   (BR)
EXTENDICARE (CANADA) INC
EXTENDICARE HAMILTON
90 Chedmac Dr Suite 2317, Hamilton, ON, L9C 7W1
(905) 318-4472
Emp Here 100
SIC 8051 Skilled nursing care facilities

D-U-N-S 25-293-9616   (BR)
HAMILTON-WENTWORTH CATHOLIC SCHOOL BOARD
REGINA MUNDI CATHOLIC SCHOOL
675 Mohawk Rd W, Hamilton, ON, L9C 1X7
(905) 383-7244
Emp Here 32
SIC 8211 Elementary and secondary schools

D-U-N-S 25-293-9681   (BR)
HAMILTON-WENTWORTH CATHOLIC SCHOOL BOARD
ST VINCENT DE PAUL CATHOLIC SCHOOL
295 Greencedar Dr, Hamilton, ON, L9C 7M9
(905) 385-3734
Emp Here 30
SIC 8211 Elementary and secondary schools

D-U-N-S 25-293-9806   (BR)
HAMILTON-WENTWORTH CATHOLIC SCHOOL BOARD
ST. TERESA OF AVILA SCHOOL
171 San Remo Dr, Hamilton, ON, L9C 6P8
(905) 385-7555
Emp Here 24
SIC 8211 Elementary and secondary schools

D-U-N-S 25-293-9640   (BR)
HAMILTON-WENTWORTH CATHOLIC SCHOOL BOARD
ANNUNCIATION OF OUR LORD
20 Gemini Dr, Hamilton, ON, L9C 5V7
(905) 389-0782
Emp Here 25
SIC 8211 Elementary and secondary schools

D-U-N-S 20-024-9659   (BR)
HAMILTON-WENTWORTH DISTRICT SCHOOL BOARD, THE
MOUNTVIEW SCHOOL
59 Karen Cres, Hamilton, ON, L9C 5M5
(905) 979-4335
Emp Here 23
SIC 8211 Elementary and secondary schools

D-U-N-S 20-138-0925   (BR)
HAMILTON-WENTWORTH DISTRICT SCHOOL BOARD, THE
CHEDOKE SCHOOL
500 Bendamere Ave, Hamilton, ON, L9C 1R3
(905) 388-5833
Emp Here 50
SIC 8211 Elementary and secondary schools

D-U-N-S 20-286-9215   (BR)
HAMILTON-WENTWORTH DISTRICT SCHOOL BOARD, THE
SIR ALLAN MACNAB
145 Magnolia Dr, Hamilton, ON, L9C 5P4
(905) 383-3337
Emp Here 90
SIC 8211 Elementary and secondary schools

D-U-N-S 20-590-5586   (BR)
HAMILTON-WENTWORTH DISTRICT SCHOOL BOARD, THE
WESTVIEW MIDDLE SCHOOL
60 Rolston Dr, Hamilton, ON, L9C 3X7

(905) 388-1502
Emp Here 30
SIC 8211 Elementary and secondary schools

D-U-N-S 20-034-2090   (BR)
HAMILTON-WENTWORTH DISTRICT SCHOOL BOARD, THE
MOUNTAIN SECONDARY SCHOOL
60 Caledon Ave, Hamilton, ON, L9C 3C8
(905) 388-2521
Emp Here 35
SIC 8211 Elementary and secondary schools

D-U-N-S 20-290-3915   (BR)
HAMILTON-WENTWORTH DISTRICT SCHOOL BOARD, THE
R. A. RIDDELL ELEMENTARY SCHOOLS
200 Cranbrook Dr, Hamilton, ON, L9C 4S9
(905) 387-3350
Emp Here 35
SIC 8211 Elementary and secondary schools

D-U-N-S 20-024-9626   (BR)
HAMILTON-WENTWORTH DISTRICT SCHOOL BOARD, THE
BUCHANAN PARK SCHOOL
30 Laurier Ave, Hamilton, ON, L9C 3R9
(905) 387-5212
Emp Here 20
SIC 8211 Elementary and secondary schools

D-U-N-S 20-590-5669   (BR)
HAMILTON-WENTWORTH DISTRICT SCHOOL BOARD, THE
WEST WOOD PUBLIC SCHOOL
9 Lynbrook Dr, Hamilton, ON, L9C 2K6
(905) 383-2143
Emp Here 25
SIC 8211 Elementary and secondary schools

D-U-N-S 20-103-8242   (BR)
HAMILTON-WENTWORTH DISTRICT SCHOOL BOARD, THE
HOLBROOK SCHOOL
450 Sanatorium Rd, Hamilton, ON, L9C 2B1
(905) 385-5369
Emp Here 20
SIC 8211 Elementary and secondary schools

D-U-N-S 24-830-6185   (BR)
HAMILTON-WENTWORTH DISTRICT SCHOOL BOARD, THE
WESTMOUNT SECONDARY SCHOOL
39 Montcalm Dr, Hamilton, ON, L9C 4B1
(905) 385-5395
Emp Here 85
SIC 8211 Elementary and secondary schools

D-U-N-S 20-161-1840   (BR)
HAMILTON-WENTWORTH DISTRICT SCHOOL BOARD, THE
GORDON PRICE SCHOOL
11 Guildwood Dr, Hamilton, ON, L9C 7K2
(905) 574-5321
Emp Here 40
SIC 8211 Elementary and secondary schools

D-U-N-S 20-024-9634   (BR)
HAMILTON-WENTWORTH DISTRICT SCHOOL BOARD, THE
JAMES MACDONALD SCHOOL
200 Chester Ave, Hamilton, ON, L9C 2X1
(905) 385-3267
Emp Here 24
SIC 8211 Elementary and secondary schools

D-U-N-S 20-741-6152   (BR)
METRO ONTARIO INC
FOOD BASICS
640 Mohawk Rd W, Hamilton, ON, L9C 1X6
(905) 388-5596
Emp Here 60
SIC 5411 Grocery stores

D-U-N-S 24-335-0415   (BR)
METRO ONTARIO INC
METRO
751 Upper James St, Hamilton, ON, L9C 3A1

(905) 575-5545
Emp Here 175
SIC 5411 Grocery stores

D-U-N-S 25-221-2915   (BR)
MOHAWK COLLEGE OF APPLIED ARTS AND TECHNOLOGY, THE
135 Fennell Ave W, Hamilton, ON, L9C 1E9
(905) 575-1212
Emp Here 1,650
SIC 8222 Junior colleges

D-U-N-S 20-004-6931   (BR)
PIONEER FAST FOODS INC
WENDY'S
(Suby of Pioneer Fast Foods Inc)
869 Upper James St, Hamilton, ON, L9C 3A3
(905) 388-9238
Emp Here 40
SIC 5812 Eating places

D-U-N-S 25-936-6276   (BR)
R DENNINGER LIMITED
DENNINGER'S
(Suby of Denninger, R Limited)
1289 Upper James St, Hamilton, ON, L9C 3B3
(905) 389-4113
Emp Here 60
SIC 2013 Sausages and other prepared meats

D-U-N-S 20-002-6297   (BR)
ROYAL BANK OF CANADA
HARVARD SQAURE SHOPPING CENTER BRANCH, THE
(Suby of Royal Bank Of Canada)
801 Mohawk Rd W, Hamilton, ON, L9C 6C2
(905) 388-8550
Emp Here 30
SIC 6021 National commercial banks

D-U-N-S 20-956-3134   (BR)
ST. JOSEPH'S HEALTHCARE FOUNDATION, HAMILTON
100 West 5th St, Hamilton, ON, L9C 0E3
(905) 388-2511
Emp Here 300
SIC 8063 Psychiatric hospitals

D-U-N-S 25-019-7399   (BR)
TORONTO-DOMINION BANK, THE
TD CANADA TRUST
(Suby of Toronto-Dominion Bank, The)
781 Mohawk Rd W, Hamilton, ON, L9C 7B7
(905) 575-9221
Emp Here 20
SIC 6021 National commercial banks

D-U-N-S 25-077-5541   (BR)
WAL-MART CANADA CORP
675 Upper James St, Hamilton, ON, L9C 2Z5
(905) 389-6333
Emp Here 250
SIC 5311 Department stores

Hammond, ON K0A
Russell County

D-U-N-S 20-349-1691   (BR)
CATHOLIC DISTRICT SCHOOL BOARD OF EASTERN ONTARIO
ST. FRANCIS XAVIER CATHOLIC HIGH SCHOOL
1235 Russell Rd, Hammond, ON, K0A 2A0
(613) 487-2913
Emp Here 38
SIC 8211 Elementary and secondary schools

D-U-N-S 20-653-4443   (BR)
CATHOLIC DISTRICT SCHOOL BOARD OF EASTERN ONTARIO
POPE JOHN PAUL II CATHOLIC ELEMENTARY SCHOOL
3818 Legault Rd, Hammond, ON, K0A 2A0
(613) 487-3075
Emp Here 22

SIC 8211 Elementary and secondary schools

D-U-N-S 25-238-6727   (BR)
CONSEIL SCOLAIRE DE DISTRICT CATHOLIQUE DE L'EST ONTARIEN
ECOLE ELEMENTAIRE SAINT MATHIEU
(*Suby of* Conseil Scolaire De District Catholique De L'Est Ontarien)
3155 Gendron St, Hammond, ON, K0A 2A0
(613) 487-2404
Emp Here 25
SIC 8211 Elementary and secondary schools

Hampton, ON L0B
Durham County

D-U-N-S 20-037-4531   (BR)
KAWARTHA PINE RIDGE DISTRICT SCHOOL BOARD
ENNISKILLEN PUBLIC SCHOOL
8145 Old Scugog Rd, Hampton, ON, L0B 1J0
(905) 263-2970
Emp Here 20
SIC 8211 Elementary and secondary schools

Hanmer, ON P3P
Sudbury County

D-U-N-S 24-174-6929   (BR)
CEDARHURST QUARRIES & CRUSHING LIMITED
BEAMISH, K. J. CONSTRUCTION
5625 Notre Dame Ave, Hanmer, ON, P3P 1P2
(705) 969-4461
Emp Here 20
SIC 1629 Heavy construction, nec

D-U-N-S 25-126-1046   (BR)
CONSEIL SCOLAIRE DE DISTRICT DU GRAND NORD DE L'ONTARIO
CONSEIL SCOLAIRE DE DISTRICT DU GRAND NORD DE L'ON
4752 Notre Dame Ave, Hanmer, ON, P3P 1X5
(705) 969-3246
Emp Here 37
SIC 8211 Elementary and secondary schools

D-U-N-S 25-228-0557   (BR)
CONSEIL SCOLAIRE DE DISTRICT DU GRAND NORD DE L'ONTARIO
CONSEIL SCOLAIRE DE DISTRICT DU GRAND NORD DE L'ON
4800 Notre Dame Ave, Hanmer, ON, P3P 1X5
(705) 969-4402
Emp Here 35
SIC 8211 Elementary and secondary schools

D-U-N-S 25-239-9696   (BR)
RAINBOW DISTRICT SCHOOL BOARD
PINECREST PUBLIC SCHOOL
(*Suby of* Rainbow District School Board)
1650 Dominion Dr, Hanmer, ON, P3P 1A1
(705) 675-0200
Emp Here 22
SIC 8211 Elementary and secondary schools

D-U-N-S 24-156-7093   (BR)
SUDBURY CATHOLIC DISTRICT SCHOOL BOARD
BISHOP ALEXANDER CARTER CATHOLIC SECONDARY SCHOOL
539 Francis St, Hanmer, ON, P3P 1E6
(705) 969-2212
Emp Here 36
SIC 8211 Elementary and secondary schools

D-U-N-S 25-239-0034   (BR)
SUDBURY CATHOLIC DISTRICT SCHOOL BOARD
ST ANNE ELEMENTARY SCHOOL
4500 St. Michel St, Hanmer, ON, P3P 1M8

(705) 969-2101
Emp Here 38
SIC 8211 Elementary and secondary schools

Hannon, ON L0R
Wentworth County

D-U-N-S 24-302-1771   (SL)
944622 ONTARIO LIMITED
CALEDONIA TRANSPORTATION CO
175 Swayze Rd, Hannon, ON, L0R 1P0
(905) 692-4488
Emp Here 110   *Sales* 3,064,349
SIC 4151 School buses

D-U-N-S 20-053-3792   (BR)
CRH CANADA GROUP INC
DUFFERIN CONCRETE
886 Nebo Rd, Hannon, ON, L0R 1P0
(905) 679-3994
Emp Here 25
SIC 5032 Brick, stone, and related material

D-U-N-S 25-255-3607   (BR)
HAMILTON-WENTWORTH CATHOLIC SCHOOL BOARD
BISHOP RYAN CATHOLIC SECONDARY SCHOOL
1824 Rymal Rd, Hannon, ON, L0R 1P0
(905) 573-2151
Emp Here 100
SIC 8211 Elementary and secondary schools

D-U-N-S 20-310-8436   (BR)
STAPLES CANADA INC
(*Suby of* Staples, Inc.)
2130 Rymal Rd Suite 103, Hannon, ON, L0R 1P0
(905) 692-7215
Emp Here 25
SIC 5943 Stationery stores

D-U-N-S 24-319-5125   (BR)
WAL-MART CANADA CORP
WALMART
2190 Rymal Rd Suite 1042, Hannon, ON, L0R 1P0
(905) 692-7000
Emp Here 120
SIC 5311 Department stores

Hanover, ON N4N
Grey County

D-U-N-S 20-590-7103   (BR)
BLUEWATER DISTRICT SCHOOL BOARD
HANOVER HEIGHTS COMMUNITY SCHOOL
524 13th St, Hanover, ON, N4N 1Y4
(519) 364-2910
Emp Here 25
SIC 8211 Elementary and secondary schools

D-U-N-S 25-238-9077   (BR)
BLUEWATER DISTRICT SCHOOL BOARD
DAWNVIEW PUBLIC SCHOOL
149 12th Ave, Hanover, ON, N4N 2S8
(519) 364-1891
Emp Here 20
SIC 8211 Elementary and secondary schools

D-U-N-S 20-590-7087   (BR)
BLUEWATER DISTRICT SCHOOL BOARD
JOHN DIEFEN BAKER SECONDARY SCHOOL
181 7th St, Hanover, ON, N4N 1G7
(519) 364-3770
Emp Here 50
SIC 8211 Elementary and secondary schools

D-U-N-S 20-710-6647   (BR)
BRUCE-GREY CATHOLIC DISTRICT SCHOOL BOARD

HOLY FAMILY SEPARATE SCHOOL
334 10th Ave, Hanover, ON, N4N 2N5
(519) 364-2760
Emp Here 50
SIC 8211 Elementary and secondary schools

D-U-N-S 20-537-1805   (BR)
CANADA POST CORPORATION
252 10th St, Hanover, ON, N4N 1N9
(519) 364-3491
Emp Here 20
SIC 4311 U.s. postal service

D-U-N-S 24-380-2803   (BR)
HANOVER NURSING HOME LIMITED
HANOVER CARE CENTRE
700 19th Ave, Hanover, ON, N4N 3S6
(519) 364-3700
Emp Here 60
SIC 8051 Skilled nursing care facilities

D-U-N-S 24-316-8143   (SL)
HANOVER, BENTINCK & BRANT AGRICULTURAL SOCIETY
HANOVER RACEWAY
265 5th St, Hanover, ON, N4N 3X3
(519) 364-2860
Emp Here 104
SIC 7948 Racing, including track operation

D-U-N-S 25-411-7674   (BR)
MAPLE LEAF FOODS INC
HORIZON POULTRY
90 10th Ave, Hanover, ON, N4N 3B8
(519) 364-3200
Emp Here 150
SIC 5144 Poultry and poultry products

D-U-N-S 25-487-1007   (BR)
NORTH WELLINGTON CO-OPERATIVE SERVICES INC
691 10th St, Hanover, ON, N4N 1S1
(519) 364-4777
Emp Here 21
SIC 5191 Farm supplies

D-U-N-S 24-523-8469   (BR)
PARRISH & HEIMBECKER, LIMITED
NEW-LIFE MILLS ANIMAL NUTRITION & FEED PRODUCTS
(*Suby of* Parrish & Heimbecker, Limited)
252 14th St, Hanover, ON, N4N 3C5
(519) 364-3263
Emp Here 30
SIC 5153 Grain and field beans

D-U-N-S 20-354-9642   (BR)
PHARMA PLUS DRUGMARTS LTD
342 10th St, Hanover, ON, N4N 1P4
(519) 364-2300
Emp Here 20
SIC 5912 Drug stores and proprietary stores

D-U-N-S 25-639-1731   (BR)
REGAL BELOIT CANADA
638 14th St, Hanover, ON, N4N 2A1
(519) 364-6024
Emp Here 20
SIC 3621 Motors and generators

D-U-N-S 20-039-7698   (BR)
REVERA INC
VILLAGE SENIORS COMMUNITY, THE
101 10th St Suite 2006, Hanover, ON, N4N 1M9
(519) 364-4320
Emp Here 100
SIC 6513 Apartment building operators

D-U-N-S 20-056-4383   (HQ)
SMITTY'S SHOPPING CENTRE LIMITED
SMITTY'S FINE FURNITURE
(*Suby of* Smitty's Holdings Inc.)
170 3rd St, Hanover, ON, N4N 1B2
(519) 364-3800
Emp Here 50   *Emp Total* 3
Sales 6,785,345
SIC 5712 Furniture stores

Lloyd Schmidt
Pr Pr Robert (Bob) Gray
Elmer Schmidt

D-U-N-S 24-727-4004   (BR)
SOBEYS CAPITAL INCORPORATED
IGA
236 10th St, Hanover, ON, N4N 1N9
(519) 364-2891
Emp Here 80
SIC 5411 Grocery stores

D-U-N-S 24-062-6960   (BR)
TELESAT CANADA
OPERATIONS NETWORK CENTRE
Gd, Hanover, ON, N4N 3C2
(519) 364-1221
Emp Here 100
SIC 4899 Communication services, nec

D-U-N-S 20-738-6454   (BR)
WAL-MART CANADA CORP
1100 10th St, Hanover, ON, N4N 3B8
(519) 364-0867
Emp Here 100
SIC 5311 Department stores

D-U-N-S 24-977-4142   (SL)
WEST FURNITURE CO INC
WEST BROS FURNITURE
582 14th St, Hanover, ON, N4N 2A1
(519) 364-7770
Emp Here 70   *Sales* 4,085,799
SIC 2511 Wood household furniture

Harriston, ON N0G
Wellington County

D-U-N-S 20-817-5349   (BR)
CARESSANT-CARE NURSING AND RETIREMENT HOMES LIMITED
24 Louise St, Harriston, ON, N0G 1Z0
(519) 338-3700
Emp Here 100
SIC 8051 Skilled nursing care facilities

D-U-N-S 20-036-9077   (BR)
UPPER GRAND DISTRICT SCHOOL BOARD, THE
MINTO-CLIFFORD PUBLIC SCHOOL
(*Suby of* Upper Grand District School Board, The)
Gd, Harriston, ON, N0G 1Z0
(519) 338-2920
Emp Here 30
SIC 8211 Elementary and secondary schools

D-U-N-S 25-845-5070   (BR)
UPPER GRAND DISTRICT SCHOOL BOARD, THE
HARRISTON SENIOR PUBLIC SCHOOL
(*Suby of* Upper Grand District School Board, The)
24 George St, Harriston, ON, N0G 1Z0
(519) 338-2920
Emp Here 20
SIC 8211 Elementary and secondary schools

Harrow, ON N0R
Essex County

D-U-N-S 25-998-5166   (SL)
AMERI-CAN INVESTMENTS INC
DELTA WIRE AND MFG
29 Delta Dr, Harrow, ON, N0R 1G0
(519) 738-3514
Emp Here 60   *Sales* 14,067,200
SIC 3496 Miscellaneous fabricated wire products
Pr Pr Howard Campbell Jr

D-U-N-S 24-506-6857   (HQ)

ATLAS TUBE CANADA ULC
200 Clark St, Harrow, ON, N0R 1G0
(519) 738-5000
Emp Here 160   *Emp Total* 600
SIC 3317 Steel pipe and tubes

D-U-N-S 25-249-2004   (BR)
GREATER ESSEX COUNTY DISTRICT SCHOOL BOARD
HARROW SENIOR PUBLIC SCHOOL
400 Centre St E, Harrow, ON, N0R 1G0
(519) 738-4921
Emp Here 40
SIC 8211 Elementary and secondary schools

D-U-N-S 25-249-1923   (BR)
GREATER ESSEX COUNTY DISTRICT SCHOOL BOARD
HARROW DISTRICT HIGH SCHOOL
45 Wellington St, Harrow, ON, N0R 1G0
(519) 738-2234
Emp Here 30
SIC 8211 Elementary and secondary schools

D-U-N-S 20-005-5940   (BR)
GREATER ESSEX COUNTY DISTRICT SCHOOL BOARD
HARROW JUNIOR PUBLIC SCHOOL
230 Center St E, Harrow, ON, N0R 1G0
(519) 738-4361
Emp Here 20
SIC 8211 Elementary and secondary schools

D-U-N-S 20-524-8438   (SL)
SELLICK EQUIPMENT LIMITED
(*Suby of* Avis Industrial Corporation)
358 Erie St N, Harrow, ON, N0R 1G0
(519) 738-2255
Emp Here 75   *Sales* 27,706,026
SIC 3537 Industrial trucks and tractors
Leland Boren
Pr Pr Howard R. Sellick
David M. Sellick
Collin Sellick

D-U-N-S 25-249-1881   (BR)
WINDSOR-ESSEX CATHOLIC DISTRICT SCHOOL BOARD, THE
ST ANTHONY SCHOOL
166 Centre St W, Harrow, ON, N0R 1G0
(519) 738-3531
Emp Here 25
SIC 8211 Elementary and secondary schools

Harrowsmith, ON K0H
Frontenac County

D-U-N-S 25-305-4696   (BR)
LIMESTONE DISTRICT SCHOOL BOARD
HARROWSMITH PUBLIC SCHOOL
4121 Colebrook Rd, Harrowsmith, ON, K0H 1V0
(613) 372-2026
Emp Here 28
SIC 8211 Elementary and secondary schools

Havelock, ON K0L
Peterborough County

D-U-N-S 25-263-5701   (BR)
KAWARTHA PINE RIDGE DISTRICT SCHOOL BOARD
HAVELOCK DELMONT PUBLIC SCHOOL
55 Mathison St E, Havelock, ON, K0L 1Z0
(705) 778-3821
Emp Here 22
SIC 8211 Elementary and secondary schools

D-U-N-S 24-104-2337   (BR)
SOBEYS CAPITAL INCORPORATED
HAVELOCK FOODLAND
38 Ottawa St E, Havelock, ON, K0L 1Z0
(705) 778-3881
Emp Here 60
SIC 5411 Grocery stores

Hawkesbury, ON K6A
Prescott County

D-U-N-S 25-322-3234   (BR)
ALGONQUIN COLLEGE OF APPLIED ARTS AND TECHNOLOGY,
1 Main St E Suite 500, Hawkesbury, ON, K6A 1A1
(613) 632-4143
Emp Here 20
SIC 8221 Colleges and universities

D-U-N-S 20-530-0945   (BR)
CANADA POST CORPORATION
HAWKESBURY POSTAL OUTLET
284 Main St E, Hawkesbury, ON, K6A 1A5
(613) 632-6792
Emp Here 20
SIC 4311 U.s. postal service

D-U-N-S 24-937-0388   (SL)
COLORAMA DYEING & FINISHING INC
1400 Aberdeen St, Hawkesbury, ON, K6A 1K7
(613) 632-0774
Emp Here 53   *Sales* 8,536,402
SIC 2261 Finishing plants, cotton
Pr Pr Julie Katz
Shalom Katz

D-U-N-S 25-238-6545   (BR)
CONSEIL SCOLAIRE DE DISTRICT CATHOLIQUE DE L'EST ONTARIEN
ECOLE PAUL VI
(*Suby of* Conseil Scolaire De District Catholique De L'Est Ontarien)
500 Main St E, Hawkesbury, ON, K6A 1A9
(613) 632-2734
Emp Here 50
SIC 8211 Elementary and secondary schools

D-U-N-S 25-238-6693   (BR)
CONSEIL SCOLAIRE DE DISTRICT CATHOLIQUE DE L'EST ONTARIEN
ECOLE ELEMENTAIRE SAINTE-MARGUERITE-BOURGEOIS
(*Suby of* Conseil Scolaire De District Catholique De L'Est Ontarien)
82 Bon Pasteur St, Hawkesbury, ON, K6A 2K5
(613) 632-7035
Emp Here 25
SIC 8211 Elementary and secondary schools

D-U-N-S 25-137-3114   (BR)
CONSEIL SCOLAIRE DE DISTRICT CATHOLIQUE DE L'EST ONTARIEN
ECOLE SECONDAIRE REGIONAL DE HAWKESBURY
(*Suby of* Conseil Scolaire De District Catholique De L'Est Ontarien)
572 Kitchener St Suite 8e, Hawkesbury, ON, K6A 2P3
(613) 632-7055
Emp Here 80
SIC 8211 Elementary and secondary schools

D-U-N-S 20-711-6760   (BR)
CONSEIL SCOLAIRE DE DISTRICT CATHOLIQUE DE L'EST ONTARIEN
ADULT EDUCATION CENTRE
429 Abbott St, Hawkesbury, ON, K6A 2E2
(613) 632-4100
Emp Here 50
SIC 8211 Elementary and secondary schools

D-U-N-S 20-575-2780   (BR)
CONSEIL DES ECOLES PUBLIQUES DE L'EST DE L'ONTARIO
ECOLE PUBLIQUE NOUVEL HORIZON
433 Cartier Blvd, Hawkesbury, ON, K6A 1V9
(613) 632-8718
Emp Here 30

SIC 8211 Elementary and secondary schools

D-U-N-S 24-095-7535   (BR)
CONSEIL DES ECOLES PUBLIQUES DE L'EST DE L'ONTARIO
ECOLE SECONDAIRE PUBLIQUE LE SOMMET
894 Cecile Blvd, Hawkesbury, ON, K6A 3R5
(613) 632-6059
Emp Here 35
SIC 8211 Elementary and secondary schools

D-U-N-S 24-382-2582   (BR)
D & W FORWARDERS INC
1490 Spence Ave, Hawkesbury, ON, K6A 3T4
(613) 632-2797
Emp Here 25
SIC 4213 Trucking, except local

D-U-N-S 25-301-4062   (BR)
DELOITTE LLP
300 Mcgill St, Hawkesbury, ON, K6A 1P8
(613) 632-4178
Emp Here 30
SIC 8721 Accounting, auditing, and book-keeping

D-U-N-S 25-896-9559   (BR)
EASTERN ONTARIO HEALTH UNIT
134 Main St E Suite 301, Hawkesbury, ON, K6A 1A3
(613) 632-4355
Emp Here 20
SIC 8621 Professional organizations

D-U-N-S 24-437-4377   (BR)
GREAT PACIFIC ENTERPRISES INC
MONTEBELLO PACKAGING
1036 Aberdeen St Suite 399, Hawkesbury, ON, K6A 1K5
(613) 632-7096
Emp Here 70
SIC 3354 Aluminum extruded products

D-U-N-S 24-313-0338   (HQ)
HEARX HEARING INC
HELIX HEARING CARE
(*Suby of* Hearx Hearing Inc)
290 Mcgill St Suite A, Hawkesbury, ON, K6A 1P8
(877) 268-1045
Emp Here 25   *Emp Total* 120
Sales 20,096,000
SIC 5999 Miscellaneous retail stores, nec
Pr Jeffrey Geigel

D-U-N-S 24-482-6962   (SL)
HOTTE AUTOMOBILE INC
HOTTE FORD
640 Main St W, Hawkesbury, ON, K6A 2J3
(613) 632-1159
Emp Here 24   *Sales* 8,755,284
SIC 5511 New and used car dealers
Pr Pr Alan Cote
Stephan Hollander

D-U-N-S 20-891-3749   (BR)
IKO INDUSTRIES LTD
ARMOROOF DIV OF
1451 Spence Ave, Hawkesbury, ON, K6A 3T4
(613) 632-8581
Emp Here 80
SIC 2952 Asphalt felts and coatings

D-U-N-S 20-774-5949   (BR)
LOBLAWS SUPERMARKETS LIMITED
LAURIN YOUR INDEPENDENT GROCER
1560 Cameron St Suite 820, Hawkesbury, ON, K6A 3S5
(613) 632-9215
Emp Here 120
SIC 5411 Grocery stores

D-U-N-S 20-506-2748   (BR)
PITTSBURGH GLASS WORKS, ULC
545 Industriel Blvd, Hawkesbury, ON, K6A 2S5
(613) 632-2711
Emp Here 300

SIC 3231 Products of purchased glass

D-U-N-S 20-577-0196   (SL)
PREMOULE PORTES THERMOPLASTIQUES INC
1245 Tessier St, Hawkesbury, ON, K6A 3R1
(613) 632-5252
Emp Here 40   *Sales* 5,928,320
SIC 3083 Laminated plastics plate and sheet
Mgr Steve Kennedy
Pr Pierre Deslauriers
Pr Louis Deslauriers

D-U-N-S 24-801-5950   (SL)
PRESCOTT & RUSSEL RESIDENCE
1020 Cartier Blvd, Hawkesbury, ON, K6A 1W7
(613) 632-2755
Emp Here 120   *Sales* 4,377,642
SIC 8361 Residential care

D-U-N-S 20-649-9105   (SL)
QUESNEL BUS LINE LTD
306 Front Rd, Hawkesbury, ON, K6A 2S9
(613) 632-7809
Emp Here 60   *Sales* 1,678,096
SIC 4151 School buses

D-U-N-S 20-704-1497   (BR)
UPPER CANADA DISTRICT SCHOOL BOARD, THE
EASTERN ONTARIO EDUCATION AND TRAINING CENTER
750 Laurier St, Hawkesbury, ON, K6A 3N9
(613) 632-4100
Emp Here 25
SIC 8211 Elementary and secondary schools

D-U-N-S 20-055-2032   (SL)
VOITH CANADA INC
VOITH PAPER FABRIC & ROLL SYSTEMS
925 Tupper St, Hawkesbury, ON, K6A 3T5
(613) 632-4163
Emp Here 64   *Sales* 27,893,282
SIC 2621 Paper mills
Opers Mgr Bernard Chaine
Genl Mgr Jean-Francois Cote

Hawkestone, ON L0L
Simcoe County

D-U-N-S 25-099-4647   (SL)
COLUMBIA TREEHOUSE INC
1015 Lakeshore Rd E Rr 2, Hawkestone, ON, L0L 1T0
(705) 722-3220
Emp Here 20   *Sales* 5,425,920
SIC 1541 Industrial buildings and warehouses
Pr Pr Vern Solomon

D-U-N-S 25-843-0396   (BR)
HAMMOND TRANSPORTATION LIMITED
(*Suby of* Hammond Transportation Limited)
136 Line 9 S Oromedon, Hawkestone, ON, L0L 1T0
(705) 325-2774
Emp Here 25
SIC 4151 School buses

D-U-N-S 25-297-6329   (BR)
SIMCOE COUNTY DISTRICT SCHOOL BOARD, THE
EAST ORO ELEMENTARY SCHOOL
(*Suby of* Simcoe County District School Board, The)
744 11 Line N, Hawkestone, ON, L0L 1T0
(705) 487-2047
Emp Here 20
SIC 8211 Elementary and secondary schools

Hearst, ON P0L
Cochrane County

D-U-N-S 25-412-9703   (SL)
865072 ONTARIO LIMITED
COMPANION HOTEL MOTEL
931 Front St, Hearst, ON, P0L 1N0
(705) 362-4304
Emp Here 50   *Sales* 1,824,018
SIC 5813 Drinking places

D-U-N-S 25-412-6659   (BR)
CONSEIL SCOLAIRE CATHOLIQUE DE DISTRICT DES GRANDES RIVIERES, LE
PAVILLON NOTRE-DAME
48 9th St, Hearst, ON, P0L 1N0
(705) 362-7121
Emp Here 35
SIC 8211 Elementary and secondary schools

D-U-N-S 20-710-4212   (BR)
CONSEIL SCOLAIRE CATHOLIQUE DE DISTRICT DES GRANDES RIVIERES, LE
ECOLE CATHOLIQUE ST ANNE
619 Allen St, Hearst, ON, P0L 1N0
(705) 362-4754
Emp Here 22
SIC 8211 Elementary and secondary schools

D-U-N-S 20-647-4400   (BR)
CONSEIL SCOLAIRE CATHOLIQUE DE DISTRICT DES GRANDES RIVIERES, LE
ST LOUISE SCHOOL
1007 Edward St, Hearst, ON, P0L 1N0
(705) 362-4804
Emp Here 30
SIC 8211 Elementary and secondary schools

D-U-N-S 24-773-1420   (BR)
DMS PROPERTY MANAGEMENT LTD
HEARST LIFELINE
925 Alexandra St, Hearst, ON, P0L 1N0
(705) 372-2822
Emp Here 100
SIC 8399 Social services, nec

D-U-N-S 20-648-3658   (BR)
DISTRICT SCHOOL BOARD ONTARIO NORTH EAST
HEARST HIGH SCHOOL
30 10th St, Hearst, ON, P0L 1N0
(705) 362-4283
Emp Here 50
SIC 8211 Elementary and secondary schools

D-U-N-S 24-174-4056   (BR)
EPCOR DISTRIBUTION & TRANSMISSION INC
Gd, Hearst, ON, P0L 1N0
(705) 463-2513
Emp Here 20
SIC 4911 Electric services

D-U-N-S 24-092-2927   (BR)
LACROIX BUS SERVICE INC
(*Suby of* Lacroix Bus Service Inc)
10 Lafond Rd, Hearst, ON, P0L 1N0
(705) 362-4845
Emp Here 30
SIC 4142 Bus charter service, except local

D-U-N-S 20-804-9507   (SL)
LAROSE HEARST RECREATION CENTRE
925 Alexander, Hearst, ON, P0L 1N0
(705) 372-2824
Emp Here 65   *Sales* 3,502,114
SIC 7999 Amusement and recreation, nec

D-U-N-S 24-086-0697   (BR)
PUROLATOR INC.
Gd, Hearst, ON, P0L 1N0
(705) 372-0020
Emp Here 25
SIC 7389 Business services, nec

Hensall, ON N0M
Huron County

D-U-N-S 20-818-4101   (SL)
PROVINCIAL LONG TERM CARE INC
QUEENSWAY NURSING & RETIREMENT HOME
100 Queen St E, Hensall, ON, N0M 1X0
(519) 262-2830
Emp Here 85   *Sales* 3,866,917
SIC 8051 Skilled nursing care facilities

D-U-N-S 20-941-4408   (BR)
THOMPSONS LIMITED
96 Nelson St, Hensall, ON, N0M 1X0
(519) 262-2527
Emp Here 49
SIC 5153 Grain and field beans

Hepworth, ON N0H
Bruce County

D-U-N-S 25-842-4340   (BR)
BLUEWATER DISTRICT SCHOOL BOARD
HEPWORTH CENTRAL SCHOOL
402 Bruce St, Hepworth, ON, N0H 1P0
(519) 935-2061
Emp Here 30
SIC 8211 Elementary and secondary schools

Hickson, ON N0J
Oxford County

D-U-N-S 20-255-7625   (BR)
DARLING INTERNATIONAL CANADA INC
ROTHSAY
(*Suby of* Darling Ingredients Inc.)
884679 Oxforf Rd Suite 8, Hickson, ON, N0J 1L0
(519) 462-2917
Emp Here 50
SIC 4953 Refuse systems

D-U-N-S 25-237-8294   (BR)
THAMES VALLEY DISTRICT SCHOOL BOARD
HICKSON CENTRAL PUBLIC SCHOOL
161 Loveys St, Hickson, ON, N0J 1L0
(519) 462-2415
Emp Here 25
SIC 8211 Elementary and secondary schools

Hillsburgh, ON N0B
Wellington County

D-U-N-S 20-162-4590   (SL)
CONRAD PAINTING LIMITED
6117 Eighth Line Rr 2, Hillsburgh, ON, N0B 1Z0
(519) 855-4807
Emp Here 50   *Sales* 4,146,248
SIC 1721 Painting and paper hanging

Hillsdale, ON L0L
Simcoe County

D-U-N-S 25-297-6139   (BR)
SIMCOE COUNTY DISTRICT SCHOOL BOARD, THE
HILLSDALE ELEMENTARY SCHOOL
(*Suby of* Simcoe County District School Board, The)
16 Albert St E, Hillsdale, ON, L0L 1V0
(705) 835-2108
Emp Here 20
SIC 8211 Elementary and secondary schools

Holland Centre, ON N0H
Grey County

D-U-N-S 24-451-1973   (BR)
BLUEWATER DISTRICT SCHOOL BOARD
HOLLAND-CHARTSWORTH CENTRAL SCHOOL
777346 10 Hwy Rr 3, Holland Centre, ON, N0H 1R0
(519) 794-2729
Emp Here 25
SIC 8211 Elementary and secondary schools

Holland Landing, ON L9N
York County

D-U-N-S 25-446-8051   (BR)
AECON CONSTRUCTION GROUP INC
AECON UTILITIES
95 Sluse Rd, Holland Landing, ON, L9N 1G8
(905) 853-7148
Emp Here 45
SIC 1541 Industrial buildings and warehouses

D-U-N-S 25-026-8778   (BR)
YORK REGION DISTRICT SCHOOL BOARD
PARK AVENUE PUBLIC SCHOOL
(*Suby of* York Region District School Board)
36 Sunrise St, Holland Landing, ON, L9N 1H5
(905) 836-5951
Emp Here 45
SIC 8211 Elementary and secondary schools

D-U-N-S 25-297-8994   (BR)
YORK REGION DISTRICT SCHOOL BOARD
HOLLAND LANDING PUBLIC SCHOOL
(*Suby of* York Region District School Board)
16 Holland River Blvd, Holland Landing, ON, L9N 1C4
(905) 836-6614
Emp Here 38
SIC 8211 Elementary and secondary schools

Honey Harbour, ON P0E
Muskoka County

D-U-N-S 25-401-7999   (SL)
1212360 ONTARIO LIMITED
DELAWANA INN & RESORT
42 Delawana Rd, Honey Harbour, ON, P0E 1E0
(705) 756-2424
Emp Here 160   *Sales* 9,423,360
SIC 7011 Hotels and motels
Fin Ex Vivian Jacques
Dir Morris Fischtein
Dir Will Fischtein

Hornby, ON L0P
Halton County

D-U-N-S 20-568-8919   (BR)
CANADIAN PACIFIC RAILWAY COMPANY
7251 Trafalgar Rd, Hornby, ON, L0P 1E0
(905) 693-1270
Emp Here 20
SIC 7011 Hotels and motels

D-U-N-S 25-845-1459   (BR)
PIONEER FOOD SERVICES LIMITED
TIM HORTONS
(*Suby of* Pioneer Food Services Limited)
4452 Trafalgar Rd, Hornby, ON, L0P 1E0
(905) 875-3799
Emp Here 40
SIC 5812 Eating places

D-U-N-S 24-078-4652   (SL)

PUTZER, M. HORNBY LIMITED
M PUTZER HORNSBY NURSERIES
7314 Sixth Line, Hornby, ON, L0P 1E0
(905) 878-7226
Emp Here 70   *Sales* 3,575,074
SIC 7389 Business services, nec

D-U-N-S 20-529-5629   (SL)
VAN DONGEN LANDSCAPING & NURSERIES LTD
VAN DONGEN TREE FARM
6750 Trafalgar Rd Suite 1, Hornby, ON, L0P 1E0
(905) 878-1105
Emp Here 40   *Sales* 9,029,050
SIC 5261 Retail nurseries and garden stores
Pr Pr Adrian Van Dongen

Hornell Heights, ON P0H
Nipissing County

D-U-N-S 20-009-8759   (BR)
ATCO FRONTEC LOGISTICS CORP
NASITTUQ
1540 Airport Rd, Hornell Heights, ON, P0H 1P0
(705) 494-2011
Emp Here 60
SIC 1731 Electrical work

Hornepayne, ON P0M
Algoma County

D-U-N-S 24-676-5270   (BR)
ALGOMA DISTRICT SCHOOL BOARD
HORNEPAYNE PUBLIC SCHOOL
(*Suby of* Algoma District School Board)
162 Fourth Ave, Hornepayne, ON, P0M 1Z0
(807) 868-2503
Emp Here 20
SIC 8211 Elementary and secondary schools

D-U-N-S 20-074-6423   (BR)
COMPAGNIE DES CHEMINS DE FER NATIONAUX DU CANADA
58 Younge St, Hornepayne, ON, P0M 1Z0
(807) 868-2902
Emp Here 250
SIC 4011 Railroads, line-haul operating

D-U-N-S 24-216-9316   (SL)
HORNEPAYNE COMMUNITY HOSPITAL
278 Front St, Hornepayne, ON, P0M 1Z0
(807) 868-2061
Emp Here 65   *Sales* 4,523,563
SIC 8062 General medical and surgical hospitals

D-U-N-S 20-785-7249   (SL)
HORNEPAYNE ROMAN CATHOLIC SEPARATE SCHOOL BOARD
59 Neesomadina, Hornepayne, ON, P0M 1Z0

Emp Here 50   *Sales* 3,356,192
SIC 8211 Elementary and secondary schools

Huntsville, ON P1H
Muskoka County

D-U-N-S 25-307-0742   (BR)
BANK OF NOVA SCOTIA, THE
SCOTIABANK
70 King William St, Huntsville, ON, P1H 2A5

Emp Here 30
SIC 6021 National commercial banks

D-U-N-S 24-045-6665   (SL)
CAMP HURONDA

Gd Stn Main, Huntsville, ON, P1H 2K2
(705) 789-7153
Emp Here 50   *Sales* 4,231,721
SIC 7032 Sporting and recreational camps

D-U-N-S 25-158-8703   (BR)
CANADA POST CORPORATION
CANADA POST HUNTSVILLE
2 Main St W, Huntsville, ON, P1H 2E1
(705) 789-2221
Emp Here 25
SIC 4311 U.s. postal service

D-U-N-S 25-830-0227   (BR)
CLUBLINK CORPORATION ULC
DELTA GRANDVIEW RESORT
(*Suby of* TWC Enterprises Limited)
939 60 Hwy, Huntsville, ON, P1H 1B2
(705) 789-4417
Emp Here 40
SIC 7992 Public golf courses

D-U-N-S 24-119-8782   (BR)
CLUBLINK CORPORATION ULC
GRANDVIEW GULF CLUB
146 Grandview Dr N, Huntsville, ON, P1H 1B4
(705) 788-9550
Emp Here 30
SIC 7997 Membership sports and recreation clubs

D-U-N-S 20-037-9498   (BR)
CORPORATION OF THE TOWN OF HUNTSVILLE, THE
CANADA SUMMIT CENTRE
20 Park Dr, Huntsville, ON, P1H 1P5
(705) 789-2927
Emp Here 30
SIC 7999 Amusement and recreation, nec

D-U-N-S 20-699-9331   (BR)
DELTA HOTELS LIMITED
DELTA GRANDVIEW RESORT (MUSKOKA)
939 60 Hwy, Huntsville, ON, P1H 1B2
(705) 789-4417
Emp Here 100
SIC 8741 Management services

D-U-N-S 20-707-7939   (BR)
EXTENDICARE (CANADA) INC
PARAMED HOME HEALTH CARE
367 Muskoka Rd 3 N Unit 6, Huntsville, ON, P1H 1H6
(705) 788-9899
Emp Here 22
SIC 8051 Skilled nursing care facilities

D-U-N-S 25-656-1846   (BR)
FAMILY, YOUTH & CHILD SERVICES OF MUSKOKA
(*Suby of* Family, Youth & Child Services of Muskoka)
81 Main St W, Huntsville, ON, P1H 1X1
(705) 789-8866
Emp Here 60
SIC 8322 Individual and family services

D-U-N-S 24-363-6821   (BR)
FANOTECH ENVIRO INC
220 Old North Rd, Huntsville, ON, P1H 2J4
(705) 645-5434
Emp Here 60
SIC 3713 Truck and bus bodies

D-U-N-S 24-211-0802   (BR)
HOME DEPOT OF CANADA INC
(*Suby of* The Home Depot Inc)
9 Ott Dr, Huntsville, ON, P1H 0A2
(705) 788-5000
Emp Here 50
SIC 5251 Hardware stores

D-U-N-S 25-615-3552   (SL)
HUNTSVILLE DISTRICT NURSING HOME INC
FAIRVERN NURSING HOME
14 Mill St Suite 101, Huntsville, ON, P1H 2A4
(705) 789-4476
Emp Here 90   *Sales* 4,085,799

SIC 8051 Skilled nursing care facilities

D-U-N-S 25-221-4044   (BR)
INNVEST PROPERTIES CORP
COMFORT INN
(*Suby of* Innvest Properties Corp)
86 King William St, Huntsville, ON, P1H 1E4
(705) 789-1701
Emp Here 24
SIC 7011 Hotels and motels

D-U-N-S 20-290-7148   (BR)
JARLETTE LTD
MUSKOKA LANDING CARE CENTRE
65 Rogers Cove Dr, Huntsville, ON, P1H 2L9
(705) 788-7713
Emp Here 100
SIC 8051 Skilled nursing care facilities

D-U-N-S 20-753-0023   (BR)
KIMBERLY-CLARK INC
(*Suby of* Kimberly-Clark Corporation)
570 Ravenscliffe Rd, Huntsville, ON, P1H 2A1
(705) 788-5200
Emp Here 220
SIC 2621 Paper mills

D-U-N-S 25-412-4456   (BR)
LAKES OF MUSKOKA REALTY INC
ROYAL LEPAGE
395 Centre St N Unit 100, Huntsville, ON, P1H 2P9
(705) 789-9677
Emp Here 20
SIC 6531 Real estate agents and managers

D-U-N-S 20-555-6397   (BR)
METRO ONTARIO INC
METRO
70 King William St Suite 5a, Huntsville, ON, P1H 2A5
(705) 789-9619
Emp Here 100
SIC 5411 Grocery stores

D-U-N-S 25-646-7291   (BR)
MUSKOKA ALGONQUIN HEALTHCARE
COMMUNITY CARE ACCESS CENTRE
8 Crescent Rd, Huntsville, ON, P1H 0B3
(705) 789-6451
Emp Here 150
SIC 8099 Health and allied services, nec

D-U-N-S 24-199-6599   (SL)
ONE KID'S PLACE
100 Frank Miller Dr Suite 2, Huntsville, ON, P1H 1H7
(705) 789-9985
Emp Here 100   *Sales* 3,939,878
SIC 8322 Individual and family services

D-U-N-S 24-092-3214   (BR)
REHAB EXPRESS INC
CLOSING THE GAP HEALTHCARE GROUP
(*Suby of* Rehab Express Inc)
367 Muskoka Rd 3 N, Huntsville, ON, P1H 1H6
(705) 788-9355
Emp Here 28
SIC 8093 Specialty outpatient clinics, nec

D-U-N-S 24-426-3336   (SL)
ROGERS COVE RETIREMENT RESIDENCE
4 Coveside Dr Suite 1, Huntsville, ON, P1H 2J9
(705) 789-1600
Emp Here 20   *Sales* 866,251
SIC 8361 Residential care

D-U-N-S 24-159-7017   (BR)
SHAWCOR LTD
CANUSA CPS
455 West Airport Rd, Huntsville, ON, P1H 1Y7
(705) 789-1787
Emp Here 166
SIC 3498 Fabricated pipe and fittings

D-U-N-S 20-711-2249   (BR)
SIMCOE MUSKOKA CATHOLIC DISTRICT

SCHOOL BOARD
ST MARYS SCHOOL
(*Suby of* Simcoe Muskoka Catholic District School Board)
36 Silverwood Dr, Huntsville, ON, P1H 1N1
(705) 789-6481
Emp Here 30
SIC 8211 Elementary and secondary schools

D-U-N-S 24-485-0793   (BR)
SOBEYS CAPITAL INCORPORATED
FRESHCO
12 Cann St, Huntsville, ON, P1H 1H3
(705) 789-9172
Emp Here 20
SIC 5411 Grocery stores

D-U-N-S 20-179-9769   (BR)
TEMBEC INC
80 Old North Rd, Huntsville, ON, P1H 2J4
(705) 789-2371
Emp Here 20
SIC 2421 Sawmills and planing mills, general

D-U-N-S 25-238-8319   (BR)
TRILLIUM LAKELANDS DISTRICT SCHOOL BOARD
SPRUCE GLEN PUBLIC SCHOOL
550 Muskoka Rd 3 N, Huntsville, ON, P1H 1C9
(705) 789-4591
Emp Here 35
SIC 8211 Elementary and secondary schools

D-U-N-S 25-238-8103   (BR)
TRILLIUM LAKELANDS DISTRICT SCHOOL BOARD
HUNTSVILLE PUBLIC SCHOOL
16 Caroline St W, Huntsville, ON, P1H 2B2
(705) 789-2318
Emp Here 35
SIC 8211 Elementary and secondary schools

D-U-N-S 25-238-8392   (BR)
TRILLIUM LAKELANDS DISTRICT SCHOOL BOARD
RIVERSIDE PUBLIC SCHOOL
755 Brunel Rd, Huntsville, ON, P1H 1Z3
(705) 789-2282
Emp Here 40
SIC 8211 Elementary and secondary schools

D-U-N-S 25-238-8434   (BR)
TRILLIUM LAKELANDS DISTRICT SCHOOL BOARD
PINE GLEN PUBLIC SCHOOL
126 West Rd, Huntsville, ON, P1H 1M5
(705) 789-4791
Emp Here 30
SIC 8211 Elementary and secondary schools

D-U-N-S 24-829-4837   (BR)
UPONOR INFRA LTD
37 Centre St N, Huntsville, ON, P1H 1X4
(705) 789-2396
Emp Here 85
SIC 3088 Plastics plumbing fixtures

D-U-N-S 24-318-0804   (BR)
WAL-MART CANADA CORP
WALMART
111 Howland Dr Unit 10, Huntsville, ON, P1H 2P4
(705) 787-1137
Emp Here 150
SIC 5311 Department stores

Huron Park, ON N0M
Huron County

D-U-N-S 24-764-7191   (SL)
GNUTTI LTD
404 Canada Ave, Huron Park, ON, N0M 1Y0
(519) 228-9494
Emp Here 150   *Sales* 30,719,925

SIC 3714 Motor vehicle parts and accessories
Paul Buchanan
Randy Francis

Ignace, ON P0T
Kenora County

D-U-N-S 20-025-1176   (BR)
CONSEIL SCOLAIRE DE DISTRICT CATHOLIQUE DES AURORES BOREALES
ECOLE IMMACULEE-CONCEPTION
(*Suby of* Conseil Scolaire De District Catholique Des Aurores Boreales)
119 Lily Pad Rd Suite 1109, Ignace, ON, P0T 1T0
(807) 934-6460
Emp Here 25
SIC 8211 Elementary and secondary schools

D-U-N-S 25-238-9929   (BR)
KEEWATIN PATRICIA DISTRICT SCHOOL BOARD
IGNACE PUBLIC SCHOOL
194 Davy Lake Rd, Ignace, ON, P0T 1T0
(807) 934-2212
Emp Here 40
SIC 8211 Elementary and secondary schools

Ilderton, ON N0M
Middlesex County

D-U-N-S 25-483-8154   (BR)
GOVERNING COUNCIL OF THE SALVATION ARMY IN CANADA, THE
GOVERNING COUNCIL OF THE SALVATION ARMY IN CANADA, THE
15000 Ilderton Rd, Ilderton, ON, N0M 2A0

Emp Here 34
SIC 8361 Residential care

D-U-N-S 20-128-4700   (SL)
SPENCER STEEL LIMITED
200 King St, Ilderton, ON, N0M 2A0

Emp Here 75   *Sales* 11,354,240
SIC 1791 Structural steel erection
Dir Richard Spencer Sr
Pr Pr Richard Spencer Jr

D-U-N-S 25-249-0289   (BR)
THAMES VALLEY DISTRICT SCHOOL BOARD
VALLEYVIEW CENTRAL SCHOOL
10339 Ilderton Rd, Ilderton, ON, N0M 2A0
(519) 666-1417
Emp Here 23
SIC 8211 Elementary and secondary schools

D-U-N-S 25-249-0594   (BR)
THAMES VALLEY DISTRICT SCHOOL BOARD
OXBOW ELEMENTARY SCHOOL
13624 Ilderton Rd, Ilderton, ON, N0M 2A0
(519) 666-0310
Emp Here 25
SIC 8211 Elementary and secondary schools

Ingersoll, ON N5C
Oxford County

D-U-N-S 24-121-1242   (SL)
ALEXANDRA HOSPITAL INGERSOLL, THE
29 Noxon St, Ingersoll, ON, N5C 1B8
(519) 485-1700
Emp Here 150   *Sales* 10,433,380
SIC 8062 General medical and surgical hospitals

Tom Mchugh

D-U-N-S 24-831-3033   (BR)
ATLANTIC PACKAGING PRODUCTS LTD
45 Chisholm Dr, Ingersoll, ON, N5C 2C7
(519) 485-4921
Emp Here 120
SIC 2653 Corrugated and solid fiber boxes

D-U-N-S 24-385-1776   (BR)
AUTO WAREHOUSING COMPANY CANADA LIMITED
(*Suby of* Auto Warehousing Co., Inc.)
274180 Wallace Line, Ingersoll, ON, N5C 3J7
(519) 485-0351
Emp Here 23
SIC 4789 Transportation services, nec

D-U-N-S 20-539-3908   (BR)
CANADA POST CORPORATION
36 Charles St W, Ingersoll, ON, N5C 2L6
(519) 485-3700
Emp Here 20
SIC 4311 U.s. postal service

D-U-N-S 25-361-7187   (HQ)
CARMEUSE LIME (CANADA) LIMITED
CARMEUSE NATURAL CHEMICALS
(*Suby of* Carmeuse Lime (Canada) Limited)
374681 County Rd 6, Ingersoll, ON, N5C 3K5
(519) 423-6283
Emp Here 175   *Emp Total* 265
SIC 3274 Lime

D-U-N-S 20-181-4063   (SL)
COILPLUS CANADA INC
COILPLUS
18 Underwood Rd, Ingersoll, ON, N5C 3V6
(519) 485-6393
Emp Here 65   *Sales* 14,286,970
SIC 5051 Metals service centers and offices
 Robert Coppens
Dir John Craig
Dir Katsuaki Horikiri
Dir Jun Takino

D-U-N-S 24-418-2536   (BR)
CORPORATION OF THE TOWN OF INGERSOLL
FUSION YOUTH CENTRE
121 Thames St N, Ingersoll, ON, N5C 3C9
(519) 485-4386
Emp Here 20
SIC 8322 Individual and family services

D-U-N-S 25-355-4380   (BR)
DIVERSICARE CANADA MANAGEMENT SERVICES CO., INC
OXFORD REGIONAL NURSING HOME
263 Wonham St S, Ingersoll, ON, N5C 3P6
(519) 485-3920
Emp Here 100
SIC 8051 Skilled nursing care facilities

D-U-N-S 25-742-4622   (SL)
ELM HURST INN
415 Harris St, Ingersoll, ON, N5C 3J8
(519) 485-5321
Emp Here 80   *Sales* 3,502,114
SIC 7011 Hotels and motels

D-U-N-S 24-404-4389   (HQ)
ERIE THAMES POWERLINES CORPORATION
143 Bell St Suite 157, Ingersoll, ON, N5C 2N9
(519) 485-1820
Emp Here 40   *Emp Total* 145
Sales 9,046,358
SIC 1623 Water, sewer, and utility lines
Pr Chris White

D-U-N-S 24-826-4397   (SL)
ERTH (HOLDINGS) INC
COULTER WATER METER SERVICE
180 Whiting St, Ingersoll, ON, N5C 3B5
(519) 485-6038
Emp Here 20   *Sales* 2,338,878
SIC 7629 Electrical repair shops

D-U-N-S 25-237-8179   (BR)
LONDON DISTRICT CATHOLIC SCHOOL BOARD
SACRED HEART CATHOLIC ELEMENTARY
121 Thames St N, Ingersoll, ON, N5C 3C9

Emp Here 22
SIC 8211 Elementary and secondary schools

D-U-N-S 24-676-5023   (BR)
LONDON DISTRICT CATHOLIC SCHOOL BOARD
ST JUDE'S SCHOOL
30 Caffyn St, Ingersoll, ON, N5C 3T9
(519) 660-2786
Emp Here 25
SIC 8211 Elementary and secondary schools

D-U-N-S 25-018-9933   (BR)
ROYAL BANK OF CANADA
RBC
(*Suby of* Royal Bank Of Canada)
156 Thames St S, Ingersoll, ON, N5C 2T4
(519) 485-3710
Emp Here 100
SIC 6021 National commercial banks

D-U-N-S 24-380-1854   (BR)
SIVACO WIRE GROUP 2004 L.P.
SIVACO ONTARIO
330 Thomas St, Ingersoll, ON, N5C 3K5
(800) 265-0418
Emp Here 80
SIC 3496 Miscellaneous fabricated wire products

D-U-N-S 20-276-7026   (BR)
TFT GLOBAL INC
(*Suby of* 1596101 Ontario Inc)
390 Thomas St Unit 1, Ingersoll, ON, N5C 2G7
(519) 842-4540
Emp Here 35
SIC 4225 General warehousing and storage

D-U-N-S 20-564-5927   (BR)
TFT GLOBAL INC
(*Suby of* 1596101 Ontario Inc)
160 Ingersoll St S, Ingersoll, ON, N5C 3J7

Emp Here 50
SIC 4789 Transportation services, nec

D-U-N-S 24-525-7402   (BR)
TFT GLOBAL INC
TFT GLOBAL NORTH
(*Suby of* 1596101 Ontario Inc)
160 Ingersoll St, Ingersoll, ON, N5C 3K3
(519) 842-4540
Emp Here 25
SIC 4225 General warehousing and storage

D-U-N-S 24-161-4820   (BR)
TFT GLOBAL INC
(*Suby of* 1596101 Ontario Inc)
160 Ingersoll St S, Ingersoll, ON, N5C 3J7
(519) 425-1289
Emp Here 20
SIC 4225 General warehousing and storage

D-U-N-S 25-249-1246   (BR)
THAMES VALLEY DISTRICT SCHOOL BOARD
HARRISFIELD PUBLIC SCHOOL
2 Caffyn St, Ingersoll, ON, N5C 3M8
(519) 485-1600
Emp Here 30
SIC 8211 Elementary and secondary schools

D-U-N-S 25-237-8377   (BR)
THAMES VALLEY DISTRICT SCHOOL BOARD
PRINCESS ELIZABETH PUBLIC SCHOOL
37 William St, Ingersoll, ON, N5C 1M2
(519) 485-4280
Emp Here 25
SIC 8211 Elementary and secondary schools

D-U-N-S 25-249-1402   (BR)
THAMES VALLEY DISTRICT SCHOOL BOARD
ROYAL ROADS PUBLIC SCHOOL
210 King St E, Ingersoll, ON, N5C 1H2
(519) 485-4849
Emp Here 20
SIC 8211 Elementary and secondary schools

D-U-N-S 25-249-1543   (BR)
THAMES VALLEY DISTRICT SCHOOL BOARD
INGERSOLL DISTRICT COLLEGIATE INSTITUTE
37 Alma St, Ingersoll, ON, N5C 1N1
(519) 485-1200
Emp Here 90
SIC 8211 Elementary and secondary schools

D-U-N-S 24-308-3123   (SL)
TORA INGERSOLL LIMITED
GIANT TIGER
111 Charles St E, Ingersoll, ON, N5C 1J9
(519) 485-0520
Emp Here 50   *Sales* 4,244,630
SIC 5311 Department stores

D-U-N-S 24-387-8134   (BR)
TRANSFREIGHT INC
300 Ingersoll St, Ingersoll, ON, N5C 3J7
(519) 485-3797
Emp Here 140
SIC 4731 Freight transportation arrangement

D-U-N-S 25-987-3560   (BR)
WESTMONT HOSPITALITY MANAGEMENT LIMITED
(*Suby of* Westmont Hospitality Management Limited)
20 Samnah Cres, Ingersoll, ON, N5C 3J7
(519) 425-1100
Emp Here 25
SIC 7011 Hotels and motels

D-U-N-S 20-960-2221   (BR)
WOODINGFORD LODGE
325 Thames St S, Ingersoll, ON, N5C 2T8
(519) 485-7053
Emp Here 40
SIC 8059 Nursing and personal care, nec

Ingleside, ON K0C
Stormont County

D-U-N-S 25-224-8901   (BR)
CATHOLIC DISTRICT SCHOOL BOARD OF EASTERN ONTARIO
OUR LADY GOOD COUNSEL SCHOOL
(*Suby of* Catholic District School Board of Eastern Ontario)
52 Dickinson Dr, Ingleside, ON, K0C 1M0
(613) 537-2556
Emp Here 20
SIC 8211 Elementary and secondary schools

D-U-N-S 24-159-7025   (BR)
KELLY SERVICES (CANADA), LTD
KELLY SERVICES
(*Suby of* Kelly Services, Inc.)
70 Dickinson Dr, Ingleside, ON, K0C 1M0
(613) 537-8491
Emp Here 80
SIC 7361 Employment agencies

D-U-N-S 25-128-8940   (BR)
UPPER CANADA DISTRICT SCHOOL BOARD, THE
ROTHEWELL-OSNABRUCK SCHOOL
(*Suby of* Upper Canada District School Board, The)
1 College St, Ingleside, ON, K0C 1M0
(613) 537-2454
Emp Here 44
SIC 8211 Elementary and secondary schools

Inglewood, ON L7C
Peel County

D-U-N-S 24-065-3902   (HQ)
CRAILIN LOGISTICS SERVICES INC
CSI LOGISTICS
14722 Heart Lake Rd, Inglewood, ON, L7C 2J7
(905) 838-3215
Emp Here 100   *Emp Total* 2
Sales 27,214,341
SIC 4731 Freight transportation arrangement
Pr Pr Craig Cottrell
 Linda Cottrell

D-U-N-S 25-996-8753   (SL)
L.N TRANSPORT INC
DISPLAY TRANSPORTATION
13904 Hurontario St Suite 1, Inglewood, ON, L7C 2B8
(905) 838-4111
Emp Here 45   *Sales* 6,879,002
SIC 4213 Trucking, except local
Pr Richard Delongete

D-U-N-S 25-297-2096   (BR)
PEEL DISTRICT SCHOOL BOARD
HERB CAMPBELL PUBLIC SCHOOL
(*Suby of* Peel District School Board)
3749 King St, Inglewood, ON, L7C 0T6
(905) 838-3952
Emp Here 60
SIC 8211 Elementary and secondary schools

Inkerman, ON K0E
Dundas County

D-U-N-S 24-991-5380   (BR)
PARRISH & HEIMBECKER, LIMITED
NEW LIFE MILLS
(*Suby of* Parrish & Heimbecker, Limited)
11489 Queen St, Inkerman, ON, K0E 1J0
(613) 989-2003
Emp Here 21
SIC 2048 Prepared feeds, nec

Innerkip, ON N0J
Oxford County

D-U-N-S 20-710-5581   (BR)
THAMES VALLEY DISTRICT SCHOOL BOARD
INNERKIP CENTRAL PUBLIC SCHOOL
180 Coleman St, Innerkip, ON, N0J 1M0
(519) 469-3435
Emp Here 25
SIC 8211 Elementary and secondary schools

Innisfil, ON L9S
Simcoe County

D-U-N-S 20-540-9654   (BR)
CANADA POST CORPORATION
INNISFIL STATION MAIN
8056 Yonge St, Innisfil, ON, L9S 1L6
(705) 436-4622
Emp Here 25
SIC 4311 U.s. postal service

D-U-N-S 25-104-1729   (SL)
CHALMERS CONSTRUCTION INC
1586 10th Line, Innisfil, ON, L9S 3P3
(705) 734-6111
Emp Here 55   *Sales* 4,012,839
SIC 1741 Masonry and other stonework

D-U-N-S 20-770-8269   (BR)

CLUBLINK CORPORATION ULC
NATIONAL PINES GOLF CLUB
8165 10 Sideroad Suite 11, Innisfil, ON, L9S
4T3
(705) 431-7000
Emp Here 200
SIC 7992 Public golf courses

D-U-N-S 24-321-8273   (BR)
DIXON GROUP CANADA LIMITED
2315 Bowman St, Innisfil, ON, L9S 3V6
(705) 436-1125
Emp Here 26
SIC 3443 Fabricated plate work (boiler shop)

D-U-N-S 20-258-6715   (SL)
INNISFIL ENERGY SERVICES LIMITED
7251 Yonge St, Innisfil, ON, L9S 0J3
(705) 431-4321
Emp Here 20   *Sales* 9,557,852
SIC 4911 Electric services
Pr Pr Wade Morris

D-U-N-S 24-179-8573   (BR)
MUSKOKA TRANSPORT LIMITED
3269 Thomas St, Innisfil, ON, L9S 3W2
(705) 431-8551
Emp Here 25
SIC 4731 Freight transportation arrangement

D-U-N-S 25-371-8829   (SL)
**NORTHERN AUTO AUCTIONS OF CANADA
INC**
NORTH TORONTO AUCTION
3230 Thomas St, Innisfil, ON, L9S 3W5
(705) 436-4111
Emp Here 75   *Sales* 4,900,111
SIC 7389 Business services, nec

D-U-N-S 20-592-0841   (BR)
**SIMCOE COUNTY DISTRICT SCHOOL
BOARD, THE**
ALCONA GLEN ELEMENTARY SCHOOL
(*Suby of* Simcoe County District School
Board, The)
1310 Innisfil Beach Rd, Innisfil, ON, L9S 4B7
(705) 431-5918
Emp Here 45
SIC 8211 Elementary and secondary schools

D-U-N-S 25-297-6733   (BR)
**SIMCOE COUNTY DISTRICT SCHOOL
BOARD, THE**
GOODFELLOW PUBLIC SCHOOL
(*Suby of* Simcoe County District School
Board, The)
827 9th Line, Innisfil, ON, L9S 1A6
(705) 436-3600
Emp Here 45
SIC 8211 Elementary and secondary schools

D-U-N-S 25-292-4709   (BR)
**SIMCOE COUNTY DISTRICT SCHOOL
BOARD, THE**
SUNNYBRAE PUBLIC SCHOOL
(*Suby of* Simcoe County District School
Board, The)
218 Sunnybrae Ave, Innisfil, ON, L9S 1H9
(705) 436-1100
Emp Here 40
SIC 8211 Elementary and secondary schools

D-U-N-S 20-711-2256   (BR)
**SIMCOE MUSKOKA CATHOLIC DISTRICT
SCHOOL BOARD**
HOLY CROSS CATHOLIC SCHOOL
(*Suby of* Simcoe Muskoka Catholic District
School Board)
910 Leslie Dr, Innisfil, ON, L9S 1A7
(705) 431-2935
Emp Here 27
SIC 8211 Elementary and secondary schools

D-U-N-S 25-293-4823   (BR)
**SIMCOE MUSKOKA CATHOLIC DISTRICT
SCHOOL BOARD**
ST FRANCIS OF ASSISI SCHOOL
(*Suby of* Simcoe Muskoka Catholic District

School Board)
1067 Anna Maria Ave, Innisfil, ON, L9S 1W2
(705) 431-5711
Emp Here 45
SIC 8211 Elementary and secondary schools

D-U-N-S 20-806-2518   (BR)
SOBEYS CAPITAL INCORPORATED
SOBEYS STORE# 7368
2080 Jans Blvd, Innisfil, ON, L9S 4Y8
(705) 431-6667
Emp Here 25
SIC 5411 Grocery stores

D-U-N-S 24-075-7505   (BR)
**UNITED LUMBER AND BUILDING SUP-
PLIES COMPANY LIMITED**
UNITED TRUSS
3325 Thomas St Suite D, Innisfil, ON, L9S
3W4
(705) 436-3425
Emp Here 25
SIC 2439 Structural wood members, nec

Iroquois, ON K0E
Dundas County

D-U-N-S 24-104-8461   (HQ)
CRAIG PACKAGING LIMITED
REPUBLIC PACKAGING OF CANADA
(*Suby of* Republic Packaging Corp.)
5911 Carmen Rd S, Iroquois, ON, K0E 1K0
(613) 652-4856
Emp Here 33   *Emp Total* 26
Sales 8,244,559
SIC 2653 Corrugated and solid fiber boxes
Pr Pr Charles Wood

D-U-N-S 20-043-5337   (SL)
UNIVERSAL TERMINALS INC
LALLY-BLANCHARD FUELS
Gd, Iroquois, ON, K0E 1K0

Emp Here 140   *Sales* 42,609,000
SIC 5983 Fuel oil dealers
  George Kaneb
Pr Pr Thomas Kaneb
Dir T Richard Hornby

D-U-N-S 20-711-5606   (BR)
**UPPER CANADA DISTRICT SCHOOL
BOARD, THE**
DIXON'S CORNER PUBLIC SCHOOL
10951 County Rd 18 Cook Rd, Iroquois, ON,
K0E 1K0

Emp Here 50
SIC 8211 Elementary and secondary schools

D-U-N-S 20-363-5581   (BR)
**UPPER CANADA DISTRICT SCHOOL
BOARD, THE**
SEAWAY DISTRICT HIGH SCHOOL
2 Beach St, Iroquois, ON, K0E 1K0
(613) 652-4878
Emp Here 50
SIC 8211 Elementary and secondary schools

D-U-N-S 20-363-5599   (BR)
**UPPER CANADA DISTRICT SCHOOL
BOARD, THE**
IROQUOIS PUBLIC SCHOOL
6 Lakeshore St, Iroquois, ON, K0E 1K0
(613) 652-4580
Emp Here 30
SIC 8211 Elementary and secondary schools

Iroquois Falls, ON P0K
Cochrane County

D-U-N-S 24-373-0848   (BR)
ANSON GENERAL HOSPITAL

SOUTH CENTENNIAL MANOR
58 Anson Dr, Iroquois Falls, ON, P0K 1E0
(705) 258-3221
Emp Here 20
SIC 8361 Residential care

D-U-N-S 25-225-1319   (BR)
**CONSEIL SCOLAIRE CATHOLIQUE DE
DISTRICT DES GRANDES RIVIERES, LE**
ECOLE SECONDAIRE L'ALLIANCE
44 Prom Anson, Iroquois Falls, ON, P0K 1E0
(705) 258-3223
Emp Here 20
SIC 8211 Elementary and secondary schools

D-U-N-S 20-515-7600   (BR)
**CONSEIL SCOLAIRE CATHOLIQUE DE
DISTRICT DES GRANDES RIVIERES, LE**
SAINT MARTYRS KENNEDY CANADIAN
Gd, Iroquois Falls, ON, P0K 1E0
(705) 232-4019
Emp Here 25
SIC 8211 Elementary and secondary schools

D-U-N-S 25-017-2988   (BR)
**DISTRICT SCHOOL BOARD ONTARIO
NORTH EAST**
IROQUOIS FALLS SECONDARY SCHOOL
44 Anson Dr, Iroquois Falls, ON, P0K 1E0
(705) 258-3921
Emp Here 39
SIC 8211 Elementary and secondary schools

D-U-N-S 20-170-2946   (BR)
**DISTRICT SCHOOL BOARD ONTARIO
NORTH EAST**
IROQUOIS FALLS PUBLIC SCHOOL
900 Centennial St, Iroquois Falls, ON, P0K
1G0
(705) 232-6651
Emp Here 22
SIC 8211 Elementary and secondary schools

D-U-N-S 25-076-4305   (BR)
LOBLAW COMPANIES LIMITED
IROQUOIS FALLS VALU-MART
320 Main St, Iroquois Falls, ON, P0K 1G0
(705) 232-5153
Emp Here 35
SIC 5411 Grocery stores

D-U-N-S 20-710-4576   (BR)
**NORTHEASTERN CATHOLIC DISTRICT
SCHOOL BOARD**
SAINT ANNE ENGLISH CATHOLIC SCHOOL
200 Church St, Iroquois Falls, ON, P0K 1E0
(705) 232-5355
Emp Here 30
SIC 8211 Elementary and secondary schools

D-U-N-S 20-754-1608   (SL)
SOUTH CENTENNIAL MANOR
240 Fyfe St, Iroquois Falls, ON, P0K 1E0
(705) 258-3836
Emp Here 55   *Sales* 2,042,900
SIC 8361 Residential care

Iroquois Falls A, ON P0K

D-U-N-S 20-558-0389   (BR)
CANADIAN RED CROSS SOCIETY, THE
Po Box 1298, Iroquois Falls A, ON, P0K 1G0
(705) 232-6537
Emp Here 42
SIC 8621 Professional organizations

Jarvis, ON N0A
Haldimand County

D-U-N-S 24-214-4459   (SL)
CAPITOL PIPE SUPPORTS LIMITED
CAPITAL EQUIPMENT RENTALS, DIV

(*Suby of* Canerector Inc)
85 Talbot St E, Jarvis, ON, N0A 1J0
(519) 587-4571
Emp Here 30   *Sales* 2,407,703
SIC 7359 Equipment rental and leasing, nec

D-U-N-S 24-126-2729   (BR)
GRAND ERIE DISTRICT SCHOOL BOARD
JARVIS PUBLIC SCHOOL
(*Suby of* Grand Erie District School Board)
14 Monson St, Jarvis, ON, N0A 1J0
(519) 587-2612
Emp Here 30
SIC 8211 Elementary and secondary schools

Jogues, ON P0L
Cochrane County

D-U-N-S 20-710-4204   (BR)
**CONSEIL SCOLAIRE CATHOLIQUE DE
DISTRICT DES GRANDES RIVIERES, LE**
HEARST HIGH SCHOOL
923 Edward St, Jogues, ON, P0L 1R0
(705) 362-4283
Emp Here 35
SIC 8211 Elementary and secondary schools

Jordan Station, ON L0R

D-U-N-S 25-990-2427   (SL)
BEST WESTERN HOTEL
BEST WESTERN BEACON HARBOUR
2793 Beacon Blvd, Jordan Station, ON, L0R
1S0
(905) 562-4155
Emp Here 60   *Sales* 2,626,585
SIC 7011 Hotels and motels

D-U-N-S 24-345-2898   (BR)
DISTRICT SCHOOL BOARD OF NIAGARA
JORDAN PUBLIC SCHOOL
2831 Victoria Ave, Jordan Station, ON, L0R
1S0

Emp Here 20
SIC 8211 Elementary and secondary schools

D-U-N-S 20-344-4930   (SL)
FLAVOUR ART NORTH AMERICA INC
2913 Leyenhorst Court, Jordan Station, ON,
L0R 1S0
(905) 397-4182
Emp Here 26   *Sales* 7,223,350
SIC 2087 Flavoring extracts and syrups, nec
Pr Shaun Casey

D-U-N-S 25-638-6541   (SL)
INN ON THE TWENTY LTD
3836 Main St, Jordan Station, ON, L0R 1S0
(905) 562-7313
Emp Here 100   *Sales* 2,991,389
SIC 5812 Eating places

D-U-N-S 20-024-9725   (BR)
**NIAGARA CATHOLIC DISTRICT SCHOOL
BOARD**
*ST EDWARD CATHOLIC ELEMENTARY
SCHOOL*
2807 Fourth Ave, Jordan Station, ON, L0R
1S0
(905) 562-5531
Emp Here 20
SIC 8211 Elementary and secondary schools

Kakabeka Falls, ON P0T
Thunder Bay County

D-U-N-S 25-238-1413   (BR)
LAKEHEAD DISTRICT SCHOOL BOARD

KAKABEKA FALLS PUBLIC SCHOOL
Gd, Kakabeka Falls, ON, P0T 1W0
(807) 473-9252
Emp Here 23
SIC 8211 Elementary and secondary schools

D-U-N-S 25-238-1017 (BR)
LAKEHEAD DISTRICT SCHOOL BOARD
WHITEFISH VALLEY PUBLIC ELEMENTARY
SCHOOL
1092 Hwy 595, Kakabeka Falls, ON, P0T 1W0
(807) 475-3181
Emp Here 23
SIC 8211 Elementary and secondary schools

Kanata, ON K2K
Carleton County

D-U-N-S 25-784-5685 (BR)
1085098 ONTARIO LTD
ROYAL OAK
329 March Rd, Kanata, ON, K2K 2E1
(613) 591-3895
Emp Here 20
SIC 5812 Eating places

D-U-N-S 25-392-5010 (SL)
ACT TELECONFERENCING CANADA IN-CORPORATED
(*Suby of* Siris Capital Group, LLC)
555 Legget Dr Suite 230, Kanata, ON, K2K
2X3
(613) 592-5752
Emp Here 50 *Sales* 2,626,585
SIC 7389 Business services, nec

D-U-N-S 24-329-8986 (BR)
AECON CONSTRUCTION GROUP INC
AECON BUILDINGS OTTAWA
495 March Rd Suite 100, Kanata, ON, K2K
3G1
(613) 591-3007
Emp Here 25
SIC 1541 Industrial buildings and warehouses

D-U-N-S 20-222-4267 (HQ)
ASTENJOHNSON, INC
(*Suby of* Astenjohnson, Inc.)
1243 Teron Rd, Kanata, ON, K2K 1X2
(613) 592-5851
Emp Here 36 *Emp Total* 1,925
Sales 44,360,106
SIC 2299 Textile goods, nec
Pr Daniel D Cappell
  William A. Finn
VP Graham Jackson
Asst VP Thomas Durkin

D-U-N-S 25-361-9134 (BR)
ASTENJOHNSON, INC
ASTENJOHNSON DRYER FABRIC
(*Suby of* Astenjohnson, Inc.)
48 Richardson Side Rd, Kanata, ON, K2K 1X2
(613) 592-5851
Emp Here 115
SIC 2221 Broadwoven fabric mills, manmade

D-U-N-S 24-155-0255 (BR)
AVAYA CANADA CORP
1135 Innovation Dr Suite 100, Kanata, ON,
K2K 3G7

Emp Here 60
SIC 7371 Custom computer programming services

D-U-N-S 20-857-6686 (HQ)
BMT FLEET TECHNOLOGY LIMITED
311 Legget Dr, Kanata, ON, K2K 1Z8
(613) 592-2830
Emp Here 67 *Emp Total* 1,276
Sales 12,474,014
SIC 8711 Engineering services
VP VP Aaron Dinovitzer
  Andrew Kendrick

VP VP David Stocks
Pr Pr Gordon Fleming
VP Opers James Buckley
VP Fin Bart Seaton
VP VP Chris Tokarchuk

D-U-N-S 25-672-4261 (SL)
BTI SYSTEMS INC
1000 Innovation Dr Unit 200, Kanata, ON, K2K
3E7
(613) 287-1700
Emp Here 100 *Sales* 52,864,657
SIC 4899 Communication services, nec
Pr Colin Doherty
  Blair Geddes
Sr VP Robert Keys
  Sally Bament

D-U-N-S 24-350-3666 (BR)
BROADRIDGE CUSTOMER COMMUNICA-TIONS CANADA, ULC
DST OUTPUT CANADA INC
31 Richardson Side Rd, Kanata, ON, K2K 0A1
(613) 739-9901
Emp Here 50
SIC 2759 Commercial printing, nec

D-U-N-S 24-985-8960 (SL)
BROGAN INC
303 Terry Fox Dr Suite 300, Kanata, ON, K2K
3J1
(613) 599-0711
Emp Here 120 *Sales* 21,301,760
SIC 8732 Commercial nonphysical research
Pr Pr Thomas Brogan
  Penny Brogan

D-U-N-S 24-011-9326 (BR)
BROOKFIELD GLOBAL INTEGRATED SO-LUTIONS CANADA LP
BLJC
350 Terry Fox Dr Suite 12, Kanata, ON, K2K
2W5
(613) 254-8834
Emp Here 20
SIC 6531 Real estate agents and managers

D-U-N-S 20-300-7760 (BR)
CAE INC
1145 Innovation Dr, Kanata, ON, K2K 3G8
(613) 225-0070
Emp Here 20
SIC 8299 Schools and educational services, nec

D-U-N-S 20-288-5141 (BR)
CAE INC
1135 Innovation Dr Suite 300, Kanata, ON,
K2K 3G7
(613) 247-0342
Emp Here 20
SIC 3699 Electrical equipment and supplies, nec

D-U-N-S 24-312-0727 (BR)
CIBC WORLD MARKETS INC
555 Legget Dr Suite 1030, Kanata, ON, K2K
2X3
(613) 783-6848
Emp Here 24
SIC 6211 Security brokers and dealers

D-U-N-S 25-150-7109 (HQ)
CALIAN LTD
SED SYSTEMS ENGINEERING, A DIV OF
340 Legget Dr Suite 101, Kanata, ON, K2K
1Y6
(613) 599-8600
Emp Here 100 *Emp Total* 2,700
Sales 484,234,309
SIC 4899 Communication services, nec
  Ray Basler
Div Pres Brent Mcconnell
VP Fin Jacqueline Gauthier
Dir Kenneth Loeb

D-U-N-S 24-325-8493 (BR)
COM DEV LTD
(*Suby of* Honeywell International Inc.)

303 Terry Fox Dr Suite 100, Kanata, ON, K2K
3J1
(613) 591-7777
Emp Here 35
SIC 3669 Communications equipment, nec

D-U-N-S 20-713-8764 (BR)
COMPUGEN INC
84 Hines Rd Suite 310, Kanata, ON, K2K 3G3
(613) 591-2200
Emp Here 20
SIC 7376 Computer facilities management

D-U-N-S 24-886-6162 (HQ)
COMPUTER SCIENCES CANADA INC
CSC
(*Suby of* Dxc Technology Company)
555 Legget Dr, Kanata, ON, K2K 2X3
(613) 591-1810
Emp Here 150 *Emp Total* 178,750
Sales 241,510,779
SIC 7373 Computer integrated systems design
Pr Pr Charles A. Whelen
  William L. Deckelman

D-U-N-S 24-322-1124 (HQ)
CONTROL MICROSYSTEMS INC
415 Legget Dr Suite 101, Kanata, ON, K2K
3R1
(613) 591-1943
Emp Here 100 *Emp Total* 2,800
Sales 33,350,664
SIC 3823 Process control instruments
VP Isabelle Tribotte
VP VP Dale A Symington
Dir Opers Lawrence Charlebois
Prd Mgr Steve Goodman
Dir Fin Dave Jeffrey

D-U-N-S 20-106-6706 (SL)
CORTINA SYSTEMS CORP
(*Suby of* Inphi Corporation)
535 Legget Dr Suite 120, Kanata, ON, K2K
3B8
(613) 595-4001
Emp Here 34 *Sales* 3,137,310
SIC 8732 Commercial nonphysical research

D-U-N-S 25-752-8984 (SL)
DECISION ACADEMIC INC
411 Legget Dr Suite 501, Kanata, ON, K2K
3C9
(613) 254-9669
Emp Here 21 *Sales* 1,532,175
SIC 7371 Custom computer programming services

D-U-N-S 25-100-5351 (HQ)
DRAGONWAVE INC
(*Suby of* DragonWave Inc)
411 Legget Dr Suite 600, Kanata, ON, K2K
3C9
(613) 599-9991
Emp Here 130 *Emp Total* 160
Sales 43,916,000
SIC 7371 Custom computer programming services
Pr Pr Peter Allen
VP Opers Dave Farrar
VP Sls Barry Dahan
VP Ingrid Mag
VP Greg Friesen
VP Tom Mclellan
CFO Patrick Houston
  Claude Haw
  Cesar Cesaratto

D-U-N-S 20-340-8612 (SL)
EMBLA SYSTEMS LTD
EMBLA SYSTEMS NATUS MEDICAL
(*Suby of* Natus Medical Incorporated)
1 Hines Rd Suite 202, Kanata, ON, K2K 3C7
(905) 829-5300
Emp Here 26 *Sales* 4,504,505
SIC 5047 Medical and hospital equipment

D-U-N-S 24-588-9274 (SL)

EMCON EMANATION CONTROL LTD
(*Suby of* Rf1 Holding Company)
360 Terry Fox Dr Suite 100, Kanata, ON, K2K
2P5
(613) 270-9009
Emp Here 40 *Sales* 5,982,777
SIC 3699 Electrical equipment and supplies,
nec
Pr Pr Peter Patterson

D-U-N-S 25-129-2173 (BR)
EMPOWERED NETWORKS INC
1 Hines Rd Suite 200, Kanata, ON, K2K 3C7
(613) 271-7970
Emp Here 27
SIC 4899 Communication services, nec

D-U-N-S 25-411-6577 (SL)
ENTRUST DATACARD LIMITED
(*Suby of* Entrust Datacard Corporation)
1000 Innovation Dr, Kanata, ON, K2K 3E7
(613) 270-3400
Emp Here 200 *Sales* 27,068,420
SIC 7371 Custom computer programming services
Pr Pr David Wagner

D-U-N-S 20-022-2276 (BR)
FARM CREDIT CANADA
FCC
309 Legget Dr Suite 102, Kanata, ON, K2K
3A3
(613) 271-7640
Emp Here 52
SIC 6159 Miscellaneous business credit institutions

D-U-N-S 24-529-8521 (BR)
GOODLIFE FITNESS CENTRES INC
555 March Rd, Kanata, ON, K2K 2M5
(613) 599-2718
Emp Here 59
SIC 7991 Physical fitness facilities

D-U-N-S 24-636-0601 (BR)
HALOGEN SOFTWARE INC
40 Hines Rd, Kanata, ON, K2K 2M5
(613) 270-1011
Emp Here 30
SIC 7372 Prepackaged software

D-U-N-S 24-858-2301 (SL)
HUAWEI TECHNOLOGIES CANADA
303 Terry Fox Dr Suite 400, Kanata, ON, K2K
3J1
(613) 595-1900
Emp Here 135 *Sales* 17,684,480
SIC 5999 Miscellaneous retail stores, nec

D-U-N-S 25-542-3527 (SL)
IDT CANADA INC
450 March Rd Suite 500, Kanata, ON, K2K
3K2
(613) 287-5100
Emp Here 40 *Sales* 3,575,074
SIC 7371 Custom computer programming services

D-U-N-S 20-552-9410 (HQ)
INNOVAPOST INC
(*Suby of* Canada Post Corporation)
365 March Rd, Kanata, ON, K2K 3N5
(613) 270-6262
Emp Here 290 *Emp Total* 63,000
Sales 156,426,614
SIC 7372 Prepackaged software
Genl Mgr David Clark

D-U-N-S 25-333-4882 (SL)
ITEX INC
ITEX ENTERPRISE SOLUTIONS
555 Legget Dr Suite 730, Kanata, ON, K2K
2X3
(613) 599-5550
Emp Here 29 *Sales* 2,991,389
SIC 5734 Computer and software stores

D-U-N-S 20-177-8177 (HQ)
JUNIPER NETWORKS CANADA INC

---

340 Terry Fox Dr, Kanata, ON, K2K 3A2
(613) 591-2700
Emp Here 47   *Emp Total* 94
Sales 13,643,651
SIC 4899 Communication services, nec
Rahim Pagerami

D-U-N-S 24-963-4007   (HQ)
KANCAR COMMUNITY CHILDRENS CEN-TRE INC
CHILDREN'S PLACE, THE
(*Suby of* Kancar Community Childrens Centre Inc)
310 Legget Dr, Kanata, ON, K2K 1Y6
(613) 591-3398
Emp Here 50   *Emp Total* 70
Sales 2,115,860
SIC 8351 Child day care services

D-U-N-S 24-308-3321   (SL)
KONGSBERG GEOSPATIAL LTD
411 Legget Dr Suite 400, Kanata, ON, K2K 3C9
(613) 271-5500
Emp Here 50   *Sales* 7,709,634
SIC 7372 Prepackaged software
Pr Ranald Mcgillis
Dir Fin Rod Hall
Tom Gerhardsen
Eirik Lie
Henry Tremblay
Tore Sannes

D-U-N-S 25-097-6107   (SL)
LPI LEVEL PLATFORMS INC
LEVEL PLATFORMS
309 Legget Dr Suite 300, Kanata, ON, K2K 3A3
(613) 232-1000
Emp Here 127   *Sales* 22,724,800
SIC 7371 Custom computer programming services
Pr Pr Peter Sandiford
VP Fin Barry Mckibbon
Dir Patrick Smith
Dir Larry Moore
Dir Jim Ambrose

D-U-N-S 24-336-8193   (BR)
LAPOINTE FISH LIMITED
LAPOINTE SEAFOOD GRILL KANATA
60 Colchester Sq Unit 1, Kanata, ON, K2K 2Z9
(613) 599-1424
Emp Here 27
SIC 5812 Eating places

D-U-N-S 20-569-9593   (SL)
MARSHES GOLF CORPORATION
MARSHES GOLF CLUB, THE
320 Terry Fox Dr, Kanata, ON, K2K 3L1
(613) 271-3377
Emp Here 50   *Sales* 2,042,900
SIC 7997 Membership sports and recreation clubs

D-U-N-S 24-191-2166   (SL)
MEAD JOHNSON NUTRITION (CANADA) CO
535 Legget Dr Suite 900, Kanata, ON, K2K 3B8
(613) 595-4700
Emp Here 110   *Sales* 15,832,472
SIC 5149 Groceries and related products, nec
Pr Stephen Golsby
Sec William P Pool
VP Fin Stanley Burhans

D-U-N-S 24-926-7162   (SL)
NUVO NETWORK MANAGEMENT INC
400 March Rd Suite 190, Kanata, ON, K2K 3H4

Emp Here 115   *Sales* 8,641,280
SIC 7376 Computer facilities management
Pr Phil Weaver
Richard Anderson
Terry Hall

Dir Peter Sommerer
Dir Barry Gekiere

D-U-N-S 20-290-6256   (BR)
OMNI HEALTH CARE LTD
FOREST HILL
6501 Campeau Dr Suite 353, Kanata, ON, K2K 3E9
(613) 599-1991
Emp Here 200
SIC 8051 Skilled nursing care facilities

D-U-N-S 24-720-0652   (HQ)
OTTAWA CARLETON LIFE SKILLS INC
(*Suby of* Ottawa Carleton Life Skills Inc)
1 Brewer Hunt Way Unit 9, Kanata, ON, K2K 2B5
(613) 254-9400
Emp Here 20   *Emp Total* 135
Sales 4,961,328
SIC 8361 Residential care

D-U-N-S 20-288-8512   (BR)
OTTAWA CATHOLIC DISTRICT SCHOOL BOARD
ALL SAINTS HIGH SCHOOL
(*Suby of* Ottawa Catholic District School Board)
5115 Kanata Ave, Kanata, ON, K2K 3K5
(613) 271-4254
Emp Here 80
SIC 8211 Elementary and secondary schools

D-U-N-S 20-711-6315   (BR)
OTTAWA CATHOLIC DISTRICT SCHOOL BOARD
GEORGES VANIER CATHOLIC SCHOOL
(*Suby of* Ottawa Catholic District School Board)
40 Varley Dr, Kanata, ON, K2K 1G5
(613) 592-4371
Emp Here 35
SIC 8211 Elementary and secondary schools

D-U-N-S 25-265-4306   (BR)
OTTAWA CATHOLIC DISTRICT SCHOOL BOARD
ST ISIDORE ELEMENTARY SCHOOL
(*Suby of* Ottawa Catholic District School Board)
1105 March Rd, Kanata, ON, K2K 1X7
(613) 592-1798
Emp Here 32
SIC 8211 Elementary and secondary schools

D-U-N-S 24-102-2904   (BR)
OTTAWA PUBLIC LIBRARY BOARD
2500 Campeau Dr, Kanata, ON, K2K 2W3

Emp Here 20
SIC 8231 Libraries

D-U-N-S 25-263-5883   (BR)
OTTAWA-CARLETON DISTRICT SCHOOL BOARD
EARL OF MARCH SECONDARY SCHOOL
4 Parkway The, Kanata, ON, K2K 1Y4
(613) 592-3361
Emp Here 90
SIC 8211 Elementary and secondary schools

D-U-N-S 24-676-3234   (BR)
OTTAWA-CARLETON DISTRICT SCHOOL BOARD
SOUTH MARCH PUBLIC SCHOOL
1032 Klonkide Rd, Kanata, ON, K2K 1X7
(613) 595-0543
Emp Here 36
SIC 8211 Elementary and secondary schools

D-U-N-S 20-081-3496   (BR)
OTTAWA-CARLETON DISTRICT SCHOOL BOARD
JOHNSTON, W ERSKINE PUBLIC SCHOOL
50 Varley Dr, Kanata, ON, K2K 1G7
(613) 592-4492
Emp Here 50
SIC 8211 Elementary and secondary schools

D-U-N-S 25-166-3142   (BR)
OTTAWA-CARLETON DISTRICT SCHOOL BOARD
ROLAND MICHENER PUBLIC SCHOOL
100 Penfield Dr, Kanata, ON, K2K 1M2
(613) 592-2126
Emp Here 30
SIC 8211 Elementary and secondary schools

D-U-N-S 25-120-2685   (SL)
PERFTECH (PTI) CANADA CORP
PERFORMANCE TECHNOLOGIES
(*Suby of* Sonus Networks, Inc.)
40 Hines Rd Suite 500, Kanata, ON, K2K 2M5
(613) 287-5344
Emp Here 40   *Sales* 3,575,074
SIC 7371 Custom computer programming services

D-U-N-S 24-107-8547   (BR)
PINCHIN LTD
(*Suby of* 2010282 Ontario Inc)
555 Legget Dr Suite 1001, Kanata, ON, K2K 2X3
(613) 592-3387
Emp Here 25
SIC 8731 Commercial physical research

D-U-N-S 24-333-2942   (BR)
QUEST SOFTWARE CANADA INC
DELL SOFTWARE CANADA INC
(*Suby of* Francisco Partners Management, L.P.)
515 Legget Dr Suite 1001, Kanata, ON, K2K 3G4
(613) 270-1500
Emp Here 150
SIC 7371 Custom computer programming services

D-U-N-S 20-003-3442   (BR)
ROYAL BANK OF CANADA
RBC
(*Suby of* Royal Bank Of Canada)
360 March Rd, Kanata, ON, K2K 2T5
(613) 592-5793
Emp Here 20
SIC 6021 National commercial banks

D-U-N-S 25-130-4556   (BR)
SCOTIA CAPITAL INC
SCOTIAMCLEOD
505 March Rd Suite 250, Kanata, ON, K2K 3A4
(613) 271-6600
Emp Here 30
SIC 6211 Security brokers and dealers

D-U-N-S 20-189-2432   (BR)
TRANSCORE LINK LOGISTICS CORPORA-TION
TRANSCORE GLOBALWAVE PRODUCTS AND SERVICES
(*Suby of* Roper Technologies, Inc.)
2 Brewer Hunt Way, Kanata, ON, K2K 2B5
(613) 591-0100
Emp Here 80
SIC 4731 Freight transportation arrangement

D-U-N-S 25-733-8871   (SL)
WATCHFIRE CORPORATION
1 Hines Rd, Kanata, ON, K2K 3C7

Emp Here 170   *Sales* 31,249,280
SIC 7372 Prepackaged software
Micheal Weider
Pr Pr Peter C Mckay
VP Fin Kenneth Macaskill
James C Mccartney
John J. Gannon

D-U-N-S 25-678-5890   (SL)
XMARK CORPORATION
STANLEY HEALTHCARE SOLUTIONS
309 Legget Dr Suite 100, Kanata, ON, K2K 3A3
(613) 592-6997
Emp Here 100   *Sales* 15,217,500

SIC 3679 Electronic components, nec
VP Opers Andrew Brazier

Kanata, ON K2L
Carleton County

D-U-N-S 25-770-0385   (SL)
1172413 ONTARIO INC
EAST SIDE MARIO'S
651 Terry Fox Dr Suite Side, Kanata, ON, K2L 4E7
(613) 836-3680
Emp Here 80   *Sales* 2,407,703
SIC 5812 Eating places

D-U-N-S 25-932-3160   (SL)
1248776 ONTARIO INC
WENDY'S OF KANATA
6 Edgewater St Suite 6458, Kanata, ON, K2L 1V8
(613) 831-9183
Emp Here 50   *Sales* 1,532,175
SIC 5812 Eating places

D-U-N-S 25-296-7310   (BR)
BANK OF NOVA SCOTIA, THE
SCOTIABANK
482 Hazeldean Rd, Kanata, ON, K2L 1V4
(613) 831-2922
Emp Here 27
SIC 6021 National commercial banks

D-U-N-S 20-965-4206   (BR)
BANQUE TORONTO-DOMINION, LA
TORONTO-DOMINION BANK, THE
(*Suby of* Toronto-Dominion Bank, The)
457 Hazeldean Rd Unit 28, Kanata, ON, K2L 1V1
(613) 592-8947
Emp Here 40
SIC 6021 National commercial banks

D-U-N-S 24-717-0793   (BR)
CML HEALTHCARE INC
150 Katimavik Rd Suite 102, Kanata, ON, K2L 2N2
(613) 592-0711
Emp Here 20
SIC 8071 Medical laboratories

D-U-N-S 24-829-4295   (BR)
CSG SECURITY CORPORATION
CHUBB SECURITY SYSTEMS, DIV OF
(*Suby of* United Technologies Corporation)
8 Hearst Way, Kanata, ON, K2L 2P4
(613) 254-7422
Emp Here 49
SIC 5099 Durable goods, nec

D-U-N-S 24-426-3526   (SL)
CSH EMPRESS KANATA INC
170 Mcgibbon Dr, Kanata, ON, K2L 4H5
(613) 271-0034
Emp Here 20   *Sales* 729,607
SIC 8361 Residential care

D-U-N-S 25-265-3209   (BR)
CONSEIL DES ECOLES CATHOLIQUES DE LANGUE FRANCAISE DU CENTRE-EST
ECOLE ROGER-SAINT-DENIS
186 Barrow Cres, Kanata, ON, K2L 2C7
(613) 592-2191
Emp Here 25
SIC 8211 Elementary and secondary schools

D-U-N-S 25-770-1409   (BR)
FARM BOY 2012 INC
FARM BOY FRESH MARKET
457 Hazeldean Rd Suite 28, Kanata, ON, K2L 1V1
(613) 836-8085
Emp Here 50
SIC 5411 Grocery stores

D-U-N-S 20-790-0429   (BR)
GOODLIFE FITNESS CENTRES INC

484 Hazeldean Rd Unit 17, Kanata, ON, K2L
1V4
(613) 831-9849
Emp Here 25
SIC 7999 Amusement and recreation, nec

D-U-N-S 25-322-3572   (BR)
HENRY SCHEIN CANADA, INC
30 Edgewater St Suite 110, Kanata, ON, K2L
1V8
(613) 836-7552
Emp Here 30
SIC 5047 Medical and hospital equipment

D-U-N-S 25-305-3136   (BR)
INNVEST PROPERTIES CORP
W-WESTMONT HOSPITALITY GROUP
(*Suby* of Innvest Properties Corp)
222 Hearst Way, Kanata, ON, K2L 3A2
(613) 592-2200
Emp Here 35
SIC 7011 Hotels and motels

D-U-N-S 25-280-8886   (SL)
MED-TEAM CLINIC INC
99 Kakulu Rd Suite 103, Kanata, ON, K2L 3C8
(613) 592-1448
Emp Here 25   *Sales* 1,532,175
SIC 8011 Offices and clinics of medical doctors

D-U-N-S 24-536-3622   (BR)
OMNI HEALTH CARE LTD
GARDEN TERRACE
100 Aird Pl, Kanata, ON, K2L 4H8
(613) 254-9702
Emp Here 200
SIC 8051 Skilled nursing care facilities

D-U-N-S 25-265-3415   (BR)
**OTTAWA CATHOLIC DISTRICT SCHOOL
BOARD**
*ST. MARTIN DE PORRES ELEMENTARY
SCHOOL*
(*Suby* of Ottawa Catholic District School
Board)
20 Mckitrick Dr, Kanata, ON, K2L 1T7
(613) 836-4754
Emp Here 25
SIC 8211 Elementary and secondary schools

D-U-N-S 25-828-5360   (BR)
**OTTAWA CATHOLIC DISTRICT SCHOOL
BOARD**
HOLY REDEEMER CATHOLIC SCHOOL
(*Suby* of Ottawa Catholic District School
Board)
75 Mccurdy Dr, Kanata, ON, K2L 3W6
(613) 591-3256
Emp Here 30
SIC 8211 Elementary and secondary schools

D-U-N-S 24-190-2357   (BR)
**OTTAWA CHILDREN'S TREATMENT CEN-
TRE**
OCTC
2 Macneil Crt, Kanata, ON, K2L 4H7
(613) 831-5098
Emp Here 24
SIC 8322 Individual and family services

D-U-N-S 25-239-5819   (BR)
**OTTAWA-CARLETON DISTRICT SCHOOL
BOARD**
KATIMAVIK ELEMENTARY SCHOOL
64 Chimo Dr, Kanata, ON, K2L 1Y9
(613) 592-5462
Emp Here 30
SIC 8211 Elementary and secondary schools

D-U-N-S 25-224-8844   (BR)
**OTTAWA-CARLETON DISTRICT SCHOOL
BOARD**
A.Y. JACKSON SECONDARY SCHOOL
150 Abbeyhill Dr, Kanata, ON, K2L 1H7
(613) 836-2527
Emp Here 75
SIC 8211 Elementary and secondary schools

D-U-N-S 25-154-1173   (BR)
**OTTAWA-CARLETON DISTRICT SCHOOL
BOARD**
GLEN CAIRIN PUBLIC SCHOOL
182 Morrena Rd, Kanata, ON, K2L 1E1
(613) 836-2342
Emp Here 30
SIC 8211 Elementary and secondary schools

D-U-N-S 20-711-6224   (BR)
**OTTAWA-CARLETON DISTRICT SCHOOL
BOARD**
JOHN YOUNG ELEMENTARY SCHOOL
5 Morton Dr, Kanata, ON, K2L 1W7
(613) 836-5987
Emp Here 50
SIC 8211 Elementary and secondary schools

D-U-N-S 20-047-1279   (BR)
**OTTAWA-CARLETON DISTRICT SCHOOL
BOARD**
CASTLEFRANK ELEMENTARY SCHOOL
55 Mccurdy Dr, Kanata, ON, K2L 4A9
(613) 592-8071
Emp Here 30
SIC 8211 Elementary and secondary schools

D-U-N-S 25-983-7912   (BR)
PRISZM LP
KFC
475 Hazeldean Rd, Kanata, ON, K2L 1V1
(613) 836-4011
Emp Here 20
SIC 5812 Eating places

D-U-N-S 25-308-4370   (BR)
ROYAL BANK OF CANADA
RBC
(*Suby* of Royal Bank Of Canada)
500 Hazeldean Rd Unit 103, Kanata, ON, K2L
2B5
(613) 831-2981
Emp Here 27
SIC 6021 National commercial banks

D-U-N-S 20-890-7725   (HQ)
ROYAL CANADIAN LEGION, THE
DOMINION COMMAND
(*Suby* of Royal Canadian Legion, The)
86 Aird Pl, Kanata, ON, K2L 0A1
(613) 591-3335
Emp Here 50   *Emp Total* 2,175
Sales 7,187,700
SIC 8641 Civic and social associations
Ch Ed J. Frost
Pr Tom Eagles
VP Dave Flannigan
VP Thomas Irvine
VP Edward Pigeau
VP Andre Paquette
Treas Mark Barham

D-U-N-S 20-806-2526   (BR)
SOBEYS CAPITAL INCORPORATED
SOBEYS STORE# 877
700 Terry Fox Dr, Kanata, ON, K2L 4H4
(613) 831-1444
Emp Here 25
SIC 5411 Grocery stores

D-U-N-S 20-278-0610   (BR)
TOROMONT INDUSTRIES LTD
TOROMONT CAT
5 Edgewater St, Kanata, ON, K2L 1V7
(613) 836-5171
Emo Here 80
SIC 5082 Construction and mining machinery

D-U-N-S 20-956-4447   (BR)
UTC FIRE & SECURITY CANADA
(*Suby* of United Technologies Corporation)
8 Hearst Way, Kanata, ON, K2L 2P4
(613) 591-0762
Emp Here 75
SIC 3699 Electrical equipment and supplies,
nec

D-U-N-S 24-187-0497   (BR)

WE CARE HEALTH SERVICES INC
WE CARE HOME HEALTH SERVICES
260 Hearst Way Suite 312, Kanata, ON, K2L
3H1
(613) 592-1182
Emp Here 20
SIC 8049 Offices of health practitioner

Kanata, ON K2M
Carleton County

D-U-N-S 20-649-8040   (HQ)
BRADLEY AIR SERVICES LIMITED
FIRST AIR
(*Suby* of Societe Makivik)
20 Cope Dr, Kanata, ON, K2M 2V8
(613) 254-6200
Emp Here 200   *Emp Total* 1,390
Sales 94,265,224
SIC 4522 Air transportation, nonscheduled
Pr Pr Kristopher Dolinki
 Pita Aatami
 Eileen Klinkig
Dir George Berthe
Dir Anthony Ittoshat
Dir Johnny Adams
Dir Michael Gordon

D-U-N-S 25-098-5421   (BR)
**CONSEIL DES ECOLES CATHOLIQUES DE
LANGUE FRANCAISE DU CENTRE-EST**
ECOLE ELISABETH-BRUYERE
100 Stonehaven Dr, Kanata, ON, K2M 2H4
(613) 271-1554
Emp Here 41
SIC 8211 Elementary and secondary schools

D-U-N-S 24-481-8175   (BR)
ELECTRICAL SAFETY AUTHORITY
FIELD EVALUATION SERVICES
1 Terence Matthews Cres Suite 130, Kanata,
ON, K2M 2G3
(613) 271-1489
Emp Here 27
SIC 7389 Business services, nec

D-U-N-S 24-383-8914   (BR)
LOBLAWS INC
REAL CANADIAN SUPERSTORE
760 Eagleson Rd, Kanata, ON, K2M 0A7
(613) 254-6050
Emp Here 150
SIC 5411 Grocery stores

D-U-N-S 25-128-7090   (BR)
METROLAND MEDIA GROUP LTD
RUNGE NEWSPAPER
240 Terence Matthews Cres Suite 202,
Kanata, ON, K2M 2C4

Emp Here 20
SIC 2711 Newspapers

D-U-N-S 24-270-8345   (HQ)
MODERN NIAGARA HVAC SERVICES INC
85 Denzil Doyle Crt, Kanata, ON, K2M 2G8
(613) 591-1338
Emp Here 20   *Emp Total* 300
Sales 8,317,520
SIC 1711 Plumbing, heating, air-conditioning
Dir Brad Mcaninch
Dir Anthony Sottile

D-U-N-S 20-590-5628   (BR)
**OTTAWA CATHOLIC DISTRICT SCHOOL
BOARD**
ST ANNE CATHOLIC SCHOOL
(*Suby* of Ottawa Catholic District School
Board)
500 Stonehaven Dr, Kanata, ON, K2M 2V6
(613) 271-0308
Emp Here 25
SIC 8211 Elementary and secondary schools

D-U-N-S 25-486-5025   (BR)

**OTTAWA CATHOLIC DISTRICT SCHOOL
BOARD**
ST JAMES SCHOOL
(*Suby* of Ottawa Catholic District School
Board)
50 Stonehaven Dr, Kanata, ON, K2M 2K6
(613) 599-6600
Emp Here 35
SIC 8211 Elementary and secondary schools

D-U-N-S 20-026-1951   (BR)
**OTTAWA-CARLETON DISTRICT SCHOOL
BOARD**
MITCHELL, W. O. ELEMENTARY SCHOOL
80 Steeple Chase Dr, Kanata, ON, K2M 2A6
(613) 271-1806
Emp Here 59
SIC 8211 Elementary and secondary schools

D-U-N-S 25-771-1911   (SL)
SARAZEN REALTY LTD
COLDWELL BANKER SARAZEN REALTY
300 Eagleson Rd Suite 46, Kanata, ON, K2M
1C9
(613) 831-4455
Emp Here 140   *Sales* 18,362,450
SIC 6531 Real estate agents and managers
Pr Pr Colin Sarazen
 Terry Sarazen

Kanata, ON K2T
Carleton County

D-U-N-S 25-770-9196   (BR)
BANK OF NOVA SCOTIA, THE
SCOTIABANK
8111 Campeau Dr, Kanata, ON, K2T 1B7
(613) 591-2020
Emp Here 25
SIC 6021 National commercial banks

D-U-N-S 20-224-5705   (SL)
BATON ROUGE RESTAURANT
790 Kanata Ave Unit M3, Kanata, ON, K2T
1H8
(613) 591-3655
Emp Here 50   *Sales* 1,532,175
SIC 5812 Eating places

D-U-N-S 24-139-5321   (BR)
BEST BUY CANADA LTD
FUTUE SHOP
(*Suby* of Best Buy Co., Inc.)
255 Kanata Ave Unit D1, Kanata, ON, K2T
1K5

Emp Here 120
SIC 5999 Miscellaneous retail stores, nec

D-U-N-S 24-363-5708   (BR)
BEST BUY CANADA LTD
BEST BUY
(*Suby* of Best Buy Co., Inc.)
745 Kanata Ave Suite Gg1, Kanata, ON, K2T
1H9
(613) 287-3912
Emp Here 100
SIC 5731 Radio, television, and electronic
stores

D-U-N-S 20-308-7882   (BR)
CARA OPERATIONS LIMITED
KELSEY'S
(*Suby* of Cara Holdings Limited)
130 Earl Grey Dr, Kanata, ON, K2T 1B6
(613) 599-4343
Emp Here 50
SIC 5812 Eating places

D-U-N-S 24-343-7394   (BR)
FGL SPORTS LTD
SPORT-CHEK KANATA CENTRUM
785 Kanata Ave Unit Q1, Kanata, ON, K2T
1H9

---

(613) 271-1513
Emp Here 25
SIC 5941 Sporting goods and bicycle shops

D-U-N-S 24-089-9661   (BR)
HUDSON'S BAY COMPANY
HOME OUTFITTERS
255 Kanata Ave Unit A, Kanata, ON, K2T 1K5
(613) 287-0140
Emp Here 25
SIC 5719 Miscellaneous homefurnishings

D-U-N-S 25-080-6874   (SL)
INN VEST HOTELS GP VIII LTD
HOLIDAY INN & SUITES SELECT OTTAWA WEST (KANATA)
101 Kanata Ave, Kanata, ON, K2T 1E6
(613) 271-3057
Emp Here 100   *Sales* 4,377,642
SIC 7011 Hotels and motels

D-U-N-S 25-170-9838   (BR)
LIQUOR CONTROL BOARD OF ONTARIO, THE
L.C.B.O.
300 Earl Grey Dr Suite 24, Kanata, ON, K2T 1B8
(613) 592-1849
Emp Here 22
SIC 5921 Liquor stores

D-U-N-S 24-252-5454   (SL)
MON 3047 INC
MONTANA'S COOK HOUSE
140 Earl Grey Dr, Kanata, ON, K2T 1B6
(613) 270-0518
Emp Here 10   *Sales* 3,283,232
SIC 5812 Eating places

D-U-N-S 24-179-3962   (SL)
RF -LAMBDA INC
91 Cambior Cres, Kanata, ON, K2T 1J3
(888) 976-8880
Emp Here 35   *Sales* 5,202,480
SIC 3679 Electronic components, nec
Pr Pr Xian Hao Liu
Sls Mgr Michael Liu

D-U-N-S 20-642-4868   (BR)
SIR CORP
JACK ASTOR'S BAR & GRILL
125 Roland Michener Dr Suite B1, Kanata, ON, K2T 1G7
(613) 271-1041
Emp Here 85
SIC 5813 Drinking places

D-U-N-S 24-340-2885   (BR)
STAPLES CANADA INC
STAPLES THE BUSINESS DEPOT
(*Suby of* Staples, Inc.)
8141 Campeau Dr, Kanata, ON, K2T 1B7
(613) 592-3538
Emp Here 20
SIC 5943 Stationery stores

D-U-N-S 25-130-5124   (BR)
STARBUCKS COFFEE CANADA, INC
STARBUCKS
(*Suby of* Starbucks Corporation)
400 Earl Grey Dr Suite 1, Kanata, ON, K2T 1B9
(613) 599-6680
Emp Here 20
SIC 5812 Eating places

D-U-N-S 24-119-2033   (BR)
TORONTO-DOMINION BANK, THE
T D CANADA TRUST
(*Suby of* Toronto-Dominion Bank, The)
110 Earl Grey Dr, Kanata, ON, K2T 1B7
(613) 599-8020
Emp Here 25
SIC 6021 National commercial banks

D-U-N-S 25-498-3141   (BR)
WAL-MART CANADA CORP
500 Earl Grey Dr, Kanata, ON, K2T 1B6

(613) 599-6765
Emp Here 150
SIC 5311 Department stores

Kanata, ON K2V
Carleton County

D-U-N-S 24-341-4385   (BR)
COSTCO WHOLESALE CANADA LTD
(*Suby of* Costco Wholesale Corporation)
770 Silver Seven Rd Suite Unit, Kanata, ON, K2V 0A1
(613) 270-5550
Emp Here 20
SIC 5099 Durable goods, nec

D-U-N-S 25-831-9995   (BR)
HOME DEPOT OF CANADA INC
HOME DEPOT
(*Suby of* The Home Depot Inc)
10 Frank Nighbor Pl Suite Frnt, Kanata, ON, K2V 1B9
(613) 271-7577
Emp Here 200
SIC 5251 Hardware stores

D-U-N-S 25-412-9653   (BR)
IBM CANADA LIMITED
IBM RATIONAL SOFTWARE
(*Suby of* International Business Machines Corporation)
770 Palladium Dr, Kanata, ON, K2V 1C8

Emp Here 170

SIC 7371 Custom computer programming services

D-U-N-S 24-103-6490   (SL)
ROBINSON CONSULTANTS INC
350 Palladium Dr Suite 210, Kanata, ON, K2V 1A8
(613) 592-6060
Emp Here 50   *Sales* 4,961,328
SIC 8711 Engineering services

D-U-N-S 24-244-9705   (BR)
SMART TECHNOLOGIES ULC
501 Palladium Dr, Kanata, ON, K2V 0A2

Emp Here 500

SIC 3674 Semiconductors and related devices

D-U-N-S 25-404-4837   (SL)
SPIRENT COMMUNICATIONS OF OTTAWA LTD
DLS, DIV OF
750 Palladium Dr Unit 310, Kanata, ON, K2V 1C7
(613) 592-2661
Emp Here 65   *Sales* 9,338,970
SIC 3669 Communications equipment, nec
Opers Mgr Jaynie Coulterman

D-U-N-S 20-551-8751   (HQ)
TELECOM OTTAWA LIMITED
(*Suby of* Telecom Ottawa Limited)
100 Maple Grove Rd, Kanata, ON, K2V 1B8
(613) 225-4631
Emp Here 50   *Emp Total* 50
Sales 3,648,035
SIC 7378 Computer maintenance and repair

D-U-N-S 24-338-5320   (HQ)
TURPIN GROUP LTD
TURPIN PONTIAC BUICK GMC
(*Suby of* Turpin Group Ltd)
2500 Palladium Dr Unit 200, Kanata, ON, K2V 1E2

Emp Here 70   *Emp Total* 100
Sales 50,240,000
SIC 5511 New and used car dealers
Pr Pr Fernand Turpin Jr

D-U-N-S 20-026-6521   (BR)
YMCA OF GREATER TORONTO

YMCA YWCA, THE
1000 Palladium Dr, Kanata, ON, K2V 1A4
(613) 599-0280
Emp Here 20
SIC 7999 Amusement and recreation, nec

Kanata, ON K2W
Carleton County

D-U-N-S 24-134-9112   (BR)
OTTAWA-CARLETON DISTRICT SCHOOL BOARD
JACK DONOHUE PUBLIC SCHOOL
101 Penrith St, Kanata, ON, K2W 1H4
(613) 271-9776
Emp Here 55
SIC 8211 Elementary and secondary schools

D-U-N-S 25-183-4458   (BR)
SOBEYS CAPITAL INCORPORATED
840 March Rd, Kanata, ON, K2W 0C9
(613) 599-8965
Emp Here 150
SIC 5411 Grocery stores

Kapuskasing, ON P5N
Cochrane County

D-U-N-S 24-420-5758   (BR)
AGRIUM INC
(*Suby of* Agrium Canada Partnership)
Gd Lcd Main, Kapuskasing, ON, P5N 2X9

Emp Here 360
SIC 2873 Nitrogenous fertilizers

D-U-N-S 20-289-9543   (BR)
CONSEIL SCOLAIRE CATHOLIQUE DE DISTRICT DES GRANDES RIVIERES, LE
75 Queen St, Kapuskasing, ON, P5N 1H5
(705) 335-6091
Emp Here 1,000
SIC 8211 Elementary and secondary schools

D-U-N-S 25-238-0944   (BR)
CONSEIL SCOLAIRE CATHOLIQUE DE DISTRICT DES GRANDES RIVIERES, LE
ECOLE CATHOLIQUE ANDRE CARY
39 Murdock St, Kapuskasing, ON, P5N 1H9
(705) 335-6197
Emp Here 25
SIC 8211 Elementary and secondary schools

D-U-N-S 20-653-7339   (BR)
CONSEIL SCOLAIRE CATHOLIQUE DE DISTRICT DES GRANDES RIVIERES, LE
CATHOLIC JACQUES CARTIER
8 Brunelle Rd S, Kapuskasing, ON, P5N 2T2
(705) 335-4013
Emp Here 25
SIC 8211 Elementary and secondary schools

D-U-N-S 25-238-0951   (BR)
CONSEIL SCOLAIRE CATHOLIQUE DE DISTRICT DES GRANDES RIVIERES, LE
ECOLE SECONDAIRE CITE DES JEUNES
10 Cite Des Jeunes Blvd Suite 1, Kapuskasing, ON, P5N 2K2
(705) 335-6057
Emp Here 50
SIC 8211 Elementary and secondary schools

D-U-N-S 24-337-1965   (BR)
DISTRICT SCHOOL BOARD ONTARIO NORTH EAST
KAPUSKASING DISTRICT HIGH SCHOOL
61 Devonshire St, Kapuskasing, ON, P5N 1C5
(705) 335-6164
Emp Here 40
SIC 8211 Elementary and secondary schools

D-U-N-S 20-551-9940   (BR)

EXTENDICARE INC
EXTENDICARE KAPUSKASING
45 Ontario St, Kapuskasing, ON, P5N 2Y5
(705) 335-8337
Emp Here 70
SIC 8051 Skilled nursing care facilities

D-U-N-S 25-033-5387   (SL)
NORTH CENTENNIAL MANOR INC
2 Kimberly Dr, Kapuskasing, ON, P5N 1L5
(705) 335-6125
Emp Here 88   *Sales* 4,012,839
SIC 8051 Skilled nursing care facilities

D-U-N-S 20-710-4550   (BR)
NORTHEASTERN CATHOLIC DISTRICT SCHOOL BOARD
ST PATRICK SCHOOL
6 Cedar St, Kapuskasing, ON, P5N 2A8
(705) 335-3241
Emp Here 30
SIC 8211 Elementary and secondary schools

D-U-N-S 25-278-5274   (BR)
ONTARIO POWER GENERATION INC
O P G
112 Government Rd W, Kapuskasing, ON, P5N 2X8
(705) 335-8403
Emp Here 35
SIC 4911 Electric services

D-U-N-S 20-761-5407   (BR)
PRIME RESTAURANTS INC
CASEY'S BAR AND GRILL
(*Suby of* Cara Holdings Limited)
106 Government Rd W, Kapuskasing, ON, P5N 2X8
(705) 337-1500
Emp Here 30
SIC 5812 Eating places

D-U-N-S 24-317-9207   (SL)
SERVICES FAMILIAUX JEANNE SAUVE
29 Mundy Ave, Kapuskasing, ON, P5N 1R1
(705) 335-8538
Emp Here 20   *Sales* 5,108,400
SIC 8399 Social services, nec
Prin Mac Hiltz

D-U-N-S 24-324-3560   (BR)
TEMBEC INC
1 Government Rd W, Kapuskasing, ON, P5N 2X8
(705) 337-9784
Emp Here 1,000
SIC 2621 Paper mills

D-U-N-S 25-297-6154   (BR)
WAL-MART CANADA CORP
350 Government Rd E, Kapuskasing, ON, P5N 2X7
(705) 335-6111
Emp Here 120
SIC 5311 Department stores

Kars, ON K0A
Carleton County

D-U-N-S 24-012-0894   (BR)
CHRISTIAN HORIZONS
(*Suby of* Christian Horizons)
1677 Century Rd Rr 1, Kars, ON, K0A 2E0
(613) 692-2445
Emp Here 20
SIC 8361 Residential care

D-U-N-S 25-265-3464   (BR)
OTTAWA-CARLETON DISTRICT SCHOOL BOARD
RIDEAU VALLEY MIDDLE SCHOOL
6680 Dorack Dr, Kars, ON, K0A 2E0
(613) 489-2024
Emp Here 25
SIC 8211 Elementary and secondary schools

D-U-N-S 25-151-3529   (SL)
SHEON ENTERPRISES INC
6047 First Line, Kars, ON, K0A 2E0
(613) 692-1011
Emp Here 55   *Sales* 1,605,135
SIC 7349 Building maintenance services, nec

Kashechewan, ON P0L
Kenora County

D-U-N-S 25-271-4175   (BR)
NORTH WEST COMPANY LP, THE
NORTHERN STORE
Gd, Kashechewan, ON, P0L 1S0
(705) 275-4574
Emp Here 50
SIC 5411 Grocery stores

Kearney, ON P0A
Parry Sound County

D-U-N-S 20-020-6287   (BR)
TORONTO DISTRICT SCHOOL BOARD
SCARBOROUGH OUTDOOR EDUCATION SCHOOL
1511 Echo Ridge Rd, Kearney, ON, P0A 1M0
(705) 636-5384
Emp Here 20
SIC 8211 Elementary and secondary schools

Keene, ON K0L
Peterborough County

D-U-N-S 20-730-0922   (SL)
ELMHIRST'S RESORT (KEENE) LIMITED
ELMHIRST'S RESORT
1045 Settlers Line Rr 1, Keene, ON, K0L 2G0
(705) 295-4591
Emp Here 50   *Sales* 2,188,821
SIC 7011 Hotels and motels

D-U-N-S 20-025-4121   (BR)
KAWARTHA PINE RIDGE DISTRICT SCHOOL BOARD
NORTH SHORE PUBLIC SCHOOL
42 Av Pinecrest, Keene, ON, K0L 2G0
(705) 295-6898
Emp Here 45
SIC 8211 Elementary and secondary schools

Keewatin, ON P0X
Kenora County

D-U-N-S 25-238-0548   (BR)
KEEWATIN PATRICIA DISTRICT SCHOOL BOARD
KEEWATIN PUBLIC SCHOOL
330 Mill St, Keewatin, ON, P0X 1C0
(807) 547-2292
Emp Here 30
SIC 8211 Elementary and secondary schools

D-U-N-S 25-238-0712   (BR)
KENORA CATHOLIC DISTRICT SCHOOL BOARD
ST LOUIS ELEMENTARY SCHOOL
(*Suby of* Kenora Catholic District School Board)
Gd, Keewatin, ON, P0X 1C0
(807) 547-2829
Emp Here 21
SIC 8211 Elementary and secondary schools

Kemble, ON N0H
Grey County

D-U-N-S 20-694-7124   (HQ)
GEORGIAN VILLAS INC
COBBLE BEACH
(*Suby of* Georgian Villas Inc)
319336 Grey Road 1, Kemble, ON, N0H 1S0
(519) 370-2173
Emp Here 20   *Emp Total* 80
Sales 3,210,271
SIC 7997 Membership sports and recreation clubs

D-U-N-S 24-805-0812   (BR)
GEORGIAN VILLAS INC
COBBLE BEACH GOLF LINKS
(*Suby of* Georgian Villas Inc)
221 Mcleese Dr Suite 3, Kemble, ON, N0H 1S0
(888) 278-8112
Emp Here 20
SIC 7997 Membership sports and recreation clubs

Kemptville, ON K0G
Grenville County

D-U-N-S 25-297-0629   (BR)
BANK OF NOVA SCOTIA, THE
SCOTIABANK
139 Prescott St, Kemptville, ON, K0G 1J0
(613) 258-5961
Emp Here 20
SIC 6021 National commercial banks

D-U-N-S 20-789-9092   (BR)
CANADIAN TIRE CORPORATION, LIMITED
CANADIAN TIRE
311 Ryans Well Dr, Kemptville, ON, K0G 1J0
(613) 258-3479
Emp Here 20
SIC 5531 Auto and home supply stores

D-U-N-S 20-286-9298   (BR)
CATHOLIC DISTRICT SCHOOL BOARD OF EASTERN ONTARIO
HOLY CROSS CATHOLIC SCHOOL
521 Clothier St W, Kemptville, ON, K0G 1J0
(613) 258-7457
Emp Here 45
SIC 8211 Elementary and secondary schools

D-U-N-S 20-711-5317   (BR)
CATHOLIC DISTRICT SCHOOL BOARD OF EASTERN ONTARIO
SAINT MICHAEL CATHOLIC HIGH SCHOOL
2755 Hwy 43, Kemptville, ON, K0G 1J0
(613) 258-7232
Emp Here 50
SIC 8211 Elementary and secondary schools

D-U-N-S 25-237-9672   (HQ)
CATHOLIC DISTRICT SCHOOL BOARD OF EASTERN ONTARIO
(*Suby of* Catholic District School Board of Eastern Ontario)
2755 Highway 43, Kemptville, ON, K0G 1J0
(613) 258-7757
Emp Here 30   *Emp Total* 1,400
Sales 128,815,360
SIC 8211 Elementary and secondary schools
Trst Ron Eamer
Dir William Gartland
Ch Bd Brant Laton

D-U-N-S 24-160-6735   (BR)
METRO ONTARIO INC
FOOD BASICS
2615 Hwy 43 Rr 5, Kemptville, ON, K0G 1J0
(613) 258-1266
Emp Here 60
SIC 5411 Grocery stores

D-U-N-S 24-634-1408   (BR)

NAVISTAR CANADA, INC
KEMPTVILLE TRUCK CENTRE
405 Van Buren St, Kemptville, ON, K0G 1J0
(613) 258-1126
Emp Here 240
SIC 3711 Motor vehicles and car bodies

D-U-N-S 24-355-3067   (BR)
UNIVERSITY OF GUELPH
KEMPTVILLE COLLEGE CAMPUS
830 Prescott St, Kemptville, ON, K0G 1J0
(613) 258-8336
Emp Here 80
SIC 8221 Colleges and universities

D-U-N-S 20-031-1426   (BR)
UPPER CANADA DISTRICT SCHOOL BOARD, THE
SOUTH BRANCH ELEMENTARY SCHOOL
2649 Concession Rd, Kemptville, ON, K0G 1J0
(613) 258-1919
Emp Here 45
SIC 8211 Elementary and secondary schools

D-U-N-S 20-785-7041   (BR)
UPPER CANADA DISTRICT SCHOOL BOARD, THE
NORTH GRENVILLE DIST HIGH SCHOOL
304 Prescott St, Kemptville, ON, K0G 1J0
(613) 258-3481
Emp Here 45
SIC 8211 Elementary and secondary schools

D-U-N-S 25-237-9649   (BR)
UPPER CANADA DISTRICT SCHOOL BOARD, THE
KEMPTVILLE PUBLIC SCHOOL
(*Suby of* Upper Canada District School Board, The)
215 Rueben Cres, Kemptville, ON, K0G 1J0
(613) 258-2206
Emp Here 30
SIC 8211 Elementary and secondary schools

D-U-N-S 20-022-2011   (SL)
VALLEY BUS LINES LTD
782 Van Buren St, Kemptville, ON, K0G 1J0
(613) 258-4022
Emp Here 75   *Sales* 3,118,504
SIC 4111 Local and suburban transit

Kenora, ON P9N
Kenora County

D-U-N-S 24-967-2841   (SL)
1526439 ONTARIO LIMITED
BEST WESTERN LAKESIDE INN
470 First Ave S, Kenora, ON, P9N 1W5
(807) 468-5521
Emp Here 65   *Sales* 2,845,467
SIC 7011 Hotels and motels

D-U-N-S 24-883-5621   (BR)
BDO CANADA LLP
KENORA ACCOUNTING
301 First Ave S Suite 300, Kenora, ON, P9N 4E9
(807) 468-5531
Emp Here 30
SIC 8721 Accounting, auditing, and bookkeeping

D-U-N-S 25-297-0389   (BR)
BANK OF NOVA SCOTIA, THE
SCOTIABANK
40 Main St S, Kenora, ON, P9N 1S7
(807) 468-6483
Emp Here 20
SIC 6021 National commercial banks

D-U-N-S 25-842-3466   (SL)
COMMUNITY CARE ACCESS CENTRE FOR KENORA & RAINY RIVER DISTRICT
Rr 1 Stn Main, Kenora, ON, P9N 3W7

Emp Here 22   *Sales* 5,626,880
SIC 8082 Home health care services
Ex Dir David Murray

D-U-N-S 25-915-1413   (BR)
CONFEDERATION COLLEGE OF APPLIED ARTS AND TECHNOLOGY, THE
900 Golf Cours Rd, Kenora, ON, P9N 3X7
(807) 468-3121
Emp Here 30
SIC 8222 Junior colleges

D-U-N-S 24-388-7069   (HQ)
COPPERFIN CREDIT UNION LIMITED
(*Suby of* Copperfin Credit Union Limited)
346 Second St S Suite 2, Kenora, ON, P9N 1G5
(807) 467-4400
Emp Here 24   *Emp Total* 50
Sales 10,999,378
SIC 6062 State credit unions
Simone Roulston
Sec Patti Edie

D-U-N-S 20-758-6900   (HQ)
DISTRICT OF KENORA HOME FOR THE AGED
PINECREST HOME FOR THE AGED
(*Suby of* District of Kenora Home for the Aged)
1220 Valley Dr, Kenora, ON, P9N 2W7
(807) 468-3165
Emp Here 188   *Emp Total* 310
Sales 15,574,400
SIC 8361 Residential care
William Mclean
Jennifer Mckibbon
Kevin Queen
Fin Ex David Gutknecht
Dir Ed Alcock
Dir Barry Sampson
Dir Lloyd Johnson
Dir Joyce Appel
Dir Lourdes Murray

D-U-N-S 20-122-5216   (SL)
EXCEL COACH LINES LTD
1350 Highway 17 E, Kenora, ON, P9N 1M2

Emp Here 50   *Sales* 1,386,253
SIC 4151 School buses

D-U-N-S 25-137-9744   (BR)
GOVERNMENT OF ONTARIO
KENORA CENTRAL AMBULANCE COMMUNICATIONS CENTRE
40 Minnesota St, Kenora, ON, P9N 3V4
(807) 467-3709
Emp Here 34
SIC 4119 Local passenger transportation, nec

D-U-N-S 24-326-1620   (BR)
GOVERNMENT OF ONTARIO
ST JOSEPH HEALTH CENTER
21 Wolsley St, Kenora, ON, P9N 3W7
(807) 467-3573
Emp Here 50
SIC 8742 Management consulting services

D-U-N-S 20-070-5098   (BR)
HUSKY OIL OPERATIONS LIMITED
KENORA HUSKY TRUCK STOP
470 Lakeview Dr, Kenora, ON, P9N 0H2
(807) 468-7740
Emp Here 20
SIC 5541 Gasoline service stations

D-U-N-S 25-868-8456   (SL)
JERITRISH COMPANY LTD
MCDONALD'S RESTAURANTS
900 Highway 17 E, Kenora, ON, P9N 1L9
(807) 468-3018
Emp Here 75   *Sales* 2,261,782
SIC 5812 Eating places

D-U-N-S 25-238-0621   (BR)
KEEWATIN PATRICIA DISTRICT SCHOOL BOARD

EVERGREEN PUBLIC SCHOOL
1 Brinkman Rd, Kenora, ON, P9N 2R5
(807) 468-8607
Emp Here 25
SIC 8211 Elementary and secondary schools

D-U-N-S 25-238-0589   (BR)
KEEWATIN PATRICIA DISTRICT SCHOOL BOARD
VALLEYVIEW ELEMENTARY SCHOOL
27 Donkirk Hts, Kenora, ON, P9N 4K3
(807) 548-4205
Emp Here 21
SIC 8211 Elementary and secondary schools

D-U-N-S 25-238-0639   (BR)
KEEWATIN PATRICIA DISTRICT SCHOOL BOARD
KING GEORGE VI ELEMENTARY SCHOOL
320 Sixth Ave S, Kenora, ON, P9N 2C3
(807) 468-7570
Emp Here 28
SIC 8211 Elementary and secondary schools

D-U-N-S 25-238-0597   (BR)
KEEWATIN PATRICIA DISTRICT SCHOOL BOARD
LAKEWOOD SCHOOL
240 Veterans Dr, Kenora, ON, P9N 3Y5
(807) 468-5571
Emp Here 70
SIC 8211 Elementary and secondary schools

D-U-N-S 25-238-0555   (BR)
KEEWATIN PATRICIA DISTRICT SCHOOL BOARD
BEAVER BRAE SECONDARY SCHOOL
1400 Ninth St N, Kenora, ON, P9N 2T7
(807) 468-6401
Emp Here 100
SIC 8211 Elementary and secondary schools

D-U-N-S 25-162-8111   (BR)
KENORA CATHOLIC DISTRICT SCHOOL BOARD
ST THOMAS AQUINAS HIGH SCHOOL
(*Suby* of Kenora Catholic District School Board)
1 Poirier Dr, Kenora, ON, P9N 4G8
(807) 548-8282
Emp Here 55
SIC 8211 Elementary and secondary schools

D-U-N-S 24-676-3200   (BR)
KENORA CATHOLIC DISTRICT SCHOOL BOARD
POPE JOHN PAUL II
(*Suby* of Kenora Catholic District School Board)
1290 Heenan Pl, Kenora, ON, P9N 2Y8
(807) 467-8910
Emp Here 50
SIC 8211 Elementary and secondary schools

D-U-N-S 20-068-4723   (BR)
KENORA CATHOLIC DISTRICT SCHOOL BOARD
ECOLE SAINTE MARGUERITE BOUR-GEOYS
(*Suby* of Kenora Catholic District School Board)
20 Gunne Cres, Kenora, ON, P9N 3N5
(807) 468-6618
Emp Here 25
SIC 8211 Elementary and secondary schools

D-U-N-S 25-399-1350   (BR)
KENORA FOREST PRODUCTS LTD
1060 Lakeview Dr, Kenora, ON, P9N 3X8
(807) 468-1550
Emp Here 120
SIC 2421 Sawmills and planing mills, general

D-U-N-S 24-742-1428   (BR)
LAKE OF THE WOODS DISTRICT HOSPITAL
MORNINGSTAR DETOX CENTRE
6 Matheson St S, Kenora, ON, P9N 1T5

(807) 468-5749
Emp Here 25
SIC 8062 General medical and surgical hospitals

D-U-N-S 25-971-6074   (BR)
LOBLAWS INC
EXTRA FOODS
538 Park St, Kenora, ON, P9N 1A1
(807) 468-4587
Emp Here 80
SIC 5411 Grocery stores

D-U-N-S 25-756-5804   (BR)
LOBLAWS INC
REAL CANADIAN WHOLESALE CLUB
16 Tenth Ave S, Kenora, ON, P9N 2J4
(807) 468-1770
Emp Here 45
SIC 5199 Nondurable goods, nec

D-U-N-S 24-331-8230   (BR)
MNP LLP
315 Main St S, Kenora, ON, P9N 1T4
(807) 468-3338
Emp Here 22
SIC 8721 Accounting, auditing, and bookkeeping

D-U-N-S 20-122-5810   (SL)
NORCOM TELECOMMUNICATIONS LIMITED
CJTV
(*Suby* of LeBlanc & Royle Enterprises Inc)
Gd Lcd Main, Kenora, ON, P9N 3W9
(807) 547-2853
Emp Here 33   *Sales* 3,109,686
SIC 4841 Cable and other pay television services

D-U-N-S 25-963-2321   (BR)
PERTH SERVICES LTD
PERTH'S CLEANERS LAUNDERERS & RENTALS
(*Suby* of Perth Services Ltd)
420 Second St S, Kenora, ON, P9N 1G6

Emp Here 30
SIC 7218 Industrial launderers

D-U-N-S 24-337-2187   (BR)
R.A.S. FOOD SERVICES INC
PIZZA HUT
(*Suby* of R.A.S. Food Services Inc)
209 Main St S, Kenora, ON, P9N 1T3
(807) 468-5732
Emp Here 22
SIC 5812 Eating places

D-U-N-S 25-957-1131   (BR)
REVERA INC
RETIREMENT RESIDENCES REAL ESTATE INVESTMENT TRUST
237 Lakeview Dr, Kenora, ON, P9N 4J7
(807) 468-9532
Emp Here 100
SIC 8051 Skilled nursing care facilities

D-U-N-S 25-963-9375   (BR)
ROYAL BANK OF CANADA
ROYAL BANK FINANCIAL GROUP
(*Suby* of Royal Bank Of Canada)
144 Main St S, Kenora, ON, P9N 1S9
(807) 468-8921
Emp Here 25
SIC 6021 National commercial banks

D-U-N-S 25-272-6112   (BR)
SOBEYS WEST INC
KENORA SAFEWAY
400 First Ave S, Kenora, ON, P9N 1W4
(807) 468-5868
Emp Here 130
SIC 5411 Grocery stores

D-U-N-S 25-083-7218   (SL)
SYLVAN LEARNING CENTRE INC
205 Second St S, Kenora, ON, P9N 1G1

Emp Here 70   *Sales* 3,793,956
SIC 8299 Schools and educational services, nec

D-U-N-S 24-329-8689   (BR)
WAL-MART CANADA CORP
24 Miikana Way Unit 1, Kenora, ON, P9N 4J1
(807) 468-6379
Emp Here 200
SIC 5311 Department stores

D-U-N-S 20-555-9540   (BR)
WEYERHAEUSER COMPANY LIMITED
I LEVEL BY WEYERHAUSER
(*Suby* of Weyerhaeuser Company)
1000 Jones Rd, Kenora, ON, P9N 3X8
(807) 548-8000
Emp Here 150
SIC 2439 Structural wood members, nec

Kent Bridge, ON N0P

D-U-N-S 20-122-6586   (BR)
THOMPSONS LIMITED
23696 Kent Bridge Rd Rr 2, Kent Bridge, ON, N0P 1V0
(519) 352-6311
Emp Here 20
SIC 5153 Grain and field beans

Keswick, ON L4P
York County

D-U-N-S 20-289-3462   (SL)
CANADA FIRE EQUIPMENT INC
31 Bache Ave, Keswick, ON, L4P 0C7
(905) 535-2777
Emp Here 3,300   *Sales* 435,220,500
SIC 5999 Miscellaneous retail stores, nec
Pr Lorne Gernstein

D-U-N-S 20-538-2513   (BR)
CANADA POST CORPORATION
KESWICK POST OFFICE
202 Church St, Keswick, ON, L4P 1J8
(905) 476-3321
Emp Here 32
SIC 4311 U.s. postal service

D-U-N-S 25-303-3237   (BR)
CANADIAN IMPERIAL BANK OF COMMERCE
CIBC
24 The Queensway S, Keswick, ON, L4P 1Y9
(905) 476-4362
Emp Here 25
SIC 6021 National commercial banks

D-U-N-S 24-659-6758   (BR)
CORPORATION OF THE TOWN OF GEORGINA, THE
RECREATION & CULTURAL OFFICE
26557 Civic Center, Keswick, ON, L4P 3G1
(705) 437-2210
Emp Here 25
SIC 7999 Amusement and recreation, nec

D-U-N-S 20-088-7482   (BR)
METRO ONTARIO INC
FOOD BASICS
199 Simcoe Ave, Keswick, ON, L4P 2H6
(905) 476-7298
Emp Here 65
SIC 5411 Grocery stores

D-U-N-S 25-469-1025   (BR)
SPECIALTY CARE INC
CEDARVALE LODGE
(*Suby* of Specialty Care Inc)
121 Morton Ave Suite 308, Keswick, ON, L4P 3T5

(905) 476-2656
Emp Here 120
SIC 8051 Skilled nursing care facilities

D-U-N-S 24-714-2669   (BR)
WAL-MART CANADA CORP
WALMART
23550 Woodbine Ave Suite 1012, Keswick, ON, L4P 0E2
(905) 476-7330
Emp Here 50
SIC 5311 Department stores

D-U-N-S 25-106-9803   (BR)
YORK CATHOLIC DISTRICT SCHOOL BOARD
OUR LADY OF THE LAKE CATHOLIC COLLEGE SCHOOL
185 Glenwoods Ave, Keswick, ON, L4P 2W6
(905) 656-9140
Emp Here 75
SIC 8211 Elementary and secondary schools

D-U-N-S 25-106-9936   (BR)
YORK CATHOLIC DISTRICT SCHOOL BOARD
ST THOMAS AQUINAS SCHOOL
262 Old Homestead Rd, Keswick, ON, L4P 3C8
(905) 476-7784
Emp Here 30
SIC 8211 Elementary and secondary schools

D-U-N-S 25-293-5705   (BR)
YORK REGION DISTRICT SCHOOL BOARD
KESWICK PUBLIC SCHOOL
(*Suby* of York Region District School Board)
25 The Queensway N, Keswick, ON, L4P 1E2
(905) 476-4377
Emp Here 20
SIC 8211 Elementary and secondary schools

D-U-N-S 25-293-5788   (BR)
YORK REGION DISTRICT SCHOOL BOARD
JERSEY PUBLIC SCHOOL
(*Suby* of York Region District School Board)
176 Glenwoods Ave, Keswick, ON, L4P 3E9
(905) 476-7777
Emp Here 45
SIC 8211 Elementary and secondary schools

D-U-N-S 25-297-9158   (BR)
YORK REGION DISTRICT SCHOOL BOARD
W J WATSON PUBLIC SCHOOL
(*Suby* of York Region District School Board)
162 Carrick Ave, Keswick, ON, L4P 3P2
(905) 476-1618
Emp Here 50
SIC 8211 Elementary and secondary schools

D-U-N-S 20-292-3459   (BR)
YORK REGION DISTRICT SCHOOL BOARD
KESWICK HIGH SCHOOL
(*Suby* of York Region District School Board)
100 Biscayne Blvd, Keswick, ON, L4P 3S2
(905) 476-0933
Emp Here 120
SIC 8211 Elementary and secondary schools

D-U-N-S 20-591-2392   (BR)
YORK REGION DISTRICT SCHOOL BOARD
FAIRWOOD PUBLIC SCHOOL
(*Suby* of York Region District School Board)
201 Fairwood Dr, Keswick, ON, L4P 3Y5
(905) 476-5447
Emp Here 38
SIC 8211 Elementary and secondary schools

D-U-N-S 20-653-2959   (BR)
YORK REGION DISTRICT SCHOOL BOARD
LAKE SIMCOE PUBLIC SCHOOL
(*Suby* of York Region District School Board)
38 Thornlodge Dr, Keswick, ON, L4P 4A3
(905) 656-5970
Emp Here 27
SIC 8211 Elementary and secondary schools

D-U-N-S 20-591-2418   (BR)
YORK REGION DISTRICT SCHOOL BOARD

▲ Public Company   ■ Public Company Family Member   **HQ** Headquarters   **BR** Branch   **SL** Single Location

LAKE SIDE PUBLIC SCHOOL
(*Suby of* York Region District School Board)
213 Shorecrest Rd, Keswick, ON, L4P 1J1
(905) 476-8369
Emp Here 50
SIC 8211 Elementary and secondary schools

D-U-N-S 20-913-6600   (BR)
YORK REGION DISTRICT SCHOOL BOARD
R. L. GRAHAM PUBLIC SCHOOL
(*Suby of* York Region District School Board)
70 Biscayne Blvd, Keswick, ON, L4P 3M8
(905) 476-9295
Emp Here 50
SIC 8211 Elementary and secondary schools

D-U-N-S 25-297-8879   (BR)
YORK REGION DISTRICT SCHOOL BOARD
DEER PARK PUBLIC SCHOOL
(*Suby of* York Region District School Board)
605 Varney Rd, Keswick, ON, L4P 3C8
(905) 476-4185
Emp Here 28
SIC 8211 Elementary and secondary schools

D-U-N-S 20-047-8886   (BR)
ZEHRMART INC
ZEHRS GREAT FOOD
24018 Woodbine Ave, Keswick, ON, L4P 3E9
(905) 476-1318
Emp Here 165
SIC 5411 Grocery stores

Kettleby, ON L0G
York County

D-U-N-S 20-195-2954   (SL)
PETER AND PAUL'S MANOR LIMITED
16750 Weston Rd, Kettleby, ON, L0G 1J0
(905) 939-2800
Emp Here 50   *Sales* 1,678,096
SIC 7299 Miscellaneous personal service

Kettleby, ON L7B
York County

D-U-N-S 25-987-4006   (SL)
SCREEMERS INC
16130 Weston Rd Suite 2, Kettleby, ON, L7B 0E7
(416) 979-3327
Emp Here 50   *Sales* 1,896,978
SIC 7996 Amusement parks

D-U-N-S 25-293-6331   (BR)
YORK REGION DISTRICT SCHOOL BOARD
KETTLEBY PUBLIC SCHOOL
(*Suby of* York Region District School Board)
3286 Lloydtown-Aurora Rd, Kettleby, ON, L7B 0H4
(905) 727-9852
Emp Here 30
SIC 8211 Elementary and secondary schools

Killaloe, ON K0J
Renfrew County

D-U-N-S 25-498-6565   (SL)
561138 ONTARIO LIMITED
HOKUM, BEN AND SONS
28 Elm St, Killaloe, ON, K0J 2A0
(613) 757-2966
Emp Here 125   *Sales* 15,359,963
SIC 2421 Sawmills and planing mills, general
Pr Pr Dean Felhaber

D-U-N-S 20-711-6885   (BR)
RENFREW COUNTY CATHOLIC DISTRICT SCHOOL BOARD

ST ANDREW SCHOOL
(*Suby of* Renfrew County Catholic District School Board)
131 Queen St, Killaloe, ON, K0J 2A0

Emp Here 50
SIC 8211 Elementary and secondary schools

D-U-N-S 20-711-6828   (BR)
RENFREW COUNTY DISTRICT SCHOOL BOARD
KILLALOE PUBLIC SCHOOL
100 Queen St, Killaloe, ON, K0J 2A0
(613) 757-2091
Emp Here 20
SIC 8211 Elementary and secondary schools

Killarney, ON P0M
Manitoulin County

D-U-N-S 25-908-1677   (BR)
UNIMIN CANADA LTD
Gd, Killarney, ON, P0M 2A0
(705) 287-2738
Emp Here 25
SIC 2819 Industrial inorganic chemicals, nec

Kimberley, ON N0C
Grey County

D-U-N-S 20-818-0695   (SL)
TALISMAN MOUNTAIN RESORT LTD
150 Talisman Blvd, Kimberley, ON, N0C 1G0

Emp Here 100   *Sales* 4,377,642
SIC 7011 Hotels and motels

Kinburn, ON K0A
Carleton County

D-U-N-S 20-049-0410   (BR)
OTTAWA-CARLETON DISTRICT SCHOOL BOARD
FITZROY CENTENNIAL SCHOOL
3765 Loggers Way, Kinburn, ON, K0A 2H0

Emp Here 20
SIC 8211 Elementary and secondary schools

D-U-N-S 20-573-8243   (BR)
ROYAL BANK OF CANADA
RBC
(*Suby of* Royal Bank Of Canada)
3803 Loggers Way, Kinburn, ON, K0A 2H0
(613) 832-2323
Emp Here 20
SIC 6021 National commercial banks

Kincardine, ON N2Z
Bruce County

D-U-N-S 20-918-1036   (BR)
BLUEWATER DISTRICT SCHOOL BOARD
KINCARDINE TOWNSHIP - TIVERTON PUBLIC SCHOOL
1805 Hwy 21 N, Kincardine, ON, N2Z 2X4
(519) 396-3371
Emo Here 20
SIC 8211 Elementary and secondary schools

D-U-N-S 25-827-8589   (BR)
BLUEWATER DISTRICT SCHOOL BOARD
HURON HEIGHTS PUBLIC SCHOOL
785 Russell St, Kincardine, ON, N2Z 1S7
(519) 396-7035
Emp Here 28

SIC 8211 Elementary and secondary schools

D-U-N-S 25-238-8772   (BR)
BLUEWATER DISTRICT SCHOOL BOARD
KINCARDINE DISTRICT SECONDARY SCHOOL
885 River Lane, Kincardine, ON, N2Z 2B9
(519) 396-9151
Emp Here 73
SIC 8211 Elementary and secondary schools

D-U-N-S 20-710-6696   (BR)
BRUCE-GREY CATHOLIC DISTRICT SCHOOL BOARD
ST ANTHONY'S SCHOOL
709 Russell St, Kincardine, ON, N2Z 1R1
(519) 396-4330
Emp Here 25
SIC 8211 Elementary and secondary schools

D-U-N-S 25-028-5244   (BR)
REVERA LONG TERM CARE INC
TRILLIUM COURT SENIORS COMMUNITY
550 Philip Pl, Kincardine, ON, N2Z 3A6
(519) 396-4400
Emp Here 95
SIC 8051 Skilled nursing care facilities

D-U-N-S 25-142-0584   (BR)
SOBEYS CAPITAL INCORPORATED
KINCARDINE SOBEYS
814 Durham St, Kincardine, ON, N2Z 3B9
(519) 395-0022
Emp Here 100
SIC 5411 Grocery stores

D-U-N-S 24-347-1641   (BR)
SOUTH BRUCE GREY HEALTH CENTRE
KINCARDINE AND DISTRICT GENERAL HOSPITAL
43 Queen St, Kincardine, ON, N2Z 1G6
(519) 396-3331
Emp Here 50
SIC 8062 General medical and surgical hospitals

D-U-N-S 25-362-4308   (HQ)
SUPERHEAT FGH CANADA INC
1463 Highway 21, Kincardine, ON, N2Z 2X3
(519) 396-1324
Emp Here 60   *Emp Total* 75
Sales 9,442,136
SIC 8711 Engineering services
 Norm Macarthur
Pr George Paul
Fin Ex Sandra Hofmann

King City, ON L7B
York County

D-U-N-S 20-595-7731   (SL)
CASEY TRANSPORTATION COMPANY LIMITED
1312 Wellington St W Suite 1, King City, ON, L7B 1K5
(905) 727-2621
Emp Here 77   *Sales* 2,188,821
SIC 4151 School buses

D-U-N-S 24-869-0356   (SL)
CLUBLINK CORPORATION ULC
BLUE SPRING GOLF CLUB
15675 Dufferin St, King City, ON, L7B 1K5
(800) 661-1818
Emp Here 50   *Sales* 2,188,821
SIC 7992 Public golf courses

D-U-N-S 20-153-9298   (BR)
CLUBLINK CORPORATION ULC
KING'S RIDING GOLD CLUB
14700 Bathurst St, King City, ON, L7B 1K5
(905) 713-6875
Emp Here 100
SIC 7992 Public golf courses

SIC 8211 Elementary and secondary schools

D-U-N-S 24-991-4284   (HQ)
CLUBLINK CORPORATION ULC
EMERALD HILLS GOLF AND COUNTRY CLUB
15675 Dufferin St, King City, ON, L7B 1K5
(905) 841-3730
Emp Here 140   *Emp Total* 550
Sales 25,554,405
SIC 7992 Public golf courses
Pr Pr K. (Rai) Sahi
VP Edge M. Caravaggio
VP Neil E. Osborne
S&M/VP Charles F. Lorimer
VP Scott A Davidson
 Robert Visentin
 Bruce S. Simmonds
 Jack D Winberg
 Patrick S. Brigham
 Donald W. Turple

D-U-N-S 20-799-8704   (BR)
CORPORATION OF THE TOWNSHIP OF KING, THE
KING TOWNSHIP PUBLIC LIBRARY
1970 King Rd, King City, ON, L7B 1K9
(905) 833-5101
Emp Here 40
SIC 8231 Libraries

D-U-N-S 25-996-0540   (HQ)
NEWLOOK INDUSTRIES CORP
(*Suby of* Dealnet Capital Corp)
3565 King Rd Suite 102, King City, ON, L7B 1M3
(905) 833-3072
Emp Here 101   *Emp Total* 5
Sales 33,158,400
SIC 4899 Communication services, nec
 Jason Moretto
Dir Carrie Weiler
CFO Gary Hokkanen
 John G Simmonds

D-U-N-S 24-117-5582   (BR)
SENECA COLLEGE OF APPLIED ARTS & TECHNOLOGY
13990 Dufferin St, King City, ON, L7B 1B3
(416) 833-3333
Emp Here 23
SIC 8221 Colleges and universities

D-U-N-S 20-646-8535   (SL)
ST THOMAS OF VILLANOVA COLLEGE
2480 15th Sideroad, King City, ON, L7B 1A4
(905) 833-1909
Emp Here 55   *Sales* 3,648,035
SIC 8211 Elementary and secondary schools

D-U-N-S 25-106-9985   (BR)
YORK CATHOLIC DISTRICT SCHOOL BOARD
HOLY NAME CATHOLIC ELEMENTARY SCHOOL
65 Spring Hill Dr, King City, ON, L7B 0B6
(905) 833-5852
Emp Here 25
SIC 8211 Elementary and secondary schools

D-U-N-S 20-591-2442   (BR)
YORK REGION DISTRICT SCHOOL BOARD
KING CITY PUBLIC SCHOOL
(*Suby of* York Region District School Board)
25 King Blvd, King City, ON, L7B 1K9
(905) 833-5115
Emp Here 25
SIC 8211 Elementary and secondary schools

D-U-N-S 20-711-4443   (BR)
YORK REGION DISTRICT SCHOOL BOARD
EVA L. DENNIS PUBLIC SCHOOL
(*Suby of* York Region District School Board)
95 Kingslynn Dr, King City, ON, L7B 1H1
(905) 833-6622
Emp Here 50
SIC 8211 Elementary and secondary schools

D-U-N-S 25-293-6422   (BR)

YORK REGION DISTRICT SCHOOL BOARD
KING CITY SECONDARY SCHOOL
(*Suby of* York Region District School Board)
2001 King Rd, King City, ON, L7B 1K2
(905) 833-5332
Emp Here 90
SIC 8211 Elementary and secondary schools

Kingston, ON K7K

D-U-N-S 25-570-4587   (SL)
976668 ONTARIO LTD
DENNY'S RESTAURANT
33 Bensor St, Kingston, ON, K7K 5W2
(613) 547-9744
Emp Here 50   *Sales* 1,532,175
SIC 5812 Eating places

D-U-N-S 25-638-7689   (SL)
995475 ONTARIO LTD
EAST SIDE MARIO'S
417 Weller Ave, Kingston, ON, K7K 6K3
(613) 547-7900
Emp Here 54   *Sales* 1,605,135
SIC 5812 Eating places

D-U-N-S 25-638-7614   (BR)
AGNEW, J. E. FOOD SERVICES LTD
TIM HORTONS
285 Ontario St, Kingston, ON, K7K 2X7

Emp Here 30
SIC 5812 Eating places

D-U-N-S 25-238-3641   (BR)
ALGONQUIN & LAKESHORE CATHOLIC DISTRICT SCHOOL BOARD
HOLY FAMILY CATHOLIC SCHOOL
114 Wiley St, Kingston, ON, K7K 5B5
(613) 546-5981
Emp Here 26
SIC 8211 Elementary and secondary schools

D-U-N-S 20-031-5500   (BR)
ALGONQUIN & LAKESHORE CATHOLIC DISTRICT SCHOOL BOARD
ST MARTHA CATHOLIC SCHOOL
455 St Martha St, Kingston, ON, K7K 7C2
(613) 544-4050
Emp Here 40
SIC 8211 Elementary and secondary schools

D-U-N-S 20-711-4914   (BR)
ALGONQUIN & LAKESHORE CATHOLIC DISTRICT SCHOOL BOARD
REGIOTOLIS-NOTRE DAME CATHOLIC HIGH SCHOOL
130 Russell St, Kingston, ON, K7K 2E9
(613) 545-1902
Emp Here 120
SIC 8211 Elementary and secondary schools

D-U-N-S 25-263-6915   (BR)
ALGONQUIN & LAKESHORE CATHOLIC DISTRICT SCHOOL BOARD
ST PATRICK CATHOLIC SCHOOL
158 Patrick St, Kingston, ON, K7K 3P5
(613) 542-1437
Emp Here 20
SIC 8211 Elementary and secondary schools

D-U-N-S 20-612-3205   (BR)
ARBOR MEMORIAL SERVICES INC
CENTRAL CHAPEL G F TOMPKINS
49 Colborne St, Kingston, ON, K7K 1C7
(613) 546-5454
Emp Here 25
SIC 7261 Funeral service and crematories

D-U-N-S 20-123-0133   (SL)
BARR, GORDON LIMITED
156 Duff St, Kingston, ON, K7K 2L5
(613) 542-4922
Emp Here 35   *Sales* 6,128,699

SIC 1623 Water, sewer, and utility lines
Pr Pr Burt Barr
  Brent Barr

D-U-N-S 20-650-9692   (SL)
BEST VALUE MOTEL INC
DAYS INN KINGSTON HOTEL & CONVENTION CENTRE
33 Benson St, Kingston, ON, K7K 5W2
(613) 546-3661
Emp Here 70   *Sales* 3,064,349
SIC 7011 Hotels and motels

D-U-N-S 25-862-3875   (BR)
BLUMETRIC ENVIRONMENTAL INC
BLUMETRIC ENVIRONMETAL INC
4 Cataraqui St, Kingston, ON, K7K 1Z7
(613) 531-2725
Emp Here 20
SIC 8748 Business consulting, nec

D-U-N-S 25-302-9557   (BR)
BREWERS RETAIL INC
BEER STORE, THE
121 Cataraqui St, Kingston, ON, K7K 1Z8
(613) 548-7786
Emp Here 30
SIC 5921 Liquor stores

D-U-N-S 25-293-8808   (BR)
CIBC WORLD MARKETS INC
WOOD GUNDY
366 King St E Suite 500, Kingston, ON, K7K 6Y3
(613) 531-5522
Emp Here 29
SIC 6282 Investment advice

D-U-N-S 24-911-4471   (HQ)
CADUCEON ENTERPRISES INC
ENVIRONMENTAL TECHNOLOGY-RESEARCH LAB
(*Suby of* Caduceon Enterprises Inc)
285 Dalton Ave, Kingston, ON, K7K 6Z1
(613) 544-2001
Emp Here 20   *Emp Total* 51
Sales 3,291,754
SIC 8731 Commercial physical research

D-U-N-S 25-928-9163   (BR)
CARA OPERATIONS LIMITED
SWISS CHALET
(*Suby of* Cara Holdings Limited)
85 Dalton Ave, Kingston, ON, K7K 6C2
(613) 547-0100
Emp Here 50
SIC 5812 Eating places

D-U-N-S 20-578-3413   (BR)
CARAUSTAR CANADA, INC
309 Dalton Ave, Kingston, ON, K7K 6Z1
(613) 548-3120
Emp Here 40
SIC 2655 Fiber cans, drums, and similar products

D-U-N-S 20-117-9095   (BR)
CORPORATION OF THE CITY OF KINGSTON, THE
RIDEAUCREST HOME FOR THE AGED
175 Rideau St Suite 416, Kingston, ON, K7K 3H6
(613) 530-2818
Emp Here 243
SIC 8361 Residential care

D-U-N-S 25-030-6859   (BR)
CORUS ENTERTAINMENT INC
CKWS-TV
170 Queen St, Kingston, ON, K7K 1B2
(613) 544-2340
Emp Here 50
SIC 7922 Theatrical producers and services

D-U-N-S 25-215-1196   (HQ)
ENGINEERING SEISMOLOGY GROUP CANADA INC
ESG SOLUTIONS

20 Hyperion Crt, Kingston, ON, K7K 7K2
(613) 548-8287
Emp Here 96   *Emp Total* 7,344
Sales 15,532,545
SIC 1382 Oil and gas exploration services
Pr Pr Ken Arnold

D-U-N-S 25-305-3078   (BR)
INNVEST PROPERTIES CORP
COMFORT INN
(*Suby of* Innvest Properties Corp)
55 Warne Cres, Kingston, ON, K7K 6Z5
(613) 546-9500
Emp Here 20
SIC 7011 Hotels and motels

D-U-N-S 20-114-5716   (HQ)
INSURANCE CENTRE INC, THE
THOMSON, JEMMETT, VOGELZANG
(*Suby of* Insurance Centre Inc, The)
321 Concession St, Kingston, ON, K7K 2B9
(613) 544-5313
Emp Here 43   *Emp Total* 53
Sales 4,742,446
SIC 6411 Insurance agents, brokers, and service

D-U-N-S 25-238-5695   (HQ)
K3C COMMUNITY COUNSELLING CENTRES
FAMILY SERVICES EMPLOYEE ASSISTANCE PROGRAMS-KINGSTON
(*Suby of* K3C Community Counselling Centres)
417 Bagot St, Kingston, ON, K7K 3C1
(613) 549-7850
Emp Here 40   *Emp Total* 80
Sales 3,137,310
SIC 8322 Individual and family services

D-U-N-S 25-263-6451   (BR)
LIMESTONE DISTRICT SCHOOL BOARD
FRONTENAC PUBLIC SCHOOL
38 Cowdy St, Kingston, ON, K7K 3V7

Emp Here 40
SIC 8211 Elementary and secondary schools

D-U-N-S 25-263-7954   (BR)
LIMESTONE DISTRICT SCHOOL BOARD
RIDEAU HEIGHTS PUBLIC SCHOOL
77 Maccauley St, Kingston, ON, K7K 2V8
(613) 542-6155
Emp Here 40
SIC 8211 Elementary and secondary schools

D-U-N-S 25-305-4647   (BR)
LIMESTONE DISTRICT SCHOOL BOARD
J E HORTON PUBLIC SCHOOL
411 Wellington St, Kingston, ON, K7K 5R5

Emp Here 40
SIC 8211 Elementary and secondary schools

D-U-N-S 25-305-5081   (BR)
LIMESTONE DISTRICT SCHOOL BOARD
ECOLE MADELEINE-DE-ROYBON
2 Montcalm Ave, Kingston, ON, K7K 7G5
(613) 547-2556
Emp Here 25
SIC 8211 Elementary and secondary schools

D-U-N-S 25-305-4779   (BR)
LIMESTONE DISTRICT SCHOOL BOARD
FIRST AVENUE PUBLIC SCHOOL
85 First Ave, Kingston, ON, K7K 2G7
(613) 542-4392
Emp Here 24
SIC 8211 Elementary and secondary schools

D-U-N-S 20-711-4773   (BR)
LIMESTONE DISTRICT SCHOOL BOARD
LUNDY'S LANE SCHOOL
57 Lundy'S Lane, Kingston, ON, K7K 5G4

Emp Here 38
SIC 8211 Elementary and secondary schools

D-U-N-S 20-289-6945   (BR)
LIMESTONE DISTRICT SCHOOL BOARD
QUEEN ELIZABETH COLLEGIATE
145 Kirkpatrick St, Kingston, ON, K7K 2P4
(613) 546-1714
Emp Here 90
SIC 8211 Elementary and secondary schools

D-U-N-S 25-318-0202   (BR)
LIQUOR CONTROL BOARD OF ONTARIO, THE
L.C.B.O.# 40
34 Barrack St, Kingston, ON, K7K 7A9
(613) 549-5092
Emp Here 25
SIC 5921 Liquor stores

D-U-N-S 24-763-8737   (HQ)
METAL CRAFT MARINE INCORPORATED
METALCRAFT FASTSHIPS
(*Suby of* Metal Craft Marine Incorporated)
347 Wellington St, Kingston, ON, K7K 6N7
(613) 549-7747
Emp Here 60   *Emp Total* 60
Sales 3,648,035
SIC 3732 Boatbuilding and repairing

D-U-N-S 20-290-7515   (BR)
METRO ONTARIO INC
FOOD BASICS
33 Barrack St Suite 949, Kingston, ON, K7K 1E7
(613) 546-7893
Emp Here 60
SIC 5141 Groceries, general line

D-U-N-S 20-647-2263   (BR)
ONGWANADA HOSPITAL
424 Montreal St, Kingston, ON, K7K 3H7
(613) 548-4417
Emp Here 100
SIC 7011 Hotels and motels

D-U-N-S 20-192-7675   (SL)
PROVIDENCE CARE
PROVIDENCE MANOR
275 Sydenham St, Kingston, ON, K7K 1G7
(613) 549-4164
Emp Here 450   *Sales* 28,564,560
SIC 8051 Skilled nursing care facilities
Pr Cathy Dunne

D-U-N-S 24-101-6377   (HQ)
ST. LAWRENCE YOUTH ASSOCIATION
(*Suby of* St. Lawrence Youth Association)
845 Division St, Kingston, ON, K7K 4C4
(613) 542-9634
Emp Here 50   *Emp Total* 94
Sales 3,720,996
SIC 8322 Individual and family services

D-U-N-S 25-213-7823   (BR)
STAPLES CANADA INC
STAPLES THE BUSINESS DEPOT
(*Suby of* Staples, Inc.)
105 Queen St, Kingston, ON, K7K 1A5
(613) 542-3585
Emp Here 50
SIC 5943 Stationery stores

D-U-N-S 25-195-3212   (HQ)
STARTEK CANADA SERVICES LTD
(*Suby of* Startek, Inc.)
100 Innovation Dr, Kingston, ON, K7K 7E7
(613) 531-6350
Emp Here 560   *Emp Total* 13,500
Sales 275,013,760
SIC 8748 Business consulting, nec
  Patrick Darby
Pr Pr William Meade

D-U-N-S 20-047-5668   (BR)
TANDET EASTERN LIMITED
TANDET KENWORTH
191 Dalton Ave, Kingston, ON, K7K 6C2
(613) 544-1212
Emp Here 20

SIC 7513 Truck rental and leasing, no drivers

D-U-N-S 25-176-0187　(BR)
TEMPLEMAN MENNINGA LLP
(*Suby of* Templeman Menninga LLP)
366 King St E Suite 401, Kingston, ON, K7K
6Y3
(613) 542-1889
Emp Here 50
SIC 8111 Legal services

D-U-N-S 24-174-3694　(BR)
TRENTWAY-WAGAR INC
COACH CANADA
1175 John Counter Blvd Unit 4, Kingston, ON,
K7K 6C7
(613) 544-3047
Emp Here 40
SIC 4142 Bus charter service, except local

D-U-N-S 24-120-3962　(BR)
UNITED PARCEL SERVICE CANADA LTD
UPS
1121 John Counter Blvd, Kingston, ON, K7K
6C7
(613) 549-7872
Emp Here 38
SIC 7389 Business services, nec

D-U-N-S 20-889-1176　(BR)
**WASTE MANAGEMENT OF CANADA COR-
PORATION**
(*Suby of* Waste Management, Inc.)
62 St Remy Pl, Kingston, ON, K7K 6C4
(613) 549-7100
Emp Here 20
SIC 4953 Refuse systems

D-U-N-S 20-084-7361　(BR)
WENDY'S RESTAURANTS OF CANADA INC
WENDY'S
(*Suby of* The Wendy's Company)
17 Warne Cres, Kingston, ON, K7K 6Z5
(613) 547-4546
Emp Here 33
SIC 5812 Eating places

D-U-N-S 20-123-7336　(BR)
WESTON BAKERIES LIMITED
MOISSON DOREE
83 Railway St, Kingston, ON, K7K 2L7
(613) 548-4434
Emp Here 100
SIC 2051 Bread, cake, and related products

D-U-N-S 25-639-7571　(BR)
WOLSELEY CANADA INC
WOLSELEY MECHANICAL GROUP
(*Suby of* WOLSELEY PLC)
75 Harvey St, Kingston, ON, K7K 5C1
(613) 546-3141
Emp Here 30
SIC 5074 Plumbing and heating equipment
and supplies (hydronics)

D-U-N-S 24-826-9730　(BR)
**WORKPLACE SAFETY & INSURANCE
BOARD, THE**
WSIB
234 Concession St Suite 304, Kingston, ON,
K7K 6W6
(613) 544-9682
Emp Here 20
SIC 8631 Labor organizations

Kingston, ON K7L

D-U-N-S 24-102-3217　(SL)
1206953 ONTARIO INC
CONFEDERATION PLACE HOTEL
237 Ontario St, Kingston, ON, K7L 2Z4
(613) 549-6300
Emp Here 60　*Sales* 2,626,585
SIC 7011 Hotels and motels

D-U-N-S 25-253-0860　(SL)
956240 ONTARIO INC
STAGES BAR & RESTAURANT
390 Princess St, Kingston, ON, K7L 1B8
(613) 547-5553
Emp Here 65　*Sales* 2,544,288
SIC 5812 Eating places

D-U-N-S 24-326-6124　(BR)
ADAMS PHARMACY LTD
SHOPPERS DRUG MART
1011 Princess St Suite 1209, Kingston, ON,
K7L 1H3
(613) 531-5373
Emp Here 50
SIC 5912 Drug stores and proprietary stores

D-U-N-S 25-638-7648　(BR)
AGNEW, J. E. FOOD SERVICES LTD
TIM HORTONS
681 Princess St, Kingston, ON, K7L 1E8
(613) 544-0201
Emp Here 22
SIC 5812 Eating places

D-U-N-S 20-011-8698　(BR)
AGNEW, J. E. FOOD SERVICES LTD
TIM HORTONS
312 Princess St, Kingston, ON, K7L 1B6
(613) 544-0563
Emp Here 20
SIC 5812 Eating places

D-U-N-S 25-263-6956　(BR)
**ALGONQUIN & LAKESHORE CATHOLIC
DISTRICT SCHOOL BOARD**
*BOA CATHOLIC ELEMENTARY SCHOOLS
HOLY NAME*
370 Kingston Mills Rd, Kingston, ON, K7L 5H6
(613) 542-8611
Emp Here 25
SIC 8211 Elementary and secondary schools

D-U-N-S 20-711-4898　(BR)
**ALGONQUIN & LAKESHORE CATHOLIC
DISTRICT SCHOOL BOARD**
ECOLE CATHEDRALE
301 Johnson St, Kingston, ON, K7L 1Y5
(613) 546-7555
Emp Here 25
SIC 8211 Elementary and secondary schools

D-U-N-S 20-891-5512　(SL)
**ALMA MATER SOCIETY OF QUEEN'S UNI-
VERSITY INCORPORATED**
AMS
99 University Ave, Kingston, ON, K7L 3N5
(613) 533-2725
Emp Here 550　*Sales* 53,202,720
SIC 8641 Civic and social associations
VP Ian Black

D-U-N-S 25-295-9416　(BR)
BANK OF NOVA SCOTIA, THE
SCOTIABANK
168 Wellington St, Kingston, ON, K7L 3E4
(613) 544-3033
Emp Here 25
SIC 6021 National commercial banks

D-U-N-S 25-297-0421　(BR)
BANK OF NOVA SCOTIA, THE
SCOTIABANK
145 Princess St Suite 143, Kingston, ON, K7L
1A8
(613) 530-2010
Emp Here 25
SIC 6021 National commercial banks

D-U-N-S 25-639-7126　(BR)
BANK OF MONTREAL
BMO
297 King St E, Kingston, ON, K7L 3B3
(613) 545-3005
Emp Here 30
SIC 6021 National commercial banks

D-U-N-S 20-589-5407　(BR)

BANQUE TORONTO-DOMINION, LA
*TD WEALTH PRIVATE INVESTMENT AD-
VISE*
(*Suby of* Toronto-Dominion Bank, The)
27 Princess St Suite 202, Kingston, ON, K7L
1A3
(613) 544-5450
Emp Here 20
SIC 6021 National commercial banks

D-U-N-S 25-639-7845　(BR)
BELL MEDIA INC
CKLC & CFLY FM
Gd, Kingston, ON, K7L 4V5
(613) 544-1380
Emp Here 25
SIC 4832 Radio broadcasting stations

D-U-N-S 20-153-3242　(BR)
CANADA POST CORPORATION
120 Clarence St, Kingston, ON, K7L 1X4
(613) 530-2260
Emp Here 90
SIC 4311 U.s. postal service

D-U-N-S 25-238-6008　(BR)
**CANADIAN IMPERIAL BANK OF COM-
MERCE**
CIBC
256 Bagot St, Kingston, ON, K7L 3G5
(613) 546-8000
Emp Here 25
SIC 6021 National commercial banks

D-U-N-S 24-382-1089　(BR)
CANCER CARE ONTARIO
KINGSTON REGIONAL CANCER CENTR
25 King St W, Kingston, ON, K7L 5P9
(613) 544-2630
Emp Here 200
SIC 8069 Specialty hospitals, except psychi-
atric

D-U-N-S 25-639-7761　(BR)
CHEZ PIGGY RESTAURANT LIMITED
PAN CHANCHO BAKERY
44 Princess St, Kingston, ON, K7L 1A4
(613) 544-7790
Emp Here 80
SIC 5461 Retail bakeries

D-U-N-S 25-238-4482　(BR)
**CORPORATION OF THE CITY OF
KINGSTON, THE**
*CITY CENTRAL WATER PURIFICATION
PLANT, UTILITIES KINGSTON*
302 King St W, Kingston, ON, K7L 2X1
(613) 542-1763
Emp Here 50
SIC 4941 Water supply

D-U-N-S 25-253-0258　(SL)
**CUNNINGHAM, SWAN, CARTY, LITTLE &
BONHAM LLP**
27 Princess St Suite 300, Kingston, ON, K7L
1A3
(613) 544-0211
Emp Here 50　*Sales* 4,304,681
SIC 8111 Legal services

D-U-N-S 25-158-8968　(BR)
EMPIRE THEATRES LIMITED
223 Princess St Suite 213, Kingston, ON, K7L
1B3

Emp Here 35
SIC 7832 Motion picture theaters, except
drive-in

D-U-N-S 25-941-2757　(BR)
GAP (CANADA) INC
GAP
(*Suby of* The Gap Inc)
230 Princess St, Kingston, ON, K7L 1B2
(613) 545-4046
Emp Here 20
SIC 5651 Family clothing stores

D-U-N-S 24-342-8278　(BR)
GOODLIFE FITNESS CENTRES INC
GOOD LIFE FITNESS CLUB
1100 Princess St, Kingston, ON, K7L 5G8
(613) 545-2499
Emp Here 35
SIC 7991 Physical fitness facilities

D-U-N-S 25-459-0532　(SL)
GRIZZLY GRILL INC, THE
GRIZZLY GRILL, THE
395 Princess St, Kingston, ON, K7L 1B9
(613) 544-7566
Emp Here 85　*Sales* 2,553,625
SIC 5812 Eating places

D-U-N-S 20-578-1305　(BR)
INNVEST PROPERTIES CORP
HOLIDAY INN HOTEL
(*Suby of* Innvest Properties Corp)
2 Princess St, Kingston, ON, K7L 1A2
(613) 549-8400
Emp Here 60
SIC 7011 Hotels and motels

D-U-N-S 20-203-4794　(HQ)
JESSUP FOOD & HERITAGE LTD
(*Suby of* Jessup Food & Heritage Ltd)
343 King St E, Kingston, ON, K7L 3B5
(613) 530-2550
Emp Here 30　*Emp Total* 100
Sales 2,991,389
SIC 5812 Eating places

D-U-N-S 24-787-8408　(BR)
JESSUP FOOD & HERITAGE LTD
(*Suby of* Jessup Food & Heritage Ltd)
1 Fort Henry Dr, Kingston, ON, K7L 4V8
(613) 530-2550
Emp Here 40
SIC 5411 Grocery stores

D-U-N-S 25-301-5481　(BR)
KPMG LLP
(*Suby of* KPMG LLP)
863 Princess St Suite 400, Kingston, ON, K7L
5N4
(613) 549-1550
Emp Here 45
SIC 8721 Accounting, auditing, and book-
keeping

D-U-N-S 24-194-1074　(BR)
KEG RESTAURANTS LTD
KEG STEAKHOUSE & BAR, THE
300 King St E, Kingston, ON, K7L 3B4
(613) 549-1333
Emp Here 63
SIC 5812 Eating places

D-U-N-S 24-242-0268　(SL)
**KINGSTON AND THE ISLANDS POLITICAL
PARTY**
LIBERAL PARTY OF ONTARIO
15 Alamein Dr, Kingston, ON, K7L 4R5
(613) 546-6081
Emp Here 200　*Sales* 26,174,100
SIC 8651 Political organizations
Pr Catherine M Milks

D-U-N-S 24-950-5611　(HQ)
**KINGSTON-FRONTENAC PUBLIC LI-
BRARY BOARD**
(*Suby of* Kingston-Frontenac Public Library
Board)
130 Johnson St, Kingston, ON, K7L 1X8
(613) 549-8888
Emp Here 100　*Emp Total* 100
Sales 6,391,350
SIC 8231 Libraries
Patricia Enright

D-U-N-S 20-563-4053　(BR)
LEXISNEXIS CANADA INC
LEXISNEXIS
2 Gore St, Kingston, ON, K7L 2L1

Emp Here 50

SIC 7372 Prepackaged software

D-U-N-S 25-305-5362 (BR)
LIMESTONE DISTRICT SCHOOL BOARD
LA SALLE SECONDARY SCHOOL
773 Highway 15, Kingston, ON, K7L 5H6
(613) 546-1737
Emp Here 75
SIC 8211 Elementary and secondary schools

D-U-N-S 25-263-7996 (BR)
LIMESTONE DISTRICT SCHOOL BOARD
RIDEAU PUBLIC SCHOOL
9 Dundas St, Kingston, ON, K7L 1N2
(613) 546-5901
Emp Here 30
SIC 8211 Elementary and secondary schools

D-U-N-S 25-263-8036 (BR)
LIMESTONE DISTRICT SCHOOL BOARD
WINSTON CHURCHILL PUBLIC SCHOOL
530 Earl St, Kingston, ON, K7L 2K3
(613) 542-6441
Emp Here 25
SIC 8211 Elementary and secondary schools

D-U-N-S 20-913-4373 (BR)
LOBLAWS SUPERMARKETS LIMITED
LOBLAWS
1100 Princess St Suite 1040, Kingston, ON, K7L 5G8
(613) 530-3861
Emp Here 30
SIC 5411 Grocery stores

D-U-N-S 24-183-3982 (BR)
LULULEMON ATHLETICA CANADA INC
LULULEMON
270 Princess St, Kingston, ON, K7L 1B5
(613) 549-3297
Emp Here 20
SIC 2339 Women's and misses' outerwear, nec

D-U-N-S 25-295-6008 (BR)
MARCH OF DIMES CANADA
920 Princess St, Kingston, ON, K7L 1H1
(613) 549-4141
Emp Here 20
SIC 8331 Job training and related services

D-U-N-S 25-974-4282 (SL)
MELO, J.S. INC
FOUR POINTS BY SHERATON KINGSTON, THE
285 King St E, Kingston, ON, K7L 3B1
(613) 544-4434
Emp Here 100   *Sales* 4,377,642
SIC 7011 Hotels and motels

D-U-N-S 25-676-1982 (BR)
METRO ONTARIO INC
METRO
310 Barrie St, Kingston, ON, K7L 5L4
(613) 542-5795
Emp Here 200
SIC 5411 Grocery stores

D-U-N-S 24-437-5135 (BR)
PHARMA PLUS DRUGMARTS LTD
1036 Princess Street Unit D101, Kingston, ON, K7L 1H2
(613) 542-1211
Emp Here 25
SIC 5912 Drug stores and proprietary stores

D-U-N-S 25-649-8098 (BR)
PHARMA PLUS DRUGMARTS LTD
1036 Princess St, Kingston, ON, K7L 1H2
(613) 542-4241
Emp Here 30
SIC 5912 Drug stores and proprietary stores

D-U-N-S 20-562-7230 (BR)
PIONEER HI-BRED LIMITED
(*Suby of* E. I. Du Pont De Nemours and Company)
461 Front Rd, Kingston, ON, K7L 5A5

(613) 548-5500
Emp Here 170
SIC 8731 Commercial physical research

D-U-N-S 25-941-1916 (BR)
PRIME RESTAURANTS INC
TIR NAN OG
(*Suby of* Cara Holdings Limited)
200 Ontario St, Kingston, ON, K7L 2Y9
(613) 544-7474
Emp Here 35
SIC 5812 Eating places

D-U-N-S 20-706-2030 (BR)
PROVIDENCE CARE CENTRE
752 King St W, Kingston, ON, K7L 4X3
(613) 548-5567
Emp Here 500
SIC 8063 Psychiatric hospitals

D-U-N-S 24-915-8192 (BR)
QUEEN'S UNIVERSITY AT KINGSTON
BAN RIGH FOUNDATION
40 University Ave, Kingston, ON, K7L 3N8
(613) 533-2976
Emp Here 25
SIC 8322 Individual and family services

D-U-N-S 24-342-2263 (BR)
QUEEN'S UNIVERSITY AT KINGSTON
PHYSICAL PLANT SERVICES
207 Stuart St, Kingston, ON, K7L 2V9
(613) 533-6075
Emp Here 200
SIC 7349 Building maintenance services, nec

D-U-N-S 24-367-3287 (BR)
QUEEN'S UNIVERSITY AT KINGSTON
INFORMATION TECHNOLOGY SERVICES
19 Division St Rm 25, Kingston, ON, K7L 3N6
(613) 533-2058
Emp Here 50
SIC 4813 Telephone communication, except radio

D-U-N-S 24-343-1975 (BR)
QUEEN'S UNIVERSITY AT KINGSTON
COLLECTION DEVELOPMENT AND E-RESOURCE MANAGEMENT
101 Union St W, Kingston, ON, K7L 2N9
(613) 533-2524
Emp Here 30
SIC 8231 Libraries

D-U-N-S 25-146-7460 (BR)
QUEEN'S UNIVERSITY AT KINGSTON
SCHOOL OF COMPUTING
25 Union St, Kingston, ON, K7L 3N5
(613) 533-6050
Emp Here 100
SIC 8221 Colleges and universities

D-U-N-S 25-193-7066 (BR)
QUEEN'S UNIVERSITY AT KINGSTON
OFFICE OF RESEARCH SERVICES
115 Barrack St, Kingston, ON, K7L 3N6
(613) 533-6081
Emp Here 30
SIC 8732 Commercial nonphysical research

D-U-N-S 25-094-9385 (BR)
QUEEN'S UNIVERSITY AT KINGSTON
SCHOOL OF NURSING
92 Barrie St, Kingston, ON, K7L 3N6
(613) 533-2668
Emp Here 50
SIC 8249 Vocational schools, nec

D-U-N-S 25-983-8639 (BR)
QUEEN'S UNIVERSITY AT KINGSTON
QUEEN'S HOUSING & ANCILLARY SERVICES
75 Bader Lane Rm D015, Kingston, ON, K7L 3N8
(613) 533-2529
Emp Here 150
SIC 8221 Colleges and universities

D-U-N-S 24-911-1436 (BR)

QUEEN'S UNIVERSITY AT KINGSTON
DONALD GORDON CENTRE
421 Union St W, Kingston, ON, K7L 2R8
(613) 533-2221
Emp Here 50
SIC 7389 Business services, nec

D-U-N-S 24-856-2709 (BR)
QUEEN'S UNIVERSITY AT KINGSTON
DEPARTMENT OF MECHANICAL & MATERIALS ENGINEERING
130 Stuart St W Rm 319, Kingston, ON, K7L 3N6
(613) 533-2575
Emp Here 40
SIC 8221 Colleges and universities

D-U-N-S 20-191-0549 (BR)
QUEEN'S UNIVERSITY AT KINGSTON
PURCHASING SERVICES
116 Barrie St, Kingston, ON, K7L 3J9
(613) 533-6000
Emp Here 30
SIC 7389 Business services, nec

D-U-N-S 25-306-0511 (BR)
RKJL FOODS LTD
MCDONALD'S
(*Suby of* RKJL Foods Ltd)
285 Princess St, Kingston, ON, K7L 1B4
(613) 533-3999
Emp Here 50
SIC 5812 Eating places

D-U-N-S 20-889-5172 (BR)
RELIGIOUS HOSPITALLERS OF SAINT JOSEPH OF THE HOTEL DIEU OF KINGSTON
166 Brock St, Kingston, ON, K7L 5G2
(613) 549-2680
Emp Here 900
SIC 8069 Specialty hospitals, except psychiatric

D-U-N-S 24-326-3238 (SL)
SHOPPERS DRUG MART
136 Princess St, Kingston, ON, K7L 1A7
(613) 544-5330
Emp Here 30   *Sales* 5,465,508
SIC 5912 Drug stores and proprietary stores
Owner Art Acharya

D-U-N-S 24-344-5116 (BR)
SODEXO CANADA LTD
75 Bader Lane, Kingston, ON, K7L 3N8
(613) 533-2953
Emp Here 500
SIC 5812 Eating places

D-U-N-S 20-057-4874 (BR)
TWD ROADS MANAGEMENT INC
1010 Middle Rd, Kingston, ON, K7L 4V3

Emp Here 120
SIC 5082 Construction and mining machinery

D-U-N-S 25-322-1949 (BR)
TORONTO-DOMINION BANK, THE
TD BANK FINANCIAL GROUP
(*Suby of* Toronto-Dominion Bank, The)
1060 Princess St, Kingston, ON, K7L 1H2
(613) 546-2666
Emp Here 35
SIC 6021 National commercial banks

D-U-N-S 25-649-7397 (BR)
WASTE CONNECTIONS OF CANADA INC
BFI CANADA
1266 Mcadoos Ln, Kingston, ON, K7L 5C7
(613) 548-4428
Emp Here 40
SIC 4953 Refuse systems

D-U-N-S 24-224-5541 (BR)
WENDY'S RESTAURANTS OF CANADA INC
WENDY'S
(*Suby of* The Wendy's Company)
1043 Princess St, Kingston, ON, K7L 1H3

(613) 549-0160
Emp Here 25
SIC 5812 Eating places

D-U-N-S 25-228-0086 (SL)
YOUNG MEN'S CHRISTIAN ASSOCIATION OF KINGSTON, THE
KINGSTON FAMILY YMCA
100 Wright Cres, Kingston, ON, K7L 4T9
(613) 546-2647
Emp Here 190   *Sales* 10,652,250
SIC 7991 Physical fitness facilities
 Mary Kloosterman
Dir Fin Eric Bogstad
Pr Pr Peter Kingston
 Tom Sullivan
 Jack Gilfillan
 Jeff Hanley

Kingston, ON K7M

D-U-N-S 24-737-1565 (BR)
1211084 ONTARIO LTD
PETRO CANADA
765 Gardiners Rd, Kingston, ON, K7M 3Y5
(613) 384-2010
Emp Here 20
SIC 5541 Gasoline service stations

D-U-N-S 25-162-0605 (SL)
1324743 ONTARIO LIMITED
MONTANA'S COOKHOUSE SALOON
630 Gardiners Rd, Kingston, ON, K7M 3X9
(613) 384-5988
Emp Here 70   *Sales* 2,115,860
SIC 5812 Eating places

D-U-N-S 20-059-3841 (SL)
1339877 ONTARIO LTD
DENNY'S RESTAURANT
670 Gardiners Rd, Kingston, ON, K7M 3X9
(613) 634-6220
Emp Here 60   *Sales* 1,824,018
SIC 5812 Eating places

D-U-N-S 25-185-0269 (SL)
1382769 ONTARIO LIMITED
KELSEY'S GARDINERS
650 Gardiners Rd, Kingston, ON, K7M 3X9
(613) 384-7784
Emp Here 70   *Sales* 1,532,175
SIC 5812 Eating places

D-U-N-S 24-437-5762 (HQ)
534118 ONTARIO CORPORATION
JEROME TAYLOR CHEVROLET GEO OLDSMOBILE CADILLAC
(*Suby of* 534118 Ontario Corporation)
2440 Princess St, Kingston, ON, K7M 3G4
(613) 549-1479
Emp Here 70   *Emp Total* 90
Sales 42,404,805
SIC 5511 New and used car dealers
Pr Pr Marilyn F. Taylor
VP Jason Taylor

D-U-N-S 20-614-0613 (BR)
AGNEW, J. E. FOOD SERVICES LTD
TIM HORTONS
4037 Bath Rd, Kingston, ON, K7M 4Y5
(613) 389-3322
Emp Here 20
SIC 5812 Eating places

D-U-N-S 25-641-5902 (BR)
AGNEW, J. E. FOOD SERVICES LTD
TIM HORTONS
2260 Princess St, Kingston, ON, K7M 3G4

Emp Here 20
SIC 5812 Eating places

D-U-N-S 25-640-7735 (BR)
AGNEW, J. E. FOOD SERVICES LTD
TIM HORTONS

---

506 Gardiners Rd, Kingston, ON, K7M 7W9
(613) 384-7137
Emp Here 22
SIC 5812 Eating places

D-U-N-S 20-711-4906   (BR)
ALGONQUIN & LAKESHORE CATHOLIC DISTRICT SCHOOL BOARD
OUR LADY OF LOURDES ELEMENTARY SCHOOL
20 Cranbrook St, Kingston, ON, K7M 4M9
(613) 389-2800
Emp Here 30
SIC 8211 Elementary and secondary schools

D-U-N-S 20-245-2137   (BR)
ALGONQUIN & LAKESHORE CATHOLIC DISTRICT SCHOOL BOARD
PLAN OPERATIONS EAST DEPARTMENT
131 Grant Timmins Dr, Kingston, ON, K7M 8N3
(613) 544-5449
Emp Here 20
SIC 7699 Repair services, nec

D-U-N-S 20-290-0283   (BR)
ALGONQUIN & LAKESHORE CATHOLIC DISTRICT SCHOOL BOARD
ST. MARGUERITE BOURGEOYS CATHOLIC SCHOOL
355 Waterloo Dr, Kingston, ON, K7M 8P5
(613) 549-4499
Emp Here 38
SIC 8211 Elementary and secondary schools

D-U-N-S 25-263-6840   (BR)
ALGONQUIN & LAKESHORE CATHOLIC DISTRICT SCHOOL BOARD
ST THOMAS MORE SEPARATE CATHOLIC SCHOOL
234 Norman Rogers Dr, Kingston, ON, K7M 2R4
(613) 542-1575
Emp Here 30
SIC 8211 Elementary and secondary schools

D-U-N-S 20-025-0533   (BR)
ALGONQUIN & LAKESHORE CATHOLIC DISTRICT SCHOOL BOARD
ST JOHN XXIII CATHOLIC SCHOOL
736 High Gate Park Dr, Kingston, ON, K7M 5Z9
(613) 389-4388
Emp Here 22
SIC 8211 Elementary and secondary schools

D-U-N-S 20-554-3304   (BR)
BMP (1985) LIMITED
ATKINSON HOME BUILDING CENTRE
731 Development Dr, Kingston, ON, K7M 4W6
(613) 389-6709
Emp Here 70
SIC 5211 Lumber and other building materials

D-U-N-S 20-535-8828   (BR)
BANK OF MONTREAL
BMO
945 Gardiners Rd, Kingston, ON, K7M 7H4
(613) 384-5634
Emp Here 20
SIC 6021 National commercial banks

D-U-N-S 25-028-5699   (BR)
BARDON SUPPLIES LIMITED
(*Suby of* Entreprises Mirca Inc, Les)
670 Progress Ave, Kingston, ON, K7M 4W9
(613) 384-5870
Emp Here 45
SIC 5074 Plumbing and heating equipment and supplies (hydronics)

D-U-N-S 24-995-8919   (BR)
BEST BUY CANADA LTD
FUTURE SHOP
(*Suby of* Best Buy Co., Inc.)
616 Gardiners Rd Unit 1, Kingston, ON, K7M 9B8

Emp Here 65
SIC 5731 Radio, television, and electronic stores

D-U-N-S 24-363-2101   (BR)
BEST BUY CANADA LTD
BEST BUY
(*Suby of* Best Buy Co., Inc.)
770 Gardiners Rd, Kingston, ON, K7M 3X9
(613) 887-2599
Emp Here 20
SIC 5731 Radio, television, and electronic stores

D-U-N-S 24-911-1675   (BR)
BOMBARDIER INC
1059 Taylor-Kidd Blvd, Kingston, ON, K7M 6J9
(613) 384-3100
Emp Here 300
SIC 2754 Commercial printing, gravure

D-U-N-S 24-987-6152   (BR)
BRICK WAREHOUSE LP, THE
BRICK, THE
770 Gardiners Rd Unit 1, Kingston, ON, K7M 3X9
(613) 634-5200
Emp Here 30
SIC 5712 Furniture stores

D-U-N-S 20-123-0612   (BR)
BRINK'S CANADA LIMITED
(*Suby of* The Brink's Company)
159 Binnington Crt, Kingston, ON, K7M 8R7
(613) 542-2185
Emp Here 30
SIC 7381 Detective and armored car services

D-U-N-S 24-437-8147   (BR)
CADILLAC FAIRVIEW CORPORATION LIMITED, THE
CATARAQUI TOWN CENTRE
945 Gardiners Rd, Kingston, ON, K7M 7H4
(613) 389-7900
Emp Here 20
SIC 6512 Nonresidential building operators

D-U-N-S 25-238-4177   (BR)
CANADIAN IMPERIAL BANK OF COMMERCE
CIBC
785 Gardiners Rd, Kingston, ON, K7M 7H8
(613) 384-2514
Emp Here 24
SIC 6021 National commercial banks

D-U-N-S 20-791-4644   (BR)
CHILDREN'S PLACE (CANADA) LP, THE
CHILDREN'S PLACE, THE
945 Gardiners Rd, Kingston, ON, K7M 7H4
(613) 634-2567
Emp Here 25
SIC 5641 Children's and infants' wear stores

D-U-N-S 24-417-5605   (BR)
CINEPLEX ODEON CORPORATION
CINEPLEX CINEMAS GARDINERS ROAD
626 Gardiners Rd, Kingston, ON, K7M 3X9
(613) 634-0152
Emp Here 40
SIC 7832 Motion picture theaters, except drive-in

D-U-N-S 25-098-5348   (BR)
CONSEIL DES ECOLES CATHOLIQUES DE LANGUE FRANCAISE DU CENTRE-EST
ECOLE MARIE-RIVIER
711 Dalton Ave, Kingston, ON, K7M 8N6
(613) 546-5270
Emp Here 28
SIC 8211 Elementary and secondary schools

D-U-N-S 20-153-5916   (SL)
CORCAN CONSTRUCTION
455 Bath Rd, Kingston, ON, K7M 7C9

Emp Here 20   *Sales* 5,478,300

SIC 1541 Industrial buildings and warehouses
Prin Chris Stein

D-U-N-S 24-207-1038   (BR)
CORPORATION OF THE CITY OF KINGSTON, THE
NORMAN ROGERS AIRPORT
1114 Len Birchall Way, Kingston, ON, K7M 9A1
(613) 389-6404
Emp Here 237
SIC 4581 Airports, flying fields, and services

D-U-N-S 25-639-0618   (BR)
CORPORATION OF THE CITY OF KINGSTON, THE
KINGSTON ACCESS SERVICES
751 Dalton Ave, Kingston, ON, K7M 8N6
(613) 542-2512
Emp Here 30
SIC 4111 Local and suburban transit

D-U-N-S 25-225-1665   (BR)
CORPORATION OF THE CITY OF KINGSTON, THE
PORTSMOUTH OLYMPIC HARBOUR
53 Yonge St Suite 14, Kingston, ON, K7M 6G4

Emp Here 20
SIC 4493 Marinas

D-U-N-S 25-999-9204   (BR)
DOLLARAMA S.E.C.
690 Gardiners Rd Unit 7, Kingston, ON, K7M 3X9
(613) 384-5680
Emp Here 40
SIC 5311 Department stores

D-U-N-S 25-941-2740   (BR)
EXTENDICARE (CANADA) INC
EXTENDICARE KINGSTON
309 Queen Mary Rd, Kingston, ON, K7M 6P4
(613) 549-5010
Emp Here 100
SIC 8051 Skilled nursing care facilities

D-U-N-S 20-889-2208   (BR)
EXTENDICARE INC
EXTENDICARE KINGSTON
309 Queen Mary Rd, Kingston, ON, K7M 6P4
(613) 549-5010
Emp Here 96
SIC 8051 Skilled nursing care facilities

D-U-N-S 24-343-7402   (BR)
FGL SPORTS LTD
SPORT CHEK CATARAQUI TOWN CENTRE
945 Gardiners Rd Suite Y006, Kingston, ON, K7M 7H4
(613) 634-0798
Emp Here 25
SIC 5941 Sporting goods and bicycle shops

D-U-N-S 24-858-2053   (SL)
FAMILY AND CHILDREN SERVICES OF FRONTENAC AND CLINICS ADDINGTON
1479 John Counter Blvd, Kingston, ON, K7M 7J3
(613) 545-3227
Emp Here 600   *Sales* 29,440,640
SIC 8399 Social services, nec

D-U-N-S 24-610-6538   (SL)
FINDLAY FOODS (KINGSTON) LTD
675 Progress Ave, Kingston, ON, K7M 0C7
(613) 384-5331
Emp Here 70   *Sales* 18,313,136
SIC 5141 Groceries, general line
Pr Pr Stewart Findlay

D-U-N-S 20-980-2404   (BR)
FIRSTCANADA ULC
FIRST STUDENT
769 Burnett St, Kingston, ON, K7M 5W2
(613) 389-8690
Emp Here 55
SIC 4151 School buses

D-U-N-S 24-176-9244   (BR)
FRECON CONSTRUCTION LIMITED
77 Grant Timmins Dr, Kingston, ON, K7M 8N3
(613) 531-1800
Emp Here 20
SIC 1542 Nonresidential construction, nec

D-U-N-S 24-089-9950   (BR)
G4S SECURE SOLUTIONS (CANADA) LTD
2437 Princess St Suite 204, Kingston, ON, K7M 3G1
(613) 389-1744
Emp Here 100
SIC 7381 Detective and armored car services

D-U-N-S 20-700-3690   (SL)
GTS HOLDINGS LIMITED
BEST WESTERN FIRESIDE INN
1217 Princess St, Kingston, ON, K7M 3E1
(613) 549-2211
Emp Here 70   *Sales* 3,064,349
SIC 7011 Hotels and motels

D-U-N-S 24-391-5597   (BR)
GOLF TOWN LIMITED
GOLF TOWN
690 Gardiners Rd Unit B003, Kingston, ON, K7M 3X9
(613) 389-3735
Emp Here 25
SIC 5941 Sporting goods and bicycle shops

D-U-N-S 25-720-1905   (BR)
GREAT-WEST LIFE ASSURANCE COMPANY, THE
1473 John Counter Blvd Suite 3, Kingston, ON, K7M 8Z6
(613) 545-5670
Emp Here 20
SIC 6311 Life insurance

D-U-N-S 25-671-4395   (BR)
HOME DEPOT OF CANADA INC
(*Suby of* The Home Depot Inc)
606 Gardiners Rd, Kingston, ON, K7M 3X9
(613) 384-3511
Emp Here 200
SIC 5251 Hardware stores

D-U-N-S 25-301-2470   (BR)
HUDSON'S BAY COMPANY
BAY, THE
945 Gardiners Rd, Kingston, ON, K7M 7H4
(613) 384-3888
Emp Here 100
SIC 5311 Department stores

D-U-N-S 24-372-2928   (BR)
HUDSON'S BAY COMPANY
HOME OUTFITTERS
770 Gardiners Rd Unit A2, Kingston, ON, K7M 3X9
(613) 384-7522
Emp Here 20
SIC 5719 Miscellaneous homefurnishings

D-U-N-S 25-213-9076   (BR)
INNVEST PROPERTIES CORP
COMFORT INN MIDTOWN
(*Suby of* Innvest Properties Corp)
1454 Princess St, Kingston, ON, K7M 3E5
(613) 549-5550
Emp Here 20
SIC 7011 Hotels and motels

D-U-N-S 25-238-5604   (BR)
KINGSTON & DISTRICT ASSOCIATION FOR COMMUNITY LIVING
COMMUNITY LIVING KINGSTON
196 Mcmichael St, Kingston, ON, K7M 1N6
(613) 547-6940
Emp Here 20
SIC 8361 Residential care

D-U-N-S 25-441-6572   (SL)
LASALLE MOTEL CO KINGSTON LTD
TRAVEL LODGE HOTEL
2360 Princess St, Kingston, ON, K7M 3G4

(613) 546-4233
Emp Here 55   *Sales* 2,407,703
SIC 7011 Hotels and motels

D-U-N-S 25-305-5115   (BR)
LIMESTONE DISTRICT SCHOOL BOARD
EDUCATIONAL SERVICES
153 Van Crder Dr, Kingston, ON, K7M 1B9
(613) 542-9871
Emp Here 100
SIC 8211 Elementary and secondary schools

D-U-N-S 25-305-5404   (BR)
LIMESTONE DISTRICT SCHOOL BOARD
LOYALIST COLLEGIATE & VOCATIONAL IN-
STITUTE
153 Van Order Dr, Kingston, ON, K7M 1B9
(613) 546-5575
Emp Here 80
SIC 8211 Elementary and secondary schools

D-U-N-S 25-263-6378   (BR)
LIMESTONE DISTRICT SCHOOL BOARD
BAYRIDGE PUBLIC SCHOOL
1066 Hudson Dr, Kingston, ON, K7M 5K8
(613) 389-6900
Emp Here 35
SIC 8211 Elementary and secondary schools

D-U-N-S 25-265-3928   (BR)
LIMESTONE DISTRICT SCHOOL BOARD
BAYRIDGE SECONDARY SCHOOL
1059 Taylcr-Kidd Blvd, Kingston, ON, K7M
6J9
(613) 389-8932
Emp Here 80
SIC 8211 Elementary and secondary schools

D-U-N-S 20-711-4765   (BR)
LIMESTONE DISTRICT SCHOOL BOARD
FRONTENAK SECONDARY SCHOOL
1789 Bath Rd, Kingston, ON, K7M 4Y3
(613) 389-2130
Emp Here 80
SIC 8211 Elementary and secondary schools

D-U-N-S 25-305-5370   (BR)
LIMESTONE DISTRICT SCHOOL BOARD
WELBORNE AVENUE PUBLIC SCHOOL
190 Welborne Ave, Kingston, ON, K7M 4G3
(613) 389-0188
Emp Here 40
SIC 8211 Elementary and secondary schools

D-U-N-S 25-263-6295   (BR)
LIMESTONE DISTRICT SCHOOL BOARD
CENTENNIAL PUBLIC SCHOOL
120 Norman Rogers Dr, Kingston, ON, K7M
2R2
(613) 544-6040
Emp Here 30
SIC 8211 Elementary and secondary schools

D-U-N-S 25-228-2215   (BR)
LIMESTONE DISTRICT SCHOOL BOARD
SINCLAIR, R GORDON MEMORIAL
SCHOOL
19 Crerar Blvd, Kingston, ON, K7M 3P7
(613) 389-0267
Emp Here 20
SIC 8211 Elementary and secondary schools

D-U-N-S 25-305-4530   (BR)
LIMESTONE DISTRICT SCHOOL BOARD
POLSON PARK PUBLIC SCHOOL
165 Robert Wallace Dr, Kingston, ON, K7M
1Y3
(613) 542-5926
Emp Here 30
SIC 8211 Elementary and secondary schools

D-U-N-S 25-305-5321   (BR)
LIMESTONE DISTRICT SCHOOL BOARD
TRUEDELL PUBLIC SCHOOL
641 Truedell Rd, Kingston, ON, K7M 6W6
(613) 389-2560
Emp Here 22
SIC 8211 Elementary and secondary schools

D-U-N-S 25-305-4928   (BR)
LIMESTONE DISTRICT SCHOOL BOARD
CALVIN PARK PUBLIC SCHOOL
153 Van Order Dr, Kingston, ON, K7M 1B9
(613) 542-0060
Emp Here 25
SIC 8211 Elementary and secondary schools

D-U-N-S 25-263-6535   (BR)
LIMESTONE DISTRICT SCHOOL BOARD
HENDERSON, JAMES R PUBLIC SCHOOL
361 Roosevelt Dr, Kingston, ON, K7M 4A8
(613) 389-2330
Emp Here 51
SIC 8211 Elementary and secondary schools

D-U-N-S 24-101-5601   (BR)
LONDON LIFE INSURANCE COMPANY
FREEDOM 55 FINANCIAL
1473 John Counter Blvd Suite 301, Kingston,
ON, K7M 8Z6
(613) 544-9600
Emp Here 30
SIC 6411 Insurance agents, brokers, and ser-
vice

D-U-N-S 20-122-9812   (SL)
M AND R MELO'S LIMITED
AMBASSADOR CONFERENCE RESORT
1550 Princess St, Kingston, ON, K7M 9E3
(613) 541-4683
Emp Here 165   *Sales* 10,043,550
SIC 7011 Hotels and motels
Pr Pr Joseph Melo
 Susan Freitas
Dir Fatima Rebelo
Dir Elisabeth Sullivan

D-U-N-S 20-789-4866   (SL)
MARTIN, BOB CONSTRUCTION CO LTD
1473 John Counter Blvd Suite 400, Kingston,
ON, K7M 8Z6
(613) 548-7136
Emp Here 40   *Sales* 5,982,777
SIC 1521 Single-family housing construction
Pr Pr Robert Martin
 Jean Martin

D-U-N-S 24-105-3651   (BR)
MEDI-SCOPE PROFESSIONAL PRODUCTS
(1987) LIMITED
SHAW KINGSTON
30 Steve Fonyo Dr, Kingston, ON, K7M 8N9
(613) 548-7854
Emp Here 28
SIC 8072 Dental laboratories

D-U-N-S 24-852-7561   (BR)
METRO ONTARIO INC
FOOD BASICS
1300 Bath Rd, Kingston, ON, K7M 4X4
(613) 544-9317
Emp Here 75
SIC 5411 Grocery stores

D-U-N-S 24-047-7252   (BR)
METRO ONTARIO INC
FOOD BASICS
1225 Princess St, Kingston, ON, K7M 3E1
(613) 544-8202
Emp Here 60
SIC 5411 Grocery stores

D-U-N-S 24-335-0506   (BR)
METRO ONTARIO INC
METRO
466 Gardiners Rd, Kingston, ON, K7M 7W8
(613) 384-6334
Emp Here 130
SIC 5411 Grocery stores

D-U-N-S 25-641-5043   (BR)
ONTARIO FEDERATION FOR CEREBRAL
PALSY
1724 Bath Rd, Kingston, ON, K7M 4Y2
(613) 384-1957
Emp Here 20

SIC 8322 Individual and family services

D-U-N-S 25-980-9945   (BR)
PROVIGO DISTRIBUTION INC
LOEB #8094
1225 Princess St, Kingston, ON, K7M 3E1
(613) 544-8202
Emp Here 130
SIC 5411 Grocery stores

D-U-N-S 25-310-8807   (BR)
RKJL FOODS LTD
MCDONALD'S
(*Suby of* RKJL Foods Ltd)
30 Beaver Cres, Kingston, ON, K7M 7C1
(613) 542-4228
Emp Here 42
SIC 5812 Eating places

D-U-N-S 24-366-7359   (BR)
ST. LAWRENCE COLLEGE OF APPLIED
ARTS AND TECHNOLOGY, THE
100 Portsmouth Ave, Kingston, ON, K7M 1G2
(613) 544-5400
Emp Here 400
SIC 8221 Colleges and universities

D-U-N-S 25-160-0219   (BR)
STAPLES CANADA INC
STAPLES THE BUSINESS DEPOT
(*Suby of* Staples, Inc.)
616 Gardiners Rd Suite 2, Kingston, ON, K7M
9B8
(613) 634-2112
Emp Here 35
SIC 5943 Stationery stores

D-U-N-S 20-426-7835   (SL)
SUBARU OF KINGSTON
399 Bath Rd, Kingston, ON, K7M 7C9
(613) 546-7000
Emp Here 39   *Sales* 14,227,337
SIC 5511 New and used car dealers
Owner Dave Tidman

D-U-N-S 25-316-8702   (BR)
SUN LIFE ASSURANCE COMPANY OF
CANADA
785 Midpark Dr, Kingston, ON, K7M 7G3
(613) 634-1664
Emp Here 22
SIC 6311 Life insurance

D-U-N-S 24-024-8968   (BR)
SUN LIFE ASSURANCE COMPANY OF
CANADA
SUN LIFE FINANCIAL
1471 John Counter Blvd Suite 101, Kingston,
ON, K7M 8S8
(613) 545-9660
Emp Here 36
SIC 6411 Insurance agents, brokers, and ser-
vice

D-U-N-S 25-639-2614   (BR)
SURGENOR PONTIAC BUICK LIMITED
SURGENOR TRUCK CENTRE
261 Binnington Crt, Kingston, ON, K7M 9H2
(613) 548-1100
Emp Here 30
SIC 5511 New and used car dealers

D-U-N-S 20-963-1543   (BR)
TACKABERRY HEATING SUPPLIES LIM-
ITED
639 Justus Dr Suite A, Kingston, ON, K7M
4H5

Emp Here 45
SIC 5075 Warm air heating and air conditioning

D-U-N-S 24-103-5898   (BR)
TAGGART CONSTRUCTION LIMITED
685 Justus Dr, Kingston, ON, K7M 4H5
(613) 389-7550
Emp Here 40
SIC 1794 Excavation work

D-U-N-S 24-951-4092   (BR)
TALLMAN TRUCK CENTRE LIMITED
KINGSTON TRUCK CENTRE
750 Dalton Ave, Kingston, ON, K7M 8N8
(613) 546-3336
Emp Here 30
SIC 5012 Automobiles and other motor vehi-
cles

D-U-N-S 25-322-2772   (BR)
TORONTO-DOMINION BANK, THE
TD CANADA TRUST
(*Suby of* Toronto-Dominion Bank, The)
750 Gardiners Rd, Kingston, ON, K7M 3X9
(613) 384-1553
Emp Here 30
SIC 6021 National commercial banks

D-U-N-S 20-177-4655   (BR)
TYCO INTEGRATED FIRE & SECURITY
CANADA, INC
SIMPLEXGRINNELL
(*Suby of* Johnson Controls, Inc.)
595 Mckay St, Kingston, ON, K7M 5V8
(613) 634-8486
Emp Here 25
SIC 7389 Business services, nec

D-U-N-S 25-158-9693   (BR)
UNIFOR
CAW LOCAL 31
728 Arlington Park Pl, Kingston, ON, K7M 8H9
(613) 542-7368
Emp Here 220
SIC 8631 Labor organizations

D-U-N-S 20-246-0510   (BR)
VALUE VILLAGE STORES, INC
(*Suby of* Savers, Inc.)
1300 Bath Rd, Kingston, ON, K7M 4X4
(613) 536-5051
Emp Here 50
SIC 5399 Miscellaneous general merchandise

D-U-N-S 25-221-2527   (BR)
WMI - 99 HOLDING COMPANY
(*Suby of* The TJX Companies Inc)
370 Select Dr, Kingston, ON, K7M 8T4

Emp Here 30
SIC 5651 Family clothing stores

D-U-N-S 24-224-5483   (BR)
WENDY'S RESTAURANTS OF CANADA INC
WENDY'S
(*Suby of* The Wendy's Company)
485 Gardiners Rd, Kingston, ON, K7M 7W9
(613) 384-6885
Emp Here 25
SIC 5812 Eating places

D-U-N-S 20-184-2981   (BR)
WINNERS MERCHANTS INTERNATIONAL
L.P.
HOMESENSE
(*Suby of* The TJX Companies Inc)
656 Gardiners Rd Unit 19, Kingston, ON, K7M
3X9
(613) 634-2696
Emp Here 40
SIC 5651 Family clothing stores

D-U-N-S 20-181-4659   (BR)
WINNERS MERCHANTS INTERNATIONAL
L.P.
WINNERS
(*Suby of* The TJX Companies Inc)
636 Gardiners Rd, Kingston, ON, K7M 3X9
(613) 389-3659
Emp Here 30
SIC 5651 Family clothing stores

Kingston, ON K7P

D-U-N-S 24-156-0684   (BR)

AECON CONSTRUCTION GROUP INC
637 Norris Crt, Kingston, ON, K7P 2R9

Emp Here 100
SIC 1522 Residential construction, nec

D-U-N-S 20-575-8886   (BR)
ALGONQUIN & LAKESHORE CATHOLIC DISTRICT SCHOOL BOARD
HOLY CROSS CATHOLIC SECONDARY SCHOOL
1085 Woodbine Rd, Kingston, ON, K7P 2V9
(613) 384-1919
Emp Here 110
SIC 8211 Elementary and secondary schools

D-U-N-S 20-653-2363   (BR)
ALGONQUIN & LAKESHORE CATHOLIC DISTRICT SCHOOL BOARD
ARCHBISHOP O'SULLIVAN CATHOLIC SCHOOL
974 Pembridge Cres, Kingston, ON, K7P 1A3
(613) 389-1891
Emp Here 37
SIC 8211 Elementary and secondary schools

D-U-N-S 20-590-6998   (BR)
ALGONQUIN & LAKESHORE CATHOLIC DISTRICT SCHOOL BOARD
MOTHER THERESA CATHOLIC SCHOOL
1044 Lancaster Dr, Kingston, ON, K7P 2L6
(613) 384-8644
Emp Here 32
SIC 8211 Elementary and secondary schools

D-U-N-S 20-245-7458   (BR)
BELL TECHNICAL SOLUTIONS INC
826 Fortune Cres Suite B, Kingston, ON, K7P 2T3
(613) 634-3357
Emp Here 40
SIC 1731 Electrical work

D-U-N-S 25-318-9989   (BR)
CO-OPERATORS GENERAL INSURANCE COMPANY
CO-OPERATORS, THE
1020 Bayridge Dr, Kingston, ON, K7P 2S2
(613) 384-4700
Emp Here 22
SIC 6411 Insurance agents, brokers, and service

D-U-N-S 25-097-2023   (BR)
COSTCO WHOLESALE CANADA LTD
COSTCO
(*Suby of* Costco Wholesale Corporation)
1015 Centennial Dr, Kingston, ON, K7P 3B7
(613) 549-2527
Emp Here 210
SIC 5141 Groceries, general line

D-U-N-S 25-643-7336   (BR)
DCB BUSINESS SYSTEMS GROUP INC
O T GROUP
(*Suby of* DCB Business Systems Group Inc)
1050 Gardiners Rd Suite 4, Kingston, ON, K7P 1R7
(905) 433-0611
Emp Here 30
SIC 5044 Office equipment

D-U-N-S 25-301-2488   (BR)
EXTENDICARE (CANADA) INC
PARAMED HOME HEALTH CARE
786 Blackburn Mews, Kingston, ON, K7P 2N7
(613) 549-0112
Emp Here 200
SIC 8051 Skilled nursing care facilities

D-U-N-S 25-986-2741   (SL)
FRULACT CANADA INC
1295 Centennial Dr, Kingston, ON, K7P 0R6
(613) 507-7500
Emp Here 30   *Sales* 6,931,267
SIC 5143 Dairy products, except dried or canned
  Benoit Keppenne

Andre Miguel Cachada Pinto Da Rocha
Duarte Nuno Da Silva Almeida Faria
Joao Evangelista Sousa Miranda

D-U-N-S 24-812-9111   (BR)
GOODLIFE FITNESS CENTRES INC
824 Norwest Rd, Kingston, ON, K7P 2N4
(613) 389-8383
Emp Here 30
SIC 7991 Physical fitness facilities

D-U-N-S 20-153-3432   (BR)
HAAKON INDUSTRIES (CANADA) LTD
HAAKON INDUSTRIES
770 Fortune Cres, Kingston, ON, K7P 2T3
(613) 634-6500
Emp Here 50
SIC 3564 Blowers and fans

D-U-N-S 25-315-7663   (BR)
INVESTORS GROUP FINANCIAL SERVICES INC
1000 Gardiners Rd Suite 100, Kingston, ON, K7P 3C4
(613) 384-8973
Emp Here 57
SIC 8741 Management services

D-U-N-S 24-435-8735   (BR)
LAFARGE PAVING & CONSTRUCTION (EASTERN) LIMITED
1600 Westbrook Rd, Kingston, ON, K7P 2Y7
(613) 389-3232
Emp Here 30
SIC 1611 Highway and street construction

D-U-N-S 25-228-0250   (BR)
LIMESTONE DISTRICT SCHOOL BOARD
CATARAQUI WOODS ELEMENTARY SCHOOL
1255 Birchwood Dr, Kingston, ON, K7P 2G6
(613) 634-4995
Emp Here 35
SIC 8211 Elementary and secondary schools

D-U-N-S 25-238-5620   (BR)
LIMESTONE DISTRICT SCHOOL BOARD
LANCASTER DRIVE PUBLIC SCHOOL
1020 Lancaster Dr, Kingston, ON, K7P 2R7
(613) 634-0470
Emp Here 35
SIC 8211 Elementary and secondary schools

D-U-N-S 25-649-7975   (BR)
LOBLAWS SUPERMARKETS LIMITED
LOBLAWS
1048 Midland Ave, Kingston, ON, K7P 2X9
(613) 389-4119
Emp Here 250
SIC 5411 Grocery stores

D-U-N-S 24-344-4861   (BR)
METRO ONTARIO INC
775 Bayridge Dr, Kingston, ON, K7P 2P1
(613) 384-8800
Emp Here 120
SIC 5411 Grocery stores

D-U-N-S 25-527-4144   (BR)
OPEN TEXT CORPORATION
1224 Gardiners Rd, Kingston, ON, K7P 0G2
(613) 548-4355
Emp Here 85
SIC 7372 Prepackaged software

D-U-N-S 24-132-1665   (BR)
PRINCESS AUTO LTD
PRINCESS AUTO
1010 Centennial Dr, Kingston, ON, K7P 2S5
(613) 530-3790
Emp Here 30
SIC 5961 Catalog and mail-order houses

D-U-N-S 25-482-4857   (BR)
PROVIGO DISTRIBUTION INC
LOEB BAYRIDGE
775 Bayridge Dr, Kingston, ON, K7P 2P1
(613) 384-8800
Emp Here 80

SIC 5141 Groceries, general line

D-U-N-S 24-764-8926   (HQ)
S.L.H. TRANSPORT INC
1585 Centennial Dr, Kingston, ON, K7P 0K4
(613) 384-9515
Emp Here 120   *Emp Total* 5,600
Sales 106,668,543
SIC 4213 Trucking, except local
Pr Pr Paul Cooper
VP Brent Fowler
Dir Fin Evelyn Dodd

D-U-N-S 24-366-4844   (BR)
SONOCO CANADA CORPORATION
(*Suby of* Sonoco Products Company)
633 Fortune Cres, Kingston, ON, K7P 2T4
(613) 389-4880
Emp Here 37
SIC 2655 Fiber cans, drums, and similar products

D-U-N-S 24-595-9671   (BR)
SYSCO CANADA, INC
SYSCO KINGSTON
(*Suby of* Sysco Corporation)
650 Cataraqui Woods Dr, Kingston, ON, K7P 2Y4
(613) 384-6666
Emp Here 170
SIC 5141 Groceries, general line

D-U-N-S 25-322-2731   (BR)
TORONTO-DOMINION BANK, THE
TD CANADA TRUST
(*Suby of* Toronto-Dominion Bank, The)
741 Bayridge Dr, Kingston, ON, K7P 2P2
(613) 384-7200
Emp Here 22
SIC 6021 National commercial banks

D-U-N-S 20-122-7514   (BR)
TOYS 'R' US (CANADA) LTD
TOYS 'R' US
(*Suby of* Toys "r" Us, Inc.)
1020 Midland Ave, Kingston, ON, K7P 2X9
(613) 634-8697
Emp Here 25
SIC 5945 Hobby, toy, and game shops

D-U-N-S 25-404-0231   (HQ)
TRANSFORMIX ENGINEERING INC
(*Suby of* Transformix Engineering Inc)
1150 Gardiners Rd, Kingston, ON, K7P 1R7
(613) 544-5970
Emp Here 40   *Emp Total* 80
Sales 8,463,441
SIC 3569 General industrial machinery, nec
Pr Pr Peng-Sang Cau
  Martin Smith
  Kenneth Nicholson
Fin Ex Charles Palmateer

D-U-N-S 25-297-6196   (BR)
WAL-MART CANADA CORP
KINGSTON SUPERCENTRE STORE- #3043
1130 Midland Ave, Kingston, ON, K7P 2X9
(613) 384-9071
Emp Here 175
SIC 5311 Department stores

D-U-N-S 24-369-2535   (BR)
WE CARE HEALTH SERVICES INC
WE CARE HOME HEALTH SERVICES
1365 Midland Ave Unit 130f, Kingston, ON, K7P 2W5

Emp Here 50
SIC 8082 Home health care services

Kingsville, ON N9Y
Essex County

D-U-N-S 20-538-8635   (BR)
CANADA POST CORPORATION

KINGSVILLE STN MAIN
28 Division St N, Kingsville, ON, N9Y 1C9
(519) 733-2343
Emp Here 22
SIC 4311 U.s. postal service

D-U-N-S 24-072-8126   (BR)
CORPORATION OF THE TOWN OF KINGSVILLE
PARKS & RECREATION DEPARTMENT
1741 Jasperson Lane, Kingsville, ON, N9Y 3J4
(519) 733-2123
Emp Here 24
SIC 7999 Amusement and recreation, nec

D-U-N-S 20-303-5894   (BR)
CORPORATION OF THE TOWN OF KINGSVILLE
KINGSVILLE FIRE DEPARTMENT
1720 Division Rd N, Kingsville, ON, N9Y 3S2
(519) 733-2314
Emp Here 56
SIC 7382 Security systems services

D-U-N-S 25-838-0955   (SL)
ERIEVIEW ACRES INC
1930 Seacliff Dr, Kingsville, ON, N9Y 2N1
(519) 326-3013
Emp Here 69   *Sales* 15,102,865
SIC 5159 Farm-product raw materials, nec
Pr Robert Hansen

D-U-N-S 25-249-1964   (BR)
GREATER ESSEX COUNTY DISTRICT SCHOOL BOARD
JACK MINER PUBLIC SCHOOL
79 Road 3 E, Kingsville, ON, N9Y 2E5
(519) 733-8875
Emp Here 30
SIC 8211 Elementary and secondary schools

D-U-N-S 25-249-2053   (BR)
GREATER ESSEX COUNTY DISTRICT SCHOOL BOARD
KINGSVILLE PUBLIC SCHOOL
36 Water St, Kingsville, ON, N9Y 1J3
(519) 733-2338
Emp Here 45
SIC 8211 Elementary and secondary schools

D-U-N-S 24-984-9431   (BR)
GREATER ESSEX COUNTY DISTRICT SCHOOL BOARD
KINGSVILLE DISTRICT HIGH SCHOOL
170 Main St E, Kingsville, ON, N9Y 1A6
(519) 733-2347
Emp Here 60
SIC 8211 Elementary and secondary schools

D-U-N-S 25-033-6021   (SL)
J-D MARKETING (LEAMINGTON) INC
2400 Graham, Kingsville, ON, N9Y 2E5
(519) 733-3663
Emp Here 60   *Sales* 14,519,179
SIC 5148 Fresh fruits and vegetables
Pr Pr James M Dimenna

D-U-N-S 24-626-4618   (SL)
LIQUI-FORCE SERVICES (ONTARIO) INC
(*Suby of* Helen Lewis Holdings Ltd)
2015 Spinks Dr Suite 2, Kingsville, ON, N9Y 2E5
(519) 322-4600
Emp Here 45   *Sales* 2,699,546
SIC 7699 Repair services, nec

D-U-N-S 24-373-0434   (SL)
PETERSON SPRING OF CANADA LIMITED
208 Wigle Ave, Kingsville, ON, N9Y 2J9
(519) 733-2358
Emp Here 60   *Sales* 2,261,782
SIC 3492 Fluid power valves and hose fittings

D-U-N-S 20-210-5248   (BR)
STEEVES & ROZEMA ENTERPRISES LIMITED
SOUTH GATE RESIDENCE

---

38 Park St, Kingsville, ON, N9Y 1N4
(519) 733-4870
Emp Here 29
SIC 8051 Skilled nursing care facilities

D-U-N-S 25-249-1816   (BR)
WINDSOR-ESSEX CATHOLIC DISTRICT SCHOOL BOARD, THE
ST JOHN DE BREBEUF SCHOOL
43 Spruce St S, Kingsville, ON, N9Y 1T8
(519) 733-6589
Emp Here 30
SIC 8211 Elementary and secondary schools

Kintore, ON N0M
Oxford County

D-U-N-S 24-668-6906   (BR)
THAMES VALLEY PROCESSORS LTD
COLD SPRINGS FARM
15 Line 155390, Kintore, ON, N0M 2C0
(519) 285-3940
Emp Here 100
SIC 2015 Poultry slaughtering and processing

Kirkfield, ON K0M

D-U-N-S 20-790-9859   (BR)
PETERBOROUGH VICTORIA NORTHUMBERLAND AND CLARINGTON CATHOLIC DISTRICT SCHOOL BOARD
ST JOHN ELEMENTARY SCHOOL
1047 Portage Rd, Kirkfield, ON, K0M 2B0
(705) 438-3181
Emp Here 25
SIC 8211 Elementary and secondary schools

D-U-N-S 20-025-4428   (BR)
TRILLIUM LAKELANDS DISTRICT SCHOOL BOARD
LADY MACKENZIE PUBLIC SCHOOL
1746 Kirkfield Rd, Kirkfield, ON, K0M 2B0
(705) 438-3371
Emp Here 35
SIC 8211 Elementary and secondary schools

Kirkland Lake, ON P0K
Timiskaming County

D-U-N-S 20-808-3191   (BR)
ST ANDREW GOLDFIELDS LTD
Hwy 101 Holloway, Kirkland Lake, ON, P0K 1N0
(705) 567-4862
Emp Here 34
SIC 1041 Gold ores

Kirkland Lake, ON P2N
Timiskaming County

D-U-N-S 24-320-2558   (SL)
161229 CANADA INC
WHELAN, PAUL MINING CONTRACTORS
21 Government Rd E, Kirkland Lake, ON, P2N 1A1

Emp Here 100
SIC 1241 Coal mining services

D-U-N-S 24-977-2950   (BR)
AEVITAS INC
455 Archer Dr, Kirkland Lake, ON, P2N 3J5
(705) 567-9997
Emp Here 22
SIC 4953 Refuse systems

D-U-N-S 20-528-1632   (BR)
CANADA POST CORPORATION
KIRKLAND LAKE POST OFFICE
15 Government Rd E, Kirkland Lake, ON, P2N 1A1
(705) 567-3333
Emp Here 20
SIC 4311 U.s. postal service

D-U-N-S 20-710-4220   (BR)
CONSEIL SCOLAIRE CATHOLIQUE DE DISTRICT DES GRANDES RIVIERES, LE
ASSUMPTION SCHOOL
31 Churchill Dr, Kirkland Lake, ON, P2N 1T8
(705) 567-5151
Emp Here 30
SIC 8211 Elementary and secondary schools

D-U-N-S 25-000-6533   (BR)
CONSEIL SCOLAIRE CATHOLIQUE DE DISTRICT DES GRANDES RIVIERES, LE
JEAN-VANIER
54 Duncan Ave S, Kirkland Lake, ON, P2N 1Y1
(705) 567-9266
Emp Here 25
SIC 8211 Elementary and secondary schools

D-U-N-S 25-228-0656   (BR)
DISTRICT SCHOOL BOARD ONTARIO NORTH EAST
KIRKLAND LAKE DISTRICT COMPOSITE SCHOOL
Gd, Kirkland Lake, ON, P2N 3P4
(705) 567-4981
Emp Here 75
SIC 8211 Elementary and secondary schools

D-U-N-S 25-228-0615   (BR)
DISTRICT SCHOOL BOARD ONTARIO NORTH EAST
FEDERAL PUBLIC SCHOOL
84 Tweedsmuir Rd, Kirkland Lake, ON, P2N 1J5
(705) 567-5288
Emp Here 20
SIC 8211 Elementary and secondary schools

D-U-N-S 20-710-4501   (BR)
DISTRICT SCHOOL BOARD ONTARIO NORTH EAST
KING GEORGE PUBLIC SCHOOL
35 Porteous Ave, Kirkland Lake, ON, P2N 1X2

Emp Here 50
SIC 8211 Elementary and secondary schools

D-U-N-S 25-228-0649   (BR)
DISTRICT SCHOOL BOARD ONTARIO NORTH EAST
CENTRAL PUBLIC SCHOOL
21 Station Rd S, Kirkland Lake, ON, P2N 3H2
(705) 567-4030
Emp Here 20
SIC 8211 Elementary and secondary schools

D-U-N-S 20-260-7250   (HQ)
DISTRICT OF TIMISKAMING SOCIAL SERVICES ADMINISTRATION BOARD
DTSSAB
29 Duncan Ave N, Kirkland Lake, ON, P2N 1X5
(705) 567-9366
Emp Here 101   *Emp Total* 90,000
Sales 15,394,708
SIC 8611 Business associations
Dir Don Studholme
Ch Bd Jim Whipple

D-U-N-S 20-086-7393   (BR)
GRANT LUMBER BUILDING CENTRES LTD
GRANT HOME HARDWARE
15 Kirkland St E, Kirkland Lake, ON, P2N 1N9
(705) 567-3383
Emp Here 28
SIC 5251 Hardware stores

D-U-N-S 25-033-5841   (BR)

GRAYDON FOODS LTD
MCDONALD'S RESTAURANT
(*Suby of* Graydon Foods Ltd)
155 Government Rd W, Kirkland Lake, ON, P2N 2E8
(705) 568-8595
Emp Here 35
SIC 5812 Eating places

D-U-N-S 20-403-5752   (SL)
HEATH & SHERWOOD (1964) LIMITED
512 Government Rd W, Kirkland Lake, ON, P2N 3J2
(705) 567-5313
Emp Here 40   *Sales* 13,695,750
SIC 3532 Mining machinery
Pr Pr J. Peter Marinigh
  Phillip Cancilla
  Michael Marinigh

D-U-N-S 24-010-7623   (SL)
KIRKLAND AND DISTRICT HOSPITAL
145 Government Rd W, Kirkland Lake, ON, P2N 2E8
(705) 567-5251
Emp Here 250   *Sales* 21,872,703
SIC 8062 General medical and surgical hospitals
Pr Pr Lois Kozak
  Cathie Horne
Dir Fin Melanie Davis
Ch Bd Patty Quinn
V Ch Bd Ted Butt
  Barry Ryan
Dir Brian Bronson
Dir Lynda Clowater
Dir David Dickinson
Dir Marcel Joliat

D-U-N-S 20-343-1721   (BR)
KIRKLAND LAKE GOLD LTD
1350 Government Rd W, Kirkland Lake, ON, P2N 3J1
(705) 567-5208
Emp Here 800
SIC 1081 Metal mining services

D-U-N-S 20-124-0439   (SL)
MCLELLAN TRANSPORTATION CO. LIMITED
MCLELLAN'S TRANSPORTATION
13 Duncan Ave S, Kirkland Lake, ON, P2N 1X2
(705) 567-3105
Emp Here 72   *Sales* 2,042,900
SIC 4151 School buses

D-U-N-S 25-239-0133   (BR)
NORTHEASTERN CATHOLIC DISTRICT SCHOOL BOARD
SACRED HEART SCHOOL
63 Churchill Dr, Kirkland Lake, ON, P2N 1T8
(705) 567-7444
Emp Here 35
SIC 8211 Elementary and secondary schools

D-U-N-S 25-239-0463   (BR)
NORTHEASTERN CATHOLIC DISTRICT SCHOOL BOARD
ST JEROME SCHOOL
128 Woods St, Kirkland Lake, ON, P2N 2S4
(705) 567-5800
Emp Here 20
SIC 8211 Elementary and secondary schools

D-U-N-S 24-184-1253   (BR)
NORTHERN COLLEGE OF APPLIED ARTS & TECHNOLOGY
140 Government Rd W, Kirkland Lake, ON, P2N 2E9
(705) 567-9291
Emp Here 80
SIC 8221 Colleges and universities

D-U-N-S 20-328-0342   (BR)
NORTHLAND POWER INC
KIRKLAND POWER STATION
505 Archers Dr, Kirkland Lake, ON, P2N 3M7

(705) 567-9501
Emp Here 35
SIC 4911 Electric services

D-U-N-S 25-297-7400   (BR)
SIEMENS CANADA LIMITED
475 Archer Dr, Kirkland Lake, ON, P2N 3H6
(705) 568-6355
Emp Here 22
SIC 7629 Electrical repair shops

D-U-N-S 25-155-1826   (BR)
TIMISKAMING HOME SUPPORT/SOUTIEN A DOMICILE
(*Suby of* Timiskaming Home Support/Soutien A Domicile)
30 Second St E Unit 2, Kirkland Lake, ON, P2N 1R1
(705) 567-7383
Emp Here 25
SIC 8059 Nursing and personal care, nec

Kitchener, ON N2A
Waterloo County

D-U-N-S 25-966-1833   (SL)
980443 ONTARIO INC
A BUCK OR TWO 45
1005 Ottawa St N Suite 72, Kitchener, ON, N2A 1H2

Emp Here 60   *Sales* 6,797,150
SIC 5399 Miscellaneous general merchandise
Pr Pr Jeff Smith

D-U-N-S 20-700-1137   (BR)
BREWERS RETAIL INC
BEER STORE, THE
1255 Weber St E, Kitchener, ON, N2A 1C2
(519) 894-9120
Emp Here 30
SIC 5921 Liquor stores

D-U-N-S 20-860-1984   (BR)
BRIDGESTONE CANADA INC
SOURCE BY CIRCUIT CITY, THE
1005 Ottawa St N Suite 26, Kitchener, ON, N2A 1H2
(519) 893-9013
Emp Here 25
SIC 5999 Miscellaneous retail stores, nec

D-U-N-S 20-124-3326   (SL)
CHARCOAL STEAK HOUSE INC
2980 King St E, Kitchener, ON, N2A 1A9
(519) 893-6570
Emp Here 150   *Sales* 5,842,440
SIC 5812 Eating places

D-U-N-S 24-436-5610   (BR)
GOODWILL INDUSTRIES, ONTARIO GREAT LAKES
GOODWILL RETAIL STORE
1348 Weber St E, Kitchener, ON, N2A 1C4
(519) 894-0628
Emp Here 35
SIC 5932 Used merchandise stores

D-U-N-S 20-733-2094   (BR)
JENKEL INVESTMENTS LTD
MCDONALDS STORE
1020 Ottawa St N Suite E, Kitchener, ON, N2A 3Z3
(519) 896-2115
Emp Here 70
SIC 5812 Eating places

D-U-N-S 20-280-7608   (BR)
JOSSLIN INSURANCE BROKERS LIMITED
(*Suby of* Josslin Insurance Brokers Limited)
1082 Weber St E, Kitchener, ON, N2A 1B8
(519) 893-7008
Emp Here 50
SIC 6411 Insurance agents, brokers, and service

D-U-N-S 20-280-7533   (BR)
OWL CHILD CARE SERVICES OF ONTARIO
75 Pebblecreek Dr, Kitchener, ON, N2A 0E3
(519) 894-0563
Emp Here 21
SIC 8351 Child day care services

D-U-N-S 25-595-4406   (BR)
PHARMA PLUS DRUGMARTS LTD
1005 Ottawa St N, Kitchener, ON, N2A 1H2
(519) 893-7171
Emp Here 21
SIC 5912 Drug stores and proprietary stores

D-U-N-S 24-338-5197   (BR)
REVERA INC
FERGUS PLACE
164 Fergus Ave, Kitchener, ON, N2A 2H2
(519) 894-9600
Emp Here 35
SIC 8361 Residential care

D-U-N-S 24-176-5127   (BR)
SUNBEAM CENTRE
26 Breckwood Pl, Kitchener, ON, N2A 4C6
(519) 894-1941
Emp Here 20
SIC 8361 Residential care

D-U-N-S 25-487-1924   (HQ)
TRAVERSE INDEPENDENCE NOT-FOR-PROFIT
(*Suby of* Traverse Independence Not-for-profit)
1382 Weber St E, Kitchener, ON, N2A 1C4
(519) 741-5845
Emp Here 20   *Emp Total* 75
Sales 2,772,507
SIC 8361 Residential care

D-U-N-S 25-310-3485   (BR)
TWINCORP INC
KFC
1020 Ottawa St N Unit D, Kitchener, ON, N2A 3Z3
(519) 894-1615
Emp Here 20
SIC 5812 Eating places

D-U-N-S 24-892-6156   (BR)
WW CANADA (ONE) NOMINEE CORP
MADISON HOTEL
2960 King St E, Kitchener, ON, N2A 1A9
(519) 894-9500
Emp Here 50
SIC 7011 Hotels and motels

D-U-N-S 20-710-7330   (BR)
WATERLOO CATHOLIC DISTRICT SCHOOL BOARD
ST PATRICK ELEMENTARY SCHOOL
50 Thaler Ave, Kitchener, ON, N2A 2V9
(519) 748-6008
Emp Here 50
SIC 8211 Elementary and secondary schools

D-U-N-S 25-228-1852   (BR)
WATERLOO CATHOLIC DISTRICT SCHOOL BOARD
ST DANIEL ELEMENTARY SCHOOL
39 Midland Dr, Kitchener, ON, N2A 2A9
(519) 893-8801
Emp Here 30
SIC 8211 Elementary and secondary schools

D-U-N-S 20-710-7017   (BR)
WATERLOO REGION DISTRICT SCHOOL BOARD
HOWARD ROBERTSON PUBLIC SCHOOL
130 Morgan Ave, Kitchener, ON, N2A 2M5
(519) 748-6161
Emp Here 50
SIC 8211 Elementary and secondary schools

D-U-N-S 20-781-6708   (BR)
WATERLOO REGION DISTRICT SCHOOL BOARD
SUNNY SIDE SENIOR PUBLIC SCHOOL

1042 Weber St E, Kitchener, ON, N2A 1B6
(519) 896-1130
Emp Here 35
SIC 8211 Elementary and secondary schools

D-U-N-S 25-237-9029   (BR)
WATERLOO REGION DISTRICT SCHOOL BOARD
FRANKLIN PUBLIC SCHOOL
371 Franklin St N, Kitchener, ON, N2A 1Y9
(519) 893-1334
Emp Here 45
SIC 8211 Elementary and secondary schools

D-U-N-S 20-591-4588   (BR)
WATERLOO REGION DISTRICT SCHOOL BOARD
CHOICES FOR YOUTH
151 Zeller Dr, Kitchener, ON, N2A 4H4
(519) 746-0140
Emp Here 25
SIC 8211 Elementary and secondary schools

D-U-N-S 25-297-8705   (BR)
ZEHRMART INC
ZEHRS MARKETS
1375 Weber St E, Kitchener, ON, N2A 3Y7
(519) 748-4570
Emp Here 150
SIC 5411 Grocery stores

Kitchener, ON N2B
Waterloo County

D-U-N-S 24-092-6993   (BR)
A & W FOOD SERVICES OF CANADA INC
A & W
933 Victoria St N, Kitchener, ON, N2B 3C6
(519) 576-1859
Emp Here 20
SIC 5812 Eating places

D-U-N-S 24-189-5817   (BR)
ABELL PEST CONTROL INC
36b Centennial Rd, Kitchener, ON, N2B 3G1
(519) 836-3800
Emp Here 20
SIC 7342 Disinfecting and pest control services

D-U-N-S 24-484-4148   (HQ)
BRICK BREWING CO. LIMITED
FORMOSA SPRINGS BREWERY
(*Suby of* Brick Brewing Co. Limited)
400 Bingemans Centre Dr, Kitchener, ON, N2B 3X9
(519) 742-2732
Emp Here 20   *Emp Total* 114
Sales 34,430,591
SIC 5921 Liquor stores
Pr Pr George H. Croft
Sean Byrne
Russell Tabata
Peter J. Schwartz
Stan G. Dunford
Edward H. Kernaghan
David R. Shaw
John Bowey

D-U-N-S 25-941-7806   (BR)
CARA OPERATIONS LIMITED
HARVEY'S RESTAURANT
(*Suby of* Cara Holdings Limited)
1157 Victoria St N, Kitchener, ON, N2B 3C8
(519) 584-2880
Emp Here 27
SIC 5812 Eating places

D-U-N-S 20-810-6224   (BR)
CORPORATION OF THE CITY OF KITCHENER
LYLE HALLMAN POOL
600 Heritage Dr, Kitchener, ON, N2B 3T9
(519) 741-2670
Emp Here 50

SIC 7999 Amusement and recreation, nec

D-U-N-S 25-977-6453   (SL)
CROSBY AUDI INC
AUDI KITCHENER-WATERLOO
(*Suby of* Crosby Holding Corporation)
2350 Shirley Dr, Kitchener, ON, N2B 3X4
(519) 514-0100
Emp Here 31   *Sales* 11,308,909
SIC 5511 New and used car dealers
Pr Pr Michael Crosby
Margaret Crosby
Kathleen Marton

D-U-N-S 20-703-7805   (SL)
CUSTOM LEATHER CANADA LIMITED
GRIZZLY FITNESS ACCESSORIES
460 Bingemans Centre Dr, Kitchener, ON, N2B 3X9
(519) 741-2070
Emp Here 120   *Sales* 16,660,949
SIC 2387 Apparel belts
Pr Pr Ken Ingram
Ric Hewson
VP Sls David Clarke
VP Cole Kennedy

D-U-N-S 20-337-6231   (SL)
ERWIN HYMER GROUP NORTH AMERICA, INC
100 Shirley Ave, Kitchener, ON, N2B 2E1
(519) 745-1169
Emp Here 50
SIC 3716 Motor homes

D-U-N-S 24-369-3095   (BR)
EXOVA CANADA INC
BODYCOTE THERMAL PROCESSING
(*Suby of* Exova, Inc.)
9 Shirley Ave, Kitchener, ON, N2B 2E6
(519) 744-6301
Emp Here 20
SIC 3398 Metal heat treating

D-U-N-S 20-923-8687   (BR)
JENKEL INVESTMENTS LTD
MCDONALD'S RESTAURANTS
1138 Victoria St N, Kitchener, ON, N2B 3C9
(519) 741-1884
Emp Here 58
SIC 5812 Eating places

D-U-N-S 20-710-7116   (BR)
LLOYDMINSTER SCHOOL DIVISION NO 99
ROSE MOUNT SCHOOL
(*Suby of* Lloydminster School Division No 99)
80 Burlington Dr, Kitchener, ON, N2B 1T5
(519) 576-6870
Emp Here 50
SIC 8211 Elementary and secondary schools

D-U-N-S 25-482-6209   (BR)
M & T INSTA-PRINT (KITCHENER-WATERLOO) LIMITED
M & T PRINTING GROUP
907 Frederick St Suite 1, Kitchener, ON, N2B 2B9
(519) 571-0101
Emp Here 40
SIC 2752 Commercial printing, lithographic

D-U-N-S 24-861-7458   (BR)
ONWARD MULTI-CORP INC
T A APPLIANCE WAREHOUSE
932 Victoria St N, Kitchener, ON, N2B 1W4
(519) 578-0300
Emp Here 30
SIC 5722 Household appliance stores

D-U-N-S 20-553-2828   (BR)
ONWARD MULTI-CORP INC
6 Shirley Ave, Kitchener, ON, N2B 2E7
(519) 772-1175
Emp Here 40
SIC 3631 Household cooking equipment

D-U-N-S 20-554-5981   (BR)
PATENE BUILDING SUPPLIES LTD

1290 Victoria St N, Kitchener, ON, N2B 3C9
(519) 745-1188
Emp Here 34
SIC 5039 Construction materials, nec

D-U-N-S 25-300-6183   (BR)
REDBERRY FRANCHISING CORP
BURGER KING
809 Victoria St N, Kitchener, ON, N2B 3C3
(519) 578-1391
Emp Here 20
SIC 5812 Eating places

D-U-N-S 24-117-3868   (BR)
SUNBEAM CENTRE
1120 Victoria St N Suite 205, Kitchener, ON, N2B 3T2
(519) 741-1121
Emp Here 30
SIC 8699 Membership organizations, nec

D-U-N-S 25-363-7243   (BR)
TCG ASPHALT & CONSTRUCTION INC
32 Forwell Rd, Kitchener, ON, N2B 3E8
(519) 578-9180
Emp Here 50
SIC 1611 Highway and street construction

D-U-N-S 20-710-7165   (BR)
WATERLOO CATHOLIC DISTRICT SCHOOL BOARD
CANADIAN MARTYRS SCHOOL
50 Confederation Dr, Kitchener, ON, N2B 2X5
(519) 578-7579
Emp Here 35
SIC 8211 Elementary and secondary schools

D-U-N-S 20-591-4596   (BR)
WATERLOO REGION DISTRICT SCHOOL BOARD
CRESTVIEW PUBLIC SCHOOL
153 Montcalm Dr, Kitchener, ON, N2B 2R6
(519) 893-1140
Emp Here 55
SIC 8211 Elementary and secondary schools

D-U-N-S 25-228-1266   (BR)
WATERLOO REGION DISTRICT SCHOOL BOARD
STANLEY PARK SENIOR PUBLIC SCHOOL
191 Hickson Dr, Kitchener, ON, N2B 2H8
(519) 578-3750
Emp Here 40
SIC 8211 Elementary and secondary schools

D-U-N-S 25-237-8898   (BR)
WATERLOO REGION DISTRICT SCHOOL BOARD
MACKENZIE KING ELEMENTARY SCHOOL
51 Natchez Rd, Kitchener, ON, N2B 3A7
(519) 745-8694
Emp Here 25
SIC 8211 Elementary and secondary schools

D-U-N-S 20-047-5676   (BR)
WATERLOO REGION DISTRICT SCHOOL BOARD
GRAND RIVER COLLEGIATE
175 Indian Rd, Kitchener, ON, N2B 2S7
(519) 576-5100
Emp Here 40
SIC 8211 Elementary and secondary schools

D-U-N-S 25-955-4921   (BR)
WATERLOO REGION DISTRICT SCHOOL BOARD
SMITHSON PUBLIC SCHOOL
150 Belleview Ave, Kitchener, ON, N2B 1G7
(519) 578-3890
Emp Here 43
SIC 8211 Elementary and secondary schools

D-U-N-S 25-034-6236   (SL)
WESTMOUNT STOREFRONT SYSTEMS LTD
20 Riverview Pl, Kitchener, ON, N2B 3X8
(519) 570-2850
Emp Here 60   *Sales* 4,377,642

▲ Public Company   ■ Public Company Family Member   **HQ** Headquarters   **BR** Branch   **SL** Single Location

SIC 1793 Glass and glazing work

D-U-N-S 24-336-4382   (BR)
WOODBRIDGE FOAM CORPORATION
MORVAL
68 Shirley Ave, Kitchener, ON, N2B 2E1
(519) 579-6100
Emp Here 60
SIC 3081 Unsupported plastics film and sheet

Kitchener, ON N2C
Waterloo County

D-U-N-S 24-339-3910   (SL)
2070403 ONTARIO INC
KINGS BUFFET - KITCHENER
509 Wilson Ave Suite 16, Kitchener, ON, N2C
2M4
(519) 893-3100
Emp Here 50   *Sales* 1,532,175
SIC 5812 Eating places

D-U-N-S 25-597-5880   (BR)
4513380 CANADA INC
LIVINGSTON INTERNATIONAL
55 Overland Dr, Kitchener, ON, N2C 2B3
(519) 743-8271
Emp Here 25
SIC 4731 Freight transportation arrangement

D-U-N-S 24-986-9843   (SL)
940734 ONTARIO LIMITED
TIM HORTONS
670 Fairway Rd S, Kitchener, ON, N2C 1X3
(519) 894-0811
Emp Here 80   *Sales* 2,407,703
SIC 5812 Eating places

D-U-N-S 24-117-4114   (BR)
BANQUE TORONTO-DOMINION, LA
TORONTO-DOMINION BANK, THE
(*Suby of* Toronto-Dominion Bank, The)
2960 Kingsway Dr, Kitchener, ON, N2C 1X1
(519) 885-8520
Emp Here 25
SIC 6021 National commercial banks

D-U-N-S 24-011-8609   (BR)
BEST BUY CANADA LTD
BEST BUY
(*Suby of* Best Buy Co., Inc.)
215 Fairway Rd S, Kitchener, ON, N2C 1X2
(519) 783-0333
Emp Here 80
SIC 5731 Radio, television, and electronic
stores

D-U-N-S 20-655-2965   (BR)
BOUTIQUE JACOB INC
(*Suby of* Boutique Jacob Inc)
2960 Kingsway Dr, Kitchener, ON, N2C 1X1

Emp Here 30
SIC 5621 Women's clothing stores

D-U-N-S 24-678-7746   (BR)
BROCK SOLUTIONS INC
90 Ardelt Ave, Kitchener, ON, N2C 2C9
(519) 571-1522
Emp Here 250
SIC 3491 Industrial valves

D-U-N-S 24-845-2682   (BR)
**CADILLAC FAIRVIEW CORPORATION LIM-
ITED, THE**
FAIRVIEW PARK
2960 Kingsway Dr, Kitchener, ON, N2C 1X1
(519) 894-2450
Emp Here 35
SIC 6512 Nonresidential building operators

D-U-N-S 20-303-3113   (BR)
CARA OPERATIONS LIMITED
KELSEY'S
(*Suby of* Cara Holdings Limited)

---

589 Fairway Rd S, Kitchener, ON, N2C 1X4
(519)
Emp Here 50
SIC 5812 Eating places

D-U-N-S 24-342-2115   (BR)
CARA OPERATIONS LIMITED
SWISS CHALET
(*Suby of* Cara Holdings Limited)
560 Fairway Rd S, Kitchener, ON, N2C 1X3
(519) 894-1311
Emp Here 30
SIC 5812 Eating places

D-U-N-S 20-294-5440   (BR)
**CHILDREN'S AID SOCIETY OF THE RE-
GIONAL MUNICIPALITY OF WATERLOO,
THE**
*FAMILY AND CHILDREN'S SERVICES OF
THE REGIONAL MUNICIPALITY OF WATER-
LOO*
200 Ardelt Ave, Kitchener, ON, N2C 2L9
(519) 772-4399
Emp Here 80
SIC 8322 Individual and family services

D-U-N-S 20-179-9850   (BR)
CONROS CORPORATION
(*Suby of* Navhein Holdings Ltd)
1 Chandaria Pl, Kitchener, ON, N2C 2S3

Emp Here 30
SIC 2499 Wood products, nec

D-U-N-S 20-124-3664   (BR)
COOKSVILLE STEEL LIMITED
80 Webster Rd, Kitchener, ON, N2C 2E6
(519) 893-7646
Emp Here 40
SIC 3441 Fabricated structural Metal

D-U-N-S 25-220-4508   (SL)
COUNTRY BOY FAMILY RESTAURANT INC
5 Manitou Dr Suite 107, Kitchener, ON, N2C
2J6
(519) 893-2120
Emp Here 60   *Sales* 2,355,823
SIC 5812 Eating places

D-U-N-S 20-800-8073   (BR)
**EXPERTECH NETWORK INSTALLATION
INC**
998 Wilson Ave, Kitchener, ON, N2C 1J3

Emp Here 29
SIC 4899 Communication services, nec

D-U-N-S 24-340-0855   (BR)
FGL SPORTS LTD
SPORT CHEK
655 Fairway Rd S, Kitchener, ON, N2C 1X4
(519) 896-2310
Emp Here 50
SIC 5941 Sporting goods and bicycle shops

D-U-N-S 25-626-1371   (HQ)
FASTENAL CANADA LTEE
900 Wabanaki Dr, Kitchener, ON, N2C 0B7
(519) 748-6566
Emp Here 100   *Emp Total* 19,624
Sales 115,124,758
SIC 5085 Industrial supplies
Dir Jeffery Watts
Dir Maximilian Bezner
Dir Darrell Cooper

D-U-N-S 24-354-8406   (BR)
FLOWSERVE CANADA CORP
CANADA ALLOY CASTING COMPANY
(*Suby of* Flowserve Corporation)
529 Manitou Dr, Kitchener, ON, N2C 1S2
(519) 895-1161
Emp Here 50
SIC 3494 Valves and pipe fittings, nec

D-U-N-S 24-792-8232   (BR)
GAP (CANADA) INC
BANANA REPUBLIC

(*Suby of* The Gap Inc)
2960 Kingsway Dr, Kitchener, ON, N2C 1X1
(519) 894-2120
Emp Here 20
SIC 5651 Family clothing stores

D-U-N-S 24-393-0364   (SL)
GAUTHIER, CHRIS J. HOLDINGS LTD
CANADIAN TIRE
385 Fairway Rd S Suite 4a, Kitchener, ON,
N2C 2N9
(519) 894-6257
Emp Here 50   *Sales* 3,575,074
SIC 5311 Department stores

D-U-N-S 20-860-5597   (BR)
GLENTEL INC
WIRELESS WAVES
2960 Kingsway Dr, Kitchener, ON, N2C 1X1
(519) 896-9283
Emp Here 20
SIC 4813 Telephone communication, except
radio

D-U-N-S 25-554-9560   (BR)
GOODLIFE FITNESS CENTRES INC
GOODLIFE FITNESS CLUBS
589 Fairway Rd S, Kitchener, ON, N2C 1X4
(519) 576-7744
Emp Here 30
SIC 7999 Amusement and recreation, nec

D-U-N-S 20-178-7798   (BR)
GRAYBAR CANADA LIMITED
GRAYBAR ELECTRIC ONTARIO
(*Suby of* Graybar Electric Company, Inc.)
130 Hayward Ave, Kitchener, ON, N2C 2E4
(519) 576-5434
Emp Here 45
SIC 5063 Electrical apparatus and equipment

D-U-N-S 20-565-2345   (SL)
GREAT CANADIAN COACHES INC
353 Manitou Dr, Kitchener, ON, N2C 1L5
(519) 896-8687
Emp Here 90   *Sales* 4,231,721
SIC 4142 Bus charter service, except local

D-U-N-S 25-407-5864   (HQ)
HERCULES TIRE INTERNATIONAL INC
HERCULES INTERNATIONAL
155 Ardelt Ave, Kitchener, ON, N2C 2E1
(519) 885-3100
Emp Here 20   *Emp Total* 150
Sales 54,720,525
SIC 5014 Tires and tubes
Pr Pr Robert Keller

D-U-N-S 24-423-7889   (SL)
J. C. VENDING (ONTARIO) LIMITED
625 Wabanaki Dr Unit 6, Kitchener, ON, N2C
2G3
(519) 893-7044
Emp Here 60   *Sales* 3,793,956
SIC 5962 Merchandising machine operators

D-U-N-S 24-924-4930   (BR)
KIRBY INTERNATIONAL TRUCKS LTD
ALTRUCK IDEALEASE
21 Ardelt Pl, Kitchener, ON, N2C 2C8
(519) 578-7040
Emp Here 25
SIC 7513 Truck rental and leasing, no drivers

D-U-N-S 24-776-0924   (SL)
KITCHENER KIA
300 Homer Watson Blvd, Kitchener, ON, N2C
2S8
(519) 571-2828
Emp Here 20   *Sales* 7,296,070
SIC 5511 New and used car dealers

D-U-N-S 20-124-7954   (SL)
KUNTZ ELECTROPLATING INC
851 Wilson Ave, Kitchener, ON, N2C 1J1
(519) 893-7680
Emp Here 850   *Sales* 57,274,150
SIC 3471 Plating and polishing

Paul Kuntz
Robert Kuntz Sr
Pr Terry Reidel
VP Sls Dave Kuntz
Treas Robert Kuntz Jr
Dir Michael Director

D-U-N-S 20-817-4805   (SL)
LEAR CORPORATION CANADA LTD
(*Suby of* Lear Corporation)
530 Manitou Dr, Kitchener, ON, N2C 1L3
(519) 895-1600
Emp Here 250   *Sales* 169,265,445
SIC 2531 Public building and related furniture

D-U-N-S 20-180-6312   (SL)
LEHMANN BOOKBINDING LTD
97 Ardelt Ave, Kitchener, ON, N2C 2E1
(519) 570-4444
Emp Here 50   *Sales* 1,824,018
SIC 2789 Bookbinding and related work

D-U-N-S 20-050-3105   (BR)
LENNOX CANADA INC
OVERLAND RNC
45 Otonabee Dr Unit C, Kitchener, ON, N2C
1L7
(519) 744-6841
Emp Here 30
SIC 5075 Warm air heating and air conditioning

D-U-N-S 25-295-5646   (BR)
LEON'S FURNITURE LIMITED
286 Fairway Rd S, Kitchener, ON, N2C 1W9
(519) 894-1850
Emp Here 70
SIC 5712 Furniture stores

D-U-N-S 24-043-7587   (BR)
METRO ONTARIO INC
FOOD BASICS
655 Fairway Rd S, Kitchener, ON, N2C 1X4
(519) 896-5100
Emp Here 100
SIC 5411 Grocery stores

D-U-N-S 20-772-5565   (BR)
PETO MACCALLUM LTD
16 Franklin St S, Kitchener, ON, N2C 1R4
(519) 893-7500
Emp Here 20
SIC 8711 Engineering services

D-U-N-S 20-959-4238   (BR)
QUINCAILLERIE RICHELIEU LTEE
ONWARD HARDWARE
800 Wilson Ave Suite 2, Kitchener, ON, N2C
0A2
(519) 578-3770
Emp Here 40
SIC 5251 Hardware stores

D-U-N-S 25-300-4956   (BR)
REDBERRY FRANCHISING CORP
BURGER KING
300 Fairway Rd S, Kitchener, ON, N2C 1W9
(519) 893-5330
Emp Here 39
SIC 5812 Eating places

D-U-N-S 24-678-2812   (SL)
ROBERTS ONSITE INC
209 Manitou Dr, Kitchener, ON, N2C 1L4
(519) 578-2230
Emp Here 350   *Sales* 30,643,494
SIC 1731 Electrical work
Pr Theodor Schlotzhauer

D-U-N-S 25-311-1405   (BR)
SEARS CANADA INC
200 Fairway Rd S, Kitchener, ON, N2C 1W9
(519) 894-2300
Emp Here 400
SIC 5311 Department stores

D-U-N-S 25-967-7599   (BR)
SUNBEAM CENTRE
SUNBEAM RESIDENTIAL GROUP HOME

---

595 Greenfield Ave Suite 43, Kitchener, ON, N2C 2N7
(519) 894-2098
Emp Here 300
SIC 8059 Nursing and personal care, nec

D-U-N-S 24-304-1159   (BR)
TEAM TRUCK CENTRES LIMITED
TEAM TRUCK AND FREIGHT LINER
599 Wabanaki Dr, Kitchener, ON, N2C 2G3
(519) 893-4150
Emp Here 31
SIC 5531 Auto and home supply stores

D-U-N-S 25-293-9418   (BR)
TOYS 'R' US (CANADA) LTD
TOYS 'R' US
(*Suby of* Toys "r" Us, Inc.)
419 Fairway Rd S, Kitchener, ON, N2C 1X4
(519) 894-8697
Emp Here 20
SIC 5945 Hobby, toy, and game shops

D-U-N-S 25-127-1300   (BR)
TWINCORP INC
KFC
951 Homer Watson Blvd, Kitchener, ON, N2C 0A7
(519) 748-9051
Emp Here 29
SIC 5812 Eating places

D-U-N-S 25-310-3832   (BR)
TWINCORP INC
KFC TACO BELL
2969 Kingsway Dr, Kitchener, ON, N2C 2H7

Emp Here 24
SIC 5812 Eating places

D-U-N-S 25-278-5621   (BR)
UNIFOR
UNIFOR LOCAL 1106
600 Wabanaki Dr, Kitchener, ON, N2C 2K4
(519) 585-3160
Emp Here 35
SIC 8631 Labor organizations

D-U-N-S 25-592-3468   (BR)
UNIFOR
CANADIAN AUTO WORKERS
1111 Homer Watson Blvd, Kitchener, ON, N2C 2P7

Emp Here 2,000
SIC 8631 Labor organizations

D-U-N-S 25-297-6279   (BR)
WAL-MART CANADA CORP
2960 Kingsway Dr Suite 3045, Kitchener, ON, N2C 1X1
(519) 894-6600
Emp Here 200
SIC 5311 Department stores

D-U-N-S 20-710-7231   (BR)
WATERLOO CATHOLIC DISTRICT SCHOOL BOARD
ST ALOYSIUS ELEMENTARY SCHOOL
504 Connaught St, Kitchener, ON, N2C 1C2
(519) 893-5830
Emp Here 47
SIC 8211 Elementary and secondary schools

D-U-N-S 20-710-7322   (BR)
WATERLOO CATHOLIC DISTRICT SCHOOL BOARD
ST MARY'S HIGH SCHOOL
1500 Block Line Rd, Kitchener, ON, N2C 2S2
(519) 745-6891
Emp Here 200
SIC 8211 Elementary and secondary schools

D-U-N-S 25-228-1233   (BR)
WATERLOO REGION DISTRICT SCHOOL BOARD
WILSON AVENUE PUBLIC SCHOOL
221 Wilson Ave, Kitchener, ON, N2C 1G9

(519) 893-7050
Emp Here 35
SIC 8211 Elementary and secondary schools

D-U-N-S 25-228-1381   (BR)
WATERLOO REGION DISTRICT SCHOOL BOARD
ROCKWAY PUBLIC SCHOOL
70 Vanier Dr, Kitchener, ON, N2C 1J5
(519) 576-5730
Emp Here 25
SIC 8211 Elementary and secondary schools

D-U-N-S 24-369-2519   (BR)
WE CARE HEALTH SERVICES INC
WE CARE HOME HEALTH SERVICES
27 Manitou Dr Unit 2ab, Kitchener, ON, N2C 1K9
(519) 576-7474
Emp Here 50
SIC 8082 Home health care services

D-U-N-S 24-224-5368   (BR)
WENDY'S RESTAURANTS OF CANADA INC
WENDY'S
(*Suby of* The Wendy's Company)
685 Fairway Rd S, Kitchener, ON, N2C 1X4

Emp Here 40
SIC 5812 Eating places

D-U-N-S 20-860-4327   (BR)
WINNERS MERCHANTS INTERNATIONAL L.P.
WINNERS
(*Suby of* The TJX Companies Inc)
655 Fairway Rd S, Kitchener, ON, N2C 1X4
(519) 893-6655
Emp Here 25
SIC 5651 Family clothing stores

Kitchener, ON N2E
Waterloo County

D-U-N-S 20-114-0899   (BR)
ACUITY BRANDS LIGHTNING, INC
ACCULITE,
219 Shoemaker St, Kitchener, ON, N2E 3B3

Emp Here 40
SIC 3648 Lighting equipment, nec

D-U-N-S 20-290-7213   (BR)
BRINK'S CANADA LIMITED
(*Suby of* The Brink's Company)
55 Trillium Park Pl, Kitchener, ON, N2E 1X1
(519) 748-5358
Emp Here 50
SIC 7381 Detective and armored car services

D-U-N-S 20-179-4406   (BR)
CANADA POST CORPORATION
KITCHENER MAIL PROCESSING PLANT
70 Trillium Dr, Kitchener, ON, N2E 0E2
(519) 748-3056
Emp Here 250
SIC 4311 U.s. postal service

D-U-N-S 25-303-6685   (BR)
CANADIAN IMPERIAL BANK OF COMMERCE
CIBC
245 Strasburg Rd Unit C, Kitchener, ON, N2E 3W7
(519) 578-2450
Emp Here 26
SIC 6021 National commercial banks

D-U-N-S 20-890-3695   (BR)
CANADIAN LINEN AND UNIFORM SERVICE CO
CANADIAN LINEN AND UNIFORM
(*Suby of* Ameripride Services, Inc.)
301 Shoemaker St, Kitchener, ON, N2E 3B3
(519) 893-3219
Emp Here 21

SIC 7213 Linen supply

D-U-N-S 20-308-7994   (BR)
CARA OPERATIONS LIMITED
KELSEY'S
(*Suby of* Cara Holdings Limited)
740 Ottawa St S, Kitchener, ON, N2E 1B6
(519) 579-0524
Emp Here 40
SIC 5812 Eating places

D-U-N-S 20-923-7481   (SL)
CAVCO FOOD SERVICES LTD
MCDONALDS RESTAURANTS
715 Ottawa St S, Kitchener, ON, N2E 3H5
(519) 569-7224
Emp Here 85   *Sales* 2,553,625
SIC 5812 Eating places

D-U-N-S 25-228-1522   (BR)
CONSEIL SCOLAIRE DE DISTRICT CATHOLIQUE CENTRE-SUD
ECOLE CARDINAL LEGER
345 The Country Way, Kitchener, ON, N2E 2S3
(519) 742-2261
Emp Here 22
SIC 8211 Elementary and secondary schools

D-U-N-S 20-200-6636   (HQ)
CORNERSTONE COURIER INC
(*Suby of* Cornerstone Courier Inc)
219 Shoemaker St, Kitchener, ON, N2E 3B3
(519) 741-0446
Emp Here 50   *Emp Total* 54
Sales 2,772,507
SIC 7389 Business services, nec

D-U-N-S 20-553-6084   (BR)
HOME DEPOT OF CANADA INC
(*Suby of* The Home Depot Inc)
1400 Ottawa St S, Kitchener, ON, N2E 4E2
(519) 569-4300
Emp Here 100
SIC 5211 Lumber and other building materials

D-U-N-S 24-654-9831   (BR)
HUDSON'S BAY COMPANY
HOME OUTFITTERS
245 Strasburg Rd, Kitchener, ON, N2E 3W7
(519) 584-2073
Emp Here 20
SIC 5311 Department stores

D-U-N-S 24-356-5301   (BR)
LOBLAW COMPANIES LIMITED
ZEHRS MARKET
750 Ottawa St S, Kitchener, ON, N2E 1B6
(519) 744-7704
Emp Here 20
SIC 5411 Grocery stores

D-U-N-S 24-334-4475   (BR)
MEIKLE AUTOMATION INC
(*Suby of* Meikle Automation Inc)
50 Groff Pl, Kitchener, ON, N2E 2L6
(519) 896-0800
Emp Here 40
SIC 3599 Industrial machinery, nec

D-U-N-S 20-017-3404   (HQ)
MEIKLE AUTOMATION INC
(*Suby of* Meikle Automation Inc)
975 Bleams Rd Unit 5-10, Kitchener, ON, N2E 3Z5
(519) 896-0800
Emp Here 40   *Emp Total* 150
Sales 15,072,000
SIC 3599 Industrial machinery, nec
Pr Pr Andrew Meikle
VP VP Andrew Stribling
 Jeff Hoffman
S&M/VP Tom Giger
VP Opers Wade Sanderson

D-U-N-S 24-204-2542   (BR)
MEIKLE AUTOMATION INC
(*Suby of* Meikle Automation Inc)

20 Steckle Pl Suite 21, Kitchener, ON, N2E 2C3
(519) 896-8001
Emp Here 35
SIC 3599 Industrial machinery, nec

D-U-N-S 24-092-6233   (BR)
OLD NAVY (CANADA) INC
(*Suby of* The Gap Inc)
1400 Ottawa St S, Kitchener, ON, N2E 4E2
(519) 568-7463
Emp Here 52
SIC 5651 Family clothing stores

D-U-N-S 24-478-4096   (HQ)
PENTAIR CANADA, INC
269 Trillium Dr, Kitchener, ON, N2E 1W9
(519) 748-5470
Emp Here 21   *Emp Total* 35
Sales 6,420,542
SIC 5084 Industrial machinery and equipment
VP Sls Alan W. Noble
Dir Ian S Mackinnon

D-U-N-S 24-134-0426   (BR)
REGIONAL MUNICIPALITY OF WATERLOO, THE
GRAND RIVER TRANSIT
250 Strasburg Rd, Kitchener, ON, N2E 3M6
(519) 585-7597
Emp Here 80
SIC 4173 Bus terminal and service facilities

D-U-N-S 20-700-6557   (BR)
REITMANS (CANADA) LIMITEE
1400 Ottawa St S Unit 7, Kitchener, ON, N2E 4E2

Emp Here 25
SIC 5621 Women's clothing stores

D-U-N-S 20-553-3458   (BR)
RYDER MATERIAL HANDLING ULC
(*Suby of* Crown Equipment Corporation)
25 Beasley Dr, Kitchener, ON, N2E 1W7
(519) 748-5252
Emp Here 20
SIC 5084 Industrial machinery and equipment

D-U-N-S 25-595-6161   (BR)
SHERIDAN NURSERIES LIMITED
100 Elmsdale Dr, Kitchener, ON, N2E 1H6
(519) 743-4146
Emp Here 25
SIC 5261 Retail nurseries and garden stores

D-U-N-S 25-560-7715   (BR)
SOBEYS CAPITAL INCORPORATED
FRESHCO
720 Westmount Rd E, Kitchener, ON, N2E 2M6
(519) 578-7851
Emp Here 70
SIC 5411 Grocery stores

D-U-N-S 20-806-2534   (BR)
SOBEYS CAPITAL INCORPORATED
SOBEYS STORE 852
1187 Fischer Hallman Rd Suite 852, Kitchener, ON, N2E 4H9
(519) 576-1280
Emp Here 200
SIC 5411 Grocery stores

D-U-N-S 25-213-7146   (BR)
STAPLES CANADA INC
STAPLES THE BUSINESS DEPOT
(*Suby of* Staples, Inc.)
245 Strasburg Rd, Kitchener, ON, N2E 3W7
(519) 571-7420
Emp Here 45
SIC 5943 Stationery stores

D-U-N-S 25-397-4638   (SL)
TECHNO-TRADE (CANADA) INC
700 Strasburg Rd Unit 31, Kitchener, ON, N2E 2M2

Emp Here 42   *Sales* 5,024,256

SIC 3571 Electronic computers
Erez Pikar
Fin Ex Lucy Siarek

D-U-N-S 25-140-4976   (BR)
UNITED PARCEL SERVICE CANADA LTD
UPS
65 Trillium Park Pl, Kitchener, ON, N2E 1X1
(519) 904-0210
Emp Here 110
SIC 7389 Business services, nec

D-U-N-S 24-319-5042   (BR)
WAL-MART CANADA CORP
WALMART
1400 Ottawa St S Unit E, Kitchener, ON, N2E 4E2
(519) 745-2297
Emp Here 120
SIC 5311 Department stores

D-U-N-S 20-025-9781   (BR)
WATERLOO CATHOLIC DISTRICT SCHOOL BOARD
BLESSED SACRAMENT SCHOOL
367 The Country Way, Kitchener, ON, N2E 2S3
(519) 745-5950
Emp Here 41
SIC 8211 Elementary and secondary schools

D-U-N-S 20-710-7280   (BR)
WATERLOO CATHOLIC DISTRICT SCHOOL BOARD
JOHN SWEENEY SCHOOL
185 Activa Ave, Kitchener, ON, N2E 4A1
(519) 579-5212
Emp Here 50
SIC 8211 Elementary and secondary schools

D-U-N-S 25-228-1621   (BR)
WATERLOO CATHOLIC DISTRICT SCHOOL BOARD
MONSIGNOR HALLER ELEMENTARY SCHOOL
118 Shea Cres, Kitchener, ON, N2E 1E8
(519) 579-1230
Emp Here 29
SIC 8211 Elementary and secondary schools

D-U-N-S 20-005-0487   (BR)
WATERLOO REGION DISTRICT SCHOOL BOARD
COUNTRY HILLS PUBLIC SCHOOL
195 Country Hill Dr, Kitchener, ON, N2E 2G7
(519) 743-6331
Emp Here 35
SIC 8211 Elementary and secondary schools

D-U-N-S 20-656-2733   (BR)
WATERLOO REGION DISTRICT SCHOOL BOARD
W T TOWNSHEND PUBLIC SCHOOL
245 Activa Ave, Kitchener, ON, N2E 4A3
(519) 579-1160
Emp Here 75
SIC 8211 Elementary and secondary schools

D-U-N-S 20-710-7157   (BR)
WATERLOO REGION DISTRICT SCHOOL BOARD
GLENCAIRN PUBLIC SCHOOL
664 Erinbrook Dr, Kitchener, ON, N2E 2R1
(519) 742-0849
Emp Here 50
SIC 8211 Elementary and secondary schools

D-U-N-S 20-710-7108   (BR)
WATERLOO REGION DISTRICT SCHOOL BOARD
ALPINE PUBLIC SCHOOL
75 Lucerne Dr, Kitchener, ON, N2E 1B4
(519) 743-4338
Emp Here 30
SIC 8211 Elementary and secondary schools

D-U-N-S 25-228-1019   (BR)
WATERLOO REGION DISTRICT SCHOOL

BOARD
TRILLIUM PUBLIC SCHOOL
79 Laurentian Dr, Kitchener, ON, N2E 1C3
(519) 743-6368
Emp Here 30
SIC 8211 Elementary and secondary schools

D-U-N-S 25-237-9151   (BR)
WATERLOO REGION DISTRICT SCHOOL BOARD
LAURENTIAN SENIOR PUBLIC SCHOOL
777 Westmount Rd E, Kitchener, ON, N2E 1J2
(519) 578-6160
Emp Here 40
SIC 8211 Elementary and secondary schools

Kitchener, ON N2G
Waterloo County

D-U-N-S 25-094-6829   (BR)
AIRBOSS OF AMERICA CORP
AIRBOSS RUBBER COMPOUNDING
101 Glasgow St, Kitchener, ON, N2G 4X8
(519) 576-5565
Emp Here 300
SIC 3069 Fabricated rubber products, nec

D-U-N-S 25-297-0504   (BR)
BANK OF NOVA SCOTIA, THE
SCOTIABANK
64 King St W, Kitchener, ON, N2G 1A3
(519) 571-6400
Emp Here 45
SIC 6021 National commercial banks

D-U-N-S 25-597-0618   (BR)
BANK OF MONTREAL
BANK OF MONTREAL
1074 King St E, Kitchener, ON, N2G 2N2
(519) 885-9262
Emp Here 22
SIC 6021 National commercial banks

D-U-N-S 20-085-6867   (BR)
BANQUE TORONTO-DOMINION, LA
TORONTO-DOMINION BANK, THE
(*Suby of* Toronto-Dominion Bank, The)
381 King St W Suite 3rd, Kitchener, ON, N2G 1B8
(519) 579-2160
Emp Here 35
SIC 6021 National commercial banks

D-U-N-S 20-292-1107   (BR)
BELL MEDIA INC
864 King St W, Kitchener, ON, N2G 1E8
(519) 578-1313
Emp Here 105
SIC 4833 Television broadcasting stations

D-U-N-S 25-407-6482   (BR)
CML HEALTHCARE INC
751 King St W Suite 104, Kitchener, ON, N2G 1E5
(519) 576-2460
Emp Here 22
SIC 8071 Medical laboratories

D-U-N-S 24-936-5164   (BR)
CTV SPECIALTY TELEVISION INC
CTV SPECIALTY TELEVISION INC/TELEVISION SPECIALISEE CTV INC
864 King St W, Kitchener, ON, N2G 1E8
(519) 578-1313
Emp Here 130
SIC 4833 Television broadcasting stations

D-U-N-S 25-303-6727   (BR)
CANADIAN IMPERIAL BANK OF COMMERCE
CIBC
1 King St E Suite 200, Kitchener, ON, N2G 2K4
(519) 742-4432
Emp Here 35

SIC 6021 National commercial banks

D-U-N-S 24-011-0619   (HQ)
CONESTOGA COLLEGE COMMUNICATIONS CORPORATION
299 Doon Valley Dr, Kitchener, ON, N2G 4M4
(519) 748-5220
Emp Here 500   *Emp Total* 700
Sales 62,892,123
SIC 8222 Junior colleges
Pr Pr John Tibbits
Kevin Mullan

D-U-N-S 25-449-8447   (BR)
CONESTOGA COLLEGE COMMUNICATIONS CORPORATION
Gd, Kitchener, ON, N2G 4M4
(519) 885-0300
Emp Here 40
SIC 8221 Colleges and universities

D-U-N-S 20-068-0283   (BR)
CORPORATION OF THE CITY OF KITCHENER
200 King St W, Kitchener, ON, N2G 4V6
(519) 741-2345
Emp Here 100
SIC 1611 Highway and street construction

D-U-N-S 20-965-5984   (HQ)
DBC SMARTSOFTWARE INC
121 Charles St W Unit C224, Kitchener, ON, N2G 1H6
(519) 893-4200
Emp Here 43   *Emp Total* 1,300
Sales 10,699,440
SIC 7371 Custom computer programming services
Henry Bonner
Kevin Hammer

D-U-N-S 24-089-9216   (BR)
DELTA HOTELS LIMITED
105 King St E, Kitchener, ON, N2G 2K8
(519) 569-4588
Emp Here 150
SIC 8741 Management services

D-U-N-S 20-937-8249   (HQ)
ECOPLANS LIMITED
72 Victoria St S Suite 100, Kitchener, ON, N2G 4Y9

Emp Here 25   *Emp Total* 350
Sales 4,669,485
SIC 8748 Business consulting, nec

D-U-N-S 20-789-9936   (BR)
ENTERPRISE RENT-A-CAR CANADA COMPANY
ENTERPRISE RENT-A-CAR
(*Suby of* The Crawford Group Inc)
505 King St E, Kitchener, ON, N2G 2L7
(519) 772-0888
Emp Here 20
SIC 7514 Passenger car rental

D-U-N-S 25-561-1550   (BR)
G4S SECURE SOLUTIONS (CANADA) LTD
1448 King St E, Kitchener, ON, N2G 2N7

Emp Here 200
SIC 7381 Detective and armored car services

D-U-N-S 20-704-2446   (BR)
GRAND RIVER HOSPITAL CORPORATION
YOUNG ADULTS PROGRAM
(*Suby of* Grand River Hospital Corporation)
850 King St W, Kitchener, ON, N2G 1E8
(519) 749-4217
Emp Here 60
SIC 8093 Specialty outpatient clinics, nec

D-U-N-S 24-009-1413   (HQ)
GRAND RIVER HOSPITAL CORPORATION
(*Suby of* Grand River Hospital Corporation)
835 King St W, Kitchener, ON, N2G 1G3

(519) 742-3611
Emp Here 1,900   *Emp Total* 2,609
Sales 312,910,166
SIC 8062 General medical and surgical hospitals
Malcolm Maxwell
Tracy Elop
Dir Jeff Evans
Dir Ted Bleaney
D'arcy Delamere
Dir Pamela Maki
Dir Ashok Sharma
Dir William Weiler
Treas David Uffelmann
CFO Barry Cheal

D-U-N-S 24-664-8372   (HQ)
KW HABILITATION SERVICES
(*Suby of* KW Habilitation Services)
108 Sydney St S, Kitchener, ON, N2G 3V2
(519) 744-6307
Emp Here 40   *Emp Total* 600
Sales 16,714,128
SIC 8361 Residential care
Ex Dir Ann Bilodeau

D-U-N-S 20-068-0317   (BR)
KIDS LINK/ NDSA
EARLY INTERVENTION SERVICES
1770 King St E Suite 5, Kitchener, ON, N2G 2P1
(519) 741-1122
Emp Here 22
SIC 8322 Individual and family services

D-U-N-S 24-336-2279   (BR)
KITCHENER WATERLOO YOUNG MENS CHRISTIAN ASSOCIATION, THE
YMCA OF KITCHENER WATERLOO
800 King St W, Kitchener, ON, N2G 1E8
(519) 579-9622
Emp Here 40
SIC 8331 Job training and related services

D-U-N-S 24-333-4984   (SL)
KITCHENER-WATERLOO SYMPHONY ORCHESTRA ASSOCIATION INC
KITCHENER-WATERLOO SYMPHONY
36 King St W, Kitchener, ON, N2G 1A3
(519) 745-4711
Emp Here 67   *Sales* 4,304,681
SIC 7929 Entertainers and entertainment groups

D-U-N-S 25-487-1932   (BR)
LUTHERWOOD
(*Suby of* Lutherwood)
165 King St E, Kitchener, ON, N2G 2K8
(519) 884-7755
Emp Here 60
SIC 8331 Job training and related services

D-U-N-S 20-943-0123   (HQ)
MTD PRODUCTS LIMITED
LES DISTRIBUTION R.V.I, DIR OF
(*Suby of* Mtd Holdings Inc.)
97 Kent Ave, Kitchener, ON, N2G 3R2
(519) 579-5500
Emp Here 173   *Emp Total* 6,000
Sales 56,257,041
SIC 5083 Farm and garden machinery
Pr Pr John Walter Norman
Edward Henderson
Robert Moll
Dir Jean Hlay

D-U-N-S 25-204-5281   (BR)
MTD PRODUCTS LIMITED
MODERN POWER PRODUCTS, DIV OF
(*Suby of* Mtd Holdings Inc.)
97 Kant Ave, Kitchener, ON, N2G 4J1
(519) 579-5500
Emp Here 100
SIC 5083 Farm and garden machinery

D-U-N-S 25-363-6963   (BR)
MANULIFE FINANCIAL CORPORATION
MANULIFE FINANCIAL

25 Water St S, Kitchener, ON, N2G 4Z4
(519) 747-7000
Emp Here 20
SIC 6311 Life insurance

D-U-N-S 24-323-4205   (BR)
MARSH CANADA LIMITED
(*Suby of* Marsh & McLennan Companies, Inc.)
55 King St W Suite 205, Kitchener, ON, N2G
4W1
(519) 585-3280
Emp Here 25
SIC 6411 Insurance agents, brokers, and service

D-U-N-S 20-084-2065   (BR)
MCCORMICK RANKIN CORPORATION
MMM GROUP
72 Victoria St S Suite 100, Kitchener, ON,
N2G 4Y9
(519) 741-1464
Emp Here 20
SIC 8711 Engineering services

D-U-N-S 24-383-3139   (BR)
METROLAND MEDIA GROUP LTD
GRAND MAGAZINE
160 King St E, Kitchener, ON, N2G 4E5
(519) 894-2250
Emp Here 20
SIC 2721 Periodicals

D-U-N-S 20-025-3537   (BR)
RAY OF HOPE INC
HOPE HARBOUR HOME
47 Madison Ave S, Kitchener, ON, N2G 3M4
(519) 741-8881
Emp Here 20
SIC 8399 Social services, nec

D-U-N-S 20-912-7237   (BR)
**REGIONAL MUNICIPALITY OF WATERLOO,
THE**
CORPORATE RESOURCES DEPARTMENT
150 Frederick Suite 5, Kitchener, ON, N2G
4J3
(519) 575-4411
Emp Here 20
SIC 8111 Legal services

D-U-N-S 25-280-5643   (BR)
REVERA INC
VICTORIA PLACE RETIREMENT RESIDENCE
290 Queen St S Suite 302, Kitchener, ON,
N2G 1W3
(519) 576-1300
Emp Here 55
SIC 8361 Residential care

D-U-N-S 25-615-6613   (BR)
RICOH CANADA INC
55 King St W Suite 800, Kitchener, ON, N2G
4W1
(519) 743-5601
Emp Here 20
SIC 5044 Office equipment

D-U-N-S 24-984-8938   (SL)
ROCKWAY GOLF & BOWLING CLUB
625 Rockway Dr, Kitchener, ON, N2G 3B5
(519) 741-2949
Emp Here 50   *Sales* 2,188,821
SIC 7992 Public golf courses

D-U-N-S 24-354-4173   (BR)
**SERVICE CORPORATION INTERNATIONAL
(CANADA) LIMITED**
RATZ-BECHTEL FUNERAL HOME
621 King St W, Kitchener, ON, N2G 1C7
(519) 745-9495
Emp Here 20
SIC 7261 Funeral service and crematories

D-U-N-S 25-593-8581   (BR)
TORONTO-DOMINION BANK, THE
TD CANADA TRUST
(*Suby of* Toronto-Dominion Bank, The)
381 King St W Suite 1, Kitchener, ON, N2G

1B8
(519) 579-2160
Emp Here 25
SIC 6021 National commercial banks

D-U-N-S 24-889-0980   (BR)
TORSTAR CORPORATION
RECORD, THE
160 King St E, Kitchener, ON, N2G 4E5
(519) 821-2022
Emp Here 375
SIC 2711 Newspapers

D-U-N-S 25-157-8860   (BR)
TRIOS TRAINING CENTRES LIMITED
TRIOS COLLEGE OF BUSINESS TECHNOLOGY AND HEALTHCARE
(*Suby of* Trios Training Centres Limited)
445 King St W, Kitchener, ON, N2G 1C2
(519) 578-0838
Emp Here 20
SIC 8221 Colleges and universities

D-U-N-S 24-736-8962   (SL)
WALPER TERRACE HOTEL INC
1 King St W, Kitchener, ON, N2G 1A1
(519) 745-4321
Emp Here 100   *Sales* 4,377,642
SIC 7011 Hotels and motels

D-U-N-S 24-159-4899   (BR)
**WATERLOO   CATHOLIC   DISTRICT
SCHOOL BOARD**
ST LOUIS ADULT LEARNING CENTRE
160 Courtland Ave E, Kitchener, ON, N2G 2V3
(519) 743-3005
Emp Here 20
SIC 8211 Elementary and secondary schools

D-U-N-S 20-710-7306   (BR)
**WATERLOO   CATHOLIC   DISTRICT
SCHOOL BOARD**
ST JOHN SCHOOL
99 Strange St, Kitchener, ON, N2G 1R4
(519) 579-0890
Emp Here 27
SIC 8211 Elementary and secondary schools

D-U-N-S 25-237-8971   (BR)
**WATERLOO REGION DISTRICT SCHOOL
BOARD**
KING EDWARD ELEMENTARY PUBLIC
709 King St W, Kitchener, ON, N2G 1E3
(519) 578-0220
Emp Here 32
SIC 8211 Elementary and secondary schools

D-U-N-S 20-710-7066   (BR)
**WATERLOO REGION DISTRICT SCHOOL
BOARD**
*KITCHENER WATERLOO COLLEGIAT AND
VOCATIONAL SCHOOL*
787 King St W, Kitchener, ON, N2G 1E3
(519) 745-6851
Emp Here 50
SIC 8211 Elementary and secondary schools

D-U-N-S 25-228-1597   (BR)
**WATERLOO REGION DISTRICT SCHOOL
BOARD**
CAMERON HEIGHTS COLLEGIATE INSTITUTE
301 Charles St E, Kitchener, ON, N2G 2P8
(519) 578-8330
Emp Here 140
SIC 8211 Elementary and secondary schools

D-U-N-S 20-591-4570   (BR)
**WATERLOO REGION DISTRICT SCHOOL
BOARD**
COURTLAND AVE PUBLIC SCHOOL
107 Courtland Ave E, Kitchener, ON, N2G 2T9
(519) 578-4690
Emp Here 28
SIC 8211 Elementary and secondary schools

D-U-N-S 25-300-6902   (BR)
WORKPLACE   SAFETY   &   INSURANCE

BOARD, THE
55 King St W Suite 502, Kitchener, ON, N2G
4W1

Emp Here 100
SIC 6331 Fire, marine, and casualty insurance

Kitchener, ON N2H
Waterloo County

D-U-N-S 24-700-9835   (BR)
CRH CANADA GROUP INC
5 Johnston St, Kitchener, ON, N2H 6N4
(519) 749-6120
Emp Here 20
SIC 5999 Miscellaneous retail stores, nec

D-U-N-S 25-303-6644   (BR)
CANADIAN IMPERIAL BANK OF COMMERCE
CIBC
385 Frederick St, Kitchener, ON, N2H 2P2
(519) 744-4151
Emp Here 20
SIC 6021 National commercial banks

D-U-N-S 25-988-7136   (BR)
CORPORATION OF THE CITY OF KITCHENER
ST PETERS LUTHERAN CEMETERY
243 Weber St E, Kitchener, ON, N2H 1E9
(519) 741-2880
Emp Here 30
SIC 6531 Real estate agents and managers

D-U-N-S 20-068-0333   (BR)
CORPORATION OF THE CITY OF KITCHENER
BREITHAUPT COMMUNITY CENTRE
350 Margaret Ave, Kitchener, ON, N2H 4J8
(519) 741-2502
Emp Here 120
SIC 8322 Individual and family services

D-U-N-S 25-272-3580   (BR)
DILLON CONSULTING LIMITED
(*Suby of* Dillon Consulting Inc)
51 Breithaupt St Suite 1, Kitchener, ON, N2H
5G5
(519) 571-9833
Emp Here 26
SIC 8711 Engineering services

D-U-N-S 20-964-8042   (BR)
DOLLARAMA S.E.C.
385 Frederick St, Kitchener, ON, N2H 2P2
(519) 579-1104
Emp Here 20
SIC 5399 Miscellaneous general merchandise

D-U-N-S 25-143-5835   (BR)
G4S CASH SOLUTIONS (CANADA) LTD
108 Ahrens St W, Kitchener, ON, N2H 4C3

Emp Here 150
SIC 7381 Detective and armored car services

D-U-N-S 24-367-0499   (BR)
GDI SERVICES (CANADA) LP
100 Campbell Ave Suite 12, Kitchener, ON,
N2H 4X8

Emp Here 100
SIC 7349 Building maintenance services, nec

D-U-N-S 24-184-0904   (BR)
GOWLING WLG (CANADA) LLP
GOWLING LAFLEUR AND HENDERSON
50 Queen St N Suite 1020, Kitchener, ON,
N2H 6P4
(519) 575-7517
Emp Here 100
SIC 8111 Legal services

D-U-N-S 24-194-0571   (BR)
GOWLING WLG (CANADA) LLP

50 Queen St N Unit 1020, Kitchener, ON, N2H
6P4
(519) 576-6910
Emp Here 110
SIC 8111 Legal services

D-U-N-S 20-057-0492   (BR)
GOWLING WLG (CANADA) LLP
GOWLINGS
50 Queen St N Suite 1020, Kitchener, ON,
N2H 6P4
(519) 576-6910
Emp Here 84
SIC 8111 Legal services

D-U-N-S 24-176-1316   (BR)
GOWLING WLG (CANADA) LLP
50 Queen St N Suite 1020, Kitchener, ON,
N2H 6P4
(519) 575-7506
Emp Here 108
SIC 8111 Legal services

D-U-N-S 25-954-2926   (BR)
GREAT-WEST LIFE ASSURANCE COMPANY, THE
RESOURCE CENTRE
101 Frederick St Suite 900, Kitchener, ON,
N2H 6R2

Emp Here 24
SIC 6411 Insurance agents, brokers, and service

D-U-N-S 24-007-9947   (HQ)
KITCHENER PUBLIC LIBRARY BOARD
(*Suby of* Kitchener Public Library Board)
85 Queen St N, Kitchener, ON, N2H 2H1
(519) 743-0271
Emp Here 125   *Emp Total* 165
Sales 9,950,816
SIC 8231 Libraries
Ch Bd Dan Carli
V Ch Bd Elizabeth Esenbergs
Ch Bd Lynn Gazzola
Trst Bruce Macneil
Trst Brian Burnley
  Berry Vrbanovic

D-U-N-S 20-184-8574   (BR)
**KITCHENER WATERLOO YOUNG MENS
CHRISTIAN ASSOCIATION, THE**
460 Frederick St Suite 203, Kitchener, ON,
N2H 2P5
(519) 584-1937
Emp Here 30
SIC 8699 Membership organizations, nec

D-U-N-S 25-239-5231   (HQ)
KITCHENER-WATERLOO YWCA
(*Suby of* Kitchener-Waterloo YWCA)
84 Frederick St, Kitchener, ON, N2H 2L7
(519) 576-8856
Emp Here 90   *Emp Total* 110
Sales 4,304,681
SIC 8322 Individual and family services

D-U-N-S 20-552-4940   (BR)
**LABOUR READY TEMPORARY SERVICES
LTD**
280 Victoria St N, Kitchener, ON, N2H 5E2
(519) 571-8817
Emp Here 60
SIC 7361 Employment agencies

D-U-N-S 24-326-9870   (BR)
MCAP SERVICE CORPORATION
101 Frederick St Suite 600, Kitchener, ON,
N2H 6R2
(519) 743-7800
Emp Here 305
SIC 6162 Mortgage bankers and loan correspondents

D-U-N-S 25-361-7294   (BR)
NCR CANADA CORP
NCR WATERLOO
(*Suby of* NCR Corporation)
580 Weber St E, Kitchener, ON, N2H 1G8

Emp Here 650
SIC 3578 Calculating and accounting equipment

D-U-N-S 20-124-9067   (SL)
NELCO MECHANICAL LIMITED
77 Edwin St, Kitchener, ON, N2H 4N7
(519) 744-6511
Emp Here 75   *Sales* 6,566,463
SIC 1711 Plumbing, heating, air-conditioning
Pr Pr Harry Vogt
VP Richard Snider
VP Michael Hobson

D-U-N-S 25-313-6329   (BR)
PLASTI-FAB LTD
1214 Union St, Kitchener, ON, N2H 6K4
(519) 571-1650
Emp Here 20
SIC 2865 Cyclic crudes and intermediates

D-U-N-S 20-004-5693   (BR)
ROGERS COMMUNICATIONS INC
(*Suby of* Rogers Communications Inc)
40 Weber St E Suite 500, Kitchener, ON, N2H 6R3
(519) 585-2400
Emp Here 535
SIC 4899 Communication services, nec

D-U-N-S 20-125-1378   (SL)
STEVE'S T.V. & APPLIANCES LIMITED
STEVE'S T.V.
385 Frederick St, Kitchener, ON, N2H 2P2
(519) 744-3528
Emp Here 50   *Sales* 4,596,524
SIC 5731 Radio, television, and electronic stores

D-U-N-S 25-954-1514   (BR)
VALUE VILLAGE STORES, INC
(*Suby of* Savers, Inc.)
120 Ottawa St N, Kitchener, ON, N2H 3K5
(519) 576-4403
Emp Here 50
SIC 5399 Miscellaneous general merchandise

D-U-N-S 20-710-7249   (BR)
WATERLOO CATHOLIC DISTRICT SCHOOL BOARD
ST. ANNE'S ELEMENTARY SCHOOL
250 East Ave, Kitchener, ON, N2H 1Z4
(519) 745-7847
Emp Here 50
SIC 8211 Elementary and secondary schools

D-U-N-S 20-710-7470   (BR)
WATERLOO CATHOLIC DISTRICT SCHOOL BOARD
ST. LOUIS KITCHENER - MAIN CAMPUS
80 Young St, Kitchener, ON, N2H 4Z1
(519) 745-1201
Emp Here 60
SIC 8211 Elementary and secondary schools

D-U-N-S 24-329-5461   (BR)
WATERLOO CATHOLIC DISTRICT SCHOOL BOARD
CATHOLIC EDUCATION CENTER
35a Weber St W, Kitchener, ON, N2H 3Z1
(519) 578-3650
Emp Here 100
SIC 8211 Elementary and secondary schools

D-U-N-S 20-710-7363   (BR)
WATERLOO CATHOLIC DISTRICT SCHOOL BOARD
ST THERESA ELEMENTARY
270 Edwin St, Kitchener, ON, N2H 4P4
(519) 743-2131
Emp Here 35
SIC 8211 Elementary and secondary schools

D-U-N-S 25-137-3916   (BR)
WATERLOO REGION DISTRICT SCHOOL BOARD
PRUTER PUBLIC SCHOOL
40 Prueter Ave, Kitchener, ON, N2H 6G6

(519) 578-0910
Emp Here 35
SIC 8211 Elementary and secondary schools

D-U-N-S 25-137-3932   (BR)
WATERLOO REGION DISTRICT SCHOOL BOARD
SHEPPARD SCHOOL
278 Weber St E, Kitchener, ON, N2H 1G2
(519) 570-0003
Emp Here 34
SIC 8211 Elementary and secondary schools

D-U-N-S 25-228-1472   (BR)
WATERLOO REGION DISTRICT SCHOOL BOARD
EASTWOOD COLLEGIATE INSTITUTE
760 Weber St E, Kitchener, ON, N2H 1H6
(519) 742-1848
Emp Here 125
SIC 8211 Elementary and secondary schools

D-U-N-S 20-228-7335   (BR)
WATERLOO REGION DISTRICT SCHOOL BOARD
MARGARET AVENUE PUBLIC SCHOOL
325 Louisa St, Kitchener, ON, N2H 5N1
(519) 578-1910
Emp Here 30
SIC 8211 Elementary and secondary schools

D-U-N-S 20-710-7033   (BR)
WATERLOO REGION DISTRICT SCHOOL BOARD
SUDDABY PUBLIC SCHOOL
171 Frederick St, Kitchener, ON, N2H 2M6
(519) 578-3840
Emp Here 40
SIC 8211 Elementary and secondary schools

D-U-N-S 24-644-5613   (BR)
WESTERN INVENTORY SERVICE LTD
WIS INTERNATIONAL
120 Ottawa St N Suite 201, Kitchener, ON, N2H 3K5
(519) 745-7160
Emp Here 30
SIC 7389 Business services, nec

D-U-N-S 25-297-8820   (BR)
ZEHRMART INC
ZEHRS MARKETS
385 Frederick St, Kitchener, ON, N2H 2P2

Emp Here 50
SIC 5411 Grocery stores

Kitchener, ON N2J
Waterloo County

D-U-N-S 24-219-3084   (HQ)
MANULIFE CANADA LTD
500 King St N, Kitchener, ON, N2J 4Z6
(519) 747-7000
Emp Here 255   *Emp Total* 34,000
Sales 467,928,720
SIC 6311 Life insurance
Pr Marianne Harrison

Kitchener, ON N2K
Waterloo County

D-U-N-S 20-302-3341   (BR)
ASSANTE CAPITAL MANAGEMENT LTD
ASSANTE WEALTH MANAGEMENT
487 Riverbend Dr, Kitchener, ON, N2K 3S3
(519) 772-5509
Emp Here 20
SIC 6211 Security brokers and dealers

D-U-N-S 24-302-1300   (HQ)
CRAWFORD & COMPANY (CANADA) INC
CRAWFORD ADJUSTERS

(*Suby of* Crawford & Company)
539 Riverbend Dr, Kitchener, ON, N2K 3S3
(519) 578-5540
Emp Here 120   *Emp Total* 9,190
Sales 96,240,486
SIC 6411 Insurance agents, brokers, and service
Dir John Sharoun
VP Fin Bob Krische

D-U-N-S 20-286-3106   (BR)
ECONOMICAL MUTUAL INSURANCE COMPANY
590 Riverbend Dr, Kitchener, ON, N2K 3S2
(519) 570-8335
Emp Here 300
SIC 6331 Fire, marine, and casualty insurance

D-U-N-S 24-411-7081   (SL)
ELDORADO PLYWOOD SPECIALTIES INC
40 Dumart Pl, Kitchener, ON, N2K 3C7
(519) 742-7011
Emp Here 20   *Sales* 5,982,777
SIC 5031 Lumber, plywood, and millwork
Pr Pr David Gould

D-U-N-S 24-845-6212   (BR)
ERNST & YOUNG LLP
(*Suby of* Ernst & Young LLP)
515 Riverbend Dr, Kitchener, ON, N2K 3S3
(519) 744-1171
Emp Here 140
SIC 8721 Accounting, auditing, and bookkeeping

D-U-N-S 24-195-3140   (SL)
GOLF'S STEAK HOUSE INC
598 Lancaster St W, Kitchener, ON, N2K 1M3
(519) 579-4050
Emp Here 65   *Sales* 1,969,939
SIC 5812 Eating places

D-U-N-S 25-560-2450   (BR)
LERON ENTERPRISES LTD
TIM HORTONS
504 Lancaster St W, Kitchener, ON, N2K 1L9
(519) 570-3186
Emp Here 25
SIC 5461 Retail bakeries

D-U-N-S 25-310-7841   (BR)
MANUFACTURERS LIFE INSURANCE COMPANY, THE
MANULIFE FINANCIAL
630 Riverbend Dr Suite 101, Kitchener, ON, N2K 3S2
(519) 571-1001
Emp Here 23
SIC 6411 Insurance agents, brokers, and service

D-U-N-S 24-827-1640   (BR)
MEDICAL PHARMACIES GROUP LIMITED
MEDICAL PHARMACY
569 Lancaster St W, Kitchener, ON, N2K 3M9
(519) 576-1001
Emp Here 25
SIC 5912 Drug stores and proprietary stores

D-U-N-S 25-034-4694   (HQ)
NAYLOR ENGINEERING ASSOCIATES LTD
353 Bridge St E, Kitchener, ON, N2K 2Y5
(519) 741-1313
Emp Here 53   *Emp Total* 6,000
Sales 6,785,345
SIC 8711 Engineering services
Sec Jean Aubuchon
Treas Marc Godin
Dir Marc Verreault

D-U-N-S 25-228-1324   (BR)
WATERLOO REGION DISTRICT SCHOOL BOARD
BRIDGEPORT ELEMENTARY SCHOOL
59 Bridge St W, Kitchener, ON, N2K 1K6
(519) 743-4318
Emp Here 28
SIC 8211 Elementary and secondary schools

D-U-N-S 20-322-1767   (HQ)
WESTPORT POWER INC
100 Hollinger Cres, Kitchener, ON, N2K 2Z3
(519) 576-4270
Emp Here 150   *Emp Total* 1,751
Sales 26,192,891
SIC 3714 Motor vehicle parts and accessories
  Mark Haskins
  Richard Nielsen
  Peter Chase

Kitchener, ON N2M
Waterloo County

D-U-N-S 25-968-3381   (BR)
1260848 ONTARIO INC
TIM HORTONS
354 Highland Rd W, Kitchener, ON, N2M 3C7
(519) 744-4427
Emp Here 25
SIC 5812 Eating places

D-U-N-S 20-864-6732   (BR)
1260848 ONTARIO INC
TIM HORTONS
700 Westmount Rd W, Kitchener, ON, N2M 1R9
(519) 581-0679
Emp Here 30
SIC 5812 Eating places

D-U-N-S 25-126-5427   (BR)
1260848 ONTARIO INC
TIM HORTONS
Westmount Rd W, Kitchener, ON, N2M 5C4
(519) 744-1585
Emp Here 34
SIC 5812 Eating places

D-U-N-S 20-588-2520   (BR)
BANQUE TORONTO-DOMINION, LA
TD CANADA TRUST
(*Suby of* Toronto-Dominion Bank, The)
272 Highland Rd W, Kitchener, ON, N2M 3C5
(519) 749-3277
Emp Here 20
SIC 6021 National commercial banks

D-U-N-S 25-625-6397   (BR)
CARA OPERATIONS LIMITED
SWISS CHALET
(*Suby of* Cara Holdings Limited)
525 Highland Rd E, Kitchener, ON, N2M 3W9
(519) 578-7030
Emp Here 60
SIC 5812 Eating places

D-U-N-S 20-308-7879   (BR)
CARA OPERATIONS LIMITED
KELSEY'S
(*Suby of* Cara Holdings Limited)
188 Highland Rd W, Kitchener, ON, N2M 3C2

Emp Here 50
SIC 5812 Eating places

D-U-N-S 25-318-1291   (BR)
CAVCO FOOD SERVICES LTD
MCDONALD'S
(*Suby of* Cavco Food Services Ltd)
431 Highland Rd W, Kitchener, ON, N2M 3C6
(519) 578-8630
Emp Here 100
SIC 5812 Eating places

D-U-N-S 25-300-0814   (SL)
CONESTOGA LODGE PARTNERSHIP
CONESTOGA LODGE RETIREMENT HOME
55 Hugo Cres Suite 322, Kitchener, ON, N2M 5J1
(519) 576-2140
Emp Here 50   *Sales* 1,824,018
SIC 8361 Residential care

D-U-N-S 25-525-6638   (BR)

DEEM MANAGEMENT SERVICES LIMITED
CONESTOGA LODGE
55 Hugo Cres, Kitchener, ON, N2M 5J1
(519) 576-2140
Emp Here 26
SIC 8051 Skilled nursing care facilities

D-U-N-S 25-925-5370   (SL)
EAST SIDE MARIO'S INC
446 Highland Rd W, Kitchener, ON, N2M 3C7

Emp Here 60   *Sales* 1,824,018
SIC 5812 Eating places

D-U-N-S 25-498-5120   (HQ)
GRAND VALLEY REAL ESTATE LIMITED
PRUDENTIAL GRAND VALLEY REALTY
(*Suby of* Grand Valley Real Estate Limited)
370 Highland Rd W Unit 15c, Kitchener, ON,
N2M 5J9
(519) 745-7000
Emp Here 36   *Emp Total* 53
Sales 4,961,328
SIC 6531 Real estate agents and managers

D-U-N-S 25-317-5616   (BR)
**LIQUOR CONTROL BOARD OF ONTARIO,
THE**
L.C.B.O.
324 Highland Rd W Unit 6, Kitchener, ON,
N2M 5G2
(519) 745-8781
Emp Here 20
SIC 5921 Liquor stores

D-U-N-S 20-622-6859   (BR)
METRO ONTARIO INC
FOOD BASICS
851 Fischer Hallman Rd, Kitchener, ON, N2M
5N8
(519) 570-2500
Emp Here 80
SIC 5411 Grocery stores

D-U-N-S 24-335-0456   (BR)
METRO ONTARIO INC
FOOD BASICS
370 Highland Rd W Suite 1, Kitchener, ON,
N2M 5J9
(519) 744-4100
Emp Here 120
SIC 5411 Grocery stores

D-U-N-S 25-300-5870   (BR)
REDBERRY FRANCHISING CORP
BURGER KING
443 Highland Rd W, Kitchener, ON, N2M 3C6

Emp Here 24
SIC 5812 Eating places

D-U-N-S 25-606-5483   (BR)
REVERA INC
HIGHLAND PLACE
20 Fieldgate St, Kitchener, ON, N2M 5K3
(519) 741-0221
Emp Here 50
SIC 6513 Apartment building operators

D-U-N-S 25-593-8177   (BR)
ROYAL BANK OF CANADA
RBC
(*Suby of* Royal Bank Of Canada)
413 Highland Rd W, Kitchener, ON, N2M 3C6
(519) 575-2280
Emp Here 20
SIC 6021 National commercial banks

D-U-N-S 25-104-1257   (BR)
**SHOPPERS HOME HEALTH CARE
(CANADA) INC**
SHOPPERS HOME HEALTH CARE
379 Gage Ave, Kitchener, ON, N2M 5E1
(519) 579-6200
Emp Here 31
SIC 5999 Miscellaneous retail stores, nec

D-U-N-S 25-393-3121   (BR)

SOBEYS CAPITAL INCORPORATED
SOBEYS
274 Highland Rd W, Kitchener, ON, N2M 3C5
(519) 744-6561
Emp Here 180
SIC 5411 Grocery stores

D-U-N-S 25-524-0723   (BR)
SOBEYS CAPITAL INCORPORATED
SOBEYS
274 Highland Rd W, Kitchener, ON, N2M 3C5
(519) 744-6561
Emp Here 200
SIC 5411 Grocery stores

D-U-N-S 20-973-5104   (BR)
SPARKLES CLEANING SERVICE LTD
300 Mill St Unit 6, Kitchener, ON, N2M 5G8
(519) 579-4845
Emp Here 20
SIC 7349 Building maintenance services, nec

D-U-N-S 25-163-6502   (BR)
TRUE NORTH IMAGING INC
*VICTORIA KITCHENER X-RAY ULTRA-
SOUND*
751 Victoria St S Suite B102, Kitchener, ON,
N2M 5N4
(519) 742-2636
Emp Here 25
SIC 8071 Medical laboratories

D-U-N-S 25-524-2901   (BR)
TWINCORP INC
TACO BELL
751 Victoria St S, Kitchener, ON, N2M 5N4

Emp Here 20
SIC 5812 Eating places

D-U-N-S 20-710-7256   (BR)
**WATERLOO CATHOLIC DISTRICT
SCHOOL BOARD**
ST BERNADETTE SCHOOL
245 Lorne Ave, Kitchener, ON, N2M 3Y9
(519) 743-1541
Emp Here 30
SIC 8211 Elementary and secondary schools

D-U-N-S 25-228-1878   (BR)
**WATERLOO CATHOLIC DISTRICT
SCHOOL BOARD**
*MONSIGNOR WILLIAM GLEASON ELE-
MENTARY SCHOOL*
155 Westwood Dr, Kitchener, ON, N2M 2K7
(519) 579-0890
Emp Here 25
SIC 8211 Elementary and secondary schools

D-U-N-S 20-710-7348   (BR)
**WATERLOO CATHOLIC DISTRICT
SCHOOL BOARD**
ST PAUL CATHOLIC SCHOOL
45 Birchcliff Ave, Kitchener, ON, N2M 4V7
(519) 743-4401
Emp Here 50
SIC 8211 Elementary and secondary schools

D-U-N-S 25-228-1084   (BR)
**WATERLOO REGION DISTRICT SCHOOL
BOARD**
WESTMOUNT PUBLIC SCHOOL
329 Glasgow St, Kitchener, ON, N2M 2M9
(519) 578-5430
Emp Here 40
SIC 8211 Elementary and secondary schools

D-U-N-S 25-228-1134   (BR)
**WATERLOO REGION DISTRICT SCHOOL
BOARD**
SOUTHRIDGE ELEMENTARY SCHOOL
1425 Queens Blvd, Kitchener, ON, N2M 5B3
(519) 576-0940
Emp Here 42
SIC 8211 Elementary and secondary schools

D-U-N-S 25-137-3809   (BR)
WATERLOO REGION DISTRICT SCHOOL

BOARD
FOREST HILL SCHOOL
255 Westmount Rd E, Kitchener, ON, N2M
4Z2
(519) 578-5480
Emp Here 40
SIC 8211 Elementary and secondary schools

D-U-N-S 25-237-8880   (BR)
**WATERLOO REGION DISTRICT SCHOOL
BOARD**
QUEENSMOUNT SENIOR PUBLIC SCHOOL
21 Westmount Rd W, Kitchener, ON, N2M 1R6
(519) 578-0400
Emp Here 35
SIC 8211 Elementary and secondary schools

D-U-N-S 25-228-1175   (BR)
**WATERLOO REGION DISTRICT SCHOOL
BOARD**
A R KAUFMAN PUBLIC SCHOOL
11 Chopin Dr, Kitchener, ON, N2M 2G3
(519) 745-7312
Emp Here 46
SIC 8211 Elementary and secondary schools

D-U-N-S 25-228-1506   (BR)
**WATERLOO REGION DISTRICT SCHOOL
BOARD**
*FOREST HEIGHTS COLLEGIATE INSTI-
TUTE*
255 Fischer Hallman Rd, Kitchener, ON, N2M
4X8
(519) 744-6567
Emp Here 160
SIC 8211 Elementary and secondary schools

D-U-N-S 25-746-6516   (BR)
**WATERLOO REGION DISTRICT SCHOOL
BOARD**
*QUEEN ELIZABETH ELEMENTARY PUBLIC
SCHOOL*
191 Hoffman St, Kitchener, ON, N2M 3N2
(519) 578-3910
Emp Here 30
SIC 8211 Elementary and secondary schools

D-U-N-S 25-237-8955   (BR)
**WATERLOO REGION DISTRICT SCHOOL
BOARD**
J F CARMICHAEL PUBLIC SCHOOL
80 Patricia Ave, Kitchener, ON, N2M 1J3
(519) 576-0123
Emp Here 58
SIC 8211 Elementary and secondary schools

D-U-N-S 20-655-8848   (BR)
WENDY'S RESTAURANTS OF CANADA INC
PIONEER FAST FOODS
(*Suby of* The Wendy's Company)
350 Westmount Rd W, Kitchener, ON, N2M
5C4
(519) 745-3786
Emp Here 32
SIC 5812 Eating places

Kitchener, ON N2N
Waterloo County

D-U-N-S 20-321-9308   (BR)
CARA OPERATIONS LIMITED
HARVEYS RESTAURANT
(*Suby of* Cara Holdings Limited)
235 Ira Needles Blvd, Kitchener, ON, N2N 0B2
(519) 568-8008
Emp Here 20
SIC 5812 Eating places

D-U-N-S 24-333-1209   (BR)
DEVTEK AEROSPACE INC.
AEROSPATIALE HOCHELAGA
1665 Highland Rd W, Kitchener, ON, N2N 3K5
(519) 576-8910
Emp Here 170
SIC 3728 Aircraft parts and equipment, nec

D-U-N-S 24-804-7990   (HQ)
DEVTEK AEROSPACE INC.
1665 Highland Rd W, Kitchener, ON, N2N 3K5
(519) 576-8910
Emp Here 179   *Emp Total* 1,500
Sales 43,046,813
SIC 3728 Aircraft parts and equipment, nec
Pr Gilles Labbe
VP Real Belanger
Sec Francois Renauld

D-U-N-S 24-382-2207   (BR)
LOBLAWS INC
REAL CANADIAN SUPERSTORE
875 Highland Rd W Suite 178, Kitchener, ON,
N2N 2Y2
(519) 745-4781
Emp Here 240
SIC 5411 Grocery stores

D-U-N-S 25-321-4290   (BR)
REVERA LONG TERM CARE INC
*FOREST HEIGHTS LONG TERM CARE
CENTER*
60 Westheights Dr, Kitchener, ON, N2N 2A8
(519) 576-2578
Emp Here 250
SIC 8051 Skilled nursing care facilities

D-U-N-S 25-471-6186   (BR)
**STEEVES & ROZEMA ENTERPRISES LIM-
ITED**
*LANARK PLACE RETIREMENT RESI-
DENCE*
44 Lanark Cres Suite 101, Kitchener, ON, N2N
2Z8
(519) 743-0121
Emp Here 55
SIC 6513 Apartment building operators

D-U-N-S 20-710-7421   (BR)
**WATERLOO CATHOLIC DISTRICT
SCHOOL BOARD**
*RESURRECION CATHOLIC SECONDARY
SCHOOL*
455 University Ave W, Kitchener, ON, N2N
3B9
(519) 741-1990
Emp Here 160
SIC 8211 Elementary and secondary schools

D-U-N-S 20-710-7371   (BR)
**WATERLOO CATHOLIC DISTRICT
SCHOOL BOARD**
ST MARKS SCHOOL
240 Autumn Hill Cres, Kitchener, ON, N2N
1K8
(519) 743-4682
Emp Here 50
SIC 8211 Elementary and secondary schools

D-U-N-S 25-137-3825   (BR)
**WATERLOO REGION DISTRICT SCHOOL
BOARD**
WESTHEIGHTS PUBLIC SCHOOL
429 Westheights Dr, Kitchener, ON, N2N 1M3
(519) 744-3549
Emp Here 50
SIC 8211 Elementary and secondary schools

D-U-N-S 20-228-7251   (BR)
**WATERLOO REGION DISTRICT SCHOOL
BOARD**
SANDHILLS PUBLIC SCHOOL
1250 Victoria St S, Kitchener, ON, N2N 3J2
(519) 744-4430
Emp Here 50
SIC 8211 Elementary and secondary schools

D-U-N-S 20-591-4604   (BR)
**WATERLOO REGION DISTRICT SCHOOL
BOARD**
JOHN DARLING PUBLIC SCHOOL
200 Rolling Meadows Dr, Kitchener, ON, N2N
3G9
(519) 749-0834
Emp Here 30
SIC 8211 Elementary and secondary schools

▲ Public Company   ■ Public Company Family Member   **HQ** Headquarters   **BR** Branch   **SL** Single Location

D-U-N-S 20-591-4620   (BR)
WATERLOO REGION DISTRICT SCHOOL BOARD
MEADOWLANE PUBLIC SCHOOL
236 Forestwood Dr, Kitchener, ON, N2N 1C1
(519) 579-5030
Emp Here 25
SIC 8211 Elementary and secondary schools

Kitchener, ON N2P
Waterloo County

D-U-N-S 24-193-7184   (SL)
742994 ONTARIO INC
EDELWEISS TAVERN
600 Doon Village Rd, Kitchener, ON, N2P 1G6
(519) 748-0221
Emp Here 55   *Sales* 1,678,096
SIC 5812 Eating places

D-U-N-S 24-978-0008   (SL)
816793 ONTARIO INC
TIM HORTONS
4396 King St E Suite 4, Kitchener, ON, N2P 2G4
(519) 650-0331
Emp Here 50   *Sales* 1,532,175
SIC 5812 Eating places

D-U-N-S 24-407-1593   (SL)
ADONAI RESIDENTIAL SERVICES INC
SUNBEAM LODGE
389 Pinnacle Dr, Kitchener, ON, N2P 2P7
(519) 896-6718
Emp Here 60   *Sales* 2,188,821
SIC 8361 Residential care

D-U-N-S 20-344-3200   (BR)
AECOM CANADA LTD
ARCHITECTURAL DIVISION
50 Sportsworld Crossing Rd Suite 290, Kitchener, ON, N2P 0A4
(519) 650-5313
Emp Here 90
SIC 8742 Management consulting services

D-U-N-S 24-389-6359   (BR)
AEROTEK ULC
4275 King St E Suite 310, Kitchener, ON, N2P 2E9
(519) 707-1025
Emp Here 25
SIC 7361 Employment agencies

D-U-N-S 20-589-4798   (BR)
BANQUE TORONTO-DOMINION, LA
TD CANADA TRUST
(*Suby of* Toronto-Dominion Bank, The)
123 Pioneer Dr Suite 1, Kitchener, ON, N2P 2A3
(519) 885-8555
Emp Here 20
SIC 6021 National commercial banks

D-U-N-S 24-995-8711   (BR)
BEST BUY CANADA LTD
FUTURE SHOP
(*Suby of* Best Buy Co., Inc.)
50 Gateway Park Dr, Kitchener, ON, N2P 2J4

Emp Here 95
SIC 5731 Radio, television, and electronic stores

D-U-N-S 25-231-7276   (BR)
BRICK WAREHOUSE LP, THE
BRICK, THE
4283 King St E, Kitchener, ON, N2P 2E9
(519) 653-1099
Emp Here 70
SIC 5712 Furniture stores

D-U-N-S 20-303-3196   (BR)
CARA OPERATIONS LIMITED
KELSEY'S

(*Suby of* Cara Holdings Limited)
4391 King St E, Kitchener, ON, N2P 2G1

Emp Here 32
SIC 5812 Eating places

D-U-N-S 24-197-5879   (HQ)
CHRISTIAN HORIZONS
(*Suby of* Christian Horizons)
25 Sportsworld Crossing Rd, Kitchener, ON, N2P 0A5
(519) 650-0966
Emp Here 50   *Emp Total* 2,900
Sales 117,631,993
SIC 8361 Residential care
Dir Janet Nolan
    Beth Woof
    Angelica Mckay

D-U-N-S 25-363-6062   (BR)
CHRISTIAN HORIZONS
WEST DISTRICT OFFICE
(*Suby of* Christian Horizons)
4275 King St E Suite 101, Kitchener, ON, N2P 2E9
(519) 650-3241
Emp Here 45
SIC 8361 Residential care

D-U-N-S 24-984-8334   (SL)
CITY OF KITCHENER COUNTRY CLUB INC
DOON VALLEY GOLF CLUB
500 Doon Valley Dr, Kitchener, ON, N2P 1B4
(519) 741-2939
Emp Here 30   *Sales* 1,313,293
SIC 7992 Public golf courses

D-U-N-S 25-524-2398   (BR)
CORPORATION OF THE CITY OF WATERLOO, THE
WATERLOO REGION MUSEUM
(*Suby of* Corporation Of The City Of Waterloo, The)
10 Huron Rd, Kitchener, ON, N2P 2R7
(519) 748-1914
Emp Here 20
SIC 8412 Museums and art galleries

D-U-N-S 24-886-0132   (BR)
COSTCO WHOLESALE CANADA LTD
COSTCO
(*Suby of* Costco Wholesale Corporation)
4438 King St E Suite 512, Kitchener, ON, N2P 2G4
(519) 650-3662
Emp Here 180
SIC 5399 Miscellaneous general merchandise

D-U-N-S 20-778-8659   (BR)
DELOITTE LLP
4210 King St E, Kitchener, ON, N2P 2G5
(519) 650-7600
Emp Here 170
SIC 8721 Accounting, auditing, and book-keeping

D-U-N-S 24-991-4771   (BR)
HOME DEPOT OF CANADA INC
(*Suby of* The Home Depot Inc)
100 Gateway Park Dr, Kitchener, ON, N2P 2J4
(519) 650-3900
Emp Here 200
SIC 5251 Hardware stores

D-U-N-S 24-682-0067   (BR)
NEIGHBOURHOOD GROUP OF COMPANIES LIMITED, THE
BOREALIS GRILLE AND BAR
4336 King St E, Kitchener, ON, N2P 3W6
(519) 219-9007
Emp Here 20
SIC 5812 Eating places

D-U-N-S 25-944-7837   (SL)
PPD CANADA, LTD
123 Pioneer Dr, Kitchener, ON, N2P 2B4
(519) 208-4222
Emp Here 55   *Sales* 9,445,120

SIC 8733 Noncommercial research organizations
Dir Matthew Parkhill

D-U-N-S 24-423-7046   (SL)
RESTAURANT INNOVATIONS INC
MOOSE WINOOSKI'S
20 Heldmann Rd, Kitchener, ON, N2P 0A6

Emp Here 80   *Sales* 2,407,703
SIC 5812 Eating places

D-U-N-S 25-498-3356   (BR)
STARBUCKS COFFEE CANADA, INC
(*Suby of* Starbucks Corporation)
135 Gateway Park Dr, Kitchener, ON, N2P 2J9
(519) 653-1333
Emp Here 20
SIC 5812 Eating places

D-U-N-S 20-710-7389   (BR)
WATERLOO CATHOLIC DISTRICT SCHOOL BOARD
ST TIMOTHYS CATHOLIC SCHOOL
15 Bechtel Dr, Kitchener, ON, N2P 1T4
(519) 748-1874
Emp Here 30
SIC 8211 Elementary and secondary schools

D-U-N-S 20-710-7447   (BR)
WATERLOO CATHOLIC DISTRICT SCHOOL BOARD
BLESSED KATERI SCHOOL
560 Pioneer Dr, Kitchener, ON, N2P 1P2
(519) 895-1716
Emp Here 331
SIC 8211 Elementary and secondary schools

D-U-N-S 25-137-3841   (BR)
WATERLOO REGION DISTRICT SCHOOL BOARD
PIONEER PARK PUBLIC SCHOOL
55 Upper Canada Dr, Kitchener, ON, N2P 1G2
(519) 748-0142
Emp Here 35
SIC 8211 Elementary and secondary schools

D-U-N-S 20-228-7269   (BR)
WATERLOO REGION DISTRICT SCHOOL BOARD
DOON PUBLIC SCHOOL
1401 Doon Village Rd, Kitchener, ON, N2P 1A8
(519) 748-1341
Emp Here 25
SIC 8211 Elementary and secondary schools

Kitchener, ON N2R
Waterloo County

D-U-N-S 24-514-0645   (SL)
1221122 ONTARIO LIMITED
KEYTECH WATER MANAGEMENT
(*Suby of* Keytech Investments Limited)
33 Mcintyre Dr Unit A, Kitchener, ON, N2R 1E4
(519) 748-4822
Emp Here 21   *Sales* 2,626,585
SIC 3589 Service industry machinery, nec

D-U-N-S 20-293-5003   (SL)
BARBARIAN SPORTSWEAR INC
575 Trillium Dr, Kitchener, ON, N2R 1J9
(519) 895-1932
Emp Here 100   *Sales* 3,939,878
SIC 2329 Men's and boy's clothing, nec

D-U-N-S 24-322-2366   (BR)
BOEHMER BOX LP
(*Suby of* Boehmer Box LP)
1560 Battler Rd, Kitchener, ON, N2R 1J6
(519) 576-2480
Emp Here 300
SIC 2652 Setup paperboard boxes

D-U-N-S 20-648-9507   (BR)

CANON CANADA INC
BUSINESS SOLUTIONS DIVISION
500 Trillium Dr Unit 23, Kitchener, ON, N2R 1E5

Emp Here 25
SIC 5044 Office equipment

D-U-N-S 20-629-6394   (SL)
CONESTOGO ELECTRIC INC
1490 Battler Rd, Kitchener, ON, N2R 1J6
(519) 748-6740
Emp Here 50   *Sales* 4,377,642
SIC 1731 Electrical work

D-U-N-S 24-652-5356   (BR)
FIRSTCANADA ULC
40 Mcbrine Dr, Kitchener, ON, N2R 1E7
(519) 748-4777
Emp Here 100
SIC 4151 School buses

D-U-N-S 25-357-7365   (SL)
HAR-HAR HOLDINGS INC
575 Trillium Dr, Kitchener, ON, N2R 1J9
(519) 895-1932
Emp Here 90   *Sales* 17,244,621
SIC 6719 Holding companies, nec
Pr Pr Robert Hartle
    Mike Hardy

D-U-N-S 20-648-3773   (BR)
HEWITT EQUIPEMENT LIMITEE
CATERPILLAR
1045 Trillium Dr Unit 1, Kitchener, ON, N2R 0A2
(519) 893-1622
Emp Here 20
SIC 4213 Trucking, except local

D-U-N-S 24-523-2934   (BR)
INTEGRATED DISTRIBUTION SYSTEMS LIMITED PARTNERSHIP
WAJAX EQUIPMENT
815 Trillium Dr, Kitchener, ON, N2R 1J9
(519) 893-2942
Emp Here 30
SIC 7538 General automotive repair shops

D-U-N-S 25-971-3477   (BR)
KUEHNE + NAGEL LTD
221b Mcintyre Dr, Kitchener, ON, N2R 1G1
(519) 893-6141
Emp Here 30
SIC 4731 Freight transportation arrangement

D-U-N-S 24-910-2765   (BR)
LIFTOW LIMITED
1465 Strasburg Rd, Kitchener, ON, N2R 1H2
(519) 748-5200
Emp Here 24
SIC 5084 Industrial machinery and equipment

D-U-N-S 24-220-6738   (HQ)
MINIT CANADA LTD
THINGS ENGRAVED, DIV OF
61 Mcbrine Pl, Kitchener, ON, N2R 1H5
(519) 748-2211
Emp Here 40   *Sales* 35,337,338
SIC 5947 Gift, novelty, and souvenir shop
Pr Pr William O'connor
Dir Fin Richard Humphrey

D-U-N-S 24-424-7185   (BR)
RYDER TRUCK RENTAL CANADA LTD
(*Suby of* Ryder System, Inc.)
80 Mcintyre Pl, Kitchener, ON, N2R 1G9
(519) 748-4767
Emp Here 35
SIC 7513 Truck rental and leasing, no drivers

D-U-N-S 24-720-6022   (BR)
SPICERS CANADA ULC
SPICERS
(*Suby of* CNG Canada Holding Inc.)
1460 Strasburg Rd, Kitchener, ON, N2R 1K1
(519) 340-1450
Emp Here 40

SIC 5111 Printing and writing paper

D-U-N-S 25-671-4759　(BR)
VENTRA GROUP CO
VENTRA PLASTIC KITCHENER
675 Trillium Dr, Kitchener, ON, N2R 1G6
(519) 895-0290
Emp Here 150
SIC 3714 Motor vehicle parts and accessories

D-U-N-S 20-605-7176　(SL)
WATERLOO BEDDING COMPANY, LIMITED
WATERLOO BEDDING
(*Suby of* Stryker Corporation)
825 Trillium Dr, Kitchener, ON, N2R 1J9
(519) 742-4447
Emp Here 105　*Sales* 21,304,500
SIC 2515 Mattresses and bedsprings
 A. Leigh Harrington
Dir George Eydt
Pr Pr Thomas Steward
Dir Habib Gorgi
 Frank Lumbar
Genl Mgr Russell Banks

D-U-N-S 24-132-0352　(BR)
WATERLOO REGION DISTRICT SCHOOL BOARD
HURON HEIGHTS SECONDARY SCHOOL
1825 Strasburg Rd, Kitchener, ON, N2R 1S3
(519) 896-2631
Emp Here 20
SIC 8211 Elementary and secondary schools

D-U-N-S 20-048-0924　(BR)
WATERLOO REGION DISTRICT SCHOOL BOARD
BRIGADOON PUBLIC SCHOOL
415 Caryndale Dr, Kitchener, ON, N2R 1J7
(519) 895-2353
Emp Here 40
SIC 8211 Elementary and secondary schools

D-U-N-S 24-858-3564　(SL)
WEBBER SUPPLY
1830 Strasburg Rd, Kitchener, ON, N2R 1E9

Emp Here 200　*Sales* 54,560,640
SIC 1541 Industrial buildings and warehouses
Owner David Webber

D-U-N-S 25-556-8727　(BR)
XEROX CANADA LTD
(*Suby of* Xerox Corporation)
31 Mcbrine Dr Unit 4, Kitchener, ON, N2R 1J1
(519) 893-6500
Emp Here 70
SIC 5044 Office equipment

Kleinburg, ON L0J
York County

D-U-N-S 24-665-7266　(SL)
666248 ONTARIO LIMITED
APRA TRUCK LINES TRANSPORT
7300 Major Mackenzie Dr, Kleinburg, ON, L0J 1C0
(905) 893-0900
Emp Here 50　*Sales* 3,939,878
SIC 4212 Local trucking, without storage

D-U-N-S 25-195-4756　(BR)
CANADIAN PACIFIC RAILWAY COMPANY
CP INTERMODAL SERVICES
6830 Rutherford Rd, Kleinburg, ON, L0J 1C0
(905) 893-5050
Emp Here 195
SIC 4011 Railroads, line-haul operating

D-U-N-S 20-821-9329　(SL)
DOCTOR'S HOUSE DINING CORP, THE
21 Nashville Rd, Kleinburg, ON, L0J 1C0
(905) 893-1615
Emp Here 70　*Sales* 2,942,050
SIC 5812 Eating places

D-U-N-S 25-297-8861　(BR)
YORK REGION DISTRICT SCHOOL BOARD
KLEINBURG PUBLIC SCHOOL
(*Suby of* York Region District School Board)
10391 Islington Ave, Kleinburg, ON, L0J 1C0
(905) 893-1142
Emp Here 40
SIC 8211 Elementary and secondary schools

Komoka, ON N0L
Middlesex County

D-U-N-S 20-750-8011　(SL)
LITTLE BEAVER ENTERPRISES LTD
LITTLE BEAVER RESTAURANT
9930 Glendon Dr, Komoka, ON, N0L 1R0
(519) 471-1200
Emp Here 65　*Sales* 4,961,328
SIC 5331 Variety stores

D-U-N-S 25-249-0776　(BR)
THAMES VALLEY DISTRICT SCHOOL BOARD
PARKVIEW PUBLIC SCHOOL
10008 Oxbow Dr, Komoka, ON, N0L 1R0
(519) 657-3868
Emp Here 26
SIC 8211 Elementary and secondary schools

L'Orignal, ON K0B
Prescott County

D-U-N-S 25-526-7536　(SL)
1024591 ONTARIO INC
BERTRAND CONSTRUCTION
56 Rue Longueil, L'Orignal, ON, K0B 1K0
(613) 675-4614
Emp Here 51　*Sales* 6,128,699
SIC 6712 Bank holding companies
Pr Raymond Bertrand

D-U-N-S 24-822-4396　(SL)
CHARTWELL SENIORS HOUSING REAL ESTATE INC
RESIDENCE CHAMPLAIN
428 Front Rd, L'Orignal, ON, K0B 1K0
(613) 675-4617
Emp Here 70　*Sales* 3,210,271
SIC 8051 Skilled nursing care facilities

D-U-N-S 25-503-9828　(HQ)
CONSEIL SCOLAIRE DE DISTRICT CATHOLIQUE DE L'EST ONTARIEN
CSDCEO
(*Suby of* Conseil Scolaire De District Catholique De L'Est Ontarien)
875 Rte 17, L'Orignal, ON, K0B 1K0
(613) 675-4691
Emp Here 100　*Emp Total* 1,400
Sales 111,053,378
SIC 8211 Elementary and secondary schools
Pr Michel Pilon
Treas Francois Bertrand
 Roger Paul
VP Georgette Sauve
 Roger Chartrand
 Andre-Paul Lalonde
 Jean Lemay
 Martial Levac
 Roger T Villeneuve
 Sergine-Rachelle Bouchard

D-U-N-S 25-238-1330　(BR)
CONSEIL SCOLAIRE DE DISTRICT CATHOLIQUE DE L'EST ONTARIEN
ECOLE ST-JEAN-BAPTISTE
(*Suby of* Conseil Scolaire De District Catholique De L'Est Ontarien)
35 Longueuil St, L'Orignal, ON, K0B 1K0
(613) 675-4878
Emp Here 30

SIC 8211 Elementary and secondary schools

D-U-N-S 24-102-6889　(SL)
IVACO ROLLING MILLS 2004 L.P.
IVACO ROLLING MILLS
1040 Hwy 17, L'Orignal, ON, K0B 1K0
(613) 675-4671
Emp Here 500　*Sales* 54,720,525
SIC 3312 Blast furnaces and steel mills
VP Luc Lachapelle
Genl Mgr Joseph Olenick

Lakefield, ON K0L
Peterborough County

D-U-N-S 20-292-0158　(BR)
EXTENDICARE INC
EXTENDICARE LAKEFIELD
19 Fraser St, Lakefield, ON, K0L 2H0
(705) 652-7112
Emp Here 120
SIC 8051 Skilled nursing care facilities

D-U-N-S 20-628-9076　(SL)
HAMILTON, ELLWOOD ENTERPRISES LTD
HAMILTON ELLWOOD BUS LINES
1325 Old Young'S Point Rd, Lakefield, ON, K0L 2H0
(705) 652-6090
Emp Here 65　*Sales* 2,324,068
SIC 4151 School buses

D-U-N-S 20-648-2791　(BR)
KAWARTHA PINE RIDGE DISTRICT SCHOOL BOARD
RIPATH MEMORIAL JUNIOR SCHOOL
39 Ermatinger St, Lakefield, ON, K0L 2H0
(705) 652-3811
Emp Here 20
SIC 8211 Elementary and secondary schools

D-U-N-S 20-047-4091　(BR)
KAWARTHA PINE RIDGE DISTRICT SCHOOL BOARD
LAKEFIELD DISTRICT SECONDARY SCHOOL
71 Bridge St, Lakefield, ON, K0L 2H0
(705) 652-3333
Emp Here 65
SIC 8211 Elementary and secondary schools

D-U-N-S 24-953-0242　(SL)
LAKEFIELD COLLEGE SCHOOL
4391 County Rd 29, Lakefield, ON, K0L 2H0
(705) 652-3324
Emp Here 50　*Sales* 4,666,700
SIC 8211 Elementary and secondary schools

D-U-N-S 25-371-5734　(BR)
PETERBOROUGH VICTORIA NORTHUMBERLAND AND CLARINGTON CATHOLIC DISTRICT SCHOOL BOARD
ST PAUL'S ELEMENTARY SCHOOL
(*Suby of* Peterborough Victoria Northumberland and Clarington Catholic District School Board)
2 Grant Ave, Lakefield, ON, K0L 2H0
(705) 652-7532
Emp Here 25
SIC 8211 Elementary and secondary schools

D-U-N-S 20-573-8425　(BR)
ROYAL BANK OF CANADA
RBC
(*Suby of* Royal Bank Of Canada)
50 Queen St, Lakefield, ON, K0L 2H0
(705) 652-6713
Emp Here 20
SIC 6021 National commercial banks

D-U-N-S 24-426-6016　(BR)
SGS CANADA INC
3347 Lakefield Rd Rr 3, Lakefield, ON, K0L 2H0

(705) 652-2000
Emp Here 350
SIC 8734 Testing laboratories

D-U-N-S 25-265-3332　(BR)
YMCA OF CENTRAL EAST ONTARIO
BALSILLIE FAMILY BRANCH
8 Caroline St, Lakefield, ON, K0L 2H0
(705) 652-7782
Emp Here 20
SIC 8351 Child day care services

Lakeside, ON N0M
Oxford County

D-U-N-S 20-179-2793　(HQ)
HUTTON TRANSPORT LIMITED
962979 19th Line, Lakeside, ON, N0M 2G0
(519) 349-2233
Emp Here 120　*Emp Total* 150
Sales 15,265,730
SIC 4212 Local trucking, without storage
Genl Mgr David Coleman
Pr Martin (Matty) Fallon

Lanark, ON K0G
Lanark County

D-U-N-S 20-711-5507　(BR)
UPPER CANADA DISTRICT SCHOOL BOARD, THE
MAPLE GROVE PUBLIC SCHOOL
151 George St, Lanark, ON, K0G 1K0
(613) 259-2777
Emp Here 50
SIC 8211 Elementary and secondary schools

Lancaster, ON K0C
Glengarry County

D-U-N-S 24-426-2973　(SL)
CSH CHATEAU GARDENS LANCASTER INC
105 Military Rd N Hwy Suite 34, Lancaster, ON, K0C 1N0
(613) 347-3016
Emp Here 20　*Sales* 729,607
SIC 8361 Residential care

Langton, ON N0E
Norfolk County

D-U-N-S 20-710-6407　(BR)
BRANT HALDIMAND NORFOLK CATHOLIC DISTRICT SCHOOL BOARD
SACRED HEART SCHOOL
26 Albert St, Langton, ON, N0E 1G0
(519) 875-2556
Emp Here 50
SIC 8211 Elementary and secondary schools

D-U-N-S 20-025-3057　(BR)
GRAND ERIE DISTRICT SCHOOL BOARD
VALLEY HEIGHTS SECONDARY SCHOOL
(*Suby of* Grand Erie District School Board)
2561 Hwy 59, Langton, ON, N0E 1G0
(519) 586-3522
Emp Here 55
SIC 8211 Elementary and secondary schools

D-U-N-S 20-086-6221　(BR)
GRAND ERIE DISTRICT SCHOOL BOARD
LANGTON PUBLIC SCHOOL
(*Suby of* Grand Erie District School Board)
23 Albert St, Langton, ON, N0E 1G0

---

(519) 875-4448
Emp Here 20
SIC 8211 Elementary and secondary schools

Lansdowne, ON K0E
Leeds County

D-U-N-S 25-238-0118   (BR)
UPPER CANADA DISTRICT SCHOOL BOARD, THE
THOUSAND ISLANDS ELEMENTARY SCHOOL
(*Suby of* Upper Canada District School Board, The)
Gd, Lansdowne, ON, K0E 1L0
(613) 659-2216
Emp Here 40
SIC 8211 Elementary and secondary schools

Lasalle, ON N9J
Essex County

D-U-N-S 25-249-1840   (BR)
WINDSOR-ESSEX CATHOLIC DISTRICT SCHOOL BOARD, THE
SACRED HEART SCHOOL
200 Kenwood Blvd, Lasalle, ON, N9J 2Z9
(519) 734-1255
Emp Here 50
SIC 8211 Elementary and secondary schools

Leamington, ON N8H
Essex County

D-U-N-S 24-021-3533   (SL)
1544982 ONTARIO INC
EWS LEAMINGTON
50 Victoria Ave N, Leamington, ON, N8H 2W1
(519) 776-9153
Emp Here 50   *Sales* 3,356,192
SIC 3471 Plating and polishing

D-U-N-S 25-644-7335   (SL)
BERGTHALER MENNONITE CHURCH
413 Wilkinson Dr, Leamington, ON, N8H 1A1
(519) 326-2152
Emp Here 70   *Sales* 4,596,524
SIC 8661 Religious organizations

D-U-N-S 20-784-6994   (BR)
CANADA POST CORPORATION
25 John St, Leamington, ON, N8H 1H3
(519) 326-2678
Emp Here 35
SIC 4311 U.s. postal service

D-U-N-S 25-303-6883   (BR)
CANADIAN IMPERIAL BANK OF COMMERCE
CIBC
69 Erie St S, Leamington, ON, N8H 3B2
(519) 326-6141
Emp Here 20
SIC 6021 National commercial banks

D-U-N-S 25-249-3846   (BR)
CONSEIL SCOLAIRE DE DISTRICT DES ECOLES CATHOLIQUES DU SUD-OUEST
ECOLE SAINT MICHEL
33 Sherman St, Leamington, ON, N8H 5H6
(519) 326-6125
Emp Here 22
SIC 8211 Elementary and secondary schools

D-U-N-S 25-361-9118   (BR)
CORPORATION OF THE COUNTY OF ESSEX, THE
SUN PARLOR HOMES
175 Talbot St E, Leamington, ON, N8H 1L9

(519) 326-5731
Emp Here 250
SIC 8361 Residential care

D-U-N-S 25-033-6096   (BR)
CORPORATION OF THE MUNICIPALITY OF LEAMINGTON, THE
LEAMINGTON MUNICIPAL MARINA
90 Robson Rd, Leamington, ON, N8H 5P3
(519) 326-0834
Emp Here 20
SIC 4493 Marinas

D-U-N-S 20-125-7479   (BR)
DIVERSICARE CANADA MANAGEMENT SERVICES CO., INC
ERIEGLEN MANNOR
119 Robson Rd, Leamington, ON, N8H 3V4
(905) 821-1161
Emp Here 32
SIC 8361 Residential care

D-U-N-S 20-175-8716   (BR)
ELRINGKLINGER CANADA, INC
15 Seneca Rd, Leamington, ON, N8H 5P2
(519) 325-0052
Emp Here 180
SIC 3053 Gaskets; packing and sealing devices

D-U-N-S 20-807-5270   (SL)
ERIE SHORE COMMUNITY TRANSIT
215 Talbot St E, Leamington, ON, N8H 3X5
(519) 326-9030
Emp Here 60   *Sales* 3,064,349
SIC 4119 Local passenger transportation, nec

D-U-N-S 24-419-6833   (SL)
GABRIELE FLOOR & HOME
55 Talbot St W, Leamington, ON, N8H 1M5
(519) 326-1859
Emp Here 45   *Sales* 6,639,424
SIC 5211 Lumber and other building materials
Pt Shelly Gale

D-U-N-S 24-525-4342   (BR)
GREATER ESSEX COUNTY DISTRICT SCHOOL BOARD
GORE HILL PUBLIC SCHOOL
1135 Mersea Road 1, Leamington, ON, N8H 3V7
(519) 326-3431
Emp Here 20
SIC 8211 Elementary and secondary schools

D-U-N-S 25-890-0620   (BR)
GREATER ESSEX COUNTY DISTRICT SCHOOL BOARD
MOUNT CARMEL BLYTHESWOOD PUBLIC SCHOOL
622 Mersea Road 5, Leamington, ON, N8H 3V5
(519) 326-7154
Emp Here 26
SIC 8211 Elementary and secondary schools

D-U-N-S 25-249-1949   (BR)
GREATER ESSEX COUNTY DISTRICT SCHOOL BOARD
MILL STREET CENTENNIAL PUBLIC SCHOOL
134 Mill St E, Leamington, ON, N8H 1S6
(519) 326-4241
Emp Here 38
SIC 8211 Elementary and secondary schools

D-U-N-S 25-249-2012   (BR)
GREATER ESSEX COUNTY DISTRICT SCHOOL BOARD
QUEEN ELIZABETH PUBLIC SCHOOL
4 Maxon Ave, Leamington, ON, N8H 2E2
(519) 322-5532
Emp Here 45
SIC 8211 Elementary and secondary schools

D-U-N-S 25-249-1931   (BR)
GREATER ESSEX COUNTY DISTRICT SCHOOL BOARD
LEAMINGTON DISTRICT SECONDARY

SCHOOL
125 Talbot St W, Leamington, ON, N8H 1N2
(519) 326-6191
Emp Here 65
SIC 8211 Elementary and secondary schools

D-U-N-S 25-249-2061   (BR)
GREATER ESSEX COUNTY DISTRICT SCHOOL BOARD
MARGARET D BENNIE PUBLIC SCHOOL
259 Sherk St, Leamington, ON, N8H 3K8
(519) 326-6603
Emp Here 35
SIC 8211 Elementary and secondary schools

D-U-N-S 24-098-0578   (BR)
LOBLAWS INC
REAL CANADIAN SUPERSTORE
201 Talbot St E, Leamington, ON, N8H 3X5

Emp Here 120
SIC 5411 Grocery stores

D-U-N-S 25-026-5212   (BR)
METRO ONTARIO INC
A & P FOOD STORES
288 Erie St S, Leamington, ON, N8H 3C5
(519) 322-1414
Emp Here 200
SIC 5411 Grocery stores

D-U-N-S 20-125-8639   (HQ)
PLANT PRODUCTS INC
(*Suby of* Morse Leasing Inc)
50 Hazelton St, Leamington, ON, N8H 1B8
(519) 326-9037
Emp Here 50   *Emp Total* 44
Sales 19,188,664
SIC 5191 Farm supplies
CEO Chris Stickles
Pr Pr Perry Stickles
 Julie Rieter

D-U-N-S 24-133-0047   (BR)
RESIDENCES ALLEGRO, S.E.C., LES
LEAMINGTON COURT RETIREMENT SUITES
(*Suby of* Residences Allegro, S.E.C., Les)
1 Henry Ave, Leamington, ON, N8H 5P1
(519) 322-0311
Emp Here 30
SIC 8059 Nursing and personal care, nec

D-U-N-S 20-573-8151   (BR)
ROYAL BANK OF CANADA
RBC
(*Suby of* Royal Bank Of Canada)
33 Princess St Suite 201, Leamington, ON, N8H 5C5

Emp Here 20
SIC 6021 National commercial banks

D-U-N-S 25-650-0687   (BR)
ROYAL BANK OF CANADA
RBC FINANCIAL GROUP
(*Suby of* Royal Bank Of Canada)
35 Talbot St W, Leamington, ON, N8H 1M3
(519) 322-2821
Emp Here 20
SIC 6021 National commercial banks

D-U-N-S 25-149-9976   (SL)
SOUTH ESSEX FABRICATING INC
4 Seneca Rd, Leamington, ON, N8H 5H7
(519) 322-5995
Emp Here 60   *Sales* 12,476,280
SIC 5191 Farm supplies
Pr Pr Peter Quiring

D-U-N-S 24-252-6932   (BR)
STAPLES CANADA INC
STAPLES THE BUSINESS DEPOT
(*Suby of* Staples, Inc.)
16 Seacliff Dr E, Leamington, ON, N8H 2L2
(519) 324-1370
Emp Here 30

SIC 5943 Stationery stores

D-U-N-S 24-310-3756   (SL)
SUN PARLOUR GROWER SUPPLY LIMITED
230 County Rd 31, Leamington, ON, N8H 3W2
(519) 326-8681
Emp Here 20   *Sales* 4,158,760
SIC 5191 Farm supplies

D-U-N-S 20-284-9873   (BR)
WFS LTD
(*Suby of* W.W. Grainger, Inc.)
213 Talbot St W, Leamington, ON, N8H 1N8
(519) 326-5767
Emp Here 25
SIC 5085 Industrial supplies

D-U-N-S 20-738-6330   (BR)
WAL-MART CANADA CORP
288 Erie St S Suite 3164, Leamington, ON, N8H 3C5
(519) 326-3900
Emp Here 200
SIC 5311 Department stores

D-U-N-S 20-710-6050   (BR)
WINDSOR-ESSEX CATHOLIC DISTRICT SCHOOL BOARD, THE
ST LOUIS CATHOLIC ELEMENTARY SCHOOL
176 Talbot St E, Leamington, ON, N8H 1M2
(519) 326-8636
Emp Here 40
SIC 8211 Elementary and secondary schools

D-U-N-S 20-710-6019   (BR)
WINDSOR-ESSEX CATHOLIC DISTRICT SCHOOL BOARD, THE
CARDINAL CARTER SECONDARY SCHOOL
120 Ellison Ave, Leamington, ON, N8H 5C7
(519) 322-2804
Emp Here 50
SIC 8211 Elementary and secondary schools

D-U-N-S 25-249-1824   (BR)
WINDSOR-ESSEX CATHOLIC DISTRICT SCHOOL BOARD, THE
QUEEN OF PEACE SCHOOL
57 Nicholas St, Leamington, ON, N8H 4B8
(519) 326-9023
Emp Here 45
SIC 8211 Elementary and secondary schools

Lefroy, ON L0L
Simcoe County

D-U-N-S 25-297-6295   (BR)
SIMCOE COUNTY DISTRICT SCHOOL BOARD, THE
KILLARLEY BEACH PUBLIC SCHOOL
(*Suby of* Simcoe County District School Board, The)
20 Side Rd Suite 850, Lefroy, ON, L0L 1W0
(705) 456-2630
Emp Here 30
SIC 8211 Elementary and secondary schools

D-U-N-S 25-297-6253   (BR)
SIMCOE COUNTY DISTRICT SCHOOL BOARD, THE
INNISFIL CENTRAL PUBLIC SCHOOL
(*Suby of* Simcoe County District School Board, The)
2075 5th Line, Lefroy, ON, L0L 1W0
(705) 456-2534
Emp Here 25
SIC 8211 Elementary and secondary schools

Levack, ON P0M
Sudbury County

D-U-N-S 25-228-0664   (BR)
RAINBOW DISTRICT SCHOOL BOARD
LEVACK PUBLIC SCHOOL
(*Suby of* Rainbow District School Board)
100 High St, Levack, ON, P0M 2C0
(705) 671-5943
Emp Here 25
SIC 8211 Elementary and secondary schools

Limoges, ON K0A
Russell County

D-U-N-S 25-238-6768   (BR)
CONSEIL SCOLAIRE DE DISTRICT CATHOLIQUE DE L'EST ONTARIEN
ECOLE ST-VIATEUR ANNEXE
(*Suby of* Conseil Scolaire De District Catholique De L'Est Ontarien)
139 Mabel Rd, Limoges, ON, K0A 2M0
(613) 443-6317
Emp Here 20
SIC 8211 Elementary and secondary schools

D-U-N-S 20-024-2779   (BR)
CONSEIL SCOLAIRE DE DISTRICT CATHOLIQUE DE L'EST ONTARIEN
ECOLE ELEMENTAIRE CATHOLIQUE SAINT-VIATEUR/ANNEXE
205 Limoges Rd, Limoges, ON, K0A 2M0
(613) 443-1976
Emp Here 26
SIC 8211 Elementary and secondary schools

D-U-N-S 20-888-9956   (SL)
GENESIS GARDENS INC
ST VIATEUR NURSING HOME
1003 Limoges Rd, Limoges, ON, K0A 2M0
(613) 443-5751
Emp Here 78   *Sales* 3,648,035
SIC 8051 Skilled nursing care facilities

Lindsay, ON K9V

D-U-N-S 20-913-9497   (BR)
BANK OF NOVA SCOTIA, THE
SCOTIABANK
165 Kent St W, Lindsay, ON, K9V 4S2
(705) 324-2123
Emp Here 30
SIC 6021 National commercial banks

D-U-N-S 20-732-5270   (BR)
CAMPBELL, JAMES INC
MCDONALD'S
(*Suby of* Campbell, James Inc)
333 Kent St W, Lindsay, ON, K9V 2Z7
(705) 324-6668
Emp Here 105
SIC 5812 Eating places

D-U-N-S 20-797-1172   (BR)
CANADIAN IMPERIAL BANK OF COMMERCE
CIBC
66 Kent St W, Lindsay, ON, K9V 2Y2
(705) 324-2183
Emp Here 35
SIC 6021 National commercial banks

D-U-N-S 20-303-3360   (BR)
CARA OPERATIONS LIMITED
KELSEY'S
(*Suby of* Cara Holdings Limited)
330 Kent St W, Lindsay, ON, K9V 4T7
(705) 324-0800
Emp Here 65
SIC 5812 Eating places

D-U-N-S 20-810-0201   (BR)
CARESSANT-CARE NURSING AND RETIREMENT HOMES LIMITED

---

114 Mclaughlin Rd, Lindsay, ON, K9V 6L1
(705) 324-0300
Emp Here 110
SIC 8051 Skilled nursing care facilities

D-U-N-S 24-316-2344   (BR)
CARESSANT-CARE NURSING AND RETIREMENT HOMES LIMITED
CARESSANT CARE LINDSAY
240 Mary St W, Lindsay, ON, K9V 5K5
(705) 324-1913
Emp Here 100
SIC 8051 Skilled nursing care facilities

D-U-N-S 25-712-2465   (BR)
CENTRAL EAST COMMUNITY CARE ACCESS CENTRE FOUNDATION
LINDSAY BRANCH
370 Kent St W, Lindsay, ON, K9V 6G8
(705) 324-9165
Emp Here 50
SIC 8059 Nursing and personal care, nec

D-U-N-S 25-481-5152   (BR)
CORPORATION OF THE CITY OF KAWARTHA LAKES, THE
VICTORIA MANOR
220 Angeline St S, Lindsay, ON, K9V 0J8
(705) 324-3558
Emp Here 175
SIC 8361 Residential care

D-U-N-S 25-184-2126   (BR)
CORPORATION OF THE CITY OF KAWARTHA LAKES, THE
COMMUNITY CARE
34 Cambridge St S, Lindsay, ON, K9V 3B8
(705) 324-7323
Emp Here 30
SIC 8322 Individual and family services

D-U-N-S 20-272-6035   (BR)
CORPORATION OF THE CITY OF KAWARTHA LAKES, THE
CITY OF KAWARTHA LAKES FIRE RESCUE SERVICE
9 Cambridge St N, Lindsay, ON, K9V 4C4
(705) 324-5731
Emp Here 400
SIC 7389 Business services, nec

D-U-N-S 25-359-6597   (BR)
CORPORATION OF THE CITY OF KAWARTHA LAKES, THE
SOCIAL SERVICES & HOUSING
322 Kent St W Suite 202, Lindsay, ON, K9V 4T7
(705) 324-9870
Emp Here 50
SIC 8399 Social services, nec

D-U-N-S 20-086-8862   (BR)
CORPORATION OF THE CITY OF KAWARTHA LAKES, THE
COMMUNITY SERVICES
180 Kent St W, Lindsay, ON, K9V 2Y6
(705) 324-9411
Emp Here 27
SIC 7389 Business services, nec

D-U-N-S 20-189-8553   (BR)
COUTTS, WILLIAM E. COMPANY, LIMITED
CRAYOLA CANADA
(*Suby of* Hallmark Cards, Incorporated)
15 Mary St W, Lindsay, ON, K9V 2N5
(705) 324-6105
Emp Here 50
SIC 3952 Lead pencils and art goods

D-U-N-S 20-292-1289   (BR)
EXTENDICARE (CANADA) INC
PARAMED HOME HEALTH CARE
108 Angeline St S Suite 1, Lindsay, ON, K9V 3L5
(705) 328-2280
Emp Here 350
SIC 8051 Skilled nursing care facilities

D-U-N-S 20-699-6634   (BR)
EXTENDICARE INC
EXTENDICARE KAWARTHA LAKES
125 Colborne St E, Lindsay, ON, K9V 6J2
(705) 878-5392
Emp Here 100
SIC 8051 Skilled nursing care facilities

D-U-N-S 25-885-4306   (BR)
FIVE COUNTIES CHILDREN'S CENTRE
9 Russell St E, Lindsay, ON, K9V 1Z7
(705) 324-1922
Emp Here 20
SIC 8699 Membership organizations, nec

D-U-N-S 25-859-1916   (BR)
HALIBURTON KAWARTHA PINE RIDGE DISTRICT HEALTH UNIT
108 Angeline St S, Lindsay, ON, K9V 3L5
(705) 324-3569
Emp Here 140
SIC 7991 Physical fitness facilities

D-U-N-S 20-291-2973   (BR)
ICT CANADA MARKETING INC
(*Suby of* Sykes Enterprises Incorporated)
370 Kent St W Unit 16, Lindsay, ON, K9V 6G8

Emp Here 250
SIC 7389 Business services, nec

D-U-N-S 25-196-5653   (BR)
KAWARTHA CHILD CARE SERVICES INC
24 Weldon Crt Suite 6, Lindsay, ON, K9V 4P1
(705) 324-8434
Emp Here 20
SIC 8351 Child day care services

D-U-N-S 25-021-4004   (BR)
LOBLAW COMPANIES LIMITED
NATIONAL GROCERS CASH & CARRY, DIV OF
55 Angeline St N, Lindsay, ON, K9V 5B7
(705) 324-5622
Emp Here 90
SIC 5411 Grocery stores

D-U-N-S 20-105-9776   (BR)
LOBLAWS SUPERMARKETS LIMITED
LOBLAWS
400 Kent St W, Lindsay, ON, K9V 6K2
(705) 878-4605
Emp Here 200
SIC 5411 Grocery stores

D-U-N-S 24-335-0480   (BR)
METRO ONTARIO INC
363 Kent St W, Lindsay, ON, K9V 2Z7
(705) 878-3300
Emp Here 100
SIC 5411 Grocery stores

D-U-N-S 20-290-8724   (BR)
METROLAND MEDIA GROUP LTD
LINDSAY THIS WEEK
192 St David St, Lindsay, ON, K9V 4Z4
(705) 324-8600
Emp Here 22
SIC 2711 Newspapers

D-U-N-S 20-126-1922   (SL)
NORTHERN CASKET (1976) LIMITED
165 St Peter St, Lindsay, ON, K9V 4S3
(705) 324-6164
Emp Here 85   *Sales* 2,845,467
SIC 3995 Burial caskets

D-U-N-S 25-182-2649   (BR)
OMNI HEALTH CARE LTD
FROST MANOR
225 Mary St W, Lindsay, ON, K9V 5K3
(705) 324-8333
Emp Here 80
SIC 8361 Residential care

D-U-N-S 20-711-6141   (BR)
PETERBOROUGH VICTORIA NORTHUMBERLAND AND CLARINGTON CATHOLIC

DISTRICT SCHOOL BOARD
ST DOMINIC CATHOLIC SCHOOL
320 Mary St W, Lindsay, ON, K9V 5X5
(705) 878-3660
Emp Here 50
SIC 8211 Elementary and secondary schools

D-U-N-S 20-653-4948   (BR)
PETERBOROUGH VICTORIA NORTHUMBERLAND AND CLARINGTON CATHOLIC DISTRICT SCHOOL BOARD
ST THOMAS AQUINAS CATHOLIC SECONDARY SCHOOL
260 Angeline St S, Lindsay, ON, K9V 0J8
(705) 878-4117
Emp Here 60
SIC 8211 Elementary and secondary schools

D-U-N-S 25-137-3627   (BR)
PETERBOROUGH VICTORIA NORTHUMBERLAND AND CLARINGTON CATHOLIC DISTRICT SCHOOL BOARD
POPE JOHN PAUL II ELEMENTARY SCHOOL
(*Suby of* Peterborough Victoria Northumberland and Clarington Catholic District School Board)
130 Orchard Park Rd, Lindsay, ON, K9V 5K1
(705) 324-7445
Emp Here 25
SIC 8211 Elementary and secondary schools

D-U-N-S 20-711-6083   (BR)
PETERBOROUGH VICTORIA NORTHUMBERLAND AND CLARINGTON CATHOLIC DISTRICT SCHOOL BOARD
ST MARY'S SCHOOL
16 St Lawrence St, Lindsay, ON, K9V 2J8
(705) 324-3113
Emp Here 50
SIC 8211 Elementary and secondary schools

D-U-N-S 25-828-2250   (BR)
PHARMA PLUS DRUGMARTS LTD
PHARMA PLUS
51 Kent St W, Lindsay, ON, K9V 2X9
(705) 328-1500
Emp Here 22
SIC 5912 Drug stores and proprietary stores

D-U-N-S 20-562-7057   (BR)
RBC DOMINION SECURITIES INC
(*Suby of* Royal Bank Of Canada)
189 Kent St W, Lindsay, ON, K9V 5G6
(705) 324-6151
Emp Here 22
SIC 6162 Mortgage bankers and loan correspondents

D-U-N-S 25-458-4386   (BR)
RESPIRON CARE-PLUS INC
CLOSING THE GAP HEALTH CARE GROUP
(*Suby of* Respiron Care-Plus Inc)
55 Mary St W Suite 205, Lindsay, ON, K9V 5Z6
(705) 324-5085
Emp Here 40
SIC 8049 Offices of health practitioner

D-U-N-S 20-563-3014   (BR)
REVERA INC
RESIDENCE ON WILLIAM ST RETIREMENT
140 William St N, Lindsay, ON, K9V 5R4
(705) 328-1016
Emp Here 55
SIC 8361 Residential care

D-U-N-S 20-860-2024   (BR)
SOURCE (BELL) ELECTRONICS INC, THE
SOURCE, THE
401 Kent St W Unit 17, Lindsay, ON, K9V 4Z1
(705) 324-1901
Emp Here 25
SIC 5999 Miscellaneous retail stores, nec

D-U-N-S 24-101-3759   (BR)
STAPLES CANADA INC
STAPLES THE BUSINESS DEPOT

(Suby of Staples, Inc.)
363 Kent St W Unit 600, Lindsay, ON, K9V 2Z7
(705) 328-3427
Emp Here 20
SIC 5943 Stationery stores

D-U-N-S 20-590-8580   (BR)
TRILLIUM LAKELANDS DISTRICT SCHOOL BOARD
LINDSAY ADULT EDUCATION TRAINING CENTER
230 Angeline St S, Lindsay, ON, K9V 0J8
(705) 324-5280
Emp Here 25
SIC 8211 Elementary and secondary schools

D-U-N-S 25-447-0503   (BR)
TRILLIUM LAKELANDS DISTRICT SCHOOL BOARD
LINDSAY COLLEGIATE AND VOCATIONAL INSTITUTE
260 Kent St W, Lindsay, ON, K9V 2Z5
(705) 324-3556
Emp Here 75
SIC 8211 Elementary and secondary schools

D-U-N-S 25-184-3371   (BR)
TRILLIUM LAKELANDS DISTRICT SCHOOL BOARD
PARKVIEW PUBLIC SCHOOL
133 Adelaide St N, Lindsay, ON, K9V 4M2
(705) 324-4558
Emp Here 45
SIC 8211 Elementary and secondary schools

D-U-N-S 25-181-3663   (BR)
TRILLIUM LAKELANDS DISTRICT SCHOOL BOARD
I E WELDON SECONDARY SCHOOL
24 Weldon Rd, Lindsay, ON, K9V 4R4
(705) 324-3585
Emp Here 160
SIC 8211 Elementary and secondary schools

D-U-N-S 25-181-6625   (BR)
TRILLIUM LAKELANDS DISTRICT SCHOOL BOARD
CENTRAL SENIOR SCHOOL
242 Kent St W, Lindsay, ON, K9V 2Z4
(705) 324-4352
Emp Here 30
SIC 8211 Elementary and secondary schools

D-U-N-S 20-590-8598   (BR)
TRILLIUM LAKELANDS DISTRICT SCHOOL BOARD
LESLIE FROST PUBLIC SCHOOL
51 Angeline St S, Lindsay, ON, K9V 3L1
(705) 324-5602
Emp Here 42
SIC 8211 Elementary and secondary schools

D-U-N-S 20-002-7329   (BR)
TRILLIUM LAKELANDS DISTRICT SCHOOL BOARD
ALEXANDRA PUBLIC SCHOOL
65 Sussex St N, Lindsay, ON, K9V 4H9
(705) 324-3313
Emp Here 25
SIC 8211 Elementary and secondary schools

D-U-N-S 24-324-2968   (BR)
TRILLIUM LAKELANDS DISTRICT SCHOOL BOARD
KING ALBERT PUBLIC SCHOOL
49 Glenelg St W, Lindsay, ON, K9V 2T9
(705) 324-3702
Emp Here 25
SIC 8211 Elementary and secondary schools

D-U-N-S 25-184-3884   (BR)
WENDY'S RESTAURANTS OF CANADA INC
WENDY'S
(Suby of The Wendy's Company)
329 Kent St W, Lindsay, ON, K9V 2Z7
(705) 878-8238
Emp Here 25

SIC 5812 Eating places

Linwood, ON N0B
Waterloo County

D-U-N-S 25-237-9185   (BR)
WATERLOO REGION DISTRICT SCHOOL BOARD
LINWOOD PUBLIC SCHOOL
50 Pine St, Linwood, ON, N0B 2A0
(519) 698-2680
Emp Here 47
SIC 8211 Elementary and secondary schools

Lions Head, ON N0H
Bruce County

D-U-N-S 20-710-6563   (BR)
BLUEWATER DISTRICT SCHOOL BOARD
BRUCE PENINSULA DISTRICT SCHOOL
5 Moore St, Lions Head, ON, N0H 1W0
(519) 793-3211
Emp Here 40
SIC 8211 Elementary and secondary schools

D-U-N-S 20-290-2438   (SL)
GOLDEN DAWN NURSING HOME
SENIOR CITIZEN HOME
80 Main St, Lions Head, ON, N0H 1W0
(519) 793-3433
Emp Here 55   *Sales* 2,480,664
SIC 8051 Skilled nursing care facilities

D-U-N-S 25-025-7326   (BR)
GREY BRUCE HEALTH SERVICES
LIONS HEAD HOSPITAL
22 Moore St Rr 3, Lions Head, ON, N0H 1W0
(519) 793-3424
Emp Here 25
SIC 8062 General medical and surgical hospitals

Listowel, ON N4W
Perth County

D-U-N-S 20-710-6811   (BR)
AVON MAITLAND DISTRICT SCHOOL BOARD
LISTOWEL CENTRAL PUBLIC SCHOOL
305 Binning St W, Listowel, ON, N4W 1G4

Emp Here 40
SIC 8211 Elementary and secondary schools

D-U-N-S 20-590-7244   (BR)
AVON MAITLAND DISTRICT SCHOOL BOARD
LISTOWEL DISTRICT SECONDARY SCHOOL
155 Maitland Ave S, Listowel, ON, N4W 2M4
(519) 291-1880
Emp Here 75
SIC 8211 Elementary and secondary schools

D-U-N-S 20-589-4822   (BR)
BANQUE TORONTO-DOMINION, LA
TD CANADA TRUST
(Suby of Toronto-Dominion Bank, The)
195 Main St E, Listowel, ON, N4W 2B5
(519) 291-2840
Emp Here 20
SIC 6021 National commercial banks

D-U-N-S 20-126-3159   (BR)
CAMPBELL COMPANY OF CANADA
(Suby of Campbell Soup Company)
1400 Mitchell Rd S, Listowel, ON, N4W 3G7

Emp Here 625

SIC 5142 Packaged frozen goods

D-U-N-S 25-303-6966   (BR)
CANADIAN IMPERIAL BANK OF COMMERCE
CIBC
105 Main St W, Listowel, ON, N4W 1A2
(519) 291-1920
Emp Here 25
SIC 6021 National commercial banks

D-U-N-S 25-915-1553   (BR)
CARESSANT-CARE NURSING AND RETIREMENT HOMES LIMITED
710 Reserve Ave S, Listowel, ON, N4W 2L1
(519) 291-1041
Emp Here 70
SIC 8051 Skilled nursing care facilities

D-U-N-S 20-791-9767   (SL)
CASSIE CO ENTERPRISES LTD
CANADIAN TIRE 57
500 Mitchell Rd S, Listowel, ON, N4W 3G7
(519) 291-1960
Emp Here 50   *Sales* 4,815,406
SIC 5251 Hardware stores

D-U-N-S 24-407-4639   (SL)
COMMUNITY LIVING NORTH PERTH
820 Main St E, Listowel, ON, N4W 3L3
(519) 291-1350
Emp Here 35   *Sales* 8,828,245
SIC 8322 Individual and family services
Treas Geoff Ramalho
Pr Bill Nauta

D-U-N-S 20-317-2044   (BR)
ERIE MEAT PRODUCTS LIMITED
LISTOWEL COLD STORAGE
(Suby of 508818 Ontario Limited)
1400 Mitchell Rd S, Listowel, ON, N4W 3G7
(519) 291-6593
Emp Here 175
SIC 2011 Meat packing plants

D-U-N-S 20-730-4007   (BR)
GRAY, L. H. & SON LIMITED
GRAY EGGS
955 Tremaine Ave S, Listowel, ON, N4W 3G9
(519) 291-5150
Emp Here 80
SIC 5995 Optical goods stores

D-U-N-S 25-407-9668   (SL)
LISTOWEL TECHNOLOGY, INC
1700 Mitchell Rd S, Listowel, ON, N4W 3H4
(519) 291-9900
Emp Here 400   *Sales* 80,214,843
SIC 3089 Plastics products, nec
Pr Shinichi Sakairi
Treas Manabue Tori
Takashi Kurita

D-U-N-S 24-344-6700   (BR)
METRO ONTARIO INC
FOOD BASICS
975 Wallace Ave N, Listowel, ON, N4W 1M6
(519) 291-5500
Emp Here 47
SIC 5411 Grocery stores

D-U-N-S 24-978-1576   (BR)
METROLAND MEDIA GROUP LTD
LISTOWEL BANNER & INDEPENDENT
185 Wallace Ave N, Listowel, ON, N4W 1K8
(519) 291-1660
Emp Here 25
SIC 2711 Newspapers

D-U-N-S 20-916-1913   (BR)
PREMIER EQUIPMENT LTD.
Gd Lcd Main, Listowel, ON, N4W 3H1
(519) 291-5390
Emp Here 25
SIC 5999 Miscellaneous retail stores, nec

D-U-N-S 25-181-4026   (BR)
QUALIDEC CORPORATION
MCDONALD'S

---

970 Wallace Ave N, Listowel, ON, N4W 1M5
(519) 291-3653
Emp Here 50
SIC 5812 Eating places

D-U-N-S 25-364-8927   (BR)
SPINRITE LIMITED PARTNERSHIP
320 Livingstone Ave S, Listowel, ON, N4W 3H3
(519) 291-3780
Emp Here 49
SIC 2282 Throwing and winding mills

D-U-N-S 24-826-2107   (SL)
STOP 23 AUTO SALES LTD
910 Wallace Ave N, Listowel, ON, N4W 1M5
(519) 291-5757
Emp Here 20   *Sales* 42,614,042
SIC 5511 New and used car dealers
Pr Pr Scott Davidson

Little Britain, ON K0M

D-U-N-S 20-031-1574   (BR)
TRILLIUM LAKELANDS DISTRICT SCHOOL BOARD
DR GEORGE HALL PUBLIC SCHOOL
374 Eldon Rd, Little Britain, ON, K0M 2C0
(705) 786-1915
Emp Here 45
SIC 8211 Elementary and secondary schools

Little Current, ON P0P
Manitoulin County

D-U-N-S 24-121-1288   (BR)
GOVERNMENT OF ONTARIO
MNAAMODZAWIN NOOJMOWIN TEG HEALTH CENTRE
48 Hillside Dr Rr 1, Little Current, ON, P0P 1K0
(705) 368-2182
Emp Here 45
SIC 8099 Health and allied services, nec

D-U-N-S 20-850-0041   (SL)
MANITOULIN CENTENNIAL MANOR
70 Robinson St, Little Current, ON, P0P 1K0
(705) 368-2710
Emp Here 65   *Sales* 2,407,703
SIC 8361 Residential care

D-U-N-S 25-238-2015   (BR)
RAINBOW DISTRICT SCHOOL BOARD
LITTLE CURRENT PUBLIC SCHOOL
(Suby of Rainbow District School Board)
18 Draper St, Little Current, ON, P0P 1K0
(705) 368-2932
Emp Here 30
SIC 8211 Elementary and secondary schools

Lively, ON P3Y
Sudbury County

D-U-N-S 24-124-4560   (BR)
ABS MANUFACTURING AND DISTRIBUTING LIMITED
ABRAFLEX SANDBLASTING & PAINTING
235 Fielding Rd, Lively, ON, P3Y 1L8

Emp Here 20
SIC 3471 Plating and polishing

D-U-N-S 25-362-4217   (BR)
AMEC FOSTER WHEELER AMERICAS LIMITED
EARTH & ENVIRONMENTAL
131 Fielding Rd, Lively, ON, P3Y 1L7

---

(705) 682-2632
Emp Here 45
SIC 8748 Business consulting, nec

D-U-N-S 24-868-7225　(BR)
ANMAR MECHANICAL AND ELECTRICAL CONTRACTORS LTD
199 Mumford Rd, Lively, ON, P3Y 0A4
(705) 692-0888
Emp Here 49
SIC 3312 Blast furnaces and steel mills

D-U-N-S 24-374-1837　(BR)
ATLAS COPCO CANADA INC
ATLAS COPCO CONSTRUCTION AND MINING CANADA, DIV OF
200 Mumford Rd Suite A, Lively, ON, P3Y 1L2
(705) 673-6711
Emp Here 150
SIC 5082 Construction and mining machinery

D-U-N-S 24-566-6677　(BR)
BREWERS RETAIL INC
BEER STORE DISTRIBUTION CENTRE, THE
50 Vagnini Crt, Lively, ON, P3Y 1K8
(705) 692-7663
Emp Here 30
SIC 5921 Liquor stores

D-U-N-S 20-155-5229　(SL)
CSH MEADOWBROOK INC
18 Jacobson Dr Suite 1, Lively, ON, P3Y 1P7
(705) 692-1832
Emp Here 24　*Sales* 1,507,726
SIC 8052 Intermediate care facilities

D-U-N-S 25-451-8744　(SL)
DEANGELO BROTHERS CORPORATION
DDI SERVICE
400 Regional Rd 55, Lively, ON, P3Y 0B1
(705) 885-1246
Emp Here 60
SIC 4173 Bus terminal and service facilities

D-U-N-S 25-641-7247　(BR)
EQUIPMENT SALES & SERVICE LIMITED
15 Mumford Rd, Lively, ON, P3Y 1K9
(705) 692-7278
Emp Here 20
SIC 5082 Construction and mining machinery

D-U-N-S 24-924-4773　(BR)
FLANAGAN FOODSERVICE INC
69 Magill St, Lively, ON, P3Y 1K6
(705) 692-5850
Emp Here 35
SIC 5141 Groceries, general line

D-U-N-S 20-321-4879　(BR)
GARDEWINE GROUP INC
30 Duhamel Rd, Lively, ON, P3Y 1L4
(705) 692-3000
Emp Here 50
SIC 4731 Freight transportation arrangement

D-U-N-S 20-057-6762　(BR)
HARRIS STEEL ULC
HARRIS REBAR
(*Suby of* Nucor Corporation)
152 Fielding Rd, Lively, ON, P3Y 1L5
(705) 682-1222
Emp Here 20
SIC 5051 Metals service centers and offices

D-U-N-S 25-116-1865　(SL)
INDUSTRIAL FABRICATION INC
240 Fielding Rd, Lively, ON, P3Y 1L6
(705) 523-1621
Emp Here 52　*Sales* 16,584,990
SIC 3532 Mining machinery
　Daryl Rautiainen
Pr Pr Paul Villgren
　Peter Villgren

D-U-N-S 20-901-3010　(BR)
INTEGRATED DISTRIBUTION SYSTEMS LIMITED PARTNERSHIP
WAJAX POWER SYSTEMS

30 Vagnini Crt, Lively, ON, P3Y 1K8
(705) 692-0707
Emp Here 27
SIC 5084 Industrial machinery and equipment

D-U-N-S 24-424-6864　(BR)
INTEGRATED DISTRIBUTION SYSTEMS LIMITED PARTNERSHIP
WAJAX EQUIPMENT
140 Magill St, Lively, ON, P3Y 1K7
(705) 692-3656
Emp Here 20
SIC 5084 Industrial machinery and equipment

D-U-N-S 20-754-5401　(SL)
LAAMANEN CONSTRUCTION LIMITED
(*Suby of* Black Lake Investments Ltd)
129 Fielding Rd, Lively, ON, P3Y 1L7

Emp Here 60　*Sales* 16,378,240
SIC 1541 Industrial buildings and warehouses
Pr Pr Risto Laamanen
　Aino Laamanen

D-U-N-S 24-246-0876　(SL)
MCDONALD GENERAL SERVICES CORP
125 Magill St Unit B, Lively, ON, P3Y 1K6
(705) 556-0172
Emp Here 51　*Sales* 4,450,603
SIC 1731 Electrical work

D-U-N-S 25-604-1252　(BR)
NORTRAX CANADA INC
(*Suby of* Deere & Company)
199 Mumford Rd Unit F, Lively, ON, P3Y 0A4
(705) 692-7272
Emp Here 20
SIC 5084 Industrial machinery and equipment

D-U-N-S 25-118-4842　(BR)
RCR INDUSTRIAL INC
25 Fielding Rd, Lively, ON, P3Y 1L7
(705) 682-0623
Emp Here 120
SIC 3532 Mining machinery

D-U-N-S 25-228-0672　(BR)
RAINBOW DISTRICT SCHOOL BOARD
LIVELY DISTRICT SECONDARY SCHOOL
(*Suby of* Rainbow District School Board)
265 Fifth Ave Suite 430, Lively, ON, P3Y 1M4
(705) 671-5940
Emp Here 45
SIC 8211 Elementary and secondary schools

D-U-N-S 20-710-3982　(BR)
RAINBOW DISTRICT SCHOOL BOARD
GEORGE VANIER PUBLIC SCHOOL
249 Sixth Ave Suite 340, Lively, ON, P3Y 1M4
(705) 692-3602
Emp Here 30
SIC 8211 Elementary and secondary schools

D-U-N-S 24-826-0890　(BR)
SANDVIK CANADA, INC
SANDVIK MINING AND CONSTRUCTION
100 Magill St, Lively, ON, P3Y 1K7
(705) 692-5881
Emp Here 100
SIC 5051 Metals service centers and offices

D-U-N-S 25-304-9175　(BR)
TOROMONT INDUSTRIES LTD
25 Mumford Rd, Lively, ON, P3Y 1K9
(705) 692-4764
Emp Here 75
SIC 5082 Construction and mining machinery

Lombardy, ON K0G
Leeds County

D-U-N-S 25-483-2173　(BR)
UPPER CANADA DISTRICT SCHOOL BOARD, THE
LOMBARDY PUBLIC SCHOOL

(*Suby of* Upper Canada District School Board, The)
596 15 Hwy, Lombardy, ON, K0G 1L0
(613) 283-0860
Emp Here 30
SIC 8211 Elementary and secondary schools

Londesborough, ON N0M
Huron County

D-U-N-S 24-053-3625　(BR)
HENSALL DISTRICT CO-OPERATIVE, INCORPORATED
HENSALL DISTRICT CO-OP
306 King St, Londesborough, ON, N0M 2H0
(519) 523-9606
Emp Here 30
SIC 2048 Prepared feeds, nec

London, ON N5V
Middlesex County

D-U-N-S 20-809-9932　(SL)
1498882 ONTARIO INC
EAST SIDE MARIO'S
1915 Dundas St Suite Side, London, ON, N5V 5J9
(519) 451-5737
Emp Here 85　*Sales* 2,553,625
SIC 5812 Eating places

D-U-N-S 24-387-4398　(BR)
3M CANADA COMPANY
(*Suby of* 3M Company)
801 Clarke Rd, London, ON, N5V 3B3
(519) 452-6139
Emp Here 20
SIC 2891 Adhesives and sealants

D-U-N-S 20-127-9676　(HQ)
3M CANADA COMPANY
(*Suby of* 3M Company)
300 Tartan Dr, London, ON, N5V 4M9
(519) 451-2500
Emp Here 1,200　*Emp Total* 91,584
Sales 145,921,400
SIC 2891 Adhesives and sealants
Pr Inge G. Thulin
　George W Buckley
　Patrick Campbell
　Linda G Alvarado
　Vance Coffman
　Michael Eskew
　W. James Farrell

D-U-N-S 24-192-5387　(SL)
469006 ONTARIO INC
METROPOLITAN MAINTENANCE
163 Stronach Cres, London, ON, N5V 3G5
(519) 679-8810
Emp Here 140　*Sales* 4,085,799
SIC 7349 Building maintenance services, nec

D-U-N-S 24-215-6776　(HQ)
947465 ONTARIO LTD
VOYAGEUR TRANSPORTATION SERVICES
573 Admiral Crt, London, ON, N5V 4L3
(519) 455-1390
Emp Here 580　*Emp Total* 1
Sales 17,218,725
SIC 4151 School buses
Pr Pr Perry Ferguson
　Dwayne Ferguson

D-U-N-S 20-059-4252　(SL)
ADJ HOLDINGS INC
AMT
(*Suby of* 1307815 Ontario Limited)
2068 Piper Ln, London, ON, N5V 3N6
(519) 455-4065
Emp Here 50　*Sales* 3,064,349

SIC 7692 Welding repair

D-U-N-S 20-547-5077　(BR)
ANAGO (NON) RESIDENTIAL RESOURCES INC
1670 Oxford St E, London, ON, N5V 3G2

Emp Here 48
SIC 8361 Residential care

D-U-N-S 24-253-1908　(BR)
ARBOR MEMORIAL SERVICES INC
FOREST LAWN MEMORIAL PROPERTY MANAGEMENT
2001 Dundas St, London, ON, N5V 1P6
(519) 451-2410
Emp Here 20
SIC 6531 Real estate agents and managers

D-U-N-S 24-378-8796　(BR)
AUTONEUM CANADA LTD
RIETER AUTOMOTIVE CANADA CARPET
1800 Huron St, London, ON, N5V 3A6
(519) 659-5752
Emp Here 300
SIC 2299 Textile goods, nec

D-U-N-S 20-126-7556　(BR)
BRINK'S CANADA LIMITED
BRINK'S
(*Suby of* The Brink's Company)
1495 Spanner St, London, ON, N5V 1Z1
(519) 659-3457
Emp Here 100
SIC 7381 Detective and armored car services

D-U-N-S 24-860-4303　(BR)
CANTWELL CULLEN & COMPANY INC
ZODIAC INTERCONNECT CANADA
10 Artisans Cres, London, ON, N5V 4N6
(519) 659-1107
Emp Here 40
SIC 3492 Fluid power valves and hose fittings

D-U-N-S 20-057-7000　(BR)
CARGILL LIMITED
CARGILL VALUE ADDED MEATS
10 Cuddy Blvd, London, ON, N5V 5E3
(519) 453-4996
Emp Here 900
SIC 2015 Poultry slaughtering and processing

D-U-N-S 24-007-4930　(HQ)
CHILDREN'S AID SOCIETY OF LONDON & MIDDLESEX
(*Suby of* Children's Aid Society of London & Middlesex)
1680 Oxford St E, London, ON, N5V 3G2
(519) 455-9000
Emp Here 250　*Emp Total* 450
Sales 24,316,160
SIC 8322 Individual and family services
Pr Peter Regier
VP Ward Coulson
Dir John Liston
Dir Fin Randy Hall

D-U-N-S 20-127-3109　(HQ)
CIE MCCORMICK CANADA CO., LA
INDUSTRIAL, DIV OF
600 Clarke Rd, London, ON, N5V 3K5
(519) 432-7311
Emp Here 415　*Emp Total* 10,500
Sales 50,707,687
SIC 2099 Food preparations, nec
Pr Pr Angela Francolini
　Frank Snyder
　Fred Fretz
VP VP David Grimshaw
　Brian E. Rainey
　Dennis R. Luc
　Carman Hamilton
　Keith Gibbons
Dir David Smith
Dir Beverley Tschirhart

D-U-N-S 24-383-8641　(BR)
CIE MCCORMICK CANADA CO., LA

600 Clarke Rd, London, ON, N5V 3K5
(519) 432-1166
Emp Here 50
SIC 4225 General warehousing and storage

D-U-N-S 24-323-5608   (HQ)
COLABOR LIMITED PARTNERSHIP
SUMMIT FOOD SERVICE DISTRIBUTORS, DIV OF
(*Suby of* Groupe Colabor Inc)
580 Industrial Rd, London, ON, N5V 1V1
(800) 265-9267
Emp Here 500   *Emp Total* 500
Sales 279 452,573
SIC 5141 Groceries, general line
Genl Mgr Claude Gariepy

D-U-N-S 20-699-1817   (BR)
COLABOR LIMITED PARTNERSHIP
SUMMIT FOOD SERVICE, A DIVISION OF COLABOR
(*Suby of* Groupe Colabor Inc)
580 Industrial Rd, London, ON, N5V 1V1
(519) 453-3410
Emp Here 150
SIC 5141 Groceries, general line

D-U-N-S 20-126-9883   (HQ)
COURTNEY WHOLESALE CONFEC-TIONERY LIMITED
(*Suby of* Courtney, L. A. Holdings Ltd)
600 Third St, London, ON, N5V 2C2
(519) 451-7440
Emp Here 89   *Emp Total* 140
Sales 24,952,559
SIC 5145 Confectionery
Pr Pr Michael Courtney
Lloyd Courtney

D-U-N-S 24-985-9356   (HQ)
CRAIG EVAN CORPORATION, THE
FLIGHTEXEC
2480 Huron St Unit 3, London, ON, N5V 0B1
(519) 455-6760
Emp Here 25   *Emp Total* 70
Sales 11,779,113
SIC 4899 Communication services, nec
Pr Pr Nick Erb
Michel Boucher

D-U-N-S 25-220-5158   (BR)
CRAWFORD METAL CORPORATION
(*Suby of* Crawford Metal Corporation)
3101 Gore Rd, London, ON, N5V 5C8
(519) 659-2080
Emp Here 40
SIC 5051 Metals service centers and offices

D-U-N-S 24-965-9145   (SL)
DIAMOND AIRCRAFT INDUSTRIES INC
1560 Cruml n, London, ON, N5V 1S2
(519) 457-4000
Emp Here 230   *Sales* 37,866,603
SIC 3721 Aircraft
Pr Peter Maurer

D-U-N-S 20-013-5569   (HQ)
DOCK PRODUCTS CANADA INC
639 Sovereign Rd Unit 3 & 4, London, ON, N5V 4K8
(519) 457-7 55
Emp Here 20   *Emp Total* 200
Sales 23,584,469
SIC 1799 Special trade contractors, nec
Kelly Esquimaux
VP VP Steven Flear
Pr Pr Keith Moore
Paul Venesky

D-U-N-S 25-729-2466   (BR)
DYNAMEX CANADA LIMITED
SAMEDAY COURIER
2515 Blair Blvd Suite B, London, ON, N5V 3Z9
(519) 659-8224
Emp Here 80
SIC 7389 Business services, nec

D-U-N-S 20-278-6443   (BR)

ELECTROZAD SUPPLY COMPANY LIM-ITED
500 Industrial Rd, London, ON, N5V 1T7
(519) 452-3444
Emp Here 25
SIC 5063 Electrical apparatus and equipment

D-U-N-S 20-127-1475   (HQ)
ELLISDON CONSTRUCTION LTD
2045 Oxford St E, London, ON, N5V 2Z7
(519) 455-6770
Emp Here 80   *Emp Total* 1,300
Sales 237,778,921
SIC 1541 Industrial buildings and warehouses
Pr Pr Geoffrey Smith
Jim King
VP Fin VP Fin John Bernhardt

D-U-N-S 24-343-7410   (BR)
FGL SPORTS LTD
SPORT CHEK ARGYLE MALL
1925 Dundas St Unit 14, London, ON, N5V 1P7
(519) 457-4848
Emp Here 25
SIC 5941 Sporting goods and bicycle shops

D-U-N-S 24-484-1250   (HQ)
FARM BUSINESS CONSULTANTS INC
FBC
2109 Oxford St E, London, ON, N5V 2Z9
(519) 453-5040
Emp Here 50   *Emp Total* 150
Sales 4,961,328
SIC 7291 Tax return preparation services

D-U-N-S 25-527-3989   (BR)
FLYNN CANADA LTD
550 Sovereign Rd, London, ON, N5V 4K5
(519) 681-0200
Emp Here 45
SIC 1761 Roofing, siding, and sheetMetal work

D-U-N-S 20-974-8334   (BR)
G&K SERVICES CANADA INC
(*Suby of* Cintas Corporation)
420 Industrial Rd, London, ON, N5V 1T5
(519) 455-4850
Emp Here 24
SIC 7213 Linen supply

D-U-N-S 24-312-1717   (BR)
GENERAL DYNAMICS LAND SYSTEMS - CANADA CORPORATION
(*Suby of* General Dynamics Corporation)
2035 Oxford St E, London, ON, N5V 2Z7
(519) 964-5900
Emp Here 350
SIC 3711 Motor vehicles and car bodies

D-U-N-S 20-175-6876   (HQ)
GENERAL DYNAMICS LAND SYSTEMS - CANADA CORPORATION
(*Suby of* General Dynamics Corporation)
1991 Oxford St E Bldg 15, London, ON, N5V 2Z7
(519) 964-5900
Emp Here 2,000   *Emp Total* 98,800
Sales 551,282,136
SIC 3711 Motor vehicles and car bodies
Dir Charles M. Hall
Dir Michael J. Mancuso
Dir David A. Savner
Dir Arthur J. Veitch

D-U-N-S 20-333-5596   (BR)
GOODLIFE FITNESS CENTRES INC
ARGYLLE CLUB
1925 Dundas St, London, ON, N5V 1P7
(519) 451-9026
Emp Here 20
SIC 7991 Physical fitness facilities

D-U-N-S 25-629-1113   (BR)
INGENIERIE CARMICHAEL LTEE
(*Suby of* Gestions Miller Carmichael Inc)
1909 Oxford St E Suite 45, London, ON, N5V

4L9
(519) 652-7667
Emp Here 25
SIC 1711 Plumbing, heating, air-conditioning

D-U-N-S 25-093-4721   (BR)
INTEGRATED DISTRIBUTION SYSTEMS LIMITED PARTNERSHIP
WAJAX POWER SYSTEMS
(*Suby of* Integrated Distribution Systems Limited Partnership)
571 Industrial Rd, London, ON, N5V 1V2
(519) 455-7410
Emp Here 21
SIC 5084 Industrial machinery and equipment

D-U-N-S 24-408-4588   (HQ)
J-AAR EXCAVATING LIMITED
AAROC EQUIPMENT
(*Suby of* J-Aar Excavating Limited)
3003 Page St, London, ON, N5V 4J1
(519) 652-2104
Emp Here 60   *Emp Total* 65
Sales 4,742,446
SIC 1794 Excavation work

D-U-N-S 20-127-7910   (SL)
J.A. MACDONALD LONDON) LIMITED
530 Admiral Dr, London, ON, N5V 0B2
(519) 453-1000
Emp Here 50   *Sales* 4,231,721
SIC 1742 Plastering, drywall, and insulation

D-U-N-S 20-589-7473   (SL)
KAISER ALUMINUM CANADA LIMITED
KAISER ALUMINUM
(*Suby of* Kaiser Aluminum Corporation)
3021 Gore Rd, London, ON, N5V 5A9
(519) 457-3610
Emp Here 200   *Sales* 33,561,922
SIC 3354 Aluminum extruded products
Pr Pr Jack Hockema
Dir Cindy Marks

D-U-N-S 24-817-1852   (BR)
LAWSON PRODUCTS INC (ONTARIO)
NEWARK ELECTRONICS
1919 Trafalgar St, London, ON, N5V 1A1
(519) 685-4280
Emp Here 20
SIC 5065 Electronic parts and equipment, nec

D-U-N-S 24-938-0601   (BR)
LEE VALLEY TOOLS LTD
2100 Oxford St E Suite 11, London, ON, N5V 4A4
(519) 659-7981
Emp Here 20
SIC 5251 Hardware stores

D-U-N-S 25-650-9639   (BR)
LONDON BRIDGE CHILD CARE SERVICES INC
HURON HEIGHTS EARLY CHILDHOOD LEARNING CENTER
1305 Webster St, London, ON, N5V 3P8
(519) 453-9570
Emp Here 26
SIC 8351 Child day care services

D-U-N-S 20-412-9811   (SL)
LONDON CAULKING AND INSTALLATIONS LIMITED
553 Clarke Rd, London, ON, N5V 2E1
(519) 451-4899
Emp Here 50   *Sales* 4,377,642
SIC 1799 Special trade contractors, nec

D-U-N-S 20-710-5177   (BR)
LONDON DISTRICT CATHOLIC SCHOOL BOARD
JOHN PAUL LL CATHOLIC SECONDARY SCHOOL
1300 Oxford St E, London, ON, N5V 4P7
(519) 675-4432
Emp Here 50
SIC 8211 Elementary and secondary schools

D-U-N-S 25-237-8740   (BR)
LONDON DISTRICT CATHOLIC SCHOOL BOARD
ST ROBERT CATHOLIC ELEMENTARY SCHOOL
1958 Duluth Cres, London, ON, N5V 1H7
(519) 453-3770
Emp Here 25
SIC 8211 Elementary and secondary schools

D-U-N-S 25-237-8443   (BR)
LONDON DISTRICT CATHOLIC SCHOOL BOARD
ST ANNES CATHOLIC SCHOOL
1366 Huron St, London, ON, N5V 2E2
(519) 675-4417
Emp Here 28
SIC 8211 Elementary and secondary schools

D-U-N-S 25-237-8526   (BR)
LONDON DISTRICT CATHOLIC SCHOOL BOARD
HOLY FAMILY ELEMENTARY SCHOOL
329 Hudson Dr, London, ON, N5V 1E4
(519) 675-4413
Emp Here 25
SIC 8211 Elementary and secondary schools

D-U-N-S 25-318-1499   (BR)
MCDONALD'S RESTAURANTS OF CANADA LIMITED
MCDONALD'S RESTAURANT
(*Suby of* McDonald's Corporation)
1950 Dundas St, London, ON, N5V 1P5
(519) 451-5590
Emp Here 20
SIC 5812 Eating places

D-U-N-S 20-175-6058   (BR)
NAV CANADA
NAV CANADA FLIGHT SERVICES
2530 Blair Blvd, London, ON, N5V 3Z9
(519) 452-4008
Emp Here 60
SIC 4899 Communication services, nec

D-U-N-S 24-425-0531   (BR)
ONTARIO LOTTERY AND GAMING CORPO-RATION
OLG LONDON DISTRIBUTION CENTRE
554 First St, London, ON, N5V 1Z3
(519) 659-1551
Emp Here 40
SIC 7999 Amusement and recreation, nec

D-U-N-S 20-859-8941   (BR)
PACIFIC LINK COMMUNICATIONS INC
BELL WORLD
1920 Dundas St, London, ON, N5V 3P1
(519) 451-5120
Emp Here 25
SIC 5999 Miscellaneous retail stores, nec

D-U-N-S 24-337-2211   (BR)
PHILON RESTAURANTS INC
PIZZA HUT
1326 Huron St, London, ON, N5V 2E2
(519) 455-0172
Emp Here 40
SIC 5812 Eating places

D-U-N-S 24-875-1182   (BR)
PRAXAIR CANADA INC
(*Suby of* Praxair, Inc.)
1910 Oxford St E, London, ON, N5V 2Z8
(519) 451-7931
Emp Here 20
SIC 5084 Industrial machinery and equipment

D-U-N-S 25-359-6035   (BR)
RICHVALE YORK BLOCK INC
1298 Clarke Rd, London, ON, N5V 3B5
(519) 455-4741
Emp Here 20
SIC 3271 Concrete block and brick

D-U-N-S 25-367-7389   (BR)
SHRED-IT INTERNATIONAL ULC

15825 Robin'S Hill Rd Unit 2, London, ON, N5V 0A5
(519) 641-8060
Emp Here 20
SIC 7389 Business services, nec

D-U-N-S 24-199-5497   (SL)
SKYLINE ELEVATOR INC
410 Industrial Rd, London, ON, N5V 1T5
(519) 659-2700
Emp Here 30   *Sales* 3,064,349
SIC 1796 Installing building equipment

D-U-N-S 24-850-5083   (HQ)
SLE-CO PLASTICS INC
1425 Creamery Rd, London, ON, N5V 5B3
(519) 451-3748
Emp Here 60   *Emp Total* 45
Sales 16,925,435
SIC 3089 Plastics products, nec
Pr Pr Jeffrey Sleegers

D-U-N-S 25-528-2428   (SL)
SPECIALIZED PACKAGING (LONDON) COMPANY ULC
(*Suby of* Sun Capital Partners, Inc.)
5 Cuddy Blvd, London, ON, N5V 3Y3
(519) 659-7011
Emp Here 200   *Sales* 20,428,996
SIC 2679 Converted paper products, nec
Pr Pr Carlton Highsmith

D-U-N-S 25-812-3363   (BR)
SPEEDY TRANSPORT GROUP INC
SPEEDY CARTAGE & TRANSPORT
535 Industrial Rd, London, ON, N5V 1T9
(519) 453-1673
Emp Here 45
SIC 4212 Local trucking, without storage

D-U-N-S 25-213-7344   (BR)
STAPLES CANADA INC
STAPLES THE BUSINESS DEPOT
(*Suby of* Staples, Inc.)
1925 Dundas St, London, ON, N5V 1P7
(519) 659-3428
Emp Here 25
SIC 5943 Stationery stores

D-U-N-S 20-806-4340   (BR)
STARBUCKS COFFEE CANADA, INC
(*Suby of* Starbucks Corporation)
162 Dundas St, London, ON, N5V 1A1
(519) 434-2424
Emp Here 25
SIC 5812 Eating places

D-U-N-S 24-153-8391   (BR)
STOCK TRANSPORTATION LTD
501 Third St, London, ON, N5V 2C1

Emp Here 200
SIC 4151 School buses

D-U-N-S 24-974-3832   (BR)
TFI INTERNATIONAL INC
TRANSFORCE INC
540 First St, London, ON, N5V 1Z3

Emp Here 20
SIC 4213 Trucking, except local

D-U-N-S 24-333-8667   (HQ)
TSC STORES L.P.
1000 Clarke Rd, London, ON, N5V 3A9
(519) 453-5270
Emp Here 80   *Emp Total* 538
Sales 114,085,257
SIC 5251 Hardware stores
David Roussy

D-U-N-S 20-068-0762   (BR)
THAMES VALLEY DISTRICT SCHOOL BOARD
HURON HEIGHTS FRENCH IMMERSION PUBLIC SCHOOL
1245 Michael St, London, ON, N5V 2H4
(519) 452-8230
Emp Here 25

SIC 8211 Elementary and secondary schools

D-U-N-S 25-239-9498   (BR)
THAMES VALLEY DISTRICT SCHOOL BOARD
JOHN P. ROBARTS ELEMENTARY PUBLIC SCHOOL
84 Bow St, London, ON, N5V 1B1
(519) 452-8270
Emp Here 50
SIC 8211 Elementary and secondary schools

D-U-N-S 20-590-5875   (BR)
THAMES VALLEY DISTRICT SCHOOL BOARD
LORD NELSON PUBLIC SCHOOL
1990 Royal Cres, London, ON, N5V 1N8
(519) 452-8320
Emp Here 25
SIC 8211 Elementary and secondary schools

D-U-N-S 20-710-5342   (BR)
THAMES VALLEY DISTRICT SCHOOL BOARD
EVELYN HARRISON PUBLIC SCHOOL
50 Tewksbury Cres, London, ON, N5V 2M8
(519) 452-8180
Emp Here 50
SIC 8211 Elementary and secondary schools

D-U-N-S 20-590-5818   (BR)
THAMES VALLEY DISTRICT SCHOOL BOARD
BONAVENTURE MEADOWS PUBLIC SCHOOL
141 Bonaventure Dr, London, ON, N5V 4S6
(519) 452-8060
Emp Here 50
SIC 8211 Elementary and secondary schools

D-U-N-S 20-070-9371   (BR)
THAMES VALLEY DISTRICT SCHOOL BOARD
ROOSEVELT PUBLIC SCHOOL
560 Second St, London, ON, N5V 2B7
(519) 452-8190
Emp Here 30
SIC 8211 Elementary and secondary schools

D-U-N-S 20-590-5719   (BR)
THAMES VALLEY DISTRICT SCHOOL BOARD
CHIPPEWA PUBLIC SCHOOL
1035 Chippewa Dr, London, ON, N5V 2T6
(519) 452-8120
Emp Here 50
SIC 8211 Elementary and secondary schools

D-U-N-S 24-195-2055   (BR)
THRIFT MAGIC LP
1345 Huron St Suite 1a, London, ON, N5V 2E3
(519) 455-1112
Emp Here 30
SIC 5651 Family clothing stores

D-U-N-S 25-283-2399   (BR)
TOROMONT INDUSTRIES LTD
BATTLEFIELD EQUIPMENT RENTALS
1901 Oxford St E, London, ON, N5V 2Z6
(519) 453-3000
Emp Here 20
SIC 7353 Heavy construction equipment rental

D-U-N-S 20-264-6258   (BR)
TRIOS COLLEGE BUSINESS TECHNOLOGY HEALTHCARE INC
520 First St Suite 1, London, ON, N5V 3C6
(519) 455-0551
Emp Here 20
SIC 8221 Colleges and universities

D-U-N-S 20-553-0657   (SL)
TRUDELL MEDICAL INTERNATIONAL EUROPE LIMITED
(*Suby of* Trudell Medical Limited)
725 Third St, London, ON, N5V 5G4

(519) 455-7060
Emp Here 30   *Sales* 5,653,974
SIC 5047 Medical and hospital equipment
Pr Mitchell Baran
VP VP Mark Pickard

D-U-N-S 24-860-9042   (HQ)
TRUDELL MEDICAL MARKETING LIMITED
(*Suby of* Trudell Medical Limited)
758 Third St, London, ON, N5V 5J7
(519) 685-8800
Emp Here 73   *Emp Total* 25
Sales 14,154,376
SIC 5047 Medical and hospital equipment
Pr Gerald Slemko

D-U-N-S 25-743-2781   (BR)
VITRAN EXPLUS CANADA
420 Industrial Rd Unit 2, London, ON, N5V 1T5
(519) 659-8505
Emp Here 25
SIC 4731 Freight transportation arrangement

D-U-N-S 24-092-9641   (BR)
VITRAN EXPRESS CANADA INC
VITRAN TRANSPORTATION
420 Industrial Rd Unit B, London, ON, N5V 1T5
(519) 659-8505
Emp Here 20
SIC 4213 Trucking, except local

D-U-N-S 24-624-0522   (HQ)
VOYAGEUR PATIENT TRANSFER SERVICES INC
573 Admiral Crt, London, ON, N5V 4L3
(519) 455-4579
Emp Here 75   *Emp Total* 1
Sales 16,981,120
SIC 4111 Local and suburban transit
Pr Pr Perry Ferguson

D-U-N-S 24-803-0202   (BR)
WABTEC CANADA INC
UNIFIN INTERNATIONAL, DIV OF
1030 Clarke Rd Suite Side, London, ON, N5V 3B2
(519) 451-0310
Emp Here 25
SIC 3564 Blowers and fans

D-U-N-S 20-184-3138   (BR)
WINNERS MERCHANTS INTERNATIONAL L.P.
WINNERS
(*Suby of* The TJX Companies Inc)
1925 Dundas St, London, ON, N5V 1P7
(519) 451-0872
Emp Here 40
SIC 5651 Family clothing stores

London, ON N5W
Middlesex County

D-U-N-S 20-345-5423   (SL)
2518879 ONTARIO INC
JUST COZY
1712 Dundas St, London, ON, N5W 3C9
(519) 659-8725
Emp Here 54   *Sales* 4,331,255
SIC 5621 Women's clothing stores

D-U-N-S 24-622-2392   (SL)
411930 ONTARIO LIMITED
H & G POWDER PAINTING, DIV OF
379 Highbury Ave N, London, ON, N5W 5K8
(519) 455-9090
Emp Here 41   *Sales* 2,845,467
SIC 3479 Metal coating and allied services

D-U-N-S 25-633-6744   (HQ)
625147 ONTARIO LTD
DOVE DENTAL CENTRE
(*Suby of* 625147 Ontario Ltd)
1657 Dundas St E, Unit # 1, London, ON, N5W

3C6
(519) 679-3683
Emp Here 30   *Emp Total* 50
Sales 2,845,467
SIC 8021 Offices and clinics of dentists

D-U-N-S 25-785-8050   (BR)
AFA FOREST PRODUCTS INC
98 Clarke Rd, London, ON, N5W 5M9
(519) 457-2311
Emp Here 20
SIC 5031 Lumber, plywood, and millwork

D-U-N-S 20-358-9051   (BR)
AGF - REBAR INC
AGF - REBAR (DIETRICH DIVISION)
120 Mcmillan St, London, ON, N5W 6C6
(519) 455-2540
Emp Here 50
SIC 1791 Structural steel erection

D-U-N-S 20-732-4273   (BR)
AIR LIQUIDE CANADA INC
351 Eleanor St, London, ON, N5W 6B7
(519) 455-3990
Emp Here 25
SIC 3548 Welding apparatus

D-U-N-S 24-976-9001   (SL)
AUTODATA SOLUTIONS COMPANY
CHROME SOLUTIONS
(*Suby of* Internet Brands, Inc.)
345 Saskatoon St, London, ON, N5W 4R4
(519) 451-2323
Emp Here 230   *Sales* 40,708,613
SIC 7371 Custom computer programming services
Pr Pr Gregory Perrier
VP Maureen Morton
VP Fin Neal James
Pt Keten Ramji
VP Hans Otten
Ex VP Chris Wedermann
Sr VP Tom Trowsdale

D-U-N-S 20-936-8757   (SL)
CASEY'S GRILL AND BAR
310 Clarke Rd, London, ON, N5W 6G4
(519) 455-4392
Emp Here 60   *Sales* 1,824,018
SIC 5812 Eating places

D-U-N-S 25-075-4335   (SL)
CHROME DATA SOLUTIONS, LP
345 Saskatoon St, London, ON, N5W 4R4
(519) 451-2323
Emp Here 240   *Sales* 42,593,271
SIC 7371 Custom computer programming services
Pr Gregory Perrier

D-U-N-S 20-190-1266   (BR)
CINTAS CANADA LIMITED
(*Suby of* Cintas Corporation)
30 Charterhouse Cres, London, ON, N5W 5V5
(519) 453-5010
Emp Here 130
SIC 7218 Industrial launderers

D-U-N-S 20-139-8919   (BR)
CITRON HYGIENE LP
CANNON HYGIENE CANADA
(*Suby of* Citron Hygiene LP)
15 Charterhouse Cresent, London, ON, N5W 5V3
(519) 471-6512
Emp Here 29
SIC 7342 Disinfecting and pest control services

D-U-N-S 20-179-3853   (BR)
CLEAN HARBORS CANADA, INC
2258 River Rd, London, ON, N5W 6C2

Emp Here 30
SIC 4953 Refuse systems

D-U-N-S 25-369-4665   (BR)
COMMISSIONAIRES GREAT LAKES

1730 Dundas St, London, ON, N5W 3E2
(519) 433-6763
Emp Here 200
SIC 7381 Detective and armored car services

D-U-N-S 25-403-7484   (BR)
**COMPAGNIE DES CHEMINS DE FER NA-
TIONAUX DU CANADA**
363 Egerton St, London, ON, N5W 6B1

Emp Here 150
SIC 7699 Repair services, nec

D-U-N-S 20-578-3215   (BR)
CONSEIL SCOLAIRE VIAMONDE
ACADEMIE DE LA TAMISE
1260 Dundas St, London, ON, N5W 5P2
(519) 659-3174
Emp Here 22
SIC 8299 Schools and educational services,
nec

D-U-N-S 25-988-4278   (BR)
CORPORATION OF THE CITY OF LONDON
RIVER ROAD GOLF COURSE
2115 River Rd, London, ON, N5W 6C4
(519) 661-1951
Emp Here 22
SIC 7992 Public golf courses

D-U-N-S 20-610-4713   (SL)
CUMBERLAND, K. W. LTD
PICADILLY SQUARE
825 Central Ave, London, ON, N5W 3R1
(519) 679-8845
Emp Here 70   *Sales* 9,739,200
SIC 5331 Variety stores
Pr Pr Ken Cumberland
VP VP Paul Yorke
    Penny Cumberland
    Gary Judd

D-U-N-S 24-602-1406   (BR)
**GOVERNING COUNCIL OF THE SALVA-
TION ARMY IN CANADA, THE**
1340 Dundas St, London, ON, N5W 3B6
(519) 455-4810
Emp Here 75
SIC 8351 Child day care services

D-U-N-S 24-315-7356   (BR)
HOME DEPOT OF CANADA INC
HOME DEPOT
(*Suby of* The Home Depot Inc)
448 Clarke Rd, London, ON, N5W 6H1
(519) 457-5800
Emp Here 100
SIC 5251 Hardware stores

D-U-N-S 20-126-5717   (SL)
HOMEWAY COMPANY LIMITED
ALUMINUM ASSOCIATES
1801 Trafalgar St, London, ON, N5W 1X7
(519) 453-6400
Emp Here 49   *Sales* 7,223,109
SIC 5211 Lumber and other building materials
Pr Pr Ian Low
    Lillian Low

D-U-N-S 20-710-5193   (BR)
**LONDON DISTRICT CATHOLIC SCHOOL
BOARD**
ST MARY SCHOOL
347 Lyle St, London, ON, N5W 3R3
(519) 675-4423
Emp Here 23
SIC 8211 Elementary and secondary schools

D-U-N-S 20-710-5110   (BR)
**LONDON DISTRICT CATHOLIC SCHOOL
BOARD**
SAINT BERNADETTE CATHOLIC SCHOOL
155 Tweedsmuir Ave, London, ON, N5W 1K9
(519) 675-4418
Emp Here 20
SIC 8211 Elementary and secondary schools

D-U-N-S 25-226-6184   (BR)

**LONDON DISTRICT CATHOLIC SCHOOL
BOARD**
ST. PIUS X SCHOOL
255 Vancouver St, London, ON, N5W 4R9
(519) 675-4427
Emp Here 26
SIC 8211 Elementary and secondary schools

D-U-N-S 20-710-5318   (BR)
**LONDON DISTRICT CATHOLIC SCHOOL
BOARD**
CENTER FOR LIFELONG LEARNING
1230 King St, London, ON, N5W 2Y2
(519) 675-4436
Emp Here 50
SIC 8211 Elementary and secondary schools

D-U-N-S 24-335-0548   (BR)
METRO ONTARIO INC
METRO
155 Clarke Rd, London, ON, N5W 5C9
(519) 455-5604
Emp Here 100
SIC 5411 Grocery stores

D-U-N-S 24-360-7848   (BR)
**ONTARIO LOTTERY AND GAMING CORPO-
RATION**
*WESTERN FAIR RACETRACK SLOTS, DIV
OF*
900 King St, London, ON, N5W 5K3
(519) 672-5394
Emp Here 30
SIC 7999 Amusement and recreation, nec

D-U-N-S 24-187-7948   (BR)
ORKIN CANADA CORPORATION
ORKIN PCO PEST CONTROL
(*Suby of* Rollins, Inc.)
65 Clarke Rd Unit 5, London, ON, N5W 5Y2
(519) 944-1001
Emp Here 27
SIC 7342 Disinfecting and pest control ser-
vices

D-U-N-S 20-974-2811   (BR)
ORKIN CANADA CORPORATION
ORKIN PEST CONTROL
(*Suby of* Rollins, Inc.)
65 Clarke Rd Unit 5, London, ON, N5W 5Y2
(519) 659-2212
Emp Here 26
SIC 7342 Disinfecting and pest control ser-
vices

D-U-N-S 25-446-9422   (BR)
PAYLESS CORP
HERBIE'S DRUG WAREHOUSE
1551 Dundas St Suite 11, London, ON, N5W
5Y5
(519) 451-0510
Emp Here 60
SIC 5912 Drug stores and proprietary stores

D-U-N-S 25-308-4347   (BR)
ROYAL BANK OF CANADA
ROYAL BANK FINANCIAL GROUP
(*Suby of* Royal Bank Of Canada)
1670 Dundas St, London, ON, N5W 3C7
(519) 457-5700
Emp Here 20
SIC 6021 National commercial banks

D-U-N-S 20-068-0796   (BR)
RUSSEL METALS INC
685 Hale St, London, ON, N5W 1J1
(519) 451-1140
Emp Here 25
SIC 5051 Metals service centers and offices

D-U-N-S 20-128-3314   (BR)
RYDER MATERIAL HANDLING ULC
RYDER LIFT TRUCKS
(*Suby of* Crown Equipment Corporation)
2390 Scanlan St, London, ON, N5W 6G8
(519) 451-1144
Emp Here 20
SIC 5084 Industrial machinery and equipment

D-U-N-S 20-590-5834   (BR)
**THAMES VALLEY DISTRICT SCHOOL
BOARD**
PRINCE CHARLES PUBLIC SCHOOL
1601 Wavell St, London, ON, N5W 2C9
(519) 452-8470
Emp Here 50
SIC 8211 Elementary and secondary schools

D-U-N-S 20-710-5409   (BR)
**THAMES VALLEY DISTRICT SCHOOL
BOARD**
*PRINCESS ANNE FRENCH IMMERSION
PUBLIC SCHOOL*
191 Dawn Dr, London, ON, N5W 4W9
(519) 452-8480
Emp Here 50
SIC 8211 Elementary and secondary schools

D-U-N-S 20-590-5727   (BR)
**THAMES VALLEY DISTRICT SCHOOL
BOARD**
FAIRMONT PUBLIC SCHOOL
1040 Hamilton Rd, London, ON, N5W 1A6
(519) 452-8200
Emp Here 50
SIC 8211 Elementary and secondary schools

D-U-N-S 20-070-0669   (BR)
**THAMES VALLEY DISTRICT SCHOOL
BOARD**
W D SUTTON SCHOOL
1250 Dundas St, London, ON, N5W 5P2
(519) 452-8740
Emp Here 42
SIC 8211 Elementary and secondary schools

D-U-N-S 25-458-0491   (BR)
**THAMES VALLEY DISTRICT SCHOOL
BOARD**
ESL ENGLISH AS A 2ND LANGUAGE
1250 Dundas St, London, ON, N5W 5P2
(519) 452-2000
Emp Here 55
SIC 8211 Elementary and secondary schools

D-U-N-S 25-239-9399   (BR)
**THAMES VALLEY DISTRICT SCHOOL
BOARD**
LORNE AVENUE PUBLIC SCHOOL
723 Lorne Ave Suite 715, London, ON, N5W
3K7

Emp Here 35
SIC 8211 Elementary and secondary schools

D-U-N-S 20-590-5990   (BR)
**THAMES VALLEY DISTRICT SCHOOL
BOARD**
TWEEDSMUIR PUBLIC SCHOOL
349 Tweedsmuir Ave, London, ON, N5W 1L5
(519) 452-8620
Emp Here 25
SIC 8211 Elementary and secondary schools

D-U-N-S 24-879-8571   (BR)
TIPPET-RICHARDSON LIMITED
DICKSON VAN LINES
1050 Brydges St, London, ON, N5W 2B4
(519) 455-0132
Emp Here 20
SIC 4212 Local trucking, without storage

D-U-N-S 25-742-6155   (BR)
TWINCORP INC
TACO BELL
1584 Dundas St, London, ON, N5W 3C1
(519) 455-1938
Emp Here 20
SIC 5812 Eating places

D-U-N-S 25-363-8316   (BR)
UAP INC
TRACTION HEAVY DUTY TRUCK PARTS
(*Suby of* Genuine Parts Company)
2405 Scanlan St, London, ON, N5W 6G9
(519) 455-3440
Emp Here 25

SIC 5013 Motor vehicle supplies and new
parts

D-U-N-S 20-783-4664   (BR)
**VICTORIAN ORDER OF NURSES FOR
CANADA**
VON MIDDLESEX-ELGIN MAIN OFFICE
1151 Florence St Suite 100, London, ON,
N5W 2M7
(519) 659-2273
Emp Here 500
SIC 8082 Home health care services

D-U-N-S 25-297-6394   (BR)
WAL-MART CANADA CORP
330 Clarke Rd, London, ON, N5W 6G4
(519) 455-8910
Emp Here 200
SIC 5311 Department stores

D-U-N-S 20-004-7525   (BR)
WENDY'S RESTAURANTS OF CANADA INC
(*Suby of* The Wendy's Company)
676 Highbury Ave N, London, ON, N5W 5R3
(519) 452-3080
Emp Here 30
SIC 5812 Eating places

D-U-N-S 20-878-4652   (SL)
WESTERN FAIR ASSOCIATION
WESTERN FAIR
316 Rectory St, London, ON, N5W 3V9
(519) 438-7203
Emp Here 60   *Sales* 3,283,232
SIC 7999 Amusement and recreation, nec

D-U-N-S 25-742-5330   (BR)
YMCA OF WESTERN ONTARIO
YMCA-YWCA OF LONDON
1050 Hamilton Rd, London, ON, N5W 1A6
(519) 451-2395
Emp Here 30
SIC 7999 Amusement and recreation, nec

London, ON N5X
Middlesex County

D-U-N-S 20-571-8534   (BR)
ARBOR MEMORIAL SERVICES INC
MEMORIAL FUNERAL HOME
1559 Fanshawe Park Rd E, London, ON, N5X
3Z9
(519) 452-3770
Emp Here 20
SIC 7261 Funeral service and crematories

D-U-N-S 20-070-1931   (BR)
BEST BUY CANADA LTD
FUTURE SHOP
(*Suby of* Best Buy Co., Inc.)
1735 Richmond St Suite 111, London, ON,
N5X 3Y2
(519) 640-2900
Emp Here 100
SIC 5731 Radio, television, and electronic
stores

D-U-N-S 25-057-6311   (BR)
CARA OPERATIONS INC
SWISS CHALET ROTISSERIE & GRIL
(*Suby of* Cara Holdings Limited)
92 Fanshawe Park Rd E, London, ON, N5X
4C5
(519) 672-0968
Emp Here 60
SIC 5812 Eating places

D-U-N-S 24-426-6172   (BR)
COCO PAVING LIMITED
1865 Clarke Rd, London, ON, N5X 3Z6
(519) 451-2750
Emp Here 20
SIC 1611 Highway and street construction

D-U-N-S 20-070-7433   (BR)
CRUISESHIPCENTERS INTERNATIONAL

INC
EXPEDIA CRUISESHIP CENTRES
(*Suby of* Cruiseshipcenters International Inc)
1735 Richmond St Unit 113, London, ON, N5X
3Y2
(519) 850-7766
Emp Here 40
SIC 4725 Tour operators

D-U-N-S 24-340-2729   (BR)
FGL SPORTS LTD
SPORT-CHEK HYLAND
1735 Richmond St Unit 3, London, ON, N5X
3Y2
(519) 645-0350
Emp Here 45
SIC 5941 Sporting goods and bicycle shops

D-U-N-S 24-315-7323   (BR)
HOME DEPOT OF CANADA INC
(*Suby of* The Home Depot Inc)
600 Fanshawe Park Rd E, London, ON, N5X
1L1
(519) 850-5900
Emp Here 50
SIC 5251 Hardware stores

D-U-N-S 25-746-3083   (SL)
KOUSINS CONSTRUCTION INC
26 Orkney Cres, London, ON, N5X 3R7
(519) 438-1558
Emp Here 20   *Sales* 5,579,750
SIC 1522 Residential construction, nec
Pr Ted Simkovich

D-U-N-S 25-226-6879   (BR)
LONDON CHILDREN'S CONNECTION INC
NORTH LONDON CHILDREN'S CENTRE
1444 Glenora Dr, London, ON, N5X 1V2
(519) 438-5977
Emp Here 20
SIC 8351 Child day care services

D-U-N-S 25-318-1531   (BR)
MCDONALD'S RESTAURANTS OF CANADA LIMITED
MCDONALD'S RESTAURANT
(*Suby of* McDonald's Corporation)
103 Fanshawe Park Rd E, London, ON, N5X
3V9
(519) 660-6950
Emp Here 50
SIC 5812 Eating places

D-U-N-S 20-068-0812   (BR)
MICHAELS OF CANADA, ULC
MICHAELS ARTS & CRAFTS
(*Suby of* The Michaels Companies Inc)
1737 Richmond St, London, ON, N5X 3Y2
(519) 661-2688
Emp Here 35
SIC 5945 Hobby, toy, and game shops

D-U-N-S 24-337-2336   (BR)
PHILON RESTAURANTS INC
PIZZA HUT
109 Fanshawe Park Rd E, London, ON, N5X
3W1
(519) 660-6545
Emp Here 30
SIC 5812 Eating places

D-U-N-S 25-057-7574   (SL)
RICHARD IVEY SCHOOL OF BUSINESS FOUNDATION
551 Windermere Rd, London, ON, N5X 2T1
(519) 679-4546
Emp Here 75   *Sales* 3,793,956
SIC 7389 Business services, nec

D-U-N-S 25-308-4461   (BR)
ROYAL BANK OF CANADA
RBC
(*Suby of* Royal Bank Of Canada)
96 Fanshawe Park Rd E, London, ON, N5X
4C5
(519) 660-4200
Emp Here 20
SIC 6021 National commercial banks

D-U-N-S 20-938-0117   (BR)
SIR CORP
JACK ASTOR'S BAR AND GRILL
88 Fanshawe Park Rd E, London, ON, N5X
4C5
(519) 663-2091
Emp Here 50
SIC 5812 Eating places

D-U-N-S 25-239-9043   (BR)
THAMES VALLEY DISTRICT SCHOOL BOARD
A. B. LUCAS SECONDARY SCHOOL
656 Tennent Ave, London, ON, N5X 1L8
(519) 452-2600
SIC 8211 Elementary and secondary schools

D-U-N-S 20-590-5933   (BR)
THAMES VALLEY DISTRICT SCHOOL BOARD
NORTHBRIDGE PUBLIC SCHOOL
25 Mclean Dr, London, ON, N5X 1Y2
(519) 452-8440
Emp Here 25
SIC 8211 Elementary and secondary schools

D-U-N-S 24-525-4268   (BR)
THAMES VALLEY DISTRICT SCHOOL BOARD
STONEY CREEK PUBLIC SCHOOL
1335 Nicole Ave, London, ON, N5X 4M7
(519) 850-8698
Emp Here 25
SIC 8211 Elementary and secondary schools

D-U-N-S 20-590-4639   (BR)
THAMES VALLEY DISTRICT SCHOOL BOARD
NORTH DALE PUBLIC SCHOOL
655 Tennent Ave, London, ON, N5X 0L2
(519) 452-8439
Emp Here 25
SIC 8211 Elementary and secondary schools

D-U-N-S 20-590-5842   (BR)
THAMES VALLEY DISTRICT SCHOOL BOARD
JACK CHAMBERS PUBLIC SCHOOL
1650 Hastings Dr, London, ON, N5X 3E3
(519) 452-8240
Emp Here 25
SIC 8211 Elementary and secondary schools

D-U-N-S 20-590-5826   (BR)
THAMES VALLEY DISTRICT SCHOOL BOARD
STONEYBROOK PUBLIC SCHOOL
1460 Stoneybrook Cres, London, ON, N5X
1C4
(519) 452-8590
Emp Here 25
SIC 8211 Elementary and secondary schools

D-U-N-S 24-207-5542   (BR)
TRILAND REALTY LTD
ROYAL LEPAGE TRILAND REALTY
235 North Centre Rd Suite 1, London, ON,
N5X 4E7
(519) 661-0380
Emp Here 90
SIC 6531 Real estate agents and managers

D-U-N-S 20-004-6964   (BR)
WENDY'S RESTAURANTS OF CANADA INC
WENDY'S
(*Suby of* The Wendy's Company)
60 North Centre Rd Unit 1, London, ON, N5X
3W1
(519) 660-8968
Emp Here 37
SIC 5812 Eating places

D-U-N-S 25-752-5469   (BR)
WESTERN AREA YOUTH SERVICES, INC
1517 Adelaide St N, London, ON, N5X 1K5
(519) 667-0714
Emp Here 50

SIC 8361 Residential care

D-U-N-S 25-221-2857   (BR)
WINNERS MERCHANTS INTERNATIONAL L.P.
WINNERS
(*Suby of* The TJX Companies Inc)
50 North Centre Rd Suite D, London, ON, N5X
3W1
(519) 645-6121
Emp Here 46
SIC 5651 Family clothing stores

London, ON N5Y
Middlesex County

D-U-N-S 25-297-1064   (BR)
BANK OF NOVA SCOTIA, THE
SCOTIABANK
1250 Highbury Ave N, London, ON, N5Y 6M7
(519) 451-4930
Emp Here 25
SIC 6021 National commercial banks

D-U-N-S 20-588-2686   (BR)
BANQUE TORONTO-DOMINION, LA
TD CANADA TRUST
(*Suby of* Toronto-Dominion Bank, The)
1314 Huron St, London, ON, N5Y 4V2
(519) 451-0453
Emp Here 20
SIC 6021 National commercial banks

D-U-N-S 20-118-3634   (BR)
BRUNSWICK CENTRES INC
BRUNSWICK HURON BOWL
(*Suby of* Brunswick Corporation)
1062 Adelaide St N, London, ON, N5Y 2N1

Emp Here 20
SIC 7933 Bowling centers

D-U-N-S 25-303-7071   (BR)
CANADIAN IMPERIAL BANK OF COMMERCE
CIBC
1299 Oxford St E, London, ON, N5Y 4W5
(519) 452-7400
Emp Here 21
SIC 6021 National commercial banks

D-U-N-S 24-227-0143   (BR)
CARA OPERATIONS LIMITED
HARVEY'S
(*Suby of* Cara Holdings Limited)
1141 Highbury Ave N, London, ON, N5Y 1A5
(519) 453-8100
Emp Here 214
SIC 5812 Eating places

D-U-N-S 24-179-7096   (BR)
CONSEIL SCOLAIRE VIAMONDE
ECOLE SECONDAIRE GABRIEL-DUMONT
920 Huron St, London, ON, N5Y 4K4
(519) 673-4552
Emp Here 25
SIC 8211 Elementary and secondary schools

D-U-N-S 25-797-2042   (BR)
CORPORATION OF THE CITY OF LONDON
CARLING HEIGHTS COMMUNITY CENTRE
656 Elizabeth St, London, ON, N5Y 6L3
(519) 661-2523
Emp Here 25
SIC 8322 Individual and family services

D-U-N-S 24-218-7763   (SL)
KELSEY'S ROAD HOUSE (LONDON) LTD
KELSEY'S RESTAURANT
900 Oxford St E Suite 18, London, ON, N5Y
5A1
(519) 455-9464
Emp Here 50   *Sales* 1,532,175
SIC 5812 Eating places

D-U-N-S 25-237-8781   (BR)

LONDON DISTRICT CATHOLIC SCHOOL BOARD
ST MICHAEL ELEMENTARY SCHOOL
926 Maitland St, London, ON, N5Y 2X1
(519) 675-4424
Emp Here 25
SIC 8211 Elementary and secondary schools

D-U-N-S 20-710-5086   (BR)
LONDON DISTRICT CATHOLIC SCHOOL BOARD
BLESSED SACRAMENT CATHOLIC SCHOOL
1063 Oxford St E, London, ON, N5Y 3L4
(519) 675-4411
Emp Here 50
SIC 8211 Elementary and secondary schools

D-U-N-S 25-310-9797   (BR)
MCDONALD'S RESTAURANTS OF CANADA LIMITED
MCDONALD'S
(*Suby of* McDonald's Corporation)
1159 Highbury Ave N, London, ON, N5Y 1A6
(519) 451-6830
Emp Here 89
SIC 5812 Eating places

D-U-N-S 25-300-0194   (BR)
METRO ONTARIO INC
METRO
1030 Adelaide St N, London, ON, N5Y 2M9
(519) 672-8994
Emp Here 200
SIC 5411 Grocery stores

D-U-N-S 24-964-9179   (BR)
METRO ONTARIO INC
FOOD BASICS
1299 Oxford St E, London, ON, N5Y 4W5
(519) 453-8510
Emp Here 80
SIC 5411 Grocery stores

D-U-N-S 25-743-0850   (HQ)
PALASAD BILLIARDS LIMITED
PALASAD WONDERLAND
(*Suby of* Palasad Billiards Limited)
777 Adelaide St N, London, ON, N5Y 2L8
(519) 649-9991
Emp Here 70   *Emp Total* 140
Sales 4,231,721
SIC 5812 Eating places

D-U-N-S 25-309-9428   (BR)
ROYAL BANK OF CANADA
RBC
(*Suby of* Royal Bank Of Canada)
621 Huron St, London, ON, N5Y 4J7
(519) 661-1144
Emp Here 67
SIC 6021 National commercial banks

D-U-N-S 25-295-3583   (BR)
SHOPPERS DRUG MART CORPORATION
SHOPPERS DRUG MART
1295 Highbury Ave N, London, ON, N5Y 5L3
(519) 453-3141
Emp Here 40
SIC 5912 Drug stores and proprietary stores

D-U-N-S 20-010-0209   (BR)
ST. JOSEPH'S HEALTH CARE, LONDON
REGIONAL MENTAL HEALTH CARE, LONDON
850 Highbury Ave N, London, ON, N5Y 1A4
(519) 455-5110
Emp Here 786
SIC 8093 Specialty outpatient clinics, nec

D-U-N-S 20-590-5776   (BR)
THAMES VALLEY DISTRICT SCHOOL BOARD
HILLCREST PUBLIC SCHOOL
1231 Fuller St, London, ON, N5Y 4P7
(519) 452-8220
Emp Here 30
SIC 8211 Elementary and secondary schools

D-U-N-S 24-126-2091 (BR)
THAMES VALLEY DISTRICT SCHOOL BOARD
LOUISE ARBOUR FRENCH IMMERSION PUBLIC SCHOOL
365 Belfield St, London, ON, N5Y 2K3
(519) 452-2820
Emp Here 60
SIC 8211 Elementary and secondary schools

D-U-N-S 25-239-9506 (BR)
THAMES VALLEY DISTRICT SCHOOL BOARD
LORD ELGIN PUBLIC SCHOOL
1100 Victoria Dr, London, ON, N5Y 4E2
(519) 452-8310
Emp Here 30
SIC 8211 Elementary and secondary schools

D-U-N-S 20-590-5750 (BR)
THAMES VALLEY DISTRICT SCHOOL BOARD
SIR JOHN A. MACDONALD PUBLIC SCHOOL
1150 Landor St, London, ON, N5Y 3W3
(519) 452-8570
Emp Here 50
SIC 8211 Elementary and secondary schools

D-U-N-S 25-239-9464 (BR)
THAMES VALLEY DISTRICT SCHOOL BOARD
MONTCALM SECONDARY SCHOOL
1350 Highbury Ave N, London, ON, N5Y 1B5
(519) 452-2730
Emp Here 100
SIC 8211 Elementary and secondary schools

D-U-N-S 25-239-9589 (BR)
THAMES VALLEY DISTRICT SCHOOL BOARD
NORTHBRAE PUBLIC SCHOOL
335 Belfield St, London, ON, N5Y 2K3
(519) 452-8420
Emp Here 30
SIC 8211 Elementary and secondary schools

D-U-N-S 25-239-9076 (BR)
THAMES VALLEY DISTRICT SCHOOL BOARD
KNOLLWOOD PARK PUBLIC SCHOOL
70 Gammage St, London, ON, N5Y 2B1
(519) 452-8290
Emp Here 40
SIC 8211 Elementary and secondary schools

D-U-N-S 20-026-2553 (BR)
THAMES VALLEY DISTRICT SCHOOL BOARD
BISHOP TOWNSEND PUBLIC SCHOOL
814 Quebec St, London, ON, N5Y 1X4
(519) 452-8050
Emp Here 26
SIC 8211 Elementary and secondary schools

D-U-N-S 20-267-2106 (BR)
TRANSFREIGHT INC
847 Highbury Ave N Unit 1, London, ON, N5Y 5B8

Emp Here 36
SIC 4731 Freight transportation arrangement

D-U-N-S 25-742-7146 (BR)
TWINCORP INC
TACO BELL
1145 Highbury Ave N, London, ON, N5Y 1A5
(519) 455-9737
Emp Here 20
SIC 5812 Eating places

D-U-N-S 20-927-3783 (BR)
WENDY'S RESTAURANTS OF CANADA INC
(*Suby of* The Wendy's Company)
1104 Adelaide St N, London, ON, N5Y 2N5
(519) 850-3535
Emp Here 30
SIC 5812 Eating places

London, ON N5Z
Middlesex County

D-U-N-S 25-751-5452 (BR)
1212551 ONTARIO INC
TIM HORTONS
(*Suby of* 1212551 Ontario Inc)
915 Commissioners Rd E, London, ON, N5Z 3H9
(519) 649-1678
Emp Here 30
SIC 5812 Eating places

D-U-N-S 25-498-5286 (HQ)
1212551 ONTARIO INC
TIM HORTONS
(*Suby of* 1212551 Ontario Inc)
95 Pond Mills Rd, London, ON, N5Z 3X3
(519) 645-1917
Emp Here 90   *Emp Total* 90
Sales 2,699,546
SIC 5812 Eating places

D-U-N-S 24-437-7094 (BR)
BANQUE TORONTO-DOMINION, LA
TORONTO-DOMINION BANK, THE
(*Suby of* Toronto-Dominion Bank, The)
1086 Commissioners Rd E, London, ON, N5Z 4W8
(519) 649-2370
Emp Here 20
SIC 6021 National commercial banks

D-U-N-S 20-126-8406 (BR)
CANADIAN LINEN AND UNIFORM SERVICE CO
(*Suby of* Ameripride Services, Inc.)
155 Adelaide St S, London, ON, N5Z 3K8
(519) 686-5000
Emp Here 150
SIC 7213 Linen supply

D-U-N-S 24-363-5281 (BR)
CANPAR TRANSPORT L.P.
(*Suby of* Canpar Transport L.P.)
3 Buchanan Crt Suite 2, London, ON, N5Z 4P9

Emp Here 40
SIC 4213 Trucking, except local

D-U-N-S 25-751-4018 (BR)
COMMUNITY LIVING LONDON INC
OPP ART
931 Leathorne St Unit C, London, ON, N5Z 3M7

Emp Here 30
SIC 7361 Employment agencies

D-U-N-S 25-481-5285 (BR)
COMMUNITY LIVING LONDON INC
OPPORTUNITY PLASTIC PACKAGING
180 Adelaide St S Suite 4, London, ON, N5Z 3L1
(519) 432-1149
Emp Here 88
SIC 8322 Individual and family services

D-U-N-S 20-704-8745 (BR)
COMSTOCK CANADA LTD
1200 Trafalgar St, London, ON, N5Z 1H5

Emp Here 300
SIC 1711 Plumbing, heating, air-conditioning

D-U-N-S 20-507-9544 (HQ)
CUDDY INTERNATIONAL CORPORATION
CUDDY FARMS
1226 Trafalgar St, London, ON, N5Z 1H5
(800) 265-1061
Emp Here 180   *Emp Total* 346
Sales 211,534,800
SIC 2015 Poultry slaughtering and processing
Pr Gerald Slemko
  Chris Palmer

D-U-N-S 24-453-7866 (BR)
EMCO CORPORATION
944 Leathorne St, London, ON, N5Z 3M5
(519) 686-7340
Emp Here 32
SIC 5074 Plumbing and heating equipment and supplies (hydronics)

D-U-N-S 24-143-6351 (BR)
GDI SERVICES (CANADA) LP
931 Leathorne St Unit E, London, ON, N5Z 3M7
(519) 681-3330
Emp Here 600
SIC 7349 Building maintenance services, nec

D-U-N-S 24-376-3864 (BR)
HALTON RECYCLING LTD
EMTERRA ENVIRONMENTAL
15 Buchanan Crt, London, ON, N5Z 4P9
(519) 690-2796
Emp Here 50
SIC 4953 Refuse systems

D-U-N-S 25-455-3381 (BR)
LAFARGE CANADA INC
100 Hume St, London, ON, N5Z 2P2
(519) 451-9240
Emp Here 45
SIC 1771 Concrete work

D-U-N-S 24-357-7603 (BR)
LONDON BRIDGE CHILD CARE SERVICES INC
ABC CHILD CARE CENTRE
189 Adelaide St S, London, ON, N5Z 3K7
(519) 685-1650
Emp Here 20
SIC 8351 Child day care services

D-U-N-S 25-237-8757 (BR)
LONDON DISTRICT CATHOLIC SCHOOL BOARD
ST SEBASTIAN ELEMENTARY SCHOOL
225 Cairn St, London, ON, N5Z 3W6
(519) 660-2791
Emp Here 30
SIC 8211 Elementary and secondary schools

D-U-N-S 24-301-8132 (HQ)
PETERBILT OF ONTARIO INC
PETERBILT OF LONDON
31 Buchanan Crt, London, ON, N5Z 4P9
(519) 686-1000
Emp Here 90   *Emp Total* 214
Sales 79,261,967
SIC 5511 New and used car dealers
Pr Pr David Climie

D-U-N-S 24-381-8544 (BR)
SOFINA FOODS INC
1226 Trafalgar St, London, ON, N5Z 1H5
(519) 455-6060
Emp Here 60
SIC 2015 Poultry slaughtering and processing

D-U-N-S 20-590-4738 (BR)
THAMES VALLEY DISTRICT SCHOOL BOARD
TRAFALGAR PUBLIC SCHOOL
919 Trafalgar St, London, ON, N5Z 1G3
(519) 452-8610
Emp Here 25
SIC 8211 Elementary and secondary schools

D-U-N-S 20-710-5391 (BR)
THAMES VALLEY DISTRICT SCHOOL BOARD
GA WHEABLE ADULT, ALTERNATIVE & CONTINUING EDUCATION
70 Jacqueline St, London, ON, N5Z 3P7
(519) 452-2660
Emp Here 50
SIC 8211 Elementary and secondary schools

D-U-N-S 20-036-9572 (BR)
THAMES VALLEY DISTRICT SCHOOL BOARD

MEDIA SERVICES DEPARTMENT
951 Leathorne St Suite 1, London, ON, N5Z 3M7
(519) 452-2573
Emp Here 30
SIC 8211 Elementary and secondary schools

D-U-N-S 20-590-5909 (BR)
THAMES VALLEY DISTRICT SCHOOL BOARD
PRINCESS ELIZABETH PUBLIC SCHOOL
247 Thompson Rd, London, ON, N5Z 2Z3
(519) 452-8490
Emp Here 50
SIC 8211 Elementary and secondary schools

D-U-N-S 20-068-0838 (BR)
THAMES VALLEY DISTRICT SCHOOL BOARD
FACILITY SERVICES DEPARTMENT
951 Leathorne St Suite 1, London, ON, N5Z 3M7
(519) 452-2444
Emp Here 100
SIC 8211 Elementary and secondary schools

D-U-N-S 20-590-4720 (BR)
THAMES VALLEY DISTRICT SCHOOL BOARD
EALING PUBLIC SCHOOL
840 Hamilton Rd, London, ON, N5Z 1V5
(519) 452-8150
Emp Here 30
SIC 8211 Elementary and secondary schools

D-U-N-S 25-239-9191 (BR)
THAMES VALLEY DISTRICT SCHOOL BOARD
C C CARROTHERS PUBLIC SCHOOL
360 Chippendale Cres, London, ON, N5Z 3G2
(519) 452-8110
Emp Here 35
SIC 8211 Elementary and secondary schools

D-U-N-S 20-029-8664 (BR)
THAMES VALLEY DISTRICT SCHOOL BOARD
GLEN CAIRN ELEMENTARY SCHOOL
53 Frontenac Rd, London, ON, N5Z 3Y5
(519) 452-8210
Emp Here 65
SIC 8211 Elementary and secondary schools

D-U-N-S 20-590-4696 (BR)
THAMES VALLEY DISTRICT SCHOOL BOARD
LESTER B PEARSON SCHOOL FOR THE ARTS
795 Trafalgar St, London, ON, N5Z 1E6
(519) 452-8300
Emp Here 25
SIC 8299 Schools and educational services, nec

London, ON N6A
Middlesex County

D-U-N-S 25-762-2498 (SL)
1069000 ONTARIO LTD
HARMONY GRAND BUFFET
304 Talbot St, London, ON, N6A 2R4

Emp Here 50   *Sales* 1,532,175
SIC 5812 Eating places

D-U-N-S 24-576-6167 (SL)
300322 ONTARIO LIMITED
150 Dufferin Ave Suite 100, London, ON, N6A 5N6
(519) 672-5272
Emp Here 90   *Sales* 17,244,621
SIC 6719 Holding companies, nec
Pr Pr Colin Cockburn
  Brian Foster

D-U-N-S 25-010-6069   (BR)
AON REED STENHOUSE INC
255 Queens Ave Suite 1400, London, ON, N6A 5R8
(519) 433-3441
Emp Here 25
SIC 6411 Insurance agents, brokers, and service

D-U-N-S 24-372-9741   (BR)
AXA INSURANCE (CANADA)
250 York St Suite 200, London, ON, N6A 6K2
(519) 679-9440
Emp Here 70
SIC 6331 Fire, marine, and casualty insurance

D-U-N-S 25-028-6580   (BR)
AECOM CANADA LTD
AECOM
250 York St Citiplaza, London, ON, N6A 6K2
(519) 673-0510
Emp Here 35
SIC 8711 Engineering services

D-U-N-S 24-201-8088   (BR)
ASTRAL MEDIA RADIO INC
STANDARD RADIO LONDON
(*Suby of* Astral Media Radio Inc)
99 Dundas St, London, ON, N6A 6K1
(519) 858-9053
Emp Here 20
SIC 4832 Radio broadcasting stations

D-U-N-S 20-979-9857   (BR)
AVIVA INSURANCE COMPANY OF CANADA
255 Queens Ave Suite 1500, London, ON, N6A 5R8
(519) 438-2981
Emp Here 75
SIC 6331 Fire, marine, and casualty insurance

D-U-N-S 25-484-0663   (BR)
BMO NESBITT BURNS INC
255 Queens Ave Suite 1900, London, ON, N6A 5R8
(519) 672-8560
Emp Here 55
SIC 6211 Security brokers and dealers

D-U-N-S 24-909-5373   (BR)
BANK OF NOVA SCOTIA, THE
SCOTIABANK
420 Richmond St, London, ON, N6A 3C9
(519) 642-5000
Emp Here 30
SIC 6021 National commercial banks

D-U-N-S 25-747-1920   (BR)
BANK OF MONTREAL
BANK OF MONTREAL
270 Dundas St, London, ON, N6A 1H3
(519) 667-6129
Emp Here 54
SIC 6021 National commercial banks

D-U-N-S 20-580-5653   (BR)
BANQUE LAURENTIENNE DU CANADA
150 Dufferin Ave, London, ON, N6A 5N6
(519) 888-1717
Emp Here 20
SIC 6021 National commercial banks

D-U-N-S 24-118-6803   (BR)
BANQUE TORONTO-DOMINION, LA
TORONTO-DOMINION BANK, THE
(*Suby of* Toronto-Dominion Bank, The)
380 Wellington St Suite 10, London, ON, N6A 5B5
(519) 640-2856
Emp Here 42
SIC 6021 National commercial banks

D-U-N-S 24-025-0969   (BR)
BANQUE TORONTO-DOMINION, LA
TORONTO-DOMINION BANK, THE
(*Suby of* Toronto-Dominion Bank, The)
220 Dundas St, London, ON, N6A 1H3

(519) 663-1560
Emp Here 30
SIC 6021 National commercial banks

D-U-N-S 24-874-7545   (BR)
BANQUE DE DEVELOPPEMENT DU CANADA
BDC
380 Wellington St, London, ON, N6A 5B5
(519) 645-4229
Emp Here 42
SIC 6141 Personal credit institutions

D-U-N-S 24-909-5944   (BR)
CBRE LIMITED
380 Wellington St Suite 30, London, ON, N6A 5B5
(519) 673-6444
Emp Here 30
SIC 6531 Real estate agents and managers

D-U-N-S 20-514-8658   (BR)
CIBC MELLON GLOBAL SECURITIES SERVICES COMPANY
150 Dufferin Ave 5th Fl, London, ON, N6A 5N6
(519) 873-2218
Emp Here 90
SIC 6091 Nondeposit trust facilities

D-U-N-S 20-911-0936   (BR)
CIBC WORLD MARKETS INC
CIBC WOODGUNDY
255 Queens Ave Suite 2200, London, ON, N6A 5R8
(519) 660-3704
Emp Here 120
SIC 6211 Security brokers and dealers

D-U-N-S 20-572-7550   (BR)
CANADA POST CORPORATION
MAIL SERVICE
255 Dufferin Ave, London, ON, N6A 4K1
(519) 435-4963
Emp Here 26
SIC 4311 U.s. postal service

D-U-N-S 24-622-2293   (SL)
CEEPS-BARNEYS LIMITED
671 Richmond St, London, ON, N6A 3G7
(519) 432-1425
Emp Here 50   *Sales* 1,824,018
SIC 5813 Drinking places

D-U-N-S 24-126-0660   (HQ)
COPP BUILDING MATERIALS LIMITED
COPP'S BUILDALL
(*Suby of* Copp Limited)
45 York St, London, ON, N6A 1A4
(519) 679-9000
Emp Here 50   *Emp Total* 3
Sales 42,099,799
SIC 5039 Construction materials, nec
Pr Pr Steven S Copp
  T Brayl Copp

D-U-N-S 25-498-2465   (BR)
CORUS ENTERTAINMENT INC
CFPL-FM
380 Wellington St Suite 222, London, ON, N6A 5B5
(519) 931-6000
Emp Here 80
SIC 7922 Theatrical producers and services

D-U-N-S 25-010-2480   (BR)
DELOITTE & TOUCHE INC
(*Suby of* Deloitte LLP)
255 Queens Ave Suite 700, London, ON, N6A 5R8
(519) 679-1880
Emp Here 70
SIC 8111 Legal services

D-U-N-S 24-756-8140   (BR)
DILLON CONSULTING LIMITED
DILLON CONSULTING MANAGEMENT
(*Suby of* Dillon Consulting Inc)
130 Dufferin Ave Suite 1400, London, ON, N6A 5R2

(519) 438-6192
Emp Here 100
SIC 8711 Engineering services

D-U-N-S 24-142-8234   (BR)
ECONOMICAL MUTUAL INSURANCE COMPANY
148 Fullarton St Suite 1200, London, ON, N6A 5P3
(519) 673-5990
Emp Here 110
SIC 6331 Fire, marine, and casualty insurance

D-U-N-S 20-849-2546   (SL)
EMBERS SERVICES LIMITED
80 Dufferin Ave, London, ON, N6A 1K4
(519) 672-4510
Emp Here 200   *Sales* 18,240,175
SIC 6512 Nonresidential building operators
Pr Pr Earl Cherniak
VP Fin Robert Moses
  Janet Stewart

D-U-N-S 25-297-1684   (BR)
ERNST & YOUNG INC
255 Queens Ave Suite 1800, London, ON, N6A 5R8
(519) 672-6100
Emp Here 100
SIC 8721 Accounting, auditing, and bookkeeping

D-U-N-S 24-337-0405   (BR)
EXTENDICARE INC
EXTENDICARE LONDON
860 Waterloo St, London, ON, N6A 3W6
(519) 433-6658
Emp Here 160
SIC 8051 Skilled nursing care facilities

D-U-N-S 24-060-2479   (BR)
FINANCIERE BANQUE NATIONALE INC
380 Wellington St Suite 802, London, ON, N6A 5B5
(519) 646-5711
Emp Here 20
SIC 6282 Investment advice

D-U-N-S 25-281-5006   (BR)
G4S SECURE SOLUTIONS (CANADA) LTD
383 Richmond St Suite 1014, London, ON, N6A 3C4

Emp Here 225
SIC 7381 Detective and armored car services

D-U-N-S 24-968-5181   (SL)
GLC ASSET MANAGEMENT GROUP LTD
255 Dufferin Ave, London, ON, N6A 4K1
(519) 432-7229
Emp Here 30   *Sales* 4,377,642
SIC 6211 Security brokers and dealers

D-U-N-S 24-324-1473   (SL)
GRACEWAY CANADA COMPANY
GRACEWAY PHARMACEUTICALS
252 Pall Mall St Suite 302, London, ON, N6A 5P6
(519) 432-7373
Emp Here 45   *Sales* 7,710,200
SIC 5122 Drugs, proprietaries, and sundries
Genl Mgr Erin Craven
Recvr David Sieradzki

D-U-N-S 25-742-6734   (BR)
GREAT-WEST LIFE ASSURANCE COMPANY, THE
140 Fullarton St Suite 1002, London, ON, N6A 5P2
(519) 434-3268
Emp Here 20
SIC 6311 Life insurance

D-U-N-S 25-747-7265   (BR)
GREYHOUND CANADA TRANSPORTATION ULC
GREYHOUND COURIER EXPRESS, DIV OF
101 York St, London, ON, N6A 1A6
(519) 434-3250
Emp Here 20

SIC 4131 Intercity and rural bus transportation

D-U-N-S 24-253-9075   (SL)
HRDOWNLOADS INC
195 Dufferin Ave Suite 500, London, ON, N6A 1K7
(519) 438-9763
Emp Here 60   *Sales* 2,699,546
SIC 8999 Services, nec

D-U-N-S 20-127-4545   (BR)
HONEYWELL LIMITED
(*Suby of* Honeywell International Inc.)
250 York St Suite 300, London, ON, N6A 6K2
(519) 640-1920
Emp Here 20
SIC 3822 Environmental controls

D-U-N-S 25-282-2051   (HQ)
ICORR PROPERTIES MANAGEMENT INC
ICORR PROPERTIES INTERNATIONAL
(*Suby of* ICORR Holdings Inc)
700 Richmond St Suite 100, London, ON, N6A 5C7
(519) 432-1888
Emp Here 25   *Emp Total* 80
Sales 7,004,227
SIC 6513 Apartment building operators
Pr Pr Ron Wolf
Fin Ex Joan Hall

D-U-N-S 20-887-6230   (SL)
INFORMATION TECHNOLOGY BUSINESS COLLEGE INC
THAMES VALLEY COLLEGE OF BUSINESS & IT
151 Dundas St Suite 501, London, ON, N6A 5R7

Emp Here 50   *Sales* 3,064,349
SIC 8244 Business and secretarial schools

D-U-N-S 20-259-4490   (SL)
INNOVATIVE SECURITY MANAGEMENT (1998) INC
ISM SECURITY
148 York St Suite 309, London, ON, N6A 1A9
(519) 858-4100
Emp Here 150   *Sales* 4,669,485
SIC 7381 Detective and armored car services

D-U-N-S 25-830-1019   (BR)
INTACT INSURANCE COMPANY
ING HALIFAX
255 Queens Ave Suite 900, London, ON, N6A 5R8
(519) 432-6721
Emp Here 172
SIC 6331 Fire, marine, and casualty insurance

D-U-N-S 25-017-0958   (BR)
INVESTORS GROUP FINANCIAL SERVICES INC
254 Pall Mall St Suite 100, London, ON, N6A 5P6
(519) 679-8993
Emp Here 70
SIC 6722 Management investment, open-end

D-U-N-S 25-053-3601   (SL)
IVEY MANAGEMENT SERVICES
EXECUTIVE BUSINESS PROGRAMM (DIV OF)
1151 Richmond St, London, ON, N6A 3K7
(519) 661-3272
Emp Here 42   *Sales* 5,985,550
SIC 8741 Management services
  Larry Wynant
  John Irwin
  Fred Longstaffe
  Rod White
  Patrick Crowley
  Carol Stephenson
  Hank Vander Laan

D-U-N-S 25-970-0722   (SL)
J B'S MONGOLIAN GRILL INC
645 Richmond St, London, ON, N6A 3G7

(519) 645-6400
Emp Here 65   *Sales* 1,969,939
SIC 5812 Eating places

D-U-N-S 24-090-1715   (BR)
JUST ENERGY ONTARIO L.P
124 Dundas St, London, ON, N6A 1G1
(519) 434-4628
Emp Here 25
SIC 5074 Plumbing and heating equipment
and supplies (hydronics)

D-U-N-S 20-651-0880   (BR)
KPMG LLP
(*Suby of* KPMG LLP)
140 Fullarton St Suite 1400, London, ON, N6A
5P2
(519) 672-4880
Emp Here 50
SIC 8721 Accounting, auditing, and book-
keeping

D-U-N-S 20-127-6078   (SL)
KINGSMILL'S, LIMITED
130 Dundas St, London, ON, N6A 1G2

Emp Here 65   *Sales* 4,669,485
SIC 5311 Department stores

D-U-N-S 25-159-6433   (SL)
**LAWYERS RESOURCE CENTRE LIMITED
PARTNERSHIP**
COHEN HIGHLEY
255 Queens Ave Suite 11, London, ON, N6A
5R8
(519) 645-6908
Emp Here 49   *Sales* 5,465,508
SIC 8111 Legal services
Ruth Hall

D-U-N-S 25-672-0475   (SL)
LEWIS BAKERIES (1996) INC
200 Albert St, London, ON, N6A 1M1
(519) 434-5252
Emp Here 75   *Sales* 3,031,879
SIC 5461 Retail bakeries

D-U-N-S 24-561-4107   (BR)
LIBRO CREDIT UNION LIMITED
167 Central Ave Suite 200, London, ON, N6A
1M6
(519) 673-4130
Emp Here 20
SIC 6062 State credit unions

D-U-N-S 20-179-1303   (SL)
LONDON CIVIC CENTRE CORPORATION
JOHN LABATT CENTRE, THE
99 Dundas St, London, ON, N6A 6K1
(519) 667-5700
Emp Here 300   *Sales* 92,536,708
SIC 7941 Sports clubs, managers, and pro-
moters
Genl Mgr Brian Ohl

D-U-N-S 25-038-7909   (BR)
LONDON HEALTH SCIENCES CENTRE
*LONDON HEALTH SCIENCE CENTER UNI-
VERSITY HOSPITAL*
339 Windermere Rd, London, ON, N6A 5A5
(519) 663-3197
Emp Here 500
SIC 8011 Offices and clinics of medical doc-
tors

D-U-N-S 24-375-5860   (BR)
LONDON HEALTH SCIENCES CENTRE
SOUTH STREET HOSPITAL
375 South St, London, ON, N6A 4G5
(519) 685-8500
Emp Here 500
SIC 8062 General medical and surgical hospi-
tals

D-U-N-S 25-303-9531   (BR)
LONDON LIFE INSURANCE COMPANY
FREEDOM 55 FINANCIAL A DIV OF
255 Queens Ave Suite 400, London, ON, N6A
5R8

(519) 435-7900
Emp Here 50
SIC 6311 Life insurance

D-U-N-S 25-281-5329   (BR)
MD MANAGEMENT LIMITED
MD FINANCIAL MANAGEMENT
(*Suby of* Canadian Medical Association)
380 Wellington St Suite 1400, London, ON,
N6A 5B5
(519) 432-0883
Emp Here 29
SIC 6722 Management investment, open-end

D-U-N-S 25-310-9730   (BR)
**MCDONALD'S   RESTAURANTS   OF
CANADA LIMITED**
MCDONALD'S
(*Suby of* McDonald's Corporation)
151 Dundas St, London, ON, N6A 5R7
(519) 661-0645
Emp Here 50
SIC 5812 Eating places

D-U-N-S 25-084-5971   (BR)
MOLLY BLOOM'S IRISH PUB INC
(*Suby of* Molly Bloom's Irish Pub Inc)
700 Richmond St Suite G, London, ON, N6A
5C7
(519) 675-1212
Emp Here 25
SIC 5812 Eating places

D-U-N-S 24-007-5267   (HQ)
**MONTESSORI HOUSE OF CHILDREN INC,
THE**
(*Suby of* Montessori House Of Children Inc,
The)
711 Waterloo St, London, ON, N6A 3W1
(519) 433-9121
Emp Here 39   *Emp Total* 60
Sales 4,012,839
SIC 8211 Elementary and secondary schools

D-U-N-S 24-776-4566   (HQ)
PWC CAPITAL INC
PACIFIC & WESTERN GROUP
(*Suby of* PWC Capital Inc)
140 Fullarton St Suite 2002, London, ON, N6A
5P2
(519) 488-1280
Emp Here 20   *Emp Total* 79
Sales 23,104
SIC 8741 Management services

D-U-N-S 25-096-9136   (SL)
**PORTFOLIO MANAGEMENT SOLUTIONS
INC**
200 Queens Ave Suite 700, London, ON, N6A
1J3
(519) 432-0075
Emp Here 119   *Sales* 6,055,738
SIC 7322 Adjustment and collection services
Pr Pr R Gerald Coffin

D-U-N-S 20-547-5093   (BR)
PRICEWATERHOUSECOOPERS LLP
PWC
465 Richmond St Suite 300, London, ON, N6A
5P4
(519) 640-8000
Emp Here 75
SIC 8721 Accounting, auditing, and book-
keeping

D-U-N-S 24-817-9525   (BR)
RBC DOMINION SECURITIES LIMITED
RBC ROYAL BANK
(*Suby of* Royal Bank Of Canada)
148 Fullarton St Suite 1900, London, ON, N6A
5P3
(519) 675-2000
Emp Here 50
SIC 6211 Security brokers and dealers

D-U-N-S 24-374-2736   (SL)
RESULTS GENERATION GROUP INC
186 King St Suite 109, London, ON, N6A 1C7

(519) 913-1545
Emp Here 100   *Sales* 5,890,507
SIC 7389 Business services, nec

D-U-N-S 24-687-6254   (SL)
ROBARTS RESEARCH INSTITUTE
100 Perth Dr, London, ON, N6A 5K8
(519) 663-5777
Emp Here 440   *Sales* 70,580,442
SIC 8733 Noncommercial research organiza-
tions
John Schucht
Pr Pr Mark Poznansky
VP Michael Crowley
VP Susan Horvath
Dir Fred Tomczyk
George Taylor
Phil Bowman
Dir Ian Bandeen
Dir Kelly Blair
Dir Serge Carriere

D-U-N-S 25-412-6261   (SL)
ROBINSON HALL LIMITED
398 Talbot St, London, ON, N6A 2R9
(519) 433-2200
Emp Here 70   *Sales* 2,553,625
SIC 5813 Drinking places

D-U-N-S 25-308-4503   (BR)
ROYAL BANK OF CANADA
ROYAL BANK FINANCIAL GROUP
(*Suby of* Royal Bank Of Canada)
383 Richmond St Suite 801, London, ON, N6A
3C4
(519) 661-1180
Emp Here 38
SIC 6021 National commercial banks

D-U-N-S 25-365-7134   (BR)
SCOTIA CAPITAL INC
SCOTIA MCLEOD
148 Fullarton St Unit 1801, London, ON, N6A
5P3
(519) 679-9490
Emp Here 50
SIC 6211 Security brokers and dealers

D-U-N-S 20-508-0617   (HQ)
SIFTON PROPERTIES LIMITED
195 Dufferin Ave Suite 800, London, ON, N6A
1K7
(519) 434-1000
Emp Here 40   *Emp Total* 1,000
Sales 327,885,386
SIC 6553 Cemetery subdividers and develop-
ers
Glen Sifton
Pr Pr Richard M. Sifton
Wayne Reid
Sec Martha Wainright
William M. Sifton
Brayl Copp
Donald N Stevens
Ian Wallace
James Harrison
Terri-Lynn Green

D-U-N-S 20-153-1659   (SL)
SOCIETY OF GRADUATE STUDENTS
UWO-UCC BUILDING
1151 Richmond St Suite 260, London, ON,
N6A 3K7
(519) 661-3394
Emp Here 30   *Sales* 5,072,500
SIC 8699 Membership organizations, nec
Owner Raquell Rodrigues

D-U-N-S 20-188-2441   (BR)
ST. JOSEPH'S HEALTH CARE, LONDON
*REGIONAL MENTAL HEALTH CARE, LON-
DON*
268 Grosvenor St, London, ON, N6A 4V2
(519) 646-6100
Emp Here 1,500
SIC 8093 Specialty outpatient clinics, nec

D-U-N-S 20-010-0159   (BR)

ST. JOSEPH'S HEALTH CARE, LONDON
*MOUNT HOPE CENTRE FOR LONG TERM
CARE*
Gd, London, ON, N6A 4V2
(519) 646-6100
Emp Here 418
SIC 8361 Residential care

D-U-N-S 25-440-7240   (BR)
ST. JOSEPH'S HEALTH CARE, LONDON
ST. JOSEPH'S HOSPITAL
298 Grosvenor St, London, ON, N6A 1Y8
(519) 646-6000
Emp Here 2,030
SIC 6324 Hospital and medical service plans

D-U-N-S 24-847-9677   (SL)
**ST. PETER'S SEMINARY CORPORATION
OF LONDON IN ONTARIO LIMITED**
SAINT PETER'S SEMINARY
1040 Waterloo St, London, ON, N6A 3Y1
(519) 432-1824
Emp Here 40   *Sales* 5,595,120
SIC 8221 Colleges and universities
Pr Steven Wlusek

D-U-N-S 24-358-2764   (BR)
STANTEC CONSULTING LTD
171 Queens Ave 6th Floor, London, ON, N6A
5J7
(519) 645-2007
Emp Here 126
SIC 8711 Engineering services

D-U-N-S 20-288-5653   (BR)
**STERICYCLE COMMUNICATION SOLU-
TIONS, ULC**
(*Suby of* Stericycle Communication Solutions,
ULC)
383 Richmond St Suite 1106, London, ON,
N6A 3C4
(519) 672-5580
Emp Here 25
SIC 4899 Communication services, nec

D-U-N-S 25-204-3443   (HQ)
**SYKES ASSISTANCE SERVICES CORPO-
RATION**
(*Suby of* Sykes Enterprises Incorporated)
248 Pall Mall St, London, ON, N6A 5P6
(519) 434-3221
Emp Here 640   *Emp Total* 55,525
Sales 109,404,397
SIC 7549 Automotive services, nec
Pr Pr Bruce Woods

D-U-N-S 24-117-4924   (BR)
TD WATERHOUSE CANADA INC
(*Suby of* Toronto-Dominion Bank, The)
380 Wellington St, London, ON, N6A 5B5
(519) 640-8530
Emp Here 32
SIC 6211 Security brokers and dealers

D-U-N-S 25-321-0587   (BR)
TNS CANADIAN FACTS INC
150 Dufferin Ave, London, ON, N6A 5N6

Emp Here 130
SIC 8732 Commercial nonphysical research

D-U-N-S 25-239-9381   (BR)
**THAMES VALLEY DISTRICT SCHOOL
BOARD**
RYERSON PUBLIC SCHOOL
940 Waterloo St, London, ON, N6A 3X3
(519) 452-8520
Emp Here 30
SIC 8211 Elementary and secondary schools

D-U-N-S 25-239-3848   (BR)
**THAMES VALLEY DISTRICT SCHOOL
BOARD**
SAINT GEORGE'S PUBLIC SCHOOL
782 Waterloo St, London, ON, N6A 3W4
(519) 452-8530
Emp Here 40
SIC 8211 Elementary and secondary schools

D-U-N-S 24-336-7732   (BR)
UNIVERSITY OF WESTERN ONTARIO, THE
DIVISION OF HOUSING AND ANCILLARY SERVICES
1151 Richmond St Suite 3, London, ON, N6A 5B9
(519) 661-3549
Emp Here 200
SIC 6531 Real estate agents and managers

D-U-N-S 20-788-0415   (BR)
UNIVERSITY OF WESTERN ONTARIO, THE
SCHULICH SCHOOL OF MEDICINE AND DENTISTRY
1151 Richmond St Rm 4, London, ON, N6A 5C1
(519) 661-3330
Emp Here 250
SIC 8062 General medical and surgical hospitals

D-U-N-S 24-317-2769   (BR)
UNIVERSITY OF WESTERN ONTARIO, THE
RICHARD IVEY SCHOOL OF BUSINESS, THE
1151 Richmond St Suite 3140, London, ON, N6A 3K7
(519) 661-3208
Emp Here 300
SIC 8748 Business consulting, nec

D-U-N-S 20-515-7576   (BR)
UNIVERSITY OF WESTERN ONTARIO, THE
PURCHASING DEPARTMENT
1151 Richmond St Suite 2, London, ON, N6A 5B8
(519) 661-2038
Emp Here 20
SIC 8221 Colleges and universities

D-U-N-S 20-297-0971   (BR)
UNIVERSITY OF WESTERN ONTARIO, THE
FACULTY OF INFORMATION AND MEDIA STUDIES
North Campus Building, Room 240, London, ON, N6A 5B7
(519) 661-3542
Emp Here 20
SIC 8221 Colleges and universities

D-U-N-S 25-688-8702   (SL)
UNIVERSITY STUDENT COUNCIL OF THE UNIVERSITY OF WESTERN ONTARIO
1151 Richmond St Rm 340, London, ON, N6A 3K7
(519) 661-3574
Emp Here 50   *Sales* 1,532,175
SIC 5812 Eating places

D-U-N-S 20-005-3382   (BR)
WENDY'S RESTAURANTS OF CANADA INC
WENDY'S
(*Suby* of The Wendy's Company)
243 Oxford St E, London, ON, N6A 1V2
(519) 434-0695
Emp Here 40
SIC 5812 Eating places

D-U-N-S 25-300-6704   (BR)
WORKPLACE SAFETY & INSURANCE BOARD, THE
WSIB
148 Fullarton St Suite 402, London, ON, N6A 5P3
(519) 663-2331
Emp Here 200
SIC 6331 Fire, marine, and casualty insurance

London, ON N6B
Middlesex County

D-U-N-S 24-411-6554   (SL)
510081 ONTARIO LIMITED
CASEYS RESTAURANT
276 Dundas St, London, ON, N6B 1T6

(519) 439-0188
Emp Here 50   *Sales* 1,978,891
SIC 5812 Eating places

D-U-N-S 20-126-5311   (HQ)
ABOUTOWN TRANSPORTATION LIMITED
1 Bathurst St, London, ON, N6B 3R2
(519) 663-2222
Emp Here 125   *Emp Total* 4
Sales 8,539,920
SIC 4151 School buses
Pr Pr James T Donnelly
Genl Mgr Stephen Smith
VP James R Donnelly
Recvr Paul Theodore Ihnatiuk

D-U-N-S 25-053-5143   (BR)
ATLIFIC INC
MARRIOTT RESIDENCE INN
(*Suby* of 3376290 Canada Inc)
383 Colborne St, London, ON, N6B 3P5
(519) 433-7222
Emp Here 44
SIC 7011 Hotels and motels

D-U-N-S 20-588-3098   (BR)
BANQUE TORONTO-DOMINION, LA
TD CANADA TRUST
(*Suby* of Toronto-Dominion Bank, The)
275 Dundas St, London, ON, N6B 3L1
(519) 663-1500
Emp Here 20
SIC 6021 National commercial banks

D-U-N-S 24-213-0763   (SL)
BOYS' & GIRLS' CLUB OF LONDON
184 Horton St E, London, ON, N6B 1K8
(519) 434-9114
Emp Here 63   *Sales* 2,553,625
SIC 7997 Membership sports and recreation clubs

D-U-N-S 24-419-4077   (SL)
CANADIAN SECURITY CONCEPTS INC
SECURITY CONCEPTS
303 Richmond St Suite 204, London, ON, N6B 2H8
(519) 642-0444
Emp Here 50   *Sales* 4,742,446
SIC 5999 Miscellaneous retail stores, nec

D-U-N-S 25-994-7570   (BR)
CHESHIRE HOMES OF LONDON INC
CHESHIRE LONDON
111 Waterloo St Suite 506, London, ON, N6B 2M4
(519) 673-6617
Emp Here 35
SIC 8051 Skilled nursing care facilities

D-U-N-S 24-420-2503   (BR)
CO-OPERATORS GROUP LIMITED, THE
CO-OPERATORS, THE
291 King St, London, ON, N6B 1R8

Emp Here 35
SIC 6331 Fire, marine, and casualty insurance

D-U-N-S 20-699-9414   (BR)
DELTA HOTELS LIMITED
325 Dundas St, London, ON, N6B 1T9
(519) 679-6111
Emp Here 200
SIC 8741 Management services

D-U-N-S 24-194-7381   (BR)
DOMINION OF CANADA GENERAL INSURANCE COMPANY, THE
DOMINION, THE
(*Suby* of The Travelers Companies Inc)
285 King St Suite 501, London, ON, N6B 3M6
(519) 433-7201
Emp Here 35
SIC 6411 Insurance agents, brokers, and service

D-U-N-S 20-096-6401   (BR)
GOODWILL INDUSTRIES, ONTARIO GREAT LAKES

GOODWILL CAREER CENTRE, THE
390 King St, London, ON, N6B 1S3
(519) 850-9675
Emp Here 200
SIC 8331 Job training and related services

D-U-N-S 20-078-5322   (BR)
GOODWILL INDUSTRIES, ONTARIO GREAT LAKES
379 Dundas St Unit 19, London, ON, N6B 1V5

Emp Here 400
SIC 7363 Help supply services

D-U-N-S 25-481-2761   (BR)
GOVERNING COUNCIL OF THE SALVATION ARMY IN CANADA, THE
GOVERNING COUNCIL OF THE SALVATION ARMY IN CANADA, THE
371 King St, London, ON, N6B 1S4
(519) 433-6106
Emp Here 40
SIC 8322 Individual and family services

D-U-N-S 24-187-0463   (BR)
GOVERNING COUNCIL OF THE SALVATION ARMY IN CANADA, THE
GOVERNING COUNCIL OF THE SALVATION ARMY IN CANADA, THE
281 Wellington St, London, ON, N6B 2L4
(519) 661-0343
Emp Here 150
SIC 8699 Membership organizations, nec

D-U-N-S 20-556-0394   (BR)
HENRY SCHEIN CANADA, INC
41 Adelaide St N Unit 57, London, ON, N6B 3P4
(519) 432-4322
Emp Here 25
SIC 5047 Medical and hospital equipment

D-U-N-S 24-336-6023   (BR)
IBM CANADA LIMITED
(*Suby* of International Business Machines Corporation)
275 Dundas St, London, ON, N6B 3L1

Emp Here 120
SIC 7379 Computer related services, nec

D-U-N-S 25-159-6813   (SL)
LAWSERVE MANAGEMENT LIMITED PARTNERSHIP
300 Dundas St, London, ON, N6B 1T6
(519) 672-5666
Emp Here 70   *Sales* 8,318,900
SIC 8111 Legal services
  Dianne Elliott

D-U-N-S 25-462-0537   (HQ)
LONDON CROSS CULTURAL LEARNER CENTRE
CCLC
(*Suby* of London Cross Cultural Learner Centre)
505 Dundas St, London, ON, N6B 1W4
(519) 432-1133
Emp Here 34   *Emp Total* 65
Sales 2,553,625
SIC 8322 Individual and family services

D-U-N-S 20-913-6824   (BR)
LONDON DISTRICT CATHOLIC SCHOOL BOARD
ST JOHN CATHOLIC FRENCH IMMERSION SCHOOL
449 Hill St, London, ON, N6B 1E5
(519) 675-4420
Emp Here 20
SIC 8211 Elementary and secondary schools

D-U-N-S 25-863-7750   (BR)
MISSION SERVICES OF LONDON
MEN'S MISSION
459 York St, London, ON, N6B 1R3
(519) 672-8500
Emp Here 30

SIC 8399 Social services, nec

D-U-N-S 20-556-1343   (BR)
PITNEY BOWES OF CANADA LTD
PITNEY BOWES LONDON
(*Suby* of Pitney Bowes Inc.)
633 Colborne St, London, ON, N6B 2V3
(519) 850-1722
Emp Here 20
SIC 5044 Office equipment

D-U-N-S 25-321-4167   (BR)
REVERA INC
279 Horton St E Suite 405, London, ON, N6B 1L3
(519) 434-4544
Emp Here 56
SIC 6513 Apartment building operators

D-U-N-S 25-147-3989   (HQ)
ST. LEONARD'S SOCIETY OF LONDON
ST LEONARD'S COMMUNITY SERVICES LONDON & REGION
(*Suby* of St. Leonard's Society of London)
405 Dundas St, London, ON, N6B 1V9
(519) 850-3777
Emp Here 25   *Emp Total* 100
Sales 14,167,680
SIC 8399 Social services, nec
Ex Dir Heather Calendar

D-U-N-S 24-382-6521   (SL)
SUNEDISON CANADIAN CONSTRUCTION LP
595 Adelaide St N Suite 400, London, ON, N6B 3J9

Emp Here 20   *Sales* 2,165,628
SIC 3433 Heating equipment, except electric

D-U-N-S 25-239-9290   (BR)
THAMES VALLEY DISTRICT SCHOOL BOARD
LONDON CENTRAL SECONDARY SCHOOL
509 Waterloo St, London, ON, N6B 2P8
(519) 452-2620
Emp Here 100
SIC 8211 Elementary and secondary schools

D-U-N-S 20-710-5375   (BR)
THAMES VALLEY DISTRICT SCHOOL BOARD
LORD ROBERTS FRENCH IMMERSION PUBLIC SCHOOL
440 Princess Ave, London, ON, N6B 2B3
(519) 452-8330
Emp Here 25
SIC 8211 Elementary and secondary schools

D-U-N-S 20-590-4605   (BR)
THAMES VALLEY DISTRICT SCHOOL BOARD
H. B. BEAL SECONDARY SCHOOL
525 Dundas St, London, ON, N6B 1W5
(519) 452-2700
Emp Here 25
SIC 8211 Elementary and secondary schools

D-U-N-S 25-239-9233   (BR)
THAMES VALLEY DISTRICT SCHOOL BOARD
ABERDEEN ELEMENTARY PUBLIC SCHOOL
580 Grey St, London, ON, N6B 1H8
(519) 452-8010
Emp Here 35
SIC 8211 Elementary and secondary schools

D-U-N-S 24-182-2907   (SL)
UNITED WAY OF LONDON & MIDDLESEX
409 King St, London, ON, N6B 1S5
(519) 438-1721
Emp Here 20   *Sales* 8,122,587
SIC 8699 Membership organizations, nec
  Andrew Lockie
  Suzanne Bembridge
  Sandy Whittall
  Phyllis Retty

Don Macdonald

D-U-N-S 20-070-4968   (BR)
WESTERN INVENTORY SERVICE LTD
WIS INTERNATIONAL
609 William St Suite 203, London, ON, N6B
3G1
(519) 433-3461
Emp Here 60
SIC 7389 Business services, nec

London, ON N6C
Middlesex County

D-U-N-S 24-874-5036   (SL)
570230 ONTARIO INC
EAST SIDE MARIO'S
387 Wellington Rd, London, ON, N6C 4P9
(519) 680-1830
Emp Here 80   *Sales* 3,109,686
SIC 5812 Eating places

D-U-N-S 20-650-9197   (BR)
BELL MEDIA INC
COUNTRY FAVOURITES BX93
743 Wellington Rd, London, ON, N6C 4R5
(519) 686-2525
Emp Here 50
SIC 4833 Television broadcasting stations

D-U-N-S 20-336-7735   (BR)
CAISSEN WATER TECHNOLOGIES INC
CULLIGAN WATER
865 Commissioners Rd E, London, ON, N6C
2V4
(519) 685-0445
Emp Here 20
SIC 5963 Direct selling establishments

D-U-N-S 25-293-4914   (BR)
**CANADIAN NATIONAL INSTITUTE FOR
THE BLIND, THE**
(*Suby of* Canadian National Institute For The
Blind, The)
749 Base Line Rd E, London, ON, N6C 2R6
(519) 685-8420
Emp Here 25
SIC 8322 Individual and family services

D-U-N-S 20-558-0462   (BR)
CANADIAN RED CROSS SOCIETY, THE
810 Commissioners Rd E, London, ON, N6C
2V5
(519) 681-7330
Emp Here 20
SIC 8399 Social services, nec

D-U-N-S 25-406-3928   (HQ)
COMCARE (CANADA) LIMITED
COMCARE HEALTH SERVICES
(*Suby of* Comcare (Canada) Limited)
339 Wellington Rd Suite 200, London, ON,
N6C 5Z9
(800) 663-5775
Emp Here 70   *Emp Total* 4,000
Sales 264,664,320
SIC 8049 Offices of health practitioner
Pr Peter Tanaka
VP Greg More
VP Wendy Theis
Jeff Bond

D-U-N-S 20-917-8909   (BR)
COMMUNITY LIFECARE INC
*GRAND WOOD PARK APARTMENTS AND
RESIDENCE*
81 Grand Ave, London, ON, N6C 1M2
(519) 432-1162
Emp Here 85
SIC 6513 Apartment building operators

D-U-N-S 24-151-7213   (BR)
DOLLARAMA S.E.C.
DOLLARAMA
395 Wellington Rd Unit 8, London, ON, N6C

5Z6
(519) 668-7837
Emp Here 20
SIC 5999 Miscellaneous retail stores, nec

D-U-N-S 24-337-2815   (BR)
FGL SPORTS LTD
NATIONAL SPORTS
332 Wellington Rd Suite 5, London, ON, N6C
4P6
(519) 858-3181
Emp Here 20
SIC 5941 Sporting goods and bicycle shops

D-U-N-S 20-824-1950   (SL)
HIGHLAND COUNTRY CLUB LTD
1922 Highland Hts, London, ON, N6C 2T4
(519) 681-8223
Emp Here 50   *Sales* 2,042,900
SIC 7997 Membership sports and recreation
clubs

D-U-N-S 24-009-1744   (BR)
LAMPLIGHTER INNS (LONDON) LIMITED
BEST WESTERN LAMPLIGHTER INN
(*Suby of* Lamplighter Inns (London) Limited)
591 Wellington Rd, London, ON, N6C 4R3
(519) 681-7151
Emp Here 100
SIC 7011 Hotels and motels

D-U-N-S 20-792-6531   (BR)
LOBLAW COMPANIES LIMITED
JOHNS VAUL-MART
179 Wortley Rd, London, ON, N6C 3P6
(519) 645-6983
Emp Here 25
SIC 5411 Grocery stores

D-U-N-S 25-755-2240   (BR)
LOBLAWS SUPERMARKETS LIMITED
GARY'S NOFRILLS
7 Base Line Rd E, London, ON, N6C 5Z8

Emp Here 100
SIC 5411 Grocery stores

D-U-N-S 25-239-4028   (BR)
**LONDON BRIDGE CHILD CARE SERVICES
INC**
*ROWNTREE PARK EARLY CHILDHOOD
CENTRE*
712 Whetter Ave, London, ON, N6C 2H2
(519) 686-8944
Emp Here 22
SIC 8351 Child day care services

D-U-N-S 25-239-3962   (BR)
**LONDON BRIDGE CHILD CARE SERVICES
INC**
ELMWOOD AVENUE DAY CARE CENTRE
89 Elmwood Ave E, London, ON, N6C 1J4
(519) 438-9141
Emp Here 20
SIC 8351 Child day care services

D-U-N-S 20-710-5094   (BR)
**LONDON DISTRICT CATHOLIC SCHOOL
BOARD**
HOLY ROSARY CATHLOIC SCHOOL
268 Herkimer St, London, ON, N6C 4S4
(519) 675-4415
Emp Here 50
SIC 8211 Elementary and secondary schools

D-U-N-S 25-237-8823   (BR)
**LONDON DISTRICT CATHOLIC SCHOOL
BOARD**
ST MARTIN ELEMENTARY SCHOOL
140 Duchess Ave, London, ON, N6C 1N9
(519) 675-4422
Emp Here 40
SIC 8211 Elementary and secondary schools

D-U-N-S 25-685-2823   (HQ)
**LONDON HEALTH SCIENCES CENTRE RE-
SEARCH INC**
LAWSON HEALTH RESEARCH INSTITUTE

(*Suby of* London Health Sciences Centre Research Inc)
750 Base Line Rd E Suite 300, London, ON,
N6C 2R5
(519) 667-6649
Emp Here 800   *Emp Total* 1,000
Sales 857,947
SIC 8733 Noncommercial research organizations

D-U-N-S 24-333-1613   (BR)
METRO ONTARIO INC
METRO
395 Wellington Rd, London, ON, N6C 5Z6
(519) 680-2317
Emp Here 100
SIC 5411 Grocery stores

D-U-N-S 25-868-1832   (BR)
MISSION SERVICES OF LONDON
ROTHOLME WOMEN'S & FAMILY SHELTER
42 Stanley St, London, ON, N6C 1B1
(519) 673-4114
Emp Here 30
SIC 8322 Individual and family services

D-U-N-S 24-803-3219   (BR)
NORDION INC
MDS LABORATORIES
746 Base Line Rd E Suite 11, London, ON,
N6C 5Z2

Emp Here 75

SIC 8071 Medical laboratories

D-U-N-S 25-312-1169   (SL)
REALTY FIRM INC, THE
395 Wellington Rd Unit 11b, London, ON, N6C
5Z6
(519) 601-1160
Emp Here 50   *Sales* 6,125,139
SIC 6531 Real estate agents and managers

D-U-N-S 25-672-8908   (BR)
RED LOBSTER HOSPITALITY LLC
RED LOBSTER RESTAURANTS
(*Suby of* Red Lobster Seafood Co., LLC)
667 Wellington Rd, London, ON, N6C 4R4
(519) 680-0220
Emp Here 100
SIC 5812 Eating places

D-U-N-S 25-361-2634   (BR)
SCM INSURANCE SERVICES INC
SCM CANADA
746 Base Line Rd E Suite 210, London, ON,
N6C 5Z2
(519) 645-6500
Emp Here 35
SIC 6411 Insurance agents, brokers, and ser-
vice

D-U-N-S 24-104-3012   (BR)
SOBEYS CAPITAL INCORPORATED
FRESHCO
645 Commissioners Rd E, London, ON, N6C
2T9
(519) 685-9581
Emp Here 20
SIC 5411 Grocery stores

D-U-N-S 25-213-7385   (BR)
STAPLES CANADA INC
STAPLES THE BUSINESS DEPOT
(*Suby of* Staples, Inc.)
332 Wellington Rd, London, ON, N6C 4P6
(519) 645-7042
Emp Here 50
SIC 5943 Stationery stores

D-U-N-S 24-125-2506   (BR)
SUN LIFE FINANCIAL TRUST INC
CLARICA LIFE FINANCIAL
1 Commissioners Rd E Unit 101, London, ON,
N6C 5Z3
(519) 680-2382
Emp Here 30
SIC 6311 Life insurance

D-U-N-S 25-239-9357   (BR)
**THAMES VALLEY DISTRICT SCHOOL
BOARD**
TECUMSEH PUBLIC SCHOOL
401 Tecumseh Ave E, London, ON, N6C 1T4
(519) 452-8600
Emp Here 27
SIC 8211 Elementary and secondary schools

D-U-N-S 25-239-9084   (BR)
**THAMES VALLEY DISTRICT SCHOOL
BOARD**
*SIR WILFRID LAURIER SECONDARY
SCHOOL*
450 Millbank Dr, London, ON, N6C 4W7
(519) 452-2840
Emp Here 100
SIC 8211 Elementary and secondary schools

D-U-N-S 25-239-9746   (BR)
**THAMES VALLEY DISTRICT SCHOOL
BOARD**
WORTLEY ROAD PUBLIC SCHOOL
301 Wortley Rd, London, ON, N6C 3R6
(519) 452-8720
Emp Here 28
SIC 8211 Elementary and secondary schools

D-U-N-S 20-590-6006   (BR)
**THAMES VALLEY DISTRICT SCHOOL
BOARD**
LONDON SOUTH SECONDARY SCHOOL
371 Tecumseh Ave E, London, ON, N6C 1T4
(519) 452-2860
Emp Here 75
SIC 8211 Elementary and secondary schools

D-U-N-S 20-590-4704   (BR)
**THAMES VALLEY DISTRICT SCHOOL
BOARD**
MOUNTSFIELD PUBLIC SCHOOL
8 Mountsfield Dr, London, ON, N6C 2S4
(519) 452-8400
Emp Here 25
SIC 8211 Elementary and secondary schools

D-U-N-S 25-239-9167   (BR)
**THAMES VALLEY DISTRICT SCHOOL
BOARD**
CLEARDALE ELEMENTARY SCHOOL
780 Dulaney Dr, London, ON, N6C 3W4
(519) 452-8140
Emp Here 35
SIC 8211 Elementary and secondary schools

D-U-N-S 20-590-4571   (BR)
**THAMES VALLEY DISTRICT SCHOOL
BOARD**
ARTHUR STRINGER PUBLIC SCHOOL
43 Shaftesbury Ave, London, ON, N6C 2Y5
(519) 452-8030
Emp Here 25
SIC 8211 Elementary and secondary schools

D-U-N-S 24-843-9051   (BR)
TRADER CORPORATION
LONDON AUTO TRADERS
332 Wellington Rd Unit 1, London, ON, N6C
4P6

Emp Here 23
SIC 2741 Miscellaneous publishing

D-U-N-S 25-838-5657   (BR)
WE CARE HEALTH SERVICES INC
190 Wortley Rd Suite 100f, London, ON, N6C
4Y7
(519) 642-1208
Emp Here 75
SIC 8322 Individual and family services

London, ON N6E
Middlesex County

D-U-N-S 25-355-0875   (BR)

3499481 CANADA INC
SUPER PET #25
765 Exeter Rd Suite F2, London, ON, N6E
3T1
(519) 681-6300
Emp Here 40
SIC 5999 Miscellaneous retail stores, nec

D-U-N-S 25-270-3319   (BR)
AMEC FOSTER WHEELER AMERICAS LIMITED
AMEC EARTH & ENVIRONMENTAL
1398 Wellington Rd S Unit 2, London, ON,
N6E 3N6
(519) 681-2400
Emp Here 22
SIC 8711 Engineering services

D-U-N-S 25-296-4556   (BR)
BANK OF NOVA SCOTIA, THE
SCOTIABANK
639 Southdale Rd E, London, ON, N6E 3M2
(519) 686-0301
Emp Here 22
SIC 6021 National commercial banks

D-U-N-S 20-003-0653   (BR)
BANQUE TORONTO-DOMINION, LA
TORONTO-DOMINION BANK, THE
(*Suby of* Toronto-Dominion Bank, The)
1420 Ernest Ave, London, ON, N6E 2H8
(519) 686-6810
Emp Here 30
SIC 6021 National commercial banks

D-U-N-S 20-797-5116   (BR)
BAYSHORE HEALTHCARE LTD.
BAYSHORE HOME HEALTH
595 Bradley Ave Suite 2, London, ON, N6E
3Z8
(519) 438-6313
Emp Here 52
SIC 8082 Home health care services

D-U-N-S 20-810-5861   (BR)
BEST BUY CANADA LTD
BEST BUY
(*Suby of* Best Buy Co., Inc.)
1080 Wellington Rd, London, ON, N6E 1M2
(519) 686-2160
Emp Here 60
SIC 5999 Miscellaneous retail stores, nec

D-U-N-S 20-321-0232   (SL)
BRADFORD COMPANY LTD
BRADFORD CANADA
4070 White Oak Rd, London, ON, N6E 0B1
(519) 451-4393
Emp Here 20   *Sales* 1,824,018
SIC 8742 Management consulting services

D-U-N-S 20-938-9576   (BR)
CSG SECURITY CORPORATION
CHUBB SECURITY SYSTEMS
(*Suby of* United Technologies Corporation)
582 Newbold St, London, ON, N6E 2W9
(519) 668-6800
Emp Here 29
SIC 1731 Electrical work

D-U-N-S 20-644-6689   (BR)
CANADIAN RED CROSS SOCIETY, THE
RED CROSS COMMUNITY HEALTH SERVICES
517 Consortium Crt, London, ON, N6E 2S8
(613) 740-1900
Emp Here 155
SIC 8093 Specialty outpatient clinics, nec

D-U-N-S 25-666-0291   (BR)
CANPAR TRANSPORT L.P.
CANPAR
(*Suby of* Canpar Transport L.P.)
3600 White Oak Rd, Suite 5, London, ON,
N6E 2Z9
(905) 430-8435
Emp Here 20
SIC 7389 Business services, nec

D-U-N-S 24-919-3194   (BR)
CARA OPERATIONS LIMITED
SWISS CHALET
(*Suby of* Cara Holdings Limited)
1067 Wellington Rd Suite 1135, London, ON,
N6E 2H5
(519) 681-1600
Emp Here 70
SIC 5812 Eating places

D-U-N-S 24-380-8016   (SL)
CASE 'N DRUM OIL LP
3462 White Oak Rd, London, ON, N6E 2Z9
(519) 681-3772
Emp Here 38   *Sales* 14,794,565
SIC 5172 Petroleum products, nec
Ch Bd Robert Sicard

D-U-N-S 25-321-1288   (BR)
CENTURA (TORONTO) LIMITED
CENTURA FLOOR AND FASHIONS
(*Suby of* Centura Limited)
993 Adelaide St S, London, ON, N6E 1R5
(519) 681-1961
Emp Here 40
SIC 5032 Brick, stone, and related material

D-U-N-S 24-893-6890   (SL)
CONKRISDA HOLDINGS LIMITED
FOUR POINTS BY SHERATON
1150 Wellington Rd, London, ON, N6E 1M3
(519) 681-0600
Emp Here 100   *Sales* 4,377,642
SIC 7011 Hotels and motels

D-U-N-S 24-874-2488   (BR)
CONTINENTAL TIRE CANADA, INC
1020 Adelaide St S, London, ON, N6E 1R6
(866) 256-3877
Emp Here 200
SIC 3714 Motor vehicle parts and accessories

D-U-N-S 25-059-4660   (BR)
CORPORATION OF THE CITY OF LONDON
THE SOUTH LONDON COMMUNITY POOL
585 Bradley Ave, London, ON, N6E 3Z8

Emp Here 20
SIC 7999 Amusement and recreation, nec

D-U-N-S 20-812-1397   (BR)
CORPORATION OF THE CITY OF LONDON
DEARNESS HOME FOR THE AGED
710 Southdale Rd E, London, ON, N6E 1R8
(519) 661-0400
Emp Here 35
SIC 8361 Residential care

D-U-N-S 20-652-1747   (BR)
COSTCO WHOLESALE CANADA LTD
COSTCO
(*Suby of* Costco Wholesale Corporation)
4313 Wellington Rd S, London, ON, N6E 2Z8
(519) 680-1027
Emp Here 200
SIC 5141 Groceries, general line

D-U-N-S 20-939-0611   (BR)
ESIT CANADA ENTERPRISE SERVICES CO
ESIT CANADA ENTERPRISE SERVICES CO
(*Suby of* Dxc Technology Company)
1100 Dearness Dr Unit 15, London, ON, N6E
1N9
(888) 447-4636
Emp Here 50
SIC 5734 Computer and software stores

D-U-N-S 24-152-6495   (BR)
EMPIRE THEATRES LIMITED
SILVERCITY LONDON
983 Wellington Rd, London, ON, N6E 3A9
(519) 673-4125
Emp Here 20
SIC 7832 Motion picture theaters, except
drive-in

D-U-N-S 20-563-3378   (BR)
ENTERPRISE RENT-A-CAR CANADA COM-

PANY
ENTERPRISE RENT-A-CAR
(*Suby of* The Crawford Group Inc)
845 Bradley Ave Unit 1, London, ON, N6E 3Z6
(519) 451-3900
Emp Here 50
SIC 7514 Passenger car rental

D-U-N-S 20-652-1796   (BR)
FAIRWEATHER LTD
INTERNATIONAL CLOTHIERS
1105 Wellington Rd, London, ON, N6E 1V4
(519) 686-7421
Emp Here 20
SIC 5621 Women's clothing stores

D-U-N-S 24-011-5688   (BR)
FIRST EFFORT INVESTMENTS LIMITED
CAMPUS CREW
1105 Wellington Rd Unit 119, London, ON,
N6E 1V4
(519) 686-4368
Emp Here 20
SIC 5651 Family clothing stores

D-U-N-S 25-321-0991   (BR)
FIRSTCANADA ULC
LAIDLAW LONDON
135 Towerline Pl, London, ON, N6E 2T3
(519) 685-6340
Emp Here 40
SIC 4151 School buses

D-U-N-S 24-924-1316   (BR)
FORD CREDIT CANADA LIMITED
(*Suby of* Ford Motor Company)
1069 Wellington Rd Suite 208, London, ON,
N6E 2H6

Emp Here 38
SIC 6141 Personal credit institutions

D-U-N-S 25-687-1575   (BR)
GAP (CANADA) INC
(*Suby of* The Gap Inc)
1105 Wellington Rd Unit 87, London, ON, N6E
1V4
(519) 685-1699
Emp Here 31
SIC 5651 Family clothing stores

D-U-N-S 25-283-9865   (BR)
GRAND & TOY LIMITED
(*Suby of* Office Depot, Inc.)
1100 Dearness Dr Unit 18, London, ON, N6E
1N9
(519) 685-2604
Emp Here 20
SIC 5943 Stationery stores

D-U-N-S 25-301-1498   (BR)
HUDSON'S BAY COMPANY
BAY, THE
1105 Wellington Rd Suite 5, London, ON, N6E
1V4
(519) 685-4100
Emp Here 250
SIC 5311 Department stores

D-U-N-S 25-094-5524   (BR)
HYDRO ONE NETWORKS INC
727 Exeter Rd, London, ON, N6E 1L3
(519) 668-5800
Emp Here 80
SIC 4911 Electric services

D-U-N-S 20-301-8382   (BR)
INDIGO BOOKS & MUSIC INC
CHAPTERS 786
(*Suby of* Indigo Books & Music Inc)
1037 Wellington Rd, London, ON, N6E 1W4
(519) 685-1008
Emp Here 25
SIC 5942 Book stores

D-U-N-S 25-305-3276   (BR)
INNVEST PROPERTIES CORP
QUALITY SUITES
(*Suby of* Innvest Properties Corp)

1120 Dearness Dr, London, ON, N6E 1N9
(519) 680-1024
Emp Here 28
SIC 7011 Hotels and motels

D-U-N-S 20-531-3711   (BR)
**JOHNSON CONTROLS NOVA SCOTIA
U.L.C.**
SYSTEMS & SERVICES
(*Suby of* Johnson Controls, Inc.)
90 Bessemer Rd, London, ON, N6E 1R1
(519) 681-1221
Emp Here 38
SIC 1711 Plumbing, heating, air-conditioning

D-U-N-S 20-127-5047   (BR)
LENNOX CANADA INC
878 Wellington Rd, London, ON, N6E 1L9
(519) 681-2450
Emp Here 40
SIC 1711 Plumbing, heating, air-conditioning

D-U-N-S 25-577-4697   (BR)
LOBLAW COMPANIES LIMITED
NATIONAL GROCERS CASH AND CARRY
1055 Hargrieve Rd Suite 244, London, ON,
N6E 1P6
(519) 686-4655
Emp Here 20
SIC 5141 Groceries, general line

D-U-N-S 25-743-3797   (BR)
LOBLAWS SUPERMARKETS LIMITED
LOBLAWS WHITE OAKS
635 Southdale Rd E, London, ON, N6E 3W6
(519) 686-8007
Emp Here 250
SIC 5411 Grocery stores

D-U-N-S 25-237-8716   (BR)
**LONDON DISTRICT CATHOLIC SCHOOL
BOARD**
ST ANTHONY CATHOLIC SCHOOL
1380 Ernest Ave, London, ON, N6E 2H8
(519) 660-2777
Emp Here 30
SIC 8351 Child day care services

D-U-N-S 20-590-9497   (BR)
**LONDON DISTRICT CATHOLIC SCHOOL
BOARD**
ARTHUR CARDI
1655 Ernest Ave, London, ON, N6E 2S3
(519) 660-2795
Emp Here 50
SIC 8211 Elementary and secondary schools

D-U-N-S 20-362-0646   (BR)
**LONDON DISTRICT CATHOLIC SCHOOL
BOARD**
ST. FRANCIS CATHOLIC SCHOOL
690 Osgoode Dr, London, ON, N6E 2G2
(519) 660-2780
Emp Here 44
SIC 8211 Elementary and secondary schools

D-U-N-S 20-581-1552   (BR)
**LONDON DISTRICT CATHOLIC SCHOOL
BOARD**
REGINA MUNDI CATHOLIC COLLEGE
5250 Wellington Rd S, London, ON, N6E 3X8
(519) 660-2797
Emp Here 84
SIC 8221 Colleges and universities

D-U-N-S 20-320-1595   (HQ)
MASTERFEEDS LP
ALLTECH, DIV OF
1020 Hargrieve Rd Suite 1, London, ON, N6E
1P5
(519) 685-4300
Emp Here 50   *Emp Total* 6,000
Sales 91,200,875
SIC 2048 Prepared feeds, nec
Pr Pr Robert Flack

D-U-N-S 25-318-1721   (BR)
MCDONALD'S   RESTAURANTS   OF

CANADA LIMITED
MCDONALD'S #8460
(*Suby of* McDonald's Corporation)
1105 Wellington Rd, London, ON, N6E 1V4
(519) 680-0503
Emp Here 40
SIC 5812 Eating places

D-U-N-S 20-641-9231   (BR)
MCDONALD'S RESTAURANTS OF CANADA LIMITED
MCDONALD'S RESTAURANTS
(*Suby of* McDonald's Corporation)
1074 Wellington Rd, London, ON, N6E 1M2
(519) 691-1042
Emp Here 106
SIC 5812 Eating places

D-U-N-S 25-318-1762   (BR)
MCDONALD'S RESTAURANTS OF CANADA LIMITED
MCDONALD'S
(*Suby of* McDonald's Corporation)
4350 Wellington Rd S, London, ON, N6E 2Z6
(519) 686-8860
Emp Here 70
SIC 5812 Eating places

D-U-N-S 20-193-7443   (BR)
MEDISYSTEM PHARMACY LIMITED
MEDISYSTEM PHARMACY
1100 Dearness Dr Unit 27-30, London, ON, N6E 1N9
(519) 681-9020
Emp Here 20
SIC 5912 Drug stores and proprietary stores

D-U-N-S 25-872-0713   (BR)
NORFOLK KNITTERS LIMITED
LEN'S MILL STORE
360 Exeter Rd Suite 2, London, ON, N6E 2Z4
(519) 686-3502
Emp Here 20
SIC 5949 Sewing, needlework, and piece goods

D-U-N-S 25-543-5026   (BR)
NORTRAX CANADA INC
(*Suby of* Deere & Company)
16 Royce Crt, London, ON, N6E 1L1
(519) 686-6400
Emp Here 39
SIC 5084 Industrial machinery and equipment

D-U-N-S 20-515-6032   (SL)
PRC BOOKS OF LONDON LIMITED
1112 Dearness Dr Unit 15, London, ON, N6E 1N9

Emp Here 120   *Sales* 7,016,633
SIC 7389 Business services, nec
Pr Pr James Geddes

D-U-N-S 24-406-6791   (BR)
PARSONS INC
DELCAN
1069 Wellington Rd Suite 214, London, ON, N6E 2H6
(519) 681-8771
Emp Here 35
SIC 8711 Engineering services

D-U-N-S 25-949-5117   (BR)
PHARMA PLUS DRUGMARTS LTD
1795 Ernest Ave, London, ON, N6E 2V5
(519) 681-0340
Emp Here 20
SIC 5912 Drug stores and proprietary stores

D-U-N-S 25-763-9385   (BR)
PHILON RESTAURANTS INC
PIZZA HUT
(*Suby of* Philon Restaurants Inc)
1300 Wellington Rd, London, ON, N6E 1M3
(519) 680-1556
Emp Here 30
SIC 5812 Eating places

D-U-N-S 24-709-1556   (SL)
PHOTON TECHNOLOGY INTERNATIONAL (CANADA) INC
P T I CANADA
(*Suby of* Cgm Us, Inc.)
347 Consortium Crt, London, ON, N6E 2S8
(519) 668-6920
Emp Here 25   *Sales* 1,732,502
SIC 3827 Optical instruments and lenses

D-U-N-S 25-033-7268   (BR)
REDBERRY FRANCHISING CORP
BURGER KING
1001 Wellington Rd Suite B, London, ON, N6E 1W4
(519) 685-9620
Emp Here 20
SIC 5812 Eating places

D-U-N-S 20-745-6752   (BR)
REID'S HERITAGE HOMES LTD
553 Southdale Rd E Suite 102, London, ON, N6E 1A2

Emp Here 20
SIC 1521 Single-family housing construction

D-U-N-S 25-949-5091   (BR)
REITMANS (CANADA) LIMITEE
PENNINGTONS
765 Exeter Rd Suite 211, London, ON, N6E 3T1
(519) 686-1782
Emp Here 20
SIC 5621 Women's clothing stores

D-U-N-S 25-372-2987   (BR)
RELIANCE COMFORT LIMITED PARTNERSHIP
RELIANCE HOME COMFORT, DIV
1045 Hargrieve Rd Suite A, London, ON, N6E 1P6
(519) 686-4942
Emp Here 60
SIC 1711 Plumbing, heating, air-conditioning

D-U-N-S 25-109-4538   (BR)
ROYAL HOST INC
TRAVELODGE LONDON
800 Exeter Rd, London, ON, N6E 1L5
(519) 681-1200
Emp Here 30
SIC 7011 Hotels and motels

D-U-N-S 25-743-0744   (BR)
SIR CORP
JACK ASTOR'S BAR & GRILL
1070 Wellington Rd Suite 1, London, ON, N6E 3V8
(519) 680-3800
Emp Here 100
SIC 5812 Eating places

D-U-N-S 24-363-4250   (BR)
SAFETY-KLEEN CANADA INC.
1020 Hargrieve Rd Suite 16, London, ON, N6E 1P5
(519) 685-3040
Emp Here 21
SIC 4953 Refuse systems

D-U-N-S 24-845-8192   (BR)
SIEMENS CANADA LIMITED
SIEMENS BUILDING TECHNOLOGIES, DIV OF
514 Newbold St Suite 514, London, ON, N6E 1K6
(519) 680-2380
Emp Here 20
SIC 4911 Electric services

D-U-N-S 20-796-7048   (BR)
SLEEP COUNTRY CANADA INC
3600 White Oak Rd Unit 5, London, ON, N6E 2Z9
(519) 691-0886
Emp Here 20
SIC 5712 Furniture stores

D-U-N-S 20-860-2107   (BR)
SOURCE (BELL) ELECTRONICS INC, THE
SOURCE, THE
1105 Wellington Rd Suite 69, London, ON, N6E 1V4
(519) 681-5914
Emp Here 25
SIC 5999 Miscellaneous retail stores, nec

D-U-N-S 25-743-7756   (BR)
STARBUCKS COFFEE CANADA, INC
(*Suby of* Starbucks Corporation)
1037 Wellington Rd Suite 2, London, ON, N6E 1W4
(519) 680-9889
Emp Here 20
SIC 5812 Eating places

D-U-N-S 25-483-7164   (SL)
TVI INC
VALUE VILLAGE
4465 Wellington Rd S, London, ON, N6E 2Z8
(519) 680-3711
Emp Here 50   *Sales* 3,575,074
SIC 5311 Department stores

D-U-N-S 25-239-9126   (BR)
THAMES VALLEY DISTRICT SCHOOL BOARD
WHITE OAKS PUBLIC SCHOOL
565 Bradley Ave, London, ON, N6E 3Z8
(519) 452-8680
Emp Here 100
SIC 8211 Elementary and secondary schools

D-U-N-S 20-590-4688   (BR)
THAMES VALLEY DISTRICT SCHOOL BOARD
RICK HANSEN PUBLIC SCHOOL
70 Ponderosa Cres, London, ON, N6E 2L7
(519) 452-8500
Emp Here 35
SIC 8211 Elementary and secondary schools

D-U-N-S 25-239-4051   (BR)
THAMES VALLEY DISTRICT SCHOOL BOARD
WILTON GROVE PUBLIC SCHOOL
626 Osgoode Dr, London, ON, N6E 1C1
(519) 452-8700
Emp Here 52
SIC 8211 Elementary and secondary schools

D-U-N-S 20-590-5768   (BR)
THAMES VALLEY DISTRICT SCHOOL BOARD
ASHLEY OAKS PUBLIC SCHOOL
121 Ashley Cres, London, ON, N6E 3W2
(519) 452-8040
Emp Here 25
SIC 8211 Elementary and secondary schools

D-U-N-S 20-710-5383   (BR)
THAMES VALLEY DISTRICT SCHOOL BOARD
NICHOLAS WILSON SCHOOL
927 Osgoode Dr, London, ON, N6E 1C9
(519) 452-8410
Emp Here 40
SIC 8211 Elementary and secondary schools

D-U-N-S 20-700-4784   (BR)
TOMMY HILFIGER CANADA INC
TOMMY HILFIGER STORE
1270 Wellington Rd Unit 101, London, ON, N6E 1M3
(519) 690-2269
Emp Here 20
SIC 5136 Men's and boy's clothing

D-U-N-S 24-124-9478   (BR)
UTC FIRE & SECURITY CANADA INC
UTC FIRE & SECURITY CANADA
(*Suby of* United Technologies Corporation)
582 Newbold St, London, ON, N6E 2W9
(519) 668-6800
Emp Here 20
SIC 1731 Electrical work

D-U-N-S 20-913-8242   (BR)
UNIFIRST CANADA LTD
(*Suby of* Unifirst Corporation)
77 Bessemer Rd Suite 15, London, ON, N6E 1P9

Emp Here 40
SIC 7213 Linen supply

D-U-N-S 24-329-6725   (BR)
WAL-MART CANADA CORP
1105 Wellington Rd Suite 3051, London, ON, N6E 1V4
(519) 681-7500
Emp Here 200
SIC 5311 Department stores

D-U-N-S 20-132-9609   (BR)
WENDY'S RESTAURANTS OF CANADA INC
WENDY'S
(*Suby of* The Wendy's Company)
1376 Wellington Rd, London, ON, N6E 1M3
(519) 681-2609
Emp Here 25
SIC 5812 Eating places

D-U-N-S 25-482-9765   (BR)
WESTMONT HOSPITALITY MANAGEMENT LIMITED
RADISSON HOTEL & SUITES LONDON
(*Suby of* Westmont Hospitality Management Limited)
855 Wellington Rd, London, ON, N6E 3N5
(519) 668-7900
Emp Here 35
SIC 7011 Hotels and motels

D-U-N-S 25-221-2402   (BR)
WINNERS MERCHANTS INTERNATIONAL L.P.
WINNERS
(*Suby of* The TJX Companies Inc)
765 Exeter Rd Unit 101, London, ON, N6E 3T1
(519) 649-2880
Emp Here 40
SIC 5651 Family clothing stores

London, ON N6G
Middlesex County

D-U-N-S 25-481-3975   (BR)
CADILLAC FAIRVIEW CORPORATION LIMITED, THE
MASONVILLE PLACE
1680 Richmond St Suite 23, London, ON, N6G 3Y9
(519) 667-4884
Emp Here 30
SIC 6512 Nonresidential building operators

D-U-N-S 24-253-5107   (BR)
CARA OPERATIONS LIMITED
MONTANA'S COOKHOUSE
(*Suby of* Cara Holdings Limited)
1335 Fanshawe Park Rd W, London, ON, N6G 0E3
(519) 473-6694
Emp Here 20
SIC 5812 Eating places

D-U-N-S 25-570-8034   (BR)
CENTRE FOR ADDICTION AND MENTAL HEALTH
100 Collip Cir Suite 200, London, ON, N6G 4X8
(519) 858-5000
Emp Here 30
SIC 8093 Specialty outpatient clinics, nec

D-U-N-S 24-074-5179   (BR)
COMMUNITY LIVING LONDON INC
99 Essex St, London, ON, N6G 1B4
(519) 434-0422
Emp Here 20

SIC 8361 Residential care

D-U-N-S 25-742-7658 (BR)
CORPORATION OF THE CITY OF LONDON
CANADA GAME AQUATIC CENTRE
1045 Wonderland Rd N, London, ON, N6G 2Y9
(519) 661-4455
Emp Here 50
SIC 7999 Amusement and recreation, nec

D-U-N-S 24-977-1952 (BR)
FGL SPORTS LTD
SPORT CHEK LONDON NW
1250 Fanshawe Park Rd W Unit 101, London, ON, N6G 5B1
(519) 641-8153
Emp Here 20
SIC 5941 Sporting goods and bicycle shops

D-U-N-S 24-251-6065 (BR)
GAP (CANADA) INC
BANANA REPUBLIC
(*Suby of* The Gap Inc)
1680 Richmond St, London, ON, N6G 3Y9
(519) 850-8820
Emp Here 32
SIC 5651 Family clothing stores

D-U-N-S 25-140-2681 (BR)
GAP (CANADA) INC
GAP
(*Suby of* The Gap Inc)
1680 Richmond St, London, ON, N6G 3Y9
(519) 673-1399
Emp Here 30
SIC 5651 Family clothing stores

D-U-N-S 24-342-8401 (BR)
GOODLIFE FITNESS CENTRES INC
GOOD LIFE FITNESS CLUB
1225 Wonderland Rd N, London, ON, N6G 2V9
(519) 641-6222
Emp Here 30
SIC 7991 Physical fitness facilities

D-U-N-S 25-729-3308 (BR)
GOODWILL INDUSTRIES, ONTARIO GREAT LAKES
GOODWILL RETAIL STORE
1225 Wonderland Rd N, London, ON, N6G 2V9
(519) 472-1959
Emp Here 29
SIC 5932 Used merchandise stores

D-U-N-S 20-304-6409 (BR)
HUDSON'S BAY COMPANY
BAY, THE
1680 Richmond St, London, ON, N6G 3Y9
(519) 675-0080
Emp Here 110
SIC 5311 Department stores

D-U-N-S 25-237-8674 (BR)
LONDON DISTRICT CATHOLIC SCHOOL BOARD
ST THOMAS MORE SCHOOL
18 Wychwood Pk, London, ON, N6G 1R5
(519) 660-2793
Emp Here 20
SIC 8211 Elementary and secondary schools

D-U-N-S 20-590-9604 (BR)
LONDON DISTRICT CATHOLIC SCHOOL BOARD
ST MARGAUERITE D'YOUVILLE
170 Hawthorne Rd, London, ON, N6G 4Z9
(519) 660-2787
Emp Here 25
SIC 8211 Elementary and secondary schools

D-U-N-S 20-710-5334 (BR)
LONDON DISTRICT CATHOLIC SCHOOL BOARD
ST CATHERINE OF SIENA CATHOLIC SCHOOL
2140 Quarrier Rd Suite Lbby, London, ON,

N6G 5L4
(519) 675-4437
Emp Here 28
SIC 8211 Elementary and secondary schools

D-U-N-S 24-803-5151 (BR)
LOWE'S COMPANIES CANADA, ULC
1335 Fanshawe Park Rd W, London, ON, N6G 0E3
(519) 474-5270
Emp Here 50
SIC 5211 Lumber and other building materials

D-U-N-S 25-318-1655 (BR)
MCDONALD'S RESTAURANTS OF CANADA LIMITED
MCDONALD'S #8854
(*Suby of* McDonald's Corporation)
1280 Fanshawe Park Rd W, London, ON, N6G 5B1
(519) 473-4043
Emp Here 50
SIC 5812 Eating places

D-U-N-S 25-300-0038 (BR)
METRO ONTARIO INC
METRO
1225 Wonderland Rd N, London, ON, N6G 2V9
(519) 472-5601
Emp Here 130
SIC 5411 Grocery stores

D-U-N-S 25-428-3807 (SL)
RABHERU, DR RITA H
LONDON PSYCHIATRIC HOSPITAL
43 Ravenglass Cres, London, ON, N6G 4K1
(519) 455-5110
Emp Here 50   *Sales* 2,991,389
SIC 8011 Offices and clinics of medical doctors

D-U-N-S 20-047-7201 (BR)
REVERA INC
MCGARREL PLACE
355 Mcgarrell Dr, London, ON, N6G 0B1
(519) 672-0500
Emp Here 170
SIC 8322 Individual and family services

D-U-N-S 20-965-8843 (BR)
SEARS CANADA INC
SEARS
1680 Richmond St Suite 2, London, ON, N6G 3Y9
(519) 660-4254
Emp Here 265
SIC 5999 Miscellaneous retail stores, nec

D-U-N-S 20-860-2057 (BR)
SOURCE (BELL) ELECTRONICS INC, THE
SOURCE, THE
1680 Richmond St Suite 190, London, ON, N6G 3Y9
(519) 660-1984
Emp Here 25
SIC 5999 Miscellaneous retail stores, nec

D-U-N-S 25-357-8116 (BR)
ST. JOSEPH'S HEALTH CARE, LONDON
ST. JOSEPH'S FAMILY MEDICAL & DENTAL CENTRE
346 Platt'S Lane, London, ON, N6G 1J1
(519) 672-9660
Emp Here 60
SIC 8093 Specialty outpatient clinics, nec

D-U-N-S 20-590-5941 (BR)
THAMES VALLEY DISTRICT SCHOOL BOARD
UNIVERSITY HEIGHTS PUBLIC SCHOOL
27 Ford Cres, London, ON, N6G 1H8
(519) 452-8630
Emp Here 25
SIC 8211 Elementary and secondary schools

D-U-N-S 25-239-9175 (BR)
THAMES VALLEY DISTRICT SCHOOL BOARD

ORCHARD PARK ELEMENTARY SCHOOL
50 Wychwood Pk, London, ON, N6G 1R6
(519) 452-8450
Emp Here 24
SIC 8211 Elementary and secondary schools

D-U-N-S 20-590-4746 (BR)
THAMES VALLEY DISTRICT SCHOOL BOARD
WILFRID JURY PUBLIC SCHOOL
950 Lawson Rd, London, ON, N6G 3M2
(519) 452-8690
Emp Here 80
SIC 8211 Elementary and secondary schools

D-U-N-S 20-590-5925 (BR)
THAMES VALLEY DISTRICT SCHOOL BOARD
MASONVILLE PUBLIC SCHOOL
25 Hillview Blvd, London, ON, N6G 3A7
(519) 452-8390
Emp Here 30
SIC 8211 Elementary and secondary schools

D-U-N-S 24-092-9971 (BR)
THAMES VALLEY DISTRICT SCHOOL BOARD
EMILY CARR PUBLIC SCHOOL
44 Hawthorne Rd, London, ON, N6G 2H5
(519) 452-8160
Emp Here 60
SIC 8211 Elementary and secondary schools

D-U-N-S 20-789-8441 (BR)
UNIVERSITY OF WESTERN ONTARIO, THE
SCHOOL OF PHYSICAL THERAPY
1201 Western Rd Suite 1588, London, ON, N6G 1H1
(519) 661-3360
Emp Here 30
SIC 8221 Colleges and universities

D-U-N-S 25-220-5398 (BR)
UNIVERSITY OF WESTERN ONTARIO, THE
SURFACE SCIENCE WESTERN
999 Collip Cir Room Ll31, London, ON, N6G 0J3
(519) 661-2173
Emp Here 20
SIC 8731 Commercial physical research

D-U-N-S 25-955-9847 (BR)
UNIVERSITY OF WESTERN ONTARIO, THE
FACULTY OF EDUCATION
1137 Western Rd Suite 1118, London, ON, N6G 1G7
(519) 661-3182
Emp Here 120
SIC 8221 Colleges and universities

D-U-N-S 20-535-5337 (BR)
UNIVERSITY OF WESTERN ONTARIO, THE
ACCOUNTS PAYABLE OFFICE
1393 Western Rd Suite 6100, London, ON, N6G 1G9
(519) 661-3024
Emp Here 60
SIC 8221 Colleges and universities

D-U-N-S 24-411-3049 (BR)
URSULINE RELIGIOUS OF THE DIOCESE OF LONDON IN ONTARIO
BRESCIA UNIVERSITY COLLEGE
(*Suby of* Ursuline Religious Of The Diocese Of London In Ontario)
1285 Western Rd, London, ON, N6G 1H2
(519) 432-8353
Emp Here 100
SIC 8221 Colleges and universities

London, ON N6H
Middlesex County

D-U-N-S 24-388-3670 (SL)
1279028 ONTARIO LIMITED

ANGELO'S BAKERY AND DELI
755 Wonderland Rd N, London, ON, N6H 4L1
(519) 473-7772
Emp Here 120   *Sales* 4,085,799
SIC 5461 Retail bakeries

D-U-N-S 24-120-9357 (BR)
BANK OF NOVA SCOTIA, THE
SCOTIABANK
301 Oxford St W, London, ON, N6H 1S6
(519) 642-5044
Emp Here 20
SIC 6021 National commercial banks

D-U-N-S 20-588-2751 (BR)
BANQUE TORONTO-DOMINION, LA
TD CANADA TRUST
(*Suby of* Toronto-Dominion Bank, The)
215 Oxford St W, London, ON, N6H 1S5
(519) 438-8311
Emp Here 20
SIC 6021 National commercial banks

D-U-N-S 24-363-5666 (BR)
BEST BUY CANADA LTD
FUTURE SHOP
(*Suby of* Best Buy Co., Inc.)
1885 Hyde Park Rd, London, ON, N6H 0A3

Emp Here 50
SIC 5731 Radio, television, and electronic stores

D-U-N-S 24-686-5062 (BR)
BULK BARN FOODS LIMITED
1965 Hyde Park Rd, London, ON, N6H 0A3
(519) 473-4897
Emp Here 20
SIC 5141 Groceries, general line

D-U-N-S 25-122-2055 (BR)
CARA OPERATIONS LIMITED
SWISS CHALET CHICKEN & RIBS
(*Suby of* Cara Holdings Limited)
735 Wonderland Rd N, London, ON, N6H 4L1
(519) 657-5241
Emp Here 55
SIC 5812 Eating places

D-U-N-S 25-981-7963 (BR)
CHESHIRE HOMES OF LONDON INC
CHESHIRE LONDON
120 Cherryhill Pl Suite 107, London, ON, N6H 4N9
(519) 438-5922
Emp Here 23
SIC 8051 Skilled nursing care facilities

D-U-N-S 25-482-8510 (HQ)
COMMUNITY CARE ACCESS CENTRE OF LONDON AND MIDDLESEX
(*Suby of* Community Care Access Centre of London and Middlesex)
356 Oxford St W, London, ON, N6H 1T3
(519) 473-2222
Emp Here 100   *Emp Total* 165
Sales 179,795,737
SIC 8059 Nursing and personal care, nec
Ex Dir Sandra Coleman
Dir Fin Terry Simpkin
Dir Kate Melito
Dir Gale Robertson

D-U-N-S 20-711-7164 (BR)
CONSEIL SCOLAIRE VIAMONDE
MARIE CURIE ELEMENTARY SCHOOL
40 Hunt Club Dr, London, ON, N6H 3Y3
(519) 471-5677
Emp Here 50
SIC 8211 Elementary and secondary schools

D-U-N-S 24-964-8338 (BR)
CORPORATION OF THE CITY OF LONDON
THAMES VALLEY GOLF & COUNTRY CLUB
850 Sunninghill Ave, London, ON, N6H 3L9
(519) 661-4440
Emp Here 20
SIC 7997 Membership sports and recreation

---

clubs

D-U-N-S 24-098-3515   (BR)
COSTCO WHOLESALE CANADA LTD
COSTCO
(*Suby of* Costco Wholesale Corporation)
693 Wonderland Rd N Suite 530, London, ON,
N6H 4L1
(519) 474-5300
Emp Here 150
SIC 5099 Durable goods, nec

D-U-N-S 24-860-4670   (SL)
CUSTOM CUISINE CATERING LIMITED
1260 Gainsborough Rd, London, ON, N6H
5K8
(519) 963-1426
Emp Here 70   *Sales* 2,115,860
SIC 5812 Eating places

D-U-N-S 24-484-0740   (BR)
**DIVERSICARE CANADA MANAGEMENT
SERVICES CO., INC**
*CHELSEY PARK RETIREMENT COMMU-
NITY*
312 Oxford St W, London, ON, N6H 4N7
(519) 432-1855
Emp Here 300
SIC 8051 Skilled nursing care facilities

D-U-N-S 20-082-3842   (SL)
DUNLINE RUBBER PRODUCTS COMPANY
*DUNLINE RUBBER PRODUCTS INTERNA-
TIONAL, DIV OF*
1579 Hyde Park Rd Suite 8, London, ON, N6H
5L4
(519) 473-1116
Emp Here 30   *Sales* 5,457,381
SIC 3069 Fabricated rubber products, nec
Alexander C Scovil
Cathy J Cronyn

D-U-N-S 25-393-0226   (BR)
ESAM CONSTRUCTION LIMITED
FLEETWAY BOWLING CENTRE
720 Proudfoot Lane, London, ON, N6H 5G5
(519) 472-9310
Emp Here 40
SIC 7933 Bowling centers

D-U-N-S 20-575-4448   (BR)
**FEDERATED INSURANCE COMPANY OF
CANADA**
735 Wonderland Rd N Suite 200, London, ON,
N6H 4L1
(519) 473-5610
Emp Here 26
SIC 6411 Insurance agents, brokers, and ser-
vice

D-U-N-S 20-177-8276   (BR)
GENERAL ELECTRIC CANADA COMPANY
(*Suby of* General Electric Company)
1510 Woodcock St Unit 1, London, ON, N6H
5S1

Emp Here 36
SIC 3625 Relays and industrial controls

D-U-N-S 24-634-2448   (SL)
**HUTTON HOUSE ASSOCIATION FOR
ADULTS WITH DISABILITIES**
HUTTON HOUSE
654 Wonderland Rd N, London, ON, N6H 3E5
(519) 472-6381
Emp Here 50   *Sales* 2,334,742
SIC 8331 Job training and related services

D-U-N-S 24-383-8948   (BR)
LOBLAWS INC
REAL CANADIAN SUPERSTORE
1205 Oxford St W, London, ON, N6H 1V9
(519) 641-3653
Emp Here 150
SIC 5411 Grocery stores

D-U-N-S 24-524-5766   (HQ)
**LONDON AGRICULTURAL COMMODITIES
INC**

LAC
(*Suby of* Michigan Agricultural Commodities,
Inc.)
1615 North Routledge Pk Unit 43, London,
ON, N6H 5L6
(519) 473-9333
Emp Here 27   *Emp Total* 100
Sales 390,107,000
SIC 6799 Investors, nec
Pr Pr Richard Smibert
Chris Mcmichael

D-U-N-S 25-237-8492   (BR)
**LONDON DISTRICT CATHOLIC SCHOOL
BOARD**
*NOTRE DAME CATHOLIC ELEMENTARY
SCHOOL*
767 Valetta St, London, ON, N6H 4N1
(519) 660-2773
Emp Here 25
SIC 8211 Elementary and secondary schools

D-U-N-S 20-710-5219   (BR)
**LONDON DISTRICT CATHOLIC SCHOOL
BOARD**
ST PAUL ELEMENTARY
1090 Guildwood Blvd, London, ON, N6H 4G6
(519) 660-2790
Emp Here 50
SIC 8211 Elementary and secondary schools

D-U-N-S 20-923-9755   (SL)
**LONDON HUNT AND COUNTRY CLUB LIM-
ITED**
1431 Oxford St W, London, ON, N6H 1W1
(519) 471-6430
Emp Here 58   *Sales* 2,334,742
SIC 7997 Membership sports and recreation
clubs

D-U-N-S 25-744-1311   (BR)
**MCG. RESTAURANTS (WONDERLAND)
INC**
OAR HOUSE SPORTS BAR & GRILL
666 Wonderland Rd N, London, ON, N6H 4K9
(519) 473-5702
Emp Here 45
SIC 5812 Eating places

D-U-N-S 24-964-9252   (BR)
METRO ONTARIO INC
METRO
301 Oxford St W, London, ON, N6H 1S6
(519) 433-1708
Emp Here 110
SIC 5411 Grocery stores

D-U-N-S 25-743-8440   (SL)
MOVATI ATHLETIC (LONDON NORTH) INC.
755 Wonderland Rd N, London, ON, N6H 4L1
(519) 471-7181
Emp Here 100   *Sales* 4,012,839
SIC 7991 Physical fitness facilities

D-U-N-S 25-203-3170   (HQ)
OXFORD LEARNING CENTRES, INC
(*Suby of* Oxford Learning Centres, Inc)
747 Hyde Park Rd Suite 230, London, ON,
N6H 3S3
(519) 473-1207
Emp Here 20   *Emp Total* 35
Sales 5,982,777
SIC 6794 Patent owners and lessors

D-U-N-S 24-409-3162   (BR)
PHARMA PLUS DRUGMARTS LTD
REXALL PHARMA PLUS
740 Hyde Park Rd, London, ON, N6H 5W9
(519) 471-1780
Emp Here 30
SIC 5912 Drug stores and proprietary stores

D-U-N-S 24-964-7611   (BR)
SEARS CANADA INC
SEARS OUTLET
530 Oxford St W, London, ON, N6H 1T6

Emp Here 100

SIC 5311 Department stores

D-U-N-S 20-128-5020   (HQ)
STERLING MARKING PRODUCTS INC
CANADA STAMP
1147 Gainsborough Rd, London, ON, N6H
5L5
(519) 434-5785
Emp Here 110   *Emp Total* 120
Sales 10,048,512
SIC 3953 Marking devices
Pr Pr Robert Schram

D-U-N-S 20-590-5891   (BR)
**THAMES VALLEY DISTRICT SCHOOL
BOARD**
EAGLE HEIGHTS PUBLIC SCHOOL
284 Oxford St W, London, ON, N6H 1S9
(519) 452-8460
Emp Here 35
SIC 8211 Elementary and secondary schools

D-U-N-S 20-653-8782   (BR)
**THAMES VALLEY DISTRICT SCHOOL
BOARD**
WESTDALE PUBLIC SCHOOL
1050 Plantation Rd, London, ON, N6H 2Y5
(519) 452-8650
Emp Here 20
SIC 8211 Elementary and secondary schools

D-U-N-S 25-239-9456   (BR)
**THAMES VALLEY DISTRICT SCHOOL
BOARD**
JOHN DEARNESS PUBLIC SCHOOL
555 Sanatorium Rd, London, ON, N6H 3W6
(519) 452-8260
Emp Here 21
SIC 8211 Elementary and secondary schools

D-U-N-S 20-590-4613   (BR)
**THAMES VALLEY DISTRICT SCHOOL
BOARD**
RIVERSIDE PUBLIC SCHOOL
550 Pinetree Dr, London, ON, N6H 3N1
(519) 452-8510
Emp Here 25
SIC 8211 Elementary and secondary schools

D-U-N-S 20-710-5425   (BR)
**THAMES VALLEY DISTRICT SCHOOL
BOARD**
*JEANNE SAUVE FRENCH IMMERSION
PUBLIC SCHOOL*
215 Wharncliffe Rd N, London, ON, N6H 2B6
(519) 452-8250
Emp Here 25
SIC 8211 Elementary and secondary schools

D-U-N-S 20-590-5735   (BR)
**THAMES VALLEY DISTRICT SCHOOL
BOARD**
OAKRIDGE SECONDARY SCHOOL
1040 Oxford St W, London, ON, N6H 1V4
(519) 452-2750
Emp Here 80
SIC 8211 Elementary and secondary schools

D-U-N-S 20-710-5441   (BR)
**THAMES VALLEY DISTRICT SCHOOL
BOARD**
MADELINE HARDY PUBLIC SCHOOL
600 Sanatorium Rd, London, ON, N6H 3W7
(519) 858-2774
Emp Here 50
SIC 8211 Elementary and secondary schools

D-U-N-S 20-005-6997   (BR)
WENDY'S RESTAURANTS OF CANADA INC
WENDY'S
(*Suby of* The Wendy's Company)
654 Wonderland Rd N, London, ON, N6H 3E5
(519) 471-4667
Emp Here 30
SIC 5812 Eating places

London, ON N6J
Middlesex County

D-U-N-S 20-547-5929   (BR)
BELL MEDIA INC
NEW PL, THE
1 Communications Rd, London, ON, N6J 4Z1
(519) 686-8810
Emp Here 175
SIC 4832 Radio broadcasting stations

D-U-N-S 20-711-7404   (BR)
**CONSEIL SCOLAIRE DE DISTRICT DES
ECOLES CATHOLIQUES DU SUD-OUEST**
ECOLE FRERE-ANDRE
400 Base Line Rd W, London, ON, N6J 1W1
(519) 471-6680
Emp Here 50
SIC 8211 Elementary and secondary schools

D-U-N-S 25-432-5645   (SL)
FINCH CHRYSLER DODGE JEEP RAM LTD
590 Wharncliffe Rd S, London, ON, N6J 2N4
(519) 686-1988
Emp Here 40   *Sales* 18,846,580
SIC 5511 New and used car dealers
Owner Dan Dale

D-U-N-S 25-462-6567   (BR)
**GOVERNING COUNCIL OF THE SALVA-
TION ARMY IN CANADA, THE**
*GOVERNING COUNCIL OF THE SALVATION
ARMY IN CANADA, THE*
54 Riverview Ave, London, ON, N6J 1A2

Emp Here 31
SIC 8322 Individual and family services

D-U-N-S 20-809-8785   (SL)
KIDLOGIC LONDON INC
750 Wharncliffe Rd S, London, ON, N6J 2N4
(519) 685-4221
Emp Here 27   *Sales* 802,568
SIC 8351 Child day care services

D-U-N-S 20-655-1611   (BR)
**LONDON DISTRICT CATHOLIC SCHOOL
BOARD**
ST. JUDE CATHOLIC SCHOOL
690 Viscount Rd, London, ON, N6J 2Y5
(519) 660-2785
Emp Here 25
SIC 8211 Elementary and secondary schools

D-U-N-S 25-237-8419   (BR)
**LONDON DISTRICT CATHOLIC SCHOOL
BOARD**
*ECOLE ELEMENTAIRE CATHOLIQUE
FRERE ANDRE*
400 Base Line Rd W, London, ON, N6J 1W1
(519) 471-6680
Emp Here 26
SIC 8211 Elementary and secondary schools

D-U-N-S 25-310-9698   (BR)
**MCDONALD'S RESTAURANTS OF
CANADA LIMITED**
MCDONALD'S
(*Suby of* McDonald's Corporation)
462 Wharncliffe Rd S, London, ON, N6J 2M9
(519) 673-0680
Emp Here 75
SIC 5812 Eating places

D-U-N-S 25-162-9416   (BR)
MERCEDES-BENZ CANADA INC
600 Wharncliffe Rd S, London, ON, N6J 2N4
(519) 668-0600
Emp Here 25
SIC 5511 New and used car dealers

D-U-N-S 25-743-6089   (BR)
METRO ONTARIO INC
FOOD BASICS
509 Commissioners Rd W, London, ON, N6J
1Y5
(519) 473-2857
Emp Here 150

SIC 5411 Grocery stores

D-U-N-S 20-059-6141   (BR)
N. TEPPERMAN LIMITED
TEPPERMAN'S
481 Wharncliffe Rd S, London, ON, N6J 2N1
(519) 433-5353
Emp Here 50
SIC 5712 Furniture stores

D-U-N-S 25-028-5293   (BR)
REVERA LONG TERM CARE INC
ELMWOOD PLACE
46 Elmwood Pl, London, ON, N6J 1J2
(519) 433-7259
Emp Here 80
SIC 8051 Skilled nursing care facilities

D-U-N-S 20-519-0171   (BR)
SEARS CANADA INC
784 Wharncliffe Rd S, London, ON, N6J 2N4
(519) 649-2796
Emp Here 33
SIC 4226 Special warehousing and storage, nec

D-U-N-S 25-255-3698   (BR)
SIFTON PROPERTIES LIMITED
BERKSHIRE CLUB
500 Berkshire Dr, London, ON, N6J 3S1
(519) 472-5665
Emp Here 20
SIC 7991 Physical fitness facilities

D-U-N-S 20-127-6300   (SL)
SOUTH WEST CHRYSLER DODGE INC
658 Wharncliffe Rd S, London, ON, N6J 2N4
(519) 649-2121
Emp Here 33   *Sales* 12,038,516
SIC 5511 New and used car dealers
Pr Pr Joseph Prossler
Genl Mgr Jeff Pressler

D-U-N-S 25-239-9753   (BR)
THAMES VALLEY DISTRICT SCHOOL BOARD
WOODLAND HEIGHTS PUBLIC SCHOOL
474 Springbank Dr, London, ON, N6J 1G8
(519) 452-8710
Emp Here 35
SIC 8211 Elementary and secondary schools

D-U-N-S 20-590-4712   (BR)
THAMES VALLEY DISTRICT SCHOOL BOARD
SIR ISAAC BROCK PUBLIC SCHOOL
80 St Lawrence Blvd, London, ON, N6J 2X1
(519) 452-8560
Emp Here 36
SIC 8211 Elementary and secondary schools

D-U-N-S 24-875-3238   (BR)
THAMES VALLEY DISTRICT SCHOOL BOARD
VICTORIA PUBLIC SCHOOL
130 Wharncliffe Rd S, London, ON, N6J 2K5
(519) 452-8640
Emp Here 25
SIC 8211 Elementary and secondary schools

D-U-N-S 20-590-5982   (BR)
THAMES VALLEY DISTRICT SCHOOL BOARD
KENSAL PARK FRENCH IMMERSION PUBLIC SCHOOL
328 Springbank Dr, London, ON, N6J 1G5
(519) 452-8280
Emp Here 25
SIC 8211 Elementary and secondary schools

D-U-N-S 25-239-9209   (BR)
THAMES VALLEY DISTRICT SCHOOL BOARD
WESTMINSTER SECONDARY SCHOOL
230 Base Line Rd W, London, ON, N6J 1W1
(519) 452-2900
Emp Here 85
SIC 8211 Elementary and secondary schools

D-U-N-S 20-590-4621   (BR)
THAMES VALLEY DISTRICT SCHOOL BOARD
ARTHUR FORD PUBLIC SCHOOL
617 Viscount Rd, London, ON, N6J 2Y4
(519) 452-8020
Emp Here 25
SIC 8211 Elementary and secondary schools

D-U-N-S 20-710-5433   (BR)
THAMES VALLEY DISTRICT SCHOOL BOARD
BRICK STREET PUBLIC SCHOOL
393 Commissioners Rd W, London, ON, N6J 1Y4

Emp Here 25
SIC 8211 Elementary and secondary schools

D-U-N-S 25-239-9514   (BR)
THAMES VALLEY DISTRICT SCHOOL BOARD
MANOR & HIGHLAND PARK PUBLIC SCHOOL
77 Tecumseh Ave W, London, ON, N6J 1K8

Emp Here 28
SIC 8211 Elementary and secondary schools

D-U-N-S 20-590-4647   (BR)
THAMES VALLEY DISTRICT SCHOOL BOARD
W SHERWOOD FOX PUBLIC SCHOOL
660 Steeplechase Dr, London, ON, N6J 3P4
(519) 452-8730
Emp Here 35
SIC 8211 Elementary and secondary schools

D-U-N-S 25-214-9141   (BR)
UNION GAS LIMITED
SPECTRA ENERGY COMPANY
109 Commissioners Rd W, London, ON, N6J 1X7
(519) 667-4100
Emp Here 225
SIC 4923 Gas transmission and distribution

D-U-N-S 20-927-3627   (BR)
WENDY'S RESTAURANTS OF CANADA INC
(Suby of The Wendy's Company)
375 Southdale Rd W, London, ON, N6J 4G8
(519) 681-0977
Emp Here 37
SIC 5812 Eating places

London, ON N6K
Middlesex County

D-U-N-S 24-418-5042   (BR)
CINEPLEX ODEON CORPORATION
CINEPLEX CINEMAS WESTMOUNT & VIP
755 Wonderland Rd S, London, ON, N6K 1M6
(519) 474-2152
Emp Here 131
SIC 7832 Motion picture theaters, except drive-in

D-U-N-S 25-054-8955   (BR)
CORPORATION OF THE CITY OF LONDON
STORY BOOK GARDENS
1958 Storybook Lane, London, ON, N6K 4Y6
(519) 661-5770
Emp Here 55
SIC 7996 Amusement parks

D-U-N-S 20-730-0992   (SL)
DIAMOND SECURITY
377 Grand View Ave, London, ON, N6K 2T1
(519) 471-8095
Emp Here 80   *Sales* 2,480,664
SIC 7381 Detective and armored car services

D-U-N-S 25-300-4964   (BR)
FABRICLAND DISTRIBUTORS INC
476 Wonderland Rd S, London, ON, N6K 3T1

(519) 641-6951
Emp Here 20
SIC 5949 Sewing, needlework, and piece goods

D-U-N-S 20-344-7847   (BR)
HOLLISWEALTH ADVISORY SERVICES INC.
HOLLIS WEALTH
785 Wonderland Rd S Suite 251, London, ON, N6K 1M6
(519) 672-8101
Emp Here 21
SIC 6282 Investment advice

D-U-N-S 24-877-1065   (HQ)
LADY'S A CHAMP (1995) LIMITED, THE
BOOMER CLUB, THE
(Suby of Lady's A Champ (1995) Limited, The)
795 Wonderland Rd S, London, ON, N6K 3C2
(519) 615-0243
Emp Here 21   *Emp Total* 50
Sales 3,648,035
SIC 5611 Men's and boys' clothing stores

D-U-N-S 20-590-9273   (BR)
LONDON DISTRICT CATHOLIC SCHOOL BOARD
ST THERESA CATHOLIC SCHOOL
108 Fairlane Ave, London, ON, N6K 3E6
(519) 660-2792
Emp Here 25
SIC 8211 Elementary and secondary schools

D-U-N-S 20-710-5102   (BR)
LONDON DISTRICT CATHOLIC SCHOOL BOARD
JEAN VANIER CATHOLIC SCHOOL
1019 Viscount Rd, London, ON, N6K 1H5
(519) 660-2771
Emp Here 50
SIC 8211 Elementary and secondary schools

D-U-N-S 24-877-0877   (BR)
LONDON HEALTH SCIENCES CENTRE
LONDON REGIONAL CANCER CENTRE
790 Commissioners Rd W, London, ON, N6K 1C2
(519) 685-8300
Emp Here 365
SIC 8011 Offices and clinics of medical doctors

D-U-N-S 25-318-1770   (BR)
MCDONALD'S RESTAURANTS OF CANADA LIMITED
MCDONALD'S 8287
(Suby of McDonald's Corporation)
1033 Wonderland Rd S, London, ON, N6K 3V1
(519) 668-0141
Emp Here 70
SIC 5812 Eating places

D-U-N-S 20-806-1270   (BR)
METRO ONTARIO INC
A & P STORES
1244 Commissioners Rd W, London, ON, N6K 1C7
(519) 473-3389
Emp Here 25
SIC 5411 Grocery stores

D-U-N-S 24-770-4187   (SL)
MOVATI ATHLETIC (HOLDINGS) INC
346 Wonderland Rd S Suite 201, London, ON, N6K 1L3
(519) 914-1730
Emp Here 50   *Sales* 2,638,521
SIC 7997 Membership sports and recreation clubs

D-U-N-S 20-862-1768   (BR)
NORTHERN REFLECTIONS LTD
785 Wonderland Rd S Unit J15, London, ON, N6K 1M6
(519) 472-3848
Emp Here 25
SIC 5621 Women's clothing stores

D-U-N-S 20-181-6928   (BR)
PALASAD BILLIARDS LIMITED
141 Pine Valley Blvd, London, ON, N6K 3T6
(519) 685-1390
Emp Here 100
SIC 5044 Office equipment

D-U-N-S 20-844-5846   (BR)
PEPSICO CANADA ULC
FRITO LAY CANADA
(Suby of Pepsico, Inc.)
104 Somerset Cres, London, ON, N6K 3M4
(519) 472-2135
Emp Here 20
SIC 2096 Potato chips and similar snacks

D-U-N-S 25-744-2053   (HQ)
PHILON RESTAURANTS INC
PIZZA HUT
(Suby of Philon Restaurants Inc)
1009 Wonderland Rd S, London, ON, N6K 3V1
(519) 649-1001
Emp Here 20   *Emp Total* 50
Sales 1,532,175
SIC 5812 Eating places

D-U-N-S 25-448-8299   (BR)
REDBERRY FRANCHISING CORP
BURGER KING 3420
660 Wonderland Rd S, London, ON, N6K 1L8

Emp Here 25
SIC 5812 Eating places

D-U-N-S 25-308-4305   (BR)
ROYAL BANK OF CANADA
RBC
(Suby of Royal Bank Of Canada)
440 Boler Rd Suite 412, London, ON, N6K 4L2
(519) 641-5000
Emp Here 20
SIC 6021 National commercial banks

D-U-N-S 20-535-8554   (BR)
SEARS CANADA INC
785 Wonderland Rd S, London, ON, N6K 1M6
(519) 641-5311
Emp Here 20
SIC 5311 Department stores

D-U-N-S 20-291-3252   (BR)
SIFTON PROPERTIES LIMITED
LONGWORTH RETIREMENT VILLAGE
600 Longworth Rd Suite 118, London, ON, N6K 4X9
(519) 472-1115
Emp Here 75
SIC 6513 Apartment building operators

D-U-N-S 20-860-2099   (BR)
SOURCE (BELL) ELECTRONICS INC, THE
SOURCE, THE
785 Wonderland Rd S, London, ON, N6K 1M6

Emp Here 25
SIC 5999 Miscellaneous retail stores, nec

D-U-N-S 24-121-4845   (SL)
SOUTHWEST OPTIMIST BASEBALL COMPLEX
785 Wonderland Rd S, London, ON, N6K 1M6
(519) 652-8571
Emp Here 20   *Sales* 6,125,139
SIC 7941 Sports clubs, managers, and promoters
Pr Chris Muscutt

D-U-N-S 20-030-1682   (BR)
THAMES VALLEY DISTRICT SCHOOL BOARD
BYRON SOMERSET PUBLIC SCHOOL
175 Whisperwood Ave, London, ON, N6K 4C6
(519) 452-8090
Emp Here 30
SIC 8211 Elementary and secondary schools

D-U-N-S 25-239-9183   (BR)

THAMES VALLEY DISTRICT SCHOOL BOARD
BYRON SOUTHWOOD ELEMENTARY SCHOOL
1379 Lola St, London, ON, N6K 3R6
(519) 452-8100
Emp Here 30
SIC 8211 Elementary and secondary schools

D-U-N-S 20-590-5800   (BR)
THAMES VALLEY DISTRICT SCHOOL BOARD
BYRON NORTHVIEW PUBLIC SCHOOL
1370 Commissioners Rd W, London, ON, N6K 1E1
(519) 452-3080
Emp Here 30
SIC 8211 Elementary and secondary schools

D-U-N-S 25-025-4760   (BR)
THAMES VALLEY DISTRICT SCHOOL BOARD
SAUNDERS SECONDARY SCHOOL
941 Viscount Rd, London, ON, N6K 1H5
(519) 452-2770
Emp Here 150
SIC 8211 Elementary and secondary schools

D-U-N-S 25-239-9134   (BR)
THAMES VALLEY DISTRICT SCHOOL BOARD
WESTMOUNT PUBLIC SCHOOL
1011 Viscount Rd, London, ON, N6K 1H5
(519) 452-8670
Emp Here 55
SIC 8211 Elementary and secondary schools

London, ON N6L
Middlesex County

D-U-N-S 20-028-7775   (BR)
BANQUE TORONTO-DOMINION, LA
TORONTO-DOMINION BANK, THE
(*Suby of* Toronto-Dominion Bank, The)
3029 Wonderland Rd S, London, ON, N6L 1R4
(519) 668-3504
Emp Here 20
SIC 6021 National commercial banks

D-U-N-S 25-231-7359   (BR)
BRICK WAREHOUSE LP, THE
1040 Wharncliffe Rd S, London, ON, N6L 1H2
(519) 649-6464
Emp Here 20
SIC 5712 Furniture stores

D-U-N-S 24-453-0879   (SL)
CANDUCT INDUSTRIES LIMITED
4575 Blakie Rd, London, ON, N6L 1P8
(519) 652-8603
Emp Here 70   *Sales* 4,417,880
SIC 2655 Fiber cans, drums, and similar products

D-U-N-S 24-751-3419   (BR)
DAVIS FUEL COMPANY LIMITED
FLYING M TRUCK STOP
7340 Colonel Talbot Rd, London, ON, N6L 1H8
(519) 652-2310
Emp Here 20
SIC 5541 Gasoline service stations

D-U-N-S 24-223-0394   (SL)
EAST SIDE MARIO'S
3079 Wonderland Rd S, London, ON, N6L 1R4
(519) 649-6566
Emp Here 50   *Sales* 1,532,175
SIC 5812 Eating places

D-U-N-S 24-086-2644   (BR)
EXPERTECH NETWORK INSTALLATION INC
220 Exeter Rd, London, ON, N6L 1A3

Emp Here 30
SIC 4899 Communication services, nec

D-U-N-S 25-708-0551   (BR)
FGL SPORTS LTD
SPORT CHEK
3165 Wonderland Road S, London, ON, N6L 1R4
(519) 668-1776
Emp Here 20
SIC 5941 Sporting goods and bicycle shops

D-U-N-S 25-321-8549   (BR)
GOLDER ASSOCIATES LTD
309 Exeter Rd Unit 1, London, ON, N6L 1C1
(519) 652-0099
Emp Here 60
SIC 8711 Engineering services

D-U-N-S 20-870-1982   (BR)
HOME DEPOT OF CANADA INC
HOME DEPOT
(*Suby of* The Home Depot Inc)
3035 Wonderland Rd S, London, ON, N6L 1R4
(519) 691-1400
Emp Here 200
SIC 5251 Hardware stores

D-U-N-S 25-759-0885   (BR)
LANGS BUS LINES LIMITED
4158 Raney Cres, London, ON, N6L 1C3
(519) 652-6994
Emp Here 30
SIC 4111 Local and suburban transit

D-U-N-S 20-773-8659   (BR)
LEON'S FURNITURE LIMITED
LEON'S
947 Wharncliffe Rd S, London, ON, N6L 1J9
(519) 680-2111
Emp Here 80
SIC 5712 Furniture stores

D-U-N-S 20-651-1052   (BR)
LINDE CANADA LIMITED
BOC GASES
234 Exeter Rd Suite A, London, ON, N6L 1A3
(519) 686-4150
Emp Here 21
SIC 5999 Miscellaneous retail stores, nec

D-U-N-S 20-781-2632   (BR)
LOBLAWS SUPERMARKETS LIMITED
LOBLAWS
3040 Wonderland Rd S, London, ON, N6L 1A6
(519) 668-5383
Emp Here 250
SIC 5411 Grocery stores

D-U-N-S 20-720-1885   (BR)
LOBLAWS SUPERMARKETS LIMITED
LOBLAWS GREAT FOOD
3040 Wonderland Rd S, London, ON, N6L 1A6
(519) 668-0719
Emp Here 350
SIC 5411 Grocery stores

D-U-N-S 20-267-8165   (BR)
MILLER PAVING LIMITED
MILLER WASTE SYSTEMS
3438 Manning Dr, London, ON, N6L 1K6
(519) 668-7894
Emp Here 40
SIC 1611 Highway and street construction

D-U-N-S 24-364-8164   (BR)
N. TEPPERMAN LIMITED
TEPPERMAN'S
1150 Wharncliffe Rd S, London, ON, N6L 1K3
(519) 433-5353
Emp Here 200
SIC 5712 Furniture stores

D-U-N-S 24-101-2140   (BR)
STAPLES CANADA INC
STAPLES THE BUSINESS DEPOT

(*Suby of* Staples, Inc.)
3080 Wonderland Rd S, London, ON, N6L 1A6
(519) 690-2049
Emp Here 40
SIC 5943 Stationery stores

D-U-N-S 20-271-6200   (BR)
THYSSENKRUPP ELEVATOR (CANADA) LIMITED
THYSSENKRUPP ELEVATOR
4096 Meadowbrook Dr Suite 133, London, ON, N6L 1G4
(519) 977-0376
Emp Here 35
SIC 7699 Repair services, nec

D-U-N-S 25-650-0786   (BR)
THYSSENKRUPP ELEVATOR (CANADA) LIMITED
4093 Meadowbrook Dr S 114, London, ON, N6L 1G2
(519) 977-0376
Emp Here 30
SIC 5084 Industrial machinery and equipment

D-U-N-S 25-366-9758   (BR)
TYCO INTEGRATED FIRE & SECURITY CANADA, INC
TYCO
(*Suby of* Johnson Controls, Inc.)
150 Exeter Rd Suite 44, London, ON, N6L 1G9
(519) 680-2001
Emp Here 21
SIC 1731 Electrical work

D-U-N-S 25-010-7356   (BR)
TYCO INTEGRATED FIRE & SECURITY CANADA, INC
SIMPLEX GRINNELL
(*Suby of* Johnson Controls, Inc.)
150 Exeter Rd Unit 44, London, ON, N6L 1G9
(519) 680-2001
Emp Here 20
SIC 7389 Business services, nec

D-U-N-S 24-923-7603   (BR)
WASTE MANAGEMENT OF CANADA CORPORATION
(*Suby of* Waste Management, Inc.)
290 Exeter Rd, London, ON, N6L 1A3
(519) 652-5299
Emp Here 65
SIC 4953 Refuse systems

D-U-N-S 20-580-4243   (BR)
WINNERS MERCHANTS INTERNATIONAL L.P.
HOMESENSE
(*Suby of* The TJX Companies Inc)
3075 Wonderland Rd S Unit E, London, ON, N6L 1R4
(519) 681-5471
Emp Here 20
SIC 5651 Family clothing stores

D-U-N-S 24-194-2403   (SL)
WONDERLAND PIZZA LTD
BOSTON PIZZA
3090 Wonderland Rd S, London, ON, N6L 1A6
(519) 472-5001
Emp Here 65   *Sales* 1,969,939
SIC 5812 Eating places

London, ON N6M
Middlesex County

D-U-N-S 24-424-4740   (BR)
0429746 B.C. LTD
(*Suby of* O.C. Holdings '87 Inc)
2825 Innovation Dr, London, ON, N6M 0B6
(519) 937-7777
Emp Here 80

SIC 5142 Packaged frozen goods

D-U-N-S 24-368-5760   (SL)
1376302 ONTARIO INC
DISTINCTIVE HOMES
329 Sovereign Rd, London, ON, N6M 1A6
(519) 859-5056
Emp Here 80   *Sales* 4,669,485
SIC 2434 Wood kitchen cabinets

D-U-N-S 20-844-0289   (BR)
BREWERS RETAIL INC
BEER STORE, THE
280 Sovereign Rd, London, ON, N6M 1B3
(519) 451-3699
Emp Here 200
SIC 5921 Liquor stores

D-U-N-S 20-773-0552   (SL)
CANADA TUBEFORM INC
2879 Innovation Dr, London, ON, N6M 0B6
(519) 451-9995
Emp Here 58   *Sales* 4,158,760
SIC 3465 Automotive stampings

D-U-N-S 24-525-4193   (BR)
CONSEIL SCOLAIRE DE DISTRICT DES ECOLES CATHOLIQUES DU SUD-OUEST
ECOLE ELEMENTAIRE CATHOLIQUE SAINT-JEAN-DE-BREBEUF
270 Chelton Rd, London, ON, N6M 0B9
(519) 963-1219
Emp Here 25
SIC 8211 Elementary and secondary schools

D-U-N-S 20-920-1719   (BR)
GENERAL ELECTRIC CANADA COMPANY
GE
(*Suby of* General Electric Company)
320 Neptune Cres Unit 1, London, ON, N6M 1A1
(519) 451-1522
Emp Here 26
SIC 3625 Relays and industrial controls

D-U-N-S 24-888-6285   (BR)
INTEGRATED DISTRIBUTION SYSTEMS LIMITED PARTNERSHIP
WAJAX EQUIPMENT
359 Tartan Dr Unit 1, London, ON, N6M 1B1
(519) 685-1172
Emp Here 20
SIC 5082 Construction and mining machinery

D-U-N-S 20-605-6327   (BR)
LIFTOW LIMITED
403 Neptune Cres, London, ON, N6M 1A2
(519) 659-0823
Emp Here 23
SIC 5084 Industrial machinery and equipment

D-U-N-S 24-346-4448   (BR)
M & T INSTA-PRINT LIMITED
318 Neptune Cres Suite 1, London, ON, N6M 1A1
(519) 455-6667
Emp Here 100
SIC 2752 Commercial printing, lithographic

London, ON N6N
Middlesex County

D-U-N-S 24-680-6041   (BR)
BRADKEN CANADA MANUFACTURED PRODUCTS LTD
BRADKEN
45 Enterprise Dr, London, ON, N6N 1C1
(519) 685-3000
Emp Here 50
SIC 3599 Industrial machinery, nec

D-U-N-S 24-849-1982   (BR)
CAISSEN WATER TECHNOLOGIES INC
CULLIGAN WATER
2800 Roxburgh Rd Unit 4, London, ON, N6N

1K9
(519) 963-0338
Emp Here 35
SIC 5963 Direct selling establishments

D-U-N-S 20-552-7778   (BR)
CANON CANADA INC
BUSINESS SOLUTIONS DIVISION
647 Wilton Grove Rd, London, ON, N6N 1N7

Emp Here 25
SIC 5044 Office equipment

D-U-N-S 20-059-6067   (BR)
COCA-COLA REFRESHMENTS CANADA COMPANY
(*Suby of* The Coca-Cola Company)
950 Green Valley Rd, London, ON, N6N 1E3
(519) 686-2100
Emp Here 160
SIC 2086 Bottled and canned soft drinks

D-U-N-S 24-926-6974   (BR)
DIVERSEY CANADA, INC
(*Suby of* Sealed Air Corporation)
1151 Green Valley Rd, London, ON, N6N 1E4
(519) 668-6211
Emp Here 100
SIC 2842 Polishes and sanitation goods

D-U-N-S 25-362-8325   (BR)
FLYING J CANADA INC
FLYING J TRAVEL PLAZA
3700 Highbury Ave S, London, ON, N6N 1P3
(519) 686-9154
Emp Here 50
SIC 5541 Gasoline service stations

D-U-N-S 20-126-6079   (SL)
FOREST CITY GRAPHICS LIMITED
982 Hubrey Rd, London, ON, N6N 1B5
(519) 668-2191
Emp Here 100
SIC 2771 Greeting cards

D-U-N-S 20-698-1446   (BR)
GEORGIAN BAY FIRE & SAFETY LTD
(*Suby of* Loti Holdings Inc)
1031 Hubrey Rd Unit 10, London, ON, N6N 1B4
(519) 686-1301
Emp Here 60
SIC 5099 Durable goods, nec

D-U-N-S 24-791-8829   (BR)
GOODWILL INDUSTRIES, ONTARIO GREAT LAKES
GOODWILL OUTLET
990 Pond Mills Rd, London, ON, N6N 1A2
(519) 685-5389
Emp Here 20
SIC 8699 Membership organizations, nec

D-U-N-S 24-336-2175   (BR)
INGREDION CANADA CORPORATION
(*Suby of* Ingredion Incorporated)
1100 Green Valley Rd, London, ON, N6N 1E3
(519) 686-3160
Emp Here 20
SIC 2063 Beet sugar

D-U-N-S 25-150-4189   (BR)
JET TRANSPORT LTD
1525 Wilton Grove Rd, London, ON, N6N 1M3
(519) 644-0183
Emp Here 60
SIC 4213 Trucking, except local

D-U-N-S 24-000-9451   (BR)
LIQUOR CONTROL BOARD OF ONTARIO, THE
LCBO
955 Wilton Grove Rd Suite 950, London, ON, N6N 1C9
(519) 681-0310
Emp Here 100
SIC 5921 Liquor stores

D-U-N-S 25-171-5561   (BR)

MAGNA SEATING INC
QUALTECH SEATING SYSTEMS DIV OF
3915 Commerce Rd, London, ON, N6N 1P4
(519) 644-1221
Emp Here 185
SIC 3714 Motor vehicle parts and accessories

D-U-N-S 20-346-3740   (BR)
MAGNA SEATING INC
QUALTECH SEATING SYSTEMS DIV OF
961 Pond Mills Rd, London, ON, N6N 1C3
(519) 808-9035
Emp Here 50
SIC 3714 Motor vehicle parts and accessories

D-U-N-S 25-503-4597   (BR)
MANITOULIN TRANSPORT INC
JET TRANSPORT
1525 Wilton Grove Rd, London, ON, N6N 1M3
(519) 644-0183
Emp Here 35
SIC 4213 Trucking, except local

D-U-N-S 20-177-9829   (HQ)
MARTINREA AUTOMOTIVE SYSTEMS CANADA LTD
MARTINREA AUTOMOTIVE SYSTEMS CANADA (LONDON)
3820 Commerce Rd, London, ON, N6N 1P6
(519) 690-5070
Emp Here 100   *Emp Total* 14,000
Sales 21,085,642
SIC 3711 Motor vehicles and car bodies
Genl Mgr Rocco Marinaccio

D-U-N-S 20-034-4081   (BR)
MASONITE INTERNATIONAL CORPORATION
HARRING DOORS DIV. OF
(*Suby of* Masonite International Corporation)
3799 Commerce Road, London, ON, N6N 1P9
(519) 644-2444
Emp Here 35
SIC 2431 Millwork

D-U-N-S 25-999-9035   (BR)
NESTLE CANADA INC
980 Wilton Grove Rd, London, ON, N6N 1C7
(519) 686-0182
Emp Here 500
SIC 2023 Dry, condensed and evaporated dairy products

D-U-N-S 24-101-2637   (BR)
PARTS CANADA DEVELOPMENT CO.
PARTS CANADA POWER TWINS
3935 Cheese Factory Rd, London, ON, N6N 1G2
(519) 644-0202
Emp Here 60
SIC 5013 Motor vehicle supplies and new parts

D-U-N-S 25-751-7763   (BR)
PATENE BUILDING SUPPLIES LTD
BEST THIER WAS
1125 Wilton Grove Rd, London, ON, N6N 1C9
(519) 649-1588
Emp Here 20
SIC 5039 Construction materials, nec

D-U-N-S 24-345-9968   (BR)
PEPSICO CANADA ULC
FRITO LAY CANADA
(*Suby of* Pepsico, Inc.)
40 Enterprise Dr Suite 2, London, ON, N6N 1A7
(519) 668-4004
Emp Here 150
SIC 5145 Confectionery

D-U-N-S 20-950-9582   (BR)
ROSEDALE TRANSPORT LIMITED
3960 Commerce Rd, London, ON, N6N 1P8
(519) 644-0330
Emp Here 25
SIC 4213 Trucking, except local

D-U-N-S 24-350-1827   (BR)

ROYAL GROUP, INC
BONCOR BUILDING PRODUCTS CO, DIV OF
3886 Commerce Rd, London, ON, N6N 1P8
(519) 644-0440
Emp Here 30
SIC 5211 Lumber and other building materials

D-U-N-S 24-425-9045   (BR)
RYDER TRUCK RENTAL CANADA LTD
RYDER CANADA
(*Suby of* Ryder System, Inc.)
2724 Roxburgh Rd Suite 7, London, ON, N6N 1K9
(519) 680-0847
Emp Here 200
SIC 7513 Truck rental and leasing, no drivers

D-U-N-S 20-880-3247   (BR)
RYDER TRUCK RENTAL CANADA LTD
(*Suby of* Ryder System, Inc.)
1459 Sise Rd, London, ON, N6N 1E1
(519) 681-0585
Emp Here 40
SIC 7513 Truck rental and leasing, no drivers

D-U-N-S 20-195-4596   (BR)
S.L.H. TRANSPORT INC
1095 Wilton Grove Rd, London, ON, N6N 1C9
(519) 681-3820
Emp Here 70
SIC 4213 Trucking, except local

D-U-N-S 24-410-5912   (SL)
SLEEGERS TANKS INC
980 Green Valley Rd, London, ON, N6N 1E3
(519) 685-7444
Emp Here 21   *Sales* 3,283,232
SIC 3443 Fabricated plate work (boiler shop)

D-U-N-S 24-336-4551   (HQ)
STIHL LIMITED
1515 Sise Rd Suite 5666, London, ON, N6N 1E1
(519) 681-3000
Emp Here 60   *Emp Total* 14,603
Sales 18,191,271
SIC 5084 Industrial machinery and equipment
Pr Pr Gregory Quigg
Dir Fin Angelo Dethomasis
Prs Mgr Elizabeth Evanski
Jack Jones
Hans Peter Stihl

D-U-N-S 20-321-3582   (BR)
SYSCO CANADA, INC
BEDELL'S (LONDON) FOOD SERVICE DISTRIBUTORS
(*Suby of* Sysco Corporation)
1011 Hubrey Rd, London, ON, N6N 1B4
(519) 680-0800
Emp Here 20
SIC 5142 Packaged frozen goods

D-U-N-S 24-924-5911   (BR)
TEAM TRUCK CENTRES LIMITED
1040 Wilton Grove Rd, London, ON, N6N 1C7
(519) 453-2970
Emp Here 160
SIC 5511 New and used car dealers

D-U-N-S 20-024-9386   (BR)
THAMES VALLEY DISTRICT SCHOOL BOARD
WESTMINSTER CENTRAL PUBLIC SCHOOL
2835 Westminster Dr, London, ON, N6N 1L7
(519) 452-8660
Emp Here 30
SIC 8211 Elementary and secondary schools

D-U-N-S 24-078-1534   (BR)
TOROMONT INDUSTRIES LTD
TOROMONT CAT
50 Enterprise Dr, London, ON, N6N 1A7
(519) 681-1900
Emp Here 50
SIC 5082 Construction and mining machinery

D-U-N-S 20-403-7071   (BR)
TOROMONT INDUSTRIES LTD
CIMCO REFRIGERATION
651 Wilton Grove Rd, London, ON, N6N 1N7
(519) 434-6444
Emp Here 20
SIC 3585 Refrigeration and heating equipment

D-U-N-S 20-100-7734   (BR)
TOROMONT INDUSTRIES LTD
CLIMATE CONTROL
651 Wilton Grove Rd Suite 1, London, ON, N6N 1N7
(519) 439-1300
Emp Here 22
SIC 1711 Plumbing, heating, air-conditioning

D-U-N-S 20-555-4145   (SL)
TRANSFORM AUTOMOTIVE CANADA LIMITED
(*Suby of* Amsted Industries Incorporated)
3745 Commerce Rd, London, ON, N6N 1R1
(519) 644-2434
Emp Here 100   *Sales* 18,797,647
SIC 3714 Motor vehicle parts and accessories
D William Shaw
Dir Denis Hartman

D-U-N-S 25-403-8128   (BR)
UNITED PARCEL SERVICE CANADA LTD
UPS
60 Midpark Rd, London, ON, N6N 1B3
(519) 686-8200
Emp Here 112
SIC 4513 Air courier services

D-U-N-S 24-124-9267   (BR)
VIPOND INC
VIPOND FIRE PROTECTION, DIV
30 Midpark Cres, London, ON, N6N 1B1
(519) 681-2233
Emp Here 20
SIC 1711 Plumbing, heating, air-conditioning

D-U-N-S 24-358-2723   (BR)
WFS LTD
WFS
(*Suby of* W.W. Grainger, Inc.)
645 Wilton Grove Rd, London, ON, N6N 1N7
(519) 681-3790
Emp Here 50
SIC 5085 Industrial supplies

D-U-N-S 20-092-3147   (BR)
WATERGROUP COMPANIES INC
CULLIGAN
(*Suby of* Clayton, Dubilier & Rice, Inc.)
2800 Roxburgh Rd Unit 4d, London, ON, N6N 1K9
(519) 685-0445
Emp Here 26
SIC 5999 Miscellaneous retail stores, nec

D-U-N-S 20-547-5960   (BR)
WOLFEDALE ELECTRIC LTD
DIAL ONE WOLFEDALE ELECTRIC
647 Wilton Grove Rd Unit 3, London, ON, N6N 1N7

Emp Here 20
SIC 1731 Electrical work

London, ON N6P
Middlesex County

D-U-N-S 25-743-4183   (BR)
ALLIED SYSTEMS (CANADA) COMPANY
6151 Colonel Talbot Rd, London, ON, N6P 1J2
(519) 652-6577
Emp Here 400
SIC 4213 Trucking, except local

D-U-N-S 20-039-7904   (BR)

CLUBLINK CORPORATION ULC
GREENHILLS GOLF CLUB
4838 Colonel Talbot Rd, London, ON, N6P 1H7
(519) 652-5033
Emp Here 60
SIC 7992 Public golf courses

D-U-N-S 24-477-9393   (SL)
G L S LEASCO CANADA
7234 Littlewood Dr, London, ON, N6P 1J7
(519) 652-2832
Emp Here 30   *Sales* 2,772,507
SIC 7513 Truck rental and leasing, no drivers

D-U-N-S 24-302-5384   (BR)
GOODLIFE FITNESS CENTRES INC
GOODLIFE FITNESS
925 Southdale Rd W Suite 2, London, ON, N6P 0B3
(519) 652-2250
Emp Here 40
SIC 7991 Physical fitness facilities

D-U-N-S 20-025-4378   (BR)
THAMES VALLEY DISTRICT SCHOOL BOARD
LAMBETH PUBLIC SCHOOL
6820 Duffield St, London, ON, N6P 1A4
(519) 652-2050
Emp Here 23
SIC 8211 Elementary and secondary schools

D-U-N-S 20-590-0645   (BR)
TORONTO-DOMINION BANK, THE
TD CANADA TRUST
(*Suby of* Toronto-Dominion Bank, The)
2478 Main St, London, ON, N6P 1R2

Emp Here 20
SIC 6021 National commercial banks

Long Sault, ON K0C
Stormont County

D-U-N-S 20-653-7859   (BR)
CONSEIL SCOLAIRE DE DISTRICT CATHOLIQUE DE L'EST ONTARIEN
ECOLE CATHOLIQUE SAINTE LUCIE
17337 Dow St, Long Sault, ON, K0C 1P0
(613) 932-9493
Emp Here 30
SIC 8211 Elementary and secondary schools

D-U-N-S 25-607-6852   (BR)
LAFARGE CANADA INC
5650 Richmond Dr, Long Sault, ON, K0C 1P0
(613) 534-2673
Emp Here 100
SIC 5039 Construction materials, nec

D-U-N-S 25-580-6192   (BR)
OMNI HEALTH CARE LTD
WOODLAND VILLA NURSING HOME
30 Mille Roches Rd Suite 388, Long Sault, ON, K0C 1P0
(613) 534-2276
Emp Here 120
SIC 8051 Skilled nursing care facilities

D-U-N-S 25-224-8661   (BR)
UPPER CANADA DISTRICT SCHOOL BOARD, THE
LONGUE SAULT PUBLIC SCHOOL
(*Suby of* Upper Canada District School Board, The)
13 Bethune St, Long Sault, ON, K0C 1P0
(613) 534-2415
Emp Here 24
SIC 8211 Elementary and secondary schools

Longlac, ON P0T
Thunder Bay County

D-U-N-S 20-705-7782   (BR)
DILICO ANISHINABEK FAMILY CARE
121 Forestry Rd Suite 2, Longlac, ON, P0T 2A0
(807) 876-2267
Emp Here 22
SIC 8322 Individual and family services

D-U-N-S 20-279-7700   (SL)
LONGLAC LUMBER INC
101 Blueberry Rd, Longlac, ON, P0T 2A0
(807) 343-6382
Emp Here 70   *Sales* 9,231,950
SIC 2421 Sawmills and planing mills, general
Pr Wolf Gericke

D-U-N-S 25-239-0000   (BR)
SUPERIOR NORTH CATHOLIC DISTRICT SCHOOL BOARD
OUR LADY OF FATIMA SCHOOL
(*Suby of* Superior North Catholic District School Board)
113 Indian Rd, Longlac, ON, P0T 2A0
(807) 876-2213
Emp Here 20
SIC 8211 Elementary and secondary schools

Loretto, ON L0G
Simcoe County

D-U-N-S 25-292-4428   (BR)
SIMCOE COUNTY DISTRICT SCHOOL BOARD, THE
ADJALA CENTRAL PUBLIC SCHOOL
(*Suby of* Simcoe County District School Board, The)
9091 County Rd 1, Loretto, ON, L0G 1L0
(905) 729-2624
Emp Here 29
SIC 8211 Elementary and secondary schools

Lucan, ON N0M
Middlesex County

D-U-N-S 25-112-9250   (SL)
CREST SUPPORT SERVICES (MEADOWCREST) INC
CREST SUPPORT SERVICES
13570 Elginfield Rd Rr 1, Lucan, ON, N0M 2J0
(519) 227-6766
Emp Here 50   *Sales* 2,544,288
SIC 8322 Individual and family services

D-U-N-S 25-237-8583   (BR)
LONDON DISTRICT CATHOLIC SCHOOL BOARD
ST PATRICK ELEMENTARY SCHOOL
33654 Roman Line, Lucan, ON, N0M 2J0
(519) 660-2789
Emp Here 23
SIC 8211 Elementary and secondary schools

D-U-N-S 25-952-0708   (BR)
MURPHY, J & T LIMITED
MURPHY BUS LINES
6214 William St, Lucan, ON, N0M 2J0
(519) 227-4427
Emp Here 43
SIC 4151 School buses

D-U-N-S 24-676-5254   (BR)
THAMES VALLEY DISTRICT SCHOOL BOARD
WILBERFORCE PUBLIC SCHOOL
340 Beech St, Lucan, ON, N0M 2J0
(519) 227-2185
Emp Here 25
SIC 8211 Elementary and secondary schools

D-U-N-S 20-590-0595   (BR)
TORONTO-DOMINION BANK, THE
TD CANADA TRUST
(*Suby of* Toronto-Dominion Bank, The)
290 Main St, Lucan, ON, N0M 2J0
(519) 227-4446
Emp Here 20
SIC 6021 National commercial banks

Lucknow, ON N0G

D-U-N-S 25-249-3788   (BR)
AVON MAITLAND DISTRICT SCHOOL BOARD
BROOKSIDE PUBLIC SCHOOL
Rr 7, Lucknow, ON, N0G 2H0
(519) 529-7900
Emp Here 22
SIC 8211 Elementary and secondary schools

D-U-N-S 25-228-1100   (BR)
BLUEWATER DISTRICT SCHOOL BOARD
LUCKNOW CENTRAL PUBLIC SCHOOL
463 Bob St, Lucknow, ON, N0G 2H0
(519) 528-3022
Emp Here 23
SIC 8211 Elementary and secondary schools

D-U-N-S 20-848-1598   (SL)
GORDON T. MONTGOMERY LIMITED
701 Campbell St, Lucknow, ON, N0G 2H0
(519) 528-2813
Emp Here 64   *Sales* 2,165,628
SIC 4151 School buses

D-U-N-S 20-557-9803   (BR)
REVERA LONG TERM CARE INC
PINECREST MANOR NURSING HOME
399 Bob St, Lucknow, ON, N0G 2H0
(519) 528-2820
Emp Here 70
SIC 8051 Skilled nursing care facilities

Lyn, ON K0E
Leeds County

D-U-N-S 20-129-0202   (HQ)
BURNBRAE FARMS LIMITED
(*Suby of* Burnbrae Holdings Ltd)
3356 County Road 27, Lyn, ON, K0E 1M0
(613) 345-5651
Emp Here 800   *Emp Total* 41
Sales 237,122,275
SIC 5144 Poultry and poultry products
  Margaret Hudson
  Donald Oddie
  VP VP Joseph Edward Hudson
  Joseph Hudson

D-U-N-S 25-486-4473   (BR)
UPPER CANADA DISTRICT SCHOOL BOARD, THE
LYN PUBLIC SCHOOL
(*Suby of* Upper Canada District School Board, The)
38 Main St E, Lyn, ON, K0E 1M0
(613) 345-1242
Emp Here 22
SIC 8211 Elementary and secondary schools

Lyndhurst, ON K0E
Leeds County

D-U-N-S 25-401-9011   (BR)
UPPER CANADA DISTRICT SCHOOL BOARD, THE
SWEETS CORNER ELEMENTARY SCHOOL
(*Suby of* Upper Canada District School Board, The)
276 Fortune Line Rd, Lyndhurst, ON, K0E 1N0
(613) 928-2777
Emp Here 25
SIC 8211 Elementary and secondary schools

M'Chigeeng, ON P0P
Manitoulin County

D-U-N-S 25-238-1975   (BR)
RAINBOW DISTRICT SCHOOL BOARD
MANITOULIN SECONDARY SCHOOL
(*Suby of* Rainbow District School Board)
107 Bay St, M'Chigeeng, ON, P0P 1G0
(705) 368-7000
Emp Here 50
SIC 8211 Elementary and secondary schools

Maberly, ON K0H
Lanark County

D-U-N-S 20-893-5270   (SL)
CRAINS' CONSTRUCTION LIMITED
1800 Mayberly 2 Elphin Rd, Maberly, ON, K0H 2B0
(613) 268-2308
Emp Here 55   *Sales* 4,012,839
SIC 1794 Excavation work

Mactier, ON P0C
Muskoka County

D-U-N-S 20-300-7484   (BR)
CANADIAN NATIONAL INSTITUTE FOR THE BLIND, THE
LAKE JOSEPH CENTER
(*Suby of* Canadian National Institute For The Blind, The)
4 Joe Finley Way #1, Parry Sound, On P2a 2w8, Mactier, ON, P0C 1H0
(705) 375-2630
Emp Here 30
SIC 8322 Individual and family services

D-U-N-S 20-589-7569   (BR)
CANADIAN PACIFIC RAILWAY COMPANY
CPR
1 Station St, Mactier, ON, P0C 1H0
(705) 375-2750
Emp Here 60
SIC 4011 Railroads, line-haul operating

Madoc, ON K0K

D-U-N-S 25-265-3662   (BR)
HASTINGS AND PRINCE EDWARD DISTRICT SCHOOL BOARD
MADOC PUBLIC SCHOOL
32 Baldwin St, Madoc, ON, K0K 2K0
(613) 473-2487
Emp Here 45
SIC 8211 Elementary and secondary schools

D-U-N-S 24-315-5228   (BR)
IKO INDUSTRIES LTD
ARMOROOF DIV OF
105084 Hwy 7, Madoc, ON, K0K 2K0
(613) 473-0430
Emp Here 110
SIC 2952 Asphalt felts and coatings

D-U-N-S 25-857-5570   (BR)
SOBEYS CAPITAL INCORPORATED
FOODLAND
40 Elgin St, Madoc, ON, K0K 2K0

(613) 473-4240
Emp Here 50
SIC 5411 Grocery stores

D-U-N-S 20-590-0462   (BR)
TORONTO-DOMINION BANK, THE
TD CANADA TRUST
(*Suby of* Toronto-Dominion Bank, The)
18 St Lawrence St W, Madoc, ON, K0K 2K0
(613) 473-4245
Emp Here 20
SIC 6021 National commercial banks

Maidstone, ON N0R
Essex County

D-U-N-S 20-153-1741   (BR)
DAY & ROSS INC
3795 Webster Cres, Maidstone, ON, N0R 1K0
(519) 737-6331
Emp Here 25
SIC 4213 Trucking, except local

D-U-N-S 20-891-5426   (BR)
TEAM TRUCK CENTRES LIMITED
4155 County Rd 46, Maidstone, ON, N0R 1K0
(519) 737-6176
Emp Here 20
SIC 5511 New and used car dealers

D-U-N-S 24-764-8033   (BR)
TOROMONT INDUSTRIES LTD
TOROMONT CAT
3740 Webster Cres Suite 3, Maidstone, ON, N0R 1K0
(519) 737-7386
Emp Here 21
SIC 5082 Construction and mining machinery

D-U-N-S 25-635-7401   (BR)
UNITED CHURCH OF CANADA, THE
BETHEL-MAIDSTONE UNITED CHURCH
933 Talbot Rd, Maidstone, ON, N0R 1K0
(519) 723-2284
Emp Here 45
SIC 8661 Religious organizations

D-U-N-S 25-636-9992   (BR)
WASTE CONNECTIONS OF CANADA INC
BFI CANADA
5000 8th Concession Rd, Maidstone, ON, N0R 1K0
(519) 737-2900
Emp Here 35
SIC 4953 Refuse systems

Maitland, ON K0E
Grenville County

D-U-N-S 24-318-0648   (BR)
ENERGIE VALERO INC
ULTRAMAR CANADA
31 Church St, Maitland, ON, K0E 1P0
(613) 348-3265
Emp Here 425
SIC 5983 Fuel oil dealers

D-U-N-S 24-844-3132   (BR)
EVONIK CANADA INC
1380 County Road 2, Maitland, ON, K0E 1P0
(613) 348-7711
Emp Here 30
SIC 2819 Industrial inorganic chemicals, nec

D-U-N-S 25-976-1872   (HQ)
EVONIK INDUSTRIES
1380 County Road 2, Maitland, ON, K0E 1P0
(613) 348-7171
Emp Here 30   *Emp Total* 11,714
Sales 46,551,053
SIC 5169 Chemicals and allied products, nec
Pr Jack Chenauld

D-U-N-S 20-563-2362   (BR)
INVISTA (CANADA) COMPANY
(*Suby of* Koch Industries, Inc.)
1400 County Rd 2, Maitland, ON, K0E 1P0
(613) 348-4204
Emp Here 80
SIC 5169 Chemicals and allied products, nec

Mallorytown, ON K0E
Leeds County

D-U-N-S 25-105-6008   (SL)
SERSA TOTAL TRACK LTD
68 County Rd 5, Mallorytown, ON, K0E 1R0
(613) 923-5702
Emp Here 54   *Sales* 4,742,446
SIC 1799 Special trade contractors, nec

Manitouwadge, ON P0T
Thunder Bay County

D-U-N-S 24-233-2356   (BR)
CANADIAN IMPERIAL BANK OF COMMERCE
CIBC 07892
34 Huron St & Barker St, Manitouwadge, ON, P0T 2C0
(807) 826-3201
Emp Here 20
SIC 6021 National commercial banks

D-U-N-S 24-169-9461   (SL)
MANITOUWADGE GENERAL HOSPITAL
1 Healthcare Cres, Manitouwadge, ON, P0T 2C0
(807) 826-3251
Emp Here 50   *Sales* 3,502,114
SIC 8062 General medical and surgical hospitals

D-U-N-S 25-863-7420   (BR)
SUPERIOR GREENSTONE DISTRICT SCHOOL BOARD
MANITOUWADGE PUBLIC SCHOOL
21 Wenonah St, Manitouwadge, ON, P0T 2C0
(807) 826-4011
Emp Here 30
SIC 8211 Elementary and secondary schools

D-U-N-S 25-265-0148   (BR)
SUPERIOR GREENSTONE DISTRICT SCHOOL BOARD
MANITOUWADGE HIGH SCHOOL
200 Manitou Rd W, Manitouwadge, ON, P0T 2C0
(807) 826-3241
Emp Here 25
SIC 8211 Elementary and secondary schools

Manotick, ON K4M
Carleton County

D-U-N-S 24-233-4550   (BR)
CITY OF OTTAWA
OTTAWA FIRE SERVICES
(*Suby of* City of Ottawa)
5669 Manotick Main St, Manotick, ON, K4M 1K1
(613) 692-3301
Emp Here 20
SIC 7389 Business services, nec

D-U-N-S 24-312-2087   (BR)
OTTAWA CATHOLIC DISTRICT SCHOOL BOARD
ST. MARK CATHOLIC HIGH SCHOOL
(*Suby of* Ottawa Catholic District School Board)
1040 Dozois Rd, Manotick, ON, K4M 1B2

(613) 692-2551
Emp Here 130
SIC 8211 Elementary and secondary schools

D-U-N-S 25-265-4058   (BR)
OTTAWA CATHOLIC DISTRICT SCHOOL BOARD
ST LEONARD SCHOOL
(*Suby of* Ottawa Catholic District School Board)
5344 Long Island Rd, Manotick, ON, K4M 1E8
(613) 692-3521
Emp Here 50
SIC 8211 Elementary and secondary schools

D-U-N-S 20-711-6182   (BR)
OTTAWA-CARLETON DISTRICT SCHOOL BOARD
MANOTICK PUBLIC SCHOOL
1075 Bridge St, Manotick, ON, K4M 1H3
(613) 692-3311
Emp Here 25
SIC 8211 Elementary and secondary schools

D-U-N-S 25-309-9402   (BR)
ROYAL BANK OF CANADA
RBC
(*Suby of* Royal Bank Of Canada)
5539 Main St, Manotick, ON, K4M 1A1
(613) 692-5400
Emp Here 20
SIC 6021 National commercial banks

D-U-N-S 24-101-2509   (SL)
SKARLAN ENTERPRISES LIMITED
1165 John St, Manotick, ON, K4M 1A5
(613) 692-2530
Emp Here 30   *Sales* 6,188,450
SIC 1521 Single-family housing construction
Pr Pr Darryl Pochailo

Maple, ON L6A
York County

D-U-N-S 25-074-1373   (SL)
ANNE & MAX TANENBAUM COMMUNITY HEBREW ACADEMY OF TORONTO
9600 Bathurst St, Maple, ON, L6A 3Z8
(905) 787-8772
Emp Here 100   *Sales* 9,333,400
SIC 8211 Elementary and secondary schools
 Ellen Chaikof
Pr Pr Leslie Fluxgold
VP VP Leanne Matlow
Dir Marcy Abramsky
 Stephen Bloom
Dir Robin Brunder
Dir Donald Carr
Dir Miray Cheskes Granovsky
Dir Lisa Dack
Dir Sara Dobner

D-U-N-S 20-589-4517   (BR)
BANQUE TORONTO-DOMINION, LA
TD BANK FINANCIAL GROUP
(*Suby of* Toronto-Dominion Bank, The)
2933 Major Mackenzie Dr, Maple, ON, L6A 3N9
(905) 832-2000
Emp Here 20
SIC 6021 National commercial banks

D-U-N-S 25-120-1968   (BR)
CANADA POST CORPORATION
MAPLE POST OFFICE
9926 Keele St, Maple, ON, L6A 3Y4
(905) 832-1435
Emp Here 40
SIC 4311 U.s. postal service

D-U-N-S 25-753-4883   (HQ)
COMMUNITY MAPLE CHILD CARE SERVICES
(*Suby of* Community Maple Child Care Services)

9350 Keele St Suite 1, Maple, ON, L6A 1P4
(905) 832-5752
Emp Here 25   *Emp Total* 80
Sales 2,858,628
SIC 8351 Child day care services

D-U-N-S 20-711-7552   (BR)
CONSEIL SCOLAIRE DE DISTRICT CATHOLIQUE CENTRE-SUD
ECOLE ELEMENTAIRE CATHOLIQUE LE-PETIT-PRINCE
79 Avro Rd, Maple, ON, L6A 1Y3
(905) 832-3153
Emp Here 25
SIC 8211 Elementary and secondary schools

D-U-N-S 25-914-9813   (BR)
CORPORATION OF THE CITY OF VAUGHAN, THE
MAPLE COMMUNITY CENTRE
10190 Keele St, Maple, ON, L6A 1R2
(905) 832-2377
Emp Here 20
SIC 8322 Individual and family services

D-U-N-S 25-935-8096   (BR)
DAVEY TREE EXPERT CO. OF CANADA, LIMITED
330 Rodinea Rd Suite 2, Maple, ON, L6A 4P5
(905) 303-7269
Emp Here 20
SIC 1422 Crushed and broken limestone

D-U-N-S 24-945-6229   (HQ)
FABCO PLASTIQUES INC
2175 Teston Rd Po Box 2175 Stn Main, Maple, ON, L6A 1T3
(905) 832-0600
Emp Here 45   *Emp Total* 50
Sales 12,695,162
SIC 5162 Plastics materials and basic shapes
Pr Pr William Kehren
Fin Ex Gary Davidson

D-U-N-S 20-649-7997   (SL)
FORTINO'S (MAJOR MACKENZIE) LTD
2911 Major Mackenzie Dr, Maple, ON, L6A 3N9
(905) 417-0484
Emp Here 350   *Sales* 66,552,480
SIC 5411 Grocery stores
Pr John Mancini

D-U-N-S 25-333-3827   (SL)
KML ENGINEERED HOMES LTD
KML BUILDING SOLUTIONS
10877 Keele St, Maple, ON, L6A 0K6

Emp Here 60   *Sales* 14,770,560
SIC 3448 Prefabricated Metal buildings and components
 John Gardner
Pr Vince Misfud

D-U-N-S 24-353-8159   (BR)
LOWE'S COMPANIES CANADA, ULC
LOWE'S OF MAPLE
200 Mcnaughton Rd E, Maple, ON, L6A 4E2
(905) 879-2450
Emp Here 100
SIC 5211 Lumber and other building materials

D-U-N-S 20-734-7118   (BR)
MCDONALD'S RESTAURANTS OF CANADA LIMITED
MCDONALD'S #8674
(*Suby of* McDonald's Corporation)
2810 Major Mackenzie Dr, Maple, ON, L6A 3L2
(905) 303-0804
Emp Here 50
SIC 5812 Eating places

D-U-N-S 24-344-3327   (BR)
MERCEDES-BENZ CANADA INC
9300 Jane St, Maple, ON, L6A 0C5
(905) 585-9300
Emp Here 40

SIC 5511 New and used car dealers

D-U-N-S 25-240-1166   (SL)
PTC AUTOMOTIVE MAPLE LTD
230 Sweetriver Blvd, Maple, ON, L6A 4V3
(905) 417-1170
Emp Here 20   *Sales* 7,296,070
SIC 5511 New and used car dealers
John Morabito

D-U-N-S 24-096-3905   (SL)
SHERWOOD COURT LONG TERM CARE CENTRE
300 Ravineview Dr Suite 1, Maple, ON, L6A 3P8
(905) 303-3565
Emp Here 76   *Sales* 3,429,153
SIC 8052 Intermediate care facilities

D-U-N-S 20-590-5404   (BR)
YORK CATHOLIC DISTRICT SCHOOL BOARD
FATHER JOHN KELLY CATHOLIC ELEMENTARY SCHOOL
9350 Keele St, Maple, ON, L6A 1P4
(905) 832-5353
Emp Here 34
SIC 8211 Elementary and secondary schools

D-U-N-S 25-151-0228   (BR)
YORK CATHOLIC DISTRICT SCHOOL BOARD
SAINT JOAN OF ARC CATHOLIC HIGH SCHOOL
1 St. Joan Of Arc Ave, Maple, ON, L6A 1W9
(905) 832-8882
Emp Here 20
SIC 8211 Elementary and secondary schools

D-U-N-S 20-590-4548   (BR)
YORK CATHOLIC DISTRICT SCHOOL BOARD
BLESSED TRINITY SCHOOL
230 Hawker Rd, Maple, ON, L6A 2R2
(905) 303-7150
Emp Here 70
SIC 8211 Elementary and secondary schools

D-U-N-S 20-977-6579   (BR)
YORK CATHOLIC DISTRICT SCHOOL BOARD
DIVINE MERCY CATHOLIC SCHOOL
251 Melville Ave, Maple, ON, L6A 1Z1
(905) 832-2555
Emp Here 20
SIC 8211 Elementary and secondary schools

D-U-N-S 20-711-4674   (BR)
YORK CATHOLIC DISTRICT SCHOOL BOARD
ST JAMES SCHOOL
171 Mast Rd, Maple, ON, L6A 3J7
(905) 832-7676
Emp Here 60
SIC 8211 Elementary and secondary schools

D-U-N-S 25-107-0264   (BR)
YORK CATHOLIC DISTRICT SCHOOL BOARD
HOLY JUBILEE
400 St. Joan Of Arc Ave, Maple, ON, L6A 2S8
(905) 303-6121
Emp Here 80
SIC 8211 Elementary and secondary schools

D-U-N-S 24-676-3390   (BR)
YORK REGION DISTRICT SCHOOL BOARD
DR. ROBERTA BONDAR PUBLIC SCHOOL
(*Suby of* York Region District School Board)
401 Av Grand Trunk, Maple, ON, L6A 0T4
(905) 417-8046
Emp Here 25
SIC 8211 Elementary and secondary schools

D-U-N-S 20-711-4351   (BR)
YORK REGION DISTRICT SCHOOL BOARD
MAPLE CREEK PUBLIC SCHOOL
(*Suby of* York Region District School Board)

210 Hawker Rd, Maple, ON, L6A 2J8
(905) 417-9177
Emp Here 50
SIC 8211 Elementary and secondary schools

D-U-N-S 20-711-4344   (BR)
YORK REGION DISTRICT SCHOOL BOARD
DISCOVERY PUBLIC SCHOOL
(*Suby of* York Region District School Board)
120 Discovery Trail, Maple, ON, L6A 2Z2
(905) 417-1622
Emp Here 50
SIC 8211 Elementary and secondary schools

D-U-N-S 24-676-5205   (BR)
YORK REGION DISTRICT SCHOOL BOARD
HERBERT H CARNEGIE PUBLIC SCHOOL
(*Suby of* York Region District School Board)
575 Via Romano Blvd, Maple, ON, L6A 0G1
(905) 417-0211
Emp Here 46
SIC 8211 Elementary and secondary schools

D-U-N-S 20-591-2608   (BR)
YORK REGION DISTRICT SCHOOL BOARD
MAPLE HIGH SCHOOL
(*Suby of* York Region District School Board)
50 Springside Rd, Maple, ON, L6A 2W5
(905) 417-9444
Emp Here 130
SIC 8211 Elementary and secondary schools

D-U-N-S 25-297-8945   (BR)
YORK REGION DISTRICT SCHOOL BOARD
JOSEPH A. GIBSON PUBLIC SCHOOL
(*Suby of* York Region District School Board)
50 Naylon St, Maple, ON, L6A 1R8
(905) 832-1291
Emp Here 28
SIC 8211 Elementary and secondary schools

D-U-N-S 24-067-9980   (BR)
YORK REGION DISTRICT SCHOOL BOARD
JULLIARD PUBLIC SCHOOL
(*Suby of* York Region District School Board)
61 Julliard Dr, Maple, ON, L6A 3W7
(905) 832-3311
Emp Here 52
SIC 8211 Elementary and secondary schools

D-U-N-S 24-676-5239   (BR)
YORK REGION DISTRICT SCHOOL BOARD
TESTON VILLAGE PUBLIC SCHOOL
(*Suby of* York Region District School Board)
80 Murray Farm Lane, Maple, ON, L6A 3G1
(905) 417-0555
Emp Here 25
SIC 8211 Elementary and secondary schools

D-U-N-S 20-288-8355   (BR)
YORK REGION DISTRICT SCHOOL BOARD
MACKENZIE GLEN PUBLIC SCHOOL
(*Suby of* York Region District School Board)
575 Melville Ave, Maple, ON, L6A 2M4
(905) 417-9771
Emp Here 48
SIC 8211 Elementary and secondary schools

Marathon, ON P0T

D-U-N-S 20-880-2186   (BR)
CANADIAN PACIFIC RAILWAY COMPANY
CPR
Gd, Marathon, ON, P0T 2E0
(807) 229-2060
Emp Here 50
SIC 4011 Railroads, line-haul operating

D-U-N-S 25-270-1776   (BR)
LOBLAWS INC
EXTRA FOODS
2 Hemlo Dr, Marathon, ON, P0T 2E0
(807) 229-8006
Emp Here 50
SIC 5411 Grocery stores

D-U-N-S 24-070-1222   (BR)
RAINONE CONSTRUCTION (2007) LIMITED
(*Suby of* Rainone Construction (2007) Limited)
86 Evergreen Dr, Marathon, ON, P0T 2E0

Emp Here 30
SIC 1623 Water, sewer, and utility lines

D-U-N-S 25-818-7004   (BR)
SUPERIOR GREENSTONE DISTRICT SCHOOL BOARD
MARGARET CHIMNEY PUBLIC SCHOOL
21 Chisholm Trl, Marathon, ON, P0T 2E0
(807) 229-3050
Emp Here 30
SIC 8211 Elementary and secondary schools

D-U-N-S 25-265-0221   (BR)
SUPERIOR GREENSTONE DISTRICT SCHOOL BOARD
MARATHON HIGH SCHOOL
14 Hemlo Dr, Marathon, ON, P0T 2E0
(807) 229-1800
Emp Here 55
SIC 8211 Elementary and secondary schools

D-U-N-S 25-486-1727   (BR)
SUPERIOR NORTH CATHOLIC DISTRICT SCHOOL BOARD
HOLY SAVIOUR SCHOOL
(*Suby of* Superior North Catholic District School Board)
23 Pennlake Rd E, Marathon, ON, P0T 2E0
(807) 229-1121
Emp Here 20
SIC 8211 Elementary and secondary schools

Markdale, ON N0C
Grey County

D-U-N-S 25-238-9036   (BR)
BLUEWATER DISTRICT SCHOOL BOARD
BEAVERCREST COMMUNITY SCHOOL
101 Main St E, Markdale, ON, N0C 1H0
(519) 986-2990
Emp Here 35
SIC 8211 Elementary and secondary schools

D-U-N-S 24-342-3709   (BR)
CHAPMAN'S, DAVID ICE CREAM LIMITED
CHAPMAN'S ICE CREAM
774792 10 Hwy, Markdale, ON, N0C 1H0
(519) 986-2915
Emp Here 30
SIC 2024 Ice cream and frozen deserts

D-U-N-S 20-585-8504   (BR)
GREY BRUCE HEALTH SERVICES
55 Isla St, Markdale, ON, N0C 1H0
(519) 986-3040
Emp Here 50
SIC 8062 General medical and surgical hospitals

D-U-N-S 25-401-9540   (HQ)
KIDS & US COMMUNITY CHILDCARE AND FAMILY EDUCATION CENTRES INCORPORATED
(*Suby of* Kids & Us Community Childcare and Family Education Centres Incorporated)
206 Toronto St S, Markdale, ON, N0C 1H0
(519) 986-3692
Emp Here 20   *Emp Total* 72
Sales 2,598,753
SIC 8351 Child day care services

D-U-N-S 25-946-1382   (HQ)
KIDS 'N US
(*Suby of* Kids 'N Us)
206 Toronto St S, Markdale, ON, N0C 1H0
(519) 986-3351
Emp Here 25   *Emp Total* 50
Sales 1,978,891
SIC 8351 Child day care services

Markham, ON L3P
York County

D-U-N-S 20-770-0894   (BR)
1326760 ONTARIO INC
TIM HORTONS
(*Suby of* 1326760 Ontario Inc)
6040 Highway 7 E Unit 1, Markham, ON, L3P 3A8
(905) 294-8736
Emp Here 20
SIC 5812 Eating places

D-U-N-S 20-289-8693   (BR)
AMICA MATURE LIFESTYLES INC
AMICA AT SWAN LAKE
6360 16th Ave Suite 336, Markham, ON, L3P 7Y6
(905) 201-6058
Emp Here 100
SIC 8361 Residential care

D-U-N-S 25-296-4754   (BR)
BANK OF NOVA SCOTIA, THE
SCOTIABANK
101 Main St N, Markham, ON, L3P 1X9
(905) 294-3113
Emp Here 40
SIC 6021 National commercial banks

D-U-N-S 24-233-0368   (SL)
CSH ROUGE VALLEY INC
ROUGE VALLEY RETIREMENT RESIDENCE
5958 16th Ave, Markham, ON, L3P 8N1
(905) 472-6811
Emp Here 21   *Sales* 952,876
SIC 8361 Residential care

D-U-N-S 24-776-6731   (BR)
CHARTWELL MASTER CARE LP
5958 16th Ave, Markham, ON, L3P 8N1
(905) 294-1114
Emp Here 52
SIC 8059 Nursing and personal care, nec

D-U-N-S 20-025-3974   (BR)
CORPORATION OF THE CITY OF MARKHAM, THE
MARKHAM MUSEUM
9350 Markham Rd, Markham, ON, L3P 3J3
(905) 294-4576
Emp Here 24
SIC 8412 Museums and art galleries

D-U-N-S 24-476-2316   (BR)
CORPORATION OF THE CITY OF MARKHAM, THE
MARKHAM PUBLIC LIBRARY
6031 Highway 7 E, Markham, ON, L3P 3A7
(905) 513-7977
Emp Here 20
SIC 8231 Libraries

D-U-N-S 24-012-3864   (BR)
DIETITIANS OF CANADA
DIETETISTES DU CANADA, LES
14 Meyer Cir, Markham, ON, L3P 4C2
(905) 471-7314
Emp Here 22
SIC 8621 Professional organizations

D-U-N-S 24-601-8402   (SL)
EMCO MASONRY LIMITED
172 Bullock Dr Unit 26, Markham, ON, L3P 7M9
(905) 294-7927
Emp Here 60   *Sales* 6,087,000
SIC 1741 Masonry and other stonework
Pr Pr Rocco Colangelo

D-U-N-S 20-216-5457   (SL)
JAYFER AUTOMOTIVE GROUP (MARKHAM) INC
MARKHAM MAZDA
5426 Highway 7 E, Markham, ON, L3P 1B7

(905) 294-1210
Emp Here 50   *Sales* 3,648,035
SIC 7538 General automotive repair shops

D-U-N-S 24-721-0131   (SL)
JIT HOLDINGS INCORPORATED
SWISS CHALET # 1166
5284 Highway 7, Markham, ON, L3P 1B9
(905) 294-6654
Emp Here 50   *Sales* 1,819,127
SIC 5812 Eating places

D-U-N-S 24-195-0240   (BR)
LOBLAWS SUPERMARKETS LIMITED
LOBLAWS
200 Bullock Dr, Markham, ON, L3P 1W2
(905) 294-6277
Emp Here 50
SIC 5411 Grocery stores

D-U-N-S 25-180-4845   (BR)
MARKHAM PUBLIC LIBRARY BOARD
*THORNHILL COMMUNITY CENTRE LI-
BRARY*
6031 Highway 7 E, Markham, ON, L3P 3A7
(905) 513-7977
Emp Here 20
SIC 8231 Libraries

D-U-N-S 20-903-6367   (SL)
MARKHAVEN, INC
54 Parkway Ave, Markham, ON, L3P 2G4
(905) 294-2233
Emp Here 65   *Sales* 2,407,703
SIC 8361 Residential care

D-U-N-S 20-550-1328   (SL)
MARKVILLE CHEVROLET INC
5336 Highway 7 E, Markham, ON, L3P 1B9
(905) 294-1440
Emp Here 38   *Sales* 18,650,400
SIC 5511 New and used car dealers
Pr Pr William Wallace

D-U-N-S 20-793-0699   (BR)
SOBEYS CAPITAL INCORPORATED
MARKHAM SOBEY'S
9580 Mccowan Rd Unit G, Markham, ON, L3P
8M1
(905) 887-4366
Emp Here 50
SIC 5411 Grocery stores

D-U-N-S 20-640-6928   (SL)
**SUPREME LIGHTING & ELECTRIC SUPPLY
LTD**
9 Laidlaw Blvd, Markham, ON, L3P 1W5
(905) 477-3113
Emp Here 25   *Sales* 5,034,288
SIC 5063 Electrical apparatus and equipment
Pr Pr Michael Stam
 Robert Lippa
Fin Ex Osman Khan

D-U-N-S 20-788-2296   (BR)
TDL GROUP CORP, THE
TIM HORTONS
1443 16th Ave, Markham, ON, L3P 7R2

Emp Here 25
SIC 5812 Eating places

D-U-N-S 25-107-0397   (BR)
**YORK CATHOLIC DISTRICT SCHOOL
BOARD**
*ST KATERI TEKAKWITHA ELEMENTARY
SCHOOL*
230 Fincham Ave, Markham, ON, L3P 4B5
(905) 472-4420
Emp Here 26
SIC 8211 Elementary and secondary schools

D-U-N-S 24-246-8127   (BR)
**YORK CATHOLIC DISTRICT SCHOOL
BOARD**
*ST PATRICK CATHOLIC ELEMENTARY
SCHOOL*
5607 Highway 7 E, Markham, ON, L3P 1B6

(905) 294-1571
Emp Here 25
SIC 8211 Elementary and secondary schools

D-U-N-S 20-711-4625   (BR)
**YORK CATHOLIC DISTRICT SCHOOL
BOARD**
BROTHER ANDRE HIGH SCHOOL
6160 16th Ave Suite 16, Markham, ON, L3P
3K8
(905) 294-7671
Emp Here 50
SIC 8211 Elementary and secondary schools

D-U-N-S 25-297-9596   (BR)
YORK REGION DISTRICT SCHOOL BOARD
WILLIAM ARMSTRONG PUBLIC SCHOOL
(*Suby of* York Region District School Board)
11 Major Button'S Dr, Markham, ON, L3P 3G6
(905) 294-1262
Emp Here 30
SIC 8211 Elementary and secondary schools

D-U-N-S 25-297-8895   (BR)
YORK REGION DISTRICT SCHOOL BOARD
MARKHAM DISTRICT HIGH SCHOOL
(*Suby of* York Region District School Board)
89 Church St, Markham, ON, L3P 2M3
(905) 294-1886
Emp Here 130
SIC 8211 Elementary and secondary schools

D-U-N-S 25-297-8887   (BR)
YORK REGION DISTRICT SCHOOL BOARD
REESOR PARK PUBLIC SCHOOL
(*Suby of* York Region District School Board)
69 Wootten Way N, Markham, ON, L3P 2Y5
(905) 294-6558
Emp Here 40
SIC 8211 Elementary and secondary schools

D-U-N-S 20-591-2749   (BR)
YORK REGION DISTRICT SCHOOL BOARD
JAMES ROBINSON PUBLIC SCHOOL
(*Suby of* York Region District School Board)
90 Robinson St, Markham, ON, L3P 1N9
(905) 294-3484
Emp Here 25
SIC 8211 Elementary and secondary schools

D-U-N-S 25-297-9240   (BR)
YORK REGION DISTRICT SCHOOL BOARD
FRANKLIN STREET PUBLIC SCHOOL
(*Suby of* York Region District School Board)
21 Franklin St, Markham, ON, L3P 2S7
(905) 294-3562
Emp Here 40
SIC 8211 Elementary and secondary schools

D-U-N-S 25-297-9281   (BR)
YORK REGION DISTRICT SCHOOL BOARD
EDWARD T. CROWLE PUBLIC SCHOOL
(*Suby of* York Region District School Board)
15 Larkin Ave, Markham, ON, L3P 4P8
(905) 471-5775
Emp Here 35
SIC 8211 Elementary and secondary schools

Markham, ON L3R
York County

D-U-N-S 25-073-6618   (SL)
1009278 ONTARIO INC
BPG GRAPHIC SOLUTIONS
800 Cochrane Dr, Markham, ON, L3R 8C9

Emp Here 55   *Sales* 4,158,760
SIC 2752 Commercial printing, lithographic

D-U-N-S 25-075-5188   (SL)
1095141 ONTARIO LIMITED
FRANKIE TOMATTOS
7225 Woodbine Ave Suite 119, Markham, ON,
L3R 1A3
(905) 940-2199
Emp Here 90   *Sales* 2,699,546

SIC 5812 Eating places

D-U-N-S 24-333-0037   (HQ)
2063412 INVESTMENT LP
LEISUREWORLD CAREGIVING CENTRE
(*Suby of* 2063412 Investment LP)
302 Town Centre Blvd Suite 200, Markham,
ON, L3R 0E8
(905) 477-4006
Emp Here 100   *Emp Total* 2,000
Sales 319,155,287
SIC 8052 Intermediate care facilities
Dir David Cutler
Dir Martin Liddell

D-U-N-S 24-333-0029   (SL)
2063414 INVESTMENT LP
LEISUREWORLD CAREGIVING CENTRES
302 Town Centre Blvd Suite 200, Markham,
ON, L3R 0E8
(905) 477-4006
Emp Here 100   *Sales* 4,523,563
SIC 8051 Skilled nursing care facilities

D-U-N-S 24-101-1639   (HQ)
2063414 ONTARIO LIMITED
LEISUREWORLD CAREGIVING CENTRES
(*Suby of* 2063414 Ontario Limited)
302 Town Centre Blvd Suite 200, Markham,
ON, L3R 0E8
(905) 477-4006
Emp Here 40   *Emp Total* 3,369
Sales 211,409,920
SIC 8051 Skilled nursing care facilities
 David Cutler
CFO Manny Difilippo
COO Paul Rushforth

D-U-N-S 24-184-6674   (SL)
438357 ONTARIO LIMITED
WYNFORD SERVICES
95 Royal Crest Crt Unit 14, Markham, ON,
L3R 9X5
(905) 940-4007
Emp Here 60   *Sales* 1,751,057
SIC 7349 Building maintenance services, nec

D-U-N-S 25-319-8014   (BR)
446987 ONTARIO INC
BOMBAY COMPANY, THE
(*Suby of* Benix & Co. Inc)
5000 Highway 7 E Suite 328, Markham, ON,
L3R 4M9
(905) 470-0604
Emp Here 20
SIC 5712 Furniture stores

D-U-N-S 24-310-3608   (HQ)
620828 N.B. INC
JANI-KING OF SOUTHERN ONTARIO
(*Suby of* 620828 N.B. Inc)
80 Acadia Ave Suite 100, Markham, ON, L3R
9V1
(905) 754-4800
Emp Here 50   *Emp Total* 50
Sales 1,459,214
SIC 7349 Building maintenance services, nec

D-U-N-S 24-598-8097   (BR)
8388059 CANADA INC
4250 14th Ave, Markham, ON, L3R 0J3
(416) 848-8500
Emp Here 450
SIC 2752 Commercial printing, lithographic

D-U-N-S 24-893-6593   (SL)
939935 ONTARIO LIMITED
MANDARIN MARKHAM RESTAURANT
7660 Woodbine Ave, Markham, ON, L3R 2N2
(905) 479-6000
Emp Here 72   *Sales* 2,188,821
SIC 5812 Eating places

D-U-N-S 25-288-0059   (BR)
A & W FOOD SERVICES OF CANADA INC
A & W RESTAURANT
5000 Highway 7 E Unit 8, Markham, ON, L3R
4M9

(905) 513-1059
Emp Here 20
SIC 5812 Eating places

D-U-N-S 20-344-3049   (HQ)
AGF - REBAR INC
2800 14th Ave Suite 204, Markham, ON, L3R
0E4
(416) 243-3903
Emp Here 20   *Emp Total* 3,000
Sales 10,944,105
SIC 3449 Miscellaneous Metalwork
 Maxime Gendron
 Serge Gendron
 Mark Clarke

D-U-N-S 24-824-9620   (BR)
**AMEC FOSTER WHEELER AMERICAS LIM-
ITED**
3190 Steeles Ave E Suite 305, Markham, ON,
L3R 1G9
(905) 415-2632
Emp Here 20
SIC 8748 Business consulting, nec

D-U-N-S 25-973-5488   (SL)
ARSYSTEMS INTERNATIONAL INC
SHOWCARE SOLUTIONS
2770 14th Ave Suite 101, Markham, ON, L3R
0J1
(905) 968-3096
Emp Here 79   *Sales* 3,939,878
SIC 7389 Business services, nec

D-U-N-S 25-536-6460   (HQ)
**ASI   COMPUTER   TECHNOLOGIES
(CANADA) CORP**
3930 14th Ave Unit 1, Markham, ON, L3R 0A8
(905) 470-1000
Emp Here 40   *Emp Total* 700
Sales 7,514,952
SIC 5045 Computers, peripherals, and soft-
ware
Pr Christine Liang
Genl Mgr Pendora Wong

D-U-N-S 25-101-3397   (HQ)
ASM CANADA, INC
*ADVANTAGE SALES AND MARKETING
CANADA*
(*Suby of* Advantage Sales & Marketing Inc.)
160 Mcnabb St Suite 330, Markham, ON, L3R
4E4
(905) 475-9623
Emp Here 110   *Emp Total* 48,000
Sales 78,432,753
SIC 5141 Groceries, general line
 Henry Gerstel

D-U-N-S 24-330-6318   (BR)
ACRODEX INC
1300 Rodick Rd Unit C, Markham, ON, L3R
8C3
(905) 752-2180
Emp Here 20
SIC 7378 Computer maintenance and repair

D-U-N-S 24-857-9760   (BR)
AECOM CANADA LTD
300 Town Centre Blvd Suite 300, Markham,
ON, L3R 5Z6

Emp Here 150
SIC 8742 Management consulting services

D-U-N-S 20-119-3963   (BR)
AGROPUR COOPERATIVE
AGROPUR NATREL, DIV OF
7100 Woodbine Ave Suite 400, Markham, ON,
L3R 5J2
(905) 947-5600
Emp Here 45
SIC 2026 Fluid milk

D-U-N-S 20-179-1550   (SL)
ALCO ELECTRONICS INC
725 Denison St, Markham, ON, L3R 1B8
(905) 477-7878
Emp Here 22   *Sales* 2,991,389

SIC 5099 Durable goods, nec

D-U-N-S 20-355-0405　(HQ)
ALLSTREAM BUSINESS INC
ENTREPRISE ALLSTREAM
7550 Birchmount Rd, Markham, ON, L3R 6C6
(905) 513-4600
Emp Here 192　*Emp Total* 2,426
Sales 17,510,568
SIC 1731 Electrical work
Kenneth Desgarennes
Dir Daniel Caruso
Michael R. Strople

D-U-N-S 25-359-3313　(HQ)
ALLSTREAM BUSINESS INC
7550 Birchmount Rd, Markham, ON, L3R 6C6
(416) 345-2000
Emp Here 2,000　*Emp Total* 48,090
Sales 1,025,535,599
SIC 4899 Communication services, nec
Pierre Bluion
Pr Kelvin Shepherd
Wayne Demkey

D-U-N-S 24-876-4995　(BR)
AMER SPORTS CANADA INC
WILSON SPORTS EQUIPMENT
2700 14th Ave Unit 1, Markham, ON, L3R 0J1
(905) 470-9966
Emp Here 20
SIC 5091 Sporting and recreation goods

D-U-N-S 24-345-7095　(BR)
AMEX CANADA INC
GLOBAL SERVICES
(*Suby of* American Express Company)
80 Micro Crt Suite 300, Markham, ON, L3R 9Z5
(905) 475-2177
Emp Here 300
SIC 6153 Short-term business credit institutions, except agricultural

D-U-N-S 20-563-2917　(BR)
ARO INC
ARO INC
7030 Woodbine Ave Suite 700, Markham, ON, L3R 6G2
(289) 789-1001
Emp Here 40
SIC 7322 Adjustment and collection services

D-U-N-S 24-977-5461　(SL)
ASSOCIATED PRO-CLEANING SERVICES CORP
3400 14th Ave Suite 39, Markham, ON, L3R 0H7
(905) 477-6966
Emp Here 75　*Sales* 2,188,821
SIC 7349 Building maintenance services, nec

D-U-N-S 24-382-5077　(BR)
AUTOLIV CANADA INC
(*Suby of* Autoliv, Inc.)
7455 Birchmount Rd, Markham, ON, L3R 5C2
(905) 475-8510
Emp Here 100
SIC 2394 Canvas and related products

D-U-N-S 20-118-9391　(SL)
AUTOLIV ELECTRONICS CANADA INC
AUTOLIV NORTH AMERICA
(*Suby of* Autoliv, Inc.)
7455 Birchmount Rd, Markham, ON, L3R 5C2
(905) 475-8510
Emp Here 330　*Sales* 42,966,050
SIC 3679 Electronic components, nec
Dir Fin Lori Valentini
Pr Pr Steve Rode

D-U-N-S 25-094-6449　(HQ)
AVAYA CANADA CORP
11 Allstate Pky Suite 300, Markham, ON, L3R 9T8
(905) 474-6000
Emp Here 310　*Emp Total* 450
Sales 80,256,770

SIC 4899 Communication services, nec
Pr Pr Mario Belanger

D-U-N-S 25-102-6563　(SL)
B.C.W. BINDERY SERVICES LTD
599 Denison St, Markham, ON, L3R 1B8
(905) 415-1900
Emp Here 68　*Sales* 2,480,664
SIC 2789 Bookbinding and related work

D-U-N-S 25-321-0298　(BR)
BDO CANADA LLP
BDO CANADA
60 Columbia Way Suite 300, Markham, ON, L3R 0C9
(905) 946-1066
Emp Here 100
SIC 8721 Accounting, auditing, and book-keeping

D-U-N-S 20-044-4727　(HQ)
BANCTEC (CANADA), INC
100 Allstate Pky Suite 400, Markham, ON, L3R 6H3
(905) 475-6060
Emp Here 24　*Emp Total* 15,000
Sales 11,673,712
SIC 7371 Custom computer programming services
Malcolm Gurney

D-U-N-S 25-296-4911　(BR)
BANK OF NOVA SCOTIA, THE
SCOTIABANK
7321 Woodbine Ave, Markham, ON, L3R 3V7
(905) 940-6350
Emp Here 25
SIC 6021 National commercial banks

D-U-N-S 25-092-6151　(BR)
BANQUE TORONTO-DOMINION, LA
TORONTO-DOMINION BANK, THE
(*Suby of* Toronto-Dominion Bank, The)
7077 Kennedy Rd, Markham, ON, L3R 0N8
(905) 946-8824
Emp Here 20
SIC 6021 National commercial banks

D-U-N-S 20-416-5088　(HQ)
BARON OUTDOOR PRODUCTS LTD
PRODUITS DE PLEIN AIR 4 ETOILES
8365 Woodbine Ave Suite 1, Markham, ON, L3R 2P4
(905) 944-0682
Emp Here 35　*Emp Total* 3
Sales 6,063,757
SIC 5941 Sporting goods and bicycle shops
Dir Sylvia Baron
Pr Pr Steven Baron
Terry Baron-Wexler

D-U-N-S 20-973-7233　(BR)
BEST BUY CANADA LTD
BEST BUY
(*Suby of* Best Buy Co., Inc.)
5000 Highway 7 E Unit D, Markham, ON, L3R 4M9
(905) 754-3025
Emp Here 50
SIC 5731 Radio, television, and electronic stores

D-U-N-S 25-310-3576　(BR)
BOUTIQUE LA VIE EN ROSE INC
BOUTIQUE LA VIE EN ROSE INC
(*Suby of* Gestion Francois Roberge Inc)
5000 Highway 7 E, Markham, ON, L3R 4M9
(905) 513-6594
Emp Here 50
SIC 5632 Women's accessory and specialty stores

D-U-N-S 24-737-5751　(HQ)
BROADRIDGE CUSTOMER COMMUNICATIONS CANADA, ULC
2601 14th Ave, Markham, ON, L3R 0H9
(905) 470-2000
Emp Here 170　*Emp Total* 10,000
Sales 17,802,411

SIC 2759 Commercial printing, nec
Joseph Faria
Andrew Idzior
Fin Ex Robert Wylie
Pr Pr Charles Schellhorn
Steve Towle

D-U-N-S 25-910-9643　(SL)
BROTHERS & WRIGHT ELECTRICAL SERVICES INC
251 Amber St Unit 1, Markham, ON, L3R 3J7

Emp Here 50　*Sales* 4,377,642
SIC 1731 Electrical work

D-U-N-S 20-547-9434　(SL)
BUBBLETEASE INC
BUBBLETEASE
400 Esna Park Dr Suite 11, Markham, ON, L3R 3K2
(905) 940-2660
Emp Here 70　*Sales* 2,512,128
SIC 5812 Eating places

D-U-N-S 25-396-8721　(BR)
BURNDY CANADA INC
FCI AUTOMOTIVE
(*Suby of* Hubbell Incorporated)
245 Renfrew Dr, Markham, ON, L3R 6G3
(905) 940-3288
Emp Here 100
SIC 3643 Current-carrying wiring devices

D-U-N-S 25-323-2615　(SL)
CBL DATA RECOVERY TECHNOLOGIES INC
CBL
590 Alden Rd Suite 105, Markham, ON, L3R 8N2
(905) 479-9938
Emp Here 82　*Sales* 4,523,563
SIC 7375 Information retrieval services

D-U-N-S 24-688-8184　(BR)
CRH CANADA GROUP INC
DUFFERIN CUSTOM CONCRETE
7655 Woodbine Ave, Markham, ON, L3R 2N4
(905) 475-6631
Emp Here 100
SIC 3273 Ready-mixed concrete

D-U-N-S 20-301-2484　(BR)
CADILLAC FAIRVIEW CORPORATION LIMITED, THE
MARKVILLE SHOPPING CENTER
5000 Highway 7 E, Markham, ON, L3R 4M9
(905) 477-6600
Emp Here 42
SIC 6512 Nonresidential building operators

D-U-N-S 24-796-2566　(BR)
CANADIAN IMPERIAL BANK OF COMMERCE
CIBC
7125 Woodbine Ave, Markham, ON, L3R 1A3
(905) 475-6754
Emp Here 30
SIC 6021 National commercial banks

D-U-N-S 24-343-1678　(BR)
CARA OPERATIONS LIMITED
SWISS CHALET
(*Suby of* Cara Holdings Limited)
7359 Woodbine Ave, Markham, ON, L3R 1A7
(905) 305-9948
Emp Here 60
SIC 5812 Eating places

D-U-N-S 20-070-3523　(BR)
CARA OPERATIONS LIMITED
KELSEY'S RESTAURANT
(*Suby of* Cara Holdings Limited)
3131 Highway 7 E, Markham, ON, L3R 0T9
(905) 470-6700
Emp Here 55
SIC 5812 Eating places

D-U-N-S 25-121-4250　(SL)

CENTURY 21 KING'S QUAY REAL ESTATE INC
CENTURY 21
7300 Warden Ave Suite 401, Markham, ON, L3R 9Z6
(905) 940-3428
Emp Here 50　*Sales* 4,742,446
SIC 6531 Real estate agents and managers

D-U-N-S 25-957-1974　(BR)
CERIDIAN CANADA LTD
CERIDIAN LIFEWORKS SERVICES
675 Cochrane Dr Suite 515n, Markham, ON, L3R 0B8
(905) 947-7000
Emp Here 100
SIC 8721 Accounting, auditing, and book-keeping

D-U-N-S 24-417-5571　(BR)
CINEPLEX ODEON CORPORATION
CINEPLEX CINEMAS FIRST MARKHAM PLACE
3275 Highway 7, Markham, ON, L3R 3P9

Emp Here 20
SIC 7832 Motion picture theaters, except drive-in

D-U-N-S 24-925-8476　(SL)
CITIZEN WATCH COMPANY OF CANADA LTD
380 Bentley St Unit 2, Markham, ON, L3R 3L2
(905) 415-1100
Emp Here 22　*Sales* 4,304,681
SIC 3873 Watches, clocks, watchcases, and parts

D-U-N-S 20-644-3868　(BR)
CLAIMSPRO LP
MCLARENS CANADA
600 Alden Rd Suite 600, Markham, ON, L3R 0E7
(519) 944-3552
Emp Here 20
SIC 6411 Insurance agents, brokers, and service

D-U-N-S 20-936-6608　(BR)
CO-OPERATORS GROUP LIMITED, THE
CO-OPERATORS, THE
7300 Warden Ave Suite 110, Markham, ON, L3R 9Z6
(905) 470-7300
Emp Here 80
SIC 6411 Insurance agents, brokers, and service

D-U-N-S 25-973-7781　(HQ)
CONEX BUSINESS SYSTEMS INC
TOSHIBA BUSINESS SOLUTIONS
191 Mcnabb St, Markham, ON, L3R 8H2
(905) 470-5400
Emp Here 70　*Emp Total* 153,492
Sales 64,392,960
SIC 5044 Office equipment
Pr Pr Boris Bratuhin
Howard Morrison

D-U-N-S 20-290-5944　(BR)
CONSEIL SCOLAIRE DE DISTRICT CATHOLIQUE CENTRE-SUD
SAINTE MARJAUET BOURGEOYS
111 John Button Blvd, Markham, ON, L3R 9C1
(905) 470-0815
Emp Here 35
SIC 8211 Elementary and secondary schools

D-U-N-S 20-646-3247　(BR)
COVER-ALL COMPUTER SERVICES CORP
1 Valleywood Dr Unit 10, Markham, ON, L3R 5L9
(905) 477-8494
Emp Here 40
SIC 7372 Prepackaged software

D-U-N-S 24-426-3724　(BR)

CRITICAL CONTROL ENERGY SERVICES CORP
2820 14th Ave Suite 100, Markham, ON, L3R 0S9
(905) 940-0190
Emp Here 60
SIC 7371 Custom computer programming services

D-U-N-S 24-662-5057 (SL)
D&M CANADA INC
DENON CANADA
505 Apple Creek Blvd Unit 5, Markham, ON, L3R 5B1
(905) 475-4085
Emp Here 30 Sales 9,266,009
SIC 5064 Electrical appliances, television and radio
Pr Doug Griesbach
VP Fin Jay Nimigon
Sec David Dunlop

D-U-N-S 20-515-2213 (BR)
DH CORPORATION
D+H
81 Whitehall Dr, Markham, ON, L3R 9T1
(905) 944-1231
Emp Here 300
SIC 6211 Security brokers and dealers

D-U-N-S 20-179-7821 (BR)
DSV SOLUTIONS INC
65 Ferrier St Suite 1, Markham, ON, L3R 3K6

Emp Here 40
SIC 4225 General warehousing and storage

D-U-N-S 20-104-1915 (BR)
DSV SOLUTIONS INC
20 Ferrier St Unit 1, Markham, ON, L3R 2Z5
(905) 479-1327
Emp Here 50
SIC 3672 Printed circuit boards

D-U-N-S 24-950-6387 (SL)
DAIWA PRECISION INDUSTRIAL LTD
361 Alden Rd, Markham, ON, L3R 3L4
(905) 940-2889
Emp Here 35 Sales 6,631,680
SIC 5045 Computers, peripherals, and software
Pinky Lau

D-U-N-S 24-834-1104 (SL)
DECOTREND HOME FASHIONS LTD
665 Hood Rd, Markham, ON, L3R 4E1
(905) 754-1798
Emp Here 22 Sales 6,044,400
SIC 2591 Drapery hardware and window blinds and shades
VP VP Jennifer Tu

D-U-N-S 20-890-3880 (SL)
DELCAN INTERNATIONAL CORPORATION
(Suby of Delcan Group Inc)
625 Cochrane Dr Suite 500, Markham, ON, L3R 9R9
(905) 943-0500
Emp Here 100 Sales 15,116,050
SIC 8711 Engineering services
James (Jim) Kerr
VP VP Jack Powers
W. Victor Anderson
Joseph K. Lam
Charles Orolowitz
VP VP Alan Rumsey
VP VP David Smith
W. James Corbett

D-U-N-S 20-301-5289 (BR)
DELOITTE LLP
DELOITTE
15 Allstate Pky Suite 400, Markham, ON, L3R 5B4

Emp Here 110
SIC 8742 Management consulting services

D-U-N-S 20-844-7680 (SL)
DEPENDABLE ANODIZING LIMITED
268 Don Park Rd Suite 1, Markham, ON, L3R 1C3
(905) 475-1229
Emp Here 65 Sales 4,377,642
SIC 3471 Plating and polishing

D-U-N-S 25-663-1854 (SL)
DIGNITY TRANSPORTATION INC
50 Mcintosh Dr Suite 110, Markham, ON, L3R 9T3
(905) 470-2399
Emp Here 80 Sales 2,845,467
SIC 4111 Local and suburban transit

D-U-N-S 24-985-2351 (SL)
DIRECT MULTI-PAK MAILING LTD
PROFESSIONAL TARGETED MARKETING
20 Torbay Rd, Markham, ON, L3R 1G6
(905) 415-1940
Emp Here 80 Sales 4,085,799
SIC 7331 Direct mail advertising services

D-U-N-S 25-418-9459 (SL)
EASTON'S 28 SERVICE CENTRE LTD
3100 Steeles Ave E Suite 401, Markham, ON, L3R 8T3
(905) 940-9409
Emp Here 50 Sales 9,333,400
SIC 5541 Gasoline service stations
Pr Pr Steve Gupta

D-U-N-S 20-547-8527 (SL)
EASTON'S TORONTO AIRPORT HOTEL (COROGA) LP
3100 Steeles Ave E, Markham, ON, L3R 8T3
(905) 940-9409
Emp Here 75 Sales 3,283,232
SIC 7011 Hotels and motels

D-U-N-S 20-052-2501 (SL)
EDJAR FOOD GROUP INC
7650 Birchmount Rd, Markham, ON, L3R 6B9
(905) 474-0710
Emp Here 70 Sales 11,066,880
SIC 6712 Bank holding companies
Daniel Chim
Pr James Chim

D-U-N-S 20-164-3921 (HQ)
ELECTRO SONIC INC
(Suby of Electro Sonic Inc)
55 Renfrew Dr Suite 100, Markham, ON, L3R 8H3
(905) 946-0100
Emp Here 165 Emp Total 210
Sales 37,333,600
SIC 5065 Electronic parts and equipment, nec
Martin Rosenthal
Joel Rosenthal
Dan Zhou

D-U-N-S 20-707-3086 (SL)
ELFA INSURANCE SERVICES INC
3950 14th Ave Unit 105, Markham, ON, L3R 0A9
(905) 470-1038
Emp Here 50 Sales 4,523,563
SIC 6411 Insurance agents, brokers, and service

D-U-N-S 25-102-1093 (SL)
ELIZABETH ARDEN (CANADA) LIMITED
505 Apple Creek Blvd Unit 2, Markham, ON, L3R 5B1
(905) 948-9990
Emp Here 45 Sales 4,961,328
SIC 5122 Drugs, proprietaries, and sundries

D-U-N-S 20-527-0622 (SL)
ELLARD-WILLSON ENGINEERING LIMITED
260 Town Centre Blvd Suite 202, Markham, ON, L3R 8H8
(905) 940-3100
Emp Here 45 Sales 5,197,506
SIC 8711 Engineering services

D-U-N-S 20-259-0055 (SL)
ENGAGE PEOPLE INC
1380 Rodick Rd Suite 300, Markham, ON, L3R 4G5
(416) 775-9180
Emp Here 121 Sales 57,569,632
SIC 7379 Computer related services, nec
Jonathan Silver
Pr Ron Benegbi
Mario Crudo
Len Covello

D-U-N-S 24-992-0216 (HQ)
ENTERPRISE RENT-A-CAR CANADA COMPANY
(Suby of The Crawford Group Inc)
200-7390 Woodbine Ave, Markham, ON, L3R 1A5
(905) 477-1688
Emp Here 40 Emp Total 68,993
Sales 49,029,590
SIC 7514 Passenger car rental
Pr Pr William W. Snyder
VP Brian M. Oddy
Andrew C. Taylor
Pamela M. Nicholson

D-U-N-S 25-517-5580 (BR)
ESTEE LAUDER COSMETICS LTD
M.A.C COSMETICS
100 Alden Rd, Markham, ON, L3R 4C1
(905) 470-7877
Emp Here 20
SIC 2844 Toilet preparations

D-U-N-S 20-366-3141 (SL)
EVERTRUST DEVELOPMENT GROUP CANADA INC
3100 Steeles Ave E Suite 302, Markham, ON, L3R 8T3
(647) 501-2345
Emp Here 3,000 Sales 556,690,141
SIC 1542 Nonresidential construction, nec
Pr Pr Jiancheng Zhou

D-U-N-S 25-101-1011 (BR)
EXCO TECHNOLOGIES LIMITED
EXCO EXTRUSION DIES
130 Spy Crt Unit 1, Markham, ON, L3R 5H6
(905) 477-1208
Emp Here 115
SIC 3544 Special dies, tools, jigs, and fixtures

D-U-N-S 24-666-5509 (HQ)
EXTENDICARE (CANADA) INC
3000 Steeles Ave E Suite 700, Markham, ON, L3R 9W2
(905) 470-1400
Emp Here 120 Emp Total 11,800
Sales 820,005,307
SIC 8051 Skilled nursing care facilities
Ch Bd Timothy Lukenda

D-U-N-S 24-340-0616 (BR)
FGL SPORTS LTD
SPORT CHEK MARKVILLE SHOPPING CENTRE
5000 Highway 7 E Unit 20a, Markham, ON, L3R 4M9
(905) 940-6400
Emp Here 35
SIC 5941 Sporting goods and bicycle shops

D-U-N-S 20-113-6418 (SL)
FIRST BASE SOLUTIONS INC
140 Renfrew Dr Suite 100, Markham, ON, L3R 6B3
(905) 477-3600
Emp Here 40 Sales 5,224,960
SIC 5999 Miscellaneous retail stores, nec
Pr Frank Mauro
John Knowles
Ron Terin
Dir Andrew Chan
Dir Gary Kirstine

D-U-N-S 24-910-3672 (BR)
FISHER SCIENTIFIC COMPANY

THERMO FISHER SCIENTIFIC
(Suby of Thermo Fisher Scientific Inc.)
145 Renfrew Dr Suite 119, Markham, ON, L3R 9R6
(905) 479-8700
Emp Here 20
SIC 5049 Professional equipment, nec

D-U-N-S 24-826-3717 (SL)
FISKARS CANADA, INC
FISKARS BRAND
675 Cochrane Dr, Markham, ON, L3R 0B8
(905) 940-8460
Emp Here 23 Sales 2,407,703
SIC 5099 Durable goods, nec

D-U-N-S 25-095-5580 (HQ)
FLEXTRONICS AUTOMOTIVE INC
450 Hood Rd, Markham, ON, L3R 9Z3
(800) 668-5649
Emp Here 45 Emp Total 1,800
Sales 5,630,632
SIC 7389 Business services, nec
Engg Mgr Greg Polityka

D-U-N-S 24-830-0428 (BR)
G.N. JOHNSTON EQUIPMENT CO. LTD
JOHNSTON EQUIPMENT
181 Whitehall Dr Suite 2, Markham, ON, L3R 9T1
(416) 798-7195
Emp Here 90
SIC 3537 Industrial trucks and tractors

D-U-N-S 25-304-7542 (BR)
GAP (CANADA) INC
GAP
(Suby of The Gap Inc)
5000 Highway 7 E, Markham, ON, L3R 4M9
(905) 513-6477
Emp Here 40
SIC 5651 Family clothing stores

D-U-N-S 20-327-4550 (BR)
GENERAL CREDIT SERVICES INC
(Suby of General Credit Services Inc)
20 Valleywood Dr Unit 101, Markham, ON, L3R 6G1

Emp Here 21
SIC 7322 Adjustment and collection services

D-U-N-S 24-827-5468 (BR)
GENESYS LABORATORIES CANADA INC
1380 Rodick Rd Suite 200, Markham, ON, L3R 4G5
(905) 968-3300
Emp Here 65
SIC 7371 Custom computer programming services

D-U-N-S 25-987-7772 (SL)
GENTEC
GENTEC INTERNATIONAL
90 Royal Crest, Markham, ON, L3R 9X6
(905) 513-7733
Emp Here 82 Sales 57,684,410
SIC 5099 Durable goods, nec
Pt Joel Siegel

D-U-N-S 20-720-4525 (SL)
GENTOX LABORATORIES INC
VITA-TECH
1345 Denison St, Markham, ON, L3R 5V2
(416) 798-4988
Emp Here 300 Sales 28,835,267
SIC 8734 Testing laboratories
Fin Ex Allan Korolnek

D-U-N-S 20-860-5845 (BR)
GLENTEL INC
WIRELESS WAVES
5000 Highway 7 E, Markham, ON, L3R 4M9
(905) 475-9283
Emp Here 25
SIC 4813 Telephone communication, except radio

D-U-N-S 24-952-4133 (SL)

GLOBAL AEROSPACE UNDERWRITING MANAGERS (CANADA) LIMITED
(*Suby of* Berkshire Hathaway Inc.)
100 Renfrew Dr Suite 200, Markham, ON, L3R 9R6
(905) 479-2244
Emp Here 25   *Sales* 2,261,782
SIC 6411 Insurance agents, brokers, and service

        D-U-N-S 24-150-3213   (SL)
GLOBAL LINK REALTY GROUP INC
340 Ferrier St Suite 8, Markham, ON, L3R 2Z5
(905) 475-0028
Emp Here 40   *Sales* 5,275,400
SIC 6531 Real estate agents and managers
Genl Mgr Dundas Kwok

        D-U-N-S 24-576-3743   (SL)
GLOBAL TRAVEL COMPUTER HOLDINGS LTD
GLOBAL MATRIX
7550 Birchmount Rd, Markham, ON, L3R 6C6
(905) 479-4949
Emp Here 60   *Sales* 3,283,232
SIC 7374 Data processing and preparation

        D-U-N-S 24-390-5796   (BR)
GOLF TOWN LIMITED
GOLF TOWN
3265 Highway 7 E Unit 1, Markham, ON, L3R 3P9
(905) 479-6978
Emp Here 50
SIC 5941 Sporting goods and bicycle shops

        D-U-N-S 20-789-1750   (BR)
GRANDI COMPANY LIMITED
WAL MART MCDONALDS
5000 Highway 7 E, Markham, ON, L3R 4M9
(905) 415-1424
Emp Here 30
SIC 5812 Eating places

        D-U-N-S 25-306-3465   (HQ)
GRAND AVIATION LTD
FLIGHTEXEC, DIV OF
(*Suby of* Grand Aviation Ltd)
330 Allstate Pky, Markham, ON, L3R 5T3
(905) 477-4434
Emp Here 45   *Emp Total* 70
Sales 16,478,720
SIC 4512 Air transportation, scheduled
Pr Pr Nick Erb

        D-U-N-S 24-964-9195   (BR)
GRANT THORNTON LLP
CAPSERVCO
15 Allstate Pky Suite 200, Markham, ON, L3R 5B4
(416) 607-2656
Emp Here 200
SIC 8721 Accounting, auditing, and bookkeeping

        D-U-N-S 20-362-1628   (BR)
GROUPE AGF ACCES INC
WINSAFE, A DIVISION OF AGF ACCESS GROUP INC
1 Valleywocd Dr Unit 1, Markham, ON, L3R 5L9
(905) 474-9340
Emp Here 45
SIC 5099 Durable goods, nec

        D-U-N-S 20-301-7343   (BR)
HSBC BANK CANADA
19 Allstate Pky Suite 2, Markham, ON, L3R 5A4
(905) 415-4723
Emp Here 70
SIC 6021 National commercial banks

        D-U-N-S 24-793-4003   (BR)
HSBC BANK CANADA
3000 Steeles Ave E, Markham, ON, L3R 4T9
(905) 475-3777
Emp Here 25

SIC 6021 National commercial banks

        D-U-N-S 25-669-0058   (BR)
HSBC BANK CANADA
4390 Steeles Ave E, Markham, ON, L3R 9V7
(905) 513-8801
Emp Here 30
SIC 6021 National commercial banks

        D-U-N-S 24-538-0548   (HQ)
HAMILTON BEACH BRANDS CANADA, INC
7300 Warden Ave Suite 201, Markham, ON, L3R 9Z6
(905) 513-6222
Emp Here 20   *Emp Total* 1,900
Sales 19,480,507
SIC 5064 Electrical appliances, television and radio
Pr Pr John Scott Seymour

        D-U-N-S 24-788-9707   (BR)
HATCH CORPORATION
15 Allstate Pky Suite 300, Markham, ON, L3R 5B4
(905) 943-9600
Emp Here 30
SIC 8711 Engineering services

        D-U-N-S 24-859-7528   (SL)
HOLMES PLASTIC BINDINGS LTD
HOLMES THE FINISHING HOUSE
200 Ferrier St, Markham, ON, L3R 2Z5
(905) 513-6211
Emp Here 100   *Sales* 3,648,035
SIC 2789 Bookbinding and related work

        D-U-N-S 25-794-3621   (BR)
HOME DEPOT OF CANADA INC
HOME DEPOT
(*Suby of* The Home Depot Inc)
3155 Highway 7 E, Markham, ON, L3R 0T9
(905) 940-5900
Emp Here 200
SIC 5251 Hardware stores

        D-U-N-S 24-374-2090   (HQ)
HUAWEI TECHNOLOGIES CANADA CO., LTD
19 Allstate Pky, Markham, ON, L3R 5A4
(905) 944-5000
Emp Here 50   *Emp Total* 500
Sales 95,287,610
SIC 4899 Communication services, nec
Dir Shengli Wang
Dir Wanzhou Meng
Dir Shaohua Ding

        D-U-N-S 24-964-9518   (BR)
HUDSON'S BAY COMPANY
BAY, THE
5000 Highway 7 E, Markham, ON, L3R 4M9
(905) 513-1770
Emp Here 100
SIC 5311 Department stores

        D-U-N-S 24-372-2944   (BR)
HUDSON'S BAY COMPANY
HOME OUTFITTERS
3275 Highway 7, Markham, ON, L3R 3P9
(905) 415-2706
Emp Here 50
SIC 5719 Miscellaneous homefurnishings

        D-U-N-S 24-925-4236   (SL)
ICON PRINT COMMUNICATIONS INC
7453 Victoria Park Ave Suite 2, Markham, ON, L3R 2Y7
(905) 513-7500
Emp Here 24
SIC 2759 Commercial printing, nec

        D-U-N-S 25-598-1664   (BR)
INDIGO BOOKS & MUSIC INC
CHAPTERS
(*Suby of* Indigo Books & Music Inc)
3175 Highway 7 E, Markham, ON, L3R 0T9
(905) 477-1756
Emp Here 50

SIC 5942 Book stores

        D-U-N-S 25-405-1204   (SL)
INTEGRATED MAINTENANCE & OPERATIONS SERVICES INC
IMOS
Gd, Markham, ON, L3R 9R8
(905) 475-6660
Emp Here 100   *Sales* 15,705,600
SIC 1611 Highway and street construction
Pr Pr Leo Mcarthur
VP VP John Karrick
  Robert Adamson
  Barrie Brayford
Sr VP Robert Bugden

        D-U-N-S 24-407-7335   (HQ)
INTERWEIGH SYSTEMS INC
(*Suby of* Interweigh Systems Inc)
51 Bentley St, Markham, ON, L3R 3L1
(416) 491-7001
Emp Here 20   *Emp Total* 35
Sales 6,407,837
SIC 3535 Conveyors and conveying equipment
Pr Pr Mark Nichol
  Bryn Savage
Dir Fin Evelyn Merker

        D-U-N-S 25-315-8950   (BR)
INVESTORS GROUP FINANCIAL SERVICES INC
675 Cochrane Dr Suite 301, Markham, ON, L3R 0B8
(905) 415-2440
Emp Here 60
SIC 6211 Security brokers and dealers

        D-U-N-S 20-125-7156   (SL)
JCTV PRODUCTIONS LTD
(*Suby of* Asian Television Network International Limited)
330 Cochrane Dr, Markham, ON, L3R 8E4
(905) 948-8199
Emp Here 72   *Sales* 7,796,259
SIC 7812 Motion picture and video production
Pr Pr Shan Chandrasekar

        D-U-N-S 24-976-5491   (SL)
JD DEVELOPMENT REGINA STREET LIMITED
3601 Highway 7 E Suite 610, Markham, ON, L3R 0M3
(905) 479-9898
Emp Here 20   *Sales* 6,347,581
SIC 6553 Cemetery subdividers and developers
Dir Yueqing Zhang

        D-U-N-S 25-283-7414   (BR)
JOHNSON & JOHNSON INC
JOHNSON & JOHNSON MEDICAL COMPANIES
(*Suby of* Johnson & Johnson)
200 Whitehall Dr, Markham, ON, L3R 0T5
(905) 946-8999
Emp Here 200
SIC 3842 Surgical appliances and supplies

        D-U-N-S 25-360-1777   (BR)
KINARK CHILD AND FAMILY SERVICES
600 Alden Rd Suite 200, Markham, ON, L3R 0E7
(905) 479-0158
Emp Here 30
SIC 8699 Membership organizations, nec

        D-U-N-S 24-506-7017   (BR)
LABORATOIRES ABBOTT LIMITEE
LABORATOIRES ABBOTT, LIMITEE
(*Suby of* Abbott Laboratories)
505 Apple Creek Blvd Suite 4, Markham, ON, L3R 5B1
(905) 947-5800
Emp Here 20
SIC 5047 Medical and hospital equipment

        D-U-N-S 20-322-6105   (BR)

LABORATOIRES ABBOTT LIMITEE
LABORATOIRES ABBOTT, LIMITEE
(*Suby of* Abbott Laboratories)
60 Columbia Way Suite 207, Markham, ON, L3R 0C9
(905) 944-2480
Emp Here 150
SIC 2834 Pharmaceutical preparations

        D-U-N-S 20-339-2316   (SL)
LINKAGE GROUP INC, THE
30 Centurian Dr Suite 200, Markham, ON, L3R 8B8
(905) 415-2300
Emp Here 400   *Sales* 72,088,169
SIC 8742 Management consulting services
Pr Pr Robert Proctor

        D-U-N-S 25-255-7525   (SL)
LITTLE GUYS DELIVERY SERVICE INC
MARS COURIER DIV
620 Alden Rd Unit 105, Markham, ON, L3R 9R7
(905) 513-9600
Emp Here 50   *Sales* 3,939,878
SIC 4212 Local trucking, without storage

        D-U-N-S 24-525-6292   (SL)
LIVING GROUP OF COMPANIES INC
7030 Woodbine Ave Suite 300, Markham, ON, L3R 6G2
(905) 477-2090
Emp Here 100   *Sales* 12,961,920
SIC 6531 Real estate agents and managers
  Stephen Wong
Pr Pr Eric Chan

        D-U-N-S 24-420-7031   (HQ)
LIVING REALTY INC
LIVING GROUPS OF COMPANIES
(*Suby of* Living Realty Inc)
7030 Woodbine Ave Suite 300, Markham, ON, L3R 6G2
(905) 474-0590
Emp Here 250   *Emp Total* 650
Sales 85,218,000
SIC 6531 Real estate agents and managers
  Steven Wong
Pr Pr Eric Chan

        D-U-N-S 25-311-1082   (BR)
LONDON LIFE INSURANCE COMPANY
FREEDOM 55 FINANCIAL
3760 14th Ave Suite 100, Markham, ON, L3R 3T7
(905) 475-0122
Emp Here 65
SIC 6311 Life insurance

        D-U-N-S 24-709-1218   (BR)
LONGO BROTHERS FRUIT MARKETS INC
LONGO'S FRUIT MARKET
3085 Highway 7 E, Markham, ON, L3R 0J5
(905) 479-8877
Emp Here 160
SIC 5411 Grocery stores

        D-U-N-S 20-695-7115   (SL)
MGA ENTERTAINMENT (CANADA) COMPANY
LITTLE TYKES COMPANY
7300 Warden Ave Suite 213, Markham, ON, L3R 9Z6
(905) 940-2700
Emp Here 30   *Sales* 1,240,332
SIC 3942 Dolls and stuffed toys

        D-U-N-S 20-184-2270   (SL)
MI5 DIGITAL COMMUNICATIONS INC
800 Cochrane Dr, Markham, ON, L3R 8C9

Emp Here 125   *Sales* 12,156,044
SIC 2752 Commercial printing, lithographic
Dir Derek Mcgeachie
Pr Pr Peter Mitchos

        D-U-N-S 24-512-6024   (BR)
MAGNA POWERTRAIN INC
PULLMATIC MANUFACTURING

430 Cochrane Dr, Markham, ON, L3R 8E3
(905) 474-0899
Emp Here 20
SIC 3714 Motor vehicle parts and accessories

D-U-N-S 20-273-9780   (SL)
MAGNASONIC INC.
SONIGEM PRODUCTS
300 Alden Rd, Markham, ON, L3R 4C1
(905) 940-5089
Emp Here 49   *Sales* 6,843,383
SIC 6712 Bank holding companies
Pr Godfrey D'cruz

D-U-N-S 20-884-4774   (BR)
MANDARIN GOLF AND COUNTRY CLUB INC, THE
MANDARIN BADMINTON CLUB
500 Esna Park Dr Unit 8, Markham, ON, L3R 1H5
(905) 940-0600
Emp Here 30
SIC 7997 Membership sports and recreation clubs

D-U-N-S 25-310-8005   (BR)
MANUFACTURERS LIFE INSURANCE COMPANY, THE
MANULIFE FINANCIAL
600 Cochrane Dr Suite 200, Markham, ON, L3R 5K3

Emp Here 30
SIC 6311 Life insurance

D-U-N-S 20-647-3832   (BR)
MANULIFE CANADA LTD
600 Cochrane Dr Suite 200, Markham, ON, L3R 5K3

Emp Here 20
SIC 6411 Insurance agents, brokers, and service

D-U-N-S 24-980-5862   (HQ)
MAQUET-DYNAMED INC
235 Shields Crt, Markham, ON, L3R 8V2
(905) 752-3300
Emp Here 50   *Emp Total* 50
Sales 13,340,265
SIC 5047 Medical and hospital equipment
Pr Peter Bennett

D-U-N-S 20-522-4780   (SL)
MARKHAM WOODBINE HOSPITALITY LTD
HOLIDAY INN HOTEL & SUITES MARKHAM
7095 Woodbine Ave, Markham, ON, L3R 1A3

Emp Here 50   *Sales* 2,188,821
SIC 7011 Hotels and motels

D-U-N-S 24-326-4665   (SL)
MARKHAM WOODBINE HOSPITALITY LTD
MARRIOTT
3100 Steeles Ave E Suite 601, Markham, ON, L3R 8T3
(905) 940-9409
Emp Here 150   *Sales* 7,796,259
SIC 7011 Hotels and motels
Pr Steve Gupta

D-U-N-S 24-524-0882   (SL)
MCATEER, J.J. & ASSOCIATES INCORPORATED
THE MCATEER GROUP
45 Mcintosh Dr, Markham, ON, L3R 8C7
(905) 946-8655
Emp Here 75   *Sales* 12,579,800
SIC 8741 Management services
Pr Susan Bird
Dir John Joseph (Jj) Mcateer
Jack Mcateer

D-U-N-S 20-163-9622   (HQ)
MCKESSON CORPORATION
GUARDIAN DRUGS
(*Suby of* McKesson Corporation)
131 Mcnabb St, Markham, ON, L3R 5V7

(905) 943-9499
Emp Here 160   *Emp Total* 83,350
Sales 29,279,284
SIC 5122 Drugs, proprietaries, and sundries
Pr Pr Andy Giancamilli
VP Fin Eugene Gidaro
Ex VP Peter Quintilliani
James Hutton
Terrence Connoy
N. Arthur Smith
Frank Tonon
Michael Brunelle
Peter Whitfield
Larry Latowsky

D-U-N-S 20-342-7810   (SL)
MCLEAN HALLMARK INSURANCE GROUP LTD
(*Suby of* Moore-McLean Corporate Insurance Ltd)
10 Konrad Cres, Markham, ON, L3R 8T7
(416) 364-4000
Emp Here 20   *Sales* 2,165,628
SIC 6411 Insurance agents, brokers, and service

D-U-N-S 20-883-6114   (HQ)
MELOCHE MONNEX FINANCIAL SERVICES INC
TD MELOCHE MONNEX
(*Suby of* Toronto-Dominion Bank, The)
101 Mcnabb St, Markham, ON, L3R 4H8
(416) 484-1112
Emp Here 200   *Emp Total* 81,233
Sales 26,995,459
SIC 6411 Insurance agents, brokers, and service
CEO Bharat Masrani
Dir William Goings
Dir Guy Vezina

D-U-N-S 24-307-5595   (SL)
MERANGUE INTERNATIONAL LIMITED
248 Steelcase Rd E, Markham, ON, L3R 1G2
(905) 946-0707
Emp Here 50   *Sales* 4,711,645
SIC 5112 Stationery and office supplies

D-U-N-S 24-826-2362   (BR)
METROLAND MEDIA GROUP LTD
MARKHAM ECONOMIST & SUN
50 Mcintosh Dr Unit 115, Markham, ON, L3R 9T3
(905) 294-2200
Emp Here 50
SIC 2711 Newspapers

D-U-N-S 20-206-4775   (BR)
MIDDLETON GROUP INC
(*Suby of* Middleton Group Inc)
226 Steelcase Rd W, Markham, ON, L3R 1B3
(905) 475-0764
Emp Here 20
SIC 2759 Commercial printing, nec

D-U-N-S 20-170-7791   (HQ)
MIDDLETON GROUP INC
(*Suby of* Middleton Group Inc)
75 Denison St Suite 6, Markham, ON, L3R 1B5
(905) 475-6556
Emp Here 80   *Emp Total* 115
Sales 5,763,895
SIC 2759 Commercial printing, nec
Robert Middleton
Pr Pr Herbert Riethmacher
Gina Jeronimo

D-U-N-S 25-696-1525   (BR)
MILLER PAVING LIMITED
MILLER WASTE SYSTEMS, DIV OF
8050 Woodbine Ave, Markham, ON, L3R 2N8
(905) 475-6356
Emo Here 50
SIC 1611 Highway and street construction

D-U-N-S 24-827-3294   (BR)
MILLER THOMSON LLP

60 Columbia Way Suite 600, Markham, ON, L3R 0C9
(905) 415-6700
Emp Here 100
SIC 8111 Legal services

D-U-N-S 20-709-3274   (BR)
MILTOM MANAGEMENT LP
MILTOM MANAGEMENT
60 Columbia Way Suite 600, Markham, ON, L3R 0C9
(905) 415-6700
Emp Here 80
SIC 8742 Management consulting services

D-U-N-S 24-183-5610   (HQ)
MITSUBISHI ELECTRIC SALES CANADA INC
4299 14th Ave, Markham, ON, L3R 0J2
(905) 475-7728
Emp Here 36   *Emp Total* 137,947
Sales 16,285,519
SIC 5075 Warm air heating and air conditioning
Pr Pr Akihiko Ninomyna
Fin Ex Francis Chan

D-U-N-S 24-365-5388   (SL)
NGK SPARK PLUGS CANADA LIMITED
275 Renfrew Dr Suite 101, Markham, ON, L3R 0C8
(905) 477-7780
Emp Here 39   *Sales* 4,742,446
SIC 5013 Motor vehicle supplies and new parts

D-U-N-S 20-160-0905   (HQ)
NEOPOST CANADA LIMITED
150 Steelcase Rd W, Markham, ON, L3R 3J9
(905) 475-3722
Emp Here 60   *Emp Total* 35
Sales 26,196,746
SIC 5044 Office equipment
Pr Lou Gizzarelli
Grant Gillhan
Sec Jules Kronis
Dir Patrick Nangle

D-U-N-S 25-178-2280   (SL)
NETWORK BUILDERS INC
NETWORKBUILDERS.COM
110 Riviera Dr Unit 14, Markham, ON, L3R 5M1
(905) 947-9201
Emp Here 60   *Sales* 8,736,240
SIC 7373 Computer integrated systems design
Pr Pr Robert Kennedy
Genl Mgr Gary Graham
Tim Stoop

D-U-N-S 24-889-2127   (HQ)
NEXANS CANADA INC
140 Allstate Pky Suite 300, Markham, ON, L3R 0Z7
(905) 944-4300
Emp Here 70   *Emp Total* 10
Sales 129,937,650
SIC 3312 Blast furnaces and steel mills
Pr Pr Steve Hall
Kevin Stinson
Sec Frank S Ryan

D-U-N-S 25-146-6298   (HQ)
NIELSEN MEDIA RESEARCH LIMITED
NIELSEN
160 Mcnabb St, Markham, ON, L3R 4B8
(905) 475-1131
Emp Here 93   *Sales* 83,333,346
SIC 8732 Commercial nonphysical research
Treas Rich Fitzgerald
Dir Ralph Hosein
Dir Harris Black
Dir David A. Schwartz-Leeper
Dir Michael Boland
Dir David Berger
Jeanne Danubio

D-U-N-S 20-151-7893   (HQ)
NORDSON CANADA, LIMITED
FINISHING, DIV OF
(*Suby of* Nordson Corporation)
1211 Denison St, Markham, ON, L3R 4B3
(905) 475-6730
Emp Here 31   *Emp Total* 6,127
Sales 9,095,636
SIC 5084 Industrial machinery and equipment
Katherine Toffan

D-U-N-S 20-276-5087   (BR)
NOVEXCO INC
LYRECO
7303 Warden Ave Suite 200, Markham, ON, L3R 5Y6
(905) 968-1320
Emp Here 20
SIC 5044 Office equipment

D-U-N-S 24-368-2932   (HQ)
OSPREY MEDIA PUBLISHING INC
(*Suby of* Placements Peladeau Inc, Les)
100 Renfrew Dr Suite 110, Markham, ON, L3R 9R6
(905) 752-1132
Emp Here 50   *Emp Total* 1
Sales 283,735,262
SIC 2711 Newspapers
Pr Michael Sifton
VP Opers Julia Kamula
Blair Mackenzie
VP Sls Shannon Mcpeak
VP Ron Laurin
VP Mike Power
VP Dan Johnson
VP Paul Mccuaig
VP Daryl Smith
Jean-Francois Pruneau

D-U-N-S 24-719-7742   (HQ)
PCI GEOMATICS ENTERPRISES INC
90 Allstate Pky Suite 501, Markham, ON, L3R 6H3
(905) 764-0614
Emp Here 40   *Emp Total* 85
Sales 12,040,889
SIC 7371 Custom computer programming services
Pr Pr Robert Moses

D-U-N-S 20-859-8586   (BR)
PACIFIC LINK COMMUNICATIONS INC
BELL WORLD
4300 Steeles Ave E, Markham, ON, L3R 0Y5
(905) 305-8700
Emp Here 25
SIC 5999 Miscellaneous retail stores, nec

D-U-N-S 20-859-8610   (BR)
PACIFIC LINK COMMUNICATIONS INC
BELL WORLD
570 Alden Rd Suite 13, Markham, ON, L3R 8N5
(905) 305-8100
Emp Here 25
SIC 5999 Miscellaneous retail stores, nec

D-U-N-S 25-203-1372   (HQ)
PACIFIC LINK COMMUNICATIONS INC
BELL MOBILITY CENTRE
(*Suby of* Pacific Link Communications Inc)
570 Alden Rd Suite 11, Markham, ON, L3R 8N5
(905) 305-8100
Emp Here 93   *Emp Total* 1,360
Sales 179,363,600
SIC 5999 Miscellaneous retail stores, nec
Pr Michael Wong
VP Benny Kwok
Treas Yin Fun Choi

D-U-N-S 20-859-9204   (BR)
PACIFIC LINK COMMUNICATIONS INC
BELL WORLD
7357 Woodbine Ave Suite 4, Markham, ON, L3R 1A7

(905) 470-2355
Emp Here 25
SIC 5999 Miscellaneous retail stores, nec

D-U-N-S 24-989-3517   (BR)
PARK PROPERTY MANAGEMENT INC
HENSEATIC HOLDINGS
16 Esna Park Dr Suite 200, Markham, ON,
L3R 5X1
(905) 940-1718
Emp Here 35
SIC 6531 Real estate agents and managers

D-U-N-S 20-408-9460   (HQ)
PARSONS INC
625 Cochrane Dr Suite 500, Markham, ON,
L3R 9R9
(905) 943-0500
Emp Here 275   *Emp Total* 15,000
Sales 87,771,722
SIC 8711 Engineering services
Pr Pr James Kerr
VP Sylvain Montminy
Sec Clyde E. Jr. Ellis
Dir Peter Marrocco
Dir Michael Johnson

D-U-N-S 20-716-3452   (SL)
PORTER, R. F. PLASTERING LIMITED
75d Konrad Cres, Markham, ON, L3R 8T8
(905) 940-4131
Emp Here 60   *Sales* 5,107,249
SIC 1742 Plastering, drywall, and insulation
Pr Pr Reginald Porter
Jean Porter

D-U-N-S 25-186-4336   (BR)
PRAXAIR CANADA INC
MEDIGAS
(*Suby of* Praxair, Inc.)
385 Bentley St, Markham, ON, L3R 9T2
(416) 365-1700
Emp Here 50
SIC 8082 Home health care services

D-U-N-S 24-024-8815   (SL)
PROPHARM LIMITED
(*Suby of* McKesson Corporation)
131 Mcnabb St, Markham, ON, L3R 5V7
(905) 943-9736
Emp Here 55   *Sales* 12,111,476
SIC 7371 Custom computer programming services
Pr Pr Larry Latowsky

D-U-N-S 24-852-8254   (BR)
PRODUITS MENAGERS FREUDENBERG INC
VILEDA PROFESSIONAL
15 Allstate Pky, Markham, ON, L3R 5B4
(905) 669-9949
Emp Here 150
SIC 5199 Nondurable goods, nec

D-U-N-S 25-053-0425   (SL)
PROTECT AIR CO
2751 John St, Markham, ON, L3R 2Y8
(905) 944-8877
Emp Here 91   *Sales* 15,214,800
SIC 8748 Business consulting, nec
Pr Pr Michael Butler
Gord Blair
VP Acctg Dave Skelton

D-U-N-S 24-525-2309   (SL)
RANKA ENTERPRISES INC
7261 Victoria Park Ave, Markham, ON, L3R 2M7
(905) 752-1081
Emp Here 70   *Sales* 3,470,686
SIC 6553 Cemetery subdividers and developers

D-U-N-S 20-224-6018   (BR)
REDBERRY FRANCHISING CORP
BURGER KING
3088 Highway 7 E, Markham, ON, L3R 5A1
(905) 479-8594
Emp Here 30

SIC 5812 Eating places

D-U-N-S 24-346-6682   (HQ)
RENTOKIL PEST CONTROL CANADA LIMITED
30 Royal Crest Crt Unit 11, Markham, ON, L3R 9W8
(416) 226-5880
Emp Here 50   *Emp Total* 29,792
Sales 3,551,629
SIC 7342 Disinfecting and pest control services

D-U-N-S 20-954-9414   (BR)
REXALL PHARMACY GROUP LTD
(*Suby of* McKesson Corporation)
131 Mcnabb St, Markham, ON, L3R 5V7
(905) 943-9499
Emp Here 170
SIC 5912 Drug stores and proprietary stores

D-U-N-S 24-965-4690   (HQ)
RISO CANADA INC
1 Valleywood Dr Unit 2, Markham, ON, L3R 5L9
(905) 475-7476
Emp Here 20   *Emp Total* 3,649
Sales 1,319,261
SIC 3579 Office machines, nec

D-U-N-S 24-579-0246   (SL)
ROLTA CANADA LTD
ORION TECHNOLOGY
140 Allstate Pky Suite 503, Markham, ON, L3R 5Y8
(905) 754-8100
Emp Here 50   *Sales* 2,699,546
SIC 8731 Commercial physical research

D-U-N-S 20-573-8342   (BR)
ROYAL BANK OF CANADA
RBC
(*Suby of* Royal Bank Of Canada)
7750 Kennedy Rd, Markham, ON, L3R 0A7
(905) 513-0309
Emp Here 20
SIC 6021 National commercial banks

D-U-N-S 25-176-0898   (BR)
ROYAL BANK OF CANADA
RBC
(*Suby of* Royal Bank Of Canada)
7481 Woodbine Ave Suite 200, Markham, ON, L3R 2W1
(905) 474-4010
Emp Here 23
SIC 6021 National commercial banks

D-U-N-S 24-850-5877   (SL)
RUBIE'S COSTUME COMPANY (CANADA)
(*Suby of* Rubie's Costume Company, Inc.)
2710 14th Ave, Markham, ON, L3R 0J1
(905) 470-0300
Emp Here 50   *Sales* 5,180,210
SIC 5099 Durable goods, nec
Pr Pr Marc Beige
Dir Michael Maskery
Howard Beige

D-U-N-S 20-699-6774   (HQ)
SRB EDUCATION SOLUTIONS INC
200 Town Centre Blvd Suite 400, Markham, ON, L3R 8G5
(905) 943-7706
Emp Here 155   *Emp Total* 255
Sales 21,231,564
SIC 7371 Custom computer programming services
Pr Steve Thompson

D-U-N-S 24-425-2862   (HQ)
SAMSON CONTROLS INC
105 Riviera Dr Unit 1, Markham, ON, L3R 5J7
(905) 474-0354
Emp Here 25   *Emp Total* 1,875
Sales 5,630,632
SIC 5084 Industrial machinery and equipment
Ch Bd Hans Grimm

Pr Pr Michael Espey

D-U-N-S 24-783-9061   (BR)
SAMUEL, SON & CO., LIMITED
ASSOCIATED TUBE CANADA, DIV OF
7455 Woodbine Ave, Markham, ON, L3R 1A7
(905) 475-6464
Emp Here 300
SIC 5051 Metals service centers and offices

D-U-N-S 25-311-1694   (BR)
SEARS CANADA INC
5000 Highway 7 E, Markham, ON, L3R 4M9

Emp Here 250
SIC 5311 Department stores

D-U-N-S 24-375-2990   (BR)
SIEMENS CANADA LIMITED
7303 Warden Ave, Markham, ON, L3R 5Y6
(905) 305-1021
Emp Here 40
SIC 3625 Relays and industrial controls

D-U-N-S 24-310-7765   (BR)
SIEMENS CANADA LIMITED
US FILTER
250 Royal Crest Crt, Markham, ON, L3R 3S1
(905) 944-2819
Emp Here 34
SIC 3589 Service industry machinery, nec

D-U-N-S 20-286-0920   (HQ)
SIGNODE PACKAGING GROUP CANADA ULC
SIGNODE CANADA
241 Gough Rd, Markham, ON, L3R 5B3
(905) 479-9754
Emp Here 50   *Sales* 17,325,020
SIC 2673 Bags: plastic, laminated, and coated
Genl Mgr Paul Cox

D-U-N-S 20-232-5031   (HQ)
SMUCKER FOODS OF CANADA CORP
ROBIN HOOD MULTIFOODS
(*Suby of* The J M Smucker Company)
80 Whitehall Dr, Markham, ON, L3R 0P3
(905) 940-9600
Emp Here 200   *Emp Total* 6,910
Sales 12,841,083
SIC 2033 Canned fruits and specialties
Pr Dave Lemmon
S&M/VP Stephen Kori
VP Opers Carl Blouin
VP Fin Aurelio Calabretta
Bobby Modi
VP Opers Todd Campbell
Adam Zitney
VP George Ellinidis
Prs Dir Melody Crawford

D-U-N-S 20-860-2149   (BR)
SOURCE (BELL) ELECTRONICS INC, THE
SOURCE, THE
5000 Highway 7 E, Markham, ON, L3R 4M9
(905) 477-0156
Emp Here 25
SIC 5999 Miscellaneous retail stores, nec

D-U-N-S 20-288-5448   (SL)
SPRINGFREE TRAMPOLINE INC
151 Whitehall Dr Unit 2, Markham, ON, L3R 9T1
(905) 948-0124
Emp Here 55   *Sales* 5,936,673
SIC 3949 Sporting and athletic goods, nec

D-U-N-S 20-107-2753   (BR)
STANTEC CONSULTING LTD
675 Cochrane Dr Suite 300 W Tower, Markham, ON, L3R 0B8
(905) 944-7777
Emp Here 300
SIC 8711 Engineering services

D-U-N-S 25-213-7666   (BR)
STAPLES CANADA INC

STAPLES THE BUSINESS DEPOT
(*Suby of* Staples, Inc.)
3175 Highway 7 E Unit 200, Markham, ON, L3R 0T9
(905) 479-3101
Emp Here 50
SIC 5943 Stationery stores

D-U-N-S 20-806-5495   (BR)
STARBUCKS COFFEE CANADA, INC
(*Suby of* Starbucks Corporation)
7333 Woodbine Ave Unit 1, Markham, ON, L3R 1A7
(905) 513-6767
Emp Here 20
SIC 5812 Eating places

D-U-N-S 25-304-1966   (BR)
SUN LIFE ASSURANCE COMPANY OF CANADA
3100 Steeles Ave E Suite 500, Markham, ON, L3R 8T3
(905) 415-9659
Emp Here 80
SIC 6311 Life insurance

D-U-N-S 24-192-1006   (HQ)
SWAROVSKI CANADA LIMITED
80 Gough Rd Unit 2, Markham, ON, L3R 6E8
(905) 752-0498
Emp Here 45   *Emp Total* 32,000
Sales 29,279,284
SIC 5944 Jewelry stores
Paula Cavaco
Dir Fin Tora Perez
S&M/VP Susan Wolf

D-U-N-S 20-015-9510   (SL)
SYNERGIO MANUFACTURING LTD
4011 14th Ave, Markham, ON, L3R 0Z9
(905) 415-1166
Emp Here 30   *Sales* 6,773,040
SIC 3571 Electronic computers
Pr Pr Frank Luk
Charlton Lam

D-U-N-S 25-929-8784   (BR)
SYSTEMES SYNTAX LTEE
SYNTAX.NET
(*Suby of* Systemes Syntax Ltee)
60 Columbia Way Suite 207, Markham, ON, L3R 0C9
(905) 709-4466
Emp Here 25
SIC 7371 Custom computer programming services

D-U-N-S 20-702-4691   (BR)
T & T SUPERMARKET INC
7070 Warden Ave, Markham, ON, L3R 5Y2
(905) 470-8113
Emp Here 50
SIC 5411 Grocery stores

D-U-N-S 20-920-0349   (SL)
TD HOME AND AUTO INSURANCE COMPANY
(*Suby of* Toronto-Dominion Bank, The)
675 Cochrane Dr Suite 100, Markham, ON, L3R 0B8
(905) 415-8400
Emp Here 50   *Sales* 5,370,756
SIC 6411 Insurance agents, brokers, and service
Pr Kenneth W. Lalonde
Sec Joanne Simard
Dir Dominic Mercuri
Dir Riaz Ahmed
Dir Mark Chauvin
Dir Susan Ann Cummings
Dir Philip C. Moore
Dir Manjit Singh
Dir Antonietta Di Girolamo

D-U-N-S 20-945-1926   (BR)
TD WATERHOUSE CANADA INC
TD WATERHOUSE PRIVATE INVESTMENT ADVICE

(Suby of Toronto-Dominion Bank, The)
3100 Steeles Ave E Suite 801, Markham, ON,
L3R 8T3
(905) 477-0676
Emp Here 20
SIC 8742 Management consulting services

D-U-N-S 24-121-0439   (BR)
TELUS COMMUNICATIONS INC
70 Gough Rd, Markham, ON, L3R 0E9

Emp Here 200
SIC 4899 Communication services, nec

D-U-N-S 24-366-2231   (HQ)
TECHTRONIC INDUSTRIES CANADA INC
TTI CANADA
7303 Warden Ave Suite 202, Markham, ON,
L3R 5Y6
(905) 479-4355
Emp Here 60   Emp Total 1,000
Sales 22,615,896
SIC 5072 Hardware
Pr Craig Baxter
VP Fin Russell Laird
 Horst Pudwill
 Gary S. Rossiter

D-U-N-S 24-752-8953   (SL)
TEMPO DRAFTING SERVICES INC
260 Town Centre Blvd Suite 300, Markham,
ON, L3R 8H8
(905) 470-7000
Emp Here 70   Sales 3,575,074
SIC 7389 Business services, nec

D-U-N-S 20-702-1015   (BR)
TEVA CANADA LIMITED
575 Hood Rd, Markham, ON, L3R 4E1
(905) 475-3370
Emp Here 180
SIC 2834 Pharmaceutical preparations

D-U-N-S 25-660-3879   (BR)
TORONTO-DOMINION BANK, THE
TD BANK
(Suby of Toronto-Dominion Bank, The)
7085 Woodbine Ave, Markham, ON, L3R 1A3
(905) 475-6291
Emp Here 30
SIC 6021 National commercial banks

D-U-N-S 25-418-4955   (HQ)
TORRES AVIATION INCORPORATED
SKYWORDS TRAFFIC NETWORK
(Suby of Torres Aviation Incorporated)
95 Royal Crest Crt Unit 5, Markham, ON, L3R
9X5
(905) 470-7655
Emp Here 25   Emp Total 60
Sales 4,377,642
SIC 7383 News syndicates

D-U-N-S 20-549-7415   (HQ)
TOSHIBA OF CANADA LIMITED
OFFICE PRODUCTS GROUP, DIV OF
75 Tiverton Crt, Markham, ON, L3R 4M8
(905) 470-3500
Emp Here 312   Emp Total 153,492
Sales 126,513,854
SIC 5064 Electrical appliances, television and
radio
Pr Ralph Hyatt
Crdt Mgr Phil Devor
 Kiyofumi Kakudo
 Osumi Masaaki
 Arthur Kitamura

D-U-N-S 25-984-5303   (BR)
TOWN SHOES LIMITED
SHOE COMPANY, THE
3175 Highway 7 E Unit 300, Markham, ON,
L3R 0T9
(905) 477-0697
Emp Here 20
SIC 5661 Shoe stores

D-U-N-S 24-927-5389   (SL)

**TOWNE MEADOW DEVELOPMENT COR-
PORATION INC**
80 Tiverton Crt Suite 300, Markham, ON, L3R
0G4
(905) 477-7609
Emp Here 50   Sales 9,611,756
SIC 1521 Single-family housing construction
Pr Sheldon Libfeld
VP VP Mark Libfeld

D-U-N-S 24-868-5323   (HQ)
TOYOTA CREDIT CANADA INC
80 Micro Crt Suite 200, Markham, ON, L3R
9Z5
(905) 513-8200
Emp Here 100   Emp Total 348,877
Sales 119,853,360
SIC 6141 Personal credit institutions
Pr Lorenzo Baldesarra
 Anthony Wearing
 Yoichi Tomihara
 Eiji Hirano
 Real Tanguay

D-U-N-S 24-212-3081   (BR)
TRANSCANADA PIPELINES LIMITED
675 Cochrane Dr Suite 701, Markham, ON,
L3R 0B8
(905) 946-7800
Emp Here 100
SIC 4922 Natural gas transmission

D-U-N-S 24-850-0584   (SL)
**TRIVISION BROADBAND AND TELECOM
INC**
7880 Woodbine Ave Suite A & B, Markham,
ON, L3R 2N7
(905) 474-1422
Emp Here 35   Sales 6,107,800
SIC 5063 Electrical apparatus and equipment
Pr Pr Qamrul Siddiqi
Fin Ex Adnan Tasadduq

D-U-N-S 20-044-1764   (HQ)
TYCO ELECTRONICS CANADA ULC
20 Esna Park Dr, Markham, ON, L3R 1E1
(905) 475-6222
Emp Here 130   Emp Total 75,000
Sales 6,493,502
SIC 3643 Current-carrying wiring devices
Pr Kevin Irons

D-U-N-S 25-509-3239   (SL)
ULTRASAVE LIGHTING LIMITED
140 Amber St Unit 12, Markham, ON, L3R 3J8
(905) 940-0888
Emp Here 23   Sales 4,596,524
SIC 5063 Electrical apparatus and equipment

D-U-N-S 25-996-9384   (BR)
UNILEVER CANADA INC
UNILEVER BEST FOODS
25 Centurian Dr Suite 101, Markham, ON,
L3R 5N8
(905) 947-9400
Emp Here 6
SIC 8742 Management consulting services

D-U-N-S 20-174-0805   (HQ)
UTHANE RESEARCH LTD
RIPPLEPAK, DIV OF
(Suby of Uthane Research Ltd)
140 Bentley St Unit 2, Markham, ON, L3R 3L2
(905) 940-2356
Emp Here 23   Emp Total 51
Sales 22,189,350
SIC 3081 Unsupported plastics film and sheet
Pr Pr Ragui Ghali

D-U-N-S 25-351-3964   (BR)
**VICTORIAN ORDER OF NURSES FOR
CANADA**
VON TORONTO-YORK REGION
7100 Woodbine Ave Suite 402, Markham, ON,
L3R 5J2
(905) 479-3201
Emp Here 300
SIC 8082 Home health care services

D-U-N-S 24-874-5044   (BR)
WSP CANADA INC
GENIVAR
600 Cochrane Dr Suite 500, Markham, ON,
L3R 5K3
(905) 475-7270
Emp Here 300
SIC 8711 Engineering services

D-U-N-S 24-793-8731   (BR)
WSP CANADA INC
600 Cochrane Dr Floor 5, Markham, ON, L3R
5K3
(905) 475-8727
Emp Here 300
SIC 7363 Help supply services

D-U-N-S 25-204-3492   (SL)
WAH LUNG LABELS (CANADA) INC
WAH LUNG LABELS
150 Telson Rd, Markham, ON, L3R 1E5
(905) 948-8877
Emp Here 75   Sales 3,064,349
SIC 2241 Narrow fabric mills

D-U-N-S 25-294-7189   (BR)
WAL-MART CANADA CORP
5000 Highway 7 E Unit Y006a, Markham, ON,
L3R 4M9
(905) 477-6060
Emp Here 200
SIC 5311 Department stores

D-U-N-S 25-973-3715   (SL)
WATER PIK TECHNOLOGIES CANADA INC
(Suby of Water Pik, Inc.)
625 Cochrane Dr, Markham, ON, L3R 9R9

Emp Here 100   Sales 18,240,175
SIC 5074 Plumbing and heating equipment
and supplies (hydronics)
VP Fin Ernest Brock
VP Sls Roger Williams
Dir Barbara Miller
Dir Anthony Prudhomme
Dir Richard Bisson
Dir Robert Rasp

D-U-N-S 20-821-0146   (HQ)
WEINS CANADA INC
MARKVILLE TOYOTA
3120 Steeles Ave E, Markham, ON, L3R 1G9
(905) 948-0977
Emp Here 190   Emp Total 113
Sales 237,122,275
SIC 5511 New and used car dealers
Pr Norio Naka
 David Lalonde
 Yoshinobu Niiro

D-U-N-S 24-310-5561   (BR)
WHITEHILL TECHNOLOGIES INC
19 Allstate Pky Suite 400, Markham, ON, L3R
5A4
(905) 475-2112
Emp Here 80
SIC 7371 Custom computer programming services

D-U-N-S 25-221-2931   (BR)
**WINNERS MERCHANTS INTERNATIONAL
L.P.**
WINNERS
(Suby of The TJX Companies Inc)
5000 Highway 7, Markham, ON, L3R 4M9
(905) 415-1441
Emp Here 120
SIC 5651 Family clothing stores

D-U-N-S 20-860-4335   (BR)
**WINNERS MERCHANTS INTERNATIONAL
L.P.**
HOMESENSE
(Suby of The TJX Companies Inc)
5000 Highway 7, Markham, ON, L3R 4M9
(905) 415-1441
Emp Here 25
SIC 5651 Family clothing stores

D-U-N-S 20-030-5477   (BR)
**WINNERS MERCHANTS INTERNATIONAL
L.P.**
WINNERS
(Suby of The TJX Companies Inc)
3105 Highway 7 E, Markham, ON, L3R 0T9
(905) 513-8464
Emp Here 65
SIC 5651 Family clothing stores

D-U-N-S 24-354-4462   (BR)
**WOODBINE TOOL & DIE MANUFACTUR-
ING LTD**
3300 14th Ave, Markham, ON, L3R 0H3
(905) 475-5223
Emp Here 75
SIC 3469 Metal stampings, nec

D-U-N-S 25-275-6358   (HQ)
**WORLDSOURCE FINANCIAL MANAGE-
MENT INC**
625 Cochrane Dr Suite 700, Markham, ON,
L3R 9R9
(905) 940-0044
Emp Here 47   Emp Total 354
Sales 14,154,376
SIC 6282 Investment advice
Ch Bd Paul Brown
Pr Andy Mitchell
VP VP Trevor Line

D-U-N-S 24-826-6801   (BR)
XEROX CANADA LTD
XEROX ENGINEERING SYSTEMS CANADA
(Suby of Xerox Corporation)
3000 Steeles Ave E Suite 200, Markham, ON,
L3R 4T9
(905) 946-7522
Emp Here 70
SIC 5049 Professional equipment, nec

D-U-N-S 25-151-0301   (BR)
**YORK CATHOLIC DISTRICT SCHOOL
BOARD**
ST JUSTIN MARTYR SCHOOL
140 Hollingham Rd, Markham, ON, L3R 8K4
(905) 947-8106
Emp Here 40
SIC 8211 Elementary and secondary schools

D-U-N-S 25-224-9875   (BR)
**YORK CATHOLIC DISTRICT SCHOOL
BOARD**
MOTHER TERESA ELEMENTARY SCHOOL
7100 Birchmount Rd, Markham, ON, L3R 4H2
(905) 475-8025
Emp Here 31
SIC 8211 Elementary and secondary schools

D-U-N-S 25-147-5232   (BR)
**YORK CATHOLIC DISTRICT SCHOOL
BOARD**
ST BENEDICT
50 Aldergrove Dr, Markham, ON, L3R 7E6
(905) 475-9646
Emp Here 30
SIC 8211 Elementary and secondary schools

D-U-N-S 25-297-9604   (BR)
YORK REGION DISTRICT SCHOOL BOARD
ALDERGROVE PUBLIC SCHOOL
(Suby of York Region District School Board)
150 Aldergrove Dr, Markham, ON, L3R 6Z8
(905) 470-2227
Emp Here 60
SIC 8211 Elementary and secondary schools

D-U-N-S 20-711-4138   (BR)
YORK REGION DISTRICT SCHOOL BOARD
COLEDALE PUBLIC SCHOOL
(Suby of York Region District School Board)
60 Coledale Rd, Markham, ON, L3R 7W8
(905) 940-0123
Emp Here 50
SIC 8211 Elementary and secondary schools

D-U-N-S 20-711-4062   (BR)
YORK REGION DISTRICT SCHOOL BOARD

UNIONVILLE HIGH SCHOOL
(Suby of York Region District School Board)
201 Town Centre Blvd, Markham, ON, L3R
8G5
(905) 479-2787
Emp Here 50
SIC 8211 Elementary and secondary schools

D-U-N-S 25-297-9125   (BR)
YORK REGION DISTRICT SCHOOL BOARD
MILLIKEN MILLS PUBLIC SCHOOL
(Suby of York Region District School Board)
289 Risebrough Circt, Markham, ON, L3R 3J3
(905) 475-8143
Emp Here 40
SIC 8211 Elementary and secondary schools

D-U-N-S 20-711-4070   (BR)
YORK REGION DISTRICT SCHOOL BOARD
HIGHGATE PUBLIC SCHOOL
(Suby of York Region District School Board)
35 Highgate Dr, Markham, ON, L3R 3R5
(905) 477-1019
Emp Here 44
SIC 8211 Elementary and secondary schools

Markham, ON L3S
York County

D-U-N-S 24-351-6106   (SL)
2419658 ONTARIO INC
BOSTON PIZZA
7680 Markham Rd Suite 1, Markham, ON,
L3S 4S1
(905) 201-0477
Emp Here 50   Sales 1,353,384
SIC 5812 Eating places

D-U-N-S 24-794-1172   (HQ)
ALPINE SYSTEMS CORPORATION
120 Travail Rd, Markham, ON, L3S 3J1
(905) 417-2766
Emp Here 20   Emp Total 557
Sales 3,866,917
SIC 3443 Fabricated plate work (boiler shop)

D-U-N-S 25-176-5780   (BR)
CORPORATION OF THE CITY OF
MARKHAM, THE
ARMADALE COMMUNITY CENTRE
2401 Denison St, Markham, ON, L3S 1G3
(905) 474-1007
Emp Here 45
SIC 8322 Individual and family services

D-U-N-S 24-354-8927   (BR)
COSTCO WHOLESALE CANADA LTD
COSTCO
(Suby of Costco Wholesale Corporation)
65 Kirkham Dr Suite 545, Markham, ON, L3S
0A9
(905) 201-3500
Emp Here 200
SIC 5099 Durable goods, nec

D-U-N-S 24-525-1822   (HQ)
ECONOLITE CANADA INC
(Suby of Econolite Control Products, Inc.)
110 Travail Rd, Markham, ON, L3S 3J1
(905) 294-9920
Emp Here 28   Emp Total 225
Sales 2,480,664
SIC 3625 Relays and industrial controls

D-U-N-S 24-391-5639   (BR)
GOLF TOWN LIMITED
GOLF TOWN
7655 Markham Rd Unit 1, Markham, ON, L3S
3J9

Emp Here 20
SIC 5941 Sporting goods and bicycle shops

D-U-N-S 24-486-6620   (HQ)
GROTE INDUSTRIES CO.

GROTE ELECTRONICS, DIV OF
230 Travail Rd, Markham, ON, L3S 3J1
(905) 209-9744
Emp Here 115   Emp Total 1,200
Sales 27,579,145
SIC 5013 Motor vehicle supplies and new
parts
Pr Pr Eric Morris

D-U-N-S 20-553-4329   (BR)
HOME DEPOT OF CANADA INC
HOME DEPOT
(Suby of The Home Depot Inc)
50 Kirkham Dr, Markham, ON, L3S 4K7
(905) 201-2590
Emp Here 150
SIC 5211 Lumber and other building materials

D-U-N-S 24-858-6708   (HQ)
ITW CANADA INC
(Suby of Illinois Tool Works Inc.)
120 Travail Rd, Markham, ON, L3S 3J1
(905) 201-8399
Emp Here 50   Emp Total 50,000
Sales 369,822,500
SIC 5084 Industrial machinery and equipment
   Mark Ristow
   Mary Ann Spiegel
   David Livingston

D-U-N-S 24-325-8865   (BR)
ITW CANADA INVESTMENTS LIMITED
PARTNERSHIP
PASLODE CANADA DIV OF
(Suby of Illinois Tool Works Inc.)
120 Travail Rd, Markham, ON, L3S 3J1
(905) 471-4250
Emp Here 150
SIC 1541 Industrial buildings and warehouses

D-U-N-S 24-318-5712   (BR)
KUBOTA CANADA LTD
5900 14th Ave, Markham, ON, L3S 4K4
(905) 294-7477
Emp Here 120
SIC 5083 Farm and garden machinery

D-U-N-S 20-920-1276   (HQ)
KUBOTA CANADA LTD
5900 14th Ave, Markham, ON, L3S 4K4
(905) 294-7477
Emp Here 91   Emp Total 38,291
Sales 19,334,586
SIC 5084 Industrial machinery and equipment
Pr Pr Ross Wallace
   Robert Hickey

D-U-N-S 24-176-5234   (BR)
MARK'S WORK WEARHOUSE LTD
WORK WORLD
7700 Markham Rd Unit 2, Markham, ON, L3S
4S1
(905) 201-6330
Emp Here 20
SIC 5651 Family clothing stores

D-U-N-S 20-923-6145   (SL)
MCDONALD'S RESTAURANTS
7630 Markham Rd, Markham, ON, L3S 4S1
(905) 472-3900
Emp Here 70   Sales 2,115,860
SIC 5812 Eating places

D-U-N-S 20-172-6205   (SL)
PARKER PAD AND PRINTING LIMITED
208 Travail Rd, Markham, ON, L3S 3J1
(905) 294-7997
Emp Here 60   Sales 4,815,406
SIC 2752 Commercial printing, lithographic

D-U-N-S 25-984-5725   (BR)
PRISZM LP
KFC
2002 Middlefield Rd Unit 2, Markham, ON,
L3S 1Y5
(905) 472-2338
Emp Here 20
SIC 5812 Eating places

D-U-N-S 20-796-4417   (BR)
STAPLES CANADA INC
STAPLES THE BUSINESS DEPOT
(Suby of Staples, Inc.)
7725 Markham Rd, Markham, ON, L3S 3J9
(905) 472-0746
Emp Here 30
SIC 5943 Stationery stores

D-U-N-S 20-344-5192   (SL)
SUPER DISCOUNT STORE INC
46 Norman Ross Dr, Markham, ON, L3S 2Z1
(416) 939-5451
Emp Here 250   Sales 3,891,960
SIC 5311 Department stores

D-U-N-S 20-340-7580   (BR)
VALUE VILLAGE STORES, INC
(Suby of Savers, Inc.)
7655 Markham Rd Units C-1 & C-2, Markham,
ON, L3S 4S1
(905) 201-6164
Emp Here 60
SIC 5399 Miscellaneous general merchandise

D-U-N-S 20-711-4567   (BR)
YORK CATHOLIC DISTRICT SCHOOL
BOARD
FR. MICHAEL MCGIVNEY CATHOLIC
ACADEMY
5300 14th Ave, Markham, ON, L3S 3K8
(905) 472-4961
Emp Here 100
SIC 8211 Elementary and secondary schools

D-U-N-S 20-914-4604   (BR)
YORK CATHOLIC DISTRICT SCHOOL
BOARD
SIR RICHARD W SCOTT
90 Roxbury St, Markham, ON, L3S 3S8
(905) 472-3964
Emp Here 44
SIC 8211 Elementary and secondary schools

D-U-N-S 25-147-5554   (BR)
YORK CATHOLIC DISTRICT SCHOOL
BOARD
ST. VINCENT DE PAUL
50 Featherstone Ave, Markham, ON, L3S 2H4
(905) 472-2420
Emp Here 37
SIC 8211 Elementary and secondary schools

D-U-N-S 20-711-4104   (BR)
YORK REGION DISTRICT SCHOOL BOARD
WILCLAY PUBLIC SCHOOL
(Suby of York Region District School Board)
60 Wilclay Ave, Markham, ON, L3S 1R4
(905) 470-1447
Emp Here 60
SIC 8211 Elementary and secondary schools

D-U-N-S 20-913-8770   (BR)
YORK REGION DISTRICT SCHOOL BOARD
PARKLAND PUBLIC SCHOOL
(Suby of York Region District School Board)
18 Coxworth Ave, Markham, ON, L3S 3B8
(905) 472-8536
Emp Here 50
SIC 8211 Elementary and secondary schools

D-U-N-S 20-299-5853   (BR)
YORK REGION DISTRICT SCHOOL BOARD
BOXWOOD PUBLIC SCHOOL
(Suby of York Region District School Board)
30 Boxwood Cres, Markham, ON, L3S 3P7
(905) 294-5563
Emp Here 30
SIC 8211 Elementary and secondary schools

D-U-N-S 20-711-4302   (BR)
YORK REGION DISTRICT SCHOOL BOARD
MARKHAM GATEWAY PUBLIC SCHOOL
(Suby of York Region District School Board)
30 Fonda Rd, Markham, ON, L3S 3X3
(905) 472-3303
Emp Here 60
SIC 8211 Elementary and secondary schools

D-U-N-S 25-297-9760   (BR)
YORK REGION DISTRICT SCHOOL BOARD
MIDDLEFIELD COLLEGIATE INSTITUTE
(Suby of York Region District School Board)
525 Highglen Ave, Markham, ON, L3S 3L5
(905) 472-8900
Emp Here 150
SIC 8211 Elementary and secondary schools

D-U-N-S 24-093-6976   (BR)
YORK REGION DISTRICT SCHOOL BOARD
ELLEN FAIRCLOUGH PUBLIC SCHOOL
(Suby of York Region District School Board)
33 Brando Ave, Markham, ON, L3S 4K9
(905) 294-9455
Emp Here 40
SIC 8211 Elementary and secondary schools

D-U-N-S 20-568-0056   (BR)
YORK REGION DISTRICT SCHOOL BOARD
CEDARWOOD PUBLIC SCHOOL
(Suby of York Region District School Board)
399 Elson St, Markham, ON, L3S 4R8
(905) 294-5756
Emp Here 60
SIC 8211 Elementary and secondary schools

D-U-N-S 20-711-4146   (BR)
YORK REGION DISTRICT SCHOOL BOARD
RANDALL PUBLIC SCHOOL
(Suby of York Region District School Board)
50 Randall Ave, Markham, ON, L3S 1E2
(905) 479-2003
Emp Here 50
SIC 8211 Elementary and secondary schools

D-U-N-S 20-591-2327   (BR)
YORK REGION DISTRICT SCHOOL BOARD
COPPARD GLEN PUBLIC SCHOOL
(Suby of York Region District School Board)
131 Coppard Ave, Markham, ON, L3S 2T5
(905) 471-0419
Emp Here 25
SIC 8211 Elementary and secondary schools

Markham, ON L3T
York County

D-U-N-S 24-313-8026   (HQ)
EVERLINK PAYMENT SERVICES INC
(Suby of Fidelity National Information Ser-
vices, Inc.)
125 Commerce Valley Dr W Suite 100,
Markham, ON, L3T 7W4
(905) 946-5898
Emp Here 45   Emp Total 55,000
Sales 25,987,530
SIC 6099 Functions related to deposit banking
Pr Pr Mark Ripplinger
Acct Mgr Duane Gomes

D-U-N-S 25-214-6766   (HQ)
MORRISON HERSHFIELD LIMITED
125 Commerce Valley Dr W Suite 300,
Markham, ON, L3T 7W4
(416) 499-3110
Emp Here 305   Emp Total 625
Sales 79,235,320
SIC 8711 Engineering services
   Anthony Karakatsanis
Pr Pr Catherine Karakatsanis
VP Fin David Pavey
VP VP James Lew
VP VP James Weir
VP VP Pierre Gallant

Markham, ON L6B
York County

D-U-N-S 25-192-2287   (BR)
CBI LIMITED

(*Suby of* CBI Limited)
110 Copper Creek Dr Suite 102, Markham,
ON, L6B 0P9
(905) 472-2273
Emp Here 20
SIC 8049 Offices of health practitioner

D-U-N-S 24-357-2646   (BR)
CHARTWELL SENIORS HOUSING REAL ESTATE INVESTMENT TRUST
WOODHAVEN, THE
380 Church St Suite 421, Markham, ON, L6B 1E1
(905) 472-3320
Emp Here 246
SIC 8059 Nursing and personal care, nec

D-U-N-S 20-770-6664   (HQ)
EBSCO CANADA LTD
(*Suby of* Ebsco Industries, Inc.)
110 Copper Creek Dr Suite 305, Markham,
ON, L6B 0P9
(416) 297-8282
Emp Here 37   *Emp Total* 6,032
Sales 2,480,664
SIC 7389 Business services, nec

D-U-N-S 24-714-2701   (BR)
WAL-MART CANADA CORP
WALMART
500 Copper Creek Dr Suite 1109, Markham,
ON, L6B 0S1
(905) 472-9582
Emp Here 50
SIC 5311 Department stores

D-U-N-S 20-288-8934   (BR)
YEE HONG CENTRE FOR GERIATRIC CARE
YEE HONG
2780 Bur Oak Ave, Markham, ON, L6B 1C9
(905) 471-3232
Emp Here 150
SIC 8059 Nursing and personal care, nec

D-U-N-S 24-676-3408   (BR)
YORK REGION DISTRICT SCHOOL BOARD
DAVID SUZUKI PUBLIC SCHOOL
(*Suby of* York Region District School Board)
45 Riverwalk Dr, Markham, ON, L6B 0L9
(905) 209-0435
Emp Here 52
SIC 8211 Elementary and secondary schools

D-U-N-S 20-711-4419   (BR)
YORK REGION DISTRICT SCHOOL BOARD
CORNELL VILLAGE PUBLIC SCHOOL
(*Suby of* York Region District School Board)
186 Country Glen Rd, Markham, ON, L6B 1B5
(905) 471-1694
Emp Here 50
SIC 8211 Elementary and secondary schools

D-U-N-S 24-676-6849   (BR)
YORK REGION DISTRICT SCHOOL BOARD
LITTLE ROUGE PUBLIC SCHOOL
(*Suby of* York Region District School Board)
571 Country Glen Rd, Markham, ON, L6B 1E8
(905) 202-5960
Emp Here 25
SIC 8211 Elementary and secondary schools

Markham, ON L6C
York County

D-U-N-S 24-622-3903   (HQ)
1300323 ONTARIO INC
AMJ CAMPBELL VAN LINES
176 Hillmount Rd, Markham, ON, L6C 1Z9
(905) 887-5557
Emp Here 300   *Emp Total* 200
Sales 34,145,608
SIC 4214 Local trucking with storage
Pr Pr Denis Frappier
VP VP Gilles Frappier

Joanne Lambert
Dir Pierre Frappier
Dir Marc Frappier
Fin Ex Carole Frappier

D-U-N-S 20-733-1351   (SL)
1373372 ONTARIO LTD
MARIO'S NO FRILLS
9255 Woodbine Ave, Markham, ON, L6C 1Y9

Emp Here 90   *Sales* 16,637,800
SIC 5411 Grocery stores
Pr Mario Natile

D-U-N-S 20-914-9686   (BR)
ARBOR MEMORIAL SERVICES INC
HIGHLAND FUNERAL HOMES
10 Cachet Woods Crt, Markham, ON, L6C 3G1
(905) 887-8600
Emp Here 20
SIC 7261 Funeral service and crematories

D-U-N-S 24-252-9845   (BR)
CARA OPERATIONS LIMITED
MONTANA'S
(*Suby of* Cara Holdings Limited)
2890 Major Mackenzie Dr E Unit C, Markham,
ON, L6C 0G6
(905) 887-1050
Emp Here 30
SIC 5812 Eating places

D-U-N-S 20-650-4875   (BR)
ENBRIDGE GAS DISTRIBUTION INC
101 Honda Blvd, Markham, ON, L6C 0M6
(905) 887-4005
Emp Here 20
SIC 4924 Natural gas distribution

D-U-N-S 24-324-3818   (BR)
FUTUREWAY COMMUNICATIONS INC
280 Hillmount Rd Unit 9, Markham, ON, L6C 3A1
(416) 987-4700
Emp Here 20
SIC 4899 Communication services, nec

D-U-N-S 24-686-2023   (HQ)
HONDA CANADA FINANCE INC
HONDA FINANCIAL SERVICES
180 Honda Blvd Suite 200, Markham, ON, L6C 0H9
(905) 888-4188
Emp Here 132   *Emp Total* 208,399
Sales 133,664,002
SIC 6141 Personal credit institutions
Pr Pr Hideo Tanaka
VP VP Hideo Moroe
Ex VP Manabu Nishimae
VP Opers Jerry Chenkin
Dir David Sudbury
VP VP Harald Ladewig

D-U-N-S 20-530-8034   (HQ)
HONDA CANADA INC
HONDA OF CANADA MANUFACTURING
180 Honda Blvd Suite 200, Markham, ON, L6C 0H9
(905) 888-8110
Emp Here 600   *Emp Total* 208,399
Sales 106,569,260
SIC 3711 Motor vehicles and car bodies
Pr Dave Gardner
Ex VP Barry Holt
Dir Mickey M. Yaksich
Dir Tsutonu Morimoto
Dir Toshiaki Mikoshiba
Dir Soichiro Takazawa
Dir Sogo Nakata

D-U-N-S 20-533-3722   (HQ)
KYLEMORE HOMES LTD
KYLEMORE COMMUNITIES
(*Suby of* Kylemore Homes Ltd)
10080 Kennedy Rd, Markham, ON, L6C 1N9

(905) 887-5799
Emp Here 20   *Emp Total* 30
Sales 6,188,450
SIC 1521 Single-family housing construction
Arthur Gordon Stollery
Cailey Stollery
Acct Mgr Barb Patterson

D-U-N-S 20-112-9678   (HQ)
LIVANOVA CANADA CORP
REGIONAL SELLING, DIVISION OF
280 Hillmount Rd Unit 8, Markham, ON, L6C 3A1
(905) 284-4245
Emp Here 50   *Emp Total* 750
Sales 26,630,656
SIC 3841 Surgical and medical instruments
Pr Eros Roncaia
VP VP Paul Parsons
Dir Fin Ken Aravindan

D-U-N-S 24-603-5794   (SL)
NIMLOK CANADA LTD
(*Suby of* Nimlok Company)
220 Markland St Unit 1, Markham, ON, L6C 1T6
(416) 798-7201
Emp Here 20   *Sales* 1,313,293
SIC 2541 Wood partitions and fixtures

D-U-N-S 24-203-9068   (SL)
NOVO PLASTICS INC
388 Markland St, Markham, ON, L6C 1Z6
(905) 887-8818
Emp Here 68   *Sales* 9,047,127
SIC 3089 Plastics products, nec
Pr Baljit Sierra
VP Joy Sarkar
VP Sunil Kumar

D-U-N-S 20-172-9944   (HQ)
PHILIPS ELECTRONICS LTD
PHILIPS HEALTH CARE, DIV OF
281 Hillmount Rd, Markham, ON, L6C 2S3
(905) 201-4100
Emp Here 300   *Emp Total* 11,357
Sales 732,934,971
SIC 5064 Electrical appliances, television and radio
Pr Pr Iain Burns
Steve Hurwitz
Danielle Lavallee
Rahul Gupta

D-U-N-S 20-275-0571   (SL)
RYASH COFFEE CORPORATION
TIM HORTONS
9251 Woodbine Ave, Markham, ON, L6C 1Y9
(905) 887-8444
Emp Here 60   *Sales* 2,042,900
SIC 5461 Retail bakeries

D-U-N-S 20-404-3392   (HQ)
SCHOLASTIC CANADA LTD
(*Suby of* Scholastic Corporation)
175 Hillmount Rd, Markham, ON, L6C 1Z7
(905) 887-7323
Emp Here 420   *Emp Total* 8,900
Sales 96,437,161
SIC 5192 Books, periodicals, and newspapers
Dir Iole Lucchese
Dir Anne Browne
Dir Nancy Pearson
Richard Robinson

D-U-N-S 24-325-9798   (SL)
WONG, VICKY C.K. DRUGS LTD
SHOPPERS DRUG MART
9255 Woodbine Ave Suite 27, Markham, ON, L6C 1Y9
(905) 887-3000
Emp Here 65   *Sales* 12,782,700
SIC 5912 Drug stores and proprietary stores
Pr Pr Vicky Wong

D-U-N-S 20-711-4666   (BR)
YORK CATHOLIC DISTRICT SCHOOL BOARD

ST AUGUSTINE CATHOLIC HIGH SCHOOL
2188 Rodick Rd, Markham, ON, L6C 1S3
(905) 887-6171
Emp Here 100
SIC 8211 Elementary and secondary schools

D-U-N-S 25-151-0343   (BR)
YORK CATHOLIC DISTRICT SCHOOL BOARD
ST MONICA CATHOLIC SCHOOL
290 Calvert Rd, Markham, ON, L6C 1V1
(905) 887-1560
Emp Here 50
SIC 8211 Elementary and secondary schools

D-U-N-S 20-288-8199   (BR)
YORK REGION DISTRICT SCHOOL BOARD
PIERRE ELLIOTT TRUDEAU HIGH SCHOOL
(*Suby of* York Region District School Board)
90 Bur Oak Ave, Markham, ON, L6C 2E6
(905) 887-2216
Emp Here 100
SIC 8211 Elementary and secondary schools

D-U-N-S 24-676-3382   (BR)
YORK REGION DISTRICT SCHOOL BOARD
LINCOLN ALEXANDER PUBLIC SCHOOL
(*Suby of* York Region District School Board)
38 Hillmount Rd, Markham, ON, L6C 2H4
(905) 284-4513
Emp Here 45
SIC 8211 Elementary and secondary schools

D-U-N-S 24-676-5171   (BR)
YORK REGION DISTRICT SCHOOL BOARD
SIR WILFRID LAURIER PUBLIC SCHOOL
(*Suby of* York Region District School Board)
160 Hazelton Ave, Markham, ON, L6C 3H6
(905) 927-1452
Emp Here 25
SIC 8211 Elementary and secondary schools

D-U-N-S 20-711-4252   (BR)
YORK REGION DISTRICT SCHOOL BOARD
ASHTON MEADOWS PUBLIC SCHOOL
(*Suby of* York Region District School Board)
230 Calvert Rd, Markham, ON, L6C 1T5
(905) 887-2656
Emp Here 50
SIC 8211 Elementary and secondary schools

D-U-N-S 20-711-4328   (BR)
YORK REGION DISTRICT SCHOOL BOARD
CASTLEMORE PUBLIC SCHOOL
(*Suby of* York Region District School Board)
256 Ridgecrest Rd, Markham, ON, L6C 2R5
(905) 887-1543
Emp Here 55
SIC 8211 Elementary and secondary schools

D-U-N-S 20-711-4401   (BR)
YORK REGION DISTRICT SCHOOL BOARD
STONEBRIGE PUBLIC SCHOOL
(*Suby of* York Region District School Board)
168 Stonebridge Dr, Markham, ON, L6C 2Z8
(905) 887-2427
Emp Here 50
SIC 8211 Elementary and secondary schools

Markham, ON L6E
York County

D-U-N-S 24-349-6283   (BR)
BRICK WAREHOUSE LP, THE
BRICK, THE
9809 Hwy 48, Markham, ON, L6E 0E5
(905) 201-3470
Emp Here 50
SIC 5712 Furniture stores

D-U-N-S 24-744-0241   (BR)
GARDEN BASKET FOOD MARKETS INCORPORATED, THE
GARDEN BASKET, THE
9271 Markham Rd, Markham, ON, L6E 1A1

---

(905) 471-0777
Emp Here 150
SIC 5411 Grocery stores

D-U-N-S 24-250-0010   (BR)
HOME DEPOT OF CANADA INC
(*Suby of* The Home Depot Inc)
1201 Castlemore Ave, Markham, ON, L6E 0G5
(905) 201-5500
Emp Here 154
SIC 5251 Hardware stores

D-U-N-S 24-843-2028   (BR)
METRO ONTARIO INC
FOOD BASICS
1220 Castlemore Ave, Markham, ON, L6E 0H7
(905) 209-9200
Emp Here 75
SIC 5411 Grocery stores

D-U-N-S 24-676-3325   (BR)
YORK CATHOLIC DISTRICT SCHOOL BOARD
SAN LORENZO RUIZ CATHOLIC ELEMENTARY SCHOOL
840 Bur Oak Ave, Markham, ON, L6E 0E1
(905) 202-2430
Emp Here 25
SIC 8211 Elementary and secondary schools

D-U-N-S 24-676-3317   (BR)
YORK CATHOLIC DISTRICT SCHOOL BOARD
ST JULIA BILLIART ELEMENTARY SCHOOL
2070 Bur Oak Ave, Markham, ON, L6E 1X5
(905) 209-1245
Emp Here 40
SIC 8211 Elementary and secondary schools

D-U-N-S 24-676-2756   (BR)
YORK REGION DISTRICT SCHOOL BOARD
DONALD COUSENS PUBLIC SCHOOL
(*Suby of* York Region District School Board)
315 Mingay Ave, Markham, ON, L6E 1T5
(905) 202-8120
Emp Here 25
SIC 8211 Elementary and secondary schools

D-U-N-S 24-097-3490   (BR)
YORK REGION DISTRICT SCHOOL BOARD
GREENSBOROUGH PUBLIC SCHOOL
(*Suby of* York Region District School Board)
80 Alfred Paterson Dr, Markham, ON, L6E 1J5
(905) 472-3474
Emp Here 42
SIC 8211 Elementary and secondary schools

D-U-N-S 20-497-6377   (BR)
YORK REGION DISTRICT SCHOOL BOARD
SAM CHAPMAN PUBLIC SCHOOL
(*Suby of* York Region District School Board)
270 Alfred Paterson Dr, Markham, ON, L6E 2G1
(905) 472-8374
Emp Here 35
SIC 8211 Elementary and secondary schools

D-U-N-S 20-568-0080   (BR)
YORK REGION DISTRICT SCHOOL BOARD
WISMER PUBLIC SCHOOL
(*Suby of* York Region District School Board)
171 Mingay Ave, Markham, ON, L6E 1H8
(905) 471-5526
Emp Here 30
SIC 8211 Elementary and secondary schools

D-U-N-S 24-676-3358   (BR)
YORK REGION DISTRICT SCHOOL BOARD
MOUNT JOY PUBLIC SCHOOL
(*Suby of* York Region District School Board)
281 Williamson Rd, Markham, ON, L6E 1X1
(905) 202-1684
Emp Here 25
SIC 8211 Elementary and secondary schools

D-U-N-S 24-676-5197   (BR)
YORK REGION DISTRICT SCHOOL BOARD

JOHN MCCRAE PUBLIC SCHOOL
(*Suby of* York Region District School Board)
565 Fred Mclaren Blvd, Markham, ON, L6E 1N7
(905) 294-9122
Emp Here 25
SIC 8211 Elementary and secondary schools

Markham, ON L6G
York County

D-U-N-S 25-535-1967   (HQ)
1059936 ONTARIO INC
TEAM INDUSTRIAL SERVICES
(*Suby of* 1059936 Ontario Inc)
25 Bodrington Crt, Markham, ON, L6G 1B6
(905) 940-9334
Emp Here 25   *Emp Total* 300
Sales 23,558,225
SIC 7699 Repair services, nec
Pr Pr Clint Griffin
Steve Griffin

D-U-N-S 20-261-4058   (SL)
1321365 ONTARIO LIMITED
HOLTZ SPA
8500 Warden Ave, Markham, ON, L6G 1A5
(905) 470-8522
Emp Here 25   *Sales* 802,568
SIC 7991 Physical fitness facilities

D-U-N-S 24-924-8485   (SL)
965046 ONTARIO INC
QUALITY ALLIED ELEVATOR
80 Citizen Crt Unit 11, Markham, ON, L6G 1A7
(905) 305-0195
Emp Here 110   *Sales* 6,712,384
SIC 7699 Repair services, nec
Pr Pr Rick Sokoloff

D-U-N-S 20-327-4808   (BR)
ACCEO SOLUTIONS INC
MULTIPOST RETAIL SYSTEMS DIV
80 Citizen Crt Suite 1, Markham, ON, L6G 1A7
(905) 477-4747
Emp Here 20
SIC 7371 Custom computer programming services

D-U-N-S 24-920-1799   (HQ)
AVIVA CANADA INC
10 Aviva Way Suite 100, Markham, ON, L6G 0G1
(416) 288-1800
Emp Here 1,250   *Emp Total* 25,581
Sales 279,220,599
SIC 6411 Insurance agents, brokers, and service
Pr Greg Somerville
Jim Falle
Dir Brian W. Barr
Dir J Charles Caty
Dir J. William Rowley

D-U-N-S 20-404-9928   (SL)
BELMONT PRESS LIMITED
5 Bodrington Crt, Markham, ON, L6G 1A6
(905) 940-4900
Emp Here 67   *Sales* 3,429,153
SIC 7389 Business services, nec

D-U-N-S 20-120-3853   (BR)
BRAMPTON BRICK LIMITED
OAKS CONCRETE PRODUCTS
455 Rodick Rd, Markham, ON, L6G 1B2
(905) 475-5900
Emp Here 30
SIC 3444 Sheet Metalwork

D-U-N-S 20-792-0112   (BR)
COSTCO WHOLESALE CANADA LTD
(*Suby of* Costco Wholesale Corporation)
1 Yorktech Dr Suite 151, Markham, ON, L6G 1A6

(905) 477-5718
Emp Here 150
SIC 5099 Durable goods, nec

D-U-N-S 20-334-3293   (BR)
CREATION TECHNOLOGIES LP
110 Clegg Rd, Markham, ON, L6G 1E1
(905) 754-0055
Emp Here 300
SIC 3679 Electronic components, nec

D-U-N-S 25-673-1803   (BR)
ESIT CANADA ENTERPRISE SERVICES CO
ESIT CANADA ENTERPRISE SERVICES CO
(*Suby of* Dxc Technology Company)
105 Clegg Rd, Markham, ON, L6G 1B9
(905) 305-7100
Emp Here 60
SIC 7376 Computer facilities management

D-U-N-S 25-320-8565   (BR)
HYDRO ONE INC
185 Clegg Rd, Markham, ON, L6G 1B7
(888) 664-9376
Emp Here 50
SIC 4911 Electric services

D-U-N-S 24-514-1171   (BR)
HYDRO ONE NETWORKS INC
185 Clegg Rd, Markham, ON, L6G 1B7
(905) 944-3200
Emp Here 200
SIC 7299 Miscellaneous personal service

D-U-N-S 24-174-1631   (BR)
MARKHAM SUITES HOTEL LIMITED
8500 Warden Ave, Markham, ON, L6G 1A5
(905) 415-7638
Emp Here 25
SIC 5812 Eating places

D-U-N-S 25-365-1707   (SL)
PLANTBEST, INC
TRADEX
170 Duffield Dr Unit 200, Markham, ON, L6G 1B5
(905) 470-0724
Emp Here 214   *Sales* 2,288,964
SIC 2879 Agricultural chemicals, nec

D-U-N-S 20-707-1965   (SL)
PREMIER SALONS CANADA INC
170 Duffield Dr Suite 200, Markham, ON, L6G 1B5

Emp Here 55   *Sales* 1,299,377
SIC 7231 Beauty shops

D-U-N-S 24-205-1519   (BR)
QUALITY MOVE MANAGEMENT INC
ALLIED INTERNATIONAL OF TORONTO
190 Duffield Dr, Markham, ON, L6G 1B5
(905) 474-2320
Emp Here 20
SIC 4214 Local trucking with storage

D-U-N-S 24-165-8926   (BR)
WHOLESOME HARVEST BAKING LTD.
CANADA FRESH BREAD
45 Bodrington Crt, Markham, ON, L6G 1C1
(905) 415-1203
Emp Here 30
SIC 2011 Meat packing plants

Markstay, ON P0M
Sudbury County

D-U-N-S 25-239-9654   (BR)
RAINBOW DISTRICT SCHOOL BOARD
MARKSTAY PUBLIC SCHOOL
(*Suby of* Rainbow District School Board)
7 Pioneer St E, Markstay, ON, P0M 2G0
(705) 671-5946
Emp Here 20
SIC 8211 Elementary and secondary schools

Marmora, ON K0K
Hastings County

D-U-N-S 25-705-9667   (BR)
CARESSANT-CARE NURSING AND RETIREMENT HOMES LIMITED
CARESSANT CARE MARMORA
58 Bursthall St, Marmora, ON, K0K 2M0
(613) 472-3130
Emp Here 110
SIC 8051 Skilled nursing care facilities

D-U-N-S 24-176-1647   (BR)
D & W FORWARDERS INC
29 Industry Lane, Marmora, ON, K0K 2M0
(613) 472-5717
Emp Here 25
SIC 4213 Trucking, except local

D-U-N-S 20-711-5069   (BR)
HASTINGS AND PRINCE EDWARD DISTRICT SCHOOL BOARD
HASTINGS AND PRINCE EDWARD DISTRICT SCHOOL BOARD
17 William St, Marmora, ON, K0K 2M0
(613) 472-2323
Emp Here 30
SIC 8211 Elementary and secondary schools

Maryhill, ON N0B
Waterloo County

D-U-N-S 25-228-1530   (BR)
WATERLOO CATHOLIC DISTRICT SCHOOL BOARD
ST BONIFACE ELEMENTARY SCHOOL
1354 Maryhill Rd, Maryhill, ON, N0B 2B0
(519) 648-2832
Emp Here 24
SIC 8211 Elementary and secondary schools

Massey, ON P0P
Sudbury County

D-U-N-S 25-255-6782   (BR)
SAGAMOK ANISHNAWBEK
BIIDAABAN ELEMENTARY SCHOOL
717 Sagamok Rd, Massey, ON, P0P 1P0
(705) 865-2421
Emp Here 27
SIC 8211 Elementary and secondary schools

D-U-N-S 25-269-8563   (BR)
SAGAMOK ANISHNAWBEK
SAGAMOK COMMUNITY WELLNESS DEPARTMENT
4005 Espaniel, Massey, ON, P0P 1P0
(705) 865-2171
Emp Here 40
SIC 8399 Social services, nec

Matachewan, ON P0K
Timiskaming County

D-U-N-S 20-282-4504   (BR)
ALAMOS GOLD INC
YOUNG-DAVIDSON MINE
259 Matheson St, Matachewan, ON, P0K 1M0
(705) 565-9800
Emp Here 500
SIC 1041 Gold ores

Matheson, ON P0K
Cochrane County

D-U-N-S 20-084-7684   (BR)
DISTRICT SCHOOL BOARD ONTARIO NORTH EAST
JOSEPH H KENNEDY PUBLIC SCHOOL
422 4th Ave, Matheson, ON, P0K 1N0
(705) 273-2324
Emp Here 29
SIC 8211 Elementary and secondary schools

D-U-N-S 24-987-6483   (BR)
ST ANDREW GOLDFIELDS LTD
489 Macdougall St, Matheson, ON, P0K 1N0
(705) 273-3030
Emp Here 55
SIC 1041 Gold ores

Mattawa, ON P0H
Nipissing County

D-U-N-S 25-238-7709   (BR)
CONSEIL SCOLAIRE CATHOLIQUE DU DISTRICT FRANCO-NORD
ECOLE STE-ANNE
(*Suby of* Conseil Scolaire Catholique Du District Franco-Nord)
298 Brydges St, Mattawa, ON, P0H 1V0
(705) 744-2441
Emp Here 25
SIC 8211 Elementary and secondary schools

D-U-N-S 20-711-7321   (BR)
CONSEIL SCOLAIRE CATHOLIQUE DU DISTRICT FRANCO-NORD
F J MCELLIGOTT
370 Pine St, Mattawa, ON, P0H 1V0
(705) 472-5398
Emp Here 50
SIC 8211 Elementary and secondary schools

D-U-N-S 25-338-2402   (SL)
HOPITAL DE MATTAWA HOSPITAL INC
215 Third St, Mattawa, ON, P0H 1V0
(705) 744-5511
Emp Here 50   *Sales* 3,502,114
SIC 8062 General medical and surgical hospitals

D-U-N-S 25-249-0545   (BR)
NEAR NORTH DISTRICT SCHOOL BOARD
MATTAWA DISTRICT PUBLIC SCHOOL
376 Park St, Mattawa, ON, P0H 1V0
(705) 472-5241
Emp Here 22
SIC 8211 Elementary and secondary schools

D-U-N-S 20-805-8508   (BR)
ONTARIO POWER GENERATION INC
O P G
770 Highway 656, Mattawa, ON, P0H 1V0
(705) 744-5591
Emp Here 25
SIC 4911 Electric services

Maxwell, ON N0C
Grey County

D-U-N-S 25-238-8970   (BR)
BLUEWATER DISTRICT SCHOOL BOARD
OSPREY   CENTRAL   ELEMENTARY SCHOOL
408053 Grey Road 4, Maxwell, ON, N0C 1J0
(519) 922-2341
Emp Here 27
SIC 8211 Elementary and secondary schools

Mcdougall, ON P2A

D-U-N-S 25-183-1855   (BR)

NEAR NORTH DISTRICT SCHOOL BOARD
MCDOUGALL PUBLIC SCHOOL
69 124 Hwy, Mcdougall, ON, P2A 2W7
(705) 746-0511
Emp Here 25
SIC 8211 Elementary and secondary schools

D-U-N-S 25-606-9840   (BR)
TIM HORTON CHILDREN'S FOUNDATION, INC
TIM HORTON MEMORIAL CAMP
550 Lorimer Lake Rd, Mcdougall, ON, P2A 2W7
(705) 389-2773
Emp Here 85
SIC 7032 Sporting and recreational camps

Meaford, ON N4L
Grey County

D-U-N-S 20-093-7790   (BR)
BLUEWATER DISTRICT SCHOOL BOARD
MEAFORD COMMUNITY SCHOOL
186 Cook St, Meaford, ON, N4L 1H2
(519) 538-2260
Emp Here 33
SIC 8211 Elementary and secondary schools

D-U-N-S 20-025-4386   (BR)
BLUEWATER DISTRICT SCHOOL BOARD
ST VINCENT EUPHRASIA
555 St Vincent St, Meaford, ON, N4L 1C6
(519) 538-1950
Emp Here 25
SIC 8211 Elementary and secondary schools

D-U-N-S 20-710-6597   (BR)
BLUEWATER DISTRICT SCHOOL BOARD
GEORGIAN BAY SECONDARY SCHOOL
125 Eliza St, Meaford, ON, N4L 1A4
(519) 538-4426
Emp Here 60
SIC 8211 Elementary and secondary schools

D-U-N-S 24-193-4561   (SL)
KNIGHTS' OF MEAFORD LIMITED
76 Edwin St E, Meaford, ON, N4L 1C2
(519) 538-1510
Emp Here 51   *Sales* 4,818,644
SIC 5211 Lumber and other building materials

D-U-N-S 20-923-7713   (BR)
MC SOUND INVESTMENTS INC
MCDONALD'S
(*Suby of* Mc Sound Investments Inc)
334 Sykes St S, Meaford, ON, N4L 1X1
(519) 538-2905
Emp Here 20
SIC 5812 Eating places

D-U-N-S 20-769-8184   (SL)
MEAFORD NURSING HOME LTD
135 William St, Meaford, ON, N4L 1T4
(519) 538-1010
Emp Here 95   *Sales* 4,304,681
SIC 8051 Skilled nursing care facilities

Meldrum Bay, ON P0P
Manitoulin County

D-U-N-S 25-447-0339   (BR)
LAFARGE CANADA INC
LAFARGE
95 Mississagi Lighthouse Rd, Meldrum Bay, ON, P0P 1R0
(705) 283-3011
Emp Here 100
SIC 1422 Crushed and broken limestone

Merrickville, ON K0G
Grenville County

D-U-N-S 20-747-7787   (SL)
HILLTOP MANOR NURSING HOME LIMITED
1005 St Lawrence St, Merrickville, ON, K0G 1N0
(613) 269-4707
Emp Here 60   *Sales* 2,699,546
SIC 8051 Skilled nursing care facilities

D-U-N-S 24-891-1208   (SL)
SAM JAKES INN INC
118 Main St, Merrickville, ON, K0G 1N0
(613) 269-3712
Emp Here 60   *Sales* 2,626,585
SIC 7011 Hotels and motels

D-U-N-S 25-263-5479   (BR)
UPPER CANADA DISTRICT SCHOOL BOARD, THE
WOLFORD PUBLIC SCHOOL
(*Suby of* Upper Canada District School Board, The)
2159 County Rd 16 Rr 2, Merrickville, ON, K0G 1N0
(613) 283-6326
Emp Here 22
SIC 8211 Elementary and secondary schools

D-U-N-S 20-711-5382   (BR)
UPPER CANADA DISTRICT SCHOOL BOARD, THE
MERRICKVILLE PUBLIC SCHOOL
2159 County Rd 16, Merrickville, ON, K0G 1N0
(613) 269-4951
Emp Here 50
SIC 8211 Elementary and secondary schools

Metcalfe, ON K0A
Carleton County

D-U-N-S 20-015-1319   (BR)
CHRISTIAN HORIZONS
(*Suby of* Christian Horizons)
6570 Bank St, Metcalfe, ON, K0A 2P0
(613) 821-3875
Emp Here 20
SIC 8361 Residential care

D-U-N-S 24-110-4574   (BR)
MATERIAUX DE CONSTRUCTION OLD-CASTLE CANADA INC, LES
MATERIAUX DE CONSTRUCTION OLDCAS-TLE CANADA INC, LE
6860 Bank St Rr 3, Metcalfe, ON, K0A 2P0
(613) 821-0898
Emp Here 30
SIC 3272 Concrete products, nec

D-U-N-S 20-711-6331   (BR)
OTTAWA CATHOLIC DISTRICT SCHOOL BOARD
ST CATHERINE SCHOOL
(*Suby of* Ottawa Catholic District School Board)
2717 8th Line Rd, Metcalfe, ON, K0A 2P0
(613) 821-1002
Emp Here 20
SIC 8211 Elementary and secondary schools

D-U-N-S 25-263-5602   (BR)
OTTAWA-CARLETON DISTRICT SCHOOL BOARD
OSGOODE TOWNSHIP HIGH SCHOOL
2800 8th Line Rd, Metcalfe, ON, K0A 2P0
(613) 821-2241
Emp Here 75
SIC 8211 Elementary and secondary schools

D-U-N-S 25-263-5446   (BR)
OTTAWA-CARLETON DISTRICT SCHOOL BOARD

METCALFE ELEMENTARY SCHOOL
2701 8th Line Rd, Metcalfe, ON, K0A 2P0
(613) 821-2261
Emp Here 40
SIC 8211 Elementary and secondary schools

D-U-N-S 24-625-9154   (SL)
TOWNSHIP OF OSGOODE CARE CENTRE
7650 Snake Island Rd Rr 3, Metcalfe, ON, K0A 2P0
Emp Here 115   *Sales* 6,992,640
SIC 8051 Skilled nursing care facilities
Murray Munro

Midhurst, ON L0L
Simcoe County

D-U-N-S 24-379-9769   (BR)
ARNOTT CONSTRUCTION LIMITED
THE EQUIPMENT SOLUTION, DIV OF
2 Bertram Industrial Pky Suite 1, Midhurst, ON, L0L 1X0
(705) 792-7620
Emp Here 20
SIC 7699 Repair services, nec

D-U-N-S 25-297-6162   (BR)
SIMCOE COUNTY DISTRICT SCHOOL BOARD, THE
FOREST HILL PUBLIC SCHOOL
(*Suby of* Simcoe County District School Board, The)
16 Doran Rd, Midhurst, ON, L0L 1X0
(705) 721-8300
Emp Here 40
SIC 8211 Elementary and secondary schools

D-U-N-S 24-008-4442   (HQ)
SIMCOE COUNTY DISTRICT SCHOOL BOARD, THE
(*Suby of* Simcoe County District School Board, The)
1170 Hwy 26, Midhurst, ON, L0L 1X0
(705) 734-6363
Emp Here 180   *Emp Total* 5,000
Sales 540,750,049
SIC 8211 Elementary and secondary schools
Ex Dir Kathi Wallace
  Peter Beacock
Dir Donna Armstrong
Dir Debra Edward
Dir Jodi Lloyd
Dir Robert North
Dir Caroline Smith
Trst Nicole Black
Trst Suzanne Lay
Trst Michelle Lock

Midland, ON L4R
Simcoe County

D-U-N-S 20-532-4700   (BR)
ADM AGRI-INDUSTRIES COMPANY
ADM MILLING CO
(*Suby of* Archer-Daniels-Midland Company)
202 First St, Midland, ON, L4R 4L1
(705) 526-7861
Emp Here 70
SIC 2041 Flour and other grain mill products

D-U-N-S 25-296-5157   (BR)
BANK OF NOVA SCOTIA, THE
SCOTIABANK
291 King St, Midland, ON, L4R 3M5
(705) 526-2237
Emp Here 25
SIC 6021 National commercial banks

D-U-N-S 24-351-6122   (SL)
BOSTON PIZZA

16835 12 Hwy, Midland, ON, L4R 0A9
(705) 526-9966
Emp Here 50   *Sales* 1,532,175
SIC 5812 Eating places

   D-U-N-S 20-583-9603   (BR)
CANADA POST CORPORATION
MIDLAND PO
525 Dominion Ave, Midland, ON, L4R 1P8
(705) 526-5571
Emp Here 20
SIC 4311 U.s. postal service

   D-U-N-S 25-303-2445   (BR)
**CANADIAN IMPERIAL BANK OF COM-
MERCE**
CIBC
274 King St, Midland, ON, L4R 3M6
(705) 526-2256
Emp Here 20
SIC 6021 National commercial banks

   D-U-N-S 20-532-8966   (BR)
GENERAL MILLS CANADA CORPORATION
(*Suby of* General Mills, Inc.)
111 Pillsbury Dr, Midland, ON, L4R 4L4

Emp Here 200
SIC 2041 Flour and other grain mill products

   D-U-N-S 20-087-4019   (BR)
**GEORGIAN COLLEGE OF APPLIED ARTS
AND TECHNOLOGY, THE**
*GEORGIAN COLLEGE ROBBERT HARTOG
MIDLAND CAMPUS*
649 Prospect Blvd, Midland, ON, L4R 4K6
(705) 526-3666
Emp Here 30
SIC 8221 Colleges and universities

   D-U-N-S 24-538-7477   (SL)
HACKER GIGNAC RICE
*COHEN, STANLEY BARRISTER & SOLICI-
TOR*
518 Yonge St, Midland, ON, L4R 2C5
(705) 526-2231
Emp Here 63   *Sales* 7,507,300
SIC 8111 Legal services
Pt Fred Hacker

   D-U-N-S 24-885-5066   (SL)
HIGHLAND INN CORPORATION
BEST WESTERN HIGHLAND INN
924 King St, Midland, ON, L4R 0B8
(705) 526-9307
Emp Here 50   *Sales* 2,188,821
SIC 7011 Hotels and motels

   D-U-N-S 24-315-7364   (BR)
HOME DEPOT OF CANADA INC
(*Suby of* The Home Depot Inc)
16775 12 Hwy, Midland, ON, L4R 0A9
(705) 527-8800
Emp Here 40
SIC 5251 Hardware stores

   D-U-N-S 24-108-8769   (BR)
LOBLAWS INC
REAL CANADIAN SUPERSTORE, THE
9292 93 Hwy, Midland, ON, L4R 4K4
(705) 527-0388
Emp Here 160
SIC 5411 Grocery stores

   D-U-N-S 25-236-5820   (BR)
MARK'S WORK WEARHOUSE LTD
MARK'S WORK WEARHOUSE 161
16825 Hwy 12, Midland, ON, L4R 0A9
(705) 526-1301
Emp Here 20
SIC 5651 Family clothing stores

   D-U-N-S 24-875-5431   (HQ)
MCAMM ENTERPRIZES LTD
MACDONALDS
(*Suby of* Mcamm Enterprizes Ltd)
9195 Hwy 93, Midland, ON, L4R 4K4

(705) 526-4631
Emp Here 80   *Emp Total* 80
Sales 2,407,703
SIC 5812 Eating places

   D-U-N-S 20-859-8495   (BR)
PACIFIC LINK COMMUNICATIONS INC
BELL WORLD
297 King St, Midland, ON, L4R 3M5
(705) 527-6424
Emp Here 25
SIC 5999 Miscellaneous retail stores, nec

   D-U-N-S 25-050-1947   (BR)
PRISZM LP
K F C
375 King St, Midland, ON, L4R 3M7
(705) 526-5522
Emp Here 22
SIC 5812 Eating places

   D-U-N-S 25-195-5126   (BR)
RAYTHEON CANADA LIMITED
*RAYTHEON ELCAN OPTICAL TECHNOLO-
GIES*
(*Suby of* Raytheon Company)
450 Leitz Rd Suite 2, Midland, ON, L4R 5B8
(705) 526-5401
Emp Here 662
SIC 3827 Optical instruments and lenses

   D-U-N-S 24-124-4482   (HQ)
REMAX GEORGIAN BAY REALTY LTD
(*Suby of* Remax Georgian Bay Realty Ltd)
833 King St, Midland, ON, L4R 0B7
(705) 526-9366
Emp Here 31   *Emp Total* 50
Sales 4,742,446
SIC 6531 Real estate agents and managers

   D-U-N-S 20-768-8917   (BR)
ROGERS COMMUNICATIONS INC
ROGERS PLUS
(*Suby of* Rogers Communications Inc)
9225 93 Hwy, Midland, ON, L4R 4K4
(705) 527-0489
Emp Here 20
SIC 7822 Motion picture and tape distribution

   D-U-N-S 25-297-6006   (BR)
**SIMCOE COUNTY DISTRICT SCHOOL
BOARD, THE**
BAYVIEW ELEMENTARY SCHOOL
(*Suby of* Simcoe County District School
Board, The)
845 Ottawa St, Midland, ON, L4R 1C9
(705) 528-6939
Emp Here 40
SIC 8211 Elementary and secondary schools

   D-U-N-S 25-297-6147   (BR)
**SIMCOE COUNTY DISTRICT SCHOOL
BOARD, THE**
MUNDY'S BAY PUBLIC SCHOOL
(*Suby of* Simcoe County District School
Board, The)
340 Sixth St, Midland, ON, L4R 3Y4
(705) 526-2091
Emp Here 25
SIC 8211 Elementary and secondary schools

   D-U-N-S 25-292-4659   (BR)
**SIMCOE COUNTY DISTRICT SCHOOL
BOARD, THE**
MIDLAND SECONDARY SCHOOL
(*Suby of* Simcoe County District School
Board, The)
865 Hugel Ave, Midland, ON, L4R 1X8
(705) 526-7817
Emp Here 95
SIC 8211 Elementary and secondary schools

   D-U-N-S 20-711-1985   (BR)
**SIMCOE COUNTY DISTRICT SCHOOL
BOARD, THE**
HURON PARK
(*Suby of* Simcoe County District School
Board, The)

425 Robert St, Midland, ON, L4R 2M2
(705) 526-5300
Emp Here 50
SIC 8211 Elementary and secondary schools

   D-U-N-S 20-711-2173   (BR)
**SIMCOE MUSKOKA CATHOLIC DISTRICT
SCHOOL BOARD**
ST. THERESA'S CATHOLIC HIGH SCHOOL
(*Suby of* Simcoe Muskoka Catholic District
School Board)
347 Galloway Blvd, Midland, ON, L4R 5B2
(705) 526-1311
Emp Here 50
SIC 8211 Elementary and secondary schools

   D-U-N-S 25-238-2445   (BR)
**SIMCOE MUSKOKA CATHOLIC DISTRICT
SCHOOL BOARD**
MONSIGNOR CASTEX CATHOLIC SCHOOL
(*Suby of* Simcoe Muskoka Catholic District
School Board)
120 Old Penetanguishene Rd, Midland, ON,
L4R 4Z6
(705) 526-2831
Emp Here 22
SIC 8211 Elementary and secondary schools

   D-U-N-S 25-293-5184   (BR)
**SIMCOE MUSKOKA CATHOLIC DISTRICT
SCHOOL BOARD**
SACRED HEART SCHOOL
(*Suby of* Simcoe Muskoka Catholic District
School Board)
241 Elizabeth St, Midland, ON, L4R 1Y5
(705) 526-0107
Emp Here 33
SIC 8211 Elementary and secondary schools

   D-U-N-S 24-058-5971   (BR)
STAPLES CANADA INC
STAPLES THE BUSINESS DEPOT
(*Suby of* Staples, Inc.)
9226 93 Hwy, Midland, ON, L4R 4K4
(705) 526-5510
Emp Here 20
SIC 5943 Stationery stores

   D-U-N-S 25-942-8399   (BR)
UNIMIN CANADA LTD
420 Bayshore Dr, Midland, ON, L4R 4K8

Emp Here 30
SIC 1429 Crushed and broken stone, nec

   D-U-N-S 24-317-1837   (BR)
WAL-MART CANADA CORP
WALMART STORE 3645
16845 12 Hwy, Midland, ON, L4R 0A9
(705) 526-4754
Emp Here 250
SIC 5311 Department stores

Millbank, ON N0K
Perth County

   D-U-N-S 20-006-8851   (SL)
**MILLBANK HOME BAKERY AND COUNTRY
CAFE LTD**
ANNA MAE'S BAKERY & RESTAURANT
4060 Perth Line Suite 72, Millbank, ON, N0K
1L0
(519) 595-4407
Emp Here 60   *Sales* 1,824,018
SIC 5812 Eating places

Millbrook, ON L0A
Durham County

   D-U-N-S 20-568-2870   (SL)
CENTENNIAL PLACE
2 Centennial Lane Rr 3, Millbrook, ON, L0A

1G0
(705) 932-4464
Emp Here 120   *Sales* 7,608,750
SIC 8051 Skilled nursing care facilities
Off Mgr Karen Wolf

   D-U-N-S 25-263-5461   (BR)
**KAWARTHA PINE RIDGE DISTRICT
SCHOOL BOARD**
*MILLBROOK SOUTH CAVAN PUBLIC
SCHOOL*
47 Tupper St, Millbrook, ON, L0A 1G0
(705) 932-2789
Emp Here 36
SIC 8211 Elementary and secondary schools

Millgrove, ON L0R
Wentworth County

   D-U-N-S 20-911-0373   (BR)
ENBRIDGE PIPELINES INC
1430 6th Concession Rd, Millgrove, ON, L0R
1V0
(905) 659-7236
Emp Here 20
SIC 4924 Natural gas distribution

   D-U-N-S 20-287-0619   (BR)
**HAMILTON-WENTWORTH DISTRICT
SCHOOL BOARD, THE**
MILLGROVE PUBLIC SCHOOL
375 Concession 5 W, Millgrove, ON, L0R 1V0
(905) 689-4544
Emp Here 20
SIC 8211 Elementary and secondary schools

   D-U-N-S 24-337-6717   (BR)
**PAN AMERICAN NURSERY PRODUCTS
INC**
525 6th Conc Rd W, Millgrove, ON, L0R 1V0
(905) 689-9919
Emp Here 50
SIC 5193 Flowers and florists supplies

Milton, ON L9E
Halton County

   D-U-N-S 24-525-4185   (BR)
**CONSEIL SCOLAIRE DE DISTRICT
CATHOLIQUE CENTRE-SUD**
EEC SAINT-NICOLAS
12705 Britannia Rd, Milton, ON, L9E 0V4
(905) 864-3025
Emp Here 25
SIC 8211 Elementary and secondary schools

   D-U-N-S 20-716-5866   (BR)
DANACA TRANSPORT MONTREAL LTEE
DANACA TRANSPORT
(*Suby of* Gestion Real Grondin Inc)
7251 Trafalgar Rd, Milton, ON, L9E 0Z9
(905) 878-8316
Emp Here 72
SIC 4225 General warehousing and storage

   D-U-N-S 25-850-1774   (BR)
PATENE BUILDING SUPPLIES LTD
PATENE'S
7085 Auburn Rd, Milton, ON, L9E 0T6
(905) 875-0279
Emp Here 30
SIC 5039 Construction materials, nec

Milton, ON L9T
Halton County

   D-U-N-S 25-110-1838   (BR)
3M CANADA COMPANY
(*Suby of* 3M Company)

2751 Peddie Rd, Milton, ON, L9T 0K1
(905) 875-2568
Emp Here 100
SIC 4225 General warehousing and storage

D-U-N-S 24-703-3830   (HQ)
ALTEC INDUSTRIES LTD
(*Suby of* Altec, Inc.)
831 Nipissing Rd, Milton, ON, L9T 4Z4
(905) 875-2000
Emp Here 25   *Emp Total* 1,550
Sales 10,654,887
SIC 5084 Industrial machinery and equipment
Pr Pr Lee J Styslinger Jr
 Jeff Benda
Fin Ex Judy Kehoe
 J Donald Williams

D-U-N-S 20-955-2301   (SL)
ASHCROFT INSTRUMENTS CANADA INC
151 Steeles Ave E, Milton, ON, L9T 1Y1
(905) 864-4989
Emp Here 20   *Sales* 4,900,111
SIC 3823 Process control instruments

D-U-N-S 24-175-9633   (BR)
BDO CANADA LLP
MILTON INSOLVENCY
14 Martin St, Milton, ON, L9T 2P9
(905) 615-8787
Emp Here 20
SIC 8721 Accounting, auditing, and book-keeping

D-U-N-S 20-588-2041   (BR)
BANQUE TORONTO-DOMINION, LA
TD CANADA TRUST
(*Suby of* Toronto-Dominion Bank, The)
252 Main St E, Milton, ON, L9T 1N8
(905) 878-2834
Emp Here 20
SIC 6021 National commercial banks

D-U-N-S 25-487-5214   (BR)
BARNES J.D., LIMITED
401 Wheelabrator Way Suite A, Milton, ON, L9T 3C1
(905) 875-9955
Emp Here 20
SIC 8713 Surveying services

D-U-N-S 24-473-6869   (SL)
BRUKER LTD
(*Suby of* Bruker Corporation)
555 Steeles Ave E, Milton, ON, L9T 1Y6
(905) 876-4641
Emp Here 29   *Sales* 4,231,721
SIC 5049 Professional equipment, nec

D-U-N-S 20-554-8571   (BR)
CRH CANADA GROUP INC
DUFFERIN AGGREGATES, DIV. OF
9410 Dublin Line, Milton, ON, L9T 2X7
(905) 878-6051
Emp Here 100
SIC 1481 NonMetallic mineral services

D-U-N-S 25-341-4478   (HQ)
CWB GROUP - INDUSTRY SERVICES
QUASAR, DIV OF
(*Suby of* CWB Group - Industry Services)
8260 Parkhill Dr, Milton, ON, L9T 5V7
(905) 542-1312
Emp Here 50   *Emp Total* 145
Sales 22,014,650
SIC 8621 Professional organizations
Pr Brian Mcqueen

D-U-N-S 20-574-9430   (BR)
CANADA POST CORPORATION
MILTON POST OFFICE
8490 Lawson Rd, Milton, ON, L9T 8T3
(905) 878-0849
Emp Here 100
SIC 4311 U.s. postal service

D-U-N-S 20-303-3121   (BR)
CARA OPERATIONS LIMITED

KELSEY'S
(*Suby of* Cara Holdings Limited)
45 Chisholm Dr, Milton, ON, L9T 4A6
(905) 876-4731
Emp Here 50
SIC 5812 Eating places

D-U-N-S 20-303-2875   (BR)
CARA OPERATIONS LIMITED
KELSEY'S
(*Suby of* Cara Holdings Limited)
1230 Steeles Ave E, Milton, ON, L9T 6R1
(905) 760-2244
Emp Here 70
SIC 5812 Eating places

D-U-N-S 25-801-4752   (HQ)
CHUDLEIGH'S LTD
(*Suby of* Chudleigh's Ltd)
8501 Chudleigh Way, Milton, ON, L9T 0L9
(905) 878-8781
Emp Here 100   *Emp Total* 120
Sales 4,085,799
SIC 5461 Retail bakeries

D-U-N-S 24-418-2924   (BR)
CINEPLEX ODEON CORPORATION
CINEPLEX CINEMAS MILTON
1175 Maple Ave, Milton, ON, L9T 0A5
(905) 864-1666
Emp Here 50
SIC 7832 Motion picture theaters, except drive-in

D-U-N-S 25-708-3027   (BR)
CLUBLINK CORPORATION ULC
GLENCAIRN GOLF CLUB
(*Suby of* TWC Enterprises Limited)
9807 Regional Road 25, Milton, ON, L9T 2X7
(905) 876-3666
Emp Here 49
SIC 7992 Public golf courses

D-U-N-S 24-194-1900   (BR)
COMMUNITY LIVING NORTH HALTON
500 Valleyview Cres, Milton, ON, L9T 3L2
(905) 693-0528
Emp Here 130
SIC 8322 Individual and family services

D-U-N-S 20-735-4424   (BR)
CONTRANS GROUP INC
PETER HODGE TRANSPORT LIMITED
100 Market Dr, Milton, ON, L9T 3H5
(905) 693-8088
Emp Here 150
SIC 4449 Water transportation of freight

D-U-N-S 25-253-2817   (BR)
DARE FOODS LIMITED
725 Steeles Ave E, Milton, ON, L9T 5H1
(905) 875-1223
Emp Here 80
SIC 2064 Candy and other confectionery products

D-U-N-S 24-767-0917   (BR)
DIVERSIFIED TRANSPORTATION LTD
MILTON TRANSIT (OPERATED BY DIVERSI-FIED)
420 Morobel Dr, Milton, ON, L9T 4N6
(905) 564-1856
Emp Here 26
SIC 4111 Local and suburban transit

D-U-N-S 24-354-6038   (HQ)
EAGLEBURGMANN CANADA INC
8699 Escarpment Way Suite 9, Milton, ON, L9T 0J5
(905) 693-8782
Emp Here 20   *Emp Total* 34,840
Sales 6,930,008
SIC 5085 Industrial supplies
Al Marques
 Sebastian Weiss

D-U-N-S 24-340-0509   (BR)
FGL SPORTS LTD

SPORT-CHEK MILTON MALL
55 Ontario St S Unit D18, Milton, ON, L9T 2M3
(905) 693-8546
Emp Here 40
SIC 5941 Sporting goods and bicycle shops

D-U-N-S 20-604-7672   (BR)
GOODLIFE FITNESS CENTRES INC
855 Steeles Ave E, Milton, ON, L9T 5H3
(905) 876-3488
Emp Here 30
SIC 7991 Physical fitness facilities

D-U-N-S 20-191-4566   (BR)
GOVERNMENT OF ONTARIO
ERNEST C DRUDY SCHOOL FOR THE DEAF, THE
255 Ontario St S, Milton, ON, L9T 2M5
(905) 878-2851
Emp Here 49
SIC 8211 Elementary and secondary schools

D-U-N-S 24-757-3652   (HQ)
GROENEVELD LUBRICATION SOLUTIONS INC
(*Suby of* The Timken Company)
8450 Lawson Rd Unit 5, Milton, ON, L9T 0J8
(905) 875-1017
Emp Here 20   *Emp Total* 14,000
Sales 5,180,210
SIC 1796 Installing building equipment
Tim Wynia
 Graham Keltie
 Johannes Van Boxtel
 Henk Groeneveld

D-U-N-S 25-806-2108   (BR)
HALTON ALCOHOL DRUG AND GAM-BLING ASSESSMENT PREVENTION AND TREATMENT SERVICES
HALTON ADAPT
245 Commercial St Unit B1, Milton, ON, L9T 2J3
(905) 639-6537
Emp Here 50
SIC 8699 Membership organizations, nec

D-U-N-S 20-711-0631   (BR)
HALTON CATHOLIC DISTRICT SCHOOL BOARD
HOLY ROSARY SCHOOL
141 Martin St, Milton, ON, L9T 2R3
(905) 876-1121
Emp Here 35
SIC 8211 Elementary and secondary schools

D-U-N-S 20-814-0264   (BR)
HALTON CATHOLIC DISTRICT SCHOOL BOARD
BISHOP P.F. REDING SECONDARY
1120 Main St E, Milton, ON, L9T 6H7
(905) 875-0124
Emp Here 125
SIC 8211 Elementary and secondary schools

D-U-N-S 20-649-5306   (BR)
HALTON CATHOLIC DISTRICT SCHOOL BOARD
GUARDIAN ANGELS ELEMENTARY SCHOOL
650 Bennett Blvd, Milton, ON, L9T 6B1
(905) 876-2386
Emp Here 40
SIC 8211 Elementary and secondary schools

D-U-N-S 24-676-3135   (BR)
HALTON CATHOLIC DISTRICT SCHOOL BOARD
OUR LADY OF FATIMA
709 Bolingbroke Dr, Milton, ON, L9T 6Z3
(905) 864-0720
Emp Here 25
SIC 8211 Elementary and secondary schools

D-U-N-S 25-165-2996   (BR)
HALTON CATHOLIC DISTRICT SCHOOL BOARD
OUR LADY OF VICTORY SCHOOL

540 Commercial St, Milton, ON, L9T 4Z3
(905) 876-4379
Emp Here 31
SIC 8211 Elementary and secondary schools

D-U-N-S 24-676-3119   (BR)
HALTON CATHOLIC DISTRICT SCHOOL BOARD
ST. ANTHONY OF PADUA CATHOLIC ELE-MENTARY SCHOOL
1240 Tupper Dr, Milton, ON, L9T 6T7
(905) 864-8272
Emp Here 25
SIC 8211 Elementary and secondary schools

D-U-N-S 20-711-0748   (BR)
HALTON CATHOLIC DISTRICT SCHOOL BOARD
ST PETER SCHOOL
137 Dixon Dr, Milton, ON, L9T 5P7
(905) 878-4626
Emp Here 30
SIC 8211 Elementary and secondary schools

D-U-N-S 20-545-2548   (BR)
HALTON DISTRICT SCHOOL BOARD
E W FOSTER PUBLIC SCHOOL
320 Coxe Blvd, Milton, ON, L9T 4M5
(905) 878-1953
Emp Here 35
SIC 8211 Elementary and secondary schools

D-U-N-S 20-711-0359   (BR)
HALTON DISTRICT SCHOOL BOARD
JM DENYES PUBLIC SCHOOL
215 Thomas St, Milton, ON, L9T 2E5
(905) 878-2379
Emp Here 50
SIC 8211 Elementary and secondary schools

D-U-N-S 24-676-4976   (BR)
HALTON DISTRICT SCHOOL BOARD
PL ROBERTSON PUBLIC SCHOOL
840 Scott Blvd, Milton, ON, L9T 2C9
(905) 878-3166
Emp Here 25
SIC 8211 Elementary and secondary schools

D-U-N-S 20-588-5457   (BR)
HALTON DISTRICT SCHOOL BOARD
CHRIS HADFIELD PUBLIC SCHOOL
1114 Woodward Ave, Milton, ON, L9T 5P5
(905) 875-1876
Emp Here 50
SIC 8211 Elementary and secondary schools

D-U-N-S 20-711-0516   (BR)
HALTON DISTRICT SCHOOL BOARD
SAM SHERRATT SCHOOL
649 Laurier Ave, Milton, ON, L9T 4N4
(905) 878-1556
Emp Here 50
SIC 8211 Elementary and secondary schools

D-U-N-S 20-711-0417   (BR)
HALTON DISTRICT SCHOOL BOARD
MARTIN STREET PUBLIC SCHOOL
184 Martin St, Milton, ON, L9T 2R4
(905) 878-8191
Emp Here 50
SIC 8211 Elementary and secondary schools

D-U-N-S 24-676-4968   (BR)
HALTON DISTRICT SCHOOL BOARD
ESCARPMENT VIEW PUBLIC SCHOOL
351 Scott Blvd, Milton, ON, L9T 0T1
(905) 878-6176
Emp Here 25
SIC 8211 Elementary and secondary schools

D-U-N-S 24-525-4367   (BR)
HALTON DISTRICT SCHOOL BOARD
BRUCE TRAIL PUBLIC SCHOOL
1199 Costigan Rd, Milton, ON, L9T 6N8
(905) 864-1300
Emp Here 25
SIC 8211 Elementary and secondary schools

D-U-N-S 20-024-9899   (BR)

HALTON DISTRICT SCHOOL BOARD
W I DICK MIDDLE SCHOOL
351 Highside Dr, Milton, ON, L9T 1W8
(905) 878-8119
Emp Here 25
SIC 8211 Elementary and secondary schools

D-U-N-S 20-711-0482   (BR)
HALTON DISTRICT SCHOOL BOARD
ROBERT BALDWIN PUBLIC SCHOOL
180 Wilson Dr, Milton, ON, L9T 3J9
(905) 878-8833
Emp Here 42
SIC 8211 Elementary and secondary schools

D-U-N-S 20-536-2853   (BR)
HALTON DISTRICT SCHOOL BOARD
MILTON DISTRICT HIGH SCHOOL
396 Williams Ave, Milton, ON, L9T 2G4
(905) 878-2839
Emp Here 80
SIC 8211 Elementary and secondary schools

D-U-N-S 24-101-5218   (BR)
HOME DEPOT OF CANADA INC
HOME DEPOT
(*Suby of* The Home Depot Inc)
1013 Maple Ave, Milton, ON, L9T 0A5
(905) 864-1200
Emp Here 140
SIC 5251 Hardware stores

D-U-N-S 24-150-6729   (BR)
JOHNSON CONTROLS NOVA SCOTIA U.L.C.
(*Suby of* Johnson Controls, Inc.)
8205 Parkhill Dr, Milton, ON, L9T 5G8
(905) 875-2128
Emp Here 200
SIC 3822 Environmental controls

D-U-N-S 25-853-9550   (SL)
KAIZEN FOODS LTD
TIM HORTONS
8501 Regional Road 25, Milton, ON, L9T 9C2
(905) 878-8712
Emp Here 62   *Sales* 1,896,978
SIC 5812 Eating places

D-U-N-S 25-747-5368   (BR)
LAFARGE CANADA INC
LAFARGE NORTH AMERICA
575 Harrop Dr, Milton, ON, L9T 3H3
(905) 876-4728
Emp Here 20
SIC 5032 Brick, stone, and related material

D-U-N-S 24-383-8971   (BR)
LOBLAWS INC
REAL CANADIAN SUPERSTORE
820 Main St E Suite 2810, Milton, ON, L9T 0J4
(905) 875-3600
Emp Here 150
SIC 5411 Grocery stores

D-U-N-S 24-045-3787   (SL)
LOGISTIC DISTRIBUTION INC
550 Industrial Dr, Milton, ON, L9T 5A6

Emp Here 50   *Sales* 3,641,637
SIC 4225 General warehousing and storage

D-U-N-S 24-643-9921   (BR)
MAGNA INTERNATIONAL INC
KARMAX HEAVY STAMPING
333 Market Dr, Milton, ON, L9T 4Z7
(905) 878-5571
Emp Here 950
SIC 3714 Motor vehicle parts and accessories

D-U-N-S 20-562-7297   (BR)
MAGNA INTERNATIONAL INC
MODATEK SYSTEMS
400 Chisholm Dr, Milton, ON, L9T 5V6
(905) 864-3400
Emp Here 400
SIC 3714 Motor vehicle parts and accessories

D-U-N-S 20-876-7590   (BR)
MANHEIM AUTO AUCTIONS COMPANY
MANHEIM TORONTO
(*Suby of* Cox Enterprises, Inc.)
8277 Lawson Rd, Milton, ON, L9T 5C7
(905) 275-3000
Emp Here 325
SIC 7389 Business services, nec

D-U-N-S 24-390-4807   (BR)
MATERIAUX DE CONSTRUCTION KP LTEE
(*Suby of* Administration F.L.T. Ltee)
2700 Highpoint Dr, Milton, ON, L9T 5G9
(905) 875-5336
Emp Here 50
SIC 5033 Roofing, siding, and insulation

D-U-N-S 24-124-5484   (BR)
MATERIAUX DE CONSTRUCTION OLD-CASTLE CANADA INC, LES
MATERIAUX DE CONSTRUCTION OLDCAS-TLE CANADA INC, LE
8375 5th Side Rd, Milton, ON, L9T 2X7
(905) 875-4215
Emp Here 50
SIC 3272 Concrete products, nec

D-U-N-S 25-364-2995   (BR)
MATTAMY HOMES LIMITED
MATTAMY HAWTHORNE VILLAGE
1550 Derry Rd, Milton, ON, L9T 1A1
(905) 875-2692
Emp Here 100
SIC 5211 Lumber and other building materials

D-U-N-S 20-718-3633   (SL)
MATTHEWS CANADA LTD
(*Suby of* Matthews International Corporation)
810 Nipissing Rd Suite 200, Milton, ON, L9T 4Z9
(905) 878-2358
Emp Here 26   *Sales* 1,240,332
SIC 3366 Copper foundries

D-U-N-S 20-182-5254   (SL)
MEADOWS, W. R. OF CANADA
(*Suby of* W. R. Meadows, Inc.)
70 Hannant Crt, Milton, ON, L9T 5C1
(905) 878-4122
Emp Here 20   *Sales* 3,769,316
SIC 5211 Lumber and other building materials

D-U-N-S 20-641-7586   (HQ)
MERCURY MARINE LIMITED
(*Suby of* Brunswick Corporation)
8698 Escarpment Way, Milton, ON, L9T 0M1
(905) 567-6372
Emp Here 48   *Emp Total* 14,415
Sales 6,785,345
SIC 5091 Sporting and recreation goods
Georges Jalbert
Marsha T Vaughn
Jim Ennis
Judy Zelisko

D-U-N-S 20-249-6162   (BR)
METRIE CANADA LTD
8100 Parkhill Dr, Milton, ON, L9T 5V7
(416) 997-0519
Emp Here 30
SIC 5031 Lumber, plywood, and millwork

D-U-N-S 24-333-1571   (BR)
METRO ONTARIO INC
FOOD BASICS
500 Laurier Ave, Milton, ON, L9T 4R3
(905) 876-1117
Emp Here 70
SIC 5411 Grocery stores

D-U-N-S 20-109-5549   (BR)
METROLAND MEDIA GROUP LTD
CANADIAN CHAMPION, THE
555 Industrial Dr, Milton, ON, L9T 5E1
(905) 878-2341
Emp Here 22
SIC 2711 Newspapers

D-U-N-S 24-561-0712   (SL)
MILTON DISTRICT HOSPITAL AUXILIARY
MILTON DIST HOSPITAL GIFT SHOP
Gd Lcd Main, Milton, ON, L9T 2Y2
(905) 878-2383
Emp Here 200   *Sales* 17,449,400
SIC 8399 Social services, nec
Pr Pr Carol Wilson

D-U-N-S 25-191-0402   (SL)
MILTON HYDRO SERVICES INC
8069 Lawson Rd, Milton, ON, L9T 5C4
(905) 876-4611
Emp Here 40   *Sales* 5,681,200
SIC 6712 Bank holding companies
VP VP Mary-Jo Corkum

D-U-N-S 24-873-5359   (SL)
MILTON PUBLIC LIBRARY BOARD
1010 Main St E, Milton, ON, L9T 6H7
(905) 875-2665
Emp Here 50   *Sales* 2,334,742
SIC 8231 Libraries

D-U-N-S 24-793-4698   (BR)
NORTHERN REFLECTIONS LTD
55 Ontario St S Unit 1, Milton, ON, L9T 2M3
(905) 875-0522
Emp Here 62
SIC 5621 Women's clothing stores

D-U-N-S 24-360-6071   (BR)
ONTARIO DOOR SALES LTD
ELTON MANUFACTURING
359 Wheelabrator Way, Milton, ON, L9T 3C1
(905) 878-5670
Emp Here 40
SIC 3442 Metal doors, sash, and trim

D-U-N-S 25-981-9357   (SL)
ONTARIO NEW ENGLAND EXPRESS INC
ONE FOR FREIGHT
8450 Lawson Rd Unit 2, Milton, ON, L9T 0J8
(905) 876-3996
Emp Here 60   *Sales* 9,517,523
SIC 4213 Trucking, except local
Pr Pr David Carruth

D-U-N-S 25-802-4108   (BR)
PADDON + YORKE INC
225 Main St E Suite 1, Milton, ON, L9T 1N9
(905) 875-0811
Emp Here 20
SIC 8111 Legal services

D-U-N-S 24-652-2569   (BR)
PARKER HANNIFIN CANADA
MOTION & CONTROL DIV
160 Chisholm Dr Suite 1, Milton, ON, L9T 3G9
(905) 693-3000
Emp Here 180
SIC 3593 Fluid power cylinders and actuators

D-U-N-S 24-253-6048   (BR)
PHELPS INVESTMENT GROUP OF COMPANIES LTD
PHELPS APARTMENT LAUNDRIES
8695 Escarpment Way Unit 6, Milton, ON, L9T 0J5
(905) 693-8666
Emp Here 30
SIC 7215 Coin-operated laundries and cleaning

D-U-N-S 24-359-0267   (BR)
PRINCESS AUTO LTD
2995 Peddie Rd, Milton, ON, L9T 0K1
(905) 875-2224
Emp Here 31
SIC 4225 General warehousing and storage

D-U-N-S 24-277-4479   (BR)
RECOCHEM INC.
CONSUMER DIVISION
8725 Holgate Cres, Milton, ON, L9T 5G7
(905) 878-5544
Emp Here 115
SIC 3221 Glass containers

D-U-N-S 20-700-6524   (BR)
REITMANS (CANADA) LIMITEE
REITMANS
1250 Steeles Ave E, Milton, ON, L9T 6R1
(905) 878-8750
Emp Here 25
SIC 5621 Women's clothing stores

D-U-N-S 24-565-9560   (BR)
RELIANCE METALS CANADA LIMITED
TEAM TUBE, DIV OF
(*Suby of* Reliance Steel & Aluminum Co.)
8055 Esquesing Line, Milton, ON, L9T 5C8
(905) 878-1156
Emp Here 20
SIC 5051 Metals service centers and offices

D-U-N-S 24-779-8994   (HQ)
ROXUL INC
8024 Esquesing Line, Milton, ON, L9T 6W3
(905) 878-8474
Emp Here 500   *Emp Total* 350
Sales 29,184,280
SIC 3296 Mineral wool
Pr Pr Trent Ogilvie

D-U-N-S 25-308-5187   (BR)
ROYAL BANK OF CANADA
RBC
(*Suby of* Royal Bank Of Canada)
55 Ontario St S, Milton, ON, L9T 2M3
(905) 875-0600
Emp Here 38
SIC 6021 National commercial banks

D-U-N-S 20-106-8553   (BR)
SOBEYS CAPITAL INCORPORATED
SOBEYS MILTON RETAIL SUPPORT CENTRE
2701 Highpoint Dr, Milton, ON, L9T 5G5

Emp Here 500
SIC 5141 Groceries, general line

D-U-N-S 20-806-2542   (BR)
SOBEYS CAPITAL INCORPORATED
SOBEYS STORE 864
20 Market Dr, Milton, ON, L9T 3H5

Emp Here 25
SIC 5411 Grocery stores

D-U-N-S 24-101-3676   (BR)
STAPLES CANADA INC
STAPLES THE BUSINESS DEPOT
(*Suby of* Staples, Inc.)
1220 Steeles Ave E Unit G6, Milton, ON, L9T 6R1
(905) 878-2434
Emp Here 20
SIC 5943 Stationery stores

D-U-N-S 20-806-5628   (BR)
STARBUCKS COFFEE CANADA, INC
(*Suby of* Starbucks Corporation)
16 Market Dr, Milton, ON, L9T 3H5
(905) 878-8300
Emp Here 20
SIC 5812 Eating places

D-U-N-S 24-844-4432   (SL)
STERITECH GROUP CORPORATION, THE
8699 Escarpment Way Suite 11, Milton, ON, L9T 0J5
(905) 878-8468
Emp Here 51   *Sales* 3,064,349
SIC 7342 Disinfecting and pest control services

D-U-N-S 24-078-5196   (BR)
TAIGA BUILDING PRODUCTS LTD
520 Harrop Dr, Milton, ON, L9T 3H2
(905) 878-8401
Emp Here 35
SIC 5031 Lumber, plywood, and millwork

D-U-N-S 24-468-0232   (BR)
TEAM INDUSTRIAL SERVICES (CANADA)

INC
430 Industrial Dr Suite 2, Milton, ON, L9T 5A6
(905) 878-7546
Emp Here 20
SIC 7363 Help supply services

D-U-N-S 25-010-8941   (BR)
UNION GAS LIMITED
8015 Esquesing Line, Milton, ON, L9T 5C8
(905) 876-3323
Emp Here 20
SIC 4923 Gas transmission and distribution

D-U-N-S 24-121-5842   (BR)
WAL-MART CANADA CORP
1280 Steeles Ave E Suite 1000, Milton, ON, L9T 6R1
(905) 864-6027
Emp Here 150
SIC 5311 Department stores

D-U-N-S 20-578-0971   (SL)
WERNER ENTERPRISES CANADA CORPORATION
(*Suby of* Werner Enterprises, Inc)
10862 Steeles Ave E, Milton, ON, L9T 2X8
(905) 693-1285
Emp Here 40   *Sales* 4,669,485
SIC 4213 Trucking, except local

Milverton, ON N0K
Perth County

D-U-N-S 25-263-5172   (BR)
AVON MAITLAND DISTRICT SCHOOL BOARD
MILVERTON PUBLIC SCHOOL
Gd, Milverton, ON, N0K 1M0
(519) 595-8859
Emp Here 20
SIC 8211 Elementary and secondary schools

D-U-N-S 20-821-5228   (SL)
KNOLLCREST LODGE
50 William St Suite 221, Milverton, ON, N0K 1M0
(519) 595-8121
Emp Here 80   *Sales* 2,918,428
SIC 8361 Residential care

Mindemoya, ON P0P
Manitoulin County

D-U-N-S 20-025-5441   (BR)
MANITOULIN HEALTH CENTRE
MINDEMOYA HOSPITAL
2120a 551 Hwy, Mindemoya, ON, P0P 1S0
(705) 377-5311
Emp Here 50
SIC 8059 Nursing and personal care, nec

Minden, ON K0M
Haliburton County

D-U-N-S 25-633-2776   (BR)
HALIBURTON HIGHLANDS HEALTH SERVICES CORPORATION
HYLAND CREST SENIOR CITIZENS HOME
30 Prentice St Rr 3, Minden, ON, K0M 2K0
(705) 286-2500
Emp Here 72
SIC 8361 Residential care

D-U-N-S 20-653-2371   (BR)
TRILLIUM LAKELANDS DISTRICT SCHOOL BOARD
STOUFFER, ARCHIE ELEMENTARY SCHOOL
12 Vintage Cres, Minden, ON, K0M 2K0

---

(705) 286-1921
Emp Here 50
SIC 8211 Elementary and secondary schools

Mine Centre, ON P0W
Rainy River County

D-U-N-S 25-265-1260   (BR)
RAINY RIVER DISTRICT SCHOOL BOARD
MINE CENTRE PUBLIC SCHOOL
123 Mine Centre Rd, Mine Centre, ON, P0W 1H0
(807) 599-2843
Emp Here 20
SIC 8211 Elementary and secondary schools

Minesing, ON L9X
Simcoe County

D-U-N-S 25-292-4824   (BR)
SIMCOE COUNTY DISTRICT SCHOOL BOARD, THE
MINESING CENTRAL PUBLIC SCHOOL
(*Suby of* Simcoe County District School Board, The)
7 Huron St, Minesing, ON, L9X 1J2
(705) 728-1944
Emp Here 30
SIC 8211 Elementary and secondary schools

Minett, ON P0B
Muskoka County

D-U-N-S 24-802-6846   (BR)
LUXURY HOTELS INTERNATIONAL OF CANADA, ULC
ROSSEAU, A JW MARRIOTT RESORT & SPA, THE
(*Suby of* Marriott International, Inc.)
1050 Paignton House Rd, Minett, ON, P0B 1G0
(705) 765-1900
Emp Here 200
SIC 7011 Hotels and motels

Mississauga, ON L4T
Peel County

D-U-N-S 25-803-6250   (BR)
718878 ONTARIO LIMITED
MESSENGERS INTERNATIONAL, THE
7485 Bath Rd, Mississauga, ON, L4T 4C1
(905) 362-0822
Emp Here 50
SIC 7389 Business services, nec

D-U-N-S 20-706-4205   (HQ)
AGRICO CANADA LIMITED
AGRICO
2896 Slough St Unit 6, Mississauga, ON, L4T 1G3
(905) 672-5700
Emp Here 22   *Emp Total* 10,079
Sales 12,387,389
SIC 5191 Farm supplies
Dir Denis Richard
Dir Luc Forget
Dir Ghislain Cloutier

D-U-N-S 24-119-6307   (BR)
AIR CANADA
2570 Britania Rd E, Mississauga, ON, L4T 3B5
(905) 694-5440
Emp Here 91
SIC 4581 Airports, flying fields, and services

D-U-N-S 20-251-6134   (BR)
ASIG CANADA LTD
ASIG
(*Suby of* Asig Canada Ltd)
7440 Torbram Rd, Mississauga, ON, L4T 1G9
(905) 694-2813
Emp Here 25
SIC 5172 Petroleum products, nec

D-U-N-S 25-296-5165   (BR)
BANK OF NOVA SCOTIA, THE
SCOTIABANK
7205 Goreway Dr Unit 39, Mississauga, ON, L4T 2T9
(905) 678-4300
Emp Here 20
SIC 6021 National commercial banks

D-U-N-S 24-816-8593   (SL)
CELTRADE CANADA INC
7566 Bath Rd, Mississauga, ON, L4T 1L2
(905) 678-1322
Emp Here 50   *Sales* 2,355,823
SIC 2035 Pickles, sauces, and salad dressings

D-U-N-S 25-819-2137   (BR)
COLISPRO INC
NATIONEX
7535 Bath Rd, Mississauga, ON, L4T 4C1

Emp Here 30
SIC 7389 Business services, nec

D-U-N-S 25-265-3076   (BR)
DUFFERIN-PEEL CATHOLIC DISTRICT SCHOOL BOARD
ST. RAPHAEL ELEMENTARY SCHOOL
3470 Clara Dr, Mississauga, ON, L4T 2C7
(905) 677-1038
Emp Here 20
SIC 8211 Elementary and secondary schools

D-U-N-S 25-265-2672   (BR)
DUFFERIN-PEEL CATHOLIC DISTRICT SCHOOL BOARD
HOLY CROSS ELEMENTARY SCHOOL
3615 Morning Star Dr, Mississauga, ON, L4T 1Y4
(905) 677-5660
Emp Here 50
SIC 8211 Elementary and secondary schools

D-U-N-S 20-913-6873   (BR)
DUFFERIN-PEEL CATHOLIC DISTRICT SCHOOL BOARD
ASCENSION OF OUR LORD SECONDARY SCHOOL
7640 Anaka Dr, Mississauga, ON, L4T 3H7
(905) 676-1287
Emp Here 70
SIC 8211 Elementary and secondary schools

D-U-N-S 25-397-2442   (SL)
INTERNATIONAL TRANSACTION SYSTEMS (CANADA) LTD
ITS CANADA
7415 Torbram Rd, Mississauga, ON, L4T 1G8
(905) 677-2088
Emp Here 52   *Sales* 3,939,878
SIC 3578 Calculating and accounting equipment

D-U-N-S 25-901-8174   (BR)
LONGO BROTHERS FRUIT MARKETS INC
LONGO'S MALTON FRUIT MARKET
7085 Goreway Dr, Mississauga, ON, L4T 3X6

Emp Here 100
SIC 5411 Grocery stores

D-U-N-S 25-886-2127   (SL)
MASTER MANUFACTURING INC
2636 Drew Rd, Mississauga, ON, L4T 3M5
(905) 673-8255
Emp Here 50   *Sales* 3,866,917
SIC 2542 Partitions and fixtures, except wood

D-U-N-S 25-310-9375   (BR)
MCDONALD'S RESTAURANTS OF CANADA LIMITED
MCDONALD'S 8108
(*Suby of* McDonald's Corporation)
3510 Derry Rd E, Mississauga, ON, L4T 3V7
(905) 677-8711
Emp Here 100
SIC 5812 Eating places

D-U-N-S 24-805-4962   (BR)
MERCEDES-BENZ CANADA INC
7380 Bren Rd Suite 2, Mississauga, ON, L4T 1H4
(905) 461-0031
Emp Here 30
SIC 5013 Motor vehicle supplies and new parts

D-U-N-S 20-596-6943   (BR)
NATIONEX INC
7535 Bath Rd, Mississauga, ON, L4T 4C1

Emp Here 35
SIC 7389 Business services, nec

D-U-N-S 24-923-5631   (HQ)
NUVO PHARMACEUTICALS INC
(*Suby of* Nuvo Pharmaceuticals Inc)
7560 Airport Rd Unit 10, Mississauga, ON, L4T 4H4
(905) 673-6980
Emp Here 42   *Emp Total* 74
Sales 19,999,261
SIC 2834 Pharmaceutical preparations
John London
Pr Jesse Ledger
Mary-Jane Burkett
Katina Loucaides
VP Mfg Cally Lunetta
Daniel Chicoine
David Copeland
Anthony Dobranowski
Jacques Messier
Robert Harris

D-U-N-S 24-663-5002   (SL)
OFFICE MOVER LTD, THE
2798 Thamesgate Dr Unit 6, Mississauga, ON, L4T 4E8
(905) 673-6683
Emp Here 50   *Sales* 3,939,878
SIC 4212 Local trucking, without storage

D-U-N-S 24-327-1108   (BR)
OLD DUTCH FOODS LTD
HUMPTY DUMPTY OLD DUTCH FOODS
(*Suby of* Old Dutch Foods Ltd)
7385 Bren Rd Suite 1, Mississauga, ON, L4T 1H3

Emp Here 30
SIC 2096 Potato chips and similar snacks

D-U-N-S 25-192-2811   (SL)
ORENDA AEROSPACE CORPORATION
MAGELLAN AEROSPACE, MISSISSAUGA
3160 Derry Rd E, Mississauga, ON, L4T 1A9
(905) 673-3250
Emp Here 320   *Sales* 23,128,902
SIC 7699 Repair services, nec

D-U-N-S 24-191-5552   (BR)
PMT INDUSTRIES LIMITED
PURE METAL GALVANIZING, DIV. OF
7470 Bren Rd, Mississauga, ON, L4T 1H4
(905) 677-7491
Emp Here 50
SIC 3479 Metal coating and allied services

D-U-N-S 25-263-7764   (BR)
PEEL DISTRICT SCHOOL BOARD
LINCOLN M. ALEXANDER SECONDARY SCHOOL
(*Suby of* Peel District School Board)
3545 Morning Star Dr, Mississauga, ON, L4T 1Y3

---

(905) 676-1191
Emp Here 135
SIC 8211 Elementary and secondary schools

D-U-N-S 25-263-8168   (BR)
PEEL DISTRICT SCHOOL BOARD
MARVIN HEIGHTS PUBLIC SCHOOL
(*Suby of* Peel District School Board)
7455 Redstone Rd, Mississauga, ON, L4T 2B3
(905) 677-1526
Emp Here 45
SIC 8211 Elementary and secondary schools

D-U-N-S 25-293-8261   (BR)
PEEL DISTRICT SCHOOL BOARD
MORNING STAR MIDDLE SCHOOL
(*Suby of* Peel District School Board)
3131 Morning Star Dr, Mississauga, ON, L4T 1X3
(905) 677-0300
Emp Here 60
SIC 8211 Elementary and secondary schools

D-U-N-S 25-278-9292   (BR)
PEEL DISTRICT SCHOOL BOARD
DARCEL AVENUE SENIOR PUBLIC SCHOOL
(*Suby of* Peel District School Board)
7635 Darcel Ave, Mississauga, ON, L4T 2Y2
(905) 677-3802
Emp Here 40
SIC 8211 Elementary and secondary schools

D-U-N-S 25-293-8113   (BR)
PEEL DISTRICT SCHOOL BOARD
DUNRANKIN DRIVE PUBLIC SCHOOL
(*Suby of* Peel District School Board)
3700 Dunrankin Dr, Mississauga, ON, L4T 1V9
(905) 677-2202
Emp Here 50
SIC 8211 Elementary and secondary schools

D-U-N-S 25-293-7727   (BR)
PEEL DISTRICT SCHOOL BOARD
LANCASTER PUBLIC SCHOOL
(*Suby of* Peel District School Board)
7425 Netherwood Rd, Mississauga, ON, L4T 2N7
(905) 677-5344
Emp Here 45
SIC 8211 Elementary and secondary schools

D-U-N-S 25-278-9136   (BR)
PEEL DISTRICT SCHOOL BOARD
BRANDON GATE PUBLIC SCHOOL
(*Suby of* Peel District School Board)
3800 Brandon Gate Dr, Mississauga, ON, L4T 3V9
(905) 677-9679
Emp Here 31
SIC 8211 Elementary and secondary schools

D-U-N-S 25-811-2093   (BR)
PRISZM LP
KFC
7161 Goreway Dr, Mississauga, ON, L4T 2T5
(905) 677-3813
Emp Here 2
SIC 5812 Eating places

D-U-N-S 20-528-0246   (SL)
PRO-X EXHIBIT INC
7621 Bath Rd, Mississauga, ON, L4T 3T1
(905) 696-0993
Emp Here 65   *Sales* 3,283,232
SIC 7389 Business services, nec

D-U-N-S 20-260-1860   (SL)
REAL ALLOY CANADA LTD
(*Suby of* Real Industry, Inc.)
7496 Torbram Rd, Mississauga, ON, L4T 1G9
(905) 672-5569
Emp Here 85   *Sales* 41,076,874
SIC 3341 Secondary nonferrous Metals
Manager Joseph Giorgio

D-U-N-S 20-260-9657   (SL)

SIX SIGMA EMPLOYMENT LTD
7160 Airport Rd Unit 2, Mississauga, ON, L4T 2H2
(905) 673-6433
Emp Here 100   *Sales* 1,752,234
SIC 7361 Employment agencies

D-U-N-S 24-421-5211   (BR)
SOBEYS CAPITAL INCORPORATED
FRESHCO
7205 Goreway Dr Unit1, Mississauga, ON, L4T 2T9
(905) 677-0239
Emp Here 80
SIC 5411 Grocery stores

D-U-N-S 20-211-6773   (BR)
SOUTHERN GRAPHIC SYSTEMS-CANADA LTD
SGS
(*Suby of* Logo Holdings I Corporation)
2620 Slough St, Mississauga, ON, L4T 3T2
(905) 405-1555
Emp Here 65
SIC 7389 Business services, nec

D-U-N-S 24-849-3459   (BR)
SPRINGWALL SLEEP PRODUCTS INC
7689 Bath Rd, Mississauga, ON, L4T 3T1
(905) 564-5008
Emp Here 55
SIC 2515 Mattresses and bedsprings

D-U-N-S 24-803-2026   (BR)
TWI FOODS INC
2600 Drew Rd, Mississauga, ON, L4T 3M5
(905) 364-3020
Emp Here 30
SIC 2051 Bread, cake, and related products

D-U-N-S 25-120-2073   (BR)
TORONTO-DOMINION BANK, THE
TD CANADA TRUST
(*Suby of* Toronto-Dominion Bank, The)
Gd, Mississauga, ON, L4T 1A1
(905) 820-7100
Emp Here 40
SIC 6021 National commercial banks

D-U-N-S 24-683-3276   (BR)
TRANSALTA GENERATION PARTNERSHIP
2740 Derry Rd E, Mississauga, ON, L4T 4J5
(905) 678-9826
Emp Here 20
SIC 4911 Electric services

D-U-N-S 24-045-9862   (BR)
WENDY'S RESTAURANTS OF CANADA INC
(*Suby of* The Wendy's Company)
3650 Derry Rd E, Mississauga, ON, L4T 3V7
(905) 671-4901
Emp Here 30
SIC 5812 Eating places

D-U-N-S 25-832-0233   (BR)
WESTERN LOGISTICS INC
7347 Kimbel St Unit B, Mississauga, ON, L4T 3M6
(905) 799-7321
Emp Here 20
SIC 4731 Freight transportation arrangement

Mississauga, ON L4V
Peel County

D-U-N-S 24-371-4792   (HQ)
1046114 ONTARIO INC
(*Suby of* 1046114 Ontario Inc)
6350 Viscount Rd, Mississauga, ON, L4V 1H3
(905) 672-0007
Emp Here 20   *Emp Total* 35
Sales 7,797,120
SIC 5085 Industrial supplies
Pr Pr Robert Craig
VP VP Janet Craig

D-U-N-S 20-734-8780   (HQ)
105675 ONTARIO LIMITED
KASTNER METALS
(*Suby of* 105675 Ontario Limited)
6577 Northwest Dr, Mississauga, ON, L4V 1L1
(905) 293-9900
Emp Here 45   *Emp Total* 55
Sales 3,720,996
SIC 3471 Plating and polishing

D-U-N-S 20-317-0493   (BR)
4513380 CANADA INC
LIVINGSTON INTERNATIONAL
6725 Airport Rd Ste 101, Mississauga, ON, L4V 1V2
(905) 676-3700
Emp Here 400
SIC 4731 Freight transportation arrangement

D-U-N-S 25-170-4771   (BR)
4513380 CANADA INC
LIVINGSTON INTERNATIONAL
6725 Airport Rd Suite 400, Mississauga, ON, L4V 1V2
(905) 676-3700
Emp Here 400
SIC 4731 Freight transportation arrangement

D-U-N-S 24-783-9681   (SL)
722140 ONTARIO LIMITED
3160 Caravelle Dr, Mississauga, ON, L4V 1K9

Emp Here 100   *Sales* 20,899,840
SIC 6712 Bank holding companies
Pr Pr Ralph Cator

D-U-N-S 24-751-8780   (BR)
ABC GROUP INC
(*Suby of* Cerberus Capital Management, L.P.)
3325 Orlando Dr, Mississauga, ON, L4V 1C5
(905) 671-0310
Emp Here 125
SIC 3089 Plastics products, nec

D-U-N-S 24-966-3139   (HQ)
ABCO INTERNATIONAL FREIGHT INC
ABCO
5945 Airport Rd Suite 338, Mississauga, ON, L4V 1R9
(905) 405-8088
Emp Here 25   *Emp Total* 80
Sales 8,536,402
SIC 4731 Freight transportation arrangement
Pr Pr Donald Lucky
VP VP Dominic Chan
John Iacuone

D-U-N-S 20-548-2339   (SL)
AMI AIR MANAGEMENT INC
AMI
3223 Orlando Dr, Mississauga, ON, L4V 1C5
(905) 694-9676
Emp Here 52   *Sales* 4,565,250
SIC 3822 Environmental controls

D-U-N-S 25-194-5283   (SL)
ADAMS CARGO LIMITED
6751 Professional Crt, Mississauga, ON, L4V 1Y3
(905) 678-0459
Emp Here 50   *Sales* 3,939,878
SIC 4212 Local trucking, without storage

D-U-N-S 24-849-6481   (HQ)
AEARO CANADA LIMITED
AO SAFETY
(*Suby of* 3M Company)
6889 Rexwood Rd Suite 8, Mississauga, ON, L4V 1R2
(905) 795-0700
Emp Here 20   *Emp Total* 91,584
Sales 3,356,192
SIC 3842 Surgical appliances and supplies

D-U-N-S 24-342-1752   (BR)
ALL WEATHER WINDOWS LTD
ALL WEATHER WINDOWS LTD.

3100 Caravelle Dr, Mississauga, ON, L4V 1K9
(905) 696-0005
Emp Here 300
SIC 3442 Metal doors, sash, and trim

D-U-N-S 20-187-3978   (SL)
BML GROUP LIMITED
5905 Campus Rd, Mississauga, ON, L4V 1P9
(905) 676-1293
Emp Here 1,000   *Sales* 234,828,387
SIC 6719 Holding companies, nec
Pr Pr Samuel Bresler
Eric Bresler
Ronald Bresler

D-U-N-S 25-296-4523   (BR)
BANK OF NOVA SCOTIA, THE
SCOTIA BANK
6725 Airport Rd Suite 100, Mississauga, ON, L4V 1V2

Emp Here 25
SIC 6021 National commercial banks

D-U-N-S 24-324-3768   (SL)
BAUER PARTNERSHIP
6490 Viscount Rd, Mississauga, ON, L4V 1H3

Emp Here 100   *Sales* 20,899,840
SIC 6712 Bank holding companies
Pt Michael Bauer

D-U-N-S 24-314-4388   (BR)
BRENNTAG CANADA INC
6395 Northwest Dr, Mississauga, ON, L4V 1K2
(905) 671-1511
Emp Here 20
SIC 5169 Chemicals and allied products, nec

D-U-N-S 20-160-8114   (SL)
BUDGET CAR RENTALS TORONTO LIMITED
5905 Campus Rd, Mississauga, ON, L4V 1P9

Emp Here 300   *Sales* 42,201,600
SIC 7514 Passenger car rental
Samuel Bresler
Pr Ray Mccarron
Rita Bresler

D-U-N-S 25-996-8261   (SL)
CASEBANK TECHNOLOGIES INC
6205 Airport Rd Bldg A Suite 200, Mississauga, ON, L4V 1E1
(905) 364-3600
Emp Here 40   *Sales* 4,244,630
SIC 7371 Custom computer programming services

D-U-N-S 25-170-4508   (BR)
COLE INTERNATIONAL INC
5955 Airport Rd Suite 223, Mississauga, ON, L4V 1R9
(905) 672-6255
Emp Here 60
SIC 4731 Freight transportation arrangement

D-U-N-S 25-915-7246   (BR)
COLGATE-PALMOLIVE CANADA INC
(*Suby of* Colgate-Palmolive Company)
6400 Northwest Dr, Mississauga, ON, L4V 1K1

Emp Here 100
SIC 2844 Toilet preparations

D-U-N-S 20-357-6608   (BR)
CONCENTRIX TECHNOLOGIES SERVICES (CANADA) LIMITED
6655 Airport Rd, Mississauga, ON, L4V 1V8
(416) 380-3800
Emp Here 82
SIC 8721 Accounting, auditing, and book-keeping

D-U-N-S 25-641-5373   (BR)
CORPORATION SERVICES MONERIS

▲ Public Company   ■ Public Company Family Member   **HQ** Headquarters   **BR** Branch   **SL** Single Location

OPTIMAL SERVICE GROUP, THE
3190 Orlando Dr, Mississauga, ON, L4V 1R5
(905) 672-1048
Emp Here 110
SIC 7378 Computer maintenance and repair

D-U-N-S 20-347-2154   (BR)
DIRECTCASH PAYMENTS INC
3269 American Dr Suite 1, Mississauga, ON,
L4V 1V4
(905) 678-7373
Emp Here 80
SIC 6099 Functions related to deposit banking

D-U-N-S 24-354-3068   (BR)
DRIVE PRODUCTS INC
DOCAP, DIV OF
6601 Goreway Dr Unit B, Mississauga, ON,
L4V 1V6
(905) 673-0000
Emp Here 30
SIC 5013 Motor vehicle supplies and new
parts

D-U-N-S 20-129-2273   (HQ)
EMI GROUP CANADA INC
EMI MUSIC CANADA, DIV OF
3109 American Dr, Mississauga, ON, L4V 0A2
(905) 677-5050
Emp Here 155   Emp Total 221
Sales 23,978,240
SIC 5099 Durable goods, nec
Pr Pr Deane Cameron
Sec Cindy Zaplachinsky

D-U-N-S 24-342-2313   (BR)
EASTON'S GROUP OF HOTELS INC
FAIRFIELD INN & SUITES BY MARRIOTT
TORONTO AIRPORT
3299 Caroga Dr, Mississauga, ON, L4V 1A3
(905) 673-9800
Emp Here 54
SIC 7011 Hotels and motels

D-U-N-S 25-840-3781   (BR)
ENTREPRISES MTY TIKI MING INC, LES
COUNTRY STYLE DONUTS
6585 Airport Rd Unit B, Mississauga, ON, L4V
1E5
(905) 678-7525
Emp Here 20
SIC 5812 Eating places

D-U-N-S 25-102-0053   (HQ)
FORSYTH HOLDINGS INC
(Suby of Forsyth Holdings Inc)
6789 Airport Rd, Mississauga, ON, L4V 1E6
(905) 362-1400
Emp Here 65   Emp Total 200
Sales 15,116,640
SIC 2321 Men's and boy's furnishings
Pr Pr Harris Hester
Oliver Morante
Thomas Siano
VP VP Wendell Wilkinson
Victor Tugwell
Michael Watt

D-U-N-S 20-558-9989   (HQ)
G&K SERVICES CANADA INC
(Suby of Cintas Corporation)
6299 Airport Rd Suite 101, Mississauga, ON,
L4V 1N3
(905) 677-6161
Emp Here 35   Emp Total 35,000
Sales 217,082,501
SIC 7213 Linen supply
Ch Bd Douglas Milroy
Pr Kevin Fancey
Jeffrey Cotter
S&M/VP David Euson
Pers/VP John Vegas

D-U-N-S 20-788-8236   (HQ)
G3 WORLDWIDE (CANADA) INC
SPRING GLOBAL MAIL
3198 Orlando Dr, Mississauga, ON, L4V 1R5

(905) 405-8900
Emp Here 40   Emp Total 23,933
Sales 2,553,625
SIC 7331 Direct mail advertising services

D-U-N-S 24-783-7438   (SL)
GAGE METAL CLADDING LIMITED
STEELTRIM MANUFACTURING
3109 American Dr, Mississauga, ON, L4V 0A2
(416) 742-0300
Emp Here 50   Sales 4,961,328
SIC 1761 Roofing, siding, and sheetMetal
work

D-U-N-S 24-493-3438   (HQ)
GEODIS WILSON CANADA LTD
3061 Orlando Dr Suite 1, Mississauga, ON,
L4V 1R4
(905) 677-5266
Emp Here 23   Sales 11,308,909
SIC 4731 Freight transportation arrangement
Pr Christopher Johnston
Brian Rusak
Gillian M Jiwani
John M Gallahan
Gerhardus Bosua

D-U-N-S 20-900-7251   (HQ)
HARTWICK O'SHEA & CARTWRIGHT LIM-
ITED
HOC GLOBAL SOLUTIONS
(Suby of Hartwick O'Shea & Cartwright Lim-
ited)
3245 American Dr, Mississauga, ON, L4V 1B8
(905) 672-5100
Emp Here 40   Emp Total 85
Sales 21,012,682
SIC 4731 Freight transportation arrangement
Pr Pr Stephen George Cartwright
Kyle Hartwick

D-U-N-S 25-948-5753   (BR)
HARTWICK O'SHEA & CARTWRIGHT LIM-
ITED
(Suby of Hartwick O'Shea & Cartwright Lim-
ited)
3350 American Dr, Mississauga, ON, L4V 1B3
(905) 676-8796
Emp Here 30
SIC 4731 Freight transportation arrangement

D-U-N-S 24-372-9931   (BR)
HILTON CANADA CO.
HILTON TORONTO AIRPORT HOTEL &
SUITES
5875 Airport Rd, Mississauga, ON, L4V 1N1
(905) 677-9900
Emp Here 220
SIC 7011 Hotels and motels

D-U-N-S 24-959-1512   (BR)
IFASTGROUPE 2004 L.P.
INFASCO NUT DIV
3990 Nashua Dr, Mississauga, ON, L4V 1P8
(905) 677-8920
Emp Here 65
SIC 3452 Bolts, nuts, rivets, and washers

D-U-N-S 24-868-9911   (SL)
IRIS POWER LP
IRIS POWER ENGINEERING
(Suby of Fortive Corporation)
3110 American Dr, Mississauga, ON, L4V 1T2
(905) 677-4824
Emp Here 20   Sales 2,918,428
SIC 3825 Instruments to measure electricity

D-U-N-S 20-642-5857   (BR)
JOHNSON CONTROLS L.P.
3255 Elmbank Rd, Mississauga, ON, L4V 1A6
(905) 676-8299
Emp Here 40
SIC 1731 Electrical work

D-U-N-S 20-335-8069   (SL)
KEYSTONE AUTOMOTIVE OPERATIONS
OF CANADA INC
3770 Nashua Dr Unit 4, Mississauga, ON, L4V

1M5
(905) 405-0999
Emp Here 80   Sales 13,055,280
SIC 5013 Motor vehicle supplies and new
parts
Edward H Orzetti
VP Sls Ralph Ruzzi
Don Grimes

D-U-N-S 24-953-8802   (HQ)
LASERNETWORKS INC
(Suby of Fcs Industries, Inc.)
6300 Viscount Rd Unit 2, Mississauga, ON,
L4V 1H3
(800) 461-4879
Emp Here 70   Emp Total 200
Sales 8,682,323
SIC 3955 Carbon paper and inked ribbons
Pr Pr Christopher Stoate

D-U-N-S 24-101-0805   (BR)
LONGO BROTHERS FRUIT MARKETS INC
LONGO'S FRUIT MARKET
6811 Goreway Dr Unit 2, Mississauga, ON,
L4V 1L9
(905) 672-7851
Emp Here 50
SIC 4225 General warehousing and storage

D-U-N-S 24-850-6813   (SL)
M3 STEEL & FABRICATION LTD
3206 Orlando Dr, Mississauga, ON, L4V 1R5
(800) 316-1074
Emp Here 30   Sales 7,950,960
SIC 1541 Industrial buildings and warehouses
Brian Fleming

D-U-N-S 24-334-6439   (BR)
MARTINREA INTERNATIONAL INC
ROLLSTAR
6655 Northwest Dr, Mississauga, ON, L4V
1L1
(905) 673-2424
Emp Here 250
SIC 3499 Fabricated Metal products, nec

D-U-N-S 20-699-6931   (BR)
MARTINREA INTERNATIONAL INC
ROLLSTAR METAL FORMING, DIV OF
6655 Northwest Dr, Mississauga, ON, L4V
1L1
(905) 673-2424
Emp Here 200
SIC 3499 Fabricated Metal products, nec

D-U-N-S 20-529-4911   (SL)
MARWICK MANUFACTURING INC
6325 Northwest Dr, Mississauga, ON, L4V
1P6
(905) 677-0677
Emp Here 90   Sales 3,283,232
SIC 2789 Bookbinding and related work

D-U-N-S 20-513-8691   (BR)
NCR CANADA CORP
SYSTEMEDIA GROUP
(Suby of NCR Corporation)
6360 Northwest Dr, Mississauga, ON, L4V
1J7
(905) 677-2223
Emp Here 60
SIC 2679 Converted paper products, nec

D-U-N-S 20-178-4233   (BR)
NESTLE CANADA INC
NESTLE ICE CREAM DISTRIBUTION CEN-
TRE
6655 Goreway Dr, Mississauga, ON, L4V 1V6

Emp Here 43
SIC 5143 Dairy products, except dried or
canned

D-U-N-S 25-249-5031   (BR)
NUANCE GROUP (CANADA) INC, THE
5925 Airport Rd Suite 300, Mississauga, ON,
L4V 1W1
(905) 673-7299
Emp Here 20

SIC 5399 Miscellaneous general merchandise

D-U-N-S 24-858-8571   (BR)
OHL CONSTRUCTION CANADA INC
5915 Airport Rd Suite 425, Mississauga, ON,
L4V 1T1
(647) 260-4880
Emp Here 30
SIC 7363 Help supply services

D-U-N-S 24-424-9561   (SL)
PCAN MAILING SOLUTIONS INC
MAILING INNOVATIONS
(Suby of Pitney Bowes Inc.)
3397 American Dr Unit 18-20, Mississauga,
ON, L4V 1T8

Emp Here 35   Sales 7,362,000
SIC 5044 Office equipment
Pr Pr Deepak Chopra

D-U-N-S 24-593-6260   (BR)
PNF HOLDINGS LIMITED
PARK 'N' FLY
(Suby of PNF Holdings Limited)
5905 Campus Rd, Mississauga, ON, L4V 1P9
(905) 676-1248
Emp Here 25
SIC 7521 Automobile parking

D-U-N-S 20-321-0992   (SL)
PIVAL INTERANTIONAL INC.
6611 Northwest Dr, Mississauga, ON, L4V
1L1
(905) 677-8179
Emp Here 25   Sales 2,772,003
SIC 8742 Management consulting services

D-U-N-S 20-714-5181   (BR)
QUINCAILLERIE RICHELIEU LTEE
RICHELIEU HARDWARE
6420 Viscount Rd, Mississauga, ON, L4V 1H3
(905) 672-1500
Emp Here 40
SIC 5251 Hardware stores

D-U-N-S 24-325-5317   (HQ)
RED APPLE STORES INC
THE BARGAIN SHOP
6877 Goreway Dr Suite 3, Mississauga, ON,
L4V 1L9
(905) 293-9700
Emp Here 100   Emp Total 15
Sales 114,694,220
SIC 5399 Miscellaneous general merchandise
Pr Clinton Wolff
VP Fin Hanspal Jando
Don Smith

D-U-N-S 24-205-9041   (BR)
ROYAL AUTOMOTIVE GROUP LTD
ROLLSTAR METAL FORMING DIV
6655 Northwest Dr, Mississauga, ON, L4V
1L1
(905) 673-5060
Emp Here 300
SIC 3499 Fabricated Metal products, nec

D-U-N-S 25-309-8685   (BR)
ROYAL BANK OF CANADA
RBC
(Suby of Royal Bank Of Canada)
6205 Airport Rd Ste 100, Mississauga, ON,
L4V 1E1
(905) 671-6262
Emp Here 30
SIC 6021 National commercial banks

D-U-N-S 20-819-4977   (HQ)
RUTHERFORD, WILLIAM L. LIMITED
RUTHERFORD INTERNATIONAL FREIGHT
SERVICE
(Suby of Rutherford, William L. Limited)
3350 Airway Dr, Mississauga, ON, L4V 1T3
(905) 673-2222
Emp Here 30   Emp Total 188
Sales 60,026,357
SIC 4731 Freight transportation arrangement

Pr Pr Romas Krilavicius
Larry Wiseman
Gwen Krilavicius
Prans Krilavicius

D-U-N-S 20-413-2179   (HQ)
SCHENKER OF CANADA LIMITED
SCHENKER DISTRIBUTION
5935 Airport Rd Suite 9, Mississauga, ON,
L4V 1W5
(905) 676-0676
Emp Here 120   *Sales* 303,187,850
SIC 4731 Freight transportation arrangement
Pr Eric Dewey
VP Opers Arnold Dasilva
Dir Thomas Lieb
Dir Heiner Murmann
Dir James J. Pelliccio
Dir Dennis Eittreim
Petra Kuester

D-U-N-S 24-093-1407   (HQ)
SEDGWICK CMS CANADA INC
CLAIMS MANAGEMENT SERVICES
(*Suby of* Sedgwick CMS Canada Inc)
5915 Airport Rd Suite 200, Mississauga, ON,
L4V 1T1
(905) 671-7800
Emp Here 30   *Emp Total* 50
Sales 4,523,563
SIC 6411 Insurance agents, brokers, and service

D-U-N-S 20-568-8323   (BR)
SINCLAIR DENTAL CO. LTD
6275 Northam Dr Unit 5, Mississauga, ON,
L4V 1Y8
(905) 740-2000
Emp Here 30
SIC 5047 Medical and hospital equipment

D-U-N-S 20-015-7753   (BR)
SOBEYS CAPITAL INCORPORATED
SOBEYS ONTARIO
6355 Viscount Rd, Mississauga, ON, L4V
1W2

Emp Here 600
SIC 5141 Groceries, general line

D-U-N-S 20-346-5687   (BR)
SOFINA FOODS INC
3340 Orlando Dr, Mississauga, ON, L4V 1C7
(905) 673-7145
Emp Here 100
SIC 2038 Frozen specialties, nec

D-U-N-S 24-045-6033   (SL)
SUNDINE PRODUCE INC
6346 Viscount Rd, Mississauga, ON, L4V 1H3
(905) 362-9400
Emp Here 20   *Sales* 5,717,257
SIC 5148 Fresh fruits and vegetables
Pr Pr Sreedhar Mundluru
Dir Divya Donthi

D-U-N-S 25-115-4456   (SL)
SYSTEM ELECTRICAL AND COMMUNICATION SERVICES INC
6354 Viscount Rd, Mississauga, ON, L4V 1H3
(905) 677-1461
Emp Here 40   *Sales* 3,502,114
SIC 1731 Electrical work

D-U-N-S 20-148-4193   (HQ)
TIMKEN CANADA LP
BEDFORD, DIV OF
(*Suby of* The Timken Company)
5955 Airport Rd Suite 100, Mississauga, ON,
L4V 1R9
(905) 826-9520
Emp Here 350   *Emp Total* 14,000
Sales 77,338,342
SIC 3562 Ball and roller bearings
Sls Mgr William Thompson

D-U-N-S 24-830-2093   (BR)
TOURAM LIMITED PARTNERSHIP

AIR CANADA VACATION
5925 Airport Rd Suite 700, Mississauga, ON,
L4V 1W1
(905) 615-8020
Emp Here 75
SIC 4724 Travel agencies

D-U-N-S 25-683-1728   (HQ)
TRANSGLOBE PROPERTY MANAGEMENT SERVICES LTD
(*Suby of* TransGlobe Property Management
Services Ltd)
5935 Airport Rd Suite 600, Mississauga, ON,
L4V 1W5

Emp Here 250   *Emp Total* 1,200
Sales 152,148,000
SIC 6531 Real estate agents and managers
Dir Kelly Hancyk
Daniel Drimmer
COO Michael Bolahood
CFO Barry Kadoch

D-U-N-S 25-031-1347   (BR)
TRENTWAY-WAGAR INC
COACH CANADA
6020 Indian Line, Mississauga, ON, L4V 1G5
(905) 677-3841
Emp Here 200
SIC 4142 Bus charter service, except local

D-U-N-S 20-789-5587   (BR)
TYCO SAFETY PRODUCTS CANADA LTD
3210 Airway Dr, Mississauga, ON, L4V 1Y6
(888) 888-7838
Emp Here 25
SIC 5099 Durable goods, nec

D-U-N-S 25-311-9184   (BR)
UPS SCS, INC
UPS SUPPLY CHAIN SOLUTION
6655 Airport Rd, Mississauga, ON, L4V 1V8
(905) 677-6735
Emp Here 235
SIC 4731 Freight transportation arrangement

D-U-N-S 24-228-6271   (BR)
UTC FIRE & SECURITY CANADA INC
UTC FIRE & SECURITY CANADA
(*Suby of* United Technologies Corporation)
6305 Northam Dr Suite 14, Mississauga, ON,
L4V 1W9
(905) 678-7650
Emp Here 50
SIC 6211 Security brokers and dealers

D-U-N-S 20-647-7270   (BR)
UNIFOR
5915 Airport Rd Suite 510, Mississauga, ON,
L4V 1T1
(905) 678-0800
Emp Here 30
SIC 8631 Labor organizations

D-U-N-S 25-988-1472   (BR)
UNITED PARCEL SERVICE CANADA LTD
UPS
3195 Airway Dr, Mississauga, ON, L4V 1C2
(905) 672-6476
Emp Here 100
SIC 7389 Business services, nec

D-U-N-S 25-511-8077   (SL)
VIDEOJET TECHNOLOGIES CANADA L.P.
VIDEOJET
(*Suby of* Danaher Corporation)
6500 Viscount Rd, Mississauga, ON, L4V 1H3
(905) 673-1341
Emp Here 42   *Sales* 20,659,800
SIC 5999 Miscellaneous retail stores, nec
Genl Mgr Michael Swevak
Fin Ex Donal Carroll

D-U-N-S 20-005-8332   (BR)
WENDY'S RESTAURANTS OF CANADA INC
WENDY'S
(*Suby of* The Wendy's Company)
6585 Airport Rd Unit B, Mississauga, ON, L4V

1E5
(905) 678-7846
Emp Here 30
SIC 5812 Eating places

D-U-N-S 20-806-5946   (HQ)
WESTERN INVENTORY SERVICE LTD
WIS INTERNATIONAL
3770 Nashua Dr Suite 5, Mississauga, ON,
L4V 1M5
(905) 677-1947
Emp Here 50   *Emp Total* 930
Sales 165,870,750
SIC 7389 Business services, nec
Pr Bret Bero
Thomas Compogiannis
Dir Helen Yang
Dir Brian Graff

D-U-N-S 20-515-9051   (BR)
WESTROCK PACKAGING COMPANY
(*Suby of* Westrock Company)
3270 American Dr, Mississauga, ON, L4V 1B5
(905) 677-3592
Emp Here 150
SIC 2679 Converted paper products, nec

D-U-N-S 20-511-7539   (BR)
WINNERS MERCHANTS INTERNATIONAL L.P.
WINNERS
(*Suby of* The TJX Companies Inc)
3185 American Dr, Mississauga, ON, L4V 1B8
(905) 672-2228
Emp Here 800
SIC 5651 Family clothing stores

D-U-N-S 20-922-4554   (BR)
XEROX CANADA LTD
(*Suby of* Xerox Corporation)
3060 Caravelle Dr, Mississauga, ON, L4V 1L7
(905) 672-4700
Emp Here 106
SIC 7374 Data processing and preparation

D-U-N-S 24-986-5775   (BR)
XEROX CANADA LTD
(*Suby of* Xerox Corporation)
5925 Airport Rd, Mississauga, ON, L4V 1W1
(905) 672-4577
Emp Here 120
SIC 5044 Office equipment

D-U-N-S 20-651-2472   (BR)
XEROX CANADA LTD
(*Suby of* Xerox Corporation)
6800 Northwest Dr, Mississauga, ON, L4V
1Z1
(905) 672-4709
Emp Here 100
SIC 5044 Office equipment

D-U-N-S 24-006-0806   (BR)
XEROX CANADA LTD
(*Suby of* Xerox Corporation)
6800 Northwest Dr, Mississauga, ON, L4V
1Z1
(905) 672-4700
Emp Here 150
SIC 5044 Office equipment

D-U-N-S 25-144-9344   (SL)
YARDI SYSTEMS
(*Suby of* Yardi Systems, Inc.)
5925 Airport Rd Suite 510, Mississauga, ON,
L4V 1W1
(905) 671-0315
Emp Here 60   *Sales* 6,493,502
SIC 7372 Prepackaged software
Lyn Capps

Mississauga, ON L4W
Peel County

D-U-N-S 24-991-5117   (SL)

1022804 ONTARIO INC
MOTOR EXPRESS TORONTO
1335 Shawson Dr, Mississauga, ON, L4W 5J6
(905) 564-0241
Emp Here 35   *Sales* 2,772,507
SIC 4212 Local trucking, without storage

D-U-N-S 25-359-5300   (BR)
115161 CANADA INC
FASHION DISTRIBUTORS, THE
2645 Skymark Ave, Mississauga, ON, L4W
4H2

Emp Here 20
SIC 4226 Special warehousing and storage,
nec

D-U-N-S 24-396-8752   (BR)
1170880 ONTARIO LIMITED
DIXIE MITSUBISHI
5525 Ambler Dr, Mississauga, ON, L4W 3Z1
(905) 282-9998
Emp Here 40
SIC 5012 Automobiles and other motor vehicles

D-U-N-S 24-317-7495   (SL)
1712790 ONTARIO LTD
DIXIE MITSUBISHI
5500 Dixie Rd, Mississauga, ON, L4W 4N3
(905) 282-9998
Emp Here 20   *Sales* 7,296,070
SIC 5511 New and used car dealers
Pr Kapdila Wri

D-U-N-S 24-355-3075   (BR)
1726837 ONTARIO INC
PARAMOUNT FINE FOOD
(*Suby of* 1726837 Ontario Inc)
1290 Crestlawn Dr Bldg 1, Mississauga, ON,
L4W 1A6
(905) 282-1600
Emp Here 30
SIC 5812 Eating places

D-U-N-S 24-355-2523   (SL)
2153463 ONTARIO INC
TOPSPEED TRANS
5185 Tomken Rd Unit 1, Mississauga, ON,
L4W 1P1

Emp Here 50   *Sales* 8,318,900
SIC 4213 Trucking, except local
Pr Pr Arsh Samra

D-U-N-S 24-688-2302   (BR)
3627730 CANADA INC
FREEMAN AUDIO VISUAL
2365 Matheson Blvd E, Mississauga, ON,
L4W 5B3
(905) 366-9200
Emp Here 250
SIC 7359 Equipment rental and leasing, nec

D-U-N-S 20-317-4123   (BR)
4542410 CANADA INC
LAURA SECORD
2700 Matheson Blvd E Suite 800, Mississauga, ON, L4W 4V9
(800) 268-6353
Emp Here 20
SIC 2066 Chocolate and cocoa products

D-U-N-S 25-996-7909   (HQ)
762695 ONTARIO LIMITED
(*Suby of* 762695 Ontario Limited)
2770 Matheson Blvd E, Mississauga, ON,
L4W 4M5
(905) 238-3466
Emp Here 65   *Emp Total* 65
Sales 11,681,040
SIC 6712 Bank holding companies
Pr Pr Robert Gorrie

D-U-N-S 20-809-4610   (BR)
ADT CANADA INC
855 Matheson Blvd E Unit 15, Mississauga,
ON, L4W 4L6

(905) 206-0430
Emp Here 50
SIC 6211 Security brokers and dealers

D-U-N-S 20-923-7015   (BR)
AECOM CANADA LTD
UMA ACOM
5080 Commerce Blvd, Mississauga, ON, L4W 4P2
(905) 238-0007
Emp Here 150
SIC 8711 Engineering services

D-U-N-S 20-183-1109   (SL)
AGILITY RECOVERY SOLUTIONS LTD
(*Suby of* Agility Recovery Solutions Inc.)
1090 Brevik Pl, Mississauga, ON, L4W 3Y5
(905) 625-7620
Emp Here 33   *Sales* 1,313,293
SIC 8322 Individual and family services

D-U-N-S 24-208-4718   (HQ)
AMDOCS CANADIAN MANAGED SERVICES INC
1705 Tech Ave Unit 2, Mississauga, ON, L4W 0A2
(905) 614-4000
Emp Here 180   *Emp Total* 20,774
Sales 26,995,459
SIC 8742 Management consulting services
Dir Paul Douglas Struthers
Dir Ronen Jacob

D-U-N-S 20-074-4436   (BR)
AMEX CANADA INC
(*Suby of* American Express Company)
5090 Explorer Dr Suite 300, Mississauga, ON, L4W 4T9

Emp Here 60
SIC 4725 Tour operators

D-U-N-S 20-158-9330   (HQ)
APPLIED ELECTRONICS LIMITED
(*Suby of* AEL Holdings Limited)
1260 Kamato Rd, Mississauga, ON, L4W 1Y1
(905) 625-4321
Emp Here 52   *Emp Total* 92
Sales 15,332,643
SIC 5065 Electronic parts and equipment, nec
Pr Pr Paul Stechly
VP VP Susan Stechly
  John Stechly
VP Fin John Leermakers

D-U-N-S 20-699-7319   (HQ)
AQUATERRA CORPORATION
CANADIAN SPRINGS
1200 Britannia Rd E, Mississauga, ON, L4W 4T5
(905) 795-6500
Emp Here 100   *Emp Total* 14,200
Sales 71,866,290
SIC 5149 Groceries and related products, nec
Pr Pr Shawn Trinier
Dir Kevin Godwin
Dir James Mcgill
Dir Daniel Samuel
Dir Storrs Mccall

D-U-N-S 24-876-3492   (SL)
ARROW TRUCK SALES CANADA, INC
1285 Shawson Dr, Mississauga, ON, L4W 1C4
(800) 311-7144
Emp Here 21   *Sales* 1,678,096
SIC 4212 Local trucking, without storage

D-U-N-S 25-319-8287   (BR)
ATLANTIC PACKAGING PRODUCTS LTD
5711 Atlantic Dr, Mississauga, ON, L4W 1H3
(905) 670-0301
Emp Here 100
SIC 2653 Corrugated and solid fiber boxes

D-U-N-S 24-212-3818   (BR)
AUTHENTIC T-SHIRT COMPANY ULC, THE
SANMAR CANADA
(*Suby of* Authentic T-Shirt Company ULC,

The)
1575 South Gateway Rd Unit D, Mississauga, ON, L4W 5J1
(905) 602-6411
Emp Here 50
SIC 5136 Men's and boy's clothing

D-U-N-S 24-420-6228   (BR)
AUTOCANADA INC
401/DIXIE HYUNDAI
5515 Ambler Dr, Mississauga, ON, L4W 3Z1
(905) 238-8080
Emp Here 50
SIC 5511 New and used car dealers

D-U-N-S 20-174-5879   (BR)
BANK OF CANADA
AGENCY OPERATIONS CENTRES DEPARTMENT OF BANKING OPERATIONS B DIV OF
5990 Explorer Dr, Mississauga, ON, L4W 5G3

Emp Here 30
SIC 6011 Federal reserve banks

D-U-N-S 25-263-8572   (SL)
BASS BUILDING MAINTENANCE LTD
1233 Aerowood Dr, Mississauga, ON, L4W 1B9
(905) 629-2277
Emp Here 50   *Sales* 1,459,214
SIC 7349 Building maintenance services, nec

D-U-N-S 24-228-5315   (BR)
BAXTER CORPORATION
(*Suby of* Baxter International Inc.)
2785 Skymark Ave Suite 14, Mississauga, ON, L4W 4Y3
(905) 290-6997
Emp Here 20
SIC 3231 Products of purchased glass

D-U-N-S 24-506-3961   (SL)
BELL CONFERENCING INC
5099 Creekbank Rd Suite B4, Mississauga, ON, L4W 5N2
(905) 602-3900
Emp Here 100   *Sales* 6,674,880
SIC 7389 Business services, nec
  Franco Sciannamblo

D-U-N-S 24-375-2826   (BR)
BELL MOBILITE INC
5055 Satellite Dr Unit 1, Mississauga, ON, L4W 5K7

Emp Here 280
SIC 5731 Radio, television, and electronic stores

D-U-N-S 20-007-3625   (HQ)
BIRD CONSTRUCTION COMPANY LIMITED
5700 Explorer Dr Suite 400, Mississauga, ON, L4W 0C6
(905) 602-4122
Emp Here 50   *Emp Total* 1,583
Sales 148,475,025
SIC 1542 Nonresidential construction, nec
  Paul A Charette
  Paul Raboud
Pr Pr Tim Talbott
Sr VP James Brennan
VP Fin Jason Trumbla
VP Opers Ken Mcclure
VP Ian Boyd
VP Ken Nakagawa
Sec Charmane L. Morrow
Dir J Richard Bird

D-U-N-S 20-811-0515   (SL)
BOSTON SCIENTIFIC LTD
(*Suby of* Boston Scientific Corporation)
5060 Spectrum Way Suite 405, Mississauga, ON, L4W 5N5
(905) 291-6900
Emp Here 45   *Sales* 4,764,381
SIC 3841 Surgical and medical instruments

D-U-N-S 25-510-5058   (HQ)
CEVA FREIGHT CANADA CORP
1880 Matheson Blvd E, Mississauga, ON, L4W 5N4
(905) 672-3456
Emp Here 100   *Emp Total* 150
Sales 37,855,169
SIC 4731 Freight transportation arrangement
  Matthew Ryan
Pr Pr Mark Carlson
Genl Mgr Marcel Brailthwaite
VP Sondra Sultemeier
VP David Souza
Sec Burch Kenneth

D-U-N-S 24-850-5620   (SL)
CHIP REIT NO 23 OPERATIONS LIMITED PARTNERSHIP
SANDALWOOD SUITES HOTEL
5050 Orbitor Dr, Mississauga, ON, L4W 4X2
(905) 238-9600
Emp Here 100   *Sales* 4,377,642
SIC 7011 Hotels and motels

D-U-N-S 20-201-6098   (BR)
CSG SECURITY CORPORATION
COUNTERFORCE
(*Suby of* United Technologies Corporation)
2740 Matheson Blvd E Unit 2a, Mississauga, ON, L4W 4X3

Emp Here 75
SIC 1731 Electrical work

D-U-N-S 20-705-8629   (HQ)
CSG SECURITY CORPORATION
CHUBB SECURITY SYSTEMS, DIV OF
(*Suby of* United Technologies Corporation)
5201 Explorer Dr, Mississauga, ON, L4W 4H1
(905) 629-1446
Emp Here 150   *Emp Total* 202,000
Sales 85,874,744
SIC 3699 Electrical equipment and supplies, nec
VP Fin Michael Pavano

D-U-N-S 24-057-6777   (BR)
CSG SECURITY CORPORATION
CHUBB SECURITY SYSTEMS
(*Suby of* United Technologies Corporation)
2740 Matheson Blvd E Unit 1, Mississauga, ON, L4W 4X3
(905) 629-2600
Emp Here 300
SIC 5065 Electronic parts and equipment, nec

D-U-N-S 20-268-6924   (HQ)
CALEA LTD
CALEA HOMECARE, DIV OF
2785 Skymark Ave Unit 2, Mississauga, ON, L4W 4Y3
(905) 238-1234
Emp Here 150   *Emp Total* 228,968
Sales 39,766,284
SIC 5122 Drugs, proprietaries, and sundries
  Matthew Rotenberg

D-U-N-S 20-572-7501   (BR)
CANADA POST CORPORATION
4567 Dixie Rd Suite 152, Mississauga, ON, L4W 1S2
(416) 979-3033
Emp Here 20
SIC 4311 U.s. postal service

D-U-N-S 20-145-2497   (HQ)
CANTEEN OF CANADA LIMITED
5560 Explorer Dr Suite 400, Mississauga, ON, L4W 5M3
(416) 258-4636
Emp Here 50   *Emp Total* 11
Sales 49,838,080
SIC 5812 Eating places
Pr Pr Gary Knox
  Manfred Dobelinger
  Steve Kelly
  Stephen Kelly

  Leslie Ann White
  Jack C. Macdonald

D-U-N-S 20-645-9005   (BR)
CARA OPERATIONS LIMITED
MONTANA'S DIXIE
(*Suby of* Cara Holdings Limited)
1495 Aerowood Dr, Mississauga, ON, L4W 1C2
(905) 206-9811
Emp Here 35
SIC 5812 Eating places

D-U-N-S 24-126-1614   (BR)
CARA OPERATIONS LIMITED
KELSEY'S RESTAURANT
(*Suby of* Cara Holdings Limited)
1485 Aerowood Dr, Mississauga, ON, L4W 1C2
(905) 624-8501
Emp Here 48
SIC 5812 Eating places

D-U-N-S 20-161-5317   (HQ)
CARLTON CARDS LIMITED
(*Suby of* Century Intermediate Holding Company)
1820 Matheson Blvd Unit B1, Mississauga, ON, L4W 0B3
(905) 219-6410
Emp Here 60   *Emp Total* 29,300
Sales 123,539,332
SIC 5112 Stationery and office supplies
Pr Roderick Sturtridge

D-U-N-S 24-376-9960   (BR)
CASCADE (CANADA) LTD
5570 Timberlea Blvd, Mississauga, ON, L4W 4M6
(905) 629-7777
Emp Here 75
SIC 3537 Industrial trucks and tractors

D-U-N-S 20-407-7051   (SL)
CENTRAL GRAPHICS AND CONTAINER GROUP LTD
5526 Timberlea Blvd Suite 217, Mississauga, ON, L4W 2T7
(905) 238-8400
Emp Here 250   *Sales* 41,368,717
SIC 2653 Corrugated and solid fiber boxes
CEO Rick M. Eastwood

D-U-N-S 25-122-1503   (BR)
CERIDIAN CANADA LTD
5600 Explorer Dr Suite 400, Mississauga, ON, L4W 4Y2
(905) 282-8100
Emp Here 150
SIC 8721 Accounting, auditing, and bookkeeping

D-U-N-S 24-125-2944   (BR)
CITIGROUP GLOBAL MARKETS CANADA INC
2920 Matheson Blvd E, Mississauga, ON, L4W 5R6
(905) 624-9889
Emp Here 1,100
SIC 6722 Management investment, open-end

D-U-N-S 20-770-4532   (BR)
COMMERCIAL SPRING AND TOOL COMPANY LIMITED
971 Matheson Blvd E, Mississauga, ON, L4W 2R7
(905) 625-3771
Emp Here 50
SIC 3089 Plastics products, nec

D-U-N-S 20-561-4092   (HQ)
COMPUCOM CANADA CO.
COMPUCOM SYSTEMS
1830 Matheson Blvd Unit 1, Mississauga, ON, L4W 0B3
(289) 261-3000
Emp Here 350   *Emp Total* 600
Sales 82,080,788
SIC 5045 Computers, peripherals, and soft-

ware
Pr Pr Jim Dixon
VP Jeffrey E Frick
VP Mike Simpson
VP VP Robert J Jourbran
Eva M Kalawski

D-U-N-S 20-132-3235   (HQ)
CONAGRA FOODS CANADA INC
ALIMENTS V-H
(*Suby of* Lamb Weston Holdings Inc)
5055 Satellite Dr Unit 1-2, Mississauga, ON, L4W 5K7
(416) 679-4200
Emp Here 120   *Emp Total* 6,400
Sales 30,570,533
SIC 2032 Canned specialties
Pr Thomas Gunter
VP Fin Brendy Sealock
VP Sls Ian Roberts
Pablo Heyman
Dir Jim Newman
Dir Christine Raptopulos
Prs Dir Tanja Fratangeli

D-U-N-S 20-690-6195   (SL)
CONNECTIONS CORPORATION
2680 Matheson Blvd E Suite 102, Mississauga, ON, L4W 0A5
(416) 858-7833
Emp Here 39   *Sales* 5,376,850
SIC 8748 Business consulting, nec
Pr Pr Jason Lightfoot
Craig Campbell

D-U-N-S 24-131-3662   (SL)
COUNSEL SELECT SMALL CAP
2680 Skymark Ave, Mississauga, ON, L4W 5L6
(905) 625-9885
Emp Here 49   *Sales* 14,592,140
SIC 6722 Management investment, open-end
Owner Christopher Reynolds

D-U-N-S 24-757-0690   (HQ)
COUNTERFORCE CORPORATION
(*Suby of* United Technologies Corporation)
2740 Matheson Blvd E Unit 2a, Mississauga, ON, L4W 4X3
(905) 282-6200
Emp Here 64   *Emp Total* 202,000
Sales 1,896,978
SIC 7382 Security systems services

D-U-N-S 24-885-2675   (SL)
CRITICAL PATH COURIERS LTD
CRITICAL PATH COURIERS
1257 Kamato Rd, Mississauga, ON, L4W 2M2
(905) 212-8333
Emp Here 50   *Sales* 2,626,585
SIC 7389 Business services, nec

D-U-N-S 24-000-8313   (BR)
DBG CANADA LIMITED
DE BIASI & ASSOCIATES
1566 Shawson Dr, Mississauga, ON, L4W 1N7
(905) 670-1555
Emp Here 60
SIC 3499 Fabricated Metal products, nec

D-U-N-S 24-873-4485   (BR)
DANONE INC
1310 Aimco Blvd, Mississauga, ON, L4W 1B2

Emp Here 50
SIC 5143 Dairy products, except dried or canned

D-U-N-S 20-564-4888   (SL)
DAY & NIGHT CARRIERS LTD
1270 Aerowood Dr, Mississauga, ON, L4W 1B7

Emp Here 80   *Sales* 13,447,920
SIC 4213 Trucking, except local
Pr Pr Tasheen Sadig

D-U-N-S 20-788-8244   (SL)
DE SOUSA PRAJA ENTERPRISES INC
SWISS CHALET
5165 Dixie Rd Suite 1, Mississauga, ON, L4W 4G1
(905) 238-0798
Emp Here 50   *Sales* 1,532,175
SIC 5812 Eating places

D-U-N-S 24-392-9812   (HQ)
DEALERTRACK CANADA INC
(*Suby of* Cox Enterprises, Inc.)
2700 Matheson Blvd E Suite 702, Mississauga, ON, L4W 4V9
(905) 281-6200
Emp Here 90   *Emp Total* 60,000
Sales 14,134,935
SIC 7372 Prepackaged software
Genl Mgr Michael Collins

D-U-N-S 20-699-9455   (BR)
DELTA HOTELS LIMITED
DELTA TORONTO AIRPORT WEST
5444 Dixie Rd Suite 47, Mississauga, ON, L4W 2L2
(905) 624-1144
Emp Here 160
SIC 8741 Management services

D-U-N-S 25-371-1758   (BR)
DESJARDINS GROUPE D'ASSURANCES GENERALES INC
5070 Dixie Rd, Mississauga, ON, L4W 1C9
(905) 366-4430
Emp Here 900
SIC 6411 Insurance agents, brokers, and service

D-U-N-S 24-927-0729   (HQ)
DIMERCO EXPRESS (CANADA) CORPORATION
5100 Orbitor Dr Suite 201, Mississauga, ON, L4W 4Z4
(905) 282-8118
Emp Here 23   *Emp Total* 144
Sales 6,785,345
SIC 4731 Freight transportation arrangement
Pr Roy Chen

D-U-N-S 24-779-9281   (HQ)
DRAEGER SAFETY CANADA LIMITED
2425 Skymark Ave Unit 1, Mississauga, ON, L4W 4Y6
(905) 212-6600
Emp Here 20   *Emp Total* 1
Sales 6,410,257
SIC 5049 Professional equipment, nec
Fin Ex Joseph Jagdeo

D-U-N-S 25-830-5382   (BR)
DUFFERIN-PEEL CATHOLIC DISTRICT SCHOOL BOARD
JOHN CABOT CATHOLIC SECONDARY
635 Willowbank Trail, Mississauga, ON, L4W 3L6
(905) 279-1554
Emp Here 100
SIC 8211 Elementary and secondary schools

D-U-N-S 25-166-6681   (BR)
DUFFERIN-PEEL CATHOLIC DISTRICT SCHOOL BOARD
ST BASIL SCHOOL
4235 Golden Orchard Dr, Mississauga, ON, L4W 3G1
(905) 624-4529
Emp Here 500
SIC 8211 Elementary and secondary schools

D-U-N-S 24-830-9395   (BR)
ERB TRANSPORT LIMITED
ERB TRANSPORT LIMITED
1889 Britannia Rd E, Mississauga, ON, L4W 1S6
(905) 670-8490
Emp Here 200
SIC 4213 Trucking, except local

D-U-N-S 25-096-2961   (BR)

ECOLAB CO.
5105 Tomken Rd, Mississauga, ON, L4W 2X5
(905) 238-0171
Emp Here 80
SIC 2841 Soap and other detergents

D-U-N-S 24-388-8448   (HQ)
ECOLAB CO.
ECOLAB
5105 Tomken Rd Suite 1, Mississauga, ON, L4W 2X5
(905) 238-0171
Emp Here 60   *Emp Total* 47,565
Sales 476,175,516
SIC 2842 Polishes and sanitation goods
Joseph Ross Rae
VP VP Michael A. Hickey
VP VP Bobby Mendez
VP VP Jill Wayant
Sec Thomas A. Mckee
David F. Duvick
Ching-Meng Chew
David J. Mitchell
Prs Dir Astrid Mitchell
Toni Del Vasto

D-U-N-S 24-827-9676   (BR)
ECOLAB CO.
4905 Timberlea Blvd, Mississauga, ON, L4W 3W4
(905) 238-0171
Emp Here 30
SIC 2842 Polishes and sanitation goods

D-U-N-S 25-462-3549   (SL)
ELITE REALTY T. W. INC
PRUDENTIAL ELITE REALTY
5090 Explorer Dr Unit 100, Mississauga, ON, L4W 4T9
(905) 629-1515
Emp Here 50   *Sales* 4,742,446
SIC 6531 Real estate agents and managers

D-U-N-S 25-167-2721   (BR)
EMERGIS INC
5090 Explorer Dr Suite 1000, Mississauga, ON, L4W 4X6
(905) 602-7350
Emp Here 150
SIC 7372 Prepackaged software

D-U-N-S 24-644-1810   (BR)
ERICSSON CANADA INC
5255 Satellite Dr, Mississauga, ON, L4W 5E3

Emp Here 120
SIC 4899 Communication services, nec

D-U-N-S 24-844-2048   (SL)
F.M.C. INVESTMENT SERVICES LIMITED
5255 Orbitor Dr, Mississauga, ON, L4W 5M6
(905) 629-8000
Emp Here 325   *Sales* 78,273,920
SIC 6712 Bank holding companies
William Waters
Pr Pr Stamos Katotakis

D-U-N-S 24-168-3598   (HQ)
FEDERAL EXPRESS CANADA CORPORATION
FEDEX
(*Suby of* Fedex Corporation)
5985 Explorer Dr Suite 313, Mississauga, ON, L4W 5K6
(800) 463-3339
Emp Here 6,000   *Emp Total* 169,000
Sales 553,260,988
SIC 4212 Local trucking, without storage
Pers/VP Sean Mcnamee
Ch Bd Fred Smith

D-U-N-S 20-413-2732   (HQ)
FEDERATED CUSTOMS BROKERS LIMITED
FEDERATED FREIGHT SERVICES, DIV OF
(*Suby of* Federated Customs Brokers Limited)
2580 Matheson Blvd E, Mississauga, ON, L4W 4J1

(905) 206-1166
Emp Here 60   *Emp Total* 110
Sales 37,479,040
SIC 4731 Freight transportation arrangement
Sr VP Sr VP Cora O Conner
Joanne Oomen
Pr Pr Richard Farrow
VP VP Joel Milgram
Robert Norris
Dir Michael J Glionna
Dir Frank Stockwell
Dir Thomas Fischer

D-U-N-S 24-045-0978   (BR)
FERRARA CANDY CO. LTD
(*Suby of* Ferrara Candy Company)
915 Matheson Blvd E, Mississauga, ON, L4W 2R7

Emp Here 25
SIC 2064 Candy and other confectionery products

D-U-N-S 24-079-7662   (HQ)
FESTO INC
5300 Explorer Dr, Mississauga, ON, L4W 5G4
(905) 624-9000
Emp Here 100   *Emp Total* 17,947
Sales 23,274,463
SIC 5085 Industrial supplies
Pr Roger Hallet
Eberhard Veit
Wilfred Stoll

D-U-N-S 20-790-6905   (BR)
FLYING J CANADA INC
1400 Britannia Rd E, Mississauga, ON, L4W 1C8
(905) 564-6216
Emp Here 40
SIC 5541 Gasoline service stations

D-U-N-S 20-010-0316   (BR)
G.N. JOHNSTON EQUIPMENT CO. LTD
RAYMOND REBUILTS
5958 Ambler Dr, Mississauga, ON, L4W 2N3
(905) 625-9311
Emp Here 40
SIC 5084 Industrial machinery and equipment

D-U-N-S 25-168-7877   (SL)
GENEX SERVICES OF CANADA INC
2800 Skymark Ave Suite 401, Mississauga, ON, L4W 5A6

Emp Here 30   *Sales* 3,486,617
SIC 6411 Insurance agents, brokers, and service

D-U-N-S 24-728-5570   (HQ)
GETINGE CANADA LIMITED
1575 South Gateway Rd Suite C, Mississauga, ON, L4W 5J1
(905) 629-8777
Emp Here 33   *Emp Total* 50
Sales 6,712,384
SIC 5047 Medical and hospital equipment
Robert Bothwell
Douglas Friesen

D-U-N-S 25-094-3958   (SL)
GIVAUDAN CANADA CO
2400 Matheson Blvd E, Mississauga, ON, L4W 5G9
(905) 282-9808
Emp Here 23   *Sales* 3,283,232
SIC 5149 Groceries and related products, nec

D-U-N-S 20-291-4461   (BR)
GOVERNMENT OF ONTARIO
SPECIAL INVESTIGATIONS UNIT
5090 Commerce Blvd Unit 100, Mississauga, ON, L4W 5M4
(416) 622-0748
Emp Here 81
SIC 7381 Detective and armored car services

D-U-N-S 20-315-9850   (BR)
GRANDMOTHER'S TOUCH INC

GRANDMOTHER'S TOUCH
(*Suby of* Grandmother's Touch Inc)
5359 Timberlea Blvd Suite 20, Mississauga,
ON, L4W 4N5
(905) 361-0485
Emp Here 30
SIC 7349 Building maintenance services, nec

D-U-N-S 24-091-6069   (SL)
GRIFOLS CANADA LIMITED
5060 Spectrum Way Suite 405, Mississauga,
ON, L4W 5N5
(905) 614-5575
Emp Here 33   *Sales* 3,939,878
SIC 2836 Biological products, except diagnostic

D-U-N-S 25-659-5968   (BR)
GROUPE EMBALLAGE SPECIALISE S.E.C.
SMITH TORONTO
930 Britannia Rd E Suite A, Mississauga,
L4W 5M7
(905) 564-6640
Emp Here 34
SIC 2449 Wood containers, nec

D-U-N-S 20-115-6960   (BR)
GROUPE EMBALLAGE SPECIALISE S.E.C.
IVEX/TORONTO
930 Britannia Rd Unit J, Mississauga, ON,
L4W 5M7
(905) 795-8887
Emp Here 31
SIC 5113 Industrial and personal service paper

D-U-N-S 24-351-6577   (SL)
HEWLETT-PACKARD FINANCIAL SERVICES CANADA COMPANY
5150 Spectrum Way Suite 101, Mississauga,
ON, L4W 5G1
(905) 206-3627
Emp Here 20   *Sales* 1,459,214
SIC 7377 Computer rental and leasing

D-U-N-S 25-360-2049   (HQ)
HILL-ROM CANADA LTD
BATESVILLE CASKET CANADA, DIV OF
(*Suby of* Hill-Rom Holdings, Inc.)
1705 Tech Ave Unit 3, Mississauga, ON, L4W
0A2
(905) 206-1355
Emp Here 58   *Emp Total* 10,000
Sales 10,214,498
SIC 5047 Medical and hospital equipment
 Wayne Flynn
Pr Peter Soderberg

D-U-N-S 24-848-6557   (BR)
HOLDING BELL MOBILITE INC
HOLDING BELL MOBILITE INC
5099 Creekbank Rd, Mississauga, ON, L4W
5N2
(416) 674-2220
Emp Here 2,000
SIC 5999 Miscellaneous retail stores, nec

D-U-N-S 25-103-7297   (SL)
INFORICA INC
5255 Orbitor Dr Suite 405, Mississauga, ON,
L4W 5M6
(905) 602-0686
Emp Here 87   *Sales* 10,506,341
SIC 7373 Computer integrated systems design
 Mario Correia
Dir Rohan D'souza
Dir Humayun Kabir
Dir Asheet Mathur

D-U-N-S 25-481-5392   (SL)
INNVEST REIT
STAYBRIDGE SUITES
5090 Explorer Dr Suite 700, Mississauga, ON,
L4W 4T9
(905) 629-3400
Emp Here 25   *Sales* 1,094,411
SIC 7011 Hotels and motels

D-U-N-S 24-304-7008   (HQ)
INTROTEL COMMUNICATIONS INC
(*Suby of* Turnpenny, Robert Limited)
5170 Timberlea Blvd Unit B, Mississauga, ON,
L4W 2S5
(905) 625-8700
Emp Here 39   *Emp Total* 40
Sales 5,107,249
SIC 5065 Electronic parts and equipment, nec
 Robert Turnpenny
 Todd Yates
 Stuart Penny
VP VP Frank Domizio
 Carlo Gentile

D-U-N-S 25-503-7012   (BR)
JOHN BROOKS COMPANY LIMITED
ARCITIC INDUSTRAIL SOLUTIONS
1260 Kamato Rd, Mississauga, ON, L4W 1Y1
(905) 624-4200
Emp Here 70
SIC 5084 Industrial machinery and equipment

D-U-N-S 20-022-3936   (BR)
KINDERSLEY TRANSPORT LTD
5355 Creekbank Rd Suite B, Mississauga,
ON, L4W 5L5
(905) 206-1377
Emp Here 20
SIC 4213 Trucking, except local

D-U-N-S 25-960-2543   (BR)
KING MARKETING LTD
1200 Aerowood Dr Unit 45, Mississauga, ON,
L4W 2S7
(905) 624-8804
Emp Here 70
SIC 7311 Advertising agencies

D-U-N-S 24-387-4471   (BR)
KITCHENER AERO AVIONICS LIMITED
MID-CANADA MOD CENTER
(*Suby of* Kitchener Aero Avionics Limited)
6120 Midfield Rd Unit 11, Mississauga, ON,
L4W 2P7
(905) 673-9918
Emp Here 30
SIC 7629 Electrical repair shops

D-U-N-S 20-964-5639   (HQ)
**KONICA MINOLTA BUSINESS SOLUTIONS
(CANADA) LTD**
IT WEAPONS DIV.
5875 Explorer Dr, Mississauga, ON, L4W 0E1
(905) 890-6600
Emp Here 100   *Emp Total* 43,979
Sales 102,582,744
SIC 5044 Office equipment
Pr Chris Dewart
 Richard Taylor

D-U-N-S 20-420-2352   (HQ)
LEDVANCE LTD
SYLVANIA LIGHTING SERVICES
5450 Explorer Dr Suite 100, Mississauga, ON,
L4W 5N1
(905) 361-9327
Emp Here 130   *Sales* 262,658,520
SIC 3641 Electric lamps
Pr John Preville
 Mattias Rosenthal

D-U-N-S 25-412-2674   (HQ)
LINK-LINE CONSTRUCTION LTD
(*Suby of* Link-Line Construction Ltd)
1625 Shawson Dr, Mississauga, ON, L4W 1T7
(905) 696-6929
Emp Here 20   *Emp Total* 350
Sales 84,403,200
SIC 1623 Water, sewer, and utility lines
Pr Pr David Civiero
Pr Pr Rick Delaney
VP Opers Glen Hansen
VP Opers Neil Waugh
 Derek Van Patter
 Michelle Shannon
Fin Ex Patrick Fung

D-U-N-S 25-361-9290   (BR)
LOBLAW COMPANIES LIMITED
NO FRILLS
925 Rathburn Rd E Unit A, Mississauga, ON,
L4W 4C3
(905) 276-6560
Emp Here 96
SIC 5411 Grocery stores

D-U-N-S 24-320-8035   (HQ)
LOWE'S COMPANIES CANADA, ULC
5150 Spectrum Way, Mississauga, ON, L4W
5G2
(905) 219-1000
Emp Here 150   *Emp Total* 290,000
Sales 880,489,728
SIC 5211 Lumber and other building materials
Pr Sylvain Prud'homme

D-U-N-S 25-998-6115   (HQ)
LOXCREEN CANADA LTD
BENGARD MANUFACTURING, DIV OF
(*Suby of* M-D Building Products, Inc.)
5720 Ambler Dr, Mississauga, ON, L4W 2B1
(905) 625-3210
Emp Here 59   *Emp Total* 600
Sales 9,047,127
SIC 3442 Metal doors, sash, and trim
 John W Parrish Jr
Pr Pr Joseph L Comitale
 Charles C Rone Jr
 Ronald B Rhymer

D-U-N-S 25-094-5581   (BR)
LOYALTYONE, CO
LOYALTY GROUP, THE
5055 Satellite Dr Unit 6, Mississauga, ON,
L4W 5K7
(905) 212-6202
Emp Here 200
SIC 8742 Management consulting services

D-U-N-S 20-169-8917   (SL)
MAGNETO ELECTRIC SERVICE CO. LIMITED
1150 Eglinton Ave E, Mississauga, ON, L4W
2M6
(905) 625-9450
Emp Here 50   *Sales* 4,521,816
SIC 7694 Armature rewinding shops

D-U-N-S 25-693-6394   (BR)
MARANELLO MOTORS LIMITED
BMW OF MISSISSAUGA
4505 Dixie Rd, Mississauga, ON, L4W 5K3
(905) 625-7533
Emp Here 80
SIC 5012 Automobiles and other motor vehicles

D-U-N-S 20-536-3245   (HQ)
MARKEM-IMAJE INC
(*Suby of* Dover Corporation)
5448 Timberlea Blvd, Mississauga, ON, L4W
2T7
(905) 624-5872
Emp Here 26   *Emp Total* 29,000
Sales 9,705,989
SIC 5084 Industrial machinery and equipment
Opers Mgr Lionel Ginisty

D-U-N-S 20-285-7843   (HQ)
MATCH DRIVE INC
(*Suby of* Beringer Group Inc)
5225 Satellite Dr, Mississauga, ON, L4W 5P9
(905) 566-2824
Emp Here 20   *Emp Total* 1
Sales 9,703,773
SIC 8742 Management consulting services
Pr Brett Farren
Ch Bd Perry Miele
Sec Andrea Nickel
Dir Bill Kostenko
Dir Michale Sifton

D-U-N-S 24-918-7204   (SL)
**MAYFIELD SUITES GENERAL PARTNER
INC**

STAGEWEST ALL SUITE HOTEL & THEATRE RESTAURANT
5400 Dixie Rd, Mississauga, ON, L4W 4T4
(905) 238-0159
Emp Here 250   *Sales* 10,944,105
SIC 7011 Hotels and motels
Pr Pr Howard Pechet
Fin Ex Marma Gamit

D-U-N-S 20-069-7055   (BR)
MCKAY-COCKER CONSTRUCTION LIMITED
5285 Solar Dr Unit 102, Mississauga, ON,
L4W 5B8
(905) 890-9193
Emp Here 80
SIC 1542 Nonresidential construction, nec

D-U-N-S 25-500-1901   (SL)
METO CANADA INC
5466 Timberlea Blvd Suite 1, Mississauga,
ON, L4W 2T7
(905) 212-9696
Emp Here 60   *Sales* 15,217,500
SIC 5084 Industrial machinery and equipment
Pr Raymond Cockell
VP Fin Robert Long

D-U-N-S 24-335-0563   (BR)
METRO ONTARIO INC
FOOD BASICS
4141 Dixie Rd Unit 2, Mississauga, ON, L4W
1V5
(905) 238-1366
Emp Here 120
SIC 5411 Grocery stores

D-U-N-S 20-059-5788   (SL)
**MITSUBISHI MOTOR SALES OF CANADA,
INC**
2090 Matheson Blvd E, Mississauga, ON,
L4W 5P8
(905) 214-9000
Emp Here 20   *Sales* 4,961,328
SIC 4731 Freight transportation arrangement

D-U-N-S 24-892-6305   (SL)
MIZUNO CANADA LTD
5206 Timberlea Blvd, Mississauga, ON, L4W
2S5
(905) 629-0500
Emp Here 28   *Sales* 4,421,120
SIC 5091 Sporting and recreation goods

D-U-N-S 24-859-1278   (HQ)
MONDELEZ CANADA INC
MONDELEZ INTERNATIONAL
2660 Matheson Blvd E Suite 100, Mississauga, ON, L4W 5M2
(289) 374-4000
Emp Here 3,200   *Emp Total* 3,600
Sales 310,155,936
SIC 2032 Canned specialties
Pr Dan Magliocco
VP Fin Brendan Flynn
VP Sls Craig Murray

D-U-N-S 20-410-6868   (BR)
MONTSHIP INC
(*Suby of* Trealmont Transport Inc)
2700 Matheson Blvd E Suite 400, Mississauga, ON, L4W 4V9
(905) 629-5900
Emp Here 25
SIC 4783 Packing and crating

D-U-N-S 25-318-3867   (BR)
NAV CANADA
TORONTO AREA CONTROL CENTRE
6055 Midfield Rd, Mississauga, ON, L4W 2P7
(905) 676-5045
Emp Here 400
SIC 4899 Communication services, nec

D-U-N-S 20-178-3672   (BR)
NAV CANADA
6110 Midfield Rd, Mississauga, ON, L4W 1S9

(905) 676-7494
Emp Here 25
SIC 4899 Communication services, nec

D-U-N-S 24-050-9265   (HQ)
NYK LINE (CANADA) INC
5090 Explorer Dr Suite 802, Mississauga, ON,
L4W 4T9
(905) 366-3542
Emp Here 20   *Emp Total* 34,276
Sales 14,119,891
SIC 4731 Freight transportation arrangement
Genl Mgr Charles Campbell

D-U-N-S 20-266-6579   (SL)
NATIONAL FIBERS INC
1655 Sismet Rd Unit 8, Mississauga, ON,
L4W 1Z4
(905) 238-6181
Emp Here 2,001   *Sales* 118,525,900
SIC 4213 Trucking, except local
Mgr John Forster

D-U-N-S 20-708-6708   (SL)
**NATIONAL INCOME PROTECTION PLAN
INC**
ONCIDIUM HEALTH GROUP
2595 Skymark Ave Unit 206, Mississauga,
ON, L4W 4L5
(905) 219-0096
Emp Here 144   *Sales* 26,377,000
SIC 8748 Business consulting, nec
VP Derrick Hamilton
Manager Hana Ifrah
Prs Dir Michelle Braga

D-U-N-S 20-917-8164   (SL)
NETSUITE INC
(*Suby of* Oracle Corporation)
5800 Explorer Dr Suite 100, Mississauga,
L4W 5K9
(905) 219-8534
Emp Here 49   *Sales* 4,669,485
SIC 5734 Computer and software stores

D-U-N-S 24-083-5355   (HQ)
NIKON CANADA INC
1366 Aerowood Dr, Mississauga, ON, L4W
1C1
(905) 625-9910
Emp Here 60   *Emp Total* 25,031
Sales 14,008,454
SIC 5043 Photographic equipment and sup-
plies
Pr Pr Michael Finch

D-U-N-S 20-114-3765   (HQ)
NISSAN CANADA INC
5290 Orbitor Dr, Mississauga, ON, L4W 4Z5
(905) 602-0792
Emp Here 250   *Emp Total* 152,421
Sales 404,507,600
SIC 5012 Automobiles and other motor vehi-
cles
Pr Joni Paiva
Marie-Claude Morrissette
Dir Christian Meunier

D-U-N-S 20-191-8104   (BR)
NORDION INC
MDS PHARMA SERVICES
1980 Matheson Blvd E Suite 1, Mississauga,
ON, L4W 5N3
(905) 206-8887
Emp Here 200
SIC 8071 Medical laboratories

D-U-N-S 24-321-4124   (HQ)
NUCLEUS DISTRIBUTION INC
*FORWARD 600 PRECISION TOOLS & MA-
CHINERY*
5220 General Rd, Mississauga, ON, L4W 1G8
(800) 263-4283
Emp Here 20   *Emp Total* 40
Sales 9,423,290
SIC 5084 Industrial machinery and equipment
Philip Jamieson
David Campbell

Pr Pr Robert Jamieson
Henry Becher
Robert Bond
Cathy Rochwerg
Debra Walton-Collings
John Wilby

D-U-N-S 24-801-7253   (SL)
OLD BRITE MAINTENANCE SERVICES LTD
5155 Spectrum Way Suite 34, Mississauga,
ON, L4W 5A1
(905) 602-5108
Emp Here 60   *Sales* 1,751,057
SIC 7349 Building maintenance services, nec

D-U-N-S 24-678-8538   (SL)
OPTIC COMMUNICATIONS CANADA INC
011 COMMUNICATIONS
2425 Matheson Blvd E, Mississauga, ON,
L4W 5K4
(888) 669-6928
Emp Here 100   *Sales* 19,828,320
SIC 4899 Communication services, nec
Dir Joseph T Koppy
Stuart M Bivans

D-U-N-S 20-106-9718   (BR)
PPG CANADA INC
PRC DESOTO INTERNATIONAL
(*Suby of* PPG Industries, Inc.)
5676 Timberlea Blvd, Mississauga, ON, L4W
4M6
(905) 629-7999
Emp Here 24
SIC 3479 Metal coating and allied services

D-U-N-S 20-322-9877   (SL)
PRACS INSTITUTE CANADA B.C. LTD.
CLINICAL DIVISION
4520 Dixie Rd, Mississauga, ON, L4W 1N2

Emp Here 200   *Sales* 22,306,560
SIC 8071 Medical laboratories
Prin Alex Quitazol
COO James Dixon

D-U-N-S 25-322-8803   (HQ)
PAGING NETWORK OF CANADA INC
PAGENET
(*Suby of* Madison Telecommunications Hold-
ings Inc)
1685 Tech Ave Suite 1, Mississauga, ON, L4W
0A7
(905) 614-3100
Emp Here 38   *Emp Total* 3
Sales 19,261,625
SIC 5065 Electronic parts and equipment, nec
Pr Pr Garry Fitzgerald
VP Fin Al Dykstra
VP Sls George Rivers

D-U-N-S 20-543-8414   (BR)
PANASONIC CANADA INC
5810 Ambler Dr Unit 4, Mississauga, ON, L4W
4J5

Emp Here 400
SIC 5065 Electronic parts and equipment, nec

D-U-N-S 20-145-5862   (HQ)
PANASONIC CANADA INC
PANASONIC
5770 Ambler Dr Suite 70, Mississauga, ON,
L4W 2T3
(905) 624-5010
Emp Here 300   *Emp Total* 249,520
Sales 183,642,082
SIC 5064 Electrical appliances, television and
radio
Pr Ian Vatcher
Ken Buschlen

D-U-N-S 24-986-7854   (BR)
PATTISON, JIM INDUSTRIES LTD
PATTISON OUTDOOR
2700 Matheson Blvd E Suite 500, Mississauga, ON, L4W 4V9

(866) 616-4448
Emp Here 100
SIC 7312 Outdoor advertising services

D-U-N-S 24-830-4719   (SL)
PAVILION ROYALE INC
5165 Dixie Rd Suite 4, Mississauga, ON, L4W
4G1
(905) 624-4009
Emp Here 60   *Sales* 1,969,939
SIC 7299 Miscellaneous personal service

D-U-N-S 20-642-0069   (SL)
PEEL TRUCK & TRAILER EQUIPMENT INC
1715 Britannia Rd E, Mississauga, ON, L4W
2A3
(905) 670-1780
Emp Here 68   *Sales* 4,961,328
SIC 7539 Automotive repair shops, nec

D-U-N-S 20-243-0208   (BR)
PENSKE TRUCK LEASING CANADA INC
(*Suby of* Penske Corporation)
1610 Enterprise Rd, Mississauga, ON, L4W
4L4
(905) 564-2176
Emp Here 50
SIC 7513 Truck rental and leasing, no drivers

D-U-N-S 25-989-4921   (HQ)
**PEPSI BOTTLING GROUP (CANADA), ULC,
THE**
PEPSICO BEVERAGES CANADA
5205 Satellite Dr, Mississauga, ON, L4W 5J7
(905) 212-7377
Emp Here 257   *Emp Total* 1
Sales 909,563,550
SIC 2086 Bottled and canned soft drinks
Pr Richard Glover
Sec Mary Manocchio
Corey Michael Baker

D-U-N-S 24-321-4116   (HQ)
PEPSICO CANADA ULC
FRITO LAY CANADA
(*Suby of* Pepsico, Inc.)
5550 Explorer Dr, Mississauga, ON, L4W 0C3
(905) 712-7377
Emp Here 80   *Emp Total* 264,000
SIC 2096 Potato chips and similar snacks

D-U-N-S 24-858-2129   (SL)
PEPSICO FOOD CANADA
5550 Explorer Dr Suite 800, Mississauga, ON,
L4W 0C3
(289) 374-5000
Emp Here 50   *Sales* 4,711,645
SIC 5963 Direct selling establishments

D-U-N-S 24-858-5999   (SL)
PERSPECSYS CORP
(*Suby of* Bain Capital, LP)
5110 Creekbank Rd Suite 500, Mississauga,
ON, L4W 0A1
(905) 282-0023
Emp Here 60   *Sales* 8,386,728
SIC 7371 Custom computer programming ser-
vices
Pr David Canellos
VP Fin Tracy Wainman

D-U-N-S 20-732-9769   (BR)
PFIZER CANADA INC
(*Suby of* Pfizer Inc.)
2400 Skymark Ave Suite 3, Mississauga, ON,
L4W 5L7

Emp Here 30
SIC 8733 Noncommercial research organizations

D-U-N-S 24-675-9026   (BR)
PITNEY BOWES OF CANADA LTD
(*Suby of* Pitney Bowes Inc.)
5500 Explorer Dr Unit 2, Mississauga, ON,
L4W 5C7
(519) 219-3000
Emp Here 200
SIC 5044 Office equipment

D-U-N-S 24-425-0325   (SL)
**PLATINUM HEALTH BENEFITS SOLU-
TIONS INC**
5090 Explorer Dr Suite 501, Mississauga, ON,
L4W 4T9
(905) 602-0404
Emp Here 25   *Sales* 59,681,853
SIC 6324 Hospital and medical service plans
Pr Barbara Mustapha

D-U-N-S 25-883-3797   (HQ)
POPPA CORN CORP
(*Suby of* Super-Pufft Snacks Corp)
5135 Creekbank Rd Unit C, Mississauga, ON,
L4W 1R3
(905) 212-9855
Emp Here 21   *Emp Total* 250
Sales 7,004,227
SIC 5145 Confectionery
Pr Pr Michel Cousineau

D-U-N-S 20-794-1746   (BR)
PREMIER HEALTH CLUBS INC
5100 Dixie Rd, Mississauga, ON, L4W 1C9

Emp Here 45
SIC 7999 Amusement and recreation, nec

D-U-N-S 24-860-9922   (BR)
PURE TECHNOLOGIES LTD
5055 Satellite Dr Unit 7, Mississauga, ON,
L4W 5K7
(905) 624-1040
Emp Here 45
SIC 4899 Communication services, nec

D-U-N-S 24-363-0741   (HQ)
RGIS CANADA ULC
2560 Matheson Blvd E Suite 224, Missis-
sauga, ON, L4W 4Y9
(905) 206-1107
Emp Here 100   *Emp Total* 2,243
Sales 128,491,440
SIC 7389 Business services, nec
Pr Nick Ford
Dir Holly Tomilson

D-U-N-S 20-702-4469   (BR)
RAYNOR CANADA CORP
5100 Timberlea Blvd Suite A, Mississauga,
ON, L4W 2S5
(905) 625-0037
Emp Here 170
SIC 3442 Metal doors, sash, and trim

D-U-N-S 24-645-5281   (HQ)
RAYNOR CANADA CORP
RICHARDS-WILCOX CANADA
5100 Timberlea Blvd Suite A, Mississauga,
ON, L4W 2S5
(905) 625-0037
Emp Here 125   *Emp Total* 1,800
Sales 24,774,779
SIC 3442 Metal doors, sash, and trim
Pr Pr Raymond Friesen
VP Sls Randolph Hiebert
VP Fin Edward Chin
Jon Keesey

D-U-N-S 25-366-7349   (BR)
READY STAFFING SOLUTIONS INC
5170 Dixie Rd Suite 202, Mississauga, ON,
L4W 1E3
(905) 625-4009
Emp Here 200
SIC 7361 Employment agencies

D-U-N-S 25-300-5037   (BR)
REDBERRY FRANCHISING CORP
BURGER KING
4141 Dixie Rd Unit 228, Mississauga, ON,
L4W 1V5
(905) 624-1664
Emp Here 40
SIC 5812 Eating places

D-U-N-S 25-272-6997   (BR)
REIMER EXPRESS LINES LTD

FAST AS FLIGHT
(*Suby of* Yrc Worldwide Inc.)
5919 Shawson Dr, Mississauga, ON, L4W 3Y2
(905) 670-9366
Emp Here 300
SIC 4213 Trucking, except local

D-U-N-S 24-345-7178   (BR)
REVERA INC
1500 Rathburn Rd E, Mississauga, ON, L4W 4L7
(905) 238-0800
Emp Here 200
SIC 6513 Apartment building operators

D-U-N-S 20-920-1891   (BR)
REVERA INC
1130 Bough Beeches Blvd, Mississauga, ON, L4W 4G3
(905) 625-2022
Emp Here 67
SIC 8361 Residential care

D-U-N-S 24-451-1143   (SL)
RICHEMONT CANADA, INC
4610 Eastgate Pky Unit 1, Mississauga, ON, L4W 3W6
(905) 602-8532
Emp Here 30   *Sales* 3,898,130
SIC 5094 Jewelry and precious stones

D-U-N-S 24-214-0135   (HQ)
RICOH CANADA INC
5560 Explorer Dr Suite 100, Mississauga, ON, L4W 5M3
(905) 795-9659
Emp Here 200   *Emp Total* 108,104
Sales 287,319,237
SIC 5044 Office equipment
Pr Pr Glenn Laverty
VP Scott Fitzgerald
  Eric Fletcher
  Martin Brodigan
Dir Dan Newman

D-U-N-S 24-079-3364   (SL)
S.D.R. DISTRIBUTION SERVICES
COLD STORAGE
1880 Matheson Blvd E, Mississauga, ON, L4W 5N4
(905) 625-7377
Emp Here 45   *Sales* 6,493,502
SIC 5137 Women's and children's clothing
Pr Pr Steve Resnick

D-U-N-S 25-153-6199   (BR)
SCM INSURANCE SERVICES INC
S C M CANADA
1550 Enterprise Rd Suite 125, Mississauga, ON, L4W 4P4
(905) 564-0654
Emp Here 30
SIC 6411 Insurance agents, brokers, and service

D-U-N-S 25-598-3694   (HQ)
SCHAWK CANADA INC
SCHAWK TRISTAR, DIV OF
(*Suby of* Matthews International Corporation)
1620 Tech Ave Suite 3, Mississauga, ON, L4W 5P4
(905) 219-1600
Emp Here 160   *Emp Total* 10,300
Sales 18,846,580
SIC 7336 Commercial art and graphic design
Pr Pr Robert Cockerill

D-U-N-S 24-153-4721   (SL)
SECAP INC
5500 Explorer Dr, Mississauga, ON, L4W 5C7
(905) 219-3000
Emp Here 30   *Sales* 1,459,214
SIC 3579 Office machines, nec

D-U-N-S 24-964-0145   (HQ)
SHOPPERS DRUG MART SPECIALTY HEALTH NETWORK INC
INFO HEALTH

1685 Tech Ave Suite 1, Mississauga, ON, L4W 0A7
(905) 212-3800
Emp Here 25   *Emp Total* 138,000
Sales 11,779,113
SIC 7363 Help supply services
Pr John Cieslowski

D-U-N-S 24-348-5807   (BR)
SOBEYS CAPITAL INCORPORATED
1680 Tech Ave Unit 1, Mississauga, ON, L4W 5S9

Emp Here 200
SIC 5411 Grocery stores

D-U-N-S 25-101-0914   (SL)
STAHLSCHMIDT LTD
STAHLSCHMIDT CABLE SYSTEMS
5208 Everest Dr, Mississauga, ON, L4W 2R4
(905) 629-4568
Emp Here 80   *Sales* 5,690,935
SIC 3465 Automotive stampings
Pr Pr George Jaeggi

D-U-N-S 20-796-7279   (BR)
STAPLES CANADA INC
STAPLES THE BUSINESS DEPOT
(*Suby of* Staples, Inc.)
1530 Aimco Blvd, Mississauga, ON, L4W 5K1
(905) 602-5889
Emp Here 20
SIC 5943 Stationery stores

D-U-N-S 24-200-8196   (BR)
STAPLES CANADA INC
STAPLES
(*Suby of* Staples, Inc.)
5170 Dixie Rd, Mississauga, ON, L4W 1E3
(905) 602-6056
Emp Here 20
SIC 5943 Stationery stores

D-U-N-S 20-145-8031   (SL)
STARRETT, L. S. CO. OF CANADA LIMITED, THE
1244 Kamato Rd, Mississauga, ON, L4W 1Y1
(905) 624-2750
Emp Here 25   *Sales* 2,407,703
SIC 5251 Hardware stores

D-U-N-S 20-288-5620   (HQ)
STERICYCLE COMMUNICATION SOLUTIONS, ULC
(*Suby of* Stericycle Communication Solutions, ULC)
2800 Skymark Ave Suite 308, Mississauga, ON, L4W 5A6
(905) 629-7190
Emp Here 20   *Emp Total* 500
Sales 2,848,319
SIC 4899 Communication services, nec

D-U-N-S 24-561-4297   (SL)
SUNGARD SHERWOOD SYSTEMS (CANADA) INC
(*Suby of* Fidelity National Information Services, Inc.)
5225 Satellite Dr, Mississauga, ON, L4W 5P9
(905) 275-2299
Emp Here 49   *Sales* 4,888,367
SIC 7372 Prepackaged software

D-U-N-S 25-709-6982   (BR)
SUPREMEX INC
(*Suby of* Supremex Inc)
5300 Tomken Rd, Mississauga, ON, L4W 1P2
(905) 624-4973
Emp Here 150
SIC 2677 Envelopes

D-U-N-S 20-112-9173   (BR)
SYMCOR INC
1625 Tech Ave, Mississauga, ON, L4W 5P5
(289) 360-2000
Emp Here 400
SIC 2752 Commercial printing, lithographic

D-U-N-S 20-705-0634   (HQ)
TST SOLUTIONS L.P.
TST AUTOMOTIVE SERVICES, DIV OF
5200 Maingate Dr, Mississauga, ON, L4W 1G5
(905) 625-7601
Emp Here 80   *Emp Total* 25,438
Sales 200,641,925
SIC 4213 Trucking, except local
Dir Alain Bedard
Pr Robert O'reilly

D-U-N-S 20-788-0779   (BR)
TST SOLUTIONS L.P.
5200 Maingate Dr, Mississauga, ON, L4W 1G5
(905) 624-7058
Emp Here 250
SIC 4731 Freight transportation arrangement

D-U-N-S 25-306-0917   (BR)
TST SOLUTIONS L.P.
TST OVERLAND EXPRESS
5200 Maingate Dr, Mississauga, ON, L4W 1G5
(905) 625-7500
Emp Here 200
SIC 4111 Local and suburban transit

D-U-N-S 25-369-0457   (SL)
TEARLAB CORPORATION
5090 Explorer Dr Suite 203, Mississauga, ON, L4W 4T9
(905) 636-0128
Emp Here 48   *Sales* 14,645,000
SIC 5048 Ophthalmic goods
  Elias Vamvakas
  William (Bill) Dumencu
  Thomas N. Davidson
  Richard Lindstrom
  Gilbert Omenn
  Adrienne Graves

D-U-N-S 24-386-7934   (BR)
TENAQUIP LIMITEE
1110 Kamato Rd Unit 18, Mississauga, ON, L4W 2P3
(905) 890-2270
Emp Here 40
SIC 5084 Industrial machinery and equipment

D-U-N-S 24-744-3765   (SL)
TERDUN MATERIAL MANAGEMENT INC
5130 Creekbank Rd, Mississauga, ON, L4W 2G2
(905) 602-4567
Emp Here 50   *Sales* 3,064,349
SIC 2675 Die-cut paper and board

D-U-N-S 25-120-2271   (BR)
TORONTO-DOMINION BANK, THE
TD CANADA TRUST
(*Suby of* Toronto-Dominion Bank, The)
925 Rathburn Rd E, Mississauga, ON, L4W 4C3
(905) 848-3390
Emp Here 20
SIC 6021 National commercial banks

D-U-N-S 25-111-9798   (SL)
TRANS-SEND FREIGHT SYSTEMS LTD
(*Suby of* 1790089 Ontario Inc)
1905 Shawson Dr, Mississauga, ON, L4W 1T9
(905) 795-0303
Emp Here 65   *Sales* 11,159,500
SIC 4213 Trucking, except local
Pr Lisa Carwardine

D-U-N-S 24-389-5989   (BR)
TRANSPORT TFI 2, S.E.C.
TRANS4 LOGISTICS
5425 Dixie Rd Suite 101, Mississauga, ON, L4W 1E6

Emp Here 31
SIC 4213 Trucking, except local

D-U-N-S 25-361-5686   (BR)
TRANSPORT TFI 5, S.E.C.

KINGSWAY TRANSPORT
1100 Haultain Crt, Mississauga, ON, L4W 2T1
(905) 624-4050
Emp Here 150
SIC 4213 Trucking, except local

D-U-N-S 24-660-2130   (BR)
TRANSPORT TFI 7 S.E.C.
UTL TRANSPORTATION SERVICES
5425 Dixie Rd, Mississauga, ON, L4W 1E6
(905) 238-6855
Emp Here 50
SIC 4212 Local trucking, without storage

D-U-N-S 20-178-2302   (HQ)
TRAVELBRANDS INC
EXOTIK TOURS
5450 Explorer Dr Suite 300, Mississauga, ON, L4W 5N1
(416) 649-3939
Emp Here 400   *Emp Total* 60
Sales 214,577,419
SIC 4725 Tour operators
Pr Pr Frank Demarinis
  Tony Saunders

D-U-N-S 25-372-4496   (BR)
TRIANGLE FREIGHT SERVICES LTD
CREEKBANK TRANSPORT, DIV OF
(*Suby of* EKS Holdings Ltd)
5355 Creekbank Rd, Mississauga, ON, L4W 5L5
(905) 624-1614
Emp Here 150
SIC 4212 Local trucking, without storage

D-U-N-S 20-150-8892   (HQ)
TYCO INTEGRATED FIRE & SECURITY CANADA, INC
(*Suby of* Johnson Controls, Inc.)
2400 Skymark Ave Suite 1, Mississauga, ON, L4W 5K5
(905) 212-4400
Emp Here 200   *Emp Total* 139,000
SIC 1731 Electrical work

D-U-N-S 25-367-3511   (HQ)
UTC FIRE & SECURITY CANADA INC
CHUBB EDWARDS SECURITY
(*Suby of* United Technologies Corporation)
5201 Explorer Dr, Mississauga, ON, L4W 4H1
(905) 629-2600
Emp Here 100   *Emp Total* 202,000
Sales 114,548,299
SIC 3669 Communications equipment, nec
VP VP Tiina Zeggil
  Mia Lalonde
  Mohit Narang

D-U-N-S 25-635-8177   (BR)
UTI, CANADA, INC
2540 Matheson Blvd E, Mississauga, ON, L4W 4Z2

Emp Here 90
SIC 4731 Freight transportation arrangement

D-U-N-S 20-732-5986   (HQ)
UNIFIRST CANADA LTD
(*Suby of* Unifirst Corporation)
5250 Orbitor Dr, Mississauga, ON, L4W 5G7
(905) 624-8525
Emp Here 40   *Emp Total* 12,700
Sales 108,541,250
SIC 7213 Linen supply
Pr Pr Ronald Croatti
  Mike Szymanski
Sec Tim Sullivan

D-U-N-S 20-181-7459   (HQ)
VALSPAR INC
PLASTI-KOTE, DIV OF
(*Suby of* The Sherwin-Williams Company)
1636 Shawson Dr, Mississauga, ON, L4W 1N7
(905) 671-8333
Emp Here 100   *Emp Total* 42,550
Sales 39,067,920

SIC 2851 Paints and allied products
Pr Gary Hendricks
Gus Amodeo

D-U-N-S 24-587-2726 (HQ)
VOLUME TANK TRANSPORT INC
1230 Shawson Dr, Mississauga, ON, L4W 1C3
(905) 670-7090
Emp Here 45   Emp Total 2
Sales 5,472,053
SIC 4212 Local trucking, without storage
Pr Pr Peter Balan
Robert Chafee

D-U-N-S 25-338-2014 (BR)
WFS LTD
(Suby of W.W. Grainger, Inc.)
1280 Aimco Blvd, Mississauga, ON, L4W 1B2
(905) 624-9546
Emp Here 20
SIC 5085 Industrial supplies

D-U-N-S 20-153-9074 (BR)
WENDY'S RESTAURANTS OF CANADA INC
WENDY'S
(Suby of The Wendy's Company)
1520 Aimco Blvd, Mississauga, ON, L4W 5K1
(905) 624-0453
Emp Here 32
SIC 5812 Eating places

D-U-N-S 24-394-4100 (SL)
WESKO LOCKS LTD
4570 Eastgate Pky, Mississauga, ON, L4W 3W6
(905) 629-3227
Emp Here 80   Sales 4,888,367
SIC 7699 Repair services, nec

D-U-N-S 20-099-9014 (BR)
WILSON, J. A. DISPLAY LTD
FIBER COATERS
1630 Matheson Blvd, Mississauga, ON, L4W 1Y4
(905) 624-1503
Emp Here 22
SIC 3312 Blast furnaces and steel mills

D-U-N-S 25-369-8260 (BR)
WILSON, J. A. DISPLAY LTD
1610 Sismet Rd, Mississauga, ON, L4W 1R4
(905) 625-6778
Emp Here 150
SIC 2542 Partitions and fixtures, except wood

D-U-N-S 20-184-3260 (BR)
WINNERS MERCHANTS INTERNATIONAL L.P.
HOMESENSE
(Suby of The TJX Companies Inc)
4141 Dixie Rd, Mississauga, ON, L4W 1V5
(905) 602-1742
Emp Here 40
SIC 5651 Family clothing stores

D-U-N-S 25-939-3296 (BR)
WINNERS MERCHANTS INTERNATIONAL L.P.
WINNERS
(Suby of The TJX Companies Inc)
4141 Dixie Rd Unit A2, Mississauga, ON, L4W 1V5
(905) 602-0941
Emp Here 40
SIC 5651 Family clothing stores

D-U-N-S 25-370-6527 (BR)
WOLSELEY CANADA INC
FRONTIER, DIV OF
(Suby of WOLSELEY PLC)
5235 Timberlea Blvd, Mississauga, ON, L4W 2S3
(905) 602-0223
Emp Here 25
SIC 5078 Refrigeration equipment and supplies

D-U-N-S 24-364-9923 (BR)

WORLEYPARSONS CANADA SERVICES LTD
2645 Skymark Ave, Mississauga, ON, L4W 4H2
(905) 614-1778
Emp Here 270
SIC 8711 Engineering services

Mississauga, ON L4X
Peel County

D-U-N-S 24-209-2666 (SL)
934571 ONTARIO LIMITED
MUDDY DUCK RESTAURANT
2200 Dundas St E Unit 1, Mississauga, ON, L4X 2V3
(905) 275-9430
Emp Here 55   Sales 1,678,096
SIC 5812 Eating places

D-U-N-S 20-936-4256 (HQ)
ABS EQUIPMENT LEASING LTD
(Suby of ABS Equipment Leasing Ltd)
1495 Sedlescomb Dr, Mississauga, ON, L4X 1M4
(905) 625-5941
Emp Here 120   Emp Total 220
Sales 28,586,283
SIC 3545 Machine tool accessories
Pr Pr Anthony Bosco

D-U-N-S 20-527-8505 (SL)
ABS MACHINING INC
(Suby of ABS Equipment Leasing Ltd)
1495 Sedlescomb Dr, Mississauga, ON, L4X 1M4
(905) 625-5941
Emp Here 20   Sales 10,395,012
SIC 3599 Industrial machinery, nec
Pr Pr Anthony Bosco

D-U-N-S 20-303-9839 (BR)
BRAND FELT OF CANADA LIMITED
(Suby of Brand Felt Of Canada Limited)
2559 Wharton Glen Ave, Mississauga, ON, L4X 2A8
(905) 279-6680
Emp Here 50
SIC 2231 Broadwoven fabric mills, wool

D-U-N-S 20-042-3622 (HQ)
BRAND FELT OF CANADA LIMITED
(Suby of Brand Felt Of Canada Limited)
2559 Wharton Glen Ave, Mississauga, ON, L4X 2A8
(905) 272-3350
Emp Here 25   Emp Total 85
SIC 2231 Broadwoven fabric mills, wool

D-U-N-S 24-488-1587 (BR)
BRICK WAREHOUSE LP, THE
THE BRICK
1607 Dundas St E, Mississauga, ON, L4X 1L5
(905) 629-2900
Emp Here 150
SIC 5712 Furniture stores

D-U-N-S 25-751-9884 (HQ)
CANADIAN EMPLOYMENT CONTRACTORS INC
(Suby of Canadian Employment Contractors Inc)
2077 Dundas St E Suite 101, Mississauga, ON, L4X 1M2
(905) 282-9578
Emp Here 200   Emp Total 400
Sales 37,693,160
SIC 7361 Employment agencies
Pr Pr Gerrie Schummer

D-U-N-S 20-754-0097 (HQ)
DAVIES AUTO ELECTRIC LIMITED
(Suby of Davies Auto Electric Limited)
2571 Wharton Glen Ave, Mississauga, ON, L4X 2A8

(905) 279-6300
Emp Here 25   Emp Total 40
Sales 14,592,140
SIC 5511 New and used car dealers
Pr Pr Andrew Davies
Chris Davies
Greta Davies

D-U-N-S 25-265-3159 (BR)
DUFFERIN-PEEL CATHOLIC DISTRICT SCHOOL BOARD
ST. ALFRED SCHOOL
3341 Havenwood Dr, Mississauga, ON, L4X 2M2
(905) 625-0584
Emp Here 50
SIC 8211 Elementary and secondary schools

D-U-N-S 20-710-9831 (BR)
DUFFERIN-PEEL CATHOLIC DISTRICT SCHOOL BOARD
ST. SOFIA BYZANTINE CATHOLIC SCHOOL
3540 Havenwood Dr, Mississauga, ON, L4X 2M9
(905) 625-0823
Emp Here 55
SIC 8211 Elementary and secondary schools

D-U-N-S 24-323-6143 (BR)
DYNAMIC TIRE CORP
3161 Wharton Way, Mississauga, ON, L4X 2B7
(905) 625-1600
Emp Here 40
SIC 5014 Tires and tubes

D-U-N-S 24-027-3250 (HQ)
ERIE MEAT PRODUCTS LIMITED
(Suby of 508818 Ontario Limited)
3240 Wharton Way, Mississauga, ON, L4X 2C1
(905) 624-3811
Emp Here 100   Emp Total 200
Sales 27,633,407
SIC 2011 Meat packing plants
Pr Pr Simon Rosen
Genl Mgr Syd Rosen

D-U-N-S 25-295-2825 (BR)
FEDERAL EXPRESS CANADA CORPORATION
FEDERAL EXPRESS CANADA LTD
(Suby of Fedex Corporation)
1450 Caterpillar Rd, Mississauga, ON, L4X 2Y1
(800) 463-3339
Emp Here 200
SIC 7389 Business services, nec

D-U-N-S 24-919-0323 (SL)
GOLDEN MAPLE MEAT PRODUCTS LTD
(Suby of 508818 Ontario Limited)
3180 Wharton Way, Mississauga, ON, L4X 2C1
(905) 624-3811
Emp Here 20   Sales 4,900,111
SIC 2015 Poultry slaughtering and processing

D-U-N-S 25-363-9975 (HQ)
INTEGRATED DISTRIBUTION SYSTEMS LIMITED PARTNERSHIP
EQUIPEMENT WAJAX
(Suby of Integrated Distribution Systems Limited Partnership)
3280 Wharton Way, Mississauga, ON, L4X 2C5
(905) 212-3300
Emp Here 50   Emp Total 1,500
Sales 273,602,625
SIC 5084 Industrial machinery and equipment
Genl Mgr Mark Foote

D-U-N-S 20-321-6809 (BR)
INTEGRATED DISTRIBUTION SYSTEMS LIMITED PARTNERSHIP
WAJAX EQUIPMENT
1865 Sharlyn Rd, Mississauga, ON, L4X 2C5
(905) 624-5611
Emp Here 100

SIC 5082 Construction and mining machinery

D-U-N-S 24-057-2276 (SL)
LK PROTECTION INC
1590 Dundas St E Suite 220, Mississauga, ON, L4X 2Z2
(905) 566-7008
Emp Here 121   Sales 4,504,505
SIC 7381 Detective and armored car services

D-U-N-S 24-418-5872 (BR)
MOORES THE SUIT PEOPLE INC
MOORES CLOTHING FOR MEN
(Suby of Tailored Brands, Inc.)
2150 Dundas St E, Mississauga, ON, L4X 1L9
(905) 276-6666
Emp Here 28
SIC 5611 Men's and boys' clothing stores

D-U-N-S 25-819-3515 (BR)
MOTION SPECIALTIES INCORPORATED
MOTION SPECIALTIES MISSISSAUGA
2130 Dundas St E, Mississauga, ON, L4X 1L9
(905) 795-0400
Emp Here 20
SIC 5047 Medical and hospital equipment

D-U-N-S 24-977-6964 (BR)
OTIS CANADA, INC
(Suby of United Technologies Corporation)
1655 Queensway E Suite 4, Mississauga, ON, L4X 2Z5
(905) 276-5577
Emp Here 30
SIC 7699 Repair services, nec

D-U-N-S 25-293-7719 (BR)
PEEL DISTRICT SCHOOL BOARD
FOREST GLEN PUBLIC SCHOOL
(Suby of Peel District School Board)
3400 Ponytrail Dr, Mississauga, ON, L4X 1V5
(905) 625-1462
Emp Here 35
SIC 8211 Elementary and secondary schools

D-U-N-S 25-263-7640 (BR)
PEEL DISTRICT SCHOOL BOARD
GLENFOREST SECONDARY SCHOOL
(Suby of Peel District School Board)
3575 Fieldgate Dr, Mississauga, ON, L4X 2J6
(905) 625-7731
Emp Here 88
SIC 8211 Elementary and secondary schools

D-U-N-S 25-293-7644 (BR)
PEEL DISTRICT SCHOOL BOARD
BRIAN W. FLEMING PUBLIC SCHOOL
(Suby of Peel District School Board)
3255 Havenwood Dr, Mississauga, ON, L4X 2M2
(905) 625-3220
Emp Here 70
SIC 8211 Elementary and secondary schools

D-U-N-S 25-137-3254 (BR)
PEEL DISTRICT SCHOOL BOARD
GLENHAVEN SENIOR PUBLIC SCHOOL
(Suby of Peel District School Board)
3570 Havenwood Dr, Mississauga, ON, L4X 2M9
(905) 625-5250
Emp Here 45
SIC 8211 Elementary and secondary schools

D-U-N-S 25-372-4074 (BR)
SHERIDAN NURSERIES LIMITED
2069 Burnhamthorpe Rd E, Mississauga, ON, L4X 2S7
(905) 624-3722
Emp Here 40
SIC 5261 Retail nurseries and garden stores

D-U-N-S 20-793-0947 (BR)
STAPLES CANADA INC
STAPLES THE BUSINESS DEPOT
(Suby of Staples, Inc.)
2040 Dundas St E Unit 1, Mississauga, ON, L4X 2X8

(905) 279-4392
Emp Here 30
SIC 5943 Stationery stores

D-U-N-S 24-336-7310   (BR)
STRONCO DESIGNS INC
CE 3
(*Suby of* Sunshine Mountain Investments Inc)
1510b Caterpillar Rd Unit B, Mississauga, ON,
L4X 2W9
(905) 270-6767
Emp Here 175
SIC 7389 Business services, nec

D-U-N-S 20-647-1344   (HQ)
UNIROPE LIMITED
3070 Universal Dr, Mississauga, ON, L4X 2C8
(905) 624-5131
Emp Here 55   *Emp Total* 1,400
Sales 7,077,188
SIC 5251 Hardware stores
Pr Pr Knut Buschmann
  Thomas Critelli

D-U-N-S 25-122-8417   (BR)
WENDY'S RESTAURANTS OF CANADA INC
WENDY'S
(*Suby of* The Wendy's Company)
1739 Dundas St E, Mississauga, ON, L4X 1L5

Emp Here 20
SIC 5812 Eating places

Mississauga, ON L4Y
Peel County

D-U-N-S 25-750-9380   (BR)
AQUARIUM SERVICES WAREHOUSE OUT-LETS INC
BIG AL AQUARIUM SERVICE WAREHOUSE
850 Dundas St E, Mississauga, ON, L4Y 2B8
(905) 276-6900
Emp Here 35
SIC 5421 Meat and fish markets

D-U-N-S 20-042-3283   (HQ)
ASTRAZENECA CANADA INC
(*Suby of* ASTRAZENECA PLC)
1004 Middlegate Rd Suite 5000, Mississauga,
ON, L4Y 1M4
(905) 277-7111
Emp Here 800   *Emp Total* 61,700
Sales 172,557,199
SIC 2834 Pharmaceutical preparations
Pr Elaine Campbell
VP Karen A. Burke
CEO Marion Mccourt
Pers/VP Laura Mably
VP Sls Mario Tremblay

D-U-N-S 25-003-5599   (BR)
BANK OF MONTREAL
BMO
985 Dundas St E, Mississauga, ON, L4Y 2B9
(905) 279-6530
Emp Here 26
SIC 6021 National commercial banks

D-U-N-S 25-122-9969   (BR)
BURGESS, JOHN WILLIAM ENTERPRISES INC
TIM HORTONS
1327 Dundas St E, Mississauga, ON, L4Y 2C7
(905) 275-6867
Emp Here 65
SIC 5812 Eating places

D-U-N-S 20-580-1637   (BR)
CANADA POST CORPORATION
1310 Dundas St E, Mississauga, ON, L4Y 2C1
(905) 279-5892
Emp Here 20
SIC 4311 U.s. postal service

D-U-N-S 25-799-5803   (BR)

CARDINAL MEAT SPECIALISTS LIMITED
CARDINAL MEAT
(*Suby of* Cardinal Meat Specialists Limited)
2396 Stanfield Rd, Mississauga, ON, L4Y 1S1
(905) 279-1734
Emp Here 35
SIC 2013 Sausages and other prepared meats

D-U-N-S 20-260-9749   (SL)
DAHNAY LOGISTICS CANADA LTD
2501 Stanfield Rd Fl 2, Mississauga, ON, L4Y
1R6
(289) 803-1982
Emp Here 25   *Sales* 6,879,002
SIC 4731 Freight transportation arrangement
Dir David Lyman

D-U-N-S 25-265-3548   (BR)
DUFFERIN-PEEL CATHOLIC DISTRICT SCHOOL BOARD
ST THOMAS MORE ELEMENTARY SCHOOL
3270 Tomken Rd, Mississauga, ON, L4Y 2Y7
(905) 279-6472
Emp Here 55
SIC 8211 Elementary and secondary schools

D-U-N-S 20-260-9079   (SL)
EVERYTHING PRODUCE LTD
FRESHLINE FOODS
2501 Stanfield Rd Unit 4, Mississauga, ON,
L4Y 1R6
(905) 615-9400
Emp Here 100   *Sales* 31,285,323
SIC 5148 Fresh fruits and vegetables
Pr James Bamford
Genl Mgr Stephen Bamford

D-U-N-S 24-684-5663   (HQ)
GARDA CANADA SECURITY CORPORA-TION
GARDA
(*Suby of* GW Intermediate Holdco Corpora-tion)
2345 Stanfield Rd Unit 400, Mississauga, ON,
L4Y 3Y3
(416) 915-9500
Emp Here 20   *Emp Total* 1
Sales 39,763,582
SIC 7349 Building maintenance services, nec
Ch Bd Stephan Cretier
Sec Pierre-Hubert Seguin

D-U-N-S 25-122-2154   (BR)
HSBC BANK CANADA
888 Dundas St E, Mississauga, ON, L4Y 4G6
(905) 277-5300
Emp Here 22
SIC 6021 National commercial banks

D-U-N-S 24-858-3366   (SL)
KAO TIRE CENTRE
2403 Stanfield Rd, Mississauga, ON, L4Y 1R6
(905) 848-3500
Emp Here 45   *Sales* 7,608,750
SIC 5531 Auto and home supply stores
Dir Rhon Perce

D-U-N-S 25-799-2727   (SL)
KINGDOM COVENANT MINISTRIES INTER-NATIONAL
1224 Dundas St E Unit 20, Mississauga, ON,
L4Y 4A2
(905) 566-1084
Emp Here 50   *Sales* 3,283,232
SIC 8661 Religious organizations

D-U-N-S 20-646-4559   (BR)
LIQUOR CONTROL BOARD OF ONTARIO, THE
LCBO
2460 Stanfield Rd Suite 941, Mississauga,
ON, L4Y 1S2
(905) 949-3522
Emp Here 40
SIC 5921 Liquor stores

D-U-N-S 25-137-9160   (BR)

LOBLAWS SUPERMARKETS LIMITED
APPLEWOOD VALUMART
1125 Bloor St, Mississauga, ON, L4Y 2N6
(905) 279-1353
Emp Here 60
SIC 5411 Grocery stores

D-U-N-S 25-236-5143   (BR)
MARK'S WORK WEARHOUSE LTD
WORK WORLD
1180 Dundas St E, Mississauga, ON, L4Y 2C1
(905) 275-6760
Emp Here 22
SIC 5651 Family clothing stores

D-U-N-S 20-294-5333   (BR)
MOTHER PARKER'S TEA & COFFEE INC
2530 Stanfield Rd, Mississauga, ON, L4Y 1S4
(905) 279-9100
Emp Here 145
SIC 2095 Roasted coffee

D-U-N-S 25-293-8030   (BR)
PEEL DISTRICT SCHOOL BOARD
DIXIE PUBLIC SCHOOL
(*Suby of* Peel District School Board)
1120 Flagship Dr, Mississauga, ON, L4Y 2K1
(905) 277-9505
Emp Here 35
SIC 8211 Elementary and secondary schools

D-U-N-S 25-265-2862   (BR)
PEEL DISTRICT SCHOOL BOARD
BURNHAMTHORPE ELEMENTARY SCHOOL
(*Suby of* Peel District School Board)
3465 Golden Orchard Dr, Mississauga, ON,
L4Y 3H7
(905) 625-0140
Emp Here 50
SIC 8211 Elementary and secondary schools

D-U-N-S 25-857-7147   (SL)
PETTOS MAINTENANCE SERVICE LTD
1090 Dundas St E Suite A, Mississauga, ON,
L4Y 2B8
(905) 275-9846
Emp Here 60   *Sales* 1,751,057
SIC 7349 Building maintenance services, nec

D-U-N-S 20-181-4006   (BR)
ROYAL BANK OF CANADA
RBC
(*Suby of* Royal Bank Of Canada)
1125 Bloor St E, Mississauga, ON, L4Y 2N6
(905) 897-8160
Emp Here 25
SIC 6021 National commercial banks

D-U-N-S 24-736-2101   (BR)
SCI GROUP INC
SCI LOGISTICS
2470 Stanfield Rd Unit A, Mississauga, ON,
L4Y 1S2
(416) 571-1410
Emp Here 30
SIC 4213 Trucking, except local

D-U-N-S 25-402-9564   (BR)
SAMUEL, SON & CO., LIMITED
SAMUEL STRAPPING SYSTEMS
2370 Dixie Rd Suite 124, Mississauga, ON,
L4Y 1Z4
(905) 279-9580
Emp Here 50
SIC 5051 Metals service centers and offices

D-U-N-S 20-074-7025   (BR)
SUNRISE NORTH ASSISTED LIVING LTD
SUNRISE SENIOR LIVING OF MISSIS-SAUGA
(*Suby of* Welltower Inc.)
1279 Burnhamthorpe Rd E Suite 220, Missis-sauga, ON, L4Y 3V7
(905) 625-1344
Emp Here 75
SIC 8361 Residential care

D-U-N-S 25-806-8592   (BR)
VALUE VILLAGE STORES, INC
(*Suby of* Savers, Inc.)
3130 Dixie Rd, Mississauga, ON, L4Y 2A6
(905) 949-4440
Emp Here 35
SIC 5399 Miscellaneous general merchandise

Mississauga, ON L4Z
Peel County

D-U-N-S 20-057-6101   (SL)
1335270 ONTARIO LTD
MANDARIN RESTAURANT
87 Matheson Blvd E, Mississauga, ON, L4Z
2Y5
(905) 502-8000
Emp Here 80   *Sales* 2,407,703
SIC 5812 Eating places

D-U-N-S 20-192-8178   (HQ)
2010282 ONTARIO INC
(*Suby of* 2010282 Ontario Inc)
5749 Coopers Ave, Mississauga, ON, L4Z
1R9

Emp Here 121   *Emp Total* 360
Sales 68,929,280
SIC 8748 Business consulting, nec
Pr Pr Donald Pinchin

D-U-N-S 25-249-5445   (BR)
A & A CONTRACT CUSTOMS BROKERS LTD
MAERSK LOGISTISCS
160 Traders Blvd E Suite 2 5, Mississauga,
ON, L4Z 3K7
(905) 507-8300
Emp Here 30
SIC 4731 Freight transportation arrangement

D-U-N-S 24-251-7295   (BR)
AGAT LABORATORIES LTD
AGAT
5835 Coopers Ave, Mississauga, ON, L4Z
1Y2
(905) 712-5100
Emp Here 120
SIC 8731 Commercial physical research

D-U-N-S 24-310-6387   (HQ)
ALLAN CANDY COMPANY LIMITED, THE
(*Suby of* Hershey Company)
3 Robert Speck Pky Suite 250, Mississauga,
ON, L4Z 2G5
(905) 270-2221
Emp Here 150   *Emp Total* 17,980
Sales 51,828,095
SIC 2064 Candy and other confectionery products
Pr Marty Thrasher
  Peter James
  David Plamondon
  Rejean Demers

D-U-N-S 24-846-3010   (BR)
BANK OF NOVA SCOTIA, THE
SCOTIABANK
49 Matheson Blvd E Suite 3, Mississauga,
ON, L4Z 2Y5

Emp Here 20
SIC 6021 National commercial banks

D-U-N-S 24-830-7878   (BR)
BANK OF NOVA SCOTIA, THE
SCOTIABANK
2 Robert Speck Pky Suite 100, Mississauga,
ON, L4Z 1H8
(905) 276-4540
Emp Here 80
SIC 6021 National commercial banks

D-U-N-S 20-339-2498   (BR)
BANQUE DE DEVELOPPEMENT DU

CANADA
BDC
4310 Sherwoodtowne Blvd, Mississauga, ON, L4Z 4C4
(905) 566-6499
Emp Here 40
SIC 6141 Personal credit institutions

D-U-N-S 20-877-6468   (SL)
BASIC PACKAGING INDUSTRIES INC
5591 Mcadam Rd, Mississauga, ON, L4Z 1N4
(905) 890-0922
Emp Here 50   *Sales* 4,888,367
SIC 2842 Polishes and sanitation goods

D-U-N-S 25-246-9036   (SL)
BELVIKA TRADE & PACKAGING LTD
340 Traders Blvd E, Mississauga, ON, L4Z 1W7
(905) 502-7444
Emp Here 75   *Sales* 4,504,505
SIC 7389 Business services, nec

D-U-N-S 20-537-2464   (BR)
CANADA POST CORPORATION
MISSISSAUGA LCD
340 Matheson Blvd E, Mississauga, ON, L4Z 1P5
(905) 755-9328
Emp Here 200
SIC 4311 U.s. postal service

D-U-N-S 20-303-3246   (BR)
CARA OPERATIONS LIMITED
MONTANAS
(*Suby of* Cara Holdings Limited)
5031 Hurontario St, Mississauga, ON, L4Z 3X7
(905) 890-6500
Emp Here 60
SIC 5812 Eating places

D-U-N-S 20-303-3139   (BR)
CARA OPERATIONS LIMITED
KELSEY'S
(*Suby of* Cara Holdings Limited)
30 Bristol Rd E, Mississauga, ON, L4Z 3K8
(905) 568-3262
Emp Here 50
SIC 5812 Eating places

D-U-N-S 25-361-1917   (BR)
CARDINAL HEALTH CANADA INC
(*Suby of* Cardinal Health, Inc.)
175 Britannia Rd E Suite 1, Mississauga, ON, L4Z 4B9
(905) 417-2900
Emp Here 70
SIC 5047 Medical and hospital equipment

D-U-N-S 20-260-6500   (BR)
CATHOLIC CROSS-CULTURAL SERVICES
LINC PROGRAM
4557 Hurontario St B11 & 12, Mississauga, ON, L4Z 3M2
(905) 272-1703
Emp Here 20
SIC 8699 Membership organizations, nec

D-U-N-S 25-312-4663   (SL)
CIBER OF CANADA INC
4 Robert Speck Pky Unit 200, Mississauga, ON, L4Z 1S1

Emp Here 20   *Sales* 1,459,214
SIC 7371 Custom computer programming services

D-U-N-S 25-274-0568   (SL)
COMMUNITY HOMEMAKERS LTD
COMMUNITY CARE SERVICES
160 Traders Blvd E Suite 103, Mississauga, ON, L4Z 3K7
(905) 275-0544
Emp Here 300   *Sales* 72,559,333
SIC 8082 Home health care services
Pr Peter Gooch

D-U-N-S 20-212-1989   (BR)

CONFISERIES REGAL INC
175 Britannia Rd E Unit 2, Mississauga, ON, L4Z 4B8
(905) 507-6868
Emp Here 20
SIC 5145 Confectionery

D-U-N-S 25-265-2995   (BR)
CONSEIL SCOLAIRE DE DISTRICT CATHOLIQUE CENTRE-SUD
ECOLE RENE LAMOUREUX
385 Meadows Blvd, Mississauga, ON, L4Z 1G5
(905) 270-0785
Emp Here 25
SIC 8211 Elementary and secondary schools

D-U-N-S 24-317-5119   (HQ)
CONTITECH CANADA, INC
GRANFORD
237 Brunel Rd, Mississauga, ON, L4Z 1X3
(905) 366-2010
Emp Here 30   *Emp Total* 220,000
Sales 152,123,060
SIC 3069 Fabricated rubber products, nec
Pr James T. Hill
VP Guy Enta

D-U-N-S 20-710-9922   (BR)
DUFFERIN-PEEL CATHOLIC DISTRICT SCHOOL BOARD
ST JUDE ELEMENTARY SCHOOL
175 Nahani Way, Mississauga, ON, L4Z 3J6
(905) 568-3720
Emp Here 50
SIC 8211 Elementary and secondary schools

D-U-N-S 20-710-9773   (BR)
DUFFERIN-PEEL CATHOLIC DISTRICT SCHOOL BOARD
ST CHARLES GARNIER ELEMENTARY SCHOOL
4233 Central Pky E, Mississauga, ON, L4Z 1M7
(905) 275-0509
Emp Here 30
SIC 8211 Elementary and secondary schools

D-U-N-S 20-711-0284   (BR)
DUFFERIN-PEEL CATHOLIC DISTRICT SCHOOL BOARD
ST. PIO OF PIETRELCINA ELEMENTARY SCHOOL
4765 Huron Heights Dr, Mississauga, ON, L4Z 4G9
(905) 361-1327
Emp Here 50
SIC 8211 Elementary and secondary schools

D-U-N-S 20-720-0945   (SL)
ELECTROTEMP TECHNOLOGIES INC
406 Watline Ave, Mississauga, ON, L4Z 1X2
(905) 361-1544
Emp Here 50   *Sales* 4,742,446
SIC 5999 Miscellaneous retail stores, nec

D-U-N-S 24-192-8662   (HQ)
ELEMENT FLEET MANAGEMENT INC
4 Robert Speck Pky Unit 900, Mississauga, ON, L4Z 1S1
(905) 366-8900
Emp Here 167   *Emp Total* 412
Sales 20,137,153
SIC 7515 Passenger car leasing
Pr Troy Campbell
VP Sls Steve Somers

D-U-N-S 25-403-9514   (BR)
FEDEX OFFICE CANADA LIMITED
FEDEX OFFICE PRINT & SHIP CENTRE
(*Suby of* Fedex Corporation)
4553 Hurontario St Suite 1, Mississauga, ON, L4Z 3L9
(905) 507-0730
Emp Here 35
SIC 7334 Photocopying and duplicating services

FLUKE ELECTRONICS CANADA LP
(*Suby of* Fortive Corporation)
400 Britannia Rd E Unit 1, Mississauga, ON, L4Z 1X9
(905) 890-7601
Emp Here 60   *Sales* 12,038,516
SIC 5084 Industrial machinery and equipment
Pr Barbara Hulit
VP VP Monti Ackerman
Sr VP Jim Cavoretto
VP Opers Daren Couture
  Clement Feng
  Tom Nealon

D-U-N-S 25-203-9789   (SL)
GEORGIAN CONSTRUCTION COMPANY LIMITED, THE
160 Traders Blvd E Suite 200, Mississauga, ON, L4Z 3K7

Emp Here 45   *Sales* 19,239,360
SIC 6552 Subdividers and developers, nec
Pr Pr Gene Maida

D-U-N-S 20-565-3442   (SL)
GEORGIAN TAYLOR WOODS INC
160 Traders Blvd E Suite 200, Mississauga, ON, L4Z 3K7

Emp Here 30   *Sales* 12,858,960
SIC 6553 Cemetery subdividers and developers
  Anthony Maida
VP VP Gene Maida
  Frank Maida

D-U-N-S 25-496-9678   (BR)
GRAYBAR CANADA LIMITED
GRAYBAR ONTARIO
(*Suby of* Graybar Electric Company, Inc.)
5895 Whittle Rd, Mississauga, ON, L4Z 2H4
(905) 507-0533
Emp Here 28
SIC 5063 Electrical apparatus and equipment

D-U-N-S 24-859-1802   (BR)
GROUPE CANTREX NATIONWIDE INC
(*Suby of* Groupe Cantrex Nationwide Inc)
405 Britannia Rd E Suite 206, Mississauga, ON, L4Z 3E6

Emp Here 20
SIC 5021 Furniture

D-U-N-S 20-191-0507   (BR)
HALF, ROBERT CANADA INC
RHI CONSULTING
(*Suby of* Robert Half International Inc.)
1 Robert Speck Pky Unit 940, Mississauga, ON, L4Z 3M3
(905) 273-4092
Emp Here 46
SIC 7361 Employment agencies

D-U-N-S 25-702-8282   (BR)
HALF, ROBERT CANADA INC
OFFICETEAM, DIV OF
(*Suby of* Robert Half International Inc.)
1 Robert Speck Pky Suite 940, Mississauga, ON, L4Z 3M3
(905) 306-8326
Emp Here 30
SIC 7361 Employment agencies

D-U-N-S 20-010-4789   (BR)
HOLDING BELL MOBILITE INC
HOLDING BELL MOBILITE INC
262 Britannia Rd E, Mississauga, ON, L4Z 1S6
(905) 890-0000
Emp Here 50
SIC 4899 Communication services, nec

D-U-N-S 25-996-6299   (BR)
HUDSON'S BAY COMPANY
4561 Hurontario St, Mississauga, ON, L4Z 3X3

(416) 789-8011
Emp Here 35
SIC 5311 Department stores

D-U-N-S 25-361-5967   (BR)
INTRIA ITEMS INC
155 Britannia Rd E Suite 200, Mississauga, ON, L4Z 4B7
(905) 502-4592
Emp Here 1,500
SIC 7374 Data processing and preparation

D-U-N-S 25-305-3367   (BR)
INNVEST PROPERTIES CORP
QUALITY INN AIRPORT WEST
(*Suby of* Innvest Properties Corp)
50 Britannia Rd E, Mississauga, ON, L4Z 2G2
(905) 890-1200
Emp Here 40
SIC 7011 Hotels and motels

D-U-N-S 20-225-2771   (HQ)
JTI-MACDONALD CORP
1 Robert Speck Pky Suite 1601, Mississauga, ON, L4Z 0A2
(905) 804-7300
Emp Here 80   *Emp Total* 44,485
Sales 18,240,175
SIC 2111 Cigarettes
Pr Michel A. Poirier
  David Marshall
  Martin-Ralph Frauendorfer
  Laura Carr

D-U-N-S 25-530-4339   (HQ)
KRG LOGISTICS INC
(*Suby of* KRG Logistics Inc)
170 Traders Blvd E, Mississauga, ON, L4Z 1W7
(905) 501-7277
Emp Here 25   *Emp Total* 31
Sales 8,480,961
SIC 4731 Freight transportation arrangement
Pr Pr Kyran Bartlett
  Ronald Alvares

D-U-N-S 24-727-1646   (SL)
KEYSER MASON BALL LLP
KMB MANAGEMENT
4 Robert Speck Pky Suite 1600, Mississauga, ON, L4Z 1S1
(905) 276-9111
Emp Here 50   *Sales* 4,304,681
SIC 8111 Legal services

D-U-N-S 20-145-5292   (HQ)
KINNEAR INDUSTRIES CORPORATION LIMITED
WAYNE-DALTON COMMERCIAL DOORS
254 Matheson Blvd E, Mississauga, ON, L4Z 1P5
(905) 890-1402
Emp Here 26   *Emp Total* 2,500
Sales 14,738,061
SIC 5031 Lumber, plywood, and millwork
Pr Pr Thomas Bennett Iii

D-U-N-S 20-159-1203   (HQ)
LARSON-JUHL CANADA LTD
LARSON JUHL
(*Suby of* Berkshire Hathaway Inc.)
416 Watline Ave, Mississauga, ON, L4Z 1X2
(905) 890-1234
Emp Here 42   *Emp Total* 331,000
Sales 10,944,105
SIC 5023 Homefurnishings
Pr Jeff Cohen

D-U-N-S 25-373-6482   (BR)
LEON'S FURNITURE LIMITED
201 Britannia Rd E, Mississauga, ON, L4Z 3X8
(905) 501-9505
Emp Here 150
SIC 5712 Furniture stores

D-U-N-S 25-988-4203   (BR)
LIQUOR CONTROL BOARD OF ONTARIO, THE

LCBO
5035 Hurontario St Unit 9, Mississauga, ON,
L4Z 3X7
(905) 501-9784
Emp Here 25
SIC 5921 Liquor stores

D-U-N-S 24-911-5403   (SL)
MACRO ENGINEERING & TECHNOLOGY INC
MACRO ENGINEERING
199 Traders Blvd E, Mississauga, ON, L4Z 2E5
(905) 507-9000
Emp Here 135   *Sales* 18,970,897
SIC 3559 Special industry machinery, nec
Pr Pr Mirek Planeta

D-U-N-S 25-504-4976   (SL)
MANTRALOGIX INC
267 Matheson Blvd E Suite 5, Mississauga,
ON, L4Z 1X8
(905) 629-3200
Emp Here 60   *Sales* 6,858,306
SIC 8741 Management services
Pr Kerry Mann

D-U-N-S 25-093-7237   (BR)
MANULIFE SECURITIES INCORPORATED
3 Robert Speck Pky Suite 200, Mississauga,
ON, L4Z 2G5
(905) 896-1822
Emp Here 27
SIC 6211 Security brokers and dealers

D-U-N-S 20-300-4374   (BR)
MANULIFE SECURITIES INVESTMENT SERVICES INC
MANULIFE SECURITIES
3 Robert Speck Pky Suite 200, Mississauga,
ON, L4Z 2G5
(905) 896-1822
Emp Here 24
SIC 6722 Management investment, open-end

D-U-N-S 20-022-4355   (BR)
MASCO CANADA LIMITED
DELTA FAUCET CANADA
(*Suby of* Masco Corporation)
395 Matheson Blvd E, Mississauga, ON, L4Z 2H2
(905) 712-3030
Emp Here 40
SIC 3432 Plumbing fixture fittings and trim

D-U-N-S 24-525-2817   (SL)
MINA MAR GROUP INC
SPOTFX
4 Robert Speck Pky 15th Floor, Mississauga,
ON, L4Z 1S1

Emp Here 78   *Sales* 25,971,200
SIC 6282 Investment advice
Dir Miro Zecevic

D-U-N-S 20-942-8952   (HQ)
NSK CANADA INC
5585 Mcadam Rd, Mississauga, ON, L4Z 1N4
(905) 890-0740
Emp Here 40   *Emp Total* 31,545
Sales 26,426,240
SIC 5085 Industrial supplies
Genl Mgr Michael St. Jacques

D-U-N-S 25-293-7800   (BR)
PEEL DISTRICT SCHOOL BOARD
NAHANI WAY PUBLIC SCHOOL
(*Suby of* Peel District School Board)
235 Nahani Way, Mississauga, ON, L4Z 3J6
(905) 507-4044
Emp Here 60
SIC 8211 Elementary and secondary schools

D-U-N-S 25-143-0781   (BR)
PEEL DISTRICT SCHOOL BOARD
BARONDALE PUBLIC SCHOOL
(*Suby of* Peel District School Board)
200 Barondale Dr, Mississauga, ON, L4Z 3N7

(905) 502-1880
Emp Here 36
SIC 8211 Elementary and secondary schools

D-U-N-S 20-878-9305   (HQ)
PERSONAL INSURANCE COMPANY, THE
PERSONNELLE, LA
3 Robert Speck Pky Suite 550, Mississauga,
ON, L4Z 3Z9
(905) 306-5252
Emp Here 355   *Emp Total* 15,000
Sales 238,946,293
SIC 6331 Fire, marine, and casualty insurance
Pr Pr Guy Cormier
VP VP Marcel Lauzon
 Stephanie Lee
 Jean Royer
Dir Clermont Tremblay
Dir Robert J. Boucher
Dir Alex Johnston
Dir Aldea Landry
Dir Andre Lord
Dir Sonia Gauthier

D-U-N-S 24-523-4245   (BR)
PFIZER CANADA INC
PFIZER CONSUMER HEALTHCARE
(*Suby of* Pfizer Inc.)
5975 Whittle Rd Suite 200, Mississauga, ON,
L4Z 3N1
(905) 507-7000
Emp Here 100
SIC 2834 Pharmaceutical preparations

D-U-N-S 24-687-8672   (SL)
PHILCOS ENTERPRISER LTD
120 Brunel Rd, Mississauga, ON, L4Z 1T5
(905) 568-1823
Emp Here 30   *Sales* 5,472,053
SIC 5136 Men's and boy's clothing
Pr Pr Satish Kumar

D-U-N-S 24-124-8868   (BR)
PRICEWATERHOUSECOOPERS LLP
1 Robert Speck Pky Suite 1100, Mississauga,
ON, L4Z 3M3

Emp Here 200
SIC 8721 Accounting, auditing, and book-keeping

D-U-N-S 25-050-6136   (SL)
QUALITY CONTINUOUS IMPROVEMENT CENTRE FOR COMMUNITY EDUCATION AND TRAINING
CENTRE FOR EDUCATION AND TRAINING
(*Suby of* Peel District School Board)
190 Robert Speck Pky, Mississauga, ON, L4Z 3K3
(905) 949-0049
Emp Here 300   *Sales* 21,108,170
SIC 3299 Schools and educational services, nec
Dir John Rhys Davies
Ch Ed Beryl Ford
Pr Pr Jim Greve
Dir Chris Besse
Dir Bob Armstrong
Dir Janet Mcdougall

D-U-N-S 25-796-6713   (BR)
RBC DOMINION SECURITIES INC
RBC INVESTMENTS
(*Suby of* Royal Bank Of Canada)
4 Robert Speck Pky Suite 1100, Mississauga,
ON, L4Z 1S1
(800) 323-6645
Emp Here 35
SIC 6211 Security brokers and dealers

D-U-N-S 25-300-6159   (BR)
REDBERRY FRANCHISING CORP
BURGER KING
5645 Hurontario St, Mississauga, ON, L4Z 1S7
(905) 890-5780
Emp Here 20
SIC 5812 Eating places

D-U-N-S 24-692-4369   (HQ)
RESOLVE CORPORATION
CANADIAN SECURITIES REGISTRATION SYSTEMS
(*Suby of* 2206997 Ontario Inc)
2 Robert Speck Pky Suite 1600, Mississauga,
ON, L4Z 1H8
(905) 306-6200
Emp Here 300   *Emp Total* 5,000
Sales 852,131,109
SIC 8748 Business consulting, nec
Pr Bruce Simmonds
Dir Gerry Mcdonald

D-U-N-S 20-354-5348   (HQ)
REXALL PHARMACY GROUP LTD
(*Suby of* McKesson Corporation)
5965 Coopers Ave, Mississauga, ON, L4Z 1R9
(905) 501-7800
Emp Here 20   *Emp Total* 83,350
Sales 141,543,758
SIC 5912 Drug stores and proprietary stores
CEO Domenic Pilla
 Todd Baldanzi
 John Saia
 Alan Champagne
Pr Barry Elliott
VP Paul Thomson
VP Fin Michael Martin
VP Opers Al Wilkie
 Ben Kachuk

D-U-N-S 20-145-7371   (HQ)
REYNOLDS AND REYNOLDS (CANADA) LIMITED
3 Robert Speck Pky Suite 700, Mississauga,
ON, L4Z 2G5
(905) 267-6000
Emp Here 150   *Emp Total* 6,000
Sales 62,626,080
SIC 5045 Computers, peripherals, and software
VP Ian Reilly

D-U-N-S 20-557-8011   (BR)
ROGERS COMMUNICATIONS INC
(*Suby of* Rogers Communications Inc)
60 Bristol Rd E Unit 1, Mississauga, ON, L4Z 3K8
(905) 568-8160
Emp Here 20
SIC 7841 Video tape rental

D-U-N-S 20-289-6523   (BR)
ROYAL EQUATOR INC
HILTON GARDEN INN TORONTO/MISSISSAUGA
100 Traders Blvd E, Mississauga, ON, L4Z 2H7
(905) 890-9110
Emp Here 60
SIC 7011 Hotels and motels

D-U-N-S 24-385-0430   (HQ)
SAPA CANADA INC
SAPA EXTRUSIONS
5675 Kennedy Rd, Mississauga, ON, L4Z 2H9
(905) 890-8821
Emp Here 50   *Emp Total* 94
Sales 75,514,325
SIC 3354 Aluminum extruded products
Genl Mgr David Mccallen

D-U-N-S 24-362-2219   (BR)
SECURITAS CANADA LIMITED
420 Britannia Rd E Suite 100, Mississauga,
ON, L4Z 3L5
(905) 272-0330
Emp Here 200
SIC 7381 Detective and armored car services

D-U-N-S 24-964-2554   (HQ)
SONOCO PLASTICS CANADA ULC
(*Suby of* Sonoco Products Company)
245 Britannia Rd E, Mississauga, ON, L4Z 4J3

(905) 624-2337
Emp Here 300   *Emp Total* 20,400
Sales 153,413,052
SIC 3089 Plastics products, nec
Pr Pr Pushminder Judge
VP Opers Marion Maclean
Dir Graeme Malloch
Fin Ex Audrey Lalande

D-U-N-S 24-644-5191   (SL)
STERIS CANADA INC
375 Britannia Rd E Unit 2, Mississauga, ON,
L4Z 3E2
(905) 677-0863
Emp Here 75   *Sales* 75,386,320
SIC 5047 Medical and hospital equipment
VP Steve Timpano
Pr Les C Vinney

D-U-N-S 25-098-6833   (SL)
STORCK CANADA INC
WERTHER'S ORIGINAL
2 Robert Speck Pky Suite 695, Mississauga,
ON, L4Z 1H8
(905) 272-4480
Emp Here 20   *Sales* 2,845,467
SIC 5149 Groceries and related products, nec

D-U-N-S 24-826-1471   (BR)
SUN LIFE ASSURANCE COMPANY OF CANADA
SUN LIFE FINANCIAL
4 Robert Speck Pky Suite 1200, Mississauga,
ON, L4Z 1S1
(905) 276-7140
Emp Here 104
SIC 6311 Life insurance

D-U-N-S 25-939-2322   (BR)
TD ASSET MANAGEMENT INC
(*Suby of* Toronto-Dominion Bank, The)
25 Watline Ave, Mississauga, ON, L4Z 2Z1
(905) 501-8200
Emp Here 24
SIC 6282 Investment advice

D-U-N-S 25-170-3922   (BR)
TRAFFIC TECH INC
(*Suby of* 2809664 Canada Inc)
550 Matheson Blvd E Suite 2, Mississauga,
ON, L4Z 4G3
(905) 629-1876
Emp Here 70
SIC 4731 Freight transportation arrangement

D-U-N-S 25-308-2333   (HQ)
TRANSCORE LINK LOGISTICS CORPORA-TION
(*Suby of* Roper Technologies, Inc.)
2 Robert Speck Pkwy Suite 900, Mississauga,
ON, L4Z 1H8
(905) 795-0580
Emp Here 25   *Emp Total* 14,205
Sales 27,214,341
SIC 4731 Freight transportation arrangement
 Claudia Malicevic

D-U-N-S 25-818-7160   (HQ)
VILLAGE ORTHODONTICS
VC ORTHODINTICS
(*Suby of* Village ORTHOdontics)
4288 Village Centre Crt, Mississauga, ON,
L4Z 1S2
(905) 275-8501
Emp Here 24   *Emp Total* 70
Sales 4,012,839
SIC 8021 Offices and clinics of dentists

D-U-N-S 20-116-7868   (HQ)
VOLT CANADA INC
VMC GAMES LABS
3 Robert Speck Pky Suite 260, Mississauga,
ON, L4Z 2G5
(905) 306-1920
Emp Here 500   *Emp Total* 25,800
Sales 47,116,450
SIC 7361 Employment agencies
Opers Mgr Jit Dhaliwal

▲ Public Company   ■ Public Company Family Member   **HQ** Headquarters   **BR** Branch   SL Single Location

Dir Howard B Weinreich
Seti Hamalian
Brahm M Gelfand

D-U-N-S 24-819-1319   (BR)
WE CARE HEALTH SERVICES INC
PROHOME HEALTH SERVICES INC DIVISION
160 Traders Blvd E Suite 208, Mississauga, ON, L4Z 3K7
(905) 275-7250
Emp Here 600
SIC 8051 Skilled nursing care facilities

D-U-N-S 24-951-7228   (SL)
WELCH ALLYN CANADA LIMITED
(*Suby of* Hill-Rom Holdings, Inc.)
160 Matheson Blvd E Unit 2, Mississauga, ON, L4Z 1V4
(905) 890-0004
Emp Here 26   *Sales* 2,334,742
SIC 3841 Surgical and medical instruments

D-U-N-S 25-853-8016   (BR)
WENDY'S RESTAURANTS OF CANADA INC
WENDY'S
(*Suby of* The Wendy's Company)
44 Britannia Rd E, Mississauga, ON, L4Z 3W7

Emp Here 43
SIC 5812 Eating places

D-U-N-S 25-997-2644   (BR)
WESTMONT HOSPITALITY MANAGEMENT LIMITED
HOLIDAY INN TORONTO WEST
(*Suby of* Westmont Hospitality Management Limited)
100 Britannia Rd E, Mississauga, ON, L4Z 2G1
(905) 890-5700
Emp Here 25
SIC 7011 Hotels and motels

Mississauga, ON L5A
Peel County

D-U-N-S 24-135-0201   (SL)
783312 ONTARIO LIMITED
TIVERON FARMS
2281 Camilla Rd, Mississauga, ON, L5A 2K2
(905) 848-4340
Emp Here 70   *Sales* 9,120,088
SIC 5411 Grocery stores
Pr Dave Tiveron

D-U-N-S 20-924-2478   (SL)
B & J MUSIC LTD
(*Suby of* Fender Musical Instruments Corporation)
2360 Tedlo St, Mississauga, ON, L5A 3V3
(905) 896-3001
Emp Here 27   *Sales* 1,969,939
SIC 5736 Musical instrument stores

D-U-N-S 20-135-6086   (SL)
BOADEN CATERING LIMITED
SOCIAL CATERING
505 Queensway E Unit 12, Mississauga, ON, L5A 4B4
(905) 276-1161
Emp Here 60   *Sales* 1,824,018
SIC 5812 Eating places

D-U-N-S 20-609-6559   (BR)
CHARTWELL RETIREMENT RESIDENCES
CHARTWELL SENIORS HOUSING REAL ESTATE INVESTMENT TRUST
590 Lolita Gdns Suite 355, Mississauga, ON, L5A 4N8
(905) 306-9934
Emp Here 225
SIC 8051 Skilled nursing care facilities

D-U-N-S 20-104-4133   (BR)

DOCK PRODUCTS CANADA INC
600 Orwell St Unit 6, Mississauga, ON, L5A 3R9
(905) 276-0565
Emp Here 20
SIC 4491 Marine cargo handling

D-U-N-S 20-965-2325   (BR)
DOLLARAMA S.E.C.
DOLLARAMA
93 Dundas St E Unit 2, Mississauga, ON, L5A 1W7
(905) 281-9895
Emp Here 20
SIC 5399 Miscellaneous general merchandise

D-U-N-S 20-291-1751   (BR)
DUFFERIN-PEEL CATHOLIC DISTRICT SCHOOL BOARD
CANADIAN MARTYRS SCHOOL
1185 Mississauga Valley Blvd, Mississauga, ON, L5A 3R7
(905) 275-0094
Emp Here 35
SIC 8211 Elementary and secondary schools

D-U-N-S 20-913-6568   (BR)
DUFFERIN-PEEL CATHOLIC DISTRICT SCHOOL BOARD
ST. TIMOTHY SEPARATE SCHOOL
2214 Cliff Rd, Mississauga, ON, L5A 2N9
(905) 277-0990
Emp Here 50
SIC 8211 Elementary and secondary schools

D-U-N-S 25-978-2225   (BR)
ENCON GROUP INC
(*Suby of* Marsh & McLennan Companies, Inc.)
55 Standish Crt Unit 600, Mississauga, ON, L5A 4R1
(905) 755-2030
Emp Here 60
SIC 6411 Insurance agents, brokers, and service

D-U-N-S 24-007-6851   (BR)
FITNESS INSTITUTE LIMITED, THE
MISSISSAUGA CLUB FITNESS INSTITUTE
2021 Cliff Rd Suite 309, Mississauga, ON, L5A 3N7
(905) 275-0182
Emp Here 25
SIC 7991 Physical fitness facilities

D-U-N-S 20-143-5294   (SL)
ILSCO OF CANADA COMPANY
615 Orwell St, Mississauga, ON, L5A 2W4
(905) 274-2341
Emp Here 140   *Sales* 6,583,508
SIC 3643 Current-carrying wiring devices
Pr James Smith
David Fitzgibbon

D-U-N-S 24-335-3042   (SL)
LOCOMOTIVE INVESTMENTS INC
SELECT BISTRO, LE
2350 Cawthra Rd, Mississauga, ON, L5A 2X1
(416) 596-6532
Emp Here 50   *Sales* 1,819,127
SIC 5812 Eating places

D-U-N-S 24-369-2394   (BR)
METRO ONTARIO INC
FOOD BASICS
377 Burnhamthorpe Rd E, Mississauga, ON, L5A 3Y1
(905) 270-2143
Emp Here 90
SIC 5411 Grocery stores

D-U-N-S 25-300-2885   (BR)
METRO ONTARIO INC
METRO
1585 Mississauga Valley Blvd, Mississauga, ON, L5A 3W9
(905) 566-9100
Emp Here 200
SIC 5411 Grocery stores

D-U-N-S 24-963-0476   (BR)
MINI-SKOOL A CHILD'S PLACE INC
CAWTHRA MINI SKOOL
3153 Cawthra Rd, Mississauga, ON, L5A 2X4
(905) 276-3933
Emp Here 30
SIC 8351 Child day care services

D-U-N-S 20-070-0156   (BR)
MORGUARD CORPORATION
ARISTA SUITES
3665 Arista Way Suite 2026, Mississauga, ON, L5A 4A3
(905) 896-6500
Emp Here 20
SIC 6513 Apartment building operators

D-U-N-S 24-693-0093   (SL)
NUSTEF FOODS LIMITED
2440 Cawthra Rd, Mississauga, ON, L5A 2X1
(905) 896-3060
Emp Here 60   *Sales* 3,137,310
SIC 2051 Bread, cake, and related products

D-U-N-S 20-322-1544   (HQ)
PCL CONSTRUCTORS CANADA INC
2085 Hurontario St Suite 400, Mississauga, ON, L5A 4G1
(905) 276-7600
Emp Here 500   *Emp Total* 16,380
Sales 881,237,142
SIC 1542 Nonresidential construction, nec
Pr Pr Chris Gower
VP Robert Martz
Frank Bison
Fin Mgr John Volcko
Fin Mgr Sean Barnes
Fin Mgr Ian Cantelon
Fin Mgr Sharon Malenki
Fin Mgr Tim Mccormick
Fin Mgr Mike Bavaro
Fin Mgr John Motter

D-U-N-S 25-263-8002   (BR)
PEEL DISTRICT SCHOOL BOARD
VALLEYS SENIOR PUBLIC SCHOOL
(*Suby of* Peel District School Board)
1235 Mississauga Valley Blvd, Mississauga, ON, L5A 3R8
(905) 275-5125
Emp Here 50
SIC 8211 Elementary and secondary schools

D-U-N-S 25-293-8477   (BR)
PEEL DISTRICT SCHOOL BOARD
CLIFTON PUBLIC SCHOOL
(*Suby of* Peel District School Board)
2389 Cliff Rd, Mississauga, ON, L5A 2P1
(905) 277-2611
Emp Here 35
SIC 8211 Elementary and secondary schools

D-U-N-S 25-265-2904   (BR)
PEEL DISTRICT SCHOOL BOARD
BRIARWOOD ELEMENTARY SCHOOL
(*Suby of* Peel District School Board)
1065 Mississauga Valley Blvd, Mississauga, ON, L5A 2A1
(905) 270-2597
Emp Here 35
SIC 8211 Elementary and secondary schools

D-U-N-S 25-278-9334   (BR)
PEEL DISTRICT SCHOOL BOARD
CORSAIR PUBLIC SCHOOL
(*Suby of* Peel District School Board)
2230 Corsair Rd, Mississauga, ON, L5A 2L9
(905) 279-1511
Emp Here 45
SIC 8211 Elementary and secondary schools

D-U-N-S 25-265-3605   (BR)
PEEL DISTRICT SCHOOL BOARD
MUNDEN PARK PUBLIC SCHOOL
(*Suby of* Peel District School Board)
515 Tedwyn Dr, Mississauga, ON, L5A 1J8
(905) 279-9251
Emp Here 22

SIC 8211 Elementary and secondary schools

D-U-N-S 25-293-8089   (BR)
PEEL DISTRICT SCHOOL BOARD
THORNWOOD PUBLIC SCHOOL
(*Suby of* Peel District School Board)
277 Mississauga Valley Blvd, Mississauga, ON, L5A 1Y6
(905) 275-4077
Emp Here 42
SIC 8211 Elementary and secondary schools

D-U-N-S 20-654-2073   (BR)
PEEL DISTRICT SCHOOL BOARD
CAMILLA ROAD SENIOR PUBLIC SCHOOL
(*Suby of* Peel District School Board)
201 Cherry Post Dr, Mississauga, ON, L5A 1J1
(905) 270-0845
Emp Here 50
SIC 8211 Elementary and secondary schools

D-U-N-S 24-800-6962   (SL)
POP ENVIRO BAGS & PRODUCTS
615 Orwell St, Mississauga, ON, L5A 2W4
(905) 272-2247
Emp Here 49   *Sales* 7,150,149
SIC 2673 Bags: plastic, laminated, and coated

D-U-N-S 25-155-7997   (HQ)
RESPIRON CARE-PLUS INC
CARE-PLUS
(*Suby of* Respiron Care-Plus Inc)
2085 Hurontario St Suite 103, Mississauga, ON, L5A 4G1
(905) 306-0204
Emp Here 300   *Emp Total* 300
Sales 53,430,054
SIC 8741 Management services
Pr Pr Connie Clerici
Jennifer Cummings

D-U-N-S 20-166-4794   (SL)
S. GUMPERT CO. OF CANADA LTD
2500 Tedlo St, Mississauga, ON, L5A 4A9
(905) 279-2600
Emp Here 60   *Sales* 2,425,503
SIC 5461 Retail bakeries

D-U-N-S 25-120-2065   (BR)
TORONTO-DOMINION BANK, THE
TD CANADA TRUST
(*Suby of* Toronto-Dominion Bank, The)
1585 Mississauga Valley Blvd, Mississauga, ON, L5A 3W9
(905) 275-0991
Emp Here 25
SIC 6021 National commercial banks

Mississauga, ON L5B
Peel County

D-U-N-S 24-660-9150   (HQ)
ACCOR CANADA INC
NOVOTEL HOTELS
3670 Hurontario St, Mississauga, ON, L5B 1P3
(905) 896-1000
Emp Here 100   *Emp Total* 1,275
Sales 13,132,926
SIC 7011 Hotels and motels
Pr Georges Le Mener
VP Robert Gauthier
VP Olivier Poirot
VP Didier Bosc
Sec Alan Rabinowitz
Treas Stephen Manthey
Asst Tr Kent Howarton

D-U-N-S 20-553-6647   (HQ)
AEROTEK ULC
AEROTEK AVIATION
350 Burnhamthorpe Rd W Suite 800, Mississauga, ON, L5B 3J1

▲ Public Company   ■ Public Company Family Member   **HQ** Headquarters   **BR** Branch   **SL** Single Location

(905) 283-1200
Emp Here 50   Emp Total 85,000
Sales 36,480,350
SIC 7361 Employment agencies
Pr Todd Mohr
VP Fin VP Fin Thomas Kelly
Sec Jeffrey W. Reichert

D-U-N-S 20-010-7287   (SL)
ALLEGIS GLOBAL SOLUTIONS CANADA CORPORATION
ALLEGIS TALENT2
350 Burnhamthorpe Rd W Unit 700, Mississauga, ON, L5B 3J1
(905) 283-1400
Emp Here 50   Sales 3,648,035
SIC 7361 Employment agencies

D-U-N-S 20-808-8588   (SL)
AMICA (CITY CENTRE) CORPORATION
380 Princess Royal Dr, Mississauga, ON, L5B 4M9
(905) 803-8100
Emp Here 50   Sales 2,165,628
SIC 8361 Residential care

D-U-N-S 24-337-3912   (BR)
APPLEONE SERVICES LTD
BILINGUALONE, DIV OF
33 City Centre Dr Suite 640, Mississauga, ON, L5B 2N5
(416) 236-0421
Emp Here 20
SIC 7361 Employment agencies

D-U-N-S 25-657-9590   (BR)
ASHLEY, WILLIAM LTD
WILLIAM ASHLEY CHINA
100 City Centre Dr, Mississauga, ON, L5B 2C9

Emp Here 20
SIC 5719 Miscellaneous homefurnishings

D-U-N-S 20-563-9060   (BR)
ASSANTE CAPITAL MANAGEMENT LTD
ASSANTE CAPITAL MANAGEMENT
350 Burnhamthorpe Rd W Suite 218, Mississauga, ON, L5B 3J1
(905) 272-2750
Emp Here 36
SIC 6211 Security brokers and dealers

D-U-N-S 20-182-9822   (BR)
ASSANTE FINANCIAL MANAGEMENT LTD
ASSANTE WEALTH MANAGEMENT
350 Burnhamthorpe Rd W Suite 218, Mississauga, ON, L5B 3J1
(905) 273-6605
Emp Here 20
SIC 8741 Management services

D-U-N-S 25-842-4084   (BR)
AVISON YOUNG COMMERCIAL REAL ESTATE (ONTARIO) INC
(Suby of AY Holdings Ontario Inc)
77 City Centre Dr Suite 301, Mississauga, ON, L5B 1M5
(905) 712-2100
Emp Here 22
SIC 6531 Real estate agents and managers

D-U-N-S 24-346-8100   (BR)
AVIVA CANADA INC
33 City Centre Dr Suite 300, Mississauga, ON, L5B 2N5
(905) 949-3900
Emp Here 40
SIC 6411 Insurance agents, brokers, and service

D-U-N-S 25-808-4102   (BR)
BDO CANADA LLP
MISSISSAUGA ACCOUNTING
1 City Centre Dr Suite 1700, Mississauga, ON, L5B 1M2
(905) 270-7700
Emp Here 80
SIC 8721 Accounting, auditing, and book-

keeping

D-U-N-S 25-845-2168   (BR)
BMO NESBITT BURNS INC
90 Burnhamthorpe Rd W Suite 210, Mississauga, ON, L5B 3C3
(905) 897-9200
Emp Here 50
SIC 6211 Security brokers and dealers

D-U-N-S 20-589-4525   (BR)
BANQUE TORONTO-DOMINION, LA
TD CANADA TRUST
(Suby of Toronto-Dominion Bank, The)
3037 Clayhill Rd, Mississauga, ON, L5B 4L2
(905) 949-6565
Emp Here 20
SIC 6021 National commercial banks

D-U-N-S 20-039-3523   (BR)
BERLITZ CANADA INC
BERLITZ LANGUAGE SCHOOL
3660 Hurontario St Suite 303, Mississauga, ON, L5B 3C4
(905) 272-5111
Emp Here 22
SIC 8299 Schools and educational services, nec

D-U-N-S 20-997-5218   (HQ)
BERLITZ CANADA INC
3660 Hurontario St Suite 302, Mississauga, ON, L5B 3C4
(905) 896-0215
Emp Here 30   Emp Total 20,145
Sales 22,507,520
SIC 8299 Schools and educational services, nec
Pr Pr Darryl Simsovic
Dir Mark Harris

D-U-N-S 25-097-8707   (SL)
BIOGEN IDEC CANADA INC
(Suby of Biogen Inc.)
90 Burnhamthorpe Rd W Suite 1100, Mississauga, ON, L5B 3C3
(905) 804-1444
Emp Here 20   Sales 2,544,288
SIC 2834 Pharmaceutical preparations

D-U-N-S 20-027-8351   (BR)
BOSTON PIZZA INTERNATIONAL INC
1 City Centre Dr Suite 708, Mississauga, ON, L5B 1M2
(905) 848-2700
Emp Here 50
SIC 6794 Patent owners and lessors

D-U-N-S 25-939-2470   (BR)
BURGESS, JOHN WILLIAM ENTERPRISES INC
TIM HORTONS
151 City Centre Dr Unit 303, Mississauga, ON, L5B 1M7
(905) 306-7942
Emp Here 20
SIC 5812 Eating places

D-U-N-S 20-573-4457   (BR)
CIBC WORLD MARKETS INC
CIBC WOOD GUNDY
1 City Centre Dr Suite 1100, Mississauga, ON, L5B 1M2
(905) 272-2200
Emp Here 50
SIC 6211 Security brokers and dealers

D-U-N-S 24-545-4699   (BR)
CANADIAN STANDARDS ASSOCIATION
QUALITY MANAGEMENT INSTITUTE
90 Burnhamthorpe Rd W Suite 300, Mississauga, ON, L5B 3C3

Emp Here 100
SIC 8741 Management services

D-U-N-S 24-456-1366   (BR)
CATHOLIC CROSS-CULTURAL SERVICES

3660 Hurontario St 7th Flr, Mississauga, ON, L5B 3C4
(905) 273-4140
Emp Here 20
SIC 8322 Individual and family services

D-U-N-S 25-938-7157   (BR)
CHILDREN'S AID SOCIETY OF THE REGION OF PEEL, THE
101 Queensway W Suite 500, Mississauga, ON, L5B 2P7

Emp Here 150
SIC 8399 Social services, nec

D-U-N-S 20-373-8856   (BR)
CINEPLEX ODEON CORPORATION
CINEPLEX CINEMAS MISSISSAUGA
309 Rathburn Rd W, Mississauga, ON, L5B 4C1
(905) 275-4969
Emp Here 130
SIC 7832 Motion picture theaters, except drive-in

D-U-N-S 20-784-1594   (HQ)
DOLLAR THRIFTY AUTOMOTIVE GROUP CANADA INC
(Suby of Hertz Global Holdings, Inc.)
3660 Hurontario St, Mississauga, ON, L5B 3C4
(905) 612-1881
Emp Here 40   Emp Total 36,000
Sales 71,015,000
SIC 7515 Passenger car leasing
Pr Pr Gary L. Paxton

D-U-N-S 24-254-2996   (SL)
DONATO ACADEMY OF HAIRSTYLING AND AESTHETICS
100 City Centre Dr, Mississauga, ON, L5B 2C9
(416) 252-8999
Emp Here 100   Sales 1,969,939
SIC 7231 Beauty shops

D-U-N-S 24-963-0732   (BR)
DUFFERIN-PEEL CATHOLIC DISTRICT SCHOOL BOARD
MARY FIX CATHOLIC SCHOOL
486 Paisley Blvd W, Mississauga, ON, L5B 2M4
(905) 270-3140
Emp Here 35
SIC 8211 Elementary and secondary schools

D-U-N-S 24-963-0583   (BR)
DUFFERIN-PEEL CATHOLIC DISTRICT SCHOOL BOARD
BISHOP SCALABRINI CATHOLIC ELEMENTARY SCHOOL
225 Central Pkwy W, Mississauga, ON, L5B 3J5
(905) 896-3665
Emp Here 50
SIC 8211 Elementary and secondary schools

D-U-N-S 25-142-4008   (BR)
DUFFERIN-PEEL CATHOLIC DISTRICT SCHOOL BOARD
FATHER MICHAEL GOETZ SECONDARY SCHOOL
330 Central Pkwy W, Mississauga, ON, L5B 3K6
(905) 277-0326
Emp Here 150
SIC 8211 Elementary and secondary schools

D-U-N-S 20-711-0110   (BR)
DUFFERIN-PEEL CATHOLIC DISTRICT SCHOOL BOARD
FATHER DANIEL ZANON ELEMENTARY SCHOOL
450 Hillcrest Ave, Mississauga, ON, L5B 4J3
(905) 279-3722
Emp Here 50
SIC 8211 Elementary and secondary schools

D-U-N-S 24-963-0773   (BR)

DUFFERIN-PEEL CATHOLIC DISTRICT SCHOOL BOARD
ST. CATHERINE OF SIENA ELEMENTARY SCHOOL
2350 Hurontario St, Mississauga, ON, L5B 1N1
(905) 277-2448
Emp Here 55
SIC 8211 Elementary and secondary schools

D-U-N-S 25-142-6821   (BR)
DUFFERIN-PEEL CATHOLIC DISTRICT SCHOOL BOARD
ST. PHILIP ELEMENTARY SCHOOL
345 Fairview Rd W, Mississauga, ON, L5B 3W5
(905) 306-8420
Emp Here 40
SIC 8211 Elementary and secondary schools

D-U-N-S 24-963-0658   (BR)
DUFFERIN-PEEL CATHOLIC DISTRICT SCHOOL BOARD
CORPUS CHRISTI SENIOR ELEMENTARY SCHOOL
4155 Elora Dr, Mississauga, ON, L5B 3N4
(905) 897-7037
Emp Here 20
SIC 8211 Elementary and secondary schools

D-U-N-S 24-424-0870   (HQ)
EASYFINANCIAL SERVICES INC
33 City Centre Dr Suite 510, Mississauga, ON, L5B 2N5
(905) 272-2788
Emp Here 57   Emp Total 1,587
Sales 227,572,454
SIC 6141 Personal credit institutions
Dir Steve Goertz

D-U-N-S 25-321-9166   (BR)
ECONOMICAL MUTUAL INSURANCE COMPANY
77 City Centre Dr Suite 400, Mississauga, ON, L5B 1M5
(905) 896-4916
Emp Here 60
SIC 6331 Fire, marine, and casualty insurance

D-U-N-S 25-254-1438   (HQ)
EDWARD D. JONES & CO. CANADA HOLDING CO., INC
EDWARD JONES
90 Burnhamthorpe Rd W Suite 902, Mississauga, ON, L5B 3C3
(905) 306-8600
Emp Here 1,600   Emp Total 41,000
Sales 4,331,255,000
SIC 6211 Security brokers and dealers
Gary Reamey
Donald J Burwell
Kevin Bastien

D-U-N-S 20-916-8256   (BR)
EMPIRE THEATRES LIMITED
MARIPLEX CONFECTIONS
100 City Centre Dr, Mississauga, ON, L5B 2C9

Emp Here 47
SIC 7832 Motion picture theaters, except drive-in

D-U-N-S 20-699-6444   (BR)
EXTENDICARE INC
COOKSVILLE CARE CENTRE
55 Queensway W, Mississauga, ON, L5B 1B5
(905) 270-0170
Emp Here 25
SIC 8051 Skilled nursing care facilities

D-U-N-S 24-847-2698   (HQ)
FAMILY SERVICES OF PEEL LTD
(Suby of Family Services of Peel Ltd)
151 City Centre Dr Suite 501, Mississauga, ON, L5B 1M7

(905) 270-2250
Emp Here 25　　　*Emp Total* 50
Sales 1,969,939
SIC 8322 Individual and family services

D-U-N-S 24-805-0820　　　(HQ)
FORSYTHE INTERNATIONAL, INC
50 Burnhamthorpe Rd W Suite 708, Mississauga, ON, L5B 3C2
(905) 283-1800
Emp Here 30　　　*Emp Total* 1,000
Sales 8,857,893
SIC 5045 Computers, peripherals, and software
Pr William P. Brennan
　　Albert L Weiss

D-U-N-S 25-403-9431　　　(BR)
GWL REALTY ADVISORS INC
1 City Centre Dr Suite 300, Mississauga, ON, L5B 1M2
(905) 275-5600
Emp Here 90
SIC 6531 Real estate agents and managers

D-U-N-S 24-321-5659　　　(BR)
GWL REALTY ADVISORS INC
50 Burnhamthorpe Rd W Suite 502, Mississauga, ON, L5B 3C2
(905) 361-3197
Emp Here 50
SIC 6282 Investment advice

D-U-N-S 20-860-5886　　　(BR)
GLENTEL INC
WIRELESS WAVES
100 City Centre Dr Unit E5, Mississauga, ON, L5B 2C9
(905) 896-9283
Emp Here 25
SIC 4813 Telephone communication, except radio

D-U-N-S 24-623-5548　　　(BR)
GOODLIFE FITNESS CENTRES INC
GOODLIFE FITNESS
100 City Centre Dr Unit R9, Mississauga, ON, L5B 2C9
(905) 804-0707
Emp Here 35
SIC 7999 Amusement and recreation, nec

D-U-N-S 20-315-9728　　　(BR)
GRANT THORNTON LLP
201 City Centre Dr Suite 501, Mississauga, ON, L5B 2T4
(416) 366-0100
Emp Here 80
SIC 8721 Accounting, auditing, and bookkeeping

D-U-N-S 24-356-1235　　　(BR)
HUDSON'S BAY COMPANY
BAY, THE
100 City Centre Dr Suite 200, Mississauga, ON, L5B 2C9
(905) 270-7600
Emp Here 100
SIC 5311 Department stores

D-U-N-S 24-575-3231　　　(HQ)
IMPACT AUTO AUCTIONS LTD
50 Burnhamthorpe Rd W Suite 800, Mississauga, ON, L5B 3C2
(905) 896-9727
Emp Here 25　　　*Emp Total* 14,400
Sales 7,806,795
SIC 7389 Business services, nec
　　Terry Daniels

D-U-N-S 25-623-6175　　　(HQ)
INDIA RAINBOW COMMUNITY SERVICES OF PEEL
RAINBOW ADULT DAY CENTRE
(*Suby of* India Rainbow Community Services of Peel)
3038 Hurontario St Suite 206, Mississauga, ON, L5B 3B9

(905) 275-2369
Emp Here 23　　　*Emp Total* 60
Sales 6,108,659
SIC 8399 Social services, nec
　　Kitty Chadda
Fin Mgr Suvarna Nimkar

D-U-N-S 25-121-4482　　　(BR)
INDIGO BOOKS & MUSIC INC
CHAPTERS
(*Suby of* Indigo Books & Music Inc)
189 Rathburn Rd W, Mississauga, ON, L5B 4C1
(905) 281-8342
Emp Here 40
SIC 5942 Book stores

D-U-N-S 20-328-3254　　　(HQ)
INGREDION CANADA CORPORATION
(*Suby of* Ingredion Incorporated)
90 Burnhamthorpe Rd W Unit 1600, Mississauga, ON, L5B 0H9
(905) 281-7950
Emp Here 100　　　*Emp Total* 11,000
Sales 4,304,681
SIC 2046 Wet corn milling

D-U-N-S 25-315-8224　　　(BR)
INVESTORS GROUP FINANCIAL SERVICES INC
1 City Centre Dr Suite 1020, Mississauga, ON, L5B 1M2
(905) 306-0031
Emp Here 55
SIC 8742 Management consulting services

D-U-N-S 24-868-2924　　　(HQ)
KNOWLEDGE FIRST FINANCIAL INC
50 Burnhamthorpe Rd W Suite 1000, Mississauga, ON, L5B 4A5
(905) 270-8777
Emp Here 120　　　*Emp Total* 130
Sales 31,154,219
SIC 6732 Trusts: educational, religious, etc.
Pr George Hopkinson
Sec Suzanne Mascarenhas

D-U-N-S 24-346-5635　　　(BR)
LAWRENZO FOODS LTD
MCDONALD'S RESTAURANT
100 City Centre Dr Suite 1031, Mississauga, ON, L5B 2C9
(905) 276-3898
Emp Here 25
SIC 5812 Eating places

D-U-N-S 20-804-4268　　　(BR)
LIQUOR CONTROL BOARD OF ONTARIO, THE
LCBO
3020 Elmcreek Rd, Mississauga, ON, L5B 4M3
(905) 949-6100
Emp Here 25
SIC 5921 Liquor stores

D-U-N-S 24-387-9418　　　(BR)
LONDON LIFE INSURANCE COMPANY
FREEDOM 55 FINANCIAL
1 City Centre Dr Suite 1600, Mississauga, ON, L5B 1M2
(905) 276-1177
Emp Here 100
SIC 6311 Life insurance

D-U-N-S 24-329-4159　　　(BR)
LUSH HANDMADE COSMETICS LTD
LUSH COSMETICS
100 City Centre Dr Suite 2422, Mississauga, ON, L5B 2C9
(905) 277-5874
Emp Here 25
SIC 5999 Miscellaneous retail stores, nec

D-U-N-S 25-686-7060　　　(BR)
MANPOWER SERVICES CANADA LIMITED
MANPOWER
201 City Centre Dr Suite 101, Mississauga, ON, L5B 2T4

(905) 276-2000
Emp Here 20
SIC 7361 Employment agencies

D-U-N-S 20-290-0598　　　(BR)
MERIT TRAVEL GROUP INC
201 City Centre Dr Unit 501, Mississauga, ON, L5B 2T4
(905) 890-8890
Emp Here 30
SIC 4724 Travel agencies

D-U-N-S 24-859-7056　　　(HQ)
MORGUARD INVESTMENTS LIMITED
MISSISSAUGA CITY CENTRE OFFICE BUILDING
55 City Centre Dr Suite 800, Mississauga, ON, L5B 1M3
(905) 281-3800
Emp Here 150　　　*Emp Total* 1,826
Sales 75,368,403
SIC 6531 Real estate agents and managers
Pr George Schott
VP David Wyatt

D-U-N-S 20-294-2637　　　(BR)
MORGUARD INVESTMENTS LIMITED
MORGUARD NORTH AMERICAN RESIDENTIAL REAL ESTATE INVESTMENT TRUST
55 City Centre Dr Suite 800, Mississauga, ON, L5B 1M3
(905) 281-3800
Emp Here 300
SIC 6798 Real estate investment trusts

D-U-N-S 24-093-1332　　　(BR)
MOXIE'S RESTAURANTS, LIMITED PARTNERSHIP
100 City Centre Dr Unit 2-730, Mississauga, ON, L5B 2C9
(905) 276-6555
Emp Here 120
SIC 5812 Eating places

D-U-N-S 20-657-9356　　　(BR)
OLD NAVY (CANADA) INC
(*Suby of* The Gap Inc)
100 City Centre Dr Unit E6, Mississauga, ON, L5B 2C9
(905) 275-5155
Emp Here 100
SIC 5651 Family clothing stores

D-U-N-S 20-655-1710　　　(BR)
ONTARIO ENGLISH CATHOLIC TEACHERS ASSOCIATION, THE
345 Fairview Rd W, Mississauga, ON, L5B 3W5
(905) 306-8420
Emp Here 35
SIC 8211 Elementary and secondary schools

D-U-N-S 25-293-8238　　　(BR)
PEEL DISTRICT SCHOOL BOARD
CASHMERE AVENUE PUBLIC SCHOOL
(*Suby of* Peel District School Board)
2455 Cashmere Ave, Mississauga, ON, L5B 2M7
(905) 276-4434
Emp Here 20
SIC 8211 Elementary and secondary schools

D-U-N-S 25-293-7834　　　(BR)
PEEL DISTRICT SCHOOL BOARD
FAIRVIEW PUBLIC SCHOOL
(*Suby of* Peel District School Board)
3590 Joan Dr, Mississauga, ON, L5B 1T8
(905) 270-0281
Emp Here 40
SIC 8211 Elementary and secondary schools

D-U-N-S 24-963-1029　　　(BR)
PEEL DISTRICT SCHOOL BOARD
FLORADALE PUBLIC SCHOOL
(*Suby of* Peel District School Board)
210 Paisley Blvd W, Mississauga, ON, L5B 2A4
(905) 275-1090
Emp Here 50

SIC 8211 Elementary and secondary schools

D-U-N-S 25-134-5245　　　(BR)
PEEL DISTRICT SCHOOL BOARD
THOMAS L KENNEDY SECONDARY SCHOOL
(*Suby of* Peel District School Board)
3100 Hurontario St, Mississauga, ON, L5B 1N7
(905) 279-6540
Emp Here 70
SIC 8211 Elementary and secondary schools

D-U-N-S 20-177-4676　　　(HQ)
PRAXAIR CANADA INC
PRAXAIR DISTRIBUTION, DIV OF
(*Suby of* Praxair, Inc.)
1 City Centre Dr Suite 1200, Mississauga, ON, L5B 1M2
(905) 803-1600
Emp Here 320　　　*Emp Total* 26,657
Sales 112,724,282
SIC 2813 Industrial gases
Pr Pr James Fuchs
Sec Sheryl Nisenbaum
Treas John Allen
Dir Robert Hossack

D-U-N-S 25-236-5531　　　(HQ)
RTO ASSET MANAGEMENT INC
33 City Centre Dr Suite 510, Mississauga, ON, L5B 2N5
(905) 272-2788
Emp Here 30　　　*Emp Total* 1,587
Sales 45,600,438
SIC 7359 Equipment rental and leasing, nec
Pr Pr David Ingram

D-U-N-S 24-447-9981　　　(BR)
RANDSTAD INTERIM INC
201 City Centre Dr, Mississauga, ON, L5B 4E4
(905) 501-7117
Emp Here 20
SIC 7361 Employment agencies

D-U-N-S 25-300-6464　　　(BR)
REDBERRY FRANCHISING CORP
BURGER KING RESTAURANT
100 City Centre Dr Unit 1-830, Mississauga, ON, L5B 2C9
(905) 279-5005
Emp Here 40
SIC 5812 Eating places

D-U-N-S 24-588-8250　　　(HQ)
RENASANT FINANCIAL PARTNERS LTD
(*Suby of* Renasant Financial Partners Ltd)
55 City Centre Dr Suite 800, Mississauga, ON, L5B 1M3
(905) 281-4758
Emp Here 85　　　*Emp Total* 110
Sales 9,528,761
SIC 7377 Computer rental and leasing

D-U-N-S 20-912-6635　　　(BR)
RICHTREE MARKET RESTAURANTS INC
OPEN KITCHENS
100 City Centre Dr Suite 138, Mississauga, ON, L5B 2C9
(905) 272-1010
Emp Here 60
SIC 5812 Eating places

D-U-N-S 20-027-9151　　　(BR)
SIR CORP
CANYON CREEK STEAK & CHOPHOUSE
299 Rathburn Rd W, Mississauga, ON, L5B 4C1
(905) 279-3342
Emp Here 100
SIC 5812 Eating places

D-U-N-S 25-786-2573　　　(BR)
SIR CORP
JACK ASTOR'S
219 Rathburn Rd W, Mississauga, ON, L5B 4C1

▲ Public Company　　■ Public Company Family Member　　**HQ** Headquarters　　**BR** Branch　　**SL** Single Location

(905) 566-4662
Emp Here 130
SIC 5812 Eating places

D-U-N-S 25-724-4830   (BR)
SIR CORP
SCADDABUSH ITALIAN KITCHEN & BAR
209 Rathburn Rd W, Mississauga, ON, L5B
4C1
(905) 281-1721
Emp Here 100
SIC 5812 Eating places

D-U-N-S 25-301-3940   (BR)
SCOTIA CAPITAL INC
SCOTIAMCLEOD
90 Burnhamthorpe Rd W Suite 1400, Mississauga, ON, L5B 3C3
(905) 848-1300
Emp Here 38
SIC 6211 Security brokers and dealers

D-U-N-S 25-311-1736   (BR)
SEARS CANADA INC
100 City Centre Dr Suite 1, Mississauga, ON,
L5B 2C9

Emp Here 300
SIC 5311 Department stores

D-U-N-S 24-760-3231   (BR)
SIENNA SENIOR LIVING INC
CAMILLA CARE COMMUNITY
2250 Hurontario St, Mississauga, ON, L5B
1M8
(905) 270-0411
Emp Here 20
SIC 8051 Skilled nursing care facilities

D-U-N-S 20-866-3588   (SL)
SIZZLING IN MISSISSAUGA INC
77 City Centre Dr Unit 100, Mississauga, ON,
L5B 1M5
(905) 897-8555
Emp Here 60   *Sales* 2,958,580
SIC 5812 Eating places

D-U-N-S 20-793-0921   (BR)
STAPLES CANADA INC
STAPLES THE BUSINESS DEPOT
(*Suby* of Staples, Inc.)
3950 Grand Park Dr Suite 1, Mississauga, ON,
L5B 4M6
(905) 306-7888
Emp Here 30
SIC 5943 Stationery stores

D-U-N-S 20-506-0259   (BR)
STARBUCKS COFFEE CANADA, INC
(*Suby* of Starbucks Corporation)
189 Rathburn Rd W, Mississauga, ON, L5B
4C1
(905) 896-7070
Emp Here 20
SIC 5812 Eating places

D-U-N-S 25-992-2409   (BR)
STARBURST COIN MACHINES INC
(*Suby* of Starburst Coin Machines Inc)
99 Rathburn Rd W, Mississauga, ON, L5B
4C1
(905) 273-9000
Emp Here 120
SIC 7999 Amusement and recreation, nec

D-U-N-S 24-363-9288   (HQ)
TEKSYSTEMS CANADA INC.
TEKSYSTEMS
350 Burnhamthorpe Rd W Suite 700, Mississauga, ON, L5B 3J1
(905) 283-1300
Emp Here 50   *Emp Total* 85,000
Sales 43,312,550
SIC 7361 Employment agencies
Pr Michael W. Salandra
VP VP Timothy W. Cerny
VP VP David J. Standeven
Sec Randall D. Sones
Treas R. Alan Butler

Dir Mike Hyatt
Dir Danny L. Chung
Dir James C. Davis

D-U-N-S 25-120-2099   (BR)
TORONTO-DOMINION BANK, THE
TD CANADA TRUST
(*Suby* of Toronto-Dominion Bank, The)
2580 Hurontario St, Mississauga, ON, L5B
1N5
(905) 277-9474
Emp Here 40
SIC 6021 National commercial banks

D-U-N-S 24-358-2954   (SL)
UNITED WAY OF PEEL REGION, THE
90 Burnhamthorpe Rd W Suite 408, Mississauga, ON, L5B 3C3
(905) 602-3650
Emp Here 45   *Sales* 20,893,320
SIC 8399 Social services, nec
Shelley White

D-U-N-S 25-460-9845   (BR)
UNIVERSITY HEALTH NETWORK
*SUSSEX CENTRE SELF CARE DIALYSIS
UNIT*
90 Burnhamthorpe Rd W Suite 208, Mississauga, ON, L5B 3C3
(905) 272-8334
Emp Here 27
SIC 8092 Kidney dialysis centers

D-U-N-S 24-327-4474   (BR)
WAL-MART CANADA CORP
100 City Centre Dr Suite 100, Mississauga,
ON, L5B 2G7
(905) 270-9300
Emp Here 150
SIC 5311 Department stores

D-U-N-S 24-214-6368   (SL)
WEST 50 POURHOUSE & GRILLE INC
50 Burnhamthorpe Rd W Suite 202, Mississauga, ON, L5B 3C2
(905) 949-9378
Emp Here 60   *Sales* 1,824,018
SIC 5812 Eating places

D-U-N-S 24-802-8354   (BR)
WHOLE FOODS MARKET CANADA INC
155 Square One Dr, Mississauga, ON, L5B
0E2
(905) 275-9393
Emp Here 50
SIC 5411 Grocery stores

D-U-N-S 24-022-7319   (BR)
**WINNERS MERCHANTS INTERNATIONAL
L.P.**
WINNERS
(*Suby* of The TJX Companies Inc)
3900 Grand Park Dr, Mississauga, ON, L5B
4M6
(905) 848-0973
Emp Here 50
SIC 5651 Family clothing stores

D-U-N-S 25-079-0219   (BR)
YM INC. (SALES)
STITCHES
100 City Centre Dr, Mississauga, ON, L5B
2C9
(905) 275-1011
Emp Here 20
SIC 5621 Women's clothing stores

D-U-N-S 24-764-8330   (BR)
YMCA OF GREATER TORONTO
MISSISSAUGA YMCA
325 Burnhamthorpe Rd W, Mississauga, ON,
L5B 3R2
(905) 897-6801
Emp Here 200
SIC 7991 Physical fitness facilities

Mississauga, ON L5C
Peel County

D-U-N-S 24-022-4808   (HQ)
ARI FINANCIAL SERVICES INC
(*Suby* of Holman Enterprises Inc.)
1270 Central Pky W Suite 600, Mississauga,
ON, L5C 4P4
(905) 803-8000
Emp Here 85   *Emp Total* 3,751
Sales 32,051,287
SIC 8741 Management services
Pr Chris Conroy
 Robert White
Sr VP Sr VP Rick Tousaw
VP Fin Gernot Leinenbach
Sr VP Tim Mchugh
Sr VP Denise Wildish

D-U-N-S 25-824-6321   (BR)
ALLIANCE FRANCAISE DE TORONTO
ALLIANCE FRANCAISE
(*Suby* of Alliance Francaise de Toronto)
1140 Burnhamthorpe Rd W Suite 111, Mississauga, ON, L5C 4E9
(905) 272-4444
Emp Here 22
SIC 8299 Schools and educational services,
nec

D-U-N-S 20-588-2231   (BR)
BANQUE TORONTO-DOMINION, LA
TD CANADA TRUST
(*Suby* of Toronto-Dominion Bank, The)
1177 Central Pky W Suite 35, Mississauga,
ON, L5C 4P3
(905) 896-3188
Emp Here 20
SIC 6021 National commercial banks

D-U-N-S 24-108-6532   (BR)
CRH CANADA GROUP INC
3649 Erindale Station Rd, Mississauga, ON,
L5C 2S9
(905) 275-2093
Emp Here 30
SIC 3272 Concrete products, nec

D-U-N-S 24-624-7720   (BR)
CANADIAN PACIFIC RAILWAY COMPANY
CPR
1290 Central Pky W Suite 800, Mississauga,
ON, L5C 4R3
(905) 803-3252
Emp Here 200
SIC 4011 Railroads, line-haul operating

D-U-N-S 25-306-4497   (BR)
**CO-OPERATORS GENERAL INSURANCE
COMPANY**
1270 Central Pky W Suite 600, Mississauga,
ON, L5C 4P4

Emp Here 90
SIC 6411 Insurance agents, brokers, and service

D-U-N-S 24-827-4024   (BR)
**COMPAGNIE DES CHEMINS DE FER NA-
TIONAUX DU CANADA**
*CN SUPPLY CHAIN SOLUTIONS CANADA,
DIV OF*
1270 Central Pky W Suite 400, Mississauga,
ON, L5C 4P4
(905) 789-4512
Emp Here 20
SIC 4731 Freight transportation arrangement

D-U-N-S 24-963-0971   (BR)
**DUFFERIN-PEEL CATHOLIC DISTRICT
SCHOOL BOARD**
SAINT GERARD CATHOLIC SCHOOL
1300 Mcbride Ave, Mississauga, ON, L5C
1M8
(905) 277-4512
Emp Here 34
SIC 8211 Elementary and secondary schools

D-U-N-S 25-224-9412   (BR)
**DUFFERIN-PEEL CATHOLIC DISTRICT
SCHOOL BOARD**
ST JEROME SCHOOL
790 Paisley Blvd W, Mississauga, ON, L5C
3P5
(905) 273-3836
Emp Here 35
SIC 8211 Elementary and secondary schools

D-U-N-S 20-653-4716   (BR)
**DUFFERIN-PEEL CATHOLIC DISTRICT
SCHOOL BOARD**
SAINT JEROME SCHOOL
790 Paisley Blvd W, Mississauga, ON, L5C
3P5
(905) 273-3836
Emp Here 20
SIC 8211 Elementary and secondary schools

D-U-N-S 24-963-0856   (BR)
**DUFFERIN-PEEL CATHOLIC DISTRICT
SCHOOL BOARD**
*ST. DAVID OF WALES ELEMENTARY
SCHOOL*
4200 Beacon Lane, Mississauga, ON, L5C
3V9
(905) 848-4200
Emp Here 40
SIC 8211 Elementary and secondary schools

D-U-N-S 24-312-3424   (BR)
**DUFFERIN-PEEL CATHOLIC DISTRICT
SCHOOL BOARD**
ST MARTINS SECONDARY SCHOOL
2470 Rosemary Dr, Mississauga, ON, L5C
1X2
(905) 279-3171
Emp Here 70
SIC 8211 Elementary and secondary schools

D-U-N-S 20-104-7094   (SL)
EDWARDS LIFESCIENCES (CANADA) INC
1290 Central Pky W Suite 300, Mississauga,
ON, L5C 4R3
(905) 273-7138
Emp Here 25   *Sales* 3,648,035
SIC 5047 Medical and hospital equipment

D-U-N-S 24-123-5956   (BR)
**ENTERPRISE RENT-A-CAR CANADA COM-
PANY**
TORONTO INTERNATIONAL AIRPORT
(*Suby* of The Crawford Group Inc)
777 Dundas St W Unit B1, Mississauga, ON,
L5C 4P6
(905) 281-0869
Emp Here 50
SIC 7514 Passenger car rental

D-U-N-S 24-318-5696   (BR)
**FIELDING CHEMICAL TECHNOLOGIES
INC**
(*Suby* of Fielding Chemical Technologies Inc)
3549 Mavis Rd, Mississauga, ON, L5C 1T7
(905) 279-5122
Emp Here 60
SIC 8731 Commercial physical research

D-U-N-S 20-073-5954   (BR)
FIRSTCANADA ULC
3599 Wolfedale Rd, Mississauga, ON, L5C
1V8
(905) 270-0561
Emp Here 235
SIC 4151 School buses

D-U-N-S 25-140-3895   (BR)
GOODLIFE FITNESS CENTRES INC
GOODLIFE FITNESS CLUBS
3045 Mavis Rd, Mississauga, ON, L5C 1T7
(905) 949-1400
Emp Here 22
SIC 7991 Physical fitness facilities

D-U-N-S 24-560-4194   (SL)
GRAHAM PACKAGING CANADA LIMITED
3174 Mavis Rd, Mississauga, ON, L5C 1T8

(905) 277-1486
Emp Here 120   *Sales* 18,167,214
SIC 3089 Plastics products, nec
  Phil Yates
Pr Roger Prevot
VP VP John Hamilton
Treas Paul Wannemacher

D-U-N-S 25-088-1794   (BR)
HOME DEPOT OF CANADA INC
HOME DEPOT
(*Suby of* The Home Depot Inc)
3065 Mavis Rd, Mississauga, ON, L5C 1T7
(905) 281-6230
Emp Here 173
SIC 5251 Hardware stores

D-U-N-S 25-333-1144   (HQ)
**INFORMATION COMMUNICATION SER-
VICES (ICS) INC**
ICS COURIER SERVICES
1290 Central Pky W Suite 50, Mississauga,
ON, L5C 4R3
(416) 642-2477
Emp Here 80   *Emp Total* 25,438
Sales 121,968,141
SIC 4212 Local trucking, without storage
Dir Chantal Martel
Dir Josiane-Melanie Langlois

D-U-N-S 25-370-3441   (BR)
LAFARGE CANADA INC
3520 Mavis Rd, Mississauga, ON, L5C 1T8
(905) 279-1608
Emp Here 35
SIC 5032 Brick, stone, and related material

D-U-N-S 25-942-3903   (BR)
LIVING REALTY INC
(*Suby of* Living Realty Inc)
1177 Central Pky W Unit 32, Mississauga,
ON, L5C 4P3
(905) 896-0002
Emp Here 100
SIC 6531 Real estate agents and managers

D-U-N-S 24-329-6931   (BR)
LOBLAWS INC
REAL CANADIAN SUPERSTORE
3045 Mavis Rd Suite 2841, Mississauga, ON,
L5C 1T7
(905) 275-6171
Emp Here 200
SIC 5411 Grocery stores

D-U-N-S 24-387-3259   (BR)
LONG & MCQUADE LIMITED
*LONG & MCQUADE MUSICAL INSTRU-
MENTS*
900 Rathburn Rd W, Mississauga, ON, L5C
4L4
(905) 273-3939
Emp Here 20
SIC 5736 Musical instrument stores

D-U-N-S 25-310-9458   (BR)
**MCDONALD'S   RESTAURANTS   OF
CANADA LIMITED**
MCDONALD'S RESTAURANTS
(*Suby of* McDonald's Corporation)
796 Burnhamthorpe Rd W Unit A, Missis-
sauga, ON, L5C 2R9
(905) 275-3011
Emp Here 70
SIC 5812 Eating places

D-U-N-S 20-805-8458   (BR)
METROLINX
GO TRANSIT
3500 Wolfedale Rd, Mississauga, ON, L5C
2V6

Emp Here 120
SIC 3743 Railroad equipment

D-U-N-S 25-755-6621   (BR)
METROLAND MEDIA GROUP LTD
MISSISSAUGA NEWS, THE
3145 Wolfedale Rd, Mississauga, ON, L5C

3A9
(905) 273-8111
Emp Here 160
SIC 2711 Newspapers

D-U-N-S 25-050-6334   (BR)
MOTORCADE INDUSTRIES LIMITED
3550 Wolfedale Rd Unit 3, Mississauga, ON,
L5C 2V6
(905) 848-1177
Emp Here 20
SIC 5013 Motor vehicle supplies and new
parts

D-U-N-S 25-293-8196   (BR)
PEEL DISTRICT SCHOOL BOARD
ELLENGALE PUBLIC SCHOOL
(*Suby of* Peel District School Board)
3480 Ellengale Dr, Mississauga, ON, L5C 1Z7
(905) 279-1555
Emp Here 24
SIC 8211 Elementary and secondary schools

D-U-N-S 25-293-7842   (BR)
PEEL DISTRICT SCHOOL BOARD
QUEENSTON DRIVE PUBLIC SCHOOL
(*Suby of* Peel District School Board)
3520 Queenston Dr, Mississauga, ON, L5C
2G6
(905) 277-9523
Emp Here 50
SIC 8211 Elementary and secondary schools

D-U-N-S 24-963-0831   (BR)
PEEL DISTRICT SCHOOL BOARD
MCBRIDE AVENUE PUBLIC SCHOOL
(*Suby of* Peel District School Board)
974 Mcbride Ave, Mississauga, ON, L5C 1L6
(905) 270-6414
Emp Here 50
SIC 8211 Elementary and secondary schools

D-U-N-S 25-220-8053   (BR)
PEEL DISTRICT SCHOOL BOARD
HAWTHORNE PUBLC SCHOOL
(*Suby of* Peel District School Board)
2473 Rosemary Dr, Mississauga, ON, L5C
1X1
(905) 277-4321
Emp Here 20
SIC 8211 Elementary and secondary schools

D-U-N-S 25-293-7610   (BR)
PEEL DISTRICT SCHOOL BOARD
WOODLANDS SCHOOL
(*Suby of* Peel District School Board)
3225 Erindale Station Rd, Mississauga, ON,
L5C 1Y5
(905) 279-0575
Emp Here 135
SIC 8211 Elementary and secondary schools

D-U-N-S 25-293-8451   (BR)
PEEL DISTRICT SCHOOL BOARD
SPRINGFIELD PUBLIC SCHOOL
(*Suby of* Peel District School Board)
3251 The Credit Woodlands, Mississauga,
ON, L5C 2J7
(905) 279-7950
Emp Here 40
SIC 8211 Elementary and secondary schools

D-U-N-S 25-317-5228   (SL)
PROG-DIE TOOL & STAMPING LTD
3161 Wolfedale Rd, Mississauga, ON, L5C
1V8
(905) 277-9187
Emp Here 60   *Sales* 6,832,640
SIC 3544 Special dies, tools, jigs, and fixtures
Pr Pr Santiago A. Almiron

D-U-N-S 20-042-7615   (HQ)
RLBS LIMITED
3350 Wolfedale Rd, Mississauga, ON, L5C
1W4
(905) 275-1800
Emp Here 175   *Emp Total* 2
Sales 87,259,665
SIC 5031 Lumber, plywood, and millwork

Pr Pr Stephen Rockett
VP Fin Aldo Bartolini

D-U-N-S 20-561-9484   (BR)
RE/MAX PERFORMANCE REALTY INC
1140 Burnhamthorpe Rd W Suite 141, Mississauga, ON, L5C 4E9
(905) 270-2000
Emp Here 130
SIC 6531 Real estate agents and managers

D-U-N-S 24-848-4255   (HQ)
RE/MAX PROFESSIONALS INC
(*Suby of* Re/Max Professionals Inc)
1645 Dundas St W, Mississauga, ON, L5C
1E3
(905) 270-8840
Emp Here 35   *Emp Total* 50
Sales 4,742,446
SIC 6531 Real estate agents and managers

D-U-N-S 25-816-0266   (BR)
REDBERRY FRANCHISING CORP
BURGER KING
769 Burnhamthorpe Rd W, Mississauga, ON,
L5C 3A6
(905) 281-0932
Emp Here 29
SIC 5812 Eating places

D-U-N-S 24-680-2693   (BR)
SILTECH CORPORATION
3265 Wolfedale Rd, Mississauga, ON, L5C
1V8
(905) 270-9328
Emp Here 42
SIC 2869 Industrial organic chemicals, nec

D-U-N-S 25-486-7328   (BR)
SOBEYS CAPITAL INCORPORATED
FRESHCO
4040 Creditview Rd, Mississauga, ON, L5C
3Y8

Emp Here 85
SIC 5411 Grocery stores

D-U-N-S 25-120-7262   (BR)
SPECTRUM HEALTH CARE LTD
*SPECTRUM HEALTH AMBULATORY CARE
CLINIC*
1290 Central Pky W Suite 302, Mississauga,
ON, L5C 4R3
(905) 272-2271
Emp Here 400
SIC 8741 Management services

D-U-N-S 25-327-6484   (SL)
SUNCORE CONSTRUCTION
3455 Wolfedale Rd, Mississauga, ON, L5C
1V8
(905) 897-1000
Emp Here 25   *Sales* 5,173,950
SIC 1521 Single-family housing construction
  Helen Jung

D-U-N-S 25-122-7948   (SL)
WALKER, J. B. & M. LIMITED
TIM HORTONS
3411 Mavis Rd, Mississauga, ON, L5C 1T7
(905) 272-4545
Emp Here 65   *Sales* 1,969,939
SIC 5812 Eating places

D-U-N-S 24-751-3955   (SL)
WHEEL CARE TRANSIT LTD
845 Central Pky W Unit 2, Mississauga, ON,
L5C 2V9

Emp Here 65   *Sales* 1,824,018
SIC 4151 School buses

Mississauga, ON L5E
Peel County

D-U-N-S 20-352-2792   (SL)

2582101 ONTARIO INC
CHANTLER PACKAGES
880 Lakeshore Rd E, Mississauga, ON, L5E
1E1
(905) 274-2533
Emp Here 35   *Sales* 5,836,856
SIC 2671 Paper; coated and laminated pack-
aging
  Roy Ferguson
  Ian Ferguson

D-U-N-S 20-790-3050   (BR)
BOUTIQUE LA VIE EN ROSE INC
BOUTIQUE LA VIE EN ROSE INC
1250 South Service Rd Suite 100, Mississauga, ON, L5E 1V4
(905) 278-2043
Emp Here 23
SIC 5632 Women's accessory and specialty
stores

D-U-N-S 24-886-4399   (SL)
C.A. FRUIT PRODUCTS LTD
(*Suby of* Sue's Produce World Ltd)
1000 Lakeshore Rd E, Mississauga, ON, L5E
1E4
(905) 271-1711
Emp Here 30   *Sales* 1,459,214
SIC 2033 Canned fruits and specialties

D-U-N-S 24-917-4574   (SL)
CHANTLER PACKAGING INC
(*Suby of* Chantler & Chantler Inc)
880 Lakeshore Rd E, Mississauga, ON, L5E
1E1
(905) 274-2533
Emp Here 35   *Sales* 6,930,008
SIC 2671 Paper; coated and laminated packaging

D-U-N-S 25-412-1932   (SL)
FILAMAT COMPOSITES INC
880 Rangeview Rd, Mississauga, ON, L5E
1G9
(905) 891-3993
Emp Here 50   *Sales* 4,711,645
SIC 3299 NonMetallic mineral products,

D-U-N-S 25-364-1104   (BR)
INTERIOR MANUFACTURING GROUP INC
850 Rangeview Rd, Mississauga, ON, L5E
1G9
(905) 278-6391
Emp Here 30
SIC 1761 Roofing, siding, and sheetMetal
work

D-U-N-S 20-768-8172   (BR)
LOBLAW PROPERTIES LIMITED
CHRIS AND STACEYS NO FRILLS
1250 South Service Rd, Mississauga, ON,
L5E 1V4
(905) 891-1021
Emp Here 49
SIC 5411 Grocery stores

D-U-N-S 25-122-3764   (BR)
**PARTICIPATION HOUSE HAMILTON AND
DISTRICT**
*PARTICIPATION   HOUSE   LAKESIDE
PROJECT*
(*Suby of* Participation House Hamilton And
District)
1022 Greaves Ave Suite 100, Mississauga,
ON, L5E 3J4
(905) 278-1112
Emp Here 21
SIC 8361 Residential care

D-U-N-S 24-962-9718   (BR)
PEEL DISTRICT SCHOOL BOARD
*ALLAN A MARTIN SENIOR PUBLIC
SCHOOL*
(*Suby of* Peel District School Board)
1390 Ogden Ave, Mississauga, ON, L5E 2H8
(905) 278-6104
Emp Here 39
SIC 8211 Elementary and secondary schools

D-U-N-S 25-293-8386   (BR)
PEEL DISTRICT SCHOOL BOARD
*GORDON GRAYDON MEMORIAL SEC-
ONDARY SCHOOL*
(*Suby of* Peel District School Board)
1490 Ogden Ave, Mississauga, ON, L5E 2H8
(905) 274-2391
Emp Here 140
SIC 8211 Elementary and secondary schools

D-U-N-S 24-704-1437   (SL)
PLASTER FORM INC
1180 Lakeshore Rd E, Mississauga, ON, L5E
1E9
(905) 891-9500
Emp Here 125
SIC 3275 Gypsum products

D-U-N-S 25-300-4584   (BR)
REDBERRY FRANCHISING CORP
BURGER KING
1490 Dixie Rd, Mississauga, ON, L5E 3E5
(905) 274-1607
Emp Here 30
SIC 5812 Eating places

D-U-N-S 20-822-4295   (SL)
TORONTO GOLF CLUB, THE
1305 Dixie Rd, Mississauga, ON, L5E 2P5
(905) 278-5255
Emp Here 97   *Sales* 4,994,344
SIC 7997 Membership sports and recreation
clubs

D-U-N-S 24-991-0498   (HQ)
WILCOX DOOR SERVICE INC
(*Suby of* Wilcox Door Service Inc)
1045 Rangeview Rd, Mississauga, ON, L5E
1H2
(905) 274-5850
Emp Here 40   *Emp Total* 60
Sales 4,377,642
SIC 1751 Carpentry work

D-U-N-S 25-221-2410   (BR)
**WINNERS MERCHANTS INTERNATIONAL
L.P.**
WINNERS
(*Suby of* The TJX Companies Inc)
1250 South Service Rd Unit 86, Mississauga,
ON, L5E 1V4
(905) 278-0030
Emp Here 60
SIC 5651 Family clothing stores

D-U-N-S 24-121-9737   (BR)
YM INC. (SALES)
URBAN PLANET
1250 South Service Rd Unit 156, Mississauga,
ON, L5E 1V4
(905) 274-9984
Emp Here 30
SIC 5621 Women's clothing stores

Mississauga, ON L5G
Peel County

D-U-N-S 24-392-6230   (BR)
CENTRE CITY CAPITAL LIMITED
WATERSIDE INN, THE
15 Stavebank Rd S Suite 804, Mississauga,
ON, L5G 2T2
(905) 891-7770
Emp Here 100
SIC 7011 Hotels and motels

D-U-N-S 20-710-9658   (BR)
**DUFFERIN-PEEL CATHOLIC DISTRICT
SCHOOL BOARD**
ST DOMINIC SCHOOL
515 Hartsdale Ave, Mississauga, ON, L5G
2G7
(905) 270-4151
Emp Here 50
SIC 8211 Elementary and secondary schools

D-U-N-S 20-352-6983   (SL)
FIRST DERIVATIVES CANADA INC
1599 Hurontario St Suite 302, Mississauga,
ON, L5G 4S1
(905) 278-9444
Emp Here 57   *Sales* 6,055,738
SIC 7371 Custom computer programming ser-
vices
Pr Hugh Hyndman
CEO Brian Conlon
 Graham Ferguson

D-U-N-S 25-202-6786   (SL)
FRAM CONSTRUCTION LIMITED
141 Lakeshore Rd E, Mississauga, ON, L5G
1E8
(905) 278-0331
Emp Here 20   *Sales* 14,724,000
SIC 1531 Operative builders
Pr Giovanni Giannone
VP Frank Giannone

D-U-N-S 25-318-7769   (BR)
**LIQUOR CONTROL BOARD OF ONTARIO,
THE**
LCBO
200 Lakeshore Rd E, Mississauga, ON, L5G
1G3
(905) 278-7931
Emp Here 20
SIC 5921 Liquor stores

D-U-N-S 20-027-3089   (BR)
MENTOR EDUCATIONAL INC
MENTOR COLLEGE PRIMARY CAMPUS
56 Cayuga Ave, Mississauga, ON, L5G 3S9
(905) 271-7100
Emp Here 43
SIC 8221 Colleges and universities

D-U-N-S 24-886-6675   (HQ)
NORMERICA INC
NORTHDOWN INDUSTRIES
1599 Hurontario St Suite 300, Mississauga,
ON, L5G 4S1
(416) 626-0556
Emp Here 50   *Emp Total* 187
Sales 31,956,787
SIC 3295 Minerals, ground or treated
 John Kimmel
Pr Colin Gleason
Ex VP Sue Sri

D-U-N-S 25-293-7883   (BR)
PEEL DISTRICT SCHOOL BOARD
*QUEEN ELIZABETH JUNIOR MIDDLE
SCHOOL*
(*Suby of* Peel District School Board)
60 South Service Rd, Mississauga, ON, L5G
2R9
(905) 278-7287
Emp Here 30
SIC 8211 Elementary and secondary schools

D-U-N-S 25-293-8360   (BR)
PEEL DISTRICT SCHOOL BOARD
MINEOLA PUBLIC SCHOOL
(*Suby of* Peel District School Board)
145 Windy Oaks, Mississauga, ON, L5G 1Z4
(905) 278-3144
Emp Here 30
SIC 8211 Elementary and secondary schools

D-U-N-S 24-963-0625   (BR)
PEEL DISTRICT SCHOOL BOARD
CAWTHRA PARK SECONDARY SCHOOL
(*Suby of* Peel District School Board)
1305 Cawthra Rd, Mississauga, ON, L5G 4L1
(905) 274-1271
Emp Here 95
SIC 8211 Elementary and secondary schools

D-U-N-S 25-293-7750   (BR)
PEEL DISTRICT SCHOOL BOARD
FOREST AVENUE PUBLIC SCHOOL
(*Suby of* Peel District School Board)
20 Forest Ave, Mississauga, ON, L5G 1K7

(905) 278-2472
Emp Here 22
SIC 8211 Elementary and secondary schools

D-U-N-S 24-346-3234   (BR)
PEEL DISTRICT SCHOOL BOARD
PORT CREDIT SECONDARY SCHOOL
(*Suby of* Peel District School Board)
70 Mineola Rd E, Mississauga, ON, L5G 2E5
(905) 278-3382
Emp Here 50
SIC 8211 Elementary and secondary schools

D-U-N-S 24-963-0872   (BR)
PEEL DISTRICT SCHOOL BOARD
LYNDWOOD PUBLIC SCHOOL
(*Suby of* Peel District School Board)
498 Hartsdale Ave, Mississauga, ON, L5G
2G6
(905) 278-6144
Emp Here 25
SIC 8211 Elementary and secondary schools

D-U-N-S 24-188-5735   (BR)
**PEEL HALTON ACQUIRED BRAIN IN-
JURIES SERVICES**
1048 Cawthra Rd, Mississauga, ON, L5G 4K2
(905) 891-8384
Emp Here 200
SIC 8093 Specialty outpatient clinics, nec

D-U-N-S 25-018-5071   (BR)
ROYAL LEPAGE LIMITED
ROYAL LEPAGE REAL ESTATE SERVICES
1654 Lakeshore Rd E, Mississauga, ON, L5G
1E2
(905) 278-5273
Emp Here 100
SIC 6531 Real estate agents and managers

D-U-N-S 25-807-3576   (SL)
SNUG HARBOUR SEAFOOD BAR & GRILL
14 Stavebank Rd S, Mississauga, ON, L5G
2T1
(905) 274-5000
Emp Here 130   *Sales* 3,939,878
SIC 5812 Eating places

D-U-N-S 24-066-0378   (SL)
TEN RESTAURANT & WINE BAR INC
139 Lakeshore Rd E, Mississauga, ON, L5G
1E5
(905) 271-0016
Emp Here 60   *Sales* 1,824,018
SIC 5812 Eating places

Mississauga, ON L5H
Peel County

D-U-N-S 24-776-6541   (BR)
CHARTWELL MASTER CARE LP
29 Mississauga Rd N, Mississauga, ON, L5H
2H7
(905) 891-2422
Emp Here 40
SIC 8322 Individual and family services

D-U-N-S 24-193-5563   (SL)
**CHARTWELL REGENCY RETIREMENT
RESIDENCE**
29 Mississauga Rd N Suite 419, Mississauga,
ON, L5H 2H7
(905) 891-2422
Emp Here 25   *Sales* 948,489
SIC 8361 Residential care

D-U-N-S 24-525-4201   (BR)
**DUFFERIN-PEEL CATHOLIC DISTRICT
SCHOOL BOARD**
*ST LUKE CATHOLIC ELEMENTARY
SCHOOL*
1280 Cobalt St, Mississauga, ON, L5H 4L8
(905) 274-2760
Emp Here 25
SIC 8211 Elementary and secondary schools

D-U-N-S 25-486-6437   (BR)
**DUFFERIN-PEEL CATHOLIC DISTRICT
SCHOOL BOARD**
HOLY NAME MARY COLLEGE SCHOOL
2241 Mississauga Rd, Mississauga, ON, L5H
2K8
(905) 891-1890
Emp Here 70
SIC 8211 Elementary and secondary schools

D-U-N-S 25-803-5039   (BR)
LOBLAWS SUPERMARKETS LIMITED
LOBLAWS
250 Lakeshore Rd W, Mississauga, ON, L5H
1G6
(905) 271-9925
Emp Here 150
SIC 5411 Grocery stores

D-U-N-S 24-963-0989   (BR)
PEEL DISTRICT SCHOOL BOARD
PARK PUBLIC SCHOOL
(*Suby of* Peel District School Board)
1325 Indian Rd, Mississauga, ON, L5H 1S3
(905) 278-8771
Emp Here 22
SIC 8211 Elementary and secondary schools

D-U-N-S 24-963-0799   (BR)
PEEL DISTRICT SCHOOL BOARD
OAKRIDGE PUBLIC SCHOOL
(*Suby of* Peel District School Board)
2060 Stonehouse Cres, Mississauga, ON,
L5H 3J1
(905) 274-3601
Emp Here 20
SIC 8211 Elementary and secondary schools

D-U-N-S 24-963-1110   (BR)
PEEL DISTRICT SCHOOL BOARD
RIVERSIDE PUBLIC SCHOOL
(*Suby of* Peel District School Board)
30 John St N, Mississauga, ON, L5H 2E8
(905) 274-1515
Emp Here 30
SIC 8211 Elementary and secondary schools

D-U-N-S 24-963-0948   (BR)
PEEL DISTRICT SCHOOL BOARD
LORNE PARK SECONDARY SCHOOL
(*Suby of* Peel District School Board)
1324 Lorne Park Rd, Mississauga, ON, L5H
3B1
(905) 278-6177
Emp Here 100
SIC 8211 Elementary and secondary schools

D-U-N-S 25-237-9813   (BR)
PEEL DISTRICT SCHOOL BOARD
TECUMSEH PUBLIC SCHOOL
(*Suby of* Peel District School Board)
1480 Chriseden Dr, Mississauga, ON, L5H
1V4
(905) 278-5594
Emp Here 35
SIC 8211 Elementary and secondary schools

D-U-N-S 20-944-5621   (BR)
STARBUCKS COFFEE CANADA, INC
(*Suby of* Starbucks Corporation)
111 Lakeshore Rd W, Mississauga, ON, L5H
1E9
(905) 278-7562
Emp Here 20
SIC 5812 Eating places

D-U-N-S 24-785-4131   (SL)
UXDU CONTRACTING INC
1235 Indian Rd, Mississauga, ON, L5H 1R8
(905) 891-5214
Emp Here 45   *Sales* 5,987,760
SIC 1761 Roofing, siding, and sheetMetal
work
Prin Roberto Roman

Mississauga, ON L5J
Peel County

D-U-N-S 20-041-2823   (BR)
CRH CANADA GROUP INC
ST-LAWRENCE CEMENT
2391 Lakeshore Rd W, Mississauga, ON, L5J 1K1
(905) 822-1653
Emp Here 300
SIC 3241 Cement, hydraulic

D-U-N-S 20-041-3094   (HQ)
CERTAINTEED GYPSUM CANADA, INC
2424 Lakeshore Rd W, Mississauga, ON, L5J 1K4
(905) 823-9881
Emp Here 150   *Emp Total* 205
SIC 3275 Gypsum products

D-U-N-S 24-919-0612   (BR)
CLEAN HARBORS CANADA, INC
551 Avonhead Rd, Mississauga, ON, L5J 4B1
(905) 822-3951
Emp Here 30
SIC 4953 Refuse systems

D-U-N-S 24-389-4644   (SL)
COHERENT CANADA INC
1222 April Dr, Mississauga, ON, L5J 3J7
(905) 823-5808
Emp Here 100   *Sales* 19,884,200
SIC 3699 Electrical equipment and supplies, nec
Pr Helene Simonet
 Bret Dimarco
VP Mitchell Mcpeek

D-U-N-S 25-512-7722   (BR)
CONTRANS FLATBED GROUP GP INC
CONTRANS FLATBED GROUP
2278 Lakeshore Rd W, Mississauga, ON, L5J 1K2
(905) 855-3906
Emp Here 50
SIC 4482 Ferries

D-U-N-S 20-041-2237   (SL)
DAHL BROTHERS (CANADA) LIMITED
2600 South Sheridan Way, Mississauga, ON, L5J 2M4
(905) 822-2330
Emp Here 140   *Sales* 23,840,924
SIC 3494 Valves and pipe fittings, nec
Pr Pr Janaike Godfree
Dir Trygve Husebye
Dir Aase Husebye

D-U-N-S 25-978-0880   (SL)
DEMYSH GROUP INC
DEMYSH METAL
2568 Royal Windsor Dr, Mississauga, ON, L5J 1K7

Emp Here 100   *Sales* 21,815,249
SIC 3612 Transformers, except electric
Pr Pr Anthony Demysh

D-U-N-S 24-157-1871   (BR)
DOLLARAMA S.E.C.
DOLLARAMA
1865 Lakeshore Rd W Suite 3, Mississauga, ON, L5J 4P1
(905) 855-9469
Emp Here 25
SIC 5311 Department stores

D-U-N-S 20-710-9997   (BR)
DUFFERIN-PEEL CATHOLIC DISTRICT SCHOOL BOARD
IONA CATHOLIC SECONDARY SCHOOL
2170 South Sheridan Way, Mississauga, ON, L5J 2M4
(905) 823-0136
Emp Here 50
SIC 8211 Elementary and secondary schools

D-U-N-S 25-265-3118   (BR)
DUFFERIN-PEEL CATHOLIC DISTRICT

SCHOOL BOARD
ST CHRISTOPHER ELEMENTARY SCHOOL
1195 Clarkson Rd N, Mississauga, ON, L5J 2W1
(905) 822-0721
Emp Here 40
SIC 8211 Elementary and secondary schools

D-U-N-S 20-041-2344   (HQ)
GRANT, JOHN HAULAGE LIMITED
(*Suby of* Grant, John Haulage Limited)
2111 Lakeshore Rd W, Mississauga, ON, L5J 1J9
(905) 849-7422
Emp Here 40   *Emp Total* 50
Sales 3,939,878
SIC 4212 Local trucking, without storage

D-U-N-S 25-724-5548   (HQ)
LOGIHEDRON INC
(*Suby of* Logihedron Inc)
1670 Finfar Crt Unit 2, Mississauga, ON, L5J 4K1
(905) 823-5767
Emp Here 60   *Emp Total* 60
Sales 8,857,893
SIC 8741 Management services
Pr Farshogar (Fred) Jasavala
VP VP Roy Gavdar

D-U-N-S 24-984-8862   (BR)
LONGYEAR CANADA, ULC
2442 South Sheridan Way, Mississauga, ON, L5J 2M7
(905) 822-7922
Emp Here 100
SIC 3532 Mining machinery

D-U-N-S 24-316-0301   (BR)
MARTINREA INTERNATIONAL INC
MJ MANUFACTURING, DIV OF
2457 Lakeshore Rd W, Mississauga, ON, L5J 1J9
(905) 403-0456
Emp Here 150
SIC 3499 Fabricated Metal products, nec

D-U-N-S 25-936-9049   (BR)
METRO ONTARIO INC
METRO
910 Southdown Rd Unit 46, Mississauga, ON, L5J 2Y4
(905) 823-4900
Emp Here 150
SIC 5411 Grocery stores

D-U-N-S 25-226-8396   (BR)
MINI-SKOOL A CHILD'S PLACE INC
MINI-SKOOL
2488 Bromsgrove Rd, Mississauga, ON, L5J 1L8
(905) 823-3000
Emp Here 35
SIC 8351 Child day care services

D-U-N-S 20-181-2562   (BR)
NESTLE CANADA INC
NESTLE PURINA PET CARE DIV OF
2500 Royal Windsor Dr, Mississauga, ON, L5J 1K8
(905) 822-1611
Emp Here 350
SIC 2047 Dog and cat food

D-U-N-S 24-632-6540   (SL)
ORC MANAGEMENT LIMITED
ONTARIO RACQUET CLUB
884 Southdown Rd, Mississauga, ON, L5J 2Y4
(905) 822-5240
Emp Here 70   *Sales* 3,828,240
SIC 7997 Membership sports and recreation clubs

D-U-N-S 20-531-3356   (BR)
PPG CANADA INC
CLARKSON DIV
(*Suby of* PPG Industries, Inc.)
84 North Bend St Suite 102, Mississauga, ON,

L5J 2Z5
(905) 823-1100
Emp Here 350
SIC 2851 Paints and allied products

D-U-N-S 25-293-7651   (BR)
PEEL DISTRICT SCHOOL BOARD
WILLOW GLEN PUBLIC SCHOOL
(*Suby of* Peel District School Board)
1301 Epton Cres, Mississauga, ON, L5J 1R9
(905) 822-4171
Emp Here 21
SIC 8211 Elementary and secondary schools

D-U-N-S 24-963-1102   (BR)
PEEL DISTRICT SCHOOL BOARD
HILLCREST PUBLIC SCHOOL
(*Suby of* Peel District School Board)
1530 Springwell Ave, Mississauga, ON, L5J 3H6
(905) 822-1657
Emp Here 26
SIC 8211 Elementary and secondary schools

D-U-N-S 25-293-8436   (BR)
PEEL DISTRICT SCHOOL BOARD
CLARKSON PUBLIC SCHOOL
(*Suby of* Peel District School Board)
888 Clarkson Rd S, Mississauga, ON, L5J 2V3
(905) 823-4470
Emp Here 20
SIC 8211 Elementary and secondary schools

D-U-N-S 25-222-0934   (BR)
PEEL DISTRICT SCHOOL BOARD
HILLSIDE SENIOR PUBLIC SCHOOL
(*Suby of* Peel District School Board)
1290 Kelly Rd, Mississauga, ON, L5J 3V1
(905) 822-0122
Emp Here 48
SIC 8211 Elementary and secondary schools

D-U-N-S 25-293-7693   (BR)
PEEL DISTRICT SCHOOL BOARD
WHITEOAKS PUBLIC SCHOOL
(*Suby of* Peel District School Board)
1690 Mazo Cres, Mississauga, ON, L5J 1Y8
(905) 822-0451
Emp Here 42
SIC 8211 Elementary and secondary schools

D-U-N-S 25-293-7958   (BR)
PEEL DISTRICT SCHOOL BOARD
ELMCREST PUBLIC SCHOOL
(*Suby of* Peel District School Board)
2620 Chalkwell Close, Mississauga, ON, L5J 2B9
(905) 822-1675
Emp Here 39
SIC 8211 Elementary and secondary schools

D-U-N-S 24-963-0559   (BR)
PEEL DISTRICT SCHOOL BOARD
CLARKSON SECONDARY SCHOOL
(*Suby of* Peel District School Board)
2524 Bromsgrove Rd, Mississauga, ON, L5J 1L8
(905) 822-6700
Emp Here 90
SIC 8211 Elementary and secondary schools

D-U-N-S 25-293-7685   (BR)
PEEL DISTRICT SCHOOL BOARD
GREEN GLADE SENIOR PUBLIC SCHOOL
(*Suby of* Peel District School Board)
1550 Green Glade, Mississauga, ON, L5J 1B5
(905) 822-8386
Emp Here 22
SIC 8211 Elementary and secondary schools

D-U-N-S 24-391-7148   (HQ)
PETRO-CANADA LUBRICANTS INC
2310 Lakeshore Rd W, Mississauga, ON, L5J 1K2
(905) 804-3600
Emp Here 83   *Emp Total* 2,676
Sales 175,470,484
SIC 5172 Petroleum products, nec

VP Howard Mcintyre

D-U-N-S 25-155-8581   (BR)
PRUDENTIAL TOWN CENTRE REALTY
1680 Lakeshore Rd W, Mississauga, ON, L5J 1J5
(905) 823-0020
Emp Here 20
SIC 6531 Real estate agents and managers

D-U-N-S 24-215-9812   (BR)
REGIONAL MUNICIPALITY OF PEEL, THE
SHERIDAN VILLA HOME FOR AGED
2460 Truscott Dr, Mississauga, ON, L5J 3Z8
(905) 791-8668
Emp Here 200
SIC 8051 Skilled nursing care facilities

D-U-N-S 20-041-2864   (BR)
SHERIDAN NURSERIES LIMITED
606 Southdown Rd Suite 32, Mississauga, ON, L5J 2Y4
(905) 822-0251
Emp Here 40
SIC 5261 Retail nurseries and garden stores

D-U-N-S 20-703-8584   (BR)
SOBEYS CAPITAL INCORPORATED
SOBEY'S
1375 Southdown Rd, Mississauga, ON, L5J 2Z1
(905) 855-1317
Emp Here 50
SIC 5411 Grocery stores

D-U-N-S 20-923-4830   (SL)
TAKARA COMPANY, CANADA, LTD
BELMONT
2076 South Sheridan Way, Mississauga, ON, L5J 2M4
(905) 822-2755
Emp Here 30   *Sales* 3,575,074
SIC 5087 Service establishment equipment

D-U-N-S 25-321-0769   (BR)
TORONTO-DOMINION BANK, THE
TD BANK
(*Suby of* Toronto-Dominion Bank, The)
2425 Truscott Dr, Mississauga, ON, L5J 2B4
(905) 822-4501
Emp Here 20
SIC 6021 National commercial banks

D-U-N-S 24-110-4822   (BR)
TURTLE JACK'S RESTAURANT INC
980 Southdown Rd Unit E1, Mississauga, ON, L5J 2Y4
(905) 822-1998
Emp Here 45
SIC 5812 Eating places

D-U-N-S 20-860-4343   (BR)
WINNERS MERCHANTS INTERNATIONAL L.P.
HOMESENSE
(*Suby of* The TJX Companies Inc)
1865 Lakeshore Rd W, Mississauga, ON, L5J 4P1
(905) 403-0049
Emp Here 25
SIC 5651 Family clothing stores

Mississauga, ON L5K
Peel County

D-U-N-S 20-551-5039   (HQ)
ALPHORA RESEARCH INC
(*Suby of* Alphora Research Inc)
2395 Speakman Dr Suite 2001, Mississauga, ON, L5K 1B3
(905) 403-0477
Emp Here 50   *Emp Total* 150
Sales 8,171,598
SIC 8731 Commercial physical research
 Isobel Ralston

D-U-N-S 25-296-4960   (BR)
BANK OF NOVA SCOTIA, THE
SCOTIABANK
2225 Erin Mills Pky Suite 1000, Mississauga,
ON, L5K 2S9
(905) 822-5354
Emp Here 40
SIC 6021 National commercial banks

D-U-N-S 20-580-2528   (BR)
CANADA POST CORPORATION
2273 Dundas St W, Mississauga, ON, L5K 2L8
(905) 828-7447
Emp Here 20
SIC 4311 U.s. postal service

D-U-N-S 20-705-6305   (BR)
CHARTWELL RETIREMENT RESIDENCES
*CHARTWELL SENIORS HOUSING REAL
ESTATE INVESTMENT TRUST*
2065 Leanne Blvd Suite 344, Mississauga,
ON, L5K 2L6
(905) 822-4663
Emp Here 20
SIC 8059 Nursing and personal care, nec

D-U-N-S 25-318-7876   (BR)
**DOVER CORPORATION (CANADA) LIM-
ITED**
LCBO
(*Suby of* Dover Corporation)
2458 Dundas St W Unit A, Mississauga, ON,
L5K 1R8
(905) 822-1776
Emp Here 20
SIC 5921 Liquor stores

D-U-N-S 20-266-8831   (BR)
ECOPLANS LIMITED
2655 North Sheridan Way Suite 280, Mississauga, ON, L5K 2P8
(905) 823-4988
Emp Here 25
SIC 8748 Business consulting, nec

D-U-N-S 24-767-0859   (SL)
ERINOAK KIDS CENTRE FOR TREATMENT
2655 North Sheridan Way Suite N, Missis-
sauga, ON, L5K 2P8
(905) 491-4439
Emp Here 41   *Sales* 5,890.507
SIC 8699 Membership organizations, nec
Owner Pamela Aasen

D-U-N-S 24-310-6510   (BR)
ETHAN ALLEN (CANADA) INC
ETHAN ALLEN HOME INTERIORS
2161 Dundas St W, Mississauga, ON, L5K
2E2
(905) 828-2264
Emp Here 25
SIC 5712 Furniture stores

D-U-N-S 24-368-1538   (HQ)
EXOVA CANADA INC
(*Suby of* Exova, Inc.)
2395 Speakman Dr Suite 583, Mississauga,
ON, L5K 1B3
(905) 822-4111
Emp Here 600   *Emp Total* 4,000
Sales 141,543,758
SIC 8734 Testing laboratories
VP Fin David Brash

D-U-N-S 24-192-1241   (BR)
**MCDONALD'S   RESTAURANTS   OF
CANADA LIMITED**
MCDONALD'S
(*Suby of* McDonald's Corporation)
2225 Erin Mills Pky, Mississauga, ON, L5K
1T9
(905) 403-8112
Emp Here 65
SIC 5812 Eating places

D-U-N-S 25-120-6215   (BR)
METRO ONTARIO INC
METRO

2225 Erin Mills Pky, Mississauga, ON, L5K
1T9
(905) 829-3737
Emp Here 250
SIC 5411 Grocery stores

D-U-N-S 24-847-9644   (SL)
NOR-SHAM HOTELS INC
HOLIDAY INN
(*Suby of* Nor-Sham Holdings Inc)
2125 North Sheridan Way, Mississauga, ON,
L5K 1A3
(905) 855-2000
Emp Here 75   *Sales* 3,283,232
SIC 7011 Hotels and motels

D-U-N-S 24-347-7382   (BR)
ONTARIO CENTRES OF EXCELLENCE INC
2655 North Sheridan Way Suite 250, Mississauga, ON, L5K 2P8
(905) 823-2020
Emp Here 25
SIC 6799 Investors, nec

D-U-N-S 20-859-8719   (BR)
PACIFIC LINK COMMUNICATIONS INC
BELL WORLD
2225 Erin Mills Pky Unit A1, Mississauga, ON,
L5K 1T9
(905) 823-1200
Emp Here 25
SIC 5999 Miscellaneous retail stores, nec

D-U-N-S 25-293-7560   (BR)
PEEL DISTRICT SCHOOL BOARD
HOMELANDS SENIOR PUBLIC SCHOOL
(*Suby of* Peel District School Board)
2420 Homelands Dr, Mississauga, ON, L5K
1H2
(905) 822-2031
Emp Here 35
SIC 8211 Elementary and secondary schools

D-U-N-S 25-293-7891   (BR)
PEEL DISTRICT SCHOOL BOARD
ERINDALE SECONDARY SCHOOL
(*Suby of* Peel District School Board)
2021 Dundas St W, Mississauga, ON, L5K
1R2
(905) 828-7206
Emp Here 100
SIC 8211 Elementary and secondary schools

D-U-N-S 24-963-1276   (BR)
PEEL DISTRICT SCHOOL BOARD
SHERIDAN PARK PUBLIC SCHOOL
(*Suby of* Peel District School Board)
2280 Perran Dr, Mississauga, ON, L5K 1M1
(905) 822-2401
Emp Here 45
SIC 8211 Elementary and secondary schools

D-U-N-S 25-238-0134   (BR)
PEEL DISTRICT SCHOOL BOARD
THORN LODGE PUBLIC SCHOOL
(*Suby of* Peel District School Board)
2730 Thorn Lodge Dr, Mississauga, ON, L5K
1L2
(905) 822-5481
Emp Here 35
SIC 8211 Elementary and secondary schools

D-U-N-S 25-528-2451   (BR)
PRISZM LP
PIZZA HUT
2125 Erin Mills Pky Unit 14a, Mississauga,
ON, L5K 1T7
(905) 858-1898
Emp Here 40
SIC 5812 Eating places

D-U-N-S 24-831-0625   (BR)
**ROYAL & SUN ALLIANCE INSURANCE
COMPANY OF CANADA**
COMMERCIAL LINES & CLAIMS
2225 Erin Mills Pky Suite 1000, Mississauga,
ON, L5K 2S9
(905) 403-2333
Emp Here 600

SIC 6331 Fire, marine, and casualty insurance

D-U-N-S 20-573-8169   (BR)
ROYAL BANK OF CANADA
RBC
(*Suby of* Royal Bank Of Canada)
2155 Leanne Blvd, Mississauga, ON, L5K 2K8

Emp Here 20
SIC 6021 National commercial banks

D-U-N-S 20-289-5095   (BR)
SIFTON PROPERTIES LIMITED
ERIN MILLS LODGE
2132 Dundas St W, Mississauga, ON, L5K
2K7
(905) 823-7273
Emp Here 160
SIC 8059 Nursing and personal care, nec

D-U-N-S 25-179-6645   (BR)
SOBEYS CAPITAL INCORPORATED
WOODCHESTER SOBEYS, DIV OF
2458 Dundas St W Unit 4, Mississauga, ON,
L5K 1R8

Emp Here 200
SIC 5411 Grocery stores

D-U-N-S 24-207-9742   (BR)
**STAR CHOICE TELEVISION NETWORK IN-
CORPORATED**
SHAW SATELLITE SERVICES
2055 Flavelle Blvd, Mississauga, ON, L5K 1Z8
(905) 403-2004
Emp Here 500
SIC 4841 Cable and other pay television ser-
vices

D-U-N-S 24-632-9783   (BR)
SUNCOR ENERGY INC
PETRO-CANADA BUSINESS CENTER
2489 North Sheridan Way, Mississauga, ON,
L5K 1A8
(905) 804-4500
Emp Here 700
SIC 1389 Oil and gas field services, nec

D-U-N-S 20-017-3032   (SL)
SURE GOOD FOODS LTD
2333 North Sheridan Way Suite 100, Missis-
sauga, ON, L5K 1A7
(905) 286-1619
Emp Here 40   *Sales* 10,287,459
SIC 5147 Meats and meat products
Pr Troy Warren

D-U-N-S 20-703-7495   (BR)
TECK METALS LTD
2380 Speakman Dr, Mississauga, ON, L5K
1B4

Emp Here 40
SIC 8731 Commercial physical research

D-U-N-S 25-939-3189   (BR)
WENDY'S RESTAURANTS OF CANADA INC
WENDY'S
(*Suby of* The Wendy's Company)
2400 Dundas St W Unit 14, Mississauga, ON,
L5K 2R8
(905) 855-8953
Emp Here 30
SIC 5812 Eating places

D-U-N-S 20-943-0453   (BR)
XEROX CANADA INC
XEROX RESEARCH CENTRE OF CDA
(*Suby of* Xerox Corporation)
2660 Speakman Dr, Mississauga, ON, L5K
2L1
(905) 823-7091
Emp Here 120
SIC 8731 Commercial physical research

Mississauga, ON L5L
Peel County

D-U-N-S 25-482-7983   (SL)
1004839 ONTARIO LIMITED
MANDARIN RESTAURANT
3105 Dundas St W Suite 101, Mississauga,
ON, L5L 3R8
(905) 569-7000
Emp Here 75   *Sales* 2,261,782
SIC 5812 Eating places

D-U-N-S 24-736-5963   (SL)
2177761 ONTARIO INC
ERIN MILLS MITSUBISHI
2477 Motorway Blvd Suite 3, Mississauga,
ON, L5L 3R2
(905) 828-8488
Emp Here 25   *Sales* 11,779,113
SIC 5511 New and used car dealers
Pr Andrew Chung

D-U-N-S 25-249-2327   (BR)
ABELL PEST CONTROL INC
3075 Ridgeway Dr Suite 27, Mississauga, ON,
L5L 5M6
(905) 828-1300
Emp Here 30
SIC 7342 Disinfecting and pest control ser-
vices

D-U-N-S 24-683-9000   (BR)
AECON GROUP INC
QX TECHNICAL SERVICES, DIV OF
4140a Sladeview Crescent, Mississauga, ON,
L5L 6A1
(905) 828-9055
Emp Here 20
SIC 4841 Cable and other pay television ser-
vices

D-U-N-S 24-363-5682   (BR)
BEST BUY CANADA LTD
FUTURE SHOP
(*Suby of* Best Buy Co., Inc.)
3050 Vega Blvd Suite 3, Mississauga, ON, L5L
5X8

Emp Here 50
SIC 5731 Radio, television, and electronic
stores

D-U-N-S 20-269-6886   (BR)
CELESTICA INC
3333 Unity Dr Suite A, Mississauga, ON, L5L
3S6
(647) 620-6864
Emp Here 25
SIC 3812 Search and navigation equipment

D-U-N-S 20-689-6297   (SL)
CERVOL SERVICE GROUP INC
2295 Dunwin Dr Unit 4, Mississauga, ON, L5L
3S4
(905) 569-0557
Emp Here 50   *Sales* 4,377,642
SIC 1711 Plumbing, heating, air-conditioning

D-U-N-S 25-139-8764   (HQ)
CLUB VALUE CLEANERS INC
TOP HAT CLEANERS, DIV OF
(*Suby of* Club Value Cleaners Inc)
3185 Unity Dr Unit 3, Mississauga, ON, L5L
4L5
(905) 607-9111
Emp Here 35   *Emp Total* 90
Sales 3,429,153
SIC 7215 Coin-operated laundries and clean-
ing

D-U-N-S 25-181-3846   (BR)
**CONSEIL   SCOLAIRE   DE   DISTRICT
CATHOLIQUE CENTRE-SUD**
*ECOLE   ELEMENTAIRE   CATHOLIQUE
SAINT-JEAN-BAPTISTE*
1910 Broad Hollow Gate, Mississauga, ON,
L5L 3T4
(905) 820-7460
Emp Here 21

SIC 8211 Elementary and secondary schools

D-U-N-S 20-810-0490   (BR)
COSTCO WHOLESALE CANADA LTD
COSTCO
(*Suby of* Costco Wholesale Corporation)
3180 Laird Rd, Mississauga, ON, L5L 6A5
(905) 828-3340
Emp Here 150
SIC 5099 Durable goods, nec

D-U-N-S 24-371-9916   (BR)
DIAGEO CANADA INC
(*Suby of* DIAGEO PLC)
2623 Dunwin Dr, Mississauga, ON, L5L 3N9
(416) 626-2000
Emp Here 40
SIC 2085 Distilled and blended liquors

D-U-N-S 24-963-1375   (BR)
**DUFFERIN-PEEL CATHOLIC DISTRICT
SCHOOL BOARD**
ST. MARK CATHOLIC SCHOOL
3675 Sawmill Valley Dr, Mississauga, ON, L5L
2Z5
(905) 820-9477
Emp Here 34
SIC 8211 Elementary and secondary schools

D-U-N-S 24-963-1136   (BR)
**DUFFERIN-PEEL CATHOLIC DISTRICT
SCHOOL BOARD**
*ST. MARGARET OF SCOTLAND ELEMEN-
TARY SCHOOL*
2266 Council Ring Rd, Mississauga, ON, L5L
1C1
(905) 820-5115
Emp Here 50
SIC 8211 Elementary and secondary schools

D-U-N-S 24-962-9833   (BR)
**DUFFERIN-PEEL CATHOLIC DISTRICT
SCHOOL BOARD**
ALL SAINTS ELEMENTARY SCHOOL
4105 Colonial Dr, Mississauga, ON, L5L 4E8
(905) 828-6348
Emp Here 45
SIC 8211 Elementary and secondary schools

D-U-N-S 24-963-0815   (BR)
**DUFFERIN-PEEL CATHOLIC DISTRICT
SCHOOL BOARD**
ST CLARE ELEMENTARY SCHOOLS
4140 Glen Erin Dr, Mississauga, ON, L5L 2Z3
(905) 820-2227
Emp Here 40
SIC 8211 Elementary and secondary schools

D-U-N-S 25-169-5177   (BR)
EMERSON ELECTRIC CANADA LIMITED
LIEBERT CANADA
(*Suby of* Emerson Electric Co.)
3580 Laird Rd Unit 1, Mississauga, ON, L5L
5Z7
(905) 569-8282
Emp Here 38
SIC 5045 Computers, peripherals, and soft-
ware

D-U-N-S 24-354-2052   (BR)
GOLF TOWN LIMITED
GOLF TOWN
3050 Vega Blvd Unit 10, Mississauga, ON,
L5L 5X8
(905) 569-2088
Emp Here 20
SIC 5941 Sporting goods and bicycle shops

D-U-N-S 24-366-7529   (SL)
GREEN IMAGING SUPPLIES INC
GIS
3330 Ridgeway Dr Unit 17, Mississauga, ON,
L5L 5Z9
(905) 607-2525
Emp Here 50   *Sales* 3,648,035
SIC 5112 Stationery and office supplies

D-U-N-S 25-405-8878   (HQ)
HOYA LENS CANADA INC

HOYA VISION CARE, CANADA
3330 Ridgeway Dr Unit 21, Mississauga, ON,
L5L 5Z9
(905) 828-3477
Emp Here 55   *Emp Total* 35,752
Sales 13,716,612
SIC 5049 Professional equipment, nec
Pr David Pietrobon

D-U-N-S 20-027-3451   (BR)
HUDSON'S BAY COMPANY
3050 Vega Blvd, Mississauga, ON, L5L 5X8
(905) 607-0909
Emp Here 50
SIC 5712 Furniture stores

D-U-N-S 25-845-3075   (BR)
INDIGO BOOKS & MUSIC INC
CHAPTERS
(*Suby of* Indigo Books & Music Inc)
3050 Vega Blvd Unit 1, Mississauga, ON, L5L
5X8
(905) 820-9910
Emp Here 40
SIC 5942 Book stores

D-U-N-S 20-805-2535   (BR)
KITCHEN STUFF PLUS INC
3050 Vega Blvd Unit 5, Mississauga, ON, L5L
5X8

Emp Here 20
SIC 5719 Miscellaneous homefurnishings

D-U-N-S 24-425-1075   (BR)
LIFTOW LIMITED
LIFTOW TRAINING CENTER
4180 Sladeview Cres Unit 3, Mississauga,
ON, L5L 0A1
(905) 461-0262
Emp Here 20
SIC 8742 Management consulting services

D-U-N-S 20-514-2222   (BR)
LONGO BROTHERS FRUIT MARKETS INC
LONGO'S FRUIT MARKET
3163 Winston Churchill Blvd, Mississauga,
ON, L5L 2W1
(905) 828-0008
Emp Here 150
SIC 5411 Grocery stores

D-U-N-S 25-797-7470   (BR)
M.D. CHARLTON CO. LTD
4100b Sladeview Cres Unit 4, Mississauga,
ON, L5L 5Z3
(905) 625-9846
Emp Here 24
SIC 5999 Miscellaneous retail stores, nec

D-U-N-S 25-785-9439   (BR)
MCI MEDICAL CLINICS INC
DOCTORS OFFICE, THE
(*Suby of* MCI Medical Clinics Inc)
4099 Erin Mills Pky Suite 7, Mississauga, ON,
L5L 3P9
(905) 820-3310
Emp Here 20
SIC 8093 Specialty outpatient clinics, nec

D-U-N-S 24-588-8136   (SL)
MANTA TEST SYSTEMS INC
(*Suby of* 6456669 Canada Inc)
4060b Sladeview Cres Unit 1, Mississauga,
ON, L5L 5Y5
(905) 828-6469
Emp Here 35   *Sales* 6,150,382
SIC 3825 Instruments to measure electricity
Pr Wayne Rabey
VP Jeffrey Minicola
  Roger Gilodo

D-U-N-S 24-093-3338   (BR)
METRO ONTARIO INC
FOOD BASICS
3476 Glen Erin Dr, Mississauga, ON, L5L 3R4
(905) 569-2162
Emp Here 93

SIC 5411 Grocery stores

D-U-N-S 20-913-7483   (BR)
METSO MINERALS CANADA INC
4050 Sladeview Cres Suite B, Mississauga,
ON, L5L 5Y5

Emp Here 25
SIC 3532 Mining machinery

D-U-N-S 25-942-3077   (BR)
**MICHAEL - ANGELO'S MARKET PLACE
INC**
4099 Erin Mills Pky Unit 14, Mississauga, ON,
L5L 3P9
(905) 820-3300
Emp Here 100
SIC 5411 Grocery stores

D-U-N-S 20-011-9670   (SL)
**NATIONAL CORPORATE HOUSEKEEPING
SERVICES INC**
NCH SERVICES
3481 Kelso Cres, Mississauga, ON, L5L 4R3
(905) 608-8004
Emp Here 100   *Sales* 2,918,428
SIC 7349 Building maintenance services, nec

D-U-N-S 24-830-0139   (HQ)
NU SKIN CANADA, INC
4085 Sladeview Cres, Mississauga, ON, L5L
5X3
(905) 569-5100
Emp Here 38   *Emp Total* 42
Sales 5,180,210
SIC 5122 Drugs, proprietaries, and sundries
Genl Mgr Paul Hanson
Pr Blake M Roney
VP VP Steven J Lund
Dir Walt Cottle

D-U-N-S 25-736-9066   (SL)
**OMCAN MANUFACTURING & DISTRIBUT-
ING COMPANY INC**
OMCAN
3115 Pepper Mill Crt, Mississauga, ON, L5L
4X5
(905) 828-0234
Emp Here 70   *Sales* 12,768,123
SIC 5084 Industrial machinery and equipment
Pr Pr Tarcisio Nella
  Lucy Nella
  Marisa Nella
  Josephine Nella

D-U-N-S 25-341-4221   (BR)
PF RESOLU CANADA INC
EDIWISE
2227 South Millway Suite 200, Mississauga,
ON, L5L 3R6
(905) 820-3084
Emp Here 21
SIC 7372 Prepackaged software

D-U-N-S 24-886-3219   (HQ)
PALL (CANADA) LIMITED
(*Suby of* Danaher Corporation)
3450 Ridgeway Dr Unit 6, Mississauga, ON,
L5L 0A2
(905) 542-0330
Emp Here 43   *Emp Total* 62,000
Sales 14,983,031
SIC 5085 Industrial supplies
  Butch Ferneyhough
Fin Ex Tom Shields

D-U-N-S 24-251-4870   (BR)
PARSONS CANADA LTD
3715 Laird Dr Suite 100, Mississauga, ON,
L5L 0A3
(905) 820-1210
Emp Here 40
SIC 8748 Business consulting, nec

D-U-N-S 20-955-4570   (BR)
PARTY CITY CANADA INC
(*Suby of* Party City Canada Inc)
3050 Vega Blvd Unit 5, Mississauga, ON, L5L

5X8
(905) 607-2789
Emp Here 30
SIC 5947 Gift, novelty, and souvenir shop

D-U-N-S 25-921-0326   (BR)
PEEL DISTRICT SCHOOL BOARD
GARTHWOOD PARK PUBLIC SCHOOL
(*Suby of* Peel District School Board)
3245 Colonial Dr, Mississauga, ON, L5L 5G2
(905) 607-0800
Emp Here 35
SIC 8211 Elementary and secondary schools

D-U-N-S 24-963-1151   (BR)
PEEL DISTRICT SCHOOL BOARD
SAWMILL VALLEY PUBLIC SCHOOL
(*Suby of* Peel District School Board)
3625 Sawmill Valley Dr, Mississauga, ON, L5L
2Z5
(905) 820-2500
Emp Here 35
SIC 8211 Elementary and secondary schools

D-U-N-S 20-711-1787   (BR)
PEEL DISTRICT SCHOOL BOARD
ERIN MILLS MIDDLE SCHOOL
(*Suby of* Peel District School Board)
3546 South Common Crt, Mississauga, ON,
L5L 2B1
(905) 820-9777
Emp Here 50
SIC 8211 Elementary and secondary schools

D-U-N-S 20-560-4655   (HQ)
SEALED AIR (CANADA) CO./CIE
CRYOVAC
(*Suby of* Sealed Air Corporation)
3755 Laird Rd Unit 10, Mississauga, ON, L5L
0B3
(905) 829-1200
Emp Here 250   *Emp Total* 23,000
Sales 67,561,608
SIC 3089 Plastics products, nec
Pr Pr Kim Leung
  Andre Schmidt

D-U-N-S 25-091-6228   (BR)
SHELL CANADA LIMITED
3255 Dundas St W, Mississauga, ON, L5L 5V7
(905) 607-0842
Emp Here 20
SIC 5541 Gasoline service stations

D-U-N-S 20-806-5503   (BR)
STARBUCKS COFFEE CANADA, INC
(*Suby of* Starbucks Corporation)
3235 Dundas St W Suite 1, Mississauga, ON,
L5L 5V7
(905) 608-0633
Emp Here 27
SIC 5812 Eating places

D-U-N-S 24-380-1771   (BR)
STARSKY FINE FOODS MISSISSAUGA INC
3115 Dundas St W, Mississauga, ON, L5L
3R8
(905) 363-2000
Emp Here 200
SIC 5411 Grocery stores

D-U-N-S 20-717-4843   (BR)
SUNRISE NORTH SENIOR LIVING LTD
SUNRISE SENIOR LIVING OF ERIN MILLS
(*Suby of* Welltower Inc.)
4046 Erin Mills Pky, Mississauga, ON, L5L
2W7
(905) 569-0004
Emp Here 150
SIC 8322 Individual and family services

D-U-N-S 25-091-8588   (SL)
**SUPER SHINE JANITORIAL SERVICES
LIMITED**
3495 Laird Rd Unit 22, Mississauga, ON, L5L
5S5
(905) 607-8200
Emp Here 140   *Sales* 4,085,799
SIC 7349 Building maintenance services, nec

D-U-N-S 25-469-0829   (HQ)
TECHSPAN INDUSTRIES INC
TECHSPAN AUTOMOTIVE
(*Suby* of Techspan Industries Inc)
3131 Pepper Mill Crt Unit 1, Mississauga, ON,
L5L 4X6
(905) 820-6150
Emp Here 66   *Emp Total* 70
Sales 3,291,754
SIC 3643 Current-carrying wiring devices

D-U-N-S 25-094-5842   (BR)
UKRAINIAN HOME FOR THE AGED
IVAN FRANKO HOME
(*Suby* of Ukrainian Home For The Aged)
3058 Winston Churchill Blvd Suite 1, Missis-
sauga, ON, L5L 3J1
(905) 820-0573
Emp Here 130
SIC 8361 Residential care

D-U-N-S 25-215-1154   (BR)
UNIFIRST CANADA LTD
(*Suby* of Unifirst Corporation)
2290 Dunwin Dr, Mississauga, ON, L5L 1C7
(905) 828-9621
Emp Here 150
SIC 7213 Linen supply

D-U-N-S 24-329-7004   (BR)
WAL-MART CANADA CORP
2150 Burnhamthorpe Rd W, Mississauga, ON,
L5L 3A2
(905) 608-0922
Emp Here 200
SIC 5311 Department stores

D-U-N-S 25-406-1237   (HQ)
YASKAWA CANADA INC
3530 Laird Rd Unit 3, Mississauga, ON, L5L
5Z7
(905) 569-6686
Emp Here 41   *Emp Total* 11,450
Sales 9,338,970
SIC 5084 Industrial machinery and equipment
Fin Ex Lianne Cutone
Genl Mgr Trevor Jones
Pr Pr Steve Barhorst

Mississauga, ON L5M
Peel County

D-U-N-S 20-172-0927   (BR)
ADM AGRI-INDUSTRIES COMPANY
ADM MILLING CO
(*Suby* of Archer-Daniels-Midland Company)
1770 Barbertown Rd, Mississauga, ON, L5M
2M5
(905) 826-2701
Emp Here 28
SIC 5149 Groceries and related products, nec

D-U-N-S 20-290-3394   (BR)
AMICA MATURE LIFESTYLES INC
AMICA AT ERIN MILLS
4620 Kimbermount Ave, Mississauga, ON,
L5M 5W5
(905) 816-9163
Emp Here 100
SIC 8361 Residential care

D-U-N-S 24-351-6197   (SL)
BOSTON PIZZA
2915 Eglinton Ave W, Mississauga, ON, L5M
6J3
(905) 569-0517
Emp Here 50   *Sales* 1,532,175
SIC 5812 Eating places

D-U-N-S 25-787-2374   (BR)
**CADILLAC FAIRVIEW CORPORATION LIM-
ITED, THE**
ERIN MILLS TOWN CENTRE
5100 Erin Mills Pky Suite 235, Mississauga,
ON, L5M 4Z5

(905) 569-1981
Emp Here 35
SIC 6512 Nonresidential building operators

D-U-N-S 25-119-1672   (BR)
CANADA POST CORPORATION
145 Queen St S, Mississauga, ON, L5M 1L1
(905) 826-3521
Emp Here 50
SIC 4311 U.s. postal service

D-U-N-S 20-809-9403   (BR)
CARA OPERATIONS LIMITED
MONTANA'S COOKHOUSE SALOON
(*Suby* of Cara Holdings Limited)
2575 Eglinton Ave W, Mississauga, ON, L5M
7E1

Emp Here 20
SIC 5812 Eating places

D-U-N-S 24-963-1250   (BR)
**DUFFERIN-PEEL CATHOLIC DISTRICT
SCHOOL BOARD**
ST JOSEPH CATHOLIC SCHOOL
249 Church St, Mississauga, ON, L5M 1N1
(905) 826-4422
Emp Here 20
SIC 8211 Elementary and secondary schools

D-U-N-S 20-653-4427   (BR)
**DUFFERIN-PEEL CATHOLIC DISTRICT
SCHOOL BOARD**
ST FAUSTINA ELEMENTARY SCHOOL
3420 Mcdowell Dr, Mississauga, ON, L5M
6R7
(905) 821-2607
Emp Here 20
SIC 8211 Elementary and secondary schools

D-U-N-S 25-166-6657   (BR)
**DUFFERIN-PEEL CATHOLIC DISTRICT
SCHOOL BOARD**
ST. DUNSTAN ELEMENTARY SCHOOL
1525 Cuthbert Ave, Mississauga, ON, L5M
3R6
(905) 567-5050
Emp Here 20
SIC 8211 Elementary and secondary schools

D-U-N-S 20-710-9898   (BR)
**DUFFERIN-PEEL CATHOLIC DISTRICT
SCHOOL BOARD**
ST ROSE OF LIMA SEPARATE SCHOOL
4590 The Gallops, Mississauga, ON, L5M 3A9
(905) 828-4076
Emp Here 50
SIC 8211 Elementary and secondary schools

D-U-N-S 20-711-0011   (BR)
**DUFFERIN-PEEL CATHOLIC DISTRICT
SCHOOL BOARD**
DIVINE MERCY SCHOOL
2840 Duncairn Dr, Mississauga, ON, L5M 5C6
(905) 812-5445
Emp Here 50
SIC 8211 Elementary and secondary schools

D-U-N-S 20-026-7792   (BR)
**DUFFERIN-PEEL CATHOLIC DISTRICT
SCHOOL BOARD**
*OUR LADY OF MERCY CATHOLIC ELEMEN-
TARY SCHOOL*
5820 Glen Erin Dr, Mississauga, ON, L5M 5J9
(905) 814-9216
Emp Here 40
SIC 8211 Elementary and secondary schools

D-U-N-S 24-346-8936   (BR)
**DUFFERIN-PEEL CATHOLIC DISTRICT
SCHOOL BOARD**
*ST. JOAN OF ARC CATHOLIC SECONDARY
SCHOOL*
3801 Thomas St, Mississauga, ON, L5M 7G2
(905) 285-0050
Emp Here 80
SIC 8211 Elementary and secondary schools

D-U-N-S 24-228-3120   (BR)

**DUFFERIN-PEEL CATHOLIC DISTRICT
SCHOOL BOARD**
*ST. BERNARD OF CLAIRVAUX CATHOLIC
SCHOOL BOARD*
3345 Escada Dr, Mississauga, ON, L5M 7V5
(905) 542-9203
Emp Here 25
SIC 8211 Elementary and secondary schools

D-U-N-S 20-294-6849   (BR)
**DUFFERIN-PEEL CATHOLIC DISTRICT
SCHOOL BOARD**
*ST. ALOYSIUS GONZAGA SECONDARY
SCHOOL*
2800 Erin Centre Blvd, Mississauga, ON, L5M
6R5
(905) 820-3900
Emp Here 100
SIC 8211 Elementary and secondary schools

D-U-N-S 25-121-9689   (BR)
**DUFFERIN-PEEL CATHOLIC DISTRICT
SCHOOL BOARD**
BLESSED TRINITY CATHOLIC SCHOOL
2495 Credit Valley Rd, Mississauga, ON, L5M
4G8
(905) 412-1000
Emp Here 45
SIC 8211 Elementary and secondary schools

D-U-N-S 24-340-0459   (BR)
FGL SPORTS LTD
SPORT-CHEK
5100 Erin Mills Pky Unit Y003, Mississauga,
ON, L5M 4Z5
(905) 828-8341
Emp Here 40
SIC 5941 Sporting goods and bicycle shops

D-U-N-S 24-337-2849   (BR)
FGL SPORTS LTD
NATIONAL SPORTS
2921 Eglinton Ave W, Mississauga, ON, L5M
6J3
(905) 820-4605
Emp Here 20
SIC 5941 Sporting goods and bicycle shops

D-U-N-S 20-790-0486   (BR)
GOODLIFE FITNESS CENTRES INC
GOODLIFE FITNESS CLUBS
5010 Glen Erin Dr, Mississauga, ON, L5M 6J3
(905) 607-2610
Emp Here 25
SIC 7999 Amusement and recreation, nec

D-U-N-S 24-126-4212   (BR)
HSBC BANK CANADA
1675 The Chase Suite 18, Mississauga, ON,
L5M 5Y7
(905) 608-0115
Emp Here 20
SIC 6021 National commercial banks

D-U-N-S 25-301-1779   (BR)
HUDSON'S BAY COMPANY
BAY, THE
5100 Erin Mills Pky Unit Y001, Mississauga,
ON, L5M 4Z5
(905) 820-8300
Emp Here 150
SIC 5311 Department stores

D-U-N-S 25-271-8031   (BR)
INDIGO BOOKS & MUSIC INC
(*Suby* of Indigo Books & Music Inc)
5015 Glen Erin Dr, Mississauga, ON, L5M 0R7
(905) 820-8336
Emp Here 35
SIC 5942 Book stores

D-U-N-S 25-372-9594   (BR)
LONGO BROTHERS FRUIT MARKETS INC
LONGO'S FRUIT MARKET
5636 Glen Erin Dr Unit 1, Mississauga, ON,
L5M 6B1
(905) 567-4450
Emp Here 200

SIC 5411 Grocery stores

D-U-N-S 24-681-6313   (BR)
**MCDONALD'S RESTAURANTS OF
CANADA LIMITED**
MCDONALD'S
(*Suby* of McDonald's Corporation)
5636 Glen Erin Dr Unit 12, Mississauga, ON,
L5M 6B1
(905) 812-7187
Emp Here 45
SIC 5812 Eating places

D-U-N-S 20-657-9604   (BR)
OLD NAVY (CANADA) INC
(*Suby* of The Gap Inc)
5100 Erin Mills Pky Unit B200a, Mississauga,
ON, L5M 4Z5
(905) 828-0521
Emp Here 65
SIC 5651 Family clothing stores

D-U-N-S 25-921-0359   (BR)
PEEL DISTRICT SCHOOL BOARD
MIDDLEBURY PUBLIC SCHOOL
(*Suby* of Peel District School Board)
5482 Middlebury Dr, Mississauga, ON, L5M
5G7
(905) 821-8585
Emp Here 38
SIC 8211 Elementary and secondary schools

D-U-N-S 25-293-8345   (BR)
PEEL DISTRICT SCHOOL BOARD
JOHN FRASER SECONDARY SCHOOL
(*Suby* of Peel District School Board)
2665 Erin Centre Blvd, Mississauga, ON, L5M
5H6
(905) 858-5910
Emp Here 100
SIC 8211 Elementary and secondary schools

D-U-N-S 25-238-0092   (BR)
PEEL DISTRICT SCHOOL BOARD
VISTA HEIGHTS PUBLIC SCHOOL
(*Suby* of Peel District School Board)
89 Vista Blvd, Mississauga, ON, L5M 1V8
(905) 826-1581
Emp Here 60
SIC 8211 Elementary and secondary schools

D-U-N-S 25-293-7578   (BR)
PEEL DISTRICT SCHOOL BOARD
WILLOW WAY PUBLIC SCHOOL
(*Suby* of Peel District School Board)
1715 Willow Way, Mississauga, ON, L5M 3W5
(905) 567-0237
Emp Here 60
SIC 8211 Elementary and secondary schools

D-U-N-S 25-265-3142   (BR)
PEEL DISTRICT SCHOOL BOARD
APPLEWOOD SCHOOL
(*Suby* of Peel District School Board)
3675 Thomas St, Mississauga, ON, L5M 7E6
(905) 363-0579
Emp Here 20
SIC 8211 Elementary and secondary schools

D-U-N-S 24-214-6145   (BR)
PEEL DISTRICT SCHOOL BOARD
ARTESIAN DRIVE PUBLIC SCHOOL
(*Suby* of Peel District School Board)
3325 Artesian Dr, Mississauga, ON, L5M 7J8
(905) 820-7786
Emp Here 50
SIC 8211 Elementary and secondary schools

D-U-N-S 24-525-4243   (BR)
PEEL DISTRICT SCHOOL BOARD
OSCAR PETERSON PUBLIC SCHOOL
(*Suby* of Peel District School Board)
5120 Perennial Dr, Mississauga, ON, L5M 7T6
(905) 569-6261
Emp Here 25
SIC 8211 Elementary and secondary schools

D-U-N-S 25-263-7723   (BR)

PEEL DISTRICT SCHOOL BOARD
STREETSVILLE SECONDARY SCHOOL
(*Suby of* Peel District School Board)
72 Joymar Dr, Mississauga, ON, L5M 1G3
(905) 826-1195
Emp Here 90
SIC 8211 Elementary and secondary schools

D-U-N-S 25-481-4429   (BR)
PEEL DISTRICT SCHOOL BOARD
HAZEL MCCALLION SENIOR PUBLIC SCHOOL
(*Suby of* Peel District School Board)
5750 River Grove Ave, Mississauga, ON, L5M 4R5
(905) 858-1133
Emp Here 70
SIC 8211 Elementary and secondary schools

D-U-N-S 24-963-1466   (BR)
PEEL DISTRICT SCHOOL BOARD
DOLPHIN SENIOR PUBLIC SCHOOL
(*Suby of* Peel District School Board)
18 Brookside Dr, Mississauga, ON, L5M 1H3
(905) 826-4247
Emp Here 40
SIC 8211 Elementary and secondary schools

D-U-N-S 24-525-4219   (BR)
PEEL DISTRICT SCHOOL BOARD
MCKINNON PUBLIC SCHOOL
(*Suby of* Peel District School Board)
3270 Tacc Dr, Mississauga, ON, L5M 0H3
(905) 812-2544
Emp Here 25
SIC 8211 Elementary and secondary schools

D-U-N-S 24-317-8766   (BR)
PEEL DISTRICT SCHOOL BOARD
STEVEN LEWIS SECONDARY SCHOOL
(*Suby of* Peel District School Board)
3675 Thomas St, Mississauga, ON, L5M 7E6
(905) 363-0289
Emp Here 50
SIC 8211 Elementary and secondary schools

D-U-N-S 24-676-3309   (BR)
PEEL DISTRICT SCHOOL BOARD
ERIN CENTRE MIDDLE SCHOOL
(*Suby of* Peel District School Board)
3240 Erin Centre Blvd, Mississauga, ON, L5M 7T9
(905) 820-5720
Emp Here 70
SIC 8211 Elementary and secondary schools

D-U-N-S 20-591-3853   (BR)
PEEL DISTRICT SCHOOL BOARD
CREDIT VALLEY PUBLIC SCHOOL
(*Suby of* Peel District School Board)
2365 Credit Valley Rd, Mississauga, ON, L5M 4E8
(905) 607-0770
Emp Here 25
SIC 8211 Elementary and secondary schools

D-U-N-S 20-711-1829   (BR)
PEEL DISTRICT SCHOOL BOARD
CASTLEBRIDGE PUBLIC SCHOOL
(*Suby of* Peel District School Board)
2801 Castlebridge Dr, Mississauga, ON, L5M 5J9
(905) 812-7906
Emp Here 50
SIC 8211 Elementary and secondary schools

D-U-N-S 20-288-2671   (BR)
PEEL DISTRICT SCHOOL BOARD
CHURCHILL MEADOWS PUBLIC SCHOOL
(*Suby of* Peel District School Board)
3310 Mcdowell Dr, Mississauga, ON, L5M 6R8
(905) 363-2338
Emp Here 60
SIC 8211 Elementary and secondary schools

D-U-N-S 20-653-4237   (BR)
PEEL DISTRICT SCHOOL BOARD

RUTH THOMPSON MIDDLE SCHOOL
(*Suby of* Peel District School Board)
5605 Freshwater Dr, Mississauga, ON, L5M 7M8
(905) 814-1729
Emp Here 45
SIC 8211 Elementary and secondary schools

D-U-N-S 25-357-4917   (BR)
PROCECO LTEE
168 Queen St S Suite 202, Mississauga, ON, L5M 1K8
(905) 828-1517
Emp Here 25
SIC 5084 Industrial machinery and equipment

D-U-N-S 25-213-2279   (BR)
RE/MAX REALTY SPECIALISTS INC
RE/MAX SPECIALISTS
(*Suby of* Re/Max Realty Specialists Inc)
2691 Credit Valley Rd Suite 101, Mississauga, ON, L5M 7A1
(905) 828-3434
Emp Here 86
SIC 6531 Real estate agents and managers

D-U-N-S 25-811-7860   (BR)
ROYAL LEPAGE LIMITED
5055 Plantation Pl Unit 1, Mississauga, ON, L5M 6J3
(905) 828-1122
Emp Here 100
SIC 6531 Real estate agents and managers

D-U-N-S 20-532-5694   (BR)
SEARS CANADA INC
5100 Erin Mills Pky Unit Y002, Mississauga, ON, L5M 4Z5
(905) 607-2300
Emp Here 30
SIC 5311 Department stores

D-U-N-S 20-793-0780   (BR)
SOBEYS CAPITAL INCORPORATED
5602 Tenth Line W, Mississauga, ON, L5M 7L9
(905) 858-2899
Emp Here 110
SIC 5411 Grocery stores

D-U-N-S 20-780-5933   (SL)
TIM HORTONS
2655 Eglinton Ave W, Mississauga, ON, L5M 7E1
(905) 828-7722
Emp Here 59   *Sales* 1,751,057
SIC 5812 Eating places

D-U-N-S 20-302-2231   (BR)
TRILLIUM HEALTH PARTNERS
2200 Eglinton Ave W Suite 905, Mississauga, ON, L5M 2N1
(905) 813-2200
Emp Here 300
SIC 8062 General medical and surgical hospitals

D-U-N-S 24-388-2735   (SL)
TROTT TRANSIT LTD
15 James St, Mississauga, ON, L5M 1R4
(905) 826-6629
Emp Here 93   *Sales* 4,377,642
SIC 4142 Bus charter service, except local

D-U-N-S 20-656-0976   (BR)
WENDY'S RESTAURANTS OF CANADA INC
WENDY'S
(*Suby of* The Wendy's Company)
2655 Eglinton Ave W, Mississauga, ON, L5M 7E1
(905) 828-2515
Emp Here 35
SIC 5812 Eating places

D-U-N-S 25-372-9099   (BR)
WINNERS MERCHANTS INTERNATIONAL L.P.
HOMESENSE
(*Suby of* The TJX Companies Inc)

2670 Erin Centre Blvd, Mississauga, ON, L5M 5P5
(905) 820-6811
Emp Here 60
SIC 5651 Family clothing stores

Mississauga, ON L5N
Peel County

D-U-N-S 24-859-3183   (SL)
2107453 ONTARIO LTD.
RELIANCE COMMODITIES CANADA
7111 Syntex Dr, Mississauga, ON, L5N 8C3
(647) 960-9377
Emp Here 25   *Sales* 19,618,752
SIC 6221 Commodity contracts brokers, dealers
Pr Pr Daljit Singh
Sec Navinder Jeet

D-U-N-S 20-228-6670   (HQ)
A. M. CASTLE & CO. (CANADA) INC
CASTLE METALS
(*Suby of* A. M. Castle & Co.)
2150 Argentia Rd, Mississauga, ON, L5N 2K7
(905) 858-3888
Emp Here 20   *Emp Total* 1,515
Sales 31,098,411
SIC 5051 Metals service centers and offices
G Thomas Mckane
Pr Michael Goldberg

D-U-N-S 20-656-1602   (BR)
ARAMARK CANADA LTD.
6880 Financial Dr Suite 200, Mississauga, ON, L5N 7Y5

Emp Here 45
SIC 5441 Candy, nut, and confectionery stores

D-U-N-S 25-148-9217   (SL)
ACTAVIS PHARMA COMPANY
6733 Mississauga Rd Suite 400, Mississauga, ON, L5N 6J5
(905) 814-1820
Emp Here 280   *Sales* 32,224,537
SIC 2834 Pharmaceutical preparations
Pr Pr Jean-Guy Goulet
   Henry Koziarski

D-U-N-S 25-530-3182   (HQ)
AGILENT TECHNOLOGIES CANADA INC
6705 Millcreek Dr Unit 5, Mississauga, ON, L5N 5M4
(289) 290-3851
Emp Here 99   *Emp Total* 11,800
Sales 41,753,298
SIC 5084 Industrial machinery and equipment
VP Fin Ronald Podio
   Andrew Harrison

D-U-N-S 25-117-5378   (BR)
AGROPUR COOPERATIVE
AGROPUR FINE CHEESE
6535 Millcreek Dr Unit 42, Mississauga, ON, L5N 2M2
(905) 812-3002
Emp Here 24
SIC 5451 Dairy products stores

D-U-N-S 24-953-5824   (HQ)
ALLIANCE CORPORATION
(*Suby of* Alliance Holdco Inc)
2395 Meadowpine Blvd, Mississauga, ON, L5N 7W6
(905) 821-4797
Emp Here 100   *Emp Total* 2
Sales 151,964,200
SIC 5065 Electronic parts and equipment, nec
Pr Pr Ron Moss
   Greg Hunter

D-U-N-S 24-384-2072   (SL)
AMA NSG INC

6699 Campobello Rd, Mississauga, ON, L5N 2L7
(905) 826-3922
Emp Here 50   *Sales* 5,399,092
SIC 8748 Business consulting, nec
   Daniel Tin Yan Cheng
Pr Pr Timothy Tin Cho Wong
   Sanny Siu Sing Wong

D-U-N-S 24-391-9433   (HQ)
ANTECH DIAGNOSTICS CANADA LTD
6625 Kitimat Rd Suite 1, Mississauga, ON, L5N 6J1
(905) 567-0597
Emp Here 20   *Emp Total* 15,150
Sales 1,094,411
SIC 8731 Commercial physical research

D-U-N-S 25-120-5597   (BR)
ATLAS COPCO CANADA INC
ATLAS COMPRESSORS CANADA
2900 Argentia Rd Unit 13, Mississauga, ON, L5N 7X9
(905) 816-9369
Emp Here 25
SIC 5084 Industrial machinery and equipment

D-U-N-S 20-421-8804   (HQ)
AVNET INTERNATIONAL (CANADA) LTD
AVNET CANADA
(*Suby of* Avnet, Inc.)
6950 Creditview Rd Unit 2, Mississauga, ON, L5N 0A6
(905) 812-4400
Emp Here 50   *Emp Total* 17,700
Sales 15,159,393
SIC 5065 Electronic parts and equipment, nec
Roy Vallee
Gavin Miller
Raymond Sadowski
David R Birk
Jun Li

D-U-N-S 24-313-5873   (BR)
BCIMC REALTY CORPORATION
6880 Financial Dr Suite 100, Mississauga, ON, L5N 7Y5
(905) 819-6750
Emp Here 20
SIC 6531 Real estate agents and managers

D-U-N-S 20-032-3889   (HQ)
BAXTER CORPORATION
(*Suby of* Baxter International Inc.)
7125 Mississauga Rd, Mississauga, ON, L5N 0C2
(905) 369-6000
Emp Here 444   *Emp Total* 48,000
Sales 113,565,506
SIC 2834 Pharmaceutical preparations
Dir Rehana Doobay
Dir Mike Oliver
Dir Michael Thuy

D-U-N-S 20-124-2229   (HQ)
BEAUTY SYSTEMS GROUP (CANADA) INC
OBSCO BEAUTY SUPPLY
2345 Argentia Rd Suite 102, Mississauga, ON, L5N 8K4
(905) 817-2200
Emp Here 80   *Emp Total* 28,330
Sales 46,456,820
SIC 5087 Service establishment equipment
Dir Julie Walton

D-U-N-S 24-524-0304   (SL)
BECKMAN COULTER CANADA INC
(*Suby of* Danaher Corporation)
7075 Financial Dr, Mississauga, ON, L5N 6V8
(905) 819-1234
Emp Here 30   *Sales* 28,308,752
SIC 5047 Medical and hospital equipment
Pr Carolyn Beaver

D-U-N-S 24-421-9882   (SL)
BECTON DICKINSON CANADA INC
BD - CANADA
(*Suby of* Becton, Dickinson and Company)

2100 Derry Rd W Suite 100, Mississauga, ON, L5N 0B3
(905) 288-6000
Emp Here 300   *Sales* 43,776,420
SIC 5047 Medical and hospital equipment
Pr Frank Florio
 David G. Butler
 Gary Defazio

D-U-N-S 24-228-1256   (BR)
BELL TECHNICAL SOLUTIONS INC
6535 Millcreek Dr, Mississauga, ON, L5N 2M2

Emp Here 120
SIC 1623 Water, sewer, and utility lines

D-U-N-S 25-362-0645   (BR)
BENTALL KENNEDY (CANADA) LIMITED PARTNERSHIP
BENTALL REAL ESTATE SERVICES
6880 Financial Dr 1 Fl, Mississauga, ON, L5N 7Y5
(905) 542-8881
Emp Here 25
SIC 6531 Real estate agents and managers

D-U-N-S 20-574-1551   (BR)
BERESKIN & PARR INC.
6733 Mississauga Rd Suite 600, Mississauga, ON, L5N 6J5
(905) 812-3600
Emp Here 25
SIC 8111 Legal services

D-U-N-S 24-363-5674   (BR)
BEST BUY CANADA LTD
FUTURE SHOP
(*Suby of* Best Buy Co., Inc.)
2975 Argentia Rd, Mississauga, ON, L5N 0A2
(905) 285-9948
Emp Here 50
SIC 5731 Radio, television, and electronic stores

D-U-N-S 24-023-7073   (HQ)
BIZERBA CANADA INC
2810 Argentia Rd Unit 9, Mississauga, ON, L5N 8L2
(905) 816-0498
Emp Here 22   *Emp Total* 3,900
Sales 7,623,009
SIC 5084 Industrial machinery and equipment
Pr Pr Robert Slykhuis

D-U-N-S 25-536-3186   (BR)
BRANDALLIANCE ONTARIO INC
W A EMBROIDERY MISSISSAUGA
6695 Millcreek Dr Suite 7, Mississauga, ON, L5N 5R8
(905) 819-0155
Emp Here 30
SIC 8743 Public relations services

D-U-N-S 20-212-8013   (HQ)
BRINK'S CANADA LIMITED
(*Suby of* The Brink's Company)
2233 Argentia Rd Suite 400, Mississauga, ON, L5N 2X7
(905) 306-9600
Emp Here 40   *Emp Total* 60,700
Sales 62,308,438
SIC 7381 Detective and armored car services
 Ronald F Rokosz
 Frank T Lennon

D-U-N-S 24-174-1300   (BR)
CDSL CANADA LIMITED
CGI
2480 Meadowvale Blvd Suite 100, Mississauga, ON, L5N 8M6
(905) 858-7100
Emp Here 2,000
SIC 7379 Computer related services, nec

D-U-N-S 24-208-8060   (HQ)
CHEP CANADA INC
7400 East Danbro Cres, Mississauga, ON, L5N 8C6

(905) 790-2437
Emp Here 140   *Emp Total* 14,500
Sales 51,628,560
SIC 7359 Equipment rental and leasing, nec
Pr Pr Michael F Dimond
 Marianne Plumb
 Scott Spivey
 Arleen Krol

D-U-N-S 24-375-0366   (BR)
CIBA VISION CANADA INC
CIBA VISION DIV.
7 Rimini Mews, Mississauga, ON, L5N 4K1
(905) 821-3661
Emp Here 300
SIC 5048 Ophthalmic goods

D-U-N-S 20-959-7140   (SL)
CLDH MEADOWVALE INC
DELTA MEADOWVALE RESORT & CONFERENCE CENTRE
(*Suby of* Host Hotels & Resorts, Inc.)
6750 Mississauga Rd, Mississauga, ON, L5N 2L3
(905) 826-0940
Emp Here 400   *Sales* 23,558,400
SIC 7011 Hotels and motels
Genl Mgr Martin Stitt
Pr W. Edward Walter
 Gregory J. Larson
Dir Ernest Mcnee
Sec David L. Buckley

D-U-N-S 24-426-3542   (SL)
CSH HERITAGE GLEN INC
HERITAGE GLEN COMMUNITY FOR SENIORS
6515 Glen Erin Dr, Mississauga, ON, L5N 8P9
(905) 567-6015
Emp Here 20   *Sales* 729,607
SIC 8361 Residential care

D-U-N-S 24-827-4383   (HQ)
CALDIC CANADA INC
6980 Creditview Rd, Mississauga, ON, L5N 8E2
(905) 812-7300
Emp Here 174   *Emp Total* 1
Sales 492,030,568
SIC 2043 Cereal breakfast foods
Pr Pr Olav Van Caldenborgah
 Steve Owen
 Jill Wuthmann
 Bernard Whitt
 Michael Lipinski

D-U-N-S 24-101-9566   (SL)
CANADIAN TEST CASE 173
(*Suby of* Canadian Test Case 8)
6750 Century Ave, Suite 305, Mississauga, ON, L5N 0B7
(905) 812-5923
Emp Here 230   *Sales* 16,632,019
SIC 3732 Boatbuilding and repairing
VP Sls Dennis Smith
 Steve Smith
 Sara Sara
 Mary Smith
 Wanda Smith
Pt Alexis French
 Bob Smith

D-U-N-S 20-320-1876   (SL)
CANADIAN TEST CASE 177 CORP
SUPERPFOOD
6750 Century Ave Suite 305, Mississauga, ON, L5N 2V8
(905) 812-5920
Emp Here 120   *Sales* 26,557,153,480
SIC 5812 Eating places
Pr Maxwell First

D-U-N-S 24-101-8766   (HQ)
CANADIAN TEST CASE 185
(*Suby of* Canadian Test Case 185)
6750 Century Ave Suite 300, Mississauga, ON, L5N 2V8

(905) 999-2222
Emp Here 300   *Emp Total* 77,000
Sales 25,186,611,516
SIC 3714 Motor vehicle parts and accessories
 John Abella
Ex VP Emmie Abello

D-U-N-S 24-101-9285   (SL)
CANADIAN TEST CASE 21
6750 Century Ave Suite 305, Mississauga, ON, L5N 2V8
(905) 999-9999
Emp Here 101   *Sales* 20,071,608
SIC 1044 Silver ores
Pr Pr Robert Lamb

D-U-N-S 24-101-8774   (SL)
CANADIAN TEST CASE 31 LTD
ARAMDOU ENGINEERING BUSINESS AND SERVICES
6750 Century Ave Suite 305, Mississauga, ON, L5N 2V8
(905) 999-9999
Emp Here 50   *Sales* 5,982,777
SIC 5199 Nondurable goods, nec
Pr Randy Ketoma

D-U-N-S 24-101-8972   (SL)
CANADIAN TEST CASE 36 LIMITED
6750 Century Ave Suite 305, Mississauga, ON, L5N 2V8
(905) 999-9999
Emp Here 30   *Sales* 9,046,358
SIC 5331 Variety stores
Pr Mike S Brown
Div VP Joel Sr Black
 Bob Silver
VP Opers Dennis White
 Peter Brown
 George Black
 William J Sr Awhite

D-U-N-S 24-101-9533   (SL)
CANADIAN TEST CASE 49 LTD
6750 Century Ave Suite 305, Mississauga, ON, L5N 2V8
(905) 999-9999
Emp Here 60   *Sales* 76,988,279
SIC 6311 Life insurance
Pr Donna Copelli
VP Zoli Simon

D-U-N-S 24-101-9301   (SL)
CANADIAN TEST CASE 65
6750 Century Ave Suite 305, Mississauga, ON, L5N 2V8
(905) 999-9999
Emp Here 70   *Sales* 15,159,393
SIC 1011 Iron ores
 Donna Copelli

D-U-N-S 24-101-9319   (SL)
CANADIAN TEST CASE 87
6750 Century Ave Suite 305, Mississauga, ON, L5N 2V8
(905) 999-9999
Emp Here 120   *Sales* 13,569,538
SIC 5932 Used merchandise stores
Pr Pr Irene Anor
VP VP Stacy Windsor
 Deva Subramanian

D-U-N-S 20-268-1987   (BR)
CANADIAN TIRE CORPORATION, LIMITED
PARTSOURCE
6400 Millcreek Dr Suite 16, Mississauga, ON, L5N 3E7
(905) 814-8578
Emp Here 45
SIC 5531 Auto and home supply stores

D-U-N-S 20-303-3089   (BR)
CARA OPERATIONS LIMITED
KELSEY'S
(*Suby of* Cara Holdings Limited)
6465 Millcreek Dr, Mississauga, ON, L5N 5R3

Emp Here 40

SIC 5812 Eating places

D-U-N-S 24-342-2172   (BR)
CARA OPERATIONS LIMITED
SWISS CHALET
(*Suby of* Cara Holdings Limited)
6430 Erin Mills Pky, Mississauga, ON, L5N 3P3
(905) 858-5849
Emp Here 50
SIC 5812 Eating places

D-U-N-S 20-796-3435   (BR)
CARA OPERATIONS LIMITED
HARVEY'S RESTAURANTS
(*Suby of* Cara Holdings Limited)
6430 Erin Mills Pky, Mississauga, ON, L5N 3P3
(905) 858-0809
Emp Here 20
SIC 5812 Eating places

D-U-N-S 20-788-3646   (HQ)
COMARK INC
RICKI'S
(*Suby of* Comark Inc)
6789 Millcreek Dr, Mississauga, ON, L5N 5M4
(905) 567-7375
Emp Here 150   *Emp Total* 4,500
Sales 273,967,429
SIC 5621 Women's clothing stores
Pr Pr Gerald Bachynski
VP Fin Bill King
 Christopher Reilly
 Dan Saucier

D-U-N-S 20-345-4418   (SL)
COMARK SERVICES INC
6789 Millcreek Dr, Mississauga, ON, L5N 5M4
(905) 567-7375
Emp Here 50   *Sales* 3,064,349
SIC 5621 Women's clothing stores

D-U-N-S 20-698-7120   (BR)
COMPAGNIE DE TELEPHONE BELL DU CANADA OU BELL CANADA, LA
BELL CANADA
7111 Syntex Dr, Mississauga, ON, L5N 8C3
(905) 614-8067
Emp Here 230
SIC 4899 Communication services, nec

D-U-N-S 24-375-5217   (HQ)
COMPASS MINERALS CANADA CORP
(*Suby of* Compass Minerals International, Inc.)
6700 Century Ave Suite 202, Mississauga, ON, L5N 6A4
(905) 567-0231
Emp Here 30   *Emp Total* 1,984
SIC 1479 Chemical and fertilizer mining

D-U-N-S 25-704-0667   (BR)
CONESTOGA COLD STORAGE (QUEBEC) LIMITED
2660 Meadowpine Blvd, Mississauga, ON, L5N 7E6
(905) 567-1144
Emp Here 60
SIC 4222 Refrigerated warehousing and storage

D-U-N-S 24-676-2723   (BR)
CONSEIL SCOLAIRE DE DISTRICT CATHOLIQUE CENTRE-SUD
EEC ANGE-GABRIEL
1830 Meadowvale Blvd, Mississauga, ON, L5N 7L2
(905) 814-9122
Emp Here 25
SIC 8211 Elementary and secondary schools

D-U-N-S 20-026-7826   (BR)
CONSEIL SCOLAIRE DE DISTRICT CATHOLIQUE CENTRE-SUD
?COLE L MENTAIRE CATHOLIQUE SAINTE-FAMILLE
1780 Meadowvale Blvd, Mississauga, ON,

L5N 7K8
(905) 814-0318
Emp Here 25
SIC 8211 Elementary and secondary schools

D-U-N-S 20-273-3655   (BR)
CONTRACT PHARMACEUTICALS LIMITED CANADA
CPL
2145 Meadowpine Blvd 1st Fl, Mississauga, ON, L5N 6R8
(905) 821-7600
Emp Here 90
SIC 2834 Pharmaceutical preparations

D-U-N-S 25-529-7970   (BR)
CREATION TECHNOLOGIES LP
6820 Creditview Rd, Mississauga, ON, L5N 0A9
(905) 814-6323
Emp Here 250
SIC 3679 Electronic components, nec

D-U-N-S 25-197-3830   (HQ)
CROSSMARK CANADA INC
2233 Argentia Rd Suite 1112, Mississauga, ON, L5N 2X7
(905) 363-1000
Emp Here 35   *Emp Total* 10,000
Sales 90,652,050
SIC 8743 Public relations services
Pr Pr Glen Wilson
 Bruce Forbes
 Brian Carley

D-U-N-S 20-248-9386   (SL)
DAIMLER TRUCKS CANADA LTD
6733 Mississauga Rd Suite 110, Mississauga, ON, L5N 6J5
(905) 812-6500
Emp Here 20   *Sales* 2,334,742
SIC 3537 Industrial trucks and tractors

D-U-N-S 20-143-4313   (SL)
DANFOSS INC
ELECTRIC FLOOR HEATING DIVISION
6711 Mississauga Rd Suite 306, Mississauga, ON, L5N 2W3
(905) 285-2050
Emp Here 22   *Sales* 4,012,839
SIC 5075 Warm air heating and air conditioning

D-U-N-S 20-321-3996   (BR)
DANIELS CORPORATION, THE
2885 Argentia Rd Unit 1, Mississauga, ON, L5N 8G6
(905) 502-5300
Emp Here 30
SIC 6553 Cemetery subdividers and developers

D-U-N-S 20-188-6384   (BR)
DATAWAVE SYSTEMS INC
(*Suby of* Incomm Holdings, Inc.)
4-6745 Century Ave, Mississauga, ON, L5N 8C9
(905) 567-5040
Emp Here 20
SIC 4813 Telephone communication, except radio

D-U-N-S 24-627-4229   (BR)
DELTA HOTELS LIMITED
TORONTO DELTA MEADOWVALE RESORT & CONFERENCE CENTRE, THE
6750 Mississauga Rd, Mississauga, ON, L5N 2L3
(905) 821-1981
Emp Here 400
SIC 8741 Management services

D-U-N-S 20-044-4214   (HQ)
DIEBOLD COMPANY OF CANADA LIMITED, THE
(*Suby of* Diebold Nixdorf, Incorporated)
6630 Campobello Rd, Mississauga, ON, L5N 2L8

(905) 817-7600
Emp Here 145   *Emp Total* 25,000
Sales 67,461,009
SIC 1731 Electrical work
VP VP Bruce Pearce
Fin Ex Rakesh Malhotra

D-U-N-S 24-312-1006   (BR)
DUFFERIN-PEEL CATHOLIC DISTRICT SCHOOL BOARD
ST RICHARD CATHOLIC ELEMENTARY SCHOOL
7270 Copenhagen Rd, Mississauga, ON, L5N 2C3
(905) 826-5572
Emp Here 25
SIC 8211 Elementary and secondary schools

D-U-N-S 24-963-0609   (BR)
DUFFERIN-PEEL CATHOLIC DISTRICT SCHOOL BOARD
ST. TERESA OF AVILA SCHOOL
6675 Montevideo Rd, Mississauga, ON, L5N 4E8
(905) 858-3462
Emp Here 40
SIC 8211 Elementary and secondary schools

D-U-N-S 24-450-9605   (BR)
DUFFERIN-PEEL CATHOLIC DISTRICT SCHOOL BOARD
ST THERESE OF THE CHILD JESUS SEPARATE SCHOOL
6930 Forest Park Dr, Mississauga, ON, L5N 6X7
(905) 785-0066
Emp Here 25
SIC 8211 Elementary and secondary schools

D-U-N-S 25-406-4959   (BR)
DUFFERIN-PEEL CATHOLIC DISTRICT SCHOOL BOARD
ST JOHN OF THE CROSS SCHOOL
3180 Aquitaine Ave, Mississauga, ON, L5N 3S5
(905) 824-3058
Emp Here 35
SIC 8211 Elementary and secondary schools

D-U-N-S 20-711-0094   (BR)
DUFFERIN-PEEL CATHOLIC DISTRICT SCHOOL BOARD
ST. ALBERT OF JERUSALEM ELEMENTARY SCHOOL
7185 Rosehurst Dr, Mississauga, ON, L5N 7G6
(905) 785-9298
Emp Here 50
SIC 8211 Elementary and secondary schools

D-U-N-S 24-963-0930   (BR)
DUFFERIN-PEEL CATHOLIC DISTRICT SCHOOL BOARD
ST. ELIZABETH SETON CATHOLIC SCHOOL
6133 Glen Erin Dr, Mississauga, ON, L5N 2T7
(905) 821-2277
Emp Here 30
SIC 8211 Elementary and secondary schools

D-U-N-S 20-299-6547   (BR)
DUFFERIN-PEEL CATHOLIC DISTRICT SCHOOL BOARD
ST. EDITH STEIN ELEMENTARY SCHOOL
6234 Osprey Blvd, Mississauga, ON, L5N 5V5
(905) 824-5777
Emp Here 50
SIC 8211 Elementary and secondary schools

D-U-N-S 20-711-0185   (BR)
DUFFERIN-PEEL CATHOLIC DISTRICT SCHOOL BOARD
ST. BARBARA ELEMENTARY SCHOOL
1455 Samuelson Cir, Mississauga, ON, L5N 7Z2
(905) 696-8860
Emp Here 50
SIC 8211 Elementary and secondary schools

D-U-N-S 24-727-2107   (HQ)
DYNAMIC PAINT PRODUCTS INC
PAINT SUNDRY PRODUCTS
7040 Financial Dr, Mississauga, ON, L5N 7H5
(905) 812-9319
Emp Here 75   *Emp Total* 401
Sales 18,451,146
SIC 5198 Paints, varnishes, and supplies
Pr Pr James Mumby, Jr

D-U-N-S 25-285-0367   (HQ)
E. & J. GALLO WINERY CANADA, LTD
(*Suby of* E. & J. Gallo Winery)
6711 Mississauga Rd Suite 202, Mississauga, ON, L5N 2W3
(905) 819-9600
Emp Here 25   *Emp Total* 6,300
Sales 20,530,149
SIC 4731 Freight transportation arrangement
 Armand G. Skol
Pr Pr Joseph E. Gallo

D-U-N-S 25-149-2435   (HQ)
ENERGIZER CANADA INC
(*Suby of* Edgewell Personal Care Company)
6733 Mississauga Rd Suite 800, Mississauga, ON, L5N 6J5
(905) 286-6175
Emp Here 20   *Emp Total* 6,000
Sales 8,244,559
SIC 3691 Storage batteries
Pr Pr Edmond Maclellan
Dir Krystine Jankowski
Dir Alan Hoskins
Dir Craig Dunaway
Dir James Macintosh

D-U-N-S 24-587-4110   (SL)
EPPENDORF CANADA LTD
2810 Argentia Rd Unit 2, Mississauga, ON, L5N 8L2
(905) 826-5525
Emp Here 30   *Sales* 6,087,000
SIC 5049 Professional equipment, nec
Pr Joseph Crowley
VP Fin Christoph Asschenfeldt
Sls Dir David Roy

D-U-N-S 24-644-0275   (HQ)
EXIDE TECHNOLOGIES CANADA CORPORATION
(*Suby of* Exide Technologies)
6950 Creditview Rd Suite 3, Mississauga, ON, L5N 0A6
(905) 817-1773
Emp Here 65   *Emp Total* 8,986
Sales 35,776,166
SIC 5063 Electrical apparatus and equipment
Dir Fin Ron Nicolson
Genl Mgr Way Sin Chan

D-U-N-S 25-990-8291   (HQ)
FNF CANADA COMPANY
2700 Argentia Rd, Mississauga, ON, L5N 5V4
(905) 813-7174
Emp Here 220   *Emp Total* 55,219
SIC 6361 Title insurance

D-U-N-S 24-631-9347   (HQ)
FANUC CANADA, LTD
6774 Financial Dr, Mississauga, ON, L5N 7J6
(905) 812-2300
Emp Here 50   *Emp Total* 6,327
Sales 9,120,088
SIC 5084 Industrial machinery and equipment
 Peter Fitzgerald

D-U-N-S 20-268-5611   (BR)
FEDEX OFFICE CANADA LIMITED
FEDEX OFFICE PRINT & SHIP CENTRE
(*Suby of* Fedex Corporation)
6974 Financial Dr Suite 1, Mississauga, ON, L5N 8J4
(905) 813-8366
Emp Here 22
SIC 7334 Photocopying and duplicating services

D-U-N-S 20-164-9951   (SL)
FEDERAL-MOGUL CANADA LIMITED
FEDERAL-MOGUL WINDSOR, DIV OF
6860 Century Ave, Mississauga, ON, L5N 2W5
(905) 761-5400
Emp Here 100   *Sales* 33,072,700
SIC 3714 Motor vehicle parts and accessories
Pr Pr Chip Mcclare
Mgr Mike Holland

D-U-N-S 24-196-8767   (HQ)
FIRST CHOICE HAIRCUTTERS LTD
REGIS CANADA
6400 Millcreek Dr, Mississauga, ON, L5N 3E7
(905) 858-8100
Emp Here 20   *Emp Total* 47,000
Sales 475,922,646
SIC 6794 Patent owners and lessors
VP Opers John Fraser

D-U-N-S 20-364-3957   (SL)
FOREVER 21
DISTRIBUTION CENTER
2450 Hogan Dr, Mississauga, ON, L5N 0G4
(905) 567-6486
Emp Here 60   *Sales* 3,648,035
SIC 5651 Family clothing stores

D-U-N-S 24-623-5498   (HQ)
FRUIT OF THE LOOM CANADA, INC
RUSSELL ATHLETIC
(*Suby of* Berkshire Hathaway Inc.)
2550 Argentia Rd Suite 207, Mississauga, ON, L5N 5R1
(905) 607-5500
Emp Here 25   *Emp Total* 331,000
Sales 2,188,821
SIC 5611 Men's and boys' clothing stores

D-U-N-S 20-075-2066   (BR)
GENERAL ELECTRIC CANADA COMPANY
(*Suby of* General Electric Company)
2300 Meadowvale Blvd Suite 200, Mississauga, ON, L5N 5P9
(905) 858-5316
Emp Here 20
SIC 3625 Relays and industrial controls

D-U-N-S 20-161-2512   (HQ)
GENERAL ELECTRIC CANADA COMPANY
GE ENERGY
(*Suby of* General Electric Company)
2300 Meadowvale Blvd Suite 100, Mississauga, ON, L5N 5P9
(905) 858-5100
Emp Here 500   *Emp Total* 295,017
Sales 770,173,149
SIC 3625 Relays and industrial controls
 Elyse Allan
VP H. Roland Hosein
 David Daubaras
 Manjit Sharma
 Bruce Futterer
Pers/VP Anna Cvecich
VP Robert Weese
VP Peter Mason

D-U-N-S 20-559-6679   (HQ)
GENERAL ELECTRIC CAPITAL CANADA
TRANSPORTATION AND INDUSTRIAL FUNDING
(*Suby of* General Electric Company)
2300 Meadowvale Blvd, Mississauga, ON, L5N 5P9
(905) 858-5100
Emp Here 250   *Emp Total* 295,017
Sales 570,187,871
SIC 6153 Short-term business credit institutions, except agricultural
Pr Pr Elyse Allan
VP VP Robert Weese
Sec David Daubaras
 Peter Donovan
 David Brennan
 Kenneth Pizer

▲ Public Company   ■ Public Company Family Member   **HQ** Headquarters   **BR** Branch   **SL** Single Location

D-U-N-S 25-570-8315   (HQ)
GIBRALTAR SOLUTIONS INC
(*Suby of* Gibraltar Solutions Inc)
6990 Creditview Rd Unit 4, Mississauga, ON,
L5N 8R9
(905) 858-9072
Emp Here 50   *Emp Total* 54
Sales 5,088,577
SIC 7379 Computer related services, nec
  Donald Lee
  Raymond Norkus
  Robert Tooth
  Trent Dilkie

D-U-N-S 24-206-8190   (SL)
GILEAD SCIENCES CANADA, INC
6711 Mississauga Rd Suite 600, Mississauga,
ON, L5N 2W3
(905) 363-8008
Emp Here 23   *Sales* 2,261,782
SIC 2834 Pharmaceutical preparations

D-U-N-S 20-191-4681   (BR)
GLAXOSMITHKLINE INC
7333 Mississauga Rd, Mississauga, ON, L5N
6L4
(905) 819-3000
Emp Here 100
SIC 2834 Pharmaceutical preparations

D-U-N-S 24-422-2118   (SL)
**GLOBAL UNIFIED SOLUTION SERVICES
INC**
6535 Millcreek Dr Unit 58, Mississauga, ON,
L5N 2M2
(905) 363-3600
Emp Here 30   *Sales* 7,208,075
SIC 8748 Business consulting, nec
Pr Pr Shaun Pinto
  Bertine Jerry
  Tammy Zuzarte

D-U-N-S 20-790-0445   (BR)
GOODLIFE FITNESS CENTRES INC
GOODLIFE FITNESS WOMEN'S CLUB
3050 Argentia Rd, Mississauga, ON, L5N 8E1
(905) 785-3213
Emp Here 25
SIC 7991 Physical fitness facilities

D-U-N-S 20-070-1618   (SL)
HMC AP CANADA COMPANY
*DELTA MEADOWVALE RESORT & CONFER-
ENCE CENTER*
(*Suby of* Host Hotels & Resorts, Inc.)
6750 Mississauga Rd, Mississauga, ON, L5N
2L3
(905) 542-4039
Emp Here 300   *Sales* 16,961,922
SIC 7011 Hotels and motels
VP VP Gregory Larson
VP VP Craig Mason
Sec William Kelso
Pr Pr Larry Harvey

D-U-N-S 24-589-2950   (SL)
**HUB PARKING TECHNOLOGY CANADA
LTD**
HUB CANADA
2900 Argentia Rd Suite 1, Mississauga, ON,
L5N 7X9
(905) 813-1966
Emp Here 21   *Sales* 2,918,428
SIC 5065 Electronic parts and equipment, nec

D-U-N-S 25-100-2689   (HQ)
HENKEL CANADA CORPORATION
HENKEL ADHESIVES TECHNOLOGIES
2515 Meadowpine Blvd Unit 1, Mississauga,
ON, L5N 6C3
(905) 814-5391
Emp Here 120   *Emp Total* 49,950
Sales 36,042,586
SIC 5169 Chemicals and allied products, nec
CEO Hans Van Bylen

D-U-N-S 24-316-0442   (SL)
HENKEL CONSUMER GOODS CANADA

INC
SCHWARTZKOPF RETAIL
2515 Meadowpine Blvd, Mississauga, ON,
L5N 6C3
(905) 814-6511
Emp Here 25   *Sales* 2,407,703
SIC 5999 Miscellaneous retail stores, nec

D-U-N-S 25-458-6498   (SL)
HILL'S PET NUTRITION CANADA INC
(*Suby of* Colgate-Palmolive Company)
6521 Mississauga Rd, Mississauga, ON, L5N
1A6
(800) 445-5777
Emp Here 30   *Sales* 3,575,074
SIC 5149 Groceries and related products, nec

D-U-N-S 20-806-3024   (HQ)
HINO MOTORS CANADA, LTD
6975 Creditview Rd Unit 2, Mississauga, ON,
L5N 8E9
(905) 670-3352
Emp Here 65   *Emp Total* 348,877
Sales 32,540,472
SIC 5012 Automobiles and other motor vehi-
cles
  Yumiko Kawamura
  Shavak Madon
  Takashi Ono
  Yoshiniro Noguchi

D-U-N-S 20-221-3096   (HQ)
HOFFMANN-LA ROCHE LIMITED
ROCHE CANADA
7070 Mississauga Rd, Mississauga, ON, L5N
5M8
(905) 542-5555
Emp Here 458   *Emp Total* 94,052
Sales 71,136,683
SIC 2834 Pharmaceutical preparations
Pr Pr Ronald Miller
VP Fin Maria Teresa Lopez
  Ian Parfrement

D-U-N-S 24-317-1779   (BR)
HOME DEPOT OF CANADA INC
HOME DEPOT
(*Suby of* The Home Depot Inc)
2920 Argentia Rd, Mississauga, ON, L5N 8C5
(905) 814-3860
Emp Here 183
SIC 5251 Hardware stores

D-U-N-S 20-191-9573   (BR)
HONEYWELL LIMITED
SYSTEM SENSOR CANADA
(*Suby of* Honeywell International Inc.)
6581 Kitimat Rd Unit 6, Mississauga, ON, L5N
3T5
(905) 812-0767
Emp Here 35
SIC 3822 Environmental controls

D-U-N-S 24-342-3873   (BR)
HUDSON'S BAY COMPANY
HOME OUTFITTERS
3135 Argentia Rd Unit 1, Mississauga, ON,
L5N 8E1
(905) 824-6653
Emp Here 42
SIC 5719 Miscellaneous homefurnishings

D-U-N-S 20-011-4572   (BR)
INTACT INSURANCE COMPANY
6925 Century Ave Suite 900, Mississauga,
ON, L5N 0E3
(905) 858-1070
Emp Here 85
SIC 6331 Fire, marine, and casualty insurance

D-U-N-S 20-361-4086   (SL)
JEAN MACHINE CLOTHING INC
6789 Millcreek Dr, Mississauga, ON, L5N 5M4
(416) 498-6601
Emp Here 50   *Sales* 3,064,349
SIC 5621 Women's clothing stores

D-U-N-S 20-251-2752   (BR)

**KINTETSU WORLD EXPRESS (CANADA)
INC**
KWE
6700 Millcreek Dr, Mississauga, ON, L5N 8B3
(905) 542-3500
Emp Here 20
SIC 4225 General warehousing and storage

D-U-N-S 20-171-1546   (HQ)
KONE INC
ASCENSEURS RE-NO
6696 Financial Dr Suite 2, Mississauga, ON,
L5N 7J6
(416) 705-1629
Emp Here 35   *Emp Total* 50,905
Sales 35,083,166
SIC 7699 Repair services, nec
  Ralf Heitz

D-U-N-S 20-264-3094   (BR)
KUEHNE + NAGEL LTD
2300 Hogan Dr, Mississauga, ON, L5N 0C8
(905) 567-4168
Emp Here 500
SIC 4731 Freight transportation arrangement

D-U-N-S 20-158-1691   (BR)
LABORATOIRES ABBOTT LIMITEE
LABORATOIRES ABBOTT, LIMITEE
(*Suby of* Abbott Laboratories)
7115 Millcreek Dr, Mississauga, ON, L5N 3R3
(905) 858-2450
Emp Here 100
SIC 2834 Pharmaceutical preparations

D-U-N-S 24-061-7829   (HQ)
LAKESIDE PROCESS CONTROLS LTD
2475 Hogan Dr, Mississauga, ON, L5N 0E9
(905) 412-0500
Emp Here 105   *Emp Total* 140
Sales 25,536,245
SIC 5084 Industrial machinery and equipment
Pr Gregory Houston
  Gregory Robertson

D-U-N-S 25-482-2166   (BR)
LAWSON PRODUCTS INC. (ONTARIO)
LAWSON PRODUCTS INC (ONTARIO)
7315 Rapistan Crt, Mississauga, ON, L5N 5Z4
(905) 567-1717
Emp Here 40
SIC 5085 Industrial supplies

D-U-N-S 24-863-1850   (SL)
LEESWOOD DESIGN/BUILD LTD
7200 West Credit Ave, Mississauga, ON, L5N
5N1
(416) 309-4482
Emp Here 50   *Sales* 5,253,170
SIC 1521 Single-family housing construction
Dir Michael Clark

D-U-N-S 25-684-6064   (HQ)
LIQUI-BOX CANADA INC
(*Suby of* E. I. Du Pont De Nemours and Com-
pany)
7070 Mississauga Rd, Mississauga, ON, L5N
5M8
(905) 821-3300
Emp Here 50   *Emp Total* 46,000
Sales 70,773,360
SIC 7389 Business services, nec
VP Opers John Foster
Dir Doug Brown
  Donald Paddock

D-U-N-S 24-195-5900   (BR)
LOBLAWS INC
REAL CANADIAN SUPERSTORE, THE
3050 Argentia Rd, Mississauga, ON, L5N 8E1
(905) 785-3150
Emp Here 50
SIC 5411 Grocery stores

D-U-N-S 20-113-2052   (HQ)
LYNDEN CANADA CO
(*Suby of* Lynden Incorporated)
6581 Kitimat Rd Unit 1-4, Mississauga, ON,

L5N 3T5
(905) 858-5058
Emp Here 25   *Emp Total* 2,500
Sales 9,611,756
SIC 4731 Freight transportation arrangement
Pr David A. Richardson

D-U-N-S 24-308-7541   (HQ)
M & M MEAT SHOPS LTD
M&M FOOD MARKET
(*Suby of* M & M Meat Shops Ltd)
2240 Argentia Rd Suite 100, Mississauga,
ON, L5N 2K7
(905) 465-6325
Emp Here 100   *Emp Total* 130
Sales 17,729,450
SIC 5411 Grocery stores
CEO Andy O' Brian

D-U-N-S 24-685-6541   (SL)
MSI STONE ULC
(*Suby of* M S International Inc)
2140 Meadowpine Blvd, Mississauga, ON,
L5N 6H6
(905) 812-6100
Emp Here 30   *Sales* 15,592,518
SIC 5032 Brick, stone, and related material
Pr Pr Manahar Shah
Dir Rajesh Shah
Dir Chandrika Shah
Dir Rupesh Shah
Brnch Mgr Raman Mangat

D-U-N-S 24-329-3631   (BR)
MANUFACTURE EXM LTEE
2450 Meadowpine Blvd, Mississauga, ON,
L5N 7X5
(905) 812-8065
Emp Here 20
SIC 3613 Switchgear and switchboard appa-
ratus

D-U-N-S 25-302-1398   (BR)
MAPLE LEAF FOODS INC
2233 Argentia Rd Suite 300, Mississauga,
ON, L5N 2X7
(905) 819-0322
Emp Here 35
SIC 8743 Public relations services

D-U-N-S 20-409-5640   (BR)
MAPLE LEAF FOODS INC
MAPLE LEAF POULTRY
2626 Argentia Rd, Mississauga, ON, L5N 5N2
(905) 890-0053
Emp Here 110
SIC 2015 Poultry slaughtering and processing

D-U-N-S 24-317-5200   (BR)
MAPLE LEAF FOODS INC
6985 Financial Dr, Mississauga, ON, L5N 0A1
(905) 285-5000
Emp Here 600
SIC 2011 Meat packing plants

D-U-N-S 20-837-4343   (BR)
MARK'S WORK WEARHOUSE LTD
IMAGEWEAR
2333 Millrace Crt Unit 2-4, Mississauga, ON,
L5N 1W2
(905) 821-6850
Emp Here 20
SIC 5136 Men's and boy's clothing

D-U-N-S 24-217-5578   (HQ)
MARTIN-BROWER OF CANADA CO
MARTIN-BROWER
6990 Creditview Rd Suite 4, Mississauga, ON,
L5N 8R9
(905) 363-7000
Emp Here 55   *Emp Total* 600
Sales 98,496,945
SIC 5113 Industrial and personal service pa-
per
Pr Peter Hobbes
VP Opers Meredith Neizer
Fin Ex Roochita Patel

D-U-N-S 24-138-5574 (HQ)
MARY KAY COSMETICS LTD
(*Suby of* Mary Kay Holding Corporation)
2020 Meadowvale Blvd, Mississauga, ON,
L5N 6Y2
(905) 858-0020
Emp Here 108　　　*Emp Total* 3,600
Sales 16,112,269
SIC 5122 Drugs, proprietaries, and sundries
Pr Ray Patrick
　Eva Liebermann
S&M/VP Linda Rose

D-U-N-S 24-382-2041 (BR)
MATRIX LOGISTICS SERVICES LIMITED
7045 Millcreek Dr, Mississauga, ON, L5N 3R3

Emp Here 30
SIC 4225 General warehousing and storage

D-U-N-S 20-105-1328 (HQ)
MAXXAM ANALYTICS INTERNATIONAL CORPORATION
MAXXAM ANALYTICS
1919 Minnesota Crt Suite 500, Mississauga,
ON, L5N 0C9
(905) 288-2150
Emp Here 90　　　*Emp Total* 8,581
Sales 194,559,975
SIC 8734 Testing laboratories
Pr Donna Garbutt
VP Steve Quon
VP VP Robert Wiebe
Pers/VP Margaret Bailey
　Danny Bharat

D-U-N-S 24-844-9522 (SL)
MEADOWVALE BIBLE BAPTIST CHURCH
2720 Gananoque Dr, Mississauga, ON, L5N
2R2
(905) 826-4114
Emp Here 60　　　*Sales* 3,939,878
SIC 8661 Religious organizations

D-U-N-S 24-953-0205 (BR)
METRO ONTARIO INC
DOMINION STORES
6677 Meadowvale Town Centre Cir, Mississauga, ON, L5N 2R5
(905) 826-2717
Emp Here 200
SIC 5411 Grocery stores

D-U-N-S 20-555-6439 (BR)
METRO ONTARIO INC
METRO
3221 Derry Rd W Suite 16, Mississauga, ON,
L5N 7L7
(905) 785-1844
Emp Here 150
SIC 5411 Grocery stores

D-U-N-S 24-545-5076 (HQ)
MICROSOFT CANADA INC
MICROSOFT
(*Suby of* Microsoft Corporation)
1950 Meadowvale Blvd, Mississauga, ON,
L5N 8L9
(905) 568-0434
Emp Here 400　　　*Emp Total* 114,124
Sales 114,869,905
SIC 5045 Computers, peripherals, and software
　Keith Dolliver
Pr Eric Gales
　Benjamin Orndorff

D-U-N-S 25-090-7714 (SL)
MISSISSAUGA CHRISTIAN ACADEMY & DAYCARE
BIBLE BAPTIST CHURCH
2690 Gananoque Dr, Mississauga, ON, L5N
2R2
(905) 826-4114
Emp Here 60　　　*Sales* 1,824,018
SIC 8351 Child day care services

D-U-N-S 25-162-9457 (BR)

MODERN NIAGARA DESIGN SERVICES INC
2240 Argentia Rd, Mississauga, ON, L5N 2K7

Emp Here 75
SIC 1711 Plumbing, heating, air-conditioning

D-U-N-S 24-421-1079 (SL)
MONESSEN HEARTH CANADA, INC
MONESSEN HEARTH SYSTEMS CO
(*Suby of* Hni Corporation)
6975 Creditview Rd Unit 2, Mississauga, ON,
L5N 8E9

Emp Here 22　　　*Sales* 5,526,400
SIC 5074 Plumbing and heating equipment
and supplies (hydronics)
Mgr Dennis Corrigan

D-U-N-S 24-388-2417 (BR)
NPL CANADA LTD
(*Suby of* Southwest Gas Holdings, Inc.)
7505 Danbro Cres, Mississauga, ON, L5N
6P9
(905) 821-8383
Emp Here 100
SIC 1623 Water, sewer, and utility lines

D-U-N-S 24-886-5156 (BR)
NTN BEARING CORPORATION OF CANADA LIMITED
NTN BEARING MANUFACTURING CANADA
6740 Kitimat Rd, Mississauga, ON, L5N 1M6
(905) 826-5500
Emp Here 115
SIC 3562 Ball and roller bearings

D-U-N-S 20-188-6756 (BR)
NOVARTIS PHARMA CANADA INC
CIBA VISION CANADA DIV
2150 Torquay Mews, Mississauga, ON, L5N
2M6

Emp Here 280
SIC 5048 Ophthalmic goods

D-U-N-S 24-393-0414 (SL)
NULOGX INC
NULOGX MANAGE TRANSPORTATION SOLUTIONS
2233 Argentia Rd Suite 202, Mississauga,
ON, L5N 2X7
(905) 486-1162
Emp Here 50　　　*Sales* 5,399,092
SIC 8742 Management consulting services
　Robert Drassinower
　Naresh Vohra
Pr Doug Payne

D-U-N-S 20-866-4524 (HQ)
PACCAR OF CANADA LTD
CANADIAN KENWORTH COMPANY
(*Suby of* Paccar Inc)
6711 Mississauga Rd Suite 500, Mississauga,
ON, L5N 4J8
(905) 858-7000
Emp Here 30　　　*Emp Total* 23,000
Sales 46,548,927
SIC 5012 Automobiles and other motor vehicles
　Mark C Piggott
Pr Thomas E. Plimpton
Dir James S. Medwid
Dir D. D. Sobic

D-U-N-S 20-104-8886 (BR)
PANASONIC CANADA INC
PANASONIC CONSUMER DISTRIBUTION CENTRE
6700 Millcreek Dr, Mississauga, ON, L5N 8B3
(905) 542-3500
Emp Here 34
SIC 4225 General warehousing and storage

D-U-N-S 24-704-8572 (SL)
PARAGON CANADA INC
6535 Millcreek Dr Unit 48, Mississauga, ON,
L5N 2M2

(905) 825-2000
Emp Here 21　　　*Sales* 1,240,332
SIC 7699 Repair services, nec

D-U-N-S 25-293-8402 (BR)
PEEL DISTRICT SCHOOL BOARD
MILLER'S GROVE PUBLIC SCHOOL
(*Suby of* Peel District School Board)
6325 Miller'S Grove, Mississauga, ON, L5N
3K2
(905) 824-3275
Emp Here 30
SIC 8211 Elementary and secondary schools

D-U-N-S 24-963-1391 (BR)
PEEL DISTRICT SCHOOL BOARD
MEADOWVALE SECONDARY SCHOOL
(*Suby of* Peel District School Board)
6700 Edenwood Dr, Mississauga, ON, L5N
3B2
(905) 824-1790
Emp Here 130
SIC 8211 Elementary and secondary schools

D-U-N-S 24-963-1193 (BR)
PEEL DISTRICT SCHOOL BOARD
SETTLER'S GREEN PUBLIC SCHOOL
(*Suby of* Peel District School Board)
5800 Montevideo Rd, Mississauga, ON, L5N
2S1
(905) 826-4947
Emp Here 50
SIC 8211 Elementary and secondary schools

D-U-N-S 25-487-5933 (BR)
PEEL DISTRICT SCHOOL BOARD
LISGAR MIDDLE SCHOOL
(*Suby of* Peel District School Board)
6755 Lisgar Dr, Mississauga, ON, L5N 6S9
(905) 785-0105
Emp Here 60
SIC 8211 Elementary and secondary schools

D-U-N-S 24-963-1078 (BR)
PEEL DISTRICT SCHOOL BOARD
RAY UNDERHILL PUBLIC SCHOOL
(*Suby of* Peel District School Board)
32 Suburban Dr, Mississauga, ON, L5N 1G6
(905) 826-1742
Emp Here 30
SIC 8211 Elementary and secondary schools

D-U-N-S 24-963-1037 (BR)
PEEL DISTRICT SCHOOL BOARD
PLOWMAN'S PARK PUBLIC SCHOOL
(*Suby of* Peel District School Board)
5940 Montevideo Rd, Mississauga, ON, L5N
3J5
(905) 821-4973
Emp Here 37
SIC 8211 Elementary and secondary schools

D-U-N-S 24-227-7270 (BR)
PEEL DISTRICT SCHOOL BOARD
KINDREE PUBLIC SCHOOL
(*Suby of* Peel District School Board)
7370 Terragar Blvd, Mississauga, ON, L5N
7L8
(905) 824-8371
Emp Here 55
SIC 8211 Elementary and secondary schools

D-U-N-S 25-921-0284 (BR)
PEEL DISTRICT SCHOOL BOARD
TRELAWNY PUBLIC SCHOOL
(*Suby of* Peel District School Board)
3420 Trelawny Cir, Mississauga, ON, L5N 6N6
(905) 824-0360
Emp Here 45
SIC 8211 Elementary and secondary schools

D-U-N-S 25-293-7925 (BR)
PEEL DISTRICT SCHOOL BOARD
PLUM TREE PARK PUBLIC SCHOOL
(*Suby of* Peel District School Board)
6855 Tenth Line W, Mississauga, ON, L5N
5R2
(905) 824-0155
Emp Here 45

SIC 8211 Elementary and secondary schools

D-U-N-S 25-293-8246 (BR)
PEEL DISTRICT SCHOOL BOARD
MAPLE WOOD PUBLIC SCHOOL
(*Suby of* Peel District School Board)
2650 Gananoque Dr, Mississauga, ON, L5N
2R2
(905) 826-3902
Emp Here 22
SIC 8211 Elementary and secondary schools

D-U-N-S 25-293-8147 (BR)
PEEL DISTRICT SCHOOL BOARD
WEST CREDIT SECONDARY SCHOOL
(*Suby of* Peel District School Board)
6325 Montevideo Rd, Mississauga, ON, L5N
4G7
(905) 858-3087
Emp Here 80
SIC 8211 Elementary and secondary schools

D-U-N-S 24-963-1383 (BR)
PEEL DISTRICT SCHOOL BOARD
EDENWOOD MIDDLE SCHOOL
(*Suby of* Peel District School Board)
6770 Edenwood Dr, Mississauga, ON, L5N
3B2
(905) 824-1020
Emp Here 40
SIC 8211 Elementary and secondary schools

D-U-N-S 20-711-1860 (BR)
PEEL DISTRICT SCHOOL BOARD
LEVI CREEK PUBLIC SCHOOL
(*Suby of* Peel District School Board)
1525 Samuelson Cir, Mississauga, ON, L5N
7Z1
(905) 564-9879
Emp Here 50
SIC 8211 Elementary and secondary schools

D-U-N-S 24-963-1235 (BR)
PEEL DISTRICT SCHOOL BOARD
SHELTER BAY PUBLIC SCHOOL
(*Suby of* Peel District School Board)
6735 Shelter Bay Rd, Mississauga, ON, L5N
2C5
(905) 826-5516
Emp Here 40
SIC 8211 Elementary and secondary schools

D-U-N-S 20-655-0597 (BR)
PEEL DISTRICT SCHOOL BOARD
OSPREY WOODS PUBLIC SCHOOL
(*Suby of* Peel District School Board)
6135 Lisgar Dr, Mississauga, ON, L5N 7V2
(905) 785-9687
Emp Here 40
SIC 8211 Elementary and secondary schools

D-U-N-S 24-452-4625 (HQ)
PINCHIN LTD
PINCHIN
(*Suby of* 2010282 Ontario Inc)
2470 Milltower Crt Suite 363, Mississauga,
ON, L5N 7W5
(905) 363-0678
Emp Here 250　　　*Emp Total* 360
Sales 61,070,696
SIC 8748 Business consulting, nec
Pr Pr Donald Pinchin
COO Jeff Grossi

D-U-N-S 20-812-1538 (BR)
PITNEY BOWES OF CANADA LTD
(*Suby of* Pitney Bowes Inc.)
6880 Financial Dr Suite 1000, Mississauga,
ON, L5N 8E8
(905) 816-2665
Emp Here 40
SIC 7389 Business services, nec

D-U-N-S 24-348-7407 (HQ)
PREMIER TECH HOME & GARDEN INC
1900 Minnesota Crt Suite 125, Mississauga,
ON, L5N 3C9

(905) 812-8556
Emp Here 30   Emp Total 50
Sales 14,293,142
SIC 5199 Nondurable goods, nec
Jean Belanger
Pr Rene Mondugo
Sec Martin Noel

D-U-N-S 24-918-8012   (HQ)
PRIMERICA LIFE INSURANCE COMPANY OF CANADA
PRIMERICA
2000 Argentia Rd Suite 5, Mississauga, ON, L5N 1P7
(905) 812-3520
Emp Here 170   Emp Total 195
Sales 193,783,619
SIC 6311 Life insurance
Dir John Adams
 Jeffrey Dumanski
 Guy Sauve
 Richard Williams
Dir Robert Mcdowell
Dir John Addison
Dir Frederick S Mallett

D-U-N-S 25-117-0767   (HQ)
RBC GENERAL INSURANCE COMPANY
(Suby of Royal Bank Of Canada)
6880 Financial Dr Suite 200, Mississauga, ON, L5N 7Y5
(905) 816-5400
Emp Here 410   Emp Total 79,000
Sales 263,860,055
SIC 6331 Fire, marine, and casualty insurance
Pr Pr Neil Skelding
CFO Katherine Gibson

D-U-N-S 20-817-0142   (HQ)
RBC INSURANCE COMPANY OF CANADA
(Suby of Royal Bank Of Canada)
6880 Financial Dr Suite 200, Mississauga, ON, L5N 7Y5
(905) 949-3663
Emp Here 120   Emp Total 79,000
Sales 20,720,839
SIC 6411 Insurance agents, brokers, and service
Pr David Lafayette
 John D Mckenna
Dir Rosemary Troiani
VP Opers Stan Seggie
 Richard Burton

D-U-N-S 20-750-8573   (HQ)
RBC LIFE INSURANCE COMPANY
(Suby of Royal Bank Of Canada)
6880 Financial Dr Suite 1000, Mississauga, ON, L5N 8E8
(905) 816-2746
Emp Here 400   Emp Total 79,000
Sales 1,579,890,998
SIC 6311 Life insurance
Pr John Young
Ch Bd Neil Skelding

D-U-N-S 24-316-2369   (HQ)
RE/MAX REALTY SPECIALISTS INC
(Suby of Re/Max Realty Specialists Inc)
6850 Millcreek Dr Unit 200, Mississauga, ON, L5N 4J9
(905) 858-3434
Emp Here 150   Emp Total 500
Sales 64,910,080
SIC 6531 Real estate agents and managers
Pr Pr Greg Gilmour

D-U-N-S 25-300-5367   (BR)
REDBERRY FRANCHISING CORP
BURGER KING
6465 Mississauga Rd, Mississauga, ON, L5N 1A6
(905) 821-3464
Emp Here 40
SIC 5812 Eating places

D-U-N-S 24-796-8241   (SL)
RESERVEAMERICA ON INC

RESERVEAMERICA
2480 Meadowvale Blvd Suite 1, Mississauga, ON, L5N 8M6
(905) 286-6600
Emp Here 130   Sales 23,110,400
SIC 7371 Custom computer programming services
 Terry Barnes
Pr Seth Rosenberg
CFO Sharon Deaver-Fisher

D-U-N-S 25-122-4358   (BR)
ROYAL BANK OF CANADA
RBC
(Suby of Royal Bank Of Canada)
6040 Glen Erin Dr Unit 7, Mississauga, ON, L5N 3M4
(905) 542-7430
Emp Here 20
SIC 6021 National commercial banks

D-U-N-S 24-663-8857   (SL)
ROYAL LEPAGE MEADOWTOWNE REALTY BROKERAGE
6948 Financial Dr, Mississauga, ON, L5N 8J4
(905) 821-3200
Emp Here 49   Sales 6,184,080
SIC 6531 Real estate agents and managers
Prin Morten Andersen

D-U-N-S 24-889-7407   (BR)
RUSSEL METALS INC
1900 Minnesota Crt Suite 210, Mississauga, ON, L5N 3C9
(905) 567-8500
Emp Here 100
SIC 5051 Metals service centers and offices

D-U-N-S 20-174-6146   (HQ)
RYDER TRUCK RENTAL CANADA LTD
RYDER CANADA
(Suby of Ryder System, Inc.)
2233 Argentia Rd Suite 300, Mississauga, ON, L5N 2X7
(905) 826-8777
Emp Here 60   Emp Total 34,500
Sales 121,844,369
SIC 7513 Truck rental and leasing, no drivers
Sr VP Todd Skiles
Sr VP John Deris
Sr VP Marc Thibeau
VP Alex Madrinkian
VP Delores Lail
VP Sls Dan Mchugh
VP Michael R. Thompson
VP Mark Edds
Dir Robert E. Sanchez

D-U-N-S 24-386-0046   (HQ)
SAMSUNG ELECTRONICS CANADA INC
2050 Derry Rd W Suite 1, Mississauga, ON, L5N 0B9
(905) 542-3535
Emp Here 182   Emp Total 94,283
Sales 223,925,884
SIC 5064 Electrical appliances, television and radio
Pr Pr Seo Gy
 Michael Sangwhun Park

D-U-N-S 24-676-9793   (SL)
SAMSUNG RENEWABLE ENERGY INC
2050 Derry Rd W 2fl, Mississauga, ON, L5N 0B9
(905) 501-4934
Emp Here 28   Sales 15,939,018
SIC 4911 Electric services
Pr Pr Jeong Tack Lee
Dir Heung-Do Kim
 Youngjin Cho

D-U-N-S 24-761-0046   (BR)
SAMUEL, SON & CO., LIMITED
ROLL FORM GROUP
6701 Financial Dr Suite 100, Mississauga, ON, L5N 7J7
(905) 270-5300
Emp Here 40

SIC 5051 Metals service centers and offices

D-U-N-S 20-719-5871   (BR)
SANDVIK CANADA, INC
SANDVIK MINING
2550 Meadowvale Blvd Unit 3, Mississauga, ON, L5N 8C2
(905) 826-8900
Emp Here 200
SIC 3312 Blast furnaces and steel mills

D-U-N-S 20-118-6488   (HQ)
SAVVIS COMMUNICATIONS CANADA, INC
(Suby of Centurylink, Inc.)
6800 Millcreek Dr, Mississauga, ON, L5N 4J9
(905) 363-3737
Emp Here 100   Emp Total 40,000
Sales 16,926,882
SIC 8741 Management services
Pr William D Fathers

D-U-N-S 25-990-2252   (HQ)
SCOTTS CANADA LTD
(Suby of The Scotts Miracle-Gro Company)
2000 Argentia Rd Suite 300, Mississauga, ON, L5N 1P7
(905) 814-7425
Emp Here 50   Emp Total 7,900
Sales 7,441,991
SIC 5199 Nondurable goods, nec
 John Warren

D-U-N-S 24-537-9631   (HQ)
SEXAUER LTD
(Suby of The Home Depot Inc)
6990 Creditview Rd Unit 4, Mississauga, ON, L5N 8R9
(905) 821-8292
Emp Here 22   Emp Total 406,000
Sales 10,068,577
SIC 5074 Plumbing and heating equipment and supplies (hydronics)
VP Sls Howard Richards

D-U-N-S 25-531-7349   (SL)
SILVER HOTEL (AMBLER) INC
FOUR POINTS BY SHERATON MISSISSAUGA MEDOWVALE
2501 Argentia Rd, Mississauga, ON, L5N 4G8
(905) 858-2424
Emp Here 100   Sales 4,377,642
SIC 7011 Hotels and motels

D-U-N-S 24-951-7640   (BR)
SMITH & NEPHEW INC
2280 Argentia Rd, Mississauga, ON, L5N 6H8
(905) 813-7770
Emp Here 30
SIC 5047 Medical and hospital equipment

D-U-N-S 25-053-7354   (BR)
SOBEYS CAPITAL INCORPORATED
PRICE SHOPPER
6040 Glen Erin Dr, Mississauga, ON, L5N 3M4
(905) 826-0582
Emp Here 140
SIC 5411 Grocery stores

D-U-N-S 20-860-2206   (BR)
SOURCE (BELL) ELECTRONICS INC, THE
SOURCE, THE
6677 Meadowvale Town Centre Cir, Mississauga, ON, L5N 2R5
(905) 369-0136
Emp Here 25
SIC 5999 Miscellaneous retail stores, nec

D-U-N-S 24-426-3781   (BR)
STANLEY BLACK & DECKER CANADA CORPORATION
STANLEY SECURITY SOLUTIONS, DIV OF
2495 Meadowpine Blvd Suite 1, Mississauga, ON, L5N 6C3
(289) 290-7100
Emp Here 65
SIC 3429 Hardware, nec

D-U-N-S 20-568-0882   (BR)

STAPLES CANADA INC
STAPLES THE BUSINESS DEPOT
(Suby of Staples, Inc.)
3135 Argentia Rd Unit 2, Mississauga, ON, L5N 8E1
(905) 785-0864
Emp Here 30
SIC 5943 Stationery stores

D-U-N-S 25-214-2237   (SL)
STARWOOD HOTEL
(Suby of Westmont Hospitality Management Limited)
2501 Argentia Rd, Mississauga, ON, L5N 4G8
(905) 858-2424
Emp Here 100   Sales 5,889,600
SIC 7011 Hotels and motels
Genl Mgr Denzul Miranda

D-U-N-S 20-955-9876   (HQ)
STRABAG INC
6790 Century Ave Suite 401, Mississauga, ON, L5N 2V8
(905) 353-5500
Emp Here 45   Emp Total 72,906
Sales 65,835,076
SIC 1541 Industrial buildings and warehouses
Dir Lloyd Furguson
 Robert Raddlinger

D-U-N-S 20-050-5381   (SL)
SUNOVION PHARMACEUTICALS CANADA INC
6790 Century Ave Suite 100, Mississauga, ON, L5N 2V8
(905) 814-9145
Emp Here 40   Sales 4,591,130
SIC 2834 Pharmaceutical preparations

D-U-N-S 20-644-3462   (SL)
SYNTHES (CANADA) LTD
(Suby of Johnson & Johnson)
2566 Meadowpine Blvd, Mississauga, ON, L5N 6P9
(905) 567-0440
Emp Here 32   Sales 4,669,485
SIC 5047 Medical and hospital equipment

D-U-N-S 20-273-8373   (SL)
SYSTEMGROUP CONSULTING INC
6701 Financial Dr Suite 200, Mississauga, ON, L5N 7J7
(647) 795-8008
Emp Here 49   Sales 6,313,604
SIC 7371 Custom computer programming services

D-U-N-S 20-072-9015   (SL)
TESTING LABORATORIES OF CANADA CORP.
1840 Argentia Rd Suite B, Mississauga, ON, L5N 1P9
(905) 812-7783
Emp Here 29   Sales 2,188,821
SIC 8734 Testing laboratories

D-U-N-S 25-245-0614   (HQ)
THOMAS & BETTS (ONTARIO) LTD
READY-LITE DIV
2233 Argentia Rd Suite 114, Mississauga, ON, L5N 2X7
(905) 858-1010
Emp Here 40   Emp Total 400
Sales 59,649,426
SIC 5063 Electrical apparatus and equipment
Pr Pr Micheal B. Kenney
 Nathalie Pilon

D-U-N-S 25-121-9804   (BR)
THOMAS & BETTS, LIMITEE
2000 Argentia Rd Suite 500, Mississauga, ON, L5N 1W1

Emp Here 20
SIC 3648 Lighting equipment, nec

D-U-N-S 24-242-2421   (SL)
TIBCO SOFTWARE CANADA INC

(Suby of Vista Equity Partners Management, LLC)
2000 Argentia Rd Suite 2, Mississauga, ON, L5N 1V8

Emp Here 25   Sales 2,450,055
SIC 7371 Custom computer programming services

D-U-N-S 25-122-7914   (SL)
TIM HORTONS
3285 Derry Rd W Suite 101, Mississauga, ON, L5N 7L7
(905) 824-2814
Emp Here 50   Sales 1,532,175
SIC 5812 Eating places

D-U-N-S 25-534-6769   (BR)
UNITED RENTALS OF CANADA, INC
UNITED RENTALS
2790 Argentia Rd Suite D, Mississauga, ON, L5N 8L2
(905) 814-3533
Emp Here 20
SIC 7353 Heavy construction equipment rental

D-U-N-S 20-403-5075   (HQ)
UPONOR INFRA LTD
6507 Mississauga Rd Unit A, Mississauga, ON, L5N 1A6
(905) 858-0206
Emp Here 25   Emp Total 3,869
Sales 35,516,291
SIC 8741 Management services
Pr Pr Paul Van Warmerdam
Dir Peter Hoglund

D-U-N-S 24-845-8069   (HQ)
VWR INTERNATIONAL CO.
(Suby of VWR Corporation)
2360 Argentia Rd, Mississauga, ON, L5N 5Z7
(905) 813-7377
Emp Here 200   Emp Total 9,426
Sales 34,650,040
SIC 5049 Professional equipment, nec
Pr Nav Arora
Dir Fin Gregory Blakely
Crdt Mgr Richard Tymczyszyn

D-U-N-S 20-177-6440   (HQ)
VANGUARD STEEL LTD
2160 Meadowpine Blvd, Mississauga, ON, L5N 6H6
(905) 821-1100
Emp Here 70   Sales 84,561,451
SIC 5051 Metals service centers and offices
Pr Pr Gary Scheichl
VP VP Craig Spence
Dir Heino Knoop
Dir Louis Kalchhauser

D-U-N-S 24-757-1250   (SL)
VIGOUR LIMITED PARTNERSHIP
2121 Argentia Rd Suite 301, Mississauga, ON, L5N 2X4
(905) 821-1161
Emp Here 1,000   Sales 62,699,520
SIC 8051 Skilled nursing care facilities
Ltd Pt Henry Alban
Ltd Pt Edward Sonshine
Ltd Pt Elizabeth O'brien

D-U-N-S 25-992-6756   (HQ)
VITALAIRE CANADA INC
VITALAIRE HEALTHCARE/SANTE
6990 Creditview Rd Unit 6, Mississauga, ON, L5N 8R9
(905) 855-0414
Emp Here 70   Emp Total 1,107
Sales 169,049,942
SIC 5169 Chemicals and allied products, nec
Pr Pr Paul Ostrowski
Jean-Pierre Girouard
Jean-Marc De Royere
Dir Pierre Dufour
Dir Oliver Petit
Dir Scott Krapf

D-U-N-S 20-402-9300   (HQ)
VOESTALPINE HIGH PERFORMACE LETALS LTD
2595 Meadowvale Blvd, Mississauga, ON, L5N 7Y3
(905) 812-9440
Emp Here 45   Emp Total 47,186
Sales 38,304,368
SIC 5051 Metals service centers and offices
Pr Paul Cavanagh

D-U-N-S 20-321-6577   (BR)
WAJAX INDUSTRIAL COMPONENTS LIMITED PARTNERSHIP
WAJAX INDUSTRIAL COMPONENTS
2250 Argentia Rd, Mississauga, ON, L5N 6A5
(905) 813-8310
Emp Here 70
SIC 5085 Industrial supplies

D-U-N-S 20-562-7313   (HQ)
WAJAX LIMITED
INDUSTRIES WAJAX
2250 Argentia Rd, Mississauga, ON, L5N 6A5
(905) 212-3300
Emp Here 25   Emp Total 2,318
Sales 21,888,210
SIC 5084 Industrial machinery and equipment
Pr Mark Foote
VP Fin John Hamilton

D-U-N-S 25-294-7346   (BR)
WAL-MART CANADA CORP
3155 Argentia Rd, Mississauga, ON, L5N 8E1
(905) 821-8150
Emp Here 300
SIC 5311 Department stores

D-U-N-S 25-294-7304   (BR)
WAL-MART CANADA CORP
1940 Argentia Rd, Mississauga, ON, L5N 1P9
(905) 821-2111
Emp Here 400
SIC 5311 Department stores

D-U-N-S 20-229-5846   (HQ)
WEIR CANADA, INC
OIL AND GAS
2360 Millrace Crt, Mississauga, ON, L5N 1W2
(905) 812-7100
Emp Here 110   Emp Total 13,245
Sales 214,285,800
SIC 5084 Industrial machinery and equipment
Pr Pr Serge Lamirande
Ian Dundee
Rui Silveira
Richard Stephenson

D-U-N-S 24-376-5828   (BR)
WEIR CANADA, INC
WEIR MINERALS
2360 Millrace Crt, Mississauga, ON, L5N 1W2
(905) 812-7100
Emp Here 100
SIC 3569 General industrial machinery, nec

D-U-N-S 20-005-4026   (BR)
WENDY'S RESTAURANTS OF CANADA INC
WENDY'S
(Suby of The Wendy's Company)
6449 Erin Mills Pky, Mississauga, ON, L5N 4H4
(905) 819-6787
Emp Here 20
SIC 5812 Eating places

D-U-N-S 20-644-9782   (BR)
WENDY'S RESTAURANTS OF CANADA INC
WENDY'S
(Suby of The Wendy's Company)
6966 Financial Dr Bldg F, Mississauga, ON, L5N 8J4
(905) 821-4538
Emp Here 32
SIC 5812 Eating places

D-U-N-S 24-827-8884   (SL)
WHIRLPOOL CANADA CO

WHIRLPOOL CANADA
(Suby of Whirlpool Corporation)
6750 Century Ave Suite 200, Mississauga, ON, L5N 0B7
(905) 821-6400
Emp Here 20   Sales 2,553,625
SIC 5065 Electronic parts and equipment, nec

D-U-N-S 20-167-5634   (HQ)
WHIRLPOOL CANADA LP
(Suby of Whirlpool Corporation)
1901 Minnesota Crt, Mississauga, ON, L5N 3C9
(905) 821-6400
Emp Here 220   Emp Total 93,000
SIC 3633 Household laundry equipment

D-U-N-S 20-184-3286   (BR)
WINNERS MERCHANTS INTERNATIONAL L.P.
WINNERS
(Suby of The TJX Companies Inc)
3135 Argentia Rd Unit G6, Mississauga, ON, L5N 8E1
(905) 785-8475
Emp Here 40
SIC 5651 Family clothing stores

D-U-N-S 24-814-9601   (HQ)
WOLVERINE WORLD WIDE CANADA ULC
HUSH PUPPIES
(Suby of Wolverine World Wide, Inc.)
6225 Millcreek Dr, Mississauga, ON, L5N 0G2
(905) 285-9560
Emp Here 50   Emp Total 5,860
Sales 24,601,528
SIC 5139 Footwear
Pr Bruke W Kruger
VP Michael D Stornant
Fotini Dermatis

D-U-N-S 20-009-9815   (BR)
YOUNG & RUBICAM GROUP OF COMPANIES ULC, THE
SUDLER & HENNESSEY MARKET FOREST, DIV OF
2121 Argentia Rd Suite 401, Mississauga, ON, L5N 2X4
(905) 581-1493
Emp Here 26
SIC 7311 Advertising agencies

D-U-N-S 24-857-3664   (SL)
ZUBLIN INC
6790 Century Ave Suite 401, Mississauga, ON, L5N 2V8
(289) 315-3972
Emp Here 20   Sales 1,459,214
SIC 1794 Excavation work

Mississauga, ON L5P
Peel County

D-U-N-S 24-093-4062   (SL)
AIRPORT TERMINAL SERVICE INC CANADIAN
6500 Silver Dart Dr Unit 211, Mississauga, ON, L5P 1B1
(905) 405-9550
Emp Here 300   Sales 189,252,480
SIC 4581 Airports, flying fields, and services
Genl Mgr Richard Chiappetta

D-U-N-S 20-251-6126   (BR)
ASIG CANADA LTD
ASIG
(Suby of Asig Canada Ltd)
5600 Silver Dart Dr, Mississauga, ON, L5P 1B2
(905) 694-2846
Emp Here 200
SIC 5172 Petroleum products, nec

D-U-N-S 20-572-2775   (BR)
BANK OF NOVA SCOTIA, THE

SCOTIABANK
6120 Midfield Rd, Mississauga, ON, L5P 1B1
(905) 677-3422
Emp Here 20
SIC 6021 National commercial banks

D-U-N-S 24-744-4227   (BR)
CLS CATERING SERVICES LTD
CLS CATERING
2950 Convair Dr, Mississauga, ON, L5P 1A2
(905) 676-3218
Emp Here 150
SIC 5812 Eating places

D-U-N-S 24-193-7130   (BR)
NUANCE GROUP (CANADA) INC, THE
SPIRIT OF THE NORTH DUTY FREE
3111 Convair Dr, Mississauga, ON, L5P 1B2
(905) 672-0591
Emp Here 50
SIC 5399 Miscellaneous general merchandise

D-U-N-S 20-275-2119   (SL)
SHERATON GATEWAY LIMITED PARTNERSHIP
6320 Silver Dart Dr, Mississauga, ON, L5P 1C4
(905) 672-7000
Emp Here 50   Sales 2,188,821
SIC 7011 Hotels and motels

D-U-N-S 20-252-3564   (HQ)
SKYSERVICE BUSINESS AVIATION INC
6120 Midfield Rd, Mississauga, ON, L5P 1B1
(905) 677-3300
Emp Here 250   Emp Total 300
Sales 48,081,101
SIC 4522 Air transportation, nonscheduled
Pr Pr Marshall Myles
Sec Emlyn David
Barbara Syrek

D-U-N-S 20-911-2114   (BR)
STARWOOD CANADA ULC
SHERATON GATEWAY HOTEL
(Suby of Marriott International, Inc.)
Gd, Mississauga, ON, L5P 1C4
(905) 672-7000
Emp Here 20
SIC 7011 Hotels and motels

D-U-N-S 24-207-0766   (HQ)
SWISSPORT CANADA HANDLING INC
6500 Silver Dart Dr, Mississauga, ON, L5P 1A2
(905) 676-2888
Emp Here 267   Emp Total 350,308
Sales 278,413,071
SIC 4581 Airports, flying fields, and services
Sec Rodrigue E Levesque
Pr Richard Van Bruygom

D-U-N-S 24-120-1040   (BR)
UNITED PARCEL SERVICE CANADA LTD
UPS
6500 Silverdart Dr Suite 104, Mississauga, ON, L5P 1B6
(905) 362-2055
Emp Here 70
SIC 4212 Local trucking, without storage

D-U-N-S 24-119-7552   (BR)
UNITED PARCEL SERVICE CANADA LTD
UPS
6500 Silver Dart Dr, Mississauga, ON, L5P 1B2
(905) 362-2040
Emp Here 50
SIC 4731 Freight transportation arrangement

Mississauga, ON L5R
Peel County

D-U-N-S 20-704-0551   (SL)
1388312 ONTARIO INC

5700 Keaton Cres Unit 1, Mississauga, ON,
L5R 3H5
(905) 272-0727
Emp Here 45   Sales 8,025,677
SIC 2531 Public building and related furniture
Pr Pr Dan Nussbaum
VP VP Pablo Reich
 Shanti Defehr
Dir Arthur Defehr

D-U-N-S 20-913-5693   (BR)
4513380 CANADA INC
LIVINGSTON INTERNATIONAL
6155 Belgrave Rd, Mississauga, ON, L5R 4E6

Emp Here 20
SIC 4731 Freight transportation arrangement

D-U-N-S 20-112-8951   (SL)
609698 ONTARIO INC
6200 Cantay Rd, Mississauga, ON, L5R 3Y9
(905) 501-9350
Emp Here 150   Sales 11,681,040
SIC 2511 Wood household furniture
Pr Pr Derek Okada

D-U-N-S 24-349-3418   (HQ)
6929818 CANADA INC
ENTREPRISES TAG, LES
(Suby of 6929818 Canada Inc)
10 Kingsbridge Garden Cir Suite 704, Mississauga, ON, L5R 3K6

Emp Here 100   Emp Total 200
Sales 26,377,000
SIC 2421 Sawmills and planing mills, general
Pr Serge Dominique
VP Christopher Bellahoussof
VP VP Jean-Yves Cardinal
 Eb Reinbergs

D-U-N-S 25-690-6470   (HQ)
AGFA HEALTHCARE INC
5975 Falbourne St Suite 2, Mississauga, ON,
L5R 3V8
(416) 241-1110
Emp Here 25   Emp Total 1,962
Sales 48,154,062
SIC 5047 Medical and hospital equipment
Pr William Corsten
Dir Gunther Mertens
Dir Peter Wilkens

D-U-N-S 20-999-3146   (HQ)
ANIXTER CANADA INC
200 Foster Cres, Mississauga, ON, L5R 3Y5
(905) 568-8999
Emp Here 450   Emp Total 8,900
Sales 147,599,496
SIC 5063 Electrical apparatus and equipment
Pr Pr Grant Gamble
VP Gary Mistak
 Marcelo Fiaes
Dir Fin Cindy Yuan
Prs Dir Brian Zolper
Dir Bradley Easton

D-U-N-S 20-210-8015   (HQ)
BASF CANADA INC
100 Milverton Dr Unit 500, Mississauga, ON,
L5R 4H1
(289) 360-1300
Emp Here 140   Emp Total 111,975
Sales 76,608,735
SIC 2821 Plastics materials and resins
Pr Marcelo Lu Navarro

D-U-N-S 20-572-2965   (BR)
BASF CANADA INC
100 Milverton Dr Floor 5, Mississauga, ON,
L5R 4H1
(289) 360-1300
Emp Here 75
SIC 2821 Plastics materials and resins

D-U-N-S 24-790-1767   (BR)
BCBG MAX AZRIA CANADA INC
BCBG MAX AZRIA

5985 Rodeo Dr Unit 9, Mississauga, ON, L5R
3X8
(905) 366-0197
Emp Here 20
SIC 5137 Women's and children's clothing

D-U-N-S 25-808-4078   (BR)
BANK OF NOVA SCOTIA, THE
SCOTIABANK
660 Eglinton Ave W, Mississauga, ON, L5R
3V2
(905) 568-4010
Emp Here 22
SIC 6021 National commercial banks

D-U-N-S 25-321-0488   (BR)
BANQUE TORONTO-DOMINION, LA
TORONTO-DOMINION BANK, THE
(Suby of Toronto-Dominion Bank, The)
20 Milverton Dr Suite 10, Mississauga, ON,
L5R 3G2
(905) 568-3600
Emp Here 75
SIC 6021 National commercial banks

D-U-N-S 25-822-3189   (BR)
BANQUE TORONTO-DOMINION, LA
TORONTO-DOMINION BANK, THE
(Suby of Toronto-Dominion Bank, The)
728 Bristol Rd W, Mississauga, ON, L5R 4A3
(905) 507-0870
Emp Here 20
SIC 6021 National commercial banks

D-U-N-S 24-116-1038   (BR)
BEST BUY CANADA LTD
(Suby of Best Buy Co., Inc.)
6075 Mavis Rd Unit 1, Mississauga, ON, L5R
4G6
(905) 361-8251
Emp Here 150
SIC 5999 Miscellaneous retail stores, nec

D-U-N-S 25-815-9128   (BR)
BOUTIQUE JACOB INC
JACOB OUTLET
(Suby of Boutique Jacob Inc)
5875 Rodeo Dr, Mississauga, ON, L5R 4C1

Emp Here 30
SIC 5621 Women's clothing stores

D-U-N-S 20-569-5898   (BR)
BRICK WAREHOUSE LP, THE
THE BRICK
5800 Mclaughlin Rd Unit 2, Mississauga, ON,
L5R 4B7
(905) 502-7500
Emp Here 30
SIC 5712 Furniture stores

D-U-N-S 20-863-2380   (HQ)
BRIDGESTONE CANADA INC
GCR TIRE CENTRES
5770 Hurontario St Suite 400, Mississauga,
ON, L5R 3G5
(877) 468-6270
Emp Here 2,100   Emp Total 142,948
Sales 1,094,410,500
SIC 5014 Tires and tubes
 Larry Magee
Dir Fin Yannick Amiot
 Pamela Scarrow
 Kenneth Weaver
 Terry Lee Reedy
 Isaku Motohashi
 Fiona Gardner
 Jim Schmidt

D-U-N-S 20-525-3912   (SL)
**BROADRIDGE INVESTOR COMMUNICA-
TIONS CORPORATION**
5970 Chedworth Way, Mississauga, ON, L5R
4G5
(905) 507-5100
Emp Here 129   Sales 16,780,961
SIC 8748 Business consulting, nec
Genl Mgr Patricia Rosch

D-U-N-S 24-925-2289   (SL)
CANADIAN HOME CARE ASSOCIATION
10 Kingsbridge Garden Cir Suite 704, Mississauga, ON, L5R 3K6

Emp Here 20   Sales 6,087,000
SIC 8399 Social services, nec
Dir Nadine Henningsen

D-U-N-S 24-331-9360   (HQ)
**CANADIAN MARKETING TEST CASE 200
LIMITED**
HIGH HOOPS
(Suby of Canadian Marketing Test Case 200
Limited)
5770 Hurontario St, Mississauga, ON, L5R
3G5
(800) 986-5569
Emp Here 150   Emp Total 170
Sales 19,681,300
SIC 3949 Sporting and athletic goods, nec
Pr Pr Don Dunker
 Sal Dunker

D-U-N-S 24-331-9402   (SL)
**CANADIAN MARKETING TEST CASE 204
LIMITED**
DOWNHILL SKIER
5770 Hurontario St, Mississauga, ON, L5R
3G5

Emp Here 25   Sales 7,350,166
SIC 5091 Sporting and recreation goods
Pr Van Couver
VP VP Regina Saskatch
Fin Ex Wes North

D-U-N-S 24-331-9501   (SL)
**CANADIAN MARKETING TEST CASE 206
LIMITED**
PRINTERS TO THE WORLD
5770 Hurontario St, Mississauga, ON, L5R
3G5
(905) 555-5555
Emp Here 20   Sales 10,797,600
SIC 2732 Book printing
Pr Pr Tim E Warner
VP Maggie Life
 Ernest Reader

D-U-N-S 20-512-5581   (BR)
CANADIAN RED CROSS SOCIETY, THE
5700 Cancross Crt, Mississauga, ON, L5R
3E9
(905) 890-1000
Emp Here 100
SIC 8322 Individual and family services

D-U-N-S 24-332-2745   (SL)
CANADIAN TEST CASE 145
MONTGOMERY PHARMA PACKAGING
5770 Hurontario St, Mississauga, ON, L5R
3G5

Emp Here 35   Sales 20,564,000
SIC 2834 Pharmaceutical preparations
Pr George Febvre
Opers Mgr David Montgomery

D-U-N-S 24-332-3123   (HQ)
CANADIAN TEST CASE 168 INC.
CANADIAN TEST CASE 169 DIV
(Suby of Canadian Test Case 168 Inc.)
5770 Hurontario St, Mississauga, ON, L5R
3G5

Emp Here 375   Emp Total 8,756
Sales 2,020,680,000
SIC 3714 Motor vehicle parts and accessories
Pr Lesley Rhodes
 Heide Paris
 Cr Sutherland
 Judy Parr
 Liz Purvis
 Maureen Ali

D-U-N-S 24-332-2547   (SL)
CANADIAN TEST CASE 193

5770 Hurontario St, Mississauga, ON, L5R
3G5

Emp Here 72   Sales 9,876,240
SIC 2331 Women's and misses' blouses and
shirts
VP James Quinn

D-U-N-S 24-331-2084   (SL)
CANADIAN TEST CASE 29-B
5770 Hurontario St, Mississauga, ON, L5R
3G5
(905) 812-5922
Emp Here 50   Sales 166,073,650
SIC 6324 Hospital and medical service plans
Pr Alexis French
Dir Jalynn Black
Dir Manfred Brown
Dir James Smith Jr
Dir Kristina Jones
Dir John Black
Dir Richard Smith
Dir Claude Jones
Dir Harry Black
Dir John Brown

D-U-N-S 24-101-8741   (SL)
CANADIAN TEST CASE 52
5770 Hurontario St, Mississauga, ON, L5R
3G5

Emp Here 80   Sales 29,799,000
SIC 3949 Sporting and athletic goods, nec
Pr Gilles Black
VP Fin Stephane White
 Jean Silver

D-U-N-S 24-148-3564   (BR)
**CENTRE FOR ADDICTION AND MENTAL
HEALTH**
CAMH PEEL
30 Eglinton Ave W Suite 801, Mississauga,
ON, L5R 3E7
(416) 535-8501
Emp Here 20
SIC 8093 Specialty outpatient clinics, nec

D-U-N-S 20-291-1496   (HQ)
CHILDREN'S PLACE (CANADA) LP, THE
6040 Cantay Rd, Mississauga, ON, L5R 4J2
(905) 502-0353
Emp Here 25   Emp Total 15,500
Sales 87,552,840
SIC 5641 Children's and infants' wear stores
 Lori Webber

D-U-N-S 24-312-0941   (BR)
COSTCO WHOLESALE CANADA LTD
(Suby of Costco Wholesale Corporation)
5900 Rodeo Dr Suite 526, Mississauga, ON,
L5R 3S9
(905) 568-4828
Emp Here 100
SIC 5099 Durable goods, nec

D-U-N-S 24-829-9018   (BR)
CUSHMAN & WAKEFIELD LTD
CUSHMAN AND WAKEFIELD LEPAGE
(Suby of Cushman & Wakefield Holdings, Inc.)
5770 Hurontario St Suite 200, Mississauga,
ON, L5R 3G5
(905) 568-9500
Emp Here 125
SIC 6531 Real estate agents and managers

D-U-N-S 25-486-9589   (BR)
**DUFFERIN-PEEL CATHOLIC DISTRICT
SCHOOL BOARD**
ST GERTRUDE ELEMENTARY SCHOOL
815 Ceremonial Dr, Mississauga, ON, L5R
3S2
(905) 568-7660
Emp Here 47
SIC 8211 Elementary and secondary schools

D-U-N-S 25-486-9597   (BR)
**DUFFERIN-PEEL CATHOLIC DISTRICT
SCHOOL BOARD**

ST HILARY ELEMENTARY SCHOOL
5070 Fairwind Dr, Mississauga, ON, L5R 2N4
(905) 568-0056
Emp Here 38
SIC 8211 Elementary and secondary schools

D-U-N-S 24-951-4423   (HQ)
ESI CANADA
C A P S S
(*Suby of* Express Scripts Holding Company)
5770 Hurontario St, Mississauga, ON, L5R 3G5
(905) 712-8615
Emp Here 120   *Emp Total* 26,050
Sales 17,151,770
SIC 6411 Insurance agents, brokers, and service
Pr Pr Jean Joubert
  Mark Murphy

D-U-N-S 24-986-3077   (HQ)
EXEL CANADA LTD
90 Matheson Blvd W Suite 111, Mississauga, ON, L5R 3R3
(905) 366-7700
Emp Here 50   *Emp Total* 498,459
Sales 67,567,578
SIC 4225 General warehousing and storage
Dir Opers Ross Weber
  Nigel Mathew
Dir Fin Paolo Mari

D-U-N-S 24-507-6039   (HQ)
EXPEDITORS CANADA INC
55 Standish Crt Suite 1100, Mississauga, ON, L5R 4A1
(905) 290-6000
Emp Here 135   *Emp Total* 16,000
Sales 80,840,456
SIC 4731 Freight transportation arrangement
Rgnl VP Ross Hurst

D-U-N-S 24-876-6453   (BR)
FAG AEROSPACE INC
6255 Cantay Rd, Mississauga, ON, L5R 3Z4
(905) 829-2750
Emp Here 45
SIC 3714 Motor vehicle parts and accessories

D-U-N-S 25-668-9522   (BR)
FEDERATED INSURANCE COMPANY OF CANADA
5770 Hurontario St Suite 710, Mississauga, ON, L5R 3G5
(905) 507-2777
Emp Here 40
SIC 6331 Fire, marine, and casualty insurance

D-U-N-S 20-760-6799   (HQ)
FUJIFILM CANADA INC
600 Suffolk Crt, Mississauga, ON, L5R 4G4
(905) 890-6611
Emp Here 120   *Emp Total* 78,665
Sales 34,996,540
SIC 5043 Photographic equipment and supplies
Pr Pr Shunji Saito
Treas Brian Boulanger

D-U-N-S 20-303-0288   (BR)
G.N. JOHNSTON EQUIPMENT CO. LTD
5990 Avebury Rd, Mississauga, ON, L5R 3R2
(905) 712-6000
Emp Here 80
SIC 5084 Industrial machinery and equipment

D-U-N-S 25-107-9893   (HQ)
GLOBALSTAR CANADA SATELLITE CO.
115 Matheson Blvd W Unit 100, Mississauga, ON, L5R 3L1
(905) 890-1377
Emp Here 60   *Emp Total* 90
Sales 10,648,318
SIC 5731 Radio, television, and electronic stores
  Steven Bell

D-U-N-S 20-349-4807   (BR)

H.B. GROUP INSURANCE MANAGEMENT LTD
5600 Cancross Crt, Mississauga, ON, L5R 3E9
(905) 507-6156
Emp Here 500
SIC 6331 Fire, marine, and casualty insurance

D-U-N-S 24-872-6804   (HQ)
H.B. GROUP INSURANCE MANAGEMENT LTD
5600 Cancross Crt Suite A, Mississauga, ON, L5R 3E9
(905) 507-6156
Emp Here 325   *Emp Total* 4,567
Sales 53,957,760
SIC 6411 Insurance agents, brokers, and service
  Karen Higgins
Dir George Hardy

D-U-N-S 25-530-9650   (BR)
HARRY ROSEN INC
ROSEN, HARRY OUTLET STORE
5985 Rodeo Dr Unit 1, Mississauga, ON, L5R 3X8
(905) 890-3100
Emp Here 30
SIC 5611 Men's and boys' clothing stores

D-U-N-S 25-418-7594   (SL)
HEALTHPRO PROCUREMENT SERVICES INC
5770 Hurontario St Suite 902, Mississauga, ON, L5R 3G5
(905) 568-3478
Emp Here 50   *Sales* 2,626,585
SIC 7389 Business services, nec

D-U-N-S 25-213-7773   (BR)
HOME DEPOT OF CANADA INC
HOME DEPOT
(*Suby of* The Home Depot Inc)
650 Matheson Blvd W, Mississauga, ON, L5R 3T2
(905) 712-5913
Emp Here 200
SIC 5251 Hardware stores

D-U-N-S 25-671-6150   (HQ)
INTRIA ITEMS INC
5705 Cancross Ct, Mississauga, ON, L5R 3E9
(905) 755-2400
Emp Here 100   *Emp Total* 44,000
Sales 131,329,260
SIC 7374 Data processing and preparation
Pr Pr Robert Bouey

D-U-N-S 24-680-5162   (HQ)
INGRAM MICRO INC
INGRAM MICRO CANADA
55 Standish Crt Suite 1, Mississauga, ON, L5R 4A1
(905) 755-5000
Emp Here 800   *Emp Total* 646
Sales 162,422,063
SIC 5045 Computers, peripherals, and software
VP VP Mark Snider

D-U-N-S 25-510-6221   (HQ)
KIA CANADA INC
KIA
180 Foster Cres, Mississauga, ON, L5R 4J5
(905) 755-6250
Emp Here 121   *Emp Total* 34,290
Sales 65,153,905
SIC 5012 Automobiles and other motor vehicles
Pr Pr Jay Chung
VP Opers Maria Soklis
Treas Harold Mun

D-U-N-S 25-304-4804   (BR)
KUEHNE + NAGEL LTD
KN TRAVEL
5800 Hurontario St Suite 1100, Mississauga, ON, L5R 4B9

(905) 502-7776
Emp Here 35
SIC 4724 Travel agencies

D-U-N-S 24-024-5936   (SL)
LIFT RITE INC
5975 Falbourne St Unit 3, Mississauga, ON, L5R 3L8
(905) 456-2603
Emp Here 90   *Sales* 11,694,389
SIC 3499 Fabricated Metal products, nec
Pr Pr Mel Griffin

D-U-N-S 20-161-3189   (HQ)
LINDE CANADA LIMITED
5860 Chedworth Way, Mississauga, ON, L5R 0A2
(905) 501-1700
Emp Here 150   *Emp Total* 60,635
Sales 285,169,829
SIC 5169 Chemicals and allied products, nec
  Bruce Hart
VP VP Christopher T Ebeling

D-U-N-S 25-087-6729   (BR)
LOBLAW COMPANIES LIMITED
LOBLAWS
5970 Mclaughlin Rd Suite A, Mississauga, ON, L5R 3X9
(905) 568-8551
Emp Here 250
SIC 5411 Grocery stores

D-U-N-S 20-337-5576   (BR)
LOWE-MARTIN COMPANY INC
5990 Falbourne St, Mississauga, ON, L5R 3S7
(905) 507-8782
Emp Here 200
SIC 2752 Commercial printing, lithographic

D-U-N-S 25-098-0083   (SL)
MDM BUSINESS SOLUTIONS INC
5900 Keaton Cres, Mississauga, ON, L5R 3K2
(905) 568-4061
Emp Here 50   *Sales* 4,742,446
SIC 4225 General warehousing and storage

D-U-N-S 20-123-2126   (BR)
MAPLE LEAF FOODS INC
30 Eglinton Ave W Suite 500, Mississauga, ON, L5R 3E7
(905) 501-3076
Emp Here 200
SIC 2011 Meat packing plants

D-U-N-S 25-295-5869   (BR)
MARCH OF DIMES CANADA
25 Glenn Hawthorne Blvd Suite 106, Mississauga, ON, L5R 3E6
(905) 568-9586
Emp Here 20
SIC 8331 Job training and related services

D-U-N-S 25-807-3568   (BR)
MCDONALD'S RESTAURANTS OF CANADA LIMITED
MCDONALD'S
(*Suby of* McDonald's Corporation)
5995 Mavis Rd, Mississauga, ON, L5R 3T7
(905) 712-4335
Emp Here 50
SIC 5812 Eating places

D-U-N-S 24-122-6091   (HQ)
MEDICAL MART SUPPLIES LIMITED
6200 Cantay Rd Suite 624, Mississauga, ON, L5R 3Y9
(905) 624-6200
Emp Here 120   *Emp Total* 2
Sales 30,318,785
SIC 5047 Medical and hospital equipment
Pr Pr Robert G West
  Robert J West
Treas Steve Currie

D-U-N-S 24-531-0979   (BR)
MELO, ALBERT FOODS LIMITED
SWISS CHALET

(*Suby of* Melo, Albert Foods Limited)
5980 Mclaughlin Rd, Mississauga, ON, L5R 3X9
(905) 507-0838
Emp Here 70
SIC 5812 Eating places

D-U-N-S 20-257-9165   (BR)
MENASHA PACKAGING CANADA L.P.
PORTABLE PACKAGING
5875 Chedworth Way, Mississauga, ON, L5R 3L9
(905) 507-3042
Emp Here 100
SIC 2653 Corrugated and solid fiber boxes

D-U-N-S 20-279-7197   (BR)
METROLAND MEDIA GROUP LTD
THE MISSISSAUGA NEWS
6255 Cantay Rd Unit 3, Mississauga, ON, L5R 3Z4
(905) 273-8100
Emp Here 250
SIC 2711 Newspapers

D-U-N-S 20-278-3874   (BR)
MOORE CANADA CORPORATION
TOPS PRODUCTS CANADA
(*Suby of* R. R. Donnelley & Sons Company)
333 Foster Cres Suite 2, Mississauga, ON, L5R 3Z9
(905) 890-1080
Emp Here 400
SIC 2782 Blankbooks and looseleaf binders

D-U-N-S 24-802-5637   (BR)
MOTOROLA SOLUTIONS CANADA INC
(*Suby of* Motorola Solutions, Inc.)
400 Matheson Blvd W, Mississauga, ON, L5R 3M1
(905) 507-7200
Emp Here 120
SIC 7379 Computer related services, nec

D-U-N-S 24-555-5818   (HQ)
NACORA INSURANCE BROKERS LTD
77 Foster Cres, Mississauga, ON, L5R 0K1
(905) 507-1551
Emp Here 34   *Emp Total* 70,000
Sales 6,323,632
SIC 6411 Insurance agents, brokers, and service
Pr Pr John Levin
VP VP David Schleifer
  Stefan Kneubuhler

D-U-N-S 25-823-9623   (BR)
NEWGEN RESTAURANT SERVICES INC
TUCKER'S MARKETPLACE
5975 Mavis Rd, Mississauga, ON, L5R 3T7
(905) 502-8555
Emp Here 100
SIC 5812 Eating places

D-U-N-S 25-366-7919   (HQ)
ORKIN CANADA CORPORATION
ORKIN PCO SERVICES
(*Suby of* Rollins, Inc.)
5840 Falbourne St, Mississauga, ON, L5R 4B5
(905) 502-9700
Emp Here 60   *Emp Total* 12,540
Sales 33,270,079
SIC 7342 Disinfecting and pest control services
Pr Pr Gary Muldoon

D-U-N-S 20-561-6006   (HQ)
PANALPINA INC
6350 Cantay Rd, Mississauga, ON, L5R 4E2
(905) 755-4500
Emp Here 250   *Emp Total* 651
Sales 95,980,611
SIC 4731 Freight transportation arrangement
VP Fin Onkar Singh Bagga
Mng Dir Jim Horgdal
Crdt Mgr Wendy D'souza

▲ Public Company   ■ Public Company Family Member   **HQ** Headquarters   **BR** Branch   **SL** Single Location

D-U-N-S 25-293-7552　(BR)
PEEL DISTRICT SCHOOL BOARD
HUNTINGTON RIDGE PUBLIC SCHOOL
(*Suby of* Peel District School Board)
345 Huntington Ridge Dr, Mississauga, ON,
L5R 1R6
(905) 890-2170
Emp Here 35
SIC 8211 Elementary and secondary schools

D-U-N-S 20-591-3911　(BR)
PEEL DISTRICT SCHOOL BOARD
COOKSVILLE CREEK PUBLIC SCHOOL
(*Suby of* Peel District School Board)
5100 Salishan Cir, Mississauga, ON, L5R 3E3
(905) 568-3402
Emp Here 25
SIC 8211 Elementary and secondary schools

D-U-N-S 24-079-5344　(HQ)
PEEL DISTRICT SCHOOL BOARD
(*Suby of* Peel District School Board)
5650 Hurontario St Suite 106, Mississauga,
ON, L5R 1C6
(905) 890-1099
Emp Here 550　　*Emp Total* 15,868
Sales 1,555,786
SIC 8211 Elementary and secondary schools

D-U-N-S 25-473-3413　(HQ)
PEEL SENIOR LINK
(*Suby of* Peel Senior Link)
30 Eglinton Ave W Suite 760, Mississauga,
ON, L5R 3E7
(905) 712-4413
Emp Here 30　　*Emp Total* 75
Sales 2,918,428
SIC 8322 Individual and family services

D-U-N-S 20-609-4203　(BR)
PEPSICO CANADA ULC
HOSTESS FRITO LAY CANADA, DIV OF
(*Suby of* Pepsico, Inc.)
55 Standish Crt Suite 700, Mississauga, ON,
L5R 4B2

Emp Here 150
SIC 2096 Potato chips and similar snacks

D-U-N-S 25-362-3292　(HQ)
PRIME RESTAURANT HOLDINGS INC
(*Suby of* Prime Restaurant Holdings Inc)
10 Kingsbridge Garden Cir Suite 600, Missis-
sauga, ON, L5R 3K6
(905) 568-0000
Emp Here 40　　*Emp Total* 220
Sales 50,356,080
SIC 6712 Bank holding companies
John A Rothschild
Pr Pr Nick Pereick
H Ross R Bain
Sec Sidney M Horn
Dir Andrew Parsons

D-U-N-S 24-334-1018　(HQ)
PRIME RESTAURANTS INC
EAST SIDE MARIO'S
(*Suby of* Cara Holdings Limited)
10 Kingsbridge Garden Cir Suite 600, Missis-
sauga, ON, L5R 3K6
(905) 568-0000
Emp Here 93　　*Emp Total* 14,038
Sales 28,672,908
SIC 5812 Eating places
Pr Nicholas M. Perpick
H. Ross R. Bain
Sr VP Grant Cobb
VP Opers Rob Carmichael
Pur/VP William Grady
VP Andrew Berzins
VP Acctg Brian Elliot
John Verdon
VP Jack Gardner
Pers/VP Nalini Barma

D-U-N-S 24-719-1877　(HQ)
PUROLATOR HOLDINGS LTD

(*Suby of* Canada Post Corporation)
5995 Avebury Rd Suite 100, Mississauga, ON,
L5R 3T8
(905) 712-1251
Emp Here 1,300　　*Emp Total* 63,000
Sales 3,158,177,896
SIC 4731 Freight transportation arrangement
Pr Pr Robert C Johnson
Sheldon Bell
Sr VP Jim Mcdade
Sr VP Brian Meagher
Pers/VP Stephen Gould
VP Opers William Henderson

D-U-N-S 20-177-2506　(HQ)
PUROLATOR INC.
PUROLATOR LOGISTICS
(*Suby of* Canada Post Corporation)
5995 Avebury Rd, Mississauga, ON, L5R 3P9
(905) 712-1084
Emp Here 350　　*Emp Total* 63,000
Sales 2,447,247,799
SIC 4731 Freight transportation arrangement
Pr Pr Patrick Nangle

D-U-N-S 25-010-5939　(BR)
RABBA, J. COMPANY LIMITED, THE
RABBA FINE FOODS
20 Kingsbridge Garden Cir Suite 1, Missis-
sauga, ON, L5R 3K7
(905) 568-3479
Emp Here 20
SIC 5411 Grocery stores

D-U-N-S 25-150-2381　(HQ)
REXEL CANADA ELECTRICAL LTD
NEDCO, DIV OF
5600 Keaton Cres, Mississauga, ON, L5R
3G3
(905) 712-4004
Emp Here 181　　*Emp Total* 3
Sales 401,648,654
SIC 5063 Electrical apparatus and equipment
Pr Roger Little
VP VP Rashid Maqsood
Rene Merat
VP Adrian Trotman
Div VP Robert Blague
Pat Foley

D-U-N-S 25-799-2644　(BR)
ROYAL BANK OF CANADA
ROYAL BANK FINANCIAL GROUP
(*Suby of* Royal Bank of Canada)
25 Milverton Dr, Mississauga, ON, L5R 3G2
(905) 568-1800
Emp Here 20
SIC 6021 National commercial banks

D-U-N-S 20-765-9673　(SL)
SORLICON MANUFACTURING INC
5770 Hurontario St, Mississauga, ON, L5R
3G5

Emp Here 70　　*Sales* 10,148,480
SIC 3444 Sheet Metalwork
Pr Donna Copelli

D-U-N-S 24-079-0779　(HQ)
SOTI INC
5770 Hurontario St Suite 1100, Mississauga,
ON, L5R 3G5
(905) 624-9828
Emp Here 205　　*Emp Total* 40
Sales 29,549,084
SIC 7371 Custom computer programming ser-
vices
Pr Pr Carl Rodrigues
Sec Lynette Rodrigues

D-U-N-S 20-860-2198　(BR)
SOURCE (BELL) ELECTRONICS INC, THE
SOURCE, THE
6045 Mavis Rd Unit 3, Mississauga, ON, L5R
4G6
(905) 890-8168
Emp Here 25

SIC 5999 Miscellaneous retail stores, nec

D-U-N-S 24-204-0728　(HQ)
SOUTHWIRE CANADA COMPANY
5705 Cancross Crt Suite 100, Mississauga,
ON, L5R 3E9
(800) 668-0303
Emp Here 100　　*Emp Total* 7,000
Sales 39,587,671
SIC 3357 Nonferrous wiredrawing and insulat-
ing
Pr Stuart W. Thorn
Ex VP J. Guyton Cochrane
Floyd Smith
Ex VP Jeff Herrin

D-U-N-S 25-296-0299　(BR)
SUNCOR ENERGY PRODUCTS INC
HUSKY
6015 Mclaughlin Rd, Mississauga, ON, L5R
1B9
(905) 507-8100
Emp Here 35
SIC 5541 Gasoline service stations

D-U-N-S 20-174-5614　(BR)
SYSTEMES CANADIEN KRONOS INC
(*Suby of* Kronos Parent Corporation)
110 Matheson Blvd W Suite 320, Mississauga,
ON, L5R 4G7
(905) 568-0101
Emp Here 26
SIC 7371 Custom computer programming ser-
vices

D-U-N-S 20-013-3580　(HQ)
TREE OF LIFE CANADA ULC
(*Suby of* Kehe Distributors, LLC)
6030 Freemont Blvd, Mississauga, ON, L5R
3X4
(905) 507-6161
Emp Here 140　　*Emp Total* 3,400
Sales 104,625,644
SIC 5141 Groceries, general line
Pr James Moody

D-U-N-S 20-178-1390　(SL)
WELLA CANADA, INC
(*Suby of* The Procter & Gamble Company)
5800 Avebury Rd Unit 1, Mississauga, ON,
L5R 3M3
(905) 568-2494
Emp Here 80　　*Sales* 15,102,865
SIC 5131 Piece goods and notions
Pr Pr David Dias
Dir Joseph Iannuzzi
Dir Rod Little
Dir Reuben Carranza
Dir Fin Zhibiao Chen

D-U-N-S 25-530-6508　(SL)
WINMAGIC INC
5600a Cancross Crt Suite A, Mississauga,
ON, L5R 3E9
(905) 502-7000
Emp Here 104　　*Sales* 12,987,005
SIC 7372 Prepackaged software
Pr Pr Thi Nguyen-Huu
Silvia Nguyen-Huu

D-U-N-S 25-221-2568　(BR)
**WINNERS MERCHANTS INTERNATIONAL
L.P.**
WINNERS
(*Suby of* The TJX Companies Inc)
650 Matheson Blvd W Suite 3, Mississauga,
ON, L5R 3T2
(905) 712-4555
Emp Here 65
SIC 5651 Family clothing stores

D-U-N-S 24-338-8944　(BR)
**WINNERS MERCHANTS INTERNATIONAL
L.P.**
WINNERS
(*Suby of* The TJX Companies Inc)
60 Standish Crt, Mississauga, ON, L5R 0G1

(905) 405-8000
Emp Here 25
SIC 5651 Family clothing stores

D-U-N-S 20-184-3146　(BR)
**WINNERS MERCHANTS INTERNATIONAL
L.P.**
HOMESENSE
(*Suby of* The TJX Companies Inc)
6075 Mavis Rd Unit 2, Mississauga, ON, L5R
4G6
(905) 502-6200
Emp Here 40
SIC 5651 Family clothing stores

D-U-N-S 20-180-5616　(HQ)
**WINNERS MERCHANTS INTERNATIONAL
L.P.**
TJX CANADA
(*Suby of* The TJX Companies Inc)
60 Standish Crt, Mississauga, ON, L5R 0G1
(905) 405-8000
Emp Here 600　　*Emp Total* 235,000
Sales 729,607,000
SIC 5651 Family clothing stores
Pr Douglas Mizzi
Jens Cermak
Douglas Moffatt

Mississauga, ON L5S
Peel County

D-U-N-S 25-370-7806　(BR)
1132694 ONTARIO INC
SPRAY-PAK INDUSTRIES
(*Suby of* Plz Aeroscience Corporation)
7550 Kimbel St, Mississauga, ON, L5S 1A2
(905) 677-1948
Emp Here 75
SIC 7389 Business services, nec

D-U-N-S 25-090-0925　(BR)
682439 ONTARIO INC
PRONORTH TRANSPORTATION
2375 Lucknow Dr, Mississauga, ON, L5S 1H9
(800) 265-9370
Emp Here 30
SIC 4213 Trucking, except local

D-U-N-S 20-694-3859　(SL)
ASD SOLUTIONS LTD
(*Suby of* Solutions 2 GO Inc)
190 Statesman Dr, Mississauga, ON, L5S 1X7
(519) 271-4900
Emp Here 60　　*Sales* 8,244,559
SIC 5045 Computers, peripherals, and soft-
ware
Pr Gabrielle Chevalier
Dir Oliver Bock

D-U-N-S 25-215-2202　(HQ)
ACE BAKERY LIMITED
580 Secretariat Crt, Mississauga, ON, L5S
2A5
(905) 565-8138
Emp Here 200　　*Emp Total* 138,000
Sales 112,782,000
SIC 5461 Retail bakeries
Pr Pr Roy Benin
Daryl Hanstead
Jason Poledano

D-U-N-S 25-312-0679　(SL)
AERO LINK CANADA INC
7035 Fir Tree Dr, Mississauga, ON, L5S 1J7
(905) 677-5362
Emp Here 55　　*Sales* 12,961,920
SIC 4512 Air transportation, scheduled
Pr Ainsworth Whyte

D-U-N-S 24-076-1754　(BR)
**AXXESS INTERNATIONAL COURTIERS EN
DOUANES INC**
(*Suby of* 6668437 Canada Inc)
1804 Alstep Dr Unit 1, Mississauga, ON, L5S

1W1
(905) 672-0270
Emp Here 112
SIC 4731 Freight transportation arrangement

D-U-N-S 24-352-6352 (BR)
BAILEY METAL PRODUCTS LIMITED
BAILEY METAL PROCESSING
(*Suby of* Bailey-Hunt Limited)
7496 Tranmere Dr, Mississauga, ON, L5S 1K4
(416) 648-0342
Emp Here 30
SIC 3312 Blast furnaces and steel mills

D-U-N-S 20-290-3816 (BR)
CAE INC
2025 Logistics Dr, Mississauga, ON, L5S 1Z9
(905) 672-3650
Emp Here 20
SIC 8742 Management consulting services

D-U-N-S 20-300-7810 (SL)
CCD LIMITED PARTNERSHIP
1115 Cardiff Blvd, Mississauga, ON, L5S 1L8
(905) 564-2115
Emp Here 75 *Sales* 14,710,250
SIC 6712 Bank holding companies
Pr William Jeffrey Lindsay
VP Fin David Bacon
S&M/VP Dave Zavitz
VP Fin Steve Sacha

D-U-N-S 24-340-8304 (SL)
CANADA CARTAGE DIVERSIFIED ULC
1115 Cardiff Blvd, Mississauga, ON, L5S 1L8
(905) 564-2115
Emp Here 51 *Sales* 4,012,839
SIC 4212 Local trucking, without storage

D-U-N-S 20-594-9407 (BR)
CASCADES CANADA ULC
CASCADE BOXBOARD GROUP, THE
7830 Tranmere Dr Suite Unit, Mississauga, ON, L5S 1L9
(905) 678-8211
Emp Here 200
SIC 7389 Business services, nec

D-U-N-S 24-466-4707 (BR)
CASCADES CANADA ULC
NORAMPAC, DIV OF
7447 Bramalea Rd, Mississauga, ON, L5S 1C4
(905) 671-2940
Emp Here 110
SIC 2631 Paperboard mills

D-U-N-S 24-123-3667 (BR)
CLARKE ROLLER & RUBBER LIMITED
PERSISTA
7075 Tomken Rd, Mississauga, ON, L5S 1R7

Emp Here 26
SIC 2821 Plastics materials and resins

D-U-N-S 20-047-6950 (HQ)
CREIGHTON ROCK DRILL LIMITED
(*Suby of* Creighton Rock Drill Limited)
2222 Drew Rd, Mississauga, ON, L5S 1B1
(905) 673-8200
Emp Here 21 *Emp Total* 43
Sales 7,879,756
SIC 5082 Construction and mining machinery
Pr Pr Robert Creighton
Treas Susan Tomowich
VP Alexander Creighton
VP James Creighton
VP Peter Creighton

D-U-N-S 24-126-4071 (BR)
DHL GLOBAL FORWARDING (CANADA) INC
1825 Alstep Dr, Mississauga, ON, L5S 1Y5

Emp Here 150
SIC 4731 Freight transportation arrangement

D-U-N-S 25-167-6599 (SL)

DATA DIRECT GROUP INC
2001 Drew Rd Unit 1, Mississauga, ON, L5S 1S4
(905) 564-0150
Emp Here 65 *Sales* 3,283,232
SIC 7331 Direct mail advertising services

D-U-N-S 24-390-7404 (SL)
DEZINECORP INC
215 Statesman Dr, Mississauga, ON, L5S 1X4
(905) 670-8741
Emp Here 35 *Sales* 5,465,508
SIC 5199 Nondurable goods, nec

D-U-N-S 20-305-3244 (BR)
E-CYCLE SOLUTIONS INC
1700 Drew Rd, Mississauga, ON, L5S 1J6
(905) 671-2900
Emp Here 60
SIC 4953 Refuse systems

D-U-N-S 24-827-5120 (BR)
EVOQUA WATER TECHNOLOGIES LTD
(*Suby of* Ewt Holdings I Corp.)
2045 Drew Rd, Mississauga, ON, L5S 1S4
(905) 890-2803
Emp Here 50
SIC 3589 Service industry machinery, nec

D-U-N-S 20-288-5232 (HQ)
EVOQUA WATER TECHNOLOGIES LTD
(*Suby of* Ewt Holdings I Corp.)
2045 Drew Rd, Mississauga, ON, L5S 1S4
(905) 890-2803
Emp Here 30 *Emp Total* 5,027
Sales 11,308,909
SIC 3589 Service industry machinery, nec
 Richard Donatelli

D-U-N-S 20-714-7617 (BR)
FEDERAL EXPRESS CANADA CORPORATION
FEDERAL EXPRESS CANADA LTD
(*Suby of* Fedex Corporation)
6895 Bramalea Rd Suite 1, Mississauga, ON, L5S 1Z7
(800) 463-3339
Emp Here 300
SIC 4215 Courier services, except by air

D-U-N-S 20-074-6670 (BR)
FORT GARRY INDUSTRIES LTD
FGI
731 Gana Crt, Mississauga, ON, L5S 1P2
(905) 564-5404
Emp Here 36
SIC 5013 Motor vehicle supplies and new parts

D-U-N-S 24-353-0206 (BR)
GROUPE ACCENT-FAIRCHILD INC
MEYERSIDE DISTRIBUTION
195 Statesman Dr, Mississauga, ON, L5S 1X4
(905) 670-0351
Emp Here 50
SIC 5023 Homefurnishings

D-U-N-S 20-041-2989 (BR)
GROUPE CANAM INC
CANAM
1739 Drew Rd, Mississauga, ON, L5S 1J5
(905) 671-3460
Emp Here 185
SIC 3441 Fabricated structural Metal

D-U-N-S 25-831-6819 (BR)
GROUPE ROBERT INC
ROBERT TRANSPORT
300 Statesman Dr, Mississauga, ON, L5S 2A2
(905) 564-9999
Emp Here 65
SIC 4213 Trucking, except local

D-U-N-S 24-871-2374 (HQ)
HELLMANN WORLDWIDE LOGISTICS INC
1375 Cardiff Blvd Unit 1, Mississauga, ON, L5S 1R1

(905) 564-6620
Emp Here 32 *Emp Total* 10,433
Sales 29,585,800
SIC 4731 Freight transportation arrangement
Pr Pr Peter Teixeira
 Benny Tom
 Julian Riches

D-U-N-S 25-117-5451 (SL)
HOMETURF LTD
HOMETURF LAWN CARE SERVICES
7123 Fir Tree Dr, Mississauga, ON, L5S 1G4
(905) 791-8873
Emp Here 20 *Sales* 9,557,852
SIC 6331 Fire, marine, and casualty insurance
Pr Pr Bruce Haastrecht

D-U-N-S 20-529-8383 (BR)
I.M.P. GROUP LIMITED
EXECAIRE
2450 Derry Rd E Unit 7, Mississauga, ON, L5S 1B2
(905) 677-2484
Emp Here 37
SIC 4522 Air transportation, nonscheduled

D-U-N-S 20-027-3576 (BR)
IN-HOUSE SOLUTIONS INC
(*Suby of* In-House Solutions Inc)
7895 Tranmere Dr Unit 6, Mississauga, ON, L5S 1V9
(905) 671-2352
Emp Here 40
SIC 7371 Custom computer programming services

D-U-N-S 24-275-6765 (HQ)
INTERMEC TECHNOLOGIES CANADA LTD
(*Suby of* Honeywell International Inc.)
7065 Tranmere Dr Unit 3, Mississauga, ON, L5S 1M2
(905) 673-9333
Emp Here 55 *Emp Total* 131,000
Sales 9,557,852
SIC 5045 Computers, peripherals, and software
Dir Fin Tony Oliverio

D-U-N-S 20-152-2088 (BR)
KITO CANADA INC
2400 Lucknow Dr Unit 36, Mississauga, ON, L5S 1T9
(905) 405-0905
Emp Here 20
SIC 5084 Industrial machinery and equipment

D-U-N-S 20-804-2999 (BR)
L-3 COMMUNICATIONS MAS (CANADA) INC
L-3 COMMUNICATIONS CMRO
(*Suby of* L3 Technologies, Inc.)
7785 Tranmere Dr, Mississauga, ON, L5S 1W5

Emp Here 75
SIC 4581 Airports, flying fields, and services

D-U-N-S 24-340-3727 (BR)
LABATT BREWING COMPANY LIMITED
445 Export Blvd, Mississauga, ON, L5S 0A1
(905) 696-3300
Emp Here 50
SIC 2082 Malt beverages

D-U-N-S 24-245-3525 (BR)
LARLYN PROPERTY MANAGEMENT LIMITED
YORK CONDOMINIUM
7370 Bramalea Rd Unit 20, Mississauga, ON, L5S 1N6
(905) 672-3355
Emp Here 30
SIC 6513 Apartment building operators

D-U-N-S 25-360-8160 (BR)
LINCOLN ELECTRIC COMPANY OF CANADA LP
INDALCO ALLOYS
(*Suby of* Lincoln Electric Holdings, Inc.)

825 Gana Crt, Mississauga, ON, L5S 1N9
(905) 564-1151
Emp Here 125
SIC 3548 Welding apparatus

D-U-N-S 20-279-6673 (BR)
LINCOLN ELECTRIC COMPANY OF CANADA LP
(*Suby of* Lincoln Electric Holdings, Inc.)
939 Gana Crt, Mississauga, ON, L5S 1N9
(905) 565-5600
Emp Here 25
SIC 5085 Industrial supplies

D-U-N-S 24-145-7105 (BR)
MCINTYRE GROUP OFFICE SERVICES INC
1625 Drew Rd, Mississauga, ON, L5S 1J5
(905) 671-2111
Emp Here 30
SIC 1799 Special trade contractors, nec

D-U-N-S 20-364-3890 (BR)
NCS INTERNATIONAL CO.
NORAMCO WIRE & CABLE
7635 Tranmere Dr, Mississauga, ON, L5S 1L4
(905) 673-3571
Emp Here 75
SIC 5063 Electrical apparatus and equipment

D-U-N-S 25-174-4905 (BR)
NCS INTERNATIONAL CO.
7635 Tranmere Dr, Mississauga, ON, L5S 1L4
(905) 673-0660
Emp Here 100
SIC 5063 Electrical apparatus and equipment

D-U-N-S 20-718-0340 (HQ)
SILGAN PLASTICS CANADA INC
1575 Drew Rd, Mississauga, ON, L5S 1S5
(905) 677-2324
Emp Here 120 *Emp Total* 9,600
Sales 138,773,410
SIC 3089 Plastics products, nec
Pr Emidio Di Meo
 Russell Gervais

D-U-N-S 24-326-7379 (BR)
SONOCO CANADA CORPORATION
(*Suby of* Sonoco Products Company)
7420a Bramalea Rd, Mississauga, ON, L5S 1W9
(905) 673-7373
Emp Here 65
SIC 2655 Fiber cans, drums, and similar products

D-U-N-S 20-291-7076 (BR)
STANLEY BLACK & DECKER CANADA CORPORATION
STANLEY ENGINEERED FASTENING
1030 Lorimar Dr, Mississauga, ON, L5S 1R8
(905) 364-0664
Emp Here 25
SIC 5085 Industrial supplies

D-U-N-S 25-511-6501 (BR)
SYSCO CANADA, INC
SYSCO TORONTO
(*Suby of* Sysco Corporation)
7055 Kennedy Rd, Mississauga, ON, L5S 1Y7
(905) 670-8605
Emp Here 30
SIC 5141 Groceries, general line

D-U-N-S 25-194-7529 (SL)
TVH CANADA LTD
TVH
1039 Cardiff Blvd, Mississauga, ON, L5S 1P4
(905) 564-0003
Emp Here 32 *Sales* 3,866,917
SIC 5013 Motor vehicle supplies and new parts

D-U-N-S 24-330-7878 (SL)
TRANSNET FREIGHT LTD
7686 Kimbel St Unit 21, Mississauga, ON, L5S 1E9

▲ Public Company ■ Public Company Family Member **HQ** Headquarters **BR** Branch **SL** Single Location

(905) 461-1558
Emp Here 27   Sales 5,763,895
SIC 4731 Freight transportation arrangement
Pr Pr Imran Mohammad

D-U-N-S 24-736-9515   (SL)
TRESMAN STEEL INDUSTRIES LTD
286 Statesman Dr, Mississauga. ON, L5S 1X7
(905) 795-8757
Emp Here 50   Sales 11,168,640
SIC 3441 Fabricated structural Metal
Pr Pr Guerrino Trentin
VP VP Ivano Trentin
   Imre Kenedi

D-U-N-S 20-628-7633   (HQ)
TSUBAKI OF CANADA LIMITED
1630 Drew Rd, Mississauga, ON, L5S 1J6
(905) 676-0400
Emp Here 120   Emp Total 7,771
Sales 32,224,537
SIC 5085 Industrial supplies
Pr Pr Masa Ushida
VP Sls Jos Sueters
   Fernando Andrade
   Miya Miyazaki

D-U-N-S 24-119-5994   (BR)
UAP INC
TRACTION
(Suby of Genuine Parts Company)
6895 Menway Crt Suite 963, Mississauga,
ON, L5S 1W2
(905) 612-0032
Emp Here 30
SIC 5013 Motor vehicle supplies and new
parts

D-U-N-S 20-703-5259   (BR)
UPS SCS, INC
UPS SUPPLY CHAIN SOLUTION
1930 Derry Rd E, Mississauga, ON, L5S 1E2
(905) 671-5454
Emp Here 170
SIC 4512 Air transportation, scheduled

D-U-N-S 20-911-3567   (BR)
UPS SCS, INC
UPS SUPPLY CHAIN SOLUTION
7315 David Hunting Dr Suite 2, Mississauga,
ON, L5S 1W3
(905) 672-9595
Emp Here 20
SIC 7389 Business services, nec

Mississauga, ON L5T
Peel County

D-U-N-S 24-936-9331   (SL)
1003274 ONTARIO LIMITED
ROCK CITY CARTAGE
1055 Courtneypark Dr E Suite A, Mississauga,
ON, L5T 1M7
(905) 565-8781
Emp Here 40   Sales 3,137,310
SIC 4212 Local trucking, without storage

D-U-N-S 24-911-8902   (SL)
1095533 ONTARIO INC
APEX GRAPHICS
320 Ambassador Dr, Mississauga, ON, L5T
2J3
(905) 795-9575
Emp Here 50   Sales 4,504,505
SIC 2752 Commercial printing, lithographic

D-U-N-S 25-089-3732   (SL)
1252537 ONTARIO LIMITED
TBN TRANSPORT
1015 Westport Cres, Mississauga, ON, L5T
1E8
(905) 670-3353
Emp Here 53   Sales 8,842,240
SIC 4213 Trucking, except local
Pr Pr Tony Nanan

VP VP Lynn Nanan

D-U-N-S 24-486-3502   (SL)
129177 CANADA INC
CAMPBELL, A M J INTERNATIONAL
1445 Courtneypark Dr E, Mississauga, ON,
L5T 2E3
(905) 670-6683
Emp Here 30   Sales 1,678,096
SIC 4214 Local trucking with storage

D-U-N-S 20-004-0520   (SL)
1327601 ONTARIO INC
BOSTON PIZZA 505
50 Courtneypark Dr E, Mississauga, ON, L5T
2Y3
(905) 565-6225
Emp Here 135   Sales 4,085,799
SIC 5812 Eating places

D-U-N-S 20-690-0602   (SL)
1333375 ONTARIO LIMITED
FOUR POINT SHERATON MISSISSAUGA
6090 Dixie Rd, Mississauga, ON, L5T 1A6
(905) 670-0050
Emp Here 60   Sales 2,626,585
SIC 7011 Hotels and motels

D-U-N-S 24-092-5792   (SL)
421229 ONTARIO LIMITED
DAPHNE FLOWER IMPORTS
7255 Pacific Cir, Mississauga, ON, L5T 1V1
(905) 564-5581
Emp Here 50   Sales 3,118,504
SIC 5992 Florists

D-U-N-S 24-140-0931   (SL)
540731 ONTARIO LIMITED
PANCOR
7105 Pacific Cir, Mississauga, ON, L5T 2A8
(905) 564-5620
Emp Here 75   Sales 4,815,406
SIC 1721 Painting and paper hanging

D-U-N-S 24-780-0360   (SL)
687336 ONTARIO LIMITED
CALIFORNIA SPA & FITNESS STORE
335 Superior Blvd, Mississauga, ON, L5T 2L6
(905) 565-6840
Emp Here 90   Sales 10,652,250
SIC 5941 Sporting goods and bicycle shops
Pr Pr Dale Papke
Dir Fred Papke

D-U-N-S 24-858-1717   (SL)
717 9472 CANADA INC
YOUNG TRANSPORTATION AMERICAN
6392 Netherhart Rd, Mississauga, ON, L5T
1A2
(905) 677-7140
Emp Here 300   Sales 32,656,000
SIC 4212 Local trucking, without storage
Pr Laurence Young

D-U-N-S 25-832-2239   (BR)
AMJ CAMPBELL INC
AMJ VAN LINES
6140 Vipond Dr, Mississauga, ON, L5T 2B2
(905) 670-7111
Emp Here 50
SIC 4214 Local trucking with storage

D-U-N-S 20-421-2336   (HQ)
AGILITY LOGISTICS, CO.
GEOLOGISTICS
185 Courtneypark Dr E Suite B, Mississauga,
ON, L5T 2T6
(905) 612-7500
Emp Here 80   Sales 53,534,312
SIC 4731 Freight transportation arrangement
VP VP Michael Shum
Dir Kate Murdoch

D-U-N-S 25-535-7840   (BR)
AIR LIQUIDE CANADA INC
MESSER CANADA
6915 Davand Dr, Mississauga, ON, L5T 1L5
(905) 670-2222
Emp Here 20

SIC 5085 Industrial supplies

D-U-N-S 20-072-5047   (BR)
ALIMENTS ULTIMA INC
YOPLAIT
6400 Shawson Dr Unit 3, Mississauga, ON,
L5T 1L8
(905) 565-8500
Emp Here 39
SIC 5143 Dairy products, except dried or
canned

D-U-N-S 24-242-4591   (BR)
ALPHA TECHNOLOGIES LTD
TORONTO SERVICE CENTRE
6740 Davand Dr Unit 4, Mississauga, ON, L5T
2K9
(416) 457-8363
Emp Here 20
SIC 7629 Electrical repair shops

D-U-N-S 24-757-6630   (SL)
ANDRON STAINLESS LTD
6170 Tomken Rd, Mississauga, ON, L5T 1X7
(905) 564-5144
Emp Here 40   Sales 5,803,882
SIC 3498 Fabricated pipe and fittings

D-U-N-S 20-214-1586   (HQ)
ARROW ELECTRONICS CANADA LTD
ARROW/BELL COMPONENTS
(Suby of Arrow Electronics, Inc.)
171 Superior Blvd Suite 2, Mississauga, ON,
L5T 2L6
(905) 564-4405
Emp Here 100   Emp Total 18,700
Sales 19,188,664
SIC 5065 Electronic parts and equipment, nec
Pr Michael Long
VP VP Paul Reilly
Sec Peter Brown

D-U-N-S 20-313-6890   (BR)
ATLAS COPCO CANADA INC
ATLAS COPCO MINING & ROCK EXCAVA-
TION TECHNIQUE CANADA
1025 Tristar Dr, Mississauga, ON, L5T 1W5
(289) 562-6126
Emp Here 75
SIC 5082 Construction and mining machinery

D-U-N-S 24-872-5533   (HQ)
ATLAS TIRE WHOLESALE INC
(Suby of Atlas Tire Wholesale Inc)
6200 Tomken Rd, Mississauga, ON, L5T 1X7
(905) 670-7354
Emp Here 61   Emp Total 140
Sales 51,072,490
SIC 5014 Tires and tubes
Pr Pr Peter Gregory
   Deborah Gregory
VP Fin Diane Tymocko

D-U-N-S 25-292-1572   (HQ)
BDI CANADA INC
6235 Tomken Rd, Mississauga, ON, L5T 1K2
(905) 238-3392
Emp Here 50   Emp Total 2,000
Sales 46,548,927
SIC 5085 Industrial supplies
Pr Pr Cameron Lawrence
VP Fin Theodore Chisholm
   Carl James
   Daniel Maisonville

D-U-N-S 25-364-4090   (BR)
BW TECHNOLOGIES LTD
ADI-BURTEK
(Suby of Honeywell International Inc.)
6510 Kennedy Rd, Mississauga, ON, L5T 2X4
(905) 564-3210
Emp Here 30
SIC 3829 Measuring and controlling devices,
nec

D-U-N-S 24-468-3673   (BR)
BAILEY METAL PRODUCTS LIMITED
(Suby of Bailey-Hunt Limited)

6920 Columbus Rd, Mississauga, ON, L5T
2G1
(905) 565-9665
Emp Here 20
SIC 3399 Primary Metal products

D-U-N-S 24-346-8266   (BR)
**BANQUE DE DEVELOPPEMENT DU
CANADA**
BDC
1450 Meyerside Dr Suite 600, Mississauga,
ON, L5T 2N5
(905) 565-9740
Emp Here 20
SIC 6141 Personal credit institutions

D-U-N-S 24-314-0626   (BR)
BEAUTY SYSTEMS GROUP (CANADA) INC
SALLY BEAUTY SUPPLY
395 Pendant Dr, Mississauga, ON, L5T 2W9
(905) 696-2600
Emp Here 40
SIC 5087 Service establishment equipment

D-U-N-S 24-307-7211   (BR)
BOLLORE LOGISTIQUES CANADA INC
S D V LOGISTICS
90 Admiral Blvd, Mississauga, ON, L5T 2W1
(905) 677-9022
Emp Here 40
SIC 4731 Freight transportation arrangement

D-U-N-S 24-978-3007   (BR)
BOMBARDIER INC
BOMBARDIER TRANSPORT
6291 Ordan Dr, Mississauga, ON, L5T 1G9
(905) 795-7869
Emp Here 80
SIC 4111 Local and suburban transit

D-U-N-S 24-830-9759   (SL)
BREADKO NATIONAL BAKING LTD
BREADKO BAKERY
6310 Kestrel Rd, Mississauga, ON, L5T 1Z3
(905) 670-4949
Emp Here 100   Sales 4,428,946
SIC 5461 Retail bakeries

D-U-N-S 24-325-5267   (BR)
BRICK WAREHOUSE LP, THE
6765 Kennedy Rd, Mississauga, ON, L5T 0A2
(905) 696-3400
Emp Here 200
SIC 5712 Furniture stores

D-U-N-S 24-372-5095   (HQ)
BRIGGS & STRATTON CANADA INC
(Suby of Briggs & Stratton Corporation)
6500 Tomken Rd, Mississauga, ON, L5T 2E9
(905) 565-0265
Emp Here 20   Emp Total 5,480
Sales 8,857,893
SIC 3524 Lawn and garden equipment
Dir Naz Virani

D-U-N-S 20-302-1183   (SL)
BUILT IT BY DESIGN INC
1580 Trinity Dr Suite 10, Mississauga, ON,
L5T 1L6
(905) 696-0468
Emp Here 22   Sales 5,277,042
SIC 1542 Nonresidential construction, nec
Dir Simon Shahin

D-U-N-S 25-148-7208   (BR)
C.H. ROBINSON PROJECT LOGISTICS LTD
6155 Tomken Rd Suite 11, Mississauga, ON,
L5T 1X3
(905) 672-2427
Emp Here 20
SIC 4731 Freight transportation arrangement

D-U-N-S 20-290-7031   (SL)
**CDC DISTRIBUTION CENTRES TORONTO
INC**
6290 Kestrel Rd, Mississauga, ON, L5T 1Z4
(905) 564-0403
Emp Here 20   Sales 2,858,628

SIC 5013 Motor vehicle supplies and new parts

D-U-N-S 24-122-7289 (SL)
CALMEC PRECISION LIMITED
1400 Bonhill Rd, Mississauga, ON, L5T 1L3
(905) 677-7976
Emp Here 20   Sales 5,326,131
SIC 3549 Metalworking machinery, nec
Pr Pr Marc Fitzner

D-U-N-S 20-015-9841 (SL)
CAMUS HYDRONICS LIMITED
(Suby of Harbour Group Ltd.)
6226 Netherhart Rd, Mississauga, ON, L5T 1B7
(905) 696-7800
Emp Here 20   Sales 2,165,628
SIC 3433 Heating equipment, except electric

D-U-N-S 25-030-7006 (BR)
CANADA BREAD COMPANY, LIMITED
DEMPSTER'S BREAD, DIV. OF
6645 Tomken Rd Unit 18, Mississauga, ON, L5T 2C3

Emp Here 20
SIC 5149 Groceries and related products, nec

D-U-N-S 20-588-3320 (BR)
CANADA POST CORPORATION
MALTON P O
6915 Dixie Rd, Mississauga, ON, L5T 2G2

Emp Here 70
SIC 4311 U.s. postal service

D-U-N-S 24-309-8469 (BR)
CARA OPERATIONS LIMITED
MONTANA'S BBQ & BAR
(Suby of Cara Holdings Limited)
60 Courtneypark Dr E Bldg G, Mississauga, ON, L5T 2Y3
(905) 564-7391
Emp Here 60
SIC 5812 Eating places

D-U-N-S 25-691-4862 (BR)
CARDINAL HEALTH CANADA INC
(Suby of Cardinal Health, Inc.)
1330 Meyerside Dr, Mississauga, ON, L5T 1C2
(905) 565-2302
Emp Here 200
SIC 5047 Medical and hospital equipment

D-U-N-S 25-202-4823 (HQ)
CHEVRON LUBRICANTS CANADA INC
(Suby of Chevron Corporation)
6975 Pacific Cir Suite A, Mississauga, ON, L5T 2H3

Emp Here 55   Emp Total 61,500
Sales 35,268,480
SIC 5172 Petroleum products, nec
Pr Pr Randy Brillhart
Dir Sandy Mcwhirter
Dir Craig Duncan
Fin Mgr Anthony Joseph
Robert C Meachen
Gail Walker
Vince P Kyle

D-U-N-S 25-167-2739 (BR)
CINTAS CANADA LIMITED
SALLY FOURMY & ASSOCIATES
(Suby of Cintas Corporation)
6300 Kennedy Rd Unit 3, Mississauga, ON, L5T 2X5
(905) 670-4409
Emp Here 40
SIC 7218 Industrial launderers

D-U-N-S 25-996-3239 (BR)
COATINGS 85 LTD
ACADIAN SALES
7007 Davand Dr, Mississauga, ON, L5T 1L5
(905) 564-1717
Emp Here 50

SIC 3479 Metal coating and allied services

D-U-N-S 20-104-4182 (BR)
COLABOR LIMITED PARTNERSHIP
SUMMIT FOOD SERVICE DISTRIBUTORS
(Suby of Groupe Colabor Inc)
6270 Kenway Dr, Mississauga, ON, L5T 2N3
(905) 795-2400
Emp Here 120
SIC 5142 Packaged frozen goods

D-U-N-S 20-014-1948 (SL)
COLOMER CANADA, LTD
1055 Courtneypark Dr E Suite A, Mississauga, ON, L5T 1M7
(905) 565-7047
Emp Here 22   Sales 4,158,760
SIC 5131 Piece goods and notions

D-U-N-S 24-859-3969 (SL)
CONXCORP LTD
VIVIX
6350 Netherhart Rd Unit 2, Mississauga, ON, L5T 1K3
(866) 815-2669
Emp Here 28   Sales 7,369,031
SIC 3648 Lighting equipment, nec
Pr Pr Jason Lightfoot

D-U-N-S 20-155-1324 (HQ)
COOPER RENTALS CANADA INC/LOCATIONS COOPER CANADA INC
COOPER EQUIPMENT RENTAL
(Suby of G. Cooper Equipment Rentals Limited)
6335 Edwards Blvd, Mississauga, ON, L5T 2W7
(289) 247-2770
Emp Here 25   Emp Total 2,000
Sales 16,124,315
SIC 7353 Heavy construction equipment rental
Pr Pr Darryl Cooper
Jim Mcinnis

D-U-N-S 20-700-2291 (BR)
CUMMINS EST DU CANADA SEC
CUMMINS EST DU CANADA SEC
7175 Pacific Cir, Mississauga, ON, L5T 2A8
(905) 795-0050
Emp Here 85
SIC 5084 Industrial machinery and equipment

D-U-N-S 24-008-0267 (HQ)
DBG CANADA LIMITED
DBG
110 Ambassador Dr, Mississauga, ON, L5T 2X8
(905) 362-2311
Emp Here 65   Emp Total 720
Sales 35,021,136
SIC 3499 Fabricated Metal products, nec
Mike De Biasi
VP VP Joseph De Biasi
VP VP Attilio De Biasi
Treas Josie De Biasi

D-U-N-S 20-177-1248 (BR)
DHL GLOBAL FORWARDING (CANADA) INC
DHL DANZAS AIR & OCEAN
6575 Davand Dr, Mississauga, ON, L5T 2M3

Emp Here 100
SIC 4731 Freight transportation arrangement

D-U-N-S 20-568-2180 (HQ)
DHL GLOBAL FORWARDING (CANADA) INC
DGF
6200 Edwards Blvd Suite 100, Mississauga, ON, L5T 2V7
(289) 562-6500
Emp Here 150   Emp Total 498,459
Sales 101,091,492
SIC 4731 Freight transportation arrangement
Pr Hans Toggweiler
VP Fin Allan Vickers

Mgr Donna Letterio
CFO Nick Verrecchia

D-U-N-S 25-293-2819 (BR)
DATA COMMUNICATIONS MANAGEMENT CORP
THE FSA GROUP
80 Ambassador Dr, Mississauga, ON, L5T 2Y9
(905) 696-8884
Emp Here 100
SIC 2759 Commercial printing, nec

D-U-N-S 24-213-0599 (SL)
DATA PARCEL EXPRESS INCORPORATED
INSTANT COURIER SERVICE
6500 Van Deemter Crt, Mississauga, ON, L5T 1S1
(905) 564-5555
Emp Here 40   Sales 8,536,402
SIC 4731 Freight transportation arrangement
Pr Pr Michael Dean

D-U-N-S 20-145-8171 (HQ)
DAYTON SUPERIOR CANADA LTD
6650 Pacific Circle, Mississauga, ON, L5T 1V6
(416) 798-2000
Emp Here 41   Emp Total 7,551
Sales 5,909,817
SIC 3444 Sheet Metalwork
Dir Brad Penn

D-U-N-S 24-752-3681 (BR)
DYNASTY FURNITURE MANUFACTURING LTD
DYNASTY FURNITURE MANUFACTURING
6830 Columbus Rd, Mississauga, ON, L5T 2G1
(905) 670-0110
Emp Here 40
SIC 2426 Hardwood dimension and flooring mills

D-U-N-S 20-313-4903 (SL)
ETG COMMODITIES INC
6220 Shawson Dr, Mississauga, ON, L5T 1J8
(416) 900-4148
Emp Here 28   Sales 20,428,996
SIC 6799 Investors, nec
Pr Pr Gaurav Kapoor
Dir Fin Anshul Nagar
Dir Ketankumar Patel
Dir Maheshkumar Patel

D-U-N-S 20-161-0573 (SL)
ENESCO CANADA CORPORATION
989 Derry Rd E Suite 303, Mississauga, ON, L5T 2J8
(905) 673-9200
Emp Here 120   Sales 13,132,926
SIC 5023 Homefurnishings
Pr Grace Kiss
VP Fin Sandy Ross

D-U-N-S 25-313-9141 (SL)
ENGLISH BAY BATTER (TORONTO) INC
6925 Invader Cres, Mississauga, ON, L5T 2B7
(905) 670-1110
Emp Here 150   Sales 27,610,240
SIC 2052 Cookies and crackers
Manager Cueonstantin Tristen

D-U-N-S 24-587-5075 (HQ)
ESAB GROUP CANADA INC
ESAB WELDING & CUTTING PRODUCTS
(Suby of Colfax Corporation)
6010 Tomken Rd, Mississauga, ON, L5T 1X9
(905) 670-0220
Emp Here 30   Emp Total 16,000
Sales 12,250,277
SIC 5084 Industrial machinery and equipment
Genl Mgr Neil Armstrong

D-U-N-S 24-175-5867 (HQ)
ESSENDANT CANADA, INC
ADOX/OKI BERING
(Suby of Essendant Inc.)

6400 Ordan Dr, Mississauga, ON, L5T 2H6
(905) 670-1223
Emp Here 35   Emp Total 6,600
Sales 5,284,131
SIC 5099 Durable goods, nec
Pr John Leclair
VP Michael Leclair

D-U-N-S 20-322-6030 (BR)
FNF CANADA COMPANY
55 Superior Blvd, Mississauga, ON, L5T 2X9
(289) 562-0088
Emp Here 200
SIC 6361 Title insurance

D-U-N-S 25-993-4321 (HQ)
FNF CANADA COMPANY
FIDELITY NATIONAL FINANCIAL CANADA
55 Superior Blvd, Mississauga, ON, L5T 2X9
(289) 562-0088
Emp Here 200   Emp Total 55,221
Sales 64,832,235
SIC 6162 Mortgage bankers and loan correspondents
Pr Dustin Allan
VP Fin Marian Poon
VP Anjaum Iqbal
VP Brian Bell
VP Craig O'brien
VP John Rider
VP Martin Drevjany
VP Steven Offer
VP Shawna Jovanovic

D-U-N-S 20-236-3404 (HQ)
FEDEX TRADE NETWORKS TRANSPORT & BROKERAGE (CANADA), INC
(Suby of Fedex Corporation)
7075 Ordan Dr, Mississauga, ON, L5T 1K6
(905) 677-7371
Emp Here 200   Emp Total 169,000
Sales 123,668,387
SIC 4731 Freight transportation arrangement
Lynn Wark

D-U-N-S 20-648-5547 (BR)
FEDEX TRADE NETWORKS TRANSPORT & BROKERAGE (CANADA), INC
FEDEX TRADE NETWORKS
(Suby of Fedex Corporation)
7075 Ordan Dr, Mississauga, ON, L5T 1K6
(800) 463-3339
Emp Here 200
SIC 4231 Trucking terminal facilities

D-U-N-S 20-171-4912 (HQ)
FILTRATION GROUP CANADA CORPORATION
(Suby of Filtration Group LLC)
6190 Kestrel Rd, Mississauga, ON, L5T 1Z1
(905) 795-9559
Emp Here 75   Emp Total 900
Sales 10,068,577
SIC 3569 General industrial machinery, nec
Pr Adrian Hanley

D-U-N-S 24-093-4757 (SL)
FIVE STAR HOUSEKEEPING SERVICES INC
6731 Columbus Rd Unit 3, Mississauga, ON, L5T 2M4
(905) 696-9449
Emp Here 50   Sales 1,732,502
SIC 7349 Building maintenance services, nec

D-U-N-S 25-076-5059 (HQ)
FORMER RESTORATION L.P.
FIRSTONSITE RESTORATION
(Suby of Interstate Restoration LLC)
60 Admiral Blvd, Mississauga, ON, L5T 2W1
(905) 696-2900
Emp Here 25   Emp Total 172
Sales 131,329,260
SIC 1771 Concrete work
CEO Dave Demos
Bruce Derraugh
Gordon Currie

D-U-N-S 20-553-8127   (SL)
FREEWAY WASHER LIMITED
(*Suby of* Freeway Corporation)
1820 Meyerside Dr, Mississauga, ON, L5T
1B4
(905) 564-2288
Emp Here 26   *Sales* 6,566,463
SIC 3452 Bolts, nuts, rivets, and washers
Pr Pr Jason Hawksworth
 Roger Alfred
 Fin Ex Neil Simpson

D-U-N-S 20-181-9856   (SL)
FREUD CANADA, INC
7450 Pacific Cir, Mississauga, ON, L5T 2A3
(905) 670-1025
Emp Here 25   *Sales* 4,596,524
SIC 5084 Industrial machinery and equipment

D-U-N-S 24-319-0662   (SL)
G.A.L. MANUFACTURING CORPORATION
(*Suby of* G.A.L. Manufacturing Corporation)
6500 Gottardo Crt, Mississauga, ON, L5T 2A2
(905) 624-6565
Emp Here 27   *Sales* 12,760,800
SIC 3699 Electrical equipment and supplies,
nec
Off Mgr Kathleen Truax
Pr Walter Glaser

D-U-N-S 20-286-1282   (BR)
**GRAHAM CONSTRUCTION AND ENGI-
NEERING INC**
6108 Edwards Blvd, Mississauga, ON, L5T
2V7
(905) 694-4000
Emp Here 40
SIC 1542 Nonresidential construction, nec

D-U-N-S 24-313-5188   (BR)
GRAHAM GROUP LTD
*GRAHAM CONSTRUCTION AND ENGI-
NEERING A JB*
6108 Edwards Blvd, Mississauga, ON, L5T
2V7
(905) 694-4000
Emp Here 20
SIC 1521 Single-family housing construction

D-U-N-S 24-463-2519   (HQ)
**HEIDELBERG CANADA GRAPHIC EQUIP-
MENT LIMITED**
6265 Kenway Dr, Mississauga, ON, L5T 2L3
(905) 362-4400
Emp Here 100   *Emp Total* 11,873
Sales 73,631,335
SIC 5084 Industrial machinery and equipment
 Niels Winther
 Robert Primeau
Pr Pr Richard Armstrong

D-U-N-S 24-761-5722   (SL)
HUDSON ENERGY CANADA CORP
6345 Dixie Rd Suite 200, Mississauga, ON,
L5T 2E6
(905) 670-4440
Emp Here 20   *Sales* 9,557,852
SIC 4911 Electric services
Dir Kate Livesey
Dir Beth Summers
Dir Ken Hartwick
Dir Rebecca Macdonald

D-U-N-S 20-016-0211   (SL)
**I.O.F. BUSINESS FURNITURE MANUFAC-
TURING INC**
1710 Bonhill Rd, Mississauga, ON, L5T 1C8
(905) 672-0942
Emp Here 50   *Sales* 3,984,755
SIC 2521 Wood office furniture

D-U-N-S 24-911-8134   (HQ)
I.R.P. INDUSTRIAL RUBBER LTD
(*Suby of* S.J.M. Products Limited)
6300 Edwards Blvd Unit 1, Mississauga, ON,
L5T 2V7

(905) 670-5700
Emp Here 50   *Emp Total* 3
Sales 2,647,265
SIC 5085 Industrial supplies
Pr Pr Richard Mallett
 Mike Mallett
VP VP Ted Flewwelling
Treas Sharon Heaman

D-U-N-S 20-603-3094   (SL)
ID TECHNOLOGY (CANADA) CORP
ID TECHNOLOGY
165 Annagem Blvd, Mississauga, ON, L5T
2V1
(905) 670-4919
Emp Here 20   *Sales* 2,115,860
SIC 3565 Packaging machinery

D-U-N-S 20-059-0037   (SL)
IMPERIAL CHILLED JUICE INC
265 Courtneypark Dr E, Mississauga, ON, L5T
2T6
(905) 565-7288
Emp Here 50   *Sales* 4,450,603
SIC 2037 Frozen fruits and vegetables

D-U-N-S 24-708-4577   (BR)
INDUSTRIES LYNX INC
(*Suby of* Industries Lynx Inc)
6311 Vipond Dr, Mississauga, ON, L5T 1T7
(416) 674-4606
Emp Here 65
SIC 3442 Metal doors, sash, and trim

D-U-N-S 25-815-9532   (SL)
INNOVATIVE FOODS CORPORATION
(*Suby of* James Richardson & Sons, Limited)
6171 Atlantic Dr, Mississauga, ON, L5T 1N7
(905) 670-8788
Emp Here 50   *Sales* 25,609,206
SIC 2079 Edible fats and oils

D-U-N-S 20-250-6945   (BR)
INTERCITY PACKERS LTD
INTERCITY PACKERS (EAST)
(*Suby of* Minto Industries Ltd)
6880 Pacific Cir, Mississauga, ON, L5T 1N8
(905) 670-1023
Emp Here 40
SIC 5147 Meats and meat products

D-U-N-S 24-182-3889   (SL)
IVOCLAR VIVADENT INC
6600 Dixie Rd Unit 1, Mississauga, ON, L5T
2Y2
(905) 670-8499
Emp Here 21   *Sales* 3,064,349
SIC 5047 Medical and hospital equipment

D-U-N-S 24-340-3743   (BR)
JUST ENERGY GROUP INC
ENERGY SAVINGS INCOME FUND
6345 Dixie Rd Suite 200, Mississauga, ON,
L5T 2E6
(905) 670-4440
Emp Here 20
SIC 6282 Investment advice

D-U-N-S 20-335-0785   (BR)
K-G SPRAY-PAK INC
K-G SPRAY-PAK INC.
(*Suby of* Plz Aeroscience Corporation)
6080 Vipond Dr, Mississauga, ON, L5T 2V4
(905) 565-1410
Emp Here 20
SIC 2813 Industrial gases

D-U-N-S 24-370-4728   (BR)
KAR INDUSTRIEL INC
6877 Edwards Blvd, Mississauga, ON, L5T
2T9
(905) 564-5587
Emp Here 22
SIC 5084 Industrial machinery and equipment

D-U-N-S 24-142-3946   (HQ)
KENNAMETAL LTD
(*Suby of* Kennametal Inc.)
1305 Meyerside Dr, Mississauga, ON, L5T

1C9

Emp Here 69   *Emp Total* 10,700
Sales 40,048,983
SIC 5084 Industrial machinery and equipment
Pr Carlos Cardoso
Genl Mgr Tom Reddick

D-U-N-S 24-319-5208   (BR)
KUEHNE + NAGEL LTD
275 Pendant Dr, Mississauga, ON, L5T 2W9
(905) 670-6901
Emp Here 20
SIC 4731 Freight transportation arrangement

D-U-N-S 25-684-2402   (BR)
KUEHNE + NAGEL LTD
6335 Edwards Blvd, Mississauga, ON, L5T
2W7
(905) 670-6901
Emp Here 100
SIC 4731 Freight transportation arrangement

D-U-N-S 24-047-9683   (HQ)
**KYOCERA DOCUMENT SOLUTIONS
CANADA, LTD**
6120 Kestrel Rd, Mississauga, ON, L5T 1S8
(905) 670-4425
Emp Here 30   *Emp Total* 70,473
Sales 5,763,895
SIC 5044 Office equipment
Pr Raymond Baraya

D-U-N-S 20-718-2366   (BR)
LEIDOS, INC
6108 Edwards Blvd, Mississauga, ON, L5T
2V7

Emp Here 110
SIC 8734 Testing laboratories

D-U-N-S 20-625-9798   (SL)
LITEFORM INTERNATIONAL INC
261 Ambassador Dr, Mississauga, ON, L5T
2J2
(905) 564-2090
Emp Here 28   *Sales* 5,318,747
SIC 3648 Lighting equipment, nec
Pr Pr Frank Porretta
 Anthony Porretta

D-U-N-S 20-013-9694   (BR)
LOWE-MARTIN COMPANY INC
LOWE-MARTIN GROUP
7330 Pacific Cir, Mississauga, ON, L5T 1V1
(905) 696-9493
Emp Here 20
SIC 2752 Commercial printing, lithographic

D-U-N-S 20-188-3076   (BR)
LOWE-MARTIN COMPANY INC
6006 Kestrel Rd, Mississauga, ON, L5T 1S8
(905) 670-7100
Emp Here 70
SIC 2752 Commercial printing, lithographic

D-U-N-S 24-770-8266   (SL)
LUMBERMEN'S CREDIT BUREAU LIMITED
1280 Courtneypark Dr E, Mississauga, ON,
L5T 1N6
(905) 283-3111
Emp Here 40   *Sales* 2,042,900
SIC 7323 Credit reporting services

D-U-N-S 20-148-4300   (HQ)
MERSEN CANADA TORONTO INC
MERSEN ELECTRONICS
6220 Kestrel Rd, Mississauga, ON, L5T 1Y9
(416) 252-9371
Emp Here 80   *Emp Total* 5
Sales 20,183,648
SIC 3679 Electronic components, nec
Dir Daniel Beaudron
Pr Gilles Boisseau
VP VP Bruce Brown

D-U-N-S 24-138-3509   (SL)
MSN WIRELESS INC
MSN

1315 Derry Rd E Suite 6a, Mississauga, ON,
L5T 1B6
(416) 745-9900
Emp Here 1,354   *Sales* 343,541,120
SIC 4899 Communication services, nec
Pr Pr Mubasshar Tahir
 Naman Tahir

D-U-N-S 20-175-1034   (BR)
MAGNA SEATING INC
MISSISAUGA SEATING SYSTEMS
400 Courtneypark Dr E Unit 1, Mississauga,
ON, L5T 2S5
(905) 696-1000
Emp Here 411
SIC 5999 Miscellaneous retail stores, nec

D-U-N-S 25-255-7723   (SL)
**MANITOULIN WAREHOUSING AND DIS-
TRIBUTION INC**
7035 Ordan Dr, Mississauga, ON, L5T 1T1
(905) 283-1630
Emp Here 40   *Sales* 3,793,956
SIC 4225 General warehousing and storage

D-U-N-S 24-684-5440   (HQ)
MARVIN WINDOWS INC
MARVIN WINDOWS & DOORS
1455 Courtneypark Dr E, Mississauga, ON,
L5T 2E3
(905) 670-5052
Emp Here 30   *Emp Total* 3,573
Sales 7,369,031
SIC 5211 Lumber and other building materials
Pr Pr Knut Holmsen

D-U-N-S 24-999-9947   (HQ)
MATRIX LOGISTICS SERVICES LIMITED
6941 Kennedy Rd, Mississauga, ON, L5T 2R6
(905) 795-2200
Emp Here 400   *Emp Total* 498,459
Sales 94,848,910
SIC 4225 General warehousing and storage
Pr Todd Yates
VP Fin Paolo Mari

D-U-N-S 20-642-6350   (SL)
MCDONALD'S RESTAURANTS
TOMKEN MCDONALDS
930 Derry Rd E, Mississauga, ON, L5T 2X6
(905) 565-7151
Emp Here 60   *Sales* 1,824,018
SIC 5812 Eating places

D-U-N-S 24-953-0395   (BR)
MOLSON CANADA 2005
MOLSON CANADA
(*Suby of* Molson Coors Brewing Company)
6300 Ordan Dr, Mississauga, ON, L5T 1W6

Emp Here 50
SIC 2082 Malt beverages

D-U-N-S 24-420-4793   (HQ)
MOORE CANADA CORPORATION
R.R. DONNELLEY
(*Suby of* R. R. Donnelley & Sons Company)
6100 Vipond Dr, Mississauga, ON, L5T 2X1
(905) 362-3100
Emp Here 400   *Emp Total* 68,400
Sales 255,873,175
SIC 6712 Bank holding companies
Pr Andrew Sullivan
VP Fin Sean Byrne

D-U-N-S 25-975-6976   (BR)
MOORE CANADA CORPORATION
ANNAN & BIRD LITHOGRAPHERS
(*Suby of* R. R. Donnelley & Sons Company)
1060 Tristar Dr, Mississauga, ON, L5T 1H9
(905) 670-0604
Emp Here 100
SIC 2752 Commercial printing, lithographic

D-U-N-S 24-388-3043   (BR)
**NATIONAL LOGISTICS SERVICES (2006)
INC**
475 Admiral Blvd Unit B, Mississauga, ON,

L5T 2N1
(905) 696-7278
Emp Here 50
SIC 5137 Women's and children's clothing

D-U-N-S 20-212-0163   (BR)
NEWARK PAPERBOARD PRODUCTS LTD
6001 Edwards Blvd, Mississauga, ON, L5T
2W7
(905) 564-0600
Emp Here 25
SIC 2655 Fiber cans, drums, and similar products

D-U-N-S 20-921-5722   (HQ)
NEWLY WEDS FOODS CO.
450 Superior Blvd, Mississauga, ON, L5T 2R9
(905) 670-7776
Emp Here 214   *Emp Total* 3,100
Sales 41,650,560
SIC 2099 Food preparations, nec
Pr Pr Charles T. Angell
VP Fin Ased Malik
  Richard Nahorniak
Dir Paul Legere
  John J. Seely

D-U-N-S 20-083-4976   (SL)
NEWMAN HATTERSLEY LTD
IMI NUCLEAR
181 Superior Blvd, Mississauga, ON, L5T 2L6
(905) 678-1240
Emp Here 25   *Sales* 3,283,232
SIC 3494 Valves and pipe fittings, nec

D-U-N-S 24-830-1095   (BR)
NIPPON EXPRESS CANADA LTD
OCEAN CARGO DIVISION
6250 Edwards Blvd, Mississauga, ON, L5T
2X3
(905) 565-7526
Emp Here 90
SIC 4731 Freight transportation arrangement

D-U-N-S 24-507-7029   (HQ)
NIPPON EXPRESS CANADA LTD
6250 Edwards Blvd, Mississauga, ON, L5T
2X3
(905) 565-7525
Emp Here 100   *Emp Total* 70,092
Sales 37,209,957
SIC 4731 Freight transportation arrangement
Pr Yoichi Satake
Sec David Street
  Peter Hayden
  Chiemi Honma

D-U-N-S 20-699-7301   (BR)
NORDION INC
MDS LABORATORIES, DIV OF
1330 Meyerside Dr, Mississauga, ON, L5T
1C2
(905) 565-2302
Emp Here 25
SIC 8071 Medical laboratories

D-U-N-S 24-382-3718   (BR)
NORDSTRONG EQUIPMENT LIMITED
(*Suby of* Canerector Inc)
400 Ambassador Dr, Mississauga, ON, L5T
2J3
(289) 562-6400
Emp Here 20
SIC 5083 Farm and garden machinery

D-U-N-S 24-987-5998   (BR)
O.K. TIRE STORES INC
520 Abilene Dr, Mississauga, ON, L5T 2H7
(905) 564-5171
Emp Here 25
SIC 5014 Tires and tubes

D-U-N-S 25-101-6754   (BR)
PACCAR OF CANADA LTD
PACCAR LEASING
(*Suby of* Paccar Inc)
6465 Van Deemter Crt, Mississauga, ON, L5T
1S1

(905) 564-2300
Emp Here 20
SIC 7513 Truck rental and leasing, no drivers

D-U-N-S 20-563-4376   (BR)
PACIFIC WESTERN TRANSPORTATION LTD
6999 Ordan Dr, Mississauga, ON, L5T 1K6
(905) 564-3232
Emp Here 70
SIC 4111 Local and suburban transit

D-U-N-S 20-640-9138   (HQ)
PAYSTATION INC
(*Suby of* Warner, Robert Holdings Limited)
6345 Dixie Rd Unit 4, Mississauga, ON, L5T
2E6
(905) 364-0700
Emp Here 43   *Emp Total* 120
Sales 16,416,158
SIC 5044 Office equipment
Dir Robert M Warner

D-U-N-S 25-511-2237   (SL)
PERFUMES ETC. LTD
6880 Columbus Rd Unit 2, Mississauga, ON,
L5T 2G1
(905) 850-8060
Emp Here 20   *Sales* 11,094,675
SIC 5122 Drugs, proprietaries, and sundries
Pr Pr Vikas Mahajan

D-U-N-S 20-246-1468   (SL)
PIRLITOR MACHINE & TOOL LIMITED
6375 Kestrel Rd, Mississauga, ON, L5T 1Z5
(905) 795-9139
Emp Here 50   *Sales* 4,711,645
SIC 3599 Industrial machinery, nec

D-U-N-S 20-145-4006   (HQ)
PRESSTEK CANADA CORP
(*Suby of* MAI Holdings, Inc.)
400 Ambassador Dr, Mississauga, ON, L5T
2J3
(905) 362-0610
Emp Here 40   *Emp Total* 384
Sales 14,592,140
SIC 5084 Industrial machinery and equipment
Dir Fred Woods
  Gerry Welstead
Pr Pr Edward Marino
  Moosa Moosa
  James Scafide

D-U-N-S 20-917-8685   (BR)
PRINCESS AUTO LTD
6608 Dixie Rd, Mississauga, ON, L5T 2Z9
(905) 564-1011
Emp Here 60
SIC 5251 Hardware stores

D-U-N-S 25-799-6124   (BR)
PRODUITS STANDARD INC
6270 Kestrel Rd, Mississauga, ON, L5T 1Z4
(905) 564-2836
Emp Here 40
SIC 7389 Business services, nec

D-U-N-S 20-076-7445   (BR)
PUROLATOR INC.
PUROLATOR INC
6520 Kestrel Rd, Mississauga, ON, L5T 1Z6
(905) 565-9306
Emp Here 200
SIC 7389 Business services, nec

D-U-N-S 20-556-8470   (SL)
QUICK CABLE CANADA LTD
6395 Kestrel Rd, Mississauga, ON, L5T 1Z5
(905) 362-1606
Emp Here 30   *Sales* 2,772,507
SIC 3694 Engine electrical equipment

D-U-N-S 20-936-7544   (BR)
REDBERRY FRANCHISING CORP
BURGER KING
6010 Dixie Rd, Mississauga, ON, L5T 1A6
(905) 670-1870
Emp Here 20

SIC 5812 Eating places

D-U-N-S 24-917-9912   (BR)
RELIANCE METALS CANADA LIMITED
EARLE M. JORGENSEN (CANADA), DIV OF
(*Suby of* Reliance Steel & Aluminum Co.)
305 Pendant Dr, Mississauga, ON, L5T 2W9
(905) 564-0866
Emp Here 39
SIC 5051 Metals service centers and offices

D-U-N-S 25-420-2732   (SL)
RENFRO CANADA CORP
(*Suby of* Renfro Corporation)
250 Admiral Blvd, Mississauga, ON, L5T 2N6
(905) 795-3130
Emp Here 21   *Sales* 1,532,175
SIC 2251 Women's hosiery, except socks

D-U-N-S 25-214-7244   (HQ)
RITTAL SYSTEMS LTD
6485 Ordan Dr, Mississauga, ON, L5T 1X2
(905) 795-0777
Emp Here 32   *Sales* 16,232,000
SIC 5063 Electrical apparatus and equipment
Genl Mgr Tony Varga

D-U-N-S 20-527-6215   (BR)
ROBCO INC
281 Ambassador Dr, Mississauga, ON, L5T
2J3
(905) 564-6555
Emp Here 35
SIC 3053 Gaskets; packing and sealing devices

D-U-N-S 25-354-9166   (HQ)
RODAIR INTERNATIONAL LTD
SEKO CANADA LOGISTICS
(*Suby of* Rodair Holdings Ltd)
350 Pendant Dr, Mississauga, ON, L5T 2W6
(905) 671-4655
Emp Here 90   *Emp Total* 2
Sales 26,630,656
SIC 4731 Freight transportation arrangement
Pr Jeffrey Cullen
VP Opers Chris Matthews
  Bryan Brooks
VP Sls Brian Schwenger

D-U-N-S 20-939-7470   (SL)
ROKAN LAMINATING CO LTD
PLAK-IT
1660 Trinity Dr, Mississauga, ON, L5T 1L6
(905) 564-7525
Emp Here 55   *Sales* 2,845,467
SIC 7389 Business services, nec

D-U-N-S 25-122-4366   (BR)
ROYAL BANK OF CANADA
RBC
(*Suby of* Royal Bank Of Canada)
6240 Dixie Rd, Mississauga, ON, L5T 1A6
(905) 564-5740
Emp Here 28
SIC 6021 National commercial banks

D-U-N-S 20-174-6120   (HQ)
RYDER MATERIAL HANDLING ULC
CRUSADER LEASING, DIV OF
(*Suby of* Crown Equipment Corporation)
210 Annagem Blvd, Mississauga, ON, L5T
2V5
(905) 565-2100
Emp Here 110   *Emp Total* 11,000
Sales 75,796,963
SIC 5084 Industrial machinery and equipment
Pr Ronald Greer
  Danny Fatigati

D-U-N-S 25-486-7559   (BR)
RYDER TRUCK RENTAL CANADA LTD
RYDER CANADA
(*Suby of* Ryder System, Inc.)
6415 Danville Rd, Mississauga, ON, L5T 2H7
(905) 564-4675
Emp Here 30
SIC 7513 Truck rental and leasing, no drivers

D-U-N-S 20-534-9053   (HQ)
SEA AIR INTERNATIONAL FORWARDERS LIMITED
(*Suby of* 1034702 Ontario Inc)
1720 Meyerside Dr, Mississauga, ON, L5T
1A3
(905) 677-7701
Emp Here 35   *Emp Total* 2
Sales 8,536,402
SIC 4731 Freight transportation arrangement
Pr Pr Peter Smith
  Geoffrey Robinson

D-U-N-S 25-223-5783   (BR)
SEIGNIORY CHEMICAL PRODUCTS LTD
(*Suby of* Seigniory Chemical Products Ltd)
6355 Kennedy Rd Unit 5, Mississauga, ON,
L5T 2L5
(905) 795-0858
Emp Here 30
SIC 2819 Industrial inorganic chemicals, nec

D-U-N-S 25-276-7751   (SL)
SELECT DRIVER SERVICES LTD
6200 Dixie Rd Suite 216, Mississauga, ON,
L5T 2E1
(905) 564-9388
Emp Here 50   *Sales* 2,699,546
SIC 8299 Schools and educational services, nec

D-U-N-S 25-063-9234   (BR)
SERVICES D'ESSAIS INTERTEK AN LTEE
INTERTEK
6225 Kenway Dr, Mississauga, ON, L5T 2L3
(905) 678-7820
Emp Here 50
SIC 8711 Engineering services

D-U-N-S 20-104-4430   (BR)
SHERWAY WAREHOUSING INC
THIRD PARTY WAREHOUSING
1055 Courtneypark Dr E Suite A, Mississauga,
ON, L5T 1M7
(905) 564-6337
Emp Here 20
SIC 4225 General warehousing and storage

D-U-N-S 20-105-7408   (BR)
SIEMENS CANADA LIMITED
SIEMENS IT SOLUTIONS AND SERVICES
6375 Shawson Dr, Mississauga, ON, L5T 1S7
(905) 819-5761
Emp Here 100
SIC 8742 Management consulting services

D-U-N-S 25-676-2162   (SL)
SIEMENS INDUSTRIES SOFTWARE LTD
SIEMENS PLM
6375 Shawson Dr, Mississauga, ON, L5T 1S7

Emp Here 39   *Sales* 5,559,741
SIC 7372 Prepackaged software
Pr Bryan Morri

D-U-N-S 20-977-2540   (SL)
SLANT/FIN LTD/LTEE
(*Suby of* Slant/Fin Corporation)
400 Ambassador Dr, Mississauga, ON, L5T
2J3
(905) 677-8400
Emp Here 45   *Sales* 3,283,232
SIC 5722 Household appliance stores

D-U-N-S 25-675-1462   (BR)
SONOCO FLEXIBLE PACKAGING CANADA CORPORATION
(*Suby of* Sonoco Products Company)
295 Superior Blvd Unit 2, Mississauga, ON,
L5T 2L6

Emp Here 35
SIC 2655 Fiber cans, drums, and similar products

D-U-N-S 20-181-4126   (HQ)
STEPHENSON'S RENTAL SERVICES INC
6895 Columbus Rd Suite 502, Mississauga,

ON, L5T 2G9
(905) 507-3650
Emp Here 25   *Emp Total* 316
Sales 28,672,908
SIC 7359 Equipment rental and leasing, nec
Pr Pr William D Swisher
James R. Mcinnis

D-U-N-S 20-057-4916   (BR)
TWD ROADS MANAGEMENT INC
6130 Edwards Blvd, Mississauga, ON, L5T 2V7
(905) 670-3080
Emp Here 22
SIC 1611 Highway and street construction

D-U-N-S 24-816-2752   (SL)
TARGUS (CANADA) LTD
6725 Edwards Blvd, Mississauga, ON, L5T 2V9
(905) 564-9300
Emp Here 35   *Sales* 4,231,721
SIC 5099 Durable goods, nec

D-U-N-S 20-917-8354   (BR)
TAYMOR INDUSTRIES LTD
6460 Kennedy Rd Suite A, Mississauga, ON, L5T 2X4
(905) 362-3660
Emp Here 30
SIC 5072 Hardware

D-U-N-S 20-547-8097   (BR)
TENCORR PACKAGING INC
1135 Courtneypark Dr E, Mississauga, ON, L5T 1S5
(905) 564-8222
Emp Here 50
SIC 2679 Converted paper products, nec

D-U-N-S 24-311-7376   (BR)
THYSSENKRUPP MATERIALS CA, LTD
ROY METAL SALES, DIV OF
6900 Davand Dr, Mississauga, ON, L5T 1J5
(905) 866-6611
Emp Here 125
SIC 3312 Blast furnaces and steel mills

D-U-N-S 20-123-1201   (SL)
TOR CAN WASTE MANAGEMENT INC
6465 Danville Rd, Mississauga, ON, L5T 2H7
(905) 856-3900
Emp Here 60   *Sales* 6,125,139
SIC 4212 Local trucking, without storage

D-U-N-S 20-879-3711   (SL)
TOTES ISOTONER CANADA LIMITED
TOTES
6335 Shawson Dr, Mississauga, ON, L5T 1S7
(905) 564-4817
Emp Here 23   *Sales* 4,304,681
SIC 5139 Footwear

D-U-N-S 24-952-3838   (HQ)
TRAILCON LEASING INC
6950 Kenderry Gate, Mississauga, ON, L5T 2S7
(905) 670-9061
Emp Here 100   *Emp Total* 1
Sales 8,609,363
SIC 7519 Utility trailer rental
Pr Alan Boughton
VP VP James Wedgewood
Dir Brent Jones

D-U-N-S 24-823-3298   (HQ)
TRANSPORT QUIK X INC
QUIK X LOGISTICS
6767 Davand Dr, Mississauga, ON, L5T 2T2
(905) 670-5770
Emp Here 200   *Emp Total* 25,438
Sales 150,554,424
SIC 4213 Trucking, except local
Josiane-M. Langlois
VP Chantal Martel
Genl Mgr Jeffery King

D-U-N-S 24-793-1249   (SL)
TRI-AD INTERNATIONAL FREIGHT FOR-

WARDING LTD
375 Annagem Blvd Unit 100, Mississauga, ON, L5T 3A7
(905) 624-8214
Emp Here 30   *Sales* 6,347,581
SIC 4731 Freight transportation arrangement
Pr Pr Linda Collier

D-U-N-S 20-106-2002   (SL)
TRI-CLEAN BUILDING SERVICES INC
1415 Bonhill Rd Unit 5, Mississauga, ON, L5T 1R2
(905) 624-6112
Emp Here 60   *Sales* 1,751,057
SIC 7349 Building maintenance services, nec

D-U-N-S 20-401-6430   (HQ)
TROPHY FOODS INC
ALIMENTS LALUMIERE
(*Suby of* Trophy Foods Inc)
71 Admiral Blvd, Mississauga, ON, L5T 2T1
(905) 564-3060
Emp Here 240   *Emp Total* 400
Sales 104,114,919
SIC 5145 Confectionery
Pr Brian Paul
Dir Fin Eva Mounsteven

D-U-N-S 24-358-2207   (SL)
TYROLIT WICKMAN INC
TYROLIT ABRASIVES CANADA
6165 Kennedy Rd, Mississauga, ON, L5T 2S8
(905) 565-9880
Emp Here 20   *Sales* 3,866,917
SIC 5085 Industrial supplies

D-U-N-S 24-314-2549   (BR)
UNIVERSITY HEALTH NETWORK
ALTUM HEALTH
989 Derry Rd E Suite 200, Mississauga, ON, L5T 2J8
(905) 564-6872
Emp Here 40
SIC 8011 Offices and clinics of medical doctors

D-U-N-S 25-397-7045   (HQ)
VIPOND INC
INTEGRATED PROTECTION
6380 Vipond Dr, Mississauga, ON, L5T 1A1
(905) 564-7060
Emp Here 120   *Emp Total* 4,237
Sales 84,853,294
SIC 3569 General industrial machinery, nec
Pr Russel Becker
VP Bernard Beliveau
VP Grant Neal

D-U-N-S 20-943-4208   (BR)
VIPOND INC
6380 Vipond Dr, Mississauga, ON, L5T 1A1
(905) 564-7060
Emp Here 30
SIC 1731 Electrical work

D-U-N-S 24-738-2740   (SL)
WEBER MARKING SYSTEMS OF (CANADA) LIMITED
6180 Danville Rd, Mississauga, ON, L5T 2H7
(905) 564-6881
Emp Here 36   *Sales* 3,648,035
SIC 2679 Converted paper products, nec

D-U-N-S 20-004-5255   (BR)
WENDY'S RESTAURANTS OF CANADA INC
WENDY'S
(*Suby of* The Wendy's Company)
1420 Mid-Way Blvd, Mississauga, ON, L5T 2S4
(905) 564-2373
Emp Here 20
SIC 5812 Eating places

D-U-N-S 20-655-8376   (BR)
WENDY'S RESTAURANTS OF CANADA INC
WENDYS INTERNATIONAL
(*Suby of* The Wendy's Company)
25 Aventura Crt Suite 6680, Mississauga, ON,

L5T 3A1
Emp Here 30
SIC 5812 Eating places

D-U-N-S 24-887-4815   (BR)
WESTPRO MACHINERY INC
6197 Kennedy Rd, Mississauga, ON, L5T 2S8
(905) 795-8577
Emp Here 25
SIC 3532 Mining machinery

D-U-N-S 24-416-5366   (BR)
WHEELS INTERNATIONAL INC
WHEELS LOGISTICS DIV
1280 Courtneypark Dr E, Mississauga, ON, L5T 1N6
(905) 565-1212
Emp Here 50
SIC 4731 Freight transportation arrangement

D-U-N-S 24-891-8190   (BR)
WHITE GLOVE TRANSPORTATION SYSTEMS LTD
6141 Vipond Dr, Mississauga, ON, L5T 2B2
(905) 565-1053
Emp Here 150
SIC 4212 Local trucking, without storage

D-U-N-S 20-185-5244   (HQ)
YELLOW TRANSPORTATION OF ONTARIO INC
YELLOW FREIGHT SYSTEM
(*Suby of* Yrc Worldwide Inc.)
6130 Netherhart Rd, Mississauga, ON, L5T 1B7
(905) 670-4445
Emp Here 125   *Emp Total* 32,000
Sales 77,082,512
SIC 4213 Trucking, except local
Dir Mark Reynolds

Mississauga, ON L5V
Peel County

D-U-N-S 20-295-9276   (SL)
2207544 ONTARIO INC
ANDERSON CONSULTING
1250 Eglinton Ave W Suite 138, Mississauga, ON, L5V 1N3
(905) 795-7781
Emp Here 112   *Sales* 25,731,432
SIC 8748 Business consulting, nec
Pr Pr Edward Anderson
Ch Bd Robert Goodwin

D-U-N-S 25-833-9449   (SL)
ACURA MAINTENANCE SERVICES LTD
4739 Rathkeale Rd, Mississauga, ON, L5V 1K3
(905) 755-0150
Emp Here 70   *Sales* 2,042,900
SIC 7349 Building maintenance services, nec

D-U-N-S 20-809-9494   (SL)
BATON ROUGE
5860 Mavis Rd, Mississauga, ON, L5V 3B7

Emp Here 50   *Sales* 1,532,175
SIC 5812 Eating places

D-U-N-S 20-338-3406   (BR)
DOLLARAMA S.E.C.
DOLLARAMA
885 Plymouth Dr Unit 1, Mississauga, ON, L5V 0B5
(905) 363-1028
Emp Here 22
SIC 5411 Grocery stores

D-U-N-S 20-711-0128   (BR)
DUFFERIN-PEEL CATHOLIC DISTRICT SCHOOL BOARD
ST HERBERT ELEMENTARY CATHOLIC SCHOOL

5180 Fallingbrook Dr, Mississauga, ON, L5V 2C6
(905) 858-1171
Emp Here 56
SIC 8211 Elementary and secondary schools

D-U-N-S 25-483-8105   (BR)
DUFFERIN-PEEL CATHOLIC DISTRICT SCHOOL BOARD
ST JOSEPH SECONDARY SCHOOL
5555 Creditview Rd, Mississauga, ON, L5V 2B9
(905) 812-1376
Emp Here 150
SIC 8211 Elementary and secondary schools

D-U-N-S 20-711-0136   (BR)
DUFFERIN-PEEL CATHOLIC DISTRICT SCHOOL BOARD
ST RAYMOND ELEMENTARY SCHOOL
5735 Whitehorn Ave, Mississauga, ON, L5V 2A9
(905) 286-1010
Emp Here 40
SIC 8211 Elementary and secondary schools

D-U-N-S 20-026-7867   (BR)
DUFFERIN-PEEL CATHOLIC DISTRICT SCHOOL BOARD
ST. BERNADETTE ELEMENTARY SCHOOL
1060 White Clover Way, Mississauga, ON, L5V 1G7
(905) 501-0906
Emp Here 40
SIC 8211 Elementary and secondary schools

D-U-N-S 20-027-7973   (BR)
DUFFERIN-PEEL CATHOLIC DISTRICT SCHOOL BOARD
ST. GREGORY ELEMENTARY SCHOOL
1075 Swinbourne Dr, Mississauga, ON, L5V 1B9
(905) 814-5237
Emp Here 55
SIC 8211 Elementary and secondary schools

D-U-N-S 24-340-0830   (BR)
FGL SPORTS LTD
SPORT CHEK HEARTLAND TOWN CENTRE
785 Britannia Rd W Unit 1, Mississauga, ON, L5V 2Y1
(905) 542-9595
Emp Here 45
SIC 5941 Sporting goods and bicycle shops

D-U-N-S 20-055-1864   (BR)
H & R BLOCK CANADA, INC
(*Suby of* H&R Block, Inc.)
801 Matheson Blvd W Unit 7, Mississauga, ON, L5V 2N6
(905) 366-0226
Emp Here 30
SIC 7291 Tax return preparation services

D-U-N-S 24-315-7372   (BR)
HOME DEPOT OF CANADA INC
(*Suby of* The Home Depot Inc)
5975 Terry Fox Way, Mississauga, ON, L5V 3E4
(905) 285-4000
Emp Here 40
SIC 5251 Hardware stores

D-U-N-S 24-372-2886   (BR)
HUDSON'S BAY COMPANY
HOME OUTFITTERS
765 Britannia Rd W Unit 1, Mississauga, ON, L5V 2Y1
(905) 363-0433
Emp Here 20
SIC 5719 Miscellaneous homefurnishings

D-U-N-S 25-755-2257   (BR)
LOBLAWS SUPERMARKETS LIMITED
LOBLAWS SUPERMARKET
6085 Creditview Rd, Mississauga, ON, L5V 2A8
(905) 607-1578
Emp Here 180

▲ Public Company   ■ Public Company Family Member   **HQ** Headquarters   **BR** Branch   **SL** Single Location

SIC 5411 Grocery stores

D-U-N-S 20-716-4083   (BR)
OMER DESERRES INC
LOOMIS ART STORE
785 Britannia Rd W, Mississauga, ON, L5V 2Y1
(905) 363-2791
Emp Here 30
SIC 5999 Miscellaneous retail stores, nec

D-U-N-S 25-921-0268   (BR)
PEEL DISTRICT SCHOOL BOARD
EDENROSE PUBLIC SCHOOL
(*Suby of* Peel District School Board)
1342 Edenrose St, Mississauga, ON, L5V 1K9
(905) 567-4296
Emp Here 60
SIC 8211 Elementary and secondary schools

D-U-N-S 20-576-9057   (BR)
PEEL DISTRICT SCHOOL BOARD
RICK HANSON SECONDARY SCHOOL
(*Suby of* Peel District School Board)
1150 Dream Crest Rd, Mississauga, ON, L5V 1N6
(905) 567-4260
Emp Here 100
SIC 8211 Elementary and secondary schools

D-U-N-S 20-591-3788   (BR)
PEEL DISTRICT SCHOOL BOARD
BRITANNIA PUBLIC SCHOOL
(*Suby of* Peel District School Board)
1145 Swinbourne Dr, Mississauga, ON, L5V 1C2
(905) 814-1146
Emp Here 50
SIC 8211 Elementary and secondary schools

D-U-N-S 20-653-8808   (BR)
PEEL DISTRICT SCHOOL BOARD
WHITEHORN PUBLIC SCHOOL
(*Suby of* Peel District School Board)
5785 Whitehorn Ave, Mississauga, ON, L5V 2A9
(905) 819-9807
Emp Here 60
SIC 8211 Elementary and secondary schools

D-U-N-S 25-137-3247   (BR)
PEEL DISTRICT SCHOOL BOARD
FALLINGBROOK MIDDLE SCHOOL
(*Suby of* Peel District School Board)
5187 Fallingbrook Dr, Mississauga, ON, L5V 1N7
(905) 812-7470
Emp Here 50
SIC 8211 Elementary and secondary schools

D-U-N-S 24-556-4898   (BR)
PEEL DISTRICT SCHOOL BOARD
SHERWOOD MILLS PUBLIC SCHOOL
(*Suby of* Peel District School Board)
1385 Sherwood Mills Blvd, Mississauga, ON, L5V 2B8
(905) 812-8265
Emp Here 49
SIC 8211 Elementary and secondary schools

D-U-N-S 25-010-5376   (BR)
PHARMA PLUS DRUGMARTS LTD
PHARMA PLUS 1321
1240 Eglinton Ave W Suite B7, Mississauga, ON, L5V 1N3
(905) 858-7903
Emp Here 20
SIC 5912 Drug stores and proprietary stores

D-U-N-S 20-818-4721   (HQ)
STAEDTLER-MARS LIMITED
850 Matheson Blvd W Unit 4, Mississauga, ON, L5V 0B4
(905) 501-9008
Emp Here 32   *Sales* 6,420,542
SIC 5199 Nondurable goods, nec
Pr Pr Diane Sant

D-U-N-S 25-213-7138   (BR)

STAPLES CANADA INC
STAPLES THE BUSINESS DEPOT
(*Suby of* Staples, Inc.)
5900 Mavis Rd, Mississauga, ON, L5V 2P5
(905) 813-3134
Emp Here 50
SIC 5943 Stationery stores

D-U-N-S 20-700-4669   (BR)
TOMMY HILFIGER CANADA INC
775 Britannia Rd W Unit 1, Mississauga, ON, L5V 2Y1
(905) 826-9645
Emp Here 80
SIC 5136 Men's and boy's clothing

D-U-N-S 25-089-7022   (BR)
TRUE NORTH RESTAURANTS INC
APPLEBEES'S NEIGHBORHOOD GRILL & BAR
(*Suby of* True North Restaurants Inc)
5700 Mavis Rd Suite 1, Mississauga, ON, L5V 2N6

Emp Here 35
SIC 5812 Eating places

D-U-N-S 24-714-2156   (BR)
WAL-MART CANADA CORP
WALMART
800 Matheson Blvd W Suite 1061, Mississauga, ON, L5V 2N6
(905) 817-9688
Emp Here 50
SIC 5311 Department stores

D-U-N-S 25-359-4436   (BR)
YEE HONG CENTRE FOR GERIATRIC CARE
YEE HONG
5510 Mavis Rd, Mississauga, ON, L5V 2X5
(905) 568-0333
Emp Here 50
SIC 8051 Skilled nursing care facilities

Mississauga, ON L5W
Peel County

D-U-N-S 24-358-6158   (BR)
4513380 CANADA INC
LIVINGSTON INTERNATIONAL
150 Courtneypark Dr W Suite C, Mississauga, ON, L5W 1Y6

Emp Here 200
SIC 4731 Freight transportation arrangement

D-U-N-S 20-918-7975   (SL)
792884 ONTARIO INC
VIBRACLEAN CORPORATE HOUSEKEEPING
257 Derry Rd W, Mississauga, ON, L5W 1G3
(905) 564-1574
Emp Here 60   *Sales* 1,751,057
SIC 7349 Building maintenance services, nec

D-U-N-S 20-588-2280   (BR)
BANQUE TORONTO-DOMINION, LA
TD CANADA TRUST
(*Suby of* Toronto-Dominion Bank, The)
7060 Mclaughlin Rd, Mississauga, ON, L5W 1W7
(905) 565-7220
Emp Here 20
SIC 6021 National commercial banks

D-U-N-S 20-255-6155   (BR)
CANADA POST CORPORATION
425 Courtneypark Dr W Unit 102, Mississauga, ON, L5W 0E4
(905) 565-6604
Emp Here 30
SIC 4311 U.s. postal service

D-U-N-S 24-228-2957   (SL)

CATERPILLAR LOGISTICS SERVICE INC
150 Courtneypark Dr W Suite C, Mississauga, ON, L5W 1Y6
(905) 564-9734
Emp Here 40   *Sales* 5,182,810
SIC 8742 Management consulting services
Prin Marty Laszlo

D-U-N-S 20-072-2457   (HQ)
COMPASS GROUP CANADA LTD
CHARTWELL
1 Prologis Blvd Suite 400, Mississauga, ON, L5W 0G2
(905) 795-5100
Emp Here 150   *Emp Total* 11
Sales 663,431,645
SIC 5812 Eating places
  Steve Kelly
  Leslie White
  Saajid Khan

D-U-N-S 20-710-9740   (BR)
DUFFERIN-PEEL CATHOLIC DISTRICT SCHOOL BOARD
ST. VERONICA ELEMENTARY SCHOOL
680 Novo Star Dr, Mississauga, ON, L5W 1C7
(905) 696-6980
Emp Here 50
SIC 8211 Elementary and secondary schools

D-U-N-S 20-711-0300   (BR)
DUFFERIN-PEEL CATHOLIC DISTRICT SCHOOL BOARD
ST JULIA ELEMENTARY SCHOOL
6770 Historic Trail, Mississauga, ON, L5W 1J3
(905) 795-2706
Emp Here 50
SIC 8211 Elementary and secondary schools

D-U-N-S 20-552-0021   (BR)
EXTENDICARE INC
EXTENDICARE MISSISSAUGA
855 John Watt Blvd, Mississauga, ON, L5W 1W4
(905) 696-0719
Emp Here 40
SIC 8051 Skilled nursing care facilities

D-U-N-S 24-757-5798   (HQ)
K C I MEDICAL CANADA INC
(*Suby of* Chiron Guernsey Holdings L.P. Inc.)
75 Courtneypark Dr W Suite 2, Mississauga, ON, L5W 0E3
(905) 565-7187
Emp Here 40   *Emp Total* 5,800
Sales 60,288,000
SIC 5047 Medical and hospital equipment
Genl Mgr Carol Robinson
Rgnl Mgr Rob Russell
VP Fin Mike Holvey

D-U-N-S 20-140-9059   (SL)
KAO CANADA INC
75 Courtneypark Dr W Unit 2, Mississauga, ON, L5W 0E3
(905) 670-7890
Emp Here 40   *Sales* 4,961,328
SIC 5122 Drugs, proprietaries, and sundries

D-U-N-S 24-078-7697   (HQ)
KENAIDAN CONTRACTING LTD
7080 Derrycrest Dr, Mississauga, ON, L5W 0G5
(905) 670-2660
Emp Here 100   *Emp Total* 14,094
Sales 40,973,672
SIC 8711 Engineering services
Pr Aidan Flatley
VP Fin Lyall Yates
Ex VP David Kirkland
  Peter Sullivan

D-U-N-S 20-852-2722   (BR)
KING'S TRANSFER VAN LINES INC
6710 Maritz Dr Unit 3, Mississauga, ON, L5W 0A1
(905) 565-9950
Emp Here 20

SIC 4213 Trucking, except local

D-U-N-S 25-204-6628   (HQ)
LA CAPITALE FINANCIAL SECURITY INSURANCE COMPANY
7150 Derrycrest Dr Suite 1150, Mississauga, ON, L5W 0E5
(905) 795-2300
Emp Here 180   *Emp Total* 3,000
Sales 463,930,850
SIC 6321 Accident and health insurance
Dir Francois Jutras
Dir Didier Ledeur
Pr Rene Rouleau
VP Dominique Dubuc
Dir Francois Latreille
Dir Richard Fiset
Dir Dominique Salvy
Dir Patrice Forget
Pr Steven Ross
Sec Pierre Marc Bellavance

D-U-N-S 20-179-0651   (BR)
LOBLAWS SUPERMARKETS LIMITED
NO FRILLS
7070 Mclaughlin Rd, Mississauga, ON, L5W 1W7
(905) 565-6490
Emp Here 70
SIC 5411 Grocery stores

D-U-N-S 20-640-5508   (HQ)
NTN BEARING CORPORATION OF CANADA LIMITED
305 Courtneypark Dr W, Mississauga, ON, L5W 1Y4
(905) 564-2700
Emp Here 60   *Emp Total* 24,738
Sales 40,712,071
SIC 5085 Industrial supplies
Pr Pr Hiroaki Tachibana
VP VP Paul Meo

D-U-N-S 20-711-1910   (BR)
PEEL DISTRICT SCHOOL BOARD
DAVID LEADER MIDDLE SCHOOL
(*Suby of* Peel District School Board)
6900 Gooderham Estate Blvd, Mississauga, ON, L5W 1B4
(905) 362-1340
Emp Here 50
SIC 8211 Elementary and secondary schools

D-U-N-S 24-344-9076   (BR)
PEEL DISTRICT SCHOOL BOARD
MISSISSAUGA SECONDARY SCHOOL
(*Suby of* Peel District School Board)
550 Courtneypark Dr W, Mississauga, ON, L5W 1L9
(905) 564-1033
Emp Here 75
SIC 8211 Elementary and secondary schools

D-U-N-S 25-293-8162   (BR)
PEEL DISTRICT SCHOOL BOARD
MEADOWVALE VILLAGE PUBLIC SCHOOL
(*Suby of* Peel District School Board)
890 Old Derry Rd, Mississauga, ON, L5W 1A1
(905) 564-5735
Emp Here 45
SIC 8211 Elementary and secondary schools

D-U-N-S 25-359-7439   (BR)
R.O.E. LOGISTICS INC
199 Longside Dr, Mississauga, ON, L5W 1Z9
(905) 625-5333
Emp Here 25
SIC 4731 Freight transportation arrangement

D-U-N-S 24-610-6140   (HQ)
RAND A TECHNOLOGY CORPORATION
RAND WORLDWIDE
151 Courtneypark Dr W Suite 201, Mississauga, ON, L5W 1Y5
(905) 565-2929
Emp Here 140   *Emp Total* 379
Sales 74,757,461
SIC 8741 Management services

Pr Marc Dulude

D-U-N-S 24-324-0723   (BR)
SOUTHWIRE CANADA COMPANY
425 Courtneypark Dr W Unit 100, Mississauga, ON, L5W 0A5
(905) 565-9798
Emp Here 50
SIC 3357 Nonferrous wiredrawing and insulating

D-U-N-S 20-968-3465   (SL)
UNICA INSURANCE INC
7150 Derrycrest Dr Suite 1, Mississauga, ON, L5W 0E5
(905) 677-9777
Emp Here 45   *Sales* 29,927,750
SIC 6331 Fire, marine, and casualty insurance
Pr Pr Martin Delage
Dir Shaun Jackson
Dir Roger Wingfield
Dir Steve Smith

D-U-N-S 20-282-4488   (HQ)
WALMART CANADA LOGISTICS ULC
6800 Maritz Dr, Mississauga, ON, L5W 1W2
(905) 670-9966
Emp Here 800   *Emp Total* 2,300,000
Sales 265,576,948
SIC 4225 General warehousing and storage
Dir Shelley Broader
Dir Ronald Strathdee
Dir William Tofflemire

D-U-N-S 24-329-9521   (BR)
WALMART CANADA LOGISTICS ULC
SUPPLY CHAIN MANAGEMENT
200 Courtneypark Dr W, Mississauga, ON, L5W 1Y6
(905) 564-1484
Emp Here 300
SIC 4225 General warehousing and storage

Mississauga, ON N5W
Peel County

D-U-N-S 25-483-3841   (HQ)
PRGX CANADA CORP
60 Courtney Park Dr W Unit 4, Mississauga, ON, N5W 0B3
(905) 670-7879
Emp Here 30   *Emp Total* 1,580
Sales 4,377,642
SIC 8721 Accounting, auditing, and bookkeeping

Mitchell, ON N0K
Perth County

D-U-N-S 24-364-6184   (BR)
ARMTEC LP
DURISOL, DIV OF
51 Arthur St, Mitchell, ON, N0K 1N0
(519) 348-8465
Emp Here 50
SIC 3312 Blast furnaces and steel mills

D-U-N-S 24-974-3139   (BR)
AVON MAITLAND DISTRICT SCHOOL BOARD
MITCHELL DISTRICT HIGH SCHOOL
95 Frances St E, Mitchell, ON. N0K 1N0
(519) 348-8495
Emp Here 59
SIC 8211 Elementary and secondary schools

D-U-N-S 25-263-5016   (BR)
AVON MAITLAND DISTRICT SCHOOL BOARD
UPPER THAMES ELEMENTARY SCHOOL
165 Frances St E Rr 5, Mitchell, ON, N0K 1N0

(519) 348-8472
Emp Here 55
SIC 8211 Elementary and secondary schools

D-U-N-S 24-386-8473   (BR)
BIO AGRI MIX LP
52 Wellington St, Mitchell, ON, N0K 1N0
(519) 348-9865
Emp Here 30
SIC 2834 Pharmaceutical preparations

D-U-N-S 24-183-1093   (SL)
M. C. MOORE HOLDINGS LTD
TIM HORTONS
235 Ontario St Ss 1, Mitchell, ON, N0K 1N0
(519) 348-0396
Emp Here 50   *Sales* 1,532,175
SIC 5812 Eating places

D-U-N-S 20-130-9739   (SL)
MITCHELL FEED MILL INC
135 Huron Rd Ss 1, Mitchell, ON, N0K 1N0
(519) 348-8752
Emp Here 22   *Sales* 6,391,350
SIC 5191 Farm supplies
Pr Pr Richard Dolmage
Bruce Dolmage
Edward Dolmage

D-U-N-S 24-208-9860   (SL)
MITCHELL NURSING HOMES LIMITED
184 Napier St Ss 1, Mitchell, ON, N0K 1N0
(519) 348-8861
Emp Here 60   *Sales* 2,699,546
SIC 8051 Skilled nursing care facilities

D-U-N-S 20-914-4141   (BR)
MURPHY, J & T LIMITED
MURPHY BUS LINES
15 Arthur St, Mitchell, ON, N0K 1N0
(519) 348-0427
Emp Here 25
SIC 4151 School buses

D-U-N-S 24-652-2858   (BR)
THOMPSONS LIMITED
3964 168 Rd, Mitchell, ON, N0K 1N0
(519) 348-8433
Emp Here 20
SIC 5153 Grain and field beans

Monkland, ON K0C
Stormont County

D-U-N-S 24-324-7330   (BR)
NUTRI-OEUF INC
ONTARIO PRIDE EGGS
(*Suby of* Nutri-Oeuf Inc)
17350 Main St, Monkland, ON, K0C 1V0
(613) 346-2154
Emp Here 24
SIC 5144 Poultry and poultry products

Moonstone, ON L0K
Simcoe County

D-U-N-S 20-711-2041   (BR)
SIMCOE COUNTY DISTRICT SCHOOL BOARD, THE
MOONSTONE ELEMENTARY
(*Suby of* Simcoe County District School Board, The)
290 Moonstone Rd E, Moonstone, ON, L0K 1N0
(705) 835-2021
Emp Here 20
SIC 8211 Elementary and secondary schools

Moorefield, ON N0G
Wellington County

D-U-N-S 24-887-9244   (BR)
DARLING INTERNATIONAL CANADA INC
ROTHSAY
(*Suby of* Darling Ingredients Inc.)
8406 Wellington County Rr, Moorefield, ON, N0G 2K0
(519) 638-3081
Emp Here 100
SIC 4953 Refuse systems

Mooretown, ON N0N
Lambton County

D-U-N-S 20-402-2586   (BR)
ENBRIDGE GAS DISTRIBUTION INC
3595 Tecumseh Rd, Mooretown, ON, N0N 1M0
(519) 862-1473
Emp Here 40
SIC 4924 Natural gas distribution

D-U-N-S 20-710-4733   (BR)
LAMBTON KENT DISTRICT SCHOOL BOARD
MOORETOWN COURTRIGHT PUBLIC SCHOOL
104 Moore Line, Mooretown, ON, N0N 1M0
(519) 867-2836
Emp Here 50
SIC 8211 Elementary and secondary schools

D-U-N-S 24-101-0722   (BR)
SUNCOR ENERGY INC
535 Rokeby Line Rr 1, Mooretown, ON, N0N 1M0
(519) 481-0454
Emp Here 100
SIC 2911 Petroleum refining

Moose Creek, ON K0C
Stormont County

D-U-N-S 20-711-6661   (BR)
CONSEIL SCOLAIRE DE DISTRICT CATHOLIQUE DE L'EST ONTARIEN
ECOLE ELEMENTAIRE CATHOLIQUE LA SOUCE
17095 Mclean Rd, Moose Creek, ON, K0C 1W0
(613) 538-2401
Emp Here 25
SIC 8211 Elementary and secondary schools

Moose Factory, ON P0L
Cochrane County

D-U-N-S 25-690-3279   (SL)
MOCREEBEC CONSUL OF THE CREE NATION
22 Nooki-June-I-Beg Rd, Moose Factory, ON, P0L 1W0
(705) 658-4769
Emp Here 40   *Sales* 12,359,040
SIC 8399 Social services, nec
Dir George Small Jr
Allan Jolly

D-U-N-S 20-029-8367   (BR)
MOOSE CREE EDUCATION AUTHORITY
DELORES D ECHUM COMPOSITE SCHOOL
28 Amisk St, Moose Factory, ON, P0L 1W0
(705) 658-5610
Emp Here 25
SIC 8211 Elementary and secondary schools

D-U-N-S 20-656-2311   (BR)
MOOSE FACTORY ISLAND DISTRICT SCHOOL AREA BOARD

MINISTIK PUBLIC SCHOOL
(*Suby of* Moose Factory Island District School Area Board)
9 Hordan St, Moose Factory, ON, P0L 1W0
(705) 658-4535
Emp Here 31
SIC 8211 Elementary and secondary schools

D-U-N-S 24-915-4584   (BR)
NORTH WEST COMPANY LP, THE
NORTHERN STORES
1 Mookijunabeg Dr, Moose Factory, ON, P0L 1W0
(705) 658-4522
Emp Here 45
SIC 5411 Grocery stores

Moosonee, ON P0L
Cochrane County

D-U-N-S 24-859-7205   (BR)
NORTH WEST COMPANY LP, THE
NORTHERN STORES
20 1st St, Moosonee, ON, P0L 1Y0
(705) 336-2280
Emp Here 65
SIC 5411 Grocery stores

D-U-N-S 24-349-9154   (BR)
NORTHEASTERN CATHOLIC DISTRICT SCHOOL BOARD
BISHOP BELLEAU SCHOOL
24 Bay Rd, Moosonee, ON, P0L 1Y0
(705) 336-2619
Emp Here 25
SIC 8211 Elementary and secondary schools

Morrisburg, ON K0C
Dundas County

D-U-N-S 20-590-7285   (BR)
CATHOLIC DISTRICT SCHOOL BOARD OF EASTERN ONTARIO
ST MARY ST CECILIA CATHOLIC SCHOOL
40 Augusta St, Morrisburg, ON, K0C 1X0
(613) 543-2907
Emp Here 25
SIC 8211 Elementary and secondary schools

D-U-N-S 20-022-8067   (BR)
CHARTWELL RETIREMENT RESIDENCES
CHARTWELL SENIORS HOUSING REAL ESTATE INVESTMENT TRUST
3 Fifth St W, Morrisburg, ON, K0C 1X0
(613) 543-3984
Emp Here 30
SIC 6513 Apartment building operators

D-U-N-S 20-577-8103   (SL)
ECKEL INDUSTRIES OF CANADA LIMITED
(*Suby of* Eckel Industries, Inc.)
35 Allison Ave, Morrisburg, ON, K0C 1X0
(613) 543-2967
Emp Here 50   *Sales* 4,591,130
SIC 3625 Relays and industrial controls

D-U-N-S 25-374-0203   (SL)
EVONIK OIL ADDITIVES CANADA IN
12695 County Road 28, Morrisburg, ON, K0C 1X0
(613) 543-2983
Emp Here 32   *Sales* 9,894,455
SIC 5169 Chemicals and allied products, nec
Pr Carmine Bonacci

D-U-N-S 25-279-6289   (BR)
INTERNATIONAL UNION OF OPERATING ENGINEERS LOCAL 793
OPERATING ENGINEERS TRAINING INSTITUTION OF ONTARIO
12580 County Road 2, Morrisburg, ON, K0C 1X0

(613) 543-2911
Emp Here 30
SIC 8331 Job training and related services

D-U-N-S 25-057-7178   (SL)
MCINTOSH COUNTRY INN INC
*MCINTOSH COUNTRY INN & CONFER-
ENCE CENTER*
12495 County Road 28, Morrisburg, ON, K0C
1X0
(613) 543-3788
Emp Here 60   *Sales* 2,626,585
SIC 7011 Hotels and motels

D-U-N-S 20-711-5648   (BR)
**UPPER CANADA DISTRICT SCHOOL
BOARD, THE**
MORRISBURG PUBLIC SCHOOL
16 Second St, Morrisburg, ON, K0C 1X0
(613) 543-3166
Emp Here 22
SIC 8211 Elementary and secondary schools

Morriston, ON N0B
Wellington County

D-U-N-S 25-726-2204   (SL)
LLEWELLYN GROUP INC, THE
107 Queen St Ss 1, Morriston, ON, N0B 2C0

Emp Here 49   *Sales* 9,847,040
SIC 6211 Security brokers and dealers
Pr Ian Mitchell

Mount Albert, ON L0G
York County

D-U-N-S 24-803-0475   (SL)
2034301 ONTARIO INC
APOGEE INTERACTIVE
(*Suby of* Seaboard Technologies Inc)
151 King St Ss 2, Mount Albert, ON, L0G 1M0
(416) 779-4879
Emp Here 200   *Sales* 13,055,280
SIC 7389 Business services, nec
Pr Pr Walter Wakulowsky
VP VP Arzu Wakulowksy

D-U-N-S 25-119-3496   (BR)
SOBEYS CAPITAL INCORPORATED
MOUNT ALBERT IGA
19263 48 Hwy, Mount Albert, ON, L0G 1M0
(905) 473-7406
Emp Here 60
SIC 5411 Grocery stores

D-U-N-S 25-293-6067   (BR)
YORK REGION DISTRICT SCHOOL BOARD
MOUNT ALBERT PUBLIC SCHOOL
(*Suby of* York Region District School Board)
5488 Mount Albert Rd, Mount Albert, ON, L0G
1M0
(905) 473-2940
Emp Here 60
SIC 8211 Elementary and secondary schools

Mount Brydges, ON N0L
Middlesex County

D-U-N-S 20-807-7078   (BR)
TT GROUP LIMITED
643 Railroad St, Mount Brydges, ON, N0L
1W0
(519) 264-1551
Emp Here 20
SIC 4783 Packing and crating

D-U-N-S 25-249-0347   (BR)
**THAMES VALLEY DISTRICT SCHOOL
BOARD**

CARADOC CENTRAL PUBLIC SCHOOL
714 Bowan St, Mount Brydges, ON, N0L 1W0
(519) 264-1630
Emp Here 27
SIC 8211 Elementary and secondary schools

Mount Elgin, ON N0J
Oxford County

D-U-N-S 24-190-0810   (HQ)
A S B GREENWORLD LTD
332911 Plank Line, Mount Elgin, ON, N0J 1N0
(519) 688-3413
Emp Here 38   *Emp Total* 232
Sales 2,921,220
SIC 1499 Miscellaneous nonMetallic minerals,
except fuels

Mount Forest, ON N0G
Wellington County

D-U-N-S 20-805-0075   (BR)
ACME UNITED LIMITED
(*Suby of* Acme United Corporation)
351 Foster St, Mount Forest, ON, N0G 2L1
(519) 323-3101
Emp Here 24
SIC 5044 Office equipment

D-U-N-S 25-634-6479   (BR)
**COMMUNITY LIVING GUELPH WELLING-
TON**
135 Fergus St S, Mount Forest, ON, N0G 2L2
(519) 323-4050
Emp Here 75
SIC 8322 Individual and family services

D-U-N-S 25-221-2147   (BR)
DANA CANADA CORPORATION
POWER TECHNOLOGIES GROUP
205 Industrial Dr, Mount Forest, ON, N0G 2L1
(519) 323-9494
Emp Here 210
SIC 3443 Fabricated plate work (boiler shop)

D-U-N-S 25-458-9088   (BR)
L & M FOOD MARKET (ONTARIO) LIMITED
445 Main St N, Mount Forest, ON, N0G 2L1

Emp Here 30
SIC 5411 Grocery stores

D-U-N-S 25-076-4164   (SL)
SAUGEEN VALLEY NURSING CENTER LTD
465 Dublin St, Mount Forest, ON, N0G 2L3
(519) 323-2140
Emp Here 85   *Sales* 3,866,917
SIC 8051 Skilled nursing care facilities

D-U-N-S 25-370-8556   (BR)
SOLOWAVE DESIGN INC
(*Suby of* Solowave Investments Limited)
375 Sligo Rd W Ss 1 Suite 1, Mount Forest,
ON, N0G 2L0
(519) 323-3833
Emp Here 96
SIC 3949 Sporting and athletic goods, nec

D-U-N-S 25-920-8312   (BR)
**UPPER GRAND DISTRICT SCHOOL
BOARD, THE**
VICTORIA CROSS PUBLIC SCHOOL
(*Suby of* Upper Grand District School Board,
The)
355 Durham St W Suite 1, Mount Forest, ON,
N0G 2L1
(519) 323-2460
Emp Here 30
SIC 8211 Elementary and secondary schools

D-U-N-S 20-861-2361   (BR)
VICTORIAN ORDER OF NURSES FOR

CANADA
SENIORS DAY OUT
392 Main St N Suite 4, Mount Forest, ON, N0G
2L2
(519) 323-9354
Emp Here 20
SIC 8082 Home health care services

D-U-N-S 24-086-4160   (BR)
VIKING-CIVES, LTD
VIKING SOUTH PLANT
555 Perth St, Mount Forest, ON, N0G 2L1
(519) 323-4137
Emp Here 125
SIC 4212 Local trucking, without storage

D-U-N-S 25-877-9081   (BR)
**WASTE MANAGEMENT OF CANADA COR-
PORATION**
(*Suby of* Waste Management, Inc.)
200 Sligo Rd W, Mount Forest, ON, N0G 2L1
(519) 323-3682
Emp Here 50
SIC 4953 Refuse systems

Mount Hope, ON L0R
Wentworth County

D-U-N-S 25-279-2879   (BR)
CARGOJET INC
CARGOJET
9300 Airport Rd Suite 320, Mount Hope, ON,
L0R 1W0
(905) 679-0038
Emp Here 200
SIC 4512 Air transportation, scheduled

D-U-N-S 20-066-8908   (BR)
CITY OF HAMILTON, THE
*DISABLED & AGED REGIONAL TRANSIT
SYSTEM*
3027 Homestead Dr, Mount Hope, ON, L0R
1W0
(905) 529-1212
Emp Here 130
SIC 4111 Local and suburban transit

D-U-N-S 20-026-6984   (BR)
**HAMILTON-WENTWORTH   DISTRICT
SCHOOL BOARD, THE**
MOUNT HOPE PUBLIC SCHOOL
9149 Airport Rd, Mount Hope, ON, L0R 1W0
(905) 977-7004
Emp Here 25
SIC 8211 Elementary and secondary schools

D-U-N-S 24-335-6628   (BR)
KELOWNA FLIGHTCRAFT LTD
9500 Airport Rd, Mount Hope, ON, L0R 1W0
(905) 679-3313
Emp Here 145
SIC 4581 Airports, flying fields, and services

D-U-N-S 24-117-4239   (BR)
PUROLATOR INC.
PUROLATOR INC
9300 Airport Rd, Mount Hope, ON, L0R 1W0
(905) 679-5722
Emp Here 150
SIC 7389 Business services, nec

D-U-N-S 20-003-0117   (BR)
UNITED PARCEL SERVICE CANADA LTD
UPS
9272 Airport Rd, Mount Hope, ON, L0R 1W0
(905) 679-7290
Emp Here 50
SIC 7389 Business services, nec

D-U-N-S 25-119-3736   (SL)
WILLOW VALLEY GOLF INC
WILLOW VALLEY GOLF COURSE
2907 Hwy 6 S, Mount Hope, ON, L0R 1W0
(905) 679-2703
Emp Here 50   *Sales* 2,188,821

SIC 7992 Public golf courses

Mountain Grove, ON K0H

D-U-N-S 20-711-4732   (BR)
LIMESTONE DISTRICT SCHOOL BOARD
LAND O LAKES SCHOOL
1447 Mountain Grove Rd, Mountain Grove,
ON, K0H 2E0
(613) 335-5254
Emp Here 20
SIC 8211 Elementary and secondary schools

Munster, ON K0A
Carleton County

D-U-N-S 25-238-1546   (BR)
**OTTAWA-CARLETON DISTRICT SCHOOL
BOARD**
MUNSTER ELEMENTARY SCHOOL
7816 Bleeks Rd, Munster, ON, K0A 3P0
(613) 838-3133
Emp Here 20
SIC 8211 Elementary and secondary schools

Nairn Centre, ON P0M
Sudbury County

D-U-N-S 24-138-5228   (BR)
EACOM TIMBER CORPORATION
EACOM TIMBER CORPORATION
100 Old Nairn Rd, Nairn Centre, ON, P0M 2L0
(705) 869-4020
Emp Here 90
SIC 2421 Sawmills and planing mills, general

D-U-N-S 24-873-4683   (BR)
NOCO CANADA INC
JEREMY'S TRUCK STOP & RESTAURANT
220 17 Hwy W, Nairn Centre, ON, P0M 2L0
(705) 869-4100
Emp Here 38
SIC 5541 Gasoline service stations

Nanticoke, ON N0A
Haldimand County

D-U-N-S 24-107-8471   (BR)
AIR PRODUCTS CANADA LTD
(*Suby of* Air Products and Chemicals, Inc.)
2100 Regional Rd 3, Nanticoke, ON, N0A 1L0
(519) 587-2401
Emp Here 50
SIC 2813 Industrial gases

D-U-N-S 24-564-7862   (BR)
CHARLES JONES INDUSTRIAL LIMITED
4 Hawk St Suite 900, Nanticoke, ON, N0A 1L0
(519) 587-2283
Emp Here 65
SIC 5085 Industrial supplies

D-U-N-S 24-318-7887   (BR)
ONTARIO POWER GENERATION INC
*ONTARIO POWER GENERATION NANTI-
COKE*
34 Regional Rd 55, Nanticoke, ON, N0A 1L0
(519) 587-2201
Emp Here 600
SIC 4911 Electric services

Napanee, ON K7R
Lennox County

D-U-N-S 25-110-5201　(BR)
ALGONQUIN & LAKESHORE CATHOLIC DISTRICT SCHOOL BOARD
J J O'NEILL CATHOLIC SCHOOL
240 Marilyn Ave, Napanee, ON, K7R 2L4
(613) 354-9500
Emp Here 25
SIC 8211 Elementary and secondary schools

D-U-N-S 20-649-3967　(SL)
BAG TO EARTH INC
201 Richmond Blvd, Napanee, ON, K7R 3Z9
(613) 354-1330
Emp Here 40　*Sales* 5,836,856
SIC 2674 Bags: uncoated paper and multiwall
Dir Louis P Meehan
Pr Pr George P Colgan
Dir Sidney Y Dick
Dir John W Welton
Dir Steve Shaver
Dir Dennis Barham
Dir David M Welton

D-U-N-S 25-862-8098　(SL)
BOYER, PETER CHEVROLET PONTIAC BUICK LTD
401 Hwy 41, Napanee, ON, K7R 3L1
(613) 354-2166
Emp Here 25　*Sales* 12,342,500
SIC 5511 New and used car dealers

D-U-N-S 25-674-0226　(BR)
C.A.T. INC
CANADIAN AMERICAN TRANSPORTATION
(*Suby of* Holding Canadian American Transportation C.A.T. Inc)
505 Goodyear Rd, Napanee, ON, K7R 3L2
(613) 354-0282
Emp Here 45
SIC 4213 Trucking, except local

D-U-N-S 20-543-1062　(BR)
CANADA POST CORPORATION
NAPANEE STATION MAIN
124 Centre St N, Napanee, ON, K7R 1N3
(613) 354-3711
Emp Here 40
SIC 4311 U.s. postal service

D-U-N-S 25-115-5479　(BR)
CINTAS CANADA LIMITED
(*Suby of* Cintas Corporation)
126 Vanluven Rd, Napanee, ON, K7R 3L2

Emp Here 30
SIC 7218 Industrial launderers

D-U-N-S 25-176-3868　(BR)
CROWN RIDGE HEALTH CARE SERVICES INC
RIVERINE, THE
328 Dundas St W Suite 222, Napanee, ON, K7R 4B5
(613) 354-8188
Emp Here 30
SIC 6513 Apartment building operators

D-U-N-S 25-842-5060　(BR)
DENCAN RESTAURANTS INC
DENNY'S RESTAURANT
(*Suby of* Northland Properties Corporation)
628 County Rd 1, Napanee, ON, K7R 3L2
(613) 354-3556
Emp Here 25
SIC 5812 Eating places

D-U-N-S 25-185-0848　(HQ)
FLYING J CANADA INC
FLYING J TRAVEL PLAZA
628 County Rd 41, Napanee, ON, K7R 3L1
(613) 354-7044
Emp Here 30　*Emp Total* 15,800
Sales 68,695,784
SIC 5541 Gasoline service stations
Genl Mgr Mark Ford

D-U-N-S 20-287-8372　(BR)

G.T. MACHINING & FABRICATING LTD
7 Kellwood Cres, Napanee, ON, K7R 4A1
(613) 354-6621
Emp Here 92
SIC 3443 Fabricated plate work (boiler shop)

D-U-N-S 24-889-5542　(BR)
GOODYEAR CANADA INC
GOODYEAR NAPANEE TIRE MANUFAC-TURING FACILITY
(*Suby of* The Goodyear Tire & Rubber Company)
388 Goodyear Rd, Napanee, ON, K7R 3L2
(613) 354-7411
Emp Here 500
SIC 3011 Tires and inner tubes

D-U-N-S 25-078-4055　(SL)
LENNOX AND ADDINGTON COUNTY GENERAL HOSPITAL ASSOCIATION
L & A HOSPITAL
8 Richmond Park Dr, Napanee, ON, K7R 2Z4
(613) 354-3301
Emp Here 175　*Sales* 21,711,878
SIC 8062 General medical and surgical hospitals
Wayne Coveyduck
Ch Bd Allan Macgregor
Treas Deb Lowry

D-U-N-S 25-263-6238　(BR)
LIMESTONE DISTRICT SCHOOL BOARD
WESTDALE PARK PUBLIC SCHOOL
12 Richmond Park Dr, Napanee, ON, K7R 2Z5
(613) 354-4596
Emp Here 30
SIC 8211 Elementary and secondary schools

D-U-N-S 25-237-9409　(BR)
LIMESTONE DISTRICT SCHOOL BOARD
H H LANGFORD PUBLIC SCHOOL
840 County Rd 8, Napanee, ON, K7R 3K7
(613) 354-5171
Emp Here 24
SIC 8211 Elementary and secondary schools

D-U-N-S 25-354-0645　(BR)
LIMESTONE DISTRICT SCHOOL BOARD
NAPANEE DISTRICT SECONDARY SCHOOL
245 Belleville Rd, Napanee, ON, K7R 3M7
(613) 354-3381
Emp Here 240
SIC 8211 Elementary and secondary schools

D-U-N-S 25-263-6279　(BR)
LIMESTONE DISTRICT SCHOOL BOARD
PRINCE CHARLES SCHOOL, THE
75 Graham St W, Napanee, ON, K7R 2J9
(613) 354-2121
Emp Here 50
SIC 8211 Elementary and secondary schools

D-U-N-S 24-009-6941　(SL)
MARTIN, C. BUS SERVICE LIMITED
MARTIN'S BUS SERVICE
106 Advance Ave, Napanee, ON, K7R 3Y6
(613) 354-7545
Emp Here 80　*Sales* 2,921,220
SIC 4151 School buses

D-U-N-S 20-131-6957　(HQ)
MCKEOWN AND WOOD FUELS LIMITED
(*Suby of* Mckeown and Wood Fuels limited)
373 Centre St N, Napanee, ON, K7R 1P7
(613) 354-6505
Emp Here 20　*Emp Total* 22
Sales 9,231,950
SIC 5172 Petroleum products, nec
Pr Pr James A Wood

D-U-N-S 25-300-0566　(BR)
METRO ONTARIO INC
METRO
35 Alkenbrack St, Napanee, ON, K7R 4C4
(613) 354-2882
Emp Here 170

SIC 5411 Grocery stores

D-U-N-S 24-845-2039　(SL)
MITECH MACHINE & FABRICATION LTD
292 Kimmet'S Side Rd, Napanee, ON, K7R 3L2
(613) 354-7403
Emp Here 25　*Sales* 2,355,823
SIC 3599 Industrial machinery, nec

D-U-N-S 24-223-2317　(BR)
PRISZM LP
PIZZA HUT
1 Richmond Blvd Unit B1, Napanee, ON, K7R 3S3
(613) 354-4344
Emp Here 30
SIC 5812 Eating places

D-U-N-S 20-968-6757　(BR)
STRATHCONA PAPER LP
77 County Rd 16, Napanee, ON, K7R 3L2
(613) 378-6672
Emp Here 172
SIC 2631 Paperboard mills

D-U-N-S 25-310-9110　(BR)
TAYLYX LTD
MCDONALD'S RESTAURANT
475 Centre St N, Napanee, ON, K7R 3S4
(613) 354-9707
Emp Here 85
SIC 5812 Eating places

D-U-N-S 25-322-2228　(BR)
TORONTO-DOMINION BANK, THE
TD BANK
(*Suby of* Toronto-Dominion Bank, The)
24 Dundas St E, Napanee, ON, K7R 1H6
(613) 354-2137
Emp Here 20
SIC 6021 National commercial banks

Navan, ON K4B
Carleton County

D-U-N-S 24-848-4099　(SL)
BRADLEY, M L LIMITED
3406 Frank Kenny Rd, Navan, ON, K4B 0C5
(613) 835-2488
Emp Here 72　*Sales* 2,553,625
SIC 4111 Local and suburban transit

D-U-N-S 25-772-1209　(BR)
CLUBLINK CORPORATION ULC
GREYHAWK GOLF CLUB
(*Suby of* TWC Enterprises Limited)
4999 Boundary Rd, Navan, ON, K4B 1P5
(613) 822-1454
Emp Here 80
SIC 7992 Public golf courses

D-U-N-S 20-556-1058　(BR)
MAPLE LEAF FOODS INC
ROTHSAY LAURENCO
5507 Boundary Rd, Navan, ON, K4B 1P6
(613) 822-6818
Emp Here 45
SIC 7359 Equipment rental and leasing, nec

D-U-N-S 24-950-5566　(BR)
WASTE CONNECTIONS OF CANADA INC
BFI CANADA
3354 Navan Rd, Navan, ON, K4B 1H9
(613) 824-7289
Emp Here 25
SIC 4953 Refuse systems

Nepean, ON K2B

D-U-N-S 20-860-4822　(BR)
BOUTIQUE LA VIE EN ROSE INC

BOUTIQUE LA VIE EN ROSE INC
100 Bayshore Dr Unit 54, Nepean, ON, K2B 8C1
(613) 828-8383
Emp Here 25
SIC 5632 Women's accessory and specialty stores

D-U-N-S 20-002-8301　(BR)
GAP (CANADA) INC
GAP
(*Suby of* The Gap Inc)
100 Bayshore Dr, Nepean, ON, K2B 8C1
(613) 828-8131
Emp Here 30
SIC 5651 Family clothing stores

D-U-N-S 20-863-0637　(BR)
GAP (CANADA) INC
BANANA REPUBLIC
(*Suby of* The Gap Inc)
100 Bayshore Dr Unit D12, Nepean, ON, K2B 8C1
(613) 721-1129
Emp Here 30
SIC 5651 Family clothing stores

D-U-N-S 25-265-2649　(BR)
OTTAWA CATHOLIC DISTRICT SCHOOL BOARD
BAYSHORE CATHOLIC SCHOOL
(*Suby of* Ottawa Catholic District School Board)
50 Bayshore Dr, Nepean, ON, K2B 6M8
(613) 828-5158
Emp Here 20
SIC 8211 Elementary and secondary schools

D-U-N-S 25-263-5875　(BR)
OTTAWA-CARLETON DISTRICT SCHOOL BOARD
BAYSHORE PUBLIC SCHOOL
145 Woodridge Cres, Nepean, ON, K2B 7T2
(613) 828-8698
Emp Here 40
SIC 8211 Elementary and secondary schools

D-U-N-S 25-983-6021　(SL)
WAHA ENTERPRISES INC
MOXIE'S CLASSIC GRILL
100 Bayshore Dr, Nepean, ON, K2B 8C1
(613) 721-2918
Emp Here 80　*Sales* 2,407,703
SIC 5812 Eating places

D-U-N-S 24-312-4356　(BR)
WINNERS MERCHANTS INTERNATIONAL L.P.
WINNERS
(*Suby of* The TJX Companies Inc)
100 Bayshore Dr, Nepean, ON, K2B 8C1
(613) 721-6451
Emp Here 80
SIC 5651 Family clothing stores

Nepean, ON K2C

D-U-N-S 20-571-8567　(BR)
ARBOR MEMORIAL SERVICES INC
CAPITOL FUNERAL & CEMETARY
3700 Prince Of Wales Dr, Nepean, ON, K2C 3H2
(613) 692-1211
Emp Here 20
SIC 7261 Funeral service and crematories

D-U-N-S 25-130-6841　(BR)
MATTAMY (MONARCH) LIMITED
MONARCH HOMES
3584 Jockvale Rd, Nepean, ON, K2C 3H2
(613) 692-8672
Emp Here 30
SIC 8742 Management consulting services

D-U-N-S 24-101-9140　(BR)

MEMORIAL GARDENS CANADA LIMITED
CAPITAL MEMORIAL GARDENS
3700 Prince Of Wales Dr, Nepean, ON, K2C
3H2
(613) 692-3588
Emp Here 23
SIC 6531 Real estate agents and managers

D-U-N-S 25-357-7274   (SL)
STAR GROUP INTERNATIONAL TRADING CORPORATION
STAR GROUP INTERNATIONAL
3971 Greenbank Rd, Nepean, ON, K2C 3H2
(613) 692-6640
Emp Here 22   *Sales* 1,313,293
SIC 8741 Management services

D-U-N-S 25-822-1167   (BR)
THEODORE RESTAURANTS INC
BROADWAY PROMOTIONS
(*Suby of* Theodore Restaurants Inc)
1896 Prince Of Wales Dr Suite 1, Nepean,
ON, K2C 3W9
(613) 224-6556
Emp Here 35
SIC 5812 Eating places

D-U-N-S 25-784-1684   (BR)
THEODORE RESTAURANTS INC
BROADWAY BAR & GRILL CENTRAL
(*Suby of* Theodore Restaurants Inc)
1896 Prince Of Wales Dr Suite 12, Nepean,
ON, K2C 3W9
(613) 224-7004
Emp Here 50
SIC 5812 Eating places

Nepean, ON K2E

D-U-N-S 25-144-0699   (SL)
1048536 ONTARIO LTD
UNICLEAN BUILDING MAINTENANCE
148 Colonnade Rd Suite 13, Nepean, ON,
K2E 7R4
(613) 727-0413
Emp Here 160   *Sales* 4,669,485
SIC 7349 Building maintenance services, nec

D-U-N-S 20-013-1584   (SL)
1120919 ONTARIO LTD
PHOENIX HOMES
18 Bentley Ave Suite A, Nepean, ON, K2E 6T8
(613) 723-9227
Emp Here 60   *Sales* 11,590,647
SIC 1521 Single-family housing construction
Pr Pr Cuckoo Kochar

D-U-N-S 20-788-8512   (SL)
1597686 ONTARIO INC
9 Antares Dr, Nepean, ON, K2E 7V5

Emp Here 70   *Sales* 8,521,800
SIC 1711 Plumbing, heating, air-conditioning
Dir Gary Beatty
Pr Pr Ken Boyd
Fin Ex Jim Wise

D-U-N-S 25-246-9028   (SL)
393450 ONTARIO LIMITED
MONTEREY INN RESORT & CONFERENCE CENTER
2259 Prince Of Wales Dr, Nepean, ON, K2E
6Z8
(613) 226-5813
Emp Here 60   *Sales* 2,626,585
SIC 7011 Hotels and motels

D-U-N-S 20-114-8678   (SL)
969200 ONTARIO LIMITED
195 Colonnade Rd, Nepean, ON, K2E 7K3
(613) 226-3830
Emp Here 49   *Sales* 6,594,250
SIC 1752 Floor laying and floor work, nec
Pr Pr Steven Kimmel

D-U-N-S 20-205-8207   (BR)
AMEC FOSTER WHEELER AMERICAS LIMITED
AMEC EARTH & ENVIRONMENTAL, DIV OF
210 Colonnade Rd Suite 300, Nepean, ON,
K2E 7L5
(613) 727-0658
Emp Here 35
SIC 8711 Engineering services

D-U-N-S 25-144-2109   (BR)
AMEC FOSTER WHEELER AMERICAS LIMITED
AMEC EARTH & ENVIRONMENTAL DIVISION
210 Colonnade Rd Unit 300, Nepean, ON,
K2E 7L5
(613) 727-0658
Emp Here 30
SIC 8748 Business consulting, nec

D-U-N-S 20-893-0602   (SL)
ADVANCE DRYWALL LTD
44 Bentley Ave, Nepean, ON, K2E 6T8
(613) 226-7722
Emp Here 50   *Sales* 4,231,721
SIC 1742 Plastering, drywall, and insulation

D-U-N-S 20-350-6923   (BR)
ALTUS GEOMATICS LIMITED PARTNERSHIP
ALTUS GROUP
14 Colonnade Rd Suite 150, Nepean, ON,
K2E 7M6
(613) 721-1333
Emp Here 25
SIC 8713 Surveying services

D-U-N-S 20-107-5715   (BR)
AVNET INTERNATIONAL (CANADA) LTD
AVNET COMPUTER ENTERPRISES SOLUTION DIVISION
(*Suby of* Avnet, Inc.)
190 Colonnade Rd Suite A, Nepean, ON, K2E
7J5
(613) 226-1700
Emp Here 20
SIC 5065 Electronic parts and equipment, nec

D-U-N-S 20-535-8810   (BR)
BANK OF MONTREAL
BMO
1454 Merivale Rd, Nepean, ON, K2E 5P1
(613) 564-6100
Emp Here 20
SIC 6021 National commercial banks

D-U-N-S 24-366-5585   (BR)
BELL MEDIA INC
BELL MEDIA INC
1504 Merivale Rd, Nepean, ON, K2E 6Z5
(613) 225-1069
Emp Here 30
SIC 4832 Radio broadcasting stations

D-U-N-S 24-375-8351   (BR)
CANADA POST CORPORATION
141 Colonnade Rd, Nepean, ON, K2E 7L9
(613) 764-1008
Emp Here 20
SIC 4311 U.s. postal service

D-U-N-S 20-105-2854   (BR)
CANADIAN BANK NOTE COMPANY, LIMITED
18 Auriga Dr Suite 200, Nepean, ON, K2E 7T9
(613) 225-3018
Emp Here 100
SIC 2796 Platemaking services

D-U-N-S 25-777-5478   (BR)
CANADIAN BANK NOTE COMPANY, LIMITED
CANADIAN BANK NOTE
18 Auriga Dr, Nepean, ON, K2E 7T9
(613) 722-6607
Emp Here 250
SIC 2759 Commercial printing, nec

D-U-N-S 24-423-6860   (SL)
CANADIAN SCIENCE PUBLISHING (CSP)
NRC RESEARCH PRESS
65 Auriga Dr Suite 203, Nepean, ON, K2E
7W6
(613) 656-9846
Emp Here 55   *Sales* 8,128,094
SIC 2721 Periodicals
Ex Dir Cameron Macdonald
Dir Michael Boroczki

D-U-N-S 25-683-7691   (HQ)
CISTEL TECHNOLOGY INC
(*Suby of* Cistel Technology Inc)
30 Concourse Gate Suite 200, Nepean, ON,
K2E 7V7
(613) 723-8344
Emp Here 27   *Emp Total* 75
Sales 7,536,000
SIC 7379 Computer related services, nec
Pr Pr Nishith Goel

D-U-N-S 25-265-2961   (BR)
CONSEIL DES ECOLES CATHOLIQUES DE LANGUE FRANCAISE DU CENTRE-EST
ECOLE LAURIER-CARRIERE
14 Four Seasons Dr, Nepean, ON, K2E 7P8

Emp Here 20
SIC 8211 Elementary and secondary schools

D-U-N-S 25-287-5349   (HQ)
COSTCO WHOLESALE CANADA LTD
(*Suby of* Costco Wholesale Corporation)
415 West Hunt Club Rd, Nepean, ON, K2E
1C5
(613) 221-2010
Emp Here 190   *Emp Total* 218,000
Sales 1,498,539,817
SIC 5099 Durable goods, nec
Dir Joseph P Portera
  Ross Hunt
Sec Joel Benoliel
Sec Richard Olin
  Richard Galanti
Dir Hubert De Suduiraut
Dir Stuart Shamis
Dir Louise Wendling

D-U-N-S 24-437-9848   (SL)
DELTA PRINTING LIMITED
47 Antares Dr, Nepean, ON, K2E 7W6
(613) 736-7777
Emp Here 60   *Sales* 2,991,389
SIC 2759 Commercial printing, nec

D-U-N-S 25-672-4634   (HQ)
DONNA CONA INC
(*Suby of* Donna Cona Enterprises Corp)
106 Colonnade Rd Suite 100, Nepean, ON,
K2E 7L6
(613) 234-5407
Emp Here 30   *Emp Total* 41
Sales 5,526,400
SIC 8742 Management consulting services
Pr Pr John Bernard
  Barry Dowdall
  Gary Fox

D-U-N-S 25-292-2398   (BR)
DYNAMEX CANADA LIMITED
60 Colonnade Rd Unit K, Nepean, ON, K2E
7J6
(613) 226-4463
Emp Here 40
SIC 7389 Business services, nec

D-U-N-S 24-662-2047   (BR)
ERB TRANSPORT LIMITED
ERB TRANSPORT LIMITED
182 Colonnade Rd, Nepean, ON, K2E 7J5
(613) 226-1358
Emp Here 73
SIC 4213 Trucking, except local

D-U-N-S 25-813-0731   (BR)
EXP SERVICES INC
154 Colonnade Rd, Nepean, ON, K2E 7J5

(613) 225-9940
Emp Here 100
SIC 8711 Engineering services

D-U-N-S 20-507-0972   (BR)
EASTERN ONTARIO WATER TECHNOLOGY LTD
OTTAWA WATER CONDITIONING
78 Auriga Dr Suite 1, Nepean, ON, K2E 7X7
(613) 225-9175
Emp Here 42
SIC 5999 Miscellaneous retail stores, nec

D-U-N-S 20-700-6115   (BR)
ENERGIE VALERO INC
ULTRAMAR
2 Gurdwara Rd Suite 400, Nepean, ON, K2E
1A2
(613) 727-5500
Emp Here 48
SIC 8741 Management services

D-U-N-S 24-369-3277   (BR)
EXOVA CANADA INC
EXOVA ACCUTEST
(*Suby of* Exova, Inc.)
146 Colonnade Rd Unit 8, Nepean, ON, K2E
7Y1
(613) 727-5692
Emp Here 50
SIC 8731 Commercial physical research

D-U-N-S 24-719-2180   (HQ)
FISHER SCIENTIFIC COMPANY
(*Suby of* Thermo Fisher Scientific Inc.)
112 Colonnade Rd, Nepean, ON, K2E 7L6
(613) 226-8874
Emp Here 180   *Emp Total* 55,000
Sales 56,909,346
SIC 5049 Professional equipment, nec
Pr John Tourlas
  Mike Aronson
  Sue Hannah
  Heidi Kornherr
  Bob Thompson

D-U-N-S 24-779-2450   (SL)
FRANCIS FUELS LTD
28 Concourse Gate Suite 105, Nepean, ON,
K2E 7T7
(613) 723-4567
Emp Here 55   *Sales* 16,196,400
SIC 5983 Fuel oil dealers
  William J Francis
Pr Brent Francis

D-U-N-S 25-361-0380   (BR)
GHD CONSULTANTS LTEE
INSPEC-SOL
179 Colonnade Rd Suite 400, Nepean, ON,
K2E 7J4
(613) 723-8182
Emp Here 20
SIC 8711 Engineering services

D-U-N-S 24-791-8753   (BR)
GOODLIFE FITNESS CENTRES INC
GOODLIFE FITNESS CLUBS
5 Roydon Pl, Nepean, ON, K2E 1A3
(613) 739-4070
Emp Here 35
SIC 7999 Amusement and recreation, nec

D-U-N-S 24-383-8679   (HQ)
INTELCAN TECHNOSYSTEMS INC
(*Suby of* Whittvest Holdings Limited)
69 Auriga Dr, Nepean, ON, K2E 7Z2
(613) 228-1150
Emp Here 40   *Emp Total* 4
Sales 6,420,542
SIC 3812 Search and navigation equipment
  Michael Lang
  Zvi Glanz
VP Fin Paulina Yee
  Philip Whittall
  Ron Weissberger

D-U-N-S 24-326-0044   (BR)
INTERMAP TECHNOLOGIES CORPORA-

TION
2 Gurdwara Rd Suite 200, Nepean, ON, K2E 1A2

Emp Here 100
SIC 7389 Business services, nec

D-U-N-S 25-315-7598   (BR)
INVESTORS GROUP FINANCIAL SERVICES INC
2 Gurdwara Rd Suite 500, Nepean, ON, K2E 1A2
(613) 723-7200
Emp Here 65
SIC 8741 Management services

D-U-N-S 20-118-7783   (SL)
LS TELCOM LIMITED
1 Antares Dr Suite 510, Nepean, ON, K2E 8C4
(613) 248-8686
Emp Here 20   Sales 1,459,214
SIC 7371 Custom computer programming services

D-U-N-S 25-836-0429   (BR)
LOBLAWS SUPERMARKETS LIMITED
ZIGGYS
1460 Merivale Rd, Nepean, ON, K2E 5P2
(613) 226-6001
Emp Here 1,500
SIC 5411 Grocery stores

D-U-N-S 25-361-5355   (SL)
LONE STAR GROUP OF COMPANIES HOLDINGS INC
32 Colonnade Rd Suite 900, Nepean, ON, K2E 7J6
(613) 727-1966
Emp Here 700   Sales 175,609,950
SIC 6712 Bank holding companies
Dir Barry Shannon

D-U-N-S 25-277-7321   (BR)
MAGASINS HART INC
COMPUSMART
3 Roydon Pl, Nepean, ON, K2E 1A3
(613) 727-0099
Emp Here 40
SIC 5734 Computer and software stores

D-U-N-S 24-827-1723   (BR)
MEDICAL PHARMACIES GROUP LIMITED
MEDICAL PHARMACY
36 Antares Dr Suite 100, Nepean, ON, K2E 7W5

Emp Here 20
SIC 5912 Drug stores and proprietary stores

D-U-N-S 20-707-0835   (BR)
NCR CANADA CORP
(Suby of NCR Corporation)
70 Bentley Ave Suite 206, Nepean, ON, K2E 6T8
(613) 745-6008
Emp Here 20
SIC 5044 Office equipment

D-U-N-S 24-224-5434   (BR)
NASCO FOOD INC
WENDY'S
430 West Hunt Club Rd, Nepean, ON, K2E 1B2
(613) 228-0684
Emp Here 25
SIC 5812 Eating places

D-U-N-S 24-109-0781   (SL)
NEWCAP RADIO OTTAWA
HOT 89 9 FM CIHT
6 Antares Dr Suite 100, Nepean, ON, K2E 8A9
(613) 723-8990
Emp Here 60   Sales 3,793,956
SIC 4832 Radio broadcasting stations

D-U-N-S 20-889-4915   (SL)
OTTAWA BUSINESS INTERIORS LTD
OBI

183 Colonnade Rd Suite 100, Nepean, ON, K2E 7J4
(613) 226-4090
Emp Here 51   Sales 4,085,799
SIC 7359 Equipment rental and leasing, nec

D-U-N-S 20-590-9158   (BR)
OTTAWA CATHOLIC DISTRICT SCHOOL BOARD
ST RITA ELEMENTARY SCHOOL
(Suby of Ottawa Catholic District School Board)
1 Inverness Ave, Nepean, ON, K2E 6N6
(613) 224-6341
Emp Here 25
SIC 8211 Elementary and secondary schools

D-U-N-S 20-802-5697   (BR)
OTTAWA COMMUNITY HOUSING CORPORATION
39 Auriga Dr, Nepean, ON, K2E 7Y8
(613) 731-7223
Emp Here 300
SIC 6531 Real estate agents and managers

D-U-N-S 25-263-5834   (BR)
OTTAWA-CARLETON DISTRICT SCHOOL BOARD
SIR WINSTON CHURCHILL PUBLIC SCHOOL
49 Mulvagh Ave, Nepean, ON, K2E 6M7
(613) 224-2336
Emp Here 35
SIC 8211 Elementary and secondary schools

D-U-N-S 25-263-5578   (BR)
OTTAWA-CARLETON DISTRICT SCHOOL BOARD
PARKWOOD HILLS PUBLIC SCHOOL
60 Tiverton Dr, Nepean, ON, K2E 6L8
(613) 823-3336
Emp Here 30
SIC 8211 Elementary and secondary schools

D-U-N-S 25-263-5925   (BR)
OTTAWA-CARLETON DISTRICT SCHOOL BOARD
CENTURY PUBLIC SCHOOL
8 Redpine Dr, Nepean, ON, K2E 6S9
(613) 224-4903
Emp Here 40
SIC 8211 Elementary and secondary schools

D-U-N-S 20-657-2427   (BR)
PCL CONSTRUCTORS CANADA INC
49 Auriga Dr, Nepean, ON, K2E 8A1
(613) 225-6130
Emp Here 150
SIC 1542 Nonresidential construction, nec

D-U-N-S 25-885-0940   (BR)
PROMARK-TELECON INC
203 Colonnade Rd Unit 10, Nepean, ON, K2E 7K3
(613) 723-9888
Emp Here 150
SIC 1623 Water, sewer, and utility lines

D-U-N-S 24-308-0710   (BR)
PYLON ELECTRONICS INC
147 Colonnade Rd, Nepean, ON, K2E 7L9
(613) 226-7920
Emp Here 45
SIC 3679 Electronic components, nec

D-U-N-S 20-522-2701   (SL)
RESEAUX MERX INC
MERX SERVICE D'APPELS D'OFFRES
38 Antares Dr Suite 1000, Nepean, ON, K2E 7V2
(613) 727-4900
Emp Here 40   Sales 2,918,428
SIC 7379 Computer related services, nec

D-U-N-S 24-105-4691   (BR)
RICOH CANADA INC
2 Gurdwara Rd Suite 102, Nepean, ON, K2E 1A2

(613) 226-8240
Emp Here 25
SIC 5044 Office equipment

D-U-N-S 20-003-8763   (BR)
ROSS VIDEO LIMITED
64 Auriga Dr Suite 1, Nepean, ON, K2E 1B8
(613) 228-0688
Emp Here 200
SIC 3663 Radio and t.v. communications equipment

D-U-N-S 24-556-7339   (BR)
SNC-LAVALIN INC
SNC LAVALIN ENVIRONMENT
20 Colonnade Rd Suite 110, Nepean, ON, K2E 7M6
(416) 635-5882
Emp Here 30
SIC 8748 Business consulting, nec

D-U-N-S 25-769-4885   (BR)
SAINT ELIZABETH HEALTH CARE
30 Colonnade Rd Suite 225, Nepean, ON, K2E 7J6
(613) 738-9661
Emp Here 100
SIC 8059 Nursing and personal care, nec

D-U-N-S 24-830-1509   (SL)
STAIRWORLD INC
110 Bentley Ave Suite 2, Nepean, ON, K2E 6T9
(613) 723-5454
Emp Here 50   Sales 4,085,799
SIC 2431 Millwork

D-U-N-S 24-344-0406   (BR)
SUPERIOR PLUS LP
63 Roydon Pl, Nepean, ON, K2E 1A3
(613) 727-8807
Emp Here 35
SIC 5984 Liquefied petroleum gas dealers

D-U-N-S 20-841-9924   (SL)
TERRAPOINT CANADA INC
1 Antares Dr Suite 140, Nepean, ON, K2E 8C4
(613) 820-4545
Emp Here 49   Sales 60,488,960
SIC 1382 Oil and gas exploration services
Pr James Ferguson
VP Opers Roger Shreenan

D-U-N-S 24-585-8923   (BR)
TYCO INTEGRATED FIRE & SECURITY CANADA, INC
ADT SECURITY SYSTEMS
(Suby of Johnson Controls, Inc.)
14 Concourse Gate Suite 100, Nepean, ON, K2E 7S6
(613) 667-9355
Emp Here 60
SIC 5065 Electronic parts and equipment, nec

D-U-N-S 20-747-0436   (BR)
VIPOND INC
VIPOND FIRE PROTECTION
34 Bentley Ave Unit 201, Nepean, ON, K2E 6T8
(613) 225-0538
Emp Here 25
SIC 7389 Business services, nec

D-U-N-S 25-392-3833   (HQ)
WINFUND SOFTWARE CORP
WINFUND SOFTWARE
2 Gurdwara Rd Suite 206, Nepean, ON, K2E 1A2
(613) 526-1969
Emp Here 45   Emp Total 95
Sales 4,304,681
SIC 7371 Custom computer programming services

Nepean, ON K2G

D-U-N-S 20-802-5820   (SL)
1514444 ONTARIO INC
EAST SIDE MARIO'S
526 West Hunt Club Rd, Nepean, ON, K2G 7B5
(613) 274-2746
Emp Here 70   Sales 2,115,860
SIC 5812 Eating places

D-U-N-S 24-330-7258   (SL)
1716530 ONTARIO INC
PRINCE OF WALES MANOR HOME
22 Barnstone Dr, Nepean, ON, K2G 2P9
(613) 843-9887
Emp Here 50   Sales 4,377,642
SIC 6513 Apartment building operators

D-U-N-S 25-355-1030   (BR)
3499481 CANADA INC
SUPER PET #22
1547 Merivale Rd, Nepean, ON, K2G 4V3
(613) 224-1212
Emp Here 30
SIC 5999 Miscellaneous retail stores, nec

D-U-N-S 25-138-2631   (BR)
429512 ONTARIO LIMITED
ROYAL OAK PUB
117 Centrepointe Dr Suite 117, Nepean, ON, K2G 5X3
(613) 695-2800
Emp Here 20
SIC 5812 Eating places

D-U-N-S 25-212-9572   (BR)
BANK OF NOVA SCOTIA, THE
SCOTIABANK
1649 Merivale Rd, Nepean, ON, K2G 3K2
(613) 226-3983
Emp Here 51
SIC 6021 National commercial banks

D-U-N-S 20-003-0364   (BR)
BANQUE TORONTO-DOMINION, LA
TORONTO-DOMINION BANK, THE
(Suby of Toronto-Dominion Bank, The)
1642 Merivale Rd, Nepean, ON, K2G 4A1
(613) 226-2224
Emp Here 25
SIC 6021 National commercial banks

D-U-N-S 20-191-7718   (BR)
BANQUE TORONTO-DOMINION, LA
TORONTO-DOMINION BANK, THE
(Suby of Toronto-Dominion Bank, The)
1547 Merivale Rd, Nepean, ON, K2G 4V3
(613) 226-7353
Emp Here 40
SIC 6021 National commercial banks

D-U-N-S 24-199-1566   (BR)
BELL TECHNICAL SOLUTIONS INC
1740 Woodroffe Ave, Nepean, ON, K2G 3R8
(613) 746-4465
Emp Here 130
SIC 4899 Communication services, nec

D-U-N-S 24-228-1231   (BR)
BEST BUY CANADA LTD
BEST BUY
(Suby of Best Buy Co., Inc.)
1701 Merivale Rd, Nepean, ON, K2G 3K2
(613) 212-0146
Emp Here 50
SIC 5999 Miscellaneous retail stores, nec

D-U-N-S 25-231-7383   (BR)
BRICK WAREHOUSE LP, THE
565 West Hunt Club Rd, Nepean, ON, K2G 5W5
(613) 225-8898
Emp Here 50
SIC 5712 Furniture stores

D-U-N-S 24-911-3051   (HQ)
CD WAREHOUSE INC
(Suby of CD Warehouse Inc)

Nepean, ON K2G

1383 Clyde Ave, Nepean, ON, K2G 3H7
(613) 225-9027
Emp Here 25   *Emp Total* 50
Sales 5,072,500
SIC 5735 Record and prerecorded tape stores
Pr Pr Janis Mcdonald
    Steven Bleeker

    D-U-N-S 20-308-7986   (BR)
CARA OPERATIONS LIMITED
KELSEY'S
(*Suby of* Cara Holdings Limited)
1711 Merivale Rd, Nepean, ON, K2G 3K2
(613) 288-0517
Emp Here 80
SIC 5812 Eating places

    D-U-N-S 24-679-8685   (BR)
CO-OPERATORS GROUP LIMITED, THE
1547 Merivale Rd Suite 40, Nepean, ON, K2G
4V3
(613) 727-3663
Emp Here 20
SIC 6331 Fire, marine, and casualty insurance

    D-U-N-S 25-529-6816   (BR)
COSTCO WHOLESALE CANADA LTD
(*Suby of* Costco Wholesale Corporation)
1849 Merivale Rd Suite 540, Nepean, ON,
K2G 1E3
(613) 727-4786
Emp Here 287
SIC 5141 Groceries, general line

    D-U-N-S 20-192-6966   (BR)
FGL SPORTS LTD
SPORT CHEK MERIVALE
1642 Merivale Rd Unit 0580, Nepean, ON,
K2G 4A1
(613) 225-6674
Emp Here 40
SIC 5941 Sporting goods and bicycle shops

    D-U-N-S 24-858-6476   (HQ)
JAM FILLED ENTERTAINMENT INC
20 Camelot Dr Suite 100, Nepean, ON, K2G
5X8
(613) 366-2550
Emp Here 35   *Emp Total* 65
Sales 25,974,009
SIC 7812 Motion picture and video production
Pr Kyle Macdougall

    D-U-N-S 25-057-7061   (SL)
**KRUPP, MASHA TRANSLATION GROUP
LTD, THE**
1547 Merivale Rd, Nepean, ON, K2G 4V3
(613) 820-4566
Emp Here 50   *Sales* 2,626,585
SIC 7389 Business services, nec

    D-U-N-S 25-279-9473   (HQ)
LOCAL HEROES INC
LOCAL HEROES BAR & GRILL
(*Suby of* Local Heroes Inc)
1400 Clyde Ave, Nepean, ON, K2G 3J2
(613) 224-3873
Emp Here 43   *Emp Total* 130
Sales 3,939,878
SIC 5812 Eating places

    D-U-N-S 24-481-9553   (SL)
M P C CIRCUITS INC
1390 Clyde Ave Suite 205, Nepean, ON, K2G
3H9
(613) 739-5060
Emp Here 60   *Sales* 9,130,500
SIC 3672 Printed circuit boards
Pr Pr Perry Pezoulas

    D-U-N-S 24-977-5623   (BR)
MAGASIN LAURA (P.V.) INC
LAURA CANADA
1667 Merivale Rd, Nepean, ON, K2G 3K2
(613) 727-9198
Emp Here 21
SIC 5621 Women's clothing stores

    D-U-N-S 25-128-8536   (BR)

**MALMBERG TRUCK TRAILER EQUIPMENT
LTD**
MALMBERG
25 Slack Rd, Nepean, ON, K2G 0B7
(613) 226-1320
Emp Here 30
SIC 5082 Construction and mining machinery

    D-U-N-S 24-346-3341   (BR)
**OTTAWA CATHOLIC DISTRICT SCHOOL
BOARD**
POPE JOHN XIII CATHOLIC SCHOOL
(*Suby of* Ottawa Catholic District School
Board)
165 Knoxdale Rd, Nepean, ON, K2G 1B1
(613) 226-6223
Emp Here 28
SIC 8211 Elementary and secondary schools

    D-U-N-S 20-894-1385   (HQ)
**OTTAWA CATHOLIC DISTRICT SCHOOL
BOARD**
OTTAWA CATHOLIC SCHOOL BOARD
(*Suby of* Ottawa Catholic District School
Board)
570 West Hunt Club Rd, Nepean, ON, K2G
3R4
(613) 224-2222
Emp Here 330   *Emp Total* 4,000
Sales 371,611,350
SIC 8211 Elementary and secondary schools
Ch Bd Ted J. Hurley
V Ch Bd Mark D Mullan

    D-U-N-S 20-711-6547   (BR)
**OTTAWA CATHOLIC DISTRICT SCHOOL
BOARD**
ST ANDREW
(*Suby of* Ottawa Catholic District School
Board)
201 Crestway Dr, Nepean, ON, K2G 6Z3
(613) 843-0050
Emp Here 45
SIC 8211 Elementary and secondary schools

    D-U-N-S 25-265-4462   (BR)
**OTTAWA CATHOLIC DISTRICT SCHOOL
BOARD**
ST. GREGORY'S SCHOOL
(*Suby of* Ottawa Catholic District School
Board)
148 Meadowlands Dr W, Nepean, ON, K2G
2S5
(613) 224-3011
Emp Here 23
SIC 8211 Elementary and secondary schools

    D-U-N-S 20-026-6463   (BR)
**OTTAWA YOUNG MEN'S AND YOUNG
WOMEN'S CHRISTIAN ASSOCIATION**
NEPEAN YMCA-YWCA
1642 Merivale Rd, Nepean, ON, K2G 4A1
(613) 727-7070
Emp Here 30
SIC 8621 Professional organizations

    D-U-N-S 25-263-5941   (BR)
**OTTAWA-CARLETON DISTRICT SCHOOL
BOARD**
BRIARGREEN PUBLIC SCHOOL
19 Parkfield Cres, Nepean, ON, K2G 0R9
(613) 828-5027
Emp Here 40
SIC 8211 Elementary and secondary schools

    D-U-N-S 25-263-6121   (BR)
**OTTAWA-CARLETON DISTRICT SCHOOL
BOARD**
MANORDALE PUBLIC SCHOOL
16 Carola St, Nepean, ON, K2G 0Y1
(613) 226-6393
Emp Here 29
SIC 8211 Elementary and secondary schools

    D-U-N-S 20-590-4910   (BR)
**OTTAWA-CARLETON DISTRICT SCHOOL
BOARD**

*ADRIAN   CLARCKSON   ELEMENTARY
SCHOOL*
170 Stoneway Dr, Nepean, ON, K2G 6R2
(613) 825-8600
Emp Here 60
SIC 8211 Elementary and secondary schools

    D-U-N-S 25-263-6402   (BR)
**OTTAWA-CARLETON DISTRICT SCHOOL
BOARD**
MERIVALE HIGH SCHOOL
1755 Merivale Rd, Nepean, ON, K2G 1E2
(613) 224-1807
Emp Here 95
SIC 8211 Elementary and secondary schools

    D-U-N-S 25-263-5537   (BR)
**OTTAWA-CARLETON DISTRICT SCHOOL
BOARD**
MEADOWLANDS PUBLIC SCHOOL
10 Fieldrow St, Nepean, ON, K2G 2Y7
(613) 224-1733
Emp Here 38
SIC 8211 Elementary and secondary schools

    D-U-N-S 24-563-0947   (BR)
**OTTAWA-CARLETON DISTRICT SCHOOL
BOARD**
FARLEY MOWAT PUBLIC SCHOOL
75 Waterbridge Dr, Nepean, ON, K2G 6T3
(613) 825-3006
Emp Here 25
SIC 8211 Elementary and secondary schools

    D-U-N-S 20-859-9022   (BR)
PACIFIC LINK COMMUNICATIONS INC
BELL WORLD
1541 Merivale Rd, Nepean, ON, K2G 5W1
(613) 723-4400
Emp Here 25
SIC 5999 Miscellaneous retail stores, nec

    D-U-N-S 20-543-6574   (BR)
PHARMA PLUS DRUGMARTS LTD
1363 Woodroffe Ave Unit B, Nepean, ON, K2G
1V7
(613) 224-7621
Emp Here 20
SIC 5912 Drug stores and proprietary stores

    D-U-N-S 24-950-3371   (SL)
PURE RENO INC
49 Roundhay Dr, Nepean, ON, K2G 1B6
(613) 851-0907
Emp Here 20   *Sales* 5,579,750
SIC 1522 Residential construction, nec
Pr Pr Giuseppe Lariccia
    Bruno Lariccia

    D-U-N-S 25-131-3110   (BR)
RED LOBSTER HOSPITALITY LLC
RED LOBSTER RESTAURANTS
(*Suby of* Red Lobster Seafood Co., LLC)
1595 Merivale Rd, Nepean, ON, K2G 3J4
(613) 727-0035
Emp Here 100
SIC 5812 Eating places

    D-U-N-S 24-801-1897   (BR)
RITCHIE FEED & SEED INC
1740 Woodroffe Ave Suite 1101, Nepean, ON,
K2G 3R8
(613) 727-4430
Emp Here 50
SIC 5191 Farm supplies

    D-U-N-S 20-002-6586   (BR)
ROYAL BANK OF CANADA
RBC
(*Suby of* Royal Bank Of Canada)
117 Centrepointe Dr, Nepean, ON, K2G 5X3
(613) 727-8130
Emp Here 32
SIC 6021 National commercial banks

    D-U-N-S 20-615-1359   (BR)
SECURITE POLYGON INC
VIKING FIRE PROTECTION

17g Enterprise Ave, Nepean, ON, K2G 0A7
(613) 225-9540
Emp Here 25
SIC 5087 Service establishment equipment

    D-U-N-S 25-213-7427   (BR)
STAPLES CANADA INC
STAPLES THE BUSINESS DEPOT
(*Suby of* Staples, Inc.)
1595 Merivale Rd, Nepean, ON, K2G 3J4
(613) 226-7989
Emp Here 50
SIC 5943 Stationery stores

    D-U-N-S 20-787-4744   (SL)
**STUDENTS ASSOCIATION OF THE ALGO-
NQUIN COLLEGE OF APPLIED ARTS AND
TECHNOLOGY CORP, THE**
ALGONQUIN STUDENTS ASSOCIATION
1385 Woodroffe Ave, Nepean, ON, K2G 1V8
(613) 727-3932
Emp Here 65   *Sales* 4,593,259
SIC 8742 Management consulting services

    D-U-N-S 20-175-3964   (BR)
SURANI, B. DRUGS LTD
SHOPPERS DRUG MART
1642 Merivale Rd Suite 910, Nepean, ON,
K2G 4A1
(613) 226-1155
Emp Here 30
SIC 5912 Drug stores and proprietary stores

    D-U-N-S 20-700-4982   (BR)
TOMMY HILFIGER CANADA INC
TOMMY HILFIGER STORE
1363 Woodroffe Ave Unit D, Nepean, ON, K2G
1V7
(613) 727-3222
Emp Here 30
SIC 5136 Men's and boy's clothing

    D-U-N-S 25-297-7996   (BR)
TOYS 'R' US (CANADA) LTD
TOYS 'R' US
(*Suby of* Toys "r" Us, Inc.)
1683 Merivale Rd, Nepean, ON, K2G 3K2
(613) 228-8697
Emp Here 25
SIC 5945 Hobby, toy, and game shops

    D-U-N-S 24-319-8400   (BR)
VALUE VILLAGE STORES, INC
(*Suby of* Savers, Inc.)
1375 Clyde Ave, Nepean, ON, K2G 3H7
(613) 288-1390
Emp Here 50
SIC 5399 Miscellaneous general merchandise

    D-U-N-S 25-221-2816   (BR)
**WINNERS MERCHANTS INTERNATIONAL
L.P.**
WINNERS
(*Suby of* The TJX Companies Inc)
1651 Merivale Rd, Nepean, ON, K2G 3K2
(613) 226-3574
Emp Here 30
SIC 5651 Family clothing stores

Nepean, ON K2H

    D-U-N-S 25-849-4947   (SL)
3349608 CANADA INC
68 Robertson Rd, Nepean, ON, K2H 5Y8
(613) 820-4000
Emp Here 47   *Sales* 6,184,080
SIC 7371 Custom computer programming services
Pr Pr Robert Hall

    D-U-N-S 20-889-3107   (BR)
**AVIVA   INSURANCE   COMPANY   OF
CANADA**
AVIVA PRODUCTS
161 Greenbank Rd Suite 250, Nepean, ON,

▲ Public Company   ■ Public Company Family Member   **HQ** Headquarters   **BR** Branch   **SL** Single Location

K2H 5V6
(613) 235-6776
Emp Here 30
SIC 6411 Insurance agents, brokers, and service

D-U-N-S 20-572-0241   (BR)
BANK OF MONTREAL
BMO
250 Greenbank Rd Suite 15, Nepean, ON, K2H 8X4
(613) 564-6490
Emp Here 20
SIC 6021 National commercial banks

D-U-N-S 25-540-9138   (BR)
BENSON GROUP INC
BENSON AUTO PARTS
(*Suby of* Benapac Inc)
34 Stafford Rd, Nepean, ON, K2H 8W1
(613) 829-9872
Emp Here 40
SIC 5013 Motor vehicle supplies and new parts

D-U-N-S 20-585-4081   (BR)
CITY OF OTTAWA
CREATIVE ARTS CENTRE
(*Suby of* City of Ottawa)
35 Stafford Rd Unit 11, Nepean, ON, K2H 8V8
(613) 596-5783
Emp Here 20
SIC 7911 Dance studios, schools, and halls

D-U-N-S 24-102-9693   (BR)
CITY OF OTTAWA
NEPEAN NATIONAL EQUESTRIAN PARK
(*Suby of* City of Ottawa)
401 Corkstown Rd, Nepean, ON, K2H 8T1

Emp Here 20
SIC 7999 Amusement and recreation, nec

D-U-N-S 20-918-9005   (SL)
COLLINS BARROW OTTAWA LLP
301 Moodie Dr Suite 400, Nepean, ON, K2H 9C4
(613) 820-8010
Emp Here 75   *Sales* 3,283,232
SIC 8721 Accounting, auditing, and bookkeeping

D-U-N-S 25-306-4208   (BR)
COMMUNITY LIFECARE INC
LYNWOOD PARK RETIREMENT LODGE
1 Eaton St Suite 517, Nepean, ON, K2H 9P1
(613) 596-6969
Emp Here 60
SIC 8361 Residential care

D-U-N-S 25-767-9662   (BR)
DAIRY QUEEN CANADA INC
BELLS CORNERS
36 Robertson Rd, Nepean, ON, K2H 5Y8
(613) 596-6447
Emp Here 20
SIC 8742 Management consulting services

D-U-N-S 24-227-7528   (BR)
EXPERTECH NETWORK INSTALLATION INC
EXPERTECH NETWORK
340 Moodie Dr, Nepean, ON, K2H 8G3

Emp Here 20
SIC 4813 Telephone communication, except radio

D-U-N-S 25-091-3993   (SL)
GRAHAM AUTOMOTIVE SALES INC
GRAHAM, TONY INFINITI NISSAN
2185 Robertson Rd, Nepean, ON, K2H 5Z2
(613) 596-1515
Emp Here 100   *Sales* 36,480,350
SIC 5511 New and used car dealers
Pr Pr Patrick Graham

D-U-N-S 25-734-3160   (SL)

GRAHAM AUTOMOTIVE SALES LTD
TONY GRAHAM NISSAN
155 Robertson Rd, Nepean, ON, K2H 5Z2
(613) 596-1515
Emp Here 50   *Sales* 23,558,225
SIC 5511 New and used car dealers
Pr Dan Sproul

D-U-N-S 25-769-5759   (BR)
LAPOINTE FISH LIMITED
194 Robertson Rd, Nepean, ON, K2H 9J5
(613) 596-9654
Emp Here 20
SIC 5812 Eating places

D-U-N-S 24-344-4929   (BR)
METRO ONTARIO INC
1811 Robertson Rd, Nepean, ON, K2H 8X3
(613) 721-7028
Emp Here 100
SIC 5141 Groceries, general line

D-U-N-S 25-797-1887   (BR)
OTTAWA CATHOLIC DISTRICT SCHOOL BOARD
ST JOHN THE APOSTLE SCHOOL
(*Suby of* Ottawa Catholic District School Board)
30 Costello Ave, Nepean, ON, K2H 7C5
(613) 828-0644
Emp Here 25
SIC 8211 Elementary and secondary schools

D-U-N-S 20-711-6323   (BR)
OTTAWA CATHOLIC DISTRICT SCHOOL BOARD
OUR LADY OF PEACE
(*Suby of* Ottawa Catholic District School Board)
3877 Old Richmond Rd, Nepean, ON, K2H 5C1
(613) 828-4037
Emp Here 33
SIC 8211 Elementary and secondary schools

D-U-N-S 24-633-6457   (SL)
OTTAWA SAFETY COUNCIL
2068 Robertson Rd Unit 105, Nepean, ON, K2H 5Y8
(613) 238-1513
Emp Here 95   *Sales* 1,895,584
SIC 8748 Business consulting, nec

D-U-N-S 25-263-6204   (BR)
OTTAWA-CARLETON DISTRICT SCHOOL BOARD
LAKEVIEW PUBLIC SCHOOL
35 Corkstown Rd, Nepean, ON, K2H 7V4
(613) 828-8077
Emp Here 20
SIC 8211 Elementary and secondary schools

D-U-N-S 25-263-6246   (BR)
OTTAWA-CARLETON DISTRICT SCHOOL BOARD
KNOXDALE PUBLIC SCHOOL
170 Greenbank Rd, Nepean, ON, K2H 5V2
(613) 828-0010
Emp Here 25
SIC 8211 Elementary and secondary schools

D-U-N-S 25-263-6287   (BR)
OTTAWA-CARLETON DISTRICT SCHOOL BOARD
GREENBANK MIDDLE SCHOOL
168 Greenbank Rd, Nepean, ON, K2H 5V2
(613) 828-4587
Emp Here 37
SIC 8211 Elementary and secondary schools

D-U-N-S 25-263-6089   (BR)
OTTAWA-CARLETON DISTRICT SCHOOL BOARD
BELL HIGH SCHOOL
40 Cassidy Rd, Nepean, ON, K2H 6K1
(613) 828-9101
Emp Here 80
SIC 8211 Elementary and secondary schools

D-U-N-S 25-263-5453   (BR)
OTTAWA-CARLETON DISTRICT SCHOOL BOARD
SIR ROBERT BORDEN HIGH SCHOOL
131 Greenbank Rd, Nepean, ON, K2H 8R1
(613) 829-5320
Emp Here 100
SIC 8211 Elementary and secondary schools

D-U-N-S 20-711-6174   (BR)
OTTAWA-CARLETON DISTRICT SCHOOL BOARD
BELL'S CORNER PUBLIC SCHOOL
3770 Old Richmond Rd, Nepean, ON, K2H 5C3
(613) 828-3100
Emp Here 50
SIC 8211 Elementary and secondary schools

D-U-N-S 25-263-5495   (BR)
OTTAWA-CARLETON DISTRICT SCHOOL BOARD
CRYSTAL BAY CENTRE FOR SPECIAL EDUCATION
31 Moodie Dr, Nepean, ON, K2H 8G1
(613) 828-5376
Emp Here 50
SIC 8211 Elementary and secondary schools

D-U-N-S 25-263-6162   (BR)
OTTAWA-CARLETON DISTRICT SCHOOL BOARD
LESLIE PARK PUBLIC SCHOOL
20 Harrison St, Nepean, ON, K2H 7N5
(613) 828-5999
Emp Here 25
SIC 8211 Elementary and secondary schools

D-U-N-S 25-771-3420   (BR)
PRIME RESTAURANTS INC
EAST SIDE MARIO'S
(*Suby of* Cara Holdings Limited)
1861 Robertson Rd, Nepean, ON, K2H 9N5
(613) 820-3278
Emp Here 40
SIC 5812 Eating places

D-U-N-S 25-775-0372   (BR)
RE/MAX METRO-CITY REALTY LTD
RE/MAX METRO-CITY
31 Northside Rd Unit 202, Nepean, ON, K2H 8S1
(613) 721-5551
Emp Here 70
SIC 6531 Real estate agents and managers

D-U-N-S 25-300-5359   (BR)
REDBERRY FRANCHISING CORP
BURGER KING
45 Robertson Rd, Nepean, ON, K2H 5Y9

Emp Here 20
SIC 5812 Eating places

D-U-N-S 25-169-7926   (SL)
RIVERPARK PLACE LIMITED PARTNERSHIP
RIVERPARK PLACE RETIREMENT RESIDENCE
1 Corkstown Rd, Nepean, ON, K2H 1B6
(613) 828-8882
Emp Here 100   *Sales* 3,648,035
SIC 8361 Residential care

D-U-N-S 20-918-8163   (HQ)
STMICROELECTRONICS (CANADA), INC
16 Fitzgerald Rd Suite 100, Nepean, ON, K2H 8R6
(613) 768-9000
Emp Here 60   *Emp Total* 43,480
Sales 23,087,061
SIC 8711 Engineering services
Dir Michel Ladouceur
Dir Ashfaq Choudhury
Dir Pierre Paulin

D-U-N-S 24-086-6140   (BR)
SOBEYS CAPITAL INCORPORATED

FRESHCO
2150 Robertson Rd Suite 1, Nepean, ON, K2H 9S1
(613) 726-8038
Emp Here 20
SIC 5411 Grocery stores

D-U-N-S 20-058-5979   (SL)
STILLWATER CREEK LIMITED PARTNERSHIP
STILLWATER CREEK RETIREMENT COMMUNITY
2018 Robertson Rd Suite 353, Nepean, ON, K2H 1C6
(613) 828-7575
Emp Here 80   *Sales* 3,793,956
SIC 8059 Nursing and personal care, nec

D-U-N-S 24-991-9341   (SL)
TEX-DON LTD
CANADIAN TIRE 272
2135 Robertson Rd, Nepean, ON, K2H 5Z2
(613) 829-9580
Emp Here 65   *Sales* 7,879,756
SIC 5531 Auto and home supply stores
Pr Donald Brooks

D-U-N-S 25-983-7805   (BR)
WINNERS MERCHANTS INTERNATIONAL L.P.
WINNERS
(*Suby of* The TJX Companies Inc)
1821 Robertson Rd Unit 4, Nepean, ON, K2H 8X3
(613) 726-6677
Emp Here 30
SIC 5651 Family clothing stores

Nepean, ON K2J

D-U-N-S 24-737-0823   (BR)
1197767 ONTARIO LTD
PETRO CANADA
3766 Fallowfield Rd, Nepean, ON, K2J 1A1
(613) 825-8765
Emp Here 20
SIC 5541 Gasoline service stations

D-U-N-S 25-495-2252   (SL)
A F C TECHNOLOGIES INC
(*Suby of* Lumentum Holdings Inc.)
61 Bill Leathem Dr, Nepean, ON, K2J 0P7
(613) 843-3000
Emp Here 25   *Sales* 2,945,253
SIC 3651 Household audio and video equipment

D-U-N-S 24-418-2734   (BR)
CINEPLEX ODEON CORPORATION
CINEPLEX CINEMAS BARRHAVEN
131 Riocan Ave, Nepean, ON, K2J 5G3
(613) 825-2463
Emp Here 20
SIC 7832 Motion picture theaters, except drive-in

D-U-N-S 25-782-5497   (BR)
CITY OF OTTAWA
WALTER BAKER SPORTS CENTRE
(*Suby of* City of Ottawa)
100 Malvern Dr, Nepean, ON, K2J 2G5
(613) 580-2788
Emp Here 60
SIC 7997 Membership sports and recreation clubs

D-U-N-S 25-099-9539   (BR)
CONSEIL DES ECOLES CATHOLIQUES DE LANGUE FRANCAISE DU CENTRE-EST
ECOLE PIERRE ELLIOTT TRUDEAU
601 Longfields Dr, Nepean, ON, K2J 4X1
(613) 521-1560
Emp Here 30
SIC 8211 Elementary and secondary schools

D-U-N-S 24-525-4169   (BR)
CONSEIL DES ECOLES PUBLIQUES DE L'EST DE L'ONTARIO
ECOLE ELEMENTAIRE PUBLIQUE MICHAELLE-JEAN
11 Claridge Dr, Nepean, ON, K2J 5A3
(613) 247-1853
Emp Here 25
SIC 8211 Elementary and secondary schools

D-U-N-S 24-069-4237   (BR)
DOLLARAMA S.E.C.
DOLLARAMA
3777 Strandherd Dr, Nepean, ON, K2J 4B1
(613) 823-2519
Emp Here 30
SIC 5399 Miscellaneous general merchandise

D-U-N-S 20-790-0452   (BR)
GOODLIFE FITNESS CENTRES INC
3201 Greenbank Rd, Nepean, ON, K2J 4H9
(613) 823-8081
Emp Here 25
SIC 7999 Amusement and recreation, nec

D-U-N-S 20-870-1990   (BR)
HOME DEPOT OF CANADA INC
(*Suby of* The Home Depot Inc)
3779 Strandherd Dr, Nepean, ON, K2J 5M4
(613) 843-7900
Emp Here 50
SIC 5251 Hardware stores

D-U-N-S 20-324-5360   (SL)
IDEABYTES INC
142 Golflinks Dr, Nepean, ON, K2J 5N5
(613) 692-9908
Emp Here 65   *Sales* 10,043,550
SIC 7371 Custom computer programming services
Pr George Philip Kongalath

D-U-N-S 24-064-5254   (BR)
K.F.S. LIMITED
TWEED & HICKORY
3161 Greenbank Rd Unit 5, Nepean, ON, K2J 4H9

Emp Here 24
SIC 5611 Men's and boys' clothing stores

D-U-N-S 24-643-2400   (BR)
KELSEY'S RESTAURANTS INC
KELSEY'S
(*Suby of* Cara Holdings Limited)
75 Marketplace Ave Suite 6, Nepean, ON, K2J 5G4
(613) 843-0662
Emp Here 50
SIC 5812 Eating places

D-U-N-S 24-318-6579   (BR)
KOTT LUMBER COMPANY
NASCOR BY KOTT
3228 Moodie Dr, Nepean, ON, K2J 4S8
(613) 838-2775
Emp Here 200
SIC 5031 Lumber, plywood, and millwork

D-U-N-S 25-801-1360   (BR)
LOBLAWS SUPERMARKETS LIMITED
LOBLAWS
3201 Greenbank Rd Suite 1035, Nepean, ON, K2J 4H9
(613) 825-0812
Emp Here 300
SIC 5411 Grocery stores

D-U-N-S 24-382-7987   (HQ)
LUMENTUM CANADA LTD
(*Suby of* Lumentum Holdings Inc.)
61 Bill Leathem Dr, Nepean, ON, K2J 0P7
(613) 843-3000
Emp Here 200   *Emp Total* 1,850
Sales 1,743,200
SIC 3827 Optical instruments and lenses

D-U-N-S 24-348-1988   (HQ)

LUMENTUM OTTAWA INC
(*Suby of* Lumentum Holdings Inc.)
61 Bill Leathem Dr, Nepean, ON, K2J 0P7
(613) 843-3000
Emp Here 45   *Emp Total* 1,850
Sales 8,489,260
SIC 3669 Communications equipment, nec
Pr Pr Alan Lowe
  Aaron Tachibana
  Christopher S Dewees
  Adam Kubelka

D-U-N-S 20-014-4769   (BR)
MATTAMY (MONARCH) LIMITED
STONEBRIDGE GOLF & COUNTRY CLUB
68 Hawktree Ridge, Nepean, ON, K2J 5N3
(613) 692-6093
Emp Here 55
SIC 7997 Membership sports and recreation clubs

D-U-N-S 20-923-9016   (BR)
MCDONALD'S RESTAURANTS OF CANADA LIMITED
MCDONALD'S
(*Suby of* McDonald's Corporation)
3340 Fallowfield Rd, Nepean, ON, K2J 5L1
(613) 843-8898
Emp Here 50
SIC 5812 Eating places

D-U-N-S 25-886-2598   (BR)
MCDONALD'S RESTAURANTS OF CANADA LIMITED
MCDONALD'S
(*Suby of* McDonald's Corporation)
3773 Strandherd Dr, Nepean, ON, K2J 4B1
(613) 823-7838
Emp Here 80
SIC 5812 Eating places

D-U-N-S 24-344-4853   (BR)
METRO ONTARIO INC
LOEB
3201 Strandherd Dr, Nepean, ON, K2J 5N1
(613) 823-8825
Emp Here 100
SIC 5411 Grocery stores

D-U-N-S 24-616-1322   (BR)
METRO ONTARIO INC
FOOD BASIC
900 Greenbank Rd, Nepean, ON, K2J 4P6
(613) 823-4458
Emp Here 75
SIC 5411 Grocery stores

D-U-N-S 20-288-9346   (BR)
OTTAWA CATHOLIC DISTRICT SCHOOL BOARD
ST JOSEPH HIGH SCHOOL
(*Suby of* Ottawa Catholic District School Board)
3333 Greenbank Rd, Nepean, ON, K2J 4J1
(613) 823-4797
Emp Here 125
SIC 8211 Elementary and secondary schools

D-U-N-S 24-500-6346   (BR)
OTTAWA CATHOLIC DISTRICT SCHOOL BOARD
ST EMILY ELEMENTARY SEPARATE SCHOOL
(*Suby of* Ottawa Catholic District School Board)
500 Chapman Mills Dr, Nepean, ON, K2J 0J2
(613) 825-4300
Emp Here 25
SIC 8211 Elementary and secondary schools

D-U-N-S 25-070-0135   (BR)
OTTAWA CATHOLIC DISTRICT SCHOOL BOARD
ST PATRICK CATHOLIC SCHOOL
(*Suby of* Ottawa Catholic District School Board)
68 Larkin Dr, Nepean, ON, K2J 1A9

---

(613) 825-4012
Emp Here 22
SIC 8211 Elementary and secondary schools

D-U-N-S 25-837-9262   (BR)
OTTAWA CATHOLIC DISTRICT SCHOOL BOARD
ST ELIZABETH ANN SETON SCHOOL
(*Suby of* Ottawa Catholic District School Board)
41 Weybridge Dr, Nepean, ON, K2J 2Z8
(613) 825-3596
Emp Here 45
SIC 8211 Elementary and secondary schools

D-U-N-S 25-238-1439   (BR)
OTTAWA CATHOLIC DISTRICT SCHOOL BOARD
ST JOSEPH INTERMEDIATE SCHOOL
(*Suby of* Ottawa Catholic District School Board)
3333 Greenbank Road, Nepean, ON, K2J 4J1
(613) 823-4797
Emp Here 35
SIC 8211 Elementary and secondary schools

D-U-N-S 20-591-5742   (BR)
OTTAWA CATHOLIC DISTRICT SCHOOL BOARD
MONSIGNOR PAUL BAXTER SCHOOL
(*Suby of* Ottawa Catholic District School Board)
333 Beatrice Dr, Nepean, ON, K2J 4W1
(613) 825-7544
Emp Here 25
SIC 8211 Elementary and secondary schools

D-U-N-S 20-711-6406   (BR)
OTTAWA CATHOLIC DISTRICT SCHOOL BOARD
ST LUKE'S SCHOOL
(*Suby of* Ottawa Catholic District School Board)
60 Mountshannon Dr, Nepean, ON, K2J 4C2
(613) 825-2520
Emp Here 50
SIC 8211 Elementary and secondary schools

D-U-N-S 20-026-2405   (BR)
OTTAWA CATHOLIC DISTRICT SCHOOL BOARD
MOTHER TERESA HIGH SCHOOL
(*Suby of* Ottawa Catholic District School Board)
440 Longfields Dr, Nepean, ON, K2J 4T1
(613) 823-1663
Emp Here 120
SIC 8211 Elementary and secondary schools

D-U-N-S 24-676-3259   (BR)
OTTAWA-CARLETON DISTRICT SCHOOL BOARD
LONGFIELDS DAVIDSON HEIGHTS INTERMEDIATE SCHOOL
149 Berrigan Dr, Nepean, ON, K2J 5C6
(613) 843-7722
Emp Here 25
SIC 8211 Elementary and secondary schools

D-U-N-S 20-021-6708   (BR)
OTTAWA-CARLETON DISTRICT SCHOOL BOARD
JOCKVALE ELEMENTARY SCHOOL
101 Malvern Dr, Nepean, ON, K2J 2S8
(613) 825-1224
Emp Here 40
SIC 8211 Elementary and secondary schools

D-U-N-S 25-130-3830   (BR)
OTTAWA-CARLETON DISTRICT SCHOOL BOARD
MARY HONEYWELL ELEMENTARY SCHOOL
54 Kennevale Dr, Nepean, ON, K2J 3B2
(613) 825-4834
Emp Here 55
SIC 8211 Elementary and secondary schools

D-U-N-S 24-229-8722   (BR)
OTTAWA-CARLETON DISTRICT SCHOOL BOARD
BERRIGAN ELEMENTARY SCHOOL
199 Berrigan Dr, Nepean, ON, K2J 5C6
(613) 825-0092
Emp Here 25
SIC 8211 Elementary and secondary schools

D-U-N-S 25-130-3822   (BR)
OTTAWA-CARLETON DISTRICT SCHOOL BOARD
CEDARVIEW MIDDLE SCHOOL
2760 Cedarview Rd, Nepean, ON, K2J 4J2
(613) 825-2185
Emp Here 50
SIC 8211 Elementary and secondary schools

D-U-N-S 20-590-4894   (BR)
OTTAWA-CARLETON DISTRICT SCHOOL BOARD
JOHN MCCRAE SECONDARY SCHOOL
103 Malvern Dr, Nepean, ON, K2J 4T2
(613) 823-0367
Emp Here 75
SIC 8211 Elementary and secondary schools

D-U-N-S 20-122-7969   (BR)
REITMANS (CANADA) LIMITEE
3161 Greenbank Rd Suite 1a, Nepean, ON, K2J 4H9
(613) 823-4053
Emp Here 20
SIC 5621 Women's clothing stores

D-U-N-S 20-796-4342   (BR)
STAPLES CANADA INC
STAPLES THE BUSINESS DEPOT
(*Suby of* Staples, Inc.)
101 Marketplace Ave, Nepean, ON, K2J 5G5
(613) 825-0457
Emp Here 30
SIC 5943 Stationery stores

D-U-N-S 24-329-7012   (BR)
WAL-MART CANADA CORP
3651 Strandherd Dr, Nepean, ON, K2J 4G8
(613) 823-8714
Emp Here 200
SIC 5311 Department stores

D-U-N-S 20-184-2841   (BR)
WINNERS MERCHANTS INTERNATIONAL L.P.
WINNERS
(*Suby of* The TJX Companies Inc)
101 Marketplace Ave Unit 2, Nepean, ON, K2J 5G5
(613) 825-2347
Emp Here 40
SIC 5651 Family clothing stores

          Nepean, ON K2R

D-U-N-S 20-136-8441   (BR)
FEDEX GROUND PACKAGE SYSTEMS LTD
FEDEX GROUND
(*Suby of* Fedex Corporation)
985 Moodie Dr Suite 3, Nepean, ON, K2R 1H4
(800) 463-3339
Emp Here 25
SIC 4215 Courier services, except by air

D-U-N-S 20-246-0569   (BR)
FIRSTCANADA ULC
FIRST STUDENT CANADA
1027 Moodie Dr, Nepean, ON, K2R 1H4

Emp Here 150
SIC 4151 School buses

D-U-N-S 25-779-5484   (BR)
TOMLINSON, R. W. LIMITED
(*Suby of* Tomlinson, R. W. Limited)
970 Moodie Dr, Nepean, ON, K2R 1H3

---

(613) 820-2332
Emp Here 30
SIC 1423 Crushed and broken granite

New Dundee, ON N0B
Waterloo County

D-U-N-S 24-348-2176   (SL)
DUNDEE COUNTRY CLUB LIMITED
1801 Queen St N, New Dundee, ON, N0B 2E0
(519) 696-3257
Emp Here 20   *Sales* 875,528
SIC 7992 Public golf courses

New Hamburg, ON N3A
Waterloo County

D-U-N-S 20-181-5388   (HQ)
ERB TRANSPORT LIMITED
290 Hamilton Rd, New Hamburg, ON, N3A 1A2
(519) 662-2710
Emp Here 75   *Emp Total* 1,200
Sales 117,290,385
SIC 4212 Local trucking, without storage
Pr Pr Wendell Erb
 Kevin Cooper
VP VP Vic Thiessen
 John Jutzi
 Vernon Erb
Dir Floyd Gerber
 Viola Erb

D-U-N-S 24-309-9715   (BR)
FORMATOP MANUFACTURING CO. LTD
(*Suby of* Formatop Manufacturing Co. Ltd)
270 Hamilton Rd, New Hamburg, ON, N3A 2K2
(519) 662-2800
Emp Here 30
SIC 2541 Wood partitions and fixtures

D-U-N-S 20-536-5323   (SL)
KLASSEN BRONZE LIMITED
30 Marvin St, New Hamburg, ON, N3A 4H8
(519) 662-1010
Emp Here 75   *Sales* 4,523,563
SIC 3993 Signs and advertising specialties

D-U-N-S 24-845-9588   (BR)
MENNONITE CENTRAL COMMITTEE CANADA
65 Heritage Dr, New Hamburg, ON, N3A 2J3
(519) 662-1879
Emp Here 45
SIC 5945 Hobby, toy, and game shops

D-U-N-S 20-734-6420   (HQ)
NACHURS ALPINE SOLUTIONS INC
ALPINE PLANT FOODS
(*Suby of* Trans-Resources, Inc.)
30 Neville St, New Hamburg, ON, N3A 4G7
(519) 662-2352
Emp Here 20   *Emp Total* 736
Sales 5,544,006
SIC 2874 Phosphatic fertilizers
 Jeff Barnes
Pr Pr Neil Dolson

D-U-N-S 20-017-3099   (BR)
SOBEYS CAPITAL INCORPORATED
338 Waterloo St Suite 3, New Hamburg, ON, N3A 0C5
(519) 662-2620
Emp Here 51
SIC 5411 Grocery stores

D-U-N-S 20-923-5886   (HQ)
TRI-COUNTY MENNONITE HOMES ASSOCIATION
NITHVIEW HOME & SENIORS VILLAGE
(*Suby of* Tri-County Mennonite Homes Asso-

ciation)
200 Boullee St, New Hamburg, ON, N3A 2K4
(519) 662-2280
Emp Here 25   *Emp Total* 200
Sales 9,816,000
SIC 8361 Residential care
Dir Rae Nafziger
Pr Dale Leis

D-U-N-S 25-228-1613   (BR)
WATERLOO REGION DISTRICT SCHOOL BOARD
FOREST GLEN PUBLIC SCHOOL
437 Waterloo St, New Hamburg, ON, N3A 1S9
(519) 662-2830
Emp Here 51
SIC 8211 Elementary and secondary schools

New Liskeard, ON P0J
Timiskaming County

D-U-N-S 25-654-2333   (BR)
756694 ONTARIO LTD
TIM HORTONS
(*Suby of* 756694 Ontario Ltd)
54 May St, New Liskeard, ON, P0J 1P0
(705) 647-4733
Emp Here 30
SIC 5812 Eating places

D-U-N-S 25-303-3013   (BR)
CANADIAN IMPERIAL BANK OF COMMERCE
CIBC
6 Armstrong St, New Liskeard, ON, P0J 1P0
(705) 647-6877
Emp Here 25
SIC 6021 National commercial banks

D-U-N-S 20-291-9044   (BR)
CANADIAN MENTAL HEALTH ASSOCIATION-COCHRANE-TIMISKAMING BRANCH
NORTHERN STAR
20 May St S, New Liskeard, ON, P0J 1P0
(705) 647-4444
Emp Here 20
SIC 8059 Nursing and personal care, nec

D-U-N-S 25-238-8152   (BR)
CONSEIL SCOLAIRE CATHOLIQUE DE DISTRICT DES GRANDES RIVIERES, LE
CATHOLIC MITHCL
998075 Hwy 11, New Liskeard, ON, P0J 1P0
(705) 647-6614
Emp Here 22
SIC 8211 Elementary and secondary schools

D-U-N-S 25-238-8277   (BR)
CONSEIL SCOLAIRE CATHOLIQUE DE DISTRICT DES GRANDES RIVIERES, LE
ECOLE SACRE COEUR
100 Lakeshore Dr, New Liskeard, ON, P0J 1P0
(705) 647-6355
Emp Here 24
SIC 8211 Elementary and secondary schools

D-U-N-S 25-263-6816   (BR)
CONSEIL SCOLAIRE CATHOLIQUE DE DISTRICT DES GRANDES RIVIERES, LE
SAINTE-MARIE ECOLE SECONDAIRE
340 Rue Hessle, New Liskeard, ON, P0J 1P0
(705) 647-7376
Emp Here 40
SIC 8211 Elementary and secondary schools

D-U-N-S 25-238-8418   (BR)
DISTRICT SCHOOL BOARD ONTARIO NORTH EAST
NEW LISKEARD PUBLIC SCHOOL
141 Dymond St, New Liskeard, ON, P0J 1P0
(705) 647-7341
Emp Here 45

SIC 8211 Elementary and secondary schools

D-U-N-S 25-238-8533   (BR)
DISTRICT SCHOOL BOARD ONTARIO NORTH EAST
TIMISKAMING DISTRICT SECONDARY SCHOOL
90 Niven St, New Liskeard, ON, P0J 1P0
(705) 647-7336
Emp Here 90
SIC 8211 Elementary and secondary schools

D-U-N-S 20-645-6795   (BR)
DISTRICT SCHOOL BOARD ONTARIO NORTH EAST
Gd, New Liskeard, ON, P0J 1P0
(705) 647-7394
Emp Here 25
SIC 8211 Elementary and secondary schools

D-U-N-S 24-384-2783   (BR)
EMPIRE THEATRES LIMITED
35 Armstrong St N, New Liskeard, ON, P0J 1P0
(705) 647-5363
Emp Here 20
SIC 7832 Motion picture theaters, except drive-in

D-U-N-S 24-417-6582   (HQ)
GRAYDON FOODS LTD
MCDONALDS RESTAURANT
(*Suby of* Graydon Foods Ltd)
11b North Hwy, New Liskeard, ON, P0J 1P0
(705) 647-8088
Emp Here 20   *Emp Total* 95
Sales 2,845,467
SIC 5812 Eating places

D-U-N-S 25-650-5066   (BR)
M. A. T. ENTERPRISES INC
WENDY'S RESTAURANT
(*Suby of* M. A. T. Enterprises Inc)
883337 Hwy 65 Dymond, New Liskeard, ON, P0J 1P0
(705) 647-5414
Emp Here 29
SIC 5812 Eating places

D-U-N-S 25-615-3826   (BR)
MANITOULIN TRANSPORT INC
399 Radley'S Hill Rd, New Liskeard, ON, P0J 1P0
(705) 647-6881
Emp Here 20
SIC 4213 Trucking, except local

D-U-N-S 24-344-4903   (BR)
METRO ONTARIO INC
FOOD BASICS
83303 Highway 11b, New Liskeard, ON, P0J 1P0
(705) 647-7649
Emp Here 45
SIC 5411 Grocery stores

D-U-N-S 20-153-6864   (BR)
MILLER GROUP INC
MILLER MAINTENANCE
704024 Rockley Rd, New Liskeard, ON, P0J 1P0
(705) 647-8299
Emp Here 30
SIC 1611 Highway and street construction

D-U-N-S 24-991-4805   (BR)
MILLER PAVING LIMITED
MILLER PAVING NORTHERN
704024 Rockley Rd, New Liskeard, ON, P0J 1P0
(705) 647-4331
Emp Here 200
SIC 1611 Highway and street construction

D-U-N-S 25-238-8236   (BR)
NORTHEASTERN CATHOLIC DISTRICT SCHOOL BOARD
ENGLISH CATHOLIC CENTRAL SCHOOL
245 Shepherdson Rd, New Liskeard, ON, P0J

1P0
(705) 647-4301
Emp Here 30
SIC 8211 Elementary and secondary schools

D-U-N-S 24-466-4301   (BR)
ONTARIO POWER GENERATION INC
1 Highway 65 W, New Liskeard, ON, P0J 1P0
(705) 647-8000
Emp Here 20
SIC 4911 Electric services

D-U-N-S 20-310-8469   (BR)
STAPLES CANADA INC
(*Suby of* Staples, Inc.)
Gd, New Liskeard, ON, P0J 1P0
(705) 647-7718
Emp Here 25
SIC 5943 Stationery stores

D-U-N-S 20-131-9456   (SL)
TEMISKAMING PRINTING COMPANY LIMITED
TEMISKAMING SPEAKER, THE
18 Wellington St, New Liskeard, ON, P0J 1P0
(705) 647-6791
Emp Here 55   *Sales* 4,596,524
SIC 2711 Newspapers

D-U-N-S 24-344-8714   (BR)
TIMISKAMING CHILD AND FAMILY SERVICES
25 Paget St, New Liskeard, ON, P0J 1P0
(705) 647-1200
Emp Here 100
SIC 8322 Individual and family services

D-U-N-S 25-146-8708   (HQ)
TIMISKAMING HOME SUPPORT/SOUTIEN A DOMICILE
(*Suby of* Timiskaming Home Support/Soutien A Domicile)
213 Whitewood Ave Suite A2, New Liskeard, ON, P0J 1P0

Emp Here 40   *Emp Total* 100
Sales 6,594,250
SIC 8059 Nursing and personal care, nec
Genl Mgr Heather St-Denis

D-U-N-S 25-294-8773   (BR)
WAL-MART CANADA CORP
133 11 Hwy N, New Liskeard, ON, P0J 1P0
(705) 647-6344
Emp Here 100
SIC 5311 Department stores

New Lowell, ON L0M
Simcoe County

D-U-N-S 20-088-1683   (BR)
LAFARGE CANADA INC
6372 County Rd 9, New Lowell, ON, L0M 1N0
(705) 446-2346
Emp Here 30
SIC 5032 Brick, stone, and related material

D-U-N-S 24-051-5440   (BR)
PHOENIX BUILDING COMPONENTS INC
2 Greengage Rd, New Lowell, ON, L0M 1N0
(705) 424-3905
Emp Here 20
SIC 1761 Roofing, siding, and sheetMetal work

D-U-N-S 25-297-6063   (BR)
RENFREW COUNTY DISTRICT SCHOOL BOARD
NEW LOWELL CENTRAL PUBLIC SCHOOL
5197 County Road 9, New Lowell, ON, L0M 1N0
(705) 424-0991
Emp Here 25
SIC 8211 Elementary and secondary schools

Newcastle, ON L1B
Durham County

D-U-N-S 20-591-6484   (BR)
KAWARTHA PINE RIDGE DISTRICT SCHOOL BOARD
NEWCASTLE PUBLIC SCHOOL
50 Glass Crt, Newcastle, ON, L1B 1M5
(905) 987-4262
Emp Here 25
SIC 8211 Elementary and secondary schools

D-U-N-S 25-265-4132   (BR)
KAWARTHA PINE RIDGE DISTRICT SCHOOL BOARD
PINES SENIOR PUBLIC SCHOOL, THE
3425 Hwy 35 & 115, Newcastle, ON, L1B 1L9
(905) 987-5232
Emp Here 25
SIC 8211 Elementary and secondary schools

D-U-N-S 20-653-7941   (BR)
PETERBOROUGH VICTORIA NORTHUMBERLAND AND CLARINGTON CATHOLIC DISTRICT SCHOOL BOARD
ST FRANCIS OF ASSISI SCHOOL
1774 Rudell Rd, Newcastle, ON, L1B 1E2
(905) 987-4797
Emp Here 46
SIC 8211 Elementary and secondary schools

D-U-N-S 25-136-6241   (BR)
REVERA LONG TERM CARE INC
FOSTERBROOKE LONG-TERM CARE FACILITY
330 King Ave W, Newcastle, ON, L1B 1G9
(905) 987-4702
Emp Here 50
SIC 8051 Skilled nursing care facilities

D-U-N-S 20-641-3093   (BR)
WILSON FOODS CENTRE LTD
MCDONALD'S
1000 Regional Rd 17, Newcastle, ON, L1B 1L9
(905) 987-0505
Emp Here 76
SIC 5812 Eating places

Newmarket, ON L3X
York County

D-U-N-S 20-780-8358   (BR)
A & W FOOD SERVICES OF CANADA INC
A&W RESTAURANT
16650 Yonge St, Newmarket, ON, L3X 2N8
(905) 868-9020
Emp Here 35
SIC 5812 Eating places

D-U-N-S 24-862-5410   (HQ)
ALLIED INTERNATIONAL CREDIT CORP
AIC
16635 Yonge St Suite 26, Newmarket, ON, L3X 1V6
(905) 470-8181
Emp Here 775   *Emp Total* 500
Sales 28,846,155
SIC 4899 Communication services, nec
Dir David Rae
Pr Kenny Johnston
  David Gallagher
  Tom Mccausland

D-U-N-S 25-361-3319   (BR)
BUCHNER MANUFACTURING INC
16650 Bayview Ave, Newmarket, ON, L3X 2S8
(905) 836-1506
Emp Here 30
SIC 3444 Sheet Metalwork

D-U-N-S 20-856-8480   (BR)

D-U-N-S 20-711-4450   (BR)
FABRICLAND DISTRIBUTORS INC
16655 Yonge St Unit 29, Newmarket, ON, L3X 1V6
(905) 898-3908
Emp Here 20
SIC 5949 Sewing, needlework, and piece goods

D-U-N-S 20-554-3762   (SL)
GLENWAY COUNTRY CLUB LIMITED
470 Crossland Gate, Newmarket, ON, L3X 1B8
(905) 235-5422
Emp Here 100   *Sales* 4,012,839
SIC 7997 Membership sports and recreation clubs

D-U-N-S 24-479-5589   (BR)
MAGNA CLOSURES INC
DORTEC INDUSTRIES, DIV OF
521 Newpark Blvd, Newmarket, ON, L3X 2S2
(905) 853-1800
Emp Here 1,000
SIC 5013 Motor vehicle supplies and new parts

D-U-N-S 24-366-6240   (BR)
MAGNA SEATING INC
CAM-SLIDE
550 Newpark Blvd, Newmarket, ON, L3X 2S2
(905) 895-4701
Emp Here 600
SIC 2531 Public building and related furniture

D-U-N-S 20-317-1590   (BR)
MAGNA SEATING INC
CAM-SLIDE
564 Newpark Blvd, Newmarket, ON, L3X 2S2
(905) 853-3604
Emp Here 600
SIC 2531 Public building and related furniture

D-U-N-S 24-249-4420   (SL)
MANDARIN RESTAURANT
16655 Yonge St Unit 100, Newmarket, ON, L3X 1V6
(905) 898-7100
Emp Here 70   *Sales* 2,115,860
SIC 5812 Eating places

D-U-N-S 20-555-6611   (BR)
METRO ONTARIO INC
METRO
16640 Yonge St Unit 1, Newmarket, ON, L3X 2N8
(905) 853-5100
Emp Here 200
SIC 5411 Grocery stores

D-U-N-S 25-396-8911   (SL)
NATURE'S EMPORIUM BULK & HEALTH FOODS LTD
NATURE'S EMPORIUM WHOLISTIC MARKET
16655 Yonge St Suite 27, Newmarket, ON, L3X 1V6
(905) 898-1844
Emp Here 50   *Sales* 2,858,628
SIC 5499 Miscellaneous food stores

D-U-N-S 20-653-8170   (BR)
YORK CATHOLIC DISTRICT SCHOOL BOARD
ST JOHN CHRYSOSTOM SCHOOL
800 Joe Persechini Dr, Newmarket, ON, L3X 2S6
(905) 836-7291
Emp Here 40
SIC 8211 Elementary and secondary schools

D-U-N-S 20-711-4575   (BR)
YORK CATHOLIC DISTRICT SCHOOL BOARD
ST NICHOLAS
480 Keith Ave, Newmarket, ON, L3X 1V5
(905) 895-3777
Emp Here 30
SIC 8211 Elementary and secondary schools

D-U-N-S 20-711-4450   (BR)
YORK CATHOLIC DISTRICT SCHOOL BOARD
NOTRE DAMME
715 Kingsmere Ave, Newmarket, ON, L3X 1L4
(905) 895-5001
Emp Here 50
SIC 8211 Elementary and secondary schools

D-U-N-S 20-711-4245   (BR)
YORK REGION DISTRICT SCHOOL BOARD
STONEHAVEN ELEMENTARY SCHOOL
(*Suby of* York Region District School Board)
875 Stonehaven Ave, Newmarket, ON, L3X 2K3
(905) 898-2077
Emp Here 50
SIC 8211 Elementary and secondary schools

D-U-N-S 24-158-2514   (BR)
YORK REGION DISTRICT SCHOOL BOARD
TERRY FOX PUBLIC SCHOOL
(*Suby of* York Region District School Board)
161 Sawmill Valley Dr, Newmarket, ON, L3X 2T1
(905) 967-0975
Emp Here 35
SIC 8211 Elementary and secondary schools

D-U-N-S 20-711-4385   (BR)
YORK REGION DISTRICT SCHOOL BOARD
POPLAR BANK PUBLIC SCHOOL
(*Suby of* York Region District School Board)
400 Woodspring Ave, Newmarket, ON, L3X 2X1
(905) 953-8995
Emp Here 50
SIC 8211 Elementary and secondary schools

D-U-N-S 24-676-5221   (BR)
YORK REGION DISTRICT SCHOOL BOARD
ALEXANDER MUIR PUBLIC SCHOOL
(*Suby of* York Region District School Board)
75 Ford Wilson Blvd, Newmarket, ON, L3X 3G1
(905) 895-9466
Emp Here 60
SIC 8211 Elementary and secondary schools

D-U-N-S 20-291-8202   (BR)
YORK REGION DISTRICT SCHOOL BOARD
SIR WILLIAM MULOCK SECONDARY SCHOOL
(*Suby of* York Region District School Board)
705 Columbus Way, Newmarket, ON, L3X 2M7
(905) 967-1045
Emp Here 150
SIC 8211 Elementary and secondary schools

D-U-N-S 20-536-4503   (BR)
YORK REGION DISTRICT SCHOOL BOARD
CLEARMEADOW PUBLIC SCHOOL
(*Suby of* York Region District School Board)
200 Clearmeadow Blvd, Newmarket, ON, L3X 2E4
(905) 868-8081
Emp Here 60
SIC 8211 Elementary and secondary schools

D-U-N-S 25-293-5812   (BR)
YORK REGION DISTRICT SCHOOL BOARD
ARMITAGE VILLAGE PUBLIC SCHOOL
(*Suby of* York Region District School Board)
125 Savage Rd, Newmarket, ON, L3X 1R3
(905) 853-3799
Emp Here 25
SIC 8211 Elementary and secondary schools

D-U-N-S 20-591-2483   (BR)
YORK REGION DISTRICT SCHOOL BOARD
CROSSLAND PUBLIC SCHOOL
(*Suby of* York Region District School Board)
255 Brimson Dr, Newmarket, ON, L3X 1H8
(905) 830-0500
Emp Here 25
SIC 8211 Elementary and secondary schools

D-U-N-S 25-984-6343   (BR)
ZAHID, M. DRUGS LTD
SHOPPERS DRUG MART
665 Stonehaven Ave, Newmarket, ON, L3X 0G2
(905) 836-9697
Emp Here 30
SIC 5912 Drug stores and proprietary stores

Newmarket, ON L3Y
York County

D-U-N-S 25-141-9180   (BR)
677957 ONTARIO INC
VINCE'S COUNTRY MARKET
869 Mulock Dr Suite 1, Newmarket, ON, L3Y 8S3
(905) 853-3356
Emp Here 35
SIC 5411 Grocery stores

D-U-N-S 24-141-0893   (SL)
87029 CANADA LTD
NEWMARKET GROUP
200 Davis Dr, Newmarket, ON, L3Y 2N4
(905) 898-5383
Emp Here 50   *Sales* 2,626,585
SIC 7389 Business services, nec

D-U-N-S 20-057-5970   (SL)
ASIAN TELEVISION NETWORK INC
(*Suby of* Asian Television Network International Limited)
130 Pony Dr, Newmarket, ON, L3Y 7B6
(905) 773-8966
Emp Here 72   *Sales* 5,465,508
SIC 4833 Television broadcasting stations
Pr Pr Subrahmanyam Chandrasekar

D-U-N-S 25-296-4739   (BR)
BANK OF NOVA SCOTIA, THE
SCOTIABANK
17900 Yonge St, Newmarket, ON, L3Y 8S1
(905) 853-7445
Emp Here 29
SIC 6021 National commercial banks

D-U-N-S 24-117-0658   (BR)
BANK OF NOVA SCOTIA, THE
SCOTIABANK
1100 Davis Dr, Newmarket, ON, L3Y 8W8
(905) 830-5900
Emp Here 40
SIC 6021 National commercial banks

D-U-N-S 20-588-2223   (BR)
BANQUE TORONTO-DOMINION, LA
TD CANADA TRUST
(*Suby of* Toronto-Dominion Bank, The)
1155 Davis Dr, Newmarket, ON, L3Y 8R1
(905) 830-9650
Emp Here 20
SIC 6021 National commercial banks

D-U-N-S 24-455-6267   (SL)
BARTON RETIREMENT INC
17290 Leslie St Suite 1, Newmarket, ON, L3Y 3E1
(905) 967-1331
Emp Here 20   *Sales* 729,607
SIC 8361 Residential care

D-U-N-S 25-997-1182   (SL)
BEAVER MACHINE CORPORATION
MACHINE-O-MATIC, DIV OF
250 Harry Walker Pkwy N Unit 1, Newmarket, ON, L3Y 7B4
(905) 836-4700
Emp Here 75
SIC 3581 Automatic vending machines

D-U-N-S 25-984-6368   (BR)
BEST BUY CANADA LTD
FUTURE SHOP
(*Suby of* Best Buy Co., Inc.)

17890 Yonge St, Newmarket, ON, L3Y 8S1

Emp Here 80
SIC 5999 Miscellaneous retail stores, nec

D-U-N-S 20-289-2670   (BR)
BRICK WAREHOUSE LP, THE
BRICK, THE
17940 Yonge St Suite A, Newmarket, ON, L3Y 8S4
(905) 830-5888
Emp Here 25
SIC 5712 Furniture stores

D-U-N-S 24-342-8104   (BR)
CARA OPERATIONS LIMITED
SWISS CHALET
(Suby of Cara Holdings Limited)
1111 Davis Dr Unit 44, Newmarket, ON, L3Y 8X2
(905) 853-3311
Emp Here 70
SIC 5812 Eating places

D-U-N-S 24-197-4885   (BR)
CARA OPERATIONS LIMITED
MILESTONE'S GRILL & BAR
(Suby of Cara Holdings Limited)
18162 Yonge St, Newmarket, ON, L3Y 4V8
(905) 853-5345
Emp Here 65
SIC 5812 Eating places

D-U-N-S 20-303-2941   (BR)
CARA OPERATIONS LIMITED
KELSEY'S RESTAURANT
(Suby of Cara Holdings Limited)
18158 Yonge St, Newmarket, ON, L3Y 4V8
(905) 895-6336
Emp Here 20
SIC 5812 Eating places

D-U-N-S 20-288-1772   (BR)
CHARTWELL RETIREMENT RESIDENCES
CHARTWELL SENIORS HOUSING REAL ESTATE INVESTMENT TRUST
17290 Leslie St Suite 1, Newmarket, ON, L3Y 3E1
(905) 967-1331
Emp Here 35
SIC 6513 Apartment building operators

D-U-N-S 20-791-4743   (BR)
CHILDREN'S PLACE (CANADA) LP, THE
17600 Yonge St, Newmarket, ON, L3Y 4Z1
(905) 953-9260
Emp Here 26
SIC 5641 Children's and infants' wear stores

D-U-N-S 24-418-1637   (BR)
CINEPLEX ODEON CORPORATION
SILVERCITY NEWMARKET CINEMAS & XS-CAPE
18151 Yonge St, Newmarket, ON, L3Y 4V8
(905) 953-2792
Emp Here 49
SIC 7832 Motion picture theaters, except drive-in

D-U-N-S 25-501-0282   (BR)
CINTAS CANADA LIMITED
SALLY FOURMY & ASSOCIATES
(Suby of Cintas Corporation)
255 Harry Walker Pky S Suite 1, Newmarket, ON, L3Y 8Z5
(905) 853-4409
Emp Here 150
SIC 7213 Linen supply

D-U-N-S 25-361-4143   (BR)
CON-PRO INDUSTRIES CANADA LTD
17075 Leslie St Suite 27, Newmarket, ON, L3Y 8E1
(905) 830-5661
Emp Here 20
SIC 1541 Industrial buildings and warehouses

D-U-N-S 24-738-3417   (BR)

EXCO TECHNOLOGIES LIMITED
EXCO ENGINEERING
1314 Ringwell Dr, Newmarket, ON, L3Y 9C6
(905) 853-8568
Emp Here 140
SIC 3544 Special dies, tools, jigs, and fixtures

D-U-N-S 25-301-2686   (BR)
EXTENDICARE (CANADA) INC
PARAMED HOME HEALTH CARE
320 Harry Walker Pky N Suite 11, Newmarket, ON, L3Y 7B4

Emp Here 80
SIC 8051 Skilled nursing care facilities

D-U-N-S 24-337-2856   (BR)
FGL SPORTS LTD
NATIONAL SPORTS
404-1111 Davis Dr, Newmarket, ON, L3Y 9E5
(905) 853-7965
Emp Here 20
SIC 5941 Sporting goods and bicycle shops

D-U-N-S 24-354-4512   (BR)
FOREVER XXI ULC
17600 Yonge St, Newmarket, ON, L3Y 4Z1
(905) 954-1359
Emp Here 40
SIC 5532 Women's accessory and specialty stores

D-U-N-S 25-304-6874   (BR)
GAP (CANADA) INC
GAP
(Suby of The Gap Inc)
17600 Yonge St, Newmarket, ON, L3Y 4Z1
(905) 336-1738
Emp Here 50
SIC 5651 Family clothing stores

D-U-N-S 25-191-1756   (BR)
GOODLIFE FITNESS CENTRES INC
20 Davis Dr, Newmarket, ON, L3Y 2M7
(905) 953-9248
Emp Here 20
SIC 7991 Physical fitness facilities

D-U-N-S 24-329-2526   (BR)
HALTON RECYCLING LTD
395 Harry Walker Pky S, Newmarket, ON, L3Y 8T3

Emp Here 30
SIC 4953 Refuse systems

D-U-N-S 25-671-4312   (BR)
HOME DEPOT OF CANADA INC
HOME DEPOT
(Suby of The Home Depot Inc)
17850 Yonge St, Newmarket, ON, L3Y 8S1
(905) 898-0090
Emp Here 200
SIC 5251 Hardware stores

D-U-N-S 25-465-7315   (BR)
IGM FINANCIAL INC
INVESTORS GROUP FINANCIAL SERVICES
17310 Yonge St Unit 10a, Newmarket, ON, L3Y 7S1
(905) 895-6718
Emp Here 70
SIC 6282 Investment advice

D-U-N-S 25-928-9551   (BR)
INDIGO BOOKS & MUSIC INC
CHAPTERS
(Suby of Indigo Books & Music Inc)
17440 Yonge St, Newmarket, ON, L3Y 6Y9
(905) 836-8508
Emp Here 50
SIC 5942 Book stores

D-U-N-S 25-305-3474   (BR)
INNVEST PROPERTIES CORP
COMFORT INN
(Suby of Innvest Properties Corp)

1230 Journey'S End Cir, Newmarket, ON, L3Y 8Z6
(905) 895-3355
Emp Here 20
SIC 7011 Hotels and motels

D-U-N-S 24-409-4561   (SL)
INSTACHANGE DISPLAYS LIMITED
360 Harry Walker Pky S Unit 1-3, Newmarket, ON, L3Y 9E9
(289) 279-1100
Emp Here 45   Sales 2,699,546
SIC 3993 Signs and advertising specialties

D-U-N-S 24-079-9614   (BR)
INVESTORS GROUP SECURITIES INC
17310 Yonge St Unit 10a, Newmarket, ON, L3Y 7S1
(905) 895-6718
Emp Here 71
SIC 6211 Security brokers and dealers

D-U-N-S 24-249-3893   (BR)
JOHNSON INC
JOHNSON INSURANCE
1111 Davis Dr Unit 42, Newmarket, ON, L3Y 8X2
(905) 952-2600
Emp Here 20
SIC 6411 Insurance agents, brokers, and service

D-U-N-S 24-340-4352   (BR)
LEON'S FURNITURE LIMITED
25 Harry Walker Pky N, Newmarket, ON, L3Y 7B3
(905) 953-1617
Emp Here 60
SIC 5712 Furniture stores

D-U-N-S 24-121-1320   (BR)
LOBLAWS SUPERMARKETS LIMITED
REAL CANADIAN SUPERSTORE
18120 Yonge St, Newmarket, ON, L3Y 4V8
(905) 830-4072
Emp Here 250
SIC 5411 Grocery stores

D-U-N-S 24-353-4471   (BR)
LOWE'S COMPANIES CANADA, ULC
LOWE'S OF E. GWILLIMBURY
18401 Yonge St, Newmarket, ON, L3Y 4V8
(905) 952-2950
Emp Here 200
SIC 5211 Lumber and other building materials

D-U-N-S 20-535-1484   (BR)
MARCH OF DIMES CANADA
MARCH OF DIMES CANADA
351 Crowder Blvd Suite 414, Newmarket, ON, L3Y 8J5
(905) 953-9700
Emp Here 20
SIC 8331 Job training and related services

D-U-N-S 25-236-5507   (BR)
MARK'S WORK WEARHOUSE LTD
MARK'S WORK WEARHOUSE NO. 151
17820 Yonge St, Newmarket, ON, L3Y 8S1
(905) 895-7707
Emp Here 20
SIC 5651 Family clothing stores

D-U-N-S 24-704-7889   (BR)
MARS CANADA INC
(Suby of Mars, Incorporated)
285 Harry Walker Pky N, Newmarket, ON, L3Y 7B3
(905) 853-6000
Emp Here 115
SIC 2064 Candy and other confectionery products

D-U-N-S 20-290-6918   (BR)
MERCEDES-BENZ CANADA INC
230 Mulock Dr, Newmarket, ON, L3Y 9B8
(905) 853-6868
Emp Here 25
SIC 5511 New and used car dealers

D-U-N-S 20-555-6579   (BR)
METRO ONTARIO INC
METRO
1111 Davis Dr, Newmarket, ON, L3Y 9E5
(905) 853-5355
Emp Here 230
SIC 5411 Grocery stores

D-U-N-S 25-300-0376   (BR)
METRO ONTARIO INC
17725 Yonge St Suite 1, Newmarket, ON, L3Y 7C1
(905) 895-9700
Emp Here 150
SIC 5411 Grocery stores

D-U-N-S 24-252-6650   (BR)
METROLAND MEDIA GROUP LTD
METROLAND
Gd Lcd 1, Newmarket, ON, L3Y 4W2

Emp Here 100
SIC 2711 Newspapers

D-U-N-S 20-699-9398   (BR)
METROLAND MEDIA GROUP LTD
NEWMARKET ERA BANNER
580 Steven Crt Unit B, Newmarket, ON, L3Y 6Z2
(905) 853-8888
Emp Here 60
SIC 2711 Newspapers

D-U-N-S 20-093-5505   (BR)
MILLER, P.G. ENTERPRISES LIMITED
MCDONALD'S RESTAURANTS
17155 Yonge St, Newmarket, ON, L3Y 5L8
(905) 895-3990
Emp Here 30
SIC 5812 Eating places

D-U-N-S 24-311-3813   (BR)
MILLER, P.G. ENTERPRISES LIMITED
MCDONALD'S
1100 Davis Dr, Newmarket, ON, L3Y 8W8
(905) 853-0118
Emp Here 90
SIC 5812 Eating places

D-U-N-S 20-801-1887   (BR)
MILLER, P.G. ENTERPRISES LIMITED
MCDONALDS
17760 Yonge St, Newmarket, ON, L3Y 8P4
(905) 895-1222
Emp Here 80
SIC 5812 Eating places

D-U-N-S 20-090-7132   (SL)
MONTANAS COOKHOUSE
17440 Yonge St, Newmarket, ON, L3Y 6Y9
(905) 898-4546
Emp Here 50   Sales 1,532,175
SIC 5812 Eating places

D-U-N-S 25-624-3627   (SL)
O'MALLEY'S CATERING & RENTAL LTD
580 Steven Crt Suite 5, Newmarket, ON, L3Y 6Z2
(905) 895-5082
Emp Here 50   Sales 1,532,175
SIC 5812 Eating places

D-U-N-S 20-808-9131   (SL)
OAK RIDGES MORAINE LAND TRUST
18462 Bathurst St, Newmarket, ON, L3Y 4V9
(905) 853-3171
Emp Here 20   Sales 17,411,645
SIC 6021 National commercial banks

D-U-N-S 20-657-9372   (BR)
OLD NAVY (CANADA) INC
(Suby of The Gap Inc)
17600 Yonge St Suite 257, Newmarket, ON, L3Y 4Z1
(905) 830-1892
Emp Here 50
SIC 5651 Family clothing stores

D-U-N-S 24-950-6825   (SL)

PFM PACKAGING MACHINERY CORPORATION
1271 Ringwell Dr, Newmarket, ON, L3Y 8T9
(905) 836-6709
Emp Here 42 *Sales* 9,480,220
SIC 3565 Packaging machinery
CEO Daniele Bisio
Sec Paolo Floravanti

D-U-N-S 25-096-9326 (BR)
PEARSON CANADA HOLDINGS INC
195 Harry Walker Pky N Suite A, Newmarket,
ON, L3Y 7B3
(905) 853-7888
Emp Here 200
SIC 2731 Book publishing

D-U-N-S 20-705-6172 (BR)
PEARSON CANADA INC
PENGUIN BOOKS CANADA
195 Harry Walker Pky N Suite A, Newmarket,
ON, L3Y 7B3
(905) 853-7888
Emp Here 700
SIC 2731 Book publishing

D-U-N-S 25-175-9072 (BR)
R.J. BURNSIDE & ASSOCIATES LIMITED
BURNSIDE, RJ INTERNATIONAL
16775 Yonge St Suite 200, Newmarket, ON,
L3Y 8J4
(905) 953-8967
Emp Here 24
SIC 8711 Engineering services

D-U-N-S 25-293-7347 (BR)
RBC DOMINION SECURITIES INC
RBC DOMINION SECURITIES
(*Suby of* Royal Bank Of Canada)
17120 Leslie St Suite 200, Newmarket, ON,
L3Y 8K7
(905) 895-2377
Emp Here 25
SIC 6211 Security brokers and dealers

D-U-N-S 20-803-8310 (BR)
REGIONAL MUNICIPALITY OF YORK, THE
COMMUNITY AND HEALTH DEPARTMENT
22 Prospect St, Newmarket, ON, L3Y 3S9
(905) 895-4512
Emp Here 35
SIC 8021 Offices and clinics of dentists

D-U-N-S 20-706-3517 (BR)
REGIONAL MUNICIPALITY OF YORK, THE
NEWMARKET HEALTH CENTRE, THE
194 Eagle St Suite 3011, Newmarket, ON,
L3Y 1J6
(905) 895-2382
Emp Here 400
SIC 8051 Skilled nursing care facilities

D-U-N-S 20-938-2964 (BR)
REVERA LONG TERM CARE INC
MACKENZIE PLCE
52 George St, Newmarket, ON, L3Y 4V3
(905) 853-3242
Emp Here 90
SIC 8059 Nursing and personal care, nec

D-U-N-S 24-334-3605 (BR)
REVERA LONG TERM CARE INC
EAGLE TERRACE
329 Eagle St, Newmarket, ON, L3Y 1K3
(905) 895-5187
Emp Here 65
SIC 8051 Skilled nursing care facilities

D-U-N-S 20-573-8136 (BR)
ROYAL BANK OF CANADA
RBC
(*Suby of* Royal Bank Of Canada)
17600 Yonge St, Newmarket, ON, L3Y 4Z1
(905) 895-5551
Emp Here 20
SIC 6021 National commercial banks

D-U-N-S 24-783-6125 (SL)

ROYAL OAK RAILING & STAIR LTD
1131 Gorham St Unit 10-15, Newmarket, ON,
L3Y 8X9
(905) 853-5727
Emp Here 50 *Sales* 4,085,799
SIC 2431 Millwork

D-U-N-S 25-294-6744 (BR)
SEARS CANADA INC
17600 Yonge St Suite 1, Newmarket, ON, L3Y
4Z1
(905) 898-2300
Emp Here 350
SIC 5311 Department stores

D-U-N-S 25-204-7006 (SL)
**SILVER LAKES GOLF & COUNTRY CLUB
INC**
21114 Yonge St, Newmarket, ON, L3Y 4V8
(905) 836-8070
Emp Here 80 *Sales* 3,210,271
SIC 7997 Membership sports and recreation
clubs

D-U-N-S 20-045-7471 (HQ)
SNAP-ON TOOLS OF CANADA LTD
SNAP-ON/SUN EQUIPMENT DIVISION
(*Suby of* Snap-On Incorporated)
1171 Gorham St, Newmarket, ON, L3Y 8Y2
(800) 665-8665
Emp Here 30 *Emp Total* 12,100
Sales 57,778,942
SIC 5013 Motor vehicle supplies and new
parts
VP VP Brian Ross
Dir Thomas J. Ward

D-U-N-S 25-915-7543 (BR)
SNAP-ON TOOLS OF CANADA LTD
SNAP-ON TOOLS
(*Suby of* Snap-On Incorporated)
145 Harry Walker Pky N, Newmarket, ON, L3Y
7B3
(905) 812-5774
Emp Here 250
SIC 3469 Metal stampings, nec

D-U-N-S 20-945-2262 (BR)
SOBEYS CAPITAL INCORPORATED
17730 Leslie St, Newmarket, ON, L3Y 3E4

Emp Here 30
SIC 5411 Grocery stores

D-U-N-S 20-699-6600 (BR)
SOUTHLAKE REGIONAL HEALTH CENTRE
SOUTHLAKE RESIDENTIAL CARE VILLAGE
640 Grace St, Newmarket, ON, L3Y 8V7
(905) 895-7661
Emp Here 25
SIC 8051 Skilled nursing care facilities

D-U-N-S 25-458-9344 (SL)
SPECIALTY PRECAST ERECTORS LIMITED
ARCHITECTURAL PRECAST
1 Bales Rd, Newmarket, ON, L3Y 4X1

Emp Here 35 *Sales* 5,202,480
SIC 1771 Concrete work
Pr Pr Dana Santoro
Vincenzo Persico

D-U-N-S 20-559-9855 (SL)
**SPECTRUM EDUCATIONAL SUPPLIES
LIMITED**
SI MANUFACTURING
(*Suby of* Geneve Holdings, Inc.)
150 Pony Dr, Newmarket, ON, L3Y 7B6
(905) 898-0031
Emp Here 70 *Sales* 7,189,883
SIC 5961 Catalog and mail-order houses
Pr Pr Brett Caldwell
Fin Ex Francis Lui

D-U-N-S 25-499-0088 (BR)
STAPLES CANADA INC
STAPLES THE BUSINESS DEPOT

(*Suby of* Staples, Inc.)
17810 Yonge St, Newmarket, ON, L3Y 8S1
(905) 898-3956
Emp Here 30
SIC 5943 Stationery stores

D-U-N-S 25-120-2057 (BR)
TORONTO-DOMINION BANK, THE
TD CANADA TRUST
(*Suby of* Toronto-Dominion Bank, The)
130 Davis Dr Suite 24, Newmarket, ON, L3Y
2N1
(905) 898-6831
Emp Here 40
SIC 6021 National commercial banks

D-U-N-S 25-405-8548 (SL)
TRI-STAR METAL STAMPINGS INC
1267 Kerrisdale Blvd Unit 2, Newmarket, ON,
L3Y 8W1
(905) 853-5583
Emp Here 50 *Sales* 4,085,799
SIC 3544 Special dies, tools, jigs, and fixtures

D-U-N-S 24-937-9439 (HQ)
TURF CARE PRODUCTS CANADA LIMITED
CANADIAN CART SALES, DIV OF
200 Pony Dr, Newmarket, ON, L3Y 7B6
(905) 836-0988
Emp Here 85 *Emp Total* 130
Sales 17,931,396
SIC 3523 Farm machinery and equipment
Pr Pr Ronald Craig
John Jarman
Jamie Worden

D-U-N-S 24-090-6284 (BR)
VALUE VILLAGE STORES, INC
(*Suby of* Savers, Inc.)
130 Davis Dr Suite 9, Newmarket, ON, L3Y
2N1
(905) 953-1344
Emp Here 55
SIC 5399 Miscellaneous general merchandise

D-U-N-S 24-851-3322 (BR)
WSP CANADA INC
GENIVAR
1091 Gorham St Suite 301, Newmarket, ON,
L3Y 8X7

Emp Here 35
SIC 8711 Engineering services

D-U-N-S 25-294-7502 (BR)
WAL-MART CANADA CORP
17940 Yonge St, Newmarket, ON, L3Y 8S4
(905) 853-8811
Emp Here 240
SIC 5311 Department stores

D-U-N-S 24-985-8861 (HQ)
WALL, BOB ENTERPRISES INC
TIM HORTONS
(*Suby of* Wall, Bob Enterprises Inc)
1111 Davis Dr Unit 5, Newmarket, ON, L3Y
8X2
(905) 853-9300
Emp Here 45 *Emp Total* 90
Sales 3,064,349
SIC 5461 Retail bakeries

D-U-N-S 20-769-0640 (BR)
WALL, BOB ENTERPRISES INC
TIM HORTONS
(*Suby of* Wall, Bob Enterprises Inc)
1166 Davis Dr, Newmarket, ON, L3Y 8X4
(905) 853-0607
Emp Here 60
SIC 5812 Eating places

D-U-N-S 24-098-3432 (BR)
WE CARE HEALTH SERVICES INC
1124 Stellar Dr, Newmarket, ON, L3Y 7B7
(905) 715-7950
Emp Here 120
SIC 8082 Home health care services

D-U-N-S 25-085-3686 (BR)

WENDY'S RESTAURANTS OF CANADA INC
WENDY'S
(*Suby of* The Wendy's Company)
17725 Yonge St, Newmarket, ON, L3Y 7C1
(905) 853-9861
Emp Here 50
SIC 5812 Eating places

D-U-N-S 24-218-8592 (BR)
WEST 49 GROUP INC
17600 Yonge St Suite 15, Newmarket, ON,
L3Y 4Z1
(905) 898-2359
Emp Here 20
SIC 5621 Women's clothing stores

D-U-N-S 25-221-2659 (BR)
**WINNERS MERCHANTS INTERNATIONAL
L.P.**
WINNERS
(*Suby of* The TJX Companies Inc)
17890 Yonge St, Newmarket, ON, L3Y 8S1
(905) 830-1815
Emp Here 50
SIC 5651 Family clothing stores

D-U-N-S 20-184-2874 (BR)
**WINNERS MERCHANTS INTERNATIONAL
L.P.**
HOMESENSE
(*Suby of* The TJX Companies Inc)
17940 Yonge St, Newmarket, ON, L3Y 8S4
(905) 830-4418
Emp Here 40
SIC 5651 Family clothing stores

D-U-N-S 25-147-3039 (BR)
**YORK CATHOLIC DISTRICT SCHOOL
BOARD**
ST. PAUL CATHOLIC SCHOOL
140 William Roe Blvd, Newmarket, ON, L3Y
1B2
(905) 895-4122
Emp Here 35
SIC 8211 Elementary and secondary schools

D-U-N-S 25-151-0327 (BR)
**YORK CATHOLIC DISTRICT SCHOOL
BOARD**
SACRED HEART HIGH SCHOOL
1 Crusader Way, Newmarket, ON, L3Y 6R2
(905) 895-3340
Emp Here 100
SIC 8211 Elementary and secondary schools

D-U-N-S 20-711-4526 (BR)
**YORK CATHOLIC DISTRICT SCHOOL
BOARD**
*CANADIAN MARTYRS ELEMENTARY
SCHOOL*
170 London Rd, Newmarket, ON, L3Y 6R5
(905) 895-8530
Emp Here 50
SIC 8211 Elementary and secondary schools

D-U-N-S 25-106-9696 (BR)
**YORK CATHOLIC DISTRICT SCHOOL
BOARD**
ST ELIZABETH SETON
960 Leslie Valley Dr, Newmarket, ON, L3Y
8B3
(905) 853-0340
Emp Here 35
SIC 8211 Elementary and secondary schools

D-U-N-S 25-931-5513 (SL)
YORK COUNTY BOWMEN INC
15887 Mccowan Rd, Newmarket, ON, L3Y
4W1

Emp Here 80 *Sales* 4,377,642
SIC 7999 Amusement and recreation, nec

D-U-N-S 20-591-2335 (BR)
YORK REGION DISTRICT SCHOOL BOARD
MAPLE LEAF PUBLIC SCHOOL
(*Suby of* York Region District School Board)
155 Longford Dr, Newmarket, ON, L3Y 2Y7

(905) 895-9681
Emp Here 40
SIC 8211 Elementary and secondary schools

D-U-N-S 20-591-2699 *(BR)*
YORK REGION DISTRICT SCHOOL BOARD
PRINCE CHARLES SCHOOL
(*Suby of* York Region District School Board)
684 Srigley St, Newmarket, ON, L3Y 1W9
(905) 895-8401
Emp Here 25
SIC 8211 Elementary and secondary schools

D-U-N-S 20-938-8318 *(BR)*
YORK REGION DISTRICT SCHOOL BOARD
MAZO DE LA ROCHE PUBLIC SCHOOL
(*Suby of* York Region District School Board)
860 Arnold Cres, Newmarket, ON, L3Y 2E2
(905) 836-1032
Emp Here 50
SIC 8211 Elementary and secondary schools

D-U-N-S 25-293-5861 *(BR)*
YORK REGION DISTRICT SCHOOL BOARD
ROGERS PUBLIC SCHOOL
(*Suby of* York Region District School Board)
256 Rogers Rd, Newmarket, ON, L3Y 1G6
(905) 895-5441
Emp Here 40
SIC 8211 Elementary and secondary schools

D-U-N-S 25-293-5895 *(BR)*
YORK REGION DISTRICT SCHOOL BOARD
HURON HEIGHTS SECONDARY SCHOOL
(*Suby of* York Region District School Board)
40 Huron Heights Dr, Newmarket, ON, L3Y 3J9
(905) 895-2384
Emp Here 175
SIC 8211 Elementary and secondary schools

D-U-N-S 25-297-8911 *(BR)*
YORK REGION DISTRICT SCHOOL BOARD
DENNE PUBLIC SCHOOL
(*Suby of* York Region District School Board)
330 Burford St, Newmarket, ON, L3Y 6L1
(905) 853-2303
Emp Here 30
SIC 8211 Elementary and secondary schools

D-U-N-S 20-291-3427 *(BR)*
YORK REGION DISTRICT SCHOOL BOARD
COMMUNITY EDUCATION CENTRE - NORTH
(*Suby of* York Region District School Board)
130 Carlson Dr, Newmarket, ON, L3Y 5H3
(905) 895-5155
Emp Here 40
SIC 8211 Elementary and secondary schools

D-U-N-S 25-297-9034 *(BR)*
YORK REGION DISTRICT SCHOOL BOARD
STUART SCOTT PUBLIC SCHOOL
(*Suby of* York Region District School Board)
247 Lorne Ave, Newmarket, ON, L3Y 4K5
(905) 895-8461
Emp Here 25
SIC 8211 Elementary and secondary schools

D-U-N-S 25-293-5978 *(BR)*
YORK REGION DISTRICT SCHOOL BOARD
DR. JOHN M. DENISON SECONDARY SCHOOL
(*Suby of* York Region District School Board)
135 Bristol Rd, Newmarket, ON, L3Y 8J7
(905) 836-0021
Emp Here 105
SIC 8211 Elementary and secondary schools

D-U-N-S 24-126-4055 *(BR)*
YORK REGION DISTRICT SCHOOL BOARD
BOGART PUBLIC SCHOOL
(*Suby of* York Region District School Board)
855 College Manor Dr, Newmarket, ON, L3Y 8G7
(905) 836-8041
Emp Here 25
SIC 8211 Elementary and secondary schools

D-U-N-S 20-711-4054 *(BR)*
YORK REGION DISTRICT SCHOOL BOARD
GLEN CEDAR PUBLIC SCHOOL
(*Suby of* York Region District School Board)
915 Wayne Dr, Newmarket, ON, L3Y 5W1
(905) 895-1500
Emp Here 25
SIC 8211 Elementary and secondary schools

D-U-N-S 25-293-5937 *(BR)*
YORK REGION DISTRICT SCHOOL BOARD
NEWMARKET HIGH SCHOOL
(*Suby of* York Region District School Board)
505 Pickering Cres, Newmarket, ON, L3Y 8H1
(905) 895-5159
Emp Here 85
SIC 8211 Elementary and secondary schools

D-U-N-S 25-293-6182 *(BR)*
YORK REGION DISTRICT SCHOOL BOARD
MEADOWBROOK PUBLIC SCHOOL
(*Suby of* York Region District School Board)
233 Patterson St, Newmarket, ON, L3Y 3L5
(905) 895-3081
Emp Here 35
SIC 8211 Elementary and secondary schools

Newtonville, ON L0A
Durham County

D-U-N-S 24-142-2810 *(BR)*
CRUICKSHANK CONSTRUCTION LIMITED
1400 Newtonville Rd, Newtonville, ON, L0A 1J0
(905) 786-2004
Emp Here 31
SIC 1611 Highway and street construction

Niagara Falls, ON L2E
Welland County

D-U-N-S 25-137-2975 *(SL)*
1346674 ONTARIO LIMITED
PERKIN'S FAMILY RESTAURANT
4800 Bender St, Niagara Falls, ON, L2E 6W7
(905) 374-4444
Emp Here 70 *Sales* 2,115,860
SIC 5812 Eating places

D-U-N-S 24-538-0837 *(SL)*
647802 ONTARIO LIMITED
SOUVENIR CITY
4199 River Rd, Niagara Falls, ON, L2E 3E7
(905) 357-1133
Emp Here 70 *Sales* 3,866,917
SIC 5947 Gift, novelty, and souvenir shop

D-U-N-S 25-478-5504 *(SL)*
867907 ONTARIO LIMITED
CHATTERS
4414 Portage Rd, Niagara Falls, ON, L2E 6A5
(905) 354-2521
Emp Here 50 *Sales* 1,532,175
SIC 5812 Eating places

D-U-N-S 24-964-2265 *(BR)*
AFFILIATED AGENTS EN DOUANES LIMITEE
AFFILIATED AGENTS EN DOUANES LIMITEE
6150 Valley Way, Niagara Falls, ON, L2E 1Y3
(905) 358-7181
Emp Here 30
SIC 4731 Freight transportation arrangement

D-U-N-S 24-176-5853 *(BR)*
ARTERRA WINES CANADA, INC
WINE RACK
(*Suby of* Arterra Wines Canada, Inc)
4887 Dorchester Rd, Niagara Falls, ON, L2E 6N8

(905) 358-7141
Emp Here 200
SIC 2084 Wines, brandy, and brandy spirits

D-U-N-S 24-362-5394 *(SL)*
CAN-ENG FURNACES INTERNATIONAL LTD
6800 Montrose Rd, Niagara Falls, ON, L2E 6V5
(905) 356-1327
Emp Here 85 *Sales* 12,257,398
SIC 3567 Industrial furnaces and ovens
Pr Pr Alan Van Geyn
John Krediet

D-U-N-S 25-706-2620 *(BR)*
CANADA POST CORPORATION
4500 Queen St, Niagara Falls, ON, L2E 2L5
(905) 374-6667
Emp Here 100
SIC 4311 U.s. postal service

D-U-N-S 20-272-7863 *(SL)*
COMPLEX SUPPLY INC
Po Box 300 Stn Main, Niagara Falls, ON, L2E 6T3
(905) 374-6928
Emp Here 100 *Sales* 6,973,235
SIC 7999 Amusement and recreation, nec
Pr Clare Copeland
Sec Bruce Clarke Caughill
Treas Kevin Wilson
Dir Art Frank

D-U-N-S 20-024-9782 *(BR)*
CONSEIL SCOLAIRE DE DISTRICT CATHOLIQUE CENTRE-SUD
ECOLE SAINT-ANTOINE
4572 Portage Rd, Niagara Falls, ON, L2E 6A8
(905) 356-2522
Emp Here 25
SIC 8211 Elementary and secondary schools

D-U-N-S 20-806-6758 *(BR)*
COUTTS, WILLIAM E. COMPANY, LIMITED
HALLMARK CARDS & GIFTS
(*Suby of* Hallmark Cards, Incorporated)
7190 Morrison St Suite 3, Niagara Falls, ON, L2E 7K5
(905) 356-5582
Emp Here 25
SIC 5947 Gift, novelty, and souvenir shop

D-U-N-S 24-507-2814 *(HQ)*
CRAWFORD SMITH & SWALLOW CHARTERED ACCOUNTANTS LLP
(*Suby of* Crawford Smith & Swallow Chartered Accountants LLP)
4741 Queen St, Niagara Falls, ON, L2E 2M2
(905) 356-4200
Emp Here 50 *Emp Total* 75
Sales 3,283,232
SIC 8721 Accounting, auditing, and bookkeeping

D-U-N-S 24-048-0793 *(SL)*
DIGITAL ATTRACTIONS INC
6650 Niagara River, Niagara Falls, ON, L2E 6T2
(905) 371-2003
Emp Here 100 *Sales* 3,939,878
SIC 7221 Photographic studios, portrait

D-U-N-S 20-710-8551 *(BR)*
DISTRICT SCHOOL BOARD OF NIAGARA
CHERRYWOOD ACRES SCHOOL
4635 Pettit Ave, Niagara Falls, ON, L2E 6L4
(905) 356-2801
Emp Here 20
SIC 8211 Elementary and secondary schools

D-U-N-S 20-710-8817 *(BR)*
DISTRICT SCHOOL BOARD OF NIAGARA
VALLEY WAY PUBLIC SCHOOL
5315 Valley Way, Niagara Falls, ON, L2E 1X4
(905) 356-6611
Emp Here 25
SIC 8211 Elementary and secondary schools

D-U-N-S 20-710-8783 *(BR)*
DISTRICT SCHOOL BOARD OF NIAGARA
SIMCOE STREET SCHOOL
4760 Simcoe St, Niagara Falls, ON, L2E 1V6
(905) 358-9121
Emp Here 20
SIC 8211 Elementary and secondary schools

D-U-N-S 24-367-1935 *(BR)*
EMCO CORPORATION
NIAGARA PLUMBING SUPPLY
4300 Stanley Ave, Niagara Falls, ON, L2E 4Z4

Emp Here 70
SIC 5074 Plumbing and heating equipment and supplies (hydronics)

D-U-N-S 24-045-0817 *(BR)*
GOVERNING COUNCIL OF THE SALVATION ARMY IN CANADA, THE
EVENTIDE HOME
5050 Jepson St, Niagara Falls, ON, L2E 1K5
(905) 356-1221
Emp Here 100
SIC 8051 Skilled nursing care facilities

D-U-N-S 24-119-3775 *(BR)*
HATCH LTD
HATCH ENERGY
4342 Queen St Suite 500, Niagara Falls, ON, L2E 7J7
(905) 374-5200
Emp Here 1,000
SIC 8711 Engineering services

D-U-N-S 20-514-9367 *(BR)*
HOME DEPOT OF CANADA INC
HOME DEPOT
(*Suby of* The Home Depot Inc)
7190 Morrison St, Niagara Falls, ON, L2E 7K5
(905) 371-7470
Emp Here 150
SIC 5211 Lumber and other building materials

D-U-N-S 25-642-2742 *(BR)*
HORTON CBI, LIMITED
4342 Queen St Suite 3, Niagara Falls, ON, L2E 7J7

Emp Here 45
SIC 1791 Structural steel erection

D-U-N-S 20-709-0759 *(BR)*
HYDRO ONE NETWORKS INC
HYDRO ONE
1210 Barron Rd, Niagara Falls, ON, L2E 6S5
(289) 439-4006
Emp Here 20
SIC 4911 Electric services

D-U-N-S 20-355-1549 *(SL)*
INTEGRATED MUNICIPAL SERVICES INC
IMS
(*Suby of* Walker Industries Holdings Limited)
2800 Thorold Town Line, Niagara Falls, ON, L2E 6S4
(905) 680-3777
Emp Here 30 *Sales* 3,291,754
SIC 8742 Management consulting services

D-U-N-S 25-315-8547 *(BR)*
INVESTORS GROUP FINANCIAL SERVICES INC
4838 Dorchester Rd Suite 100, Niagara Falls, ON, L2E 6N9
(905) 374-2842
Emp Here 40
SIC 8742 Management consulting services

D-U-N-S 25-642-3195 *(BR)*
MARINELAND OF CANADA INC
KING WALDORF'S TENT & TRAILER
(*Suby of* Marineland of Canada Inc)
9015 Stanley Ave, Niagara Falls, ON, L2E 6X8
(905) 295-8191
Emp Here 20
SIC 7033 Trailer parks and campsites

D-U-N-S 24-938-0643   (BR)
MERIDIAN CREDIT UNION LIMITED
4780 Portage Rd, Niagara Falls, ON, L2E 6A8
(905) 356-2275
Emp Here 20
SIC 6062 State credit unions

D-U-N-S 25-688-3604   (SL)
NEW YORK HOSPITALITY INC
PLANET HOLLYWOOD
4608 Bender St, Niagara Falls, ON, L2E 6V7
(905) 374-8332
Emp Here 50   *Sales* 1,532,175
SIC 5812 Eating places

D-U-N-S 20-710-9005   (BR)
NIAGARA CATHOLIC DISTRICT SCHOOL BOARD
ST MARY CATHOLIC SCHOOL
5719 Morrison St, Niagara Falls, ON, L2E 2E8
(905) 354-7744
Emp Here 25
SIC 8211 Elementary and secondary schools

D-U-N-S 20-024-9774   (BR)
NIAGARA CATHOLIC DISTRICT SCHOOL BOARD
ST ANN ADULT LEARNING CENTRE
4700 Epworth Cir, Niagara Falls, ON, L2E 1C6
(905) 354-3531
Emp Here 30
SIC 8211 Elementary and secondary schools

D-U-N-S 20-939-9583   (HQ)
NIAGARA FALLS PUBLIC LIBRARY
(*Suby of* Niagara Falls Public Library)
4848 Victoria Ave, Niagara Falls, ON, L2E 4C5
(905) 356-8080
Emp Here 30   *Emp Total* 80
Sales 3,720,996
SIC 8231 Libraries

D-U-N-S 24-803-2815   (SL)
NIAGARA FALLS TRANSIT
NIAGARA TRANSIT
4320 Bridge St, Niagara Falls, ON, L2E 2R7
(905) 356-1179
Emp Here 60   *Sales* 2,115,860
SIC 4111 Local and suburban transit

D-U-N-S 25-835-6682   (BR)
NIAGARA PARKS COMMISSION, THE
QUEEN VICTORIA PLACE
6345 Niagara Pkwy, Niagara Falls, ON, L2E 6T2
(905) 356-2217
Emp Here 90
SIC 5812 Eating places

D-U-N-S 20-009-8023   (BR)
NIAGARA PARKS COMMISSION, THE
ELEMENTS ON THE FALLS RESTAURANT
6650 Niagara Pky, Niagara Falls, ON, L2E 6T2
(905) 354-3631
Emp Here 100
SIC 5812 Eating places

D-U-N-S 20-157-3326   (SL)
NIAGARA WASTE SYSTEMS LIMITED
(*Suby of* Walker Industries Holdings Limited)
2800 Thorold Town Line, Niagara Falls, ON, L2E 6S4
(905) 227-4142
Emp Here 27
SIC 1422 Crushed and broken limestone

D-U-N-S 20-357-7028   (BR)
ONTARIO LOTTERY AND GAMING CORPORATION
DELTA BINGO AND GAMING NIAGARA FALLS
4735 Drummond Rd, Niagara Falls, ON, L2E 6C8
(905) 356-8109
Emp Here 42
SIC 7999 Amusement and recreation, nec

D-U-N-S 20-124-5503   (HQ)

POLYONE CANADA INC
940 Chippawa Creek Rd, Niagara Falls, ON, L2E 6S5
(905) 353-4200
Emp Here 50   *Emp Total* 200
Sales 21,888,210
SIC 2821 Plastics materials and resins
Pr Thomas Waltermire
Dir Michel Roy
   Mario Tremblay

D-U-N-S 25-689-5145   (BR)
STAPLES CANADA INC
STAPLES THE BUSINESS DEPOT
(*Suby of* Staples, Inc.)
7190 Morrison St, Niagara Falls, ON, L2E 7K5
(905) 358-0650
Emp Here 30
SIC 5943 Stationery stores

D-U-N-S 24-572-5200   (BR)
TRENTWAY-WAGAR INC
4555 Erie Ave, Niagara Falls, ON, L2E 7G9
(905) 358-7230
Emp Here 100
SIC 4111 Local and suburban transit

D-U-N-S 24-329-6972   (BR)
WAL-MART CANADA CORP
7190 Morrison St, Niagara Falls, ON, L2E 7K5
(905) 371-3999
Emp Here 200
SIC 5311 Department stores

D-U-N-S 24-868-5737   (HQ)
WALKER INDUSTRIES HOLDINGS LIMITED
(*Suby of* Walker Industries Holdings Limited)
2800 Thorold Town Line, Niagara Falls, ON, L2E 6S4
(905) 227-4142
Emp Here 50   *Emp Total* 400
SIC 1411 Dimension stone

D-U-N-S 24-664-1021   (SL)
WASHINGTON MILLS ELECTRO MINERALS CORPORATION
7780 Stanley Ave, Niagara Falls, ON, L2E 6X8
(905) 357-5500
Emp Here 100   *Sales* 8,922,385
SIC 3291 Abrasive products
Dir Sandro Borghesi
Treas Michael Sproule
Pr Pr Ronald Campbell
Asst Tr Aldon Harris
Sec Warner Fletcher
Sec Nancy Gates

Niagara Falls, ON L2G
Welland County

D-U-N-S 20-844-3622   (SL)
289900 ONTARIO LIMITED
BETTY'S RESTAURANT & TAVERN
8921 Sodom Rd, Niagara Falls, ON, L2G 0T4
(905) 295-4436
Emp Here 50   *Sales* 1,532,175
SIC 5812 Eating places

D-U-N-S 24-313-6376   (BR)
ARROW GAMES CORPORATION
BAZAAR & NOVELTY
6199 Don Murie St, Niagara Falls, ON, L2G 0B1
(905) 354-7300
Emp Here 85
SIC 5092 Toys and hobby goods and supplies

D-U-N-S 25-293-2744   (BR)
ATLIFIC INC
COMFORT INN NIAGARA FALLS
(*Suby of* 3376290 Canada Inc)
4960 Clifton Hill, Niagara Falls, ON, L2G 3N4
(905) 358-3293
Emp Here 1,000

SIC 7011 Hotels and motels

D-U-N-S 20-742-8777   (SL)
BELLA SENIOR CARE RESIDENCES INC
8720 Willoughby Dr, Niagara Falls, ON, L2G 7X3
(905) 295-2727
Emp Here 65   *Sales* 2,991,389
SIC 8051 Skilled nursing care facilities

D-U-N-S 24-822-9833   (SL)
CADE HOLDING INC
BEST WESTERN CAIRN CROFT HOTEL
6400 Lundy'S Lane, Niagara Falls, ON, L2G 1T6
(905) 356-1161
Emp Here 100   *Sales* 4,377,642
SIC 7011 Hotels and motels

D-U-N-S 20-086-9258   (BR)
CANADIAN NIAGARA HOTELS INC
SHERATON ON THE FALLS
5875 Falls Ave, Niagara Falls, ON, L2G 3K7
(905) 374-4445
Emp Here 100
SIC 7011 Hotels and motels

D-U-N-S 20-303-2982   (BR)
CARA OPERATIONS LIMITED
KELSEY'S
(*Suby of* Cara Holdings Limited)
4960 Clifton Hill, Niagara Falls, ON, L2G 3N4
(905) 353-0051
Emp Here 130
SIC 5812 Eating places

D-U-N-S 24-371-7738   (BR)
CARA OPERATIONS LIMITED
SWISS CHALET
(*Suby of* Cara Holdings Limited)
6666 Lundy'S Lane, Niagara Falls, ON, L2G 1V5
(905) 356-1028
Emp Here 40
SIC 5812 Eating places

D-U-N-S 25-984-9172   (BR)
CASINO NIAGARA LIMITED
(*Suby of* Casino Niagara Limited)
5705 Falls Ave, Niagara Falls, ON, L2G 3K6
(905) 374-3598
Emp Here 3,000
SIC 7999 Amusement and recreation, nec

D-U-N-S 25-359-7124   (BR)
CHARTWELL SENIORS HOUSING REAL ESTATE INVESTMENT TRUST
WILLOUGHBY MANOR RETIREMENT RESIDENCE
3584 Bridgewater St, Niagara Falls, ON, L2G 6H1
(905) 295-6288
Emp Here 20
SIC 6513 Apartment building operators

D-U-N-S 20-711-7446   (BR)
CONSEIL SCOLAIRE DE DISTRICT CATHOLIQUE CENTRE-SUD
ELEMENTARY SCHOOL CATHOLIC NOTRE-DAME-DE-LA-JEUNES
7374 Wilson Cres, Niagara Falls, ON, L2G 4S1
(905) 357-2311
Emp Here 50
SIC 8211 Elementary and secondary schools

D-U-N-S 20-292-1248   (BR)
DISTRICT SCHOOL BOARD OF NIAGARA
PRINCESS MARGARET ELEMENTARY
6624 Culp St, Niagara Falls, ON, L2G 2C4
(905) 354-2333
Emp Here 40
SIC 8211 Elementary and secondary schools

D-U-N-S 20-710-8635   (BR)
DISTRICT SCHOOL BOARD OF NIAGARA
JAMES MORDEN PUBLIC SCHOOL
7112 Dorchester Rd, Niagara Falls, ON, L2G 5V6

(905) 358-5011
Emp Here 50
SIC 8211 Elementary and secondary schools

D-U-N-S 20-710-8791   (BR)
DISTRICT SCHOOL BOARD OF NIAGARA
STANFORD COLLEGIATE
5775 Drummond Rd, Niagara Falls, ON, L2G 4L2
(905) 354-7409
Emp Here 50
SIC 8211 Elementary and secondary schools

D-U-N-S 24-972-3529   (BR)
DISTRICT SCHOOL BOARD OF NIAGARA
HEXIMER AVENUE PUPLIC SCHOOL
6727 Heximer Ave, Niagara Falls, ON, L2G 4T1
(905) 356-0932
Emp Here 22
SIC 8211 Elementary and secondary schools

D-U-N-S 25-642-0894   (BR)
DIVERSICARE CANADA MANAGEMENT SERVICES CO., INC
CAVENDISH MANOR RETIREMENT HOME
5781 Dunn St, Niagara Falls, ON, L2G 2N9
(905) 354-2733
Emp Here 33
SIC 6513 Apartment building operators

D-U-N-S 25-525-0144   (SL)
DYACO CANADA INC
5955 Don Murie St, Niagara Falls, ON, L2G 0A9
(905) 353-8955
Emp Here 26   *Sales* 2,918,428
SIC 5091 Sporting and recreation goods

D-U-N-S 24-097-4126   (SL)
FAMOUS COFFEE SHOP, THE
6380 Fallsview Blvd Unit R 1, Niagara Falls, ON, L2G 7Y6
(905) 354-7775
Emp Here 80   *Sales* 2,407,703
SIC 5812 Eating places

D-U-N-S 24-602-7072   (SL)
FOOD ROLL SALES (NIAGARA) LTD
8464 Earl Thomas Ave, Niagara Falls, ON, L2G 0B6
(905) 358-5747
Emp Here 50   *Sales* 3,648,035
SIC 2038 Frozen specialties, nec

D-U-N-S 20-747-4755   (SL)
FRANK'S FEATHER AND FIN LIMITED
TIM HORTONS
5470 Drummond Rd Unit 1, Niagara Falls, ON, L2G 4K9
(905) 353-8550
Emp Here 60   *Sales* 1,824,018
SIC 5812 Eating places

D-U-N-S 20-943-5507   (SL)
HARD ROCK CAFE
5685 Falls Ave, Niagara Falls, ON, L2G 3K6
(905) 356-7625
Emp Here 80   *Sales* 2,407,703
SIC 5812 Eating places

D-U-N-S 20-774-5907   (BR)
HOCO LIMITED
4946 Clifton Hill, Niagara Falls, ON, L2G 3N4
(905) 357-5911
Emp Here 400
SIC 5812 Eating places

D-U-N-S 20-132-5602   (SL)
HOLIDAY INN (NIAGARA FALLS) LIMITED
HOLIDAY INN BY THE FALLS
5339 Murray St, Niagara Falls, ON, L2G 2J3
(905) 356-1333
Emp Here 80   *Sales* 3,502,114
SIC 7011 Hotels and motels

D-U-N-S 24-356-4304   (SL)
LUNDY'S REGENCY ARMS CORP
DAYS INN

(*Suby of* Ciminelli Real Estate Corporation)
7280 Lundy'S Lane, Niagara Falls, ON, L2G
1W2
(905) 358-3621
Emp Here 42   *Sales* 1,824,018
SIC 7011 Hotels and motels

D-U-N-S 24-318-0965   (HQ)
MARINELAND OF CANADA INC
(*Suby of* Marineland of Canada Inc)
7885 Stanley Ave, Niagara Falls, ON, L2G
0C7
(905) 356-8250
Emp Here 70   *Emp Total* 100
Sales 3,793,956
SIC 7996 Amusement parks

D-U-N-S 20-413-2211   (SL)
MODERN MOSAIC LIMITED
8620 Oakwood Dr, Niagara Falls, ON, L2G
0J2
(905) 356-3045
Emp Here 50   *Sales* 7,369,031
SIC 5211 Lumber and other building materials
Pr Pr Herbert Nemeth
  Anthony Digiacomo

D-U-N-S 20-132-9091   (HQ)
MYER SALIT LIMITED
SALIT STEEL
(*Suby of* Myer Salit Limited)
7771 Stanley Ave, Niagara Falls, ON, L2G
0C7
(905) 354-5691
Emp Here 126   *Emp Total* 150
Sales 60,411,460
SIC 5051 Metals service centers and offices
  Steven Cohen
  Laurence Cohen
  Marlene Cohen
  Joy Cohen

D-U-N-S 20-563-4210   (BR)
NIAGARA 21ST GROUP INC
*MARRIOTT NIAGARA FALLS FALLSVIEW
HOTEL & SPA*
6740 Fallsview Blvd, Niagara Falls, ON, L2G
3W6
(905) 357-7300
Emp Here 1,500
SIC 7011 Hotels and motels

D-U-N-S 20-591-5783   (BR)
**NIAGARA CATHOLIC DISTRICT SCHOOL
BOARD**
*SACRED HEART CATHOLIC ELEMENTARY
SCHOOL*
8450 Oliver St, Niagara Falls, ON, L2G 6Z2
(905) 295-3732
Emp Here 25
SIC 8211 Elementary and secondary schools

D-U-N-S 20-710-8973   (BR)
**NIAGARA CATHOLIC DISTRICT SCHOOL
BOARD**
ST JOSEPH SCHOOL
5895 North St, Niagara Falls, ON, L2G 1J7
(905) 354-3531
Emp Here 50
SIC 8211 Elementary and secondary schools

D-U-N-S 25-138-2685   (BR)
**NIAGARA CATHOLIC DISTRICT SCHOOL
BOARD**
ST THOMAS MORE SCHOOL
6642 Schanklee St, Niagara Falls, ON, L2G
5N4

Emp Here 30
SIC 8211 Elementary and secondary schools

D-U-N-S 20-075-3288   (BR)
**NIAGARA COLLEGE OF APPLIED ARTS &
TECHNOLOGY**
MAID OF THE MIST CAMPUS
5881 Dunn St, Niagara Falls, ON, L2G 2N9
(905) 374-7454
Emp Here 600

SIC 8221 Colleges and universities

D-U-N-S 24-858-6278   (SL)
NIAGARA CONVENTION & CIVIC CENTER
SCOTIABANK CONVENTION CENTER
6815 Stanley Ave, Niagara Falls, ON, L2G 3Y9
(905) 357-6222
Emp Here 150   *Sales* 4,961,328
SIC 7299 Miscellaneous personal service

D-U-N-S 20-647-5709   (SL)
NIAGARA FASTENERS INC
6095 Progress St, Niagara Falls, ON, L2G 0C2
(905) 356-6887
Emp Here 30   *Sales* 7,587,913
SIC 3452 Bolts, nuts, rivets, and washers
Pr Dean Zaniol
Owner Leanne Russell

D-U-N-S 20-013-2079   (BR)
NIAGARA HEALTH SYSTEM
*THE GREATER NIAGARA GENERAL HOSPI-
TAL*
5546 Portage Rd, Niagara Falls, ON, L2G 5X8
(905) 378-4647
Emp Here 950
SIC 8062 General medical and surgical hospi-
tals

D-U-N-S 20-403-9234   (SL)
NIAGARA IMPERIAL MOTEL LIMITED
5851 Victoria Ave, Niagara Falls, ON, L2G 3L6
(905) 356-2648
Emp Here 55   *Sales* 2,858,628
SIC 7011 Hotels and motels

D-U-N-S 20-554-9488   (HQ)
ONEIDA CANADA, LIMITED
(*Suby of* Everyware Global, Inc.)
8699 Stanley Ave, Niagara Falls, ON, L2G 0E1
(905) 356-1591
Emp Here 27   *Emp Total* 1,663
Sales 3,064,349
SIC 5094 Jewelry and precious stones

D-U-N-S 25-366-5095   (BR)
**ONTARIO LOTTERY AND GAMING CORPO-
RATION**
NIAGARA FALLSVIEW CASINO RESORT
6380 Fallsview Blvd, Niagara Falls, ON, L2G
7X5
(905) 358-7654
Emp Here 4,500
SIC 7999 Amusement and recreation, nec

D-U-N-S 24-844-7088   (HQ)
PALFINGER INC
7942 Dorchester Rd, Niagara Falls, ON, L2G
7W7
(905) 374-3363
Emp Here 45   *Emp Total* 8
Sales 11,892,594
SIC 5084 Industrial machinery and equipment
Pr Pr Mark Woody
  Hubert Palfinger

D-U-N-S 25-180-1031   (SL)
PERKINS RESTAURANT
5685 Falls Ave, Niagara Falls, ON, L2G 3K6
(905) 371-8688
Emp Here 65   *Sales* 1,969,939
SIC 5812 Eating places

D-U-N-S 20-792-7950   (BR)
PHARMA PLUS DRUGMARTS LTD
PHARMA PLUS
6484 Lundy'S Lane, Niagara Falls, ON, L2G
1T6
(905) 354-3314
Emp Here 25
SIC 5912 Drug stores and proprietary stores

D-U-N-S 25-179-6348   (BR)
PRISZM LP
KFC
6566 Lundy'S Lane, Niagara Falls, ON, L2G
1V2

Emp Here 20

SIC 5812 Eating places

D-U-N-S 25-705-1342   (BR)
RED LOBSTER HOSPITALITY LLC
RED LOBSTER RESTAURANTS
(*Suby of* Red Lobster Seafood Co., LLC)
6220 Lundy'S Ln, Niagara Falls, ON, L2G 1T6
(905) 357-1303
Emp Here 80
SIC 5812 Eating places

D-U-N-S 20-084-5019   (BR)
REDBERRY FRANCHISING CORP
BURGER KING
6235 Lundy'S Lane, Niagara Falls, ON, L2G
1T5
(905) 357-3210
Emp Here 20
SIC 5812 Eating places

D-U-N-S 25-989-2156   (BR)
**REGIONAL MUNICIPALITY OF NIAGARA,
THE**
*NIAGARA FALLS WATER TREATMENT
PLANT*
3599 Macklem St, Niagara Falls, ON, L2G 6C7
(905) 295-4831
Emp Here 20
SIC 4971 Irrigation systems

D-U-N-S 24-150-1886   (BR)
ROYAL BANK OF CANADA
RBC
(*Suby of* Royal Bank Of Canada)
6518 Lundy'S Lane, Niagara Falls, ON, L2G
1T6
(905) 356-7313
Emp Here 20
SIC 8742 Management consulting services

D-U-N-S 24-655-8659   (BR)
SIR CORP
CANYON CREEK CHOP HOUSE
6380 Fallsview Blvd, Niagara Falls, ON, L2G
7X5
(905) 354-0030
Emp Here 40
SIC 5812 Eating places

D-U-N-S 25-330-4687   (SL)
**SAINT-GOBAIN CERAMIC MATERIALS
CANADA INC**
8001 Daly St, Niagara Falls, ON, L2G 6S2
(905) 295-4311
Emp Here 40   *Sales* 2,991,389
SIC 3291 Abrasive products

D-U-N-S 20-940-5521   (BR)
ST. JOHN COUNCIL FOR ONTARIO
ST JOHN AMBULANCE NIAGARA FALLS
5734 Glenholme Ave, Niagara Falls, ON, L2G
4Y3
(905) 356-7340
Emp Here 30
SIC 8611 Business associations

D-U-N-S 25-115-3706   (SL)
STELCRETE INDUSTRIES LTD
(*Suby of* Myer Salit Limited)
7771 Stanley Ave, Niagara Falls, ON, L2G
0C7
(905) 354-5691
Emp Here 20   *Sales* 1,472,627
SIC 7692 Welding repair

D-U-N-S 25-642-2346   (BR)
THE GOLDEN GRIDDLE CORPORATION
GOLDEN GRIDDLE FAMILY RESTAURANT
4946 Clifton Hill, Niagara Falls, ON, L2G 3N4
(905) 358-3601
Emp Here 100
SIC 5812 Eating places

D-U-N-S 25-185-6043   (BR)
VALUE VILLAGE STORES, INC
VALUE VILLAGE # 2077
(*Suby of* Savers, Inc.)
6278 Lundy'S Lane, Niagara Falls, ON, L2G
1T5

(905) 354-6336
Emp Here 30
SIC 5399 Miscellaneous general merchandise

D-U-N-S 24-926-6115   (SL)
WALTER, L. & SONS EXCAVATING LTD
7527 Stanley Ave, Niagara Falls, ON, L2G
0C7
(905) 371-1300
Emp Here 50   *Sales* 5,024,000
SIC 1794 Excavation work
Pr Stefan Walter
Ch Bd Louis Walter
Treas Jeff Walter
Off Mgr Joanne Bauer

D-U-N-S 25-639-0832   (BR)
WENDY'S RESTAURANTS OF CANADA INC
(*Suby of* The Wendy's Company)
6948 Mcleod Rd, Niagara Falls, ON, L2G 7K3

Emp Here 30
SIC 5812 Eating places

D-U-N-S 20-005-2137   (BR)
WENDY'S RESTAURANTS OF CANADA INC
(*Suby of* The Wendy's Company)
6363 Lundy'S Lane, Niagara Falls, ON, L2G
1T8
(905) 357-0666
Emp Here 25
SIC 5812 Eating places

D-U-N-S 24-224-5491   (BR)
WENDY'S RESTAURANTS OF CANADA INC
WENDY'S
(*Suby of* The Wendy's Company)
4850 Clifton Hill, Niagara Falls, ON, L2G 3N4
(905) 358-4789
Emp Here 30
SIC 5812 Eating places

Niagara Falls, ON L2H
Welland County

D-U-N-S 25-641-9763   (BR)
5-0 TAXI CO. INC.
CENTRAL TAXI
(*Suby of* 5-0 Taxi Co. Inc.)
8236 Beaverdams Rd, Niagara Falls, ON, L2H
3K8
(905) 358-3232
Emp Here 60
SIC 4121 Taxicabs

D-U-N-S 24-879-1969   (BR)
ACADIAN COACH LINES LP
(*Suby of* Acadian Coach Lines LP)
7500 Lundy'S Lane, Niagara Falls, ON, L2H
1G8
(905) 353-9782
Emp Here 100
SIC 4142 Bus charter service, except local

D-U-N-S 20-026-7172   (BR)
ADIDAS CANADA LIMITED
7500 Lundy'S Ln Suite B12b19, Niagara Falls,
ON, L2H 1G8
(289) 341-0003
Emp Here 20
SIC 5661 Shoe stores

D-U-N-S 20-021-7581   (SL)
BIAMONTE INVESTMENTS LTD
MICK & ANGELO'S EATERY AND BAR
7600 Lundy'S Lane, Niagara Falls, ON, L2H
1H1
(905) 354-2211
Emp Here 80   *Sales* 2,407,703
SIC 5812 Eating places

D-U-N-S 24-342-2107   (BR)
CARA OPERATIONS LIMITED
SWISS CHALET
(*Suby of* Cara Holdings Limited)
3770 Montrose Rd Suite 6, Niagara Falls, ON,

L2H 3K3
(905) 354-9660
Emp Here 40
SIC 5812 Eating places

D-U-N-S 20-848-1296   (BR)
CENTURY 21 TODAY REALTY LTD
8123 Lundy'S Lane Suite 10, Niagara Falls,
ON, L2H 1H3
(905) 356-9100
Emp Here 20
SIC 6531 Real estate agents and managers

D-U-N-S 24-097-6779   (HQ)
CIRCUS WORLD DISPLAYS LIMITED
SVAT ELECTRONICS
(*Suby of* Circus World Displays Limited)
4080 Montrose Rd, Niagara Falls, ON, L2H
1J9
(905) 353-0732
Emp Here 86   *Emp Total* 100
Sales 9,849,695
SIC 3651 Household audio and video equip-
ment
Ch Bd Ramesh C Jain
Sec Sujata Jain
     Deepak Jain
     Rajesh Jain

D-U-N-S 20-561-2083   (BR)
CIRCUS WORLD DISPLAYS LIMITED
SVAT ELECTRONICS (DIV)
(*Suby of* Circus World Displays Limited)
4080 Montrose Rd, Niagara Falls, ON, L2H
1J9
(905) 353-0732
Emp Here 20
SIC 3699 Electrical equipment and supplies,
nec

D-U-N-S 25-278-7726   (SL)
**CLUB ITALIA,NIAGARA, ORDER SONS OF
ITALY OF CANADA**
CLUB ITALIA LODGE NO 5
2525 Montrose Rd, Niagara Falls, ON, L2H
0T9
(905) 374-7388
Emp Here 100   *Sales* 3,283,232
SIC 7299 Miscellaneous personal service

D-U-N-S 20-710-8650   (BR)
DISTRICT SCHOOL BOARD OF NIAGARA
DURDAN, KATE S PUBLIC SCHOOL
6855 Kalar Rd, Niagara Falls, ON, L2H 2T3
(905) 356-0488
Emp Here 50
SIC 8211 Elementary and secondary schools

D-U-N-S 24-253-1916   (BR)
DISTRICT SCHOOL BOARD OF NIAGARA
FORESTVIEW PUBLIC SCHOOL
8406 Forestview Blvd, Niagara Falls, ON, L2H
0B9
(905) 354-6261
Emp Here 40
SIC 8211 Elementary and secondary schools

D-U-N-S 20-026-3213   (BR)
DISTRICT SCHOOL BOARD OF NIAGARA
WESTLANE SECONDARY SCHOOL
5960 Pitton Rd, Niagara Falls, ON, L2H 1T5
(905) 356-2401
Emp Here 90
SIC 8211 Elementary and secondary schools

D-U-N-S 24-972-3651   (BR)
DISTRICT SCHOOL BOARD OF NIAGARA
GREENDALE PUBLIC SCHOOL
5504 Montrose Rd, Niagara Falls, ON, L2H
1K7
(905) 358-8111
Emp Here 35
SIC 8211 Elementary and secondary schools

D-U-N-S 20-132-4811   (BR)
E.S. FOX LIMITED
4935 Kent Ave, Niagara Falls, ON, L2H 1J5

Emp Here 20

SIC 1711 Plumbing, heating, air-conditioning

D-U-N-S 24-337-3144   (BR)
FGL SPORTS LTD
SPORT CHEK NIAGARA SQUARE
7555 Montrose Rd Suite A30, Niagara Falls,
ON, L2H 2E9
(905) 354-6239
Emp Here 30
SIC 5941 Sporting goods and bicycle shops

D-U-N-S 24-858-2178   (BR)
LOWE'S COMPANIES CANADA, ULC
7959 Mcleod Rd, Niagara Falls, ON, L2H 0G5
(905) 374-5520
Emp Here 150
SIC 5211 Lumber and other building materials

D-U-N-S 25-651-7368   (BR)
METRO ONTARIO INC
A & P
3770 Montrose Rd, Niagara Falls, ON, L2H
3C8
(905) 371-3200
Emp Here 150
SIC 5411 Grocery stores

D-U-N-S 24-758-0947   (SL)
NIAGARA AIR BUS INC
8626 Lundy'S Lane, Niagara Falls, ON, L2H
1H4
(905) 374-8111
Emp Here 75   *Sales* 2,626,585
SIC 4111 Local and suburban transit

D-U-N-S 20-132-7566   (SL)
**NIAGARA ARTCRAFT WOODWORK COM-
PANY LIMITED, THE**
ARTCRAFT KITCHENS
4417 Kent Ave, Niagara Falls, ON, L2H 1J1
(905) 354-5657
Emp Here 60   *Sales* 4,523,179
SIC 2434 Wood kitchen cabinets

D-U-N-S 20-591-6062   (BR)
**NIAGARA CATHOLIC DISTRICT SCHOOL
BOARD**
ST MICHAEL CATHOLIC HIGH SCHOOL
8699 Mcleod Rd, Niagara Falls, ON, L2H 0Z2
(905) 356-5155
Emp Here 80
SIC 8211 Elementary and secondary schools

D-U-N-S 25-137-4112   (BR)
**NIAGARA CATHOLIC DISTRICT SCHOOL
BOARD**
CARDINAL NEWMAN SCHOOL
8120 Beaverdams Rd, Niagara Falls, ON, L2H
1R8
(905) 354-9033
Emp Here 37
SIC 8211 Elementary and secondary schools

D-U-N-S 25-181-5809   (BR)
**NIAGARA CATHOLIC DISTRICT SCHOOL
BOARD**
*LORETTO   CATHOLIC   ELEMENTARY
SCHOOL*
6855 Kalar Rd, Niagara Falls, ON, L2H 2T3
(905) 356-4175
Emp Here 35
SIC 8211 Elementary and secondary schools

D-U-N-S 25-527-7907   (BR)
NIKE CANADA CORP
NIKE NIAGARA FACTORY STORE
(*Suby of* Nike, Inc.)
7500 Lundy'S Lane Suite B2, Niagara Falls,
ON, L2H 1G8
(905) 374-4420
Emp Here 60
SIC 5091 Sporting and recreation goods

D-U-N-S 20-862-1826   (BR)
NORTHERN REFLECTIONS LTD
7555 Montrose Rd, Niagara Falls, ON, L2H
2E9
(905) 374-6531
Emp Here 25

SIC 5621 Women's clothing stores

D-U-N-S 25-204-3518   (BR)
**REGIONAL MUNICIPALITY OF NIAGARA,
THE**
MEADOWS DORCHESTER, THE
6623 Kalar Rd Suite 312, Niagara Falls, ON,
L2H 2T3
(905) 357-1911
Emp Here 116
SIC 8051 Skilled nursing care facilities

D-U-N-S 20-405-6865   (SL)
**RESORTS INTERNATIONAL (NIAGARA)
INC**
*AMERICANA CONFERENCE RESORT &
SPA*
8444 Lundy'S Lane, Niagara Falls, ON, L2H
1H4
(905) 356-8444
Emp Here 50   *Sales* 2,826,987
SIC 7011 Hotels and motels

D-U-N-S 25-653-0841   (BR)
REVERA INC
LUNDY MANOR RETIREMENT RESIDENCE
7860 Lundy'S Lane Suite 205, Niagara Falls,
ON, L2H 1H1
(905) 356-1511
Emp Here 30
SIC 6513 Apartment building operators

D-U-N-S 25-811-7837   (BR)
**ROYAL LEPAGE NIAGARA REAL ESTATE
CENTRE**
3770 Montrose Rd Suite 1, Niagara Falls, ON,
L2H 3K3
(905) 357-3000
Emp Here 50
SIC 6531 Real estate agents and managers

D-U-N-S 20-974-6163   (SL)
SWS STAR WARNING SYSTEMS INC
7695 Blackburn Pky, Niagara Falls, ON, L2H
0A6
(905) 357-0222
Emp Here 62
SIC 3647 Vehicular lighting equipment

D-U-N-S 25-671-4767   (BR)
TOMMY HILFIGER CANADA INC
TOMMY HILFIGER CANADA ONE FACTORY
7500 Lundy'S Lane Suite B5, Niagara Falls,
ON, L2H 1G8
(905) 354-6194
Emp Here 40
SIC 5611 Men's and boys' clothing stores

D-U-N-S 25-931-4441   (BR)
**WINNERS MERCHANTS INTERNATIONAL
L.P.**
WINNERS
(*Suby of* The TJX Companies Inc)
7555 Montrose Rd Suite A3, Niagara Falls,
ON, L2H 2E9
(905) 358-8893
Emp Here 30
SIC 5651 Family clothing stores

D-U-N-S 24-159-7512   (BR)
YM INC. (SALES)
URBAN PLANET
7500 Lundy'S Lane Unit 11c, Niagara Falls,
ON, L2H 1G8
(905) 371-3287
Emp Here 20
SIC 5621 Women's clothing stores

Niagara Falls, ON L2J
Welland County

D-U-N-S 24-819-1582   (SL)
1788741 ONTARIO INC
COMMISSO'S FRESH FOODS
6161 Thorold Stone Rd Suite 3, Niagara Falls,

ON, L2J 1A4
(905) 357-6600
Emp Here 130   *Sales* 4,450,603
SIC 5461 Retail bakeries

D-U-N-S 25-296-4655   (BR)
BANK OF NOVA SCOTIA, THE
SCOTIABANK
6225 Thorold Stone Rd, Niagara Falls, ON,
L2J 1A6
(905) 356-4495
Emp Here 20
SIC 6021 National commercial banks

D-U-N-S 20-020-4035   (BR)
DISTRICT SCHOOL BOARD OF NIAGARA
*MARTHA   CULLIMORE   ELEMENTARY
SCHOOL*
3155 St Andrew Ave, Niagara Falls, ON, L2J
2R7
(905) 358-5142
Emp Here 23
SIC 8211 Elementary and secondary schools

D-U-N-S 20-710-8718   (BR)
DISTRICT SCHOOL BOARD OF NIAGARA
PRINCE PHILIPS SCHOOL
3112 Dorchester Rd, Niagara Falls, ON, L2J
2Z7
(905) 356-0521
Emp Here 25
SIC 8211 Elementary and secondary schools

D-U-N-S 20-710-8684   (BR)
DISTRICT SCHOOL BOARD OF NIAGARA
ORCHARD PARK PUBLIC SCHOOL
3691 Dorchester Rd, Niagara Falls, ON, L2J
3A6
(905) 354-3916
Emp Here 50
SIC 8211 Elementary and secondary schools

D-U-N-S 20-769-1952   (SL)
GENERATION 3 HOLDINGS INC
MCDONALD'S
6161 Thorold Stone Rd Unit 15, Niagara Falls,
ON, L2J 1A4
(905) 356-9823
Emp Here 50   *Sales* 1,532,175
SIC 5812 Eating places

D-U-N-S 20-710-8866   (BR)
**NIAGARA CATHOLIC DISTRICT SCHOOL
BOARD**
MARY WARD CATHOLIC SCHOOL
2999 Dorchester Rd, Niagara Falls, ON, L2J
2Z9
(905) 354-9221
Emp Here 35
SIC 8211 Elementary and secondary schools

D-U-N-S 25-137-4120   (BR)
**NIAGARA CATHOLIC DISTRICT SCHOOL
BOARD**
ST GABRIEL
6121 Vine St, Niagara Falls, ON, L2J 1L4
(905) 354-5422
Emp Here 24
SIC 8211 Elementary and secondary schools

D-U-N-S 25-224-9453   (BR)
**NIAGARA CATHOLIC DISTRICT SCHOOL
BOARD**
SAINT PAUL CATHOLIC HIGH SCHOOL
3834 Windermere Rd, Niagara Falls, ON, L2J
2Y5
(905) 356-4313
Emp Here 80
SIC 8211 Elementary and secondary schools

D-U-N-S 24-972-3644   (BR)
**NIAGARA CATHOLIC DISTRICT SCHOOL
BOARD**
NOTRE DAME ELEMENTARY SCHOOL
6559 Caswell St, Niagara Falls, ON, L2J 1C2
(905) 358-3861
Emp Here 28
SIC 8211 Elementary and secondary schools

D-U-N-S 20-859-9188   (BR)
PACIFIC LINK COMMUNICATIONS INC
BELL WORLD
3714 Portage Rd Suite 11, Niagara Falls, ON,
L2J 2K9
(905) 357-7225
Emp Here 25
SIC 5999 Miscellaneous retail stores, nec

D-U-N-S 24-008-8039   (SL)
SIRA RESTAURANTS LTD
MCDONALDS DRIVE-IN RESTAURANT
6161 Thorold Stone Rd, Niagara Falls, ON,
L2J 1A4
(905) 356-8856
Emp Here 68   *Sales* 2,042,900
SIC 5812 Eating places

D-U-N-S 25-934-7441   (BR)
SOBEYS CAPITAL INCORPORATED
3714 Portage Rd, Niagara Falls, ON, L2J 2K9
(905) 371-2270
Emp Here 160
SIC 5411 Grocery stores

D-U-N-S 25-634-1116   (SL)
STRANGES, N.J. DRYWALL & CONSTRUC-
TION LTD
2577 Claude Ave, Niagara Falls, ON, L2J 2C7
(905) 356-3299
Emp Here 50   *Sales* 4,231,721
SIC 1742 Plastering, drywall, and insulation

D-U-N-S 25-357-3752   (BR)
TORONTO-DOMINION BANK, THE
TD CANADA TRUST
(*Suby of* Toronto-Dominion Bank, The)
3643 Portage Rd, Niagara Falls, ON, L2J 2K8
(905) 356-6931
Emp Here 24
SIC 6021 National commercial banks

Niagara On The Lake, ON L0S
Lincoln County

D-U-N-S 25-637-8050   (BR)
591182 ONTARIO LIMITED
WOLVERINE FREIGHT SYSTEMS
56 Niagara Stone Rd, Niagara On The Lake,
ON, L0S 1J0
(905) 685-4544
Emp Here 45
SIC 4213 Trucking, except local

D-U-N-S 25-086-6571   (BR)
ANDREW PELLER LIMITED
HILLEBRAND WINERY
1249 Niagara Stone Rd, Niagara On The
Lake, ON, L0S 1J0
(905) 468-3201
Emp Here 70
SIC 2084 Wines, brandy, and brandy spirits

D-U-N-S 25-670-1178   (BR)
ANDREW PELLER LIMITED
TRIUS WINERY - HILLEBRAND
1249 Niagara Stone Rd, Niagara On The
Lake, ON, L0S 1J0
(905) 468-7123
Emp Here 120
SIC 2084 Wines, brandy, and brandy spirits

D-U-N-S 24-322-0485   (BR)
ARTERRA WINES CANADA, INC
JACKSON TRIGGS NIAGARA ESTATE WIN-
ERY
(*Suby of* Arterra Wines Canada, Inc)
Gd, Niagara On The Lake, ON, L0S 1J0
(905) 468-4637
Emp Here 25
SIC 2084 Wines, brandy, and brandy spirits

D-U-N-S 24-197-5838   (HQ)
CN WORLDWIDE DISTRIBUTION SER-
VICES (CANADA) INC

IBS INTERNATIONAL BULK SERVICES OF
CANADA
303 Townline Rd Suite 200, Niagara On The
Lake, ON, L0S 1J0
(905) 684-5098
Emp Here 20   *Emp Total* 23,172
Sales 22,522,526
SIC 4225 General warehousing and storage
Pr Keith Reardon
Genl Mgr Mike Karshaw
Genl Mgr Timothy Yetsick
Sebastien Labbe

D-U-N-S 25-461-0603   (BR)
CHARTWELL RETIREMENT RESIDENCES
CHARTWELL SENIORS HOUSING REAL
ESTATE INVESTMENT TRUST
120 Wellngton St, Niagara On The Lake, ON,
L0S 1J0
(905) 468-2111
Emp Here 150
SIC 8051 Skilled nursing care facilities

D-U-N-S 24-373-5110   (BR)
DIAMOND ESTATES WINES & SPIRITS LTD
1067 Niagara Stone Rd, Niagara On The
Lake, ON, L0S 1J0
(905) 641-1042
Emp Here 50
SIC 2084 Wines, brandy, and brandy spirits

D-U-N-S 25-895-7992   (BR)
DISTRICT SCHOOL BOARD OF NIAGARA
NIAGARA DISTRICT SECONDARY SCHOOL
1875 Niagara Stone Rd, Niagara On The
Lake, ON, L0S 1J0
(905) 468-7793
Emp Here 40
SIC 8211 Elementary and secondary schools

D-U-N-S 24-345-2906   (BR)
DISTRICT SCHOOL BOARD OF NIAGARA
PARLIAMENT OAK ELEMENTRY SCHOOL
565 East West Line Rd, Niagara On The Lake,
ON, L0S 1J0

Emp Here 50
SIC 8211 Elementary and secondary schools

D-U-N-S 20-704-3048   (BR)
DISTRICT SCHOOL BOARD OF NIAGARA
COLONEL JOHN BUTLER PUBLIC SCHOOL
565 East West Line Rd, Niagara On The Lake,
ON, L0S 1J0
(905) 468-5651
Emp Here 20
SIC 8211 Elementary and secondary schools

D-U-N-S 25-301-2884   (BR)
EXTENDICARE (CANADA) INC
PARAMED HOME HEALTH CARE
509 Glendale Ave Suite 200, Niagara On The
Lake, ON, L0S 1J0
(905) 682-6555
Emp Here 500
SIC 8051 Skilled nursing care facilities

D-U-N-S 25-321-0389   (BR)
FIRSTCANADA ULC
LAIDLAW EDUCATIONAL SERVICES
349 Airport Rd, Niagara On The Lake, ON,
L0S 1J0
(905) 688-9600
Emp Here 160
SIC 4151 School buses

D-U-N-S 24-164-2636   (HQ)
HENRY SCHEIN CANADA, INC
345 Townline Rd Ss 4, Niagara On The Lake,
ON, L0S 1J0
(905) 646-1711
Emp Here 260   *Emp Total* 12,200
Sales 164,587,690
SIC 5047 Medical and hospital equipment
Dir Stanley Bergman
Joe Robertson
Pr Cyril F. Elborne
Glen Watson

Peter D. Jugoon
Ex VP Mark Mlotek
Ex VP Steven Paladino

D-U-N-S 24-577-4885   (BR)
HORTON CBI, LIMITED
303 Townline Rd Suite 100, Niagara On The
Lake, ON, L0S 1J0
(905) 684-0012
Emp Here 52
SIC 5051 Metals service centers and offices

D-U-N-S 25-180-1304   (BR)
KANEFF PROPERTIES LIMITED
ROYAL NIAGARA GOLF CLUB
1 Niagara On The Green Blvd, Niagara On
The Lake, ON, L0S 1J0
(905) 685-9501
Emp Here 40
SIC 7992 Public golf courses

D-U-N-S 20-183-4707   (BR)
LAIS HOTEL PROPERTIES LIMITED
PRINCE OF WALES HOTEL
6 Pinot Trail, Niagara On The Lake, ON, L0S
1J0
(905) 468-3246
Emp Here 160
SIC 7011 Hotels and motels

D-U-N-S 25-638-4777   (SL)
LAKEVIEW CELLARS ESTATE WINERY
LIMITED
20 BEES WINERY
1067 Niagara Stone Rd, Niagara On The
Lake, ON, L0S 1J0
(905) 641-1042
Emp Here 50   *Sales* 1,459,214
SIC 2084 Wines, brandy, and brandy spirits

D-U-N-S 20-175-7262   (BR)
LEON'S FURNITURE LIMITED
440 Taylor Rd, Niagara On The Lake, ON, L0S
1J0
(905) 682-8519
Emp Here 100
SIC 5712 Furniture stores

D-U-N-S 20-792-5319   (BR)
MCDONALD'S   RESTAURANTS   OF
CANADA LIMITED
MCDONALD'S #8848
(*Suby of* McDonald's Corporation)
1835 Niagara Stone Rd, Niagara On The
Lake, ON, L0S 1J0

Emp Here 50
SIC 5812 Eating places

D-U-N-S 24-395-9553   (BR)
MILLER PAVING LIMITED
MILLER MAINTENANCE
571 York Rd, Niagara On The Lake, ON, L0S
1J0
(905) 685-4352
Emp Here 40
SIC 1611 Highway and street construction

D-U-N-S 25-224-8513   (BR)
NIAGARA CATHOLIC DISTRICT SCHOOL
BOARD
ST. MICHAEL ELEMENTERY SCHOOL
387 3 Line, Niagara On The Lake, ON, L0S
1J0
(905) 684-1051
Emp Here 26
SIC 8211 Elementary and secondary schools

D-U-N-S 20-945-2247   (BR)
NIAGARA HEALTH SYSTEM
NIAGARA ON THE LAKE GENERAL HOSPI-
TAL
176 Wellington St, Niagara On The Lake, ON,
L0S 1J0
(905) 378-4647
Emp Here 100
SIC 8062 General medical and surgical hospi-
tals

D-U-N-S 25-642-4524   (BR)
NIAGARA PARKS COMMISSION, THE
QUEENSTON HEIGHTS RESTAURANT
14184 Niagara River Pkwy, Niagara On The
Lake, ON, L0S 1J0
(905) 262-4274
Emp Here 40
SIC 5812 Eating places

D-U-N-S 24-853-0425   (SL)
NIAGARA PATIENT TRANSFER INC
454 Mississauga Rd Unit 373, Niagara On The
Lake, ON, L0S 1J0
(905) 228-0314
Emp Here 50   *Sales* 2,411,520
SIC 4111 Local and suburban transit

D-U-N-S 24-206-4439   (BR)
ONTARIO POWER GENERATION INC
O P G
14000 Niagara River Pky Suite 1, Niagara On
The Lake, ON, L0S 1J0
(905) 357-0322
Emp Here 225
SIC 4911 Electric services

D-U-N-S 25-318-5367   (BR)
REGIONAL MUNICIPALITY OF NIAGARA,
THE
UPPER CANADA LODGE
272 Wellington St, Niagara On The Lake, ON,
L0S 1J0
(905) 468-4208
Emp Here 60
SIC 8742 Management consulting services

D-U-N-S 24-676-2103   (SL)
SMJR HOLDINGS LTD
HILTON GARDEN INN
500 York Rd Suite 4, Niagara On The Lake,
ON, L0S 1J0
(905) 984-4200
Emp Here 50   *Sales* 2,188,821
SIC 7011 Hotels and motels

D-U-N-S 24-348-1905   (BR)
UTI, CANADA, INC
Gd, Niagara On The Lake, ON, L0S 1J0
(905) 262-5078
Emp Here 20
SIC 4731 Freight transportation arrangement

D-U-N-S 24-075-4531   (SL)
WHITE OAKS TENNIS WORLD INC
WHITE OAKS CONFERENCE RESORT &
SPA
253 Taylor Rd Ss 4, Niagara On The Lake, ON,
L0S 1J0
(905) 688-2550
Emp Here 350   *Sales* 22,674,960
SIC 7389 Business services, nec
Pr Pr George Wakil
  Ameer Wakil
VP VP Michael Wakil
Dir Jasmine Wakil-Tonnos
Dir Adelene Wakil-Booth
VP Fin John Holjak

Nipigon, ON P0T
Thunder Bay County

D-U-N-S 20-291-4607   (BR)
DILICO ANISHINABEK FAMILY CARE
112 4th St, Nipigon, ON, P0T 2J0
(807) 887-2514
Emp Here 22
SIC 8322 Individual and family services

D-U-N-S 25-194-1563   (BR)
ONTARIO POWER GENERATION INC
Hwy 585, Nipigon, ON, P0T 2J0
(807) 887-3658
Emp Here 26
SIC 4911 Electric services

Nobel, ON P0G
Parry Sound County

D-U-N-S 20-009-6555   (BR)
NEAR NORTH DISTRICT SCHOOL BOARD
NOBEL SCHOOL
140 Hammel Ave, Nobel, ON, P0G 1G0
(705) 342-5251
Emp Here 25
SIC 8211 Elementary and secondary schools

D-U-N-S 25-604-1344   (BR)
SELKIRK CANADA CORPORATION
(*Suby of* Selkirk Americas, L.P.)
21 Woods Rd, Nobel, ON, P0G 1G0
(705) 342-5236
Emp Here 110
SIC 3259 Structural clay products, nec

D-U-N-S 24-350-2114   (BR)
YORK PROFESSIONAL CARE & EDUCA-TION INC
HIDDEN BAY LEADERSHIP CAMP
200 Shebeshekong Rd S, Nobel, ON, P0G 1G0
(705) 342-7345
Emp Here 20
SIC 7032 Sporting and recreational camps

Nobleton, ON L0G
York County

D-U-N-S 24-335-3497   (SL)
COLUMBIA MASONRY LTD
14320 Highway 27, Nobleton, ON, L0G 1N0
(905) 859-7315
Emp Here 50   *Sales* 3,648,035
SIC 1741 Masonry and other stonework

D-U-N-S 24-339-7697   (BR)
SOBEYS CAPITAL INCORPORATED
13305 Highway 27 Unit 1, Nobleton, ON, L0G 1N0

Emp Here 50
SIC 5411 Grocery stores

D-U-N-S 20-711-4609   (BR)
YORK CATHOLIC DISTRICT SCHOOL BOARD
ST MARY CATHOLIC SCHOOL
75 Greenside Dr, Nobleton, ON, L0G 1N0
(905) 859-3336
Emp Here 50
SIC 8211 Elementary and secondary schools

D-U-N-S 25-293-6133   (BR)
YORK REGION DISTRICT SCHOOL BOARD
NOBLETON PUBLIC SCHOOL
(*Suby of* York Region District School Board)
13375 Highway 27, Nobleton, ON, L0G 1N0
(905) 859-4590
Emp Here 30
SIC 8211 Elementary and secondary schools

Noelville, ON P0M
Sudbury County

D-U-N-S 20-133-2582   (BR)
CO-OPERATIVE REGIONALE DE NIPISSING-SUDBURY LIMITED
NOELVILLE CO-OP
22 Notre Dame St W, Noelville, ON, P0M 2N0
(705) 898-2226
Emp Here 25
SIC 5411 Grocery stores

D-U-N-S 25-238-9994   (BR)
CONSEIL SCOLAIRE DE DISTRICT CATHOLIQUE DU NOUVEL-ONTARIO,

LE
ECOLE SAINT ANTOINE
28 Saint-Antoine St, Noelville, ON, P0M 2N0
(705) 898-2205
Emp Here 20
SIC 8211 Elementary and secondary schools

North Bay, ON P1A
Nipissing County

D-U-N-S 20-770-4334   (SL)
1510610 ONTARIO INC
CENTRAL WELDING & IRON WORKS
1811 Seymour St, North Bay, ON, P1A 0C7
(705) 474-0350
Emp Here 50   *Sales* 3,064,349
SIC 7692 Welding repair

D-U-N-S 24-216-9977   (BR)
2063414 ONTARIO LIMITED
WATERS EDGE CARE COMMUNITY
(*Suby of* 2063414 Ontario Limited)
401 William St, North Bay, ON, P1A 1X5
(705) 476-2602
Emp Here 140
SIC 8051 Skilled nursing care facilities

D-U-N-S 20-581-2423   (HQ)
611421 ONTARIO INC.
BAYWOOD ENTERPRISES
(*Suby of* 611421 Ontario Inc.)
119 Progress Crt, North Bay, ON, P1A 0C1
(705) 476-4222
Emp Here 50   *Emp Total* 54
Sales 5,024,000
SIC 3799 Transportation equipment, nec
Pr Pr Carl Crewson
   Gloria Crewson
   David Crewson
   Sherri Crewson

D-U-N-S 24-919-3616   (HQ)
682439 ONTARIO INC
PRONORTH TRANSPORTATION
348 Birchs Rd Suite 824, North Bay, ON, P1A 4A9
(705) 476-0444
Emp Here 255   *Emp Total* 535
Sales 47,587,615
SIC 4213 Trucking, except local
Pr Pr Brian Glass
   Dale Glass
   Bill Ayers

D-U-N-S 20-002-9424   (BR)
BANQUE TORONTO-DOMINION, LA
TORONTO-DOMINION BANK, THE
(*Suby of* Toronto-Dominion Bank, The)
300 Lakeshore Dr, North Bay, ON, P1A 3V2
(705) 474-1724
Emp Here 23
SIC 6021 National commercial banks

D-U-N-S 24-340-5946   (BR)
CANADA BREAD COMPANY, LIMITED
1704 Seymour St, North Bay, ON, P1A 0E1
(705) 474-3970
Emp Here 75
SIC 2051 Bread, cake, and related products

D-U-N-S 24-392-3828   (SL)
CARDINAL EQUIPMENT INC
161 Ferris Dr Suite 7, North Bay, ON, P1A 4K2
(705) 840-2056
Emp Here 40   *Sales* 7,733,834
SIC 5085 Industrial supplies
Pr Jean Paul Perron

D-U-N-S 20-778-8949   (BR)
CHISHOLM, R. FOOD SERVICES INC
MCDONALD'S RESTAURANTS
(*Suby of* Chisholm, R. Food Services Inc)
140 Lakeshore Dr, North Bay, ON, P1A 2A8
(705) 474-9770
Emp Here 100

SIC 5812 Eating places

D-U-N-S 24-418-2940   (BR)
CINEPLEX ODEON CORPORATION
GALAXY CINEMAS NORTH BAY
300 Lakeshore Dr, North Bay, ON, P1A 3V2
(705) 476-6410
Emp Here 20
SIC 7832 Motion picture theaters, except drive-in

D-U-N-S 25-818-8812   (BR)
COMMUNITY LIVING NORTH BAY
NBDACL/BANNER RESIDENCE
(*Suby of* Community Living North Bay)
624 Banner Ave, North Bay, ON, P1A 1X8
(705) 472-4844
Emp Here 21
SIC 8361 Residential care

D-U-N-S 20-068-1414   (BR)
COMMUNITY LIVING NORTH BAY
BIRCH'S RESIDENCE
(*Suby of* Community Living North Bay)
168 Birchs Rd, North Bay, ON, P1A 3Z8
(705) 476-5401
Emp Here 20
SIC 8361 Residential care

D-U-N-S 25-263-1296   (BR)
COMMUNITY LIVING NORTH BAY
S-J DELANDRED PLACE COUNTRY HER-ITAGE
(*Suby of* Community Living North Bay)
741 Wallace Rd, North Bay, ON, P1A 0E6
(705) 476-3280
Emp Here 25
SIC 8322 Individual and family services

D-U-N-S 25-321-8655   (BR)
ERB TRANSPORT LIMITED
ERB TRANSPORT LIMITED
4 Commerce Cres, North Bay, ON, P1A 0B4
(705) 476-7077
Emp Here 50
SIC 4212 Local trucking, without storage

D-U-N-S 25-278-6025   (SL)
EAST SIDE MARIO'S
285 Lakeshore Dr, North Bay, ON, P1A 2B9
(705) 497-9555
Emp Here 55   *Sales* 1,678,096
SIC 5812 Eating places

D-U-N-S 24-337-3219   (BR)
FGL SPORTS LTD
SPORT-CHEK NEW NORTH BAY MALL
300 Lakeshore Dr Unit 101, North Bay, ON, P1A 3V2
(705) 840-5007
Emp Here 20
SIC 5941 Sporting goods and bicycle shops

D-U-N-S 24-321-1724   (HQ)
FORACO CANADA LTD
1839 Seymour St, North Bay, ON, P1A 0C7
(705) 495-6363
Emp Here 90   *Emp Total* 2
Sales 8,755,284
SIC 1799 Special trade contractors, nec
Dir Timothy Bremner

D-U-N-S 24-009-6354   (SL)
INVEST REIT
BEST WESTERN NORTH BAY HOTEL AND CONFERENCE CENTRE, THE
700 Lakeshore Dr, North Bay, ON, P1A 2G4
(705) 474-5800
Emp Here 90   *Sales* 3,939,878
SIC 7011 Hotels and motels

D-U-N-S 25-742-5132   (BR)
METRO ONTARIO INC
METRO
390 Lakeshore Dr, North Bay, ON, P1A 2C7
(705) 840-2424
Emp Here 220
SIC 5411 Grocery stores

D-U-N-S 25-975-9033   (BR)
METSO MINERALS CANADA INC
28 Commerce Cres, North Bay, ON, P1A 0B4
(705) 476-1331
Emp Here 68
SIC 3532 Mining machinery

D-U-N-S 25-249-0271   (BR)
NEAR NORTH DISTRICT SCHOOL BOARD
TWEED SMUIR PUBLIC SCHOOL
176 Lakeshore Dr, North Bay, ON, P1A 2A8

Emp Here 21
SIC 8211 Elementary and secondary schools

D-U-N-S 25-238-6842   (BR)
NEAR NORTH DISTRICT SCHOOL BOARD
MARSHALL PARK PUBLIC SCHOOL
4 Marshall Park Dr, North Bay, ON, P1A 2N9

Emp Here 23
SIC 8211 Elementary and secondary schools

D-U-N-S 25-249-0461   (BR)
NEAR NORTH DISTRICT SCHOOL BOARD
E. W. NORMAN PUBLIC SCHOOL
599 Lake Heights Rd, North Bay, ON, P1A 3A1
(705) 472-5534
Emp Here 23
SIC 8211 Elementary and secondary schools

D-U-N-S 25-249-0214   (BR)
NEAR NORTH DISTRICT SCHOOL BOARD
WEST FERRIS SECONDARY SCHOOL
60 Marshall Park Dr, North Bay, ON, P1A 2P2
(705) 475-2333
Emp Here 70
SIC 8211 Elementary and secondary schools

D-U-N-S 25-249-0313   (BR)
NEAR NORTH DISTRICT SCHOOL BOARD
SILVER BIRCHES ELEMENTARY SCHOOL
65 Marshall Ave E, North Bay, ON, P1A 3L4
(705) 475-2322
Emp Here 25
SIC 8211 Elementary and secondary schools

D-U-N-S 25-238-8335   (BR)
NIPISSING PARRY SOUND CATHOLIC DIS-TRICT SCHOOL BOARD
OUR LADY OF FATIMA SCHOOL
60 Marshall Ave E, North Bay, ON, P1A 1R1
(705) 472-7280
Emp Here 21
SIC 8211 Elementary and secondary schools

D-U-N-S 25-238-7428   (BR)
NIPISSING PARRY SOUND CATHOLIC DIS-TRICT SCHOOL BOARD
JOHN XXIII SEPERATE SCHOOL
602 Lake Heights Rd, North Bay, ON, P1A 2Z8
(705) 472-6380
Emp Here 25
SIC 8211 Elementary and secondary schools

D-U-N-S 20-133-6575   (SL)
NORTH BAY CHRYSLER LTD
352 Lakeshore Dr, North Bay, ON, P1A 2C2
(705) 472-0820
Emp Here 40   *Sales* 14,592,140
SIC 5511 New and used car dealers
Pr Pr Steven Farquhar

D-U-N-S 20-697-3674   (BR)
PIONEER CONSTRUCTION INC
175 Progress Rd, North Bay, ON, P1A 0B8
(705) 472-0890
Emp Here 100
SIC 1611 Highway and street construction

D-U-N-S 24-227-5514   (BR)
STOCK TRANSPORTATION LTD
59 Commerce Cres, North Bay, ON, P1A 0B3
(705) 474-4370
Emp Here 150
SIC 4151 School buses

D-U-N-S 20-614-6073   (BR)
TORBA RESTAURANTS INC
WENDY'S RESTAURANTS
368 Lakeshore Dr, North Bay, ON, P1A 2C2
(705) 472-7240
Emp Here 25
SIC 5812 Eating places

D-U-N-S 24-125-9100   (BR)
UNION GAS LIMITED
SPECTRA ENERGY COMPANY
36 Charles St E, North Bay, ON, P1A 1E9

Emp Here 140
SIC 4923 Gas transmission and distribution

D-U-N-S 25-174-3464   (BR)
VALUE VILLAGE STORES, INC
(*Suby of* Savers, Inc.)
390 Lakeshore Dr, North Bay, ON, P1A 2C7
(705) 476-1888
Emp Here 30
SIC 5399 Miscellaneous general merchandise

North Bay, ON P1B
Nipissing County

D-U-N-S 25-730-5334   (BR)
ARAMARK CANADA LTD.
100 College Dr, North Bay, ON, P1B 8K9
(705) 472-7548
Emp Here 45
SIC 5812 Eating places

D-U-N-S 20-340-4640   (BR)
ASSANTE FINANCIAL MANAGEMENT LTD
ASSANTE WEALTH MANAGEMENT
101 Mcintyre St W, North Bay, ON, P1B 2Y5
(705) 476-5422
Emp Here 49
SIC 8748 Business consulting, nec

D-U-N-S 25-296-4812   (BR)
BANK OF NOVA SCOTIA, THE
SCOTIABANK
204 Main St W, North Bay, ON, P1B 2T7
(705) 494-4689
Emp Here 35
SIC 6021 National commercial banks

D-U-N-S 25-296-4853   (BR)
BANK OF NOVA SCOTIA, THE
SCOTIABANK
1500 Fisher St, North Bay, ON, P1B 2H3
(705) 472-5680
Emp Here 30
SIC 6021 National commercial banks

D-U-N-S 24-975-4086   (BR)
BANK OF MONTREAL
BMO
154 Main St E, North Bay, ON, P1B 1A8
(705) 472-2620
Emp Here 20
SIC 6021 National commercial banks

D-U-N-S 20-005-3184   (BR)
BANQUE TORONTO-DOMINION, LA
TORONTO-DOMINION BANK, THE
(*Suby of* Toronto-Dominion Bank, The)
240 Main St E, North Bay, ON, P1B 1B1
(705) 472-4370
Emp Here 30
SIC 6021 National commercial banks

D-U-N-S 25-745-4256   (BR)
BELL MEDIA INC
245 Oak St E, North Bay, ON, P1B 8P8
(705) 476-3111
Emp Here 40
SIC 4833 Television broadcasting stations

D-U-N-S 24-363-5724   (BR)
BEST BUY CANADA LTD
FUTURE SHOP

(*Suby of* Best Buy Co., Inc.)
1500 Fisher St, North Bay, ON, P1B 2H3
(705) 472-2126
Emp Here 55
SIC 5731 Radio, television, and electronic stores

D-U-N-S 25-974-9455   (SL)
BLACK SAXON III INC
CLARION RESORT
201 Pinewood Park Dr, North Bay, ON, P1B 8Z4
(705) 472-0810
Emp Here 75   *Sales* 3,283,232
SIC 7011 Hotels and motels

D-U-N-S 24-803-5045   (BR)
BOART LONGYEAR CANADA
1111 Main St W, North Bay, ON, P1B 2W4
(705) 474-2800
Emp Here 20
SIC 1799 Special trade contractors, nec

D-U-N-S 25-093-2444   (BR)
BOMBARDIER INC
BOMBARDIER AERONAUTIQUE
1500 Airport Rd, North Bay, ON, P1B 8G2

Emp Here 500
SIC 8711 Engineering services

D-U-N-S 20-196-8927   (BR)
BRAMBURYTOWN HOLDINGS CORP
KELSEY'S RESTAURANT
(*Suby of* Bramburytown Holdings Corp)
1899 Algonquin Ave, North Bay, ON, P1B 4Y8

Emp Here 30
SIC 5812 Eating places

D-U-N-S 25-303-6420   (BR)
CANADIAN IMPERIAL BANK OF COMMERCE
CIBC
195 Main St W, North Bay, ON, P1B 2T6
(705) 474-8900
Emp Here 30
SIC 6021 National commercial banks

D-U-N-S 20-588-8493   (BR)
CANADIAN PACIFIC RAILWAY COMPANY
CPR
100 Ferguson St, North Bay, ON, P1B 1W8
(705) 472-6200
Emp Here 20
SIC 4011 Railroads, line-haul operating

D-U-N-S 24-419-6247   (BR)
CANADIAN TIRE CORPORATION, LIMITED
PARTSOURCE
1016 Fisher St Suite 782, North Bay, ON, P1B 2G4
(705) 476-2162
Emp Here 20
SIC 5531 Auto and home supply stores

D-U-N-S 24-889-2023   (BR)
CAPSERVCO LIMITED PARTNERSHIP
(*Suby of* CapServCo Limited Partnership)
222 Mcintyre St W Suite 200, North Bay, ON, P1B 2Y8
(705) 472-6500
Emp Here 20
SIC 8721 Accounting, auditing, and bookkeeping

D-U-N-S 20-648-5315   (BR)
CARA OPERATIONS LIMITED
SWISS CHALET
(*Suby of* Cara Holdings Limited)
1899 Algonquin Ave, North Bay, ON, P1B 4Y8
(705) 474-7191
Emp Here 20
SIC 5812 Eating places

D-U-N-S 24-773-0943   (HQ)
CEMENTATION CANADA INC
(*Suby of* Cementation Canada Inc)

590 Graham Dr, North Bay, ON, P1B 7S1
(705) 472-3381
Emp Here 140   *Emp Total* 170
SIC 1241 Coal mining services

D-U-N-S 20-923-8760   (BR)
CHISHOLM, R. FOOD SERVICES INC
MCDONALD'S RESTAURANTS
(*Suby of* Chisholm, R. Food Services Inc)
1500 Fisher St, North Bay, ON, P1B 2H3
(705) 494-6003
Emp Here 41
SIC 5812 Eating places

D-U-N-S 20-068-1455   (BR)
COMMUNITY LIVING NORTH BAY
CEDARVIEW RESIDENCE
(*Suby of* Community Living North Bay)
105 Larocque Rd, North Bay, ON, P1B 8G3

Emp Here 22
SIC 8361 Residential care

D-U-N-S 20-573-3293   (BR)
COMPAGNIE DES CHEMINS DE FER NATIONAUX DU CANADA
915 Mcintyre St W, North Bay, ON, P1B 3A5
(705) 472-4500
Emp Here 20
SIC 4011 Railroads, line-haul operating

D-U-N-S 20-711-7313   (BR)
CONSEIL SCOLAIRE CATHOLIQUE DU DISTRICT FRANCO-NORD
CITE DES JEUNES
681b Chippewa St W, North Bay, ON, P1B 6G8
(705) 472-4963
Emp Here 22
SIC 8211 Elementary and secondary schools

D-U-N-S 25-121-5489   (BR)
CONSEIL SCOLAIRE CATHOLIQUE DU DISTRICT FRANCO-NORD
L'ICOLE SECONDAIRE CATHOLIQUE ALGONQUIN
(*Suby of* Conseil Scolaire Catholique Du District Franco-Nord)
555 Algonquin Ave, North Bay, ON, P1B 4W8
(705) 472-8240
Emp Here 70
SIC 8211 Elementary and secondary schools

D-U-N-S 25-263-8101   (BR)
CONSEIL SCOLAIRE CATHOLIQUE DU DISTRICT FRANCO-NORD
ECOLE ST VINCENT
(*Suby of* Conseil Scolaire Catholique Du District Franco-Nord)
124 King St E, North Bay, ON, P1B 1P2
(705) 474-6740
Emp Here 22
SIC 8211 Elementary and secondary schools

D-U-N-S 25-263-8069   (BR)
CONSEIL SCOLAIRE CATHOLIQUE DU DISTRICT FRANCO-NORD
ECOLE STE ANNE
(*Suby of* Conseil Scolaire Catholique Du District Franco-Nord)
235 Albert Ave, North Bay, ON, P1B 7J6

Emp Here 20
SIC 8211 Elementary and secondary schools

D-U-N-S 20-072-4073   (BR)
CORPORATION OF THE CITY OF NORTH BAY, THE
NORTH BAY FIRE DEPARTMENT, THE
119 Princess St W, North Bay, ON, P1B 6C2
(705) 474-5662
Emp Here 87
SIC 7389 Business services, nec

D-U-N-S 24-096-6155   (BR)
CORPORATION OF THE CITY OF NORTH BAY, THE
NORTH BAY MEMORIAL GARDENS

SPORTS ARENA
100 Chippewa St W, North Bay, ON, P1B 6G2
(705) 474-3770
Emp Here 20
SIC 7941 Sports clubs, managers, and promoters

D-U-N-S 25-760-7754   (BR)
CRISIS CENTRE NORTH BAY
NIPISSING CUSTODY RESIDENCE
214 Second Ave W, North Bay, ON, P1B 3K9

Emp Here 44
SIC 8399 Social services, nec

D-U-N-S 25-473-4957   (BR)
CRISIS CENTRE NORTH BAY
NIPISSING DETENTION CENTRE
45 Pinewood Park Dr, North Bay, ON, P1B 8Z4
(705) 474-6488
Emp Here 59
SIC 8361 Residential care

D-U-N-S 20-549-8624   (SL)
EMPIRE LIVING CENTRE INC
EMPIRE TERRACE SUITES
425 Fraser St Suite 505, North Bay, ON, P1B 3X1
(705) 474-9555
Emp Here 50   *Sales* 4,377,642
SIC 6513 Apartment building operators

D-U-N-S 25-301-2728   (BR)
EXTENDICARE (CANADA) INC
PARAMED HOME HEALTH CARE
222 Mcintyre St W Suite 202, North Bay, ON, P1B 2Y8
(705) 495-4391
Emp Here 165
SIC 8051 Skilled nursing care facilities

D-U-N-S 24-660-4821   (HQ)
FABRENE, INC
FABRENE
240 Dupont Rd, North Bay, ON, P1B 8Z4
(705) 476-7057
Emp Here 220   *Emp Total* 21,000
Sales 26,160,780
SIC 2221 Broadwoven fabric mills, manmade
VP VP John Spencer
  Eric Henderson

D-U-N-S 20-085-4573   (SL)
FIRST CANADIAN PERSONAL ALARM & EMERGENCY HOME RESPONSE SYSTEM
FIRST RESPONSE
1033 Hammond St Suite 97, North Bay, ON, P1B 2H7
(705) 495-2792
Emp Here 40   *Sales* 5,275,400
SIC 5999 Miscellaneous retail stores, nec
Pt John Hinkley

D-U-N-S 20-227-3012   (BR)
GAP (CANADA) INC
GAP
(*Suby of* The Gap Inc)
1500 Fisher St, North Bay, ON, P1B 2H3
(705) 498-6589
Emp Here 30
SIC 5651 Family clothing stores

D-U-N-S 25-945-4809   (BR)
GARDEWINE GROUP INC
8 Ferris Dr, North Bay, ON, P1B 8Z4
(705) 476-0140
Emp Here 20
SIC 4731 Freight transportation arrangement

D-U-N-S 20-645-2729   (BR)
GOODYEAR CANADA INC
GOODYEAR OTR CENTER
(*Suby of* The Goodyear Tire & Rubber Company)
100 Booth Rd, North Bay, ON, P1B 0B3
(705) 476-9184
Emp Here 50
SIC 7534 Tire retreading and repair shops

▲ Public Company   ■ Public Company Family Member   **HQ** Headquarters   **BR** Branch   **SL** Single Location

D-U-N-S 25-074-9884　　　(BR)
GOVERNMENT OF ONTARIO
CENTRAL AMBULANCE COMMUNICA-TIONS CENTRE
50 College Dr, North Bay, ON, P1B 0A4
(705) 474-7426
Emp Here 25
SIC 4119 Local passenger transportation, nec

D-U-N-S 25-124-9827　　　(HQ)
HANDS THEFAMILYHELPNETWORK.CA
(*Suby of* Hands TheFamilyHelpNetwork.ca)
222 Main St E, North Bay, ON, P1B 1B1
(705) 476-2293
Emp Here 25　　　*Emp Total* 50
Sales 1,969,939
SIC 8322 Individual and family services

D-U-N-S 20-553-6365　　　(BR)
HOME DEPOT OF CANADA INC
(*Suby of* The Home Depot Inc)
1275 Seymour St, North Bay, ON, P1B 9V6
(705) 845-2300
Emp Here 100
SIC 5251 Hardware stores

D-U-N-S 24-222-5969　　　(SL)
HOPPER PONTIAC BUICK GMC
HOPPER BUICK GMC
550 Mckecwn Ave, North Bay, ON, P1B 7M2
(705) 472-3110
Emp Here 50　　　*Sales* 18,240,175
SIC 5511 New and used car dealers
　Stuart Hopper
Pr Pr John Hopper

D-U-N-S 24-337-0223　　　(BR)
HUSQVARNA CANADA CORP
HUSQVARNA CONSTRUCTION PROD-UCTS CANADA
2077 Bond St, North Bay, ON, P1B 4V7
(705) 476-2705
Emp Here 28
SIC 3425 Saw blades and handsaws

D-U-N-S 24-339-7341　　　(BR)
INNVEST HOTELS LP
HOLIDAY INN EXPRESS
1325 Seymour St, North Bay, ON, P1B 9V6
(705) 476-7700
Emp Here 25
SIC 7011 Hotels and motels

D-U-N-S 25-305-2732　　　(BR)
INNVEST PROPERTIES CORP
WESTMONT HOSPITALITY GROUP
(*Suby of* Innvest Properties Corp)
1200 O'Brien St, North Bay, ON, P1B 9B3
(905) 624-7801
Emp Here 21
SIC 7011 Hotels and motels

D-U-N-S 25-300-5615　　　(BR)
KPMG LLP
K P M G
(*Suby of* KPMG LLP)
925 Stockdale Rd Suite 300, North Bay, ON, P1B 9N5
(705) 472-5110
Emp Here 30
SIC 8721 Accounting, auditing, and book-keeping

D-U-N-S 25-361-0539　　　(BR)
KNIGHT PIESOLD LTD
1650 Main St W, North Bay, ON, P1B 8G5
(705) 476-2165
Emp Here 23
SIC 8711 Engineering services

D-U-N-S 24-744-5067　　　(SL)
MAIN STREET AUTO IMPORTERS LTD
GOLDFLEET SUBARU
600 Mckeown Ave, North Bay, ON, P1B 7M2
(705) 472-2222
Emp Here 20　　　*Sales* 7,296,070
SIC 5511 New and used car dealers
　Clifford E Pilon

D-U-N-S 25-730-3883　　　(BR)
MANITOULIN TRANSPORT INC
180 Ferris Dr, North Bay, ON, P1B 8Z4
(705) 476-1333
Emp Here 30
SIC 4213 Trucking, except local

D-U-N-S 20-119-8517　　　(BR)
MILLER TECHNOLOGY INCORPORATED
175 Eloy Rd, North Bay, ON, P1B 9T9
(705) 476-4501
Emp Here 55
SIC 5084 Industrial machinery and equipment

D-U-N-S 24-218-1402　　　(BR)
MORGUARD INVESTMENTS LIMITED
NORTHGATE SHOPPING CENTRE
1500 Fisher St Suite 200, North Bay, ON, P1B 2H3
(705) 472-8110
Emp Here 25
SIC 6512 Nonresidential building operators

D-U-N-S 25-166-5766　　　(BR)
MOTION INDUSTRIES (CANADA), INC
(*Suby of* Genuine Parts Company)
600 Gormanville Rd, North Bay, ON, P1B 9S7
(705) 476-3109
Emp Here 35
SIC 5084 Industrial machinery and equipment

D-U-N-S 25-375-3990　　　(BR)
MUSKOKA AUTO PARTS LIMITED
H.E. BROWN SUPPLY
150 Mcintyre St E, North Bay, ON, P1B 1C4
(705) 472-4165
Emp Here 30
SIC 5013 Motor vehicle supplies and new parts

D-U-N-S 20-589-9144　　　(BR)
NAV CANADA
50 Terminal St Suite 2, North Bay, ON, P1B 8G2
(705) 476-1788
Emp Here 47
SIC 3812 Search and navigation equipment

D-U-N-S 25-249-0420　　　(BR)
NEAR NORTH DISTRICT SCHOOL BOARD
E T CARMICHAEL ELEMENTARY SCHOOL
1351 Chapais St, North Bay, ON, P1B 6M6
(705) 472-5502
Emp Here 21
SIC 8211 Elementary and secondary schools

D-U-N-S 25-249-0321　　　(BR)
NEAR NORTH DISTRICT SCHOOL BOARD
ALLIANCE PUBLIC SCHOOL
700 Stones St, North Bay, ON, P1B 6C1
(705) 475-2326
Emp Here 30
SIC 8211 Elementary and secondary schools

D-U-N-S 25-249-0628　　　(BR)
NEAR NORTH DISTRICT SCHOOL BOARD
PINEWOOD PUBLIC SCHOOL
1325 Cedargrove Dr, North Bay, ON, P1B 4S3
(705) 472-9251
Emp Here 20
SIC 8211 Elementary and secondary schools

D-U-N-S 25-249-0230　　　(BR)
NEAR NORTH DISTRICT SCHOOL BOARD
SUNSET PARK PUBLIC SCHOOL
1191 Lakeshore Dr, North Bay, ON, P1B 8Z4
(705) 475-2330
Emp Here 30
SIC 8211 Elementary and secondary schools

D-U-N-S 20-279-7320　　　(BR)
NEAR NORTH DISTRICT SCHOOL BOARD
CHIPPEWA INTERMEDIATE SCHOOL
539 Chippewa St W, North Bay, ON, P1B 6G8
(705) 475-2341
Emp Here 30
SIC 8211 Elementary and secondary schools

D-U-N-S 25-249-0503　　　(BR)
NEAR NORTH DISTRICT SCHOOL BOARD
J W TRUSLER PUBLIC SCHOOL
111 Cartier St, North Bay, ON, P1B 4Z4
(705) 472-5459
Emp Here 22
SIC 8211 Elementary and secondary schools

D-U-N-S 25-253-6297　　　(BR)
NEAR NORTH DISTRICT SCHOOL BOARD
KING GEORGE PUBLIC SCHOOL
550 Harvey St, North Bay, ON, P1B 4H3
(705) 472-5448
Emp Here 20
SIC 8211 Elementary and secondary schools

D-U-N-S 25-249-4018　　　(BR)
NEAR NORTH DISTRICT SCHOOL BOARD
WIDDIFIELD SECONDARY SCHOOL
320 Ski Club Rd, North Bay, ON, P1B 7R2
(705) 472-5711
Emp Here 70
SIC 8211 Elementary and secondary schools

D-U-N-S 20-653-3411　　　(BR)
NIPISSING PARRY SOUND CATHOLIC DIS-TRICT SCHOOL BOARD
MOTHER ST. BRIDE CATHOLIC ELEMEN-TARY SCHOOL
414 Second Ave W, North Bay, ON, P1B 3L2
(705) 472-1524
Emp Here 35
SIC 8211 Elementary and secondary schools

D-U-N-S 20-710-4428　　　(BR)
NIPISSING PARRY SOUND CATHOLIC DIS-TRICT SCHOOL BOARD
ST ALEXANDER SCHOOL
900 Bloem St, North Bay, ON, P1B 4Z8
(705) 472-9141
Emp Here 30
SIC 8211 Elementary and secondary schools

D-U-N-S 25-238-8038　　　(BR)
NIPISSING PARRY SOUND CATHOLIC DIS-TRICT SCHOOL BOARD
ST LUKE CATHOLIC ELEMENTARY SCHOOL
225 Milani Rd, North Bay, ON, P1B 7P4
(705) 472-6690
Emp Here 20
SIC 8211 Elementary and secondary schools

D-U-N-S 20-710-4436　　　(BR)
NIPISSING PARRY SOUND CATHOLIC DIS-TRICT SCHOOL BOARD
ST HUBERT CATHOLIC SCHOOL
850 Lorne Ave, North Bay, ON, P1B 8M2
(705) 472-2770
Emp Here 30
SIC 8211 Elementary and secondary schools

D-U-N-S 25-828-1377　　　(BR)
NORTH BAY REGIONAL HEALTH CENTRE
NORTHEAST MENTAL HEALTH CENTRE
200 First Ave W, North Bay, ON, P1B 3B9
(705) 494-3050
Emp Here 20
SIC 8062 General medical and surgical hospitals

D-U-N-S 24-719-9461　　　(BR)
NORTH BAY REGIONAL HEALTH CENTRE
147 Mcintyre St W, North Bay, ON, P1B 2Y5
(705) 474-8600
Emp Here 22
SIC 8062 General medical and surgical hospitals

D-U-N-S 25-745-9701　　　(BR)
NORTH BAY REGIONAL HEALTH CENTRE
NORTH BAY DISTRICT AMBULANCE SER-VICE
750 Scollard St, North Bay, ON, P1B 5A4
(705) 474-4130
Emp Here 44
SIC 4119 Local passenger transportation, nec

D-U-N-S 25-743-3334　　　(BR)
NORTH EAST COMMUNITY CARE ACCESS CENTRE
(*Suby of* North East Community Care Access Centre)
1164 Devonshire Ave, North Bay, ON, P1B 6X7
(705) 474-5885
Emp Here 100
SIC 8059 Nursing and personal care, nec

D-U-N-S 25-282-5179　　　(SL)
NORTH EAST MENTAL HEALTH CENTRE (NORTH BAY CAMPUS)
4700 Highway 11 N, North Bay, ON, P1B 8G3
(705) 474-1200
Emp Here 575　　　*Sales* 57,072,640
SIC 8063 Psychiatric hospitals
Dir Robert Cunningham

D-U-N-S 20-629-3495　　　(SL)
O.N. TEL INC
555 Oak St E, North Bay, ON, P1B 8E3
(705) 472-4500
Emp Here 50　　　*Sales* 4,742,446
SIC 4813 Telephone communication, except radio

D-U-N-S 20-133-6849　　　(BR)
ONTARIO ELECTRICAL CONSTRUCTION COMPANY, LIMITED
(*Suby of* Ontario Electrical Construction Company, Limited)
211 Airport Rd, North Bay, ON, P1B 8W7
(705) 474-3040
Emp Here 40
SIC 1731 Electrical work

D-U-N-S 25-945-9972　　　(BR)
ONTARIO ENGLISH CATHOLIC TEACHERS ASSOCIATION, THE
387 Algonquin Ave, North Bay, ON, P1B 4W4
(705) 495-4433
Emp Here 158
SIC 8631 Labor organizations

D-U-N-S 20-133-6864　　　(HQ)
ONTARIO NORTHLAND TRANSPORTA-TION COMMISSION
ONTARIO NORTHLAND RAILWAY
555 Oak St E, North Bay, ON, P1B 8E3
(705) 472-4500
Emp Here 600　　　*Emp Total* 90,000
Sales 183,204,318
SIC 4899 Communication services, nec
Pr Corina Moore
VP John Thub
Dir Opers Dennis Higgs
Dir Chad Evans
Dir Tracy Macphee
　Rebecca Mcglynn
Prs Dir Greg Stuart

D-U-N-S 20-808-1591　　　(BR)
ONTARIO POWER GENERATION INC
O P G
133 Eloy Rd, North Bay, ON, P1B 9T9
(705) 474-2364
Emp Here 25
SIC 4911 Electric services

D-U-N-S 25-411-3657　　　(BR)
PETERBILT OF ONTARIO INC
PETERBILT OF NORTH BAY
3410 Highway 11 N, North Bay, ON, P1B 8G3
(705) 472-4000
Emp Here 20
SIC 5511 New and used car dealers

D-U-N-S 25-687-6756　　　(BR)
PHARMA PLUS DRUGMARTS LTD
1500 Fisher St, North Bay, ON, P1B 2H3
(705) 476-2205
Emp Here 20
SIC 5912 Drug stores and proprietary stores

D-U-N-S 25-743-2849　　　(BR)
RCR INDUSTRIAL INC

21 Exeter St, North Bay, ON, P1B 8K6
(705) 472-5207
Emp Here 70
SIC 7699 Repair services, nec

D-U-N-S 20-415-6905   (HQ)
REDPATH CANADA LIMITED
REDPATH GROUP
101 Worthington St E 3rd Fl, North Bay, ON,
P1B 1G5
(705) 474-2461
Emp Here 60   *Emp Total* 1
Sales 6,639,424
SIC 1081 Metal mining services
Pr Pr George Flumerfelt
  Martin A. Hunka

D-U-N-S 24-079-1785   (BR)
RESEAU TEL-SYNERGIE INC
DOLLARAMA
(*Suby of* Reseau Tel-Synergie Inc)
1500 Fisher St, North Bay, ON, P1B 2H3
(705) 840-1027
Emp Here 24
SIC 5311 Department stores

D-U-N-S 24-316-9687   (BR)
ROGERS MEDIA INC
CKAT-AM
(*Suby of* Rogers Communications Inc)
743 Main St E, North Bay, ON, P1B 1C2
(705) 474-2000
Emp Here 32
SIC 4832 Radio broadcasting stations

D-U-N-S 25-742-5009   (BR)
ROYAL BANK OF CANADA
RBC
(*Suby of* Royal Bank Of Canada)
105 Main St W, North Bay, ON, P1B 2T6
(705) 472-5470
Emp Here 21
SIC 6021 National commercial banks

D-U-N-S 24-367-6207   (BR)
SANDVIK CANADA, INC
SANDVIK MINING AND CONSTRUCTION
400 Kirkpatrick St Suite B, North Bay, ON, P1B
8G5

Emp Here 85
SIC 5082 Construction and mining machinery

D-U-N-S 25-743-5875   (BR)
SOBEYS CAPITAL INCORPORATED
FRESHCO
2555 Trout Lake Rd, North Bay, ON, P1B 7S8
(705) 495-4221
Emp Here 75
SIC 5141 Groceries, general line

D-U-N-S 25-743-5883   (BR)
SOBEYS CAPITAL INCORPORATED
1899 Algonquin Ave, North Bay, ON, P1B 4Y8
(705) 472-4001
Emp Here 200
SIC 5411 Grocery stores

D-U-N-S 25-184-7195   (BR)
**STANTEC CONSULTING INTERNATIONAL
LTD**
147 Mcintyre St W Suite 200, North Bay, ON,
P1B 2Y5
(705) 494-8255
Emp Here 108
SIC 8711 Engineering services

D-U-N-S 20-352-6959   (BR)
STANTEC CONSULTING LTD
147 Mcintyre St W Suite 200, North Bay, ON,
P1B 2Y5
(705) 494-8255
Emp Here 41
SIC 8711 Engineering services

D-U-N-S 25-498-9445   (BR)
STAPLES CANADA INC
STAPLES THE BUSINESS DEPOT

(*Suby of* Staples, Inc.)
1899 Algonquin Ave, North Bay, ON, P1B 4Y8
(705) 472-7223
Emp Here 50
SIC 5943 Stationery stores

D-U-N-S 24-343-9994   (BR)
SUPERIOR PLUS LP
SUPERIOR PROPANE
1366 Main St W, North Bay, ON, P1B 2W6
(705) 494-6000
Emp Here 30
SIC 5984 Liquefied petroleum gas dealers

D-U-N-S 20-115-1631   (BR)
**SYKES ASSISTANCE SERVICES CORPO-
RATION**
SYKES TELEHEALTH
(*Suby of* Sykes Enterprises Incorporated)
555 Oak St E, North Bay, ON, P1B 8E3
(705) 840-1350
Emp Here 100
SIC 8099 Health and allied services, nec

D-U-N-S 24-329-6998   (BR)
WAL-MART CANADA CORP
1500 Fisher St Suite 102, North Bay, ON, P1B
2H3
(705) 472-1704
Emp Here 200
SIC 5311 Department stores

D-U-N-S 25-829-6995   (BR)
WENDY'S RESTAURANTS OF CANADA INC
WENDY'S
(*Suby of* The Wendy's Company)
925 Mckeown Ave, North Bay, ON, P1B 9P3
(705) 476-1937
Emp Here 30
SIC 5812 Eating places

D-U-N-S 20-184-1538   (BR)
**WINNERS MERCHANTS INTERNATIONAL
L.P.**
WINNERS
(*Suby of* The TJX Companies Inc)
850 Mckeown Ave, North Bay, ON, P1B 8M1
(705) 475-9292
Emp Here 22
SIC 5651 Family clothing stores

North Bay, ON P1C
Nipissing County

D-U-N-S 25-249-0396   (BR)
NEAR NORTH DISTRICT SCHOOL BOARD
VINCENT MASSEY PUBLIC SCHOOL
15 Janey Ave, North Bay, ON, P1C 1N1
(705) 475-2340
Emp Here 30
SIC 8211 Elementary and secondary schools

North Gower, ON K0A
Carleton County

D-U-N-S 25-263-5487   (BR)
**OTTAWA-CARLETON DISTRICT SCHOOL
BOARD**
*NORTH GOWER-MARLBOROUGH PUBLIC
SCHOOL*
2403 Church St, North Gower, ON, K0A 2T0
(613) 489-3375
Emp Here 21
SIC 8211 Elementary and secondary schools

D-U-N-S 20-890-4748   (SL)
STRATHMERE FARM INC
STRATHMERE
1980 Phelan Rd W, North Gower, ON, K0A
2T0
(613) 489-2409
Emp Here 50   *Sales* 2,188,821

SIC 7011 Hotels and motels

North Lancaster, ON K0C
Glengarry County

D-U-N-S 20-592-0494   (BR)
**CONSEIL SCOLAIRE DE DISTRICT
CATHOLIQUE DE L'EST ONTARIEN**
*ECOLE ELEMENTAIRE CATHOLIQUE DE
L'ANGE-GARDIEN*
4831 2nd Line Rd, North Lancaster, ON, K0C
1Z0
(613) 347-2728
Emp Here 30
SIC 8211 Elementary and secondary schools

North York, ON M2H
York County

D-U-N-S 20-571-8559   (BR)
ARBOR MEMORIAL SERVICES INC
ARBOUR MEMORIAL
33 Memory Gardens Lane, North York, ON,
M2H 3K4
(416) 493-9580
Emp Here 40
SIC 6712 Bank holding companies

D-U-N-S 24-117-5590   (BR)
BANQUE TORONTO-DOMINION, LA
TORONTO-DOMINION BANK, THE
(*Suby of* Toronto-Dominion Bank, The)
3555 Don Mills Rd, North York, ON, M2H 3N3
(416) 498-3331
Emp Here 20
SIC 6021 National commercial banks

D-U-N-S 20-584-9743   (BR)
CANADA POST CORPORATION
WILLOWDALE DEPOT
101 Placer Crt, North York, ON, M2H 3H9

Emp Here 125
SIC 4311 U.s. postal service

D-U-N-S 25-868-9215   (BR)
**CHARTWELL SENIORS HOUSING REAL
ESTATE INVESTMENT TRUST**
CHARTWELL SENIOR HOUSING
1925 Steeles Ave E, North York, ON, M2H
2H3
(416) 493-4666
Emp Here 300
SIC 8322 Individual and family services

D-U-N-S 20-112-6559   (SL)
CHEMTRADE LOGISTICS (US) INC
155 Gordon Baker Rd Suite 300, North York,
ON, M2H 3N5
(416) 496-5856
Emp Here 450   *Sales* 145,374,960
SIC 5169 Chemicals and allied products, nec
Pr Mark Davis
Crdt Mgr Tom Briand

D-U-N-S 24-805-0358   (BR)
CHEMTRADE LOGISTICS INC
111 Gordon Baker Rd Suite 300, North York,
ON, M2H 3R1
(416) 496-9655
Emp Here 20
SIC 2819 Industrial inorganic chemicals, nec

D-U-N-S 20-180-1144   (SL)
**CHEMTRADE PERFORMANCE CHEMI-
CALS US, LLC**
155 Gordon Baker Rd Suite 300, North York,
ON, M2H 3N5
(416) 496-5856
Emp Here 75   *Sales* 23,275,526
SIC 5169 Chemicals and allied products, nec
  Mark Davis

Crdt Mgr Tom Briand

D-U-N-S 20-708-6401   (BR)
COCA-COLA LTD
(*Suby of* The Coca-Cola Company)
3389 Steeles Ave E Suite 500, North York,
ON, M2H 3S8

Emp Here 150
SIC 5149 Groceries and related products, nec

D-U-N-S 25-531-9949   (SL)
DYADEM INTERNATIONAL LTD
155 Gordon Baker Rd Suite 401, North York,
ON, M2H 3N5
(416) 649-9200
Emp Here 105   *Sales* 18,563,881
SIC 5045 Computers, peripherals, and soft-
ware
Pr Pr Kevin North
  Andrew Shannon
  Sam Zawaideh

D-U-N-S 24-355-3190   (SL)
EMBANET ULC
EMBANETCOMPASS
105 Gordon Baker Rd Suite 300, North York,
ON, M2H 3P8
(416) 494-6622
Emp Here 200   *Sales* 37,177,600
SIC 8748 Business consulting, nec
  Steve Fireng
CFO Patrick Donoghue
  Gloria Pickar
COO Paul Gleason
  Mike Purcell
Pers/VP Nikki Zinman

D-U-N-S 25-406-3183   (SL)
**GLOBAL   PAYMENT   SYSTEMS   OF
CANADA, LTD**
(*Suby of* Global Payments Inc.)
3381 Steeles Ave E Suite 200, North York,
ON, M2H 3S7
(416) 644-5959
Emp Here 60   *Sales* 3,064,349
SIC 7389 Business services, nec

D-U-N-S 25-270-3384   (BR)
HSBC BANK CANADA
3640 Victoria Park Ave Suite 301, North York,
ON, M2H 3B2
(416) 756-2333
Emp Here 40
SIC 6021 National commercial banks

D-U-N-S 25-794-0239   (BR)
J.F. & L. RESTAURANTS LIMITED
PICKLE BARREL RESTAURANT, THE
(*Suby of* J.F. & L. Restaurants Limited)
5941 Leslie St, North York, ON, M2H 1J8
(416) 493-4444
Emp Here 150
SIC 5812 Eating places

D-U-N-S 24-795-1445   (HQ)
LEXISNEXIS CANADA INC
111 Gordon Baker Road Suite 900, North
York, ON, M2H 3R1
(905) 479-2665
Emp Here 200   *Emp Total* 115
Sales 17,584,895
SIC 2731 Book publishing
Dir Patrick Collins
VP Linda Kee
VP Sls Antoine Shiu

D-U-N-S 20-140-2265   (BR)
MEMORIAL GARDENS CANADA LIMITED
HIGHLAND MEMORY GARDEN
33 Memory Gardens Lane, North York, ON,
M2H 3K4
(416) 493-9580
Emp Here 50
SIC 6553 Cemetery subdividers and develop-
ers

D-U-N-S 25-255-0421   (BR)

METROLAND MEDIA GROUP LTD
NORTH YORK MIRROR
175 Gordon Baker Rd, North York, ON, M2H 2N7
(416) 493-4400
Emp Here 68
SIC 2711 Newspapers

D-U-N-S 24-023-4562 (SL)
PEOPLELOGIC CORP
250 Tempo Ave, North York, ON, M2H 2N8

Emp Here 450 *Sales* 86,714,240
SIC 8748 Business consulting, nec
Pr Pr Naeem Bhatti

D-U-N-S 25-805-3156 (BR)
PHARMA PLUS DRUGMARTS LTD
3555 Don Mills Rd, North York, ON, M2H 3N3
(416) 494-8102
Emp Here 20
SIC 5912 Drug stores and proprietary stores

D-U-N-S 20-271-8060 (SL)
PROVALUE GROUP INC
3750 Victoria Park Ave Unit 208, North York, ON, M2H 3S2
(416) 496-8899
Emp Here 400 *Sales* 37,693,160
SIC 7361 Employment agencies
Pr Pr Yun Lin Chen

D-U-N-S 24-636-8398 (BR)
SHOPPERS DRUG MART INC
SHOPPERS HOME HEALTHCARE
202 Sparks Ave, North York, ON, M2H 2S4
(416) 701-1351
Emp Here 60
SIC 5912 Drug stores and proprietary stores

D-U-N-S 20-638-6737 (BR)
SO, JAMES REALTY LTD
3790 Victoria Park Ave Suite 200, North York, ON, M2H 3H7

Emp Here 30
SIC 6531 Real estate agents and managers

D-U-N-S 24-384-2981 (SL)
SONY INTERACTIVE ENTERTAINMENT CANADA INC
115 Gordon Baker Rd, North York, ON, M2H 3R6
(416) 499-1414
Emp Here 20 *Sales* 2,918,428
SIC 5092 Toys and hobby goods and supplies

D-U-N-S 25-532-0251 (SL)
SONY PICTURES HOME ENTERTAINMENT CANADA LTD
115 Gordon Baker Rd, North York, ON, M2H 3R6
(416) 221-8660
Emp Here 44 *Sales* 1,605,135
SIC 7841 Video tape rental

D-U-N-S 20-948-7966 (HQ)
SONY OF CANADA LTD
SONY STORES, THE
115 Gordon Baker Rd, North York, ON, M2H 3R6
(416) 499-1414
Emp Here 200 *Emp Total* 125,300
Sales 293,139,338
SIC 5064 Electrical appliances, television and radio
Howard Stringer
Pr Pr Douglas Wilson
Barry Hasler
Tariq Shameem
VP Diana Zangrilli
Pers/VP Susan Bean
Div VP Anil Sethi
Martin Huntington
Raj Rawara
Ravi Nookala

D-U-N-S 20-176-5468 (HQ)

TAB PRODUCTS OF CANADA, CO.
TAB CANADA
136 Sparks Ave, North York, ON, M2H 2S4
(416) 497-1552
Emp Here 75 *Sales* 20,501,957
SIC 5044 Office equipment
Pr Pr John Palmer
VP Sls Janet Campbell
  Ross Nepean
Sr VP Jonathon Shea
VP Sls Jonathan Cowie
VP Brad Hicks
  Aggie Koniak Jaggers
VP VP Henry Van Pypen

D-U-N-S 25-684-2485 (BR)
THYSSENKRUPP ELEVATOR (CANADA) LIMITED
THYSSEN KRUPP ELEVATOR
517 Mcnicoll Ave, North York, ON, M2H 2C9
(416) 496-6000
Emp Here 20
SIC 3534 Elevators and moving stairways

D-U-N-S 20-026-0326 (BR)
TORONTO DISTRICT SCHOOL BOARD
CHEROKEE PUBLIC SCHOOL
390 Cherokee Blvd, North York, ON, M2H 2W7
(416) 395-2190
Emp Here 20
SIC 8211 Elementary and secondary schools

D-U-N-S 20-035-4699 (BR)
TORONTO DISTRICT SCHOOL BOARD
ZION HEIGHTS JUNIOR HIGH SCHOOL
5900 Leslie St, North York, ON, M2H 1J9
(416) 395-3120
Emp Here 40
SIC 8211 Elementary and secondary schools

D-U-N-S 20-700-2663 (BR)
TORONTO DISTRICT SCHOOL BOARD
A Y JACKSON SECONDARY SCHOOL
50 Francine Dr, North York, ON, M2H 2G6
(416) 395-3140
Emp Here 75
SIC 8211 Elementary and secondary schools

D-U-N-S 20-025-9617 (BR)
TORONTO DISTRICT SCHOOL BOARD
ARBOR GLEN PUBLIC SCHOOL
55 Freshmeadow Dr, North York, ON, M2H 3H6
(416) 395-3020
Emp Here 22
SIC 8211 Elementary and secondary schools

D-U-N-S 20-044-6367 (HQ)
WRIGLEY CANADA INC
(*Suby of* Mars, Incorporated)
3389 Steeles Ave E, North York, ON, M2H 3S8
(416) 449-8600
Emp Here 500 *Emp Total* 80,000
SIC 2067 Chewing gum

D-U-N-S 20-795-1393 (HQ)
YAMAHA MOTOR CANADA LTD
480 Gordon Baker Rd, North York, ON, M2H 3B4
(416) 498-1911
Emp Here 120 *Emp Total* 53,125
Sales 21,569,650
SIC 5091 Sporting and recreation goods
Pr Yoichiro Kojima
Treas Steve Tanaka
  Peter R Braund
  William T Pashby

D-U-N-S 24-205-5973 (SL)
YESUP ECOMMERCE SOLUTIONS INC
YES ADVERTISING
565 Gordon Baker Rd, North York, ON, M2H 2W2
(416) 499-8009
Emp Here 50 *Sales* 2,699,546
SIC 8731 Commercial physical research

North York, ON M2J
York County

D-U-N-S 20-283-4693 (HQ)
ARZ GROUP LIMITED
279 Yorkland Blvd, North York, ON, M2J 1S5
(416) 847-0350
Emp Here 120 *Emp Total* 138,000
Sales 13,424,769
SIC 5099 Durable goods, nec
Pr Armand Boyadjian

D-U-N-S 25-511-5867 (SL)
ADVANCED UTILITY SYSTEMS CORPORATION
2235 Sheppard Ave E Suite 1400, North York, ON, M2J 5B5
(416) 496-0149
Emp Here 70 *Sales* 7,952,716
SIC 7371 Custom computer programming services
VP VP Philip Playfair
VP VP Steven Hammond

D-U-N-S 24-209-1028 (BR)
ARITZIA LP
1800 Sheppard E, North York, ON, M2J 5A7
(416) 494-5166
Emp Here 30
SIC 5963 Direct selling establishments

D-U-N-S 20-101-7816 (BR)
CBRE LIMITED
2001 Sheppard Ave E Suite 300, North York, ON, M2J 4Z8
(416) 494-0600
Emp Here 100
SIC 6531 Real estate agents and managers

D-U-N-S 20-848-9518 (HQ)
CH2M HILL CANADA LIMITED
(*Suby of* Ch2m Hill Companies, Ltd.)
245 Consumers Rd Suite 400, North York, ON, M2J 1R3
(416) 499-9000
Emp Here 250 *Emp Total* 22,000
Sales 85,436,980
SIC 8711 Engineering services
Pr Peter Nicol
VP Andrew Phillip
  David Larter
Sr VP Bruce Tucker
VP Fin VP Fin Dottie Swallow
Sr VP Gary Webster
Sr VP Shawn Gibbons
  William T. Dohn
  M. Catherine Santee
  Ronald A. Campbell

D-U-N-S 25-950-9354 (SL)
CANADIAN HEART RESEARCH CENTRE
259 Yorkland Rd Suite 200, North York, ON, M2J 0B5
(416) 977-8010
Emp Here 65 *Sales* 3,502,114
SIC 8731 Commercial physical research

D-U-N-S 24-418-2809 (BR)
CINEPLEX ODEON CORPORATION
SILVERCITY FAIRVIEW MALL
1800 Sheppard Ave E, North York, ON, M2J 5A7
(416) 644-7746
Emp Here 20
SIC 7832 Motion picture theaters, except drive-in

D-U-N-S 20-780-0405 (BR)
CLUB MONACO CORP
CLUB MONACO
(*Suby of* Ralph Lauren Corporation)
1800 Sheppard Ave E Suite 138, North York, ON, M2J 5A7
(416) 499-1266
Emp Here 40
SIC 5621 Women's clothing stores

D-U-N-S 25-273-7911 (BR)
COLLIERS MACAULAY NICOLLS INC
COLLIERS INTERNATIONAL
245 Yorkland Blvd Suite 200, North York, ON, M2J 4W9
(416) 492-2000
Emp Here 40
SIC 6531 Real estate agents and managers

D-U-N-S 25-504-5494 (BR)
COMCARE (CANADA) LIMITED
(*Suby of* Comcare (Canada) Limited)
255 Consumers Rd Suite 120, North York, ON, M2J 1R4
(416) 929-3364
Emp Here 30
SIC 7361 Employment agencies

D-U-N-S 25-226-3520 (BR)
CORPORATION OF THE CITY OF TORONTO
ORIOLE RESOURCES CENTRE
2975 Don Mills Rd, North York, ON, M2J 3B7
(416) 395-7855
Emp Here 20
SIC 7999 Amusement and recreation, nec

D-U-N-S 20-162-7221 (HQ)
COUTTS, WILLIAM E. COMPANY, LIMITED
HAPPY HOUR CARD'N PARTY SHOPS
(*Suby of* Hallmark Cards, Incorporated)
501 Consumers Rd, North York, ON, M2J 5E2
(416) 492-1300
Emp Here 900 *Emp Total* 27,000
SIC 2771 Greeting cards

D-U-N-S 20-817-2528 (HQ)
CROSSEY ENGINEERING LTD
(*Suby of* Lacela Holdings Corp)
2255 Sheppard Ave E Suite E 331, North York, ON, M2J 4Y1
(416) 497-3111
Emp Here 134 *Emp Total* 100
Sales 18,537,771
SIC 8711 Engineering services
Dir Wallace Eley
Pr Clive Lacey
VP Andrew Pratt
VP Duane Waite

D-U-N-S 20-127-0626 (HQ)
DILLON CONSULTING LIMITED
(*Suby of* Dillon Consulting Inc)
235 Yorkland Blvd Suite 800, North York, ON, M2J 4Y8
(416) 229-4646
Emp Here 77 *Emp Total* 700
Sales 79,608,467
SIC 8711 Engineering services
Jim R Balfour
Patrick J Wright
Alan K Mitchell
David J Clark
Andrew Blackmer
Paul R Schaap
Gary Komar
Owen Wilson
Jeffrey Matthews
Terry Boutilier

D-U-N-S 24-314-4982 (BR)
DIRECT ENERGY MARKETING LIMITED
DIRECT ENERGY HOME ESSENTIALS, DIV OF
2225 Sheppard Ave E Suite 100, North York, ON, M2J 5C2
(905) 944-9944
Emp Here 50
SIC 4911 Electric services

D-U-N-S 25-294-7932 (BR)
EMPIRE LIFE INSURANCE COMPANY, THE
EMPIRE FINANCAL GROUP
2550 Victoria Park Ave Suite 800, North York, ON, M2J 5A9
(416) 494-6834
Emp Here 40

SIC 6311 Life insurance

D-U-N-S 25-998-1058   (SL)
ENBRIDGE COMMERCIAL SERVICES INC
500 Consumers Rd, North York, ON, M2J 1P8
(416) 492-5000
Emp Here 1,000   Sales 210,553,200
SIC 8741 Management services
Pr Pr Dwight Willett
VP Paul Dalglish

D-U-N-S 25-679-6798   (HQ)
ENBRIDGE ENERGY DISTRIBUTION INC
500 Consumers Rd, North York, ON, M2J 1P8
(416) 492-5000
Emp Here 400   Emp Total 7,733
Sales 1,012,061,346
SIC 4924 Natural gas distribution
Pr Pr D. Guy Jarvis
 J. Richard Bird
Dir J. Lorne Braithwaite
Dir David Leslie
Dir Al Monaco

D-U-N-S 24-977-2034   (BR)
FGL SPORTS LTD
SPORT CHEK FAIRVIEW MALL
1800 Sheppard Ave E Unit 2074, North York, ON, M2J 5A7
(416) 502-2931
Emp Here 35
SIC 5941 Sporting goods and bicycle shops

D-U-N-S 24-830-4537   (HQ)
FERRING INC
FERRING PHARMACEUTICALS
200 Yorkland Blvd Suite 500, North York, ON, M2J 5C1
(416) 490-0121
Emp Here 30   Emp Total 5,000
Sales 7,369,031
SIC 5122 Drugs, proprietaries, and sundries
Genl Mgr Rick Jeysman
 Michel Pettigrew
 Michael Penman

D-U-N-S 20-822-7710   (HQ)
FITNESS INSTITUTE LIMITED, THE
FITNESS INSTITUTE, THE
2235 Sheppard Ave E Suite 901, North York, ON, M2J 5B5
(416) 492-7611
Emp Here 200   Emp Total 450
Sales 27,632,000
SIC 7991 Physical fitness facilities
Pr Clive Caldwell
VP Steve Roest

D-U-N-S 24-795-5482   (BR)
FOREVER XXI ULC
1800 Sheppard Ave E, North York, ON, M2J 5A7
(416) 494-6363
Emp Here 80
SIC 5651 Family clothing stores

D-U-N-S 20-226-6024   (SL)
FROST & SULLIVAN CANADA INC
2001 Sheppard Ave E Suite 504, North York, ON, M2J 4Z8
(416) 490-1511
Emp Here 40   Sales 4,012,839
SIC 8732 Commercial nonphysical research

D-U-N-S 25-696-2143   (BR)
G4S SECURE SOLUTIONS (CANADA) LTD
2 Lansing Sq Suite 204, North York, ON, M2J 4P8
(416) 490-8329
Emp Here 800
SIC 7381 Detective and armored car services

D-U-N-S 25-373-8306   (SL)
GENERATION 5 MATHEMATICAL TECHNOLOGIES INC
515 Consumers Rd Suite 600, North York, ON, M2J 4Z2

Emp Here 49   Sales 7,304,400

SIC 8732 Commercial nonphysical research
Pr Pr Milorad Krneta

D-U-N-S 20-046-4522   (BR)
GREAT-WEST LIFE ASSURANCE COMPANY, THE
SALES AND MARKTING TORONTO
2005 Sheppard Ave E Suite 600, North York, ON, M2J 5B4
(416) 492-4300
Emp Here 60
SIC 6159 Miscellaneous business credit institutions

D-U-N-S 20-700-8830   (BR)
HUDSON'S BAY COMPANY
THE BAY
1800 Sheppard Ave E Suite 1, North York, ON, M2J 5A7
(416) 491-2010
Emp Here 450
SIC 5311 Department stores

D-U-N-S 20-105-9248   (BR)
IBM CANADA LIMITED
ACCOUNTS RECEIVABLE DEPT
(Suby of International Business Machines Corporation)
245 Consumers Rd, North York, ON, M2J 1R3
(905) 316-7785
Emp Here 60
SIC 8721 Accounting, auditing, and bookkeeping

D-U-N-S 25-315-7515   (BR)
INVESTORS GROUP FINANCIAL SERVICES INC
200 Yorkland Blvd Suite 300, North York, ON, M2J 5C1
(416) 491-7400
Emp Here 80
SIC 8741 Management services

D-U-N-S 25-830-3312   (BR)
INVESTORS GROUP TRUST CO. LTD
INVESTORS GROUP FINANCIAL SERVICE
200 Yorkland Blvd Unit 300, North York, ON, M2J 5C1

Emp Here 120
SIC 6282 Investment advice

D-U-N-S 24-387-2769   (HQ)
JUVENILE DIABETES RESEARCH FOUNDATION CANADA
(Suby of Juvenile Diabetes Research Foundation Canada)
2550 Victoria Park Ave Suite 800, North York, ON, M2J 5A9
(647) 789-2000
Emp Here 45   Emp Total 100
Sales 10,287,459
SIC 8399 Social services, nec
Pr Andrew Mckee
Dir Fin Myra Scott
 Aubrey Baillie
 David Kozloff
 Alex Davidson

D-U-N-S 24-626-0343   (SL)
LIPTON CHARTERED ACCOUNTANTS LLP
245 Fairview Mall Dr Suite 600, North York, ON, M2J 4T1
(416) 496-2900
Emp Here 50   Sales 2,188,821
SIC 8721 Accounting, auditing, and bookkeeping

D-U-N-S 24-570-3322   (BR)
MAGASIN LAURA (P.V.) INC
LAURA, LAURA PETITES, LAURA PLUS
1800 Sheppard Ave E Suite 218, North York, ON, M2J 5A7
(416) 490-6326
Emp Here 45
SIC 5621 Women's clothing stores

D-U-N-S 24-126-1598   (BR)

MANUFACTURERS LIFE INSURANCE COMPANY, THE
MANULIFE FINANCIAL
4 Lansing Sq Suite 201, North York, ON, M2J 5A2
(416) 496-1602
Emp Here 60
SIC 6321 Accident and health insurance

D-U-N-S 24-333-1712   (BR)
METRO ONTARIO INC
FOOD BASICS
2452 Sheppard Ave E, North York, ON, M2J 1X1
(416) 756-2513
Emp Here 150
SIC 5411 Grocery stores

D-U-N-S 24-668-6526   (SL)
METTKO CONSTRUCTION INC
200 Yorkland Blvd Suite 610, North York, ON, M2J 5C1
(416) 444-9600
Emp Here 20   Sales 7,460,160
SIC 1542 Nonresidential construction, nec
Pr Pr Mo Ettehadieh

D-U-N-S 24-927-7898   (HQ)
NORSTAN CANADA LTD
BLACK BOX NETWORK SERVICES
(Suby of Black Box Corporation)
2225 Sheppard Ave E Suite 1600, North York, ON, M2J 5C2
(416) 490-9500
Emp Here 61   Emp Total 3,488
Sales 12,111,476
SIC 5065 Electronic parts and equipment, nec
 Brian Genderon
 Dan Tyndale

D-U-N-S 24-925-0234   (SL)
NORTH AMERICAN RECEIVABLE MANAGEMENT SERVICES COMPANY
255 Consumers Rd Suite 250, North York, ON, M2J 1R4
(800) 387-0912
Emp Here 50   Sales 3,298,152
SIC 7322 Adjustment and collection services

D-U-N-S 25-989-8609   (SL)
NORTH TORONTO CHRISTIAN SCHOOL
(Suby of North Toronto Christian School (Interdenominational)
255 Yorkland Blvd, North York, ON, M2J 1S3
(416) 491-7667
Emp Here 30   Sales 1,969,939
SIC 8661 Religious organizations

D-U-N-S 20-876-7418   (HQ)
R. V. ANDERSON ASSOCIATES LIMITED
TOUCHIE ENGINEERING, DIV OF
(Suby of Arval Holdings Limited)
2001 Sheppard Ave E Suite 400, North York, ON, M2J 4Z8
(416) 497-8600
Emp Here 150   Emp Total 200
Sales 26,940,406
SIC 8711 Engineering services
Pr Pr Kenneth Morrison
VP VP Reginald J Andres
VP VP Kenneth Campbell
 Gary Farrell
Dir T Harold Mccolm
Pastor Vaino Raun
Dir Allan R Perks
Dir Vincent Nazareth
Dir Zoran Filinov

D-U-N-S 20-573-8318   (BR)
ROYAL BANK OF CANADA
RBC
(Suby of Royal Bank Of Canada)
1510 Finch Ave E, North York, ON, M2J 4Y6
(416) 491-0050
Emp Here 20
SIC 6021 National commercial banks

D-U-N-S 20-268-0299   (SL)

ROYAL LIFE SAVING SOCIETY CANADA, ONTARIO BRANCH, THE
LIFESAVING SOCIETY
400 Consumers Rd, North York, ON, M2J 1P8
(416) 494-1024
Emp Here 37   Sales 5,800,482
SIC 7999 Amusement and recreation, nec
Ex Dir Douglas Ferguson

D-U-N-S 20-113-4850   (BR)
ROYAL LIFE SAVINGS SOCIETY CANADA, THE
LIFE SAVINGS SOCIETY
400 Consumers Rd, North York, ON, M2J 1P8

Emp Here 30
SIC 7999 Amusement and recreation, nec

D-U-N-S 20-267-6743   (BR)
SAINT ELIZABETH HEALTH CARE
2 Lansing Sq Suite 600, North York, ON, M2J 4P8
(416) 498-8600
Emp Here 20
SIC 8011 Offices and clinics of medical doctors

D-U-N-S 20-270-5930   (BR)
SEARS CANADA INC
1800 Sheppard Ave E Unit 200, North York, ON, M2J 5A7
(416) 502-3737
Emp Here 300
SIC 5311 Department stores

D-U-N-S 20-634-4970   (HQ)
SECURITAS CANADA LIMITED
265 Yorkland Blvd Suite 500, North York, ON, M2J 1S5
(416) 774-2500
Emp Here 45   Emp Total 50
Sales 249,160,791
SIC 7381 Detective and armored car services
Pr Perry Clarke
Pers/VP John Coletti
VP Tim Beaver
VP Lance Kelly
VP Trevor Thompson
VP Rowan Hamilton
VP Dustin Lambert
Rgnl VP Kim Hunt

D-U-N-S 24-596-9506   (SL)
SEGAL LLP
2005 Sheppard Ave E Suite 500, North York, ON, M2J 5B4
(416) 391-4499
Emp Here 60   Sales 2,626,585
SIC 8721 Accounting, auditing, and bookkeeping

D-U-N-S 25-991-0156   (HQ)
SHOPPERS DRUG MART CORPORATION
SHOPPERS DRUG MART
243 Consumers Rd, North York, ON, M2J 4W8
(416) 493-1220
Emp Here 100   Emp Total 138,000
Sales 164,234,536
SIC 5912 Drug stores and proprietary stores
Pr Pr Domenic Pilla
Ex VP Dorian Lo
 Bradley Lukow
Ex VP Michael Motz
Ex VP Frank Pedinelli
Pers/VP Mary-Alice Vuicic
 James Hankinson
 Sarah Raiss
 Beth Pritchard
 Johanna Waterous

D-U-N-S 20-969-2537   (SL)
SMITH & BROOKS SERVICES INC
250 Consumers Rd Suite 508, North York, ON, M2J 4V6
(866) 974-6373
Emp Here 60   Sales 1,751,057
SIC 7349 Building maintenance services, nec

D-U-N-S 25-109-4223   (SL)
SO CANADA INC
2005 Sheppard Ave E Suite 100, North York, ON, M2J 5B4

Emp Here 90   *Sales* 4,888,367
SIC 8731 Commercial physical research

D-U-N-S 25-204-3542   (BR)
SUN LIFE ASSURANCE COMPANY OF CANADA
SUN LIFE FINANCIAL
2255 Sheppard Ave E Suite 135a, North York, ON, M2J 4Y1
(416) 496-4500
Emp Here 800
SIC 6311 Life insurance

D-U-N-S 25-704-5880   (SL)
TENDER RETAIL SYSTEMS INC
2 Lansing Sq Suite 400, North York, ON, M2J 4P8
(416) 498-1200
Emp Here 25   *Sales* 1,896,978
SIC 7371 Custom computer programming services

D-U-N-S 24-394-0363   (SL)
TODDGLEN ILOFTS LIMITED
2225 Sheppard Ave E Suite 1100, North York, ON, M2J 5C2
(416) 492-2450
Emp Here 50   *Sales* 8,551,680
SIC 1521 Single-family housing construction
Pr Pr John Todd

D-U-N-S 24-784-3998   (SL)
TODDGLEN MANAGEMENT LIMITED
2225 Sheppard Ave E Suite 1100, North York, ON, M2J 5C2
(416) 492-2450
Emp Here 68   *Sales* 11,052,800
SIC 8741 Management services
 John Todd
Sr VP Brian Dunslow

D-U-N-S 24-334-1158   (SL)
TODDGLEN WINDERMERE LIMITED
2225 Sheppard Ave E Suite 1100, North York, ON, M2J 5C2
(416) 492-2450
Emp Here 70   *Sales* 11,454,720
SIC 8742 Management consulting services
Pr Pr John Todd

D-U-N-S 20-700-2192   (BR)
TORONTO CATHOLIC DISTRICT SCHOOL BOARD
OUR LADY OF GUADALUPE CATHOLIC SCHOOL
3105 Don Mills Rd, North York, ON, M2J 3C2
(416) 393-5342
Emp Here 20
SIC 8211 Elementary and secondary schools

D-U-N-S 20-711-1399   (BR)
TORONTO CATHOLIC DISTRICT SCHOOL BOARD
ST. MATTHIAS CATHOLIC SCHOOL
101 Van Horne Ave, North York, ON, M2J 2S8
(416) 393-5357
Emp Here 20
SIC 8211 Elementary and secondary schools

D-U-N-S 20-711-1506   (BR)
TORONTO CATHOLIC DISTRICT SCHOOL BOARD
ST. TIMOTHY CATHOLIC SCHOOL
25 Rochelle Cres, North York, ON, M2J 1Y3
(416) 393-5298
Emp Here 50
SIC 8211 Elementary and secondary schools

D-U-N-S 20-711-2983   (BR)
TORONTO DISTRICT SCHOOL BOARD
DALLINGTON PUBLIC SCHOOL
18 Dallington Dr, North York, ON, M2J 2G3

(416) 395-2270
Emp Here 50
SIC 8211 Elementary and secondary schools

D-U-N-S 20-025-3248   (BR)
TORONTO DISTRICT SCHOOL BOARD
MUIRHEAD PUBLIC SCHOOL
25 Muirhead Rd, North York, ON, M2J 3W3
(416) 395-2710
Emp Here 20
SIC 8211 Elementary and secondary schools

D-U-N-S 25-237-7791   (BR)
TORONTO DISTRICT SCHOOL BOARD
FOREST MANOR ELEMENTARY SCHOOL
25 Forest Manor Rd, North York, ON, M2J 1M4
(416) 395-2440
Emp Here 60
SIC 8211 Elementary and secondary schools

D-U-N-S 20-711-2660   (BR)
TORONTO DISTRICT SCHOOL BOARD
BLOORVIEW SCHOOL
25 Buchan Crt, North York, ON, M2J 1V2
(416) 753-6090
Emp Here 50
SIC 8211 Elementary and secondary schools

D-U-N-S 25-237-8195   (BR)
TORONTO DISTRICT SCHOOL BOARD
CRESTVIEW ELEMENTARY SCHOOL
101 Seneca Hill Dr, North York, ON, M2J 2W3
(416) 395-2253
Emp Here 35
SIC 8211 Elementary and secondary schools

D-U-N-S 20-711-3080   (BR)
TORONTO DISTRICT SCHOOL BOARD
LECSON PUBLIC ELEMENTARY SCHOOL
34 Lescon Rd, North York, ON, M2J 2G6
(416) 395-2640
Emp Here 50
SIC 8211 Elementary and secondary schools

D-U-N-S 20-346-6966   (BR)
TORONTO DISTRICT SCHOOL BOARD
BRIAN PUBLIC SCHOOL
95 Brian Dr, North York, ON, M2J 3Y6
(416) 395-2080
Emp Here 50
SIC 8211 Elementary and secondary schools

D-U-N-S 20-029-8474   (BR)
TORONTO DISTRICT SCHOOL BOARD
DON VALLEY JUNIOR HIGH SCHOOL
3100 Don Mills Rd, North York, ON, M2J 3C3
(416) 395-3010
Emp Here 35
SIC 8211 Elementary and secondary schools

D-U-N-S 20-025-2455   (BR)
TORONTO DISTRICT SCHOOL BOARD
PLEASANT VIEW JUNIOR HIGH SCHOOL
175 Brian Dr, North York, ON, M2J 3Y8
(416) 395-3080
Emp Here 35
SIC 8211 Elementary and secondary schools

D-U-N-S 24-823-1268   (BR)
TORONTO-DOMINION BANK, THE
TD BANK
(*Suby of* Toronto-Dominion Bank, The)
1800 Sheppard Ave E Suite 1, North York, ON, M2J 5A7
(416) 491-0567
Emp Here 20
SIC 6021 National commercial banks

D-U-N-S 25-474-0145   (BR)
TROPICANA COMMUNITY SERVICES ORGANIZATION OF SCARBOROUGH, THE
ALTERNATIVE YOUTH CENTRE
505 Consumers Rd Suite 102, North York, ON, M2J 4V8
(416) 491-7000
Emp Here 30
SIC 8322 Individual and family services

D-U-N-S 24-665-8009   (HQ)
UNISYS CANADA INC
2001 Sheppard Ave E Suite 200, North York, ON, M2J 4Z8
(416) 495-0515
Emp Here 20   *Emp Total* 21,000
Sales 47,884,400
SIC 7371 Custom computer programming services
 Mary Joynt
Dir Tim Feick
Sec Gregory Bergman

D-U-N-S 25-813-1390   (HQ)
UNIVERSAL MUSIC CANADA INC
VIVENDI VISUAL ENTERTAINMENT
2450 Victoria Park Ave Suite 1, North York, ON, M2J 5H3
(416) 718-4000
Emp Here 190   *Emp Total* 221
Sales 26,667,911
SIC 5099 Durable goods, nec
Pr Randy Lennox
Sr VP Sarah Scott
VP Fin VP Fin Mark Jones

D-U-N-S 25-475-3072   (BR)
UPPER CANADA CREATIVE CHILD CARE CENTRES OF ONTARIO
UPPER CANADA CHILDCARE CENTRE
(*Suby of* Upper Canada Creative Child Care Centres Of Ontario)
30 Shaughnessy Blvd, North York, ON, M2J 1H5
(416) 499-6500
Emp Here 23
SIC 8351 Child day care services

D-U-N-S 24-427-5579   (BR)
UPTOWN COMMUNICATION HOUSE INC
ROGERS UPTOWN COMMUNICATION
1800 Sheppard Ave E Suite 217, North York, ON, M2J 5A7
(416) 492-8800
Emp Here 20
SIC 5999 Miscellaneous retail stores, nec

D-U-N-S 20-077-3195   (BR)
VALUE VILLAGE STORES, INC
(*Suby of* Savers, Inc.)
2776 Victoria Park Ave, North York, ON, M2J 4A8
(416) 499-4041
Emp Here 46
SIC 5399 Miscellaneous general merchandise

D-U-N-S 25-099-1817   (BR)
WW HOTELS CORP
RADISSON HOTEL TORONTO EAST
(*Suby of* WW Hotels Corp)
55 Hallcrown Pl, North York, ON, M2J 4R1
(416) 493-7000
Emp Here 110
SIC 7011 Hotels and motels

D-U-N-S 25-508-6977   (HQ)
WELLS FARGO EQUIPMENT FINANCE COMPANY
WELLS FARGO EQUIPMENT FINANCING
(*Suby of* Wells Fargo & Company)
2550 Victoria Park Ave Suite 700, North York, ON, M2J 5A9
(416) 498-6464
Emp Here 36   *Emp Total* 273,100
Sales 4,523,563
SIC 6159 Miscellaneous business credit institutions

D-U-N-S 25-221-2535   (BR)
WINNERS MERCHANTS INTERNATIONAL L.P.
WINNERS
(*Suby of* The TJX Companies Inc)
2450 Sheppard Ave E, North York, ON, M2J 1X1
(416) 502-2248
Emp Here 60

SIC 5651 Family clothing stores

North York, ON M2K
York County

D-U-N-S 20-773-6898   (BR)
1094285 ONTARIO LIMITED
II FORNELLO RESTAURANTS
2901 Bayview Ave Suite 107, North York, ON, M2K 1E6
(416) 227-1271
Emp Here 45
SIC 5812 Eating places

D-U-N-S 24-314-6771   (BR)
AMICA MATURE LIFESTYLES INC
AMICA AT BAYVIEW GARDENS
19 Rean Dr, North York, ON, M2K 0A4
(647) 286-7935
Emp Here 25
SIC 8361 Residential care

D-U-N-S 20-647-1653   (BR)
ASSANTE CAPITAL MANAGEMENT LTD
ASSANTE WEALTH MANAGEMENT
1210 Sheppard Ave E Suite 307, North York, ON, M2K 1E3
(416) 494-2300
Emp Here 25
SIC 6211 Security brokers and dealers

D-U-N-S 25-296-8565   (BR)
BANK OF NOVA SCOTIA, THE
SCOTIABANK
2901 Bayview Ave Suite 109, North York, ON, M2K 1E6
(416) 590-7910
Emp Here 30
SIC 6021 National commercial banks

D-U-N-S 24-343-1348   (BR)
CARA OPERATIONS LIMITED
SWISS CHALET
(*Suby of* Cara Holdings Limited)
3253 Bayview Ave, North York, ON, M2K 1G4
(416) 250-0050
Emp Here 50
SIC 5812 Eating places

D-U-N-S 25-790-6966   (BR)
CARA OPERATIONS LIMITED
HARVEY'S RESTAURANTS
(*Suby of* Cara Holdings Limited)
3343 Bayview Ave, North York, ON, M2K 1G4
(416) 730-9599
Emp Here 20
SIC 5812 Eating places

D-U-N-S 25-666-9680   (BR)
EXTENDICARE (CANADA) INC
BAYVIEW VILLA NURSING HOME
550 Cummer Ave, North York, ON, M2K 2M2
(416) 226-1331
Emp Here 200
SIC 8051 Skilled nursing care facilities

D-U-N-S 20-699-6519   (BR)
EXTENDICARE INC
EXTENDICARE BAYVIEW
550 Cummer Ave, North York, ON, M2K 2M2
(416) 226-1331
Emp Here 300
SIC 8051 Skilled nursing care facilities

D-U-N-S 24-745-4028   (SL)
FABRICVILLE MARITIMES INC
1210 Sheppard Ave E Suite 304, North York, ON, M2K 1E3
(416) 658-2200
Emp Here 150   *Sales* 7,608,750
SIC 5949 Sewing, needlework, and piece goods
Pr Pr Murray Morgan
 Marcel Fuhrer

D-U-N-S 20-228-0868   (BR)

GAP (CANADA) INC
BANANA REPUBLIC
(*Suby of* The Gap Inc)
2901 Bayview Ave Suite 41, North York, ON,
M2K 1E6
(416) 733-0021
Emp Here 35
SIC 5651 Family clothing stores

D-U-N-S 25-304-7427   (BR)
GAP (CANADA) INC
GAP
(*Suby of* The Gap Inc)
2901 Bayview Ave, North York, ON, M2K 1E6
(416) 250-1958
Emp Here 65
SIC 5651 Family clothing stores

D-U-N-S 24-435-0364   (BR)
GAP (CANADA) INC
GAP
(*Suby of* The Gap Inc)
2901 Bayview Ave Suite 41, North York, ON,
M2K 1E6
(416) 250-1958
Emp Here 40
SIC 5651 Family clothing stores

D-U-N-S 20-942-1635   (HQ)
GREENWICH ASSOCIATES ULC
RESEARCH BY NET
(*Suby of* Greenwich Associates LLC)
1220 Sheppard Ave E Suite 201, North York,
ON, M2K 2S5
(416) 493-6111
Emp Here 62   *Emp Total* 200
Sales 165,001,808
SIC 8732 Commercial nonphysical research
Pr Derek Bildfell
 Don W. Ambrose
Ch Bd Bonna Brows
 Joseph Herbert
 Jay Bennett
 David Fox

D-U-N-S 20-651-2076   (BR)
INDIGO BOOKS & MUSIC INC
CHAPTERS
(*Suby of* Indigo Books & Music Inc)
2901 Bayview Ave Suite 132, North York, ON,
M2K 1E6
(416) 222-6323
Emp Here 60
SIC 5942 Book stores

D-U-N-S 24-424-4679   (SL)
INSTITUTE OF NATUROPATHIC EDUCA-TION AND RESEARCH
CANADIAN COLLEGE OF NATUROPATHIC MEDICINE
1255 Sheppard Ave E, North York, ON, M2K
1E2
(416) 498-1255
Emp Here 200   *Sales* 14,768,043
SIC 8221 Colleges and universities
Pr Robert Bernhardt
 Barbara Weissr
 Malcolm Heins

D-U-N-S 20-077-3617   (BR)
LIVING REALTY INC
(*Suby of* Living Realty Inc)
685 Sheppard Ave E Suite 501, North York,
ON, M2K 1B6
(416) 223-8833
Emp Here 50
SIC 6531 Real estate agents and managers

D-U-N-S 25-310-8930   (BR)
MCDONALD'S RESTAURANTS OF CANADA LIMITED
MCDONALD'S
(*Suby of* McDonald's Corporation)
1125 Sheppard Ave E, North York, ON, M2K
1C5
(416) 224-1145
Emp Here 90
SIC 5812 Eating places

D-U-N-S 25-721-1615   (BR)
ORLANDO CORPORATION
BAYVIEW VILLAGE SHOPPING CENTRE
2901 Bayview Ave Suite 32, North York, ON,
M2K 1E6
(416) 226-0404
Emp Here 20
SIC 6512 Nonresidential building operators

D-U-N-S 24-125-3087   (HQ)
PARAGON PROTECTION LTD
PARAGON SECURITY
1210 Sheppard Ave E Suite 488, North York,
ON, M2K 1E3
(416) 498-4000
Emp Here 70   *Emp Total* 650
Sales 3,724,879
SIC 7381 Detective and armored car services

D-U-N-S 24-120-8714   (BR)
PITNEY BOWES OF CANADA LTD
(*Suby of* Pitney Bowes Inc.)
1200 Sheppard Ave E Suite 400, North York,
ON, M2K 2S5

Emp Here 75
SIC 5044 Office equipment

D-U-N-S 20-555-4228   (BR)
SHERIDAN NURSERIES LIMITED
784 Sheppard Ave E, North York, ON, M2K
1C3

Emp Here 50
SIC 5261 Retail nurseries and garden stores

D-U-N-S 24-248-9743   (BR)
TORONTO CATHOLIC DISTRICT SCHOOL BOARD
BLESSED TRINITY ELEMENTARY SCHOOL
3205 Bayview Ave, North York, ON, M2K 1G3
(416) 226-3336
Emp Here 35
SIC 8211 Elementary and secondary schools

D-U-N-S 20-025-2935   (BR)
TORONTO DISTRICT SCHOOL BOARD
ELKHORN PUBLIC SCHOOL
10 Elkhorn Dr, North York, ON, M2K 1J3
(416) 395-9500
Emp Here 25
SIC 8211 Elementary and secondary schools

D-U-N-S 25-120-2198   (BR)
TORONTO-DOMINION BANK, THE
TD BANK
(*Suby of* Toronto-Dominion Bank, The)
686 Finch Ave E, North York, ON, M2K 2E6
(416) 225-7791
Emp Here 20
SIC 6021 National commercial banks

D-U-N-S 25-994-8818   (BR)
TORONTO-DOMINION BANK, THE
TD BANK
(*Suby of* Toronto-Dominion Bank, The)
2885 Bayview Ave, North York, ON, M2K 0A3
(416) 733-1015
Emp Here 5,000
SIC 6021 National commercial banks

D-U-N-S 24-876-3021   (SL)
VILLAGE SPA LIMITED, THE
2901 Bayview Ave Suite 43, North York, ON,
M2K 1E6
(416) 224-1101
Emp Here 58   *Sales* 1,896,978
SIC 7991 Physical fitness facilities

North York, ON M2L
York County

D-U-N-S 24-992-2246   (BR)
BANQUE TORONTO-DOMINION, LA
TD CANADA TRUST

(*Suby of* Toronto-Dominion Bank, The)
2518 Bayview Ave, North York, ON, M2L 1A9
(416) 444-4457
Emp Here 30
SIC 6021 National commercial banks

D-U-N-S 24-763-3964   (BR)
CORPORATION OF THE CITY OF TORONTO
FIREHALL 122
2545 Bayview Ave, North York, ON, M2L 1B4
(416) 338-9122
Emp Here 24
SIC 7389 Business services, nec

D-U-N-S 25-534-9037   (BR)
METRO ONTARIO INC
DOMINION
291 York Mills Rd, North York, ON, M2L 1L3
(416) 444-5809
Emp Here 150
SIC 5411 Grocery stores

D-U-N-S 25-411-8581   (BR)
ROYAL BANK OF CANADA
RBC
(*Suby of* Royal Bank Of Canada)
2514 Bayview Ave, North York, ON, M2L 1A9
(416) 510-3080
Emp Here 35
SIC 6021 National commercial banks

D-U-N-S 25-237-7981   (BR)
TORONTO DISTRICT SCHOOL BOARD
HARRISON PUBLIC SCHOOL
81 Harrison Rd, North York, ON, M2L 1V9
(416) 395-2530
Emp Here 30
SIC 8211 Elementary and secondary schools

North York, ON M2M
York County

D-U-N-S 25-106-7583   (HQ)
AXA INSURANCE (CANADA)
5700 Yonge St Suite 1400, North York, ON,
M2M 4K2
(416) 218-4175
Emp Here 200   *Emp Total* 2,000
Sales 277,704,356
SIC 6331 Fire, marine, and casualty insurance
Ch Bd Jean-Denis Talon
Pr Pr Jean-Francois Blais
Ex VP Mathieu Lamy
VP Fin Joseph Fung
Sr VP Carmen Crigg
Fin Mgr Tenny Yeung
 Paule Dore
 Francois De Meneval
 Pierre Monahan
 Gilles G Charette

D-U-N-S 25-296-3780   (BR)
BANK OF NOVA SCOTIA, THE
SCOTIABANK
6416 Yonge St, North York, ON, M2M 3X4
(416) 590-7488
Emp Here 34
SIC 6021 National commercial banks

D-U-N-S 20-572-1298   (BR)
BANK OF MONTREAL
BMO
5925 Yonge St, North York, ON, M2M 3V7
(416) 221-5561
Emp Here 20
SIC 6021 National commercial banks

D-U-N-S 20-580-5679   (BR)
BANQUE LAURENTIENNE DU CANADA
TD CANADA TRUST BANK
5615 Yonge St, North York, ON, M2M 4G3
(416) 250-8080
Emp Here 20

SIC 6021 National commercial banks

D-U-N-S 25-094-5037   (BR)
CANADIAN IMPERIAL BANK OF COM-MERCE
TORONTO CUSTOMER CONTACT CENTRE
5650 Yonge St Suite 1400, North York, ON,
M2M 4G3
(416) 218-9922
Emp Here 1,500
SIC 4899 Communication services, nec

D-U-N-S 25-940-3418   (HQ)
CONSEIL SCOLAIRE CATHOLIQUE DU DISTRICT FRANCO-NORD
(*Suby of* Conseil Scolaire Catholique Du Dis-trict Franco-Nord)
110 Drewry Ave, North York, ON, M2M 1C8
(416) 397-6564
Emp Here 35   *Emp Total* 500
Sales 43,158,668
SIC 8211 Elementary and secondary schools
Pr Pr Roland Demers
VP VP Diane Corriveau
Dir Francois Rivet
Fin Mgr Pierre Chaput
Dir Nicole Fournier
Dir Stephan Poulin
Dir Roland Rochon
 Cynthia Roveda

D-U-N-S 20-709-0551   (BR)
CORPORATION OF THE CITY OF TORONTO
GOULDING COMMUNITY CENTRE
45 Goulding Ave, North York, ON, M2M 1K8
(416) 395-7826
Emp Here 30
SIC 7999 Amusement and recreation, nec

D-U-N-S 25-321-8945   (BR)
ECONOMICAL MUTUAL INSURANCE COM-PANY
ECONOMICAL INSURANCE GROUP
5700 Yonge St Suite 1600, North York, ON,
M2M 4K2
(416) 590-9040
Emp Here 125
SIC 6331 Fire, marine, and casualty insurance

D-U-N-S 24-488-0126   (HQ)
EQUIFAX CANADA CO.
INSURANCE INFORMATION SERVICES
5700 Yonge St Suite 1700, North York, ON,
M2M 4K2
(800) 278-0278
Emp Here 200   *Emp Total* 9,500
Sales 36,382,542
SIC 7323 Credit reporting services
Pr Carol Gray
Dir Robert M.A. Brabers
Dir Rodolfo Ploder
Dir Joel Heft

D-U-N-S 20-108-0020   (HQ)
GARTNER CANADA CO. INC
5700 Yonge St Suite 1205, North York, ON,
M2M 4K2
(416) 222-7900
Emp Here 25   *Emp Total* 8,813
Sales 3,429,153
SIC 7379 Computer related services, nec

D-U-N-S 24-636-5659   (BR)
GOODLIFE FITNESS CENTRES INC
5650 Yonge St, North York, ON, M2M 4G3
(416) 222-9500
Emp Here 40
SIC 7991 Physical fitness facilities

D-U-N-S 20-868-4493   (BR)
GOVERNMENT OF ONTARIO
EMERGENCY HEALTH SERVICES BRANCH
5700 Yonge St 6th Fl, North York, ON, M2M
4K5
(416) 327-7900
Emp Here 25
SIC 4119 Local passenger transportation, nec

D-U-N-S 25-301-1696   (BR)
HUDSON'S BAY COMPANY
6500 Yonge St, North York, ON, M2M 3X4
(416) 226-4202
Emp Here 100
SIC 5311 Department stores

D-U-N-S 20-051-1017   (SL)
MUZYK, D.J. DRUGS LTD
SHOPPERS DRUG MART
1515 Steeles Ave E, North York, ON, M2M 3Y7
(416) 226-1313
Emp Here 50   *Sales* 7,077,188
SIC 5912 Drug stores and proprietary stores
Pr Dan Muzyk

D-U-N-S 20-859-9436   (BR)
PACIFIC LINK COMMUNICATIONS INC
BELL WORLD
6252 Yonge St, North York, ON, M2M 3X4
(416) 221-3222
Emp Here 25
SIC 5999 Miscellaneous retail stores, nec

D-U-N-S 25-996-9863   (SL)
PRUDENTIAL RELOCATION CANADA LTD
(*Suby of* Prudential Financial, Inc.)
5700 Yonge St Suite 1110, North York, ON, M2M 4K2

Emp Here 60   *Sales* 3,064,349
SIC 7389 Business services, nec

D-U-N-S 25-308-5005   (BR)
ROYAL BANK OF CANADA
RBC ROYAL BANK
(*Suby of* Royal Bank Of Canada)
1545 Steeles Ave E, North York, ON, M2M 3Y7
(416) 512-4680
Emp Here 20
SIC 6021 National commercial banks

D-U-N-S 24-027-0934   (SL)
ST JOHN'S REHABILITATION HOSPITAL
ST JOHN'S REHAB HOSPITAL
285 Cummer Ave, North York, ON, M2M 2G1
(416) 226-6780
Emp Here 400   *Sales* 33,923,844
SIC 8093 Specialty outpatient clinics, nec
Pr Malcolm Moffat
Ch Bd Charles Seguin
  Sally M Horsfall

D-U-N-S 20-918-8437   (BR)
TORONTO CATHOLIC DISTRICT SCHOOL BOARD
BREBEUF COLLEGE SECONDARY SCHOOL
211 Steeles Ave E, North York, ON, M2M 3Y6
(416) 393-5508
Emp Here 75
SIC 8211 Elementary and secondary schools

D-U-N-S 20-025-5425   (BR)
TORONTO CATHOLIC DISTRICT SCHOOL BOARD
ST. JOSEPH MORROW PARK CATHOLIC SECONDARY SCHOOL
3379 Bayview Ave, North York, ON, M2M 3S4
(416) 393-5516
Emp Here 75
SIC 8211 Elementary and secondary schools

D-U-N-S 20-700-2432   (BR)
TORONTO CATHOLIC DISTRICT SCHOOL BOARD
ST. PASCHAL BAYLON CATHOLIC SCHOOL
15 St Paschal Crt, North York, ON, M2M 1X6
(416) 393-5283
Emp Here 50
SIC 8211 Elementary and secondary schools

D-U-N-S 20-711-2975   (BR)
TORONTO DISTRICT SCHOOL BOARD
CUMMER VALLEY MIDDLE SCHOOL
70 Maxome Ave, North York, ON, M2M 3K1

(416) 395-2260
Emp Here 30
SIC 8211 Elementary and secondary schools

D-U-N-S 20-035-4822   (BR)
TORONTO DISTRICT SCHOOL BOARD
STEELESVIEW PUBLIC SCHOOL
105 Bestview Dr, North York, ON, M2M 2Y1
(416) 395-2900
Emp Here 28
SIC 8211 Elementary and secondary schools

D-U-N-S 20-025-1796   (BR)
TORONTO DISTRICT SCHOOL BOARD
NEWTONBROOK SECONDARY SCHOOL
155 Hilda Ave, North York, ON, M2M 1V6
(416) 395-3280
Emp Here 120
SIC 8211 Elementary and secondary schools

D-U-N-S 25-237-7866   (BR)
TORONTO DISTRICT SCHOOL BOARD
DREWRY SECONDARY SCHOOL
70 Drewry Ave Suite 313, North York, ON, M2M 1C8
(416) 395-3260
Emp Here 36
SIC 8211 Elementary and secondary schools

D-U-N-S 24-000-4817   (BR)
TORONTO HYDRO-ELECTRIC SYSTEM LIMITED
TORONTO HYDRO
5800 Yonge St, North York, ON, M2M 3T3
(416) 542-3564
Emp Here 375
SIC 4911 Electric services

D-U-N-S 24-938-0049   (HQ)
XEROX CANADA LTD
(*Suby of* Xerox Corporation)
5650 Yonge St Suite 900, North York, ON, M2M 4G7
(416) 733-6501
Emp Here 350   *Emp Total* 37,900
Sales 426,820,095
SIC 5999 Miscellaneous retail stores, nec
Pr Pr Mandy Shapansky

North York, ON M2N
York County

D-U-N-S 25-370-8705   (HQ)
4386396 CANADA INC
2 Sheppard Ave E Suite 2000, North York, ON, M2N 5Y7
(416) 225-9900
Emp Here 170   *Emp Total* 180
Sales 13,132,926
SIC 7361 Employment agencies
Pr Pr Rag Singh
  Robert Prentice

D-U-N-S 25-536-4275   (HQ)
AMERESCO CANADA INC
90 Sheppard Ave E Suite 7, North York, ON, M2N 6X3
(416) 512-7700
Emp Here 74   *Emp Total* 1,037
Sales 22,695,776
SIC 3825 Instruments to measure electricity
Pr Robert Mccullough
Ex VP Louis Maltezos
Sr VP Tim Dettlaff

D-U-N-S 25-693-4928   (BR)
BMO NESBITT BURNS INC
4881 Yonge St 9th Flr, North York, ON, M2N 5X3
(416) 590-7600
Emp Here 50
SIC 6211 Security brokers and dealers

D-U-N-S 25-793-7789   (BR)
BANK OF NOVA SCOTIA, THE
SCOTIABANK

5075 Yonge St, North York, ON, M2N 6C6
(416) 590-7320
Emp Here 20
SIC 6021 National commercial banks

D-U-N-S 20-572-1025   (BR)
BANK OF MONTREAL
BANK OF MONTREAL
4881 Yonge St, North York, ON, M2N 5X3
(416) 549-6592
Emp Here 20
SIC 6021 National commercial banks

D-U-N-S 25-955-0697   (BR)
BANQUE TORONTO-DOMINION, LA
TORONTO-DOMINION BANK, THE
(*Suby of* Toronto-Dominion Bank, The)
4950 Yonge St Suite 1600, North York, ON, M2N 6K1
(416) 512-6788
Emp Here 42
SIC 6211 Security brokers and dealers

D-U-N-S 20-697-3229   (BR)
BEST BUY CANADA LTD
FUTURE SHOP
(*Suby of* Best Buy Co., Inc.)
5095 Yonge St Unit A14, North York, ON, M2N 6Z4
(416) 642-7980
Emp Here 70
SIC 5999 Miscellaneous retail stores, nec

D-U-N-S 20-876-7327   (SL)
BETH TIKVAH SYNAGOGUE
3080 Bayview Ave, North York, ON, M2N 5L3
(416) 221-3433
Emp Here 55   *Sales* 3,648,035
SIC 8661 Religious organizations

D-U-N-S 24-000-4387   (BR)
CANADIAN IMPERIAL BANK OF COMMERCE
CIBC
5255 Yonge St, North York, ON, M2N 6P4
(416) 223-8772
Emp Here 20
SIC 6021 National commercial banks

D-U-N-S 25-303-0118   (BR)
CANADIAN IMPERIAL BANK OF COMMERCE
CIBC
4841 Yonge St, North York, ON, M2N 5X2
(416) 223-7361
Emp Here 30
SIC 6021 National commercial banks

D-U-N-S 20-987-0240   (BR)
CARA OPERATIONS LIMITED
MILESTONES BAR & GRILL
(*Suby of* Cara Holdings Limited)
5095 Yonge St Unit A13, North York, ON, M2N 6Z4

Emp Here 60
SIC 5812 Eating places

D-U-N-S 25-369-4541   (BR)
CENTRAL MONTESSORI SCHOOLS INC
CENTRAL MONTESSORI SCHOOL
200 Sheppard Ave E, North York, ON, M2N 3A9
(416) 222-5940
Emp Here 85
SIC 8211 Elementary and secondary schools

D-U-N-S 20-077-8103   (BR)
CINEPLEX ODEON CORPORATION
CINEPLEX CINEMAS EMPRESS WALK
5095 Yonge St, North York, ON, M2N 6Z4
(416) 847-0087
Emp Here 50
SIC 7832 Motion picture theaters, except drive-in

D-U-N-S 20-704-4590   (BR)
CORPORATION OF THE CITY OF

TORONTO
MITCHELL FIELD COMMUNITY CENTRE
89 Church Ave, North York, ON, M2N 6C9
(416) 395-0262
Emp Here 46
SIC 7999 Amusement and recreation, nec

D-U-N-S 20-818-1164   (HQ)
CRAWFORD METAL CORPORATION
(*Suby of* Crawford Metal Corporation)
132 Sheppard Ave W Suite 200, North York, ON, M2N 1M5
(416) 224-1515
Emp Here 20   *Emp Total* 175
Sales 70,480,036
SIC 5051 Metals service centers and offices
Dir Gary Stern
Pr Pr Sidney Spiegel
  Naomi Spiegel

D-U-N-S 24-874-7503   (BR)
DELOITTE LLP
5140 Yonge St Suite 1700, North York, ON, M2N 6L7
(416) 601-6150
Emp Here 327
SIC 8721 Accounting, auditing, and bookkeeping

D-U-N-S 25-695-9867   (BR)
FOREST HILL REAL ESTATE INC
500 Sheppard Ave E Suite 201, North York, ON, M2N 6H7
(416) 226-1987
Emp Here 200
SIC 6531 Real estate agents and managers

D-U-N-S 24-576-4373   (BR)
GOODLIFE FITNESS CENTRES INC
50 Sheppard Ave E, North York, ON, M2N 2Z7
(416) 221-3488
Emp Here 30
SIC 7991 Physical fitness facilities

D-U-N-S 20-762-4354   (HQ)
GUARANTEE COMPANY OF NORTH AMERICA, THE
4950 Yonge St Suite 1400, North York, ON, M2N 6K1
(416) 223-9580
Emp Here 96   *Emp Total* 390
Sales 291,472
SIC 6411 Insurance agents, brokers, and service

D-U-N-S 24-075-0182   (BR)
GUARANTEE COMPANY OF NORTH AMERICA, THE
GARANTIE COMPAGNIE D'ASSURANCE DE L'AMERIQUE DU NORD, LA
4950 Yonge St Suite 1400, North York, ON, M2N 6K1
(416) 223-9582
Emp Here 45
SIC 6411 Insurance agents, brokers, and service

D-U-N-S 24-242-6216   (BR)
HALF, ROBERT CANADA INC
(*Suby of* Robert Half International Inc.)
5140 Yonge St Suite 1500, North York, ON, M2N 6L7
(416) 226-4570
Emp Here 40
SIC 7361 Employment agencies

D-U-N-S 24-303-2075   (HQ)
HEWITT ASSOCIATES CORP
(*Suby of* Tempo Acquisition, LLC)
2 Sheppard Ave E Suite 1500, North York, ON, M2N 7A4
(416) 225-5001
Emp Here 50   *Emp Total* 62,055
Sales 220,027,754
SIC 8748 Business consulting, nec
Pr Anthony Gaffney
VP James Hubbard
VP Jean-Francois Chartray

▲ Public Company   ■ Public Company Family Member   **HQ** Headquarters   **BR** Branch   **SL** Single Location

Dir Terri-Lynne Devonish
Sr VP Rejean Tremblay
Sr VP Martin Papillion
Sr VP Scott Bunker

D-U-N-S 20-010-1587   (HQ)
INFOSYS LIMITED
5140 Yonge St Suite 1400, North York, ON,
M2N 6L7
(416) 224-7400
Emp Here 50   *Emp Total* 200,364
Sales 15,592,518
SIC 7379 Computer related services, nec
Mgr Divakar Shenoy
Mgr Andrew Shnuriwsky

D-U-N-S 25-528-7104   (HQ)
INVESCO CANADA LTD
TRIMARK
5140 Yonge St Suite 800, North York, ON,
M2N 6X7
(800) 874-6275
Emp Here 800   *Emp Total* 6,790
Sales 145,921,400
SIC 6211 Security brokers and dealers
Pr Pietro Intraligi
  Philip A Taylor
VP Fin David Warren

D-U-N-S 25-315-7788   (BR)
**INVESTORS GROUP FINANCIAL SER-
VICES INC**
*INVESTORS FINANCIAL PLANNING CEN-
TRE DIV OF*
4950 Yonge St Unit 2100, North York, ON,
M2N 6K1
(416) 733-4722
Emp Here 40
SIC 8741 Management services

D-U-N-S 24-047-5434   (HQ)
IVARI CANADA ULC
IVARI
(*Suby of* Wilton RE Ltd)
5000 Yonge St Suite 500, North York, ON,
M2N 7E9
(416) 883-5000
Emp Here 500   *Emp Total* 114
Sales 589,916,931
SIC 6311 Life insurance
Pr Douglas Brooks
Sr VP Richard Sachs
VP Dan Mackenzie
VP Mark Jackson
  Glen Daniels
Ex VP Karen L Gavan
Asst VP Patrick Wolfe
Dir David E Gooding
Dir Ronald Corey

D-U-N-S 20-934-3714   (HQ)
KEB HANA BANK CANADA
4950 Yonge St Suite 103, North York, ON,
M2N 6K1
(416) 222-5200
Emp Here 35   *Emp Total* 112
Sales 32,072,891
SIC 6021 National commercial banks
Pr Pr Larry Klane
Ch Bd Richard Wacker
  Jang Myoung Kee

D-U-N-S 24-977-5834   (SL)
KIMATSU ENTERPRISES
KIMATSU INTERNATIONAL
5334 Yonge St, North York, ON, M2N 6V1

Emp Here 66   *Sales* 56,192,400
SIC 6799 Investors, nec
Pr Yon Kuchi
VP John Yamamoto
Acct Mgr Jack Taylor
Opers Mgr Greg Richie

D-U-N-S 24-411-1022   (BR)
LOBLAWS SUPERMARKETS LIMITED
LOBLAWS
5095 Yonge St, North York, ON, M2N 6Z4

(416) 512-9430
Emp Here 20
SIC 5411 Grocery stores

D-U-N-S 25-702-7334   (BR)
LONDON LIFE INSURANCE COMPANY
FREEDOM 55 FINANCIAL
2 Sheppard Ave E Suite 600, North York, ON,
M2N 5Y7
(416) 250-5520
Emp Here 40
SIC 8742 Management consulting services

D-U-N-S 20-875-4440   (HQ)
MANPOWER SERVICES CANADA LIMITED
MANPOWER TEMPORARY SERVICES
4950 Yonge St Suite 700, North York, ON,
M2N 6K1
(416) 225-4455
Emp Here 40   *Emp Total* 28,000
Sales 21,656,275
SIC 7363 Help supply services
VP VP Nadia Clani
VP Richard Pett
  Mike Vanhandel
Dir Fin Sandra Clarke
Prs Dir Jo-Anne Yanuziello
  Stephen Walker

D-U-N-S 24-728-3955   (BR)
MAPLE LEAF FOODS INC
*MAPLE LEAF FOODS INTERNATIONAL, DIV
OF*
5160 Yonge St Suite 300, North York, ON,
M2N 6L9

Emp Here 60
SIC 5147 Meats and meat products

D-U-N-S 20-912-5900   (SL)
MAPLERIDGE CAPITAL CORPORATION
5000 Yonge St Suite 1408, North York, ON,
M2N 7E9

Emp Here 30   *Sales* 7,350,166
SIC 6162 Mortgage bankers and loan corre-
spondents
  Pierre Villeneuve
  Randal Selkirk

D-U-N-S 20-552-8669   (BR)
METRO ONTARIO INC
METRO
20 Church Ave, North York, ON, M2N 0B7
(416) 229-6200
Emp Here 300
SIC 5411 Grocery stores

D-U-N-S 25-274-6383   (HQ)
MILLWARD BROWN CANADA, INC
MILLWARD BROWN
4950 Yonge St Suite 600, North York, ON,
M2N 6K1
(416) 221-9200
Emp Here 50   *Emp Total* 124,930
Sales 6,407,837
SIC 7374 Data processing and preparation
  Chuck Chakrapani
Pr Pr William Ratcliffe
  David Sandberg

D-U-N-S 20-120-6591   (HQ)
MINTO APARTMENTS LIMITED
(*Suby of* Minto Apartments Limited)
90 Sheppard Ave E Suite 500, North York, ON,
M2N 3A1
(416) 977-0777
Emp Here 500   *Emp Total* 1,200
Sales 113,089,085
SIC 6531 Real estate agents and managers
Pr Pr Roger Greenberg
Dir Peter Goring
Dir Alan Greenberg
  Daniel Greenberg
Dir J Eric Mckinney
Dir Andrew Price

D-U-N-S 20-272-1338   (SL)
MONEY EXPRESS POS SOLUTIONS INC

MONEXGROUP
5075 Yonge St Suite 301, North York, ON,
M2N 6C6
(866) 286-7787
Emp Here 50   *Sales* 4,900,111
SIC 3578 Calculating and accounting equipment

D-U-N-S 24-067-2167   (BR)
**MOXIE'S RESTAURANTS, LIMITED PART-
NERSHIP**
MOXIE'S
4950 Yonge St Suite 105, North York, ON,
M2N 6K1
(416) 226-3217
Emp Here 100
SIC 5812 Eating places

D-U-N-S 20-553-8283   (HQ)
MR. SUBMARINE LIMITED
MR. SUB
4576 Yonge St Suite 600, North York, ON,
M2N 6N4
(416) 225-5545
Emp Here 26   *Emp Total* 450
Sales 7,033,600
SIC 6794 Patent owners and lessors
  Jack Levinson
Dir Fin Barry Wilde
Dir Earl Linzon
Dir Bernard Levinson
Dir Jerald Shuman
Dir Jess Collins

D-U-N-S 24-822-8129   (SL)
NATIONAL ENERGY CORPORATION
NATIONAL HOME SERVICES
25 Sheppard Ave W Suite 1700, North York,
ON, M2N 6S6
(416) 673-1162
Emp Here 190   *Sales* 19,750,523
SIC 1711 Plumbing, heating, air-conditioning
Pr Pr Lewis James
VP Jonah Davids
  Patrick Mccullough
  Gord Potter
Dir Deborah Merril

D-U-N-S 24-075-4275   (HQ)
NESTLE CANADA INC
NESPRESSO
25 Sheppard Ave W Suite 1700, North York,
ON, M2N 6S6
(416) 512-9000
Emp Here 300   *Emp Total* 9,000
Sales 76,827,617
SIC 2095 Roasted coffee
Pr Shelley Martin
  Gavin Wright
Sec Daniel Holden

D-U-N-S 25-051-7695   (BR)
PHARMA PLUS DRUGMARTS LTD
PHARMA PLUS #0885
288 Sheppard Ave E, North York, ON, M2N
3B1
(416) 222-5454
Emp Here 24
SIC 5912 Drug stores and proprietary stores

D-U-N-S 25-370-8853   (BR)
PROCTER & GAMBLE INC
(*Suby of* The Procter & Gamble Company)
4711 Yonge St, North York, ON, M2N 6K8
(416) 730-4141
Emp Here 100
SIC 5169 Chemicals and allied products, nec

D-U-N-S 20-173-4217   (HQ)
PROCTER & GAMBLE INC
(*Suby of* The Procter & Gamble Company)
4711 Yonge St, North York, ON, M2N 6K8
(416) 730-4711
Emp Here 700   *Emp Total* 105,000
Sales 38,158,446
SIC 2841 Soap and other detergents
Pr Pr Timothy H Penner

Sec Eric Glass

D-U-N-S 24-381-3180   (BR)
RBC DOMINION SECURITIES INC
RBC ROYAL BANK
(*Suby of* Royal Bank Of Canada)
5140 Yonge St Unit 1100, North York, ON,
M2N 6L7
(416) 733-5200
Emp Here 70
SIC 6282 Investment advice

D-U-N-S 20-077-4029   (BR)
RE/MAX REALTRON REALTY INC
183 Willowdale Ave, North York, ON, M2N 4Y9
(416) 225-4900
Emp Here 169
SIC 6531 Real estate agents and managers

D-U-N-S 24-891-5712   (SL)
S. F. PARTNERSHIP LLP
4950 Yonge St Suite 400, North York, ON,
M2N 6K1
(416) 250-1212
Emp Here 65   *Sales* 2,845,467
SIC 8721 Accounting, auditing, and book-
keeping

D-U-N-S 24-157-4537   (BR)
SMG ADVISORS INC
170 Sheppard Ave E Suite 101, North York,
ON, M2N 3A4
(416) 223-5880
Emp Here 20
SIC 8742 Management consulting services

D-U-N-S 20-578-0455   (HQ)
SMSI TRAVEL CENTRES INC
HMS HOST
45 Sheppard Ave E Suite 302, North York, ON,
M2N 5W9
(416) 221-4900
Emp Here 25   *Emp Total* 18
Sales 48,227,023
SIC 5812 Eating places
VP Fin Vijay Francis
VP Opers Bruce Carbone
  Bernard Brown

D-U-N-S 20-649-9738   (BR)
SSQ SOCIETE D'ASSURANCE-VIE INC
SSQ FINANCIAL GROUP
110 Sheppard Ave E Unit 500, North York, ON,
M2N 6Y8
(416) 221-3477
Emp Here 150
SIC 6351 Surety insurance

D-U-N-S 24-192-2822   (BR)
SCOTIA CAPITAL INC
SCOTIA MCLEOD
4950 Yonge St Suite 1200, North York, ON,
M2N 6K1
(416) 226-9505
Emp Here 60
SIC 6211 Security brokers and dealers

D-U-N-S 24-097-2174   (SL)
SELECTACARE LIMITED
139 Sheppard Ave E, North York, ON, M2N
3A6
(416) 225-8900
Emp Here 50   *Sales* 2,334,742
SIC 8059 Nursing and personal care, nec

D-U-N-S 24-169-4111   (BR)
SHELL CANADA LIMITED
SHELL CANADA PRODUCTS
90 Sheppard Ave E Suite 600, North York, ON,
M2N 6Y2
(416) 227-7111
Emp Here 40
SIC 5172 Petroleum products, nec

D-U-N-S 20-192-5893   (HQ)
STARBUCKS COFFEE CANADA, INC
STARBUCKS COFFEE COMPANY
(*Suby of* Starbucks Corporation)
5140 Yonge St Suite 1205, North York, ON,

M2N 6L7
(416) 228-7300
Emp Here 100   *Emp Total* 254,000
Sales 150 809,767
SIC 5812 Eating places
Pr Rossann Williams
Ex VP Clifford Burrows

D-U-N-S 24-349-6705   (BR)
TD WATERHOUSE CANADA INC
(*Suby of* Toronto-Dominion Bank, The)
4950 Yonge St Suite 1600, North York, ON,
M2N 6K1
(416) 512-6776
Emp Here 45
SIC 6211 Security brokers and dealers

D-U-N-S 20-912-2550   (BR)
TARION WARRANTY CORPORATION
5160 Yonge St, North York, ON, M2N 6L9
(416) 229-9200
Emp Here 20
SIC 6351 Surety insurance

D-U-N-S 20-177-5777   (SL)
THOUGHTCORP SYSTEMS INC
(*Suby of* Epam Systems, Inc.)
4950 Yonge St Suite 1700, North York, ON,
M2N 6K1
(416) 591-4004
Emp Here 100   *Sales* 7,296,070
SIC 7379 Computer related services, nec
Dir David Bercovitch
Dir Kirk Robinson

D-U-N-S 20-077-8483   (BR)
TORONTO CATHOLIC DISTRICT SCHOOL BOARD
ST. GABRIEL CATHOLIC SCHOOL
396 Spring Garden Ave, North York, ON, M2N 3H5
(416) 393-5256
Emp Here 35
SIC 8211 Elementary and secondary schools

D-U-N-S 20-035-4889   (BR)
TORONTO CATHOLIC DISTRICT SCHOOL BOARD
ST. ANTOINE DANIEL CATHOLIC SCHOOL
160 Finch Ave W, North York, ON, M2N 2J2
(416) 393-5339
Emp Here 22
SIC 8211 Elementary and secondary schools

D-U-N-S 20-591-1907   (BR)
TORONTO CATHOLIC DISTRICT SCHOOL BOARD
TORONTO CATHOLIC DISTRICT SCHOOL BOARD GENERAL INQUIRY CENTER
5050 Yonge St, North York, ON, M2N 5N8
(416) 397-3000
Emp Here 25
SIC 8211 Elementary and secondary schools

D-U-N-S 20-711-1670   (BR)
TORONTO CATHOLIC DISTRICT SCHOOL BOARD
SPECIAL SERVICES CATHOLIC EDUCA-TION CENTRE
80 Sheppard Ave E Suite 222, North York, ON,
M2N 6E8
(416) 222-8282
Emp Here 80
SIC 8211 Elementary and secondary schools

D-U-N-S 20-913-6931   (BR)
TORONTO DISTRICT SCHOOL BOARD
MCKEE PUBLIC SCHOOL
35 Church Ave, North York, ON, M2N 6X6
(416) 395-2680
Emp Here 60
SIC 8211 Elementary and secondary schools

D-U-N-S 25-237-7874   (BR)
TORONTO DISTRICT SCHOOL BOARD
CHURCHILL PUBLIC SCHOOL
188 Churchill Ave, North York, ON, M2N 1Z5
(416) 395-2200
Emp Here 35

SIC 8211 Elementary and secondary schools

D-U-N-S 20-913-6451   (BR)
TORONTO DISTRICT SCHOOL BOARD
AVONDALE PUBLIC SCHOOL
171 Avondale Ave, North York, ON, M2N 2V4
(416) 395-3130
Emp Here 20
SIC 8211 Elementary and secondary schools

D-U-N-S 20-035-4905   (BR)
TORONTO DISTRICT SCHOOL BOARD
CLAUDE WATSON SCHOOL FOR THE ARTS
130 Doris Ave, North York, ON, M2N 0A8
(416) 395-3180
Emp Here 40
SIC 8211 Elementary and secondary schools

D-U-N-S 24-174-8362   (BR)
TORONTO DISTRICT SCHOOL BOARD
MONO CLIFFS OUTDOOR EDUCATION CENTRE
5050 Yonge St, North York, ON, M2N 5N8
(519) 942-0330
Emp Here 26
SIC 7389 Business services, nec

D-U-N-S 24-500-2865   (SL)
TREASURY WINE ESTATES INC
5255 Yonge St Suite 1111, North York, ON,
M2N 6P4
(416) 504-3830
Emp Here 25   *Sales* 729,607
SIC 2084 Wines, brandy, and brandy spirits

D-U-N-S 20-651-2183   (BR)
WENDY'S RESTAURANTS OF CANADA INC
WENDY'S
(*Suby of* The Wendy's Company)
5095 Yonge St Unit 12a, North York, ON, M2N 6Z4
(416) 221-4866
Emp Here 32
SIC 5812 Eating places

D-U-N-S 20-044-2325   (HQ)
WOLTERS KLUWER CANADA LIMITED
90 Sheppard Ave E Suite 300, North York, ON,
M2N 6X1
(416) 224-2224
Emp Here 200   *Emp Total* 191
Sales 39,241,170
SIC 2721 Periodicals
Pr Doug Finley
VP Fin Allan Orr

North York, ON M2P
York County

D-U-N-S 25-106-2378   (SL)
1428228 ONTARIO INC
VISION 2000 TRAVEL GROUP
4141 Yonge St Suite 301, North York, ON,
M2P 2A8
(416) 221-6411
Emp Here 36   *Sales* 11,856,640
SIC 4724 Travel agencies
Dir Arend Roos
Pr Brian Robertson
Ex VP Stephanie Anevich

D-U-N-S 20-553-3685   (SL)
AUBERGE DU POMMIER INC
4150 Yonge St, North York, ON, M2P 2C6
(416) 222-2220
Emp Here 70   *Sales* 2,115,860
SIC 5812 Eating places

D-U-N-S 25-315-8695   (BR)
CIBC WORLD MARKETS INC
CIBC WOOD GUNDY
4110 Yonge St Suite 600, North York, ON,
M2P 2B7
(416) 229-5900
Emp Here 40

SIC 6211 Security brokers and dealers

D-U-N-S 20-036-6453   (SL)
GALLAGHER BASSETT CANADA INC
(*Suby of* Arthur J. Gallagher & Co.)
4311 Yonge St Suite 404, North York, ON,
M2P 1N6
(416) 861-8212
Emp Here 20   *Sales* 2,536,250
SIC 6411 Insurance agents, brokers, and service

D-U-N-S 24-948-1573   (SL)
HUGH WOOD CANADA LTD
4120 Yonge St Suite 201, North York, ON,
M2P 2B8
(416) 229-6600
Emp Here 50   *Sales* 5,842,440
SIC 6411 Insurance agents, brokers, and service

D-U-N-S 25-300-6415   (BR)
KPMG LLP
(*Suby of* KPMG LLP)
4100 Yonge St Unit 200, North York, ON, M2P 2H3
(416) 228-7000
Emp Here 170
SIC 8721 Accounting, auditing, and book-keeping

D-U-N-S 25-367-8098   (HQ)
LENOVO (CANADA) INC
10 York Mills Rd Suite 400, North York, ON,
M2P 2G4
(855) 253-6686
Emp Here 500   *Emp Total* 52,000
Sales 55,523,093
SIC 3571 Electronic computers
 Murray Wright
 Verne Deneault

D-U-N-S 25-149-8234   (HQ)
ONTARIO LOTTERY AND GAMING CORPO-RATION
OLG
4120 Yonge St Suite 420, North York, ON,
M2P 2B8
(416) 224-1772
Emp Here 300   *Emp Total* 90,000
Sales 380,344,129
SIC 7999 Amusement and recreation, nec
Pr Stephen Rigby
 Paul V. Godfrey
Dir Shirley Hoy
Dir Dale Lastman
Dir Anthony Melman
Dir Thomas O'brien
Dir William Swirsky
Dir Ron Carinci
Dir Jan Westcott
Dir Charlotte Burke

D-U-N-S 24-981-3481   (BR)
RICOH CANADA INC
DOCUMENT DIRECTION
4100 Yonge St Suite 600, North York, ON,
M2P 2B5
(416) 218-4360
Emp Here 130
SIC 5044 Office equipment

D-U-N-S 24-830-1251   (HQ)
SAP CANADA INC
4120 Yonge St Suite 600, North York, ON,
M2P 2B8
(416) 229-0574
Emp Here 304   *Emp Total* 80,609
Sales 409,253,485
SIC 7372 Prepackaged software
Pr Mark Aboud

D-U-N-S 20-784-5215   (HQ)
SAVE THE CHILDREN CANADA
(*Suby of* Save The Children Canada)
4141 Yonge St Suite 300, North York, ON,
M2P 2A8

(416) 221-5501
Emp Here 29   *Emp Total* 105
Sales 42,317,773
SIC 8399 Social services, nec
Pr David Morley
Ch Bd William Chambers
Dir Dan Legault

D-U-N-S 25-296-1230   (BR)
SUNCOR ENERGY PRODUCTS INC
36 York Mills Rd Suite 110, North York, ON,
M2P 2E9
(416) 498-7751
Emp Here 250
SIC 2911 Petroleum refining

D-U-N-S 20-646-8709   (BR)
VOXDATA SOLUTIONS INC
VOXDATA CALL CENTER
20 York Mills Rd Suite 201, North York, ON,
M2P 2C2

Emp Here 200
SIC 4899 Communication services, nec

D-U-N-S 24-915-5623   (BR)
WAWANESA LIFE INSURANCE COMPANY, THE
(*Suby of* Wawanesa Mutual Insurance Company, The)
4110 Yonge St Suite 100, North York, ON,
M2P 2B7
(519) 886-4320
Emp Here 150
SIC 6311 Life insurance

D-U-N-S 20-934-1585   (BR)
WAWANESA MUTUAL INSURANCE COM-PANY, THE
(*Suby of* Wawanesa Mutual Insurance Company, The)
4110 Yonge St Suite 100, North York, ON,
M2P 2B7
(416) 250-9292
Emp Here 180
SIC 6331 Fire, marine, and casualty insurance

North York, ON M2R
York County

D-U-N-S 20-583-9546   (BR)
CANADA POST CORPORATION
WILLOWDALE DEPOT D
6035 Bathurst St, North York, ON, M2R 1Z3
(416) 226-1717
Emp Here 45
SIC 4311 U.s. postal service

D-U-N-S 24-011-3907   (BR)
HOLLISWEALTH ADVISORY SERVICES INC.
200 Finch Ave W Suite 390, North York, ON,
M2R 3W4

Emp Here 20
SIC 6282 Investment advice

D-U-N-S 20-011-3855   (SL)
INTERNATIONAL ECONOMY SERVICES INC
1057 Steeles Ave W Suite 1, North York, ON,
M2R 2S9
(416) 725-1294
Emp Here 103   *Sales* 13,059,965
SIC 8742 Management consulting services
Pr Pr Rouslan Moroz
Dir Scott Mccleod
Dir Caroline Cummings

D-U-N-S 25-998-5786   (BR)
NORTH YORK GENERAL HOSPITAL
555 Finch Ave W Suite 262, North York, ON,
M2R 1N5
(416) 633-9420
Emp Here 500
SIC 8062 General medical and surgical hospi-

---

tals

D-U-N-S 25-896-3883   (BR)
SOBEYS CAPITAL INCORPORATED
PRICE CHOPPER
6201 Bathurst St, North York, ON, M2R 2A5
(416) 223-8585
Emp Here 81
SIC 5411 Grocery stores

D-U-N-S 20-025-2125   (BR)
TORONTO DISTRICT SCHOOL BOARD
NORTHVIEW HEIGHTS SS
550 Finch Ave W, North York, ON, M2R 1N6
(416) 395-3290
Emp Here 20
SIC 8211 Elementary and secondary schools

D-U-N-S 20-035-4988   (BR)
TORONTO DISTRICT SCHOOL BOARD
ROCKFORD PUBLIC SCHOOL
60 Rockford Rd, North York, ON, M2R 3A7
(416) 395-2820
Emp Here 55
SIC 8211 Elementary and secondary schools

D-U-N-S 20-003-5330   (BR)
TORONTO DISTRICT SCHOOL BOARD
PLEASANT PUBLIC SCHOOL
288 Pleasant Ave, North York, ON, M2R 2R1
(416) 395-2770
Emp Here 26
SIC 8211 Elementary and secondary schools

D-U-N-S 20-026-1993   (BR)
TORONTO DISTRICT SCHOOL BOARD
FISHERVILLE JUNIOR HIGH SCHOOL
425 Patricia Ave, North York, ON, M2R 2N1
(416) 395-3030
Emp Here 40
SIC 8211 Elementary and secondary schools

D-U-N-S 20-711-3130   (BR)
TORONTO DISTRICT SCHOOL BOARD
WILLOWDALE MIDDLE SCHOOL
225 Senlac Rd, North York, ON, M2R 1P6
(416) 395-2970
Emp Here 50
SIC 8211 Elementary and secondary schools

North York, ON M3A
York County

D-U-N-S 20-323-0263   (SL)
2179321 ONTARIO LIMITED
NATIONAL SERVICES
27 Larabee Cres, North York, ON, M3A 3E6
(416) 219-1050
Emp Here 25   *Sales* 6,330,240
SIC 5074 Plumbing and heating equipment
and supplies (hydronics)
Pt Joseph Del Mortal
Pt Leo Liao

D-U-N-S 20-038-6667   (BR)
COMMISSION SCOLAIRE DU CHEMIN-DU-ROY
ECOLE SAINTE MADELEINE
1 Ness Dr, North York, ON, M3A 2W1
(416) 393-5312
Emp Here 30
SIC 8211 Elementary and secondary schools

D-U-N-S 20-824-0788   (SL)
DONALDA CLUB
12 Bushbury Dr, North York, ON, M3A 2Z7
(416) 447-5575
Emp Here 100   *Sales* 4,012,839
SIC 7997 Membership sports and recreation
clubs

D-U-N-S 24-976-8383   (BR)
FIRSTCANADA ULC
AIRPORTER, SERVICE, DIV OF
103 Railside Rd, North York, ON, M3A 1B2

(416) 444-7030
Emp Here 212
SIC 4151 School buses

D-U-N-S 20-310-9558   (BR)
INFOSYS LIMITED
66 Parkwoods Village Dr, North York, ON,
M3A 2X6
(416) 224-7400
Emp Here 20
SIC 7379 Computer related services, nec

D-U-N-S 24-768-7747   (BR)
METRO ONTARIO INC
FOOD BASICS
1277 York Mills Rd, North York, ON, M3A 1Z5
(416) 444-7921
Emp Here 75
SIC 5411 Grocery stores

D-U-N-S 20-711-1142   (BR)
**TORONTO CATHOLIC DISTRICT SCHOOL
BOARD**
ST. CATHERINE CATHOLIC SCHOOL
30 Roanoke Rd, North York, ON, M3A 1E9
(416) 393-5316
Emp Here 20
SIC 8211 Elementary and secondary schools

D-U-N-S 20-035-5027   (BR)
**TORONTO CATHOLIC DISTRICT SCHOOL
BOARD**
ST. ISAAC JOGUES CATHOLIC SCHOOL
1330 York Mills Rd, North York, ON, M3A 1Z8
(416) 393-5315
Emp Here 25
SIC 8211 Elementary and secondary schools

D-U-N-S 24-972-4550   (BR)
TORONTO DISTRICT SCHOOL BOARD
VICTORIA PARK COLLEGIATE INSTITUTE
15 Wallingford Rd, North York, ON, M3A 2V1
(416) 395-3310
Emp Here 100
SIC 8211 Elementary and secondary schools

D-U-N-S 20-025-0111   (BR)
TORONTO DISTRICT SCHOOL BOARD
RANCHDALE ELEMENTARY SCHOOL
60 Ranchdale Cres, North York, ON, M3A 2M3
(416) 395-2800
Emp Here 30
SIC 8211 Elementary and secondary schools

D-U-N-S 20-035-5001   (BR)
TORONTO DISTRICT SCHOOL BOARD
BROADLANDS PUBLIC SCHOOL
106 Broadlands Blvd, North York, ON, M3A
1J7
(416) 395-2090
Emp Here 25
SIC 8211 Elementary and secondary schools

D-U-N-S 20-913-7954   (BR)
TORONTO DISTRICT SCHOOL BOARD
DONVIEW MIDDLE SCHOOL
20 Evermede Dr, North York, ON, M3A 2S3
(416) 395-2330
Emp Here 40
SIC 8211 Elementary and secondary schools

D-U-N-S 20-025-2448   (BR)
TORONTO DISTRICT SCHOOL BOARD
GEORGE S HENRY ACADEMY
200 Graydon Hall Dr, North York, ON, M3A
3A6
(416) 395-3240
Emp Here 49
SIC 8211 Elementary and secondary schools

D-U-N-S 20-169-6648   (SL)
W.T. LYNCH FOODS LIMITED
LYNCH FOOD
72 Railside Rd, North York, ON, M3A 1A3
(416) 449-5464
Emp Here 50   *Sales* 14,592,140
SIC 2099 Food preparations, nec
Walker Lynch
Pr Pr Scott Lynch

Douglas Roger Nowlan

North York, ON M3B
York County

D-U-N-S 20-314-4126   (SL)
458984 ONTARIO LIMITED
DAVID DUNCAN HOUSE, THE
125 Moatfield Dr, North York, ON, M3B 3L6
(416) 391-1424
Emp Here 50   *Sales* 1,532,175
SIC 5812 Eating places

D-U-N-S 25-704-7134   (SL)
592534 ONTARIO INC
CARE 2000 HEALTH SERVICES
1262 Don Mills Rd Suite 202, North York, ON,
M3B 2W7
(416) 447-8409
Emp Here 50   *Sales* 2,334,742
SIC 8059 Nursing and personal care, nec

D-U-N-S 25-405-3010   (HQ)
A RIGHT TO LEARN INC
WILLOWWOOD SCHOOL
(*Suby of* A Right To Learn Inc)
55 Scarsdale Rd, North York, ON, M3B 2R3
(416) 444-7644
Emp Here 20   *Emp Total* 50
Sales 4,334,713
SIC 8211 Elementary and secondary schools

D-U-N-S 24-371-3976   (SL)
**ACHIEVO NETSTAR SOLUTIONS COM-
PANY**
(*Suby of* Achievo Corporation)
220 Duncan Mill Rd Suite 505, North York,
ON, M3B 3J5
(416) 383-1818
Emp Here 80   *Sales* 9,411,930
SIC 7371 Custom computer programming ser-
vices
Pr Pr Nestor Cruz
Sing Cheong Chan
Dir Jeffrey Tung
Dir Julio Leung

D-U-N-S 20-852-6590   (HQ)
ALPHA LABORATORIES INC
(*Suby of* 600144 Ontario Inc)
1262 Don Mills Rd Suite 103, North York, ON,
M3B 2W7
(416) 449-2166
Emp Here 30   *Emp Total* 60
Sales 4,888,367
SIC 8071 Medical laboratories

D-U-N-S 25-404-7954   (SL)
AVANTE SECURITY INC
1959 Leslie St, North York, ON, M3B 2M3
(416) 923-2435
Emp Here 60   *Sales* 1,896,978
SIC 7382 Security systems services

D-U-N-S 25-795-8157   (SL)
BBM ANALYTICS INC
NLOGIC
1500 Don Mills Rd 3rd Fl, North York, ON,
M3B 3L7
(416) 445-8881
Emp Here 25   *Sales* 2,334,742
SIC 8732 Commercial nonphysical research

D-U-N-S 25-367-6688   (BR)
BELL EXPRESSVU INC
115 Scarsdale Rd, North York, ON, M3B 2R2
(416) 383-6299
Emp Here 150
SIC 4899 Communication services, nec

D-U-N-S 24-181-7022   (SL)
BLIZZARD COURIER SERVICE LTD
1937 Leslie St, North York, ON, M3B 2M3
(416) 444-0596
Emp Here 75   *Sales* 3,793,956

SIC 7389 Business services, nec

D-U-N-S 25-909-6204   (BR)
BODY SHOP CANADA LIMITED, THE
BODY SHOP, THE
33 Kern Rd, North York, ON, M3B 1S9

Emp Here 21
SIC 5999 Miscellaneous retail stores, nec

D-U-N-S 20-112-3770   (HQ)
BYRON-HILL GROUP CANADA INC
(*Suby of* Byron-Hill Group Canada Inc)
255 Duncan Mill Rd Suite 310, North York,
ON, M3B 3H9
(416) 590-1555
Emp Here 20   *Emp Total* 55
Sales 24,115,200
SIC 6553 Cemetery subdividers and develop-
ers
Pr K.M. (Greg) Sarkissian
Ex VP George Haroutunian

D-U-N-S 24-248-2938   (BR)
CARA OPERATIONS LIMITED
KELSEYS
(*Suby of* Cara Holdings Limited)
861 York Mills Rd Suite 1, North York, ON,
M3B 1Y2

Emp Here 50
SIC 5812 Eating places

D-U-N-S 20-587-2364   (BR)
**CORPORATION OF THE CITY OF
TORONTO**
*TORONTO PRESCHOOL SPEECH AND
LANGUAGE SEVICES*
225 Duncan Mill Rd Suite 201, North York,
ON, M3B 3K9
(416) 338-8255
Emp Here 20
SIC 8351 Child day care services

D-U-N-S 20-709-6798   (HQ)
ERSKINE GREEN LIMITED
1 Valleybrook Dr Suite 201, North York, ON,
M3B 2S7
(416) 487-3883
Emp Here 196   *Emp Total* 1,200
Sales 11,159,500
SIC 6519 Real property lessors, nec
Pr Pr Miriam Green
VP Cary Joseph Green
VP Kevin Marc Green

D-U-N-S 25-531-4874   (BR)
**EVA'S INITIATIVES FOR HOMELESS
YOUTH**
EVA'S PLACE
360 Lesmill Rd, North York, ON, M3B 2T5
(416) 441-4060
Emp Here 30
SIC 8361 Residential care

D-U-N-S 24-910-2906   (SL)
HSBC RETAIL SERVICES LIMITED
101 Duncan Mill Rd Suite 500, North York,
ON, M3B 1Z3
(416) 443-3600
Emp Here 190   *Sales* 90,252,386
SIC 6153 Short-term business credit institu-
tions, except agricultural
Pr Pr Tom Kimble

D-U-N-S 25-109-3068   (HQ)
**HAYS SPECIALIST RECRUITMENT
(CANADA) INC**
HAYS PERSONNEL
1500 Don Mills Rd Suite 402, North York, ON,
M3B 3K4
(416) 203-1925
Emp Here 26   *Emp Total* 7,996
Sales 6,670,133
SIC 7299 Miscellaneous personal service
Pr Rowan O'grady
Douglas Evans

▲ Public Company   ■ Public Company Family Member   **HQ** Headquarters   **BR** Branch   **SL** Single Location

D-U-N-S 24-644-1414 (SL)
HOLMAN EXHIBITS LIMITED
160 Lesmill Rd, North York, ON, M3B 2T5
(416) 441-1877
Emp Here 70 *Sales* 4,231,721
SIC 3993 Signs and advertising specialties

D-U-N-S 25-094-7470 (BR)
IBM CANADA LIMITED
(*Suby of* International Business Machines
Corporation)
105 Moatfield Dr Suite 100, North York, ON,
M3B 0A4
(905) 316-5000
Emp Here 1,500
SIC 7299 Miscellaneous personal service

D-U-N-S 20-305-0745 (SL)
**ICC IMAGINE COMMUNICATIONS CANADA
LTD**
IMAGINE COMMUNICATIONS
(*Suby of* The Gores Group LLC)
25 Dyas Rd, North York, ON, M3B 1V7
(416) 445-9640
Emp Here 330 *Sales* 68,347,204
SIC 3663 Radio and t.v. communications
equipment
Dir Charlie Vogt
Dir Fin Filbert Cozier
 Michael Behling

D-U-N-S 20-299-7243 (SL)
KEDDCO USA INC.
23 Lesmill Rd Suite 201, North York, ON, M3B
3P6
(416) 508-3000
Emp Here 40 *Sales* 8,420,350
SIC 3061 Mechanical rubber goods
Pr Scott Ruston

D-U-N-S 25-849-7932 (BR)
KEG RESTAURANTS LTD
KEG STEAKHOUSE & BAR, THE
1977 Leslie St, North York, ON, M3B 2M3
(416) 446-1045
Emp Here 100
SIC 5812 Eating places

D-U-N-S 20-165-7681 (HQ)
KRAFT HEINZ CANADA ULC
CLASSICO GOURMET
95 Moatfield Dr Suite 316, North York, ON,
M3B 3L6
(416) 441-5000
Emp Here 350 *Sales* 9,277,025,966
SIC 2043 Cereal breakfast foods
Sec Av Maharaj
Dir Carlos Piani
Dir Taryn Miller

D-U-N-S 24-688-2203 (SL)
MAGSTAR INC
240 Duncan Mill Rd Suite 502, North York,
ON, M3B 3S6
(416) 447-1442
Emp Here 34 *Sales* 3,205,129
SIC 7371 Custom computer programming ser-
vices

D-U-N-S 20-059-6935 (HQ)
MEDISYSTEM PHARMACY LIMITED
75 Lesmill Rd Suite 3, North York, ON, M3B
2T8
(416) 441-2293
Emp Here 250 *Emp Total* 138,000
Sales 77,102,000
SIC 5122 Drugs, proprietaries, and sundries
Pr Helen Huh
Dir Fred Bruns

D-U-N-S 24-575-4551 (HQ)
MOTION SPECIALTIES INCORPORATED
1925 Leslie St, North York, ON, M3B 2M3
(416) 441-3585
Emp Here 35 *Emp Total* 449
Sales 6,596,303
SIC 5047 Medical and hospital equipment
Pr Pr David Harding

VP VP Douglas Kerr
 Janet Kerr

D-U-N-S 25-116-3499 (BR)
**MOUNT PLEASANT GROUP OF CEMETER-
IES**
SIMPLE ALTERNATIVE CENTRE, THE
275 Lesmill Rd, North York, ON, M3B 2V1
(416) 441-1580
Emp Here 37
SIC 7261 Funeral service and crematories

D-U-N-S 24-341-4229 (SL)
ONTARIO TELEMEDICINE NETWORK
OTN
105 Moatfield Dr Suite 1100, North York, ON,
M3B 0A2
(416) 446-4110
Emp Here 187 *Sales* 15,674,880
SIC 7363 Help supply services
Pr Edward Brown
VP Neil Maclean
Ch Bd Raymond Marshall

D-U-N-S 24-386-5201 (SL)
**PAISLEY-MANOR INSURANCE BROKERS
INC**
1446 Don Mills Rd Suite 110, North York, ON,
M3B 3N3
(416) 510-1177
Emp Here 50 *Sales* 4,523,563
SIC 6411 Insurance agents, brokers, and ser-
vice

D-U-N-S 24-356-5905 (BR)
POSTMEDIA NETWORK INC
FPINFOMART
1450 Don Mills Rd, North York, ON, M3B 0B3
(416) 442-2121
Emp Here 20
SIC 2711 Newspapers

D-U-N-S 20-191-9433 (SL)
POTSDAM TOWNHOUSES LIMITED
100 Scarsdale Rd Suite 100, North York, ON,
M3B 2R8
(416) 449-3300
Emp Here 30 *Sales* 11,347,888
SIC 6552 Subdividers and developers, nec
Pr Ralph Halbert

D-U-N-S 24-720-9703 (SL)
REGENCY APPAREL CO LTD
255 Duncan Mill Rd Suite 303, North York,
ON, M3B 3H9
(416) 504-6090
Emp Here 100 *Sales* 4,677,755
SIC 2329 Men's and boy's clothing, nec

D-U-N-S 24-665-8041 (HQ)
ROTHMANS, BENSON & HEDGES INC
(*Suby of* Philip Morris International Inc.)
1500 Don Mills Rd Suite 900, North York, ON,
M3B 3L1
(416) 449-5525
Emp Here 145 *Emp Total* 80,200
Sales 57,055,267
SIC 2111 Cigarettes
Pr Pr John R Barnett
Pers/VP Faryl A Hausman
 Robert J Carew
Dir Brenda J Moher

D-U-N-S 24-383-7056 (BR)
SNC-LAVALIN INC
235 Lesmill Rd, North York, ON, M3B 2V1
(416) 445-8255
Emp Here 50
SIC 8711 Engineering services

D-U-N-S 24-320-8357 (BR)
SCHAWK CANADA INC
SCHAWK CACTUS IMAGING CENTRE
(*Suby of* Matthews International Corporation)
54 Lesmill Rd, North York, ON, M3B 2T5

Emp Here 36
SIC 2752 Commercial printing, lithographic

D-U-N-S 20-556-0621 (SL)
SECURE 724 LTD
AVANTE SECURITY
1959 Leslie St, North York, ON, M3B 2M3
(416) 923-6984
Emp Here 50 *Sales* 7,150,149
SIC 3699 Electrical equipment and supplies,
nec
Pr Emmanuel Mounouchos

D-U-N-S 24-632-8983 (SL)
SHELLEY, R G ENTERPRISES (1990) INC
41 Coldwater Rd, North York, ON, M3B 1Y8
(416) 447-6471
Emp Here 55 *Sales* 13,004,140
SIC 5084 Industrial machinery and equipment
Pr Pr Robert G Shelley
 Peter G Shelley
Dir Brian R Shelley

D-U-N-S 24-351-2295 (BR)
ST. JOSEPH PRINTING LIMITED
ST. JOSEPH COMMUNICATIONS
236 Lesmill Rd, North York, ON, M3B 2T5
(416) 449-4579
Emp Here 200
SIC 2711 Newspapers

D-U-N-S 24-311-6295 (BR)
**STERICYCLE COMMUNICATION SOLU-
TIONS, ULC**
(*Suby of* Stericycle Communication Solutions,
ULC)
2 Duncan Mill Rd, North York, ON, M3B 1Z4

Emp Here 80
SIC 4899 Communication services, nec

D-U-N-S 25-475-8113 (SL)
T.L.W. ENTERPRISE INC
255 Duncan Mill Rd Suite 312, North York,
ON, M3B 3H9
(416) 510-3011
Emp Here 50 *Sales* 3,648,035
SIC 7379 Computer related services, nec

D-U-N-S 20-192-3682 (HQ)
THALES CANADA INC
*THALES CANADA, DIVISION AERONAU-
TIQUE*
105 Moatfield Dr Suite 100, North York, ON,
M3B 0A4
(416) 742-3900
Emp Here 151 *Emp Total* 852
Sales 53,620,937
SIC 8711 Engineering services
Pr Pr Guy Baruchel
 Dave Spagnolo
VP Fin Sergio Vettese
 Luc Vigneron
Sec Martine Funston
 Michel Lamarche
 Allain Boursier
 Gabriel De Quatrebarbes

D-U-N-S 20-913-6469 (BR)
TORONTO DISTRICT SCHOOL BOARD
DENLOW PUBLIC SCHOOL
50 Denlow Blvd, North York, ON, M3B 1P7
(416) 395-2300
Emp Here 25
SIC 8211 Elementary and secondary schools

D-U-N-S 20-025-0129 (BR)
TORONTO DISTRICT SCHOOL BOARD
RIPPLETON ELEMENTARY SCHOOL
21 Rippleton Rd, North York, ON, M3B 1H4
(416) 395-2810
Emp Here 30
SIC 8211 Elementary and secondary schools

D-U-N-S 20-927-3882 (BR)
WENDY'S RESTAURANTS OF CANADA INC
WENDY'S
(*Suby of* The Wendy's Company)
861 York Mills Rd Unit 1, North York, ON, M3B
1Y2

Emp Here 32
SIC 5812 Eating places

D-U-N-S 24-387-6190 (SL)
**ZUCHTER BERK CREATIVE CATERERS
INC**
1895 Leslie St, North York, ON, M3B 2M3
(416) 386-1086
Emp Here 60 *Sales* 4,159,450
SIC 5812 Eating places

North York, ON M3C
York County

D-U-N-S 24-304-8808 (SL)
429616 ONTARIO LIMITED
GREENVIEW LODGE
880 Lawrence Ave E, North York, ON, M3C
1P6
(416) 445-2255
Emp Here 60 *Sales* 2,188,821
SIC 8361 Residential care

D-U-N-S 25-825-2527 (BR)
ARAMARK CANADA LTD.
CLASSIC FARE CATERING DIV OF
770 Don Mills Rd, North York, ON, M3C 1T3
(416) 696-5530
Emp Here 60
SIC 5812 Eating places

D-U-N-S 25-662-7365 (BR)
ACCESS INDEPENDENT LIVING SERVICES
ACCESS ST MARK'S
(*Suby of* Access Independent Living Services)
7 The Donway E Suite 403, North York, ON,
M3C 3P8
(416) 443-1701
Emp Here 26
SIC 8621 Professional organizations

D-U-N-S 25-252-9615 (HQ)
ACCESSIBLE MEDIA INC
VOICE PRINT, DIV OF
(*Suby of* Accessible Media Inc)
1090 Don Mills Rd Suite 200, North York, ON,
M3C 3R6
(416) 422-4222
Emp Here 40 *Emp Total* 60
Sales 4,669,485
SIC 7812 Motion picture and video production

D-U-N-S 24-889-3802 (SL)
ALLIED DON VALLEY HOTEL INC
DON VALLEY HOTEL
(*Suby of* Allied Holdings Ltd)
175 Wynford Dr, North York, ON, M3C 1J3
(416) 449-4111
Emp Here 206 *Sales* 9,047,127
SIC 7011 Hotels and motels
Genl Mgr Kevin Porter

D-U-N-S 25-168-9626 (HQ)
BGRS LIMITED
39 Wynford Dr, North York, ON, M3C 3K5
(416) 510-5600
Emp Here 100 *Emp Total* 55,700
Sales 9,703,773
SIC 7389 Business services, nec
Pr Pr Traci Morris
VP VP Michael Bonin
 Richard Ballot
 Kent Williams
 Thomas Hogan

D-U-N-S 25-296-8870 (BR)
BANK OF NOVA SCOTIA, THE
SCOTIABANK
885 Lawrence Ave E, North York, ON, M3C
1P7
(416) 448-7050
Emp Here 20
SIC 6021 National commercial banks

D-U-N-S 25-274-7084 (HQ)

BELL EXPRESSVU INC
100 Wynford Dr Suite 300, North York, ON, M3C 4B4
(416) 383-6600
Emp Here 1,170   *Emp Total* 48,090
Sales 377,425,200
SIC 4841 Cable and other pay television services
Wade Oosterman
George A. Cope
Alexander J. Du

D-U-N-S 25-403-8821   (SL)
BETTER LIVING AT THOMPSON HOUSE
THOMPSON HOUSE
1 Overland Dr, North York, ON, M3C 2C3
(416) 447-7244
Emp Here 50   *Sales* 2,261,782
SIC 8051 Skilled nursing care facilities

D-U-N-S 20-847-5780   (HQ)
BOWDENS MEDIA MONITORING LIMITED
(*Suby of* Bowdens Media Monitoring Limited)
150 Ferrand Dr Suite 1100, North York, ON, M3C 3E5
(416) 750-2220
Emp Here 100   *Emp Total* 320
Sales 80,384,000
SIC 7319 Advertising, nec
Pr Pr John Weinseis
VP Ernie Dewal
VP Gary Larose
VP Phil Crompton
S&M/VP Nicolas Sleeth

D-U-N-S 25-462-4687   (SL)
CPAS SYSTEMS INC
(*Suby of* Conduent Incorporated)
250 Ferrand Dr 7th Floor, North York, ON, M3C 3G8
(416) 422-0563
Emp Here 85   *Sales* 10,141,537
SIC 7371 Custom computer programming services
Pr Pr David Rive
VP Fin Liam Robertson
S&M/VP Jeanette Willis
James Higginson-Rollins

D-U-N-S 20-920-0588   (BR)
CADILLAC FAIRVIEW CORPORATION LIMITED, THE
SHOPS AT DON MILLS
75 The Donway W Suite 910, North York, ON, M3C 2E9
(416) 447-6087
Emp Here 30
SIC 6512 Nonresidential building operators

D-U-N-S 24-453-6264   (BR)
CANADA POST CORPORATION
169 The Donway W, North York, ON, M3C 4G6
(416) 444-6271
Emp Here 200
SIC 4311 U.s. postal service

D-U-N-S 24-358-2926   (BR)
CELESTICA INC
12 Concorde Pl Suite 500, North York, ON, M3C 3R8
(416) 448-5800
Emp Here 25
SIC 3679 Electronic components, nec

D-U-N-S 25-815-7734   (SL)
CENTENNIAL CENTRE OF SCIENCE AND TECHNOLOGY
ONTARIO SCIENCE CENTRE
770 Don Mills Rd, North York, ON, M3C 1T3
(416) 429-4100
Emp Here 300   *Sales* 29,494,898
SIC 8412 Museums and art galleries
Mark Cohon
Dir Robert J. Macdonald
Dir Robert Miller
Dir Sarah Mitchell
Dir Gail Obrien

Dir Sam L. Zuk
V Ch Bd Peter Irwin
Dir John R.G Challis
Dir Anthony Cohen
Dir Mary Anne Crummond

D-U-N-S 20-708-2590   (HQ)
CENTRACT SETTLEMENT SERVICES INC
39 Wynford Dr, North York, ON, M3C 3K5
(416) 510-5300
Emp Here 106   *Emp Total* 55,700
Sales 15,574,400
SIC 6531 Real estate agents and managers
Pr Graham Badun
Fin Ex Richard Collins

D-U-N-S 20-162-2578   (HQ)
COLGATE-PALMOLIVE CANADA INC
(*Suby of* Colgate-Palmolive Company)
895 Don Mills Rd, North York, ON, M3C 1W3
(416) 421-6000
Emp Here 80   *Emp Total* 36,700
Sales 9,875,261
SIC 2844 Toilet preparations
Pr Pr Scott Geffery

D-U-N-S 24-238-3169   (BR)
COMMUNITY LIVING ONTARIO
29 Gervais Dr Suite 208, North York, ON, M3C 1Y9
(416) 446-1620
Emp Here 20
SIC 8322 Individual and family services

D-U-N-S 20-029-4481   (BR)
CORPORATION OF THE CITY OF TORONTO
DENNIS R. TIMBRELL RESOURCE CENTRE
29 St Dennis Dr, North York, ON, M3C 3J3
(416) 395-7974
Emp Here 31
SIC 7999 Amusement and recreation, nec

D-U-N-S 25-663-2050   (BR)
CORUS MEDIA HOLDINGS INC
SHAW MEDIA INC
81 Barber Greene Rd, North York, ON, M3C 2A2
(416) 446-5311
Emp Here 250
SIC 4833 Television broadcasting stations

D-U-N-S 24-390-4245   (BR)
DELOITTE & TOUCHE MANAGEMENT CONSULTANTS
(*Suby of* Deloitte & Touche Management Consultants)
1 Concorde Gate Suite 200, North York, ON, M3C 3N6
(416) 775-4700
Emp Here 100
SIC 8111 Legal services

D-U-N-S 24-185-1633   (SL)
DON MILLS SURGICAL UNIT LIMITED
SURGICAL UNIT
20 Wynford Dr Suite 208, North York, ON, M3C 1J4
(416) 441-2111
Emp Here 20   *Sales* 1,605,135
SIC 8069 Specialty hospitals, except psychiatric

D-U-N-S 24-207-9015   (HQ)
G4S CASH SOLUTIONS (CANADA) LTD
G4S SECURICOR
150 Ferrand Dr Suite 600, North York, ON, M3C 3E5
(416) 645-5555
Emp Here 50   *Emp Total* 592,897
Sales 120,712,345
SIC 7381 Detective and armored car services
Dir Edward Jamieson
Dir Han Koren
Dir Alain Roy

D-U-N-S 25-352-9952   (HQ)

GLASSHOUSE SYSTEMS INC
(*Suby of* Glasshouse Systems Inc)
885 Don Mills Road, North York, ON, M3C 1V9
(416) 229-2950
Emp Here 25   *Emp Total* 48
Sales 6,566,463
SIC 5045 Computers, peripherals, and software
Pr Pr David Antebi

D-U-N-S 24-170-3938   (BR)
GOODLIFE FITNESS CENTRES INC
825 Don Mills Rd Suite 300, North York, ON, M3C 1V4
(416) 383-1816
Emp Here 20
SIC 7999 Amusement and recreation, nec

D-U-N-S 20-413-9083   (HQ)
GRAND & TOY LIMITED
OFFICEMAXMD GRAND&TOY
(*Suby of* Office Depot, Inc.)
33 Green Belt Dr, North York, ON, M3C 1M1
(416) 391-8100
Emp Here 210   *Emp Total* 38,000
Sales 123,741,347
SIC 5943 Stationery stores
VP John Baigrie
Pers/VP Marla Allan
VP Sls Stan Dabic
Sec Darlene Quashie Henry

D-U-N-S 24-885-4796   (HQ)
HOME DEPOT OF CANADA INC
(*Suby of* The Home Depot Inc)
1 Concorde Gate Suite 900, North York, ON, M3C 4H9
(416) 609-0852
Emp Here 110   *Emp Total* 406,000
Sales 1,729,168,590
SIC 5251 Hardware stores
Jocelyn J Hunter
Carol Tome
Michael F Rowe

D-U-N-S 24-632-5831   (SL)
HOMESERVE TECHNOLOGIES INC
39 Wynford Dr, North York, ON, M3C 3K5
(416) 510-5722
Emp Here 20   *Sales* 1,459,214
SIC 7371 Custom computer programming services

D-U-N-S 20-556-0415   (HQ)
ICICI BANK CANADA
150 Ferrand Dr Suite 1200, North York, ON, M3C 3E5
(416) 847-7881
Emp Here 120   *Emp Total* 81,129
Sales 52,458,743
SIC 6021 National commercial banks
Pr Pr Sriram Iyer

D-U-N-S 25-664-9617   (BR)
LA FONDATION CANADIENNE DU REIN
CENTRAL ONTARIO BRANCH
15 Gervais Dr Unit 700, North York, ON, M3C 1Y8
(416) 445-0373
Emp Here 25
SIC 8621 Professional organizations

D-U-N-S 24-607-0333   (BR)
LOBLAWS INC
REAL CANDIAN SUPERSTORE
825 Don Mills Rd Suite 1077, North York, ON, M3C 1V4
(416) 391-0080
Emp Here 25
SIC 5411 Grocery stores

D-U-N-S 25-318-1846   (BR)
MCDONALD'S RESTAURANTS OF CANADA LIMITED
MCDONALD'S
(*Suby of* McDonald's Corporation)
747 Don Mills Rd Suite 13, North York, ON, M3C 1T2

(416) 429-1266
Emp Here 80
SIC 5812 Eating places

D-U-N-S 20-774-2982   (HQ)
MCDONALD'S RESTAURANTS OF CANADA LIMITED
(*Suby of* McDonald's Corporation)
1 Mcdonalds Pl, North York, ON, M3C 3L4
(416) 443-1000
Emp Here 300   *Emp Total* 375,000
Sales 417,043,361
SIC 5812 Eating places
Pr John Betts
VP VP Jeff Mclean
Dir Michael Flores
VP VP Dave Simsons

D-U-N-S 20-968-0867   (HQ)
MILLS, BRYAN IRODESSO CORP
1129 Leslie St, North York, ON, M3C 2K5
(416) 447-4740
Emp Here 25   *Emp Total* 5,690
Sales 5,399,092
SIC 8748 Business consulting, nec
Nancy Ladenheim
Ex VP Michael Bertouche
VP Allan Austin
VP Shelley Marchant
VP Glen Nelson
VP Chris Oberg
VP Bruce Wigle
Geoffrey Vanderburg
Brenda Hanchar
Jeffrey Martin

D-U-N-S 24-903-2061   (HQ)
PANAVISION (CANADA) CORPORATION
900a Don Mills Rd Suite 100, North York, ON, M3C 1V6
(416) 444-7000
Emp Here 60   *Emp Total* 70
Sales 4,591,130
SIC 7819 Services allied to motion pictures

D-U-N-S 24-826-3246   (SL)
PARETO INC
1 Concorde Gate Suite 200, North York, ON, M3C 4G4

Emp Here 60   *Sales* 9,717,840
SIC 7311 Advertising agencies
Pr Pr Micheal Collin

D-U-N-S 20-044-1723   (HQ)
PEARSON CANADA HOLDINGS INC
PEARSON EDUCATION CANADA
26 Prince Andrew Pl, North York, ON, M3C 2H4
(416) 447-5101
Emp Here 260   *Emp Total* 36,317
Sales 44,611,927
SIC 2731 Book publishing
Pr Pr Allan Reynolds

D-U-N-S 20-177-3673   (BR)
RR DONELLEY CANADA FINANCIAL COMPANY
COMPOSITE DIV OF
(*Suby of* R. R. Donnelley & Sons Company)
60 Gervais Dr, North York, ON, M3C 1Z3

Emp Here 100
SIC 2752 Commercial printing, lithographic

D-U-N-S 24-826-6264   (HQ)
RR DONELLEY CANADA FINANCIAL COMPANY
BOWNE ENTERPRISE SOLUTIONS, DIV OF
(*Suby of* R. R. Donnelley & Sons Company)
60 Gervais Dr, North York, ON, M3C 1Z3

Emp Here 300   *Emp Total* 68,400
Sales 36,373,760
SIC 2752 Commercial printing, lithographic
Robert Kadis
VP Opers Robert Hayes
VP Sls Barry Scruton

▲ Public Company   ■ Public Company Family Member   **HQ** Headquarters   **BR** Branch   **SL** Single Location

VP Opers Loren Patterson
Pr Bill Penders

D-U-N-S 25-704-3562   (BR)
REVERA INC
DONWAY PLACE
8 The Donway E Suite 557, North York, ON, M3C 3R7
(416) 445-7555
Emp Here 120
SIC 8051 Skilled nursing care facilities

D-U-N-S 24-362-9057   (HQ)
SHI CANADA ULC
895 Don Mills Rd Suite 200, North York, ON, M3C 1W3
(888) 235-3871
Emp Here 30   *Emp Total* 3,800
Sales 5,277,042
SIC 5045 Computers, peripherals, and software
Genl Mgr Adam Belzycki

D-U-N-S 20-519-5154   (BR)
SNC-LAVALIN INTERNATIONAL INC
SNC -LAVALIN PHARMA
789 Don Mills Rd Suite 1000, North York, ON, M3C 1T5
(416) 422-4056
Emp Here 60
SIC 8711 Engineering services

D-U-N-S 25-317-2639   (HQ)
SHEPELL FGI LP
(*Suby of* Morneau Shepell Inc)
895 Don Mills Rd, North York, ON, M3C 1W3
(416) 961-0023
Emp Here 90   *Emp Total* 4,300
Sales 126,837,483
SIC 8322 Individual and family services
Ch Bd William Morneau
CEO Alen Torrie
VP Scott Milligen
VP Paula Allen
VP Michae Lin
VP Sls Neil King
VP Opers Rita Fridella

D-U-N-S 24-688-0710   (HQ)
SONY MUSIC ENTERTAINMENT CANADA INC
RCA RECORDS
150 Ferrand Dr Suite 300, North York, ON, M3C 3E5
(416) 589-3171
Emp Here 100   *Emp Total* 125,300
Sales 13,424,769
SIC 5099 Durable goods, nec
Pr Shane Carter
VP VP Stephen Simon
VP VP Larry Mcrae
Pr Neil Foster

D-U-N-S 20-733-2110   (BR)
SYMCOR INC
8 Prince Andrew Pl, North York, ON, M3C 2H4
(905) 273-1000
Emp Here 800
SIC 8741 Management services

D-U-N-S 20-035-5084   (BR)
TORONTO CATHOLIC DISTRICT SCHOOL BOARD
ST. BONAVENTURE CATHOLIC SCHOOL
1340 Leslie St, North York, ON, M3C 2K9
(416) 393-5263
Emp Here 30
SIC 8211 Elementary and secondary schools

D-U-N-S 25-509-3718   (BR)
TORONTO DISTRICT SCHOOL BOARD
OVERLAND LEARNING CENTRE
55 Overland Dr, North York, ON, M3C 2C3
(416) 395-5080
Emp Here 100
SIC 8211 Elementary and secondary schools

D-U-N-S 20-025-0053   (BR)

TORONTO DISTRICT SCHOOL BOARD
GREENLAND PUBLIC SCHOOL
15 Greenland Rd, North York, ON, M3C 1N1
(416) 395-2500
Emp Here 25
SIC 8211 Elementary and secondary schools

D-U-N-S 25-237-8039   (BR)
TORONTO DISTRICT SCHOOL BOARD
GRENOBLE PUBLIC SCHOOL
9 Grenoble Dr, North York, ON, M3C 1C3
(416) 397-2900
Emp Here 80
SIC 8211 Elementary and secondary schools

D-U-N-S 25-237-7742   (BR)
TORONTO DISTRICT SCHOOL BOARD
GATEWAY PUBLIC SCHOOL
55 Gateway Blvd, North York, ON, M3C 1B4
(416) 397-2970
Emp Here 70
SIC 8211 Elementary and secondary schools

D-U-N-S 24-830-4362   (SL)
TROJAN CONSOLIDATED INVESTMENTS LIMITED
DIAMOND & DIAMOND CERTIFIED MG
18 Wynford Dr Suite 516, North York, ON, M3C 3S2
(416) 785-3961
Emp Here 160   *Sales* 21,231,564
SIC 8742 Management consulting services
Pr Pr Stephen Robinson
Robert Kleinfeldt
Arthur Paul
Aaron Stein
A Mendelson
Helmut Stern
Arthur Paulson

D-U-N-S 20-039-6583   (BR)
WASTE CONNECTIONS OF CANADA INC
BFI CANADA
75 The Donway W Suite 714, North York, ON, M3C 2E9
(905) 389-2422
Emp Here 25
SIC 4953 Refuse systems

D-U-N-S 20-650-7225   (HQ)
ISKIN INC
(*Suby of* iSkin Inc)
3 Concorde Gate Unit 311, North York, ON, M3C 3N7
(416) 924-9607
Emp Here 50   *Emp Total* 60
Sales 3,283,232
SIC 8731 Commercial physical research

North York, ON M3H
York County

D-U-N-S 24-209-0876   (SL)
ANNE AND MAX TANENBAUN HEBREW ACADEMY OF TORONTO
200 Wilmington Ave, North York, ON, M3H 5J8
(416) 636-5984
Emp Here 220   *Sales* 20,391,450
SIC 8211 Elementary and secondary schools
Ex Dir Rhona Birenbaum
Dir Paul Shaviv
Pr Pr Judy Engel
Dir Lori Disenhouse

D-U-N-S 24-140-0035   (SL)
BETH EMETH BAIS YEHUDA SYNAGOGUE
100 Elder St, North York, ON, M3H 5G7
(416) 633-3838
Emp Here 50   *Sales* 3,283,232
SIC 8661 Religious organizations

D-U-N-S 24-118-2406   (BR)
BRICK WAREHOUSE LP, THE
BRICK STORE, THE
4250 Dufferin St, North York, ON, M3H 5W4

(416) 635-5522
Emp Here 20
SIC 5712 Furniture stores

D-U-N-S 24-411-4138   (SL)
CATERERS (YORK) LIMITED
SWEET YORK DESSERTS
37 Southbourne Ave, North York, ON, M3H 1A4
(416) 783-4293
Emp Here 100   *Sales* 2,991,389
SIC 5812 Eating places

D-U-N-S 20-967-3867   (SL)
CONDOR SECURITY
4610 Dufferin St Unit 1b, North York, ON, M3H 5S4
(416) 410-4035
Emp Here 70   *Sales* 2,188,821
SIC 7381 Detective and armored car services

D-U-N-S 24-764-8421   (BR)
CORPORATION OF THE CITY OF TORONTO
TORONTO PARAMEDICS SERVICES
4330 Dufferin St Suite 28, North York, ON, M3H 5R9
(416) 392-2000
Emp Here 1,000
SIC 4119 Local passenger transportation, nec

D-U-N-S 20-709-5717   (BR)
DEL MANAGEMENT SOLUTIONS INC
DMS PROPERTY MANAGEMENT
4810 Dufferin St Suite E, North York, ON, M3H 5S8
(416) 661-3070
Emp Here 45
SIC 8741 Management services

D-U-N-S 25-406-0908   (SL)
EDI CUSTOMS BROKERS INC
2 Tippet Rd, North York, ON, M3H 2V2
(416) 630-3000
Emp Here 57   *Sales* 19,392,640
SIC 4731 Freight transportation arrangement
Pr Pr Rajiv Manucha
VP VP Maria Shepherd
Ann Smokorowski
Acct Mgr Selina Kwan

D-U-N-S 20-194-3607   (BR)
GOVERNING COUNCIL OF THE UNIVERSITY OF TORONTO
INSTITUTE FOR AERO SPACE STUDIES
4925 Dufferin St, North York, ON, M3H 5T6
(416) 667-7700
Emp Here 100
SIC 8221 Colleges and universities

D-U-N-S 20-966-5850   (SL)
HENNICK, NATHAN & CO. LTD
6 Tippett Rd, North York, ON, M3H 2V2
(416) 636-4040
Emp Here 65   *Sales* 4,742,446
SIC 3911 Jewelry, precious Metal

D-U-N-S 20-746-1836   (SL)
KENSINGTON PLACE RETIREMENT RESIDENCE
866 Sheppard Ave W Suite 415, North York, ON, M3H 2T5
(416) 636-9555
Emp Here 50   *Sales* 1,824,018
SIC 8361 Residential care

D-U-N-S 20-559-4281   (SL)
MANSIONS OF HUMBERWOOD INC
4800 Dufferin St Suite 200, North York, ON, M3H 5S9
(416) 661-9290
Emp Here 20   *Sales* 5,398,800
SIC 1522 Residential construction, nec
Pr Pr Marian (Murphy) Hull

D-U-N-S 25-300-3198   (BR)
METRO ONTARIO INC
METRO
600 Sheppard Ave W, North York, ON, M3H

2S1
(416) 636-5136
Emp Here 130
SIC 5411 Grocery stores

D-U-N-S 20-408-1863   (SL)
NEW YORK WINDOW CLEANING COMPANY, LIMITED
3793 Bathurst St, North York, ON, M3H 3N1
(416) 635-0765
Emp Here 70   *Sales* 1,313,293
SIC 7349 Building maintenance services, nec

D-U-N-S 25-221-4937   (SL)
NORTOWN ELECTRICAL CONTRACTORS ASSOCIATES
3845 Bathurst St Suite 102, North York, ON, M3H 3N2
(416) 638-6700
Emp Here 180   *Sales* 15,759,511
SIC 1731 Electrical work
Pt Harry Marder
Pt Shirley Marder

D-U-N-S 20-046-3391   (SL)
PAESE RISTORANTE KING ST. LTD
PAESE RISTORANTE
3829 Bathurst St, North York, ON, M3H 3N1
(416) 631-6585
Emp Here 50   *Sales* 1,532,175
SIC 5812 Eating places

D-U-N-S 20-200-3088   (SL)
PAYLESS TRAVEL INC
CORPORATE TRAVEL MANAGEMENT SOLUTIONS
5000 Dufferin St Suite 219, North York, ON, M3H 5T5
(416) 665-1010
Emp Here 20   *Sales* 6,594,250
SIC 4724 Travel agencies
Pr Pr Gerry Osovitzki
Dir Galia Osovitzki

D-U-N-S 24-845-1569   (SL)
PROBE INVESTIGATION AND SECURITY SERVICES LTD
PROBE SECURITY
3995 Bathurst St Suite 301, North York, ON, M3H 5V3
(416) 636-7000
Emp Here 75   *Sales* 2,334,742
SIC 7381 Detective and armored car services

D-U-N-S 24-206-7549   (SL)
QUALICARE INC
3910 Bathurst St Suite 304, North York, ON, M3H 5Z3
(416) 630-0202
Emp Here 85   *Sales* 4,012,839
SIC 8059 Nursing and personal care, nec

D-U-N-S 20-711-1464   (BR)
TORONTO CATHOLIC DISTRICT SCHOOL BOARD
ST. ROBERT ELEMENTARY CATHOLIC SCHOOL
70 Bainbridge Ave, North York, ON, M3H 2K2
(416) 393-5297
Emp Here 50
SIC 8211 Elementary and secondary schools

D-U-N-S 20-025-0210   (BR)
TORONTO DISTRICT SCHOOL BOARD
DUBLIN HEIGHTS ELEMENTARY & MIDDLE SCHOOL
100 Bainbridge Ave, North York, ON, M3H 2K2
(416) 395-2360
Emp Here 59
SIC 8211 Elementary and secondary schools

D-U-N-S 20-025-0707   (BR)
TORONTO DISTRICT SCHOOL BOARD
WILMINGTON ELEMENTARY SCHOOL
330 Wilmington Ave, North York, ON, M3H 5L1
(416) 395-2180
Emp Here 25

▲ Public Company   ■ Public Company Family Member   **HQ** Headquarters   **BR** Branch   **SL** Single Location

SIC 8211 Elementary and secondary schools

D-U-N-S 20-025-2463   (BR)
TORONTO DISTRICT SCHOOL BOARD
CHARLES H BEST MIDDLE SCHOOL
285 Wilmington Ave, North York, ON, M3H 5K8
(416) 395-2170
Emp Here 35
SIC 8211 Elementary and secondary schools

D-U-N-S 25-263-3581   (BR)
TYCO INTEGRATED FIRE & SECURITY CANADA, INC
SIMPLEXGRINNELL
(*Suby of* Johnson Controls, Inc.)
5000 Dufferin St, North York, ON, M3H 5T5

Emp Here 100
SIC 7381 Detective and armored car services

D-U-N-S 20-693-7281   (BR)
UNIVERSITY OF TORONTO PRESS
UTP DISTRIBUTION, DIV OF
5201 Dufferin St, North York, ON, M3H 5T8
(416) 667-7777
Emp Here 150
SIC 2731 Book publishing

D-U-N-S 20-980-7551   (BR)
UNIVERSITY OF TORONTO PRESS
UTP NORTH YORK, DIV OF
5201 Dufferin St, North York, ON, M3H 5T8
(416) 667-7810
Emp Here 150
SIC 2731 Book publishing

D-U-N-S 24-171-8134   (HQ)
YUMMY MARKET INC
(*Suby of* Yummy Market Inc)
4400 Dufferin St Unit B-4, North York, ON, M3H 6A8
(416) 665-0040
Emp Here 150   *Emp Total* 380
Sales 53,844,997
SIC 5411 Grocery stores
VP Alexei Tsvetkov
Pr Anna Tsvetkov
Dir Fin Mila Sak

North York, ON M3J
York County

D-U-N-S 24-830-2804   (SL)
824416 ONTARIO LTD
MANDARIN RESTAURANT
1027 Finch Ave W, North York, ON, M3J 2C7
(416) 736-6000
Emp Here 65   *Sales* 1,969,939
SIC 5812 Eating places

D-U-N-S 24-420-1885   (SL)
ARRAY SYSTEMS COMPUTING INC
1120 Finch Ave W, North York, ON, M3J 3H7
(416) 736-0900
Emp Here 45   *Sales* 5,791,440
SIC 7371 Custom computer programming services
Pr Pr Stuart Berkowitz

D-U-N-S 25-790-7295   (BR)
BANK OF NOVA SCOTIA, THE
SCOTIABANK
845 Finch Ave W, North York, ON, M3J 2C7
(416) 665-8742
Emp Here 20
SIC 6021 National commercial banks

D-U-N-S 20-174-8316   (HQ)
C.G. MAINTENANCE & SANITARY PRODUCTS INC
CG MAINTENANCE
(*Suby of* C.G. Maintenance & Sanitary Products Inc)
40 Saint Regis Cres, North York, ON, M3J 1Y5

Emp Here 30   *Emp Total* 40
Sales 6,478,560
SIC 5087 Service establishment equipment

D-U-N-S 24-173-5021   (BR)
CANADA FIBERS LTD
CMC PAPER CONVERERS
35 Vanley Cres Suite 500, North York, ON, M3J 2B7
(416) 398-7989
Emp Here 100
SIC 4953 Refuse systems

D-U-N-S 20-074-5235   (BR)
CANLAN ICE SPORTS CORP
989 Murray Ross Pky, North York, ON, M3J 3M4
(416) 661-4423
Emp Here 60
SIC 5812 Eating places

D-U-N-S 20-920-0075   (BR)
CARA OPERATIONS LIMITED
(*Suby of* Cara Holdings Limited)
1113 Finch Ave W, North York, ON, M3J 2P7

Emp Here 25
SIC 5812 Eating places

D-U-N-S 20-797-3988   (SL)
CHOICE OFFICE INSTALLATIONS INC
201 Limestone Cres, North York, ON, M3J 2R1
(416) 645-8095
Emp Here 50   *Sales* 4,377,642
SIC 1799 Special trade contractors, nec

D-U-N-S 20-059-4856   (SL)
CITIWELL INTERNATIONAL INC
401 Magnetic Dr Unit 9, North York, ON, M3J 3H9
(905) 760-9686
Emp Here 162   *Sales* 32,869,800
SIC 5092 Toys and hobby goods and supplies
Pr Pr Brenda Ehrentreu
CEO David Rosenberg

D-U-N-S 24-220-1101   (SL)
COLUMBIA BUILDING MAINTENANCE CO LTD
65 Martin Ross Ave Unit 1, North York, ON, M3J 2L6
(416) 663-5020
Emp Here 100   *Sales* 2,918,428
SIC 7349 Building maintenance services, nec

D-U-N-S 25-239-8888   (BR)
COMMUNITY LIVING TORONTO
NORTH YORK EARLY CHILDHOOD
1122 Finch Ave W Unit 18, North York, ON, M3J 3J5
(416) 225-7166
Emp Here 100
SIC 8322 Individual and family services

D-U-N-S 24-248-8992   (BR)
COMPAGNIE DE TELEPHONE BELL DU CANADA OU BELL CANADA, LA
BELL CANADA FLEET
1101 Alness St Suite 1, North York, ON, M3J 2J1
(416) 650-6439
Emp Here 30
SIC 4813 Telephone communication, except radio

D-U-N-S 20-784-7377   (BR)
COONEY TRANSPORT LTD
1133 Finch Ave W, North York, ON, M3J 2E8
(416) 630-7042
Emp Here 30
SIC 4213 Trucking, except local

D-U-N-S 20-087-9919   (BR)
CORPORATION OF THE CITY OF TORONTO
GRANDRAVINE COMMUNITY CENTRE
23 Grandravine Dr, North York, ON, M3J 1B3

(416) 395-6171
Emp Here 25
SIC 8322 Individual and family services

D-U-N-S 20-549-7357   (HQ)
D'AVERSA, NINO BAKERY LIMITED
(*Suby of* D'Aversa, Nino Bakery Limited)
1 Toro Rd, North York, ON, M3J 2A4
(416) 638-3271
Emp Here 60   *Emp Total* 85
Sales 2,918,428
SIC 5461 Retail bakeries

D-U-N-S 20-610-7047   (SL)
DOWNSVIEW CHRYSLER PLYMOUTH (1964) LTD
(*Suby of* Walsh, N.L. Holdings Limited)
199 Rimrock Rd, North York, ON, M3J 3C6
(416) 635-1660
Emp Here 100   *Sales* 49,080,000
SIC 5511 New and used car dealers
Pr Pr Peter Kepecs
Treas David Mckerracher
Dir Wesley Scott
Dir Neil Walsh

D-U-N-S 20-857-9636   (BR)
ESTEE LAUDER COSMETICS LTD
MAC COSMETICS
550 Petrolia Rd, North York, ON, M3J 2W3
(905) 944-7600
Emp Here 20
SIC 5122 Drugs, proprietaries, and sundries

D-U-N-S 24-463-7773   (SL)
FIRWIN CORP
DIESELTECH
1685 Flint Rd, North York, ON, M3J 2W8
(416) 907-4093
Emp Here 50   *Sales* 4,847,019
SIC 3086 Plastics foam products

D-U-N-S 25-099-4100   (BR)
GANZ CANADA
TIME AND AGAIN
(*Suby of* Ganz)
100 Brisbane Rd, North York, ON, M3J 2K2
(416) 663-7401
Emp Here 25
SIC 3999 Manufacturing industries, nec

D-U-N-S 20-017-3305   (BR)
GLOBAL CONTRACT INC
EVOLVE SYSTEMS
555 Petrolia Rd Suite 1, North York, ON, M3J 2X8
(416) 739-5000
Emp Here 60
SIC 2522 Office furniture, except wood

D-U-N-S 24-343-4136   (BR)
GLOBAL UPHOLSTERY CO. INC
THE GLOBAL GROUP
1350 Flint Rd, North York, ON, M3J 2J7
(416) 661-3660
Emp Here 80
SIC 6719 Holding companies, nec

D-U-N-S 20-913-8218   (BR)
GLOBAL UPHOLSTERY CO. INC
565 Petrolia Rd, North York, ON, M3J 2X8
(416) 739-5000
Emp Here 550
SIC 2522 Office furniture, except wood

D-U-N-S 20-697-5364   (BR)
GLOBAL UPHOLSTERY CO. INC
GLOBAL TOTAL OFFICE
596 Supertest Rd, North York, ON, M3J 2M5
(416) 661-3660
Emp Here 50
SIC 2522 Office furniture, except wood

D-U-N-S 25-409-8320   (SL)
HAN MINH MACHINE WORKS LTD
1100 Lodestar Rd Unit 5, North York, ON, M3J 2Z4
(416) 636-0660
Emp Here 50   *Sales* 3,648,035

SIC 3599 Industrial machinery, nec

D-U-N-S 25-365-8660   (BR)
HOME DEPOT OF CANADA INC
HOME DEPOT
(*Suby of* The Home Depot Inc)
2375 Steeles Ave W, North York, ON, M3J 3A8
(416) 664-9800
Emp Here 100
SIC 5251 Hardware stores

D-U-N-S 25-403-9340   (SL)
HOUSE INC, THE
620 Supertest Rd Unit 9, North York, ON, M3J 2M5

Emp Here 30   *Sales* 7,608,750
SIC 5136 Men's and boy's clothing
Pr Pr Steve Kumar
 Danielle Rabinowitz
 Sandeep (Sonny) Luthra

D-U-N-S 24-044-5184   (HQ)
INTERNATIONAL AQUATIC SERVICES LTD
POOL OF EXPERTS
4496 Chesswood Dr, North York, ON, M3J 2B9
(416) 665-6400
Emp Here 125   *Emp Total* 3
Sales 35,458,900
SIC 5999 Miscellaneous retail stores, nec
Dir Greg Cook

D-U-N-S 20-974-0240   (HQ)
JOHNVINCE FOODS
PLANTERS PEANUTS
(*Suby of* Johnvince Foods)
555 Steeprock Dr, North York, ON, M3J 2Z6
(416) 636-6146
Emp Here 400   *Emp Total* 550
Sales 143,148,893
SIC 5145 Confectionery
Pt Vincent Pulla
Pt Pt Joe Pulla
S&M/VP Don Lock
 Vincent Cosentino

D-U-N-S 20-012-8101   (BR)
LIBERTE NATURAL FOODS INC
LIBERTE NATURAL FOODS
60 Brisbane Rd, North York, ON, M3J 2K2
(416) 661-0582
Emp Here 50
SIC 2026 Fluid milk

D-U-N-S 24-117-0419   (BR)
LOBLAWS INC
REAL CANADIAN SUPERSTORE
51 Gerry Fitzgerald Dr Suite 1033, North York, ON, M3J 3N4
(416) 665-7636
Emp Here 280
SIC 5411 Grocery stores

D-U-N-S 25-476-0234   (BR)
LOBLAWS SUPERMARKETS LIMITED
NO FRILLS
3685 Keele St, North York, ON, M3J 3H6
(416) 398-3021
Emp Here 50
SIC 5411 Grocery stores

D-U-N-S 25-213-0109   (BR)
LONG & MCQUADE LIMITED
LONG & MCQUADE MUSICAL INSTRUMENTS
2777 Steeles Ave W Suite 5, North York, ON, M3J 3K5
(416) 663-8612
Emp Here 30
SIC 5736 Musical instrument stores

D-U-N-S 24-760-4718   (BR)
LOVELY IMPORTS & RETAILS LTD
PETRO CANADA
3720 Keele St, North York, ON, M3J 2V9
(416) 636-0568
Emp Here 80

SIC 5541 Gasoline service stations

D-U-N-S 24-185-4124 (SL)
M & A TILE COMPANY LIMITED
1155 Petrolia Rd, North York, ON, M3J 2X7

Emp Here 50   Sales 6,631,680
SIC 1752 Floor laying and floor work, nec
Pr Pr Mario Amelio

D-U-N-S 20-590-2443 (SL)
MARTIN ROSS GROUP INC
MASTER DESIGN
250 Canarctic Dr, North York, ON, M3J 2P4

Emp Here 46   Sales 7,000,050
SIC 5094 Jewelry and precious stones
Dir Allan Shechtman

D-U-N-S 20-923-7663 (BR)
MCDONALD'S RESTAURANTS OF CANADA LIMITED
MCDONALD'S RESTAURANT
(Suby of McDonald's Corporation)
150 Rimrock Rd, North York, ON, M3J 3A6
(416) 630-8381
Emp Here 85
SIC 5812 Eating places

D-U-N-S 24-892-9841 (BR)
METROLINX
200 Steeprock Dr, North York, ON, M3J 2T4

Emp Here 700
SIC 4011 Railroads, line-haul operating

D-U-N-S 20-058-9369 (SL)
MIRATEL SOLUTIONS INC
2501 Steeles Ave W Suite 200, North York, ON, M3J 2P1
(416) 650-7850
Emp Here 100   Sales 4,961,328
SIC 7389 Business services, nec

D-U-N-S 20-555-7853 (HQ)
MODERN NIAGARA TORONTO INC
695 Flint Rd, North York, ON, M3J 2T7
(416) 749-6031
Emp Here 25   Emp Total 300
Sales 13,132,926
SIC 1711 Plumbing, heating, air-conditioning
Pr Craig Pickering
   Robert Silberstein

D-U-N-S 20-859-9477 (BR)
PACIFIC LINK COMMUNICATIONS INC
BELL WORLD
170 Rimrock Rd, North York, ON, M3J 3A6
(416) 667-1489
Emp Here 25
SIC 5999 Miscellaneous retail stores, nec

D-U-N-S 25-118-7753 (BR)
PETRO PARTNERS LIMITED
PETRO CANADA
3993 Keele St, North York, ON, M3J 2X6
(416) 461-0991
Emp Here 20
SIC 1311 Crude petroleum and natural gas

D-U-N-S 24-915-2539 (BR)
PRO AUTO LTD
PRO BODY PARTS
301 Flint Rd Unit 2, North York, ON, M3J 2J2
(416) 739-7735
Emp Here 25
SIC 5531 Auto and home supply stores

D-U-N-S 24-977-8093 (BR)
PROGRESS LUV2PAK INTERNATIONAL LTD
20 Tangiers Rd, North York, ON, M3J 2B2
(416) 638-1221
Emp Here 50
SIC 5113 Industrial and personal service paper

D-U-N-S 20-174-7305 (SL)
SMS MODERN CLEANING SERVICE (AL-

BERTA) INC
777 Supertest Rd, North York, ON, M3J 2M9
(416) 736-1144
Emp Here 378   Sales 15,318,950
SIC 7349 Building maintenance services, nec
Pr Pr Glenn Mccurzy

D-U-N-S 24-216-8847 (BR)
SCOUTS CANADA
SCOUTS CANADA CENTRAL ONTARIO
10 Kodiak Cres Unit 120, North York, ON, M3J 3G5
(416) 490-6364
Emp Here 20
SIC 8641 Civic and social associations

D-U-N-S 20-117-6497 (SL)
SIGA INTERNATIONAL
81 Saint Regis Cres S, North York, ON, M3J 1Y6
(416) 504-7442
Emp Here 45   Sales 8,244,559
SIC 5136 Men's and boy's clothing
Pt Mark Lucas

D-U-N-S 24-395-5825 (SL)
SIGMACON ESTHETICS CORPORATION
436 Limestone Cres, North York, ON, M3J 2S4
(416) 665-6616
Emp Here 40   Sales 6,674,880
SIC 5122 Drugs, proprietaries, and sundries
Pr Paul Levy

D-U-N-S 24-389-6628 (SL)
SUPERIOR MEDICAL LIMITED
520 Champagne Dr, North York, M3J 2T9
(416) 635-9797
Emp Here 25   Sales 5,545,013
SIC 5047 Medical and hospital equipment
Pr Pr Ron Kilius

D-U-N-S 20-629-5706 (SL)
SYNERGY MARKETING CONSULTANTS INC
10 Kodiak Cres Suite 101, North York, ON, M3J 3G5
(416) 398-5660
Emp Here 115   Sales 19,174,050
SIC 7311 Advertising agencies
Pr Jeffrey Szenes

D-U-N-S 20-913-7251 (BR)
TAYMOR INDUSTRIES LTD
205 Limestone Cres, North York, ON, M3J 2R1
(416) 661-0292
Emp Here 25
SIC 5072 Hardware

D-U-N-S 20-058-1010 (HQ)
TEKNION FURNITURE SYSTEMS CO. LIMITED
1150 Flint Rd, North York, ON, M3J 2J5
(416) 661-3370
Emp Here 90   Emp Total 8,930
Sales 41,406,798
SIC 5021 Furniture
Pr Pr David Feldberg
Sr VP Joe Regan
Sr VP Scott Deugo

D-U-N-S 20-108-3495 (BR)
TEKNION LIMITED
TEKNION FURNITURE SYSTEMS, DIV OF
1150 Flint Rd, North York, ON, M3J 2J5
(416) 661-3370
Emp Here 150
SIC 2522 Office furniture, except wood

D-U-N-S 25-360-0019 (BR)
TEKNION LIMITED
STAMPTEK
555 Petrolia Rd Unit 3, North York, ON, M3J 2X8
(416) 663-5442
Emp Here 120
SIC 2522 Office furniture, except wood

D-U-N-S 24-362-4249 (BR)
TEKNION LIMITED
TEKWOOD
607 Canarctic Dr, North York, ON, M3J 2P9
(416) 665-7802
Emp Here 200
SIC 2522 Office furniture, except wood

D-U-N-S 24-463-8532 (HQ)
TEL-E CONNECT SYSTEMS LTD
CANADA PURE SPRING WATER, DIV OF
(Suby of Tel-e Connect Systems Ltd)
7 Kodiak Cres, North York, ON, M3J 3E5
(416) 635-1234
Emp Here 50   Emp Total 150
Sales 16,961,922
SIC 1731 Electrical work
Pr Pr David Tavares

D-U-N-S 25-853-0708 (BR)
TEL-E CONNECT SYSTEMS LTD
(Suby of Tel-e Connect Systems Ltd)
7 Kodiak Cres, North York, ON, M3J 3E5
(416) 635-1234
Emp Here 20
SIC 1731 Electrical work

D-U-N-S 20-591-1576 (BR)
TORONTO CATHOLIC DISTRICT SCHOOL BOARD
ST. WILFRID CATHOLIC SCHOOL
1685 Finch Ave W, North York, ON, M3J 2G8
(416) 393-5313
Emp Here 55
SIC 8211 Elementary and secondary schools

D-U-N-S 20-026-1191 (BR)
TORONTO CATHOLIC DISTRICT SCHOOL BOARD
JAMES CARDINAL MCGUIGAN CATHOLIC SCHOOL
1440 Finch Ave W, North York, ON, M3J 3G3
(416) 393-5527
Emp Here 100
SIC 8211 Elementary and secondary schools

D-U-N-S 20-711-3007 (BR)
TORONTO DISTRICT SCHOOL BOARD
DERRYDOWN PUBLIC SCHOOL
120 Derrydown Rd, North York, ON, M3J 1R7
(416) 395-2310
Emp Here 50
SIC 8211 Elementary and secondary schools

D-U-N-S 20-711-2959 (BR)
TORONTO DISTRICT SCHOOL BOARD
C W JEFFERYS CI
340 Sentinel Rd, North York, ON, M3J 1T9
(416) 395-3170
Emp Here 50
SIC 8211 Elementary and secondary schools

D-U-N-S 20-698-7260 (BR)
TORONTO DISTRICT SCHOOL BOARD
ELIA MIDDLE SCHOOL
215 Sentinel Rd, North York, ON, M3J 1T7
(416) 395-3020
Emp Here 45
SIC 8211 Elementary and secondary schools

D-U-N-S 25-793-8597 (BR)
TORONTO AND REGION CONSERVATION AUTHORITY
BLACK CREEK PIONEER VILLAGE
(Suby of Toronto and Region Conservation Authority)
1000 Murray Ross Pky, North York, ON, M3J 2P3
(416) 736-1740
Emp Here 120
SIC 8412 Museums and art galleries

D-U-N-S 24-205-1972 (SL)
TRANSATLANTIC INC
3875 Keele St Suite 401, North York, ON, M3J 1N6

Emp Here 28   Sales 8,318,900

SIC 4731 Freight transportation arrangement
Pr Pr Rafael Rakhmankulov
   Alexander Abramov
   Turgun Shakhabiddinov
   Fedor Ossinin

D-U-N-S 20-936-6574 (HQ)
VPC GROUP INC
ENGINEERED FOAM PRODUCTS CANADA, DIV
(Suby of VPC Group Inc)
150 Toro Rd, North York, ON, M3J 2A9
(416) 630-6633
Emp Here 128   Emp Total 284
Sales 12,403,319
SIC 2824 Organic fibers, noncellulosic
Pr Peter Farah
   Kevin Day

D-U-N-S 20-004-4936 (BR)
WENDY'S RESTAURANTS OF CANADA INC
WENDY'S
(Suby of The Wendy's Company)
1050 Finch Ave W, North York, ON, M3J 2E2

Emp Here 35
SIC 5812 Eating places

D-U-N-S 25-221-2618 (BR)
WINNERS MERCHANTS INTERNATIONAL L.P.
WINNERS
(Suby of The TJX Companies Inc)
81 Gerry Fitzgerald, North York, ON, M3J 3N4
(416) 665-7380
Emp Here 50
SIC 5651 Family clothing stores

D-U-N-S 20-861-2817 (BR)
YORK UNIVERSITY
COGNITIVE SCIENCE PROGRAM
4700 Keele St Rm 428, North York, ON, M3J 1P3
(416) 736-5113
Emp Here 20
SIC 8221 Colleges and universities

D-U-N-S 24-308-4550 (BR)
YORK UNIVERSITY
DEPARTMENT OF POLITICAL SCIENCE FACILITY OF ARTS
4700 Keele St S672 R, North York, ON, M3J 1P3
(416) 736-5265
Emp Here 55
SIC 8221 Colleges and universities

D-U-N-S 20-035-5118 (BR)
YORK UNIVERSITY
INSTITUTE FOR SOCIAL RESEARCH, DIV. OF
4700 Keele St Suite 5075, North York, ON, M3J 1P3
(416) 736-5061
Emp Here 120
SIC 8742 Management consulting services

D-U-N-S 25-059-3282 (BR)
YORK UNIVERSITY
YORK UNIVERSITY BOOKSTORE
4700 Keele St Suite 335, North York, ON, M3J 1P3
(416) 736-5024
Emp Here 50
SIC 5942 Book stores

North York, ON M3K
York County

D-U-N-S 24-383-4921 (SL)
2069718 ONTARIO LIMITED
BAYWOOD HOMES
1140 Sheppard Ave W Unit 13, North York, ON, M3K 2A2

(416) 633-7333
Emp Here 110   *Sales* 21,202,403
SIC 1521 Single-family housing construction
Pr Pr Frank Canonaco

D-U-N-S 24-023-3064   (SL)
BATISE INVESTMENTS LIMITED
3625 Dufferin St Suite 503, North York, ON,
M3K 1Z2
(416) 635-7520
Emp Here 120   *Sales* 51,435,840
SIC 6553 Cemetery subdividers and developers
Pr Pr Sandor Hofstader
  George Hofstader

D-U-N-S 20-973-9593   (BR)
BEST BUY CANADA LTD
BEST BUY
(*Suby of* Best Buy Co., Inc.)
695 Wilson Ave, North York, ON, M3K 1E3
(416) 635-6574
Emp Here 50
SIC 5731 Radio, television, and electronic stores

D-U-N-S 25-203-5027   (BR)
BOMBARDIER INC
BOMBARDIER AERONAUTIQUE
123 Garratt Blvd, North York, ON, M3K 1Y5
(416) 633-7310
Emp Here 5,000
SIC 3721 Aircraft

D-U-N-S 24-120-1214   (BR)
COSTCO WHOLESALE CANADA LTD
(*Suby of* Costco Wholesale Corporation)
100 Billy Bishop Way Suite 535, North York,
ON, M3K 2C8
(416) 635-8175
Emp Here 20
SIC 5399 Miscellaneous general merchandise

D-U-N-S 24-950-3046   (HQ)
FEDEX FREIGHT CANADA, CORP
(*Suby of* Fedex Corporation)
1011 Wilson Ave, North York, ON, M3K 1G1
(800) 463-3339
Emp Here 80   *Emp Total* 169,000
Sales 8,317,520
SIC 4212 Local trucking, without storage
Ch Bd Doug Duncan
Pr Pat Reed

D-U-N-S 24-709-3685   (HQ)
H&R PROPERTY MANAGEMENT LTD
(*Suby of* H&R Property Management Ltd)
3625 Dufferin St Suite 409, North York, ON,
M3K 1Z2
(416) 635-0163
Emp Here 60   *Emp Total* 100
Sales 9,411,930
SIC 6531 Real estate agents and managers
Pr Pr Robert Rubinstein
VP Fin Larry Froom

D-U-N-S 25-171-5595   (BR)
HOME DEPOT OF CANADA INC
(*Suby of* The Home Depot Inc)
90 Billy Bishop Way, North York, ON, M3K 2C8
(416) 373-6000
Emp Here 100
SIC 5251 Hardware stores

D-U-N-S 24-247-6781   (SL)
HOUSING SERVICES INC
HSI SOLUTIONS
35 Carl Hall Rd Suite 1, North York, ON, M3K
2B6
(416) 921-3625
Emp Here 300   *Sales* 25,362,500
SIC 8741 Management services
Ch Bd Antoinnette Tummillo
  Len Koroneos

D-U-N-S 20-272-9583   (BR)
LAFARGE CANADA INC
LAFARGE PAVING & CONSTRUCTION, DIV OF

949 Wilson Ave, North York, ON, M3K 1G2
(416) 635-6002
Emp Here 150
SIC 1611 Highway and street construction

D-U-N-S 24-228-5877   (BR)
LIQUOR CONTROL BOARD OF ONTARIO, THE
LCBO
675 Wilson Ave, North York, ON, M3K 1E3
(416) 636-5349
Emp Here 27
SIC 5921 Liquor stores

D-U-N-S 25-300-3073   (BR)
METRO ONTARIO INC
METRO
1090 Wilson Ave, North York, ON, M3K 1G6
(416) 635-0284
Emp Here 100
SIC 5411 Grocery stores

D-U-N-S 24-441-1695   (BR)
REDBERRY FRANCHISING CORP
BURGER KING
1077 Wilson Ave, North York, ON, M3K 1G7
(416) 638-2222
Emp Here 35
SIC 5812 Eating places

D-U-N-S 25-093-4572   (BR)
SGS CANADA INC
1140 Sheppard Ave W Suite 6, North York,
ON, M3K 2A2
(416) 633-9400
Emp Here 20
SIC 8748 Business consulting, nec

D-U-N-S 20-045-8032   (SL)
TESKEY CONSTRUCTION COMPANY LTD
20 Murray Rd, North York, ON, M3K 1T2
(416) 638-0340
Emp Here 60   *Sales* 4,377,642
SIC 1794 Excavation work

D-U-N-S 20-035-5167   (BR)
TORONTO DISTRICT SCHOOL BOARD
DOWNSVIEW SECONDARY SCHOOL
7 Hawksdale Rd, North York, ON, M3K 1W3
(416) 395-3200
Emp Here 75
SIC 8211 Elementary and secondary schools

D-U-N-S 20-057-6630   (SL)
TWO BLOOR RESIDENCES LIMITED
3625 Dufferin St Suite 500, North York, ON,
M3K 1Z2
(416) 635-7520
Emp Here 200   *Sales* 51,451,163
SIC 1522 Residential construction, nec
Pr Pr Mark Mandelbaum

D-U-N-S 24-074-9742   (BR)
VALUE VILLAGE STORES, INC
(*Suby of* Savers, Inc.)
1030 Wilson Ave, North York, ON, M3K 1G6
(416) 633-2623
Emp Here 30
SIC 5399 Miscellaneous general merchandise

North York, ON M3L
York County

D-U-N-S 20-536-5260   (BR)
BANK OF MONTREAL
BMO
1951 Sheppard Ave W, North York, ON, M3L
1Y8
(416) 743-0222
Emp Here 20
SIC 6021 National commercial banks

D-U-N-S 20-301-9927   (BR)
BANK OF MONTREAL
BMO
1700 Wilson Ave, North York, ON, M3L 1B2

(416) 247-6281
Emp Here 22
SIC 6021 National commercial banks

D-U-N-S 24-227-8906   (BR)
CANADIAN IMPERIAL BANK OF COMMERCE
CIBC #00922
1700 Wilson Ave, North York, ON, M3L 1B2
(416) 244-5632
Emp Here 20
SIC 6021 National commercial banks

D-U-N-S 25-198-9422   (BR)
SERVICE CORPORATION INTERNATIONAL (CANADA) LIMITED
DELMORO FUNERAL HOME
61 Beverly Hills Dr, North York, ON, M3L 1A2
(416) 249-4499
Emp Here 25
SIC 7261 Funeral service and crematories

D-U-N-S 20-035-5225   (BR)
TORONTO CATHOLIC DISTRICT SCHOOL BOARD
ST. JANE FRANCES ELEMENTARY SCHOOL
2745 Jane St, North York, ON, M3L 2E8
(416) 393-5296
Emp Here 34
SIC 8211 Elementary and secondary schools

D-U-N-S 24-231-8108   (BR)
TORONTO CATHOLIC DISTRICT SCHOOL BOARD
WEST FACILITIES SERVICES
18 Beverly Hills Dr, North York, ON, M3L 1A1
(416) 393-5100
Emp Here 40
SIC 8211 Elementary and secondary schools

D-U-N-S 20-647-4806   (BR)
TORONTO DISTRICT SCHOOL BOARD
CALICO PUBLIC SCHOOL
35 Calico Dr, North York, ON, M3L 1V5
(416) 395-2130
Emp Here 60
SIC 8211 Elementary and secondary schools

D-U-N-S 20-811-2289   (SL)
VIRK HOSPITALITY CORP
THE TORONTO PLAZA HOTEL
1677 Wilson Ave, North York, ON, M3L 1A5
(416) 249-8171
Emp Here 50   *Sales* 2,826,987
SIC 7011 Hotels and motels

D-U-N-S 20-184-3161   (BR)
WINNERS MERCHANTS INTERNATIONAL L.P.
WINNERS
(*Suby of* The TJX Companies Inc)
1700 Wilson Ave, North York, ON, M3L 1B2
(416) 235-0286
Emp Here 40
SIC 5651 Family clothing stores

North York, ON M3M
York County

D-U-N-S 25-651-1254   (BR)
BENEFIT PLAN ADMINISTRATORS LIMITED
(*Suby of* Benefit Plan Administrators Limited)
1263 Wilson Ave Suite 205, North York, ON,
M3M 3G2
(416) 240-7480
Emp Here 20
SIC 6321 Accident and health insurance

D-U-N-S 25-303-0357   (BR)
CANADIAN IMPERIAL BANK OF COMMERCE
CIBC
1098 Wilson Ave, North York, ON, M3M 1G7

(416) 633-9156
Emp Here 50
SIC 6021 National commercial banks

D-U-N-S 24-008-0564   (HQ)
HINCKS-DELLCREST TREATMENT CENTRE, THE
(*Suby of* Hincks-Dellcrest Treatment Centre,
The)
1645 Sheppard Ave W, North York, ON, M3M
2X4
(416) 633-0515
Emp Here 350   *Emp Total* 375
Sales 33,861,760
SIC 8093 Specialty outpatient clinics, nec
Ex Dir John S Speckkens
Fin Ex Lucy D'souza

D-U-N-S 20-593-2739   (BR)
METRO ONTARIO INC
METRO
2200 Jane St, North York, ON, M3M 1A4
(416) 241-5732
Emp Here 120
SIC 5411 Grocery stores

D-U-N-S 20-879-5286   (HQ)
OAKDALE GOLF AND COUNTRY CLUB, LIMITED,THE
(*Suby of* Oakdale Golf and Country Club, Limited,The)
2388 Jane St, North York, ON, M3M 1A8
(416) 245-3500
Emp Here 40   *Emp Total* 60
Sales 2,407,703
SIC 7997 Membership sports and recreation clubs

D-U-N-S 24-368-1587   (BR)
OAKDALE GOLF AND COUNTRY CLUB, LIMITED,THE
OAKDALE PRO SHOP
(*Suby of* Oakdale Golf and Country Club, Limited,The)
2388 Jane St, North York, ON, M3M 1A8
(416) 245-7361
Emp Here 20
SIC 5941 Sporting goods and bicycle shops

D-U-N-S 20-711-3015   (BR)
TORONTO DISTRICT SCHOOL BOARD
DOWNSVIEW PUBLIC SCHOOL
2829 Keele St, North York, ON, M3M 2G7
(416) 395-2340
Emp Here 50
SIC 8211 Elementary and secondary schools

D-U-N-S 20-025-3594   (BR)
TORONTO DISTRICT SCHOOL BOARD
PIERRE LAPORTE MIDDLE SCHOOL
1270 Wilson Ave, North York, ON, M3M 1H5
(416) 395-3070
Emp Here 35
SIC 8211 Elementary and secondary schools

D-U-N-S 20-700-2101   (BR)
TORONTO DISTRICT SCHOOL BOARD
SHEPPARD PUBLIC SCHOOL
1430 Sheppard Ave W, North York, ON, M3M
2W9
(416) 395-2860
Emp Here 40
SIC 8211 Elementary and secondary schools

D-U-N-S 25-265-2664   (BR)
TORONTO DISTRICT SCHOOL BOARD
BLAYDON PUBLIC SCHOOL
25 Blaydon Ave, North York, ON, M3M 2C9
(416) 395-2070
Emp Here 20
SIC 8211 Elementary and secondary schools

North York, ON M3N
York County

D-U-N-S 20-708-6765   (BR)

2063414 ONTARIO LIMITED
LEISURE WORLD CAREGIVING CENTRE NORFINCH
(*Suby of* 2063414 Ontario Limited)
22 Norfinch Dr, North York, ON, M3N 1X1
(416) 623-1120
Emp Here 150
SIC 8051 Skilled nursing care facilities

    D-U-N-S 20-227-8284   (SL)
B&M EMPLOYMENT INC
168 Oakdale Rd Unit 8, North York, ON, M3N 2S5
(416) 747-5359
Emp Here 50   *Sales* 3,648,035
SIC 7361 Employment agencies

    D-U-N-S 20-044-8611   (HQ)
BIC INC
BIC SPORT
155 Oakdale Rd, North York, ON, M3N 1W2
(416) 742-9173
Emp Here 87   *Emp Total* 2
Sales 14,323,401
SIC 5122 Drugs, proprietaries, and sundries
S&M/VP Kevin Murphy
Fin Ex Angelo Di Placido

    D-U-N-S 20-211-1522   (SL)
CANADIAN UNIFORM LIMITED
75 Norfinch Dr, North York, ON, M3N 1W8
(416) 252-9321
Emp Here 45   *Sales* 3,724,879
SIC 5699 Miscellaneous apparel and accessory stores

    D-U-N-S 25-143-2555   (BR)
CASA BELLA WINDOWS INC
124 Norfinch Dr, North York, ON, M3N 1X1
(416) 650-1033
Emp Here 80
SIC 2431 Millwork

    D-U-N-S 24-031-5858   (BR)
CHAMPION PRODUCTS CORP
350 Norfinch Dr, North York, ON, M3N 1Y4
(416) 749-4242
Emp Here 25
SIC 5087 Service establishment equipment

    D-U-N-S 24-247-3382   (BR)
CORPORATION OF THE CITY OF TORONTO
RECREATION
4401 Jane St, North York, ON, M3N 2K3
(416) 395-7944
Emp Here 48
SIC 8322 Individual and family services

    D-U-N-S 24-394-9794   (BR)
CROWN FOOD SERVICE EQUIPMENT LTD
320 Oakdale Rd, North York, ON, M3N 1W5
(416) 377-1500
Emp Here 40
SIC 3589 Service industry machinery, nec

    D-U-N-S 20-804-0134   (SL)
DEEPER LIFE BIBLE CHURCH
750 Oakdale Rd Suite 46, North York, ON, M3N 2Z4
(416) 740-7023
Emp Here 50   *Sales* 3,283,232
SIC 8661 Religious organizations

    D-U-N-S 24-886-7137   (HQ)
DRECHSEL INCORPORATED
DRECHSEL BUSINESS INTERIORS
(*Suby of* Drechsel Incorporated)
400 Oakdale Rd, North York, ON, M3N 1W5
(416) 740-7120
Emp Here 45   *Emp Total* 50
Sales 4,764,381
SIC 7359 Equipment rental and leasing, nec

    D-U-N-S 24-463-5025   (SL)
GARDWELL SECURITY AGENCY INC
168 Oakdale Rd Suite 6b, North York, ON, M3N 2S5

(416) 746-6007
Emp Here 65   *Sales* 2,042,900
SIC 7381 Detective and armored car services

    D-U-N-S 20-579-4147   (BR)
GOVERNMENT OF ONTARIO
PROBATION AND PAROLE FIELD OFFICES
2065 Finch Ave W, North York, ON, M3N 2V7
(416) 314-9531
Emp Here 24
SIC 8322 Individual and family services

    D-U-N-S 25-305-3201   (BR)
INNVEST PROPERTIES CORP
COMFORT INN TORONTO NORTH
(*Suby of* Innvest Properties Corp)
66 Norfinch Dr Suite 115, North York, ON, M3N 1X1
(416) 736-4700
Emp Here 25
SIC 7011 Hotels and motels

    D-U-N-S 24-371-2499   (SL)
J ANN J CLEANING SERVICES
64 Flax Garden Way, North York, ON, M3N 2H5
(647) 233-2029
Emp Here 50   *Sales* 1,459,214
SIC 7349 Building maintenance services, nec

    D-U-N-S 25-310-8849   (BR)
MCDONALD'S RESTAURANTS OF CANADA LIMITED
MCDONALD'S
(*Suby of* McDonald's Corporation)
1831 Finch Ave W Suite 56, North York, ON, M3N 2V2
(416) 636-7601
Emp Here 75
SIC 5812 Eating places

    D-U-N-S 20-191-2479   (SL)
OAKDALE KITCHENS INC
92 Oakdale Rd, North York, ON, M3N 1V9
(416) 741-1122
Emp Here 60   *Sales* 3,502,114
SIC 2434 Wood kitchen cabinets

    D-U-N-S 20-859-8909   (BR)
PACIFIC LINK COMMUNICATIONS INC
BELL WORLD
1 York Gate Blvd, North York, ON, M3N 3A1

Emp Here 25
SIC 5999 Miscellaneous retail stores, nec

    D-U-N-S 20-860-2412   (BR)
SOURCE (BELL) ELECTRONICS INC, THE
SOURCE, THE
1 York Gate Blvd Suite 109, North York, ON, M3N 3A1

Emp Here 25
SIC 5999 Miscellaneous retail stores, nec

    D-U-N-S 20-711-1654   (BR)
TORONTO CATHOLIC DISTRICT SCHOOL BOARD
MONSIGNOR FRASER COLLEGE - NORFINCH
45 Norfinch Dr, North York, ON, M3N 1W8
(416) 393-5558
Emp Here 30
SIC 8211 Elementary and secondary schools

    D-U-N-S 20-698-6916   (BR)
TORONTO CATHOLIC DISTRICT SCHOOL BOARD
ST. FRANCIS DE SALES SCHOOL
333 Firgrove Cres, North York, ON, M3N 1K9
(416) 393-5366
Emp Here 50
SIC 8211 Elementary and secondary schools

    D-U-N-S 25-237-7833   (BR)
TORONTO DISTRICT SCHOOL BOARD
FIRGROVE PUBLIC SCHOOL
270 Firgrove Cres, North York, ON, M3N 1K8

(416) 395-2420
Emp Here 65
SIC 8211 Elementary and secondary schools

    D-U-N-S 20-543-8026   (BR)
TORONTO DISTRICT SCHOOL BOARD
WESTVIEW CENTENNIAL SECONDARY SCHOOL
755 Oakdale Rd, North York, ON, M3N 1W7
(416) 395-3320
Emp Here 20
SIC 8211 Elementary and secondary schools

    D-U-N-S 20-591-5171   (BR)
TORONTO DISTRICT SCHOOL BOARD
YORKWOODS PUBLIC SCHOOL
25 Yorkwoods Gate, North York, ON, M3N 1K1
(416) 395-2990
Emp Here 40
SIC 8211 Elementary and secondary schools

    D-U-N-S 20-025-3552   (BR)
TORONTO DISTRICT SCHOOL BOARD
BROOKVIEW MIDDLE SCHOOL
4505 Jane St, North York, ON, M3N 2K7
(416) 395-2120
Emp Here 50
SIC 8211 Elementary and secondary schools

    D-U-N-S 20-025-0160   (BR)
TORONTO DISTRICT SCHOOL BOARD
STANLEY PUBLIC SCHOOL
75 Stanley Rd, North York, ON, M3N 1C2
(416) 395-2890
Emp Here 40
SIC 8211 Elementary and secondary schools

    D-U-N-S 20-025-3529   (BR)
TORONTO DISTRICT SCHOOL BOARD
TOPCLIFF ELEMENTARY SCHOOL
65 Topcliff Ave, North York, ON, M3N 1L6
(416) 395-2940
Emp Here 50
SIC 8211 Elementary and secondary schools

    D-U-N-S 20-624-9013   (HQ)
ULBRICH OF CANADA INC
DIVERSIFIED ULBRICH - TORONTO
(*Suby of* Ulbrich Stainless Steels & Special Metals, Inc.)
98 Norfinch Dr, North York, ON, M3N 1X1
(416) 663-7130
Emp Here 23   *Emp Total* 623
Sales 18,094,254
SIC 5051 Metals service centers and offices
Sec S Fay Sulley
  Barry S Arbus
Pr Frederick C Ulbrich LII
Sec Frederick C Ulbrich Jr
Treas John J Cei Jr

    D-U-N-S 24-174-8503   (BR)
WW HOTELS CORP
HOLIDAY INN EXPRESS
30 Norfinch Dr, North York, ON, M3N 1X1
(416) 665-3500
Emp Here 20
SIC 7011 Hotels and motels

North York, ON M4A
York County

    D-U-N-S 20-158-4323   (HQ)
AINSWORTH INC
NATIONAL REFRIGERATION HEATING
131 Bermondsey Rd, North York, ON, M4A 1X4
(416) 751-4420
Emp Here 130   *Emp Total* 13,000
Sales 77,962,590
SIC 1731 Electrical work
Pr Craig Stanford

    D-U-N-S 24-345-9117   (BR)
CONROS CORPORATION
(*Suby of* Navhein Holdings Ltd)

125 Bermondsey Rd, North York, ON, M4A 1X3
(416) 285-9222
Emp Here 30
SIC 2499 Wood products, nec

    D-U-N-S 20-706-2378   (BR)
CORPORATION OF THE CITY OF TORONTO
O'CONNOR COMMUNITY CENTER
1386 Victoria Park Ave, North York, ON, M4A 2L8
(416) 395-7957
Emp Here 40
SIC 8322 Individual and family services

    D-U-N-S 20-585-4123   (BR)
CORPORATION OF THE CITY OF TORONTO
SOLID WASTE MANAGEMENT OF CITY OF TORONTO
188 Bermondsey Rd, North York, ON, M4A 1Y1
(416) 392-3131
Emp Here 31
SIC 4212 Local trucking, without storage

    D-U-N-S 20-165-4654   (HQ)
FREEMAN FORMALWEAR LIMITED
(*Suby of* Freeman Formalwear Limited)
111 Bermondsey Rd, North York, ON, M4A 2T7
(416) 288-1222
Emp Here 90   *Emp Total* 130
Sales 4,304,681
SIC 7299 Miscellaneous personal service

    D-U-N-S 24-487-4368   (SL)
GRIFFIN HOUSE GRAPHICS LIMITED
35 Mobile Dr, North York, ON, M4A 2P6
(416) 596-8800
Emp Here 60   *Sales* 4,523,563
SIC 2752 Commercial printing, lithographic

    D-U-N-S 24-422-7484   (SL)
METROPOLITAN PREPARATORY ACADEMY INC
49 Mobile Dr, North York, ON, M4A 1H5
(416) 285-0870
Emp Here 50   *Sales* 3,356,192
SIC 8211 Elementary and secondary schools

    D-U-N-S 20-851-1881   (HQ)
ONTARIO SECONDARY SCHOOL TEACHERS' FEDERATION, THE
OSSTF
(*Suby of* Ontario Secondary School Teachers' Federation, The)
60 Mobile Dr Suite 100, North York, ON, M4A 2P3
(416) 751-8300
Emp Here 30   *Emp Total* 120
Sales 13,132,926
SIC 8621 Professional organizations
Sec Pierre Cote
Treas Earl Burt
  James Spray

    D-U-N-S 25-710-1329   (BR)
PARKWAY AUTOMOTIVE SALES LIMITED
PARKWAY LEASING
1681 Eglinton Ave E, North York, ON, M4A 1J6
(416) 752-1485
Emp Here 193
SIC 7515 Passenger car leasing

    D-U-N-S 20-717-0499   (HQ)
SHOPPERS HOME HEALTH CARE (ONTARIO) INC
104 Bartley Dr, North York, ON, M4A 1C5
(416) 752-8885
Emp Here 63   *Emp Total* 138,000
Sales 11,684,880
SIC 5999 Miscellaneous retail stores, nec
Genl Mgr Micheal Mores

    D-U-N-S 24-784-6470   (BR)
THOMSON REUTERS CANADA LIMITED

▲ Public Company   ■ Public Company Family Member   **HQ** Headquarters   **BR** Branch   **SL** Single Location

245 Bartley Dr, North York, ON, M4A 2V8
(416) 759-6707
Emp Here 30
SIC 2731 Book publishing

D-U-N-S 20-047-1121   (BR)
TORONTO DISTRICT SCHOOL BOARD
VICTORIA VILLAGE PUBLIC SCHOOL
88 Sweeney Dr, North York, ON, M4A 1T7
(416) 397-2930
Emp Here 35
SIC 8211 Elementary and secondary schools

D-U-N-S 20-698-8086   (BR)
TORONTO DISTRICT SCHOOL BOARD
O'CONNOR PUBLIC SCHOOL
1665 O'Connor Dr, North York, ON, M4A 1W5
(416) 397-2980
Emp Here 20
SIC 8211 Elementary and secondary schools

North York, ON M4N
York County

D-U-N-S 24-329-6865   (BR)
LOBLAWS INC
LOBLAWS
3501 Yonge St, North York, ON, M4N 2N5
(416) 481-8105
Emp Here 200
SIC 5411 Grocery stores

D-U-N-S 20-698-7732   (BR)
TORONTO DISTRICT SCHOOL BOARD
SUNNY VIEW PUBLIC SCHOOL
450 Blythwood Rd, North York, ON, M4N 1A9
(416) 393-9275
Emp Here 100
SIC 8211 Elementary and secondary schools

North York, ON M5M
York County

D-U-N-S 24-761-9294   (BR)
PUSATERI'S LIMITED
1539 Avenue Rd, North York, ON, M5M 3X4
(416) 785-9124
Emp Here 300
SIC 5411 Grocery stores

D-U-N-S 20-818-6858   (SL)
TEMPLE SINAI CONGREGATION OF TORONTO
210 Wilson Ave, North York, ON, M5M 3B1
(416) 487-4161
Emp Here 50   *Sales* 3,283,232
SIC 8661 Religious organizations

D-U-N-S 20-799-0412   (BR)
TORONTO CATHOLIC DISTRICT SCHOOL BOARD
ST. MARGARET CATHOLIC SCHOOL
85 Carmichael Ave, North York, ON, M5M 2X1
(416) 393-5249
Emp Here 25
SIC 8211 Elementary and secondary schools

D-U-N-S 20-656-2360   (BR)
TORONTO CATHOLIC DISTRICT SCHOOL BOARD
LORETTO ABBEY HIGHSCHOOL
101 Mason Blvd, North York, ON, M5M 3E2
(416) 393-5510
Emp Here 75
SIC 8211 Elementary and secondary schools

D-U-N-S 20-700-2622   (BR)
TORONTO DISTRICT SCHOOL BOARD
ARMOUR HEIGHTS PS
148 Wilson Ave, North York, ON, M5M 3A5
(416) 397-2950
Emp Here 30

SIC 8211 Elementary and secondary schools

D-U-N-S 20-809-8322   (SL)
TRAVEL DISCOUNTERS
2019 Avenue Rd, North York, ON, M5M 4A5
(416) 481-6701
Emp Here 50   *Sales* 2,626,585
SIC 7389 Business services, nec

North York, ON M5N
York County

D-U-N-S 24-078-3290   (SL)
SAM FIRESTONE CATERERS LIMITED
470 Glencairn Ave, North York, ON, M5N 1V8
(416) 782-8022
Emp Here 60   *Sales* 1,824,018
SIC 5812 Eating places

North York, ON M6A
York County

D-U-N-S 25-709-0787   (SL)
1056934 ONTARIO LTD
RINX, THE
65 Orfus Rd, North York, ON, M6A 1L7
(416) 410-7469
Emp Here 60   *Sales* 3,283,232
SIC 7999 Amusement and recreation, nec

D-U-N-S 24-938-1278   (SL)
1456882 ONTARIO LTD
MICHEL'S BAGUETTE
3401 Dufferin St, North York, ON, M6A 2T9
(416) 789-3533
Emp Here 50   *Sales* 1,678,096
SIC 5461 Retail bakeries

D-U-N-S 20-266-6103   (HQ)
3127885 CANADA INC
LIMITE
(*Suby of* Isaac Bennet Sales Agencies Inc)
111 Orfus Rd, North York, ON, M6A 1M4
(416) 785-1771
Emp Here 50   *Emp Total* 1
Sales 18,104,646
SIC 5621 Women's clothing stores
  Isaac Benitah

D-U-N-S 20-704-6629   (BR)
ARAMARK CANADA LTD.
750 Lawrence Ave W Suite 2623, North York, ON, M6A 1B8
(416) 784-7714
Emp Here 21
SIC 5962 Merchandising machine operators

D-U-N-S 24-991-6222   (HQ)
BENIX & CO. INC
BARNES & CASTLE
(*Suby of* Benix & Co. Inc)
98 Orfus Rd, North York, ON, M6A 1L9
(416) 784-0732
Emp Here 25   *Emp Total* 922
Sales 98,913,750
SIC 5719 Miscellaneous homefurnishings
Pr Pr Fred Benitah

D-U-N-S 24-386-8481   (HQ)
BODY SHOP CANADA LIMITED, THE
1 Yorkdale Rd Suite 510, North York, ON, M6A 3A1
(416) 782-2948
Emp Here 35   *Emp Total* 6,653
Sales 66,961,202
SIC 6794 Patent owners and lessors
  Andrea Goldner
  Jayme Jenkins
Dir Indra Chanicka

D-U-N-S 25-847-7397   (BR)
BOUTIQUE JACOB INC

(*Suby of* Boutique Jacob Inc)
3401 Dufferin St, North York, ON, M6A 2T9

Emp Here 35
SIC 5621 Women's clothing stores

D-U-N-S 20-754-2416   (BR)
CANSEW INC
28 Apex Rd, North York, ON, M6A 2V2
(416) 782-1124
Emp Here 20
SIC 5131 Piece goods and notions

D-U-N-S 20-070-3531   (BR)
CARA OPERATIONS LIMITED
SWISS CHALET
(*Suby of* Cara Holdings Limited)
950 Lawrence Ave W, North York, ON, M6A 1C4
(416) 783-8262
Emp Here 50
SIC 5812 Eating places

D-U-N-S 20-792-5665   (BR)
CARA OPERATIONS LIMITED
MILESTONE'S GRILL & BAR
(*Suby of* Cara Holdings Limited)
3401 Dufferin St Suite 17, North York, ON, M6A 2T9

Emp Here 20
SIC 5812 Eating places

D-U-N-S 20-161-7610   (HQ)
CENTURA (TORONTO) LIMITED
CENTURA FLOOR AND WALL FASHIONS
(*Suby of* Centura Limited)
53 Apex Rd, North York, ON, M6A 2V6
(416) 785-5165
Emp Here 100   *Emp Total* 400
Sales 83,394,080
SIC 5032 Brick, stone, and related material
Pr Pr Brian Cowie

D-U-N-S 25-052-3776   (BR)
CHAUSSURES BROWNS INC
BROWNS SHOE
(*Suby of* 90401 Canada Ltee)
3401 Dufferin St Suite 100, North York, ON, M6A 2T9
(416) 787-0313
Emp Here 25
SIC 5661 Shoe stores

D-U-N-S 24-351-4796   (BR)
CRYSTAL TILE & MARBLE LTD
CRYSTAL DISTRIBUTION
(*Suby of* Crystal Tile & Marble Ltd)
27 Dufflaw Rd, North York, ON, M6A 2W2
(416) 782-4380
Emp Here 50
SIC 5032 Brick, stone, and related material

D-U-N-S 20-655-7035   (BR)
DOLLARAMA S.E.C.
DOLLARAMA
20 Orfus Rd, North York, ON, M6A 1L6
(416) 782-1273
Emp Here 21
SIC 5331 Variety stores

D-U-N-S 25-319-7248   (BR)
DON MICHAEL HOLDINGS INC
ROOTS
3401 Dufferin St Suite 117, North York, ON, M6A 2T9
(416) 783-3371
Emp Here 20
SIC 5651 Family clothing stores

D-U-N-S 20-358-6248   (SL)
EUROPEAN & CO. INC
EUROPEAN JEWELLERY
1 Yorkdale Rd Unit 402, North York, ON, M6A 3A1
(416) 785-8801
Emp Here 55   *Sales* 4,961,328
SIC 5944 Jewelry stores

D-U-N-S 25-143-9717   (BR)
FITNESS ONE SPORTS CLUB FOR WOMEN INC
(*Suby of* Fitness One Sports Club for Women Inc)
700 Lawrence Ave W Suite 235, North York, ON, M6A 3B4

Emp Here 20
SIC 7999 Amusement and recreation, nec

D-U-N-S 25-172-1767   (SL)
FRAMEWORTH CUSTOM FRAMING INC
1198 Caledonia Rd Unit B, North York, ON, M6A 2W5
(416) 784-5292
Emp Here 75   *Sales* 4,523,563
SIC 7699 Repair services, nec

D-U-N-S 24-094-5431   (BR)
FRENCH CONNECTION (CANADA) LIMITED
(*Suby of* FRENCH CONNECTION GROUP PLC)
3401 Dufferin St Suite 132, North York, ON, M6A 2T9

Emp Here 25
SIC 7389 Business services, nec

D-U-N-S 25-118-1400   (BR)
GAP (CANADA) INC
BANANA REPUBLIC
(*Suby of* The Gap Inc)
3401 Dufferin St Suite 12d, North York, ON, M6A 2T9
(416) 782-0814
Emp Here 70
SIC 5651 Family clothing stores

D-U-N-S 25-687-1617   (BR)
GAP (CANADA) INC
GAPKIDS
(*Suby of* The Gap Inc)
3401 Dufferin St Suite 12, North York, ON, M6A 2T9
(416) 783-2995
Emp Here 34
SIC 5651 Family clothing stores

D-U-N-S 24-098-2728   (SL)
GIFFIN CONTRACTORS
133 Bridgeland Ave, North York, ON, M6A 1Y7
(416) 781-6166
Emp Here 50
SIC 3499 Fabricated Metal products, nec

D-U-N-S 25-747-2936   (BR)
GRANDE CHEESE COMPANY LIMITED
22 Orfus Rd, North York, ON, M6A 1L6
(416) 787-7670
Emp Here 25
SIC 5411 Grocery stores

D-U-N-S 25-309-4080   (BR)
GROUPE ALDO INC, LE
3401 Dufferin St Suite 114, North York, ON, M6A 2T9
(416) 783-9472
Emp Here 28
SIC 5661 Shoe stores

D-U-N-S 24-047-2118   (SL)
HANKOOK ILBO & THE KOREA TIMES LIMITED
HANKOOK ILBO KOREA DAILY TIMES
287 Bridgeland Ave, North York, ON, M6A 1Z6
(416) 787-1111
Emp Here 75   *Sales* 4,158,760
SIC 2711 Newspapers

D-U-N-S 20-553-8135   (BR)
HARRY ROSEN INC
HARRY ROSEN MENS WEAR
3401 Dufferin St Suite 37, North York, ON, M6A 2T9
(416) 787-4231
Emp Here 27

SIC 5611 Men's and boys' clothing stores

D-U-N-S 25-360-1330   (BR)
HUDSON'S BAY COMPANY
698 Lawrence Ave W, North York, ON, M6A 3A5
(416) 256-3200
Emp Here 50
SIC 5311 Department stores

D-U-N-S 25-301-1894   (BR)
HUDSON'S BAY COMPANY
BAY, THE
3401 Dufferin St, North York, ON, M6A 2T9
(416) 789-8011
Emp Here 100
SIC 5311 Department stores

D-U-N-S 25-082-5718   (BR)
INDIGO BOOKS & MUSIC INC
INDIGO
(*Suby of* Indigo Books & Music Inc)
3401 Dufferin St Suite 29, North York, ON, M6A 2T9
(416) 781-6660
Emp Here 60
SIC 5942 Book stores

D-U-N-S 20-533-2641   (SL)
KASHRUTH COUNCIL OF CANADA
3200 Dufferin St Suite 308, North York, ON, M6A 3B2
(416) 635-9550
Emp Here 65   *Sales* 4,815,406
SIC 8734 Testing laboratories

D-U-N-S 20-921-7173   (BR)
LONDON LIFE INSURANCE COMPANY
FREEDOM 55 FINANCIAL
970 Lawrence Ave W Suite 600, North York, ON, M6A 3B6
(416) 789-4527
Emp Here 75
SIC 6311 Life insurance

D-U-N-S 20-169-5525   (SL)
LOUIS INTERIORS INC
1283 Caledonia Rd, North York, ON, M6A 2X7
(416) 785-9909
Emp Here 48   *Sales* 5,110,881
SIC 2512 Upholstered household furniture

D-U-N-S 25-841-7203   (BR)
MAGASIN LAURA (P.V.) INC
MELANIE LYNE
3401 Dufferin St, North York, ON, M6A 2T9
(416) 256-9831
Emp Here 27
SIC 5621 Women's clothing stores

D-U-N-S 20-220-6137   (BR)
MAPLE LEAF FOODS INC
92 Cartwright Ave, North York, ON, M6A 1V2
(416) 633-0389
Emp Here 30
SIC 5147 Meats and meat products

D-U-N-S 25-500-8609   (HQ)
MEDALLION PROPERTIES INC
970 Lawrence Ave W Suite 304, North York, ON, M6A 3B6
(416) 256-3900
Emp Here 65   *Emp Total* 80
Sales 8,575,885
SIC 6531 Real estate agents and managers
Pr Pr Abraham Bleeman
VP VP Nathan Bleeman
VP VP Aaron Bleeman

D-U-N-S 20-552-8479   (BR)
METRO ONTARIO INC
METRO
3090 Bathurst St, North York, ON, M6A 2A1
(416) 783-1227
Emp Here 300
SIC 5411 Grocery stores

D-U-N-S 25-662-3562   (SL)
MONTAGE   SUPPORT   SERVICES   OF

METROPOLITAN TORONTO
700 Lawrence Ave W Suite 325, North York, ON, M6A 3B4
(416) 780-9630
Emp Here 135   *Sales* 4,961,328
SIC 8361 Residential care

D-U-N-S 24-170-1486   (BR)
PACE INDEPENDENT LIVING
3270 Bathurst St Suite 715, North York, ON, M6A 3A8
(416) 785-9904
Emp Here 20
SIC 8399 Social services, nec

D-U-N-S 20-859-8883   (BR)
PACIFIC LINK COMMUNICATIONS INC
BELL WORLD
3401 Dufferin St, North York, ON, M6A 2T9

Emp Here 25
SIC 5999 Miscellaneous retail stores, nec

D-U-N-S 25-099-8200   (HQ)
RANDY RIVER INC
(*Suby of* Isaac Bennet Sales Agencies Inc)
107a Orfus Rd, North York, ON, M6A 1M4
(416) 785-1771
Emp Here 20   *Emp Total* 1
Sales 26,160,780
SIC 5611 Men's and boys' clothing stores
Pr Pr Isaac Benitah
   Michael Goldgrub

D-U-N-S 25-711-6921   (BR)
RED LOBSTER HOSPITALITY LLC
RED LOBSTER RESTAURANTS
(*Suby of* Red Lobster Seafood Co., LLC)
3200 Dufferin St, North York, ON, M6A 3B2
(416) 785-7930
Emp Here 200
SIC 5812 Eating places

D-U-N-S 25-300-4709   (BR)
REDBERRY FRANCHISING CORP
BURGER KING
940 Lawrence Ave W Suite 709, North York, ON, M6A 1C4
(416) 256-9439
Emp Here 35
SIC 5812 Eating places

D-U-N-S 20-707-9612   (BR)
REVERA INC
3705 Bathurst St, North York, ON, M6A 2E8
(416) 789-7670
Emp Here 50
SIC 6513 Apartment building operators

D-U-N-S 20-012-1825   (HQ)
RIOCAN PROPERTY SERVICES INC
700 Lawrence Ave W Suite 315, North York, ON, M6A 3B4
(416) 256-0256
Emp Here 50   *Emp Total* 669
Sales 60,874,453
SIC 6531 Real estate agents and managers
Pr Pr Edward Sonshine
VP Opers Frederic Waks
   Robert Wolf

D-U-N-S 25-311-1892   (BR)
SEARS CANADA INC
SEARS
3401 Dufferin St Suite 1, North York, ON, M6A 2T9

Emp Here 300
SIC 5311 Department stores

D-U-N-S 20-860-2396   (BR)
SOURCE (BELL) ELECTRONICS INC, THE
SOURCE, THE
700 Lawrence Ave W Suite 120, North York, ON, M6A 3B4
(416) 256-7282
Emp Here 25
SIC 5999 Miscellaneous retail stores, nec

D-U-N-S 20-860-3220   (BR)
SOURCE (BELL) ELECTRONICS INC, THE
SOURCE, THE
526 Lawrence Ave W, North York, ON, M6A 1A1
(416) 782-6379
Emp Here 25
SIC 5999 Miscellaneous retail stores, nec

D-U-N-S 25-213-7500   (BR)
STAPLES CANADA INC
STAPLES THE BUSINESS DEPOT
(*Suby of* Staples, Inc.)
3150 Dufferin St, North York, ON, M6A 2T1
(416) 785-5335
Emp Here 40
SIC 5943 Stationery stores

D-U-N-S 24-324-7272   (BR)
STEPHENSON'S RENTAL SERVICES INC
278 Bridgeland Ave, North York, ON, M6A 1Z4
(416) 781-5244
Emp Here 50
SIC 7359 Equipment rental and leasing, nec

D-U-N-S 25-119-4692   (SL)
STERLING HALL SCHOOL, THE
99 Cartwright Ave, North York, ON, M6A 1V4
(416) 785-3410
Emp Here 55   *Sales* 3,648,035
SIC 8211 Elementary and secondary schools

D-U-N-S 24-097-3719   (SL)
TAUB, BERNARD & COMPANY
1167 Caledonia Rd, North York, ON, M6A 2X1
(416) 785-5353
Emp Here 75   *Sales* 3,283,232
SIC 8721 Accounting, auditing, and book-keeping

D-U-N-S 25-107-7541   (BR)
TORONTO DISTRICT SCHOOL BOARD
YORKDALE ADULT LEARNING CENTRE & SECONDARY SCHOOL
38 Orfus Rd, North York, ON, M6A 1L6
(416) 395-3350
Emp Here 75
SIC 8211 Elementary and secondary schools

D-U-N-S 20-038-4399   (BR)
TORONTO DISTRICT SCHOOL BOARD
VISION PROGRAM
38 Orfus Rd Rm 158, North York, ON, M6A 1L6
(416) 395-2145
Emp Here 26
SIC 8361 Residential care

D-U-N-S 20-698-7666   (BR)
TORONTO DISTRICT SCHOOL BOARD
FLEMINGTON PUBLIC SCHOOL
10 Flemington Rd, North York, ON, M6A 2N4
(416) 395-2430
Emp Here 50
SIC 8211 Elementary and secondary schools

D-U-N-S 25-265-2748   (BR)
TORONTO DISTRICT SCHOOL BOARD
BAYCREST PUBLIC SCHOOL
145 Baycrest Ave, North York, ON, M6A 1W4
(416) 395-2040
Emp Here 22
SIC 8211 Elementary and secondary schools

D-U-N-S 20-346-7006   (BR)
TORONTO DISTRICT SCHOOL BOARD
JOHN POLANYI COLLEGIATE INSTITUTE
640 Lawrence Ave W, North York, ON, M6A 1B1
(416) 395-3303
Emp Here 80
SIC 8211 Elementary and secondary schools

D-U-N-S 24-098-2897   (BR)
TORONTO PUBLIC LIBRARY BOARD
BARBARA FRUM BRANCH
20 Covington Rd, North York, ON, M6A 3C1
(416) 395-5440
Emp Here 26

SIC 8231 Libraries

D-U-N-S 25-684-5108   (BR)
TORONTO-DOMINION BANK, THE
TD CANADA TRUST
(*Suby of* Toronto-Dominion Bank, The)
3401 Dufferin St, North York, ON, M6A 2T9

Emp Here 25
SIC 6021 National commercial banks

D-U-N-S 20-860-5290   (BR)
TOWN SHOES LIMITED
SHOE COMPANY, THE
3110 Bathurst St Unit 7b, North York, ON, M6A 2A1
(416) 787-5136
Emp Here 25
SIC 5661 Shoe stores

D-U-N-S 20-191-7940   (BR)
TRADER CORPORATION
970 Lawrence Ave W Suite 500, North York, ON, M6A 3B6
(416) 784-5494
Emp Here 30
SIC 2721 Periodicals

D-U-N-S 24-360-6089   (BR)
TYCO SAFETY PRODUCTS CANADA LTD
DSC
95 Bridgeland Ave, North York, ON, M6A 1Y7
(905) 760-3000
Emp Here 600
SIC 3699 Electrical equipment and supplies, nec

D-U-N-S 24-862-1542   (SL)
U.B. RESTAURANT INC
UNITED BAKERS DAIRY RESTAURANT
506 Lawrence Ave W, North York, ON, M6A 1A1
(416) 789-0519
Emp Here 60   *Sales* 1,824,018
SIC 5812 Eating places

D-U-N-S 24-094-8617   (BR)
VENTE AU DETAIL PARASUCO INC
PARASUCO JEANS
3401 Dufferin St Unit 321, North York, ON, M6A 2T9

Emp Here 20
SIC 5651 Family clothing stores

D-U-N-S 20-153-0586   (BR)
WENDY'S RESTAURANTS OF CANADA INC
WENDY S
(*Suby of* The Wendy's Company)
1002 Lawrence Ave W, North York, ON, M6A 1C8
(416) 783-2574
Emp Here 39
SIC 5812 Eating places

D-U-N-S 20-982-4580   (BR)
WESTERN INVENTORY SERVICE LTD
192 Bridgeland Ave, North York, ON, M6A 1Z4
(416) 781-5563
Emp Here 30
SIC 7389 Business services, nec

D-U-N-S 24-779-0538   (BR)
WINNERS   MERCHANTS   INTERNATIONAL L.P.
WINNERS
(*Suby of* The TJX Companies Inc)
3090 Bathurst St Suite 1, North York, ON, M6A 2A1
(416) 782-4469
Emp Here 110
SIC 5651 Family clothing stores

D-U-N-S 25-054-7106   (BR)
YM INC. (SALES)
SIRENS
3401 Dufferin St Suite 104, North York, ON, M6A 2T9

(416) 789-7819
Emp Here 20
SIC 5621 Women's clothing stores

D-U-N-S 20-048-6236   (BR)
YORKDALE CAFE LTD
TIM HORTONS
1 Yorkdale Rd Suite 1574, North York, ON,
M6A 3A1
(416) 787-6268
Emp Here 25
SIC 5812 Eating places

D-U-N-S 25-282-6748   (SL)
ZEIFMANS LLP
201 Bridgeland Ave Suite 1, North York, ON,
M6A 1Y7
(416) 256-4000
Emp Here 85   *Sales* 4,805,878
SIC 8721 Accounting, auditing, and book-
keeping

North York, ON M6B
York County

D-U-N-S 20-572-0365   (BR)
BANK OF MONTREAL
BMO
2953 Bathurst St, North York, ON, M6B 3B2
(416) 789-7915
Emp Here 20
SIC 6021 National commercial banks

D-U-N-S 25-921-6703   (SL)
CHD MAINTENANCE LIMITED
274 Viewmount Ave, North York, ON, M6B
1V2
(416) 782-5071
Emp Here 100   *Sales* 2,918,428
SIC 7349 Building maintenance services, nec

D-U-N-S 20-965-4719   (BR)
**CANADIAN IMPERIAL BANK OF COM-
MERCE**
CIBC
2866 Dufferin St, North York, ON, M6B 3S6
(416) 781-5610
Emp Here 23
SIC 6021 National commercial banks

D-U-N-S 20-041-1333   (BR)
**CORPORATION OF THE CITY OF
TORONTO**
COMMUNITY CENTRE
35 Glen Long Ave, North York, ON, M6B 2M1
(416) 395-7961
Emp Here 25
SIC 7999 Amusement and recreation, nec

D-U-N-S 25-370-3201   (BR)
DARE FOODS LIMITED
143 Tycos Dr, North York, ON, M6B 1W6
(416) 787-0253
Emp Here 60
SIC 2064 Candy and other confectionery
products

D-U-N-S 25-926-6203   (BR)
DON MICHAEL HOLDINGS INC
ROOTS
75 Tycos Dr, North York, ON, M6B 1W3
(416) 781-7540
Emp Here 100
SIC 5651 Family clothing stores

D-U-N-S 20-004-0686   (BR)
HOME DEPOT OF CANADA INC
HOME DEPOT
(*Suby of* The Home Depot Inc)
825 Caledonia Rd, North York, ON, M6B 3X8
(416) 780-4730
Emp Here 150
SIC 5251 Hardware stores

D-U-N-S 25-185-5631   (BR)
JEWISH FAMILY AND CHILD SERVICE OF

GREATER TORONTO
EITZ CHAIM SCHOOL
1 Viewmount Ave, North York, ON, M6B 1T2
(416) 789-4366
Emp Here 50
SIC 8211 Elementary and secondary schools

D-U-N-S 20-172-8896   (SL)
PERL'S MEAT PRODUCTS LIMITED
3015 Bathurst St, North York, ON, M6B 3B5
(416) 787-4234
Emp Here 57   *Sales* 5,545,013
SIC 5421 Meat and fish markets
Pr Pr Herman Perl
VP VP Brian Perl
Elliot Perl

D-U-N-S 24-364-8271   (HQ)
PITTSBURGH GLASS WORKS, ULC
PGW CANADA
834 Caledonia Rd, North York, ON, M6B 3X9
(888) 774-2886
Emp Here 45   *Emp Total* 10,744
Sales 66,102,394
SIC 3714 Motor vehicle parts and accessories
Pr Christoper Lacovara

D-U-N-S 24-095-4552   (HQ)
PRISMATIQUE DESIGNS LTD
97 Wingold Ave, North York, ON, M6B 1P8
(416) 787-6182
Emp Here 46   *Emp Total* 51
Sales 3,429,153
SIC 2521 Wood office furniture

D-U-N-S 25-173-9009   (SL)
RADICAL DESIGN LTD
2888 Bathurst St Suite 123, North York, ON,
M6B 4H6
(416) 787-1350
Emp Here 75   *Sales* 3,769,316
SIC 2329 Men's and boy's clothing, nec

D-U-N-S 20-922-6401   (SL)
RE/MAX REALTRON REALTY INC
2815 Bathurst St, North York, ON, M6B 3A4
(416) 782-8882
Emp Here 50   *Sales* 4,742,446
SIC 6531 Real estate agents and managers

D-U-N-S 25-019-0444   (BR)
ROYAL BANK OF CANADA
RBC
(*Suby of* Royal Bank Of Canada)
2765 Dufferin St, North York, ON, M6B 3R6
(416) 789-7637
Emp Here 25
SIC 6021 National commercial banks

D-U-N-S 24-551-1183   (SL)
STUDLEY CANADA LIMITED
(*Suby of* Studley Products, Inc)
900a Caledonia Rd, North York, ON, M6B 3Y1
(416) 787-1441
Emp Here 20   *Sales* 2,407,703
SIC 5087 Service establishment equipment

D-U-N-S 20-067-8782   (BR)
TLS FASHIONS INC
ORIGINAL LEVI'S STORE, THE
2782a Dufferin St, North York, ON, M6B 3R7
(416) 293-4044
Emp Here 29
SIC 5651 Family clothing stores

D-U-N-S 20-698-6684   (BR)
**TORONTO CATHOLIC DISTRICT SCHOOL
BOARD**
DANTE ALIGHIERI ACADEMY SCHOOL
60 Playfair Ave, North York, ON, M6B 2P9
(416) 393-5522
Emp Here 50
SIC 8211 Elementary and secondary schools

D-U-N-S 20-711-1159   (BR)
**TORONTO CATHOLIC DISTRICT SCHOOL
BOARD**
ST. CHARLES CATHOLIC SCHOOL

---

50 Claver Ave, North York, ON, M6B 2W1
(416) 393-5250
Emp Here 50
SIC 8211 Elementary and secondary schools

D-U-N-S 20-026-4310   (BR)
**TORONTO CATHOLIC DISTRICT SCHOOL
BOARD**
REGINA MUNDI CATHOLIC SCHOOL
70 Playfair Ave, North York, ON, M6B 2P9
(416) 393-5362
Emp Here 35
SIC 8211 Elementary and secondary schools

D-U-N-S 20-025-0087   (BR)
TORONTO DISTRICT SCHOOL BOARD
JOYCE PUBLIC SCHOOL
26 Joyce Pky, North York, ON, M6B 2S9
(416) 395-2600
Emp Here 25
SIC 8211 Elementary and secondary schools

D-U-N-S 25-321-1544   (BR)
TORONTO-DOMINION BANK, THE
TD BANK
(*Suby of* Toronto-Dominion Bank, The)
2793 Bathurst St, North York, ON, M6B 3A4
(416) 781-6131
Emp Here 20
SIC 6021 National commercial banks

North York, ON M6L
York County

D-U-N-S 25-016-8044   (BR)
**CANADIAN IMPERIAL BANK OF COM-
MERCE**
CIBC
1400 Lawrence Ave W, North York, ON, M6L
1A7
(416) 235-2387
Emp Here 40
SIC 6021 National commercial banks

D-U-N-S 20-081-3462   (BR)
**CORPORATION OF THE CITY OF
TORONTO**
FALSTAFF CHILD CARE CENTRE
10 Falstaff Ave, North York, ON, M6L 2C7
(416) 392-5688
Emp Here 20
SIC 8351 Child day care services

D-U-N-S 20-655-8822   (BR)
**CORPORATION OF THE CITY OF
TORONTO**
FALSTAFF COMMUNITY CENTRE
50 Falstaff Ave, North York, ON, M6L 2C7
(416) 395-7924
Emp Here 40
SIC 7999 Amusement and recreation, nec

D-U-N-S 20-982-2261   (SL)
NORTH PARK NURSING HOME LIMITED
450 Rustic Rd, North York, ON, M6L 1W9
(416) 247-0531
Emp Here 80   *Sales* 3,648,035
SIC 8051 Skilled nursing care facilities

D-U-N-S 25-805-3404   (BR)
PRISZM LP
PIZZA HUT
1635 Lawrence Ave W Suite 13, North York,
ON, M6L 3C9
(416) 241-6006
Emp Here 25
SIC 5812 Eating places

D-U-N-S 20-711-1209   (BR)
**TORONTO CATHOLIC DISTRICT SCHOOL
BOARD**
ST. FRANCIS XAVIER CATHOLIC SCHOOL
53 Gracefield Ave, North York, ON, M6L 1L3
(416) 393-5271
Emp Here 50

SIC 8211 Elementary and secondary schools

D-U-N-S 20-698-6676   (BR)
**TORONTO CATHOLIC DISTRICT SCHOOL
BOARD**
CHAMINADE COLLEGE SCHOOL
490 Queens Dr, North York, ON, M6L 1M8
(416) 393-5509
Emp Here 70
SIC 8211 Elementary and secondary schools

D-U-N-S 24-677-1294   (BR)
TORONTO DISTRICT SCHOOL BOARD
GRACEFIELD PUBLIC SCHOOL
177 Gracefield Ave, North York, ON, M6L 1L7
(416) 395-2490
Emp Here 40
SIC 8211 Elementary and secondary schools

D-U-N-S 20-700-2580   (BR)
TORONTO DISTRICT SCHOOL BOARD
AMESBURY MIDDLE SCHOOL
201 Gracefield Ave, North York, ON, M6L 1L7
(416) 395-2000
Emp Here 20
SIC 8211 Elementary and secondary schools

D-U-N-S 20-079-2807   (BR)
TORONTO DISTRICT SCHOOL BOARD
*NELSON A BOYLEN COLLEGIATE INSTI-
TUTE*
155 Falstaff Ave, North York, ON, M6L 2E5
(416) 395-3270
Emp Here 50
SIC 8211 Elementary and secondary schools

North York, ON M6M
York County

D-U-N-S 25-967-8170   (BR)
ACE BAKERY LIMITED
1 Hafis Rd, North York, ON, M6M 2V6
(416) 241-3600
Emp Here 20
SIC 5461 Retail bakeries

D-U-N-S 20-169-8313   (SL)
MAC MOR OF CANADA LTD
21 Benton Rd, North York, ON, M6M 3G2
(416) 596-8237
Emp Here 120   *Sales* 4,742,446
SIC 2329 Men's and boy's clothing, nec

D-U-N-S 24-964-4584   (SL)
MELLOW WALK FOOTWEAR INC
17 Milford Ave, North York, ON, M6M 2W1
(416) 241-1312
Emp Here 53   *Sales* 948,489
SIC 3143 Men's footwear, except athletic

D-U-N-S 24-977-9943   (SL)
ST. JOSEPH PRINTING LIMITED
ST JOSEPH PI MEDIA
15 Benton Rd, North York, ON, M6M 3G2
(416) 248-4868
Emp Here 300
SIC 2752 Commercial printing, lithographic

D-U-N-S 24-451-2070   (BR)
**TORONTO CATHOLIC DISTRICT SCHOOL
BOARD**
*IMMACULATE CONCEPTION SEPARATE
SCHOOL*
23 Comay Rd, North York, ON, M6M 2K9
(416) 393-5281
Emp Here 25
SIC 8211 Elementary and secondary schools

D-U-N-S 20-711-3056   (BR)
TORONTO DISTRICT SCHOOL BOARD
GEORGE ANDERSON PUBLIC SCHOOL
30 George Anderson Dr, North York, ON, M6M
2Y8
(416) 395-5000
Emp Here 20

SIC 8211 Elementary and secondary schools

North York, ON M9L
York County

D-U-N-S 25-332-9742   (SL)
1100378 ONTARIO LIMITED
WILSON WINDINGS, DIV OF
805 Fenmar Dr, North York, ON, M9L 1C8
(416) 746-7704
Emp Here 50   *Sales* 4,596,524
SIC 3694 Engine electrical equipment

D-U-N-S 24-025-0852   (BR)
3225537 NOVA SCOTIA LIMITED
WILSON AUTO ELECTRIC
805 Fenmar Dr, North York, ON, M9L 1C8

Emp Here 42
SIC 3694 Engine electrical equipment

D-U-N-S 25-824-9614   (SL)
933796 ONTARIO INC
CARMEN CARTAGE
3700 Weston Rd, North York, ON, M9L 2Z4
(416) 667-9700
Emp Here 50   *Sales* 3,939,878
SIC 4212 Local trucking, without storage

D-U-N-S 25-664-8767   (SL)
A Z BUS TOURS INC
(*Suby of* Tai Pan Vacations Inc)
3666 Weston Rd, North York, ON, M9L 1W2
(416) 748-8828
Emp Here 70   *Sales* 3,283,232
SIC 4142 Bus charter service, except local

D-U-N-S 24-421-5893   (HQ)
ABC GROUP INC
(*Suby of* Cerberus Capital Management, L.P.)
2 Norelco Dr, North York, ON, M9L 2X6
(416) 246-1782
Emp Here 150   *Emp Total* 143,502
Sales 1,124,981,033
SIC 3089 Plastics products, nec
CEO Mary Anne Bueschkens
Pr Derrick Phelps
Ex VP Mark Poynton
Ex VP Robert Kunihiro
VP Timothy Schmidt

D-U-N-S 24-621-7376   (SL)
ABC GROUP RESEARCH & DEVELOPMENT LTD
2 Norelco Dr, North York, ON, M9L 2X6
(416) 742-4037
Emp Here 55   *Sales* 3,551,629
SIC 8731 Commercial physical research

D-U-N-S 25-117-4330   (BR)
AIR LIQUIDE CANADA INC
CAMCARB COMPRESSED GASES
155 Signet Dr, North York, ON, M9L 1V1
(416) 745-1304
Emp Here 27
SIC 2813 Industrial gases

D-U-N-S 24-360-2021   (BR)
ANIXTER POWER SOLUTIONS CANADA INC
SESCO
601 Ormont Dr, North York, ON, M9L 2W6
(416) 745-9292
Emp Here 60
SIC 5085 Industrial supplies

D-U-N-S 20-187-8407   (SL)
ANKOR ENGINEERING SYSTEMS LTD
32 Penn Dr, North York, ON, M9L 2A9
(416) 740-5671
Emp Here 50   *Sales* 5,401,673
SIC 8748 Business consulting, nec
Pr Pr Jozef Budziak

D-U-N-S 24-310-3699   (BR)

APOTEX INC
APOBIOLOGIX
200 Barmac Dr, North York, ON, M9L 2Z7
(800) 268-4623
Emp Here 4,000
SIC 2834 Pharmaceutical preparations

D-U-N-S 20-320-1673   (BR)
APOTEX INC
285 Garyray Dr, North York, ON, M9L 1P2
(416) 749-9300
Emp Here 500
SIC 2834 Pharmaceutical preparations

D-U-N-S 24-117-0013   (BR)
BANK OF NOVA SCOTIA, THE
SCOTIABANK
2 Toryork Dr, North York, ON, M9L 1X6
(416) 749-4900
Emp Here 20
SIC 6021 National commercial banks

D-U-N-S 24-796-3317   (BR)
COCA-COLA REFRESHMENTS CANADA COMPANY
(*Suby of* The Coca-Cola Company)
24 Fenmar Dr, North York, ON, M9L 1L8
(416) 749-0440
Emp Here 130
SIC 2086 Bottled and canned soft drinks

D-U-N-S 24-329-6717   (BR)
DIRECT ENERGY MARKETING LIMITED
ELECTRON CANADA
30 High Meadow Pl, North York, ON, M9L 2Z5
(416) 780-2800
Emp Here 20
SIC 1731 Electrical work

D-U-N-S 25-077-2852   (BR)
DOVERCO INC
5783 Steeles Ave W, North York, ON, M9L 2W3

Emp Here 20
SIC 5113 Industrial and personal service paper

D-U-N-S 24-737-1417   (BR)
FGF BRANDS INC
1295 Ormont Dr, North York, ON, M9L 2W6
(416) 742-7434
Emp Here 80
SIC 5149 Groceries and related products, nec

D-U-N-S 24-679-4056   (HQ)
FOOT LOCKER CANADA CO
230 Barmac Dr, North York, ON, M9L 2Z3
(416) 748-4210
Emp Here 40   *Emp Total* 50,168
Sales 183,277,278
SIC 5661 Shoe stores
  Ken C. Hicks
  Giovanna Cipriano
  Paulette Alviti
  Jeffrey L. Berk
  John A. Maurer
  Phillip Reiprich
  Lauren B. Peters
  Robert W. Mchugh
  Jeremy Nowak
VP VP Patricia A. Peck

D-U-N-S 20-518-0557   (SL)
G III LTD
150 Klondike Dr, North York, ON, M9L 1X3
(416) 747-7769
Emp Here 35   *Sales* 7,405,850
SIC 3069 Fabricated rubber products, nec
  Herb Singer
  Sol Kanee
Dir Abe M Globerman
Dir Norman Humby
Recvr Bryan Adam Gelman

D-U-N-S 20-647-0296   (SL)
GIB-SAN POOLS LIMITED
59 Milvan Dr, North York, ON, M9L 1Y8

---

(416) 749-4361
Emp Here 50   *Sales* 4,377,642
SIC 1799 Special trade contractors, nec

D-U-N-S 20-182-3796   (SL)
INGOT METAL COMPANY LIMITED
111 Fenmar Dr, North York, ON, M9L 1M3
(416) 749-1372
Emp Here 50   *Sales* 24,149,992
SIC 3341 Secondary nonferrous Metals
Pr Pr Mendel Shore
  Ivan Betcherman
Treas Hy Shore
Dir David Shore

D-U-N-S 25-203-5787   (BR)
LEE VALLEY TOOLS LTD
5701 Steeles Ave W, North York, ON, M9L 1S7
(416) 746-0850
Emp Here 30
SIC 5084 Industrial machinery and equipment

D-U-N-S 25-496-5585   (SL)
LINKS CONTRACT FURNITURE INC
131 Ormont Dr, North York, ON, M9L 2S3
(416) 745-8910
Emp Here 51   *Sales* 3,429,153
SIC 2521 Wood office furniture

D-U-N-S 24-555-8234   (SL)
P & P PROJECTS INC
233 Signet Dr Suite 1, North York, ON, M9L 1V3
(416) 398-6197
Emp Here 60   *Sales* 3,064,349
SIC 7389 Business services, nec

D-U-N-S 20-015-1160   (BR)
PHILIPS ELECTRONICS LTD
SAECO
5171 Steeles Ave W, North York, ON, M9L 1R5

Emp Here 20
SIC 5046 Commercial equipment, nec

D-U-N-S 25-107-9539   (SL)
PRECISION COMMUNICATION SERVICES CORP
TELMAR NETWORK TECHNOLOGY
99 Signet Dr Unit 200, North York, ON, M9L 1T6
(416) 749-0110
Emp Here 70   *Sales* 8,317,520
SIC 8748 Business consulting, nec
Pr Hartmut Liebel
Dir Arthur Smid

D-U-N-S 24-141-5004   (SL)
RENBALDO HOLDINGS INC
5395 Steeles Ave W, North York, ON, M9L 1R6
(416) 749-9522
Emp Here 30   *Sales* 8,038,400
SIC 5521 Used car dealers
Pr Renzo Moser

D-U-N-S 24-390-0656   (BR)
RICHARDS PACKAGING INC
REXPLAS
500 Barmac Dr Unit 1, North York, ON, M9L 2X8
(416) 745-6643
Emp Here 44
SIC 2821 Plastics materials and resins

D-U-N-S 24-244-9663   (BR)
SATIN FINISH HARDWOOD FLOORING, LIMITED
15 Fenmar Dr, North York, ON, M9L 1L4
(416) 747-9924
Emp Here 130
SIC 2426 Hardwood dimension and flooring mills

D-U-N-S 24-816-1648   (SL)
SIGNET DEVELOPMENT CORPORATION
150 Signet Dr, North York, ON, M9L 1T9
(416) 749-9300
Emp Here 1,700   *Sales* 728,150,880

SIC 6553 Cemetery subdividers and developers
Pr Pr Bernard Sherman
Acct Mgr Katrin Schmidt

D-U-N-S 25-212-6883   (HQ)
TAI PAN VACATIONS INC
(*Suby of* Tai Pan Vacations Inc)
3668 Weston Rd Unit A, North York, ON, M9L 1W2
(416) 646-8828
Emp Here 20   *Emp Total* 170
Sales 52,299,260
SIC 4724 Travel agencies
Acct Mgr Miranda Cheung

D-U-N-S 24-848-3380   (HQ)
TELELATINO NETWORK INC
TLN
5125 Steeles Ave W, North York, ON, M9L 1R5
(416) 744-8200
Emp Here 45   *Emp Total* 1,900
Sales 2,845,467
SIC 4833 Television broadcasting stations

D-U-N-S 25-690-7999   (SL)
TEMPO TILE LTD
853 Garyray Dr, North York, ON, M9L 1R2
(416) 663-5065
Emp Here 21   *Sales* 6,087,000
SIC 5032 Brick, stone, and related material
Pr Pr Gina Cacchione

D-U-N-S 20-025-0806   (BR)
TORONTO DISTRICT SCHOOL BOARD
HUMBER SUMMIT MIDDLE SCHOOL
60 Pearldale Ave, North York, ON, M9L 2G9
(416) 395-2570
Emp Here 50
SIC 8211 Elementary and secondary schools

D-U-N-S 24-816-2885   (SL)
TRI-TINA FORMING INC
4701 Steeles Ave W Suite 220, North York, ON, M9L 1X2
(416) 746-1501
Emp Here 50   *Sales* 7,067,468
SIC 1771 Concrete work
  Carlo Plastina

D-U-N-S 24-391-2842   (BR)
TRIUMPH GEAR SYSTEMS-TORONTO ULC
GENERAL GEAR
11 Fenmar Dr, North York, ON, M9L 1L5
(416) 743-4410
Emp Here 100
SIC 3089 Plastics products, nec

D-U-N-S 24-045-4629   (SL)
TUFF CONTROL SYSTEMS LIMITED
5145 Steeles Ave W Suite 201, North York, ON, M9L 1R5

Emp Here 120   *Sales* 5,173,950
SIC 7381 Detective and armored car services
Pr Pr Michael Hearsum
  Debi Bellis

D-U-N-S 20-789-2048   (BR)
UNITED STEELWORKERS OF AMERICA
(*Suby of* United Steelworkers)
21 Fenmar Dr, North York, ON, M9L 2Y9

Emp Here 20
SIC 8631 Labor organizations

D-U-N-S 20-145-8619   (SL)
VAUGHAN METAL POLISHING LTD
206 Milvan Dr, North York, ON, M9L 1Z9
(416) 743-7500
Emp Here 60   *Sales* 4,012,839
SIC 3471 Plating and polishing

D-U-N-S 25-404-0926   (SL)
VEGFRESH INC
1290 Ormont Dr, North York, ON, M9L 2V4
(416) 667-0518
Emp Here 65   *Sales* 2,188,821

SIC 5461 Retail bakeries

North York, ON M9M
York County

D-U-N-S 20-327-7959   (BR)
2168587 ONTARIO LTD
UPPER CRUST
50 Marmora St, North York, ON, M9M 2X5
(416) 661-7744
Emp Here 900
SIC 2053 Frozen bakery products, except
bread

D-U-N-S 25-374-1953   (BR)
ABC GROUP INC
SALFLEX POLYMERS
(*Suby of* Cerberus Capital Management, L.P.)
1925 Wilson Ave, North York, ON, M9M 1A9
(416) 741-0273
Emp Here 60
SIC 3087 Custom compound purchased
resins

D-U-N-S 25-836-2342   (BR)
BINGO COUNTRY HOLDINGS LIMITED
(*Suby of* Bingo Country Holdings Limited)
2424 Finch Ave W, North York, ON, M9M 2E3

Emp Here 20
SIC 7999 Amusement and recreation, nec

D-U-N-S 20-049-1152   (BR)
CANADIAN DIABETES ASSOCIATION
CLOTHESLINE
2300 Sheppard Ave W Suite 201, North York,
ON, M9M 3A4
(416) 746-5757
Emp Here 20
SIC 8699 Membership organizations, nec

D-U-N-S 25-303-1421   (BR)
**CANADIAN IMPERIAL BANK OF COM-
MERCE**
CIBC
2340 Finch Ave W, North York, ON, M9M 2C7
(416) 749-6062
Emp Here 20
SIC 6021 National commercial banks

D-U-N-S 20-176-7050   (HQ)
**CHARLES   TENNANT   &   COMPANY
(CANADA) LIMITED**
TENNANT, CHARLES & COMPANY
34 Clayson Rd, North York, ON, M9M 2G8
(416) 741-9264
Emp Here 30   *Emp Total* 867
Sales 64,842,534
SIC 5169 Chemicals and allied products, nec
Pr Pr Robert Macphail
 Marcelo Ulloa
 William Paul Alexander
 Andrew Gingell

D-U-N-S 24-937-3838   (BR)
CHRISTIAN HORIZONS
CENTRAL DISTRICT OFFICE
(*Suby of* Christian Horizons)
155 Deerhide Cres, North York, ON, M9M 2Z2
(416) 630-3646
Emp Here 50
SIC 8361 Residential care

D-U-N-S 20-182-1956   (BR)
DOW CHEMICAL CANADA ULC
PACKAGING DIVISION
(*Suby of* The Dow Chemical Company)
122 Arrow Rd, North York, ON, M9M 2M1

Emp Here 200
SIC 3081 Unsupported plastics film and sheet

D-U-N-S 20-583-1936   (BR)
EMCO CORPORATION
EMCO

65 Huxley Rd, North York, ON, M9M 1H5
(416) 742-6220
Emp Here 50
SIC 5074 Plumbing and heating equipment
and supplies (hydronics)

D-U-N-S 24-308-8825   (SL)
FALBO ALUMINUM SYSTEMS LTD
66 Rivalda Rd, North York, ON, M9M 2M3
(416) 740-9304
Emp Here 40   *Sales* 5,545,013
SIC 3442 Metal doors, sash, and trim
Pr Isaac Walter
Dir Eli Fataei

D-U-N-S 20-535-5733   (BR)
GOVERNMENT OF ONTARIO
*LAWRENCE SQUARE EMPLOYMENT & SO-
CIAL SERVICES*
1860 Wilson Ave Suite 100, North York, ON,
M9M 3A7
(416) 392-6500
Emp Here 100
SIC 8399 Social services, nec

D-U-N-S 24-858-2087   (BR)
HOME DEPOT OF CANADA INC
IMPORT DISTRIBUTION CENTER
(*Suby of* The Home Depot Inc)
2233 Sheppard Ave W, North York, ON, M9M
2Z7

Emp Here 110
SIC 5251 Hardware stores

D-U-N-S 20-182-7037   (HQ)
KNOLL NORTH AMERICA CORP
1000 Arrow Rd, North York, ON, M9M 2Y7
(416) 741-5453
Emp Here 900   *Emp Total* 3,471
Sales 79,521,842
SIC 2521 Wood office furniture
Sec Gary D Graham

D-U-N-S 20-182-3887   (SL)
LEDA FURNITURE LTD
350 Clayson Rd, North York, ON, M9M 2H2

Emp Here 50   *Sales* 2,918,428
SIC 2511 Wood household furniture

D-U-N-S 24-783-5366   (SL)
MANOUCHER FINE FOODS INC
703 Clayson Rd, North York, ON, M9M 2H4
(416) 747-1234
Emp Here 50   *Sales* 2,626,585
SIC 2051 Bread, cake, and related products

D-U-N-S 20-294-2082   (BR)
NAILOR INDUSTRIES INC
18 Gail Grove, North York, ON, M9M 1M4
(416) 744-3300
Emp Here 30
SIC 4225 General warehousing and storage

D-U-N-S 25-320-8920   (BR)
PUROLATOR INC.
PUROLATOR INC
1100 Arrow Rd, North York, ON, M9M 2Z1
(416) 241-4496
Emp Here 250
SIC 4731 Freight transportation arrangement

D-U-N-S 25-300-4634   (BR)
REDBERRY FRANCHISING CORP
BURGER KING
2372 Finch Ave W, North York, ON, M9M 2C7
(416) 749-9087
Emp Here 40
SIC 5812 Eating places

D-U-N-S 25-726-1222   (SL)
RELIABLE TOY CORP
707 Arrow Rd, North York, ON, M9M 2L4
(415) 762-1111
Emp Here 75   *Sales* 9,536,300
SIC 3944 Games, toys, and children's vehicles
Pr Pr Ronald Bruhm

Todd Bruhm
Trudy Bruhm

D-U-N-S 24-320-3101   (BR)
**SOMERVILLE   NATIONAL   LEASING &
RENTALS LTD**
(*Suby of* Somerville, William H. Holdings Inc)
75 Arrow Rd, North York, ON, M9M 2L4
(416) 747-7578
Emp Here 40
SIC 7515 Passenger car leasing

D-U-N-S 25-373-6722   (BR)
SUN-BRITE FOODS INC
PRIMO FOODS
56 Huxley Rd, North York, ON, M9M 1H2
(416) 741-9300
Emp Here 40
SIC 2098 Macaroni and spaghetti

D-U-N-S 20-364-6174   (BR)
THOMSON TERMINALS LIMITED
700 Clayson Rd Exit Ramp, North York, ON,
M9M 0A8
(416) 240-4459
Emp Here 40
SIC 4213 Trucking, except local

D-U-N-S 24-044-5036   (HQ)
TOPCUTS INC
88 Arrow Rd, North York, ON, M9M 2L8
(416) 223-1700
Emp Here 64   *Emp Total* 200
Sales 2,073,124
SIC 7231 Beauty shops

D-U-N-S 20-698-7237   (BR)
TORONTO DISTRICT SCHOOL BOARD
GULFSTREAM PUBLIC SCHOOL
20 Gulfstream Rd, North York, ON, M9M 1S3
(416) 395-2520
Emp Here 70
SIC 8211 Elementary and secondary schools

D-U-N-S 25-237-8187   (BR)
TORONTO DISTRICT SCHOOL BOARD
DAYSTROM ELEMENTARY SCHOOL
25 Daystrom Dr, North York, ON, M9M 2A8
(416) 395-2280
Emp Here 48
SIC 8211 Elementary and secondary schools

D-U-N-S 25-361-4549   (BR)
UNIVAR CANADA LTD
64 Arrow Rd, North York, ON, M9M 2L9
(416) 740-5300
Emp Here 200
SIC 5169 Chemicals and allied products, nec

D-U-N-S 25-406-4116   (BR)
VAN-ROB INC
114 Clayson Rd, North York, ON, M9M 2H2
(416) 740-2656
Emp Here 250
SIC 3469 Metal stampings, nec

D-U-N-S 20-237-1860   (HQ)
WALTER, E. F. INC
WALCO-INDUSTRIAL PRODUCTS
(*Suby of* Walter, E. F. Inc)
180 Bartor Rd, North York, ON, M9M 2W6
(416) 782-4492
Emp Here 40   *Emp Total* 54
Sales 2,261,782
SIC 2299 Textile goods, nec

North York, ON M9N
York County

D-U-N-S 25-795-7589   (BR)
770976 ONTARIO LIMITED
TIM HORTONS
(*Suby of* 770976 Ontario Limited)
2625g Weston Rd, North York, ON, M9N 3X2
(416) 242-5090
Emp Here 50

SIC 5812 Eating places

D-U-N-S 24-995-8794   (BR)
BEST BUY CANADA LTD
(*Suby of* Best Buy Co., Inc.)
2625a Weston Rd, North York, ON, M9N 3V8
(416) 242-6162
Emp Here 80
SIC 5731 Radio, television, and electronic
stores

D-U-N-S 25-231-7664   (BR)
BRICK WAREHOUSE LP, THE
BRICK, THE
2625b Weston Rd Unit 7, North York, ON,
M9N 3W1
(416) 249-1211
Emp Here 50
SIC 5712 Furniture stores

D-U-N-S 25-060-5789   (BR)
**LIQUOR CONTROL BOARD OF ONTARIO,
THE**
LCBO STORE 1
2625d Weston Rd, North York, ON, M9N 3W2
(416) 243-3320
Emp Here 38
SIC 5921 Liquor stores

D-U-N-S 25-310-9169   (BR)
**MCDONALD'S   RESTAURANTS   OF
CANADA LIMITED**
MCDONALD'S RESTAURANT
(*Suby of* McDonald's Corporation)
2625f Weston Rd, North York, ON, M9N 3X2
(416) 241-5505
Emp Here 85
SIC 5812 Eating places

D-U-N-S 25-318-2174   (BR)
**MCDONALD'S   RESTAURANTS   OF
CANADA LIMITED**
MCDONALD'S
(*Suby of* McDonald's Corporation)
2020 Jane St, North York, ON, M9N 2V3
(416) 248-6648
Emp Here 110
SIC 5812 Eating places

D-U-N-S 20-698-7336   (BR)
TORONTO DISTRICT SCHOOL BOARD
PELMO PARK PS
180 Gary Dr, North York, ON, M9N 2M1
(416) 395-2750
Emp Here 40
SIC 8211 Elementary and secondary schools

Northbrook, ON K0H
Addington County

D-U-N-S 20-699-6568   (BR)
EXTENDICARE (CANADA) INC
PARAMED HOME HEALTH CARE
124 Lloyd St Rr 1, Northbrook, ON, K0H 2G0
(613) 336-9120
Emp Here 87
SIC 8051 Skilled nursing care facilities

Norwich, ON N0J
Oxford County

D-U-N-S 20-714-1628   (SL)
**REHOBOTH REFORMED SCHOOL SOCI-
ETY**
REHOBOTH CHRISTIAN SCHOOL
43 Main St E, Norwich, ON, N0J 1P0
(519) 863-2403
Emp Here 50   *Sales* 3,356,192
SIC 8211 Elementary and secondary schools

D-U-N-S 25-901-5220   (BR)
TOWNSHIP OF NORWICH

NORWICH COMMUNITY CENTRE
(*Suby of* Township of Norwich)
53 1/2 Stover St S, Norwich, ON, N0J 1P0
(519) 863-3733
Emp Here 20
SIC 8322 Individual and family services

Norwood, ON K0L
Peterborough County

D-U-N-S 20-711-5952 (BR)
KAWARTHA PINE RIDGE DISTRICT SCHOOL BOARD
NORWOOD DISTRICT HIGHSCHOOL
44 Elm St, Norwood, ON, K0L 2V0
(705) 639-5332
Emp Here 45
SIC 8211 Elementary and secondary schools

D-U-N-S 20-938-3236 (BR)
KAWARTHA PINE RIDGE DISTRICT SCHOOL BOARD
NORWOOD ELEMENTARY SCHOOL
24 Flora St, Norwood, ON, K0L 2V0
(705) 639-5382
Emp Here 35
SIC 8211 Elementary and secondary schools

D-U-N-S 24-912-2185 (BR)
OMNI HEALTH CARE LTD
PLEASANT MEADOW MANOR
99 Alma St, Norwood, ON, K0L 2V0
(705) 639-5590
Emp Here 70
SIC 8051 Skilled nursing care facilities

D-U-N-S 25-137-9731 (BR)
PETERBOROUGH VICTORIA NORTHUMBERLAND AND CLARINGTON CATHOLIC DISTRICT SCHOOL BOARD
ST PAUL ELEMENTARY SCHOOL NORWOOD
(*Suby of* Peterborough Victoria Northumberland and Clarington Catholic District School Board)
55 Oak St, Norwood, ON, K0L 2V0
(705) 639-2191
Emp Here 23
SIC 8211 Elementary and secondary schools

D-U-N-S 20-537-2787 (BR)
UNIVERSAL INDUSTRIAL SUPPLY GROUP INC
NAPA AUTO PARTS
Gd, Norwood, ON, K0L 2V0
(705) 639-5452
Emp Here 20
SIC 5531 Auto and home supply stores

Oakville, ON L6H
Halton County

D-U-N-S 20-792-8479 (SL)
1298051 ONTARIO INC
EAST SIDE MARIO'S
2035 Winston Park Dr, Oakville, ON, L6H 6P5
(905) 829-3233
Emp Here 60 *Sales* 1,824,018
SIC 5812 Eating places

D-U-N-S 24-339-5170 (BR)
446987 ONTARIO INC
BOMBAY COMPANY, THE
(*Suby of* Benix & Co. Inc)
2501 Hyde Park Gate, Oakville, ON, L6H 6G6
(905) 829-2988
Emp Here 23
SIC 5712 Furniture stores

D-U-N-S 20-012-0751 (BR)
AMEC FOSTER WHEELER INC
AMEC EC SERVICES
2020 Winston Park Dr Suite 700, Oakville, ON, L6H 6X7
(905) 829-5400
Emp Here 350
SIC 8711 Engineering services

D-U-N-S 20-065-3459 (HQ)
AMEC FOSTER WHEELER INC
2020 Winston Park Dr Suite 700, Oakville, ON, L6H 6X7
(905) 829-5400
Emp Here 535 *Emp Total* 34,013
Sales 1,263,097,792
SIC 6719 Holding companies, nec
Fin Ex Grant Ling

D-U-N-S 20-026-2108 (BR)
AMJ CAMPBELL INC
AMJ CAMPBELL VAN LINES OAKVILLE
2695 Bristol Cir Unit 2, Oakville, ON, L6H 6X5
(905) 829-1233
Emp Here 20
SIC 4214 Local trucking with storage

D-U-N-S 24-318-2453 (BR)
AON REED STENHOUSE INC
2010 Winston Park Dr Suite 200, Oakville, ON, L6H 6A3
(905) 829-5008
Emp Here 30
SIC 6411 Insurance agents, brokers, and service

D-U-N-S 20-180-4507 (HQ)
ATC-FROST MAGNETICS INC
(*Suby of* Standex International Corporation)
1130 Eighth Line, Oakville, ON, L6H 2R4
(905) 844-6681
Emp Here 34 *Emp Total* 5,300
Sales 66,394,237
SIC 3677 Electronic coils and transformers
VP Opers Rick Sherrill

D-U-N-S 20-305-1842 (BR)
ACCURISTIX
(*Suby of* Accuristix)
2905 Bristol Cir, Oakville, ON, L6H 6Z5
(905) 829-9927
Emp Here 25
SIC 6712 Bank holding companies

D-U-N-S 24-389-5310 (BR)
ALPHORA RESEARCH INC
(*Suby of* Alphora Research Inc)
2884 Portland Dr, Oakville, ON, L6H 5W8
(905) 829-9704
Emp Here 80
SIC 8731 Commercial physical research

D-U-N-S 20-589-4491 (BR)
BANQUE TORONTO-DOMINION, LA
TD CANADA TRUST
(*Suby of* Toronto-Dominion Bank, The)
2325 Trafalgar Rd, Oakville, ON, L6H 6N9
(905) 257-0255
Emp Here 20
SIC 6021 National commercial banks

D-U-N-S 20-343-6878 (BR)
BATH & BODY WORKS INC
(*Suby of* Bath & Body Works Inc)
240 Leighland Ave Suite 228, Oakville, ON, L6H 3H6
(905) 845-3385
Emp Here 30
SIC 5719 Miscellaneous homefurnishings

D-U-N-S 20-574-1304 (BR)
BREWERS RETAIL INC
BEER STORE, THE
2923 Portland Dr, Oakville, ON, L6H 5S4
(905) 829-9015
Emp Here 20
SIC 7699 Repair services, nec

D-U-N-S 20-176-0191 (BR)
CCI THERMAL TECHNOLOGIES INC
2721 Plymouth Dr, Oakville, ON, L6H 5R5

(905) 829-4422
Emp Here 120
SIC 3443 Fabricated plate work (boiler shop)

D-U-N-S 20-535-9359 (HQ)
CTL CORP
CORPORATION CTL
1660 North Service Rd E Suite 102, Oakville, ON, L6H 7G3
(905) 815-9510
Emp Here 45 *Emp Total* 5,350
Sales 35,677,782
SIC 6159 Miscellaneous business credit institutions
Pr Pr Sean O'brien
  Amelie Cantin
Dir Douglas A. Carrothers
Dir Denis Ricard
Dir Normand Pepin
Dir Michel St-Francois
Dir Gerald Bouwers
Dir Edmee Metivier
Dir Jeffrey Newhouse

D-U-N-S 24-424-1936 (SL)
CANADA LOYAL FINANCIAL LIMITED
2866 Portland Dr, Oakville, ON, L6H 5W8
(905) 829-5514
Emp Here 60 *Sales* 80,196,720
SIC 6311 Life insurance
Pr Pr Lawrence Fuller
Sec Debra Fuller

D-U-N-S 20-303-3238 (BR)
CARA OPERATIONS LIMITED
KELSEY'S
(*Suby of* Cara Holdings Limited)
2530 Hyde Park Gate, Oakville, ON, L6H 6M2
(905) 829-9932
Emp Here 50
SIC 5812 Eating places

D-U-N-S 20-566-3474 (SL)
CARLSBERG CANADA INC
2650 Bristol Cir Suite 100, Oakville, ON, L6H 6Z7
(905) 829-0299
Emp Here 27 *Sales* 2,480,664
SIC 8743 Public relations services

D-U-N-S 24-284-4520 (HQ)
CLARION CANADA INC
2239 Winston Park Dr, Oakville, ON, L6H 5R1
(905) 829-4600
Emp Here 30 *Emp Total* 335,244
Sales 9,266,009
SIC 5064 Electrical appliances, television and radio
Dir Philip Albanese
Pr Pr Hiro Murakami

D-U-N-S 24-704-1726 (HQ)
COMNETIX INC
2872 Bristol Cir Suite 100, Oakville, ON, L6H 6G4
(905) 829-9988
Emp Here 40 *Emp Total* 1,577
Sales 12,403,319
SIC 7371 Custom computer programming services
Dir Neil Wiener
Dir James Depalma
Dir Robert Lapenta

D-U-N-S 24-347-1054 (BR)
DIRECT LIMITED PARTNERSHIP
DIRECT DISTRIBUTION CENTRES
2340 Winston Park Dr Suite 2, Oakville, ON, L6H 7T7

Emp Here 21
SIC 4225 General warehousing and storage

D-U-N-S 24-677-8216 (SL)
ENCORE FIELD MARKETING SOLUTIONS INC
ENCORE MARKET ENGAGEMENT
2421 Bristol Cir Suite 101, Oakville, ON, L6H

5S9
(289) 999-5128
Emp Here 80 *Sales* 12,532,976
SIC 8743 Public relations services
Pr Pr Ken Pickthall
  Gary Nagasuye

D-U-N-S 20-107-8974 (SL)
EVAULT CANADA INC
(*Suby of* Carbonite, Inc.)
2315 Bristol Cir Unit 200, Oakville, ON, L6H 6P8
(905) 287-2600
Emp Here 100 *Sales* 12,403,319
SIC 7371 Custom computer programming services
Pr Terry Cunningham

D-U-N-S 24-340-0574 (BR)
FGL SPORTS LTD
SPORT-CHEK
2460 Winston Churchill Blvd Unit 2, Oakville, ON, L6H 6J5
(905) 829-4721
Emp Here 40
SIC 5941 Sporting goods and bicycle shops

D-U-N-S 24-340-0749 (BR)
FGL SPORTS LTD
SPORT MART
261 Oak Walk Dr Unit 1, Oakville, ON, L6H 6M3
(905) 257-7538
Emp Here 20
SIC 5941 Sporting goods and bicycle shops

D-U-N-S 24-757-9857 (HQ)
FERN HILL SCHOOL MISSISSAUGA INC
(*Suby of* Fern Hill School Mississauga Inc)
3300 Ninth Line, Oakville, ON, L6H 7A8
(905) 257-0022
Emp Here 48 *Emp Total* 60
Sales 4,012,839
SIC 8211 Elementary and secondary schools

D-U-N-S 20-966-4858 (HQ)
GENWORTH FINANCIAL MORTGAGE INSURANCE COMPANY CANADA
GENWORTH MORTGAGE INSURANCE CANADA
2060 Winston Park Dr Suite 300, Oakville, ON, L6H 5R7
(905) 287-5300
Emp Here 275 *Emp Total* 4,100
Sales 33,350,664
SIC 6351 Surety insurance
  Brian Hurley
  Philip Mayers

D-U-N-S 20-181-9950 (BR)
GLAXOSMITHKLINE INC
2030 Bristol Cir, Oakville, ON, L6H 0H2
(416) 738-1041
Emp Here 150
SIC 2834 Pharmaceutical preparations

D-U-N-S 20-719-2092 (SL)
GLAXOSMITHKLINE CONSUMER HEALTHCARE INC
2030 Bristol Cir, Oakville, ON, L6H 0H2

Emp Here 150 *Sales* 24,834,480
SIC 5122 Drugs, proprietaries, and sundries
Dir Jennifer Denomme
  Diane Williams
Dir Fin Diane Daniel
Dir W. E. Morris
  Karen Scollick

D-U-N-S 24-529-8547 (BR)
GOODLIFE FITNESS CENTRES INC
201 Oak Walk Dr, Oakville, ON, L6H 6M3

Emp Here 35
SIC 7991 Physical fitness facilities

D-U-N-S 20-195-1352 (BR)
GROUPE PHOENICIA INC

1303 North Service Rd E Unit 4, Oakville, ON, L6H 1A7
(905) 829-2488
Emp Here 20
SIC 5149 Groceries and related products, nec

D-U-N-S 20-591-3689　(BR)
HALTON CATHOLIC DISTRICT SCHOOL BOARD
OUR LADY OF PEACE ELEMENTARY SCHOOL.
391 River Glen Blvd, Oakville, ON, L6H 5X5
(905) 257-2791
Emp Here 25
SIC 8211 Elementary and secondary schools

D-U-N-S 20-711-0680　(BR)
HALTON CATHOLIC DISTRICT SCHOOL BOARD
ST. MICHAEL SCHOOL
165 Sewell Dr, Oakville, ON, L6H 1E3
(905) 844-6811
Emp Here 25
SIC 8211 Elementary and secondary schools

D-U-N-S 25-174-4264　(BR)
HALTON CATHOLIC DISTRICT SCHOOL BOARD
ST JOHN ELEMENTARY SCHOOL
1480 Mansfield Dr, Oakville, ON, L6H 1K4
(905) 844-3111
Emp Here 20
SIC 8211 Elementary and secondary schools

D-U-N-S 20-591-2343　(BR)
HALTON CATHOLIC DISTRICT SCHOOL BOARD
ST MARGARETTE DEUVILLE
1359 Bayshire Dr, Oakville, ON, L6H 6C7
(905) 849-7772
Emp Here 50
SIC 8211 Elementary and secondary schools

D-U-N-S 20-591-2574　(BR)
HALTON CATHOLIC DISTRICT SCHOOL BOARD
ST ANDREW CATHOLIC SCHOOL
145 Millbank Dr, Oakville, ON, L6H 6G3
(905) 257-7102
Emp Here 55
SIC 8211 Elementary and secondary schools

D-U-N-S 20-711-0755　(BR)
HALTON CATHOLIC DISTRICT SCHOOL BOARD
HOLY FAMILY SCHOOL
1420 Grosvenor St, Oakville, ON, L6H 2X8
(905) 845-6987
Emp Here 27
SIC 8211 Elementary and secondary schools

D-U-N-S 20-711-0425　(BR)
HALTON DISTRICT SCHOOL BOARD
MUNNS ELEMENTARY SCHOOL
1511 Sixth Line, Oakville, ON, L6H 1X8
(905) 844-9461
Emp Here 50
SIC 8211 Elementary and secondary schools

D-U-N-S 20-289-1128　(BR)
HALTON DISTRICT SCHOOL BOARD
IROQUOIS RIDGE SECONDARY SCHOOL
1123 Glenashton Dr, Oakville, ON, L6H 5M1
(905) 845-0012
Emp Here 100
SIC 8211 Elementary and secondary schools

D-U-N-S 25-143-3660　(BR)
HALTON DISTRICT SCHOOL BOARD
RIVER OAKS PUBLIC SCHOOL
2173 Munn'S Ave, Oakville, ON, L6H 3S9
(905) 842-7430
Emp Here 50
SIC 8211 Elementary and secondary schools

D-U-N-S 25-143-3629　(BR)
HALTON DISTRICT SCHOOL BOARD
FALGARWOOD PUBLIC SCHOOL

1385 Gainsborough Dr, Oakville, ON, L6H 2H7
(905) 845-7478
Emp Here 50
SIC 8211 Elementary and secondary schools

D-U-N-S 20-024-9881　(BR)
HALTON DISTRICT SCHOOL BOARD
SUNNINGDALE PUBLIC SCHOOL
1434 Oxford Ave, Oakville, ON, L6H 1T4
(905) 844-9941
Emp Here 50
SIC 8211 Elementary and secondary schools

D-U-N-S 20-545-2530　(BR)
HALTON DISTRICT SCHOOL BOARD
SYL APPS SCHOOL
475 Iroquois Shore Rd Suite 2199, Oakville, ON, L6H 1M3
(905) 844-4110
Emp Here 40
SIC 8322 Individual and family services

D-U-N-S 20-711-0540　(BR)
HALTON DISTRICT SCHOOL BOARD
POST'S CORNERS PUBLIC SCHOOL
2220 Caldwell Dr, Oakville, ON, L6H 6B5
(905) 845-1661
Emp Here 60
SIC 8211 Elementary and secondary schools

D-U-N-S 25-134-7944　(BR)
HALTON DISTRICT SCHOOL BOARD
SHERIDAN SCHOOL
1555 Lancaster Dr, Oakville, ON, L6H 3H4
(905) 845-3925
Emp Here 27
SIC 8211 Elementary and secondary schools

D-U-N-S 24-596-2261　(SL)
HAYWARD POOL PRODUCTS CANADA, INC
(*Suby of* Hayward Industries, Inc.)
2880 Plymouth Dr, Oakville, ON, L6H 5R4
(905) 829-2880
Emp Here 55　　*Sales* 4,596,524
SIC 3949 Sporting and athletic goods, nec

D-U-N-S 20-026-3478　(SL)
HIP RESTAURANTS LTD
1011 Upper Middle Rd E Suite C3, Oakville, ON, L6H 5Z9
(647) 403-2494
Emp Here 100　　*Sales* 3,551,629
SIC 5812 Eating places

D-U-N-S 25-514-2895　(BR)
HOME DEPOT OF CANADA INC
HOME DEPOT
(*Suby of* The Home Depot Inc)
2555 Bristol Cir, Oakville, ON, L6H 5W9
(905) 829-5900
Emp Here 250
SIC 5251 Hardware stores

D-U-N-S 25-301-1852　(BR)
HUDSON'S BAY COMPANY
BAY, THE
240 Leighland Ave, Oakville, ON, L6H 3H6
(905) 842-4811
Emp Here 150
SIC 5311 Department stores

D-U-N-S 24-574-0035　(BR)
IMVESCOR RESTAURANT GROUP INC
BATON ROUGE RESTAURANTS
2005 Winston Park Dr, Oakville, ON, L6H 6P5
(905) 829-2279
Emp Here 30
SIC 5812 Eating places

D-U-N-S 20-631-4259　(SL)
KP PORTFOLIO INC
TIM HORTONS
2355 Trafalgar Rd, Oakville, ON, L6H 6N9
(905) 257-1294
Emp Here 50　　*Sales* 1,532,175
SIC 5812 Eating places

D-U-N-S 24-249-3943　(SL)
KEG RESTAURANTS LTD
KEG STEAKHOUSE & BAR, THE
300 Hays Blvd, Oakville, ON, L6H 7P3
(905) 257-2700
Emp Here 90　　*Sales* 2,699,546
SIC 5812 Eating places

D-U-N-S 20-645-8205　(BR)
KINARK CHILD AND FAMILY SERVICES
SYLAPPS YOUTH CENTER
475 Iroquois Shore Rd, Oakville, ON, L6H 1M3
(905) 844-4110
Emp Here 250
SIC 8322 Individual and family services

D-U-N-S 25-318-7488　(BR)
LIQUOR CONTROL BOARD OF ONTARIO, THE
L.C.B.O. #179
1011 Upper Middle Rd E, Oakville, ON, L6H 5Z9
(905) 849-9934
Emp Here 20
SIC 5921 Liquor stores

D-U-N-S 24-383-8823　(BR)
LOBLAWS INC
REAL CANADIAN SUPERSTORE
201 Oak Park Blvd Suite 1024, Oakville, ON, L6H 7T4
(905) 257-9330
Emp Here 100
SIC 5411 Grocery stores

D-U-N-S 24-389-6073　(BR)
LONGO BROTHERS FRUIT MARKETS INC
LONGO'S OAKVILLE FRUIT MARKET
338 Dundas St E, Oakville, ON, L6H 6Z9
(905) 257-5633
Emp Here 230
SIC 5431 Fruit and vegetable markets

D-U-N-S 24-758-0491　(SL)
MAGNUM 2000 INC
1137 North Service Rd E, Oakville, ON, L6H 1A7
(905) 339-1104
Emp Here 65　　*Sales* 4,742,446
SIC 7539 Automotive repair shops, nec

D-U-N-S 25-368-2231　(BR)
MARGARINE GOLDEN GATE-MICHCA INC
GOLDEN GATE MARGARINE
(*Suby of* James Richardson & Sons, Limited)
2835 Bristol Cir, Oakville, ON, L6H 6X5
(905) 829-2942
Emp Here 60
SIC 2079 Edible fats and oils

D-U-N-S 25-236-6414　(BR)
MARK'S WORK WEARHOUSE LTD
WORK WORLD
2501 Hyde Park Gate, Oakville, ON, L6H 6G6
(905) 829-0844
Emp Here 20
SIC 5651 Family clothing stores

D-U-N-S 25-149-8721　(SL)
MATTAMY (UPPER GLEN ABBEY) LIMITED
2360 Bristol Cir Suite 100, Oakville, ON, L6H 6M5
(905) 829-7604
Emp Here 300　　*Sales* 61,795,200
SIC 1521 Single-family housing construction
　Peter Gilgan
VP Fin Donald Walker

D-U-N-S 24-830-5039　(SL)
MAXAN DRYWALL LIMITED
2770 Brighton Rd, Oakville, ON, L6H 5T4
(905) 829-0070
Emp Here 55　　*Sales* 4,669,485
SIC 1742 Plastering, drywall, and insulation

D-U-N-S 20-704-3688　(SL)
MCDERMID PAPER CONVERTERS LIMITED

2951 Bristol Cir Unit B, Oakville, ON, L6H 6P9
(905) 829-9899
Emp Here 40　　*Sales* 15,715,860
SIC 2679 Converted paper products, nec

D-U-N-S 20-792-5335　(BR)
MCDONALD'S RESTAURANTS OF CANADA LIMITED
MCDONALD'S #8446
(*Suby of* McDonald's Corporation)
2510 Hampshire Gate, Oakville, ON, L6H 6A2
(905) 829-1227
Emp Here 50
SIC 5812 Eating places

D-U-N-S 24-319-5927　(HQ)
MCFADDEN'S HARDWOOD & HARDWARE INC
2323 Winston Park Dr Suite 1, Oakville, ON, L6H 6R7
(416) 674-3333
Emp Here 35　　*Emp Total* 70,553
Sales 18,532,018
SIC 5072 Hardware
Pr John Stafford

D-U-N-S 20-316-4553　(SL)
MEETING HOUSE, THE
MEETING HOUSE CHURCH FAMILY, THE
2700 Bristol Cir, Oakville, ON, L6H 6E1
(905) 287-7000
Emp Here 60　　*Sales* 3,939,878
SIC 8661 Religious organizations

D-U-N-S 25-721-1037　(BR)
MEMORIAL GARDENS CANADA LIMITED
GLEN OAKS MEMORIAL
3164 Ninth Line. Oakville, ON, L6H 7A8
(905) 257-8822
Emp Here 30
SIC 6553 Cemetery subdividers and developers

D-U-N-S 25-311-9689　(BR)
METRO ONTARIO INC
METRO
1011 Upper Middle Rd E Suite 412, Oakville, ON, L6H 5Z9
(905) 849-4911
Emp Here 250
SIC 5411 Grocery stores

D-U-N-S 20-552-8628　(BR)
METRO ONTARIO INC
FOOD BASICS
478 Dundas St W, Oakville, ON, L6H 6Y3
(905) 257-2500
Emp Here 70
SIC 5411 Grocery stores

D-U-N-S 24-199-3591　(HQ)
MIELZYNSKI, PETER AGENCIES LIMITED
PMA CANADA
231 Oak Park Blvd Suite 400, Oakville, ON, L6H 7S8
(905) 257-2116
Emp Here 40　　*Emp Total* 1,467
Sales 11,527,791
SIC 5182 Wine and distilled beverages
Pr Pr Peter D Mielznyski Jr
　Peter G Mielzynski Sr
　Simon J. Hunt
　John Torella
　Grant Farrow
　Walter Perchal
　Cary Kurz
　Gian Alfonso Negretti
　David Mcconnell
　Paul H. Rochford

D-U-N-S 24-316-4758　(SL)
MIRROR INTERIORS INC
2504 Bristol Cir, Oakville, ON, L6H 5S1
(416) 740-7932
Emp Here 50　　*Sales* 4,596,524
SIC 3231 Products of purchased glass

D-U-N-S 20-731-2299　(HQ)

MOEN INC
(*Suby of* Fortune Brands Home & Security, Inc.)
2816 Bristol Cir, Oakville, ON, L6H 5S7
(905) 829-3400
Emp Here 120   *Emp Total* 22,700
Sales 25,536,245
SIC 5074 Plumbing and heating equipment and supplies (hydronics)
Pr Pr Michael J Dennis
VP Sls John Hammill

D-U-N-S 20-522-3717   (SL)
MOLNLYCKE HEALTH CARE INC
2010 Winston Park Dr Suite 100, Oakville, ON, L6H 6A3
(905) 829-1502
Emp Here 22   *Sales* 3,811,504
SIC 5047 Medical and hospital equipment

D-U-N-S 20-789-2881   (BR)
NEZIOL INSURANCE BROKERS LTD
NEZIOL GROUP, THE
(*Suby of* Neziol Insurance Brokers Ltd)
2421 Bristol Cir Unit 203, Oakville, ON, L6H 5S9
(905) 274-8840
Emp Here 30
SIC 6411 Insurance agents, brokers, and service

D-U-N-S 20-292-0190   (SL)
NORTHRIDGE LONGTERM CARE CENTER
496 Postridge Dr, Oakville, ON, L6H 7A2
(905) 257-9382
Emp Here 78   *Sales* 3,648,035
SIC 8059 Nursing and personal care, nec

D-U-N-S 20-887-1173   (SL)
OAKVILLE ACADEMY FOR THE ARTS LTD, THE
1011 Upper Middle Rd E Suite E, Oakville, ON, L6H 5Z9
(905) 844-2787
Emp Here 67   *Sales* 1,167,371
SIC 7911 Dance studios, schools, and halls

D-U-N-S 24-062-9139   (SL)
OAKVILLE GOLF CLUB LIMITED, THE
1154 Sixth Line, Oakville, ON, L6H 6M1
(905) 845-8321
Emp Here 60   *Sales* 2,407,703
SIC 7997 Membership sports and recreation clubs

D-U-N-S 25-477-0290   (BR)
OMER DESERRES INC
LOOMIS ART STORE
2501 Hyde Park Gate, Oakville, ON, L6H 6G6
(905) 829-9181
Emp Here 20
SIC 5999 Miscellaneous retail stores, nec

D-U-N-S 24-352-8465   (BR)
OTTO BOCK HEALTHCARE CANADA LTD
2897 Brighton Rd, Oakville, ON, L6H 6C9

Emp Here 87
SIC 5047 Medical and hospital equipment

D-U-N-S 24-847-1542   (HQ)
PELMOREX WEATHER NETWORKS (TELEVISION) INC
WEATHER NETWORK, THE
2655 Bristol Cir, Oakville, ON, L6H 7W1
(905) 829-1159
Emp Here 117   *Emp Total* 166
Sales 11,090.026
SIC 4833 Television broadcasting stations
Ch Bd Ch Bd Pierre Morrissette
Carlos Astorqui
Bala Gopalakrishnan
VP Fin Tawnie Mcnabb
Maureen Rogers
Roy Bliss
Geoff Browne
John Dionne
Francis Fox

R. Kelly Shaughnessy

D-U-N-S 25-799-6884   (SL)
PING CANADA CORPORATION
PING CANADA
2790 Brighton Rd, Oakville, ON, L6H 5T4
(905) 829-8004
Emp Here 30   *Sales* 3,429,153
SIC 5091 Sporting and recreation goods

D-U-N-S 24-327-4458   (BR)
PINTY'S DELICIOUS FOODS INC
2714 Bristol Cir, Oakville, ON, L6H 6A1
(905) 319-5300
Emp Here 100
SIC 2015 Poultry slaughtering and processing

D-U-N-S 24-311-0207   (HQ)
PIPER FOODS INC
MCDONALD'S
(*Suby of* Piper Foods Inc)
375 Iroquois Shore Rd, Oakville, ON, L6H 1M3
(905) 842-6865
Emp Here 40   *Emp Total* 50
Sales 1,532,175
SIC 5812 Eating places

D-U-N-S 20-774-8919   (BR)
PREMIER HEALTH CLUBS INC
PREMIERE FITNESS
474 Iroquois Shore Rd, Oakville, ON, L6H 2Y7
(905) 842-2366
Emp Here 20
SIC 7999 Amusement and recreation, nec

D-U-N-S 25-796-4643   (BR)
RABBA, J. COMPANY LIMITED, THE
RABBA FINE FOODS
1289 Marlborough Crt Unit 5, Oakville, ON, L6H 2R9
(905) 815-8279
Emp Here 37
SIC 5411 Grocery stores

D-U-N-S 25-845-2937   (BR)
REDBERRY FRANCHISING CORP
BURGER KING
2460 Winston Churchill Blvd Suite 1, Oakville, ON, L6H 6J5
(905) 829-4792
Emp Here 25
SIC 5812 Eating places

D-U-N-S 25-882-9092   (BR)
ROYAL BANK OF CANADA
RBC
(*Suby of* Royal Bank Of Canada)
2460 Winston Churchill Blvd Suite 5, Oakville, ON, L6H 6J5
(905) 829-8665
Emp Here 50
SIC 6021 National commercial banks

D-U-N-S 24-364-5020   (BR)
SIR CORP
ALICE FAZOOLI'S
2015 Winston Park Dr, Oakville, ON, L6H 6P5
(905) 829-3250
Emp Here 50
SIC 5812 Eating places

D-U-N-S 24-953-5915   (HQ)
SMC PNEUMATICS (CANADA) LTD
2715 Bristol Cir Suite 2, Oakville, ON, L6H 6X5
(905) 812-0400
Emp Here 150   *Emp Total* 19,191
Sales 45,600,438
SIC 5084 Industrial machinery and equipment
Mgr Dave Armstrong
Pr Pr Yoshiki Takada

D-U-N-S 24-389-5419   (BR)
SNC-LAVALIN INTERNATIONAL INC
SLII
2275 Upper Middle Rd E, Oakville, ON, L6H 0C3

(905) 829-8808
Emp Here 250
SIC 8711 Engineering services

D-U-N-S 20-763-4684   (HQ)
SNC-LAVALIN NUCLEAR INC
2275 Upper Middle Rd E, Oakville, ON, L6H 0C3
(905) 829-8808
Emp Here 80   *Emp Total* 33,000
Sales 16,198,894
SIC 8999 Services, nec
VP VP Patrick Lamarre
Dir Gilles Laramee
Dir Rejean Goulet

D-U-N-S 20-911-0183   (BR)
SCHAEFFLER CANADA INC
2871 Plymouth Dr, Oakville, ON, L6H 5S5
(905) 829-2750
Emp Here 60
SIC 5085 Industrial supplies

D-U-N-S 20-913-9778   (BR)
SEARS CANADA INC
240 Leighland Ave Suite 142, Oakville, ON, L6H 3H6
(905) 842-9410
Emp Here 200
SIC 5311 Department stores

D-U-N-S 20-703-3205   (BR)
SHERIDAN COLLEGE INSTITUTE OF TECHNOLOGY AND ADVANCED LEARNING
1430 Trafalgar Rd, Oakville, ON, L6H 2L1
(905) 845-9430
Emp Here 50
SIC 8331 Job training and related services

D-U-N-S 20-234-2051   (HQ)
SIEMENS CANADA LIMITED
SIEMENS NETWORK OF CARING
1577 North Service Rd E, Oakville, ON, L6H 0H6
(905) 465-8000
Emp Here 300   *Emp Total* 351,000
Sales 369,691,867
SIC 3625 Relays and industrial controls
Pr Pr Robert Hardt
VP Fin Maria Ferraro
Sec Richard Brait
Sec Christa Wessel
Dir Peter Solmssen
Uriel Sharef

D-U-N-S 25-398-5964   (SL)
SILVER HOTEL (OAKVILLE) INC
RAMADA INN & CONVENTION CENTRE
360 Oakville Place Dr, Oakville, ON, L6H 6K8
(905) 845-7561
Emp Here 50   *Sales* 2,626,585
SIC 7011 Hotels and motels

D-U-N-S 25-312-6767   (BR)
STAPLES CANADA INC
STAPLES THE BUSINESS DEPOT
(*Suby of* Staples, Inc.)
2460 Winston Churchill Blvd, Oakville, ON, L6H 6J5
(905) 829-1960
Emp Here 45
SIC 5943 Stationery stores

D-U-N-S 20-506-0705   (BR)
STARBUCKS COFFEE CANADA, INC
(*Suby of* Starbucks Corporation)
330 Dundas St E Unit 5, Oakville, ON, L6H 6Z9
(905) 257-4244
Emp Here 22
SIC 5812 Eating places

D-U-N-S 24-097-1270   (SL)
STERIMAX INC
2770 Portland Dr, Oakville, ON, L6H 6R4
(905) 890-0661
Emp Here 60   *Sales* 3,283,232
SIC 8731 Commercial physical research

D-U-N-S 20-596-2017   (BR)
STOCK TRANSPORTATION LTD
2741 Plymouth Dr, Oakville, ON, L6H 5R5
(905) 829-2040
Emp Here 20
SIC 4151 School buses

D-U-N-S 25-369-8930   (BR)
SUNGARD AVAILABILITY SERVICES (CANADA) LTD
(*Suby of* Fidelity National Information Services, Inc.)
2010 Winston Park Dr Suite 400, Oakville, ON, L6H 6A3
(905) 287-4000
Emp Here 35
SIC 7371 Custom computer programming services

D-U-N-S 25-626-1363   (BR)
SWISH MAINTENANCE LIMITED
2512 Bristol Cir, Oakville, ON, L6H 5S1
(905) 829-9366
Emp Here 22
SIC 5087 Service establishment equipment

D-U-N-S 20-425-2068   (BR)
SWISH MAINTENANCE LIMITED
2600 Bristol Cir Unit 1, Oakville, ON, L6H 6Z7
(519) 340-3010
Emp Here 40
SIC 5087 Service establishment equipment

D-U-N-S 25-477-8624   (BR)
THURBER ENGINEERING LTD
THURBER MANAGEMENT
2010 Winston Park Dr Suite 103, Oakville, ON, L6H 5R7
(905) 829-8666
Emp Here 21
SIC 8711 Engineering services

D-U-N-S 25-120-2305   (BR)
TORONTO-DOMINION BANK, THE
TD CANADA TRUST
(*Suby of* Toronto-Dominion Bank, The)
321 Iroquois Shore Rd, Oakville, ON, L6H 1M3
(905) 845-6621
Emp Here 28
SIC 6021 National commercial banks

D-U-N-S 24-171-2087   (SL)
TURNPIKE GLOBAL TECHNOLOGIES INC
2401 Bristol Cir Suite C 100, Oakville, ON, L6H 5S9
(905) 829-9204
Emp Here 30   *Sales* 4,304,681
SIC 3663 Radio and t.v. communications equipment

D-U-N-S 20-174-8477   (BR)
UPS SCS, INC
UPS SUPPLY CHAIN SOLUTION
1595 North Service Rd E, Oakville, ON, L6H 7L9
(905) 338-2523
Emp Here 70
SIC 4225 General warehousing and storage

D-U-N-S 25-474-1572   (SL)
ULTIMATE TRAVEL GROUP INC
ULTIMATE GOLF VACATIONS
1660 North Service Rd E Suite 101, Oakville, ON, L6H 7G3
(905) 755-0999
Emp Here 21   *Sales* 5,034,288
SIC 4725 Tour operators
Pr Ron Dawick

D-U-N-S 25-693-3987   (BR)
WIKA INSTRUMENTS LTD
2679 Bristol Cir Unit 1, Oakville, ON, L6H 6Z8
(905) 337-1611
Emp Here 35
SIC 3823 Process control instruments

D-U-N-S 25-498-3349   (BR)
WAL-MART CANADA CORP

▲ Public Company   ■ Public Company Family Member   **HQ** Headquarters   **BR** Branch   **SL** Single Location

234 Hays Blvd, Oakville, ON, L6H 6M4
(905) 257-5740
Emp Here 200
SIC 5311 Department stores

D-U-N-S 20-850-7269   (HQ)
WEIGHT WATCHERS CANADA, LTD
(*Suby of* Weight Watchers International, Inc.)
2295 Bristol Cir Unit 200, Oakville, ON, L6H 6P8
(905) 491-2100
Emp Here 120   *Emp Total* 18,000
Sales 466,547,088
SIC 8099 Health and allied services, nec
Pr Stacey Mowbray

D-U-N-S 20-251-9856   (SL)
WELLSPRING PHARMA SERVICES INC
400 Iroquois Shore Rd, Oakville, ON, L6H 1M5
(905) 337-4500
Emp Here 130   *Sales* 12,622,201
SIC 2834 Pharmaceutical preparations
Pr Sam Ricchezza
Dir Sharon Sasranyos

D-U-N-S 25-221-2576   (BR)
WINNERS MERCHANTS INTERNATIONAL L.P.
WINNERS
(*Suby of* The TJX Companies Inc)
2460 Winston Churchill Blvd Suite 1, Oakville, ON, L6H 6J5
(905) 829-9086
Emp Here 100
SIC 5651 Family clothing stores

D-U-N-S 20-860-4350   (BR)
WINNERS MERCHANTS INTERNATIONAL L.P.
WINNERS
(*Suby of* The TJX Companies Inc)
2431 Trafalgar Rd, Oakville, ON, L6H 6K7
(905) 257-2104
Emp Here 25
SIC 5651 Family clothing stores

D-U-N-S 25-081-2039   (SL)
WINSTON CHURCHILL PIZZA LIMITED
BOSTON PIZZA
2011 Winston Park Dr, Oakville, ON, L6H 6P5
(905) 829-8370
Emp Here 50   *Sales* 1,532,175
SIC 5812 Eating places

Oakville, ON L6J
Halton County

D-U-N-S 24-368-5679   (SL)
ACI BRANDS INC
2616 Sheridan Garden Dr, Oakville, ON, L6J 7Z2
(905) 829-1566
Emp Here 160   *Sales* 19,188,664
SIC 5137 Women's and children's clothing
Pr John A Goraieb
Pr Pr Jeffrey G Goraieb
VP Fin Jeffrey Berk
Fin Ex Wayne Onishi
Dir Paul Eldridge
Dir John Philp

D-U-N-S 25-797-6639   (BR)
BMO NESBITT BURNS INC
132 Trafalgar Rd, Oakville, ON, L6J 3G5
(905) 337-2000
Emp Here 29
SIC 6211 Security brokers and dealers

D-U-N-S 24-469-2018   (SL)
BURNSTEIN, DR. & ASSOCIATES
CHISHOLM CENTRE
1484 Cornwall Rd, Oakville, ON, L6J 7W5

Emp Here 63   *Sales* 3,429,153

SIC 8299 Schools and educational services, nec

D-U-N-S 20-562-1761   (BR)
CCTF CORPORATION
1387 Cornwall Rd, Oakville, ON, L6J 7T5

Emp Here 40
SIC 5074 Plumbing and heating equipment and supplies (hydronics)

D-U-N-S 20-576-1070   (BR)
CIBC WORLD MARKETS INC
CIBC WOOD GUNDY
277 Lakeshore Rd E Suite 905, Oakville, ON, L6J 6J3
(905) 842-6770
Emp Here 20
SIC 6211 Security brokers and dealers

D-U-N-S 20-589-7395   (BR)
CANADIAN IMPERIAL BANK OF COMMERCE
CIBC
197 Lakeshore Rd E, Oakville, ON, L6J 1H5
(905) 845-4327
Emp Here 20
SIC 6021 National commercial banks

D-U-N-S 25-796-6382   (BR)
COLLEGA INTERNATIONAL INC
CIVELLO SALON-SPA
145 Lakeshore Rd E, Oakville, ON, L6J 1H3
(905) 842-4222
Emp Here 20
SIC 7991 Physical fitness facilities

D-U-N-S 24-120-1958   (BR)
COMPAGNIE DES CHEMINS DE FER NATIONAUX DU CANADA
C N
553 Chartwell Rd, Oakville, ON, L6J 4A8
(905) 844-5047
Emp Here 21
SIC 4789 Transportation services, nec

D-U-N-S 24-523-8337   (SL)
ESCAPE PROOF INC
ESCAPE PROOF QUALITY INSPECTION SERVICES
1496 Durham St, Oakville, ON, L6J 2P3
(905) 815-2452
Emp Here 50   *Sales* 2,991,389
SIC 7549 Automotive services, nec

D-U-N-S 20-699-6295   (BR)
EXTENDICARE INC
WYNDHAM MANOR LONG-TERM CARE CENTRE
291 Reynolds St Suite 128, Oakville, ON, L6J 3L5
(905) 849-7766
Emp Here 200
SIC 8051 Skilled nursing care facilities

D-U-N-S 24-076-0103   (BR)
FINANCIERE BANQUE NATIONALE INC
105 Robinson St, Oakville, ON, L6J 1G1
(905) 842-1925
Emp Here 22
SIC 6211 Security brokers and dealers

D-U-N-S 25-539-1559   (HQ)
FIRST CANADIAN TITLE COMPANY LIMITED
2235 Sheridan Garden Dr Suite 745, Oakville, ON, L6J 7Y5
(905) 287-1000
Emp Here 300   *Emp Total* 600
SIC 6361 Title insurance

D-U-N-S 20-134-2466   (HQ)
FORD CREDIT CANADA LIMITED
(*Suby of* Ford Motor Company)
The Canadian Rd, Oakville, ON, L6J 5C7
(905) 845-2511
Emp Here 27   *Emp Total* 201,000
Sales 318,984,180
SIC 6141 Personal credit institutions

Pr Charles Bilyeu
John Noone
Mark Mueller
VP Norman Stewart
Paul Pandos
Michael Herniak
Paul Micallef

D-U-N-S 20-711-0722   (BR)
HALTON CATHOLIC DISTRICT SCHOOL BOARD
ST. VINCENT ELEMENTARY SCHOOL
1280 Braeside Dr, Oakville, ON, L6J 2A4
(905) 849-0777
Emp Here 50
SIC 8211 Elementary and secondary schools

D-U-N-S 20-591-3457   (BR)
HALTON CATHOLIC DISTRICT SCHOOL BOARD
ST LUKE ELEMENTARY SCHOOL
2750 Kingsway Dr, Oakville, ON, L6J 7G5
(905) 829-1700
Emp Here 25
SIC 8211 Elementary and secondary schools

D-U-N-S 25-143-3611   (BR)
HALTON DISTRICT SCHOOL BOARD
LINBROOK PUBLIC SCHOOL
1079 Linbrook Rd, Oakville, ON, L6J 2L2

Emp Here 24
SIC 8211 Elementary and secondary schools

D-U-N-S 25-153-9557   (BR)
HALTON DISTRICT SCHOOL BOARD
BRANTWOOD PUBLIC SCHOOL
221 Allan St, Oakville, ON, L6J 3P2
(905) 337-9232
Emp Here 20
SIC 8211 Elementary and secondary schools

D-U-N-S 20-026-7891   (BR)
HALTON DISTRICT SCHOOL BOARD
MAPLE GROVE PUBLIC SCHOOL
165 Charnwood Dr, Oakville, ON, L6J 5H2
(905) 844-2963
Emp Here 26
SIC 8211 Elementary and secondary schools

D-U-N-S 25-143-3678   (BR)
HALTON DISTRICT SCHOOL BOARD
E J JAMES PUBLIC SCHOOL
338 Cairncroft Rd, Oakville, ON, L6J 4M6
(905) 845-2015
Emp Here 30
SIC 8211 Elementary and secondary schools

D-U-N-S 20-291-6479   (BR)
HALTON DISTRICT SCHOOL BOARD
MAPLE GROVE PUBLIC SCHOOL
288 Maple Grove Dr, Oakville, ON, L6J 4V5
(905) 844-9322
Emp Here 20
SIC 8211 Elementary and secondary schools

D-U-N-S 24-875-2024   (BR)
HENNIGES AUTOMOTIVE SCHLEGEL CANADA INC
2360 Cornwall Rd Unit 1, Oakville, ON, L6J 7T9
(905) 338-3082
Emp Here 20
SIC 3069 Fabricated rubber products, nec

D-U-N-S 20-107-1268   (BR)
HOME DEPOT OF CANADA INC
HOME DEPOT
(*Suby of* The Home Depot Inc)
99 Cross Ave, Oakville, ON, L6J 2W7
(905) 815-5000
Emp Here 170
SIC 5251 Hardware stores

D-U-N-S 25-403-1719   (HQ)
KELSEY'S RESTAURANTS INC
MONTANA'S
(*Suby of* Cara Holdings Limited)

387 Gloucester Ave, Oakville, ON, L6J 3X3

Emp Here 40   *Emp Total* 14,038
Sales 584,243,980
SIC 5812 Eating places
Ch Bd Don Robinson
Pr Nils Kravis
Dir Leslie Buist

D-U-N-S 24-346-5155   (SL)
KIDLOGIC OAKVILLE INC
580 Argus Rd, Oakville, ON, L6J 3J3
(905) 842-6280
Emp Here 22   *Sales* 663,942
SIC 8351 Child day care services

D-U-N-S 24-094-9961   (BR)
LULULEMON ATHLETICA CANADA INC
LULULEMON
291 Lakeshore Rd E, Oakville, ON, L6J 1J3
(905) 338-9449
Emp Here 20
SIC 2339 Women's and misses' outerwear, nec

D-U-N-S 24-333-1415   (BR)
MAPLE LEAF FOODS INC
MAPLE LEAF FRESH FOODS
178 South Service Rd E, Oakville, ON, L6J 0A5
(905) 815-6500
Emp Here 200
SIC 5141 Groceries, general line

D-U-N-S 25-295-6024   (BR)
MARCH OF DIMES CANADA
259 Robinson St, Oakville, ON, L6J 6G8
(905) 845-7412
Emp Here 30
SIC 8059 Nursing and personal care, nec

D-U-N-S 24-593-7672   (SL)
MARQUEE HOTELS OAKVILLE INC
HILTON GARDEN INN TORONTO/OAKVILLE
2774 South Sheridan Way, Oakville, ON, L6J 7T4
(905) 829-1145
Emp Here 55   *Sales* 2,407,703
SIC 7011 Hotels and motels

D-U-N-S 24-198-2388   (SL)
MCDONALD, D. SALES & MERCHANDISING LIMITED
2861 Sherwood Heights Dr Unit 28, Oakville, ON, L6J 7K1
(905) 855-8550
Emp Here 50   *Sales* 2,626,585
SIC 7389 Business services, nec

D-U-N-S 20-324-9982   (BR)
NBM ENGINEERING INC
1525 Cornwall Rd, U 27, Oakville, ON, L6J 0B2
(905) 845-7770
Emp Here 40
SIC 8711 Engineering services

D-U-N-S 20-772-6662   (SL)
OAKVILLE CLUB, LIMITED, THE
56 Water St, Oakville, ON, L6J 2Y3
(905) 845-0231
Emp Here 50   *Sales* 2,042,900
SIC 7997 Membership sports and recreation clubs

D-U-N-S 20-792-4924   (BR)
PIPER FOODS INC
MCDONALD'S
(*Suby of* Piper Foods Inc)
227 Cross Ave, Oakville, ON, L6J 2W9
(905) 337-2976
Emp Here 50
SIC 5812 Eating places

D-U-N-S 25-254-6627   (BR)
REVERA INC
CHURCHILL PLACE
345 Church St, Oakville, ON, L6J 7G4

(905) 338-3311
Emp Here 20
SIC 8051 Skilled nursing care facilities

D-U-N-S 25-803-2838   (BR)
REVERA INC
TRAFALGAR LODGE RETIREMENT RESI-
DENCE
299 Randall St, Oakville, ON, L6J 6B4
(905) 842-8408
Emp Here 40
SIC 8051 Skilled nursing care facilities

D-U-N-S 25-477-9614   (SL)
RISTORANTE PARADISO (2000) LIMITED
PARADISO RESTAURANT
125 Lakeshore Rd E, Oakville, ON, L6J 1H3
(905) 338-1594
Emp Here 110   *Sales* 4,521,600
SIC 5812 Eating places

D-U-N-S 24-972-8841   (BR)
ROYAL BANK OF CANADA
ROYAL BANK FINANCIAL GROUP
(*Suby of* Royal Bank Of Canada)
279 Lakeshore Rd E, Oakville, ON, L6J 1H9
(905) 845-4224
Emp Here 25
SIC 6021 National commercial banks

D-U-N-S 25-990-8556   (BR)
ROYAL HOST INC
HOLIDAY INN
590 Argus Rd, Oakville, ON, L6J 3J3
(905) 842-5000
Emp Here 30
SIC 7011 Hotels and motels

D-U-N-S 25-402-8558   (BR)
ROYAL LEPAGE LIMITED
ROYAL LEPAGE RESIDENTIAL REAL ES-
TATE SERVICES
326 Lakeshore Rd E, Oakville, ON, L6J 1J6
(905) 845-4267
Emp Here 95
SIC 6531 Feal estate agents and managers

D-U-N-S 25-598-5434   (SL)
SHRED-IT AMERICA INC
2794 South Sheridan Way, Oakville, ON, L6J
7T4
(905) 829-2794
Emp Here 27   *Sales* 4,596,524
SIC 6794 Patent owners and lessors

D-U-N-S 25-802-9834   (BR)
SOBEYS CAPITAL INCORPORATED
MAPLE GROVE SOBEYS
511 Maple Grove Dr Suite 4, Oakville, ON, L6J
6X8
(905) 849-0691
Emp Here 180
SIC 5411 Grocery stores

D-U-N-S 20-806-5586   (BR)
STARBUCKS COFFEE CANADA, INC
(*Suby of* Starbucks Corporation)
321 Cornwall Rd Unit 114, Oakville, ON, L6J
7Z5
(905) 844-8668
Emp Here 20
SIC 5812 Eating places

D-U-N-S 20-527-6236   (BR)
SUNRISE NORTH SENIOR LIVING LTD
(*Suby of* Welltower Inc.)
456 Trafalgar Rd Suite 312, Oakville, ON, L6J
7X1
(905) 337-1145
Emp Here 100
SIC 8361 Residential care

D-U-N-S 20-328-3221   (BR)
TDL GROUP CORP, THE
TIM HORTONS
135 Trafalgar Rd, Oakville, ON, L6J 3G4
(905) 845-0421
Emp Here 25
SIC 5812 Eating places

D-U-N-S 25-684-1990   (SL)
TT ESSEX INC
TWISTEE TREAT
1400 Cornwall Rd Unit 5, Oakville, ON, L6J
7W5
(905) 829-8686
Emp Here 50   *Sales* 11,768,200
SIC 6794 Patent owners and lessors
Pr Pr Mark Liptok
Sec Janet Liptok

D-U-N-S 25-278-0861   (BR)
TWINCORP INC
TACO BELL
546 Trafalgar Rd, Oakville, ON, L6J 3J2

Emp Here 20
SIC 5812 Eating places

D-U-N-S 25-065-5297   (BR)
VIA RAIL CANADA INC
200 Cross Ave, Oakville, ON, L6J 2W6
(888) 842-7245
Emp Here 100
SIC 4111 Local and suburban transit

D-U-N-S 20-927-4161   (BR)
WENDY'S RESTAURANTS OF CANADA INC
WENDY'S
(*Suby of* The Wendy's Company)
2304 Royal Windsor Dr, Oakville, ON, L6J 7Y1
(905) 845-8094
Emp Here 25
SIC 5812 Eating places

D-U-N-S 25-796-3926   (BR)
WENDY'S RESTAURANTS OF CANADA INC
WENDY'S
(*Suby of* The Wendy's Company)
2960 South Sheridan Way, Oakville, ON, L6J
7T4
(905) 829-9139
Emp Here 28
SIC 5812 Eating places

Oakville, ON L6K
Halton County

D-U-N-S 24-380-9782   (SL)
123 BUSY BEAVERS LEARNING CENTRES INC
690 Dorval Dr Suite 400, Oakville, ON, L6K
3W7

Emp Here 50   *Sales* 1,978,891
SIC 8351 Child day care services

D-U-N-S 25-099-5537   (SL)
ACCESS FLOWER TRADING INC
FLOWERBUYER.COM
700 Dorval Dr Suite 405, Oakville, ON, L6K
3V3
(905) 849-1343
Emp Here 30   *Sales* 3,575,074
SIC 5193 Flowers and florists supplies

D-U-N-S 24-335-5898   (BR)
CRH CANADA GROUP INC
DUFFERIN CONSTRUCTION COMPANY,
DIV OF
690 Dorval Dr Suite 200, Oakville, ON, L6K
3W7
(905) 842-2741
Emp Here 150
SIC 8711 Engineering services

D-U-N-S 20-303-3352   (BR)
CARA OPERATIONS LIMITED
KELSEY'S
(*Suby of* Cara Holdings Limited)
450 South Service Rd W, Oakville, ON, L6K
2H4
(905) 842-5510
Emp Here 20
SIC 5812 Eating places

D-U-N-S 20-291-0217   (BR)
CONSEIL SCOLAIRE DE DISTRICT CATHOLIQUE CENTRE-SUD
ECOLE ELEMENTAIRE CATHOLIQUE
SAINTE-MARIE
336 Maurice Dr, Oakville, ON, L6K 2X3
(905) 845-4472
Emp Here 27
SIC 8211 Elementary and secondary schools

D-U-N-S 24-910-6576   (SL)
CONSTELLATION FINANCING SYSTEMS CORP
690 Dorval Dr Suite 405, Oakville, ON, L6K
3W7
(289) 291-4999
Emp Here 20   *Sales* 1,884,658
SIC 7371 Custom computer programming services

D-U-N-S 20-566-3235   (SL)
CORBETT'S SKIS & SNOWBOARDS INC
144 Speers Rd, Oakville, ON, L6K 2E7
(905) 845-1566
Emp Here 50   *Sales* 4,231,721
SIC 5941 Sporting goods and bicycle shops

D-U-N-S 20-157-2450   (HQ)
DANA CANADA CORPORATION
SERVICE PARTS DIVISION
656 Kerr St, Oakville, ON, L6K 3E4
(905) 849-1200
Emp Here 60   *Emp Total* 24,900
Sales 376,472,685
SIC 3714 Motor vehicle parts and accessories
 Paul Teeple
 Rodney R Filcek
Sec Paul Fudacz
Sec Rodney W.J. Seyfert
 William A Jocsak
Treas Teresa Mulawa
Asst Tr David J Watson
 Gilberto Ceratti

D-U-N-S 25-301-2967   (BR)
EXTENDICARE (CANADA) INC
PARAMED HOME HEALTH CARE
700 Dorval Sr Suite 111, Oakville, ON, L6K
3V3
(905) 847-1025
Emp Here 500
SIC 8051 Skilled nursing care facilities

D-U-N-S 24-823-6762   (SL)
FANTASY FRUIT MARKET (1987) LTD.
427 Speers Rd Unit 1, Oakville, ON, L6K 3S8

Emp Here 80   *Sales* 9,536,300
SIC 5431 Fruit and vegetable markets
Pr Pr Danny Mazzilli
 Lenny Mazzilli
Dir Mike Dinadis
Dir Frank Bellissimo

D-U-N-S 20-290-8104   (BR)
HALTON CATHOLIC DISTRICT SCHOOL BOARD
THOMAS MERTON CENTRE FOR CONED
(OAKVILLE)
171 Speers Rd, Oakville, ON, L6K 3W8
(905) 849-7555
Emp Here 50
SIC 8211 Elementary and secondary schools

D-U-N-S 20-591-9629   (BR)
HALTON CATHOLIC DISTRICT SCHOOL BOARD
ST JAMES ELEMENTARY
255 Morden Rd, Oakville, ON, L6K 2S2
(905) 339-0731
Emp Here 40
SIC 8211 Elementary and secondary schools

D-U-N-S 20-025-4485   (BR)
HALTON CATHOLIC DISTRICT SCHOOL BOARD
ST THOMAS AQUINAS SECONDARY
SCHOOL

124 Dorval Dr, Oakville, ON, L6K 2W1
(905) 842-9494
Emp Here 110
SIC 8211 Elementary and secondary schools

D-U-N-S 25-143-3645   (BR)
HALTON DISTRICT SCHOOL BOARD
W.H. MORDEN SCHOOL
180 Morden Rd, Oakville, ON, L6K 2S3
(905) 844-9612
Emp Here 45
SIC 8211 Elementary and secondary schools

D-U-N-S 20-408-1848   (HQ)
IAN MARTIN LIMITED
(*Suby of* Martin, Ian Technology Staffing Limited)
465 Morden Rd, Oakville, ON, L6K 3W6
(905) 815-1600
Emp Here 60   *Emp Total* 1,000
Sales 72,960,700
SIC 7361 Employment agencies
Pr Pr William Masson
Dir Robert G. Witterick
Dir Ratnasingham Singaratnam

D-U-N-S 24-577-0300   (SL)
INNOVATIVE FOOD BRANDS INC
(*Suby of* Donato Group Inc, The)
700 Kerr St W, Oakville, ON, L6K 3W5
(905) 337-7777
Emp Here 20   *Sales* 1,459,214
SIC 2038 Frozen specialties, nec

D-U-N-S 20-897-4308   (BR)
LEE HECHT HARRISON-CANADA CORP
LEE HECHT HARRISON KNIGHTSBRIDGE
710 Dorval Dr Suite 108, Oakville, ON, L6K
3V7
(905) 338-7679
Emp Here 30
SIC 8742 Management consulting services

D-U-N-S 25-079-0474   (BR)
LOBLAWS SUPERMARKETS LIMITED
LOBLAWS 190
173 Lakeshore Rd W, Oakville, ON, L6K 1E7
(905) 845-4946
Emp Here 200
SIC 5411 Grocery stores

D-U-N-S 25-237-0259   (BR)
MANULIFE SECURITIES INVESTMENT SERVICES INC
MANULIFE SECURITIES
710 Dorval Dr Unit 505, Oakville, ON, L6K 3V7

Emp Here 45
SIC 6211 Security brokers and dealers

D-U-N-S 25-300-2802   (BR)
METRO ONTARIO INC
FOOD BASICS
530 Kerr St, Oakville, ON, L6K 3C7

Emp Here 50
SIC 5411 Grocery stores

D-U-N-S 24-486-8543   (BR)
METROLAND MEDIA GROUP LTD
OAKVILLE BEAVER
467 Speers Rd Suite 1, Oakville, ON, L6K 3S4
(905) 845-3824
Emp Here 100
SIC 2711 Newspapers

D-U-N-S 20-514-0655   (BR)
OPEN SOLUTIONS CANADA INC
DATA WEST SOLUTIONS
(*Suby of* Fiserv, Inc.)
700 Dorval Dr Suite 202, Oakville, ON, L6K
3V3
(905) 849-1390
Emp Here 85
SIC 8741 Management services

D-U-N-S 24-115-6400   (BR)
PEEL HALTON ACQUIRED BRAIN IN-

JURIES SERVICES
37 Bond St, Oakville, ON, L6K 1L8
(905) 844-2240
Emp Here 30
SIC 8621 Professional organizations

D-U-N-S 25-944-4024   (BR)
REVERA INC
THE KENSINGTON VICTORIA
25 Lakeshore Rd W Suite 509, Oakville, ON,
L6K 3X8
(905) 844-4000
Emp Here 62
SIC 8051 Skilled nursing care facilities

D-U-N-S 25-165-3531   (SL)
ROCK CONCRETE FORMING LTD
547 Speers Rd, Oakville, ON, L6K 2G4

Emp Here 40   *Sales* 5,653,974
SIC 1771 Concrete work
Pr Adelino Dasilva

D-U-N-S 24-050-1288   (HQ)
WENDY'S RESTAURANTS OF CANADA INC
WENDY'S OLD FASHION HAMBURGERS
(*Suby of* The Wendy's Company)
240 Wyecroft Rd, Oakville, ON, L6K 2G7
(905) 337-8041
Emp Here 100   *Emp Total* 23,000
Sales 214,191,382
SIC 5812 Eating places
Neil Lester
VP VP John Brownley
Lawrence Laudick

Oakville, ON L6L
Halton County

D-U-N-S 24-802-7026   (BR)
178028 CANADA INC
PLACAGE AU CHROME DE L'ONTARIO
(*Suby of* 178028 Canada Inc)
1328 Speers Rd, Oakville, ON, L6L 2X4
(905) 825-1995
Emp Here 20
SIC 3471 Plating and polishing

D-U-N-S 20-697-8376   (SL)
2088343 ONTARIO LIMITED
CARTER GROUP
2125 Wyecroft Rd, Oakville, ON, L6L 5L7

Emp Here 45   *Sales* 6,832,640
SIC 3679 Electronic components, nec
Pr Butch Carter

D-U-N-S 24-689-2053   (SL)
678114 ONTARIO INC
VISTAMERE, THE
380 Sherin Dr, Oakville, ON, L6L 4J3
(905) 847-1413
Emp Here 50   *Sales* 5,889,600
SIC 6513 Apartment building operators
Pr Pr John Pennington
Robert Fasken

D-U-N-S 25-722-3958   (SL)
981543 ONTARIO INC
A C EXPRESS DIV
1150 South Service Rd W, Oakville, ON, L6L
5T7
(905) 827-1669
Emp Here 50   *Sales* 8,239,360
SIC 4213 Trucking, except local
Pr Pr Ian Smith
VP VP Georgine Smith
VP Opers Norm Rego
Acct Mgr Antonella Gismondi

D-U-N-S 24-310-4051   (SL)
ACCLAIM HEALTH COMMUNITY CARE SERVICES
ACCLAIM HEALTH
2370 Speers Rd, Oakville, ON, L6L 5M2

(905) 827-8800
Emp Here 350   *Sales* 91,102,100
SIC 8082 Home health care services
Dir Angela Brewer
Pr Gerald Park

D-U-N-S 20-918-5896   (BR)
ACUREN GROUP INC
(*Suby of* Rockwood Service Corporation)
2190 Speers Rd, Oakville, ON, L6L 2X8
(905) 825-8595
Emp Here 40
SIC 8734 Testing laboratories

D-U-N-S 20-174-9392   (SL)
ARCH CHEMICALS CANADA, INC
QUATIC CONSUMER PRODUCTS
160 Warner Dr, Oakville, ON, L6L 6E7
(905) 847-9878
Emp Here 20   *Sales* 33,377,050
SIC 5169 Chemicals and allied products, nec
Dir Larry Mcgregor

D-U-N-S 20-134-1310   (HQ)
BOT CONSTRUCTION LIMITED
(*Suby of* S. Bot & Sons Enterprises Limited)
1224 Speers Rd, Oakville, ON, L6L 5B6
(905) 827-4167
Emp Here 22   *Emp Total* 3
Sales 6,274,620
SIC 1611 Highway and street construction
Pr Pr Roy Bot
Steve Bot

D-U-N-S 25-659-5356   (SL)
BUDD BROTHERS HOLDING COMPANY LTD
BUDD'S SATURN SAAB OF OAKVILLE
2400 South Service Rd W, Oakville, ON, L6L
5M9
(905) 845-1610
Emp Here 35   *Sales* 18,261,000
SIC 5511 New and used car dealers
Pr Pr Christopher Budd

D-U-N-S 25-560-0884   (BR)
BUDD, STUART & SONS LIMITED
BUDD'S IMPORTED CARS
2430 South Service Rd W, Oakville, ON, L6L
5M9
(905) 845-1443
Emp Here 40
SIC 5511 New and used car dealers

D-U-N-S 25-362-7517   (BR)
CRH CANADA GROUP INC
DUFFERIN CONSTRUCTION COMPANY MAINTENANCE SHOP
731 Third Line, Oakville, ON, L6L 4B2
(905) 827-5750
Emp Here 50
SIC 7699 Repair services, nec

D-U-N-S 20-297-0906   (BR)
CANADA POST CORPORATION
1130 Speers Rd, Oakville, ON, L6L 2X4
(905) 338-1199
Emp Here 97
SIC 4311 U.s. postal service

D-U-N-S 25-303-6503   (BR)
CANADIAN IMPERIAL BANK OF COMMERCE
CIBC
1515 Rebecca St, Oakville, ON, L6L 5G8
(800) 465-2422
Emp Here 20
SIC 6021 National commercial banks

D-U-N-S 25-695-8885   (BR)
CANADIAN STEBBINS ENGINEERING & MFG CO LIMITED
BIGELOW LIPTAK OF CANADA, DIV OF
(*Suby of* The Stebbins Engineering and Manufacturing Company)
2384 Speers Rd, Oakville, ON, L6L 5M2
(905) 825-1800
Emp Here 22

SIC 8711 Engineering services

D-U-N-S 24-469-6068   (HQ)
CANTWELL CULLEN & COMPANY INC
1131 South Service Rd W, Oakville, ON, L6L
6K4
(905) 825-3255
Emp Here 128   *Emp Total* 241
Sales 17,510,568
SIC 3679 Electronic components, nec
Pr Pr Ted Perdue
S&M/VP Stuart Robertson

D-U-N-S 24-252-5165   (BR)
CARA OPERATIONS LIMITED
KELSEY'S
(*Suby of* Cara Holdings Limited)
3549 Wyecroft Rd, Oakville, ON, L6L 0B7
(905) 825-9134
Emp Here 40
SIC 5812 Eating places

D-U-N-S 24-255-3258   (BR)
CARA OPERATIONS LIMITED
MONTANA'S COOKHOUSE
(*Suby of* Cara Holdings Limited)
3537 Wyecroft Rd Suite 3041, Oakville, ON,
L6L 0B7
(905) 827-1691
Emp Here 40
SIC 5812 Eating places

D-U-N-S 24-418-2866   (BR)
CINEPLEX ODEON CORPORATION
CINEPLEX CINEMAS OAKVILLE & VIP
3531 Wyecroft Rd, Oakville, ON, L6L 0B7
(905) 827-7173
Emp Here 20
SIC 7832 Motion picture theaters, except drive-in

D-U-N-S 20-711-7230   (BR)
CONSEIL SCOLAIRE VIAMONDE
PATRICIA PICKNELL SCHOOL
1257 Sedgewick Cres, Oakville, ON, L6L 1X5
(905) 465-0512
Emp Here 26
SIC 8211 Elementary and secondary schools

D-U-N-S 20-800-5897   (BR)
CORPORATION OF THE TOWN OF OAKVILLE, THE
KINOAK ARENA
363 Warminster Dr, Oakville, ON, L6L 4N1
(905) 338-4191
Emp Here 20
SIC 7999 Amusement and recreation, nec

D-U-N-S 20-752-4927   (HQ)
DAEMAR INC
861 Cranberry Crt, Oakville, ON, L6L 6J7
(905) 847-6500
Emp Here 22   *Emp Total* 20
Sales 7,687,973
SIC 5085 Industrial supplies
William Pirie
Pr Pr Craig Pirie
VP VP David Copping
Alan Puls
Donna Pirie
Karen Unsworth

D-U-N-S 25-404-3110   (BR)
DANA CANADA CORPORATION
THERMAL PRODUCTS - LONG MANUFACTURING
1400 Advance Rd, Oakville, ON, L6L 6L6
(905) 825-8856
Emp Here 150
SIC 3443 Fabricated plate work (boiler shop)

D-U-N-S 25-966-8759   (SL)
EL-CON CONSTRUCTION INC
2231 Wyecroft Rd, Oakville, ON, L6L 5L7
(905) 825-4461
Emp Here 25   *Sales* 1,824,018
SIC 1794 Excavation work

D-U-N-S 24-977-1937   (BR)
FGL SPORTS LTD
SPORT CHEK BURLOAK
3465 Wyecroft Rd Unit B, Oakville, ON, L6L
0B6
(905) 847-9445
Emp Here 30
SIC 5941 Sporting goods and bicycle shops

D-U-N-S 24-984-7849   (BR)
GENERAL ELECTRIC CANADA COMPANY
GE LIGHTING CANADA
(*Suby of* General Electric Company)
1290 S Service Rd W, Oakville, ON, L6L 5T7
(905) 849-5048
Emp Here 500
SIC 3625 Relays and industrial controls

D-U-N-S 24-239-1506   (BR)
GENERAL ELECTRIC CANADA COMPANY
GE
(*Suby of* General Electric Company)
1290 South Service Rd W, Oakville, ON, L6L
5T7

Emp Here 40

SIC 3625 Relays and industrial controls

D-U-N-S 20-707-0830   (HQ)
GOODRICH AEROSPACE CANADA LTD
GOODRICH LANDING GEAR
(*Suby of* United Technologies Corporation)
1400 South Service Rd W, Oakville, ON, L6L
5Y7
(905) 827-7777
Emp Here 580   *Emp Total* 202,000
Sales 150,590,885
SIC 3728 Aircraft parts and equipment, nec
VP Frank Karakas
Tim Whittier
Fabrice Rancoeur
Bob Corbell

D-U-N-S 25-340-5898   (BR)
GOVERNING COUNCIL OF THE SALVATION ARMY IN CANADA, THE
GOVERNING COUNCIL OF THE SALVATION ARMY IN CANADA, THE
2360 South Service Rd W, Oakville, ON, L6L
5M9
(905) 825-9208
Emp Here 50
SIC 8322 Individual and family services

D-U-N-S 25-084-4487   (SL)
HALTON ALARM RESPONSE & PROTECTION LTD
HARP SECURITY
760 Pacific Rd Unit 21, Oakville, ON, L6L 6M5
(905) 827-6655
Emp Here 60   *Sales* 1,896,978
SIC 7382 Security systems services

D-U-N-S 25-149-6097   (BR)
HALTON CATHOLIC DISTRICT SCHOOL BOARD
ST DOMINIC ELEMENTARY SCHOOL
2405 Rebecca St, Oakville, ON, L6L 2B1
(905) 827-4401
Emp Here 40
SIC 8211 Elementary and secondary schools

D-U-N-S 20-711-0672   (BR)
HALTON CATHOLIC DISTRICT SCHOOL BOARD
ST. JOSEPH (OAKVILLE) ELEMENTARY SCHOOL
477 Warminster Dr, Oakville, ON, L6L 4N4
(905) 827-4231
Emp Here 37
SIC 8211 Elementary and secondary schools

D-U-N-S 24-193-6561   (BR)
HALTON DISTRICT SCHOOL BOARD
1474 Wallace Rd, Oakville, ON, L6L 2Y2

Emp Here 4,000
SIC 8211 Elementary and secondary schools

▲ Public Company   ■ Public Company Family Member   **HQ** Headquarters   **BR** Branch   **SL** Single Location

D-U-N-S 25-143-3652   (BR)
HALTON DISTRICT SCHOOL BOARD
GLADYS SPEERS PUBLIC SCHOOL
2150 Samway Rd, Oakville, ON, L6L 2P6
(905) 827-4841
Emp Here 30
SIC 8211 Elementary and secondary schools

D-U-N-S 20-081-7000   (BR)
HALTON DISTRICT SCHOOL BOARD
EASTVIEW PUBLIC SCHOOL
2266 Hixon St, Oakville, ON, L6L 1T4
(905) 827-1541
Emp Here 35
SIC 8211 Elementary and secondary schools

D-U-N-S 20-009-7033   (BR)
HALTON DISTRICT SCHOOL BOARD
BROOKDALE PULBIC SCHOOL
1195 Bridge Rd, Oakville, ON, L6L 2C3
(905) 827-2741
Emp Here 35
SIC 8211 Elementary and secondary schools

D-U-N-S 20-024-9873   (BR)
HALTON DISTRICT SCHOOL BOARD
ECOLE PINE GROVE SCHOOL
529 Fourth Line, Oakville, ON, L6L 5A8
(905) 844-6371
Emp Here 50
SIC 8211 Elementary and secondary schools

D-U-N-S 25-459-2736   (SL)
HALTON MULTICULTURAL COUNCIL INC
1092 Speers Rd, Oakville, ON, L6L 2X4
(905) 842-2486
Emp Here 50   *Sales* 2,712,960
SIC 8322 Individual and family services

D-U-N-S 20-338-5067   (BR)
HEARN INDUSTRIAL SERVICES INC
2189 Speers Rd, Oakville, ON, L6L 2X9
(226) 340-1147
Emp Here 75
SIC 4225 General warehousing and storage

D-U-N-S 24-361-7250   (BR)
HOME DEPOT OF CANADA INC
HOME DEPOT
(*Suby of* The Home Depot Inc)
3300 South Service Rd W, Oakville, ON, L6L 0B1
(905) 469-7110
Emp Here 200
SIC 5251 Hardware stores

D-U-N-S 20-052-2097   (SL)
INNOMAR STRATEGIES INC
3470 Superior Crt Suite 2, Oakville, ON, L6L 0C4
(905) 847-4310
Emp Here 30   *Sales* 2,772,507
SIC 8741 Management services

D-U-N-S 20-134-6475   (BR)
JEMPAK GK INC
1485 Speers Rd, Oakville, ON, L6L 2X5
(905) 827-1123
Emp Here 80
SIC 2841 Soap and other detergents

D-U-N-S 24-850-1728   (HQ)
JOHN DEERE FINANCIAL INC
3430 Superior Crt, Oakville, ON, L6L 0C4
(905) 319-9100
Emp Here 130   *Emp Total* 913
Sales 101,524,617
SIC 6153 Short-term business credit institutions, except agricultural
    David C. Gilmore
Pr Pr Teresa Garside
VP VP W. John Grosso
    Thomas C. Spitzfaden
    Steve A. Watson
Dir Bret C. Thomas

D-U-N-S 24-575-4502   (BR)
KEG RESTAURANTS LTD

KEG STEAKHOUSE AND BAR, THE
3130 South Service Rd W, Oakville, ON, L6L 6T1
(905) 681-1810
Emp Here 85
SIC 5812 Eating places

D-U-N-S 25-318-7561   (BR)
LIQUOR CONTROL BOARD OF ONTARIO, THE
L.C.B.O. #437
1527 Rebecca St, Oakville, ON, L6L 1Z8
(905) 827-5072
Emp Here 20
SIC 5921 Liquor stores

D-U-N-S 20-280-8218   (SL)
MACHINABILITY AUTOMATION CORP
1045 South Service Rd W, Oakville, ON, L6L 6K3
(905) 618-0187
Emp Here 50   *Sales* 4,961,328
SIC 8711 Engineering services

D-U-N-S 20-555-6314   (BR)
METRO ONTARIO INC
METRO
1521 Rebecca St, Oakville, ON, L6L 1Z8
(905) 827-5421
Emp Here 150
SIC 5411 Grocery stores

D-U-N-S 25-192-9386   (BR)
METROLAND MEDIA GROUP LTD
QE WEB
1158 South Service Rd W, Oakville, ON, L6L 5T7

Emp Here 30
SIC 2759 Commercial printing, nec

D-U-N-S 25-538-3671   (SL)
MOUNTAIN INN AT RIBBON CREEK LIMITED PARTNERSHIP, THE
380 Sherin Dr, Oakville, ON, L6L 4J3
(905) 847-6120
Emp Here 50   *Sales* 2,188,821
SIC 7011 Hotels and motels

D-U-N-S 24-800-0478   (BR)
NIKE CANADA CORP
(*Suby of* Nike, Inc.)
3509 Wyecroft Rd Suite J, Oakville, ON, L6L 0B6
(905) 827-4677
Emp Here 30
SIC 5091 Sporting and recreation goods

D-U-N-S 24-860-3250   (BR)
NORTHAMPTON INNS (OAKVILLE) INC
QUALITY HOTEL & SUITES
(*Suby of* Northampton Inns (Oakville) Inc)
754 Bronte Rd, Oakville, ON, L6L 6R8
(905) 847-6667
Emp Here 40
SIC 7011 Hotels and motels

D-U-N-S 20-181-4931   (HQ)
OAKVILLE ENTERPRISES CORPORATION
861 Redwood Sq Suite 1900, Oakville, ON, L6L 6R6
(905) 825-9400
Emp Here 150   *Emp Total* 4,500
Sales 85,152,473
SIC 4911 Electric services
Pr Alex Bystrin
    Gary Burkett
    David Sweezie
    Gary Kain

D-U-N-S 25-512-2376   (BR)
PLASTIQUES BERRY CANADA INC
MAC WATERLOO
2250 South Service Rd W, Oakville, ON, L6L 5N1
(905) 827-8600
Emp Here 50
SIC 3089 Plastics products, nec

D-U-N-S 20-528-6883   (BR)
PRAXAIR CANADA INC
(*Suby of* Praxair, Inc.)
2393 Speers Rd, Oakville, ON, L6L 2X9
(905) 827-4321
Emp Here 40
SIC 2813 Industrial gases

D-U-N-S 24-827-3187   (BR)
ROPAK CANADA INC
BWAY PACKAGING CANADA
(*Suby of* Stone Canyon Industries LLC)
2240 Wyecroft Rd, Oakville, ON, L6L 6M1
(905) 827-9340
Emp Here 135
SIC 3089 Plastics products, nec

D-U-N-S 20-569-9007   (BR)
ROYAL BANK OF CANADA
RBC
(*Suby of* Royal Bank Of Canada)
1005 Speers Rd, Oakville, ON, L6L 2X5
(905) 842-2360
Emp Here 20
SIC 6021 National commercial banks

D-U-N-S 24-523-8530   (HQ)
SM CYCLO OF CANADA, LTD
SUMITOMO DRIVE TECHNOLOGIES
1045 South Service Rd W, Oakville, ON, L6L 6K3
(905) 469-1050
Emp Here 20   *Emp Total* 19,321
Sales 6,330,240
SIC 3462 Iron and steel forgings
VP Opers Ian Wells
Pr Greg Banero

D-U-N-S 24-842-4991   (SL)
SAINT-GOBAIN SOLAR GUARD, INC
760 Pacific Rd Unit 1, Oakville, ON, L6L 6M5
(905) 847-2790
Emp Here 50   *Sales* 9,423,290
SIC 2899 Chemical preparations, nec
Dir Thomas Kinisky
Genl Mgr Frank Mackay
Sec Timothy Feagans
Dir Jean-Pierre Floris
Dir Lisa Grossi
CFO M.Shawn Puccio
Treas John Sweeney

D-U-N-S 25-053-7404   (BR)
SOBEYS CAPITAL INCORPORATED
2441 Lakeshore Rd W, Oakville, ON, L6L 5V5
(905) 825-2278
Emp Here 120
SIC 5411 Grocery stores

D-U-N-S 20-860-2446   (BR)
SOURCE (BELL) ELECTRONICS INC, THE
SOURCE, THE
1515 Rebecca St Suite 34, Oakville, ON, L6L 5G8
(905) 825-5778
Emp Here 25
SIC 5999 Miscellaneous retail stores, nec

D-U-N-S 25-910-5794   (SL)
STRATOSPHERE QUALITY, INC
1515 Rebecca St, Oakville, ON, L6L 1Z8
(877) 224-8584
Emp Here 354   *Sales* 17,218,725
SIC 4785 Inspection and fixed facilities
VP VP Tammy Mcewen

D-U-N-S 25-418-6570   (BR)
SUNCOR ENERGY INC
3275 Rebecca St, Oakville, ON, L6L 6N5
(905) 804-7152
Emp Here 200
SIC 2911 Petroleum refining

D-U-N-S 24-847-5915   (HQ)
SUPERIOR SOLUTIONS LTD
(*Suby of* Superior Solutions Ltd)
851 Progress Crt, Oakville, ON, L6L 6K1

(800) 921-5527
Emp Here 30   *Emp Total* 36
Sales 5,559,741
SIC 5087 Service establishment equipment

D-U-N-S 20-845-6624   (HQ)
TISI CANADA INC
781 Westgate Rd, Oakville, ON, L6L 6R7
(905) 845-9542
Emp Here 50   *Emp Total* 7,400
Sales 27,806,657
SIC 3398 Metal heat treating
VP Fin Charles Slater
    Martin Decamp
Dir John E. G. Gilgan
    Authur F Victorson
Sr VP David C. Palmore
Sr VP Peter W. Wallace Jr
    Ted W. Owen
VP James Campbell

D-U-N-S 25-531-0401   (HQ)
TANDET NATIONALEASE LTD
1351 Speers Rd, Oakville, ON, L6L 2X5
(905) 827-4200
Emp Here 25   *Emp Total* 355
Sales 3,210,271
SIC 7513 Truck rental and leasing, no drivers

D-U-N-S 20-891-8714   (HQ)
THERMADYNE WELDING PRODUCTS CANADA LIMITED
(*Suby of* Colfax Corporation)
2070 Wyecroft Rd, Oakville, ON, L6L 5V6
(905) 827-1111
Emp Here 50   *Emp Total* 16,000
Sales 18,752,347
SIC 5085 Industrial supplies
Pr Pr Betty Robertson

D-U-N-S 25-322-2566   (BR)
TORONTO-DOMINION BANK, THE
TD BANK FINANCIAL GROUP
(*Suby of* Toronto-Dominion Bank, The)
1515 Rebecca St Suite 36, Oakville, ON, L6L 5G8
(905) 827-1107
Emp Here 22
SIC 6021 National commercial banks

D-U-N-S 25-796-2795   (HQ)
TOTAL TECH POOLS INC
(*Suby of* Total Tech Pools Inc)
1380 Speers Rd Suite 1, Oakville, ON, L6L 5V3
(905) 825-1389
Emp Here 23   *Emp Total* 50
Sales 2,626,585
SIC 7389 Business services, nec

D-U-N-S 20-279-3279   (SL)
VICTOR TECHNOLOGIES CANADA LTD
(*Suby of* Colfax Corporation)
2070 Wyecroft Rd, Oakville, ON, L6L 5V6
(905) 827-7777
Emp Here 30   *Sales* 3,210,271
SIC 3569 General industrial machinery, nec

D-U-N-S 24-130-8472   (HQ)
VICWEST INC
VICWEST BUILDING PRODUCTS
(*Suby of* Vicwest Inc)
1296 South Service Rd W, Oakville, ON, L6L 5T7
(905) 825-2252
Emp Here 50   *Emp Total* 406
Sales 42,682,010
SIC 3444 Sheet Metalwork
Pr Paul Lobb
Sec Ronan Dowling
Dir Fin Jason Fortuna
    Russell Shiels

D-U-N-S 24-927-2212   (BR)
WALLACE & CAREY INC
2226 South Service Rd W, Oakville, ON, L6L 5N1
(905) 825-9640
Emp Here 50

SIC 5099 Durable goods, nec

D-U-N-S 24-524-5659   (BR)
WASTE MANAGEMENT OF CANADA COR-PORATION
WASTE MANAGEMENT OF CANADA COR-PORATION
(*Suby of* Waste Management, Inc.)
3275 Rebecca St, Oakville, ON, L6L 6N5
(905) 433-5077
Emp Here 30
SIC 4953 Refuse systems

D-U-N-S 24-358-4849   (BR)
WOLSELEY CANADA INC
REGIONAL DISTRIBUTION CENTER
(*Suby of* WOLSELEY PLC)
1330 South Service Rd W, Oakville, ON, L6L 5T7

Emp Here 50
SIC 5074 Plumbing and heating equipment and supplies (hydronics)

Oakville, ON L6M
Halton County

D-U-N-S 25-295-7519   (BR)
BANK OF NOVA SCOTIA, THE
SCOTIABANK
1500 Upper Middle Rd W Unit 10, Oakville, ON, L6M 3G3
(905) 847-0220
Emp Here 23
SIC 6021 National commercial banks

D-U-N-S 20-554-7594   (BR)
CHARTWELL RETIREMENT RESIDENCES
CHARTWELL SENIORS HOUSING REAL ESTATE INVESTMENT TRUST
2140 Baronwood Dr Suite 225, Oakville, ON, L6M 4V6
(905) 827-2405
Emp Here 100
SIC 8059 Nursing and personal care, nec

D-U-N-S 25-369-5290   (BR)
DILLON CONSULTING LIMITED
(*Suby of* Dillon Consulting Inc)
1155 North Service Rd W Unit 14, Oakville, ON, L6M 3E3

Emp Here 20
SIC 8711 Engineering services

D-U-N-S 20-209-1679   (BR)
DOLLARAMA S.E.C.
DOLLARAMA
290 North Service Rd W, Oakville, ON, L6M 2S2
(905) 337-8104
Emp Here 20
SIC 5399 Miscellaneous general merchandise

D-U-N-S 24-735-9656   (BR)
DOMINION OF CANADA GENERAL INSUR-ANCE COMPANY, THE
(*Suby of* The Travelers Companies Inc)
1275 North Service Rd W Suite 103, Oakville, ON, L6M 3G4
(905) 825-6400
Emp Here 350
SIC 6411 Insurance agents, brokers, and service

D-U-N-S 24-337-3037   (BR)
FGL SPORTS LTD
SPORT CHECK
270 North Service Rd W Unit C08, Oakville, ON, L6M 2R8
(905) 338-7224
Emp Here 20
SIC 5941 Sporting goods and bicycle shops

D-U-N-S 20-790-0494   (BR)

GOODLIFE FITNESS CENTRES INC
300 North Service Rd W, Oakville, ON, L6M 2S1
(905) 337-7244
Emp Here 20
SIC 7999 Amusement and recreation, nec

D-U-N-S 20-591-3572   (BR)
HALTON CATHOLIC DISTRICT SCHOOL BOARD
ST JOAN OF ARC
2912 Westoak Trails Blvd, Oakville, ON, L6M 4T7
(905) 847-3581
Emp Here 50
SIC 8211 Elementary and secondary schools

D-U-N-S 20-711-0797   (BR)
HALTON CATHOLIC DISTRICT SCHOOL BOARD
ST BERNADETTE CATHOLIC SCHOOL
1201 Heritage Way, Oakville, ON, L6M 3A4
(905) 827-7235
Emp Here 55
SIC 8211 Elementary and secondary schools

D-U-N-S 20-591-2236   (BR)
HALTON CATHOLIC DISTRICT SCHOOL BOARD
MOTHER TERESA ELEMENTARY SCHOOL
1190 Westview Terr, Oakville, ON, L6M 3N2
(905) 325-6382
Emp Here 25
SIC 8211 Elementary and secondary schools

D-U-N-S 20-711-0763   (BR)
HALTON CATHOLIC DISTRICT SCHOOL BOARD
ST. MATTHEW CATHOLIC ELEMENTARY SCHOOL
1050 Nottinghill Gate, Oakville, ON, L6M 2G3
(905) 847-0088
Emp Here 50
SIC 8211 Elementary and secondary schools

D-U-N-S 24-525-4375   (BR)
HALTON DISTRICT SCHOOL BOARD
FOREST TRAIL PUBLIC ELEMENTARY SCHOOL
1406 Pine Glen Rd, Oakville, ON, L6M 4B9
(905) 469-0341
Emp Here 25
SIC 8211 Elementary and secondary schools

D-U-N-S 24-525-4391   (BR)
HALTON DISTRICT SCHOOL BOARD
EMILY CARR PUBLIC SCHOOL
2255 Pine Glen Rd, Oakville, ON, L6M 0G5
(905) 827-3928
Emp Here 25
SIC 8211 Elementary and secondary schools

D-U-N-S 20-591-2848   (BR)
HALTON DISTRICT SCHOOL BOARD
PILGRIM WOOD SCHOOL
1551 Pilgrims Way, Oakville, ON, L6M 2W7
(905) 825-9808
Emp Here 43
SIC 8211 Elementary and secondary schools

D-U-N-S 20-711-0581   (BR)
HALTON DISTRICT SCHOOL BOARD
CAPTAIN R WILSON PUBLIC SCHOOL
2145 Grand Oak Trail, Oakville, ON, L6M 4S7
(905) 465-3881
Emp Here 40
SIC 8211 Elementary and secondary schools

D-U-N-S 20-711-0557   (BR)
HALTON DISTRICT SCHOOL BOARD
WEST OAK PUBLIC SCHOOL
2071 Fourth Line, Oakville, ON, L6M 3K1
(905) 469-6119
Emp Here 65
SIC 8211 Elementary and secondary schools

D-U-N-S 25-143-3637   (BR)
HALTON DISTRICT SCHOOL BOARD

HERITAGE GLEN PUBLIC SCHOOL
1641 Heritage Way, Oakville, ON, L6M 2Z4
(905) 847-5496
Emp Here 53
SIC 8211 Elementary and secondary schools

D-U-N-S 25-138-3717   (BR)
HALTON DISTRICT SCHOOL BOARD
ABBEY PARK HIGH SCHOOL
1455 Glen Abbey Gate, Oakville, ON, L6M 2G5
(905) 827-4101
Emp Here 100
SIC 8211 Elementary and secondary schools

D-U-N-S 20-876-7863   (SL)
HORIBA AUTOMOTIVE TEST SYSTEMS, INC
1115 North Service Rd W, Oakville, ON, L6M 2V9
(905) 827-7755
Emp Here 45   *Sales* 5,559,741
SIC 7371 Custom computer programming services
Genl Mgr Brian Mcfadyen
Pr Rex Tapp

D-U-N-S 25-595-4885   (BR)
INDIGO BOOKS & MUSIC INC
CHAPTERS
(*Suby of* Indigo Books & Music Inc)
310 North Service Rd W Unit G, Oakville, ON, L6M 2R7
(905) 815-8197
Emp Here 45
SIC 5942 Book stores

D-U-N-S 25-315-7622   (BR)
INVESTORS GROUP FINANCIAL SER-VICES INC
INVESTORS FINANCIAL PLANNING CEN-TRE DIV OF
1275 North Service Rd W Unit 100, Oakville, ON, L6M 3G4
(905) 847-7776
Emp Here 70
SIC 8741 Management services

D-U-N-S 20-084-7551   (BR)
LICK'S ICE CREAM & BURGER SHOPS INC
LICK'S RESTAURANT
(*Suby of* Lick's Ice Cream & Burger Shops Inc)
270 North Service Rd W, Oakville, ON, L6M 2R8

Emp Here 35
SIC 5812 Eating places

D-U-N-S 25-803-1293   (BR)
MCG. RESTAURANTS (WONDERLAND) INC
OAR HOUSE SPORTS BAR & GRILL
270 North Service Rd W, Oakville, ON, L6M 2R8
(905) 338-1422
Emp Here 40
SIC 5812 Eating places

D-U-N-S 25-136-9955   (BR)
METRO ONTARIO PHARMACIES LIMITED
METRO
280 North Service Rd W, Oakville, ON, L6M 2S2
(905) 337-7694
Emp Here 200
SIC 5411 Grocery stores

D-U-N-S 24-985-6352   (BR)
MICHAELS OF CANADA, ULC
MICHAELS
(*Suby of* The Michaels Companies Inc)
200 North Service Rd W, Oakville, ON, L6M 2Y1
(905) 842-1555
Emp Here 30
SIC 5945 Hobby, toy, and game shops

D-U-N-S 24-771-4579   (SL)
OAKVILLE GYMNASTIC CLUB

1415 Third Line, Oakville, ON, L6M 3G2
(905) 847-7747
Emp Here 80   *Sales* 4,377,642
SIC 7999 Amusement and recreation, nec

D-U-N-S 20-576-7598   (BR)
OAKVILLE PUBLIC LIBRARY BOARD, THE
GLEN ABBEY BRANCH
1415 Third Line, Oakville, ON, L6M 3G2
(905) 815-2039
Emp Here 20
SIC 8231 Libraries

D-U-N-S 20-637-8296   (BR)
PIONEER FOOD SERVICES LIMITED
WENDY'S RESTAURANTS
(*Suby of* Pioneer Food Services Limited)
1530 North Service Rd W, Oakville, ON, L6M 4A1
(905) 465-3989
Emp Here 30
SIC 5812 Eating places

D-U-N-S 25-745-5931   (BR)
RBC DOMINION SECURITIES LIMITED
RBC INVESTMENTS
(*Suby of* Royal Bank Of Canada)
435 North Service Rd W Suite 101, Oakville, ON, L6M 4X8
(905) 469-7000
Emp Here 30
SIC 6211 Security brokers and dealers

D-U-N-S 20-978-4367   (BR)
REVERA LONG TERM CARE INC
2370 Third Line, Oakville, ON, L6M 4E2
(905) 469-3294
Emp Here 250
SIC 8059 Nursing and personal care, nec

D-U-N-S 24-010-4646   (SL)
ROSCETTI DRYWALL LIMITED
2495 Old Bronte Rd, Oakville, ON, L6M 4J2
(905) 827-8305
Emp Here 50   *Sales* 5,465,508
SIC 1742 Plastering, drywall, and insulation
Pr Pr Giacomo (Jack) Roscetti
Valerio Roscetti

D-U-N-S 25-301-1043   (BR)
SCOTIA CAPITAL INC
SCOTIA MCLEOD
1235 North Service Rd W Suite 200, Oakville, ON, L6M 2W2
(905) 842-9000
Emp Here 44
SIC 6211 Security brokers and dealers

D-U-N-S 25-987-4170   (BR)
SOBEYS CAPITAL INCORPORATED
SOBEYS NO 777
1500 Upper Middle Rd W, Oakville, ON, L6M 0C2
(905) 847-1909
Emp Here 200
SIC 5411 Grocery stores

D-U-N-S 25-806-4856   (BR)
SOBEYS CAPITAL INCORPORATED
SOBEY'S STORE 777
1500 Upper Middle Rd W, Oakville, ON, L6M 0C2
(905) 847-1909
Emp Here 200
SIC 5411 Grocery stores

D-U-N-S 24-389-3802   (BR)
STAPLES CANADA INC
STAPLES THE BUSINESS DEPOT
(*Suby of* Staples, Inc.)
320 North Service Rd W, Oakville, ON, L6M 2R7
(905) 338-6535
Emp Here 20
SIC 5943 Stationery stores

D-U-N-S 25-796-5749   (BR)
STARBUCKS COFFEE CANADA, INC
(*Suby of* Starbucks Corporation)

223 North Service Rd W Unit A, Oakville, ON, L6M 3R2
(905) 815-8551
Emp Here 21
SIC 5812 Eating places

D-U-N-S 24-545-1091   (SL)
TEMPO CANADA INC
1175 North Service Rd W Suite 200, Oakville, ON, L6M 2W1
(905) 339-3309
Emp Here 28   *Sales* 9,333,400
SIC 5169 Chemicals and allied products, nec
Pr Pr Carlo Agro
VP VP Bob Vaughan
VP VP Glen Hildebrand
   Joseph Agro

D-U-N-S 24-250-2081   (SL)
TOOR & ASSOCIATES INC
BOSTON PIZZA
270 North Service Rd W, Oakville, ON, L6M 2R8
(905) 849-8100
Emp Here 150   *Sales* 4,523,563
SIC 5812 Eating places

D-U-N-S 20-122-7498   (BR)
TOYS 'R' US (CANADA) LTD
TOYS 'R' US
(*Suby of* Toys "r" Us, Inc.)
290 North Service Rd W, Oakville, ON, L6M 2S2
(905) 849-1860
Emp Here 25
SIC 5945 Hobby, toy, and game shops

D-U-N-S 25-221-2493   (BR)
WINNERS MERCHANTS INTERNATIONAL L.P.
WINNERS
(*Suby of* The TJX Companies Inc)
200 North Service Rd W, Oakville, ON, L6M 2Y1
(905) 338-5700
Emp Here 40
SIC 5651 Family clothing stores

Oakwood, ON K0M

D-U-N-S 25-081-5230   (BR)
TRILLIUM LAKELANDS DISTRICT SCHOOL BOARD
MARIPOSA ELEMENTARY SCHOOL
755 Eldon Rd, Oakwood, ON, K0M 2M0
(705) 953-9740
Emp Here 40
SIC 8211 Elementary and secondary schools

Odessa, ON K0H
Lennox County

D-U-N-S 20-799-6930   (BR)
CORPORATION OF LOYALIST TOWNSHIP, THE
263 Main St, Odessa, ON, K0H 2H0
(613) 386-7351
Emp Here 50
SIC 4941 Water supply

D-U-N-S 24-507-6526   (SL)
DOORNEKAMP, H. R. CONSTRUCTION LTD
588 Scotland Rd, Odessa, ON, K0H 2H0
(613) 386-3033
Emp Here 60   *Sales* 14,417,634
SIC 1542 Nonresidential construction, nec
Pr Pr Henrick R Doornekamp
   Sheri Doornekamp

D-U-N-S 25-237-9441   (BR)
LIMESTONE DISTRICT SCHOOL BOARD
ODESSA PUBLIC SCHOOL

10 North St, Odessa, ON, K0H 2H0
(613) 386-3022
Emp Here 55
SIC 8211 Elementary and secondary schools

D-U-N-S 20-025-9906   (BR)
LIMESTONE DISTRICT SCHOOL BOARD
ERNESTOWN SECONDARY SCHOOL
50 Main St, Odessa, ON, K0H 2H0
(613) 386-3054
Emp Here 70
SIC 8211 Elementary and secondary schools

D-U-N-S 25-310-9151   (BR)
RKJL FOODS LTD
MCDONALD'S
(*Suby of* RKJL Foods Ltd)
Hwy 401 W, Odessa, ON, K0H 2H0

Emp Here 90
SIC 5812 Eating places

D-U-N-S 25-067-1922   (BR)
UNITED CHURCH OF CANADA, THE
EMMANUEL UNITED CHURCH
63 Factory St, Odessa, ON, K0H 2H0
(613) 386-7125
Emp Here 20
SIC 8661 Religious organizations

Ohsweken, ON N0A
Brant County

D-U-N-S 25-828-5469   (BR)
CHILDRENS AID SOCIETY OF BRANT
NATIVE SERVICES BRANCH
16 Sunrise Crt Suite 600, Ohsweken, ON, N0A 1M0
(519) 753-8681
Emp Here 24
SIC 8322 Individual and family services

D-U-N-S 25-477-8194   (SL)
IROQUOIS LODGE
1755 Chiefswood Rd, Ohsweken, ON, N0A 1M0
(519) 445-2224
Emp Here 60   *Sales* 2,699,546
SIC 8051 Skilled nursing care facilities

D-U-N-S 20-260-9736   (BR)
SIX NATIONS COUNCIL
CHILD & FAMILY SERVICES
15 Sunrise Crt, Ohsweken, ON, N0A 1M0
(519) 445-0230
Emp Here 35
SIC 8322 Individual and family services

D-U-N-S 20-654-8070   (BR)
SIX NATIONS COUNCIL
I L THOMAS ELEMENTARY SCHOOL
2120 Cayuga Rd, Ohsweken, ON, N0A 1M0
(519) 445-0433
Emp Here 25
SIC 8211 Elementary and secondary schools

D-U-N-S 25-362-5107   (BR)
SIX NATIONS COUNCIL
SIX NATIONS BINGO HALL
2469 Fourthline, Ohsweken, ON, N0A 1M0
(519) 753-3574
Emp Here 37
SIC 7999 Amusement and recreation, nec

Oldcastle, ON N0R
Essex County

D-U-N-S 25-687-9818   (SL)
1732187 ONTARIO INC
TOOL-PLAS
1905 Blackacre Dr Rr 1, Oldcastle, ON, N0R 1L0

(519) 737-9948
Emp Here 1,200   *Sales* 127,685,580
SIC 3544 Special dies, tools, jigs, and fixtures
Pr Pr Robert Claeys

D-U-N-S 25-459-0136   (HQ)
ADVANTAGE ENGINEERING INC
5000 Regal Dr, Oldcastle, ON, N0R 1L0
(519) 737-7535
Emp Here 110   *Emp Total* 120
Sales 23,463,992
SIC 3089 Plastics products, nec
Pr Pr Steve Hengsperger
VP Fin Lynda Dettinger

D-U-N-S 25-647-4008   (SL)
CON-TACT MASONRY LTD
2504 Binder Cres Suite 1, Oldcastle, ON, N0R 1L0
(519) 737-1852
Emp Here 50   *Sales* 3,648,035
SIC 1741 Masonry and other stonework

D-U-N-S 24-142-0558   (SL)
CREST MOLD TECHNOLOGY INC
2055 Blackacre Dr Rr 1, Oldcastle, ON, N0R 1L0
(519) 737-1546
Emp Here 52   *Sales* 6,201,660
SIC 3089 Plastics products, nec
Pr Pr William Cipkar

D-U-N-S 25-312-0661   (SL)
DELL WILL CUSTOMS BROKERS INC
3455 N Talbot Rd, Oldcastle, ON, N0R 1L0
(519) 736-6480
Emp Here 30   *Sales* 10,347,900
SIC 4731 Freight transportation arrangement
Pr Pr Richard Will
VP VP David Mcmillan

D-U-N-S 24-310-3145   (BR)
ITW CANADA INC
TREGASKISS WELDING PRODUCTS, DIV OF
(*Suby of* Illinois Tool Works Inc.)
2570 North Talbot Rd, Oldcastle, ON, N0R 1L0
(519) 737-6966
Emp Here 178
SIC 3548 Welding apparatus

D-U-N-S 20-011-1990   (BR)
LAKESIDE PLASTICS LIMITED
5186 O'Neil Dr Rr 1, Oldcastle, ON, N0R 1L0
(519) 737-1271
Emp Here 300
SIC 3089 Plastics products, nec

D-U-N-S 25-057-4142   (BR)
MEMORIAL GARDENS CANADA LIMITED
VICTORIA MEMORIAL GARDENS
1185 3 Hwy, Oldcastle, ON, N0R 1L0
(519) 969-6340
Emp Here 20
SIC 6553 Cemetery subdividers and developers

D-U-N-S 20-192-1157   (SL)
PANGEO CORPORATION
3440 North Talbot Rd, Oldcastle, ON, N0R 1L0
(519) 737-1678
Emp Here 30   *Sales* 4,331,255
SIC 5013 Motor vehicle supplies and new parts

D-U-N-S 25-093-1581   (SL)
PHILLIPS TOOL & MOULD (WINDSOR) LIMITED
5810 Outer Dr, Oldcastle, ON, N0R 1L0

Emp Here 157   *Sales* 17,374,320
SIC 3544 Special dies, tools, jigs, and fixtures
Pr Pr Otto Phillips
Treas Joseph Phillips

D-U-N-S 24-390-8501   (BR)
RELIANCE COMFORT LIMITED PARTNER-

SHIP
RELIANCE HOME COMFORT, DIV OF
1900 Blackacre Dr Rr 1, Oldcastle, ON, N0R 1L0
(519) 737-0334
Emp Here 60
SIC 1711 Plumbing, heating, air-conditioning

D-U-N-S 24-381-1101   (SL)
REVSTONE PLASTICS CANADA INC
2045 Solar Cres Rr 1, Oldcastle, ON, N0R 1L0
(519) 737-1201
Emp Here 200   *Sales* 19,577,273
SIC 3544 Special dies, tools, jigs, and fixtures
Dir George S Hofmeister
Dir Richard E Clark

D-U-N-S 20-117-5929   (SL)
SIGMA ENGINEERING (WINDSOR) INC
5101 Ure St, Oldcastle, ON, N0R 1L0
(519) 737-7538
Emp Here 40   *Sales* 3,283,232
SIC 3544 Special dies, tools, jigs, and fixtures

D-U-N-S 20-104-2988   (SL)
WINDSOR METAL TECHNOLOGIES INC
3900 Delduca Dr, Oldcastle, ON, N0R 1L0
(519) 737-7611
Emp Here 60   *Sales* 17,875,372
SIC 3544 Special dies, tools, jigs, and fixtures
Pr Pr John Spidalieri
   Mike Spidalieri

Omemee, ON K0L

D-U-N-S 20-410-9862   (BR)
GOVERNMENT OF ONTARIO
EMILY PROVINCIAL PARK
797 Emily Park Rd, Omemee, ON, K0L 2W0
(705) 799-5170
Emp Here 35
SIC 7033 Trailer parks and campsites

D-U-N-S 24-523-3130   (BR)
GREEN TRACTORS INC
114 Heights Rd, Omemee, ON, K0L 2W0
(705) 799-2427
Emp Here 25
SIC 5999 Miscellaneous retail stores, nec

D-U-N-S 25-920-6670   (BR)
TRILLIUM LAKELANDS DISTRICT SCHOOL BOARD
LADY EATON ELEMENTARY SCHOOL
17 James St, Omemee, ON, K0L 2W0
(705) 799-5292
Emp Here 33
SIC 8211 Elementary and secondary schools

D-U-N-S 20-025-4030   (BR)
TRILLIUM LAKELANDS DISTRICT SCHOOL BOARD
YOUNG, SCOTT PUBLIC SCHOOL
27 Walnut St, Omemee, ON, K0L 2W0
(705) 799-5133
Emp Here 28
SIC 8211 Elementary and secondary schools

Orangeville, ON L9W
Dufferin County

D-U-N-S 24-795-9034   (SL)
488491 ONTARIO INC
AVALON RETIREMENT CENTER
355 Broadway Suite 1, Orangeville, ON, L9W 3Y3
(519) 941-5161
Emp Here 250   *Sales* 21,888,210
SIC 6513 Apartment building operators
Pr Alex Jarlette
Treas Erna Baniulis

D-U-N-S 25-306-1055   (BR)
ARMTEC LP
BIG O
33 Centennial Rd, Orangeville, ON, L9W 1R1
(519) 942-2643
Emp Here 25
SIC 3088 Plastics plumbing fixtures

D-U-N-S 25-171-1545   (BR)
BANK OF NOVA SCOTIA, THE
SCOTIABANK
97 First St, Orangeville, ON, L9W 2E8
(519) 941-5544
Emp Here 26
SIC 6021 National commercial banks

D-U-N-S 20-698-7062   (BR)
BEST BUY CANADA LTD
FUTURE SHOP
(*Suby of* Best Buy Co., Inc.)
99 First St, Orangeville, ON, L9W 2E8
(519) 940-8206
Emp Here 70
SIC 5731 Radio, television, and electronic stores

D-U-N-S 24-545-5865   (SL)
CCI RESEARCH INC
CCI RESEARCH
71 Broadway, Orangeville, ON, L9W 1K1
(519) 938-9552
Emp Here 50   *Sales* 5,399,092
SIC 8732 Commercial nonphysical research
Pr Ian Macfarlane
Dir Andrew Blunden

D-U-N-S 20-537-7281   (BR)
CANADA POST CORPORATION
ORANGEVILLE MALL P.O.
150 First St, Orangeville, ON, L9W 3T7
(519) 940-9740
Emp Here 20
SIC 4311 U.s. postal service

D-U-N-S 20-303-3428   (BR)
CARA OPERATIONS LIMITED
KELSEY'S
(*Suby of* Cara Holdings Limited)
115 Fifth Ave, Orangeville, ON, L9W 5B7
(519) 940-4004
Emp Here 75
SIC 5812 Eating places

D-U-N-S 24-418-2718   (BR)
CINEPLEX ODEON CORPORATION
GALAXY CINEMAS ORANGEVILLE
85 Fifth Ave, Orangeville, ON, L9W 5B7
(519) 941-4970
Emp Here 20
SIC 7832 Motion picture theaters, except drive-in

D-U-N-S 24-910-3979   (BR)
CLOROX COMPANY OF CANADA, LTD, THE
(*Suby of* The Clorox Company)
101 John St, Orangeville, ON, L9W 2R1
(519) 941-0720
Emp Here 300
SIC 2673 Bags: plastic, laminated, and coated

D-U-N-S 24-525-7311   (BR)
CONSEIL SCOLAIRE VIAMONDE
ECOLE ELEMENTAIRE DES QUATRE-RIVIERES
60 Century Dr, Orangeville, ON, L9W 3K4
(519) 940-5145
Emp Here 20
SIC 8211 Elementary and secondary schools

D-U-N-S 24-420-5824   (BR)
CORPORATION OF THE COUNTY OF DUFFERIN, THE
DUFFERIN COUNTY AMBULANCE SERVICE
325 Blind Line, Orangeville, ON, L9W 5J8

(519) 941-9608
Emp Here 32
SIC 4119 Local passenger transportation, nec

D-U-N-S 24-199-7795   (BR)
CORPORATION OF THE COUNTY OF DUFFERIN, THE
DUFFERIN COMMUNITY SERVICES
30 Centre St, Orangeville, ON, L9W 2X1
(519) 941-6991
Emp Here 20
SIC 8322 Individual and family services

D-U-N-S 20-846-8165   (SL)
DUFFERIN SHEET METAL LTD
D S M
14 Robb Blvd, Orangeville, ON, L9W 3L2
(519) 941-8177
Emp Here 50   *Sales* 4,742,446
SIC 4225 General warehousing and storage

D-U-N-S 25-225-0220   (BR)
DUFFERIN-PEEL CATHOLIC DISTRICT SCHOOL BOARD
ST ANDREW SCHOOL
50 Meadow Dr, Orangeville, ON, L9W 4C8
(519) 942-0262
Emp Here 40
SIC 8211 Elementary and secondary schools

D-U-N-S 25-143-2936   (BR)
DUFFERIN-PEEL CATHOLIC DISTRICT SCHOOL BOARD
ST. BENEDICT SCHOOL
345 Blind Line, Orangeville, ON, L9W 4X1
(519) 942-5980
Emp Here 33
SIC 8211 Elementary and secondary schools

D-U-N-S 25-265-2656   (BR)
DUFFERIN-PEEL CATHOLIC DISTRICT SCHOOL BOARD
ST PETER ELEMENTARY SCHOOL
46 Dawson Rd, Orangeville, ON, L9W 2W3
(519) 941-2741
Emp Here 30
SIC 8211 Elementary and secondary schools

D-U-N-S 25-182-6330   (BR)
GOODLIFE FITNESS CENTRES INC
50 Fourth Ave, Orangeville, ON, L9W 4P1
(519) 943-0600
Emp Here 30
SIC 7991 Physical fitness facilities

D-U-N-S 20-801-3701   (SL)
GREENWOOD READY MIX LIMITED
Hwy 9, Orangeville, ON, L9W 2Y9
(519) 941-0710
Emp Here 80   *Sales* 20,594,350
SIC 1542 Nonresidential construction, nec
Pr Pr John Samuel Greenwood
Sec Cheryl Irene Greenwood
Treas Joseph Greenwood

D-U-N-S 24-387-5569   (SL)
HOFMANN, E. PLASTICS, INC
51 Centennial Rd, Orangeville, ON, L9W 3R1
(519) 943-5050
Emp Here 125   *Sales* 29,145,634
SIC 3089 Plastics products, nec
Pr Pr Paul Kalia

D-U-N-S 20-192-4045   (BR)
HOME DEPOT OF CANADA INC
HOME DEPOT
(*Suby of* The Home Depot Inc)
49 Fourth Ave, Orangeville, ON, L9W 1G7
(519) 940-9061
Emp Here 150
SIC 5251 Hardware stores

D-U-N-S 20-650-9577   (BR)
HYDRO ONE INC
125 C Line, Orangeville, ON, L9W 3V2
(519) 942-4148
Emp Here 60
SIC 4911 Electric services

D-U-N-S 24-684-4203   (BR)
JOHNSON CONTROLS NOVA SCOTIA U.L.C.
AUTOMOTIVE SYSTEMS GROUP
(*Suby of* Johnson Controls, Inc.)
120 C Line, Orangeville, ON, L9W 3Z8

Emp Here 350
SIC 2531 Public building and related furniture

D-U-N-S 20-024-1565   (SL)
JOPAMAR HOLDINGS INC
HARVEY'S/SWISS CHALET
93 First St, Orangeville, ON, L9W 2E8
(519) 941-4009
Emp Here 78   *Sales* 2,334,742
SIC 5812 Eating places

D-U-N-S 25-155-2279   (BR)
MCDONALD'S RESTAURANTS OF CANADA LIMITED
MCDONALD'S
(*Suby of* McDonald's Corporation)
95 First St, Orangeville, ON, L9W 2E8
(519) 940-0197
Emp Here 90
SIC 5812 Eating places

D-U-N-S 25-676-1867   (BR)
METRO ONTARIO INC
METRO
150 First St Suite 7, Orangeville, ON, L9W 3T7
(519) 941-6391
Emp Here 140
SIC 5411 Grocery stores

D-U-N-S 20-699-8879   (BR)
METROLAND MEDIA GROUP LTD
ORANGEVILLE BANNER
37 Mill St, Orangeville, ON, L9W 2M4
(519) 941-1350
Emp Here 30
SIC 2752 Commercial printing, lithographic

D-U-N-S 25-221-4549   (SL)
ORANGEVILLE CHRYSLER LIMITED
207 163 Hwy Suite 9, Orangeville, ON, L9W 2Z7
(519) 942-8400
Emp Here 30   *Sales* 10,944,105
SIC 5511 New and used car dealers
Owner Danny Brackett

D-U-N-S 24-364-1896   (BR)
PFIZER CANADA INC
PFIZER GLOBAL MANUFACTURING
(*Suby of* Pfizer Inc.)
40 Centennial Rd, Orangeville, ON, L9W 3T3
(519) 949-1030
Emp Here 20
SIC 2834 Pharmaceutical preparations

D-U-N-S 25-274-5260   (BR)
RESOLVE CORPORATION
(*Suby of* 2206997 Ontario Inc)
695 Riddell Rd, Orangeville, ON, L9W 4Z5
(519) 941-9800
Emp Here 200
SIC 7374 Data processing and preparation

D-U-N-S 25-499-7588   (SL)
SANOH CANADA, LTD
300 C Line, Orangeville, ON, L9W 3Z8
(519) 941-2229
Emp Here 120   *Sales* 14,592,140
SIC 5013 Motor vehicle supplies and new parts
Genl Mgr Connie Fraser

D-U-N-S 24-326-0291   (BR)
SOBEYS CAPITAL INCORPORATED
500 Riddell Rd, Orangeville, ON, L9W 5L1
(519) 941-1339
Emp Here 150
SIC 5411 Grocery stores

D-U-N-S 25-370-1197   (BR)
STAPLES CANADA INC

STAPLES THE BUSINESS DEPOT
(*Suby of* Staples, Inc.)
88 First St, Orangeville, ON, L9W 3J6
(519) 942-1360
Emp Here 30
SIC 5943 Stationery stores

D-U-N-S 24-145-3799   (BR)
TSC STORES L.P.
207211 Hwy 9 E, Orangeville, ON, L9W 2Z2
(519) 940-8810
Emp Here 25
SIC 5251 Hardware stores

D-U-N-S 25-322-0917   (BR)
TORONTO-DOMINION BANK, THE
TD BANK
(*Suby of* Toronto-Dominion Bank, The)
89 Broadway Ave, Orangeville, ON, L9W 1K2
(519) 941-1850
Emp Here 25
SIC 6021 National commercial banks

D-U-N-S 20-026-0003   (BR)
UPPER GRAND DISTRICT SCHOOL BOARD, THE
MONO-AMARANTH PUBLIC SCHOOL
(*Suby of* Upper Grand District School Board, The)
60 Century Dr, Orangeville, ON, L9W 3K4
(519) 941-5555
Emp Here 40
SIC 8211 Elementary and secondary schools

D-U-N-S 20-710-7678   (BR)
UPPER GRAND DISTRICT SCHOOL BOARD, THE
MONTGOMERY VILLAGE PUBLIC SCHOOL
(*Suby of* Upper Grand District School Board, The)
70 Montgomery Blvd, Orangeville, ON, L9W 5H6
(519) 940-3002
Emp Here 50
SIC 8211 Elementary and secondary schools

D-U-N-S 20-004-8531   (BR)
UPPER GRAND DISTRICT SCHOOL BOARD, THE
PRINCESS MARGARET PUBLIC SCHOOL
(*Suby of* Upper Grand District School Board, The)
51 Wellington St, Orangeville, ON, L9W 2L6
(519) 941-3731
Emp Here 35
SIC 8211 Elementary and secondary schools

D-U-N-S 20-710-7645   (BR)
UPPER GRAND DISTRICT SCHOOL BOARD, THE
CREDIT MEADOWS ELEMENTARY SCHOOL
(*Suby of* Upper Grand District School Board, The)
220 Blind Line, Orangeville, ON, L9W 4V2
(519) 941-7487
Emp Here 50
SIC 8211 Elementary and secondary schools

D-U-N-S 20-004-8523   (BR)
UPPER GRAND DISTRICT SCHOOL BOARD, THE
PARKINSON CENTENNIAL PUBLIC SCHOOL
(*Suby of* Upper Grand District School Board, The)
120 Lawrence Ave, Orangeville, ON, L9W 1S8
(519) 941-2461
Emp Here 50
SIC 8211 Elementary and secondary schools

D-U-N-S 25-143-0740   (BR)
UPPER GRAND DISTRICT SCHOOL BOARD, THE
WESTSIDE SECONDARY SCHOOL
(*Suby of* Upper Grand District School Board, The)

300 Alder St, Orangeville, ON, L9W 5A2
(519) 938-9355
Emp Here 75
SIC 8211 Elementary and secondary schools

D-U-N-S 24-197-1402   (BR)
UPPER GRAND DISTRICT SCHOOL BOARD, THE
LAURELWOODS ELEMENTARY SCHOOL
(*Suby of* Upper Grand District School Board, The)
Gd, Orangeville, ON, L9W 2Z4
(519) 940-3666
Emp Here 25
SIC 8211 Elementary and secondary schools

D-U-N-S 20-710-7660   (BR)
UPPER GRAND DISTRICT SCHOOL BOARD, THE
ORANGEVILLE DISTRICT SECONDARY SCHOOL
(*Suby of* Upper Grand District School Board, The)
22 Faulkner St, Orangeville, ON, L9W 2G7
(519) 941-0491
Emp Here 50
SIC 8211 Elementary and secondary schools

D-U-N-S 25-154-0829   (BR)
UPPER GRAND DISTRICT SCHOOL BOARD, THE
PRINCESS ELIZABETH SCHOOL
(*Suby of* Upper Grand District School Board, The)
51 Elizabeth St, Orangeville, ON, L9W 1C5
(519) 941-0220
Emp Here 50
SIC 8211 Elementary and secondary schools

D-U-N-S 20-719-9824   (BR)
WAL-MART CANADA CORP
WALMART
95 First St Suite 3142, Orangeville, ON, L9W 2E8
(519) 940-9558
Emp Here 50
SIC 5912 Drug stores and proprietary stores

D-U-N-S 20-555-9722   (BR)
WINNERS MERCHANTS INTERNATIONAL L.P.
WINNERS
(*Suby of* The TJX Companies Inc)
55 Fourth St, Orangeville, ON, L9W 1G7
(519) 943-1240
Emp Here 50
SIC 5651 Family clothing stores

Orillia, ON L3V
Simcoe County

D-U-N-S 24-823-4379   (SL)
126074 ONTARIO INC
ORILLIA ASSOCIATION FOR THE HANDI-CAPPED
6 Kitchener St, Orillia, ON, L3V 6Z9
(705) 327-2232
Emp Here 115   *Sales* 4,231,721
SIC 8361 Residential care

D-U-N-S 24-232-5681   (SL)
1646419 ONTARIO INC
BEST WESTERN PLUS MARIPOSA INN AND CONFERENCE CENTRE
400 Memorial Ave, Orillia, ON, L3V 0T7
(705) 325-9511
Emp Here 100   *Sales* 6,087,000
SIC 7011 Hotels and motels
Sls Dir Steven Ollerenshaw

D-U-N-S 24-368-1496   (SL)
ACCUTRAC CAPITAL SOLUTIONS INC
174 West St S 2 Fl, Orillia, ON, L3V 6L4
(866) 531-2615
Emp Here 30   *Sales* 14,227,337

SIC 6153 Short-term business credit institutions, except agricultural
Charles Sheppard
CEO Kenneth Judd
    Oscar Rombola
    Amar Sandhu
    Harry Singh

D-U-N-S 24-352-2419   (BR)
BDO CANADA LLP
19 Front St N, Orillia, ON, L3V 4R6
(705) 325-1386
Emp Here 25
SIC 8721 Accounting, auditing, and bookkeeping

D-U-N-S 25-296-5017   (BR)
BANK OF NOVA SCOTIA, THE
SCOTIABANK
56 Mississaga St E, Orillia, ON, L3V 1V5
(705) 325-1341
Emp Here 22
SIC 6021 National commercial banks

D-U-N-S 24-363-5641   (BR)
BEST BUY CANADA LTD
FUTURE SHOP
(*Suby of* Best Buy Co., Inc.)
3200 Monarch Dr Unit 1, Orillia, ON, L3V 8A2
(705) 325-0519
Emp Here 42
SIC 5731 Radio, television, and electronic stores

D-U-N-S 24-364-4770   (BR)
CCI THERMAL TECHNOLOGIES INC
CALORITECH
1 Hunter Valley Rd, Orillia, ON, L3V 0Y7
(705) 325-3473
Emp Here 190
SIC 3567 Industrial furnaces and ovens

D-U-N-S 25-303-6784   (BR)
CANADIAN IMPERIAL BANK OF COMMERCE
CIBC
1 Mississaga St W, Orillia, ON, L3V 3A5
(705) 325-4441
Emp Here 32
SIC 6021 National commercial banks

D-U-N-S 25-955-4103   (BR)
CARA OPERATIONS LIMITED
SWISS CHALET
(*Suby of* Cara Holdings Limited)
390 Memorial Ave, Orillia, ON, L3V 0T7
(705) 327-6667
Emp Here 50
SIC 5812 Eating places

D-U-N-S 25-157-4661   (SL)
CHAMPLAIN MANOR RETIREMENT RESIDENCE
65 Fittons Rd W, Orillia, ON, L3V 3V2
(705) 326-8597
Emp Here 50   *Sales* 2,334,742
SIC 8059 Nursing and personal care, nec

D-U-N-S 24-418-2932   (BR)
CINEPLEX ODEON CORPORATION
GALAXY CINEMAS ORILLIA
865 West Ridge Blvd, Orillia, ON, L3V 8B3
(705) 325-3661
Emp Here 20
SIC 7832 Motion picture theaters, except drive-in

D-U-N-S 24-346-4372   (BR)
CORPORATION OF THE COUNTY OF SIMCOE
TRILLIUM MANOR HOME FOR THE AGED
12 Grace Ave, Orillia, ON, L3V 2K2
(705) 325-1504
Emp Here 150
SIC 8361 Residential care

D-U-N-S 24-095-1082   (BR)
DOLLARAMA S.E.C.

DOLLARAMA
187 Memorial Ave Suite 289, Orillia, ON, L3V 5X7
(705) 327-2659
Emp Here 20
SIC 5999 Miscellaneous retail stores, nec

D-U-N-S 24-153-6726   (SL)
EAST SIDE MARIO'S
315 Memorial Ave, Orillia, ON, L3V 5Y1
(705) 329-2800
Emp Here 55   *Sales* 1,678,096
SIC 5812 Eating places

D-U-N-S 20-699-0876   (BR)
FGL SPORTS LTD
SPORT CHEK WEST RIDGE PLACE
3275 Monarch Dr Unit 1, Orillia, ON, L3V 7Z4
(705) 326-4411
Emp Here 40
SIC 5941 Sporting goods and bicycle shops

D-U-N-S 20-556-3380   (SL)
FERN RESORT LTD
4432 Fern Resort Rd, Orillia, ON, L3V 6H5
(705) 325-2256
Emp Here 60   *Sales* 2,626,585
SIC 7011 Hotels and motels

D-U-N-S 24-707-8660   (BR)
FIRSTCANADA ULC
FIRST STUDENT CANADA
445 Laclie St, Orillia, ON, L3V 4P7
(705) 326-7376
Emp Here 85
SIC 4151 School buses

D-U-N-S 25-878-7035   (BR)
HANSON RESTAURANTS INC
ARBY'S
(*Suby of* Hanson Restaurants Inc)
385 Memorial Ave Suite 2039, Orillia, ON, L3V 0T7
(705) 326-2667
Emp Here 21
SIC 5812 Eating places

D-U-N-S 25-171-5793   (BR)
HOME DEPOT OF CANADA INC
HOME DEPOT
(*Suby of* The Home Depot Inc)
3225 Monarch Dr, Orillia, ON, L3V 7Z4
(705) 327-6500
Emp Here 150
SIC 5261 Retail nurseries and garden stores

D-U-N-S 25-305-2815   (BR)
INNVEST PROPERTIES CORP
COMFORT INN
(*Suby of* Innvest Properties Corp)
75 Progress Dr, Orillia, ON, L3V 0T7
(705) 327-7444
Emp Here 20
SIC 7011 Hotels and motels

D-U-N-S 25-273-6392   (SL)
JTS INC
JACKSON TRANSPORTATION SYSTEMS
475 Memorial Ave, Orillia, ON, L3V 6H1
(705) 326-8888
Emp Here 50   *Sales* 7,727,098
SIC 4213 Trucking, except local
Pr Pr Paul Jackson

D-U-N-S 20-290-6249   (BR)
JARLETTE LTD
LEACOCK CARE CENTRE
25 Museum Dr Suite 204, Orillia, ON, L3V 7T9
(705) 325-9181
Emp Here 160
SIC 8051 Skilled nursing care facilities

D-U-N-S 24-919-5488   (SL)
JIM WILSON CHEVROLET BUICK GMC INC
20 Mulcahy Ct, Orillia, ON, L3V 6H9
(705) 329-2000
Emp Here 65   *Sales* 23,712,228
SIC 5511 New and used car dealers

Pr Pr Jim Wilson

D-U-N-S 20-811-4863   (BR)
K.J BEAMISH CONSTRUCTION CO. LTD
BEAMISH
4293 Fairgrounds Rd, Orillia, ON, L3V 6H2
(705) 325-7447
Emp Here 20
SIC 1611 Highway and street construction

D-U-N-S 25-058-3960   (SL)
KELSEY'S RESTAURANT (ORILLIA) LTD
KELSEY'S
405 Memorial Ave Suite 2, Orillia, ON, L3V 0T7
(705) 327-2900
Emp Here 52   *Sales* 1,532,175
SIC 5812 Eating places

D-U-N-S 25-946-1416   (BR)
LAFLECHE ROOFING (1992) LIMITED
144 Forest Plain Rd, Orillia, ON, L3V 6H1
(705) 329-4485
Emp Here 26
SIC 1761 Roofing, siding, and sheetMetal work

D-U-N-S 20-927-3999   (BR)
M. A. T. ENTERPRISES INC
WENDY'S
(*Suby of* M. A. T. Enterprises Inc)
545 Memorial Ave, Orillia, ON, L3V 7Z5
(705) 325-5550
Emp Here 40
SIC 5812 Eating places

D-U-N-S 24-911-0669   (SL)
MARIPOSA MARKET LTD
MARIPOSA MARKET
109 Mississaga St E, Orillia, ON, L3V 1V6
(705) 325-8885
Emp Here 55   *Sales* 2,991,389
SIC 5947 Gift, novelty, and souvenir shop

D-U-N-S 24-326-5845   (BR)
MATTHEWS, MARK PHARMACY LTD
SHOPPERS DRUG MART
4435 Burnside Line, Orillia, ON, L3V 7X8
(705) 326-7373
Emp Here 30
SIC 5912 Drug stores and proprietary stores

D-U-N-S 24-333-1696   (BR)
METRO ONTARIO INC
METRO
70 Front St N, Orillia, ON, L3V 4R8
(705) 323-9334
Emp Here 100
SIC 5411 Grocery stores

D-U-N-S 20-793-1952   (BR)
METRO ONTARIO INC
FOOD BASICS
975 West Ridge Blvd, Orillia, ON, L3V 8A3
(705) 326-5200
Emp Here 45
SIC 5411 Grocery stores

D-U-N-S 25-457-8453   (BR)
NEW PATH YOUTH & FAMILY COUNSELLING SERVICES OF SIMCOE COUNTY
(*Suby of* New Path Youth & Family Counselling Services Of Simcoe County)
359 West St N, Orillia, ON, L3V 5E5
(705) 325-6161
Emp Here 40
SIC 8322 Individual and family services

D-U-N-S 20-195-2475   (BR)
PARKER HANNIFIN CANADA
255 Hughes Rd, Orillia, ON, L3V 2M2
(705) 325-2391
Emp Here 70
SIC 3559 Special industry machinery, nec

D-U-N-S 20-028-4912   (BR)
PATTISON, JIM INDUSTRIES LTD
ILLUMINATED SCIENCE
580 Harvie Settlement Rd, Orillia, ON, L3V

0Y7
(705) 325-2799
Emp Here 70
SIC 3993 Signs and advertising specialties

D-U-N-S 24-364-4481   (SL)
PEARN, ROY E. ENTERPRISES LIMITED
MCDONALD'S RESTAURANT
320 Memorial Ave, Orillia, ON, L3V 5X6
(705) 325-9851
Emp Here 100   *Sales* 2,991,389
SIC 5812 Eating places

D-U-N-S 20-515-6727   (BR)
PLASTIQUES BERRY CANADA INC
301 Forest Ave, Orillia, ON, L3V 3Y7
(705) 326-8921
Emp Here 100
SIC 3081 Unsupported plastics film and sheet

D-U-N-S 20-820-2023   (BR)
R & F CONSTRUCTION INC
Gd Lcd Main, Orillia, ON, L3V 6H8
(705) 326-7169
Emp Here 60
SIC 1521 Single-family housing construction

D-U-N-S 25-283-1219   (BR)
REVERA INC
OAK TERRACE
291 Mississaga St W Suite 106, Orillia, ON,
L3V 3B9
(705) 325-2289
Emp Here 95
SIC 8051 Skilled nursing care facilities

D-U-N-S 20-078-1743   (BR)
ROYAL BANK OF CANADA
RBC ROYAL BANK
(*Suby of* Royal Bank Of Canada)
40 Peter St S, Orillia, ON, L3V 5A9
(705) 326-6417
Emp Here 31
SIC 6021 National commercial banks

D-U-N-S 24-061-8186   (BR)
SARJEANT COMPANY LIMITED, THE
CUSTOM CONCRETE NORTHERN
82 Forest Plain Rd, Orillia, ON, L3V 6H1
(705) 325-2492
Emp Here 20
SIC 3273 Ready-mixed concrete

D-U-N-S 20-026-6869   (BR)
**SIMCOE COUNTY DISTRICT SCHOOL
BOARD, THE**
ARDTREA CUMBERLAND BEACH SCHOOL
(*Suby of* Simcoe County District School
Board, The)
3797 Telford Line, Orillia, ON, L3V 6H3
(705) 327-1321
Emp Here 22
SIC 8211 Elementary and secondary schools

D-U-N-S 25-238-2841   (BR)
**SIMCOE COUNTY DISTRICT SCHOOL
BOARD, THE**
*ORILLIA DISTRICT COLLEGIATE & VOCA-
TIONAL INSTITUTE*
(*Suby of* Simcoe County District School
Board, The)
2 Borland St E, Orillia, ON, L3V 2B4

Emp Here 90
SIC 8211 Elementary and secondary schools

D-U-N-S 24-525-4136   (BR)
**SIMCOE COUNTY DISTRICT SCHOOL
BOARD, THE**
LIONS OVAL PUBLIC SCHOOL
(*Suby of* Simcoe County District School
Board, The)
25 Brant St W, Orillia, ON, L3V 3N6
(705) 325-5031
Emp Here 30
SIC 8211 Elementary and secondary schools

D-U-N-S 25-263-7160   (BR)
SIMCOE COUNTY DISTRICT SCHOOL

BOARD, THE
COUCHICHING HEIGHTS PUBLIC SCHOOL
(*Suby of* Simcoe County District School
Board, The)
455 Laclie St, Orillia, ON, L3V 4P7
(705) 325-9311
Emp Here 35
SIC 8211 Elementary and secondary schools

D-U-N-S 25-297-6402   (BR)
**SIMCOE COUNTY DISTRICT SCHOOL
BOARD, THE**
DAVID H CHURCH PUBLIC SCHOOL
(*Suby of* Simcoe County District School
Board, The)
230 James St E, Orillia, ON, L3V 1M2

Emp Here 24
SIC 8211 Elementary and secondary schools

D-U-N-S 25-297-6667   (BR)
**SIMCOE COUNTY DISTRICT SCHOOL
BOARD, THE**
REGENT PARK PUBLIC SCHOOL
(*Suby of* Simcoe County District School
Board The)
485 Regent St, Orillia, ON, L3V 4E2
(705) 326-7481
Emp Here 35
SIC 8211 Elementary and secondary schools

D-U-N-S 25-292-4774   (BR)
**SIMCOE COUNTY DISTRICT SCHOOL
BOARD, THE**
UPTERGROVE PUBLIC SCHOOL
(*Suby of* Simcoe County District School
Board, The)
4833 Muley Point Rd Suite 7, Orillia, ON, L3V
6H7
(705) 326-4332
Emp Here 25
SIC 8211 Elementary and secondary schools

D-U-N-S 25-292-4980   (BR)
**SIMCOE COUNTY DISTRICT SCHOOL
BOARD, THE**
TWINS LAKES SECONDARY SCHOOL
(*Suby of* Simcoe County District School
Board, The)
381 Birch St, Orillia, ON, L3V 2P5
(705) 325-1318
Emp Here 85
SIC 8211 Elementary and secondary schools

D-U-N-S 25-297-6014   (BR)
**SIMCOE COUNTY DISTRICT SCHOOL
BOARD, THE**
HARRIETT TODD PUBLIC SCHOOL
(*Suby of* Simcoe County District School
Board, The)
11 George St, Orillia, ON, L3V 2V1
(705) 325-9388
Emp Here 50
SIC 8211 Elementary and secondary schools

D-U-N-S 25-238-3070   (BR)
**SIMCOE COUNTY DISTRICT SCHOOL
BOARD, THE**
PARK STREET COLLEGIATE INST
(*Suby of* Simcoe County District School
Board, The)
233 Park St, Orillia, ON, L3V 5W1

Emp Here 95
SIC 8211 Elementary and secondary schools

D-U-N-S 25-297-6105   (BR)
**SIMCOE COUNTY DISTRICT SCHOOL
BOARD, THE**
ORCHARD PARK PUBLIC SCHOOL
(*Suby of* Simcoe County District School
Board, The)
24 Calverley St, Orillia, ON, L3V 3T4
(705) 325-7772
Emp Here 50
SIC 8211 Elementary and secondary schools

D-U-N-S 20-711-2025   (BR)
**SIMCOE COUNTY DISTRICT SCHOOL
BOARD, THE**
MOUNT SLAVEN PUBLIC SCHOOL
(*Suby of* Simcoe County District School
Board, The)
50 Westmount Dr N, Orillia, ON, L3V 6C1
(705) 728-7570
Emp Here 50
SIC 8211 Elementary and secondary schools

D-U-N-S 25-297-6535   (BR)
**SIMCOE COUNTY DISTRICT SCHOOL
BOARD, THE**
MARCHMONT PUBLIC SCHOOL
(*Suby of* Simcoe County District School
Board, The)
1902 Division Rd W, Orillia, ON, L3V 6H2
(705) 326-7652
Emp Here 30
SIC 8211 Elementary and secondary schools

D-U-N-S 20-291-1256   (BR)
**SIMCOE COUNTY DISTRICT SCHOOL
BOARD, THE**
ORILLIA LEARNING CENTRE
(*Suby of* Simcoe County District School
Board, The)
575 West St S Unit 15, Orillia, ON, L3V 7N6
(705) 325-9279
Emp Here 25
SIC 8211 Elementary and secondary schools

D-U-N-S 20-711-2231   (BR)
**SIMCOE MUSKOKA CATHOLIC DISTRICT
SCHOOL BOARD**
NOTRE DAME SCHOOL
(*Suby of* Simcoe Muskoka Catholic District
School Board)
140 Atlantis Dr, Orillia, ON, L3V 0A8
(705) 326-0979
Emp Here 50
SIC 8211 Elementary and secondary schools

D-U-N-S 25-238-3153   (BR)
**SIMCOE MUSKOKA CATHOLIC DISTRICT
SCHOOL BOARD**
*MONSIGNOR LEE ROMAN CATHOLIC
SCHOOL*
(*Suby of* Simcoe Muskoka Catholic District
School Board)
14 Fittons Rd E, Orillia, ON, L3V 2H9
(705) 326-3601
Emp Here 33
SIC 8211 Elementary and secondary schools

D-U-N-S 24-964-4592   (BR)
**SIMCOE MUSKOKA CATHOLIC DISTRICT
SCHOOL BOARD**
PATRICK FOGARTY SECONDARY SCHOOL
(*Suby of* Simcoe Muskoka Catholic District
School Board)
15 Commerce Rd, Orillia, ON, L3V 0Z2
(705) 325-9372
Emp Here 70
SIC 8211 Elementary and secondary schools

D-U-N-S 25-293-5259   (BR)
**SIMCOE MUSKOKA CATHOLIC DISTRICT
SCHOOL BOARD**
ST BERNARD SCHOOL
(*Suby of* Simcoe Muskoka Catholic District
School Board)
255 Oxford St, Orillia, ON, L3V 1H6
(705) 326-2331
Emp Here 30
SIC 8211 Elementary and secondary schools

D-U-N-S 20-127-4938   (BR)
**SIMCOE MUSKOKA DISTRICT HEALTH
UNIT**
169 Front St S Unit 120, Orillia, ON, L3V 4S8
(705) 325-9565
Emp Here 25
SIC 8011 Offices and clinics of medical doc-
tors

D-U-N-S 25-498-9635   (BR)

STAPLES CANADA INC
STAPLES THE BUSINESS DEPOT
(*Suby of* Staples, Inc.)
135 Murphy Rd, Orillia, ON, L3V 0B5
(705) 329-3074
Emp Here 30
SIC 5943 Stationery stores

D-U-N-S 24-478-0391   (SL)
STORBURN CONSTRUCTION LTD
MCGILL FORMING, DIV OF
Po Box 157 Stn Main, Orillia, ON, L3V 6J3
(705) 326-4140
Emp Here 30   *Sales* 5,545,013
SIC 1542 Nonresidential construction, nec
Pr Pr Frank Burns

D-U-N-S 20-328-3101   (BR)
TDL GROUP CORP, THE
TIM HORTONS
352 Bay St, Orillia, ON, L3V 3X4
(705) 327-3645
Emp Here 25
SIC 5812 Eating places

D-U-N-S 24-390-9160   (BR)
TI AUTOMOTIVE CANADA INC
35 Progress Dr, Orillia, ON, L3V 0T7

Emp Here 95
SIC 3465 Automotive stampings

D-U-N-S 24-124-1587   (SL)
THOR MOTORS ORILLIA (1978) LTD
201 Gill St, Orillia, ON, L3V 6K7
(705) 326-6447
Emp Here 30   *Sales* 20,096,000
SIC 5511 New and used car dealers
Pr Pr Kris Thor
  Henry Thor
VP VP Robert Brown

D-U-N-S 20-177-8078   (BR)
TOROMONT INDUSTRIES LTD
TOROMONT CAT
8 Forestview Rd, Orillia, ON, L3V 6H1
(705) 327-1801
Emp Here 22
SIC 5082 Construction and mining machinery

D-U-N-S 25-498-2663   (BR)
WAL-MART CANADA CORP
175 Murphy Rd, Orillia, ON, L3V 0B5
(705) 325-7403
Emp Here 200
SIC 5311 Department stores

D-U-N-S 25-398-5352   (SL)
YMCA OF SIMCOE/MUSKOKA
300 Peter St N, Orillia, ON, L3V 5A2
(705) 325-6168
Emp Here 70   *Sales* 2,115,860
SIC 8351 Child day care services

D-U-N-S 24-390-5002   (BR)
YMCA OF SIMCOE/MUSKOKA
YMCA GENEVA PARK
Gd, Orillia, ON, L3V 6H8
(705) 325-2253
Emp Here 50
SIC 8641 Civic and social associations

Orleans, ON K1C
Carleton County

D-U-N-S 25-890-7914   (SL)
AMOS, DR H M
*ARGYLE ASSOCIATES ORAL MAXILOFA-
CIAL SURGERY*
2555 St. Joseph Blvd Suite 304, Orleans, ON,
K1C 1S6
(613) 837-4207
Emp Here 50   *Sales* 2,991,389
SIC 8011 Offices and clinics of medical doc-
tors

D-U-N-S 25-296-5173   (BR)
BANK OF NOVA SCOTIA, THE
SCOTIABANK
110 Place D'Orleans Dr, Orleans, ON, K1C 2L9
(613) 824-6691
Emp Here 40
SIC 6021 National commercial banks

D-U-N-S 25-769-7185   (BR)
BANQUE NATIONALE DU CANADA
NATIONAL BANK OF CANADA
5929 Jeanne D'Arc Blvd S Suite Aa, Orleans, ON, K1C 6V8
(613) 830-9327
Emp Here 20
SIC 6021 National commercial banks

D-U-N-S 25-769-7573   (BR)
BEL-AIR AUTOMOBILES INC
BEL AIR ORLEANS TOYOTA
(*Suby of* 95661 Canada Ltd)
1485 Youville Dr, Orleans, ON, K1C 4R1
(613) 830-3401
Emp Here 34
SIC 5511 New and used car dealers

D-U-N-S 24-112-7401   (BR)
BISHOP HAMILTON MONTESSORI SCHOOL
1395 Youville Dr, Orleans, ON, K1C 4R1
(613) 834-6265
Emp Here 20
SIC 8299 Schools and educational services, nec

D-U-N-S 20-711-7065   (BR)
CONSEIL DES ECOLES CATHOLIQUES DE LANGUE FRANCAISE DU CENTRE-EST
ECOLE ELEMENTAIRE CATHOLIQUE SAINT-JOSEPH D'ORLEAN
6664 Carrière St, Orleans, ON, K1C 1J4

Emp Here 50
SIC 8211 Elementary and secondary schools

D-U-N-S 25-099-9653   (BR)
CONSEIL DES ECOLES CATHOLIQUES DE LANGUE FRANCAISE DU CENTRE-EST
ECOLE L'ETOILE DE L'EST
6220 Beausejour Dr, Orleans, ON, K1C 8E4
(613) 744-5713
Emp Here 35
SIC 8211 Elementary and secondary schools

D-U-N-S 20-574-8887   (BR)
CONSEIL DES ECOLES PUBLIQUES DE L'EST DE L'ONTARIO
ECOLE ELEMENTAIRE PUBLIQUE L'ODYSSEE
1770 Grey Nuns Dr, Orleans, ON, K1C 1C3
(613) 834-2097
Emp Here 35
SIC 8211 Elementary and secondary schools

D-U-N-S 24-340-0483   (BR)
FGL SPORTS LTD
SPORT CHEK PLACE D'ORLEANS
110 Place D'Orleans Dr Unit 2400, Orleans, ON, K1C 2L9
(613) 824-9933
Emp Here 40
SIC 5941 Sporting goods and bicycle shops

D-U-N-S 25-301-2637   (BR)
HUDSON'S BAY COMPANY
110 Place D'Orleans Dr, Orleans, ON, K1C 2L9
(613) 837-8274
Emp Here 200
SIC 5311 Department stores

D-U-N-S 25-769-3655   (BR)
LOBLAWS SUPERMARKETS LIMITED
LOBLAWS
1226 Place D'Orleans Dr Suite 3935, Orleans, ON, K1C 7K3

(613) 834-4074
Emp Here 100
SIC 5411 Grocery stores

D-U-N-S 25-279-5190   (BR)
MCDONALD'S RESTAURANTS OF CANADA LIMITED
MCDONALD'S
(*Suby of* McDonald's Corporation)
2643 St. Joseph Blvd, Orleans, ON, K1C 1G4
(613) 837-2866
Emp Here 55
SIC 5812 Eating places

D-U-N-S 24-344-4960   (BR)
METRO ONTARIO INC
6509 Jeanne D'Arc Blvd N, Orleans, ON, K1C 2R1
(613) 837-1170
Emp Here 45
SIC 5411 Grocery stores

D-U-N-S 25-132-9058   (BR)
OTTAWA CATHOLIC DISTRICT SCHOOL BOARD
CHAPPEL HILL CATHOLIC SCHOOL
(*Suby of* Ottawa Catholic District School Board)
1534 Forest Valley Dr, Orleans, ON, K1C 6G9
(613) 837-3773
Emp Here 30
SIC 8211 Elementary and secondary schools

D-U-N-S 25-926-3457   (BR)
OTTAWA CATHOLIC DISTRICT SCHOOL BOARD
ST MATTHEW HIGH SCHOOL
(*Suby of* Ottawa Catholic District School Board)
6550 Bilberry Dr, Orleans, ON, K1C 2S9
(613) 837-3161
Emp Here 100
SIC 8211 Elementary and secondary schools

D-U-N-S 20-025-4006   (BR)
OTTAWA CATHOLIC DISTRICT SCHOOL BOARD
BLESSED KATERI TEKAKWITHA SCHOOL
(*Suby of* Ottawa Catholic District School Board)
6400 Beausejour Dr, Orleans, ON, K1C 4W2
(613) 830-2454
Emp Here 26
SIC 8211 Elementary and secondary schools

D-U-N-S 20-024-3280   (BR)
OTTAWA PUBLIC LIBRARY BOARD
ORLEANS BRANCH LIBRARY
1705 Orleans Blvd, Orleans, ON, K1C 4W2

Emp Here 21
SIC 8231 Libraries

D-U-N-S 25-131-4472   (BR)
OTTAWA-CARLETON DISTRICT SCHOOL BOARD
LARSEN, HENRY ELEMENTARY SCHOOL
1750 Sunview Dr, Orleans, ON, K1C 5B3
(613) 830-4634
Emp Here 35
SIC 8211 Elementary and secondary schools

D-U-N-S 25-156-2104   (BR)
OTTAWA-CARLETON DISTRICT SCHOOL BOARD
FOREST VALLEY ELEMENTARY SCHOOL
1570 Forest Valley Dr, Orleans, ON, K1C 6X7
(613) 824-0733
Emp Here 42
SIC 8211 Elementary and secondary schools

D-U-N-S 20-711-6232   (BR)
OTTAWA-CARLETON DISTRICT SCHOOL BOARD
TERRY FOX ELEMENTARY SCHOOL
6400 Jeanne D'Arc Blvd N, Orleans, ON, K1C 2S7
(613) 837-3251
Emp Here 50

SIC 8211 Elementary and secondary schools

D-U-N-S 25-265-3852   (BR)
OTTAWA-CARLETON DISTRICT SCHOOL BOARD
CAIRINE WILSON SECONDARY SCHOOL
975 Orleans Blvd, Orleans, ON, K1C 2Z5
(613) 824-4411
Emp Here 60
SIC 8211 Elementary and secondary schools

D-U-N-S 25-224-9131   (BR)
OTTAWA-CARLETON DISTRICT SCHOOL BOARD
ORLEANS WOOD ELEMENTARY SCHOOL
7859 Decarie Dr, Orleans, ON, K1C 2J4
(613) 837-4622
Emp Here 29
SIC 8211 Elementary and secondary schools

D-U-N-S 24-054-1743   (BR)
PATTISON, JIM INDUSTRIES LTD
CANADIAN FISHING COMPANY
1652 Sansonnet St, Orleans, ON, K1C 5Y3
(613) 841-0608
Emp Here 200
SIC 2091 Canned and cured fish and seafoods

D-U-N-S 20-298-7314   (BR)
RE/MAX METRO-CITY REALTY LTD
2315 St. Joseph Blvd, Orleans, ON, K1C 1E7
(613) 841-2111
Emp Here 50
SIC 6531 Real estate agents and managers

D-U-N-S 25-983-5007   (BR)
ROGERS COMMUNICATIONS INC
ROGERS PLUS
(*Suby of* Rogers Communications Inc)
1615 Orleans Blvd Suite 3, Orleans, ON, K1C 7E2
(613) 830-6820
Emp Here 20
SIC 7841 Video tape rental

D-U-N-S 24-227-9631   (BR)
SOBEYS CAPITAL INCORPORATED
FRESHCO
1887 St. Joseph Blvd, Orleans, ON, K1C 7J2
(613) 590-0993
Emp Here 32
SIC 5411 Grocery stores

D-U-N-S 24-684-9587   (BR)
SOEURS DE LA CHARITE D'OTTAWA, LES
SOEURS DE LA CHARITE D'OTTAWA, LES
879 Hiawatha Park Rd, Orleans, ON, K1C 2Z6
(613) 562-6262
Emp Here 170
SIC 8361 Residential care

D-U-N-S 20-860-2511   (BR)
SOURCE (BELL) ELECTRONICS INC, THE
SOURCE, THE
110 Place D'Orleans Dr Suite 3, Orleans, ON, K1C 2L9
(613) 830-4606
Emp Here 25
SIC 5999 Miscellaneous retail stores, nec

Orleans, ON K1E
Carleton County

D-U-N-S 24-876-4474   (SL)
841065 ONTARIO INC
EAST SIDE MARIOS
250 Centrum Blvd Suite Side, Orleans, ON, K1E 3J1
(613) 834-0088
Emp Here 75   *Sales* 2,685,378
SIC 5812 Eating places

D-U-N-S 20-916-1475   (BR)
EMPIRE THEATRES LIMITED
MARIPLEX CONFECTIONS

250 Centrum Blvd, Orleans, ON, K1E 3J1

Emp Here 26
SIC 7832 Motion picture theaters, except drive-in

D-U-N-S 24-344-5058   (BR)
METRO ONTARIO INC
LOEB FALLINGBROOK
1675e Tenth Line Rd, Orleans, ON, K1E 3P6
(613) 837-2614
Emp Here 120
SIC 5411 Grocery stores

D-U-N-S 25-265-4207   (BR)
OTTAWA CATHOLIC DISTRICT SCHOOL BOARD
OUR LADY OF WISDOM
(*Suby of* Ottawa Catholic District School Board)
1565 St. Georges St, Orleans, ON, K1E 1R2
(613) 824-9700
Emp Here 30
SIC 8211 Elementary and secondary schools

D-U-N-S 20-861-2411   (BR)
OTTAWA YOUNG MEN'S AND YOUNG WOMEN'S CHRISTIAN ASSOCIATION
YMCA
265 Centrum Blvd, Orleans, ON, K1E 3X7
(613) 830-4199
Emp Here 50
SIC 7999 Amusement and recreation, nec

D-U-N-S 25-263-6048   (BR)
OTTAWA-CARLETON DISTRICT SCHOOL BOARD
QUEENSWOOD PUBLIC SCHOOL
1445 Duford Dr, Orleans, ON, K1E 1E8

Emp Here 30
SIC 8211 Elementary and secondary schools

D-U-N-S 25-131-4464   (BR)
OTTAWA-CARLETON DISTRICT SCHOOL BOARD
DUNNING-FOUBERT ELEMENTARY SCHOOL
1610 Prestwick Dr, Orleans, ON, K1E 2N1
(613) 824-5800
Emp Here 30
SIC 8211 Elementary and secondary schools

D-U-N-S 25-825-6932   (BR)
ROGERS COMMUNICATIONS INC
ROGERS RETAIL
(*Suby of* Rogers Communications Inc)
1675b Tenth Line Rd Suite 4, Orleans, ON, K1E 3P6
(613) 841-8485
Emp Here 21
SIC 7841 Video tape rental

D-U-N-S 25-769-3085   (BR)
ROYAL LEPAGE LIMITED
ROYAL LEPAGE PERFORMANCE REALTY
250 Centrum Blvd Suite 107, Orleans, ON, K1E 3J1
(613) 446-5544
Emp Here 80
SIC 6531 Real estate agents and managers

Orleans, ON K1W
Carleton County

D-U-N-S 24-350-2627   (SL)
BOSTON PIZZA ORLEANS
3884 Innes Rd, Orleans, ON, K1W 1K9
(613) 590-0881
Emp Here 80   *Sales* 2,407,703
SIC 5812 Eating places

D-U-N-S 20-648-7733   (BR)
CONSEIL DES ECOLES PUBLIQUES DE L'EST DE L'ONTARIO

ECOLE ELEMENTAIRE PUBLIQUE LE PRE-LUDE
6025 Longleaf Dr, Orleans, ON, K1W 1J2
(613) 834-8411
Emp Here 25
SIC 8211 Elementary and secondary schools

D-U-N-S 24-803-7504   (BR)
LOWE'S COMPANIES CANADA, ULC
3828 Innes Rd, Orleans, ON, K1W 0C8
(613) 830-6370
Emp Here 100
SIC 5211 Lumber and other building materials

D-U-N-S 25-294-8104   (BR)
WAL-MART CANADA CORP
3900 Innes Rd, Orleans, ON, K1W 1K9
(613) 837-9399
Emp Here 200
SIC 5311 Department stores

Orleans, ON K4A
Carleton County

D-U-N-S 20-048-4744   (BR)
AGROPUR COOPERATIVE
NATREL
1001 Dairy Dr, Orleans, ON, K4A 3N3
(613) 834-5700
Emp Here 100
SIC 5143 Dairy products, except dried or canned

D-U-N-S 24-363-5658   (BR)
BEST BUY CANADA LTD
FUTURE SHOP
(Suby of Best Buy Co., Inc.)
2020 Mer Bleue Rd Unit C2, Orleans, ON, K4A 0G2
(613) 830-2706
Emp Here 50
SIC 5731 Radio, television, and electronic stores

D-U-N-S 24-112-0463   (BR)
CITY OF OTTAWA
OTTAWA FIRE DEPARTMENT
(Suby of City of Ottawa)
500 Charlemagne Blvd, Orleans, ON, K4A 1S2
(613) 580-2860
Emp Here 40
SIC 7389 Business services, nec

D-U-N-S 25-098-5074   (BR)
CONSEIL DES ECOLES CATHOLIQUES DE LANGUE FRANCAISE DU CENTRE-EST
ECOLE ARC-EN-CIEL
1830 Portobello Blvd, Orleans, ON, K4A 3T6
(613) 744-0486
Emp Here 46
SIC 8211 Elementary and secondary schools

D-U-N-S 25-095-5648   (BR)
HOME DEPOT OF CANADA INC
HOME DEPOT
(Suby of The Home Depot Inc)
2121 Tenth Line Rd Suite 1, Orleans, ON, K4A 4C5
(613) 590-2030
Emp Here 200
SIC 5251 Hardware stores

D-U-N-S 24-309-9228   (SL)
INNOVATIVE COMMUNITY SUPPORT SERVICES
ICSS
2025 Lanthier Dr Suite A, Orleans, ON, K4A 3V3
(613) 824-8434
Emp Here 60   Sales 2,188,821
SIC 8361 Residential care

D-U-N-S 24-118-1721   (BR)
LOBLAWS INC

REAL CANADIAN SUPERSTORE, THE
4270 Innes Rd Suite 1071, Orleans, ON, K4A 5E6
(613) 824-8914
Emp Here 50
SIC 5411 Grocery stores

D-U-N-S 20-805-8060   (BR)
MARK'S WORK WEARHOUSE LTD
WORK WORLD
2055 Tenth Line Rd Suite 7, Orleans, ON, K4A 4C5
(613) 824-7729
Emp Here 20
SIC 5699 Miscellaneous apparel and accessory stores

D-U-N-S 25-311-0175   (BR)
MCDONALD'S   RESTAURANTS   OF CANADA LIMITED
MCDONALD'S #8490
(Suby of McDonald's Corporation)
4416 Innes Rd, Orleans, ON, K4A 3W3
(613) 841-6633
Emp Here 85
SIC 5812 Eating places

D-U-N-S 24-228-3880   (BR)
METRO ONTARIO INC
4510 Innes Rd, Orleans, ON, K4A 4C5
(613) 824-8850
Emp Here 100
SIC 5141 Groceries, general line

D-U-N-S 24-656-4939   (BR)
MICHAELS OF CANADA, ULC
MICHAELS ARTS & CRAFTS
(Suby of The Michaels Companies Inc)
4220 Innes Rd Suite 2, Orleans, ON, K4A 5E6
(613) 590-1813
Emp Here 30
SIC 5945 Hobby, toy, and game shops

D-U-N-S 25-804-3579   (BR)
OTTAWA CATHOLIC DISTRICT SCHOOL BOARD
ST CLARE CATHOLIC SCHOOL
(Suby of Ottawa Catholic District School Board)
2133 Gardenway Dr, Orleans, ON, K4A 3M2
(613) 834-6334
Emp Here 35
SIC 8211 Elementary and secondary schools

D-U-N-S 20-290-6868   (BR)
OTTAWA CATHOLIC DISTRICT SCHOOL BOARD
ST. PETER CATHOLIC HIGH SCHOOL
(Suby of Ottawa Catholic District School Board)
750 Charlemagne Blvd, Orleans, ON, K4A 3M4
(613) 837-9377
Emp Here 120
SIC 8211 Elementary and secondary schools

D-U-N-S 25-828-5402   (BR)
OTTAWA CATHOLIC DISTRICT SCHOOL BOARD
ST FRANCIS OF ASSISI CATHOLIC SCHOOL
(Suby of Ottawa Catholic District School Board)
795b Watters Rd, Orleans, ON, K4A 2T2
(613) 830-7239
Emp Here 40
SIC 8211 Elementary and secondary schools

D-U-N-S 20-591-3564   (BR)
OTTAWA CATHOLIC DISTRICT SCHOOL BOARD
ST THERESA SCHOOL
(Suby of Ottawa Catholic District School Board)
2000 Portobello Blvd, Orleans, ON, K4A 4M9
(613) 837-4114
Emp Here 35
SIC 8211 Elementary and secondary schools

D-U-N-S 24-676-3267   (BR)
OTTAWA-CARLETON DISTRICT SCHOOL BOARD
AVALON PUBLIC SCHOOL
2080 Portobello Blvd, Orleans, ON, K4A 0K5
(613) 834-7313
Emp Here 46
SIC 8211 Elementary and secondary schools

D-U-N-S 25-131-4456   (BR)
OTTAWA-CARLETON DISTRICT SCHOOL BOARD
TRILLIUM ELEMENTARY SCHOOL
1515 Varennes Blvd, Orleans, ON, K4A 3S1
(613) 841-7393
Emp Here 50
SIC 8211 Elementary and secondary schools

D-U-N-S 20-590-4886   (BR)
OTTAWA-CARLETON DISTRICT SCHOOL BOARD
MAPLE RIDGE ELEMENTARY SCHOOL
1000 Valin St, Orleans, ON, K4A 4B5
(613) 834-1927
Emp Here 65
SIC 8211 Elementary and secondary schools

D-U-N-S 24-101-3791   (BR)
STAPLES CANADA INC
STAPLES THE BUSINESS DEPOT
(Suby of Staples, Inc.)
2085 Tenth Line Rd, Orleans, ON, K4A 4C5
(613) 830-8100
Emp Here 20
SIC 5943 Stationery stores

D-U-N-S 24-251-9564   (SL)
TIM HORTONS
2020 Trim Rd, Orleans, ON, K4A 0G4
(613) 830-2712
Emp Here 50   Sales 1,532,175
SIC 5812 Eating places

D-U-N-S 25-134-3653   (HQ)
TODAY'S COLONIAL FURNITURE 2000 INC
TODAY'S COLONIAL FURNITURE
(Suby of Today's Colonial Furniture 2000 Inc)
1680 Vimont Crt Suite 100, Orleans, ON, K4A 3M3
(613) 837-5900
Emp Here 50   Emp Total 90
Sales 14,067,200
SIC 5712 Furniture stores
Pr Pr Jim Demers
VP Opers Terry Cole
Vicki Demers
Prin Cyndi Demers

D-U-N-S 20-003-2886   (BR)
VALUE VILLAGE STORES, INC
(Suby of Savers, Inc.)
4420 Innes Rd, Orleans, ON, K4A 3W3
(613) 837-9080
Emp Here 20
SIC 5399 Miscellaneous general merchandise

D-U-N-S 20-106-2952   (BR)
WINNERS MERCHANTS INTERNATIONAL L.P.
WINNERS
(Suby of The TJX Companies Inc)
4220 Innes Rd Suite 4, Orleans, ON, K4A 5E6
(613) 834-9722
Emp Here 35
SIC 5651 Family clothing stores

Oro Station, ON L0L
Simcoe County

D-U-N-S 24-761-0533   (BR)
CORPORATION OF THE COUNTY OF SIMCOE
ORO LANDFIL SITE 11
610 Old Barrie Rd, Oro Station, ON, L0L 2E0

(705) 735-6901
Emp Here 20
SIC 4953 Refuse systems

D-U-N-S 24-345-0934   (BR)
RENFREW COUNTY DISTRICT SCHOOL BOARD
GUTHRIE PUBLIC SCHOOL
22 5 Line S, Oro Station, ON, L0L 2E0
(705) 487-2532
Emp Here 43
SIC 8211 Elementary and secondary schools

Orono, ON L0B
Durham County

D-U-N-S 25-157-1105   (BR)
CRH CANADA GROUP INC
DUFFERIN AGGREGATES
3565 Durham Rd Suite 20, Orono, ON, L0B 1M0
(905) 983-9289
Emp Here 20
SIC 3532 Mining machinery

D-U-N-S 20-067-0011   (BR)
CORPORATION OF THE REGIONAL MUNICIPALITY OF DURHAM, THE
WORKS DEPARTMENT OF ORONO DEPOT
3480 Taunton Rd, Orono, ON, L0B 1M0
(905) 983-5116
Emp Here 40
SIC 4959 Sanitary services, nec

D-U-N-S 25-340-7456   (SL)
DURHAM CUSTOM MILLWORK INC
19 Tamblyn Rd, Orono, ON, L0B 1M0
(905) 683-8444
Emp Here 70   Sales 3,793,956
SIC 2599 Furniture and fixtures, nec

D-U-N-S 24-544-1969   (SL)
R.A.C.E. MECHANICAL SYSTEMS INC
9 Cobbledick St, Orono, ON, L0B 1M0
(905) 983-9800
Emp Here 50   Sales 3,648,035
SIC 5722 Household appliance stores

Orton, ON L0N

D-U-N-S 20-641-9744   (BR)
UPPER   GRAND   DISTRICT   SCHOOL BOARD, THE
EAST GARAFRAXA CENTRAL PUBLIC SCHOOL
(Suby of Upper Grand District School Board, The)
Gd, Orton, ON, L0N 1N0
(519) 855-4484
Emp Here 25
SIC 8211 Elementary and secondary schools

Osgoode, ON K0A
Carleton County

D-U-N-S 25-263-6006   (BR)
OTTAWA-CARLETON DISTRICT SCHOOL BOARD
OSGOODE PUBLIC SCHOOL
5590 Osgoode Main St, Osgoode, ON, K0A 2W0
(613) 826-2550
Emp Here 22
SIC 8211 Elementary and secondary schools

Oshawa, ON L1G

D-U-N-S 24-334-1919   (BR)
BAYSHORE HEALTHCARE LTD.
BAYSHORE HOME HEALTH
1 Mary St N Unit C, Oshawa, ON, L1G 7W8
(905) 433-4002
Emp Here 50
SIC 8082 Home health care services

D-U-N-S 25-306-7631   (BR)
BINGO COUNTRY HOLDINGS LIMITED
(*Suby of* Bingo Country Holdings Limited)
285 Taunton Rd E, Oshawa, ON, L1G 3V2

Emp Here 33
SIC 7999 Amusement and recreation, nec

D-U-N-S 24-426-1959   (SL)
CSH CENTENNIAL INC
CENTENNIAL RETIREMENT RESIDENCE
259 Hillcroft St Suite 214, Oshawa, ON, L1G 8E4
(905) 436-1901
Emp Here 20   *Sales* 729,607
SIC 8361 Residential care

D-U-N-S 25-301-5226   (BR)
CANADIAN MENTAL HEALTH ASSOCIATION TORONTO BRANCH, THE
CMHA
60 Bond St W, Oshawa, ON, L1G 1A5
(905) 436-8760
Emp Here 100
SIC 8011 Offices and clinics of medical doctors

D-U-N-S 25-667-7766   (BR)
CORPORATION OF THE CITY OF OSHAWA
NORTH VIEW COMMUNITY CENTER
150 Beatrice St E, Oshawa, ON, L1G 7T6
(905) 432-1984
Emp Here 20
SIC 8322 Individual and family services

D-U-N-S 24-805-2453   (BR)
CORPORATION OF THE REGIONAL MUNICIPALITY OF DURHAM, THE
HILLSDALE TERRACES
600 Oshawa Blvd N Suite 208, Oshawa, ON, L1G 5T9
(905) 579-3313
Emp Here 300
SIC 8741 Management services

D-U-N-S 20-711-3627   (BR)
DURHAM CATHOLIC DISTRICT SCHOOL BOARD
CENINI, FR JOSEPH CATHOLIC SCHOOL
120 Glovers Rd, Oshawa, ON, L1G 3X9
(905) 723-2421
Emp Here 50
SIC 8211 Elementary and secondary schools

D-U-N-S 25-265-2193   (BR)
DURHAM CATHOLIC DISTRICT SCHOOL BOARD
ST JOSEPH CATHOLIC SCHOOL
1037 Simcoe St N, Oshawa, ON, L1G 4W3
(905) 725-6751
Emp Here 25
SIC 8211 Elementary and secondary schools

D-U-N-S 25-263-7368   (BR)
DURHAM DISTRICT SCHOOL BOARD
HARRIS, WALTER E PUBLIC SCHOOL
495 Central Park Blvd N, Oshawa, ON, L1G 6A2
(905) 728-4532
Emp Here 30
SIC 8211 Elementary and secondary schools

D-U-N-S 25-300-7991   (BR)
DURHAM DISTRICT SCHOOL BOARD
MARY STREET COMMUNITY SCHOOL
110 Mary St N, Oshawa, ON, L1G 7S2
(905) 433-8910
Emp Here 20
SIC 8211 Elementary and secondary schools

D-U-N-S 25-300-7819   (BR)
DURHAM DISTRICT SCHOOL BOARD
CORONATION PUBLIC SCHOOL
441 Adelaide Ave E, Oshawa, ON, L1G 2A4
(905) 725-2032
Emp Here 32
SIC 8211 Elementary and secondary schools

D-U-N-S 25-263-7327   (BR)
DURHAM DISTRICT SCHOOL BOARD
QUEEN ELIZABETH PUBLIC SCHOOL
1205 Simcoe St N, Oshawa, ON, L1G 4X1
(905) 723-7042
Emp Here 45
SIC 8211 Elementary and secondary schools

D-U-N-S 20-711-3460   (BR)
DURHAM DISTRICT SCHOOL BOARD
DR. S J PHILLIPS PUBLIC SCHOOL
625 Simcoe St N, Oshawa, ON, L1G 4V5
(905) 725-4232
Emp Here 40
SIC 8211 Elementary and secondary schools

D-U-N-S 25-263-7020   (BR)
DURHAM DISTRICT SCHOOL BOARD
SUNSET HEIGHTS PUBLIC SCHOOL
1130 Mohawk St, Oshawa, ON, L1G 4G7
(905) 723-9223
Emp Here 30
SIC 8211 Elementary and secondary schools

D-U-N-S 25-263-6980   (BR)
DURHAM DISTRICT SCHOOL BOARD
VINCENT MASSEY PUBLIC SCHOOL
211 Harmony Rd N, Oshawa, ON, L1G 6L4
(905) 728-0681
Emp Here 37
SIC 8211 Elementary and secondary schools

D-U-N-S 25-300-8296   (BR)
DURHAM DISTRICT SCHOOL BOARD
O'NEILL COLLEGIATE & VOCATIONAL
301 Simcoe St N, Oshawa, ON, L1G 4T2
(905) 728-7531
Emp Here 93
SIC 8211 Elementary and secondary schools

D-U-N-S 20-711-3510   (BR)
DURHAM DISTRICT SCHOOL BOARD
EASTDALE COLLEGIATE & VOCATIONAL INSTITUTE
265 Harmony Rd N, Oshawa, ON, L1G 6L4
(905) 723-8157
Emp Here 100
SIC 8211 Elementary and secondary schools

D-U-N-S 24-337-2864   (BR)
FGL SPORTS LTD
NATIONAL SPORTS
285 Taunton Rd E, Oshawa, ON, L1G 3V2
(905) 434-3998
Emp Here 25
SIC 5941 Sporting goods and bicycle shops

D-U-N-S 20-347-0497   (BR)
JYSK LINEN'N FURNITURE INC
1199 Ritson Rd N, Oshawa, ON, L1G 8B9
(905) 233-7227
Emp Here 20
SIC 5712 Furniture stores

D-U-N-S 20-084-5068   (BR)
LAKERIDGE HEALTH
LAKERIDGE HEALTH OSHAWA
(*Suby of* Lakeridge Health)
1 Hospital Crt, Oshawa, ON, L1G 2B9
(905) 576-8711
Emp Here 100
SIC 6324 Hospital and medical service plans

D-U-N-S 25-429-4051   (BR)
LAKERIDGE HEALTH
MENTAL HEALTH DEPARTMENT
(*Suby of* Lakeridge Health)
1 Hospital Crt, Oshawa, ON, L1G 2B9
(905) 576-8711
Emp Here 50

SIC 8011 Offices and clinics of medical doctors

D-U-N-S 25-321-7400   (BR)
LONG & MCQUADE LIMITED
LONG & MCQUADE MUSICAL INSTRUMENTS
902 Simcoe St N, Oshawa, ON, L1G 4W2
(905) 434-1773
Emp Here 20
SIC 5736 Musical instrument stores

D-U-N-S 24-140-7712   (SL)
M2 SOLUTIONS INC
M2 FINANCIAL SOLUTIONS
628 Beechwood St, Oshawa, ON, L1G 2R9
(905) 436-1784
Emp Here 100   *Sales* 4,377,642
SIC 8721 Accounting, auditing, and bookkeeping

D-U-N-S 25-300-0707   (BR)
METRO ONTARIO INC
METRO
285 Taunton Rd E Suite 4, Oshawa, ON, L1G 3V2
(905) 432-2197
Emp Here 190
SIC 5411 Grocery stores

D-U-N-S 20-550-3485   (SL)
OSHAWA GOLF CLUB LIMITED
OSHAWA GOLF & CURLING CLUB
160 Alexandra St, Oshawa, ON, L1G 2C4
(905) 723-4681
Emp Here 55   *Sales* 2,188,821
SIC 7997 Membership sports and recreation clubs

D-U-N-S 20-135-9742   (SL)
PEACOCK LUMBER LIMITED
328 Ritson Rd N, Oshawa, ON, L1G 5P8
(905) 725-4744
Emp Here 30   *Sales* 5,653,974
SIC 5211 Lumber and other building materials

D-U-N-S 24-363-0881   (BR)
RGIS CANADA ULC
946 Simcoe St N, Oshawa, ON, L1G 4W2
(905) 571-7807
Emp Here 75
SIC 7389 Business services, nec

D-U-N-S 25-300-5110   (BR)
REDBERRY FRANCHISING CORP
BURGER KING
1327 Simcoe St N, Oshawa, ON, L1G 4X1

Emp Here 25
SIC 5812 Eating places

D-U-N-S 25-947-7230   (BR)
ROYAL BANK OF CANADA
RBC
(*Suby of* Royal Bank Of Canada)
1050 Simcoe St N, Oshawa, ON, L1G 4W5
(905) 576-6010
Emp Here 20
SIC 6021 National commercial banks

D-U-N-S 25-662-5161   (BR)
ROYAL BANK OF CANADA
RBC
(*Suby of* Royal Bank Of Canada)
27 Simcoe St N, Oshawa, ON, L1G 4R7
(905) 723-8511
Emp Here 20
SIC 6021 National commercial banks

D-U-N-S 24-111-1694   (BR)
SOBEYS CAPITAL INCORPORATED
FRESHCO
1150 Simcoe St N, Oshawa, ON, L1G 4W7
(905) 576-9562
Emp Here 25
SIC 5411 Grocery stores

D-U-N-S 20-860-2578   (BR)
SOURCE (BELL) ELECTRONICS INC, THE

SOURCE, THE
1100 Simcoe St N, Oshawa, ON, L1G 4W6
(905) 725-6775
Emp Here 25
SIC 5999 Miscellaneous retail stores, nec

D-U-N-S 25-977-8199   (BR)
STERICYCLE COMMUNICATION SOLUTIONS, ULC
(*Suby of* Stericycle Communication Solutions, ULC)
44 Richmond St W Unit 105, Oshawa, ON, L1G 1C7
(905) 428-2337
Emp Here 30
SIC 4899 Communication services, nec

D-U-N-S 25-363-6864   (BR)
VICTORIAN ORDER OF NURSES FOR CANADA
VON DURHAM REGION DISTRICT
50 Richmond St E Suite 116, Oshawa, ON, L1G 7C7
(905) 571-3151
Emp Here 20
SIC 8082 Home health care services

Oshawa, ON L1H

D-U-N-S 20-021-7235   (SL)
2020799 ONTARIO LIMITED
GRANDVIEW FOODLAND
600 Grandview St S Suite 17, Oshawa, ON, L1H 8P4
(905) 728-8401
Emp Here 40   *Sales* 6,594,250
SIC 5411 Grocery stores
Pt Fred Seymour

D-U-N-S 25-027-9106   (SL)
473980 ONTARIO LTD
DURHAMWAY BUS LINES, DIV OF
485 Waterloo Crt, Oshawa, ON, L1H 3X2
(905) 433-1392
Emp Here 175   *Sales* 4,961,328
SIC 4151 School buses

D-U-N-S 24-279-1648   (BR)
A.G. SIMPSON AUTOMOTIVE INC
OSHAWA PLANT
901 Simcoe St S, Oshawa, ON, L1H 4L1
(905) 571-2121
Emp Here 510
SIC 3465 Automotive stampings

D-U-N-S 25-296-4507   (BR)
BANK OF NOVA SCOTIA, THE
SCOTIABANK
75 King St W, Oshawa, ON, L1H 8W7
(905) 723-1630
Emp Here 40
SIC 6021 National commercial banks

D-U-N-S 25-694-8779   (BR)
BANK OF MONTREAL
BMO
600 King St E, Oshawa, ON, L1H 1G6

Emp Here 20
SIC 6021 National commercial banks

D-U-N-S 25-662-6946   (BR)
BANK OF MONTREAL
BANK OF MONTREAL
38 Simcoe St S, Oshawa, ON, L1H 4G2
(905) 432-6700
Emp Here 20
SIC 6021 National commercial banks

D-U-N-S 25-371-1592   (BR)
BEST BUY CANADA LTD
FUTURE SHOP
(*Suby of* Best Buy Co., Inc.)
1471 Harmony Rd N, Oshawa, ON, L1H 7K5

(905) 433-4455
Emp Here 100
SIC 5731 Radio, television, and electronic stores

D-U-N-S 20-860-4897   (BR)
BOUTIQUE LA VIE EN ROSE INC
BOUTIQUE LA VIE EN ROSE INC
1471 Harmony Rd N Unit 2, Oshawa, ON, L1H 7K5
(905) 429-2066
Emp Here 25
SIC 5632 Women's accessory and specialty stores

D-U-N-S 25-226-9824   (SL)
BOYS' & GIRLS' CLUB OF DURHAM
HANSEL & GRETEL NURSERY SCHOOL, DIV. OF
433 Eulalie Ave, Oshawa, ON, L1H 2C6
(905) 728-5121
Emp Here 60   *Sales* 1,824,018
SIC 8351 Child day care services

D-U-N-S 20-648-2056   (BR)
CAISSE POPULAIRE DES VOYAGEURS INC
(*Suby of* Caaisse Populaire des Voyageurs Inc)
600 Grandview St S, Oshawa, ON, L1H 8P4
(905) 432-7336
Emp Here 40
SIC 6062 State credit unions

D-U-N-S 25-448-5832   (SL)
CAMASTRA DISANTO RHODES DENTISTRY PROFESSIONAL CORPORATION
KING RITSON DENTAL CLINIC
255 King St E, Oshawa, ON, L1H 1C5
(905) 579-5464
Emp Here 50   *Sales* 2,845,467
SIC 8021 Offices and clinics of dentists

D-U-N-S 24-924-5143   (BR)
CANFAB PACKAGING INC
(*Suby of* Canfab Packaging Inc)
707 Raleigh Ave, Oshawa, ON, L1H 8T4
(905) 404-2023
Emp Here 25
SIC 2655 Fiber cans, drums, and similar products

D-U-N-S 24-182-4866   (SL)
CANNON SECURITY AND PATROL SERVICES
23 Simcoe St S Fl 2, Oshawa, ON, L1H 4G1
(416) 742-9994
Emp Here 150   *Sales* 4,669,485
SIC 7381 Detective and armored car services

D-U-N-S 25-652-9561   (BR)
CARA OPERATIONS LIMITED
SWISS CHALET
(*Suby of* Cara Holdings Limited)
555 Simcoe St S, Oshawa, ON, L1H 8K8
(905) 728-8833
Emp Here 60
SIC 5812 Eating places

D-U-N-S 20-558-6035   (SL)
CARLOS ELECTRIC LIMITED
105 Olive Ave, Oshawa, ON, L1H 2P1
(905) 728-7361
Emp Here 50   *Sales* 4,377,642
SIC 1731 Electrical work

D-U-N-S 20-935-6179   (HQ)
COMMUNITY   LIVING   OSHAWA/CLARINGTON
CLOC
(*Suby   of   Community   Living   Oshawa/Clarington)
39 Wellington Ave E, Oshawa, ON, L1H 3Y1
(905) 576-3011
Emp Here 27   *Emp Total* 360
Sales 18,086,400
SIC 8361 Residential care
Dir Fin Barbara Feyko
Ex Dir Steven Findlay

D-U-N-S 20-651-9329   (BR)
COMPAGNIE DE TELEPHONE BELL DU CANADA OU BELL CANADA, LA
BELL CANADA
15 Victoria St Suite 2, Oshawa, ON, L1H 8W9
(905) 433-3369
Emp Here 30
SIC 4813 Telephone communication, except radio

D-U-N-S 25-027-9015   (SL)
CORNERSTONE COMMUNITY ASSOCIATION DURHAM INC
133 Simcoe St S, Oshawa, ON, L1H 4G8
(905) 433-0254
Emp Here 50   *Sales* 2,334,742
SIC 8059 Nursing and personal care, nec

D-U-N-S 20-591-5528   (BR)
DURHAM CATHOLIC DISTRICT SCHOOL BOARD
421 Olive Ave, Oshawa, ON, L1H 2R2
(905) 728-5521
Emp Here 25
SIC 8211 Elementary and secondary schools

D-U-N-S 20-711-3791   (BR)
DURHAM CATHOLIC DISTRICT SCHOOL BOARD
CONTINUING AND ALTERNATIVE EDUCATION
692 King St E, Oshawa, ON, L1H 1G5
(905) 438-0570
Emp Here 50
SIC 8211 Elementary and secondary schools

D-U-N-S 25-265-3472   (BR)
DURHAM CATHOLIC DISTRICT SCHOOL BOARD
HOLY CROSS CATHOLIC SCHOOL
357 Simcoe St S, Oshawa, ON, L1H 4J2
(905) 723-5259
Emp Here 25
SIC 8211 Elementary and secondary schools

D-U-N-S 25-265-3555   (BR)
DURHAM CATHOLIC DISTRICT SCHOOL BOARD
MONSIGNOR   JOHN   PEREYMA   SECONDARY
316 Conant St, Oshawa, ON, L1H 3S6
(905) 432-8470
Emp Here 20
SIC 8211 Elementary and secondary schools

D-U-N-S 25-265-1641   (BR)
DURHAM CATHOLIC DISTRICT SCHOOL BOARD
JOHN XXIII CATHOLIC SCHOOL
195 Athabasca St, Oshawa, ON, L1H 7J2
(905) 723-1991
Emp Here 25
SIC 8211 Elementary and secondary schools

D-U-N-S 25-373-8462   (SL)
DURHAM CHILDREN'S AID SOCIETY
1320 Airport Blvd, Oshawa, ON, L1H 7K4
(905) 433-1551
Emp Here 350   *Sales* 75,691,523
SIC 8322 Individual and family services
Ch Bd Ch Bd Peter Spratt
VP Paul Martin
Esrick Quintyn
David Wade
Dir Ted Aldridge
Dir Heather Boissoin
Dir Valerie Mcintyre
Dir Audra Mikaly

D-U-N-S 20-025-2406   (BR)
DURHAM DISTRICT SCHOOL BOARD
GROVE SCHOOL
1356 Simcoe St S, Oshawa, ON, L1H 4M4
(905) 725-7042
Emp Here 80
SIC 8211 Elementary and secondary schools

D-U-N-S 25-265-2243   (BR)

DURHAM DISTRICT SCHOOL BOARD
DUKE EDINBURGH PUBLIC SCHOOL
610 Taylor Ave, Oshawa, ON, L1H 2E7

Emp Here 20
SIC 8211 Elementary and secondary schools

D-U-N-S 25-300-7934   (BR)
DURHAM DISTRICT SCHOOL BOARD
BOBBY ORR PUBLIC SCHOOL
7 Waterloo St, Oshawa, ON, L1H 8V9
(905) 723-3621
Emp Here 35
SIC 8211 Elementary and secondary schools

D-U-N-S 20-913-6592   (BR)
DURHAM DISTRICT SCHOOL BOARD
T R MCEWEN PUBLIC SCHOOL
460 Wilson Rd S, Oshawa, ON, L1H 6C9

Emp Here 25
SIC 8211 Elementary and secondary schools

D-U-N-S 25-300-7538   (BR)
DURHAM DISTRICT SCHOOL BOARD
GERTRUDE COLPUS PUBLIC SCHOOL
570 Shakespeare Ave, Oshawa, ON, L1H 3H6
(905) 436-5039
Emp Here 40
SIC 8211 Elementary and secondary schools

D-U-N-S 25-300-7637   (BR)
DURHAM DISTRICT SCHOOL BOARD
FOREST VIEW PUBLIC SCHOOL
285 Grandview St, Oshawa, ON, L1H 7C6
(905) 723-8233
Emp Here 30
SIC 8211 Elementary and secondary schools

D-U-N-S 25-095-1746   (BR)
DURHAM DISTRICT SCHOOL BOARD
VILLAGE UNION PUBLIC SCHOOL
240 Simcoe St S, Oshawa, ON, L1H 4H4
(905) 725-1622
Emp Here 40
SIC 8211 Elementary and secondary schools

D-U-N-S 25-300-8221   (BR)
DURHAM DISTRICT SCHOOL BOARD
KEDRON PUBLIC SCHOOL
1935 Ritson Rd N, Oshawa, ON, L1H 7K5
(905) 728-2851
Emp Here 30
SIC 8211 Elementary and secondary schools

D-U-N-S 25-300-7967   (BR)
DURHAM DISTRICT SCHOOL BOARD
GRANDVIEW PUBLIC SCHOOL
285 Grandview St S, Oshawa, ON, L1H 7C6
(905) 728-5791
Emp Here 32
SIC 8211 Elementary and secondary schools

D-U-N-S 25-300-8171   (BR)
DURHAM DISTRICT SCHOOL BOARD
DR F. J. DONEVAN COLLEGIATE INSTITUTE
250 Harmony Rd S, Oshawa, ON, L1H 6T9
(905) 728-7315
Emp Here 50
SIC 8211 Elementary and secondary schools

D-U-N-S 24-190-1532   (BR)
ENTERPHASE CHILD AND FAMILY SERVICES INC
250 Harmony Rd S, Oshawa, ON, L1H 6T9
(905) 725-6387
Emp Here 100
SIC 8299 Schools and educational services, nec

D-U-N-S 25-842-4246   (BR)
FASTENAL CANADA LTEE
350 Wentworth St E Suite 1, Oshawa, ON, L1H 7R7
(905) 443-0428
Emp Here 37
SIC 5085 Industrial supplies

D-U-N-S 20-260-7573   (HQ)

FRONTENAC YOUTH SERVICES
(*Suby of* Frontenac Youth Services)
1160 Simcoe St S, Oshawa, ON, L1H 5L8
(905) 579-1551
Emp Here 30   *Emp Total* 100
Sales 4,677,755
SIC 8322 Individual and family services

D-U-N-S 20-709-0577   (BR)
G&K SERVICES CANADA INC
(*Suby of* Cintas Corporation)
984 Farewell St Unit 1, Oshawa, ON, L1H 6N6
(905) 433-9453
Emp Here 20
SIC 7213 Linen supply

D-U-N-S 25-666-7270   (BR)
G4S SECURE SOLUTIONS (CANADA) LTD
214 King St E, Oshawa, ON, L1H 1C7
(905) 579-8020
Emp Here 250
SIC 7381 Detective and armored car services

D-U-N-S 20-135-6847   (HQ)
GENERAL MOTORS OF CANADA COMPANY
OSHAWA SOUTH STAMPING PLANT
1908 Colonel Sam Dr, Oshawa, ON, L1H 8P7
(905) 644-5000
Emp Here 450   *Emp Total* 225,000
Sales 2,110,607,130
SIC 3711 Motor vehicles and car bodies
Stephen Carlisle
John Roth
VP Peter Cho
Ines Craviotto

D-U-N-S 25-318-5169   (SL)
GLAZIER MEDICAL CENTRE
11 Gibb St, Oshawa, ON, L1H 2J9
(905) 728-3668
Emp Here 50   *Sales* 2,991,389
SIC 8011 Offices and clinics of medical doctors

D-U-N-S 24-319-0998   (BR)
GREAT-WEST LIFE ASSURANCE COMPANY, THE
CENTRAL ONTARIO RESOURCE CENTRE
2 Simcoe St S Suite 400, Oshawa, ON, L1H 8C1
(905) 571-2676
Emp Here 20
SIC 6311 Life insurance

D-U-N-S 20-177-1503   (BR)
H & R BLOCK CANADA, INC
(*Suby of* H&R Block, Inc.)
40 King St W, Oshawa, ON, L1H 1A4
(905) 436-9882
Emp Here 20
SIC 7291 Tax return preparation services

D-U-N-S 24-874-2405   (BR)
HARPER TRUCK CENTRES INC
PREMIER TRUCK GROUP
(*Suby of* Harper Truck Centres Inc)
720 Wilson Rd S, Oshawa, ON, L1H 6E8
(905) 432-3838
Emp Here 40
SIC 5084 Industrial machinery and equipment

D-U-N-S 25-171-5538   (BR)
HOME DEPOT OF CANADA INC
HOME DEPOT
(*Suby of* The Home Depot Inc)
1481 Harmony Rd N, Oshawa, ON, L1H 7K5
(905) 743-5600
Emp Here 200
SIC 5231 Paint, glass, and wallpaper stores

D-U-N-S 20-264-2997   (BR)
HUDSON'S BAY COMPANY
HUDSON'S BAY CO
555 Simcoe St S Unit 16, Oshawa, ON, L1H 8K8
(905) 571-2326
Emp Here 30

SIC 4225 General warehousing and storage

D-U-N-S 24-470-9077   (HQ)
KERR INDUSTRIES LIMITED
(Suby of Baybriar Management Services Limited)
635 Farewell St, Oshawa, ON, L1H 6N2
(905) 725-6561
Emp Here 75   Emp Total 4
Sales 12,171,840
SIC 7549 Automotive services, nec
Pr Bradley Baker

D-U-N-S 24-344-7260   (BR)
LAFARGE CANADA INC
LAFARGE PAVING & CONSTRUCTION, DIV OF
1255 Wilson Rd N, Oshawa, ON, L1H 7L3
(905) 728-4661
Emp Here 75
SIC 1611 Highway and street construction

D-U-N-S 24-718-9595   (BR)
LAKERIDGE HEALTH
GLAZIER MEDICAL CENTER
(Suby of Lakeridge Health)
11 Gibb St, Oshawa, ON, L1H 2J9
(905) 579-1212
Emp Here 100
SIC 8011 Offices and clinics of medical doctors

D-U-N-S 25-637-9470   (BR)
LAKERIDGE HEALTH
PINEWOOD CENTRE
(Suby of Lakeridge Health)
300 Centre St S, Oshawa, ON, L1H 4B2
(905) 576-8711
Emp Here 70
SIC 8361 Residential care

D-U-N-S 20-183-1299   (BR)
LENNOX CANADA INC
LIMCAN HEATING & AIR CONDITIONING
330 Marwood Dr Unit 1, Oshawa, ON, L1H 8B4
(905) 579-6616
Emp Here 20
SIC 1711 Plumbing, heating, air-conditioning

D-U-N-S 25-659-2064   (BR)
LIFETOUCH CANADA INC
(Suby of Lifetouch Inc.)
320 Marwood Dr Unit 6, Oshawa, ON, L1H 8B4
(905) 571-1103
Emp Here 40
SIC 7221 Photographic studios, portrait

D-U-N-S 24-383-8963   (BR)
LOBLAWS INC
REAL CANADIAN SUPERSTORE
1385 Harmony Rd N Suite 1043, Oshawa, ON, L1H 7K5
(905) 433-9569
Emp Here 150
SIC 5411 Grocery stores

D-U-N-S 20-135-8496   (SL)
MARACLE PRESS LIMITED
1156 King St E, Oshawa, ON, L1H 1H8
(905) 723-3438
Emp Here 60   Sales 4,523,563
SIC 2752 Commercial printing, lithographic

D-U-N-S 24-418-4227   (BR)
MARK'S WORK WEARHOUSE LTD
WORK WORLD
1397 Harmony Rd N, Oshawa, ON, L1H 7K5
(905) 571-5992
Emp Here 20
SIC 5699 Miscellaneous apparel and accessory stores

D-U-N-S 20-005-3614   (BR)
MEDICAL PHARMACIES GROUP LIMITED
CLINIC PHARMACY
117 King St E, Oshawa, ON, L1H 1B9

(905) 576-9090
Emp Here 20
SIC 5912 Drug stores and proprietary stores

D-U-N-S 24-086-8179   (BR)
METROLAND MEDIA GROUP LTD
OSHAWA THIS WEEK
865 Farewell St, Oshawa, ON, L1H 6N8
(905) 579-4400
Emp Here 200
SIC 2711 Newspapers

D-U-N-S 24-119-3924   (BR)
METROLAND MEDIA GROUP LTD
845 Farewell St, Oshawa, ON, L1H 6N8
(905) 579-4400
Emp Here 150
SIC 2711 Newspapers

D-U-N-S 24-817-1639   (SL)
NORVAN LIMITED
CLINTAR GROUNDSKEEPING SERVICES
712 Wilson Rd S, Oshawa, ON, L1H 8R3

Emp Here 80   Sales 8,826,150
SIC 4212 Local trucking, without storage
Pr Pr Steven Gamsby

D-U-N-S 24-205-9207   (BR)
OSSO HOLDINGS LTD
OSSONA PARK CANADA, DIVISION OF
(Suby of Osso Holdings Ltd)
209 Bloor St E, Oshawa, ON, L1H 3M3
(905) 576-4166
Emp Here 20
SIC 5063 Electrical apparatus and equipment

D-U-N-S 25-361-2568   (SL)
PENSKE VEHICLE SERVICES (CANADA), INC
(Suby of Penske Corporation)
850 Wilson Rd S, Oshawa, ON, L1H 6E8
(905) 432-3388
Emp Here 34   Sales 2,480,664
SIC 7538 General automotive repair shops

D-U-N-S 20-708-6179   (BR)
ROYAL BANK OF CANADA
RBC FINANCIAL GROUP
(Suby of Royal Bank Of Canada)
40 King St W Suite 800, Oshawa, ON, L1H 1A4

Emp Here 25
SIC 6021 National commercial banks

D-U-N-S 25-667-8665   (SL)
SEVENTH-DAY ADVENTISTS COMMUNITY SERVICE
1170 King St E, Oshawa, ON, L1H 1H9
(905) 433-8800
Emp Here 50   Sales 1,969,939
SIC 8322 Individual and family services

D-U-N-S 20-644-3272   (BR)
SOBEYS CAPITAL INCORPORATED
FRESHCO
564 King St E, Oshawa, ON, L1H 1G5
(905) 571-4835
Emp Here 100
SIC 5411 Grocery stores

D-U-N-S 24-207-0949   (BR)
TIERCON CORP
901 Simcoe St S, Oshawa, ON, L1H 4L1
(905) 728-5887
Emp Here 49
SIC 3714 Motor vehicle parts and accessories

D-U-N-S 24-118-2646   (BR)
TORONTO-DOMINION BANK, THE
TD BANK
(Suby of Toronto-Dominion Bank, The)
4 King St W, Oshawa, ON, L1H 1A3
(905) 576-6281
Emp Here 20
SIC 6021 National commercial banks

D-U-N-S 20-086-9373   (BR)

TORSTAR CORPORATION
OSHAWA THIS WEEK NEWSPAPER
865 Farewell St, Oshawa, ON, L1H 6N8
(905) 579-4400
Emp Here 100
SIC 2711 Newspapers

D-U-N-S 20-789-7518   (BR)
WAL-MART CANADA CORP
1471 Harmony Rd N Suite 3161, Oshawa, ON, L1H 7K5
(905) 404-6581
Emp Here 200
SIC 5311 Department stores

D-U-N-S 20-732-9470   (BR)
WILSON FOODS CENTRE LTD
MCDONALDS RESTAURANT
1369 Harmony Rd N, Oshawa, ON, L1H 7K5
(905) 436-6277
Emp Here 70
SIC 5812 Eating places

D-U-N-S 25-321-5685   (SL)
WILSON FOODS KINGSWAY LTD
MCDONALD'S 7403
1300 King St E, Oshawa, ON, L1H 8J4
(905) 434-7111
Emp Here 90   Sales 2,699,546
SIC 5812 Eating places

D-U-N-S 20-106-3000   (BR)
WINNERS MERCHANTS INTERNATIONAL L.P.
WINNERS
(Suby of The TJX Companies Inc)
891 Taunton Rd E, Oshawa, ON, L1H 7K5
(905) 433-8181
Emp Here 24
SIC 5651 Family clothing stores

D-U-N-S 20-638-8121   (SL)
YOUTH CONNECTIONS INC
YOUTH CONNECTIONS
762 King St E Suite 1, Oshawa, ON, L1H 1G9
(905) 579-0057
Emp Here 50   Sales 1,824,018
SIC 8361 Residential care

Oshawa, ON L1J

D-U-N-S 20-755-3934   (HQ)
AUTO   WAREHOUSING   COMPANY CANADA LIMITED
(Suby of Auto Warehousing Co., Inc.)
1150 Stevenson Rd S Suite 1, Oshawa, ON, L1J 0B3
(905) 725-6549
Emp Here 200   Emp Total 1,000
Sales 28,454,673
SIC 4789 Transportation services, nec
Pr Stephen Seher
VP VP Brian Taylor
Fin Ex Belinda Woodford

D-U-N-S 25-296-4580   (BR)
BANK OF NOVA SCOTIA, THE
SCOTIABANK
800 King St W, Oshawa, ON, L1J 2L5
(905) 404-6950
Emp Here 20
SIC 6021 National commercial banks

D-U-N-S 25-992-2730   (BR)
BELL MOBILITE INC
BELL WORLD
419 King St W, Oshawa, ON, L1J 2K5
(905) 579-4026
Emp Here 20
SIC 4899 Communication services, nec

D-U-N-S 25-409-7009   (SL)
CANADIAN FLIGHT ACADEMY LTD
(Suby of Armadale Co. Limited)
1250 Airport Blvd, Oshawa, ON, L1J 8P5

(905) 404-9252
Emp Here 25   Sales 1,386,253
SIC 8299 Schools and educational services, nec

D-U-N-S 25-303-6941   (BR)
CANADIAN IMPERIAL BANK OF COMMERCE
CIBC
419 King St W, Oshawa, ON, L1J 2K5
(905) 576-9560
Emp Here 30
SIC 6021 National commercial banks

D-U-N-S 25-650-3632   (SL)
CASEY'S GRILLHOUSE & BEVERAGE CO
CASEY'S BAR GRILL
419 King St W, Oshawa, ON, L1J 2K5
(905) 576-3333
Emp Here 65   Sales 1,969,939
SIC 5812 Eating places

D-U-N-S 20-573-3160   (BR)
COMPAGNIE DES CHEMINS DE FER NATIONAUX DU CANADA
CN RAIL
767 Thornton Rd S, Oshawa, ON, L1J 8M6
(905) 436-4218
Emp Here 35
SIC 4011 Railroads, line-haul operating

D-U-N-S 25-359-9237   (BR)
CONSEIL   SCOLAIRE   DE   DISTRICT CATHOLIQUE CENTRE-SUD
ECOLE CORPUS CHRISTI
362 Hillside Ave, Oshawa, ON, L1J 6L7
(905) 728-0491
Emp Here 28
SIC 8211 Elementary and secondary schools

D-U-N-S 20-794-6190   (BR)
CORPORATION OF THE CITY OF OSHAWA
OSHAWA FIRE SERVICES
199 Adelaide Ave W, Oshawa, ON, L1J 7B1
(905) 433-1239
Emp Here 200
SIC 7389 Business services, nec

D-U-N-S 25-361-4721   (BR)
CORPORATION OF THE REGIONAL MUNICIPALITY OF DURHAM, THE
DEPARTMENT OF SOCIAL SERVICES
505 Wentworth St W, Oshawa, ON, L1J 6G5
(905) 436-6747
Emp Here 60
SIC 8399 Social services, nec

D-U-N-S 20-711-3635   (BR)
DURHAM CATHOLIC DISTRICT SCHOOL BOARD
MONT SENOR PHILLIP COSSEY CATHOLIC SCHOOL
1324 Oxford St, Oshawa, ON, L1J 3W6
(905) 723-4241
Emp Here 50
SIC 8211 Elementary and secondary schools

D-U-N-S 20-711-3643   (BR)
DURHAM CATHOLIC DISTRICT SCHOOL BOARD
MONSIGNOR PAUL DWYER CATHOLIC HIGH SCHOOL
700 Stevenson Rd N, Oshawa, ON, L1J 5P5
(905) 723-5255
Emp Here 50
SIC 8211 Elementary and secondary schools

D-U-N-S 25-265-1997   (BR)
DURHAM CATHOLIC DISTRICT SCHOOL BOARD
ST. CHRISTOPHER CATHOLIC SCHOOL
431 Annapolis Ave, Oshawa, ON, L1J 2Y5
(905) 725-7672
Emp Here 35
SIC 8211 Elementary and secondary schools

D-U-N-S 25-265-1831   (BR)
DURHAM CATHOLIC DISTRICT SCHOOL BOARD

ST THOMAS AQUINAS CATHOLIC SCHOOL
400 Pacific Ave, Oshawa, ON, L1J 1V9
(905) 723-1921
Emp Here 35
SIC 8211 Elementary and secondary schools

D-U-N-S 25-265-2235   (BR)
**DURHAM CATHOLIC DISTRICT SCHOOL
BOARD**
ST MICHAEL'S CATHOLIC SCHOOL
50 Vancouver Crt, Oshawa, ON, L1J 5X2
(905) 728-5333
Emp Here 30
SIC 8211 Elementary and secondary schools

D-U-N-S 25-018-0767   (BR)
DURHAM DISTRICT SCHOOL BOARD
OSHAWA CENTRAL COLLEGIATE
155 Gibb St, Oshawa, ON, L1J 1Y4
(905) 723-4678
Emp Here 75
SIC 8211 Elementary and secondary schools

D-U-N-S 25-300-7850   (BR)
DURHAM DISTRICT SCHOOL BOARD
COLLEGE HILL PUBLIC SCHOOL
530 Laval St, Oshawa, ON, L1J 6R2
(905) 723-2876
Emp Here 21
SIC 8211 Elementary and secondary schools

D-U-N-S 25-300-8015   (BR)
DURHAM DISTRICT SCHOOL BOARD
WOODCREST PUBLIC SCHOOL
506 Woodcrest Ave, Oshawa, ON, L1J 2T8
(905) 725-1031
Emp Here 25
SIC 8211 Elementary and secondary schools

D-U-N-S 25-300-8155   (BR)
DURHAM DISTRICT SCHOOL BOARD
LAKEWOODS PUBLIC SCHOOL
323 Chaleur Ave, Oshawa, ON, L1J 1G5
(905) 576-8820
Emp Here 40
SIC 8211 Elementary and secondary schools

D-U-N-S 25-300-7660   (BR)
DURHAM DISTRICT SCHOOL BOARD
*ADELAIDE MCLAUGHLIN ELEMENTARY
SCHOOL*
630 Stevenson Rd N, Oshawa, ON, L1J 5P1
(905) 728-0521
Emp Here 29
SIC 8211 Elementary and secondary schools

D-U-N-S 24-796-5049   (BR)
DURHAM DISTRICT SCHOOL BOARD
*MCLAUGHLIN, R S COLLEGIATE & VOCA-
TIONAL INSTITUTE*
570 Stevenson Rd N, Oshawa, ON, L1J 5P1
(905) 728-9407
Emp Here 80
SIC 8211 Elementary and secondary schools

D-U-N-S 20-711-3452   (BR)
DURHAM DISTRICT SCHOOL BOARD
CANNON, DR C F SCHOOL
1196 Cedar St, Oshawa, ON, L1J 3S2
(905) 725-0344
Emp Here 50
SIC 8211 Elementary and secondary schools

D-U-N-S 25-301-7073   (BR)
DURHAM DISTRICT SCHOOL BOARD
WAVERLY PUBLIC SCHOOL
100 Waverly St S, Oshawa, ON, L1J 5V1
(905) 728-4461
Emp Here 35
SIC 8211 Elementary and secondary schools

D-U-N-S 25-300-7496   (BR)
DURHAM DISTRICT SCHOOL BOARD
GLEN STREET PUBLIC SCHOOL
929 Glen St, Oshawa, ON, L1J 3T9
(905) 723-8821
Emp Here 40
SIC 8211 Elementary and secondary schools

D-U-N-S 20-807-3721   (SL)
DURHAM RADIO INC
ROCK 94.9 FM, THE
1200 Airport Blvd Suite 207, Oshawa, ON, L1J
8P5
(905) 571-0949
Emp Here 50   *Sales* 3,137,310
SIC 4832 Radio broadcasting stations

D-U-N-S 25-301-3163   (BR)
EXTENDICARE (CANADA) INC
PARAMED HOME HEALTH CARE
1143 Wentworth St W Ste 201, Oshawa, ON,
L1J 8P7
(905) 433-7600
Emp Here 20
SIC 8741 Management services

D-U-N-S 25-694-8118   (BR)
GAP (CANADA) INC
GAP
(*Suby of* The Gap Inc)
419 King St W, Oshawa, ON, L1J 2K5
(905) 438-0865
Emp Here 70
SIC 5651 Family clothing stores

D-U-N-S 20-820-7535   (BR)
GOODLIFE FITNESS CENTRES INC
GOODLIFE FITNESS
419 King St W, Oshawa, ON, L1J 2K5
(905) 433-1665
Emp Here 20
SIC 7999 Amusement and recreation, nec

D-U-N-S 25-998-3260   (BR)
HUDSON'S BAY COMPANY
BAY, THE
419 King St W, Oshawa, ON, L1J 2K5
(905) 571-1211
Emp Here 100
SIC 5311 Department stores

D-U-N-S 25-170-4615   (BR)
**IFS INTERNATIONAL FREIGHT SYSTEMS
INC**
INTERNATIONAL FREIGHT SYSTEMS
280 Cordova Rd, Oshawa, ON, L1J 1N9
(905) 436-1218
Emp Here 70
SIC 4213 Trucking, except local

D-U-N-S 24-512-0530   (BR)
INDIGO BOOKS & MUSIC INC
CHAPTERS
(*Suby of* Indigo Books & Music Inc)
419 King St W Suite 1135, Oshawa, ON, L1J
2K5
(905) 438-8593
Emp Here 40
SIC 5942 Book stores

D-U-N-S 24-651-9565   (BR)
INNVEST PROPERTIES CORP
COMFORT INN OSHAWA
(*Suby of* Innvest Properties Corp)
605 Bloor St W, Oshawa, ON, L1J 5Y6
(905) 434-5000
Emp Here 25
SIC 7011 Hotels and motels

D-U-N-S 24-624-9452   (BR)
KEG RESTAURANTS LTD
KEG STEAKHOUSE & BAR, THE
255 Stevenson Rd S, Oshawa, ON, L1J 6Y4
(905) 571-3212
Emp Here 60
SIC 5812 Eating places

D-U-N-S 24-028-6559   (HQ)
LAKERIDGE HEALTH
LAKERIDGE HEALTH OSHAWA
(*Suby of* Lakeridge Health)
850 1/4 Champlain Ave, Oshawa, ON, L1J
8R2
(905) 576-8711
Emp Here 200   *Emp Total* 3,000
Sales 208,740,563

SIC 8062 General medical and surgical hospi-
tals
VP Fin Natalie Hovey
Dir Fin Terry Caputo

D-U-N-S 25-947-7198   (BR)
LOBLAWS SUPERMARKETS LIMITED
REAL CANADIAN SUPERSTORE
481 Gibb St, Oshawa, ON, L1J 1Z4
(905) 743-0043
Emp Here 400
SIC 5411 Grocery stores

D-U-N-S 20-966-6627   (HQ)
**MACKIE MOVING SYSTEMS CORPORA-
TION**
MACKIE GROUP, THE
933 Bloor St W, Oshawa, ON, L1J 5Y7
(905) 728-2400
Emp Here 400   *Emp Total* 200
Sales 35,677,782
SIC 4231 Trucking terminal facilities
 Ross Mackie
Pr Jilles Bernier
VP Donald Bain
VP Mike Farger
 Dean Mackie
 Scott Mackie
Dir Paul Mackie
Dir Norman Mackie

D-U-N-S 25-141-9289   (SL)
**MENTOR MEDICAL SYSTEMS (CANADA)
INC**
(*Suby of* Johnson & Johnson)
1129 Wentworth St W Unit B2, Oshawa, ON,
L1J 8P7

Emp Here 23   *Sales* 2,626,585
SIC 4213 Trucking, except local

D-U-N-S 25-676-2022   (BR)
METRO ONTARIO INC
METRO
149 Midtown Dr, Oshawa, ON, L1J 3Z7
(905) 723-7731
Emp Here 100
SIC 5411 Grocery stores

D-U-N-S 20-772-7660   (BR)
MOORE CANADA CORPORATION
(*Suby of* R. R. Donnelley & Sons Company)
1100 Thornton Rd S, Oshawa, ON, L1J 7E2
(905) 579-2461
Emp Here 70
SIC 2761 Manifold business forms

D-U-N-S 25-953-6464   (BR)
**MUNICIPAL PROPERTY ASSESSMENT
CORPORATION**
MUNICIPAL PROPERTY ASSESSMENT
419 King St W Suite 170, Oshawa, ON, L1J
2K5
(905) 432-9470
Emp Here 70
SIC 7389 Business services, nec

D-U-N-S 20-434-0863   (SL)
NORMARK INC
1350 Phillip Murray Ave, Oshawa, ON, L1J
6Z9
(905) 571-3001
Emp Here 20   *Sales* 2,261,782
SIC 5091 Sporting and recreation goods

D-U-N-S 20-052-8953   (SL)
NU FLOW TECHNOLOGIES (2000) INC
1313 Boundary Rd, Oshawa, ON, L1J 6Z7
(905) 433-5510
Emp Here 31   *Sales* 2,699,546
SIC 1799 Special trade contractors, nec

D-U-N-S 25-096-1695   (BR)
PENSKE TRUCK LEASING CANADA INC
(*Suby of* Penske Corporation)
850 Champlain Ave, Oshawa, ON, L1J 8C3
(905) 436-0171
Emp Here 30

SIC 7513 Truck rental and leasing, no drivers

D-U-N-S 25-665-0367   (BR)
PHARMA PLUS DRUGMARTS LTD
419 King St W, Oshawa, ON, L1J 2K5
(905) 728-5101
Emp Here 35
SIC 5912 Drug stores and proprietary stores

D-U-N-S 25-364-9206   (BR)
PIVAL INTERNATIONAL INC
1001 Thornton Rd S, Oshawa, ON, L1J 0B1
(905) 579-1402
Emp Here 35
SIC 4226 Special warehousing and storage,
nec

D-U-N-S 20-271-5988   (BR)
RE/MAX ABILITY REAL ESTATE LTD
379 Bond St W Suite 300, Oshawa, ON, L1J
8R7
(905) 434-7777
Emp Here 60
SIC 6531 Real estate agents and managers

D-U-N-S 25-662-4578   (BR)
RED LOBSTER HOSPITALITY LLC
RED LOBSTER RESTAURANTS
(*Suby of* Red Lobster Seafood Co., LLC)
311 King St W, Oshawa, ON, L1J 2J8
(905) 434-1143
Emp Here 74
SIC 5812 Eating places

D-U-N-S 25-300-5078   (BR)
REDBERRY FRANCHISING CORP
BURGER KING
338 King St W, Oshawa, ON, L1J 2J9
(905) 571-2334
Emp Here 30
SIC 5812 Eating places

D-U-N-S 24-726-7420   (BR)
REVERA LONG TERM CARE INC
*THORNTONVIEW LONG TERM CARE RES-
IDENCE*
186 Thornton Rd S Suite 1103, Oshawa, ON,
L1J 5Y2
(905) 576-5181
Emp Here 100
SIC 8051 Skilled nursing care facilities

D-U-N-S 20-974-5694   (BR)
SEARS CANADA INC
419 King St W Suite 1, Oshawa, ON, L1J 2K5
(905) 576-1711
Emp Here 100
SIC 5311 Department stores

D-U-N-S 24-622-2681   (SL)
SOUTHERN SUPPLIES LIMITED
(*Suby of* Wegmart Ltd)
323 Bloor St W, Oshawa, ON, L1J 6X4
(905) 728-6216
Emp Here 25   *Sales* 6,420,542
SIC 5075 Warm air heating and air condition-
ing
Pr Pr Walter H Libby
VP VP Gordon M Libby
 Walter E Libby
Dir Marie Libby
Dir Joanne M Littlejohn
Dir Leanna Meier

D-U-N-S 24-389-4990   (SL)
**SPECIALIZED TRANSPORTATION AGENT
GROUP - CANADA CORP**
SPECIALIZED TRANSPORTATION
(*Suby of* CRST International, Inc.)
933 Bloor St W, Oshawa, ON, L1J 5Y7
(905) 728-4506
Emp Here 50   *Sales* 3,939,878
SIC 4212 Local trucking, without storage

D-U-N-S 20-107-1276   (BR)
STAPLES CANADA INC
STAPLES THE BUSINESS DEPOT
(*Suby of* Staples, Inc.)

▲ Public Company   ■ Public Company Family Member   **HQ** Headquarters   **BR** Branch   **SL** Single Location

410 Gibb St W, Oshawa, ON, L1J 0B2
(905) 404-4392
Emp Here 37
SIC 5943 Stationery stores

D-U-N-S 20-806-5461　　(BR)
STARBUCKS COFFEE CANADA, INC
(*Suby of* Starbucks Corporation)
419 King St W Suite 1135, Oshawa, ON, L1J 2K5
(905) 438-9838
Emp Here 21
SIC 5812 Eating places

D-U-N-S 20-108-9815　　(HQ)
SYNCREON CANADA INC
SYNCREON
999 Boundary Rd, Oshawa, ON, L1J 8P8
(905) 743-6277
Emp Here 44　　　　*Emp Total* 4
Sales 164,161,575
SIC 4783 Packing and crating
Pr Pr Brian Enright
Kenneth Pocius
Carine Vanlandschoot
Ex VP Michael Neumann
Ex VP Julian Mordaunt
VP Don Heath

D-U-N-S 25-203-0572　　(SL)
T.T.O.C.S. LIMITED
EAST SIDE MARIO'S #640
419 King St W Suite Side, Oshawa, ON, L1J 2K5

Emp Here 100　　*Sales* 2,991,389
SIC 5812 Eating places

D-U-N-S 25-527-8020　　(BR)
TST SOLUTIONS L.P.
TST OVERLAND EXPRESS, DIV OF
1250 Thornton Rd S, Oshawa, ON, L1J 7E2
(905) 728-7329
Emp Here 60
SIC 4212 Local trucking, without storage

D-U-N-S 24-892-1806　　(BR)
TALLMAN TRUCK CENTRE LIMITED
787 Bloor St W, Oshawa, ON, L1J 5Y6
(905) 436-9292
Emp Here 20
SIC 4212 Local trucking, without storage

D-U-N-S 25-120-2081　　(BR)
TORONTO-DOMINION BANK, THE
TD CANADA TRUST
(*Suby of* Toronto-Dominion Bank, The)
22 Stevenson Rd S, Oshawa, ON, L1J 5L9
(905) 427-7870
Emp Here 23
SIC 6021 National commercial banks

D-U-N-S 25-027-7902　　(BR)
TWINCORP INC
PIZZA HUT
299 King St W, Oshawa, ON, L1J 2J8
(905) 721-7525
Emp Here 25
SIC 5812 Eating places

D-U-N-S 24-219-7887　　(SL)
TZOGAS ENTERPRISES INC
TEDDY'S RESTAURANT & DELI
245 King St W Suite 15, Oshawa, ON, L1J 2J7
(905) 579-5529
Emp Here 60　　*Sales* 1,824,018
SIC 5812 Eating places

D-U-N-S 25-705-0856　　(BR)
UNIFOR
CAW LOCAL 222
1425 Phillip Murray Ave Suite 1, Oshawa, ON, L1J 8L4
(905) 723-1187
Emp Here 32
SIC 8631 Labor organizations

D-U-N-S 24-991-2452　　(HQ)

VELCAN FOREST PRODUCTS INC
(*Suby of* Velcan Forest Products Inc)
1240 Skae Dr, Oshawa, ON, L1J 7A1
(905) 571-2477
Emp Here 90　　　　*Emp Total* 90
Sales 27,068,420
SIC 5031 Lumber, plywood, and millwork
Joseph Carpino
Pr Pr Hovan Tchaglassian

D-U-N-S 24-609-2097　　(BR)
WAL-MART CANADA CORP
WAL-MART
680 Laval Dr Suite 1056, Oshawa, ON, L1J 0B5
(905) 438-1400
Emp Here 50
SIC 5311 Department stores

D-U-N-S 20-005-2178　　(BR)
WENDY'S RESTAURANTS OF CANADA INC
WENDY'S
(*Suby of* The Wendy's Company)
323 King St W, Oshawa, ON, L1J 2J8
(905) 579-9750
Emp Here 38
SIC 5812 Eating places

D-U-N-S 20-343-2039　　(BR)
WESTERN INVENTORY SERVICE LTD
199 Wentworth St W Suite 4, Oshawa, ON, L1J 6P4
(905) 571-6436
Emp Here 20
SIC 8748 Business consulting, nec

D-U-N-S 25-873-7626　　(BR)
WILSON FOODS CENTRE LTD
MCDONALD S RESTAURANT NO 14535
419 King St W, Oshawa, ON, L1J 2K5
(905) 576-3400
Emp Here 41
SIC 5812 Eating places

D-U-N-S 25-695-0270　　(BR)
YM INC. (SALES)
BLUENOTES
419 King St W, Oshawa, ON, L1J 2K5
(905) 579-5756
Emp Here 20
SIC 5621 Women's clothing stores

Oshawa, ON L1K

D-U-N-S 24-418-2742　　(BR)
CINEPLEX ODEON CORPORATION
CINEPLEX CINEMAS OSHAWA
1351 Grandview St N, Oshawa, ON, L1K 0G1
(905) 432-3486
Emp Here 20
SIC 7832 Motion picture theaters, except drive-in

D-U-N-S 20-711-3809　　(BR)
DURHAM CATHOLIC DISTRICT SCHOOL BOARD
ST JOHN BOSCO CATHOLIC SCHOOL
1600 Clearbrook Dr, Oshawa, ON, L1K 2P6
(905) 743-6223
Emp Here 50
SIC 8211 Elementary and secondary schools

D-U-N-S 24-111-1884　　(BR)
DURHAM DISTRICT SCHOOL BOARD
NORMAN G POWERS PUBLIC SCHOOL
1555 Coldstream Dr, Oshawa, ON, L1K 3B5
(905) 728-5448
Emp Here 35
SIC 8211 Elementary and secondary schools

D-U-N-S 20-653-4518　　(BR)
DURHAM DISTRICT SCHOOL BOARD
SHERWOOD PUBLIC SCHOOL
633 Ormond Dr, Oshawa, ON, L1K 2W6

(905) 728-9283
Emp Here 50
SIC 8211 Elementary and secondary schools

D-U-N-S 25-300-7926　　(BR)
DURHAM DISTRICT SCHOOL BOARD
ATTERSLEY, GORDON B. PUBLIC SCHOOL
1110 Attersley Dr, Oshawa, ON, L1K 1X8
(905) 576-8901
Emp Here 45
SIC 8211 Elementary and secondary schools

D-U-N-S 25-300-8387　　(BR)
DURHAM DISTRICT SCHOOL BOARD
HARMONY HEIGHTS PUBLIC SCHOOL
590 Galahad Dr, Oshawa, ON, L1K 1M2
(905) 433-8933
Emp Here 25
SIC 8211 Elementary and secondary schools

D-U-N-S 20-655-0704　　(BR)
DURHAM DISTRICT SCHOOL BOARD
PIERRE ELLIOTT TRUDEAU PUBLIC SCHOOL
1111 Beatrice St E, Oshawa, ON, L1K 2S7
(905) 725-7353
Emp Here 40
SIC 8211 Elementary and secondary schools

D-U-N-S 25-057-7517　　(BR)
METRO ONTARIO INC
A & P FOOD STORES
555 Rossland Rd E, Oshawa, ON, L1K 1K8
(905) 579-5862
Emp Here 200
SIC 5411 Grocery stores

D-U-N-S 20-793-0756　　(BR)
SOBEYS CAPITAL INCORPORATED
SOBEYS
1377 Wilson Rd N, Oshawa, ON, L1K 2Z5
(905) 440-4687
Emp Here 100
SIC 5411 Grocery stores

D-U-N-S 24-977-2554　　(BR)
STARBUCKS COFFEE CANADA, INC
(*Suby of* Starbucks Corporation)
1365 Wilson Rd N, Oshawa, ON, L1K 2Z5
(905) 728-8312
Emp Here 20
SIC 5812 Eating places

Otonabee, ON K9J

D-U-N-S 20-141-0875　　(SL)
287912 ONTARIO LTD
2193 Keene Rd, Otonabee, ON, K9J 6X7
(705) 743-6141
Emp Here 41　　*Sales* 5,803,882
SIC 5411 Grocery stores

Ottawa, ON K0A
Carleton County

D-U-N-S 24-686-4573　　(SL)
BLACK ELECTRIC LTD
217 Cardevco Road, Ottawa, ON, K0A 1L0
(613) 738-0705
Emp Here 25　　*Sales* 2,188,821
SIC 1731 Electrical work

Ottawa, ON K1A
Carleton County

D-U-N-S 20-537-1748　　(BR)
CANADA POST CORPORATION
BOWDEN PO
2701 Riverside Dr, Ottawa, ON, K1A 0B1

(613) 734-8440
Emp Here 3,000
SIC 4311 U.s. postal service

D-U-N-S 20-580-2965　　(BR)
CANADA POST CORPORATION
1400 Merivale Rd, Ottawa, ON, K1A 0Y9

Emp Here 20
SIC 4311 U.s. postal service

D-U-N-S 24-269-8181　　(HQ)
CANADA POST CORPORATION
INNOVAPOST
(*Suby of* Canada Post Corporation)
2701 Riverside Dr, Ottawa, ON, K1A 1L5
(613) 734-8440
Emp Here 2,500　　*Emp Total* 63,000
Sales 6,019,551,280
SIC 4311 U.s. postal service
Pr Deepak Chopra
Wayne Cheeseman
Jacques Cote
Kerry Munro
VP Douglas Greaves
Sr VP Andre Turgeon
Sr VP Cal Hart
Andre Joron
VP Sls Peter Melanson
Sr VP Mary Traversy

D-U-N-S 20-652-9815　　(BR)
CANADA POST CORPORATION
2701 Riverside Dr Suite 604, Ottawa, ON, K1A 1L9
(613) 734-1017
Emp Here 100
SIC 4311 U.s. postal service

D-U-N-S 20-787-7507　　(HQ)
EXPORT DEVELOPMENT CANADA
EDC
150 Slater St, Ottawa, ON, K1A 1K3
(613) 598-2500
Emp Here 1,000　　*Emp Total* 570,000
Sales 1,163,910,240
SIC 6111 Federal and federally sponsored credit agencies
Pr Benoit Daignault
Ch Bd Kevin Warn-Shindel
VP Fin Carl Burlock
Sr VP Catherine Decarie
Sr VP Al Hamdani
VP Fin Ken Kember
Sr VP Mairead Lavery
Sr VP Derek Layne
Jim Mcardle
Sr VP Clive Witter

D-U-N-S 20-362-4296　　(SL)
MASTER GARDENERS OF OTTAWA-CARLETON
930 Carling Ave, Ottawa, ON, K1A 0C6
(613) 236-0034
Emp Here 28　　*Sales* 5,370,756
SIC 5261 Retail nurseries and garden stores

D-U-N-S 20-552-4759　　(BR)
NATIONAL RESEARCH COUNCIL CANADA
NRC-FINANCE BRANCH
1200 Montreal Rd Suite 207, Ottawa, ON, K1A 0R6
(613) 993-9200
Emp Here 150
SIC 8741 Management services

D-U-N-S 20-889-3875　　(HQ)
ROYAL CANADIAN MINT
320 Sussex Dr, Ottawa, ON, K1A 0G8
(613) 993-3500
Emp Here 400　　*Emp Total* 570,000
Sales 117,463,636
SIC 5094 Jewelry and precious stones
Pr Pr Sandra Harrington
Jennifer Camelon
Pers/VP Michel Boucher
VP Opers Sean Byrne
VP Simon Kamel

VP Sls John Moore

D-U-N-S 24-324-1713   (BR)
SNC-LAVALIN OPERATIONS & MAINTE-NANCE INC
SNC-LAVALIN PROFAC
150 Tunney'S Pasture Drwy, Ottawa, ON, K1A 0T6

Emp Here 20
SIC 6531 Real estate agents and managers

D-U-N-S 20-789-6259   (BR)
SODEXO CANADA LTD
125 Sussex Dr, Ottawa, ON, K1A 0G2
(613) 789-9389
Emp Here 20
SIC 5812 Eating places

D-U-N-S 20-716-9231   (BR)
ST. JOSEPH CORPORATION
E-PRINT IT
120 Parkdale Ave Rm 0122 C, Ottawa, ON, K1A 1K6

Emp Here 20
SIC 2269 Finishing plants, nec

Ottawa, ON K1B
Carleton County

D-U-N-S 20-893-2210   (SL)
126677 CANADA LIMITED
LOLACHERS CATERING DIV. OF
1620 Michael St, Ottawa, ON, K1B 3T7
(613) 741-2800
Emp Here 125   Sales 3,793,956
SIC 5812 Eating places

D-U-N-S 24-685-4632   (SL)
718009 ONTARIO INC
SPRINT COURIER
2617 Edinburgh Pl, Ottawa, ON, K1B 5M1
(613) 742-7171
Emp Here 75   Sales 3,793,956
SIC 7389 Business services, nec

D-U-N-S 24-662-1353   (SL)
AQUATECK WATER SYSTEMS DISTRIBU-TORS LTD
2700 Lancaster Rd Suite 116, Ottawa, ON, K1B 4T7
(613) 526-4613
Emp Here 35   Sales 8,927,600
SIC 5084 Industrial machinery and equipment
Pr Pr Jed Dreifke
Dir Ronald Dreifke
Sls Mgr Stewart Makinson

D-U-N-S 20-615-9931   (SL)
ARCELORMITTAL OTTAWA INC
BAKERMET
2555 Sheffield Rd, Ottawa, ON, K1B 3V6
(613) 745-6000
Emp Here 50   Sales 14,466,392
SIC 5093 Scrap and waste materials

D-U-N-S 25-570-3910   (SL)
BLONDEAU TAXI LIMITEE
BLONDEAU TRANSPORTATION
2161 Bantree St, Ottawa, ON, K1B 4X3

Emp Here 170   Sales 4,815,406
SIC 4151 School buses

D-U-N-S 20-136-5616   (HQ)
BOYD MOVING & STORAGE LTD
1255 Leeds Ave Unit 1, Ottawa, ON, K1B 3W2
(613) 244-4444
Emp Here 99   Emp Total 25
Sales 5,690,935
SIC 4214 Local trucking with storage
Vera Klein
Dom Mccormick

D-U-N-S 20-136-5830   (BR)

BRINK'S CANADA LIMITED
BRINK'S CANADA
(Suby of The Brink's Company)
2755 Lancaster Rd, Ottawa, ON, K1B 4V8
(613) 521-8650
Emp Here 120
SIC 7381 Detective and armored car services

D-U-N-S 24-892-8772   (HQ)
CANADA SCIENCE AND TECHNOLOGY MUSEUMS CORPORATION
CANADA AVIATION AND SPACE MUSEUM
2421 Lancaster Rd, Ottawa, ON, K1B 4L5
(613) 991-3044
Emp Here 55   Emp Total 570,000
Sales 14,812,892
SIC 8412 Museums and art galleries
Pr Denise Amyot
Ch Bd Gary Polonsky

D-U-N-S 20-574-4878   (BR)
CARDINAL COURIERS LTD
2715 Sheffield Rd Suite B, Ottawa, ON, K1B 3V8
(613) 228-0519
Emp Here 25
SIC 7389 Business services, nec

D-U-N-S 24-844-9746   (HQ)
DRAIN-ALL LTD
ROOTER OTTAWA
1611 Liverpool Crt, Ottawa, ON, K1B 4L1
(613) 739-1070
Emp Here 87   Emp Total 115
Sales 25,565,400
SIC 4953 Refuse systems
Pr Pr Frank Cardinali
VP Clara Cardinali

D-U-N-S 24-330-7980   (BR)
FLYNN CANADA LTD
2780 Sheffield Rd, Ottawa, ON, K1B 3V9
(613) 696-0086
Emp Here 100
SIC 1761 Roofing, siding, and sheetMetal work

D-U-N-S 25-718-7427   (BR)
FOURNITURES DE BUREAU DENIS INC
DENIS OFFICE SUPPLIES
(Suby of Placements Denis Latulippe Inc, Les)
2500 Lancaster Rd, Ottawa, ON, K1B 4S5
(613) 739-8900
Emp Here 20
SIC 5712 Furniture stores

D-U-N-S 20-616-1580   (BR)
G&K SERVICES CANADA INC
WHISTLE KLEEN
(Suby of Cintas Corporation)
201 Innes Park Way Unit 280, Ottawa, ON, K1B 1E3
(613) 746-7160
Emp Here 45
SIC 2326 Men's and boy's work clothing

D-U-N-S 24-965-8188   (BR)
G.N. JOHNSTON EQUIPMENT CO. LTD
JOHNSTON EQUIPMENT
2100 Bantree St Unit 10, Ottawa, ON, K1B 5R4
(613) 745-0744
Emp Here 30
SIC 5084 Industrial machinery and equipment

D-U-N-S 20-702-8346   (BR)
G.T. WHOLESALE LIMITED
GIANT TIGER WAREHOUSE
(Suby of Giant Tiger Stores Limited)
2001 Bantree St, Ottawa, ON, K1B 4X3
(613) 747-6702
Emp Here 50
SIC 5099 Durable goods, nec

D-U-N-S 25-726-2790   (SL)
GPEC INTERNATIONAL LTD
2880 Sheffield Rd Suite 3, Ottawa, ON, K1B 1A4

---

(613) 747-1788
Emp Here 50   Sales 4,961,328
SIC 8711 Engineering services

D-U-N-S 25-371-6500   (BR)
GRAYBAR CANADA LIMITED
(Suby of Graybar Electric Company, Inc.)
1730 Bantree St Unit 2, Ottawa, ON, K1B 3W4
(613) 688-0124
Emp Here 21
SIC 5063 Electrical apparatus and equipment

D-U-N-S 20-788-5807   (SL)
GUARDIAN OVERSEAS SHIPPING LTD
2222 Gladwin Cres, Ottawa, ON, K1B 4S6
(613) 523-5855
Emp Here 20   Sales 6,407,837
SIC 4731 Freight transportation arrangement
Pr Pr Robert Mcrae

D-U-N-S 24-336-9451   (HQ)
KEYSTONE AUTOMOTIVE INDUSTRIES ON INC
KEYSTONE AUTOMOTIVE
1230 Old Innes Rd Suite 401, Ottawa, ON, K1B 3V3
(613) 745-4088
Emp Here 22   Emp Total 42,500
Sales 7,296,070
SIC 5013 Motor vehicle supplies and new parts
Genl Mgr Phil St.Pierre

D-U-N-S 20-084-9037   (BR)
KING'S TRANSFER VAN LINES INC
1290 Old Innes Rd Unit 710, Ottawa, ON, K1B 5M6

Emp Here 22
SIC 4214 Local trucking with storage

D-U-N-S 25-975-1675   (BR)
LENNOX CANADA INC
DEARIE CONTRACTING
(Suby of Lennox Canada Inc)
101 Innes Park Way Unit 190, Ottawa, ON, K1B 1E3
(613) 739-1715
Emp Here 60
SIC 1731 Electrical work

D-U-N-S 25-459-8246   (SL)
LEXON TRANSPORT INC
1132 Old Innes Rd, Ottawa, ON, K1B 3V2
(613) 741-2696
Emp Here 35   Sales 4,012,839
SIC 4213 Trucking, except local

D-U-N-S 24-103-0824   (BR)
LOBLAWS INC
LOBLAW COMPANIES EAST, DIV OF
2625 Sheffield Rd, Ottawa, ON, K1B 1A8
(613) 741-4756
Emp Here 400
SIC 5141 Groceries, general line

D-U-N-S 24-344-5009   (BR)
METRO ONTARIO INC
1184 Old Innes Rd, Ottawa, ON, K1B 3V3
(613) 747-2328
Emp Here 70
SIC 5141 Groceries, general line

D-U-N-S 20-347-1107   (BR)
MILLER PAVING LIMITED
MILLER WASTE SYSTEMS
1815 Bantree St, Ottawa, ON, K1B 4L6
(613) 749-2222
Emp Here 100
SIC 4953 Refuse systems

D-U-N-S 20-893-3960   (SL)
O A C HOLDINGS LIMITED
OTTAWA ATHLETIC CLUB
2525 Lancaster Rd, Ottawa, ON, K1B 4L5
(613) 523-1540
Emp Here 100   Sales 4,012,839
SIC 7991 Physical fitness facilities

D-U-N-S 20-788-2531   (SL)
P.V.L. MOVING AND STORAGE LTD
PARKWAY VAN LINES
1199 Newmarket St, Ottawa, ON, K1B 3V1
(613) 744-4781
Emp Here 53   Sales 2,991,389
SIC 4214 Local trucking with storage

D-U-N-S 25-277-5945   (BR)
PINKHAM & SONS BUILDING MAINTE-NANCE INC
(Suby of Pinkham & Sons Building Mainte-nance Inc)
1181m Newmarket St, Ottawa, ON, K1B 3V1
(613) 745-7753
Emp Here 80
SIC 7349 Building maintenance services, nec

D-U-N-S 25-392-3528   (BR)
POSTMEDIA NETWORK INC
FLYER FORCE, THE
1230 Old Innes Rd Suite 407, Ottawa, ON, K1B 3V3
(613) 287-3318
Emp Here 70
SIC 4212 Local trucking, without storage

D-U-N-S 20-890-2015   (BR)
RYDER TRUCK RENTAL CANADA LTD
(Suby of Ryder System, Inc.)
1515 Michael St, Ottawa, ON, K1B 4T3
(613) 741-1000
Emp Here 35
SIC 7513 Truck rental and leasing, no drivers

D-U-N-S 24-210-5471   (BR)
SHRED-IT INTERNATIONAL ULC
SHRED-IT OTTAWA
1171 Kenaston St, Ottawa, ON, K1B 3N9
(613) 742-0101
Emp Here 50
SIC 7389 Business services, nec

D-U-N-S 24-752-7401   (SL)
SIERRA SUNROOMS INC
FOUR SEASONS SUNROOMS
(Suby of Four Seasons Solar Products, LLC)
2450 Lancaster Rd Unit 31, Ottawa, ON, K1B 5N3
(613) 738-8055
Emp Here 20   Sales 3,720,996
SIC 1542 Nonresidential construction, nec

D-U-N-S 25-065-1593   (SL)
SIMPLEX INDUSTRIES INC
2762 Sheffield Rd, Ottawa, ON, K1B 3V9
(613) 244-0586
Emp Here 80   Sales 4,523,563
SIC 4214 Local trucking with storage

D-U-N-S 20-748-0521   (SL)
SOLTA ENTERPRISES INC
SWISS CHALET PLUS
1899 Cyrville Rd, Ottawa, ON, K1B 1A9

Emp Here 70   Sales 2,115,860
SIC 5812 Eating places

D-U-N-S 24-437-2090   (BR)
SOLUTIONS DE MAINTENANCE AP-PLIQUEES (AMS) INC
SOLUTIONS DE MAINTENANCE AP-PLIQUEES (AMS) INC
1470 Triole St, Ottawa, ON, K1B 3S6
(613) 241-7794
Emp Here 300
SIC 7349 Building maintenance services, nec

D-U-N-S 25-357-3174   (BR)
SURGENOR PONTIAC BUICK LIMITED
SURGENOR TRUCK CENTRE
1571 Liverpool Crt, Ottawa, ON, K1B 4L1
(613) 745-0024
Emp Here 92
SIC 5511 New and used car dealers

D-U-N-S 24-383-6665   (BR)
TALLMAN TRUCK CENTRE LIMITED

OTTAWA TRUCK CENTRE, DIV OF
2716 Sheffield Rd, Ottawa, ON, K1B 3V9
(613) 741-1231
Emp Here 58
SIC 5511 New and used car dealers

D-U-N-S 20-580-3310   (BR)
UNITED RENTALS OF CANADA, INC
2660 Sheffield Rd, Ottawa, ON, K1B 3V7
(613) 745-3060
Emp Here 22
SIC 7359 Equipment rental and leasing, nec

D-U-N-S 24-807-2311   (SL)
UTILITY SERVICES LTD.
1611 Liverpool Crt, Ottawa, ON, K1B 4L1
(613) 746-9192
Emp Here 49   *Sales* 7,296,070
SIC 1521 Single-family housing construction
Pr Frank Cardinali

D-U-N-S 24-156-5121   (BR)
VISUAL DEFENCE INC
2450 Lancaster Rd Unit 40, Ottawa, ON, K1B
5N3
(613) 226-6661
Emp Here 120
SIC 7382 Security systems services

D-U-N-S 24-309-9665   (BR)
WASTE CONNECTIONS OF CANADA INC
BFI CANADA
1152 Kenaston St, Ottawa, ON, K1B 3P5
(613) 749-8000
Emp Here 300
SIC 4953 Refuse systems

D-U-N-S 20-860-4368   (BR)
**WINNERS MERCHANTS INTERNATIONAL
L.P.**
HOMESENSE
(*Suby of* The TJX Companies Inc)
1501 Innes Rd Suite 417, Ottawa, ON, K1B
1C5
(613) 740-1299
Emp Here 25
SIC 5651 Family clothing stores

Ottawa, ON K1C
Carleton County

D-U-N-S 20-281-1733   (BR)
CITY OF OTTAWA
*BOB MACQUARRIE RECREATION COM-
PLEX - ORLEANS*
(*Suby of* City of Ottawa)
1490 Youville Dr, Ottawa, ON, K1C 2X8
(613) 824-0819
Emp Here 75
SIC 7999 Amusement and recreation, nec

D-U-N-S 25-265-4264   (BR)
**OTTAWA CATHOLIC DISTRICT SCHOOL
BOARD**
CONVENT GLEN CATHOLIC SCHOOL
(*Suby of* Ottawa Catholic District School
Board)
6212 Jeanne D'Arc Blvd N, Ottawa, ON, K1C
2M4
(613) 824-8541
Emp Here 25
SIC 8211 Elementary and secondary schools

D-U-N-S 25-263-5529   (BR)
**OTTAWA-CARLETON DISTRICT SCHOOL
BOARD**
CONVENT GLEN ELEMENTARY SCHOOL
1708 Grey Nuns Dr, Ottawa, ON, K1C 1C1
(613) 824-8177
Emp Here 25
SIC 8211 Elementary and secondary schools

Ottawa, ON K1E
Carleton County

D-U-N-S 25-129-1258   (BR)
NASCO FOOD INC
TIM HORTONS
(*Suby of* Nasco Food Inc)
1675e Tenth Line Rd, Ottawa, ON, K1E 3P6
(613) 834-6638
Emp Here 35
SIC 5812 Eating places

Ottawa, ON K1G
Carleton County

D-U-N-S 25-495-4753   (SL)
1222010 ONTARIO INC
AKRAN MARKETING
2000 Thurston Dr Unit 12, Ottawa, ON, K1G
4K7
(613) 739-4000
Emp Here 55   *Sales* 6,639,424
SIC 7311 Advertising agencies
Pr Raman Agarwal

D-U-N-S 25-359-4162   (SL)
1550825 ONTARIO INC
MANOIR ALTA VISTA MANOR
751 Peter Morand Cres, Ottawa, ON, K1G 6S9
(613) 739-0909
Emp Here 60   *Sales* 2,845,467
SIC 8059 Nursing and personal care, nec

D-U-N-S 24-917-4681   (BR)
3627730 CANADA INC
FREEMAN AUDIO VISUAL
3020 Hawthorne Rd Suite 300, Ottawa, ON,
K1G 3J6
(613) 526-3121
Emp Here 80
SIC 7389 Business services, nec

D-U-N-S 20-116-1853   (BR)
AMJ CAMPBELL INC
A M J CAMPBELL VAN LINES
2710 Stevenage Dr, Ottawa, ON, K1G 3N2
(613) 737-0000
Emp Here 50
SIC 4214 Local trucking with storage

D-U-N-S 24-269-8629   (BR)
ACKLANDS - GRAINGER INC
AGI
(*Suby of* W.W. Grainger, Inc.)
3020 Hawthorne Rd, Ottawa, ON, K1G 3J6
(613) 744-5012
Emp Here 20
SIC 5085 Industrial supplies

D-U-N-S 20-257-6229   (BR)
ALL CANADIAN COURIER CORP
380 Terminal Ave Suite 200, Ottawa, ON, K1G
0Z3
(613) 688-3001
Emp Here 25
SIC 7389 Business services, nec

D-U-N-S 25-724-0820   (BR)
ARCHITECTURE49 INC
200 Tremblay Rd Suite 152, Ottawa, ON, K1G
3H5
(613) 238-0440
Emp Here 60
SIC 8712 Architectural services

D-U-N-S 25-318-5193   (BR)
BENSON GROUP INC
BENSON AUTO PARTS
(*Suby of* Benapac Inc)
1400 Ages Dr, Ottawa, ON, K1G 5T4
(613) 746-5353
Emp Here 35
SIC 5013 Motor vehicle supplies and new
parts

D-U-N-S 20-856-6708   (BR)

BREWERS RETAIL INC
BEER STORE, THE
2750 Swansea Cres, Ottawa, ON, K1G 6R8
(613) 738-8615
Emp Here 100
SIC 5921 Liquor stores

D-U-N-S 20-788-0766   (HQ)
CAA NORTH & EAST ONTARIO
CAA
(*Suby of* CAA North & East Ontario)
2151 Thurston Dr, Ottawa, ON, K1G 6C9
(613) 820-1890
Emp Here 100   *Emp Total* 171
Sales 23,099,553
SIC 8699 Membership organizations, nec
Pr Pr Christina Hlusko
  Robert Keeper
  Peter Mcintosh
  Vicky Paine-Mantha
Dir Jack Campbell
Dir John Morton
Dir Richard Nowak
Dir Kate Wright
Dir Line Villeneuve
Dir Gerry Brown

D-U-N-S 25-541-7685   (HQ)
CANADIAN BLOOD SERVICES
(*Suby of* Canadian Blood Services)
1800 Alta Vista Dr, Ottawa, ON, K1G 4J5
(613) 739-2300
Emp Here 400   *Emp Total* 4,000
Sales 830,976,351
SIC 8099 Health and allied services, nec
  Graham D Sher
VP Christian Choquet
  Pauline Port
Div VP Dana Devine

D-U-N-S 20-136-6986   (BR)
**CANADIAN LINEN AND UNIFORM SER-
VICE CO**
*CANADIAN LINEN AND UNIFORM SERVICE
CO*
(*Suby of* Ameripride Services, Inc.)
1695 Russell Rd, Ottawa, ON, K1G 0N1
(613) 736-9975
Emp Here 160
SIC 7213 Linen supply

D-U-N-S 24-642-9737   (BR)
CANON CANADA INC
CANON DIRECT SALES DIV
2260 Walkley Rd, Ottawa, ON, K1G 6A8
(613) 248-8060
Emp Here 38
SIC 5044 Office equipment

D-U-N-S 20-303-2826   (BR)
CARA OPERATIONS LIMITED
KELSEY'S
(*Suby of* Cara Holdings Limited)
1910 St. Laurent Blvd, Ottawa, ON, K1G 1A4
(613) 733-2200
Emp Here 40
SIC 5812 Eating places

D-U-N-S 20-013-5775   (BR)
CITY OF OTTAWA
*OTTAWA-CARLETON REGIONAL TRANSIT
COMMISSION*
(*Suby of* City of Ottawa)
1500 St. Laurent Blvd, Ottawa, ON, K1G 0Z8
(613) 741-6440
Emp Here 4,000
SIC 4111 Local and suburban transit

D-U-N-S 24-891-3600   (BR)
COLABOR LIMITED PARTNERSHIP
SUMMIT FOOD
(*Suby of* Groupe Colabor Inc)
100 Legacy Rd, Ottawa, ON, K1G 5T8
(613) 737-7000
Emp Here 200
SIC 5141 Groceries, general line

D-U-N-S 25-302-1414   (BR)
**CONSEIL DES ECOLES CATHOLIQUES DE
LANGUE FRANCAISE DU CENTRE-EST**
ECOLE SECONDAIRE FRANCO-CIT
623 Smyth Rd, Ottawa, ON, K1G 1N7
(613) 521-4999
Emp Here 65
SIC 8211 Elementary and secondary schools

D-U-N-S 25-302-0978   (BR)
**CONSEIL DES ECOLES CATHOLIQUES DE
LANGUE FRANCAISE DU CENTRE-EST**
SAINTE-GENEVIEVE
2198 Arch St, Ottawa, ON, K1G 2H7
(613) 733-9729
Emp Here 40
SIC 8211 Elementary and secondary schools

D-U-N-S 25-132-3325   (BR)
**CONSEIL DES ECOLES PUBLIQUES DE
L'EST DE L'ONTARIO**
*ECOLE ELEMENTAIRE PUBLIQUE MARIE
CURIE*
860 Colson Ave, Ottawa, ON, K1G 1R7
(613) 523-4975
Emp Here 36
SIC 8211 Elementary and secondary schools

D-U-N-S 20-020-5636   (BR)
**CONSEIL DES ECOLES PUBLIQUES DE
L'EST DE L'ONTARIO**
CARREFOUR, LE
2445 St. Laurent Blvd Suite 613, Ottawa, ON,
K1G 6C3
(613) 731-7212
Emp Here 70
SIC 8211 Elementary and secondary schools

D-U-N-S 24-126-6753   (BR)
CUMMINS EST DU CANADA SEC
CUMMINS EST DU CANADA SEC
3189 Swansea Cres, Ottawa, ON, K1G 3W5
(613) 736-1146
Emp Here 20
SIC 5084 Industrial machinery and equipment

D-U-N-S 24-362-8836   (HQ)
**DEW ENGINEERING AND DEVELOPMENT
ULC**
(*Suby of* Keystone Holdings, LLC)
3429 Hawthorne Rd, Ottawa, ON, K1G 4G2
(613) 736-5100
Emp Here 200   *Emp Total* 6,102
SIC 3795 Tanks and tank components

D-U-N-S 25-358-3009   (BR)
DST CONSULTING ENGINEERS INC
2150 Thurston Dr Unit 203, Ottawa, ON, K1G
5T9
(613) 748-1415
Emp Here 34
SIC 8748 Business consulting, nec

D-U-N-S 24-311-7913   (BR)
DRAIN-ALL LTD
2705 Stevenage Dr, Ottawa, ON, K1G 3N2
(800) 265-3868
Emp Here 40
SIC 4953 Refuse systems

D-U-N-S 24-437-6497   (SL)
DUSTBANE PRODUCTS LIMITED
25 Pickering Pl, Ottawa, ON, K1G 5P4
(613) 745-6861
Emp Here 50   *Sales* 6,797,150
SIC 2842 Polishes and sanitation goods
Pr Pr John French
  Pierre Perron
  Normand Perron

D-U-N-S 20-714-7096   (BR)
**DYNACARE-GAMMA LABORATORY PART-
NERSHIP**
750 Peter Morand Cres, Ottawa, ON, K1G 6S4
(613) 729-0200
Emp Here 200
SIC 8071 Medical laboratories

D-U-N-S 20-181-6316   (BR)
FREEMAN EXPOSITIONS, LTD
FREEMAN ELECTRICAL
940 Belfast Rd, Ottawa, ON, K1G 4A2
(613) 748-7180
Emp Here 70
SIC 7359 Equipment rental and leasing, nec

D-U-N-S 24-269-2507   (HQ)
G.T. WHOLESALE LIMITED
G.T. TABACCO
(*Suby of* Giant Tiger Stores Limited)
2480 Walkley Rd, Ottawa, ON, K1G 6A9
(613) 521-8222
Emp Here 220   *Emp Total* 400
Sales 81,643,023
SIC 5194 Tobacco and tobacco products
Pr Pr Gordon Reid
 Greg Farrell

D-U-N-S 25-283-8370   (BR)
GDI SERVICES (CANADA) LP
GDI INTEGRATED FACILITY SERVICES
800 Industrial Ave Suite 12, Ottawa, ON, K1G 4B8
(613) 247-0065
Emp Here 250
SIC 7349 Building maintenance services, nec

D-U-N-S 20-649-7513   (HQ)
GIANT TIGER STORES LIMITED
GIANT TIGER
(*Suby of* Giant Tiger Stores Limited)
2480 Walkley Rd, Ottawa, ON, K1G 6A9
(613) 521-8222
Emp Here 350   *Emp Total* 400
Sales 28,673,555
SIC 5311 Department stores
 Andrew Gross
 Gordon Reid
Pr Pr Greg Farrell
 Michael Lewis
 Leatrice Reid
 Blake Reid
 Scott Reid
 Jacqueline Vasile

D-U-N-S 24-390-5838   (BR)
GOLF TOWN LIMITED
GOLF TOWN
500 Terminal Ave Unit A20, Ottawa, ON, K1G 0Z3
(613) 241-9859
Emp Here 20
SIC 5941 Sporting goods and bicycle shops

D-U-N-S 24-112-0539   (BR)
GORDON FOOD SERVICE CANADA LTD
1435 Sandford Fleming Ave Unit 120, Ottawa, ON, K1G 3H3
(613) 842-9162
Emp Here 30
SIC 5141 Groceries, general line

D-U-N-S 20-443-0672   (BR)
GRAND & TOY LIMITED
(*Suby of* Office Depot, Inc.)
900 Belfast Rd, Ottawa, ON, K1G 0Z6
(613) 244-1212
Emp Here 140
SIC 5112 Stationery and office supplies

D-U-N-S 20-578-1693   (BR)
INTEGRATED DISTRIBUTION SYSTEMS LIMITED PARTNERSHIP
WAJAX POWER SYSTEMS
2450 Stevenage Dr, Ottawa, ON, K1G 3W3
(613) 736-6060
Emp Here 35
SIC 5084 Industrial machinery and equipment

D-U-N-S 20-789-1409   (SL)
KOYMAN GALLERIES LIMITED
KOYMAN GALLERIES
1771 St. Laurent Blvd, Ottawa, ON, K1G 3V4
(613) 526-1562
Emp Here 50   *Sales* 6,531,200
SIC 5999 Miscellaneous retail stores, nec

Pr Pr Marie Koyman
 Benjamin Koyman

D-U-N-S 25-365-1939   (BR)
LAFARGE PAVING & CONSTRUCTION (EASTERN) LIMITED
1651 Bearbrook Rd, Ottawa, ON, K1G 3K2
(613) 830-3060
Emp Here 100
SIC 1611 Highway and street construction

D-U-N-S 25-130-6726   (SL)
LATCON LTD
3387 Hawthorne Rd, Ottawa, ON, K1G 4G2
(613) 738-9061
Emp Here 65   *Sales* 6,712,384
SIC 1795 Wrecking and demolition work
Pr Pr Leonard Graham
 Robert Desormeaux
 Vivianne Duval

D-U-N-S 24-194-5505   (BR)
LOCAL HEROES INC
LOCAL HEROES BAR & GRILL
1760 St. Laurent Blvd, Ottawa, ON, K1G 1A2
(613) 737-9292
Emp Here 50
SIC 5812 Eating places

D-U-N-S 24-267-7490   (HQ)
MD MANAGEMENT LIMITED
MD EQUITY FUND
(*Suby of* Canadian Medical Association)
1870 Alta Vista Dr Suite 1, Ottawa, ON, K1G 6R7
(613) 731-4552
Emp Here 20   *Emp Total* 160
Sales 90,652,050
SIC 8741 Management services
Pr Brian Peters
VP Lindsay Hugenholtz
Ex VP Michelle Masson
Dir Daniel Labonte
 John Riviere

D-U-N-S 24-344-4887   (BR)
METRO ONTARIO INC
METRO
490 Industrial Ave, Ottawa, ON, K1G 0Y9
(613) 737-1410
Emp Here 100
SIC 5141 Groceries, general line

D-U-N-S 24-708-9659   (SL)
MIDEAST FOOD DISTRIBUTORS (1987) LTD
MID EAST FOOD CENTRE
1010 Belfast Rd, Ottawa, ON, K1G 4A2
(613) 244-2525
Emp Here 50   *Sales* 2,407,703
SIC 5499 Miscellaneous food stores

D-U-N-S 25-995-9096   (BR)
NESTLE CANADA INC
2370 Walkley Rd, Ottawa, ON, K1G 4H9

Emp Here 20
SIC 5143 Dairy products, except dried or canned

D-U-N-S 20-615-9295   (SL)
ON CALL CENTRE INC
2405 St. Laurent Blvd Unit B, Ottawa, ON, K1G 5B4
(613) 238-3262
Emp Here 50   *Sales* 2,626,585
SIC 7389 Business services, nec

D-U-N-S 25-238-2932   (BR)
OTTAWA CATHOLIC DISTRICT SCHOOL BOARD
ST LUKE SCHOOL
(*Suby of* Ottawa Catholic District School Board)
2485 Dwight Cres, Ottawa, ON, K1G 1C7
(613) 731-3541
Emp Here 23
SIC 8211 Elementary and secondary schools

D-U-N-S 20-711-6471   (BR)
OTTAWA CATHOLIC DISTRICT SCHOOL BOARD
ST. THOMAS MORE ELEMENTARY SCHOOL
(*Suby of* Ottawa Catholic District School Board)
1620 Blohm Dr, Ottawa, ON, K1G 5N6
(613) 739-7131
Emp Here 40
SIC 8211 Elementary and secondary schools

D-U-N-S 25-142-8652   (SL)
OTTAWA MONTESSORI SCHOOL / ECOLE MONTESSORI D'OTTAWA
335 Lindsay St, Ottawa, ON, K1G 0L6
(613) 521-5185
Emp Here 59   *Sales* 3,939,878
SIC 8211 Elementary and secondary schools

D-U-N-S 25-504-0891   (BR)
OTTAWA-CARLETON DISTRICT SCHOOL BOARD
CANTERBURY HIGH SCHOOL
900 Canterbury Ave, Ottawa, ON, K1G 3A7
(613) 731-1191
Emp Here 100
SIC 8211 Elementary and secondary schools

D-U-N-S 25-504-0610   (BR)
OTTAWA-CARLETON DISTRICT SCHOOL BOARD
MASSEY, VINCENT PUBLIC SCHOOL
745 Smyth Rd, Ottawa, ON, K1G 1N9
(613) 733-5955
Emp Here 65
SIC 8211 Elementary and secondary schools

D-U-N-S 20-009-6662   (BR)
OTTAWA-CARLETON DISTRICT SCHOOL BOARD
ROBERT BATEMAN PUBLIC SCHOOL
1250 Blohm Dr, Ottawa, ON, K1G 5R8
(613) 737-3169
Emp Here 55
SIC 8211 Elementary and secondary schools

D-U-N-S 25-501-6172   (BR)
OTTAWA-CARLETON DISTRICT SCHOOL BOARD
ARCH STREET PUBLIC SCHOOL
2129 Arch St, Ottawa, ON, K1G 2H5
(613) 733-0205
Emp Here 25
SIC 8211 Elementary and secondary schools

D-U-N-S 25-504-0644   (BR)
OTTAWA-CARLETON DISTRICT SCHOOL BOARD
HAWTHORNE PUBLIC SCHOOL
2158 St. Laurent Blvd, Ottawa, ON, K1G 1A9
(613) 733-6221
Emp Here 45
SIC 8211 Elementary and secondary schools

D-U-N-S 25-504-0974   (BR)
OTTAWA-CARLETON DISTRICT SCHOOL BOARD
HILLCREST HIGH SCHOOL
1900 Dauphin Rd, Ottawa, ON, K1G 2L7
(613) 733-1755
Emp Here 90
SIC 8211 Elementary and secondary schools

D-U-N-S 25-504-0339   (BR)
OTTAWA-CARLETON DISTRICT SCHOOL BOARD
RIVERVIEW ALTERNATIVE SCHOOL
260 Knox Cres, Ottawa, ON, K1G 0K8
(613) 733-6898
Emp Here 20
SIC 8211 Elementary and secondary schools

D-U-N-S 25-129-1910   (BR)
PENSKE TRUCK LEASING CANADA INC
PENSKE TRUCK RENTAL & LEASING
(*Suby of* Penske Corporation)
2323 Stevenage Dr, Ottawa, ON, K1G 3W1

(613) 731-9998
Emp Here 20
SIC 7513 Truck rental and leasing, no drivers

D-U-N-S 24-595-5919   (BR)
PIZZA PIZZA LIMITED
770 Industrial Ave Suite 8, Ottawa, ON, K1G 4H3
(613) 737-1111
Emp Here 80
SIC 5812 Eating places

D-U-N-S 24-859-8609   (BR)
PRAXAIR CANADA INC
MEDIGAS
(*Suby of* Praxair, Inc.)
900 Ages Dr, Ottawa, ON, K1G 6B3
(613) 733-8201
Emp Here 25
SIC 5047 Medical and hospital equipment

D-U-N-S 25-772-8089   (BR)
PRINCESS AUTO LTD
1111 Ages Dr, Ottawa, ON, K1G 6L3
(613) 247-1651
Emp Here 30
SIC 5251 Hardware stores

D-U-N-S 24-771-0338   (BR)
PROVIGO DISTRIBUTION INC
LOEB
2261 Walkley Rd, Ottawa, ON, K1G 3G8
(613) 526-5994
Emp Here 70
SIC 5411 Grocery stores

D-U-N-S 20-553-5243   (BR)
RAIL-TERM INC
200 Tremblay Rd, Ottawa, ON, K1G 3H5
(613) 569-6344
Emp Here 20
SIC 4111 Local and suburban transit

D-U-N-S 25-772-8543   (BR)
RED LOBSTER HOSPITALITY LLC
RED LOBSTER RESTAURANTS
(*Suby of* Red Lobster Seafood Co., LLC)
1499 St. Laurent Blvd, Ottawa, ON, K1G 0Z9
(613) 744-7560
Emp Here 96
SIC 5812 Eating places

D-U-N-S 25-601-6155   (BR)
ROGERS MEDIA INC
Y101 FM CKBY
(*Suby of* Rogers Communications Inc)
2001 Thurston Dr, Ottawa, ON, K1G 6C9
(613) 736-2001
Emp Here 20
SIC 4832 Radio broadcasting stations

D-U-N-S 25-542-9003   (BR)
RUSSEL METALS INC
2420 Stevenage Dr, Ottawa, ON, K1G 3W3
(613) 738-2961
Emp Here 40
SIC 5051 Metals service centers and offices

D-U-N-S 25-674-3550   (BR)
RYDER MATERIAL HANDLING ULC
(*Suby of* Crown Equipment Corporation)
2188 Thurston Dr, Ottawa, ON, K1G 6E1
(613) 739-1484
Emp Here 20
SIC 5084 Industrial machinery and equipment

D-U-N-S 24-312-3069   (BR)
SCHINDLER ELEVATOR CORPORATION
2200a Thurston Dr, Ottawa, ON, K1G 6E1
(613) 727-1289
Emp Here 20
SIC 5084 Industrial machinery and equipment

D-U-N-S 20-732-3986   (BR)
SHOPPERS DRUG MART (LONDON) LIMITED
SHOPPERS HOME HEALTH CARE
2405 St Laurent Blvd, Ottawa, ON, K1G 5B4

(613) 737-6335
Emp Here 20
SIC 8051 Skilled nursing care facilities

D-U-N-S 20-568-7747   (BR)
SHOPPERS HOME HEALTH CARE (CANADA) INC
SHOPPERS HOME HEALTHCARE
2405 St Laurent Blvd, Ottawa, ON, K1G 5B4
(613) 737-6335
Emp Here 20
SIC 5999 Miscellaneous retail stores, nec

D-U-N-S 20-787-7903   (HQ)
TANNIS TRADING INC
TANNIS FOOD DISTRIBUTORS
(*Suby of* Sysco Corporation)
2390 Stevenage Dr, Ottawa, ON, K1G 3W3
(613) 736-6000
Emp Here 120   *Emp Total* 51,900
Sales 29,683,364
SIC 5149 Groceries and related products, nec
Pr Pr Theo Tannis
VP VP Michael Tannis
  Eli Tannis
Dir Kammal Tannis

D-U-N-S 20-442-5144   (HQ)
TOMLINSON, R. W. LIMITED
ONTARIO TRAP ROCK, DIV OF
(*Suby of* Tomlinson, R. W. Limited)
5597 Power Rd, Ottawa, ON, K1G 3N4
(613) 822-1867
Emp Here 250   *Emp Total* 500
SIC 1411 Dimension stone

D-U-N-S 24-701-7101   (BR)
TOMMY HILFIGER CANADA INC
550 Terminal Ave Suite B20, Ottawa, ON, K1G 0Z3
(613) 789-6185
Emp Here 40
SIC 5651 Family clothing stores

D-U-N-S 24-045-7155   (BR)
TOSHIBA OF CANADA LIMITED
695 Industrial Ave, Ottawa, ON, K1G 0Z1
(613) 249-9900
Emp Here 40
SIC 5999 Miscellaneous retail stores, nec

D-U-N-S 20-798-8697   (BR)
UNITED PARCEL SERVICE CANADA LTD
UPS
2281 Stevenage Dr, Ottawa, ON, K1G 3W1
(613) 670-6061
Emp Here 300
SIC 4215 Courier services, except by air

D-U-N-S 24-365-9120   (BR)
VEOLIA ES CANADA SERVICES INDUS-TRIELS INC
4140 Belgreen Dr, Ottawa, ON, K1G 3N2
(613) 739-1150
Emp Here 98
SIC 7389 Business services, nec

D-U-N-S 25-471-0486   (BR)
VIA RAIL CANADA INC
200 Tremblay Rd, Ottawa, ON, K1G 3H5
(877) 711-9079
Emp Here 43
SIC 4111 Local and suburban transit

D-U-N-S 24-319-5174   (BR)
WAL-MART CANADA CORP
450 Termina Ave Suite 1031, Ottawa, ON, K1G 0Z3
(613) 562-0500
Emp Here 120
SIC 5311 Department stores

D-U-N-S 20-839-1685   (SL)
WALKER YOUTH HOMES INC
2162 Haig Dr, Ottawa, ON, K1G 2L2

Emp Here 25   *Sales* 5,006,160
SIC 1521 Single-family housing construction

D-U-N-S 20-861-2536   (BR)
YOUTH SERVICES BUREAU OF OTTAWA
WILLIAM E HAY CENTRE
3000 Hawthorne Rd, Ottawa, ON, K1G 5Y3
(613) 738-7776
Emp Here 90
SIC 8322 Individual and family services

Ottawa, ON K1H
Carleton County

D-U-N-S 20-714-1164   (SL)
ALEXANDER MONTESSORI SCHOOL INC
188 Billings Ave, Ottawa, ON, K1H 5K9
(613) 733-6137
Emp Here 50   *Sales* 3,356,192
SIC 8211 Elementary and secondary schools

D-U-N-S 24-103-4719   (BR)
BLACK & MCDONALD LIMITED
2460 Don Reid Dr, Ottawa, ON, K1H 1E1
(613) 526-1226
Emp Here 135
SIC 1731 Electrical work

D-U-N-S 25-175-1228   (SL)
BRUMICAL INVESTMENTS LIMITED
BILLINGS LODGE RETIREMENT COMMU-NITY
1180 Belanger Ave, Ottawa, ON, K1H 8N2
(613) 737-7877
Emp Here 60   *Sales* 2,188,821
SIC 8361 Residential care

D-U-N-S 20-522-7593   (SL)
CANADIAN APPRENTICESHIP FORUM
FORUM   CANADIEN   SUR L'APPRENTISSAGE
2197 Riverside Dr Suite 404, Ottawa, ON, K1H 7X3
(613) 235-4004
Emp Here 57   *Sales* 3,502,114
SIC 8249 Vocational schools, nec

D-U-N-S 25-304-9621   (BR)
CANADIAN HEARING SOCIETY
2197 Riverside Dr Suite 600, Ottawa, ON, K1H 7X3
(613) 521-0509
Emp Here 26
SIC 8099 Health and allied services, nec

D-U-N-S 20-587-1978   (BR)
CANADIAN IMPERIAL BANK OF COM-MERCE
CIBC
2217 Riverside Dr E, Ottawa, ON, K1H 1A1
(613) 736-6010
Emp Here 20
SIC 6021 National commercial banks

D-U-N-S 24-102-9149   (BR)
CANADIAN NATIONAL INSTITUTE FOR THE BLIND, THE
CNIB
(*Suby of* Canadian National Institute For The Blind, The)
1355 Bank St Suite 101, Ottawa, ON, K1H 8K7
(613) 563-4021
Emp Here 46
SIC 8093 Specialty outpatient clinics, nec

D-U-N-S 25-371-0115   (BR)
COMPAGNIE DE TELEPHONE BELL DU CANADA OU BELL CANADA, LA
1501 Bank St, Ottawa, ON, K1H 7Z1

Emp Here 20
SIC 4899 Communication services, nec

D-U-N-S 24-619-0701   (SL)
DWP SOLUTIONS INC
2012 Norway Cres, Ottawa, ON, K1H 5N7
(613) 738-9574
Emp Here 30   *Sales* 2,772,507

SIC 8741 Management services

D-U-N-S 24-104-7356   (HQ)
LARNY HOLDINGS LIMITED
QUICKIE CONVENIENCE STORES
(*Suby of* Larny Holdings Limited)
2520 St. Laurent Blvd Suite 201, Ottawa, ON, K1H 1B1
(613) 736-7962
Emp Here 20   *Emp Total* 450
Sales 88,020,480
SIC 5411 Grocery stores
  Arnold Kimmel
Pr Pr Lawrence Hartman
Prin Christopher Wilcox

D-U-N-S 20-153-5973   (SL)
M & J GALLANT FOODS INC
WENDY'S
1950 Walkley Rd, Ottawa, ON, K1H 1W1
(613) 739-0311
Emp Here 55   *Sales* 1,678,096
SIC 5812 Eating places

D-U-N-S 20-918-6845   (BR)
MORRISON HERSHFIELD LIMITED
2440 Don Reid Dr Suite 200, Ottawa, ON, K1H 1E1
(613) 739-2910
Emp Here 70
SIC 7363 Help supply services

D-U-N-S 25-238-1470   (BR)
OTTAWA CATHOLIC DISTRICT SCHOOL BOARD
MCMASTER CATHOLIC SCHOOL
(*Suby of* Ottawa Catholic District School Board)
1760 Mcmaster Ave, Ottawa, ON, K1H 6R8
(613) 731-8841
Emp Here 21
SIC 8211 Elementary and secondary schools

D-U-N-S 24-387-3101   (BR)
OTTAWA CHILDREN'S TREATMENT CEN-TRE
401 Smyth Rd, Ottawa, ON, K1H 8L1
(613) 737-2286
Emp Here 27
SIC 8322 Individual and family services

D-U-N-S 20-714-7161   (BR)
OTTAWA HOSPITAL, THE
RIVERSIDE CAMPUS
1967 Riverside Dr Suite 323, Ottawa, ON, K1H 7W9
(613) 738-7100
Emp Here 550
SIC 8062 General medical and surgical hospi-tals

D-U-N-S 25-504-0099   (BR)
OTTAWA-CARLETON DISTRICT SCHOOL BOARD
PLEASANT PARK PUBLIC SCHOOL
564 Pleasant Park Rd, Ottawa, ON, K1H 5N1
(613) 733-5253
Emp Here 30
SIC 8211 Elementary and secondary schools

D-U-N-S 25-501-6131   (BR)
OTTAWA-CARLETON DISTRICT SCHOOL BOARD
ALTA VISTA PUBLIC SCHOOL
1349 Randall Ave, Ottawa, ON, K1H 7R2
(613) 733-7124
Emp Here 50
SIC 8211 Elementary and secondary schools

D-U-N-S 25-504-0362   (BR)
OTTAWA-CARLETON DISTRICT SCHOOL BOARD
FEATHERSTON DRIVE PUBLIC SCHOOL
1801 Featherston Dr, Ottawa, ON, K1H 6P4
(613) 731-3357
Emp Here 55
SIC 8211 Elementary and secondary schools

D-U-N-S 24-363-0840   (BR)

RGIS CANADA ULC
2197 Riverside Dr Suite 305, Ottawa, ON, K1H 7X3
(613) 226-4086
Emp Here 100
SIC 7389 Business services, nec

D-U-N-S 20-002-6552   (BR)
ROYAL BANK OF CANADA
RBC
(*Suby of* Royal Bank Of Canada)
1535 Bank St, Ottawa, ON, K1H 7Z1
(613) 733-7993
Emp Here 46
SIC 6021 National commercial banks

D-U-N-S 25-222-0306   (SL)
SOUTH-EAST OTTAWA COMMUNITY HEALTH SERVICES
1355 Bank St Suite 600, Ottawa, ON, K1H 8K7
(613) 737-5115
Emp Here 60   *Sales* 2,699,546
SIC 8051 Skilled nursing care facilities

D-U-N-S 25-767-8995   (BR)
SPACE MAINTAINERS LAB CANADA LTD
SPACE MAINTAINERS LAB (OTTAWA)
1175 Cecil Ave, Ottawa, ON, K1H 7Z6
(613) 736-1946
Emp Here 20
SIC 3843 Dental equipment and supplies

D-U-N-S 24-965-5721   (BR)
TORONTO-DOMINION BANK, THE
TD CANADA TRUST
(*Suby of* Toronto-Dominion Bank, The)
2269 Riverside Dr Suite 1, Ottawa, ON, K1H 8K2
(613) 731-4220
Emp Here 20
SIC 6021 National commercial banks

D-U-N-S 20-860-5324   (BR)
TOWN SHOES LIMITED
SHOE COMPANY, THE
2277 Riverside Dr Unit 40, Ottawa, ON, K1H 7X6
(613) 731-8858
Emp Here 25
SIC 5661 Shoe stores

D-U-N-S 25-361-2345   (BR)
UNIVERSITY OF OTTAWA
DEPARTMENT EPIDEMIOLOGY & COMMU-NITY MEDICINE
451 Smyth Rd Unit 3105, Ottawa, ON, K1H 8M5
(613) 562-5410
Emp Here 35
SIC 8221 Colleges and universities

D-U-N-S 24-424-9020   (BR)
UNIVERSITY OF OTTAWA
FACULTY OF MEDICINE
451 Smyth Rd Suite Rgn, Ottawa, ON, K1H 8M5
(613) 562-5800
Emp Here 1,000
SIC 8221 Colleges and universities

D-U-N-S 25-128-7272   (BR)
IMARKETING SOLUTIONS GROUP INC
(*Suby of* iMarketing Solutions Group Inc)
2197 Riverside Dr Suite 203, Ottawa, ON, K1H 7X3
(613) 733-1091
Emp Here 40
SIC 8399 Social services, nec

Ottawa, ON K1J
Carleton County

D-U-N-S 20-347-2899   (BR)
COLLIERS PROJECT LEADERS INC
1900 City Park Dr Suite 402, Ottawa, ON, K1J

1A3
(613) 216-4345
Emp Here 65
SIC 8741 Management services

D-U-N-S 24-844-4945   (HQ)
ELECTRONIC WARFARE ASSOCIATES-CANADA LTD
EWA-CANADA
1223 Michael St Suite 200, Ottawa, ON, K1J 7T2
(613) 230-6067
Emp Here 34   *Emp Total* 400
Sales 4,504,505
SIC 8734 Testing laboratories

D-U-N-S 25-779-0451   (BR)
LONE STAR GROUP OF COMPANIES LIMITED
LONESTAR TEXAS GRILL
1211 Lemieux St, Ottawa, ON, K1J 1A2
(613) 742-9378
Emp Here 150
SIC 5812 Eating places

D-U-N-S 25-263-6063   (BR)
OTTAWA-CARLETON DISTRICT SCHOOL BOARD
PHARE ELEMENTARY SCHOOL, LE
1965 Naskapi Dr, Ottawa, ON, K1J 8M9
(613) 744-2597
Emp Here 20
SIC 8211 Elementary and secondary schools

D-U-N-S 25-213-7583   (BR)
STAPLES CANADA INC
STAPLES THE BUSINESS DEPOT
(*Suby of* Staples, Inc.)
1233 Donald St Unit 20, Ottawa, ON, K1J 8W3
(613) 745-4773
Emp Here 50
SIC 5943 Stationery stores

D-U-N-S 20-355-0058   (BR)
VIAS CANADA, INC
1223 Michael St, Ottawa, ON, K1J 7T2
(613) 656-8427
Emp Here 40
SIC 1629 Heavy construction, nec

D-U-N-S 25-203-1026   (BR)
WINNERS MERCHANTS INTERNATIONAL L.P.
WINNERS
(*Suby of* The TJX Companies Inc)
1235 Donald St, Ottawa, ON, K1J 8W3
(613) 746-0727
Emp Here 45
SIC 5651 Family clothing stores

Ottawa, ON K1K
Carleton County

D-U-N-S 25-203-0655   (SL)
914068 ONTARIO INC
EAST SIDE MARIO'S 631
1200 St. Laurent Blvd Suite 500, Ottawa, ON, K1K 3B8
(613) 747-0888
Emp Here 55   *Sales* 1,678,096
SIC 5812 Eating places

D-U-N-S 25-288-0828   (BR)
A & W FOOD SERVICES OF CANADA INC
A & W
1200 St. Laurent Blvd Unit 607, Ottawa, ON, K1K 3B8
(613) 741-8950
Emp Here 20
SIC 5812 Eating places

D-U-N-S 20-717-1641   (SL)
ASSOCIATION ETUDIANTE CITE COLLEGIAL
801 Aviation Pky, Ottawa, ON, K1K 4R3

(613) 742-2493
Emp Here 200   *Sales* 28,171,920
SIC 8222 Junior colleges
Dir Mona Fortier

D-U-N-S 24-117-6879   (BR)
BANQUE TORONTO-DOMINION, LA
TORONTO-DOMINION BANK, THE
(*Suby of* Toronto-Dominion Bank, The)
525 Coventry Rd, Ottawa, ON, K1K 2C5
(613) 782-1219
Emp Here 30
SIC 6021 National commercial banks

D-U-N-S 20-913-9794   (BR)
BANQUE TORONTO-DOMINION, LA
TORONTO-DOMINION BANK, THE
(*Suby of* Toronto-Dominion Bank, The)
562 Montreal Rd, Ottawa, ON, K1K 0T9
(613) 783-6210
Emp Here 20
SIC 6021 National commercial banks

D-U-N-S 20-577-2601   (HQ)
BEL-AIR AUTOMOBILES INC
(*Suby of* 95661 Canada Ltd)
450 Mcarthur Ave, Ottawa, ON, K1K 1G4
(613) 741-3270
Emp Here 130   *Emp Total* 146
Sales 68,318,853
SIC 5511 New and used car dealers
Pr Pr Roland Parent
Robert Parent
Michel Parent

D-U-N-S 24-011-8641   (BR)
BEST BUY CANADA LTD
BEST BUY
(*Suby of* Best Buy Co., Inc.)
380 Coventry Rd, Ottawa, ON, K1K 2C6
(613) 212-0333
Emp Here 100
SIC 5731 Radio, television, and electronic stores

D-U-N-S 20-529-2902   (BR)
CANADA SCIENCE AND TECHNOLOGY MUSEUMS CORPORATION
CANADA AVIATION AND SPACE MUSEUM
11 Aviation Pkwy, Ottawa, ON, K1K 2X5
(613) 993-2010
Emp Here 20
SIC 8412 Museums and art galleries

D-U-N-S 25-770-7422   (SL)
CANADIAN DINERS (1995) L.P. LTD
PERKINS FAMILY RESTAURANT
1130 St. Laurent Blvd, Ottawa, ON, K1K 3B6
(613) 747-9190
Emp Here 90   *Sales* 2,699,546
SIC 5812 Eating places

D-U-N-S 20-791-4388   (BR)
CHILDREN'S PLACE (CANADA) LP, THE
CHILDREN'S PLACE, THE
1200 St. Laurent Blvd Suite 535, Ottawa, ON, K1K 3B8
(613) 741-4547
Emp Here 50
SIC 5641 Children's and infants' wear stores

D-U-N-S 25-321-4639   (BR)
CLUB MONACO CORP
(*Suby of* Ralph Lauren Corporation)
1200 St. Laurent Blvd Suite 314, Ottawa, ON, K1K 3B8
(613) 741-0886
Emp Here 20
SIC 5621 Women's clothing stores

D-U-N-S 20-070-2517   (BR)
CONSEIL DES ECOLES CATHOLIQUES DE LANGUE FRANCAISE DU CENTRE-EST
COLLEGE CATHOLIC SAMUEL-GENEST
704 Carson'S Rd, Ottawa, ON, K1K 2H3
(613) 744-8344
Emp Here 120
SIC 8211 Elementary and secondary schools

D-U-N-S 25-238-1306   (BR)
CONSEIL DES ECOLES CATHOLIQUES DE LANGUE FRANCAISE DU CENTRE-EST
ECOLE MONTFORT
641 Sladen Ave, Ottawa, ON, K1K 2S8
(613) 745-3310
Emp Here 35
SIC 8211 Elementary and secondary schools

D-U-N-S 20-711-7107   (BR)
CONSEIL DES ECOLES CATHOLIQUES DE LANGUE FRANCAISE DU CENTRE-EST
181 Donald St, Ottawa, ON, K1K 1N1
(613) 741-2304
Emp Here 50
SIC 8211 Elementary and secondary schools

D-U-N-S 20-137-3107   (BR)
EMCO CORPORATION
EMCO SUPPLY
535 Coventry Rd, Ottawa, ON, K1K 2C5

Emp Here 27
SIC 5074 Plumbing and heating equipment and supplies (hydronics)

D-U-N-S 24-964-9021   (BR)
ENBRIDGE GAS DISTRIBUTION INC
400 Coventry Rd, Ottawa, ON, K1K 2C7
(613) 741-5800
Emp Here 269
SIC 4924 Natural gas distribution

D-U-N-S 25-783-7419   (BR)
FARM BOY 2012 INC
FARM BOY FRESH MARKETS
585 Montreal Rd, Ottawa, ON, K1K 4K4
(613) 744-3463
Emp Here 70
SIC 5431 Fruit and vegetable markets

D-U-N-S 25-769-6336   (BR)
GAP (CANADA) INC
GAP
(*Suby of* The Gap Inc)
1200 St. Laurent Blvd, Ottawa, ON, K1K 3B8
(613) 746-1070
Emp Here 45
SIC 5651 Family clothing stores

D-U-N-S 24-269-4255   (BR)
HERZING INSTITUTES OF CANADA INC
HERZING COLLEGE
1200 St. Laurent Blvd Suite 408, Ottawa, ON, K1K 3B8
(613) 742-8099
Emp Here 25
SIC 8221 Colleges and universities

D-U-N-S 25-401-9052   (BR)
HUDSON'S BAY COMPANY
THE BAY
1200 St. Laurent Blvd, Ottawa, ON, K1K 3B8
(613) 748-6105
Emp Here 200
SIC 5311 Department stores

D-U-N-S 25-365-3430   (BR)
IBM CANADA LIMITED
IBM GLOBAL SERVICES
(*Suby of* International Business Machines Corporation)
1400 St. Laurent Blvd Suite 500, Ottawa, ON, K1K 4H4

Emp Here 100
SIC 3571 Electronic computers

D-U-N-S 24-267-6716   (BR)
INTACT INSURANCE COMPANY
ING DIRECT
1400 St. Laurent Blvd Suite 300, Ottawa, ON, K1K 4H4
(613) 748-3000
Emp Here 100
SIC 6331 Fire, marine, and casualty insurance

D-U-N-S 20-174-1662   (SL)
LIXAR I.T. INC

373 Coventry Rd, Ottawa, ON, K1K 2C5
(613) 722-0688
Emp Here 80   *Sales* 4,377,642
SIC 7374 Data processing and preparation

D-U-N-S 20-442-8833   (HQ)
MARK MOTORS OF OTTAWA (1987) LIMITED
MARK MOTORS OF OTTAWA
(*Suby of* Mark Holdings Inc)
611 Montreal Rd Suite 1, Ottawa, ON, K1K 0T8
(613) 749-4275
Emp Here 22   *Emp Total* 2
Sales 18,969,782
SIC 5511 New and used car dealers
Pr Pr Louis Mrak
Marguerite Mrak

D-U-N-S 24-103-9700   (BR)
MCDONALD'S RESTAURANTS OF CANADA LIMITED
MCDONALD'S 8092
(*Suby of* McDonald's Corporation)
594 Montreal Rd, Ottawa, ON, K1K 0T9
(613) 741-0093
Emp Here 85
SIC 5812 Eating places

D-U-N-S 25-771-1101   (BR)
MORGUARD INVESTMENTS LIMITED
CENTRE ST-LAURENT
1200 St. Laurent Blvd Suite 199, Ottawa, ON, K1K 3B8
(613) 745-6858
Emp Here 40
SIC 6512 Nonresidential building operators

D-U-N-S 25-238-1660   (BR)
OTTAWA CATHOLIC DISTRICT SCHOOL BOARD
OUR LADY OF MOUNT CARMEL SCHOOL
(*Suby of* Ottawa Catholic District School Board)
675 Gardenvale Rd, Ottawa, ON, K1K 1C9
(613) 745-4884
Emp Here 25
SIC 8211 Elementary and secondary schools

D-U-N-S 20-711-6422   (BR)
OTTAWA CATHOLIC DISTRICT SCHOOL BOARD
MS MCHUGH
(*Suby of* Ottawa Catholic District School Board)
437 Donald St, Ottawa, ON, K1K 1L8
(613) 747-6885
Emp Here 50
SIC 8211 Elementary and secondary schools

D-U-N-S 25-131-2989   (BR)
OTTAWA CATHOLIC DISTRICT SCHOOL BOARD
ST MICHAEL CATHOLIC SCHOOL
(*Suby of* Ottawa Catholic District School Board)
437 Donald St, Ottawa, ON, K1K 1L8
(613) 749-1642
Emp Here 21
SIC 8211 Elementary and secondary schools

D-U-N-S 20-805-9266   (BR)
OTTAWA-CARLETON ASSOCIATION FOR PERSONS WITH DEVELOPMENTAL DISABILITIES
171 Donald St, Ottawa, ON, K1K 1N1
(613) 744-8504
Emp Here 20
SIC 6321 Accident and health insurance

D-U-N-S 25-504-0131   (BR)
OTTAWA-CARLETON DISTRICT SCHOOL BOARD
QUEEN ELIZABETH PUBLIC SCHOOL
689 St. Laurent Blvd, Ottawa, ON, K1K 3A6
(613) 746-3246
Emp Here 60
SIC 8211 Elementary and secondary schools

D-U-N-S 25-504-0172   (BR)
OTTAWA-CARLETON DISTRICT SCHOOL BOARD
QUEEN MARY STREET PUBLIC SCHOOL
557 Queen Mary St, Ottawa, ON, K1K 1V9
(613) 749-1692
Emp Here 30
SIC 8211 Elementary and secondary schools

D-U-N-S 25-504-0800   (BR)
OTTAWA-CARLETON DISTRICT SCHOOL BOARD
MANOR PARK PUBLIC SCHOOL
100 Braemar St, Ottawa, ON, K1K 3C9
(613) 746-3131
Emp Here 45
SIC 8211 Elementary and secondary schools

D-U-N-S 25-504-0149   (BR)
OTTAWA-CARLETON DISTRICT SCHOOL BOARD
OTTAWA TECHNICAL LEARNING CENTRE
485 Donald St, Ottawa, ON, K1K 1L8
(613) 745-0347
Emp Here 60
SIC 8211 Elementary and secondary schools

D-U-N-S 25-504-0222   (BR)
OTTAWA-CARLETON DISTRICT SCHOOL BOARD
RIDEAU HIGH SCHOOL
815 St. Laurent Blvd, Ottawa, ON, K1K 3A7
(613) 746-8196
Emp Here 80
SIC 8211 Elementary and secondary schools

D-U-N-S 20-859-8768   (BR)
PACIFIC LINK COMMUNICATIONS INC
BELL WORLD
1200 St. Laurent Blvd Suite 21, Ottawa, ON, K1K 3B8
(613) 741-8029
Emp Here 25
SIC 5999 Miscellaneous retail stores, nec

D-U-N-S 25-981-9589   (BR)
ROGERS COMMUNICATIONS INC
ROGERS PLUS
(*Suby of* Rogers Communications Inc)
530 Montreal Rd Suite 526, Ottawa, ON, K1K 0T9
(613) 745-6800
Emp Here 20
SIC 7841 Video tape rental

D-U-N-S 20-003-0729   (BR)
ROYAL BANK OF CANADA
RBC
(*Suby of* Royal Bank Of Canada)
551 Montreal Rd, Ottawa, ON, K1K 0V1
(613) 749-4579
Emp Here 25
SIC 6021 National commercial banks

D-U-N-S 20-528-3653   (BR)
SEARS CANADA INC
1250 St. Laurent Blvd, Ottawa, ON, K1K 3B9
(613) 746-4311
Emp Here 30
SIC 5311 Department stores

D-U-N-S 20-860-2594   (BR)
SOURCE (BELL) ELECTRONICS INC, THE
SOURCE, THE
1045 St. Laurent Blvd, Ottawa, ON, K1K 3B1

Emp Here 25
SIC 5999 Miscellaneous retail stores, nec

D-U-N-S 24-379-8043   (BR)
TOURS NEW YORK INC
ALIOTOURS
1400 St. Laurent Blvd, Ottawa, ON, K1K 4H4
(613) 748-7759
Emp Here 20
SIC 4725 Tour operators

D-U-N-S 20-122-7571   (BR)

TOYS 'R' US (CANADA) LTD
TOYS 'R' US
(*Suby of* Toys "r" Us, Inc.)
1200 St. Laurent Blvd Suite 77, Ottawa, ON, K1K 3B8
(613) 749-8697
Emp Here 25
SIC 5945 Hobby, toy, and game shops

D-U-N-S 20-789-6952   (SL)
UNITED WAY/CENTRAIDE OTTAWA
363 Coventry Rd, Ottawa, ON, K1K 2C5
(613) 228-6700
Emp Here 95   *Sales* 28,275,816
SIC 6732 Trusts: educational, religious, etc.
Pr Pr Michael Allen
VP Opers Edward Wolkowycki
 Dennis Jackson
 Eric Girard

D-U-N-S 25-773-7080   (BR)
VITALAIRE CANADA INC
VITALAIRE
1155 Lola St Suite 2, Ottawa, ON, K1K 4C1
(613) 741-0202
Emp Here 30
SIC 5169 Chemicals and allied products, nec

D-U-N-S 25-970-7990   (BR)
WESTERN INVENTORY SERVICE LTD
W I S INTERNATIONAL
435 St. Laurent Blvd Suite 203, Ottawa, ON, K1K 2Z8
(613) 744-2450
Emp Here 50
SIC 7389 Business services, nec

D-U-N-S 20-793-3644   (BR)
YM INC. (SALES)
SUZY SHIER
1200 St. Laurent Blvd, Ottawa, ON, K1K 3B8
(613) 749-4691
Emp Here 21
SIC 5621 Women's clothing stores

Ottawa, ON K1L
Carleton County

D-U-N-S 20-711-7099   (BR)
CONSEIL DES ECOLES CATHOLIQUES DE LANGUE FRANCAISE DU CENTRE-EST
ECOLE LE PETITE TIRNCE
349 Olmstead St, Ottawa, ON, K1L 1B1
(613) 741-8515
Emp Here 50
SIC 8211 Elementary and secondary schools

D-U-N-S 24-174-7729   (BR)
SOBEYS CAPITAL INCORPORATED
FRESHCO
318 Mcarthur Ave, Ottawa, ON, K1L 6N8
(613) 744-4343
Emp Here 50
SIC 5411 Grocery stores

Ottawa, ON K1M
Carleton County

D-U-N-S 20-774-2268   (SL)
3782981 CANADA INC.
A.M.S. ENTERPRISES
125 Beechwood Ave, Ottawa, ON, K1M 1L5
(613) 744-6896
Emp Here 25   *Sales* 6,674,880
SIC 1541 Industrial buildings and warehouses
Owner Tony Fa

D-U-N-S 20-289-8503   (SL)
CSH NEW EDINBURGH SQUARE INC
NEW EDINBURGH SQUARE
420 Mackay St Suite 904, Ottawa, ON, K1M 2C4

(613) 744-0901
Emp Here 20   *Sales* 942,329
SIC 8361 Residential care

D-U-N-S 25-238-1272   (BR)
OTTAWA CATHOLIC DISTRICT SCHOOL BOARD
ST BRIGID SCHOOL
(*Suby of* Ottawa Catholic District School Board)
200 Springfield Rd, Ottawa, ON, K1M 1C2
(613) 746-4888
Emp Here 22
SIC 8211 Elementary and secondary schools

D-U-N-S 25-455-6715   (BR)
REVERA INC
EDINBURGH RETIREMENT RESIDENCE
10 Vaughan St Suite 703, Ottawa, ON, K1M 2H6
(613) 747-2233
Emp Here 50
SIC 8051 Skilled nursing care facilities

D-U-N-S 20-890-3232   (SL)
SISTERS OF CHARITY OF OTTAWA, THE
COUVENT MONT SAINT JOSEPH
50 Maple Lane, Ottawa, ON, K1M 1G8
(613) 745-1584
Emp Here 75   *Sales* 4,961,328
SIC 8661 Religious organizations

Ottawa, ON K1N
Carleton County

D-U-N-S 25-770-0120   (SL)
1202937 ONTARIO INC.
FISH MARKET RESTAURANT, THE
54 York St, Ottawa, ON, K1N 5T1
(613) 241-3474
Emp Here 50   *Sales* 1,819,127
SIC 5812 Eating places

D-U-N-S 25-526-0010   (SL)
1248741 ONTARIO LTD
EMPIRE GRILL, THE
47 Clarence St, Ottawa, ON, K1N 9K1
(613) 241-1343
Emp Here 80   *Sales* 3,109,686
SIC 5812 Eating places

D-U-N-S 24-926-7600   (SL)
977619 ONTARIO INC
HEART & CROWN PUB, THE
67 Clarence St, Ottawa, ON, K1N 5P5
(613) 562-0674
Emp Here 50   *Sales* 1,532,175
SIC 5812 Eating places

D-U-N-S 25-288-0679   (BR)
A & W FOOD SERVICES OF CANADA INC
A & W RESTAURANT
50 Rideau St Unit J, Ottawa, ON, K1N 9J7
(613) 230-2753
Emp Here 24
SIC 5812 Eating places

D-U-N-S 25-777-5361   (BR)
ACCOR CANADA INC
CAFE NICOLE BISTRO
33 Nicholas St, Ottawa, ON, K1N 9M7
(613) 760-4771
Emp Here 25
SIC 5812 Eating places

D-U-N-S 20-735-9790   (BR)
ACCOR CANADA INC
NOVOTEL OTTAWA
33 Nicholas St, Ottawa, ON, K1N 9M7
(613) 760-4771
Emp Here 75
SIC 7011 Hotels and motels

D-U-N-S 25-239-6221   (BR)
ANDREW FLECK CHILD CARE SERVICES
(*Suby of* Andrew Fleck Child Care Services)

195 George St, Ottawa, ON, K1N 5W6
(613) 789-4100
Emp Here 25
SIC 8351 Child day care services

D-U-N-S 20-790-4678   (SL)
AULDE DOUBLINER
62 William St, Ottawa, ON, K1N 7A3
(613) 241-0066
Emp Here 55   *Sales* 1,678,096
SIC 5812 Eating places

D-U-N-S 20-108-8494   (BR)
BMO NESBITT BURNS INC
303 Dalhousie St Suite 300, Ottawa, ON, K1N 7E8
(613) 562-6400
Emp Here 80
SIC 6211 Security brokers and dealers

D-U-N-S 24-482-1013   (BR)
BANQUE NATIONALE DU CANADA
242 Rideau St, Ottawa, ON, K1N 0B7
(613) 241-9110
Emp Here 22
SIC 6021 National commercial banks

D-U-N-S 20-292-1172   (BR)
BELL MEDIA INC
CFRA
87 George St, Ottawa, ON, K1N 9H7
(613) 789-0606
Emp Here 74
SIC 4833 Television broadcasting stations

D-U-N-S 25-769-3218   (BR)
BELL MEDIA INC
CTV OTTAWA
87 George St, Ottawa, ON, K1N 9H7
(613) 224-1313
Emp Here 100
SIC 4833 Television broadcasting stations

D-U-N-S 25-798-0979   (BR)
BOUTIQUE JACOB INC
JACOB
(*Suby of* Boutique Jacob Inc)
50 Rideau St Suite 275, Ottawa, ON, K1N 9J7

Emp Here 45
SIC 5621 Women's clothing stores

D-U-N-S 25-195-2974   (BR)
BOUTIQUE TRISTAN & ISEUT INC
RIDEAU CENTRE RETAIL TRISTAN & AMERICA
50 Rideau St Suite 300, Ottawa, ON, K1N 9J7
(613) 567-5507
Emp Here 20
SIC 5611 Men's and boys' clothing stores

D-U-N-S 20-860-4814   (BR)
BOUTIQUE LA VIE EN ROSE INC
BOUTIQUE LA VIE EN ROSE INC
50 Rideau St, Ottawa, ON, K1N 9J7
(613) 563-2959
Emp Here 25
SIC 5632 Women's accessory and specialty stores

D-U-N-S 24-426-3500   (SL)
CSH RIDEAU PLACE INC
CHARTWELL CLASSIC RIDEAU PLACE-ON-THE-RIVER
550 Wilbrod St, Ottawa, ON, K1N 9M3
(613) 234-6003
Emp Here 20   *Sales* 729,607
SIC 8361 Residential care

D-U-N-S 24-084-1226   (BR)
CARA OPERATIONS LIMITED
MILESTONE
(*Suby of* Cara Holdings Limited)
700 Sussex Dr Unit 201, Ottawa, ON, K1N 1K4
(613) 789-5432
Emp Here 50
SIC 5812 Eating places

D-U-N-S 24-910-7467 (BR)
CITY OF OTTAWA
SANDY HILL COMMUNITY CENTRE
(*Suby of* City of Ottawa)
250 Somerset St E, Ottawa, ON, K1N 6V6
(613) 564-1062
Emp Here 50
SIC 8322 Individual and family services

D-U-N-S 20-787-5428 (BR)
CLS-LEXI TECH LTD.
(*Suby of* LBT Acquisition, Inc.)
126 York St Suite 500, Ottawa, ON, K1N 5T5
(613) 234-5312
Emp Here 52
SIC 7389 Business services, nec

D-U-N-S 25-321-4753 (BR)
CLUB MONACO CORP
(*Suby of* Ralph Lauren Corporation)
50 Rideau St Suite 347, Ottawa, ON, K1N 9J7
(613) 230-0245
Emp Here 30
SIC 5651 Family clothing stores

D-U-N-S 20-058-5508 (BR)
COMPAGNIE DE TELEPHONE BELL DU CANADA OU BELL CANADA, LA
393 Rideau St, Ottawa, ON, K1N 1H1
(613) 244-6100
Emp Here 50
SIC 4813 Telephone communication, except radio

D-U-N-S 25-263-6576 (BR)
CONSEIL DES ECOLES PUBLIQUES DE L'EST DE L'ONTARIO
FRANCOJEUNESSE PUBLIC SCHOOL
119 Osgoode St, Ottawa, ON, K1N 6S3
(613) 232-0020
Emp Here 36
SIC 8211 Elementary and secondary schools

D-U-N-S 20-810-6703 (BR)
EDDIE BAUER OF CANADA INC
(*Suby of* Golden Gate Capital LP)
50 Rideau St Unit 308, Ottawa, ON, K1N 9J7
(613) 567-3010
Emp Here 20
SIC 5651 Family clothing stores

D-U-N-S 20-714-8466 (BR)
ESTEE LAUDER COSMETICS LTD
73 Rideau St, Ottawa, ON, K1N 5W8
(613) 241-7511
Emp Here 50
SIC 5999 Miscellaneous retail stores, nec

D-U-N-S 25-361-4101 (BR)
FAIRMONT HOTELS & RESORTS INC
FAIRMONT CHATEAU LAURIER
1 Rideau St, Ottawa, ON, K1N 8S7
(613) 241-1414
Emp Here 500
SIC 7011 Hotels and motels

D-U-N-S 24-047-1073 (BR)
FAIRWEATHER LTD
50 Rideau St Unit 216, Ottawa, ON, K1N 9J7

Emp Here 20
SIC 5621 Women's clothing stores

D-U-N-S 25-784-2997 (BR)
FOOT LOCKER CANADA CO.
50 Rideau St Suite 108, Ottawa, ON, K1N 9J7
(613) 563-2884
Emp Here 20
SIC 5651 Family clothing stores

D-U-N-S 24-195-6569 (SL)
FOUNDATION RESTAURANT
18 York St Suite B, Ottawa, ON, K1N 5S6
(613) 562-9331
Emp Here 50   *Sales* 1,532,175
SIC 5812 Eating places

D-U-N-S 25-689-6093 (BR)
GAP (CANADA) INC

GAP
(*Suby of* The Gap Inc)
50 Rideau St Suite 213, Ottawa, ON, K1N 9J7
(613) 569-4100
Emp Here 50
SIC 5651 Family clothing stores

D-U-N-S 25-449-3075 (BR)
GESCA LTEE
QUOTIDIEN DROIT DIV OF
(*Suby of* Gesca Ltee)
47 Clarence St Suite 222, Ottawa, ON, K1N 9K1
(613) 562-0111
Emp Here 100
SIC 2711 Newspapers

D-U-N-S 25-777-7433 (BR)
GOODLIFE FITNESS CENTRES INC
50 Rideau St Suite 118, Ottawa, ON, K1N 9J7
(613) 567-0037
Emp Here 20
SIC 7991 Physical fitness facilities

D-U-N-S 20-652-1879 (BR)
GOVERNING COUNCIL OF THE SALVA-TION ARMY IN CANADA, THE
171 George St, Ottawa, ON, K1N 5W5
(613) 241-1573
Emp Here 150
SIC 8399 Social services, nec

D-U-N-S 25-775-0513 (BR)
GREENPEACE CANADA
GREENPEACE OTTAWA
110 Clarence St Suite 5, Ottawa, ON, K1N 5P6
(416) 597-8408
Emp Here 23
SIC 8699 Membership organizations, nec

D-U-N-S 25-769-8969 (BR)
GROUPE BIRKS INC
BIRKS JEWELLERS
50 Rideau St Suite 333, Ottawa, ON, K1N 9J7
(613) 236-3641
Emp Here 25
SIC 5944 Jewelry stores

D-U-N-S 25-769-3606 (BR)
HARRY ROSEN INC
50 Rideau St Suite 329, Ottawa, ON, K1N 9J7
(416) 935-9200
Emp Here 25
SIC 5611 Men's and boys' clothing stores

D-U-N-S 24-421-5492 (BR)
HOCKEY CANADA
801 King Edward Ave Suite N204, Ottawa, ON, K1N 6N5

Emp Here 90
SIC 8699 Membership organizations, nec

D-U-N-S 20-696-4251 (BR)
HUDSON'S BAY COMPANY
BAY, THE
73 Rideau St, Ottawa, ON, K1N 5W8
(613) 241-7511
Emp Here 100
SIC 5311 Department stores

D-U-N-S 20-651-0484 (BR)
KEG RESTAURANTS LTD
KEG STEAKHOUSE & BAR, THE
75 York St, Ottawa, ON, K1N 5T2
(613) 241-8514
Emp Here 100
SIC 5812 Eating places

D-U-N-S 25-085-1581 (HQ)
KIVUTO SOLUTIONS INC
(*Suby of* Kivuto Solutions Inc)
126 York St Suite 200, Ottawa, ON, K1N 5T5
(613) 526-3005
Emp Here 80   *Emp Total* 80
Sales 9,411,930
SIC 7372 Prepackaged software

Pr Pr Ram Raju
Rick White

D-U-N-S 25-317-5863 (BR)
LIQUOR CONTROL BOARD OF ONTARIO, THE
L.C.B.O.
275 Rideau St, Ottawa, ON, K1N 5Y2
(613) 789-5226
Emp Here 60
SIC 5921 Liquor stores

D-U-N-S 25-092-7360 (BR)
LULULEMON ATHLETICA CANADA INC
LULULEMON
50 Rideau St 3rd Fl, Ottawa, ON, K1N 9J7
(613) 230-6633
Emp Here 40
SIC 2339 Women's and misses' outerwear, nec

D-U-N-S 25-812-4445 (BR)
MAGASIN DE MUSIQUE STEVE INC
STEVE'S MUSIC
308 Rideau St, Ottawa, ON, K1N 5Y5
(613) 789-1131
Emp Here 30
SIC 5736 Musical instrument stores

D-U-N-S 25-310-9433 (BR)
MCDONALD'S RESTAURANTS OF CANADA LIMITED
MCDONALD'S RESTAURANTS
(*Suby of* McDonald's Corporation)
99 Rideau St, Ottawa, ON, K1N 9L8
(613) 241-4414
Emp Here 50
SIC 5812 Eating places

D-U-N-S 25-771-2950 (BR)
MEDICAL PHARMACIES GROUP LIMITED
ONTARIO MEDICAL SUPPLIES
298 Dalhousie St, Ottawa, ON, K1N 7E7
(613) 241-1871
Emp Here 25
SIC 5122 Drugs, proprietaries, and sundries

D-U-N-S 20-805-0471 (SL)
MONTFORT RENAISSANCE INC
162 Murray St, Ottawa, ON, K1N 5M8
(613) 789-5144
Emp Here 50   *Sales* 4,742,446
SIC 6531 Real estate agents and managers

D-U-N-S 24-380-9261 (BR)
NORR LIMITED
55 Murray St Suite 600, Ottawa, ON, K1N 5M3
(613) 241-5300
Emp Here 25
SIC 8712 Architectural services

D-U-N-S 25-775-4366 (BR)
NEWGEN RESTAURANT SERVICES INC
TUCKER'S MARKETPLACE
61 York St, Ottawa, ON, K1N 5T2
(613) 241-6525
Emp Here 80
SIC 5812 Eating places

D-U-N-S 25-726-3764 (SL)
PHASE 5 CONSULTING GROUP INC
PHASE 5
109 Murray St Suite 4, Ottawa, ON, K1N 5M5
(613) 241-7555
Emp Here 24   *Sales* 5,079,395
SIC 8732 Commercial nonphysical research
Pr Pr Carol Blackie
VP VP Douglas Church
 Andreas Noe
 Michael Dolenko
 Arnab Guha

D-U-N-S 24-111-2148 (BR)
REITMANS (CANADA) LIMITEE
SMARTSET
50 Rideau St, Ottawa, ON, K1N 9J7

Emp Here 25

SIC 5621 Women's clothing stores

D-U-N-S 20-245-2715 (BR)
REVERA INC
SANDY HILL RETIREMENT RESIDENCE
353 Friel St, Ottawa, ON, K1N 7W7

Emp Here 35
SIC 8051 Skilled nursing care facilities

D-U-N-S 25-079-7057 (BR)
RICHTREE MARKET RESTAURANTS INC
MARCHELINO RESTAURANT
50 Rideau St Suite 115, Ottawa, ON, K1N 9J7

Emp Here 80
SIC 5812 Eating places

D-U-N-S 25-784-3334 (SL)
ROCK THE BYWARD MARKET CORPORA-TION
HARD ROCK CAFE
73 York St, Ottawa, ON, K1N 5T2
(613) 241-2442
Emp Here 100   *Sales* 3,551,629
SIC 5812 Eating places

D-U-N-S 25-784-5750 (BR)
SAP CANADA INC
100 Murray St Suite 200, Ottawa, ON, K1N 0A1

Emp Here 55
SIC 7371 Custom computer programming services

D-U-N-S 20-520-5110 (BR)
SEARS CANADA INC
CATALOGUE
50 Rideau St Suite 113, Ottawa, ON, K1N 9J7

Emp Here 200
SIC 5961 Catalog and mail-order houses

D-U-N-S 25-843-3986 (BR)
SHEPHERDS OF GOOD HOPE
SHEPHERDS OF GOOD HOPE
(*Suby of* Shepherds Of Good Hope)
256 King Edward Ave, Ottawa, ON, K1N 7M1
(613) 789-8210
Emp Here 100
SIC 8322 Individual and family services

D-U-N-S 24-965-0029 (BR)
SOEURS DE LA CHARITE D'OTTAWA, LES
ELIZABETH BRUYERE HEALTH CENTRE
43 Bruyere St, Ottawa, ON, K1N 5C8
(613) 562-0050
Emp Here 950
SIC 8661 Religious organizations

D-U-N-S 25-373-4750 (BR)
STARBUCKS COFFEE CANADA, INC
STARBUCKS COFFEE CO
(*Suby of* Starbucks Corporation)
47 Rideau St, Ottawa, ON, K1N 5W8
(613) 562-0588
Emp Here 27
SIC 5812 Eating places

D-U-N-S 20-180-4619 (BR)
STARWOOD CANADA ULC
WESTIN OTTAWA, THE
(*Suby of* Marriott International, Inc.)
11 Colonel By Dr, Ottawa, ON, K1N 9H4
(613) 560-7000
Emp Here 400
SIC 7011 Hotels and motels

D-U-N-S 24-386-6753 (SL)
STEPHEN MACDONALD PHARMACY INC
SHOPPERS DRUG MART
334 Cumberland St, Ottawa, ON, K1N 7J2
(705) 325-2377
Emp Here 50   *Sales* 7,077,188
SIC 5912 Drug stores and proprietary stores
Pr Stephen Macdonald

D-U-N-S 20-789-6812 (HQ)

▲ Public Company   ■ Public Company Family Member   **HQ** Headquarters   **BR** Branch   **SL** Single Location

STUDENTS' FEDERATION OF THE UNIVERSITY OF OTTAWA, THE
PIVIK, LE
(*Suby of* Students' Federation of The University of Ottawa, The)
85 Universite Pvt Suite 07, Ottawa, ON, K1N 6N5
(613) 562-5966
Emp Here 55   *Emp Total* 60
Sales 4,304,681
SIC 8641 Civic and social associations

    D-U-N-S 24-065-9875   (BR)
TOMMY HILFIGER CANADA INC
50 Rideau St Unit 205, Ottawa, ON, K1N 9J7

Emp Here 30
SIC 5651 Family clothing stores

    D-U-N-S 24-766-9901   (BR)
UNIVERSITY OF OTTAWA
FACULTY OF ART
70 Laurier Ave E Suite 338, Ottawa, ON, K1N 6N6
(613) 562-5715
Emp Here 54
SIC 8221 Colleges and universities

    D-U-N-S 20-536-3232   (BR)
UNIVERSITY OF OTTAWA
161 Louis-Pasteur Pvt Suite A306, Ottawa, ON, K1N 6N5
(613) 562-5800
Emp Here 25
SIC 8221 Colleges and universities

    D-U-N-S 24-422-8040   (BR)
UNIVERSITY OF OTTAWA
FINANCIAL AID & AWARD SERVICE
85 Universite Pvt Unit 102, Ottawa, ON, K1N 6N5
(613) 562-5734
Emp Here 21
SIC 8221 Colleges and universities

    D-U-N-S 24-425-8906   (BR)
UNIVERSITY OF OTTAWA
HISTORY DEPARTMENT
147 Seraphin-Marion Pvt, Ottawa, ON, K1N 6N5
(613) 562-5800
Emp Here 30
SIC 8221 Colleges and universities

    D-U-N-S 25-352-6362   (BR)
UNIVERSITY OF OTTAWA
FACULTY OF ENGINEERING DIV SITE
800 King Edward Ave Suite 2002, Ottawa, ON, K1N 6N5
(613) 562-5800
Emp Here 110
SIC 8221 Colleges and universities

    D-U-N-S 25-092-0373   (BR)
UNIVERSITY OF OTTAWA
SCHOOL OF INTERNATIONAL DEVELOPMENT AND GLOBAL STUDIESEDIM/SIDGS
550 Cumberland St Suite 378, Ottawa, ON, K1N 6N5
(613) 562-5800
Emp Here 40
SIC 8221 Colleges and universities

    D-U-N-S 25-993-3955   (BR)
UNIVERSITY OF OTTAWA
FACULTY OF SOCIAL SCIENCES
120 Universite Pvt Unit 3010, Ottawa, ON, K1N 6N5
(613) 562-5800
Emp Here 400
SIC 8221 Colleges and universities

    D-U-N-S 24-320-8472   (BR)
UNIVERSITY OF OTTAWA
SCHOOL OF MANAGEMENT
55 Laurier Ave E Suite 5105, Ottawa, ON, K1N 6N5
(613) 562-5731
Emp Here 150

SIC 8221 Colleges and universities

    D-U-N-S 25-246-3583   (SL)
YORK STREET HOSPITALITY LTD
73 York St, Ottawa, ON, K1N 5T2
(613) 599-0230
Emp Here 256   *Sales* 9,988,687
SIC 5812 Eating places
Pr Pr Keith Taggart
VP Opers John Thompson

    D-U-N-S 25-773-7536   (BR)
YOUTH SERVICES BUREAU OF OTTAWA
DOWNTOWN SERVICES & DROP IN
147 Besserer St, Ottawa, ON, K1N 6A7
(613) 241-7788
Emp Here 25
SIC 8322 Individual and family services

    D-U-N-S 20-888-8300   (BR)
YOUTH SERVICES BUREAU OF OTTAWA
YOUNG WOMEN'S EMERGENCY SHELTER
433 Nelson St, Ottawa, ON, K1N 7S6
(613) 789-8220
Emp Here 30
SIC 8322 Individual and family services

Ottawa, ON K1P
Carleton County

    D-U-N-S 24-426-2676   (SL)
7073674 CANADA LTD
MCDONALD'S
77 Bank St, Ottawa, ON, K1P 5N2
(613) 831-2235
Emp Here 100   *Sales* 2,991,389
SIC 5812 Eating places

    D-U-N-S 25-624-4138   (SL)
ANTHONY MACAULEY ASSOCIATES INC
85 Albert St Suite 605, Ottawa, ON, K1P 6A4
(613) 230-3833
Emp Here 40   *Sales* 5,579,750
SIC 8741 Management services
Pr Pr Bob Rutherford
  Bob Macdonald
  John Punnett

    D-U-N-S 24-268-2755   (BR)
BMO NESBITT BURNS INC
269 Laurier Ave W Suite 201, Ottawa, ON, K1P 5J9
(613) 567-6232
Emp Here 25
SIC 6211 Security brokers and dealers

    D-U-N-S 25-296-4945   (BR)
BANK OF NOVA SCOTIA, THE
SCOTIABANK
119 Queen St Suite 501, Ottawa, ON, K1P 6L8
(613) 564-7974
Emp Here 40
SIC 6021 National commercial banks

    D-U-N-S 24-080-3692   (BR)
BANK OF NOVA SCOTIA, THE
SCOTIABANK
118 Sparks St, Ottawa, ON, K1P 5B6
(613) 564-5100
Emp Here 150
SIC 6021 National commercial banks

    D-U-N-S 20-891-0190   (BR)
BANQUE DE DEVELOPPEMENT DU CANADA
BDC
55 Metcalfe St Suite 1400, Ottawa, ON, K1P 6L5
(877) 232-2269
Emp Here 50
SIC 6141 Personal credit institutions

    D-U-N-S 24-046-2064   (BR)
BELL MEDIA INC
GLOBAL & MAIL, THE

---

100 Queen St Suite 1400, Ottawa, ON, K1P 1J9
(613) 566-3600
Emp Here 20
SIC 2711 Newspapers

    D-U-N-S 25-769-7532   (BR)
BELL MEDIA INC
BELL GLOBE MEDIA
100 Queen St Suite 1400, Ottawa, ON, K1P 1J9
(613) 236-7343
Emp Here 25
SIC 4833 Television broadcasting stations

    D-U-N-S 24-787-2687   (BR)
BENNETT JONES LLP
45 O'Connor St Suite 1900, Ottawa, ON, K1P 1A4
(613) 683-2300
Emp Here 50
SIC 8111 Legal services

    D-U-N-S 24-525-7576   (BR)
BENTALL KENNEDY (CANADA) LIMITED PARTNERSHIP
BENTALL REAL ESTATE SERVICES
50 O'Connor St Suite 315, Ottawa, ON, K1P 6L2
(613) 236-6452
Emp Here 20
SIC 6531 Real estate agents and managers

    D-U-N-S 25-093-2386   (BR)
BOMBARDIER INC
50 O'Connor St Suite 1425, Ottawa, ON, K1P 6L2
(613) 237-4050
Emp Here 40
SIC 5088 Transportation equipment and supplies

    D-U-N-S 20-268-0505   (BR)
BORDEN LADNER GERVAIS LLP
BLG
100 Queen St Suite 1100, Ottawa, ON, K1P 1J9
(613) 237-5160
Emp Here 250
SIC 8111 Legal services

    D-U-N-S 24-227-8104   (BR)
BROOKFIELD PROPERTIES LTD
BROOKFIELD OFFICE PROPERTIES MANAGEMENT
112 Kent St Suite 480, Ottawa, ON, K1P 5P2
(613) 783-0930
Emp Here 50
SIC 8741 Management services

    D-U-N-S 24-403-0321   (BR)
CES ENERGY SOLUTIONS CORP
AES DRILLING FLUIDS
234 Laurier Ave W, Ottawa, ON, K1P 6K6
(613) 233-2177
Emp Here 30
SIC 1382 Oil and gas exploration services

    D-U-N-S 20-576-7312   (BR)
CIBC WORLD MARKETS INC
CIBC WOOD GUNDY
50 O'Connor St Suite 800, Ottawa, ON, K1P 6L2
(613) 237-5775
Emp Here 100
SIC 6211 Security brokers and dealers

    D-U-N-S 25-956-0142   (SL)
CORADIX TECHNOLOGY CONSULTING LTD
151 Slater St Suite 1010, Ottawa, ON, K1P 5H3
(613) 234-0800
Emp Here 50   *Sales* 3,648,035
SIC 7379 Computer related services, nec

    D-U-N-S 24-059-7943   (SL)
CSL BEHRING CANADA, INC
55 Metcalfe St Suite 1460, Ottawa, ON, K1P

6L5
(613) 232-3111
Emp Here 28   *Sales* 2,407,703
SIC 5961 Catalog and mail-order houses

    D-U-N-S 20-707-1809   (BR)
CTV SPECIALTY TELEVISION INC
CTV SPECIALTY TELEVISION INC/TELEVISION SPECIALISEE CTV INC
100 Queen St Suite 1400, Ottawa, ON, K1P 1J9
(613) 236-7343
Emp Here 40
SIC 4832 Radio broadcasting stations

    D-U-N-S 24-948-1128   (SL)
CABLE PUBLIC AFFAIRS CHANNEL INC
CPAC
45 O'Connor St Suite 1750, Ottawa, ON, K1P 1A4
(613) 567-2722
Emp Here 76   *Sales* 4,450,603
SIC 4841 Cable and other pay television services

    D-U-N-S 20-298-4766   (BR)
CANACCORD GENUITY CORP
(*Suby of* Canaccord Genuity Group Inc)
45 O'Connor St Suite 830, Ottawa, ON, K1P 1A4

Emp Here 26
SIC 6733 Trusts, nec

    D-U-N-S 20-530-6637   (BR)
CANADIAN DEVELOPMENT CONSULTANTS INTERNATIONAL INC
CDCI
246 Queen St Suite 300, Ottawa, ON, K1P 5E4
(613) 234-1849
Emp Here 40
SIC 8748 Business consulting, nec

    D-U-N-S 24-102-2375   (BR)
CANADIAN IMPERIAL BANK OF COMMERCE
CIBC
119 Sparks St, Ottawa, ON, K1P 5B5
(613) 564-8600
Emp Here 30
SIC 6021 National commercial banks

    D-U-N-S 24-124-8736   (BR)
CANADIAN IMPERIAL BANK OF COMMERCE
CIBC
50 O'Connor St Suite 800, Ottawa, ON, K1P 6L2
(613) 783-7344
Emp Here 130
SIC 6211 Security brokers and dealers

    D-U-N-S 20-278-7586   (SL)
COMMISSIONER FOR COMPLAINTS FOR TELECOMMUNICATIONS SERVICES INC
Gd, Ottawa, ON, K1P 1B1
(888) 221-1687
Emp Here 50   *Sales* 6,410,257
SIC 4899 Communication services, nec

    D-U-N-S 20-059-5572   (BR)
COMPAGNIE DE TELEPHONE BELL DU CANADA OU BELL CANADA, LA
GROUP TELECOM
270 Albert St, Ottawa, ON, K1P 6N7

Emp Here 25
SIC 4899 Communication services, nec

    D-U-N-S 25-748-1838   (BR)
CORUS MEDIA HOLDINGS INC
SHAW MEDIA INC
150 Wellington St Suite 501, Ottawa, ON, K1P 5A4
(613) 232-6078
Emp Here 22
SIC 4833 Television broadcasting stations

D-U-N-S 20-105-8802 (BR)
CRAWFORD & COMPANY (CANADA) INC
(Suby of Crawford & Company)
151 Slater St Suite 900, Ottawa, ON, K1P 5H3
(613) 564-7182
Emp Here 28
SIC 8111 Legal services

D-U-N-S 25-769-4547 (BR)
CUSHMAN & WAKEFIELD LTD
(Suby of Cushman & Wakefield Holdings, Inc.)
99 Bank St Suite 700, Ottawa, ON, K1P 6B9
(613) 236-7777
Emp Here 33
SIC 6531 Real estate agents and managers

D-U-N-S 20-789-4296 (BR)
DELOITTE LLP
DELOITTE & TOUCHE MANAGEMENT CONSULTANTS
100 Queen St Suite 800, Ottawa, ON, K1P 5T8
(613) 751-5449
Emp Here 400
SIC 8741 Management services

D-U-N-S 20-894-5956 (BR)
DELOITTE LLP
100 Queen St Suite 1600, Ottawa, ON, K1P 1J9
(613) 236-2442
Emp Here 300
SIC 8721 Accounting, auditing, and bookkeeping

D-U-N-S 24-992-0273 (BR)
DENTONS CANADA LLP
(Suby of Dentons Canada LLP)
99 Bank St Suite 1420, Ottawa, ON, K1P 1H4
(613) 783-9600
Emp Here 75
SIC 8111 Legal services

D-U-N-S 20-889-3768 (BR)
DOMINION OF CANADA GENERAL INSURANCE COMPANY, THE
(Suby of The Travelers Companies Inc)
155 Queen St Suite 300, Ottawa, ON, K1P 6L1
(613) 233-1363
Emp Here 65
SIC 6411 Insurance agents, brokers, and service

D-U-N-S 20-609-7201 (BR)
ESIT CANADA ENTERPRISE SERVICES CO
ESIT CANADA ENTERPRISE SERVICES CO
(Suby of Dxc Technology Company)
50 O'Connor St Suite 500, Ottawa, ON, K1P 6L2
(613) 266-9442
Emp Here 400
SIC 7376 Computer facilities management

D-U-N-S 24-220-8101 (SL)
ELEMENTAL DATA COLLECTION INC
170 Laurier Ave W Suite 400, Ottawa, ON, K1P 5V5
(613) 667-9352
Emp Here 200   Sales 26,995,459
SIC 8732 Commercial nonphysical research
Pt Colin Kiviaho
Pt Darcy Zwetko
Mgr Rick Lyster

D-U-N-S 24-417-2636 (BR)
EMPIRE THEATRES LIMITED
111 Albert St, Ottawa, ON, K1P 1A5

Emp Here 30
SIC 7832 Motion picture theaters, except drive-in

D-U-N-S 20-890-6917 (BR)
ERNST & YOUNG LLP
EY
(Suby of Ernst & Young LLP)
99 Bank St Suite 1600, Ottawa, ON, K1P 6B9

(613) 232-1511
Emp Here 184
SIC 8721 Accounting, auditing, and bookkeeping

D-U-N-S 24-375-7593 (BR)
FASKEN MARTINEAU DUMOULIN LLP
FASKEN MARTINEAU
55 Metcalfe St Suite 1300, Ottawa, ON, K1P 6L5
(613) 236-3882
Emp Here 20
SIC 8111 Legal services

D-U-N-S 25-092-3328 (BR)
FIDUCIAIRES DU FONDS DE PLACEMENT IMMOBILIER COMINAR, LES
FIDUCIAIRES DU FONDS DE PLACEMENT IMMOBILIER COMIN
222 Queen St Suite 300, Ottawa, ON, K1P 5V9
(613) 569-8151
Emp Here 28
SIC 6719 Holding companies, nec

D-U-N-S 20-056-7852 (BR)
FLEETWAY INC
141 Laurier Ave W Suite 800, Ottawa, ON, K1P 5J3
(613) 236-6048
Emp Here 75
SIC 8711 Engineering services

D-U-N-S 25-363-7391 (BR)
FLEISHMAN HILLARD CANADA CORP
(Suby of Omnicom Group Inc.)
1200-45 O'Connor S, Ottawa, ON, K1P 1A4
(613) 238-2090
Emp Here 30
SIC 8741 Management services

D-U-N-S 25-769-7524 (BR)
FUJITSU CONSEIL (CANADA) INC
FUJITSU CONSEIL
55 Metcalfe St Suite 530, Ottawa, ON, K1P 6L5
(613) 238-2697
Emp Here 100
SIC 8741 Management services

D-U-N-S 24-338-3101 (BR)
GOVERNMENT OF ONTARIO
OFFICE OF THE OMBUDSMAN
100 Metcalfe St, Ottawa, ON, K1P 5M1
(613) 992-0787
Emp Here 50
SIC 7389 Business services, nec

D-U-N-S 25-193-7660 (SL)
GRANTIUM INC
279 Laurier Ave W Suite 200, Ottawa, ON, K1P 5J9

Emp Here 41   Sales 5,928,320
SIC 7371 Custom computer programming services
Peter Andrews
VP Fin Catherine Sterling

D-U-N-S 24-736-0738 (BR)
HSBC BANK CANADA
HSBC SECURITIES
30 Metcalfe St, Ottawa, ON, K1P 5L4
(613) 238-3331
Emp Here 40
SIC 6099 Functions related to deposit banking

D-U-N-S 24-765-3285 (BR)
HSBC BANK CANADA
131 Queen St, Ottawa, ON, K1P 0A1
(613) 238-3331
Emp Here 22
SIC 6021 National commercial banks

D-U-N-S 24-503-9628 (BR)
HSBC SECURITIES (CANADA) INC
NATIONAL BANK FINANCIAL
50 O'Corner St Suit 1602, Ottawa, ON, K1P 6L2

(613) 236-0103
Emp Here 30
SIC 6211 Security brokers and dealers

D-U-N-S 25-132-9280 (BR)
HEENAN BLAIKIE S.E.N.C.R.L.
55 Metcalfe St Suite 300, Ottawa, ON, K1P 6L5

Emp Here 35
SIC 8111 Legal services

D-U-N-S 25-408-5400 (HQ)
HIGH ROAD COMMUNICATIONS CORP
(Suby of Omnicom Group Inc.)
45 O'Connor St Suite 1200, Ottawa, ON, K1P 1A4
(613) 236-0909
Emp Here 24   Emp Total 74,900
Sales 8,317,520
SIC 8743 Public relations services
Dir Katherine Fletcher

D-U-N-S 24-102-8620 (BR)
HOLT, RENFREW & CIE, LIMITEE
HOLT RENFREW
240 Sparks St, Ottawa, ON, K1P 6C9
(905) 922-4658
Emp Here 90
SIC 5621 Women's clothing stores

D-U-N-S 24-482-9206 (BR)
HY'S OF CANADA LTD
HY'S STEAK HOUSE
170 Queen St, Ottawa, ON, K1P 5E1
(613) 234-4545
Emp Here 53
SIC 5812 Eating places

D-U-N-S 20-056-1715 (BR)
INFRASTRUCTURE AND COMMUNITIES CANADA
INFRASTRUCTURE OF CANADA, OFFICE OF
180 Kent St Suite 1100, Ottawa, ON, K1P 0B6
(613) 948-1148
Emp Here 70
SIC 1522 Residential construction, nec

D-U-N-S 20-345-4210 (BR)
INNVEST HOTELS LP
OTTAWA MARRIOTT
100 Kent St, Ottawa, ON, K1P 5R7
(613) 238-1122
Emp Here 258
SIC 7011 Hotels and motels

D-U-N-S 20-891-7088 (SL)
INUIT TAPIRIIT KANATAMI
75 Albert St Suite 1101, Ottawa, ON, K1P 5E7
(613) 238-8181
Emp Here 40   Sales 6,027,300
SIC 8699 Membership organizations, nec
Pr Duane Smith
VP Kirt Ejesiak
VP Terry Audla
Dir Cathy Towtongie
Dir Jobie Tukkiapik
Dir Sarah Leo
Dir Nellie Cournoyea
Dir Rebecca Kudloo
Dir Thomas Anguti Johnston

D-U-N-S 25-543-0100 (SL)
KIMWEST HOTELS ENTERPRISES LTD
ARC THE HOTEL
140 Slater St, Ottawa, ON, K1P 5H6
(613) 238-2888
Emp Here 60   Sales 2,626,585
SIC 7011 Hotels and motels

D-U-N-S 24-060-4004 (SL)
KNOWLEDGE CIRCLE LEARNING SERVICES INC
KNOWLEDGE CIRCLE
130 Slater St Suite 850, Ottawa, ON, K1P 6E2
(613) 233-2112
Emp Here 50   Sales 2,699,546
SIC 8299 Schools and educational services,

nec

D-U-N-S 24-483-6300 (HQ)
LOCKHEED MARTIN CANADA INC
45 O'Connor St Suite 870, Ottawa, ON, K1P 1A4
(613) 688-0698
Emp Here 600   Emp Total 97,000
Sales 77,046,499
SIC 3625 Relays and industrial controls
Dir Felix Montanaro
Rosemary Chapdelaine

D-U-N-S 25-359-7595 (BR)
LUXURY HOTELS INTERNATIONAL OF CANADA, ULC
RESIDENCE INN OTTAWA
(Suby of Marriott International, Inc.)
161 Laurier Ave W, Ottawa, ON, K1P 5J2
(613) 231-2020
Emp Here 50
SIC 7011 Hotels and motels

D-U-N-S 25-726-4481 (HQ)
MBM INTELLECTUAL PROPERTY LAW LLP
MBM & CO
(Suby of MBM Intellectual Property Law LLP)
275 Slater St Suite 1400, Ottawa, ON, K1P 5H9
(613) 567-0762
Emp Here 50   Emp Total 55
Sales 4,742,446
SIC 8111 Legal services

D-U-N-S 24-247-4356 (BR)
MALATEST, R. A. & ASSOCIATES LTD
294 Albert St Suite 500, Ottawa, ON, K1P 6E6
(613) 688-1847
Emp Here 50
SIC 8732 Commercial nonphysical research

D-U-N-S 20-384-8333 (BR)
MCMILLAN LLP
45 O'Connor St Suite 2000, Ottawa, ON, K1P 1A4
(613) 232-7171
Emp Here 38
SIC 8111 Legal services

D-U-N-S 24-817-0540 (SL)
METROPOLITAN LIFE HOLDINGS LIMITED
99 Bank St, Ottawa, ON, K1P 6B9
(613) 560-7446
Emp Here 800   Sales 103,795,840
SIC 6531 Real estate agents and managers
Pr Pr William Toppeta

D-U-N-S 20-801-1044 (SL)
METVIEW REALTY LIMITED
130 Albert St Suite 210, Ottawa, ON, K1P 5G4
(613) 230-5174
Emp Here 50   Sales 4,742,446
SIC 6531 Real estate agents and managers

D-U-N-S 24-991-5216 (BR)
MICROSOFT CANADA INC
(Suby of Microsoft Corporation)
100 Queen St Suite 500, Ottawa, ON, K1P 1J9
(613) 232-0484
Emp Here 60
SIC 5045 Computers, peripherals, and software

D-U-N-S 25-130-3301 (SL)
MICROTIME INC
(Suby of Tca Consulting Group, Inc.)
116 Albert St Suite 701, Ottawa, ON, K1P 5G3
(613) 234-2345
Emp Here 29   Sales 2,188,821
SIC 7379 Computer related services, nec

D-U-N-S 25-772-5622 (HQ)
MINTO PROPERTIES INC
MINTO COMMERCIAL
180 Kent St Suite 200, Ottawa, ON, K1P 0B6
(613) 786-3000
Emp Here 30   Emp Total 1,140
Sales 10,648,318

SIC 6512 Nonresidential building operators
Pr Pr Roger Greenberg

D-U-N-S 25-264-8225   (BR)
MODIS CANADA INC
AJILON COUSULTING
155 Queen St Suite 1206, Ottawa, ON, K1P
6L1
(613) 786-3106
Emp Here 30
SIC 7361 Employment agencies

D-U-N-S 25-789-0145   (BR)
MOMENTIS CANADA CORP
130 Slater St Suite 1100, Ottawa, ON, K1P
6E2
(613) 233-8483
Emp Here 40
SIC 5085 Industrial supplies

D-U-N-S 20-697-8764   (BR)
NAV CANADA
77 Metcalf St, Ottawa, ON, K1P 1L6
(613) 563-5949
Emp Here 25
SIC 4899 Communication services, nec

D-U-N-S 20-587-5110   (BR)
NAV CANADA
Gd, Ottawa, ON, K1P 5L6

Emp Here 20
SIC 7389 Business services, nec

D-U-N-S 24-924-7180   (BR)
**NORTON ROSE FULBRIGHT CANADA
S.E.N.C.R.L., S.R.L.**
NORTON ROSE FULBRIGHT
45 O'Connor St Suite 1600, Ottawa, ON, K1P
1A4
(613) 780-8661
Emp Here 100
SIC 8111 Legal services

D-U-N-S 24-830-8355   (BR)
ORACLE CANADA ULC
(*Suby of* Oracle Corporation)
45 O'Connor St Suite 400, Ottawa, ON, K1P
1A4
(613) 569-0001
Emp Here 120
SIC 7371 Custom computer programming services

D-U-N-S 25-130-7922   (BR)
**OTTAWA YOUNG MEN'S AND YOUNG
WOMEN'S CHRISTIAN ASSOCIATION**
*OTTAWA YOUNG MEN'S AND YOUNG
WOMEN'S CHRISTIAN ASSOCIATION*
99 Bank St Suite 1, Ottawa, ON, K1P 6B9
(613) 233-9331
Emp Here 35
SIC 8621 Professional organizations

D-U-N-S 20-569-3513   (SL)
PARLIAMENTARY CENTRE
255 Albert St Suite 802, Ottawa, ON, K1P 6A9
(613) 237-0143
Emp Here 40   *Sales* 6,797,150
SIC 8699 Membership organizations, nec
Ch Bd Michael Murphy
Pr Jean-Paul Ruszkowski
Dir David Schijns
Dir Peter C Dobell
Angela Madge

D-U-N-S 24-437-6067   (BR)
PRICEWATERHOUSECOOPERS LLP
99 Bank St Suite 800, Ottawa, ON, K1P 1E4
(613) 237-3702
Emp Here 150
SIC 8721 Accounting, auditing, and book-
keeping

D-U-N-S 25-770-0492   (BR)
PRIME RESTAURANTS INC
DARCY MCGEE'S IRISH PUB
(*Suby of* Cara Holdings Limited)
44 Sparks St, Ottawa, ON, K1P 5A8

(613) 230-4433
Emp Here 55
SIC 5812 Eating places

D-U-N-S 24-481-0289   (BR)
RBC DOMINION SECURITIES INC
(*Suby of* Royal Bank Of Canada)
45 O'Connor St Suite 900, Ottawa, ON, K1P
1A4
(613) 566-7500
Emp Here 78
SIC 6211 Security brokers and dealers

D-U-N-S 24-465-5523   (BR)
**RAYMOND CHABOT GRANT THORNTON
S.E.N.C.R.L.**
116 Albert St Suite 1000, Ottawa, ON, K1P
5G3
(613) 760-3500
Emp Here 60
SIC 8721 Accounting, auditing, and book-
keeping

D-U-N-S 24-977-5821   (BR)
RAYMOND JAMES (USA) LTD
RAYMOND JAMES LTD
(*Suby of* Raymond James Financial, Inc.)
45 O'Connor St Suite 750, Ottawa, ON, K1P
1A4
(613) 369-4600
Emp Here 25
SIC 6211 Security brokers and dealers

D-U-N-S 24-103-6862   (SL)
RIDEAU CLUB LIMITED
99 Bank St Suite 1500, Ottawa, ON, K1P 6B9
(613) 233-7787
Emp Here 45   *Sales* 5,472,053
SIC 8699 Membership organizations, nec
Genl Mgr Robert Lams
Dir Carol Pink

D-U-N-S 20-136-4189   (SL)
RODAS INVESTMENTS LIMITED
CAPITAL HILL HOTEL & SUITES
88 Albert St, Ottawa, ON, K1P 5E9
(613) 235-1413
Emp Here 60   *Sales* 2,626,585
SIC 7011 Hotels and motels

D-U-N-S 20-889-4444   (BR)
ROYAL BANK OF CANADA
ROYAL BANK FINANCIAL GROUP
(*Suby of* Royal Bank Of Canada)
90 Sparks St Suite 300, Ottawa, ON, K1P 5B4
(613) 564-3100
Emp Here 725
SIC 6021 National commercial banks

D-U-N-S 20-550-5568   (SL)
SNC-LAVALIN PAE INC
170 Laurier Ave W Suite 1104, Ottawa, ON,
K1P 5V5

Emp Here 300   *Sales* 44,572,162
SIC 8711 Engineering services
Ian Malcolm

D-U-N-S 25-412-4423   (BR)
**SERVICES DE GESTION QUANTUM LIMI-
TEE, LES**
275 Slater St Suite 500, Ottawa, ON, K1P 5H9
(613) 237-8888
Emp Here 25
SIC 7361 Employment agencies

D-U-N-S 25-128-8312   (BR)
SIERRA SYSTEMS GROUP INC
220 Laurier Ave W Suite 800, Ottawa, ON,
K1P 5Z9
(613) 236-7888
Emp Here 93
SIC 7379 Computer related services, nec

D-U-N-S 24-977-5438   (HQ)
SONOVISION CANADA INC
85 Albert St Suite 400, Ottawa, ON, K1P 6A4
(613) 234-4849
Emp Here 35   *Emp Total* 1
Sales 5,589,420

SIC 8999 Services, nec
Pr Pr Rick Temelini
Bertrand Doucet

D-U-N-S 25-306-1907   (BR)
STIKEMAN ELLIOTT LLP
50 O'Connor St Suite 1600, Ottawa, ON, K1P
6L2
(613) 234-4555
Emp Here 55
SIC 8111 Legal services

D-U-N-S 24-267-8266   (BR)
TORONTO-DOMINION BANK, THE
TD CANADA TRUST
(*Suby of* Toronto-Dominion Bank, The)
45 O'Connor St Suite 1100, Ottawa, ON, K1P
1A4
(613) 782-1201
Emp Here 25
SIC 6021 National commercial banks

D-U-N-S 20-112-3481   (HQ)
VALCOM CONSULTING GROUP INC
85 Albert St Suite 300, Ottawa, ON, K1P 6A4
(613) 594-5200
Emp Here 392   *Emp Total* 50
Sales 59,932,124
SIC 8711 Engineering services
Pr Pr Paul Macpherson

D-U-N-S 24-666-4296   (BR)
**WPP GROUP CANADA COMMUNICATIONS
LIMITED**
HILL & KNOWLTON CANADA
55 Metcalfe St Suite 1100, Ottawa, ON, K1P
6L5
(613) 238-4371
Emp Here 70
SIC 8741 Management services

D-U-N-S 25-300-6621   (BR)
**WORKPLACE SAFETY & INSURANCE
BOARD, THE**
WSIB
180 Kent St Suite 400, Ottawa, ON, K1P 0B6
(416) 344-1000
Emp Here 200
SIC 6331 Fire, marine, and casualty insurance

D-U-N-S 25-360-1488   (BR)
ZAYO CANADA INC
45 O'Connor St Suite 1400, Ottawa, ON, K1P
1A4
(613) 688-4688
Emp Here 110
SIC 4899 Communication services, nec

Ottawa, ON K1R
Carleton County

D-U-N-S 24-802-3918   (SL)
ALBERT AT BAY SUITE HOTEL LTD
435 Albert St, Ottawa, ON, K1R 7X4
(613) 238-8858
Emp Here 50   *Sales* 2,598,753
SIC 7011 Hotels and motels

D-U-N-S 24-663-3619   (SL)
ART-IS-IN BAKERY INC
250 City Centre Ave Unit 112, Ottawa, ON,
K1R 6K7
(613) 695-1226
Emp Here 50   *Sales* 2,167,357
SIC 5461 Retail bakeries

D-U-N-S 25-499-7026   (BR)
AUTODESK CANADA CIE
(*Suby of* Autodesk, Inc.)
427 Laurier Ave W Suite 500, Ottawa, ON,
K1R 7Y2
(613) 755-5000
Emp Here 35
SIC 7372 Prepackaged software

D-U-N-S 20-517-7772   (BR)

BANQUE TORONTO-DOMINION, LA
TORONTO-DOMINION BANK, THE
(*Suby of* Toronto-Dominion Bank, The)
360 Albert St Suite 1100, Ottawa, ON, K1R
7X7
(613) 783-1993
Emp Here 60
SIC 6021 National commercial banks

D-U-N-S 25-213-3269   (SL)
BAY STREET BISTRO INC
160 Bay St, Ottawa, ON, K1R 7X8

Emp Here 50   *Sales* 1,532,175
SIC 5812 Eating places

D-U-N-S 20-200-0931   (HQ)
BELLAI BROTHERS CONSTRUCTION LTD
440 Laurier Ave W, Ottawa, ON, K1R 7X6
(613) 782-2932
Emp Here 295   *Emp Total* 325
Sales 84,459,473
SIC 1771 Concrete work
Pietro Bellai
Pr Pr Gianni Bellai

D-U-N-S 24-874-8220   (BR)
BERLITZ CANADA INC
BERLITZ LANGUAGE CENTRES
350 Sparks St Suite 1001, Ottawa, ON, K1R
7S8
(613) 234-8686
Emp Here 30
SIC 8299 Schools and educational services,
nec

D-U-N-S 24-104-1052   (HQ)
**BROWN'S CLEANERS AND TAILORS LIM-
ITED**
BROWN'S CLEANERS
(*Suby of* Brown's Cleaners and Tailors Lim-
ited)
270 City Centre Ave, Ottawa, ON, K1R 7R7
(613) 235-5181
Emp Here 50   *Emp Total* 102
Sales 2,918,428
SIC 7216 Drycleaning plants, except rugs

D-U-N-S 20-573-0422   (BR)
CANADA POST CORPORATION
797 Somerset St W Suite 14, Ottawa, ON,
K1R 6R3
(613) 729-6761
Emp Here 20
SIC 4311 U.s. postal service

D-U-N-S 20-892-2237   (SL)
CANADIAN INSTITUTE OF ACTUARIES
360 Albert St Suite 1740, Ottawa, ON, K1R
7X7
(613) 236-8196
Emp Here 21   *Sales* 5,250,815
SIC 8621 Professional organizations
Pr Robert Howard
Ex Dir Daniel Lapointe
Dir Opers Rosemary Leu
Normand Gendron

D-U-N-S 24-175-6902   (BR)
CISCO SYSTEMS CANADA CO
(*Suby of* Cisco Systems, Inc.)
340 Albert St Suite 1710, Ottawa, ON, K1R
7Y6
(613) 788-7200
Emp Here 38
SIC 7373 Computer integrated systems design

D-U-N-S 20-291-2163   (BR)
COLLIERS MACAULAY NICOLLS INC
COLLIERS INTERNATIONAL
340 Albert St Suite 930, Ottawa, ON, K1R 7Y6
(613) 567-8050
Emp Here 26
SIC 6531 Real estate agents and managers

D-U-N-S 20-789-6002   (HQ)
DEFENCE CONSTRUCTION (1951) LIM-

ITED
DEFENCE CONSTRUCTION CANADA
350 Albert St Suite 1900, Ottawa, ON, K1R 1A4
(613) 998-9548
Emp Here 120   *Emp Total* 570,000
Sales 168,745,695
SIC 8741 Management services
Pr James Paul
VP Opers Ronald De Vries
VP Opers Daniel Benjamin
VP Opers Randy Mcgee
VP Angelo Ottoni
Robert Presser

D-U-N-S 20-699-9497   (BR)
DELTA HOTELS LIMITED
DELTA OTTAWA HOTEL AND SUITES
361 Queen St, Ottawa, ON, K1R 7S9

Emp Here 200
SIC 8741 Management services

D-U-N-S 24-633-6952   (SL)
EVRIPOS JANITORIAL SERVICES LTD
136 Flora St Suite 1, Ottawa, ON, K1R 5R5
(613) 232-9069
Emp Here 150   *Sales* 4,377,642
SIC 7349 Building maintenance services, nec

D-U-N-S 25-772-1217   (BR)
GREYHOUND CANADA TRANSPORTA-TION ULC
GREYHOUND COURIER EXPRESS DIV OF
265 Catherine St, Ottawa, ON, K1R 7S5
(613) 234-5115
Emp Here 25
SIC 4731 Freight transportation arrangement

D-U-N-S 20-511-7018   (BR)
GROUPE PAGES JAUNES CORP
1 Raymond St Suite 300, Ottawa, ON, K1R 1A2
(888) 909-0930
Emp Here 50
SIC 4899 Communication services, nec

D-U-N-S 24-924-0003   (BR)
HALF, ROBERT CANADA INC
(*Suby of* Robert Half International Inc.)
360 Albert St Suite 520, Ottawa, ON, K1R 7X7
(613) 236-4253
Emp Here 40
SIC 7361 Employment agencies

D-U-N-S 20-890-9809   (BR)
INNVEST PROPERTIES CORP
RADISSON HOTEL OTTAWA PARLIAMENT HILL
(*Suby of* Innvest Properties Corp)
402 Queen St, Ottawa, ON, K1R 5A7
(613) 236-1133
Emp Here 20
SIC 7011 Hotels and motels

D-U-N-S 24-112-1206   (SL)
JANI QUEEN
250 Rochester St, Ottawa, ON, K1R 7N1

Emp Here 60   *Sales* 1,751,057
SIC 7349 Building maintenance services, nec

D-U-N-S 25-344-5126   (SL)
MACERA & JARZYNA LLP
427 Laurier Ave W Suite 1200, Ottawa, ON, K1R 7Y2
(613) 238-8173
Emp Here 50   *Sales* 4,304,681
SIC 8111 Legal services

D-U-N-S 25-302-2271   (SL)
MACY HOLDINGS LIMITED
435 Albert St, Ottawa, ON, K1R 7X4
(613) 238-8858
Emp Here 80   *Sales* 4,158,005
SIC 7011 Hotels and motels

D-U-N-S 25-540-7017   (BR)
MERCER (CANADA) LIMITED

(*Suby of* Marsh & McLennan Companies, Inc.)
360 Albert St Suite 701, Ottawa, ON, K1R 7X7
(613) 230-9348
Emp Here 58
SIC 8742 Management consulting services

D-U-N-S 24-952-2665   (SL)
METROPOLITAN LIFE INSURANCE COM-PANY
METLIFE
360 Albert St Suite 1750, Ottawa, ON, K1R 7X7

Emp Here 22   *Sales* 30,144,000
SIC 6311 Life insurance
CFO P James Anderson
Karen Sauve

D-U-N-S 24-345-8291   (BR)
MORGUARD CORPORATION
350 Sparks St Suite 402, Ottawa, ON, K1R 7S8
(613) 237-6373
Emp Here 140
SIC 6519 Real property lessors, nec

D-U-N-S 25-028-6713   (BR)
MORGUARD INVESTMENTS LIMITED
350 Sparks St Suite 402, Ottawa, ON, K1R 7S8
(613) 237-6373
Emp Here 30
SIC 6531 Real estate agents and managers

D-U-N-S 25-028-6754   (BR)
OSLER, HOSKIN & HARCOURT LLP
CARTHO SERVICES
340 Albert St Suite 1900, Ottawa, ON, K1R 7Y6
(613) 235-7234
Emp Here 94
SIC 8111 Legal services

D-U-N-S 25-131-2898   (BR)
OTTAWA CATHOLIC DISTRICT SCHOOL BOARD
ST PATRICK ADULT SCHOOL
(*Suby of* Ottawa Catholic District School Board)
290 Nepean St, Ottawa, ON, K1R 5G3
(613) 594-5773
Emp Here 30
SIC 8211 Elementary and secondary schools

D-U-N-S 25-501-6370   (BR)
OTTAWA-CARLETON DISTRICT SCHOOL BOARD
CENTENNIAL PUBLIC SCHOOL
376 Gloucester St, Ottawa, ON, K1R 5E8
(613) 239-2277
Emp Here 45
SIC 8211 Elementary and secondary schools

D-U-N-S 25-263-8143   (BR)
OTTAWA-CARLETON DISTRICT SCHOOL BOARD
RICHARD PFAFF ALTERNATIVE PROGRAM
160 Percy St, Ottawa, ON, K1R 6E5
(613) 594-8020
Emp Here 21
SIC 8211 Elementary and secondary schools

D-U-N-S 25-238-1355   (BR)
OTTAWA-CARLETON DISTRICT SCHOOL BOARD
ST ANTHONY SCHOOL
391 Booth St, Ottawa, ON, K1R 7K5
(613) 235-0340
Emp Here 30
SIC 8211 Elementary and secondary schools

D-U-N-S 20-711-6265   (BR)
OTTAWA-CARLETON DISTRICT SCHOOL BOARD
CAMBRIDGE STREET COMMUNITY PUB-LIC SCHOOL
250 Cambridge St N, Ottawa, ON, K1R 7B2
(613) 239-2216
Emp Here 27

SIC 8211 Elementary and secondary schools

D-U-N-S 25-481-2746   (BR)
OTTAWA-CARLETON DISTRICT SCHOOL BOARD
ADULT HIGH SCHOOL
300 Rochester St Suite 302, Ottawa, ON, K1R 7N4
(613) 239-2416
Emp Here 100
SIC 8211 Elementary and secondary schools

D-U-N-S 20-645-5763   (BR)
OXFORD PROPERTIES GROUP INC
350 Albert St Suite 200, Ottawa, ON, K1R 1A4
(613) 594-0238
Emp Here 20
SIC 6512 Nonresidential building operators

D-U-N-S 25-769-4968   (BR)
ROGERS COMMUNICATIONS INC
(*Suby of* Rogers Communications Inc)
360 Albert St Suite 1010, Ottawa, ON, K1R 7X7
(613) 688-5569
Emp Here 20
SIC 4899 Communication services, nec

D-U-N-S 25-774-6131   (BR)
SAS INSTITUTE (CANADA) INC
SAS
(*Suby of* Sas Institute Inc.)
360 Albert St Suite 1600, Ottawa, ON, K1R 7X7
(613) 231-8503
Emp Here 21
SIC 7371 Custom computer programming services

D-U-N-S 24-436-3974   (BR)
SCOTIA CAPITAL INC
SCOTIA MCLEOD
350 Albert St Suite 2100, Ottawa, ON, K1R 1A4
(613) 563-0991
Emp Here 80
SIC 6211 Security brokers and dealers

D-U-N-S 20-137-1937   (SL)
SLAU LIMITED
YANGTZE RESTAURANT
700 Somerset St W, Ottawa, ON, K1R 6P6
(613) 236-0555
Emp Here 60   *Sales* 1,824,018
SIC 5812 Eating places

D-U-N-S 25-778-8422   (SL)
SOMERSET WEST COMMUNITY HEALTH CENTRE
SOMERSET WEST CHC
55 Eccles St, Ottawa, ON, K1R 6S3
(613) 238-8210
Emp Here 90   *Sales* 3,502,114
SIC 8322 Individual and family services

D-U-N-S 25-010-7869   (BR)
TD ASSET MANAGEMENT INC
TD WATERHOUSE PRIVATE INVESTMENT ADVICE
(*Suby of* Toronto-Dominion Bank, The)
360 Albert St Suite 1100, Ottawa, ON, K1R 7X7
(613) 783-6197
Emp Here 60
SIC 6211 Security brokers and dealers

D-U-N-S 25-087-3791   (BR)
TANNIS TRADING INC
TANNIS FOOD DISTRIBUTORS
(*Suby of* Sysco Corporation)
288 Catherine St, Ottawa, ON, K1R 5T3
(613) 236-9572
Emp Here 20
SIC 5194 Tobacco and tobacco products

D-U-N-S 24-101-9934   (SL)
VISITING HOMEMAKERS ASSOCIATON OF OTTAWA
VHA HEALTH & HOME SUPPORT

250 City Centre Ave Unit 7, Ottawa, ON, K1R 6K7
(613) 238-8420
Emp Here 300   *Sales* 15,265,730
SIC 8322 Individual and family services
Ex Dir Valerie Bishop-Deyoung
Dir Louise Senechal

Ottawa, ON K1S
Carleton County

D-U-N-S 24-794-1925   (SL)
1039658 ONTARIO INC
WEST COAST VIDEO
1123 Bank St, Ottawa, ON, K1S 3X4

Emp Here 50   *Sales* 4,596,524
SIC 5731 Radio, television, and electronic stores

D-U-N-S 25-767-9571   (BR)
429512 ONTARIO LIMITED
ROYAL OAK PUB
779 Bank St, Ottawa, ON, K1S 3V5
(613) 235-2624
Emp Here 20
SIC 5812 Eating places

D-U-N-S 25-305-0496   (BR)
AON REED STENHOUSE INC
333 Preston St Suite 600 Preston Sq Tower 1, Ottawa, ON, K1S 5N4
(613) 722-7070
Emp Here 30
SIC 6411 Insurance agents, brokers, and service

D-U-N-S 24-436-7421   (HQ)
ADOBE SYSTEMS CANADA INC
343 Preston St, Ottawa, ON, K1S 1N4
(613) 940-3676
Emp Here 320   *Emp Total* 13,893
Sales 65,613,440
SIC 7372 Prepackaged software
Pr Pr Shantanu Narayen

D-U-N-S 25-296-4622   (BR)
BANK OF NOVA SCOTIA, THE
SCOTIABANK
828 Bank St, Ottawa, ON, K1S 3W1
(613) 564-5333
Emp Here 20
SIC 6021 National commercial banks

D-U-N-S 20-588-2330   (BR)
BANQUE TORONTO-DOMINION, LA
TD CANADA TRUST
(*Suby of* Toronto-Dominion Bank, The)
1158 Bank St, Ottawa, ON, K1S 3X8
(613) 783-6222
Emp Here 20
SIC 6021 National commercial banks

D-U-N-S 20-699-1866   (BR)
CB RICHARD ELLIS GLOBAL CORPORATE SERVICES LTD
TEMPEST MANAGEMENT CORPC
1125 Colonel By Dr Suite 4400, Ottawa, ON, K1S 5R1
(613) 231-3875
Emp Here 50
SIC 8742 Management consulting services

D-U-N-S 24-106-0268   (HQ)
CANADIAN BAR ASSOCIATION, THE
(*Suby of* Canadian Bar Association, The)
865 Carling Ave Suite 500, Ottawa, ON, K1S 5S8
(613) 237-2925
Emp Here 72   *Emp Total* 120
Sales 16,961,922
SIC 8621 Professional organizations
John Hoyles
Pr Pr Fred Headon
Michele H. Hollins

Janet M. Fuhrer
Annette J.R. Horst
Robert C. Brun

D-U-N-S 24-365-5789   (SL)
CANADIAN INTERNATIONAL COUNCIL
NATIONAL CAPITAL BRANCH
1125 Colonel By Dr, Ottawa, ON, K1S 5B6
(613) 903-4011
Emp Here 350   *Sales* 66,919,680
SIC 8732 Commercial nonphysical research
Ch Bd Jim Balsillie
Pr John Noble
Craig Hunter

D-U-N-S 24-830-2937   (SL)
CANADIAN MEDICAL PROTECTIVE ASSO-CIATION, THE
875 Carling Ave Suite 928, Ottawa, ON, K1S 5P1
(613) 725-2000
Emp Here 287   *Sales* 37,941,794
SIC 8621 Professional organizations
Pr Pr Hartley Stern
E. Douglas Bell
Stephen Eryan
Cory Garbolinsky

D-U-N-S 20-362-5350   (BR)
CANADIAN UNION OF PUBLIC EMPLOY-EES
CUPE LOCAL 4000
182 Isabella St, Ottawa, ON, K1S 1V7
(613) 722-0652
Emp Here 20
SIC 8631 Labor organizations

D-U-N-S 24-105-0293   (SL)
CARLETON UNIVERSITY STUDENTS' AS-SOCIATION
CUSA
1125 Colonel By Dr Rm 401, Ottawa, ON, K1S 5B6
(613) 520-6688
Emp Here 300   *Sales* 48,981,840
SIC 8699 Membership organizations, nec
Carl Kazmierczak
VP Kimberly Bryce
Ex Dir Robert Jamieson
Pr Obed Okyere

D-U-N-S 25-129-4583   (BR)
CERIDIAN CANADA LTD
343 Preston St Suite 1000, Ottawa, ON, K1S 1N4
(613) 228-0222
Emp Here 30
SIC 8721 Accounting, auditing, and book-keeping

D-U-N-S 25-513-6624   (BR)
CITY OF OTTAWA
ARENAS AND ICE RINKS CITY OF OTTAWA PUBLIC SKATING CIVIC CENTRE LANS-DOWNE PARK
(*Suby of* City of Ottawa)
1015 Bank St, Ottawa, ON, K1S 3W7
(613) 580-2429
Emp Here 50
SIC 7299 Miscellaneous personal service

D-U-N-S 20-029-6445   (BR)
CITY OF OTTAWA
BREWER POOLS
(*Suby of* City of Ottawa)
100 Brewer Way, Ottawa, ON, K1S 5R2
(613) 247-4938
Emp Here 25
SIC 7999 Amusement and recreation, nec

D-U-N-S 20-797-1388   (BR)
DAIRY QUEEN CANADA INC
1272 Bank St, Ottawa, ON, K1S 3Y4
(613) 738-7146
Emp Here 22
SIC 8742 Management consulting services

D-U-N-S 24-383-7932   (BR)

DYMON STORAGE CORPORATION
LORD LANSDOWNE RETIREMENT RESI-DENCE
920 Bank St Suite 711, Ottawa, ON, K1S 1M8
(613) 230-9900
Emp Here 50
SIC 6513 Apartment building operators

D-U-N-S 20-891-5608   (BR)
ECONOMICAL MUTUAL INSURANCE COM-PANY
ECONOMICAL INSURANCE GROUP
343 Preston St Suite 500, Ottawa, ON, K1S 1N4
(613) 567-7060
Emp Here 145
SIC 6331 Fire, marine, and casualty insurance

D-U-N-S 20-876-2245   (SL)
FLOWERS CANADA INC
99 Fifth Ave Suite 305, Ottawa, ON, K1S 5K4
(800) 447-5147
Emp Here 958   *Sales* 132,417,840
SIC 8611 Business associations
Ex Dir Arman Patel

D-U-N-S 20-137-7405   (SL)
HUTCHINGS & PATRICK INC
100 Champagne Ave S, Ottawa, ON, K1S 4P4
(613) 728-5803
Emp Here 31   *Sales* 30,132,769
SIC 2678 Stationery products

D-U-N-S 24-589-0959   (HQ)
INVEST OTTAWA
O C R I
(*Suby of* Invest Ottawa)
80 Aberdeen St Suite 100, Ottawa, ON, K1S 5R5
(613) 828-6274
Emp Here 32   *Emp Total* 35
Sales 11,402,181
SIC 8399 Social services, nec
Pr Bruce Lazenby
Margot Sunter

D-U-N-S 25-203-2693   (SL)
LANGUAGES OF LIFE INC
99 Fifth Ave Suite 14, Ottawa, ON, K1S 5K4
(613) 232-9770
Emp Here 600   *Sales* 37,221,996
SIC 7389 Business services, nec
Pr Pr Bryna Monson

D-U-N-S 20-788-1736   (BR)
LOBLAW COMPANIES LIMITED
LOBLAWS
64 Isabella St, Ottawa, ON, K1S 1V4
(613) 232-4831
Emp Here 140
SIC 5411 Grocery stores

D-U-N-S 25-131-2906   (BR)
OTTAWA CATHOLIC DISTRICT SCHOOL BOARD
CORPUS CHRISTI SCHOOL
(*Suby of* Ottawa Catholic District School Board)
798 Lyon St S, Ottawa, ON, K1S 5H5
(613) 232-9743
Emp Here 21
SIC 8211 Elementary and secondary schools

D-U-N-S 25-515-8958   (BR)
OTTAWA CATHOLIC DISTRICT SCHOOL BOARD
IMMACULATA HIGH SCHOOL
(*Suby of* Ottawa Catholic District School Board)
140 Main St, Ottawa, ON, K1S 5P4
(613) 237-2001
Emp Here 125
SIC 8211 Elementary and secondary schools

D-U-N-S 24-855-6321   (BR)
OTTAWA SALUS CORPORATION
111 Grove Ave, Ottawa, ON, K1S 3A9

(613) 523-3232
Emp Here 20
SIC 8361 Residential care

D-U-N-S 25-504-0446   (BR)
OTTAWA-CARLETON DISTRICT SCHOOL BOARD
FIRST AVENUE PUBLIC SCHOOL
73 First Ave, Ottawa, ON, K1S 2G1
(613) 239-2261
Emp Here 23
SIC 8211 Elementary and secondary schools

D-U-N-S 25-504-0925   (BR)
OTTAWA-CARLETON DISTRICT SCHOOL BOARD
MUTCHMOR PUBLIC SCHOOL
185 Fifth Ave, Ottawa, ON, K1S 2N1
(613) 239-2267
Emp Here 30
SIC 8211 Elementary and secondary schools

D-U-N-S 25-026-7622   (BR)
OTTAWA-CARLETON DISTRICT SCHOOL BOARD
GLEBE COLLEGIATE INSTITUTE
212 Glebe Ave, Ottawa, ON, K1S 2C9
(613) 239-2424
Emp Here 110
SIC 8211 Elementary and secondary schools

D-U-N-S 25-263-7665   (BR)
OTTAWA-CARLETON DISTRICT SCHOOL BOARD
HOPEWELL AVENUE PUBLIC SCHOOL
17 Hopewell Ave, Ottawa, ON, K1S 2Y7
(613) 239-2348
Emp Here 30
SIC 8211 Elementary and secondary schools

D-U-N-S 24-796-1329   (SL)
OWL RAFTING INC
39 First Ave, Ottawa, ON, K1S 2G1
(613) 238-7238
Emp Here 80   *Sales* 4,377,642
SIC 7999 Amusement and recreation, nec

D-U-N-S 25-772-7917   (BR)
POMERLEAU INC
POMERLEAU
343 Preston St Suite 220, Ottawa, ON, K1S 1N4
(613) 244-4323
Emp Here 35
SIC 1541 Industrial buildings and warehouses

D-U-N-S 20-709-2003   (BR)
RBC DOMINION SECURITIES INC
(*Suby of* Royal Bank Of Canada)
333 Preston St Suite 1100, Ottawa, ON, K1S 5N4
(613) 564-4800
Emp Here 50
SIC 6282 Investment advice

D-U-N-S 20-289-8172   (BR)
REVERA INC
COLONEL BY RETIREMENT RESIDENCE, THE
43 Aylmer Ave Suite 358, Ottawa, ON, K1S 5R4
(613) 730-2002
Emp Here 50
SIC 8051 Skilled nursing care facilities

D-U-N-S 24-891-9474   (SL)
ROYAL COLLEGE OF PHYSICIANS AND SURGEONS OF CANADA, THE
774 Echo Dr, Ottawa, ON, K1S 5N8
(613) 730-8177
Emp Here 300   *Sales* 38,044,662
SIC 8621 Professional organizations
Dir Andrew Padmos
Pr Francoise Chagnon

D-U-N-S 20-890-7212   (SL)
SAINT PAUL UNIVERSITY
CANTERBURY HOUSE BOOKSTORE
223 Main St Suite 267, Ottawa, ON, K1S 1C4

(613) 236-1393
Emp Here 275   *Sales* 36,939,297
SIC 8221 Colleges and universities
Dir Chantal Beauvais
Dir Fin Lyne Paris

D-U-N-S 20-580-6263   (BR)
SUN LIFE ASSURANCE COMPANY OF CANADA
333 Preston St Suite 800, Ottawa, ON, K1S 5N4
(613) 567-9700
Emp Here 70
SIC 6311 Life insurance

D-U-N-S 20-580-6289   (BR)
SUN LIFE ASSURANCE COMPANY OF CANADA
SUN LIFE
865 Carling Ave Suite 400, Ottawa, ON, K1S 5S8
(613) 728-1223
Emp Here 20
SIC 6311 Life insurance

D-U-N-S 24-125-9733   (BR)
XEROX CANADA LTD
(*Suby of* Xerox Corporation)
333 Preston St Suite 1000, Ottawa, ON, K1S 5N4
(613) 230-1002
Emp Here 150
SIC 5044 Office equipment

Ottawa, ON K1T
Carleton County

D-U-N-S 20-591-2459   (BR)
OTTAWA CATHOLIC DISTRICT SCHOOL BOARD
ST BERNARD SCHOOL
(*Suby of* Ottawa Catholic District School Board)
1722 St. Bernard St, Ottawa, ON, K1T 1K8
(613) 521-5894
Emp Here 45
SIC 8211 Elementary and secondary schools

D-U-N-S 20-711-6455   (BR)
OTTAWA CATHOLIC DISTRICT SCHOOL BOARD
ST. MARGUERITE D'YOUVILLE SCHOOL
(*Suby of* Ottawa Catholic District School Board)
89 Lorry Greenberg Dr, Ottawa, ON, K1T 3J6
(613) 737-1141
Emp Here 50
SIC 8211 Elementary and secondary schools

D-U-N-S 25-504-0453   (BR)
OTTAWA-CARLETON DISTRICT SCHOOL BOARD
BONDAR, ROBERTA PUBLIC SCHOOL
159 Lorry Greenberg Dr, Ottawa, ON, K1T 3J6
(613) 736-7334
Emp Here 55
SIC 8211 Elementary and secondary schools

D-U-N-S 24-466-4442   (HQ)
W.O. STINSON & SON LIMITED
4728 Bank St, Ottawa, ON, K1T 3W7
(613) 822-7400
Emp Here 100   *Emp Total* 175
Sales 39,934,171
SIC 5541 Gasoline service stations
Pr Pr David Stinson
Eric Stinson

Ottawa, ON K1V
Carleton County

D-U-N-S 20-698-8334   (BR)

AIR CANADA
AIR CANADA CARGO
900 Airport Parkway Pvt, Ottawa, ON, K1V 2E7
(613) 783-6463
Emp Here 30
SIC 4512 Air transportation, scheduled

D-U-N-S 20-123-0955   (BR)
AVISCAR INC
AVIS
(*Suby of* Avis Budget Group, Inc.)
180 Paul Benoit Dr, Ottawa, ON, K1V 2E5
(613) 521-7541
Emp Here 100
SIC 7514 Passenger car rental

D-U-N-S 25-296-5371   (BR)
BANK OF NOVA SCOTIA, THE
SCOTIABANK
2714 Alta Vista Dr, Ottawa, ON, K1V 7T4
(613) 731-3660
Emp Here 25
SIC 6021 National commercial banks

D-U-N-S 20-002-8152   (BR)
BANQUE TORONTO-DOMINION, LA
TORONTO-DOMINION BANK, THE
(*Suby of* Toronto-Dominion Bank, The)
2470 Bank St, Ottawa, ON, K1V 8S2
(613) 526-2128
Emp Here 31
SIC 6021 National commercial banks

D-U-N-S 25-777-8100   (BR)
BAYSHORE HEALTHCARE LTD.
BAYSHORE HOME HEALTH
310 Hunt Club Rd Suite 202, Ottawa, ON, K1V 1C1
(613) 733-4408
Emp Here 200
SIC 8082 Home health care services

D-U-N-S 25-131-4043   (BR)
BEST BUY CANADA LTD
FUTURE SHOP
(*Suby of* Best Buy Co., Inc.)
2210 Bank St Unit B1, Ottawa, ON, K1V 1J5
(613) 526-7450
Emp Here 120
SIC 5731 Radio, television, and electronic stores

D-U-N-S 24-986-8829   (BR)
BRADLEY AIR SERVICES LIMITED
FIRST AIR
(*Suby of* Societe Makivik)
100 Thad Johnson Pvt, Ottawa, ON, K1V 0R1
(613) 254-6200
Emp Here 300
SIC 8322 Individual and family services

D-U-N-S 24-595-3935   (BR)
CADUCEON ENTERPRISES INC
(*Suby of* Caduceon Enterprises Inc)
2378 Holly Lane, Ottawa, ON, K1V 7P1
(613) 526-0123
Emp Here 24
SIC 8731 Commercial physical research

D-U-N-S 24-440-8915   (BR)
CARA OPERATIONS LIMITED
MONTANA'S COOKHOUSE
(*Suby of* Cara Holdings Limited)
2216 Bank St, Ottawa, ON, K1V 1J6
(613) 731-3058
Emp Here 40
SIC 5812 Eating places

D-U-N-S 24-417-5589   (BR)
CINEPLEX ODEON CORPORATION
CINEPLEX CINEMAS SOUTH KEYS
2214 Bank St, Ottawa, ON, K1V 1J6
(613) 736-1115
Emp Here 20
SIC 7832 Motion picture theaters, except drive-in

D-U-N-S 20-707-1221   (BR)
CITY OF OTTAWA
HOCKEY ARENA
(*Suby of* City of Ottawa)
1265 Walkley Rd, Ottawa, ON, K1V 6P9
(613) 247-4811
Emp Here 20
SIC 7999 Amusement and recreation, nec

D-U-N-S 25-238-3005   (BR)
CONSEIL DES ECOLES CATHOLIQUES DE LANGUE FRANCAISE DU CENTRE-EST
ECOLE LAMOUREUX
2540 Kaladar Ave, Ottawa, ON, K1V 8C5
(613) 731-3713
Emp Here 30
SIC 8211 Elementary and secondary schools

D-U-N-S 25-238-1421   (BR)
CONSEIL DES ECOLES CATHOLIQUES DE LANGUE FRANCAISE DU CENTRE-EST
ECOLE GEORGES ETIENNE-CARTIER
880 Thorndale Dr, Ottawa, ON, K1V 6Y3
(613) 731-6007
Emp Here 22
SIC 8211 Elementary and secondary schools

D-U-N-S 25-238-1348   (BR)
CONSEIL DES ECOLES CATHOLIQUES DE LANGUE FRANCAISE DU CENTRE-EST
ECOLE MARIUS-BARBEAU
1345 Notting Hill Ave, Ottawa, ON, K1V 6T3
(613) 737-4404
Emp Here 30
SIC 8211 Elementary and secondary schools

D-U-N-S 20-958-3520   (BR)
DOLLARAMA S.E.C.
DOLLARAMA
1670 Heron Rd Unit 150, Ottawa, ON, K1V 0C2
(613) 247-1692
Emp Here 25
SIC 5399 Miscellaneous general merchandise

D-U-N-S 24-847-2334   (SL)
DONNELLY PONTIAC BUICK GMC LTD
2496 Bank St, Ottawa, ON, K1V 8S2
(613) 737-5000
Emp Here 68   *Sales* 24,806,638
SIC 5511 New and used car dealers
Pr Pr Thomas Donnelly
Dan Mckenna

D-U-N-S 24-827-2197   (BR)
EXTENDICARE (CANADA) INC
PARAMED HOME HEALTH CARE
1145 Hunt Club Rd Suite 400, Ottawa, ON, K1V 0Y3
(613) 728-7080
Emp Here 30
SIC 8051 Skilled nursing care facilities

D-U-N-S 25-853-0781   (BR)
GOODFELLOW INC
3091 Albion Rd N, Ottawa, ON, K1V 9V9
(613) 244-3169
Emp Here 20
SIC 5031 Lumber, plywood, and millwork

D-U-N-S 20-176-2114   (BR)
HOME DEPOT OF CANADA INC
HOME DEPOT
(*Suby of* The Home Depot Inc)
2056 Bank St, Ottawa, ON, K1V 7Z8
(613) 739-5300
Emp Here 125
SIC 5251 Hardware stores

D-U-N-S 25-623-8122   (SL)
HUNT CLUB RIVERSIDE COMMUNITY CENTRE INC
3320 Paul Anka Dr, Ottawa, ON, K1V 0J9
(613) 260-1299
Emp Here 70   *Sales* 2,772,507
SIC 8322 Individual and family services

D-U-N-S 25-501-8590   (BR)

INDIGO BOOKS & MUSIC INC
CHAPTERS
(*Suby of* Indigo Books & Music Inc)
2210 Bank St, Ottawa, ON, K1V 1J5
(613) 521-9199
Emp Here 60
SIC 5942 Book stores

D-U-N-S 20-697-3633   (BR)
IOGEN BIO-PRODUCTS CORPORATION
300 Hunt Club Rd, Ottawa, K1V 1C1
(613) 733-9830
Emp Here 200
SIC 2869 Industrial organic chemicals, nec

D-U-N-S 20-552-0286   (HQ)
IOGEN BIO-PRODUCTS CORPORATION
310 Hunt Club Rd, Ottawa, ON, K1V 1C1
(613) 733-9830
Emp Here 200   *Emp Total* 278
Sales 53,430,054
SIC 8732 Commercial nonphysical research
Pr Pr Brian E Foody
William Waller
Patrick J Jr Foody

D-U-N-S 24-419-3541   (BR)
IOGEN CORPORATION
310 Hunt Club Rd, Ottawa, ON, K1V 1C1
(613) 733-9830
Emp Here 100
SIC 2869 Industrial organic chemicals, nec

D-U-N-S 25-091-6884   (SL)
JAZZWORKS
1234 Ridgemont Ave, Ottawa, ON, K1V 6E7
(613) 523-0316
Emp Here 75   *Sales* 4,815,406
SIC 7929 Entertainers and entertainment groups

D-U-N-S 20-578-5827   (BR)
LEON'S FURNITURE LIMITED
1718 Heron Rd, Ottawa, ON, K1V 6A1
(613) 737-3530
Emp Here 20
SIC 5712 Furniture stores

D-U-N-S 25-797-7280   (BR)
LICK'S ICE CREAM & BURGER SHOPS INC
(*Suby of* Lick's Ice Cream & Burger Shops Inc)
1788 Bank St, Ottawa, ON, K1V 7Y6

Emp Here 21
SIC 5812 Eating places

D-U-N-S 25-317-5665   (BR)
LIQUOR CONTROL BOARD OF ONTARIO, THE
L.C.B.O.
1980 Bank St, Ottawa, ON, K1V 0E8
(613) 523-7763
Emp Here 27
SIC 5921 Liquor stores

D-U-N-S 25-137-2330   (BR)
LIQUOR CONTROL BOARD OF ONTARIO, THE
LCBO OTTAWA RETAIL SERVICE CENTRE
1980 Bank St, Ottawa, ON, K1V 0E8
(613) 733-6322
Emp Here 115
SIC 5181 Beer and ale

D-U-N-S 25-784-6873   (BR)
LOBLAWS INC
LOBLAWS
2210c Bank St Suite 1188, Ottawa, ON, K1V 1J5
(613) 733-1377
Emp Here 300
SIC 5411 Grocery stores

D-U-N-S 20-790-3159   (BR)
LONG & MCQUADE LIMITED
LONG & MCQUADE MUSICAL INSTRUMENTS
2631 Alta Vista Dr, Ottawa, ON, K1V 7T5

(613) 521-1909
Emp Here 20
SIC 5099 Durable goods, nec

D-U-N-S 20-789-1433   (HQ)
LOWE-MARTIN COMPANY INC
LOWE-MARTIN GROUP, THE
400 Hunt Club Rd, Ottawa, ON, K1V 1C1
(613) 741-0962
Emp Here 290   *Emp Total* 320
Sales 37,720,682
SIC 2752 Commercial printing, lithographic
Pr Pr Ward Griffin
Tracy Griffin

D-U-N-S 20-665-9492   (BR)
LUXURY HOTELS INTERNATIONAL OF CANADA, ULC
(*Suby of* Marriott International, Inc.)
1172 Walkley Rd, Ottawa, ON, K1V 2P7
(613) 523-9600
Emp Here 25
SIC 7011 Hotels and motels

D-U-N-S 25-772-4880   (BR)
MARK'S WORK WEARHOUSE LTD
MARK'S WORK WEARHOUSE 175
2210 Bank St, Ottawa, ON, K1V 1J5
(613) 733-8648
Emp Here 25
SIC 5651 Family clothing stores

D-U-N-S 20-104-2426   (BR)
MCCORMICK RANKIN CORPORATION
1145 Hunt Club Rd Suite 300, Ottawa, ON, K1V 0Y3
(613) 736-7200
Emp Here 65
SIC 8711 Engineering services

D-U-N-S 25-129-4468   (BR)
MCDONALD'S RESTAURANTS OF CANADA LIMITED
MCDONALD'S 8571
(*Suby of* McDonald's Corporation)
1771 Walkley Rd, Ottawa, ON, K1V 1L2
(613) 733-8354
Emp Here 100
SIC 5812 Eating places

D-U-N-S 25-310-9094   (BR)
MCDONALD'S RESTAURANTS OF CANADA LIMITED
MCDONALD'S RESTAURANTS OF CANADA LIMITED
(*Suby of* McDonald's Corporation)
2380 Bank St, Ottawa, ON, K1V 8S1
(613) 526-1258
Emp Here 130
SIC 5812 Eating places

D-U-N-S 24-103-2572   (SL)
MENDES MOTORS LTD
MENDES TOYOTA SALES
1811 Bank St, Ottawa, ON, K1V 7Z6
(613) 523-8666
Emp Here 50   *Sales* 3,648,035
SIC 7538 General automotive repair shops

D-U-N-S 24-344-4952   (BR)
METRO ONTARIO INC
LOEB
2515 Bank St, Ottawa, ON, K1V 0Y4
(613) 731-7410
Emp Here 120
SIC 5411 Grocery stores

D-U-N-S 25-292-3495   (BR)
METRO ONTARIO INC
METRO
3310 Mccarthy Rd, Ottawa, ON, K1V 9S1
(613) 523-2774
Emp Here 85
SIC 5411 Grocery stores

D-U-N-S 25-676-2063   (BR)
METRO ONTARIO INC
METRO
1670 Heron Rd, Ottawa, ON, K1V 0C2

(613) 731-0066
Emp Here 94
SIC 5411 Grocery stores

D-U-N-S 25-671-9329   (BR)
MICON SPORTS LTD
PLAY IT AGAIN SPORTS
(*Suby of* Micon Sports Ltd)
1701 Bank St, Ottawa, ON, K1V 7Z4
(613) 731-6006
Emp Here 30
SIC 5941 Sporting goods and bicycle shops

D-U-N-S 24-247-7516   (BR)
OTTAWA CARLETON LIFE SKILLS INC
(*Suby of* Ottawa Carleton Life Skills Inc)
3041 Upper Otterson Pl, Ottawa, ON, K1V 7B5
(613) 523-7220
Emp Here 30
SIC 8322 Individual and family services

D-U-N-S 25-238-2973   (BR)
OTTAWA CATHOLIC DISTRICT SCHOOL BOARD
ST PATRICK INTERMEDIATE SCHOOL
(*Suby of* Ottawa Catholic District School Board)
1485 Heron Rd, Ottawa, ON, K1V 6A6
(613) 733-3736
Emp Here 50
SIC 8211 Elementary and secondary schools

D-U-N-S 20-711-6414   (BR)
OTTAWA CATHOLIC DISTRICT SCHOOL BOARD
HOLY FAMILY SCHOOL
(*Suby of* Ottawa Catholic District School Board)
245 Owl Dr, Ottawa, ON, K1V 9K3
(613) 521-0475
Emp Here 25
SIC 8211 Elementary and secondary schools

D-U-N-S 20-711-6430   (BR)
OTTAWA CATHOLIC DISTRICT SCHOOL BOARD
QUEEN OF THE ANGELS SCHOOL
(*Suby of* Ottawa Catholic District School Board)
1461 Heron Rd, Ottawa, ON, K1V 6A6
(613) 731-3237
Emp Here 30
SIC 8211 Elementary and secondary schools

D-U-N-S 25-131-4423   (BR)
OTTAWA CATHOLIC DISTRICT SCHOOL BOARD
DUNLOP PUBLIC SCHOOL
(*Suby of* Ottawa Catholic District School Board)
1310 Pebble Rd, Ottawa, ON, K1V 7R8
(613) 521-4611
Emp Here 30
SIC 8211 Elementary and secondary schools

D-U-N-S 25-238-3179   (BR)
OTTAWA CATHOLIC DISTRICT SCHOOL BOARD
PRINCE OF PEACE SCHOOL
(*Suby of* Ottawa Catholic District School Board)
1620 Heatherington Rd, Ottawa, ON, K1V 9P5
(613) 731-4733
Emp Here 25
SIC 8211 Elementary and secondary schools

D-U-N-S 20-591-4661   (BR)
OTTAWA CATHOLIC DISTRICT SCHOOL BOARD
HOLY CROSS SCHOOL
(*Suby of* Ottawa Catholic District School Board)
2820 Springland Dr, Ottawa, ON, K1V 6M4
(613) 733-5887
Emp Here 25
SIC 8211 Elementary and secondary schools

D-U-N-S 20-711-6463   (BR)
OTTAWA CATHOLIC DISTRICT SCHOOL BOARD
ST PATRICK HIGHSCHOOL
(*Suby of* Ottawa Catholic District School Board)
2525 Alta Vista Dr, Ottawa, ON, K1V 7T3
(613) 733-0501
Emp Here 50
SIC 8211 Elementary and secondary schools

D-U-N-S 20-889-2257   (SL)
OTTAWA HUNT AND GOLF CLUB, LIMITED
1 Hunt Club Rd, Ottawa, ON, K1V 1B9
(613) 736-1102
Emp Here 50   *Sales* 2,042,900
SIC 7997 Membership sports and recreation clubs

D-U-N-S 20-797-8607   (BR)
OTTAWA MOTOR SALES (1987) LIMITED
(*Suby of* Ottawa Motor Sales (1987) Limited)
1325 Johnston Rd, Ottawa, ON, K1V 8Z1
(613) 521-8370
Emp Here 70
SIC 7532 Top and body repair and paint shops

D-U-N-S 25-886-5963   (BR)
OTTAWA MOTOR SALES (1987) LIMITED
DONNELLY'S OTTAWA FORD SALES
(*Suby of* Ottawa Motor Sales (1987) Limited)
2496 Bank St, Ottawa, ON, K1V 8S2
(613) 523-5230
Emp Here 50
SIC 5511 New and used car dealers

D-U-N-S 25-504-0859   (BR)
OTTAWA-CARLETON DISTRICT SCHOOL BOARD
BROOKFIELD HIGH SCHOOL
824 Brookfield Rd, Ottawa, ON, K1V 6J3
(613) 733-0610
Emp Here 85
SIC 8211 Elementary and secondary schools

D-U-N-S 25-504-0255   (BR)
OTTAWA-CARLETON DISTRICT SCHOOL BOARD
CURRY, R. BYRNS PUBLIC SCHOOL
185 Owl Dr, Ottawa, ON, K1V 9K3

Emp Here 25
SIC 8211 Elementary and secondary schools

D-U-N-S 25-504-0263   (BR)
OTTAWA-CARLETON DISTRICT SCHOOL BOARD
RIDGEMONT HIGH SCHOOL
2597 Alta Vista Dr, Ottawa, ON, K1V 7T3
(613) 733-4860
Emp Here 100
SIC 8211 Elementary and secondary schools

D-U-N-S 25-501-6214   (BR)
OTTAWA-CARLETON DISTRICT SCHOOL BOARD
BAYVIEW PUBLIC SCHOOL
185 Owl Dr, Ottawa, ON, K1V 9K3
(613) 733-4726
Emp Here 40
SIC 8211 Elementary and secondary schools

D-U-N-S 25-504-0040   (BR)
OTTAWA-CARLETON DISTRICT SCHOOL BOARD
CLIFFORD BOWEY PUBLIC SCHOOL
1300 Kitchener Ave, Ottawa, ON, K1V 6W2
(613) 737-4401
Emp Here 65
SIC 8211 Elementary and secondary schools

D-U-N-S 25-501-6412   (BR)
OTTAWA-CARLETON DISTRICT SCHOOL BOARD
CHARLES H HULSE PUBLIC SCHOOL
2605 Alta Vista Dr, Ottawa, ON, K1V 7T3
(613) 521-8535
Emp Here 50

SIC 8211 Elementary and secondary schools

D-U-N-S 20-166-2843   (BR)
PLH AVIATION SERVICES INC
265 Leckie Pvt, Ottawa, ON, K1V 1S3
(613) 247-8722
Emp Here 23
SIC 5172 Petroleum products, nec

D-U-N-S 25-129-0748   (BR)
PATTISON, JIM INDUSTRIES LTD
PATTISON SIGN GROUP DIV OF.
2421 Holly Lane, Ottawa, ON, K1V 7P2
(613) 247-7762
Emp Here 30
SIC 3993 Signs and advertising specialties

D-U-N-S 25-542-9888   (BR)
PHARMA PLUS DRUGMARTS LTD
1670 Heron Rd, Ottawa, ON, K1V 0C2
(613) 731-8087
Emp Here 22
SIC 5912 Drug stores and proprietary stores

D-U-N-S 20-649-8503   (BR)
PITNEY BOWES OF CANADA LTD
(*Suby of* Pitney Bowes Inc.)
1145 Hunt Club Rd Suite 520, Ottawa, ON, K1V 0Y3
(613) 247-1631
Emp Here 60
SIC 5044 Office equipment

D-U-N-S 25-483-4492   (BR)
RE/MAX METRO-CITY REALTY LTD
1217 Walkley Rd, Ottawa, ON, K1V 6P9
(613) 737-7200
Emp Here 20
SIC 6531 Real estate agents and managers

D-U-N-S 25-297-7640   (BR)
SIEMENS CANADA LIMITED
SIEMENS WESTINGHOUSE
2435 Holly Ln, Ottawa, ON, K1V 7P2
(613) 737-6072
Emp Here 60
SIC 7629 Electrical repair shops

D-U-N-S 25-769-7078   (BR)
SIEMENS CANADA LIMITED
BUILDING AUTOMATION
2435 Holly Lane, Ottawa, ON, K1V 7P2
(613) 733-9781
Emp Here 110
SIC 1711 Plumbing, heating, air-conditioning

D-U-N-S 25-125-6772   (SL)
ST PATRICK'S HOME OF OTTAWA INC
2865 Riverside Dr, Ottawa, ON, K1V 8N5
(613) 731-4660
Emp Here 255   *Sales* 15,607,440
SIC 8051 Skilled nursing care facilities
VP Fin VP Fin Marilyn Willms
   Donald Burke
   Lyla Graham
   Mary Whelan
   Alberta Casey
   John Duvernet
   Linda Chapmin

D-U-N-S 25-771-0061   (BR)
STAPLES CANADA INC
STAPLES THE BUSINESS DEPOT
(*Suby of* Staples, Inc.)
2210 Bank St, Ottawa, ON, K1V 1J5
(613) 521-3030
Emp Here 60
SIC 5943 Stationery stores

D-U-N-S 25-824-5257   (BR)
STARBUCKS COFFEE CANADA, INC
(*Suby of* Starbucks Corporation)
2210 Bank St, Ottawa, ON, K1V 1J5
(613) 733-3227
Emp Here 23
SIC 5812 Eating places

D-U-N-S 24-595-6867   (BR)
SWISSPORT CANADA INC

SIC 8211 Elementary and secondary schools

SWISSPORT
130 Thad Johnson Rd, Ottawa, ON, K1V 0X1
(613) 521-4730
Emp Here 110
SIC 4581 Airports, flying fields, and services

D-U-N-S 24-937-5734   (SL)
SYNERGY PRINT AND COPY INC
400 Hunt Club Rd, Ottawa, ON, K1V 1C1
(613) 749-9382
Emp Here 100   *Sales* 9,423,290
SIC 2752 Commercial printing, lithographic
Pr Pr Ward Griffin
Dir Tracy Griffin

D-U-N-S 25-407-5468   (BR)
TOROMONT INDUSTRIES LTD
MECHRON POWER SYSTEMS
2437 Kaladar Ave, Ottawa, ON, K1V 8B9
(613) 733-3855
Emp Here 50
SIC 3621 Motors and generators

D-U-N-S 25-769-8514   (BR)
VALUE VILLAGE STORES, INC
SAVERS
(*Suby of* Savers, Inc.)
1824 Bank St, Ottawa, ON, K1V 7Y6
(613) 526-5551
Emp Here 35
SIC 5399 Miscellaneous general merchandise

D-U-N-S 25-773-7148   (BR)
WAL-MART CANADA CORP
2210 Bank St, Ottawa, ON, K1V 1J5
(613) 247-1184
Emp Here 311
SIC 5311 Department stores

D-U-N-S 24-224-5640   (BR)
WENDY'S RESTAURANTS OF CANADA INC
WENDY'S
(*Suby of* The Wendy's Company)
2456 Bank St, Ottawa, ON, K1V 8S2
(613) 738-7980
Emp Here 25
SIC 5812 Eating places

D-U-N-S 25-983-5692   (BR)
WINNERS MERCHANTS INTERNATIONAL L.P.
WINNERS
(*Suby of* The TJX Companies Inc)
2210 Bank St, Ottawa, ON, K1V 1J5
(613) 736-6588
Emp Here 60
SIC 5651 Family clothing stores

Ottawa, ON K1Y
Carleton County

D-U-N-S 24-745-7559   (SL)
ARTECH DIGITAL ENTERTAINMENT INC
ARTECH STUDIOS
6 Hamilton Ave N, Ottawa, ON, K1Y 4R1
(613) 728-4880
Emp Here 70   *Sales* 7,952,716
SIC 7371 Custom computer programming services
Dir Rick Banks
Dir Paul Butler

D-U-N-S 20-797-1164   (BR)
BANK OF MONTREAL
BMO
1247 Wellington St W, Ottawa, ON, K1Y 3A3
(613) 564-6090
Emp Here 20
SIC 6021 National commercial banks

D-U-N-S 20-589-5464   (BR)
BANQUE TORONTO-DOMINION, LA
TD CANADA TRUST
(*Suby of* Toronto-Dominion Bank, The)
1620 Scott St, Ottawa, ON, K1Y 4S7

Emp Here 20
SIC 6021 National commercial banks

D-U-N-S 24-372-4676 (SL)
BESTORA INC
18 Burnside Ave Suite 601, Ottawa, ON, K1Y 4V7

Emp Here 35 Sales 5,693,280
SIC 7311 Advertising agencies
Pr Pr Patrick Versailles

D-U-N-S 25-099-9711 (BR)
CONSEIL DES ECOLES CATHOLIQUES DE LANGUE FRANCAISE DU CENTRE-EST
ECOLE SAINT-FRANCOIS-D'ASSISE
35 Melrose Ave, Ottawa, ON, K1Y 1T8
(613) 729-1463
Emp Here 30
SIC 8211 Elementary and secondary schools

D-U-N-S 24-364-4478 (BR)
GENERAL ELECTRIC CANADA COMPANY
GE HEALTHCARE
(Suby of General Electric Company)
1053 Carling Ave, Ottawa, ON, K1Y 4E9
(613) 761-5370
Emp Here 50
SIC 3625 Relays and industrial controls

D-U-N-S 25-092-7196 (BR)
GLOBAL KNOWLEDGE NETWORK (CANADA) INC
1600 Scott St Suite 300, Ottawa, ON, K1Y 4N7
(613) 288-0451
Emp Here 49
SIC 8741 Management services

D-U-N-S 20-651-1391 (BR)
GOVERNING COUNCIL OF THE SALVATION ARMY IN CANADA, THE
GOVERNING COUNCIL OF THE SALVATION ARMY IN CANADA, THE
1156 Wellington St W Suite 613, Ottawa, ON, K1Y 2Z3
(613) 722-8025
Emp Here 250
SIC 8051 Skilled nursing care facilities

D-U-N-S 24-950-4200 (BR)
GREAT-WEST LIFE ASSURANCE COMPANY, THE
GREAT WEST LIFE
11 Holland Ave Suite 300, Ottawa, ON, K1Y 4W4
(613) 761-3940
Emp Here 60
SIC 6321 Accident and health insurance

D-U-N-S 20-275-4057 (BR)
GREAT-WEST LIFE ASSURANCE COMPANY, THE
11 Holland Ave Unit 410, Ottawa, ON, K1Y 4S1
(613) 761-3950
Emp Here 25
SIC 6311 Life insurance

D-U-N-S 25-529-8473 (BR)
HIGH ROAD COMMUNICATIONS CORP
(Suby of Omnicom Group Inc.)
11 Holland Ave Suite 715, Ottawa, ON, K1Y 4S1
(613) 236-0909
Emp Here 24
SIC 8743 Public relations services

D-U-N-S 25-495-5412 (SL)
OTTAWA HEART INSTITUTE RESEARCH CORPORATION
40 Ruskin St, Ottawa, ON, K1Y 4W7
(613) 761-5000
Emp Here 350 Sales 30,666,056
SIC 8733 Noncommercial research organizations
Marion Fraser

D-U-N-S 20-709-1989 (BR)
OTTAWA HOSPITAL, THE
OTTAWA HEALTH RESEARCH INSTITUTE
725 Parkdale Ave, Ottawa, ON, K1Y 4E9
(613) 761-4395
Emp Here 1,300
SIC 8733 Noncommercial research organizations

D-U-N-S 25-359-5532 (BR)
OTTAWA HOSPITAL, THE
OTTAWA REGIONAL CANCER CENTRE
200 Melrose Ave, Ottawa, ON, K1Y 4K7
(613) 737-7700
Emp Here 100
SIC 8069 Specialty hospitals, except psychiatric

D-U-N-S 24-455-3413 (BR)
OTTAWA HOSPITAL, THE
1053 Carling Ave Suite 119, Ottawa, ON, K1Y 4E9
(613) 722-7000
Emp Here 12,000
SIC 8062 General medical and surgical hospitals

D-U-N-S 25-504-0487 (BR)
OTTAWA-CARLETON DISTRICT SCHOOL BOARD
FISHER PARK SUMMIT SCHOOL
250 Holland Ave Suite 109, Ottawa, ON, K1Y 0Y5
(613) 729-5054
Emp Here 50
SIC 8211 Elementary and secondary schools

D-U-N-S 25-504-0081 (BR)
OTTAWA-CARLETON DISTRICT SCHOOL BOARD
CONNAUGHT PUBLIC SCHOOL
1149 Gladstone Ave, Ottawa, ON, K1Y 3H7
(613) 728-4671
Emp Here 40
SIC 8211 Elementary and secondary schools

D-U-N-S 20-590-4928 (BR)
OTTAWA-CARLETON DISTRICT SCHOOL BOARD
ELM DALE PUBLIC SCHOOL
49 Iona St, Ottawa, ON, K1Y 3L9
(613) 728-4653
Emp Here 25
SIC 8211 Elementary and secondary schools

D-U-N-S 25-248-6899 (BR)
PROVIGO DISTRIBUTION INC
LOEB ISLANDPARK
345 Carleton Ave, Ottawa, ON, K1Y 0K3
(613) 725-3065
Emp Here 60
SIC 5411 Grocery stores

D-U-N-S 20-070-2483 (BR)
ROYAL BANK OF CANADA
RBC
(Suby of Royal Bank Of Canada)
1145 Wellington St W, Ottawa, ON, K1Y 2Y9
(613) 722-8351
Emp Here 24
SIC 6021 National commercial banks

D-U-N-S 24-436-2539 (BR)
TRADER CORPORATION
AUTO TRADER
950 Gladstone Ave, Ottawa, ON, K1Y 3E6

Emp Here 30
SIC 5963 Direct selling establishments

D-U-N-S 20-288-9234 (SL)
WORKSHOPX INC
6 Hamilton Ave N Suite 004, Ottawa, ON, K1Y 4R1
(613) 860-7000
Emp Here 65 Sales 4,869,600
SIC 8731 Commercial physical research

Ottawa, ON K1Z
Carleton County

D-U-N-S 24-268-8927 (BR)
299208 ONTARIO INC
NEILSON DAIRY, DIV OF
861 Clyde Ave, Ottawa, ON, K1Z 5A4
(613) 728-1751
Emp Here 100
SIC 2026 Fluid milk

D-U-N-S 24-318-6819 (BR)
3M CANADA COMPANY
(Suby of 3M Company)
1545 Carling Ave Suite 700, Ottawa, ON, K1Z 8P9
(613) 722-2070
Emp Here 100
SIC 5065 Electronic parts and equipment, nec

D-U-N-S 20-633-8829 (BR)
ADT CANADA INC
HOME SECURITY DEALER
1600 Laperriere Ave Suite 200, Ottawa, ON, K1Z 1B7
(613) 228-6000
Emp Here 70
SIC 5072 Hardware

D-U-N-S 20-571-8831 (BR)
AVIVA CANADA INC
1545 Carling Ave, Ottawa, ON, K1Z 8P9
(416) 288-5205
Emp Here 20
SIC 8741 Management services

D-U-N-S 20-890-3315 (BR)
BMO NESBITT BURNS INC
1600 Carling Ave Suite 700, Ottawa, ON, K1Z 1B4
(613) 798-4200
Emp Here 40
SIC 6211 Security brokers and dealers

D-U-N-S 20-945-2775 (BR)
BANQUE TORONTO-DOMINION, LA
TORONTO-DOMINION BANK, THE
(Suby of Toronto-Dominion Bank, The)
1309 Carling Ave, Ottawa, ON, K1Z 7L3
(613) 728-2681
Emp Here 20
SIC 6021 National commercial banks

D-U-N-S 20-796-8269 (BR)
BUDGET CAR & TRUCK RENTALS OF OTTAWA LTD
1551 Laperriere Ave, Ottawa, ON, K1Z 7T1
(613) 729-6666
Emp Here 40
SIC 7514 Passenger car rental

D-U-N-S 25-086-6209 (SL)
BUSHTUKAH INC
203 Richmond Rd, Ottawa, ON, K1Z 6W4
(613) 232-0211
Emp Here 50 Sales 4,231,721
SIC 5941 Sporting goods and bicycle shops

D-U-N-S 24-343-1660 (BR)
CARA OPERATIONS LIMITED
SWISS CHALET
(Suby of Cara Holdings Limited)
675 Kirkwood Ave, Ottawa, ON, K1Z 8N7

Emp Here 50
SIC 5812 Eating places

D-U-N-S 24-330-0725 (BR)
CARILLION CANADA INC
CARILLION SERVICE ROH
1145 Carling Ave Suite 1317, Ottawa, ON, K1Z 7K4
(613) 722-6521
Emp Here 100
SIC 8741 Management services

D-U-N-S 24-597-4035 (HQ)

COREL CORPORATION
COREL COMPUTER
(Suby of Vector Capital Management, L.P.)
1600 Carling Ave Suite 100, Ottawa, ON, K1Z 8R7
(613) 728-8200
Emp Here 450 Emp Total 915
Sales 154,279,303
SIC 7371 Custom computer programming services
Pr Patrick Nichols
CEO Tom Berquist
Chris Debiase
VP Opers Malgosia Plucinska
Ex VP Nich Davies
VP Sls Jussi Arovaara
VP Mark Fernandes

D-U-N-S 20-700-7543 (SL)
EMBASSY WEST HOTEL
EMBASSY WEST HOTEL CONFERENCE CENTRE
1400 Carling Ave Suite 517, Ottawa, ON, K1Z 7L8
(613) 729-4321
Emp Here 60 Sales 2,626,585
SIC 7011 Hotels and motels

D-U-N-S 25-771-4014 (BR)
ESRI CANADA LIMITED
ESRI CANADA LIMITED
1600 Carling Ave Suite 430, Ottawa, ON, K1Z 1G3
(613) 234-2103
Emp Here 34
SIC 8243 Data processing schools

D-U-N-S 20-937-4979 (SL)
FRATELLI GOUP INC
FRATELLI RESTAURANTS
309 Richmond Rd, Ottawa, ON, K1Z 6X3
(613) 722-6772
Emp Here 80 Sales 2,407,703
SIC 5812 Eating places

D-U-N-S 24-364-2217 (HQ)
HDR CORPORATION
(Suby of Hdr, Inc.)
1545 Carling Ave Suite 410, Ottawa, ON, K1Z 8P9
(613) 234-7575
Emp Here 53 Emp Total 10,000
Sales 19,837,148
SIC 8712 Architectural services
Sr VP David Lewis

D-U-N-S 25-477-6537 (BR)
KANCAR COMMUNITY CHILDRENS CENTRE INC
CHILDREN'S PLACE, THE
(Suby of Kancar Community Childrens Centre Inc)
1150 Carling Ave, Ottawa, ON, K1Z 7K5
(613) 729-1222
Emp Here 30
SIC 8351 Child day care services

D-U-N-S 24-383-9011 (BR)
LOBLAWS INC
REAL CANADIAN SUPERSTORE
190 Richmond Rd Suite 1009, Ottawa, ON, K1Z 6W6
(613) 722-5890
Emp Here 200
SIC 5411 Grocery stores

D-U-N-S 20-647-1893 (BR)
MD MANAGEMENT LIMITED
MD FINANCIAL
(Suby of Canadian Medical Association)
1565 Carling Ave Suite 200, Ottawa, ON, K1Z 8R1
(613) 722-7688
Emp Here 30
SIC 6722 Management investment, open-end

D-U-N-S 25-310-7734 (BR)
MANUFACTURERS LIFE INSURANCE

COMPANY, THE
MANULIFE FINANCIAL
1525 Carling Ave Suite 600, Ottawa, ON, K1Z 8R9
(613) 724-6200
Emp Here 20
SIC 6311 Life insurance

D-U-N-S 20-785-6852   (BR)
OTTAWA CATHOLIC DISTRICT SCHOOL BOARD
ST NICHOLAS ADULT HIGH SCHOOL
(*Suby of* Ottawa Catholic District School Board)
893 Admiral Ave, Ottawa, ON, K1Z 6L6
(613) 228-8888
Emp Here 25
SIC 8211 Elementary and secondary schools

D-U-N-S 25-238-1629   (BR)
OTTAWA CATHOLIC DISTRICT SCHOOL BOARD
ST. ELIZABETH SCHOOL
(*Suby of* Ottawa Catholic District School Board)
1366 Coldrey Ave, Ottawa, ON, K1Z 7P5
(613) 728-4744
Emp Here 25
SIC 8211 Elementary and secondary schools

D-U-N-S 25-128-7827   (HQ)
OTTAWA SALUS CORPORATION
(*Suby of* Ottawa Salus Corporation)
2000 Scott St, Ottawa, ON, K1Z 6T2
(613) 729-0123
Emp Here 25   *Emp Total* 80
Sales 3,769,316
SIC 8361 Residential care

D-U-N-S 24-465-1431   (BR)
OTTAWA SALUS CORPORATION
1006 Fisher Ave, Ottawa, ON, K1Z 6P5
(613) 722-3305
Emp Here 25
SIC 8611 Business associations

D-U-N-S 25-504-0685   (BR)
OTTAWA-CARLETON DISTRICT SCHOOL BOARD
HILSON AVENUE PUBLIC SCHOOL
407 Hilson Ave, Ottawa, ON, K1Z 6B9
(613) 728-4607
Emp Here 20
SIC 8211 Elementary and secondary schools

D-U-N-S 25-504-0693   (BR)
OTTAWA-CARLETON DISTRICT SCHOOL BOARD
GOWLING, W.E. PUBLIC SCHOOL
250 Anna Ave, Ottawa, ON, K1Z 7V6
(613) 728-3537
Emp Here 40
SIC 8211 Elementary and secondary schools

D-U-N-S 24-101-0763   (BR)
SNC-LAVALIN OPERATIONS & MAINTENANCE INC
1600 Carling Ave Suite 800, Ottawa, ON, K1Z 1G3

Emp Here 100
SIC 8741 Management services

D-U-N-S 25-623-7967   (BR)
SMITH AND ANDERSEN CONSULTING ENGINEERING
1600 Carling Ave Suite 530, Ottawa, ON, K1Z 1G3
(613) 230-1186
Emp Here 25
SIC 8711 Engineering services

D-U-N-S 24-421-5229   (BR)
TECHNOLOGIES METAFORE INC
1545 Carling Ave Suite 110, Ottawa, ON, K1Z 8P9
(613) 727-0386
Emp Here 20

SIC 5734 Computer and software stores

D-U-N-S 25-773-6587   (BR)
TURPIN GROUP LTD
TURPIN PAINT & COLLISION CENTRE
(*Suby of* Turpin Group Ltd)
1615 Laperriere Ave, Ottawa, ON, K1Z 8S7
(613) 728-1908
Emp Here 50
SIC 7532 Top and body repair and paint shops

D-U-N-S 24-246-9331   (BR)
YOUTH SERVICES BUREAU OF OTTAWA
1199 Carling Ave Unit B, Ottawa, ON, K1Z 8N3
(613) 722-4802
Emp Here 75
SIC 8641 Civic and social associations

Ottawa, ON K2A
Carleton County

D-U-N-S 24-436-4733   (BR)
20 VIC MANAGEMENT INC
CARLINGWOOD SHOPPING CENTRE
2121 Carling Ave Suite 201, Ottawa, ON, K2A 1H2
(613) 725-1546
Emp Here 20
SIC 6512 Nonresidential building operators

D-U-N-S 25-401-8591   (SL)
ABILITY JANITORIAL SERVICES LIMITED
870 Campbell Ave Suite 2, Ottawa, ON, K2A 2C5

Emp Here 500   *Sales* 19,632,000
SIC 7349 Building maintenance services, nec
Pr Pr Simos Xarchos
VP VP Jim Reklitis
VP VP Gus Xarchos

D-U-N-S 25-296-4663   (BR)
BANK OF NOVA SCOTIA, THE
SCOTIABANK
2121 Carling Ave, Ottawa, ON, K2A 1S3
(613) 798-2000
Emp Here 50
SIC 6021 National commercial banks

D-U-N-S 20-588-2389   (BR)
BANQUE TORONTO-DOMINION, LA
TD CANADA TRUST
(*Suby of* Toronto-Dominion Bank, The)
1800 Carling Ave, Ottawa, ON, K2A 1E2
(613) 728-1802
Emp Here 20
SIC 6021 National commercial banks

D-U-N-S 20-791-4719   (BR)
CHILDREN'S PLACE (CANADA) LP, THE
92-2121 Carling Ave, Ottawa, ON, K2A 1S3
(613) 798-9339
Emp Here 24
SIC 5641 Children's and infants' wear stores

D-U-N-S 25-773-4731   (BR)
HOMESTEAD LAND HOLDINGS LIMITED
2001 Carling Ave, Ottawa, ON, K2A 3W5
(613) 729-4115
Emp Here 50
SIC 6513 Apartment building operators

D-U-N-S 24-112-1123   (BR)
LABOUR READY TEMPORARY SERVICES LTD
1659 Carling Ave, Ottawa, ON, K2A 1C4
(613) 829-8174
Emp Here 40
SIC 7361 Employment agencies

D-U-N-S 20-945-9564   (SL)
MKI TRAVEL AND CONFERENCE MANAGEMENT INC
SOL'EX TRAVEL/ VOYAGES SOL'EX

(*Suby of* 1437041 Ontario Inc)
2121 Carling Ave Suite 202, Ottawa, ON, K2A 1H2

Emp Here 27   *Sales* 14,135,040
SIC 4724 Travel agencies
Pr Pr Ronald Greenwood
VP VP Christopher Greenwood
  Mikael Greenwood
Recvr Paul E Salewski
Recvr Alan Herbert Page

D-U-N-S 25-775-3269   (BR)
MOUNTAIN EQUIPMENT CO-OPERATIVE
MOUNTAIN EQUIPMENT CO-OPERATIVE
366 Richmond Rd, Ottawa, ON, K2A 0E8
(613) 729-2700
Emp Here 120
SIC 5941 Sporting goods and bicycle shops

D-U-N-S 25-263-6659   (BR)
OTTAWA CATHOLIC DISTRICT SCHOOL BOARD
NOTRE DAME INTERMEDIATE SCHOOL
(*Suby of* Ottawa Catholic District School Board)
710 Broadview Ave, Ottawa, ON, K2A 2M2
(613) 722-6565
Emp Here 100
SIC 8211 Elementary and secondary schools

D-U-N-S 25-131-2955   (BR)
OTTAWA CATHOLIC DISTRICT SCHOOL BOARD
OUR LADY OF FATIMA SCHOOL
(*Suby of* Ottawa Catholic District School Board)
2135 Knightsbridge Rd, Ottawa, ON, K2A 0R3
(613) 722-4075
Emp Here 26
SIC 8211 Elementary and secondary schools

D-U-N-S 25-215-2020   (SL)
OTTAWA FAMILY CINEMA FOUNDATION
OTTAWA FAMILY CINEMA
710 Broadview Ave, Ottawa, ON, K2A 2M2
(613) 722-8218
Emp Here 50   *Sales* 4,158,760
SIC 7822 Motion picture and tape distribution

D-U-N-S 25-128-7157   (BR)
OTTAWA YOUNG MEN'S AND YOUNG WOMEN'S CHRISTIAN ASSOCIATION
YMCA-YWCA OF THE NATIONAL CAPITAL REGION
200 Lockhart Ave, Ottawa, ON, K2A 4C6

Emp Here 30
SIC 8699 Membership organizations, nec

D-U-N-S 25-504-0164   (BR)
OTTAWA-CARLETON DISTRICT SCHOOL BOARD
D. ROYKENNEDY PUBLIC SCHOOL
919 Woodroffe Ave, Ottawa, ON, K2A 3G9
(613) 728-1993
Emp Here 50
SIC 8211 Elementary and secondary schools

D-U-N-S 25-501-6495   (BR)
OTTAWA-CARLETON DISTRICT SCHOOL BOARD
CHURCHILL ALTERNATIVE SCHOOL
345 Ravenhill Ave, Ottawa, ON, K2A 0J5
(613) 722-4474
Emp Here 35
SIC 8211 Elementary and secondary schools

D-U-N-S 25-504-0776   (BR)
OTTAWA-CARLETON DISTRICT SCHOOL BOARD
WOODROFFE AVENUE PUBLIC SCHOOL
235 Woodroffe Ave, Ottawa, ON, K2A 3V3
(613) 722-6585
Emp Here 30
SIC 8211 Elementary and secondary schools

D-U-N-S 25-504-0180   (BR)

OTTAWA-CARLETON DISTRICT SCHOOL BOARD
NEPEAN HIGH SCHOOL
574 Broadview Ave, Ottawa, ON, K2A 3V8
(613) 722-6551
Emp Here 110
SIC 8211 Elementary and secondary schools

D-U-N-S 25-501-6255   (BR)
OTTAWA-CARLETON DISTRICT SCHOOL BOARD
BROADVIEW PUBLIC SCHOOL
590 Broadview Ave, Ottawa, ON, K2A 2L8
(613) 728-1721
Emp Here 80
SIC 8211 Elementary and secondary schools

D-U-N-S 20-804-0274   (BR)
PHARMA PLUS DRUGMARTS LTD
2121
2121 Carling Ave Unit 34, Ottawa, ON, K2A 1S3
(613) 722-4588
Emp Here 25
SIC 5912 Drug stores and proprietary stores

D-U-N-S 24-243-9342   (BR)
RINALDO HAIR DESIGNERS & SPA LIMITED
RINALDO'S
(*Suby of* Rinaldo Hair Designers & Spa Limited)
2121 Carling Ave Suite 24 C, Ottawa, ON, K2A 1S3
(613) 761-6800
Emp Here 20
SIC 7991 Physical fitness facilities

D-U-N-S 20-084-7304   (BR)
ROYAL BANK OF CANADA
RBC
(*Suby of* Royal Bank Of Canada)
2158 Carling Ave, Ottawa, ON, K2A 1H1
(613) 725-3145
Emp Here 24
SIC 6021 National commercial banks

D-U-N-S 20-019-6363   (BR)
ROYAL BANK OF CANADA
ROYAL BANK-CARLINGWOOD
(*Suby of* Royal Bank Of Canada)
2121 Carling Ave Suite 34, Ottawa, ON, K2A 1S3
(613) 725-3181
Emp Here 40
SIC 6021 National commercial banks

D-U-N-S 20-532-5587   (BR)
SEARS CANADA INC
SEARS CARLINGWOOD
2165 Carling Ave, Ottawa, ON, K2A 1H2
(613) 729-2561
Emp Here 30
SIC 5311 Department stores

D-U-N-S 20-860-2602   (BR)
SOURCE (BELL) ELECTRONICS INC, THE
SOURCE, THE
2121 Carling Ave, Ottawa, ON, K2A 1S3
(613) 722-6052
Emp Here 25
SIC 5999 Miscellaneous retail stores, nec

D-U-N-S 20-806-5180   (BR)
STARBUCKS COFFEE CANADA, INC
(*Suby of* Starbucks Corporation)
421 Richmond Rd Suite 101, Ottawa, ON, K2A 4H1
(613) 715-9796
Emp Here 28
SIC 5812 Eating places

D-U-N-S 20-789-6531   (SL)
SYNAGOGUE AND JEWISH COMMUNITY CENTRE OF OTTAWA
SOLOWAY JCC
21 Nadolny Sachs Pvt, Ottawa, ON, K2A 1R9

▲ Public Company   ■ Public Company Family Member   **HQ** Headquarters   **BR** Branch   **SL** Single Location

(613) 798-9818
Emp Here 60   *Sales* 3,939,878
SIC 8661 Religious organizations

D-U-N-S 20-889-5342   (HQ)
TUBMAN FUNERAL HOMES & CREMA-TION LTD
TUBMAN FUNERAL HOMES
(*Suby of* Park Lawn Corporation)
403 Richmond Rd, Ottawa, ON, K2A 0E9
(613) 722-6559
Emp Here 20   *Emp Total* 93
Sales 4,417,880
SIC 7261 Funeral service and crematories

Ottawa, ON K2B
Carleton County

D-U-N-S 20-580-1702   (BR)
CANADA POST CORPORATION
1355 Richmond Rd, Ottawa, ON, K2B 6R7
(613) 828-2672
Emp Here 20
SIC 4311 U.s. postal service

D-U-N-S 20-343-0608   (BR)
CAREFOR HEALTH & COMMUNITY SER-VICES
CARLING DAY PROGRAM
2576 Carling Ave, Ottawa, ON, K2B 7H5
(613) 721-6496
Emp Here 40
SIC 8621 Professional organizations

D-U-N-S 20-891-5566   (BR)
DESSAU INC
2625 Queensview Dr Suite 105, Ottawa, ON, K2B 8K2
(613) 226-9667
Emp Here 30
SIC 8711 Engineering services

D-U-N-S 24-111-2726   (BR)
ELLISDON INC
2680 Queensview Dr, Ottawa, ON, K2B 8J9
(613) 565-2680
Emp Here 25
SIC 8741 Management services

D-U-N-S 25-982-4589   (BR)
GOODLIFE FITNESS CENTRES INC
2655 Queensview Dr, Ottawa, ON, K2B 8K2
(613) 820-9531
Emp Here 100
SIC 7991 Physical fitness facilities

D-U-N-S 20-011-0067   (SL)
HIGHROADS CANADA INC
2650 Queensview Dr Suite 270, Ottawa, ON, K2B 8H6
(613) 234-2426
Emp Here 20   *Sales* 1,459,214
SIC 7371 Custom computer programming services

D-U-N-S 25-869-6665   (BR)
LEON'S FURNITURE LIMITED
2600 Queensview Dr, Ottawa, ON, K2B 8H6
(613) 820-6446
Emp Here 90
SIC 5712 Furniture stores

D-U-N-S 24-344-4945   (BR)
METRO ONTARIO INC
LOEB CANADA
1360 Richmond Rd, Ottawa, ON, K2B 8L4
(613) 828-4207
Emp Here 80
SIC 5141 Groceries, general line

D-U-N-S 25-772-5887   (BR)
MOORES THE SUIT PEOPLE INC
MOORES CLOTHING FOR MEN
(*Suby of* Tailored Brands, Inc.)
2525 Carling Ave, Ottawa, ON, K2B 7Z2

(613) 726-0450
Emp Here 25
SIC 5611 Men's and boys' clothing stores

D-U-N-S 25-238-1595   (BR)
OTTAWA CATHOLIC DISTRICT SCHOOL BOARD
DR F J MCDONALD CATHOLIC SCHOOL
(*Suby of* Ottawa Catholic District School Board)
2860 Ahearn Ave, Ottawa, ON, K2B 6Z9
(613) 829-3878
Emp Here 23
SIC 8211 Elementary and secondary schools

D-U-N-S 20-711-6281   (BR)
OTTAWA-CARLETON DISTRICT SCHOOL BOARD
REGINA STREET PUBLIC SCHOOL
2599 Regina St, Ottawa, ON, K2B 8B6
(613) 829-8777
Emp Here 50
SIC 8211 Elementary and secondary schools

D-U-N-S 25-504-0602   (BR)
OTTAWA-CARLETON DISTRICT SCHOOL BOARD
GRANT ALTERNATIVE SCHOOL
2720 Richmond Rd, Ottawa, ON, K2B 6S2
(613) 596-0188
Emp Here 20
SIC 8211 Elementary and secondary schools

D-U-N-S 25-263-4498   (BR)
OTTAWA-CARLETON DISTRICT SCHOOL BOARD
WOODROFFE SECONDARY HIGH SCHOOL
2410 Georgina Dr, Ottawa, ON, K2B 7M8
(613) 820-7186
Emp Here 80
SIC 8211 Elementary and secondary schools

D-U-N-S 25-504-0537   (BR)
OTTAWA-CARLETON DISTRICT SCHOOL BOARD
SEVERN AVENUE PUBLIC SCHOOL
2553 Severn Ave, Ottawa, ON, K2B 7V8
(613) 828-3039
Emp Here 35
SIC 8211 Elementary and secondary schools

D-U-N-S 24-345-7061   (BR)
REVERA LONG TERM CARE INC
CARLINGVIEW MANOR
2330 Carling Ave, Ottawa, ON, K2B 7H1
(613) 820-9328
Emp Here 400
SIC 8051 Skilled nursing care facilities

D-U-N-S 24-773-0281   (BR)
REXALL PHARMACY GROUP LTD
PHARMA PLUS 1362
(*Suby of* McKesson Corporation)
2525 Carling Ave, Ottawa, ON, K2B 7Z2
(613) 828-1119
Emp Here 20
SIC 5912 Drug stores and proprietary stores

D-U-N-S 24-862-3555   (SL)
SARAZEN REALTY LTD
COLDWELL BANKER SARAZEN REALTY BROKERAGE
1090 Ambleside Dr Suite 108, Ottawa, ON, K2B 8G7
(613) 596-4133
Emp Here 195   *Sales* 25,565,400
SIC 6531 Real estate agents and managers
Pr Pr Colin Sarazen
Terry Sarazen

D-U-N-S 24-476-1735   (BR)
WSP CANADA INC
GENIVAR
2611 Queensview Dr Suite 300, Ottawa, ON, K2B 8K2
(613) 829-2800
Emp Here 175
SIC 8711 Engineering services

D-U-N-S 24-224-5400   (BR)
WENDY'S RESTAURANTS OF CANADA INC
WENDY'S
(*Suby of* The Wendy's Company)
2545 Carling Ave, Ottawa, ON, K2B 7H6
(613) 829-4429
Emp Here 25
SIC 5812 Eating places

D-U-N-S 20-106-5989   (SL)
WORLDREACH SOFTWARE CORPORA-TION
2650 Queensview Dr Suite 250, Ottawa, ON, K2B 8H6
(613) 742-6482
Emp Here 34   *Sales* 2,699,546
SIC 7371 Custom computer programming services

Ottawa, ON K2C
Carleton County

D-U-N-S 20-610-0583   (SL)
1230172 ONTARIO INC
PARK PLACE RETIREMENT RESIDENCE
110 Central Park Dr Suite 512, Ottawa, ON, K2C 4G3
(613) 727-2773
Emp Here 55   *Sales* 4,815,406
SIC 6513 Apartment building operators

D-U-N-S 24-309-0391   (BR)
AMEX CANADA INC
AMERICAN EXPRESS
(*Suby of* American Express Company)
1840 Woodward Dr, Ottawa, ON, K2C 0P7
(613) 226-8641
Emp Here 20
SIC 6099 Functions related to deposit banking

D-U-N-S 25-649-0723   (HQ)
BISHOP HAMILTON MONTESSORI SCHOOL
BISHOP HAMILTON CHRISTIAN MONTES-SORI SCHOOL
(*Suby of* Bishop Hamilton Montessori School)
2199 Regency Terr, Ottawa, ON, K2C 1H2
(613) 596-4013
Emp Here 50   *Emp Total* 60
Sales 4,012,839
SIC 8211 Elementary and secondary schools

D-U-N-S 20-533-4639   (BR)
CH2M HILL CANADA LIMITED
(*Suby of* Ch2m Hill Companies, Ltd.)
1101 Prince Of Wales Dr Unit 330, Ottawa, ON, K2C 3W7
(613) 723-8700
Emp Here 30
SIC 8711 Engineering services

D-U-N-S 20-303-3378   (BR)
CARA OPERATIONS LIMITED
KELSEY'S
(*Suby of* Cara Holdings Limited)
1100 Baxter Rd, Ottawa, ON, K2C 4B1

Emp Here 80
SIC 5812 Eating places

D-U-N-S 24-197-1881   (BR)
CARA OPERATIONS LIMITED
MILESTONE'S GRILL & BAR
(*Suby of* Cara Holdings Limited)
1080 Baxter Rd, Ottawa, ON, K2C 4B1
(613) 721-1373
Emp Here 20
SIC 5812 Eating places

D-U-N-S 20-615-3546   (BR)
CARLSON WAGONLIT CANADA
CARLSON WAGONLIT TRAVEL
885 Meadowlands Dr Suite 401, Ottawa, ON, K2C 3N2

(613) 274-6969
Emp Here 80
SIC 4724 Travel agencies

D-U-N-S 24-121-2641   (BR)
CARLSON WAGONLIT CANADA
CARLSON WAGONLIT TRAVEL
885 Meadowlands Dr Suite 500, Ottawa, ON, K2C 3N2
(613) 274-4561
Emp Here 60
SIC 4724 Travel agencies

D-U-N-S 20-576-7569   (BR)
CARRIER ENTERPRISE CANADA, L.P.
CARRIER ENTERPRISE CANADA, L.P
1050 Baxter Rd, Ottawa, ON, K2C 3P1
(613) 820-0720
Emp Here 30
SIC 5075 Warm air heating and air conditioning

D-U-N-S 25-362-6006   (BR)
CITY OF OTTAWA
CARLETON LODGE
(*Suby of* City of Ottawa)
55 Lodge Rd Suite 1, Ottawa, ON, K2C 3H1
(613) 825-3763
Emp Here 200
SIC 8361 Residential care

D-U-N-S 24-992-8151   (HQ)
COLLIERS PROJECT LEADERS INC
2720 Iris St, Ottawa, ON, K2C 1E6
(613) 820-6610
Emp Here 31   *Emp Total* 10,035
Sales 39,690,621
SIC 8741 Management services
Pr Pr Franklin Holtforster

D-U-N-S 20-032-2332   (BR)
COMPAGNIE D'ASSURANCE BELAIR INC, LA
BELAIR DIRECT
1111 Prince Of Wales Dr Suite 200, Ottawa, ON, K2C 3T2
(613) 744-3279
Emp Here 100
SIC 6411 Insurance agents, brokers, and service

D-U-N-S 20-648-7725   (BR)
CONSEIL DES ECOLES CATHOLIQUES DE LANGUE FRANCAISE DU CENTRE-EST
1303 Fellows Rd, Ottawa, ON, K2C 2V8
(613) 820-2121
Emp Here 40
SIC 7999 Amusement and recreation, nec

D-U-N-S 20-025-0871   (BR)
CONSEIL DES ECOLES PUBLIQUES DE L'EST DE L'ONTARIO
ECOLE PUBLIQUE CHARLOTTE-LEMIEUX
2093 Bel-Air Dr, Ottawa, ON, K2C 0X2
(613) 225-1113
Emp Here 50
SIC 8211 Elementary and secondary schools

D-U-N-S 25-311-1231   (BR)
CRAWFORD & COMPANY (CANADA) INC
CRAWFORD ADJUSTERS CANADA
(*Suby of* Crawford & Company)
955 Green Valley Cres Suite 285, Ottawa, ON, K2C 3V4
(613) 233-5661
Emp Here 22
SIC 6411 Insurance agents, brokers, and service

D-U-N-S 20-575-1147   (BR)
DESLAURIER CUSTOM CABINETS INC
1050 Baxter Rd Unit 7cd, Ottawa, ON, K2C 3P1
(613) 596-5155
Emp Here 25
SIC 5712 Furniture stores

D-U-N-S 20-699-6675   (BR)
EXTENDICARE INC

EXTENDICARE MEDEX
1865 Baseline Rd, Ottawa, ON, K2C 3K6
(613) 225-5650
Emp Here 25
SIC 8051 Skilled nursing care facilities

D-U-N-S 24-437-8741   (BR)
EXTENDICARE INC
EXTENDICARE WEST END VILLA
2179 Elmira Dr, Ottawa, ON, K2C 3S1
(613) 829-3501
Emp Here 225
SIC 8051 Skilled nursing care facilities

D-U-N-S 25-128-7892   (BR)
GILMORE GLOBAL LOGISTICS SERVICES INC
GILMORE INVESTMENTS
1636 Woodward Dr, Ottawa, ON, K2C 3R8
(613) 599-5065
Emp Here 20
SIC 2752 Commercial printing, lithographic

D-U-N-S 25-852-4214   (BR)
GILMORE, R. E. INVESTMENTS CORP
GILMORE REPRODUCTIONS
1636 Woodward Dr, Ottawa, ON, K2C 3R8
(613) 727-5610
Emp Here 20
SIC 2752 Commercial printing, lithographic

D-U-N-S 20-790-0460   (BR)
GOODLIFE FITNESS CENTRES INC
1980 Baseline Rd, Ottawa, ON, K2C 0C6
(613) 226-2638
Emp Here 25
SIC 7999 Amusement and recreation, nec

D-U-N-S 25-130-6551   (BR)
GROUPE ALDO INC, LE
2685 Iris St, Ottawa, ON, K2C 3S4
(613) 820-1682
Emp Here 25
SIC 5661 Shoe stores

D-U-N-S 25-772-2025   (BR)
HTS ENGINEERING LTD
1646 Woodward Dr, Ottawa, ON, K2C 3R8
(613) 728-7400
Emp Here 40
SIC 5075 Warm air heating and air conditioning

D-U-N-S 25-749-4435   (BR)
HOME DEPOT OF CANADA INC
HOME DEPOT
(*Suby of* The Home Depot Inc)
1900 Baseline Rd, Ottawa, ON, K2C 3Z6
(613) 723-5900
Emp Here 300
SIC 5211 Lumber and other building materials

D-U-N-S 20-137-7074   (BR)
HONEYWELL LIMITED
(*Suby of* Honeywell International Inc.)
1682 Woodward Dr, Ottawa, ON, K2C 3R8
(613) 595-7611
Emp Here 30
SIC 3822 Environmental controls

D-U-N-S 20-892-3169   (BR)
KONE INC
1735 Courtwood Cres Suite 1, Ottawa, ON, K2C 3J2
(613) 225-8222
Emp Here 35
SIC 5084 Industrial machinery and equipment

D-U-N-S 24-117-0708   (BR)
LOBLAWS SUPERMARKETS LIMITED
LOBLAWS
1980 Baseline Rd, Ottawa, ON, K2C 0C6
(613) 723-3200
Emp Here 100
SIC 5411 Grocery stores

D-U-N-S 25-238-1314   (BR)
OTTAWA CATHOLIC DISTRICT SCHOOL BOARD

ST AUGUSTINE SCHOOL
(*Suby of* Ottawa Catholic District School Board)
1009 Arnot Rd, Ottawa, ON, K2C 0H5
(613) 225-8020
Emp Here 24
SIC 8211 Elementary and secondary schools

D-U-N-S 25-131-2963   (BR)
OTTAWA CATHOLIC DISTRICT SCHOOL BOARD
OUR LADY VICTORY SCHOOL
(*Suby of* Ottawa Catholic District School Board)
1175 Soderlind St, Ottawa, ON, K2C 3B3
(613) 828-5594
Emp Here 20
SIC 8211 Elementary and secondary schools

D-U-N-S 25-265-4348   (BR)
OTTAWA CATHOLIC DISTRICT SCHOOL BOARD
ST. PIUS X HIGH SCHOOL
(*Suby of* Ottawa Catholic District School Board)
1481 Fisher Ave, Ottawa, ON, K2C 1X4
(613) 225-8105
Emp Here 145
SIC 8211 Elementary and secondary schools

D-U-N-S 20-706-0430   (SL)
OTTAWA GRAPHIC SYSTEMS
GILMORE REPRODUCTIONS
1636 Woodward Dr, Ottawa, ON, K2C 3R8
(613) 727-5610
Emp Here 50   *Sales* 4,961,328
SIC 7334 Photocopying and duplicating services

D-U-N-S 25-504-0727   (BR)
OTTAWA-CARLETON DISTRICT SCHOOL BOARD
J.H. PUTMAN PUBLIC SCHOOL
2051 Bel-Air Dr, Ottawa, ON, K2C 0X2
(613) 225-4646
Emp Here 26
SIC 8211 Elementary and secondary schools

D-U-N-S 25-504-0842   (BR)
OTTAWA-CARLETON DISTRICT SCHOOL BOARD
MCGREGOR EASSON PUBLIC SCHOOL
991 Dynes Rd, Ottawa, ON, K2C 0H2
(613) 225-8033
Emp Here 25
SIC 8211 Elementary and secondary schools

D-U-N-S 25-501-6099   (BR)
OTTAWA-CARLETON DISTRICT SCHOOL BOARD
AGINCOURT ROAD PUBLIC SCHOOL
1250 Agincourt Rd, Ottawa, ON, K2C 2J2
(613) 225-2750
Emp Here 40
SIC 8211 Elementary and secondary schools

D-U-N-S 25-501-6339   (BR)
OTTAWA-CARLETON DISTRICT SCHOOL BOARD
CARLETON HEIGHTS PUBLIC SCHOOL
1660 Prince Of Wales Dr, Ottawa, ON, K2C 1P4
(613) 224-7922
Emp Here 25
SIC 8211 Elementary and secondary schools

D-U-N-S 25-504-0057   (BR)
OTTAWA-CARLETON DISTRICT SCHOOL BOARD
PINECREST PUBLIC SCHOOL
1281 Mcwatters Rd, Ottawa, ON, K2C 3E7
(613) 828-5115
Emp Here 40
SIC 8211 Elementary and secondary schools

D-U-N-S 25-070-5548   (HQ)
PEARSON CENTRE INC
PEARSON CENTRE

(*Suby of* Pearson Centre Inc)
1101 Prince Of Wales Dr Suite 135, Ottawa, ON, K2C 3W7
(613) 800-8950
Emp Here 41   *Emp Total* 85
Sales 9,459,133
SIC 8299 Schools and educational services, nec
Pr Kevin Mcgarr
  Louise Frechette
Dir Yves Gauthier
Dir David Campbell Halton
Dir Fen Osler Hampson
Dir Ewan Hare
Dir Arthur Defehr

D-U-N-S 20-139-0929   (BR)
POSTMEDIA NETWORK INC
OTTAWA CITIZEN, THE
1101 Baxter Rd, Ottawa, ON, K2C 3M4
(613) 829-9100
Emp Here 300
SIC 2711 Newspapers

D-U-N-S 24-407-2349   (BR)
SCM INSURANCE SERVICES INC
CLAIMSPRO
1737 Woodward Dr Suite 103, Ottawa, ON, K2C 0P9
(613) 798-1998
Emp Here 30
SIC 6411 Insurance agents, brokers, and service

D-U-N-S 20-300-7166   (BR)
STANTEC ARCHITECTURE LTD
1331 Clyde Ave Suite 400, Ottawa, ON, K2C 3G4
(613) 722-4420
Emp Here 275
SIC 8712 Architectural services

D-U-N-S 20-515-7725   (SL)
TRIALSTAT CORPORATION
955 Green Valley Cres Suite 280, Ottawa, ON, K2C 3V4
(613) 741-9909
Emp Here 58   *Sales* 6,201,660
SIC 7372 Prepackaged software
VP VP Peter O'blenis

D-U-N-S 25-279-4847   (SL)
UNICAD CANADA LTD
(*Suby of* Cadence Design Systems, Inc.)
2745 Iris St Suite 1, Ottawa, ON, K2C 3V5
(613) 596-9091
Emp Here 37   *Sales* 3,137,310
SIC 7371 Custom computer programming services

Ottawa, ON K2E
Carleton County

D-U-N-S 20-955-1436   (HQ)
IRONHORSE CORPORATION
IRONHORSE GROUP, THE
(*Suby of* Ironhorse Corporation)
9 Capella Crt Suite 200, Ottawa, ON, K2E 8A7
(613) 228-2813
Emp Here 600   *Emp Total* 800
Sales 51,534,000
SIC 7389 Business services, nec
Pr Pr Robin St Martin

D-U-N-S 20-120-7631   (SL)
LUMENERA CORPORATION
(*Suby of* Roper Technologies, Inc.)
7 Capella Crt, Ottawa, ON, K2E 8A7
(613) 736-4077
Emp Here 65   *Sales* 3,429,153
SIC 3861 Photographic equipment and supplies

D-U-N-S 24-380-2415   (BR)
OTTAWA CATHOLIC DISTRICT SCHOOL

BOARD
FRANK RYAN SENIOR ELEMENTARY
(*Suby of* Ottawa Catholic District School Board)
128 Chesterton Dr, Ottawa, ON, K2E 5T8
(613) 224-8833
Emp Here 45
SIC 8211 Elementary and secondary schools

D-U-N-S 24-566-1657   (SL)
OTTAWA HUMANE SOCIETY
SPA D' OTTAWA
245 West Hunt Club Rd, Ottawa, ON, K2E 1A6
(613) 725-3166
Emp Here 102   *Sales* 9,244,382
SIC 8699 Membership organizations, nec
Dir Bruce Roney

Ottawa, ON K2G
Carleton County

D-U-N-S 24-437-7214   (SL)
119155 CANADA LIMITED
DAQUIN SALES
159 Cleopatra Dr Suite 100, Ottawa, ON, K2G 5X4
(613) 226-8680
Emp Here 40   *Sales* 7,296,070
SIC 5136 Men's and boy's clothing
Pr Pr Randy Goyette
  Michael Dupuis

D-U-N-S 20-699-6204   (BR)
EXTENDICARE INC
EXTENDICARE STARWOOD
114 Starwood Rd, Ottawa, ON, K2G 3N5
(613) 224-3960
Emp Here 20
SIC 8051 Skilled nursing care facilities

D-U-N-S 25-279-4516   (BR)
LENNOX CANADA INC
HOME ENVIRONMENT CENTRE, THE
(*Suby of* Lennox Canada Inc)
1926 Merivale Rd Suite 105, Ottawa, ON, K2G 1E8
(613) 723-4700
Emp Here 40
SIC 1711 Plumbing, heating, air-conditioning

D-U-N-S 25-295-5968   (BR)
MARCH OF DIMES CANADA
117 Centrepointe Dr Suite 250, Ottawa, ON, K2G 5X3
(613) 596-3463
Emp Here 20
SIC 8331 Job training and related services

D-U-N-S 24-595-5653   (SL)
OTTAWA RESTAURANT INVESTMENTS LIMITED
CHANCES 'R' RESTAURANT
1363 Woodroffe Ave Suite B, Ottawa, ON, K2G 1V7
(613) 225-6887
Emp Here 64   *Sales* 1,896,978
SIC 5812 Eating places

D-U-N-S 20-711-6240   (BR)
OTTAWA-CARLETON DISTRICT SCHOOL BOARD
SIR GUY CARLTON SECONDARY SCHOOL
55 Centrepointe Dr, Ottawa, ON, K2G 5L4
(613) 723-5136
Emp Here 85
SIC 8211 Elementary and secondary schools

D-U-N-S 24-482-2698   (BR)
PEPSICO CANADA ULC
FRITO-LAY CANADA, DIV OF
(*Suby of* Pepsico, Inc.)
37 Enterprise Ave, Ottawa, ON, K2G 0A7
(613) 226-7301
Emp Here 65
SIC 5145 Confectionery

D-U-N-S 24-065-9297   (BR)
PLAN GROUP INC
2081 Merivale Rd Unit 100, Ottawa, ON, K2G
1G9
(613) 274-2716
Emp Here 20
SIC 4899 Communication services, nec

Ottawa, ON K2H
Carleton County

D-U-N-S 20-247-7519   (SL)
8603600 CANADA INC
MONSTER HOLLOWEEN
27 Northside Rd Unit 2710, Ottawa, ON, K2H
8S1
(613) 265-4095
Emp Here 50   *Sales* 2,772,507
SIC 5947 Gift, novelty, and souvenir shop

D-U-N-S 24-120-5900   (BR)
AECOM CANADA LTD
1150 Morrison Dr Suite 302, Ottawa, ON, K2H
8S9
(613) 820-8282
Emp Here 35
SIC 8711 Engineering services

D-U-N-S 24-850-7035   (SL)
**ALION SCIENCE AND TECHNOLOGY
(CANADA) CORPORATION**
(*Suby of* Alion Science and Technology Cor-
poration)
303 Moodie Dr, Ottawa, ON, K2H 9R4
(613) 751-2812
Emp Here 50   *Sales* 5,197,506
SIC 3731 Shipbuilding and repairing
Bahman Atefi
Barry Broadus
Sr VP Kathy Madaleno

D-U-N-S 24-119-6232   (BR)
**ALTERNA SAVINGS AND CREDIT UNION
LIMITED**
ALTERNA BANK
90k Robertson Rd, Ottawa, ON, K2H 5Z1
(613) 560-0100
Emp Here 20
SIC 6062 State credit unions

D-U-N-S 25-315-9305   (BR)
ASSANTE CAPITAL MANAGEMENT LTD
ASSANTE WEALTH MANAGEMENT
301 Moodie Dr Suite 121, Ottawa, ON, K2H
9C4
(613) 729-7526
Emp Here 20
SIC 6211 Security brokers and dealers

D-U-N-S 25-131-0181   (SL)
ATREUS SYSTEMS CORP
(*Suby of* Sonus Networks, Inc.)
1130 Morrison Dr Suite 300, Ottawa, ON, K2H
9N6

Emp Here 90   *Sales* 15,072,000
SIC 7371 Custom computer programming ser-
vices
Pr Andrea Babtiset
Ex VP Douglas Bellinger
Ronald Blair

D-U-N-S 25-408-2084   (SL)
**CADENCE DESIGN SYSTEMS (CANADA)
LTD**
(*Suby of* Cadence Design Systems, Inc.)
1130 Morrison Dr Suite 240, Ottawa, ON, K2H
9N6
(613) 828-5626
Emp Here 60   *Sales* 3,064,349
SIC 7389 Business services, nec

D-U-N-S 24-910-4951   (BR)
**CONSEIL DES ECOLES CATHOLIQUES DE
LANGUE FRANCAISE DU CENTRE-EST**

**COLLEGE SCOLAIRE CATHOLIQUE
FRANCO OUEST**
2675 Draper Ave, Ottawa, ON, K2H 7A1
(613) 820-2920
Emp Here 90
SIC 8211 Elementary and secondary schools

D-U-N-S 20-257-1972   (BR)
**GENERAL DYNAMICS LAND SYSTEMS -
CANADA CORPORATION**
*GENERAL DYNAMICS MISSION SYSTEMS-
CANADA, DIV OF*
(*Suby of* General Dynamics Corporation)
1941 Robertson Rd, Ottawa, ON, K2H 5B7
(613) 596-7222
Emp Here 1,500
SIC 3711 Motor vehicles and car bodies

D-U-N-S 24-985-0561   (BR)
GOLDER ASSOCIATES LTD
1931 Robertson Rd, Ottawa, ON, K2H 5B7
(613) 592-9600
Emp Here 160
SIC 8711 Engineering services

D-U-N-S 24-101-0958   (HQ)
LEE VALLEY TOOLS LTD
1090 Morrison Dr, Ottawa, ON, K2H 1C2
(613) 596-0350
Emp Here 500   *Emp Total* 1,000
Sales 101,524,617
SIC 5251 Hardware stores
Pr Pr Robin Lee
Ian Campbell
Lillian Lee
Leonard Lee

D-U-N-S 25-027-7852   (BR)
LOBLAWS INC
LOBLAWS
2065a Robertson Rd, Ottawa, ON, K2H 5Y9
(613) 829-9770
Emp Here 170
SIC 5141 Groceries, general line

D-U-N-S 20-787-5634   (BR)
MARSH CANADA LIMITED
(*Suby of* Marsh & McLennan Companies, Inc.)
1130 Morrison Dr Suite 280, Ottawa, ON, K2H
9N6
(613) 725-5050
Emp Here 26
SIC 6411 Insurance agents, brokers, and service

D-U-N-S 25-130-3772   (BR)
**OTTAWA CATHOLIC DISTRICT SCHOOL
BOARD**
ST PAUL CATHOLIC HIGH SCHOOL
(*Suby of* Ottawa Catholic District School
Board)
2675 Draper Ave, Ottawa, ON, K2H 7A1
(613) 820-9705
Emp Here 100
SIC 8211 Elementary and secondary schools

D-U-N-S 25-501-6453   (BR)
**OTTAWA-CARLETON DISTRICT SCHOOL
BOARD**
CHRISTIE PUBLIC SCHOOL
2625 Draper Ave, Ottawa, ON, K2H 7A1
(613) 596-8211
Emp Here 25
SIC 8211 Elementary and secondary schools

D-U-N-S 25-263-6329   (BR)
**OTTAWA-CARLETON DISTRICT SCHOOL
BOARD**
*AUBREY D MOODIE INTERMEDIATE
SCHOOL*
595 Moodie Dr, Ottawa, ON, K2H 8A8
(613) 829-4080
Emp Here 35
SIC 8211 Elementary and secondary schools

D-U-N-S 20-026-6489   (BR)
RBC DOMINION SECURITIES INC
(*Suby of* Royal Bank Of Canada)

303 Moodie Dr Ste 5500, Ottawa, ON, K2H
9R4
(613) 721-4670
Emp Here 26
SIC 6211 Security brokers and dealers

Ottawa, ON K2J
Carleton County

D-U-N-S 20-893-1550   (SL)
GOLDIE MOHR LTD
3862 Moodie Dr, Ottawa, ON, K2J 4A9
(613) 838-5042
Emp Here 50   *Sales* 4,377,642
SIC 1799 Special trade contractors, nec

D-U-N-S 25-263-6022   (BR)
**OTTAWA-CARLETON DISTRICT SCHOOL
BOARD**
BARRHAVEN PUBLIC SCHOOL
80 Larkin Dr, Ottawa, ON, K2J 1B7
(613) 825-2691
Emp Here 45
SIC 8211 Elementary and secondary schools

Ottawa, ON K2K
Carleton County

D-U-N-S 24-744-7035   (SL)
BTG INTERNATIONAL CANADA INC
11 Hines Rd Suite 200, Ottawa, ON, K2K 2X1
(613) 801-1880
Emp Here 35   *Sales* 3,137,310
SIC 3841 Surgical and medical instruments

D-U-N-S 20-288-3708   (BR)
CMC ELECTRONIQUE INC
(*Suby of* Esterline Technologies Corp)
415 Legget Dr, Ottawa, ON, K2K 2B2
(613) 592-6500
Emp Here 120
SIC 8711 Engineering services

D-U-N-S 25-098-3251   (SL)
CIENA CANADA, INC
385 Terry Fox Dr, Ottawa, ON, K2K 0L1
(613) 670-2000
Emp Here 342   *Sales* 34,510,411
SIC 3571 Electronic computers
Pr Gary Smith
Sr VP Stephen Alexander
Sr VP David Rothenstein
James Jr Moylan
Sr VP James Frodsham
Pers/VP Jane Hobbs
Sr VP Scott Mcfeely
S&M/VP Jason Phipps
Sr VP Rick Hamilton
Andrew Petrik

D-U-N-S 25-401-8302   (BR)
ESIT CANADA ENTERPRISE SERVICES CO
ESIT CANADA ENTERPRISE SERVICES CO
(*Suby of* Dxc Technology Company)
100 Herzberg Rd, Ottawa, ON, K2K 3B7
(613) 592-5111
Emp Here 325
SIC 5045 Computers, peripherals, and soft-
ware

D-U-N-S 24-708-7377   (BR)
HERJAVEC GROUP INC, THE
555 Legget Dr Suite 530, Ottawa, ON, K2K
2X3
(613) 271-2400
Emp Here 160
SIC 5045 Computers, peripherals, and software

D-U-N-S 25-263-5727   (BR)
**OTTAWA-CARLETON DISTRICT SCHOOL
BOARD**

STEPHEN LEACOCK PUBLIC SCHOOL
25 Leacock Dr, Ottawa, ON, K2K 1S2
(613) 592-2261
Emp Here 48
SIC 8211 Elementary and secondary schools

Ottawa, ON K2M
Carleton County

D-U-N-S 24-189-5239   (BR)
**OTTAWA-CARLETON DISTRICT SCHOOL
BOARD**
ROCH CARRIER ELEMENTARY SCHOOL
401 Stonehaven Dr, Ottawa, ON, K2M 3B5
(613) 254-8400
Emp Here 45
SIC 8211 Elementary and secondary schools

Ottawa, ON K2P
Carleton County

D-U-N-S 24-438-4574   (SL)
1175328 ONTARIO LIMITED
HOLIDAY INN HOTELS & SUITES OTTAWA
111 Cooper St, Ottawa, ON, K2P 2E3
(613) 238-1331
Emp Here 50   *Sales* 2,188,821
SIC 7011 Hotels and motels

D-U-N-S 25-296-5066   (BR)
BANK OF NOVA SCOTIA, THE
SCOTIABANK
186 Bank St, Ottawa, ON, K2P 1W6
(613) 564-5307
Emp Here 38
SIC 6021 National commercial banks

D-U-N-S 20-535-8950   (BR)
BANK OF MONTREAL
BMO
160 Elgin St Suite 200, Ottawa, ON, K2P 2C4
(613) 564-6037
Emp Here 20
SIC 6021 National commercial banks

D-U-N-S 20-589-4558   (BR)
BANQUE TORONTO-DOMINION, LA
TD CANADA TRUST
(*Suby of* Toronto-Dominion Bank, The)
263 Elgin St, Ottawa, ON, K2P 1L8
(613) 783-6260
Emp Here 20
SIC 6021 National commercial banks

D-U-N-S 24-892-6966   (HQ)
CANADIAN MUSEUM OF NATURE
240 Mcleod St, Ottawa, ON, K2P 2R1
(613) 566-4700
Emp Here 40   *Emp Total* 570,000
Sales 12,549,240
SIC 8412 Museums and art galleries
Ch Bd Florence Minz

D-U-N-S 25-132-3390   (SL)
**CATHOLIC IMMIGRATION CENTRE OT-
TAWA**
219 Argyle Ave Suite 500, Ottawa, ON, K2P
2H4
(613) 232-9634
Emp Here 80   *Sales* 5,275,400
SIC 8331 Job training and related services
Ex Dir Carl Nicholson

D-U-N-S 20-025-1713   (BR)
CITY OF OTTAWA
JACK PURCELL COMMUNITY CENTRE
(*Suby of* City of Ottawa)
320 Jack Purcell Lane, Ottawa, ON, K2P 2J5
(613) 564-1050
Emp Here 40
SIC 7999 Amusement and recreation, nec

D-U-N-S 24-847-4322   (HQ)
DECIMA INC
(*Suby of* Decima Inc)
160 Elgin St Suite 1800, Ottawa, ON, K2P 2P7
(613) 230-2200
Emp Here 500   *Emp Total* 1,000
Sales 191,215,680
SIC 8732 Commercial nonphysical research
VP VP Kerri Loiselle

D-U-N-S 20-316-5790   (SL)
DEVENCORE REAL ESTATE SERVICES LTD./DEVENCORE SERVICES IMMOBILIERS LTEE
150 Metcalfe St Suite 1401, Ottawa, ON, K2P 1P1
(613) 235-1330
Emp Here 20   *Sales* 2,450,055
SIC 6531 Real estate agents and managers

D-U-N-S 25-571-6250   (BR)
DISTRIBUTEL COMMUNICATIONS LIMITED
177 Nepean St Unit 300, Ottawa, ON, K2P 0B4
(613) 237-7055
Emp Here 100
SIC 4899 Communication services, nec

D-U-N-S 25-357-7472   (SL)
ELGIN STREET HOLDINGS INC
LIEUTENANT'S PUMP
361 Elgin St Unit 1, Ottawa, ON, K2P 1M7
(613) 238-2949
Emp Here 52   *Sales* 1,532,175
SIC 5812 Eating places

D-U-N-S 25-857-2577   (HQ)
ESPIAL GROUP INC
(*Suby of* Espial Group Inc)
200 Elgin St Suite 900, Ottawa, ON, K2P 1L5
(613) 230-4770
Emp Here 55   *Emp Total* 201
Sales 21,186,813
SIC 7371 Custom computer programming services
Pr Pr Jaison Dolvane
Carl Smith
Yvonne Holand
VP Sls Peter Szalay
VP Junaid Muzaffar
VP Michael Mccluskey
VP Madani Bougnounou
VP Engg Dilshan De Silva
Kirk Edwardson

D-U-N-S 20-534-5981   (BR)
FIDELITAS HOLDING COMPANY LIMITED
CARTIER PLACE SUITE HOTEL
30 Cartier St, Ottawa, ON, K2P 2E7
(613) 238-8040
Emp Here 20
SIC 7011 Hotels and motels

D-U-N-S 24-116-9940   (BR)
GOVERNMENT OF ONTARIO
MINISTRY OF COMMUNITY SAFETY AND CORRECTIONAL SERVICES
161 Elgin St Rm 3211, Ottawa, ON, K2P 2K1
(613) 239-1100
Emp Here 28
SIC 8322 Individual and family services

D-U-N-S 25-198-2989   (BR)
HICKS MORLEY HAMILTON STEWART STORIE LLP
HICKS MORLEY
150 Metcalfe St Suite 2000, Ottawa, ON, K2P 1P1
(613) 234-0336
Emp Here 20
SIC 8111 Legal services

D-U-N-S 20-137-7306   (HQ)
HULSE PLAYFAIR & MCGARRY HOLDINGS LTD
(*Suby of* Hulse Playfair & McGarry Holdings Ltd)

315 Mcleod St, Ottawa, ON, K2P 1A2
(613) 233-1143
Emp Here 20   *Emp Total* 63
Sales 4,596,524
SIC 7261 Funeral service and crematories

D-U-N-S 20-321-3103   (SL)
IT/NET-OTTAWA INC
(*Suby of* KPMG LLP)
150 Elgin St Suite 1800, Ottawa, ON, K2P 2P8
(613) 234-8638
Emp Here 30   *Sales* 2,772,507
SIC 8748 Business consulting, nec

D-U-N-S 24-523-8444   (SL)
JOYING CANADA INC
71 Somerset St W Suite 1750, Ottawa, ON, K2P 2G2
(613) 238-7743
Emp Here 100   *Sales* 11,025,249
SIC 5941 Sporting goods and bicycle shops
Pr Pr Li Zheng
Roberto Carretero
Dir Wilhelm Liedemann

D-U-N-S 20-918-8320   (BR)
KPMG LLP
(*Suby of* KPMG LLP)
160 Elgin St Suite 2000, Ottawa, ON, K2P 2P7
(613) 212-5764
Emp Here 200
SIC 8721 Accounting, auditing, and bookkeeping

D-U-N-S 24-438-4103   (SL)
MARBEK RESOURCE CONSULTANTS LTD
(*Suby of* Icf International, Inc.)
222 Somerset St W Suite 300, Ottawa, ON, K2P 2G3
(613) 523-0784
Emp Here 32   *Sales* 3,551,629
SIC 8748 Business consulting, nec

D-U-N-S 25-770-0021   (BR)
MCDONALD'S RESTAURANTS OF CANADA LIMITED
MCDONALD'S #22248
(*Suby of* McDonald's Corporation)
252 Elgin St, Ottawa, ON, K2P 1L9
(613) 236-6769
Emp Here 30
SIC 5812 Eating places

D-U-N-S 20-718-9437   (SL)
NUTRITION INTERNATIONAL
180 Elgin St 10 Fl, Ottawa, ON, K2P 2K3
(613) 782-6800
Emp Here 70   *Sales* 3,575,074
SIC 7389 Business services, nec

D-U-N-S 20-116-0145   (HQ)
OPINION SEARCH INC
(*Suby of* Decima Inc)
160 Elgin St Suite 1800, Ottawa, ON, K2P 2P7
(613) 230-9109
Emp Here 400   *Emp Total* 1,000
Sales 136,250,880
SIC 8732 Commercial nonphysical research
Pr Pr Edward Hum
VP VP Janette Niwa
VP VP Sarah Greenberg
Dir Michel Lucas
Dir Kevin Loiselle

D-U-N-S 25-504-0107   (BR)
OTTAWA-CARLETON DISTRICT SCHOOL BOARD
LISGAR COLLEGIATE INSTITUTE
29 Lisgar St, Ottawa, ON, K2P 0B9
(613) 239-2696
Emp Here 85
SIC 8211 Elementary and secondary schools

D-U-N-S 25-504-0289   (BR)
OTTAWA-CARLETON DISTRICT SCHOOL BOARD
ELGIN STREET PUBLIC SCHOOL
310 Elgin St, Ottawa, ON, K2P 1M4

(613) 239-2231
Emp Here 24
SIC 8211 Elementary and secondary schools

D-U-N-S 25-504-0560   (BR)
OTTAWA-CARLETON DISTRICT SCHOOL BOARD
GLASHAN INTERMEDIATE SCHOOL
28 Arlington Ave, Ottawa, ON, K2P 1C2
(613) 239-2264
Emp Here 33
SIC 8211 Elementary and secondary schools

D-U-N-S 24-975-0860   (BR)
RE/MAX METRO-CITY REALTY LTD
344 O'Connor St, Ottawa, ON, K2P 1W1
(613) 563-1155
Emp Here 50
SIC 6531 Real estate agents and managers

D-U-N-S 20-795-9045   (BR)
ROGERS COMMUNICATIONS INC
(*Suby of* Rogers Communications Inc)
363 Bank St Suite 359, Ottawa, ON, K2P 1X9
(613) 594-4555
Emp Here 40
SIC 4899 Communication services, nec

D-U-N-S 25-103-7222   (SL)
SOCIETE GAMMA INC
240 Bank St Suite 600, Ottawa, ON, K2P 1X4
(613) 233-4407
Emp Here 75   *Sales* 3,793,956
SIC 7389 Business services, nec

D-U-N-S 20-580-7667   (BR)
STAPLES CANADA INC
(*Suby of* Staples, Inc.)
403 Bank St, Ottawa, ON, K2P 1Y6
(613) 235-2525
Emp Here 30
SIC 5943 Stationery stores

Ottawa, ON K2R
Carleton County

D-U-N-S 25-365-2010   (BR)
LAFARGE PAVING & CONSTRUCTION (EASTERN) LIMITED
LAFARGE
998 Moodie Dr, Ottawa, ON, K2R 1H3
(613) 829-1770
Emp Here 40
SIC 1611 Highway and street construction

D-U-N-S 20-352-3345   (SL)
MOTOR WORKS ONE HOLDINGS INC
BARRHAVEN CHRYSLER DODGE JEEP RAM
510 Motor Works Pvt, Ottawa, ON, K2R 0A5
(613) 656-6526
Emp Here 40   *Sales* 14,592,140
SIC 5511 New and used car dealers
Pr Shiv Dilawri

D-U-N-S 20-352-3329   (SL)
MOTOR WORKS TWO HOLDINGS INC
BARRHAVEN MAZDA
520 Motor Works Pvt, Ottawa, ON, K2R 0A5
(613) 656-6536
Emp Here 40   *Sales* 14,592,140
SIC 5511 New and used car dealers
Pr Shiv Dilawri

Ottawa, ON K2S
Carleton County

D-U-N-S 20-262-5653   (SL)
8677018 CANADA INC
(*Suby of* Emballages GAB Ltee, Les)
140 Iber Rd, Ottawa, ON, K2S 1E9
(613) 742-6766
Emp Here 45   *Sales* 4,961,328

SIC 3086 Plastics foam products

Ottawa, ON K2T
Carleton County

D-U-N-S 20-621-9011   (SL)
O'CONNOR'S IRISH PUB
650 Kanata Ave, Ottawa, ON, K2T 1H6
(613) 270-0367
Emp Here 60   *Sales* 2,188,821
SIC 5813 Drinking places

Ottawa, ON K4A
Carleton County

D-U-N-S 24-334-3451   (BR)
CONSEIL DES ECOLES PUBLIQUES DE L'EST DE L'ONTARIO
ECOLE SECONDAIRE PUBLIQUE GISELE-LALONDE
500 Millennium Blvd, Ottawa, ON, K4A 4X3
(613) 833-0018
Emp Here 100
SIC 8211 Elementary and secondary schools

D-U-N-S 20-615-0948   (SL)
INFORMATION SCIENCE INDUSTRIES (CANADA) LIMITED
AM PRODUCTIONS
530 Lacolle Way, Ottawa, ON, K4A 0N9
(613) 745-3098
Emp Here 90   *Sales* 2,553,625
SIC 2731 Book publishing

D-U-N-S 25-317-6077   (BR)
LIQUOR CONTROL BOARD OF ONTARIO, THE
LCBO
4220 Innes Rd Unit 2, Ottawa, ON, K4A 5E6
(613) 837-5527
Emp Here 28
SIC 5921 Liquor stores

Otterville, ON N0J
Oxford County

D-U-N-S 24-938-1062   (BR)
FLEETWOOD METAL INDUSTRIES INC
71 Dover St, Otterville, ON, N0J 1R0
(519) 879-6577
Emp Here 90
SIC 3469 Metal stampings, nec

D-U-N-S 20-710-5599   (BR)
THAMES VALLEY DISTRICT SCHOOL BOARD
OTTERVILLE PUBLIC SCHOOL
318 Main St, Otterville, ON, N0J 1R0
(519) 879-1109
Emp Here 50
SIC 8211 Elementary and secondary schools

Owen Sound, ON N4K
Grey County

D-U-N-S 24-222-3167   (SL)
1638825 ONTARIO LTD
BOSTON PIZZA
1605 16th St E, Owen Sound, ON, N4K 5N3
(519) 370-2003
Emp Here 50   *Sales* 1,532,175
SIC 5812 Eating places

D-U-N-S 24-757-7885   (BR)
BDO CANADA LLP
OWEN SOUND ACCOUNTING

1717 2nd Ave E Suite 200, Owen Sound, ON, N4K 6V4
(519) 376-6110
Emp Here 36
SIC 8721 Accounting, auditing, and book-keeping

D-U-N-S 25-296-3632   (BR)
BANK OF NOVA SCOTIA, THE
SCOTIABANK
857 2nd Ave E, Owen Sound, ON, N4K 2H2
(519) 376-8480
Emp Here 50
SIC 6021 National commercial banks

D-U-N-S 24-974-3501   (BR)
BANK OF MONTREAL
BANK OF MONTREAL
899 2nd Ave E, Owen Sound, ON, N4K 2H2
(519) 376-4130
Emp Here 22
SIC 6021 National commercial banks

D-U-N-S 25-004-2272   (BR)
BANQUE TORONTO-DOMINION, LA
TD CANADA TRUST
(*Suby of* Toronto-Dominion Bank, The)
985 2nd Ave E Suite 101, Owen Sound, ON, N4K 2H5
(519) 376-2535
Emp Here 21
SIC 6021 National commercial banks

D-U-N-S 24-437-8415   (BR)
BANQUE TORONTO-DOMINION, LA
TORONTO-DOMINION BANK, THE
(*Suby of* Toronto-Dominion Bank, The)
901 2nd Ave E, Owen Sound, ON, N4K 2H5
(519) 376-6510
Emp Here 38
SIC 6021 National commercial banks

D-U-N-S 24-826-5746   (HQ)
BAYSHORE BROADCASTING CORPORATION
CFOS RADIO
(*Suby of* Bayshore Broadcasting Corporation)
270 9 St E, Owen Sound, ON, N4K 5P5
(519) 376-2030
Emp Here 40   *Emp Total* 60
Sales 3,793,956
SIC 4832 Radio broadcasting stations

D-U-N-S 24-269-8236   (BR)
BELLWYCK PACKAGING INC
BELLWYCK PACKAGING SOLUTIONS
Gd, Owen Sound, ON, N4K 5N9
(800) 265-3708
Emp Here 150
SIC 2657 Folding paperboard boxes

D-U-N-S 25-238-8954   (BR)
BLUEWATER DISTRICT SCHOOL BOARD
BAYVIEW PUBLIC SCHOOL
615 6th St E, Owen Sound, ON, N4K 1G5
(519) 376-6665
Emp Here 35
SIC 8211 Elementary and secondary schools

D-U-N-S 25-238-8624   (BR)
BLUEWATER DISTRICT SCHOOL BOARD
SYDENHAM COMMUNITY SCHOOL
1130 8th St E, Owen Sound, ON, N4K 1M7
(519) 376-2851
Emp Here 25
SIC 8211 Elementary and secondary schools

D-U-N-S 20-648-7626   (BR)
BLUEWATER DISTRICT SCHOOL BOARD
1550 8th St E, Owen Sound, ON, N4K 0A2
(519) 376-2010
Emp Here 100
SIC 8211 Elementary and secondary schools

D-U-N-S 24-391-0929   (BR)
BLUEWATER DISTRICT SCHOOL BOARD
ALEXANDRA COMMUNITY ELEMENTARY SCHOOL
1525 7th Ave E, Owen Sound, ON, N4K 2Z3

(519) 376-6306
Emp Here 25
SIC 8211 Elementary and secondary schools

D-U-N-S 20-025-1481   (BR)
BLUEWATER DISTRICT SCHOOL BOARD
HILLCREST ELEMENTARY SCHOOL
501 8th St W, Owen Sound, ON, N4K 3M8
(519) 376-1771
Emp Here 64
SIC 8211 Elementary and secondary schools

D-U-N-S 24-174-8867   (BR)
BRICK WAREHOUSE LP, THE
1125 8th St E, Owen Sound, ON, N4K 1M5
(519) 371-8061
Emp Here 20
SIC 5712 Furniture stores

D-U-N-S 20-590-7202   (BR)
BRUCE-GREY CATHOLIC DISTRICT SCHOOL BOARD
NOTRE DAME CATHOLIC SCHOOL
885 25th St E, Owen Sound, ON, N4K 6X6
(519) 371-0161
Emp Here 39
SIC 8211 Elementary and secondary schools

D-U-N-S 20-710-6662   (BR)
BRUCE-GREY CATHOLIC DISTRICT SCHOOL BOARD
ST BASIL'S CATHOLIC SCHOOL
925 9th Ave W, Owen Sound, ON, N4K 4N8
(519) 376-9370
Emp Here 30
SIC 8211 Elementary and secondary schools

D-U-N-S 25-920-9807   (BR)
BRUCE-GREY CATHOLIC DISTRICT SCHOOL BOARD
ST. MARY'S HIGH SCHOOL
555 15th St E Suite 5, Owen Sound, ON, N4K 1X2
(519) 376-4278
Emp Here 40
SIC 8211 Elementary and secondary schools

D-U-N-S 20-088-8027   (BR)
CARA OPERATIONS LIMITED
KELSEY'S RESTAURANT
(*Suby of* Cara Holdings Limited)
1350 16th St E, Owen Sound, ON, N4K 6N7
(519) 372-1992
Emp Here 40
SIC 5812 Eating places

D-U-N-S 25-923-7121   (SL)
CENTRAL PLACE RETIREMENT COMMUNITY LTD
LANDEN GROUP OF HOMES
855 3rd Ave E, Owen Sound, ON, N4K 2K6
(519) 371-1968
Emp Here 50   *Sales* 1,824,018
SIC 8361 Residential care

D-U-N-S 20-916-2101   (BR)
CHIRO FOODS LIMITED
A & W RESTAURANT
1313 16th St E, Owen Sound, ON, N4K 1Z4
(519) 371-8009
Emp Here 30
SIC 5812 Eating places

D-U-N-S 24-936-5917   (BR)
COCA-COLA REFRESHMENTS CANADA COMPANY
(*Suby of* The Coca-Cola Company)
1795 23rd St E, Owen Sound, ON, N4K 5P5
(519) 376-3593
Emp Here 20
SIC 4925 Gas production and/or distribution

D-U-N-S 20-560-2790   (BR)
CONTITECH CANADA, INC
3225 3rd Ave E, Owen Sound, ON, N4K 5N3

Emp Here 120
SIC 3714 Motor vehicle parts and accessories

D-U-N-S 24-340-2661   (BR)
FGL SPORTS LTD
SPORT CHEK HERITAGE PLACE
1350 16th St E, Owen Sound, ON, N4K 6N7
(519) 371-5114
Emp Here 30
SIC 5941 Sporting goods and bicycle shops

D-U-N-S 24-125-8805   (BR)
FIRSTCANADA ULC
FIRST STUDENT CANADA
2180 20th St E, Owen Sound, ON, N4K 5P7
(519) 376-5712
Emp Here 75
SIC 4151 School buses

D-U-N-S 24-577-2090   (BR)
FLANAGAN FOODSERVICE INC
16 East Ave Suite 2125, Owen Sound, ON, N4K 5P5
(519) 376-8407
Emp Here 40
SIC 5141 Groceries, general line

D-U-N-S 24-324-7157   (BR)
G4S CASH SOLUTIONS (CANADA) LTD
GARDA WORLD CASH SERVICES
2020 20th St E Suite 1, Owen Sound, ON, N4K 5N3
(519) 372-0299
Emp Here 25
SIC 7381 Detective and armored car services

D-U-N-S 24-077-2210   (BR)
GEORGIAN COLLEGE OF APPLIED ARTS AND TECHNOLOGY, THE
1450 8th St E Gd Lcd Main Gd Lcd Main, Owen Sound, ON, N4K 5N9
(519) 376-0840
Emp Here 70
SIC 8221 Colleges and universities

D-U-N-S 25-361-9688   (BR)
GOVERNING COUNCIL OF THE SALVATION ARMY IN CANADA, THE
GOVERNING COUNCIL OF THE SALVATION ARMY IN CANADA, THE
365 14th St W, Owen Sound, ON, N4K 3X9
(519) 376-5699
Emp Here 21
SIC 8351 Child day care services

D-U-N-S 20-787-6350   (SL)
HIRE RITE PERSONNEL LTD
366 9th St E, Owen Sound, ON, N4K 1P1
(519) 376-6662
Emp Here 95   *Sales* 2,991,389
SIC 7381 Detective and armored car services

D-U-N-S 20-107-1185   (BR)
HOME DEPOT OF CANADA INC
HOME DEPOT
(*Suby of* The Home Depot Inc)
1590 20th Ave E, Owen Sound, ON, N4K 5N3
(519) 372-3970
Emp Here 150
SIC 5251 Hardware stores

D-U-N-S 25-463-6350   (BR)
HOPEGREYBRUCE MENTAL HEALTH AND ADDICTIONS SERVICES
NEW DIRECTIONS FOR ALCHOOL, DRUGS & GAMBLING PROBLEMS
1101 2nd Ave E Suite 207, Owen Sound, ON, N4K 2J1
(519) 371-1232
Emp Here 20
SIC 8322 Individual and family services

D-U-N-S 25-174-0031   (BR)
ITW CANADA INC
HOBART FOOD EQUIPMENT GROUP (OWEN SOUND) DIV OF
(*Suby of* Illinois Tool Works Inc.)
2875 East Bay Shore Road, Owen Sound, ON, N4K 5P5
(519) 376-8886
Emp Here 200

SIC 3639 Household appliances, nec

D-U-N-S 24-412-7445   (BR)
IMPRIMERIES TRANSCONTINENTAL 2005 S.E.N.C.
RBW GRAPHICS
2049 20th St E, Owen Sound, ON, N4K 5R2
(519) 376-8330
Emp Here 600
SIC 2732 Book printing

D-U-N-S 25-315-7929   (BR)
INVESTORS GROUP FINANCIAL SERVICES INC
733 9th Ave E Suite 1, Owen Sound, ON, N4K 3E6
(519) 372-1177
Emp Here 30
SIC 8741 Management services

D-U-N-S 24-419-4606   (BR)
MARK'S WORK WEARHOUSE LTD
WORK WORLD
1605 16th St E, Owen Sound, ON, N4K 5N3
(519) 376-2677
Emp Here 25
SIC 5699 Miscellaneous apparel and accessory stores

D-U-N-S 24-248-0742   (HQ)
MC SOUND INVESTMENTS INC
MCDONALD RESTAURANT
(*Suby of* Mc Sound Investments Inc)
1015 10th St W, Owen Sound, ON, N4K 5S2
(519) 371-3363
Emp Here 60   *Emp Total* 120
Sales 3,648,035
SIC 5812 Eating places

D-U-N-S 24-974-3477   (BR)
MCINTEE , WILFRED & CO. LIMITED
733 9th Ave E Suite 3, Owen Sound, ON, N4K 3E6

Emp Here 23
SIC 6531 Real estate agents and managers

D-U-N-S 25-320-4861   (SL)
MCSOUND INVESTMENTS INC
MACDONALD'S RESTAURANT
1015 10th St W, Owen Sound, ON, N4K 5S2
(519) 371-8948
Emp Here 140   *Sales* 4,231,721
SIC 5812 Eating places

D-U-N-S 24-421-5187   (BR)
METRO ONTARIO INC
FOOD BASICS
1350 16th St E, Owen Sound, ON, N4K 6N7
(519) 376-9261
Emp Here 55
SIC 5411 Grocery stores

D-U-N-S 25-300-0731   (BR)
METRO ONTARIO INC
METRO
1070 2nd Ave E, Owen Sound, ON, N4K 2H7
(519) 371-0222
Emp Here 85
SIC 5411 Grocery stores

D-U-N-S 24-321-1302   (BR)
MILLER PAVING LIMITED
MILLER WASTE SYSTEMS
2085 20th Ave E, Owen Sound, ON, N4K 5N3
(519) 372-1855
Emp Here 20
SIC 4212 Local trucking, without storage

D-U-N-S 20-139-7734   (HQ)
OWEN SOUND LEDGEROCK LIMITED
(*Suby of* Owen Sound Ledgerock Limited)
138436 Ledgerock Rd, Owen Sound, ON, N4K 5P7
(519) 376-0366
Emp Here 70   *Emp Total* 75
Sales 4,815,406
SIC 3281 Cut stone and stone products

D-U-N-S 24-026-9746   (SL)
OWESON LTD
945 3rd Ave E Suite 212, Owen Sound, ON, N4K 2K8
(519) 376-7612
Emp Here 35   *Sales* 4,240,481
SIC 8741 Management services

D-U-N-S 20-531-1749   (BR)
PPG CANADA INC
(*Suby of* FPG Industries, Inc.)
1799 20th St E, Owen Sound, ON, N4K 2C3

Emp Here 180
SIC 3211 Flat glass

D-U-N-S 20-139-6926   (SL)
PENINSULA MOTOR SALES LTD
PENINSULA FORD LINCOLN
202392 Sunset Strip, Owen Sound, ON, N4K 5N7
(519) 376-3252
Emp Here 62   *Sales* 45,652,500
SIC 5511 New and used car dealers
Pr Pr Kelly Jennings
VP VP Brian Leggat
  Craig Beck

D-U-N-S 24-112-2030   (BR)
REHAB EXPRESS INC
(*Suby of* Rehab Express Inc)
733 9th Ave E Unit 4, Owen Sound, ON, N4K 3E6
(519) 370-2165
Emp Here 50
SIC 8049 Offices of health practitioner

D-U-N-S 20-006-6269   (BR)
REVERA LONG TERM CARE INC
1029 4th Ave W, Owen Sound, ON, N4K 4W1
(519) 376-2522
Emp Here 25
SIC 8051 Skilled nursing care facilities

D-U-N-S 24-119-3007   (BR)
REVERA LONG TERM CARE INC
SUMMIT PLACE
850 4th St E, Owen Sound, ON, N4K 6A3
(519) 376-3213
Emp Here 200
SIC 8051 Skilled nursing care facilities

D-U-N-S 25-311-1488   (BR)
SEARS CANADA INC
1350 16th St E Suite 1, Owen Sound, ON, N4K 6P9
(519) 376-8080
Emp Here 100
SIC 5311 Department stores

D-U-N-S 25-741-1777   (BR)
SOBEYS CAPITAL INCORPORATED
IGA
915 10th St W, Owen Sound, ON, N4K 5S2
(519) 376-8872
Emp Here 20
SIC 5411 Grocery stores

D-U-N-S 25-687-2284   (BR)
STAPLES CANADA INC
STAPLES THE BUSINESS DEPOT
(*Suby of* Staples, Inc.)
1077 10th St W, Owen Sound, ON, N4K 5S2
(519) 372-2228
Emp Here 30
SIC 5943 Stationery stores

D-U-N-S 25-316-8371   (BR)
SUN LIFE ASSURANCE COMPANY OF CANADA
CLARICA
1000 1st Ave W, Owen Sound, ON, N4K 4K5
(519) 376-6850
Emp Here 28
SIC 6311 Life insurance

D-U-N-S 25-861-9576   (BR)
TRANSCONTINENTAL PRINTING INC
RBW GRAPHICS

1590 20th St E, Owen Sound, ON, N4K 5R2
(519) 371-5171
Emp Here 600
SIC 2752 Commercial printing, lithographic

D-U-N-S 24-120-5892   (BR)
UNITED PARCEL SERVICE CANADA LTD
UPS
1349 2nd Ave E, Owen Sound, ON, N4K 2J5
(519) 376-3386
Emp Here 20
SIC 7389 Business services, nec

D-U-N-S 24-098-7227   (BR)
VICTORIAN ORDER OF NURSES FOR CANADA
VON GREY BRUCE DISTRICT
1280 20th St E, Owen Sound, ON, N4K 6H6
(519) 376-5895
Emp Here 150
SIC 8611 Business associations

D-U-N-S 24-860-4998   (BR)
WSP CANADA INC
GENIVAR
1450 1st Ave W Suite 101, Owen Sound, ON, N4K 6W2
(519) 376-7612
Emp Here 55
SIC 8711 Engineering services

D-U-N-S 25-946-1853   (BR)
WAL-MART CANADA CORP
WAL MART
1555 18th Ave E, Owen Sound, ON, N4K 6Y3
(519) 371-6900
Emp Here 250
SIC 5311 Department stores

Oxford Mills, ON K0G
Grenville County

D-U-N-S 20-711-5416   (BR)
UPPER CANADA DISTRICT SCHOOL BOARD, THE
OXFORD ON RIDEAU PUBLIC SCHOOL
50 Water St, Oxford Mills, ON, K0G 1S0
(613) 258-3141
Emp Here 22
SIC 8211 Elementary and secondary schools

Pain Court, ON N0P

D-U-N-S 20-711-7396   (BR)
CONSEIL SCOLAIRE DE DISTRICT DES ECOLES CATHOLIQUES DU SUD-OUEST
PAIN COURT SECONDARY SCHOOL
C.P. 70, Pain Court, ON, N0P 1Z0
(519) 352-1614
Emp Here 40
SIC 8211 Elementary and secondary schools

D-U-N-S 25-249-3234   (BR)
CONSEIL SCOLAIRE DE DISTRICT DES ECOLES CATHOLIQUES DU SUD-OUEST
ECOLE SAINTE-CATHERINE
24162 Winter Line Rd, Pain Court, ON, N0P 1Z0
(519) 354-2913
Emp Here 25
SIC 8211 Elementary and secondary schools

D-U-N-S 20-299-5846   (BR)
CONSEIL SCOLAIRE DE DISTRICT DES ECOLES CATHOLIQUES DU SUD-OUEST
SCHOOL SECONDARY CATHOLIC PAIN COURT
14 Notre Dame St, Pain Court, ON, N0P 1Z0
(519) 948-9227
Emp Here 35
SIC 8211 Elementary and secondary schools

Palgrave, ON L7E
Peel County

D-U-N-S 25-297-1429   (BR)
PEEL DISTRICT SCHOOL BOARD
PALGRAVE PUBLIC SCHOOL
(*Suby of* Peel District School Board)
8962 Patterson Sideroad, Palgrave, ON, L7E 0L2
(905) 880-0361
Emp Here 28
SIC 8211 Elementary and secondary schools

Palmerston, ON N0G
Wellington County

D-U-N-S 24-830-9049   (BR)
L & M FOOD MARKET (ONTARIO) LIMITED
150 Main W, Palmerston, ON, N0G 2P0
(519) 343-2266
Emp Here 30
SIC 5411 Grocery stores

D-U-N-S 20-816-8013   (SL)
SHANTI ENTERPRISES LIMITED
ROYAL TERRACE
600 Whites Rd Rr 3, Palmerston, ON, N0G 2P0
(519) 343-2611
Emp Here 80   *Sales* 3,648,035
SIC 8051 Skilled nursing care facilities

D-U-N-S 20-024-9477   (BR)
UPPER GRAND DISTRICT SCHOOL BOARD, THE
PALMERSTON PUBLIC SCHOOL
(*Suby of* Upper Grand District School Board, The)
530 Prospect St, Palmerston, ON, N0G 2P0
(519) 343-3520
Emp Here 35
SIC 8211 Elementary and secondary schools

D-U-N-S 20-024-9501   (BR)
UPPER GRAND DISTRICT SCHOOL BOARD, THE
NORWELL DISTRICT SECONDARY SCHOOL
(*Suby of* Upper Grand District School Board, The)
Po Box 160, Palmerston, ON, N0G 2P0
(519) 343-3107
Emp Here 80
SIC 8211 Elementary and secondary schools

Paris, ON N3L
Brant County

D-U-N-S 25-869-0783   (SL)
BEAUMAC MANAGEMENT LIMITED
MCDONALD'S RESTAURANTS
307 Grand River St N, Paris, ON, N3L 2N9
(519) 442-5964
Emp Here 55   *Sales* 1,678,096
SIC 5812 Eating places

D-U-N-S 20-125-9491   (BR)
BERRY, DON HOLDINGS INC
TIM HORTONS
(*Suby of* Berry, Don Holdings Inc)
194 Grand River St N, Paris, ON, N3L 2N3

Emp Here 49
SIC 5461 Retail bakeries

D-U-N-S 20-710-6365   (BR)
BRANT HALDIMAND NORFOLK CATHOLIC DISTRICT SCHOOL BOARD
HOLY FAMILY SCHOOL
20 Sunset Dr, Paris, ON, N3L 3W4

(519) 442-5333
Emp Here 20
SIC 8211 Elementary and secondary schools

D-U-N-S 24-571-4030   (SL)
CALENDAR CLUB OF CANADA LIMITED PARTNERSHIP
CALENDAR CLUB OF CANADA
6 Adams St Suite A, Paris, ON, N3L 3X4
(519) 442-8355
Emp Here 50   *Sales* 4,417,880
SIC 5945 Hobby, toy, and game shops

D-U-N-S 24-560-4582   (SL)
DARBY SPORTSWEAR CO. LTD
100 Dundas St E, Paris, ON, N3L 3H6
(519) 442-4423
Emp Here 60   *Sales* 2,334,742
SIC 2329 Men's and boy's clothing, nec

D-U-N-S 24-767-9694   (BR)
FIRSTCANADA ULC
FIRST STUDENT CANADA
829 Rest Acres Rd, Paris, ON, N3L 3E3
(519) 442-2258
Emp Here 134
SIC 4142 Bus charter service, except local

D-U-N-S 20-710-6217   (BR)
GRAND ERIE DISTRICT SCHOOL BOARD
PARIS CENTRAL SCHOOL
(*Suby of* Grand Erie District School Board)
7 Broadway St E, Paris, ON, N3L 2R2
(519) 442-4163
Emp Here 20
SIC 8211 Elementary and secondary schools

D-U-N-S 20-710-6142   (BR)
GRAND ERIE DISTRICT SCHOOL BOARD
NORTH WARD PUBLIC SCHOOL
(*Suby of* Grand Erie District School Board)
107 Silver St, Paris, ON, N3L 1V2
(519) 442-2311
Emp Here 40
SIC 8211 Elementary and secondary schools

D-U-N-S 20-738-6553   (BR)
PHARMA PLUS DRUGMARTS LTD
72 Grand River St N, Paris, ON, N3L 2M2
(519) 442-2203
Emp Here 20
SIC 5912 Drug stores and proprietary stores

D-U-N-S 20-266-8310   (BR)
PRAXAIR CANADA INC
(*Suby of* Praxair, Inc.)
15 Consolidated Dr, Paris, ON, N3L 3G2
(519) 442-6373
Emp Here 50
SIC 2813 Industrial gases

D-U-N-S 20-733-2532   (BR)
SOBEYS CAPITAL INCORPORATED
307 Grand River St N, Paris, ON, N3L 2N9
(519) 442-4485
Emp Here 250
SIC 5411 Grocery stores

Parkhill, ON N0M
Middlesex County

D-U-N-S 24-000-2688   (BR)
B & C DALLNER HOLDINGS INC
TIM HORTONS
2227 Elginfield Rd Rr 5, Parkhill, ON, N0M 2K0
(519) 294-1052
Emp Here 25
SIC 5812 Eating places

D-U-N-S 20-738-6306   (SL)
CSH CHATEAU GARDENS PARKHILL INC
250 Tain St Rr 3, Parkhill, ON, N0M 2K0
(519) 294-6342
Emp Here 49   *Sales* 1,824,018
SIC 8361 Residential care

D-U-N-S 25-249-0636   (BR)
THAMES VALLEY DISTRICT SCHOOL BOARD
PARKHILL-WEST WILLIAMS PUBLIC SCHOOL
204 Mcleod St, Parkhill, ON, N0M 2K0
(519) 294-1117
Emp Here 25
SIC 8211 Elementary and secondary schools

D-U-N-S 25-249-3549   (BR)
THAMES VALLEY DISTRICT SCHOOL BOARD
NORTH MIDDLESEX DISTRICT HIGH SCHOOL
100 Main St, Parkhill, ON, N0M 2K0
(519) 294-1128
Emp Here 35
SIC 8211 Elementary and secondary schools

Parry Sound, ON P2A
Parry Sound County

D-U-N-S 24-253-1130   (SL)
DON CHERRY'S SPORTS GRILL INC
DON CHERRY'S
72 James St, Parry Sound, ON, P2A 1T5
(705) 746-1270
Emp Here 60   *Sales* 2,536,250
SIC 5812 Eating places

D-U-N-S 20-912-9381   (SL)
G & B MCNABB LUMBER COMPANY LIMITED
G & B BUILDING CENTRE
22 Seguin St, Parry Sound, ON, P2A 1B1
(705) 746-5825
Emp Here 50   *Sales* 4,304,681
SIC 3429 Hardware, nec

D-U-N-S 20-528-6631   (SL)
GIBSON'S, TIM HOLDINGS PARRY SOUND LTD
1 Mall Dr, Parry Sound, ON, P2A 3A9
(705) 746-8467
Emp Here 100   *Sales* 2,991,389
SIC 5812 Eating places

D-U-N-S 20-216-7867   (BR)
HAMMOND TRANSPORTATION LIMITED
(*Suby of* Hammond Transportation Limited)
6 Mill Lake Rd, Parry Sound, ON, P2A 2X9
(705) 746-5430
Emp Here 45
SIC 4142 Bus charter service, except local

D-U-N-S 20-004-1887   (BR)
KPMG INC
84 James St, Parry Sound, ON, P2A 1T9
(705) 746-9346
Emp Here 280
SIC 8741 Management services

D-U-N-S 25-605-0642   (BR)
MUSKOKA-PARRY SOUND COMMUNITY MENTAL HEALTH SERVICES
(*Suby of* Muskoka-Parry Sound Community Mental Health Services)
26 James St Suite 3, Parry Sound, ON, P2A 1T5
(705) 746-4264
Emp Here 20
SIC 8049 Offices of health practitioner

D-U-N-S 20-024-9311   (BR)
NEAR NORTH DISTRICT SCHOOL BOARD
VICTORY PUBLIC SCHOOL
15 Forest St, Parry Sound, ON, P2A 2R1
(705) 746-5691
Emp Here 25
SIC 8211 Elementary and secondary schools

D-U-N-S 20-710-4402   (BR)
NEAR NORTH DISTRICT SCHOOL BOARD
WILLIAM BEATTY PUBLIC SCHOOL

82 Gibson St, Parry Sound, ON, P2A 1X5
(705) 746-9333
Emp Here 40
SIC 8211 Elementary and secondary schools

D-U-N-S 20-710-4360   (BR)
NEAR NORTH DISTRICT SCHOOL BOARD
HUMPHREY PUBLIC SCHOOL
141 Bon Echo Rd, Parry Sound, ON, P2A 2W8
(705) 746-0511
Emp Here 25
SIC 8211 Elementary and secondary schools

D-U-N-S 20-862-1818   (BR)
NORTHERN REFLECTIONS LTD
70 Joseph St Unit 301, Parry Sound, ON, P2A 2G5
(705) 746-4248
Emp Here 25
SIC 5621 Women's clothing stores

D-U-N-S 20-519-4280   (BR)
SHAW-ALMEX INDUSTRIES LIMITED
17 Shaw Almex Dr, Parry Sound, ON, P2A 2X4
(705) 746-5884
Emp Here 75
SIC 3535 Conveyors and conveying equipment

D-U-N-S 20-591-8845   (BR)
SIMCOE MUSKOKA CATHOLIC DISTRICT SCHOOL BOARD
ST PETER THE APOSTLE SCHOOL
(*Suby of* Simcoe Muskoka Catholic District Schoo Board)
134 William St Unit A, Parry Sound, ON, P2A 1W2
(705) 746-7196
Emp Here 20
SIC 8211 Elementary and secondary schools

D-U-N-S 20-806-2567   (BR)
SOBEYS CAPITAL INCORPORATED
SOBEYS STORE
25 Pine Dr, Parry Sound, ON, P2A 3B7
(705) 746-4809
Emp Here 25
SIC 5411 Grocery stores

D-U-N-S 24-317-1852   (BR)
WAL-MART CANADA CORP
WALMART
1 Pine Dr, Parry Sound, ON, P2A 3C3
(705) 746-1573
Emp Here 130
SIC 5311 Department stores

D-U-N-S 25-305-3250   (BR)
WESTMONT HOSPITALITY MANAGEMENT LIMITED
COMFORT INN, THE
(*Suby of* Westmont Hospitality Management Limited)
120 Bowes St, Parry Sound, ON, P2A 2L7
(705) 746-6221
Emp Here 21
SIC 7011 Hotels and motels

D-U-N-S 25-746-2242   (BR)
YOUNG WOMEN'S CHRISTIAN ASSOCIATION OF GREATER TORONTO
CAMP TAPAWINGO
Gd, Parry Sound, ON, P2A 2X1
(705) 746-5455
Emp Here 35
SIC 7032 Sporting and recreational camps

Pefferlaw, ON L0E
York County

D-U-N-S 25-293-6141   (BR)
YORK REGION DISTRICT SCHOOL BOARD
MORNING GLORY PUBLIC SCHOOL
(*Suby of* York Region District School Board)

29478 48 Hwy, Pefferlaw, ON, L0E 1N0
(705) 437-1537
Emp Here 50
SIC 8211 Elementary and secondary schools

Pembroke, ON K8A
Renfrew County

D-U-N-S 25-486-4762   (SL)
1048271 ONTARIO INC
MONCION GROCERS RIVERSIDE MARKET
1200 Pembroke St W, Pembroke, ON, K8A 7T1
(613) 735-5335
Emp Here 65   *Sales* 8,390,481
SIC 5411 Grocery stores
Pr Pr Pierre Moncion
  Colleen Moncion

D-U-N-S 25-664-4832   (SL)
1213874 ONTARIO INC
EASTSIDE MARIO'S
100 Pembroke St E, Pembroke, ON, K8A 8A3
(613) 732-9955
Emp Here 50   *Sales* 1,532,175
SIC 5812 Eating places

D-U-N-S 20-514-5878   (BR)
1555314 ONTARIO INC
EASTWAY
100 Crandall St Suite 100, Pembroke, ON, K8A 6X8
(613) 735-4593
Emp Here 20
SIC 7532 Top and body repair and paint shops

D-U-N-S 24-383-5519   (SL)
506555 ONTARIO LIMITED
EDWARDS MAZDA
1356 Pembroke St E, Pembroke, ON, K8A 6W2
(613) 735-0166
Emp Here 23   *Sales* 12,681,250
SIC 5511 New and used car dealers
Pr Pr Edward John Poirier

D-U-N-S 20-251-5503   (BR)
ACCESS HEALTHCARE SERVICES INC
458 Pembroke St E, Pembroke, ON, K8A 3L2
(613) 732-4713
Emp Here 55
SIC 8082 Home health care services

D-U-N-S 24-889-6953   (BR)
BANK OF NOVA SCOTIA, THE
SCOTIABANK
81 Pembroke St W, Pembroke, ON, K8A 5M7
(613) 732-2826
Emp Here 35
SIC 6021 National commercial banks

D-U-N-S 24-270-5804   (BR)
BELL MEDIA INC
NEW RO, THE
611 Tv Tower Rd, Pembroke, ON, K8A 6Y6

Emp Here 40
SIC 4833 Television broadcasting stations

D-U-N-S 24-269-6201   (HQ)
BUTLER CHEVROLET PONTIAC BUICK CADILLAC LTD
(*Suby of* C B Holdings Ltd)
1370 Pembroke St W, Pembroke, ON, K8A 7M3
(613) 735-3147
Emp Here 43   *Emp Total* 70
Sales 25,536,245
SIC 5511 New and used car dealers
Pr Pr Charles Butler
  Charlotte Macintosh

D-U-N-S 20-530-1034   (BR)
CANADA POST CORPORATION
162 Pembroke St W, Pembroke, ON, K8A 5M8

(613) 732-2411
Emp Here 50
SIC 4311 U.s. postal service

D-U-N-S 24-567-5892   (BR)
CARA OPERATIONS LIMITED
HARVEY'S
(*Suby of* Cara Holdings Limited)
1290 Pembroke St W, Pembroke, ON, K8A 7A2
(613) 735-3279
Emp Here 20
SIC 5812 Eating places

D-U-N-S 24-341-0573   (BR)
CAREFOR HEALTH & COMMUNITY SERVICES
CAREFOR HEALTH AND COMMUNITY SERVICES
425 Cecelia St, Pembroke, ON, K8A 1S7
(613) 732-9993
Emp Here 100
SIC 8082 Home health care services

D-U-N-S 24-310-6858   (BR)
CHAMPLAIN COMMUNITY CARE ACCESS CENTRE
1100 Pembroke St E, Pembroke, ON, K8A 6Y7
(613) 732-7007
Emp Here 50
SIC 8082 Home health care services

D-U-N-S 24-776-6822   (BR)
CHARTWELL MASTER CARE LP
1022 Pembroke St E, Pembroke, ON, K8A 8A7
(613) 735-4056
Emp Here 30
SIC 8322 Individual and family services

D-U-N-S 20-809-0980   (BR)
CHILDREN'S AID SOCIETY OF THE COUNTY OF RENFREW
77 Mary St, Pembroke, ON, K8A 5V4
(613) 735-6866
Emp Here 20
SIC 8322 Individual and family services

D-U-N-S 25-027-7605   (BR)
CHILDREN'S AID SOCIETY OF TORONTO
FAMILY AND CHILDREN'S SERVICES
77 Mary St Suite 100, Pembroke, ON, K8A 5V4
(613) 735-6866
Emp Here 200
SIC 8322 Individual and family services

D-U-N-S 24-984-8508   (BR)
COMPAGNIE COMMONWEALTH PLYWOOD LTEE, LA
794 River Rd, Pembroke, ON, K8A 6X7
(613) 735-6801
Emp Here 30
SIC 2435 Hardwood veneer and plywood

D-U-N-S 25-302-0929   (BR)
CONSEIL DES ECOLES CATHOLIQUES DE LANGUE FRANCAISE DU CENTRE-EST
CENTRE SCOLAIRE SEC JEANNE LAJOIE
1257 Pembroke St W, Pembroke, ON, K8A 8T1
(613) 735-3948
Emp Here 45
SIC 8211 Elementary and secondary schools

D-U-N-S 25-224-8125   (BR)
CONSEIL DES ECOLES CATHOLIQUES DE LANGUE FRANCAISE DU CENTRE-EST
ECOLE SAINT-JEAN-BAPTISTE
464 Isabella St, Pembroke, ON, K8A 5T9
(613) 732-8302
Emp Here 25
SIC 8211 Elementary and secondary schools

D-U-N-S 20-653-4385   (BR)
CONSEIL DES ECOLES PUBLIQUES DE L'EST DE L'ONTARIO
SECONDAIRE PUBLIQUE L' QUINOXE

▲ Public Company   ■ Public Company Family Member   **HQ** Headquarters   **BR** Branch   **SL** Single Location

412 Pembroke St W, Pembroke, ON, K8A 5N6
(613) 732-1525
Emp Here 40
SIC 8211 Elementary and secondary schools

D-U-N-S 20-573-6254   (BR)
ESIT CANADA ENTERPRISE SERVICES CO
ESIT CANADA ENTERPRISE SERVICES CO
(*Suby of* Dxc Technology Company)
235 Pembroke St E, Pembroke, ON, K8A 3J8

Emp Here 20
SIC 5734 Computer and software stores

D-U-N-S 25-301-3080   (BR)
EXTENDICARE (CANADA) INC
PARAMED HOME HEALTH CARE
595 Pembroke St E, Pembroke, ON, K8A 3L7
(613) 735-4165
Emp Here 150
SIC 8059 Nursing and personal care, nec

D-U-N-S 24-337-3300   (BR)
FGL SPORTS LTD
SPORT-CHEK PEMBROKE MALL
1100 Pembroke St E Unit 503, Pembroke, ON,
K8A 6Y7
(613) 735-3016
Emp Here 30
SIC 5941 Sporting goods and bicycle shops

D-U-N-S 24-102-0098   (SL)
**GREY SISTERS OF THE IMMACULATE
CONCEPTION**
700 Mackay St, Pembroke, ON, K8A 1G6
(613) 735-4111
Emp Here 58   *Sales* 3,793,956
SIC 8661 Religious organizations

D-U-N-S 20-639-5373   (SL)
HCN LESSEY (PEMBROKE) LP
PEMBROKE HERITAGE MANOR
1111 Pembroke St W Suite 238, Pembroke,
ON, K8A 8P6
(613) 635-7926
Emp Here 50   *Sales* 2,188,821
SIC 8361 Residential care

D-U-N-S 24-426-7055   (BR)
HGS CANADA INC
ONLINE SUPPORT
100 Crandall St Suite 100, Pembroke, ON,
K8A 6X8
(613) 633-4600
Emp Here 455
SIC 7379 Computer related services, nec

D-U-N-S 24-361-7268   (BR)
HOME DEPOT OF CANADA INC
HOME DEPOT
(*Suby of* The Home Depot Inc)
27 Robinson Lane, Pembroke, ON, K8A 0A5
(613) 732-6550
Emp Here 100
SIC 5251 Hardware stores

D-U-N-S 20-366-1087   (SL)
KI CANADA CORPORATION
1000 Olympic Drive, Pembroke, ON, K8A 0E1
(613) 735-5566
Emp Here 200   *Sales* 14,592,140
SIC 2514 Metal household furniture
Pr Pr Richard Resch
   Michael Pum
   Kelly J. Andersen

D-U-N-S 24-925-2834   (SL)
KI PEMBROKE LP
KICI
1000 Olympic Dr, Pembroke, ON, K8A 0E1
(613) 735-5566
Emp Here 310   *Sales* 57,345,816
SIC 2522 Office furniture, except wood

D-U-N-S 24-381-6621   (SL)
KRUEGER PEMBROKE LP
1000 Olympic Dr, Pembroke, ON, K8A 0E1

Emp Here 275   *Sales* 57,619,920

SIC 2522 Office furniture, except wood
Fin Ex Rudy Witlox

D-U-N-S 25-365-4404   (BR)
LEHIGH HANSON MATERIALS LIMITED
ESSROC-ITALCEMENTI GROUP
2065a Petawawa Blvd, Pembroke, ON, K8A
7G8
(613) 741-1212
Emp Here 20
SIC 3241 Cement, hydraulic

D-U-N-S 25-292-3370   (BR)
METRO ONTARIO INC
FOOD BASICS
1100 Pembroke St E Suite 891, Pembroke,
ON, K8A 6Y7
(613) 735-1846
Emp Here 80
SIC 5411 Grocery stores

D-U-N-S 20-859-8925   (BR)
PACIFIC LINK COMMUNICATIONS INC
BELL WORLD
1018 Pembroke St E, Pembroke, ON, K8A
3M2
(613) 732-2825
Emp Here 25
SIC 5999 Miscellaneous retail stores, nec

D-U-N-S 20-711-7024   (BR)
**RENFREW COUNTY CATHOLIC DISTRICT
SCHOOL BOARD**
BISHOP SMITH ALTERNATE SCHOOL
(*Suby of* Renfrew County Catholic District
School Board)
222 Church St, Pembroke, ON, K8A 4K9

Emp Here 25
SIC 8211 Elementary and secondary schools

D-U-N-S 20-026-6687   (HQ)
**RENFREW COUNTY CATHOLIC DISTRICT
SCHOOL BOARD**
(*Suby of* Renfrew County Catholic District
School Board)
499 Pembroke St W, Pembroke, ON, K8A 5P1
(613) 735-1031
Emp Here 100   *Emp Total* 500
Sales 58,343,672
SIC 8211 Elementary and secondary schools
Superintnt Michele Arbour
   Mary Lynn Schauer
   Bob Schreader
   Judy Ellis
   Andrew Bray
   David Howard
   Marlene Borutski
   Bob Michaud
   Anne Smith
   Ashley Stroud

D-U-N-S 20-891-5350   (BR)
**RENFREW COUNTY CATHOLIC DISTRICT
SCHOOL BOARD**
MARY STREET EDUCATION CENTRE
(*Suby of* Renfrew County Catholic District
School Board)
1270 Pembroke St W, Pembroke, ON, K8A
4G4
(613) 735-0151
Emp Here 50
SIC 8211 Elementary and secondary schools

D-U-N-S 20-711-6877   (BR)
**RENFREW COUNTY CATHOLIC DISTRICT
SCHOOL BOARD**
HOLY NAME SCHOOL
(*Suby of* Renfrew County Catholic District
School Board)
299 First Ave, Pembroke, ON, K8A 5C3
(613) 732-2248
Emp Here 35
SIC 8211 Elementary and secondary schools

D-U-N-S 20-711-6802   (BR)
**RENFREW COUNTY DISTRICT SCHOOL
BOARD**

HIGHVIEW PUBLIC SCHOOL
320 Herbert St, Pembroke, ON, K8A 2Y4
(613) 732-8761
Emp Here 60
SIC 8211 Elementary and secondary schools

D-U-N-S 20-590-8572   (BR)
**RENFREW COUNTY DISTRICT SCHOOL
BOARD**
FELLOWES HIGH SCHOOL
420 Bell St, Pembroke, ON, K8A 2K5
(613) 735-6858
Emp Here 125
SIC 8211 Elementary and secondary schools

D-U-N-S 25-238-6479   (BR)
**RENFREW COUNTY DISTRICT SCHOOL
BOARD**
LAURENTIAN ELEMENTARY SCHOOL
412 Pembroke St W, Pembroke, ON, K8A 5N6
(613) 732-9401
Emp Here 40
SIC 8211 Elementary and secondary schools

D-U-N-S 20-227-2071   (BR)
**RENFREW COUNTY DISTRICT SCHOOL
BOARD**
CONTINUING & COMMUNITY EDUCATION
480 Mary St, Pembroke, ON, K8A 5W9
(613) 732-8105
Emp Here 23
SIC 8211 Elementary and secondary schools

D-U-N-S 25-486-3996   (BR)
**RENFREW COUNTY DISTRICT SCHOOL
BOARD**
CHAMPLAIN DISCOVERY PUBLIC SCHOOL
390 Bell St, Pembroke, ON, K8A 2K5
(613) 735-6575
Emp Here 60
SIC 8211 Elementary and secondary schools

D-U-N-S 25-238-6446   (BR)
**RENFREW COUNTY DISTRICT SCHOOL
BOARD**
ROCKWOOD PUBLIC SCHOOL
11588 Round Lake Rd, Pembroke, ON, K8A
0K8
(613) 732-3789
Emp Here 30
SIC 8211 Elementary and secondary schools

D-U-N-S 24-847-0379   (SL)
SRB TECHNOLOGIES (CANADA) INC
320 Boundary Rd E Suite 140, Pembroke, ON,
K8A 6W5
(613) 732-0055
Emp Here 42   *Sales* 2,553,625
SIC 3993 Signs and advertising specialties

D-U-N-S 20-545-1441   (BR)
STAPLES CANADA INC
STAPLES 233
(*Suby of* Staples, Inc.)
1100 Pembroke St E Suite 100, Pembroke,
ON, K8A 6Y7
(613) 735-0437
Emp Here 30
SIC 5943 Stationery stores

D-U-N-S 20-077-1702   (BR)
WAL-MART CANADA CORP
WAL MART
1108 Pembroke St E, Pembroke, ON, K8A
8P7
(613) 735-4997
Emp Here 200
SIC 5311 Department stores

───────────────────────

Pembroke, ON K8B
Renfrew County

D-U-N-S 24-104-6184   (BR)
PUROLATOR INC.
PUROLATOR INC

980 Cecelia St, Pembroke, ON, K8B 1A7
(888) 744-7123
Emp Here 26
SIC 7389 Business services, nec

───────────────────────

Penetanguishene, ON L9M
Simcoe County

D-U-N-S 24-544-5911   (SL)
1711085 ONTARIO INC
BEACON BAY MARINA
37 Champlain Rd Suite 1, Penetanguishene,
ON, L9M 1S1
(705) 549-2075
Emp Here 25   *Sales* 1,532,175
SIC 3732 Boatbuilding and repairing

D-U-N-S 25-311-9952   (SL)
**ASSOCIATION CANADIENNE-FRANCAISE
DE L'ONTARIO/HURONIE**
ACFO-HURONIE
(*Suby of* La Cle d'la Baie en Huronie- Associ-
ation Culturelle Francophone)
63 Main St, Penetanguishene, ON, L9M 1S8
(705) 549-3116
Emp Here 60   *Sales* 12,961,920
SIC 8399 Social services, nec
Pr Claudette Paquim
Genl Mgr Pierre Casaulc
Treas Lionel Gignac

D-U-N-S 25-239-5801   (BR)
**CONSEIL   SCOLAIRE   DE   DISTRICT
CATHOLIQUE CENTRE-SUD**
ECOLE SAINT LOUIS
54 Dufferin St, Penetanguishene, ON, L9M
1H4
(705) 549-3677
Emp Here 28
SIC 8211 Elementary and secondary schools

D-U-N-S 20-026-8154   (BR)
CONSEIL SCOLAIRE VIAMONDE
ECOLE SECONDAIRE LE CARON
22 John St, Penetanguishene, ON, L9M 1N8
(705) 549-3202
Emp Here 30
SIC 8211 Elementary and secondary schools

D-U-N-S 20-267-9841   (BR)
MAGNA CLOSURES INC
TECHFORM
11 Centennial Dr Suite 1, Penetanguishene,
ON, L9M 1G8
(705) 549-7406
Emp Here 350
SIC 5013 Motor vehicle supplies and new
parts

D-U-N-S 24-354-3761   (BR)
SHOPPERS DRUG MART CORPORATION
88 Main St Suite 1004, Penetanguishene, ON,
L9M 1T4
(705) 549-2332
Emp Here 20
SIC 5912 Drug stores and proprietary stores

D-U-N-S 25-263-7202   (BR)
**SIMCOE COUNTY DISTRICT SCHOOL
BOARD, THE**
JAMES KEATING ELEMENTARY SCHOOL
(*Suby of* Simcoe County District School
Board, The)
20 Lorne Ave, Penetanguishene, ON, L9M
1B2
(705) 549-8381
Emp Here 30
SIC 8211 Elementary and secondary schools

D-U-N-S 20-591-4885   (BR)
**SIMCOE MUSKOKA CATHOLIC DISTRICT
SCHOOL BOARD**
CANADIAN MARTYRS CATHOLIC SCHOOL
(*Suby of* Simcoe Muskoka Catholic District
School Board)

───────────────────────

7 Bellisle Rd, Penetanguishene, ON, L9M 1N6
(705) 549-1877
Emp Here 25
SIC 8211 Elementary and secondary schools

D-U-N-S 20-711-2181 (BR)
SIMCOE MUSKOKA CATHOLIC DISTRICT SCHOOL BOARD
ST ANN SCHOOL
(*Suby* of Simcoe Muskoka Catholic District School Board)
5 Dunlop St, Penetanguishene, ON, L9M 1J2
(705) 549-3101
Emp Here 32
SIC 8211 Elementary and secondary schools

Perth, ON K7H

D-U-N-S 24-268-6376 (BR)
3M CANADA COMPANY
(*Suby* of 3M Company)
2 Craig St, Perth, ON, K7H 3E2
(613) 267-5300
Emp Here 200
SIC 2672 Paper; coated and laminated, nec

D-U-N-S 25-569-5959 (SL)
535688 ONTARIO LTD
TIM HORTONS
98 Dufferin St, Perth, ON, K7H 3A7
(613) 267-3353
Emp Here 50   *Sales* 1,532,175
SIC 5812 Eating places

D-U-N-S 24-104-5681 (BR)
ALBANY INTERNATIONAL CANADA CORP
(*Suby* of Albany International Corp.)
Rideau Perry Rd, Perth, ON, K7H 3E3
(613) 267-6600
Emp Here 170
SIC 2231 Broadwoven fabric mills, wool

D-U-N-S 20-140-8499 (HQ)
CALERES CANADA, INC
NATURALIZER
(*Suby* of Caleres, Inc.)
1857 Rogers Rd, Perth, ON, K7H 1P7
(613) 267-0348
Emp Here 35   *Emp Total* 12,000
Sales 219,091,493
SIC 5139 Footwear
Dir Brian Bingley

D-U-N-S 20-573-0463 (BR)
CANADA POST CORPORATION
PERTH POST OFFICE
7 Beckwith St E, Perth, ON, K7H 1B2
(613) 267-1608
Emp Here 21
SIC 4311 U.s. postal service

D-U-N-S 25-237-9599 (BR)
CATHOLIC DISTRICT SCHOOL BOARD OF EASTERN ONTARIO
ST JOHN CATHOLIC HIGH SCHOOL
(*Suby* of Catholic District School Board of Eastern Ontario)
2066 Scotch Line Rd, Perth, ON, K7H 3C5
(613) 267-4724
Emp Here 70
SIC 8211 Elementary and secondary schools

D-U-N-S 20-711-5143 (BR)
CATHOLIC DISTRICT SCHOOL BOARD OF EASTERN ONTARIO
ST JOHN ELEMENTARY SCHOOL
34 Wilson St E, Perth, ON, K7H 1L6
(613) 267-2865
Emp Here 50
SIC 8211 Elementary and secondary schools

D-U-N-S 25-101-6770 (BR)
CONTRANS GROUP INC
GLEN TAY TRANSPORTATION
42 Lanark Rd, Perth, ON, K7H 3K5

(613) 267-2007
Emp Here 85
SIC 4482 Ferries

D-U-N-S 24-666-2118 (HQ)
CRAIN & SCHOOLEY INSURANCE BROKERS LTD
81 Gore St E, Perth, ON, K7H 1J1
(613) 267-1194
Emp Here 28   *Emp Total* 22,078
Sales 7,852,800
SIC 6411 Insurance agents, brokers, and service
Richard Schooley
Pr Pr Megan Schooley
VP VP Peter Mast
VP VP Jason Schooley
George Mclennan

D-U-N-S 24-355-4396 (SL)
ELMSLEY LOMBARDY PASTORAL CHARGE
1502 Rideau Ferry Rd, Perth, ON, K7H 3C7
(613) 267-3855
Emp Here 120   *Sales* 10,601,280
SIC 8661 Religious organizations
Minister Elizabeth Tucker
Sec Joyce Firlotte

D-U-N-S 20-556-1975 (BR)
HYDRO ONE NETWORKS INC
99 Drummond St W, Perth, ON, K7H 3E7
(613) 267-6473
Emp Here 100
SIC 4911 Electric services

D-U-N-S 20-890-5885 (SL)
LANARK LODGE
115 Christie Lake Rd Suite 223, Perth, ON, K7H 3C6
(613) 267-4225
Emp Here 180   *Sales* 6,566,463
SIC 8361 Residential care
Dir Debroah Pidgeon

D-U-N-S 24-805-4830 (BR)
MAGNA STRUCTURAL SYSTEMS INC
GRENVILLE CASTINGS, DIV OF
1 Conlon Dr, Perth, ON, K7H 3N1
(613) 267-7557
Emp Here 500
SIC 3365 Aluminum foundries

D-U-N-S 20-033-2534 (HQ)
OMYA CANADA INC
SNOWHITE
18595 Hwy 7 W, Perth, ON, K7H 3E4
(613) 267-5367
Emp Here 100   *Emp Total* 8,000
Sales 5,909,817
SIC 1499 Miscellaneous nonMetallic minerals, except fuels
Berndt Kanduth

D-U-N-S 20-140-8911 (SL)
PERTH DOWNTOWN PHARMASAVE (PAMELA NEWTON) LTD
57 Foster St Suite 762, Perth, ON, K7H 1R9
(613) 267-1578
Emp Here 28   *Sales* 5,425,920
SIC 5912 Drug stores and proprietary stores
Pr Pr Pamela Newton
VP VP Robin Newton

D-U-N-S 24-381-4188 (SL)
PERTH SOAP MANUFACTURING INC
PERTH SOAP, DIV OF
(*Suby* of Body Care Innovations Inc)
5 Herriott St, Perth, ON, K7H 3E5
(613) 267-1881
Emp Here 65   *Sales* 1,313,293
SIC 2841 Soap and other detergents

D-U-N-S 24-350-8087 (BR)
PERTH AND SMITHS FALLS DISTRICT HOSPITAL
GREAT WAR MEMORIAL
(*Suby* of Perth And Smiths Falls District Hos-

pital)
33 Drummond St W, Perth, ON, K7H 2K1
(613) 267-1500
Emp Here 270
SIC 8062 General medical and surgical hospitals

D-U-N-S 24-344-9068 (BR)
PERTH, CORPORATION OF THE TOWN OF
PERTH & DISTRICT INDOOR SWIMMING POOL
(*Suby* of Perth, Corporation Of The Town Of)
3 Sunset Blvd, Perth, ON, K7H 0A1
(613) 267-5302
Emp Here 20
SIC 7999 Amusement and recreation, nec

D-U-N-S 25-580-6820 (BR)
TAYSIDE COMMUNITY RESIDENTIAL & SUPPORT OPTIONS
BRADY HOUSE
(*Suby* of Tayside Community Residential & Support Options)
58 South St, Perth, ON, K7H 2G7
(613) 264-9242
Emp Here 22
SIC 8361 Residential care

D-U-N-S 20-422-7607 (BR)
THE COMMONWELL MUTUAL INSURANCE GROUP
(*Suby* of Commonwell Mutual Insurance Group, The)
96 South St, Perth, ON, K7H 0A2
(613) 267-5561
Emp Here 42
SIC 6411 Insurance agents, brokers, and service

D-U-N-S 20-026-6596 (BR)
UPPER CANADA DISTRICT SCHOOL BOARD, THE
GLEN TAY PUBLIC SCHOOL
155 Harper Rd, Perth, ON, K7H 3C6
(613) 267-1909
Emp Here 26
SIC 8211 Elementary and secondary schools

D-U-N-S 20-000-9913 (BR)
UPPER CANADA DISTRICT SCHOOL BOARD, THE
PERTH & DISTRICT COLLEGIATE INSTITUTE
13 Victoria St, Perth, ON, K7H 2H3
(613) 267-3051
Emp Here 60
SIC 8211 Elementary and secondary schools

D-U-N-S 25-188-7097 (BR)
UPPER CANADA DISTRICT SCHOOL BOARD, THE
THE STEWART SCHOOL
(*Suby* of Upper Canada District School Board, The)
80 Wilson St W, Perth, ON, K7H 2N6
(613) 267-2940
Emp Here 32
SIC 8211 Elementary and secondary schools

Perth Road, ON K0H

D-U-N-S 25-263-7913 (BR)
LIMESTONE DISTRICT SCHOOL BOARD
PERTH ROAD PUBLIC SCHOOL
1084 Walsh Lane, Perth Road, ON, K0H 2L0
(613) 353-2151
Emp Here 28
SIC 8211 Elementary and secondary schools

Petawawa, ON K8H

Renfrew County

D-U-N-S 20-560-0708 (SL)
1534825 ONTARIO INC
KELSEY'S PETAWAWA
3119 Petawawa Blvd, Petawawa, ON, K8H 1X9
(613) 687-0841
Emp Here 55   *Sales* 1,678,096
SIC 5812 Eating places

D-U-N-S 20-191-1190 (SL)
558297 ONTARIO INC
MONCION GROCERS PETAWAWA MARKET
3025 Petawawa Blvd Suite 6, Petawawa, ON, K8H 1X9
(613) 687-5000
Emp Here 110   *Sales* 19,223,512
SIC 5411 Grocery stores
Pr Pr Denis Moncion
Debra Moncion

D-U-N-S 20-711-6984 (BR)
RENFREW COUNTY CATHOLIC DISTRICT SCHOOL BOARD
SAINT FRANCIS OF ASSISI CATHOLIC ELEMENTARY SCHOOL
(*Suby* of Renfrew County Catholic District School Board)
22 Leeder Lane, Petawawa, ON, K8H 0B8
(613) 687-4167
Emp Here 50
SIC 8211 Elementary and secondary schools

D-U-N-S 25-994-5780 (BR)
RENFREW COUNTY CATHOLIC DISTRICT SCHOOL BOARD
OUR LADY OF SORROWS SEPARATE SCHOOL
(*Suby* of Renfrew County Catholic District School Board)
19 Mohns Ave, Petawawa, ON, K8H 2G7
(613) 687-5918
Emp Here 25
SIC 8211 Elementary and secondary schools

D-U-N-S 25-588-2136 (BR)
RENFREW COUNTY DISTRICT SCHOOL BOARD
PINECREST PUBLIC SCHOOL
43 Ypres Blvd, Petawawa, ON, K8H 1E5
(613) 687-4211
Emp Here 20
SIC 8211 Elementary and secondary schools

D-U-N-S 20-026-2546 (BR)
RENFREW COUNTY DISTRICT SCHOOL BOARD
GENERAL PANET HIGH SCHOOL
14 Ypres Blvd, Petawawa, ON, K8H 1C6

Emp Here 45
SIC 8211 Elementary and secondary schools

D-U-N-S 25-238-6289 (BR)
RENFREW COUNTY DISTRICT SCHOOL BOARD
HERMAN STREET PUBLIC SCHOOL
15 Herman St, Petawawa, ON, K8H 1W1
(613) 687-2457
Emp Here 24
SIC 8211 Elementary and secondary schools

D-U-N-S 20-590-8556 (BR)
RENFREW COUNTY DISTRICT SCHOOL BOARD
GENERAL LAKE SCHOOL
1900 Borden Ave, Petawawa, ON, K8H 2T6
(613) 687-2404
Emp Here 25
SIC 8211 Elementary and secondary schools

D-U-N-S 25-667-6672 (BR)
RENFREW COUNTY DISTRICT SCHOOL BOARD
VALOUR JK-12 SCHOOL
19 Leeder Lane, Petawawa, ON, K8H 0B8
(613) 687-2121
Emp Here 49

SIC 8211 Elementary and secondary schools

Peterborough, ON K9H
Peterborough County

D-U-N-S 24-549-8043   (BR)
BANK OF NOVA SCOTIA, THE
SCOTIABANK
111 Hunter St W, Peterborough, ON, K9H 7G5
(705) 748-2886
Emp Here 60
SIC 6021 National commercial banks

D-U-N-S 20-010-5638   (SL)
CSH JACKSON CREEK INC
*JACKSON CREEK RETIREMENT RESI-
DENCE*
481 Reid St, Peterborough, ON, K9H 7R9
(705) 742-0411
Emp Here 20   *Sales* 729,607
SIC 8361 Residential care

D-U-N-S 24-426-3310   (SL)
CSH PETERBOROUGH MANOR INC
1039 Water St, Peterborough, ON, K9H 3P5
(705) 748-5343
Emp Here 20   *Sales* 729,607
SIC 8361 Residential care

D-U-N-S 20-800-5632   (BR)
CAMPBELL, JAMES INC
MCDONALD'S
(*Suby of* Campbell, James Inc)
360 George St N, Peterborough, ON, K9H 7E7
(705) 876-6227
Emp Here 23
SIC 5812 Eating places

D-U-N-S 24-418-2700   (BR)
CINEPLEX ODEON CORPORATION
GALAXY CINEMAS PETERBOROUGH
320 Water St, Peterborough, ON, K9H 7N9
(705) 749-2000
Emp Here 20
SIC 7832 Motion picture theaters, except
drive-in

D-U-N-S 24-211-7935   (BR)
**CORPORATION OF THE CITY OF PETER-
BOROUGH, THE**
CITY OF PETERBOROUGH TRANSIT
190 Simcoe St, Peterborough, ON, K9H 2H7
(705) 745-0525
Emp Here 60
SIC 4111 Local and suburban transit

D-U-N-S 20-079-8549   (BR)
**CORPORATION OF THE CITY OF PETER-
BOROUGH, THE**
LANG PIONEER VILLAGE
470 Water St, Peterborough, ON, K9H 3M3
(705) 295-6694
Emp Here 25
SIC 8412 Museums and art galleries

D-U-N-S 20-845-0965   (SL)
FAIRHAVEN
881 Dutton Rd, Peterborough, ON, K9H 7S4
(705) 743-4265
Emp Here 280   *Sales* 17,584,000
SIC 8051 Skilled nursing care facilities
Ex Dir Joy Husack
Dir Opers Mary-Lynn Koekkoek

D-U-N-S 24-023-8415   (BR)
**GOVERNING COUNCIL OF THE SALVA-
TION ARMY IN CANADA, THE**
*GOVERNING COUNCIL OF THE SALVATION
ARMY IN CANADA, THE*
219 Simcoe St, Peterborough, ON, K9H 2H6

Emp Here 28
SIC 8661 Religious organizations

D-U-N-S 20-614-3914   (SL)

HOT BELLY MAMAS
OLD STONE BRING COMPANY, THE
380 George St N, Peterborough, ON, K9H
3R3
(705) 745-3544
Emp Here 50   *Sales* 1,532,175
SIC 5812 Eating places

D-U-N-S 20-088-6070   (BR)
**KAWARTHA PINE RIDGE DISTRICT
SCHOOL BOARD**
HIGHLAND HEIGHTS PUBLIC SCHOOL
430 Highland Rd, Peterborough, ON, K9H 5J7
(705) 742-8321
Emp Here 22
SIC 8211 Elementary and secondary schools

D-U-N-S 20-938-3194   (BR)
**KAWARTHA PINE RIDGE DISTRICT
SCHOOL BOARD**
EDMISON HEIGHTS PUBLIC SCHOOL
1111 Royal Dr, Peterborough, ON, K9H 6P9
(705) 745-0722
Emp Here 25
SIC 8211 Elementary and secondary schools

D-U-N-S 24-676-5007   (BR)
**KAWARTHA PINE RIDGE DISTRICT
SCHOOL BOARD**
KING GEORGE PUBLIC SCHOOL
220 Hunter St E, Peterborough, ON, K9H 1H1
(705) 745-7462
Emp Here 25
SIC 8211 Elementary and secondary schools

D-U-N-S 25-263-5958   (BR)
**KAWARTHA PINE RIDGE DISTRICT
SCHOOL BOARD**
QUEEN ELIZABETH PUBLIC SCHOOL
830 Barnardo Ave, Peterborough, ON, K9H
5V9
(705) 742-6331
Emp Here 30
SIC 8211 Elementary and secondary schools

D-U-N-S 24-048-1866   (BR)
**KAWARTHA PINE RIDGE DISTRICT
SCHOOL BOARD**
*THOMAS A. STEWART SECONDARY
SCHOOL*
1009 Armour Rd, Peterborough, ON, K9H 7H2
(705) 743-5230
Emp Here 20
SIC 8211 Elementary and secondary schools

D-U-N-S 20-711-5911   (BR)
**KAWARTHA PINE RIDGE DISTRICT
SCHOOL BOARD**
ARMOUR HEIGHT PUBLIC SCHOOL
245 Mcfarlane St, Peterborough, ON, K9H
1K1
(705) 742-6001
Emp Here 27
SIC 8211 Elementary and secondary schools

D-U-N-S 25-082-0594   (SL)
**KAWARTHA-HALIBURTON CHILDREN'S
AID SOCIETY, THE**
1100 Chemong Rd, Peterborough, ON, K9H
7S2
(705) 743-9751
Emp Here 114   *Sales* 4,450,603
SIC 8322 Individual and family services

D-U-N-S 20-086-7716   (SL)
LLF LAWYERS LLP
332 Aylmer St N, Peterborough, ON, K9H 3V6
(705) 742-1674
Emp Here 50   *Sales* 4,304,681
SIC 8111 Legal services

D-U-N-S 25-292-3578   (BR)
METRO ONTARIO INC
METRO
1154 Chemong Rd Suite 9, Peterborough,
ON, K9H 7J6
(705) 745-3381
Emp Here 100

SIC 5411 Grocery stores

D-U-N-S 24-677-0353   (BR)
**OMNI HEALTH CARE LIMITED PARTNER-
SHIP**
RIVERVIEW MANOR NURSING HOME
(*Suby of* Omni Health Care Limited Partner-
ship)
1155 Water St, Peterborough, ON, K9H 3P8
(705) 748-6706
Emp Here 150
SIC 8051 Skilled nursing care facilities

D-U-N-S 20-303-9466   (BR)
OPEN TEXT CORPORATION
194 Sophia St, Peterborough, ON, K9H 1E5
(705) 745-6605
Emp Here 30
SIC 7372 Prepackaged software

D-U-N-S 24-409-9453   (SL)
**PETERBOROUGH PUBLIC LIBRARY
BOARD**
345 Aylmer St N, Peterborough, ON, K9H 3V7
(705) 745-5560
Emp Here 45   *Sales* 2,334,742
SIC 8231 Libraries

D-U-N-S 25-263-5818   (BR)
**PETERBOROUGH VICTORIA NORTHUM-
BERLAND AND CLARINGTON CATHOLIC
DISTRICT SCHOOL BOARD**
ST ANNE'S ELEMENTARY SCHOOL
(*Suby of* Peterborough Victoria Northumber-
land and Clarington Catholic District School
Board)
240 Bellevue St, Peterborough, ON, K9H 5E5
(705) 742-3342
Emp Here 40
SIC 8211 Elementary and secondary schools

D-U-N-S 20-009-9047   (BR)
**PETERBOROUGH VICTORIA NORTHUM-
BERLAND AND CLARINGTON CATHOLIC
DISTRICT SCHOOL BOARD**
*ST PAUL CATHOLIC ELEMENTARY
SCHOOL*
1101 Hilliard St, Peterborough, ON, K9H 5S3
(705) 742-2991
Emp Here 31
SIC 8211 Elementary and secondary schools

D-U-N-S 25-263-5891   (BR)
**PETERBOROUGH VICTORIA NORTHUM-
BERLAND AND CLARINGTON CATHOLIC
DISTRICT SCHOOL BOARD**
*IMMACULATE CONCEPTION ELEMENTARY
SCHOOL*
(*Suby of* Peterborough Victoria Northumber-
land and Clarington Catholic District School
Board)
76 Robinson St, Peterborough, ON, K9H 1E8
(705) 745-6777
Emp Here 24
SIC 8211 Elementary and secondary schools

D-U-N-S 25-980-7188   (BR)
PRISZM LP
KFC
786 Chemong Rd, Peterborough, ON, K9H
5Z3
(705) 742-2519
Emp Here 25
SIC 5812 Eating places

D-U-N-S 20-519-9891   (BR)
RBC DOMINION SECURITIES INC
(*Suby of* Royal Bank Of Canada)
60 Hunter St E, Peterborough, ON, K9H 1G5
(705) 743-4275
Emp Here 22
SIC 6282 Investment advice

D-U-N-S 25-281-2854   (BR)
SECURITAS CANADA LIMITED
349a George St N Suite 206, Peterborough,
ON, K9H 3P9

---

(705) 743-8026
Emp Here 115
SIC 7381 Detective and armored car services

D-U-N-S 24-692-9483   (BR)
SHOPPERS DRUG MART CORPORATION
865 Chemong Rd, Peterborough, ON, K9H
5Z5
(705) 745-2401
Emp Here 40
SIC 5912 Drug stores and proprietary stores

D-U-N-S 25-027-8124   (BR)
**VICTORIAN ORDER OF NURSES FOR
CANADA**
*VON   PETERBOROUGH-VICTORIA-
HALIBURTON DISTRICT*
360 George St N Suite 25, Peterborough, ON,
K9H 7E7
(705) 745-9155
Emp Here 100
SIC 8082 Home health care services

D-U-N-S 25-294-7908   (BR)
WAL-MART CANADA CORP
1002 Chemong Rd Suite 3071, Peterborough,
ON, K9H 7E2
(705) 742-1685
Emp Here 300
SIC 5311 Department stores

D-U-N-S 20-806-3151   (BR)
YM INC. (SALES)
BLUENOTES
360 George St N, Peterborough, ON, K9H 7E7
(705) 741-2901
Emp Here 25
SIC 5621 Women's clothing stores

Peterborough, ON K9J
Peterborough County

D-U-N-S 25-530-3315   (SL)
990628 ONTARIO INC
RUBIDGE RETIREMENT RESIDENCE
270 Rubidge St Suite 246, Peterborough, ON,
K9J 3P2
(705) 748-4000
Emp Here 50   *Sales* 1,824,018
SIC 8361 Residential care

D-U-N-S 24-849-5814   (HQ)
AON GROUP INC
(*Suby of* AON Group Inc)
307 Aylmer St N, Peterborough, ON, K9J 7M4
(705) 742-3801
Emp Here 20   *Emp Total* 300
Sales 70,282,560
SIC 6712 Bank holding companies
Pr Pr Ross Smith
Dir Hugh Smith
Bradley Smith

D-U-N-S 20-967-0934   (HQ)
AON INC
(*Suby of* AON Group Inc)
307 Aylmer St N, Peterborough, ON, K9J 7M4
(705) 742-5445
Emp Here 60   *Emp Total* 300
Sales 223,568,000
SIC 6553 Cemetery subdividers and develop-
ers
Pr Pr Ross Smith
VP VP Brad Smith
Todd Smith
Fin Ex Domenic Idesanya

D-U-N-S 25-487-4381   (BR)
AON INC
EMPRESS GARDENS
(*Suby of* AON Group Inc)
131 Charlotte St Suite 333, Peterborough, ON,
K9J 2T6
(705) 876-1314
Emp Here 45

SIC 6513 Apartment building operators

D-U-N-S 20-141-0230   (SL)
ADAMSON & DOBBIN LIMITED
407 Pido Rd, Peterborough, ON, K9J 6X7
(705) 745-5751
Emp Here 52   *Sales* 4,523,563
SIC 1711 Plumbing, heating, air-conditioning

D-U-N-S 25-468-0556   (SL)
ALTERNATIVES COMMUNITY PROGRAM PETERBOROUGH SERVICES INC
267 Stewart St, Peterborough, ON, K9J 3M8
(705) 742-7038
Emp Here 23   *Sales* 7,067,520
SIC 8399 Social services, nec
Ex Dir Vikki Etchells

D-U-N-S 25-296-8938   (BR)
BANK OF NOVA SCOTIA, THE
SCOTIABANK
780 Clonsilla Ave, Peterborough, ON, K9J 5Y3
(705) 748-5681
Emp Here 26
SIC 6021 National commercial banks

D-U-N-S 25-019-5278   (BR)
BANQUE TORONTO-DOMINION, LA
TD FINANCIAL GROUP
(*Suby of* Toronto-Dominion Bank, The)
Gd, Peterborough, ON, K9J 7H7
(705) 745-5777
Emp Here 40
SIC 6021 National commercial banks

D-U-N-S 25-010-2340   (BR)
BELL MEDIA INC
COUNTRY UNIFIED
59 George St N, Peterborough, ON, K9J 3G2
(705) 742-8844
Emp Here 35
SIC 4832 Radio broadcasting stations

D-U-N-S 24-356-2571   (SL)
BOROUGHQUEST LIMITED
RICKY'S ALL DAY GRILL
898 Monaghan Rd Unit 4b, Peterborough, ON, K9J 5K4
(705) 749-1100
Emp Here 70   *Sales* 2,115,860
SIC 5812 Eating places

D-U-N-S 24-222-9941   (BR)
BOSTON PIZZA INTERNATIONAL INC
BOSTON PIZZA
821 Rye St, Peterborough, ON, K9J 6X1
(705) 740-2775
Emp Here 90
SIC 5812 Eating places

D-U-N-S 25-027-7639   (BR)
BRICK WAREHOUSE LP, THE
1200 Lansdowne St W, Peterborough, ON, K9J 2A1
(705) 743-8676
Emp Here 30
SIC 5712 Furniture stores

D-U-N-S 25-310-7981   (BR)
BRINK'S CANADA LIMITED
(*Suby of* The Brink's Company)
920 Major Bennett Dr, Peterborough, ON, K9J 6X6
(705) 742-8961
Emp Here 50
SIC 7381 Detective and armored car services

D-U-N-S 20-881-0838   (SL)
CALL-A-CAB LIMITED
2026 Bensfort Rd, Peterborough, ON, K9J 0G7
(705) 745-2424
Emp Here 56   *Sales* 1,605,135
SIC 4151 School buses

D-U-N-S 20-084-2289   (BR)
CAMPBELL, JAMES INC
MCDONALD'S
(*Suby of* Campbell, James Inc)

978 Lansdowne St W, Peterborough, ON, K9J 1Z9
(705) 743-6731
Emp Here 116
SIC 5812 Eating places

D-U-N-S 24-975-5307   (BR)
CANADA BREAD COMPANY, LIMITED
CANADA BREAD
774 Rye St Unit 17, Peterborough, ON, K9J 6W9
(705) 745-6753
Emp Here 20
SIC 5149 Groceries and related products, nec

D-U-N-S 24-669-4850   (BR)
CANADA BROKERLINK INC
201 George St N Unit 201, Peterborough, ON, K9J 3G7
(705) 743-4211
Emp Here 20
SIC 6411 Insurance agents, brokers, and service

D-U-N-S 24-104-5298   (BR)
CANADA POST CORPORATION
795 Rye St, Peterborough, ON, K9J 6X1

Emp Here 175
SIC 4311 U.s. postal service

D-U-N-S 25-303-6024   (BR)
CANADIAN IMPERIAL BANK OF COMMERCE
CIBC
825 Monaghan Rd, Peterborough, ON, K9J 5K2
(705) 742-0445
Emp Here 20
SIC 6021 National commercial banks

D-U-N-S 25-914-4731   (BR)
CANADIAN PACIFIC RAILWAY COMPANY
KAWARTHA LAKES RAILWAY
270 George St N, Peterborough, ON, K9J 3H1
(705) 745-1211
Emp Here 20
SIC 4011 Railroads, line-haul operating

D-U-N-S 20-321-8433   (BR)
CARA OPERATIONS LIMITED
MONTANA'S COOKHOUSE
(*Suby of* Cara Holdings Limited)
870 The Parkway, Peterborough, ON, K9J 8S5
(705) 743-9385
Emp Here 40
SIC 5812 Eating places

D-U-N-S 20-624-9831   (BR)
CASCADES CANADA ULC
NORAMPAC-PETERBOROUGH, DIV OF
105 Park St S, Peterborough, ON, K9J 3R8

Emp Here 30
SIC 2653 Corrugated and solid fiber boxes

D-U-N-S 24-560-7296   (SL)
CENTURY AIRLINE SERVICES INC
COACH CANADA
779 Erskine Ave, Peterborough, ON, K9J 5V1

Emp Here 35   *Sales* 1,724,650
SIC 4111 Local and suburban transit

D-U-N-S 24-829-3359   (SL)
CHARLOTTE PRODUCTS LTD
2060 Fisher Dr, Peterborough, ON, K9J 6X6
(705) 740-2880
Emp Here 43   *Sales* 4,158,760
SIC 2842 Polishes and sanitation goods

D-U-N-S 24-670-0277   (BR)
CITY OF PETERBOROUGH HOLDINGS INC
PETERBOROUGH REGIONAL HEALTH CENTRE
1 Hospital Dr, Peterborough, ON, K9J 7C6
(705) 740-8326
Emp Here 20

SIC 8062 General medical and surgical hospitals

D-U-N-S 24-154-3342   (BR)
COCO PAVING INC
2317 Television Rd, Peterborough, ON, K9J 6X8
(705) 742-4448
Emp Here 30
SIC 1611 Highway and street construction

D-U-N-S 20-881-5738   (HQ)
COLLINS BARROW KAWARTHAS LLP
(*Suby of* Collins Barrow Kawarthas LLP)
272 Charlotte St, Peterborough, ON, K9J 2V4
(705) 742-3418
Emp Here 45   *Emp Total* 70
Sales 3,064,349
SIC 8721 Accounting, auditing, and book-keeping

D-U-N-S 24-602-4806   (SL)
COMPLETE AVIATION SERVICES LTD
Ss 5 Stn Delivery Centre, Peterborough, ON, K9J 6X6
(705) 745-8626
Emp Here 30   *Sales* 9,047,127
SIC 5172 Petroleum products, nec
Pr Pr George Johnston

D-U-N-S 20-087-9851   (BR)
CORPORATION OF THE CITY OF PETERBOROUGH, THE
EVINRUDE CENTRE, THE
911 Monaghan Rd, Peterborough, ON, K9J 5K5
(705) 876-8121
Emp Here 50
SIC 7389 Business services, nec

D-U-N-S 25-478-8599   (BR)
CORPORATION OF THE CITY OF PETERBOROUGH, THE
PETERBOROUGH MEMORIAL CENTRE
151 Lansdowne St W, Peterborough, ON, K9J 1Y4
(705) 743-3561
Emp Here 75
SIC 8322 Individual and family services

D-U-N-S 25-143-1896   (BR)
CORUS ENTERTAINMENT INC
CKRU-FM
159 King St, Peterborough, ON, K9J 2R8
(705) 748-6101
Emp Here 30
SIC 7922 Theatrical producers and services

D-U-N-S 25-106-6064   (BR)
CORUS ENTERTAINMENT INC
CHEX-TV
743 Monaghan Rd, Peterborough, ON, K9J 5K2
(705) 742-0451
Emp Here 80
SIC 7922 Theatrical producers and services

D-U-N-S 24-369-9183   (BR)
COSTCO WHOLESALE CANADA LTD
COSTCO
(*Suby of* Costco Wholesale Corporation)
485 The Parkway, Peterborough, ON, K9J 0B3
(705) 750-2600
Emp Here 250
SIC 5199 Nondurable goods, nec

D-U-N-S 24-308-9737   (HQ)
DARLING INSURANCE AND REALTY LIMITED
(*Suby of* Darling Insurance And Realty Limited)
193 Aylmer St N, Peterborough, ON, K9J 3K2
(705) 742-4245
Emp Here 43   *Emp Total* 50
Sales 6,229,760
SIC 6411 Insurance agents, brokers, and service
Pr Pr Peter Blodgett

D-U-N-S 25-357-8090   (BR)
DYNACARE-GAMMA LABORATORY PARTNERSHIP
GAMMA-DYNACARE MEDICAL LAB
26 Hospital Dr Suite 5, Peterborough, ON, K9J 7C3
(705) 876-7313
Emp Here 22
SIC 8071 Medical laboratories

D-U-N-S 25-305-3334   (BR)
EASTON & YORK ENTERPRISES INC
QUALITY INN
1074 Lansdowne St W, Peterborough, ON, K9J 1Z9
(705) 748-6801
Emp Here 35
SIC 7011 Hotels and motels

D-U-N-S 20-551-9981   (BR)
EXTENDICARE (CANADA) INC
EXTENDICARE PETERBOROUGH
80 Alexander Ave, Peterborough, ON, K9J 6B4
(705) 743-7552
Emp Here 200
SIC 8051 Skilled nursing care facilities

D-U-N-S 24-340-0848   (BR)
FGL SPORTS LTD
SPORT-CHEK LANSDOWNE PLACE
645 Lansdowne St W Unit L019a, Peterborough, ON, K9J 7Y5
(705) 742-8951
Emp Here 25
SIC 5941 Sporting goods and bicycle shops

D-U-N-S 24-337-2872   (BR)
FGL SPORTS LTD
NATIONAL SPORTS
81 George St N, Peterborough, ON, K9J 3G3
(705) 740-9770
Emp Here 20
SIC 5941 Sporting goods and bicycle shops

D-U-N-S 24-925-4426   (SL)
FARMBOY MARKETS LIMITED
754 Lansdowne St W, Peterborough, ON, K9J 1Z3
(705) 745-2811
Emp Here 42   *Sales* 5,034,288
SIC 5411 Grocery stores
Pr Pr John Strano
  Bill Strano

D-U-N-S 25-527-3500   (BR)
FLEX-N-GATE CANADA COMPANY
VENTRA PLASTICS PETERBOROUGH
775 Technology Dr, Peterborough, ON, K9J 6Z8
(705) 742-3534
Emp Here 500
SIC 3714 Motor vehicle parts and accessories

D-U-N-S 25-361-1594   (BR)
G4S CASH SOLUTIONS (CANADA) LTD
GARDA WORLD
785 The Queensway Suite D, Peterborough, ON, K9J 6W7
(705) 741-4137
Emp Here 27
SIC 7381 Detective and armored car services

D-U-N-S 20-141-1063   (BR)
GENERAL ELECTRIC CANADA COMPANY
GE CANADA
(*Suby of* General Electric Company)
107 Park St N Suite 2, Peterborough, ON, K9J 7B5
(705) 748-8486
Emp Here 1,300
SIC 3625 Relays and industrial controls

D-U-N-S 20-968-4799   (SL)
GILL TECHNOLOGIES GLOBAL COMMUNICATIONS INC
150 King St, Peterborough, ON, K9J 2R9
(877) 507-6988
Emp Here 200   *Sales* 43,252,901

SIC 4899 Communication services, nec
Pr George Gill

D-U-N-S 20-813-1677   (SL)
GLOBAL TELESALES OF CANADA INC
1900 Fisher Dr, Peterborough, ON, K9J 6X6
(705) 872-3021
Emp Here 165   *Sales* 8,098,638
SIC 7389 Business services, nec
Genl Mgr Andreas Gruenewald

D-U-N-S 20-294-8852   (BR)
GOOD WATER COMPANY LTD, THE
CULLIGAN
620 Cameron Pl, Peterborough, ON, K9J 5T8
(705) 745-6962
Emp Here 30
SIC 7389 Business services, nec

D-U-N-S 25-868-8910   (BR)
GOODLIFE FITNESS CENTRES INC
PETERBOROUGH GOODLIFE FITNESS
200 Charlotte St, Peterborough, ON, K9J 2T8
(705) 876-1822
Emp Here 20
SIC 7991 Physical fitness facilities

D-U-N-S 24-461-9250   (BR)
GREAT PACIFIC ENTERPRISES LIMITED PARTNERSHIP
GENPAK
25 Aylmer St N, Peterborough, ON, K9J 3J2
(705) 743-4733
Emp Here 50
SIC 3081 Unsupported plastics film and sheet

D-U-N-S 20-212-7671   (BR)
HGC MANAGEMENT INC
390 Pido Rd, Peterborough, ON, K9J 6X7
(705) 876-1600
Emp Here 30
SIC 4953 Refuse systems

D-U-N-S 25-882-4812   (BR)
HANSON RESTAURANTS INC
ARBY'S ROAST BEEF RESTAURANT
(*Suby of* Hanson Restaurants Inc)
1165 Lansdowne St W, Peterborough, ON, K9J 7M2

Emp Here 20
SIC 5812 Eating places

D-U-N-S 25-088-1786   (BR)
HOME DEPOT OF CANADA INC
HOME DEPOT
(*Suby of* The Home Depot Inc)
500 Lansdowne St W, Peterborough, ON, K9J 8J7
(705) 876-4560
Emp Here 300
SIC 5211 Lumber and other building materials

D-U-N-S 20-003-8912   (BR)
INDIGO BOOKS & MUSIC INC
CHAPTERS
(*Suby of* Indigo Books & Music Inc)
873 Lansdowne St W, Peterborough, ON, K9J 1Z5
(705) 740-2272
Emp Here 40
SIC 5942 Book stores

D-U-N-S 25-239-6999   (BR)
KAWARTHA CHILD CARE SERVICES INC
733 Parkhill Rd W, Peterborough, ON, K9J 8M4
(705) 740-9439
Emp Here 20
SIC 8351 Child day care services

D-U-N-S 20-800-5640   (BR)
KAWARTHA CREDIT UNION LIMITED
645 Lansdowne St W, Peterborough, ON, K9J 7Y5
(705) 743-1630
Emp Here 20
SIC 6062 State credit unions

D-U-N-S 20-025-0608   (BR)
KAWARTHA PINE RIDGE DISTRICT SCHOOL BOARD
KENNER COLLEGIATE VOCATIONAL SCHOOL
633 Monaghan Rd, Peterborough, ON, K9J 5J2
(705) 743-2181
Emp Here 150
SIC 8211 Elementary and secondary schools

D-U-N-S 25-263-6170   (BR)
KAWARTHA PINE RIDGE DISTRICT SCHOOL BOARD
KING GEORGE PUBLIC SCHOOL
1994 Fisher Dr Suite K9j, Peterborough, ON, K9J 6X6
(705) 742-9773
Emp Here 25
SIC 8211 Elementary and secondary schools

D-U-N-S 20-711-5929   (BR)
KAWARTHA PINE RIDGE DISTRICT SCHOOL BOARD
ROGER NEILSON PUBLIC SCHOOL
550 Erskine Ave, Peterborough, ON, K9J 5T4
(705) 745-6456
Emp Here 30
SIC 8211 Elementary and secondary schools

D-U-N-S 25-263-6097   (BR)
KAWARTHA PINE RIDGE DISTRICT SCHOOL BOARD
KEITH WHITEMAN PUBLIC SCHOOL
860 St Mary'S St, Peterborough, ON, K9J 4H6
(705) 745-7775
Emp Here 24
SIC 8211 Elementary and secondary schools

D-U-N-S 20-290-4095   (BR)
KAWARTHA PINE RIDGE DISTRICT SCHOOL BOARD
PRINCE OF WALES PUBLIC SCHOOL
1211 Monaghan Rd, Peterborough, ON, K9J 5L4
(705) 743-8595
Emp Here 50
SIC 8211 Elementary and secondary schools

D-U-N-S 25-263-6055   (BR)
KAWARTHA PINE RIDGE DISTRICT SCHOOL BOARD
KAWARTHA HEIGHTS ELEMENTARY SCHOOL
11 Kawartha Heights Blvd, Peterborough, ON, K9J 1N4
(705) 742-7521
Emp Here 30
SIC 8211 Elementary and secondary schools

D-U-N-S 25-263-6071   (BR)
KAWARTHA PINE RIDGE DISTRICT SCHOOL BOARD
QUEEN MARY PUBLIC SCHOOL
1445 Monaghan Rd, Peterborough, ON, K9J 5M8
(705) 745-1353
Emp Here 35
SIC 8211 Elementary and secondary schools

D-U-N-S 25-809-9845   (BR)
KAWARTHA PINE RIDGE DISTRICT SCHOOL BOARD
WESTMOUNT PUBLIC SCHOOL
1520 Sherwood Cres, Peterborough, ON, K9J 6T8
(705) 742-7871
Emp Here 30
SIC 8211 Elementary and secondary schools

D-U-N-S 25-263-5990   (BR)
KAWARTHA PINE RIDGE DISTRICT SCHOOL BOARD
OTONABEE VALLEY PUBLIC SCHOOL
580 River Rd S, Peterborough, ON, K9J 1E7
(705) 745-0651
Emp Here 50
SIC 8211 Elementary and secondary schools

D-U-N-S 24-850-2762   (HQ)
KONRAD GROUP, INC
(*Suby of* Konrad Group Corporation)
1726 Henderson Line, Peterborough, ON, K9J 6X8
(416) 551-3684
Emp Here 100   *Emp Total* 1
Sales 12,993,765
SIC 7374 Data processing and preparation
Pr Pr George Konrad
Pr Pr Bill Konrad
   Hooman Bahador

D-U-N-S 20-070-9009   (BR)
LABOUR READY TEMPORARY SERVICES LTD
306 George St N Unit 6, Peterborough, ON, K9J 3H2
(705) 760-9111
Emp Here 100
SIC 7361 Employment agencies

D-U-N-S 20-361-9143   (SL)
LANSDOWNE MALL INC
LANSDOWNE PLACE
645 Lansdowne St W, Peterborough, ON, K9J 7Y5
(705) 748-2961
Emp Here 50   *Sales* 4,596,524
SIC 6512 Nonresidential building operators

D-U-N-S 25-322-3770   (BR)
LIFELABS LP
LIFELABS MEDICAL LABORATORY
849 Alexander Crt Suite 106, Peterborough, ON, K9J 7H8

Emp Here 43
SIC 8071 Medical laboratories

D-U-N-S 25-996-5846   (BR)
LOBLAW PROPERTIES LIMITED
769 Borden Ave, Peterborough, ON, K9J 0B6
(705) 748-6020
Emp Here 80
SIC 6512 Nonresidential building operators

D-U-N-S 24-632-2861   (SL)
MASTERBRAND CABINETS INC
944 Crawford Dr, Peterborough, ON, K9J 3X2
(705) 749-1201
Emp Here 400   *Sales* 32,153,600
SIC 2434 Wood kitchen cabinets
Dir Shanon Grauer
Dir Gregory Stoner
Dir Richard Forbes

D-U-N-S 24-737-4564   (SL)
MAXAMA PROTECTION INC
234 Romaine St, Peterborough, ON, K9J 2C5
(705) 745-7500
Emp Here 70   *Sales* 2,188,821
SIC 7381 Detective and armored car services

D-U-N-S 24-964-2661   (BR)
METROLAND MEDIA GROUP LTD
PETERBOROUGH THIS WEEK
884 Ford St, Peterborough, ON, K9J 5V3
(705) 749-3383
Emp Here 120
SIC 2711 Newspapers

D-U-N-S 20-981-1827   (HQ)
MINUTE MAID COMPANY CANADA INC, THE
(*Suby of* The Coca-Cola Company)
781 Lansdowne St W, Peterborough, ON, K9J 1Z2
(705) 742-8011
Emp Here 100   *Emp Total* 100,300
Sales 51,729,136
SIC 2086 Bottled and canned soft drinks
Pr Vincent R. Timpano
   Spencer Enright
Dir Fin Sivarajah Faiyanthan

D-U-N-S 25-282-4842   (BR)
MINUTE MAID COMPANY CANADA INC,

THE
MINUTE MAID
(*Suby of* The Coca-Cola Company)
781 Lansdowne St W, Peterborough, ON, K9J 1Z2
(705) 742-8011
Emp Here 80
SIC 2037 Frozen fruits and vegetables

D-U-N-S 24-585-8659   (HQ)
NEFAB INC
211 Jameson Dr, Peterborough, ON, K9J 6X6
(705) 748-4888
Emp Here 83   *Emp Total* 2,350
Sales 10,654,887
SIC 2441 Nailed wood boxes and shook
Pr Pr Mark Robinson
   Rui Garrido
Treas Frank Slovacek

D-U-N-S 25-459-5010   (SL)
NIGHTINGALE NURSING REGISTRY LTD
2948 Lakefield Rd, Peterborough, ON, K9J 6X5
(705) 652-6118
Emp Here 100   *Sales* 4,742,446
SIC 8059 Nursing and personal care, nec

D-U-N-S 25-361-4119   (BR)
OMNI HEALTH CARE LTD
SPRINGDALE COUNTRY MANOR
2020 Fisher Dr, Peterborough, ON, K9J 6X6

Emp Here 75
SIC 8051 Skilled nursing care facilities

D-U-N-S 20-859-9758   (BR)
PACIFIC LINK COMMUNICATIONS INC
BELL WORLD
645 Lansdowne St W, Peterborough, ON, K9J 7Y5
(705) 742-2555
Emp Here 25
SIC 5999 Miscellaneous retail stores, nec

D-U-N-S 24-662-8515   (HQ)
PAULMAC'S PET FOOD INC
2365 Whittington Dr, Peterborough, ON, K9J 0G5
(905) 946-1200
Emp Here 40   *Emp Total* 550
Sales 13,192,606
SIC 5149 Groceries and related products, nec
Pr Geoffrey Holt
   Tony Iordanis
VP VP John Fleming
VP Fin Sharla Trudell
   Wade Jamieson
Treas Carole Holt

D-U-N-S 24-111-4284   (BR)
PEPSICO CANADA ULC
FRITO LAY CANADA
(*Suby of* Pepsico, Inc.)
686 Rye St, Peterborough, ON, K9J 6W9
(705) 748-6162
Emp Here 20
SIC 5145 Confectionery

D-U-N-S 20-176-9630   (BR)
PEPSICO CANADA ULC
PEPSI QTG CANADA
(*Suby of* Pepsico, Inc.)
14 Hunter St E, Peterborough, ON, K9J 7B2
(705) 743-6330
Emp Here 700
SIC 2043 Cereal breakfast foods

D-U-N-S 25-263-5859   (BR)
PETERBOROUGH VICTORIA NORTHUMBERLAND AND CLARINGTON CATHOLIC DISTRICT SCHOOL BOARD
ST ALPHONSUS ELEMENTARY SCHOOL
(*Suby of* Peterborough Victoria Northumberland and Clarington Catholic District School Board)
875 St Mary'S St, Peterborough, ON, K9J 4H7

(705) 742-0594
Emp Here 31
SIC 8211 Elementary and secondary schools

D-U-N-S 25-487-4209   (BR)
**PETERBOROUGH VICTORIA NORTHUM-
BERLAND AND CLARINGTON CATHOLIC
DISTRICT SCHOOL BOARD**
*ST TERESA'S CATHOLIC ELEMENTARY
SCHOOL*
(*Suby of* Peterborough Victoria Northumber-
land and Clarington Catholic District School
Board)
1525 Fairmount Blvd, Peterborough, ON, K9J
6S9
(705) 745-0332
Emp Here 25
SIC 8211 Elementary and secondary schools

D-U-N-S 25-402-0761   (HQ)
**PETERBOROUGH VICTORIA NORTHUM-
BERLAND AND CLARINGTON CATHOLIC
DISTRICT SCHOOL BOARD**
*PVNC CATHOLIC DISTRICT SCHOOL
BOARD*
(*Suby of* Peterborough Victoria Northumber-
land and Clarington Catholic District School
Board)
1355 Lansdowne St W, Peterborough, ON,
K9J 7M3
(705) 748-4861
Emp Here 70   *Emp Total* 2,257
Sales 194,779,404
SIC 8211 Elementary and secondary schools
Ch Bd Joseph Whibbs
Ch Bd Margaret Godawa
V Ch Bd Christine Dunn
V Ch Bd Francis Flagler
John Mackle

D-U-N-S 25-263-5776   (BR)
**PETERBOROUGH VICTORIA NORTHUM-
BERLAND AND CLARINGTON CATHOLIC
DISTRICT SCHOOL BOARD**
ST JOHN'S ELEMENTARY SCHOOL
(*Suby of* Peterborough Victoria Northumber-
land and Clarington Catholic District School
Board)
746 Park St S, Peterborough, ON, K9J 3T4
(705) 745-4113
Emp Here 25
SIC 8211 Elementary and secondary schools

D-U-N-S 24-370-4470   (BR)
POLYTUBES 2009 INC
POLYTUBES PETERBOROUGH
416 Pido Rd, Peterborough, ON, K9J 6X7
(705) 740-2872
Emp Here 104
SIC 3084 Plastics pipe

D-U-N-S 20-734-5062   (BR)
POSI-SLOPE ENTERPRISES INC
(*Suby of* Beacon Roofing Supply, Inc.)
615 The Kingsway, Peterborough, ON, K9J
7G2
(705) 743-5013
Emp Here 50
SIC 2493 Reconstituted wood products

D-U-N-S 24-792-9409   (SL)
QUICKMILL INC
760 Rye St, Peterborough, ON, K9J 6W9
(705) 745-2961
Emp Here 40   *Sales* 6,670,133
SIC 3541 Machine tools, Metal cutting type
Pr Pr Gord Buchholz
VP VP David Piggott
VP Fin Joe Hall

D-U-N-S 25-172-5040   (BR)
RED LOBSTER HOSPITALITY LLC
RED LOBSTER RESTAURANTS
(*Suby of* Red Lobster Seafood Co., LLC)
870 Lansdowne St W, Peterborough, ON, K9J
1Z7
(705) 876-1840
Emp Here 35

SIC 5812 Eating places

D-U-N-S 24-679-3025   (BR)
ROLLS-ROYCE CANADA LIMITEE
597 The Queensway, Peterborough, ON, K9J
7J6
(705) 743-9249
Emp Here 50
SIC 5551 Boat dealers

D-U-N-S 20-164-3702   (SL)
**ROYAL GARDENS RETIREMENT RESI-
DENCE INC**
*ROYAL GARDENS RETIREMENT COMMU-
NITY*
(*Suby of* AON Group Inc)
1160 Clonsilla Ave, Peterborough, ON, K9J
8P8
(705) 741-6036
Emp Here 50   *Sales* 1,824,018
SIC 8361 Residential care

D-U-N-S 24-764-7928   (BR)
SEARS CANADA INC
637 Lansdowne St W, Peterborough, ON, K9J
7C5
(705) 743-6611
Emp Here 260
SIC 5311 Department stores

D-U-N-S 24-516-5204   (SL)
SHIMANO CANADA LTD
427 Pido Rd, Peterborough, ON, K9J 6X7
(705) 745-3232
Emp Here 30   *Sales* 3,429,153
SIC 5091 Sporting and recreation goods

D-U-N-S 24-805-1034   (BR)
SIEMENS CANADA LIMITED
*SIEMENS MILLTRONICS PROCESS IN-
STRUMENTS*
1954 Technology Dr, Peterborough, ON, K9J
6X7
(705) 745-2431
Emp Here 350
SIC 3823 Process control instruments

D-U-N-S 25-278-9045   (BR)
SOBEYS CAPITAL INCORPORATED
FRESHCO
950 Lansdowne St W, Peterborough, ON, K9J
1Z9

Emp Here 140
SIC 5411 Grocery stores

D-U-N-S 25-139-8756   (BR)
STAPLES CANADA INC
STAPLES THE BUSINESS DEPOT
(*Suby of* Staples, Inc.)
109 Park St S Suite 160, Peterborough, ON,
K9J 3R8
(705) 741-1130
Emp Here 40
SIC 5943 Stationery stores

D-U-N-S 20-580-6305   (BR)
**SUN LIFE ASSURANCE COMPANY OF
CANADA**
SUNLIFE FINANCIAL
950 Lansdowne St W, Peterborough, ON, K9J
1Z9
(705) 742-0474
Emp Here 20
SIC 6311 Life insurance

D-U-N-S 20-552-8263   (BR)
SYSCO CANADA, INC
SYSCO FOOD SERVICES OF ONTARIO
(*Suby of* Sysco Corporation)
65 Elmdale Rd, Peterborough, ON, K9J 6X4
(705) 748-6701
Emp Here 450
SIC 5141 Groceries, general line

D-U-N-S 20-803-2842   (SL)
T L C NURSING LTD
1434 Chemong Rd Suite 14, Peterborough,
ON, K9J 6X2

Emp Here 45   *Sales* 5,544,006
SIC 8741 Management services

D-U-N-S 20-141-6948   (HQ)
TRENTWAY-WAGAR INC
COACH CANADA
791 Webber Ave, Peterborough, ON, K9J 8N3
(705) 748-6411
Emp Here 200   *Emp Total* 31,799
Sales 54,580,100
SIC 4131 Intercity and rural bus transportation
Pr Pr James Devlin
VP VP Ron English
Dir Ross Kinnear

D-U-N-S 24-757-1540   (BR)
UNILEVER CANADA INC
715 Neal Dr, Peterborough, ON, K9J 6X7

Emp Here 32
SIC 2033 Canned fruits and specialties

D-U-N-S 25-981-7997   (BR)
UNITED PARCEL SERVICE CANADA LTD
UPS
634 Neal Dr, Peterborough, ON, K9J 6X7
(705) 743-3432
Emp Here 35
SIC 7389 Business services, nec

D-U-N-S 24-319-8392   (BR)
VALUE VILLAGE STORES, INC
(*Suby of* Savers, Inc.)
1101 Lansdowne St W, Peterborough, ON,
K9J 7M2
(705) 741-2644
Emp Here 70
SIC 5399 Miscellaneous general merchandise

D-U-N-S 25-671-9345   (BR)
WASTE CONNECTIONS OF CANADA INC
BFI CANADA
688 Harper Rd, Peterborough, ON, K9J 6X6
(705) 742-4268
Emp Here 30
SIC 4953 Refuse systems

D-U-N-S 20-164-3355   (BR)
WENDY'S RESTAURANTS OF CANADA INC
(*Suby of* The Wendy's Company)
1124 Chemong Rd, Peterborough, ON, K9J
6X2
(705) 745-7629
Emp Here 42
SIC 5812 Eating places

D-U-N-S 25-398-9743   (BR)
WENDY'S RESTAURANTS OF CANADA INC
WENDY'S
(*Suby of* The Wendy's Company)
961 Lansdowne St W, Peterborough, ON, K9J
1Z5
(705) 745-5253
Emp Here 30
SIC 5812 Eating places

D-U-N-S 20-644-3777   (BR)
WESTERN INVENTORY SERVICE LTD
727 Lansdowne St W, Peterborough, ON, K9J
1Z2
(705) 748-0623
Emp Here 20
SIC 7389 Business services, nec

D-U-N-S 20-184-2882   (BR)
**WINNERS MERCHANTS INTERNATIONAL
L.P.**
WINNERS
(*Suby of* The TJX Companies Inc)
950 Lansdowne St W, Peterborough, ON, K9J
1Z9
(705) 876-7722
Emp Here 40
SIC 5651 Family clothing stores

D-U-N-S 20-806-3144   (BR)
YM INC. (SALES)
STITCHES

L 026b-645 Lansdowne St W, Peterborough,
ON, K9J 7Y5
(705) 740-2061
Emp Here 25
SIC 5621 Women's clothing stores

D-U-N-S 20-401-7206   (SL)
YOUNG, ROBERT E CONSTRUCTION LTD
1488 Chemong Rd, Peterborough, ON, K9J
6X2
(705) 745-1488
Emp Here 50   *Sales* 4,523,563
SIC 1442 Construction sand and gravel

Peterborough, ON K9K
Peterborough County

D-U-N-S 25-194-2942   (SL)
**AMERICREDIT FINANCIAL SERVICES OF
CANADA LTD**
200 Jameson Dr, Peterborough, ON, K9K 2N3
(705) 876-3900
Emp Here 450   *Sales* 345,269,346
SIC 6141 Personal credit institutions
VP VP Michael Allman

D-U-N-S 24-012-1025   (BR)
CHRISTIAN HORIZONS
(*Suby of* Christian Horizons)
1289 Kawartha Cres, Peterborough, ON, K9K
1G4
(705) 876-0700
Emp Here 25
SIC 8361 Residential care

D-U-N-S 25-315-7903   (BR)
**INVESTORS GROUP FINANCIAL SER-
VICES INC**
1743 Lansdowne St W, Peterborough, ON,
K9K 1R2
(705) 876-1282
Emp Here 50
SIC 8742 Management consulting services

D-U-N-S 20-026-0508   (BR)
**KAWARTHA PINE RIDGE DISTRICT
SCHOOL BOARD**
JAMES STRATH PUBLIC SCHOOL
1175 Brealey Dr, Peterborough, ON, K9K 0C1
(705) 742-8090
Emp Here 40
SIC 8211 Elementary and secondary schools

D-U-N-S 20-812-8285   (BR)
**NEW HORIZONS CAR & TRUCK RENTALS
LTD**
DISCOUNT CAR & TRUCK RENTALS
1585 Lansdowne St W, Peterborough, ON,
K9K 1R2
(705) 749-6116
Emp Here 30
SIC 7514 Passenger car rental

D-U-N-S 24-320-7847   (SL)
OMNI HOLDINGS INC
1840 Lansdowne St W Unit 12, Peterborough,
ON, K9K 2M9
(705) 748-6631
Emp Here 1,300   *Sales* 81,589,760
SIC 8051 Skilled nursing care facilities
Fraser Wilson

D-U-N-S 25-487-4175   (BR)
**PETERBOROUGH VICTORIA NORTHUM-
BERLAND AND CLARINGTON CATHOLIC
DISTRICT SCHOOL BOARD**
*ST CATHERINE CATHOLIC ELEMENTARY
SCHOOL*
(*Suby of* Peterborough Victoria Northumber-
land and Clarington Catholic District School
Board)
1575 Glenforest Blvd, Peterborough, ON, K9K
2J6
(705) 742-6109
Emp Here 55

SIC 8211 Elementary and secondary schools

D-U-N-S 25-295-3807   (BR)
SHOPPERS DRUG MART CORPORATION
SHOPPERS DRUG MART
1840 Lansdowne St W, Peterborough, ON,
K9K 2M9
(705) 749-6547
Emp Here 25
SIC 5912 Drug stores and proprietary stores

Peterborough, ON K9L
Peterborough County

D-U-N-S 24-418-2833   (BR)
ARAMARK CANADA LTD.
OTONABEE MARKETPLACE
2151 East Bank Dr, Peterborough, ON, K9L
1Z8
(705) 741-0399
Emp Here 90
SIC 5812 Eating places

D-U-N-S 20-923-8844   (BR)
CAMPBELL, JAMES INC
MCDONALD'S RESTAURANTS
(Suby of Campbell, James Inc)
400 Lansdowne St E, Peterborough, ON, K9L
0B2
(705) 741-2887
Emp Here 50
SIC 5812 Eating places

D-U-N-S 20-037-4721   (BR)
KINGDON LUMBER LIMITED
KINGDON TIM-BR MART
309 Lansdowne St E, Peterborough, ON, K9L
2A3
(705) 749-1144
Emp Here 20
SIC 5211 Lumber and other building materials

D-U-N-S 20-655-0340   (BR)
**PETERBOROUGH VICTORIA NORTHUM-
BERLAND AND CLARINGTON CATHOLIC
DISTRICT SCHOOL BOARD**
*MONSIGNOR O'DONOGHUE CATHOLIC
ELEMENTARY SCHOOL*
2400 Marsdale Dr, Peterborough, ON, K9L
1Z2
(705) 743-9851
Emp Here 35
SIC 8211 Elementary and secondary schools

D-U-N-S 20-164-3348   (BR)
WENDY'S RESTAURANTS OF CANADA INC
WENDY'S
(Suby of The Wendy's Company)
705 Ashburnham Dr, Peterborough, ON, K9L
1P7
(705) 749-2335
Emp Here 29
SIC 5812 Eating places

D-U-N-S 25-293-8949   (BR)
WESTON BAKERIES LIMITED
678 Ashburnham Dr, Peterborough, ON, K9L
1T7
(905) 373-7089
Emp Here 40
SIC 2051 Bread, cake, and related products

Petrolia, ON N0N
Lambton County

D-U-N-S 20-552-7315   (BR)
BLUEWATER HEALTH
450 Blanche St, Petrolia, ON, N0N 1R0
(519) 464-4400
Emp Here 160
SIC 8062 General medical and surgical hospitals

D-U-N-S 24-420-5667   (BR)
**CORPORATION OF THE COUNTY OF
LAMBTON**
EMERGENCY MEDICAL SERVICES
3958 Petrolia Line Rr 4, Petrolia, ON, N0N
1R0
(519) 882-3797
Emp Here 150
SIC 4119 Local passenger transportation, nec

D-U-N-S 25-249-3838   (BR)
**LAMBTON KENT DISTRICT SCHOOL
BOARD**
QUEEN ELIZABETH II SCHOOL
363 Kerby St, Petrolia, ON, N0N 1R0
(519) 882-2123
Emp Here 30
SIC 8211 Elementary and secondary schools

D-U-N-S 20-710-4725   (BR)
**LAMBTON KENT DISTRICT SCHOOL
BOARD**
*LAMBTON CENTENNIAL ELEMENTARY
SCHOOL*
Gd, Petrolia, ON, N0N 1R0
(519) 882-0138
Emp Here 30
SIC 8211 Elementary and secondary schools

D-U-N-S 25-249-3804   (BR)
**LAMBTON KENT DISTRICT SCHOOL
BOARD**
*LAMBTON CENTRAL COLLEGIATE & VOCA-
TIONAL INSTITUTE*
4141 Dufferin St, Petrolia, ON, N0N 1R0
(519) 882-1910
Emp Here 115
SIC 8211 Elementary and secondary schools

D-U-N-S 20-710-4998   (BR)
**ST. CLAIR CATHOLIC DISTRICT SCHOOL
BOARD**
SAINT PHILIPS SCHOOL
420 Queen St, Petrolia, ON, N0N 1R0
(519) 882-1520
Emp Here 20
SIC 8211 Elementary and secondary schools

D-U-N-S 24-234-5556   (BR)
**ST. FRANCIS ADVOCATES FOR THE
AUTISTIC & DEVELOPMENTALLY DIS-
ABLED (SARNIA) INC**
ST FRANCIS ADVOCATEE
(Suby of St. Francis Advocates For The Autis-
tic & Developmentally Disabled (Sarnia) Inc)
Gd, Petrolia, ON, N0N 1R0
(519) 296-5544
Emp Here 20
SIC 8361 Residential care

D-U-N-S 25-687-4421   (BR)
WATERVILLE TG INC
4491 Discovery Line, Petrolia, ON, N0N 1R0
(519) 882-4366
Emp Here 205
SIC 3069 Fabricated rubber products, nec

Pickering, ON L1V

D-U-N-S 24-992-5132   (SL)
1051107 ONTARIO LTD
MANDARIN RESTAURANT
1725 Kingston Rd Suite 25, Pickering, ON,
L1V 4L9
(905) 619-1000
Emp Here 80   *Sales* 2,407,703
SIC 5812 Eating places

D-U-N-S 25-712-2325   (BR)
1561716 ONTARIO LTD
LONE STAR TEXAS GRILL
(Suby of 1561716 Ontario Ltd)
705 Kingston Rd, Pickering, ON, L1V 6K3
(905) 420-3334
Emp Here 80

SIC 5812 Eating places

D-U-N-S 20-805-8763   (BR)
20 VIC MANAGEMENT INC
20 VIC INDUSTRIAL
1355 Kingston Rd Suite 20, Pickering, ON,
L1V 1B8
(905) 831-6066
Emp Here 30
SIC 6512 Nonresidential building operators

D-U-N-S 25-194-2769   (SL)
CSH PARKWAY INC
PARKWAY RETIREMENT HOME, THE
1645 Pickering Pky, Pickering, ON, L1V 7E9
(905) 426-6603
Emp Here 20   *Sales* 1,751,057
SIC 6513 Apartment building operators

D-U-N-S 25-303-5869   (BR)
**CANADIAN IMPERIAL BANK OF COM-
MERCE**
CIBC
376 Kingston Rd Suite 1, Pickering, ON, L1V
6K4
(905) 509-2560
Emp Here 20
SIC 6021 National commercial banks

D-U-N-S 24-419-4382   (BR)
CANADIAN TIRE CORPORATION, LIMITED
PARTSOURCE
1095 Kingston Rd, Pickering, ON, L1V 1B5
(905) 420-1332
Emp Here 28
SIC 5531 Auto and home supply stores

D-U-N-S 24-776-7069   (BR)
CHARTWELL MASTER CARE LP
*CHARTWELL SELECT PICKERING CITY
CENTRE*
1801 Valley Farm Rd, Pickering, ON, L1V 0A5
(905) 420-3369
Emp Here 40
SIC 8322 Individual and family services

D-U-N-S 24-242-4369   (BR)
CHARTWELL RETIREMENT RESIDENCES
*CHARTWELL SENIORS HOUSING REAL
ESTATE INVESTMENT TRUST*
1801 Valley Farm Rd Suite 700, Pickering,
ON, L1V 0A5
(905) 420-3369
Emp Here 35
SIC 8059 Nursing and personal care, nec

D-U-N-S 25-666-6843   (SL)
CHERRY TREE ENTERPRISES INC
DAIRY QUEEN PICKERING
1099 Kingston Rd Suite 1, Pickering, ON, L1V
1B5
(905) 831-2665
Emp Here 60   *Sales* 1,824,018
SIC 5812 Eating places

D-U-N-S 20-791-4867   (BR)
CHILDREN'S PLACE (CANADA) LP, THE
1355 Kingston Rd, Pickering, ON, L1V 1B8
(905) 420-5624
Emp Here 20
SIC 5641 Children's and infants' wear stores

D-U-N-S 24-336-8904   (BR)
**CORPORATION OF THE CITY OF PICKER-
ING, THE**
PICKERING OPERATIONS CENTRE
2570 Tillings Rd, Pickering, ON, L1V 2P8
(905) 683-7575
Emp Here 60
SIC 8743 Public relations services

D-U-N-S 20-591-5312   (BR)
**DURHAM CATHOLIC DISTRICT SCHOOL
BOARD**
ST MARGUERITE COURGEOYF
1765 Meadowview Ave, Pickering, ON, L1V
3G7

Emp Here 25

SIC 8211 Elementary and secondary schools

D-U-N-S 20-711-3692   (BR)
**DURHAM CATHOLIC DISTRICT SCHOOL
BOARD**
*ST MARGUERITE BOURGEOYS CATHOLIC
SCHOOL*
1765 Meadowview Ave, Pickering, ON, L1V
3G7

Emp Here 50
SIC 8211 Elementary and secondary schools

D-U-N-S 20-591-4984   (BR)
**DURHAM CATHOLIC DISTRICT SCHOOL
BOARD**
1166 Finch Ave, Pickering, ON, L1V 1J6
(905) 839-1844
Emp Here 25
SIC 8211 Elementary and secondary schools

D-U-N-S 25-126-1160   (BR)
**DURHAM CATHOLIC DISTRICT SCHOOL
BOARD**
SAINT MONICA CATHOLIC SCHOOL
275 Twyn Rivers Dr, Pickering, ON, L1V 1E3
(905) 509-6691
Emp Here 44
SIC 8211 Elementary and secondary schools

D-U-N-S 25-068-0378   (BR)
**DURHAM CATHOLIC DISTRICT SCHOOL
BOARD**
*ST. ELIZABETH SETON CATHOLIC
SCHOOL*
490 Strouds Lane, Pickering, ON, L1V 6W7
(905) 831-9724
Emp Here 60
SIC 8211 Elementary and secondary schools

D-U-N-S 25-300-7652   (BR)
DURHAM DISTRICT SCHOOL BOARD
ELIZABETH B PHIN PUBLIC SCHOOL
1500 Rougemount Dr, Pickering, ON, L1V
1N1
(905) 509-2277
Emp Here 30
SIC 8211 Elementary and secondary schools

D-U-N-S 25-263-8051   (BR)
DURHAM DISTRICT SCHOOL BOARD
VAUGHAN WILLARD SCHOOL
1911 Dixie Rd, Pickering, ON, L1V 1V4
(905) 839-1931
Emp Here 30
SIC 8211 Elementary and secondary schools

D-U-N-S 25-300-7975   (BR)
DURHAM DISTRICT SCHOOL BOARD
DUNBAR, WILLIAM PUBLIC SCHOOL
1030 Glenanna Rd, Pickering, ON, L1V 5E5
(905) 420-5745
Emp Here 40
SIC 8211 Elementary and secondary schools

D-U-N-S 25-300-8312   (BR)
DURHAM DISTRICT SCHOOL BOARD
HIGHBUSH PUBLIC SCHOOL
605 Strouds Lane, Pickering, ON, L1V 5M5
(905) 839-5289
Emp Here 50
SIC 8211 Elementary and secondary schools

D-U-N-S 25-300-7561   (BR)
DURHAM DISTRICT SCHOOL BOARD
GANDATSETIAGON PUBLIC SCHOOL
1868 Parkside Dr, Pickering, ON, L1V 3R2
(905) 831-1868
Emp Here 35
SIC 8211 Elementary and secondary schools

D-U-N-S 25-300-7488   (BR)
DURHAM DISTRICT SCHOOL BOARD
GLENGROVE PUBLIC SCHOOL
1934 Glengrove Rd, Pickering, ON, L1V 1X2
(905) 839-1771
Emp Here 35
SIC 8211 Elementary and secondary schools

D-U-N-S 25-300-8163   (BR)
DURHAM DISTRICT SCHOOL BOARD
DUNBARTON HIGH SCHOOL
655 Sheppard Ave, Pickering, ON, L1V 1G2
(905) 839-1125
Emp Here 140
SIC 8211 Elementary and secondary schools

D-U-N-S 20-206-7406   (BR)
DURHAM DISTRICT SCHOOL BOARD
ALTONA FOREST PUBLIC SCHOOL
405 Woodsmere Cres, Pickering, ON, L1V 7A3
(905) 839-9900
Emp Here 40
SIC 8211 Elementary and secondary schools

D-U-N-S 20-650-9213   (BR)
DURHAM DISTRICT SCHOOL BOARD
WESTCREEK PUBLIC SCHOOL
1779 Westcreek Dr, Pickering, ON, L1V 6M9
(905) 509-5437
Emp Here 40
SIC 8211 Elementary and secondary schools

D-U-N-S 25-169-2653   (SL)
EAST SIDE MARIO'S
1355 Kingston Rd Suite 101, Pickering, ON, L1V 1B8
(905) 839-5811
Emp Here 65   *Sales* 1,969,939
SIC 5812 Eating places

D-U-N-S 25-708-9151   (BR)
FGL SPORTS LTD
SPORT-CHEK
1355 Kingston Rd Suite 120, Pickering, ON, L1V 1B8
(905) 420-1208
Emp Here 60
SIC 5699 Miscellaneous apparel and accessory stores

D-U-N-S 24-337-2906   (BR)
FGL SPORTS LTD
NATIONAL SPORTS
699 Kingston Rd, Pickering, ON, L1V 3N7
(905) 831-6360
Emp Here 20
SIC 5941 Sporting goods and bicycle shops

D-U-N-S 24-977-2612   (BR)
FGL SPORTS LTD
SPORT CHEK
1355 Kingston Rd Unit 120, Pickering, ON, L1V 1B8
(905) 420-1208
Emp Here 47
SIC 5941 Sporting goods and bicycle shops

D-U-N-S 24-760-2506   (BR)
HOME DEPOT OF CANADA INC
PICKERING HOME DEPOT
(*Suby of* The Home Depot Inc)
1105a Kingston Rd, Pickering, ON, L1V 1B5
(905) 421-2000
Emp Here 160
SIC 5251 Hardware stores

D-U-N-S 25-865-6776   (BR)
HONDA CANADA INC
PICKERING HONDA
1800 Kingston Rd, Pickering, ON, L1V 1C6
(905) 831-5400
Emp Here 25
SIC 5511 New and used car dealers

D-U-N-S 24-119-4963   (BR)
HUDSON'S BAY COMPANY
HOME OUTFITTERS
1300 Kingston Rd, Pickering, ON, L1V 3M9
(905) 831-8506
Emp Here 30
SIC 5251 Hardware stores

D-U-N-S 24-576-1531   (BR)
INNVEST PROPERTIES CORP
COMFORT INN

(*Suby of* Innvest Properties Corp)
533 Kingston Rd, Pickering, ON, L1V 3N7
(905) 831-6200
Emp Here 30
SIC 7011 Hotels and motels

D-U-N-S 25-315-8786   (BR)
INVESTORS GROUP FINANCIAL SERVICES INC
INVESTORS FINANCIAL SERVICES PLANNING CENTRE, DIVISION OF
1550 Kingston Rd Suite 313, Pickering, ON, L1V 1C3
(905) 831-0034
Emp Here 30
SIC 8741 Management services

D-U-N-S 20-708-7912   (BR)
LOBLAWS SUPERMARKETS LIMITED
LOBLAWS
1792 Liverpool Rd, Pickering, ON, L1V 4G6
(905) 831-6301
Emp Here 400
SIC 5411 Grocery stores

D-U-N-S 25-303-9309   (BR)
LONDON LIFE INSURANCE COMPANY
FREEDOM 55 FINANCIAL
1465 Pickering Pky Suite 300, Pickering, ON, L1V 7G7
(905) 831-3600
Emp Here 35
SIC 6411 Insurance agents, brokers, and service

D-U-N-S 24-802-8123   (BR)
LOWE'S COMPANIES CANADA, ULC
1899 Brock Rd, Pickering, ON, L1V 4H7
(905) 619-7530
Emp Here 100
SIC 5211 Lumber and other building materials

D-U-N-S 25-310-9219   (BR)
MCDONALD'S RESTAURANTS OF CANADA LIMITED
MCDONALD'S
(*Suby of* McDonald's Corporation)
1300 Kingston Rd, Pickering, ON, L1V 3M9
(905) 839-5665
Emp Here 100
SIC 5812 Eating places

D-U-N-S 25-366-1185   (BR)
MCDONALD'S RESTAURANTS OF CANADA LIMITED
MCDONALD'S
(*Suby of* McDonald's Corporation)
1899 Brock Rd, Pickering, ON, L1V 4H7
(905) 683-0944
Emp Here 100
SIC 5812 Eating places

D-U-N-S 20-076-9268   (BR)
MERIDIAN CREDIT UNION LIMITED
1550 Kingston Rd Unit 25, Pickering, ON, L1V 1C3
(905) 831-1121
Emp Here 25
SIC 6062 State credit unions

D-U-N-S 20-555-6355   (BR)
METRO ONTARIO INC
METRO
1822 Whites Rd Suite 11, Pickering, ON, L1V 4M1
(905) 420-8838
Emp Here 208
SIC 5411 Grocery stores

D-U-N-S 24-122-3387   (BR)
ONTARIO POWER GENERATION INC
O P G
1675 Montgomery Park Rd, Pickering, ON, L1V 2R5
(905) 839-1151
Emp Here 3,600
SIC 4911 Electric services

D-U-N-S 20-859-8602   (BR)

PACIFIC LINK COMMUNICATIONS INC
BELL WORLD
1355 Kingston Rd, Pickering, ON, L1V 1B8
(905) 837-1212
Emp Here 25
SIC 5999 Miscellaneous retail stores, nec

D-U-N-S 25-662-4412   (BR)
PHARMA PLUS DRUGMARTS LTD
1900 Dixie Rd, Pickering, ON, L1V 6M4
(905) 420-8735
Emp Here 25
SIC 5912 Drug stores and proprietary stores

D-U-N-S 24-803-1882   (SL)
PICKERING PUBLIC LIBRARY BOARD
1 The Esplanade, Pickering, ON, L1V 6K7
(905) 831-6265
Emp Here 65   *Sales* 2,991,389
SIC 8231 Libraries

D-U-N-S 24-823-4093   (SL)
PROFORMANCE ADJUSTING SOLUTIONS
1101 Kingston Rd Suite 280, Pickering, ON, L1V 1B5
(905) 420-3111
Emp Here 30   *Sales* 66,624,320
SIC 6321 Accident and health insurance
Owner Tammie Norn

D-U-N-S 24-845-8044   (BR)
SEARS CANADA INC
SEARS PICKERING #1034
1355 Kingston Rd, Pickering, ON, L1V 1B8
(905) 420-8000
Emp Here 300
SIC 5311 Department stores

D-U-N-S 20-806-2591   (BR)
SOBEYS CAPITAL INCORPORATED
SOBEYS STORE# 858
1899 Brock Rd Suite F, Pickering, ON, L1V 4H7
(905) 619-9130
Emp Here 25
SIC 5411 Grocery stores

D-U-N-S 20-077-8004   (BR)
SOBEYS CAPITAL INCORPORATED
FRESHCO
650 Kingston Rd, Pickering, ON, L1V 1A6
(905) 837-8611
Emp Here 100
SIC 5411 Grocery stores

D-U-N-S 24-101-2918   (BR)
STAPLES CANADA INC
STAPLES THE BUSINESS DEPOT
(*Suby of* Staples, Inc.)
1755 Pickering Pky, Pickering, ON, L1V 6K5
(905) 683-4620
Emp Here 25
SIC 5943 Stationery stores

D-U-N-S 20-700-5021   (BR)
TOMMY HILFIGER CANADA INC
TOMMY HILFIGER STORE
1899 Brock Rd Suite G12, Pickering, ON, L1V 4H7
(905) 426-9677
Emp Here 22
SIC 5651 Family clothing stores

D-U-N-S 24-971-6705   (BR)
TORONTO-DOMINION BANK, THE
T D BANK
(*Suby of* Toronto-Dominion Bank, The)
1822 Whites Rd Suite 1, Pickering, ON, L1V 4M1
(905) 420-8312
Emp Here 23
SIC 6021 National commercial banks

D-U-N-S 25-092-7514   (BR)
TORONTO-DOMINION BANK, THE
TD CANADA TRUST
(*Suby of* Toronto-Dominion Bank, The)
1794 Liverpool Rd, Pickering, ON, L1V 4G7

(905) 831-6114
Emp Here 30
SIC 6021 National commercial banks

D-U-N-S 25-322-1337   (BR)
TORONTO-DOMINION BANK, THE
TD BANK
(*Suby of* Toronto-Dominion Bank, The)
1355 Kingston Rd, Pickering, ON, L1V 1B8
(905) 831-2873
Emp Here 35
SIC 6021 National commercial banks

D-U-N-S 20-106-5260   (BR)
VERIDIAN CORPORATION
ENERGY BILLING CENTRE
1465 Pickering Pky Suite 2, Pickering, ON, L1V 7G7
(905) 420-8440
Emp Here 60
SIC 8721 Accounting, auditing, and bookkeeping

D-U-N-S 24-166-0435   (BR)
WAL-MART CANADA CORP
1899 Brock Rd Unit B, Pickering, ON, L1V 4H7
(905) 619-9588
Emp Here 200
SIC 5311 Department stores

D-U-N-S 24-224-5327   (BR)
WENDY'S RESTAURANTS OF CANADA INC
WENDY'S
(*Suby of* The Wendy's Company)
742 Kingston Rd, Pickering, ON, L1V 1A8
(905) 421-9266
Emp Here 25
SIC 5812 Eating places

D-U-N-S 25-372-9057   (BR)
WINNERS MERCHANTS INTERNATIONAL L.P.
WINNERS
(*Suby of* The TJX Companies Inc)
1899 Brock Rd, Pickering, ON, L1V 4H7
(905) 683-9819
Emp Here 20
SIC 5651 Family clothing stores

Pickering, ON L1W

D-U-N-S 20-205-8579   (SL)
1023248 ONTARIO INC
K & K RECYCLING SERVICES
870 Mckay Rd, Pickering, ON, L1W 2Y4
(905) 426-8989
Emp Here 65   *Sales* 3,283,232
SIC 7389 Business services, nec

D-U-N-S 20-965-4164   (BR)
ACTION VAN & TRUCK WORLD LTD
ACTION CAR AND TRUCK ACCESSORIES
1050 Squires Beach Rd, Pickering, ON, L1W 3N8
(905) 428-7373
Emp Here 25
SIC 5531 Auto and home supply stores

D-U-N-S 24-181-8228   (SL)
ALLIED CONVEYORS LIMITED
902 Dillingham Rd, Pickering, ON, L1W 1Z6
(905) 839-5196
Emp Here 50   *Sales* 8,749,135
SIC 3535 Conveyors and conveying equipment

D-U-N-S 20-267-0654   (HQ)
AREVA NP CANADA LTD
925 Brock Rd Suite B, Pickering, ON, L1W 2X9
(905) 421-2600
Emp Here 33   *Sales* 6,128,699
SIC 1629 Heavy construction, nec
Pr Pr Gary Mignogna
VP Opers William Cooper

D-U-N-S 20-314-5958   (SL)
AUTOLUX LTD
1550 Bayly St Unit 45, Pickering, ON, L1W 3W1

Emp Here 120   Sales 4,231,721
SIC 4111 Local and suburban transit

D-U-N-S 24-586-1083   (SL)
BEDWELL MOVERS LTD
BEDWELL MANAGEMENT SYSTEMS
1051 Toy Ave, Pickering, ON, L1W 3N9
(905) 686-0002
Emp Here 50   Sales 5,088,577
SIC 4212 Local trucking, without storage
Pr Pr James R Bedwell

D-U-N-S 20-781-0743   (SL)
BEDWELL VAN LINES LIMITED
1051 Toy Ave, Pickering, ON, L1W 3N9
(416) 283-9667
Emp Here 75   Sales 4,304,681
SIC 4214 Local trucking with storage

D-U-N-S 24-720-5966   (SL)
BRADFORD DIRECT INC
1920 Clements Rd, Pickering, ON, L1W 3V6
(416) 789-7411
Emp Here 50   Sales 3,031,879
SIC 7331 Direct mail advertising services

D-U-N-S 20-150-5260   (HQ)
BURNDY CANADA INC
(Suby of Hubbell Incorporated)
870 Brock Rd, Pickering, ON, L1W 1Z8
(905) 752-5400
Emp Here 60   Emp Total 17,425
Sales 14,323,401
SIC 3643 Current-carrying wiring devices
Fin Ex Albert He
Dir Richard W Davies
 Paul J Ashworth

D-U-N-S 20-348-3698   (SL)
CANADA HOUSE WELLNESS GROUP INC.
CHV
1773 Bayly St, Pickering, ON, L1W 2Y7
(905) 492-9420
Emp Here 50   Sales 3,898,130
SIC 8011 Offices and clinics of medical doctors

D-U-N-S 24-101-1860   (BR)
CONCENTRIX TECHNOLOGIES SERVICES (CANADA) LIMITED
MINACS GROUP INC, THE
915 Sandy Beach Rd, Pickering, ON, L1W 1Z5
(905) 837-6000
Emp Here 380
SIC 4899 Communication services, nec

D-U-N-S 24-992-4481   (SL)
DURADIE TECHNOLOGIES INC
1940 Clements Rd, Pickering, ON, L1W 4A1
(905) 426-9990
Emp Here 50   Sales 4,085,799
SIC 3544 Special dies, tools, jigs, and fixtures

D-U-N-S 25-265-1872   (BR)
DURHAM CATHOLIC DISTRICT SCHOOL BOARD
OUR LADY OF THE BAY CATHOLIC SCHOOL
795 Eyer Dr, Pickering, ON, L1W 2K2

Emp Here 26
SIC 8211 Elementary and secondary schools

D-U-N-S 25-265-3514   (BR)
DURHAM CATHOLIC DISTRICT SCHOOL BOARD
HOLY REDEEMER CATHOLIC SCHOOL
747 Liverpool Rd, Pickering, ON, L1W 1R8
(905) 839-5409
Emp Here 35
SIC 8211 Elementary and secondary schools

D-U-N-S 25-300-7611   (BR)
DURHAM DISTRICT SCHOOL BOARD
FAIRPORT BEACH PUBLIC SCHOOL
754 Oklahoma Dr, Pickering, ON, L1W 2H5
(905) 839-1451
Emp Here 30
SIC 8211 Elementary and secondary schools

D-U-N-S 25-300-7629   (BR)
DURHAM DISTRICT SCHOOL BOARD
BAYVIEW HEIGHTS PUBLIC SCHOOL
1400 Garvolin Ave, Pickering, ON, L1W 1J6
(905) 839-1146
Emp Here 46
SIC 8211 Elementary and secondary schools

D-U-N-S 25-300-7579   (BR)
DURHAM DISTRICT SCHOOL BOARD
FRENCHMAN'S BAY PUBLIC SCHOOL
920 Oklahoma Dr, Pickering, ON, L1W 2H7
(905) 839-1131
Emp Here 45
SIC 8211 Elementary and secondary schools

D-U-N-S 25-300-7710   (BR)
DURHAM DISTRICT SCHOOL BOARD
ROSEBANK ROAD PUBLIC SCHOOL
591 Rosebank Rd, Pickering, ON, L1W 2N6
(905) 509-2274
Emp Here 20
SIC 8211 Elementary and secondary schools

D-U-N-S 20-711-3494   (BR)
DURHAM DISTRICT SCHOOL BOARD
SIR JOHN A MACDONALD PUBLIC SCHOOL
777 Balaton Ave, Pickering, ON, L1W 1W7
(905) 839-1159
Emp Here 50
SIC 8211 Elementary and secondary schools

D-U-N-S 24-889-6730   (BR)
GENERAL ELECTRIC CANADA COMPANY
GE SILICONES OF CANADA
(Suby of General Electric Company)
1920 Silicone Dr, Pickering, ON, L1W 3V7
(905) 427-5656
Emp Here 35
SIC 3625 Relays and industrial controls

D-U-N-S 25-865-4763   (BR)
HARPER TRUCK CENTRES INC
(Suby of Harper Truck Centres Inc)
1555 Sandy Beach Rd, Pickering, ON, L1W 3S2

Emp Here 40
SIC 5511 New and used car dealers

D-U-N-S 24-360-2252   (BR)
HATCH CORPORATION
1815 Ironstone Manor Suite 10, Pickering, ON, L1W 3W9
(902) 564-5583
Emp Here 25
SIC 8711 Engineering services

D-U-N-S 20-940-8970   (HQ)
HOLMES & BRAKEL LIMITED
(Suby of Holmes & Brakel Limited)
830 Brock Rd, Pickering, ON, L1W 1Z8
(416) 798-7255
Emp Here 40   Emp Total 100
Sales 4,961,328
SIC 7389 Business services, nec

D-U-N-S 24-468-3913   (BR)
JORIKI INC
JORIKI FOOD AND BEVERAGE
(Suby of Joriki Inc)
885 Sandy Beach Rd, Pickering, ON, L1W 3N6
(905) 420-0188
Emp Here 100
SIC 2024 Ice cream and frozen deserts

D-U-N-S 25-667-4631   (SL)
KNIGHTS ON GUARD SECURITY SURVEIL-

LANCE SYSTEMS CORPORATION
KNIGHTS ON GUARD PROTECTIVES SERVICES
1048 Toy Ave Suite 101, Pickering, ON, L1W 3P1
(905) 427-7863
Emp Here 325   Sales 13,644,240
SIC 7381 Detective and armored car services
Pr Pr Steve Dimkovski

D-U-N-S 24-122-8147   (HQ)
LENBROOK INDUSTRIES LIMITED
PSB INTERNATIONAL
633 Granite Crt, Pickering, ON, L1W 3K1
(905) 831-6555
Emp Here 82   Emp Total 130
Sales 12,841,083
SIC 3651 Household audio and video equipment
Pr Pr Gordon Simmonds
 Dennis Hill
 Terry Mccrae

D-U-N-S 24-937-4117   (BR)
LONG & MCQUADE LIMITED
YORKVILLE SOUND
550 Granite Crt, Pickering, ON, L1W 3Y8
(905) 839-8816
Emp Here 200
SIC 3651 Household audio and video equipment

D-U-N-S 24-352-8457   (BR)
OTTO BOCK HEALTHCARE CANADA LTD
901 Dillingham Rd, Pickering, ON, L1W 2Y5

Emp Here 87
SIC 3842 Surgical appliances and supplies

D-U-N-S 24-822-5468   (BR)
PITNEY BOWES OF CANADA LTD
(Suby of Pitney Bowes Inc.)
1550 Bayly St, Pickering, ON, L1W 3W1
(416) 281-2777
Emp Here 20
SIC 5044 Office equipment

D-U-N-S 24-977-1312   (BR)
PITNEY BOWES OF CANADA LTD
POSTAGE BY PHONE
(Suby of Pitney Bowes Inc.)
1550 Bayly St, Pickering, ON, L1W 3W1

Emp Here 32
SIC 5044 Office equipment

D-U-N-S 24-278-6192   (BR)
PUROLATOR INC.
PUROLATOR INC
1075 Squires Beach Rd, Pickering, ON, L1W 3S3
(905) 686-1973
Emp Here 200
SIC 4731 Freight transportation arrangement

D-U-N-S 20-119-7550   (HQ)
RCM TECHNOLOGIES CANADA CORP
(Suby of RCM Technologies, Inc.)
895 Brock Rd, Pickering, ON, L1W 3C1
(905) 837-8333
Emp Here 30   Emp Total 2,368
Sales 6,785,345
SIC 8999 Services, nec
 Rocco Campanelli
Sr VP Danny White
VP Engg Robert Black
VP VP Craig Sellers
Dir Fin Juan Laverde

D-U-N-S 25-145-6927   (SL)
RECOVERCORP INC
RCI
1735 Bayly St Suite 8c, Pickering, ON, L1W 3G7

Emp Here 25   Sales 1,559,252
SIC 7322 Adjustment and collection services

D-U-N-S 25-170-4219   (BR)
RYDER TRUCK RENTAL CANADA LTD
RYDER INTEGRATED LOGISTICS, DIV OF
(Suby of Ryder System, Inc.)
910 Mckay Rd, Pickering, ON, L1W 3X8
(905) 428-9711
Emp Here 30
SIC 7513 Truck rental and leasing, no drivers

D-U-N-S 25-360-7584   (BR)
STATE FARM INSURANCE
1845 Clements Rd Suite 200, Pickering, ON, L1W 3R8
(905) 420-8500
Emp Here 25
SIC 6411 Insurance agents, brokers, and service

D-U-N-S 20-176-5385   (SL)
TML INDUSTRIES LTD
1745 Mcpherson Crt, Pickering, ON, L1W 3E9
(905) 831-7525
Emp Here 50
SIC 3411 Metal cans

D-U-N-S 20-341-7779   (BR)
TRENCH LIMITED
1865 Clements Rd, Pickering, ON, L1W 3R8
(647) 925-9760
Emp Here 20
SIC 3699 Electrical equipment and supplies, nec

D-U-N-S 25-282-4446   (BR)
UNILOCK LTD
1890 Clements Rd, Pickering, ON, L1W 3R8
(905) 427-2082
Emp Here 30
SIC 3272 Concrete products, nec

D-U-N-S 20-914-5809   (BR)
UNISYS CANADA INC
925 Brock Rd, Pickering, ON, L1W 2X9
(905) 837-1811
Emp Here 150
SIC 7371 Custom computer programming services

D-U-N-S 24-365-9138   (BR)
VEOLIA ES CANADA SERVICES INDUSTRIELS INC
820 Mckay Rd, Pickering, ON, L1W 2Y4

Emp Here 30
SIC 7389 Business services, nec

Pickering, ON L1X

D-U-N-S 20-025-3446   (BR)
DURHAM CATHOLIC DISTRICT SCHOOL BOARD
ST ANTHONY DANIEL CATHOLIC SCHOOL
2090 Duberry Dr, Pickering, ON, L1X 1Y5

Emp Here 35
SIC 8211 Elementary and secondary schools

D-U-N-S 20-711-3734   (BR)
DURHAM CATHOLIC DISTRICT SCHOOL BOARD
ST. WILFRID CATHOLIC SCHOOL
2360 Southcott Rd, Pickering, ON, L1X 2S9
(905) 427-6225
Emp Here 50
SIC 8211 Elementary and secondary schools

D-U-N-S 25-300-8338   (BR)
DURHAM DISTRICT SCHOOL BOARD
PINE RIDGE SECONDARY SCHOOL
2155 Liverpool Rd, Pickering, ON, L1X 1V4
(905) 420-1885
Emp Here 200
SIC 8211 Elementary and secondary schools

D-U-N-S 25-301-7180   (BR)

DURHAM DISTRICT SCHOOL BOARD
VALLEY FARM PUBLIC SCHOOL
1615 Pepperwood Gate, Pickering, ON, L1X 2K5
(905) 428-6337
Emp Here 50
SIC 8211 Elementary and secondary schools

D-U-N-S 25-300-8023   (BR)
DURHAM DISTRICT SCHOOL BOARD
MAPLE RIDGE PUBLIC SCHOOL
2010 Bushmill St, Pickering, ON, L1X 2M2
(905) 420-4103
Emp Here 30
SIC 8211 Elementary and secondary schools

Pickering, ON L1Y

D-U-N-S 20-811-4129   (SL)
BROOKLIN MEWS INC
WATSONS GLEN GOLF COURSE
3430 Seventh Concession Rd, Pickering, ON, L1Y 1C6
(905) 655-9187
Emp Here 52   *Sales* 2,261,782
SIC 7992 Public golf courses

D-U-N-S 20-709-1484   (BR)
CHRISTIAN HORIZONS
(*Suby of* Christian Horizons)
4342 Sideline 2 Suite 2, Pickering, ON, L1Y 1G2
(905) 649-5716
Emp Here 20
SIC 8361 Residential care

Pickle Lake, ON P0V
Kenora County

D-U-N-S 25-238-0381   (BR)
KEEWATIN PATRICIA DISTRICT SCHOOL BOARD
CROLANCIA ELEMENTARY SECONDARY SCHOOL
1 E St, Pickle Lake, ON, P0V 3A0
(807) 928-2381
Emp Here 25
SIC 8211 Elementary and secondary schools

D-U-N-S 24-227-6173   (BR)
WASAYA AIRWAYS LIMITED PARTNERSHIP
6 Airport Rd, Pickle Lake, ON, P0V 3A0
(807) 928-2244
Emp Here 30
SIC 4581 Airports, flying fields, and services

Picton, ON K0K
Prince Edward County

D-U-N-S 25-296-8854   (BR)
BANK OF NOVA SCOTIA, THE
SCOTIABANK
211 Main St, Picton, ON, K0K 2T0
(613) 476-3207
Emp Here 20
SIC 6021 National commercial banks

D-U-N-S 20-794-8550   (BR)
CANADIAN TIRE CORPORATION, LIMITED
CANADIAN TIRE ASSOCIATE STORE
13321 Loyalist Pky Rr 1, Picton, ON, K0K 2T0
(613) 476-7407
Emp Here 30
SIC 5531 Auto and home supply stores

D-U-N-S 25-456-5369   (BR)
CORPORATION OF THE COUNTY OF PRINCE EDWARD, THE

WATER PURIFICATION PLANT
30 Spencer St, Picton, ON, K0K 2T0
(613) 476-2337
Emp Here 20
SIC 4941 Water supply

D-U-N-S 25-318-9666   (BR)
FIRSTCANADA ULC
LAIDLAW EDUCATION SERVICES
3 Macsteven Dr, Picton, ON, K0K 2T0
(613) 476-7466
Emp Here 40
SIC 4151 School buses

D-U-N-S 20-583-3783   (BR)
HAMILTON BEACH BRANDS CANADA, INC
10 Mcfarland Dr Suite 201, Picton, ON, K0K 2T0
(613) 476-2191
Emp Here 75
SIC 3634 Electric housewares and fans

D-U-N-S 25-810-0890   (BR)
HASTINGS AND PRINCE EDWARD DISTRICT SCHOOL BOARD
QUEEN ELIZABETH SCHOOL
35 Barker St, Picton, ON, K0K 2T0
(613) 476-6475
Emp Here 20
SIC 8211 Elementary and secondary schools

D-U-N-S 20-711-5135   (BR)
HASTINGS AND PRINCE EDWARD DISTRICT SCHOOL BOARD
PRINCE EDWARD AND COLLEGIATE
41 Barker St, Picton, ON, K0K 2T0
(613) 476-2196
Emp Here 100
SIC 8211 Elementary and secondary schools

D-U-N-S 25-468-0192   (SL)
PICTON MANOR NURSING HOME LIMITED
9 Hill St, Picton, ON, K0K 2T0

Emp Here 90   *Sales* 4,085,799
SIC 8051 Skilled nursing care facilities

D-U-N-S 20-347-5707   (BR)
QUINTE HEALTHCARE CORPORATION
QUINTE HEALTHCARE PRINCE EDWARD COUNTY MEMORIAL
403 Picton Main St, Picton, ON, K0K 2T0
(613) 476-1008
Emp Here 100
SIC 8621 Professional organizations

D-U-N-S 25-461-8416   (BR)
REVERA LONG TERM CARE INC
VERSA-CARE HALLOWELL HOUSE
13628 Loyalist Pky Rr 1, Picton, ON, K0K 2T0
(613) 476-6233
Emp Here 100
SIC 8051 Skilled nursing care facilities

D-U-N-S 24-537-8146   (SL)
WARING HOUSE RESTAURANT AND INN
395 Sandy Hook Rd, Picton, ON, K0K 2T0
(613) 476-7492
Emp Here 72   *Sales* 2,826,987
SIC 5812 Eating places

D-U-N-S 20-245-8621   (SL)
YEO, JAMIE SUPERMARKET LTD
PICTON SOBEYS
97 Main St, Picton, ON, K0K 2T0
(613) 476-3246
Emp Here 49   *Sales* 7,821,331
SIC 5411 Grocery stores
Pt Jamie Yeo

Pikangikum, ON P0V
Kenora County

D-U-N-S 25-987-5938   (BR)
NORTH WEST COMPANY LP, THE

Gd, Pikangikum, ON, P0V 2L0
(807) 773-5913
Emp Here 30
SIC 5411 Grocery stores

D-U-N-S 25-142-6805   (BR)
PIKANGIKUM FIRST NATION
EENCHOKAY BIRCHSTICK SCHOOL
Gd, Pikangikum, ON, P0V 2L0
(807) 773-5561
Emp Here 55
SIC 8211 Elementary and secondary schools

Plantagenet, ON K0B
Prescott County

D-U-N-S 20-889-9476   (SL)
656955 ONTARIO LIMITED
PINECREST NURSING HOME
101 Parent St, Plantagenet, ON, K0B 1L0
(613) 673-4835
Emp Here 75   *Sales* 3,429,153
SIC 8051 Skilled nursing care facilities

D-U-N-S 20-711-6653   (BR)
CONSEIL SCOLAIRE DE DISTRICT CATHOLIQUE DE L'EST ONTARIEN
ECOLE SECONDAIRE CATHOLIQUE PAVILLON PLANTAGENET
6150 County Rd 17 Rr 1, Plantagenet, ON, K0B 1L0
(613) 673-5124
Emp Here 60
SIC 8211 Elementary and secondary schools

Plattsville, ON N0J
Oxford County

D-U-N-S 24-966-1851   (HQ)
SAINT-GOBAIN CANADA INC
28 Albert St W, Plattsville, ON, N0J 1S0
(519) 684-7441
Emp Here 100   *Emp Total* 205
Sales 17,948,332
SIC 3291 Abrasive products
 Sheri Y Olinyk
 John T Crowe
Pr Pr Mark E Mathieson

D-U-N-S 25-237-8336   (BR)
THAMES VALLEY DISTRICT SCHOOL BOARD
PLATTSVILLE & DISTRICT PUBLIC SCHOOL
112 Mill St E, Plattsville, ON, N0J 1S0
(519) 684-7390
Emp Here 20
SIC 8211 Elementary and secondary schools

D-U-N-S 20-903-2510   (BR)
UNIFOR
CEP LOCAL 12
28 Dup Albert W, Plattsville, ON, N0J 1S0
(519) 684-7346
Emp Here 119
SIC 8631 Labor organizations

Point Edward, ON N7T
Lambton County

D-U-N-S 24-028-6377   (SL)
BLUE WATER BRIDGE CANADA
BLUE WATER BRIDGE AUTHORITY
1555 Venetian Blvd Suite 436, Point Edward, ON, N7T 0A9
(519) 336-2720
Emp Here 73   *Sales* 23,808,251
SIC 4785 Inspection and fixed facilities

Pr Chuck Chrapko
Ch Bd Cathy Newman
 David Joy
VP Opers Stan Korosec

D-U-N-S 20-177-1560   (BR)
DHL GLOBAL FORWARDING (CANADA) INC
1555 Venetian Blvd Suite 12, Point Edward, ON, N7T 0A9
(519) 336-4194
Emp Here 20
SIC 4731 Freight transportation arrangement

D-U-N-S 24-305-7106   (SL)
GUILDWOOD INN LIMITED, THE
BEST WESTERN GUILDWOOD INN
1400 Venetian Blvd, Point Edward, ON, N7T 7W6
(519) 337-7577
Emp Here 75   *Sales* 3,283,232
SIC 7011 Hotels and motels

D-U-N-S 20-788-4052   (BR)
UPS SCS, INC
UPS SUPPLY CHAIN SOLUTIONS
1555 Venetian Blvd Suite 13, Point Edward, ON, N7T 0A9
(519) 337-1883
Emp Here 23
SIC 4731 Freight transportation arrangement

Point Edward, ON N7V
Lambton County

D-U-N-S 24-101-0391   (HQ)
ADVANCED EMISSIONS TECHNOLOGIES LTD
(*Suby of* Car-Ber Investments Inc)
128 Kendall St, Point Edward, ON, N7V 4G5
(519) 336-4498
Emp Here 30   *Emp Total* 460
Sales 5,088,577
SIC 7549 Automotive services, nec
Pr Pr James Nattier
 Bob Pullar
Dir Glenn Carson

D-U-N-S 25-283-5996   (HQ)
CAR-BER TESTING SERVICES INC
CAR-BER TESTING SERVICES
(*Suby of* Car-Ber Investments Inc)
911 Michigan Ave, Point Edward, ON, N7V 1H2
(519) 336-7775
Emp Here 63   *Emp Total* 460
Sales 4,815,406
SIC 8734 Testing laboratories

D-U-N-S 25-238-6750   (BR)
LAMBTON KENT DISTRICT SCHOOL BOARD
BRIDGEVIEW ELEMENTARY SCHOOL
205 Albert St, Point Edward, ON, N7V 1R4
(519) 337-3295
Emp Here 30
SIC 8211 Elementary and secondary schools

Porcupine, ON P0N
Cochrane County

D-U-N-S 20-710-4253   (BR)
CONSEIL SCOLAIRE CATHOLIQUE DE DISTRICT DES GRANDES RIVIERES, LE
ST JUDE
225 Dixon St, Porcupine, ON, P0N 1C0
(705) 235-2411
Emp Here 28
SIC 8211 Elementary and secondary schools

D-U-N-S 25-238-9861   (BR)
DISTRICT SCHOOL BOARD ONTARIO

NORTH EAST
FRANK P KRZNARIC WHITNEY PUBLIC SCHOOL
712 Earl St E, Porcupine, ON, P0N 1C0
(705) 235-8050
Emp Here 20
SIC 8211 Elementary and secondary schools

D-U-N-S 24-410-4568   (SL)
GORF CONTRACTING (1982) LTD
6588 Hwy 101 E, Porcupine, ON, P0N 1C0
(705) 235-3278
Emp Here 20   *Sales* 5,478,300
SIC 1541 Industrial buildings and warehouses
Pr Pr Mark Norkum
   Enrique Gaces
   Tom Laughren

Port Burwell, ON N0J
Elgin County

D-U-N-S 25-238-8004   (BR)
THAMES VALLEY DISTRICT SCHOOL BOARD
PORT BURWELL PUBLIC SCHOOL
30 Strachan St, Port Burwell, ON, N0J 1T0
(519) 874-4558
Emp Here 20
SIC 8211 Elementary and secondary schools

Port Carling, ON P0B
Muskoka County

D-U-N-S 24-676-5148   (BR)
TRILLIUM LAKELANDS DISTRICT SCHOOL BOARD
GLEN ORCHARD/HONEY HARBOUR PUBLIC SCHOOL
3954 Muskoka Rd 169, Port Carling, ON, P0B 1J0
(705) 765-3144
Emp Here 24
SIC 8211 Elementary and secondary schools

Port Colborne, ON L3K
Welland County

D-U-N-S 20-288-2630   (SL)
1448170 ONTARIO LIMITED
ITT ONTARIO PRO SERVICE
(*Suby of* ITT Inc.)
12 Petersburg Cir, Port Colborne, ON, L3K 5V4
(905) 835-6761
Emp Here 23   *Sales* 1,386,253
SIC 7699 Repair services, nec

D-U-N-S 24-986-4737   (BR)
ALGOMA CENTRAL CORPORATION
FRASER MARINE & INDUSTRIAL, DIV. OF
1 Chestnut St, Port Colborne, ON, L3K 1R3
(905) 834-4549
Emp Here 100
SIC 3731 Shipbuilding and repairing

D-U-N-S 24-374-1290   (SL)
ALLIED MARINE & INDUSTRIAL INC
1 Lake Rd, Port Colborne, ON, L3K 1A2
(905) 834-8275
Emp Here 50   *Sales* 3,638,254
SIC 7699 Repair services, nec

D-U-N-S 20-538-0418   (BR)
CANADA POST CORPORATION
PORT COLBORNE STATION MAIN
184 Elm St, Port Colborne, ON, L3K 4N8
(905) 834-3331
Emp Here 28
SIC 4311 U.s. postal service

D-U-N-S 20-980-7239   (SL)
CLAIRE'S DELIVERY SERVICE LIMITED
33 Stonebridge Dr, Port Colborne, ON, L3K 5V5
(905) 835-2222
Emp Here 50   *Sales* 3,939,878
SIC 4212 Local trucking, without storage

D-U-N-S 25-214-5214   (HQ)
COMMUNITY LIVING PORT COLBORNE-WAINFLEET
(*Suby of* Community Living Port Colborne-Wainfleet)
100 Mcrae Ave, Port Colborne, ON, L3K 2A8
(905) 835-8941
Emp Here 30   *Emp Total* 150
Sales 7,536,000
SIC 8361 Residential care
Ex Dir Vickie Moreland
   Dianne Cornwall
Pr Pr Pat Davis
   Jean Adams
   Larry Boggio

D-U-N-S 25-179-4590   (BR)
DISTRICT SCHOOL BOARD OF NIAGARA
MCKAY SCHOOL
320 Fielden Ave, Port Colborne, ON, L3K 4T7
(905) 834-4753
Emp Here 30
SIC 8211 Elementary and secondary schools

D-U-N-S 20-710-8577   (BR)
DISTRICT SCHOOL BOARD OF NIAGARA
DEWITT CARTER PUBLIC SCHOOL
435 Fares St, Port Colborne, ON, L3K 1X4
(905) 834-7440
Emp Here 50
SIC 8211 Elementary and secondary schools

D-U-N-S 20-025-2208   (BR)
DISTRICT SCHOOL BOARD OF NIAGARA
PORT COLBORNE HIGH SCHOOL
211 Elgin St, Port Colborne, ON, L3K 3K4
(905) 835-1186
Emp Here 70
SIC 8211 Elementary and secondary schools

D-U-N-S 20-710-8809   (BR)
DISTRICT SCHOOL BOARD OF NIAGARA
STEELE STREET PUBLIC SCHOOL
214 Steele St, Port Colborne, ON, L3K 4X7
(905) 834-4333
Emp Here 50
SIC 8211 Elementary and secondary schools

D-U-N-S 25-179-4541   (BR)
DISTRICT SCHOOL BOARD OF NIAGARA
OAKWOOD PUBLIC SCHOOL
255 Omer Ave, Port Colborne, ON, L3K 3Z1
(905) 834-9732
Emp Here 300
SIC 8211 Elementary and secondary schools

D-U-N-S 24-953-1583   (BR)
IMT PARTNERSHIP
PC FORGE
837 Reuter Rd, Port Colborne, ON, L3K 5V7
(905) 834-7211
Emp Here 115
SIC 3444 Sheet Metalwork

D-U-N-S 25-300-0046   (BR)
METRO ONTARIO INC
METRO
124 Clarence St, Port Colborne, ON, L3K 3G3
(905) 834-8800
Emp Here 100
SIC 5411 Grocery stores

D-U-N-S 25-137-6513   (BR)
NIAGARA CATHOLIC DISTRICT SCHOOL BOARD
ST JOHN BOSCO SCHOOL
191 Highland Ave, Port Colborne, ON, L3K 3S7
(905) 835-1930
Emp Here 25

SIC 8211 Elementary and secondary schools

D-U-N-S 25-137-3999   (BR)
NIAGARA CATHOLIC DISTRICT SCHOOL BOARD
LAKESHORE CATHOLIC HIGH SCHOOL
150 Janet St, Port Colborne, ON, L3K 2E7
(905) 835-2451
Emp Here 150
SIC 8211 Elementary and secondary schools

D-U-N-S 20-710-9013   (BR)
NIAGARA CATHOLIC DISTRICT SCHOOL BOARD
ST PATRICK SCHOOL
266 Rosemount Ave, Port Colborne, ON, L3K 5R4
(905) 835-1091
Emp Here 50
SIC 8211 Elementary and secondary schools

D-U-N-S 20-710-8874   (BR)
NIAGARA CATHOLIC DISTRICT SCHOOL BOARD
ST THERESE SCHOOL
530 Killaly St E, Port Colborne, ON, L3K 1P5
(905) 835-8082
Emp Here 30
SIC 8211 Elementary and secondary schools

D-U-N-S 24-644-2586   (BR)
NIAGARA HEALTH SYSTEM
PORT COLBORNE GENERAL HOSPITAL
260 Sugarloaf St, Port Colborne, ON, L3K 2N7
(905) 834-4501
Emp Here 250
SIC 8062 General medical and surgical hospitals

D-U-N-S 25-641-1810   (BR)
NORMA DONUTS LIMITED
TIM HORTONS
429 Main St W, Port Colborne, ON, L3K 3W2
(905) 834-7484
Emp Here 20
SIC 5812 Eating places

D-U-N-S 25-694-3069   (SL)
PORT COLBORNE COMMUNITY ASSOCIATION FOR RESOURCE EXTENSION
PORT CARES
92 Charlotte St, Port Colborne, ON, L3K 3E1
(905) 834-3629
Emp Here 53   *Sales* 12,760,960
SIC 8399 Social services, nec
Ex Dir Lynda Reinhart
Fin Mgr Leane Carpenter

D-U-N-S 25-368-6760   (BR)
SMUCKER FOODS OF CANADA CORP
(*Suby of* The J M Smucker Company)
2 Second Ave, Port Colborne, ON, L3K 5P1

Emp Here 80
SIC 2041 Flour and other grain mill products

D-U-N-S 20-610-1495   (SL)
THURSTON MACHINE COMPANY LIMITED
(*Suby of* Canerector Inc)
45 Invertose Dr, Port Colborne, ON, L3K 5V8
(905) 834-3606
Emp Here 82   *Sales* 97,256,613
SIC 3547 Rolling mill machinery
Pr Cecil Hawkins
Div Mgr Mark Yallin
Div Mgr Mark Nevar

D-U-N-S 24-117-6119   (BR)
TORONTO-DOMINION BANK, THE
TD BANK
(*Suby of* Toronto-Dominion Bank, The)
45 Clarence St, Port Colborne, ON, L3K 3G1
(905) 835-2437
Emp Here 20
SIC 6021 National commercial banks

Port Dover, ON N0A
Norfolk County

D-U-N-S 20-710-6415   (BR)
BRANT HALDIMAND NORFOLK CATHOLIC DISTRICT SCHOOL BOARD
ST CECELIA CATHOLIC SCHOOL
3 Lynn Park Ave, Port Dover, ON, N0A 1N5
(519) 583-0231
Emp Here 50
SIC 8211 Elementary and secondary schools

D-U-N-S 20-143-8033   (SL)
ERIE BEACH HOTEL LIMITED
19 Walker St, Port Dover, ON, N0A 1N0
(519) 583-1391
Emp Here 100   *Sales* 4,377,642
SIC 7011 Hotels and motels

D-U-N-S 20-143-8017   (HQ)
F. W. KNECHTEL FOODS LTD
DOVER DAIRY BAR
(*Suby of* F. W. Knechtel Foods Ltd)
214 Main St, Port Dover, ON, N0A 1N0
(519) 583-1048
Emp Here 20   *Emp Total* 60
Sales 1,824,018
SIC 5812 Eating places

D-U-N-S 20-024-9758   (BR)
GRAND ERIE DISTRICT SCHOOL BOARD
DOVERWOOD PUBLIC SCHOOL
(*Suby of* Grand Erie District School Board)
109 Hamilton Plank Rd, Port Dover, ON, N0A 1N7
(519) 583-0830
Emp Here 30
SIC 8211 Elementary and secondary schools

D-U-N-S 25-944-6003   (BR)
REVERA LONG TERM CARE INC
DOVER CLIFFS
501 St George St, Port Dover, ON, N0A 1N0
(519) 583-1422
Emp Here 75
SIC 8051 Skilled nursing care facilities

Port Elgin, ON N0H
Bruce County

D-U-N-S 25-238-8756   (BR)
BLUEWATER DISTRICT SCHOOL BOARD
SAUGEEN DIST SECONDARY SCHOOL
780 Gustavus St Ss 4, Port Elgin, ON, N0H 2C4
(519) 832-2091
Emp Here 90
SIC 8211 Elementary and secondary schools

D-U-N-S 20-710-6555   (BR)
BLUEWATER DISTRICT SCHOOL BOARD
PORT ELGIN SAUGEEN CENTRAL PUBLIC SCHOOL
504 Catherine St Ss 1, Port Elgin, ON, N0H 2C1
(519) 832-2038
Emp Here 50
SIC 8211 Elementary and secondary schools

D-U-N-S 20-036-9291   (BR)
BRUCE-GREY CATHOLIC DISTRICT SCHOOL BOARD
ST JOSEPH SCHOOL
584 Stafford St, Port Elgin, ON, N0H 2C1
(519) 389-5495
Emp Here 25
SIC 8211 Elementary and secondary schools

D-U-N-S 25-940-6270   (BR)
SAUGEEN SHORES, TOWN OF
CENTENNIAL POOL
780 Gustavus St Ss 4, Port Elgin, ON, N0H 2C4

---

(519) 832-2627
Emp Here 30
SIC 7999 Amusement and recreation, nec

D-U-N-S 24-849-8727   (BR)
UNIFOR
UNIFOR FAMILY EDUCATION CENTER
115 Shipley Ave, Port Elgin, ON, N0H 2C5
(519) 389-3200
Emp Here 100
SIC 8631 Labor organizations

D-U-N-S 24-606-2009   (BR)
WAL-MART CANADA CORP
5122 Hwy 21, Port Elgin, ON, N0H 2C0
(519) 389-6150
Emp Here 40
SIC 5311 Department stores

Port Hope, ON L1A

D-U-N-S 25-949-2650   (BR)
1036028 ONTARIO LIMITED
WENDY'S
Gd Lcd Main, Port Hope, ON, L1A 3V4

Emp Here 120
SIC 5812 Eating places

D-U-N-S 24-388-2065   (SL)
ACCESS COMMUNITY SERVICES INC
160 Walton St, Port Hope, ON, L1A 1N6
(905) 885-6358
Emp Here 85   *Sales* 3,137,310
SIC 8361 Residential care

D-U-N-S 20-571-8740   (BR)
ATOMIC ENERGY OF CANADA LIMITED
AECL
110 Walton St, Port Hope, ON, L1A 1N5
(905) 885-8830
Emp Here 20
SIC 2819 Industrial inorganic chemicals, nec

D-U-N-S 24-347-9305   (BR)
CENTRAL EAST COMMUNITY CARE AC-CESS CENTRE FOUNDATION
ACCESS CENTRE
151 Rose Glen Rd, Port Hope, ON, L1A 3V6
(905) 885-6600
Emp Here 20
SIC 8059 Nursing and personal care, nec

D-U-N-S 24-844-0380   (SL)
EASTON'S 28 RESTAURANTS LTD
HARVEY'S
Hwy 28 & 401, Port Hope, ON, L1A 3V6
(905) 885-1400
Emp Here 160   *Sales* 4,815,406
SIC 5812 Eating places

D-U-N-S 20-143-9742   (BR)
ESCO LIMITED
(*Suby of* Esco Corporation)
185 Hope St S, Port Hope, ON, L1A 4C2
(905) 885-6301
Emp Here 150
SIC 3325 Steel foundries, nec

D-U-N-S 20-708-2657   (BR)
EXTENDICARE INC
EXTENDICARE PORT HOPE
360 Croft St Suite 1124, Port Hope, ON, L1A 4K8
(905) 885-1266
Emp Here 100
SIC 8051 Skilled nursing care facilities

D-U-N-S 20-717-3964   (SL)
GILMER'S BUILDING CENTRE LIMITED
GILMER'S HOME CENTRE
177 Toronto Rd Suite 1, Port Hope, ON, L1A 3V5
(905) 885-4568
Emp Here 50   *Sales* 4,815,406
SIC 5251 Hardware stores

D-U-N-S 25-238-0274   (BR)
KAWARTHA PINE RIDGE DISTRICT SCHOOL BOARD
DR M S HAWKINS SENIOR PUBLIC SCHOOL
130 Highland Dr, Port Hope, ON, L1A 2A3
(905) 885-6346
Emp Here 20
SIC 8211 Elementary and secondary schools

D-U-N-S 20-711-5887   (BR)
KAWARTHA PINE RIDGE DISTRICT SCHOOL BOARD
BEATRICE STRONG PUBLIC SCHOOL
90 Rose Glen Rd, Port Hope, ON, L1A 3V6
(905) 885-9399
Emp Here 36
SIC 8211 Elementary and secondary schools

D-U-N-S 20-348-3615   (BR)
KAWARTHA PINE RIDGE DISTRICT SCHOOL BOARD
KAWARTA PINE RIDGE DISTRICT SCHOOL BOARD
130 Highland Dr, Port Hope, ON, L1A 2A3
(905) 885-6346
Emp Here 40
SIC 8211 Elementary and secondary schools

D-U-N-S 20-736-5185   (SL)
MCDONALD'S RESTAURANTS
175 Rose Glen Rd, Port Hope, ON, L1A 3V6
(905) 885-2480
Emp Here 80   *Sales* 2,407,703
SIC 5812 Eating places

D-U-N-S 24-335-0423   (BR)
METRO ONTARIO INC
METRO
125 Hope St S, Port Hope, ON, L1A 4C2
(905) 885-8194
Emp Here 70
SIC 5411 Grocery stores

D-U-N-S 20-653-4591   (BR)
PETERBOROUGH VICTORIA NORTHUM-BERLAND AND CLARINGTON CATHOLIC DISTRICT SCHOOL BOARD
ST ANTHONY'S ELEMENTARY SCHOOL
74 Toronto Rd, Port Hope, ON, L1A 3R9
(905) 885-4583
Emp Here 20
SIC 8211 Elementary and secondary schools

D-U-N-S 25-182-6277   (BR)
SAINT ELIZABETH HEALTH CARE
100 Peter St, Port Hope, ON, L1A 1C3

Emp Here 250
SIC 8322 Individual and family services

Port Mcnicoll, ON L0K
Simcoe County

D-U-N-S 25-297-6188   (BR)
SIMCOE COUNTY DISTRICT SCHOOL BOARD, THE
PORT MCNICOLL PUBLIC SCHOOL
(*Suby of* Simcoe County District School Board, The)
722 Seventh Ave, Port Mcnicoll, ON, L0K 1R0

Emp Here 24
SIC 8211 Elementary and secondary schools

Port Perry, ON L9L

D-U-N-S 20-538-1010   (BR)
CANADA POST CORPORATION
CANADA POST
192 Queen St, Port Perry, ON, L9L 1B9

Emp Here 30
SIC 4311 U.s. postal service

D-U-N-S 25-303-5281   (BR)
CANADIAN IMPERIAL BANK OF COM-MERCE
CIBC
145 Queen St, Port Perry, ON, L9L 1B8
(905) 985-4444
Emp Here 32
SIC 6021 National commercial banks

D-U-N-S 20-591-5205   (BR)
DURHAM CATHOLIC DISTRICT SCHOOL BOARD
GOOD SHEPHERD CATHOLIC SCHOOL
1650 Reach St, Port Perry, ON, L9L 1T1
(905) 985-7829
Emp Here 25
SIC 8211 Elementary and secondary schools

D-U-N-S 25-300-8361   (BR)
DURHAM DISTRICT SCHOOL BOARD
PORT PERRY HIGH SCHOOL
160 Rosa St, Port Perry, ON, L9L 1L7
(905) 985-7337
Emp Here 105
SIC 8211 Elementary and secondary schools

D-U-N-S 25-301-7396   (BR)
DURHAM DISTRICT SCHOOL BOARD
S. A. CAWKER PUBLIC SCHOOL
16200 Old Simcoe Rd, Port Perry, ON, L9L 1P3
(905) 985-4491
Emp Here 50
SIC 8211 Elementary and secondary schools

D-U-N-S 25-300-7793   (BR)
DURHAM DISTRICT SCHOOL BOARD
R H CORNISH PUBLIC SCHOOL
494 Queen St, Port Perry, ON, L9L 1K2
(905) 985-4468
Emp Here 74
SIC 8211 Elementary and secondary schools

D-U-N-S 25-265-2250   (BR)
DURHAM DISTRICT SCHOOL BOARD
PRINCE ALBERT PUBLIC SCHOOL
13700 Old Simcoe Rd, Port Perry, ON, L9L 1A1
(905) 985-2877
Emp Here 30
SIC 8211 Elementary and secondary schools

D-U-N-S 24-153-6593   (BR)
DYNACARE-GAMMA LABORATORY PART-NERSHIP
GAMMA-DYNACARE MEDICAL LABORATO-RIES
462 Paxton St, Port Perry, ON, L9L 1L9
(905) 985-8048
Emp Here 20
SIC 8071 Medical laboratories

D-U-N-S 25-695-0080   (SL)
HAUGENS BBQ. LTD
HAUGEN'S CHICKEN BARBECUE
13801 Hwy 7 & 12, Port Perry, ON, L9L 1B5
(905) 985-2402
Emp Here 65   *Sales* 1,969,939
SIC 5812 Eating places

D-U-N-S 25-187-2099   (BR)
LAKERIDGE HEALTH
(*Suby of* Lakeridge Health)
451 Paxton St, Port Perry, ON, L9L 1L9
(905) 985-7321
Emp Here 160
SIC 8062 General medical and surgical hospi-tals

D-U-N-S 25-302-1190   (BR)
MAPLE LEAF FOODS INC
SCHNEIDER FOODS
15350 Old Simcoe Rd, Port Perry, ON, L9L 1L8

(905) 985-7373
Emp Here 100
SIC 2038 Frozen specialties, nec

D-U-N-S 25-190-0861   (BR)
PROMARK-TELECON INC
96 North Port Rd, Unit 4, Port Perry, ON, L9L 1B2
(905) 982-1413
Emp Here 30
SIC 4899 Communication services, nec

D-U-N-S 24-114-4430   (BR)
R M R REAL ESTATE LIMITED
COLDWELL BANKER RMR REAL ESTATE
1894 Scugog St Suite 1, Port Perry, ON, L9L 1H7
(905) 985-9777
Emp Here 22
SIC 6531 Real estate agents and managers

D-U-N-S 24-046-3369   (SL)
RIDGELAND DEVELOPMENTS LTD
OAKRIDGE GOLF CLUB
35 Lauren Rd, Port Perry, ON, L9L 2A7
(905) 985-8390
Emp Here 50   *Sales* 2,042,900
SIC 7997 Membership sports and recreation clubs

D-U-N-S 25-658-0200   (BR)
ROYAL BANK OF CANADA
RBC
(*Suby of* Royal Bank Of Canada)
210 Queen St, Port Perry, ON, L9L 1B9
(905) 985-7316
Emp Here 23
SIC 6021 National commercial banks

Port Robinson, ON L0S
Welland County

D-U-N-S 24-745-5827   (HQ)
ARROW GAMES CORPORATION
9515 Montrose Rd Unit 2, Port Robinson, ON, L0S 1K0
(905) 354-7300
Emp Here 60   *Emp Total* 1,161
Sales 29,184,280
SIC 5092 Toys and hobby goods and supplies
Pr Pr John E Gallagher Jr
  John E Gallagher Sr
  Ron Kelly

D-U-N-S 20-573-2188   (BR)
COMPAGNIE DES CHEMINS DE FER NA-TIONAUX DU CANADA
10 Canby Rd, Port Robinson, ON, L0S 1K0

Emp Here 20
SIC 4011 Railroads, line-haul operating

D-U-N-S 25-372-8398   (BR)
E.S. FOX LIMITED
1201 Egerter Rd, Port Robinson, ON, L0S 1K0
(905) 384-2761
Emp Here 65
SIC 3441 Fabricated structural Metal

D-U-N-S 25-186-6476   (BR)
MORRISON HERSHFIELD LIMITED
9515 Montrose Rd, Port Robinson, ON, L0S 1K0
(905) 394-3900
Emp Here 650
SIC 4899 Communication services, nec

Port Rowan, ON N0E
Norfolk County

D-U-N-S 20-710-6290   (BR)
GRAND ERIE DISTRICT SCHOOL BOARD
PORT ROWAN PUBLIC SCHOOL

(Suby of Grand Erie District School Board)
48 College Ave, Port Rowan, ON, N0E 1M0
(519) 586-3541
Emp Here 20
SIC 8211 Elementary and secondary schools

Port Severn, ON L0K

D-U-N-S 20-144-3157   (SL)
SEVERN LODGE LIMITED, THE
SEVERN LODGE
116 Gloucester Trail, Port Severn, ON, L0K 1S0
(705) 756-2722
Emp Here 60   Sales 2,626,585
SIC 7011 Hotels and motels

Port Stanley, ON N5L
Elgin County

D-U-N-S 25-095-1431   (BR)
EXTENDICARE INC
EXTENDICARE PORT STANLEY
4551 East St, Port Stanley, ON, N5L 1J6
(519) 782-3339
Emp Here 70
SIC 8051 Skilled nursing care facilities

D-U-N-S 20-965-2288   (SL)
L. R. JACKSON FISHERIES LIMITED
172 Main St, Port Stanley, ON, N5L 1H6
(519) 782-3562
Emp Here 25   Sales 9,120,088
SIC 5146 Fish and seafoods
Pr Pr Larry Jackson
Bonnie Jackson

D-U-N-S 20-653-4021   (BR)
THAMES VALLEY DISTRICT SCHOOL BOARD
PORT STANLEY PUBLIC SCHOOL
350 Carlow Rd, Port Stanley, ON, N5L 1B6
(519) 782-3983
Emp Here 20
SIC 8211 Elementary and secondary schools

Port Sydney, ON P0B
Muskoka County

D-U-N-S 24-212-2885   (BR)
INTER-VARSITY CHRISTIAN FELLOWSHIP OF CANADA
ONTARIO PIONEER CAMP
942 Clearwater Lake Rd Rr 2, Port Sydney, ON, P0B 1L0
(705) 385-2370
Emp Here 25
SIC 8661 Religious organizations

Powassan, ON P0H
Parry Sound County

D-U-N-S 24-215-5398   (SL)
EASTHOLME HOME FOR THE AGED
62 Big Bend Ave, Powassan, ON, P0H 1Z0
(705) 724-2005
Emp Here 119   Sales 4,377,642
SIC 8361 Residential care

D-U-N-S 25-946-8510   (BR)
NEAR NORTH DISTRICT SCHOOL BOARD
MAPLERIDGE PUBLIC SCHOOL
171 Edward St, Powassan, ON, P0H 1Z0
(705) 472-5751
Emp Here 20

SIC 8211 Elementary and secondary schools

D-U-N-S 25-633-1844   (BR)
NIPISSING PARRY SOUND CATHOLIC DISTRICT SCHOOL BOARD
ST GREGORY SCHOOL
152 Fairview Lane, Powassan, ON, P0H 1Z0
(705) 724-3482
Emp Here 25
SIC 8211 Elementary and secondary schools

D-U-N-S 24-461-8088   (SL)
QUALITY HARDWOODS LTD
196 Latour Cres Rr 3, Powassan, ON, P0H 1Z0
(705) 724-2424
Emp Here 45   Sales 15,029,904
SIC 5031 Lumber, plywood, and millwork
Pr Pr Paul Brooks

Prescott, ON K0E
Grenville County

D-U-N-S 24-426-3302   (SL)
CSH MAYFIELD RETIREMENT HOME INC
MAYFIELD RETIREMENT RESIDENCE
248 Park St W, Prescott, ON, K0E 1T0
(613) 925-3784
Emp Here 20   Sales 729,607
SIC 8361 Residential care

D-U-N-S 24-737-0344   (BR)
DEEM MANAGEMENT SERVICES LIMITED
WELLINGTON HOUSE
990 Edward St, Prescott, ON, K0E 1T0
(613) 925-2834
Emp Here 100
SIC 8051 Skilled nursing care facilities

D-U-N-S 24-363-6698   (BR)
GREENFIELD GLOBAL, INC
141 Commerce Pl, Prescott, ON, K0E 1T0
(613) 925-1385
Emp Here 40
SIC 2869 Industrial organic chemicals, nec

D-U-N-S 25-089-8624   (SL)
IDEAL BUILDING FASTENERS INC
(Suby of Lewis, Jospe et Associes Ltee)
855 Edward St, Prescott, ON, K0E 1T0
(613) 925-1191
Emp Here 32   Sales 10,365,619
SIC 3452 Bolts, nuts, rivets, and washers
Pr Pr Joseph Jospe
Sammy Toldanno
Genl Mgr Adrian Macdonald

D-U-N-S 24-269-8454   (BR)
SYSTEMES ET CABLES PRYSMIAN CANADA LTEE
PRYSMIAN CABLES AND SYSTEMS CANADA LTD
137 Commerce Dr, Prescott, ON, K0E 1T0
(613) 925-5913
Emp Here 23
SIC 3496 Miscellaneous fabricated wire products

D-U-N-S 25-237-9532   (BR)
UPPER CANADA DISTRICT SCHOOL BOARD, THE
CENTRAL PUBLIC SCHOOL
(Suby of Upper Canada District School Board, The)
490 Jessup St, Prescott, ON, K0E 1T0
(613) 925-1834
Emp Here 20
SIC 8211 Elementary and secondary schools

D-U-N-S 25-263-5511   (BR)
UPPER CANADA DISTRICT SCHOOL BOARD, THE
MAYNARD PUBLIC SCHOOL
(Suby of Upper Canada District School Board, The)

---

21 Stewart St Rr 2, Prescott, ON, K0E 1T0
(613) 925-4291
Emp Here 33
SIC 8211 Elementary and secondary schools

D-U-N-S 20-047-8589   (BR)
UPPER CANADA DISTRICT SCHOOL BOARD, THE
SOUTH GRENVILLE DISTRICT HIGH SCHOOL
1000 Edward St, Prescott, ON, K0E 1T0
(613) 925-2855
Emp Here 70
SIC 7389 Business services, nec

D-U-N-S 25-238-0191   (BR)
UPPER CANADA DISTRICT SCHOOL BOARD, THE
BOUNDARY STREET ELEMENTARY SCHOOL
(Suby of Upper Canada District School Board, The)
920 Boundary St, Prescott, ON, K0E 1T0
(613) 925-2803
Emp Here 25
SIC 8211 Elementary and secondary schools

Princeton, ON N0J
Oxford County

D-U-N-S 20-710-5276   (BR)
LONDON DISTRICT CATHOLIC SCHOOL BOARD
Gd, Princeton, ON, N0J 1V0
(519) 663-2088
Emp Here 20
SIC 8211 Elementary and secondary schools

D-U-N-S 25-249-1444   (BR)
THAMES VALLEY DISTRICT SCHOOL BOARD
PRINCETON PUBLIC SCHOOL
40 Elgin St E, Princeton, ON, N0J 1V0
(519) 458-4315
Emp Here 25
SIC 8211 Elementary and secondary schools

Puslinch, ON N0B
Wellington County

D-U-N-S 25-595-7235   (BR)
PRESBYTERIAN CHURCH IN CANADA, THE
CRIEFF HILLS COMMUNITY RETREAT & CONFERENCE CENTRE
7098 Concession 1, Puslinch, ON, N0B 2J0
(519) 824-7898
Emp Here 20
SIC 8322 Individual and family services

D-U-N-S 24-375-5225   (BR)
TRANSX LTD
TRANSX LOGISTICS
7459 Mclean Rd W, Puslinch, ON, N0B 2J0
(519) 763-9330
Emp Here 30
SIC 4213 Trucking, except local

Putnam, ON N0L
Middlesex County

D-U-N-S 24-539-3822   (HQ)
SYLVITE AGRI-SERVICES LTD
SYLVITE TRANSPORTATION GROUP, DIV OF
(Suby of Sylvite Holdings Inc)
2740 Couch Rd, Putnam, ON, N0L 2B0

---

(519) 485-5770
Emp Here 40   Emp Total 110
Sales 20,866,760
SIC 5191 Farm supplies
Bob Mcnaughton

Queensville, ON L0G
York County

D-U-N-S 25-861-1110   (BR)
KERRY'S PLACE AUTISM SERVICES
(Suby of Kerry's Place Autism Services)
19660 Warden Ave, Queensville, ON, L0G 1R0
(905) 478-1482
Emp Here 20
SIC 8399 Social services, nec

Quinte West, ON K0K

D-U-N-S 20-923-1690   (SL)
AS CUSTOM CONTRACTING LTD
41a Elizabeth St, Quinte West, ON, K0K 1H0

Emp Here 25   Sales 5,173,950
SIC 1521 Single-family housing construction
Pr Doug Leblanc

Rainy River, ON P0W
Rainy River County

D-U-N-S 25-237-9359   (BR)
RAINY RIVER DISTRICT SCHOOL BOARD
RAINY RIVER HIGH SCHOOL
1 Mill Ave, Rainy River, ON, P0W 1L0
(807) 852-3284
Emp Here 30
SIC 8211 Elementary and secondary schools

Red Lake, ON P0V
Kenora County

D-U-N-S 25-830-2132   (BR)
DISTRICT OF KENORA HOME FOR THE AGED
NORTHWOOD LODGE HOME FOR THE AGED
(Suby of District of Kenora Home for the Aged)
51 Hwy 105, Red Lake, ON, P0V 2M0
(807) 727-2323
Emp Here 42
SIC 8361 Residential care

D-U-N-S 25-265-1112   (BR)
KEEWATIN PATRICIA DISTRICT SCHOOL BOARD
RED LAKE DISTRICT HIGH SCHOOL
Gd, Red Lake, ON, P0V 2M0
(807) 727-2092
Emp Here 50
SIC 8211 Elementary and secondary schools

D-U-N-S 20-026-4005   (BR)
KEEWATIN PATRICIA DISTRICT SCHOOL BOARD
RED LAKE-MADSEN PUBLIC SCHOOL
201 Howey St, Red Lake, ON, P0V 2M0
(807) 727-2331
Emp Here 20
SIC 8211 Elementary and secondary schools

D-U-N-S 20-124-8239   (BR)
KENORA CATHOLIC DISTRICT SCHOOL BOARD
ST JOHN'S SEPARATE SCHOOL
(Suby of Kenora Catholic District School

Board)
54 Discovery Rd, Red Lake, ON, P0V 2M0
(807) 727-3470
Emp Here 25
SIC 8211 Elementary and secondary schools

D-U-N-S 20-183-7502   (BR)
SGS CANADA INC
16a Young St, Red Lake, ON, P0V 2M0
(807) 727-2939
Emp Here 28
SIC 8734 Testing laboratories

Red Rock, ON P0T

D-U-N-S 20-710-3453   (BR)
**SUPERIOR   GREENSTONE   DISTRICT
SCHOOL BOARD**
RED ROCK PUBLIC SCHOOL
46 Salls St, Red Rock, ON, P0T 2P0
(807) 886-2253
Emp Here 20
SIC 8211 Elementary and secondary schools

Renfrew, ON K7V
Renfrew County

D-U-N-S 25-296-8490   (BR)
BANK OF NOVA SCOTIA, THE
SCOTIABANK
215 Raglan St S, Renfrew, ON, K7V 1R2
(613) 432-5818
Emp Here 30
SIC 6021 National commercial banks

D-U-N-S 20-589-4566   (BR)
BANQUE TORONTO-DOMINION, LA
TD CANADA TRUST
(*Suby of* Toronto-Dominion Bank, The)
270 Raglan St S, Renfrew, ON, K7V 1R4
(613) 432-3682
Emp Here 20
SIC 6021 National commercial banks

D-U-N-S 20-538-6597   (BR)
CANADA POST CORPORATION
RENFREW STN MAIN
249 Raglan St S, Renfrew, ON, K7V 1R3
(613) 432-3384
Emp Here 23
SIC 4311 U.s. postal service

D-U-N-S 25-853-3132   (BR)
CHILDREN'S AID SOCIETY OF TORONTO
FAMILLY & CHILDREN'S SERVICES
331 Martin St, Renfrew, ON, K7V 1A1
(613) 432-4821
Emp Here 20
SIC 8322 Individual and family services

D-U-N-S 20-770-5604   (BR)
**CORPORATION OF THE TOWN OF REN-
FREW, THE**
RENFREW FIRE DEPARTMENT
152 Plaunt St S, Renfrew, ON, K7V 1M8
(613) 432-4962
Emp Here 25
SIC 7389 Business services, nec

D-U-N-S 20-787-7804   (BR)
**CORPORATION OF THE COUNTY OF REN-
FREW**
BONNECHERE MANOR
(*Suby of* Corporation of the County of Ren-
frew)
470 Albert St, Renfrew, ON, K7V 4L5
(613) 432-4873
Emp Here 200
SIC 8361 Residential care

D-U-N-S 24-112-4390   (BR)
CORPORATION OF THE COUNTY OF REN-

FREW
(*Suby of* Corporation of the County of Renfrew)
450 O'Brien Rd Suite 105, Renfrew, ON, K7V
3Z2
(613) 432-3679
Emp Here 29
SIC 6531 Real estate agents and managers

D-U-N-S 24-312-1212   (BR)
E.T.M. INDUSTRIES INC
(*Suby of* E.T.M. Industries Inc)
266 Hall Ave E Suite 610, Renfrew, ON, K7V
2S5
(613) 432-6136
Emp Here 70
SIC 7539 Automotive repair shops, nec

D-U-N-S 24-102-1328   (HQ)
E.T.M. INDUSTRIES INC
(*Suby of* E.T.M. Industries Inc)
310 Hall Ave E, Renfrew, ON, K7V 2S5
(613) 432-6136
Emp Here 40   *Emp Total* 90
Sales 6,566,463
SIC 3599 Industrial machinery, nec
Pr Pr Jeffrey Campbell
VP VP John Paul Leclair
   John Robertson

D-U-N-S 20-282-1179   (BR)
GEM HEALTH CARE GROUP LIMITED
470 Raglan St N, Renfrew, ON, K7V 1P5
(613) 432-5823
Emp Here 120
SIC 8051 Skilled nursing care facilities

D-U-N-S 20-227-2204   (SL)
KENOPIC, W. V. & SONS LIMITED
*CANADIAN TIRE CORPORATION ASSO-
CIATES STORE*
1050 O'Brien Rd, Renfrew, ON, K7V 0B4
(613) 432-8117
Emp Here 54   *Sales* 9,130,500
SIC 5531 Auto and home supply stores
Pr Pr William V Kenopic

D-U-N-S 20-923-7564   (BR)
**MCDONALD'S   RESTAURANTS   OF
CANADA LIMITED**
MCDONALD'S
(*Suby of* McDonald's Corporation)
980 O'Brien Rd, Renfrew, ON, K7V 0B4
(613) 433-9546
Emp Here 50
SIC 5812 Eating places

D-U-N-S 24-344-4895   (BR)
METRO ONTARIO INC
LOEB
83 Raglan St S, Renfrew, ON, K7V 1P8
(613) 432-3013
Emp Here 50
SIC 5411 Grocery stores

D-U-N-S 25-682-8526   (BR)
ONTARIO POWER GENERATION INC
O P G
2 Innovation Dr, Renfrew, ON, K7V 0C2
(613) 433-9673
Emp Here 50
SIC 4911 Electric services

D-U-N-S 24-393-9514   (BR)
PHILIPS LIGHTING CANADA LTD
USS MANUFACTURING DIV OF
64 Ma-Te-Way Park Dr, Renfrew, ON, K7V 2L5
(613) 432-3653
Emp Here 36
SIC 3446 Architectural Metalwork

D-U-N-S 20-711-6943   (BR)
**RENFREW COUNTY CATHOLIC DISTRICT
SCHOOL BOARD**
ST JOSEPH HIGH SCHOOL
(*Suby of* Renfrew County Catholic District
School Board)
835 First St, Renfrew, ON, K7V 4E1

(613) 432-5846
Emp Here 50
SIC 8211 Elementary and secondary schools

D-U-N-S 20-026-6679   (BR)
**RENFREW COUNTY CATHOLIC DISTRICT
SCHOOL BOARD**
OUR LADY OF FATIMA
(*Suby of* Renfrew County Catholic District
School Board)
228 Mason Ave, Renfrew, ON, K7V 3Y3
(613) 432-4351
Emp Here 20
SIC 8211 Elementary and secondary schools

D-U-N-S 25-224-8620   (BR)
**RENFREW COUNTY CATHOLIC DISTRICT
SCHOOL BOARD**
ST THOMAS THE APOSTLE SCHOOL
(*Suby of* Renfrew County Catholic District
School Board)
41 Bolger Lane, Renfrew, ON, K7V 2M9
(613) 432-3137
Emp Here 21
SIC 8211 Elementary and secondary schools

D-U-N-S 20-711-6992   (BR)
**RENFREW COUNTY CATHOLIC DISTRICT
SCHOOL BOARD**
RENFREW COLLEGIATE INSTITUTE
(*Suby of* Renfrew County Catholic District
School Board)
184 Bonnechere St S, Renfrew, ON, K7V 1Z5
(613) 432-4858
Emp Here 50
SIC 8211 Elementary and secondary schools

D-U-N-S 20-711-6778   (BR)
**RENFREW COUNTY DISTRICT SCHOOL
BOARD**
CENTRAL PUBLIC SCHOOL
140 Munroe Ave E, Renfrew, ON, K7V 3K4
(613) 432-3627
Emp Here 25
SIC 8211 Elementary and secondary schools

D-U-N-S 20-634-1450   (SL)
TIM HORTONS
780 O'Brien Rd, Renfrew, ON, K7V 3Z4
(613) 432-9071
Emp Here 60   *Sales* 1,824,018
SIC 5812 Eating places

D-U-N-S 25-294-7783   (BR)
WAL-MART CANADA CORP
WAL MART
980 O'Brien Rd Suite 1, Renfrew, ON, K7V
0B4
(613) 432-4676
Emp Here 200
SIC 5311 Department stores

Richmond, ON K0A
Carleton County

D-U-N-S 25-360-5240   (SL)
**FIND-A-CAR AUTO SALES & BROKERING
INC**
6104 Perth St, Richmond, ON, K0A 2Z0

Emp Here 35   *Sales* 9,434,850
SIC 5521 Used car dealers
Pr Pr Ryan O'connor

D-U-N-S 25-070-0150   (BR)
**OTTAWA CATHOLIC DISTRICT SCHOOL
BOARD**
*ST.   PHILIP   CATHOLIC   ELEMENTARY
SCHOOL*
(*Suby of* Ottawa Catholic District School
Board)
79 Maitland St, Richmond, ON, K0A 2Z0
(613) 838-2466
Emp Here 24
SIC 8211 Elementary and secondary schools

D-U-N-S 25-263-5560   (BR)
**OTTAWA-CARLETON DISTRICT SCHOOL
BOARD**
SOUTH CARLETON HIGH SCHOOL
3673 Mcbean St, Richmond, ON, K0A 2Z0
(613) 838-2212
Emp Here 110
SIC 8211 Elementary and secondary schools

D-U-N-S 25-263-5404   (BR)
**OTTAWA-CARLETON DISTRICT SCHOOL
BOARD**
RICHMOND PUBLIC SCHOOL
3499 Mcbean St, Richmond, ON, K0A 2Z0
(613) 838-2371
Emp Here 20
SIC 8211 Elementary and secondary schools

D-U-N-S 20-891-8813   (SL)
RAB DEDESCO LTD
(*Suby of* Quatrosense Environmental Ltd)
5935 Ottawa St, Richmond, ON, K0A 2Z0
(613) 838-4005
Emp Here 23   *Sales* 6,714,320
SIC 3823 Process control instruments
Pr Pr David Jenkins
   Bern Currie

Richmond Hill, ON L4B
York County

D-U-N-S 25-246-7485   (SL)
1078505 ONTARIO INC
ROCKY MOUNTAIN HIGH RESTAURANT
125 York Blvd, Richmond Hill, ON, L4B 3B4

Emp Here 85   *Sales* 3,031,879
SIC 5812 Eating places

D-U-N-S 25-355-0883   (BR)
1325994 ONTARIO LIMITED
WORLD BOWL
9 East Wilmot St Suite 2, Richmond Hill, ON,
L4B 1A3
(905) 881-5927
Emp Here 20
SIC 7933 Bowling centers

D-U-N-S 20-709-0627   (BR)
2063414 ONTARIO LIMITED
LEISUREWORLD CAREGIVING CENTRE
(*Suby of* 2063414 Ontario Limited)
170 Red Maple Rd, Richmond Hill, ON, L4B
4T8
(905) 731-2273
Emp Here 160
SIC 8051 Skilled nursing care facilities

D-U-N-S 24-351-5033   (SL)
2101440 ONTARIO INC
MODERN REQUIREMENTS
30 East Beaver Creek Rd Suite 204, Richmond Hill, ON, L4B 1J2
(416) 469-3131
Emp Here 70   *Sales* 7,952,716
SIC 7371 Custom computer programming services
Pr Pr Asif Sharif

D-U-N-S 20-317-2077   (HQ)
AVI-SPL CANADA LTD
AVI-SPL
35 East Beaver Creek Rd Suite 1, Richmond
Hill, ON, L4B 1B3
(866) 797-5635
Emp Here 75   *Emp Total* 2,000
Sales 332,919,674
SIC 4813 Telephone communication, except
radio
Pr Pr John Zettel
Dir Boris Koechlin

D-U-N-S 24-365-6647   (SL)
ACCOLADE GROUP INC
ACCOLADE GROUP

---

66 West Beaver Creek Rd, Richmond Hill, ON, L4B 1G5
(416) 465-7211
Emp Here 100   *Sales* 4,677,755
SIC 2329 Men's and boy's clothing, nec

D-U-N-S 25-405-4463   (SL)
APPLANIX CORPORATION
(Suby of Trimble Inc.)
85 Leek Cres, Richmond Hill, ON, L4B 3B3
(289) 695-6000
Emp Here 100   *Sales* 17,931,396
SIC 3829 Measuring and controlling devices, nec
Pr Steve Woolven
  Bruno Scherzinger
Dir Fin Peter Teixeira
Sls Dir Eric Liberty
Prs Dir Michelle Papanikolov

D-U-N-S 20-251-1986   (BR)
ARCADIS CANADA INC
121 Granton Dr Unit 12, Richmond Hill, ON, L4B 3N4
(905) 764-9380
Emp Here 100
SIC 8748 Business consulting, nec

D-U-N-S 25-507-5475   (HQ)
ARTAFLEX INC
(Suby of Artaflex Inc)
174 West Beaver Creek Rd, Richmond Hill, ON, L4B 1B4
(905) 470-0109
Emp Here 220   *Emp Total* 250
Sales 27,433,223
SIC 3679 Electronic components, nec
Ch Bd Paul Walker
Ex VP Trent Carruthers
Dir Shmulik Vlodinger

D-U-N-S 20-563-8831   (BR)
ASSANTE CAPITAL MANAGEMENT LTD
ASSANTE WEALTH MANAGEMENT
550 Highway 7 E Suite 328, Richmond Hill, ON, L4B 3Z4
(905) 771-1535
Emp Here 20
SIC 6211 Security brokers and dealers

D-U-N-S 24-795-9521   (HQ)
AVENUE INDUSTRIAL SUPPLY COMPANY LIMITED
GLOBAL INDUSTRIAL CANADA
35 Staples Ave Suite 110, Richmond Hill, ON, L4B 4W6
(905) 780-2200
Emp Here 35   *Emp Total* 50
Sales 10,828,138
SIC 5084 Industrial machinery and equipment
  Nelson Rivers
Treas Robert Setnyk

D-U-N-S 20-807-4364   (BR)
BDO CANADA LIMITED
BDO DUNWOODY
45 Vogell Rd Unit 300, Richmond Hill, ON, L4B 3P6
(905) 508-0080
Emp Here 20
SIC 8111 Legal services

D-U-N-S 20-939-6501   (BR)
BANK OF NOVA SCOTIA, THE
SCOTIABANK
420 Highway 7 E Unit 38, Richmond Hill, ON, L4B 3K2
(905) 731-6915
Emp Here 30
SIC 6021 National commercial banks

D-U-N-S 24-437-5494   (BR)
BANQUE TORONTO-DOMINION, LA
TORONTO-DOMINION BANK, THE
(Suby of Toronto-Dominion Bank, The)
200-500 Highway 7 E, Richmond Hill, ON, L4B 1J1
(905) 764-7730
Emp Here 59

SIC 6021 National commercial banks

D-U-N-S 24-803-0335   (HQ)
BELL AND HOWELL CANADA LTD
(Suby of Bell and Howell Canada Ltd)
30 Mural St Unit 6, Richmond Hill, ON, L4B 1B5
(416) 746-2200
Emp Here 50   *Emp Total* 110
Sales 4,304,681
SIC 7629 Electrical repair shops

D-U-N-S 20-255-6858   (BR)
BENTO NOUVEAU LTD
BENTO SUSHI
50 West Pearce St Unit 17, Richmond Hill, ON, L4B 1C5
(905) 881-7772
Emp Here 20
SIC 4225 General warehousing and storage

D-U-N-S 24-213-6641   (BR)
BEST BUY CANADA LTD
BEST BUY
(Suby of Best Buy Co., Inc.)
225 High Tech Rd Unit C, Richmond Hill, ON, L4B 0A6
(905) 695-3906
Emp Here 50
SIC 5731 Radio, television, and electronic stores

D-U-N-S 20-038-1432   (HQ)
BLACK & DECKER CANADA INC
125 Mural St, Richmond Hill, ON, L4B 1M4
(905) 886-9511
Emp Here 100   *Emp Total* 54,023
Sales 76,564,800
SIC 5072 Hardware
Pr Pr David Howe
VP VP Robert Burke
  Joe Dillio
  William Owen

D-U-N-S 20-260-7230   (SL)
CTL-WDW LTD
9130 Leslie St Ste 204, Richmond Hill, ON, L4B 0B9
(416) 781-3635
Emp Here 50   *Sales* 2,553,625
SIC 7322 Adjustment and collection services

D-U-N-S 20-363-9968   (SL)
CWB MAXIUM FINANCIAL INC
30 Vogell Rd Suite 1, Richmond Hill, ON, L4B 3K6
(905) 780-6150
Emp Here 55   *Sales* 6,566,463
SIC 6159 Miscellaneous business credit institutions
Pr Daryl Mccollum

D-U-N-S 20-107-6465   (HQ)
CANADIAN CONTRACT CLEANING SPECIALISTS, INC
CCCSI
10 East Wilmot St Unit 25, Richmond Hill, ON, L4B 1G9
(905) 707-0410
Emp Here 285   *Emp Total* 12,924
Sales 19,230,772
SIC 7349 Building maintenance services, nec
Pr Pr Jeffrey Kaiser
VP VP Edward Lam
  Ceanne Kaiser

D-U-N-S 25-274-7753   (HQ)
CANADIAN HICKORY FARMS LTD
200 West Beaver Creek Rd Unit 14, Richmond Hill, ON, L4B 1B4
(905) 669-5929
Emp Here 30   *Emp Total* 95
Sales 24,587,756
SIC 5499 Miscellaneous food stores
VP Sls James O'neil

D-U-N-S 25-303-4482   (BR)
CANADIAN IMPERIAL BANK OF COMMERCE

CIBC
300 West Beaver Creek Rd Suite 201, Richmond Hill, ON, L4B 3B1
(905) 886-1370
Emp Here 22
SIC 6021 National commercial banks

D-U-N-S 24-341-0821   (BR)
COMPAGNIE DE TELEPHONE BELL DU CANADA OU BELL CANADA, LA
INFOSTREAM, DIV OF
9133 Leslie St, Richmond Hill, ON, L4B 4N1
(905) 762-9137
Emp Here 100
SIC 7379 Computer related services, nec

D-U-N-S 25-362-0272   (BR)
COMPUTERSHARE TRUST COMPANY OF CANADA
88a East Beaver Creek Rd Unit 3, Richmond Hill, ON, L4B 4A8
(905) 771-4390
Emp Here 40
SIC 6289 Security and commodity service

D-U-N-S 24-991-1103   (HQ)
CONNEX ONTARIO INC
44 East Beaver Creek Rd Unit 16, Richmond Hill, ON, L4B 1G8
(905) 944-6500
Emp Here 50   *Emp Total* 87
Sales 13,860,016
SIC 4899 Communication services, nec
Pr Pr Sayan Navaratnam
  Heung Hung Lee
  Sammy Kumaresh
VP Opers Pierre Ouellet

D-U-N-S 25-244-2991   (HQ)
CROCS CANADA INC
1455 16th Ave Unit 7, Richmond Hill, ON, L4B 4W5
(905) 747-3366
Emp Here 80   *Emp Total* 5,068
SIC 3021 Rubber and plastics footwear

D-U-N-S 24-610-4640   (HQ)
DECISIONONE CORPORATION
(Suby of D1 Holdings, LLC)
44 East Beaver Creek Rd Unit 19, Richmond Hill, ON, L4B 1G8
(905) 882-1555
Emp Here 50   *Emp Total* 275
Sales 12,768,123
SIC 7378 Computer maintenance and repair
VP VP Paul Lachance
Fin Ex Don Hamilton

D-U-N-S 20-129-6043   (HQ)
EMERSON ELECTRIC CANADA LIMITED
EMERSON POWER TRANSMISSION, DIV OF
(Suby of Emerson Electric Co.)
66 Leek Crescent, Richmond Hill, ON, L4B 1H1
(905) 948-3401
Emp Here 3,000   *Emp Total* 110,800
Sales 653,727,872
SIC 5063 Electrical apparatus and equipment
Pr Pr Michael Cousineau
  David Distler
  John Shivey
Prs Dir Douglas W Kelly

D-U-N-S 25-366-1953   (SL)
FLEXITY SOLUTIONS INC
45 Vogell Rd, Richmond Hill, ON, L4B 3P6
(905) 787-3500
Emp Here 50   *Sales* 4,711,645
SIC 7379 Computer related services, nec

D-U-N-S 25-189-6056   (HQ)
FRESENIUS MEDICAL CARE CANADA INC
45 Staples Ave Suite 110, Richmond Hill, ON, L4B 4W6
(905) 770-0855
Emp Here 75   *Emp Total* 107,354
Sales 11,673,712

SIC 5047 Medical and hospital equipment
Dir John N. Mcfarlane

D-U-N-S 24-993-3334   (HQ)
FUJITEC CANADA, INC
15 East Wilmot St, Richmond Hill, ON, L4B 1A3
(905) 731-8681
Emp Here 66   *Emp Total* 9,486
Sales 30,278,691
SIC 5084 Industrial machinery and equipment
Pr Ralph Wischnewski
Ex VP Masaaki Kubo
  Takakazu Uchiyama
  Katsuji Okuda

D-U-N-S 20-651-1490   (BR)
GAMBRO INC
(Suby of Baxter International Inc.)
2 East Beaver Creek Rd Suite 4, Richmond Hill, ON, L4B 2N3

Emp Here 35
SIC 5047 Medical and hospital equipment

D-U-N-S 24-319-1785   (HQ)
GRIFFIN JEWELLERY DESIGNS INC
(Suby of Griffin Jewellery Designs Inc)
50 West Wilmot St Suite 201, Richmond Hill, ON, L4B 1M5
(905) 882-0004
Emp Here 50   *Emp Total* 60
Sales 3,283,232
SIC 5944 Jewelry stores

D-U-N-S 24-525-1108   (BR)
HDR CORPORATION
(Suby of Hdr, Inc.)
100 York Blvd Suite 300, Richmond Hill, ON, L4B 1J8
(289) 695-4600
Emp Here 58
SIC 8711 Engineering services

D-U-N-S 25-270-3145   (BR)
HSBC BANK CANADA
330 Highway 7 E Suite 111, Richmond Hill, ON, L4B 3P8
(905) 881-7007
Emp Here 25
SIC 6021 National commercial banks

D-U-N-S 20-151-2050   (SL)
HANDLEMAN COMPANY OF CANADA LIMITED
60 Leek Cres, Richmond Hill, ON, L4B 1H1
(905) 763-1999
Emp Here 180   *Sales* 25,030,800
SIC 5099 Durable goods, nec
  Ned Talmey

D-U-N-S 25-832-0621   (BR)
HOME DEPOT OF CANADA INC
HOME DEPOT
(Suby of The Home Depot Inc)
50 Red Maple Rd, Richmond Hill, ON, L4B 4K1
(905) 763-2311
Emp Here 200
SIC 5251 Hardware stores

D-U-N-S 20-346-5307   (SL)
INNOVAGE CANADA LP
35 Fulton Way Suite 200, Richmond Hill, ON, L4B 2N4
(905) 738-9950
Emp Here 60   *Sales* 7,276,508
SIC 8611 Business associations

D-U-N-S 20-168-0766   (HQ)
JOHNSON CONTROLS NOVA SCOTIA U.L.C.
JOHNSON CONTROLS
56 Leek Cres, Richmond Hill, ON, L4B 1H1
(866) 468-1484
Emp Here 200   *Emp Total* 3,000
Sales 534,656,010
SIC 2531 Public building and related furniture

Pr Pr Alex A. Molinaroli
VP Brian Cadwallader
Pers/VP Susan Davis
Jerome Okarma
VP VP Frank Voltolina
Brian Stief
CFO R. Bruce Mcdonald

D-U-N-S 24-330-6219   (BR)
JOHNSON INC
1595 16th Ave Suite 700, Richmond Hill, ON, L4B 3S5
(905) 764-4900
Emp Here 160
SIC 6411 Insurance agents, brokers, and service

D-U-N-S 25-272-8548   (BR)
KEG RESTAURANTS LTD
KEG STEAKHOUSE & BAR, THE
162 York Blvd, Richmond Hill, ON, L4B 3J6
(905) 882-0500
Emp Here 50
SIC 5812 Eating places

D-U-N-S 24-668-6344   (BR)
KUMON CANADA INC
88b East Beaver Creek Rd Unit 4, Richmond Hill, ON, L4B 4W2
(905) 763-8911
Emp Here 30
SIC 6794 Patent owners and lessors

D-U-N-S 24-244-5211   (SL)
LITELINE CORPORATION
90 West Beaver Creek Rd, Richmond Hill, ON, L4B 1E7
(416) 996-1856
Emp Here 110   *Sales* 16,416,158
SIC 3089 Plastics products, nec
Pr Pr Steven Silverstein
VP Opers Daniel Silverstein
S&M/VP Mark Silverstein
Treas Helen Silverstein

D-U-N-S 20-181-3115   (SL)
M.I.S. ELECTRONICS INC
174 West Beaver Creek Rd, Richmond Hill, ON, L4B 1B4
(905) 707-2305
Emp Here 65   *Sales* 4,320,097
SIC 3679 Electronic components, nec

D-U-N-S 20-116-9104   (SL)
MERA NETWORKS INC
15 Wertheim Crt Suite 306, Richmond Hill, ON, L4B 3H7
(905) 882-4443
Emp Here 1,500   *Sales* 24,778,416
SIC 7371 Custom computer programming services
Pr Pr Marc Granic
Dir Opers Andrei Kostiounine

D-U-N-S 20-026-7495   (SL)
MID-LAND GROUP REALTY INC
330 Highway 7 E Suite 502, Richmond Hill, ON, L4B 3P8
(905) 709-0828
Emp Here 50   *Sales* 4,742,446
SIC 6531 Real estate agents and managers

D-U-N-S 20-589-2248   (BR)
NAV CANADA
1595 16th Ave Suite 100, Richmond Hill, ON, L4B 3N9
(905) 771-2872
Emp Here 20
SIC 4899 Communication services, nec

D-U-N-S 25-368-3049   (BR)
NTT DATA CANADA, INC.
30 East Beaver Creek Rd Ste 206, Richmond Hill, ON, L4B 1J2
(905) 695-1804
Emp Here 150
SIC 7371 Custom computer programming services

D-U-N-S 25-109-7473   (BR)
NAYLOR GROUP INCORPORATED
120 West Beaver Creek Rd Unit 6, Richmond Hill, ON, L4B 1L2
(905) 764-0913
Emp Here 30
SIC 1711 Plumbing, heating, air-conditioning

D-U-N-S 24-744-1215   (SL)
NORTHERN RESPONSE (INTERNATIONAL) LTD
50 Staples Ave, Richmond Hill, ON, L4B 0A7
(905) 737-6698
Emp Here 52   *Sales* 3,793,956
SIC 5963 Direct selling establishments

D-U-N-S 25-341-4916   (SL)
OMEGA DIRECT RESPONSE INC
30 Wertheim Crt Unit 12, Richmond Hill, ON, L4B 1B9
(416) 733-9911
Emp Here 825   *Sales* 54,884,450
SIC 7389 Business services, nec
Pr Pr Bharat Hansraj
Everton Thompson

D-U-N-S 24-764-1863   (HQ)
PACTIV CANADA INC
33 Staples Ave, Richmond Hill, ON, L4B 4W6
(905) 770-8810
Emp Here 25   *Sales* 59,098,167
SIC 5113 Industrial and personal service paper
Dir Opers Ken Bumstead
Fin Ex Emiljia Georgievski

D-U-N-S 24-348-5831   (SL)
PARETO RETAIL SERVICES INC
56 Leek Cres, Richmond Hill, ON, L4B 1H1

Emp Here 80   *Sales* 12,532,976
SIC 8732 Commercial nonphysical research
Karen Trudell

D-U-N-S 24-365-1838   (BR)
PLAN GROUP INC
DELTA MECHANICAL, DIV OF
100 West Beaver Creek Rd Unit 9, Richmond Hill, ON, L4B 1H4
(905) 771-0777
Emp Here 55
SIC 1711 Plumbing, heating, air-conditioning

D-U-N-S 25-992-3969   (SL)
PREMIER BOOKS DIRECT LTD
(*Suby of* Innovage Canada Limited)
29 East Wilmot St, Richmond Hill, ON, L4B 1A3
(905) 738-9200
Emp Here 50   *Sales* 12,270,000
SIC 7319 Advertising, nec
Pr Allan Bessada

D-U-N-S 20-983-4175   (HQ)
QUALITY UNDERWRITING SERVICES LTD
(*Suby of* Quality Underwriting Services Ltd)
111 Granton Dr Suite 105, Richmond Hill, ON, L4B 1L5
(905) 762-9827
Emp Here 45   *Emp Total* 300
Sales 20,613,600
SIC 7323 Credit reporting services
Dir Alan Shinton
Pr Pr Greg Shinton

D-U-N-S 25-191-7696   (BR)
RBC DOMINION SECURITIES INC
RBC DOMINION SECURITIES
(*Suby of* Royal Bank Of Canada)
260 East Beaver Creek Rd Suite 500, Richmond Hill, ON, L4B 3M3
(905) 764-6404
Emp Here 38
SIC 6282 Investment advice

D-U-N-S 20-804-3252   (BR)
SIR CORP
JACK ASTOR'S BAR & GRILL

155 York Blvd, Richmond Hill, ON, L4B 3B4
(905) 771-9191
Emp Here 70
SIC 5812 Eating places

D-U-N-S 20-405-1064   (BR)
SANDERSON-HAROLD COMPANY LIMITED, THE
PARIS KITCHENS
245 West Beaver Creek Rd Unit 2, Richmond Hill, ON, L4B 1L1
(905) 886-5751
Emp Here 20
SIC 2434 Wood kitchen cabinets

D-U-N-S 24-374-1407   (HQ)
SICK LTD
2 East Beaver Creek Rd Building #3, Richmond Hill, ON, L4B 2N3
(905) 771-1444
Emp Here 30   *Emp Total* 5,674
Sales 8,575,885
SIC 5084 Industrial machinery and equipment
Pr Pr Craig Smith
Off Mgr Eileen Bogo
Robert Barniskis
Dir Alberto Bertomeu

D-U-N-S 20-058-7009   (SL)
SPECTRAL APPLIED RESEARCH INC
2 East Beaver Creek Rd, Richmond Hill, ON, L4B 2N3
(905) 326-5040
Emp Here 30   *Sales* 3,283,232
SIC 3545 Machine tool accessories

D-U-N-S 25-114-8169   (BR)
ST JOSEPH PRINT GROUP INC
ST JOSEPH DOCUMENTS
70 West Wilmot St, Richmond Hill, ON, L4B 1H8

Emp Here 22
SIC 2752 Commercial printing, lithographic

D-U-N-S 20-647-6004   (HQ)
STRAUSS, LEVI & CO. (CANADA) INC
LEVI-STRAUSS
1725 16th Ave Suite 200, Richmond Hill, ON, L4B 4C6
(905) 763-4400
Emp Here 50   *Emp Total* 13,200
Sales 11,867,639
SIC 5632 Women's accessory and specialty stores
Diana Dimitian
Dir Fin Donna Keon

D-U-N-S 24-683-3326   (SL)
SUMMERCOVE ESTATES INC
30 Wertheim Crt Suite 9, Richmond Hill, ON, L4B 1B9
(905) 881-1026
Emp Here 20   *Sales* 5,579,750
SIC 1522 Residential construction, nec
Shahrokh Nourmansouri
Azim Azimi

D-U-N-S 24-125-2217   (BR)
SUN LIFE ASSURANCE COMPANY OF CANADA
225 East Beaver Creek Rd Suite 720, Richmond Hill, ON, L4B 3P4
(905) 763-8188
Emp Here 40
SIC 6311 Life insurance

D-U-N-S 20-310-8055   (BR)
SUPREME OFFICE PRODUCTS LIMITED
SUPREME BASICS
(*Suby of* Placements Denis Latulippe Inc, Les)
40 West Beaver Creek Rd, Richmond Hill, ON, L4B 1G5
(905) 762-7100
Emp Here 40
SIC 5112 Stationery and office supplies

D-U-N-S 24-395-3895   (SL)

SUZUKI CANADA (ES2-S1) INC
100 East Beaver Creek Rd, Richmond Hill, ON, L4B 1J6
(905) 889-2677
Emp Here 49   *Sales* 24,049,200
SIC 5511 New and used car dealers

D-U-N-S 20-528-8210   (SL)
SWISS NATURAL A DIVISION OF ALEANT PHARMACEUTICALS INT'L INC
35 Fulton Way, Richmond Hill, ON, L4B 2N4
(905) 886-9500
Emp Here 100   *Sales* 12,330,358
SIC 5122 Drugs, proprietaries, and sundries
Pr John Ferris
Ch Bd Steve Mckerrell
Dir John Annett
Dir David Bloom
Dir Michael Eustace

D-U-N-S 25-404-1593   (SL)
SYM-TECH INC
SYM-TECH AUTOMOTIVE PROTECTION
150 West Beaver Creek, Richmond Hill, ON, L4B 1B4
(905) 889-5390
Emp Here 125   *Sales* 15,159,393
SIC 6399 Insurance carriers, nec
CEO Brad Wells
Pr Chris Cawston
Geoff Seely

D-U-N-S 24-876-2650   (SL)
TILWOOD DIRECT MARKETING INC
81 Granton Dr Suite 1, Richmond Hill, ON, L4B 2N5

Emp Here 85   *Sales* 9,333,400
SIC 4226 Special warehousing and storage, nec
Pr Pr Costas Menegakis
VP VP Francis Gallera
Dir Fin John Kapsalis

D-U-N-S 20-177-2423   (HQ)
TRANS-NORTHERN PIPELINES INC
(*Suby of* Trans-Northern Pipelines Inc)
45 Vogell Rd Suite 310, Richmond Hill, ON, L4B 3P6
(905) 770-3353
Emp Here 38   *Emp Total* 69
SIC 4613 Refined petroleum pipelines

D-U-N-S 24-415-1205   (HQ)
TRANSPLACE CANADA LTD
45a West Wilmot St Unit 213, Richmond Hill, ON, L4B 1K1
(905) 771-7111
Emp Here 26   *Emp Total* 1,000
Sales 7,441,991
SIC 4731 Freight transportation arrangement
Thomas Sanderson
Frank Mcguigan
Jay Baker
VP Sls Michael Chapman
Mike Dieter
George Abernathy
Steven Crowther

D-U-N-S 20-101-7980   (BR)
TRENT METALS (2012) LIMITED
30 Mural St Unit 1, Richmond Hill, ON, L4B 1B5
(905) 886-5442
Emp Here 30
SIC 5075 Warm air heating and air conditioning

D-U-N-S 24-093-4778   (HQ)
TUXEDO ROYALE LIMITED
TUXEDO ROYALE FORMAL WEAR
(*Suby of* Tuxedo Royale Limited)
9078 Leslie St Unit 5, Richmond Hill, ON, L4B 3L8
(416) 798-7617
Emp Here 20   *Emp Total* 140
Sales 4,669,485
SIC 7299 Miscellaneous personal service

D-U-N-S 24-121-6030   (BR)
WAL-MART CANADA CORP
SAM'S CLUB 4848
255 Silver Linden Dr, Richmond Hill, ON, L4B 4V5
(905) 747-0628
Emp Here 25
SIC 5311 Department stores

D-U-N-S 20-755-4221   (SL)
WATSON GROUP LTD, THE
95 West Beaver Creek Rd Unit 10, Richmond Hill, ON, L4B 1H2
(905) 889-9119
Emp Here 55   *Sales* 4,815,406
SIC 1711 Plumbing, heating, air-conditioning

D-U-N-S 24-312-3119   (BR)
WESTERN WAFFLES CORP
20 Sims Cres Suite 2, Richmond Hill, ON, L4B 2N9
(905) 889-1190
Emp Here 50
SIC 2052 Cookies and crackers

D-U-N-S 20-106-3570   (BR)
WINNERS MERCHANTS INTERNATIONAL L.P.
WINNERS
(*Suby of* The TJX Companies Inc)
45 Red Maple Rd Unit 7, Richmond Hill, ON, L4B 4M6
(905) 889-5456
Emp Here 50
SIC 5651 Family clothing stores

D-U-N-S 20-711-4716   (BR)
YORK CATHOLIC DISTRICT SCHOOL BOARD
POPE JOHN PAUL II SCHOOL
155 Red Maple Rd, Richmond Hill, ON, L4B 4P9
(905) 709-3134
Emp Here 50
SIC 8211 Elementary and secondary schools

D-U-N-S 20-711-4153   (BR)
YORK REGION DISTRICT SCHOOL BOARD
BAYVIEW HILL ELEMENTARY SCHOOL
(*Suby of* York Region District School Board)
81 Strathearn Ave, Richmond Hill, ON, L4B 2J5
(905) 508-0806
Emp Here 75
SIC 8211 Elementary and secondary schools

D-U-N-S 20-711-3965   (BR)
YORK REGION DISTRICT SCHOOL BOARD
ADRIENNE CLARKSON PUBLIC SCHOOL
(*Suby of* York Region District School Board)
68 Queens College Dr, Richmond Hill, ON, L4B 1X3
(905) 709-3554
Emp Here 50
SIC 8211 Elementary and secondary schools

D-U-N-S 25-297-9224   (BR)
YORK REGION DISTRICT SCHOOL BOARD
DONCREST PUBLIC SCHOOL
(*Suby of* York Region District School Board)
124 Blackmore Ave, Richmond Hill, ON, L4B 2B1
(905) 882-4480
Emp Here 50
SIC 8211 Elementary and secondary schools

D-U-N-S 24-470-1736   (SL)
ZAN-NOR CONSTRUCTION & MANAGEMENT LIMITED
50 West Beaver Creek Rd Unit B, Richmond Hill, ON, L4B 1G5
(905) 707-1130
Emp Here 35   *Sales* 6,594,250
SIC 5541 Gasoline service stations
Pr Pr Bella Ziering

Richmond Hill, ON L4C
York County

D-U-N-S 25-509-2496   (BR)
APOTEX INC
380 Elgin Mills Rd E, Richmond Hill, ON, L4C 5H2
(905) 884-2050
Emp Here 520
SIC 2834 Pharmaceutical preparations

D-U-N-S 25-524-2646   (SL)
AVANTE AUTOMOBILE CORPORATION
AVANTE MAZDA
10414 Yonge St, Richmond Hill, ON, L4C 3C3
(905) 780-9999
Emp Here 44   *Sales* 22,319,000
SIC 5511 New and used car dealers
Pr Pr Frank Serpa

D-U-N-S 25-296-7260   (BR)
BANK OF NOVA SCOTIA, THE
SCOTIABANK
10355 Yonge St, Richmond Hill, ON, L4C 3C1
(905) 884-1107
Emp Here 21
SIC 6021 National commercial banks

D-U-N-S 20-845-6371   (SL)
BASIC MORTGAGE CORP
10211 Yonge St Unit 201, Richmond Hill, ON, L4C 3B3
(905) 508-6300
Emp Here 20   *Sales* 5,104,320
SIC 6162 Mortgage bankers and loan correspondents
Prin Adolf Kleiner

D-U-N-S 25-060-0640   (BR)
BULK BARN FOODS LIMITED
9350 Yonge St Suite A6, Richmond Hill, ON, L4C 5G2
(905) 883-3036
Emp Here 20
SIC 5411 Grocery stores

D-U-N-S 20-074-5680   (BR)
CANADA POST CORPORATION
21 Arnold Cres, Richmond Hill, ON, L4C 3R6
(905) 884-9424
Emp Here 100
SIC 4311 U.s. postal service

D-U-N-S 20-352-8641   (SL)
CANADIAN AID ORGANIZATION FOR IRAQI SOCIETY REHAB. (CAOFISR)
CAOFISR
8 Lawson Crt, Richmond Hill, ON, L4C 8L6
(647) 449-1621
Emp Here 166   *Sales* 11,746,673
SIC 8399 Social services, nec
Ch Bd Majid Shamil

D-U-N-S 25-303-4441   (BR)
CANADIAN IMPERIAL BANK OF COMMERCE
CIBC
9335 Yonge St, Richmond Hill, ON, L4C 1V4
(905) 884-4460
Emp Here 28
SIC 6021 National commercial banks

D-U-N-S 24-342-2180   (BR)
CARA OPERATIONS LIMITED
SWISS CHALET
(*Suby of* Cara Holdings Limited)
9350 Yonge St Suite 1209, Richmond Hill, ON, L4C 5G2
(905) 737-4307
Emp Here 50
SIC 5812 Eating places

D-U-N-S 24-469-2802   (BR)
CARA OPERATIONS LIMITED
SWISS CHALET
(*Suby of* Cara Holdings Limited)
9625 Yonge St, Richmond Hill, ON, L4C 5T2
(905) 884-1515
Emp Here 60

SIC 5812 Eating places

D-U-N-S 20-779-8237   (BR)
CHILDREN'S PLACE (CANADA) LP, THE
CHILDREN'S PLACE, THE
9350 Yonge St, Richmond Hill, ON, L4C 5G2
(905) 884-4991
Emp Here 25
SIC 5641 Children's and infants' wear stores

D-U-N-S 20-005-9371   (BR)
CINEPLEX ODEON CORPORATION
SILVERCITY RICHMOND HILL
8725 Yonge St, Richmond Hill, ON, L4C 6Z1
(905) 709-0025
Emp Here 20
SIC 7832 Motion picture theaters, except drive-in

D-U-N-S 24-345-5297   (BR)
CORPORATION OF THE TOWN OF RICHMOND HILL, THE
ELGIN WEST COMMUNITY CENTRE & POOL
11099 Bathurst St, Richmond Hill, ON, L4C 0N2
(905) 508-7012
Emp Here 60
SIC 7999 Amusement and recreation, nec

D-U-N-S 25-729-3225   (BR)
CORPORATION OF THE TOWN OF RICHMOND HILL, THE
WAVE POOL, THE
5 Hopkins St, Richmond Hill, ON, L4C 0C1
(905) 508-9283
Emp Here 50
SIC 7999 Amusement and recreation, nec

D-U-N-S 24-728-6057   (BR)
COSTI IMMIGRANT SERVICES
WELCOME CENTRE IMMIGRANT REFUGEE SERVICES
9325 Yonge St Suite 31a, Richmond Hill, ON, L4C 0A8
(289) 842-3124
Emp Here 30
SIC 8322 Individual and family services

D-U-N-S 20-407-4777   (SL)
CUSCO FABRICATORS LLC
305 Enford Rd, Richmond Hill, ON, L4C 3E9
(905) 883-1214
Emp Here 75   *Sales* 10,271,386
SIC 3569 General industrial machinery, nec
Pr Pr Stephen Godwin

D-U-N-S 20-806-0678   (SL)
DELMANOR ELGIN MILLS
80 Elgin Mills Rd E, Richmond Hill, ON, L4C 0L3
(905) 770-7963
Emp Here 50   *Sales* 1,824,018
SIC 8361 Residential care

D-U-N-S 25-999-8602   (BR)
DOLLARAMA S.E.C.
606 Major Mackenzie Dr E, Richmond Hill, ON, L4C 1J9
(905) 883-3859
Emp Here 27
SIC 5331 Variety stores

D-U-N-S 20-708-1253   (BR)
ENBRIDGE INC
93 Edward Ave, Richmond Hill, ON, L4C 5E5

Emp Here 55
SIC 4612 Crude petroleum pipelines

D-U-N-S 24-342-8427   (BR)
GOODLIFE FITNESS CENTRES INC
GOODLIFE FITNESS CLUB
9350 Yonge St, Richmond Hill, ON, L4C 5G2
(905) 884-5769
Emp Here 40
SIC 7991 Physical fitness facilities

D-U-N-S 25-301-1373   (BR)

HUDSON'S BAY COMPANY
BAY, THE
9350 Yonge St Suite 1999, Richmond Hill, ON, L4C 5G2
(905) 883-1222
Emp Here 250
SIC 5311 Department stores

D-U-N-S 24-987-6319   (BR)
LAFARGE CANADA INC
INNOCON
50 Newkirk Rd, Richmond Hill, ON, L4C 3G3
(905) 508-7676
Emp Here 200
SIC 3273 Ready-mixed concrete

D-U-N-S 25-295-5604   (BR)
LEON'S FURNITURE LIMITED
10875 Yonge St, Richmond Hill, ON, L4C 3E3
(905) 770-4424
Emp Here 35
SIC 5712 Furniture stores

D-U-N-S 25-317-7331   (BR)
LIQUOR CONTROL BOARD OF ONTARIO, THE
L.C.B.O. #623
8783 Yonge St, Richmond Hill, ON, L4C 6Z1
(905) 886-3511
Emp Here 23
SIC 5921 Liquor stores

D-U-N-S 20-747-0605   (BR)
LOBLAWS SUPERMARKETS LIMITED
LOBLAWS
10909 Yonge St, Richmond Hill, ON, L4C 3E3
(905) 737-1222
Emp Here 20
SIC 5411 Grocery stores

D-U-N-S 20-097-6764   (BR)
LOBLAWS SUPERMARKETS LIMITED
ENZO'S NOFRILLS
9325 Yonge St, Richmond Hill, ON, L4C 0A8
(905) 737-1988
Emp Here 20
SIC 5411 Grocery stores

D-U-N-S 20-699-6337   (BR)
MACKENZIE HEALTH
YORK CENTRAL HOSPITAL
10 Trench St, Richmond Hill, ON, L4C 4Z3
(905) 883-1212
Emp Here 25
SIC 8062 General medical and surgical hospitals

D-U-N-S 20-341-6813   (BR)
MAGNA EXTERIORS INC
POLYBRITE, DIV OF
254 Centre St E, Richmond Hill, ON, L4C 1A8
(905) 883-3600
Emp Here 125
SIC 3089 Plastics products, nec

D-U-N-S 24-045-4876   (BR)
MAGNA INTERNATIONAL INC
POLYBRITE DIV OF
254 Centre St E, Richmond Hill, ON, L4C 1A8
(905) 883-3600
Emp Here 150
SIC 3465 Automotive stampings

D-U-N-S 25-295-5943   (BR)
MARCH OF DIMES CANADA
25 Marshall St Suite 100, Richmond Hill, ON, L4C 0A3
(905) 508-5555
Emp Here 22
SIC 8331 Job training and related services

D-U-N-S 20-783-3591   (SL)
MARIANN NURSING HOME AND RESIDENCE
MARIANN HOME
9915 Yonge St, Richmond Hill, ON, L4C 1V1
(905) 884-9276
Emp Here 100   *Sales* 4,523,563

SIC 8051 Skilled nursing care facilities

D-U-N-S 20-779-4244　　(BR)
MASTERMIND LP
9350 Yonge St, Richmond Hill, ON, L4C 5G2
(905) 508-5001
Emp Here 30
SIC 5945 Hobby, toy, and game shops

D-U-N-S 24-313-0643　　(BR)
MEDITRUST PHARMACY SERVICES INC
MEDITRUST PHARMACY
9665 Bayview Ave Unit 27, Richmond Hill, ON, L4C 9V4
(905) 770-6618
Emp Here 20
SIC 5912 Drug stores and proprietary stores

D-U-N-S 25-597-9403　　(SL)
ONTREA INC
CADILLAR FAIRVIEW
9350 Yonge St Suite 205, Richmond Hill, ON, L4C 5G2
(905) 883-1400
Emp Here 30　　　*Sales* 1,668,720
SIC 6519 Real property lessors, nec

D-U-N-S 20-703-4021　　(BR)
PHARMA PLUS DRUGMARTS LTD
MEDITRUST
9665 Bayview Ave, Richmond Hill, ON, L4C 9V4
(905) 770-7377
Emp Here 30
SIC 5912 Drug stores and proprietary stores

D-U-N-S 25-859-1858　　(BR)
PHARMA PLUS DRUGMARTS LTD
PHARM PLUS
9325 Yonge St, Richmond Hill, ON, L4C 0A8
(905) 508-5958
Emp Here 20
SIC 5912 Drug stores and proprietary stores

D-U-N-S 24-395-3770　　(BR)
REXALL PHARMACY GROUP LTD
REXALL 1313
(*Suby of* McKesson Corporation)
10870 Yonge St, Richmond Hill, ON, L4C 3E4
(905) 508-5395
Emp Here 22
SIC 5912 Drug stores and proprietary stores

D-U-N-S 25-800-6071　　(HQ)
RICHMOND HILL ARENA ASSOCIATION
ELGIN BARROW ARENA COMPLEX
(*Suby of* Richmond Hill Arena Association)
43 Church St S, Richmond Hill, ON, L4C 1W1
(905) 884-1368
Emp Here 25　　　*Emp Total* 60
Sales 3,283,232
SIC 7999 Amusement and recreation, nec

D-U-N-S 25-049-6866　　(BR)
RICHMOND HILL ARENA ASSOCIATION
STOJKO, ELVIS ARENA
(*Suby of* Richmond Hill Arena Association)
350 16th Ave, Richmond Hill, ON, L4C 7A9
(905) 884-6776
Emp Here 24
SIC 7999 Amusement and recreation, nec

D-U-N-S 25-507-6739　　(SL)
**RICHMOND HILL MONTESSORI & ELE-
MENTARY PRIVATE SCHOOL**
189 Weldrick Rd E, Richmond Hill, ON, L4C 0A6
(905) 508-2228
Emp Here 70　　　*Sales* 4,669,485
SIC 8211 Elementary and secondary schools

D-U-N-S 20-080-1541　　(BR)
ROYAL BANK OF CANADA
RBC
(*Suby of* Royal Bank Of Canada)
9555 Yonge St Suite 25, Richmond Hill, ON, L4C 9M5
(905) 780-8100
Emp Here 30

SIC 6021 National commercial banks

D-U-N-S 20-643-7902　　(BR)
STARBUCKS COFFEE CANADA, INC
(*Suby of* Starbucks Corporation)
10520 Yonge St Suite 35b, Richmond Hill, ON, L4C 3C7
(905) 508-7474
Emp Here 30
SIC 5812 Eating places

D-U-N-S 24-174-5517　　(BR)
STOCK TRANSPORTATION LTD
550 Edward Ave, Richmond Hill, ON, L4C 3K4
(905) 883-6665
Emp Here 250
SIC 4151 School buses

D-U-N-S 25-180-5271　　(BR)
SUNRISE NORTH ASSISTED LIVING LTD
SUNRISE ASSISTED LIVING OF RICH-MOND HILL
(*Suby of* Welltower Inc.)
9800 Yonge St Suite 101, Richmond Hill, ON, L4C 0P5
(905) 383-6963
Emp Here 75
SIC 8361 Residential care

D-U-N-S 25-321-1809　　(BR)
TORONTO-DOMINION BANK, THE
TD BANK FINANCIAL GROUP
(*Suby of* Toronto-Dominion Bank, The)
10909 Yonge St Suite 13, Richmond Hill, ON, L4C 3E3
(905) 508-4511
Emp Here 30
SIC 6021 National commercial banks

D-U-N-S 25-807-4236　　(BR)
VALUE VILLAGE STORES, INC
(*Suby of* Savers, Inc.)
10620 Yonge St, Richmond Hill, ON, L4C 3C8
(905) 737-7444
Emp Here 30
SIC 5399 Miscellaneous general merchandise

D-U-N-S 20-182-9272　　(HQ)
VICTAULIC COMPANY OF CANADA ULC
(*Suby of* Victaulic Company)
123 Newkirk Rd, Richmond Hill, ON, L4C 3G5
(905) 884-7444
Emp Here 450　　　*Emp Total* 3,000
Sales 65,883,512
SIC 3494 Valves and pipe fittings, nec
Ch Bd Joseph M Trachtenburg
Pr Gary Moore
VP VP Tim Meadows
　Mario D'ambrosio
　John Malloy

D-U-N-S 25-221-2691　　(BR)
WINNERS MERCHANTS INTERNATIONAL L.P.
WINNERS
(*Suby of* The TJX Companies Inc)
10520 Yonge St Suite 35b, Richmond Hill, ON, L4C 3C7
(905) 770-8754
Emp Here 35
SIC 5651 Family clothing stores

D-U-N-S 25-147-3492　　(BR)
YORK CATHOLIC DISTRICT SCHOOL BOARD
ST. JOSEPH RICHMOND HILL
301 Roney Ave, Richmond Hill, ON, L4C 2H4
(905) 884-5077
Emp Here 40
SIC 8211 Elementary and secondary schools

D-U-N-S 25-147-3468　　(BR)
YORK CATHOLIC DISTRICT SCHOOL BOARD
ST. CHARLES GARNIER CATHOLIC ELE-MENTARY SCHOOL
16 Castle Rock Dr, Richmond Hill, ON, L4C 5H5

---

(905) 884-0223
Emp Here 34
SIC 8211 Elementary and secondary schools

D-U-N-S 25-147-3450　　(BR)
YORK CATHOLIC DISTRICT SCHOOL BOARD
ST ANNE CATHOLIC SCHOOL
105 Don Head Village Blvd, Richmond Hill, ON, L4C 7N1
(905) 883-0311
Emp Here 33
SIC 8211 Elementary and secondary schools

D-U-N-S 25-147-3518　　(BR)
YORK CATHOLIC DISTRICT SCHOOL BOARD
ST. MARY IMMACULATE SCHOOL
161 Regent St, Richmond Hill, ON, L4C 9N9
(905) 884-5381
Emp Here 40
SIC 8211 Elementary and secondary schools

D-U-N-S 20-711-4617　　(BR)
YORK CATHOLIC DISTRICT SCHOOL BOARD
HENRI NOUWEN ELEMENTARY SCHOOL
121 Larratt Lane, Richmond Hill, ON, L4C 0E6
(905) 884-8086
Emp Here 50
SIC 8211 Elementary and secondary schools

D-U-N-S 25-293-6539　　(BR)
YORK REGION DISTRICT SCHOOL BOARD
CROSBY HEIGHTS PUBLIC SCHOOL
(*Suby of* York Region District School Board)
190 Neal Dr, Richmond Hill, ON, L4C 3K7
(905) 884-5281
Emp Here 60
SIC 8211 Elementary and secondary schools

D-U-N-S 25-297-9133　　(BR)
YORK REGION DISTRICT SCHOOL BOARD
ROSS DOAN PUBLIC SCHOOL
(*Suby of* York Region District School Board)
101 Weldrick Rd W, Richmond Hill, ON, L4C 3T9
(905) 884-4022
Emp Here 35
SIC 8211 Elementary and secondary schools

D-U-N-S 25-297-9018　　(BR)
YORK REGION DISTRICT SCHOOL BOARD
SIXTEENTH AVENUE PUBLIC SCHOOL
(*Suby of* York Region District School Board)
400 16th Ave, Richmond Hill, ON, L4C 7A9
(905) 884-5598
Emp Here 55
SIC 8211 Elementary and secondary schools

D-U-N-S 20-591-2590　　(BR)
YORK REGION DISTRICT SCHOOL BOARD
ROSTLAWN PUBLIC SCHOOL
(*Suby of* York Region District School Board)
422 Carrville Rd, Richmond Hill, ON, L4C 6E6
(905) 884-5934
Emp Here 35
SIC 8211 Elementary and secondary schools

D-U-N-S 25-297-8978　　(BR)
YORK REGION DISTRICT SCHOOL BOARD
WALTER SCOTT PUBLIC SCHOOL
(*Suby of* York Region District School Board)
500 Major Mackenzie Dr E, Richmond Hill, ON, L4C 1J2
(905) 884-2693
Emp Here 50
SIC 8211 Elementary and secondary schools

D-U-N-S 20-291-3435　　(BR)
YORK REGION DISTRICT SCHOOL BOARD
COMMUNITY EDUCATIONAL CENTRE - CENTRAL
(*Suby of* York Region District School Board)
317 Centre St E, Richmond Hill, ON, L4C 1B3
(905) 884-4477
Emp Here 30
SIC 8211 Elementary and secondary schools

D-U-N-S 25-297-9059　　(BR)
YORK REGION DISTRICT SCHOOL BOARD
SILVER PINES PUBLIC SCHOOL
(*Suby of* York Region District School Board)
112 Stave Cres, Richmond Hill, ON, L4C 9J2
(905) 508-6698
Emp Here 60
SIC 8211 Elementary and secondary schools

D-U-N-S 24-227-8096　　(BR)
YORK REGION DISTRICT SCHOOL BOARD
PLEASANTVILLE PUBLIC SCHOOL
(*Suby of* York Region District School Board)
400 Mill St, Richmond Hill, ON, L4C 4B9
(905) 884-7431
Emp Here 35
SIC 8211 Elementary and secondary schools

D-U-N-S 25-293-6349　　(BR)
YORK REGION DISTRICT SCHOOL BOARD
BAYVIEW SECONDARY SCHOOL
(*Suby of* York Region District School Board)
10077 Bayview Ave, Richmond Hill, ON, L4C 2L4
(905) 884-4453
Emp Here 135
SIC 8211 Elementary and secondary schools

D-U-N-S 25-297-9307　　(BR)
YORK REGION DISTRICT SCHOOL BOARD
CHARLES HOWITT PUBLIC SCHOOL
(*Suby of* York Region District School Board)
30 Pearson Ave, Richmond Hill, ON, L4C 6T7
(905) 889-2522
Emp Here 45
SIC 8211 Elementary and secondary schools

D-U-N-S 25-293-6265　　(BR)
YORK REGION DISTRICT SCHOOL BOARD
ALEXANDER MACKENZIE HIGH SCHOOL
(*Suby of* York Region District School Board)
300 Major Mackenzie Dr W, Richmond Hill, ON, L4C 3S3
(905) 884-0554
Emp Here 125
SIC 8211 Elementary and secondary schools

D-U-N-S 20-591-2509　　(BR)
YORK REGION DISTRICT SCHOOL BOARD
BEVERLY ACRES PUBLIC SCHOOL
(*Suby of* York Region District School Board)
283 Neal Dr, Richmond Hill, ON, L4C 3L3
(905) 884-5059
Emp Here 30
SIC 8211 Elementary and secondary schools

D-U-N-S 20-711-4047　　(BR)
YORK REGION DISTRICT SCHOOL BOARD
MACKILLOP, O M PUBLIC SCHOOL
(*Suby of* York Region District School Board)
206 Lucas St, Richmond Hill, ON, L4C 4P7
(905) 884-5711
Emp Here 32
SIC 8211 Elementary and secondary schools

D-U-N-S 25-221-4606　　(BR)
YORK REGION DISTRICT SCHOOL BOARD
LANGSTAFF SECONDARY SCHOOL
(*Suby of* York Region District School Board)
106 Garden Ave, Richmond Hill, ON, L4C 6M1
(905) 889-6266
Emp Here 100
SIC 8211 Elementary and secondary schools

Richmond Hill, ON L4E
York County

D-U-N-S 24-342-7940　　(BR)
CARA OPERATIONS LIMITED
HARVEY'S
(*Suby of* Cara Holdings Limited)
13085 Yonge St, Richmond Hill, ON, L4E 3S8
(905) 773-1988
Emp Here 30
SIC 5812 Eating places

▲ Public Company　　■ Public Company Family Member　　**HQ** Headquarters　　**BR** Branch　　**SL** Single Location

D-U-N-S 20-026-7511   (BR)
CLUBLINK CORPORATION ULC
DIAMOND BACK GOLF CLUB
13300 Leslie St, Richmond Hill, ON, L4E 1A2
(905) 888-9612
Emp Here 50
SIC 7992 Public golf courses

D-U-N-S 25-419-2289   (BR)
CONCORD FOOD CENTRE INC
OAK RIDGES
13144 Yonge St, Richmond Hill, ON, L4E 1A4
(905) 773-5212
Emp Here 30
SIC 5411 Grocery stores

D-U-N-S 20-582-0710   (BR)
CONSEIL SCOLAIRE VIAMONDE
ACADEMIE DE LA NORAINE
13200 Yonge St, Richmond Hill, ON, L4E 2T2
(905) 773-7616
Emp Here 20
SIC 8211 Elementary and secondary schools

D-U-N-S 20-251-3839   (BR)
MARCH OF DIMES CANADA
13311 Yonge St Suite 202, Richmond Hill, ON, L4E 3L6
(905) 773-7758
Emp Here 25
SIC 8331 Job training and related services

D-U-N-S 24-122-2624   (BR)
MILLER, P.G. ENTERPRISES LIMITED
MCDONALD'S
13081 Yonge St, Richmond Hill, ON, L4E 3M2
(905) 773-6777
Emp Here 64
SIC 5812 Eating places

D-U-N-S 25-084-1871   (BR)
TORONTO AND REGION CONSERVATION AUTHORITY
BATHURST GLEN GOLF CLUB
(*Suby of* Toronto and Region Conservation Authority)
12481 Bathurst St, Richmond Hill, ON, L4E 2B4
(905) 773-4334
Emp Here 20
SIC 7992 Public golf courses

D-U-N-S 25-028-5657   (BR)
UNILOCK LTD
37 Gormley Rd E, Richmond Hill, ON, L4E 1A2
(905) 887-1717
Emp Here 20
SIC 3271 Concrete block and brick

D-U-N-S 20-182-1209   (BR)
WEINS CANADA INC
LEXUS OF RICHMOND HILL
11552 Yonge St, Richmond Hill, ON, L4E 3N7
(905) 883-8812
Emp Here 20
SIC 5511 New and used car dealers

D-U-N-S 25-147-3377   (BR)
YORK CATHOLIC DISTRICT SCHOOL BOARD
OUR LADY OF THE ANNUNCIATION
30 Bayswater Ave, Richmond Hill, ON, L4E 2L3
(905) 773-3283
Emp Here 35
SIC 8211 Elementary and secondary schools

D-U-N-S 20-590-5297   (BR)
YORK CATHOLIC DISTRICT SCHOOL BOARD
OUR LADY OF HOPE CATHOLIC ELEMENTARY SCHOOL
80 Red Cardinal Trail, Richmond Hill, ON, L4E 4B8
(905) 773-1383
Emp Here 25
SIC 8211 Elementary and secondary schools

D-U-N-S 24-525-4284   (BR)
YORK CATHOLIC DISTRICT SCHOOL BOARD
ST MARGUERITE D'YOUVILLE CATHOLIC ELMENTARY SCHOOL
121 Rollinghill Rd, Richmond Hill, ON, L4E 4L2
(905) 883-5221
Emp Here 45
SIC 8211 Elementary and secondary schools

D-U-N-S 24-676-3333   (BR)
YORK REGION DISTRICT SCHOOL BOARD
MACLEOD'S LANDING PUBLIC SCHOOL
(*Suby of* York Region District School Board)
195 Silver Maple Rd, Richmond Hill, ON, L4E 4Z1
(905) 398-7945
Emp Here 25
SIC 8211 Elementary and secondary schools

D-U-N-S 24-676-3341   (BR)
YORK REGION DISTRICT SCHOOL BOARD
BOND LAKE PUBLIC SCHOOL
(*Suby of* York Region District School Board)
245 Old Colony Rd, Richmond Hill, ON, L4E 5B9
(905) 313-8693
Emp Here 25
SIC 8211 Elementary and secondary schools

D-U-N-S 25-293-6216   (BR)
YORK REGION DISTRICT SCHOOL BOARD
LAKE WILCOX PUBLIC SCHOOL
(*Suby of* York Region District School Board)
80 Wildwood Ave, Richmond Hill, ON, L4E 3B5
(905) 773-5381
Emp Here 60
SIC 8211 Elementary and secondary schools

D-U-N-S 25-083-9966   (BR)
YORK REGION DISTRICT SCHOOL BOARD
YORK REGION CONTINUING EDUCATION
(*Suby of* York Region District School Board)
36 Regatta Ave, Richmond Hill, ON, L4E 4R1
(905) 884-3434
Emp Here 20
SIC 8211 Elementary and secondary schools

D-U-N-S 25-293-6059   (BR)
YORK REGION DISTRICT SCHOOL BOARD
OAK RIDGES PUBLIC SCHOOL
(*Suby of* York Region District School Board)
160 Coon'S Rd, Richmond Hill, ON, L4E 2P7
(905) 773-5572
Emp Here 40
SIC 8211 Elementary and secondary schools

D-U-N-S 24-247-5031   (BR)
YORK REGION DISTRICT SCHOOL BOARD
MORAINE HILLS PUBLIC SCHOOL
(*Suby of* York Region District School Board)
85 Rollinghill Rd, Richmond Hill, ON, L4E 4C7
(905) 292-0530
Emp Here 25
SIC 8211 Elementary and secondary schools

D-U-N-S 24-676-5213   (BR)
YORK REGION DISTRICT SCHOOL BOARD
KETTLE LAKES PUBLIC SCHOOL
(*Suby of* York Region District School Board)
62 Kingshill Rd, Richmond Hill, ON, L4E 4X5
(905) 313-8406
Emp Here 25
SIC 8211 Elementary and secondary schools

Richmond Hill, ON L4S
York County

D-U-N-S 24-485-8536   (SL)
ARCHE DAYBREAK, L'
11339 Yonge St, Richmond Hill, ON, L4S 1L1
(905) 884-3454
Emp Here 100   *Sales* 3,648,035

SIC 8361 Residential care

D-U-N-S 20-561-2856   (HQ)
BMW CANADA INC
BMW GROUP CANADA
50 Ultimate Dr, Richmond Hill, ON, L4S 0C8
(905) 770-1758
Emp Here 203   *Emp Total* 123,755
Sales 183,905,087
SIC 5012 Automobiles and other motor vehicles
Pr Pr Hendrik Von Kuenheim
  Adam Zimmerman
VP VP Walter Schauer
Dir Tom Purves

D-U-N-S 24-253-3789   (SL)
CARA FOODS INTERNATIONAL LTD
KELSEY'S
1620 Elgin Mills Rd E, Richmond Hill, ON, L4S 0B2
(905) 508-4139
Emp Here 100   *Sales* 2,991,389
SIC 5812 Eating places

D-U-N-S 25-998-3203   (HQ)
COMPUGEN INC
100 Via Renzo Dr, Richmond Hill, ON, L4S 0B8
(905) 707-2000
Emp Here 210   *Emp Total* 400
Sales 58,660,403
SIC 7373 Computer integrated systems design
Pr Pr Harry Zarek
  David Austin
VP Michael Charter
Sr VP Steve Glover
VP Sls Brian Macintosh
VP Opers Karen Atkinson

D-U-N-S 24-358-6042   (BR)
COSTCO WHOLESALE CANADA LTD
COSTCO
(*Suby of* Costco Wholesale Corporation)
35 John Birchall Rd Suite 592, Richmond Hill, ON, L4S 0B2
(905) 780-2100
Emp Here 200
SIC 5099 Durable goods, nec

D-U-N-S 24-361-7284   (BR)
HOME DEPOT OF CANADA INC
HOME DEPOT
(*Suby of* The Home Depot Inc)
1706 Elgin Mills Rd E, Richmond Hill, ON, L4S 1M6
(905) 787-7200
Emp Here 100
SIC 5251 Hardware stores

D-U-N-S 24-796-2301   (SL)
ISERVE INC
30 Via Renzo Dr Unit 1, Richmond Hill, ON, L4S 0B8
(905) 709-1130
Emp Here 25   *Sales* 12,977,991
SIC 5045 Computers, peripherals, and software
Pr Mel Clarke
VP Altaf Sayani
Treas William Breuls

D-U-N-S 20-552-8545   (BR)
METRO ONTARIO INC
METRO
1070 Major Mackenzie Dr E, Richmond Hill, ON, L4S 1P3
(905) 770-1400
Emp Here 300
SIC 5411 Grocery stores

D-U-N-S 20-292-0364   (BR)
MOUNT PLEASANT GROUP OF CEMETERIES
ELGIN MILLS CEMETERY, VISITATION, CHAPEL AND RECEPTION CENTER
1591 Elgin Mills Rd E, Richmond Hill, ON, L4S

1M9
(905) 737-1720
Emp Here 20
SIC 6531 Real estate agents and managers

D-U-N-S 24-215-3679   (HQ)
RCM AEROSERVICES LTD
(*Suby of* RCM Aeroservices Ltd)
89 Mojave Cres, Richmond Hill, ON, L4S 1R7
(905) 264-7501
Emp Here 34   *Emp Total* 62
Sales 9,942,100
SIC 8742 Management consulting services
Pr Pr Paul Vascotto
  Jaspar Phull

D-U-N-S 25-292-1374   (BR)
REVERA INC
BROOKSIDE RETIREMENT RESIDENCE
980 Elgin Mills Rd E, Richmond Hill, ON, L4S 1M4
(905) 884-9248
Emp Here 80
SIC 8361 Residential care

D-U-N-S 20-609-2681   (BR)
REVERA LONG TERM CARE INC
ELGINWOOD LONG TERM CARE
182 Yorkland St Suite 1, Richmond Hill, ON, L4S 2M9
(905) 737-0858
Emp Here 150
SIC 8051 Skilled nursing care facilities

D-U-N-S 24-112-5173   (BR)
SOBEYS CAPITAL INCORPORATED
FRESHCO
1430 Major Mackenzie Dr E, Richmond Hill, ON, L4S 0A1
(905) 770-9370
Emp Here 50
SIC 5411 Grocery stores

D-U-N-S 20-310-8758   (BR)
STAPLES CANADA INC
(*Suby of* Staples, Inc.)
1700 Elgin Mills Rd E Suite 2, Richmond Hill, ON, L4S 0B2
(905) 770-1600
Emp Here 25
SIC 5943 Stationery stores

D-U-N-S 25-147-3419   (BR)
YORK CATHOLIC DISTRICT SCHOOL BOARD
OUR LADY HELP OF CHRISTIANS
275 Redstone Rd, Richmond Hill, ON, L4S 2H1
(905) 884-4023
Emp Here 40
SIC 8211 Elementary and secondary schools

D-U-N-S 24-112-5116   (BR)
YORK REGION DISTRICT SCHOOL BOARD
REDSTONE PUBLIC SCHOOL
(*Suby of* York Region District School Board)
235 Redstone Rd, Richmond Hill, ON, L4S 2E2
(905) 508-1073
Emp Here 50
SIC 8211 Elementary and secondary schools

D-U-N-S 24-676-3366   (BR)
YORK REGION DISTRICT SCHOOL BOARD
MICHAELLE JEAN PUBLIC SCHOOL
(*Suby of* York Region District School Board)
320 Shirley Dr, Richmond Hill, ON, L4S 2P1
(905) 770-6507
Emp Here 25
SIC 8211 Elementary and secondary schools

D-U-N-S 20-711-4369   (BR)
YORK REGION DISTRICT SCHOOL BOARD
SILVER STREAM PUBLIC SCHOOL
(*Suby of* York Region District School Board)
180 Farmstead Rd, Richmond Hill, ON, L4S 2K9
(905) 508-5696
Emp Here 50

SIC 8211 Elementary and secondary schools

D-U-N-S 24-111-6594   (BR)
YORK REGION DISTRICT SCHOOL BOARD
RICHMOND GREEN SENIOR SCHOOL
(*Suby of* York Region District School Board)
1 William F Bell Pky, Richmond Hill, ON, L4S 2T9
(905) 780-7858
Emp Here 50
SIC 8211 Elementary and secondary schools

D-U-N-S 20-568-0049   (BR)
YORK REGION DISTRICT SCHOOL BOARD
TRILLIUM WOODS PUBLIC SCHOOL
(*Suby of* York Region District School Board)
18 Alamo Heights Dr, Richmond Hill, ON, L4S 2P3
(905) 508-5215
Emp Here 30
SIC 8211 Elementary and secondary schools

D-U-N-S 20-711-4237   (BR)
YORK REGION DISTRICT SCHOOL BOARD
H G BERNARD PUBLIC SCHOOL
(*Suby of* York Region District School Board)
245 Bernard Ave, Richmond Hill, ON, L4S 1E1
(905) 508-7009
Emp Here 50
SIC 8211 Elementary and secondary schools

Ridgetown, ON N0P

D-U-N-S 20-146-2561   (SL)
DANIELS SERVICE CENTRE LTD
21180 Victoria Rd, Ridgetown, ON, N0P 2C0
(519) 674-5493
Emp Here 50   *Sales* 3,648,035
SIC 7538 General automotive repair shops

D-U-N-S 20-325-9262   (SL)
KSR BRAZIL, LLC
95 Erie St S, Ridgetown, ON, N0P 2C0
(519) 674-5413
Emp Here 150   *Sales* 25,120,000
SIC 5013 Motor vehicle supplies and new parts
 Jeffrey De Liberato

D-U-N-S 25-503-1544   (HQ)
KSR INTERNATIONAL INC
DRESDEN INDUSTRIAL
(*Suby of* KSR International Inc)
95 Erie St S, Ridgetown, ON, N0P 2C0
(519) 674-5413
Emp Here 450   *Emp Total* 770
Sales 122,063,251
SIC 3714 Motor vehicle parts and accessories
Pr Pr Rodney Nunn

D-U-N-S 20-710-4907   (BR)
LAMBTON KENT DISTRICT SCHOOL BOARD
RICHTOWN DISTRICT HIGH SCHOOL
9 Harold St North, Ridgetown, ON, N0P 2C0
(519) 674-5449
Emp Here 20
SIC 8211 Elementary and secondary schools

D-U-N-S 20-004-8465   (BR)
LAMBTON KENT DISTRICT SCHOOL BOARD
RICHVIEW MORAVIAN ELEMENTARY SCHOOL
20473 Victoria Rd, Ridgetown, ON, N0P 2C0
(519) 674-3173
Emp Here 30
SIC 8211 Elementary and secondary schools

D-U-N-S 20-024-9352   (BR)
LAMBTON KENT DISTRICT SCHOOL BOARD
RIDGETOWN DISTRICT HIGH SCHOOL
9 Harold St N, Ridgetown, ON, N0P 2C0

(519) 674-5449
Emp Here 45
SIC 8211 Elementary and secondary schools

D-U-N-S 20-710-4881   (BR)
LAMBTON KENT DISTRICT SCHOOL BOARD
RIDGEVIEW MORAVIAN ELEMENTARY SCHOOL
73 Victoria Rd Suite 204, Ridgetown, ON, N0P 2C0
(519) 674-3173
Emp Here 50
SIC 8211 Elementary and secondary schools

D-U-N-S 24-087-0480   (BR)
LOBLAWS SUPERMARKETS LIMITED
BARTLETT'S VALUE MART
46 Main St W, Ridgetown, ON, N0P 2C0
(519) 674-3473
Emp Here 25
SIC 5411 Grocery stores

D-U-N-S 20-652-1101   (BR)
REVERA INC
VILLAGE RETIREMENT, THE
9 Myrtle St, Ridgetown, ON, N0P 2C0
(519) 674-5427
Emp Here 100
SIC 8051 Skilled nursing care facilities

D-U-N-S 25-249-3242   (BR)
ST. CLAIR CATHOLIC DISTRICT SCHOOL BOARD
ST MICHAEL ELEMENTARY SCHOOL
(*Suby of* St. Clair Catholic District School Board)
25 Maple St S, Ridgetown, ON, N0P 2C0
(519) 674-3475
Emp Here 20
SIC 8211 Elementary and secondary schools

D-U-N-S 25-605-5245   (BR)
UNIVERSITY OF GUELPH
RIDGETOWN COLLEGE
120 Main St, Ridgetown, ON, N0P 2C0
(519) 674-1500
Emp Here 100
SIC 8221 Colleges and universities

D-U-N-S 25-908-4358   (BR)
VENTRA GROUP CO
VENTRA RIDGETOWN
74 Marsh St, Ridgetown, ON, N0P 2C0
(519) 674-2323
Emp Here 35
SIC 3714 Motor vehicle parts and accessories

Ridgeway, ON L0S
Welland County

D-U-N-S 20-848-2083   (SL)
BUFFALO CANOE CLUB
4475 Erie Rd Suite 1, Ridgeway, ON, L0S 1N0
(905) 894-2750
Emp Here 85   *Sales* 3,429,153
SIC 7997 Membership sports and recreation clubs

D-U-N-S 20-852-4066   (SL)
CHERRY HILL CLUB, LIMITED
912 Cherry Hill Blvd, Ridgeway, ON, L0S 1N0
(905) 894-1122
Emp Here 110   *Sales* 4,450,603
SIC 7997 Membership sports and recreation clubs

D-U-N-S 20-710-8759   (BR)
DISTRICT SCHOOL BOARD OF NIAGARA
RIDGEWAY CRYSTAL BEACH SECONDARY SCHOOL
576 Ridge Rd N, Ridgeway, ON, L0S 1N0
(905) 894-3461
Emp Here 50
SIC 8211 Elementary and secondary schools

D-U-N-S 20-710-8544   (BR)
DISTRICT SCHOOL BOARD OF NIAGARA
BERTIE PUBLIC SCHOOL
3770 Hazel St, Ridgeway, ON, L0S 1N0
(905) 894-0313
Emp Here 21
SIC 8211 Elementary and secondary schools

D-U-N-S 25-179-4558   (BR)
DISTRICT SCHOOL BOARD OF NIAGARA
RIDGEWAY PUBLIC SCHOOL
143 Ridge Rd N, Ridgeway, ON, L0S 1N0
(905) 894-3751
Emp Here 25
SIC 8211 Elementary and secondary schools

Rockcliffe, ON K1M
Carleton County

D-U-N-S 25-504-0495   (BR)
OTTAWA-CARLETON DISTRICT SCHOOL BOARD
ROCKCLIFFE PARK PUBLIC SCHOOL
350 Buena Vista Rd, Rockcliffe, ON, K1M 1C1
(613) 749-5387
Emp Here 38
SIC 8211 Elementary and secondary schools

Rockland, ON K4K
Russell County

D-U-N-S 24-252-9357   (SL)
2158390 ONTARIO INC
BOSTON PIZZA ROCKLAND
3002 Richelieu St, Rockland, ON, K4K 0B5
(613) 446-7772
Emp Here 70   *Sales* 2,115,860
SIC 5812 Eating places

D-U-N-S 25-484-1877   (BR)
CATHOLIC DISTRICT SCHOOL BOARD OF EASTERN ONTARIO
ST PATRICK CATHOLIC ELEMENTARY SCHOOL
(*Suby of* Catholic District School Board of Eastern Ontario)
1001 Heritage Rd, Rockland, ON, K4K 1R2
(613) 446-7215
Emp Here 30
SIC 8211 Elementary and secondary schools

D-U-N-S 24-975-1744   (BR)
CONSEIL SCOLAIRE DE DISTRICT CATHOLIQUE DE L'EST ONTARIEN
ECOLE INTERMEDIAIRE CATHOLIQUE-PAVILLON ROCKLAND
1535 Du Parc Ave, Rockland, ON, K4K 1C3
(613) 446-5169
Emp Here 80
SIC 8211 Elementary and secondary schools

D-U-N-S 20-711-6646   (BR)
CONSEIL SCOLAIRE DE DISTRICT CATHOLIQUE DE L'EST ONTARIEN
ECOLE ST TRINITE
879 Saint-Joseph St, Rockland, ON, K4K 1C2
(613) 446-5128
Emp Here 50
SIC 8211 Elementary and secondary schools

D-U-N-S 20-009-7694   (BR)
CONSEIL DES ECOLES PUBLIQUES DE L'EST DE L'ONTARIO
ECOLE PUBLIQUE ELEMENTAIRE CAR-REFOUR JEUNESSE
927 St Jean St, Rockland, ON, K4K 1P4
(613) 446-1248
Emp Here 30
SIC 8211 Elementary and secondary schools

D-U-N-S 24-393-2451   (SL)
JEMARICA INC

CANADIAN TIRE
9040 County Road 17 Suite 623, Rockland, ON, K4K 1V5
(613) 446-4410
Emp Here 50   *Sales* 4,815,406
SIC 5251 Hardware stores

D-U-N-S 24-102-1906   (SL)
LEDUC BUS LINES LTD
8467 County Road 17, Rockland, ON, K4K 1K7
(613) 446-0606
Emp Here 58   *Sales* 2,772,507
SIC 4142 Bus charter service, except local

D-U-N-S 24-076-8999   (BR)
METRO ONTARIO INC
FOOD BASICS
9030 County Road 17, Rockland, ON, K4K 1V5
(613) 446-2825
Emp Here 50
SIC 5411 Grocery stores

D-U-N-S 20-590-7079   (BR)
UPPER CANADA DISTRICT SCHOOL BOARD, THE
ROCKLAND PUBLIC SCHOOL
999 Giroux St, Rockland, ON, K4K 1C2
(613) 446-6001
Emp Here 40
SIC 8211 Elementary and secondary schools

D-U-N-S 20-805-8953   (BR)
UPPER CANADA DISTRICT SCHOOL BOARD, THE
CENTRE DE L EDUCATION DE FORMATION DE L EST ONTARIO
2303 Rue Laurier, Rockland, ON, K4K 1K4
(613) 446-9842
Emp Here 20
SIC 8211 Elementary and secondary schools

D-U-N-S 20-914-0743   (BR)
UPPER CANADA DISTRICT SCHOOL BOARD, THE
ROCKLAND DISTRICT HIGH SCHOOL
1004 Saint-Joseph St, Rockland, ON, K4K 1P6
(613) 446-7347
Emp Here 49
SIC 8211 Elementary and secondary schools

D-U-N-S 24-251-9853   (BR)
WAL-MART CANADA CORP
WALMART
3001 Richelieu St, Rockland, ON, K4K 0B5
(613) 446-5730
Emp Here 150
SIC 5399 Miscellaneous general merchandise

Rockport, ON K0E
Leeds County

D-U-N-S 20-700-4011   (SL)
ROCKPORT BOAT LINE (1994) LIMITED
23 Front St, Rockport, ON, K0E 1V0
(613) 659-3402
Emp Here 75   *Sales* 4,768,150
SIC 4489 Water passenger transportation

Rockwood, ON N0B
Wellington County

D-U-N-S 20-545-2407   (BR)
UPPER GRAND DISTRICT SCHOOL BOARD, THE
ROCKWOOD CENTENNIAL PUBLIC SCHOOL
(*Suby of* Upper Grand District School Board, The)
137 Kasmore St, Rockwood, ON, N0B 2K0

---

(519) 856-9556
Emp Here 40
SIC 8211 Elementary and secondary schools

Rodney, ON N0L
Elgin County

D-U-N-S 24-990-6280   (BR)
KSR INTERNATIONAL CO
DRESDEN INDUSTRIAL, DIV OF
172 Centre St, Rodney, ON, N0L 2C0
(519) 785-0121
Emp Here 320
SIC 3714 Motor vehicle parts and accessories

D-U-N-S 25-238-8178   (BR)
**THAMES VALLEY DISTRICT SCHOOL
BOARD**
ALDBOROUGH PUBLIC SCHOOL
11443 Furnival Rd, Rodney, ON, N0L 2C0
(519) 785-0811
Emp Here 25
SIC 8211 Elementary and secondary schools

Roseneath, ON K0K

D-U-N-S 20-711-5846   (BR)
**KAWARTHA PINE RIDGE DISTRICT
SCHOOL BOARD**
*ROSENEATH CENTENNIAL PUBLIC
SCHOOL*
9047 County Road 45 Rr 4, Roseneath, ON,
K0K 2X0
(905) 352-2161
Emp Here 35
SIC 8211 Elementary and secondary schools

Rosseau, ON P0C
Parry Sound County

D-U-N-S 24-120-7146   (BR)
MUSKOKA WOODS YOUTH CAMP INC
MUSKOKA WOODS SPORT RESORT
(Suby of Boddy, John Albert Youth Foundation)
4585 Hwy 141, Rosseau, ON, P0C 1J0
(705) 732-4373
Emp Here 50
SIC 7032 Sporting and recreational camps

Rosslyn, ON P7K

D-U-N-S 25-054-8336   (SL)
**THUNDER BAY DISTRICT CRIME STOP-
PERS INC**
CRIME STOPPERS
3267 Highway 130, Rosslyn, ON, P7K 0B1
(807) 623-8477
Emp Here 20   Sales 5,197,506
SIC 8399 Social services, nec

Russell, ON K4R
Russell County

D-U-N-S 25-296-7302   (BR)
BANK OF NOVA SCOTIA, THE
SCOTIABANK
1116 Concession St, Russell, ON, K4R 1C8
(613) 445-2880
Emp Here 20
SIC 6021 National commercial banks

D-U-N-S 25-464-1822   (BR)

**CATHOLIC DISTRICT SCHOOL BOARD OF
EASTERN ONTARIO**
MOTHER TERESA CATHOLIC SCHOOL
(Suby of Catholic District School Board of
Eastern Ontario)
1035 Concession St, Russell, ON, K4R 1G7
(613) 445-3788
Emp Here 40
SIC 8211 Elementary and secondary schools

D-U-N-S 20-711-6588   (BR)
**CONSEIL SCOLAIRE DE DISTRICT
CATHOLIQUE DE L'EST ONTARIEN**
*ECOLE ELEMENTAIRE CATHOLIQUE
SAINT-JOSEPH*
1008 Russell Rd N, Russell, ON, K4R 1G7
(613) 445-2947
Emp Here 50
SIC 8211 Elementary and secondary schools

D-U-N-S 25-867-1924   (BR)
SOBEYS CAPITAL INCORPORATED
FOODLAND
124 Craig St, Russell, ON, K4R 1A1
(613) 445-5308
Emp Here 24
SIC 5411 Grocery stores

D-U-N-S 20-711-5671   (BR)
**UPPER CANADA DISTRICT SCHOOL
BOARD, THE**
RUSSELL HIGH SCHOOL
982n North Russell Rd, Russell, ON, K4R 1C8
(613) 445-2659
Emp Here 30
SIC 8211 Elementary and secondary schools

D-U-N-S 25-238-6651   (BR)
**UPPER CANADA DISTRICT SCHOOL
BOARD, THE**
RUSSELL PUBLIC SCHOOL
(Suby of Upper Canada District School Board,
The)
14 Mill St, Russell, ON, K4R 1A6
(613) 445-2190
Emp Here 35
SIC 8211 Elementary and secondary schools

Ruthven, ON N0P
Essex County

D-U-N-S 24-356-1896   (SL)
1046201 ONTARIO LIMITED
ERIE SHORES TRUCKING
1577 County Road 34, Ruthven, ON, N0P 2G0
(519) 322-2328
Emp Here 70   Sales 11,681,040
SIC 4213 Trucking, except local
Pr Pr Gene Ingratta
Dir Jamie Mastronardi
VP VP Agostino Ingratta
VP VP Luis Chibante

D-U-N-S 24-736-8744   (HQ)
745822 ONTARIO LIMITED
(Suby of 745822 Ontario Limited)
1593 Essex County Rd 34, Ruthven, ON, N0P
2G0
(519) 326-5743
Emp Here 145   Emp Total 150
Sales 69,780,604
SIC 5148 Fresh fruits and vegetables
Gerry Mastronardi

D-U-N-S 25-221-4689   (SL)
971016 ONTARIO LIMITED
RED ZOO MARKETING
1621 Road 3, Ruthven, ON, N0P 2G0

Emp Here 75   Sales 25,019,520
SIC 5148 Fresh fruits and vegetables
Pr Pr Jay Colasanti
Ron Colasanti
William K. Colasanti

D-U-N-S 25-249-3093   (BR)
**GREATER ESSEX COUNTY DISTRICT
SCHOOL BOARD**
RUTHVEN PUBLIC SCHOOL
1664 Talbot Rd, Ruthven, ON, N0P 2G0

Emp Here 25
SIC 8211 Elementary and secondary schools

D-U-N-S 20-146-7271   (HQ)
LAKE ERIE MANAGEMENT INC
(Suby of 745822 Ontario Limited)
1593 Essex County Rd 34, Ruthven, ON, N0P
2G0
(519) 326-5743
Emp Here 145   Emp Total 150
Sales 43,139,300
SIC 5148 Fresh fruits and vegetables
Pr Gerry Mastronardi
 Guy Totaro
Dir David Mastronardi
Sec Steve Mastronardi
Dir Ake Mastronardi
Dir Angelo Mastronardi
Recvr Susan Lynn Mingie

Sandford, ON L0C

D-U-N-S 25-265-2573   (BR)
DURHAM DISTRICT SCHOOL BOARD
SCOTT CENTRAL PUBLIC SCHOOL
421 Regional Rd 11, Sandford, ON, L0C 1E0
(905) 852-9751
Emp Here 33
SIC 8211 Elementary and secondary schools

Sandy Lake, ON P0V
Kenora County

D-U-N-S 25-271-4365   (BR)
NORTH WEST COMPANY LP, THE
SANDY LAKE NORTHERN STORE
Gd, Sandy Lake, ON, P0V 1V0
(807) 774-4451
Emp Here 40
SIC 5411 Grocery stores

D-U-N-S 20-998-2813   (BR)
TIKINAGAN CHILD & FAMILY SERVICES
(Suby of Tikinagan Child & Family Services)
Gd, Sandy Lake, ON, P0V 1V0
(807) 771-1149
Emp Here 20
SIC 8322 Individual and family services

Sarnia, ON N7S
Lambton County

D-U-N-S 20-701-5827   (SL)
B & D INSULATION INC
1351 Lougar Ave, Sarnia, ON, N7S 5N5
(519) 344-5287
Emp Here 50   Sales 4,377,642
SIC 1799 Special trade contractors, nec

D-U-N-S 20-698-7104   (BR)
BEST BUY CANADA LTD
FUTURE SHOP
(Suby of Best Buy Co., Inc.)
1380 Exmouth St, Sarnia, ON, N7S 3X9
(519) 542-4388
Emp Here 100
SIC 5731 Radio, television, and electronic
stores

D-U-N-S 25-231-7508   (BR)
BRICK WAREHOUSE LP, THE
BRICK, THE

1379 London Rd Suite 3, Sarnia, ON, N7S
1P6
(519) 542-1461
Emp Here 20
SIC 5712 Furniture stores

D-U-N-S 25-016-9653   (BR)
**CANADIAN IMPERIAL BANK OF COM-
MERCE**
CIBC
1170 London Rd, Sarnia, ON, N7S 1P4
(519) 337-0373
Emp Here 20
SIC 6021 National commercial banks

D-U-N-S 25-449-6508   (BR)
CINEPLEX ODEON CORPORATION
GALAXY CINEMAS SARNIA
1450 London Rd, Sarnia, ON, N7S 1P7
(519) 541-0959
Emp Here 20
SIC 7832 Motion picture theaters, except
drive-in

D-U-N-S 25-172-1788   (BR)
CLEAN HARBORS CANADA, INC
1166 Michener Rd, Sarnia, ON, N7S 4B1
(519) 339-9855
Emp Here 70
SIC 2819 Industrial inorganic chemicals, nec

D-U-N-S 25-116-7433   (BR)
COGECO COMMUNICATIONS INC
1421 Confederation St, Sarnia, ON, N7S 5N9
(519) 336-0443
Emp Here 20
SIC 4841 Cable and other pay television services

D-U-N-S 20-005-2665   (BR)
**CONSEIL SCOLAIRE DE DISTRICT DES
ECOLES CATHOLIQUES DU SUD-OUEST**
ST FRANCIS OF XAVIER
901 The Rapids Pky, Sarnia, ON, N7S 6K2
(519) 542-1055
Emp Here 25
SIC 8211 Elementary and secondary schools

D-U-N-S 24-828-8649   (BR)
CORPORATION OF THE CITY OF SARNIA
SARNIA TRANSIT
1169 Michener Rd, Sarnia, ON, N7S 4W3
(519) 336-3271
Emp Here 50
SIC 4111 Local and suburban transit

D-U-N-S 24-602-0184   (SL)
DANTE CLUB INC
1330 London Rd, Sarnia, ON, N7S 1P7
(519) 542-8578
Emp Here 50   Sales 1,678,096
SIC 7299 Miscellaneous personal service

D-U-N-S 20-817-1207   (BR)
ENBRIDGE PIPELINES INC
1086 Modeland Rd Suite 1, Sarnia, ON, N7S
6L2
(519) 339-0500
Emp Here 36
SIC 4612 Crude petroleum pipelines

D-U-N-S 24-340-0863   (BR)
FGL SPORTS LTD
SPORT-CHEK SARNIA
595 Murphy Rd, Sarnia, ON, N7S 6K1
(519) 344-8140
Emp Here 40
SIC 5941 Sporting goods and bicycle shops

D-U-N-S 24-616-0969   (BR)
FIRSTCANADA ULC
FIRST STUDENT CANADA
1430 Lougar Ave, Sarnia, ON, N7S 5N4
(519) 336-0077
Emp Here 55
SIC 4142 Bus charter service, except local

D-U-N-S 20-108-5557   (BR)
HOME DEPOT OF CANADA INC

HOME DEPOT
(Suby of The Home Depot Inc)
1350 Quinn Dr, Sarnia, ON, N7S 6L5
(519) 333-2302
Emp Here 150
SIC 5251 Hardware stores

D-U-N-S 20-071-0791   (BR)
LAMBTON FINANCIAL CREDIT UNION LIMITED
LAMBTON FINANCIAL
(Suby of Lambton Financial Credit Union Limited)
1295 London Rd, Sarnia, ON, N7S 1P6
(519) 542-9059
Emp Here 70
SIC 6062 State credit unions

D-U-N-S 25-249-3440   (BR)
LAMBTON KENT DISTRICT SCHOOL BOARD
LANSDOWNE PUBLIC SCHOOL
95 Lansdowne Ave S, Sarnia, ON, N7S 1G7
(519) 336-2111
Emp Here 37
SIC 8211 Elementary and secondary schools

D-U-N-S 24-420-0031   (BR)
LAMBTON KENT DISTRICT SCHOOL BOARD
ST. CLAIR SECONDARY SCHOOL
340 Murphy Rd, Sarnia, ON, N7S 2X1
(519) 332-1140
Emp Here 75
SIC 8211 Elementary and secondary schools

D-U-N-S 24-312-0933   (BR)
LAMBTON KENT DISTRICT SCHOOL BOARD
NORTHERN COLLEGIATE INSTITUTE & VOCATIONAL SCHOOL
940 Michigan Ave, Sarnia, ON, N7S 2B1
(519) 542-5545
Emp Here 50
SIC 8211 Elementary and secondary schools

D-U-N-S 25-238-6974   (BR)
LAMBTON KENT DISTRICT SCHOOL BOARD
CATHCART BOULEVARD PUBLIC SCHOOL
1219 Cathcart Blvd, Sarnia, ON, N7S 2H7
(519) 542-5651
Emp Here 20
SIC 8211 Elementary and secondary schools

D-U-N-S 20-710-4659   (BR)
LAMBTON KENT DISTRICT SCHOOL BOARD
ERROL ROAD PUBLIC SCHOOL
989 Errol Rd E, Sarnia, ON, N7S 2E6
(519) 542-9341
Emp Here 40
SIC 8211 Elementary and secondary schools

D-U-N-S 25-249-3705   (BR)
LAMBTON KENT DISTRICT SCHOOL BOARD
ALEXANDER MACKENZIE SECONDARY SCHOOL
1257 Michigan Ave, Sarnia, ON, N7S 3Y3
(519) 542-5505
Emp Here 80
SIC 8211 Elementary and secondary schools

D-U-N-S 20-710-4709   (BR)
LAMBTON KENT DISTRICT SCHOOL BOARD
HIGH PARK PUBLIC SCHOOL
757 Kember Ave, Sarnia, ON, N7S 2T3
(519) 332-0474
Emp Here 35
SIC 8211 Elementary and secondary schools

D-U-N-S 25-249-3283   (BR)
LAMBTON KENT DISTRICT SCHOOL BOARD
QUEEN ELIZABETH II SCHOOL
60 Aberdeen Ave, Sarnia, ON, N7S 2N8

(519) 344-0801
Emp Here 35
SIC 8211 Elementary and secondary schools

D-U-N-S 20-837-3782   (BR)
LANGS BUS LINES LIMITED
1370 Lougar Ave, Sarnia, ON, N7S 5N7
(519) 383-1221
Emp Here 33
SIC 4151 School buses

D-U-N-S 25-018-5865   (BR)
LIBRO CREDIT UNION LIMITED
1315 Exmouth St, Sarnia, ON, N7S 3Y1
(519) 542-5578
Emp Here 20
SIC 6062 State credit unions

D-U-N-S 25-297-8697   (BR)
LOBLAWS INC
REAL CANADIAN SUPERSTORE, THE
600 Murphy Rd, Sarnia, ON, N7S 5T7
(519) 383-8300
Emp Here 301
SIC 5411 Grocery stores

D-U-N-S 25-360-2981   (BR)
LUXURY HOTELS INTERNATIONAL OF CANADA, ULC
MARRIOTT WORLDWIDE RESERVATIONS
(Suby of Marriott International, Inc.)
1337 London Rd, Sarnia, ON, N7S 1P6
(519) 346-4551
Emp Here 350
SIC 7389 Business services, nec

D-U-N-S 25-236-5069   (BR)
MARK'S WORK WEARHOUSE LTD
MARK'S WORK WEARHOUSE 79
1380 London Rd, Sarnia, ON, N7S 1P8
(519) 542-3429
Emp Here 25
SIC 5651 Family clothing stores

D-U-N-S 25-666-2149   (BR)
N. TEPPERMAN LIMITED
TEPPERMAN'S FURNITURE APPLIANCES & ELECTRONICS
1380 London Rd, Sarnia, ON, N7S 1P8
(519) 541-0100
Emp Here 24
SIC 5722 Household appliance stores

D-U-N-S 20-859-9741   (BR)
PACIFIC LINK COMMUNICATIONS INC
BELL WORLD
1380 London Rd, Sarnia, ON, N7S 1P8
(519) 542-1864
Emp Here 25
SIC 5999 Miscellaneous retail stores, nec

D-U-N-S 25-265-3225   (SL)
PATHWAYS HEALTH CENTRE FOR CHILDREN
1240 Murphy Rd, Sarnia, ON, N7S 2Y6
(519) 542-3471
Emp Here 120   Sales 4,742,446
SIC 8322 Individual and family services

D-U-N-S 24-319-0423   (BR)
PRINCESS AUTO LTD
1370 Quinn Dr, Sarnia, ON, N7S 6M8
(519) 542-1661
Emp Here 40
SIC 5251 Hardware stores

D-U-N-S 25-028-5210   (BR)
REVERA LONG TERM CARE INC
SUMAC LODGE
1464 Blackwell Rd, Sarnia, ON, N7S 5M4
(519) 542-3421
Emp Here 103
SIC 8051 Skilled nursing care facilities

D-U-N-S 20-769-4733   (SL)
SARNIA PIZZA LIMITED
BOSTON PIZZA
1400 Exmouth St, Sarnia, ON, N7S 3X9

(519) 542-7500
Emp Here 70   Sales 2,115,860
SIC 5812 Eating places

D-U-N-S 25-740-3055   (BR)
SARNIA AND DISTRICT ASSOCIATION FOR COMMUNITY LIVING
WAWANOSH INDUSTRIAL SERVICES, DIV OF
1315 Lougar Ave, Sarnia, ON, N7S 5N5
(519) 336-9825
Emp Here 40
SIC 8322 Individual and family services

D-U-N-S 25-311-1215   (BR)
SEARS CANADA INC
1380 London Rd Unit 3, Sarnia, ON, N7S 1P8
(519) 542-2121
Emp Here 200
SIC 5311 Department stores

D-U-N-S 24-377-1834   (BR)
SERVICES FINANCIERS NCO, INC
(Suby of Egs Shell Company, Inc.)
1086 Modeland Rd, Sarnia, ON, N7S 6L2

Emp Here 50
SIC 7322 Adjustment and collection services

D-U-N-S 20-640-7301   (BR)
SOBEYS CAPITAL INCORPORATED
FRESHCO
1330 Exmouth St, Sarnia, ON, N7S 3X9

Emp Here 50
SIC 5411 Grocery stores

D-U-N-S 20-710-5003   (BR)
ST. CLAIR CATHOLIC DISTRICT SCHOOL BOARD
ST. CHRISTOPHER'S SECONDARY SCHOOL
1001 The Rapids Pky, Sarnia, ON, N7S 6K2
(519) 332-3976
Emp Here 90
SIC 8211 Elementary and secondary schools

D-U-N-S 20-092-0242   (BR)
ST. CLAIR CATHOLIC DISTRICT SCHOOL BOARD
ST. ANNE'S SCHOOL
1000 The Rapids Pky, Sarnia, ON, N7S 6K3
(519) 542-2710
Emp Here 25
SIC 8211 Elementary and secondary schools

D-U-N-S 25-249-3853   (BR)
ST. CLAIR CATHOLIC DISTRICT SCHOOL BOARD
GREGORY A HOGAN ELEMENTARY SCHOOL
(Suby of St. Clair Catholic District School Board)
1825 Hogan Dr, Sarnia, ON, N7S 6G9
(519) 542-8190
Emp Here 40
SIC 8211 Elementary and secondary schools

D-U-N-S 25-740-5415   (BR)
STAPLES CANADA INC
STAPLES THE BUSINESS DEPOT
(Suby of Staples, Inc.)
1379 London Rd Suite 2, Sarnia, ON, N7S 1P6
(519) 542-4461
Emp Here 35
SIC 5943 Stationery stores

D-U-N-S 25-140-5676   (BR)
STEEVES & ROZEMA ENTERPRISES LIMITED
TRILLIUM VILLA NURSING HOME
1221 Michigan Ave, Sarnia, ON, N7S 3Y3
(519) 542-5529
Emp Here 180
SIC 8051 Skilled nursing care facilities

D-U-N-S 25-740-4558   (BR)
STEEVES & ROZEMA ENTERPRISES LIMITED

ITED
TWIN LAKES TERRACE
1310 Murphy Rd Suite 216, Sarnia, ON, N7S 6K5
(519) 542-2939
Emp Here 100
SIC 8059 Nursing and personal care, nec

D-U-N-S 20-608-1150   (SL)
TREL OF SARNIA LIMITED
1165 Confederation St, Sarnia, ON, N7S 3Y5
(519) 344-7025
Emp Here 60   Sales 4,377,642
SIC 3599 Industrial machinery, nec

D-U-N-S 20-549-7902   (BR)
TEAM TRUCK CENTRES LIMITED
1453 Confederation St, Sarnia, ON, N7S 5N9
(519) 332-2622
Emp Here 20
SIC 7538 General automotive repair shops

D-U-N-S 25-571-0295   (BR)
TORNADO INSULATION LTD
781 Roper St, Sarnia, ON, N7S 6G7
(519) 344-3603
Emp Here 70
SIC 1742 Plastering, drywall, and insulation

D-U-N-S 25-321-2005   (BR)
TORONTO-DOMINION BANK, THE
TD BANK
(Suby of Toronto-Dominion Bank, The)
1210 London Rd, Sarnia, ON, N7S 1P4
(519) 383-8320
Emp Here 35
SIC 6021 National commercial banks

D-U-N-S 20-793-1077   (BR)
TWINCORP INC
TACO BELL
1182 London Rd, Sarnia, ON, N7S 1P4
(519) 383-7875
Emp Here 20
SIC 5812 Eating places

D-U-N-S 25-740-6751   (BR)
VALUE VILLAGE STORES, INC
(Suby of Savers, Inc.)
1379 London Rd, Sarnia, ON, N7S 1P6
(519) 541-0153
Emp Here 30
SIC 5399 Miscellaneous general merchandise

D-U-N-S 24-329-6956   (BR)
WAL-MART CANADA CORP
1444 Quinn Dr, Sarnia, ON, N7S 6M8
(519) 542-4272
Emp Here 200
SIC 5311 Department stores

D-U-N-S 25-221-2329   (BR)
WINNERS MERCHANTS INTERNATIONAL L.P.
WINNERS
(Suby of The TJX Companies Inc)
1470 Quinn Dr, Sarnia, ON, N7S 6M8
(519) 383-1613
Emp Here 30
SIC 5651 Family clothing stores

D-U-N-S 25-355-4356   (BR)
WORLEYPARSONS CANADA SERVICES LTD
1086 Modeland Rd Bldg 1050, Sarnia, ON, N7S 6L2
(519) 332-0160
Emp Here 340
SIC 8742 Management consulting services

Sarnia, ON N7T
Lambton County

D-U-N-S 25-525-6604   (SL)
1210632 ONTARIO INC
DRAWBRIDGE INN

---

283 Christina St N, Sarnia, ON, N7T 5V4
(519) 337-7571
Emp Here 50   *Sales* 2,188,821
SIC 7011 Hotels and motels

    D-U-N-S 25-078-9450   (BR)
4513380 CANADA INC
LIVINGSTON INTERNATIONAL
4676 Brigden Rd, Sarnia, ON, N7T 7H3
(519) 332-2633
Emp Here 20
SIC 4731 Freight transportation arrangement

    D-U-N-S 20-285-0483   (BR)
518162 ALBERTA INC
CROSSROADS C & I DISTRIBUTORS INC
272 St Andrew St, Sarnia, ON, N7T 8G8
(519) 336-9590
Emp Here 25
SIC 5033 Roofing, siding, and insulation

    D-U-N-S 25-252-9961   (SL)
581821 ONTARIO LIMITED
C&C ENTERPRISES ELECTRICAL CON-STRUCTION
126 Green St, Sarnia, ON, N7T 2K5
(519) 336-3430
Emp Here 50   *Sales* 6,028,800
SIC 1731 Electrical work
Pr Pr Edmond Braithwaite

    D-U-N-S 25-362-8739   (HQ)
ARLANXEO CANADA INC
ENERGIZING CHEMISTRY
1265 Vidal St S, Sarnia, ON, N7T 7M2
(519) 337-8251
Emp Here 500   *Emp Total* 8
Sales 90,179,425
SIC 2822 Synthetic rubber
Dirk Fischer
John Sawyer
Sharon Guo

    D-U-N-S 24-873-2000   (BR)
ACUREN GROUP INC
CANSPEC GROUP I
(*Suby of* Rockwood Service Corporation)
396 Mcgregor Side Rd Suite 1, Sarnia, ON,
N7T 7H5
(519) 336-3021
Emp Here 29
SIC 8734 Testing laboratories

    D-U-N-S 24-408-6138   (BR)
AIR PRODUCTS CANADA LTD
AIR PRODUCTS
(*Suby of* Air Products and Chemicals, Inc.)
20 Indian Rd, Sarnia, ON, N7T 7K2
(519) 332-1500
Emp Here 35
SIC 2813 Industrial gases

    D-U-N-S 20-965-2767   (BR)
BDO CANADA LLP
SARNIA ACCOUNTING
250 Christina St N, Sarnia, ON, N7T 7V3
(519) 337-5500
Emp Here 35
SIC 8721 Accounting, auditing, and book-keeping

    D-U-N-S 25-316-0980   (BR)
BP CANADA ENERGY COMPANY
(*Suby of* BP P.L.C.)
201 Front St N Suite 1405, Sarnia, ON, N7T
7T9
(519) 383-3500
Emp Here 70
SIC 1311 Crude petroleum and natural gas

    D-U-N-S 25-296-6668   (BR)
BANK OF NOVA SCOTIA, THE
SCOTIABANK
560 Exmouth St, Sarnia, ON, N7T 5P5
(519) 339-1300
Emp Here 34
SIC 6021 National commercial banks

    D-U-N-S 20-071-0759   (BR)
BANK OF NOVA SCOTIA, THE
SCOTIABANK
238 Indian Rd S, Sarnia, ON, N7T 3W4
(519) 339-1330
Emp Here 30
SIC 6021 National commercial banks

    D-U-N-S 24-976-3384   (BR)
BAYER INC
BAYER HEALTHCARE
1265 Vidal St S, Sarnia, ON, N7T 7M2
(519) 337-8251
Emp Here 900
SIC 2822 Synthetic rubber

    D-U-N-S 24-339-6236   (BR)
CANADA IMPERIAL OIL LIMITED
(*Suby of* Exxon Mobil Corporation)
602 Christina St S, Sarnia, ON, N7T 7M5
(519) 339-2000
Emp Here 1,000
SIC 5172 Petroleum products, nec

    D-U-N-S 20-572-9317   (BR)
CANADA POST CORPORATION
242 Indian Rd S, Sarnia, ON, N7T 3W4

Emp Here 20
SIC 4311 U.s. postal service

    D-U-N-S 20-539-7230   (BR)
CANADA POST CORPORATION
SARNIA STATION MAIN
105 Christina St S, Sarnia, ON, N7T 2M7
(519) 344-7074
Emp Here 100
SIC 4311 U.s. postal service

    D-U-N-S 25-303-5547   (BR)
CANADIAN IMPERIAL BANK OF COM-MERCE
CIBC
478 Exmouth St, Sarnia, ON, N7T 5P3
(519) 336-2276
Emp Here 20
SIC 6021 National commercial banks

    D-U-N-S 24-760-2803   (BR)
CANADIAN MENTAL HEALTH ASSOCIA-TION, THE
LAMBTON COUNTY BRANCH
(*Suby of* Canadian Mental Health Association, The)
210 Lochiel St, Sarnia, ON, N7T 4C7
(519) 337-5411
Emp Here 45
SIC 8621 Professional organizations

    D-U-N-S 20-734-6065   (BR)
CARGILL LIMITED
CARGILL SARNIA
101 Exmouth St, Sarnia, ON, N7T 5M2
(519) 337-5428
Emp Here 24
SIC 4221 Farm product warehousing and storage

    D-U-N-S 24-452-2454   (SL)
CENTRAL MACHINE & MARINE INC
(*Suby of* Canerector Inc)
649 Mcgregor Rd, Sarnia, ON, N7T 7H5
(519) 337-3722
Emp Here 75   *Sales* 7,067,468
SIC 3599 Industrial machinery, nec

    D-U-N-S 24-365-7327   (BR)
COMPAGNIE DES CHEMINS DE FER NA-TIONAUX DU CANADA
C N RAIL
699 Macgregor Rd, Sarnia, ON, N7T 7H8
(519) 339-1253
Emp Here 270
SIC 4011 Railroads, line-haul operating

    D-U-N-S 24-850-3760   (BR)
COMPAGNIE DES CHEMINS DE FER NA-TIONAUX DU CANADA

CANADIAN NATIONAL RAILWAY CO
699 Mcgregor Rd, Sarnia, ON, N7T 7H8
(519) 339-1216
Emp Here 300
SIC 4011 Railroads, line-haul operating

    D-U-N-S 25-457-8511   (BR)
CORPORATION OF THE COUNTY OF LAMBTON
MARSHALL GOWLAND MANOR
749 Devine St, Sarnia, ON, N7T 1X3

Emp Here 141
SIC 8361 Residential care

    D-U-N-S 25-749-3601   (BR)
CORPORATION OF THE COUNTY OF LAMBTON
CORPORATION OF THE COUNTY OF LAMBTON
150 Christina St N Suite 1b, Sarnia, ON, N7T
8H3
(519) 332-0998
Emp Here 30
SIC 8399 Social services, nec

    D-U-N-S 20-104-3119   (BR)
DOW CHEMICAL CANADA ULC
(*Suby of* The Dow Chemical Company)
1425 St Videl S, Sarnia, ON, N7T 8K6

Emp Here 60
SIC 2899 Chemical preparations, nec

    D-U-N-S 25-212-8202   (BR)
DOWLER-KARN LIMITED
DOWLER KARN PROPANE
1494 Plank Rd, Sarnia, ON, N7T 7H3
(519) 332-3481
Emp Here 24
SIC 5984 Liquefied petroleum gas dealers

    D-U-N-S 25-946-7579   (BR)
ELYOD INVESTMENTS LIMITED
TIM HORTONS
(*Suby of* Elyod Investments Limited)
137 Indian Rd S, Sarnia, ON, N7T 3W3
(519) 344-0262
Emp Here 25
SIC 5812 Eating places

    D-U-N-S 24-987-4918   (HQ)
ELYOD INVESTMENTS LIMITED
TIM HORTONS
(*Suby of* Elyod Investments Limited)
775 Exmouth St, Sarnia, ON, N7T 5P7
(519) 332-6741
Emp Here 30   *Emp Total* 62
Sales 2,115,860
SIC 5461 Retail bakeries

    D-U-N-S 24-424-8758   (BR)
ENBRIDGE PIPELINES INC
1010 Plank Rd, Sarnia, ON, N7T 7H3
(519) 332-4700
Emp Here 20
SIC 4612 Crude petroleum pipelines

    D-U-N-S 25-733-2155   (BR)
FAMZ RESTAURANT (1985) LIMITEDPART-NERSHIP
HARVEY'S
321 Christina St N, Sarnia, ON, N7T 5V6
(519) 344-1911
Emp Here 20
SIC 5812 Eating places

    D-U-N-S 20-213-8637   (BR)
GLASSCELL ISOFAB INC
SARNIA INSULATION SUPPLY
272 St Andrew St, Sarnia, ON, N7T 8G8
(519) 336-6444
Emp Here 25
SIC 5033 Roofing, siding, and insulation

    D-U-N-S 24-341-5218   (SL)
H.C. STARCK CANADA INC
933 Vidal St S, Sarnia, ON, N7T 8H8

(519) 346-4300
Emp Here 30   *Sales* 6,274,620
SIC 2819 Industrial inorganic chemicals, nec
Dir Carol Gilmurray
Dir Karlheinz Riechert
Dir Ludger Heuberg

    D-U-N-S 20-914-4794   (BR)
HSBC BANK CANADA
889 Exmouth St Unit 5, Sarnia, ON, N7T 5R3

Emp Here 20
SIC 6141 Personal credit institutions

    D-U-N-S 24-179-6965   (BR)
HARRIS STEEL ULC
(*Suby of* Nucor Corporation)
5334 Brigden Rd, Sarnia, ON, N7T 7H3
(519) 383-8260
Emp Here 20
SIC 3316 Cold finishing of steel shapes

    D-U-N-S 20-802-5259   (BR)
HYDRO ONE INC
HYDRO ONE SCOTT TRANSFORMER STA-TION
110 Scott Rd, Sarnia, ON, N7T 7H5
(519) 332-6060
Emp Here 20
SIC 4911 Electric services

    D-U-N-S 25-203-5506   (BR)
IMPERIAL OIL LIMITED
PRODUCTS & CHEMICALS, DIV OF
(*Suby of* Exxon Mobil Corporation)
453 Christina St, Sarnia, ON, N7T 5W3
(519) 339-2712
Emp Here 110
SIC 2911 Petroleum refining

    D-U-N-S 24-681-1749   (SL)
IMPERIAL OIL LIMITED
Po Box 3004 Stn Main, Sarnia, ON, N7T 7M5
(519) 339-4015
Emp Here 950   *Sales* 1,398,780,000
SIC 2911 Petroleum refining
Jon Harding

    D-U-N-S 25-315-8984   (BR)
INVESTORS GROUP FINANCIAL SER-VICES INC
201 Front St N Unit 1410, Sarnia, ON, N7T
7T9
(519) 336-4262
Emp Here 25
SIC 8741 Management services

    D-U-N-S 24-827-1756   (HQ)
KEDDCO MFG. (2011) LTD
(*Suby of* Canerector Inc)
645 Keddco St, Sarnia, ON, N7T 7H5
(519) 336-2960
Emp Here 27   *Emp Total* 3,000
Sales 4,511,280
SIC 3462 Iron and steel forgings

    D-U-N-S 25-341-4452   (BR)
LAMBTON COUNTY LIBRARY
SARNIA LIBRARY
124 Christina St S, Sarnia, ON, N7T 8E1
(519) 337-3291
Emp Here 50
SIC 8231 Libraries

    D-U-N-S 25-249-3325   (BR)
LAMBTON KENT DISTRICT SCHOOL BOARD
LONDON ROAD PUBLIC SCHOOL
240 London Rd, Sarnia, ON, N7T 4V8
(519) 344-5741
Emp Here 20
SIC 8211 Elementary and secondary schools

    D-U-N-S 25-238-7006   (BR)
LAMBTON KENT DISTRICT SCHOOL BOARD
JOHNSTON MEMORIAL PUBLIC SCHOOL
217 Russell St S, Sarnia, ON, N7T 3L6

(519) 344-4371
Emp Here 35
SIC 8211 Elementary and secondary schools

D-U-N-S 25-249-3523   (BR)
LAMBTON KENT DISTRICT SCHOOL BOARD
SARNIA COLLEGIATE INSTITUTE & TECHNICAL SCHOOL
275 Wellington St, Sarnia, ON, N7T 1H1
(519) 336-6131
Emp Here 100
SIC 8211 Elementary and secondary schools

D-U-N-S 20-710-4626   (BR)
LAMBTON KENT DISTRICT SCHOOL BOARD
CONFEDERATION CENTRAL ELEMENTARY SCHOOL
2500 Confederation Line, Sarnia, ON, N7T 7H3
(519) 383-7004
Emp Here 30
SIC 8211 Elementary and secondary schools

D-U-N-S 20-710-4683   (BR)
LAMBTON KENT DISTRICT SCHOOL BOARD
HANNA MEMORIAL PUBLIC SCHOOL
369 Maria St, Sarnia, ON, N7T 4T7
(519) 344-7631
Emp Here 40
SIC 8211 Elementary and secondary schools

D-U-N-S 25-732-4970   (BR)
LONDON BRIDGE CHILD CARE SERVICES INC
A B C CHILD CARE CENTRE
811 London Rd, Sarnia, ON, N7T 4X7
(519) 337-8668
Emp Here 28
SIC 8351 Child day care services

D-U-N-S 25-311-0720   (BR)
LONDON LIFE INSURANCE COMPANY
FREEDOM 55 FINANCIAL
265 Front St N Suite 505, Sarnia, ON, N7T 7X1
(519) 336-5540
Emp Here 28
SIC 6311 Life insurance

D-U-N-S 25-695-5279   (BR)
MAGIC REALTY INC
380 London Rd, Sarnia, ON, N7T 4W7
(519) 542-4005
Emp Here 90
SIC 6531 Real estate agents and managers

D-U-N-S 24-333-1746   (BR)
METRO ONTARIO INC
METRO
560 Exmouth St, Sarnia, ON, N7T 5P5
(519) 337-8308
Emp Here 110
SIC 5411 Grocery stores

D-U-N-S 24-333-1720   (BR)
METRO ONTARIO INC
FOOD BASIC
191 Indian Rd S, Sarnia, ON, N7T 3W3
(519) 344-1500
Emp Here 80
SIC 5411 Grocery stores

D-U-N-S 24-381-1689   (BR)
ONTARIO ENGLISH CATHOLIC TEACHERS ASSOCIATION, THE
ST CLAIR SECONDARY OECTA
281 East St N, Sarnia, ON, N7T 6X8
(519) 332-4550
Emp Here 175
SIC 8641 Civic and social associations

D-U-N-S 20-608-1770   (BR)
PLAINS MIDSTREAM CANADA ULC
BP CANADA
1182 Plank Rd, Sarnia, ON, N7T 7H9

(519) 336-4270
Emp Here 75
SIC 4923 Gas transmission and distribution

D-U-N-S 25-051-9097   (BR)
PRIME RESTAURANTS INC
PADDY FLAHERTY'S IRISH PUB
(Suby of Cara Holdings Limited)
130 Seaway Rd, Sarnia, ON, N7T 8A5
(519) 336-1999
Emp Here 25
SIC 5812 Eating places

D-U-N-S 25-028-6424   (BR)
PROCOR LIMITED
PROCOR
(Suby of Berkshire Hathaway Inc.)
725 Procor Dr, Sarnia, ON, N7T 7H3
(519) 384-0741
Emp Here 40
SIC 4741 Rental of railroad cars

D-U-N-S 24-319-3849   (BR)
ROYAL GROUP, INC
ROYAL POLYMERS CO, DIV OF
900 South Vidal St, Sarnia, ON, N7T 8G1

Emp Here 74
SIC 3089 Plastics products, nec

D-U-N-S 20-517-7988   (BR)
SNC-LAVALIN INTERNATIONAL INC
SNC LAVALIN ENGINEERS & CONSTRUCTORS
265 Front St N Suite 301, Sarnia, ON, N7X 7X1
(519) 336-0201
Emp Here 300
SIC 8711 Engineering services

D-U-N-S 24-370-0825   (BR)
ST. CLAIR CATHOLIC DISTRICT SCHOOL BOARD
ST MARGARET ELEMENTARY SCHOOL
720 Devine St, Sarnia, ON, N7T 1X2
(519) 332-4300
Emp Here 25
SIC 8211 Elementary and secondary schools

D-U-N-S 24-420-0106   (BR)
ST. CLAIR CATHOLIC DISTRICT SCHOOL BOARD
ST PATRICK'S CATHOLIC HIGH SCHOOL
281 East St N, Sarnia, ON, N7T 6X8
(519) 541-1465
Emp Here 61
SIC 8211 Elementary and secondary schools

D-U-N-S 20-535-7010   (BR)
STEEVES & ROZEMA ENTERPRISES LIMITED
RESIDENCE ON ST CLAIR
170 Front St S Suite 340, Sarnia, ON, N7T 2M5
(519) 336-1455
Emp Here 40
SIC 8361 Residential care

D-U-N-S 25-278-8013   (BR)
STEEVES & ROZEMA ENTERPRISES LIMITED
ROSEWOOD MANOR RETIREMENT COMMUNITY
711 Indian Rd N, Sarnia, ON, N7T 7Z5
(519) 332-8877
Emp Here 40
SIC 6513 Apartment building operators

D-U-N-S 20-795-4525   (BR)
SUNCOR ENERGY PRODUCTS INC
1900 River Rd, Sarnia, ON, N7T 7J3
(519) 337-2301
Emp Here 350
SIC 5172 Petroleum products, nec

D-U-N-S 25-481-5194   (BR)
TANDET MANAGEMENT INC
TANDET LOGISTICS
1006 Prescott Dr Suite 2, Sarnia, ON, N7T

7H3
(519) 332-6000
Emp Here 50
SIC 7513 Truck rental and leasing, no drivers

D-U-N-S 24-124-9544   (BR)
TEAM INDUSTRIAL SERVICES (CANADA) INC
893 Campbell St, Sarnia, ON, N7T 2J9
(519) 337-2375
Emp Here 50
SIC 7389 Business services, nec

D-U-N-S 24-772-2077   (SL)
TECSAR ENGINEERING INC
117 Front St N, Sarnia, ON, N7T 0B3
(519) 383-8028
Emp Here 50   *Sales* 4,961,328
SIC 8711 Engineering services

D-U-N-S 24-097-8650   (SL)
TEE JAY INSTRUMENTATION SERVICES LTD
TJI
1014 Prescott Dr, Sarnia, ON, N7T 7H3
(519) 332-8120
Emp Here 50   *Sales* 4,377,642
SIC 1731 Electrical work

D-U-N-S 24-348-6870   (SL)
TODA ADVANCED MATERIALS INC
933 Vidal St, Sarnia, ON, N7T 7K2
(519) 346-4331
Emp Here 35   *Sales* 8,749,135
SIC 2819 Industrial inorganic chemicals, nec
Pr Kazuyoshi Murashige
VP Opers Michael Kruft
Dir Tadashi Kubota
Dir Kenji Ogisu
Dir Osamu Oishi
Dir Junichi Nakano
Dir Ulrich Koemm

D-U-N-S 24-387-3093   (BR)
VEOLIA ES CANADA SERVICES INDUSTRIELS INC
VEOLIA ENVIRONMENTAL SERVICES
605 Scott Rd, Sarnia, ON, N7T 8G3
(519) 336-3330
Emp Here 20
SIC 7349 Building maintenance services, nec

D-U-N-S 25-940-7385   (BR)
WAL-MART CANADA CORP
Gd Lcd Main, Sarnia, ON, N7T 7H7
(519) 542-1854
Emp Here 150
SIC 5311 Department stores

Sarnia, ON N7V
Lambton County

D-U-N-S 25-237-8542   (BR)
CONSEIL SCOLAIRE DE DISTRICT DES ECOLES CATHOLIQUES DU SUD-OUEST
ECOLE ST THOMAS D'AQUIN
931 Champlain Rd, Sarnia, ON, N7V 2E9
(519) 542-5423
Emp Here 40
SIC 8211 Elementary and secondary schools

D-U-N-S 20-591-6401   (BR)
LAMBTON KENT DISTRICT SCHOOL BOARD
KING GEORGE VI SCHOOL
585 O'Dell St, Sarnia, ON, N7V 4H7
(519) 344-2942
Emp Here 25
SIC 8211 Elementary and secondary schools

D-U-N-S 25-249-3366   (BR)
LAMBTON KENT DISTRICT SCHOOL BOARD
ROSEDALE SCHOOL
1018 Indian Rd N, Sarnia, ON, N7V 4C5

(519) 542-4552
Emp Here 30
SIC 8211 Elementary and secondary schools

D-U-N-S 20-974-2548   (BR)
LEGAL AID ONTARIO
SARNIA DUTY COUNSEL OFFICE
700 Christina St N, Sarnia, ON, N7V 3C2
(519) 337-1210
Emp Here 30
SIC 8111 Legal services

D-U-N-S 20-047-1030   (BR)
ST. CLAIR CATHOLIC DISTRICT SCHOOL BOARD
SACRED HEART SCHOOL
1411 Lecaron Ave, Sarnia, ON, N7V 3J1
(519) 344-1601
Emp Here 30
SIC 8211 Elementary and secondary schools

D-U-N-S 20-965-5208   (HQ)
ST. CLAIR CHILD & YOUTH SERVICES
(Suby of St. Clair Child & Youth Services)
129 Kendall St, Sarnia, ON, N7V 4G6
(519) 337-3701
Emp Here 45   *Emp Total* 65
Sales 2,553,625
SIC 8322 Individual and family services

D-U-N-S 20-179-5585   (BR)
WINDSOR-ESSEX CHILDREN'S AID SOCIETY
CHILDREN'S AID SOCIETY
161 Kendall St, Sarnia, ON, N7V 4G6
(519) 336-0623
Emp Here 83
SIC 8399 Social services, nec

D-U-N-S 25-740-3899   (BR)
YMCAS ACROSS SOUTHWESTERN ONTARIO
ESSO YMCA LEARNING AND CAREER CENTRE
660 Oakdale Ave, Sarnia, ON, N7V 2A9
(519) 336-5950
Emp Here 24
SIC 8399 Social services, nec

Sarnia, ON N7W
Lambton County

D-U-N-S 25-203-1422   (SL)
405730 ONTARIO LIMITED
HIAWATHA HORSE PARK & ENTERMAINENT CENTRE
1730 London Line, Sarnia, ON, N7W 1A1
(519) 542-5543
Emp Here 60
SIC 7948 Racing, including track operation

D-U-N-S 20-149-3830   (SL)
JOHN'S RESTAURANT & GIFTS (SARNIA) LIMITED
JOHN'S RESTAURANT & GIFTS
1643 London Line, Sarnia, ON, N7W 1A9
(519) 542-9821
Emp Here 50   *Sales* 1,532,175
SIC 5812 Eating places

D-U-N-S 20-048-4749   (SL)
LAMONS CANADA LIMITED
LAMONS
835 Upper Canada Dr, Sarnia, ON, N7W 1A3
(519) 332-1800
Emp Here 22   *Sales* 3,064,349
SIC 3499 Fabricated Metal products, nec

D-U-N-S 24-313-4066   (BR)
PARKBRIDGE LIFESTYLE COMMUNITIES INC
BLUEWATER ADULT LEISURE LIVING
5700 Blackwell Siderd, Sarnia, ON, N7W 1B7
(519) 542-7800
Emp Here 20

SIC 6719 Holding companies, nec

D-U-N-S 20-100-5076   (BR)
VICTORIAN ORDER OF NURSES FOR CANADA
VON BATHURST DISTRICT
1705 Loncon Line, Sarnia, ON, N7W 1B2
(519) 542-2310
Emp Here 120
SIC 8082 Home health care services

Sarsfield, ON K0A
Carleton County

D-U-N-S 25-464-3612   (BR)
REVERA INC
CENTRAL PARK LODGES
2781 Colonial Rd, Sarsfield, ON, K0A 3E0
(613) 835-2977
Emp Here 50
SIC 8051 Skilled nursing care facilities

Sault Ste. Marie, ON P6A
Algoma County

D-U-N-S 25-238-9366   (BR)
ALGOMA DISTRICT SCHOOL BOARD
GREENWOOD PUBLIC SCHOOL
(*Suby of* Algoma District School Board)
8 Fourth Line W, Sault Ste. Marie, ON, P6A 0B5
(705) 945-7118
Emp Here 22
SIC 8211 Elementary and secondary schools

D-U-N-S 25-238-9143   (BR)
ALGOMA DISTRICT SCHOOL BOARD
ANNA MCCREA PUBLIC SCHOOL
(*Suby of* Algoma District School Board)
250 Mark St, Sault Ste. Marie, ON, P6A 3M7
(705) 945-7106
Emp Here 33
SIC 8211 Elementary and secondary schools

D-U-N-S 20-710-3701   (BR)
ALGOMA DISTRICT SCHOOL BOARD
EAST VIEW SCHOOL
(*Suby of* Algoma District School Board)
75 Arizona Ave, Sault Ste. Marie, ON, P6A 4L9
(705) 945-7115
Emp Here 50
SIC 8211 Elementary and secondary schools

D-U-N-S 24-012-2031   (BR)
ALGOMA DISTRICT SCHOOL BOARD
MICHIPICOTEN HIGH SCHOOL
(*Suby of* Algoma District School Board)
84 Albert St E, Sault Ste. Marie, ON, P6A 2H9
(705) 856-4464
Emp Here 50
SIC 8211 Elementary and secondary schools

D-U-N-S 25-238-9044   (BR)
ALGOMA DISTRICT SCHOOL BOARD
R.M. MOORE PUBLIC SCHOOL
(*Suby of* Algoma District School Board)
1272 Base Line, Sault Ste. Marie, ON, P6A 5K6
(705) 945-7135
Emp Here 25
SIC 8211 Elementary and secondary schools

D-U-N-S 25-239-0729   (BR)
ALGOMA DISTRICT SCHOOL BOARD
SIR JAMES DUNN COLLEGIATE & VOCATIONAL
(*Suby of* Algoma District School Board)
1601 Wellington St E, Sault Ste. Marie, ON, P6A 2R8
(705) 945-7177
Emp Here 100

SIC 8211 Elementary and secondary schools

D-U-N-S 20-010-0514   (BR)
ALGOMA DISTRICT SCHOOL BOARD
PINEWOOD PUBLIC SCHOOL
(*Suby of* Algoma District School Board)
3924 Queen St E, Sault Ste. Marie, ON, P6A 5K9
(705) 945-7133
Emp Here 20
SIC 8211 Elementary and secondary schools

D-U-N-S 20-913-6782   (BR)
ALGOMA DISTRICT SCHOOL BOARD
QUEEN ELIZABETH PUBLIC SCHOOL
(*Suby of* Algoma District School Board)
139 Elizabeth St, Sault Ste. Marie, ON, P6A 3Z5
(705) 945-7132
Emp Here 30
SIC 8211 Elementary and secondary schools

D-U-N-S 24-097-8239   (HQ)
ALGOMA DISTRICT SCHOOL BOARD
(*Suby of* Algoma District School Board)
644 Albert St E, Sault Ste. Marie, ON, P6A 2K7
(705) 945-7111
Emp Here 60   *Emp Total* 2,600
Sales 224,368,535
SIC 8211 Elementary and secondary schools
Dir Mario Turco
Superintnt Joe Santa Maria
Superintnt Joe Maurice
Superintnt Lucia Reece
Superintnt Kime Collver
Superintnt Asima Vezina

D-U-N-S 20-037-3756   (BR)
ALGOMA DISTRICT SCHOOL BOARD
PARKLAND PUBLIC SCHOOL
(*Suby of* Algoma District School Board)
54 Amber St, Sault Ste. Marie, ON, P6A 5G1
(705) 945-7129
Emp Here 42
SIC 8211 Elementary and secondary schools

D-U-N-S 20-710-3719   (BR)
ALGOMA DISTRICT SCHOOL BOARD
GRAND VIEW PUBLIC SCHOOL
(*Suby of* Algoma District School Board)
161 Denwood Dr, Sault Ste. Marie, ON, P6A 5R4
(705) 945-7148
Emp Here 50
SIC 8211 Elementary and secondary schools

D-U-N-S 20-025-3198   (BR)
ALGOMA DISTRICT SCHOOL BOARD
WHITE PINES COLLEGIATE & VOCATIONAL SCHOOL
(*Suby of* Algoma District School Board)
1007 Trunk Rd, Sault Ste. Marie, ON, P6A 5K9
(705) 945-7181
Emp Here 70
SIC 8211 Elementary and secondary schools

D-U-N-S 24-507-9889   (SL)
ALGOMA STEEL INC
105 West St, Sault Ste. Marie, ON, P6A 7B4
(705) 945-2351
Emp Here 2,300   *Sales* 1,288,313,550
SIC 5051 Metals service centers and offices
Prin Paul Finley

D-U-N-S 24-179-4812   (BR)
AVERY CONSTRUCTION LIMITED
1109 Allen'S Side Rd, Sault Ste. Marie, ON, P6A 5K8

Emp Here 50
SIC 1611 Highway and street construction

D-U-N-S 25-321-0306   (BR)
BDO CANADA LLP
SAULT STE. MARIE ACCOUNTING
747 Queen St E Suite 1109, Sault Ste. Marie, ON, P6A 2A8

(705) 945-0990
Emp Here 40
SIC 8721 Accounting, auditing, and bookkeeping

D-U-N-S 25-296-6783   (BR)
BANK OF NOVA SCOTIA, THE
SCOTIABANK
293 Bay St Suite 79, Sault Ste. Marie, ON, P6A 1X3
(705) 254-7660
Emp Here 35
SIC 6021 National commercial banks

D-U-N-S 20-000-7669   (BR)
BAYSHORE HEALTHCARE LTD.
BAYSHORE HOME HEALTH
390 Bay St Suite 304, Sault Ste. Marie, ON, P6A 1X2
(705) 942-3232
Emp Here 60
SIC 8082 Home health care services

D-U-N-S 25-303-5349   (BR)
CANADIAN IMPERIAL BANK OF COMMERCE
CIBC
530 Queen St E Suite 100, Sault Ste. Marie, ON, P6A 2A1
(705) 254-6633
Emp Here 33
SIC 6021 National commercial banks

D-U-N-S 20-526-5981   (BR)
CANADIAN RED CROSS SOCIETY, THE
COMMUNITY HEALTH SERVICES
390 Bay St Suite 305, Sault Ste. Marie, ON, P6A 1X2

Emp Here 120
SIC 8322 Individual and family services

D-U-N-S 20-968-6534   (BR)
COMMONWEALTH HOSPITALITY LTD
HOLIDAY INN SAULT SAINTE MARIE WATERFRONT
(*Suby of* WXI/WWH Parallel Amalco (Ontario) Ltd)
208 St Mary'S River Dr, Sault Ste. Marie, ON, P6A 5V4
(705) 945-6950
Emp Here 70
SIC 7011 Hotels and motels

D-U-N-S 24-057-7911   (BR)
COMMUNITY LIVING ALGOMA
59 Lewis Rd Suite 3, Sault Ste. Marie, ON, P6A 4G3
(705) 759-6810
Emp Here 20
SIC 8322 Individual and family services

D-U-N-S 24-179-4804   (BR)
COMMUNITY LIVING ALGOMA
1020 Queen St E, Sault Ste. Marie, ON, P6A 2C6
(705) 942-1960
Emp Here 23
SIC 8641 Civic and social associations

D-U-N-S 25-643-8177   (BR)
CORPORATION OF THE CITY OF SAULT STE MARIE, THE
SAULT STE MARIE PUBLIC LIBRARY
50 East St, Sault Ste. Marie, ON, P6A 3C3
(705) 759-5230
Emp Here 60
SIC 8231 Libraries

D-U-N-S 25-134-3711   (BR)
CORPORATION OF THE CITY OF SAULT STE MARIE, THE
SPORTS AND ENTERTAINMENT CENTER
269 Queen St E, Sault Ste. Marie, ON, P6A 1Y9
(705) 759-5251
Emp Here 150
SIC 7389 Business services, nec

D-U-N-S 24-892-6339   (BR)

G&K SERVICES CANADA INC
G & K SERVICES
(*Suby of* Cintas Corporation)
121 Queen St E, Sault Ste. Marie, ON, P6A 1Y6
(705) 253-1131
Emp Here 35
SIC 7299 Miscellaneous personal service

D-U-N-S 20-588-1654   (BR)
GOVERNMENT OF ONTARIO
ALGOMA UNIVERSITY
1520 Queen St E, Sault Ste. Marie, ON, P6A 2G4
(705) 949-2301
Emp Here 200
SIC 8221 Colleges and universities

D-U-N-S 25-641-8021   (BR)
GREAT-WEST LIFE ASSURANCE COMPANY, THE
421 Bay St Suite 606, Sault Ste. Marie, ON, P6A 1X3

Emp Here 30
SIC 6311 Life insurance

D-U-N-S 20-710-3925   (BR)
HURON-SUPERIOR CATHOLIC DISTRICT SCHOOL BOARD
ST MARYS FRENCH IMMERSION
124 Gibbs St, Sault Ste. Marie, ON, P6A 5H6
(705) 945-5531
Emp Here 25
SIC 8211 Elementary and secondary schools

D-U-N-S 20-710-3891   (BR)
HURON-SUPERIOR CATHOLIC DISTRICT SCHOOL BOARD
ST HUBERT ELEMENTARY SCHOOL
207 Dacey Rd, Sault Ste. Marie, ON, P6A 5J8
(705) 945-5526
Emp Here 50
SIC 8211 Elementary and secondary schools

D-U-N-S 20-710-3917   (BR)
HURON-SUPERIOR CATHOLIC DISTRICT SCHOOL BOARD
ECHO-DES-RAPIDES PUBLIC SCHOOL
145 Hugill St, Sault Ste. Marie, ON, P6A 4E9

Emp Here 50
SIC 8211 Elementary and secondary schools

D-U-N-S 20-652-2257   (BR)
HURON-SUPERIOR CATHOLIC DISTRICT SCHOOL BOARD
ST PATRICK CATHOLIC SCHOOL
178 Glen Ave, Sault Ste. Marie, ON, P6A 5E2
(705) 945-5532
Emp Here 30
SIC 8211 Elementary and secondary schools

D-U-N-S 25-225-0089   (BR)
HURON-SUPERIOR CATHOLIC DISTRICT SCHOOL BOARD
ST MARY'S COLLEGE
130 Wellington St E, Sault Ste. Marie, ON, P6A 2L5
(705) 945-5540
Emp Here 65
SIC 8211 Elementary and secondary schools

D-U-N-S 25-238-8905   (BR)
HURON-SUPERIOR CATHOLIC DISTRICT SCHOOL BOARD
SISTER MARY CLARE ELEMENTARY SCHOOL
178 Glen Ave, Sault Ste. Marie, ON, P6A 5E2

Emp Here 22
SIC 8211 Elementary and secondary schools

D-U-N-S 25-315-8422   (BR)
INVESTORS GROUP FINANCIAL SERVICES INC
855 Queen St E Suite 100, Sault Ste. Marie, ON, P6A 2B3

---

(705) 759-0220
Emp Here 20
SIC 8741 Management services

D-U-N-S 25-300-6134   (BR)
KPMG LLP
(Suby of KPMG LLP)
111 Elgin St Suite 200, Sault Ste. Marie, ON, P6A 6L6
(705) 949-5811
Emp Here 20
SIC 8721 Accounting, auditing, and book-keeping

D-U-N-S 25-303-9259   (BR)
LONDON LIFE INSURANCE COMPANY
FREEDOM 55 FINANCIAL
477 Queen St E, Sault Ste. Marie, ON, P6A 1Z5
(705) 256-5618
Emp Here 40
SIC 6311 Life insurance

D-U-N-S 20-787-4368   (BR)
METRO ONTARIO INC
FOOD BASICS
625 Trunk Rd, Sault Ste. Marie, ON, P6A 3T1
(705) 949-7260
Emp Here 110
SIC 5411 Grocery stores

D-U-N-S 24-333-1647   (BR)
METRO ONTARIO INC
150 Churchill Blvd, Sault Ste. Marie, ON, P6A 3Z9
(705) 254-7070
Emp Here 100
SIC 5411 Grocery stores

D-U-N-S 20-175-0614   (BR)
NAV CANADA
FLIGHT SERVICES
475 Airport Rd Suite 1, Sault Ste. Marie, ON, P6A 5K6
(705) 779-3838
Emp Here 21
SIC 4581 Airports, flying fields, and services

D-U-N-S 24-345-4712   (BR)
NORTH EAST COMMUNITY CARE ACCESS CENTRE
SAULT STE MARIE MAIN OFFICE
(Suby of North East Community Care Access Centre)
390 Bay St, Sault Ste. Marie, ON, P6A 1X2
(705) 949-1650
Emp Here 85
SIC 8322 Individual and family services

D-U-N-S 24-378-8598   (BR)
ONTARIO LOTTERY AND GAMING CORPO-RATION
OLG CASINO SAULT STE MARIE
30 Bay St W, Sault Ste. Marie, ON, P6A 7A6
(705) 759-0100
Emp Here 360
SIC 7999 Amusement and recreation, nec

D-U-N-S 20-120-7367   (BR)
ONTARIO LOTTERY AND GAMING CORPO-RATION
70 Foster Dr Suite 800, Sault Ste. Marie, ON, P6A 6V2
(705) 946-6464
Emp Here 500
SIC 7999 Amusement and recreation, nec

D-U-N-S 20-647-5696   (BR)
OPERATION SPRINGBOARD
136 Pilgrim St, Sault Ste. Marie, ON, P6A 3E9

Emp Here 20
SIC 8361 Residential care

D-U-N-S 25-649-3446   (BR)
ORANO LIMITED
STATION MALL DRUG MART
293 Bay St Suite 1, Sault Ste. Marie, ON, P6A 1X3

(705) 949-7331
Emp Here 20
SIC 5912 Drug stores and proprietary stores

D-U-N-S 20-183-8732   (SL)
PUC DISTRIBUTION INC
765 Queen St E, Sault Ste. Marie, ON, P6A 2A8
(705) 759-6500
Emp Here 100   Sales 18,261,000
SIC 4971 Irrigation systems
Pr Pr Brian Curran
Terry Greco
VP VP Dominic Parella

D-U-N-S 20-183-8690   (SL)
PUC ENERGIES INC
765 Queen St E, Sault Ste. Marie, ON, P6A 2A8
(705) 759-6500
Emp Here 50   Sales 7,263,840
SIC 8748 Business consulting, nec
Pr Pr Brian Curran

D-U-N-S 20-149-9696   (SL)
PALMER CONSTRUCTION GROUP INC
258 Queen St E Suite 301, Sault Ste. Marie, ON, P6A 1Y7
(705) 254-1644
Emp Here 86   Sales 9,995,616
SIC 1611 Highway and street construction
Terry Rainone

D-U-N-S 25-841-9670   (BR)
PHARMA PLUS DRUGMARTS LTD
REXALL PHARMA PLUS
129 Trunk Rd, Sault Ste. Marie, ON, P6A 3S4
(705) 253-3254
Emp Here 25
SIC 5912 Drug stores and proprietary stores

D-U-N-S 24-345-9646   (BR)
PIONEER CONSTRUCTION INC
845 Old Goulais Bay Rd Suite 3, Sault Ste. Marie, ON, P6A 0B5
(705) 541-2250
Emp Here 30
SIC 1611 Highway and street construction

D-U-N-S 20-150-1558   (BR)
PRAXAIR CANADA INC
(Suby of Praxair, Inc.)
1 Patrick St, Sault Ste. Marie, ON, P6A 5N5
(705) 759-2103
Emp Here 20
SIC 2813 Industrial gases

D-U-N-S 25-079-7412   (BR)
PRISZM LP
KFC
161 Trunk Rd, Sault Ste. Marie, ON, P6A 3S5
(705) 946-2792
Emp Here 21
SIC 5812 Eating places

D-U-N-S 24-817-1865   (BR)
PROCRANE INC
STERLING CRANE DIV
(Suby of Berkshire Hathaway Inc.)
Baseline Rd, Sault Ste. Marie, ON, P6A 5L1
(705) 945-5099
Emp Here 20
SIC 7353 Heavy construction equipment rental

D-U-N-S 20-150-0055   (SL)
ROBINSON, ELLWOOD LIMITED
2075 Great Northern Rd, Sault Ste. Marie, ON, P6A 5K7
(705) 759-1759
Emp Here 30   Sales 4,823,040
SIC 1611 Highway and street construction

D-U-N-S 20-535-7598   (BR)
ROYAL BANK OF CANADA
RBC ROYAL BANK
(Suby of Royal Bank Of Canada)
602 Queen St E, Sault Ste. Marie, ON, P6A 2A4

(705) 759-7000
Emp Here 20
SIC 6021 National commercial banks

D-U-N-S 25-109-5428   (SL)
SAULT & DISTRICT PERSONNEL SER-VICES
1719 Trunk Rd, Sault Ste. Marie, ON, P6A 6X9
(705) 759-6191
Emp Here 60   Sales 4,377,642
SIC 7361 Employment agencies

D-U-N-S 24-123-4228   (SL)
SAULT STE MARIE HOUSING CORPORA-TION
180 Brock St, Sault Ste. Marie, ON, P6A 3B7
(705) 946-2077
Emp Here 50   Sales 4,742,446
SIC 6531 Real estate agents and managers

D-U-N-S 25-713-7992   (SL)
SAULT STE. MARIE GOLF CLUB
1804 Queen St E, Sault Ste. Marie, ON, P6A 2H1
(705) 759-5133
Emp Here 50   Sales 2,042,900
SIC 7997 Membership sports and recreation clubs

D-U-N-S 24-764-8082   (BR)
SEARS CANADA INC
293 Bay St, Sault Ste. Marie, ON, P6A 1X3
(705) 949-7611
Emp Here 220
SIC 5311 Department stores

D-U-N-S 25-250-3073   (BR)
SERVICE CORPORATION INTERNATIONAL (CANADA) LIMITED
ARTHUR FUNERAL & CREAMATION CEN-TRE
492 Wellington St E, Sault Ste. Marie, ON, P6A 2L9
(705) 759-2522
Emp Here 35
SIC 7261 Funeral service and crematories

D-U-N-S 25-255-7467   (BR)
SERVICE CORPORATION INTERNATIONAL (CANADA) LIMITED
BARTON & KITELEY FUNERAL HOME & CREMATION CENTRE
165 Brock St, Sault Ste. Marie, ON, P6A 3B8
(705) 759-2114
Emp Here 25
SIC 7261 Funeral service and crematories

D-U-N-S 20-639-0150   (BR)
SERVICES FINANCIERS NCO, INC
AGENCE DE RECOUVREMENT
(Suby of Egs Shell Company, Inc.)
345 Queen St E, Sault Ste. Marie, ON, P6A 1Z2

Emp Here 800
SIC 7389 Business services, nec

D-U-N-S 25-301-3577   (BR)
UNITED STEELWORKERS OF AMERICA
USWA
(Suby of United Steelworkers)
68 Dennis St, Sault Ste. Marie, ON, P6A 2W9
(705) 759-4945
Emp Here 20
SIC 8631 Labor organizations

D-U-N-S 24-187-0505   (BR)
WE CARE HEALTH SERVICES INC
369 Queen St E Suite 201, Sault Ste. Marie, ON, P6A 1Z4
(705) 941-5222
Emp Here 70
SIC 8049 Offices of health practitioner

Sault Ste. Marie, ON P6B
Algoma County

D-U-N-S 25-931-2882   (SL)
985907 ONTARIO LIMITED
WENDY'S RESTAURANT
389 Great Northern Rd, Sault Ste. Marie, ON, P6B 4Z8
(705) 941-9999
Emp Here 90   Sales 2,699,546
SIC 5812 Eating places

D-U-N-S 25-237-2040   (BR)
A.J. BUS LINES LIMITED
A.J. BUS LINES
132 Industrial Park Cres, Sault Ste. Marie, ON, P6B 5P2
(705) 759-1228
Emp Here 20
SIC 4119 Local passenger transportation, nec

D-U-N-S 20-710-3735   (BR)
ALGOMA DISTRICT SCHOOL BOARD
NORTHERN HEIGHTS PUBLIC SCHOOL
(Suby of Algoma District School Board)
210 Grand Blvd, Sault Ste. Marie, ON, P6B 4S8
(705) 945-7128
Emp Here 50
SIC 8211 Elementary and secondary schools

D-U-N-S 20-710-3768   (BR)
ALGOMA DISTRICT SCHOOL BOARD
ROSEVILLE PUBLIC SCHOOL
(Suby of Algoma District School Board)
90 Chapple Ave, Sault Ste. Marie, ON, P6B 3N9
(705) 945-7149
Emp Here 25
SIC 8211 Elementary and secondary schools

D-U-N-S 20-589-3076   (BR)
ALGOMA DISTRICT SCHOOL BOARD
SUPERIOR HEIGHTS COLLEGIATE & VO-CATIONAL SCHOOL
(Suby of Algoma District School Board)
750 North St, Sault Ste. Marie, ON, P6B 2C5
(705) 945-7177
Emp Here 50
SIC 8211 Elementary and secondary schools

D-U-N-S 25-238-9200   (BR)
ALGOMA DISTRICT SCHOOL BOARD
MANITOU PARK ELEMENTARY SCHOOL
(Suby of Algoma District School Board)
92 Manitou Dr, Sault Ste. Marie, ON, P6B 5K6
(705) 945-7125
Emp Here 20
SIC 8211 Elementary and secondary schools

D-U-N-S 20-025-9567   (BR)
ALGOMA DISTRICT SCHOOL BOARD
F.H. CLERGUE PUBLIC SCHOOL
(Suby of Algoma District School Board)
80 Weldon Ave, Sault Ste. Marie, ON, P6B 3C6
(705) 945-7136
Emp Here 25
SIC 8211 Elementary and secondary schools

D-U-N-S 25-238-8889   (BR)
ALGOMA DISTRICT SCHOOL BOARD
BEN R MCMULLIN ELEMENTARY SCHOOL
(Suby of Algoma District School Board)
24 Paradise Ave, Sault Ste. Marie, ON, P6B 5K2
(705) 945-7108
Emp Here 25
SIC 8211 Elementary and secondary schools

D-U-N-S 25-238-9002   (BR)
ALGOMA DISTRICT SCHOOL BOARD
RIVER VIEW PUBLIC SCHOOL
(Suby of Algoma District School Board)
51 Wireless Ave, Sault Ste. Marie, ON, P6B 1L4
(705) 945-7134
Emp Here 35
SIC 8211 Elementary and secondary schools

D-U-N-S 25-238-9242   (BR)
ALGOMA DISTRICT SCHOOL BOARD
KIWEDIN PUBLIC SCHOOL
(*Suby of* Algoma District School Board)
735 North St, Sault Ste. Marie, ON, P6B 2C4
(705) 945-7124
Emp Here 25
SIC 8211 Elementary and secondary schools

D-U-N-S 20-710-3750   (BR)
ALGOMA DISTRICT SCHOOL BOARD
ALEXANDER HENRY HIGH SCHOOL
(*Suby of* Algoma District School Board)
232 Northern Ave E, Sault Ste. Marie, ON, P6B 4H6

Emp Here 50
SIC 8211 Elementary and secondary schools

D-U-N-S 25-239-0646   (BR)
ALGOMA DISTRICT SCHOOL BOARD
BAWATING COLLEGIATE & VOCATION SCHOOL
(*Suby of* Algoma District School Board)
750 North St, Sault Ste. Marie, ON, P6B 2C5
(705) 945-7177
Emp Here 75
SIC 8211 Elementary and secondary schools

D-U-N-S 25-239-0489   (BR)
ALGOMA DISTRICT SCHOOL BOARD
TARENTORUS PUBLIC SCHOOL
(*Suby of* Algoma District School Board)
96 Northwood St, Sault Ste. Marie, ON, P6B 4M4
(705) 945-7138
Emp Here 40
SIC 8211 Elementary and secondary schools

D-U-N-S 20-002-6438   (BR)
BANQUE TORONTO-DOMINION, LA
TORONTO-DOMINION BANK, THE
(*Suby of* Toronto-Dominion Bank, The)
44 Great Northern Rd, Sault Ste. Marie, ON, P6B 4Y5
(705) 254-7355
Emp Here 35
SIC 6021 National commercial banks

D-U-N-S 20-700-0022   (BR)
BANQUE DE DEVELOPPEMENT DU CANADA
BDC
153 Great Northern Rd, Sault Ste. Marie, ON, P6B 4Y9
(877) 232-2269
Emp Here 40
SIC 6141 Personal credit institutions

D-U-N-S 24-335-9218   (BR)
BEST BUY CANADA LTD
FUTURE SHOP
(*Suby of* Best Buy Co., Inc.)
548 Great Northern Rd, Sault Ste. Marie, ON, P6B 4Z9
(705) 942-0722
Emp Here 40
SIC 5731 Radio, television, and electronic stores

D-U-N-S 25-648-1995   (SL)
BIOFOREST TECHNOLOGIES INC
59 Industrial Park Cres Unit 1, Sault Ste. Marie, ON, P6B 5P3
(705) 942-5824
Emp Here 25   *Sales* 2,334,742
SIC 8741 Management services

D-U-N-S 24-966-1471   (HQ)
BOARD OF HEALTH FOR THE DISTRICT OF ALGOMA HEALTH UNIT
ALGOMA PUBLIC HEALTH
(*Suby of* Board of Health for the District of Algoma Health Unit)
294 Willow Ave, Sault Ste. Marie, ON, P6B 0A9
(705) 942-4646
Emp Here 116   *Emp Total* 170
Sales 16,707,430

SIC 8011 Offices and clinics of medical doctors
Jeffrey Holmes

D-U-N-S 24-841-1014   (BR)
BOSTON PIZZA INTERNATIONAL INC
601 Great Northern Rd, Sault Ste. Marie, ON, P6B 5A1
(705) 949-5560
Emp Here 30
SIC 5812 Eating places

D-U-N-S 25-369-5217   (BR)
CARA OPERATIONS LIMITED
SWISS CHALET
(*Suby of* Cara Holdings Limited)
332 Great Northern Rd, Sault Ste. Marie, ON, P6B 4Z7
(705) 256-2677
Emp Here 60
SIC 5812 Eating places

D-U-N-S 24-349-0641   (BR)
CHARTWELL SENIORS HOUSING REAL ESTATE INVESTMENT TRUST
COLLEGIATE HEIGHTS RETIREMENT HOME
95 Fauquier Ave, Sault Ste. Marie, ON, P6B 2P2
(705) 253-1667
Emp Here 35
SIC 8322 Individual and family services

D-U-N-S 25-174-8224   (BR)
COMCARE (CANADA) LIMITED
COMCARE HEALTH SERVICES
(*Suby of* Comcare (Canada) Limited)
370 Lake St, Sault Ste. Marie, ON, P6B 3L1
(705) 759-0110
Emp Here 60
SIC 8051 Skilled nursing care facilities

D-U-N-S 20-354-8750   (BR)
COMMUNITY LIVING ALGOMA
SOOGOMA INDUSTRIES
105 White Oak Dr E, Sault Ste. Marie, ON, P6B 4J7
(705) 946-0931
Emp Here 60
SIC 8322 Individual and family services

D-U-N-S 25-641-8690   (BR)
COMMUNITY LIVING ONTARIO
RECYCLING MATTERS
253 Bruce St, Sault Ste. Marie, ON, P6B 1P3
(705) 945-1030
Emp Here 21
SIC 8399 Social services, nec

D-U-N-S 20-025-0830   (BR)
CONSEIL SCOLAIRE DE DISTRICT CATHOLIQUE DU NOUVEL-ONTARIO, LE
NOTRE-DAME-DU-SAULT
600 North St, Sault Ste. Marie, ON, P6B 2B9
(705) 945-5520
Emp Here 45
SIC 8211 Elementary and secondary schools

D-U-N-S 24-466-4335   (BR)
ENERGIE RENOUVELABLE BROOKFIELD INC
HYDRO-PONTIAC INC.
243 Industrial Park Cres, Sault Ste. Marie, ON, P6B 5P3
(705) 256-7575
Emp Here 20
SIC 4911 Electric services

D-U-N-S 20-047-4794   (BR)
EXTENDICARE INC
EXTENDICARE VAN DAELE
39 Van Daele St, Sault Ste. Marie, ON, P6B 4V3
(705) 949-7934
Emp Here 170
SIC 8051 Skilled nursing care facilities

D-U-N-S 20-753-7267   (BR)

FIRSTCANADA ULC
LAIDLAW TRANSIT
70 Industrial Court A, Sault Ste. Marie, ON, P6B 5W6
(705) 759-2192
Emp Here 130
SIC 4151 School buses

D-U-N-S 20-553-6076   (BR)
HOME DEPOT OF CANADA INC
HOME DEPOT
(*Suby of* The Home Depot Inc)
530 Great Northern Rd, Sault Ste. Marie, ON, P6B 4Z9
(705) 254-1150
Emp Here 150
SIC 5251 Hardware stores

D-U-N-S 25-238-9853   (BR)
HURON-SUPERIOR CATHOLIC DISTRICT SCHOOL BOARD
ST PIUS X CATHOLIC SCHOOL
48 Oryme Ave, Sault Ste. Marie, ON, P6B 4C3
(705) 945-5534
Emp Here 25
SIC 8211 Elementary and secondary schools

D-U-N-S 20-289-9253   (BR)
HURON-SUPERIOR CATHOLIC DISTRICT SCHOOL BOARD
ST. BASIL SECONDARY
250 St George'S Ave E, Sault Ste. Marie, ON, P6B 1X5
(705) 945-5542
Emp Here 60
SIC 8211 Elementary and secondary schools

D-U-N-S 25-238-9812   (BR)
HURON-SUPERIOR CATHOLIC DISTRICT SCHOOL BOARD
ST PAUL ELEMENTARY SCHOOL
78 Dablon St, Sault Ste. Marie, ON, P6B 5E6
(705) 945-5533
Emp Here 40
SIC 8211 Elementary and secondary schools

D-U-N-S 25-225-0154   (BR)
HURON-SUPERIOR CATHOLIC DISTRICT SCHOOL BOARD
MOUNT ST JOSEPH COLLEGE
100 Ontario Ave, Sault Ste. Marie, ON, P6B 1E3
(705) 945-5650
Emp Here 45
SIC 8211 Elementary and secondary schools

D-U-N-S 25-238-8822   (BR)
HURON-SUPERIOR CATHOLIC DISTRICT SCHOOL BOARD
ST BERNADETTE ELEMENTARY SCHOOL
462 Mcnabb St, Sault Ste. Marie, ON, P6B 1Z3
(705) 945-5524
Emp Here 25
SIC 8211 Elementary and secondary schools

D-U-N-S 20-349-9301   (SL)
HYDRO ONE SAULT STE. MARIE LP
2 Sackville Rd Suite B, Sault Ste. Marie, ON, P6B 6J6
(705) 254-7444
Emp Here 55   *Sales* 26,265,852
SIC 4911 Electric services

D-U-N-S 25-305-3532   (BR)
INNVEST PROPERTIES CORP
COMFORT INN
(*Suby of* Innvest Properties Corp)
333 Great Northern Rd Suite 293, Sault Ste. Marie, ON, P6B 4Z8
(705) 759-8000
Emp Here 22
SIC 7011 Hotels and motels

D-U-N-S 20-020-0421   (BR)
J.J.'S HOSPITALITY LIMITED
PAVILION, THE
360 Great Northern Rd Suite 787, Sault Ste.

Marie, ON, P6B 4Z7
(705) 945-7614
Emp Here 150
SIC 7011 Hotels and motels

D-U-N-S 25-650-7070   (SL)
KITANA INCORPORATED
HUSKY HOUSE NORTH
458 Great Northern Rd, Sault Ste. Marie, ON, P6B 4Z9

Emp Here 60   *Sales* 1,824,018
SIC 5812 Eating places

D-U-N-S 24-023-8477   (BR)
LEON'S FURNITURE LIMITED
682 Second Line E, Sault Ste. Marie, ON, P6B 4K3
(705) 946-2510
Emp Here 30
SIC 5712 Furniture stores

D-U-N-S 20-225-2578   (BR)
LOBLAW COMPANIES LIMITED
NATIONAL GROCERS CASH & CARRY
173 Trelawne Ave, Sault Ste. Marie, ON, P6B 2N3
(705) 946-5462
Emp Here 20
SIC 5141 Groceries, general line

D-U-N-S 25-295-6065   (BR)
MARCH OF DIMES CANADA
277 Northern Ave E, Sault Ste. Marie, ON, P6B 6E1
(705) 759-0328
Emp Here 32
SIC 8331 Job training and related services

D-U-N-S 24-118-5375   (BR)
MARCH OF DIMES CANADA
31 Old Garden River Rd Suite 122, Sault Ste. Marie, ON, P6B 5Y7
(705) 254-1099
Emp Here 20
SIC 8331 Job training and related services

D-U-N-S 24-544-4617   (BR)
MARK'S WORK WEARHOUSE LTD
MARK'S
548 Great Northern Rd, Sault Ste. Marie, ON, P6B 4Z9
(705) 256-2247
Emp Here 20
SIC 5651 Family clothing stores

D-U-N-S 25-446-8887   (BR)
PRISZM LP
KFC
389 Great Northern Rd, Sault Ste. Marie, ON, P6B 4Z8
(705) 946-2791
Emp Here 22
SIC 5812 Eating places

D-U-N-S 24-202-5349   (BR)
PUROLATOR INC.
PUROLATOR INC
40 Industrial Court A, Sault Ste. Marie, ON, P6B 5W6
(705) 949-5862
Emp Here 30
SIC 7389 Business services, nec

D-U-N-S 24-186-1819   (SL)
R F CONTRACTING INC
116 Industrial Park Cres, Sault Ste. Marie, ON, P6B 5P2
(705) 253-1151
Emp Here 50   *Sales* 4,377,642
SIC 1711 Plumbing, heating, air-conditioning

D-U-N-S 24-174-1151   (BR)
ROGERS MEDIA INC
Q 104 FM RADDIO
(*Suby of* Rogers Communications Inc)
642 Great Northern Rd, Sault Ste. Marie, ON, P6B 4Z9
(705) 759-9200
Emp Here 30

SIC 4832 Radio broadcasting stations

D-U-N-S 25-083-4926   (SL)
ROMES YOUR INDEPENDANT GROCER INC
44 Great Northern Rd, Sault Ste. Marie, ON, P6B 4Y5
(705) 253-1726
Emp Here 350   *Sales* 66,552,480
SIC 5411 Grocery stores
Pr Pr Steve Romes
 Kelly Romes

D-U-N-S 24-408-2806   (SL)
ROYAL TIRE SERVICE LTD
55 Black Rd, Sault Ste. Marie, ON, P6B 0A3
(705) 254-6664
Emp Here 33   *Sales* 6,125,139
SIC 5531 Auto and home supply stores
Dir Phil Shaw
Dir Gary Foley
Opers Mgr Hans Christian Klemm

D-U-N-S 24-141-5660   (HQ)
SAULT AREA HOSPITAL
(*Suby of* Sault Area Hospital)
750 Great Northern Rd Suite 1, Sault Ste. Marie, ON, P6B 0A8
(705) 759-3434
Emp Here 1,292   *Emp Total* 1,300
Sales 90,471,268
SIC 8062 General medical and surgical hospitals
 Ron Gagnon
 Rick Cooper
Prs Dir Teresa D'angelo
 Elaine Pitcher
 Ralph Barker

D-U-N-S 24-333-1795   (BR)
SEARS CANADA INC
SEARS SERVICE
45 White Oak Dr E, Sault Ste. Marie, ON, P6B 4J7
(800) 469-4663
Emp Here 20
SIC 7629 Electrical repair shops

D-U-N-S 20-657-9828   (BR)
SEARS CANADA INC
D AND L INVESTMENT
115a Northern Ave E Suite A, Sault Ste. Marie, ON, P6B 4H5

Emp Here 25
SIC 5311 Department stores

D-U-N-S 25-271-5826   (BR)
SHAW COMMUNICATIONS INC
23 Manitou Dr, Sault Ste. Marie, ON, P6B 6G9
(705) 946-2234
Emp Here 20
SIC 4841 Cable and other pay television services

D-U-N-S 20-150-0816   (HQ)
SOO MILL & LUMBER COMPANY LIMITED
(*Suby of* Soo Mill Holdings Limited)
539 Great Northern Rd, Sault Ste. Marie, ON, P6B 5A1
(705) 759-0533
Emp Here 85   *Emp Total* 80
Sales 17,411,645
SIC 5211 Lumber and other building materials
Pr Pr D Lynn Hollingsworth
VP VP Scott Macpillivray
 Ann Melville
 John Hollingsworth

D-U-N-S 25-282-7787   (SL)
SOONOR RETIREMENT CORPORATION
GREAT NORTHERN RETIREMENT HOME
760 Great Northern Rd Suite 137, Sault Ste. Marie, ON, P6B 0B5
(705) 945-9405
Emp Here 55   *Sales* 2,425,503
SIC 8361 Residential care

D-U-N-S 20-822-1952   (BR)
TOROMONT INDUSTRIES LTD
1207 Great Northern Rd, Sault Ste. Marie, ON, P6B 0B9
(705) 759-2444
Emp Here 27
SIC 5082 Construction and mining machinery

D-U-N-S 25-483-5150   (BR)
VALUE VILLAGE STORES, INC
(*Suby of* Savers, Inc.)
248 Northern Ave E, Sault Ste. Marie, ON, P6B 4H6
(705) 256-1801
Emp Here 30
SIC 5399 Miscellaneous general merchandise

D-U-N-S 20-101-9804   (BR)
WASTE MANAGEMENT OF CANADA CORPORATION
(*Suby of* Waste Management, Inc.)
120 Industrial Court A, Sault Ste. Marie, ON, P6B 5W6
(705) 254-5050
Emp Here 20
SIC 4212 Local trucking, without storage

D-U-N-S 20-106-3497   (BR)
WINNERS MERCHANTS INTERNATIONAL L.P.
WINNERS
(*Suby of* The TJX Companies Inc)
44 Great Northern Rd, Sault Ste. Marie, ON, P6B 4Y5
(705) 942-0266
Emp Here 40
SIC 5651 Family clothing stores

D-U-N-S 25-643-9118   (BR)
YMCA OF GREATER TORONTO
YMCA
235 Mcnabb St, Sault Ste. Marie, ON, P6B 1Y3
(705) 945-5178
Emp Here 55
SIC 8641 Civic and social associations

Sault Ste. Marie, ON P6C
Algoma County

D-U-N-S 24-135-8808   (SL)
1022239 ONTARIO INC
7500 TAXI
633 Wallace Terr, Sault Ste. Marie, ON, P6C 6A2
(705) 945-7500
Emp Here 60   *Sales* 1,824,018
SIC 4121 Taxicabs

D-U-N-S 24-135-0562   (BR)
ALGOMA DISTRICT SCHOOL BOARD
WM. MERRIFIELD V.C. PUBLIC SCHOOL
(*Suby of* Algoma District School Board)
331 Patrick St, Sault Ste. Marie, ON, P6C 3Y9

Emp Here 35
SIC 8211 Elementary and secondary schools

D-U-N-S 25-239-0687   (BR)
ALGOMA DISTRICT SCHOOL BOARD
KORAH COLLEGIATE AND VOCATIONAL SCHOOL
(*Suby of* Algoma District School Board)
636 Goulais Ave, Sault Ste. Marie, ON, P6C 5A7
(705) 945-7180
Emp Here 80
SIC 8211 Elementary and secondary schools

D-U-N-S 20-710-3727   (BR)
ALGOMA DISTRICT SCHOOL BOARD
H M ROBINS PUBLIC SCHOOL
(*Suby of* Algoma District School Board)
83 East Balfour St, Sault Ste. Marie, ON, P6C 1X4

(705) 945-7119
Emp Here 26
SIC 8211 Elementary and secondary schools

D-U-N-S 20-763-6551   (SL)
BIASUCCI DEVELOPMENTS INC
544 Wellington St W, Sault Ste. Marie, ON, P6C 3T6
(705) 946-8701
Emp Here 26   *Sales* 5,717,257
SIC 1542 Nonresidential construction, nec

D-U-N-S 25-162-7899   (SL)
CHILDREN'S REHABILITATION CENTRE ALGOMA
74 Johnson Ave, Sault Ste. Marie, ON, P6C 2V5
(705) 759-1131
Emp Here 50   *Sales* 3,283,232
SIC 8093 Specialty outpatient clinics, nec

D-U-N-S 20-337-8708   (BR)
EACOM TIMBER CORPORATION
POWER JOISTS
1195 Peoples Rd, Sault Ste. Marie, ON, P6C 3W7
(705) 254-7597
Emp Here 50
SIC 2499 Wood products, nec

D-U-N-S 20-710-3875   (BR)
HURON-SUPERIOR CATHOLIC DISTRICT SCHOOL BOARD
HOLY FAMILY CATHOLIC SCHOOL
42 Rushmere Dr, Sault Ste. Marie, ON, P6C 2T4
(705) 945-5519
Emp Here 20
SIC 8211 Elementary and secondary schools

D-U-N-S 25-238-8863   (BR)
HURON-SUPERIOR CATHOLIC DISTRICT SCHOOL BOARD
ST ANN CATHOLIC SCHOOL
139 White Oak Dr W, Sault Ste. Marie, ON, P6C 2H7
(705) 945-5523
Emp Here 20
SIC 8211 Elementary and secondary schools

D-U-N-S 25-238-9895   (BR)
HURON-SUPERIOR CATHOLIC DISTRICT SCHOOL BOARD
ST THERESA ELEMENTARY SCHOOL
100 Estelle St, Sault Ste. Marie, ON, P6C 2C2
(705) 945-5535
Emp Here 32
SIC 8211 Elementary and secondary schools

D-U-N-S 20-710-3909   (BR)
HURON-SUPERIOR CATHOLIC DISTRICT SCHOOL BOARD
ST JOHN SCHOOL
100 Churchill Ave, Sault Ste. Marie, ON, P6C 2R2

Emp Here 50
SIC 8211 Elementary and secondary schools

D-U-N-S 25-239-0109   (BR)
HURON-SUPERIOR CATHOLIC DISTRICT SCHOOL BOARD
OUR LADY OF LOURDES CATHOLIC SCHOOL
319 Prentice Ave, Sault Ste. Marie, ON, P6C 4R7
(705) 945-5521
Emp Here 45
SIC 8211 Elementary and secondary schools

D-U-N-S 20-710-3883   (BR)
HURON-SUPERIOR CATHOLIC DISTRICT SCHOOL BOARD
ST FRANCIS CATHOLIC SCHOOL
147 Brookfield Ave, Sault Ste. Marie, ON, P6C 5P2
(705) 945-5525
Emp Here 20
SIC 8211 Elementary and secondary schools

D-U-N-S 25-300-0699   (BR)
METRO ONTARIO INC
METRO
275 Second Line W, Sault Ste. Marie, ON, P6C 2J4
(705) 949-0350
Emp Here 75
SIC 5411 Grocery stores

D-U-N-S 25-648-1730   (BR)
REXALL PHARMACY GROUP LTD
SECOND LINE REXALL DRUG STORE
(*Suby of* McKesson Corporation)
612 Second Line W, Sault Ste. Marie, ON, P6C 2K7
(705) 759-3115
Emp Here 25
SIC 5912 Drug stores and proprietary stores

Savant Lake, ON P0V
Thunder Bay County

D-U-N-S 25-238-1058   (BR)
KEEWATIN PATRICIA DISTRICT SCHOOL BOARD
SAVANT LAKE PUBLIC SCHOOL
Gd, Savant Lake, ON, P0V 2S0
(807) 584-2242
Emp Here 25
SIC 8211 Elementary and secondary schools

Scarborough, ON L9W
York County

D-U-N-S 20-512-2836   (HQ)
AVERTEX UTILITY SOLUTIONS INC
205235 County Rd 109, Scarborough, ON, L9W 0T8
(519) 942-3030
Emp Here 75   *Emp Total* 1
Sales 48,647,330
SIC 1623 Water, sewer, and utility lines
Pr Pr Jack Kottelenberg
VP VP Andrew Blokker
 Grant Kottelenberg

Scarborough, ON M1B
York County

D-U-N-S 24-862-2771   (HQ)
A/D FIRE PROTECTION SYSTEMS INC
(*Suby of* RPM International Inc.)
420 Tapscott Rd Unit 5, Scarborough, ON, M1B 1Y4
(416) 292-2361
Emp Here 50   *Emp Total* 14,318
Sales 5,827,840
SIC 3479 Metal coating and allied services
VP Bruno Stieg

D-U-N-S 20-159-3019   (HQ)
ALTROM AUTO GROUP LTD
(*Suby of* Genuine Parts Company)
1995 Markham Rd, Scarborough, ON, M1B 2W3
(416) 281-8600
Emp Here 80   *Emp Total* 40,000
Sales 24,295,913
SIC 5015 Motor vehicle parts, used
Pr Pr Dieter Gamm
 Thomas Seidel

D-U-N-S 24-792-8641   (HQ)
AMPHENOL CANADA CORP
605 Milner Ave, Scarborough, ON, M1B 5X6
(416) 291-4401
Emp Here 160   *Emp Total* 62,000
Sales 25,536,245
SIC 5065 Electronic parts and equipment, nec

Dir Fin Anthony Davidson
Genl Mgr Andrew Toffelmire

D-U-N-S 25-359-5128   (BR)
BANQUE DE DEVELOPPEMENT DU CANADA
BUSINESS DEVELOPMENT BANK OF CANADA
305 Milner Ave Suite 112, Scarborough, ON, M1B 3V4
(416) 952-7900
Emp Here 35
SIC 6141 Personal credit institutions

D-U-N-S 20-251-1994   (BR)
CLT LOGISTICS, INC
CLT INTERNATIONAL
5900 Finch Ave E Unit 1, Scarborough, ON, M1B 5P8
(416) 686-4199
Emp Here 40
SIC 4225 General warehousing and storage

D-U-N-S 25-167-2895   (BR)
CASCADES CANADA ULC
NORAMPAC-LITHOTECH
5910 Finch Ave E, Scarborough, ON, M1B 5P8
(416) 412-3500
Emp Here 110
SIC 2679 Converted paper products, nec

D-U-N-S 25-925-3508   (BR)
CINEPLEX ODEON CORPORATION
CINEPLEX CINEMAS MORNINGSIDE
785 Milner Ave, Scarborough, ON, M1B 3C3
(416) 281-1444
Emp Here 20
SIC 7832 Motion picture theaters, except drive-in

D-U-N-S 20-703-5754   (BR)
CLAYBAR CONTRACTING INC
91 Melford Dr, Scarborough, ON, M1B 2G6
(416) 298-1144
Emp Here 25
SIC 1799 Special trade contractors, nec

D-U-N-S 24-577-1832   (BR)
COMMUNITY LIVING TORONTO
70 Forest Creek Ptway, Scarborough, ON, M1B 5K8
(416) 724-8757
Emp Here 30
SIC 8322 Individual and family services

D-U-N-S 20-039-6724   (BR)
CORPORATION OF THE CITY OF TORONTO
MALVERN RECREATION CENTRE
30 Sewells Rd, Scarborough, ON, M1B 3G5
(416) 396-8969
Emp Here 35
SIC 7999 Amusement and recreation, nec

D-U-N-S 24-119-6224   (BR)
CORPORATION OF THE CITY OF TORONTO
HEALTH DEPARTMENT, CITY OF
1530 Markham Rd, Scarborough, ON, M1B 3G4
(416) 338-7680
Emp Here 20
SIC 8322 Individual and family services

D-U-N-S 20-151-5509   (HQ)
DART CANADA INC
2121 Markham Rd, Scarborough, ON, M1B 2W3
(416) 293-2877
Emp Here 410   *Emp Total* 450
SIC 2656 Sanitary food containers

D-U-N-S 20-288-9242   (HQ)
EOS CANADA INC
EOS NCN
325 Milner Ave Suite 1111, Scarborough, ON, M1B 5N1

(647) 436-2605
Emp Here 96   *Emp Total* 1
Sales 8,835,760
SIC 7322 Adjustment and collection services
Pr Paul Leary Jr
Dir Paul Leary Sr.
  Jim Shaw
Dir Fin Abdul Wahid

D-U-N-S 20-699-6717   (BR)
EXTENDICARE INC
EXTENDICARE ROUGE VALLEY
551 Conlins Rd, Scarborough, ON, M1B 5S1
(416) 282-6768
Emp Here 25
SIC 8051 Skilled nursing care facilities

D-U-N-S 24-652-9499   (BR)
GROUPE PAGES JAUNES CORP
325 Milner Ave Suite 4, Scarborough, ON, M1B 5S8
(416) 412-5000
Emp Here 100
SIC 2741 Miscellaneous publishing

D-U-N-S 25-514-3091   (BR)
HOME DEPOT OF CANADA INC
HOME DEPOT
(*Suby of* The Home Depot Inc)
60 Grand Marshall Dr, Scarborough, ON, M1B 5N6
(416) 283-3166
Emp Here 100
SIC 5251 Hardware stores

D-U-N-S 25-109-1575   (BR)
HUDSON'S BAY COMPANY
HUDSON BAY REG CREDIT OFFICE
603 Milner Ave, Scarborough, ON, M1B 5Z9

Emp Here 250
SIC 7389 Business services, nec

D-U-N-S 25-323-4082   (BR)
INNVEST PROPERTIES CORP
TRAVEL LODGE
(*Suby of* Innvest Properties Corp)
20 Milner Business Crt, Scarborough, ON, M1B 3M6
(416) 299-9500
Emp Here 20
SIC 7011 Hotels and motels

D-U-N-S 25-315-9065   (BR)
INVESTORS GROUP FINANCIAL SERVICES INC
305 Milner Ave Suite 701, Scarborough, ON, M1B 3V4
(416) 292-7229
Emp Here 50
SIC 8741 Management services

D-U-N-S 20-648-6354   (BR)
INVESTORS GROUP INC
INVESTORS GROUP FINANCIAL SERVICES
305 Milner Ave Suite 701, Scarborough, ON, M1B 3V4
(416) 292-7229
Emp Here 100
SIC 6162 Mortgage bankers and loan correspondents

D-U-N-S 25-634-3575   (BR)
LEE VALLEY TOOLS LTD
1275 Morningside Ave Suite 1, Scarborough, ON, M1B 3W1
(416) 286-7574
Emp Here 20
SIC 5251 Hardware stores

D-U-N-S 24-757-5947   (BR)
LEON'S FURNITURE LIMITED
20 Mclevin Ave, Scarborough, ON, M1B 2V5
(416) 291-3818
Emp Here 300
SIC 5712 Furniture stores

D-U-N-S 24-242-3317   (HQ)

OMRON CANADA INC
885 Milner Ave, Scarborough, ON, M1B 5V8
(416) 286-6465
Emp Here 70   *Emp Total* 36,944
Sales 22,238,964
SIC 5065 Electronic parts and equipment, nec
Pr Pr Ted Butson
Dir Arthur Kitamura
Dir John A Abraham
Dir J Mark Stinson
Dir Fin Deepak Sharma

D-U-N-S 24-383-1315   (SL)
OMRON ELECTRONIC COMPONENTS CANADA, INC
100 Consilium Pl Suite 802, Scarborough, ON, M1B 3E3
(416) 286-6465
Emp Here 50   *Sales* 6,420,542
SIC 5065 Electronic parts and equipment, nec
  Michael Snow
Genl Mgr Ron Gee

D-U-N-S 20-859-8446   (BR)
PACIFIC LINK COMMUNICATIONS INC
BELL WORLD
31 Tapscott Rd Suite 25, Scarborough, ON, M1B 4Y7

Emp Here 25
SIC 5999 Miscellaneous retail stores, nec

D-U-N-S 20-911-3864   (BR)
PEPSICO CANADA ULC
FRITO LAY CANADA
(*Suby of* Pepsico, Inc.)
1 Water Tower Gate, Scarborough, ON, M1B 6C5
(416) 284-3200
Emp Here 210
SIC 5145 Confectionery

D-U-N-S 24-365-8924   (SL)
PHOENIX RESTORATION INC
27 Casebridge Crt Unit 7, Scarborough, ON, M1B 4Y4
(416) 208-7700
Emp Here 40   *Sales* 7,952,716
SIC 1541 Industrial buildings and warehouses
Pr Pr Vincent Brannigan
  Michael Brannigan

D-U-N-S 24-964-3255   (BR)
PIONEER HI-BRED LIMITED
TONA LOGISTICS
(*Suby of* E. I. Du Pont De Nemours and Company)
75 Venture Dr, Scarborough, ON, M1B 3E8
(416) 287-1661
Emp Here 45
SIC 4225 General warehousing and storage

D-U-N-S 24-346-3192   (BR)
RE/MAX ROUGE RIVER REALTY LTD
31 Tapscott Rd Suite 37, Scarborough, ON, M1B 4Y7

Emp Here 50
SIC 6531 Real estate agents and managers

D-U-N-S 20-174-0698   (BR)
S-A-S PETROLEUM TECHNOLOGIES INC
91 Melford Dr, Scarborough, ON, M1B 2G6
(416) 298-1145
Emp Here 30
SIC 1799 Special trade contractors, nec

D-U-N-S 20-082-7751   (BR)
SOBEYS CAPITAL INCORPORATED
SOBEY'S MORNINGSIDE
1150 Morningside Ave, Scarborough, ON, M1B 3A4
(416) 284-8864
Emp Here 130
SIC 5411 Grocery stores

D-U-N-S 25-710-4281   (SL)
SOMERVILLE MERCHANDISING INC

5760 Finch Ave E, Scarborough, ON, M1B 5J9
(416) 754-7228
Emp Here 70   *Sales* 4,231,721
SIC 3993 Signs and advertising specialties

D-U-N-S 20-077-8574   (SL)
STAIN GUARD ENTERPRISES LIMITED
525 Milner Ave Unit 5, Scarborough, ON, M1B 2K4
(416) 297-5525
Emp Here 20   *Sales* 5,024,256
SIC 2819 Industrial inorganic chemicals, nec

D-U-N-S 25-498-9551   (BR)
STAPLES CANADA INC
STAPLES THE BUSINESS DEPOT
(*Suby of* Staples, Inc.)
850 Milner Ave, Scarborough, ON, M1B 5N7
(416) 208-7728
Emp Here 30
SIC 5943 Stationery stores

D-U-N-S 25-202-8337   (SL)
STEELCASE CONSTRUCTION INC
50 Venture Dr Unit 11, Scarborough, ON, M1B 3L6
(416) 282-4888
Emp Here 25   *Sales* 6,030,906
SIC 1542 Nonresidential construction, nec
Pr Pr Themis Tzovolos

D-U-N-S 20-922-1811   (HQ)
TAPP LABEL LTD
999 Progress Ave, Scarborough, ON, M1B 6J1
(416) 292-6600
Emp Here 120   *Emp Total* 280
Sales 20,866,760
SIC 2672 Paper; coated and laminated, nec
Pr Pr David Bowyer
  Gerard Hauprich

D-U-N-S 20-151-8008   (HQ)
TEVA CANADA LIMITED
TEVA NOVOPHARM
30 Novopharm Crt, Scarborough, ON, M1B 2K9
(416) 291-8876
Emp Here 300   *Emp Total* 44,945
Sales 161,036,061
SIC 2834 Pharmaceutical preparations
Pr Barry Fishman
VP Opers Ed Hogan
  Dan Youtoff

D-U-N-S 20-714-1743   (SL)
THREE FISHES CHRISTIAN ELEMENTARY SCHOOL
30 Dean Park Rd, Scarborough, ON, M1B 3H1
(416) 284-9003
Emp Here 50   *Sales* 3,356,192
SIC 8211 Elementary and secondary schools

D-U-N-S 24-222-9875   (SL)
TOOR RESTAURANTS MANAGEMENT INC
BOSTON PIZZA
785 Milner Ave, Scarborough, ON, M1B 3C3
(416) 282-0770
Emp Here 50   *Sales* 1,532,175
SIC 5812 Eating places

D-U-N-S 20-711-1597   (BR)
TORONTO CATHOLIC DISTRICT SCHOOL BOARD
ST. FLORENCE CATHOLIC SCHOOL
101 Murison Blvd, Scarborough, ON, M1B 2L6
(416) 393-5385
Emp Here 50
SIC 8211 Elementary and secondary schools

D-U-N-S 20-913-7194   (BR)
TORONTO CATHOLIC DISTRICT SCHOOL BOARD
ST. GABRIEL LALEMANT ELEMENTARY SCHOOL
160 Crow Trail, Scarborough, ON, M1B 1Y3
(416) 393-5377
Emp Here 20

SIC 8211 Elementary and secondary schools

D-U-N-S 20-711-1647 (BR)
TORONTO CATHOLIC DISTRICT SCHOOL BOARD
BLESSED MOTHER TERESA SECONDARY SCHOOL
40 Sewells Rd, Scarborough, ON, M1B 3G5
(416) 393-5538
Emp Here 50
SIC 8211 Elementary and secondary schools

D-U-N-S 25-224-9909 (BR)
TORONTO CATHOLIC DISTRICT SCHOOL BOARD
ST. JEAN DE BREBEUF CATHOLIC SCHOOL
101 Dean Park Rd, Scarborough, ON, M1B 2X2
(416) 393-5394
Emp Here 20
SIC 8211 Elementary and secondary schools

D-U-N-S 25-224-8810 (BR)
TORONTO DISTRICT SCHOOL BOARD
CHIEF DAN GEORGE ELEMENTARY SCHOOL
185 Generation Blvd, Scarborough, ON, M1B 2K5
(416) 396-6150
Emp Here 25
SIC 8211 Elementary and secondary schools

D-U-N-S 20-913-6477 (BR)
TORONTO DISTRICT SCHOOL BOARD
EMILY CARR PS
90 John Tabor Trail, Scarborough, ON, M1B 2V2
(416) 396-6230
Emp Here 30
SIC 8211 Elementary and secondary schools

D-U-N-S 20-346-6941 (BR)
TORONTO DISTRICT SCHOOL BOARD
ALVIN CURLING PUBLIC SCHOOL
50 Upper Rouge Trl, Scarborough, ON, M1B 6K4
(416) 396-7850
Emp Here 40
SIC 8211 Elementary and secondary schools

D-U-N-S 20-025-1556 (BR)
TORONTO DISTRICT SCHOOL BOARD
FLEMING PUBLIC SCHOOL
20 Littles Rd, Scarborough, ON, M1B 5B5
(416) 396-6862
Emp Here 35
SIC 8211 Elementary and secondary schools

D-U-N-S 24-676-5080 (BR)
TORONTO DISTRICT SCHOOL BOARD
BERNER TRAIL JUNIOR ELEMENTARY SCHOOL
120 Berner Trail, Scarborough, ON, M1B 1B3
(416) 396-6050
Emp Here 25
SIC 8211 Elementary and secondary schools

D-U-N-S 20-026-8253 (BR)
TORONTO DISTRICT SCHOOL BOARD
LUCY MAUD MONTGOMERY ELEMENTARY
95 Murison Blvd, Scarborough, ON, M1B 2L6
(416) 396-6838
Emp Here 30
SIC 8211 Elementary and secondary schools

D-U-N-S 20-026-8303 (BR)
TORONTO DISTRICT SCHOOL BOARD
ROUGE VALLEY PUBLIC SCHOOL
30 Durnford Rd, Scarborough, ON, M1B 4X3
(416) 396-6433
Emp Here 25
SIC 8211 Elementary and secondary schools

D-U-N-S 20-037-7013 (BR)
TORONTO PUBLIC LIBRARY BOARD
MALVERN BRANCH

30 Sewells Rd, Scarborough, ON, M1B 3G5
(416) 396-8969
Emp Here 30
SIC 8231 Libraries

D-U-N-S 25-294-8179 (BR)
WAL-MART CANADA CORP
785 Milner Ave, Scarborough, ON, M1B 3C3
(416) 281-2929
Emp Here 250
SIC 5311 Department stores

D-U-N-S 20-789-3087 (BR)
XEROX CANADA LTD
XEROX
(Suby of Xerox Corporation)
120 Mclevin Ave Unit 4, Scarborough, ON, M1B 3E9
(416) 733-6296
Emp Here 30
SIC 7334 Photocopying and duplicating services

D-U-N-S 20-546-1994 (BR)
YMCA OF GREATER TORONTO
10 Milner Business Crt Suite 600, Scarborough, ON, M1B 3C6
(416) 609-9622
Emp Here 32
SIC 8331 Job training and related services

Scarborough, ON M1C
York County

D-U-N-S 25-186-3163 (BR)
ARAMARK CANADA LTD.
ARAMARK REFRESHMENT SERVICES CANADA
105 East Ave Unit 1, Scarborough, ON, M1C 3K9
(416) 649-2051
Emp Here 50
SIC 5962 Merchandising machine operators

D-U-N-S 25-303-6669 (BR)
CANADIAN IMPERIAL BANK OF COMMERCE
CIBC
371 Old Kingston Rd, Scarborough, ON, M1C 1B7
(416) 282-1477
Emp Here 25
SIC 6021 National commercial banks

D-U-N-S 20-026-8337 (BR)
CORPORATION OF THE CITY OF TORONTO
PORT UNION SENIORS
5450 Lawrence Ave E, Scarborough, ON, M1C 3B2
(416) 396-4034
Emp Here 25
SIC 8322 Individual and family services

D-U-N-S 24-936-5610 (BR)
GOVERNING COUNCIL OF THE UNIVERSITY OF TORONTO
UNIVERSITY OF TORONTO
1265 Military Trail Suite 303, Scarborough, ON, M1C 1A4
(416) 287-7033
Emp Here 500
SIC 8221 Colleges and universities

D-U-N-S 25-300-0418 (BR)
METRO ONTARIO INC
METRO
261 Port Union Rd, Scarborough, ON, M1C 2L3
(416) 284-7792
Emp Here 130
SIC 5411 Grocery stores

D-U-N-S 25-898-4467 (SL)
NEBRASKA COLLISION CENTRE INC

6511 Kingston Rd, Scarborough, ON, M1C 1L5
(416) 282-5794
Emp Here 50   *Sales* 3,575,074
SIC 7532 Top and body repair and paint shops

D-U-N-S 20-651-1896 (BR)
RE/MAX WEST REALTY INC
6074 Kingston Rd, Scarborough, ON, M1C 1K4
(416) 281-0027
Emp Here 37
SIC 6531 Real estate agents and managers

D-U-N-S 24-337-0673 (SL)
ROYAL CANADIAN LEGION DISTRICT D CARE CENTRES
TONY STACEY CENTRE FOR VETERANS CARE
59 Lawson Rd, Scarborough, ON, M1C 2J1
(416) 284-9235
Emp Here 120   *Sales* 4,377,642
SIC 8361 Residential care

D-U-N-S 20-034-2132 (BR)
TORONTO CATHOLIC DISTRICT SCHOOL BOARD
ST. BRENDAN CATHOLIC SCHOOL
186 Centennial Rd, Scarborough, ON, M1C 1Z9
(416) 393-5359
Emp Here 45
SIC 8211 Elementary and secondary schools

D-U-N-S 24-242-3197 (BR)
TORONTO CATHOLIC DISTRICT SCHOOL BOARD
HIGHLAND CREEK PUBLIC SCHOOL
1410 Military Trail, Scarborough, ON, M1C 1A8
(416) 396-6330
Emp Here 50
SIC 8211 Elementary and secondary schools

D-U-N-S 20-591-5007 (BR)
TORONTO DISTRICT SCHOOL BOARD
WILLIAM D DAVIS JUNIOR PUBLIC SCHOOL
128 East Ave, Scarborough, ON, M1C 3L6
(416) 396-6650
Emp Here 25
SIC 8211 Elementary and secondary schools

D-U-N-S 20-698-7641 (BR)
TORONTO DISTRICT SCHOOL BOARD
MEADOWVALE PRE SCHOOL
761 Meadowvale Rd, Scarborough, ON, M1C 1T1
(416) 396-6470
Emp Here 25
SIC 8211 Elementary and secondary schools

D-U-N-S 20-025-0905 (BR)
TORONTO DISTRICT SCHOOL BOARD
MORRISH PUBLIC SCHOOL
61 Canmore Blvd, Scarborough, ON, M1C 3T7
(416) 396-6730
Emp Here 30
SIC 8211 Elementary and secondary schools

D-U-N-S 20-025-3776 (BR)
TORONTO DISTRICT SCHOOL BOARD
SIR OLIVER MOWAT C I
5400 Lawrence Ave E, Scarborough, ON, M1C 2C6
(416) 396-6802
Emp Here 100
SIC 8211 Elementary and secondary schools

Scarborough, ON M1E
York County

D-U-N-S 20-790-2219 (SL)
1594414 ONTARIO LIMITED
FRANK'S NO FRILLS

4473 Kingston Rd, Scarborough, ON, M1E 2N7
(416) 281-9140
Emp Here 45   *Sales* 7,536,000
SIC 5411 Grocery stores
Pr Frank Palmieri

D-U-N-S 24-760-1359 (SL)
1694863 ONTARIO INC
HOWARD JOHNSON SCARBOROUGH
4694 Kingston Rd, Scarborough, ON, M1E 2P9
(416) 913-7184
Emp Here 50   *Sales* 2,188,821
SIC 7011 Hotels and motels

D-U-N-S 25-403-5132 (HQ)
BERRY PLASTICS CANADA INC
595 Coronation Dr, Scarborough, ON, M1E 2K4
(416) 281-6000
Emp Here 86   *Emp Total* 21,000
Sales 12,695,162
SIC 3081 Unsupported plastics film and sheet
Fin Ex David Lai Thom
Pr Brendan Barba
S&M/Mgr Nat Mcgrath
Manager Dave Oxley
Paul Feeney
VP Larry Noll

D-U-N-S 24-322-3885 (BR)
CARA OPERATIONS LIMITED
(Suby of Cara Holdings Limited)
4410 Kingston Rd Suite 201, Scarborough, ON, M1E 2N5
(416) 281-0230
Emp Here 20
SIC 5812 Eating places

D-U-N-S 24-920-0221 (BR)
CHEMTURA CANADA CO./CIE
CROMPTON CO
10 Chemical Crt, Scarborough, ON, M1E 3X7
(416) 284-1662
Emp Here 40
SIC 2992 Lubricating oils and greases

D-U-N-S 25-359-6456 (BR)
CHEMTURA CANADA CO./CIE
CROMPTON CO./CIE
565 Coronation Dr, Scarborough, ON, M1E 2K3
(416) 284-1661
Emp Here 40
SIC 2992 Lubricating oils and greases

D-U-N-S 24-649-2669 (BR)
COMMUNITY LIVING TORONTO
4617 Kingston Rd, Scarborough, ON, M1E 2P5
(416) 283-1640
Emp Here 25
SIC 8322 Individual and family services

D-U-N-S 25-213-8359 (BR)
CORPORATION OF THE CITY OF TORONTO
TAM HEATHER CURLING & TENNIS CLUB
730 Military Trail, Scarborough, ON, M1E 4P7
(416) 284-9251
Emp Here 29
SIC 7997 Membership sports and recreation clubs

D-U-N-S 20-958-4064 (BR)
DOLLARAMA S.E.C.
DOLLARAMA
2900 Ellesmere Rd, Scarborough, ON, M1E 4B8
(416) 283-3091
Emp Here 20
SIC 5399 Miscellaneous general merchandise

D-U-N-S 25-021-5902 (SL)
EHATARE RETIREMENT & NURSING HOME
40 Old Kingston Rd, Scarborough, ON, M1E

3J5
(416) 284-0828
Emp Here 70   *Sales* 3,210,271
SIC 8051 Skilled nursing care facilities

D-U-N-S 25-691-5315   (BR)
EXTENDICARE (CANADA) INC
EXTENDICARE GUILDWOOD
60 Guildwood Pky Suite 327, Scarborough,
ON, M1E 1N9
(416) 266-7711
Emp Here 200
SIC 8051 Skilled nursing care facilities

D-U-N-S 20-923-9573   (BR)
EXTENDICARE INC
EXTENDICARE GUILDWOOD
60 Guildwood Pky Suite 327, Scarborough,
ON, M1E 1N9
(416) 266-7711
Emp Here 182
SIC 8051 Skilled nursing care facilities

D-U-N-S 25-365-5450   (HQ)
HENRY COMPANY CANADA INC
15 Wallsend Dr, Scarborough, ON, M1E 3X6
(416) 724-2000
Emp Here 25   *Emp Total* 560
Sales 11,867,639
SIC 2851 Paints and allied products
Dir Brooke Wade
Dir Michael J. Kenny

D-U-N-S 24-885-7948   (BR)
LICK'S ICE CREAM & BURGER SHOPS INC
LICK'S
(*Suby of* Lick's Ice Cream & Burger Shops Inc)
4543 Kingston Rd, Scarborough, ON, M1E
2P1
(416) 287-9300
Emp Here 32
SIC 5812 Eating places

D-U-N-S 24-609-6486   (BR)
METRO ONTARIO INC
FOOD BASIC
255 Morningside Ave, Scarborough, ON, M1E
3E6
(416) 284-2158
Emp Here 50
SIC 5411 Grocery stores

D-U-N-S 24-953-0320   (BR)
METRO ONTARIO INC
FOOD BASICS
2900 Ellesmere Rd Suite 587, Scarborough,
ON, M1E 4B8
(416) 284-5320
Emp Here 122
SIC 5411 Grocery stores

D-U-N-S 25-405-2558   (SL)
S G ENTERPRISES INC
570 Coronation Dr, Scarborough, ON, M1E
2K1
(416) 724-5950
Emp Here 50   *Sales* 4,377,642
SIC 5932 Used merchandise stores

D-U-N-S 20-698-6841   (BR)
**TORONTO CATHOLIC DISTRICT SCHOOL
BOARD**
*ST. EDMUND CAMPION CATHOLIC
SCHOOL*
30 Highcastle Rd, Scarborough, ON, M1E
4N1
(416) 393-5356
Emp Here 30
SIC 8211 Elementary and secondary schools

D-U-N-S 20-700-2358   (BR)
**TORONTO CATHOLIC DISTRICT SCHOOL
BOARD**
*ST. JOHN PAUL LL CATHOLIC SECONDARY
SCHOOL*
685 Military Trail, Scarborough, ON, M1E 4P6
(416) 393-5531
Emp Here 130

SIC 8211 Elementary and secondary schools

D-U-N-S 20-081-0401   (BR)
**TORONTO CATHOLIC DISTRICT SCHOOL
BOARD**
*ST. MARTIN DE PORRES CATHOLIC
SCHOOL*
230 Morningside Ave, Scarborough, ON, M1E
3E1
(416) 393-5286
Emp Here 40
SIC 8211 Elementary and secondary schools

D-U-N-S 20-078-8979   (BR)
**TORONTO CATHOLIC DISTRICT SCHOOL
BOARD**
ST. MALACHY CATHOLIC SCHOOL
80 Bennett Rd, Scarborough, ON, M1E 3Y3
(416) 393-5336
Emp Here 32
SIC 8211 Elementary and secondary schools

D-U-N-S 20-047-1543   (BR)
TORONTO DISTRICT SCHOOL BOARD
GALLOWAY ROAD PUBLIC SCHOOL
192 Galloway Rd, Scarborough, ON, M1E 1X2
(416) 396-6245
Emp Here 25
SIC 8211 Elementary and secondary schools

D-U-N-S 20-025-2976   (BR)
TORONTO DISTRICT SCHOOL BOARD
JOSEPH BRANT PUBLIC SCHOOL
270 Manse Rd, Scarborough, ON, M1E 3V4
(416) 396-6400
Emp Here 27
SIC 8211 Elementary and secondary schools

D-U-N-S 20-025-1085   (BR)
TORONTO DISTRICT SCHOOL BOARD
WEST HILL COLLEGIATE INSTITUTE
350 Morningside Ave, Scarborough, ON, M1E
3G3
(416) 396-6864
Emp Here 100
SIC 8211 Elementary and secondary schools

D-U-N-S 20-591-5213   (BR)
TORONTO DISTRICT SCHOOL BOARD
WEST HILL PUBLIC SCHOOL
299 Morningside Ave, Scarborough, ON, M1E
3G1
(416) 396-6630
Emp Here 25
SIC 8211 Elementary and secondary schools

D-U-N-S 20-025-5201   (BR)
TORONTO DISTRICT SCHOOL BOARD
*ELIZABETH SIMCOE JUNIOR PUBLIC
SCHOOL*
166 Sylvan Ave, Scarborough, ON, M1E 1A3
(416) 396-6220
Emp Here 24
SIC 8211 Elementary and secondary schools

D-U-N-S 25-153-1372   (BR)
TORONTO DISTRICT SCHOOL BOARD
MAPLEWOOD HIGH SCHOOL
120 Galloway Rd, Scarborough, ON, M1E
1W7
(416) 396-6765
Emp Here 100
SIC 8211 Elementary and secondary schools

D-U-N-S 20-026-8352   (BR)
TORONTO DISTRICT SCHOOL BOARD
*EASTVIEW JUNIOR ELEMENTARY
SCHOOL*
20 Waldock St, Scarborough, ON, M1E 2E5
(416) 396-6210
Emp Here 30
SIC 8211 Elementary and secondary schools

D-U-N-S 20-698-7682   (BR)
TORONTO DISTRICT SCHOOL BOARD
MILITARY TRAIL PS
701 Military Trail, Scarborough, ON, M1E 4P6
(416) 396-6475
Emp Here 50

SIC 8211 Elementary and secondary schools

D-U-N-S 25-684-3863   (BR)
TORONTO-DOMINION BANK, THE
TD CANADA TRUST
(*Suby of* Toronto-Dominion Bank, The)
4515 Kingston Rd, Scarborough, ON, M1E
2P1
(416) 281-6701
Emp Here 20
SIC 6021 National commercial banks

D-U-N-S 20-654-8369   (BR)
WENDY'S RESTAURANTS OF CANADA INC
WENDY'S 6401
(*Suby of* The Wendy's Company)
2908 Ellesmere Rd, Scarborough, ON, M1E
4B8
(416) 208-9902
Emp Here 35
SIC 5812 Eating places

Scarborough, ON M1G
York County

D-U-N-S 25-222-1890   (BR)
EXTENDICARE (CANADA) INC
EXTENDICARE SCARBOROUGH
3830 Lawrence Ave E Suite 103, Scarbor-
ough, ON, M1G 1R6
(416) 439-1243
Emp Here 160
SIC 8051 Skilled nursing care facilities

D-U-N-S 25-363-8985   (BR)
SOBEYS CAPITAL INCORPORATED
3750 Lawrence Ave E, Scarborough, ON,
M1G 1R1

Emp Here 20
SIC 5411 Grocery stores

D-U-N-S 20-024-9949   (BR)
**TORONTO CATHOLIC DISTRICT SCHOOL
BOARD**
*ST. BARBARA CATHOLIC ELEMENTARY
SCHOOL*
25 Janray Dr, Scarborough, ON, M1G 1Y2
(416) 393-5274
Emp Here 35
SIC 8211 Elementary and secondary schools

D-U-N-S 20-025-0442   (BR)
TORONTO DISTRICT SCHOOL BOARD
TECUMSEH SENIOR PUBLIC SCHOOL
720 Scarborough Golf Club Rd, Scarborough,
ON, M1G 1H7
(416) 396-6590
Emp Here 24
SIC 8211 Elementary and secondary schools

D-U-N-S 20-025-0483   (BR)
TORONTO DISTRICT SCHOOL BOARD
WILLOW PARK JR PUBLIC SCHOOL
45 Windover Dr, Scarborough, ON, M1G 1P1
(416) 396-6665
Emp Here 45
SIC 8211 Elementary and secondary schools

D-U-N-S 24-875-5290   (BR)
TORONTO DISTRICT SCHOOL BOARD
WOBURN COLLEGIATE INSTITUTE
2222 Ellesmere Rd, Scarborough, ON, M1G
3M3
(416) 396-4575
Emp Here 100
SIC 8211 Elementary and secondary schools

D-U-N-S 20-024-9980   (BR)
TORONTO DISTRICT SCHOOL BOARD
GEORGE B. LITTLE PUBLIC SCHOOL
125 Orton Park Rd, Scarborough, ON, M1G
3G9
(416) 396-6260
Emp Here 45

SIC 8211 Elementary and secondary schools

D-U-N-S 20-711-3213   (BR)
TORONTO DISTRICT SCHOOL BOARD
GOLF ROAD JUNIOR PUBLIC SCHOOL
730 Scarborough Golf Club Rd, Scarborough,
ON, M1G 1H7
(416) 396-6285
Emp Here 30
SIC 8211 Elementary and secondary schools

D-U-N-S 24-321-4652   (BR)
VALUE VILLAGE STORES, INC
(*Suby of* Savers, Inc.)
3701 Lawrence Ave E Suite 1, Scarborough,
ON, M1G 1P7
(416) 439-4464
Emp Here 30
SIC 5399 Miscellaneous general merchandise

Scarborough, ON M1H
York County

D-U-N-S 25-815-3097   (SL)
1034881 ONTARIO INC
SOON LEE SUPERMARKET
629 Markham Rd, Scarborough, ON, M1H
2A4
(416) 439-3333
Emp Here 43   *Sales* 7,202,950
SIC 5411 Grocery stores
Pr Pauong Lam
Treas Lien Chiem

D-U-N-S 25-739-9378   (SL)
ABLE CLOTHING INC
2050 Ellesmere Rd Unit 8, Scarborough, ON,
M1H 3A9

Emp Here 80   *Sales* 3,724,879
SIC 2329 Men's and boy's clothing, nec

D-U-N-S 20-105-2177   (BR)
ATLAS COPCO CANADA INC
755 Progress Ave, Scarborough, ON, M1H
2W7
(416) 439-4181
Emp Here 35
SIC 5085 Industrial supplies

D-U-N-S 25-704-3190   (BR)
BMO NESBITT BURNS INC
100 Consilium Pl Suite 106, Scarborough, ON,
M1H 3E3
(416) 296-0040
Emp Here 25
SIC 6211 Security brokers and dealers

D-U-N-S 25-296-9126   (BR)
BANK OF NOVA SCOTIA, THE
SCOTIABANK
3475 Lawrence Ave E, Scarborough, ON,
M1H 1B2
(416) 439-2333
Emp Here 42
SIC 6021 National commercial banks

D-U-N-S 20-080-3968   (BR)
BANK OF MONTREAL
BANK OF MONTREAL
1225 Mccowan Rd Suite 2986, Scarborough,
ON, M1H 3K3
(416) 438-9900
Emp Here 20
SIC 6021 National commercial banks

D-U-N-S 24-121-0967   (BR)
BANQUE TORONTO-DOMINION, LA
TORONTO-DOMINION BANK, THE
(*Suby of* Toronto-Dominion Bank, The)
740 Progress Ave, Scarborough, ON, M1H
2X3
(416) 983-5204
Emp Here 20
SIC 6021 National commercial banks

D-U-N-S 20-079-1106   (BR)
CANADIAN MENTAL HEALTH ASSOCIA-TION TORONTO BRANCH, THE
CMHA
1200 Markham Rd Suite 500, Scarborough, ON, M1H 3C3
(416) 289-6285
Emp Here 20
SIC 8011 Offices and clinics of medical doctors

D-U-N-S 20-029-2378   (BR)
CATHOLIC CROSS-CULTURAL SERVICES
1200 Markham Rd Suite 503, Scarborough, ON, M1H 3C3
(416) 289-6766
Emp Here 35
SIC 8699 Membership organizations, nec

D-U-N-S 25-088-3360   (BR)
CORPORATION OF THE CITY OF TORONTO
SCARBOROUGH CENTENNIAL RECREATION CENTRE
1967 Ellesmere Rd, Scarborough, ON, M1H 2W5
(416) 396-4057
Emp Here 50
SIC 8322 Individual and family services

D-U-N-S 20-077-3203   (BR)
DOMINION OF CANADA GENERAL INSURANCE COMPANY, THE
(*Suby of* The Travelers Companies Inc)
300 Consilium Pl Suite 300, Scarborough, ON, M1H 3G2
(289) 333-2000
Emp Here 70
SIC 6411 Insurance agents, brokers, and service

D-U-N-S 20-807-2681   (BR)
EXTREME FITNESS GROUP INC
BALLY TOTAL FITNESS
(*Suby of* Extreme Fitness Group Inc)
3495 Lawrence Ave E, Scarborough, ON, M1H 1B3
(416) 646-2925
Emp Here 30
SIC 7991 Physical fitness facilities

D-U-N-S 25-227-0236   (SL)
GROWING TYKES CHILD CARE
GROWING TYKES LEARNING CENTRE
910 Markham Rd, Scarborough, ON, M1H 2Y2
(416) 438-4088
Emp Here 85   *Sales* 2,553,625
SIC 8351 Child day care services

D-U-N-S 25-272-8589   (BR)
KEG RESTAURANTS LTD
KEG STEAKHOUSE & BAR, THE
60 Estate Dr, Scarborough, ON, M1H 2Z1
(416) 438-1452
Emp Here 100
SIC 5812 Eating places

D-U-N-S 24-837-6654   (SL)
KOODO MOBILE-SCARBOROUGH
TELUS MOBILITY
200 Consilium Pl Suite 1600, Scarborough, ON, M1H 3J3
(647) 837-6252
Emp Here 40,000   *Sales* 10,405,523,600
SIC 4899 Communication services, nec
Mgr Michael Ying

D-U-N-S 25-318-7371   (BR)
LIQUOR CONTROL BOARD OF ONTARIO, THE
L.C.B.O. #269
3441 Lawrence Ave E, Scarborough, ON, M1H 1B2
(416) 431-0791
Emp Here 20
SIC 5921 Liquor stores

D-U-N-S 25-944-3349   (BR)
LOBLAWS SUPERMARKETS LIMITED
LOBLAWS NO 105
3401 Lawrence Ave E, Scarborough, ON, M1H 1B2
(416) 438-4392
Emp Here 450
SIC 5411 Grocery stores

D-U-N-S 25-310-9813   (BR)
MCDONALD'S RESTAURANTS OF CANADA LIMITED
MCDONALD'S RESTAURANT
(*Suby of* McDonald's Corporation)
1280 Markham Rd, Scarborough, ON, M1H 2Y9
(416) 438-3344
Emp Here 70
SIC 5812 Eating places

D-U-N-S 24-622-0672   (BR)
RBC DOMINION SECURITIES INC
RBC INVESTMENTS
(*Suby of* Royal Bank Of Canada)
111 Grangeway Ave Suite 2, Scarborough, ON, M1H 3E9
(416) 289-2886
Emp Here 22
SIC 6282 Investment advice

D-U-N-S 20-708-9744   (BR)
RBC GENERAL INSURANCE COMPANY
RBC LIFE INSURANCE
(*Suby of* Royal Bank Of Canada)
111 Grangeway Ave Suite 400, Scarborough, ON, M1H 3E9
(416) 289-5600
Emp Here 22
SIC 6311 Life insurance

D-U-N-S 25-319-9723   (BR)
RE/MAX REALTRON REALTY INC
885 Progress Ave Suite 209, Scarborough, ON, M1H 3G3
(416) 289-3333
Emp Here 40
SIC 6531 Real estate agents and managers

D-U-N-S 20-700-6342   (BR)
REITMANS (CANADA) LIMITEE
3495 Lawrence Ave E, Scarborough, ON, M1H 1B3
(416) 431-0271
Emp Here 25
SIC 5621 Women's clothing stores

D-U-N-S 24-965-9855   (BR)
SCOTIA CAPITAL INC
SCCTIAMCLEOD
300 Consilium Pl Suite 101, Scarborough, ON, M1H 3G2
(416) 296-0043
Emp Here 30
SIC 6211 Security brokers and dealers

D-U-N-S 20-553-3511   (BR)
SHERIDAN NURSERIES LIMITED
WEALL AND CULLEN
1774 Ellesmere Rd, Scarborough, ON, M1H 2V5
(416) 438-6931
Emp Here 20
SIC 5261 Retail nurseries and garden stores

D-U-N-S 24-001-9518   (BR)
SOBEYS CAPITAL INCORPORATED
FRESHCO
1255 Mccowan Rd, Scarborough, ON, M1H 3K3
(416) 431-2555
Emp Here 80
SIC 5411 Grocery stores

D-U-N-S 25-620-0247   (HQ)
SOUTH ASIAN FAMILY SUPPORT SERVICES OF SCARBOROUGH
(*Suby of* South Asian Family Support Services Of Scarborough)
1200 Markham Rd Suite 214, Scarborough, ON, M1H 3C3
(416) 431-5170
Emp Here 22   *Emp Total* 50
Sales 1,969,939
SIC 8322 Individual and family services

D-U-N-S 20-030-5592   (BR)
TORONTO CATHOLIC DISTRICT SCHOOL BOARD
ST. ROSE OF LIMA CATHOLIC SCHOOL
3220 Lawrence Ave E, Scarborough, ON, M1H 1A4
(416) 393-5269
Emp Here 40
SIC 8211 Elementary and secondary schools

D-U-N-S 20-025-0475   (BR)
TORONTO DISTRICT SCHOOL BOARD
TREDWAY WOODSWORTH PUBLIC SCHOOL
112 Sedgemount Dr, Scarborough, ON, M1H 1X9
(416) 396-6660
Emp Here 42
SIC 8211 Elementary and secondary schools

D-U-N-S 20-711-3304   (BR)
TORONTO DISTRICT SCHOOL BOARD
NORTH BENDAILE JUNIOR PUBLIC SCHOOL
29 Aveline Cres, Scarborough, ON, M1H 2P4
(416) 396-6495
Emp Here 50
SIC 8211 Elementary and secondary schools

D-U-N-S 20-025-2893   (BR)
TORONTO DISTRICT SCHOOL BOARD
CEDARBRAE COLLEGIATE INSTITUTE
550 Markham Rd, Scarborough, ON, M1H 2A2
(416) 396-4400
Emp Here 120
SIC 8211 Elementary and secondary schools

D-U-N-S 20-642-7192   (BR)
TORONTO DISTRICT SCHOOL BOARD
BENDALE JUNIOR PUBLIC SCHOOL
61 Benshire Dr, Scarborough, ON, M1H 1M4
(416) 396-6045
Emp Here 30
SIC 8211 Elementary and secondary schools

D-U-N-S 20-698-7716   (BR)
TORONTO DISTRICT SCHOOL BOARD
JS WOODSWORTH SR PUBLIC SCHOOL
120 Sedgemount Dr, Scarborough, ON, M1H 1X9
(416) 396-6370
Emp Here 20
SIC 8211 Elementary and secondary schools

D-U-N-S 25-684-2972   (BR)
TORONTO-DOMINION BANK, THE
TD CANADA TRUST
(*Suby of* Toronto-Dominion Bank, The)
680 Markham Rd, Scarborough, ON, M1H 2A7
(416) 439-5534
Emp Here 30
SIC 6021 National commercial banks

D-U-N-S 20-704-6228   (HQ)
TOYOTA CANADA INC
1 Toyota Pl, Scarborough, ON, M1H 1H9
(416) 438-6320
Emp Here 425   *Emp Total* 348,877
Sales 414,154,603
SIC 5012 Automobiles and other motor vehicles
Pr Larry Hutchinson
Dir Donald Campbell
Dir Larry Baldesarra
Dir Tetsuo Komuro
Dir Real Tanguay

D-U-N-S 25-221-2444   (BR)
WINNERS MERCHANTS INTERNATIONAL L.P.

WINNERS
(*Suby of* The TJX Companies Inc)
3495 Lawrence Ave E, Scarborough, ON, M1H 1B3
(416) 289-1145
Emp Here 35
SIC 5651 Family clothing stores

Scarborough, ON M1J
York County

D-U-N-S 20-730-5475   (SL)
EASTWAY CHRYSLER DODGE JEEP LTD
2851 Eglinton Ave E, Scarborough, ON, M1J 2E2
(416) 264-2501
Emp Here 40   *Sales* 14,592,140
SIC 5511 New and used car dealers
Pr Craig Hind

D-U-N-S 25-171-5488   (BR)
HOME DEPOT OF CANADA INC
HOME DEPOT
(*Suby of* The Home Depot Inc)
2911 Eglinton Ave E, Scarborough, ON, M1J 2E5
(416) 289-2500
Emp Here 150
SIC 5231 Paint, glass, and wallpaper stores

D-U-N-S 20-152-2604   (SL)
JOE & ANH ENTERPRISES INC
2990 Eglinton Ave E, Scarborough, ON, M1J 2E7

Emp Here 52   *Sales* 1,819,127
SIC 5812 Eating places

D-U-N-S 24-380-0930   (BR)
LOBLAWS INC
REAL CANADIAN SUPERSTORE
755 Brimley Rd, Scarborough, ON, M1J 1C5
(416) 279-0802
Emp Here 75
SIC 5411 Grocery stores

D-U-N-S 25-300-2737   (BR)
METRO ONTARIO INC
METRO
3221 Eglinton Ave E, Scarborough, ON, M1J 2H7
(416) 261-4204
Emp Here 300
SIC 5411 Grocery stores

D-U-N-S 20-904-2811   (SL)
SCARBORO GOLF & COUNTRY CLUB LTD, THE
SCARBORO GOLF CLUB
321 Scarborough Golf Club Rd, Scarborough, ON, M1J 3H2
(416) 261-3393
Emp Here 50   *Sales* 2,042,900
SIC 7997 Membership sports and recreation clubs

D-U-N-S 20-711-1415   (BR)
TORONTO CATHOLIC DISTRICT SCHOOL BOARD
ST. NICHOLAS CATHOLIC SCHOOL
33 Amarillo Dr, Scarborough, ON, M1J 2P7
(416) 393-5308
Emp Here 30
SIC 8211 Elementary and secondary schools

D-U-N-S 20-025-0418   (BR)
TORONTO DISTRICT SCHOOL BOARD
JOHN MCCRAE PUBLIC SCHOOL
431 Mccowan Rd, Scarborough, ON, M1J 1J1
(416) 396-6395
Emp Here 63
SIC 8211 Elementary and secondary schools

D-U-N-S 20-698-7203   (BR)
TORONTO DISTRICT SCHOOL BOARD

KNOB HILL JR PUBLIC SCHOOL
25 Seminole Ave, Scarborough, ON, M1J 1M8
(416) 396-6415
Emp Here 50
SIC 8211 Elementary and secondary schools

D-U-N-S 25-321-2377   (BR)
TORONTO-DOMINION BANK, THE
TD BANK
(Suby of Toronto-Dominion Bank, The)
697 Mccowan Rd, Scarborough, ON, M1J 1K2
(416) 431-4810
Emp Here 20
SIC 6021 National commercial banks

Scarborough, ON M1K
York County

D-U-N-S 20-007-9700   (BR)
BANK OF NOVA SCOTIA, THE
SCOTIABANK
2668 Eglinton Ave E, Scarborough, ON, M1K
2S3
(416) 266-4446
Emp Here 20
SIC 6021 National commercial banks

D-U-N-S 20-535-8794   (BR)
BANK OF MONTREAL
BMO
2739 Eglinton Ave E, Scarborough, ON, M1K
2S2
(416) 267-1157
Emp Here 20
SIC 6021 National commercial banks

D-U-N-S 20-588-2082   (BR)
BANQUE TORONTO-DOMINION, LA
TD CANADA TRUST
(Suby of Toronto-Dominion Bank, The)
2428 Eglinton Ave E, Scarborough, ON, M1K
2P7
(416) 751-3810
Emp Here 20
SIC 6021 National commercial banks

D-U-N-S 24-317-4344   (BR)
CLT LOGISTICS, INC
CLT INTERNATIONAL
1020 Birchmount Rd Door 48, Scarborough,
ON, M1K 1S1
(416) 686-1140
Emp Here 50
SIC 5122 Drugs, proprietaries, and sundries

D-U-N-S 25-303-1033   (BR)
CANADIAN IMPERIAL BANK OF COM-
MERCE
CIBC
2705 Eglinton Ave E, Scarborough, ON, M1K
2S2
(416) 266-5314
Emp Here 22
SIC 6021 National commercial banks

D-U-N-S 24-375-7205   (BR)
HILLMAN GROUP CANADA ULC, THE
376 Birchmount Rd, Scarborough, ON, M1K
1M6
(416) 694-3351
Emp Here 25
SIC 5085 Industrial supplies

D-U-N-S 20-077-8764   (BR)
MERRITHEW CORPORATION
770 Birchmount Rd Unit 17, Scarborough, ON,
M1K 5H3
(416) 752-1169
Emp Here 30
SIC 5091 Sporting and recreation goods

D-U-N-S 20-711-1076   (BR)
TORONTO CATHOLIC DISTRICT SCHOOL
BOARD
ST. ALBERT CATHOLIC SCHOOL
1125 Midland Ave, Scarborough, ON, M1K

4H2
(416) 393-5335
Emp Here 50
SIC 8211 Elementary and secondary schools

D-U-N-S 20-003-5348   (BR)
TORONTO DISTRICT SCHOOL BOARD
J G WORKMAN ELEMENTARY SCHOOL
487 Birchmount Rd, Scarborough, ON, M1K
1N7
(416) 396-6365
Emp Here 20
SIC 8211 Elementary and secondary schools

D-U-N-S 20-711-3205   (BR)
TORONTO DISTRICT SCHOOL BOARD
CORVETTE JUNIOR PUBLIC SCHOOL
30 Corvette Ave, Scarborough, ON, M1K 3G2
(416) 396-6180
Emp Here 50
SIC 8211 Elementary and secondary schools

D-U-N-S 20-591-5346   (BR)
TORONTO DISTRICT SCHOOL BOARD
IONVIEW PUBLIC SCHOOL
90 Ionview Rd, Scarborough, ON, M1K 2Z9
(416) 396-6350
Emp Here 35
SIC 8211 Elementary and secondary schools

D-U-N-S 20-025-0301   (BR)
TORONTO DISTRICT SCHOOL BOARD
CHARLES GORDON SENIOR ELEMEN-
TARY SCHOOL
25 Marcos Blvd, Scarborough, ON, M1K 5A7
(416) 396-6130
Emp Here 32
SIC 8211 Elementary and secondary schools

D-U-N-S 25-359-5540   (BR)
TORONTO DISTRICT SCHOOL BOARD
HUNTER'S GLEN JUNIOR PUBLIC SCHOOL
16 Haileybury Dr, Scarborough, ON, M1K 4X5
(416) 396-6340
Emp Here 28
SIC 8211 Elementary and secondary schools

D-U-N-S 20-698-7369   (BR)
TORONTO DISTRICT SCHOOL BOARD
LORD ROBERTS PUBLIC SCHOOL
165 Lord Roberts Dr, Scarborough, ON, M1K
3W5
(416) 396-6420
Emp Here 30
SIC 8211 Elementary and secondary schools

D-U-N-S 25-360-2544   (BR)
UAP INC
NAPA
(Suby of Genuine Parts Company)
750 Birchmount Rd Suite 53, Scarborough,
ON, M1K 5H7
(416) 752-8543
Emp Here 20
SIC 5013 Motor vehicle supplies and new
parts

Scarborough, ON M1L
York County

D-U-N-S 24-822-5807   (SL)
820229 ONTARIO LIMITED
MANDARIN RESTAURANT
2206 Eglinton Ave E, Scarborough, ON, M1L
4S7
(416) 288-1177
Emp Here 70   Sales 2,115,860
SIC 5812 Eating places

D-U-N-S 20-771-1508   (HQ)
AVIVA INSURANCE COMPANY OF
CANADA
2206 Eglinton Ave E Suite 160, Scarborough,
ON, M1L 4S8

(416) 288-1800
Emp Here 20   Emp Total 25,581
Sales 61,722,550
SIC 6331 Fire, marine, and casualty insurance
Pr Pr Igal Mayer
 A Warren Moysey
Sr VP Karl Driedger
 Carol A Berger
Sr VP Michael D Marco
Dir J William Rowley
Dir Mark Dearsley
Dir Philip G. Scott
Dir Louise Vaillancourt-Chatillon
Dir C Wesley Scott

D-U-N-S 20-104-2772   (BR)
BANK OF NOVA SCOTIA, THE
SCOTIABANK
2201 Eglinton Ave E Suite 1, Scarborough,
ON, M1L 4S2
(416) 701-7307
Emp Here 2,500
SIC 6021 National commercial banks

D-U-N-S 20-072-6045   (BR)
BANK OF NOVA SCOTIA, THE
SCOTIABANK
1940 Eglinton Ave E, Scarborough, ON, M1L
4R1
(416) 288-4645
Emp Here 100
SIC 6021 National commercial banks

D-U-N-S 20-535-7804   (BR)
BANK OF MONTREAL
BMO
627 Pharmacy Ave, Scarborough, ON, M1L
3H3
(416) 759-9371
Emp Here 20
SIC 6021 National commercial banks

D-U-N-S 24-336-3129   (BR)
BEST BUY CANADA LTD
BEST BUY
(Suby of Best Buy Co., Inc.)
50 Ashtonbee Rd Unit 2, Scarborough, ON,
M1L 4R5
(416) 615-2879
Emp Here 50
SIC 5731 Radio, television, and electronic
stores

D-U-N-S 20-008-9113   (BR)
CANADIAN IMPERIAL BANK OF COM-
MERCE
CIBC
2 Lebovic Ave, Scarborough, ON, M1L 4V9
(416) 757-6780
Emp Here 30
SIC 6021 National commercial banks

D-U-N-S 24-319-3799   (BR)
CENTENNIAL COLLEGE OF APPLIED
ARTS & TECHNOLOGY, THE
1960 Eglinton Ave E, Scarborough, ON, M1L
2M5

Emp Here 20
SIC 8222 Junior colleges

D-U-N-S 25-139-8343   (SL)
DEBMAR HOLDINGS LIMITED
CASEY'S BAR & GRILL RESTAURANT
10 Lebovic Ave, Scarborough, ON, M1L 4V9

Emp Here 55   Sales 1,678,096
SIC 5812 Eating places

D-U-N-S 24-124-6875   (SL)
DONWAY FORD SALES LIMITED
DONWAY LEASING
1975 Eglinton Ave E, Scarborough, ON, M1L
2N1
(416) 751-2200
Emp Here 90   Sales 32,832,315
SIC 5511 New and used car dealers
Pr Pr Paul Lenneard

Terry Fisher
Matthew Fisher

D-U-N-S 25-197-7179   (BR)
FABRICLAND DISTRIBUTORS INC
FABRICLAND
1980 Eglinton Ave E, Scarborough, ON, M1L
2M6
(416) 752-8119
Emp Here 21
SIC 5949 Sewing, needlework, and piece
goods

D-U-N-S 24-172-9685   (BR)
FAMILY SERVICE TORONTO
FAMILY SERVICE CHANNEL TORONTO
747 Warden Ave, Scarborough, ON, M1L 4A8
(416) 755-5565
Emp Here 25
SIC 8322 Individual and family services

D-U-N-S 24-892-6172   (BR)
G&K SERVICES CANADA INC
(Suby of Cintas Corporation)
940 Warden Ave Suite 1, Scarborough, ON,
M1L 4C9
(647) 933-2627
Emp Here 150
SIC 2326 Men's and boy's work clothing

D-U-N-S 25-214-7335   (BR)
GAP (CANADA) INC
GAP OUTLET
(Suby of The Gap Inc)
1900 Eglinton Ave E, Scarborough, ON, M1L
2L9
(416) 285-8915
Emp Here 45
SIC 5651 Family clothing stores

D-U-N-S 24-830-7712   (BR)
HSBC BANK CANADA
1940 Eglinton Ave E Suite 1, Scarborough,
ON, M1L 4R1
(416) 752-8910
Emp Here 27
SIC 6021 National commercial banks

D-U-N-S 25-301-1613   (BR)
HUDSON'S BAY COMPANY
BAY, THE
1 Eglinton Sq, Scarborough, ON, M1L 2K1
(416) 759-4771
Emp Here 300
SIC 5311 Department stores

D-U-N-S 20-026-8436   (BR)
LIQUOR CONTROL BOARD OF ONTARIO,
THE
LCBO
3111 Danforth Ave, Scarborough, ON, M1L
1A9
(416) 699-7003
Emp Here 20
SIC 5921 Liquor stores

D-U-N-S 24-937-2061   (SL)
M T N ENTERPRISES INC
120 Sinnott Rd, Scarborough, ON, M1L 4N1
(416) 285-2051
Emp Here 300   Sales 70,282,560
SIC 6712 Bank holding companies
Pr Pr James B Neil

D-U-N-S 24-764-8298   (BR)
MARK'S WORK WEARHOUSE LTD
MARK'S WORK WEARHOUSE 74
1900 Eglinton Ave E, Scarborough, ON, M1L
2L9
(416) 759-4124
Emp Here 20
SIC 5651 Family clothing stores

D-U-N-S 25-310-8971   (BR)
MCDONALD'S RESTAURANTS OF
CANADA LIMITED
MCDONALDS
(Suby of McDonald's Corporation)
3150 St Clair Ave E, Scarborough, ON, M1L

1V6
(416) 751-9014
Emp Here 94
SIC 5812 Eating places

D-U-N-S 24-205-9900   (SL)
NOBLE CULINARY INC
NOBLE CULINARY CREATIONS CATERING
127 Manville Rd Suite 14, Scarborough, ON,
M1L 4J7
(416) 288-9713
Emp Here 90   *Sales* 9,043,200
SIC 5963 Direct selling establishments
Pr Neal Noble

D-U-N-S 25-531-7067   (HQ)
OAK LEAF CONFECTIONS CO.
440 Comstock Rd, Scarborough, ON, M1L
2H6
(416) 751-0740
Emp Here 200   *Emp Total* 87,414
Sales 16,780,961
SIC 2064 Candy and other confectionery
products
Pr Pr Philip Terranova

D-U-N-S 24-426-5711   (BR)
OAK LEAF CONFECTIONS CO.
110 Sinnott Rd, Scarborough, ON, M1L 4S6
(416) 751-0895
Emp Here 230
SIC 2064 Candy and other confectionery
products

D-U-N-S 24-719-1786   (SL)
POLYDEX PHARMACEUTICALS LIMITED
421 Comstock Rd, Scarborough, ON, M1L
2H5
(416) 755-2231
Emp Here 22   *Sales* 5,963,784
SIC 2834 Pharmaceutical preparations
George Usher
John A Luce
Sharon Wardlaw
Joseph Buchman
Derek Lederer
Martin Lipper

D-U-N-S 25-084-5534   (BR)
PRIME RESTAURANTS INC
EAST SIDE MARIO'S
(*Suby of* Cara Holdings Limited)
12 Lebovic Ave Suite 9, Scarborough, ON,
M1L 4V9
(416) 285-6631
Emp Here 75
SIC 5812 Eating places

D-U-N-S 24-191-8739   (BR)
RYDER TRUCK RENTAL CANADA LTD
*RYDER LOGISTICS AND TRANSPORTA-
TION*
(*Suby of* Ryder System, Inc.)
39 Comstock Rd, Scarborough, ON, M1L 2G6
(416) 752-3446
Emp Here 31
SIC 7538 General automotive repair shops

D-U-N-S 24-285-4669   (SL)
SOLARFECTIVE PRODUCTS LIMITED
55 Hymus Rd, Scarborough, ON, M1L 2C6
(416) 421-3800
Emp Here 65   *Sales* 4,071,380
SIC 3861 Photographic equipment and supplies

D-U-N-S 25-213-7377   (BR)
STAPLES CANADA INC
STAPLES THE BUSINESS DEPOT
(*Suby of* Staples, Inc.)
1980 Eglinton Ave E, Scarborough, ON, M1L
2M6
(416) 752-1091
Emp Here 50
SIC 5943 Stationery stores

D-U-N-S 24-986-2293   (BR)
STOCK TRANSPORTATION LTD

17 Upton Rd, Scarborough, ON, M1L 2C1
(416) 754-4949
Emp Here 253
SIC 4151 School buses

D-U-N-S 25-395-4135   (BR)
SUNCOR ENERGY INC
1896 Eglinton Ave E, Scarborough, ON, M1L
2L9
(416) 751-8896
Emp Here 32
SIC 5541 Gasoline service stations

D-U-N-S 24-172-1450   (BR)
**TORONTO CATHOLIC DISTRICT SCHOOL
BOARD**
OUR LADY OF FATIMA CATHOLIC SCHOOL
3176 St Clair Ave E, Scarborough, ON, M1L
1V6
(416) 393-5252
Emp Here 50
SIC 8211 Elementary and secondary schools

D-U-N-S 20-003-9977   (BR)
TORONTO DISTRICT SCHOOL BOARD
*REGENT HEIGHTS JUNIOR PUBLIC
SCHOOL*
555 Pharmacy Ave, Scarborough, ON, M1L
3H1
(416) 396-6535
Emp Here 35
SIC 8211 Elementary and secondary schools

D-U-N-S 20-025-0459   (BR)
TORONTO DISTRICT SCHOOL BOARD
*WARDEN AVENUE JUNIOR PUBLIC
SCHOOL*
644 Warden Ave, Scarborough, ON, M1L 3Z3
(416) 396-6625
Emp Here 40
SIC 8211 Elementary and secondary schools

D-U-N-S 20-025-0491   (BR)
TORONTO DISTRICT SCHOOL BOARD
*SATEC @ W.A. PORTER COLLEGIATE IN-
STITUTE*
40 Fairfax Cres, Scarborough, ON, M1L 1Z9
(416) 396-3365
Emp Here 70
SIC 8211 Elementary and secondary schools

D-U-N-S 24-319-8418   (BR)
VALUE VILLAGE STORES, INC
(*Suby of* Savers, Inc.)
1525 Victoria Park Ave, Scarborough, ON,
M1L 2T3
(416) 752-0060
Emp Here 50
SIC 5399 Miscellaneous general merchandise

D-U-N-S 25-498-2705   (BR)
WAL-MART CANADA CORP
800 Warden Ave, Scarborough, ON, M1L 4T7
(416) 615-2697
Emp Here 170
SIC 5311 Department stores

D-U-N-S 25-193-5656   (HQ)
WARDEN WOODS COMMUNITY CENTRE
(*Suby of* Warden Woods Community Centre)
74 Firvalley Crt, Scarborough, ON, M1N 1N9
(416) 694-1138
Emp Here 42   *Emp Total* 80
Sales 3,137,310
SIC 8322 Individual and family services

D-U-N-S 20-273-3213   (BR)
WENDY'S RESTAURANTS OF CANADA INC
WENDY'S 6669
(*Suby of* The Wendy's Company)
4 Lebovic Ave, Scarborough, ON, M1L 4V9
(416) 751-4834
Emp Here 30
SIC 5812 Eating places

D-U-N-S 20-005-3374   (BR)
WENDY'S RESTAURANTS OF CANADA INC
WENDY'S

(*Suby of* The Wendy's Company)
960 Warden Ave, Scarborough, ON, M1L 4C9

Emp Here 27
SIC 5812 Eating places

D-U-N-S 24-357-2638   (BR)
**WINNERS MERCHANTS INTERNATIONAL
L.P.**
HOMESENSE
(*Suby of* The TJX Companies Inc)
50 Ashtonbee Rd, Scarborough, ON, M1L
4R5
(416) 750-8066
Emp Here 45
SIC 5651 Family clothing stores

D-U-N-S 25-864-6314   (SL)
YOUTHLINK
747 Warden Ave, Scarborough, ON, M1L 4A8
(416) 967-1773
Emp Here 60   *Sales* 3,246,400
SIC 8322 Individual and family services

Scarborough, ON M1M
York County

D-U-N-S 20-016-3702   (BR)
ATLANTIC PACKAGING PRODUCTS LTD
GRAN PACKAGING
255 Brimley Rd Suite 1, Scarborough, ON,
M1M 3J2
(416) 261-2356
Emp Here 65
SIC 3081 Unsupported plastics film and sheet

D-U-N-S 24-720-9281   (SL)
INTELLIGARDE INTERNATIONAL INC
3090 Kingston Rd Suite 400, Scarborough,
ON, M1M 1P2
(416) 760-0000
Emp Here 130   *Sales* 4,764,381
SIC 7381 Detective and armored car services

D-U-N-S 20-106-4826   (BR)
NIKE CANADA CORP
(*Suby of* Nike, Inc.)
260 Brimley Rd, Scarborough, ON, M1M 3H8
(416) 264-8505
Emp Here 250
SIC 5091 Sporting and recreation goods

D-U-N-S 25-003-4006   (SL)
**ST.   AUGUSTINE'S   SEMINARY   OF
TORONTO**
2661 Kingston Rd, Scarborough, ON, M1M
1M3
(416) 261-7207
Emp Here 65   *Sales* 4,304,681
SIC 8661 Religious organizations

D-U-N-S 20-079-2583   (BR)
**TORONTO CATHOLIC DISTRICT SCHOOL
BOARD**
*BLESSED CARDINAL NEWMAN SEC-
ONDARY SCHOOL*
100 Brimley Rd S, Scarborough, ON, M1M
3X4
(416) 393-5519
Emp Here 100
SIC 8211 Elementary and secondary schools

D-U-N-S 20-698-6593   (BR)
**TORONTO CATHOLIC DISTRICT SCHOOL
BOARD**
ST. BONIFACE ELEMENTARY SCHOOL
20 Markanna Dr, Scarborough, ON, M1M 2J1
(416) 393-5277
Emp Here 30
SIC 8211 Elementary and secondary schools

D-U-N-S 20-026-8469   (BR)
**TORONTO CATHOLIC DISTRICT SCHOOL
BOARD**
ST. THERESA SHRINE SCHOOL

2665 Kingston Rd, Scarborough, ON, M1M
1M2
(416) 393-5248
Emp Here 26
SIC 8211 Elementary and secondary schools

D-U-N-S 20-025-0277   (BR)
TORONTO DISTRICT SCHOOL BOARD
BLISS CARMAN SENIOR PUBLIC SCHOOL
10 Bellamy Rd S, Scarborough, ON, M1M 3N8
(416) 396-6075
Emp Here 50
SIC 8211 Elementary and secondary schools

D-U-N-S 20-711-3239   (BR)
TORONTO DISTRICT SCHOOL BOARD
HA HALBERT JR SCHOOL
31 Mccowan Rd, Scarborough, ON, M1M 3L7
(416) 396-6300
Emp Here 40
SIC 8211 Elementary and secondary schools

D-U-N-S 20-591-5338   (BR)
TORONTO DISTRICT SCHOOL BOARD
MASON ROAD
78 Mason Rd, Scarborough, ON, M1M 3R2
(416) 396-6460
Emp Here 50
SIC 8211 Elementary and secondary schools

D-U-N-S 20-178-2260   (BR)
TRAVELBRANDS INC
TRAVELBRANDS INC
2975 Kingston Rd, Scarborough, ON, M1M
1P1
(416) 265-3100
Emp Here 20
SIC 4724 Travel agencies

D-U-N-S 24-684-7966   (SL)
VERSATECH MECHANICAL LTD
50 Skagway Ave Suite A, Scarborough, ON,
M1M 3V1
(416) 292-9220
Emp Here 50   *Sales* 4,377,642
SIC 1711 Plumbing, heating, air-conditioning

D-U-N-S 25-577-7971   (SL)
WEST HILL COMMUNITY SERVICES
3545 Kingston Rd, Scarborough, ON, M1M
1R6
(416) 284-6439
Emp Here 75   *Sales* 9,776,734
SIC 8399 Social services, nec
Pr Len Forde
VP VP Bob Lopston
Treas Carol Smith
Treas Bryan Stewart

Scarborough, ON M1N
York County

D-U-N-S 20-618-5410   (BR)
CANADA POST CORPORATION
1085 Kingston Rd, Scarborough, ON, M1N
4E3
(416) 699-5355
Emp Here 20
SIC 4311 U.s. postal service

D-U-N-S 25-303-0746   (BR)
**CANADIAN IMPERIAL BANK OF COM-
MERCE**
CIBC
2472 Kingston Rd, Scarborough, ON, M1N
1V3
(800) 465-2422
Emp Here 30
SIC 6021 National commercial banks

D-U-N-S 20-875-3095   (SL)
CRAIGLEE NURSING HOME LIMITED
102 Craiglee Dr, Scarborough, ON, M1N 2M7
(416) 264-2260
Emp Here 60   *Sales* 3,486,617

SIC 8051 Skilled nursing care facilities

D-U-N-S 20-151-5491   (HQ)
ELI LILLY CANADA INC
LILLY ANALYTICAL RESEARCH LAB
(*Suby of* Eli Lilly and Company)
3650 Danforth Ave Suite 1907, Scarborough, ON, M1N 2E8
(416) 694-3221
Emp Here 400   *Emp Total* 41,975
Sales 38,742,132
SIC 2834 Pharmaceutical preparations
Pr Lisa Elias Matar
VP Fin Nicholas B. Lemen
VP Lauren Fischer
Pers/VP Karen Mckay
VP Doron Sagman

D-U-N-S 24-171-8381   (BR)
PHARMA PLUS DRUGMARTS LTD
2447 Kingston Rd Unit 103, Scarborough, ON, M1N 1V4
(416) 264-2444
Emp Here 20
SIC 5912 Drug stores and proprietary stores

D-U-N-S 24-425-1591   (HQ)
SOLAR GROUP INC, THE
(*Suby of* Solar Group Inc, The)
2481 Kingston Rd Suite 203, Scarborough, ON, M1N 1V4
(416) 269-2288
Emp Here 67   *Emp Total* 69
Sales 1,708,160
SIC 7349 Building maintenance services, nec

D-U-N-S 25-886-2671   (SL)
SQUARE ARCH LTD
MCDONALD'S RESTAURANTS
2480 Gerrard St E, Scarborough, ON, M1N 4C3
(416) 690-3658
Emp Here 60   *Sales* 1,824,018
SIC 5812 Eating places

D-U-N-S 25-265-2318   (BR)
TORONTO CATHOLIC DISTRICT SCHOOL BOARD
IMMACULATE HEART MARY SCHOOL
101 Birchmount Rd, Scarborough, ON, M1N 3J7
(416) 393-5272
Emp Here 24
SIC 8211 Elementary and secondary schools

D-U-N-S 20-025-0269   (BR)
TORONTO DISTRICT SCHOOL BOARD
BLANTYRE PUBLIC SCHOOL
290 Blantyre Ave, Scarborough, ON, M1N 2S4
(416) 396-6070
Emp Here 23
SIC 8211 Elementary and secondary schools

D-U-N-S 24-172-2540   (BR)
TORONTO DISTRICT SCHOOL BOARD
BIRCH CLIFF PUBLIC SCHOOL
1650 Kingston Rd, Scarborough, ON, M1N 1S2
(416) 396-6060
Emp Here 25
SIC 8211 Elementary and secondary schools

D-U-N-S 20-700-2911   (BR)
TORONTO DISTRICT SCHOOL BOARD
BIRCHMOUNT PARK COLLEGIATE INSTITUTE
3663 Danforth Ave, Scarborough, ON, M1N 2G2
(416) 396-6704
Emp Here 20
SIC 8211 Elementary and secondary schools

Scarborough, ON M1P
York County

D-U-N-S 24-182-8040   (SL)
1351786 ONTARIO LTD
CASEY'S BAR & GRILL
37 William Kitchen Rd, Scarborough, ON, M1P 5B7
(800) 361-3111
Emp Here 50   *Sales* 1,532,175
SIC 5812 Eating places

D-U-N-S 20-974-3587   (BR)
2063414 ONTARIO LIMITED
LEISUREWORLD CAREGIVING CENTRE
(*Suby of* 2063414 Ontario Limited)
1000 Ellesmere Rd Suite 333, Scarborough, ON, M1P 5G2
(416) 291-0222
Emp Here 75
SIC 8051 Skilled nursing care facilities

D-U-N-S 25-344-0358   (SL)
ANDERSON LEARNING INC
BOND INTERNATIONAL COLLEGE
1500 Birchmount Rd, Scarborough, ON, M1P 2G5
(416) 266-8878
Emp Here 70   *Sales* 4,557,599
SIC 8211 Elementary and secondary schools

D-U-N-S 25-529-8846   (BR)
AQUARIUM SERVICES WAREHOUSE OUTLETS INC
BIG AL'S
1295 Kennedy Rd, Scarborough, ON, M1P 2L4
(416) 757-3281
Emp Here 24
SIC 5999 Miscellaneous retail stores, nec

D-U-N-S 25-095-5564   (BR)
ATLANTIC PACKAGING PRODUCTS LTD
350 Midwest Rd, Scarborough, ON, M1P 3A9
(416) 642-1236
Emp Here 60
SIC 2653 Corrugated and solid fiber boxes

D-U-N-S 24-692-0623   (BR)
ATLANTIC PACKAGING PRODUCTS LTD
COLOR PAK, DIV OF
80 Progress Ave Suite Side, Scarborough, ON, M1P 2Z1
(416) 642-1090
Emp Here 25
SIC 2396 Automotive and apparel trimmings

D-U-N-S 20-544-0808   (BR)
ATLANTIC PACKAGING PRODUCTS LTD
111 Progress Ave, Scarborough, ON, M1P 2Y9
(416) 298-5456
Emp Here 200
SIC 2679 Converted paper products, nec

D-U-N-S 25-704-9353   (BR)
BAD BOY FURNITURE WAREHOUSE LIMITED
LAST MEN'S BAD BOY
1119 Kennedy Rd, Scarborough, ON, M1P 2K8
(416) 750-8888
Emp Here 30
SIC 5712 Furniture stores

D-U-N-S 25-306-9405   (BR)
BANK OF NOVA SCOTIA, THE
SCOTIABANK
300 Borough Dr Unit 2, Scarborough, ON, M1P 4P5
(416) 296-5626
Emp Here 20
SIC 6021 National commercial banks

D-U-N-S 24-437-7664   (BR)
BANQUE TORONTO-DOMINION, LA
TORONTO-DOMINION BANK, THE
(*Suby of* Toronto-Dominion Bank, The)
26 William Kitchen Rd, Scarborough, ON, M1P 5B7
(416) 292-2201
Emp Here 25

SIC 6021 National commercial banks

D-U-N-S 25-371-1717   (BR)
BEST BUY CANADA LTD
BEST BUY
(*Suby of* Best Buy Co., Inc.)
480 Progress Ave, Scarborough, ON, M1P 5J1
(416) 296-7020
Emp Here 170
SIC 5731 Radio, television, and electronic stores

D-U-N-S 20-006-1682   (BR)
BRICK WAREHOUSE LP, THE
1165 Kennedy Rd, Scarborough, ON, M1P 2K8
(416) 751-2150
Emp Here 35
SIC 5712 Furniture stores

D-U-N-S 20-409-4643   (BR)
BRICK WAREHOUSE LP, THE
19 William Kitchen Rd, Scarborough, ON, M1P 5B7
(416) 751-3383
Emp Here 80
SIC 5712 Furniture stores

D-U-N-S 24-173-4305   (BR)
BULK BARN FOODS LIMITED
300 Borough Dr Suite 2, Scarborough, ON, M1P 4P5
(416) 279-1180
Emp Here 25
SIC 5411 Grocery stores

D-U-N-S 25-120-6512   (BR)
CANADA POST CORPORATION
SCARBOROUGH STATION D
280 Progress Ave, Scarborough, ON, M1P 2Z4
(416) 299-4577
Emp Here 500
SIC 4311 U.s. postal service

D-U-N-S 24-172-2276   (BR)
CARA OPERATIONS LIMITED
MILESTONE'S GRILL & BAR
(*Suby of* Cara Holdings Limited)
300 Borough Dr Suite 2, Scarborough, ON, M1P 4P5
(416) 290-0464
Emp Here 45
SIC 5812 Eating places

D-U-N-S 25-508-2158   (SL)
CASE REALTY LIMITED
55 Town Centre Crt Suite 100, Scarborough, ON, M1P 4X4
(416) 751-6533
Emp Here 260   *Sales* 33,761,280
SIC 6531 Real estate agents and managers
VP Frank Mihalek

D-U-N-S 25-531-1516   (HQ)
CHAIRMAN'S BRAND CORPORATION
COFFEE TIME
(*Suby of* Chairman's Brand Corporation)
77 Progress Ave, Scarborough, ON, M1P 2Y7
(416) 288-8515
Emp Here 50   *Emp Total* 150
Sales 3,027
SIC 6794 Patent owners and lessors

D-U-N-S 20-648-4227   (BR)
CINEPLEX ODEON CORPORATION
CINEPLEX CINEMAS SCARBOROUGH
300 Borough Dr Unit 765, Scarborough, ON, M1P 4P5
(416) 290-5217
Emp Here 20
SIC 7832 Motion picture theaters, except drive-in

D-U-N-S 24-860-0397   (SL)
CITIGUARD SECURITY SERVICES INC
1560 Brimley Rd Suite 201, Scarborough, ON, M1P 3G9

(416) 431-6888
Emp Here 150   *Sales* 4,669,485
SIC 7381 Detective and armored car services

D-U-N-S 20-598-1426   (SL)
CLIFFORD MASONRY LIMITED
1190 Birchmount Rd, Scarborough, ON, M1P 2B8
(416) 691-2341
Emp Here 30   *Sales* 2,188,821
SIC 1741 Masonry and other stonework

D-U-N-S 25-321-4951   (BR)
CLUB MONACO CORP
CLUB MONACO SCARBOROUGH
(*Suby of* Ralph Lauren Corporation)
300 Borough Dr Suite 302, Scarborough, ON, M1P 4P5

Emp Here 20
SIC 5621 Women's clothing stores

D-U-N-S 20-031-1699   (BR)
CORPORATION OF THE CITY OF TORONTO
TORONTO HOME FOR THE AGED (COMMUNITY SERVICES)
2920 Lawrence Ave E, Scarborough, ON, M1P 2T8
(416) 397-7000
Emp Here 300
SIC 8361 Residential care

D-U-N-S 25-978-7497   (SL)
DYNAMIC TEAM SPORTS CANADA CO
(*Suby of* Dynamic Team Sports, Inc.)
1870 Birchmount Rd, Scarborough, ON, M1P 2J7
(416) 496-8600
Emp Here 100   *Sales* 3,939,878
SIC 2329 Men's and boy's clothing, nec

D-U-N-S 24-171-4497   (SL)
EAGLE RESTAURANT MANAGEMENT INC
BOSTON PIZZA
400 Progress Ave, Scarborough, ON, M1P 5J1
(416) 290-0029
Emp Here 60   *Sales* 1,824,018
SIC 5812 Eating places

D-U-N-S 20-641-6562   (SL)
ECON-O-PAC LIMITED
490 Midwest Rd, Scarborough, ON, M1P 3A9
(416) 750-7200
Emp Here 175   *Sales* 8,536,402
SIC 7389 Business services, nec
Pr Pr Howard Nisenbaum
Elliott Warsh
Irving Walsh
Nathan Hartley
Norman Scolnick

D-U-N-S 24-343-7436   (BR)
FGL SPORTS LTD
SPORT-CHEK
300 Borough Dr Suite 2, Scarborough, ON, M1P 4P5
(416) 296-0413
Emp Here 25
SIC 5941 Sporting goods and bicycle shops

D-U-N-S 25-051-6580   (BR)
FOOT LOCKER CANADA CO.
FOOTLOCKER
300 Borough Dr Suite 2, Scarborough, ON, M1P 4P5
(416) 296-2137
Emp Here 25
SIC 5661 Shoe stores

D-U-N-S 24-195-3538   (SL)
FORTESCUE BINDERY LIMITED
285 Nantucket Blvd, Scarborough, ON, M1P 2P2
(416) 701-1673
Emp Here 50   *Sales* 1,824,018
SIC 2789 Bookbinding and related work

D-U-N-S 24-208-8086   (HQ)

FORTRAN TRAFFIC SYSTEMS LIMITED
470 Midwest Rd, Scarborough, ON, M1P 4Y5
(416) 288-1320
Emp Here 50   *Emp Total* 650
Sales 7,150,149
SIC 3669 Communications equipment, nec
  Peter Lengyel
Pr Pr Andrew Lengyel

  D-U-N-S 25-897-0185   (BR)
GAP (CANADA) INC
GAP
(*Suby of* The Gap Inc)
300 Borough Dr Suite 2, Scarborough, ON,
M1P 4P5
(416) 296-0528
Emp Here 65
SIC 5651 Family clothing stores

  D-U-N-S 24-390-5770   (BR)
GOLF TOWN LIMITED
GOLF TOWN
23 William Kitchen Rd, Scarborough, ON,
M1P 5B7
(416) 335-4888
Emp Here 25
SIC 5941 Sporting goods and bicycle shops

  D-U-N-S 24-253-2294   (BR)
GOODLIFE FITNESS CENTRES INC
1755 Brimley Rd, Scarborough, ON, M1P 0A3
(416) 296-1276
Emp Here 20
SIC 7991 Physical fitness facilities

  D-U-N-S 20-511-6978   (BR)
**GREYHOUND CANADA TRANSPORTA-
TION ULC**
300 Borough Dr Suite 2, Scarborough, ON,
M1P 4P5
(416) 296-9301
Emp Here 50
SIC 4131 Intercity and rural bus transportation

  D-U-N-S 20-837-1737   (SL)
HENNES & MAURITZ
H & M
300 Borough Dr Unit 2, Scarborough, ON,
M1P 4P5
(416) 290-6670
Emp Here 50   *Sales* 3,064,349
SIC 5621 Women's clothing stores

  D-U-N-S 24-910-5602   (BR)
HEROUX-DEVTEK INC
MAGTRON
1480 Birchmount Rd, Scarborough, ON, M1P
2E3
(416) 757-2366
Emp Here 75
SIC 3443 Fabricated plate work (boiler shop)

  D-U-N-S 25-667-3427   (BR)
HONDA CANADA INC
ROADSPORT HONDA
940 Ellesmere Rd, Scarborough, ON, M1P
2W8
(416) 291-9501
Emp Here 50
SIC 7515 Passenger car leasing

  D-U-N-S 24-120-1180   (BR)
HUDSON'S BAY COMPANY
300 Borough Dr Suite 2, Scarborough, ON,
M1P 4P5
(416) 296-0555
Emp Here 300
SIC 5311 Department stores

  D-U-N-S 24-972-4469   (BR)
INDIGO BOOKS & MUSIC INC
COLES STORE
(*Suby of* Indigo Books & Music Inc)
300 Borough Dr Suite 2, Scarborough, ON,
M1P 4P5

Emp Here 20
SIC 5942 Book stores

  D-U-N-S 24-228-2387   (BR)
INDIGO BOOKS & MUSIC INC
CHAPTERS
(*Suby of* Indigo Books & Music Inc)
20 William Kitchen Rd, Scarborough, ON,
M1P 5B7
(416) 335-4311
Emp Here 30
SIC 5942 Book stores

  D-U-N-S 25-062-2164   (BR)
KITCHEN STUFF PLUS INC
KITCHEN STUFF PLUS
(*Suby of* Halpern, Mark Holdings Inc)
29 William Kitchen Rd Unit J3, Scarborough,
ON, M1P 5B7
(416) 291-0533
Emp Here 42
SIC 5719 Miscellaneous homefurnishings

  D-U-N-S 25-059-2532   (BR)
LE CHATEAU INC
(*Suby of* Le Chateau Inc)
300 Borough Dr Suite 2, Scarborough, ON,
M1P 4P5
(416) 296-3434
Emp Here 24
SIC 5651 Family clothing stores

  D-U-N-S 20-151-5467   (SL)
LEWIS MOVERS LIMITED
106 Ridgetop Rd, Scarborough, ON, M1P 2J9
(416) 438-6805
Emp Here 30   *Sales* 2,334,742
SIC 4212 Local trucking, without storage

  D-U-N-S 25-536-0083   (SL)
LINCARE LTD
332 Nantucket Blvd, Scarborough, ON, M1P
2P4
(416) 759-7777
Emp Here 80   *Sales* 2,407,703
SIC 7211 Power laundries, family and commercial

  D-U-N-S 24-670-6308   (BR)
MAGASIN LAURA (P.V.) INC
LAURA, LAURA PETITES, LAURA PLUS
300 Borough Dr, Scarborough, ON, M1P 4P5
(416) 296-1064
Emp Here 35
SIC 5621 Women's clothing stores

  D-U-N-S 24-170-6477   (BR)
**MCDONALD'S   RESTAURANTS   OF
CANADA LIMITED**
MCDONALD'S
(*Suby of* McDonald's Corporation)
300 Borough Dr Suite 2, Scarborough, ON,
M1P 4P5
(416) 279-0722
Emp Here 20
SIC 5812 Eating places

  D-U-N-S 20-771-5918   (BR)
**MCDONALD'S   RESTAURANTS   OF
CANADA LIMITED**
MCDONALD'S 8018
(*Suby of* McDonald's Corporation)
2701 Lawrence Ave E, Scarborough, ON, M1P
2S2
(416) 752-2610
Emp Here 30
SIC 5812 Eating places

  D-U-N-S 25-499-8073   (HQ)
MEGLEEN INC
TIM HORTONS
(*Suby of* Megleen Inc)
1 William Kitchen Rd Suite 1, Scarborough,
ON, M1P 5B7
(416) 293-1010
Emp Here 35   *Emp Total* 60
Sales 2,042,900
SIC 5461 Retail bakeries

  D-U-N-S 20-078-7625   (BR)
METRO ONTARIO INC

METRO
16 William Kitchen Rd Suite 535, Scarborough, ON, M1P 5B7
(416) 321-0500
Emp Here 240
SIC 5411 Grocery stores

  D-U-N-S 24-194-2481   (HQ)
MISTER COFFEE & SERVICES INC
(*Suby of* Mister Coffee & Services Inc)
2045 Midland Ave Suite 1, Scarborough, ON,
M1P 3E2
(416) 293-3333
Emp Here 68   *Emp Total* 76
Sales 3,866,917
SIC 7389 Business services, nec

  D-U-N-S 25-293-6513   (BR)
NESTLE CANADA INC
1500 Birchmount Rd, Scarborough, ON, M1P
2G5

Emp Here 160
SIC 2066 Chocolate and cocoa products

  D-U-N-S 25-226-4080   (BR)
O'NEIL, EARL ELECTRIC SUPPLY LIMITED
O'NEIL ELECTRIC SUPPLY
85 Progress Ave, Scarborough, ON, M1P 2Y7
(416) 609-1010
Emp Here 20
SIC 5999 Miscellaneous retail stores, nec

  D-U-N-S 20-657-9505   (BR)
OLD NAVY (CANADA) INC
(*Suby of* The Gap Inc)
300 Borough Dr Suite 2, Scarborough, ON,
M1P 4P5
(416) 279-1143
Emp Here 35
SIC 5651 Family clothing stores

  D-U-N-S 20-151-9907   (SL)
**RAPID   REFRIGERATION   MANUFACTUR-
ING COMPANY LIMITED**
1550 Birchmount Rd, Scarborough, ON, M1P
2H1
(416) 285-8282
Emp Here 75   *Sales* 9,484,891
SIC 3585 Refrigeration and heating equip-
ment
Pr Pr Albert Sausik
VP VP Albert Sausik Jr
  Hilda Sausik

  D-U-N-S 20-047-8084   (BR)
REVERA LONG TERM CARE INC
KENNEDY LODGE NURSING HOME
1400 Kennedy Rd, Scarborough, ON, M1P
4V6
(416) 752-8282
Emp Here 200
SIC 8051 Skilled nursing care facilities

  D-U-N-S 24-097-4402   (BR)
RYDER TRUCK RENTAL CANADA LTD
(*Suby of* Ryder System, Inc.)
1249 Kennedy Rd, Scarborough, ON, M1P
2L4
(416) 752-2931
Emp Here 20
SIC 7513 Truck rental and leasing, no drivers

  D-U-N-S 25-186-2256   (BR)
SIR CORP
JACK ASTOR'S BAR AND GRILL
580 Progress Ave, Scarborough, ON, M1P
2K2
(416) 296-0965
Emp Here 50
SIC 5812 Eating places

  D-U-N-S 25-311-1819   (BR)
SEARS CANADA INC
300 Borough Dr Suite 2, Scarborough, ON,
M1P 4P5
(416) 296-0171
Emp Here 400
SIC 5311 Department stores

  D-U-N-S 20-610-7880   (HQ)
**SHOREWOOD   PACKAGING   CORP.   OF
CANADA LIMITED**
AGI SHOREWOOD
(*Suby of* Multi Packaging Solutions, Inc.)
2220 Midland Ave Unit 50, Scarborough, ON,
M1P 3E6
(416) 940-2400
Emp Here 300   *Emp Total* 10
Sales 71,552,333
SIC 2657 Folding paperboard boxes
Pr Pr Fernando Pimentel

  D-U-N-S 25-812-1490   (BR)
SILGAN PLASTICS CANADA INC
1200 Ellesmere Rd, Scarborough, ON, M1P
2X4
(416) 293-8233
Emp Here 120
SIC 3089 Plastics products, nec

  D-U-N-S 24-870-0838   (SL)
SRV INDUSTRIAL SUPPLY INC
2500 Lawrence Ave E Suite 12, Scarborough,
ON, M1P 2R7
(416) 757-1020
Emp Here 40   *Sales* 12,532,976
SIC 5093 Scrap and waste materials
Pr Sam Ragah

  D-U-N-S 25-849-5571   (SL)
**TCS   ENTERTAINMENT   ONE   CORPORA-
TION**
KOCH ENTERTAINMENT
1220 Ellesmere Rd Unit 8, Scarborough, ON,
M1P 2X5
(416) 292-8111
Emp Here 42   *Sales* 2,480,664
SIC 2782 Blankbooks and looseleaf binders

  D-U-N-S 20-120-0404   (BR)
TEKNION LIMITED
WIREFAB INDUSTRIES, DIV OF
195 Nantucket Blvd, Scarborough, ON, M1P
2P2
(416) 751-9900
Emp Here 75
SIC 2522 Office furniture, except wood

  D-U-N-S 20-027-1059   (BR)
**TORONTO CATHOLIC DISTRICT SCHOOL
BOARD**
ST. LAWRENCE CATHOLIC SCHOOL
2216 Lawrence Ave E, Scarborough, ON, M1P
2P9
(416) 393-5264
Emp Here 40
SIC 8211 Elementary and secondary schools

  D-U-N-S 20-025-0855   (BR)
TORONTO DISTRICT SCHOOL BOARD
*DAVID & MARY THOMSON COLLEGIATE IN-
STITUTE*
2740 Lawrence Ave E, Scarborough, ON, M1P
2S7
(416) 396-5525
Emp Here 100
SIC 8221 Colleges and universities

  D-U-N-S 20-025-0384   (BR)
TORONTO DISTRICT SCHOOL BOARD
ELLESMERE-STATTON PUBLIC SCHOOL
739 Ellesmere Rd, Scarborough, ON, M1P
2W1
(416) 396-6225
Emp Here 50
SIC 8211 Elementary and secondary schools

  D-U-N-S 20-026-8501   (BR)
TORONTO DISTRICT SCHOOL BOARD
*BENDALE BUSINESS & TECHNICAL INSTI-
TUTE*
1555 Midland Ave, Scarborough, ON, M1P
3C1
(416) 396-6695
Emp Here 100
SIC 8211 Elementary and secondary schools

  D-U-N-S 20-025-0368   (BR)

TORONTO DISTRICT SCHOOL BOARD
DORSET PARK ELEMENTARY SCHOOL
28 Blaisdale Rd, Scarborough, ON, M1P 1V6
(416) 396-6205
Emp Here 30
SIC 8211 Elementary and secondary schools

D-U-N-S 25-065-4118   (HQ)
TRANSPHARM CANADA INC
*TORONTO INSTITUTE OF PHARMACEUTI-
CAL TECHNOLOGY*
(*Suby of* Transpharm Canada Inc)
55 Town Centre Crt Suite 200, Scarborough,
ON, M1P 4X4
(416) 296-3860
Emp Here 39   *Emp Total* 54
Sales 3,356,192
SIC 8249 Vocational schools, nec

D-U-N-S 24-330-0469   (BR)
WAL-MART CANADA CORP
300 Borough Dr Suite 2, Scarborough, ON,
M1P 4P5
(416) 290-1916
Emp Here 200
SIC 5311 Department stores

D-U-N-S 20-005-6989   (BR)
WENDY'S RESTAURANTS OF CANADA INC
WENDY'S
(*Suby of* The Wendy's Company)
1460 Kennedy Rd, Scarborough, ON, M1P
2L7
(416) 752-8195
Emp Here 30
SIC 5812 Eating places

D-U-N-S 20-806-3201   (BR)
YM INC. (SALES)
STITCHES
2300 Lawrence Ave E Unit 15, Scarborough,
ON, M1P 2R2
(416) 752-7772
Emp Here 25
SIC 5621 Women's clothing stores

D-U-N-S 20-857-0601   (BR)
YM INC. (SALES)
SIRENS
300 Borough Dr Suite 204, Scarborough, ON,
M1P 4P5
(416) 296-0203
Emp Here 20
SIC 5621 Women's clothing stores

D-U-N-S 20-788-2924   (BR)
YORKDALE CAFE LTD
TIM HORTON DONUTS
300 Borough Dr Suite 2, Scarborough, ON,
M1P 4P5

Emp Here 32
SIC 5812 Eating places

Scarborough, ON M1R
York County

D-U-N-S 25-270-3350   (BR)
**AMEC FOSTER WHEELER AMERICAS LIM-
ITED**
AMEC EARTH & ENVIRONMENTAL, DIV OF
104 Crockford Blvd, Scarborough, ON, M1R
3C3
(416) 751-6565
Emp Here 100
SIC 8711 Engineering services

D-U-N-S 25-881-9051   (BR)
ACCESS INDEPENDENT LIVING SERVICES
(*Suby of* Access Independent Living Services)
2155 Lawrence Ave E Suite 623, Scarbor-
ough, ON, M1R 5G9
(416) 752-2490
Emp Here 60
SIC 8361 Residential care

D-U-N-S 25-117-4181   (BR)
ADVANTAGE PERSONNEL LTD
2130 Lawrence Ave E Suite 310, Scarborough, ON, M1R 3A6
(416) 288-0368
Emp Here 50
SIC 7361 Employment agencies

D-U-N-S 24-632-1335   (SL)
**AFRICA INLAND MISSION INTERNA-
TIONAL (CANADA)**
1641 Victoria Park Ave, Scarborough, ON,
M1R 1P8
(416) 751-6077
Emp Here 130   *Sales* 11,869,650
SIC 8661 Religious organizations
Dir John P Brown
Dir Robert Macdonald
Dir Ian Campbell
Dir Kichner Firmin
Dir Robin Goudie
Dir Muriel Harbourne
Dir Warren Kroeker
 Brad Cole
Dir Wayne Farquhar
 Paul Frew

D-U-N-S 24-437-6591   (BR)
BANQUE TORONTO-DOMINION, LA
TORONTO-DOMINION BANK, THE
(*Suby of* Toronto-Dominion Bank, The)
85 Ellesmere Rd, Scarborough, ON, M1R 4B7
(416) 441-2041
Emp Here 30
SIC 6021 National commercial banks

D-U-N-S 20-717-6538   (SL)
**BOBRICK WASHROOM EQUIPMENT COM-
PANY**
(*Suby of* The Bobrick Corporation)
45 Rolark Dr, Scarborough, ON, M1R 3B1
(416) 298-1611
Emp Here 70
SIC 3431 Metal sanitary ware

D-U-N-S 20-098-4370   (BR)
CON-WAY FREIGHT-CANADA INC
99 Howden Rd, Scarborough, ON, M1R 3C7
(416) 285-5399
Emp Here 30
SIC 4213 Trucking, except local

D-U-N-S 25-756-3999   (BR)
COSTCO WHOLESALE CANADA LTD
PRICE CLUB SCARBOROUGH
(*Suby of* Costco Wholesale Corporation)
1411 Warden Ave Suite 537, Scarborough,
ON, M1R 2S3
(416) 288-0033
Emp Here 75
SIC 5099 Durable goods, nec

D-U-N-S 20-769-4410   (BR)
**GOVERNING COUNCIL OF THE SALVA-
TION ARMY IN CANADA, THE**
*GOVERNING COUNCIL OF THE SALVATION
ARMY IN CANADA, THE*
1645 Warden Ave, Scarborough, ON, M1R
5B3
(416) 335-8618
Emp Here 38
SIC 8742 Management consulting services

D-U-N-S 25-234-5103   (BR)
**GOVERNING COUNCIL OF THE SALVA-
TION ARMY IN CANADA, THE**
*GOVERNING COUNCIL OF THE SALVATION
ARMY IN CANADA, THE*
1645 Warden Ave Suite 105, Scarborough,
ON, M1R 5B3
(416) 321-2654
Emp Here 50
SIC 8322 Individual and family services

D-U-N-S 25-289-2419   (SL)
HAMILTON, T & SON ROOFING INC
42 Crockford Blvd, Scarborough, ON, M1R

3C3
(416) 755-5522
Emp Here 53   *Sales* 5,253,170
SIC 1761 Roofing, siding, and sheetMetal
work
Pr Pr Tom Hamilton

D-U-N-S 24-892-9309   (SL)
HUME MEDIA INC
HUME IMAGING
66 Crockford Blvd, Scarborough, ON, M1R
3C3
(416) 921-7204
Emp Here 50   *Sales* 2,480,664
SIC 2759 Commercial printing, nec

D-U-N-S 25-306-1758   (HQ)
**ICOM INFORMATION & COMMUNICATIONS
L.P.**
EPSILON TARGETING, DIV OF
41 Metropolitan Rd, Scarborough, ON, M1R
2T5
(416) 297-7887
Emp Here 250   *Emp Total* 17,000
Sales 44,383,696
SIC 8732 Commercial nonphysical research
Pr Catherine Mcintyre

D-U-N-S 25-880-3642   (HQ)
INSURANCELAND INC
(*Suby of* Insuranceland Inc)
85 Ellesmere Rd Unit F10, Scarborough, ON,
M1R 4B7
(416) 449-5125
Emp Here 50   *Emp Total* 55
Sales 4,961,328
SIC 6411 Insurance agents, brokers, and ser-
vice

D-U-N-S 24-596-6866   (SL)
**INTERNATIONAL CUSTOM PRODUCTS
INC**
AEROSPACE & DEFENCE
49 Howden Rd, Scarborough, ON, M1R 3C7
(416) 285-4311
Emp Here 100   *Sales* 3,898,130
SIC 7299 Miscellaneous personal service

D-U-N-S 25-300-3388   (BR)
METRO ONTARIO INC
METRO
15 Ellesmere Rd, Scarborough, ON, M1R 4B7
(416) 391-0626
Emp Here 200
SIC 5411 Grocery stores

D-U-N-S 24-079-9825   (BR)
PATTISON, JIM INDUSTRIES LTD
PATTISON SIGN GROUP, DIV OF
555 Ellesmere Rd, Scarborough, ON, M1R
4E8
(416) 759-1111
Emp Here 130
SIC 3993 Signs and advertising specialties

D-U-N-S 24-828-0497   (SL)
PROGRESSIVE ANODIZERS INC
41 Crockford Blvd, Scarborough, ON, M1R
3B7
(416) 751-5487
Emp Here 60   *Sales* 4,012,839
SIC 3471 Plating and polishing

D-U-N-S 25-351-8583   (SL)
RAE BROTHERS LTD
60 Modern Rd, Scarborough, ON, M1R 3B6

Emp Here 50   *Sales* 13,349,760
SIC 1541 Industrial buildings and warehouses
Pr Pr David Wilkie
VP VP John Brennen

D-U-N-S 25-708-2297   (SL)
SHURWAY CONTRACTING LTD
72 Crockford Blvd, Scarborough, ON, M1R
3C3
(416) 750-4204
Emp Here 30   *Sales* 5,909,817

SIC 1541 Industrial buildings and warehouses
Pr Pr Kevin Gallant
 Paul Wright
 Dale Gallant

D-U-N-S 24-032-0775   (BR)
STAPLES CANADA INC
STAPLES THE BUSINESS DEPOT
(*Suby of* Staples, Inc.)
95 Ellesmere Rd, Scarborough, ON, M1R 4B7
(416) 444-5237
Emp Here 20
SIC 5943 Stationery stores

D-U-N-S 20-346-6974   (BR)
TORONTO DISTRICT SCHOOL BOARD
BUCHANAN PUBLIC SCHOOL
4 Bucannan Rd, Scarborough, ON, M1R 3V3
(416) 396-6100
Emp Here 45
SIC 8211 Elementary and secondary schools

D-U-N-S 20-025-0467   (BR)
TORONTO DISTRICT SCHOOL BOARD
WEXFORD PUBLIC SCHOOL
1050 Pharmacy Ave, Scarborough, ON, M1R
2H1
(416) 396-6640
Emp Here 45
SIC 8211 Elementary and secondary schools

D-U-N-S 20-688-9342   (BR)
TORONTO DISTRICT SCHOOL BOARD
WEXFORD CI
1176 Pharmacy Ave, Scarborough, ON, M1R
2H7
(416) 396-6874
Emp Here 40
SIC 8211 Elementary and secondary schools

D-U-N-S 25-932-3970   (BR)
**WOODGREEN RED DOOR FAMILY SHEL-
TER INC**
FAMILY SHELTER
(*Suby of* Woodgreen Red Door Family Shel-
ter)
1731 Lawrence Ave E, Scarborough, ON,
M1R 2X7
(416) 750-3800
Emp Here 20
SIC 8361 Residential care

Scarborough, ON M1S
York County

D-U-N-S 24-736-4318   (SL)
1061890 ONTARIO LTD
PANDA SPORTSWEAR
1361 Huntingwood Dr Unit 6, Scarborough,
ON, M1S 3J1
(416) 298-8918
Emp Here 60   *Sales* 3,720,996
SIC 2339 Women's and misses' outerwear,
nec

D-U-N-S 24-632-0469   (SL)
602390 ONTARIO LIMITED
OCEAN SEAFOOD COMPANY
81 Scottfield Dr, Scarborough, ON, M1S 5R4
(416) 740-9000
Emp Here 35   *Sales* 12,768,123
SIC 5146 Fish and seafoods
Pr Pr Patrick Lay
 Amy Lay

D-U-N-S 25-974-1585   (HQ)
ALFA LAVAL INC
101 Milner Ave, Scarborough, ON, M1S 4S6
(416) 299-6101
Emp Here 50   *Emp Total* 17,305
Sales 25,065,951
SIC 5085 Industrial supplies
Pr Pr Ashley Davis

D-U-N-S 20-150-3562   (SL)

AUTOMATIC COATING LIMITED
211 Nugget Ave, Scarborough, ON, M1S 3B1
(416) 335-7500
Emp Here 60   Sales 4,231,721
SIC 3479 Metal coating and allied services

D-U-N-S 24-387-5577   (SL)
AXISOURCE HOLDINGS INC
45 Commander Blvd Suite 1, Scarborough, ON, M1S 3Y3

Emp Here 130   Sales 22,992,828
SIC 5045 Computers, peripherals, and software
Dir Ken Mcmillen
Dir Thomas Carre
Dir Neal Cohen
Dir Ashraf Gerges
Dir Andrina Rose

D-U-N-S 25-369-4764   (BR)
BELL MEDIA INC
9 Channel Nine Crt, Scarborough, ON, M1S 4B5
(416) 332-5000
Emp Here 2,000
SIC 4833 Television broadcasting stations

D-U-N-S 24-013-2506   (BR)
CRH CANADA GROUP INC
1940 Mccowan Rd, Scarborough, ON, M1S 4K1
(416) 293-4147
Emp Here 30
SIC 3241 Cement, hydraulic

D-U-N-S 20-321-8466   (BR)
CARA OPERATIONS LIMITED
MONTANA'S COOKHOUSE
(Suby of Cara Holdings Limited)
41 Milner Ave, Scarborough, ON, M1S 3P6
(416) 321-5684
Emp Here 40
SIC 5812 Eating places

D-U-N-S 20-134-3014   (SL)
CENTURY 21 REGAL REALTY INC
4030 Sheppard Ave E Suite 2, Scarborough, ON, M1S 1S6
(416) 291-0929
Emp Here 140   Sales 18,362,450
SIC 6531 Real estate agents and managers
Pr John D'andrade
Dir Jennifer D'andrade

D-U-N-S 24-000-2951   (BR)
CINRAM CANADA OPERATIONS ULC
400 Nugget Ave, Scarborough, ON, M1S 4A4
(416) 332-9000
Emp Here 500
SIC 3652 Prerecorded records and tapes

D-U-N-S 20-056-4891   (SL)
DERMA SCIENCES CANADA INC
(Suby of Derma Sciences, Inc.)
104 Shorting Rd, Scarborough, ON, M1S 3S4
(416) 299-4003
Emp Here 115   Sales 11,162,987
SIC 2834 Pharmaceutical preparations
Ex VP Ex VP Frederic Eigner
Stephen T. Wills
Fin Ex Geoff Reid

D-U-N-S 24-597-3003   (SL)
DUVET COMFORT INC
130 Commander Blvd, Scarborough, ON, M1S 3H7
(416) 754-1455
Emp Here 75   Sales 2,918,428
SIC 2329 Men's and boy's clothing, nec

D-U-N-S 24-684-9343   (SL)
ENCHANTRESS HOSIERY CORPORATION OF CANADA LTD
ENCHANTRESS
70 Weybright Crt Unit 1, Scarborough, ON, M1S 4E4

(416) 292-3330
Emp Here 25   Sales 4,711,645
SIC 5137 Women's and children's clothing

D-U-N-S 25-092-6276   (BR)
ESTEE LAUDER COSMETICS LTD
161 Commander Blvd, Scarborough, ON, M1S 3K9
(416) 292-1111
Emp Here 200
SIC 5122 Drugs, proprietaries, and sundries

D-U-N-S 20-188-7317   (SL)
EXPLORATION PRODUCTION INC
9 Channel Nine Crt, Scarborough, ON, M1S 4B5
(416) 332-5700
Emp Here 20   Sales 1,824,018
SIC 7812 Motion picture and video production

D-U-N-S 20-770-2341   (HQ)
GRAIN PROCESS ENTERPRISES LIMITED
(Suby of Grain Process Enterprises Limited)
105 Commander Blvd, Scarborough, ON, M1S 3M7
(416) 291-3226
Emp Here 30   Emp Total 50
Sales 22,904,250
SIC 2041 Flour and other grain mill products
Pr Pr George Birinyi Sr
VP VP George Birinyi Jr
VP VP Irene Evans
Irene Birinyi

D-U-N-S 25-222-1734   (BR)
HSBC BANK CANADA
4438 Sheppard Ave E Suite 102a, Scarborough, ON, M1S 5V9
(416) 291-5717
Emp Here 29
SIC 6021 National commercial banks

D-U-N-S 20-183-0903   (SL)
HIGHLAND FEATHER MANUFACTURING INC
171 Nugget Ave, Scarborough, ON, M1S 3B1
(416) 754-7443
Emp Here 40   Sales 4,377,642
SIC 5023 Homefurnishings

D-U-N-S 20-400-2208   (SL)
HOGAN CHEVROLET BUICK GMC LIMITED
5000 Sheppard Ave E, Scarborough, ON, M1S 4L9
(416) 291-5054
Emp Here 110   Sales 55,797,500
SIC 5511 New and used car dealers
Drew Foss
Roy Foss

D-U-N-S 25-590-5010   (BR)
HONDA CANADA INC
300 Middlefield Rd, Scarborough, ON, M1S 5B1

Emp Here 180
SIC 5012 Automobiles and other motor vehicles

D-U-N-S 24-000-8529   (BR)
IMPRIMERIE SOLISCO INC
(Suby of 2856-8848 Quebec Inc)
330 Middlefield Rd, Scarborough, ON, M1S 5B1

Emp Here 60
SIC 2732 Book printing

D-U-N-S 24-346-3283   (BR)
INFORMATION COMMUNICATION SERVICES (ICS) INC
ICS COURIER SERVICES
80 Cowdray Crt, Scarborough, ON, M1S 4N1
(416) 642-2477
Emp Here 100
SIC 7389 Business services, nec

D-U-N-S 25-246-5398   (SL)
INVESTIGATORS GROUP INC, THE

2061 Mccowan Rd Suite 2, Scarborough, ON, M1S 3Y6
(416) 955-9450
Emp Here 100   Sales 3,137,310
SIC 7381 Detective and armored car services

D-U-N-S 20-709-2524   (BR)
IRON MOUNTAIN CANADA OPERATIONS ULC
ARCHIVES IRON MOUNTAIN
2388 Midland Ave, Scarborough, ON, M1S 1P8
(416) 291-7522
Emp Here 30
SIC 4226 Special warehousing and storage, nec

D-U-N-S 20-291-7873   (SL)
JERICO SPORTSWEAR LTD
120 Commander Blvd, Scarborough, ON, M1S 3H7
(416) 288-0822
Emp Here 75   Sales 4,669,485
SIC 2339 Women's and misses' outerwear, nec

D-U-N-S 25-876-3739   (BR)
LIFETOUCH CANADA INC
(Suby of Lifetouch Inc.)
140 Shorting Rd, Scarborough, ON, M1S 3S6
(416) 298-1842
Emp Here 25
SIC 7221 Photographic studios, portrait

D-U-N-S 24-415-3193   (SL)
M.S. EMPLOYMENT CONSULTANTS LTD
43 Havenview Rd, Scarborough, ON, M1S 3A4
(416) 299-1070
Emp Here 60   Sales 4,377,642
SIC 7361 Employment agencies

D-U-N-S 24-462-0258   (SL)
MAJOR D. S. SERVICES LIMITED
TECHNICAN INTERNATIONAL
55 Nugget Ave Unit 229, Scarborough, ON, M1S 3L1
(416) 292-6300
Emp Here 50   Sales 4,961,328
SIC 8711 Engineering services

D-U-N-S 20-138-3742   (HQ)
MORRISON LAMOTHE INC
(Suby of Pigott Hale & Cook Investment Limited)
5240 Finch Ave E Unit 2, Scarborough, ON, M1S 5A2
(416) 291-6762
Emp Here 50   Emp Total 2
Sales 30,318,785
SIC 2038 Frozen specialties, nec
Pr Pr John M Pigott
David Williams
Dir David C Pigott
Dir Kelly Kubrick
Allan Halter

D-U-N-S 20-172-2055   (HQ)
ONTARIO ELECTRICAL CONSTRUCTION COMPANY, LIMITED
(Suby of Ontario Electrical Construction Company, Limited)
7 Compass Crt, Scarborough, ON, M1S 5N3
(416) 363-5741
Emp Here 35   Emp Total 50
Sales 4,377,642
SIC 1731 Electrical work

D-U-N-S 20-153-0537   (BR)
ORKIN CANADA CORPORATION
ORKIN PCO SERVICES
(Suby of Rollins, Inc.)
1361 Huntingwood Dr Unit 3, Scarborough, ON, M1S 3J1
(416) 754-7339
Emp Here 70
SIC 7342 Disinfecting and pest control services

D-U-N-S 24-425-6827   (BR)
PRODUITS LABELINK INC, LES
LABELINK PRODUCTS INC
5240 Finch Ave E Unit 10, Scarborough, ON, M1S 5A3
(416) 913-0572
Emp Here 20
SIC 2759 Commercial printing, nec

D-U-N-S 24-122-5614   (BR)
ROLF C. HAGEN INC
5230 Finch Ave E Suite 8, Scarborough, ON, M1S 5A1

Emp Here 30
SIC 5149 Groceries and related products, nec

D-U-N-S 20-610-8797   (HQ)
SKF CANADA LIMITED
40 Executive Crt, Scarborough, ON, M1S 4N4
(416) 299-1220
Emp Here 90   Emp Total 500
Sales 37,768,544
SIC 5085 Industrial supplies
Pr Pr Joao Ricciarelli
Paul Winter
VP Sls Tom Karch
VP Opers Frank Bijnens

D-U-N-S 24-555-9893   (SL)
SATISFASHION INC
33 Commander Blvd Suite 1, Scarborough, ON, M1S 3E7
(416) 291-9626
Emp Here 80   Sales 5,836,856
SIC 2337 Women's and misses' suits and coats
Pr Pr Kelly Wong
Wayne Wong

D-U-N-S 24-048-2906   (BR)
SOBEYS CAPITAL INCORPORATED
FRESHCO
2361 Brimley Rd, Scarborough, ON, M1S 3L6

Emp Here 60
SIC 5411 Grocery stores

D-U-N-S 20-260-5739   (BR)
SOFINA FOODS INC
VIENNA MEAT PRODUCTS
170 Nugget Ave, Scarborough, ON, M1S 3A7
(416) 297-1062
Emp Here 100
SIC 2013 Sausages and other prepared meats

D-U-N-S 25-790-9770   (SL)
TIAN BAO TRAVEL CO INC
4002 Sheppard Ave E Unit 106a, Scarborough, ON, M1S 4R5

Emp Here 30   Sales 7,150,149
SIC 4724 Travel agencies
Pr Pr Kim Zhang

D-U-N-S 20-081-0377   (BR)
TORONTO CATHOLIC DISTRICT SCHOOL BOARD
ST. ELIZABETH SETON CATHOLIC SCHOOL
25 Havenview Rd, Scarborough, ON, M1S 3A4
(416) 393-5386
Emp Here 25
SIC 8211 Elementary and secondary schools

D-U-N-S 20-653-7636   (BR)
TORONTO CATHOLIC DISTRICT SCHOOL BOARD
MONSIGNOR FRASER COLLEGE - MIDLAND
2900 Midland Ave, Scarborough, ON, M1S 3K8
(416) 393-5532
Emp Here 35
SIC 8211 Elementary and secondary schools

D-U-N-S 24-976-1107   (BR)
TORONTO CATHOLIC DISTRICT SCHOOL BOARD
FRANCIS LIBERMANN CATHOLIC SCHOOL
4640 Finch Ave E, Scarborough, ON, M1S 4G2
(416) 393-5524
Emp Here 60
SIC 8211 Elementary and secondary schools

D-U-N-S 20-034-2264   (BR)
TORONTO CATHOLIC DISTRICT SCHOOL BOARD
ST. BARTHOLOMEW ELEMENTARY SCHOOL
51 Heather Rd, Scarborough, ON, M1S 2E2
(416) 393-5334
Emp Here 20
SIC 8211 Elementary and secondary schools

D-U-N-S 20-535-5501   (BR)
TORONTO CATHOLIC DISTRICT SCHOOL BOARD
ST. IGNATIUS OF LOYOLA CATHOLIC SCHOOL
2350 Mccowan Rd, Scarborough, ON, M1S 4B4
(416) 393-5365
Emp Here 30
SIC 8211 Elementary and secondary schools

D-U-N-S 20-034-2272   (BR)
TORONTO DISTRICT SCHOOL BOARD
SIR ALEXANDER MACKENZIE SR PUBLIC SCHOOL
33 Heather Rd, Scarborough, ON, M1S 2E2
(416) 396-6570
Emp Here 33
SIC 8211 Elementary and secondary schools

D-U-N-S 20-700-2598   (BR)
TORONTO DISTRICT SCHOOL BOARD
ANSON S TAYLOR JUNIOR PUBLIC SCHOOL
20 Placentia Blvd, Scarborough, ON, M1S 4C5
(416) 396-6035
Emp Here 20
SIC 8211 Elementary and secondary schools

D-U-N-S 20-700-2648   (BR)
TORONTO DISTRICT SCHOOL BOARD
C D FARQUHARSON JUNIOR ELEMENTARY SCHOOL
1965 Brimley Rd, Scarborough, ON, M1S 2B1
(647) 438-7124
Emp Here 27
SIC 8211 Elementary and secondary schools

D-U-N-S 20-119-8251   (BR)
TORONTO DISTRICT SCHOOL BOARD
52 Mcgriskin Rd, Scarborough, ON, M1S 5C5
(416) 396-7610
Emp Here 100
SIC 8211 Elementary and secondary schools

D-U-N-S 25-355-0347   (SL)
TRIMONT MFG. INC
TS TECH CO
115 Milner Ave Suite 2, Scarborough, ON, M1S 4L7
(416) 640-2045
Emp Here 120   *Sales* 33,923,844
SIC 2211 Broadwoven fabric mills, cotton
Pr Pr Steven Li

D-U-N-S 25-712-6128   (BR)
TWINCORP INC
PIZZA HUT
4186 Finch Ave E Suite 30, Scarborough, ON, M1S 4T5
(416) 292-1447
Emp Here 35
SIC 5812 Eating places

D-U-N-S 25-686-5403   (BR)
VIPOND INC
VIPOND FIRE PROTECTION

210 Milner Ave Suite 1, Scarborough, ON, M1S 4M7

Emp Here 23
SIC 3569 General industrial machinery, nec

D-U-N-S 20-194-3631   (BR)
WENDY'S RESTAURANTS OF CANADA INC
WENDY'S RESTAURANTS OF CANADA INC
(*Suby of* The Wendy's Company)
438 Nugget Ave, Scarborough, ON, M1S 4A4
(416) 754-2196
Emp Here 25
SIC 5812 Eating places

D-U-N-S 25-059-2813   (BR)
WINNERS MERCHANTS INTERNATIONAL L.P.
WINNERS
(*Suby of* The TJX Companies Inc)
47 Milner Ave, Scarborough, ON, M1S 3P6
(416) 754-1215
Emp Here 40
SIC 5651 Family clothing stores

D-U-N-S 24-010-3697   (HQ)
YAMAHA CANADA MUSIC LTD
135 Milner Ave, Scarborough, ON, M1S 3R1
(416) 298-1311
Emp Here 80   *Emp Total* 20,175
Sales 10,944,105
SIC 5099 Durable goods, nec
Pr Pr Yosuke Mikami
Dir John R Finley
Yoshihiro Doi

D-U-N-S 25-360-1850   (BR)
YEE HONG CENTRE FOR GERIATRIC CARE
YEE HONG CENTRE SCARBOROUGH FINCH
60 Scottfield Dr Suite 428, Scarborough, ON, M1S 5T7
(416) 321-3000
Emp Here 200
SIC 8059 Nursing and personal care, nec

Scarborough, ON M1T
York County

D-U-N-S 20-031-8996   (SL)
AGINCOURT AUTOHAUS INC
3450 Sheppard Ave E, Scarborough, ON, M1T 3K4

Emp Here 78   *Sales* 39,565,500
SIC 5511 New and used car dealers
Pr Pr Ken Laird
M John Fingret

D-U-N-S 25-140-4406   (BR)
ARBOR MEMORIAL SERVICES INC
HIGHLAND FUNERAL HOME
3280 Sheppard Ave E, Scarborough, ON, M1T 3K3
(416) 773-0933
Emp Here 20
SIC 7261 Funeral service and crematories

D-U-N-S 20-301-2757   (BR)
BANK OF MONTREAL
BMO
2350 Kennedy Rd, Scarborough, ON, M1T 3H1
(416) 291-7987
Emp Here 20
SIC 6021 National commercial banks

D-U-N-S 24-972-3313   (BR)
BANQUE TORONTO-DOMINION, LA
TORONTO-DOMINION BANK, THE
(*Suby of* Toronto-Dominion Bank, The)
3477 Sheppard Ave E, Scarborough, ON, M1T 3K6

(416) 291-9566
Emp Here 22
SIC 6021 National commercial banks

D-U-N-S 24-173-4883   (BR)
CARA OPERATIONS LIMITED
SWISS CHALET ROTISSERIE GRILL
(*Suby of* Cara Holdings Limited)
2555 Victoria Park Ave Suite 19, Scarborough, ON, M1T 1A3
(416) 494-9693
Emp Here 80
SIC 5812 Eating places

D-U-N-S 20-699-8721   (BR)
DELTA HOTELS LIMITED
DELTA TORONTO EAST
2035 Kennedy Rd, Scarborough, ON, M1T 3G2
(416) 299-1500
Emp Here 50
SIC 8741 Management services

D-U-N-S 20-074-0301   (BR)
HOLLISWEALTH INC
DUNDEE SECURITY
2075 Kennedy Rd Suite 500, Scarborough, ON, M1T 3V3
(416) 292-0869
Emp Here 75
SIC 8742 Management consulting services

D-U-N-S 20-650-7613   (BR)
JCC RESTAURANT SERVICES LIMITED
MCDONALD'S
3305 Sheppard Ave E, Scarborough, ON, M1T 3K2
(416) 491-7751
Emp Here 60
SIC 5812 Eating places

D-U-N-S 24-228-4326   (BR)
LONDON LIFE INSURANCE COMPANY
2075 Kennedy Rd Suite 300, Scarborough, ON, M1T 3V3
(416) 291-0451
Emp Here 100
SIC 6411 Insurance agents, brokers, and service

D-U-N-S 25-310-8815   (BR)
MCDONALD'S RESTAURANTS OF CANADA LIMITED
MCDONALD'S
(*Suby of* McDonald's Corporation)
3850 Sheppard Ave E Suite 222, Scarborough, ON, M1T 3L4
(416) 754-4337
Emp Here 45
SIC 5812 Eating places

D-U-N-S 25-137-5366   (SL)
NURSING & HOMEMAKERS INC
NHI
2347 Kennedy Rd Suite 204, Scarborough, ON, M1T 3T8
(416) 754-0700
Emp Here 350   *Sales* 20,448,539
SIC 8399 Social services, nec
Pr Delores Lawrence

D-U-N-S 25-172-5487   (BR)
RED LOBSTER HOSPITALITY LLC
RED LOBSTER RESTAURANTS
(*Suby of* Red Lobster Seafood Co., LLC)
3252 Sheppard Ave E, Scarborough, ON, M1T 3K3
(416) 491-2507
Emp Here 90
SIC 5812 Eating places

D-U-N-S 20-536-6250   (BR)
ROYAL BANK OF CANADA
RBC LIFE INSURANCE
(*Suby of* Royal Bank Of Canada)
2075 Kennedy Rd Suite 600, Scarborough, ON, M1T 3V3
(416) 292-6466
Emp Here 20

SIC 6021 National commercial banks

D-U-N-S 25-316-8645   (BR)
SUN LIFE ASSURANCE COMPANY OF CANADA
SUN LIFE FINANCIAL
2075 Kennedy Rd Suite 1300, Scarborough, ON, M1T 3V3
(416) 412-0401
Emp Here 50
SIC 6311 Life insurance

D-U-N-S 20-711-0953   (BR)
TORONTO CATHOLIC DISTRICT SCHOOL BOARD
HOLY SPIRIT CATHOLIC SCHOOL
3530 Sheppard Ave E, Scarborough, ON, M1T 3K7
(416) 393-5282
Emp Here 50
SIC 8211 Elementary and secondary schools

D-U-N-S 20-079-2864   (BR)
TORONTO DISTRICT SCHOOL BOARD
HIGHLAND HEIGHTS JR PUBLIC SCHOOL
35 Glendower Circt, Scarborough, ON, M1T 2Z3
(416) 396-6335
Emp Here 40
SIC 8211 Elementary and secondary schools

D-U-N-S 20-711-3189   (BR)
TORONTO DISTRICT SCHOOL BOARD
BRIDLEWOOD JUNIOR PUBLIC SCHOOL
60 Bridlewood Blvd, Scarborough, ON, M1T 1P7
(416) 396-6080
Emp Here 20
SIC 8211 Elementary and secondary schools

D-U-N-S 20-025-5862   (BR)
TORONTO DISTRICT SCHOOL BOARD
STEPHEN LEACOCK COLLEGIATE INSTITUTE
2450 Birchmount Rd, Scarborough, ON, M1T 2M5
(416) 396-8000
Emp Here 100
SIC 8211 Elementary and secondary schools

D-U-N-S 20-079-2880   (BR)
TORONTO DISTRICT SCHOOL BOARD
LYNNGATE JUNIOR PUBLIC SCHOOL
129 Cass Ave, Scarborough, ON, M1T 2B5
(416) 396-6425
Emp Here 20
SIC 8211 Elementary and secondary schools

D-U-N-S 20-711-3387   (BR)
TORONTO DISTRICT SCHOOL BOARD
VRADENBURG JUNIOR PUBLIC SCHOOL
50 Vradenberg Dr, Scarborough, ON, M1T 1M6
(416) 396-6615
Emp Here 50
SIC 8211 Elementary and secondary schools

D-U-N-S 25-297-7772   (BR)
WAL-MART CANADA CORP
WALMART
3850 Sheppard Ave E Suite 3000, Scarborough, ON, M1T 3L4
(416) 291-4100
Emp Here 420
SIC 5311 Department stores

Scarborough, ON M1V
York County

D-U-N-S 25-825-3301   (BR)
ALL-WELD COMPANY LIMITED
14 Passmore Ave, Scarborough, ON, M1V 2R6
(416) 293-3638
Emp Here 80
SIC 7539 Automotive repair shops, nec

D-U-N-S 25-117-9024   (SL)
ARSENAL CLEANING SERVICES LTD
80 Nashdene Rd Unit 7, Scarborough, ON,
M1V 5E4
(416) 321-8777
Emp Here 110   *Sales* 3,210,271
SIC 7349 Building maintenance services, nec

D-U-N-S 24-639-7215   (BR)
ATLANTIC PACKAGING PRODUCTS LTD
ADD INK
118 Tiffield Rd, Scarborough, ON, M1V 5N2
(416) 421-3636
Emp Here 75
SIC 2653 Corrugated and solid fiber boxes

D-U-N-S 24-207-1004   (BR)
ATLANTIC PACKAGING PRODUCTS LTD
55 Milliken Blvd, Scarborough, ON, M1V 1V3
(416) 298-5508
Emp Here 100
SIC 2653 Corrugated and solid fiber boxes

D-U-N-S 24-098-2822   (BR)
ATLANTIC PACKAGING PRODUCTS LTD
45 Milliken Blvd, Scarborough, ON, M1V 1V3
(416) 298-5566
Emp Here 150
SIC 2676 Sanitary paper products

D-U-N-S 25-296-3962   (BR)
BANK OF NOVA SCOTIA, THE
SCOTIABANK
250 Alton Towers Cir Suite 1, Scarborough,
ON, M1V 3Z4
(416) 297-6500
Emp Here 25
SIC 6021 National commercial banks

D-U-N-S 20-937-5393   (SL)
CARDINAL CARETAKERS CO LIMITED
80 Dynamic Dr, Scarborough, ON, M1V 2V1
(416) 292-7701
Emp Here 80   *Sales* 2,334,742
SIC 7349 Building maintenance services, nec

D-U-N-S 24-688-7517   (SL)
CESARONI CONTRACTING INC
3015 Kennedy Rd Suite 101, Scarborough,
ON, M1V 1E7
(416) 292-2225
Emp Here 50   *Sales* 4,231,721
SIC 1742 Plastering, drywall, and insulation

D-U-N-S 20-190-6018   (BR)
CONEX BUSINESS SYSTEMS INC
50 Tiffield Rd, Scarborough, ON, M1V 5B7
(416) 321-8392
Emp Here 20
SIC 5044 Office equipment

D-U-N-S 20-034-2405   (BR)
**CORPORATION OF THE CITY OF
TORONTO**
*L'AMOREAUX COMMUNITY RECREATION
CENTRE*
2000 Mcnicoll Ave, Scarborough, ON, M1V
5E9
(416) 396-4510
Emp Here 50
SIC 8322 Individual and family services

D-U-N-S 20-650-5021   (HQ)
D. CRUPI & SONS LIMITED
CRUPI GROUP, THE
(*Suby of* Crupi Holdings Limited)
85 Passmore Ave, Scarborough, ON, M1V
4S9
(416) 291-1986
Emp Here 120   *Emp Total* 50
Sales 41,580,048
SIC 1611 Highway and street construction
Pr Pr Cosimo Crupi

D-U-N-S 24-576-0418   (BR)
DE LUXE PRODUITS DE PAPIER INC
DE LUXE PAPER PRODUCTS
35 Dynamic Dr, Scarborough, ON, M1V 2W2

(416) 754-4633
Emp Here 30
SIC 2621 Paper mills

D-U-N-S 25-977-6586   (BR)
ECI TECHNOLOGY GROUP INC
115 Select Ave Suite 1, Scarborough, ON,
M1V 4A5
(416) 754-7539
Emp Here 21
SIC 3679 Electronic components, nec

D-U-N-S 24-784-0119   (SL)
FLAVORCHEM INTERNATIONAL INC
145 Dynamic Dr Suite 100, Scarborough, ON,
M1V 5L8
(416) 321-2124
Emp Here 28   *Sales* 5,782,650
SIC 2869 Industrial organic chemicals, nec
Pr Pr Louis Gorassi

D-U-N-S 24-308-9591   (BR)
FLEXTRONICS AUTOMOTIVE INC
85 Select Ave, Scarborough, ON, M1V 4A9

Emp Here 30
SIC 3679 Electronic components, nec

D-U-N-S 25-330-5775   (HQ)
GROUPE SEB CANADA INC
345 Passmore Ave, Scarborough, ON, M1V
3N8
(416) 297-4131
Emp Here 47   *Emp Total* 2
Sales 19,977,375
SIC 5064 Electrical appliances, television and
radio
Pr Pr Marc Turgeon

D-U-N-S 25-270-3186   (BR)
HSBC BANK CANADA
15 Milliken Blvd, Scarborough, ON, M1V 1V3
(416) 321-8017
Emp Here 40
SIC 6021 National commercial banks

D-U-N-S 25-404-1304   (SL)
**HIGH LIFE HEATING, AIR CONDITIONING &
SECURITY INC**
102 Passmore Ave, Scarborough, ON, M1V
4S9
(416) 298-2987
Emp Here 50   *Sales* 6,087,000
SIC 1711 Plumbing, heating, air-conditioning
Pr Pr Stephen Yeung
 Rosanna Yeung

D-U-N-S 20-152-2380   (SL)
KINEDYNE CANADA LIMITED
10 Maybrook Dr, Scarborough, ON, M1V 4B6
(416) 291-7168
Emp Here 40   *Sales* 1,605,135
SIC 2241 Narrow fabric mills

D-U-N-S 20-707-8903   (BR)
LIFTOW LIMITED
145 Select Ave Unit 8, Scarborough, ON, M1V
5M8
(416) 745-9770
Emp Here 25
SIC 5084 Industrial machinery and equipment

D-U-N-S 24-727-5563   (BR)
LIFTOW LIMITED
145 Select Ave Unit 8, Scarborough, ON, M1V
5M8
(416) 298-7119
Emp Here 25
SIC 5084 Industrial machinery and equipment

D-U-N-S 24-858-2210   (BR)
LOWE'S COMPANIES CANADA, ULC
6005 Steeles Ave E, Scarborough, ON, M1V
5P7
(416) 940-4827
Emp Here 150
SIC 5211 Lumber and other building materials

D-U-N-S 25-318-1978   (BR)
MCDONALD'S RESTAURANTS OF

CANADA LIMITED
MCDONALD'S # 8030
(*Suby of* McDonald's Corporation)
1571 Sandhurst Cir Suite 102, Scarborough,
ON, M1V 1V2
(416) 292-6706
Emp Here 50
SIC 5812 Eating places

D-U-N-S 24-845-1908   (BR)
MIRTREN CONTRACTORS LIMITED
MIRTREN CONSTRUCTION
50 Nashdene Rd Suite 110, Scarborough, ON,
M1V 5J2
(416) 292-9393
Emp Here 20
SIC 1542 Nonresidential construction, nec

D-U-N-S 20-990-6846   (BR)
MON SHEONG FOUNDATION
(*Suby of* Mon Sheong Foundation)
2030 Mcnicoll Ave, Scarborough, ON, M1V
5P4
(416) 291-3898
Emp Here 160
SIC 8051 Skilled nursing care facilities

D-U-N-S 20-859-9139   (BR)
PACIFIC LINK COMMUNICATIONS INC
BELL WORLD
1571 Sandhurst Cir, Scarborough, ON, M1V
1V2
(416) 298-9800
Emp Here 25
SIC 5999 Miscellaneous retail stores, nec

D-U-N-S 24-478-9855   (BR)
PUROLATOR INC.
PUROLATOR INC
90 Silver Star Blvd, Scarborough, ON, M1V
4V8
(416) 298-6881
Emp Here 300
SIC 4731 Freight transportation arrangement

D-U-N-S 24-338-0453   (BR)
RJM56 INVESTMENTS INC
RJ MCCARTHY UNIFORMS
12 Trojan Gate, Scarborough, ON, M1V 3B8
(416) 492-3311
Emp Here 30
SIC 5699 Miscellaneous apparel and acces-
sory stores

D-U-N-S 20-580-6057   (BR)
ROYAL BANK OF CANADA
RBC
(*Suby of* Royal Bank Of Canada)
4751 Steeles Ave E, Scarborough, ON, M1V
4S5
(416) 412-6900
Emp Here 20
SIC 6021 National commercial banks

D-U-N-S 20-355-8007   (SL)
STAR WALK BUFFET INC
648 Silver Star Blvd, Scarborough, ON, M1V
5N1
(416) 299-0928
Emp Here 50   *Sales* 1,532,175
SIC 5812 Eating places

D-U-N-S 20-108-3107   (BR)
TEKNION LIMITED
ERGOTECH
851 Middlefield Rd, Scarborough, ON, M1V
2R2
(416) 291-6530
Emp Here 70
SIC 2522 Office furniture, except wood

D-U-N-S 24-851-0146   (BR)
THOMAS & BETTS, LIMITEE
AMERACE
120 Nashdene Rd, Scarborough, ON, M1V
2W3
(416) 292-9782
Emp Here 57
SIC 5063 Electrical apparatus and equipment

D-U-N-S 25-092-1194   (HQ)
**THYSSENKRUPP ELEVATOR (CANADA)
LIMITED**
THYSSENKRUPP ELEVATOR
410 Passmore Ave Unit 1, Scarborough, ON,
M1V 5C3
(416) 291-2000
Emp Here 150   *Emp Total* 155,584
Sales 123,522,465
SIC 1796 Installing building equipment
Pr Ryan Wilson
Dir Richard T. Hussey

D-U-N-S 24-688-6899   (SL)
TIP TOP BINDERY LTD
335 Passmore Ave, Scarborough, ON, M1V
4B5
(416) 609-3281
Emp Here 500   *Sales* 23,558,225
SIC 2789 Bookbinding and related work
Pr Pr Cal Johnson
Treas Dean Johnson

D-U-N-S 20-034-2363   (BR)
**TORONTO CATHOLIC DISTRICT SCHOOL
BOARD**
PRINCE OF PEACE CATHOLIC SCHOOL
255 Alton Towers Cir, Scarborough, ON, M1V
4E7
(416) 393-5416
Emp Here 25
SIC 8211 Elementary and secondary schools

D-U-N-S 24-243-6496   (BR)
**TORONTO CATHOLIC DISTRICT SCHOOL
BOARD**
MARY WARD CATHOLIC HIGH SCHOOL
3200 Kennedy Rd, Scarborough, ON, M1V
3S8
(416) 393-5544
Emp Here 100
SIC 8211 Elementary and secondary schools

D-U-N-S 20-526-8019   (BR)
**TORONTO CATHOLIC DISTRICT SCHOOL
BOARD**
*ST. MARGUERITE BOURGEOYS CATHOLIC
SCHOOL*
75 Alexmuir Blvd, Scarborough, ON, M1V 1H6
(416) 393-5381
Emp Here 20
SIC 8211 Elementary and secondary schools

D-U-N-S 20-077-8558   (BR)
**TORONTO CATHOLIC DISTRICT SCHOOL
BOARD**
ST. SYLVESTER CATHOLIC SCHOOL
260 Silver Springs Blvd, Scarborough, ON,
M1V 1S4
(416) 393-5373
Emp Here 20
SIC 8211 Elementary and secondary schools

D-U-N-S 20-084-0838   (BR)
**TORONTO CATHOLIC DISTRICT SCHOOL
BOARD**
ST. RENE GOUPIL ELEMENTARY SCHOOL
44 Port Royal Trail, Scarborough, ON, M1V
2G8
(416) 393-5408
Emp Here 20
SIC 8211 Elementary and secondary schools

D-U-N-S 20-025-9724   (BR)
TORONTO DISTRICT SCHOOL BOARD
KENNEDY PUBLIC SCHOOL
20 Elmfield Cres, Scarborough, ON, M1V 2Y6
(416) 396-6410
Emp Here 35
SIC 8211 Elementary and secondary schools

D-U-N-S 20-711-3353   (BR)
TORONTO DISTRICT SCHOOL BOARD
SILVER SPRINGS PS
222 Silver Springs Blvd, Scarborough, ON,
M1V 1S4
(416) 396-6565
Emp Here 50

SIC 8211 Elementary and secondary schools

D-U-N-S 20-100-1166 (BR)
TORONTO DISTRICT SCHOOL BOARD
ALBERT CAMPBELL C.I.
1550 Sandhurst Cir, Scarborough, ON, M1V 1S6
(416) 396-6684
Emp Here 120
SIC 8211 Elementary and secondary schools

D-U-N-S 20-025-2695 (BR)
TORONTO DISTRICT SCHOOL BOARD
ALEXMUIR JUNIOR ELEMENTARY SCHOOL
95 Alexmuir Blvd, Scarborough, ON, M1V 1H6
(416) 396-6025
Emp Here 37
SIC 8211 Elementary and secondary schools

D-U-N-S 20-700-2705 (BR)
TORONTO DISTRICT SCHOOL BOARD
BANTING & BEST PUBLIC SCHOOL
380 Goldhawk Trail, Scarborough, ON, M1V 4E7
(416) 396-5800
Emp Here 20
SIC 8211 Elementary and secondary schools

D-U-N-S 20-025-3396 (BR)
TORONTO DISTRICT SCHOOL BOARD
PORT ROYAL PUBLIC SCHOOL
408 Port Royal Trail, Scarborough, ON, M1V 4R1
(416) 396-5595
Emp Here 30
SIC 8211 Elementary and secondary schools

D-U-N-S 20-524-5087 (HQ)
TRENCH LIMITED
TRENCH CANADA COIL PRODUCTS
71 Maybrook Dr, Scarborough, ON, M1V 4B6
(416) 298-8108
Emp Here 300   *Emp Total* 351,000
Sales 219,767,879
SIC 3699 Electrical equipment and supplies, nec
Marco Michel
Norman Hyde-Whipp

D-U-N-S 24-765-3061 (BR)
WAL-MART CANADA CORP
5995 Steeles Ave E Suite Side, Scarborough, ON, M1V 5P7
(416) 297-5330
Emp Here 200
SIC 5311 Department stores

D-U-N-S 24-964-4253 (SL)
WRIGHT, GEORGE A. & SON (TORONTO) LIMITED
21 State Crown Blvd, Scarborough, ON, M1V 4B1
(416) 261-6499
Emp Here 55   *Sales* 4,012,839
SIC 3599 Industrial machinery, nec

Scarborough, ON M1W
York County

D-U-N-S 25-306-9447 (BR)
BANK OF NOVA SCOTIA, THE
SCOTIABANK
2900 Warden Ave, Scarborough, ON, M1W 2S8
(416) 497-7012
Emp Here 20
SIC 6021 National commercial banks

D-U-N-S 20-333-2395 (BR)
BANK OF MONTREAL
4100 Gordon Baker Rd, Scarborough, ON, M1W 3E8
(416) 508-7618
Emp Here 3,000
SIC 8731 Commercial physical research

D-U-N-S 25-406-9115 (BR)
BANK OF MONTREAL
BANK OF MONTREAL INSTITUTE FOR LEARNING
3550 Pharmacy Ave, Scarborough, ON, M1W 3Z3
(416) 490-4300
Emp Here 100
SIC 6021 National commercial banks

D-U-N-S 25-703-7721 (BR)
EXTENDICARE INC
TENDERCARE NURSING HOME
1020 Mcnicoll Ave Suite 547, Scarborough, ON, M1W 2J6
(416) 499-2020
Emp Here 300
SIC 8051 Skilled nursing care facilities

D-U-N-S 25-310-7957 (BR)
HOOPER-HOLMES CANADA LIMITED
PORTAMEDIC
1059 Mcnicoll Ave, Scarborough, ON, M1W 3W6
(416) 493-2800
Emp Here 100
SIC 6411 Insurance agents, brokers, and service

D-U-N-S 20-556-0043 (BR)
JCC RESTAURANT SERVICES LIMITED
MCDONALD'S
2936 Finch Ave E, Scarborough, ON, M1W 2T4
(416) 497-2166
Emp Here 40
SIC 5812 Eating places

D-U-N-S 24-752-9084 (SL)
KAY CEE KAY RESTAURANTS LIMITED
DEVONSLEIGH PLACE RESTAURANT, THE
4125 Steeles Ave E, Scarborough, ON, M1W 3T4

Emp Here 50   *Sales* 1,532,175
SIC 5812 Eating places

D-U-N-S 25-300-2810 (BR)
METRO ONTARIO INC
METRO
2900 Warden Ave, Scarborough, ON, M1W 2S8
(416) 497-6734
Emp Here 120
SIC 5411 Grocery stores

D-U-N-S 24-307-3939 (HQ)
MUSKOKA WOODS YOUTH CAMP INC
(*Suby of* Boddy, John Albert Youth Foundation)
20 Bamburgh Cir Suite 200, Scarborough, ON, M1W 3Y5
(416) 495-6960
Emp Here 25   *Emp Total* 50
Sales 3,866,917
SIC 7032 Sporting and recreational camps

D-U-N-S 20-699-6485 (BR)
TENDERCARE NURSING HOMES LIMITED
MOLL BERCZY HAUS
1020 Mcnicoll Ave Suite 436, Scarborough, ON, M1W 2J6
(416) 497-3639
Emp Here 275
SIC 8051 Skilled nursing care facilities

D-U-N-S 20-698-6809 (BR)
TORONTO CATHOLIC DISTRICT SCHOOL BOARD
EPIPHANY OF OUR LORD CATHOLIC ACADEMY
3150 Pharmacy Ave, Scarborough, ON, M1W 3J5
(416) 393-5378
Emp Here 50
SIC 8211 Elementary and secondary schools

D-U-N-S 20-711-1613 (BR)
TORONTO CATHOLIC DISTRICT SCHOOL BOARD
ST. HENRY CATHOLIC SCHOOL
100 Bamburgh Cir, Scarborough, ON, M1W 3R3
(416) 393-5395
Emp Here 50
SIC 8211 Elementary and secondary schools

D-U-N-S 20-807-4281 (BR)
TORONTO CATHOLIC DISTRICT SCHOOL BOARD
SPECIAL SERVICES - EAST REGION
100 Fundy Bay Blvd, Scarborough, ON, M1W 3G1
(416) 393-5404
Emp Here 60
SIC 8211 Elementary and secondary schools

D-U-N-S 24-676-2731 (BR)
TORONTO DISTRICT SCHOOL BOARD
FAIRGLEN JUNIOR PUBLIC SCHOOL
2200 Pharmacy Ave, Scarborough, ON, M1W 1H8
(416) 396-6235
Emp Here 25
SIC 8211 Elementary and secondary schools

D-U-N-S 20-913-5677 (BR)
TORONTO DISTRICT SCHOOL BOARD
BROOKMILL BOULEVARD JUNIOR PUBLIC SCHOOL
25 Brookmill Blvd, Scarborough, ON, M1W 2L5
(416) 396-6090
Emp Here 35
SIC 8211 Elementary and secondary schools

D-U-N-S 20-025-1077 (BR)
TORONTO DISTRICT SCHOOL BOARD
TIMOTHY EATON BTI
1251 Bridletowne Cir, Scarborough, ON, M1W 1S7

Emp Here 85
SIC 8211 Elementary and secondary schools

D-U-N-S 20-698-7880 (BR)
TORONTO DISTRICT SCHOOL BOARD
NORTH BRIDLEWOOD JR PS
50 Collingsbrook Blvd, Scarborough, ON, M1W 1L7
(416) 396-6500
Emp Here 25
SIC 8211 Elementary and secondary schools

D-U-N-S 20-653-8394 (BR)
TORONTO DISTRICT SCHOOL BOARD
DAVID LEWIS ELEMENTARY SCHOOL
130 Fundy Bay Blvd, Scarborough, ON, M1W 3G1
(416) 396-5810
Emp Here 20
SIC 8211 Elementary and secondary schools

D-U-N-S 20-158-7524 (HQ)
TRANE CANADA ULC
4051 Gordon Baker Rd, Scarborough, ON, M1W 2P3
(416) 499-3600
Emp Here 120   *Emp Total* 500
Sales 63,475,809
SIC 3585 Refrigeration and heating equipment
Dir Vic Smith

D-U-N-S 24-985-9547 (SL)
TRIPLEWELL ENTERPRISES LTD
3440 Pharmacy Ave Unit 9, Scarborough, ON, M1W 2P8
(416) 498-5637
Emp Here 450   *Sales* 95,457,928
SIC 2399 Fabricated textile products, nec
Pr Pr Lincoln Wong

Scarborough, ON M1X
York County

BOARD

D-U-N-S 24-964-3396 (HQ)
BERENDSEN FLUID POWER LTD
35a Ironside Cres Suite 1, Scarborough, ON, M1X 1G5
(416) 335-5557
Emp Here 45   *Emp Total* 200
Sales 47,116,450
SIC 5084 Industrial machinery and equipment
Anthony Foster
Ex VP Valerie Lister

D-U-N-S 24-383-8732 (BR)
BLACK & MCDONALD LIMITED
31 Pullman Crt, Scarborough, ON, M1X 1E4
(416) 298-9977
Emp Here 500
SIC 1711 Plumbing, heating, air-conditioning

D-U-N-S 25-370-8085 (BR)
BLACK & MCDONALD LIMITED
BLACK & MCDONALD SHEET METAL AND CUSTOM FABRICATION
35 Pullman Crt, Scarborough, ON, M1X 1E4
(416) 291-8200
Emp Here 200
SIC 1711 Plumbing, heating, air-conditioning

D-U-N-S 24-727-1554 (SL)
DURAPAINT INDUSTRIES LIMITED
247 Finchdene Sq Suite 1, Scarborough, ON, M1X 1B9
(416) 754-3664
Emp Here 65   *Sales* 4,377,642
SIC 3471 Plating and polishing

D-U-N-S 24-948-0708 (SL)
G & P MILLWORK LTD
40 Pullman Crt, Scarborough, ON, M1X 1E4
(416) 298-4204
Emp Here 50   *Sales* 4,851,006
SIC 2431 Millwork

D-U-N-S 24-361-6328 (HQ)
NUTRALAB CANADA CORP
980 Tapscott Rd, Scarborough, ON, M1X 1C3
(905) 752-1823
Emp Here 50   *Emp Total* 5
Sales 5,836,856
SIC 2834 Pharmaceutical preparations
Pr Pr Peter Ou

D-U-N-S 20-010-1868 (BR)
ORKIN CANADA CORPORATION
ORKIN PCO SERVICES
(*Suby of* Rollins, Inc.)
720 Tapscott Rd Unit 2, Scarborough, ON, M1X 1C6
(416) 363-8821
Emp Here 35
SIC 7342 Disinfecting and pest control services

D-U-N-S 24-365-5748 (SL)
SSAB CENTRAL INC
1051 Tapscott Rd, Scarborough, ON, M1X 1A1
(416) 321-4949
Emp Here 34   *Sales* 4,417,880
SIC 3312 Blast furnaces and steel mills

D-U-N-S 20-596-3945 (HQ)
SCHINDLER ELEVATOR CORPORATION
3640a Mcnicoll Ave Suite A, Scarborough, ON, M1X 1G5
(416) 332-8280
Emp Here 100   *Emp Total* 58,271
Sales 53,794,187
SIC 1796 Installing building equipment
Pr Pr Jeff Coles
VP Fin Thomas Koch

D-U-N-S 24-820-0862 (BR)
STERICYCLE, ULC
25 Ironside Cres, Scarborough, ON, M1X 1G5

Emp Here 60
SIC 4953 Refuse systems

D-U-N-S 24-006-5920   (HQ)
TFI FOODS LTD
2900 Markham Rd, Scarborough, ON, M1X
1E6
(416) 299-7575
Emp Here 55   *Emp Total* 97
Sales 34,656,333
SIC 5146 Fish and seafoods
Pr Pr David Lam
Dir Sherman Lam

D-U-N-S 24-676-5114   (BR)
TORONTO DISTRICT SCHOOL BOARD
THOMAS L WELLS PUBLIC SCHOOL
69 Nightstar Rd, Scarborough, ON, M1X 1V6
(416) 396-3040
Emp Here 70
SIC 8211 Elementary and secondary schools

D-U-N-S 24-676-5122   (BR)
TORONTO DISTRICT SCHOOL BOARD
BROOKSIDE PUBLIC SCHOOL
75 Oasis Blvd, Scarborough, ON, M1X 0A3
(416) 396-5757
Emp Here 25
SIC 8211 Elementary and secondary schools

D-U-N-S 20-851-7359   (HQ)
TRANSCENDIA CANADA LTD
(*Suby of* Transcendia, Inc.)
333 Finchdene Sq, Scarborough, ON, M1X
1B9
(416) 292-6000
Emp Here 22   *Emp Total* 823
Sales 5,977,132
SIC 2671 Paper; coated and laminated packaging
Pr Pr Andy Brewer
Fin Mgr Lori Joyce

D-U-N-S 25-386-6149   (HQ)
VIVA MEDIA PACKAGING (CANADA) LTD
1663 Neilson Rd Suite 13, Scarborough, ON,
M1X 1T1
(416) 321-0622
Emp Here 50   *Emp Total* 500
Sales 118,392,150
SIC 3089 Plastics products, nec
Dir May Chan
Pr Pr Ky Choi

Scarborough, ON M4E
York County

D-U-N-S 25-486-7112   (BR)
**TORONTO CATHOLIC DISTRICT SCHOOL
BOARD**
NEIL MCNEIL HIGH SCHOOL
127 Victoria Park Ave, Scarborough, ON, M4E
3S2
(416) 393-5502
Emp Here 38
SIC 8211 Elementary and secondary schools

Schomberg, ON L0G
York County

D-U-N-S 24-418-5620   (BR)
SILANI SWEET CHEESE LIMITED
(*Suby of* Silani Sweet Cheese Limited)
Gd, Schomberg, ON, L0G 1T0
(416) 324-3290
Emp Here 185
SIC 2022 Cheese; natural and processed

D-U-N-S 25-364-3076   (BR)
YMCA OF GREATER TORONTO
YMCA CEDAR GLEN
13300 11th Conc, Schomberg, ON, L0G 1T0
(905) 859-9622
Emp Here 20
SIC 7011 Hotels and motels

D-U-N-S 20-653-4880   (BR)
**YORK CATHOLIC DISTRICT SCHOOL
BOARD**
*ST PATRICK CATHOLIC ELEMENTARY
SCHOOL*
51 Western Ave, Schomberg, ON, L0G 1T0
(905) 939-7753
Emp Here 21
SIC 8211 Elementary and secondary schools

Schreiber, ON P0T
Thunder Bay County

D-U-N-S 20-589-7551   (BR)
CANADIAN PACIFIC RAILWAY COMPANY
CPR
219 Brunswick St, Schreiber, ON, P0T 2S0
(807) 824-2054
Emp Here 20
SIC 4011 Railroads, line-haul operating

Schumacher, ON P0N
Cochrane County

D-U-N-S 25-238-9879   (BR)
**DISTRICT SCHOOL BOARD ONTARIO
NORTH EAST**
SCHUMACHER PUBLIC SCHOOL
64 Croatia Ave, Schumacher, ON, P0N 1G0
(705) 360-1780
Emp Here 32
SIC 8211 Elementary and secondary schools

D-U-N-S 20-710-4519   (BR)
**DISTRICT SCHOOL BOARD ONTARIO
NORTH EAST**
*KIRKLAND LAKE COLLEGIATE VOCA-
TIONAL INSTITUTE*
153 Croatia Ave, Schumacher, ON, P0N 1G0
(705) 360-1151
Emp Here 50
SIC 8211 Elementary and secondary schools

D-U-N-S 20-037-8698   (BR)
EXTENDICARE (CANADA) INC
EXTENDICARE TIMMINS
15 Hollinger Lane, Schumacher, ON, P0N
1G0
(705) 360-1913
Emp Here 147
SIC 8059 Nursing and personal care, nec

Seaforth, ON N0K
Huron County

D-U-N-S 20-518-1287   (SL)
450252 ONTARIO LTD
SEAFORTH FOOD MARKET
95 Main St S, Seaforth, ON, N0K 1W0
(519) 527-1631
Emp Here 50   *Sales* 8,343,600
SIC 5411 Grocery stores
Pr Pr Stephen Delchiaro
Barbara Delchiaro

D-U-N-S 20-710-6977   (BR)
**AVON MAITLAND DISTRICT SCHOOL
BOARD**
SEAFORTH PUBLIC SCHOOL
58 Chalk St N, Seaforth, ON, N0K 1W0
(519) 527-0790
Emp Here 40
SIC 8211 Elementary and secondary schools

D-U-N-S 24-333-2256   (SL)
E.D. SMITH & SONS, LP
151 Main St S, Seaforth, ON, N0K 1W0

Emp Here 185   *Sales* 8,763,660

SIC 2035 Pickles, sauces, and salad dressings
Ex Dir Mike Barr

D-U-N-S 25-228-1704   (BR)
**HURON PERTH CATHOLIC DISTRICT
SCHOOL BOARD**
ST JAMES SCHOOL
62 Chalk St, Seaforth, ON, N0K 1W0
(519) 527-0321
Emp Here 20
SIC 8211 Elementary and secondary schools

D-U-N-S 25-460-7948   (SL)
**PROVINCIAL NURSING HOME LIMITED
PARTNERSHIP**
*SEAFORTH MANOR RETIREMENT LIVING
AND LONG TERM CARE*
100 James St, Seaforth, ON, N0K 1W0
(519) 527-0030
Emp Here 75   *Sales* 4,071,380
SIC 8051 Skilled nursing care facilities

D-U-N-S 20-876-1015   (SL)
SEAFORTH COMMUNITY HOSPITAL
*A MEMBER OF HURON PERTH HEALTH-
CARE ALLIANCE*
24 Centennial Dr, Seaforth, ON, N0K 1W0
(519) 527-1650
Emp Here 50   *Sales* 3,502,114
SIC 8062 General medical and surgical hospitals

D-U-N-S 24-947-4321   (SL)
**VINCENT FARM EQUIPMENT (SEAFORTH)
INC**
42787 Hydroline Rd, Seaforth, ON, N0K 1W0
(519) 527-0120
Emp Here 20   *Sales* 6,028,800
SIC 5083 Farm and garden machinery
Pr Pr Marlen Vincent
VP VP Bryan Vincent
Barry Vincent

Searchmont, ON P0S
Algoma County

D-U-N-S 24-356-2860   (HQ)
SEARCHMONT SKI ASSOCIATION INC
SEARCHMONT RESORT
(*Suby of* Searchmont Ski Association Inc)
103 Searchmont Resort Rd, Searchmont, ON,
P0S 1J0
(705) 781-2340
Emp Here 158   *Emp Total* 160
Sales 839,710
SIC 7011 Hotels and motels

Sebringville, ON N0K
Perth County

D-U-N-S 20-710-6860   (BR)
**AVON MAITLAND DISTRICT SCHOOL
BOARD**
CENTRAL PERTH ELEMENTARY SCHOOL
4663 Road 135, Sebringville, ON, N0K 1X0
(519) 393-5300
Emp Here 50
SIC 8211 Elementary and secondary schools

D-U-N-S 20-607-5616   (HQ)
LUCKHART TRANSPORT LTD
(*Suby of* Luckhart Transport Ltd)
4049 Perth County Rd 135, Sebringville, ON,
N0K 1X0
(519) 393-6128
Emp Here 79   *Emp Total* 80
Sales 6,347,581
SIC 4212 Local trucking, without storage
Pr Pr Douglas Luckhart
VP VP Thomas Luckhart

Dir Howard Luckhart
Treas Marjorie Luckhart

D-U-N-S 24-476-8255   (SL)
NUHN INDUSTRIES LTD
(*Suby of* Nuhn Holdings Ltd)
4816 Perth Line Suite 34, Sebringville, ON,
N0K 1X0
(519) 393-6284
Emp Here 40   *Sales* 6,219,371
SIC 3523 Farm machinery and equipment

Seguin, ON P2A

D-U-N-S 24-114-4646   (SL)
CAMP GEORGE
45 Good Fellowship Rd, Seguin, ON, P2A 0B2
(705) 732-6964
Emp Here 49   *Sales* 5,595,120
SIC 7032 Sporting and recreational camps
Dir Jeff Rose

Selby, ON K0K
Lennox County

D-U-N-S 20-655-1173   (BR)
LIMESTONE DISTRICT SCHOOL BOARD
SELBY PUBLIC SCHOOL
1623 County Rd 41, Selby, ON, K0K 2Z0
(613) 388-2670
Emp Here 25
SIC 8211 Elementary and secondary schools

D-U-N-S 25-198-3110   (BR)
OMNI HEALTH CARE LTD
VILLAGE GREEN NURSING
166 Pleasant Dr Rr 1, Selby, ON, K0K 2Z0
(613) 388-2693
Emp Here 60
SIC 8051 Skilled nursing care facilities

Serpent River, ON P0P
Algoma County

D-U-N-S 25-000-6459   (BR)
ALGOMA DISTRICT SCHOOL BOARD
*ROCKHAVEN SCHOOL FOR EXCEPTIONAL
CHILDREN*
(*Suby of* Algoma District School Board)
1459 Riverview Rd, Serpent River, ON, P0P
1V0
(705) 844-2168
Emp Here 26
SIC 8211 Elementary and secondary schools

Severn Bridge, ON P0E
Muskoka County

D-U-N-S 20-608-6068   (SL)
BAYVIEW WILDWOOD RESORT LIMITED
COTTAGES OF PORT STANTON
1500 Port Stanton Pky Rr 1, Severn Bridge,
ON, P0E 1N0
(705) 689-2338
Emp Here 55   *Sales* 2,407,703
SIC 7011 Hotels and motels

D-U-N-S 20-711-3890   (BR)
**TRILLIUM LAKELANDS DISTRICT
SCHOOL BOARD**
K P MANSON PUBLIC SCHOOL
1017 Graham Rd, Severn Bridge, ON, P0E
1N0
(705) 689-2612
Emp Here 35
SIC 8211 Elementary and secondary schools

Shakespeare, ON N0B
Perth County

D-U-N-S 25-249-1253   (BR)
AVON MAITLAND DISTRICT SCHOOL BOARD
SPRUCEDALE PUBLIC SCHOOL
2215 Fraser St, Shakespeare, ON, N0B 2P0
(519) 625-8722
Emp Here 20
SIC 8211 Elementary and secondary schools

Shannonville, ON K0K
Hastings County

D-U-N-S 24-450-8342   (BR)
HASTINGS AND PRINCE EDWARD DISTRICT SCHOOL BOARD
TYENDINAGA PUBLIC SCHOOL
650 Shannonville Rd Rr 1, Shannonville, ON, K0K 3A0
(613) 962-4447
Emp Here 25
SIC 8211 Elementary and secondary schools

D-U-N-S 20-031-1517   (SL)
MOHAWKS OF THE BAY OF QUINTE
RED CEDARS SHELTER
(*Suby of* Mohawks Of The Bay Of Quinte)
Gd, Shannonville, ON, K0K 3A0
(613) 967-2003
Emp Here 20   *Sales* 4,377,642
SIC 8322 Individual and family services

Shanty Bay, ON L0L
Simcoe County

D-U-N-S 24-120-4986   (SL)
CARRIAGE HILLS VACATION OWNERS ASSOCIATION
90 Highland Dr, Shanty Bay, ON, L0L 2L0
(705) 835-5858
Emp Here 137   *Sales* 8,318,900
SIC 7011 Hotels and motels
Emily Burns

Sharbot Lake, ON K0H

D-U-N-S 20-049-0204   (BR)
LIMESTONE DISTRICT SCHOOL BOARD
SHARBOT LAKE HIGH SCHOOL
24719 Hwy 7, Sharbot Lake, ON, K0H 2P0
(613) 279-2131
Emp Here 50
SIC 8211 Elementary and secondary schools

D-U-N-S 24-268-5717   (SL)
ROBINSON, W. A. & ASSOCIATES LTD
Gd, Sharbot Lake, ON, K0H 2P0
(613) 279-2116
Emp Here 23   *Sales* 7,536,000
SIC 6282 Investment advice
Pr Pr Wayne Robinson
VP VP Matthew Robinson
David Robinson

D-U-N-S 20-568-7721   (BR)
ROYAL BANK OF CANADA
RBC
(*Suby of* Royal Bank Of Canada)
1043 Elizabeth St, Sharbot Lake, ON, K0H 2P0
(613) 279-3191
Emp Here 20
SIC 6021 National commercial banks

Sharon, ON L0G

D-U-N-S 20-577-7431   (BR)
TANDET MANAGEMENT INC
2510 Davis Dr, Sharon, ON, L0G 1V0
(905) 953-5457
Emp Here 300
SIC 4212 Local trucking, without storage

D-U-N-S 25-293-5820   (BR)
YORK REGION DISTRICT SCHOOL BOARD
SHARON PUBLIC SHOOL
(*Suby of* York Region District School Board)
18532 Leslie St, Sharon, ON, L0G 1V0
(905) 478-4952
Emp Here 20
SIC 8211 Elementary and secondary schools

Sheffield, ON L0R
Wentworth County

D-U-N-S 20-651-2027   (BR)
HAMILTON-WENTWORTH DISTRICT SCHOOL BOARD, THE
DR JOHN G. SEATON SENIOR PUBLIC SCHOOL
1279 Seaton Rd, Sheffield, ON, L0R 1Z0
(519) 647-3471
Emp Here 20
SIC 8211 Elementary and secondary schools

Shelburne, ON L0N
Dufferin County

D-U-N-S 20-026-1720   (BR)
UPPER GRAND DISTRICT SCHOOL BOARD, THE
PRIMROSE ELEMENTARY SCHOOL
(*Suby of* Upper Grand District School Board, The)
Gd, Shelburne, ON, L0N 1S8
(519) 925-3939
Emp Here 35
SIC 8211 Elementary and secondary schools

Shelburne, ON L9V
Dufferin County

D-U-N-S 20-349-8456   (BR)
CORPORATION OF THE COUNTY OF DUFFERIN, THE
DUFFERIN OAKS HOME FOR SENIOR CITIZENS
151 Centre St, Shelburne, ON, L9V 3R7
(519) 925-2140
Emp Here 164
SIC 8322 Individual and family services

D-U-N-S 20-914-0511   (BR)
HEADWATERS HEALTH CARE CENTRE
301 First Ave E, Shelburne, ON, L9V 3W3
(519) 941-2410
Emp Here 100
SIC 8069 Specialty hospitals, except psychiatric

D-U-N-S 25-510-1982   (SL)
KTH SHELBURNE MFG. INC
(*Suby of* Kth Parts Industries, Inc.)
300 2nd Line, Shelburne, ON, L9V 3N4
(519) 925-3030
Emp Here 430   *Sales* 68,145,294
SIC 3714 Motor vehicle parts and accessories
Pr Yosuke Sewa
Ted Scott
Tim Inoue

D-U-N-S 20-024-9808   (BR)
UPPER GRAND DISTRICT SCHOOL BOARD, THE
CENTENNIAL HYLANDS ELEMENTARY SCHOOL
(*Suby of* Upper Grand District School Board, The)
35 School Rd, Shelburne, ON, L9V 3S5
(519) 925-2142
Emp Here 35
SIC 8211 Elementary and secondary schools

D-U-N-S 20-590-4837   (BR)
UPPER GRAND DISTRICT SCHOOL BOARD, THE
HYLAND HEIGHTS ELEMENTARY SCHOOL
(*Suby of* Upper Grand District School Board, The)
200 Fourth Ave, Shelburne, ON, L9V 3R9
(519) 925-3745
Emp Here 35
SIC 8211 Elementary and secondary schools

D-U-N-S 24-974-5993   (BR)
UPPER GRAND DISTRICT SCHOOL BOARD, THE
CENTRE DUFFERIN DISTRICT HIGH SCHOOL
(*Suby of* Upper Grand District School Board, The)
150 Fourth Ave, Shelburne, ON, L9V 3R5
(519) 925-3834
Emp Here 100
SIC 8211 Elementary and secondary schools

Shining Tree, ON P0M
Sudbury County

D-U-N-S 24-369-2188   (BR)
RAINBOW DISTRICT SCHOOL BOARD
M W MOORE PUBLIC SCHOOL
106 Lakeshore Rd, Shining Tree, ON, P0M 2X0
(705) 263-2038
Emp Here 25
SIC 8211 Elementary and secondary schools

Shuniah, ON P7A

D-U-N-S 25-238-0852   (BR)
LAKEHEAD DISTRICT SCHOOL BOARD
MCKENZIE PUBLIC SCHOOL
1625 Lakeshore Dr, Shuniah, ON, P7A 0T2
(807) 983-2355
Emp Here 20
SIC 8211 Elementary and secondary schools

Simcoe, ON N3Y

D-U-N-S 24-693-1617   (BR)
1003694 ONTARIO INC
CARE PARTNERS-SIMCOE
(*Suby of* 1003694 Ontario Inc)
69 Talbot St S, Simcoe, ON, N3Y 2Z4
(519) 428-1161
Emp Here 30
SIC 8059 Nursing and personal care, nec

D-U-N-S 20-589-5274   (BR)
BANQUE TORONTO-DOMINION, LA
TD CANADA TRUST
(*Suby of* Toronto-Dominion Bank, The)
135 Queensway E, Simcoe, ON, N3Y 4M5
(519) 426-9230
Emp Here 20
SIC 6021 National commercial banks

D-U-N-S 20-293-1056   (BR)

BRANT HALDIMAND NORFOLK CATHOLIC DISTRICT SCHOOL BOARD
HOLY TRINITY CATHOLIC HIGH SCHOOL
128 Evergreen Hill Rd, Simcoe, ON, N3Y 4K1
(519) 429-3600
Emp Here 125
SIC 8211 Elementary and secondary schools

D-U-N-S 20-590-7178   (BR)
BRANT HALDIMAND NORFOLK CATHOLIC DISTRICT SCHOOL BOARD
ST JOSEPH'S SCHOOL
34 Potts Rd, Simcoe, ON, N3Y 2S8
(519) 426-0820
Emp Here 45
SIC 8211 Elementary and secondary schools

D-U-N-S 20-543-1112   (BR)
CANADA POST CORPORATION
SIMCOE STN MAIN
124 Norfolk St N, Simcoe, ON, N3Y 3N8
(519) 426-1365
Emp Here 30
SIC 4311 U.s. postal service

D-U-N-S 25-303-5059   (BR)
CANADIAN IMPERIAL BANK OF COMMERCE
CIBC
5 Norfolk St S, Simcoe, ON, N3Y 2V8
(519) 426-4630
Emp Here 35
SIC 6021 National commercial banks

D-U-N-S 24-011-7213   (BR)
COMCARE (CANADA) LIMITED
COMCARE HEALTH SERVICES
8 Queensway E Suite 4, Simcoe, ON, N3Y 4M3
(519) 426-5122
Emp Here 80
SIC 8059 Nursing and personal care, nec

D-U-N-S 20-025-3339   (BR)
CORPORATION OF NORFOLK COUNTY
SIMCOE RECREATION CENTRE
182 South Dr, Simcoe, ON, N3Y 1G5
(519) 426-8866
Emp Here 35
SIC 7999 Amusement and recreation, nec

D-U-N-S 20-845-3241   (BR)
CORPORATION OF NORFOLK COUNTY
NORVIEW LODGE
44 Rob Blake Way, Simcoe, ON, N3Y 0E3
(519) 426-0902
Emp Here 110
SIC 8051 Skilled nursing care facilities

D-U-N-S 24-119-5291   (BR)
CORPORATION OF NORFOLK COUNTY
PUBLIC WORKS DEPT ROADS DIVISION
8 Schellburg Ave, Simcoe, ON, N3Y 2J4
(519) 426-4377
Emp Here 29
SIC 7389 Business services, nec

D-U-N-S 24-044-8332   (SL)
D.G.S. DEVELOPMENT INC
GREENS AT RENTON, THE
Gd Lcd Main, Simcoe, ON, N3Y 4K7
(519) 426-3308
Emp Here 60   *Sales* 2,553,625
SIC 7992 Public golf courses

D-U-N-S 24-347-6327   (SL)
ESSEX GROUP CANADA INC
SUPERIOR ESSEX
20 Gilbertson Dr Suite 20, Simcoe, ON, N3Y 4L5
(519) 428-3900
Emp Here 147
SIC 3351 Copper rolling and drawing

D-U-N-S 20-523-5349   (BR)
GOVERNMENT OF ONTARIO
ONTARIO WORKS & SOCIAL SERVICES DIVISION

12 Gilbertson Dr, Simcoe, ON, N3Y 4N5
(519) 426-6170
Emp Here 40
SIC 8399 Social services, nec

D-U-N-S 25-137-3502   (BR)
GRAND ERIE DISTRICT SCHOOL BOARD
SPRUCEDALE SECONDARY SCHOOL
(*Suby of* Grand Erie District School Board)
660 Ireland Rd, Simcoe, ON, N3Y 4K2
(519) 426-8400
Emp Here 21
SIC 8211 Elementary and secondary schools

D-U-N-S 20-024-9766   (BR)
GRAND ERIE DISTRICT SCHOOL BOARD
SIMCOE COMPOSITE SCHOOL
(*Suby of* Grand Erie District School Board)
40 Wilson Ave, Simcoe, ON, N3Y 2E5
(519) 426-4664
Emp Here 100
SIC 8211 Elementary and secondary schools

D-U-N-S 20-037-4085   (BR)
GRAND ERIE DISTRICT SCHOOL BOARD
WALSH PUBLIC SCHOOL
(*Suby of* Grand Erie District School Board)
933 St John'S Rd W, Simcoe, ON, N3Y 4K1
(519) 426-3716
Emp Here 36
SIC 8211 Elementary and secondary schools

D-U-N-S 20-920-9670   (BR)
GRAND ERIE DISTRICT SCHOOL BOARD
ELGIN AVENUE ELEMENTARY SCHOOL
(*Suby of* Grand Erie District School Board)
80 Elgin Ave, Simcoe, ON, N3Y 4A8
(519) 426-4628
Emp Here 20
SIC 8211 Elementary and secondary schools

D-U-N-S 25-137-3528   (BR)
GRAND ERIE DISTRICT SCHOOL BOARD
WEST LYNN PUBLIC SCHOOL
(*Suby of* Grand Erie District School Board)
18 Parker Dr, Simcoe, ON, N3Y 1A1
(519) 426-0688
Emp Here 25
SIC 8211 Elementary and secondary schools

D-U-N-S 20-035-1554   (BR)
GRAND ERIE DISTRICT SCHOOL BOARD
LYNNDALE HEIGHTS PUBLIC SCHOOL
(*Suby of* Grand Erie District School Board)
55 Donly Dr S, Simcoe, ON, N3Y 5G7
(519) 429-2997
Emp Here 32
SIC 8211 Elementary and secondary schools

D-U-N-S 24-220-2419   (BR)
HGC MANAGEMENT INC
456 Queensway W, Simcoe, ON, N3Y 2N3
(519) 426-1633
Emp Here 20
SIC 4953 Refuse systems

D-U-N-S 25-300-2703   (BR)
METRO ONTARIO INC
FOOD BASICS
150 West St, Simcoe, ON, N3Y 5C1
(519) 426-2010
Emp Here 75
SIC 5411 Grocery stores

D-U-N-S 24-116-8553   (BR)
METRO ONTARIO INC
140 Queensway E, Simcoe, ON, N3Y 4Y7
(519) 426-8092
Emp Here 20
SIC 5411 Grocery stores

D-U-N-S 24-892-4227   (BR)
MUELLER CANADA LTD
ANVIL INTERNATIONAL
(*Suby of* Mueller Water Products, Inc.)
390 2nd Ave, Simcoe, ON, N3Y 4K9
(519) 426-4551
Emp Here 50

SIC 5074 Plumbing and heating equipment and supplies (hydronics)

D-U-N-S 24-977-1338   (SL)
NELSON, NELSON FOODS INC
TIM HORTONS
15 Queensway E, Simcoe, ON, N3Y 4Y2
(519) 428-0101
Emp Here 50   *Sales* 1,678,096
SIC 5461 Retail bakeries

D-U-N-S 25-918-0834   (BR)
NORFOLK ASSOCIATION FOR COMMUNITY LIVING
JOB LINKS
5 Queensway E, Simcoe, ON, N3Y 5K2
(519) 428-4069
Emp Here 20
SIC 8331 Job training and related services

D-U-N-S 20-001-0226   (BR)
NORFOLK ASSOCIATION FOR COMMUNITY LIVING
BUSINESS SUPPORT SERVICE
12 Argyle St, Simcoe, ON, N3Y 1V5
(519) 428-2932
Emp Here 25
SIC 7363 Help supply services

D-U-N-S 24-334-1500   (SL)
NORFOLK FAMILY RESTAURANTS LTD
MCDONALDS
77 Queensway E, Simcoe, ON, N3Y 4M5
(519) 426-8084
Emp Here 70   *Sales* 2,115,860
SIC 5812 Eating places

D-U-N-S 25-034-3829   (HQ)
NORFOLK POWER INC
70 Victoria St, Simcoe, ON, N3Y 1L5

Emp Here 42   *Emp Total* 1,000
Sales 26,994,000
SIC 4911 Electric services
Dir Brad Randal
Pr Martin Malinowski
 Fred Druyf

D-U-N-S 25-359-7116   (BR)
ROULSTON'S DISCOUNT DRUGS LIMITED
140 Queensway E, Simcoe, ON, N3Y 4Y7
(519) 426-8011
Emp Here 35
SIC 5912 Drug stores and proprietary stores

D-U-N-S 25-309-1870   (BR)
SOBEYS CAPITAL INCORPORATED
SOBEYS
438 Norfolk St S, Simcoe, ON, N3Y 2X3
(519) 426-4799
Emp Here 125
SIC 5411 Grocery stores

D-U-N-S 20-980-7015   (BR)
UNILEVER CANADA INC
GOOD HUMOR BREYERS
175 Union St, Simcoe, ON, N3Y 2B1
(519) 426-1673
Emp Here 350
SIC 2024 Ice cream and frozen deserts

D-U-N-S 24-606-2090   (BR)
WAL-MART CANADA CORP
160 Queensway E, Simcoe, ON, N3Y 0A8
(519) 426-6900
Emp Here 40
SIC 5311 Department stores

D-U-N-S 24-165-7191   (BR)
WENDCORP HOLDINGS INC
WENDY'S OLD FASHIONED HAMBURGERS
413 Norfolk St N Unit 6399, Simcoe, ON, N3Y 3P4
(519) 426-4800
Emp Here 50
SIC 5812 Eating places

D-U-N-S 20-004-0660   (BR)

ZEHRMART INC
REAL CANADIAN SUPERSTORE
125 Queensway E, Simcoe, ON, N3Y 5M7
(519) 426-7743
Emp Here 220
SIC 5411 Grocery stores

Sioux Lookout, ON P8T
Kenora County

D-U-N-S 24-966-8930   (BR)
BEARSKIN LAKE AIR SERVICE LP
BEARSKIN AIRLINES
7 Airport Rd, Sioux Lookout, ON, P8T 1J6
(807) 737-3473
Emp Here 110
SIC 4522 Air transportation, nonscheduled

D-U-N-S 20-007-9650   (BR)
CANADIAN IMPERIAL BANK OF COMMERCE
CIBC
50 Front, Sioux Lookout, ON, P8T 1A1
(807) 737-2331
Emp Here 25
SIC 6021 National commercial banks

D-U-N-S 25-927-8562   (BR)
KEEWATIN PATRICIA DISTRICT SCHOOL BOARD
QUEEN ELIZABETH DISTRICT NIGHT SCHOOL
15 Fair St, Sioux Lookout, ON, P8T 1A9
(807) 737-3500
Emp Here 55
SIC 8211 Elementary and secondary schools

D-U-N-S 20-705-2684   (BR)
NORTHERN NISHNAWBE EDUCATION COUNCIL
PELICAN FALLS FIRST NATIONS HIGH SCHOOL
650 Pelican Falls Rd, Sioux Lookout, ON, P8T 0A7
(807) 737-1110
Emp Here 35
SIC 8211 Elementary and secondary schools

D-U-N-S 20-291-4649   (BR)
NORTHERN NISHNAWBE EDUCATION COUNCIL
WAHSA DISTANCE EDUCATION CENTRE
74 Front St, Sioux Lookout, ON, P8T 1B7
(807) 737-1488
Emp Here 25
SIC 8211 Elementary and secondary schools

D-U-N-S 20-710-3313   (BR)
NORTHWEST CATHOLIC DISTRICT SCHOOL BOARD, THE
SACRED HEART SCHOOL
41 Eighth Ave, Sioux Lookout, ON, P8T 1B7
(807) 737-1121
Emp Here 38
SIC 8211 Elementary and secondary schools

D-U-N-S 24-059-8800   (BR)
SIOUX LOOKOUT FIRST NATIONS HEALTH AUTHORITY
76 7 Ave, Sioux Lookout, ON, P8T 1B8
(807) 737-3850
Emp Here 50
SIC 7011 Hotels and motels

D-U-N-S 20-119-5844   (BR)
SIOUX LOOKOUT MENO-YA-WIN HEALTH CENTRE PLANNING CORPORATION
(*Suby of* Sioux Lookout Meno-Ya-Win Health Centre Planning Corporation)
1 Meno Ya Win Way, Sioux Lookout, ON, P8T 1B4
(807) 737-3030
Emp Here 50
SIC 7389 Business services, nec

D-U-N-S 20-180-8040   (HQ)
SIOUX LOOKOUT MENO-YA-WIN HEALTH CENTRE PLANNING CORPORATION
WILLIAM A.(BILL) GEORGE EXTENDED CARE FACILITY
(*Suby of* Sioux Lookout Meno-Ya-Win Health Centre Planning Corporation)
1 Meno Ya Win Way, Sioux Lookout, ON, P8T 1B4
(807) 737-3030
Emp Here 100   *Emp Total* 275
Sales 19,115,703
SIC 8062 General medical and surgical hospitals
Pr Roger Walker
Dir Fin Gordon Hill
Treas Knowles Mcgill

D-U-N-S 20-260-1241   (BR)
WASAYA AIRWAYS LIMITED PARTNERSHIP
17 Airport Rd, Sioux Lookout, ON, P8T 1J6
(807) 737-7124
Emp Here 40
SIC 4512 Air transportation, scheduled

Smiths Falls, ON K7A
Lanark County

D-U-N-S 20-291-2841   (BR)
ACCESS CENTRE FOR COMMUNITY CARE IN LANARK, LEEDS AND GRENVILLE
52 Abbott St N, Smiths Falls, ON, K7A 1W3
(613) 283-8012
Emp Here 35
SIC 8059 Nursing and personal care, nec

D-U-N-S 25-296-6585   (BR)
BANK OF NOVA SCOTIA, THE
SCOTIABANK
92 Lombard St, Smiths Falls, ON, K7A 4G5
(613) 284-4111
Emp Here 22
SIC 6021 National commercial banks

D-U-N-S 20-708-7037   (BR)
BAYSHORE HEALTHCARE LTD.
BAYSHORE HOME HEALTH
94 Beckwith St N, Smiths Falls, ON, K7A 2C1
(613) 283-1400
Emp Here 200
SIC 8082 Home health care services

D-U-N-S 25-572-5277   (SL)
BROADVIEW NURSING CENTRE LIMITED
210 Brockville St, Smiths Falls, ON, K7A 3Z4
(613) 283-1845
Emp Here 85   *Sales* 3,866,917
SIC 8051 Skilled nursing care facilities

D-U-N-S 20-537-9220   (BR)
CANADA POST CORPORATION
SMITHS FALLS STN MAIN
17 Church St E, Smiths Falls, ON, K7A 1H1

Emp Here 33
SIC 4311 U.s. postal service

D-U-N-S 25-237-9623   (BR)
CATHOLIC DISTRICT SCHOOL BOARD OF EASTERN ONTARIO
ST. JAMES THE GREATER SCHOOL
(*Suby of* Catholic District School Board of Eastern Ontario)
5 Catherine St, Smiths Falls, ON, K7A 3Z9
(613) 283-1848
Emp Here 20
SIC 8211 Elementary and secondary schools

D-U-N-S 25-237-9961   (BR)
CATHOLIC DISTRICT SCHOOL BOARD OF EASTERN ONTARIO
ST FRANCIS DE SALES SCHOOL
(*Suby of* Catholic District School Board of Eastern Ontario)

43 Russell St E, Smiths Falls, ON, K7A 1G2
(613) 283-6101
Emp Here 25
SIC 8211 Elementary and secondary schools

D-U-N-S 20-711-5325   (BR)
CATHOLIC DISTRICT SCHOOL BOARD OF EASTERN ONTARIO
SAINT JOHN EDUCATION CENTER
4 Ross St, Smiths Falls, ON, K7A 4L5
(613) 283-4477
Emp Here 25
SIC 8211 Elementary and secondary schools

D-U-N-S 20-646-1514   (BR)
CATHOLIC DISTRICT SCHOOL BOARD OF EASTERN ONTARIO
WESTERN REGION EDUCATION CENTRE
385 Highway 29, Smiths Falls, ON, K7A 4W7
(613) 283-5007
Emp Here 35
SIC 8211 Elementary and secondary schools

D-U-N-S 24-776-7028   (BR)
CHARTWELL MASTER CARE LP
CHARTWELL VAN HORNE RETIREMENT
25 Van Horne Ave, Smiths Falls, ON, K7A 5L2
(613) 284-8080
Emp Here 35
SIC 8322 Individual and family services

D-U-N-S 20-008-6135   (BR)
COMCARE (CANADA) LIMITED
COMCARE HEALTH SERVICES
52 Abbott St N Unit 3, Smiths Falls, ON, K7A 1W3
Emp Here 80
SIC 7363 Help supply services

D-U-N-S 25-832-9234   (BR)
CORPORATION LEEDS GRENVILLE & LANARK DISTRICT HEALTH UNIT, THE
52 Abbott St N Suite 2, Smiths Falls, ON, K7A 1W3
(613) 283-2740
Emp Here 20
SIC 8621 Professional organizations

D-U-N-S 20-588-9160   (BR)
ECONOMICAL MUTUAL INSURANCE COMPANY
ECONOMICAL INSURANCE
100 Elmsley St N, Smiths Falls, ON, K7A 2H2
Emp Here 20
SIC 6331 Fire, marine, and casualty insurance

D-U-N-S 20-153-4765   (SL)
HEALEY TRANSPORTATION LIMITED
10 Gile St, Smiths Falls, ON, K7A 3C2
(613) 283-3518
Emp Here 53   *Sales* 1,605,135
SIC 4151 School buses

D-U-N-S 24-826-7551   (BR)
HERSHEY CANADA INC
(*Suby of* Hershey Company)
1 Hershey Dr, Smiths Falls, ON, K7A 4T8
Emp Here 500
SIC 2066 Chocolate and cocoa products

D-U-N-S 24-633-9568   (BR)
KAYCAN LTEE
WEATHERSTRONG BUILDING PRODUCTS
(*Suby of* Administration F.L.T. Ltee)
37 Union St, Smiths Falls, ON, K7A 4Z4
(613) 283-0999
Emp Here 40
SIC 3479 Metal coating and allied services

D-U-N-S 24-188-8770   (SL)
MCDONALDS RESTAURANT
81 Lombard St, Smiths Falls, ON, K7A 4Y9
(613) 283-8633
Emp Here 60   *Sales* 1,824,018
SIC 5812 Eating places

D-U-N-S 24-607-7692   (BR)
METRO ONTARIO INC
FOOD BASICS
275 Brockville St Suite 4, Smiths Falls, ON, K7A 4Z6
(613) 283-5858
Emp Here 50
SIC 5411 Grocery stores

D-U-N-S 20-334-6866   (BR)
METROLAND MEDIA GROUP LTD
PERFORMANCE PRINTING
65 Lorne St, Smiths Falls, ON, K7A 3K8
(800) 267-7936
Emp Here 150
SIC 2711 Newspapers

D-U-N-S 24-103-5401   (HQ)
PERTH AND SMITHS FALLS DISTRICT HOSPITAL
(*Suby of* Perth And Smiths Falls District Hospital)
60 Cornelia St W, Smiths Falls, ON, K7A 2H9
(613) 283-2330
Emp Here 270   *Emp Total* 540
Sales 39,799,194
SIC 8062 General medical and surgical hospitals
  Beverley Mcfarlane
V Ch Bd Wayne Johnson
V Ch Bd Cheryl Becket
  Michele Bellows
  Jay Brennan
  Leslie Drynan
  John Fenik
  Warren Hollis
  Anil Kuchinad
  Bruce Laing

D-U-N-S 20-506-3704   (BR)
ROGERS MEDIA INC
CJET
(*Suby of* Rogers Communications Inc)
6 Beckwith St N Unit A, Smiths Falls, ON, K7A 2B1
(613) 283-4630
Emp Here 25
SIC 4832 Radio broadcasting stations

D-U-N-S 25-121-5935   (BR)
UPPER CANADA DISTRICT SCHOOL BOARD, THE
TR LEGER SCHOOL OF ADULT ALTERNATIVE & CONTINUING EDUCATION
(*Suby of* Upper Canada District School Board, The)
10 Ontario St, Smiths Falls, ON, K7A 4K7
(613) 283-5418
Emp Here 20
SIC 8211 Elementary and secondary schools

D-U-N-S 25-956-6974   (BR)
UPPER CANADA DISTRICT SCHOOL BOARD, THE
CHIMO ELEMENTARY SCHOOL
(*Suby of* Upper Canada District School Board, The)
11 Ross St, Smiths Falls, ON, K7A 4V7
(613) 283-1761
Emp Here 41
SIC 8211 Elementary and secondary schools

D-U-N-S 20-648-4391   (BR)
UPPER CANADA DISTRICT SCHOOL BOARD, THE
MONTAGUE CENTRAL ELEMENTARY SCHOOL
1200 Rosedale Rd N Gd Stn Main Gd Lcd Main, Smiths Falls, ON, K7A 4S8
(613) 283-6426
Emp Here 20
SIC 8211 Elementary and secondary schools

D-U-N-S 25-914-5720   (BR)
UPPER CANADA DISTRICT SCHOOL BOARD, THE
SMITH FALLS AND DISTRICT COLLEGIATE INSTITUTE
(*Suby of* Upper Canada District School Board, The)
299 Percy St, Smiths Falls, ON, K7A 5M2
(613) 283-0288
Emp Here 73
SIC 8211 Elementary and secondary schools

D-U-N-S 20-031-5484   (BR)
UPPER CANADA DISTRICT SCHOOL BOARD, THE
DUNCAN J SCHOULAR PUBLIC SCHOOL
41 Mcgill St S, Smiths Falls, ON, K7A 3M9
(613) 283-1367
Emp Here 40
SIC 8211 Elementary and secondary schools

D-U-N-S 24-318-0812   (BR)
WAL-MART CANADA CORP
WALMART
114 Lombard St, Smiths Falls, ON, K7A 5B8
(613) 284-0838
Emp Here 120
SIC 5311 Department stores

D-U-N-S 20-153-5895   (HQ)
WILLS TRANSFER LIMITED
(*Suby of* Wills Transfer Limited)
146 Hwy 15, Smiths Falls, ON, K7A 4T2
(613) 283-0225
Emp Here 62   *Emp Total* 151
Sales 14,300,297
SIC 4225 General warehousing and storage
Pr Pr Terry Wills
VP VP Heather Wills

Smithville, ON L0R

D-U-N-S 20-773-2822   (BR)
1010360 ONTARIO INC
G-TEL ENGINEERING
2952 Thompson Rd, Smithville, ON, L0R 2A0
Emp Here 20
SIC 1623 Water, sewer, and utility lines

D-U-N-S 24-736-9601   (HQ)
CROSS ISLAND INC
(*Suby of* Cross Island Inc)
4972 Spring Creek Rd, Smithville, ON, L0R 2A0
(905) 957-3326
Emp Here 180   *Emp Total* 280
Sales 65,276,400
SIC 6712 Bank holding companies
Pr Pr Stephen Witt
Sec Andrew Witt
Treas Matthew Witt

D-U-N-S 20-009-6597   (BR)
DISTRICT SCHOOL BOARD OF NIAGARA
SOUTH LINCOLN HIGH SCHOOL
260 Canborough St, Smithville, ON, L0R 2A0
(905) 957-3359
Emp Here 40
SIC 8211 Elementary and secondary schools

D-U-N-S 20-710-8379   (BR)
DISTRICT SCHOOL BOARD OF NIAGARA
COLLEGE STREET ELEMENTARY SCHOOL
132 College St, Smithville, ON, L0R 2A0
(905) 957-7024
Emp Here 50
SIC 8211 Elementary and secondary schools

D-U-N-S 24-219-9110   (BR)
GREELY CONSTRUCTION INC
2952 Thompson Rd, Smithville, ON, L0R 2A0
(905) 643-7687
Emp Here 30
SIC 1623 Water, sewer, and utility lines

D-U-N-S 24-363-3760   (HQ)
HARBISONWALKER INTERNATIONAL CORP
(*Suby of* Harbisonwalker International Holdings, Inc.)
2689 Industrial Park Rd, Smithville, ON, L0R 2A0
(905) 957-3311
Emp Here 30   *Emp Total* 1,700
SIC 3297 Nonclay refractories

D-U-N-S 25-144-3545   (BR)
NIAGARA CATHOLIC DISTRICT SCHOOL BOARD
ST MARTIN SCHOOL
186 Margaret St, Smithville, ON, L0R 2A0
(905) 957-3032
Emp Here 38
SIC 8211 Elementary and secondary schools

D-U-N-S 20-051-3414   (HQ)
NIAGARA GRAIN & FEED (1984) LIMITED
157 Griffin St S, Smithville, ON, L0R 2A0
(905) 957-3336
Emp Here 20   *Emp Total* 1,300
Sales 11,088,013
SIC 2048 Prepared feeds, nec
  Micheal Burrows
Sec Wendy Robson
Dir Larry May
Dir Robert May
Dir Elizabeth May
Dir Jack May
Dir Debi Kee
  Kathy Wienhold
Dir Jean May
Dir Greg Scott

D-U-N-S 25-093-1854   (BR)
NIAGARA PISTON INC
MAPLE MANUFACTURING
(*Suby of* 33139 Ontario Limited)
6275 Spring Creek Rd, Smithville, ON, L0R 2A0
(905) 957-1984
Emp Here 53
SIC 3592 Carburetors, pistons, piston rings and valves

D-U-N-S 20-153-6307   (BR)
REXALL PHARMACY GROUP LTD
REXALL
(*Suby of* McKesson Corporation)
144 Griffin St S, Smithville, ON, L0R 2A0
(905) 957-3943
Emp Here 20
SIC 5912 Drug stores and proprietary stores

D-U-N-S 20-533-9054   (SL)
SICARD HOLIDAY CAMPERS LIMITED
SICARD RV
7526 Regional Road 20, Smithville, ON, L0R 2A0
(905) 957-3344
Emp Here 75   *Sales* 15,832,472
SIC 5561 Recreational vehicle dealers
Pr Pr Gary Sicard
  Blair Sicard

D-U-N-S 25-248-7707   (BR)
SOBEYS CAPITAL INCORPORATED
FOODLAND
176 Griffin St N Unit 174, Smithville, ON, L0R 2A0
Emp Here 50
SIC 5411 Grocery stores

Smooth Rock Falls, ON P0L
Cochrane County

D-U-N-S 25-239-0216   (BR)
CONSEIL SCOLAIRE CATHOLIQUE DE DISTRICT DES GRANDES RIVIERES, LE
ECOLE SECONDAIRE GEORGES VANIER
120 Ross St, Smooth Rock Falls, ON, P0L 2B0
(705) 338-2787
Emp Here 21

SIC 8211 Elementary and secondary schools

D-U-N-S 20-075-4518   (BR)
DISTRICT SCHOOL BOARD ONTARIO NORTH EAST
SMOOTH ROCK FALLS PUBLIC SCHOOL
50 3rd St, Smooth Rock Falls, ON, P0L 2B0
(705) 338-2755
Emp Here 20
SIC 8211 Elementary and secondary schools

South Bruce Peninsula, ON N0H

D-U-N-S 20-090-8999   (BR)
OWEN SOUND LEDGEROCK LIMITED
(*Suby of* Owen Sound Ledgerock Limited)
3476 Bruce Road 13 Rr 3, South Bruce Peninsula, ON, N0H 2T0
(519) 534-0444
Emp Here 25
SIC 1422 Crushed and broken limestone

South Mountain, ON K0E
Dundas County

D-U-N-S 25-224-8679   (BR)
UPPER CANADA DISTRICT SCHOOL BOARD, THE
NATIONVIEW PUBLIC SCHOOL
(*Suby of* Upper Canada District School Board, The)
3045 County Rd 1, South Mountain, ON, K0E 1W0
(613) 989-2600
Emp Here 25
SIC 8211 Elementary and secondary schools

South Porcupine, ON P0N
Cochrane County

D-U-N-S 25-238-9838   (BR)
DISTRICT SCHOOL BOARD ONTARIO NORTH EAST
ROLAND MICHENER SECONDARY SCHOOL
155 Legion Dr, South Porcupine, ON, P0N 1H0
(705) 360-8056
Emp Here 33
SIC 8211 Elementary and secondary schools

D-U-N-S 25-238-9101   (BR)
DISTRICT SCHOOL BOARD ONTARIO NORTH EAST
GOLDEN AVENUE PUBLIC SCHOOL
117 Golden Ave, South Porcupine, ON, P0N 1H0
(705) 360-8054
Emp Here 30
SIC 8211 Elementary and secondary schools

D-U-N-S 24-059-2001   (BR)
DOLLARAMA S.E.C.
DOLLARAMA
4858 Hwy 101 E Suite 104, South Porcupine, ON, P0N 1K0
(705) 235-0831
Emp Here 20
SIC 5311 Department stores

D-U-N-S 20-153-8055   (BR)
GOLDCORP CANADA LTD
PORCUPINE JOINT VENTURE
4315 Goldmine Rd, South Porcupine, ON, P0N 1H0
(705) 235-3221
Emp Here 510
SIC 1041 Gold ores

D-U-N-S 20-007-9072   (BR)
KINROSS GOLD CORPORATION
PROCUPINE JOINT VENTURES
4315 Goldmine Rd, South Porcupine, ON, P0N 1H0
Emp Here 285
SIC 1041 Gold ores

D-U-N-S 24-344-4911   (BR)
METRO ONTARIO INC
Gd, South Porcupine, ON, P0N 1K0
(705) 235-3535
Emp Here 60
SIC 5411 Grocery stores

South River, ON P0A
Parry Sound County

D-U-N-S 25-975-7180   (BR)
PHOENIX BUILDING COMPONENTS INC
93 Ottawa Ave, South River, ON, P0A 1X0
(705) 386-0007
Emp Here 100
SIC 2439 Structural wood members, nec

South Woodslee, ON N0R
Essex County

D-U-N-S 25-249-1774   (BR)
WINDSOR-ESSEX CATHOLIC DISTRICT SCHOOL BOARD, THE
ST JOHN THE EVANGELIST SCHOOL
1473 West Belle River Rd, South Woodslee, ON, N0R 1V0
(519) 723-4403
Emp Here 20
SIC 8211 Elementary and secondary schools

Southampton, ON N0H
Bruce County

D-U-N-S 25-228-1027   (BR)
BLUEWATER DISTRICT SCHOOL BOARD
G C HUSTON
61 Victoria St, Southampton, ON, N0H 2L0
(519) 797-3241
Emp Here 24
SIC 8211 Elementary and secondary schools

D-U-N-S 20-647-9151   (BR)
PHARMA PLUS DRUGMARTS LTD
REXALL DRUG STORE 1644
174 Albert St S, Southampton, ON, N0H 2L0
(519) 797-2113
Emp Here 20
SIC 5912 Drug stores and proprietary stores

D-U-N-S 24-120-7984   (SL)
SOUTHAMPTON CARE CENTRE INC
140 Grey St S, Southampton, ON, N0H 2L0
(519) 797-3220
Emp Here 80   *Sales* 3,648,035
SIC 8051 Skilled nursing care facilities

Southwold, ON N0L
Elgin County

D-U-N-S 20-022-8281   (BR)
ONEIDA NATION OF THE THAMES
STANDING STONE ELEMENTARY SCHOOL
2315 Keystone Pl, Southwold, ON, N0L 2G0
(519) 652-3271
Emp Here 30
SIC 8211 Elementary and secondary schools

Spanish, ON P0P
Algoma County

D-U-N-S 20-710-3867   (BR)
ALGOMA DISTRICT SCHOOL BOARD
SPANISH PUBLIC SCHOOL
(*Suby of* Algoma District School Board)
35 John St, Spanish, ON, P0P 2A0
(705) 844-1098
Emp Here 50
SIC 8211 Elementary and secondary schools

Sparta, ON N0L
Elgin County

D-U-N-S 20-024-9329   (BR)
THAMES VALLEY DISTRICT SCHOOL BOARD
SPARTA PUBLIC SCHOOL
45885 Sparta Line, Sparta, ON, N0L 2H0
(519) 775-2541
Emp Here 23
SIC 8211 Elementary and secondary schools

St Agatha, ON N0B
Waterloo County

D-U-N-S 20-975-5222   (BR)
ANGIE'S KITCHEN LIMITED
(*Suby of* Angie's Kitchen Limited)
1761 Erbs Rd W, St Agatha, ON, N0B 2L0
(519) 747-1700
Emp Here 90
SIC 5812 Eating places

D-U-N-S 24-587-5505   (SL)
KENNEDY'S TAVERN AND CATERING INCORPORATED
1750 Erb Rd W, St Agatha, ON, N0B 2L0
(519) 747-1313
Emp Here 50   *Sales* 1,824,018
SIC 5813 Drinking places

St Albert, ON K0A
Russell County

D-U-N-S 20-934-7728   (BR)
CONSEIL SCOLAIRE DE DISTRICT CATHOLIQUE DE L'EST ONTARIEN
ECOLE ELEMENTAIRE CATHOLIQUE SAINT-ALBERT
116 Principale St, St Albert, ON, K0A 3C0
(613) 987-2157
Emp Here 25
SIC 8211 Elementary and secondary schools

St Andrews West, ON K0C
Stormont County

D-U-N-S 20-711-5192   (BR)
CATHOLIC DISTRICT SCHOOL BOARD OF EASTERN ONTARIO
SAINT ANDREWS CATHOLIC SCHOOL
17283 County Rd 18, St Andrews West, ON, K0C 2A0
(613) 932-6592
Emp Here 27
SIC 8211 Elementary and secondary schools

D-U-N-S 24-666-9535   (SL)
KIRKEY RACING FABRICATION INC
5215 Hwy 138, St Andrews West, ON, K0C 2A0
(613) 938-4885
Emp Here 27   *Sales* 5,717,257
SIC 2531 Public building and related furniture

St Anns, ON L0R
Lincoln County

D-U-N-S 20-710-8429   (BR)
DISTRICT SCHOOL BOARD OF NIAGARA
GAINSBORO ELEMENTARY
5459 Regional Rd 20, St Anns, ON, L0R 1Y0
(905) 386-6223
Emp Here 30
SIC 8211 Elementary and secondary schools

St Catharines, ON L2M
Lincoln County

D-U-N-S 24-319-4169   (SL)
ALIKAT ENTERPRISES INC
17 Keefer Rd, St Catharines, ON, L2M 6K4
(905) 684-8134
Emp Here 50   *Sales* 3,638,254
SIC 5621 Women's clothing stores

D-U-N-S 20-588-2975   (BR)
BANQUE TORONTO-DOMINION, LA
TD CANADA TRUST
(*Suby of* Toronto-Dominion Bank, The)
364 Scott St, St Catharines, ON, L2M 3W4
(905) 934-6225
Emp Here 20
SIC 6021 National commercial banks

D-U-N-S 20-572-7329   (BR)
CANADA POST CORPORATION
234 Bunting Rd, St Catharines, ON, L2M 3Y1
(905) 688-7765
Emp Here 100
SIC 4311 U.s. postal service

D-U-N-S 24-385-4465   (HQ)
DENDRES CORP
MCDONALD'S RESTAURANT
(*Suby of* Dendres Corp)
500 Welland Ave, St Catharines, ON, L2M 5V5
(905) 688-5461
Emp Here 25   *Emp Total* 100
Sales 2,991,389
SIC 5812 Eating places

D-U-N-S 20-914-5395   (BR)
DENDRES CORP
MCDONALD'S
(*Suby of* Dendres Corp)
525 Welland Ave, St Catharines, ON, L2M 6P3
(905) 688-5461
Emp Here 70
SIC 5812 Eating places

D-U-N-S 25-144-3487   (BR)
DISTRICT SCHOOL BOARD OF NIAGARA
LAURA SECORD SECONDARY SCHOOL
349 Niagara St, St Catharines, ON, L2M 4V9
(905) 934-8501
Emp Here 60
SIC 8211 Elementary and secondary schools

D-U-N-S 20-920-1990   (BR)
DISTRICT SCHOOL BOARD OF NIAGARA
LOCKVIEW ELEMENTARY SCHOOL
505 Bunting Rd, St Catharines, ON, L2M 3A9
(905) 934-3331
Emp Here 34
SIC 8211 Elementary and secondary schools

D-U-N-S 24-347-5436   (BR)
DISTRICT SCHOOL BOARD OF NIAGARA
PRINCE OF WALES SCHOOL
95 Facer St, St Catharines, ON, L2M 5J6
(905) 937-2225
Emp Here 20

▲ Public Company   ■ Public Company Family Member   **HQ** Headquarters   **BR** Branch   **SL** Single Location

SIC 8211 Elementary and secondary schools

D-U-N-S 25-178-5143   (BR)
DISTRICT SCHOOL BOARD OF NIAGARA
CARLETON PUBLIC SCHOOL
1 Carlton Park Dr, St Catharines, ON, L2M
4M9
(905) 934-5243
Emp Here 24
SIC 8211 Elementary and secondary schools

D-U-N-S 20-710-8403   (BR)
DISTRICT SCHOOL BOARD OF NIAGARA
E I MCCULLEY PUBLIC SCHOOL
16 Berkley Dr, St Catharines, ON, L2M 6B8
(905) 934-7344
Emp Here 50
SIC 8211 Elementary and secondary schools

D-U-N-S 25-922-0184   (BR)
DISTRICT SCHOOL BOARD OF NIAGARA
PRINCE PHILIP SCHOOL
600 Vine St, St Catharines, ON, L2M 3V1
(905) 934-2525
Emp Here 35
SIC 8211 Elementary and secondary schools

D-U-N-S 20-591-3143   (BR)
DISTRICT SCHOOL BOARD OF NIAGARA
PORT WELLER PUBLIC SCHOOL
273 Parnell Rd, St Catharines, ON, L2M 1W4
(905) 934-3322
Emp Here 30
SIC 8211 Elementary and secondary schools

D-U-N-S 25-137-3460   (BR)
DISTRICT SCHOOL BOARD OF NIAGARA
ST ALFRED'S SCHOOL
280 Vine St, St Catharines, ON, L2M 4T3
(905) 934-9922
Emp Here 30
SIC 8211 Elementary and secondary schools

D-U-N-S 20-116-5324   (SL)
DLB ELECTRIC INC
113 Cushman Rd Unit 15, St Catharines, ON,
L2M 6S9
(905) 682-4447
Emp Here 23   *Sales* 5,034,288
SIC 4931 Electric and other services combined
Owner Derek Beauchamp

D-U-N-S 25-350-7651   (BR)
ELMWOOD GROUP LIMITED, THE
ELMWOOD KITCHEN
570 Welland Ave, St Catharines, ON, L2M 5V6
(905) 688-5205
Emp Here 75
SIC 3429 Hardware, nec

D-U-N-S 20-267-3930   (BR)
FEDERAL EXPRESS CANADA CORPORATION
FEDERAL EXPRESS CANADA LTD
(*Suby of* Fedex Corporation)
495 Eastchester Ave E Unit 1, St Catharines,
ON, L2M 6S2
(800) 463-3339
Emp Here 35
SIC 4212 Local trucking, without storage

D-U-N-S 20-878-9532   (BR)
**GOODWILL INDUSTRIES OF ALBERTA
(REGISTERED SOCIETY)**
525 Welland Ave, St Catharines, ON, L2M 6P3
(905) 684-7741
Emp Here 20
SIC 3999 Manufacturing industries, nec

D-U-N-S 20-342-4341   (SL)
HERB LODDE & SONS ROOFING LTD
QUALITY EXTERIOR SYSTEMS
17 Neilson Ave, St Catharines, ON, L2M 5V9
(905) 935-7571
Emp Here 50   *Sales* 4,961,328
SIC 1761 Roofing, siding, and sheetMetal
work

D-U-N-S 20-707-7285   (BR)
MARCH OF DIMES CANADA
436 Scott St Unit 3, St Catharines, ON, L2M
3W6
(905) 938-2888
Emp Here 30
SIC 8331 Job training and related services

D-U-N-S 25-010-4817   (BR)
MERIDIAN CREDIT UNION LIMITED
400 Scott St, St Catharines, ON, L2M 3W4
(905) 934-9561
Emp Here 30
SIC 6062 State credit unions

D-U-N-S 20-282-8687   (SL)
NEPTUNUS YACHTS INTERNATIONAL INC
8 Keefer Rd, St Catharines, ON, L2M 7N9
(905) 937-3737
Emp Here 57   *Sales* 4,961,328
SIC 3731 Shipbuilding and repairing

D-U-N-S 25-866-6379   (BR)
**NIAGARA CATHOLIC DISTRICT SCHOOL
BOARD**
HOLY CROSS SECONDARY SCHOOL
460 Linwell Rd, St Catharines, ON, L2M 2P9
(905) 937-6446
Emp Here 100
SIC 8211 Elementary and secondary schools

D-U-N-S 25-144-3578   (BR)
**NIAGARA CATHOLIC DISTRICT SCHOOL
BOARD**
ASSUMPTION CATHOLIC SCHOOL
225 Parnell Rd, St Catharines, ON, L2M 1W3
(905) 935-5281
Emp Here 27
SIC 8211 Elementary and secondary schools

D-U-N-S 20-710-9104   (BR)
**NIAGARA CATHOLIC DISTRICT SCHOOL
BOARD**
ST ALFRED SCHOOL
280 Vine St, St Catharines, ON, L2M 4T3
(905) 934-9922
Emp Here 30
SIC 8211 Elementary and secondary schools

D-U-N-S 24-972-9740   (BR)
**NIAGARA CATHOLIC DISTRICT SCHOOL
BOARD**
CANADIAN MARTYRS CATHOLIC SCHOOL
502 Scott St, St Catharines, ON, L2M 3X2
(905) 934-9972
Emp Here 40
SIC 8211 Elementary and secondary schools

D-U-N-S 25-137-3486   (BR)
**NIAGARA CATHOLIC DISTRICT SCHOOL
BOARD**
OUR LADY OF FATIMA SCHOOL
439 Vine St, St Catharines, ON, L2M 3S6
(905) 935-4343
Emp Here 22
SIC 8211 Elementary and secondary schools

D-U-N-S 24-058-0530   (SL)
**NIAGARA INA GRAFTON GAGE HOME OF
THE UNITED CHURCH**
NIAGARA INA GRAFTON GAGE VILLAGE
413 Linwell Rd Suite 4212, St Catharines, ON,
L2M 7Y2
(905) 935-6822
Emp Here 100   *Sales* 3,648,035
SIC 8361 Residential care

D-U-N-S 24-421-5534   (BR)
PARTY CITY CANADA INC
(*Suby of* Party City Canada Inc)
286 Bunting Rd Suite 26, St Catharines, ON,
L2M 7S5
(905) 684-8795
Emp Here 20
SIC 5947 Gift, novelty, and souvenir shop

D-U-N-S 20-909-6366   (BR)
PREMIER HEALTH CLUBS INC
PREMIER HEALTH & FITNESS

366 Bunting Rd, St Catharines, ON, L2M 3Y6
Emp Here 26
SIC 7991 Physical fitness facilities

D-U-N-S 25-309-9170   (BR)
ROYAL BANK OF CANADA
RBC
(*Suby of* Royal Bank Of Canada)
380 Scott St, St Catharines, ON, L2M 3W4
(905) 934-4303
Emp Here 45
SIC 6021 National commercial banks

D-U-N-S 25-178-8246   (BR)
SAINT ELIZABETH HEALTH CARE
444 Scott St Unit 5, St Catharines, ON, L2M
3W6

Emp Here 70
SIC 8322 Individual and family services

D-U-N-S 20-755-0856   (SL)
**SEAPARK INDUSTRIAL DRY CLEANERS
LIMITED**
SEAPARK INDUSTRIAL GLOVE RECYCLING
147 Cushman Rd, St Catharines, ON, L2M
6T2
(905) 688-1671
Emp Here 60   *Sales* 3,429,153
SIC 7218 Industrial launderers

D-U-N-S 25-295-3336   (BR)
SHOPPERS DRUG MART CORPORATION
286 Bunting Rd Suite 22, St Catharines, ON,
L2M 7S5
(905) 688-6733
Emp Here 25
SIC 5912 Drug stores and proprietary stores

D-U-N-S 20-769-8205   (BR)
SOBEYS CAPITAL INCORPORATED
400 Scott St, St Catharines, ON, L2M 3W4
(905) 935-9974
Emp Here 150
SIC 5411 Grocery stores

D-U-N-S 25-204-2874   (BR)
STAPLES CANADA INC
STAPLES BUSINESS DEPOT
(*Suby of* Staples, Inc.)
185 Bunting Rd, St Catharines, ON, L2M 3Y2
(905) 685-4921
Emp Here 40
SIC 5943 Stationery stores

D-U-N-S 24-197-2129   (BR)
TST SOLUTIONS L.P.
*ST CATHARINES SUFFERANCE WARE-
HOUSE*
191 Bunting Rd, St Catharines, ON, L2M 3Y2
(905) 688-1698
Emp Here 20
SIC 4213 Trucking, except local

D-U-N-S 25-254-9423   (BR)
TST SOLUTIONS L.P.
TST OVERLAND EXPRESS
191 Bunting Rd, St Catharines, ON, L2M 3Y2
(905) 688-1882
Emp Here 25
SIC 4213 Trucking, except local

D-U-N-S 20-788-2221   (SL)
TIM HORTONS
579 Carlton St, St Catharines, ON, L2M 4Y1
(905) 937-3900
Emp Here 50   *Sales* 1,532,175
SIC 5812 Eating places

D-U-N-S 25-369-0994   (BR)
TORA INVESTMENTS INC
453 Eastchester Ave E, St Catharines, ON,
L2M 6S2
(905) 685-5409
Emp Here 80
SIC 7549 Automotive services, nec

D-U-N-S 24-218-2301   (SL)
**VON CANADA-ONTARIO GREATER NIA-
GARA**
A-7 Neilson Ave, St Catharines, ON, L2M 5V9
(905) 641-0630
Emp Here 65   *Sales* 7,587,913
SIC 8741 Management services
David Gooch

D-U-N-S 25-498-3224   (BR)
WAL-MART CANADA CORP
525 Welland Ave, St Catharines, ON, L2M 6P3
(905) 685-4100
Emp Here 200
SIC 5311 Department stores

D-U-N-S 25-652-3671   (BR)
**WASTE MANAGEMENT OF CANADA COR-
PORATION**
(*Suby of* Waste Management, Inc.)
124 Cushman Rd, St Catharines, ON, L2M
6T6
(905) 687-9605
Emp Here 85
SIC 4953 Refuse systems

D-U-N-S 25-638-5030   (BR)
WENDY'S RESTAURANTS OF CANADA INC
WENDY'S
(*Suby of* The Wendy's Company)
525 Welland Ave, St Catharines, ON, L2M 6P3

Emp Here 35
SIC 5812 Eating places

St Catharines, ON L2N
Lincoln County

D-U-N-S 25-647-2572   (BR)
968563 ONTARIO INC
TIM HORTONS
498 Ontario St, St Catharines, ON, L2N 4N1
(905) 937-7070
Emp Here 25
SIC 5812 Eating places

D-U-N-S 20-588-2801   (BR)
BANQUE TORONTO-DOMINION, LA
TD CANADA TRUST
(*Suby of* Toronto-Dominion Bank, The)
37 Lakeshore Rd, St Catharines, ON, L2N 2T2
(905) 646-4141
Emp Here 20
SIC 6021 National commercial banks

D-U-N-S 25-147-7014   (BR)
BAYSHORE HEALTHCARE LTD.
BAYSHORE HEALTH GROUP
282 Linwell Rd Suite 205, St Catharines, ON,
L2N 6N5
(905) 688-5214
Emp Here 125
SIC 8322 Individual and family services

D-U-N-S 24-121-3425   (BR)
CANADA POST CORPORATION
CANADA POST
163 Scott St, St Catharines, ON, L2N 1H3
(905) 934-9792
Emp Here 90
SIC 4311 U.s. postal service

D-U-N-S 20-303-3410   (BR)
CARA OPERATIONS LIMITED
MONTANA'S
(*Suby of* Cara Holdings Limited)
327 Lake St, St Catharines, ON, L2N 7T3
(905) 938-7050
Emp Here 35
SIC 5812 Eating places

D-U-N-S 20-308-7981   (BR)
CARA OPERATIONS LIMITED
KELSEY'S
(*Suby of* Cara Holdings Limited)

10 Ymca Dr, St Catharines, ON, L2N 7R6
(905) 646-5200
Emp Here 50
SIC 5812 Eating places

D-U-N-S 24-451-1122   (BR)
CONSEIL SCOLAIRE VIAMONDE
ECOLE ELEMENTAIRE L'HERITAGE
35 Prince Charles Dr, St Catharines, ON, L2N 3Y8
(905) 937-4608
Emp Here 25
SIC 8211 Elementary and secondary schools

D-U-N-S 25-529-3144   (BR)
COSTCO WHOLESALE CANADA LTD
COSTCO
(*Suby of* Costco Wholesale Corporation)
3 North Service Rd, St Catharines, ON, L2N 7R1
(905) 646-2008
Emp Here 225
SIC 5141 Groceries, general line

D-U-N-S 20-024-9709   (BR)
DISTRICT SCHOOL BOARD OF NIAGARA
GOVERNOR SIMCOE SECONDARY SCHOOL
15 Glenview Ave, St Catharines, ON, L2N 2Z7
(905) 227-6641
Emp Here 60
SIC 8211 Elementary and secondary schools

D-U-N-S 24-316-5974   (BR)
DISTRICT SCHOOL BOARD OF NIAGARA
EDEN HIGH SCHOOL
535 Lake St Unit 1, St Catharines, ON, L2N 4H7
(905) 641-1550
Emp Here 44
SIC 8211 Elementary and secondary schools

D-U-N-S 20-289-1177   (BR)
DISTRICT SCHOOL BOARD OF NIAGARA
LIFETIME LEARNING CENTRE
535 Lake St, St Catharines, ON, L2N 4H7
(905) 646-3737
Emp Here 20
SIC 8211 Elementary and secondary schools

D-U-N-S 20-710-8510   (BR)
DISTRICT SCHOOL BOARD OF NIAGARA
SHERIDAN PARK PUBLIC SCHOOL
114 Linwell Rd, St Catharines, ON, L2N 6N8
(905) 937-0510
Emp Here 28
SIC 8211 Elementary and secondary schools

D-U-N-S 20-710-8387   (BR)
DISTRICT SCHOOL BOARD OF NIAGARA
DALEWOOD PUBLIC SCHOOL
61 Duncan Dr, St Catharines, ON, L2N 3P3
(905) 934-3325
Emp Here 20
SIC 8211 Elementary and secondary schools

D-U-N-S 25-137-3395   (BR)
DISTRICT SCHOOL BOARD OF NIAGARA
PARNALL PUBLIC SCHOOL
507 Geneva St, St Catharines, ON, L2N 2H7
(905) 934-3348
Emp Here 25
SIC 8211 Elementary and secondary schools

D-U-N-S 25-144-3461   (BR)
DISTRICT SCHOOL BOARD OF NIAGARA
LINCOLN CENTENIAL PUBLIC SCHOOL
348 Scott St, St Catharines, ON, L2N 1J5
(905) 937-5110
Emp Here 30
SIC 8211 Elementary and secondary schools

D-U-N-S 25-065-3631   (SL)
FIVE BROTHERS HOSPITALITY PARTNER-SHIP
HOLIDAY INN
2 North Service Rd, St Catharines, ON, L2N 4G9

(905) 934-8000
Emp Here 90   *Sales* 3,939,878
SIC 7011 Hotels and motels

D-U-N-S 25-354-9703   (BR)
HOME DEPOT OF CANADA INC
HOME DEPOT
(*Suby of* The Home Depot Inc)
20 Ymca Dr, St Catharines, ON, L2N 7R6
(905) 937-5900
Emp Here 250
SIC 5251 Hardware stores

D-U-N-S 25-651-7442   (SL)
JOHN BEAR BUICK GMC LTD
333 Lake St, St Catharines, ON, L2N 7T3
(905) 934-2571
Emp Here 70   *Sales* 35,507,500
SIC 5511 New and used car dealers
Pr Pr John Bear
VP Jamie Lalande

D-U-N-S 25-818-4399   (BR)
LENNOX CANADA INC
SERVICE EXPERT OF NIAGARA, DIV. OF
(*Suby of* Lennox Canada Inc)
177 Scott St, St Catharines, ON, L2N 1H4
(905) 937-6011
Emp Here 20
SIC 1711 Plumbing, heating, air-conditioning

D-U-N-S 24-550-7306   (BR)
MARK'S WORK WEARHOUSE LTD
MARK'S WORK WEARHOUSE 78
285 Geneva St, St Catharines, ON, L2N 2G1
(905) 934-6464
Emp Here 20
SIC 5651 Family clothing stores

D-U-N-S 25-674-7411   (BR)
MERIDIAN CREDIT UNION LIMITED
531 Lake St, St Catharines, ON, L2N 4H6
(905) 937-7111
Emp Here 28
SIC 6062 State credit unions

D-U-N-S 25-292-3735   (BR)
METRO ONTARIO INC
METRO
101 Lakeshore Rd, St Catharines, ON, L2N 2T6
(905) 934-0131
Emp Here 130
SIC 5411 Grocery stores

D-U-N-S 25-129-5796   (HQ)
MORZOC INVESTMENT INC
TIM HORTONS
(*Suby of* Morzoc Investment Inc)
275 Geneva St, St Catharines, ON, L2N 2E9
(905) 935-0071
Emp Here 25   *Emp Total* 50
Sales 1,678,096
SIC 5461 Retail bakeries

D-U-N-S 20-710-9146   (BR)
NIAGARA CATHOLIC DISTRICT SCHOOL BOARD
ST JAMES SCHOOL
615 Geneva St, St Catharines, ON, L2N 2J3
(905) 934-3112
Emp Here 50
SIC 8211 Elementary and secondary schools

D-U-N-S 20-710-9112   (BR)
NIAGARA CATHOLIC DISTRICT SCHOOL BOARD
ST ANN CATHOLIC SCHOOL
218 Main St, St Catharines, ON, L2N 4W1
(905) 934-1755
Emp Here 25
SIC 8211 Elementary and secondary schools

D-U-N-S 20-710-9138   (BR)
NIAGARA CATHOLIC DISTRICT SCHOOL BOARD
ST FRANCIS SECONDARY SCHOOL
541 Lake St, St Catharines, ON, L2N 4H7

(905) 646-2002
Emp Here 55
SIC 8211 Elementary and secondary schools

D-U-N-S 24-875-0093   (SL)
PERFORMANCE TOYOTA LTD
PERFORMANCE LEXUS TOYOTA
262 Lake St, St Catharines, ON, L2N 4H1
(905) 934-7246
Emp Here 55   *Sales* 26,994,000
SIC 5511 New and used car dealers
Pr Pr Campbell Champion
 John Mann
Genl Mgr David Reilley

D-U-N-S 25-529-0140   (BR)
PRISZM LP
PIZZA HUT
294 Lake St, St Catharines, ON, L2N 4H2
(905) 934-3972
Emp Here 20
SIC 5812 Eating places

D-U-N-S 25-028-5202   (BR)
REVERA LONG TERM CARE INC
VERSA CARE CENTER
168 Scott St, St Catharines, ON, L2N 1H2
(905) 934-3321
Emp Here 240
SIC 8051 Skilled nursing care facilities

D-U-N-S 20-793-8825   (BR)
ROYAL CANADIAN LEGION, THE
(*Suby of* Royal Canadian Legion, The)
600 Ontario St, St Catharines, ON, L2N 7H8
(905) 934-1261
Emp Here 50
SIC 8641 Civic and social associations

D-U-N-S 20-310-8019   (BR)
STAPLES CANADA INC
(*Suby of* Staples, Inc.)
10 Ymca Dr, St Catharines, ON, L2N 7R6
(905) 937-4292
Emp Here 30
SIC 5943 Stationery stores

D-U-N-S 20-506-1265   (BR)
STARBUCKS COFFEE CANADA, INC
STARBUCKS
(*Suby of* Starbucks Corporation)
285 Geneva St, St Catharines, ON, L2N 2G1
(905) 935-0330
Emp Here 20
SIC 5812 Eating places

D-U-N-S 24-200-3379   (BR)
TORONTO-DOMINION BANK, THE
TD CANADA TRUST
(*Suby of* Toronto-Dominion Bank, The)
270 Geneva St, St Catharines, ON, L2N 2E8

Emp Here 20
SIC 6021 National commercial banks

D-U-N-S 25-297-8150   (BR)
TOYS 'R' US (CANADA) LTD
TOYS 'R' US
(*Suby of* Toys "r" Us, Inc.)
87 Meadowvale Dr, St Catharines, ON, L2N 3Z8
(905) 646-8697
Emp Here 30
SIC 5945 Hobby, toy, and game shops

D-U-N-S 25-638-5022   (BR)
WENDY'S RESTAURANTS OF CANADA INC
WENDY'S RESTAURANT
(*Suby of* The Wendy's Company)
342 Lake St, St Catharines, ON, L2N 4H4
(905) 934-6421
Emp Here 45
SIC 5812 Eating places

D-U-N-S 24-936-5859   (BR)
ZEHRMART INC
ZEHRS MARKETS
285 Geneva St, St Catharines, ON, L2N 2G1

(905) 646-7420
Emp Here 200
SIC 5411 Grocery stores

St Catharines, ON L2P
Lincoln County

D-U-N-S 20-147-3709   (BR)
ASAHI REFINING CANADA LTD
NIAGARA INVESTMENT CASTINGS, DIV OF
16 Smith St Suite 1, St Catharines, ON, L2P 3J1
(905) 682-9258
Emp Here 60
SIC 3366 Copper foundries

D-U-N-S 25-655-7513   (BR)
DENDRES CORP
MCDONALD'S RESTAURANT
(*Suby of* Dendres Corp)
95 Hartzel Rd, St Catharines, ON, L2P 1N2

Emp Here 48
SIC 5812 Eating places

D-U-N-S 20-009-6589   (BR)
DISTRICT SCHOOL BOARD OF NIAGARA
FERNDALE PUBLIC SCHOOL
35 Ferndale Ave, St Catharines, ON, L2P 1V8
(905) 684-1101
Emp Here 45
SIC 8211 Elementary and secondary schools

D-U-N-S 20-289-8834   (BR)
DISTRICT SCHOOL BOARD OF NIAGARA
KERNAHAN PARK SECONDARY SCHOOL
91 Bunting Rd, St Catharines, ON, L2P 3G8
(905) 684-9461
Emp Here 75
SIC 8211 Elementary and secondary schools

D-U-N-S 20-893-7388   (SL)
HELPING LIMITED
SERVICEMASTER CLEAN OF NIAGARA
114 Dunkirk Road Unit 1, St Catharines, ON, L2P 3H5
(905) 646-9890
Emp Here 88   *Sales* 2,553,625
SIC 7349 Building maintenance services, nec

D-U-N-S 20-877-6919   (BR)
INTERNATIONAL MARINE SALVAGE INC
GLENDALE METALS
424 Glendale Ave, St Catharines, ON, L2P 3Y1
(905) 680-0801
Emp Here 30
SIC 4789 Transportation services, nec

D-U-N-S 25-398-2482   (SL)
KRAUN ELECTRIC INC
45 Wright St, St Catharines, ON, L2P 3J5
(905) 684-6895
Emp Here 50   *Sales* 4,377,642
SIC 1731 Electrical work

D-U-N-S 25-652-4976   (BR)
MORZOC INVESTMENT INC
TIM HORTONS
(*Suby of* Morzoc Investment Inc)
145 Hartzel Rd, St Catharines, ON, L2P 1N6
(905) 684-6253
Emp Here 40
SIC 5812 Eating places

D-U-N-S 25-137-3494   (BR)
NIAGARA CATHOLIC DISTRICT SCHOOL BOARD
ST CHRISTOPHER CATHOLIC SCHOOL
33 Woodrow St, St Catharines, ON, L2P 2A1
(905) 684-3963
Emp Here 20
SIC 8211 Elementary and secondary schools

D-U-N-S 20-710-9211   (BR)

NIAGARA CATHOLIC DISTRICT SCHOOL BOARD
ST THERESA SCHOOL
58 Seymour Ave, St Catharines, ON, L2P 1A7
(905) 682-0244
Emp Here 20
SIC 8211 Elementary and secondary schools

D-U-N-S 25-309-8909   (BR)
ROYAL BANK OF CANADA
RBC
(*Suby of* Royal Bank Of Canada)
108 Hartzel Rd, St Catharines, ON, L2P 1N4
(905) 688-3350
Emp Here 20
SIC 6021 National commercial banks

D-U-N-S 24-776-0916   (SL)
SILVERLINE GROUP INC
144 Dunkirk Rd, St Catharines, ON, L2P 3H6
(905) 680-6002
Emp Here 49   *Sales* 6,973,235
SIC 1771 Concrete work
Dir Phil Parlatore

D-U-N-S 24-387-8415   (HQ)
TIW STEEL PLATEWORK INC
(*Suby of* Canerector Inc)
23 Smith St, St Catharines, ON, L2P 3J7
(905) 684-9421
Emp Here 30   *Emp Total* 3,000
Sales 20,720,839
SIC 3441 Fabricated structural Metal
Pr Jacques Dion

D-U-N-S 25-169-7454   (SL)
TUFFORD NURSING HOME LTD
312 Queenston St, St Catharines, ON, L2P 2X4
(905) 682-0411
Emp Here 85   *Sales* 3,866,917
SIC 8051 Skilled nursing care facilities

D-U-N-S 25-934-0453   (BR)
UNGER NURSING HOMES LIMITED
TUFFORD NURSING HOME
(*Suby of* Unger Nursing Homes Limited)
312 Queenston St, St Catharines, ON, L2P 2X4
(905) 682-0503
Emp Here 90
SIC 8051 Skilled nursing care facilities

D-U-N-S 20-005-1147   (BR)
WENDY'S RESTAURANTS OF CANADA INC
WENDY'S OLD FASHIONED HAMBURGERS
(*Suby of* The Wendy's Company)
145 Hartzel Rd, St Catharines, ON, L2P 1N6
(905) 704-1010
Emp Here 30
SIC 5812 Eating places

St Catharines, ON L2R
Lincoln County

D-U-N-S 24-853-6448   (SL)
1814124 ONTARIO INC
NIAGARA GARDENS
181 Niagara St, St Catharines, ON, L2R 4M1
(905) 687-3388
Emp Here 60   *Sales* 3,014,400
SIC 8361 Residential care

D-U-N-S 20-878-1898   (SL)
295823 ONTARIO INC
TROJAN SECURITY AND INVESTIGATION SERVICES
31 Raymond St, St Catharines, ON, L2R 2T3
(905) 685-4279
Emp Here 75   *Sales* 2,334,742
SIC 7381 Detective and armored car services

D-U-N-S 25-648-5533   (HQ)
5-0 TAXI CO. INC.
(*Suby of* 5-0 Taxi Co. Inc.)

16 Mitchell St, St Catharines, ON, L2R 3W4
(905) 685-5464
Emp Here 40   *Emp Total* 100
Sales 2,991,389
SIC 4121 Taxicabs

D-U-N-S 25-330-5742   (BR)
ALGOMA CENTRAL CORPORATION
ALGOMA CENTRAL MARINE
63 Church St Suite 600, St Catharines, ON, L2R 3C4
(905) 687-7888
Emp Here 100
SIC 4432 Freight transportation on the great lakes

D-U-N-S 20-280-3573   (SL)
APEX-NIAGARA TOOL LTD
(*Suby of* Bain Capital, LP)
54 Catherine St, St Catharines, ON, L2R 7R5
(905) 704-1797
Emp Here 43   *Sales* 4,937,631
SIC 5251 Hardware stores

D-U-N-S 24-700-2798   (BR)
ASTRAL MEDIA RADIO INC
ENERGIE
(*Suby of* Astral Media Radio Inc)
12 Yates St, St Catharines, ON, L2R 5R2
(905) 684-1174
Emp Here 60
SIC 4832 Radio broadcasting stations

D-U-N-S 25-296-7104   (BR)
BANK OF NOVA SCOTIA, THE
SCOTIABANK
185 St. Paul St Ste 177, St Catharines, ON, L2R 3M5
(905) 684-2021
Emp Here 30
SIC 6021 National commercial banks

D-U-N-S 20-797-1040   (BR)
BANK OF MONTREAL
BMO
191 Welland Ave, St Catharines, ON, L2R 2P2

Emp Here 20
SIC 6021 National commercial banks

D-U-N-S 24-193-1844   (HQ)
CANADIAN MENTAL HEALTH ASSOCIATION, NIAGARA BRANCH
CMHA
(*Suby of* Canadian Mental Health Association, Niagara Branch)
15 Wellington St, St Catharines, ON, L2R 5P7
(905) 641-5222
Emp Here 20   *Emp Total* 70
Sales 4,596,524
SIC 8011 Offices and clinics of medical doctors

D-U-N-S 25-178-9160   (SL)
CANTEC SECURITY SERVICES INC
140 Welland Ave Unit 5, St Catharines, ON, L2R 2N6
(905) 687-9500
Emp Here 318   *Sales* 13,349,760
SIC 7381 Detective and armored car services
Pr Pr Gregory Hoadley

D-U-N-S 25-179-4103   (BR)
CONSEIL SCOLAIRE DE DISTRICT CATHOLIQUE CENTRE-SUD
ECOLE ELEMENTAIRE CATHOLIQUE IMMACULEE-CONCEPTION
153 Church St, St Catharines, ON, L2R 3E2
(905) 682-6732
Emp Here 20
SIC 8211 Elementary and secondary schools

D-U-N-S 25-985-5682   (SL)
COPPOLA'S RISTORANTE
203 Carlton St, St Catharines, ON, L2R 1S1
(905) 688-6694
Emp Here 50   *Sales* 1,532,175
SIC 5812 Eating places

D-U-N-S 25-297-3383   (BR)
CRAWFORD & COMPANY (CANADA) INC
CRAWFORD AND COMPANY
(*Suby of* Crawford & Company)
55 King St Suite 300, St Catharines, ON, L2R 3H5
(905) 688-6391
Emp Here 20
SIC 6411 Insurance agents, brokers, and service

D-U-N-S 25-643-9621   (BR)
CRAWFORD SMITH & SWALLOW CHARTERED ACCOUNTANTS LLP
(*Suby of* Crawford Smith & Swallow Chartered Accountants LLP)
43 Church St Suite 400, St Catharines, ON, L2R 7E1
(905) 937-2100
Emp Here 24
SIC 8721 Accounting, auditing, and bookkeeping

D-U-N-S 25-869-7051   (BR)
DISTRICT SCHOOL BOARD OF NIAGARA
ALEXANDRA SCHOOL
84 Henry St, St Catharines, ON, L2R 5V4
(905) 685-5489
Emp Here 28
SIC 8211 Elementary and secondary schools

D-U-N-S 20-710-8460   (BR)
DISTRICT SCHOOL BOARD OF NIAGARA
QUEEN MARY PUBLIC SCHOOL
185 Carlton St, St Catharines, ON, L2R 1S1

Emp Here 50
SIC 8211 Elementary and secondary schools

D-U-N-S 25-755-1986   (BR)
DISTRICT SCHOOL BOARD OF NIAGARA
ST CATHARINES COLLEGIATE
34 Catherine St, St Catharines, ON, L2R 5E7
(905) 687-7301
Emp Here 90
SIC 8211 Elementary and secondary schools

D-U-N-S 25-143-8792   (BR)
DISTRICT SCHOOL BOARD OF NIAGARA
CONNAUGHT PUBLIC SCHOOL
28 Prince St, St Catharines, ON, L2R 3X7
(905) 682-6609
Emp Here 21
SIC 8211 Elementary and secondary schools

D-U-N-S 20-026-7198   (BR)
DISTRICT SCHOOL BOARD OF NIAGARA
WOODLAND PUBLIC SCHOOL
1511 Seventh St, St Catharines, ON, L2R 6P9
(905) 685-1331
Emp Here 20
SIC 8211 Elementary and secondary schools

D-U-N-S 25-913-2728   (BR)
DISTRICT SCHOOL BOARD OF NIAGARA
MEMORIAL SCHOOL
17 Welland Ave, St Catharines, ON, L2R 2M1

Emp Here 26
SIC 8211 Elementary and secondary schools

D-U-N-S 20-031-5658   (BR)
DISTRICT SCHOOL BOARD OF NIAGARA
GRAPEVIEW PUBLIC SCHOOL
106 First St Louth, St Catharines, ON, L2R 6P9
(905) 984-5517
Emp Here 40
SIC 8211 Elementary and secondary schools

D-U-N-S 25-876-2392   (BR)
DISTRICT SCHOOL BOARD OF NIAGARA
MAYWOOD ELEMENTARY
140 Haig St, St Catharines, ON, L2R 6L3

Emp Here 30
SIC 8211 Elementary and secondary schools

D-U-N-S 20-710-8437   (BR)

DISTRICT SCHOOL BOARD OF NIAGARA
GLEN RIDGE SCHOOL
101 South Dr, St Catharines, ON, L2R 4V7
(905) 685-9586
Emp Here 50
SIC 8211 Elementary and secondary schools

D-U-N-S 20-824-1992   (HQ)
DIXON COMMERCIAL INVESTIGATORS (1982) INC
(*Suby of* Dixon Commercial Investigators (1982) Inc)
91 Geneva St, St Catharines, ON, L2R 4M9
(905) 688-0447
Emp Here 49   *Emp Total* 50
Sales 2,553,625
SIC 7322 Adjustment and collection services

D-U-N-S 20-892-5029   (BR)
DURWARD JONES BARKWELL & COMPANY LLP
(*Suby of* Durward Jones Barkwell & Company LLP)
69 Ontario St, St Catharines, ON, L2R 5J5
(905) 684-9221
Emp Here 40
SIC 8721 Accounting, auditing, and bookkeeping

D-U-N-S 24-873-0947   (BR)
ESIT CANADA ENTERPRISE SERVICES CO
ESIT CANADA ENTERPRISE SERVICES CO
(*Suby of* Dxc Technology Company)
570 Glendale Ave, St Catharines, ON, L2R 7B3
(905) 641-4241
Emp Here 50
SIC 8741 Management services

D-U-N-S 25-178-8279   (SL)
EAST SIDE MARIOS
332 Ontario St, St Catharines, ON, L2R 5L8

Emp Here 55   *Sales* 1,678,096
SIC 5812 Eating places

D-U-N-S 20-563-3931   (BR)
EVONIK INDUSTRIES
321 Welland Ave, St Catharines, ON, L2R 2R2
(905) 688-6470
Emp Here 20
SIC 2899 Chemical preparations, nec

D-U-N-S 25-638-4876   (BR)
FIRSTONTARIO CREDIT UNION LIMITED
148 Niagara St, St Catharines, ON, L2R 4L4
(905) 685-5555
Emp Here 300
SIC 6062 State credit unions

D-U-N-S 20-793-8833   (BR)
GOVERNING COUNCIL OF THE SALVATION ARMY IN CANADA, THE
SALVATION ARMY BOOTH CENTER
184 Church St, St Catharines, ON, L2R 3E7
(905) 684-7813
Emp Here 20
SIC 8322 Individual and family services

D-U-N-S 25-365-7852   (BR)
HOME TRUST COMPANY
15 Church St Suite 100, St Catharines, ON, L2R 3B5

Emp Here 20
SIC 6021 National commercial banks

D-U-N-S 24-198-1232   (SL)
HOTEL DIEU HEALTH SCIENCES HOSPITAL, NIAGARA
ST CATHARINES DISTRICT AMBULANCE SERVICE
155 Ontario St, St Catharines, ON, L2R 5K2

Emp Here 1,015   *Sales* 91,217,447
SIC 8062 General medical and surgical hospitals
Ex Dir Frank Vetrano

D-U-N-S 20-642-3720   (SL)
INTELESERVICES CANADA INC
15 Church St, St Catharines, ON, L2R 3B5
(905) 684-7273
Emp Here 350   *Sales* 35,168,000
SIC 5963 Direct selling establishments
Pr Pr Ronald Benson

D-U-N-S 20-607-4270   (HQ)
JACK VAN KLAVEREN LIMITED
J V K
1894 Seventh St, St Catharines, ON, L2R 6P9
(905) 641-5599
Emp Here 50   *Emp Total* 2
Sales 14,592,140
SIC 5191 Farm supplies
Pr Pr Robert Murch
VP Glenn Fozard

D-U-N-S 25-978-6754   (HQ)
JOHN HOWARD SOCIETY OF NIAGARA
(*Suby of* John Howard Society of Niagara)
210 King St, St Catharines, ON, L2R 3J9
(905) 682-2657
Emp Here 47   *Emp Total* 76
Sales 1,101,828
SIC 8399 Social services, nec

D-U-N-S 20-422-1068   (BR)
KEMIRA WATER SOLUTIONS CANADA INC
KEMIRA PAPER CHEMICALS CANADA
321 Welland Ave, St Catharines, ON, L2R 2R2
(905) 688-6470
Emp Here 23
SIC 2899 Chemical preparations, nec

D-U-N-S 24-246-9476   (BR)
M. VAN NOORT & SONS BULB COMPANY LIMITED
3930 Ninth St, St Catharines, ON, L2R 6P9
(905) 641-2152
Emp Here 35
SIC 5191 Farm supplies

D-U-N-S 20-800-5723   (SL)
MCDONALD'S RESTAURANTS
385 Ontario St, St Catharines, ON, L2R 5L3
(905) 688-0244
Emp Here 80   *Sales* 2,407,703
SIC 5812 Eating places

D-U-N-S 20-710-9195   (BR)
NIAGARA CATHOLIC DISTRICT SCHOOL BOARD
ST. NICHOLAS CATHOLIC ELEMENTARY SCHOOL
149 Church St, St Catharines, ON, L2R 3E2
(905) 685-7764
Emp Here 50
SIC 8211 Elementary and secondary schools

D-U-N-S 24-180-1583   (BR)
NIAGARA CATHOLIC DISTRICT SCHOOL BOARD
MOTHER TERESA SCHOOL
125 First St Louth, St Catharines, ON, L2R 6P9
(905) 682-6862
Emp Here 25
SIC 8211 Elementary and secondary schools

D-U-N-S 25-144-3560   (BR)
NIAGARA CATHOLIC DISTRICT SCHOOL BOARD
ST JOHN ADULT LEARNING CENTRE
145 Niagara St, St Catharines, ON, L2R 4L7
(905) 682-3360
Emp Here 40
SIC 8211 Elementary and secondary schools

D-U-N-S 20-710-9120   (BR)
NIAGARA CATHOLIC DISTRICT SCHOOL BOARD
ST DENNIS SCHOOL
175 Carlton St, St Catharines, ON, L2R 1S1
(905) 682-4156
Emp Here 50
SIC 8211 Elementary and secondary schools

D-U-N-S 24-355-3166   (BR)
NIAGARA HEALTH SYSTEM
ST. CATHARINES GENERAL SITE
142 Queenston St, St Catharines, ON, L2R 2Z7
(905) 684-7271
Emp Here 800
SIC 8062 General medical and surgical hospitals

D-U-N-S 24-000-8453   (BR)
PROCESS DEVELOPMENT CANADA CORP
6 Davidson St, St Catharines, ON, L2R 2V4

Emp Here 25
SIC 7389 Business services, nec

D-U-N-S 25-651-6279   (BR)
RBC DOMINION SECURITIES INC
(*Suby of* Royal Bank Of Canada)
63 Church St Suite 400, St Catharines, ON, L2R 3C4
(905) 988-5888
Emp Here 28
SIC 6211 Security brokers and dealers

D-U-N-S 25-638-8646   (BR)
REVERA INC
CENTRAL PARK LODGES
190 King St, St Catharines, ON, L2R 7N2
(905) 641-4422
Emp Here 40
SIC 8361 Residential care

D-U-N-S 20-614-3997   (BR)
SIR CORP
JACK ASTOR'S BAR AND GRILL
400 Ontario St, St Catharines, ON, L2R 5L8
(905) 988-5677
Emp Here 50
SIC 5812 Eating places

D-U-N-S 25-178-7511   (BR)
SCOTIA CAPITAL INC
SCOTIA MCLEOD
80 King St Suite 705, St Catharines, ON, L2R 7G1
(905) 641-7700
Emp Here 20
SIC 6211 Security brokers and dealers

D-U-N-S 25-684-0224   (BR)
ST. LAWRENCE SEAWAY MANAGEMENT CORPORATION, THE
508 Glendale Ave, St Catharines, ON, L2R 6V8
(905) 641-1932
Emp Here 200
SIC 4432 Freight transportation on the great lakes

D-U-N-S 24-308-3222   (SL)
TORA ST CATHARINES (WELLAND) LIMITED
GIANT TIGER
120 Welland Ave, St Catharines, ON, L2R 2N3
(905) 685-1167
Emp Here 50   *Sales* 3,575,074
SIC 5311 Department stores

D-U-N-S 25-637-7615   (BR)
VALUE VILLAGE STORES, INC
(*Suby of* Savers, Inc.)
360 Ontario St, St Catharines, ON, L2R 5L8
(905) 688-7764
Emp Here 40
SIC 5399 Miscellaneous general merchandise

D-U-N-S 24-859-8559   (HQ)
W. S. TYLER CANADA LTD
225 Ontario St, St Catharines, ON, L2R 7J2
(905) 688-2644
Emp Here 83   *Emp Total* 3,005
Sales 15,248,786
SIC 3496 Miscellaneous fabricated wire products
Pr Florian Festge

Randy Bakeberg
Caroline Mann

D-U-N-S 25-178-7768   (BR)
WE CARE HEALTH SERVICES INC
WE CARE HOME HEALTH SERVICES
277 Welland Ave, St Catharines, ON, L2R 2P7
(905) 988-5262
Emp Here 60
SIC 8082 Home health care services

D-U-N-S 25-720-2861   (BR)
WESTERN INVENTORY SERVICE LTD
WIS INTERNATIONAL
140 Welland Ave Unit 15a, St Catharines, ON, L2R 2N6
(905) 646-0796
Emp Here 25
SIC 7389 Business services, nec

D-U-N-S 25-305-3458   (BR)
WESTMONT HOSPITALITY MANAGEMENT LIMITED
COMFORT INN
(*Suby of* Westmont Hospitality Management Limited)
2 Dunlop Dr Suite 1, St Catharines, ON, L2R 1A2
(905) 687-8890
Emp Here 22
SIC 7011 Hotels and motels

D-U-N-S 25-300-6860   (BR)
WORKPLACE SAFETY & INSURANCE BOARD, THE
301 St. Paul St Suite 1, St Catharines, ON, L2R 7R4

Emp Here 30
SIC 6331 Fire, marine, and casualty insurance

St Catharines, ON L2S
Lincoln County

D-U-N-S 20-572-2676   (BR)
BANK OF NOVA SCOTIA, THE
SCOTIABANK
500 Glenridge Ave, St Catharines, ON, L2S 3A1
(905) 684-6988
Emp Here 20
SIC 6021 National commercial banks

D-U-N-S 20-146-8782   (HQ)
BEATTIE STATIONERY LIMITED
BEATTIE'S BASICS
(*Suby of* Beattie Stationery Limited)
399 Vansickle Rd Suite 3056, St Catharines, ON, L2S 3T4
(905) 688-4040
Emp Here 60   *Emp Total* 130
Sales 11,090,026
SIC 5943 Stationery stores
Pr Pr Ted Hoxie
  Trevor Henry

D-U-N-S 24-011-8674   (BR)
BEST BUY CANADA LTD
BEST BUY
(*Suby of* Best Buy Co., Inc.)
420 Vansickle Rd Suite 1, St Catharines, ON, L2S 0C7
(905) 378-0333
Emp Here 50
SIC 5731 Radio, television, and electronic stores

D-U-N-S 24-543-9682   (SL)
DBN DRYWALL & ACOUSTICS LIMITED
200 Louth St, St Catharines, ON, L2S 2R6
(905) 684-3271
Emp Here 50   *Sales* 4,231,721
SIC 1742 Plastering, drywall, and insulation

D-U-N-S 25-010-2456   (BR)
DELOITTE LLP

3rd Fl, St Catharines, ON, L2S 3W2
(905) 323-6000
Emp Here 40
SIC 8721 Accounting, auditing, and bookkeeping

D-U-N-S 20-710-8486   (BR)
DISTRICT SCHOOL BOARD OF NIAGARA
WESTDALE PUBLIC ELEMENTARY SCHOOL
130 Rykert St, St Catharines, ON, L2S 2B4
(905) 682-9284
Emp Here 50
SIC 8211 Elementary and secondary schools

D-U-N-S 20-710-8411   (BR)
DISTRICT SCHOOL BOARD OF NIAGARA
EDITH CAVELL ELEMENTARY SCHOOL
1 Monck St, St Catharines, ON, L2S 1L5
(905) 684-6545
Emp Here 50
SIC 8211 Elementary and secondary schools

D-U-N-S 20-710-8452   (BR)
DISTRICT SCHOOL BOARD OF NIAGARA
POWER GLEN PUBLIC SCHOOL
34 Westland St, St Catharines, ON, L2S 4C1
(905) 684-7429
Emp Here 50
SIC 8211 Elementary and secondary schools

D-U-N-S 24-470-8533   (HQ)
DURWARD JONES BARKWELL & COMPANY LLP
DJB
(*Suby of* Durward Jones Barkwell & Company LLP)
20 Corporate Park Dr Suite 300, St Catharines, ON, L2S 3W2
(905) 684-9221
Emp Here 30   *Emp Total* 126
Sales 5,545,013
SIC 8721 Accounting, auditing, and bookkeeping
Pt Brent Pyper
Pt Mark Brohman
Pt Robert Niell
Pt Kim Boutin
Pt Gregory Sawatsky
Pt Darryl Teutenberg
Pt Dwane Pyper
Pt Andrew Walker
Pt Terry Suess
Pt Amanda Pyper

D-U-N-S 25-280-0990   (BR)
EXTENDICARE INC
EXTENDICARE ST. CATHERINES
283 Pelham Rd, St Catharines, ON, L2S 1X7
(905) 688-3311
Emp Here 265
SIC 8051 Skilled nursing care facilities

D-U-N-S 24-992-0679   (BR)
FIRSTONTARIO CREDIT UNION LIMITED
275 4th Ave Suite D006, St Catharines, ON, L2S 0C2
(905) 685-5555
Emp Here 40
SIC 6062 State credit unions

D-U-N-S 24-523-9483   (BR)
GLOBAL VINTNERS INC
WINEXPERTS
301 Louth St Unit B3, St Catharines, ON, L2S 3V6
(905) 708-6680
Emp Here 20
SIC 5921 Liquor stores

D-U-N-S 24-391-5571   (BR)
GOLF TOWN LIMITED
GOLF TOWN
275 Fourth Ave Unit 300, St Catharines, ON, L2S 0C2
(905) 641-1599
Emp Here 50
SIC 5941 Sporting goods and bicycle shops

D-U-N-S 24-373-0905   (BR)
HUDSON'S BAY COMPANY
HOME OUTFITTERS
399 Louth St Unit 2, St Catharines, ON, L2S 4A2
(905) 346-0958
Emp Here 21
SIC 5719 Miscellaneous homefurnishings

D-U-N-S 20-155-3315   (BR)
LONDON LIFE INSURANCE COMPANY
FREEDOM 55 FINANCIAL
24 Park Dr Suite 200, St Catharines, ON, L2S 2W2
(905) 688-0864
Emp Here 70
SIC 6311 Life insurance

D-U-N-S 24-424-7250   (BR)
MAGNA INTERNATIONAL INC
VENEST INDUSTRIES DIV OF
2032 First St Louth, St Catharines, ON, L2S 0C5
(905) 641-9110
Emp Here 200
SIC 3714 Motor vehicle parts and accessories

D-U-N-S 25-295-6214   (BR)
MARCH OF DIMES CANADA
448 Louth St Suite 103, St Catharines, ON, L2S 3S9
(905) 641-4911
Emp Here 40
SIC 8331 Job training and related services

D-U-N-S 20-798-4845   (BR)
MCDONALD'S RESTAURANTS OF CANADA LIMITED
MCDONALD'S
(*Suby of* McDonald's Corporation)
420 Vansickle Rd, St Catharines, ON, L2S 0C7
(905) 687-8820
Emp Here 60
SIC 5812 Eating places

D-U-N-S 25-162-9812   (BR)
NIAGARA CATHOLIC DISTRICT SCHOOL BOARD
ST ANTHONY CATHOLIC ELEMENTARY SCHOOL
81 Rykert St, St Catharines, ON, L2S 1Z2
(905) 685-8859
Emp Here 55
SIC 8211 Elementary and secondary schools

D-U-N-S 24-218-7979   (HQ)
RANKIN CONSTRUCTION INC
222 Martindale Rd, St Catharines, ON, L2S 0B2
(905) 684-1111
Emp Here 60   *Emp Total* 60
Sales 4,377,642
SIC 1794 Excavation work

D-U-N-S 25-862-3599   (BR)
TD WATERHOUSE CANADA INC
TD WEALTH PRIVATE INVESTMENT AD-VICE
(*Suby of* Toronto-Dominion Bank, The)
25 Corporate Park Dr Suite 101, St Catharines, ON, L2S 3W2
(905) 704-1405
Emp Here 20
SIC 6211 Security brokers and dealers

D-U-N-S 20-042-7821   (SL)
VWR EDUCATION, LTD
BOREAL NORTHWEST
(*Suby of* VWR Corporation)
399 Vansickle Rd, St Catharines, ON, L2S 3T4
(800) 387-9393
Emp Here 22   *Sales* 3,210,271
SIC 5049 Professional equipment, nec

D-U-N-S 24-329-6840   (BR)
WAL-MART CANADA CORP
420 Vansickle Rd Suite 2, St Catharines, ON, L2S 0C7

(905) 687-9212
Emp Here 200
SIC 5311 Department stores

St Catharines, ON L2T
Lincoln County

D-U-N-S 20-917-9170   (BR)
20 VIC MANAGEMENT INC
PEN CENTRE, THE
221 Glendale Ave, St Catharines, ON, L2T 2K9
(905) 687-6622
Emp Here 20
SIC 6531 Real estate agents and managers

D-U-N-S 25-288-0729   (BR)
A & W FOOD SERVICES OF CANADA INC
A & W
221 Glendale Ave Suite 1009, St Catharines, ON, L2T 2K9
(905) 684-1884
Emp Here 20
SIC 5812 Eating places

D-U-N-S 20-260-8659   (BR)
ARLIE'S SPORT SHOP (DOWNTOWN) LTD
BOATHOUSE
221 Glendale Ave, St Catharines, ON, L2T 2K9
(905) 684-8730
Emp Here 42
SIC 5941 Sporting goods and bicycle shops

D-U-N-S 20-588-2777   (BR)
BANQUE TORONTO-DOMINION, LA
TD CANADA TRUST
(*Suby of* Toronto-Dominion Bank, The)
240 Glendale Ave, St Catharines, ON, L2T 2L2
(905) 684-8719
Emp Here 20
SIC 6021 National commercial banks

D-U-N-S 24-342-2131   (BR)
CARA OPERATIONS LIMITED
SWISS CHALET
(*Suby of* Cara Holdings Limited)
221 Glendale Ave Unit 60a, St Catharines, ON, L2T 2K9

Emp Here 36
SIC 5812 Eating places

D-U-N-S 20-303-3451   (BR)
CARA OPERATIONS LIMITED
KELSEY'S
(*Suby of* Cara Holdings Limited)
221 Glendale Ave, St Catharines, ON, L2T 2K9
(905) 684-1145
Emp Here 50
SIC 5812 Eating places

D-U-N-S 20-024-9733   (BR)
CONSEIL SCOLAIRE DE DISTRICT CATHOLIQUE CENTRE-SUD
ECOLE ELEMENTAIRE CATHOLIQUE SAINTE-MARGUERITE-BOURGEOYS
12 Burleigh Hill Dr, St Catharines, ON, L2T 2V5
(905) 227-4002
Emp Here 20
SIC 8211 Elementary and secondary schools

D-U-N-S 20-732-5288   (BR)
DENDRES CORP
MCDONALD'S RESTAURANT
(*Suby of* Dendres Corp)
210 Glendale Ave, St Catharines, ON, L2T 3Y6
(905) 688-8877
Emp Here 70
SIC 5812 Eating places

D-U-N-S 25-755-1978   (BR)

DISTRICT SCHOOL BOARD OF NIAGARA
OAKRIDGE PUBLIC SCHOOL
1 Caroline St Suite A, St Catharines, ON, L2T 3E9
(905) 684-9259
Emp Here 27
SIC 8211 Elementary and secondary schools

D-U-N-S 20-710-8353   (BR)
DISTRICT SCHOOL BOARD OF NIAGARA
BURLEIGH HILL PUBLIC SCHOOL
15 Burleigh Hill Dr, St Catharines, ON, L2T 2V6
(905) 227-6641
Emp Here 50
SIC 8211 Elementary and secondary schools

D-U-N-S 25-143-8776   (BR)
DISTRICT SCHOOL BOARD OF NIAGARA
OAKRIDGE PUBLIC SCHOOL
1 Marsdale Dr, St Catharines, ON, L2T 3R7
(905) 684-6589
Emp Here 25
SIC 8211 Elementary and secondary schools

D-U-N-S 25-926-3309   (BR)
DISTRICT SCHOOL BOARD OF NIAGARA
SIR WINSTON CHURCHHILL SECONDARY SCHOOL
101 Glen Morris Dr, St Catharines, ON, L2T 2N1
(905) 684-6349
Emp Here 55
SIC 8211 Elementary and secondary schools

D-U-N-S 20-917-8230   (BR)
EMPIRE THEATRES LIMITED
221 Glendale Ave, St Catharines, ON, L2T 2K9
(905) 682-8843
Emp Here 20
SIC 7832 Motion picture theaters, except drive-in

D-U-N-S 24-337-3326   (BR)
FGL SPORTS LTD
SPORT-CHEK
221 Glendale Ave Unit 119, St Catharines, ON, L2T 2K9
(905) 687-4808
Emp Here 40
SIC 5941 Sporting goods and bicycle shops

D-U-N-S 25-301-2058   (BR)
HUDSON'S BAY COMPANY
BAY, THE
221 Glendale Ave, St Catharines, ON, L2T 2K9
(905) 688-4441
Emp Here 200
SIC 5311 Department stores

D-U-N-S 24-157-7431   (BR)
KEG RESTAURANTS LTD
344 Glendale Ave, St Catharines, ON, L2T 4E3
(905) 680-4585
Emp Here 100
SIC 5812 Eating places

D-U-N-S 25-984-4900   (BR)
LE CHATEAU INC
LE CHATEAU #92
(*Suby of* Le Chateau Inc)
221 Glendale Ave, St Catharines, ON, L2T 2K9
(905) 682-7046
Emp Here 20
SIC 5621 Women's clothing stores

D-U-N-S 25-162-9788   (BR)
NIAGARA CATHOLIC DISTRICT SCHOOL BOARD
DENIS MORRIS CATHOLIC HIGH SCHOOL
40 Glen Morris Dr, St Catharines, ON, L2T 2M9
(905) 684-8731
Emp Here 90
SIC 8211 Elementary and secondary schools

D-U-N-S 20-710-9203   (BR)
NIAGARA CATHOLIC DISTRICT SCHOOL BOARD
ST PETER CATHOLIC ELEMENTARY SCHOOL
7 Aberdeen Cir, St Catharines, ON, L2T 2B7
(905) 984-3040
Emp Here 50
SIC 8211 Elementary and secondary schools

D-U-N-S 24-321-4645   (BR)
PF RESOLU CANADA INC
ABITIBI BOWATER
2 Allanburg Rd S, St Catharines, ON, L2T 3W9
(905) 227-5000
Emp Here 125
SIC 2621 Paper mills

D-U-N-S 24-159-2554   (SL)
PENCE RESTAURANT SERVICES LTD
BOSTON PIZZA
221 Glendale Ave, St Catharines, ON, L2T 2K9
(905) 687-1991
Emp Here 50   *Sales* 1,532,175
SIC 5812 Eating places

D-U-N-S 24-598-2959   (BR)
SOBEYS CAPITAL INCORPORATED
SOBEYS
344 Glendale Ave, St Catharines, ON, L2T 4E3
(905) 680-8563
Emp Here 25
SIC 5411 Grocery stores

D-U-N-S 20-205-7977   (BR)
UNIFOR
CAW LOCAL 4401
20 Walnut St, St Catharines, ON, L2T 1H5
(905) 227-7717
Emp Here 600
SIC 8631 Labor organizations

D-U-N-S 20-860-4392   (BR)
WINNERS MERCHANTS INTERNATIONAL L.P.
HOMESENSE
(*Suby of* The TJX Companies Inc)
221 Glendale Ave, St Catharines, ON, L2T 2K9
(905) 684-3657
Emp Here 25
SIC 5651 Family clothing stores

D-U-N-S 20-184-2932   (BR)
WINNERS MERCHANTS INTERNATIONAL L.P.
WINNERS
(*Suby of* The TJX Companies Inc)
221 Glendale Ave Unit 6151, St Catharines, ON, L2T 2K9
(905) 641-9481
Emp Here 40
SIC 5651 Family clothing stores

St Catharines, ON L2W
Lincoln County

D-U-N-S 25-826-8291   (BR)
AECOM CANADA LTD
SWAN HILLS TREATMENT CENTER
30 Hannover Dr Suite 3, St Catharines, ON, L2W 1A3
(905) 688-4272
Emp Here 20
SIC 8711 Engineering services

D-U-N-S 24-388-9938   (HQ)
LADSON PROPERTIES LIMITED
CHARTER BUILDING CO DIV OF
235 Martindale Rd Unit 14, St Catharines, ON, L2W 1A5

---

(905) 684-6542
Emp Here 21   *Emp Total* 31
Sales 5,545,013
SIC 1542 Nonresidential construction, nec
Pr Pr Donald Ward
Fin Ex Jeff Gradner

D-U-N-S 20-613-8237   (BR)
SAINT ELIZABETH REHAB
COMMUNITY REHAB
110b Hannover Dr Suite 105, St Catharines, ON, L2W 1A4
(905) 988-9198
Emp Here 50
SIC 8399 Social services, nec

St Clements, ON N0B
Waterloo County

D-U-N-S 20-848-6030   (BR)
JONES FEED MILLS LIMITED
MILLERS STONE, THE
2755 Lobsinger Line, St Clements, ON, N0B 2M0
(519) 699-5200
Emp Here 20
SIC 5999 Miscellaneous retail stores, nec

D-U-N-S 20-129-5029   (HQ)
STEED & EVANS LIMITED
(*Suby of* Steed & Evans Limited)
3000 Ament Line, St Clements, ON, N0B 2M0
(519) 744-7315
Emp Here 20   *Emp Total* 200
Sales 23,347,424
SIC 1611 Highway and street construction
Pr Pr Malcolm Matheson

D-U-N-S 25-228-1902   (BR)
WATERLOO   CATHOLIC   DISTRICT SCHOOL BOARD
ST CLEMENT ELEMENTARY SCHOOL
3639 Lobsinger Line, St Clements, ON, N0B 2M0
(519) 699-5271
Emp Here 21
SIC 8211 Elementary and secondary schools

St Davids, ON L0S
Lincoln County

D-U-N-S 25-137-3411   (BR)
DISTRICT SCHOOL BOARD OF NIAGARA
ST DAVIDS SCHOOL
1344 York St, St Davids, ON, L0S 1P0
(905) 262-4533
Emp Here 20
SIC 8211 Elementary and secondary schools

D-U-N-S 25-702-4794   (SL)
ORCHARD GLEN GARDEN FRESH TRADITIONS INC
ORCHARD GLEN
Gd, St Davids, ON, L0S 1P0
(905) 262-5531
Emp Here 35   *Sales* 5,782,650
SIC 5411 Grocery stores
Pr Moe Iaanchuk

St Eugene, ON K0B
Prescott County

D-U-N-S 24-885-7443   (SL)
1048547 ONTARIO INC
SKOTIDAKIS GOAT FARM
185 County Rd 10, St Eugene, ON, K0B 1P0
(613) 674-3183
Emp Here 180   *Sales* 17,510,568
SIC 2022 Cheese; natural and processed

Pr Pr John Skotidakis
Antigoni Skotidakis

D-U-N-S 20-711-6562   (BR)
CONSEIL   SCOLAIRE   DE   DISTRICT CATHOLIQUE DE L'EST ONTARIEN
ECOLE   ELEMENTAIRE   CATHOLIQUE CURE-LABROSSE
5050 Fatima St Bureau 130, St Eugene, ON, K0B 1P0
(613) 674-2145
Emp Here 50
SIC 8211 Elementary and secondary schools

St George Brant, ON N0E
Brant County

D-U-N-S 20-710-6191   (BR)
GRAND ERIE DISTRICT SCHOOL BOARD
ST GEORGE-GERMAN SCHOOL.
(*Suby of* Grand Erie District School Board)
3 College, St George Brant, ON, N0E 1N0
(519) 448-1493
Emp Here 22
SIC 8211 Elementary and secondary schools

D-U-N-S 20-316-0044   (BR)
TIM HORTON CHILDREN'S FOUNDATION, INC
TIM HORTON ONONDAGA FARMS
264 Glen Morris Rd E, St George Brant, ON, N0E 1N0
(519) 448-1264
Emp Here 95
SIC 7032 Sporting and recreational camps

St Isidore, ON K0C
Prescott County

D-U-N-S 25-126-3836   (BR)
CONSEIL   SCOLAIRE   DE   DISTRICT CATHOLIQUE DE L'EST ONTARIEN
ECOLE   ELEMENTAIRE   CATHOLIQUE SAINT-ISIDORE
(*Suby of* Conseil Scolaire De District Catholique De L'Est Ontarien)
20 Rue De L'Ecole, St Isidore, ON, K0C 2B0
(613) 524-2945
Emp Here 30
SIC 8211 Elementary and secondary schools

D-U-N-S 24-377-5116   (BR)
CORPORATION OF THE NATION MUNICIPALITY
ST ISIDORE RECREATION CENTRE
20 Arena St, St Isidore, ON, K0C 2B0
(613) 524-2522
Emp Here 20
SIC 7999 Amusement and recreation, nec

D-U-N-S 24-886-1627   (HQ)
PETROLE LEVAC PETROLEUM INC
(*Suby of* Petrole Levac Petroleum Inc)
5552 Rue St Catharine, St Isidore, ON, K0C 2B0
(613) 524-2079
Emp Here 45   *Emp Total* 75
Sales 13,546,080
SIC 5984 Liquefied petroleum gas dealers
Pr Pr Jean-Marc Levac
Allan Macewen

St Jacobs, ON N0B
Waterloo County

D-U-N-S 20-170-3225   (HQ)
1003694 ONTARIO INC
CARE PARTNERS
(*Suby of* 1003694 Ontario Inc)

1580 King St N, St Jacobs, ON, N0B 2N0
(519) 664-0756
Emp Here 100   *Emp Total* 400
Sales 100,810,320
SIC 8082 Home health care services
Pr Pr Linda Knight

D-U-N-S 20-783-3286   (SL)
DERBECKER'S HERITAGE HOUSE LIMITED
HERITAGE HOUSE NURSING HOME
54 Eby St, St Jacobs, ON, N0B 2N0
(519) 664-2921
Emp Here 60   *Sales* 2,699,546
SIC 8051 Skilled nursing care facilities

D-U-N-S 24-007-1530   (SL)
MERCEDES CORP
1386 King St N, St Jacobs, ON, N0B 2N0
(519) 664-2293
Emp Here 350   *Sales* 54,661,120
SIC 5712 Furniture stores
Pr Pr Marcus Shantz
Ross Shantz
Treas David Howey

D-U-N-S 24-617-8383   (BR)
QUARRY   INTEGRATED   COMMUNICATIONS INC
1440 King St N Suite 1, St Jacobs, ON, N0B 2N0

Emp Here 80
SIC 7311 Advertising agencies

D-U-N-S 24-467-9606   (SL)
STEED AND EVANS LIMITED
3000 Ament Line Rr 1, St Jacobs, ON, N0B 2N0

Emp Here 49   *Sales* 7,656,480
SIC 1611 Highway and street construction

D-U-N-S 25-943-4447   (BR)
STONE CROCK INC, THE
VIDALIA'S MARKET DINING
1398 King St N, St Jacobs, ON, N0B 2N0
(519) 664-2575
Emp Here 60
SIC 5812 Eating places

D-U-N-S 25-228-1340   (BR)
WATERLOO REGION DISTRICT SCHOOL BOARD
ST. JACOBS PUBLIC SCHOOL
72 Queensway Dr, St Jacobs, ON, N0B 2N0
(519) 664-2272
Emp Here 30
SIC 8211 Elementary and secondary schools

St Joachim, ON N0R
Essex County

D-U-N-S 25-249-1956   (BR)
CONSEIL SCOLAIRE DE DISTRICT DES ECOLES CATHOLIQUES DU SUD-OUEST
ECOLE L MENTAIRE CATHOLIQUE SAINT-AMBROISE
2716 Rd 42, St Joachim, ON, N0R 1S0
(519) 728-2010
Emp Here 25
SIC 8211 Elementary and secondary schools

St Marys, ON N4X
Perth County

D-U-N-S 25-294-0739   (SL)
2008788 ONTARIO LIMITED
CALEDON TUBING, DIV OF
(*Suby of* Martinrea International Inc)
580 James St S, St Marys, ON, N4X 1C6

(519) 349-2850
Emp Here 66
SIC 3317 Steel pipe and tubes

D-U-N-S 25-263-5099   (BR)
AVON   MAITLAND   DISTRICT   SCHOOL BOARD
ST MARY'S COLLEGIATE & VOCATIONAL INSTITUTE
338 Elizabeth St, St Marys, ON, N4X 1B6
(519) 284-1731
Emp Here 45
SIC 8211 Elementary and secondary schools

D-U-N-S 20-710-6894   (BR)
AVON   MAITLAND   DISTRICT   SCHOOL BOARD
ARTHUR MEIGHEN PUBLIC SCHOOL
151 Water St N, St Marys, ON, N4X 1B8

Emp Here 25
SIC 8211 Elementary and secondary schools

D-U-N-S 24-335-0357   (BR)
CASCADES CANADA ULC
NORAMPAC ST. MARYS
304 James St S, St Marys, ON, N4X 1B7
(519) 284-1840
Emp Here 151
SIC 2653 Corrugated and solid fiber boxes

D-U-N-S 25-842-2666   (BR)
HURON   PERTH   CATHOLIC   DISTRICT SCHOOL BOARD
HOLY NAME OF MARY SCHOOL
161 Peel St N, St Marys, ON, N4X 1B2
(519) 284-2170
Emp Here 40
SIC 8211 Elementary and secondary schools

D-U-N-S 20-818-9308   (SL)
KINGSWAY LODGE ST. MARYS LTD
310 Queen St E, St Marys, ON, N4X 1C8
(519) 284-2921
Emp Here 78   *Sales* 3,575,074
SIC 8051 Skilled nursing care facilities

D-U-N-S 20-178-3722   (BR)
MAPLE LEAF FOODS INC
SCHNEIDER FOODS
Gd, St Marys, ON, N4X 1B7
(519) 229-8900
Emp Here 400
SIC 2015 Poultry slaughtering and processing

D-U-N-S 25-515-9840   (BR)
MURPHY, J & T LIMITED
MURPHY BUS LINES
Gd, St Marys, ON, N4X 1C8
(519) 229-8956
Emp Here 70
SIC 4151 School buses

D-U-N-S 25-306-1261   (SL)
SUPER STAR HOCKEY LIMITED
RIVER VALLEY GOLF & COUNTRY CLUB
4725 Line 1, St Marys, ON, N4X 1C6
(519) 225-2329
Emp Here 65   *Sales* 2,772,507
SIC 7992 Public golf courses

D-U-N-S 20-975-4027   (SL)
WILDWOOD CARE CENTRE INC
100 Ann St, St Marys, ON, N4X 1A1
(519) 284-3628
Emp Here 70   *Sales* 4,146,248
SIC 8051 Skilled nursing care facilities

St Thomas, ON N5P
Elgin County

D-U-N-S 20-119-1488   (SL)
552429 ONTARIO LIMITED
ALE WALKER TRANSPORT
389 South Edgeware Rd, St Thomas, ON,

N5P 4C5

Emp Here 300   *Sales* 53,202,720
SIC 4213 Trucking, except local
Pr Pr Julie Tanguay
  Laurie Bearss
VP VP Jean Walker

D-U-N-S 20-515-5992   (SL)
AMINO NORTH AMERICA CORPORATION
15 Highbury Ave, St Thomas, ON, N5P 4M1
(519) 637-2156
Emp Here 49   *Sales* 4,158,005
SIC 3465 Automotive stampings

D-U-N-S 25-306-7086   (BR)
BINGO COUNTRY HOLDINGS LIMITED
ST THOMAS BINGO COUNTRY
(*Suby of* Bingo Country Holdings Limited)
140 Edward St, St Thomas, ON, N5P 1Z3
(519) 633-1984
Emp Here 30
SIC 7999 Amusement and recreation, nec

D-U-N-S 20-692-7712   (HQ)
CANADIAN IPG CORPORATION
CANADIAN IPG
130 Woodworth Ave, St Thomas, ON, N5P
3K1
(519) 637-1945
Emp Here 38   *Emp Total* 4
Sales 8,390,481
SIC 5084 Industrial machinery and equipment
Pr Pr Rodney Malloy
VP VP Dale Stewart
VP Opers Paul Heddele
Dir William Buckborough

D-U-N-S 25-003-1663   (BR)
CANADIAN IMPERIAL BANK OF COM-MERCE
CIBC
440 Talbot St, St Thomas, ON, N5P 1B9
(519) 631-1280
Emp Here 25
SIC 6021 National commercial banks

D-U-N-S 25-517-7693   (SL)
CARING CUPBOARD, THE
803 Talbot St, St Thomas, ON, N5P 1E4
(519) 633-5308
Emp Here 49   *Sales* 11,873,345
SIC 8399 Social services, nec
Ch Bd Jim Miller

D-U-N-S 24-045-6595   (SL)
CIRCLE CORTINA INDUSTRIES CANADA LTD
195 Edward St, St Thomas, ON, N5P 1Z4
(519) 631-2900
Emp Here 49   *Sales* 9,423,360
SIC 3669 Communications equipment, nec
Genl Mgr Dave Wilkens

D-U-N-S 20-903-7407   (HQ)
COMMUNITY LIVING ELGIN
ELGIN A.C.L.
(*Suby of* Community Living Elgin)
400 Talbot St, St Thomas, ON, N5P 1B8
(519) 631-9222
Emp Here 20   *Emp Total* 260
Sales 13,062,400
SIC 8361 Residential care
Ex Dir Tom Mccallum
Dir Fin David Round
Dir Mary Cosyns

D-U-N-S 25-800-6022   (BR)
COMMUNITY LIVING ELGIN
FRIENDCO PACKAGING & ASSEMBLY
(*Suby of* Community Living Elgin)
5 Frisch St, St Thomas, ON, N5P 3N3
(519) 631-1721
Emp Here 24
SIC 7389 Business services, nec

D-U-N-S 24-248-6434   (BR)
CORPORATION OF THE CITY OF ST.

THOMAS, THE
VALLEYVIEW HOME
350 Burwell Rd, St Thomas, ON, N5P 0A3
(519) 631-1030
Emp Here 20
SIC 8051 Skilled nursing care facilities

D-U-N-S 25-517-8436   (BR)
CORPORATION OF THE COUNTY OF EL-GIN
ELGIN MANOR HOME FOR SENIORS
39232 Fingal Line, St Thomas, ON, N5P 3S5
(519) 631-0620
Emp Here 110
SIC 8361 Residential care

D-U-N-S 24-118-5748   (BR)
DOLLARAMA S.E.C.
DOLLARAMA
1010 Talbot St, St Thomas, ON, N5P 4N2
(519) 633-3457
Emp Here 22
SIC 5311 Department stores

D-U-N-S 24-026-9050   (SL)
ELGIN MANOR HOME FOR SR CITIZENS
A COUNTY OF ELGIN
39262 Fingal Line, St Thomas, ON, N5P 3S5
(519) 631-0620
Emp Here 100   *Sales* 4,331,255
SIC 8361 Residential care

D-U-N-S 20-511-9337   (BR)
FORD MOTOR COMPANY OF CANADA, LIMITED
(*Suby of* Ford Motor Company)
1188 Ford Sunset Rd, St Thomas, ON, N5P
3W1
(519) 637-5332
Emp Here 20
SIC 3711 Motor vehicles and car bodies

D-U-N-S 20-706-0682   (BR)
FORD MOTOR COMPANY OF CANADA, LIMITED
(*Suby of* Ford Motor Company)
Gd, St Thomas, ON, N5P 3W1

Emp Here 1,500
SIC 3711 Motor vehicles and car bodies

D-U-N-S 20-553-1630   (SL)
FOREST CITY CASTINGS INC
10 Highbury Ave, St Thomas, ON, N5P 4C7
(519) 633-2999
Emp Here 80   *Sales* 8,901,205
SIC 3365 Aluminum foundries
Pr Pr Michael Vandenboom
  Scott Mcrae

D-U-N-S 20-148-5257   (SL)
GORMAN-RUPP OF CANADA LIMITED
(*Suby of* Gorman-Rupp Company)
70 Burwell Rd, St Thomas, ON, N5P 3R7
(519) 631-2870
Emp Here 46   *Sales* 1,021,450
SIC 3561 Pumps and pumping equipment

D-U-N-S 20-918-6159   (BR)
HURON TRACTOR LTD
CAN-EAST EQUIPMENT
43900 Talbot Line, St Thomas, ON, N5P 3S7
(519) 631-7230
Emp Here 22
SIC 5083 Farm and garden machinery

D-U-N-S 20-189-7100   (BR)
LEAR CANADA
10 Highbury Ave, St Thomas, ON, N5P 4C7

Emp Here 320
SIC 2531 Public building and related furniture

D-U-N-S 20-148-5554   (BR)
LENNOX CANADA INC
INCH, ROY & SONS SERVICE EXPERTS
283 Talbot St, St Thomas, ON, N5P 1B3
(519) 631-7140
Emp Here 30

SIC 1711 Plumbing, heating, air-conditioning

D-U-N-S 24-326-2719   (BR)
LOBLAWS INC
REAL CANADIAN SUPERSTORE
1063 Talbot St Unit 50, St Thomas, ON, N5P
1G4
(519) 637-6358
Emp Here 200
SIC 5411 Grocery stores

D-U-N-S 24-361-4872   (BR)
MAGNA INTERNATIONAL INC
PRESSTRAN INDUSTRIES
170 Edward St, St Thomas, ON, N5P 4B4
(519) 633-7080
Emp Here 500
SIC 3714 Motor vehicle parts and accessories

D-U-N-S 25-399-0576   (BR)
MAGNA INTERNATIONAL INC
FORMET INDUSTRIES
1 Cosma Crt, St Thomas, ON, N5P 4J5
(519) 633-8400
Emp Here 1,000
SIC 3714 Motor vehicle parts and accessories

D-U-N-S 24-346-4554   (BR)
MASCO CANADA LIMITED
(*Suby of* Masco Corporation)
35 Currah Rd, St Thomas, ON, N5P 3R2

Emp Here 100
SIC 3432 Plumbing fixture fittings and trim

D-U-N-S 24-953-7002   (HQ)
MASCO CANADA LIMITED
DELTA FAUCET CANADA
(*Suby of* Masco Corporation)
350 South Edgeware Rd, St Thomas, ON,
N5P 4L1
(519) 633-5050
Emp Here 410   *Emp Total* 26,000
Sales 159,065,135
SIC 3432 Plumbing fixture fittings and trim
Pr Rod Pullen
VP Fin William Simpson

D-U-N-S 24-576-5896   (SL)
NORTH STAR MANUFACTURING (LON-DON) LTD
NORTH STAR VINYL WINDOWS AND DOORS
(*Suby of* Atrium Corporation)
40684 Talbot Line, St Thomas, ON, N5P 3T2
(519) 637-7899
Emp Here 210   *Sales* 40,453,922
SIC 3089 Plastics products, nec
Pr Pr Ron Cauchi
Dir Fin Pat Rooke

D-U-N-S 25-220-7022   (BR)
RAM-LP INC
ST THOMAS SANITARY COLLECTION SER-VICES
(*Suby of* Ram-LP Inc)
38590 Third Line, St Thomas, ON, N5P 3T2

Emp Here 65
SIC 4953 Refuse systems

D-U-N-S 25-309-9493   (BR)
ROYAL BANK OF CANADA
RBC
(*Suby of* Royal Bank Of Canada)
1099 Talbot St, St Thomas, ON, N5P 1G4
(519) 631-7369
Emp Here 40
SIC 6021 National commercial banks

D-U-N-S 25-623-2703   (BR)
ROYAL BANK OF CANADA
RBC
(*Suby of* Royal Bank Of Canada)
367 Talbot St, St Thomas, ON, N5P 1B7

Emp Here 20
SIC 6021 National commercial banks

D-U-N-S 24-336-3293   (BR)
SMP MOTOR PRODUCTS LTD
UNIMOTOR, DIVISION OF
(*Suby of* Standard Motor Products, Inc.)
33 Gaylord Rd, St Thomas, ON, N5P 3R9
(519) 633-8422
Emp Here 170
SIC 3621 Motors and generators

D-U-N-S 20-920-0042   (BR)
ST. JOHN COUNCIL FOR ONTARIO
ST. JOHN AMBULANCE
656 Talbot St, St Thomas, ON, N5P 1C8
(519) 633-2290
Emp Here 20
SIC 4119 Local passenger transportation, nec

D-U-N-S 20-010-0241   (BR)
ST. JOSEPH'S HEALTH CARE, LONDON
REGIONAL MENTAL HEALTH CARE, ST THOMAS
Gd, St Thomas, ON, N5P 3V9
(519) 631-8510
Emp Here 667
SIC 8093 Specialty outpatient clinics, nec

D-U-N-S 24-347-1542   (BR)
ST. THOMAS FORD LINCOLN SALES LIM-ITED
ST THOMAS FORD COLLISION
700 Talbot St, St Thomas, ON, N5P 1E2

Emp Here 53
SIC 7532 Top and body repair and paint shops

D-U-N-S 20-310-8477   (BR)
STAPLES CANADA INC
(*Suby of* Staples, Inc.)
1063 Talbot St Suite 3, St Thomas, ON, N5P
1G4
(519) 631-1810
Emp Here 25
SIC 5943 Stationery stores

D-U-N-S 25-238-8400   (BR)
THAMES VALLEY DISTRICT SCHOOL BOARD
BALACLAVA STREET ADULT AND ALTER-NATIVE EDUCATION CENTRE
20 Balaclava St, St Thomas, ON, N5P 3C2
(519) 631-1006
Emp Here 25
SIC 8211 Elementary and secondary schools

D-U-N-S 25-263-7533   (BR)
THAMES VALLEY DISTRICT SCHOOL BOARD
SCOTT STREET PUBLIC SCHOOL
50 Scott St, St Thomas, ON, N5P 1K6
(519) 631-1382
Emp Here 20
SIC 8211 Elementary and secondary schools

D-U-N-S 25-033-7631   (BR)
THAMES VALLEY DISTRICT SCHOOL BOARD
ARTHUR VOADEN SECONDARY SCHOOL
41 Flora St, St Thomas, ON, N5P 2X5
(519) 631-3770
Emp Here 80
SIC 8211 Elementary and secondary schools

D-U-N-S 25-238-8327   (BR)
THAMES VALLEY DISTRICT SCHOOL BOARD
JUNE ROSE CALLWOOD PUBLIC SCHOOL
84 Edward St, St Thomas, ON, N5P 1Y7
(519) 631-5010
Emp Here 45
SIC 8211 Elementary and secondary schools

D-U-N-S 20-710-5482   (BR)
THAMES VALLEY DISTRICT SCHOOL BOARD
NEW SARUM PUBLIC SCHOOL
9473 Belmont Rd Suite 3, St Thomas, ON,
N5P 3S7

(519) 773-5185
Emp Here 50
SIC 8211 Elementary and secondary schools

D-U-N-S 25-238-8202   (BR)
THAMES VALLEY DISTRICT SCHOOL BOARD
LOCKES PUBLIC SCHOOL
22 South Edgeware Rd, St Thomas, ON, N5P 2H2
(519) 631-8890
Emp Here 42
SIC 8211 Elementary and secondary schools

D-U-N-S 25-238-8046   (BR)
THAMES VALLEY DISTRICT SCHOOL BOARD
SOUTHWOLD PUBLIC SCHOOL
39261 Fingal Line, St Thomas, ON, N5P 3S5
(519) 631-5997
Emp Here 45
SIC 8211 Elementary and secondary schools

D-U-N-S 25-516-1812   (BR)
VICTORIAN ORDER OF NURSES FOR CANADA
V O N
175 South Edgeware Rd, St Thomas, ON, N5P 4C4
(519) 637-6408
Emp Here 50
SIC 8082 Home health care services

D-U-N-S 24-329-0256   (BR)
WAL-MART CANADA CORP
1063 Talbot St Unit 60, St Thomas, ON, N5P 1G4
(519) 637-7100
Emp Here 200
SIC 5311 Department stores

St Thomas, ON N5R
Elgin County

D-U-N-S 20-303-2925   (BR)
CARA OPERATIONS LIMITED
KELSEY'S
(*Suby of* Cara Holdings Limited)
415 Wellington St, St Thomas, ON, N5R 5K5
(519) 637-8962
Emp Here 50
SIC 5812 Eating places

D-U-N-S 25-347-6287   (BR)
CARESSANT-CARE NURSING AND RE-TIREMENT HOMES LIMITED
15 Bonnie Pl, St Thomas, ON, N5R 5T8
(519) 633-6493
Emp Here 100
SIC 8051 Skilled nursing care facilities

D-U-N-S 24-505-6247   (BR)
CARESSANT-CARE NURSING AND RE-TIREMENT HOMES LIMITED
4 Mary Bucke St, St Thomas, ON, N5R 5J6
(519) 633-3164
Emp Here 60
SIC 8051 Skilled nursing care facilities

D-U-N-S 25-940-3772   (BR)
CHESHIRE HOMES OF LONDON INC
ELGIN OUTREACH ATTENDANT SERVICES
200 Chestnut St Suite 110, St Thomas, ON, N5R 5P3
(519) 631-9097
Emp Here 28
SIC 8399 Social services, nec

D-U-N-S 25-419-3790   (BR)
DIVERSICARE CANADA MANAGEMENT SERVICES CO., INC
METCALFE GARDENS RETIREMENT RESI-DENCE
45 Metcalfe St, St Thomas, ON, N5R 5Y1
(519) 631-9393
Emp Here 51

SIC 6513 Apartment building operators

D-U-N-S 25-987-2497   (BR)
FANSHAWE COLLEGE OF APPLIED ARTS AND TECHNOLOGY, T
120 Bill Martyn Pky, St Thomas, ON, N5R 6A7
(519) 633-2030
Emp Here 55
SIC 8221 Colleges and universities

D-U-N-S 24-000-5392   (SL)
GEERLINKS BUILDING CENTRE AND FUR-NITURE LIMITED
GEERLINKS HOME HARDWARE BUILDING CENTRE AND FURNITURE STORE
295 Wellington St, St Thomas, ON, N5R 2S6
(519) 631-0095
Emp Here 50   *Sales* 4,815,406
SIC 5251 Hardware stores

D-U-N-S 20-710-5250   (BR)
LONDON DISTRICT CATHOLIC SCHOOL BOARD
ST RAPHAEL'S CATHOLIC SCHOOL
84 Park Ave, St Thomas, ON, N5R 4W1
(519) 675-4428
Emp Here 24
SIC 8211 Elementary and secondary schools

D-U-N-S 25-300-0590   (BR)
METRO ONTARIO INC
METRO
417 Wellington St Suite 1, St Thomas, ON, N5R 5J5
(519) 633-8780
Emp Here 80
SIC 5411 Grocery stores

D-U-N-S 25-295-2932   (BR)
SHOPPERS DRUG MART CORPORATION
204 First Ave, St Thomas, ON, N5R 4P5
(519) 633-1146
Emp Here 65
SIC 5912 Drug stores and proprietary stores

D-U-N-S 24-676-2715   (BR)
THAMES VALLEY DISTRICT SCHOOL BOARD
MITCHELL HEPBURN PUBLIC SCHOOL
95 Raven Ave, St Thomas, ON, N5R 0C2
(519) 631-3370
Emp Here 25
SIC 8211 Elementary and secondary schools

D-U-N-S 25-263-7491   (BR)
THAMES VALLEY DISTRICT SCHOOL BOARD
FOREST PARK PUBLIC SCHOOL
295 Forest Ave, St Thomas, ON, N5R 2K5
(519) 631-3563
Emp Here 40
SIC 8211 Elementary and secondary schools

D-U-N-S 25-238-8285   (BR)
THAMES VALLEY DISTRICT SCHOOL BOARD
ELGIN COURT PUBLIC SCHOOL
254 First Ave, St Thomas, ON, N5R 4P5
(519) 631-7118
Emp Here 23
SIC 8211 Elementary and secondary schools

D-U-N-S 20-068-0747   (BR)
THAMES VALLEY DISTRICT SCHOOL BOARD
PARKSIDE COLLEGIATE INSTITUTE
241 Sunset Dr, St Thomas, ON, N5R 3C2
(519) 633-0090
Emp Here 80
SIC 8211 Elementary and secondary schools

D-U-N-S 24-676-2699   (BR)
THAMES VALLEY DISTRICT SCHOOL BOARD
JOHN WISE PUBLIC SCHOOL
100 Parkside Dr, St Thomas, ON, N5R 3T9
(519) 633-1611
Emp Here 25

SIC 8211 Elementary and secondary schools

D-U-N-S 20-710-5458   (BR)
THAMES VALLEY DISTRICT SCHOOL BOARD
PIERRE ELLIOTT TRUDEAU FRENCH IM-MERSION
112 Churchill Cres, St Thomas, ON, N5R 1R1
(519) 631-7820
Emp Here 50
SIC 8211 Elementary and secondary schools

D-U-N-S 20-068-0739   (BR)
THAMES VALLEY DISTRICT SCHOOL BOARD
CENTRAL ELGIN COLLEGIATE INSTITUTE
201 Chestnut St, St Thomas, ON, N5R 2B5
(519) 631-4460
Emp Here 70
SIC 8211 Elementary and secondary schools

St. Pauls, ON N0K

D-U-N-S 20-094-8169   (BR)
AVON MAITLAND DISTRICT SCHOOL BOARD
DOWNIE CENTRAL PUBLIC SCHOOL
4384 First Line 20, St. Pauls, ON, N0K 1V0
(519) 393-6196
Emp Here 27
SIC 8211 Elementary and secondary schools

Stayner, ON L0M
Simcoe County

D-U-N-S 20-921-0442   (BR)
REINHART FOODS LIMITED
7449 Hwy 26, Stayner, ON, L0M 1S0
(705) 428-2422
Emp Here 110
SIC 2099 Food preparations, nec

D-U-N-S 25-264-2798   (BR)
REVERA INC
BLUE MOUNTAIN MANOR RETIREMENT HOME
236 Weir St, Stayner, ON, L0M 1S0
(705) 428-3240
Emp Here 50
SIC 8361 Residential care

D-U-N-S 25-297-6493   (BR)
SIMCOE COUNTY DISTRICT SCHOOL BOARD, THE
BYNG PUBLIC SCHOOL
(*Suby of* Simcoe County District School Board, The)
Gd, Stayner, ON, L0M 1S0
(705) 428-2245
Emp Here 25
SIC 8211 Elementary and secondary schools

D-U-N-S 25-297-6501   (BR)
SIMCOE COUNTY DISTRICT SCHOOL BOARD, THE
STAYNER COLLEGIATE INSTITUTE
(*Suby of* Simcoe County District School Board, The)
7578 26 Hwy, Stayner, ON, L0M 1S0
(705) 428-2639
Emp Here 50
SIC 8211 Elementary and secondary schools

D-U-N-S 24-378-3615   (SL)
TUNDRA STRATEGIES, INC
TUNDRA
1393 Centre Line Rd, Stayner, ON, L0M 1S0
(705) 734-7700
Emp Here 55   *Sales* 8,521,800
SIC 8742 Management consulting services
CEO Rob Macintyre

Stella, ON K0H
Lennox County

D-U-N-S 20-024-2662   (BR)
CORPORATION OF LOYALIST TOWNSHIP, THE
AMHERST ISLAND FERRY
955 Stella 40 Foot Rd, Stella, ON, K0H 2S0
(613) 389-3393
Emp Here 27
SIC 4482 Ferries

Stevensville, ON L0S
Welland County

D-U-N-S 20-290-7056   (SL)
1492332 ONTARIO LIMITED
ZOOZ
2821 Stevensville Rd, Stevensville, ON, L0S 1S0
(905) 382-9669
Emp Here 70   *Sales* 2,699,546
SIC 7996 Amusement parks

D-U-N-S 20-903-1871   (SL)
BLACK CREEK METAL INC
2991 Townline Rd, Stevensville, ON, L0S 1S0
(905) 382-3152
Emp Here 40   *Sales* 5,239,129
SIC 3441 Fabricated structural Metal
Pr Pr Marvin Beam
Merle Beam

D-U-N-S 24-101-4849   (SL)
DMI CANADA INC
2677 Winger Rd, Stevensville, ON, L0S 1S0
(905) 382-5793
Emp Here 142   *Sales* 20,356,899
SIC 3523 Farm machinery and equipment
Genl Mgr Paul Smith

D-U-N-S 20-286-9264   (BR)
DISTRICT SCHOOL BOARD OF NIAGARA
STEVENSVILLE PUBLIC SCHOOL
3521 Main St E, Stevensville, ON, L0S 1S0
(905) 382-3122
Emp Here 30
SIC 8211 Elementary and secondary schools

D-U-N-S 24-664-4819   (BR)
MAPLE LEAF FOODS INC
SHUR-GAIN FEEDS, DIV OF
2736 Stevensville Rd, Stevensville, ON, L0S 1S0

Emp Here 22
SIC 2048 Prepared feeds, nec

D-U-N-S 20-270-3534   (BR)
ZAVCOR TRUCKING LIMITED
ZAVCOR LOGISTICS
3650 Eagle St, Stevensville, ON, L0S 1S0
(905) 382-3444
Emp Here 120
SIC 4213 Trucking, except local

Stirling, ON K0K
Hastings County

D-U-N-S 24-363-1178   (SL)
GRANOVITA CANADA LTD
166 North St, Stirling, ON, K0K 3E0
(613) 395-9800
Emp Here 20   *Sales* 2,918,428
SIC 2023 Dry, condensed and evaporated dairy products

D-U-N-S 25-265-4355   (BR)
HASTINGS AND PRINCE EDWARD DIS-TRICT SCHOOL BOARD

STIRLING JUNIOR SCHOOL
84 Church St, Stirling, ON, K0K 3E0

Emp Here 28
SIC 8211 Elementary and secondary schools

D-U-N-S 20-649-5041   (BR)
**HASTINGS AND PRINCE EDWARD DIS-
TRICT SCHOOL BOARD**
STIRLING PUBLIC SHOOL
107 St James St, Stirling, ON, K0K 3E0
(613) 395-3389
Emp Here 25
SIC 8211 Elementary and secondary schools

D-U-N-S 25-119-5400   (SL)
MANORCARE PARTNERS
STIRLING MANOR NURSING HOME
218 Edward St, Stirling, ON, K0K 3E0
(613) 395-2596
Emp Here 85   Sales 3,866,917
SIC 8051 Skilled nursing care facilities

Stittsville, ON K2K
Carleton County

D-U-N-S 25-078-8189   (BR)
CLUBLINK CORPORATION ULC
KANATA GOLF & COUNTRY CLUB
(*Suby of* TWC Enterprises Limited)
Gd, Stittsville, ON, K2K 1X5
(613) 592-9417
Emp Here 70
SIC 7992 Public golf courses

Stittsville, ON K2S
Carleton County

D-U-N-S 25-292-3123   (HQ)
1024399 ONTARIO INC
BEDDINGTON'S BED & BATH
(*Suby of* 1024399 Ontario Inc)
3 Iber Rd Unit 2, Stittsville, ON, K2S 1E6
(613) 836-4488
Emp Here 21   Emp Total 85
Sales 8,480,961
SIC 5719 Miscellaneous homefurnishings
Pr Pr Murray Wall
VP VP Lynn Soucie
Jordan Rosove

D-U-N-S 24-682-2691   (SL)
1803661 ONTARIO INC
BEDDINGTON'S BED & BATH
3 Iber Rd Unit 2, Stittsville, ON, K2S 1E6
(613) 836-4488
Emp Here 80   Sales 9,988,687
SIC 5719 Miscellaneous homefurnishings
Dir Murray Wall
Dir Lynn Soucie

D-U-N-S 24-327-8699   (BR)
CARLETON PLACE DRUG MART INC
STITTSVILLE IDA PHARMACY
1250c Stittsville Main St Suite 21, Stittsville,
ON, K2S 1S9
(613) 836-3881
Emp Here 20
SIC 5912 Drug stores and proprietary stores

D-U-N-S 24-520-2820   (SL)
DKL ELECTRIC ENTERPRISES LTD
155 Iber Rd, Stittsville, ON, K2S 1E7
(613) 836-4311
Emp Here 49   Sales 5,985,550
SIC 1731 Electrical work
Pr David Lindsey

D-U-N-S 20-705-7212   (SL)
GOULBOURN RECREATION COMPLEX
1500 Shea Rd, Stittsville, ON, K2S 0B2

---

(613) 831-1169
Emp Here 60   Sales 3,283,232
SIC 7999 Amusement and recreation, nec

D-U-N-S 24-422-1086   (BR)
GROUPE EMBALLAGE SPECIALISE S.E.C.
SMITH INDUSPAC OTTAWA
140 Iber Rd, Stittsville, ON, K2S 1E9
(613) 742-6766
Emp Here 90
SIC 3086 Plastics foam products

D-U-N-S 20-804-4342   (SL)
MAHOGANY SALON & SPA LTD
1261 Stittsville Main St Unit 1, Stittsville, ON,
K2S 2E4

Emp Here 90   Sales 2,991,389
SIC 7991 Physical fitness facilities

D-U-N-S 24-847-0825   (SL)
MOR-WEN RESTAURANTS LTD
GLEN SCOTTISH PUB & RESTAURANT
1010 Stittsville Main St, Stittsville, ON, K2S
1B9
(613) 831-2738
Emp Here 80   Sales 2,407,703
SIC 5812 Eating places

D-U-N-S 24-676-3226   (BR)
**OTTAWA CATHOLIC DISTRICT SCHOOL
BOARD**
*ST. STEPHEN CATHOLIC ELEMENTARY
SCHOOL*
(*Suby of* Ottawa Catholic District School
Board)
1145 Stittsville Main St, Stittsville, ON, K2S
0M5
(613) 831-8844
Emp Here 40
SIC 8211 Elementary and secondary schools

D-U-N-S 25-081-4696   (BR)
**OTTAWA CATHOLIC DISTRICT SCHOOL
BOARD**
HOLY SPIRIT ELEMENTARY SCHOOL
(*Suby of* Ottawa Catholic District School
Board)
1383 Stittsville Main Street, Stittsville, ON,
K2S 1A6
(613) 831-1853
Emp Here 25
SIC 8211 Elementary and secondary schools

D-U-N-S 20-711-6505   (BR)
**OTTAWA CATHOLIC DISTRICT SCHOOL
BOARD**
GUARDIAN ANGELS CATHOLIC SCHOOL
(*Suby of* Ottawa Catholic District School
Board)
4 Baywood Dr, Stittsville, ON, K2S 1K5
(613) 836-7423
Emp Here 54
SIC 8211 Elementary and secondary schools

D-U-N-S 25-131-3003   (BR)
**OTTAWA CATHOLIC DISTRICT SCHOOL
BOARD**
SACRED HEART CATHOLIC HIGH SCHOOL
(*Suby of* Ottawa Catholic District School
Board)
Sacred Heart Catholic High School, Stittsville,
ON, K2S 1X4
(613) 831-6643
Emp Here 130
SIC 8211 Elementary and secondary schools

D-U-N-S 20-837-3915   (BR)
**OTTAWA-CARLETON DISTRICT SCHOOL
BOARD**
STITTSVILLE PUBLIC SCHOOL
40 Granite Ridge Dr, Stittsville, ON, K2S 1Y9
(613) 836-2818
Emp Here 45
SIC 8211 Elementary and secondary schools

D-U-N-S 25-130-3855   (BR)
**OTTAWA-CARLETON DISTRICT SCHOOL
BOARD**

A. CASSIDY LORNE ELEMENTARY
SCHOOL
27 Hobin St, Stittsville, ON, K2S 1G8
(613) 831-3434
Emp Here 55
SIC 8211 Elementary and secondary schools

D-U-N-S 25-130-3806   (BR)
**OTTAWA-CARLETON DISTRICT SCHOOL
BOARD**
*FREDERICK BANTING ALTERNATE PRO-
GRAM*
1453 Stittsville Main St, Stittsville, ON, K2S
1A6
(613) 591-7678
Emp Here 20
SIC 8211 Elementary and secondary schools

D-U-N-S 25-263-5644   (BR)
**OTTAWA-CARLETON DISTRICT SCHOOL
BOARD**
GOULBOURN MIDDLE SCHOOL
2176 Huntley Rd, Stittsville, ON, K2S 1B8
(613) 836-1312
Emp Here 34
SIC 8211 Elementary and secondary schools

D-U-N-S 25-769-8621   (BR)
REVERA INC
*STITTSVILLE VILLA RETIREMENT COMMU-
NITY*
1354 Stittsville Main St Suite 102, Stittsville,
ON, K2S 1V4
(613) 836-2216
Emp Here 50
SIC 6513 Apartment building operators

D-U-N-S 24-370-4686   (BR)
SAAND INC
EASTERN FLOAT GLASS, DIV OF
2448 Huntley Rd, Stittsville, ON, K2S 1B8
(613) 838-3373
Emp Here 63
SIC 3211 Flat glass

D-U-N-S 20-288-9197   (BR)
SPECIALTY CARE INC
SPECIALTY CARE FAMILY
(*Suby of* Specialty Care Inc)
5501 Abbott St E, Stittsville, ON, K2S 2C5
(613) 836-0331
Emp Here 100
SIC 8051 Skilled nursing care facilities

D-U-N-S 24-091-5418   (BR)
THEODORE RESTAURANTS INC
(*Suby of* Theodore Restaurants Inc)
1261 Stittsville Main St, Stittsville, ON, K2S
2E4
(613) 831-1841
Emp Here 30
SIC 5812 Eating places

Stoney Creek, ON L8E
Wentworth County

D-U-N-S 20-698-2022   (BR)
1589711 ONTARIO INC
WENTWORTH MOLD, DIV OF
566 Arvin Ave, Stoney Creek, ON, L8E 5P1
(905) 643-9044
Emp Here 130
SIC 3544 Special dies, tools, jigs, and fixtures

D-U-N-S 20-524-2758   (BR)
ARAMARK CANADA LTD.
ARAMARK MANAGED SERVICES
903 Barton St Suite 5, Stoney Creek, ON, L8E
5P5
(905) 643-4550
Emp Here 20
SIC 5962 Merchandising machine operators

D-U-N-S 20-836-0540   (SL)
AESTHETICS LANDSCAPE CONTRAC-

TORS
1092 Highway 8, Stoney Creek, ON, L8E 5H8
(905) 643-9933
Emp Here 30   Sales 8,643,680
SIC 5083 Farm and garden machinery
Owner Greg Davis

D-U-N-S 24-924-8626   (SL)
ALPHAGARY (CANADA) LIMITED
5 Pinelands Ave, Stoney Creek, ON, L8E 3A4

Emp Here 30   Sales 5,399,092
SIC 2822 Synthetic rubber
Pr Pr Ariff Wakani
  Charles Cross
  Terry Kimball

D-U-N-S 24-314-0600   (BR)
BARTEK INGREDIENTS INC
690 South Service Rd, Stoney Creek, ON,
L8E 5M5
(905) 643-1286
Emp Here 40
SIC 2865 Cyclic crudes and intermediates

D-U-N-S 25-530-7936   (BR)
BARTON AUTO PARTS LIMITED
201 Barton St Suite 1, Stoney Creek, ON, L8E
2K3
(905) 662-9266
Emp Here 20
SIC 5013 Motor vehicle supplies and new
parts

D-U-N-S 25-359-8734   (SL)
**BEVERLEY HILLS HOME IMPROVEMENTS
INC**
201 Barton St Unit 3, Stoney Creek, ON, L8E
2K3
(905) 578-2292
Emp Here 25   Sales 5,124,480
SIC 1521 Single-family housing construction
Pr Pr Richard Hames

D-U-N-S 24-381-7975   (BR)
BLACK & MCDONALD LIMITED
328 Green Rd, Stoney Creek, ON, L8E 5T7
(905) 560-3100
Emp Here 20
SIC 1711 Plumbing, heating, air-conditioning

D-U-N-S 25-294-9185   (BR)
BREWERS RETAIL INC
BEER STORE, THE
414 Dewitt Rd, Stoney Creek, ON, L8E 4B7
(905) 664-7921
Emp Here 100
SIC 5921 Liquor stores

D-U-N-S 20-572-8624   (BR)
CANADA POST CORPORATION
HAMILTON MAIL PROCESSING PLANT
393 Millen Rd, Stoney Creek, ON, L8E 5A8
(905) 664-0009
Emp Here 600
SIC 4311 U.s. postal service

D-U-N-S 20-054-2074   (HQ)
CHARLES JONES INDUSTRIAL LIMITED
237 Arvin Ave, Stoney Creek, ON, L8E 5S6
(905) 664-8448
Emp Here 34   Emp Total 115
Sales 58,202,700
SIC 5085 Industrial supplies
Pr Pr William Baird Jones
VP Fin Syd Wilkinson

D-U-N-S 25-786-0726   (BR)
COLEMAN, DOUG TRUCKING LTD
330 South Service Rd, Stoney Creek, ON,
L8E 2R4
(905) 664-9477
Emp Here 20
SIC 4212 Local trucking, without storage

D-U-N-S 24-601-8964   (BR)
CRANE, JOHN CANADA INC
423 Green Rd N, Stoney Creek, ON, L8E 3A1

---

(905) 662-6191
Emp Here 90
SIC 3061 Mechanical rubber goods

D-U-N-S 20-053-1812   (HQ)
CRANE, JOHN CANADA INC
423 Green Rd, Stoney Creek, ON, L8E 3A1
(905) 662-6191
Emp Here 120   *Emp Total* 50
Sales 26,767,156
SIC 3499 Fabricated Metal products, nec
Sls Dir Chris Steele
Dir Opers Fern Lebeille

D-U-N-S 25-911-6028   (BR)
EXTENDICARE INC
STONEY CREEK LIFECARE CENTRE
199 Glover Rd, Stoney Creek, ON, L8E 5J2
(905) 643-1795
Emp Here 80
SIC 8051 Skilled nursing care facilities

D-U-N-S 24-952-4943   (BR)
FLOCOR INC
FLOCOR
(*Suby of* Entreprises Mirca Inc, Les)
470 Seaman St, Stoney Creek, ON, L8E 2V9
(905) 664-9230
Emp Here 35
SIC 3498 Fabricated pipe and fittings

D-U-N-S 24-390-6539   (HQ)
FLOCOR INC
FLOCOR, LES SPECIALISTES DE LA TUYAUTERIE
(*Suby of* Entreprises Mirca Inc, Les)
470 Seaman St, Stoney Creek, ON, L8E 2V9
(905) 664-9230
Emp Here 50   *Emp Total* 1,342
Sales 43,347,134
SIC 5074 Plumbing and heating equipment and supplies (hydronics)
Pr Martin Deschenes
VP Francois Deschenes
Sec Marc Lapierre
Dir Jacques Deschenes
Dir Brian Findlay
Dir Wayne Walker
Genl Mgr Joe Senese

D-U-N-S 20-708-1832   (BR)
FLYNN CANADA LTD
890 Arvin Ave, Stoney Creek, ON, L8E 5Y8
(905) 643-9515
Emp Here 90
SIC 1761 Roofing, siding, and sheetMetal work

D-U-N-S 25-214-4969   (SL)
GARRTECH INC
910 Arvin Ave, Stoney Creek, ON, L8E 5Y8
(905) 643-6414
Emp Here 60   *Sales* 4,961,328
SIC 3544 Special dies, tools, jigs, and fixtures

D-U-N-S 24-342-1406   (BR)
GENERAL ELECTRIC CANADA COMPANY
GE ENERGY SERVICES
(*Suby of* General Electric Company)
180 Constellation Dr, Stoney Creek, ON, L8E 6B2
(905) 335-6301
Emp Here 20
SIC 3625 Relays and industrial controls

D-U-N-S 25-098-0539   (SL)
GRAND OLYMPIA HOSPITALITY & CONVENTION CENTER INC, THE
660 Barton St, Stoney Creek, ON, L8E 5L6
(905) 643-4291
Emp Here 50   *Sales* 1,678,096
SIC 7299 Miscellaneous personal service

D-U-N-S 24-923-5987   (SL)
GRECO MANAGEMENT INC
21 Teal Ave, Stoney Creek, ON, L8E 2P1
(905) 560-0661
Emp Here 65   *Sales* 2,845,467

SIC 8721 Accounting, auditing, and bookkeeping

D-U-N-S 24-818-6590   (BR)
HAMILTON HEALTH SCIENCES CORPORATION
CENTER FOR PARAMEDIC EDUCATION AND RESEARCH
(*Suby of* Hamilton Health Sciences Corporation)
430 Mcneilly Rd Suite 201, Stoney Creek, ON, L8E 5E3

Emp Here 50
SIC 8049 Offices of health practitioner

D-U-N-S 20-653-7198   (BR)
HAMILTON-WENTWORTH CATHOLIC SCHOOL BOARD
IMMACULATE HEART OF MARY
190 Glover Rd, Stoney Creek, ON, L8E 5J2
(905) 523-2332
Emp Here 60
SIC 8211 Elementary and secondary schools

D-U-N-S 20-655-0621   (BR)
HAMILTON-WENTWORTH CATHOLIC SCHOOL BOARD
OUR LADY OF PEACE CATHOLIC SCHOOL
252 Dewitt Rd, Stoney Creek, ON, L8E 2R1
(905) 664-3806
Emp Here 35
SIC 8211 Elementary and secondary schools

D-U-N-S 20-138-0933   (BR)
HAMILTON-WENTWORTH DISTRICT SCHOOL BOARD, THE
EASTDALE PUBLIC SCHOOL
275 Lincoln Rd, Stoney Creek, ON, L8E 1Z4
(905) 662-4363
Emp Here 22
SIC 8211 Elementary and secondary schools

D-U-N-S 20-026-0490   (BR)
HAMILTON-WENTWORTH DISTRICT SCHOOL BOARD, THE
WINONA PUBLIC SCHOOL
255 Winona Rd, Stoney Creek, ON, L8E 5L3
(905) 979-5317
Emp Here 37
SIC 8211 Elementary and secondary schools

D-U-N-S 20-590-5503   (BR)
HAMILTON-WENTWORTH DISTRICT SCHOOL BOARD, THE
MOUNTAIN VIEW SCHOOL
299 Barton St, Stoney Creek, ON, L8E 2K7
(905) 662-6939
Emp Here 30
SIC 8211 Elementary and secondary schools

D-U-N-S 20-136-4598   (BR)
HAMILTON-WENTWORTH DISTRICT SCHOOL BOARD, THE
ORCHARD PARK SECONDARY SCHOOL
200 Dewitt Rd, Stoney Creek, ON, L8E 4M5
(905) 573-3550
Emp Here 90
SIC 8211 Elementary and secondary schools

D-U-N-S 25-118-4743   (BR)
HEWITT MATERIAL HANDLING INC
CATERPILLAR
369 Glover Rd Unit 2, Stoney Creek, ON, L8E 6C9
(905) 643-6072
Emp Here 25
SIC 7699 Repair services, nec

D-U-N-S 25-367-7868   (BR)
HONEYWELL LIMITED
(*Suby of* Honeywell International Inc.)
430 Mcneilly Rd Unit 4, Stoney Creek, ON, L8E 5E3
(905) 643-5560
Emp Here 35
SIC 3822 Environmental controls

D-U-N-S 20-321-6705   (BR)
INTEGRATED DISTRIBUTION SYSTEMS LIMITED PARTNERSHIP
WAJAX POWER SYSTEMS
324 South Service Rd, Stoney Creek, ON, L8E 2R4
(905) 561-9721
Emp Here 20
SIC 5084 Industrial machinery and equipment

D-U-N-S 24-384-1132   (BR)
IONBOND INC
295 Arvin Ave, Stoney Creek, ON, L8E 2M3
(905) 664-1996
Emp Here 25
SIC 3398 Metal heat treating

D-U-N-S 24-827-0142   (SL)
JANCO STEEL LTD
925 Arvin Ave, Stoney Creek, ON, L8E 5N9
(905) 643-3535
Emp Here 140   *Sales* 56,398,621
SIC 5051 Metals service centers and offices
Pr Pr Allan Schutten

D-U-N-S 24-751-5521   (SL)
JAYNE INDUSTRIES INC
550 Seaman St, Stoney Creek, ON, L8E 3X7
(905) 643-9200
Emp Here 64
SIC 3297 Nonclay refractories

D-U-N-S 24-751-8913   (SL)
KLINGSPOR INC
KLINGSPOR ENGINEERED ABBRASIVES
1175 Barton St Unit 1, Stoney Creek, ON, L8E 5H1
(905) 643-0770
Emp Here 36   *Sales* 9,646,080
SIC 5085 Industrial supplies
Pr Jim Doherty
Fin Mgr Jim Gallino

D-U-N-S 25-815-4095   (BR)
KUBES STEEL INC
930 Arvin Ave, Stoney Creek, ON, L8E 5Y8
(905) 643-1229
Emp Here 50
SIC 3499 Fabricated Metal products, nec

D-U-N-S 25-332-3406   (SL)
L.P. CUSTOM MACHINING LTD
211 Barton St, Stoney Creek, ON, L8E 2K3
(905) 664-9445
Emp Here 80   *Sales* 5,836,856
SIC 3599 Industrial machinery, nec
Pr Pr David Singh

D-U-N-S 24-339-8760   (BR)
MATERIAUX DE CONSTRUCTION OLDCASTLE CANADA INC, LES
DECOR PRECAST, DIV OF
682 Arvin Ave, Stoney Creek, ON, L8E 5R4

Emp Here 80
SIC 3272 Concrete products, nec

D-U-N-S 24-199-7493   (SL)
MEAT FACTORY LIMITED, THE
TMF FOODS
46 Community Ave, Stoney Creek, ON, L8E 2Y3
(905) 664-2126
Emp Here 100   *Sales* 4,377,642
SIC 2013 Sausages and other prepared meats

D-U-N-S 24-337-2971   (BR)
METROLAND MEDIA GROUP LTD
HAMILTON WEB PRINTING
333 Arvin Ave, Stoney Creek, ON, L8E 2M6
(905) 664-2660
Emp Here 30
SIC 2752 Commercial printing, lithographic

D-U-N-S 20-708-2343   (BR)
MINTECH CANADA INC
19 Community Ave Unit 5, Stoney Creek, ON,

L8E 2X9
(905) 664-2222
Emp Here 25
SIC 1741 Masonry and other stonework

D-U-N-S 24-964-7009   (BR)
MOHAWK COLLEGE OF APPLIED ARTS AND TECHNOLOGY, THE
MOHAWK COLLEGE STARRT INSTITUTE
481 Barton St, Stoney Creek, ON, L8E 2L7
(905) 575-1212
Emp Here 80
SIC 8222 Junior colleges

D-U-N-S 24-581-7940   (BR)
NORTRAX CANADA INC
(*Suby of* Deere & Company)
760 South Service Rd, Stoney Creek, ON, L8E 5M6
(905) 643-4166
Emp Here 40
SIC 1794 Excavation work

D-U-N-S 24-316-2278   (SL)
NU-LINE PRODUCTS INC
(*Suby of* Berkshire Hathaway Inc.)
891 Arvin Ave, Stoney Creek, ON, L8E 5N9
(905) 643-5375
Emp Here 32   *Sales* 4,450,603
SIC 3441 Fabricated structural Metal

D-U-N-S 20-708-2574   (BR)
ORKIN CANADA CORPORATION
(*Suby of* Rollins, Inc.)
237 Barton St, Stoney Creek, ON, L8E 2K4
(905) 662-8494
Emp Here 30
SIC 7342 Disinfecting and pest control services

D-U-N-S 24-302-9360   (BR)
ORLICK INDUSTRIES LIMITED
359 Millen Rd, Stoney Creek, ON, L8E 2H4
(905) 664-3990
Emp Here 43
SIC 3365 Aluminum foundries

D-U-N-S 25-306-2715   (BR)
ORLICK INDUSTRIES LIMITED
500 Seaman St, Stoney Creek, ON, L8E 2V9
(905) 662-5954
Emp Here 200
SIC 3365 Aluminum foundries

D-U-N-S 24-417-0937   (BR)
QM LP
10 Kenmore Ave Suite 4, Stoney Creek, ON, L8E 5N1
(905) 388-4444
Emp Here 20
SIC 1795 Wrecking and demolition work

D-U-N-S 20-292-8602   (SL)
RADWELL INTERNATIONAL CANADA - AUTOMATION ULC
(*Suby of* Radwell International Inc.)
1100 South Service Rd Unit 101, Stoney Creek, ON, L8E 0C5

Emp Here 27   *Sales* 1,021,450
SIC 7629 Electrical repair shops

D-U-N-S 25-220-8707   (BR)
RUSSEL METALS INC
MCCABE STEEL
687 Arvin Ave, Stoney Creek, ON, L8E 5R2
(905) 643-4271
Emp Here 29
SIC 3499 Fabricated Metal products, nec

D-U-N-S 24-779-2260   (BR)
RUSSEL METALS INC
B & T STEEL
1052 Service Rd S, Stoney Creek, ON, L8E 6G3
(905) 643-3008
Emp Here 60
SIC 7389 Business services, nec

D-U-N-S 20-794-3007   (BR)
SAMUEL, SON & CO., LIMITED
SAMUEL PLATE SALES
12 Teal Ave, Stoney Creek, ON, L8E 3Y5
(905) 561-8228
Emp Here 160
SIC 5051 Metals service centers and offices

D-U-N-S 25-362-9505   (BR)
SAMUEL, SON & CO., LIMITED
NELSON STEEL
400 Glover Rd, Stoney Creek, ON, L8E 5X1
(905) 662-1404
Emp Here 100
SIC 3479 Metal coating and allied services

D-U-N-S 25-673-5572   (HQ)
SELKIRK CANADA CORPORATION
(*Suby of* Selkirk Americas, L.P.)
375 Green Rd Suite 1, Stoney Creek, ON, L8E 4A5
(905) 662-6600
Emp Here 50   *Emp Total* 767
SIC 3259 Structural clay products, nec

D-U-N-S 24-586-8831   (BR)
SERVICES D'ESSAIS INTERTEK AN LTEE
710 South Service Rd Unit 1, Stoney Creek, ON, L8E 5S7
(905) 529-0090
Emp Here 30
SIC 8734 Testing laboratories

D-U-N-S 20-571-9644   (BR)
SIEMENS CANADA LIMITED
SIEMENS BUILDING TECHNOLOGIES LTD
735 South Service Rd Suite 3, Stoney Creek, ON, L8E 5Z2
(905) 643-2200
Emp Here 40
SIC 1711 Plumbing, heating, air-conditioning

D-U-N-S 20-555-3683   (BR)
STONEY CREEK FURNITURE LIMITED
360 Lewis Rd Suite 10, Stoney Creek, ON, L8E 5Y7
(905) 643-0500
Emp Here 20
SIC 4225 General warehousing and storage

D-U-N-S 20-336-9590   (BR)
TAYLOR STEEL INC
395 Green Rd, Stoney Creek, ON, L8E 5V4
(905) 662-5555
Emp Here 80
SIC 4225 General warehousing and storage

D-U-N-S 20-812-5646   (SL)
THERMAL DEBURRING CANADA INC
MAGNA-TECH CANADA
921 Barton St, Stoney Creek, ON, L8E 5P5
(905) 643-2990
Emp Here 35   *Sales* 4,888,367
SIC 3541 Machine tools, Metal cutting type

D-U-N-S 20-320-1736   (BR)
TIERCON CORP
352 Arvin Ave, Stoney Creek, ON, L8E 2M4
(905) 662-1097
Emp Here 100
SIC 3714 Motor vehicle parts and accessories

D-U-N-S 20-921-0454   (BR)
TOROMONT INDUSTRIES LTD
BATTLEFIELD EQUIPMENT RENTALS
880 South Service Rd, Stoney Creek, ON, L8E 5M7
(905) 643-9410
Emp Here 80
SIC 7359 Equipment rental and leasing, nec

D-U-N-S 24-007-7388   (BR)
TOROMONT INDUSTRIES LTD
460 South Service Rd, Stoney Creek, ON, L8E 2P8
(905) 662-8080
Emp Here 80
SIC 7699 Repair services, nec

D-U-N-S 25-999-2600   (BR)
UNITED RENTALS OF CANADA, INC
45 Oriole Ave, Stoney Creek, ON, L8E 5C4
(905) 664-5007
Emp Here 50
SIC 7353 Heavy construction equipment rental

D-U-N-S 20-508-2290   (HQ)
VSL CANADA LTD
(*Suby of* Nucor Corporation)
318 Arvin Ave, Stoney Creek, ON, L8E 2M2
(905) 662-0611
Emp Here 80   *Emp Total* 23,900
Sales 45,216,000
SIC 1771 Concrete work
Pr Pr John Harris
 Douglas Deighton
 Milton Harris

D-U-N-S 24-198-9615   (HQ)
VENETOR CRANE LTD
(*Suby of* 1090319 Ontario Inc)
45 Oriole Ave, Stoney Creek, ON, L8E 5C4
(905) 664-5007
Emp Here 170   *Emp Total* 2
Sales 20,825,471
SIC 7353 Heavy construction equipment rental
Pr Pr Louis Beraldo
 Miranda Beraldo

D-U-N-S 24-069-5838   (BR)
VIPOND INC
807 South Service Rd, Stoney Creek, ON, L8E 5Z2
(905) 643-6006
Emp Here 20
SIC 3569 General industrial machinery, nec

D-U-N-S 25-510-4036   (BR)
W.J. DEANS TRANSPORTATION INC
371 Jones Rd, Stoney Creek, ON, L8E 5N2
(905) 643-9405
Emp Here 50
SIC 4214 Local trucking with storage

D-U-N-S 24-564-6476   (BR)
WASTE MANAGEMENT OF CANADA COR-PORATION
(*Suby of* Waste Management, Inc.)
407 Mcneilly Rd, Stoney Creek, ON, L8E 5E3
(905) 643-1202
Emp Here 50
SIC 4953 Refuse systems

D-U-N-S 20-116-6621   (SL)
ZELUS MATERIAL HANDLING INC
730 South Service Rd, Stoney Creek, ON, L8E 5S7
(905) 643-4928
Emp Here 38   *Sales* 3,957,782
SIC 7699 Repair services, nec

D-U-N-S 25-320-3657   (BR)
EXP SERVICES INC
EXP SERVICES INC
428 Millen Rd Suite 1, Stoney Creek, ON, L8E 3N9
(905) 664-3300
Emp Here 20
SIC 8711 Engineering services

Stoney Creek, ON L8G
Wentworth County

D-U-N-S 25-360-6354   (BR)
BANK OF MONTREAL
BMO
10 Queenston Rd, Stoney Creek, ON, L8G 1B5
(905) 662-4903
Emp Here 22
SIC 6021 National commercial banks

D-U-N-S 24-437-8498   (BR)
BANQUE TORONTO-DOMINION, LA
TORONTO-DOMINION BANK, THE
(*Suby of* Toronto-Dominion Bank, The)
800 Queenston Rd, Stoney Creek, ON, L8G 1A7
(905) 664-6510
Emp Here 41
SIC 6021 National commercial banks

D-U-N-S 25-598-0120   (HQ)
COMPLETE COMMUNICATION SYSTEMS INC
ROGERS WIRELESS
(*Suby of* Complete Communication Systems Inc)
905 Queenston Rd, Stoney Creek, ON, L8G 1B6
(905) 664-1158
Emp Here 20   *Emp Total* 50
Sales 4,742,446
SIC 5999 Miscellaneous retail stores, nec

D-U-N-S 20-940-4974   (BR)
FORTINOS SUPERMARKET LTD
102 Highway 8, Stoney Creek, ON, L8G 4H3
(905) 664-2886
Emp Here 250
SIC 5141 Groceries, general line

D-U-N-S 25-293-9533   (BR)
HAMILTON-WENTWORTH CATHOLIC SCHOOL BOARD
OUR LADY OF PEACE SCHOOL
185 Glenashton Dr, Stoney Creek, ON, L8G 4E7
(905) 664-8148
Emp Here 25
SIC 8211 Elementary and secondary schools

D-U-N-S 25-292-6829   (BR)
HAMILTON-WENTWORTH CATHOLIC SCHOOL BOARD
CARDINAL NEWMAN SECONDARY SCHOOL
127 Gray Rd, Stoney Creek, ON, L8G 3V3
(905) 523-2314
Emp Here 120
SIC 8211 Elementary and secondary schools

D-U-N-S 20-710-8270   (BR)
HAMILTON-WENTWORTH DISTRICT SCHOOL BOARD, THE
RL HYSLOP SCHOOL
20 Lake Ave S, Stoney Creek, ON, L8G 1P3
(905) 662-8425
Emp Here 25
SIC 8211 Elementary and secondary schools

D-U-N-S 25-000-3142   (BR)
HAMILTON-WENTWORTH DISTRICT SCHOOL BOARD, THE
MEMORIAL SCHOOL
211 Memorial Ave, Stoney Creek, ON, L8G 3B2
(905) 979-6595
Emp Here 25
SIC 8211 Elementary and secondary schools

D-U-N-S 20-291-1892   (BR)
HAMILTON-WENTWORTH DISTRICT SCHOOL BOARD, THE
GREEN ACRES PUBLIC SCHOOL
45 Randall Ave, Stoney Creek, ON, L8G 2K8
(905) 662-7021
Emp Here 30
SIC 8211 Elementary and secondary schools

D-U-N-S 20-710-8304   (BR)
HAMILTON-WENTWORTH DISTRICT SCHOOL BOARD, THE
CCE REDHILL LEARNING CENTER
910 Queenston Rd, Stoney Creek, ON, L8G 1B5
(905) 573-3144
Emp Here 50
SIC 8211 Elementary and secondary schools

D-U-N-S 20-160-6642   (BR)
HAMILTON-WENTWORTH DISTRICT SCHOOL BOARD, THE
COLLEGIATE AVENUE ELEMENTARY SCHOOL
49 Collegiate Ave, Stoney Creek, ON, L8G 3L5
(905) 662-2990
Emp Here 25
SIC 8211 Elementary and secondary schools

D-U-N-S 20-705-1488   (BR)
MCDONALD'S RESTAURANTS OF CANADA LIMITED
MCDONALD'S 8357
(*Suby of* McDonald's Corporation)
385 Highway 8, Stoney Creek, ON, L8G 5A2
(905) 662-1423
Emp Here 65
SIC 5812 Eating places

D-U-N-S 20-004-7426   (SL)
NARDINI, JOHN DRUGS LIMITED
SHOPPERS DRUG MART
377 Highway 8, Stoney Creek, ON, L8G 1E7
(905) 662-9996
Emp Here 30   *Sales* 5,024,256
SIC 5912 Drug stores and proprietary stores

D-U-N-S 25-811-7381   (BR)
ROYAL BANK OF CANADA
RBC
(*Suby of* Royal Bank Of Canada)
917 Queenston Rd, Stoney Creek, ON, L8G 1B8
(905) 664-6412
Emp Here 30
SIC 6021 National commercial banks

D-U-N-S 20-944-6058   (BR)
STARBUCKS COFFEE CANADA, INC
(*Suby of* Starbucks Corporation)
377 Highway 8 Suite 369, Stoney Creek, ON, L8G 1E7
(905) 664-9494
Emp Here 20
SIC 5812 Eating places

D-U-N-S 25-987-3313   (BR)
VALUE VILLAGE STORES, INC
VALUE VILLAGE 2025
(*Suby of* Savers, Inc.)
840 Queenston Rd, Stoney Creek, ON, L8G 4A8
(905) 664-8884
Emp Here 45
SIC 5399 Miscellaneous general merchandise

D-U-N-S 25-051-1664   (BR)
WINNERS MERCHANTS INTERNATIONAL L.P.
WINNERS
(*Suby of* The TJX Companies Inc)
75 Centennial Pky N, Stoney Creek, ON, L8G 2C7
(905) 560-7366
Emp Here 50
SIC 5651 Family clothing stores

Stoney Creek, ON L8J
Wentworth County

D-U-N-S 24-418-2817   (BR)
CINEPLEX ODEON CORPORATION
SILVERCITY HAMILTON MOUNTAIN
795 Paramount Dr, Stoney Creek, ON, L8J 0B4
(905) 560-0239
Emp Here 20
SIC 7832 Motion picture theaters, except drive-in

D-U-N-S 25-293-9723   (BR)
HAMILTON-WENTWORTH CATHOLIC SCHOOL BOARD

ST JAMES THE APOSTLE CATHOLIC ELE-
MENTARY SCHOOL
29 John Murray St, Stoney Creek, ON, L8J
1C5
(905) 560-2700
Emp Here 30
SIC 8211 Elementary and secondary schools

D-U-N-S 20-653-3858   (BR)
HAMILTON-WENTWORTH   CATHOLIC
SCHOOL BOARD
OUR LADY OF THE ASSUMPTION SEPA-
RATE SCHOOL
55 Regional Rd 20, Stoney Creek, ON, L8J
2W9
(905) 523-2329
Emp Here 35
SIC 8211 Elementary and secondary schools

D-U-N-S 24-676-3150   (BR)
HAMILTON-WENTWORTH   CATHOLIC
SCHOOL BOARD
GATESTONE   PUBLIC   ELEMENTARY
SCHOOL
127 Gatestone Dr, Stoney Creek, ON, L8J 3Z5
(905) 573-7731
Emp Here 25
SIC 8211 Elementary and secondary schools

D-U-N-S 25-293-9731   (BR)
HAMILTON-WENTWORTH   CATHOLIC
SCHOOL BOARD
ST PAUL'S SCHOOL
24 Amberwood St, Stoney Creek, ON, L8J
2H9
(905) 578-2117
Emp Here 35
SIC 8211 Elementary and secondary schools

D-U-N-S 20-590-7632   (BR)
HAMILTON-WENTWORTH   CATHOLIC
SCHOOL BOARD
ST. MARK ELEMENTARY SCHOOL
43 Whitedeer Rd, Stoney Creek, ON, L8J 2V8
(905) 560-0032
Emp Here 40
SIC 8211 Elementary and secondary schools

D-U-N-S 20-710-8288   (BR)
HAMILTON-WENTWORTH   DISTRICT
SCHOOL BOARD, THE
SALTFLEET DISTRICT HIGH SCHOOL
108 Highland Rd W, Stoney Creek, ON, L8J
2T2
(905) 573-3000
Emp Here 100
SIC 8211 Elementary and secondary schools

D-U-N-S 20-290-6165   (BR)
HAMILTON-WENTWORTH   DISTRICT
SCHOOL BOARD, THE
JANET LEE ELEMENTARY SCHOOL
291 Winterberry Dr, Stoney Creek, ON, L8J
2N5
(905) 573-9113
Emp Here 38
SIC 8211 Elementary and secondary schools

D-U-N-S 20-592-1146   (BR)
HAMILTON-WENTWORTH   DISTRICT
SCHOOL BOARD, THE
BILLY GREEN ELEMENTARY SCHOOL
1105 Paramount Dr, Stoney Creek, ON, L8J
1W2
(905) 573-3505
Emp Here 30
SIC 8211 Elementary and secondary schools

D-U-N-S 20-291-1900   (BR)
HAMILTON-WENTWORTH   DISTRICT
SCHOOL BOARD, THE
TAPLEYTOWN ELEMENTARY
390 Mud St E, Stoney Creek, ON, L8J 3C6
(905) 662-2297
Emp Here 22
SIC 8211 Elementary and secondary schools

D-U-N-S 20-100-5050   (BR)

MAPLE LEAF FOODS INC
92 Highland Rd E, Stoney Creek, ON, L8J
2W6
(905) 662-8883
Emp Here 100
SIC 2015 Poultry slaughtering and processing

D-U-N-S 20-927-4005   (BR)
PRIME ENTERPRISES INC
WENDY'S RESTAURANT
(Suby of Prime Enterprises Inc)
244 Upper Centennial Pky, Stoney Creek, ON,
L8J 2V6
(905) 662-0462
Emp Here 40
SIC 5812 Eating places

D-U-N-S 20-644-7463   (BR)
REVERA LONG TERM CARE INC
RIDGEVIEW LONG TERM CARE CENTER
385 Highland Rd W, Stoney Creek, ON, L8J
3X9
(905) 561-3332
Emp Here 100
SIC 8051 Skilled nursing care facilities

D-U-N-S 20-300-7000   (BR)
STANTEC CONSULTING LTD
835 Paramount Dr Suite 200, Stoney Creek,
ON, L8J 0B4
(905) 385-3234
Emp Here 80
SIC 8711 Engineering services

D-U-N-S 24-503-5022   (BR)
TURTLE JACK'S RESTAURANT INC
143 Upper Centennial Pky, Stoney Creek, ON,
L8J 0B2
(905) 662-3120
Emp Here 30
SIC 5812 Eating places

D-U-N-S 24-972-5219   (SL)
VALLEY PARK COMMUNITY CENTRE
970 Paramount Dr, Stoney Creek, ON, L8J
1Y2
(905) 573-3600
Emp Here 50   Sales 1,969,939
SIC 8322 Individual and family services

Stouffville, ON L4A
York County

D-U-N-S 20-537-2654   (BR)
CANADA POST CORPORATION
STOUFFVILLE STN MAIN
6379 Main St, Stouffville, ON, L4A 1G4
(905) 640-2466
Emp Here 30
SIC 4311 U.s. postal service

D-U-N-S 20-812-1470   (BR)
CLUBLINK CORPORATION ULC
EMERALD HILLS GOLF & COUNTRY CLUB
14001 Warden Ave, Stouffville, ON, L4A 3T4
(905) 888-1100
Emp Here 100
SIC 7992 Public golf courses

D-U-N-S 20-076-0028   (BR)
CLUBLINK CORPORATION ULC
ROLLING HILLS GOLF CLUB
128081 Warden Ave, Stouffville, ON, L4A 7X5
(905) 888-1955
Emp Here 70
SIC 7992 Public golf courses

D-U-N-S 24-075-2782   (SL)
COOK (CANADA) INC
(Suby of Cook Group Incorporated)
165 Mostar St, Stouffville, ON, L4A 0Y2
(905) 640-7110
Emp Here 69   Sales 10,068,577
SIC 5047 Medical and hospital equipment
Pr Pr William Bobbie
Ch Bd Carl Cook

D-U-N-S 20-884-9385   (BR)
CORPORATION OF THE TOWN OF
WHITCHURCH STOUFFVILLE
LEBOVIC LEISURE CENTRE
30 Burkholder St, Stouffville, ON, L4A 4K1
(905) 642-7529
Emp Here 30
SIC 7999 Amusement and recreation, nec

D-U-N-S 24-250-4848   (BR)
DIVERSICARE CANADA MANAGEMENT
SERVICES CO., INC
STOUFFVILLE CREEK RETIREMENT RESI-
DENCE
40 Freel Lane Suite 412, Stouffville, ON, L4A
0P5
(905) 642-2902
Emp Here 45
SIC 6513 Apartment building operators

D-U-N-S 25-967-9025   (BR)
FGL SPORTS LTD
SPORT CHEK
1010 Hoover Park Dr Unit 3, Stouffville, ON,
L4A 0K2
(905) 640-3919
Emp Here 20
SIC 5941 Sporting goods and bicycle shops

D-U-N-S 20-805-3574   (SL)
GRANITE GOLF CLUB
2699 Durham Rd 30, Stouffville, ON, L4A 7X4
(905) 642-4416
Emp Here 50   Sales 2,042,900
SIC 7997 Membership sports and recreation
clubs

D-U-N-S 20-291-8467   (BR)
LAFARGE CANADA INC
LAFARGE AGGREGATES
14204 Durham Rd 30, Stouffville, ON, L4A
3L4
(905) 738-7050
Emp Here 50
SIC 5032 Brick, stone, and related material

D-U-N-S 20-552-8586   (BR)
METRO ONTARIO INC
METRO
5612 Main St, Stouffville, ON, L4A 8B7
(905) 642-8600
Emp Here 30
SIC 5411 Grocery stores

D-U-N-S 20-708-8159   (SL)
MYRSA MANAGEMENT SERVICES LTD
LOAD LISTER
3 Anderson Blvd Suite 1, Stouffville, ON, L4A
7X4
(416) 291-9756
Emp Here 41   Sales 5,465,508
SIC 6712 Bank holding companies
Pr Headley Thomas

D-U-N-S 20-693-2514   (SL)
PARKVIEW VILLAGE RETIREMENT COM-
MUNITY ASSOCIATION OF YORK REGION
PARKVIEW VILLAGE
12184 Ninth Line Suite A103, Stouffville, ON,
L4A 3N6
(905) 640-1940
Emp Here 50   Sales 1,824,018
SIC 8361 Residential care

D-U-N-S 25-365-9882   (BR)
SOBEYS CAPITAL INCORPORATED
STOUFFVILLE SOBEY'S
5857 Main St, Stouffville, ON, L4A 2S9
(905) 640-0883
Emp Here 100
SIC 5411 Grocery stores

D-U-N-S 25-911-5707   (SL)
SPRING LAKES GOLF CLUB
4632 Stouffville Rd, Stouffville, ON, L4A 3X4
(905) 640-3633
Emp Here 70   Sales 2,845,467
SIC 7997 Membership sports and recreation

clubs

D-U-N-S 24-757-0476   (SL)
ST. ANDREWS EAST GOLF & COUNTRY
CLUB
14022 Mccowan Rd, Stouffville, ON, L4A 7X5
(905) 640-4444
Emp Here 56   Sales 2,261,782
SIC 7997 Membership sports and recreation
clubs

D-U-N-S 24-344-0117   (BR)
SUPERIOR PLUS LP
SPECIALTY PRODUCTS AND INSULATION
6 Sangster Rd, Stouffville, ON, L4A 7X4
(905) 640-6811
Emp Here 29
SIC 5033 Roofing, siding, and insulation

D-U-N-S 25-321-9422   (BR)
TEVA CANADA LIMITED
5691 Main St, Stouffville, ON, L4A 1H5
(416) 291-8888
Emp Here 110
SIC 2834 Pharmaceutical preparations

D-U-N-S 24-121-1205   (BR)
TORONTO-DOMINION BANK, THE
TD CANADA TRUST
(Suby of Toronto-Dominion Bank, The)
5887 Main St Suite 1, Stouffville, ON, L4A 1N2
(905) 640-4000
Emp Here 20
SIC 6021 National commercial banks

D-U-N-S 24-329-8705   (BR)
WAL-MART CANADA CORP
1050 Hoover Park Dr, Stouffville, ON, L4A 0K2
(905) 640-8848
Emp Here 200
SIC 5311 Department stores

D-U-N-S 20-591-6716   (BR)
YORK CATHOLIC DISTRICT SCHOOL
BOARD
ST BRIGID CATHOLIC ELEMENTARY
SCHOOL
223 Millard St, Stouffville, ON, L4A 5S2
(905) 642-5100
Emp Here 25
SIC 8211 Elementary and secondary schools

D-U-N-S 25-147-3617   (BR)
YORK CATHOLIC DISTRICT SCHOOL
BOARD
ST. MARK ELEMENTARY SCHOOL
333 Glad Park Ave, Stouffville, ON, L4A 1E4
(905) 640-2915
Emp Here 30
SIC 8211 Elementary and secondary schools

D-U-N-S 25-297-9687   (BR)
YORK REGION DISTRICT SCHOOL BOARD
STOUFFVILLE   DISTRICT   SECONDARY
SCHOOL
(Suby of York Region District School Board)
801 Hoover Park Dr, Stouffville, ON, L4A 0A4
(905) 640-1433
Emp Here 80
SIC 8211 Elementary and secondary schools

D-U-N-S 25-297-9521   (BR)
YORK REGION DISTRICT SCHOOL BOARD
BALLANTRAE PUBLIC SCHOOL
(Suby of York Region District School Board)
5632 Aurora Rd, Stouffville, ON, L4A 3K3
(905) 640-2232
Emp Here 25
SIC 8211 Elementary and secondary schools

D-U-N-S 20-711-3973   (BR)
YORK REGION DISTRICT SCHOOL BOARD
SUMMIT VIEW PUBLIC SCHOOL
(Suby of York Region District School Board)
6551 Main St, Stouffville, ON, L4A 5Z4
(905) 640-1102
Emp Here 50
SIC 8211 Elementary and secondary schools

▲ Public Company   ■ Public Company Family Member   **HQ** Headquarters   **BR** Branch   **SL** Single Location

D-U-N-S 24-676-4943   (BR)
YORK REGION DISTRICT SCHOOL BOARD
HARRY BOWES PUBLIC SCHOOL
(*Suby of* York Region District School Board)
90 Greenwood Rd, Stouffville, ON, L4A 0N8
(905) 640-9856
Emp Here 25
SIC 8211 Elementary and secondary schools

D-U-N-S 20-591-2525   (BR)
YORK REGION DISTRICT SCHOOL BOARD
GLAD PARK PUBLIC SCHOOL
(*Suby of* York Region District School Board)
300 Glad Park Ave, Stouffville, ON, L4A 1E5
(905) 642-0224
Emp Here 25
SIC 8211 Elementary and secondary schools

D-U-N-S 24-676-5247   (BR)
YORK REGION DISTRICT SCHOOL BOARD
OSCAR PETERSON PUBLIC SCHOOL
(*Suby of* York Region District School Board)
850 Hoover Park Dr, Stouffville, ON, L4A 0E7
(905) 642-1236
Emp Here 25
SIC 8211 Elementary and secondary schools

Straffordville, ON N0J
Elgin County

D-U-N-S 20-710-5490   (BR)
THAMES VALLEY DISTRICT SCHOOL BOARD
STRAFFORDVILLE PUBLIC SCHOOL
9188 Plank Rd, Straffordville, ON, N0J 1Y0
(519) 866-3021
Emp Here 45
SIC 8211 Elementary and secondary schools

Stratford, ON N4Z
Perth County

D-U-N-S 24-424-5705   (BR)
A.O. SMITH ENTERPRISES LTD
A.O. SMITH ENTERPRISES STRATFORD WATER SYSTEM DIV.,
(*Suby of* A. O. Smith Corporation)
768 Erie St, Stratford, ON, N4Z 1A2
(519) 271-5800
Emp Here 25
SIC 5074 Plumbing and heating equipment and supplies (hydronics)

D-U-N-S 24-348-7464   (HQ)
BALDOR ELECTRIC CANADA INC
BALDOR DODGE RELIANCE
678 Erie St, Stratford, ON, N4Z 1A2
(519) 271-3630
Emp Here 105   *Emp Total* 400
Sales 22,398,935
SIC 3621 Motors and generators
Pr Nathalie Pilon
VP Fannie Fannie
  Guy Dionne
  Guido Mussehl

D-U-N-S 20-104-9207   (SL)
C. R. PLASTIC PRODUCTS INC
CRP PRODUCTS
1172 Erie St Stratford, Stratford, ON, N4Z 0A1
(519) 271-1283
Emp Here 72   *Sales* 2,772,003
SIC 2519 Household furniture, nec

D-U-N-S 25-194-2595   (BR)
FAG AEROSPACE INC
151 Wright Blvd, Stratford, ON, N4Z 1H3
(519) 271-3230
Emp Here 250
SIC 3369 Nonferrous foundries, nec

D-U-N-S 24-846-0701   (BR)

SOBEYS CAPITAL INCORPORATED
SOBEYS
30 Queensland Rd, Stratford, ON, N4Z 1H4
(519) 273-2631
Emp Here 140
SIC 5411 Grocery stores

Stratford, ON N5A
Perth County

D-U-N-S 24-477-2349   (SL)
1427732 ONTARIO INC
TIM HORTONS
1067 Ontario St Suite 2, Stratford, ON, N5A 6W6
(519) 272-2701
Emp Here 70   *Sales* 2,115,860
SIC 5812 Eating places

D-U-N-S 20-913-6857   (BR)
AVON MAITLAND DISTRICT SCHOOL BOARD
STRATFORD NORTHWESTERN SECONDARY SCHOOL
428 Forman Ave, Stratford, ON, N5A 6R7
(519) 271-9740
Emp Here 100
SIC 8211 Elementary and secondary schools

D-U-N-S 25-249-1220   (BR)
AVON MAITLAND DISTRICT SCHOOL BOARD
HAMLET ELEMENTARY SCHOOL
315 West Gore St, Stratford, ON, N5A 7N4
(519) 271-2826
Emp Here 20
SIC 8211 Elementary and secondary schools

D-U-N-S 24-245-8888   (BR)
AVON MAITLAND DISTRICT SCHOOL BOARD
STRATFORD CENTRAL SECONDARY SCHOOL
60 St Andrew St, Stratford, ON, N5A 1A3
(519) 271-4500
Emp Here 20
SIC 8211 Elementary and secondary schools

D-U-N-S 20-590-7251   (BR)
AVON MAITLAND DISTRICT SCHOOL BOARD
ROMEO PUBLIC SHOOL
49 Rebecca St, Stratford, ON, N5A 3P2
(519) 271-4487
Emp Here 20
SIC 8211 Elementary and secondary schools

D-U-N-S 20-024-9410   (BR)
AVON MAITLAND DISTRICT SCHOOL BOARD
BEDFORD PUBLIC SCHOOL
59 Bedford Dr, Stratford, ON, N5A 5J7
(519) 273-1190
Emp Here 28
SIC 8211 Elementary and secondary schools

D-U-N-S 20-913-6840   (BR)
AVON MAITLAND DISTRICT SCHOOL BOARD
347 Brunswick St, Stratford, ON, N5A 3N1

Emp Here 25

SIC 8211 Elementary and secondary schools

D-U-N-S 20-710-6803   (BR)
AVON MAITLAND DISTRICT SCHOOL BOARD
ANNE HATHWAY PUBLIC SCHOOL
77 Bruce St, Stratford, ON, N5A 4A2
(519) 271-8576
Emp Here 50
SIC 8211 Elementary and secondary schools

D-U-N-S 25-263-4894   (BR)
AVON MAITLAND DISTRICT SCHOOL

BOARD
SHAKESPEARE PUBLIC SCHOOL
35 Mowat St, Stratford, ON, N5A 2B8
(519) 271-3727
Emp Here 30
SIC 8211 Elementary and secondary schools

D-U-N-S 25-296-7138   (BR)
BANK OF NOVA SCOTIA, THE
SCOTIABANK
1 Ontario St, Stratford, ON, N5A 3G7
(519) 272-8250
Emp Here 35
SIC 6021 National commercial banks

D-U-N-S 25-004-1696   (BR)
BANQUE TORONTO-DOMINION, LA
TD CANADA TRUST
(*Suby of* Toronto-Dominion Bank, The)
41 Downie St, Stratford, ON, N5A 1W7
(519) 271-4160
Emp Here 30
SIC 6021 National commercial banks

D-U-N-S 24-761-2133   (BR)
BELFOR (CANADA) INC
BELFOR PROPERTY RESTORATION
457 Douro St, Stratford, ON, N5A 3S9
(519) 271-1129
Emp Here 20
SIC 1799 Special trade contractors, nec

D-U-N-S 24-289-1505   (SL)
BENTLEY'S HOSPITALITY INC
BENTLEY'S INN BAR & RESTAURANT
99 Ontario St, Stratford, ON, N5A 3H1
(519) 271-1121
Emp Here 50   *Sales* 2,130,450
SIC 5812 Eating places

D-U-N-S 20-540-8797   (BR)
CANADA POST CORPORATION
STRATFORD STN MAIN
75 Waterloo St S, Stratford, ON, N5A 7B2
(519) 271-1282
Emp Here 50
SIC 4311 U.s. postal service

D-U-N-S 25-303-5299   (BR)
CANADIAN IMPERIAL BANK OF COMMERCE
CIBC
30 Downie St, Stratford, ON, N5A 1W5
(519) 271-0920
Emp Here 25
SIC 6021 National commercial banks

D-U-N-S 20-041-4741   (BR)
CARA OPERATIONS LIMITED
SWISS CHALET ROTISSERIE & GRILL
(*Suby of* Cara Holdings Limited)
684 Ontario St, Stratford, ON, N5A 3J7
(519) 271-2171
Emp Here 60
SIC 5812 Eating places

D-U-N-S 20-154-6678   (HQ)
CLEAVER-BROOKS OF CANADA LIMITED
NATCOM
(*Suby of* Harbour Group Ltd.)
161 Lorne Ave W, Stratford, ON, N5A 6S4
(519) 271-9220
Emp Here 117   *Emp Total* 5,250
Sales 19,407,546
SIC 3443 Fabricated plate work (boiler shop)
Pr Pr Robert St Denis
  Richard Williamson
CFO Rick Williamson

D-U-N-S 20-794-1605   (BR)
COMMUNITY LIVING STRATFORD AND AREA
STRATFORD AREA ASSOCIATION FOR COMMUNITY LIVING
400 Huron St, Stratford, ON, N5A 5T5
(519) 271-9751
Emp Here 125
SIC 8322 Individual and family services

D-U-N-S 25-372-8414   (BR)
COOPER-STANDARD AUTOMOTIVE CANADA LIMITED
341 Erie St, Stratford, ON, N5A 2N3
(519) 271-3360
Emp Here 70
SIC 3069 Fabricated rubber products, nec

D-U-N-S 25-664-9263   (BR)
COOPER-STANDARD AUTOMOTIVE CANADA LIMITED
SEALING SYSTEMS GROUP
703 Douro St, Stratford, ON, N5A 3T1
(519) 271-3360
Emp Here 369
SIC 2891 Adhesives and sealants

D-U-N-S 25-226-6085   (BR)
CORPORATION OF THE CITY OF STRATFORD
ANNE HATHAWAY DAY CARE CENTRE
103 Bruce St, Stratford, ON, N5A 4A2
(519) 273-1803
Emp Here 30
SIC 8351 Child day care services

D-U-N-S 25-911-1151   (BR)
CORPORATION OF THE CITY OF STRATFORD
FESTIVAL HYDRO
187 Erie St, Stratford, ON, N5A 2M6
(519) 271-4700
Emp Here 53
SIC 4911 Electric services

D-U-N-S 20-955-9108   (HQ)
CRANE PLUMBING CANADA CORP
FIAT PRODUCTS, A DIV OF
(*Suby of* Crane Plumbing Canada Corp)
15 Crane Ave, Stratford, ON, N5A 6S4
(519) 271-6150
Emp Here 130   *Emp Total* 195
SIC 3431 Metal sanitary ware

D-U-N-S 25-822-5580   (SL)
CREDIT BUREAU OF STRATFORD (1970) LTD
CREDIT RISK MANAGEMENT CANADA
61 Lorne Ave E Suite 96, Stratford, ON, N5A 6S4
(519) 271-6211
Emp Here 50   *Sales* 2,553,625
SIC 7323 Credit reporting services

D-U-N-S 25-301-2801   (BR)
EXTENDICARE (CANADA) INC
PARAMED HOME HEALTH CARE
55 Lorne Ave E Suite 4, Stratford, ON, N5A 6S4

Emp Here 60
SIC 8051 Skilled nursing care facilities

D-U-N-S 24-677-3753   (BR)
F&P MFG., INC
DYNA-MIG
275 Wright Blvd, Stratford, ON, N5A 7Y1

Emp Here 500
SIC 3714 Motor vehicle parts and accessories

D-U-N-S 24-343-7345   (BR)
FGL SPORTS LTD
SPORT-CHEK FESTIVAL MARKET PLACE
1067 Ontario St Unit S2, Stratford, ON, N5A 6W6
(519) 273-4838
Emp Here 20
SIC 5941 Sporting goods and bicycle shops

D-U-N-S 25-035-2515   (HQ)
FAMME & CO. PROFESSIONAL CORPORATION
(*Suby of* Famme & Co. Professional Corporation)
125 Ontario St, Stratford, ON, N5A 3H1
(519) 271-7581
Emp Here 40   *Emp Total* 60
Sales 2,626,585

SIC 8721 Accounting, auditing, and book-keeping

D-U-N-S 24-564-7060   (BR)
FIRSTCANADA ULC
FIRST STUDENT CANADA
4321 Line 34, Stratford, ON, N5A 6S7

Emp Here 80
SIC 4151 School buses

D-U-N-S 20-017-9740   (BR)
GEORGIAN BAY FIRE & SAFETY LTD
(*Suby of* Loti Holdings Inc)
51 Griffith Rd Suite 3, Stratford, ON, N5A 6S4
(519) 725-2206
Emp Here 20
SIC 5099 Durable goods, nec

D-U-N-S 24-947-3851   (HQ)
GODERICH-EXETER RAILWAY COMPANY LIMITED
(*Suby of* Genesee & Wyoming Inc.)
101 Shakespeare St Suite 2, Stratford, ON, N5A 3W5
(519) 271-4441
Emp Here 42   *Emp Total* 7,516
Sales 24,818,560
SIC 4011 Railroads, line-haul operating
Pr Doug Mackenzie
 Sherri Haggith

D-U-N-S 20-154-7510   (HQ)
HENDRICKSON CANADA ULC
HENDRICKSON SPRING
(*Suby of* The Boler Company)
532 Romeo St S, Stratford, ON, N5A 4V4
(519) 271-4840
Emp Here 250   *Emp Total* 3,000
Sales 14,319,256
SIC 3493 Steel springs, except wire
Pr Pr Matthew Boler
Dir Matthew Joy
Dir Paul Schouwstra

D-U-N-S 20-353-1272   (BR)
HURON PERTH CATHOLIC DISTRICT SCHOOL BOARD
JEANNE SAUVE ELEMENTARY SCHOOL
8 Grange St, Stratford, ON, N5A 3P6
(519) 273-3396
Emp Here 30
SIC 8211 Elementary and secondary schools

D-U-N-S 25-228-1639   (BR)
HURON PERTH CATHOLIC DISTRICT SCHOOL BOARD
ST AMBROSE ELEMENTARY SCHOOL
181 Louise St, Stratford, ON, N5A 2E6
(519) 271-7544
Emp Here 35
SIC 8211 Elementary and secondary schools

D-U-N-S 25-228-1753   (BR)
HURON PERTH CATHOLIC DISTRICT SCHOOL BOARD
ST ALOYSIUS ELEMENTARY SCHOOL
228 Avondale Ave, Stratford, ON, N5A 6N4
(519) 271-3636
Emp Here 35
SIC 8211 Elementary and secondary schools

D-U-N-S 20-710-6753   (BR)
HURON PERTH CATHOLIC DISTRICT SCHOOL BOARD
SAINT JOSEPH SCHOOL
363 St Vincent St S, Stratford, ON, N5A 2Y2
(519) 271-3574
Emp Here 20
SIC 8211 Elementary and secondary schools

D-U-N-S 20-047-7565   (SL)
HURON-PERTH CHILDREN'S AID SOCIETY
FINANCIAL PLAN AND OFFICE
639 Lorne Ave E, Stratford, ON, N5A 6S4
(519) 271-5290
Emp Here 110   *Sales* 4,304,681
SIC 8322 Individual and family services

D-U-N-S 20-051-3161   (BR)
INDUSTRIES SPECTRA PREMIUM INC, LES
SPI
533 Romeo St S, Stratford, ON, N5A 4V3
(519) 275-3802
Emp Here 250
SIC 3714 Motor vehicle parts and accessories

D-U-N-S 20-719-0633   (BR)
MASTERFEEDS INC
DACO ANIMAL NUTRITION SAA
1131 Erie St, Stratford, ON, N5A 6S4
(519) 272-1768
Emp Here 50
SIC 8734 Testing laboratories

D-U-N-S 24-909-5118   (BR)
MASTERFEEDS INC
130 Park St, Stratford, ON, N5A 3W8
(519) 273-1810
Emp Here 25
SIC 2048 Prepared feeds, nec

D-U-N-S 24-467-6792   (BR)
ONTARIO CLEAN WATER AGENCY
701 West Gore St, Stratford, ON, N5A 1L4
(519) 271-9071
Emp Here 49
SIC 4941 Water supply

D-U-N-S 20-845-6673   (SL)
PEOPLECARE STRATFORD INC
198 Mornington St, Stratford, ON, N5A 5G3
(519) 271-4440
Emp Here 72   *Sales* 3,429,153
SIC 8051 Skilled nursing care facilities

D-U-N-S 24-873-4667   (BR)
POLYONE DSS CANADA INC
SPARTECH COLOR
577 Erie St, Stratford, ON, N5A 2N7

Emp Here 100
SIC 2821 Plastics materials and resins

D-U-N-S 25-462-6112   (HQ)
POWERHOUSE CONTROLS LIMITED
(*Suby of* Powerhouse Controls Limited)
89 Lorne Ave E Unit 2, Stratford, ON, N5A 6S4
(519) 273-6602
Emp Here 47   *Emp Total* 50
Sales 4,961,328
SIC 8711 Engineering services

D-U-N-S 20-108-3305   (BR)
PRECISE CASTINGS INC
ENGINEERED PRODUCTS DIVISION
251 O'Loane Ave, Stratford, ON, N5A 6S4
(519) 273-6613
Emp Here 45
SIC 3324 Steel investment foundries

D-U-N-S 25-320-9910   (BR)
PUROLATOR INC.
PUROLATOR INC
753a Ontario St, Stratford, ON, N5A 7Y2
(888) 744-7123
Emp Here 35
SIC 4731 Freight transportation arrangement

D-U-N-S 24-924-3379   (HQ)
RE/MAX A-B REALTY LTD
(*Suby of* Re/Max A-B Realty Ltd)
88 Wellington St, Stratford, ON, N5A 2L2
(519) 273-2821
Emp Here 42   *Emp Total* 50
Sales 4,742,446
SIC 6531 Real estate agents and managers

D-U-N-S 20-700-6474   (BR)
REITMANS (CANADA) LIMITEE
1067 Ontario St, Stratford, ON, N5A 6W6
(519) 273-5940
Emp Here 25
SIC 5621 Women's clothing stores

D-U-N-S 24-387-3119   (BR)
REVERA LONG TERM CARE INC

HILLSIDE MANOR
5066 Line 34 Hwy Suite 8, Stratford, ON, N5A 6S6
(519) 393-5132
Emp Here 86
SIC 8051 Skilled nursing care facilities

D-U-N-S 24-829-2823   (HQ)
SAMSONITE CANADA INC
753 Ontario St, Stratford, ON, N5A 7Y2
(519) 271-5040
Emp Here 40   *Emp Total* 1
Sales 8,669,427
SIC 5099 Durable goods, nec
Dir Fin Keith Pehlke
S&M/Dir Paul Hanley
Genl Mgr Paul Decorso

D-U-N-S 20-154-7189   (HQ)
SCHAEFFLER CANADA INC
801 Ontario St, Stratford, ON, N5A 7Y2
(519) 271-3231
Emp Here 375   *Emp Total* 273,484
Sales 54,720,525
SIC 3562 Ball and roller bearings
Ch Bd Juergen Geissinger
Acct Mgr Ralph Moore
 Bob Hillstrom
Dir Frank Lange
Dir Ella Bernhard
Dir Bruce Warmbold
Fin Ex Kelly Walsh

D-U-N-S 25-311-1256   (BR)
SEARS CANADA INC
SEARS
1067 Ontario St, Stratford, ON, N5A 6W6
(519) 273-1630
Emp Here 50
SIC 5311 Department stores

D-U-N-S 24-101-2348   (BR)
STAPLES CANADA INC
STAPLES THE BUSINESS DEPOT
(*Suby of* Staples, Inc.)
1076 Ontario St, Stratford, ON, N5A 6Z3
(519) 273-5305
Emp Here 25
SIC 5943 Stationery stores

D-U-N-S 24-420-5894   (SL)
STRATFORD HOTEL LIMITED
107 Erie St, Stratford, ON, N5A 2M5
(519) 273-3666
Emp Here 59   *Sales* 2,553,625
SIC 7011 Hotels and motels

D-U-N-S 24-845-4480   (SL)
STRATFORD PUBLIC LIBRARY
19 St Andrew St, Stratford, ON, N5A 1A2
(519) 271-0220
Emp Here 30   *Sales* 1,386,253
SIC 8231 Libraries

D-U-N-S 25-819-9884   (SL)
STRATFORD-PERTH FAMILY YMCA
204 Downie St, Stratford, ON, N5A 1X4
(519) 271-0480
Emp Here 100   *Sales* 4,012,839
SIC 7997 Membership sports and recreation clubs

D-U-N-S 20-006-5824   (BR)
SUN LIFE ASSURANCE COMPANY OF CANADA
CLARICA LIFE FINANCIAL
342 Erie St Suite 107, Stratford, ON, N5A 2N4
(519) 271-0740
Emp Here 40
SIC 6411 Insurance agents, brokers, and service

D-U-N-S 25-910-7621   (BR)
TAILWIND INVESTMENTS LTD
BOWERS PROCESS EQUIPMENT
(*Suby of* Tailwind Investments Ltd)
487 Lorne Ave E, Stratford, ON, N5A 6S4

(519) 271-4757
Emp Here 30
SIC 3523 Farm machinery and equipment

D-U-N-S 24-151-5852   (SL)
TIM HORTONS
166 Ontario St, Stratford, ON, N5A 3H4
(519) 273-2421
Emp Here 125   *Sales* 4,231,721
SIC 5461 Retail bakeries

D-U-N-S 25-347-6550   (SL)
TORA STRATFORD LIMITED
GIANT TIGER
477 Huron St, Stratford, ON, N5A 5T8
(519) 272-2029
Emp Here 60   *Sales* 4,888,367
SIC 5399 Miscellaneous general merchandise

D-U-N-S 20-025-6258   (BR)
TRI-COUNTY MENNONITE HOMES ASSOCIATION
GREENWOOD COURT, DIV OF
(*Suby of* Tri-County Mennonite Homes Association)
90 Greenwood Dr Suite 117, Stratford, ON, N5A 7W5
(519) 273-4662
Emp Here 85
SIC 8059 Nursing and personal care, nec

D-U-N-S 25-310-4038   (BR)
TWINCORP INC
KFC TACOBELL
1067 Ontario St, Stratford, ON, N5A 6W6

Emp Here 23
SIC 5812 Eating places

D-U-N-S 20-789-6023   (BR)
UNITED PARCEL SERVICE CANADA LTD
UPS
9 Griffith Rd, Stratford, ON, N5A 6S4
(519) 271-9610
Emp Here 27
SIC 4212 Local trucking, without storage

D-U-N-S 25-357-8306   (BR)
VICTORIAN ORDER OF NURSES FOR CANADA
VON PERTH-HURON DISTRICT
40 Long Dr Suite 111, Stratford, ON, N5A 8A3
(519) 271-7991
Emp Here 65
SIC 8082 Home health care services

D-U-N-S 20-303-3972   (BR)
VICWEST INC
(*Suby of* Vicwest Inc)
362 Lorne Ave E, Stratford, ON, N5A 6S4
(519) 271-5553
Emp Here 75
SIC 3444 Sheet Metalwork

Strathroy, ON N7G
Middlesex County

D-U-N-S 24-394-4050   (BR)
ACCUCAPS INDUSTRIES LIMITED
ACCUCAPS STRATHROY OPERATIONS
720 Wright St, Strathroy, ON, N7G 3H8
(519) 245-8880
Emp Here 50
SIC 2899 Chemical preparations, nec

D-U-N-S 24-469-5953   (HQ)
BONDUELLE ONTARIO INC
225 Lothian Ave, Strathroy, ON, N7G 4J1
(519) 245-4600
Emp Here 100   *Sales* 8,828,245
SIC 2037 Frozen fruits and vegetables
 Robert Shareck
Pr Pr Marcel Ostiguy
 Claude Ostiguy

D-U-N-S 20-292-5298   (BR)

CANADA POST CORPORATION
62 Frank St, Strathroy, ON, N7G 2R4
(519) 245-1461
Emp Here 35
SIC 4311 J.s. postal service

D-U-N-S 20-015-4479   (BR)
CARGILL LIMITED
CARGILL ANIMAL NUTRITION DIV
127 Zimmerman St, Strathroy, ON, N7G 2G7
(519) 245-9600
Emp Here 30
SIC 5191 Farm supplies

D-U-N-S 25-147-4573   (BR)
CORPORATION OF THE COUNTY OF MID-DLESEX
STRATHMERE LODGE
(*Suby of* Corporation of The County of Middlesex)
599 Albert St, Strathroy, ON, N7G 1X1
(519) 245-2520
Emp Here 160
SIC 8361 Residential care

D-U-N-S 24-977-5383   (BR)
DOLLARAMA S.E.C.
70 Carroll St E, Strathroy, ON, N7G 4G2
(519) 245-7439
Emp Here 20
SIC 5331 Variety stores

D-U-N-S 25-625-0150   (BR)
EXTENDICARE (CANADA) INC
PARAMED HOME HEALTH CARE
323 Caradcc St S, Strathroy, ON, N7G 2P3

Emp Here 45
SIC 8051 Skilled nursing care facilities

D-U-N-S 20-146-2678   (HQ)
GRAY, L. H. & SON LIMITED
GRAY RIDGE EGGS
644 Wright St, Strathroy, ON, N7G 3H8
(519) 245-0480
Emp Here 100   *Emp Total* 240
Sales 56,909,346
SIC 5144 Poultry and poultry products
  William Gray
S&M/VP Mike Walsh
VP Opers Scott Brookshaw
VP Fin Brent Drew

D-U-N-S 25-482-9724   (BR)
LIBRO CREDIT UNION LIMITED
72 Front St W, Strathroy, ON, N7G 1X7
(519) 245-1261
Emp Here 20
SIC 6062 State credit unions

D-U-N-S 20-590-9810   (BR)
LONDON DISTRICT CATHOLIC SCHOOL BOARD
HOLY CROSS CATHOLIC SECONDARY SCHOOL
367 Second St, Strathroy, ON, N7G 4K6
(519) 245-8488
Emp Here 33
SIC 8211 Elementary and secondary schools

D-U-N-S 20-362-0661   (BR)
LONDON DISTRICT CATHOLIC SCHOOL BOARD
ST. VINCENT DE PAUL CATHOLIC SCHOOL
286 Mckellar St, Strathroy, ON, N7G 2Y5
(519) 660-2794
Emp Here 36
SIC 8211 Elementary and secondary schools

D-U-N-S 25-237-8633   (BR)
LONDON DISTRICT CATHOLIC SCHOOL BOARD
OUR LADY IMMACULATE CATHOLIC SCHOOL
75 Head St N, Strathroy, ON, N7G 2J6
(519) 660-2774
Emp Here 33

SIC 8211 Elementary and secondary schools

D-U-N-S 24-369-4036   (HQ)
MERIDIAN LIGHTWEIGHT TECHNOLO-GIES HOLDINGS INC
25 Mcnab St, Strathroy, ON, N7G 4H6
(519) 246-9600
Emp Here 30   *Emp Total* 10,000
Sales 34,563,415
SIC 3364 Nonferrous die-castings except aluminum
CEO Terry Luo

D-U-N-S 24-359-8765   (HQ)
MERIDIAN LIGHTWEIGHT TECHNOLO-GIES INC
MAGNESIUM PRODUCTS
25 Mcnab St, Strathroy, ON, N7G 4H6
(519) 246-9600
Emp Here 35   *Emp Total* 10,000
Sales 29,972,285
SIC 3364 Nonferrous die-castings except aluminum
Pr Pr Terry Luo
Dir Frank Chen

D-U-N-S 24-826-4509   (BR)
MERIDIAN LIGHTWEIGHT TECHNOLO-GIES INC
MAGNESIUM PRODUCTS DIVISION
155 High St E, Strathroy, ON, N7G 1H4
(519) 245-4040
Emp Here 400
SIC 3364 Nonferrous die-castings except aluminum

D-U-N-S 25-018-9883   (BR)
ROYAL BANK OF CANADA
RBC
(*Suby of* Royal Bank Of Canada)
38 Front St W, Strathroy, ON, N7G 1X4
(519) 245-1420
Emp Here 24
SIC 6021 National commercial banks

D-U-N-S 25-629-1915   (BR)
STRATHROY-CARADOC, MUNICIPALITY OF
WEST MIDDLESEX MEMORIAL CENTRE
334 Metcalfe St W, Strathroy, ON, N7G 1N5
(519) 245-2971
Emp Here 23
SIC 7999 Amusement and recreation, nec

D-U-N-S 24-118-5631   (BR)
STRATHROY-CARADOC, MUNICIPALITY OF
GEMINI SPORTSPLEX
667 Adair Blvd, Strathroy, ON, N7G 3H8
(519) 245-7557
Emp Here 25
SIC 7299 Miscellaneous personal service

D-U-N-S 20-710-5623   (BR)
THAMES VALLEY DISTRICT SCHOOL BOARD
NORTH MEADOWS PUBLIC SCHOOL
82 Middlesex Dr, Strathroy, ON, N7G 4G5
(519) 245-7373
Emp Here 50
SIC 8211 Elementary and secondary schools

D-U-N-S 25-249-0818   (BR)
THAMES VALLEY DISTRICT SCHOOL BOARD
ADELAIDE W.G. MACDONALD PUBLIC SCHOOL
29059 School Rd, Strathroy, ON, N7G 3H6
(519) 247-3369
Emp Here 25
SIC 8211 Elementary and secondary schools

D-U-N-S 25-249-0495   (BR)
THAMES VALLEY DISTRICT SCHOOL BOARD
COLBORNE PUBLIC SCHOOL
25 Colborne St, Strathroy, ON, N7G 2M1

(519) 245-2044
Emp Here 40
SIC 8211 Elementary and secondary schools

D-U-N-S 20-710-5631   (BR)
THAMES VALLEY DISTRICT SCHOOL BOARD
STRATHROY ADULT LEARNING CENTRE
51 Front St E, Strathroy, ON, N7G 1Y5
(519) 245-3900
Emp Here 50
SIC 8211 Elementary and secondary schools

D-U-N-S 25-249-0669   (BR)
THAMES VALLEY DISTRICT SCHOOL BOARD
CARADOC NORTH PUBLIC SCHOOL
Gd Lcd Main, Strathroy, ON, N7G 3H9
(519) 245-2085
Emp Here 22
SIC 8211 Elementary and secondary schools

D-U-N-S 20-710-5540   (BR)
THAMES VALLEY DISTRICT SCHOOL BOARD
STRATHROY DISTRICT COLLEGIATE INSTI-TUTE
361 Second St, Strathroy, ON, N7G 4J8
(519) 245-2680
Emp Here 50
SIC 8211 Elementary and secondary schools

D-U-N-S 25-249-0248   (BR)
THAMES VALLEY DISTRICT SCHOOL BOARD
J.S. BUCHANAN FRENCH IMMERSION PUBLIC SCHOOL
248 Keefer St, Strathroy, ON, N7G 1E2
(519) 245-0473
Emp Here 24
SIC 8211 Elementary and secondary schools

D-U-N-S 24-319-5190   (BR)
WAL-MART CANADA CORP
WALMART
150 Carroll St E, Strathroy, ON, N7G 4G2
(519) 245-7200
Emp Here 125
SIC 5311 Department stores

Stratton, ON P0W
Rainy River County

D-U-N-S 20-710-3388   (BR)
RAINY RIVER DISTRICT SCHOOL BOARD
STURGEON CREEK ALTERNATIVE PRO-GRAM
270 Hwy 617, Stratton, ON, P0W 1N0

Emp Here 21
SIC 8211 Elementary and secondary schools

Sturgeon Falls, ON P2B
Nipissing County

D-U-N-S 20-155-3575   (SL)
ALOUETTE BUS LINES LTD
194 Front St Suite Front, Sturgeon Falls, ON, P2B 2J3
(705) 753-3911
Emp Here 100   *Sales* 2,845,467
SIC 4151 School buses

D-U-N-S 20-070-2848   (BR)
CHISHOLM, R. FOOD SERVICES INC
MCDONALD'S RESTAURANTS
(*Suby of* Chisholm, R. Food Services Inc)
195 Front St, Sturgeon Falls, ON, P2B 2J4
(705) 753-5155
Emp Here 30
SIC 5812 Eating places

D-U-N-S 25-478-8722   (HQ)
COMMUNITY LIVING WEST NIPISSING
(*Suby of* Community Living West Nipissing)
75 Railway St, Sturgeon Falls, ON, P2B 3A1
(705) 753-1665
Emp Here 48   *Emp Total* 95
Sales 5,480,771
SIC 8399 Social services, nec
Ex Dir Sylvie Belanger
Dir Fin Armande Jodouin
Pr Pr Sandra Massicoppe
  Louise Gauthier

D-U-N-S 24-178-8145   (BR)
COMMUNITY LIVING WEST NIPISSING
120 Nipissing St, Sturgeon Falls, ON, P2B 1J6
(705) 753-3143
Emp Here 100
SIC 8059 Nursing and personal care, nec

D-U-N-S 20-913-6808   (BR)
CONSEIL SCOLAIRE CATHOLIQUE DU DISTRICT FRANCO-NORD
ECOLE ELEMENTAIRE CATHOLIQUE SAINT-JOSEPH
150 Levesque St, Sturgeon Falls, ON, P2B 1M1
(705) 753-0750
Emp Here 30
SIC 8211 Elementary and secondary schools

D-U-N-S 20-648-2965   (BR)
CONSEIL SCOLAIRE CATHOLIQUE DU DISTRICT FRANCO-NORD
ECOLE SEPAREE LA RESURRECTION
136 Third St Suite 120, Sturgeon Falls, ON, P2B 3C6
(705) 753-1100
Emp Here 34
SIC 8211 Elementary and secondary schools

D-U-N-S 25-238-7626   (BR)
CONSEIL SCOLAIRE CATHOLIQUE DU DISTRICT FRANCO-NORD
ECOLE SECONDAIRE FRANCO CITE
(*Suby of* Conseil Scolaire Catholique Du District Franco-Nord)
90 Main St, Sturgeon Falls, ON, P2B 2Z7
(705) 753-1510
Emp Here 50
SIC 8211 Elementary and secondary schools

D-U-N-S 25-263-7988   (BR)
CONSEIL SCOLAIRE CATHOLIQUE DU DISTRICT FRANCO-NORD
ECOLE ECHO JEUNESSE
(*Suby of* Conseil Scolaire Catholique Du District Franco-Nord)
99 Michaud St, Sturgeon Falls, ON, P2B 1B9

Emp Here 20
SIC 8211 Elementary and secondary schools

D-U-N-S 20-789-7955   (BR)
MUNICIPALITY OF WEST NIPISSING
WEST NIPISSING RECREATION CENTRE
219 O'Hara St Unit A, Sturgeon Falls, ON, P2B 1A2
(705) 753-0160
Emp Here 30
SIC 7999 Amusement and recreation, nec

D-U-N-S 25-249-0362   (BR)
NEAR NORTH DISTRICT SCHOOL BOARD
WHITE WOODS PUBLIC SCHOOL
177 Ethel St, Sturgeon Falls, ON, P2B 2Z8
(705) 472-4224
Emp Here 25
SIC 8211 Elementary and secondary schools

D-U-N-S 25-238-8376   (BR)
NIPISSING PARRY SOUND CATHOLIC DIS-TRICT SCHOOL BOARD
OUR LADY OF SORROWS SCHOOL
680 Coursol Rd, Sturgeon Falls, ON, P2B 3L1
(705) 753-2590
Emp Here 30
SIC 8211 Elementary and secondary schools

D-U-N-S 25-292-5185 (BR)
REXALL PHARMACY GROUP LTD
REXALL 8176
(*Suby of* McKesson Corporation)
228 King St, Sturgeon Falls, ON, P2B 1R9
(705) 753-0150
Emp Here 30
SIC 5912 Drug stores and proprietary stores

D-U-N-S 24-121-6795 (SL)
STURGEON FALLS BRUSH SPRAYING AND CUTTING LIMITED
125 Lisgar St, Sturgeon Falls, ON, P2B 3H4
(705) 753-3883
Emp Here 30   *Sales* 5,496,960
SIC 1629 Heavy construction, nec

D-U-N-S 24-796-0016 (BR)
SYSCO CANADA, INC
SYSCO FOOD SERVICES
(*Suby of* Sysco Corporation)
106 Bay St, Sturgeon Falls, ON, P2B 3G6
(705) 753-4444
Emp Here 95
SIC 5141 Groceries, general line

D-U-N-S 20-950-3056 (BR)
WADLAND PHARMACY LIMITED
LOBLAW
12035 Highway 17 E, Sturgeon Falls, ON, P2B 2S6
(705) 753-5850
Emp Here 20
SIC 5912 Drug stores and proprietary stores

Sudbury, ON P3A
Sudbury County

D-U-N-S 24-858-3424 (BR)
510172 ONTARIO LTD
DIESEL ELECTRIC SERVICES
100 Rr1 Foundry St, Sudbury, ON, P3A 4R7
(705) 674-5626
Emp Here 30
SIC 3743 Railroad equipment

D-U-N-S 24-177-5522 (BR)
ALS CANADA LTD
ALS CHEMEX
1512 Old Falconbridge Rd, Sudbury, ON, P3A 4N8
(705) 560-7225
Emp Here 20
SIC 8731 Commercial physical research

D-U-N-S 25-769-9272 (BR)
BANK OF NOVA SCOTIA, THE
SCOTIABANK
1094 Barrydowne Rd, Sudbury, ON, P3A 3V3
(705) 560-2700
Emp Here 23
SIC 6021 National commercial banks

D-U-N-S 24-227-4277 (BR)
BELL TECHNICAL SOLUTIONS INC
1771 Old Falconbridge Rd, Sudbury, ON, P3A 4R7
(705) 566-6122
Emp Here 20
SIC 4899 Communication services, nec

D-U-N-S 20-402-0820 (SL)
BENC HOTEL HOLDINGS LIMITED
AMBASSADOR MOTOR HOTEL
225 Falconbridge Rd, Sudbury, ON, P3A 5K4
(705) 566-3601
Emp Here 50   *Sales* 2,188,821
SIC 7011 Hotels and motels

D-U-N-S 24-425-0924 (SL)
BINGO ONE LIMITED
BOARDWALK GAMING CENTER
940 Newgate Ave, Sudbury, ON, P3A 5J9
(705) 560-4243
Emp Here 50   *Sales* 2,699,546

SIC 7999 Amusement and recreation, nec

D-U-N-S 25-231-7540 (BR)
BRICK WAREHOUSE LP, THE
BRICK, THE
747 Notre Dame Ave, Sudbury, ON, P3A 2T2
(705) 560-9911
Emp Here 50
SIC 5712 Furniture stores

D-U-N-S 20-155-4722 (BR)
BRINK'S CANADA LIMITED
(*Suby of* The Brink's Company)
2423 Lasalle Blvd, Sudbury, ON, P3A 2A9
(705) 560-7007
Emp Here 23
SIC 7381 Detective and armored car services

D-U-N-S 24-426-3518 (SL)
CSH WESTMOUNT INC
WESTMOUNT RETIREMENT RESIDENCE
599 William Ave Suite 77, Sudbury, ON, P3A 5W3
(705) 566-6221
Emp Here 20   *Sales* 729,607
SIC 8361 Residential care

D-U-N-S 24-773-1206 (BR)
CAISSE POPULAIRE DES VOYAGEURS INC
(*Suby of* Caisse Populaire des Voyageurs Inc)
1380 Lasalle Blvd, Sudbury, ON, P3A 1Z6
(705) 566-3644
Emp Here 25
SIC 6062 State credit unions

D-U-N-S 20-845-0049 (HQ)
CAMBRIAN COLLEGE OF APPLIED ARTS & TECHNOLOGY, THE
(*Suby of* Cambrian College of Applied Arts & Technology, The)
1400 Barrydowne Rd, Sudbury, ON, P3A 3V8
(705) 566-8101
Emp Here 830   *Emp Total* 850
Sales 123,870,450
SIC 8222 Junior colleges
Pr Pr Sylvia Barnard
VP Sonia Delmissier
VP Betty Freelandt
Dir Fin Glenn Toikka

D-U-N-S 24-414-4234 (BR)
CANADIAN BLOOD SERVICES
944 Barrydowne Rd, Sudbury, ON, P3A 3V3
(705) 674-2636
Emp Here 35
SIC 3099 Health and allied services, nec

D-U-N-S 25-303-4490 (BR)
CANADIAN IMPERIAL BANK OF COMMERCE
CIBC
1349 Lasalle Blvd, Sudbury, ON, P3A 1Z2
(705) 566-2458
Emp Here 30
SIC 6021 National commercial banks

D-U-N-S 24-418-6560 (BR)
CATERPILLAR MINING CANADA ULC
2555 Maley Dr Suite 3, Sudbury, ON, P3A 4R7

Emp Here 20
SIC 5082 Construction and mining machinery

D-U-N-S 20-791-4362 (BR)
CHILDREN'S PLACE (CANADA) LP, THE
1349 Lasalle Blvd, Sudbury, ON, P3A 1Z2
(705) 524-9645
Emp Here 20
SIC 5641 Children's and infants' wear stores

D-U-N-S 24-977-7178 (BR)
CITY OF GREATER SUDBURY, THE
PIONEER MANOR DIVISION
(*Suby of* City of Greater Sudbury, The)
960 Notre Dame Ave Suite D, Sudbury, ON, P3A 2T4

(705) 566-4270
Emp Here 400
SIC 8059 Nursing and personal care, nec

D-U-N-S 24-214-8315 (BR)
CO-OPERATORS GROUP LIMITED, THE
CO-OPERATORS, THE
363 Falconbridge Rd Suite 1, Sudbury, ON, P3A 5K5
(705) 566-1300
Emp Here 50
SIC 6411 Insurance agents, brokers, and service

D-U-N-S 24-182-9175 (HQ)
COLLINS BARROW, SUDBURY - NIPISSING LLP
(*Suby of* Collins Barrow, Sudbury - Nipissing LLP)
1174 St. Jerome St, Sudbury, ON, P3A 2V9
(705) 560-5592
Emp Here 60   *Emp Total* 70
Sales 3,064,349
SIC 8721 Accounting, auditing, and bookkeeping

D-U-N-S 25-239-0620 (BR)
CONSEIL SCOLAIRE DE DISTRICT CATHOLIQUE DU NOUVEL-ONTARIO, LE
ECOLE FELIX RICARD
691 Lasalle Blvd, Sudbury, ON, P3A 1X3
(705) 566-8300
Emp Here 40
SIC 8211 Elementary and secondary schools

D-U-N-S 25-239-0190 (BR)
CONSEIL SCOLAIRE DE DISTRICT CATHOLIQUE DU NOUVEL-ONTARIO, LE
ECOLE ST DOMINIQUE
2096 Montfort St, Sudbury, ON, P3A 2K8
(705) 566-2616
Emp Here 25
SIC 8211 Elementary and secondary schools

D-U-N-S 25-137-3106 (BR)
CONSEIL SCOLAIRE DE DISTRICT DU GRAND NORD DE L'ONTARIO
CONSEIL SCOLAIRE DE DISTRICT DU GRAND NORD DE L'ON
2190 Lasalle Blvd, Sudbury, ON, P3A 2A8
(705) 566-1071
Emp Here 20
SIC 8211 Elementary and secondary schools

D-U-N-S 20-716-8928 (BR)
CONSEIL SCOLAIRE DE DISTRICT DU GRAND NORD DE L'ONTARIO
CONSEIL SCOLAIRE DE DISTRICT DU GRAND NORD DE L'ON
37 Lasalle Blvd, Sudbury, ON, P3A 1W1
(705) 566-7660
Emp Here 50
SIC 8211 Elementary and secondary schools

D-U-N-S 20-715-6068 (SL)
CROSSTOWN OLDSMOBILE CHEVROLET LTD
280 Falconbridge Rd, Sudbury, ON, P3A 5K3
(705) 566-4804
Emp Here 60   *Sales* 21,888,210
SIC 5511 New and used car dealers
Pr Pr Merle Gray
Vince Pollesel

D-U-N-S 20-127-8467 (BR)
DYNAMEX CANADA LIMITED
1785 Frobisher St Unit 3, Sudbury, ON, P3A 6C8
(705) 524-0400
Emp Here 20
SIC 7389 Business services, nec

D-U-N-S 24-523-3064 (BR)
EASTON'S GROUP OF HOTELS INC
TOWNEPLACE SUITES SUDBURY
1710 The Kingsway, Sudbury, ON, P3A 0A3

(705) 525-7700
Emp Here 50
SIC 7011 Hotels and motels

D-U-N-S 20-020-6253 (BR)
EXTENDICARE INC
EXTENDICARE FALCONBRIDGE
281 Falconbridge Rd, Sudbury, ON, P3A 5K4
(705) 566-7980
Emp Here 200
SIC 8051 Skilled nursing care facilities

D-U-N-S 24-340-2539 (BR)
FGL SPORTS LTD
SPORT CHEK NEW SUDBURY CENTRE
1349 Lasalle Blvd, Sudbury, ON, P3A 1Z2
(705) 525-8181
Emp Here 50
SIC 5941 Sporting goods and bicycle shops

D-U-N-S 25-146-9045 (BR)
HALIBURTON BROADCASTING GROUP INC
NEWHOT93.5FM
493 Barrydowne Rd, Sudbury, ON, P3A 3T4
(705) 560-8323
Emp Here 25
SIC 4832 Radio broadcasting stations

D-U-N-S 20-155-7238 (BR)
HONEYWELL LIMITED
(*Suby of* Honeywell International Inc.)
1500 Fairburn St, Sudbury, ON, P3A 1N7
(705) 566-6730
Emp Here 24
SIC 3822 Environmental controls

D-U-N-S 20-717-1377 (BR)
HYDRO ONE INC
957 Falconbridge Rd, Sudbury, ON, P3A 5K8
(705) 566-8955
Emp Here 50
SIC 4911 Electric services

D-U-N-S 20-190-4245 (BR)
HYDRO ONE NETWORKS INC
957 Falconbridge Rd, Sudbury, ON, P3A 5K8
(705) 566-8955
Emp Here 100
SIC 4911 Electric services

D-U-N-S 25-309-7372 (BR)
INDUSTRIELLE ALLIANCE, ASSURANCE ET SERVICES FINANCIERS INC
1210 Lasalle Blvd, Sudbury, ON, P3A 1Y5
(705) 524-5755
Emp Here 100
SIC 6411 Insurance agents, brokers, and service

D-U-N-S 24-344-7732 (BR)
KAVERIT CRANES & SERVICE ULC
AONES CRANES
598 Falconbridge Rd Unit 12, Sudbury, ON, P3A 5K6
(705) 521-0953
Emp Here 20
SIC 7389 Business services, nec

D-U-N-S 24-677-1567 (BR)
KONECRANES CANADA INC
598 Falconbridge Rd Unit 12, Sudbury, ON, P3A 5K6
(705) 521-0953
Emp Here 20
SIC 7699 Repair services, nec

D-U-N-S 25-295-5489 (BR)
LEON'S FURNITURE LIMITED
LEON'S
817 Notre Dame Ave, Sudbury, ON, P3A 2T2
(705) 524-5366
Emp Here 60
SIC 5712 Furniture stores

D-U-N-S 24-377-0042 (BR)
LOBLAWS INC
REAL CANADIAN SUPERSTORE
1485 Lasalle Blvd, Sudbury, ON, P3A 5H7

---

(705) 560-4961
Emp Here 200
SIC 5411 Grocery stores

D-U-N-S 24-476-5236   (SL)
LYNSOS INC
PAT & MARIO'S RESTAURANT
1463 Lasalle Blvd, Sudbury, ON, P3A 1Z8
(705) 560-2500
Emp Here 90   Sales 2,699,546
SIC 5812 Eating places

D-U-N-S 25-282-8637   (BR)
MAC'S CONVENIENCE STORES INC
MAC'S CONVENIENCE STORES
2142 Lasalle Blvd, Sudbury, ON, P3A 2A7
(705) 560-2399
Emp Here 60
SIC 5411 Grocery stores

D-U-N-S 24-116-7902   (BR)
MAJOR DRILLING GROUP INTERNA-TIONAL INC
(Suby of Major Drilling Group International Inc)
598 Falconbridge Rd Unit 1, Sudbury, ON, P3A 5K6
(705) 560-5995
Emp Here 50
SIC 1481 NonMetallic mineral services

D-U-N-S 24-795-9117   (BR)
MCKESSON CORPORATION
PHARMA PLUS DRUGMART
(Suby of McKesson Corporation)
555 Barrydowne Rd, Sudbury, ON, P3A 3T4
(705) 566-5200
Emp Here 20
SIC 5912 Drug stores and proprietary stores

D-U-N-S 24-610-4454   (BR)
METRO ONTARIO INC
900 Lasalle Blvd, Sudbury, ON, P3A 5W8
(705) 560-9500
Emp Here 49
SIC 5411 Grocery stores

D-U-N-S 20-918-8478   (BR)
ORKIN CANADA CORPORATION
(Suby of Rollins, Inc.)
760 Notre Dame Ave, Sudbury, ON, P3A 2T4
(705) 524-2847
Emp Here 23
SIC 7342 Disinfecting and pest control services

D-U-N-S 25-828-2268   (BR)
PHARMA PLUS DRUGMARTS LTD
555 Barrydowne Rd, Sudbury, ON, P3A 3T4
(705) 566-0220
Emp Here 25
SIC 5912 Drug stores and proprietary stores

D-U-N-S 24-891-2693   (BR)
R. V. ANDERSON ASSOCIATES LIMITED
DENNIS CONSULTANTS
(Suby of Arval Holdings Limited)
436 Westmount Ave Suite 6, Sudbury, ON, P3A 5Z8
(705) 560-5555
Emp Here 25
SIC 8711 Engineering services

D-U-N-S 20-156-0463   (HQ)
RAINBOW CONCRETE INDUSTRIES LIM-ITED
(Suby of Concrete Holdings Ltd)
2477 Maley Dr, Sudbury, ON, P3A 4R7
(705) 566-1740
Emp Here 90   Emp Total 127
Sales 16,999,843
SIC 3271 Concrete block and brick
Pr Pr Boris Naneff
VP Rade Brujic

D-U-N-S 20-710-3974   (BR)
RAINBOW DISTRICT SCHOOL BOARD
CYRIL VARNEY PUBLIC SCHOOL
1545 Gary Ave, Sudbury, ON, P3A 4G5

(705) 566-2424
Emp Here 40
SIC 8211 Elementary and secondary schools

D-U-N-S 25-239-9969   (BR)
RAINBOW DISTRICT SCHOOL BOARD
LASALLE SECONDARY SCHOOL
(Suby of Rainbow District School Board)
1545 Kennedy St, Sudbury, ON, P3A 2G1
(705) 688-0888
Emp Here 100
SIC 8211 Elementary and secondary schools

D-U-N-S 25-239-9878   (BR)
RAINBOW DISTRICT SCHOOL BOARD
CARL A. NESBITT PUBLIC SCHOOL
(Suby of Rainbow District School Board)
1241 Roy Ave, Sudbury, ON, P3A 3M5
(705) 566-3935
Emp Here 20
SIC 8211 Elementary and secondary schools

D-U-N-S 25-228-0797   (BR)
RAINBOW DISTRICT SCHOOL BOARD
CHURCHILL PUBLIC SCHOOL
(Suby of Rainbow District School Board)
1722 Fielding St, Sudbury, ON, P3A 1P1
(705) 566-5130
Emp Here 30
SIC 8211 Elementary and secondary schools

D-U-N-S 24-423-7488   (BR)
RED LOBSTER HOSPITALITY LLC
RED LOBSTER RESTAURANTS
(Suby of Red Lobster Seafood Co., LLC)
1600 Lasalle Blvd, Sudbury, ON, P3A 1Z7

Emp Here 60
SIC 5812 Eating places

D-U-N-S 25-018-9545   (BR)
ROYAL BANK OF CANADA
RBC
(Suby of Royal Bank Of Canada)
1720 Lasalle Blvd, Sudbury, ON, P3A 2A1
(705) 566-1710
Emp Here 45
SIC 6021 National commercial banks

D-U-N-S 24-354-1369   (HQ)
SKL 4 EVER LTD
MCDONALD'S RESTAURANT
(Suby of SKL 4 Ever Ltd)
914 Newgate Ave, Sudbury, ON, P3A 5J9
(705) 560-3030
Emp Here 20   Emp Total 50
Sales 1,532,175
SIC 5812 Eating places

D-U-N-S 25-311-1298   (BR)
SEARS CANADA INC
1349 Lasalle Blvd Suite 50, Sudbury, ON, P3A 1Z3
(705) 566-4000
Emp Here 350
SIC 5311 Department stores

D-U-N-S 25-281-2896   (BR)
SECURITAS CANADA LIMITED
767 Barrydowne Rd Suite 301, Sudbury, ON, P3A 3T6
(705) 675-3654
Emp Here 130
SIC 7381 Detective and armored car services

D-U-N-S 25-419-2958   (SL)
SMITH'S MARKETS INC
971 Lasalle Blvd, Sudbury, ON, P3A 1X7
(705) 560-3663
Emp Here 50   Sales 4,304,681
SIC 5431 Fruit and vegetable markets

D-U-N-S 25-213-7229   (BR)
STAPLES CANADA INC
STAPLES THE BUSINESS DEPOT
(Suby of Staples, Inc.)
747 Notre Dame Ave, Sudbury, ON, P3A 2T2
(705) 525-1180
Emp Here 40

SIC 5943 Stationery stores

D-U-N-S 25-239-0786   (BR)
SUDBURY CATHOLIC DISTRICT SCHOOL BOARD
ST. RAPHAEL ELEMENTARY SCHOOL
1096 Dublin St, Sudbury, ON, P3A 1R6

Emp Here 55
SIC 8211 Elementary and secondary schools

D-U-N-S 25-239-0075   (BR)
SUDBURY CATHOLIC DISTRICT SCHOOL BOARD
ST ANDREW ELEMENTARY SCHOOL
1305 Holland Rd, Sudbury, ON, P3A 3R4

Emp Here 20
SIC 8211 Elementary and secondary schools

D-U-N-S 20-851-6831   (SL)
SUDBURY MANAGEMENT SERVICES LIM-ITED
MANPOWER
1901 Lasalle Blvd, Sudbury, ON, P3A 2A3
(705) 525-4357
Emp Here 50   Sales 3,648,035
SIC 7363 Help supply services

D-U-N-S 25-322-1477   (BR)
TORONTO-DOMINION BANK, THE
TD BANK
(Suby of Toronto-Dominion Bank, The)
2208 Lasalle Blvd, Sudbury, ON, P3A 2A8
(705) 566-2313
Emp Here 30
SIC 6021 National commercial banks

D-U-N-S 24-302-6648   (HQ)
TRACKS & WHEELS EQUIPMENT BRO-KERS INC
GENERAL BREAKERS CANADA
(Suby of Tracks & Wheels Equipment Brokers Inc)
400 Hwy 69 N, Sudbury, ON, P3A 4S9
(705) 566-5438
Emp Here 80   Emp Total 100
Sales 18,240,175
SIC 5082 Construction and mining machinery
Conrad Houle
Pr Roger Coggins
Sheila Houle

D-U-N-S 25-293-5598   (BR)
UNION GAS LIMITED
828 Falconbridge Rd, Sudbury, ON, P3A 4S4
(705) 566-4301
Emp Here 102
SIC 4924 Natural gas distribution

D-U-N-S 25-807-4491   (BR)
VALUE VILLAGE STORES, INC
(Suby of Savers, Inc.)
799 Notre Dame Ave, Sudbury, ON, P3A 2T2
(705) 525-2339
Emp Here 35
SIC 5399 Miscellaneous general merchandise

D-U-N-S 25-294-8625   (BR)
WAL-MART CANADA CORP
1349 Lasalle Blvd Suite 3097, Sudbury, ON, P3A 1Z2
(705) 566-3700
Emp Here 250
SIC 5311 Department stores

D-U-N-S 20-769-2005   (BR)
WASTE MANAGEMENT OF CANADA COR-PORATION
(Suby of Waste Management, Inc.)
1865 Lasalle Blvd, Sudbury, ON, P3A 2A3
(705) 566-8444
Emp Here 60
SIC 4953 Refuse systems

D-U-N-S 24-194-0696   (BR)
XS CARGO GP INC
(Suby of XSC Canada Holdings Inc)

900 Lasalle Blvd, Sudbury, ON, P3A 5W8

Emp Here 20
SIC 5399 Miscellaneous general merchandise

Sudbury, ON P3B
Sudbury County

D-U-N-S 20-700-0105   (BR)
BANQUE DE DEVELOPPEMENT DU CANADA
BDC
233 Brady St E Unit 10, Sudbury, ON, P3B 4H5
(888) 463-6232
Emp Here 40
SIC 6141 Personal credit institutions

D-U-N-S 25-278-5639   (BR)
CARA OPERATIONS LIMITED
HARVEY'S
(Suby of Cara Holdings Limited)
894 Kingsway, Sudbury, ON, P3B 2E5
(519) 679-9660
Emp Here 20
SIC 5812 Eating places

D-U-N-S 20-021-7961   (BR)
CONSEIL SCOLAIRE DE DISTRICT DU GRAND NORD DE L'ONTARIO
CONSEIL SCOLAIRE DE DISTRICT DU GRAND NORD DE L'ON
300 Van Horne St, Sudbury, ON, P3B 1H9
(705) 675-1613
Emp Here 25
SIC 8211 Elementary and secondary schools

D-U-N-S 25-097-2320   (BR)
COSTCO WHOLESALE CANADA LTD
COSTCO
(Suby of Costco Wholesale Corporation)
1465 Kingsway, Sudbury, ON, P3B 0A5
(705) 524-8255
Emp Here 200
SIC 5141 Groceries, general line

D-U-N-S 25-394-1546   (BR)
ENDURAPAK INC
(Suby of Endurapak Inc)
360 Mountain St, Sudbury, ON, P3B 2T7
(705) 673-7777
Emp Here 20
SIC 2673 Bags: plastic, laminated, and coated

D-U-N-S 25-184-3905   (BR)
GAP (CANADA) INC
(Suby of The Gap Inc)
110 Donna St, Sudbury, ON, P3B 4K6
(705) 524-5469
Emp Here 65
SIC 5651 Family clothing stores

D-U-N-S 25-171-5678   (BR)
HOME DEPOT OF CANADA INC
HOME DEPOT
(Suby of The Home Depot Inc)
1500 Marcus Dr, Sudbury, ON, P3B 4K5
(705) 525-2960
Emp Here 100
SIC 5251 Hardware stores

D-U-N-S 25-092-5708   (BR)
INDIGO BOOKS & MUSIC INC
CHAPTERS
(Suby of Indigo Books & Music Inc)
1425 Kingsway, Sudbury, ON, P3B 0A2
(705) 525-5616
Emp Here 50
SIC 5942 Book stores

D-U-N-S 25-305-2807   (BR)
INNVEST PROPERTIES CORP
COMFORT INN EAST
(Suby of Innvest Properties Corp)

440 Second Ave N, Sudbury, ON, P3B 4A4
(705) 560-4502
Emp Here 20
SIC 7011 Hotels and motels

D-U-N-S 20-155-7568   (SL)
JUTRAS, PHIL & SON LIMITED
JUTRAS AUTO SALES
(*Suby of* Transporation Jutras Transporation Inc)
2042 Kingsway, Sudbury, ON, P3B 4J8
(705) 525-5560
Emp Here 45   *Sales* 6,229,760
SIC 4212 Local trucking, without storage
Dir Denise Jutras

D-U-N-S 24-858-2194   (BR)
LOWE'S COMPANIES CANADA, ULC
1199 Marcus Dr, Sudbury, ON, P3B 4K6
(705) 521-7200
Emp Here 150
SIC 5211 Lumber and other building materials

D-U-N-S 25-305-0389   (BR)
MANUFACTURERS LIFE INSURANCE COMPANY, THE
FAIELLA FINANCIAL GROUP, THE
272 Larch St, Sudbury, ON, P3B 1M1
(705) 674-1974
Emp Here 30
SIC 6411 Insurance agents, brokers, and service

D-U-N-S 24-189-1790   (BR)
OLD NAVY (CANADA) INC
OLD NAVY
(*Suby of* The Gap Inc)
1599 Marcus Dr Unit 1, Sudbury, ON, P3B 4K6
(705) 525-8233
Emp Here 50
SIC 5651 Family clothing stores

D-U-N-S 25-769-7219   (BR)
PRIME RESTAURANTS INC
CASEY'S GRILL HOUSE & BEVERAGE
(*Suby of* Cara Holdings Limited)
1070 Kingsway, Sudbury, ON, P3B 2E5
(705) 560-6888
Emp Here 55
SIC 5812 Eating places

D-U-N-S 25-228-0581   (BR)
RAINBOW DISTRICT SCHOOL BOARD
ADAMSDALE ELEMENTARY SCHOOL
(*Suby of* Rainbow District School Board)
181 First Ave, Sudbury, ON, P3B 3L3
(705) 566-6020
Emp Here 21
SIC 8211 Elementary and secondary schools

D-U-N-S 20-700-6482   (BR)
REITMANS (CANADA) LIMITEE
1599 Marcus Dr Suite 3, Sudbury, ON, P3B 4K6
(705) 560-0102
Emp Here 25
SIC 5621 Women's clothing stores

D-U-N-S 24-062-0299   (BR)
ROYAL J & M DISTRIBUTING INC
3085 Kingsway, Sudbury, ON, P3B 2G5
(705) 566-8111
Emp Here 23
SIC 5571 Motorcycle dealers

D-U-N-S 20-703-8084   (BR)
SENATOR HOTELS LIMITED
QUALITY INN
(*Suby of* Senator Hotels Limited)
390 Elgin St, Sudbury, ON, P3B 1B1
(705) 675-1273
Emp Here 50
SIC 7011 Hotels and motels

D-U-N-S 20-543-7200   (BR)
STAPLES CANADA INC
STAPLES THE BUSINESS DEPOT
(*Suby of* Staples, Inc.)

1425 Kingsway Suite 146, Sudbury, ON, P3B 0A2
(705) 524-6227
Emp Here 30
SIC 5943 Stationery stores

D-U-N-S 20-806-5248   (BR)
STARBUCKS COFFEE CANADA, INC
(*Suby of* Starbucks Corporation)
1425 Kingsway, Sudbury, ON, P3B 0A2
(705) 525-5060
Emp Here 20
SIC 5812 Eating places

D-U-N-S 25-239-0158   (BR)
SUDBURY CATHOLIC DISTRICT SCHOOL BOARD
ST ALBERT ADULT LEARNING CENTRE
504 St. Raphael St, Sudbury, ON, P3B 1M4
(705) 673-3031
Emp Here 20
SIC 8211 Elementary and secondary schools

D-U-N-S 20-042-7115   (BR)
SUDBURY CATHOLIC DISTRICT SCHOOL BOARD
PIUS XII
44 Third Ave, Sudbury, ON, P3B 3P8
(705) 566-6080
Emp Here 35
SIC 8211 Elementary and secondary schools

D-U-N-S 24-199-5588   (SL)
SUDBURY CYCLE CENTRE INC
SUDBURY CYCLE & MARINE
3085 Kingsway, Sudbury, ON, P3B 2G5

Emp Here 29   *Sales* 5,617,280
SIC 5551 Boat dealers
Pr Pr Lorenzo Temelini
VP VP Luciano Temelini

D-U-N-S 20-555-9680   (BR)
WINNERS MERCHANTS INTERNATIONAL L.P.
HOMESENSE
(*Suby of* The TJX Companies Inc)
1499 Marcus Dr Suite 2, Sudbury, ON, P3B 4K6
(705) 560-7883
Emp Here 44
SIC 5651 Family clothing stores

D-U-N-S 20-161-4463   (BR)
WINNERS MERCHANTS INTERNATIONAL L.P.
WINNERS
(*Suby of* The TJX Companies Inc)
1399 Marcus Dr, Sudbury, ON, P3B 4K6
(705) 521-1522
Emp Here 30
SIC 5651 Family clothing stores

Sudbury, ON P3C
Sudbury County

D-U-N-S 24-312-1899   (BR)
ACCESSIBLE MEDIA INC
VOICE PRINT DIV OF
40 Elm St Unit M 300, Sudbury, ON, P3C 1S8

Emp Here 25
SIC 7389 Business services, nec

D-U-N-S 20-007-9205   (BR)
CTV SPECIALTY TELEVISION INC
CTV SPECIALTY TELEVISION INC/TELEVISION SPECIALISEE CTV INC
699 Frood Rd, Sudbury, ON, P3C 5A3
(705) 674-8301
Emp Here 75
SIC 4833 Television broadcasting stations

D-U-N-S 20-510-9791   (BR)
CANADIAN BLOOD SERVICES

NATIONAL CONTACT CENTRE SUDBURY
300 Elm St, Sudbury, ON, P3C 1V4
(705) 688-3300
Emp Here 50
SIC 8099 Health and allied services, nec

D-U-N-S 24-196-0434   (BR)
CANADIAN BROADCASTING CORPORATION
CBC
15 Mackenzie St, Sudbury, ON, P3C 4Y1
(705) 688-3232
Emp Here 60
SIC 4832 Radio broadcasting stations

D-U-N-S 25-488-4653   (BR)
CLAIMSECURE INC
40 Elm St Suite 225, Sudbury, ON, P3C 0A2
(705) 673-2541
Emp Here 100
SIC 6324 Hospital and medical service plans

D-U-N-S 24-703-6932   (BR)
COCA-COLA REFRESHMENTS CANADA COMPANY
(*Suby of* The Coca-Cola Company)
970 Lorne St, Sudbury, ON, P3C 4R9
(705) 675-2404
Emp Here 50
SIC 5149 Groceries and related products, nec

D-U-N-S 20-710-4097   (BR)
CONSEIL SCOLAIRE DE DISTRICT CATHOLIQUE DU NOUVEL-ONTARIO, LE
201 Jogues St, Sudbury, ON, P3C 5L7
(705) 675-5626
Emp Here 100
SIC 8211 Elementary and secondary schools

D-U-N-S 25-099-9067   (BR)
CONSEIL SCOLAIRE DE DISTRICT CATHOLIQUE DU NOUVEL-ONTARIO, LE
ECOLE SECONDAIRE DU SACRE-COEUR
261 Notre Dame Ave, Sudbury, ON, P3C 5K4
(705) 566-5511
Emp Here 40
SIC 8211 Elementary and secondary schools

D-U-N-S 25-482-9799   (BR)
CONSEIL SCOLAIRE DE DISTRICT CATHOLIQUE DU NOUVEL-ONTARIO, LE
COLLEGE NOTRE-DAME
100 Levis St, Sudbury, ON, P3C 2H1
(705) 674-7484
Emp Here 80
SIC 8211 Elementary and secondary schools

D-U-N-S 25-752-9826   (SL)
DIBRINA SURE FINANCIAL GROUP INC
62 Frood Rd Suite 302, Sudbury, ON, P3C 4Z3
(705) 688-9011
Emp Here 35   *Sales* 11,288,400
SIC 6282 Investment advice
Pr Pr Michael Dibrina

D-U-N-S 24-345-9687   (BR)
G4S SECURE SOLUTIONS (CANADA) LTD
238 Elm St Suite 200, Sudbury, ON, P3C 1V3
(705) 524-1519
Emp Here 350
SIC 7381 Detective and armored car services

D-U-N-S 25-321-8770   (BR)
GOLDER ASSOCIATES LTD
33 Mackenzie St Suite 100, Sudbury, ON, P3C 4Y1
(705) 524-6861
Emp Here 100
SIC 8711 Engineering services

D-U-N-S 25-891-1759   (BR)
HATCH LTD
HATCH
128 Pine St Suite 103, Sudbury, ON, P3C 1X3

(705) 688-0250
Emp Here 50
SIC 8711 Engineering services

D-U-N-S 24-951-7319   (SL)
ICAN INDEPENDENCE CENTRE AND NETWORK
765 Brennan Rd, Sudbury, ON, P3C 1C4
(705) 673-0655
Emp Here 77   *Sales* 3,502,114
SIC 8051 Skilled nursing care facilities

D-U-N-S 25-315-7341   (BR)
INVESTORS GROUP FINANCIAL SERVICES INC
INVESTORS GROUP
144 Pine St Suite 101, Sudbury, ON, P3C 1X3
(705) 674-4551
Emp Here 52
SIC 8741 Management services

D-U-N-S 25-196-1319   (BR)
KPMG LLP
BISSONETTE, LAURIE CA
(*Suby of* KPMG LLP)
144 Pine St Suite 4, Sudbury, ON, P3C 1X3
(705) 675-8500
Emp Here 60
SIC 8721 Accounting, auditing, and book-keeping

D-U-N-S 25-194-4331   (SL)
KOVIT ENGINEERING LIMITED
OUTOTEC
31 Dean Ave, Sudbury, ON, P3C 3B8
(705) 523-1040
Emp Here 29   *Sales* 2,553,625
SIC 8711 Engineering services

D-U-N-S 20-008-1060   (BR)
LOBLAW PROPERTIES LIMITED
NATIONAL GROCERS
1160 Lorne St, Sudbury, ON, P3C 4T2

Emp Here 100
SIC 5141 Groceries, general line

D-U-N-S 25-311-1058   (BR)
LONDON LIFE INSURANCE COMPANY
FREEDOM 55 FINANCIAL
144 Pine St Suite 600, Sudbury, ON, P3C 1X3
(705) 675-8341
Emp Here 30
SIC 6311 Life insurance

D-U-N-S 24-323-8024   (BR)
MAGIC LANTERN THEATRES LTD
RAINBOW CINEMAS
40 Elm St, Sudbury, ON, P3C 1S8

Emp Here 20
SIC 7832 Motion picture theaters, except drive-in

D-U-N-S 24-896-4272   (BR)
METRO ONTARIO INC
FOOD BASICS
400 Notre Dame Ave, Sudbury, ON, P3C 5K5
(705) 675-5845
Emp Here 120
SIC 5411 Grocery stores

D-U-N-S 24-664-8679   (BR)
ORICA CANADA INC
62 Frood Rd, Sudbury, ON, P3C 4Z3
(705) 674-1913
Emp Here 42
SIC 5169 Chemicals and allied products, nec

D-U-N-S 20-156-0398   (SL)
PROSPERI CO. LTD
299 Willow St, Sudbury, ON, P3C 1K2
(705) 673-1376
Emp Here 50   *Sales* 4,231,721
SIC 1742 Plastering, drywall, and insulation

D-U-N-S 25-239-9738   (BR)
RAINBOW DISTRICT SCHOOL BOARD
PRINCESS ANNE PUBLIC SCHOOL

(Suby of Rainbow District School Board)
500 Douglas St, Sudbury, ON, P3C 1H7
(705) 673-6516
Emp Here 20
SIC 8211 Elementary and secondary schools

D-U-N-S 20-590-4779   (BR)
RAINBOW DISTRICT SCHOOL BOARD
LANSDOWNE   PUBLIC   ELEMENTARY
SCHOOL
185 Lansdowne St, Sudbury, ON, P3C 4M1
(705) 675-6451
Emp Here 35
SIC 8211 Elementary and secondary schools

D-U-N-S 25-228-0755   (BR)
RAINBOW DISTRICT SCHOOL BOARD
GATCHELL SCHOOL
(Suby of Rainbow District School Board)
31 Tuddenham Ave, Sudbury, ON, P3C 3E9
(705) 674-1221
Emp Here 25
SIC 8211 Elementary and secondary schools

D-U-N-S 25-239-9761   (BR)
RAINBOW DISTRICT SCHOOL BOARD
QUEEN ELIZABETH II PUBLIC SCHOOL
(Suby of Rainbow District School Board)
32 Dell St, Sudbury, ON, P3C 2X8
(705) 675-6198
Emp Here 25
SIC 8211 Elementary and secondary schools

D-U-N-S 20-710-4014   (BR)
RAINBOW DISTRICT SCHOOL BOARD
SUDBURY SECONDARY SCHOOL
154 College St, Sudbury, ON, P3C 4Y2
(705) 674-7551
Emp Here 40
SIC 8211 Elementary and secondary schools

D-U-N-S 20-104-6146   (BR)
**RELIABLE WINDOW CLEANERS (SUD-
BURY) LIMITED**
RELIABLE CLEANING SERVICES
(Suby of Reliable Trivestments Limited)
345 Regent St, Sudbury, ON, P3C 4E1
(705) 675-5281
Emp Here 100
SIC 7349 Building maintenance services, nec

D-U-N-S 20-156-0620   (HQ)
**RELIABLE WINDOW CLEANERS (SUD-
BURY) LIMITED**
RELIABLE MAINTENANCE PRODUCT
(Suby of Reliable Trivestments Limited)
345 Regent St, Sudbury, ON, P3C 4E1
(705) 675-5281
Emp Here 130   Emp Total 172
Sales 24,514,903
SIC 5087 Service establishment equipment
Pr Pr Albert Bertuzzi
 Robert Bertuzzi
 Noah Jr Bertuzzi

D-U-N-S 20-731-6782   (BR)
**RELIANCE COMFORT LIMITED PARTNER-
SHIP**
RELIANCE HOME COMFORT, DIV OF
955 Cambrian Heights Dr, Sudbury, ON, P3C
5M6
(705) 566-1919
Emp Here 35
SIC 1711 Plumbing, heating, air-conditioning

D-U-N-S 20-711-7594   (BR)
**SUDBURY CATHOLIC DISTRICT SCHOOL
BOARD**
ST DAVID CATHOLIC SCHOOL
350 Jean St, Sudbury, ON, P3C 2S8
(705) 674-4096
Emp Here 20
SIC 8211 Elementary and secondary schools

D-U-N-S 20-597-2466   (BR)
TORONTO-DOMINION BANK, THE
TD BANK FINANCIAL GROUP
(Suby of Toronto-Dominion Bank, The)

43 Elm St Suite 210, Sudbury, ON, P3C 1S4
(705) 669-4000
Emp Here 25
SIC 6021 National commercial banks

D-U-N-S 25-865-8079   (BR)
VIPOND INC
VIPOND FIRE PROTECTION
95 Pacific Ave, Sudbury, ON, P3C 3J1
(705) 675-2705
Emp Here 25
SIC 5063 Electrical apparatus and equipment

D-U-N-S 24-335-1421   (BR)
YOUNG MENS CHRISTIAN ASSOCIATION
YMCA EMPLOYMENT AND CAREER SER-
VICES
10 Elm St Suite 112, Sudbury, ON, P3C 5N3
(705) 674-2324
Emp Here 30
SIC 8641 Civic and social associations

Sudbury, ON P3E
Sudbury County

D-U-N-S 24-418-3096   (BR)
ARAMARK CANADA LTD.
ARAMARK HIGHER EDUCATION
935 Ramsey Lake Rd Suite 705, Sudbury, ON,
P3E 2C6
(705) 673-6559
Emp Here 40
SIC 5812 Eating places

D-U-N-S 24-975-4912   (BR)
AECOM CANADA LTD
SWAN HILLS TREATMENT CENTER
1361 Paris St Suite 105, Sudbury, ON, P3E
3B6
(705) 674-8343
Emp Here 20
SIC 8711 Engineering services

D-U-N-S 20-177-0026   (SL)
BM METALS SERVICES INC
2502 Elm St, Sudbury, ON, P3E 4R6
(705) 682-9277
Emp Here 40   Sales 3,724,879
SIC 4212 Local trucking, without storage

D-U-N-S 25-783-9480   (BR)
BANK OF MONTREAL
BMO
2017 Long Lake Rd, Sudbury, ON, P3E 4M8
(705) 522-2090
Emp Here 20
SIC 6021 National commercial banks

D-U-N-S 25-002-4502   (BR)
BANK OF MONTREAL
BMO
79 Durham St, Sudbury, ON, P3E 3M5
(705) 670-2235
Emp Here 20
SIC 6021 National commercial banks

D-U-N-S 24-437-7433   (BR)
BANQUE TORONTO-DOMINION, LA
TORONTO-DOMINION BANK, THE
(Suby of Toronto-Dominion Bank, The)
1935 Paris St Suite 3, Sudbury, ON, P3E 3C6
(705) 522-2370
Emp Here 30
SIC 6021 National commercial banks

D-U-N-S 24-344-5165   (BR)
BAYSHORE HEALTHCARE LTD.
BAYSHORE HOME HEALTH
2120 Regent St Suite 8, Sudbury, ON, P3E
3Z9
(705) 523-6668
Emp Here 300
SIC 8082 Home health care services

D-U-N-S 20-736-0640   (SL)

**CSH   SOUTHWIND   RETIREMENT   RESI-
DENCE INC**
SOUTHWIND RETIREMENT RESIDENCE
1645 Paris St Suite 205, Sudbury, ON, P3E
0A5
(705) 521-1443
Emp Here 30   Sales 1,094,411
SIC 8361 Residential care

D-U-N-S 25-304-9381   (BR)
CANADIAN HEARING SOCIETY
1233 Paris St, Sudbury, ON, P3E 3B6
(705) 522-1020
Emp Here 25
SIC 8399 Social services, nec

D-U-N-S 24-531-0847   (BR)
CARA OPERATIONS LIMITED
HARVEY'S
(Suby of Cara Holdings Limited)
2169 Regent St, Sudbury, ON, P3E 5V3
(705) 523-1222
Emp Here 35
SIC 5812 Eating places

D-U-N-S 20-586-8156   (BR)
CITY OF GREATER SUDBURY, THE
GREATER SUDBURY TRANSIT
(Suby of City of Greater Sudbury, The)
1700 Kingsway Rd, Sudbury, ON, P3E 3L7
(705) 675-3333
Emp Here 150
SIC 4111 Local and suburban transit

D-U-N-S 20-088-0578   (BR)
COMMUNITY LIVING GREATER SUDBURY
GRANDVIEW RESIDENCE
303 York St Unit 241, Sudbury, ON, P3E 2A5
(705) 897-2298
Emp Here 22
SIC 8361 Residential care

D-U-N-S 25-239-0232   (BR)
**CONSEIL   SCOLAIRE   DE   DISTRICT
CATHOLIQUE   DU   NOUVEL-ONTARIO,
LE**
ECOLE ST-DENIS
347 Hyland Dr, Sudbury, ON, P3E 0G6
(705) 675-1201
Emp Here 25
SIC 8211 Elementary and secondary schools

D-U-N-S 24-317-4773   (BR)
**CONSEIL SCOLAIRE DE DISTRICT DU
GRAND NORD DE L'ONTARIO**
CONSEIL SCOLAIRE DE DISTRICT DU
GRAND NORD DE L'ON
190 Larch St, Sudbury, ON, P3E 1C5
(705) 671-1533
Emp Here 20
SIC 8211 Elementary and secondary schools

D-U-N-S 25-541-5895   (SL)
**CONSOLIDATED DRILLING AND BLAST-
ING INC**
2502 Elm St, Sudbury, ON, P3E 4R6
(705) 682-9900
Emp Here 150   Sales 28,507,450
SIC 1629 Heavy construction, nec
Pr Pr Milad Mansour

D-U-N-S 24-345-4571   (SL)
**CONSOLIDATED INDUSTRIAL PRODUCTS
INC**
2502 Elm St, Sudbury, ON, P3E 4R6
(705) 682-3387
Emp Here 20   Sales 3,866,917
SIC 5085 Industrial supplies

D-U-N-S 24-626-4936   (BR)
E.S. FOX LIMITED
1349 Kelly Lake Rd Suite 1, Sudbury, ON, P3E
5P5
(705) 522-3357
Emp Here 100
SIC 1541 Industrial buildings and warehouses

D-U-N-S 24-919-0844   (BR)

EXP SERVICES INC
885 Regent St Suite 3-6a, Sudbury, ON, P3E
5M4
(705) 674-9681
Emp Here 30
SIC 8711 Engineering services

D-U-N-S 25-868-6955   (BR)
EXTENDICARE INC
EXTENDICARE YORK
333 York St, Sudbury, ON, P3E 5J3
(705) 674-4221
Emp Here 300
SIC 8051 Skilled nursing care facilities

D-U-N-S 20-891-6192   (BR)
GOVERNMENT OF ONTARIO
NORTHERN DEVELOPMENT AND MINES
199 Larch St Suite 803, Sudbury, ON, P3E
5P9
(705) 564-0060
Emp Here 25
SIC 1481 NonMetallic mineral services

D-U-N-S 20-575-8944   (BR)
HEALTH SCIENCES NORTH
SUDBURY MEMORIAL HOSPITAL
865 Regent St Suite 426, Sudbury, ON, P3E
3Y9
(705) 523-7100
Emp Here 30
SIC 8062 General medical and surgical hospitals

D-U-N-S 20-042-2629   (BR)
J.L. RICHARDS & ASSOCIATES LIMITED
314 Countryside Dr, Sudbury, ON, P3E 6G2
(705) 522-8174
Emp Here 58
SIC 8711 Engineering services

D-U-N-S 20-742-6177   (BR)
KGHM INTERNATIONAL LTD
1300 Kelly Lake Rd, Sudbury, ON, P3E 5P4
(705) 671-1779
Emp Here 30
SIC 1081 Metal mining services

D-U-N-S 25-479-4977   (BR)
KLOHN CRIPPEN BERGER LTD
(Suby of Klohn Crippen Berger Holdings Ltd)
1361 Paris St Unit 101, Sudbury, ON, P3E 3B6
(705) 522-1367
Emp Here 20
SIC 8711 Engineering services

D-U-N-S 24-333-1662   (BR)
METRO ONTARIO INC
1933 Regent St, Sudbury, ON, P3E 5R2

Emp Here 85
SIC 5411 Grocery stores

D-U-N-S 24-893-3165   (SL)
MILMAN INDUSTRIES INC
2502 Elm St, Sudbury, ON, P3E 4R6
(705) 682-9277
Emp Here 200   Sales 24,540,000
SIC 6512 Nonresidential building operators
VP Gilles Lebeau

D-U-N-S 24-337-5677   (BR)
NORTH BAY REGIONAL HEALTH CENTRE
NORTHEAST MENTAL HEALTH CENTRE
680 Kirkwood Dr, Sudbury, ON, P3E 1X3
(705) 675-9193
Emp Here 60
SIC 8062 General medical and surgical hospi-
tals

D-U-N-S 25-860-8314   (BR)
NORTH-WEST TRANSPORT INC
(Suby of North-West Transport Inc)
250 Wilson St, Sudbury, ON, P3E 2S2
(705) 523-5618
Emp Here 30
SIC 4213 Trucking, except local

D-U-N-S 20-730-3843   (SL)

NORTHBURY HOTEL LIMITED
HOWARD JOHNSON PLAZA
50 Brady St, Sudbury, ON, P3E 1C8
(705) 675-5602
Emp Here 55   *Sales* 2,407,703
SIC 7011 Hotels and motels

D-U-N-S 24-175-3388   (BR)
NORTHERN ONTARIO SCHOOL OF MEDICINE
935 Ramsey Lake Rd, Sudbury, ON, P3E 2C6
(705) 675-4883
Emp Here 110
SIC 8221 Colleges and universities

D-U-N-S 24-060-9131   (BR)
PUROLATOR INC.
PUROLATOR INC
1300 Kelly Lake Rd, Sudbury, ON, P3E 5P4
(705) 671-1224
Emp Here 60
SIC 7389 Business services, nec

D-U-N-S 20-590-4753   (BR)
RAINBOW DISTRICT SCHOOL BOARD
R L B D PUBLIC SCHOOL
102 Loach'S Rd, Sudbury, ON, P3E 2P7
(705) 522-7178
Emp Here 25
SIC 8211 Elementary and secondary schools

D-U-N-S 25-239-9720   (BR)
RAINBOW DISTRICT SCHOOL BOARD
WEMBLEY PUBLIC SCHOOL
(*Suby of* Rainbow District School Board)
408 Wembley Dr, Sudbury, ON, P3E 1P2
(705) 673-1381
Emp Here 40
SIC 8211 Elementary and secondary schools

D-U-N-S 25-228-0706   (BR)
RAINBOW DISTRICT SCHOOL BOARD
LO-ELLEN PARK SECONDARY SCHOOL
(*Suby of* Rainbow District School Board)
275 Loach'S Rd, Sudbury, ON, P3E 2P8
(705) 522-2320
Emp Here 55
SIC 8211 Elementary and secondary schools

D-U-N-S 25-542-6736   (HQ)
RAINBOW DISTRICT SCHOOL BOARD
(*Suby of* Rainbow District School Board)
69 Young St, Sudbury, ON, P3E 3G5
(705) 377-4615
Emp Here 50   *Emp Total* 1,400
Sales 172,438,480
SIC 8211 Elementary and secondary schools
Tyler Campbell

D-U-N-S 25-228-0714   (BR)
RAINBOW DISTRICT SCHOOL BOARD
LOCKERBY COMPOSITE SECONDARY SCHOOL
(*Suby of* Rainbow District School Board)
1391 Ramsey View Crt, Sudbury, ON, P3E 5T4
(705) 522-9968
Emp Here 70
SIC 8211 Elementary and secondary schools

D-U-N-S 25-228-0631   (BR)
RAINBOW DISTRICT SCHOOL BOARD
ALGONQUIN ROAD PUBLIC SCHOOL
(*Suby of* Rainbow District School Board)
2650 Algonquin Rd, Sudbury, ON, P3E 4X6
(705) 522-3171
Emp Here 20
SIC 8211 Elementary and secondary schools

D-U-N-S 20-938-3699   (BR)
RAINBOW DISTRICT SCHOOL BOARD
GORD EWIN CENTRE FOR EDUCATION
275 Loach'S Rd, Sudbury, ON, P3E 2P8
(705) 523-3308
Emp Here 40
SIC 8733 Noncommercial research organizations

D-U-N-S 25-807-5555   (BR)
ROYAL BANK OF CANADA
RBC
(*Suby of* Royal Bank Of Canada)
72 Durham St, Sudbury, ON, P3E 3M6
(705) 688-4710
Emp Here 25
SIC 6021 National commercial banks

D-U-N-S 25-019-1251   (BR)
ROYAL BANK OF CANADA
RBC
(*Suby of* Royal Bank Of Canada)
1879 Regent St, Sudbury, ON, P3E 3Z7
(705) 522-7170
Emp Here 28
SIC 6021 National commercial banks

D-U-N-S 20-300-7026   (BR)
STANTEC CONSULTING LTD
1760 Regent St, Sudbury, ON, P3E 3Z8
(705) 566-6891
Emp Here 67
SIC 8711 Engineering services

D-U-N-S 20-711-7602   (BR)
SUDBURY CATHOLIC DISTRICT SCHOOL BOARD
ST FRANCIS SCHOOL
691 Lilac St, Sudbury, ON, P3E 4E2
(705) 674-0701
Emp Here 30
SIC 8211 Elementary and secondary schools

D-U-N-S 24-048-1523   (SL)
SUDBURY HOSPITAL SERVICES
363 York St, Sudbury, ON, P3E 2A8
(705) 674-2158
Emp Here 90   *Sales* 2,845,467
SIC 7219 Laundry and garment services, nec

D-U-N-S 24-380-7356   (SL)
SUDBURY REGENT STREET INC
HOMEWOOD SUITES BY HILTON
2270 Regent St, Sudbury, ON, P3E 0B4
(705) 523-8100
Emp Here 100   *Sales* 6,028,800
SIC 7011 Hotels and motels
Darko Vranich

D-U-N-S 24-308-3529   (BR)
SYKES ASSISTANCE SERVICES CORPORATION
SYKES TELEHEALTH
(*Suby of* Sykes Enterprises Incorporated)
1361 Paris St Suite 102, Sudbury, ON, P3E 3B6

Emp Here 40
SIC 8099 Health and allied services, nec

D-U-N-S 20-116-0988   (SL)
VISTA SUDBURY HOTEL INC
RADISSON HOTEL SUDBURY
85 Ste Anne Rd, Sudbury, ON, P3E 4S4
(705) 675-1123
Emp Here 75   *Sales* 3,283,232
SIC 7011 Hotels and motels

D-U-N-S 20-155-5955   (BR)
WE CARE HEALTH SERVICES INC
2140 Regent St Unit 6, Sudbury, ON, P3E 5S8
(705) 523-4008
Emp Here 40
SIC 8011 Offices and clinics of medical doctors

D-U-N-S 25-643-9084   (BR)
WESTERN INVENTORY SERVICE LTD
WIS INTERNATIONAL
1351d Kelly Lake Rd, Sudbury, ON, P3E 5P5
(705) 523-3332
Emo Here 30
SIC 7389 Business services, nec

D-U-N-S 25-300-6787   (BR)
WORKPLACE SAFETY & INSURANCE BOARD, THE

30 Cedar St, Sudbury, ON, P3E 1A4
(705) 677-4260
Emp Here 130
SIC 6331 Fire, marine, and casualty insurance

Sudbury, ON P3G
Sudbury County

D-U-N-S 20-710-4048   (BR)
RAINBOW DISTRICT SCHOOL BOARD
RAINBOW ALTERNATIVE SECONDARY SCHOOL
2500 South Lane Rd, Sudbury, ON, P3G 1C8

Emp Here 24
SIC 8211 Elementary and secondary schools

Sudbury, ON P3Y
Sudbury County

D-U-N-S 20-139-9180   (SL)
TECHNICA GROUP INC
TECHNICA MINING
225 Fielding Rd, Sudbury, ON, P3Y 1L8
(705) 692-2204
Emp Here 50   *Sales* 3,551,629
SIC 1499 Miscellaneous nonMetallic minerals, except fuels

Summerstown, ON K0C
Glengarry County

D-U-N-S 20-890-8889   (BR)
NESEL FAST FREIGHT INCORPORATED
19216 Hay Rd, Summerstown, ON, K0C 2E0

Emp Here 100
SIC 4213 Trucking, except local

Sunderland, ON L0C

D-U-N-S 25-265-1799   (BR)
DURHAM DISTRICT SCHOOL BOARD
SUNDERLAND PUBLIC SCHOOL
41 Albert St, Sunderland, ON, L0C 1H0
(705) 357-3975
Emp Here 35
SIC 8211 Elementary and secondary schools

D-U-N-S 24-785-1124   (SL)
MC G. POLE LINE LTD
167005 Sideroad 17a, Sunderland, ON, L0C 1H0

Emp Here 50   *Sales* 4,377,642
SIC 1731 Electrical work

D-U-N-S 25-352-0506   (BR)
STOCK TRANSPORTATION LTD
36 12 Hwy, Sunderland, ON, L0C 1H0
(705) 357-3187
Emp Here 250
SIC 4151 School buses

Sundridge, ON P0A
Parry Sound County

D-U-N-S 20-156-3574   (SL)
LANG, MAC SUNDRIDGE LIMITED
(*Suby of* Farquhar, Thomas & Son Co. Limited)
156 Main St Suite 539, Sundridge, ON, P0A

1Z0
(705) 384-5352
Emp Here 25   *Sales* 12,560,000
SIC 5511 New and used car dealers
Pr Pr John Farquhar
John E Farquhar

Sutton West, ON L0E
York County

D-U-N-S 20-354-6650   (SL)
2521153 ONTARIO INC
WPSL SECURITY SOLUTIONS
17 Beechener St, Sutton West, ON, L0E 1R0
(416) 222-7144
Emp Here 130   *Sales* 4,012,839
SIC 7381 Detective and armored car services

D-U-N-S 24-345-9604   (BR)
CORPORATION OF THE TOWN OF GEORGINA, THE
COMMUNITY LIVING GEORGINA
26943 48 Hwy Rr 2, Sutton West, ON, L0E 1R0
(905) 722-8947
Emp Here 100
SIC 8361 Residential care

D-U-N-S 25-147-3633   (BR)
YORK CATHOLIC DISTRICT SCHOOL BOARD
ST BERNADETTE CATHOLIC ELEMENTARY SCHOOL
5279 Black River Rd, Sutton West, ON, L0E 1R0
(905) 722-6226
Emp Here 20
SIC 8211 Elementary and secondary schools

D-U-N-S 25-293-5853   (BR)
YORK REGION DISTRICT SCHOOL BOARD
SUTTON DISTRICT HIGH SCHOOL
(*Suby of* York Region District School Board)
20798 Dalton Rd, Sutton West, ON, L0E 1R0
(905) 722-3281
Emp Here 150
SIC 8211 Elementary and secondary schools

D-U-N-S 20-591-2616   (BR)
YORK REGION DISTRICT SCHOOL BOARD
BLACK RIVER PUBLIC SCHOOL
(*Suby of* York Region District School Board)
26465 Park Rd Rr 2, Sutton West, ON, L0E 1R0
(905) 722-5889
Emp Here 45
SIC 8211 Elementary and secondary schools

D-U-N-S 25-297-9117   (BR)
YORK REGION DISTRICT SCHOOL BOARD
SUTTON PUBLIC SCHOOL
(*Suby of* York Region District School Board)
26465 Park Rd Rr 2, Sutton West, ON, L0E 1R0
(905) 722-3782
Emp Here 40
SIC 8211 Elementary and secondary schools

Sydenham, ON K0H

D-U-N-S 25-305-4605   (BR)
LIMESTONE DISTRICT SCHOOL BOARD
LOUGHBOROUGH PUBLIC SCHOOL
4330 Wheatley St, Sydenham, ON, K0H 2T0
(613) 376-3848
Emp Here 35
SIC 8211 Elementary and secondary schools

D-U-N-S 25-305-4993   (BR)
LIMESTONE DISTRICT SCHOOL BOARD
SYDENHAM HIGH SCHOOL
2860 Rutledge Rd, Sydenham, ON, K0H 2T0

▲ Public Company   ■ Public Company Family Member   **HQ** Headquarters   **BR** Branch   **SL** Single Location

(613) 376-3612
Emp Here 80
SIC 8211 Elementary and secondary schools

Tamworth, ON K0K
Addington County

D-U-N-S 20-711-4831   (BR)
LIMESTONE DISTRICT SCHOOL BOARD
TAMWORTH ELEMENTARY SCHOOL
6668 Wheeler St, Tamworth, ON, K0K 3G0
(613) 379-2317
Emp Here 20
SIC 8211 Elementary and secondary schools

Tavistock, ON N0B
Oxford County

D-U-N-S 24-627-4104   (BR)
ALIMENTS SAPUTO LIMITEE
SAPUTO
284 Hope St W, Tavistock, ON, N0B 2R0
(519) 655-2337
Emp Here 240
SIC 2022 Cheese; natural and processed

D-U-N-S 25-469-0035   (BR)
CARESSANT-CARE NURSING AND RE-TIREMENT HOMES LIMITED
MAPLES HOME FOR SENIORS, THE
94 William St S Suite 202, Tavistock, ON, N0B 2R0
(519) 655-2344
Emp Here 75
SIC 8051 Skilled nursing care facilities

D-U-N-S 24-095-3760   (SL)
PEOPLE CARE CENTRES INC
PEOPLE CARE TAVISTOCK
28 William St N, Tavistock, ON, N0B 2R0
(519) 655-2031
Emp Here 100   *Sales* 4,523,563
SIC 8051 Skilled nursing care facilities

D-U-N-S 24-862-0882   (BR)
REVERA LONG TERM CARE INC
BONNIE BRAE HEALTH CARE
55 Woodstock St N, Tavistock, ON, N0B 2R0

Emp Here 50
SIC 8051 Skilled nursing care facilities

D-U-N-S 25-249-1527   (BR)
THAMES VALLEY DISTRICT SCHOOL BOARD
TAVISTOCK PUBLIC SCHOOL
79 Maria St, Tavistock, ON, N0B 2R0
(519) 655-2350
Emp Here 25
SIC 8211 Elementary and secondary schools

Tecumseh, ON N8N
Essex County

D-U-N-S 20-549-8442   (BR)
A.P. PLASMAN INC.
A.P. PLASMAN TECUMSEH PLANT
418 Silver Creek Industrial Dr Rr1, Tecumseh, ON, N8N 4Y3
(519) 727-4545
Emp Here 520
SIC 3089 Plastics products, nec

D-U-N-S 20-306-6683   (BR)
COCO PAVING INC
485 Little Baseline Rd Suite 1, Tecumseh, ON, N8N 2L9
(519) 727-3838
Emp Here 20
SIC 1611 Highway and street construction

D-U-N-S 24-538-1660   (SL)
DUNN PAVING LIMITED
485 Little Baseline Rd, Tecumseh, ON, N8N 2L9
(519) 727-3838
Emp Here 70   *Sales* 8,171,598
SIC 1611 Highway and street construction
Pr Michael Dunn

D-U-N-S 20-699-6246   (BR)
EXTENDICARE INC
EXTENDICARE TECUMSEH
2475 St. Alphonse St Suite 1238, Tecumseh, ON, N8N 2X2
(519) 739-2998
Emp Here 100
SIC 8051 Skilled nursing care facilities

D-U-N-S 20-530-2136   (HQ)
G.W. ANGLIN MANUFACTURING INC
220 Patillo Rd Suite 1, Tecumseh, ON, N8N 2L9
(519) 727-4398
Emp Here 70   *Emp Total* 70
Sales 13,132,926
SIC 3499 Fabricated Metal products, nec
Pr Pr Loris Boschin

D-U-N-S 24-390-5887   (BR)
GOLF TOWN LIMITED
GOLF TOWN
1695 Manning Rd, Tecumseh, ON, N8N 2L9
(519) 739-9707
Emp Here 20
SIC 5941 Sporting goods and bicycle shops

D-U-N-S 24-984-9472   (BR)
GREATER ESSEX COUNTY DISTRICT SCHOOL BOARD
D M EAGLE ELEMENTARY SCHOOL
14194 Tecumseh Rd E, Tecumseh, ON, N8N 1M7
(519) 979-8186
Emp Here 25
SIC 8211 Elementary and secondary schools

D-U-N-S 25-294-0911   (SL)
INNOVATIVE APPLIED TECHNOLOGIES, INC
IAT GLOBAL
288 Patillo Rd, Tecumseh, ON, N8N 2L9
(519) 737-0303
Emp Here 23   *Sales* 2,535,341
SIC 3599 Industrial machinery, nec

D-U-N-S 20-917-9360   (BR)
MAGNA SEATING INC
INTEGRAM-WINDSOR SEATING DIV OF
201 Patillo Rd, Tecumseh, ON, N8N 2L9
(519) 727-6222
Emp Here 750
SIC 2531 Public building and related furniture

D-U-N-S 20-792-5285   (BR)
MCDONALD'S RESTAURANTS OF CANADA LIMITED
MCDONALD'S
(Suby of McDonald's Corporation)
1631 Manning Rd, Tecumseh, ON, N8N 2L9
(519) 735-8122
Emp Here 80
SIC 5812 Eating places

D-U-N-S 20-192-7543   (HQ)
TRQSS, INC
QUALITY SAFETY SYSTEMS COMPANY
255 Patillo Rd, Tecumseh, ON, N8N 2L9
(519) 973-7400
Emp Here 700   *Emp Total* 18,668
Sales 175,415,828
SIC 2399 Fabricated textile products, nec
Pr Pr Mark Dolsen
Fin Mgr John Dinardo
Dir Yasutaka Watanabe
Dir Kouji Buma
Dir Mikio Kato

D-U-N-S 25-249-1808   (BR)

WINDSOR-ESSEX CATHOLIC DISTRICT SCHOOL BOARD, THE
ST PETER SCHOOL
2451 St. Alphonse St, Tecumseh, ON, N8N 2X2
(519) 735-2666
Emp Here 40
SIC 8211 Elementary and secondary schools

Tecumseh, ON N9A
Essex County

D-U-N-S 20-336-4880   (BR)
ESSEX WELD SOLUTIONS LTD
WINDSOR MANAGEMENT
1720 North Talbot Rd, Tecumseh, ON, N9A 6J3
(519) 776-9153
Emp Here 50
SIC 3499 Fabricated Metal products, nec

Teeswater, ON N0G
Bruce County

D-U-N-S 20-156-6734   (BR)
GAY LEA FOODS CO-OPERATIVE LIMITED
21 Clinton St, Teeswater, ON, N0G 2S0
(519) 392-6864
Emp Here 65
SIC 2023 Dry, condensed and evaporated dairy products

Temagami, ON P0H
Nipissing County

D-U-N-S 20-287-3428   (SL)
TEMAGAMI BOAT MANUFACTURING INC
NADEN BOATS
52 Temagami Marine Rd, Temagami, ON, P0H 2H0
(705) 569-3520
Emp Here 50   *Sales* 4,260,900
SIC 3732 Boatbuilding and repairing

Terrace Bay, ON P0T
Thunder Bay County

D-U-N-S 20-919-2843   (SL)
MCCAUSLAND HOSPITAL, THE
2b Cartier Dr, Terrace Bay, ON, P0T 2W0
(807) 825-3273
Emp Here 90   *Sales* 8,724,700
SIC 8062 General medical and surgical hospitals
Pr Ms. Danielle Boulianne
VP Bob Hopper
Treas Sheri Notarbartolo
Sec Paul Paradis
Prs Mgr Suzanne Bouchard
   Mary Lynn Dingwell
   Rita Mcbride
   John Mckinnon
   Jason Nesbitt
   Benoit Rioux

D-U-N-S 20-980-8166   (BR)
SUPERIOR GREENSTONE DISTRICT SCHOOL BOARD
TERRACE BAY PUBLIC SCHOOL
9 Selkirk St, Terrace Bay, ON, P0T 2W0
(807) 825-3253
Emp Here 20
SIC 8211 Elementary and secondary schools

D-U-N-S 20-653-2967   (BR)

SUPERIOR GREENSTONE DISTRICT SCHOOL BOARD
LAKE SUPERIOR HIGH SCHOOL
19 Hudson St, Terrace Bay, ON, P0T 2W0
(807) 825-3271
Emp Here 30
SIC 8211 Elementary and secondary schools

D-U-N-S 24-323-6366   (SL)
TERRACE BAY PULP INC
(Suby of Lucky Star Holdings Inc)
21 Mill Rd, Terrace Bay, ON, P0T 2W0

Emp Here 50   *Sales* 2,512,128
SIC 2611 Pulp mills

Thamesford, ON N0M
Oxford County

D-U-N-S 25-471-8232   (BR)
ELGIE BUS LINES LIMITED
5137 Cobblehill Rd, Thamesford, ON, N0M 2M0
(519) 461-1227
Emp Here 55
SIC 4151 School buses

D-U-N-S 25-487-0769   (BR)
HURON TRACTOR LTD
HURON TRACTOR & LAWN EQUIPMENT
37 Elgin Rd, Thamesford, ON, N0M 2M0
(519) 285-3845
Emp Here 25
SIC 5999 Miscellaneous retail stores, nec

D-U-N-S 20-710-5284   (BR)
LONDON DISTRICT CATHOLIC SCHOOL BOARD
ST JOSEPH CATHOLIC SCHOOL
154978 15th Line, Thamesford, ON, N0M 2M0

Emp Here 50
SIC 8211 Elementary and secondary schools

D-U-N-S 25-249-1584   (BR)
THAMES VALLEY DISTRICT SCHOOL BOARD
THAMESFORD PUBLIC SCHOOL
130 Mccarty St, Thamesford, ON, N0M 2M0
(519) 285-2043
Emp Here 30
SIC 8211 Elementary and secondary schools

Thamesville, ON N0P

D-U-N-S 25-173-5809   (SL)
768308 ONTARIO INC
SUNSHINE ASPARAGUS FARMS
30043 Jane Rd, Thamesville, ON, N0P 2K0
(519) 692-4416
Emp Here 50   *Sales* 1,824,018
SIC 2035 Pickles, sauces, and salad dressings

D-U-N-S 24-277-8173   (SL)
ERICKSON, B. MANUFACTURING LTD
ERICKSON MANUFACTURING
11297 Merritt Line Rr 6, Thamesville, ON, N0P 2K0
(519) 352-2259
Emp Here 50   *Sales* 2,042,900
SIC 2241 Narrow fabric mills

Thedford, ON N0M
Lambton County

D-U-N-S 25-238-7014   (BR)
LAMBTON KENT DISTRICT SCHOOL BOARD

BOSANQUET CENTRAL SCHOOL
8766 Northville Rd, Thedford, ON, N0M 2N0
(519) 296-4962
Emp Here 25
SIC 8211 Elementary and secondary schools

Thessalon, ON P0R
Algoma County

D-U-N-S 25-238-2122   (BR)
ALGOMA DISTRICT SCHOOL BOARD
THESSALON PUBLIC SCHOOL
(*Suby of* Algoma District School Board)
90 Station Rd, Thessalon, ON, P0R 1L0
(705) 842-2410
Emp Here 20
SIC 8211 Elementary and secondary schools

D-U-N-S 25-481-2514   (SL)
ALGOMA MANOR NURSING HOME
ALGOMA MANOR
145 Dawson St, Thessalon, ON, P0R 1L0
(705) 842-2840
Emp Here 110   *Sales* 4,012,839
SIC 8361 Residential care

D-U-N-S 24-522-0095   (BR)
BIRCHLAND PLYWOOD - VENEER LIMITED
12564 Hwy 17 E, Thessalon, ON, P0R 1L0
(705) 842-2430
Emp Here 20
SIC 2435 Hardwood veneer and plywood

D-U-N-S 25-003-7785   (BR)
SAULT AREA HOSPITAL
THESSALON HOSPITAL
(*Suby of* Sault Area Hospital)
135 Dawson St, Thessalon, ON, P0R 1L0
(705) 842-2014
Emp Here 20
SIC 8062 General medical and surgical hospitals

Thomasburg, ON K0K
Hastings County

D-U-N-S 25-473-4346   (BR)
KERRY'S PLACE AUTISM SERVICES
KERRY'S PLACE HASTINGS
(*Suby of* Kerry's Place Autism Services)
200 Thomasburg Rd Rr 1, Thomasburg, ON, K0K 3H0

Emp Here 50
SIC 8322 Individual and family services

Thornbury, ON N0H
Grey County

D-U-N-S 25-019-5005   (BR)
BANQUE TORONTO-DOMINION, LA
TD BANK
(*Suby of* Toronto-Dominion Bank, The)
67 Bruce St, Thornbury, ON, N0H 2P0
(519) 599-2622
Emp Here 2
SIC 6021 National commercial banks

D-U-N-S 25-238-8996   (BR)
BLUEWATER DISTRICT SCHOOL BOARD
BEAVER VALLEY COMMUNITY SCHOOL
189 Bruce St S, Thornbury, ON, N0H 2P0
(519) 599-5991
Emp Here 35
SIC 8211 Elementary and secondary schools

D-U-N-S 25-834-8648   (SL)
PROVINCIAL LONGTERM CARE INC
ERRINRUNG RETIREMENT & NURSING

HOME
67 Bruce St S, Thornbury, ON, N0H 2P0
(519) 599-2737
Emp Here 60   *Sales* 2,699,546
SIC 8051 Skilled nursing care facilities

Thorndale, ON N0M
Middlesex County

D-U-N-S 24-676-5262   (BR)
THAMES VALLEY DISTRICT SCHOOL BOARD
WEST NISSOURI PUBLIC SCHOOL
37 Elliott Trail, Thorndale, ON, N0M 2P0
(519) 461-9575
Emp Here 25
SIC 8211 Elementary and secondary schools

Thornhill, ON L3T
York County

D-U-N-S 20-117-0920   (HQ)
AT&T GLOBAL SERVICES CANADA CO
(*Suby of* AT&T Inc.)
55 Commerce Valley Dr W Suite 700, Thornhill, ON, L3T 7V9
(905) 762-7390
Emp Here 100   *Emp Total* 268,000
Sales 17,498,270
SIC 4899 Communication services, nec
Ch Bd Ch Bd David Dorman
Genl Mgr David Stroud
VP Opers Justin Simms
VP VP Mary Livingston
VP Sls David Aspinall

D-U-N-S 24-610-2081   (HQ)
ATI TECHNOLOGIES ULC
(*Suby of* ATI Technologies ULC)
1 Commerce Valley Dr E, Thornhill, ON, L3T 7X6
(905) 882-7589
Emp Here 1,200   *Emp Total* 4,100
Sales 413,833,090
SIC 3577 Computer peripheral equipment, nec
Michael J Woollems
Benjamin Bar-Haim

D-U-N-S 24-321-7929   (HQ)
ACCELLOS CANADA, INC
125 Commerce Valley Dr W Suite 700, Thornhill, ON, L3T 7W4
(905) 695-9999
Emp Here 90   *Emp Total* 771
Sales 19,091,200
SIC 7371 Custom computer programming services
Ch Bd Michael Cornell
Ross Elliott
Edward Flint Seaton
Joel Kremke
VP Sls Matthew Petty
Matthew Turner
Svc Mgr Brian Jamieson

D-U-N-S 20-982-8826   (BR)
ACKLANDS - GRAINGER INC
AGI
(*Suby of* W.W. Grainger, Inc.)
50 Minthorn Blvd, Thornhill, ON, L3T 7X8
(905) 763-3474
Emp Here 500
SIC 5084 Industrial machinery and equipment

D-U-N-S 24-425-1109   (BR)
AECOM CANADA LTD
105 Commerce Valley Dr W, Thornhill, ON, L3T 7W3
(905) 886-7022
Emp Here 50

SIC 8742 Management consulting services

D-U-N-S 25-890-8409   (HQ)
BMC SOFTWARE CANADA INC
(*Suby of* Boxer Parent Company Inc.)
50 Minthorn Blvd Suite 200, Thornhill, ON, L3T 7X8
(905) 707-4600
Emp Here 45   *Emp Total* 6,900
Sales 5,034,288
SIC 7372 Prepackaged software
Dir Paul Capombassis

D-U-N-S 24-951-3763   (HQ)
BANK OF CHINA (CANADA)
50 Minthorn Blvd Suite 600, Thornhill, ON, L3T 7X8
(905) 771-6886
Emp Here 32   *Emp Total* 1,200
Sales 13,351,808
SIC 6021 National commercial banks
Brnch Mgr Qing Uyu

D-U-N-S 20-708-1568   (BR)
BANK OF MONTREAL
BMO NESTBITT BURNS
8500 Leslie St Suite 101, Thornhill, ON, L3T 7M8

Emp Here 30
SIC 6021 National commercial banks

D-U-N-S 24-437-7037   (BR)
BANQUE TORONTO-DOMINION, LA
TORONTO-DOMINION BANK, THE
(*Suby of* Toronto-Dominion Bank, The)
7967 Yonge St, Thornhill, ON, L3T 2C4
(905) 881-3252
Emp Here 25
SIC 6021 National commercial banks

D-U-N-S 20-844-8977   (SL)
BAYVIEW GOLF & COUNTRY CLUB LIMITED
25 Fairway Heights Dr, Thornhill, ON, L3T 3X1
(905) 889-4833
Emp Here 60   *Sales* 2,407,703
SIC 7997 Membership sports and recreation clubs

D-U-N-S 20-573-4416   (BR)
CIBC WORLD MARKETS INC
CIBC WOOD GUNDY
123 Commerce Valley Dr E Suite 100, Thornhill, ON, L3T 7W8
(905) 762-2300
Emp Here 90
SIC 6211 Security brokers and dealers

D-U-N-S 24-342-2149   (BR)
CARA OPERATIONS LIMITED
MONTANA'S COOKHOUSE
(*Suby of* Cara Holdings Limited)
2910 Steeles Ave E, Thornhill, ON, L3T 7X1
(905) 709-0550
Emp Here 75
SIC 5812 Eating places

D-U-N-S 24-206-8091   (BR)
CEREBRAL PALSY PARENT COUNCIL OF TORONTO
PARTICIPATION HOUSE ST. LUKES
49 Green Lane Unit 251, Thornhill, ON, L3T 7M9
(905) 731-0792
Emp Here 25
SIC 8059 Nursing and personal care, nec

D-U-N-S 20-011-7658   (SL)
CONTENT MANAGEMENT CORPORATION
MULTIVIEW CANADA
(*Suby of* Multi-View, Inc.)
50 Minthorn Blvd Suite 800, Thornhill, ON, L3T 7X8
(905) 889-6555
Emp Here 100   *Sales* 5,472,053
SIC 7376 Computer facilities management
Ex Dir Scott Bedford

Pr Pr Dan Maitland

D-U-N-S 25-300-1671   (BR)
DUNDEE SECURITIES CORPORATION
DUNDEE WEALTH MANAGEMENT
105 Commerce Valley Dr W Suite 408, Thornhill, ON, L3T 7W3
(905) 763-2339
Emp Here 20
SIC 6211 Security brokers and dealers

D-U-N-S 20-153-8811   (BR)
EXP SERVICES INC
220 Commerce Valley Dr W Suite 500, Thornhill, ON, L3T 0A8
(905) 695-3217
Emp Here 35
SIC 8711 Engineering services

D-U-N-S 24-707-5039   (BR)
ERNST & YOUNG LLP
(*Suby of* Ernst & Young LLP)
175 Commerce Valley Dr W Suite 600, Thornhill, ON, L3T 7P6
(905) 731-1500
Emp Here 125
SIC 8721 Accounting, auditing, and bookkeeping

D-U-N-S 24-345-9661   (BR)
EXECUTIVE WOODWORK LTD
(*Suby of* Executive Woodwork Ltd)
110 Confederation Way, Thornhill, ON, L3T 5R5
(905) 660-5995
Emp Here 50
SIC 7389 Business services, nec

D-U-N-S 20-070-8167   (HQ)
EXTREME FITNESS GROUP INC
(*Suby of* Extreme Fitness Group Inc)
8281 Yonge St, Thornhill, ON, L3T 2C7
(905) 709-1248
Emp Here 140   *Emp Total* 250
Sales 13,546,080
SIC 7991 Physical fitness facilities
Pr Pr Steven Colivas
Stephen Dacosta

D-U-N-S 20-206-7950   (SL)
FAGA GROUP INC
137 Langstaff Rd E, Thornhill, ON, L3T 3M6
(905) 881-2552
Emp Here 50   *Sales* 4,331,255
SIC 1794 Excavation work

D-U-N-S 25-318-9708   (BR)
FIRSTCANADA ULC
1ST STUDENT CANADA
120 Doncaster Ave, Thornhill, ON, L3T 1L3
(905) 764-6662
Emp Here 200
SIC 4151 School buses

D-U-N-S 24-872-4908   (SL)
GALDERMA CANADA INC
105 Commerce Valley Dr W Suite 300, Thornhill, ON, L3T 7W3
(905) 762-2500
Emp Here 62   *Sales* 61,654,160
SIC 5122 Drugs, proprietaries, and sundries
Genl Mgr Wendy Adams

D-U-N-S 20-055-3506   (BR)
H & R BLOCK CANADA, INC
(*Suby of* H&R Block, Inc.)
8199 Yonge St, Thornhill, ON, L3T 2C6
(905) 707-7785
Emp Here 20
SIC 7291 Tax return preparation services

D-U-N-S 20-295-4301   (SL)
HUBHEAD CORP
50 Minthorn Blvd Suite 500, Thornhill, ON, L3T 7X8
(905) 707-1288
Emp Here 50   *Sales* 3,648,035
SIC 7379 Computer related services, nec

D-U-N-S 20-288-1616   (HQ)
ILLUMITI INC
123 Commerce Valley Dr E Suite 500, Thornhill, ON, L3T 7W8
(905) 737-1066
Emp Here 20   *Emp Total* 1
Sales 11,162,987
SIC 8748 Business consulting, nec
Pr Pr Nir Orbach
Dror Orbach

D-U-N-S 24-351-9191   (SL)
INNOVATION GROUP (CANADA) LIMITED, THE
175 Commerce Valley Dr W Suite 108, Thornhill, ON, L3T 7P6
(905) 771-5110
Emp Here 50   *Sales* 3,392,384
SIC 7389 Business services, nec

D-U-N-S 24-876-8095   (HQ)
LEXMARK CANADA INC
125 Commerce Valley Dr W Unit 600, Thornhill, ON, L3T 7W4
(905) 763-0560
Emp Here 135   *Emp Total* 13,600
Sales 37,075,543
SIC 5045 Computers, peripherals, and software
Pr Todd Hamblin
Dir Todd Greenwood
Dir Matthew Barnicoat

D-U-N-S 20-635-0949   (SL)
MEDICLEAN INCORPORATED
60 Bradgate Dr, Thornhill, ON, L3T 7L9
(905) 886-4305
Emp Here 60   *Sales* 2,261,590
SIC 7349 Building maintenance services, nec

D-U-N-S 25-672-3362   (BR)
METRO ONTARIO INC
FOOD BASICS
8190 Bayview Ave, Thornhill, ON, L3T 2S2
(905) 731-2300
Emp Here 80
SIC 5411 Grocery stores

D-U-N-S 25-300-2976   (BR)
METRO ONTARIO INC
FOOD BASICS
300 John St, Thornhill, ON, L3T 5W4
(905) 886-0983
Emp Here 70
SIC 5411 Grocery stores

D-U-N-S 24-032-1567   (BR)
METRO ONTARIO INC
300 John St, Thornhill, ON, L3T 5W4
(905) 886-0983
Emp Here 100
SIC 5411 Grocery stores

D-U-N-S 20-251-0223   (SL)
ON TRACK SAFETY LTD
29 Ruggles Ave, Thornhill, ON, L3T 3S4
(905) 660-5969
Emp Here 70   *Sales* 4,244,630
SIC 7389 Business services, nec

D-U-N-S 24-310-6924   (HQ)
ONX ENTERPRISE SOLUTIONS LTD
165 Commerce Valley Dr W Suite 300, Thornhill, ON, L3T 7V8
(905) 881-4414
Emp Here 125   *Emp Total* 8,300
Sales 68,145,294
SIC 5045 Computers, peripherals, and software
CEO Tom Signorello
Pr Pr Dave Hansen
Sec Stephen Johnson
Rosalind Lehman
Paul Khawaja
Patrick Doherty
Michael Aniballi

D-U-N-S 24-247-8613   (BR)

PROCTER & GAMBLE INC
(*Suby of* The Procter & Gamble Company)
211 Bayview Fairways Dr, Thornhill, ON, L3T 2Z1
(416) 730-4872
Emp Here 600
SIC 5099 Durable goods, nec

D-U-N-S 25-735-5560   (BR)
RED LOBSTER HOSPITALITY LLC
RED LOBSTER RESTAURANTS
(*Suby of* Red Lobster Seafood Co., LLC)
7291 Yonge St, Thornhill, ON, L3T 2A9
(905) 731-3550
Emp Here 80
SIC 5812 Eating places

D-U-N-S 25-794-9735   (BR)
REVERA INC
GLYNNWOOD
7700 Bayview Ave Suite 518, Thornhill, ON, L3T 5W1
(905) 881-9475
Emp Here 110
SIC 8051 Skilled nursing care facilities

D-U-N-S 25-297-1544   (BR)
ROYAL BANK OF CANADA
RBC AUTOMOTIVE FINANCE
(*Suby of* Royal Bank Of Canada)
8500 Leslie St Suite 400, Thornhill, ON, L3T 7P8
(905) 882-3900
Emp Here 45
SIC 6411 Insurance agents, brokers, and service

D-U-N-S 25-311-1652   (BR)
SEARS CANADA INC
2900 Steeles Ave E, Thornhill, ON, L3T 4X1

Emp Here 50
SIC 5311 Department stores

D-U-N-S 20-234-1400   (HQ)
SHERWIN-WILLIAMS CANADA INC
DIVERSIFIED BRANDS DIV OF
(*Suby of* The Sherwin-Williams Company)
8500 Leslie St Suite 220, Thornhill, ON, L3T 7M8
(905) 761-9185
Emp Here 40   *Emp Total* 42,550
Sales 23,042,277
SIC 5198 Paints, varnishes, and supplies
Ch Bd Christopher M Connor
Dir Judy Belaske
Dir John L Ault
VP Fin VP Fin Sean Hennessey
Pers/VP Thomas E Hopkins
Dir Robert Liebel

D-U-N-S 25-362-0900   (BR)
SIEMENS CANADA LIMITED
SIEMENS TANGO SOFTWARE
55 Commerce Valley Dr W Suite 400, Thornhill, ON, L3T 7V9

Emp Here 170
SIC 7371 Custom computer programming services

D-U-N-S 20-506-0416   (BR)
STARBUCKS COFFEE CANADA, INC
STARBUCKS
(*Suby of* Starbucks Corporation)
7355 Bayview Ave Suite 1b, Thornhill, ON, L3T 5Z2
(905) 771-9229
Emp Here 20
SIC 5812 Eating places

D-U-N-S 20-301-3805   (BR)
TD WATERHOUSE CANADA INC
TD WATERHOUSE PRIVATE INVESTMENT ADVICE
(*Suby of* Toronto-Dominion Bank, The)
220 Commerce Valley Dr W Unit 100, Thornhill, ON, L3T 0A8

(905) 764-7730
Emp Here 25
SIC 6211 Security brokers and dealers

D-U-N-S 25-531-2845   (BR)
TELUS CORPORATION
120 Commerce Valley Dr E Suite 1, Thornhill, ON, L3T 7R2
(905) 707-4000
Emp Here 150
SIC 7371 Custom computer programming services

D-U-N-S 20-700-5773   (HQ)
TERAGO INC
(*Suby of* TeraGo Inc)
55 Commerce Valley Dr W Suite 800, Thornhill, ON, L3T 7V9
(905) 326-8711
Emp Here 33   *Emp Total* 180
Sales 43,702,664
SIC 4813 Telephone communication, except radio
Pr Pr Antonio Ciciretto
Ron Perrotta
VP Sls Daren Hanson
VP Jeffrey Yim
Matthew Gerber
Jerry Grafstein
Michael Martin
Richard Brekka
Jim Sanger
Gary Sherlock

D-U-N-S 25-101-1771   (HQ)
TERAGO NETWORKS INC
TERAGO
(*Suby of* TeraGo Inc)
55 Commerce Valley Dr W Suite 800, Thornhill, ON, L3T 7V9
(866) 837-2461
Emp Here 55   *Emp Total* 180
Sales 26,420,656
SIC 4813 Telephone communication, except radio
Pr Stewart Lyons
Joe Frodan
Ryan Lausman
VP Jeffrey Yim

D-U-N-S 20-708-1998   (BR)
TRADEWORLD REALTY INC
300 John St Unit 500, Thornhill, ON, L3T 5W4
(416) 250-1323
Emp Here 20
SIC 6531 Real estate agents and managers

D-U-N-S 25-657-6406   (BR)
WEINS CANADA INC
DON VALLEY NORTH & MARKVILLE TOYOTA
391 John St, Thornhill, ON, L3T 5W5
(905) 886-0434
Emp Here 23
SIC 7532 Top and body repair and paint shops

D-U-N-S 25-151-0376   (BR)
YORK CATHOLIC DISTRICT SCHOOL BOARD
ST ROBERT CATHOLIC HIGH SCHOOL
8101 Leslie St, Thornhill, ON, L3T 7P4
(905) 889-4982
Emp Here 140
SIC 8211 Elementary and secondary schools

D-U-N-S 25-151-0137   (BR)
YORK CATHOLIC DISTRICT SCHOOL BOARD
ST MICHAEL CATHOLIC ACADEMY
41 Simonston Blvd, Thornhill, ON, L3T 4R6
(905) 889-4816
Emp Here 20
SIC 8211 Elementary and secondary schools

D-U-N-S 25-225-2457   (BR)
YORK CATHOLIC DISTRICT SCHOOL BOARD
ST RENE GOUPIL CATHOLIC SCHOOL

135 Green Lane, Thornhill, ON, L3T 6K7
(905) 881-2300
Emp Here 20
SIC 8211 Elementary and secondary schools

D-U-N-S 20-711-4468   (BR)
YORK CATHOLIC DISTRICT SCHOOL BOARD
ST. ANTHONY CATHOLIC ELEMENTARY SCHOOL
141 Kirk Dr, Thornhill, ON, L3T 3L3
(905) 889-7420
Emp Here 50
SIC 8211 Elementary and secondary schools

D-U-N-S 25-297-9315   (BR)
YORK REGION DISTRICT SCHOOL BOARD
BAYTHORN PUBLIC SCHOOL
(*Suby of* York Region District School Board)
201 Bay Thorn Dr, Thornhill, ON, L3T 3V2
(905) 889-7992
Emp Here 25
SIC 8211 Elementary and secondary schools

D-U-N-S 25-297-9026   (BR)
YORK REGION DISTRICT SCHOOL BOARD
HENDERSON AVENUE PUBLIC SCHOOL
(*Suby of* York Region District School Board)
66 Henderson Ave, Thornhill, ON, L3T 2K7
(905) 889-3132
Emp Here 28
SIC 8211 Elementary and secondary schools

D-U-N-S 25-297-9232   (BR)
YORK REGION DISTRICT SCHOOL BOARD
BAYVIEW GLEN PUBLIC SCHOOL
(*Suby of* York Region District School Board)
42 Limcombe Dr, Thornhill, ON, L3T 2V5
(905) 889-2448
Emp Here 20
SIC 8211 Elementary and secondary schools

D-U-N-S 25-297-9612   (BR)
YORK REGION DISTRICT SCHOOL BOARD
STORNOWAY CRESCENT PUBIC SCHOOL
(*Suby of* York Region District School Board)
36 Stornoway Cres, Thornhill, ON, L3T 3X7
(905) 889-9535
Emp Here 20
SIC 8211 Elementary and secondary schools

D-U-N-S 25-297-9471   (BR)
YORK REGION DISTRICT SCHOOL BOARD
THORNLEA SECONDARY SCHOOL
(*Suby of* York Region District School Board)
8075 Bayview Ave, Thornhill, ON, L3T 4N4
(905) 889-9696
Emp Here 120
SIC 8211 Elementary and secondary schools

D-U-N-S 25-297-9372   (BR)
YORK REGION DISTRICT SCHOOL BOARD
WOODLAND PUBLIC SCHOOL
(*Suby of* York Region District School Board)
120 Royal Orchard Blvd, Thornhill, ON, L3T 3C9
(905) 889-4910
Emp Here 23
SIC 8211 Elementary and secondary schools

D-U-N-S 20-591-2582   (BR)
YORK REGION DISTRICT SCHOOL BOARD
JOHN VIEW VILLAGE PUBLIC SCHOOL
(*Suby of* York Region District School Board)
41 Porterfield Cres, Thornhill, ON, L3T 5C3
(905) 881-3360
Emp Here 25
SIC 8211 Elementary and secondary schools

D-U-N-S 20-591-2368   (BR)
YORK REGION DISTRICT SCHOOL BOARD
E J SAND PUBLIC SCHOOL
(*Suby of* York Region District School Board)
160 Henderson Ave, Thornhill, ON, L3T 2L5
(905) 889-2753
Emp Here 25
SIC 8211 Elementary and secondary schools

D-U-N-S 20-711-4021   (BR)
YORK REGION DISTRICT SCHOOL BOARD
THORNHILL SECONDARY SCHOOL
(*Suby of* York Region District School Board)
167 Dudley Ave, Thornhill, ON, L3T 2E5
(905) 889-5453
Emp Here 50
SIC 8211 Elementary and secondary schools

D-U-N-S 20-292-0265   (BR)
YORK REGION DISTRICT SCHOOL BOARD
COMMUNITY EDUCATION CENTER - WEST
(*Suby of* York Region District School Board)
36 Stornoway Cres, Thornhill, ON, L3T 3X7
(905) 764-6830
Emp Here 30
SIC 8211 Elementary and secondary schools

D-U-N-S 25-297-9497   (BR)
YORK REGION DISTRICT SCHOOL BOARD
WILLOWBROOK PUBLIC SCHOOL
(*Suby of* York Region District School Board)
45 Willowbrook Rd, Thornhill, ON, L3T 4X6
(905) 886-0743
Emp Here 35
SIC 8211 Elementary and secondary schools

D-U-N-S 20-711-3932   (BR)
YORK REGION DISTRICT SCHOOL BOARD
BAYVIEW FAIRWAYS PUBLIC SCHOOL
(*Suby of* York Region District School Board)
255 Bayview Fairways Dr, Thornhill, ON, L3T 2Z6
(905) 889-1858
Emp Here 25
SIC 8211 Elementary and secondary schools

D-U-N-S 20-711-4088   (BR)
YORK REGION DISTRICT SCHOOL BOARD
GIANT STEPS TORONTO
(*Suby of* York Region District School Board)
35 Flowervale Rd, Thornhill, ON, L3T 4J3
(905) 881-3104
Emp Here 30
SIC 8211 Elementary and secondary schools

Thornhill, ON L4J
York County

D-U-N-S 25-513-0130   (SL)
1177972 ONTARIO LIMITED
HUNTER AUTOMATICS
221 Racco Pky Unit A, Thornhill, ON, L4J 8X9
(416) 674-8880
Emp Here 22   *Sales* 1,645,877
SIC 5962 Merchandising machine operators

D-U-N-S 25-296-6890   (BR)
BANK OF NOVA SCOTIA, THE
SCOTIABANK
7700 Bathurst St Suite 18, Thornhill, ON, L4J 7Y3
(905) 731-8009
Emp Here 25
SIC 6021 National commercial banks

D-U-N-S 24-693-8245   (BR)
BOUTIQUE JACOB INC
JACOB ANNEXE
(*Suby of* Boutique Jacob Inc)
1 Promenade Cir, Thornhill, ON, L4J 4P8

Emp Here 34
SIC 5621 Women's clothing stores

D-U-N-S 20-965-4743   (BR)
CANADIAN IMPERIAL BANK OF COMMERCE
CIBC
800 Steeles Ave W Suite 712, Thornhill, ON, L4J 7L2
(905) 660-3476
Emp Here 20
SIC 6021 National commercial banks

D-U-N-S 25-369-4509   (BR)
CENTRAL MONTESSORI SCHOOLS INC
CENTRAL MONTESSORI SCHOOL
72 Steeles Ave W, Thornhill, ON, L4J 1A1
(905) 889-0012
Emp Here 43
SIC 8211 Elementary and secondary schools

D-U-N-S 20-253-7234   (SL)
CHABAD AT FLAMINGO INC
8001 Bathurst St, Thornhill, ON, L4J 8L5
(905) 763-4040
Emp Here 50   *Sales* 3,283,232
SIC 8661 Religious organizations

D-U-N-S 25-075-1625   (BR)
CHARTWELL MASTER CARE LP
784 Centre St, Thornhill, ON, L4J 9G7
(905) 771-1013
Emp Here 50
SIC 6513 Apartment building operators

D-U-N-S 24-193-5498   (BR)
CHARTWELL RETIREMENT RESIDENCES
CHARTWELL SENIORS HOUSING REAL ESTATE INVESTMENT TRUST
784 Centre St Suite 404, Thornhill, ON, L4J 9G7
(905) 771-1013
Emp Here 40
SIC 6513 Apartment building operators

D-U-N-S 25-092-6776   (SL)
CODEVALUE CANADA INC.
173 Charles St, Thornhill, ON, L4J 3A2
(647) 834-1888
Emp Here 50   *Sales* 6,933,120
SIC 7371 Custom computer programming services
  Aaron Etchin

D-U-N-S 20-268-3769   (SL)
CROWN MOVING
800 Steeles Ave W Unit D-10181, Thornhill, ON, L4J 7L2
(416) 831-0489
Emp Here 87   *Sales* 5,527,332
SIC 4731 Freight transportation arrangement
Pt Conroy Gord
Pt Banks Ralph
Pt Montana Renfrew

D-U-N-S 24-343-7329   (BR)
FGL SPORTS LTD
SPORT CHEK THE PROMENADE
1 Promenade Cir Unit 117 8, Thornhill, ON, L4J 4P8
(905) 707-0557
Emp Here 50
SIC 5941 Sporting goods and bicycle shops

D-U-N-S 20-587-9757   (BR)
GAP (CANADA) INC
GAP
(*Suby of* The Gap Inc)
1 Promenade Cir, Thornhill, ON, L4J 4P8
(905) 886-9509
Emp Here 25
SIC 5651 Family clothing stores

D-U-N-S 25-318-4634   (BR)
HOLT, RENFREW & CIE, LIMITEE
LAST CALL
370 Steeles Ave W, Thornhill, ON, L4J 6X1
(905) 886-7444
Emp Here 30
SIC 5311 Department stores

D-U-N-S 24-169-7106   (SL)
HOMELIFE FRONTIER REALTY INC
7620 Yonge St Suite 400, Thornhill, ON, L4J 1V9
(416) 218-8800
Emp Here 50   *Sales* 4,742,446
SIC 6531 Real estate agents and managers

D-U-N-S 20-081-9634   (BR)
J.F. & L. RESTAURANTS LIMITED
PICKLE BARREL RESTAURANT

(*Suby of* J.F. & L. Restaurants Limited)
1 Promenade Cir, Thornhill, ON, L4J 4P8
(905) 764-3444
Emp Here 100
SIC 5812 Eating places

D-U-N-S 24-826-4293   (SL)
JACOBS CATERING LTD
613 Clark Ave W, Thornhill, ON, L4J 5V3
(905) 886-3832
Emp Here 106   *Sales* 3,210,271
SIC 5812 Eating places

D-U-N-S 20-967-4139   (BR)
MCI MEDICAL CLINICS INC
DOCTOR'S OFFICE, THE
(*Suby of* MCI Medical Clinics Inc)
800 Steeles Ave W Suite 4a, Thornhill, ON, L4J 7L2
(905) 660-6228
Emp Here 30
SIC 8011 Offices and clinics of medical doctors

D-U-N-S 24-489-1487   (BR)
MAC'S CONVENIENCE STORES INC
7241 Bathurst St Suite 2, Thornhill, ON, L4J 3W1
(905) 731-0013
Emp Here 25
SIC 5411 Grocery stores

D-U-N-S 20-793-1945   (BR)
METRO ONTARIO INC
FOOD BASICS
800 Steeles Ave W, Thornhill, ON, L4J 7L2

Emp Here 50
SIC 5411 Grocery stores

D-U-N-S 24-124-8061   (SL)
OR-HAEMET SEPHARDIC SCHOOL
7026 Bathurst St, Thornhill, ON, L4J 8K3
(905) 669-7653
Emp Here 50   *Sales* 3,356,192
SIC 8211 Elementary and secondary schools

D-U-N-S 20-859-8636   (BR)
PACIFIC LINK COMMUNICATIONS INC
BELL WORLD
1 Promenade Cir, Thornhill, ON, L4J 4P8

Emp Here 25
SIC 5999 Miscellaneous retail stores, nec

D-U-N-S 24-991-2098   (SL)
PEERLESS TRAVEL INC
PEERLESS TRAVEL RUTHERFORD VILLAGE
7117 Bathurst St Suite 200, Thornhill, ON, L4J 2J6
(905) 886-5610
Emp Here 60   *Sales* 19,694,080
SIC 4724 Travel agencies
Pr Pr Ehud Telem

D-U-N-S 25-659-5802   (BR)
PHARMA PLUS DRUGMARTS LTD
1 Promenade Cir, Thornhill, ON, L4J 4P8
(905) 764-0620
Emp Here 35
SIC 5912 Drug stores and proprietary stores

D-U-N-S 25-117-2342   (BR)
RE/MAX REALTRON REALTY INC
7646 Yonge St, Thornhill, ON, L4J 1V9
(905) 764-6000
Emp Here 85
SIC 6531 Real estate agents and managers

D-U-N-S 20-806-2609   (BR)
SOBEYS CAPITAL INCORPORATED
SOBEYS STORE 794
9200 Bathurst St, Thornhill, ON, L4J 8W1
(905) 731-7600
Emp Here 100
SIC 5411 Grocery stores

D-U-N-S 24-101-3460   (BR)

D-U-N-S STAPLES CANADA INC
STAPLES CANADA INC
STAPLES THE BUSINESS DEPOT
(*Suby of* Staples, Inc.)
1450 Clark Ave W Suite 1, Thornhill, ON, L4J 7R5
(905) 669-5096
Emp Here 20
SIC 5943 Stationery stores

D-U-N-S 20-944-5779   (BR)
STARBUCKS COFFEE CANADA, INC
(*Suby of* Starbucks Corporation)
7077 Bathurst St Suite 6, Thornhill, ON, L4J 2J6
(905) 764-2332
Emp Here 20
SIC 5812 Eating places

D-U-N-S 20-185-0810   (BR)
T & T SUPERMARKET INC
1 Promenade Cir, Thornhill, ON, L4J 4P8
(905) 763-8113
Emp Here 200
SIC 5411 Grocery stores

D-U-N-S 20-874-6180   (SL)
TORONTO WALDORF SCHOOL, THE
9100 Bathurst St Unit 1, Thornhill, ON, L4J 8C7
(905) 881-1611
Emp Here 60   *Sales* 4,012,839
SIC 8211 Elementary and secondary schools

D-U-N-S 25-092-8892   (BR)
TORONTO-DOMINION BANK, THE
TD CANADA TRUST
(*Suby of* Toronto-Dominion Bank, The)
100 Steeles Ave W Suite 1, Thornhill, ON, L4J 7Y1
(905) 882-0300
Emp Here 25
SIC 6021 National commercial banks

D-U-N-S 25-297-8317   (BR)
TOYS 'R' US (CANADA) LTD
TOYS 'R' US
(*Suby of* Toys "r" Us, Inc.)
300 Steeles Ave W, Thornhill, ON, L4J 1A1
(416) 222-8697
Emp Here 40
SIC 5945 Hobby, toy, and game shops

D-U-N-S 25-979-6670   (SL)
VAUGHAN PROMENADE SHOPPING CENTRE INC
1 Promenade Cir Suite 316, Thornhill, ON, L4J 4P8
(905) 764-0022
Emp Here 30   *Sales* 3,291,754
SIC 6512 Nonresidential building operators

D-U-N-S 25-221-2337   (BR)
WINNERS MERCHANTS INTERNATIONAL L.P.
WINNERS
(*Suby of* The TJX Companies Inc)
1054 Centre St, Thornhill, ON, L4J 3M8
(905) 731-3201
Emp Here 30
SIC 5651 Family clothing stores

D-U-N-S 25-151-0079   (BR)
YORK CATHOLIC DISTRICT SCHOOL BOARD
ST JOSEPH THE WORKER CATHOLIC SCHOOL
475 Brownridge Dr, Thornhill, ON, L4J 5Y6
(905) 738-5703
Emp Here 40
SIC 8211 Elementary and secondary schools

D-U-N-S 20-590-5081   (BR)
YORK CATHOLIC DISTRICT SCHOOL BOARD
ST ELIZABETH CATHOLIC HIGH SCHOOL
525 New Westminster Dr, Thornhill, ON, L4J 7X3
(905) 882-1460
Emp Here 25

SIC 8211 Elementary and secondary schools

D-U-N-S 25-151-0012 (BR)
YORK CATHOLIC DISTRICT SCHOOL BOARD
BISHOP SCALABRINI ELEMENTARY SCHOOL
290 York Hill Blvd, Thornhill, ON, L4J 3B6
(905) 886-3272
Emp Here 21
SIC 8211 Elementary and secondary schools

D-U-N-S 20-914-4612 (BR)
YORK CATHOLIC DISTRICT SCHOOL BOARD
HOLY FAMILY ELEMENTARY SCHOOL
21 Mullen Dr, Thornhill, ON, L4J 2T6
(905) 731-7682
Emp Here 35
SIC 8211 Elementary and secondary schools

D-U-N-S 24-676-5189 (BR)
YORK REGION DISTRICT SCHOOL BOARD
CARRVILLE MILLS PUBLIC SCHOOL
(*Suby of* York Region District School Board)
270 Apple Blossom Dr, Thornhill, ON, L4J 8W5
(905) 709-2646
Emp Here 50
SIC 8211 Elementary and secondary schools

D-U-N-S 20-031-5708 (BR)
YORK REGION DISTRICT SCHOOL BOARD
VENTURA PARK PUBLIC SCHOOL
(*Suby of* York Region District School Board)
121 Worth Blvd, Thornhill, ON, L4J 7V5
(905) 707-6488
Emp Here 40
SIC 8211 Elementary and secondary schools

D-U-N-S 25-297-9430 (BR)
YORK REGION DISTRICT SCHOOL BOARD
VAUGHAN SECONDARY SCHOOL
(*Suby of* York Region District School Board)
1401 Clark Ave W, Thornhill, ON, L4J 7R4
(905) 660-1397
Emp Here 120
SIC 8211 Elementary and secondary schools

D-U-N-S 20-591-2566 (BR)
YORK REGION DISTRICT SCHOOL BOARD
YORKHILL ELEMENTARY SCHOOL
(*Suby of* York Region District School Board)
350 Hilda Ave, Thornhill, ON, L4J 5K2
(905) 764-5292
Emp Here 50
SIC 8211 Elementary and secondary schools

D-U-N-S 20-653-8915 (BR)
YORK REGION DISTRICT SCHOOL BOARD
UPLANDS COMMUNITY LEARNING CENTRE
(*Suby of* York Region District School Board)
8210 Yonge St, Thornhill, ON, L4J 1W6
(905) 731-9557
Emp Here 30
SIC 8211 Elementary and secondary schools

D-U-N-S 25-297-9455 (BR)
YORK REGION DISTRICT SCHOOL BOARD
WILSHIRE ELEMENTARY SCHOOL
(*Suby of* York Region District School Board)
265 Beverley Glen Blvd, Thornhill, ON, L4J 7S8
(905) 889-6767
Emp Here 35
SIC 8211 Elementary and secondary schools

D-U-N-S 24-676-3374 (BR)
YORK REGION DISTRICT SCHOOL BOARD
THORNHILL WOODS PUBLIC SCHOOL
(*Suby of* York Region District School Board)
341 Thornhill Woods Dr, Thornhill, ON, L4J 8V6
(905) 326-8626
Emp Here 25
SIC 8211 Elementary and secondary schools

D-U-N-S 20-711-4112 (BR)

YORK REGION DISTRICT SCHOOL BOARD
CHARLTON PUBLIC SCHOOL
(*Suby of* York Region District School Board)
121 Joseph Aaron Blvd, Thornhill, ON, L4J 6J5
(905) 738-5497
Emp Here 50
SIC 8211 Elementary and secondary schools

D-U-N-S 25-224-8372 (BR)
YORK REGION DISTRICT SCHOOL BOARD
WESTMINSTER PUBLIC SCHOOL
(*Suby of* York Region District School Board)
366 Mullen Dr, Thornhill, ON, L4J 2P3
(905) 731-2963
Emp Here 30
SIC 8211 Elementary and secondary schools

D-U-N-S 25-297-9778 (BR)
YORK REGION DISTRICT SCHOOL BOARD
LOUIS-HONORE FRECHETTE PUBLIC SCHOOL
(*Suby of* York Region District School Board)
40 New Westminster Dr, Thornhill, ON, L4J 7Z8
(905) 738-1724
Emp Here 41
SIC 8211 Elementary and secondary schools

D-U-N-S 25-297-9695 (BR)
YORK REGION DISTRICT SCHOOL BOARD
ROSEDALE HEIGHTS PUBLIC SCHOOL
(*Suby of* York Region District School Board)
300 Rosedale Heights Dr, Thornhill, ON, L4J 6Y8
(905) 882-1864
Emp Here 42
SIC 8211 Elementary and secondary schools

D-U-N-S 20-711-4161 (BR)
YORK REGION DISTRICT SCHOOL BOARD
BROWNRIDGE PUBLIC SCHOOL
(*Suby of* York Region District School Board)
65 Brownridge Dr, Thornhill, ON, L4J 7R8
(905) 660-3083
Emp Here 50
SIC 8211 Elementary and secondary schools

Thorold, ON L2V
Welland County

D-U-N-S 25-087-5929 (SL)
1364084 ONTARIO INC
FOUR POINTS BY SHERATON ST CATHARINES NIAGARA SUITES
3530 Schmon Pky Suite 11, Thorold, ON, L2V 4Y6
(905) 984-8484
Emp Here 65   *Sales* 2,845,467
SIC 7011 Hotels and motels

D-U-N-S 25-403-6676 (BR)
AMEC FOSTER WHEELER AMERICAS LIMITED
AMEC EARTH & ENVIRONMENTAL, DIV OF
3300 Merrittville Hwy Unit 5, Thorold, ON, L2V 4Y6
(905) 687-6616
Emp Here 20
SIC 8711 Engineering services

D-U-N-S 25-282-7993 (HQ)
BRAIN INJURY COMMUNITY RE-ENTRY (NIAGARA) INC
(*Suby of* Brain Injury Community Re-Entry (Niagara) Inc)
3340 Schmon Pkwy Unit 2, Thorold, ON, L2V 4Y6
(905) 687-6788
Emp Here 30   *Emp Total* 137
Sales 11,090,026
SIC 8399 Social services, nec
Pr Nick Ostryhon
Dir Fin Sandra Harding
CEO Frank Greco

D-U-N-S 25-826-8531 (BR)
CANPAR TRANSPORT L.P.
(*Suby of* Canpar Transport L.P.)
320 Collier Rd S, Thorold, ON, L2V 5B6
(905) 227-9733
Emp Here 26
SIC 7389 Business services, nec

D-U-N-S 24-937-2053 (BR)
CLEAN HARBORS CANADA, INC
1829 Allanport Rd, Thorold, ON, L2V 3Y9
(905) 227-7872
Emp Here 35
SIC 4953 Refuse systems

D-U-N-S 24-386-1838 (BR)
COMCARE (CANADA) LIMITED
COMCARE HEALTH SERVICE
3550 Schmon Pky Suite 4, Thorold, ON, L2V 4Y6
(905) 685-6501
Emp Here 175
SIC 8049 Offices of health practitioner

D-U-N-S 24-336-9746 (BR)
DANA CANADA CORPORATION
SPICER DRIVESHAFT, DIV OF
90 Hayes Rd, Thorold, ON, L2V 0C3

Emp Here 200
SIC 3714 Motor vehicle parts and accessories

D-U-N-S 20-710-8676 (BR)
DISTRICT SCHOOL BOARD OF NIAGARA
ONTARIO PUBLIC SCHOOL
550 Allanburg Rd, Thorold, ON, L2V 1A8
(905) 227-2851
Emp Here 50
SIC 8211 Elementary and secondary schools

D-U-N-S 20-026-7230 (BR)
DISTRICT SCHOOL BOARD OF NIAGARA
RICHMOND STREET PUBLIC SCHOOL
153 Richmond St, Thorold, ON, L2V 3H3
(905) 227-2971
Emp Here 30
SIC 8211 Elementary and secondary schools

D-U-N-S 20-286-9256 (BR)
DISTRICT SCHOOL BOARD OF NIAGARA
PRINCE OF WALES ELEMENTARY SCHOOL
40 Pine St S, Thorold, ON, L2V 3L4
(905) 227-1321
Emp Here 25
SIC 8211 Elementary and secondary schools

D-U-N-S 20-009-6605 (BR)
DISTRICT SCHOOL BOARD OF NIAGARA
THOROLD SECONDARY SCHOOL
50 Ormond St N, Thorold, ON, L2V 1Z1
(905) 227-1188
Emp Here 50
SIC 8211 Elementary and secondary schools

D-U-N-S 20-031-5666 (BR)
DISTRICT SCHOOL BOARD OF NIAGARA
WESTMOUNT ELEMENTARY SCHOOL
73 Ann St, Thorold, ON, L2V 2J8
(905) 227-3827
Emp Here 27
SIC 8211 Elementary and secondary schools

D-U-N-S 24-760-2571 (HQ)
GEORGIA-PACIFIC CANADA LP
(*Suby of* Koch Industries, Inc.)
319 Allanburg Rd, Thorold, ON, L2V 5C3
(905) 227-6651
Emp Here 100   *Emp Total* 70,000
Sales 61,286,988
SIC 2679 Converted paper products, nec
Genl Mgr Gerald Finlayson

D-U-N-S 20-157-2468 (SL)
HENDERSON'S PHARMACY LIMITED
HENDERSON'S PHARMASAVE
15 Front St S, Thorold, ON, L2V 1W8
(905) 227-2511
Emp Here 50   *Sales* 7,077,188

SIC 5912 Drug stores and proprietary stores
Pr Pr John E Henderson

D-U-N-S 25-137-6497 (BR)
NIAGARA CATHOLIC DISTRICT SCHOOL BOARD
MONSEIGNEUR CLANCY CATHOLIC ELEMENTARY SCHOOL
41 Collier Rd S, Thorold, ON, L2V 3S9
(905) 227-4910
Emp Here 25
SIC 8211 Elementary and secondary schools

D-U-N-S 20-710-8858 (BR)
NIAGARA CATHOLIC DISTRICT SCHOOL BOARD
ST CHARLES CATHOLIC ELEMENTARY SCHOOL
25 Whyte Ave N, Thorold, ON, L2V 2T4
(905) 227-3522
Emp Here 45
SIC 8211 Elementary and secondary schools

D-U-N-S 24-771-5261 (HQ)
NIAGARA CHILD AND YOUTH SERVICES
NCYS
(*Suby of* Niagara Child and Youth Services)
3340 Schmon Pky, Thorold, ON, L2V 4Y6
(905) 688-6850
Emp Here 50   *Emp Total* 120
Sales 4,742,446
SIC 8322 Individual and family services

D-U-N-S 20-132-4308 (BR)
STEED & EVANS LIMITED
(*Suby of* Steed & Evans Limited)
3551 Wesleslie St, Thorold, ON, L2V 3Y7
(905) 227-2994
Emp Here 40
SIC 1611 Highway and street construction

D-U-N-S 24-369-4150 (BR)
V.K. MASON CONSTRUCTION LTD
(*Suby of* V.K. Mason Construction Ltd)
Gd, Thorold, ON, L2V 3Y9

Emp Here 200
SIC 1541 Industrial buildings and warehouses

Thunder Bay, ON P7A
Thunder Bay County

D-U-N-S 25-613-8884 (BR)
BRAIN INJURY SERVICES OF NORTHERN ONTARIO
(*Suby of* Brain Injury Services Of Northern Ontario)
130 Castlegreen Dr, Thunder Bay, ON, P7A 7T9
(807) 768-1881
Emp Here 50
SIC 8361 Residential care

D-U-N-S 20-568-9425 (BR)
BREWERS RETAIL INC
BEER STORE, THE
184 Camelot St, Thunder Bay, ON, P7A 4A9
(807) 345-3561
Emp Here 20
SIC 5181 Beer and ale

D-U-N-S 24-535-5800 (BR)
COMMUNITY LIVING THUNDER BAY
CLTB
(*Suby of* Community Living Thunder Bay)
246 Market St, Thunder Bay, ON, P7A 8A5
(807) 767-7322
Emp Here 58
SIC 8059 Nursing and personal care, nec

D-U-N-S 25-238-1074 (BR)
CONSEIL SCOLAIRE DE DISTRICT CATHOLIQUE DES AURORES BOREALES
ECOLE FRANCO-SUPERIEUR
(*Suby of* Conseil Scolaire De District

Catholique Des Aurores Boreales)
220 Elgin St, Thunder Bay, ON, P7A 0A4
(807) 344-1169
Emp Here 33
SIC 8211 Elementary and secondary schools

D-U-N-S 24-775-4666   (BR)
CORPORATION OF THE CITY OF THUN-DER BAY, THE
DAWSON COURT HOME FOR THE AGED
523 Algoma St N, Thunder Bay, ON, P7A 5C2
(807) 684-2926
Emp Here 225
SIC 8361 Residential care

D-U-N-S 20-891-7232   (BR)
GOVERNMENT OF ONTARIO
THUNDER BAY & DISTRICT EN-TREPRENEUR CENTRE, THE
34 Cumberland St N Suite 816, Thunder Bay, ON, P7A 4L3
(807) 625-3972
Emp Here 25
SIC 8748 Business consulting, nec

D-U-N-S 25-265-1393   (BR)
LAKEHEAD DISTRICT SCHOOL BOARD
CLAUDE GARTON ELEMENTARY SCHOOL
414 Grenville Ave, Thunder Bay, ON, P7A 1X9
(807) 683-6289
Emp Here 40
SIC 8211 Elementary and secondary schools

D-U-N-S 25-238-1223   (BR)
LAKEHEAD DISTRICT SCHOOL BOARD
HILLCREST HIGH SCHOOL
96 High St N, Thunder Bay, ON, P7A 5R3
(807) 625-5100
Emp Here 65
SIC 8211 Elementary and secondary schools

D-U-N-S 25-238-1124   (BR)
LAKEHEAD DISTRICT SCHOOL BOARD
SIR JOHN A MACDONALD ELEMENTARY
160 Logan Ave, Thunder Bay, ON, P7A 6R1
(807) 345-2375
Emp Here 20
SIC 8211 Elementary and secondary schools

D-U-N-S 25-238-0803   (BR)
LAKEHEAD DISTRICT SCHOOL BOARD
C D HOWE PUBLIC SCHOOL
30 Wishart Cres, Thunder Bay, ON, P7A 6G3
(807) 767-6244
Emp Here 25
SIC 8211 Elementary and secondary schools

D-U-N-S 20-710-3503   (BR)
LAKEHEAD DISTRICT SCHOOL BOARD
ST JAMES ELEMENTARY SCHOOL
243 St. James St, Thunder Bay, ON, P7A 3P1
(807) 345-7191
Emp Here 50
SIC 8211 Elementary and secondary schools

D-U-N-S 25-238-0969   (BR)
LAKEHEAD DISTRICT SCHOOL BOARD
VANCE CHAPMAN ELEMENTARY SCHOOL
1000 Huron Ave, Thunder Bay, ON, P7A 6L4
(807) 344-8661
Emp Here 30
SIC 8211 Elementary and secondary schools

D-U-N-S 24-967-0183   (BR)
MARCH OF DIMES CANADA
237 Camelot St, Thunder Bay, ON, P7A 4B2
(807) 345-6595
Emp Here 50
SIC 8331 Job training and related services

D-U-N-S 25-787-2689   (BR)
MCDONALD'S RESTAURANTS OF CANADA LIMITED
MCDONALD'S
(*Suby of* McDonald's Corporation)
81 Cumberland St N, Thunder Bay, ON, P7A 4M1

(807) 344-1513
Emp Here 70
SIC 5812 Eating places

D-U-N-S 24-333-1589   (BR)
METRO ONTARIO INC
METRO
640 River St, Thunder Bay, ON, P7A 3S4
(807) 345-8342
Emp Here 300
SIC 5411 Grocery stores

D-U-N-S 20-948-1241   (SL)
PORT ARTHUR HEALTH CENTRE INC, THE
194 Court St N, Thunder Bay, ON, P7A 4V7
(807) 345-2332
Emp Here 75   *Sales* 4,523,563
SIC 8011 Offices and clinics of medical doctors

D-U-N-S 24-115-8138   (SL)
PRINCE ARTHUR HOTEL (1983) LTD
THE PRINCE ARTHUR WATERFRONT HO-TEL & SUITES
17 Cumberland St N, Thunder Bay, ON, P7A 4K8
(807) 345-5411
Emp Here 60   *Sales* 2,626,585
SIC 7011 Hotels and motels

D-U-N-S 20-142-8463   (BR)
RICHARDSON INTERNATIONAL LIMITED
181 North Water St, Thunder Bay, ON, P7A 8C2
(807) 343-5570
Emp Here 63
SIC 4221 Farm product warehousing and storage

D-U-N-S 24-917-3022   (SL)
ROACH'S TAXI (1988) LTD
CALL ROACH'S YELLOW TAXI
216 Camelot St, Thunder Bay, ON, P7A 4B1
(807) 344-8481
Emp Here 100   *Sales* 2,991,389
SIC 4121 Taxicabs

D-U-N-S 25-265-0460   (BR)
THUNDER BAY CATHOLIC DISTRICT SCHOOL BOARD
ST MARGARET ELEMENTARY SCHOOL
(*Suby of* Thunder Bay Catholic District School Board)
89 Clayte St, Thunder Bay, ON, P7A 6S4
(807) 344-4701
Emp Here 35
SIC 8211 Elementary and secondary schools

D-U-N-S 25-264-9983   (BR)
THUNDER BAY CATHOLIC DISTRICT SCHOOL BOARD
ST IGNATIUS HIGH SCHOOL
(*Suby of* Thunder Bay Catholic District School Board)
285 Gibson St, Thunder Bay, ON, P7A 2J6
(807) 344-8433
Emp Here 105
SIC 8211 Elementary and secondary schools

D-U-N-S 20-591-4232   (BR)
THUNDER BAY CATHOLIC DISTRICT SCHOOL BOARD
ST BERNARD SCHOOL
(*Suby of* Thunder Bay Catholic District School Board)
655 River St, Thunder Bay, ON, P7A 3S5
(807) 344-8321
Emp Here 25
SIC 8211 Elementary and secondary schools

D-U-N-S 20-591-4018   (BR)
THUNDER BAY CATHOLIC DISTRICT SCHOOL BOARD
OUR LADY OF CHARITY SCHOOL
(*Suby of* Thunder Bay Catholic District School Board)
370 County Blvd, Thunder Bay, ON, P7A 7P5
(807) 768-9363
Emp Here 25

SIC 8211 Elementary and secondary schools

Thunder Bay, ON P7B
Thunder Bay County

D-U-N-S 25-116-5049   (SL)
1204626 ONTARIO INC
MAKKINGA CONTRACTING & EQUIPMENT RENTAL
570 Squier Pl, Thunder Bay, ON, P7B 6M2
(807) 935-2792
Emp Here 50   *Sales* 3,648,035
SIC 1794 Excavation work

D-U-N-S 25-386-9242   (BR)
ALS CANADA LTD
1081 Barton St, Thunder Bay, ON, P7B 5N3
(807) 623-6463
Emp Here 25
SIC 8731 Commercial physical research

D-U-N-S 25-848-9137   (BR)
AON REED STENHOUSE INC
1205 Amber Dr Unit 100, Thunder Bay, ON, P7B 6M4
(807) 346-7450
Emp Here 23
SIC 6411 Insurance agents, brokers, and service

D-U-N-S 24-032-1583   (BR)
ARAMARK CANADA LTD.
ARAMARK MANAGED SERVICES
955 Oliver Rd, Thunder Bay, ON, P7B 5E1
(807) 343-8337
Emp Here 100
SIC 5812 Eating places

D-U-N-S 24-883-5787   (BR)
BDO CANADA LLP
THUNDER BAY ACCOUNTING
1095 Barton St, Thunder Bay, ON, P7B 5N3
(807) 625-4444
Emp Here 67
SIC 8721 Accounting, auditing, and bookkeeping

D-U-N-S 24-376-5310   (BR)
BMO NESBITT BURNS INC
BMO NESBITT BURNS PRIVATE CLIENT
1139 Alloy Dr Suite 210, Thunder Bay, ON, P7B 6M8
(807) 343-1900
Emp Here 20
SIC 6211 Security brokers and dealers

D-U-N-S 25-296-6817   (BR)
BANK OF NOVA SCOTIA, THE
SCOTIABANK
745 Hewitson St, Thunder Bay, ON, P7B 6B5
(807) 623-5626
Emp Here 28
SIC 6021 National commercial banks

D-U-N-S 20-944-5485   (BR)
BANK OF NOVA SCOTIA, THE
SCOTIABANK
225 Red River Rd, Thunder Bay, ON, P7B 1A7
(807) 343-5600
Emp Here 31
SIC 6021 National commercial banks

D-U-N-S 24-467-0899   (BR)
BANK OF MONTREAL
BMO BANK OF MONTREAL
256 Red River Rd, Thunder Bay, ON, P7B 1A8
(807) 343-1450
Emp Here 25
SIC 6021 National commercial banks

D-U-N-S 25-613-0659   (BR)
BEST BUY CANADA LTD
FUTURE SHOP
(*Suby of* Best Buy Co., Inc.)
767 Memorial Ave Suite 1, Thunder Bay, ON,

SIC 8211 Elementary and secondary schools

P7B 3Z7
(807) 346-1900
Emp Here 50
SIC 5999 Miscellaneous retail stores, nec

D-U-N-S 25-613-8835   (BR)
BOOTLEGGER CLOTHING INC
BOOTLEGGER
1000 Fort William Rd Unit 1, Thunder Bay, ON, P7B 6B9
(807) 623-1103
Emp Here 20
SIC 5651 Family clothing stores

D-U-N-S 25-231-7581   (BR)
BRICK WAREHOUSE LP, THE
BRICK, THE
869 Fort William Rd, Thunder Bay, ON, P7B 0A9
(807) 475-7300
Emp Here 35
SIC 5712 Furniture stores

D-U-N-S 20-142-3753   (BR)
BRINK'S CANADA LIMITED
(*Suby of* The Brink's Company)
887a Tungsten St, Thunder Bay, ON, P7B 6H2
(807) 623-2999
Emp Here 30
SIC 7381 Detective and armored car services

D-U-N-S 25-148-1123   (BR)
CAA NORTH & EAST ONTARIO
CAA
(*Suby of* CAA North & East Ontario)
585 Memorial Ave, Thunder Bay, ON, P7B 3Z1
(807) 345-1261
Emp Here 20
SIC 8699 Membership organizations, nec

D-U-N-S 25-613-1467   (BR)
CANADA BROKERLINK (ONTARIO) INC
1139 Alloy Dr Suite 110, Thunder Bay, ON, P7B 6M8
(807) 622-6155
Emp Here 39
SIC 6411 Insurance agents, brokers, and service

D-U-N-S 25-196-8272   (BR)
CANADA BROKERLINK INC
1139 Alloy Dr Suite 110, Thunder Bay, ON, P7B 6M8
(807) 623-4343
Emp Here 40
SIC 6411 Insurance agents, brokers, and service

D-U-N-S 20-944-5436   (BR)
CANADIAN IMPERIAL BANK OF COM-MERCE
CIBC
2 Cumberland St S, Thunder Bay, ON, P7B 2T2
(807) 343-3710
Emp Here 29
SIC 6021 National commercial banks

D-U-N-S 20-568-7846   (BR)
CANADIAN PACIFIC RAILWAY COMPANY
949 Fort William Rd, Thunder Bay, ON, P7B 3A6
(807) 625-5665
Emp Here 20
SIC 4111 Local and suburban transit

D-U-N-S 24-915-7942   (BR)
CANCER CARE ONTARIO
NORTHWESTERN ONTARIO REGIONAL CANCER CENTRE
980 Oliver Rd, Thunder Bay, ON, P7B 6V4
(807) 343-1610
Emp Here 150
SIC 8731 Commercial physical research

D-U-N-S 20-945-2288   (BR)
CANCER CARE ONTARIO
NORTHWESTERN ONTARIO BREAST SCREENING PROGRAM

984 Oliver Rd Suite 401, Thunder Bay, ON, P7B 7C7
(807) 684-7777
Emp Here 25
SIC 8069 Specialty hospitals, except psychiatric

D-U-N-S 24-420-1450   (BR)
CAPSERVCO LIMITED PARTNERSHIP
(*Suby of* CapServCo Limited Partnership)
979 Alloy Dr Suite 300, Thunder Bay, ON, P7B 5Z8
(807) 345-6571
Emp Here 60
SIC 8721 Accounting, auditing, and bookkeeping

D-U-N-S 20-867-2365   (BR)
CARA OPERATIONS LIMITED
MONTANA'S COOKHOUSE
(*Suby of* Cara Holdings Limited)
615 Sibley Dr, Thunder Bay, ON, P7B 6Z8
(807) 622-1000
Emp Here 30
SIC 5812 Eating places

D-U-N-S 20-303-3006   (BR)
CARA OPERATIONS LIMITED
KELSEY'S
(*Suby of* Cara Holdings Limited)
805 Memorial Ave, Thunder Bay, ON, P7B 3Z7
(807) 345-0400
Emp Here 65
SIC 5812 Eating places

D-U-N-S 20-948-7958   (BR)
CARGILL LIMITED
140 Darrel Ave, Thunder Bay, ON, P7B 6T8
(807) 623-6724
Emp Here 50
SIC 4221 Farm product warehousing and storage

D-U-N-S 25-614-9246   (BR)
COMCARE (CANADA) LIMITED
REVERA - RETIREMENT LIVING
(*Suby of* Comcare (Canada) Limited)
91 Cumberland St S Suite 200, Thunder Bay, ON, P7B 6A7
(807) 346-0633
Emp Here 20
SIC 8051 Skilled nursing care facilities

D-U-N-S 20-545-2092   (BR)
CONTINENTAL NEWSPAPERS (CANADA) LTD
CHRONICLE JOURNAL, THE
75 Cumberland St S, Thunder Bay, ON, P7B 1A3
(807) 343-6200
Emp Here 20
SIC 2711 Newspapers

D-U-N-S 25-612-7184   (BR)
CORPORATION OF THE CITY OF THUNDER BAY, THE
TBAY TEL MOBILITY
1046 Lithium Dr, Thunder Bay, ON, P7B 6G3
(807) 623-4400
Emp Here 400
SIC 4899 Communication services, nec

D-U-N-S 24-818-9698   (HQ)
CROOKS, J R HEALTH CARE SERVICES INC
SHOPPERS HOME HEALTH CARE
285 Memorial Ave, Thunder Bay, ON, P7B 6H4
(807) 345-6564
Emp Here 48   *Emp Total* 70
Sales 7,623,009
SIC 5999 Miscellaneous retail stores, nec
Pr Pr Jim Crooks
Suzanne Crooks

D-U-N-S 24-235-2987   (BR)
ERB TRANSPORT LIMITED
ERB TRANSPORT LIMITED

580 Eighth Ave, Thunder Bay, ON, P7B 6B2
(807) 344-2323
Emp Here 30
SIC 4213 Trucking, except local

D-U-N-S 24-818-8740   (BR)
EMCO CORPORATION
WESTERN SUPPLIES
933 Tungsten St, Thunder Bay, ON, P7B 5Z3
(807) 345-6543
Emp Here 22
SIC 5074 Plumbing and heating equipment and supplies (hydronics)

D-U-N-S 25-301-5010   (BR)
FABRICLAND DISTRIBUTORS INC
FABRICLAND
1186 Memorial Ave, Thunder Bay, ON, P7B 5K5
(807) 622-4111
Emp Here 20
SIC 5949 Sewing, needlework, and piece goods

D-U-N-S 24-017-1673   (BR)
GAP (CANADA) INC
GAP OUTLET
(*Suby of* The Gap Inc)
339 Main St, Thunder Bay, ON, P7B 5L6
(807) 344-6344
Emp Here 20
SIC 5651 Family clothing stores

D-U-N-S 20-106-9783   (BR)
GAP (CANADA) INC
(*Suby of* The Gap Inc)
1000 Fort William Rd, Thunder Bay, ON, P7B 6B9
(807) 624-0500
Emp Here 20
SIC 5651 Family clothing stores

D-U-N-S 25-318-9740   (BR)
GREYHOUND CANADA TRANSPORTATION ULC
GREYHOUND CANADA
815 Fort William Rd, Thunder Bay, ON, P7B 3A4
(807) 345-2194
Emp Here 35
SIC 4173 Bus terminal and service facilities

D-U-N-S 20-042-1779   (SL)
HOCKENHULL LAND & CATTLE CO. LTD
PROSPECTOR STEAKHOUSE
27 Cumberland St S, Thunder Bay, ON, P7B 2T3
(807) 345-5833
Emp Here 60   *Sales* 1,824,018
SIC 5812 Eating places

D-U-N-S 20-142-5709   (SL)
HOITO RESTAURANT LTD
314 Bay St, Thunder Bay, ON, P7B 1S1
(807) 345-6323
Emp Here 65   *Sales* 1,969,939
SIC 5812 Eating places

D-U-N-S 20-556-0688   (BR)
HOME DEPOT OF CANADA INC
HOME DEPOT
(*Suby of* The Home Depot Inc)
359 Main St, Thunder Bay, ON, P7B 5L6
(807) 624-1100
Emp Here 175
SIC 5251 Hardware stores

D-U-N-S 24-631-0221   (HQ)
HOOD LOGGING EQUIPMENT CANADA INCORPORATED
(*Suby of* Hood Logging Equipment Canada Incorporated)
Gd Stn Csc, Thunder Bay, ON, P7B 5E6
(807) 939-2641
Emp Here 35   *Emp Total* 38
Sales 6,931,267
SIC 5082 Construction and mining machinery
Pr Pr Bruce Hynnes

Beverley Hynnes

D-U-N-S 25-315-7861   (BR)
INVESTORS GROUP FINANCIAL SERVICES INC
1113 Jade Crt Suite 100, Thunder Bay, ON, P7B 6M7
(807) 345-6363
Emp Here 65
SIC 8741 Management services

D-U-N-S 20-834-7419   (HQ)
IRON RANGE SCHOOL BUS LINES INC
IRON RANGE
1141 Golf Links Rd, Thunder Bay, ON, P7B 7A3
(807) 345-7387
Emp Here 98   *Emp Total* 250
Sales 9,611,756
SIC 4151 School buses
Pr Jason Logozzo
VP VP Joseph Logozzo

D-U-N-S 20-775-2101   (BR)
KAL TIRE LTD
590 Central Ave, Thunder Bay, ON, P7B 6B2
(807) 345-0600
Emp Here 30
SIC 5531 Auto and home supply stores

D-U-N-S 24-427-0658   (BR)
KEG RESTAURANTS LTD
KEG STEAKHOUSE & BAR, THE
735 Hewitson St, Thunder Bay, ON, P7B 6B5
(807) 623-1960
Emp Here 100
SIC 5812 Eating places

D-U-N-S 20-009-7850   (BR)
KONTZAMANIS GRAUMANN SMITH MACMILLAN INC
KGS GROUP
1001 William St Suite 301a, Thunder Bay, ON, P7B 6M1
(807) 623-2195
Emp Here 40
SIC 8711 Engineering services

D-U-N-S 25-238-1991   (BR)
LAKEHEAD DISTRICT SCHOOL BOARD
ALGONQUIN AVENUE ELEMENTARY SCHOOL
160 Algonquin Ave S, Thunder Bay, ON, P7B 4T1
(807) 767-3881
Emp Here 25
SIC 8211 Elementary and secondary schools

D-U-N-S 25-238-2064   (BR)
LAKEHEAD DISTRICT SCHOOL BOARD
OLIVER ROAD ELEMENTARY SCHOOL
500 Oliver Rd, Thunder Bay, ON, P7B 2H1
(807) 345-8503
Emp Here 23
SIC 8211 Elementary and secondary schools

D-U-N-S 25-238-1520   (BR)
LAKEHEAD DISTRICT SCHOOL BOARD
FOREST PARK PUBLIC SCHOOL
270 Windsor St, Thunder Bay, ON, P7B 1V6
(807) 767-1696
Emp Here 43
SIC 8211 Elementary and secondary schools

D-U-N-S 20-591-7383   (BR)
LAKEHEAD DISTRICT SCHOOL BOARD
ECOLE GRON MORGAN PUBLIC SCHOOL
174 Marlborough St, Thunder Bay, ON, P7B 4G4
(807) 345-1468
Emp Here 85
SIC 8211 Elementary and secondary schools

D-U-N-S 25-238-1231   (BR)
LAKEHEAD DISTRICT SCHOOL BOARD
HAMMARSKJOLD HIGH SCHOOL
80 Clarkson St S, Thunder Bay, ON, P7B 4W8
(807) 767-1631
Emp Here 155

SIC 8211 Elementary and secondary schools

D-U-N-S 24-852-6881   (HQ)
LAKEHEAD FREIGHTWAYS INC
774 Field St, Thunder Bay, ON, P7B 3W3
(807) 345-6501
Emp Here 40   *Emp Total* 100
Sales 14,081,415
SIC 4213 Trucking, except local
Pr Pr Doug Smith

D-U-N-S 20-073-7927   (BR)
LAKEHEAD UNIVERSITY
955 Oliver Rd Suite 2008, Thunder Bay, ON, P7B 5E1
(807) 343-8110
Emp Here 2,000
SIC 8221 Colleges and universities

D-U-N-S 25-834-9547   (SL)
LAKEHEAD UNIVERSITY STUDENT UNION
OUTPOST, THE
955 Oliver Rd, Thunder Bay, ON, P7B 5E1
(807) 343-8551
Emp Here 80   *Sales* 2,407,703
SIC 5812 Eating places

D-U-N-S 24-391-2453   (SL)
LANDMARK INN LEASING CORPORATION
1010 Dawson Rd, Thunder Bay, ON, P7B 5J4
(807) 767-1681
Emp Here 70   *Sales* 3,064,349
SIC 7011 Hotels and motels

D-U-N-S 25-317-7612   (BR)
LIQUOR CONTROL BOARD OF ONTARIO, THE
L.C.B.O. #501
1010 Dawson Rd, Thunder Bay, ON, P7B 5J4
(807) 767-8882
Emp Here 20
SIC 5921 Liquor stores

D-U-N-S 25-270-1503   (BR)
LOBLAWS INC
REAL CANADIAN SUPERSTORE 1504
600 Harbour Expy, Thunder Bay, ON, P7B 6P4
(807) 343-4500
Emp Here 300
SIC 5411 Grocery stores

D-U-N-S 25-413-2780   (BR)
LOBLAWS INC
REAL CANADIAN WHOLESALE CLUB
319 Fort William Rd, Thunder Bay, ON, P7B 2Z2
(807) 346-4669
Emp Here 37
SIC 5141 Groceries, general line

D-U-N-S 20-142-6772   (HQ)
LOWERYS, LIMITED
LOWERYS BASICS
540 Central Ave, Thunder Bay, ON, P7B 6B4
(807) 344-6666
Emp Here 38   *Emp Total* 65
Sales 5,545,013
SIC 5943 Stationery stores
Pr Pr Brian L Christie
Dir Kim Christie
Dir Andrew Christie
Dir Shawn Christie

D-U-N-S 25-236-6828   (BR)
MARK'S WORK WEARHOUSE LTD
MARK'S WORK WEARHOUSE #66
969 Fort William Rd Unit 1, Thunder Bay, ON, P7B 3A6
(807) 344-1634
Emp Here 20
SIC 5651 Family clothing stores

D-U-N-S 25-630-2688   (BR)
MCDONALD'S RESTAURANTS OF CANADA LIMITED
MCDONALD S
(*Suby of* McDonald's Corporation)
853 Red River Rd, Thunder Bay, ON, P7B 1K3

(807) 767-7551
Emp Here 50
SIC 5812 Eating places

D-U-N-S 20-142-7218　(HQ)
MCKEVITT TRUCKING LIMITED
1200 Carrick St, Thunder Bay, ON, P7B 5P9
(807) 623-0054
Emp Here 140　*Emp Total* 2
Sales 20,793,800
SIC 4213 Trucking, except local
Pr Pr John Mckevitt Sr
　Shirley Mckevitt

D-U-N-S 24-203-1149　(SL)
METALS CREEK RESOURCES CORP
1100 Memorial Ave Suite 329, Thunder Bay, ON, P7B 4A3
(807) 345-4990
Emp Here 50　*Sales* 5,465,508
SIC 1081 Metal mining services
Pr Pr Alexander Sandy Stares
VP Michael Macisaac
　Nikolaos Tsimidis
Dir Wayne Reid
Dir Michael Stares
Dir Richard Nemis
Dir Malvin Spooner
Dir Pat Mohan

D-U-N-S 24-779-5771　(BR)
OLD NAVY (CANADA) INC
(*Suby of* The Gap Inc)
389 Main St, Thunder Bay, ON, P7B 5L6
(807) 622-8800
Emp Here 35
SIC 5651 Family clothing stores

D-U-N-S 20-245-7318　(BR)
ONTARIO LOTTERY AND GAMING CORPO-RATION
THUNDER BAY CHARITY CASINO
50 Cumberland St S, Thunder Bay, ON, P7B 5L4
(807) 683-1935
Emp Here 460
SIC 7999 Amusement and recreation, nec

D-U-N-S 20-059-0805　(BR)
ONTARIO POWER GENERATION INC
O P G
167 Burwood Rd, Thunder Bay, ON, P7B 6C2
(807) 346-3900
Emp Here 25
SIC 4911 Electric services

D-U-N-S 20-938-9753　(BR)
ONTARIO POWER GENERATION INC
OPG
108 Ave, Thunder Bay, ON, P7B 6T7
(807) 625-6400
Emp Here 145
SIC 4911 Electric services

D-U-N-S 24-467-6268　(BR)
PERTH SERVICES LTD
PERTH'S
(*Suby of* Perth Services Ltd)
339 Memorial Ave, Thunder Bay, ON, P7B 3Y4
(807) 345-2295
Emp Here 30
SIC 7216 Drycleaning plants, except rugs

D-U-N-S 25-353-2535　(SL)
PIONEER RIDGE HOME FOR THE AGED
750 Tungsten St, Thunder Bay, ON, P7B 6R1
(807) 684-3910
Emp Here 80　*Sales* 2,918,428
SIC 8361 Residential care

D-U-N-S 20-965-7845　(BR)
PUROLATOR INC.
PUROLATOR INC
140 Main St, Thunder Bay, ON, P7B 6S4
(807) 623-4058
Emp Here 45
SIC 7389 Business services, nec

D-U-N-S 24-337-2161　(BR)
R.A.S. FOOD SERVICES INC
PIZZA HUT
(*Suby of* R.A.S. Food Services Inc)
807 Red River Rd, Thunder Bay, ON, P7B 1K3
(807) 767-5360
Emp Here 25
SIC 5812 Eating places

D-U-N-S 25-810-2656　(BR)
RBC DOMINION SECURITIES INC
(*Suby of* Royal Bank Of Canada)
1001 William St Suite 300, Thunder Bay, ON, P7B 6M1
(807) 343-2042
Emp Here 22
SIC 6211 Security brokers and dealers

D-U-N-S 24-376-4086　(SL)
RED METAL RESOURCES LTD
195 Park Ave, Thunder Bay, ON, P7B 1B9
(807) 345-7384
Emp Here 50　*Sales* 471
SIC 1081 Metal mining services

D-U-N-S 20-292-3723　(BR)
SAINT ELIZABETH HEALTH CARE
920 Tungsten St Suite 103, Thunder Bay, ON, P7B 5Z6
(807) 344-2002
Emp Here 25
SIC 8082 Home health care services

D-U-N-S 20-918-9054　(BR)
SEARS CANADA INC
880 Fort William Rd, Thunder Bay, ON, P7B 2S4
(807) 622-6811
Emp Here 200
SIC 5999 Miscellaneous retail stores, nec

D-U-N-S 24-375-1732　(SL)
SOHI HOLDINGS INC
TACO TIME
679 Memorial Ave, Thunder Bay, ON, P7B 3Z6
(807) 345-4096
Emp Here 60　*Sales* 1,824,018
SIC 5812 Eating places

D-U-N-S 20-860-3063　(BR)
SOURCE (BELL) ELECTRONICS INC, THE
SOURCE, THE
1020 Dawson Rd, Thunder Bay, ON, P7B 1K6

Emp Here 25
SIC 5999 Miscellaneous retail stores, nec

D-U-N-S 20-860-3071　(BR)
SOURCE (BELL) ELECTRONICS INC, THE
SOURCE, THE
1000 Fort William Rd Suite 32a, Thunder Bay, ON, P7B 6B9
(807) 622-8530
Emp Here 25
SIC 5999 Miscellaneous retail stores, nec

D-U-N-S 25-213-7179　(BR)
STAPLES CANADA INC
STAPLES THE BUSINESS DEPOT
(*Suby of* Staples, Inc.)
767 Memorial Ave Suite 37, Thunder Bay, ON, P7B 3Z7
(807) 343-2506
Emp Here 45
SIC 5943 Stationery stores

D-U-N-S 25-244-2637　(BR)
STUART OLSON CONSTRUCTION LTD
INDUSTRIAL CONSTRUCTORS DIVISION
946 Cobalt Cres Unit 1, Thunder Bay, ON, P7B 5W3
(807) 768-9753
Emp Here 20
SIC 1522 Residential construction, nec

D-U-N-S 20-832-8997　(HQ)
SUPERIOR SAFETY INC
782 Macdonell St, Thunder Bay, ON, P7B 4A6

(807) 344-3473
Emp Here 36　*Emp Total* 1
Sales 8,755,284
SIC 5099 Durable goods, nec
Pr Pr Douglas Coppin
　Susan Coppin

D-U-N-S 25-613-8538　(SL)
THUNDER APPLE NORTH INC
APPLEBEE'S NEIGHBOURHOOD GRILL & BAR
1155 Alloy Dr, Thunder Bay, ON, P7B 6M8
(807) 346-5994
Emp Here 70　*Sales* 2,115,860
SIC 5812 Eating places

D-U-N-S 25-265-0304　(BR)
THUNDER BAY CATHOLIC DISTRICT SCHOOL BOARD
ST PIUS X SCHOOL
(*Suby of* Thunder Bay Catholic District School Board)
140 Clarkson St S, Thunder Bay, ON, P7B 4W8
(807) 767-3061
Emp Here 20
SIC 8211 Elementary and secondary schools

D-U-N-S 20-710-3594　(BR)
THUNDER BAY CATHOLIC DISTRICT SCHOOL BOARD
ST JOHN SCHOOL
(*Suby of* Thunder Bay Catholic District School Board)
380 Ray Blvd, Thunder Bay, ON, P7B 4E6
(807) 344-7691
Emp Here 22
SIC 8211 Elementary and secondary schools

D-U-N-S 20-710-3552　(BR)
THUNDER BAY CATHOLIC DISTRICT SCHOOL BOARD
CORPUS CHRISTI SCHOOL
(*Suby of* Thunder Bay Catholic District School Board)
110 Marlborough St, Thunder Bay, ON, P7B 4G4
(807) 345-9782
Emp Here 50
SIC 8211 Elementary and secondary schools

D-U-N-S 20-644-3967　(BR)
TORONTO-DOMINION BANK, THE
TD CANADA TRUST
(*Suby of* Toronto-Dominion Bank, The)
231 Red River Rd, Thunder Bay, ON, P7B 1A7
(807) 346-3175
Emp Here 20
SIC 6021 National commercial banks

D-U-N-S 25-171-6176　(BR)
TORONTO-DOMINION BANK, THE
TD BANK
(*Suby of* Toronto-Dominion Bank, The)
1039 Memorial Ave, Thunder Bay, ON, P7B 4A4
(807) 626-1565
Emp Here 35
SIC 6021 National commercial banks

D-U-N-S 20-286-5262　(BR)
UNION GAS LIMITED
1211 Amber Dr, Thunder Bay, ON, P7B 6M4
(705) 232-4250
Emp Here 100
SIC 4923 Gas transmission and distribution

D-U-N-S 25-332-6763　(BR)
VALMET LTEE
400 Memorial Ave, Thunder Bay, ON, P7B 3Y5
(807) 346-7100
Emp Here 32
SIC 8742 Management consulting services

D-U-N-S 20-966-0864　(BR)
VALUE VILLAGE STORES, INC
(*Suby of* Savers, Inc.)
915 Memorial Ave, Thunder Bay, ON, P7B 4A1

(807) 345-3232
Emp Here 40
SIC 5399 Miscellaneous general merchandise

D-U-N-S 24-367-4152　(BR)
VECTOR CONSTRUCTION LTD
(*Suby of* Vector Management Ltd)
359 Burbidge St, Thunder Bay, ON, P7B 5R3
(807) 346-4405
Emp Here 50
SIC 1541 Industrial buildings and warehouses

D-U-N-S 24-851-3371　(BR)
WSP CANADA INC
GENIVAR
1269 Premier Way, Thunder Bay, ON, P7B 0A3
(807) 625-6700
Emp Here 140
SIC 8711 Engineering services

D-U-N-S 25-294-8617　(BR)
WAL-MART CANADA CORP
777 Memorial Ave, Thunder Bay, ON, P7B 6S2
(807) 346-9441
Emp Here 400
SIC 5311 Department stores

D-U-N-S 25-618-9127　(BR)
WENDY'S RESTAURANTS OF CANADA INC
WENDY'S
(*Suby of* The Wendy's Company)
950 Memorial Ave, Thunder Bay, ON, P7B 4A2
(807) 343-0406
Emp Here 60
SIC 5812 Eating places

D-U-N-S 24-312-4349　(BR)
WINNERS MERCHANTS INTERNATIONAL L.P.
HOMESENSE
(*Suby of* The TJX Companies Inc)
1000 Fort William Rd, Thunder Bay, ON, P7B 6B9
(807) 622-8866
Emp Here 30
SIC 5651 Family clothing stores

D-U-N-S 20-106-3737　(BR)
WINNERS MERCHANTS INTERNATIONAL L.P.
WINNERS
(*Suby of* The TJX Companies Inc)
777 Memorial Ave, Thunder Bay, ON, P7B 6S2
(807) 346-6886
Emp Here 50
SIC 5651 Family clothing stores

Thunder Bay, ON P7C
Thunder Bay County

D-U-N-S 24-035-1957　(SL)
1333482 ONTARIO LIMITED
DIAMOND /LACEY TAXI
113 Leith St, Thunder Bay, ON, P7C 1M7
(807) 623-4968
Emp Here 70　*Sales* 2,115,860
SIC 4121 Taxicabs

D-U-N-S 24-913-6797　(BR)
BOMBARDIER TRANSPORTATION CANADA INC
BOMBARIDER TRANSPORT
1001 Montreal St, Thunder Bay, ON, P7C 4V6
(807) 475-2810
Emp Here 650
SIC 3743 Railroad equipment

D-U-N-S 25-097-2718　(BR)
CANADIAN PACIFIC RAILWAY COMPANY
CPR
500 Mcnaughton St, Thunder Bay, ON, P7C 5Z3
(807) 625-5679
Emp Here 80

▲ Public Company　■ Public Company Family Member　**HQ** Headquarters　**BR** Branch　**SL** Single Location

SIC 4011 Railroads, line-haul operating

D-U-N-S 25-612-5592   (BR)
CANADIAN UNION OF POSTAL WORKERS
CUPW
212 Miles St E Suite 102, Thunder Bay, ON,
P7C 1J6
(807) 624-9131
Emp Here 250
SIC 8631 Labor organizations

D-U-N-S 25-614-1896   (BR)
CORPORATION OF THE CITY OF THUN-DER BAY, THE
SIR WINSTON CHURCHILL POOL
130 Churchill Dr W, Thunder Bay, ON, P7C
1V5
(807) 577-2538
Emp Here 36
SIC 7999 Amusement and recreation, nec

D-U-N-S 24-819-9580   (HQ)
COURTESY FREIGHT SYSTEMS LTD
340 Simpson St, Thunder Bay, ON, P7C 3H7
(807) 623-3278
Emp Here 30   *Emp Total* 5,515
Sales 6,420,542
SIC 4231 Trucking terminal facilities
  Ron Speziale

D-U-N-S 25-611-7730   (BR)
DHL EXPRESS (CANADA) LTD
645 Norah Cres, Thunder Bay, ON, P7C 5H9

Emp Here 20
SIC 7389 Business services, nec

D-U-N-S 24-496-3013   (SL)
GEORGE JEFFREY CHILDREN'S CENTRE
507 Lillie St N, Thunder Bay, ON, P7C 4Y8
(807) 623-4381
Emp Here 60   *Sales* 1,824,018
SIC 8351 Child day care services

D-U-N-S 25-612-8984   (BR)
HUSKY OIL OPERATIONS LIMITED
SANTORELLI'S TRUCK STOP
3131 Arthur St W, Thunder Bay, ON, P7C 4B1
(807) 939-2619
Emp Here 30
SIC 5541 Gasoline service stations

D-U-N-S 25-026-6293   (BR)
LAKEHEAD DISTRICT SCHOOL BOARD
SIR WINSTON CHURCHILL C. & V.I.
130 Churchill Dr W, Thunder Bay, ON, P7C
1V5
(807) 473-8100
Emp Here 100
SIC 8211 Elementary and secondary schools

D-U-N-S 25-137-3312   (BR)
LAKEHEAD DISTRICT SCHOOL BOARD
AGNEW   JOHNSTONE   ELEMENTARY SCHOOL
145 Churchill Dr W, Thunder Bay, ON, P7C
1V6
(807) 577-6448
Emp Here 55
SIC 8211 Elementary and secondary schools

D-U-N-S 25-137-3338   (BR)
LAKEHEAD DISTRICT SCHOOL BOARD
EDGEWATER PARK SCHOOL
511 Victoria Ave W, Thunder Bay, ON, P7C
1H2
(807) 577-7551
Emp Here 30
SIC 8211 Elementary and secondary schools

D-U-N-S 25-238-0886   (BR)
LAKEHEAD DISTRICT SCHOOL BOARD
OGDEN COMMUNITY SCHOOL
600 Mckenzie St, Thunder Bay, ON, P7C 4Z3
(807) 622-9513
Emp Here 24
SIC 8211 Elementary and secondary schools

D-U-N-S 25-912-9831   (BR)

LAKEHEAD DISTRICT SCHOOL BOARD
MCKELLAR PARK CENTRAL SCHOOL
301 Archibald St N, Thunder Bay, ON, P7C
3Y3
(807) 623-2289
Emp Here 25

D-U-N-S 25-912-9856   (BR)
LAKEHEAD DISTRICT SCHOOL BOARD
SHERBROOKE PUBLIC SCHOOL
110 Sherbrooke St, Thunder Bay, ON, P7C
4R6
(807) 625-6793
Emp Here 24
SIC 8211 Elementary and secondary schools

D-U-N-S 24-915-3508   (SL)
PEROGY - POLISH HALL
818 Spring St, Thunder Bay, ON, P7C 3L6
(807) 623-8613
Emp Here 49   *Sales* 5,982,777
SIC 8699 Membership organizations, nec
Dir Jan Slis

D-U-N-S 25-612-6285   (BR)
ROYAL BANK OF CANADA
RBC ROYAL BANK
(*Suby of* Royal Bank Of Canada)
504 Edward St N, Thunder Bay, ON, P7C 4P9
(807) 473-1700
Emp Here 20
SIC 6021 National commercial banks

D-U-N-S 24-242-1761   (BR)
SAFETY NET SECURITY LTD
857 May St N, Thunder Bay, ON, P7C 3S2
(807) 623-1844
Emp Here 100
SIC 5065 Electronic parts and equipment, nec

D-U-N-S 25-332-7308   (BR)
SYSCO CANADA, INC
SYSCO THUNDER BAY
(*Suby of* Sysco Corporation)
840 Mckellar St N, Thunder Bay, ON, P7C 4A8
(807) 623-2331
Emp Here 50
SIC 5141 Groceries, general line

D-U-N-S 24-819-0217   (HQ)
THUNDER BAY CATHOLIC DISTRICT SCHOOL BOARD
(*Suby of* Thunder Bay Catholic District School
Board)
459 Victoria Ave W, Thunder Bay, ON, P7C
0A4
(807) 625-1555
Emp Here 67   *Emp Total* 1,000
Sales 97,241,305
SIC 8211 Elementary and secondary schools
  John De Faveri
Svc Mgr Tom Mustapic
Fin Mgr David Fulton
  Bob Hupka
  Tony Romeo
  Eleanor Ashe
  Doug Demeo
  Phil Colosimo
  Kathy O'brien
  Philip Pelletier

D-U-N-S 25-265-0387   (BR)
THUNDER BAY CATHOLIC DISTRICT SCHOOL BOARD
ST VINCENT ELEMENTARY SCHOOL
(*Suby of* Thunder Bay Catholic District School
Board)
150 Redwood Ave W, Thunder Bay, ON, P7C
1Z6
(807) 577-3823
Emp Here 20
SIC 8211 Elementary and secondary schools

D-U-N-S 25-265-0544   (BR)
THUNDER BAY CATHOLIC DISTRICT SCHOOL BOARD
ST JUDE ELEMENTARY SCHOOL

(*Suby of* Thunder Bay Catholic District School
Board)
345 Ogden St, Thunder Bay, ON, P7C 2N4
(807) 623-5989
Emp Here 25
SIC 8211 Elementary and secondary schools

D-U-N-S 20-591-4125   (BR)
THUNDER BAY CATHOLIC DISTRICT SCHOOL BOARD
ST FRANCIS
(*Suby of* Thunder Bay Catholic District School
Board)
600 Redwood Ave W, Thunder Bay, ON, P7C
5G1
(807) 577-8565
Emp Here 25
SIC 8211 Elementary and secondary schools

D-U-N-S 20-835-1296   (SL)
THUNDER BAY TERMINALS LTD
Gd, Thunder Bay, ON, P7C 5J7
(807) 625-7800
Emp Here 25   *Sales* 4,504,505
SIC 4491 Marine cargo handling

Thunder Bay, ON P7E
Thunder Bay County

D-U-N-S 24-426-7944   (BR)
BEARSKIN LAKE AIR SERVICE LP
BEARSKIN AIRLINES
216 Round Blvd Suite 2, Thunder Bay, ON,
P7E 3N9
(807) 475-0006
Emp Here 160
SIC 4512 Air transportation, scheduled

D-U-N-S 24-826-3381   (HQ)
BEARSKIN LAKE AIR SERVICE LP
BEARSKIN AIRLINES
1475 Walsh St W, Thunder Bay, ON, P7E 4X6
(807) 577-1141
Emp Here 100   *Emp Total* 3,951
Sales 40,540,547
SIC 4512 Air transportation, scheduled
Pr Brad Martin

D-U-N-S 25-017-0032   (BR)
CANADIAN IMPERIAL BANK OF COM-MERCE
CIBC
127 Arthur St W, Thunder Bay, ON, P7E 5P7
(807) 474-3600
Emp Here 20
SIC 6021 National commercial banks

D-U-N-S 24-233-5685   (BR)
CANADIAN PACIFIC RAILWAY COMPANY
CPR
440 Syndicate Ave S, Thunder Bay, ON, P7E
1E5
(807) 625-5601
Emp Here 350
SIC 4011 Railroads, line-haul operating

D-U-N-S 24-172-1810   (HQ)
CLARA INDUSTRIAL SERVICES LIMITED
(*Suby of* Clara Industrial Services Limited)
1130 Commerce St, Thunder Bay, ON, P7E
6E9
(807) 475-4608
Emp Here 30   *Emp Total* 70
Sales 4,523,563
SIC 1721 Painting and paper hanging

D-U-N-S 24-851-9142   (BR)
COCA-COLA REFRESHMENTS CANADA COMPANY
(*Suby of* The Coca-Cola Company)
615 Beaverhall Pl, Thunder Bay, ON, P7E 3N1
(807) 577-6406
Emp Here 20
SIC 5149 Groceries and related products, nec

D-U-N-S 24-717-9807   (BR)
COMPAGNIE DE TELEPHONE BELL DU CANADA OU BELL CANADA, LA
229 Vickers St S, Thunder Bay, ON, P7E 7J9
(807) 625-1981
Emp Here 200
SIC 4813 Telephone communication, except
radio

D-U-N-S 20-797-8516   (BR)
COMPAGNIE DE TELEPHONE BELL DU CANADA OU BELL CANADA, LA
605 Beaverhall Pl, Thunder Bay, ON, P7E 3N1

Emp Here 20
SIC 4813 Telephone communication, except
radio

D-U-N-S 24-236-8454   (SL)
COUNTRY GOOD MEATS & DELI-CATESSEN LTD
MEAT STORE, THE
310 Mountdale Ave, Thunder Bay, ON, P7E
6G8

Emp Here 40   *Sales* 5,325,440
SIC 5421 Meat and fish markets
Pr Pr Aaro Nuutinen
  Sandra Nuutinen

D-U-N-S 25-297-5750   (BR)
FEDERAL EXPRESS CANADA CORPORA-TION
FEDERAL EXPRESS CANADA LTD
(*Suby of* Fedex Corporation)
305 Hector Dougall Way, Thunder Bay, ON,
P7E 6M5
(800) 463-3339
Emp Here 50
SIC 7389 Business services, nec

D-U-N-S 24-691-1762   (BR)
FORT GARRY INDUSTRIES LTD
FGI
915 Walsh St W, Thunder Bay, ON, P7E 4X5
(807) 577-5724
Emp Here 22
SIC 5013 Motor vehicle supplies and new
parts

D-U-N-S 24-497-8292   (BR)
GENERAL SCRAP PARTNERSHIP
LAKEHEAD SCRAP METAL
305 106th St, Thunder Bay, ON, P7E 0A3
(807) 623-4559
Emp Here 28
SIC 5093 Scrap and waste materials

D-U-N-S 20-694-9526   (SL)
GRID LINK CORP
1499 Rosslyn Rd, Thunder Bay, ON, P7E 6W1
(807) 683-0350
Emp Here 70   *Sales* 6,128,699
SIC 1731 Electrical work
Pr Pr Jody Bernst
  Neal Stubbs

D-U-N-S 20-179-6542   (BR)
HYDRO ONE REMOTE COMMUNITIES INC
680 Beaverhall Pl, Thunder Bay, ON, P7E 6G9
(807) 474-2837
Emp Here 41
SIC 4911 Electric services

D-U-N-S 25-305-2849   (BR)
INNVEST PROPERTIES CORP
COMFORT INN
(*Suby of* Innvest Properties Corp)
660 Arthur St W Suite 307, Thunder Bay, ON,
P7E 5R8
(807) 475-3155
Emp Here 25
SIC 7011 Hotels and motels

D-U-N-S 20-835-3292   (SL)
ITALIAN SOCIETY PRINCIPE DI PIEMONTE
DAVINCI CENTRE
340 Waterloo St S, Thunder Bay, ON, P7E

6H9
(807) 623-2415
Emp Here 60   Sales 1,824,018
SIC 5812 Eating places

D-U-N-S 20-710-3545   (BR)
LAKEHEAD DISTRICT SCHOOL BOARD
HIGH PARK SCHOOL
2040 Walsh St E, Thunder Bay, ON, P7E 4W2
(807) 623-1541
Emp Here 27
SIC 8211 Elementary and secondary schools

D-U-N-S 25-238-1454   (BR)
LAKEHEAD DISTRICT SCHOOL BOARD
HEATH PARK ELEMENTARY SCHOOL
1115 Yonge St, Thunder Bay, ON, P7E 2T6
(807) 625-5268
Emp Here 35
SIC 8211 Elementary and secondary schools

D-U-N-S 25-238-1082   (BR)
LAKEHEAD DISTRICT SCHOOL BOARD
FORT WILLIAM COLLEGIATE INSTITUT
512 Marks St S, Thunder Bay, ON, P7E 1M7

Emp Here 55
SIC 8211 Elementary and secondary schools

D-U-N-S 20-710-3537   (BR)
LAKEHEAD DISTRICT SCHOOL BOARD
WEST GATE COLLEGIATE VOCATIONAL IN-STITUTE
707 James St S, Thunder Bay, ON, P7E 2V9
(807) 577-4251
Emp Here 50
SIC 8211 Elementary and secondary schools

D-U-N-S 20-710-3529   (BR)
LAKEHEAD DISTRICT SCHOOL BOARD
WESTMOUNT PUBLIC SCHOOL
120 Begin St W, Thunder Bay, ON, P7E 5M4
(807) 623-7715
Emp Here 50
SIC 8211 Elementary and secondary schools

D-U-N-S 20-321-8045   (BR)
MAC'S CONVENIENCE STORES INC
MAC'S CONVENIENCE STORE
1315 Arthur St E, Thunder Bay, ON, P7E 5N3
(807) 623-9419
Emp Here 35
SIC 5411 Grocery stores

D-U-N-S 25-614-9212   (BR)
MCDONALD'S RESTAURANTS OF CANADA LIMITED
MCDONALD'S
(Suby of McDonald's Corporation)
201 Arthur St W, Thunder Bay, ON, P7E 5P7
(807) 577-8718
Emp Here 60
SIC 5812 Eating places

D-U-N-S 24-333-1597   (BR)
METRO ONTARIO INC
505 Arthur St W, Thunder Bay, ON, P7E 5R5
(807) 475-0276
Emp Here 250
SIC 5411 Grocery stores

D-U-N-S 24-333-1605   (BR)
METRO ONTARIO INC
METRO (SUPERMARKETS)
1101 Arthur St W, Thunder Bay, ON, P7E 5S2
(807) 577-3910
Emp Here 100
SIC 5411 Grocery stores

D-U-N-S 20-281-5460   (SL)
MOVATI ATHLETIC (THUNDER BAY) INC.
1185 Arthur St W, Thunder Bay, ON, P7E 6E2
(807) 623-6223
Emp Here 75   Sales 3,551,629
SIC 7991 Physical fitness facilities

D-U-N-S 20-529-6291   (BR)
NAV CANADA

343 Hector Dougall W, Thunder Bay, ON, P7E 6M5
(807) 474-4247
Emp Here 20
SIC 4899 Communication services, nec

D-U-N-S 24-174-9626   (BR)
NORTHERN CREDIT UNION LIMITED
111 Frederica St W, Thunder Bay, ON, P7E 3V8
(807) 475-5817
Emp Here 20
SIC 6062 State credit unions

D-U-N-S 25-119-7299   (BR)
NORTRAX CANADA INC
(Suby of Deere & Company)
1450 Walsh St W, Thunder Bay, ON, P7E 6H6
(807) 474-2530
Emp Here 30
SIC 5084 Industrial machinery and equipment

D-U-N-S 24-208-9899   (BR)
PF RESOLU CANADA INC
RESOLUTE FORCE PRODUCT
2001 Neebing Ave, Thunder Bay, ON, P7E 6S3
(807) 475-2400
Emp Here 1,000
SIC 2621 Paper mills

D-U-N-S 20-278-9988   (BR)
PFI FUELS INC
1250 Rosslyn Rd, Thunder Bay, ON, P7E 6V9
(807) 475-7667
Emp Here 20
SIC 5172 Petroleum products, nec

D-U-N-S 24-337-2179   (BR)
R.A.S. FOOD SERVICES INC
PIZZA HUT
(Suby of R.A.S. Food Services Inc)
635 Arthur St W, Thunder Bay, ON, P7E 5R6
(807) 475-7516
Emp Here 20
SIC 5812 Eating places

D-U-N-S 24-352-1429   (BR)
REVERA LONG TERM CARE INC
PINEWOOD COURT
2625 Walsh St E Suite 1127, Thunder Bay, ON, P7E 2E5
(807) 577-1127
Emp Here 95
SIC 8361 Residential care

D-U-N-S 20-913-8317   (BR)
RIO TINTO EXPLORATION CANADA INC
KENNECOTT CANADA EXPLORATION INC
(Suby of RIO TINTO PLC)
1300 Walsh St W, Thunder Bay, ON, P7E 4X4
(807) 473-5558
Emp Here 25
SIC 1081 Metal mining services

D-U-N-S 25-612-6293   (BR)
ROYAL BANK OF CANADA
RBC
(Suby of Royal Bank Of Canada)
201 Frederica St W, Thunder Bay, ON, P7E 3W1

Emp Here 24
SIC 6021 National commercial banks

D-U-N-S 20-064-3067   (BR)
THUNDER BAY CATHOLIC DISTRICT SCHOOL BOARD
ST THOMAS AQUINAS SCHOOL
(Suby of Thunder Bay Catholic District School Board)
2645 Donald St E, Thunder Bay, ON, P7E 5X5
(807) 577-1835
Emp Here 30
SIC 8211 Elementary and secondary schools

D-U-N-S 25-265-0585   (BR)
THUNDER BAY CATHOLIC DISTRICT

SCHOOL BOARD
ST ANN ELEMENTARY SCHOOL
(Suby of Thunder Bay Catholic District School Board)
1130 Georgina Ave, Thunder Bay, ON, P7E 3J1
(807) 577-7211
Emp Here 25
SIC 8211 Elementary and secondary schools

D-U-N-S 25-224-8653   (BR)
THUNDER BAY CATHOLIC DISTRICT SCHOOL BOARD
POPE JOHN PAUL II SENIOR ELEMENTARY SCHOOL
(Suby of Thunder Bay Catholic District School Board)
205 Franklin St S, Thunder Bay, ON, P7E 1R2
(807) 623-2324
Emp Here 60
SIC 8211 Elementary and secondary schools

D-U-N-S 25-224-9230   (BR)
THUNDER BAY CATHOLIC DISTRICT SCHOOL BOARD
ST PATRICK HIGH SCHOOL
(Suby of Thunder Bay Catholic District School Board)
621 Selkirk St S, Thunder Bay, ON, P7E 1T9
(807) 623-5218
Emp Here 150
SIC 8211 Elementary and secondary schools

D-U-N-S 25-237-7502   (BR)
THUNDER BAY PUBLIC LIBRARY BOARD
BRODIE RESOURCE BRANCH LIBRARY
(Suby of Thunder Bay Public Library Board)
216 Brodie St S, Thunder Bay, ON, P7E 1C2
(807) 345-8275
Emp Here 30
SIC 8231 Libraries

D-U-N-S 20-944-6202   (HQ)
THUNDER BAY TRUCK CENTRE INC
PETERBILT
(Suby of Thunder Bay Truck Centre Holdings Inc)
1145 Commerce St, Thunder Bay, ON, P7E 6E8
(807) 577-5793
Emp Here 28   Emp Total 36
Sales 21,673,567
SIC 5012 Automobiles and other motor vehicles
VP VP Carolyn Igo
Pr Pr Theodore Kaemingh

D-U-N-S 25-360-3299   (BR)
TOROMONT INDUSTRIES LTD
TOROMONT CAT
620 Beaverhall Pl, Thunder Bay, ON, P7E 6G9
(807) 475-7535
Emp Here 60
SIC 5082 Construction and mining machinery

D-U-N-S 20-778-4559   (BR)
UNIFOR
CAW LOCAL 1075
112 Gore St W, Thunder Bay, ON, P7E 3V9
(807) 475-2829
Emp Here 36
SIC 8631 Labor organizations

D-U-N-S 20-861-2593   (BR)
WESTJET AIRLINES LTD
100 Princess St Suite 160, Thunder Bay, ON, P7E 6S2
(807) 473-1825
Emp Here 20
SIC 4512 Air transportation, scheduled

Thunder Bay, ON P7G
Thunder Bay County

D-U-N-S 20-176-2106   (SL)

GRANITE ELECTRICAL LTD
GRANITE SYSTEMS
430 Wardrope Ave, Thunder Bay, ON, P7G 2C9
(807) 346-0996
Emp Here 50   Sales 4,377,642
SIC 1731 Electrical work

D-U-N-S 20-710-3461   (BR)
LAKEHEAD DISTRICT SCHOOL BOARD
FIVE MILES SCHOOL
2025 Dawson Rd, Thunder Bay, ON, P7G 2E9
(807) 767-1411
Emp Here 50
SIC 8211 Elementary and secondary schools

D-U-N-S 24-676-3218   (BR)
LAKEHEAD DISTRICT SCHOOL BOARD
WOODCREST PUBLIC SCHOOL
867 Woodcrest Rd, Thunder Bay, ON, P7G 0A3
(807) 346-9396
Emp Here 25
SIC 8211 Elementary and secondary schools

D-U-N-S 20-646-4294   (BR)
PIONEER CONSTRUCTION INC
1344 Oliver Rd, Thunder Bay, ON, P7G 1K4
(807) 345-2338
Emp Here 100
SIC 1611 Highway and street construction

Thunder Bay, ON P7J
Thunder Bay County

D-U-N-S 20-758-6645   (SL)
GOOSE CREEK INVESTMENTS LIMITED
NEEBING ROADHOUSE, THE
2121 Highway 61, Thunder Bay, ON, P7J 1G4
(807) 623-3544
Emp Here 55   Sales 1,678,096
SIC 5812 Eating places

D-U-N-S 25-137-3320   (BR)
LAKEHEAD DISTRICT SCHOOL BOARD
VALLEY CENTRAL ELEMENTARY SCHOOL
563 Candy Mountain Dr, Thunder Bay, ON, P7J 0B8
(807) 473-5810
Emp Here 23
SIC 8211 Elementary and secondary schools

D-U-N-S 24-348-7118   (BR)
PF RESOLU CANADA INC
156 Darrel Ave, Thunder Bay, ON, P7J 1L7
(807) 624-9400
Emp Here 216
SIC 2421 Sawmills and planing mills, general

Thunder Bay, ON P7K
Thunder Bay County

D-U-N-S 24-378-6691   (BR)
CN WORLDWIDE AMERIQUE DU NORD (CANADA) INC
1825 Broadway Ave, Thunder Bay, ON, P7K 1M8
(807) 475-6775
Emp Here 50
SIC 4011 Railroads, line-haul operating

D-U-N-S 24-426-6763   (BR)
COMPAGNIE DES CHEMINS DE FER NATIONAUX DU CANADA
C N
1825 Broadway Ave, Thunder Bay, ON, P7K 1M8

Emp Here 85
SIC 4011 Railroads, line-haul operating

D-U-N-S 25-265-1633   (BR)

THUNDER BAY CATHOLIC DISTRICT SCHOOL BOARD
HOLY FAMILY ELEMENTARY SCHOOL
(*Suby of* Thunder Bay Catholic District School Board)
2075 Rosslyn Rd, Thunder Bay, ON, P7K 1H7
(807) 473-4900
Emp Here 21
SIC 8211 Elementary and secondary schools

Tilbury, ON N0P

D-U-N-S 24-120-1230   (BR)
A.P. PLASMAN INC.
A.P. PLASMAN TILBURY
24 Industrial Park Rd, Tilbury, ON, N0P 2L0
(519) 682-1155
Emp Here 120
SIC 7532 Top and body repair and paint shops

D-U-N-S 24-017-1517   (BR)
ADESA AUCTIONS CANADA CORPORATION
18800 County Road 42 Rr 5, Tilbury, ON, N0P 2L0
(519) 682-9500
Emp Here 20
SIC 5012 Automobiles and other motor vehicles

D-U-N-S 25-647-3047   (SL)
ACCESS FIRE
28 Mill Street W, Tilbury, ON, N0P 2L0

Emp Here 49   *Sales* 5,559,741
SIC 1711 Plumbing, heating, air-conditioning

D-U-N-S 20-113-1120   (BR)
ANCHOR DANLY INC
95 Lyon Ave N, Tilbury, ON, N0P 2L0
(519) 682-0470
Emp Here 60
SIC 3499 Fabricated Metal products, nec

D-U-N-S 25-534-3741   (HQ)
AUTOLIV CANADA INC
(*Suby of* Autoliv, Inc.)
20 Autoliv Dr, Tilbury, ON, N0P 2L0
(519) 682-1083
Emp Here 491   *Emp Total* 61,500
Sales 26,411,773
SIC 2394 Canvas and related products
Pr Jan Carlson
   Lars Westerberg

D-U-N-S 20-940-0030   (BR)
AUTOLIV CANADA INC
(*Suby of* Autoliv, Inc.)
351 Queen St N, Tilbury, ON, N0P 2L0
(519) 682-9501
Emp Here 640
SIC 3089 Plastics products, nec

D-U-N-S 25-249-3473   (BR)
CONSEIL SCOLAIRE DE DISTRICT DES ECOLES CATHOLIQUES DU SUD-OUEST
ST FRANCIS ELEMENTARY SCHOOL
11 St Clair St, Tilbury, ON, N0P 2L0
(519) 682-3243
Emp Here 21
SIC 8211 Elementary and secondary schools

D-U-N-S 24-032-8216   (BR)
DIVERSICARE CANADA MANAGEMENT SERVICES CO., INC
TILBURY MANOR NURSING HOME
16 Fort St, Tilbury, ON, N0P 2L0
(519) 682-0243
Emp Here 84
SIC 8059 Nursing and personal care, nec

D-U-N-S 20-026-1480   (BR)
DIVERSICARE CANADA MANAGEMENT SERVICES CO., INC
HUDSON MANOR RETIREMENT RESI-

DENCE
36 Lawson St Rr 3, Tilbury, ON, N0P 2L0
(519) 682-3366
Emp Here 32
SIC 8361 Residential care

D-U-N-S 20-718-6891   (BR)
FLEETWOOD METAL INDUSTRIES INC
22 Industrial Park Rd, Tilbury, ON, N0P 2L0
(519) 682-2220
Emp Here 150
SIC 3469 Metal stampings, nec

D-U-N-S 24-651-6074   (HQ)
KS CENTOCO LTD
(*Suby of* KS Centoco Ltd)
26 Industrial Pk Rd, Tilbury, ON, N0P 2L0

Emp Here 175   *Emp Total* 250
Sales 56,570,240
SIC 3089 Plastics products, nec
Pr Anthony P Toldo

D-U-N-S 25-215-4724   (SL)
LALLY FORD SALES
78 Mill St W, Tilbury, ON, N0P 2L0
(519) 969-3673
Emp Here 25   *Sales* 9,120,088
SIC 5511 New and used car dealers
Pr Vince Lally

D-U-N-S 20-024-9360   (BR)
LAMBTON KENT DISTRICT SCHOOL BOARD
TILBURY DISTRICT HIGH SCHOOL
97 Queen St S, Tilbury, ON, N0P 2L0
(519) 682-0751
Emp Here 45
SIC 8211 Elementary and secondary schools

D-U-N-S 20-005-0446   (BR)
LAMBTON KENT DISTRICT SCHOOL BOARD
TILBURY AREA PUBLIC SCHOOL
5 Mable St, Tilbury, ON, N0P 2L0
(519) 682-2260
Emp Here 40
SIC 8211 Elementary and secondary schools

D-U-N-S 24-310-6015   (BR)
MAHLE FILTER SYSTEMS CANADA ULC
18 Industrial Park Rd, Tilbury, ON, N0P 2L0
(519) 682-0444
Emp Here 50
SIC 3089 Plastics products, nec

D-U-N-S 24-188-3672   (BR)
ST. CLAIR CATHOLIC DISTRICT SCHOOL BOARD
ST JOSEPH CATHOLIC SCHOOL
43 St Clair, Tilbury, ON, N0P 2L0
(519) 682-2790
Emp Here 34
SIC 8211 Elementary and secondary schools

D-U-N-S 24-388-2367   (BR)
WINDSOR MACHINE & STAMPING LTD
WINDSOR MACHINE & STAMPING (2009) LTD
14 Industrial Park Rd, Tilbury, ON, N0P 2L0

Emp Here 95
SIC 3499 Fabricated Metal products, nec

D-U-N-S 25-406-9784   (BR)
WOODBRIDGE FOAM CORPORATION
ENERFLEX DIV.
189 Queen St N, Tilbury, ON, N0P 2L0

Emp Here 127
SIC 3086 Plastics foam products

D-U-N-S 24-361-4013   (BR)
WOODBRIDGE FOAM CORPORATION
MOULDED FOAM DIV.
189 Queen St N, Tilbury, ON, N0P 2L0
(519) 682-3080
Emp Here 160

SIC 2851 Paints and allied products

D-U-N-S 20-977-0577   (SL)
WORTHINGTON INDUSTRIES OF CANADA INC
(*Suby of* Worthington Industries, Inc.)
97 Lyon Ave, Tilbury, ON, N0P 2L0
(519) 682-1313
Emp Here 140   *Sales* 72,842,032
SIC 5051 Metals service centers and offices
Genl Mgr Mike Moss

Tillsonburg, ON N4G
Oxford County

D-U-N-S 25-168-6754   (SL)
1295224 ONTARIO LIMITED
KELSEY'S RESTAURANT
258 Broadway St, Tillsonburg, ON, N4G 3R4
(519) 688-7674
Emp Here 70   *Sales* 2,732,754
SIC 5812 Eating places

D-U-N-S 20-532-1953   (HQ)
AUTONEUM CANADA LTD
1451 Bell Mill Sideroad, Tillsonburg, ON, N4G 4H8
(519) 842-6411
Emp Here 40   *Emp Total* 11,423
Sales 16,718,644
SIC 2299 Textile goods, nec
   Richard Derr
   John Lenga
   Scott Cole
   Jeffrey S Miller

D-U-N-S 25-296-6775   (BR)
BANK OF NOVA SCOTIA, THE
SCOTIABANK
199 Broadway St, Tillsonburg, ON, N4G 3P9
(519) 688-6400
Emp Here 25
SIC 6021 National commercial banks

D-U-N-S 20-588-2744   (BR)
BANQUE TORONTO-DOMINION, LA
TD BANK
(*Suby of* Toronto-Dominion Bank, The)
200 Broadway St Suite 205, Tillsonburg, ON, N4G 5A7
(519) 842-8401
Emp Here 20
SIC 6021 National commercial banks

D-U-N-S 20-540-2469   (BR)
CANADA POST CORPORATION
TILLSONBURG STN MAIN PO
54 Brock St W, Tillsonburg, ON, N4G 2A5
(519) 688-1119
Emp Here 35
SIC 4311 U.s. postal service

D-U-N-S 25-303-4987   (BR)
CANADIAN IMPERIAL BANK OF COMMERCE
CIBC
200 Broadway St, Tillsonburg, ON, N4G 5A7
(519) 842-7331
Emp Here 35
SIC 6021 National commercial banks

D-U-N-S 20-575-4588   (BR)
COMPAGNIE D'ASSURANCE SONNET
38 Brock St E, Tillsonburg, ON, N4G 1Z5
(519) 688-3344
Emp Here 28
SIC 6411 Insurance agents, brokers, and service

D-U-N-S 20-778-7289   (BR)
E. & E. MCLAUGHLIN LTD
500 Hwy 3, Tillsonburg, ON, N4G 4G8
(519) 842-3363
Emp Here 20
SIC 1541 Industrial buildings and warehouses

D-U-N-S 20-413-1874   (SL)
EBERHARD HARDWARE MANUFACTURING LIMITED
COMPOSITE PANEL TECHNOLOGY
(*Suby of* The Eastern Company)
1523 Bell Mill Sideroad, Tillsonburg, ON, N4G 0C9
(519) 688-3443
Emp Here 34   *Sales* 3,465,004
SIC 3429 Hardware, nec

D-U-N-S 25-022-4896   (BR)
FANSHAWE COLLEGE OF APPLIED ARTS AND TECHNOLOGY, T
FANSHAWE COLLEGE OF TILLSONBURG
90 Tillson Ave, Tillsonburg, ON, N4G 3A1
(519) 842-9000
Emp Here 20
SIC 8222 Junior colleges

D-U-N-S 20-812-0498   (BR)
FLEETWOOD METAL INDUSTRIES INC
21 Clearview Dr, Tillsonburg, ON, N4G 4H5
(519) 737-1919
Emp Here 280
SIC 3469 Metal stampings, nec

D-U-N-S 20-628-8599   (HQ)
GUARDIAN INDUSTRIES CANADA CORP
(*Suby of* Koch Industries, Inc.)
10 Rouse St, Tillsonburg, ON, N4G 5W8

Emp Here 175   *Emp Total* 70,000
Sales 61,884,500
SIC 3211 Flat glass
Pr Pr James Boudreault
Fin Ex Dave Zanin

D-U-N-S 25-092-2742   (BR)
HOOVER ENTERPRISES INC
81 Lincoln St, Tillsonburg, ON, N4G 5Y4
(519) 842-2890
Emp Here 66
SIC 3441 Fabricated structural Metal

D-U-N-S 25-124-3429   (SL)
INTERNATIONAL BEAMS INC
10 Rouse St, Tillsonburg, ON, N4G 5W8
(519) 842-2700
Emp Here 64   *Sales* 9,615,386
SIC 3272 Concrete products, nec

D-U-N-S 20-536-5505   (BR)
JOHNSON CONTROLS NOVA SCOTIA U.L.C.
(*Suby of* Johnson Controls, Inc.)
100 Townline Rd, Tillsonburg, ON, N4G 2R7
(519) 842-5971
Emp Here 350
SIC 2531 Public building and related furniture

D-U-N-S 20-710-5268   (BR)
LONDON DISTRICT CATHOLIC SCHOOL BOARD
JH O NEIL CATHOLIC SCHOOL
250 Quarter Town Line, Tillsonburg, ON, N4G 4G8
(519) 842-5588
Emp Here 25
SIC 8211 Elementary and secondary schools

D-U-N-S 24-350-9994   (BR)
MAPLEWOOD NURSING HOME LIMITED
73 Bidwell St, Tillsonburg, ON, N4G 3T8
(519) 842-3563
Emp Here 120
SIC 8051 Skilled nursing care facilities

D-U-N-S 24-380-0021   (BR)
MARTINREA INTERNATIONAL INC
MARTINREA TILLSONBURG
301 Tillson Ave Unit 12, Tillsonburg, ON, N4G 5E5
(519) 688-3693
Emp Here 50
SIC 3499 Fabricated Metal products, nec

D-U-N-S 24-677-3407   (BR)

MARWOOD METAL FABRICATION LIMITED
(*Suby of* 1058347 Ontario Limited)
101 Townline Rd, Tillsonburg, ON, N4G 5Y2
(519) 688-1144
Emp Here 40
SIC 3714 Motor vehicle parts and accessories

D-U-N-S 24-685-2862   (BR)
MARWOOD METAL FABRICATION LIMITED
(*Suby of* 1058347 Ontario Limited)
105 Spruce St, Tillsonburg, ON, N4G 5C4
(519) 688-1144
Emp Here 20
SIC 3714 Motor vehicle parts and accessories

D-U-N-S 25-300-0350   (BR)
METRO ONTARIO INC
225 Broadway St, Tillsonburg, ON, N4G 3R2
(519) 842-3625
Emp Here 150
SIC 5411 Grocery stores

D-U-N-S 20-945-2106   (BR)
ROYAL BANK OF CANADA
RBC
(*Suby of* Royal Bank Of Canada)
121 Broadway St, Tillsonburg, ON, N4G 3P7
(519) 842-7321
Emp Here 25
SIC 6021 National commercial banks

D-U-N-S 20-793-0715   (BR)
SOBEYS CAPITAL INCORPORATED
678 Broadway St, Tillsonburg, ON, N4G 3S9
(519) 688-1734
Emp Here 100
SIC 5411 Grocery stores

D-U-N-S 20-793-0889   (BR)
STAPLES CANADA INC
STAPLES THE BUSINESS DEPOT
(*Suby of* Staples, Inc.)
200 Broadway St, Tillsonburg, ON, N4G 5A7
(519) 688-2196
Emp Here 20
SIC 5943 Stationery stores

D-U-N-S 20-358-2838   (BR)
THK RHYTHM AUTOMOTIVE CANADA LIMITED
1417 Bell Mill Side Rd, Tillsonburg, ON, N4G 4G9
(519) 688-4200
Emp Here 200
SIC 3089 Plastics products, nec

D-U-N-S 25-301-3346   (BR)
TSC STORES L.P.
121 Concession St E, Tillsonburg, ON, N4G 4W4
(519) 842-7001
Emp Here 20
SIC 5251 Hardware stores

D-U-N-S 25-237-8369   (BR)
THAMES VALLEY DISTRICT SCHOOL BOARD
ROLPH STREET PUBLIC SCHOOL
83 Rolph St, Tillsonburg, ON, N4G 3Y2
(519) 842-4323
Emp Here 25
SIC 8211 Elementary and secondary schools

D-U-N-S 20-710-5557   (BR)
THAMES VALLEY DISTRICT SCHOOL BOARD
ANANDALE SCHOOL
60 Tillson Ave, Tillsonburg, ON, N4G 3A1
(519) 688-3498
Emp Here 50
SIC 8211 Elementary and secondary schools

D-U-N-S 25-237-8252   (BR)
THAMES VALLEY DISTRICT SCHOOL BOARD
MAPLE LANE PUBLIC SCHOOL
25 Maple Lane, Tillsonburg, ON, N4G 2Y8

(519) 688-0197
Emp Here 30
SIC 8211 Elementary and secondary schools

D-U-N-S 25-249-1469   (BR)
THAMES VALLEY DISTRICT SCHOOL BOARD
GLENDALE HIGH SCHOOL
37 Glendale Dr Suite 16, Tillsonburg, ON, N4G 1J6
(519) 842-4207
Emp Here 80
SIC 8211 Elementary and secondary schools

D-U-N-S 20-554-9590   (BR)
THAMES VALLEY DISTRICT SCHOOL BOARD
SOUTH RIDGE PUBLIC SCHOOL
10 South Ridge Rd, Tillsonburg, ON, N4G 0C1
(519) 842-7319
Emp Here 30
SIC 8211 Elementary and secondary schools

D-U-N-S 20-157-5289   (SL)
TILLSONBURG RECREATION & INDUSTRIAL PRODUCTS ULC
RIPCO
(*Suby of* Worth Investment Group)
111 Townline Rd, Tillsonburg, ON, N4G 5Y2
(519) 842-5941
Emp Here 21   *Sales* 2,334,742
SIC 3499 Fabricated Metal products, nec

D-U-N-S 25-857-9481   (SL)
TILLSONBURG RETIREMENT CENTRE
183 Rolph St Suite 230, Tillsonburg, ON, N4G 3Y9
(519) 688-0347
Emp Here 20   *Sales* 729,607
SIC 8361 Residential care

D-U-N-S 24-872-3843   (BR)
TILLSONBURG AND DISTRICT ASSOCIATION FOR COMMUNITY LIVING
A R C INDUSTRIES
(*Suby of* Tillsonburg and District Association
For Community Living)
126 Concession St E Suite 6, Tillsonburg, ON, N4G 1P7
(519) 842-8406
Emp Here 20
SIC 2448 Wood pallets and skids

D-U-N-S 25-294-8864   (BR)
WAL-MART CANADA CORP
400 Simcoe St, Tillsonburg, ON, N4G 4X1
(519) 842-7770
Emp Here 100
SIC 5311 Department stores

Timmins, ON P4N
Cochrane County

D-U-N-S 24-477-1598   (SL)
510487 ONTARIO LIMITED
CASEY'S RESTAURANT
760 Algonquin Blvd, Timmins, ON, P4N 7E3
(705) 267-6467
Emp Here 65   *Sales* 1,969,939
SIC 5812 Eating places

D-U-N-S 20-014-0346   (BR)
768812 ONTARIO INC
VIANET
363 Algonquin Blvd W, Timmins, ON, P4N 2S3
(705) 269-9996
Emp Here 50
SIC 4899 Communication services, nec

D-U-N-S 24-585-7891   (SL)
ACCESS BETTER LIVING INC
733 Ross Ave E Suite 3, Timmins, ON, P4N 8S8
(705) 268-2240
Emp Here 60   *Sales* 2,188,821
SIC 8361 Residential care

D-U-N-S 25-373-4701   (BR)
AIR CREEBEC INC
(*Suby of* Cree Regional Economic Enterprises
Company (Cree Co) Inc)
Gd Lcd Main, Timmins, ON, P4N 7C4
(705) 264-9521
Emp Here 140
SIC 4512 Air transportation, scheduled

D-U-N-S 24-964-0814   (BR)
ATLIFIC INC
SUPER 8
(*Suby of* 3376290 Canada Inc)
Algonquin Po Box 730 Stn Main, Timmins, ON, P4N 7G2
(705) 268-7171
Emp Here 50
SIC 7011 Hotels and motels

D-U-N-S 25-320-5181   (HQ)
AUBE, J.-P. RESTAURANT SERVICES LTD
MCDONALDS
(*Suby of* Aube, J.-P. Restaurant Services Ltd)
522 Algonquin Blvd E Unit 520, Timmins, ON, P4N 1B7
(705) 264-7323
Emp Here 80   *Emp Total* 100
Sales 2,991,389
SIC 5812 Eating places

D-U-N-S 25-296-8292   (BR)
BANK OF NOVA SCOTIA, THE
SCOTIABANK
1 Pine St S Suite Bank, Timmins, ON, P4N 2J9
(705) 268-8030
Emp Here 36
SIC 6021 National commercial banks

D-U-N-S 20-911-0662   (BR)
BAYSHORE HEALTHCARE LTD.
BAYSHORE HOME HEALTH
119 Pine St S Suite 202, Timmins, ON, P4N 2K3
(705) 268-6088
Emp Here 30
SIC 8082 Home health care services

D-U-N-S 20-188-7432   (BR)
BELL MEDIA INC
CTV NORTHERN ONTARIO
681 Pine St N, Timmins, ON, P4N 7L6
(705) 264-4211
Emp Here 30
SIC 4833 Television broadcasting stations

D-U-N-S 20-519-7952   (SL)
CSH GEORGIAN RESIDENCE INC
CHATEAU GEORGIAN RETIREMENT
455 Cedar St N, Timmins, ON, P4N 8K4
(705) 267-7935
Emp Here 20   *Sales* 729,607
SIC 8361 Residential care

D-U-N-S 25-174-1203   (HQ)
CAISSE POPULAIRE DE TIMMINS LIMITEE, LA
SUCCURSALE D'IROQUOIS FALLS
(*Suby of* Caisse Populaire De Timmins Limitee, La)
45 Mountjoy St N, Timmins, ON, P4N 8H7
(705) 268-9724
Emp Here 22   *Emp Total* 32
Sales 6,229,760
SIC 6062 State credit unions
Genl Mgr Jocelyn St-Pierre
Pr Marcel Gendron
VP Michel Fecteau

D-U-N-S 20-047-5700   (BR)
CANADA POST CORPORATION
140 Second Ave, Timmins, ON, P4N 1E9
(705) 268-2951
Emp Here 60
SIC 4311 U.s. postal service

D-U-N-S 25-017-0461   (BR)
CANADIAN IMPERIAL BANK OF COM-

MERCE
CIBC
236 Third Ave, Timmins, ON, P4N 1E1
(705) 264-4234
Emp Here 37
SIC 6021 National commercial banks

D-U-N-S 20-978-4300   (BR)
CANADIAN RED CROSS SOCIETY, THE
60 Wilson Ave Suite 201, Timmins, ON, P4N 2S7
(705) 267-6085
Emp Here 25
SIC 8621 Professional organizations

D-U-N-S 24-419-6072   (BR)
CANADIAN TIRE CORPORATION, LIMITED
PARTSOURCE
234 Spruce St S Suite 783, Timmins, ON, P4N 2M5
(705) 264-4400
Emp Here 20
SIC 5531 Auto and home supply stores

D-U-N-S 20-965-2668   (HQ)
COCHRANE TEMISKAMING RESOURCE CENTRE
INFANCY AND EARLY CHILDHOOD SERVICES
(*Suby of* Cochrane Temiskaming Resource
Centre)
600 Toke St, Timmins, ON, P4N 6W1
(705) 267-8181
Emp Here 50   *Emp Total* 175
Sales 11,354,240
SIC 8052 Intermediate care facilities
Fin Mgr Clair Dorval
Wade Durling

D-U-N-S 20-099-5848   (BR)
COLLEGE BOREAL D'ARTS APPLIQUES ET DE TECHNOLOGIE
395 Theriault Blvd, Timmins, ON, P4N 0A8
(705) 267-5850
Emp Here 25
SIC 8221 Colleges and universities

D-U-N-S 25-238-9465   (BR)
CONSEIL SCOLAIRE CATHOLIQUE DE DISTRICT DES GRANDES RIVIERES, LE
ECOLE CATHOLIQUE ST DOMINIQUE
855 Park Ave, Timmins, ON, P4N 8G2
(705) 264-7188
Emp Here 40
SIC 8211 Elementary and secondary schools

D-U-N-S 20-555-5357   (BR)
CONSEIL SCOLAIRE CATHOLIQUE DE DISTRICT DES GRANDES RIVIERES, LE
ECOLE ST-CHARLES
120 Kent Ave, Timmins, ON, P4N 7S4

Emp Here 30
SIC 8211 Elementary and secondary schools

D-U-N-S 20-515-7568   (BR)
CONSEIL SCOLAIRE CATHOLIQUE DE DISTRICT DES GRANDES RIVIERES, LE
ECOLE SACRE COEUR
560 Dieppe St, Timmins, ON, P4N 7N4
(705) 264-7004
Emp Here 25
SIC 8211 Elementary and secondary schools

D-U-N-S 20-651-5178   (BR)
CONSEIL SCOLAIRE CATHOLIQUE DE DISTRICT DES GRANDES RIVIERES, LE
CATHOLIC SAINT GERARD
59 Sterling Ave E, Timmins, ON, P4N 1R7
(705) 264-2615
Emp Here 31
SIC 8211 Elementary and secondary schools

D-U-N-S 25-238-9705   (BR)
CONSEIL SCOLAIRE CATHOLIQUE DE DISTRICT DES GRANDES RIVIERES, LE
ECOLE JACQUES-CARTIER
377 Maple St N, Timmins, ON, P4N 6C4

(705) 264-3534
Emp Here 23
SIC 8211 Elementary and secondary schools

D-U-N-S 24-020-3575　　(BR)
DE BEERS CANADA INC
119 Pine St S Suite 310, Timmins, ON, P4N 2K3
(705) 268-0988
Emp Here 20
SIC 1499 Miscellaneous nonMetallic minerals, except fuels

D-U-N-S 20-710-4493　　(BR)
DISTRICT SCHOOL BOARD ONTARIO NORTH EAST
TIMMINS HIGH & VOCATIONAL SCHOOL
451 Theriault Blvd, Timmins, ON, P4N 8B2
(705) 360-1411
Emp Here 50
SIC 8211 Elementary and secondary schools

D-U-N-S 25-238-8988　　(BR)
DISTRICT SCHOOL BOARD ONTARIO NORTH EAST
QUEEN ELIZABETH PUBLIC SCHOOL
383 Birch St N, Timmins, ON, P4N 6E8
(705) 267-1186
Emp Here 25
SIC 8211 Elementary and secondary schools

D-U-N-S 25-225-1541　　(BR)
DISTRICT SCHOOL BOARD ONTARIO NORTH EAST
MILLER, W EARLE PUBLIC SCHOOL
200 Victoria Ave, Timmins, ON, P4N 8G9
(705) 268-5555
Emp Here 30
SIC 8211 Elementary and secondary schools

D-U-N-S 25-238-8947　　(BR)
DISTRICT SCHOOL BOARD ONTARIO NORTH EAST
ROSS BEATTIE SENIOR PUBLIC SCHOOL
300 Pearl Ave, Timmins, ON, P4N 7X5
(705) 264-9438
Emp Here 30
SIC 8211 Elementary and secondary schools

D-U-N-S 20-709-6715　　(BR)
EACOM TIMBER CORPORATION
EACOM TIMBER CORPORATION
823 Birch St, Timmins, ON, P4N 7E3
(705) 267-1000
Emp Here 25
SIC 5031 Lumber, plywood, and millwork

D-U-N-S 24-762-7321　　(BR)
FORMER RESTORATION L.P.
340 Pine St N, Timmins, ON, P4N 6L3
(705) 264-5985
Emp Here 20
SIC 1771 Concrete work

D-U-N-S 24-228-1553　　(BR)
G4S SECURE SOLUTIONS (CANADA) LTD
211 Craig St, Timmins, ON, P4N 4A2
(705) 268-7040
Emp Here 80
SIC 7381 Detective and armored car services

D-U-N-S 20-102-5470　　(BR)
GARDEWINE GROUP INC
1780 Hwy 655, Timmins, ON, P4N 7J5
(705) 264-5336
Emp Here 20
SIC 4731 Freight transportation arrangement

D-U-N-S 24-329-2211　　(BR)
GROUPE RESTAURANTS IMVESCOR INC
MIKES RESTAURANT
355 Algonquin Blvd E, Timmins, ON, P4N 1B5
(705) 264-3000
Emp Here 20
SIC 5812 Eating places

D-U-N-S 20-157-7350　　(BR)
K.F.S. LIMITED
TWEED AND HICKORY

227 Third Ave, Timmins, ON, P4N 1C9

Emp Here 32
SIC 5311 Department stores

D-U-N-S 24-008-1018　　(BR)
LONDON LIFE INSURANCE COMPANY
80 Mountjoy St N Suite A, Timmins, ON, P4N 4V7
(705) 264-2204
Emp Here 29
SIC 6141 Personal credit institutions

D-U-N-S 24-964-3826　　(HQ)
M. A. T. ENTERPRISES INC
WENDY'S
(*Suby of* M. A. T. Enterprises Inc)
54 Waterloo Rd Suite 3, Timmins, ON, P4N 8P3
(705) 267-4150
Emp Here 60　　*Emp Total* 120
Sales 3,648,035
SIC 5812 Eating places

D-U-N-S 24-344-4978　　(BR)
METRO ONTARIO INC
FOOD BASICS
105 Brunette Rd, Timmins, ON, P4N 2R1
(705) 268-9922
Emp Here 51
SIC 5411 Grocery stores

D-U-N-S 25-292-3651　　(BR)
METRO ONTARIO INC
140 Algonquin Blvd W, Timmins, ON, P4N 8M2
(705) 268-5481
Emp Here 70
SIC 5411 Grocery stores

D-U-N-S 24-035-2455　　(BR)
NEAR NORTH DISTRICT SCHOOL BOARD
ECOLE PUBLIQUE LIONEL GAUTHIER
88 Rea St S, Timmins, ON, P4N 3P9
(705) 264-3858
Emp Here 35
SIC 8211 Elementary and secondary schools

D-U-N-S 25-238-9382　　(BR)
NORTHEASTERN CATHOLIC DISTRICT SCHOOL BOARD
ST. PAUL ELEMENTARY SCHOOL
387 Balsam St N, Timmins, ON, P4N 6H5
(705) 264-5620
Emp Here 30
SIC 8211 Elementary and secondary schools

D-U-N-S 25-238-9937　　(BR)
NORTHEASTERN CATHOLIC DISTRICT SCHOOL BOARD
O'GORMAN HIGH SCHOOL
150 George Ave, Timmins, ON, P4N 4M1
(705) 268-4501
Emp Here 50
SIC 8211 Elementary and secondary schools

D-U-N-S 24-576-9521　　(BR)
NORTHEASTERN CATHOLIC DISTRICT SCHOOL BOARD
O'GORMAN INTERMEDIATE
490 Maclean Dr, Timmins, ON, P4N 4W6
(705) 264-6555
Emp Here 26
SIC 8211 Elementary and secondary schools

D-U-N-S 25-238-9580　　(BR)
NORTHEASTERN CATHOLIC DISTRICT SCHOOL BOARD
SACRED HEART ELEMENTARY SCHOOL
401 Cedar St S, Timmins, ON, P4N 2H7
(705) 264-5869
Emp Here 25
SIC 8211 Elementary and secondary schools

D-U-N-S 25-355-4232　　(BR)
NORTHERNTEL LIMITED PARTNERSHIP
850 Birch St S, Timmins, ON, P4N 7J4
(705) 360-8555
Emp Here 50

SIC 4813 Telephone communication, except radio

D-U-N-S 25-248-7178　　(BR)
NORTRAX CANADA INC
(*Suby of* Deere & Company)
101 Hwy W Suite 4087, Timmins, ON, P4N 7X8
(705) 268-7933
Emp Here 25
SIC 5084 Industrial machinery and equipment

D-U-N-S 20-703-1654　　(BR)
ONTARIO NORTHLAND TRANSPORTATION COMMISSION
ONTERA
160 Cedar St S, Timmins, ON, P4N 2G8
(705) 268-2400
Emp Here 25
SIC 4899 Communication services, nec

D-U-N-S 25-320-9993　　(BR)
PUROLATOR INC.
PUROLATOR INC
804 Mountjoy St S, Timmins, ON, P4N 7W7
(888) 744-7123
Emp Here 35
SIC 7389 Business services, nec

D-U-N-S 20-753-8513　　(HQ)
RLP MACHINE & STEEL FABRICATION INC
RLP MACHINE
(*Suby of* RLP Machine & Steel Fabrication Inc)
259 Reliable Lane, Timmins, ON, P4N 7W7
(705) 267-1445
Emp Here 50　　*Emp Total* 200
Sales 38,081,920
SIC 3441 Fabricated structural Metal
Pr Pr Stephen Symes
VP VP Robert Parcey
　Monica Parcey

D-U-N-S 20-081-4791　　(BR)
RELIABLE WINDOW CLEANERS (SUDBURY) LIMITED
RELIABLE CLEANING SERVICES
(*Suby of* Reliable Trivestments Limited)
167 Wilson Ave, Timmins, ON, P4N 2T2
(705) 360-1194
Emp Here 100
SIC 1799 Special trade contractors, nec

D-U-N-S 24-859-2669　　(BR)
ROGERS MEDIA INC
CKGB
(*Suby of* Rogers Communications Inc)
260 Second Ave, Timmins, ON, P4N 8A4
(705) 264-2351
Emp Here 24
SIC 4832 Radio broadcasting stations

D-U-N-S 25-309-9618　　(BR)
ROYAL BANK OF CANADA
RBC
(*Suby of* Royal Bank Of Canada)
38 Pine St N Suite 101, Timmins, ON, P4N 6K6
(705) 267-7171
Emp Here 20
SIC 6021 National commercial banks

D-U-N-S 24-626-3909　　(BR)
SARJEANT COMPANY LIMITED, THE
CUSTOM CONCRETE NORTHERN
2416 655 Hwy, Timmins, ON, P4N 8R9
(705) 264-2264
Emp Here 40
SIC 5211 Lumber and other building materials

D-U-N-S 20-157-9885　　(HQ)
SENATOR HOTELS LIMITED
DAYS INN
(*Suby of* Senator Hotels Limited)
14 Mountjoy St S, Timmins, ON, P4N 1S4
(705) 267-6211
Emp Here 80　　*Emp Total* 110
Sales 4,815,406

SIC 7011 Hotels and motels

D-U-N-S 20-881-3600　　(SL)
SPRUCE NEEDLES INC
SPRUCE NEEDLES GOLF CLUB
2400 Dalton Rd, Timmins, ON, P4N 7C2
(705) 267-1332
Emp Here 65　　*Sales* 2,626,585
SIC 7997 Membership sports and recreation clubs

D-U-N-S 20-273-2330　　(BR)
TEMBEC INC
5310 Hwy 101 W, Timmins, ON, P4N 7J3
(705) 268-1462
Emp Here 200
SIC 2611 Pulp mills

D-U-N-S 20-745-6398　　(BR)
UNION GAS LIMITED
SPECTRA ENERGY COMPANY
615 Moneta Ave, Timmins, ON, P4N 7X4
(705) 268-6141
Emp Here 20
SIC 4924 Natural gas distribution

D-U-N-S 20-787-0119　　(BR)
VICTORIAN ORDER OF NURSES FOR CANADA
VON PORCUPINE DISTRICT
38 Pine St N Suite 139, Timmins, ON, P4N 6K6
(705) 267-8444
Emp Here 45
SIC 8082 Home health care services

Timmins, ON P4P
Cochrane County

D-U-N-S 20-651-8214　　(BR)
CONSEIL SCOLAIRE CATHOLIQUE DE DISTRICT DES GRANDES RIVIERES, LE
ECOLE CATHOLIQUE DON-BOSCO
400 Lonergan Blvd, Timmins, ON, P4P 1C7
(705) 268-5611
Emp Here 25
SIC 8211 Elementary and secondary schools

D-U-N-S 24-324-2596　　(BR)
EXP SERVICES INC
690 River Park Rd Suite 401, Timmins, ON, P4P 1B4
(705) 268-4351
Emp Here 20
SIC 8711 Engineering services

Timmins, ON P4R
Cochrane County

D-U-N-S 20-140-1044　　(SL)
957358 ONTARIO INC
EAST SIDE MARIOS
1120 Riverside Dr, Timmins, ON, P4R 1A2
(705) 268-9555
Emp Here 55　　*Sales* 1,678,096
SIC 5812 Eating places

D-U-N-S 24-330-3232　　(BR)
ALS CANADA LTD
A L S CHEMEX
2090 Riverside Dr Unit 10, Timmins, ON, P4R 0A2
(705) 360-1987
Emp Here 25
SIC 8734 Testing laboratories

D-U-N-S 20-644-3124　　(BR)
AUBE, J.-P. RESTAURANT SERVICES LTD
MCDONALD'S
1870 Riverside Dr, Timmins, ON, P4R 1N7
(705) 267-4411
Emp Here 50

SIC 5812 Eating places

D-U-N-S 24-816-5391   (HQ)
BUCKET SHOP INC, THE
STEELTEC, DIV OF
24 Government Rd S, Timmins, ON, P4R 1N4
(705) 531-2658
Emp Here 45   *Emp Total* 35
Sales 19,407,546
SIC 5085 Industrial supplies
Pr Pr Ross Woodward
VP Paul Woodward

D-U-N-S 20-303-3436   (BR)
CARA OPERATIONS LIMITED
MONTANA'S TIMMINS
(*Suby of* Cara Holdings Limited)
1500 Riverside Dr, Timmins, ON, P4R 1A1
(705) 360-5999
Emp Here 45
SIC 5812 Eating places

D-U-N-S 20-808-5295   (BR)
COCHRANE TEMISKAMING RESOURCE CENTRE
(*Suby of* Cochrane Temiskaming Resource Centre)
141 Philip St, Timmins, ON, P4R 1J5
(705) 268-7333
Emp Here 50
SIC 8361 Residential care

D-U-N-S 25-238-9788   (BR)
CONSEIL SCOLAIRE CATHOLIQUE DE DISTRICT DES GRANDES RIVIERES, LE
ECOLE ANICET-MORIN
1070 Power Ave, Timmins, ON, P4R 1B4
(705) 264-4533
Emp Here 40
SIC 8211 Elementary and secondary schools

D-U-N-S 25-819-5395   (BR)
DAY, WILLIAM CONSTRUCTION LIMITED
125 Kamiskotia Rd, Timmins, ON, P4R 0B3
(705) 268-7250
Emp Here 20
SIC 4212 Local trucking, without storage

D-U-N-S 20-859-8156   (BR)
FGL SPORTS LTD
ATHLETES WORLD
1500 Riverside Dr, Timmins, ON, P4R 1A1
(705) 268-5972
Emp Here 25
SIC 5661 Shoe stores

D-U-N-S 24-196-9336   (BR)
FOUNTAIN TIRE LTD
ROYAL TIRE SERVICE
2090 Riverside Dr Suite 26, Timmins, ON, P4R 0A2
(705) 267-8473
Emp Here 30
SIC 5531 Auto and home supply stores

D-U-N-S 24-361-7300   (BR)
HOME DEPOT OF CANADA INC
HOME DEPOT
(*Suby of* The Home Depot Inc)
2143 Riverside Dr, Timmins, ON, P4R 0A1
(705) 360-8750
Emp Here 100
SIC 5251 Hardware stores

D-U-N-S 25-311-1330   (BR)
SEARS CANADA INC
1500 Riverside Dr, Timmins, ON, P4R 1A1
(705) 268-8788
Emp Here 125
SIC 5311 Department stores

D-U-N-S 20-747-9887   (BR)
STAPLES CANADA INC
STAPLES THE BUSINESS DEPOT
(*Suby of* Staples, Inc.)
1485 Riverside Dr Suite 97, Timmins, ON, P4R 1M8
(705) 360-4200
Emp Here 35

SIC 5943 Stationery stores

D-U-N-S 24-684-7813   (BR)
TOROMONT INDUSTRIES LTD
99 Jaguar Dr, Timmins, ON, P4R 0A9
(705) 268-9900
Emp Here 50
SIC 5082 Construction and mining machinery

D-U-N-S 24-599-1893   (BR)
WAL-MART CANADA CORP
WALMART
1870 Riverside Dr, Timmins, ON, P4R 1N7
(705) 267-6451
Emp Here 50
SIC 5311 Department stores

D-U-N-S 24-312-4281   (BR)
WINNERS MERCHANTS INTERNATIONAL L.P.
WINNERS
(*Suby of* The TJX Companies Inc)
1500 Riverside Dr Suite 1, Timmins, ON, P4R 1A1
(705) 267-6082
Emp Here 30
SIC 5651 Family clothing stores

D-U-N-S 20-806-3243   (BR)
YM INC. (SALES)
STITCHES
1500 Riverside Dr Unit 49, Timmins, ON, P4R 1A1
(705) 264-2770
Emp Here 25
SIC 5621 Women's clothing stores

Tiverton, ON N0G
Bruce County

D-U-N-S 24-346-4596   (BR)
ATOMIC ENERGY OF CANADA LIMITED
AECL
Gd, Tiverton, ON, N0G 2T0

Emp Here 190
SIC 2819 Industrial inorganic chemicals, nec

D-U-N-S 24-847-0288   (BR)
GREENFIELD GLOBAL, INC
COMMERCIAL ALCOHOLS
5 Farrell Dr 4th Conc, Tiverton, ON, N0G 2T0
(519) 368-7723
Emp Here 30
SIC 2869 Industrial organic chemicals, nec

D-U-N-S 20-943-4042   (BR)
MUNICIPALITY OF KINCARDINE, THE
BRUCE TELECOM
3145 Hwy 21 N, Tiverton, ON, N0G 2T0
(519) 368-2000
Emp Here 80
SIC 4813 Telephone communication, except radio

D-U-N-S 20-015-7431   (BR)
ONTARIO POWER GENERATION INC
WESTERN WASTE MANAGEMENT FACILITY
Gd, Tiverton, ON, N0G 2T0
(519) 361-6414
Emp Here 200
SIC 8741 Management services

Tobermory, ON N0H
Bruce County

D-U-N-S 25-060-7603   (BR)
ONTARIO NORTHLAND TRANSPORTATION COMMISSION
8 Eliza St, Tobermory, ON, N0H 2R0
(519) 596-2510
Emp Here 20

SIC 4899 Communication services, nec

Toronto, ON M1B
York County

D-U-N-S 24-118-2182   (BR)
CASCADES CANADA ULC
CASCADES RECOVERY+
45 Thornmount Dr, Toronto, ON, M1B 5P5
(416) 292-5149
Emp Here 35
SIC 4953 Refuse systems

D-U-N-S 20-128-4213   (HQ)
MAC'S CONVENIENCE STORES INC
DEPANNEURS MAC'S, LES
305 Milner Ave Suite 400, Toronto, ON, M1B 0A5
(416) 291-4441
Emp Here 110   *Emp Total* 65,000
Sales 526,776,254
SIC 5411 Grocery stores
Pr Jean Bernier
Sec Sylvain Aubry
Treas Karinne Bouchard
Dir Fin Claude Tessier

D-U-N-S 25-310-9201   (BR)
MCDONALD'S RESTAURANTS OF CANADA LIMITED
MCDONALD'S
(*Suby of* McDonald's Corporation)
31 Tapscott Rd, Toronto, ON, M1B 4Y7
(416) 754-8071
Emp Here 45
SIC 5812 Eating places

D-U-N-S 24-309-0474   (BR)
MUNICIPAL PROPERTY ASSESSMENT CORPORATION
601 Milner Ave Suite 200, Toronto, ON, M1B 6B8
(416) 299-0313
Emp Here 20
SIC 6531 Real estate agents and managers

D-U-N-S 20-860-2826   (BR)
SOURCE (BELL) ELECTRONICS INC, THE
SOURCE, THE
31 Tapscott Rd, Toronto, ON, M1B 4Y7
(416) 754-8419
Emp Here 25
SIC 5999 Miscellaneous retail stores, nec

D-U-N-S 24-172-2359   (BR)
TORONTO CATHOLIC DISTRICT SCHOOL BOARD
ST. BARNABAS CATHOLIC SCHOOL
30 Washburn Way, Toronto, ON, M1B 1H3
(416) 393-5351
Emp Here 40
SIC 8211 Elementary and secondary schools

D-U-N-S 20-698-6791   (BR)
TORONTO CATHOLIC DISTRICT SCHOOL BOARD
ST. DOMINIC SAVIO
50 Tideswell Blvd, Toronto, ON, M1B 5X3
(416) 393-5467
Emp Here 30
SIC 8211 Elementary and secondary schools

D-U-N-S 20-698-6569   (BR)
TORONTO CATHOLIC DISTRICT SCHOOL BOARD
ST. COLUMBA CATHOLIC SCHOOL
10 John Tabor Trail, Toronto, ON, M1B 1M9
(416) 393-5380
Emp Here 35
SIC 8211 Elementary and secondary schools

D-U-N-S 20-698-6510   (BR)
TORONTO CATHOLIC DISTRICT SCHOOL BOARD
ST. BEDE CATHOLIC SCHOOL

521 Sewells Rd, Toronto, ON, M1B 5H3
(416) 393-5425
Emp Here 26
SIC 8211 Elementary and secondary schools

D-U-N-S 20-698-7757   (BR)
TORONTO DISTRICT SCHOOL BOARD
JOHN G DIEFENBAKER PUBLIC SCHOOL
70 Dean Park Rd, Toronto, ON, M1B 2X3
(416) 396-6390
Emp Here 35
SIC 8211 Elementary and secondary schools

D-U-N-S 25-224-8687   (BR)
TORONTO DISTRICT SCHOOL BOARD
ALEXANDER STIRLING PUBLIC SCHOOL
70 Fawcett Trail, Toronto, ON, M1B 3A9
(416) 396-6020
Emp Here 50
SIC 8211 Elementary and secondary schools

D-U-N-S 20-698-7856   (BR)
TORONTO DISTRICT SCHOOL BOARD
TOM LONGBOAT JR PUBLIC SCHOOL
37 Crow Trail, Toronto, ON, M1B 1X6
(416) 396-6610
Emp Here 20
SIC 8211 Elementary and secondary schools

D-U-N-S 20-026-8238   (BR)
TORONTO DISTRICT SCHOOL BOARD
MALVERN JUNIOR PUBLIC SCHOOL
70 Mammoth Hall Trail, Toronto, ON, M1B 1P6
(416) 396-6440
Emp Here 35
SIC 8211 Elementary and secondary schools

D-U-N-S 20-698-7153   (BR)
TORONTO DISTRICT SCHOOL BOARD
GREY OWL JR PS
150 Wickson Trail, Toronto, ON, M1B 1M4
(416) 396-6290
Emp Here 30
SIC 8211 Elementary and secondary schools

D-U-N-S 20-025-2851   (BR)
TORONTO DISTRICT SCHOOL BOARD
HERITAGE PARK PUBLIC SCHOOL
80 Old Finch Ave, Toronto, ON, M1B 5J2
(416) 396-6207
Emp Here 30
SIC 8211 Elementary and secondary schools

D-U-N-S 20-025-0723   (BR)
TORONTO DISTRICT SCHOOL BOARD
LESTER B PEARSON COLLEGIATE INSTITUTE
150 Tapscott Rd, Toronto, ON, M1B 2L2
(416) 396-5892
Emp Here 114
SIC 8211 Elementary and secondary schools

D-U-N-S 20-025-1093   (BR)
TORONTO DISTRICT SCHOOL BOARD
BURROWS HALL JUNIOR PUBLIC SCHOOL
151 Burrows Hall Blvd, Toronto, ON, M1B 1M5
(416) 396-6105
Emp Here 20
SIC 8211 Elementary and secondary schools

D-U-N-S 20-711-3270   (BR)
TORONTO DISTRICT SCHOOL BOARD
SHADD, MARY ELEMENTARY
135 Hupfield Trail, Toronto, ON, M1B 4R6
(416) 396-6450
Emp Here 50
SIC 8211 Elementary and secondary schools

D-U-N-S 20-714-0315   (SL)
TORONTO FREE PRESBYTERIAN CHURCH
WHITEFIELD CHRISTIAN SCHOOLS
5808 Finch Ave E, Toronto, ON, M1B 4Y6
(416) 297-1212
Emp Here 50   *Sales* 3,356,192
SIC 8211 Elementary and secondary schools

D-U-N-S 24-393-6924   (SL)
VIASYSTEMS TORONTO, INC

MEMBER OF TTM TECHNOLOGIES
8150 Sheppard Ave E, Toronto, ON, M1B 5K2
(416) 208-2100
Emp Here 485   *Sales* 63,149,698
SIC 3672 Printed circuit boards
CEO Thomas Edman
VP Fin Wayne Slomsky

Toronto, ON M1C
York County

D-U-N-S 20-026-8345   (BR)
TORONTO CATHOLIC DISTRICT SCHOOL BOARD
CARDINAL LEGER CATHOLIC SCHOOL
600 Morrish Rd, Toronto, ON, M1C 4Y1
(416) 393-5419
Emp Here 45
SIC 8211 Elementary and secondary schools

D-U-N-S 20-081-2316   (BR)
TORONTO DISTRICT SCHOOL BOARD
CENTENNIAL ROAD JUNIOR ELEMENTARY SCHOOL
271 Centennial Rd, Toronto, ON, M1C 2A2
(416) 396-6125
Emp Here 22
SIC 8211 Elementary and secondary schools

D-U-N-S 20-025-2612   (BR)
TORONTO DISTRICT SCHOOL BOARD
JOSEPH HOWE SENIOR PUBLIC SCHOOL
20 Winter Gardens Trail, Toronto, ON, M1C 3E7
(416) 396-6405
Emp Here 35
SIC 8211 Elementary and secondary schools

Toronto, ON M1E
York County

D-U-N-S 20-738-4962   (BR)
MEGLEEN INC
TIM HORTONS
2862 Ellesmere Rd Suite 2, Toronto, ON, M1E 4B8
(416) 282-1499
Emp Here 50
SIC 5812 Eating places

D-U-N-S 24-219-6108   (BR)
RESIDENCES ALLEGRO, S.E.C., LES
CHARTWELL GUILDWOOD RETIREMENT RESIDENCE
(*Suby of* Residences Allegro, S.E.C., Les)
65 Livingston Rd, Toronto, ON, M1E 1L1
(416) 264-4348
Emp Here 45
SIC 6513 Apartment building operators

D-U-N-S 20-711-1514   (BR)
TORONTO CATHOLIC DISTRICT SCHOOL BOARD
ST. URSULA CATHOLIC SCHOOL
215 Livingston Rd, Toronto, ON, M1E 1L8
(416) 393-5306
Emp Here 25
SIC 8211 Elementary and secondary schools

D-U-N-S 20-698-7195   (BR)
TORONTO DISTRICT SCHOOL BOARD
GUILDWOOD JR PUBLIC SCHOOL
225 Livingston Rd, Toronto, ON, M1E 1L8
(416) 396-6295
Emp Here 30
SIC 8211 Elementary and secondary schools

D-U-N-S 20-077-8525   (BR)
TORONTO DISTRICT SCHOOL BOARD
ST MARGARET'S PUBLIC SCHOOL
235 Galloway Rd, Toronto, ON, M1E 1X5

(416) 396-6550
Emp Here 30
SIC 8211 Elementary and secondary schools

D-U-N-S 20-025-2489   (BR)
TORONTO DISTRICT SCHOOL BOARD
SIR WILFRID LAURIER COLLEGIATE INSTITUTE
145 Guildwood Pky, Toronto, ON, M1E 1P5
(416) 396-6820
Emp Here 100
SIC 8211 Elementary and secondary schools

D-U-N-S 20-025-1036   (BR)
TORONTO DISTRICT SCHOOL BOARD
BROOKS ROAD ELEMENTARY SCHOOL
85 Keeler Blvd, Toronto, ON, M1E 4K6
(416) 396-6739
Emp Here 34
SIC 8211 Elementary and secondary schools

D-U-N-S 20-025-1044   (BR)
TORONTO DISTRICT SCHOOL BOARD
HIGHCASTLE PUBLIC SCHOOL
370 Military Trail, Toronto, ON, M1E 4E6
(416) 396-6325
Emp Here 25
SIC 8211 Elementary and secondary schools

Toronto, ON M1G
York County

D-U-N-S 20-657-1239   (BR)
CORPORATION OF THE CITY OF TORONTO
CEDAR RIDGE CREATIVE CENTER
225 Confederation Dr, Toronto, ON, M1G 1B2
(416) 396-4026
Emp Here 30
SIC 8699 Membership organizations, nec

D-U-N-S 20-082-2273   (BR)
TORONTO CATHOLIC DISTRICT SCHOOL BOARD
ST. THOMAS MORE CATHOLIC ELEMENTARY SCHOOL
2300 Ellesmere Rd, Toronto, ON, M1G 3M7
(416) 393-5322
Emp Here 30
SIC 8211 Elementary and secondary schools

D-U-N-S 20-025-0400   (BR)
TORONTO DISTRICT SCHOOL BOARD
HEATHER HEIGHTS JUNIOR PUBLIC SCHOOL
80 Slan Ave, Toronto, ON, M1G 3B5
(416) 396-6305
Emp Here 30
SIC 8211 Elementary and secondary schools

D-U-N-S 20-025-9641   (BR)
TORONTO DISTRICT SCHOOL BOARD
WOBURN JUNIOR PUBLIC SCHOOL
40 Dormington Dr, Toronto, ON, M1G 3N2
(416) 396-6670
Emp Here 42
SIC 8211 Elementary and secondary schools

D-U-N-S 25-226-0302   (BR)
TORONTO DISTRICT SCHOOL BOARD
HENRY HUDSON SENIOR PUBLIC SCHOOL
350 Orton Park Rd, Toronto, ON, M1G 3H4
(416) 396-6310
Emp Here 45
SIC 8211 Elementary and secondary schools

D-U-N-S 20-034-2157   (BR)
TORONTO DISTRICT SCHOOL BOARD
CHURCHILL HEIGHTS ELEMENTARY SCHOOL
749 Brimorton Dr, Toronto, ON, M1G 2S4
(416) 396-6160
Emp Here 39
SIC 8211 Elementary and secondary schools

Toronto, ON M1H
York County

D-U-N-S 24-793-0522   (BR)
HAKIM OPTICAL LABORATORY LIMITED
HAKIM OPTICAL FACTORY OUTLET
3430 Lawrence Ave E, Toronto, ON, M1H 1A9
(416) 439-5351
Emp Here 25
SIC 5995 Optical goods stores

D-U-N-S 20-711-1431   (BR)
TORONTO CATHOLIC DISTRICT SCHOOL BOARD
ST. RICHARD CATHOLIC SCHOOL
960 Bellamy Rd N, Toronto, ON, M1H 1H1
(416) 393-5301
Emp Here 50
SIC 8211 Elementary and secondary schools

D-U-N-S 20-025-0244   (BR)
TORONTO DISTRICT SCHOOL BOARD
BELLMERE JUNIOR ELEMENTARY SCHOOL
470 Brimorton Dr, Toronto, ON, M1H 2E6
(416) 396-6040
Emp Here 44
SIC 8211 Elementary and secondary schools

D-U-N-S 24-369-2543   (BR)
WE CARE HEALTH SERVICES INC
WE CARE HOME HEALTH SERVICES
1200 Markham Rd Suite 220, Toronto, ON, M1H 3C3
(416) 438-4577
Emp Here 50
SIC 8082 Home health care services

Toronto, ON M1J
York County

D-U-N-S 20-025-0293   (BR)
TORONTO DISTRICT SCHOOL BOARD
CEDARBROOK PUBLIC SCHOOL
56 Nelson St, Toronto, ON, M1J 2V6
(416) 396-6115
Emp Here 20
SIC 8211 Elementary and secondary schools

D-U-N-S 20-025-0285   (BR)
TORONTO DISTRICT SCHOOL BOARD
CEDAR DRIVE JUNIOR PUBLIC SCHOOL
21 Gatesview Ave, Toronto, ON, M1J 3G4
(416) 396-6120
Emp Here 80
SIC 8211 Elementary and secondary schools

Toronto, ON M1K
York County

D-U-N-S 20-797-0059   (BR)
CORPORATION OF THE CITY OF TORONTO
NSK
20 Gordonridge Pl, Toronto, ON, M1K 4H5
(416) 392-5698
Emp Here 20
SIC 8351 Child day care services

D-U-N-S 25-682-9102   (BR)
ENBRIDGE GAS DISTRIBUTION INC
Scarborough, Toronto, ON, M1K 5E3
(416) 492-5000
Emp Here 2,000
SIC 4612 Crude petroleum pipelines

D-U-N-S 25-794-1336   (BR)
MOUNT PLEASANT GROUP OF CEMETERIES
PINE HILL CEMETERY

625 Birchmount Rd, Toronto, ON, M1K 1R1
(416) 267-8229
Emp Here 35
SIC 6531 Real estate agents and managers

D-U-N-S 20-711-1365   (BR)
TORONTO CATHOLIC DISTRICT SCHOOL BOARD
ST. MARIA GORETTI CATHOLIC SCHOOL
21 Kenmark Blvd, Toronto, ON, M1K 3N8
(416) 393-5260
Emp Here 70
SIC 8211 Elementary and secondary schools

D-U-N-S 20-025-0426   (BR)
TORONTO DISTRICT SCHOOL BOARD
ROBERT SERVICE SENIOR PUBLIC SCHOOL
945 Danforth Rd, Toronto, ON, M1K 1J2
(416) 396-6540
Emp Here 25
SIC 8211 Elementary and secondary schools

D-U-N-S 20-025-0509   (BR)
TORONTO DISTRICT SCHOOL BOARD
GLEN RAVINE JR PUBLIC SCHOOL
11 Gadsby Dr, Toronto, ON, M1K 4V4
(416) 396-6280
Emp Here 32
SIC 8211 Elementary and secondary schools

D-U-N-S 20-026-0318   (BR)
TORONTO DISTRICT SCHOOL BOARD
WALTER PERRY JR PUBLIC SCHOOL
45 Falmouth Ave, Toronto, ON, M1K 4M7
(416) 396-6620
Emp Here 35
SIC 8211 Elementary and secondary schools

Toronto, ON M1L
York County

D-U-N-S 24-049-9426   (SL)
CANADIAN KAWASAKI MOTORS INC
101 Thermos Rd, Toronto, ON, M1L 4W8
(416) 445-7775
Emp Here 50   *Sales* 23,274,463
SIC 5012 Automobiles and other motor vehicles
Pr Goro Takahashi
VP VP Pat Chambers
Stephen Pike
Dir Shinichi Juri

D-U-N-S 20-657-9612   (BR)
OLD NAVY (CANADA) INC
(*Suby of* The Gap Inc)
6 Lebovic Ave Unit 1, Toronto, ON, M1L 4V9
(416) 757-1481
Emp Here 50
SIC 5651 Family clothing stores

D-U-N-S 20-078-8946   (BR)
TORONTO CATHOLIC DISTRICT SCHOOL BOARD
ST. DUNSTAN ELEMENTARY SCHOOL
14 Pharmacy Ave, Toronto, ON, M1L 3E4
(416) 393-5241
Emp Here 50
SIC 8211 Elementary and secondary schools

D-U-N-S 20-026-2231   (BR)
TORONTO DISTRICT SCHOOL BOARD
DANFORTH GARDENS ELEMENTARY SCHOOL
20 Santamonica Blvd, Toronto, ON, M1L 4H4
(416) 396-6190
Emp Here 30
SIC 8211 Elementary and secondary schools

D-U-N-S 20-025-9633   (BR)
TORONTO DISTRICT SCHOOL BOARD
OAKRIDGE JUNIOR PUBLIC SCHOOL
110 Byng Ave, Toronto, ON, M1L 3P1

(416) 396-6505
Emp Here 24
SIC 8211 Elementary and secondary schools

D-U-N-S 20-081-2241   (BR)
TORONTO DISTRICT SCHOOL BOARD
HEARNE, SAMUEL SENIOR PUBLIC SCHOOL
21 Newport Ave, Toronto, ON, M1L 4N7
(416) 396-6555
Emp Here 30
SIC 8211 Elementary and secondary schools

D-U-N-S 20-698-7781   (BR)
TORONTO DISTRICT SCHOOL BOARD
GENERAL BROCK PS
140 Chestnut Cres, Toronto, ON, M1L 1Y5
(416) 396-6250
Emp Here 40
SIC 8211 Elementary and secondary schools

D-U-N-S 20-106-3695   (BR)
WINNERS MERCHANTS INTERNATIONAL L.P.
WINNERS
(*Suby of* The TJX Companies Inc)
1900 Eglinton Ave E, Toronto, ON, M1L 2L9
(416) 757-6420
Emp Here 45
SIC 5651 Family clothing stores

Toronto, ON M1M
York County

D-U-N-S 20-738-4947   (BR)
MEMORIAL GARDENS CANADA LIMITED
RESTHAVEN MEMORIAL GARDENS
2700 Kingston Rd, Toronto, ON, M1M 1M5
(416) 267-4653
Emp Here 20
SIC 6531 Real estate agents and managers

D-U-N-S 20-711-1050   (BR)
TORONTO CATHOLIC DISTRICT SCHOOL BOARD
ST. AGATHA CATHOLIC SCHOOL
49 Cathedral Bluffs Dr, Toronto, ON, M1M 2T6
(416) 393-5302
Emp Here 20
SIC 8211 Elementary and secondary schools

D-U-N-S 20-698-7542   (BR)
TORONTO DISTRICT SCHOOL BOARD
FAIRMOUNT JR. PUBLIC SCHOOL
31 Sloley Rd, Toronto, ON, M1M 1C7
(416) 396-6240
Emp Here 30
SIC 8211 Elementary and secondary schools

D-U-N-S 20-025-2943   (BR)
TORONTO DISTRICT SCHOOL BOARD
R. H. KING ACADEMY
3800 St Clair Ave E, Toronto, ON, M1M 1V3
(416) 396-5550
Emp Here 100
SIC 8211 Elementary and secondary schools

D-U-N-S 20-025-0236   (BR)
TORONTO DISTRICT SCHOOL BOARD
ANSON PARK PUBLIC SCHOOL
30 Macduff Cres, Toronto, ON, M1M 1X5
(416) 396-6030
Emp Here 20
SIC 8211 Elementary and secondary schools

Toronto, ON M1N
York County

D-U-N-S 20-025-3131   (BR)
TORONTO DISTRICT SCHOOL BOARD
BIRCH CLIFF HEIGHTS PUBLIC SCHOOL
120 Highview Ave, Toronto, ON, M1N 2J1

(416) 396-6065
Emp Here 25
SIC 8211 Elementary and secondary schools

Toronto, ON M1P
York County

D-U-N-S 25-059-2490   (BR)
857780 ONTARIO LIMITED
PREMIER FITNESS CLUB
1399 Kennedy Rd Suite 22, Toronto, ON, M1P 2L6

Emp Here 50
SIC 7991 Physical fitness facilities

D-U-N-S 25-717-8707   (BR)
GOODLIFE FITNESS CENTRES INC
1911 Kennedy Rd, Toronto, ON, M1P 2L9
(416) 297-7279
Emp Here 165
SIC 7991 Physical fitness facilities

D-U-N-S 24-892-6677   (BR)
HIGHLAND FARMS INC
HIGHLAND FARMS SUPERMARKETS
850 Ellesmere Rd, Toronto, ON, M1P 2W5
(416) 298-1999
Emp Here 125
SIC 5411 Grocery stores

D-U-N-S 24-805-5209   (BR)
NUCAP INDUSTRIES INC
115 Ridgetop Rd, Toronto, ON, M1P 4W9
(416) 494-1444
Emp Here 100
SIC 3714 Motor vehicle parts and accessories

D-U-N-S 25-300-5516   (BR)
REDBERRY FRANCHISING CORP
BURGER KING
2571 Lawrence Ave E, Toronto, ON, M1P 4W5
(416) 757-2401
Emp Here 30
SIC 5812 Eating places

D-U-N-S 20-643-1533   (BR)
REDBERRY FRANCHISING CORP
BURGER KING
1607 Birchmount Rd, Toronto, ON, M1P 2J3
(416) 292-8840
Emp Here 29
SIC 5812 Eating places

D-U-N-S 25-292-5227   (BR)
REXALL PHARMACY GROUP LTD
SGH REXALL DRUG STORE 6909
(*Suby of* McKesson Corporation)
3030 Lawrence Ave E Suite 316, Toronto, ON, M1P 2T7
(416) 438-6668
Emp Here 20
SIC 5912 Drug stores and proprietary stores

D-U-N-S 24-170-9000   (BR)
SIR CORP
CANYON CREEK CHOP HOUSE
430 Progress Ave Unit 10, Toronto, ON, M1P 5J1
(416) 296-1400
Emp Here 45
SIC 5812 Eating places

D-U-N-S 24-242-3015   (BR)
TEKNION FURNITURE SYSTEMS CO. LIMITED
ESMOND MANUFACTURING
195 Nantucket Blvd, Toronto, ON, M1P 2P2
(416) 759-3573
Emp Here 100
SIC 5063 Electrical apparatus and equipment

D-U-N-S 20-711-1522   (BR)
TORONTO CATHOLIC DISTRICT SCHOOL BOARD
ST. VICTOR CATHOLIC SCHOOL

20 Bernadine St, Toronto, ON, M1P 4M2
(416) 393-5338
Emp Here 37
SIC 8211 Elementary and secondary schools

D-U-N-S 20-003-9969   (BR)
TORONTO DISTRICT SCHOOL BOARD
DONWOOD PARK JUNIOR PUBLIC SCHOOL
61 Dorcot Ave, Toronto, ON, M1P 3K5
(416) 396-6201
Emp Here 37
SIC 8211 Elementary and secondary schools

D-U-N-S 20-698-7823   (BR)
TORONTO DISTRICT SCHOOL BOARD
GENERAL CRERAR PUBLIC SCHOOL
30 Mcgregor Rd, Toronto, ON, M1P 1C8
(416) 396-6255
Emp Here 29
SIC 8211 Elementary and secondary schools

D-U-N-S 20-025-0376   (BR)
TORONTO DISTRICT SCHOOL BOARD
EDGEWOOD PUBLIC SCHOOL
230 Birkdale Rd, Toronto, ON, M1P 3S4
(416) 396-6215
Emp Here 30
SIC 8211 Elementary and secondary schools

D-U-N-S 24-424-2624   (BR)
TRENCH LIMITED
390 Midwest Rd, Toronto, ON, M1P 3B5
(416) 751-8570
Emp Here 175
SIC 3612 Transformers, except electric

Toronto, ON M1R
York County

D-U-N-S 20-078-8961   (BR)
TORONTO CATHOLIC DISTRICT SCHOOL BOARD
ST. KEVIN CATHOLIC ELEMENTARY SCHOOL
15 Murray Glen Dr, Toronto, ON, M1R 3J6
(416) 393-5300
Emp Here 30
SIC 8211 Elementary and secondary schools

D-U-N-S 20-535-5576   (BR)
TORONTO CATHOLIC DISTRICT SCHOOL BOARD
OUR LADY OF WISDOM CATHOLIC SCHOOL
10 Japonica Rd, Toronto, ON, M1R 4R7
(416) 393-5273
Emp Here 25
SIC 8211 Elementary and secondary schools

D-U-N-S 20-034-2207   (BR)
TORONTO CATHOLIC DISTRICT SCHOOL BOARD
PRECIOUS BLOOD CATHOLIC SCHOOL
1035 Pharmacy Ave, Toronto, ON, M1R 2G8
(416) 393-5258
Emp Here 42
SIC 8211 Elementary and secondary schools

D-U-N-S 20-698-7526   (BR)
TORONTO DISTRICT SCHOOL BOARD
MARYVALE PUBLIC SCHOOL
1325 Pharmacy Ave, Toronto, ON, M1R 2J1
(416) 396-6455
Emp Here 35
SIC 8211 Elementary and secondary schools

D-U-N-S 20-081-3488   (BR)
TORONTO DISTRICT SCHOOL BOARD
MANHATTAN PARK JUNIOR PUBLIC SCHOOL
90 Manhattan Dr, Toronto, ON, M1R 3V8
(416) 396-6445
Emp Here 33
SIC 8211 Elementary and secondary schools

D-U-N-S 20-079-2922   (BR)
TORONTO DISTRICT SCHOOL BOARD
GEORGE PECK PUBLIC SCHOOL
1 Wayne Ave, Toronto, ON, M1R 1Y1
(416) 396-6270
Emp Here 27
SIC 8211 Elementary and secondary schools

D-U-N-S 20-785-7827   (SL)
UHAUL COMPANY OF EASTERN ONTARIO
1555 Warden Ave, Toronto, ON, M1R 2S9
(416) 335-1250
Emp Here 60   *Sales* 4,815,406
SIC 7359 Equipment rental and leasing, nec

Toronto, ON M1S
York County

D-U-N-S 24-079-8350   (SL)
2138894 ONTARIO INC
METRO PROTECTIVE SERVICES
140 Shorting Rd, Toronto, ON, M1S 3S6
(416) 240-0911
Emp Here 151   *Sales* 4,669,485
SIC 7381 Detective and armored car services

D-U-N-S 24-337-2914   (BR)
FGL SPORTS LTD
NATIONAL SPORTS
1455 Mccowan Rd, Toronto, ON, M1S 5K7
(416) 335-7227
Emp Here 20
SIC 5941 Sporting goods and bicycle shops

D-U-N-S 20-552-6796   (BR)
FIRAN TECHNOLOGY GROUP CORPORATION
FTG AEROSPACE
10 Commander Blvd, Toronto, ON, M1S 3T2
(416) 438-6076
Emp Here 60
SIC 3613 Switchgear and switchboard apparatus

D-U-N-S 24-393-5694   (BR)
PHARMA MEDICA RESEARCH INC
4770 Sheppard Ave E Suite 2, Toronto, ON, M1S 3V6
(416) 759-4111
Emp Here 263
SIC 8731 Commercial physical research

D-U-N-S 20-008-0690   (BR)
TD WATERHOUSE CANADA INC
(*Suby of* Toronto-Dominion Bank, The)
60 Wind Pl N, Toronto, ON, M1S 5L5

Emp Here 100
SIC 6211 Security brokers and dealers

D-U-N-S 20-269-3669   (SL)
TIELMAN NORTH AMERICA LTD
180 Middlefield Rd, Toronto, ON, M1S 4M6
(416) 297-9775
Emp Here 34   *Sales* 4,244,630
SIC 3565 Packaging machinery

D-U-N-S 20-711-3296   (BR)
TORONTO DISTRICT SCHOOL BOARD
NORTH AGENCY COURT JUNIOR PUBLIC SCHOOL
60 Moran Rd, Toronto, ON, M1S 2J3
(416) 396-6490
Emp Here 20
SIC 8211 Elementary and secondary schools

D-U-N-S 20-025-3768   (BR)
TORONTO DISTRICT SCHOOL BOARD
HENRY KELSEY SR PUBLIC SCHOOL
1200 Huntingwood Dr, Toronto, ON, M1S 1K7
(416) 396-6315
Emp Here 40
SIC 8211 Elementary and secondary schools

D-U-N-S 20-077-8160   (BR)

TORONTO DISTRICT SCHOOL BOARD
SIR WILLIAM OSLER HIGH SCHOOL
1050 Huntingwood Dr, Toronto, ON, M1S 3H5
(416) 396-6830
Emp Here 102
SIC 8211 Elementary and secondary schools

D-U-N-S 20-711-3148   (BR)
TORONTO DISTRICT SCHOOL BOARD
AGINCOURT COLLEGIATE INSTITUTE
2621 Midland Ave, Toronto, ON, M1S 1R6
(416) 396-6675
Emp Here 120
SIC 8211 Elementary and secondary schools

D-U-N-S 20-698-7997   (BR)
TORONTO DISTRICT SCHOOL BOARD
IROQUOIS JR PUBLIC SCHOOL
265 Chartland Blvd S, Toronto, ON, M1S 2S6
(416) 396-6355
Emp Here 23
SIC 8211 Elementary and secondary schools

Toronto, ON M1T
York County

D-U-N-S 20-711-3361   (BR)
TORONTO DISTRICT SCHOOL BOARD
TAM O'SHANTER JUNIOR PUBLIC SCHOOL
21 King Henrys Blvd, Toronto, ON, M1T 2V3
(416) 396-6585
Emp Here 50
SIC 8211 Elementary and secondary schools

D-U-N-S 20-025-1051   (BR)
TORONTO DISTRICT SCHOOL BOARD
INGLEWOOD HEIGHTS JR PUBLIC SCHOOL
45 Dempster St, Toronto, ON, M1T 2T6
(416) 396-6345
Emp Here 25
SIC 8211 Elementary and secondary schools

Toronto, ON M1V
York County

D-U-N-S 20-771-5751   (SL)
GRAND BACCUS LIMITED
*GRAND BACCUS BANQUET AND CONFER-
ENCE CENTRE*
2155 Mcnicoll Ave, Toronto, ON, M1V 5P1
(416) 299-0077
Emp Here 75   *Sales* 2,480,664
SIC 7299 Miscellaneous personal service

D-U-N-S 24-885-6346   (HQ)
STONEMILL BAKEHOUSE LIMITED, THE
365 Passmore Ave, Toronto, ON, M1V 4B3
(416) 757-0582
Emp Here 75   *Emp Total* 130,913
Sales 14,373,258
SIC 5149 Groceries and related products, nec
Pr Pr Gottfried Boehringer
   Gustav Boehringer

D-U-N-S 20-079-3615   (BR)
**TORONTO CATHOLIC DISTRICT SCHOOL
BOARD**
THE DIVINE INFANT CATHOLIC SCHOOL
30 Ingleton Blvd, Toronto, ON, M1V 3H7
(416) 393-5414
Emp Here 20
SIC 8211 Elementary and secondary schools

D-U-N-S 20-591-1121   (BR)
**TORONTO CATHOLIC DISTRICT SCHOOL
BOARD**
OUR LADY OF GRACE CATHOLIC SCHOOL
121 Brimwood Blvd, Toronto, ON, M1V 1E5
(416) 393-5372
Emp Here 23
SIC 8211 Elementary and secondary schools

D-U-N-S 20-025-2687   (BR)
TORONTO DISTRICT SCHOOL BOARD
AGNES MACPHAIL ELEMENTARY SCHOOL
112 Goldhawk Trail, Toronto, ON, M1V 1W5
(416) 396-6015
Emp Here 24
SIC 8211 Elementary and secondary schools

D-U-N-S 20-081-3579   (BR)
TORONTO DISTRICT SCHOOL BOARD
MILLIKEN PUBLIC SCHOOL
130 Port Royal Trail, Toronto, ON, M1V 2T4
(416) 396-6480
Emp Here 30
SIC 8211 Elementary and secondary schools

D-U-N-S 20-025-1028   (BR)
TORONTO DISTRICT SCHOOL BOARD
*BRIMWOOD BOULEVARD JUNIOR PUBLIC
SCHOOL*
151 Brimwood Blvd, Toronto, ON, M1V 1E5
(416) 396-6085
Emp Here 25

D-U-N-S 25-224-8331   (BR)
TORONTO DISTRICT SCHOOL BOARD
MACKLIN PUBLIC SCHOOL
136 Ingleton Blvd, Toronto, ON, M1V 2Y4
(416) 396-6435
Emp Here 40
SIC 8211 Elementary and secondary schools

D-U-N-S 20-034-2355   (BR)
TORONTO DISTRICT SCHOOL BOARD
PERCY WILLIAMS JR PUBLIC SCHOOL
35 White Heather Blvd, Toronto, ON, M1V 1P6
(416) 396-6515
Emp Here 35
SIC 8211 Elementary and secondary schools

D-U-N-S 24-097-5367   (BR)
WAR AMPUTATIONS OF CANADA, THE
KEY TAG SERVICE
1 Maybrook Dr, Toronto, ON, M1V 5K9
(416) 412-0600
Emp Here 100
SIC 8699 Membership organizations, nec

Toronto, ON M1W
York County

D-U-N-S 20-079-2930   (BR)
TORONTO DISTRICT SCHOOL BOARD
BEVERLY GLEN JUNIOR PUBLIC SCHOOL
85 Beverly Glen Blvd, Toronto, ON, M1W 1W4
(416) 396-6055
Emp Here 35
SIC 8211 Elementary and secondary schools

D-U-N-S 24-248-3530   (BR)
TORONTO DISTRICT SCHOOL BOARD
SIR ERNEST MACMILLAN PUBLIC SCHOOL
149 Huntsmill Blvd, Toronto, ON, M1W 2Y2
(416) 396-6575
Emp Here 20
SIC 8211 Elementary and secondary schools

D-U-N-S 20-711-3197   (BR)
TORONTO DISTRICT SCHOOL BOARD
CHESTER LE JUNOIR PUBLIC SCHOOL
201 Chester Le Blvd, Toronto, ON, M1W 2K7
(416) 396-6145
Emp Here 20
SIC 8211 Elementary and secondary schools

D-U-N-S 20-079-2898   (BR)
TORONTO DISTRICT SCHOOL BOARD
L'AMOREAUX COLLEGIATE INSTITUTE
2501 Bridletowne Cir, Toronto, ON, M1W 2K1
(416) 396-6745
Emp Here 100
SIC 8211 Elementary and secondary schools

D-U-N-S 20-008-1987   (BR)

TORONTO DISTRICT SCHOOL BOARD
FOX, TERRY PUBLIC SCHOOL
185 Wintermute Blvd, Toronto, ON, M1W 3M9
(416) 396-6600
Emp Here 27
SIC 8211 Elementary and secondary schools

D-U-N-S 20-698-7872   (BR)
TORONTO DISTRICT SCHOOL BOARD
J B TYRRELL SENIOR PUBLIC SCHOOL
10 Corinthian Blvd, Toronto, ON, M1W 1B3
(416) 396-6360
Emp Here 70
SIC 8211 Elementary and secondary schools

D-U-N-S 24-247-7375   (BR)
TORONTO DISTRICT SCHOOL BOARD
*SIR SAMUEL B STEELE JR PUBLIC
SCHOOL*
131 Huntsmill Blvd, Toronto, ON, M1W 2Y2
(416) 396-6580
Emp Here 25
SIC 8211 Elementary and secondary schools

D-U-N-S 20-591-5056   (BR)
TORONTO DISTRICT SCHOOL BOARD
TIMBERBANK JUNIOR PUBLIC SCHOOL
170 Timberbank Blvd, Toronto, ON, M1W 2A3
(416) 396-6605
Emp Here 20
SIC 8211 Elementary and secondary schools

Toronto, ON M1X
York County

D-U-N-S 20-903-3935   (SL)
FELLOWES CANADA LTD
1261 Tapscott Rd, Toronto, ON, M1X 1S9
(905) 475-6320
Emp Here 45   *Sales* 7,369,031
SIC 5113 Industrial and personal service pa-
per
Pr Pr James Edmonds
   James E Fellowes

D-U-N-S 25-094-9161   (SL)
MADISON SECURITY
1080 Tapscott Rd Suite 17, Toronto, ON, M1X
1E7
(416) 421-0666
Emp Here 50   *Sales* 1,532,175
SIC 7381 Detective and armored car services

D-U-N-S 20-259-5872   (SL)
NUGALE PHARMACEUTICAL INC
41 Pullman Crt, Toronto, ON, M1X 1E4
(416) 298-7275
Emp Here 50   *Sales* 6,219,371
SIC 2834 Pharmaceutical preparations
Pr Pr Wynn Xie

D-U-N-S 20-599-6023   (BR)
WGI MANUFACTURING INC
WALKER GROUP
3 Pullman Crt, Toronto, ON, M1X 1E4
(416) 412-2966
Emp Here 20
SIC 2899 Chemical preparations, nec

Toronto, ON M2H
York County

D-U-N-S 24-044-4765   (SL)
CARNEGIE, SHAUN
PRIMERICA FINANCIAL SERVICES
716 Gordon Baker Rd, Toronto, ON, M2H 3B4

Emp Here 50   *Sales* 7,435,520
SIC 8742 Management consulting services
Owner Shaun Carnegie

D-U-N-S 20-705-8574   (BR)

**CORPORATION OF THE CITY OF
TORONTO**
3350 Victoria Park Ave, Toronto, ON, M2H 3K5
(416) 392-3023
Emp Here 20
SIC 4212 Local trucking, without storage

D-U-N-S 25-685-3912   (SL)
DAPASOFT INC
111 Gordon Baker Suite 600, Toronto, ON,
M2H 3R1
(416) 847-4080
Emp Here 100   *Sales* 12,403,319
SIC 7371 Custom computer programming ser-
vices
Dir Stephen Chan
   Elaine Chan

D-U-N-S 20-188-1948   (BR)
ITW CANADA INC
*HOBART FOOD EQUIPMENT GROUP
CANADA, DIV OF*
(*Suby of* Illinois Tool Works Inc.)
105 Gordon Baker Rd Suite 801, Toronto, ON,
M2H 3P8
(416) 447-6432
Emp Here 20
SIC 1799 Special trade contractors, nec

D-U-N-S 24-323-5988   (BR)
METROLAND MEDIA GROUP LTD
10 Tempo Ave, Toronto, ON, M2H 2N8
(416) 493-1300
Emp Here 25
SIC 2711 Newspapers

D-U-N-S 20-025-0061   (BR)
TORONTO DISTRICT SCHOOL BOARD
HILLMOUNT ELEMENTARY SCHOOL
245 Mcnicoll Ave, Toronto, ON, M2H 2C6
(416) 395-2550
Emp Here 20
SIC 8211 Elementary and secondary schools

D-U-N-S 20-047-4851   (BR)
TORONTO DISTRICT SCHOOL BOARD
CLIFFWOOD PUBLIC SCHOOL
140 Cliffwood Rd, Toronto, ON, M2H 2E4
(416) 395-2230
Emp Here 28
SIC 8211 Elementary and secondary schools

D-U-N-S 20-711-3114   (BR)
TORONTO DISTRICT SCHOOL BOARD
PINEWAY PUBLIC SCHOOL
110 Pineway Blvd, Toronto, ON, M2H 1A8
(416) 395-2760
Emp Here 30
SIC 8211 Elementary and secondary schools

D-U-N-S 24-805-6991   (HQ)
**XPERA RISK MITIGATION & INVESTIGA-
TION LP**
CKR GLOBAL
155 Gordon Baker Rd Suite 101, Toronto, ON,
M2H 3N5
(416) 449-8677
Emp Here 150   *Emp Total* 550
Sales 81,322,993
SIC 8741 Management services
Pr Robert Burns
Ch Bd Brian D. King
VP Ken M. Cahoon
VP Nino G. Calabrese
VP Royston Colbourne
VP Jason J Dumbreck
VP Matt Henschel
VP Opers Tim Houghton
   Paul Mcparlan

Toronto, ON M2J
York County

D-U-N-S 25-300-3628   (HQ)
A.G. SIMPSON AUTOMOTIVE INC

AGS AUTOMOTIVE SYSTEMS
200 Yorkland Blvd Suite 800, Toronto, ON, M2J 5C1
(416) 438-6650
Emp Here 120   *Emp Total* 1,000
Sales 121,114,762
SIC 3714 Motor vehicle parts and accessories
Pr Joseph Loparco
VP Joseph Leon

D-U-N-S 20-558-9757   (HQ)
AMEX CANADA INC
AMERICAN EXPRESS
(*Suby of* American Express Company)
2225 Sheppard Ave E, Toronto, ON, M2J 5C2
(905) 474-8000
Emp Here 2,000   *Emp Total* 56,400
Sales 912,008,750
SIC 6099 Functions related to deposit banking
Pr Rob Mcclean
  Shawn Klerer
VP Opers Betty Daruwala
  David Barnes

D-U-N-S 24-874-7669   (HQ)
BOYS AND GIRLS CLUBS OF CANADA
(*Suby of* Boys And Girls Clubs Of Canada)
2005 Sheppard Ave E Suite 400, Toronto, ON, M2J 5B4
(905) 477-7272
Emp Here 32   *Emp Total* 8,000
Sales 10,118,519
SIC 8641 Civic and social associations
Dir David Ingram
Dir David Mather
Dir Donald Smith
Dir James Rice
Dir Paul E Brace
Dir Peter Wallace
Dir Peter Webster
Dir Stephen Voisin
Ch Bd Daniel Laprade

D-U-N-S 24-714-7700   (BR)
DIRECT ENERGY MARKETING LIMITED
2225 Sheppard Ave E Suite 5C2, Toronto, ON, M2J 5C2
(416) 758-8700
Emp Here 42
SIC 1711 Plumbing, heating, air-conditioning

D-U-N-S 24-862-0791   (HQ)
DOMINION COLOUR CORPORATION
DCC
(*Suby of* H.I.G. Capital, L.L.C.)
515 Consumers Rd Suite 700, Toronto, ON, M2J 4Z2
(416) 791-4200
Emp Here 25   *Emp Total* 6,181
Sales 58,368,560
SIC 2816 Inorganic pigments
Pr Mark Vincent
  Graham Dickie
  Probyn Forbes
VP Sls Peter Baggen

D-U-N-S 20-780-1163   (BR)
FRUITS & PASSION BOUTIQUES INC
1800 Sheppard Ave E Suite 33, Toronto, ON, M2J 5A7
(416) 491-4622
Emp Here 20
SIC 5122 Drugs, proprietaries, and sundries

D-U-N-S 20-285-0814   (SL)
GENERAL MOTORS FINANCIAL OF CANADA, LTD.
GM FINANCIAL
2001 Sheppard Ave E Suite 600, Toronto, ON, M2J 4Z8
(416) 753-4000
Emp Here 200   *Sales* 141,025,663
SIC 6159 Miscellaneous business credit institutions
Sr VP Howard Cobham
Genl Mgr Jennifer Hardy-Ogle

D-U-N-S 24-284-4835   (BR)
INSURANCE BUREAU OF CANADA

(*Suby of* Insurance Bureau of Canada)
2235 Sheppard Ave E Suite 1100, Toronto, ON, M2J 5B5
(416) 445-5912
Emp Here 170
SIC 6411 Insurance agents, brokers, and service

D-U-N-S 20-300-2340   (BR)
NTT DATA CANADA, INC.
251 Consumers Rd Suite 300, Toronto, ON, M2J 4R3
(416) 572-8533
Emp Here 50
SIC 7379 Computer related services, nec

D-U-N-S 24-171-5767   (SL)
SENIORS HEALTH CENTRE OF NORTH YORK GENERAL HOSPITAL
2 Buchan Crt, Toronto, ON, M2J 5A3
(416) 756-1040
Emp Here 80   *Sales* 3,648,035
SIC 8051 Skilled nursing care facilities

D-U-N-S 20-025-1101   (BR)
TORONTO CATHOLIC DISTRICT SCHOOL BOARD
BLESSED KATERI TEKAKWITHA
70 Margaret Ave, Toronto, ON, M2J 4C5
(416) 393-5393
Emp Here 25
SIC 8211 Elementary and secondary schools

D-U-N-S 20-035-4756   (BR)
TORONTO CATHOLIC DISTRICT SCHOOL BOARD
ST. GERALD CATHOLIC SCHOOL
200 Old Sheppard Ave, Toronto, ON, M2J 3L9
(416) 393-5319
Emp Here 28
SIC 8211 Elementary and secondary schools

D-U-N-S 20-035-4764   (BR)
TORONTO DISTRICT SCHOOL BOARD
ERNEST ELEMENTARY SCHOOL
150 Cherokee Blvd, Toronto, ON, M2J 4A4
(416) 395-2380
Emp Here 35
SIC 8211 Elementary and secondary schools

D-U-N-S 20-025-0145   (BR)
TORONTO DISTRICT SCHOOL BOARD
SENECA HILL PUBLIC SCHOOL
625 Seneca Hill Dr, Toronto, ON, M2J 2W6
(416) 395-2840
Emp Here 22
SIC 8211 Elementary and secondary schools

Toronto, ON M2K
York County

D-U-N-S 24-745-7096   (BR)
YMCA OF GREATER TORONTO
YMCA
567 Sheppard Ave E, Toronto, ON, M2K 1B2
(416) 225-7773
Emp Here 250
SIC 8351 Child day care services

Toronto, ON M2L
York County

D-U-N-S 20-711-3031   (BR)
TORONTO DISTRICT SCHOOL BOARD
DUNLACE PUBLIC SCHOOL
20 Dunlace Dr, Toronto, ON, M2L 2S1
(416) 395-2370
Emp Here 25
SIC 8211 Elementary and secondary schools

D-U-N-S 20-784-3397   (BR)
TORONTO DISTRICT SCHOOL BOARD

WINDFIELDS JUNIOR HIGH SCHOOL
375 Banbury Rd, Toronto, ON, M2L 2V2
(416) 395-3100
Emp Here 40
SIC 8211 Elementary and secondary schools

Toronto, ON M2M
York County

D-U-N-S 20-026-1845   (BR)
CATHOLIC CHILDREN'S AID SOCIETY OF TORONTO, THE
30 Drewry Ave, Toronto, ON, M2M 4C4
(416) 395-1700
Emp Here 70
SIC 8322 Individual and family services

D-U-N-S 24-375-4129   (HQ)
HALLCON CORPORATION
5775 Yonge St Suite 1010, Toronto, ON, M2M 4J1
(416) 964-9191
Emp Here 250   *Emp Total* 90
SIC 4741 Rental of railroad cars

D-U-N-S 25-535-4441   (BR)
TD SECURITIES INC
TD SECURITIES
(*Suby of* Toronto-Dominion Bank, The)
5700 Yonge St, Toronto, ON, M2M 4K2
(416) 512-6611
Emp Here 28
SIC 6211 Security brokers and dealers

D-U-N-S 20-038-4993   (BR)
TORONTO CATHOLIC DISTRICT SCHOOL BOARD
ST. AGNES ELEMENTARY SCHOOL
280 Otonabee Ave, Toronto, ON, M2M 2T2
(416) 393-5345
Emp Here 20
SIC 8211 Elementary and secondary schools

D-U-N-S 20-025-0202   (BR)
TORONTO DISTRICT SCHOOL BOARD
R. J. LANG ELEMENTARY & MIDDLE SCHOOL
227 Drewry Ave, Toronto, ON, M2M 1E3
(416) 395-2780
Emp Here 60
SIC 8211 Elementary and secondary schools

Toronto, ON M2N
York County

D-U-N-S 20-652-1119   (BR)
ACCOR CANADA INC
NOVOTEL TORONTO NORTH YORK
3 Park Home Ave, Toronto, ON, M2N 6L3
(416) 733-2929
Emp Here 75
SIC 7011 Hotels and motels

D-U-N-S 20-353-4540   (SL)
BLADDER CANCER CANADA
4936 Yonge St Suite 1000, Toronto, ON, M2N 6S3
(866) 974-8889
Emp Here 50   *Sales* 455,730
SIC 8399 Social services, nec

D-U-N-S 24-337-2948   (BR)
FGL SPORTS LTD
NATIONAL SPORTS
4783 Yonge St, Toronto, ON, M2N 5M5
(416) 225-0929
Emp Here 20
SIC 5941 Sporting goods and bicycle shops

D-U-N-S 25-487-2476   (BR)
MOUNT PLEASANT GROUP OF CEMETERIES

YORK CEMETERY VISITATION, CHAPEL AND RECEPTION CENTRE
160 Beecroft Rd, Toronto, ON, M2N 5Z5
(416) 221-3404
Emp Here 25
SIC 6553 Cemetery subdividers and developers

D-U-N-S 25-843-3713   (BR)
SECOND CUP LTD, THE
5095 Yonge St, Toronto, ON, M2N 6Z4
(416) 227-9332
Emp Here 226
SIC 5812 Eating places

D-U-N-S 25-225-9908   (BR)
TORONTO CATHOLIC DISTRICT SCHOOL BOARD
ST. CYRIL CATHOLIC SCHOOL
18 Kempford Blvd, Toronto, ON, M2N 2B9
(416) 393-5270
Emp Here 25
SIC 8211 Elementary and secondary schools

D-U-N-S 25-265-3456   (BR)
TORONTO DISTRICT SCHOOL BOARD
CAMERON PUBLIC SCHOOL
211 Cameron Ave, Toronto, ON, M2N 1E8
(416) 395-2140
Emp Here 35
SIC 8211 Elementary and secondary schools

D-U-N-S 20-025-1259   (BR)
TORONTO DISTRICT SCHOOL BOARD
EARL HAIG SECONDARY SCHOOL
100 Princess Ave, Toronto, ON, M2N 3R7
(416) 395-3210
Emp Here 150
SIC 8211 Elementary and secondary schools

D-U-N-S 25-684-3335   (BR)
TORONTO-DOMINION BANK, THE
TD CANADA TRUST
(*Suby of* Toronto-Dominion Bank, The)
5400 Yonge St, Toronto, ON, M2N 5R5
(416) 225-5767
Emp Here 25
SIC 6021 National commercial banks

Toronto, ON M2P
York County

D-U-N-S 20-025-3438   (BR)
TORONTO DISTRICT SCHOOL BOARD
ST ANDREW'S JUNIOR HIGH SCHOOL
131 Fenn Ave, Toronto, ON, M2P 1X7
(416) 395-3090
Emp Here 20
SIC 8211 Elementary and secondary schools

D-U-N-S 20-698-7294   (BR)
TORONTO DISTRICT SCHOOL BOARD
OWEN PUBLIC SCHOOL
111 Owen Blvd, Toronto, ON, M2P 1G6
(416) 395-2740
Emp Here 31
SIC 8211 Elementary and secondary schools

Toronto, ON M2R
York County

D-U-N-S 25-852-3612   (BR)
DIVERSICARE CANADA MANAGEMENT SERVICES CO., INC
CHELTENHAM NURSING HOME
5935 Bathurst St, Toronto, ON, M2R 1Y8
(416) 223-4050
Emp Here 160
SIC 8051 Skilled nursing care facilities

D-U-N-S 20-610-7856   (BR)
MCDONALD'S RESTAURANTS OF

CANADA LIMITED
MCDONALD'S
(*Suby of* McDonald's Corporation)
6170 Bathurst St, Toronto, ON, M2R 2A2
(416) 226-0351
Emp Here 55
SIC 5812 Eating places

D-U-N-S 20-700-1715   (BR)
TORONTO DISTRICT SCHOOL BOARD
YORKVIEW PUBLIC SCHOOL
130 Yorkview Dr, Toronto, ON, M2R 1K1
(416) 395-2980
Emp Here 50
SIC 8211 Elementary and secondary schools

Toronto, ON M3A
York County

D-U-N-S 20-059-2090   (SL)
CRESTWOOD PREPARATORY COLLEGE INC
217 Brookbanks Dr, Toronto, ON, M3A 2T7
(416) 444-6230
Emp Here 50   *Sales* 3,356,192
SIC 8211 Elementary and secondary schools

D-U-N-S 20-025-6076   (BR)
TORONTO CATHOLIC DISTRICT SCHOOL BOARD
ANNUNCIATION CATHOLIC SCHOOL
65 Avonwick Gate, Toronto, ON, M3A 2M8
(416) 393-5299
Emp Here 20
SIC 8211 Elementary and secondary schools

D-U-N-S 20-064-1475   (BR)
TORONTO DISTRICT SCHOOL BOARD
MILNE VALLEY MIDDLE SCHOOL
100 Underhill Dr, Toronto, ON, M3A 2J9
(416) 395-2700
Emp Here 40
SIC 8211 Elementary and secondary schools

D-U-N-S 20-025-0137   (BR)
TORONTO DISTRICT SCHOOL BOARD
ROYWOOD PUBLIC SCHOOL
11 Roywood Dr, Toronto, ON, M3A 2C7
(416) 395-2830
Emp Here 30
SIC 8211 Elementary and secondary schools

D-U-N-S 20-038-7418   (BR)
TORONTO DISTRICT SCHOOL BOARD
RENE GORDON ELEMENTARY SCHOOL
20 Karen Rd, Toronto, ON, M3A 3L6
(416) 395-2790
Emp Here 40
SIC 8211 Elementary and secondary schools

D-U-N-S 20-025-3024   (BR)
TORONTO DISTRICT SCHOOL BOARD
FENSIDE PUBLIC SCHOOL
131 Fenside Dr, Toronto, ON, M3A 2V9
(416) 395-2400
Emp Here 28
SIC 8211 Elementary and secondary schools

Toronto, ON M3B
York County

D-U-N-S 20-333-5211   (BR)
MOORE CANADA CORPORATION
RR DONNELLEY MIL
(*Suby of* R. R. Donnelley & Sons Company)
180 Bond Ave, Toronto, ON, M3B 3P3
(416) 445-8800
Emp Here 200
SIC 2752 Commercial printing, lithographic

D-U-N-S 24-794-4077   (BR)
SGS CANADA INC

S G S MINERALS SERVICES
1885 Leslie St, Toronto, ON, M3B 2M3
(416) 736-2782
Emp Here 100
SIC 8734 Testing laboratories

D-U-N-S 20-698-7849   (BR)
TORONTO DISTRICT SCHOOL BOARD
INGRAM, NORMAN PUBLIC SCHOOL
50 Duncairn Rd, Toronto, ON, M3B 1C8
(416) 395-2720
Emp Here 27
SIC 8211 Elementary and secondary schools

D-U-N-S 20-035-5043   (BR)
TORONTO DISTRICT SCHOOL BOARD
YORK MILLS COLLEGIATE INSTITUTE
490 York Mills Rd, Toronto, ON, M3B 1W6
(416) 395-3340
Emp Here 84
SIC 8211 Elementary and secondary schools

D-U-N-S 24-379-9264   (SL)
XYLITOL CANADA INC
41 Lesmill Rd, Toronto, ON, M3B 2T3
(416) 288-1019
Emp Here 20   *Sales* 5,153,197
SIC 2869 Industrial organic chemicals, nec
Pr Pr Andrew Reid
CFO Kyle Appelby
VP Matt Willer
Sec Josh Arbuckle
   Thomas Kierans
   Roger Daher
   Muneeb Yusef

Toronto, ON M3C
York County

D-U-N-S 24-626-4394   (SL)
MASTERFILE CORPORATION
3 Concorde Gate Floor 4, Toronto, ON, M3C 3N7
(416) 929-3000
Emp Here 50   *Sales* 2,626,585
SIC 7389 Business services, nec

D-U-N-S 20-711-0987   (BR)
TORONTO CATHOLIC DISTRICT SCHOOL BOARD
ST. JOHN XXIII ELEMENTARY SCHOOL
175 Grenoble Dr, Toronto, ON, M3C 3E7
(416) 393-5348
Emp Here 60
SIC 8211 Elementary and secondary schools

D-U-N-S 20-047-1535   (BR)
TORONTO DISTRICT SCHOOL BOARD
VALLEY PARK MIDDLE SCHOOL
130 Overlea Blvd, Toronto, ON, M3C 1B2
(416) 396-2465
Emp Here 95
SIC 8211 Elementary and secondary schools

D-U-N-S 20-039-1253   (BR)
TORONTO DISTRICT SCHOOL BOARD
MARC GARNEAU COLLEGIATE INSTITUTE
135 Overlea Blvd, Toronto, ON, M3C 1B3
(416) 396-2410
Emp Here 140
SIC 8211 Elementary and secondary schools

D-U-N-S 24-676-5098   (BR)
TORONTO DISTRICT SCHOOL BOARD
DON MILLS MIDDLE SCHOOL
17 The Donway E, Toronto, ON, M3C 1X6
(416) 395-2320
Emp Here 25
SIC 8211 Elementary and secondary schools

D-U-N-S 24-364-7398   (BR)
TORONTO-DOMINION BANK, THE
TD BANK
(*Suby of* Toronto-Dominion Bank, The)
12 Concord Pl, Toronto, ON, M3C 2R8

(416) 462-2054
Emp Here 800
SIC 6021 National commercial banks

Toronto, ON M3H
York County

D-U-N-S 24-425-1059   (BR)
CROWN METAL PACKAGING CANADA LP
(*Suby of* Crown Holdings Inc.)
51 Signet Dr, Toronto, ON, M3H 2W0
(416) 747-5513
Emp Here 25
SIC 4225 General warehousing and storage

Toronto, ON M3J
York County

D-U-N-S 20-190-1209   (SL)
APOLLO HEALTH AND BEAUTY CARE INC
(*Suby of* Acasta Enterprises Inc)
1 Apollo Pl, Toronto, ON, M3J 0H2
(416) 758-3700
Emp Here 300   *Sales* 30,643,494
SIC 2679 Converted paper products, nec

D-U-N-S 25-249-6914   (SL)
ASKAN ARTS LIMITED
PICTURE DEPOT
20 Toro Rd, Toronto, ON, M3J 2A7
(416) 398-2333
Emp Here 110   *Sales* 9,333,400
SIC 7699 Repair services, nec
Pr Pr Sam Alavy

D-U-N-S 20-708-2939   (BR)
BUCKINGHAM SPORTS PROPERTIES COMPANY
CHESSWOOD ARENAS
4000 Chesswood Dr, Toronto, ON, M3J 2B9
(416) 630-8114
Emp Here 40
SIC 7941 Sports clubs, managers, and promoters

D-U-N-S 24-346-3218   (BR)
CHILDREN'S AID SOCIETY OF TORONTO
20 De Boers Dr Suite 250, Toronto, ON, M3J 0H1
(416) 924-4646
Emp Here 150
SIC 8322 Individual and family services

D-U-N-S 20-810-7123   (BR)
GLEN CORPORATION
624 Magnetic Dr, Toronto, ON, M3J 2C4
(416) 663-4664
Emp Here 67
SIC 7349 Building maintenance services, nec

D-U-N-S 24-815-2436   (SL)
MOUSE MARKETING INC
5 Kodiak Cres Suite 4-5, Toronto, ON, M3J 3E5
(416) 398-4334
Emp Here 175   *Sales* 1,571,739
SIC 8742 Management consulting services

D-U-N-S 20-273-6823   (BR)
PARTY CITY CANADA INC
(*Suby of* Party City Canada Inc)
1225 Finch Ave W, Toronto, ON, M3J 2E8
(416) 631-7688
Emp Here 25
SIC 5947 Gift, novelty, and souvenir shop

D-U-N-S 24-079-1368   (SL)
PICADILLY FASHIONS
4050 Chesswood Dr, Toronto, ON, M3J 2B9
(416) 783-1889
Emp Here 58   *Sales* 3,575,074
SIC 2339 Women's and misses' outerwear, nec

D-U-N-S 20-104-3580   (BR)
TEKNION LIMITED
FILE CO
1150 Flint Rd, Toronto, ON, M3J 2J5
(416) 661-3370
Emp Here 400
SIC 2522 Office furniture, except wood

D-U-N-S 20-084-0861   (BR)
TORONTO CATHOLIC DISTRICT SCHOOL BOARD
ST. JEROME CATHOLIC ELEMENTARY SCHOOL
111 Sharpecroft Blvd, Toronto, ON, M3J 1P5
(416) 393-5294
Emp Here 35
SIC 8211 Elementary and secondary schools

D-U-N-S 20-700-1749   (BR)
TORONTO DISTRICT SCHOOL BOARD
STILECROFT PS
50 Stilecroft Dr, Toronto, ON, M3J 1A7
(416) 395-2910
Emp Here 50
SIC 8211 Elementary and secondary schools

D-U-N-S 20-711-3072   (BR)
TORONTO DISTRICT SCHOOL BOARD
LAMBERTON PUBLIC ELEMENTARY SCHOOL
33 Lamberton Blvd, Toronto, ON, M3J 1G6
(416) 395-9570
Emp Here 40
SIC 8211 Elementary and secondary schools

D-U-N-S 20-284-8784   (BR)
UNIVAR CANADA LTD
777 Supertest Rd, Toronto, ON, M3J 2M9
(416) 740-5300
Emp Here 59
SIC 4225 General warehousing and storage

D-U-N-S 20-346-1637   (SL)
VITABATH INC
(*Suby of* 570746 Ontario Inc)
333 Rimrock Rd, Toronto, ON, M3J 3J9
(416) 373-4459
Emp Here 20   *Sales* 2,945,253
SIC 5122 Drugs, proprietaries, and sundries

Toronto, ON M3K
York County

D-U-N-S 24-688-6261   (BR)
FLIGHTSAFETY CANADA LTD
FLIGHTSAFETY INTERNATIONAL CANADA
(*Suby of* Berkshire Hathaway Inc.)
95 Garratt Blvd, Toronto, ON, M3K 2A5
(416) 638-9313
Emp Here 90
SIC 8299 Schools and educational services, nec

D-U-N-S 20-035-5159   (BR)
TORONTO CATHOLIC DISTRICT SCHOOL BOARD
SAINT NORBERT ELEMENTARY
60 Maniza Rd, Toronto, ON, M3K 1R6
(416) 393-5309
Emp Here 30
SIC 8211 Elementary and secondary schools

D-U-N-S 20-076-9854   (BR)
TORONTO CATHOLIC DISTRICT SCHOOL BOARD
MADONNA CATHOLIC SECONDARY SCHOOL
20 Dubray Ave, Toronto, ON, M3K 1V5
(416) 393-5506
Emp Here 50
SIC 8211 Elementary and secondary schools

Toronto, ON M3L
York County

D-U-N-S 20-081-3561 (BR)
TORONTO CATHOLIC DISTRICT SCHOOL BOARD
BLESSED MARGHERITA OF CITT DI CASTELLO SCHOOL
108 Spenvalley Dr, Toronto, ON, M3L 1Z5
(416) 393-5409
Emp Here 45
SIC 8211 Elementary and secondary schools

D-U-N-S 20-035-5217 (BR)
TORONTO CATHOLIC DISTRICT SCHOOL BOARD
ST. MARTHA CATHOLIC SCHOOL
1865 Sheppard Ave W, Toronto, ON, M3L 1Y5
(416) 393-5344
Emp Here 25
SIC 8211 Elementary and secondary schools

Toronto, ON M3M
York County

D-U-N-S 24-011-9722 (BR)
CANADA POST CORPORATION
2800 Keele St, Toronto, ON, M3M 2G4

Emp Here 500
SIC 4311 U.s. postal service

D-U-N-S 20-698-6601 (BR)
TORONTO CATHOLIC DISTRICT SCHOOL BOARD
ST. CONRAD CATHOLIC SCHOOL
610 Roding St, Toronto, ON, M3M 2A5
(416) 393-5396
Emp Here 50
SIC 8211 Elementary and secondary schools

D-U-N-S 20-515-0357 (BR)
TORONTO CATHOLIC DISTRICT SCHOOL BOARD
ST. RAPHAEL ELEMENTARY SCHOOL
3 Gade Dr, Toronto, ON, M3M 2K2
(416) 393-5285
Emp Here 50
SIC 8211 Elementary and secondary schools

D-U-N-S 25-237-7957 (BR)
TORONTO DISTRICT SCHOOL BOARD
HIGHVIEW PUBLIC SCHOOL
22 Highview Ave, Toronto, ON, M3M 1C4
(416) 395-2540
Emp Here 30
SIC 8211 Elementary and secondary schools

D-U-N-S 20-700-2838 (BR)
TORONTO DISTRICT SCHOOL BOARD
BEVERLEY HEIGHTS MIDDLE SCHOOL
26 Troutbrooke Dr, Toronto, ON, M3M 1S5
(416) 395-3000
Emp Here 50
SIC 8211 Elementary and secondary schools

Toronto, ON M3N
York County

D-U-N-S 24-850-3430 (BR)
CANADIAN LINEN AND UNIFORM SERVICE CO
(*Suby of* Ameripride Services, Inc.)
75 Norfinch Dr Suite 1, Toronto, ON, M3N 1W8
(416) 849-5100
Emp Here 140
SIC 7218 Industrial launderers

D-U-N-S 20-513-9806 (BR)
CINTAS CANADA LIMITED
SALLY FOURMY & ASSOCIATES
(*Suby of* Cintas Corporation)

149 Eddystone Ave, Toronto, ON, M3N 1H5
(416) 743-5070
Emp Here 100
SIC 7218 Industrial launderers

D-U-N-S 20-699-6378 (BR)
EXTENDICARE INC
YORKVIEW LIFECARE CENTRE
2045 Finch Ave W, Toronto, ON, M3N 1M9
(416) 745-0811
Emp Here 25
SIC 8051 Skilled nursing care facilities

D-U-N-S 20-690-1659 (BR)
HUMBER RIVER HOSPITAL
2111 Finch Ave W, Toronto, ON, M3N 1N1
(416) 744-2500
Emp Here 800
SIC 8062 General medical and surgical hospitals

D-U-N-S 20-012-2591 (SL)
SUNRISE MEDICAL HCM INC
(*Suby of* V.S.M. Investors, LLC)
355 Norfinch Dr, Toronto, ON, M3N 1Y7
(416) 739-8333
Emp Here 25   *Sales* 3,109,686
SIC 3842 Surgical appliances and supplies

D-U-N-S 20-035-5274 (BR)
TORONTO CATHOLIC DISTRICT SCHOOL BOARD
ST. AUGUSTINE CATHOLIC SCHOOL
98 Shoreham Dr, Toronto, ON, M3N 1S9
(416) 393-5328
Emp Here 50
SIC 8211 Elementary and secondary schools

D-U-N-S 25-237-7908 (BR)
TORONTO DISTRICT SCHOOL BOARD
DRIFTWOOD PUBLIC SCHOOL
265 Driftwood Ave, Toronto, ON, M3N 2N6
(416) 395-2350
Emp Here 60
SIC 8211 Elementary and secondary schools

D-U-N-S 20-025-0152 (BR)
TORONTO DISTRICT SCHOOL BOARD
SHOREHAM PUBLIC SPORTS AND WELLNESS ACADEMY
31 Shoreham Dr, Toronto, ON, M3N 2S6
(416) 395-2870
Emp Here 50
SIC 8211 Elementary and secondary schools

D-U-N-S 20-711-3064 (BR)
TORONTO DISTRICT SCHOOL BOARD
GOSFORD PUBLIC SCHOOL
30 Gosford Blvd, Toronto, ON, M3N 2G8
(416) 395-2470
Emp Here 28
SIC 8211 Elementary and secondary schools

D-U-N-S 20-035-5266 (BR)
TORONTO DISTRICT SCHOOL BOARD
OAKDALE PARK MIDDLE SCHOOL
315 Grandravine Dr, Toronto, ON, M3N 1J5
(416) 395-3060
Emp Here 52
SIC 8211 Elementary and secondary schools

D-U-N-S 20-064-1517 (BR)
TORONTO DISTRICT SCHOOL BOARD
BLACKSMITH PUBLIC SCHOOL
45 Blacksmith Cres, Toronto, ON, M3N 1V5
(416) 395-2060
Emp Here 30
SIC 8211 Elementary and secondary schools

Toronto, ON M4A
York County

D-U-N-S 20-512-2703 (SL)
COMET ENTERTAINMENT INC
1880 O'Connor Dr Suite 204, Toronto, ON,

M4A 1W9
(416) 421-4229
Emp Here 50   *Sales* 3,866,917
SIC 7812 Motion picture and video production

D-U-N-S 20-704-5910 (BR)
CORPORATION OF THE CITY OF TORONTO
PRINTING AND DISTRIBUTION SERVICES
2 Hobson Ave, Toronto, ON, M4A 1Y2
(416) 392-8940
Emp Here 20
SIC 2741 Miscellaneous publishing

D-U-N-S 20-016-2522 (BR)
CORPORATION OF THE CITY OF TORONTO
TORONTO DESIGN & REPRODUCTION SERVICES
2 Hobson Ave, Toronto, ON, M4A 1Y2
(416) 392-8940
Emp Here 28
SIC 7336 Commercial art and graphic design

D-U-N-S 24-173-0279 (BR)
GOODLIFE FITNESS CENTRES INC
1448 Lawrence Ave E Unit 17, Toronto, ON, M4A 2V6
(416) 615-1185
Emp Here 30
SIC 7991 Physical fitness facilities

D-U-N-S 24-318-0309 (BR)
SHOPPERS DRUG MART CORPORATION
SHOPPERS HOME HEALTHCARE
104 Bartley Dr, Toronto, ON, M4A 1C5
(416) 752-8885
Emp Here 90
SIC 5999 Miscellaneous retail stores, nec

D-U-N-S 20-035-5282 (BR)
TORONTO DISTRICT SCHOOL BOARD
SLOANE PUBLIC SCHOOL
110 Sloane Ave, Toronto, ON, M4A 2B1
(416) 397-2920
Emp Here 30
SIC 8211 Elementary and secondary schools

Toronto, ON M4B
York County

D-U-N-S 24-537-6777 (HQ)
AVIDA HEALTHWEAR INC
(*Suby of* Avida Healthwear Inc)
87 Northline Rd, Toronto, ON, M4B 3E9
(416) 751-5874
Emp Here 43   *Emp Total* 50
Sales 3,648,035
SIC 2337 Women's and misses' suits and coats

D-U-N-S 20-328-7177 (SL)
B & R HOLDINGS INC
32 Cranfield Rd, Toronto, ON, M4B 3H3
(416) 701-9800
Emp Here 100   *Sales* 16,708,000
SIC 2672 Paper; coated and laminated, nec
  Rhys Seymour

D-U-N-S 24-437-8332 (BR)
BANQUE TORONTO-DOMINION, LA
TORONTO-DOMINION BANK, THE
(*Suby of* Toronto-Dominion Bank, The)
801 O'Connor Dr, Toronto, ON, M4B 2S7
(416) 757-1361
Emp Here 25
SIC 6021 National commercial banks

D-U-N-S 25-667-2312 (SL)
CITY WIDE GROUP INC, THE
CITY WIDE CONSTRUCTION
25 Hollinger Rd Unit 3, Toronto, ON, M4B 3N4
(416) 881-6379
Emp Here 50   *Sales* 1,459,214
SIC 1799 Special trade contractors, nec

D-U-N-S 20-691-4058 (SL)
EVAGELOU ENTERPRISES INC
CRANFIELD GENERAL CONTRACTING
39 Cranfield Rd, Toronto, ON, M4B 3H6
(416) 285-4774
Emp Here 150   *Sales* 4,961,328
SIC 7299 Miscellaneous personal service

D-U-N-S 20-172-2188 (BR)
GREAT CANADIAN SOX CO. INC, THE
J.B. FIELDS
25 Waterman Ave, Toronto, ON, M4B 1Y6
(416) 288-0028
Emp Here 57   *Sales* 2,165,628
SIC 2252 Hosiery, nec

D-U-N-S 24-418-0501 (SL)
KIANGTEX COMPANY LIMITED
46 Hollinger Rd, Toronto, ON, M4B 3G5
(416) 750-3771
Emp Here 120   *Sales* 17,364,647
SIC 5137 Women's and children's clothing
Pr Pr Anna Kiang
  Raymond Kiang

D-U-N-S 20-079-3862 (BR)
LOBLAWS SUPERMARKETS LIMITED
TOM FRILLS
1150 Victoria Park Ave, Toronto, ON, M4B 2K4
(416) 755-5661
Emp Here 49
SIC 5411 Grocery stores

D-U-N-S 24-682-0273 (BR)
MEDIACO THE PRESENTATION COMPANY INC
(*Suby of* Mediaco The Presentation Company Inc)
6 Curity Ave Unit B, Toronto, ON, M4B 1X2
(416) 405-9797
Emp Here 30
SIC 7359 Equipment rental and leasing, nec

D-U-N-S 24-927-0216 (SL)
SKYREACH WINDOW AND BUILDING SERVICES INC
SKYREACH WINDOW CLEANING
2857 St Clair Ave E Suite A, Toronto, ON, M4B 1N4
(416) 285-6312
Emp Here 60   *Sales* 1,094,411
SIC 7349 Building maintenance services, nec

D-U-N-S 24-469-7124 (SL)
ST. CLAIR O'CONNOR COMMUNITY INC
2701 St Clair Ave E Suite 211, Toronto, ON, M4B 1M5
(416) 757-8757
Emp Here 80   *Sales* 2,918,428
SIC 8361 Residential care

D-U-N-S 24-287-0962 (SL)
TANG APPAREL CO. LIMITED
50 Northline Rd, Toronto, ON, M4B 3E2
(416) 603-0021
Emp Here 80   *Sales* 5,836,856
SIC 2337 Women's and misses' suits and coats
Pr Pr James Tang

D-U-N-S 25-265-0957 (BR)
TORONTO DISTRICT SCHOOL BOARD
SELWYN ELEMENTARY SCHOOL
1 Selwyn Ave, Toronto, ON, M4B 3J9
(416) 396-2455
Emp Here 25
SIC 8211 Elementary and secondary schools

D-U-N-S 20-913-6907 (BR)
TORONTO DISTRICT SCHOOL BOARD
GORDON A BROWN MIDDLE SCHOOL
2800 St Clair Ave E, Toronto, ON, M4B 1N2
(416) 396-2440
Emp Here 55
SIC 8211 Elementary and secondary schools

D-U-N-S 20-711-2892 (BR)
TORONTO DISTRICT SCHOOL BOARD

GEORGE WEBSTER SCHOOL
2 Cedarcrest Blvd, Toronto, ON, M4B 2N9
(416) 396-2375
Emp Here 40
SIC 8211 Elementary and secondary schools

D-U-N-S 25-265-1625   (BR)
TORONTO DISTRICT SCHOOL BOARD
VICTORIA PARK ELEMENTARY SCHOOL
145 Tiago Ave, Toronto, ON, M4B 2A6
(416) 396-2475
Emp Here 22
SIC 8211 Elementary and secondary schools

D-U-N-S 25-265-0833   (BR)
TORONTO DISTRICT SCHOOL BOARD
PRESTEIGN HEIGHTS ELEMENTARY
SCHOOL
2570 St Clair Ave E, Toronto, ON, M4B 1M3
(416) 396-2430
Emp Here 24
SIC 8211 Elementary and secondary schools

Toronto, ON M4C
York County

D-U-N-S 25-275-7000   (SL)
A WAY EXPRESS COURIER SERVICE
2168 Danforth Ave, Toronto, ON, M4C 1K3
(416) 424-4471
Emp Here 60   Sales 3,064,349
SIC 7389 Business services, nec

D-U-N-S 25-296-8953   (BR)
BANK OF NOVA SCOTIA, THE
SCOTIABANK
2072 Danforth Ave, Toronto, ON, M4C 1J6
(416) 425-8444
Emp Here 28
SIC 6021 National commercial banks

D-U-N-S 20-538-5540   (BR)
CANADA POST CORPORATION
2315 Danforth Ave, Toronto, ON, M4C 1K5

Emp Here 60
SIC 4311 U.s. postal service

D-U-N-S 20-812-8079   (BR)
CORPORATION OF THE CITY OF
TORONTO
EAST YOPK FIRE FIGHTERS ASSOCIA-
TION
1313 Woodbine Ave, Toronto, ON, M4C 4E9
(416) 338-9224
Emp Here 45
SIC 7389 Business services, nec

D-U-N-S 24-018-0419   (BR)
DOLLARAMA S.E.C.
DOLLARAMA
3003 Danforth Ave Suite 230, Toronto, ON,
M4C 1M9
(416) 691-7607
Emp Here 32
SIC 5999 Miscellaneous retail stores, nec

D-U-N-S 20-708-3440   (SL)
FAMILIES FOR CHILDREN INC
111 Roseheath Ave, Toronto, ON, M4C 3P6
(416) 686-1688
Emp Here 50   Sales 2,355,823
SIC 8361 Residential care

D-U-N-S 25-295-5521   (BR)
LEON'S FURNITURE LIMITED
LEON'S
2872 Danforth Ave, Toronto, ON, M4C 1M1
(416) 699-7143
Emp Here 25
SIC 5712 Furniture stores

D-U-N-S 24-024-0973   (BR)
METRO ONTARIO INC
DOMINION

1500 Woodbine Ave, Toronto, ON, M4C 4G9
(416) 422-0076
Emp Here 100
SIC 5411 Grocery stores

D-U-N-S 25-692-9332   (BR)
NEIGHBOURHOOD GROUP COMMUNITY
SERVICES, THE
STEPHENSON SENIOR LINK HOME
(Suby of Neighbourhood Group Community
Services, The)
11 Coatsworth Cres, Toronto, ON, M4C 5P8
(416) 691-7407
Emp Here 105
SIC 8322 Individual and family services

D-U-N-S 25-795-5831   (BR)
OMER DESERRES INC
LOOMIS ART STORE
2056 Danforth Ave, Toronto, ON, M4C 1J6
(416) 422-2443
Emp Here 25
SIC 5999 Miscellaneous retail stores, nec

D-U-N-S 25-092-6284   (BR)
OPERATION SPRINGBOARD
BLUE JAYS LODGE
51 Dawes Rd, Toronto, ON, M4C 5B1
(416) 698-0047
Emp Here 23
SIC 8322 Individual and family services

D-U-N-S 25-090-2947   (BR)
SOBEYS CAPITAL INCORPORATED
2451 Danforth Ave Suite 938, Toronto, ON,
M4C 1L1
(416) 698-6868
Emp Here 120
SIC 5411 Grocery stores

D-U-N-S 20-860-3261   (BR)
SOURCE (BELL) ELECTRONICS INC, THE
SOURCE, THE
3003 Danforth Ave, Toronto, ON, M4C 1M9
(416) 699-9794
Emp Here 25
SIC 5999 Miscellaneous retail stores, nec

D-U-N-S 25-143-4718   (BR)
STAPLES CANADA INC
STAPLES THE BUSINESS DEPOT
(Suby of Staples, Inc.)
3003 Danforth Ave, Toronto, ON, M4C 1M9
(416) 686-4711
Emp Here 20
SIC 5943 Stationery stores

D-U-N-S 20-711-1126   (BR)
TORONTO CATHOLIC DISTRICT SCHOOL
BOARD
ST. BRIGID CATHOLIC SCHOOL
50 Woodmount Ave, Toronto, ON, M4C 3X9
(416) 393-5235
Emp Here 50
SIC 8211 Elementary and secondary schools

D-U-N-S 25-265-3944   (BR)
TORONTO CATHOLIC DISTRICT SCHOOL
BOARD
CANADIAN MARTYRS CATHOLIC SCHOOL
520 Plains Rd, Toronto, ON, M4C 2Z1
(416) 393-5251
Emp Here 35
SIC 8211 Elementary and secondary schools

D-U-N-S 20-700-3398   (BR)
TORONTO DISTRICT SCHOOL BOARD
EARL HAIG PUBLIC SCHOOL
15 Earl Haig Ave, Toronto, ON, M4C 1E2
(416) 393-1640
Emp Here 50
SIC 8211 Elementary and secondary schools

D-U-N-S 25-265-0999   (BR)
TORONTO DISTRICT SCHOOL BOARD
SECORD ELEMENTARY SCHOOL
101 Barrington Ave, Toronto, ON, M4C 4Y9
(416) 396-2450
Emp Here 70

SIC 8211 Elementary and secondary schools

D-U-N-S 25-265-1542   (BR)
TORONTO DISTRICT SCHOOL BOARD
D. A. MORRISON MIDDLE SCHOOL
271 Gledhill Ave, Toronto, ON, M4C 4L2
(416) 396-2400
Emp Here 40
SIC 8211 Elementary and secondary schools

D-U-N-S 25-139-0597   (BR)
TORONTO DISTRICT SCHOOL BOARD
EAST YORK COLLEGIATE INSTITUTE
650 Cosburn Ave, Toronto, ON, M4C 2V2
(416) 396-2355
Emp Here 200
SIC 8211 Elementary and secondary schools

D-U-N-S 20-914-4901   (BR)
TORONTO DISTRICT SCHOOL BOARD
GLEDHILL JUNIOR PUBLIC SCHOOL
2 Gledhill Ave, Toronto, ON, M4C 5K6
(416) 393-1745
Emp Here 45
SIC 8211 Elementary and secondary schools

D-U-N-S 20-700-1558   (BR)
TORONTO DISTRICT SCHOOL BOARD
WILLIAM J MCCORDIC SCHOOL
45 Balfour Ave, Toronto, ON, M4C 1T4
(416) 397-2720
Emp Here 60
SIC 8211 Elementary and secondary schools

D-U-N-S 20-046-2005   (BR)
TORONTO DISTRICT SCHOOL BOARD
CRESCENT TOWN ELEMENTARY SCHOOL
4 Massey Sq, Toronto, ON, M4C 5M9
(416) 396-2340
Emp Here 70
SIC 8211 Elementary and secondary schools

D-U-N-S 20-819-7541   (SL)
TORONTO EAST GENERAL GIFT SHOP
825 Coxwell Ave, Toronto, ON, M4C 3E7
(416) 469-6050
Emp Here 61   Sales 3,356,192
SIC 5947 Gift, novelty, and souvenir shop

D-U-N-S 25-684-3160   (BR)
TORONTO-DOMINION BANK, THE
TD CANADA TRUST
(Suby of Toronto-Dominion Bank, The)
3060 Danforth Ave, Toronto, ON, M4C 1N2
(416) 698-2871
Emp Here 30
SIC 6021 National commercial banks

D-U-N-S 25-684-3129   (BR)
TORONTO-DOMINION BANK, THE
TD CANADA TRUST
(Suby of Toronto-Dominion Bank, The)
1684 Danforth Ave Suite 1, Toronto, ON, M4C
1H6
(416) 466-2317
Emp Here 20
SIC 6021 National commercial banks

D-U-N-S 25-487-2922   (BR)
VALUE VILLAGE STORES, INC
(Suby of Savers, Inc.)
2119 Danforth Ave, Toronto, ON, M4C 1K1
(416) 698-0621
Emp Here 25
SIC 5399 Miscellaneous general merchandise

D-U-N-S 20-049-6854   (BR)
VICTORIA VILLAGE CHILDREN'S SER-
VICES LTD
MUPPETS CHILDRENS CENTER
314 Main St, Toronto, ON, M4C 4X7
(416) 690-8668
Emp Here 30
SIC 8351 Child day care services

D-U-N-S 25-917-9703   (BR)
VICTORIA VILLAGE CHILDREN'S SER-
VICES LTD
MUPPETS CHILDREN'S CENTRE

312 Main St, Toronto, ON, M4C 4X7
(416) 693-9879
Emp Here 40
SIC 8351 Child day care services

Toronto, ON M4E
York County

D-U-N-S 20-574-4522   (SL)
CANADIAN COAST GUARD AUXILIARY
(CENTRAL AND ARCTIC) INC
577 Kingston Rd Suite 206, Toronto, ON, M4E
1R3
(416) 463-7283
Emp Here 811   Sales 132,516,000
SIC 8699 Membership organizations, nec
Pr Pr Jack Kruger
VP VP Leslie Reading
 Lou Lochner
Dir Rick Oldale
Dir Shannon Laird

D-U-N-S 24-964-4204   (SL)
DAVIS & WILLMOT INC
2060 Queen St E Suite 51504, Toronto, ON,
M4E 1C9

Emp Here 75   Sales 9,620,820
SIC 5094 Jewelry and precious stones
Dir David Dobbs

D-U-N-S 24-119-2330   (BR)
LOBLAW COMPANIES LIMITED
LOBLAWS
50 Musgrave St, Toronto, ON, M4E 3W2
(416) 694-6263
Emp Here 200
SIC 5411 Grocery stores

D-U-N-S 20-088-4562   (SL)
NATIONAL RESERVATION CENTRE FOR
AVIS
132 Brookside Dr, Toronto, ON, M4E 2M2
(416) 213-8400
Emp Here 450   Sales 107,976,000
SIC 4899 Communication services, nec
Pr Henry Silverman

D-U-N-S 25-531-6911   (BR)
RE/MAX HALLMARK REALTY LTD
2237 Queen St E, Toronto, ON, M4E 1G1
(416) 357-1059
Emp Here 130
SIC 6531 Real estate agents and managers

D-U-N-S 24-306-4797   (BR)
REVERA LONG TERM CARE INC
VERSA CARE
77 Main St, Toronto, ON, M4E 2V6
(416) 690-3001
Emp Here 120
SIC 8051 Skilled nursing care facilities

D-U-N-S 20-711-1274   (BR)
TORONTO CATHOLIC DISTRICT SCHOOL
BOARD
ST. JOHN CATHOLIC SCHOOL
780 Kingston Rd, Toronto, ON, M4E 1R7
(416) 393-5220
Emp Here 20
SIC 8211 Elementary and secondary schools

D-U-N-S 20-711-2546   (BR)
TORONTO DISTRICT SCHOOL BOARD
WILLIAMSON ROAD JR PS
24 Williamson Rd, Toronto, ON, M4E 1K5
(416) 393-1740
Emp Here 50
SIC 8211 Elementary and secondary schools

D-U-N-S 20-700-2747   (BR)
TORONTO DISTRICT SCHOOL BOARD
BEACHES ALTERNATIVE SCHOOL
50 Swanwick Ave, Toronto, ON, M4E 1Z5
(416) 393-1451
Emp Here 20

SIC 8211 Elementary and secondary schools

D-U-N-S 20-700-2671   (BR)
TORONTO DISTRICT SCHOOL BOARD
BALMY BEACH COMMUNITY SCHOOL
14 Pine Ave Suite 107, Toronto, ON, M4E 1L6
(416) 393-1565
Emp Here 20
SIC 8211 Elementary and secondary schools

D-U-N-S 20-700-2507   (BR)
TORONTO DISTRICT SCHOOL BOARD
ADAM BECK JUNIOR PUBLIC SCHOOL
400 Scarborough Rd, Toronto, ON, M4E 3M8
(416) 393-1682
Emp Here 30
SIC 8211 Elementary and secondary schools

Toronto, ON M4G
York County

D-U-N-S 24-154-6691   (BR)
122164 CANADA LIMITED
NEW YORK FRIES & SOUTH STREET BURGER
(*Suby of* 122164 Canada Limited)
45 Wicksteed Ave, Toronto, ON, M4G 4H9
(416) 421-8559
Emp Here 25
SIC 5812 Eating places

D-U-N-S 20-808-9255   (SL)
ACCORD SPECIALIZED INVESTIGATIONS & SECURITY
1560 Bayview Ave Ste 300, Toronto, ON, M4G 3B8
(416) 461-2774
Emp Here 75   *Sales* 2,334,742
SIC 7382 Security systems services

D-U-N-S 25-214-6444   (SL)
BELLWOOD HEALTH SERVICES INC
BELLWOOD HEALTH SERVICES
175 Brentcliffe Rd, Toronto, ON, M4G 0C5
(416) 495-0926
Emp Here 55   *Sales* 4,450,603
SIC 8069 Specialty hospitals, except psychiatric

D-U-N-S 20-934-4717   (BR)
BEST BUY CANADA LTD
FUTURE SHOP
(*Suby of* Best Buy Co., Inc.)
845 Eglinton Ave E, Toronto, ON, M4G 4G9
(647) 253-1270
Emp Here 70
SIC 5999 Miscellaneous retail stores, nec

D-U-N-S 20-199-5623   (BR)
CANADA POST CORPORATION
2 Laird Dr, Toronto, ON, M4G 4K6

Emp Here 28
SIC 4311 U.s. postal service

D-U-N-S 20-552-9126   (HQ)
CANADIAN NATIONAL INSTITUTE FOR THE BLIND, THE
CNIB
(*Suby of* Canadian National Institute For The Blind, The)
1929 Bayview Ave, Toronto, ON, M4G 3E8
(416) 486-2500
Emp Here 250   *Emp Total* 750
Sales 61,178,367
SIC 8331 Job training and related services
Pr Pr John M. Rafferty
  Craig Lillico
  Pamela Gow-Boyd
  Len Baker
  John Mulka
  Rob Hindley
VP VP Keith Gordon
VP VP Garry Nenson
VP VP Maria Ash

Victoria Pearson

D-U-N-S 20-073-3843   (BR)
CENTRE FOR ADDICTION AND MENTAL HEALTH
QUEEN STREET MENTAL HEALTH
175 Brentcliffe Rd, Toronto, ON, M4G 0C5
(416) 425-3930
Emp Here 1,000
SIC 8093 Specialty outpatient clinics, nec

D-U-N-S 24-366-1373   (HQ)
DEL EQUIPMENT LIMITED
139 Laird Dr, Toronto, ON, M4G 3V6
(416) 421-5851
Emp Here 80   *Emp Total* 210
Sales 30,058,910
SIC 3713 Truck and bus bodies
Pr Paul Martin
  Doug Lucky

D-U-N-S 24-977-1945   (BR)
FGL SPORTS LTD
SPORT CHEK LEASIDE
B3 147 Laird Dr Unit 300, Toronto, ON, M4G 4K1
(416) 421-6093
Emp Here 20
SIC 5941 Sporting goods and bicycle shops

D-U-N-S 20-108-5318   (BR)
HOME DEPOT OF CANADA INC
HOME DEPOT
(*Suby of* The Home Depot Inc)
101 Wicksteed Ave, Toronto, ON, M4G 4H9
(416) 467-2300
Emp Here 200
SIC 5251 Hardware stores

D-U-N-S 25-318-2000   (BR)
HU-A-KAM ENTERPRISES INC
MCDONALD'S
(*Suby of* Hu-A-Kam Enterprises Inc)
1787 Bayview Ave, Toronto, ON, M4G 3C5
(416) 292-0459
Emp Here 76
SIC 5812 Eating places

D-U-N-S 20-167-3613   (SL)
HUMPHREY FUNERAL HOME & A.W. MILES CHAPEL LIMITED
1403 Bayview Ave, Toronto, ON, M4G 3A8
(416) 487-4523
Emp Here 50   *Sales* 3,648,035
SIC 7261 Funeral service and crematories

D-U-N-S 24-845-3896   (BR)
LEVITT-SAFETY LIMITED
NL TECHNOLOGIES, DIV OF
33 Laird Dr, Toronto, ON, M4G 3S8
(416) 425-6559
Emp Here 37
SIC 3648 Lighting equipment, nec

D-U-N-S 24-859-1810   (BR)
LEVITT-SAFETY LIMITED
NL TECHNOLOGIES
33 Laird Dr, Toronto, ON, M4G 3S8
(416) 425-6659
Emp Here 300
SIC 5999 Miscellaneous retail stores, nec

D-U-N-S 20-002-8269   (BR)
LIQUOR CONTROL BOARD OF ONTARIO, THE
LCBO 164
147 Laird Dr Unit 2, Toronto, ON, M4G 4K1
(416) 425-6282
Emp Here 27
SIC 5921 Liquor stores

D-U-N-S 25-504-5338   (BR)
LOBLAWS SUPERMARKETS LIMITED
LOBLAWS
301 Moore Ave, Toronto, ON, M4G 1E1
(416) 425-0604
Emp Here 100
SIC 5411 Grocery stores

D-U-N-S 20-170-6223   (HQ)
MERCEDES-BENZ CANADA INC
98 Vanderhoof Ave, Toronto, ON, M4G 4C9
(416) 425-3550
Emp Here 289   *Emp Total* 284,960
Sales 744,199,140
SIC 5012 Automobiles and other motor vehicles
Pr Brian Fulton
Dir Hannu Ylanko
Dir Christian Spelter
Dir Tim A Reuss
Dir James C M Rossitier
  Joachim Schmidt

D-U-N-S 25-711-6525   (BR)
PHARMA PLUS DRUGMARTS LTD
325 Moore Ave, Toronto, ON, M4G 3T6
(416) 423-5201
Emp Here 20
SIC 5912 Drug stores and proprietary stores

D-U-N-S 24-355-7308   (BR)
RESOLVE CORPORATION
(*Suby of* 2206997 Ontario Inc)
210 Wicksteed Ave, Toronto, ON, M4G 2C3

Emp Here 130
SIC 8743 Public relations services

D-U-N-S 20-174-7268   (HQ)
ST. MARYS CEMENT INC. (CANADA)
ST. MARYS CEMENT CO
55 Industrial St, Toronto, ON, M4G 3W9
(416) 423-1300
Emp Here 75   *Emp Total* 1,400
SIC 3241 Cement, hydraulic

D-U-N-S 25-213-7062   (BR)
STAPLES CANADA INC
STAPLES THE BUSINESS DEPOT
(*Suby of* Staples, Inc.)
945 Eglinton Ave E, Toronto, ON, M4G 4B5
(416) 696-0043
Emp Here 60
SIC 5943 Stationery stores

D-U-N-S 20-711-1100   (BR)
TORONTO CATHOLIC DISTRICT SCHOOL BOARD
ST. ANSELM CATHOLIC ELEMENTARY SCHOOL
182 Bessborough Dr, Toronto, ON, M4G 4H5
(416) 393-5243
Emp Here 50
SIC 8211 Elementary and secondary schools

D-U-N-S 20-700-2796   (BR)
TORONTO DISTRICT SCHOOL BOARD
BESSBOROUGH DRIVE ELEMENTARY & MIDDLE SCHOOL
211 Bessborough Dr, Toronto, ON, M4G 3K2
(416) 396-2315
Emp Here 20
SIC 8211 Elementary and secondary schools

D-U-N-S 20-048-5238   (BR)
TORONTO DISTRICT SCHOOL BOARD
NORTHLEA ELEMENTARY & MIDDLE SCHOOL
305 Rumsey Rd, Toronto, ON, M4G 1R4
(416) 396-2395
Emp Here 75
SIC 8211 Elementary and secondary schools

D-U-N-S 25-265-0759   (BR)
TORONTO DISTRICT SCHOOL BOARD
ROLPH ROAD ELEMENTARY SCHOOL
31 Rolph Rd, Toronto, ON, M4G 3M5
(416) 396-2435
Emp Here 27
SIC 8211 Elementary and secondary schools

D-U-N-S 25-692-5504   (SL)
TORONTO FINNISH CANADIAN SENIOR CENTRE
SUOMI-KOTI
795 Eglinton Ave E Suite 105, Toronto, ON,

M4G 4E4
(416) 425-4134
Emp Here 50   *Sales* 1,824,018
SIC 8361 Residential care

D-U-N-S 24-347-9982   (BR)
TORONTO REHABILITATION INSTITUTE
520 Sutherland Dr, Toronto, ON, M4G 3V9
(416) 597-3422
Emp Here 500
SIC 8093 Specialty outpatient clinics, nec

D-U-N-S 25-138-1521   (BR)
WASTE MANAGEMENT OF CANADA CORPORATION
(*Suby of* Waste Management, Inc.)
20 Esandar Dr, Toronto, ON, M4G 1Y2
(416) 423-6396
Emp Here 40
SIC 4953 Refuse systems

D-U-N-S 25-221-3210   (BR)
WINNERS MERCHANTS INTERNATIONAL L.P.
WINNERS
(*Suby of* The TJX Companies Inc)
147 Laird Dr, Toronto, ON, M4G 4K1
(416) 425-2777
Emp Here 40
SIC 5651 Family clothing stores

Toronto, ON M4H
York County

D-U-N-S 25-092-6557   (BR)
ALPHA LABORATORIES INC
(*Suby of* 600144 Ontario Inc)
45 Overlea Blvd Suite 2, Toronto, ON, M4H 1C3
(416) 421-9414
Emp Here 50
SIC 8071 Medical laboratories

D-U-N-S 24-342-8112   (BR)
CARA OPERATIONS LIMITED
SWISS CHALET
(*Suby of* Cara Holdings Limited)
60 Overlea Blvd Suite 1208, Toronto, ON, M4H 1B6
(416) 696-2268
Emp Here 30
SIC 5812 Eating places

D-U-N-S 20-050-2180   (BR)
DOLLARAMA S.E.C.
DOLLARAMA
45 Overlea Blvd Suite 2, Toronto, ON, M4H 1C3
(416) 425-2830
Emp Here 25
SIC 5311 Department stores

D-U-N-S 24-625-1078   (HQ)
GREEK COMMUNITY OF TORONTO
(*Suby of* Greek Community of Toronto)
30 Thorncliffe Park Dr, Toronto, ON, M4H 1H8
(416) 425-2485
Emp Here 55   *Emp Total* 80
Sales 3,137,310
SIC 8322 Individual and family services

D-U-N-S 25-318-2018   (BR)
MCDONALD'S RESTAURANTS OF CANADA LIMITED
MCDONALD'S
(*Suby of* McDonald's Corporation)
45 Overlea Blvd Suite 2, Toronto, ON, M4H 1C3

Emp Here 45
SIC 5812 Eating places

D-U-N-S 25-300-3461   (BR)
METRO ONTARIO INC
FOOD BASICS
45 Overlea Blvd Suite 2, Toronto, ON, M4H

1C3
(416) 421-1732
Emp Here 180
SIC 5411 Grocery stores

D-U-N-S 20-651-2886   (BR)
MORGUARD CORPORATION
MORGUARD RESIDENTIAL
47 Thorncliffe Park Dr Suite 105, Toronto, ON, M4H 1J5
(416) 421-3109
Emp Here 30
SIC 8741 Management services

D-U-N-S 20-166-9249   (SL)
R.G. HENDERSON & SON LIMITED
FOOD EQUIPMENT PARTS & SERVICE
100 Thorncliffe Park Dr Suite 416, Toronto, ON, M4H 1L9
(416) 422-5580
Emp Here 64   *Sales* 3,866,917
SIC 7699 Repair services, nec

D-U-N-S 25-193-0806   (HQ)
RPM CANADA
TREMCO CANADA
(*Suby of* RPM International Inc.)
220 Wicksteed Ave, Toronto, ON, M4H 1G7
(416) 421-3300
Emp Here 450   *Emp Total* 14,318
Sales 127,512,147
SIC 2851 Paints and allied products
Mgr Kathie Rogers

D-U-N-S 25-911-0674   (BR)
REDBERRY FRANCHISING CORP
BURGER KING
66 Overlea Blvd, Toronto, ON, M4H 1C4

Emp Here 20
SIC 5812 Eating places

D-U-N-S 25-321-4894   (BR)
REVERA INC
LEASIDE RETIREMENT RESIDENCE
14 William Morgan Dr Suite 2716, Toronto, ON, M4H 1E8
(416) 422-1320
Emp Here 50
SIC 8051 Skilled nursing care facilities

D-U-N-S 25-321-4852   (BR)
REVERA INC
LEASIDE RETIREMENT RESIDENCE II
10 William Morgan Dr, Toronto, ON, M4H 1E7
(416) 425-3722
Emp Here 60
SIC 8051 Skilled nursing care facilities

D-U-N-S 24-843-7303   (SL)
ROSE REISMAN CATERING INC
18 Banigan Dr, Toronto, ON, M4H 1E9
(416) 467-7758
Emp Here 70   *Sales* 2,115,860
SIC 5812 Eating places

D-U-N-S 25-220-3260   (BR)
STERLING MARKING PRODUCTS INC
CANADA STAMP
4 William Morgan Dr, Toronto, ON, M4H 1E6
(416) 425-4140
Emp Here 30
SIC 3953 Marking devices

D-U-N-S 24-096-7257   (BR)
STERLING MARKING PRODUCTS INC
TORONTO W, DIV OF
4 William Morgan Dr, Toronto, ON, M4H 1E6
(416) 255-3401
Emp Here 20
SIC 3953 Marking devices

D-U-N-S 25-265-0791   (BR)
TORONTO DISTRICT SCHOOL BOARD
THORNCLIFFE PARK PUBLIC SCHOOL
80 Thorncliffe Park Dr, Toronto, ON, M4H 1K3
(416) 396-2460
Emp Here 110

SIC 8211 Elementary and secondary schools

Toronto, ON M4J
York County

D-U-N-S 25-882-4341   (SL)
AMPHORA MAINTENANCE SERVICES INC
707a Danforth Ave, Toronto, ON, M4J 1L2
(416) 461-0401
Emp Here 95   *Sales* 2,772,507
SIC 7349 Building maintenance services, nec

D-U-N-S 24-476-2084   (BR)
BANK OF NOVA SCOTIA, THE
SCOTIABANK
661 Danforth Ave, Toronto, ON, M4J 1L2

Emp Here 20
SIC 6021 National commercial banks

D-U-N-S 24-525-7352   (BR)
CONSEIL SCOLAIRE VIAMONDE
ECOLE ELEMENTAIRE LA MOSA QUE
80 Queensdale Ave, Toronto, ON, M4J 1Y3
(416) 465-5757
Emp Here 40
SIC 8211 Elementary and secondary schools

D-U-N-S 25-512-3135   (SL)
DAILY SEAFOOD INC
135 Blake St, Toronto, ON, M4J 3E2
(416) 461-9449
Emp Here 35   *Sales* 12,768,123
SIC 5146 Fish and seafoods
Pr Pr Timen Ho
  Jessie Ho

D-U-N-S 24-311-6220   (SL)
GRIDUS TECHNOLOGY INC
127 Torrens Ave, Toronto, ON, M4J 2P6
(416) 716-0735
Emp Here 20   *Sales* 5,376,850
SIC 5085 Industrial supplies
  Yanlin Chen
Dir Tong Hu

D-U-N-S 20-994-7105   (BR)
LICK'S ICE CREAM & BURGER SHOPS INC
LICK'S HOMEBURGERS & ICE CREAM SHOPS
(*Suby of* Lick's Ice Cream & Burger Shops Inc)
654 Danforth Ave, Toronto, ON, M4J 1L1

Emp Here 20
SIC 5812 Eating places

D-U-N-S 20-697-6230   (BR)
TORONTO CATHOLIC DISTRICT SCHOOL BOARD
ST. PATRICK CATHOLIC SECONDARY SCHOOL
49 Felstead Ave, Toronto, ON, M4J 1G3
(416) 393-5546
Emp Here 75
SIC 8211 Elementary and secondary schools

D-U-N-S 20-711-1266   (BR)
TORONTO CATHOLIC DISTRICT SCHOOL BOARD
ST. JOACHIM CATHOLIC SCHOOL
343 Jones Ave, Toronto, ON, M4J 3G4
(416) 393-5292
Emp Here 20
SIC 8211 Elementary and secondary schools

D-U-N-S 20-035-5399   (BR)
TORONTO CATHOLIC DISTRICT SCHOOL BOARD
HOLY CROSS CATHOLIC ELEMENTARY SCHOOL
299a Donlands Ave, Toronto, ON, M4J 3R7
(416) 393-5242
Emp Here 30
SIC 8211 Elementary and secondary schools

D-U-N-S 20-572-4516   (BR)
TORONTO DISTRICT SCHOOL BOARD
ADULT CENTER
540 Jones Ave, Toronto, ON, M4J 3G9
(416) 393-9645
Emp Here 35
SIC 8211 Elementary and secondary schools

D-U-N-S 20-025-2471   (BR)
TORONTO DISTRICT SCHOOL BOARD
BLAKE STREET JUNIOR PUBLIC SCHOOL
21 Boultbee Ave, Toronto, ON, M4J 1A7
(416) 393-9415
Emp Here 35
SIC 8211 Elementary and secondary schools

D-U-N-S 20-026-1779   (BR)
TORONTO DISTRICT SCHOOL BOARD
EARL GREY ELEMENTARY SCHOOL
100 Strathcona Ave, Toronto, ON, M4J 1G8
(416) 393-9545
Emp Here 50
SIC 8211 Elementary and secondary schools

D-U-N-S 25-531-1607   (BR)
TORONTO DISTRICT SCHOOL BOARD
MONARCH PARK COLLEGIATE
1 Hanson St, Toronto, ON, M4J 1G6
(416) 393-0190
Emp Here 90
SIC 8211 Elementary and secondary schools

D-U-N-S 20-700-3430   (BR)
TORONTO DISTRICT SCHOOL BOARD
GREENWOOD SECONDARY SCHOOL
24 Mountjoy Ave, Toronto, ON, M4J 1J6
(416) 226-0494
Emp Here 40
SIC 8211 Elementary and secondary schools

D-U-N-S 20-711-2942   (BR)
TORONTO DISTRICT SCHOOL BOARD
WILLIAM BURGESS ELEMENTARY SCHOOL
100 Torrens Ave, Toronto, ON, M4J 2P5
(416) 396-2490
Emp Here 35
SIC 8211 Elementary and secondary schools

D-U-N-S 25-265-1039   (BR)
TORONTO DISTRICT SCHOOL BOARD
DIEFENBAKER ELEMENTARY SCHOOL
175 Plains Rd, Toronto, ON, M4J 2R2
(416) 396-2350
Emp Here 30
SIC 8211 Elementary and secondary schools

D-U-N-S 25-357-8231   (BR)
TORONTO EAST GENERAL HOSPITAL
WITHDRAWAL MANAGEMENT CENTRE
985 Danforth Ave, Toronto, ON, M4J 1M1
(416) 461-2010
Emp Here 25
SIC 8069 Specialty hospitals, except psychiatric

D-U-N-S 25-319-8733   (BR)
TORONTO TRANSIT COMMISSION
400 Greenwood Ave, Toronto, ON, M4J 4Y5
(416) 393-3176
Emp Here 200
SIC 4111 Local and suburban transit

D-U-N-S 24-608-9858   (HQ)
WOODGREEN COMMUNITY SERVICES
(*Suby of* Woodgreen Community Services)
815 Danforth Ave Suite 100, Toronto, ON, M4J 1L2
(416) 645-6000
Emp Here 50   *Emp Total* 330
Sales 21,201,280
SIC 8399 Social services, nec
Pr Brian Smith
  Thomas Hofmann
Dir Fin Larry Whatmore

Toronto, ON M4K
York County

D-U-N-S 25-341-3264   (SL)
1073197 ONTARIO LTD
IL FORNELLO RESTAURANT
576 Danforth Ave, Toronto, ON, M4K 1R1
(416) 466-2931
Emp Here 50   *Sales* 1,532,175
SIC 5812 Eating places

D-U-N-S 24-545-3667   (SL)
546073 ONTARIO LIMITED
BIG CARROT NATURAL FOOD MARKET
348 Danforth Ave Suite 8, Toronto, ON, M4K 1N8
(416) 466-2129
Emp Here 100   *Sales* 4,888,367
SIC 5499 Miscellaneous food stores

D-U-N-S 25-227-4923   (BR)
BANK OF NOVA SCOTIA, THE
SCOTIABANK
363 Broadview Ave, Toronto, ON, M4K 2M7
(416) 465-3531
Emp Here 25
SIC 6021 National commercial banks

D-U-N-S 20-580-1314   (BR)
CANADA POST CORPORATION
1032 Pape Ave, Toronto, ON, M4K 3W2
(416) 423-4661
Emp Here 20
SIC 4311 U.s. postal service

D-U-N-S 20-039-7003   (BR)
CORPORATION OF THE CITY OF TORONTO
EASTERN COMMUNITY CENTRE
1081 1/2 Pape Ave, Toronto, ON, M4K 3W6
(416) 396-2880
Emp Here 50
SIC 8322 Individual and family services

D-U-N-S 25-340-6052   (BR)
GOVERNING COUNCIL OF THE SALVATION ARMY IN CANADA, THE
HARBOUR LIGHT CENTRE, THE
450 Pape Ave, Toronto, ON, M4K 3P7
(416) 363-6880
Emp Here 35
SIC 8361 Residential care

D-U-N-S 25-520-4380   (BR)
GOVERNING COUNCIL OF THE SALVATION ARMY IN CANADA, THE
GOVERNING COUNCIL OF THE SALVATION ARMY IN CANADA, THE
1132 Broadview Ave, Toronto, ON, M4K 2S5
(416) 425-1052
Emp Here 120
SIC 8399 Social services, nec

D-U-N-S 24-382-3288   (BR)
LOBLAWS INC
LOBLAWS
720 Broadview Ave, Toronto, ON, M4K 2P1
(416) 778-8762
Emp Here 100
SIC 5411 Grocery stores

D-U-N-S 24-874-7289   (SL)
MASCAREN INTERNATIONAL INC
500a Danforth Ave Suite 304, Toronto, ON, M4K 1P6
(416) 465-6690
Emp Here 1,000   *Sales* 98,160,000
SIC 7363 Help supply services
Pr Pr Heather Mascaren

D-U-N-S 20-800-6226   (BR)
MCDONALD'S RESTAURANTS OF CANADA LIMITED
MCDONALD'S
(*Suby of* McDonald's Corporation)
1045 Pape Ave, Toronto, ON, M4K 3W3

---

(416) 423-3475
Emp Here 30
SIC 5812 Eating places

D-U-N-S 25-412-8382   (BR)
METRO ONTARIO INC
FOOD BASICS
1070 Pape Ave, Toronto, ON, M4K 3W5
(416) 467-8519
Emp Here 58
SIC 5411 Grocery stores

D-U-N-S 24-010-6435   (SL)
MONTCREST SCHOOL
4 Montcrest Blvd, Toronto, ON, M4K 1J7
(416) 469-2008
Emp Here 60   *Sales* 4,012,839
SIC 8211 Elementary and secondary schools

D-U-N-S 20-784-3632   (SL)
NISBET LODGE
740 Pape Ave, Toronto, ON, M4K 3S7
(416) 469-1105
Emp Here 100   *Sales* 3,648,035
SIC 8361 Residential care

D-U-N-S 24-315-7351   (SL)
PRO-ART DENTAL LABORATORY LTD
855 Broadview Ave Suite 408, Toronto, ON,
M4K 3Z1
(416) 469-4121
Emp Here 65   *Sales* 3,793,956
SIC 8072 Dental laboratories

D-U-N-S 25-988-4245   (BR)
SOBEYS CAPITAL INCORPORATED
SOBEYS 611
1015 Broadview Ave Suite 718, Toronto, ON,
M4K 2S1
(416) 421-5906
Emp Here 130
SIC 5141 Groceries, general line

D-U-N-S 20-711-0920   (BR)
**TORONTO CATHOLIC DISTRICT SCHOOL
BOARD**
HOLY NAME CATHOLIC SCHOOL
690 Carlaw Ave, Toronto, ON, M4K 3K9
(416) 393-5215
Emp Here 45
SIC 8211 Elementary and secondary schools

D-U-N-S 20-035-5415   (BR)
TORONTO DISTRICT SCHOOL BOARD
PAPE AVENUE PUBLIC SCHOOL
220 Langley Ave, Toronto, ON, M4K 1B9
(416) 393-9470
Emp Here 30
SIC 8211 Elementary and secondary schools

D-U-N-S 20-711-2876   (BR)
TORONTO DISTRICT SCHOOL BOARD
CHESTER ELEMENTARY SCHOOL
115 Gowan Ave, Toronto, ON, M4K 2E4
(416) 396-2325
Emp Here 50
SIC 8211 Elementary and secondary schools

D-U-N-S 20-711-2579   (BR)
TORONTO DISTRICT SCHOOL BOARD
WITHROW AVENUE PUBLIC SCHOOL
25 Bain Ave, Toronto, ON, M4K 1E5
(416) 393-9440
Emp Here 45
SIC 8211 Elementary and secondary schools

D-U-N-S 25-237-9391   (BR)
TORONTO DISTRICT SCHOOL BOARD
CITY ADULT LEARNING CENTRE
1 Danforth Ave, Toronto, ON, M4K 1M8
(416) 393-9740
Emp Here 100
SIC 8211 Elementary and secondary schools

D-U-N-S 20-025-3081   (BR)
TORONTO DISTRICT SCHOOL BOARD
JACKMAN AVE PUBLIC SCHOOL
79 Jackman Ave, Toronto, ON, M4K 2X5
(416) 393-9710
Emp Here 52

SIC 8211 Elementary and secondary schools

D-U-N-S 20-012-5305   (BR)
TORONTO EAST GENERAL HOSPITAL
COMMUNITY OUTREACH SERVICES
177 Danforth Ave Suite 203, Toronto, ON,
M4K 1N2
(416) 461-2000
Emp Here 27
SIC 8322 Individual and family services

D-U-N-S 20-650-5583   (BR)
TURNING POINT YOUTH SERVICES
WITHROW
(*Suby of* Turning Point Youth Services)
1 Wroxeter Ave, Toronto, ON, M4K 1J5
(416) 466-9730
Emp Here 30
SIC 8361 Residential care

D-U-N-S 24-826-7791   (SL)
V A V HOLDINGS LIMITED
MISTER GREEK
568 Danforth Ave, Toronto, ON, M4K 1R1
(416) 461-5470
Emp Here 50   *Sales* 1,532,175
SIC 5812 Eating places

Toronto, ON M4L
York County

D-U-N-S 25-471-8794   (SL)
BEACH ARMS RETIREMENT LODGE INC
505 Kingston Rd, Toronto, ON, M4L 1V5
(416) 698-0414
Emp Here 31   *Sales* 2,699,546
SIC 6513 Apartment building operators

D-U-N-S 24-825-9673   (SL)
CANCORE BUILDING SERVICES LTD
1306 Queen St E, Toronto, ON, M4L 1C4
(416) 406-1900
Emp Here 60   *Sales* 1,751,057
SIC 7349 Building maintenance services, nec

D-U-N-S 25-265-4140   (BR)
**CONSEIL SCOLAIRE DE DISTRICT
CATHOLIQUE CENTRE-SUD**
*ECOLE ELEMENTAIRE CATHOLIQUE
GEORGES-ETIENNE-CARTIER*
250 Gainsborough Rd, Toronto, ON, M4L 3C6
(416) 393-5314
Emp Here 25
SIC 8211 Elementary and secondary schools

D-U-N-S 20-705-8525   (BR)
**CORPORATION OF THE CITY OF
TORONTO**
FLEET SERVICES
843 Eastern Ave, Toronto, ON, M4L 1A2
(416) 392-7791
Emp Here 200
SIC 7699 Repair services, nec

D-U-N-S 20-717-1633   (BR)
CORUS MEDIA HOLDINGS INC
SHAW MEDIA INC
1651 Queen St E, Toronto, ON, M4L 1G5
(416) 699-1327
Emp Here 50
SIC 7832 Motion picture theaters, except
drive-in

D-U-N-S 24-486-2306   (BR)
G4S CASH SOLUTIONS (CANADA) LTD
7 Woodfield Rd, Toronto, ON, M4L 2W1

Emp Here 400
SIC 7381 Detective and armored car services

D-U-N-S 20-781-2681   (BR)
G4S CASH SOLUTIONS (CANADA) LTD
GROUP 4 SECURICOR-CASH SERVICE
1 Woodfield Rd, Toronto, ON, M4L 2W1
(416) 406-4926
Emp Here 40

SIC 7381 Detective and armored car services

D-U-N-S 24-690-4879   (BR)
GOODLIFE FITNESS CENTRES INC
280 Coxwell Ave, Toronto, ON, M4L 3B6
(416) 466-8699
Emp Here 40
SIC 7991 Physical fitness facilities

D-U-N-S 24-779-6972   (SL)
HALO SECURITY INC
SECURITY MANAGEMENT SERVICES
1574 Queen St E Suite 1, Toronto, ON, M4L
1G1
(416) 360-1902
Emp Here 150   *Sales* 4,669,485
SIC 7381 Detective and armored car services

D-U-N-S 25-321-7988   (BR)
LICK'S ICE CREAM & BURGER SHOPS INC
(*Suby of* Lick's Ice Cream & Burger Shops Inc)
1960 Queen St E, Toronto, ON, M4L 1H8

Emp Here 30
SIC 5812 Eating places

D-U-N-S 20-346-6990   (BR)
TORONTO DISTRICT SCHOOL BOARD
*EQUINOX HOLISTIC ALTERNATIVE
SCHOOL*
151 Hiawatha Rd, Toronto, ON, M4L 2Y1
(416) 393-8274
Emp Here 22
SIC 8211 Elementary and secondary schools

D-U-N-S 25-111-2140   (BR)
TORONTO DISTRICT SCHOOL BOARD
NORWAY JUNIOR PUBLIC SCHOOL
390 Kingston Rd, Toronto, ON, M4L 1T9
(416) 393-1700
Emp Here 30
SIC 8211 Elementary and secondary schools

D-U-N-S 20-648-5760   (BR)
TORONTO DISTRICT SCHOOL BOARD
RODEN JUNIOR PUBLIC SCHOOL
151 Hiawatha Rd, Toronto, ON, M4L 2Y1
(416) 393-9555
Emp Here 35
SIC 8211 Elementary and secondary schools

D-U-N-S 20-700-3158   (BR)
TORONTO DISTRICT SCHOOL BOARD
*BOWMORE JUNIOR & SENIOR PUBLIC
SCHOOL*
80 Bowmore Rd, Toronto, ON, M4L 3J2
(416) 393-9450
Emp Here 20
SIC 8211 Elementary and secondary schools

D-U-N-S 20-913-6584   (BR)
TORONTO DISTRICT SCHOOL BOARD
*DUKE OF CONNAUGHT JUNIOR & SENIOR
PUBLIC SCHOOL*
70 Woodfield Rd, Toronto, ON, M4L 2W6
(416) 393-9455
Emp Here 50
SIC 8211 Elementary and secondary schools

D-U-N-S 20-025-3073   (BR)
TORONTO DISTRICT SCHOOL BOARD
KEW BEACH JUNIOR PUBLIC SCHOOL
101 Kippendavie Ave, Toronto, ON, M4L 3R3
(416) 393-1810
Emp Here 30
SIC 8211 Elementary and secondary schools

D-U-N-S 20-714-5231   (BR)
WOODBINE ENTERTAINMENT GROUP
ONTARIO JOCKEY CLUB
(*Suby of* Woodbine Entertainment Group)
1661 Queen St E, Toronto, ON, M4L 1G5
(416) 698-3136
Emp Here 20
SIC 7999 Amusement and recreation, nec

Toronto, ON M4M
York County

D-U-N-S 20-522-3089   (BR)
BRAMBLES CANADA INC
*RECALL TOTAL INFORMATION MANAGE-
MENT*
77 East Don Roadway, Toronto, ON, M4M 2A5
(416) 424-3087
Emp Here 20
SIC 4226 Special warehousing and storage,
nec

D-U-N-S 20-984-1639   (BR)
CRH CANADA GROUP INC
DUFFERIN CONCRETE PRODUCTS
650 Commissioners St, Toronto, ON, M4M
1A7
(416) 465-3300
Emp Here 30
SIC 3531 Construction machinery

D-U-N-S 20-580-1371   (BR)
CANADA POST CORPORATION
1075 Queen St E, Toronto, ON, M4M 0C1

Emp Here 75
SIC 4311 U.s. postal service

D-U-N-S 24-452-4377   (HQ)
CANROOF CORPORATION INC
560 Commissioners St, Toronto, ON, M4M
1A7
(416) 461-8122
Emp Here 95   *Emp Total* 100
Sales 16,124,315
SIC 5211 Lumber and other building materials
Pr Pr Saul Koschitzky
　　Martin Vaughn
　　Henry Koschitzky

D-U-N-S 24-793-4813   (BR)
CASCADES CANADA ULC
*CASCADES BOXBOARD GROUP
TORONTO*
495 Commissioners St, Toronto, ON, M4M
1A5

Emp Here 150
SIC 2631 Paperboard mills

D-U-N-S 24-795-1460   (SL)
CHAI POULTRY INC
HIGH KOSHER POULTRY
115 Saulter St S, Toronto, ON, M4M 3K8
(416) 462-1313
Emp Here 100   *Sales* 32,971,250
SIC 5144 Poultry and poultry products
Pr Pr Charles Weinburg

D-U-N-S 25-999-6585   (BR)
**CORPORATION OF THE CITY OF
TORONTO**
ASHBRIDGES BAY TREATMENT PLANT
9 Leslie St, Toronto, ON, M4M 3M9
(416) 392-5153
Emp Here 220
SIC 4953 Refuse systems

D-U-N-S 20-041-1226   (BR)
**CORPORATION OF THE CITY OF
TORONTO**
MATTY ECKLER RECREATION CENTRE
953 Gerrard St E, Toronto, ON, M4M 1Z4
(416) 392-0750
Emp Here 50
SIC 7999 Amusement and recreation, nec

D-U-N-S 20-176-7691   (BR)
**CORPORATION OF THE CITY OF
TORONTO**
WASTE MANAGEMENT FACILITY
400 Commissioners St, Toronto, ON, M4M
3K2
(416) 392-5890
Emp Here 20
SIC 4953 Refuse systems

D-U-N-S 24-826-2490   (SL)

DIGITAL GENERATION ULC
EXTREME REACH CANADA
635 Queen St E, Toronto, ON, M4M 1G4
(647) 436-0563
Emp Here 50   *Sales* 4,596,524
SIC 7812 Motion picture and video production

D-U-N-S 20-777-0020   (SL)
EAST-YORK & EAST-TORONTO FAMILY RESOURCES ORGANIZATION
947 Queen St E, Toronto, ON, M4M 1J9
(416) 686-3390
Emp Here 54   *Sales* 2,115,860
SIC 8322 Individual and family services

D-U-N-S 25-721-2563   (BR)
GREYHOUND CANADA TRANSPORTATION ULC
GREYHOUND MAINTENANCE
685 Lake Shore Blvd E, Toronto, ON, M4M 3J9
(416) 465-4049
Emp Here 60
SIC 7538 General automotive repair shops

D-U-N-S 20-553-6324   (BR)
HOME DEPOT OF CANADA INC
HOME DEPOT
(*Suby of* The Home Depot Inc)
1000 Gerrard St E Suite 366, Toronto, ON, M4M 3G6
(416) 462-6270
Emp Here 50
SIC 5211 Lumber and other building materials

D-U-N-S 20-039-7029   (BR)
LOBLAWS INC
LOBLAWS
17 Leslie St, Toronto, ON, M4M 3H9
(416) 469-2897
Emp Here 300
SIC 5411 Grocery stores

D-U-N-S 25-139-8095   (BR)
MAYFAIR TENNIS COURTS LIMITED
MAYFAIR RAQUET & FITNESS CLUBS
801 Lake Shore Blvd E, Toronto, ON, M4M 1A9
(416) 466-3770
Emp Here 80
SIC 7997 Membership sports and recreation clubs

D-U-N-S 24-344-5140   (BR)
METROLINX
GO TRANSIT
580 Commissioners St, Toronto, ON, M4M 1A7
(416) 393-4111
Emp Here 350
SIC 4131 Intercity and rural bus transportation

D-U-N-S 20-209-3410   (BR)
PUROLATOR INC.
PUROLATOR INC
20 Morse St, Toronto, ON, M4M 2P6
(416) 461-9031
Emp Here 350
SIC 4731 Freight transportation arrangement

D-U-N-S 25-300-5169   (BR)
REDBERRY FRANCHISING CORP
BURGER KING
11 Leslie St, Toronto, ON, M4M 3H9
(416) 462-0264
Emp Here 25
SIC 5812 Eating places

D-U-N-S 24-101-2389   (BR)
STAPLES CANADA INC
STAPLES THE BUSINESS DEPOT
(*Suby of* Staples, Inc.)
1000 Gerrard St E Unit Dd16, Toronto, ON, M4M 3G6
(416) 466-4900
Emp Here 30
SIC 5943 Stationery stores

D-U-N-S 24-569-0990   (SL)
TD AUTO FINANCE (CANADA) INC.

TD AUTO FINANCE
(*Suby of* Toronto-Dominion Bank, The)
25 Booth Ave Suite 101, Toronto, ON, M4M 2M3
(416) 463-4422
Emp Here 32   *Sales* 19,042,743
SIC 6159 Miscellaneous business credit institutions
Dir Sandra Mundy
Dir Timothy Hockey
Dir Paul Vessey
Dir Shailesh Kotwal
Dir Richard Mathes
Dir David Sloan

D-U-N-S 25-341-0708   (HQ)
TD FINANCING SERVICES HOME INC
(*Suby of* Toronto-Dominion Bank, The)
25 Booth Ave Suite 101, Toronto, ON, M4M 2M3
(416) 463-4422
Emp Here 200   *Emp Total* 81,233
Sales 178,242,990
SIC 6141 Personal credit institutions
Dir Erik De Witte
Dir Shailesh Kotwal
Dir Christine Morris
Dir Manjit Singh
Dir Raymond Chun
Dir Mark Clearihue
Dir Sandra Mundy
Dir Catherine Sampson

D-U-N-S 20-738-5266   (SL)
TIM HORTONS INVESTMENTS INC
TIM HORTONS
731 Eastern Ave, Toronto, ON, M4M 3H6
(416) 466-3580
Emp Here 70   *Sales* 2,115,860
SIC 5812 Eating places

D-U-N-S 25-486-9605   (BR)
TORONTO CATHOLIC DISTRICT SCHOOL BOARD
ST. JOSEPH'S ELEMENTARY SCHOOL
176 Leslie St, Toronto, ON, M4M 3C7
(416) 393-5209
Emp Here 25
SIC 8211 Elementary and secondary schools

D-U-N-S 25-447-1006   (BR)
TORONTO DISTRICT SCHOOL BOARD
LESLIEVILLE PUBLIC SCHOOL
254 Leslie St, Toronto, ON, M4M 3C9
(416) 393-9480
Emp Here 40
SIC 8211 Elementary and secondary schools

D-U-N-S 20-591-5320   (BR)
TORONTO DISTRICT SCHOOL BOARD
EASTDALE CI
701 Gerrard St E, Toronto, ON, M4M 1Y4
(416) 393-9630
Emp Here 44
SIC 8211 Elementary and secondary schools

D-U-N-S 20-698-7450   (BR)
TORONTO DISTRICT SCHOOL BOARD
QUEEN ALEXANDRA MIDDLE SCHOOL
181 Broadview Ave, Toronto, ON, M4M 2G3
(416) 393-9535
Emp Here 40
SIC 8211 Elementary and secondary schools

D-U-N-S 25-237-9425   (BR)
TORONTO DISTRICT SCHOOL BOARD
RIVERDALE COLLEGIATE INSTITUTE
1094 Gerrard St E, Toronto, ON, M4M 2A1
(416) 393-9820
Emp Here 101
SIC 8211 Elementary and secondary schools

D-U-N-S 20-654-9441   (BR)
TORONTO DISTRICT SCHOOL BOARD
DUNDAS JUNIOR PUBLIC SCHOOL
935 Dundas St E, Toronto, ON, M4M 1R4
(416) 393-9565
Emp Here 20

SIC 8211 Elementary and secondary schools

D-U-N-S 20-698-7765   (BR)
TORONTO DISTRICT SCHOOL BOARD
MORSE ST PS
180 Carlaw Ave, Toronto, ON, M4M 2R9
(416) 393-9494
Emp Here 30
SIC 8211 Elementary and secondary schools

D-U-N-S 20-700-2606   (BR)
TORONTO DISTRICT SCHOOL BOARD
BRUCE JUNIOR PUBLIC SCHOOL
51 Larchmount Ave, Toronto, ON, M4M 2Y6
(416) 393-0670
Emp Here 35
SIC 8211 Elementary and secondary schools

D-U-N-S 25-513-8026   (SL)
URBACON BUILDINGS GROUP CORP
URBACON
(*Suby of* Renzo Holdings Limited)
750 Lake Shore Blvd E, Toronto, ON, M4M 3M3
(416) 865-9405
Emp Here 70   *Sales* 9,703,773
SIC 8741 Management services
Pr Pr Marco Mancini
   Ron Carinci

D-U-N-S 20-804-5331   (BR)
URBACON LIMITED/URBACON LIMITEE
750 Lake Shore Blvd E, Toronto, ON, M4M 3M3
(416) 865-9405
Emp Here 80
SIC 1541 Industrial buildings and warehouses

D-U-N-S 25-487-8093   (BR)
VALUE VILLAGE STORES, INC
(*Suby of* Savers, Inc.)
924 Queen St E, Toronto, ON, M4M 1J5
(416) 778-4818
Emp Here 26
SIC 5399 Miscellaneous general merchandise

D-U-N-S 20-005-4018   (BR)
WENDY'S RESTAURANTS OF CANADA INC
(*Suby of* The Wendy's Company)
731 Eastern Ave, Toronto, ON, M4M 3H6
(416) 465-9904
Emp Here 50
SIC 5812 Eating places

D-U-N-S 25-293-8865   (BR)
WESTON BAKERIES LIMITED
MOISSON DOREE
462 Eastern Ave, Toronto, ON, M4M 1C3

Emp Here 150
SIC 2051 Bread, cake, and related products

D-U-N-S 24-074-8749   (SL)
WINGBACK ENTERPRISES LIMITED
ADELAIDE CLUB, THE
1 First Ave, Toronto, ON, M4M 1W7
(416) 367-9957
Emp Here 80   *Sales* 3,210,271
SIC 7991 Physical fitness facilities

D-U-N-S 24-312-4307   (BR)
WINNERS MERCHANTS INTERNATIONAL L.P.
WINNERS
(*Suby of* The TJX Companies Inc)
1000 Gerrard St E, Toronto, ON, M4M 3G6
(416) 466-2796
Emp Here 30
SIC 5651 Family clothing stores

D-U-N-S 25-359-5219   (BR)
WOODGREEN COMMUNITY SERVICES
(*Suby of* Woodgreen Community Services)
835 Queen St E, Toronto, ON, M4M 1H9
(416) 469-5211
Emp Here 25
SIC 8351 Child day care services

D-U-N-S 25-686-8647   (HQ)

WOODGREEN RED DOOR FAMILY SHELTER
FAMILY SHELTER
(*Suby of* Woodgreen Red Door Family Shelter)
21 Carlaw Ave, Toronto, ON, M4M 2R6
(416) 915-5671
Emp Here 50   *Emp Total* 100
Sales 3,970,892
SIC 8322 Individual and family services

Toronto, ON M4N
York County

D-U-N-S 25-940-6817   (SL)
CSH FOUR TEDDINGTON PARK INC
CHARTWELL SENIOR HOUSING
4 Teddington Park Ave, Toronto, ON, M4N 2C3
(416) 481-2986
Emp Here 47   *Sales* 4,085,799
SIC 6513 Apartment building operators

D-U-N-S 25-119-5640   (BR)
CANADA POST CORPORATION
2708 Yonge St, Toronto, ON, M4N 2H9
(416) 483-7122
Emp Here 60
SIC 4311 U.s. postal service

D-U-N-S 25-138-5035   (SL)
ESTATES OF SUNNYBROOK, THE
2075 Bayview Ave, Toronto, ON, M4N 3M5
(416) 487-3841
Emp Here 62   *Sales* 2,042,900
SIC 7299 Miscellaneous personal service

D-U-N-S 20-521-8311   (SL)
FIRST CANADIAN HEALTH MANAGEMENT CORPORATION
3080 Yonge St Suite 3002, Toronto, ON, M4N 3N1

Emp Here 60   *Sales* 3,064,349
SIC 7389 Business services, nec

D-U-N-S 25-425-4899   (SL)
HANNA, WEDAD MEDICINE PROFESSIONAL CORPORATION
SUNNYBROOK HOSPITAL
2075 Bayview Ave Unit E432, Toronto, ON, M4N 3M5
(416) 480-6100
Emp Here 57   *Sales* 4,071,380
SIC 8011 Offices and clinics of medical doctors

D-U-N-S 25-692-9308   (BR)
MASTERMIND LP
MASTERMIND EDUCATIONAL
3350 Yonge St, Toronto, ON, M4N 2M7
(416) 487-7177
Emp Here 25
SIC 5945 Hobby, toy, and game shops

D-U-N-S 25-300-0210   (BR)
METRO ONTARIO INC
3142 Yonge St, Toronto, ON, M4N 2K6
(416) 484-0750
Emp Here 70
SIC 5411 Grocery stores

D-U-N-S 24-382-2223   (SL)
RESEARCH NOW INC
E-REWARDS
(*Suby of* Research Now Group, Inc.)
3080 Yonge St Suite 2000, Toronto, ON, M4N 3N1
(800) 599-7938
Emp Here 152   *Sales* 11,463,850
SIC 8731 Commercial physical research
CEO Kurt Knapton

D-U-N-S 25-512-2400   (BR)
ROYAL LEPAGE LIMITED
LEPAGE ON YONGE

3080 Yonge St Suite 2060, Toronto, ON, M4N
3N1
(416) 487-4311
Emp Here 96
SIC 6531 Real estate agents and managers

D-U-N-S 25-031-5736   (BR)
SHERIDAN NURSERIES LIMITED
2827 Yonge St, Toronto, ON, M4N 2J4
(416) 481-6429
Emp Here 20
SIC 5261 Retail nurseries and garden stores

D-U-N-S 20-046-6345   (HQ)
**SUNNYBROOK HEALTH SCIENCES CEN-
TRE FOUNDATION**
SUNNYBROOK FOUNDATION
(*Suby of* Sunnybrook Health Sciences Centre
Foundation)
2075 Bayview Ave Suite 747, Toronto, ON,
M4N 3M5
(416) 480-6100
Emp Here 7,000   *Emp Total* 10,000
Sales 803,787,987
SIC 8011 Offices and clinics of medical doc-
tors
Pr Barry A Mclellan
 David A Leslie
 J David A Jackson

D-U-N-S 24-684-0065   (SL)
SUNNYBROOK RESEARCH INSTITUTE
2075 Bayview Ave, Toronto, ON, M4N 3M5
(416) 480-6100
Emp Here 480   *Sales* 90,503,520
SIC 8732 Commercial nonphysical research
VP Michael Julius
Ex Dir Grace Cheng

D-U-N-S 20-700-2994   (BR)
TORONTO DISTRICT SCHOOL BOARD
BLYTHWOOD JUNIOR PUBLIC SCHOOL
2 Strathgowan Cres, Toronto, ON, M4N 2Z5
(416) 393-9105
Emp Here 20
SIC 8211 Elementary and secondary schools

Toronto, ON M4P
York County

D-U-N-S 20-113-9297   (SL)
1118174 ONTARIO LIMITED
*BEST WESTERN ROEHAMPTON HOTEL &
SUITES*
808 Mount Pleasant Rd, Toronto, ON, M4P
2L2
(416) 487-5101
Emp Here 50   *Sales* 2,188,821
SIC 7011 Hotels and motels

D-U-N-S 20-286-6067   (SL)
2188262 ONTARIO LTD
AVANT SLEEP
586 Eglinton Ave E Unit 208, Toronto, ON,
M4P 1P2
(416) 802-2382
Emp Here 50   *Sales* 10,145,000
SIC 5047 Medical and hospital equipment
Kostas Tsambourlianos

D-U-N-S 24-437-7474   (BR)
BANQUE TORONTO-DOMINION, LA
TORONTO-DOMINION BANK, THE
(*Suby of* Toronto-Dominion Bank, The)
2453 Yonge St, Toronto, ON, M4P 2H6
(416) 932-1500
Emp Here 30
SIC 6021 National commercial banks

D-U-N-S 20-113-5667   (BR)
BELL MEDIA INC
ASTRAL TELEVISION NETWORK, DIV OF
50 Eglinton Ave E Suite 1, Toronto, ON, M4P
1A6

(416) 924-6664
Emp Here 175
SIC 4833 Television broadcasting stations

D-U-N-S 20-919-2454   (BR)
BEST BUY CANADA LTD
FUTURE SHOP
(*Suby of* Best Buy Co., Inc.)
2400 Yonge St, Toronto, ON, M4P 2H4
(416) 489-4726
Emp Here 50
SIC 5731 Radio, television, and electronic
stores

D-U-N-S 24-645-9135   (SL)
CS & P ARCHITECTS INC
CS & P
2345 Yonge St Suite 200, Toronto, ON, M4P
2E5
(416) 482-5002
Emp Here 50   *Sales* 4,961,328
SIC 8712 Architectural services

D-U-N-S 24-985-2039   (BR)
**CANADIAN INSTITUTE FOR HEALTH IN-
FORMATION**
CIHI
90 Eglinton Ave E Suite 300, Toronto, ON,
M4P 2Y3
(416) 481-2002
Emp Here 300
SIC 8361 Residential care

D-U-N-S 20-566-1353   (SL)
CARD ONE PLUS LTD
40 Eglinton Ave E Suite 502, Toronto, ON,
M4P 3A2

Emp Here 20   *Sales* 9,423,290
SIC 6099 Functions related to deposit banking
Pr Pr Kevin Lewis

D-U-N-S 24-418-2858   (BR)
CINEPLEX ODEON CORPORATION
SILVERCITY YONGE (EGLINTON CENTRE)
2300 Yonge St Suite 2307, Toronto, ON, M4P
1E4
(416) 544-1236
Emp Here 20
SIC 7832 Motion picture theaters, except
drive-in

D-U-N-S 25-321-6568   (BR)
CLUB MONACO CORP
(*Suby of* Ralph Lauren Corporation)
2610 Yonge St, Toronto, ON, M4P 2J4
(416) 487-0841
Emp Here 20
SIC 5611 Men's and boys' clothing stores

D-U-N-S 24-555-7384   (SL)
CUSTOM MAIDS INCORPORATED
55 Eglinton Ave E Suite 706, Toronto, ON,
M4P 1G8
(416) 488-5254
Emp Here 50   *Sales* 1,459,214
SIC 7349 Building maintenance services, nec

D-U-N-S 25-510-7716   (BR)
DECIMA INC
OPINION SEARCH (OSI)
(*Suby of* Decima Inc)
2345 Yonge St Suite 704, Toronto, ON, M4P
2E5
(416) 962-9109
Emp Here 90
SIC 8732 Commercial nonphysical research

D-U-N-S 25-319-7529   (BR)
DON MICHAEL HOLDINGS INC
ROOTS CANADA
2670 Yonge St, Toronto, ON, M4P 2J5
(416) 482-6773
Emp Here 20
SIC 5651 Family clothing stores

D-U-N-S 25-951-2184   (SL)
ELDERCARE HOME HEALTH INC
234 Eglinton Ave E Unit 207, Toronto, ON,

M4P 1K5
(416) 482-8292
Emp Here 60   *Sales* 2,334,742
SIC 8322 Individual and family services

D-U-N-S 25-304-6916   (BR)
GAP (CANADA) INC
GAP
(*Suby of* The Gap Inc)
2635 Yonge St, Toronto, ON, M4P 2J6
(416) 487-1583
Emp Here 30
SIC 5651 Family clothing stores

D-U-N-S 25-702-7417   (BR)
GAP (CANADA) INC
GAPKIDS
(*Suby of* The Gap Inc)
2574 Yonge St, Toronto, ON, M4P 2J3
(416) 440-0187
Emp Here 20
SIC 5651 Family clothing stores

D-U-N-S 24-143-2087   (HQ)
**HANSA   LANGUAGE   CENTRE   OF
TORONTO INC**
(*Suby of* Hansa Language Centre Of Toronto
Inc)
51 Eglinton Ave E Suite 200, Toronto, ON,
M4P 1G7
(416) 487-8643
Emp Here 50   *Emp Total* 75
Sales 4,851,006
SIC 8299 Schools and educational services,
nec

D-U-N-S 24-858-5940   (SL)
HARRIS/DECIMA
(*Suby of* NIELSEN HOLDINGS PLC)
2345 Yonge St Suite 405, Toronto, ON, M4P
2E5
(416) 716-4903
Emp Here 100   *Sales* 12,622,201
SIC 8732 Commercial nonphysical research
VP VP Richard Cooper

D-U-N-S 24-346-7664   (BR)
HU-A-KAM ENTERPRISES INC
MCDONALD'S
(*Suby of* Hu-A-Kam Enterprises Inc)
20 Eglinton Ave E, Toronto, ON, M4P 1A9
(416) 489-3773
Emp Here 46
SIC 5812 Eating places

D-U-N-S 25-708-5068   (BR)
IMAGO RESTAURANTS INC
SUMMIT HOUSE GRILL
(*Suby of* Imago Restaurants Inc)
40 Eglinton Ave E, Toronto, ON, M4P 3A2

Emp Here 50
SIC 5812 Eating places

D-U-N-S 20-812-0324   (SL)
K & G APARTMENT HOLDINGS INC
299 Roehampton Ave, Toronto, ON, M4P 1S2
(416) 487-2844
Emp Here 50   *Sales* 4,742,446
SIC 6531 Real estate agents and managers

D-U-N-S 25-804-8438   (BR)
KITCHEN STUFF PLUS INC
(*Suby of* Halpern, Mark Holdings Inc)
2287 Yonge St Suite 200, Toronto, ON, M4P
2C6

Emp Here 25
SIC 5719 Miscellaneous homefurnishings

D-U-N-S 25-951-3778   (SL)
LABRASH SECURITY SERVICES LTD
55 Eglinton Ave E Suite 403, Toronto, ON,
M4P 1G8
(416) 487-4864
Emp Here 120   *Sales* 3,720,996
SIC 7381 Detective and armored car services

D-U-N-S 24-763-4350   (SL)

MKTG CANADA CORP
MKTG
1 Eglinton Ave E Suite 800, Toronto, ON, M4P
3A1
(416) 250-0321
Emp Here 30   *Sales* 3,476,332
SIC 8748 Business consulting, nec

D-U-N-S 24-525-3013   (HQ)
MMCC SOLUTIONS CANADA COMPANY
TELEPERFORMANCE CANADA
75 Eglinton Ave E, Toronto, ON, M4P 3A4
(416) 922-3519
Emp Here 500   *Emp Total* 47
Sales 71,647,407
SIC 7389 Business services, nec
 Dean Duncan
Genl Mgr Jeffrey K. Balagna

D-U-N-S 24-556-6419   (HQ)
MARKET PROBE CANADA COMPANY
40 Eglinton Ave E Suite 501, Toronto, ON,
M4P 3A2
(416) 487-4144
Emp Here 20   *Emp Total* 240
Sales 1,824,018
SIC 8732 Commercial nonphysical research

D-U-N-S 20-923-8984   (BR)
**MCDONALD'S   RESTAURANTS   OF
CANADA LIMITED**
MCDONALD'S
(*Suby of* McDonald's Corporation)
1 Eglinton Ave E, Toronto, ON, M4P 3A1
(416) 701-9560
Emp Here 30
SIC 5812 Eating places

D-U-N-S 20-552-8552   (BR)
METRO ONTARIO INC
DOMINION
2300 Yonge St Suite 752, Toronto, ON, M4P
1E4
(416) 483-7340
Emp Here 250
SIC 5411 Grocery stores

D-U-N-S 20-552-8784   (BR)
METRO ONTARIO INC
METRO
656 Eglinton Ave E, Toronto, ON, M4P 1P1
(416) 482-7422
Emp Here 300
SIC 5411 Grocery stores

D-U-N-S 24-335-0530   (BR)
METRO ONTARIO INC
METRO
40 Eglinton Ave E, Toronto, ON, M4P 3A2
(416) 759-1952
Emp Here 150
SIC 5411 Grocery stores

D-U-N-S 20-859-9261   (BR)
PACIFIC LINK COMMUNICATIONS INC
BELL WORLD
2323 Yonge St Unit 101, Toronto, ON, M4P
2C9
(416) 322-7091
Emp Here 25
SIC 5999 Miscellaneous retail stores, nec

D-U-N-S 24-349-0377   (HQ)
PIVOTAL PROJECTS INCORPORATED
2300 Yonge St Suite 2202, Toronto, ON, M4P
1E4
(416) 847-0018
Emp Here 20   *Emp Total* 15,000
Sales 4,012,839
SIC 8742 Management consulting services

D-U-N-S 25-943-3365   (BR)
RBC DOMINION SECURITIES INC
RBC DOMINION SECURITIES
(*Suby of* Royal Bank Of Canada)
2345 Yonge St Suite 1000, Toronto, ON, M4P
2E5
(416) 974-0202
Emp Here 45

SIC 6282 Investment advice

D-U-N-S 25-147-7055   (SL)
RSM RICHTER & ASSOCIATES INC
90 Eglinton Ave E Suite 700, Toronto, ON, M4P 2Y3
(416) 932-8000
Emp Here 160   *Sales* 24,397,440
SIC 8742 Management consulting services
Dir Joel Cohen
Dir Robert Harlang
Dir Peter Farkas
Dir Leonard Bore

D-U-N-S 25-474-7942   (BR)
SCM INSURANCE SERVICES INC
SCM CANADA
2323 Yonge St Suite 501, Toronto, ON, M4P 2C9
(416) 360-7434
Emp Here 20
SIC 6411 Insurance agents, brokers, and service

D-U-N-S 25-691-2775   (BR)
SCHWARTZ   LEVITSKY   FELDMAN S.E.N.C.R.L.
2300 Yonge St Suite 1500, Toronto, ON, M4P 1E4
(416) 785-5353
Emp Here 80
SIC 8721 Accounting, auditing, and book-keeping

D-U-N-S 25-791-2410   (BR)
SCOTIA CAPITAL INC
SCOTIA MCLEOD
2300 Yonge St Suite 2000, Toronto, ON, M4P 1E4
(416) 945-4840
Emp Here 29
SIC 6211 Security brokers and dealers

D-U-N-S 20-743-2597   (BR)
SENIOR PEOPLES' RESOURCES IN NORTH TORONTO INCORPORATED
MONTGOMERY PLACE SPRINT SUPPORT-IVE HOUSING
(*Suby of* Senior Peoples' Resources In North Toronto Incorporated)
130 Eglinton Ave E Suite 1304, Toronto, ON, M4P 2X9
(416) 481-3225
Emp Here 20
SIC 8051 Skilled nursing care facilities

D-U-N-S 24-752-4853   (SL)
SPAGO RESTAURANT INC
CENTRO GRILL & WINE BAR
2472 Yonge St, Toronto, ON, M4P 2H5

Emp Here 50   *Sales* 1,532,175
SIC 5812 Eating places

D-U-N-S 25-905-6364   (BR)
SPORTING LIFE INC
2454 Yonge St, Toronto, ON, M4P 2H5
(416) 485-4440
Emp Here 50
SIC 5941 Sporting goods and bicycle shops

D-U-N-S 20-337-8760   (SL)
STAGNITO PARTNERS CANADA INC
ENSEMBLEiQ
2300 Yonge St Suite 1510, Toronto, ON, M4P 1E4
(416) 256-9908
Emp Here 25   *Sales* 5,982,777
SIC 7311 Advertising agencies
Pr Korry Stagnito
Sec Kyle Stagnito

D-U-N-S 20-711-1407   (BR)
TORONTO CATHOLIC DISTRICT SCHOOL BOARD
ST. MONICA CATHOLIC SCHOOL
14 Broadway Ave, Toronto, ON, M4P 1T4
(416) 393-5224
Emp Here 40

SIC 8211 Elementary and secondary schools

D-U-N-S 25-422-4041   (BR)
TORONTO DISTRICT SCHOOL BOARD
JOHN FISHER JUNIOR PUBLIC SCHOOL
40 Erskine Ave, Toronto, ON, M4P 1Y2
(416) 393-9325
Emp Here 30
SIC 8211 Elementary and secondary schools

D-U-N-S 20-698-8003   (BR)
TORONTO DISTRICT SCHOOL BOARD
NORTH TORONTO COLLEGIATE INSTI-TUTE
17 Broadway Ave, Toronto, ON, M4P 1T7
(416) 393-9180
Emp Here 100
SIC 8211 Elementary and secondary schools

D-U-N-S 24-242-3171   (BR)
TORONTO DISTRICT SCHOOL BOARD
EGLINTON JUNIOR PUBLIC SCHOOL
223 Eglinton Ave E, Toronto, ON, M4P 1L1
(416) 393-9315
Emp Here 40
SIC 8211 Elementary and secondary schools

D-U-N-S 25-019-5062   (BR)
TORONTO DISTRICT SCHOOL BOARD
NORTHERN SECONDARY SCHOOL
851 Mount Pleasant Rd, Toronto, ON, M4P 2L5
(416) 393-0270
Emp Here 200
SIC 8211 Elementary and secondary schools

D-U-N-S 25-321-3128   (BR)
TORONTO-DOMINION BANK, THE
TD CANADA TRUST
(*Suby of* Toronto-Dominion Bank, The)
2263 Yonge St, Toronto, ON, M4P 2C6
(416) 932-1500
Emp Here 35
SIC 6021 National commercial banks

D-U-N-S 25-092-7100   (BR)
TOYS 'R' US (CANADA) LTD
TOYS 'R' US
(*Suby of* Toys "r" Us, Inc.)
2300 Yonge St, Toronto, ON, M4P 1E4
(416) 322-1599
Emp Here 75
SIC 5945 Hobby, toy, and game shops

D-U-N-S 25-362-1403   (BR)
TRAVELBRANDS INC
TRAVELBRANDS INC
75 Eglinton Ave E, Toronto, ON, M4P 3A4
(416) 921-7923
Emp Here 60
SIC 4729 Passenger transportation arrangement

D-U-N-S 20-818-6106   (HQ)
UNITED STEELWORKERS OF AMERICA
(*Suby of* United Steelworkers)
234 Eglinton Ave E Suite 800, Toronto, ON, M4P 1K7
(416) 487-1571
Emp Here 50   *Emp Total* 1,800
Sales 26,484,734
SIC 8631 Labor organizations
Dir Ken Newmann

D-U-N-S 25-343-4559   (HQ)
YORKDALE CAFE LTD
TIM HORTONS
(*Suby of* Yorkdale Cafe Ltd)
2377 Yonge St Suite 823, Toronto, ON, M4P 2C8
(416) 484-4231
Emp Here 25   *Emp Total* 145
Sales 4,961,328
SIC 5461 Retail bakeries

Toronto, ON M4R
York County

D-U-N-S 25-092-4144   (BR)
HAVERGAL COLLEGE
460 Rosewell Ave, Toronto, ON, M4R 2H5
(416) 483-3843
Emp Here 50
SIC 8211 Elementary and secondary schools

D-U-N-S 20-818-1214   (HQ)
PILOT INSURANCE COMPANY
90 Eglinton Ave W Suite 102, Toronto, ON, M4R 2E4
(416) 487-5141
Emp Here 150   *Emp Total* 25,581
Sales 329,088,755
SIC 6331 Fire, marine, and casualty insurance
Pr Maurice Tulloch

D-U-N-S 25-338-1248   (SL)
THE RESPONSIVE MARKETING GROUP INC
(*Suby of* iMarketing Solutions Group Inc)
90 Eglinton Ave W Suite 300, Toronto, ON, M4R 2E4
(416) 921-6595
Emp Here 400   *Sales* 26,782,800
SIC 7389 Business services, nec
Pr Pr Michael Davis
  Kenneth Dewey
  Christopher Mccarthy

D-U-N-S 20-711-2611   (BR)
TORONTO DISTRICT SCHOOL BOARD
LAWRENCE PARK COLLEGITE INSTITUTE
125 Chatsworth Dr, Toronto, ON, M4R 1S1
(416) 393-9500
Emp Here 50
SIC 8211 Elementary and secondary schools

Toronto, ON M4S
York County

D-U-N-S 20-057-6143   (SL)
1381111 ONTARIO LTD
MANDARIN RESTAURANT-YONGE
2200 Yonge St Suite 603, Toronto, ON, M4S 2C6
(416) 486-2222
Emp Here 70   *Sales* 2,115,860
SIC 5812 Eating places

D-U-N-S 25-169-1275   (SL)
ACCLAIM SBA DISABILITY MANAGEMENT INC
250 Merton St Unit 503, Toronto, ON, M4S 1B1
(800) 565-2857
Emp Here 125   *Sales* 7,016,633
SIC 8331 Job training and related services

D-U-N-S 24-196-3594   (BR)
BANK OF MONTREAL
BMO
2210 Yonge St, Toronto, ON, M4S 2B8
(416) 488-1145
Emp Here 35
SIC 6021 National commercial banks

D-U-N-S 24-992-9431   (BR)
BANQUE TORONTO-DOMINION, LA
TD CANADA TRUST
(*Suby of* Toronto-Dominion Bank, The)
1955 Yonge St, Toronto, ON, M4S 1Z6
(416) 481-4423
Emp Here 20
SIC 6021 National commercial banks

D-U-N-S 24-761-8341   (HQ)
CANADIAN HOME INCOME PLAN CORPO-RATION
C H I P CORP
1881 Yonge St Suite 300, Toronto, ON, M4S 3C4

(416) 925-2447
Emp Here 45   *Emp Total* 35
Sales 14,033,266
SIC 6162 Mortgage bankers and loan correspondents
Pr Steve Ranson
Ch Bd Daniel Jauernig
VP Fin Scott G Cameron
VP VP Wendy Dryden

D-U-N-S 25-405-0263   (HQ)
CANADIAN TIRE REAL ESTATE LIMITED
2180 Yonge St, Toronto, ON, M4S 2B9
(416) 480-3000
Emp Here 70   *Emp Total* 12,356
Sales 7,514,952
SIC 6531 Real estate agents and managers
Pr Pr Ken Silver

D-U-N-S 24-418-2825   (BR)
CINEPLEX ODEON CORPORATION
FAMOUS PLAYERS CANADA SQUARE
2190 Yonge St, Toronto, ON, M4S 2B8
(416) 646-2913
Emp Here 20
SIC 7832 Motion picture theaters, except drive-in

D-U-N-S 25-274-7100   (SL)
DO PROCESS SOFTWARE LTD
(*Suby of* Teranet Inc)
2200 Yonge St Suite 1300, Toronto, ON, M4S 2C6
(416) 322-6111
Emp Here 25   *Sales* 1,896,978
SIC 7372 Prepackaged software

D-U-N-S 25-461-4035   (SL)
EASTER SEALS CANADA
40 Holly St Suite 401, Toronto, ON, M4S 3C3
(416) 932-8382
Emp Here 200   *Sales* 4,444,761
SIC 8699 Membership organizations, nec

D-U-N-S 20-038-7640   (BR)
FJORDS PROCESSING CANADA INC
1920 Yonge St Suite 301, Toronto, ON, M4S 3E2
(416) 343-9223
Emp Here 50
SIC 8711 Engineering services

D-U-N-S 24-343-2288   (SL)
FLEXTRACK INC
(*Suby of* Keal Inc)
2200 Yonge St Suite 801, Toronto, ON, M4S 2C6
(416) 545-5288
Emp Here 45   *Sales* 4,669,485
SIC 8741 Management services

D-U-N-S 24-198-7171   (SL)
GENEVA CENTRE FOR AUTISM
112 Merton St, Toronto, ON, M4S 2Z8
(416) 322-7877
Emp Here 60   *Sales* 2,918,428
SIC 8049 Offices of health practitioner

D-U-N-S 24-858-6146   (SL)
GLASSBOX TV INC
130 Merton St, Toronto, ON, M4S 1A4

Emp Here 49   *Sales* 12,478,350
SIC 7319 Advertising, nec
  Raja Khana
Pr Jeffrey Elliot
  Joseph Arcuri

D-U-N-S 20-180-6135   (SL)
GREENWOOD COLLEGE SCHOOL
443 Mount Pleasant Rd, Toronto, ON, M4S 2L8
(416) 482-9811
Emp Here 68   *Sales* 4,523,563
SIC 8211 Elementary and secondary schools

D-U-N-S 20-514-8484   (BR)
GREY ADVERTISING ULC
GCI GROUPE

40 Holly St Suite 600, Toronto, ON, M4S 3C3
(416) 486-7200
Emp Here 25
SIC 8743 Public relations services

HANSA LANGUAGE CENTRE OF TORONTO INC
D-U-N-S 25-754-1664   (BR)
(*Suby of* Hansa Language Centre Of Toronto Inc)
2160 Yonge St, Toronto, ON, M4S 2A8
(416) 485-1410
Emp Here 30
SIC 8299 Schools and educational services, nec

MERRITHEW INTERNATIONAL INC
D-U-N-S 25-460-1727   (SL)
(*Suby of* Merrithew Corporation)
2200 Yonge St Suite 500, Toronto, ON, M4S 2C6
(416) 482-4050
Emp Here 75   *Sales* 4,085,799
SIC 8299 Schools and educational services, nec

NEIGHBOURHOOD GROUP OF COMPANIES LIMITED, THE
D-U-N-S 25-342-1374   (BR)
BOW AND ARROW PUB, THE
(*Suby of* Neighbourhood Group Of Companies Limited, The)
1954 Yonge St, Toronto, ON, M4S 1Z4
(519) 836-3948
Emp Here 25
SIC 5813 Drinking places

NORTHERN ETHANOL (SARNIA) INC
D-U-N-S 24-388-5915   (SL)
(*Suby of* Sarnia Biofuels Inc)
225 Merton St Unit 320, Toronto, ON, M4S 3H1
(416) 917-4672
Emp Here 40   *Sales* 63,812,050
SIC 1321 Natural gas liquids
Pr Gordon Laschinger

ONTARIO CINEMAS INC
D-U-N-S 24-757-8008   (SL)
LANSDOWNE CINEMA
745 Mount Pleasant Rd Suite 300, Toronto, ON, M4S 2N4
(416) 481-1186
Emp Here 100   *Sales* 4,994,344
SIC 7832 Motion picture theaters, except drive-in

PITNEY BOWES OF CANADA LTD
D-U-N-S 24-079-6748   (BR)
(*Suby of* Pitney Bowes Inc.)
2200 Yonge St Suite 100, Toronto, ON, M4S 2C6
(416) 484-3807
Emp Here 20
SIC 5044 Office equipment

POLY PLACEMENTS INC
D-U-N-S 24-616-8251   (SL)
1920 Yonge St Suite 200, Toronto, ON, M4S 3E2
(416) 440-3362
Emp Here 55   *Sales* 4,012,839
SIC 7361 Employment agencies

QUALITY RESPONSE INC
D-U-N-S 25-530-5799   (SL)
2200 Yonge St Suite 903, Toronto, ON, M4S 2C6
(416) 484-0072
Emp Here 40   *Sales* 5,182,810
SIC 8732 Commercial nonphysical research
Pr Joan Pingitore

REUVEN INTERNATIONAL LIMITED
D-U-N-S 24-222-6611   (SL)
ROXBOROUGH POULTRY
1881 Yonge St Suite 201, Toronto, ON, M4S 3C4

(416) 929-1496
Emp Here 30   *Sales* 67,525,338
SIC 5142 Packaged frozen goods
Pr Pr Paul Stott
 John Barker

ROYAL LEPAGE LIMITED
D-U-N-S 20-709-2532   (BR)
477 Mount Pleasant Rd Unit 210, Toronto, ON, M4S 2L9
(416) 489-2121
Emp Here 250
SIC 7389 Business services, nec

ROYAL LEPAGE LIMITED
D-U-N-S 20-004-5941   (BR)
JOHNSTON & DANIEL
477 Mount Pleasant Rd, Toronto, ON, M4S 2L9
(416) 268-9420
Emp Here 160
SIC 6531 Real estate agents and managers

RUTLEDGE FLOWERS AT YORKDALE INC
D-U-N-S 20-645-5987   (SL)
635 Mount Pleasant Rd Suite A, Toronto, ON, M4S 2M9
(416) 783-6355
Emp Here 85   *Sales* 4,523,563
SIC 5992 Florists

SPORTING LIFE INC
D-U-N-S 24-181-4516   (HQ)
130 Merton St 6th Fl, Toronto, ON, M4S 1A4
(416) 485-1685
Emp Here 240   *Emp Total* 23,576
Sales 65,661,826
SIC 5941 Sporting goods and bicycle shops
 Brian Mcgrath
Pr Pr David Russell
 Patty Russell
 Sharon Mcgrath

T.E.S. CONTRACT SERVICES INC
D-U-N-S 20-939-6332   (HQ)
EMPLOYMENT SOLUTION, THE
(*Suby of* T.E.S. Contract Services Inc)
40 Holly St Suite 500, Toronto, ON, M4S 3C3
(416) 482-2420
Emp Here 45   *Emp Total* 100
Sales 9,816,000
SIC 7361 Employment agencies
Pr Pr Frank A. Wilson
VP Fin Christina Lusignan
 Raymond Moscoe

TORONTO DISTRICT SCHOOL BOARD
D-U-N-S 20-035-5464   (BR)
HODGSON SENIOR PUBLIC SCHOOL
282 Davisville Ave, Toronto, ON, M4S 1H2
(416) 393-0390
Emp Here 25
SIC 8211 Elementary and secondary schools

UPPER LAKES GROUP INC
D-U-N-S 24-783-8949   (HQ)
(*Suby of* Upper Lakes Group Inc)
250 Merton St Suite 403, Toronto, ON, M4S 1B1
(416) 920-7610
Emp Here 35   *Emp Total* 1,000
Sales 201,152,650
SIC 4432 Freight transportation on the great lakes
 John D Leitch
Pers/VP Eva Chudecki
 Pat Loduca
 Robert G Dale
Dir Jim Gillies
Dir John Hillicker
Dir Dan Barraclough

VHA HOME HEALTHCARE
D-U-N-S 24-097-5722   (HQ)
(*Suby of* VHA Home Healthcare)
30 Soudan Ave Suite 500, Toronto, ON, M4S 1V6

(416) 489-2500
Emp Here 100   *Emp Total* 1,000
Sales 63,509,520
SIC 8059 Nursing and personal care, nec
Pr Carol Annett
Dir Alan Ely
Dir Susan Houston
Dir Catherine Seguin
Dir Diane Pirner
Dir Joel Kohm
Dir Denis Long
Dir Donna-Dale Smith
 Vikas Sharma
Dir Jeff Litwin

Toronto, ON M4T
York County

1094285 ONTARIO LIMITED
D-U-N-S 25-487-2971   (BR)
IL FORNELLO RESTAURANT
(*Suby of* 1094285 Ontario Limited)
1560 Yonge St, Toronto, ON, M4T 2S9
(905) 338-5233
Emp Here 30
SIC 5812 Eating places

1404136 ONTARIO LIMITED
D-U-N-S 20-290-4954   (HQ)
NEW BALANCE TORONTO
(*Suby of* 1404136 Ontario Limited)
1510 Yonge St, Toronto, ON, M4T 1Z6
(416) 962-8662
Emp Here 35   *Emp Total* 70
Sales 4,231,721
SIC 5651 Family clothing stores

ASQUITH INTERIOR DIMENSIONS INC
D-U-N-S 24-046-1384   (SL)
INTERIOR DIMENSIONS
(*Suby of* 1381077 Onario Inc)
21 St Clair Ave E Suite 700, Toronto, ON, M4T 1L9
Emp Here 20   *Sales* 5,006,160
SIC 1542 Nonresidential construction, nec
Pr Pr Robert Horwitz
 Yalta Horwitz

BANQUE TORONTO-DOMINION, LA
D-U-N-S 25-321-2484   (BR)
TORONTO-DOMINION BANK, THE
(*Suby of* Toronto-Dominion Bank, The)
2 St Clair Ave E Suite 100, Toronto, ON, M4T 2T5
(416) 944-4054
Emp Here 35
SIC 6021 National commercial banks

CANADIAN OLYMPIC COMMITTEE
D-U-N-S 20-762-3380   (HQ)
(*Suby of* Canadian Olympic Committee)
21 St Clair Ave E Suite 900, Toronto, ON, M4T 1L9
(416) 962-0262
Emp Here 40   *Emp Total* 70
Sales 59,200,401
SIC 8699 Membership organizations, nec
 Christopher Overholt
Pr Marcel Aubut
VP VP Gordon Peterson
Dir Trisha Smith
Treas Wayne Russell

DELISLE CLUB
D-U-N-S 20-704-5928   (SL)
EXTREME FITNESS
1521 Yonge St Suite 303, Toronto, ON, M4T 1Z2
(416) 922-9624
Emp Here 75   *Sales* 2,991,389
SIC 7991 Physical fitness facilities

EMPIRE LIFE INSURANCE COMPANY, THE
D-U-N-S 20-817-8350   (BR)

EMPIRE LIFE
2 St Clair Ave E 5th Flr, Toronto, ON, M4T 2T5
(416) 494-4431
Emp Here 50
SIC 6311 Life insurance

EXTREME FITNESS GROUP INC
D-U-N-S 24-320-1980   (BR)
(*Suby of* Extreme Fitness Group Inc)
1521 Yonge St, Toronto, ON, M4T 1Z2
(416) 922-9624
Emp Here 30
SIC 7991 Physical fitness facilities

FEDSEC CORPORATION
D-U-N-S 24-380-9311   (SL)
FEDERAL FORCE PROTECTION SERVICE
60 St Clair Ave E Suite 1000, Toronto, ON, M4T 1N5
(416) 323-9911
Emp Here 500   *Sales* 20,908,080
SIC 7381 Detective and armored car services
Pr Arthur H. Peckham

FRONTIER COLLEGE
D-U-N-S 20-878-8216   (HQ)
(*Suby of* Frontier College)
35 Jackes Ave, Toronto, ON, M4T 1E2
(416) 923-3591
Emp Here 25   *Emp Total* 56
Sales 3,064,349
SIC 8299 Schools and educational services, nec

GENESIS MEDIA INC
D-U-N-S 24-256-2676   (SL)
AEGIS GROUP
22 St Clair Ave E Suite 500, Toronto, ON, M4T 2S3
(416) 967-7282
Emp Here 66   *Sales* 16,739,250
SIC 7319 Advertising, nec
Pr Pr Annette Warring
VP VP Lisa Hudson
Dir Azim Alibhai
Dir Derek Bhopalsingh
Dir Scott Stewart

GOODLIFE FITNESS CENTRES INC
D-U-N-S 25-704-8025   (BR)
12 St Clair Ave E, Toronto, ON, M4T 1L7
(416) 927-8042
Emp Here 25
SIC 7991 Physical fitness facilities

IQPC WORLDWIDE COMPANY
D-U-N-S 25-052-1101   (SL)
INTERNATIONAL QUALITY AND PRODUCTIVITY CENTRE
60 St Clair Ave E Suite 304, Toronto, ON, M4T 1N5
(416) 597-4700
Emp Here 75   *Sales* 3,793,956
SIC 7389 Business services, nec

LOBLAWS SUPERMARKETS LIMITED
D-U-N-S 25-306-1741   (BR)
ST CLAIR MARKET
12 St Clair Ave E, Toronto, ON, M4T 1L7
(416) 960-8108
Emp Here 100
SIC 5411 Grocery stores

MCDONALD'S RESTAURANTS OF CANADA LIMITED
D-U-N-S 25-318-1937   (BR)
MCDONALD'S #8431
(*Suby of* McDonald's Corporation)
11 St Clair Ave E, Toronto, ON, M4T 1L8
(416) 323-3173
Emp Here 30
SIC 5812 Eating places

NATIONAL GROCERS CO. LTD
D-U-N-S 24-310-7880   (HQ)
22 St Clair Ave E Suite 1901, Toronto, ON, M4T 2S7

(416) 922-2500
Emp Here 50   *Emp Total* 138,000
Sales 31,011,786
SIC 5141 Groceries, general line
   Robert A. Balcom
   Leo Buge,a
   Carmen Fortino
   VP VP Louise Lacchin
   Stephen A. Smith
   Richard P. Mavrinac

D-U-N-S 25-707-5119   (BR)
PHARMA PLUS DRUGMARTS LTD
1481 Yonge St, Toronto, ON, M4T 1Z2
(416) 921-2171
Emp Here 20
SIC 5912 Drug stores and proprietary stores

D-U-N-S 20-199-7256   (SL)
PINE RIVER INSTITUTE
2 St Clair Ave E Suite 800, Toronto, ON, M4T 2T5
(416) 955-1453
Emp Here 58   *Sales* 2,261,782
SIC 8322 Individual and family services

D-U-N-S 25-308-4966   (BR)
ROYAL BANK OF CANADA
RBC
(*Suby of* Foyal Bank Of Canada)
26 St Clair Ave E, Toronto, ON, M4T 1L7
(416) 974-7840
Emp Here 20
SIC 6021 National commercial banks

D-U-N-S 20-806-2625   (BR)
SOBEYS CAPITAL INCORPORATED
SOBEYS STORE# 693
81 St Clair Ave E Suite 693, Toronto, ON, M4T 1M7
(416) 413-0594
Emp Here 25
SIC 5411 Grocery stores

D-U-N-S 24-227-3758   (BR)
TD ASSET MANAGEMENT INC
T D WATERHOUSE
(*Suby of* Toronto-Dominion Bank, The)
2 St Clair Ave E 6th Fl, Toronto, ON, M4T 2T5
(416) 983-0239
Emp Here 30
SIC 6211 Security brokers and dealers

D-U-N-S 20-700-3232   (BR)
TORONTO DISTRICT SCHOOL BOARD
DEER PARK JUNIOR & SENIOR SCHOOL
23 Ferndale Ave Suite 105, Toronto, ON, M4T 2B4
(416) 393-1550
Emp Here 50
SIC 8211 Elementary and secondary schools

D-U-N-S 20-711-2538   (BR)
TORONTO DISTRICT SCHOOL BOARD
WHITNEY JUNIOR PUBLIC SCHOOL
119 Rosedale Heights Dr, Toronto, ON, M4T 1C7
(416) 393-9380
Emp Here 50
SIC 8211 Elementary and secondary schools

D-U-N-S 25-315-9222   (BR)
UNITED FINANCIAL CORPORATION
(*Suby of* United Financial Corporation)
21 St Clair Ave E Suite 204, Toronto, ON, M4T 1L9
(416) 968-2310
Emp Here 20
SIC 6211 Security brokers and dealers

D-U-N-S 20-273-2173   (BR)
WSP CANADA INC
GENIVAR
1300 Yonge St Suite 801, Toronto, ON, M4T 1X3
(416) 484-4200
Emp Here 52
SIC 8711 Engineering services

D-U-N-S 20-845-8109   (SL)
WITTINGTON PROPERTIES LIMITED
22 St Clair Ave E Suite 400, Toronto, ON, M4T 2S3
(416) 967-7923
Emp Here 30   *Sales* 3,730,080
SIC 6512 Nonresidential building operators

D-U-N-S 24-424-5721   (SL)
WORLD FISHING NETWORK ULC
(*Suby of* Insight Sports Ltd)
60 St Clair Ave E Suite 400, Toronto, ON, M4T 1N5
(416) 593-0915
Emp Here 30   *Sales* 1,751,057
SIC 4833 Television broadcasting stations

D-U-N-S 24-910-9521   (SL)
YORK SCHOOL, THE
1320 Yonge St, Toronto, ON, M4T 1X2
(416) 926-1325
Emp Here 90   *Sales* 16,191,228
SIC 8211 Elementary and secondary schools
   Stephen Karam
   Sara Bellamy
   Warren Bongard
   John Brown
   Lynn Clarfield
   Joel Feldberg
   Andrew Kay
   Gene Mcburney
   Allison Menkes
   Lloyd A. Perlmutter

D-U-N-S 20-077-6453   (BR)
YOUNG WOMEN'S CHRISTIAN ASSOCIATION OF GREATER TORONTO
YWCA INTERNATIONAL BOUTIQUE
81 St Clair Ave E, Toronto, ON, M4T 1M7
(416) 924-4762
Emp Here 40
SIC 8699 Membership organizations, nec

Toronto, ON M4V
York County

D-U-N-S 25-459-1506   (SL)
1121859 ONTARIO LIMITED
SCARAMOUCHE RESTAURANT
1 Benvenuto Pl Suite 220, Toronto, ON, M4V 2L1
(416) 961-8011
Emp Here 59   *Sales* 1,751,057
SIC 5812 Eating places

D-U-N-S 25-708-6819   (BR)
AMICA MATURE LIFESTYLES INC
AMICA AT THE BALMORAL CLUB
155 Balmoral Ave Suite 130, Toronto, ON, M4V 1J5
(416) 927-0055
Emp Here 30
SIC 8361 Residential care

D-U-N-S 25-695-9073   (BR)
ANGLICAN CHURCH OF CANADA
GRACE CHURCH ON THE HILL
300 Lonsdale Rd, Toronto, ON, M4V 1X4
(416) 488-7884
Emp Here 30
SIC 8661 Religious organizations

D-U-N-S 25-360-7667   (BR)
ASTRAL MEDIA AFFICHAGE, S.E.C.
OUTDOOR DIVISION
2 St Clair Ave W Suite 2000, Toronto, ON, M4V 1L5
(416) 924-6664
Emp Here 50
SIC 7312 Outdoor advertising services

D-U-N-S 24-390-9046   (BR)
ASTRAL MEDIA RADIO INC
(*Suby of* Astral Media Radio Inc)
2 St Clair Ave W Suite 200, Toronto, ON, M4V

1L6
(416) 323-5200
Emp Here 150
SIC 4832 Radio broadcasting stations

D-U-N-S 20-646-9413   (SL)
BADMINTON AND RACQUET CLUB OF TORONTO, THE
25 St Clair Ave W, Toronto, ON, M4V 1K6
(416) 921-2159
Emp Here 100   *Sales* 4,764,381
SIC 7997 Membership sports and recreation clubs

D-U-N-S 20-012-1858   (BR)
CANADIAN CANCER SOCIETY
ONTARIO DIVISION
55 St Clair Ave W Suite 500, Toronto, ON, M4V 2Y7
(416) 488-5400
Emp Here 200
SIC 8399 Social services, nec

D-U-N-S 25-693-0769   (HQ)
CANADIAN MOTHERCRAFT SOCIETY
BREAKING THE CYCLE
(*Suby of* Canadian Mothercraft Society)
32 Heath St W, Toronto, ON, M4V 1T3
(416) 920-3515
Emp Here 40   *Emp Total* 120
Sales 3,648,035
SIC 8351 Child day care services

D-U-N-S 25-370-1668   (BR)
CORPORATION OF THE CITY OF TORONTO
TORONTO WATER
235 Cottingham St, Toronto, ON, M4V 1C7
(416) 397-0187
Emp Here 40
SIC 4941 Water supply

D-U-N-S 20-285-1465   (BR)
DESJARDINS SECURITE FINANCIERE, COMPAGNIE D'ASSURANCE VIE
DESJARDINS FINANCIAL SECURITY
95 St Clair Ave W Suite 100, Toronto, ON, M4V 1N7
(416) 926-2700
Emp Here 460
SIC 6311 Life insurance

D-U-N-S 24-097-5300   (SL)
DONOVAN DATA SYSTEMS CANADA LTD
DDS CANADA
2 St Clair Ave W Suite 1500, Toronto, ON, M4V 1L5
(416) 929-3372
Emp Here 34   *Sales* 1,896,978
SIC 7374 Data processing and preparation

D-U-N-S 20-003-8581   (BR)
GIRL GUIDES OF CANADA/GUIDES DU CANADA
GIRL GUIDES OF CANADA ONTARIO COUNCIL
14 Birch Ave, Toronto, ON, M4V 1C8
(416) 920-6666
Emp Here 26
SIC 8641 Civic and social associations

D-U-N-S 20-303-4640   (BR)
IBI GROUP INC
IBI GROUP
95 St Clair Ave W Suite 200, Toronto, ON, M4V 1N6
(416) 924-9966
Emp Here 125
SIC 8712 Architectural services

D-U-N-S 24-286-1834   (BR)
NEWCAP INC
FLOW 93-5
2 St Clair Ave W, Toronto, ON, M4V 1L5
(416) 482-0973
Emp Here 60
SIC 4832 Radio broadcasting stations

D-U-N-S 20-279-7247   (SL)

NORTHLAND POWER SOLAR FINANCE ONE LP
30 St Clair Ave W, Toronto, ON, M4V 3A1
(416) 962-6262
Emp Here 100   *Sales* 66,449,750
SIC 4911 Electric services
   Pr Sean Durfy

D-U-N-S 20-911-1835   (BR)
REVERA INC
BRADGATE ARMS
54 Foxbar Rd, Toronto, ON, M4V 2G6
(416) 968-1331
Emp Here 50
SIC 6513 Apartment building operators

D-U-N-S 20-408-5419   (SL)
ROLEX CANADA LTD
50 St Clair Ave W, Toronto, ON, M4V 3B7
(416) 968-1100
Emp Here 36   *Sales* 3,939,878
SIC 5094 Jewelry and precious stones

D-U-N-S 20-711-2363   (BR)
TORONTO DISTRICT SCHOOL BOARD
BROWN JUNIOR PUBLIC SCHOOL
454 Avenue Rd, Toronto, ON, M4V 2J1
(416) 393-1560
Emp Here 50
SIC 8211 Elementary and secondary schools

D-U-N-S 20-591-7110   (BR)
TORONTO DISTRICT SCHOOL BOARD
COTTINGHAM JUNIOR PUBLIC SCHOOL
85 Birch Ave, Toronto, ON, M4V 1E3
(416) 393-1895
Emp Here 20
SIC 8211 Elementary and secondary schools

D-U-N-S 20-114-1236   (BR)
TOTUM LIFE SCIENCE INC
(*Suby of* Totum Life Science Inc)
200 St Clair Ave W Suite 108, Toronto, ON, M4V 1R1
(416) 960-3636
Emp Here 70
SIC 7999 Amusement and recreation, nec

Toronto, ON M4W
York County

D-U-N-S 20-159-1518   (HQ)
333308 ONTARIO LTD
55 Bloor St W Suite 506, Toronto, ON, M4W 1A5
(416) 964-2900
Emp Here 90   *Emp Total* 23,576
Sales 9,266,009
SIC 5719 Miscellaneous homefurnishings
   Pr Pr Alan J Stark

D-U-N-S 20-322-9117   (SL)
5TOUCH SOLUTIONS INC
EVENTMOBI
14th Floor, Toronto, ON, M4W 3R8
(647) 496-5623
Emp Here 80   *Sales* 4,377,642
SIC 7374 Data processing and preparation

D-U-N-S 24-032-2003   (SL)
6142974 CANADA INC
LUSIGHT RESEARCH
175 Bloor St E Suite 606, Toronto, ON, M4W 3R8
(416) 934-1436
Emp Here 40   *Sales* 13,289,950
SIC 6282 Investment advice
   Prin Paul Warme
   Prin Philip Harrison
   Prin Paul Sparrow

D-U-N-S 20-651-1508   (BR)
ARAMARK CANADA LTD.
200 Bloor St E Suite 1, Toronto, ON, M4W 1E5
(416) 926-3654
Emp Here 45

SIC 5812 Eating places

D-U-N-S 24-952-8688 (SL)
ALL HEALTH SERVICES INC
PARMED ACADEMY
66 Collier St Unit 9d, Toronto, ON, M4W 1L9
(416) 515-1151
Emp Here 50   *Sales* 3,648,035
SIC 7361 Employment agencies

D-U-N-S 24-204-9232 (HQ)
ALL SENIORS CARE LIVING CENTRES LTD
ALL SENIORS CARE ASC
(*Suby of* All Seniors Care Holdings Inc)
175 Bloor St E Suite 601, Toronto, ON, M4W 3R8
(416) 323-3773
Emp Here 30   *Emp Total* 2,000
Sales 175,105,680
SIC 6513 Apartment building operators
Pr Pr George Uhl
Micheal Kuhl
VP Opers Joshua Kuhl
Lily Goodman
Michael Fraser

D-U-N-S 25-364-1609 (BR)
AMDOCS CANADIAN MANAGED SERVICES INC
2 Bloor St E Suite 3100, Toronto, ON, M4W 1A8

Emp Here 20
SIC 7371 Custom computer programming services

D-U-N-S 25-359-7934 (BR)
BBDO CANADA CORP
PROXIMITY CANADA, DIV OF
(*Suby of* Omnicom Group Inc.)
2 Bloor St W Suite 2900, Toronto, ON, M4W 3E2
(416) 323-9162
Emp Here 200
SIC 7311 Advertising agencies

D-U-N-S 24-822-7118 (SL)
BAIN & COMPANY CANADA, INC
(*Suby of* Bain & Company, Inc.)
2 Bloor St E, Toronto, ON, M4W 1A8
(416) 929-1888
Emp Here 80   *Sales* 9,703,773
SIC 8742 Management consulting services
VP VP Pierre Lavallee
Genl Mgr Michael Collins
Ch Bd Orit Gadish

D-U-N-S 25-997-3410 (BR)
BAYSHORE HEALTHCARE LTD.
BAYSHORE HOME HEALTH
345 Bloor St E Unit 1b, Toronto, ON, M4W 3J6
(416) 927-7850
Emp Here 150
SIC 8082 Home health care services

D-U-N-S 24-309-8501 (BR)
BOUTIQUE JACOB INC
JACOB CONNEXION
(*Suby of* Boutique Jacob Inc)
55 Bloor St W, Toronto, ON, M4W 1A5

Emp Here 50
SIC 5621 Women's clothing stores

D-U-N-S 24-388-4988 (HQ)
CANADA COLORS AND CHEMICALS (EASTERN) LIMITED
175 Bloor St E Suite 1300, Toronto, ON, M4W 3R8
(416) 443-5500
Emp Here 24   *Emp Total* 350
Sales 78,067,949
SIC 5169 Chemicals and allied products, nec
Pr Pr Brian Job
Carol Maclean

D-U-N-S 24-207-0923 (BR)

CANADIAN TIRE CORPORATION, LIMITED
839 Yonge St Suite 150, Toronto, ON, M4W 2H2
(416) 925-9592
Emp Here 20
SIC 5531 Auto and home supply stores

D-U-N-S 25-473-3280 (BR)
CANON CANADA INC
BUSINESS SOLUTIONS DIVISION
175 Bloor St E Suite 1200, Toronto, ON, M4W 3R8
(416) 491-9330
Emp Here 225
SIC 5999 Miscellaneous retail stores, nec

D-U-N-S 20-074-4741 (BR)
COLLEGA INTERNATIONAL INC
CIVELLO SALON & SPA
887 Yonge St, Toronto, ON, M4W 2H2
(416) 924-9244
Emp Here 50
SIC 7231 Beauty shops

D-U-N-S 25-757-7866 (BR)
CORPORATION OF THE CITY OF TORONTO
TORONTO PUBLIC LIBRARY
789 Yonge St, Toronto, ON, M4W 2G8
(416) 393-7131
Emp Here 600
SIC 8231 Libraries

D-U-N-S 24-676-8381 (HQ)
CORUS MEDIA HOLDINGS INC
GLOBAL TELEVISION
121 Bloor St E Suite 1500, Toronto, ON, M4W 3M5
(416) 967-1174
Emp Here 250   *Emp Total* 14,000
Sales 128,410,832
SIC 4833 Television broadcasting stations
Paul Robertson
VP Fin Michael French

D-U-N-S 20-810-0540 (BR)
DIALOG
DIALOG DESIGN
2 Bloor St E Suite 1000, Toronto, ON, M4W 1A8
(416) 966-0220
Emp Here 100
SIC 7361 Employment agencies

D-U-N-S 24-321-5071 (SL)
DYNEXA CORPORATION
2 Bloor St W Suite 903, Toronto, ON, M4W 3E2
(416) 646-4746
Emp Here 40   *Sales* 5,526,400
SIC 8243 Data processing schools
Pr Pravin Patel
Dir Peter Di Santo
Mgr Alexey Zelenov
Genl Mgr Vishwas Sawant

D-U-N-S 20-260-2694 (SL)
EAB NORTH AMERICA INC
2 Bloor St W Suite 2120, Toronto, ON, M4W 3E2
(905) 570-5200
Emp Here 20   *Sales* 2,772,507
SIC 3441 Fabricated structural Metal

D-U-N-S 25-530-9791 (SL)
ELLIOTT & PAGE LIMITED
MANULIFE MUTUAL FUNDS
200 Bloor St E Suite 1, Toronto, ON, M4W 1E5
(416) 581-8300
Emp Here 345   *Sales* 141,475,840
SIC 6722 Management investment, open-end
Dir Roy Firth

D-U-N-S 24-551-9371 (SL)
FRESHII INC
1055 Yonge St, Toronto, ON, M4W 2L2
(647) 350-2001
Emp Here 50   *Sales* 16,118,000

SIC 5812 Eating places
Matthew Corrin
CFO Craig De Pratto
Adam Corrin
VP Ashley Dalziel
VP Jenny Hoshoian
Melissa Gallagher
Michael Allen
Sean Berry
Jeffrey Burchell
Marc Kielburger

D-U-N-S 20-015-2036 (SL)
GCI COMMUNICATIONS INC
160 Bloor St E Fl 8, Toronto, ON, M4W 3P7
(416) 486-7200
Emp Here 27   *Sales* 2,480,664
SIC 8743 Public relations services

D-U-N-S 24-844-9845 (HQ)
GAP (CANADA) INC
(*Suby of* The Gap Inc)
60 Bloor St W Suite 1501, Toronto, ON, M4W 3B8
(416) 921-2225
Emp Here 65   *Emp Total* 135,000
Sales 364,803,500
SIC 5651 Family clothing stores
Pr Pr Pierre Pronovost

D-U-N-S 20-384-1028 (BR)
GOODLIFE FITNESS CENTRES INC
8 Park Rd, Toronto, ON, M4W 3S5
(416) 922-1262
Emp Here 25
SIC 7991 Physical fitness facilities

D-U-N-S 20-868-7959 (BR)
GOVERNMENT OF ONTARIO
MUNICIPAL ISSUES
2 Bloor St W Suite 2500, Toronto, ON, M4W 3E2
(416) 212-1253
Emp Here 300
SIC 8399 Social services, nec

D-U-N-S 20-699-6584 (BR)
GROUPE BIRKS INC
55 Bloor St W Unit 152, Toronto, ON, M4W 1A5
(416) 922-2266
Emp Here 30
SIC 5944 Jewelry stores

D-U-N-S 25-984-8641 (SL)
GROUPEX INC
GROUPEX-SOLUTIONS
3 Rowanwood Ave, Toronto, ON, M4W 1Y5
(416) 968-0000
Emp Here 94   *Sales* 11,746,673
SIC 8748 Business consulting, nec
Laurie Dudo
Theodore Smith
Farham Khan
Aman Dassi

D-U-N-S 25-508-3446 (SL)
HGTV CANADA INC
121 Bloor St E Suite 1500, Toronto, ON, M4W 3M5
(416) 967-0022
Emp Here 60   *Sales* 4,158,005
SIC 4833 Television broadcasting stations

D-U-N-S 20-044-2671 (HQ)
HARPERCOLLINS CANADA LIMITED
2 Bloor St E 20th Fl, Toronto, ON, M4W 1A8
(416) 975-9334
Emp Here 100   *Emp Total* 4,725
Sales 22,262,651
SIC 5192 Books, periodicals, and newspapers
Pr Pr David Kent
VP Fin Wayne Playter

D-U-N-S 24-826-5415 (BR)
HARPERCOLLINS CANADA LIMITED
(*Suby of* News Corporation)
2 Bloor St E 20th Fl, Toronto, ON, M4W 1A8

(416) 975-9334
Emp Here 35
SIC 2731 Book publishing

D-U-N-S 20-221-3484 (HQ)
HOLT, RENFREW & CIE, LIMITEE
CAFE HOLT TMA482, 017
60 Bloor St W Suite 1100, Toronto, ON, M4W 3B8
(416) 922-2333
Emp Here 200   *Emp Total* 2,300
Sales 140,011,583
SIC 5621 Women's clothing stores
Pr Mark Derbyshire
Sec Lorraine E Kuska
Hilary Weston
Isabelle Hudon
Alannah Weston
Paul Kelly
Anthony R Graham
Robert John Dart
Galen W.G Weston

D-U-N-S 25-104-4806 (BR)
HOLT, RENFREW & CIE, LIMITEE
HOLT RENFREW
50 Bloor St W Suite 200, Toronto, ON, M4W 1A1
(416) 922-2333
Emp Here 100
SIC 5621 Women's clothing stores

D-U-N-S 24-681-6933 (BR)
HU-A-KAM ENTERPRISES INC
MCDONALD'S
(*Suby of* Hu-A-Kam Enterprises Inc)
345 Bloor St E Suite 1, Toronto, ON, M4W 3J6
(416) 967-1081
Emp Here 43
SIC 5812 Eating places

D-U-N-S 25-721-1524 (BR)
HUDSON'S BAY COMPANY
THE BAY
2 Bloor St E Suite 52, Toronto, ON, M4W 3H7
(416) 972-3313
Emp Here 600
SIC 5311 Department stores

D-U-N-S 20-702-8288 (BR)
HUDSON'S BAY COMPANY
2 Bloor St E Suite 52, Toronto, ON, M4W 3H7
(416) 972-3333
Emp Here 300
SIC 5311 Department stores

D-U-N-S 20-005-4034 (BR)
INDIGO BOOKS & MUSIC INC
INDIGO BOOKS MUSIC & MORE
(*Suby of* Indigo Books & Music Inc)
55 Bloor St W, Toronto, ON, M4W 1A5
(416) 925-3536
Emp Here 100
SIC 5942 Book stores

D-U-N-S 24-684-7818 (SL)
INTERBRAND CANADA INC
(*Suby of* Omnicom Group Inc.)
33 Bloor St E Suite 1400, Toronto, ON, M4W 3H1
(416) 366-7100
Emp Here 24   *Sales* 1,824,018
SIC 8748 Business consulting, nec

D-U-N-S 25-990-6402 (HQ)
INTERNATIONAL LANGUAGE ACADEMY OF CANADA INC
ILAC
(*Suby of* International Language Academy Of Canada Inc)
920 Yonge St, Toronto, ON, M4W 3C7
(416) 961-5375
Emp Here 48   *Emp Total* 60
Sales 4,417,200
SIC 8299 Schools and educational services, nec

D-U-N-S 20-176-7894 (HQ)
J. WALTER THOMPSON COMPANY LIM-

ITED
JWT
160 Bloor St E Suite 11, Toronto, ON, M4W
1B9
(416) 926-7300
Emp Here 150   *Emp Total* 124,930
Sales 31,002,624
SIC 7311 Advertising agencies
Pr Pr Tony Pigott
 Anthony Futa
Ex VP Martin Shewchuk

D-U-N-S 25-213-1362   (SL)
LIFE NETWORK INC
SLICE
121 Bloor St E Suite 1500, Toronto, ON, M4W
3M5
(416) 967-0022
Emp Here 50   *Sales* 3,465,004
SIC 4833 Television broadcasting stations

D-U-N-S 25-317-8099   (BR)
**LIQUOR CONTROL BOARD OF ONTARIO,
THE**
L.C.B.O. #528
55 Bloor St W Unit 200, Toronto, ON, M4W
1A5
(416) 925-5266
Emp Here 25
SIC 5921 Liquor stores

D-U-N-S 24-005-7372   (HQ)
MARITZ RESEARCH COMPANY
*MARITZ AUTOMOTIVE RESEARCH GROUP
DIV OF*
425 Bloor St E, Toronto, ON, M4W 3R4
(416) 922-8014
Emp Here 40   *Emp Total* 4,646
Sales 34,218,568
SIC 8732 Commercial nonphysical research
 John Risberg
 Rick Ramos

D-U-N-S 20-338-4045   (SL)
MARU GROUP CANADA INC
MARU VCR & C
2 Bloor St E Suite 1600, Toronto, ON, M4W
1A8
(647) 258-1416
Emp Here 80   *Sales* 11,521,138
SIC 8732 Commercial nonphysical research
Pr Edward Morawski
 Amanda Rem

D-U-N-S 25-109-2409   (SL)
MILLENNIUM RESEARCH GROUP INC
175 Bloor St E Suite 701, Toronto, ON, M4W
3R8
(416) 364-7776
Emp Here 180   *Sales* 24,149,992
SIC 8748 Business consulting, nec
Pr Pr Shahir Kassam-Adams
VP VP Mary Argent-Katwala
Dir Ken Mclaren

D-U-N-S 24-094-7606   (BR)
NAYLOR (CANADA), INC
(*Suby of* Naylor (Canada), Inc)
2 Bloor St W Suite 2001, Toronto, ON, M4W
3E2

Emp Here 25
SIC 2721 Periodicals

D-U-N-S 24-319-0381   (BR)
NEXIENT LEARNING CANADA INC
2 Bloor St W Suite 1200, Toronto, ON, M4W
3E2
(416) 964-8664
Emp Here 50
SIC 8243 Data processing schools

D-U-N-S 24-789-3634   (BR)
OMNICOM CANADA CORP
KETCHUM PUBLIC RELATIONS CANADA
(*Suby of* Omnicom Group Inc.)
33 Bloor St E Suite 1607, Toronto, ON, M4W
3H1

(416) 544-4912
Emp Here 25
SIC 8743 Public relations services

D-U-N-S 25-362-9307   (BR)
OMNICOM CANADA CORP
PORTER NOVELLI CANADA
(*Suby of* Omnicom Group Inc.)
2 Bloor St W Suite 2202, Toronto, ON, M4W
3E2
(416) 423-6605
Emp Here 20
SIC 8743 Public relations services

D-U-N-S 25-000-4207   (BR)
OMNICOM CANADA CORP
ANDERSON DDB HEALTH & LIFESTYLE
(*Suby of* Omnicom Group Inc.)
33 Bloor St E Suite 1300, Toronto, ON, M4W
3H1
(416) 960-3830
Emp Here 80
SIC 7311 Advertising agencies

D-U-N-S 25-520-5908   (BR)
ONTARIO MEDICAL ASSOCIATION
*QUALITY MANAGEMENT PROGRAM-
LABORATORY SERVICES*
250 Bloor St E Suite 1510, Toronto, ON, M4W
1E6
(416) 323-9540
Emp Here 28
SIC 8621 Professional organizations

D-U-N-S 25-343-3049   (BR)
OXFORD PROPERTIES GROUP INC
160 Bloor St E Unit 1000, Toronto, ON, M4W
1B9
(416) 927-7274
Emp Here 20
SIC 6512 Nonresidential building operators

D-U-N-S 25-530-5443   (SL)
PLAZA II CORPORATION, THE
TORONTO MARRIOTT BLOOR YORKVILLE
(*Suby of* Larco Investments Ltd)
90 Bloor St E, Toronto, ON, M4W 1A7
(416) 961-8000
Emp Here 100   *Sales* 4,377,642
SIC 7011 Hotels and motels

D-U-N-S 24-322-6524   (BR)
POST ROAD HEALTH & DIET INC
*BERNSTRIN'S DR STANLEY K HEALTH &
DIET CLINICS*
11 Yorkville Ave, Toronto, ON, M4W 1L2
(416) 922-9777
Emp Here 46
SIC 7299 Miscellaneous personal service

D-U-N-S 24-424-3254   (HQ)
POSTMEDIA NETWORK INC
POSTMEDIA INTEGRATED ADVERTISING
365 Bloor St E Suite 1601, Toronto, ON, M4W
3L4
(416) 383-2300
Emp Here 200   *Emp Total* 4,733
Sales 414,562,697
SIC 2711 Newspapers
Pr Pr Paul Godfrey
VP Brenda Lazare
 Doug Lamb
 Robert Steacy
 Peter Sharpe
 Steven Shapiro
 Graham Savage
 John Paton
 David Emerson
 Hugh Dow

D-U-N-S 25-010-5970   (BR)
RABBA, J. COMPANY LIMITED, THE
RABBA FINE FOODS STORES
40 Asquith Ave, Toronto, ON, M4W 1J6
(416) 967-5326
Emp Here 20
SIC 5411 Grocery stores

D-U-N-S 24-383-3154   (BR)

RANDSTAD INTERIM INC
RANDSTAD CANADA GROUP
60 Bloor St W Suite 1400, Toronto, ON, M4W
3B8
(416) 962-9262
Emp Here 50
SIC 7361 Employment agencies

D-U-N-S 24-352-0645   (BR)
RANDSTAD INTERIM INC
ORIGINHR CANADA, DIV OF
60 Bloor St W Suite 505, Toronto, ON, M4W
3B8
(416) 962-8133
Emp Here 20
SIC 7361 Employment agencies

D-U-N-S 24-487-7429   (BR)
**READER'S   DIGEST   ASSOCIATION
(CANADA) ULC, THE**
250 Bloor St E Suite 502, Toronto, ON, M4W
1E6
(416) 925-8941
Emp Here 20
SIC 2731 Book publishing

D-U-N-S 25-362-4670   (HQ)
RIGHT MANAGEMENT CANADA, INC
2 Bloor St E, Toronto, ON, M4W 1A8
(416) 926-1324
Emp Here 35   *Emp Total* 28,000
Sales 9,703,773
SIC 8741 Management services
Pr Jonas Prising
Ex VP Theodore A Young
Ex VP Brian Clapp
Ex VP George Herrmann
Sr VP Joe Catrino
Sr VP Paul Straub
VP VP Frank P Louchheim
VP VP John Bourbeau
Genl Mgr Bram Lowsky

D-U-N-S 20-164-9068   (HQ)
ROGERS COMMUNICATIONS INC
ROGERS COMMUNICATIONS PARTNERS
(*Suby of* Rogers Communications Inc)
333 Bloor St E 10 Fl, Toronto, ON, M4W 1G9
(416) 935-2303
Emp Here 5,000   *Emp Total* 25,200
SIC 4899 Communication services, nec

D-U-N-S 20-606-1855   (HQ)
RONALD A. CHISHOLM LIMITED
(*Suby of* Ronald A. Chisholm Limited)
2 Bloor St W Suite 3300, Toronto, ON, M4W
3K3
(416) 967-6000
Emp Here 115   *Emp Total* 250
Sales 65,372,787
SIC 5141 Groceries, general line
VP VP Stephen R Chisholm
VP VP Timothy Frith
VP VP Paul Buzbuzian
VP VP Zoran Perusina
 Gregg Badger
Dir Yuval Hason
 Jeffrey S. Ryley

D-U-N-S 24-252-1081   (BR)
RYERSON UNIVERSITY
GERRARD RESOURCE CENTRE
525 Bloor St E, Toronto, ON, M4W 1J1
(416) 972-1319
Emp Here 30
SIC 8322 Individual and family services

D-U-N-S 20-588-7446   (BR)
SAP CANADA INC
2 Bloor St E Suite 1600, Toronto, ON, M4W
1A8

Emp Here 40
SIC 8299 Schools and educational services,
nec

D-U-N-S 25-530-7811   (SL)
SFP INC

175 Bloor St E Suite 900, Toronto, ON, M4W
3R9
(416) 203-2300
Emp Here 35   *Sales* 3,298,152
SIC 7336 Commercial art and graphic design

D-U-N-S 25-283-4403   (HQ)
SPAFAX CANADA INC
2 Bloor St E Suite 1020, Toronto, ON, M4W
1A8
(416) 350-2425
Emp Here 20   *Emp Total* 124,930
Sales 8,390,481
SIC 5199 Nondurable goods, nec
Pr Pr Richard Staunton
 Simon Ogden

D-U-N-S 24-985-0363   (HQ)
SPIN MASTER LTD
SPIN MASTER FILM PRODUCTION
(*Suby of* Spin Master Corp)
121 Bloor St E, Toronto, ON, M4W 3M5
(416) 364-6002
Emp Here 300   *Emp Total* 1,426
Sales 36,480,350
SIC 3944 Games, toys, and children's vehicles
Dir Ronnen Harary
Pr Pr Anton Rabie
Ex VP Ben Varadi
S&M/VP Chris Beardall

D-U-N-S 20-537-0252   (BR)
ST. JOHN COUNCIL FOR ONTARIO
ST JOHN AMBULANCE
365 Bloor St E Suite 900, Toronto, ON, M4W
3L4
(416) 967-4244
Emp Here 20
SIC 8611 Business associations

D-U-N-S 25-498-9379   (BR)
STAPLES CANADA INC
STAPLES/BUSINESS DEPOT
(*Suby of* Staples, Inc.)
1140 Yonge St, Toronto, ON, M4W 2L8
(416) 961-4949
Emp Here 30
SIC 5943 Stationery stores

D-U-N-S 20-414-1360   (SL)
STOLLERY, FRANK LIMITED
STOLLERY'S
1 Bloor St W, Toronto, ON, M4W 1A3

Emp Here 56   *Sales* 4,085,799
SIC 5611 Men's and boys' clothing stores

D-U-N-S 20-115-2282   (HQ)
**TORONTO COMMUNITY HOUSING COR-
PORATION**
931 Yonge St Suite 400, Toronto, ON, M4W
2H2
(416) 981-5500
Emp Here 50   *Emp Total* 39,000
Sales 131,912,946
SIC 6531 Real estate agents and managers
 Len Koroneos
VP Bronwyn Krog
 Howie Wong
 Deborah Simon
 Mitzie Hunter
Genl Mgr Michelle Haney-Kileeg

D-U-N-S 20-292-0711   (BR)
TORONTO DISTRICT SCHOOL BOARD
*ROSEDALE HEIGHTS SCHOOL OF THE
ARTS*
711 Bloor St E, Toronto, ON, M4W 1J4
(416) 393-1580
Emp Here 85
SIC 8211 Elementary and secondary schools

D-U-N-S 20-817-7618   (SL)
**TORONTO LAWN TENNIS CLUB, LIMITED,
THE**
44 Price St, Toronto, ON, M4W 1Z4
(416) 922-1105
Emp Here 60   *Sales* 2,407,703

SIC 7997 Membership sports and recreation clubs

D-U-N-S 20-114-7100   (HQ)
TOTUM LIFE SCIENCE INC
(Suby of Totum Life Science Inc)
2 Roxborough St E Unit 2, Toronto, ON, M4W 3V7
(416) 925-5706
Emp Here 40   Emp Total 90
Sales 4,888,367
SIC 7999 Amusement and recreation, nec

D-U-N-S 20-921-8387   (HQ)
TOWERS WATSON CANADA INC
175 Bloor St E Suite 1701, Toronto, ON, M4W 3T6
(416) 960-2700
Emp Here 50   Emp Total 100
Sales 5,370,756
SIC 8999 Services, nec
Dir Kevin Aselstine
Dir William Gulliver

D-U-N-S 20-009-1999   (HQ)
TOWLE, RUSSELL L ENTERPRISES LTD
MARVEL BEAUTY SCHOOL
(Suby of Towle, Russell L Enterprises Ltd)
25 Yorkville Ave, Toronto, ON, M4W 1L1
(416) 923-0993
Emp Here 140   Emp Total 150
Sales 2,991,389
SIC 7231 Beauty shops

D-U-N-S 24-418-2861   (HQ)
UNILEVER CANADA INC
UNILEVER BEST FOODS
160 Bloor St E Suite 1400, Toronto, ON, M4W 3R2
(416) 964-1857
Emp Here 200   Emp Total 200
Sales 354,151,238
SIC 2099 Food preparations, nec
Pr John Leboutillier
John Coyne
VP Fin VP Fin Paulo Decastro

D-U-N-S 24-171-0420   (BR)
VALUMART LTD
VALUMART
(Suby of Valumart Ltd)
55 Bloor St W, Toronto, ON, M4W 1A5
(416) 923-8831
Emp Here 100
SIC 5411 Grocery stores

D-U-N-S 25-318-5490   (SL)
VETERINARY REFERRAL CLINIC
920 Yonge St Suite 117, Toronto, ON, M4W 3C7
(416) 920-2002
Emp Here 50   Sales 4,417,880
SIC 8734 Testing laboratories

D-U-N-S 25-203-5738   (BR)
XEROX CANADA LTD
(Suby of Xerox Corporation)
33 Bloor St E, Toronto, ON, M4W 3H1

Emp Here 500
SIC 5044 Office equipment

D-U-N-S 25-469-8061   (BR)
YOUNG & RUBICAM GROUP OF COMPANIES ULC, THE
BLUE HIVE
60 Bloor St W Suite 8, Toronto, ON, M4W 3B8
(416) 640-4484
Emp Here 102
SIC 7311 Advertising agencies

Toronto, ON M4X
York County

D-U-N-S 20-075-7123   (BR)

CORPORATION OF THE CITY OF TORONTO
ECONOMIC DEVELOPMENT, CULTURE & TOURISM DEPARTMENT
495 Sherbourne St, Toronto, ON, M4X 1K7
(416) 392-0227
Emp Here 30
SIC 7999 Amusement and recreation, nec

D-U-N-S 24-034-1292   (BR)
CORPORATION OF THE CITY OF TORONTO
FUDGER HOUSE
439 Sherbourne St Suite 301, Toronto, ON, M4X 1K6
(416) 392-5252
Emp Here 150
SIC 8059 Nursing and personal care, nec

D-U-N-S 24-952-0560   (SL)
FIFE HOUSE FOUNDATION INC
490 Sherbourne St 2nd Fl, Toronto, ON, M4X 1K9
(416) 205-9888
Emp Here 65   Sales 3,064,349
SIC 8051 Skilled nursing care facilities

D-U-N-S 25-263-1825   (SL)
HOMELIFE REALTY ONE LTD
501 Parliament St, Toronto, ON, M4X 1P3
(416) 922-5533
Emp Here 68   Sales 8,927,600
SIC 6531 Real estate agents and managers
Owner Linda Thompson

D-U-N-S 20-543-7549   (BR)
TORONTO CATHOLIC DISTRICT SCHOOL BOARD
OUR LADY OF LOURDES CATHOLIC SCHOOL
444 Sherbourne St, Toronto, ON, M4X 1K2
(416) 393-5221
Emp Here 60
SIC 8211 Elementary and secondary schools

D-U-N-S 20-711-2553   (BR)
TORONTO DISTRICT SCHOOL BOARD
WINCHESTER JUNIOR AND SENIOR PUBLIC SCHOOL
15 Prospect St, Toronto, ON, M4X 1C7
(416) 393-1270
Emp Here 50
SIC 8211 Elementary and secondary schools

D-U-N-S 20-064-1566   (BR)
TORONTO DISTRICT SCHOOL BOARD
ROSE AVENUE PUBLIC SCHOOL
675 Ontario St, Toronto, ON, M4X 1N4
(416) 393-1260
Emp Here 60
SIC 8211 Elementary and secondary schools

Toronto, ON M4Y
York County

D-U-N-S 24-822-9791   (SL)
826788 ONTARIO LTD
WOODY'S
467 Church St Suite 3, Toronto, ON, M4Y 2C5
(416) 972-0887
Emp Here 50   Sales 1,532,175
SIC 5812 Eating places

D-U-N-S 24-213-9819   (BR)
ARAMARK CANADA LTD.
ROGERS ARAMARK
1 Mount Pleasant Rd, Toronto, ON, M4Y 2Y5
(416) 935-7487
Emp Here 60
SIC 5812 Eating places

D-U-N-S 25-296-3822   (BR)
BANK OF NOVA SCOTIA, THE
SCOTIABANK
555 Yonge St, Toronto, ON, M4Y 3A6

---

(416) 515-2800
Emp Here 25
SIC 6021 National commercial banks

D-U-N-S 25-929-4762   (SL)
CYM HOSPITALITY INC
475 Yonge St, Toronto, ON, M4Y 1X7
(416) 924-0611
Emp Here 50   Sales 2,188,821
SIC 7011 Hotels and motels

D-U-N-S 20-086-8169   (BR)
CANADA POST CORPORATION
50 Charles St E, Toronto, ON, M4Y 1T1
(416) 413-4815
Emp Here 100
SIC 4311 U.s. postal service

D-U-N-S 20-850-6238   (SL)
CANADA'S NATIONAL BALLET SCHOOL
400 Jarvis St, Toronto, ON, M4Y 2G6
(416) 964-3780
Emp Here 150   Sales 2,699,546
SIC 7911 Dance studios, schools, and halls

D-U-N-S 24-046-0261   (HQ)
CANADIAN UNIVERSITIES TRAVEL SERVICE LIMITED
TRAVEL CUTS
(Suby of Canadian Federation Of Students)
45 Charles St W Suite 200, Toronto, ON, M4Y 2R4

Emp Here 45   Emp Total 8
Sales 63,669,449
SIC 4724 Travel agencies
Pr Pr Rodney Hurd
  Simon Simangan
Ch Bd Dave Hare

D-U-N-S 24-704-4985   (SL)
CASEY HOUSE HOSPICE INC
9 Huntley St, Toronto, ON, M4Y 2K8
(416) 962-7600
Emp Here 80   Sales 3,648,035
SIC 8051 Skilled nursing care facilities

D-U-N-S 20-785-4738   (HQ)
CHURCH OF SCIENTOLOGY OF TORONTO
(Suby of Church Of Scientology Of Toronto)
696 Yonge St, Toronto, ON, M4Y 2A7
(416) 925-2146
Emp Here 60   Emp Total 100
Sales 9,130,500
SIC 8661 Religious organizations
Pr Pr Yvette Shank

D-U-N-S 25-956-0675   (BR)
ELEMENTARY TEACHERS FEDERATION OF ONTARIO
136 Isabella St, Toronto, ON, M4Y 0B5
(416) 926-0295
Emp Here 120
SIC 8631 Labor organizations

D-U-N-S 20-187-9694   (HQ)
FREE DAILY NEWS GROUP INC
METRO TORONTO
(Suby of Free Daily News Group Inc)
625 Church St Suite 400, Toronto, ON, M4Y 2G1
(416) 486-4900
Emp Here 60   Emp Total 60
Sales 4,961,328
SIC 2711 Newspapers

D-U-N-S 24-242-5069   (BR)
GOVERNING COUNCIL OF THE UNIVERSITY OF TORONTO
10 St Mary St Suite 700, Toronto, ON, M4Y 2W8
(416) 978-1000
Emp Here 200
SIC 8221 Colleges and universities

D-U-N-S 24-346-7672   (BR)
HU-A-KAM ENTERPRISES INC
MCDONALD'S
(Suby of Hu-A-Kam Enterprises Inc)

---

675 Yonge St, Toronto, ON, M4Y 2B2
(416) 413-1442
Emp Here 40
SIC 5812 Eating places

D-U-N-S 25-272-8621   (BR)
KEG RESTAURANTS LTD
KEG STEAKHOUSE & BAR, THE
515 Jarvis St, Toronto, ON, M4Y 2H7
(416) 964-6609
Emp Here 100
SIC 5812 Eating places

D-U-N-S 25-867-8374   (BR)
KITCHEN STUFF PLUS INC
KITCHEN STUFF PLUS
(Suby of Halpern, Mark Holdings Inc)
703 Yonge St, Toronto, ON, M4Y 2B2
(416) 944-2718
Emp Here 30
SIC 5719 Miscellaneous homefurnishings

D-U-N-S 25-924-5058   (BR)
PHARMA PLUS DRUGMARTS LTD
63 Wellesley St E, Toronto, ON, M4Y 1G7
(416) 924-7760
Emp Here 25
SIC 5912 Drug stores and proprietary stores

D-U-N-S 20-021-5754   (BR)
RABBA, J. COMPANY LIMITED, THE
RABBA FINE FOODS STORES
148 Wellesley St E, Toronto, ON, M4Y 1J3
(416) 925-2100
Emp Here 22
SIC 5411 Grocery stores

D-U-N-S 25-669-1403   (BR)
RABBA, J. COMPANY LIMITED, THE
RABBA FINE FOODS
9 Isabella St, Toronto, ON, M4Y 1M7
(416) 928-2300
Emp Here 25
SIC 5411 Grocery stores

D-U-N-S 24-315-8243   (BR)
RABBA, J. COMPANY LIMITED, THE
RABBA FINE FOODS
37 Charles St W, Toronto, ON, M4Y 2R4
(416) 964-3409
Emp Here 20
SIC 5411 Grocery stores

D-U-N-S 20-112-1618   (BR)
ROGERS COMMUNICATIONS CANADA INC
(Suby of Rogers Communications Inc)
1 Mount Pleasant Rd Suite 115, Toronto, ON, M4Y 2Y5
(416) 935-1100
Emp Here 3,000
SIC 6712 Bank holding companies

D-U-N-S 20-709-5964   (BR)
ROGERS MEDIA INC
TODAY'S PARENT
(Suby of Rogers Communications Inc)
1 Mount Pleasant Rd, Toronto, ON, M4Y 2Y5
(416) 764-2000
Emp Here 40
SIC 2721 Periodicals

D-U-N-S 20-003-0596   (BR)
ROYAL BANK OF CANADA
RBC
(Suby of Royal Bank Of Canada)
468 Yonge St, Toronto, ON, M4Y 1X3
(416) 974-7763
Emp Here 23
SIC 6021 National commercial banks

D-U-N-S 24-772-3935   (SL)
SALVATION ARMY TORONTO GRACE HEALTH CENTER, THE
650 Church St, Toronto, ON, M4Y 2G5
(416) 925-2251
Emp Here 275   Sales 17,195,686
SIC 8051 Skilled nursing care facilities
Pr Marilyn Rook

D-U-N-S 20-506-0101 (BR)
STARBUCKS COFFEE CANADA, INC
(Suby of Starbucks Corporation)
450 Yonge St, Toronto, ON, M4Y 1W9
(416) 922-6696
Emp Here 25
SIC 5812 Eating places

D-U-N-S 20-506-0648 (BR)
STARBUCKS COFFEE CANADA, INC
(Suby of Starbucks Corporation)
8 Wellesley St E Suite 1105, Toronto, ON, M4Y 3B2
(416) 927-3277
Emp Here 20
SIC 5812 Eating places

D-U-N-S 25-531-1904 (BR)
SUNNYBROOK HEALTH SCIENCES CENTRE FOUNDATION
ORTHOPAEDIC & ATHRITIC CAMPUS
(Suby of Sunnybrook Health Sciences Centre Foundation)
43 Wellesley St E Suite 327, Toronto, ON, M4Y 1H1
(416) 967-8500
Emp Here 350
SIC 8069 Specialty hospitals, except psychiatric

D-U-N-S 24-248-5907 (BR)
TORONTO CATHOLIC DISTRICT SCHOOL BOARD
MONSIGNOR FRASER COLLEGE - ISABELLA
146 Isabella St, Toronto, ON, M4Y 1P6
(416) 393-5533
Emp Here 30
SIC 8211 Elementary and secondary schools

D-U-N-S 20-711-2603 (BR)
TORONTO DISTRICT SCHOOL BOARD
JARVIS COLLEGIATE INSTITUTE
495 Jarvis St, Toronto, ON, M4Y 2G8
(416) 393-0140
Emp Here 100
SIC 8211 Elementary and secondary schools

D-U-N-S 20-700-2846 (BR)
TORONTO DISTRICT SCHOOL BOARD
CHURCH STREET JUNIOR PUBLIC SCHOOL
83 Alexander St, Toronto, ON, M4Y 1B7
(416) 393-1250
Emp Here 30
SIC 8211 Elementary and secondary schools

D-U-N-S 25-167-4743 (BR)
TORONTO STAR NEWSPAPERS LIMITED
STAR MEDIA GROUP
625 Church St Suite 600, Toronto, ON, M4Y 2G1

Emp Here 90
SIC 2711 Newspapers

D-U-N-S 24-337-8643 (HQ)
TURNING POINT YOUTH SERVICES
(Suby of Turning Point Youth Services)
95 Wellesley St E, Toronto, ON, M4Y 2X9
(416) 925-9250
Emp Here 60   Emp Total 260
Sales 14,067,200
SIC 8322 Individual and family services
Opers Mgr Jeanetta Hoffman
Ex Dir Colin Dart

D-U-N-S 25-131-4902 (HQ)
UNIVERSITY OF TORONTO PRESS
(Suby of University of Toronto Press)
10 St Mary St Suite 700, Toronto, ON, M4Y 2W8
(416) 978-2239
Emp Here 200   Emp Total 250
Sales 14,227,337
SIC 2731 Book publishing
Pr Pr John Yates
Roger Parkinson

Dir Frank Anderson
Dir Carol Moore
Dir Catherine Riggall

D-U-N-S 20-651-2191 (BR)
WENDY'S RESTAURANTS OF CANADA INC
WENDY'S
(Suby of The Wendy's Company)
475 Yonge St, Toronto, ON, M4Y 1X7
(416) 921-9045
Emp Here 27
SIC 5812 Eating places

Toronto, ON M5A
York County

D-U-N-S 20-356-2058 (SL)
3981240 CANADA INC
DOWNTOWN MAZDA
259 Lake Shore Blvd E, Toronto, ON, M5A 3T7

Emp Here 25   Sales 12,681,250
SIC 5511 New and used car dealers
Genl Mgr John Farley

D-U-N-S 24-421-8140 (SL)
ABS-CBN CANADA, ULC
411 Richmond St E Suite 203, Toronto, ON, M5A 3S5
(800) 345-2465
Emp Here 50   Sales 5,371,275
SIC 7822 Motion picture and tape distribution
Dir Marco Amoranto

D-U-N-S 24-128-3543 (BR)
AUTODESK CANADA CIE
(Suby of Autodesk, Inc.)
210 King St E, Toronto, ON, M5A 1J7
(416) 362-9181
Emp Here 275
SIC 7371 Custom computer programming services

D-U-N-S 24-207-5104 (HQ)
CANOE INC
RESEAU CANOE
(Suby of Placements Peladeau Inc, Les)
333 King St E Suite 1, Toronto, ON, M5A 3X5
(416) 947-2154
Emp Here 440   Emp Total 1
Sales 101,206,135
SIC 4813 Telephone communication, except radio
Pr Pr Pierre K Peladeau
Sec Claudine Tremblay
Serge Gouin
Jean-Francois Pruneau

D-U-N-S 20-088-4927 (BR)
CLARENDON FOUNDATION (CHESHIRE HOMES) INC
(Suby of Clarendon Foundation (Cheshire Homes) Inc)
25 Henry Lane Terr Suite 442, Toronto, ON, M5A 4B6

Emp Here 80
SIC 8699 Membership organizations, nec

D-U-N-S 20-179-4039 (HQ)
COCA-COLA REFRESHMENTS CANADA COMPANY
COCA-COLA BOTTLING
(Suby of The Coca-Cola Company)
335 King St E, Toronto, ON, M5A 1L1
(416) 424-6000
Emp Here 383   Emp Total 100,300
Sales 715,014,860
SIC 2086 Bottled and canned soft drinks
Pr Pr Kevin Warren
Jeffrey Kirsh
Dir Kathy Loveless
Ed Walker
Dir Christopher Nolan

D-U-N-S 24-172-9961 (BR)
COMPAGNIE DES CHEMINS DE FER NATIONAUX DU CANADA
CN RAILS
277 Front St W, Toronto, ON, M5A 1E1
(888) 888-5909
Emp Here 21,967
SIC 4111 Local and suburban transit

D-U-N-S 24-345-0322 (BR)
CONSEIL SCOLAIRE VIAMONDE
ECOLE GABRIELLE-ROY
14 Pembroke St, Toronto, ON, M5A 2N7
(416) 393-1360
Emp Here 25
SIC 8211 Elementary and secondary schools

D-U-N-S 20-585-4180 (BR)
CORPORATION OF THE CITY OF TORONTO
ROBERTSON HOUSE
291 Sherbourne St, Toronto, ON, M5A 2R9
(416) 392-5662
Emp Here 60
SIC 8322 Individual and family services

D-U-N-S 24-619-9058 (BR)
CORUS ENTERTAINMENT INC
CFMJ-AM
25 Dockside Dr, Toronto, ON, M5A 0B5
(416) 642-3770
Emp Here 250
SIC 7922 Theatrical producers and services

D-U-N-S 20-109-6380 (BR)
CORUS ENTERTAINMENT INC
Q107 FM
25 Dockside Dr Suite 25, Toronto, ON, M5A 0B5
(416) 221-0107
Emp Here 175
SIC 7922 Theatrical producers and services

D-U-N-S 24-409-0114 (SL)
DANIEL ET DANIEL CATERING INC
248 Carlton St, Toronto, ON, M5A 2L1
(416) 968-9275
Emp Here 90   Sales 2,699,546
SIC 5812 Eating places

D-U-N-S 25-461-9604 (SL)
DELMAGE, J A PRODUCTIONS LTD
512 King St E Suite 310, Toronto, ON, M5A 1M1

Emp Here 50   Sales 6,184,080
SIC 7812 Motion picture and video production
John A Delmage
Dir Neil Court
Dir Beth Stevenson
Dir Steven Denure

D-U-N-S 24-138-2584 (SL)
DIGNITAS INTERNATIONAL
550 Queen St E Suite 335, Toronto, ON, M5A 1V2
(416) 260-3100
Emp Here 190   Sales 42,273,049
SIC 8099 Health and allied services, nec

D-U-N-S 20-788-3013 (BR)
DIXON HALL
SCHOOL HOUSE EMERGENCY SHELTER
349 George St, Toronto, ON, M5A 2N2
(416) 960-9240
Emp Here 20
SIC 8399 Social services, nec

D-U-N-S 24-045-4330 (SL)
DOWNTOWN FINE CARS INC
DOWNTOWN PORCHE
68 Parliament St, Toronto, ON, M5A 0B2
(416) 363-2818
Emp Here 80   Sales 40,580,000
SIC 5511 New and used car dealers
Dir Peter A Kircher
Pr Pr Helen Ching

D-U-N-S 24-977-1960 (BR)

FGL SPORTS LTD
SPORT CHEK SHERWAY
167 Queen St E Unit B1, Toronto, ON, M5A 1S2
(416) 621-6796
Emp Here 20
SIC 5941 Sporting goods and bicycle shops

D-U-N-S 25-405-1337 (SL)
FIREWORKS MEDIA INC
111 George St, Toronto, ON, M5A 2N4
(416) 360-4321
Emp Here 70   Sales 6,177,930
SIC 7812 Motion picture and video production
Ch Bd Jay Firestone
Pr Pr Adam Haight
VP Fin Blake Tohana
Sr VP John Robinson

D-U-N-S 20-716-2848 (BR)
GOVERNING COUNCIL OF THE UNIVERSITY OF TORONTO
DEPARTMENT OF HISTORY & ART
100 St. George St Suite 6036, Toronto, ON, M5A 2M4
(416) 978-7892
Emp Here 50
SIC 8221 Colleges and universities

D-U-N-S 20-074-5383 (BR)
GREYHOUND CANADA TRANSPORTATION ULC
GREYHOUND COURIER EXPRESS
154 Front St E, Toronto, ON, M5A 1E5
(416) 594-1311
Emp Here 30
SIC 4131 Intercity and rural bus transportation

D-U-N-S 24-822-6227 (SL)
HARRIS INSTITUTE FOR THE ARTS INCORPORATED, THE
118 Sherbourne St, Toronto, ON, M5A 2R2
(416) 367-0162
Emp Here 75   Sales 4,669,485
SIC 8249 Vocational schools, nec

D-U-N-S 25-460-9183 (SL)
INFOMART DIALOG LTD
INFOMART
333 King St E Suite 300, Toronto, ON, M5A 0E1

Emp Here 59   Sales 5,030,400
SIC 7379 Computer related services, nec
Pr Andrew Martin

D-U-N-S 25-246-4268 (SL)
INFONEX INC
INFONEX DEFENSE
145 Berkeley St Suite 200, Toronto, ON, M5A 2X1
(416) 971-4177
Emp Here 60   Sales 3,283,232
SIC 8299 Schools and educational services, nec

D-U-N-S 24-182-4580 (SL)
KIDS CAN PRESS LTD
CORUS QUAY
25 Dockside Dr, Toronto, ON, M5A 0B5
(416) 479-7191
Emp Here 45   Sales 2,553,625
SIC 2731 Book publishing

D-U-N-S 20-648-4011 (BR)
MARCH OF DIMES CANADA
30 Saint Lawrence St Suite A3, Toronto, ON, M5A 3C5
(416) 703-8781
Emp Here 20
SIC 8331 Job training and related services

D-U-N-S 24-418-5661 (BR)
MARK'S WORK WEARHOUSE LTD
WORK WORLD
167 Queen St E, Toronto, ON, M5A 1S2
(416) 626-2729
Emp Here 25

SIC 5699 Miscellaneous apparel and accessory stores

D-U-N-S 20-923-8547 (BR)
MCDONALD'S RESTAURANTS OF CANADA LIMITED
MCDONALD'S
(*Suby of* McDonald's Corporation)
121 Front St E, Toronto, ON, M5A 4S5
(416) 868-9998
Emp Here 60
SIC 5812 Eating places

D-U-N-S 24-336-2287 (BR)
MERCEDES-BENZ CANADA INC
761 Dundas St E, Toronto, ON, M5A 4N5
(416) 947-9000
Emp Here 40
SIC 5012 Automobiles and other motor vehicles

D-U-N-S 20-774-2065 (HQ)
P.S. PRODUCTION SERVICES LTD
80 Commissioners St, Toronto, ON, M5A 1A8
(416) 466-0037
Emp Here 84   *Emp Total* 125
Sales 8,952,126
SIC 7819 Services allied to motion pictures
Pr Pr Douglas Dales
Sr VP Rae Thurston
 Douglas Barrett
VP Fin Alex Sandahl

D-U-N-S 24-039-4465 (BR)
PATHWAYS TO EDUCATION CANADA
PATHWAYS TO EDUCATION
411 Parliament St 2nd Fl, Toronto, ON, M5A 3A1
(416) 642-1570
Emp Here 40
SIC 8211 Elementary and secondary schools

D-U-N-S 25-311-7444 (SL)
PEBBLEHUT ELLIE SERVICES INC
63 Polson St, Toronto, ON, M5A 1A4
(416) 778-6800
Emp Here 80   *Sales* 9,423,290
SIC 7812 Motion picture and video production

D-U-N-S 24-022-2989 (SL)
PEEKS SOCIAL LTD
184 Front St E Suite 701, Toronto, ON, M5A 4N3
(416) 639-5335
Emp Here 50   *Sales* 134,779
SIC 1382 Oil and gas exploration services

D-U-N-S 20-188-4983 (SL)
PLATESPIN LTD
340 King St E Suite 200, Toronto, ON, M5A 1K8

Emp Here 21   *Sales* 1,532,175
SIC 7372 Prepackaged software

D-U-N-S 24-319-1231 (SL)
PRICING SOLUTIONS LTD
106 Front St E Suite 300, Toronto, ON, M5A 1E1
(416) 943-0505
Emp Here 20   *Sales* 1,824,018
SIC 8741 Management services

D-U-N-S 20-691-6152 (SL)
PROOFPOINT CANADA, INC.
(*Suby of* Proofpoint, Inc.)
210 King St E Suite 300, Toronto, ON, M5A 1J7
(416) 366-6666
Emp Here 25   *Sales* 2,425,503
SIC 7372 Prepackaged software

D-U-N-S 25-108-0487 (HQ)
QUEST SOFTWARE CANADA INC
FASTLANE TECHNOLOGIES
(*Suby of* Francisco Partners Management, L.P.)
260 King St E 4th Flr, Toronto, ON, M5A 4L5

(416) 933-5000
Emp Here 150   *Emp Total* 6,405
Sales 49,686,237
SIC 7371 Custom computer programming services
Pr Douglas F. Garn
Dir J Michael Vaughn
 Enrico D'amico
 Vincent Smith

D-U-N-S 25-868-2202 (BR)
REGENT PARK COMMUNITY HEALTH CENTRE
PARENTS FOR BETTER BEGINNINGS
(*Suby of* Regent Park Community Health Centre)
38 Regent St Suite 2, Toronto, ON, M5A 3N7
(416) 362-0805
Emp Here 20
SIC 8399 Social services, nec

D-U-N-S 25-708-4137 (BR)
S B R INTERNATIONAL INC
S B R GLOBAL
173 Queen St E, Toronto, ON, M5A 1S2

Emp Here 50
SIC 8741 Management services

D-U-N-S 24-828-2907 (HQ)
SAS INSTITUTE (CANADA) INC
(*Suby of* Sas Institute Inc.)
280 King St E Suite 500, Toronto, ON, M5A 1K4
(416) 363-4424
Emp Here 200   *Emp Total* 13,147
Sales 54,833,688
SIC 7372 Prepackaged software
Pr Carl Farrell
VP Fin VP Fin Stuart Bowden
Dir James Goodnight

D-U-N-S 20-802-4278 (SL)
SOMERSET CHEVROLET CORVETTE LTD
SOMERSET CHEV
291 Lake Shore Blvd E, Toronto, ON, M5A 1B9
(416) 368-8878
Emp Here 25   *Sales* 11,779,113
SIC 5511 New and used car dealers
Sec Sadelone Nympfha

D-U-N-S 24-486-9053 (SL)
ST. LAWRENCE CO-OPERATIVE DAY CARE INC
SCHOOL AGE CENTRE
230 The Esplanade, Toronto, ON, M5A 4J6
(416) 363-9425
Emp Here 50   *Sales* 1,532,175
SIC 8351 Child day care services

D-U-N-S 25-531-8057 (BR)
ST. MICHAEL'S HOSPITAL
ANCHOR PERSON PROJECT
(*Suby of* St. Michael's Hospital)
135 Sherbourne St, Toronto, ON, M5A 2R5
(416) 864-5873
Emp Here 20
SIC 8322 Individual and family services

D-U-N-S 25-213-6973 (BR)
STAPLES CANADA INC
STAPLES/BUSINESS DEPOT
(*Suby of* Staples, Inc.)
250 Front St E, Toronto, ON, M5A 1E9
(416) 368-3331
Emp Here 20
SIC 5943 Stationery stores

D-U-N-S 24-676-9314 (SL)
SUPREME MUNSINGWEAR CANADA INC
(*Suby of* Perry Ellis International Inc)
2 Berkeley St Suite 4, Toronto, ON, M5A 4J5
(647) 344-2026
Emp Here 20   *Sales* 1,240,332
SIC 5651 Family clothing stores

D-U-N-S 24-329-0009 (BR)
TECHNICOLOR SERVICES CREATIFS

CANADA INC
49 Ontario St, Toronto, ON, M5A 2V1
(416) 585-9995
Emp Here 50
SIC 7819 Services allied to motion pictures

D-U-N-S 24-006-7876 (SL)
THE LITTLE BROTHERS OF THE GOOD SHEPHERD (CANADA)
412 Queen St E, Toronto, ON, M5A 1T3
(416) 869-3619
Emp Here 60   *Sales* 3,939,878
SIC 8661 Religious organizations

D-U-N-S 24-977-6626 (BR)
TOROMONT INDUSTRIES LTD
CIMCO REFRIGERATION
65 Villiers St, Toronto, ON, M5A 3S1
(416) 465-7581
Emp Here 850
SIC 3585 Refrigeration and heating equipment

D-U-N-S 20-711-1605 (BR)
TORONTO CATHOLIC DISTRICT SCHOOL BOARD
ST. MICHAEL CATHOLIC SCHOOL
50 George St S, Toronto, ON, M5A 4B2
(416) 393-5387
Emp Here 50
SIC 8211 Elementary and secondary schools

D-U-N-S 20-711-1423 (BR)
TORONTO CATHOLIC DISTRICT SCHOOL BOARD
ST PAUL CATHOLIC ELEMENTARY SCHOOL
80 Sackville St, Toronto, ON, M5A 3E5
(416) 393-5204
Emp Here 50
SIC 8211 Elementary and secondary schools

D-U-N-S 20-035-5605 (BR)
TORONTO DISTRICT SCHOOL BOARD
LORD DUFFERIN PUBLIC SCHOOL
350 Parliament St, Toronto, ON, M5A 2Z7
(416) 393-1760
Emp Here 70
SIC 8211 Elementary and secondary schools

D-U-N-S 20-698-7443 (BR)
TORONTO DISTRICT SCHOOL BOARD
MARKET LANE JUNIOR AND SENIOR PUBLIC SCHOOL
246 The Esplanade, Toronto, ON, M5A 4J6
(416) 393-1300
Emp Here 60
SIC 8211 Elementary and secondary schools

D-U-N-S 20-700-1863 (BR)
TORONTO DISTRICT SCHOOL BOARD
SPRUCECOURT PUBLIC SCHOOL
70 Spruce St, Toronto, ON, M5A 2J1
(416) 393-1522
Emp Here 40
SIC 8211 Elementary and secondary schools

D-U-N-S 20-025-9955 (BR)
TORONTO DISTRICT SCHOOL BOARD
NELSON MANDELA PARK PUBLIC SCHOOL
440 Shuter St, Toronto, ON, M5A 1X6
(416) 393-1620
Emp Here 61
SIC 8211 Elementary and secondary schools

D-U-N-S 20-902-0999 (SL)
TORONTO HUMANE SOCIETY, THE
11 River St, Toronto, ON, M5A 4C2
(416) 392-2273
Emp Here 100   *Sales* 9,503,658
SIC 8699 Membership organizations, nec
Dir Jacques Messier
 David Bronskill
Pr Pr Marcie Laking
VP VP Elizabeth Cabral
VP VP Dean Maher
VP VP Peter Newell
VP VP Crystal Tomusiak

 Lisa Gibbens
 Stephen Steele
Ex Dir Barbara Steinhoff

D-U-N-S 20-787-3774 (BR)
TORONTO PORT AUTHORITY
62 Villiers St, Toronto, ON, M5A 1B1
(416) 462-1261
Emp Here 35
SIC 4491 Marine cargo handling

D-U-N-S 24-727-3972 (BR)
TORONTO PUBLIC LIBRARY BOARD
BIBLIOGRAPHIC SERVICES DEPARTMENT
281 Front St E, Toronto, ON, M5A 4L2
(416) 393-7215
Emp Here 120
SIC 8231 Libraries

D-U-N-S 25-720-3047 (SL)
TRANSASIAN FINE CARS LTD
DOWNTOWN ACURA
183 Front St E, Toronto, ON, M5A 1E7
(416) 867-1577
Emp Here 35   *Sales* 12,768,123
SIC 5511 New and used car dealers
Pr Sylvester Chuang

D-U-N-S 25-217-3992 (SL)
W NETWORK INC
25 Dockside Dr, Toronto, ON, M5A 0B5
(416) 530-2329
Emp Here 50   *Sales* 2,918,428
SIC 4833 Television broadcasting stations

D-U-N-S 20-113-4785 (BR)
WATT INTERNATIONAL INC
WATT IDG
(*Suby of* Watt International Inc)
300 Bayview Ave, Toronto, ON, M5A 3R7
(416) 364-9384
Emp Here 30
SIC 7389 Business services, nec

D-U-N-S 20-290-7353 (HQ)
WEBER SHANDWICK WORLDWIDE (CANADA) INC
GOLLIN HARRIS
(*Suby of* The Interpublic Group of Companies Inc)
351 King St E Suite 800, Toronto, ON, M5A 0L6
(416) 964-6444
Emp Here 48   *Emp Total* 49,800
Sales 6,858,306
SIC 8743 Public relations services
Pr Pr Greg Power

D-U-N-S 24-704-8481 (SL)
WING MACHINE INC, THE
246 Parliament St, Toronto, ON, M5A 3A4
(416) 961-1000
Emp Here 150   *Sales* 6,289,900
SIC 5812 Eating places
Pr Pr Joseph Schiavone
 Frank Schiavone
 Vito Schiavone

Toronto, ON M5B
York County

D-U-N-S 25-249-4760 (SL)
AIDS COMMITTEE OF TORONTO
399 Church St Suite 400, Toronto, ON, M5B 2J6
(416) 340-2437
Emp Here 50   *Sales* 1,969,939
SIC 8322 Individual and family services

D-U-N-S 24-001-9096 (BR)
ARAMARK CANADA LTD.
ARAMARK MANAGED SERVICES
290 Yonge St Suite 600, Toronto, ON, M5B 1C8
(416) 204-1802
Emp Here 26

SIC 5812 Eating places

D-U-N-S 25-824-1939 (BR)
ADIDAS CANADA LIMITED
10 Dundas St E, Toronto, ON, M5B 2G9
(416) 915-8140
Emp Here 40
SIC 5941 Sporting goods and bicycle shops

D-U-N-S 25-342-9021 (BR)
AMATO PIZZA INC
(Suby of Amato Pizza Inc)
429a Yonge St, Toronto, ON, M5B 1T1
(416) 977-8989
Emp Here 22
SIC 5812 Eating places

D-U-N-S 24-206-6673 (BR)
BCBG MAX AZRIA CANADA INC
218 Yonge St, Toronto, ON, M5B 2H6
(416) 640-2766
Emp Here 20
SIC 5611 Men's and boys' clothing stores

D-U-N-S 20-981-9465 (SL)
BOND PLACE HOTEL LTD
65 Dundas St E, Toronto, ON, M5B 2G8
(416) 362-6061
Emp Here 80   Sales 3,502,114
SIC 7011 Hotels and motels

D-U-N-S 25-310-3618 (BR)
BOUTIQUE LA VIE EN ROSE INC
BOUTIQUE LA VIE EN ROSE INC
(Suby of Gestion Francois Roberge Inc)
218 Yonge St, Toronto, ON, M5B 2H6
(416) 595-0898
Emp Here 23
SIC 5632 Women's accessory and specialty stores

D-U-N-S 24-833-3358 (BR)
BRASSEURS RJ INC, LES
BREWERS
275 Yonge St, Toronto, ON, M5B 1N8
(647) 347-6286
Emp Here 40
SIC 2082 Malt beverages

D-U-N-S 25-520-3192 (BR)
CADILLAC FAIRVIEW CORPORATION LIMITED, THE
TORONTO EATON CENTRE
220 Yonge St Suite 110, Toronto, ON, M5B 2H1
(416) 598-8700
Emp Here 140
SIC 6512 Nonresidential building operators

D-U-N-S 25-520-5643 (BR)
CADILLAC FAIRVIEW CORPORATION LIMITED, THE
250 Yonge St Suite 610, Toronto, ON, M5B 2L7
(416) 598-8500
Emp Here 35
SIC 6553 Cemetery subdividers and developers

D-U-N-S 20-776-9568 (BR)
CINEPLEX ODEON CORPORATION
MAGIC LANTERN CARLTON CINEMA
20 Carlton St, Toronto, ON, M5B 2H5
(416) 494-9371
Emp Here 20
SIC 7832 Motion picture theaters, except drive-in

D-U-N-S 20-653-0466 (BR)
CONSEIL SCOLAIRE VIAMONDE
CONSEIL SCOLAIRE VIAMONDE
100 Carlton St, Toronto, ON, M5B 1M3
(416) 393-0175
Emp Here 45
SIC 8211 Elementary and secondary schools

D-U-N-S 25-972-4706 (BR)
CONSEILLERS EN GESTION ET INFORMATIQUE CGI INC

CGI
250 Yonge St Suite 2000, Toronto, ON, M5B 2L7
(416) 363-7827
Emp Here 400
SIC 8741 Management services

D-U-N-S 24-387-1076 (SL)
COVENANT HOUSE TORONTO
20 Gerrard St E, Toronto, ON, M5B 2P3
(416) 598-4898
Emp Here 150   Sales 20,123,868
SIC 8322 Individual and family services
Ex Dir Ruth Dacosta
Ex Dir Cindy Metzler

D-U-N-S 25-518-5456 (HQ)
DION, DURRELL & ASSOCIATES INC
(Suby of Dion, Durrell & Associates Inc)
250 Yonge St Suite 2, Toronto, ON, M5B 2L7
(416) 408-2626
Emp Here 70   Emp Total 100
Sales 4,523,563
SIC 8999 Services, nec

D-U-N-S 20-779-8633 (BR)
DON MICHAEL HOLDINGS INC
ROOTS
220 Yonge St, Toronto, ON, M5B 2H1
(416) 593-9640
Emp Here 50
SIC 5651 Family clothing stores

D-U-N-S 25-702-8258 (BR)
FGL SPORTS LTD
ATHLETES WORLD
260 Yonge St Suite 18, Toronto, ON, M5B 2L9
(416) 598-2456
Emp Here 30
SIC 5661 Shoe stores

D-U-N-S 24-787-8908 (BR)
FGL SPORTS LTD
COAST MOUNTAIN
220 Yonge St, Toronto, ON, M5B 2H1
(416) 598-1626
Emp Here 50
SIC 5941 Sporting goods and bicycle shops

D-U-N-S 24-308-9922 (BR)
FIDELITY INVESTMENTS CANADA ULC
(Suby of Fmr LLC)
250 Yonge St Suite 700, Toronto, ON, M5B 2L7
(416) 307-5478
Emp Here 250
SIC 6722 Management investment, open-end

D-U-N-S 20-553-9245 (BR)
FOOT LOCKER CANADA CO.
FOOT LOCKER
247 Yonge St, Toronto, ON, M5B 1N8
(416) 368-4569
Emp Here 20
SIC 5661 Shoe stores

D-U-N-S 20-780-4100 (BR)
FOOT LOCKER CANADA CO.
FOOT LOCKER
218 Yonge St Unit 2022, Toronto, ON, M5B 2H6
(416) 598-1860
Emp Here 25
SIC 5661 Shoe stores

D-U-N-S 25-366-3462 (SL)
GFX PARTNERS INC
229 Yonge St Suite 502, Toronto, ON, M5B 1N9
(416) 217-3088
Emp Here 28   Sales 61,072,900
SIC 6099 Functions related to deposit banking
Pr Michael Smith

D-U-N-S 25-304-6833 (BR)
GAP (CANADA) INC
GAP
(Suby of The Gap Inc)

260 Yonge St, Toronto, ON, M5B 2L9
(416) 599-8802
Emp Here 160
SIC 5651 Family clothing stores

D-U-N-S 25-721-2035 (BR)
GAP (CANADA) INC
BANANA REPUBLIC
(Suby of The Gap Inc)
220 Yonge St, Toronto, ON, M5B 2H1
(416) 595-6336
Emp Here 75
SIC 5651 Family clothing stores

D-U-N-S 25-687-1690 (BR)
GAP (CANADA) INC
BABYGAP
(Suby of The Gap Inc)
220 Yonge St, Toronto, ON, M5B 2H1
(416) 591-0512
Emp Here 20
SIC 5651 Family clothing stores

D-U-N-S 25-371-3143 (SL)
GOODLAW SERVICES LIMITED PARTNERSHIP
250 Yonge St Suite 2400, Toronto, ON, M5B 2L7
(416) 979-2211
Emp Here 300   Sales 55,656,720
SIC 8741 Management services
Dir Byron Sonberg

D-U-N-S 25-852-6615 (BR)
GROUPE ALDO INC, LE
ALDO SHOES
332 Yonge St, Toronto, ON, M5B 1R8
(416) 596-1390
Emp Here 27
SIC 5661 Shoe stores

D-U-N-S 25-309-4429 (BR)
GROUPE ALDO INC, LE
ALDO
220 Yonge St Suite 600, Toronto, ON, M5B 2H1
(416) 979-2477
Emp Here 25
SIC 5661 Shoe stores

D-U-N-S 24-140-3013 (HQ)
HRC CANADA INC
HARD ROCK CAFE CANADA
(Suby of Hard Rock Heals Foundation, Inc.)
279 Yonge St, Toronto, ON, M5B 1N8
(416) 362-3636
Emp Here 80   Emp Total 3,000
Sales 8,025,677
SIC 5813 Drinking places
Pr Hamish Dodds

D-U-N-S 25-795-5229 (BR)
HARRY ROSEN INC
ROSEN, HARRY GENTLEMEN'S APPAREL
218 Yonge St Suite 3015, Toronto, ON, M5B 2H6
(416) 598-8885
Emp Here 25
SIC 5611 Men's and boys' clothing stores

D-U-N-S 20-770-0675 (HQ)
HERZING INSTITUTES OF CANADA INC
HERZING COLLEGE
220 Yonge St Suite 202, Toronto, ON, M5B 2H1
(416) 599-6996
Emp Here 25   Emp Total 475
Sales 8,339,840
SIC 8244 Business and secretarial schools
Henry Herzing
Pr Pr George Hood

D-U-N-S 25-707-5259 (BR)
IMAGO RESTAURANTS INC
CITY GRILL RESTAURANT
(Suby of Imago Restaurants Inc)
220 Yonge St, Toronto, ON, M5B 2H1

Emp Here 30
SIC 5812 Eating places

D-U-N-S 25-082-6435 (BR)
INDIGO BOOKS & MUSIC INC
INDIGO
(Suby of Indigo Books & Music Inc)
220 Yonge St Suite 103, Toronto, ON, M5B 2H1
(416) 591-3622
Emp Here 100
SIC 5942 Book stores

D-U-N-S 20-772-2831 (SL)
KANATA ENTERTAINMENT HOLDINGS INC
10 Dundas St E Suite 1002, Toronto, ON, M5B 2G9
(416) 408-3080
Emp Here 20   Sales 6,347,581
SIC 6553 Cemetery subdividers and developers
Pr David Johnson

D-U-N-S 25-061-3064 (BR)
LE CHATEAU INC
ANABANANA & DESIGN (HORIZONTAL)
(Suby of Le Chateau Inc)
220 Yonge St Unit B 10-12, Toronto, ON, M5B 2H1
(416) 979-3122
Emp Here 30
SIC 5651 Family clothing stores

D-U-N-S 25-362-3664 (BR)
LOFT COMMUNITY SERVICES
COLLEGE VIEW SUPPORTIVE HOUSING SERVICES
423 Yonge St 2nd Fl, Toronto, ON, M5B 1T2
(416) 340-7222
Emp Here 25
SIC 8059 Nursing and personal care, nec

D-U-N-S 24-386-0939 (SL)
MAGNUM PROTECTIVE SERVICES LIMITED
27 Carlton St Unit 203, Toronto, ON, M5B 1L2
(416) 591-1566
Emp Here 100   Sales 3,137,310
SIC 7381 Detective and armored car services

D-U-N-S 25-310-9128 (BR)
MCDONALD'S RESTAURANTS OF CANADA LIMITED
MCDONALD'S
(Suby of McDonald's Corporation)
218 Yonge St, Toronto, ON, M5B 2H6
(416) 422-7500
Emp Here 50
SIC 5812 Eating places

D-U-N-S 24-335-0571 (BR)
METRO ONTARIO INC
METRO
89 Gould St, Toronto, ON, M5B 2R1
(416) 862-7171
Emp Here 160
SIC 5411 Grocery stores

D-U-N-S 25-147-8889 (SL)
MILESTONE RADIO INC
FLOW 93.5 FM
211 Yonge St Suite 400, Toronto, ON, M5B 1M4
(416) 214-5000
Emp Here 50   Sales 3,137,310
SIC 4832 Radio broadcasting stations

D-U-N-S 20-859-9592 (BR)
PACIFIC LINK COMMUNICATIONS INC
BELL CENTRE
218 Yonge St, Toronto, ON, M5B 2H6
(416) 596-1006
Emp Here 25
SIC 5999 Miscellaneous retail stores, nec

D-U-N-S 24-062-5301 (SL)
PALIN FOUNDATION, THE
OAKHAM HOUSE

63 Gould St, Toronto, ON, M5B 1E9
(416) 979-5250
Emp Here 130   *Sales* 4,304,681
SIC 7299 Miscellaneous personal service

D-U-N-S 25-300-4626   (BR)
REDBERRY FRANCHISING CORP
BURGER KING
243 Yonge St, Toronto, ON, M5B 1N8
(416) 368-7190
Emp Here 26
SIC 5812 Eating places

D-U-N-S 25-659-5703   (BR)
REITMANS (CANADA) LIMITEE
REITMANS
218 Yonge St, Toronto, ON, M5B 2H6
(416) 598-3563
Emp Here 25
SIC 5621 Women's clothing stores

D-U-N-S 25-947-4286   (BR)
RICHTREE MARKET RESTAURANTS INC
MARCHELINO RESTAURANTS
220 Yonge St, Toronto, ON, M5B 2H1
(416) 506-0113
Emp Here 49
SIC 5812 Eating places

D-U-N-S 20-306-5149   (BR)
RYERSON UNIVERSITY
AEROSPACE ENGINEERING, SCHOOL OF
245 Church St, Toronto, ON, M5B 2K3
(416) 979-5016
Emp Here 26
SIC 8221 Colleges and universities

D-U-N-S 20-543-6710   (BR)
SIR CORP
DUKE'S REFRESHER
382 Yonge St Unit 8, Toronto, ON, M5B 1S8
(416) 597-8838
Emp Here 20
SIC 5812 Eating places

D-U-N-S 24-848-3989   (BR)
SEARS CANADA INC
SEARS CANADA-ACCOUNTS PAYABLE
290 Yonge St Suite 700, Toronto, ON, M5B 2C3
(416) 941-2253
Emp Here 25
SIC 5311 Department stores

D-U-N-S 20-860-3295   (BR)
SOURCE (BELL) ELECTRONICS INC, THE
SOURCE, THE
220 Yonge St Suite 201, Toronto, ON, M5B 2H1
(416) 979-7776
Emp Here 25
SIC 5999 Miscellaneous retail stores, nec

D-U-N-S 25-894-4073   (BR)
ST VINCENT DE PAUL SOCIETY
MARY'S HOME
70 Gerrard St E, Toronto, ON, M5B 1G6
(416) 595-1578
Emp Here 22
SIC 8399 Social services, nec

D-U-N-S 24-629-6847   (BR)
STARBUCKS COFFEE CANADA, INC
(*Suby of* Starbucks Corporation)
10 Dundas St E Suite 128, Toronto, ON, M5B 2G9
(416) 593-9790
Emp Here 20
SIC 5812 Eating places

D-U-N-S 24-693-9508   (SL)
TEPLITSKY, COLSON LLP BARRISTERS
70 Bond St Suite 200, Toronto, ON, M5B 1X3
(416) 365-9320
Emp Here 54   *Sales* 4,596,524
SIC 8111 Legal services

D-U-N-S 20-077-8988   (BR)
TOBIAS HOUSE ATTENDANT CARE INC

84 Carlton St Suite 306, Toronto, ON, M5B 2P4

Emp Here 25
SIC 8361 Residential care

D-U-N-S 20-700-2036   (BR)
TORONTO CATHOLIC DISTRICT SCHOOL BOARD
ST. MICHAEL'S CHOIR SCHOOL
67 Bond St, Toronto, ON, M5B 1X5
(416) 393-5217
Emp Here 30
SIC 8211 Elementary and secondary schools

D-U-N-S 20-521-7552   (HQ)
TORONTO HYDRO-ELECTRIC SYSTEM LIMITED
14 Carlton St, Toronto, ON, M5B 1K5
(416) 542-3100
Emp Here 170   *Emp Total* 1,480
Sales 741,280,712
SIC 4911 Electric services
Pr Anthony Haines
 Jean-Sebastien Couillard

D-U-N-S 20-753-0049   (SL)
VOLUNTEER ASSOCIATION FROM THE ST MICHAELS HOSPITAL, THE
THE VOLUNTEER ASSOCIATION GIFT SHOP
30 Bond St, Toronto, ON, M5B 1W8
(416) 864-5859
Emp Here 400   *Sales* 38,675,040
SIC 8641 Civic and social associations
Pr Margaret Coates

D-U-N-S 20-106-3562   (BR)
WINNERS MERCHANTS INTERNATIONAL L.P.
WINNERS
(*Suby of* The TJX Companies Inc)
444 Yonge St Unit G3, Toronto, ON, M5B 2H4
(416) 598-8800
Emp Here 175
SIC 5651 Family clothing stores

D-U-N-S 24-357-2398   (BR)
WINNERS MERCHANTS INTERNATIONAL L.P.
HOMESENSE
(*Suby of* The TJX Companies Inc)
195 Yonge St, Toronto, ON, M5B 1M4
(416) 941-9185
Emp Here 32
SIC 5651 Family clothing stores

D-U-N-S 20-550-3324   (SL)
WORLD TRADE GROUP (NORTH AMERICA) INC
WORLD TRADE GROUP
211 Yonge St, Toronto, ON, M5B 1M4
(416) 214-3400
Emp Here 75   *Sales* 3,793,956
SIC 7389 Business services, nec

D-U-N-S 20-780-1866   (BR)
YM INC. (SALES)
BLUENOTES
220 Yonge St Suite 125, Toronto, ON, M5B 2H1
(416) 598-9428
Emp Here 20
SIC 5621 Women's clothing stores

D-U-N-S 25-846-9394   (BR)
YONGE STREET MISSION, THE
EVERGREEN CENTRE FOR STREET YOUTH
(*Suby of* Yonge Street Mission, The)
381 Yonge St, Toronto, ON, M5B 1S1
(416) 977-7259
Emp Here 20
SIC 8322 Individual and family services

D-U-N-S 20-178-8395   (SL)
ZANTAV LIMITED
ZANZIBAR CIRCUS TAVERN

359 Yonge St, Toronto, ON, M5B 1S1

Emp Here 50   *Sales* 1,824,018
SIC 5813 Drinking places

Toronto, ON M5C
York County

D-U-N-S 24-787-9443   (SL)
24/7 CUSTOMER CANADA, INC
20 Toronto St Suite 530, Toronto, ON, M5C 2B8
(416) 214-9337
Emp Here 125   *Sales* 14,726,267
SIC 7371 Custom computer programming services
VP Fin David Richardson
 David Lloyd

D-U-N-S 20-955-4653   (BR)
AJILON STAFFING OF CANADA LIMITED
1 Adelaide St E Suite 2500, Toronto, ON, M5C 2V9

Emp Here 30
SIC 7361 Employment agencies

D-U-N-S 24-627-4062   (BR)
AMEX CANADA INC
AMERICAN EXPRESS TRAVEL
(*Suby of* American Express Company)
100 Yonge St Suite 1600, Toronto, ON, M5C 2W1

Emp Here 50
SIC 4724 Travel agencies

D-U-N-S 24-338-1303   (SL)
ARROW CAPITAL MANAGEMENT INC
36 Toronto St Suite 750, Toronto, ON, M5C 2C5
(416) 323-0477
Emp Here 30   *Sales* 5,889,600
SIC 6211 Security brokers and dealers
 James Mcgovern

D-U-N-S 20-300-2969   (SL)
ARROW DIVERSIFIED FUND
36 Toronto St Suite 750, Toronto, ON, M5C 2C5
(416) 323-0477
Emp Here 30   *Sales* 8,901,205
SIC 6722 Management investment, open-end
Dir Tim Mc Govern

D-U-N-S 25-183-6532   (BR)
ARTSMARKETING SERVICES INC
100 Lombard St Suite 105, Toronto, ON, M5C 1M3
(416) 941-9000
Emp Here 20
SIC 7389 Business services, nec

D-U-N-S 20-915-8638   (SL)
ASSANTE WEALTH MANAGEMENT LTD
(*Suby of* CI Financial Corp)
20 Queen St E, Toronto, ON, M5C 3G7
(416) 364-1145
Emp Here 500   *Sales* 94,429,920
SIC 8742 Management consulting services
Dir William Holland

D-U-N-S 24-565-1872   (SL)
ASSET COMPUTER PERSONNEL LTD
(*Suby of* CDI Corp.)
700-110 Yonge St, Toronto, ON, M5C 1T4
(416) 777-1717
Emp Here 46   *Sales* 3,356,192
SIC 7361 Employment agencies

D-U-N-S 20-076-9276   (BR)
BANK OF NOVA SCOTIA, THE
SCOTIA INSURANCE
100 Yonge St Suite 1801, Toronto, ON, M5C 2W1

(416) 866-7075
Emp Here 60
SIC 6021 National commercial banks

D-U-N-S 24-119-1837   (BR)
BANK OF NOVA SCOTIA, THE
SCOTIA LEASING
20 Adelaide St E Suite 601, Toronto, ON, M5C 2T6
(416) 866-4666
Emp Here 30
SIC 6021 National commercial banks

D-U-N-S 20-639-6736   (HQ)
BROADGRAIN COMMODITIES INC
(*Suby of* BroadGrain Holdings Inc)
18 King St E Suite 900, Toronto, ON, M5C 1C4
(416) 504-0070
Emp Here 55   *Emp Total* 1
Sales 494,437,800
SIC 5153 Grain and field beans
Pr Pr Zaid Qadoumi
 Ghazi Qadoumi
 David Hanna
Sr VP Brian Hazzard

D-U-N-S 20-551-9791   (HQ)
CI FINANCIAL CORP
(*Suby of* CI Financial Corp)
2 Queen St E, Toronto, ON, M5C 3G7
(416) 364-1145
Emp Here 500   *Emp Total* 1,364
Sales 1,441,050,354
SIC 6282 Investment advice
 Peter Anderson
 William Holland
Pr Sheila Murray
 Douglas Jamieson
Ex VP David Pauli
 Paul W. Derksen
 Stephen T. Moore
 Sonia A Baxendale
 David Miller
 Tom Muir

D-U-N-S 20-283-4453   (SL)
CPP INVESTMENT BOARD PRIVATE HOLDINGS (2) INC.
One Queen St E Suite 2500, Toronto, ON, M5C 2W5
(416) 868-4075
Emp Here 886   *Sales* 154,305,450
SIC 6371 Pension, health, and welfare funds
CEO Mark Wiseman

D-U-N-S 24-425-9433   (SL)
CPPIB ZAMBEZI HOLDINGS INC
1 Queen St E Suite 2600, Toronto, ON, M5C 2W5
(416) 868-4075
Emp Here 2,000   *Sales* 688,033,900
SIC 4731 Freight transportation arrangement
VP John Butler
VP David Denison

D-U-N-S 24-199-2213   (BR)
CANADIAN BAR ASSOCIATION, THE
ONTARIO BAR ASSOCIATION
(*Suby of* Canadian Bar Association, The)
20 Toronto St Suite 300, Toronto, ON, M5C 2B8
(416) 869-1047
Emp Here 45
SIC 8621 Professional organizations

D-U-N-S 20-899-4116   (BR)
CANADIAN BREAST CANCER FOUNDATION
CANADIAN BREAST CANCER FOUNDATION ONTARIO CHAPTER
20 Victoria St Suite 600, Toronto, ON, M5C 2N8
(416) 815-1313
Emp Here 40
SIC 8399 Social services, nec

D-U-N-S 20-944-1211   (HQ)
CHUBB INSURANCE COMPANY OF

CANADA
1 Adelaide St E Suite 1500, Toronto, ON, M5C 2V9
(416) 863-0550
Emp Here 250 *Emp Total* 10
Sales 238,305,650
SIC 6331 Fire, marine, and casualty insurance
Janice M Tomlinson
Crawford W Spratt
Dir Dennis Brown
Dir Barry T Grant
Dir Jim Thorndycraft
Pr Pr Ellen Moore
D Udo Nixdorf
Diane Baxter
Sr VP Susan Vella
Giovanni Damiani

D-U-N-S 24-861-8043 (BR)
CITIBANK CANADA
CITIBANK VISA
1 Toronto St Suite 1200, Toronto, ON, M5C 2V6
(416) 369-6399
Emp Here 400
SIC 6153 Short-term business credit institutions, except agricultural

D-U-N-S 20-810-0516 (BR)
CUNNINGHAM LINDSEY CANADA LIMITED
2 Toronto St, Toronto, ON, M5C 2B6
(416) 869-3232
Emp Here 20
SIC 6411 Insurance agents, brokers, and service

D-U-N-S 20-360-0320 (SL)
DREAM OFFICE LP
30 Adelaide St E Suite 301, Toronto, ON, M5C 3H1
(416) 365-3535
Emp Here 200 *Sales* 18,823,861
SIC 6531 Real estate agents and managers
Pt Jane Gavan

D-U-N-S 24-684-9665 (HQ)
DREAM OFFICE MANAGEMENT CORP
(*Suby of* Dundee Real Estate Investment Trust)
30 Adelaide St E Suite 301, Toronto, ON, M5C 3H1
(416) 365-3535
Emp Here 50 *Emp Total* 1
Sales 11,174,638
SIC 6531 Real estate agents and managers
Pr Pr Michael J. Cooper
Michael Knowlton
Jean Gavan
Div VP Jo Ladeluca
Div VP John Page
Div VP Chris Holtved
Div VP Randy Cameron

D-U-N-S 24-851-6127 (SL)
DUNDEE CAPITAL MARKETS INC
(*Suby of* Dundee Corporation)
1 Adelaide St E Suite 2100, Toronto, ON, M5C 2V9
(416) 350-3388
Emp Here 29 *Sales* 8,229,385
SIC 6282 Investment advice
Pr Mark Attanasio
Dir Tony Loria
Sls Dir Patrick Mcbride
Dir Fin Donato Sferra

D-U-N-S 20-806-0686 (SL)
EH MANAGEMENT LIMITED
ADAIR MORSE
1 Queen St E Suite 1800, Toronto, ON, M5C 2Y5
(416) 863-1230
Emp Here 49 *Sales* 5,632,960
SIC 8111 Legal services
Pt Jeffery Adair

D-U-N-S 20-697-0233 (HQ)
EAUX VIVES WATER INC

ESKA WATER
(*Suby of* Morgan Stanley)
25 Adelaide St E Suite 1000, Toronto, ON, M5C 3A1
(416) 504-2222
Emp Here 20 *Emp Total* 55,311
Sales 29,184,280
SIC 3221 Glass containers
Pr Pr James Delsnyder
Michael Mcgrath

D-U-N-S 25-096-2347 (SL)
EXCHANGE SOLUTIONS INC
36 Toronto St Suite 1200, Toronto, ON, M5C 2C5
(416) 646-7000
Emp Here 100 *Sales* 16,302,292
SIC 8741 Management services
Pr Steven Hoffman
Dir Fin Maureen Drew

D-U-N-S 24-989-3509 (BR)
GOODLIFE FITNESS CENTRES INC
GOODLIFE FITNESS CLUBS
137 Yonge St, Toronto, ON, M5C 1W6
(416) 599-0430
Emp Here 30
SIC 7999 Amusement and recreation, nec

D-U-N-S 24-409-4764 (BR)
GOODLIFE FITNESS CENTRES INC
100 Yonge St Suite 2, Toronto, ON, M5C 2W1
(416) 869-3900
Emp Here 30
SIC 7999 Amusement and recreation, nec

D-U-N-S 24-763-2214 (SL)
H2 MARKETING & COMMUNICATIONS
36 Toronto St Suite 800, Toronto, ON, M5C 2C5
(416) 862-2800
Emp Here 43 *Sales* 5,748,207
SIC 8732 Commercial nonphysical research
Owner Elizabeth Hoyle

D-U-N-S 20-180-4155 (SL)
HMZ METALS INC
2 Toronto St Suite 500, Toronto, ON, M5C 2B6

Emp Here 400 *Sales* 164,686,720
SIC 3339 Primary nonferrous Metals, nec
Pr Pr Kerry Smith
Stephen Wilkinson
Birks Bovaird
Brian Cloney
CFO Timothy Campbell

D-U-N-S 24-373-1101 (BR)
HAYS SPECIALIST RECRUITMENT (CANADA) INC
HAYS RECRUITMENT
6 Adelaide St E Suite 600, Toronto, ON, M5C 1H6
(416) 367-4297
Emp Here 30
SIC 7361 Employment agencies

D-U-N-S 20-174-0318 (HQ)
HOLLISWEALTH ADVISORY SERVICES INC.
1 Adelaide St E Suite 2700, Toronto, ON, M5C 2V9
(416) 350-3250
Emp Here 200 *Emp Total* 68,000
Sales 773,275,177
SIC 6282 Investment advice
Pr Kym Anthony
Robert Sellars

D-U-N-S 24-363-4057 (SL)
HUDSON HIGHLAND GROUP SEARCH, INC
HUDSON
(*Suby of* Hudson Global, Inc.)
20 Adelaide St E Suite 401, Toronto, ON, M5C 2T6

Emp Here 30 *Sales* 2,188,821

SIC 7361 Employment agencies

D-U-N-S 25-354-9034 (BR)
HUDSON'S BAY COMPANY
BAY, THE
176 Yonge St, Toronto, ON, M5C 2L7
(416) 861-9111
Emp Here 1,200
SIC 5311 Department stores

D-U-N-S 24-523-0672 (SL)
IFG - INTERNATIONAL FINANCIAL GROUP LTD
100 Yonge St Suite 1501, Toronto, ON, M5C 2W1
(416) 645-2434
Emp Here 110 *Sales* 4,815,406
SIC 8721 Accounting, auditing, and bookkeeping

D-U-N-S 25-305-2963 (BR)
INNVEST PROPERTIES CORP
QUALITY HOTEL
(*Suby of* Innvest Properties Corp)
111 Lombard St, Toronto, ON, M5C 2T9
(416) 367-5555
Emp Here 80
SIC 7011 Hotels and motels

D-U-N-S 25-255-0371 (SL)
INTERNATIONAL CHAMPIONSHIP MANAGEMENT LIMITED
MARCUS EVANS
20 Toronto St, Toronto, ON, M5C 2B8
(416) 955-0375
Emp Here 120 *Sales* 37,033,530
SIC 7941 Sports clubs, managers, and promoters
Pr Marcus Evan

D-U-N-S 24-130-8191 (SL)
MAVRIX AMERICAN GROWTH FUND
MATRIX ASSET MANAGEMENT
36 Lombard St Suite 2200, Toronto, ON, M5C 2X3
(416) 362-3077
Emp Here 26 *Sales* 9,988,687
SIC 6722 Management investment, open-end
Pr Dvid Levi

D-U-N-S 20-334-7872 (SL)
MELTWATER NEWS CANADA INC.
8 King St E Suite 1300, Toronto, ON, M5C 1B5
(647) 258-1726
Emp Here 25 *Sales* 1,896,978
SIC 7372 Prepackaged software

D-U-N-S 20-250-7323 (SL)
MOMENTUM DIGITAL SOLUTIONS INC
MOMENTUM
20 Toronto St Suite 1100, Toronto, ON, M5C 2B8
(416) 971-6612
Emp Here 54 *Sales* 2,991,389
SIC 7374 Data processing and preparation

D-U-N-S 20-108-8221 (HQ)
NAVIGANT CONSULTING LTD
LAC
(*Suby of* Navigant Consulting, Inc.)
1 Adelaide St E Suite 3000, Toronto, ON, M5C 2V9
(416) 777-2440
Emp Here 35 *Emp Total* 5,768
Sales 11,162,987
SIC 8742 Management consulting services
Pr William Goodyear
Richard Fischer
VP VP Ben Perks
Dir Wayne Koprowski
Dir Robert Macdonald

D-U-N-S 20-702-3453 (BR)
NORTHGATE MINERALS CORPORATION
110 Yonge St Suite 1601, Toronto, ON, M5C 1T4

Emp Here 50

SIC 1021 Copper ores

D-U-N-S 25-369-7619 (BR)
ORANGE BUSINESS SERVICES CANADA INC
ORANGE BUSINESS SERVICES
36 Lombard St Suite 500, Toronto, ON, M5C 2X3
(416) 362-9255
Emp Here 20
SIC 4899 Communication services, nec

D-U-N-S 25-669-0876 (BR)
PENGUIN RANDOM HOUSE CANADA LIMITED
1 Toronto St Suite 300, Toronto, ON, M5C 2V6
(416) 364-4449
Emp Here 60
SIC 2731 Book publishing

D-U-N-S 20-879-4107 (SL)
PRESS NEWS LIMITED
36 King St E Suite 301, Toronto, ON, M5C 2L9
(416) 364-3172
Emp Here 300 *Sales* 29,622,000
SIC 7383 News syndicates
Pr Eric Morrison
VP Wayne Waldroff

D-U-N-S 24-893-8776 (HQ)
PRIMARIS MANAGEMENT INC
1 Adelaide St E Suite 900, Toronto, ON, M5C 2V9
(416) 642-7800
Emp Here 75 *Emp Total* 8
Sales 48,591,826
SIC 8741 Management services
Pr Pr Tom Hofstedter
VP Fin Lesley Gibson
Sr VP Toran Eggert
Pers/VP Brenda Huggins
Larry Froom
Patrick Sullivan
Mordecai Bobrowsky
Robyn Kestenberg

D-U-N-S 20-323-0487 (SL)
PROFESSIONAL THOUGHT LEADERS ACADEMY LTD
PTLA
151 Yonge St 19th Floor, Toronto, ON, M5C 2W7
(416) 216-5481
Emp Here 40 *Sales* 5,579,750
SIC 8742 Management consulting services
Pr Ship Heflin

D-U-N-S 25-530-0519 (SL)
REGAL CONSOLIDATED VENTURES LIMITED
20 Adelaide St E Suite 1100, Toronto, ON, M5C 2T6
(416) 642-0602
Emp Here 50 *Sales* 4,231,721
SIC 1081 Metal mining services

D-U-N-S 20-349-6799 (SL)
SITEIMPROVE INC
110 Yonge St Suite 700, Toronto, ON, M5C 1T4
(647) 797-3640
Emp Here 20 *Sales* 1,459,214
SIC 7371 Custom computer programming services

D-U-N-S 20-544-5880 (BR)
STAPLES CANADA INC
STAPLES THE BUSINESS DEPOT
(*Suby of* Staples, Inc.)
89 Yonge St, Toronto, ON, M5C 1S8
(416) 203-3525
Emp Here 30
SIC 5943 Stationery stores

D-U-N-S 24-877-2345 (HQ)
STATE STREET TRUST COMPANY CANADA
STATE STREET FUND SERVICES

(*Suby of* State Street Corporation)
30 Adelaide St E Suite 1100, Toronto, ON,
M5C 3G8
(416) 362-1100
Emp Here 900   *Emp Total* 33,783
Sales 326,861,440
SIC 6719 Holding companies, nec
Pr Stephen Smit

D-U-N-S 20-193-7948   (BR)
TERANET INC
(*Suby of* Teranet Inc)
1 Adelaide St E Suite 600, Toronto, ON, M5C
2V9
(416) 360-5263
Emp Here 300
SIC 7371 Custom computer programming services

D-U-N-S 25-340-9858   (BR)
TONY MAC LIMITED
MCDONALD'S
(*Suby of* Tony Mac Limited)
127 Church St, Toronto, ON, M5C 2G5
(416) 368-1562
Emp Here 50
SIC 5812 Eating places

D-U-N-S 20-077-4789   (BR)
TORONTO-DOMINION BANK, THE
TD BANK
(*Suby of* Toronto-Dominion Bank, The)
110 Yonge St Suite 2587, Toronto, ON, M5C
1T4
(416) 361-8600
Emp Here 20
SIC 6021 National commercial banks

D-U-N-S 20-105-8190   (HQ)
TRAVELEX CANADA LIMITED
TRAVELEX GLOBAL BUSINESS PAYMENTS
100 Yonge St, Toronto, ON, M5C 2W1
(416) 359-3700
Emp Here 500   *Emp Total* 4
Sales 790,602,145
SIC 6099 Functions related to deposit banking
VP Fin Judy Adams

D-U-N-S 20-769-7330   (SL)
WW HOTELS TORONTO
HOLIDAY INN EXPRESS
111 Lombard St, Toronto, ON, M5C 2T9
(416) 367-5555
Emp Here 50   *Sales* 2,188,821
SIC 7011 Hotels and motels

D-U-N-S 25-986-7369   (HQ)
XL SPECIALTY INSURANCE COMPANY
100 Yonge St Ste 1200, Toronto, ON, M5C
2W1
(416) 363-7818
Emp Here 52   *Emp Total* 57
Sales 6,063,757
SIC 6411 Insurance agents, brokers, and service
Mgr Nick Greggains
Off Mgr Heather Cunningham

D-U-N-S 20-107-5673   (HQ)
ZENITHOPTIMEDIA CANADA INC
OPTIMEDIA
111 Queen St E Suite 200, Toronto, ON, M5C
1S2
(416) 925-7277
Emp Here 80   *Emp Total* 17
Sales 14,293,142
SIC 7311 Advertising agencies
Pr Pr Sunni Boot
Dir Fin Navil Bajina

Toronto, ON M5E
York County

D-U-N-S 25-496-9363   (BR)
1772887 ONTARIO LIMITED

WHERE TORONTO DIV
6 Church St Suite 200, Toronto, ON, M5E 1M1
(416) 364-3336
Emp Here 30
SIC 2721 Periodicals

D-U-N-S 24-525-5559   (HQ)
AMI PARTNERS INC
(*Suby of* AMI Partners Inc)
26 Wellington St E Suite 800, Toronto, ON,
M5E 1S2

Emp Here 24   *Emp Total* 32
Sales 9,557,852
SIC 6722 Management investment, open-end
Pr Pr Robert Gibson
  Douglas Thomas
  Larry Avant
  Ronald Patton

D-U-N-S 25-710-0396   (BR)
ACCOR CANADA INC
NOVOTEL TORONTO CENTER
45 The Esplanade, Toronto, ON, M5E 1W2
(416) 367-8900
Emp Here 50
SIC 7011 Hotels and motels

D-U-N-S 24-857-2633   (SL)
ALPHAPRO MANAGEMENT INC
26 Wellington St E Suite 700, Toronto, ON,
M5E 1S2
(416) 933-5745
Emp Here 45   *Sales* 17,338,854
SIC 6722 Management investment, open-end
Pr Mark Arthur

D-U-N-S 24-805-6934   (BR)
ALTUS GEOMATICS LIMITED PARTNERSHIP
ALTUS GROUP
33 Yonge St Suite 500, Toronto, ON, M5E 1G4
(416) 641-9500
Emp Here 250
SIC 8713 Surveying services

D-U-N-S 24-850-7563   (SL)
ASSOCIATION OF MUNICIPAL EMERGENCY MEDICAL SERVICES OF ONTARIO
AMEMSO
1 Yonge St Suite 1801, Toronto, ON, M5E 1W7

Emp Here 50   *Sales* 3,031,879
SIC 4119 Local passenger transportation, nec

D-U-N-S 25-821-4550   (HQ)
BMO LIFE ASSURANCE COMPANY
60 Yonge St, Toronto, ON, M5E 1H5
(416) 596-3900
Emp Here 230   *Emp Total* 46,000
Sales 22,544,856
SIC 6411 Insurance agents, brokers, and service
Pr Pr Peter C Mccarthy
Ch Bd Myra Cridland
Sec Paul Dubal
Dir Fin David Mackie
Dir Crawford William Spratt
Dir J. Peter Eccleton
Dir Maurice Hudon
Dir Thomas Brian
Dir Charyl Gaplin
Dir Rebecca Tascona

D-U-N-S 24-172-6087   (BR)
BRICK WAREHOUSE LP, THE
63 Yonge St, Toronto, ON, M5E 1Z1

Emp Here 20
SIC 5712 Furniture stores

D-U-N-S 20-911-1710   (HQ)
CIBC PRIVATE INVESTMENT COUNSEL INC
55 Yonge St Suite 700, Toronto, ON, M5E 1J4
(416) 980-8651
Emp Here 25   *Emp Total* 44,000
Sales 7,727,098

SIC 6282 Investment advice
Dir Victor Dodig
Dir Daniel Donnelly
Dir Thomas Mccready
Dir John Braive
Dir Gary Whitfield
Dir Norah Mccarthy
Dir Stephen Geist

D-U-N-S 25-072-4820   (BR)
CANADA BROKERLINK INC
48 Yonge St Suite 700, Toronto, ON, M5E 1G6
(416) 368-6511
Emp Here 25
SIC 6411 Insurance agents, brokers, and service

D-U-N-S 25-602-4910   (HQ)
CANADIAN APARTMENT PROPERTIES REAL ESTATE INVESTMENT TRUST
CAP REIT
(*Suby of* Canadian Apartment Properties Real Estate Investment Trust)
11 Church St Suite 401, Toronto, ON, M5E 1W1
(416) 861-5771
Emp Here 125   *Emp Total* 991
Sales 441,443,065
SIC 6722 Management investment, open-end
Pr Pr Thomas Schwartz
  Michael L. Stein
Sr VP Maria Amaral
Sec Corinne Pruzanski
  Mark Kenney
  Richard Smith
Trst Paul Harris
Trst Edwin Hawken
Trst Stanley Swartzman
Trst David Sloan

D-U-N-S 20-912-3418   (BR)
CANADIAN IMPERIAL BANK OF COMMERCE
CIBC
33 Yonge St Suite 700, Toronto, ON, M5E 1G4
(416) 980-3799
Emp Here 21
SIC 6021 National commercial banks

D-U-N-S 20-693-6432   (SL)
COSMOPOLITAN SUITES & SPA
8 Colborne St, Toronto, ON, M5E 1E1
(416) 350-2000
Emp Here 50   *Sales* 2,826,987
SIC 7011 Hotels and motels

D-U-N-S 25-340-6912   (HQ)
CUSHMAN & WAKEFIELD LTD
(*Suby of* Cushman & Wakefield Holdings, Inc.)
33 Yonge St Suite 1000, Toronto, ON, M5E 1S9
(416) 862-0611
Emp Here 200   *Emp Total* 43,000
Sales 70,512,831
SIC 6531 Real estate agents and managers
Pr Pr Edward Forst

D-U-N-S 24-140-9650   (BR)
EAGLE PROFESSIONAL RESOURCES INC
67 Yonge St Suite 200, Toronto, ON, M5E 1J8
(416) 861-1492
Emp Here 100
SIC 7361 Employment agencies

D-U-N-S 20-573-5884   (BR)
FLIGHT SHOPS INC, THE
41 Colborne St, Toronto, ON, M5E 1E3
(877) 967-5302
Emp Here 20
SIC 4724 Travel agencies

D-U-N-S 24-788-8592   (BR)
GREAT-WEST LIFE ASSURANCE COMPANY, THE
GREAT WEST LIFE REALITY ADVISORS
33 Yonge St Suite 105, Toronto, ON, M5E 1G4
(416) 359-2929
Emp Here 40

SIC 6321 Accident and health insurance

D-U-N-S 20-300-6036   (SL)
HORIZONS ACTIVE DIVERSIFIED INCOME ETF INC
26 Wellington St E Suite 700, Toronto, ON,
M5E 1S2
(416) 933-5745
Emp Here 45   *Sales* 6,030,906
SIC 8742 Management consulting services
Pr Adam Felesky

D-U-N-S 24-513-2006   (SL)
HOT HOUSE RESTAURANT AND BAR
35 Church St, Toronto, ON, M5E 1T3
(416) 366-7800
Emp Here 95   *Sales* 2,845,467
SIC 5812 Eating places

D-U-N-S 25-085-5236   (SL)
HUGHES AMYS LLP
48 Yonge St Suite 200, Toronto, ON, M5E 1G6
(416) 367-1608
Emp Here 80   *Sales* 9,536,300
SIC 8111 Legal services
Sr Pt Jack F. Fitch
Pt William S Chalmers
Pt James V. Maloney
Pt Jennifer M. Malchuk
Pt Michael T.J. Mcgoey
Pt Pamela M. Stevens
Pt Mary A. Teal

D-U-N-S 20-012-2062   (BR)
JENNINGS CAPITAL INC
33 Yonge St Suite 320, Toronto, ON, M5E 1G4
(416) 304-2195
Emp Here 20
SIC 6211 Security brokers and dealers

D-U-N-S 24-588-5041   (BR)
KEG RESTAURANTS LTD
KEG STEAKHOUSE & BAR, THE
56 The Esplanade, Toronto, ON, M5E 1A7
(416) 367-0685
Emp Here 95
SIC 5812 Eating places

D-U-N-S 20-818-5843   (HQ)
LIQUOR CONTROL BOARD OF ONTARIO, THE
55 Lake Shore Blvd E Suite 874, Toronto, ON,
M5E 1A4
(416) 365-5900
Emp Here 100   *Emp Total* 90,000
Sales 4,174,116,090
SIC 5921 Liquor stores
Ch Bd Bonnie Brooks
Pr George Soleas
Sr VP Rob Dutton
Sr VP Nancy Cardinal
VP Opers Bob Clevely
Pers/VP Bob Downey
Sr VP Penny Wyger
Sr VP Pat Ford
Sr VP Michael Eubanks

D-U-N-S 20-641-4638   (BR)
LIQUOR CONTROL BOARD OF ONTARIO, THE
LCBO, THE
55 Lake Shore Blvd E Suite 886, Toronto, ON,
M5E 1A4
(416) 864-6777
Emp Here 50
SIC 5921 Liquor stores

D-U-N-S 20-703-5226   (BR)
LIQUOR CONTROL BOARD OF ONTARIO, THE
VINTAGES
43 Freeland St, Toronto, ON, M5E 1L7
(416) 365-5863
Emp Here 180
SIC 5921 Liquor stores

D-U-N-S 24-121-0942   (BR)
LIQUOR CONTROL BOARD OF ONTARIO,

THE
LCBO FINANCIAL OFFICE
1 Yonge St 13th Floor, Toronto, ON, M5E 1E5
(416) 365-5778
Emp Here 85
SIC 5921 Liquor stores

D-U-N-S 25-052-1036   (BR)
LOBLAW COMPANIES LIMITED
LOBLAW BRANDS, DIV OF
10 Lower Jarvis St, Toronto, ON, M5E 1Z2
(416) 304-0611
Emp Here 300
SIC 5411 Grocery stores

D-U-N-S 20-181-7231   (HQ)
MGI SECURITIES INC
26 Wellington St E Suite 900, Toronto, ON, M5E 1S2
(416) 864-6477
Emp Here 60   *Emp Total* 600
Sales 17,510,568
SIC 6211 Security brokers and dealers
Pr Pr Andrea Jones
 Donald Mcfarlane
 Gordon Crawford

D-U-N-S 20-289-4247   (BR)
MACQUARIE CAPITAL MARKETS CANADA LTD
26 Wellington St E Suite 300, Toronto, ON, M5E 1S2

Emp Here 100
SIC 6211 Security brokers and dealers

D-U-N-S 20-779-4830   (BR)
MAGIC LANTERN THEATRES LTD
RAINBOW CINEMAS
80 Front St E, Toronto, ON, M5E 1T4
(416) 214-7006
Emp Here 20
SIC 7832 Motion picture theaters, except drive-in

D-U-N-S 24-333-1563   (BR)
METRO ONTARIO INC
METRO
80 Front St E Suite 804, Toronto, ON, M5E 1T4
(416) 703-9393
Emp Here 220
SIC 5411 Grocery stores

D-U-N-S 20-108-2570   (BR)
MONSTER WORLDWIDE CANADA INC
TMP WORLDWIDE ADVERTISING & COMMUNICATIONS
47 Colborne St Suite 301, Toronto, ON, M5E 1P8
(416) 861-8679
Emp Here 21
SIC 7311 Advertising agencies

D-U-N-S 20-073-4502   (SL)
NEXUS PROTECTIVE SERVICES LTD
56 The Esplanade Suite 200, Toronto, ON, M5E 1A7
(416) 815-7575
Emp Here 75   *Sales* 2,334,742
SIC 7381 Detective and armored car services

D-U-N-S 25-322-9785   (HQ)
ONTARIO CLEAN WATER AGENCY
OCWA
1 Yonge St Suite 1700, Toronto, ON, M5E 1E5
(416) 314-5600
Emp Here 100   *Emp Total* 90,000
Sales 131,200,052
SIC 4941 Water supply
Dir Elizabeth Mclaren
 Michael R. Garrett
 Art Leitch
Dir Juli Abouchar
Dir John Bergsma
Dir Susan Fletcher
Dir Allan Gunn
Dir Doug Lawson

Dir Gino Nicolini

D-U-N-S 20-293-0975   (SL)
ONTARIO RIBS INC
TONY ROMA'S
56 The Esplanade Suite 201, Toronto, ON, M5E 1A7
(416) 864-9775
Emp Here 500   *Sales* 21,000,150
SIC 5812 Eating places
Pr Peter Hnatiw

D-U-N-S 20-299-9421   (SL)
PICTON MAHONEY GLOBAL LONG SHORT EQUITY FUND
PICTON MAHONEY ASSET MANAGEMENT
33 Yonge St Suite 830, Toronto, ON, M5E 1G4
(416) 955-4108
Emp Here 49   *Sales* 14,592,140
SIC 6722 Management investment, open-end
Dir David Picton

D-U-N-S 20-912-6189   (BR)
ROYAL & SUN ALLIANCE INSURANCE COMPANY OF CANADA
10 Wellington St E, Toronto, ON, M5E 1C5
(416) 366-7511
Emp Here 20
SIC 6411 Insurance agents, brokers, and service

D-U-N-S 20-352-3659   (SL)
ROYAL LEGAL SOLUTIONS P.C. INC
1 Yonge St Suite 1801, Toronto, ON, M5E 1W7
(416) 619-9197
Emp Here 490   *Sales* 41,952,403
SIC 8111 Legal services
Pr Pr Ahmed Ali

D-U-N-S 24-341-8881   (BR)
STATPRO CANADA INC
33 Yonge St Suite 2701, Toronto, ON, M5E 1G4
(416) 619-3999
Emp Here 20
SIC 8742 Management consulting services

D-U-N-S 20-986-9770   (BR)
STONEMILL BAKEHOUSE LIMITED, THE
92 Front St E Unit B27, Toronto, ON, M5E 1C4
(416) 601-1853
Emp Here 20
SIC 5461 Retail bakeries

D-U-N-S 24-082-8012   (HQ)
T.E. FINANCIAL CONSULTANTS LTD
T.E. WEALTH
26 Wellington St E Unit 710, Toronto, ON, M5E 1S2
(416) 366-1451
Emp Here 46   *Emp Total* 600
Sales 25,171,442
SIC 6282 Investment advice
Pr Mark Arthur
VP Fin Gerry Deboer
 Timothy Egan
Dir Steven Belchetz

D-U-N-S 20-328-3130   (BR)
TDL GROUP CORP, THE
TIM HORTONS
73 Front St E Unit 8, Toronto, ON, M5E 1B8
(416) 363-1055
Emp Here 30
SIC 5812 Eating places

D-U-N-S 25-849-3709   (BR)
TRANSCANADA PIPELINES LIMITED
55 Yonge St Suite 800, Toronto, ON, M5E 1J4
(416) 869-2000
Emp Here 25
SIC 4922 Natural gas transmission

D-U-N-S 20-114-1244   (BR)
TRAVELBRANDS INC
TRAVELBRANDS INC
26 Wellington St E, Toronto, ON, M5E 1S2
(416) 364-5100
Emp Here 500

SIC 4725 Tour operators

D-U-N-S 25-862-8676   (BR)
UNION SECURITIES LTD
33 Yonge St Suite 901, Toronto, ON, M5E 1G4
(416) 777-0600
Emp Here 30
SIC 6211 Security brokers and dealers

D-U-N-S 25-191-0360   (BR)
WPP GROUP CANADA COMMUNICATIONS LIMITED
OGILVY & ACTION DIV
33 Yonge St Suite 1100, Toronto, ON, M5E 1X6
(416) 945-2360
Emp Here 236
SIC 7311 Advertising agencies

D-U-N-S 24-859-3233   (SL)
XMG STUDIO INC
67 Yonge St Suite 1600, Toronto, ON, M5E 1J8
(416) 619-0700
Emp Here 45   *Sales* 5,985,550
SIC 5734 Computer and software stores
 Ray Sharma
VP Fin Irving Ho
Treas Mansoor Ahmed

Toronto, ON M5G
York County

D-U-N-S 24-167-3347   (SL)
678925 ONTARIO INC
S B R GLOBAL
14 College St, Toronto, ON, M5G 1K2
(416) 962-7500
Emp Here 50   *Sales* 3,064,349
SIC 8741 Management services

D-U-N-S 24-204-7152   (HQ)
AMEC NCL LIMITED
AMEC
700 University Ave Suite 200, Toronto, ON, M5G 1X6
(416) 592-2102
Emp Here 308   *Emp Total* 34,013
Sales 17,238,395
SIC 8999 Services, nec
Dir Charles Caza
Dir Charles Mountain
Pr James P Rippon

D-U-N-S 24-120-8813   (BR)
ART INSTITUTE OF VANCOUVER INC, THE
ART INSTITUTE OF TORONTO, THE
655 Bay St Suite 200, Toronto, ON, M5G 2K4
(416) 351-7273
Emp Here 35
SIC 8299 Schools and educational services, nec

D-U-N-S 20-571-8963   (BR)
AVIVA CANADA INC
500 University Ave, Toronto, ON, M5G 1V7
(416) 288-5202
Emp Here 20
SIC 8741 Management services

D-U-N-S 24-422-7450   (SL)
B2B BANK FINANCIAL SERVICES INC
B2B BANK DEALER SERVICES
199 Bay St Suite 610, Toronto, ON, M5G 1M5
(416) 926-0221
Emp Here 335   *Sales* 48,883,669
SIC 6282 Investment advice
 Deborah Rose
Pr Pr Francois Desjardins
Dir Fin Diane Lafresnaye
Dir Theodore Ikonomou

D-U-N-S 25-571-0279   (SL)
BANGKOK GARDEN INC
(*Suby of* Brydson Group Inc)

18 Elm St, Toronto, ON, M5G 1G7
(416) 977-6748
Emp Here 35   *Sales* 1,021,450
SIC 5812 Eating places

D-U-N-S 25-721-3058   (BR)
BANK OF MONTREAL
BANK OF MONTREAL
700 University Ave Suite 1, Toronto, ON, M5G 1X7
(416) 867-5330
Emp Here 24
SIC 6021 National commercial banks

D-U-N-S 24-363-0766   (BR)
BEST BUY CANADA LTD
BEST BUY
(*Suby of* Best Buy Co., Inc.)
65 Dundas St W, Toronto, ON, M5G 2C3
(416) 642-8321
Emp Here 50
SIC 5731 Radio, television, and electronic stores

D-U-N-S 25-787-2890   (BR)
BOUYGUES BUILDING CANADA INC
180 Dundas St W Suite 2605, Toronto, ON, M5G 1Z8

Emp Here 50
SIC 1541 Industrial buildings and warehouses

D-U-N-S 20-291-8962   (BR)
BRUCE POWER L.P.
700 University Ave Suite 200, Toronto, ON, M5G 1X6
(519) 361-2673
Emp Here 3,700
SIC 4911 Electric services

D-U-N-S 25-649-2307   (BR)
CTC TRAINCANADA INC
595 Bay St Unit 302, Toronto, ON, M5G 2C2
(416) 214-1090
Emp Here 20
SIC 8243 Data processing schools

D-U-N-S 20-984-0891   (SL)
CANADA LIFE MORTGAGE SERVICES LTD
330 University Ave, Toronto, ON, M5G 1R8
(416) 597-6981
Emp Here 50   *Sales* 9,120,088
SIC 6163 Loan brokers
Dir Brian R. Allison
Dir David N. Grieve
Dir Kenneth W. Jack

D-U-N-S 20-587-4717   (BR)
CANADA POST CORPORATION
1 Dundas St W Suite 500, Toronto, ON, M5G 2L5

Emp Here 20
SIC 4311 U.s. postal service

D-U-N-S 25-504-4018   (HQ)
CANADIAN BREAST CANCER FOUNDATION
(*Suby of* Canadian Breast Cancer Foundation)
375 University Ave Suite 301, Toronto, ON, M5G 2J5
(416) 596-6773
Emp Here 50   *Emp Total* 75
Sales 41,281,461
SIC 8399 Social services, nec

D-U-N-S 25-512-0321   (HQ)
CLEAR CHANNEL OUTDOOR COMPANY CANADA
20 Dundas St W Suite 1001, Toronto, ON, M5G 2C2
(416) 408-0800
Emp Here 21   *Emp Total* 14,300
Sales 11,308,909
SIC 7312 Outdoor advertising services
Dir Mark P Mays
 Randall Mays

D-U-N-S 25-311-9812   (BR)
COMPAGNIE D'ASSURANCE BELAIR INC, LA
BELAIR DIRECT
700 University Ave Suite 1100, Toronto, ON, M5G 0A2
(416) 250-6363
Emp Here 300
SIC 6331 Fire, marine, and casualty insurance

D-U-N-S 20-077-1850   (BR)
CORUS PREMIUM CORPORATION
CFMJ AM 640 MOJO RADIO TALK RADIO FOR GUYS
1 Dundas St W Suite 1600, Toronto, ON, M5G 1Z3
(416) 221-0107
Emp Here 60
SIC 4832 Radio broadcasting stations

D-U-N-S 24-247-3242   (BR)
ESIT CANADA ENTERPRISE SERVICES CO
ESIT CANADA ENTERPRISE SERVICES CO
(*Suby of* Dxc Technology Company)
700 University Ave Suite 27, Toronto, ON, M5G 1Z5
(416) 592-2140
Emp Here 20
SIC 7379 Computer related services, nec

D-U-N-S 20-699-6493   (BR)
EXTENDICARE (CANADA) INC
EXTENDICARE TORONTO
480 University Ave Suite 708, Toronto, ON, M5G 1V2
(416) 977-5008
Emp Here 35
SIC 8051 Skilled nursing care facilities

D-U-N-S 20-042-2165   (BR)
FEDEX OFFICE CANADA LIMITED
FEDEX OFFICE PRINT & SHIP CENTRE
(*Suby of* Fedex Corporation)
505 University Ave, Toronto, ON, M5G 2P2
(416) 979-8447
Emp Here 40
SIC 2752 Commercial printing, lithographic

D-U-N-S 20-652-4691   (BR)
FETHERSTONHAUGH & CO.
BIGGAR
438 University Ave Suite 1500, Toronto, ON, M5G 2K8
(416) 598-4209
Emp Here 85
SIC 8111 Legal services

D-U-N-S 20-259-5054   (SL)
FIDELITY CANADA ULC
FIDELITY INVESTMENTS
483 Bay St Suite 300, Toronto, ON, M5G 2N7
(416) 307-5200
Emp Here 49   *Sales* 14,592,140
SIC 6722 Management investment, open-end

D-U-N-S 24-721-2046   (HQ)
FIDELITY INVESTMENTS CANADA ULC
(*Suby of* Fmr LLC)
483 Bay St Suite 200, Toronto, ON, M5G 2N7
(416) 307-5200
Emp Here 600   *Emp Total* 41,350
Sales 231,577,262
SIC 6722 Management investment, open-end
Pr Robert Strickland

D-U-N-S 25-079-2140   (BR)
GOVERNING COUNCIL OF THE UNIVERSITY OF TORONTO
FACULTY OF DENTISTRY
124 Edward St Suite 511, Toronto, ON, M5G 1G6
(416) 979-4900
Emp Here 100
SIC 8221 Colleges and universities

D-U-N-S 24-345-5271   (BR)
GOVERNING COUNCIL OF THE UNIVERSITY OF TORONTO

FACULTY OF MEDICINE CONTINUING EDUCATION
500 University Ave Suite 650, Toronto, ON, M5G 1V7

Emp Here 21
SIC 8221 Colleges and universities

D-U-N-S 20-794-4112   (BR)
GOVERNING COUNCIL OF THE UNIVERSITY OF TORONTO
REHABILITATION SCIENCES SECTOR OF THE FACULTY OF MEDICINE
500 University Ave Suite 160, Toronto, ON, M5G 1V7
(416) 978-0300
Emp Here 120
SIC 8221 Colleges and universities

D-U-N-S 24-174-9501   (BR)
GOVERNING COUNCIL OF THE UNIVERSITY OF TORONTO
DEPARTMENT OF MEDICAL BIOPHYSICS
610 University Ave, Toronto, ON, M5G 2M9
(416) 946-4501
Emp Here 200
SIC 8221 Colleges and universities

D-U-N-S 24-276-6905   (BR)
GOVERNING COUNCIL OF THE UNIVERSITY OF TORONTO
INNOVATIONS FOUNDATION
101 College St Suite 320, Toronto, ON, M5G 1L7
(416) 946-7342
Emp Here 30
SIC 8221 Colleges and universities

D-U-N-S 25-362-0363   (BR)
GOVERNING COUNCIL OF THE UNIVERSITY OF TORONTO
REHABILITATION SCIENCES
500 University Ave Suite 160, Toronto, ON, M5G 1V7
(416) 946-8554
Emp Here 70
SIC 8221 Colleges and universities

D-U-N-S 20-911-3005   (BR)
GOVERNING COUNCIL OF THE UNIVERSITY OF TORONTO
THE TORONTO GENERAL HOSPITAL
190 Elizabeth St, Toronto, ON, M5G 2C4
(416) 978-8383
Emp Here 500
SIC 8221 Colleges and universities

D-U-N-S 20-868-6407   (BR)
GOVERNMENT OF ONTARIO
SUPERIOR COURT OF JUSTICE, CRIMINAL - COURT SUPPORT
361 University Ave Suite 315, Toronto, ON, M5G 1T3
(416) 327-5558
Emp Here 25
SIC 7338 Secretarial and court reporting

D-U-N-S 20-918-8676   (BR)
GREAT-WEST LIFE ASSURANCE COMPANY, THE
330 University Ave Suite 400, Toronto, ON, M5G 1R7
(416) 552-5050
Emp Here 100
SIC 6311 Life insurance

D-U-N-S 20-179-5387   (BR)
GREYHOUND CANADA TRANSPORTATION ULC
180 Dundas St W Suite 300, Toronto, ON, M5G 1Z8
(416) 594-0343
Emp Here 20
SIC 4111 Local and suburban transit

D-U-N-S 20-547-8766   (HQ)
H&M HENNES & MAURITZ INC
1 Dundas St W Suite 1808, Toronto, ON, M5G 1Z3

(416) 623-4300
Emp Here 30   *Sales* 121,625,487
SIC 5651 Family clothing stores
  Chelsia Wharton
  Toni Galli
Dir Jyrki Peter Tervonen
Dir Karl-Johan Persson

D-U-N-S 24-953-6830   (HQ)
HOK ARCHITECTS CORPORATION
(*Suby of* Hok Group, Inc)
400 University Ave Suite 2200, Toronto, ON, M5G 1S5
(416) 203-9993
Emp Here 102   *Emp Total* 1,839
Sales 15,540,629
SIC 8712 Architectural services
Sr VP Gordon Stratford
Pr Pr William Valentine

D-U-N-S 25-094-5458   (HQ)
HYDRO ONE NETWORKS INC
483 Bay St Suite 1000, Toronto, ON, M5G 2P5
(416) 345-5000
Emp Here 500   *Emp Total* 5,500
Sales 1,897,124,121
SIC 4911 Electric services
Pr Laura Formusa

D-U-N-S 25-507-9642   (SL)
HYGEIA CORPORATION
(*Suby of* Unitedhealth Group Incorporated)
777 Bay St Suite 2700, Toronto, ON, M5G 2C8
(888) 249-4342
Emp Here 24   *Sales* 2,188,821
SIC 6411 Insurance agents, brokers, and service

D-U-N-S 24-131-3811   (HQ)
IA CLARINGTON INVESTMENTS INC
JOVFINANCIAL
522 University Ave Suite 700, Toronto, ON, M5G 1W7
(416) 860-9880
Emp Here 80   *Emp Total* 5,350
Sales 11,673,712
SIC 6282 Investment advice
  Normand Pepin
Pr Pr Carl Mustos
VP VP Yvon Charest
  Amelie Cantin
Dir Theresa Currie
Dir Andre Dubuc
Dir Lisa Pankratz
Dir Gerald Bouwers

D-U-N-S 20-027-5357   (SL)
ILSC (TORONTO) INC
INTERNATIONAL LANGUAGE SCHOOLS OF CANADA
443 University Ave Suite 3, Toronto, ON, M5G 2H6
(416) 323-1770
Emp Here 60   *Sales* 3,283,232
SIC 8299 Schools and educational services, nec

D-U-N-S 25-529-0041   (HQ)
INDEPENDENT ELECTRICITY SYSTEM OPERATOR
IESO
(*Suby of* Independent Electricity System Operator)
655 Bay St Suite 410, Toronto, ON, M5G 2K4
(905) 855-6100
Emp Here 20   *Emp Total* 410
Sales 35,223
SIC 4911 Electric services

D-U-N-S 24-194-4982   (BR)
INDIGO BOOKS & MUSIC INC
WORLD BIGGEST BOOK STORE
(*Suby of* Indigo Books & Music Inc)
20 Edward St, Toronto, ON, M5G 1C9
(416) 977-7009
Emp Here 60
SIC 5942 Book stores

D-U-N-S 25-309-7661   (BR)
INDUSTRIELLE ALLIANCE, ASSURANCE ET SERVICES FINANCIERS INC
522 University Ave Suite 400, Toronto, ON, M5G 1Y7
(416) 487-0242
Emp Here 25
SIC 6311 Life insurance

D-U-N-S 25-804-4940   (SL)
INSTITUTE FOR WORK & HEALTH
481 University Ave Suite 800, Toronto, ON, M5G 2E9
(416) 927-2027
Emp Here 88   *Sales* 13,898,650
SIC 8399 Social services, nec
Pr Pr Cameron Mustard
Svc Mgr Mary Cicinelli
  Roland Hosein

D-U-N-S 20-820-6482   (HQ)
INSURANCE BUREAU OF CANADA
INSURANCE INFORMATION DIVISION
(*Suby of* Insurance Bureau of Canada)
777 Bay St Suite 2400, Toronto, ON, M5G 2C8
(416) 362-2031
Emp Here 35   *Emp Total* 300
Sales 26,995,459
SIC 6411 Insurance agents, brokers, and service
Pr Pr Don Forgeron
Sr VP David Mcgown
VP Sally Turney
VP Kim Donaldson
VP Craig Stewart
VP Bill Adams
VP Amanda Dean
VP Johanne Lamanque
VP Aaron Sutherland
  Kenn Lalonde

D-U-N-S 20-771-6473   (HQ)
INTACT INSURANCE COMPANY
700 University Ave Suite 1500, Toronto, ON, M5G 0A1
(416) 341-1464
Emp Here 200   *Emp Total* 11,000
Sales 1,720,267,385
SIC 6331 Fire, marine, and casualty insurance
  Charles Brindamour
Pr Pr Louis Gagnon
Sec Francoise Guenette
  Yves Brouillette
  Stephen G Snyder
  Marcel Cote
  Eileen Mercier
  Timothy H Penner
  Louise Roy
  Claude Dussault

D-U-N-S 25-100-8520   (BR)
INTACT INSURANCE COMPANY
SURETY DEPARTMENT
700 University Ave Suite 1500, Toronto, ON, M5G 0A1
(416) 341-1464
Emp Here 20
SIC 6311 Life insurance

D-U-N-S 20-078-0273   (BR)
LEGAL AID ONTARIO
CLINIC RESOURCE OFFICE
40 Dundas St W Suite 200, Toronto, ON, M5G 2H1
(416) 204-5420
Emp Here 20
SIC 8111 Legal services

D-U-N-S 25-117-4272   (BR)
LEGAL AID ONTARIO
TORONTO DUTY COUNSEL OFFICE
375 University Ave Suite 304, Toronto, ON, M5G 2J5
(416) 979-1446
Emp Here 46
SIC 8111 Legal services

D-U-N-S 20-921-7298   (BR)

LONDON LIFE INSURANCE COMPANY
FREEDOM 55 FINANCIAL
330 University Ave Suite 110, Toronto, ON, M5G 1R7
(416) 366-2971
Emp Here 20
SIC 6311 Life insurance

D-U-N-S 24-334-1547   (SL)
LUNENFELD RESEARCH INSTITUTE
600 University Ave Rm 982, Toronto, ON, M5G 1X5
(416) 586-8811
Emp Here 49   *Sales* 7,821,331
SIC 8733 Noncommercial research organizations
Dir James Woodgett

D-U-N-S 24-926-4813   (BR)
LUXURY HOTELS INTERNATIONAL OF CANADA, ULC
TORONTO MARRIOTT EATON CENTRE
(*Suby of* Marriott International, Inc.)
525 Bay St, Toronto, ON, M5G 2L2
(416) 597-9200
Emp Here 350
SIC 7011 Hotels and motels

D-U-N-S 24-931-2661   (SL)
MBAC FERTILIZER CORP
1 Dundas St W Suite 2500, Toronto, ON, M5G 1Z3
(416) 367-2200
Emp Here 50
SIC 1475 Phosphate rock

D-U-N-S 20-303-5915   (BR)
MD MANAGEMENT LIMITED
MD FINANCIAL
(*Suby of* Canadian Medical Association)
522 University Ave Suite 1100, Toronto, ON, M5G 1W7
(416) 598-1442
Emp Here 30
SIC 6722 Management investment, open-end

D-U-N-S 20-771-9378   (HQ)
MEDIA BUYING SERVICES ULC
(*Suby of* Media Buying Services ULC)
1 Dundas St W Suite 2800, Toronto, ON, M5G 1Z3
(416) 961-1255
Emp Here 50   *Emp Total* 100
Sales 25,362,500
SIC 7319 Advertising, nec
Pr Pr David Campbell
VP VP Marilyn Dixon

D-U-N-S 24-181-6144   (BR)
MERIDIAN CREDIT UNION LIMITED
777 Bay St Suite 118, Toronto, ON, M5G 2C8
(416) 597-4400
Emp Here 160
SIC 6062 State credit unions

D-U-N-S 24-000-9196   (SL)
OLSON CANADA, INC
(*Suby of* Icf International, Inc.)
17 Fl, Toronto, ON, M5G 1S5
(416) 848-4115
Emp Here 25   *Sales* 2,991,389
SIC 7311 Advertising agencies

D-U-N-S 20-912-2907   (BR)
ONTARIO INSTITUTE FOR STUDIES IN EDUCATION OF THE UNIVERSITY OF TORONTO
FAMILY & COMMUNITY MEDICINE
500 University Ave Suite 602, Toronto, ON, M5G 1V7
(416) 946-5938
Emp Here 55
SIC 8641 Civic and social associations

D-U-N-S 20-718-4073   (BR)
RBC GENERAL INSURANCE COMPANY
(*Suby of* Royal Bank Of Canada)
483 Bay St Suite 1000, Toronto, ON, M5G 2E7

(416) 777-4594
Emp Here 70
SIC 6331 Fire, marine, and casualty insurance

D-U-N-S 20-344-4344   (HQ)
RED LOBSTER HOSPITALITY LLC
RED LOBSTER RESTAURANTS
(*Suby of* Red Lobster Seafood Co., LLC)
20 Dundas St W, Toronto, ON, M5G 2C2
(416) 348-8938
Emp Here 20   *Emp Total* 62,000
Sales 3,551,629
SIC 5812 Eating places

D-U-N-S 25-512-3838   (SL)
SAMUEL LUNENFELD RESEARCH INSTITUTE OF MOUNT SINAI HOSPITAL
600 University Ave Suite 1078, Toronto, ON, M5G 1X5
(416) 596-4200
Emp Here 400   *Sales* 29,251,680
SIC 8731 Commercial physical research
Dir James Woodgett

D-U-N-S 20-105-9214   (SL)
SELECTCARE WORLDWIDE CORP
438 University Ave Suite 1201, Toronto, ON, M5G 2K8
(416) 340-7265
Emp Here 25   *Sales* 57,474,560
SIC 6321 Accident and health insurance
Pr Mark Sylvia
Acct Mgr Sunder Mayuran

D-U-N-S 20-176-2239   (BR)
SMART & BIGGAR
438 University Ave Suite 1500, Toronto, ON, M5G 2K8
(416) 593-5514
Emp Here 70
SIC 8111 Legal services

D-U-N-S 25-213-7906   (BR)
STAPLES CANADA INC
STAPLES THE BUSINESS DEPOT
(*Suby of* Staples, Inc.)
375 University Ave, Toronto, ON, M5G 2J5
(416) 598-4818
Emp Here 40
SIC 5943 Stationery stores

D-U-N-S 24-345-0900   (BR)
SUNNYBROOK HEALTH SCIENCES CENTRE FOUNDATION
BAY CENTRE FOR BIRTH CONTROL
(*Suby of* Sunnybrook Health Sciences Centre Foundation)
790 Bay St Suite 536, Toronto, ON, M5G 1N8
(416) 351-3700
Emp Here 45
SIC 8093 Specialty outpatient clinics, nec

D-U-N-S 24-911-4182   (SL)
THE PRINCESS MARGARET CANCER FOUNDATION
700 University Ave Suite 1056, Toronto, ON, M5G 1Z5
(416) 946-6560
Emp Here 36   *Sales* 85,944,401
SIC 8399 Social services, nec
Pr Paul Alofs
Stephen Bear
Treas Asha Raheja
Sec Margo Clarke
Robert Bell
John Bowey
Sean Boyd
Tom Ehrlich
Marnie Escaf
Janice Fukakusa

D-U-N-S 24-358-2215   (BR)
TORONTO REHABILITATION INSTITUTE
550 University Ave Suite 123, Toronto, ON, M5G 2A2
(416) 597-3422
Emp Here 40
SIC 8742 Management consulting services

D-U-N-S 24-119-2751   (BR)
TORONTO-DOMINION BANK, THE
TD BANK
(*Suby of* Toronto-Dominion Bank, The)
777 Bay St Suite 248, Toronto, ON, M5G 2C8
(416) 982-4364
Emp Here 20
SIC 6021 National commercial banks

D-U-N-S 24-386-8556   (HQ)
TOTTEN INSURANCE GROUP INC
20 Dundas St W Suite 910, Toronto, ON, M5G 2C2
(416) 342-1159
Emp Here 20   *Emp Total* 100
Sales 10,654,887
SIC 6411 Insurance agents, brokers, and service
Pr Heather Masterson
Ex VP Theresa Teixeira
VP Gerry Kennedy
VP Barb Dinan
Rgnl VP Richard Belanger
Rgnl VP John Rhuland
Rgnl VP Terry Gudmundson
Marco Andolfatto

D-U-N-S 24-180-3659   (SL)
UNIVERSITY CLUB OF TORONTO, THE
380 University Ave, Toronto, ON, M5G 1R6
(416) 597-1336
Emp Here 50   *Sales* 3,575,074
SIC 8641 Civic and social associations

D-U-N-S 25-361-7237   (BR)
UNIVERSITY HEALTH NETWORK
ADVANCED MEDICAL DISCOVERIES INSTITUTE
620 University Ave Suite 706, Toronto, ON, M5G 2C1
(416) 946-2294
Emp Here 90
SIC 8733 Noncommercial research organizations

D-U-N-S 25-426-3726   (BR)
UNIVERSITY HEALTH NETWORK
TORONTO GENERAL HOSPITAL
200 Elizabeth St Suite 224, Toronto, ON, M5G 2C4

Emp Here 200
SIC 8011 Offices and clinics of medical doctors

D-U-N-S 24-345-0553   (BR)
UNIVERSITY HEALTH NETWORK
DEPARTMENT OF PSYCHIATRY
200 Elizabeth St Suite 235, Toronto, ON, M5G 2C4
(416) 340-3155
Emp Here 40
SIC 8011 Offices and clinics of medical doctors

D-U-N-S 24-388-9107   (BR)
WOMEN'S COLLEGE HOSPITAL
WOMEN'S COLLEGE RESEARCH INSTITUTE
790 Bay St Suite 750, Toronto, ON, M5G 1N8
(416) 351-2535
Emp Here 50
SIC 8071 Medical laboratories

D-U-N-S 20-302-9835   (BR)
YORK UNIVERSITY
OSWALD PROFESSIONAL SERVICES
1 Dundas St W Suite 2602, Toronto, ON, M5G 1Z3
(416) 597-9724
Emp Here 30
SIC 8221 Colleges and universities

Toronto, ON M5H
York County

D-U-N-S 25-418-6158   (BR)
1561716 ONTARIO LTD
LONE STAR ACCESS GRILL
(*Suby of* 1561716 Ontario Ltd)
212 King St W, Toronto, ON, M5H 1K5
(416) 408-4064
Emp Here 60
SIC 5812 Eating places

D-U-N-S 20-328-4989   (SL)
500PX, INC
20 Duncan St Suite 1, Toronto, ON, M5H 3G8
(647) 465-1033
Emp Here 67   *Sales* 3,759,400
SIC 4813 Telephone communication, except radio

D-U-N-S 24-130-9280   (SL)
ACKER FINLEY CANADA FOCUS FUND
181 University Ave Suite 1400, Toronto, ON, M5H 3M7
(416) 777-9005
Emp Here 20   *Sales* 8,318,900
SIC 6722 Management investment, open-end
Owner Brian Acker

D-U-N-S 20-571-8138   (BR)
AMEX CANADA INC
AMERICAN EXPRESS
(*Suby of* American Express Company)
121 Richmond St W, Toronto, ON, M5H 2K1
(416) 868-4992
Emp Here 20
SIC 4724 Travel agencies

D-U-N-S 24-966-3840   (SL)
ASSOCIATION OF MUNICIPALITIES OF ONTARIO
AMO
200 University Ave Suite 801, Toronto, ON, M5H 3C6
(416) 971-9856
Emp Here 28   *Sales* 9,244,160
SIC 6282 Investment advice
Pr Pr Russ Powers
Ex Dir Patricia Vanini
Nancy Plumridge

D-U-N-S 20-650-4537   (SL)
AUDICO SERVICES LIMITED PARTNERSHIP
SMITH NIXON
390 Bay St Suite 1900, Toronto, ON, M5H 2Y2
(416) 361-1622
Emp Here 75   *Sales* 3,283,232
SIC 8721 Accounting, auditing, and bookkeeping

D-U-N-S 25-214-5289   (BR)
AVIVA INSURANCE COMPANY OF CANADA
121 King St W Suite 1400, Toronto, ON, M5H 3T9
(416) 363-9363
Emp Here 130
SIC 6411 Insurance agents, brokers, and service

D-U-N-S 20-819-6691   (HQ)
BAGG INC
THE BAGG GROUP
(*Suby of* Bagg Inc)
372 Bay St Suite 2100, Toronto, ON, M5H 2W9
(416) 863-1800
Emp Here 40   *Emp Total* 50
Sales 3,648,035
SIC 7361 Employment agencies

D-U-N-S 20-709-0155   (BR)
BANK OF NOVA SCOTIA, THE
SCOTIABANK
40 King St W Suite 1500, Toronto, ON, M5H 3Y2
(416) 933-1392
Emp Here 60
SIC 6021 National commercial banks

D-U-N-S 25-735-5677 (BR)
BANK OF NOVA SCOTIA, THE
SCOTIABANK
392 Bay St, Toronto, ON, M5H 3K5
(416) 866-5700
Emp Here 26
SIC 6021 National commercial banks

D-U-N-S 25-721-2316 (BR)
BANK OF MONTREAL
BMO
6 King St W, Toronto, ON, M5H 1C3
(416) 867-6636
Emp Here 23
SIC 6021 National commercial banks

D-U-N-S 24-683-2336 (BR)
BANQUE NATIONALE DU CANADA
145 King St W Suite 710, Toronto, ON, M5H 1J8
(416) 864-7981
Emp Here 20
SIC 6021 National commercial banks

D-U-N-S 24-874-8519 (BR)
BANQUE NATIONALE DU CANADA
121 King St W Suite 1700, Toronto, ON, M5H 3T9
(416) 864-7791
Emp Here 20
SIC 6021 National commercial banks

D-U-N-S 20-588-2884 (BR)
BANQUE TORONTO-DOMINION, LA
TD CANADA TRUST
(*Suby of* Toronto-Dominion Bank, The)
11 King St W, Toronto, ON, M5H 4C7

Emp Here 20
SIC 6021 National commercial banks

D-U-N-S 24-861-8001 (BR)
BANQUE DE DEVELOPPEMENT DU CANADA
BUSINESS DEVELOPMENT BANK OF CANADA
121 King St W Suite 1200, Toronto, ON, M5H 3T9
(416) 973-0341
Emp Here 25
SIC 6141 Personal credit institutions

D-U-N-S 25-674-3311 (SL)
BELO SUN MINING CORP
65 Queen St W Suite 800, Toronto, ON, M5H 2M5
(416) 309-2137
Emp Here 70   *Sales* 7,587,913
SIC 1041 Gold ores
Pr Pr Peter Tagliamonte
Ian Pritchard
Ryan Ptolemy
Joe Milbourne
VP Stephane Amireault
Sec Patrick Gleeson
Mark Eaton
Stan Bharti
Carol Fries
William Clarke

D-U-N-S 20-771-1813 (HQ)
BOILER INSPECTION AND INSURANCE COMPANY OF CANADA, THE
HSB BI&I
390 Bay St Suite 2000, Toronto, ON, M5H 2Y2
(416) 363-5491
Emp Here 100   *Emp Total* 43,428
Sales 78,870,517
SIC 6331 Fire, marine, and casualty insurance
Pr Pr John Mulvihill
Sr VP Sr VP Dave Picot
VP Derrick Hughes
VP Jean Dubois
Asst VP Brian Storey
VP David Pivato
Asst VP Barbara Hanley
Mark Moore

D-U-N-S 25-102-8973 (HQ)
BORDEN LADNER GERVAIS LLP
BLG
(*Suby of* Borden Ladner Gervais LLP)
22 Adelaide St W Suite 3400, Toronto, ON, M5H 4E3
(416) 367-6000
Emp Here 600   *Emp Total* 1,800
Sales 347,633,150
SIC 8111 Legal services
Pt Pt Sean Weir
Genl Mgr William Bryden
Ch Bd Melinda Park
Robert Morris
James Hubbard

D-U-N-S 25-536-1263 (BR)
BROADRIDGE SOFTWARE LIMITED
A D P DATAPHIE
4 King St W Suite 500, Toronto, ON, M5H 1B6
(416) 350-0999
Emp Here 100
SIC 7371 Custom computer programming services

D-U-N-S 24-421-0472 (HQ)
CBRE LIMITED
CBRE
145 King St W Suite 1100, Toronto, ON, M5H 1J8
(416) 362-2244
Emp Here 1,800   *Emp Total* 75,000
Sales 4,459,066,141
SIC 8748 Business consulting, nec
Pr Pr Mark Renzoni
VP Greg Moore
Gerald Mccrindle
Maureen Ehrenberg
Brad Henderson
John Gallagher
Glenn Ducan
John O'toole

D-U-N-S 24-206-9446 (BR)
CBRE LIMITED
CBRE
40 King St W Suite 4100, Toronto, ON, M5H 3Y4
(416) 947-7661
Emp Here 80
SIC 6531 Real estate agents and managers

D-U-N-S 20-007-9387 (BR)
CIBC WORLD MARKETS INC
CIBC WOOD GUNDY
200 King St W Suite 800, Toronto, ON, M5H 3T4
(416) 594-8999
Emp Here 130
SIC 6211 Security brokers and dealers

D-U-N-S 20-706-4973 (BR)
CIBC WORLD MARKETS INC
100 Simcoe St Suite 200, Toronto, ON, M5H 3G2
(416) 594-7950
Emp Here 50
SIC 6211 Security brokers and dealers

D-U-N-S 25-487-2591 (HQ)
CSI CONSULTING INC
(*Suby of* CSI Consulting Inc)
150 York St Suite 1612, Toronto, ON, M5H 3S5
(416) 364-6376
Emp Here 47   *Emp Total* 55
Sales 7,444,399
SIC 7371 Custom computer programming services
Pr Pr Ajit Someshwar

D-U-N-S 20-160-9823 (HQ)
CADILLAC FAIRVIEW CORPORATION LIMITED, THE
20 Queen St W Suite 500, Toronto, ON, M5H 3R4

(416) 598-8200
Emp Here 200   *Emp Total* 13,865
Sales 134,101,767
SIC 6512 Nonresidential building operators
Pr Pr John Sullivan
Cathal O'connor
Robert Michaels
Robert G Bertram
Barbara Zvan
Chuck Crovitz
Craig Macnab
Jane Rowe
John Curtin Jr.
Nora Aufreiter

D-U-N-S 24-817-6877 (BR)
CANADA LIFE ASSURANCE COMPANY, THE
REGIONAL ACCOUNTS MARKETING DIVISION
390 Bay St Suite 1100, Toronto, ON, M5H 2Y2
(416) 342-5406
Emp Here 20
SIC 6311 Life insurance

D-U-N-S 24-120-1859 (BR)
CANADIAN IMPERIAL BANK OF COMMERCE
CIBC
150 York St Suite 300, Toronto, ON, M5H 3S5
(416) 307-3563
Emp Here 100
SIC 6021 National commercial banks

D-U-N-S 24-791-6716 (BR)
CANADIAN OPERA COMPANY
FOUR SEASONS CENTRE PERFORMING ARTS
145 Queen St W, Toronto, ON, M5H 4G1
(416) 363-6671
Emp Here 20
SIC 7922 Theatrical producers and services

D-U-N-S 20-813-2592 (SL)
CANADIAN PUBLIC ACCOUNTABILITY BOARD
CPAB
150 York St Suite 900, Toronto, ON, M5H 3S5
(416) 913-8260
Emp Here 25   *Sales* 14,139,865
SIC 8721 Accounting, auditing, and bookkeeping
Brian A Hunt
Sr VP Keneth J.A. Vallilee
VP Fin Glen Fagan
VP Kam Grewal

D-U-N-S 24-682-1313 (SL)
CANADIAN STOCK TRANSFER COMPANY INC
320 Bay St Suite 1000, Toronto, ON, M5H 4A6
(888) 402-1644
Emp Here 20   *Sales* 10,449,920
SIC 6231 Security and commodity exchanges
Pr Pr Mark C Healy
CFO Marty Flanigan
COO Robert M Carney Sr.
Vincient J. Ioria
Dir Bill Spiers

D-U-N-S 20-797-0752 (BR)
CANNON DESIGN ARCHITECTURE INC
200 University Ave Suite 1200, Toronto, ON, M5H 3C6
(416) 915-0121
Emp Here 20
SIC 8712 Architectural services

D-U-N-S 24-243-2149 (SL)
CAPITAL MARKETS COMPANY LIMITED, THE
CAPCO
(*Suby of* Fidelity National Information Services, Inc.)
360 Bay St Suite 600, Toronto, ON, M5H 2V6
(416) 923-4570
Emp Here 40   *Sales* 4,012,839
SIC 8742 Management consulting services

D-U-N-S 24-130-8530 (SL)
CLAYMORE CANADIAN FINANCIAL MONTHLY INCOME ETF
CLAYMORE ADVANTAGED SHORT DURATION HIGH INCOME ETF CSD
200 University Ave Suite 13th, Toronto, ON, M5H 3C6

Emp Here 25   *Sales* 10,347,900
SIC 6722 Management investment, open-end
Pr Pr Som Seif
VP Jeffrey Logan

D-U-N-S 24-387-5916 (BR)
COMPAGNIE DE TELEPHONE BELL DU CANADA OU BELL CANADA, LA
76 Adelaide St W, Toronto, ON, M5H 1P6

Emp Here 100
SIC 4899 Communication services, nec

D-U-N-S 24-858-4174 (BR)
CONNOR, CLARK & LUNN FINANCIAL GROUP
181 University Ave Suite 300, Toronto, ON, M5H 3M7
(416) 862-2020
Emp Here 50
SIC 8732 Commercial nonphysical research

D-U-N-S 25-835-8969 (BR)
CONNOR, CLARK & LUNN INVESTMENT MANAGEMENT LTD
(*Suby of* Connor, Clark & Lunn Investment Management Ltd)
181 University Ave Suite 300, Toronto, ON, M5H 3M7
(416) 862-2020
Emp Here 32
SIC 6282 Investment advice

D-U-N-S 20-985-3915 (BR)
CORPORATION OF THE CITY OF TORONTO
TORONTO FIRE SERVICES
260 Adelaide St W, Toronto, ON, M5H 1X6
(416) 338-9356
Emp Here 25
SIC 7389 Business services, nec

D-U-N-S 20-291-5844 (BR)
CUSTOM HOUSE ULC
330 Bay St Suite 300, Toronto, ON, M5H 2S8
(905) 882-6004
Emp Here 20
SIC 6099 Functions related to deposit banking

D-U-N-S 24-209-8981 (BR)
CUSTOM HOUSE ULC
330 Bay St Suite 405, Toronto, ON, M5H 2S8
(905) 949-6000
Emp Here 35
SIC 6099 Functions related to deposit banking

D-U-N-S 24-000-3025 (BR)
DELOITTE LLP
DELOITTE MANAGEMENT SERVICES
22 Adelaide St W Suite 200, Toronto, ON, M5H 0A9
(416) 601-6150
Emp Here 350
SIC 8721 Accounting, auditing, and bookkeeping

D-U-N-S 24-677-0437 (SL)
DELOITTE MANAGEMENT SERVICES LP
DELOITTE
121 King St W Suite 300, Toronto, ON, M5H 3T9
(416) 775-2364
Emp Here 400   *Sales* 306,434,940
SIC 8721 Accounting, auditing, and bookkeeping
Pt Frank Vettese

D-U-N-S 20-573-5280 (BR)
DESJARDINS SECURITE FINANCIERE, COMPAGNIE D'ASSURANCE VIE

145 King St W Suite 2750, Toronto, ON, M5H 1J8

Emp Here 100
SIC 6311 Life insurance

    D-U-N-S 24-324-7728   (BR)
DOMINION OF CANADA GENERAL INSUR-ANCE COMPANY, THE
(*Suby of* The Travelers Companies Inc)
165 Unversity Ave, Toronto, ON, M5H 3R3
(416) 362-7231
Emp Here 200
SIC 6411 Insurance agents, brokers, and service

    D-U-N-S 24-024-6504   (HQ)
DOMINION OF CANADA GENERAL INSUR-ANCE COMPANY, THE
(*Suby of* The Travelers Companies Inc)
165 University Ave Suite 101, Toronto, ON, M5H 3B9
(416) 362-7231
Emp Here 200   *Emp Total* 30,900
Sales 477,892,585
SIC 6331 Fire, marine, and casualty insurance
Pr Pr Brigid Murphy
   Duncan Nr Jackman
   Mark J Fuller
   Deanna Rosenswig
   Mark M Taylor
   Clive Rowe
   Douglas Townsend

    D-U-N-S 20-562-1782   (HQ)
DOW JONES CANADA, INC
(*Suby of* News Corporation)
145 King St W Suite 730, Toronto, ON, M5H 1J8
(416) 306-2100
Emp Here 20   *Emp Total* 25,000
Sales 1,459,214
SIC 7383 News syndicates

    D-U-N-S 24-195-0146   (SL)
DUCARTOR HOLDINGS LTD
130 Adelaide St W Suite 701, Toronto, ON, M5H 2K4
(416) 593-5555
Emp Here 80   *Sales* 11,150,720
SIC 8741 Management services
   Julie Holmes

    D-U-N-S 20-174-7180   (HQ)
EDGESTONE CAPITAL PARTNERS, INC
141 Adelaide St W Suite 1002, Toronto, ON, M5H 3L5
(416) 860-3740
Emp Here 34   *Emp Total* 316
Sales 4,158,005
SIC 6719 Holding companies, nec

    D-U-N-S 24-477-0707   (HQ)
ENWAVE ENERGY CORPORATION
333 Bay St Suite 710, Toronto, ON, M5H 2R2
(416) 392-6838
Emp Here 30   *Emp Total* 55,700
Sales 14,883,983
SIC 4961 Steam and air-conditioning supply
Pr Dennis Fotinos
Dir Opers Graham Harding

    D-U-N-S 20-880-6323   (BR)
EXPORT DEVELOPMENT CANADA
EDC
150 York St Suite 810, Toronto, ON, M5H 3S5
(416) 640-7600
Emp Here 20
SIC 6111 Federal and federally sponsored credit agencies

    D-U-N-S 24-382-9640   (SL)
FIVE MOBILE INC
218 Adelaide St W Suite 400, Toronto, ON, M5H 1W7
(416) 479-0334
Emp Here 30   *Sales* 2,921,220
SIC 7371 Custom computer programming ser-

vices

    D-U-N-S 25-682-0986   (HQ)
FRONTERA ENERGY CORPORATION
(*Suby of* Frontera Energy Corporation)
333 Bay St Suite 1100, Toronto, ON, M5H 2R2
(416) 362-7735
Emp Here 30   *Emp Total* 1,376
Sales 1,411,711,000
SIC 1381 Drilling oil and gas wells
   Barry Larson
   Camilo Mcallister
VP Opers Camilo Valencia
VP Renata Campagnaro
VP Erik Lyngberg
Sec Peter Volk
   Gabriel De Alba
   Luis Alarcon
   W. Ellis Armstrong
   Raymond Bromark

    D-U-N-S 24-562-8433   (HQ)
FUJITSU CANADA, INC
155 University Ave Suite 1600, Toronto, ON, M5H 3B7
(905) 286-9666
Emp Here 50   *Emp Total* 156,515
Sales 16,773,456
SIC 5045 Computers, peripherals, and software
Ex VP David Shearer
VP Fin Danielle Parent

    D-U-N-S 25-520-4927   (HQ)
FUTURPRENEUR CANADA
YOUTH BUSINESS
(*Suby of* Futurpreneur Canada)
100 Adelaide St W, Toronto, ON, M5H 1S3
(416) 408-2923
Emp Here 20   *Emp Total* 50
Sales 15,454,196
SIC 6732 Trusts: educational, religious, etc.
   Vivian Prokop
   John Risley
   John Clark
V Ch Bd David Stewart-Patterson
Treas Jonathan Simmons
Sec Steve Farlow
   David Aisenstat
   Harry Chemko
   Ronnen Harary
   Michel Kelly-Gagnon

    D-U-N-S 25-273-8190   (HQ)
GMP SECURITIES L.P.
(*Suby of* GMP Corp)
145 King St W Suite 300, Toronto, ON, M5H 1J8
(416) 367-8600
Emp Here 100   *Emp Total* 5
Sales 41,650,942
SIC 6211 Security brokers and dealers
Dir Kevin M Sullivan
   J. Robert Fraser
Dir Eugene C Mcburney
Dir Mark Wellings
Dir Lorne M. Sugarman
Dir Jason J. Robertson
Sr VP Bob Bastianon
Dir Ed Charron
   Leo Ciccone

    D-U-N-S 25-094-7595   (BR)
GENERAL ELECTRIC CAPITAL EQUIP-MENT FINANCE INC
CORPORATE LENDING GROUP
(*Suby of* General Electric Company)
11 King St W Suite 1500, Toronto, ON, M5H 4C7
(416) 646-8370
Emp Here 40
SIC 6159 Miscellaneous business credit institutions

    D-U-N-S 24-525-3260   (SL)
GLOBAL   CROSSING TELECOMMUNICATIONS-CANADA, LTD

(*Suby of* Level 3 Communications, Inc.)
120 Adelaide St W Suite 2119, Toronto, ON, M5H 1T1
(416) 216-2011
Emp Here 30   *Sales* 2,512,128
SIC 4899 Communication services, nec

    D-U-N-S 20-077-4052   (SL)
GLOBAL SKILLS INC
366 Bay St 10th Fl, Toronto, ON, M5H 4B2
(416) 907-8400
Emp Here 50   *Sales* 3,648,035
SIC 7361 Employment agencies

    D-U-N-S 24-388-0143   (BR)
GREAT-WEST LIFE ASSURANCE COMPANY, THE
200 King St W Suite 400, Toronto, ON, M5H 3T4

Emp Here 80
SIC 6311 Life insurance

    D-U-N-S 20-341-1095   (SL)
GREEN ESSENTIAL SERVICES INC
250 University Ave Suite 200, Toronto, ON, M5H 3E5
(866) 820-2284
Emp Here 50   *Sales* 4,742,446
SIC 5999 Miscellaneous retail stores, nec

    D-U-N-S 20-544-9510   (BR)
GREEN SHIELD CANADA
155 University Ave, Toronto, ON, M5H 3B7
(416) 867-1777
Emp Here 30
SIC 6324 Hospital and medical service plans

    D-U-N-S 24-685-5097   (BR)
HDR CORPORATION
(*Suby of* Hdr, Inc.)
255 Adelaide St W, Toronto, ON, M5H 1X9
(647) 777-4900
Emp Here 55
SIC 8711 Engineering services

    D-U-N-S 25-255-0298   (BR)
HEENAN BLAIKIE S.E.N.C.R.L.
333 Bay St Suite 2900, Toronto, ON, M5H 2R2

Emp Here 300
SIC 8111 Legal services

    D-U-N-S 24-810-6742   (HQ)
HITACHI DATA SYSTEMS INC
11 King St W Suite 1400, Toronto, ON, M5H 4C7
(416) 494-4114
Emp Here 95   *Emp Total* 335,244
Sales 11,673,712
SIC 7372 Prepackaged software
Pr Pr Minoru Kosuge
   Barry Morrison

    D-U-N-S 20-077-3401   (HQ)
HOME TRUST COMPANY
145 King St W Suite 2300, Toronto, ON, M5H 1J8
(416) 360-4663
Emp Here 300   *Emp Total* 916
Sales 279,220,599
SIC 6021 National commercial banks
   Gerald Soloway
Pr Yousry Bissada
VP VP Chris Ahlvik
VP Fin Cathy Sutherland
Sr VP John Harry
   Brian Mosko
   William Davis

    D-U-N-S 20-772-5123   (BR)
HUDSON'S BAY COMPANY
HBC
401 Bay St Suite 601, Toronto, ON, M5H 2Y4
(416) 861-6728
Emp Here 80
SIC 5719 Miscellaneous homefurnishings

    D-U-N-S 20-009-1189   (HQ)

HUDSON'S BAY COMPANY
401 Bay St Suite 500, Toronto, ON, M5H 2Y4
(800) 521-2364
Emp Here 600   *Emp Total* 9,000
Sales 11,016,690,335
SIC 5311 Department stores
   Richard Baker
   Bonnie Brooks
Pr Elizabeth Rodbell
   Robert Baker
   David Leith
   William Mack
   Lee Neibart
   Denise Pickett
   Wayne Pommen
   Earl Rotman

    D-U-N-S 20-356-0177   (SL)
HY'S STEAK HOUSE EASTERN
120 Adelaide St W, Toronto, ON, M5H 1T1
(416) 364-6600
Emp Here 70   *Sales* 2,115,860
SIC 5812 Eating places

    D-U-N-S 20-770-1616   (BR)
HY'S OF CANADA LTD
HY'S STEAKHOUSE
120 Adelaide St W Suite 101, Toronto, ON, M5H 1T1
(416) 364-6600
Emp Here 100
SIC 5812 Eating places

    D-U-N-S 25-278-1042   (HQ)
INDUSTRIAL AND COMMERCIAL BANK OF CHINA (CANADA)
333 Bay St Suite 3710, Toronto, ON, M5H 2R2
(416) 366-5588
Emp Here 40   *Emp Total* 461,749
Sales 26,265,852
SIC 6021 National commercial banks
   Cedric Ng
   David K.P. Li

    D-U-N-S 20-706-0158   (BR)
INFOROUTE SANTE DU CANADA INC
CANADA HEALTH INFOWAY
150 King St W Suite 1308, Toronto, ON, M5H 1J9
(416) 979-4606
Emp Here 75
SIC 7338 Secretarial and court reporting

    D-U-N-S 24-027-0561   (BR)
INVESTORS GROUP FINANCIAL SER-VICES INC
INVESTORS FINANCIAL SERVICES PLAN-NING CENTRE
145 King St W Suite 2800, Toronto, ON, M5H 1J8
(416) 860-1668
Emp Here 60
SIC 8741 Management services

    D-U-N-S 20-563-3899   (BR)
JARISLOWSKY, FRASER LIMITEE
20 Queen St W Suite 3100, Toronto, ON, M5H 3R3
(416) 363-7417
Emp Here 50
SIC 6722 Management investment, open-end

    D-U-N-S 25-975-9603   (HQ)
JONES LANG LASALLE REAL ESTATE SERVICES, INC
(*Suby of* Jones Lang Lasalle Incorporated)
22 Adelaide St W 26th Fl East Tower, Toronto, ON, M5H 4E3
(416) 304-6000
Emp Here 50   *Emp Total* 77,300
Sales 9,411,930
SIC 6531 Real estate agents and managers
VP Rick Urbanczyk

    D-U-N-S 20-847-4585   (HQ)
KJA CONSULTANTS INC
(*Suby of* KJA Consultants Inc)
85 Richmond St W, Toronto, ON, M5H 2C9

(416) 961-3938
Emp Here 25   *Emp Total* 50
Sales 4,961,328
SIC 8711 Engineering services

D-U-N-S 24-000-3546   (SL)
KOEI CANADA INC
257 Adelaide St W Suite 500, Toronto, ON,
M5H 1X9

Emp Here 42   *Sales* 5,376,850
SIC 7371 Custom computer programming services
VP VP Hidenori Taniguchi

D-U-N-S 20-770-4156   (HQ)
KPMG LLP
(*Suby of* KPMG LLP)
333 Bay St Suite 4600, Toronto, ON, M5H 2S5
(416) 777-8500
Emp Here 150   *Emp Total* 5,000
Sales 218,882,100
SIC 8721 Accounting, auditing, and bookkeeping
Sr Pt Bill Thomas
  Mary Lou Maher
  Mario Paron
Pt Peter Doyle
Pt Axel Thesburg
Pt John Herhalt
Pt Greg Wiebe
Pt Jean-Pierre Desrosiers
Pt Beth Wilson

D-U-N-S 24-120-3525   (BR)
LAW SOCIETY OF UPPER CANADA, THE
BARREAU DU HAUT CANADA
130 Queen St W Suite 100, Toronto, ON, M5H
2N6
(416) 947-3315
Emp Here 525
SIC 8111 Legal services

D-U-N-S 24-610-4830   (SL)
LAXTON GLASS LLP
390 Bay St Suite 200, Toronto, ON, M5H 2B1
(416) 363-2353
Emp Here 50   *Sales* 4,304,681
SIC 8111 Legal services

D-U-N-S 25-185-0301   (SL)
LEGAL LINK CORPORATION, THE
333 Bay St Suite 400, Toronto, ON, M5H 2R2
(416) 348-0432
Emp Here 55   *Sales* 8,245,440
SIC 8732 Commercial nonphysical research
Pr Pr Vince Saroli

D-U-N-S 25-520-3879   (BR)
LERNERS LLP
130 Adelaide St W Suite 2400, Toronto, ON,
M5H 3P5
(416) 867-3076
Emp Here 150
SIC 8111 Legal services

D-U-N-S 25-221-3509   (HQ)
LINDT & SPRUNGLI (CANADA), INC
181 University Ave Suite 900, Toronto, ON,
M5H 3M7
(416) 351-8566
Emp Here 73   *Emp Total* 10
Sales 30,248,761
SIC 5145 Confectionery
Pr Rudi Blatter
  Cyndi Culp

D-U-N-S 20-059-2710   (SL)
LIVE NATION TOURING (CANADA), INC
214 King St W Suite 510, Toronto, ON, M5H
3S6
(416) 922-5290
Emp Here 30   *Sales* 4,428,946
SIC 7922 Theatrical producers and services

D-U-N-S 20-288-5336   (SL)
LONGBAR MANAGEMENT SERVICES LIMITED PARTNERSHIP
250 University Ave Suite 700, Toronto, ON,

M5H 3E5
(416) 214-5200
Emp Here 41   *Sales* 5,371,275
SIC 8742 Management consulting services

D-U-N-S 24-763-7239   (BR)
MCAP FINANCIAL CORPORATION
MCAP
200 King St W Suite 400, Toronto, ON, M5H
3T4
(416) 368-8844
Emp Here 50
SIC 6163 Loan brokers

D-U-N-S 24-366-0532   (BR)
MNP LLP
111 Richmond St W Suite 300, Toronto, ON,
M5H 2G4
(416) 596-1711
Emp Here 100
SIC 8721 Accounting, auditing, and bookkeeping

D-U-N-S 20-320-1772   (SL)
MRP RECRUITING INC
JOBSPRING PARTNERS
200 University Ave Suite 1302, Toronto, ON,
M5H 3C6
(647) 499-8100
Emp Here 30   *Sales* 2,598,753
SIC 7361 Employment agencies

D-U-N-S 24-764-2312   (BR)
MACDOUGALL, MACDOUGALL & MACTIER INC
3 MACS
200 King St W Suite 1806, Toronto, ON, M5H
3T4
(416) 597-7900
Emp Here 45
SIC 6211 Security brokers and dealers

D-U-N-S 20-553-6738   (BR)
MARSH CANADA LIMITED
(*Suby of* Marsh & McLennan Companies, Inc.)
200 King St W Suite 1806, Toronto, ON, M5H
3T4
(416) 979-0123
Emp Here 30
SIC 6411 Insurance agents, brokers, and service

D-U-N-S 24-130-8324   (SL)
MCLEAN BUDDEN GLOBAL EQUITY FUND
145 King St W Suite 2525, Toronto, ON, M5H
1J8
(416) 862-9800
Emp Here 49   *Sales* 19,632,000
SIC 6722 Management investment, open-end
Pr Roger Bauchemin

D-U-N-S 24-131-4413   (SL)
MCLEAN BUDDEN LTD
MCLEAN BUDDEN HIGH INCOME EQUITY FUND
145 King St W Suite 2525, Toronto, ON, M5H
1J8
(416) 862-9800
Emp Here 45   *Sales* 18,061,440
SIC 6722 Management investment, open-end
Pr Roger Beauchemin

D-U-N-S 20-278-8055   (SL)
MINCORE INC
80 Richmond St W Suite 1502, Toronto, ON,
M5H 2A4
(416) 214-1766
Emp Here 50   *Sales* 4,231,721
SIC 1081 Metal mining services

D-U-N-S 25-213-4069   (SL)
MINCORP EXCHANGE INC
20 Queen St W Unit 702, Toronto, ON, M5H
3R3

Emp Here 112   *Sales* 236,369,280
SIC 6099 Functions related to deposit banking
Pr Pr Karim Manji
  Mina Manji

D-U-N-S 24-829-4381   (SL)
MONITOR COMPANY CANADA
(*Suby of* Deloitte LLP)
100 Simcoe St Suite 500, Toronto, ON, M5H
3G2
(416) 408-4800
Emp Here 70   *Sales* 8,317,520
SIC 8741 Management services
Dir Michael Wenban
Dir Jonathan Goodman

D-U-N-S 24-379-0099   (BR)
MORNINGSTAR RESEARCH INC
C.P.M.S.
(*Suby of* Morningstar, Inc.)
141 Adelaide St W Suite 910, Toronto, ON,
M5H 3L5
(416) 366-4253
Emp Here 40
SIC 8732 Commercial nonphysical research

D-U-N-S 20-771-6879   (HQ)
MUNICH REINSURANCE COMPANY OF CANADA
390 Bay St Suite 2300, Toronto, ON, M5H 2Y2
(416) 366-9206
Emp Here 110   *Emp Total* 43,428
Sales 62,089,556
SIC 6331 Fire, marine, and casualty insurance
Pr Pr Kenneth Irvin
  D. Murray Paton
VP Opers John Lower
  Gary Gray
  Peter Mccutcheon
  Robert Jemmett
  James Brierley
  Anthony Fall
V Ch Bd John Phelan

D-U-N-S 20-785-3409   (SL)
MUNICH-CANADA MANAGEMENT CORPORATION LTD
MUNICH RE
390 Bay St Suite 2200, Toronto, ON, M5H 2Y2
(416) 359-2147
Emp Here 20   *Sales* 1,969,939
SIC 6712 Bank holding companies

D-U-N-S 24-576-2984   (SL)
NT GLOBAL ADVISORS INC
(*Suby of* Northern Trust Corporation)
145 King St W Suite 1910, Toronto, ON, M5H
1J8
(416) 366-2020
Emp Here 20   *Sales* 4,815,406
SIC 6282 Investment advice

D-U-N-S 24-602-8799   (HQ)
NATIONAL BANK FINANCIAL LTD
121 King St W Suite 600, Toronto, ON, M5H
3T9
(877) 864-1859
Emp Here 25   *Emp Total* 20,000
Sales 92,319,500
SIC 6211 Security brokers and dealers
Pr Pr Luc Paiment
Sec Melanie Frappier
  Alain Legris
  Brian Davis
Dir Ricardo Pascoe

D-U-N-S 25-805-1804   (BR)
NIAGARA KANKO TOURS INC
218 Adelaide St W, Toronto, ON, M5H 1W7

Emp Here 30
SIC 4725 Tour operators

D-U-N-S 24-006-4923   (HQ)
NORTHBRIDGE COMMERCIAL INSURANCE CORPORATION
105 Adelaide St W, Toronto, ON, M5H 1P9
(416) 350-4400
Emp Here 66   *Emp Total* 23,576
Sales 79,435,217
SIC 6331 Fire, marine, and casualty insurance
Pr Pr Mark Ram

V Prem Watsa

D-U-N-S 25-405-6195   (BR)
NORTHBRIDGE GENERAL INSURANCE CORPORATION
105 Adelaide St W Suit 700, Toronto, ON,
M5H 1P9
(416) 350-4400
Emp Here 600
SIC 6331 Fire, marine, and casualty insurance

D-U-N-S 25-097-1736   (HQ)
NORTHERN FINANCIAL CORPORATION
(*Suby of* Northern Financial Corporation)
145 King St W Suite 2020, Toronto, ON, M5H
1J8

Emp Here 24   *Emp Total* 104
Sales 12,278,783
SIC 6211 Security brokers and dealers
  Vic Alboini
  Don Chornoboy
Dir R Ian Bradley
Dir William Grant
Dir Wesley Roitman

D-U-N-S 25-195-2834   (HQ)
NORTHERN SECURITIES INC
(*Suby of* Northern Financial Corporation)
145 King St W Suite 2020, Toronto, ON, M5H
1J8

Emp Here 40   *Emp Total* 104
Sales 11,673,712
SIC 6211 Security brokers and dealers
Pr Vic Alboini

D-U-N-S 25-535-4813   (HQ)
NORTHGATEARINSO CANADA INC
121 King St W Suite 2220, Toronto, ON, M5H
3T9
(416) 622-9559
Emp Here 25   *Emp Total* 7
Sales 16,019,593
SIC 7372 Prepackaged software
  Pierre Rochette

D-U-N-S 24-376-3708   (BR)
NORTHSTAR HOSPITALITY LIMITED PARTNERSHIP
HILTON TORONTO, THE
(*Suby of* Northstar Hospitality Limited Partnership)
145 Richmond St W Suite 212, Toronto, ON,
M5H 2L2
(416) 869-3456
Emp Here 100
SIC 7011 Hotels and motels

D-U-N-S 25-530-9940   (HQ)
OMD CANADA
(*Suby of* Omnicom Group Inc.)
67 Richmond St W Suite 2, Toronto, ON, M5H
1Z5
(416) 681-5600
Emp Here 175   *Emp Total* 74,900
Sales 54,183,918
SIC 7319 Advertising, nec
Pr Cathy Collier
CFO Michael Pitre
  Lorraine Hughes
Genl Mgr Frank Palmer

D-U-N-S 24-733-7350   (SL)
OXCAP INC
130 Adelaide St W Suite 1100, Toronto, ON,
M5H 3P5
(416) 865-8264
Emp Here 375   *Sales* 47,509,440
SIC 6531 Real estate agents and managers
Genl Mgr Ron Perlmutter

D-U-N-S 24-620-1474   (BR)
PI FINANCIAL CORP
40 King St W Suite 3401, Toronto, ON, M5H
3Y2
(416) 883-9040
Emp Here 29

SIC 6211 Security brokers and dealers

D-U-N-S 20-526-8852   (SL)
PLUSONE INC
347 Bay St Suite 506, Toronto, ON, M5H 2R7
(416) 861-1662
Emp Here 68   *Sales* 11,159,500
SIC 8741 Management services
Pr Don Mccaw
Dir Joseph Brandt

D-U-N-S 25-676-6395   (HQ)
QMX GOLD CORPORATION
(*Suby of* CMX Gold Corporation)
65 Queen St W Suite 815, Toronto, ON, M5H 2M5
(416) 861-5889
Emp Here 30   *Emp Total* 131
Sales 11,263,103
SIC 1081 Metal mining services

D-U-N-S 25-150-2597   (SL)
RSM RUV MANAGEMENT
200 King St W Suite 1100, Toronto, ON, M5H 3T4
(416) 932-8000
Emp Here 170   *Sales* 29,306,432
SIC 8741 Management services
Sr Pt Joel Cohen

D-U-N-S 25-361-7161   (SL)
RSM RICHTER LLP
200 King St W Suite 1100, Toronto, ON, M5H 3T4
(416) 932-8000
Emp Here 100   *Sales* 4,377,642
SIC 8721 Accounting, auditing, and bookkeeping

D-U-N-S 20-278-5887   (SL)
RX GOLD & SILVER INC
145 King St W Suite 2870, Toronto, ON, M5H 1J8
(416) 848-9503
Emp Here 40   *Sales* 3,356,192
SIC 1081 Metal mining services

D-U-N-S 20-609-8019   (BR)
RAYMOND JAMES (USA) LTD
(*Suby of* Raymond James Financial, Inc.)
40 King St W Suite 5300, Toronto, ON, M5H 3Y2
(416) 777-7000
Emp Here 20
SIC 8742 Management consulting services

D-U-N-S 20-307-0248   (BR)
RELIANT WEB HOSTING INC
TENZING MANAGED IT SERVICES
85 Richmond St W Suite 510, Toronto, ON, M5H 2C9
(877) 767-5577
Emp Here 26
SIC 7371 Custom computer programming services

D-U-N-S 24-991-1918   (SL)
RETAIL READY FOODS INC
130 Adelaide St W Suite 810, Toronto, ON, M5H 3P5
(905) 812-8555
Emp Here 39   *Sales* 9,995,616
SIC 5147 Meats and meat products
Pr John Ferraro

D-U-N-S 25-528-9092   (SL)
ROXGOLD INC
360 Bay St Suite 500, Toronto, ON, M5H 2V6
(416) 203-6401
Emp Here 171   *Sales* 41,385,000
SIC 1081 Metal mining services
Pr Pr John Dorward
Natacha Garoute
VP Yan Bourassa
Paul Criddle
Ch Bd Oliver Lennox-King
Richard Colterjohn
John Knowles
Kate Harcourt

Robin Mills
Norm Pitcher

D-U-N-S 20-188-4876   (HQ)
ROYNAT CAPITAL INC
40 King St W, Toronto, ON, M5H 3Y2
(416) 933-2730
Emp Here 25   *Emp Total* 68,000
Sales 17,875,372
SIC 6159 Miscellaneous business credit institutions
Pr Pr Renie Llewellyn
Sr VP Jeff Chernin
VP VP Wray Stannard

D-U-N-S 20-200-4078   (BR)
SCOTIA CAPITAL INC
SCOTIA MCLEOD
40 King St W Suite Lower, Toronto, ON, M5H 3Y2
(416) 863-7072
Emp Here 50
SIC 6211 Security brokers and dealers

D-U-N-S 24-377-3848   (BR)
SIERRA SYSTEMS GROUP INC
SIERRA SYSTEMS
150 York St Suite 1910, Toronto, ON, M5H 3S5
(416) 777-1212
Emp Here 105
SIC 7379 Computer related services, nec

D-U-N-S 25-283-3314   (SL)
SIZZLING IN TORONTO, INC
RUTH'S CHRIS STEAK HOUSE
145 Richmond St W, Toronto, ON, M5H 2L2
(416) 955-1455
Emp Here 60   *Sales* 1,824,018
SIC 5812 Eating places

D-U-N-S 20-804-3112   (SL)
SOLUTIA SDO LTD
14 Duncan St Suite 209, Toronto, ON, M5H 3G8
(416) 204-9797
Emp Here 85   *Sales* 9,261,811
SIC 8742 Management consulting services
Pr Pr Sam D'aurizio
Jackie Clark
VP VP Troy Loder
VP VP Robert Emer
VP VP Frank D'addio

D-U-N-S 25-498-2994   (BR)
STARBUCKS COFFEE CANADA, INC
STARBUCKS
(*Suby of* Starbucks Corporation)
4 King St W, Toronto, ON, M5H 1B6
(416) 363-5983
Emp Here 25
SIC 5812 Eating places

D-U-N-S 20-034-5820   (SL)
STRATIX TECHNOLOGIES INC
STRATIX CONSULTING
(*Suby of* Fidelity National Information Services, Inc.)
150 King St W Suite 2110, Toronto, ON, M5H 1J9
(416) 865-3310
Emp Here 20   *Sales* 1,824,018
SIC 8742 Management consulting services

D-U-N-S 20-773-1845   (HQ)
SWISS REINSURANCE COMPANY CANADA
150 King St W Suite 2200, Toronto, ON, M5H 1J9
(416) 408-0272
Emp Here 71   *Emp Total* 14,053
Sales 37,282,918
SIC 6331 Fire, marine, and casualty insurance
Peter Forstmoser
Dir Benedict Hentsch
Dir Bob Scott
Dir John Jr Smith
Dir Kasper Villiger

Sec Thomas Hodler
Dir Walter Kielholz
Dir Jakob Baer
Dir Thomas Bechtler
Dir Raymund Breu

D-U-N-S 24-337-4824   (SL)
T GP MANAGEMENT
150 York Street Unit 1801, Toronto, ON, M5H 3S5
(416) 507-1800
Emp Here 49   *Sales* 6,784,769
SIC 8741 Management services
Owner Alex Pettinvill

D-U-N-S 25-684-5801   (BR)
TELUS COMMUNICATIONS INC
11 King St W Suite C115, Toronto, ON, M5H 4C7
(416) 507-7400
Emp Here 600
SIC 4899 Communication services, nec

D-U-N-S 24-364-4320   (BR)
TEKSYSTEMS CANADA INC.
TEKSYSTEMS CANADA INC./SOCIETE TEKSYSTEMS CANADA INC
150 York St Suite 501, Toronto, ON, M5H 3S5
(416) 342-5000
Emp Here 40
SIC 7361 Employment agencies

D-U-N-S 24-126-9948   (SL)
TEMPLETON, FRANKLIN MUTUAL BEACON FUND
200 King St W Suite 1500, Toronto, ON, M5H 3T4
(416) 957-6000
Emp Here 700   *Sales* 280,344,960
SIC 6722 Management investment, open-end
CEO Don Reed

D-U-N-S 20-646-7628   (BR)
THOMSON REUTERS CANADA LIMITED
333 Bay St Suite 400, Toronto, ON, M5H 2R2
(416) 687-7500
Emp Here 300
SIC 8732 Commercial nonphysical research

D-U-N-S 20-876-7736   (SL)
THOMSON, WILLIAM E ASSOCIATES INC
THOMSON ASSOCIATES
390 Bay St Suite 1102, Toronto, ON, M5H 2Y2
(416) 947-1300
Emp Here 35   *Sales* 6,871,200
SIC 6211 Security brokers and dealers
Pr William Thomson

D-U-N-S 25-496-9355   (BR)
TORONTO-DOMINION BANK, THE
TD CANADA TRUST
(*Suby of* Toronto-Dominion Bank, The)
141 Adelaide St W Suite 1700, Toronto, ON, M5H 3L5
(416) 982-8768
Emp Here 40
SIC 6021 National commercial banks

D-U-N-S 20-280-7707   (BR)
TRAVELERS INSURANCE COMPANY OF CANADA
165 University Ave Suite 101, Toronto, ON, M5H 3B9
(416) 362-7231
Emp Here 500
SIC 6351 Surety insurance

D-U-N-S 24-850-6433   (SL)
TRENT RAPIDS POWER CORP
4 King St W Suite 1230, Toronto, ON, M5H 1B6
(416) 640-0503
Emp Here 20   *Sales* 12,858,960
SIC 4911 Electric services
Pr Pr Robert Lake

D-U-N-S 24-334-3027   (HQ)
UBS BANK (CANADA)
154 University Ave Suite 700, Toronto, ON,

M5H 3Y9
(416) 343-1800
Emp Here 82   *Emp Total* 59,387
Sales 27,798,027
SIC 6021 National commercial banks
Pr Sarah Bevin
Ch Bd Martin Liechti
Dir John F. Angus
Dir Geoffrey R. Walker

D-U-N-S 24-312-8993   (HQ)
URANIUM ONE INC
333 Bay St Suite 1200, Toronto, ON, M5H 2R2
(647) 788-8500
Emp Here 22   *Emp Total* 3,000
Sales 314,600,000
SIC 1094 Uranium-radium-vanadium ores
Eduards Smirnovs
VP Jane Luck
Ch Bd Vasily Konstantinov
Feroz Ashraf
Guerman Kornilov
Vladimir Hlavinka

D-U-N-S 24-947-5393   (HQ)
WILDEBOER DELLELCE LLP
(*Suby of* Wildeboer Dellelce LLP)
365 Bay St Suite 800, Toronto, ON, M5H 2V1
(416) 361-3121
Emp Here 45   *Emp Total* 50
Sales 4,304,681
SIC 8111 Legal services

D-U-N-S 24-792-7882   (SL)
WILLMS & SHIER ENVIRONMENTAL LAWYERS LLP
4 King St W Suite 900, Toronto, ON, M5H 1B6
(416) 863-0711
Emp Here 50   *Sales* 4,304,681
SIC 8111 Legal services

D-U-N-S 20-250-5848   (SL)
WORLDGAMING NETWORK INC
WORLDGAMING
208 Adelaide St W Suite 200, Toronto, ON, M5H 1W7
(416) 800-4263
Emp Here 35   *Sales* 3,675,083
SIC 7372 Prepackaged software

D-U-N-S 25-942-3697   (SL)
XCEED MORTGAGE CORPORATION
200 King St W Suite 600, Toronto, ON, M5H 3T4
(416) 203-5933
Emp Here 130   *Sales* 33,075,748
SIC 6162 Mortgage bankers and loan correspondents
Ivan Wahl
Dir Thomas R Alton
Dir Thomas A Di Giacomo
Dir William Mulvihill
Dir Melvyn P Rubinoff
Dir W James Taylor

Toronto, ON M5J
York County

D-U-N-S 20-937-9457   (BR)
1094285 ONTARIO LIMITED
IL FORNELLO RESTAURANT
207 Queens Quay W, Toronto, ON, M5J 1A7

Emp Here 50
SIC 5812 Eating places

D-U-N-S 24-219-6702   (SL)
1548383 ONTARIO INC
RADISSONADMIRAL HOTEL
249 Queens Quay W Suite 109, Toronto, ON, M5J 2N5
(416) 203-3333
Emp Here 110   *Sales* 4,815,406
SIC 7011 Hotels and motels

D-U-N-S 25-203-0606   (SL)
164074 CANADA INC
EAST SIDE MARIO'S
151 Front St W, Toronto, ON, M5J 2N1

Emp Here 70   *Sales* 2,115,860
SIC 5812 Eating places

D-U-N-S 25-302-2859   (BR)
4513380 CANADA INC
LIVINGSTON EVENT LOGISTICS
40 University Ave Suite 602, Toronto, ON, M5J 1J9
(416) 863-9339
Emp Here 25
SIC 4731 Freight transportation arrangement

D-U-N-S 24-848-8145   (SL)
530093 ONTARIO LIMITED
PEARL HARBOURFRONT CHINESE CUISINE
207 Queens Quay W Suite 200, Toronto, ON, M5J 1A7
(416) 203-1233
Emp Here 50   *Sales* 1,532,175
SIC 5812 Eating places

D-U-N-S 24-951-9604   (SL)
979786 ONTARIO LIMITED
LOOSE MOOSE TAP & GRILL, THE
146 Front St W, Toronto, ON, M5J 1G2
(416) 977-8840
Emp Here 110   *Sales* 3,283,232
SIC 5812 Eating places

D-U-N-S 20-848-9823   (SL)
AGF ALL WORLD TAX ADVANTAGE GROUP LIMITED
Gd, Toronto, ON, M5J 2W7
(416) 367-1900
Emp Here 500   *Sales* 200,246,400
SIC 6722 Management investment, open-end
Pr Pr Robert Farquharson
Edwin Wing
Philippe Casgrain
Warren Goldring
Ian H Macdonald
Allan Manford

D-U-N-S 20-771-6994   (HQ)
AON CONSULTING INC
145 Wellington St W Suite 300, Toronto, ON, M5J 1H8
(416) 542-5500
Emp Here 180   *Emp Total* 67,562
Sales 43,139,300
SIC 8999 Services, nec
Ashim Khemani
Louis Gagnon
Kaylynn M Schroeder
VP Fin Jim Hubbard

D-U-N-S 20-786-9884   (HQ)
AON REED STENHOUSE INC
20 Bay St Suite 2400, Toronto, ON, M5J 2N8
(416) 868-5500
Emp Here 314   *Emp Total* 67,562
Sales 160,429,685
SIC 6411 Insurance agents, brokers, and service
Pr Pr Christine Lithgow
Ex VP Gilles Corriveau
James Millard
Grant Assman
Lily Choo
James A. Hubbard
Jonh W. King

D-U-N-S 20-911-7308   (HQ)
ADECCO EMPLOYMENT SERVICES LIMITED
HOLLOWAY SCHULZ
20 Bay St Suite 800, Toronto, ON, M5J 2N8
(416) 646-3322
Emp Here 40   *Emp Total* 576
Sales 36,772,193
SIC 7361 Employment agencies

Pr Pr Sandra Hokannson
VP Opers Carol Gilchrist
VP Fin Douglas Hamlyn

D-U-N-S 20-704-9714   (BR)
ADECCO EMPLOYMENT SERVICES LIMITED
ADECCO
20 Bay St Suite 800, Toronto, ON, M5J 2N8
(416) 646-3322
Emp Here 35
SIC 7361 Employment agencies

D-U-N-S 25-691-5018   (BR)
AINSWORTH INC
161 Bay St Suite 527, Toronto, ON, M5J 2S1
(416) 594-8451
Emp Here 40
SIC 1731 Electrical work

D-U-N-S 24-218-3440   (HQ)
APPLE CANADA INC
APPLE STORE
(*Suby of* Apple Inc.)
120 Bremner Blvd Suite 1600, Toronto, ON, M5J 0A8
(647) 943-4400
Emp Here 100   *Emp Total* 116,000
Sales 20,501,957
SIC 5045 Computers, peripherals, and software
John Hagias
Derek Smith

D-U-N-S 25-483-6687   (SL)
ARONOVITCH MACAULAY ROLLO LLP
145 Wellington St W Suite 300, Toronto, ON, M5J 1H8
(416) 369-9393
Emp Here 56   *Sales* 4,815,406
SIC 8111 Legal services

D-U-N-S 24-933-7973   (HQ)
ASTRAL BROADCASTING GROUP INC
VIEWER'S CHOICE CANADA
(*Suby of* Astral Broadcasting Group Inc)
181 Bay St Unit 100, Toronto, ON, M5J 2T3
(416) 956-2010
Emp Here 204   *Emp Total* 314
Sales 37,033,530
SIC 7812 Motion picture and video production
Pr Pr Ian Greenberg
Andre Bureau
VP Fin Claude Gagnon

D-U-N-S 24-087-2122   (BR)
BDO CANADA LLP
123 Front St W Suite 1100, Toronto, ON, M5J 2M2
(416) 865-0210
Emp Here 48
SIC 8111 Legal services

D-U-N-S 25-790-5232   (SL)
BADALI'S, JOE PIAZZA ON FRONT INC
BADALI'S, JOE ITALIAN RESTAURANT & BAR
156 Front St W, Toronto, ON, M5J 2L6
(416) 977-3064
Emp Here 85   *Sales* 2,553,625
SIC 5812 Eating places

D-U-N-S 20-796-0159   (BR)
BANK OF NOVA SCOTIA, THE
SCOTIA BANK REAL ESTATE
61 Front St W Suite 120, Toronto, ON, M5J 1E5
(416) 866-7871
Emp Here 125
SIC 6531 Real estate agents and managers

D-U-N-S 24-360-1593   (HQ)
BANK OF TOKYO-MITSUBISHI UFJ (CANADA)
200 Bay St Suite 1700, Toronto, ON, M5J 2J1
(416) 865-0220
Emp Here 72   *Emp Total* 115,276
Sales 14,899,517

SIC 6211 Security brokers and dealers
Pr Pr Takashi Ando
Sr VP Angelo Bisutti
Dir Normand Bernier
Dir William Saywell
Dir John A Paterson
Dir M Joseph Regan
Dir James Kennedy
Dir Donald Brown

D-U-N-S 20-079-2021   (BR)
BANQUE TORONTO-DOMINION, LA
TORONTO-DOMINION BANK, THE
(*Suby of* Toronto-Dominion Bank, The)
161 Bay St Suite 3200, Toronto, ON, M5J 2T2
(416) 361-5400
Emp Here 40
SIC 6021 National commercial banks

D-U-N-S 25-915-7519   (SL)
BEAZLEY CANADA LIMITED
(*Suby of* BEAZLEY IRELAND HOLDINGS PLC)
55 University Ave Suite 550, Toronto, ON, M5J 2H7
(416) 601-2155
Emp Here 25   *Sales* 2,261,782
SIC 6411 Insurance agents, brokers, and service

D-U-N-S 20-176-0993   (SL)
BENTAL REAL ESTATE SERVICES LP
55 University Ave Suite 300, Toronto, ON, M5J 2H7

Emp Here 50   *Sales* 4,742,446
SIC 6531 Real estate agents and managers

D-U-N-S 24-344-7559   (BR)
BENTALL KENNEDY (CANADA) LIMITED PARTNERSHIP
1 York St Suite 1100, Toronto, ON, M5J 2L9
(416) 681-3400
Emp Here 150
SIC 6531 Real estate agents and managers

D-U-N-S 25-991-6484   (BR)
BLUE TREE HOTELS INVESTMENT (CANADA), LTD
WESTIN HARBOUR CASTLE
Westin Harbour Castle, Toronto, ON, M5J 1A6
(416) 869-1600
Emp Here 750
SIC 7011 Hotels and motels

D-U-N-S 20-818-5942   (SL)
BOSTON CONSULTING GROUP OF CANADA LIMITED, THE
(*Suby of* The Boston Consulting Group Inc)
181 Bay St Suite 2400, Toronto, ON, M5J 2T3
(416) 955-4200
Emp Here 125   *Sales* 16,197,275
SIC 8741 Management services
Peter Stanger
VP VP George Stalk
VP VP David Pecaut
VP VP Joe Manget
Pr Hans-Paul Buerknar

D-U-N-S 24-130-7326   (SL)
BRANDES U.S. SMALL CAP EQUITY FUND
20 Bay St Suite 400, Toronto, ON, M5J 2N8
(416) 306-5700
Emp Here 49   *Sales* 20,290,000
SIC 6722 Management investment, open-end
Genl Mgr Carol Lynde

D-U-N-S 20-284-9071   (SL)
BRIDGEHOUSE ASSET MANAGERS
20 Bay St Suite 400, Toronto, ON, M5J 2N8
(416) 306-5700
Emp Here 50   *Sales* 20,695,800
SIC 6722 Management investment, open-end
CEO Oliver Murray

D-U-N-S 24-805-6413   (HQ)
BROOKFIELD PROPERTIES (CDHI) LTD
181 Bay St Suite 330, Toronto, ON, M5J 2T3

(416) 363-9491
Emp Here 90   *Emp Total* 55,700
Sales 73,030,498
SIC 6531 Real estate agents and managers
Pr Jan Sucharda
VP VP Keith Hyde
VP Michelle Campbell
Bryan Davis
Brett Fox

D-U-N-S 24-120-4432   (BR)
BROOKFIELD PROPERTIES LTD
BROOKFIELD PLACE MANAGEMENT OFFICE
181 Bay St Suite 220, Toronto, ON, M5J 2T3
(416) 777-6480
Emp Here 20
SIC 6531 Real estate agents and managers

D-U-N-S 24-859-6819   (HQ)
BROOKFIELD PROPERTIES LTD
181 Bay St Suite 330, Toronto, ON, M5J 2T3
(416) 369-2300
Emp Here 100   *Emp Total* 55,700
Sales 270,703,438
SIC 6512 Nonresidential building operators
Pr Pr Richard Clark
Gordon Arnell
John Zuccotti
Samuel Pollock
William Wheaton
Bruce Flatt
Jack Cockwell
Lance Liebman
Robert Mccaig
Paul Mcfarlane

D-U-N-S 20-139-7028   (BR)
BROOKFIELD RESIDENTIAL SERVICES LTD
NUMBER ONE YORK QUAY
99 Harbour Sq Suite 77, Toronto, ON, M5J 2H2
(416) 203-2004
Emp Here 20
SIC 6531 Real estate agents and managers

D-U-N-S 20-410-2917   (HQ)
CIBC WORLD MARKETS INC
161 Bay St Suite 700, Toronto, ON, M5J 2S1
(416) 594-7000
Emp Here 50   *Emp Total* 44,000
Sales 433,125,500
SIC 6211 Security brokers and dealers
Pr Pr Gary Brown
Scott Bere
Richard Venn

D-U-N-S 20-522-2891   (BR)
CIBC WORLD MARKETS INC
CIBC WOOD GUNDY
22 Front St W Suite 700, Toronto, ON, M5J 2W5
(416) 956-3766
Emp Here 20
SIC 6211 Security brokers and dealers

D-U-N-S 20-152-9737   (BR)
CIBC WORLD MARKETS INC
CIBC WOOD GUNDY
181 Bay St Suite 600, Toronto, ON, M5J 2T3
(416) 369-8100
Emp Here 65
SIC 6211 Security brokers and dealers

D-U-N-S 25-483-1985   (BR)
CIBC WORLD MARKETS INC
COPY CENTRE, DIV OF
161 Bay St Suite 400, Toronto, ON, M5J 2S8
(416) 594-7312
Emp Here 30
SIC 2759 Commercial printing, nec

D-U-N-S 25-406-4413   (HQ)
CIT FINANCIAL LTD
CIT ENERGY AND INFRASTRUCTURE, CANADA
207 Queens Quay W Suite 700, Toronto, ON,

M5J 1A7
(416) 507-2400
Emp Here 300   *Emp Total* 4,080
Sales 3,102,824,457
SIC 6153 Short-term business credit institutions, except agricultural

D-U-N-S 25-320-7849   (HQ)
CANADA LANDS COMPANY CLC LIMITED
CN TOWER
1 University Ave Suite 1200, Toronto, ON, M5J 2P1
(416) 952-6100
Emp Here 40   *Emp Total* 570,000
Sales 42,900,892
SIC 6531 Real estate agents and managers
Pr John Mcbain
  Matthew Topscott
  Neil Jones
Pers/VP Teresa Law
VP Rodger Martin
VP Basil Cavis
Sec Greg Barker
  Grant Walsh
  Clint Hames

D-U-N-S 20-587-2067   (BR)
CANADIAN IMPERIAL BANK OF COMMERCE
CIBC
20 Bay St Suite 416, Toronto, ON, M5J 2N8
(416) 980-3699
Emp Here 20
SIC 6021 National commercial banks

D-U-N-S 20-181-2901   (BR)
CANADIAN PACIFIC RAILWAY COMPANY
AVENDRA
70 York St Suite 1200, Toronto, ON, M5J 1S9

Emp Here 20
SIC 7011 Hotels and motels

D-U-N-S 20-514-3048   (BR)
CANADIAN PACIFIC RAILWAY COMPANY
CPR
40 University Ave Suite 200, Toronto, ON, M5J 1T1
(705) 233-2898
Emp Here 90
SIC 4011 Railroads, line-haul operating

D-U-N-S 24-720-2849   (BR)
CARLSON WAGONLIT CANADA
CARLSON WAGONLIT TRAVEL
40 University Ave Suite 1100, Toronto, ON, M5J 1T1

Emp Here 50
SIC 4724 Travel agencies

D-U-N-S 25-852-7688   (HQ)
CENTERRA GOLD INC
(*Suby of* Centerra Gold Inc)
1 University Ave Suite 1500, Toronto, ON, M5J 2P1
(416) 204-1241
Emp Here 50   *Emp Total* 2,582
Sales 760,758,000
SIC 1081 Metal mining services
  Scott Perry
Pr Frank Herbert
  Gordon Reid
  Darren Millman
VP Dennis Kwong
  Stephen Lang
  Bruce Walter
  Sheryl Pressler
  Terry Rogers
  Richard Connor

D-U-N-S 20-914-6492   (BR)
CIGNA LIFE INSURANCE COMPANY OF CANADA
CHUBB INSURANCE COMPANY OF CANADA
(*Suby of* Cigna Corporation)

25 York St Suite 1400, Toronto, ON, M5J 2V5
(416) 368-2911
Emp Here 150
SIC 6321 Accident and health insurance

D-U-N-S 24-877-1776   (HQ)
CISCO SYSTEMS CANADA CO
(*Suby of* Cisco Systems, Inc.)
88 Queens Quay W Suite 2700, Toronto, ON, M5J 0B8
(416) 306-7000
Emp Here 200   *Emp Total* 71,858
Sales 60,265,538
SIC 5065 Electronic parts and equipment, nec
Pr Nitin Kawale
  Lui Fogolini
  Pierre Paul Allard
  John P Mogridge

D-U-N-S 24-873-3479   (SL)
CITICAPITAL LIMITED
123 Front St W Suite 1500, Toronto, ON, M5J 2M3
(800) 991-4046
Emp Here 42   *Sales* 5,034,288
SIC 6159 Miscellaneous business credit institutions
VP VP John Maydanski
VP Fin Don Jenkin

D-U-N-S 24-985-0454   (HQ)
CITICORP VENDOR FINANCE, LTD
CITICAPITAL
123 Front St W Suite 1500, Toronto, ON, M5J 2M3
(800) 991-4046
Emp Here 82   *Emp Total* 231,000
Sales 11,017,066
SIC 6159 Miscellaneous business credit institutions
Pr Steve Klein
Crdt Mgr Michael Lin

D-U-N-S 24-952-7375   (HQ)
CITIGROUP GLOBAL MARKETS CANADA INC
161 Bay St Suite 4600, Toronto, ON, M5J 2S1
(416) 866-2300
Emp Here 39   *Emp Total* 231,000
Sales 5,836,856
SIC 6211 Security brokers and dealers
Pr Pr Robert J Gemmell
  Stanley Hartt

D-U-N-S 24-859-0965   (SL)
COMMONWEALTH
(*Suby of* The Interpublic Group of Companies Inc)
10 Bay St Suite 1300, Toronto, ON, M5J 2R8
(416) 594-6774
Emp Here 435   *Sales* 72,638,200
SIC 7311 Advertising agencies
Fin Ex Tracie Ma

D-U-N-S 20-180-5640   (HQ)
COMMONWEALTH LEGAL INC
RICOH CANADA, DIV OF
145 Wellington St W Suite 901, Toronto, ON, M5J 1H8
(416) 703-3755
Emp Here 40   *Emp Total* 240
Sales 5,982,777
SIC 8111 Legal services
Pr Pr Karen Brookman
Dir Martin Felsky

D-U-N-S 25-115-7004   (HQ)
COMPUTERSHARE TRUST COMPANY OF CANADA
100 University Ave Suite 800, Toronto, ON, M5J 2Y1
(416) 263-9200
Emp Here 400   *Emp Total* 17,839
Sales 207,792,074
SIC 6733 Trusts, nec
Pr Pr Wayne Newling
VP Fin Sharon Tulloch
VP VP Lindsay Horwood

Dir Paul H Farrar
Dir William Braithwaite
Dir Robert Fairweather
Dir Brian Puckier
Dir Hector Mcfadyen
Dir Steve Rothbloom

D-U-N-S 24-816-7272   (BR)
CRAWFORD & COMPANY (CANADA) INC
CRAWFORD ADJUSTERS CANADA
(*Suby of* Crawford & Company)
123 Front St W Suite 300, Toronto, ON, M5J 2M2
(416) 867-1188
Emp Here 70
SIC 6411 Insurance agents, brokers, and service

D-U-N-S 24-857-2625   (SL)
CRITERION GLOBAL DIVIDEND FUND
95 Wellington St W Suite 1400, Toronto, ON, M5J 2N7
(416) 642-5998
Emp Here 25   *Sales* 10,347,900
SIC 6722 Management investment, open-end
  Robert Macniven

D-U-N-S 20-077-3583   (BR)
CUNNINGHAM LINDSEY CANADA LIMITED
70 University Ave Suite 1000, Toronto, ON, M5J 2M4
(416) 596-8020
Emp Here 25
SIC 6411 Insurance agents, brokers, and service

D-U-N-S 20-547-4120   (HQ)
D+H LIMITED PARTNERSHIP
DAVIS HENDERSON INTERCHEQUES
120 Bremner Blvd 30th Fl, Toronto, ON, M5J 0A8
(416) 696-7700
Emp Here 500   *Emp Total* 5,500
Sales 393,987,780
SIC 6211 Security brokers and dealers
Pr Pr Gerrard Schmid
  Paul Damp
Ex VP Young Park
VP Fin Brian Kyle
VP Opers Yves Denomme
Pers/VP Bob Noftall
  David Caldwell

D-U-N-S 20-772-6779   (HQ)
DTZ BARNICKE LIMITED
161 Bay St Suite 4040, Toronto, ON, M5J 2S1
(416) 863-1215
Emp Here 40   *Emp Total* 4
Sales 27,979,907
SIC 6531 Real estate agents and managers
Pr Pr Christopher Ridabock
Pr Colin Ross
CFO Laurie Mcgee
  Thomas Mccarthy

D-U-N-S 24-376-4029   (SL)
DATA & AUDIO-VISUAL ENTERPRISES HOLDINGS INC
MOBILICITY
161 Bay St Suite 2300, Toronto, ON, M5J 2S1
(416) 361-1959
Emp Here 200   *Sales* 45,349,920
SIC 6712 Bank holding companies
Dir John Bitove
Dir Frank Penny
Dir Stewart Lyons

D-U-N-S 20-790-6736   (HQ)
DELOITTE & TOUCHE MANAGEMENT CONSULTANTS
(*Suby of* Deloitte & Touche Management Consultants)
181 Bay St Suite 1400, Toronto, ON, M5J 2V1
(416) 601-6150
Emp Here 120   *Emp Total* 338
Sales 60,497,522
SIC 8741 Management services

  Kate Peacock

D-U-N-S 24-355-8710   (SL)
DIGITAL WYZDOM INC
161 Bay St 27 Fl, Toronto, ON, M5J 2S1
(416) 304-3934
Emp Here 88   *Sales* 6,695,700
SIC 7375 Information retrieval services
Pr Pr Daniel Tobok

D-U-N-S 24-564-5437   (HQ)
DUMAS CONTRACTING LTD
DUMAS MINING
200 Bay St Suite 2301, Toronto, ON, M5J 2J1
(416) 594-2525
Emp Here 20   *Sales* 110,706,878
SIC 1081 Metal mining services
Dir Daniel Dumas
  Steven Chambers
VP Wayne Mohns
VP Larry Zuccherato
VP Michael Psihogios
CFO Steven Chambers

D-U-N-S 24-194-2184   (BR)
EGON ZEHNDER INTERNATIONAL INC
181 Bay St Suite 3920, Toronto, ON, M5J 2T3
(416) 364-0222
Emp Here 26
SIC 8741 Management services

D-U-N-S 25-351-4905   (SL)
ENTRO COMMUNICATIONS INC
33 Harbour Sq Suite 202, Toronto, ON, M5J 2G2
(416) 368-6988
Emp Here 50   *Sales* 3,064,349
SIC 3993 Signs and advertising specialties

D-U-N-S 20-912-2543   (BR)
FAIRFAX FINANCIAL HOLDINGS LIMITED
95 Wellington Street West Suite 800, Toronto, ON, M5J 2N7
(416) 367-4941
Emp Here 50
SIC 6411 Insurance agents, brokers, and service

D-U-N-S 24-813-5696   (SL)
FRAGOMEN (CANADA) CO
55 York St Suite 1500, Toronto, ON, M5J 1R7
(416) 504-3838
Emp Here 49   *Sales* 4,231,721
SIC 8111 Legal services

D-U-N-S 24-152-5414   (HQ)
GENIVAR CONSTRUCTION LTD
60 Harbour St, Toronto, ON, M5J 1B7
(416) 977-9666
Emp Here 30   *Emp Total* 15,000
Sales 4,058,000
SIC 8741 Management services

D-U-N-S 25-405-4349   (SL)
GEORGESON SHAREHOLDER COMMUNICATIONS CANADA INC
100 University Ave Unit 1100, Toronto, ON, M5J 1V6
(416) 862-8088
Emp Here 50   *Sales* 2,626,585
SIC 7389 Business services, nec

D-U-N-S 24-796-1910   (SL)
GEOSOFT INC
207 Queens Quay W Suite 810, Toronto, ON, M5J 1A7
(416) 369-0111
Emp Here 49   *Sales* 6,313,604
SIC 7372 Prepackaged software
Pr Tim Dobush

D-U-N-S 24-489-1271   (BR)
GESTION D'ACTIFS CIBC INC
CIBC
161 Bay St Suite 2320, Toronto, ON, M5J 2S1
(416) 364-5620
Emp Here 60
SIC 6726 Investment offices, nec

▲ Public Company   ■ Public Company Family Member   **HQ** Headquarters   **BR** Branch   **SL** Single Location

D-U-N-S 24-689-0276 (BR)
GOODLIFE FITNESS CENTRES INC
GOOD LIFE FITNESS CLUBS
7 Station St, Toronto, ON, M5J 1C3
(416) 964-1821
Emp Here 20
SIC 7991 Physical fitness facilities

D-U-N-S 24-947-9171 (BR)
GRANARD MANAGEMENT LIMITED PART-NERSHIP
181 Bay St Suite 3300, Toronto, ON, M5J 2T3
(416) 864-0829
Emp Here 22
SIC 8111 Legal services

D-U-N-S 25-839-3313 (SL)
GREAT LAKES SCHOONER COMPANY LIMITED
249 Queens Quay W Suite 111, Toronto, ON, M5J 2N5
(416) 260-6355
Emp Here 55   *Sales* 2,480,664
SIC 4489 Water passenger transportation

D-U-N-S 20-784-4471 (SL)
GUY CARPENTER & COMPANY LTD
(*Suby of* Marsh & McLennan Companies, Inc.)
120 Bremner Blvd Suite 800, Toronto, ON, M5J 0A8
(416) 979-0123
Emp Here 23   *Sales* 2,638,521
SIC 6411 Insurance agents, brokers, and service

D-U-N-S 24-910-6832 (BR)
HSBC BANK CANADA
70 York St Suite 800, Toronto, ON, M5J 1S9
(416) 868-8000
Emp Here 300
SIC 6021 National commercial banks

D-U-N-S 20-526-8196 (HQ)
HSBC SECURITIES (CANADA) INC
HSBC INVESTDIRECT
70 York St, Toronto, ON, M5J 1S9
(416) 947-2700
Emp Here 75   *Emp Total* 284,186
Sales 19,577,273
SIC 6211 Security brokers and dealers
Pr Simon Edwards
Dir Youssef Nasr
Dir Mac Nisker
Dir James O'donnell
Dir Brian Robertson
Ex VP Randy Ambroise
Dir Donald Pangman
Dir George Hartman
Dir Douglas Pocock
Dir Frank Mayer

D-U-N-S 25-116-1204 (BR)
HSBC SECURITIES (CANADA) INC
HSBC
70 York St Suite 800, Toronto, ON, M5J 1S9
(416) 868-8000
Emp Here 110
SIC 6211 Security brokers and dealers

D-U-N-S 20-849-7818 (HQ)
HALF, ROBERT CANADA INC
ACCOUNTEMPS, DIV OF
(*Suby of* Robert Half International Inc.)
181 Bay St Suite 820, Toronto, ON, M5J 2T3
(416) 203-7656
Emp Here 375   *Emp Total* 16,400
Sales 43,312,550
SIC 7361 Employment agencies
 Greg Scileppi
Dir David King

D-U-N-S 24-815-8305 (SL)
HAMBLIN, WATSA INVESTMENT COUNSEL LTD
95 Wellington St W Suite 802, Toronto, ON, M5J 2N7
(416) 366-9544
Emp Here 20   *Sales* 4,815,406

SIC 6282 Investment advice

D-U-N-S 20-321-5082 (BR)
HAYWOOD SECURITIES INC
181 Bay St Unit 2910, Toronto, ON, M5J 2T3
(416) 507-2300
Emp Here 50
SIC 6211 Security brokers and dealers

D-U-N-S 20-700-7647 (SL)
HEMLO PROPERTY
161 Bay St, Toronto, ON, M5J 2S1
(416) 861-9911
Emp Here 50   *Sales* 7,536,000
SIC 1041 Gold ores
Pr Pr Gregory C. Wilkins

D-U-N-S 20-081-1755 (SL)
HENIN BLAKEY
Po Box 185 Stn Royal Bank, Toronto, ON, M5J 2J4

Emp Here 49   *Sales* 5,693,280
SIC 8111 Legal services
Genl Mgr Daryl Craig

D-U-N-S 20-912-6940 (SL)
HOWSON TATTERSALL INVESTMENT COUNSEL LIM
MUTUAL FUNDS
70 University Ave Suite 1100, Toronto, ON, M5J 2M4

Emp Here 48   *Sales* 16,029,100
SIC 6282 Investment advice

D-U-N-S 25-991-5478 (SL)
INDEPENDENT LEARNING CENTER
20 Bay St Suite 600, Toronto, ON, M5J 2W3
(416) 484-2704
Emp Here 75   *Sales* 2,858,628
SIC 8249 Vocational schools, nec

D-U-N-S 24-771-4298 (HQ)
INNVEST PROPERTIES CORP
(*Suby of* Innvest Properties Corp)
200 Bay St Suite 2200, Toronto, ON, M5J 2J2
(416) 607-7100
Emp Here 70   *Emp Total* 4,500
Sales 196,993,890
SIC 7011 Hotels and motels
Pr Anthony Messiana
 George Koszwika

D-U-N-S 20-269-0038 (BR)
INTERPUBLIC GROUP OF COMPANIES CANADA, INC, THE
UM CANADA
(*Suby of* The Interpublic Group of Companies Inc)
207 Queens Quay W Suite 2, Toronto, ON, M5J 1A7
(647) 260-2116
Emp Here 105
SIC 7336 Commercial art and graphic design

D-U-N-S 25-598-1730 (BR)
IVANHOE CAMBRIDGE INC
IVANHOE CAMBRIDGE INC
95 Wellington St W Suite 300, Toronto, ON, M5J 2R2
(416) 369-1200
Emp Here 150
SIC 6719 Holding companies, nec

D-U-N-S 25-398-9313 (BR)
JARDINE LLOYD THOMPSON CANADA INC
JLT CANADA
55 University Ave Suite 800, Toronto, ON, M5J 2H7
(416) 941-9551
Emp Here 60
SIC 6411 Insurance agents, brokers, and service

D-U-N-S 24-337-5099 (BR)
KINROSS GOLD CORPORATION
25 York St Suite 17, Toronto, ON, M5J 2V5

(416) 365-5123
Emp Here 49
SIC 1041 Gold ores

D-U-N-S 20-295-7569 (SL)
KOODO MOBILE
25 York St Suite 1900, Toronto, ON, M5J 2V5
(647) 454-5286
Emp Here 125   *Sales* 26,110,560
SIC 4899 Communication services, nec
Pr Kevin Banderk

D-U-N-S 24-368-9135 (HQ)
KORN/FERRY INTERNATIONAL, FUTURESTEP (CANADA) INC
181 Bay St Suite 3810, Toronto, ON, M5J 2T3
(416) 342-5182
Emp Here 20   *Emp Total* 6,947
Sales 3,957,782
SIC 7361 Employment agencies

D-U-N-S 24-888-1450 (SL)
LARGO RESOURCES LTD
55 University Ave Suite 1101, Toronto, ON, M5J 2H7
(416) 861-9797
Emp Here 333   *Sales* 60,083,582
SIC 1094 Uranium-radium-vanadium ores
Pr Pr Mark Brennan
 Ernest Cleave
VP Robert Campbell
VP Luciano Chaves
 Alberto Arias
 Daniel Tellechea
 David Brace
 Alberto Beeck
 Sam Abraham
 Koko Yamamoto

D-U-N-S 24-171-9686 (BR)
MACQUARIE CAPITAL MARKETS CANADA LTD
181 Bay St Suite 900, Toronto, ON, M5J 2T3
(416) 848-3500
Emp Here 125
SIC 6211 Security brokers and dealers

D-U-N-S 20-921-3370 (HQ)
MACQUARIE CAPITAL MARKETS CANADA LTD
181 Bay St Suite 3100, Toronto, ON, M5J 2T3
(416) 848-3500
Emp Here 100   *Emp Total* 13,500
Sales 21,656,275
SIC 6211 Security brokers and dealers
Pr Pr John Budreski
Dir Fin Chris Salapoutis

D-U-N-S 20-026-0409 (HQ)
MACQUARIE NORTH AMERICA LTD
MACQUARIE CAPITAL MARKETS CANADA
181 Bay St Suite 3100, Toronto, ON, M5J 2T3
(416) 607-5000
Emp Here 59   *Emp Total* 13,500
Sales 9,995,616
SIC 8742 Management consulting services
Dir Gregory Smith
Dir Michael Bernstein
 David Fleck
 Nicholas Hann
 Matthew Rady

D-U-N-S 24-768-9768 (BR)
MAPLE LEAF SPORTS & ENTERTAINMENT LTD
MAPLE LEAF SPORTS & ENTERTAINMENT PARTNERSHIP
40 Bay St Suite 300, Toronto, ON, M5J 2X2
(416) 815-5400
Emp Here 50
SIC 7941 Sports clubs, managers, and promoters

D-U-N-S 20-300-1458 (SL)
MARQUEST CANADIAN EQUITY INCOME FUND
161 Bay St Suite 4420, Toronto, ON, M5J 2S1

(416) 777-7350
Emp Here 20   *Sales* 8,318,900
SIC 6722 Management investment, open-end
Genl Mgr Gerry Brocksby

D-U-N-S 20-769-5347 (HQ)
MARSH CANADA LIMITED
(*Suby of* Marsh & McLennan Companies, Inc.)
120 Bremner Blvd Suite 800, Toronto, ON, M5J 0A8
(416) 868-2600
Emp Here 500   *Emp Total* 60,000
Sales 106,895,373
SIC 6411 Insurance agents, brokers, and service
Pr Alan Garner
V Ch Bd Peter Cleyn
VP Fin VP Fin James Abernethy

D-U-N-S 25-687-1799 (BR)
MARSH CANADA LIMITED
(*Suby of* Marsh & McLennan Companies, Inc.)
120 Bremner Blvd Suite 800, Toronto, ON, M5J 0A8
(416) 349-4700
Emp Here 250
SIC 6411 Insurance agents, brokers, and service

D-U-N-S 20-412-5777 (HQ)
MCKAY, W. G. LIMITED
(*Suby of* McKay, W. G. Limited)
40 University Ave Suite 602, Toronto, ON, M5J 1T1
(416) 593-1380
Emp Here 35   *Emp Total* 65
Sales 16,051,354
SIC 4731 Freight transportation arrangement
 Winfield C Mckay
Pr Pr Winfield L Mckay
VP VP Ken Tracy
VP Opers Cheryl D Dottin
 Noreen Mckay

D-U-N-S 24-425-6269 (SL)
MELLOY MANAGEMENT LIMITED
95 Wellington St W Suite 1200, Toronto, ON, M5J 2Z9
(416) 864-9700
Emp Here 150   *Sales* 26,699,520
SIC 8741 Management services
Genl Mgr Karen Schremps

D-U-N-S 24-126-9401 (BR)
MERCER (CANADA) LIMITED
(*Suby of* Marsh & McLennan Companies, Inc.)
70 University Ave Suite 900, Toronto, ON, M5J 2M4
(416) 868-2000
Emp Here 100
SIC 8742 Management consulting services

D-U-N-S 20-731-5169 (HQ)
MERRILL LYNCH CANADA INC
MERRILL LYNCH FUTURES
(*Suby of* Bank of America Corporation)
181 Bay St Suite 400, Toronto, ON, M5J 2V8
(416) 369-7400
Emp Here 200   *Emp Total* 208,000
Sales 43,776,420
SIC 6211 Security brokers and dealers
Pr Pr Lynn Paterson
 Mark Dickerson

D-U-N-S 24-367-4376 (BR)
METROLINX
GO TRANSIT
20 Bay St Suite 901, Toronto, ON, M5J 2N8
(416) 874-5900
Emp Here 500
SIC 4011 Railroads, line-haul operating

D-U-N-S 25-352-3948 (HQ)
MODIS CANADA INC
10 Bay St Suite 700, Toronto, ON, M5J 2R8
(416) 367-2020
Emp Here 80   *Emp Total* 576
Sales 13,188,500

SIC 7361 Employment agencies
Lynn Bouchard
Dir Nicolette Mueller
Dir Fin Rakesh Das

D-U-N-S 25-318-3529   (SL)
MOODY'S CANADA INC
MOODY'S INVESTORS SERVICE
(*Suby of* Moody's Corporation)
70 York St Suite 1400, Toronto, ON, M5J 1S9
(416) 214-1635
Emp Here 30   *Sales* 1,532,175
SIC 7323 Credit reporting services

D-U-N-S 24-356-8396   (BR)
MOORE CANADA CORPORATION
(*Suby of* R. R. Donnelley & Sons Company)
220 Bay St Suite 200, Toronto, ON, M5J 2W4
(416) 599-0011
Emp Here 25
SIC 2761 Manifold business forms

D-U-N-S 20-013-0784   (BR)
MUGGS, J J INC
HARBOUR SIXTY STEAK HOUSE
(*Suby of* Muggs, J J Inc)
60 Harbour St, Toronto, ON, M5J 1B7
(416) 777-2111
Emp Here 50
SIC 5812 Eating places

D-U-N-S 25-360-0803   (BR)
NATIONAL FILM BOARD OF CANADA
ONTARIO STUDIO
145 Wellington St Suite 1010, Toronto, ON, M5J 1H8
(416) 973-5344
Emp Here 40
SIC 7812 Motion picture and video production

D-U-N-S 24-376-3955   (SL)
NERIUM BIOTECHNOLOGY, INC
220 Bay St Unit 500, Toronto, ON, M5J 2W4
(416) 862-7330
Emp Here 100   *Sales* 311,498
SIC 8731 Commercial physical research

D-U-N-S 25-318-5045   (HQ)
NORTHWATER CAPITAL MANAGEMENT INC
NORTHWATER
(*Suby of* Northwater Capital Inc)
181 Bay St Suite 4700, Toronto, ON, M5J 2T3
(416) 360-5435
Emp Here 60   *Emp Total* 100
Sales 27,331,840
SIC 6722 Management investment, open-end
David Patterson
Pr Paul Robson

D-U-N-S 24-326-4020   (BR)
NORTON ROSE FULBRIGHT CANADA S.E.N.C.R.L., S.R.L.
200 Bay St Suite 3800, Toronto, ON, M5J 2Z4
(416) 216-4000
Emp Here 300
SIC 8111 Legal services

D-U-N-S 24-394-1874   (BR)
OXFORD PROPERTIES GROUP INC
200 Bay St Suite 1305, Toronto, ON, M5J 2J1
(416) 865-8300
Emp Here 30
SIC 6531 Real estate agents and managers

D-U-N-S 20-639-6756   (HQ)
OXFORD PROPERTIES GROUP INC
200 Bay St Suite 900, Toronto, ON, M5J 2J2
(416) 865-8300
Emp Here 100   *Emp Total* 2,500
Sales 118,561,138
SIC 6512 Nonresidential building operators
Pr Blake Hutcheson
Colin Loudon
Ex VP Robert Aziz
Ex VP Michael Kitt
VP Ann Clavelle

D-U-N-S 25-517-4492   (BR)
OXFORD PROPERTIES GROUP INC
WATERPARK PLACE
10 Bay St Suite 810, Toronto, ON, M5J 2R8
(416) 360-4611
Emp Here 20
SIC 6512 Nonresidential building operators

D-U-N-S 20-698-4515   (HQ)
PARAMOUNT PICTURES ENTERTAINMENT CANADA INC
PARAMOUNT HOME ENTERTAINMENT (DIV)
40 University Ave Suite 900, Toronto, ON, M5J 1T1
(416) 969-9901
Emp Here 29   *Emp Total* 9,200
Sales 4,523,563
SIC 3651 Household audio and video equipment

D-U-N-S 20-706-6098   (SL)
PEOPLES FINANCIAL CORPORATION
95 Wellington St W Suite 915, Toronto, ON, M5J 2N7
(416) 861-1315
Emp Here 100   *Sales* 23,639,267
SIC 6162 Mortgage bankers and loan correspondents
Pr Pr Grant Mackenzie
Dir Frank Ganis
Dir Mike Barrett

D-U-N-S 20-692-1921   (SL)
PERIMETER FINANCIAL CORP
PERIMETER MARKETS
(*Suby of* CI Financial Corp)
15 York St Suite 200, Toronto, ON, M5J 0A3
(416) 703-7800
Emp Here 25   *Sales* 2,772,003
SIC 8742 Management consulting services

D-U-N-S 24-350-4037   (SL)
PINNACLE CATERERS LTD
40 Bay St Suite 300, Toronto, ON, M5J 2X2
(416) 815-5720
Emp Here 100   *Sales* 2,991,389
SIC 5812 Eating places

D-U-N-S 24-892-8509   (SL)
POWER PLANT CONTEMPORARY ART GALLERY, THE
THE POWER PLANT
231 Queens Quay W, Toronto, ON, M5J 2G8
(416) 973-4949
Emp Here 25   *Sales* 1,896,978
SIC 8412 Museums and art galleries

D-U-N-S 20-104-3507   (HQ)
PRESIDENT'S CHOICE BANK
PRESIDENTS CHOICE FINANCIAL
25 York St Suite 7fl, Toronto, ON, M5J 2V5
(416) 204-2600
Emp Here 62   *Emp Total* 138,000
Sales 26,995,459
SIC 8742 Management consulting services
Pr Pr Donald Reid
Anthony Graham
Sr VP David Boone
VP Fin Kevin Lengyell
VP VP Lisa Swartzman

D-U-N-S 20-077-3872   (BR)
PRICEWATERHOUSECOOPERS LLP
18 York St Suite 2600, Toronto, ON, M5J 0B2
(416) 869-1130
Emp Here 20
SIC 8721 Accounting, auditing, and bookkeeping

D-U-N-S 25-693-4894   (BR)
PRIME RESTAURANTS INC
CASEY'S
(*Suby of* Cara Holdings Limited)
123 Front St W, Toronto, ON, M5J 2M2

Emp Here 60
SIC 5812 Eating places

D-U-N-S 25-509-2769   (SL)
QUALCOMM ATHEROS CANADA CORPORATION
QCA CANADA
144 Front St W Suite 385, Toronto, ON, M5J 2L7

Emp Here 50   *Sales* 3,392,384
SIC 7389 Business services, nec

D-U-N-S 20-764-9351   (HQ)
RBC CAPITAL MARKETS REAL ESTATE GROUP INC
(*Suby of* Royal Bank Of Canada)
200 Bay St, Toronto, ON, M5J 2W7
(416) 842-8900
Emp Here 20   *Emp Total* 79,000
Sales 5,630,632
SIC 6159 Miscellaneous business credit institutions
Pr Mark Standish
Doug Mcgregor

D-U-N-S 20-561-2849   (HQ)
RBC DOMINION SECURITIES INC
RBC CAPITAL MARKETS
(*Suby of* Royal Bank Of Canada)
200 Bay St, Toronto, ON, M5J 2W7
(416) 842-2000
Emp Here 1,000   *Emp Total* 79,000
Sales 1,507,016,865
SIC 6282 Investment advice
Anthony Fell
Dir David John Agnew
Dir A. Douglas Mcgregor
Dir Wayne Bossert
Dir V. Troy Maxwell
Donald Bruce Macdonald

D-U-N-S 24-365-4741   (BR)
RBC INVESTOR SERVICES TRUST
(*Suby of* Royal Bank Of Canada)
200 Bay St, Toronto, ON, M5J 2J5

Emp Here 100
SIC 6282 Investment advice

D-U-N-S 20-787-0403   (BR)
READ JONES CHRISTOFFERSEN LTD
RJC
144 Front St W Suite 500, Toronto, ON, M5J 2L7
(416) 977-5335
Emp Here 60
SIC 8711 Engineering services

D-U-N-S 20-026-1118   (BR)
RICHTREE MARKET RESTAURANTS INC
MARCHELINO RESTAURANT MOVENPICK
181 Bay St Suite 867, Toronto, ON, M5J 2T3
(416) 366-8122
Emp Here 20
SIC 5812 Eating places

D-U-N-S 20-700-7597   (SL)
ROMANEX INTERNATIONAL LIMITED
161 Bay St Suite 3700, Toronto, ON, M5J 2S1
(416) 861-9911
Emp Here 50   *Sales* 7,362,000
SIC 1041 Gold ores
Pr Pr J Michael Kenyon

D-U-N-S 20-524-7372   (HQ)
ROYAL BANK OF CANADA
(*Suby of* Royal Bank Of Canada)
200 Bay St, Toronto, ON, M5J 2J5
(416) 974-3940
Emp Here 500   *Emp Total* 79,000
Sales 20,724,267,953
SIC 6021 National commercial banks
Pr Pr David Mckay
Rod Bolger
Kathleen P. Taylor
David Denison
Richard George
Alice D. Laberge
Michael H. Mccain

Heather Munroe-Blum
Bridget Van Kralingen
Andrew Chisholm

D-U-N-S 20-333-2952   (BR)
ROYAL BANK OF CANADA
RBC AUTOMOTIVE FINANCE
(*Suby of* Royal Bank Of Canada)
88 Queens Quay W Suite 300, Toronto, ON, M5J 0B8
(416) 313-5378
Emp Here 150
SIC 6021 National commercial banks

D-U-N-S 24-828-6577   (SL)
ROYAL BANK VENTURES INC
(*Suby of* Royal Bank Of Canada)
200 Bay St, Toronto, ON, M5J 2J5
(416) 974-2493
Emp Here 30   *Sales* 8,489,260
SIC 6282 Investment advice
Peter Currie

D-U-N-S 20-511-7315   (BR)
SAP CANADA INC
181 Bay St, Toronto, ON, M5J 2T3

Emp Here 20
SIC 7371 Custom computer programming services

D-U-N-S 20-877-1352   (HQ)
SEI INVESTMENTS CANADA COMPANY
(*Suby of* SEI Investments Company)
70 York St Suite 1600, Toronto, ON, M5J 1S9
(416) 777-9700
Emp Here 28   *Emp Total* 2,985
Sales 3,898,130
SIC 8741 Management services

D-U-N-S 20-938-0133   (BR)
SIR CORP
JACK ASTOR'S BAR AND GRILL
144 Front St W, Toronto, ON, M5J 2L7
(416) 585-2121
Emp Here 195
SIC 5812 Eating places

D-U-N-S 25-340-4586   (BR)
SECOND CUP LTD, THE
SECOND CUP, THE
145 Queens Quay W, Toronto, ON, M5J 2H4
(416) 203-7880
Emp Here 20
SIC 5812 Eating places

D-U-N-S 24-077-2087   (BR)
SERVICES DE GESTION QUANTUM LIMITEE, LES
55 University Ave Suite 950, Toronto, ON, M5J 2H7
(416) 366-3660
Emp Here 30
SIC 8741 Management services

D-U-N-S 24-556-7479   (BR)
SOBEYS CAPITAL INCORPORATED
SOBEY'S
207 Queens Quay W Suite 867, Toronto, ON, M5J 1A7
(416) 603-8689
Emp Here 25
SIC 5411 Grocery stores

D-U-N-S 24-130-3747   (SL)
SPROTT BULL/BEAR RSP
200 Bay St Suite 2700, Toronto, ON, M5J 2J1
(416) 943-6707
Emp Here 49   *Sales* 14,592,140
SIC 6722 Management investment, open-end
Owner Eric Sprott

D-U-N-S 24-248-0510   (BR)
STANDARD PARKING OF CANADA LTD
(*Suby of* Sp Plus Corporation)
181 Bay St Suite P1, Toronto, ON, M5J 2T3
(416) 777-6468
Emp Here 50

SIC 1799 Special trade contractors, nec

D-U-N-S 24-307-8763   (BR)
SUN LIFE ASSURANCE COMPANY OF CANADA
1 University Ave Suite 201, Toronto, ON, M5J 2P1
(416) 366-8771
Emp Here 40
SIC 6311 Life insurance

D-U-N-S 24-378-4217   (SL)
TDAM USA INC
(Suby of Toronto-Dominion Bank, The)
161 Bay St Suite 3200, Toronto, ON, M5J 2T2
(416) 982-6681
Emp Here 20   Sales 5,982,777
SIC 6722 Management investment, open-end
 Barbara Palk

D-U-N-S 20-328-3205   (BR)
TDL GROUP CORP, THE
TIM HORTONS
207 Queens Quay W, Toronto, ON, M5J 1A7
(416) 214-9474
Emp Here 30
SIC 5812 Eating places

D-U-N-S 24-911-2640   (HQ)
TERANET INC
(Suby of Teranet Inc)
123 Front St W Suite 700, Toronto, ON, M5J 2M2
(416) 360-5263
Emp Here 250   Emp Total 800
Sales 115,277,906
SIC 7371 Custom computer programming services
Pr Elgin Farewell
Sr VP Peter Vukanovich
VP Eduardo Alzamora
 Kerri Brass
VP Greg Kowal
Sec Agostino Russo
 Julia Reed
 Dennis Barnhart
 Ryan Doersam

D-U-N-S 25-663-3744   (BR)
TILLEY ENDURABLES, INC
207 Queens Quay W Suite 108, Toronto, ON, M5J 1A7
(416) 203-0463
Emp Here 20
SIC 5651 Family clothing stores

D-U-N-S 25-056-7633   (SL)
TORONTO CLUB
107 Wellington St W, Toronto, ON, M5J 1H1
(416) 362-2751
Emp Here 50   Sales 3,575,074
SIC 8641 Civic and social associations

D-U-N-S 20-698-7955   (BR)
TORONTO DISTRICT SCHOOL BOARD
ISLAND PUBLIC NATURAL SCIENCE SCHOOL
30 Centre Island Pk, Toronto, ON, M5J 2E9
(416) 393-1910
Emp Here 30
SIC 8211 Elementary and secondary schools

D-U-N-S 20-647-0536   (HQ)
TORONTO PORT AUTHORITY
PORTS TORONTO
60 Harbour St, Toronto, ON, M5J 1B7
(416) 203-6942
Emp Here 80   Emp Total 39,000
Sales 44,257,050
SIC 4581 Airports, flying fields, and services
Pr Geoffrey A. Wilson
VP Alan J. Paul
 Jeremy Adams
 G. Mark Curry
 Jan Innes
 Sean L. Morley
 Craig Rix
 Jim Ginou

Ch Bd Mark R Mcqueen

D-U-N-S 25-798-8592   (BR)
TORONTO-DOMINION BANK, THE
TD BANK
(Suby of Toronto-Dominion Bank, The)
70 University Ave Suite 1105, Toronto, ON, M5J 2M4
(416) 982-2322
Emp Here 25
SIC 6021 National commercial banks

D-U-N-S 25-172-3680   (SL)
TRILOGY RETAIL ENTERPRISES L.P
161 Bay St Suite 4900, Toronto, ON, M5J 2S1
(416) 943-4110
Emp Here 6,000   Sales 1,540,112,450
SIC 6712 Bank holding companies
Dir Heather Reisman
Dir Gerald Schwartz

D-U-N-S 25-167-2838   (HQ)
TRIOVEST REALTY ADVISORS INC
40 University Ave Suite 1200, Toronto, ON, M5J 1T1
(416) 362-0045
Emp Here 50   Emp Total 1,100
Sales 58,879,285
SIC 6531 Real estate agents and managers
Pr Vince Brown
 David Robins
 Yves-Andre Godon
 Scott Ball

D-U-N-S 24-873-8031   (HQ)
UBS GLOBAL ASSET MANAGEMENT (CANADA) INC
161 Bay St Suite 4000, Toronto, ON, M5J 2S1
(416) 681-5200
Emp Here 20   Emp Total 59,387
Sales 4,815,406
SIC 6282 Investment advice

D-U-N-S 24-327-6073   (HQ)
VALE CANADA LIMITED
200 Bay St Suite 1600, Toronto, ON, M5J 2K2
(416) 361-7511
Emp Here 200   Emp Total 10,534
Sales 1,441,411,589
SIC 1629 Heavy construction, nec
Pr Pr Peter Poppinga
 Roberto Moretzsohn
 Jennifer Maki
 Mark Travers

D-U-N-S 24-142-0371   (BR)
VIA RAIL CANADA INC
65 Front St W Suite 222, Toronto, ON, M5J 1E6
(888) 842-7245
Emp Here 600
SIC 4111 Local and suburban transit

D-U-N-S 20-988-6840   (SL)
WATTS' GROUP LIMITED
156 Front St W Suite 610, Toronto, ON, M5J 2L6
(416) 755-1374
Emp Here 120   Sales 3,648,035
SIC 5812 Eating places

D-U-N-S 20-786-9801   (HQ)
YOLLES PARTNERSHIP INC
YOLLES, CH2M HILL COMPANY
(Suby of Ch2m Hill Companies, Ltd.)
207 Queens Quay W Suite 550, Toronto, ON, M5J 1A7
(416) 363-8123
Emp Here 220   Emp Total 22,000
Sales 33,358,447
SIC 8711 Engineering services
Dir Eric Gordon

D-U-N-S 25-093-4325   (SL)
ISHARES DEX ALL CORPORATE BOND INDEX FUND
161 Bay St Suite 2500, Toronto, ON, M5J 2S1
(866) 486-4874
Emp Here 200   Sales 81,991,680

SIC 6722 Management investment, open-end
Pt Larry Fink

Toronto, ON M5K
York County

D-U-N-S 20-560-1250   (SL)
2004995 ONTARIO LIMITED
BYMARK RESTAURANT & BAR
66 Wellington St W, Toronto, ON, M5K 1J3
(416) 777-1144
Emp Here 65   Sales 1,969,939
SIC 5812 Eating places

D-U-N-S 24-423-8648   (SL)
373813 ONTARIO LIMITED
TORYCO SERVICES
Gd, Toronto, ON, M5K 1N2
(416) 865-0040
Emp Here 250   Sales 46,037,040
SIC 8741 Management services
Dir Les Viner

D-U-N-S 24-130-8597   (SL)
AGF CANADIAN RESOURCES FUND LIMITED
66 Wellington St W, Toronto, ON, M5K 1E9
(800) 268-8583
Emp Here 500   Sales 204,979,200
SIC 6722 Management investment, open-end
Sr VP Robert Lyon

D-U-N-S 20-275-3232   (BR)
BDO CANADA LLP
66 Wellington St W Suite 3600, Toronto, ON, M5K 1H1
(416) 865-0200
Emp Here 180
SIC 8748 Business consulting, nec

D-U-N-S 24-079-7027   (BR)
BNP PARIBAS (CANADA)
77 King St W Suite 4100, Toronto, ON, M5K 2A1
(416) 365-9600
Emp Here 28
SIC 6021 National commercial banks

D-U-N-S 20-588-3106   (BR)
BANQUE TORONTO-DOMINION, LA
TD CANADA TRUST
(Suby of Toronto-Dominion Bank, The)
100 Wellington St, Toronto, ON, M5K 1A2
(416) 982-8910
Emp Here 20
SIC 6021 National commercial banks

D-U-N-S 24-118-6365   (BR)
BANQUE TORONTO-DOMINION, LA
TORONTO-DOMINION BANK, THE
(Suby of Toronto-Dominion Bank, The)
100 Wellington St W, Toronto, ON, M5K 1Y6
(416) 982-5146
Emp Here 100
SIC 6021 National commercial banks

D-U-N-S 24-121-0561   (BR)
BANQUE TORONTO-DOMINION, LA
TORONTO-DOMINION BANK, THE
(Suby of Toronto-Dominion Bank, The)
79 Wellington St W, Toronto, ON, M5K 1A2
(416) 982-8990
Emp Here 2,000
SIC 6021 National commercial banks

D-U-N-S 24-118-1630   (BR)
BANQUE TORONTO-DOMINION, LA
TORONTO-DOMINION BANK, THE
(Suby of Toronto-Dominion Bank, The)
15th St, Toronto, ON, M5K 1A2
(416) 982-6703
Emp Here 25
SIC 6021 National commercial banks

D-U-N-S 20-589-5555   (BR)

BANQUE TORONTO-DOMINION, LA
TD CANADA TRUST
(Suby of Toronto-Dominion Bank, The)
55 King St W, Toronto, ON, M5K 1A2
(416) 982-2322
Emp Here 7,000
SIC 6021 National commercial banks

D-U-N-S 24-118-1226   (BR)
BANQUE TORONTO-DOMINION, LA
TORONTO-DOMINION BANK, THE
(Suby of Toronto-Dominion Bank, The)
66 Wellington St West Rd, Toronto, ON, M5K 1A2
(416) 982-8641
Emp Here 25
SIC 6021 National commercial banks

D-U-N-S 24-118-0475   (BR)
BANQUE TORONTO-DOMINION, LA
TORONTO-DOMINION BANK, THE
(Suby of Toronto-Dominion Bank, The)
66 Wellington St W, Toronto, ON, M5K 1A2
(416) 982-7650
Emp Here 100
SIC 6021 National commercial banks

D-U-N-S 24-117-5863   (BR)
BANQUE TORONTO-DOMINION, LA
TORONTO-DOMINION BANK, THE
(Suby of Toronto-Dominion Bank, The)
Gd, Toronto, ON, M5K 1A2
(416) 982-4888
Emp Here 25
SIC 6021 National commercial banks

D-U-N-S 24-120-8854   (BR)
BANQUE TORONTO-DOMINION, LA
TORONTO-DOMINION BANK, THE
(Suby of Toronto-Dominion Bank, The)
77 King St W Suite 3000, Toronto, ON, M5K 2A1
(416) 864-6448
Emp Here 35
SIC 6021 National commercial banks

D-U-N-S 20-552-1177   (SL)
BIRCH HILL EQUITY PARTNERS II LTD
(Suby of Toronto-Dominion Bank, The)
100 Wellington St W Suite 2300, Toronto, ON, M5K 1B7
(416) 775-3800
Emp Here 50   Sales 7,296,070
SIC 6211 Security brokers and dealers
 Joseph P Wiley
 Stephen J Dent
Pr Pr John B Macintyre
CFO Peter Zissis
COO Pierre J Schuurmans
Sr VP Michael R Mazan
Sr VP Michael J Salamon
Sr VP Paul R Henry
Sr VP David G Samuel
Sr VP William A Lambert

D-U-N-S 20-267-1249   (HQ)
CNA CANADA
(Suby of Loews Corporation)
66 Wellington St W Suite 3700, Toronto, ON, M5K 1J5
(416) 542-7300
Emp Here 90   Emp Total 15,800
Sales 12,214,139
SIC 6411 Insurance agents, brokers, and service
Pr Gary Owcar
VP Denis Dei Cont
CFO Gale Lockbaum

D-U-N-S 20-111-2278   (SL)
CT FINANCIAL ASSURANCE COMPANY
(Suby of Toronto-Dominion Bank, The)
55 King St W, Toronto, ON, M5K 1A2

Emp Here 500   Sales 45,016,752
SIC 6411 Insurance agents, brokers, and service

Pr Sean Kilburn
  Bernard T. Dorval
Sec Joanne Simard
Dir Alain Thibault
Dir William J. Fulton
Dir Damain Macnamee
Dir Teri Currie
Dir Dominic Mercuri
Dir Heather Ross
Dir Suzanne Deuel

    D-U-N-S 24-736-9945   (BR)
CADILLAC FAIRVIEW CORPORATION LIMITED, THE
CADILLAC FAIRVIEW TD CENTRE, THE
66 Wellington St W Suite 3800, Toronto, ON, M5K 1A1
(416) 869-1144
Emp Here 175
SIC 6512 Nonresidential building operators

    D-U-N-S 25-528-5892   (HQ)
CONTINENTAL CASUALTY COMPANY
CNA CANADA
(*Suby of* Loews Corporation)
66 Wellington St W Suite 3700, Toronto, ON, M5K 1E9
(416) 542-7300
Emp Here 135   *Emp Total* 15,800
Sales 102,130,993
SIC 6331 Fire, marine, and casualty insurance
Pr Gary Owcar

    D-U-N-S 20-587-5149   (HQ)
DELTA HOTELS LIMITED
77 King St W Suite 2300, Toronto, ON, M5K 2A1
(416) 874-2000
Emp Here 750   *Emp Total* 60,000
Sales 357,945,194
SIC 8741 Management services
Pr Pr Hank Stackhouse
  Ken Lambert

    D-U-N-S 20-784-7062   (HQ)
DENTONS CANADA LLP
F M C
(*Suby of* Dentons Canada LLP)
77 King St W Suite 400, Toronto, ON, M5K 2A1
(416) 863-4511
Emp Here 504   *Emp Total* 1,379
Sales 118,123,373
SIC 8111 Legal services
Pr Pr Beth Wilson
  Chris Pinnington

    D-U-N-S 20-818-2006   (HQ)
ERNST & YOUNG LLP
EY
(*Suby of* Ernst & Young LLP)
222 Bay St 21 Fl, Toronto, ON, M5K 1J7
(416) 864-1234
Emp Here 3,000   *Emp Total* 27,390
Sales 144,462,186
SIC 8721 Accounting, auditing, and bookkeeping
Pt Eric Rawlinson

    D-U-N-S 24-331-0229   (BR)
ERNST & YOUNG LLP
ORENDA CORPORATE FINANCE
(*Suby of* Ernst & Young LLP)
222 Bay St, Toronto, ON, M5K 1J7
(416) 943-2040
Emp Here 200
SIC 8721 Accounting, auditing, and bookkeeping

    D-U-N-S 24-891-7119   (SL)
FTI CONSULTING CANADA INC
(*Suby of* Fti Consulting, Inc.)
79 Wellington St W Suite 2010, Toronto, ON, M5K 1G8
(416) 649-8041
Emp Here 34   *Sales* 3,724,879
SIC 8748 Business consulting, nec

    D-U-N-S 24-335-5521   (SL)
FIRST URANIUM CORPORATION
77 King St W Suite 400, Toronto, ON, M5K 0A1
(416) 306-3072
Emp Here 500   *Sales* 458,254,593
SIC 1094 Uranium-radium-vanadium ores
Pr Mary Batoff
  Emma Oosthuizen

    D-U-N-S 24-564-6914   (BR)
FITNESS INSTITUTE LIMITED, THE
THE TORONTO ATHLETIC CLUB
79 Wellington St. W 36th Fl, Toronto, ON, M5K 1J5
(416) 865-0900
Emp Here 75
SIC 7991 Physical fitness facilities

    D-U-N-S 24-130-1733   (SL)
HILLSDALE CANADIAN PERFORMANCE EQUITY
100 Wellington St W Suite 2100, Toronto, ON, M5K 1J3
(416) 913-3900
Emp Here 30   *Sales* 8,901,205
SIC 6722 Management investment, open-end
Pr Christoper Guthrie

    D-U-N-S 24-645-0969   (SL)
LANNICK GROUP INC
LANNICK ASSOCIATES
77 King St W Suite 4110, Toronto, ON, M5K 2A1
(416) 340-1500
Emp Here 45   *Sales* 4,742,446
SIC 7361 Employment agencies

    D-U-N-S 20-299-7953   (SL)
LOGIQ ASSET MANAGEMENT INC
77 King Street W 21st Floor, Toronto, ON, M5K 2A1
(416) 597-9595
Emp Here 49   *Sales* 14,592,140
SIC 6722 Management investment, open-end

    D-U-N-S 20-764-3024   (HQ)
MFS INVESTMENT MANAGEMENT CANADA LIMITED
77 King St W Suite 3500, Toronto, ON, M5K 2A1
(416) 862-9800
Emp Here 70   *Emp Total* 20,980
Sales 19,188,664
SIC 6282 Investment advice
Dir Peter Kotsopoulos

    D-U-N-S 20-548-3907   (BR)
MACLEOD DIXON LLP
(*Suby of* Macleod Dixon LLP)
100 Wellington St, Toronto, ON, M5K 1H1
(416) 360-8511
Emp Here 40
SIC 8111 Legal services

    D-U-N-S 24-174-8990   (BR)
MICROSOFT CANADA INC
MSN
(*Suby of* Microsoft Corporation)
22 Bay St Suite 12, Toronto, ON, M5K 1E7
(416) 349-3620
Emp Here 60
SIC 7372 Prepackaged software

    D-U-N-S 24-387-6336   (BR)
Q9 NETWORKS INC
100 Wellington St W, Toronto, ON, M5K 1J3
(416) 365-7200
Emp Here 99
SIC 4813 Telephone communication, except radio

    D-U-N-S 24-363-0634   (SL)
STIFEL NICOLAUS CANADA INC
(*Suby of* Stifel Financial Corp.)
79 Wellington W, Toronto, ON, M5K 1K7
Emp Here 70   *Sales* 10,742,551

SIC 8742 Management consulting services
Dir Mark Philip Fisher
Dir David Fowler

    D-U-N-S 20-562-2629   (SL)
TD ASSET FINANCE CORP
(*Suby of* Toronto-Dominion Bank, The)
55 King St W, Toronto, ON, M5K 1A2

Emp Here 100   *Sales* 11,965,555
SIC 6159 Miscellaneous business credit institutions
  Jane Stubbington

    D-U-N-S 25-692-7716   (BR)
TD ASSET MANAGEMENT INC
TD WATERHOUSE PRIVATE INVESTMENT ADVICE
(*Suby of* Toronto-Dominion Bank, The)
79 Wellington St W, Toronto, ON, M5K 1A1
(416) 307-6672
Emp Here 63
SIC 6719 Holding companies, nec

    D-U-N-S 24-860-8549   (SL)
TD CAPITAL GROUP LIMITED
(*Suby of* Toronto-Dominion Bank, The)
100 Wellington St W, Toronto, ON, M5K 1A2
(800) 430-6095
Emp Here 25   *Sales* 2,991,389
SIC 6211 Security brokers and dealers

    D-U-N-S 20-552-1250   (SL)
TD CAPITAL TRUST
(*Suby of* Toronto-Dominion Bank, The)
55 King St W, Toronto, ON, M5K 1A2

Emp Here 100   *Sales* 14,592,140
SIC 6211 Security brokers and dealers
Pr Edmund Clark

    D-U-N-S 20-562-2660   (SL)
TD DIRECT INSURANCE INC
(*Suby of* Toronto-Dominion Bank, The)
55 King St W, Toronto, ON, M5K 1A2

Emp Here 50   *Sales* 6,085,920
SIC 6411 Insurance agents, brokers, and service
Pr Alain Thibault

    D-U-N-S 20-552-1334   (SL)
TD INVESTMENT SERVICES INC
(*Suby of* Toronto-Dominion Bank, The)
55 King St W, Toronto, ON, M5K 1A2
(416) 944-5728
Emp Here 50   *Sales* 7,296,070
SIC 6282 Investment advice
Pr William Hatanaka

    D-U-N-S 25-193-8544   (SL)
TD LIFE INSURANCE COMPANY
TD INSURANCE
(*Suby of* Toronto-Dominion Bank, The)
55 King St W, Toronto, ON, M5K 1A2

Emp Here 200   *Sales* 198,744,947
SIC 6311 Life insurance
Pr Pr Sean E. Kilburn
Ch Bd Bernard T. Dorval
Dir Jim Senn
Dir David G. Duncan

    D-U-N-S 24-323-0757   (SL)
TD PARALLEL PRIVATE EQUITY INVESTORS LTD
(*Suby of* Toronto-Dominion Bank, The)
55 King St, Toronto, ON, M5K 1A2

Emp Here 50   *Sales* 7,296,070
SIC 6211 Security brokers and dealers
Pr Edmund Clark

    D-U-N-S 24-889-5799   (HQ)
TD SECURITIES INC
(*Suby of* Toronto-Dominion Bank, The)
66 Wellington St W, Toronto, ON, M5K 1A2

(416) 307-8500
Emp Here 1,600   *Emp Total* 81,233
Sales 364,803,500
SIC 6211 Security brokers and dealers
Ch Bd Ch Bd Bob Dorrance
  John F. Coombs
V Ch Bd William J. (Bill) Furlong

    D-U-N-S 20-865-2727   (BR)
TD WATERHOUSE CANADA INC
TD WEALTH
(*Suby of* Toronto-Dominion Bank, The)
79 Wellington W, Toronto, ON, M5K 1A1
(416) 307-6672
Emp Here 97
SIC 6211 Security brokers and dealers

    D-U-N-S 25-996-5820   (SL)
TORONTO DOMINION LIFE INSURANCE COMPANY
(*Suby of* Toronto-Dominion Bank, The)
55 King St W, Toronto, ON, M5K 1A2
(416) 982-8222
Emp Here 50   *Sales* 13,132,926
SIC 6021 National commercial banks
  Charles Baillie

    D-U-N-S 24-121-0322   (BR)
TORONTO-DOMINION BANK, THE
TD CANADA TRUST
(*Suby of* Toronto-Dominion Bank, The)
55 King St, Toronto, ON, M5K 1A2
(416) 982-5084
Emp Here 25
SIC 6021 National commercial banks

    D-U-N-S 20-268-6150   (HQ)
TORONTO-DOMINION BANK, THE
TD CANADA TRUST
(*Suby of* Toronto-Dominion Bank, The)
55 King St W, Toronto, ON, M5K 1A2
(416) 982-5722
Emp Here 5,000   *Emp Total* 81,233
Sales 27,356,640,075
SIC 6021 National commercial banks
Ch Bd Brian M. Levitt
D Ch Bd Frank Mckenna
Pr Bharat B Masrani
Ex VP Paul Douglas
Ex VP Greg Braca
Ex VP Kenn Lalonde
Ex VP Leo Salom
Pers/VP Sue Cummings
Sec Philip C Moore
Dir William E Bennett

    D-U-N-S 24-118-7108   (BR)
TORONTO-DOMINION BANK, THE
TD CANADA TRUST
(*Suby of* Toronto-Dominion Bank, The)
55 King St W, Toronto, ON, M5K 1A2
(416) 983-3434
Emp Here 25
SIC 6021 National commercial banks

    D-U-N-S 24-855-0225   (BR)
TORONTO-DOMINION BANK, THE
TD BANK
(*Suby of* Toronto-Dominion Bank, The)
66 Wellington St W, Toronto, ON, M5K 1A2
(416) 944-5746
Emp Here 40,000
SIC 6021 National commercial banks

    D-U-N-S 25-684-3178   (BR)
TORONTO-DOMINION BANK, THE
TD CANADA TRUST
(*Suby of* Toronto-Dominion Bank, The)
55 King St W, Toronto, ON, M5K 1A2
(416) 982-2322
Emp Here 30
SIC 6021 National commercial banks

    D-U-N-S 20-308-3928   (SL)
VISA CANADA CORPORATION
VISA CANADA
77 King W Suite 4400, Toronto, ON, M5K 1J5

(416) 367-8472
Emp Here 30   *Sales* 3,291,754
SIC 8741 Management services

D-U-N-S 20-104-1345   (BR)
YORK UNIVERSITY
SCHULICH SCHOOL OF BUSINESS
222 Bay St Suite 500, Toronto, ON, M5K 1K2
(416) 360-8850
Emp Here 20
SIC 7389 Business services, nec

Toronto, ON M5L
York County

D-U-N-S 20-587-2083   (BR)
CIBC WORLD MARKETS INC
199 Bay St, Toronto, ON, M5L 1A2
(416) 304-2680
Emp Here 35
SIC 6211 Security brokers and dealers

D-U-N-S 20-714-8441   (BR)
CANADIAN IMPERIAL BANK OF COMMERCE
CIBC
199 Bay St, Toronto, ON, M5L 1G9
(416) 980-7777
Emp Here 100
SIC 6021 National commercial banks

D-U-N-S 20-587-2034   (BR)
CANADIAN IMPERIAL BANK OF COMMERCE
CIBC
25 King St Crt, Toronto, ON, M5L 1A2
(416) 980-4552
Emp Here 20
SIC 6021 National commercial banks

D-U-N-S 24-324-6522   (HQ)
DETOUR GOLD CORPORATION
(*Suby of* Detour Gold Corporation)
199 Bay St Suite 4100, Toronto, ON, M5L 1E2
(416) 304-0800
Emp Here 425   *Emp Total* 817
Sales 658,286,000
SIC 1081 Metal mining services
Pr Pr Paul Martin
CFO James Mavor
 Pierre Beaudoin
Sec Julie Galloway
Sr VP Drew Anwyll
Sr VP Derek Teevan
VP Jean Francois Metail
VP Ruben Wallin
VP Laurie Gaborit
 Michael Kenyon

D-U-N-S 20-304-3620   (BR)
GWL REALTY ADVISORS INC
25 King St W, Toronto, ON, M5L 2A1
(416) 364-2281
Emp Here 40
SIC 6282 Investment advice

D-U-N-S 20-783-9614   (SL)
INCURSUS LIMITED
21 Melinda St Suite 805, Toronto, ON, M5L 1G4
(416) 365-3313
Emp Here 64   *Sales* 11,869,650
SIC 6712 Bank holding companies
Pr Pr Murray Pollitt

D-U-N-S 24-034-7885   (HQ)
INTEGRO (CANADA) LTD
INTEGRO INSURANCE BROKERS
199 Bay St Suite 4800, Toronto, ON, M5L 1E8
(416) 619-8000
Emp Here 35   *Emp Total* 468
Sales 4,961,328
SIC 6411 Insurance agents, brokers, and service

D-U-N-S 20-702-3730   (HQ)
MACKIE RESEACH CAPITAL CORPORATION
MRCC
199 Bay St Suite 4500, Toronto, ON, M5L 1G2
(416) 860-7600
Emp Here 150   *Emp Total* 310
Sales 60,637,570
SIC 6211 Security brokers and dealers
 Patrick Walsh
Pr Pr Geoffrey Whitlam
 Andrew Selbie

Toronto, ON M5M
York County

D-U-N-S 25-059-3688   (BR)
LIQUOR CONTROL BOARD OF ONTARIO, THE
LCBO
1717 Avenue Rd Suite 307, Toronto, ON, M5M 0A2
(416) 785-6389
Emp Here 30
SIC 5921 Liquor stores

D-U-N-S 25-202-4658   (BR)
RICHTREE MARKET RESTAURANTS INC
MARCHE MOVENPICK
40 Yonge Blvd, Toronto, ON, M5M 3G5
(416) 366-8986
Emp Here 200
SIC 5812 Eating places

D-U-N-S 25-265-3985   (BR)
TORONTO CATHOLIC DISTRICT SCHOOL BOARD
BLESSED SACRAMENT CATHOLIC SCHOOL
24 Bedford Park Ave, Toronto, ON, M5M 1H9
(416) 393-5226
Emp Here 30
SIC 8211 Elementary and secondary schools

D-U-N-S 20-025-0186   (BR)
TORONTO DISTRICT SCHOOL BOARD
LEDBURY PARK ELEMENTARY AND MIDDLE SCHOOL
95 Falkirk St, Toronto, ON, M5M 4K1
(416) 395-2630
Emp Here 25
SIC 8211 Elementary and secondary schools

D-U-N-S 20-572-4888   (BR)
TORONTO DISTRICT SCHOOL BOARD
JOHN WANLESS PUBLIC SCHOOL
245 Fairlawn Ave, Toronto, ON, M5M 1T2
(416) 393-9350
Emp Here 60
SIC 8211 Elementary and secondary schools

Toronto, ON M5N
York County

D-U-N-S 25-619-6866   (SL)
GROSSMAN, LARRY FOREST HILL MEMORIAL ARENA, THE
340 Chaplin Cres, Toronto, ON, M5N 2N3
(416) 488-1800
Emp Here 25   *Sales* 1,386,253
SIC 7999 Amusement and recreation, nec

D-U-N-S 24-104-4655   (SL)
MAVI DEVELOPMENTS INC
TAS DESIGNBUILD
491 Eglinton Ave W Suite 503, Toronto, ON, M5N 1A8
(416) 510-8181
Emp Here 20   *Sales* 6,347,581
SIC 6552 Subdividers and developers, nec
 Babak Mortazavi

V Ch Bd Tooran Mortazavi
Pr Pr Mazyar Mortazavi
 Dino Divito

D-U-N-S 25-254-5983   (BR)
REVERA INC
FOREST HILL PLACE
645 Castlefield Ave Suite 716, Toronto, ON, M5N 3A5
(416) 785-1511
Emp Here 120
SIC 8051 Skilled nursing care facilities

D-U-N-S 20-711-1696   (BR)
TORONTO CATHOLIC DISTRICT SCHOOL BOARD
MARSHALL MCLUHAN CATHOLIC SECONDARY SCHOOL
1107 Avenue Rd, Toronto, ON, M5N 3B1
(416) 393-5561
Emp Here 50
SIC 8211 Elementary and secondary schools

D-U-N-S 20-700-2515   (BR)
TORONTO DISTRICT SCHOOL BOARD
ALLENBY JR PS
391 St Clements Ave, Toronto, ON, M5N 1M2
(416) 393-9115
Emp Here 20
SIC 8211 Elementary and secondary schools

D-U-N-S 20-700-2549   (BR)
TORONTO DISTRICT SCHOOL BOARD
ALTERNATIVE PRIMARY SCHOOL JR
1100 Spadina Rd, Toronto, ON, M5N 2M6
(416) 393-9199
Emp Here 20
SIC 8211 Elementary and secondary schools

D-U-N-S 20-025-4063   (BR)
TORONTO DISTRICT SCHOOL BOARD
FOREST HILL COLLEGIATE INSTITUTE
730 Eglinton Ave W, Toronto, ON, M5N 1B9
(416) 393-1860
Emp Here 65
SIC 8211 Elementary and secondary schools

Toronto, ON M5P
York County

D-U-N-S 24-610-6082   (SL)
1162006 ONTARIO LTD
CROSSTOWN CAR WASH
1467 Bathurst St, Toronto, ON, M5P 3G8
(416) 653-1144
Emp Here 40   *Sales* 7,435,520
SIC 5541 Gasoline service stations
Pr Pr Donato Dimonte
VP VP Domenic Dimonte
Dir Sergio Dimonte
Dir Maria Sgro
Dir Iole Dimonte

D-U-N-S 24-564-3754   (SL)
ADVOCATE HEALTH CARE PARTNERSHIP (NO. 1)
LINCOLN PLACE NURSING HOME
429 Walmer Rd, Toronto, ON, M5P 2X9
(416) 967-6949
Emp Here 500   *Sales* 29,400,665
SIC 8051 Skilled nursing care facilities
VP Opers William Dillane
Dir Fin Enzo Catini

D-U-N-S 25-303-0043   (BR)
CANADIAN IMPERIAL BANK OF COMMERCE
CIBC
462 Spadina Rd, Toronto, ON, M5P 2W4
(416) 487-1396
Emp Here 23
SIC 6021 National commercial banks

D-U-N-S 20-985-7635   (BR)
CANADIAN UNION OF PUBLIC EMPLOY-

EES
CUPE LOCAL 4400
1482 Bathurst St Suite 200, Toronto, ON, M5P 3H1
(416) 393-0440
Emp Here 20
SIC 8631 Labor organizations

D-U-N-S 20-299-6075   (BR)
TORONTO CATHOLIC DISTRICT SCHOOL BOARD
HOLY ROSARY CATHOLIC SCHOOL
308 Tweedsmuir Ave, Toronto, ON, M5P 2Y1
(416) 393-5225
Emp Here 25
SIC 8211 Elementary and secondary schools

D-U-N-S 20-029-8433   (BR)
TORONTO DISTRICT SCHOOL BOARD
ORIOLE PARK ELEMENTARY SCHOOL
80 Braemar Ave, Toronto, ON, M5P 2L4
(416) 393-9215
Emp Here 20
SIC 8211 Elementary and secondary schools

D-U-N-S 25-237-9474   (BR)
TORONTO DISTRICT SCHOOL BOARD
FOREST HILL JUNIOR & SENIOR PUBLIC SCHOOL
78 Dunloe Rd, Toronto, ON, M5P 2T6
(416) 393-9335
Emp Here 45
SIC 8211 Elementary and secondary schools

Toronto, ON M5R
York County

D-U-N-S 20-176-9119   (SL)
1561109 ONTARIO INC
PRODUCT EXCELLENCE
40 Bernard Ave, Toronto, ON, M5R 1R2
(416) 460-0980
Emp Here 30   *Sales* 5,173,950
SIC 5122 Drugs, proprietaries, and sundries
Dir Norman Paul
Dir Fin Ralph Phillips
VP Sls Annette Ryan
VP Opers Shiam Pasupathay

D-U-N-S 25-321-7525   (BR)
2063414 ONTARIO LIMITED
LEISUREWORLD CAREGIVING CENTRE
(*Suby of* 2063414 Ontario Limited)
225 St. George St, Toronto, ON, M5R 2M2
(416) 967-3985
Emp Here 200
SIC 8051 Skilled nursing care facilities

D-U-N-S 25-404-7129   (SL)
924169 ONTARIO LIMITED
SPAMEDICA CANADA
66 Avenue Rd Unit 4, Toronto, ON, M5R 3N8
(416) 922-2868
Emp Here 60   *Sales* 4,331,255
SIC 8011 Offices and clinics of medical doctors

D-U-N-S 20-106-7563   (SL)
ACCERTACLAIM SERVICORP INC
4 New St, Toronto, ON, M5R 1P6
(416) 922-6565
Emp Here 25   *Sales* 1,905,752
SIC 8011 Offices and clinics of medical doctors

D-U-N-S 24-045-8737   (HQ)
ALLIANCE FRANCAISE DE TORONTO
(*Suby of* Alliance Francaise de Toronto)
24 Spadina Rd, Toronto, ON, M5R 2S7
(416) 922-2014
Emp Here 40   *Emp Total* 100
Sales 34,282,500
SIC 8299 Schools and educational services, nec
Ex Dir Patrick Riba

D-U-N-S 20-202-0256 (SL)
CCI ENTERTAINMENT LTD
18 Dupont St, Toronto, ON, M5R 1V2
(416) 964-8750
Emp Here 60   *Sales* 10,404,960
SIC 6712 Bank holding companies
Pr Arnie Zipursky
Dir Charles Salzon
 Gordon Mcilquham
 Murray Palay

D-U-N-S 24-013-4457 (BR)
CML HEALTHCARE INC
ENDODONTIC SPECIALISTS
1235 Bay St Suite 201, Toronto, ON, M5R 3K4
(416) 963-9988
Emp Here 25
SIC 8071 Medical laboratories

D-U-N-S 20-979-6833 (BR)
CENTRECORP MANAGEMENT SERVICES LIMITED
STERLING DIVISION
94 Cumberland St Suite 600, Toronto, ON, M5R 1A3
(416) 972-1803
Emp Here 20
SIC 6531 Real estate agents and managers

D-U-N-S 25-693-5446 (BR)
CINEPLEX ODEON CORPORATION
FAMOUS PLAYERS
159 Cumberland St, Toronto, ON, M5R 1A2
(416) 699-5971
Emp Here 20
SIC 7832 Motion picture theaters, except drive-in

D-U-N-S 20-803-8476 (BR)
COMMUNITY LIVING TORONTO
20 Spadina Rd Suite 257, Toronto, ON, M5R 2S7
(416) 968-0650
Emp Here 100
SIC 8742 Management consulting services

D-U-N-S 24-004-3534 (BR)
CORPORATION OF THE CITY OF TORONTO
FIREHALL NO 344
240 Howland Ave, Toronto, ON, M5R 3B6
(416) 338-9344
Emp Here 30
SIC 7389 Business services, nec

D-U-N-S 25-359-3289 (BR)
DIVERSICARE CANADA MANAGEMENT SERVICES CO., INC
HAZELTON PLACE
111 Avenue Rd Suite 322, Toronto, ON, M5R 3J8
(416) 928-0111
Emp Here 55
SIC 8361 Residential care

D-U-N-S 24-966-0226 (BR)
GEORGE BROWN COLLEGE OF APPLIED ARTS AND TECHNOLOGY, THE
BROWN, GEORGE COLLEGE OF APPLIED ARTS AND TECHNOLOGY, THE
160 Kendal Ave Suite C420, Toronto, ON, M5R 1M3
(416) 415-2000
Emp Here 100
SIC 8222 Junior colleges

D-U-N-S 25-790-2080 (BR)
IMAGO RESTAURANTS INC
DUKE OF YORK
(*Suby of* Imago Restaurants Inc)
39 Prince Arthur Ave, Toronto, ON, M5R 1B2
(416) 964-2441
Emp Here 55
SIC 5812 Eating places

D-U-N-S 24-337-4949 (SL)
KIWANIS CLUB OF CASA LOMA, TORONTO

CASA LOMA
1 Austin Terr, Toronto, ON, M5R 1X8
(416) 925-1588
Emp Here 50   *Sales* 3,575,074
SIC 8641 Civic and social associations

D-U-N-S 25-317-8248 (BR)
LIQUOR CONTROL BOARD OF ONTARIO, THE
L.C.B.O. #15
232 Dupont St, Toronto, ON, M5R 1V7
(416) 922-7066
Emp Here 30
SIC 5921 Liquor stores

D-U-N-S 24-198-8427 (SL)
MCSHEEP INVESTMENTS INC
HEMINGWAYS RESTAURANT
142 Cumberland St, Toronto, ON, M5R 1A8
(416) 968-2828
Emp Here 50   *Sales* 1,532,175
SIC 5812 Eating places

D-U-N-S 25-989-0721 (SL)
MORTON'S OF CHICAGO/CANADA, INC
MORTONS OF CHICAGO/TORONTO
4 Avenue Rd, Toronto, ON, M5R 2E8
(416) 925-0648
Emp Here 70   *Sales* 2,115,860
SIC 5812 Eating places

D-U-N-S 25-052-1358 (SL)
PRINCETON REVIEW CANADA INC, THE
PRINCETON REVIEW, THE
1255 Bay St Suite 550, Toronto, ON, M5R 2A9
(416) 944-8001
Emp Here 70   *Sales* 26,995,459
SIC 8748 Business consulting, nec
Ex Dir Blaise Moritz

D-U-N-S 24-793-0043 (SL)
RAINBOW NURSING REGISTRY LTD
344 Dupont St Suite 402c, Toronto, ON, M5R 1V9
(416) 922-7616
Emp Here 100   *Sales* 4,815,406
SIC 8049 Offices of health practitioner

D-U-N-S 25-695-7713 (SL)
RESTAURANTS ON THE GO INC
ORDERIT.CA
1200 Bay St Suite 504, Toronto, ON, M5R 2A5
(416) 932-3999
Emp Here 20   *Sales* 605,574
SIC 5812 Eating places

D-U-N-S 25-321-4811 (BR)
REVERA INC
CENTRAL PARK LODGES
123 Spadina Rd Suite 308, Toronto, ON, M5R 2T1
(416) 961-6446
Emp Here 40
SIC 8051 Skilled nursing care facilities

D-U-N-S 20-821-6457 (SL)
ROYAL CANADIAN YACHT CLUB, THE
141 St. George St Suite 218, Toronto, ON, M5R 2L8
(416) 967-7245
Emp Here 120   *Sales* 4,815,406
SIC 7997 Membership sports and recreation clubs

D-U-N-S 25-721-0583 (SL)
SOTTO SOTTO RISTORANTE LIMITED
116a Avenue Rd, Toronto, ON, M5R 2H4
(416) 962-0011
Emp Here 80   *Sales* 3,239,280
SIC 5812 Eating places

D-U-N-S 25-092-5534 (BR)
ST STEPHENS COMMUNITY HOUSE
ST STEPHENS EMPLOYMENT AND TRAINING CENTER
1415 Bathurst St Suite 201, Toronto, ON, M5R 3H8
(416) 531-4631
Emp Here 30

SIC 8361 Residential care

D-U-N-S 20-257-4174 (SL)
TEAM CANADA LLC
360 Davenport Rd, Toronto, ON, M5R 1K6
(416) 603-6144
Emp Here 28   *Sales* 1,601,959
SIC 8721 Accounting, auditing, and bookkeeping

D-U-N-S 20-711-2462 (BR)
TORONTO DISTRICT SCHOOL BOARD
HILLCREST COMMUNITY SCHOOL
44 Hilton Ave, Toronto, ON, M5R 3E6
(416) 393-9700
Emp Here 35
SIC 8211 Elementary and secondary schools

D-U-N-S 20-025-1929 (BR)
TORONTO DISTRICT SCHOOL BOARD
JESSE KETCHUM PUBLIC SCHOOL
61 Davenport Rd, Toronto, ON, M5R 1H4
(416) 393-1530
Emp Here 43
SIC 8211 Elementary and secondary schools

D-U-N-S 20-698-8078 (BR)
TORONTO DISTRICT SCHOOL BOARD
HURON STREET JR PS
541 Huron St, Toronto, ON, M5R 2R6
(416) 393-1570
Emp Here 35
SIC 8211 Elementary and secondary schools

D-U-N-S 24-925-7387 (BR)
TORONTO TRANSIT COMMISSION
MATERIALS AND PROCUREMENT DEPARTMENT
1138 Bathurst St, Toronto, ON, M5R 3H2
(416) 393-3546
Emp Here 40
SIC 7389 Business services, nec

D-U-N-S 20-172-6473 (SL)
VILLAGE MANOR (TO) LTD
MADISON AVENUE PUB
(*Suby of* Village Manor Ltd)
14 Madison Ave, Toronto, ON, M5R 2S1
(416) 927-1722
Emp Here 100   *Sales* 3,648,035
SIC 5813 Drinking places

D-U-N-S 20-178-5185 (HQ)
WING HING LUNG LIMITED
WINGS FOOD PRODUCTS
275 Albany Ave, Toronto, ON, M5R 3E1
(416) 531-5768
Emp Here 50   *Emp Total* 60
Sales 7,004,227
SIC 2098 Macaroni and spaghetti
Pr Pr Kenneth Lee

D-U-N-S 24-123-4434 (SL)
YORK CLUB, THE
135 St. George St Suite 218, Toronto, ON, M5R 2L8
(416) 922-3101
Emp Here 50   *Sales* 3,575,074
SIC 8641 Civic and social associations

Toronto, ON M5S
York County

D-U-N-S 20-316-7713 (SL)
6926614 CANADA INC
ENTREPRISES TAG
(*Suby of* 6929818 Canada Inc)
80 Bloor St W Suite 1800, Toronto, ON, M5S 2V1
(416) 892-2071
Emp Here 20   *Sales* 44,662,800
SIC 2421 Sawmills and planing mills, general
Pr Pr Serge Dominique
Ex VP Jean-Yves Cardinal
Fin Ex Vittoria Fortunato

Guy Bonneau

D-U-N-S 24-794-5418 (BR)
ARAMARK CANADA LTD.
21 Classic Ave Suite 1008, Toronto, ON, M5S 2Z3

Emp Here 85
SIC 5812 Eating places

D-U-N-S 24-620-5996 (BR)
ARAMARK CANADA LTD.
100 St. George St, Toronto, ON, M5S 3G3
(416) 591-6557
Emp Here 25
SIC 5812 Eating places

D-U-N-S 24-061-0618 (HQ)
ACCORD FINANCIAL LTD
77 Bloor St W Suite 1803, Toronto, ON, M5S 1M2
(416) 961-0007
Emp Here 20   *Emp Total* 93
Sales 2,638,521
SIC 8741 Management services

D-U-N-S 20-590-3250 (BR)
ALTERNA SAVINGS
(*Suby of* Alterna Savings)
800 Bay St, Toronto, ON, M5S 3A9
(416) 252-5621
Emp Here 22
SIC 6062 State credit unions

D-U-N-S 25-354-8242 (HQ)
AQUENT INC
AQUENT
(*Suby of* Tri Ventures, Inc.)
77 Bloor St W Suite 1405, Toronto, ON, M5S 1M2
(416) 323-0600
Emp Here 285   *Emp Total* 5,700
Sales 32,321,885
SIC 8999 Services, nec
Pr John Chuang
VP VP Steve Kapner
VP VP Mia Wenjen

D-U-N-S 20-978-5737 (BR)
CANDEREL STONERIDGE EQUITY GROUP INC
(*Suby of* Entreprises Canderel Inc)
130 Bloor St W Suite 502, Toronto, ON, M5S 1N5
(416) 922-4579
Emp Here 20
SIC 6553 Cemetery subdividers and developers

D-U-N-S 25-512-1006 (HQ)
CANDEREL STONERIDGE EQUITY GROUP INC
(*Suby of* Entreprises Canderel Inc)
1075 Bay St Suite 400, Toronto, ON, M5S 2B1
(416) 593-6366
Emp Here 33   *Emp Total* 100
Sales 19,115,703
SIC 6553 Cemetery subdividers and developers
 Jonathan Wener
Pr Michael Labrier
Treas David Hawrysh

D-U-N-S 25-790-9879 (BR)
CARA OPERATIONS LIMITED
HARVEY'S
(*Suby of* Cara Holdings Limited)
238 Bloor St W, Toronto, ON, M5S 1T8

Emp Here 30
SIC 5812 Eating places

D-U-N-S 20-515-1934 (BR)
CENTRE FOR ADDICTION AND MENTAL HEALTH
33 Russell St, Toronto, ON, M5S 2S1
(416) 535-8501
Emp Here 250

SIC 8093 Specialty outpatient clinics, nec

D-U-N-S 24-737-7310   (HQ)
CLUB MONACO CORP
CABAN
(Suby of Ralph Lauren Corporation)
157 Bloor St W, Toronto, ON, M5S 1P7
(416) 591-8837
Emp Here 150   *Emp Total* 23,300
Sales 79,162,360
SIC 5621 Women's clothing stores
Pr Pr John Mehas
  Gary Miller

D-U-N-S 20-005-0339   (BR)
COSTI IMMIGRANT SERVICES
COSTI RECEPTION CENTRE
100 Lippincott St, Toronto, ON, M5S 2P1
(416) 922-6688
Emp Here 20
SIC 8322 Individual and family services

D-U-N-S 25-319-7339   (BR)
DON MICHAEL HOLDINGS INC
80 Bloor St W, Toronto, ON, M5S 2V1
(416) 323-3289
Emp Here 25
SIC 5651 Family clothing stores

D-U-N-S 20-305-5645   (SL)
EDGEPOINT CANADIAN PORTFOLIO
150 Bloor St W Suite 200, Toronto, ON, M5S
2X9
(416) 963-9353
Emp Here 39   *Sales* 11,600,751
SIC 6722 Management investment, open-end
Pr Patrick Farmer

D-U-N-S 25-447-0347   (BR)
FEDEX OFFICE CANADA LIMITED
FEDEX OFFICE PRINT & SHIP CENTRE
(Suby of Fedex Corporation)
459 Bloor St W, Toronto, ON, M5S 1X9
(416) 928-0110
Emp Here 30
SIC 7334 Photocopying and duplicating services

D-U-N-S 25-511-6204   (SL)
FORUM RESEARCH INC
180 Bloor St W Suite 1401, Toronto, ON, M5S
2V6
(416) 960-3153
Emp Here 300   *Sales* 55,656,720
SIC 8732 Commercial nonphysical research
Pr Lorne Bozinoff

D-U-N-S 20-848-5052   (SL)
FULLER LANDAU LLP
151 Bloor St W, Toronto, ON, M5S 1S4
(416) 645-6500
Emp Here 50   *Sales* 2,188,821
SIC 8721 Accounting, auditing, and bookkeeping

D-U-N-S 25-882-6502   (BR)
GAP (CANADA) INC
BANANA REPUBLIC
(Suby of The Gap Inc)
80 Bloor St W, Toronto, ON, M5S 2V1
(416) 515-0018
Emp Here 70
SIC 5651 Family clothing stores

D-U-N-S 25-940-8128   (BR)
GAP (CANADA) INC
GAPKIDS
(Suby of The Gap Inc)
80 Bloor St W, Toronto, ON, M5S 2V1

Emp Here 50
SIC 5651 Family clothing stores

D-U-N-S 25-138-4814   (BR)
GOVERNING COUNCIL OF THE UNIVERSITY OF TORONTO
OFFICE OF UNIVERSITY OPERATIONS
27 King'S College Cir, Toronto, ON, M5S 1A1

(416) 978-5850
Emp Here 2,500
SIC 8221 Colleges and universities

D-U-N-S 24-312-5403   (BR)
GOVERNING COUNCIL OF THE UNIVERSITY OF TORONTO
DEPARTMENT OF COMPUTER SCIENCE
10 King'S College Rd Suite 3302, Toronto, ON, M5S 3G4
(416) 978-6025
Emp Here 300
SIC 8221 Colleges and universities

D-U-N-S 20-188-5642   (BR)
GOVERNING COUNCIL OF THE UNIVERSITY OF TORONTO
CAMPUS POLICE
21 Sussex Ave Suite 100, Toronto, ON, M5S 1J6
(416) 978-2323
Emp Here 50
SIC 8221 Colleges and universities

D-U-N-S 24-926-3005   (BR)
GOVERNING COUNCIL OF THE UNIVERSITY OF TORONTO
JOSEPH L. ROTMAN SCHOOL OF MANAGEMENT
105 St. George St Suite 340, Toronto, ON, M5S 3E6
(416) 978-3423
Emp Here 150
SIC 8221 Colleges and universities

D-U-N-S 20-912-2295   (BR)
GOVERNING COUNCIL OF THE UNIVERSITY OF TORONTO
UC FOOD SERVICES
75 St. George St, Toronto, ON, M5S 2E5
(416) 978-7269
Emp Here 65
SIC 8221 Colleges and universities

D-U-N-S 20-357-9615   (BR)
GOVERNING COUNCIL OF THE UNIVERSITY OF TORONTO
164 College St Room 407, Toronto, ON, M5S 3G9
(416) 978-7459
Emp Here 49
SIC 8221 Colleges and universities

D-U-N-S 25-999-9779   (BR)
GOVERNING COUNCIL OF THE UNIVERSITY OF TORONTO
UNIVERSITY TORONTO RESEARCH
27 King'S College Cir, Toronto, ON, M5S 1A1
(416) 978-2116
Emp Here 85
SIC 8221 Colleges and universities

D-U-N-S 25-127-1052   (BR)
GOVERNING COUNCIL OF THE UNIVERSITY OF TORONTO
BLUE SKY SOLAR RACING
10 King'S College Rd, Toronto, ON, M5S 3E5
(416) 978-2820
Emp Here 49
SIC 8711 Engineering services

D-U-N-S 20-192-5513   (BR)
GOVERNING COUNCIL OF THE UNIVERSITY OF TORONTO
FACULTY OF MEDICINE
1 King'S College Cir Suite 2109, Toronto, ON, M5S 1A8
(416) 978-1000
Emp Here 200
SIC 8733 Noncommercial research organizations

D-U-N-S 20-344-6430   (BR)
GOVERNING COUNCIL OF THE UNIVERSITY OF TORONTO
UNIVERSITY OF TORONTO
725 Spadina Ave, Toronto, ON, M5S 2J4

(416) 946-4058
Emp Here 100
SIC 8221 Colleges and universities

D-U-N-S 20-077-5083   (BR)
GOVERNING COUNCIL OF THE UNIVERSITY OF TORONTO
MATERIAL SCIENCE AND ENGINEERING
184 College St Rm 140, Toronto, ON, M5S 3E4
(416) 978-3012
Emp Here 20
SIC 8221 Colleges and universities

D-U-N-S 20-124-7827   (BR)
GOVERNING COUNCIL OF THE UNIVERSITY OF TORONTO
DEPARTMENT OF CHEMICAL ENGINEERING & APPLIED CHEMISTRY
200 College St Unit 217, Toronto, ON, M5S 3E5
(416) 978-6204
Emp Here 120
SIC 8221 Colleges and universities

D-U-N-S 24-205-8787   (BR)
GOVERNING COUNCIL OF THE UNIVERSITY OF TORONTO
DEPARTMENT OF CIVIL ENGINEERING
35 St. George St Suite 173, Toronto, ON, M5S 1A4
(416) 978-0120
Emp Here 100
SIC 8221 Colleges and universities

D-U-N-S 24-764-8413   (BR)
GOVERNING COUNCIL OF THE UNIVERSITY OF TORONTO
STUDENT ACCOUNTS
215 Huron St, Toronto, ON, M5S 1A2
(416) 978-2142
Emp Here 500
SIC 8221 Colleges and universities

D-U-N-S 25-486-5702   (BR)
GOVERNING COUNCIL OF THE UNIVERSITY OF TORONTO
CAMPUS BEVERAGE SERVICES
252 Bloor St W Suite 100, Toronto, ON, M5S 1V6
(416) 978-6415
Emp Here 55
SIC 8221 Colleges and universities

D-U-N-S 20-200-9911   (BR)
GOVERNING COUNCIL OF THE UNIVERSITY OF TORONTO
DEPARTMENT OF ASTRONOMY & ASTROPHYSICS
50 St. George St Suite 101, Toronto, ON, M5S 3H4
(416) 946-7119
Emp Here 20
SIC 8221 Colleges and universities

D-U-N-S 20-714-0299   (BR)
GOVERNING COUNCIL OF THE UNIVERSITY OF TORONTO
FACULTY OF EDUCATION
252 Bloor Street W, Toronto, ON, M5S 1V6
(416) 978-0005
Emp Here 50
SIC 8221 Colleges and universities

D-U-N-S 24-174-2217   (BR)
GOVERNING COUNCIL OF THE UNIVERSITY OF TORONTO
NEAR & MIDDLE EASTERN CIVILIZATIONS DEPT
4 Bancroft Ave Suite 103, Toronto, ON, M5S 1C1
(416) 978-3306
Emp Here 30
SIC 8221 Colleges and universities

D-U-N-S 20-790-7507   (BR)
GOVERNING COUNCIL OF THE UNIVERSITY OF TORONTO
UNIVERSITY OF TORONTO

100 St. George St, Toronto, ON, M5S 3G3
(416) 978-3450
Emp Here 50
SIC 8221 Colleges and universities

D-U-N-S 25-987-9799   (BR)
GOVERNING COUNCIL OF THE UNIVERSITY OF TORONTO
FACULTY OF PHYSICAL EDUCATION AND HEALTH
55 Harbord St Suite 1048, Toronto, ON, M5S 2W6
(416) 978-7375
Emp Here 1,500
SIC 8221 Colleges and universities

D-U-N-S 20-535-9552   (BR)
GOVERNING COUNCIL OF THE UNIVERSITY OF TORONTO
DEPARTMENT OF CELL & SYSTEMS BIOLOGY
25 Harbord St Suite 401, Toronto, ON, M5S 3G5
(416) 946-3692
Emp Here 150
SIC 8221 Colleges and universities

D-U-N-S 20-716-4364   (BR)
GOVERNING COUNCIL OF THE UNIVERSITY OF TORONTO
GEOGRAPHY DEPARTMENT
184 College St, Toronto, ON, M5S 3E4
(416) 978-3375
Emp Here 60
SIC 8221 Colleges and universities

D-U-N-S 20-718-1038   (BR)
GOVERNING COUNCIL OF THE UNIVERSITY OF TORONTO
FACULTY OF FORESTRY
33 Willcocks St Suite 1019, Toronto, ON, M5S 3B3
(416) 978-6184
Emp Here 30
SIC 8221 Colleges and universities

D-U-N-S 20-512-6076   (BR)
GOVERNING COUNCIL OF THE UNIVERSITY OF TORONTO
ROTMAN SCHOOL OF MANAGEMENT
105 St. George St Suite 275, Toronto, ON, M5S 3E6
(416) 978-4574
Emp Here 300
SIC 8221 Colleges and universities

D-U-N-S 20-295-9230   (BR)
GOVERNING COUNCIL OF THE UNIVERSITY OF TORONTO
ADMISSIONS & AWARDS DEPARTMENT
315 Bloor St W, Toronto, ON, M5S 0A7
(416) 978-7960
Emp Here 80
SIC 8742 Management consulting services

D-U-N-S 24-986-5668   (BR)
GOVERNING COUNCIL OF THE UNIVERSITY OF TORONTO
SCHOOL OF CONTINUING STUDIES
158 St. George St, Toronto, ON, M5S 2V8
(416) 978-2400
Emp Here 40
SIC 8221 Colleges and universities

D-U-N-S 20-153-1212   (BR)
GOVERNING COUNCIL OF THE UNIVERSITY OF TORONTO
DEPARTMENT OF ELECTRICAL COMPUTER & ENGINEERING
10 King'S College Rd Rm 1024, Toronto, ON, M5S 3H5
(416) 978-3112
Emp Here 125
SIC 8711 Engineering services

D-U-N-S 20-190-8402   (BR)
GOVERNING COUNCIL OF THE UNIVERSITY OF TORONTO

MUNK SCHOOL OF GLOBAL AFFAIRS
1 Devonshire Pl, Toronto, ON, M5S 3K7
(416) 946-8926
Emp Here 100
SIC 8732 Commercial nonphysical research

D-U-N-S 20-153-1147   (BR)
GOVERNING COUNCIL OF THE UNIVERSITY OF TORONTO
DEPARTMENT OF GEOLOGY
22 Russell St Suite 1066, Toronto, ON, M5S 3B1
(416) 978-3022
Emp Here 40
SIC 8221 Colleges and universities

D-U-N-S 20-912-3244   (BR)
GOVERNING COUNCIL OF THE UNIVERSITY OF TORONTO
GRADUATE HOUSE
60 Harbord St, Toronto, ON, M5S 3L1
(416) 946-3882
Emp Here 20
SIC 8221 Colleges and universities

D-U-N-S 24-124-6920   (BR)
GOVERNING COUNCIL OF THE UNIVERSITY OF TORONTO
JOHN P ROBARTS LIBRARY OF UNIVERSITY OF TORONTO
130 St. George St, Toronto, ON, M5S 1A5
(416) 978-4357
Emp Here 20
SIC 8231 Libraries

D-U-N-S 20-555-0812   (BR)
GOVERNING COUNCIL OF THE UNIVERSITY OF TORONTO
DEPARTMENT OF ECONOMICS
150 St. George St Suite 1, Toronto, ON, M5S 3G7
(416) 978-4622
Emp Here 100
SIC 8221 Colleges and universities

D-U-N-S 24-777-2960   (BR)
GOVERNING COUNCIL OF THE UNIVERSITY OF TORONTO
DEPARTMENT OF FINANCIAL SERVICES
215 Huron St Suite 525, Toronto, ON, M5S 1A2
(416) 978-2148
Emp Here 35
SIC 8221 Colleges and universities

D-U-N-S 24-319-9366   (BR)
GOVERNING COUNCIL OF THE UNIVERSITY OF TORONTO
WOODSWORTH COLLEGE
119 St. George St Suite 236, Toronto, ON, M5S 1A9
(416) 946-7146
Emp Here 40
SIC 8221 Colleges and universities

D-U-N-S 24-677-3647   (BR)
GOVERNING COUNCIL OF THE UNIVERSITY OF TORONTO
GOVERNING COUNCIL OF THE UNIVERSITY OF TORONTO, THE
27 King'S College Cir Rm 106, Toronto, ON, M5S 1A1
(416) 978-6576
Emp Here 20
SIC 8299 Schools and educational services, nec

D-U-N-S 20-153-1139   (BR)
GOVERNING COUNCIL OF THE UNIVERSITY OF TORONTO
DEPARTMENT OF COMPUTING & NETWORKING SERVICES
4 Bancroft Ave Suite 120, Toronto, ON, M5S 1C1

Emp Here 80
SIC 8221 Colleges and universities

D-U-N-S 24-227-7643   (BR)

GOVERNING COUNCIL OF THE UNIVERSITY OF TORONTO
LESLIE DAN FACULTY OF PHARMACY
144 College St Suite 805, Toronto, ON, M5S 3M2
(416) 978-2889
Emp Here 150
SIC 8221 Colleges and universities

D-U-N-S 20-648-5653   (BR)
GOVERNING COUNCIL OF THE UNIVERSITY OF TORONTO
PARKING SERVICES
1 Spadina Cres Suite 105, Toronto, ON, M5S 2J5
(416) 978-0469
Emp Here 25
SIC 8221 Colleges and universities

D-U-N-S 20-732-6989   (BR)
GOVERNING COUNCIL OF THE UNIVERSITY OF TORONTO
FACTOR INWENTASH FACULTY OF SOCIAL WORK
246 Bloor St W Rm 250, Toronto, ON, M5S 1V4
(416) 978-6314
Emp Here 60
SIC 8221 Colleges and universities

D-U-N-S 20-911-2775   (BR)
GOVERNING COUNCIL OF THE UNIVERSITY OF TORONTO
SCHOOL OF CONTINUING EDUCATION
252 Bloor St W Suite 4106, Toronto, ON, M5S 1V6
(416) 978-5104
Emp Here 30
SIC 8221 Colleges and universities

D-U-N-S 24-119-9756   (BR)
GOVERNING COUNCIL OF THE UNIVERSITY OF TORONTO
DEPARTMENT OF ELECTRICAL ENGINEERS
40 St. George St Rm 4113, Toronto, ON, M5S 2E4
(416) 978-1655
Emp Here 100
SIC 8221 Colleges and universities

D-U-N-S 20-042-8014   (BR)
GOVERNING COUNCIL OF THE UNIVERSITY OF TORONTO
HART HOUSE THEATRE
7 Hart House Cir, Toronto, ON, M5S 3H3
(416) 978-8668
Emp Here 20
SIC 8221 Colleges and universities

D-U-N-S 20-580-3708   (BR)
GOVERNING COUNCIL OF THE UNIVERSITY OF TORONTO
DEPARTMENT OF STATISTICS
100 St. George St Suite 6018, Toronto, ON, M5S 3G3
(416) 978-3452
Emp Here 25
SIC 8732 Commercial nonphysical research

D-U-N-S 24-117-4593   (BR)
GOVERNMENT OF ONTARIO
MINISTRY OF LABOR
151 Bloor St W Suite 704, Toronto, ON, M5S 1S4
(416) 327-0020
Emp Here 25
SIC 6331 Fire, marine, and casualty insurance

D-U-N-S 25-109-5659   (BR)
HSBC BANK CANADA
150 Bloor St W Suite 116, Toronto, ON, M5S 2X9
(416) 968-7622
Emp Here 22
SIC 6021 National commercial banks

D-U-N-S 25-293-7289   (BR)
HARRY ROSEN INC

HARRY ROSEN MENS WEAR
82 Bloor St W, Toronto, ON, M5S 1L9
(416) 972-0556
Emp Here 100
SIC 5611 Men's and boys' clothing stores

D-U-N-S 24-389-8319   (SL)
LANGUAGE WORKSHOP INC, THE
180 Bloor St W Suite 202, Toronto, ON, M5S 2V6
(416) 968-1405
Emp Here 55   *Sales* 2,991,389
SIC 8299 Schools and educational services, nec

D-U-N-S 20-290-7978   (BR)
LE GROUPE VOYAGES VISION 2000 INC
VISION TRAVEL
1075 Bay St, Toronto, ON, M5S 2B1
(416) 928-3113
Emp Here 70
SIC 4724 Travel agencies

D-U-N-S 24-388-7817   (SL)
MASTER AND FELLOWS OF MASSEY COLLEGE, THE
MASSEY COLLEGE
4 Devonshire Pl, Toronto, ON, M5S 2E1
(416) 978-2892
Emp Here 50   *Sales* 4,888,367
SIC 6514 Dwelling operators, except apartments

D-U-N-S 24-172-6376   (BR)
MCDONALD'S RESTAURANTS OF CANADA LIMITED
MCDONALD'S
(*Suby of* McDonald's Corporation)
192a Bloor St W, Toronto, ON, M5S 1T8

Emp Here 50
SIC 5812 Eating places

D-U-N-S 20-552-8701   (BR)
METRO ONTARIO INC
METRO
425 Bloor St W, Toronto, ON, M5S 1X6
(416) 923-9099
Emp Here 300
SIC 5411 Grocery stores

D-U-N-S 20-913-4357   (SL)
MILES NADAL JEWISH COMMUNITY CENTRE
750 Spadina Ave, Toronto, ON, M5S 2J2
(416) 944-8002
Emp Here 100   *Sales* 5,088,577
SIC 8322 Individual and family services

D-U-N-S 25-359-9765   (BR)
MORGUARD INVESTMENTS LIMITED
77 Bloor Street W Suite 1704, Toronto, ON, M5S 1M2
(416) 921-3149
Emp Here 50
SIC 6531 Real estate agents and managers

D-U-N-S 20-004-5222   (BR)
NIKE CANADA CORP
(*Suby of* Nike, Inc.)
110 Bloor St W, Toronto, ON, M5S 2W7

Emp Here 80
SIC 5941 Sporting goods and bicycle shops

D-U-N-S 20-200-2544   (BR)
SODEXO CANADA LTD
SODEXHO
21 Sussex Ave Unit 3, Toronto, ON, M5S 1J6
(416) 598-2820
Emp Here 180
SIC 5812 Eating places

D-U-N-S 20-977-0820   (BR)
SODEXO CANADA LTD
41 Classic Ave, Toronto, ON, M5S 2Z3
(416) 598-2029
Emp Here 80

SIC 5812 Eating places

D-U-N-S 25-226-6671   (BR)
ST STEPHENS COMMUNITY HOUSE
ST STEPHEN'S KING EDWARD DAY CARE CENTRE
112 Lippincott St Suite 4, Toronto, ON, M5S 2P1
(416) 922-8705
Emp Here 21
SIC 8351 Child day care services

D-U-N-S 20-506-0689   (BR)
STARBUCKS COFFEE CANADA, INC
(*Suby of* Starbucks Corporation)
110 Bloor St W, Toronto, ON, M5S 2W7
(416) 921-2525
Emp Here 24
SIC 5812 Eating places

D-U-N-S 20-806-4142   (BR)
STARBUCKS COFFEE CANADA, INC
(*Suby of* Starbucks Corporation)
55 Harbord St, Toronto, ON, M5S 2W6
(416) 598-2220
Emp Here 22
SIC 5812 Eating places

D-U-N-S 25-359-7090   (BR)
SUTTON PLACE GRANDE LIMITED
THE SUTTON PLACE HOTEL TORONTO
(*Suby of* Northland Properties Corporation)
955 Bay St, Toronto, ON, M5S 2A2

Emp Here 250
SIC 7011 Hotels and motels

D-U-N-S 24-506-3607   (HQ)
TD WATERHOUSE CANADA INC
(*Suby of* Toronto-Dominion Bank, The)
77 Bloor St W Suite 3, Toronto, ON, M5S 1M2
(416) 982-7686
Emp Here 1,200   *Emp Total* 81,233
Sales 291,842,800
SIC 6211 Security brokers and dealers
Pr Pr John See
Ex VP Gerry O'mahoney
Ex VP Bruce Shewfelt
Dir Fin Kathleen Devenny

D-U-N-S 20-811-3527   (BR)
TD WATERHOUSE CANADA INC
(*Suby of* Toronto-Dominion Bank, The)
77 Bloor St W Suite 3, Toronto, ON, M5S 1M2
(416) 542-0971
Emp Here 20
SIC 8742 Management consulting services

D-U-N-S 24-886-1320   (HQ)
TIFFANY & CO. CANADA
(*Suby of* Tiffany & Co.)
150 Bloor St W Suite M108, Toronto, ON, M5S 2X9
(416) 921-3900
Emp Here 65   *Emp Total* 11,900
Sales 8,104,029
SIC 5944 Jewelry stores
VP VP Andrea Hopson

D-U-N-S 20-655-1587   (BR)
TORONTO CATHOLIC DISTRICT SCHOOL BOARD
ST JOSEPH COLLEGE SCHOOL
74 Wellesley St W, Toronto, ON, M5S 1C4
(416) 393-5514
Emp Here 50
SIC 8211 Elementary and secondary schools

D-U-N-S 24-247-3358   (SL)
TORONTO COMMUNITY HOSTELS
344 Bloor St W Suite 402, Toronto, ON, M5S 3A7
(416) 963-0043
Emp Here 20   *Sales* 6,087,000
SIC 8399 Social services, nec
Ex Dir Donna Johnson
Prin Edward Marchewka

D-U-N-S 20-698-7328   (BR)

TORONTO DISTRICT SCHOOL BOARD
LORD LANSDOWNE PUBLIC SCHOOL
33 Robert St, Toronto, ON, M5S 2K2
(416) 393-1350
Emp Here 25
SIC 8211 Elementary and secondary schools

D-U-N-S 25-092-8124   (BR)
TORONTO DISTRICT SCHOOL BOARD
CENTRAL TECHNICAL SCHOOL
725 Bathurst St, Toronto, ON, M5S 2R5
(416) 393-0060
Emp Here 220
SIC 8211 Elementary and secondary schools

D-U-N-S 20-698-7559   (BR)
TORONTO DISTRICT SCHOOL BOARD
KING EDWARD JR & SR PUBLIC SCHOOL
112 Lippincott St, Toronto, ON, M5S 2P1
(416) 393-1325
Emp Here 60
SIC 8211 Elementary and secondary schools

D-U-N-S 25-684-5264   (BR)
TORONTO-DOMINION BANK, THE
TD CANADA TRUST
(*Suby of* Toronto-Dominion Bank, The)
220 Bloor St W, Toronto, ON, M5S 3B7
(416) 766-9200
Emp Here 20
SIC 6021 National commercial banks

D-U-N-S 20-105-2904   (BR)
VICTORIA UNIVERSITY
NORTHROP FRYE HALL
75 Queen'S Park Cres E, Toronto, ON, M5S 1K7
(416) 585-4467
Emp Here 150
SIC 8742 Management consulting services

D-U-N-S 25-332-4446   (SL)
WINDSOR ARMS DEVELOPMENT CORPO-RATION
THE WINDSOR ARMS HOTEL
18 Saint Thomas St, Toronto, ON, M5S 3E7
(416) 971-9666
Emp Here 100   *Sales* 4,377,642
SIC 7011 Hotels and motels

D-U-N-S 24-312-4315   (BR)
WINNERS MERCHANTS INTERNATIONAL L.P.
WINNERS
(*Suby of* The TJX Companies Inc)
110 Bloor St W, Toronto, ON, M5S 2W7
(416) 920-0193
Emp Here 30
SIC 5651 Family clothing stores

D-U-N-S 24-119-9327   (BR)
IMARKETING SOLUTIONS GROUP INC
80 Bloor St W Suite 601, Toronto, ON, M5S 2V1
(416) 646-3128
Emp Here 250
SIC 8399 Social services, nec

Toronto, ON M5T
York County

D-U-N-S 20-786-8639   (SL)
ART GALLERY OF ONTARIO
317 Dundas St W Suite 535, Toronto, ON, M5T 1G4
(416) 977-0414
Emp Here 475   *Sales* 36,188,507
SIC 8412 Museums and art galleries
 Matthew Teitelbaum

D-U-N-S 25-296-8649   (BR)
BANK OF NOVA SCOTIA, THE
BANK OF NOVA SCOTIA, THE
347 Bathurst St, Toronto, ON, M5T 2S7
(416) 866-6651
Emp Here 22

SIC 6021 National commercial banks

D-U-N-S 25-296-3699   (BR)
BANK OF NOVA SCOTIA, THE
SCOTIABANK
292 Spadina Ave, Toronto, ON, M5T 2E7
(416) 866-4612
Emp Here 20
SIC 6021 National commercial banks

D-U-N-S 24-752-8110   (SL)
CAVALLUZZO, HAYES, SHILTON, MCIN-TYRE & CORNISH LLP
474 Bathurst St Suite 300, Toronto, ON, M5T 2S6
(416) 964-1115
Emp Here 50   *Sales* 4,304,681
SIC 8111 Legal services

D-U-N-S 24-409-6707   (HQ)
COMPUTER SYSTEMS CENTRE CORP
JUMP+
(*Suby of* Computer Systems Centre Corp)
275 College St, Toronto, ON, M5T 1S2
(416) 927-8000
Emp Here 20   *Emp Total* 42
Sales 5,763,895
SIC 5045 Computers, peripherals, and soft-ware
 Daniel Schneeweiss
 Pr Pr Joseph Schneeweiss

D-U-N-S 20-587-2281   (BR)
CORPORATION OF THE CITY OF TORONTO
WOMEN'S RESIDENCE
674 Dundas St W, Toronto, ON, M5T 1H9
(416) 392-5500
Emp Here 20
SIC 8322 Individual and family services

D-U-N-S 20-293-8184   (BR)
GOVERNING COUNCIL OF THE UNIVER-SITY OF TORONTO
U OF T SCHOOL OF ARCHITECTURE
230 College St Suite 120, Toronto, ON, M5T 1R2
(416) 978-5038
Emp Here 25
SIC 8712 Architectural services

D-U-N-S 20-291-8855   (BR)
GOVERNING COUNCIL OF THE UNIVER-SITY OF TORONTO
LAWRENCE S. BLOOMBERG FACULTY OF NURSING
155 College St Suite 130, Toronto, ON, M5T 1P8
(416) 978-6058
Emp Here 120
SIC 8221 Colleges and universities

D-U-N-S 24-345-0355   (BR)
GOVERNING COUNCIL OF THE UNIVER-SITY OF TORONTO
DEPARTMENT OF OPHTHALMOLOGY & VI-SION SCIENCES
399 Bathurst St, Toronto, ON, M5T 2S8
(416) 978-4321
Emp Here 150
SIC 8221 Colleges and universities

D-U-N-S 25-360-9424   (BR)
GREAT-WEST LIFE ASSURANCE COM-PANY, THE
CANADA LIFE
190 Simcoe St, Toronto, ON, M5T 3M3
(416) 597-1440
Emp Here 2,000
SIC 6311 Life insurance

D-U-N-S 25-735-5651   (BR)
HSBC BANK CANADA
421 Dundas St W, Toronto, ON, M5T 2W4
(416) 598-3982
Emp Here 20
SIC 6021 National commercial banks

D-U-N-S 25-270-3343   (BR)

HSBC BANK CANADA
222 Spadina Ave Unite 101, Toronto, ON, M5T 3B3
(416) 348-8888
Emp Here 25
SIC 6021 National commercial banks

D-U-N-S 24-028-8969   (SL)
K.M. BAKERY
KIM MOON BAKERY
438 Dundas St W, Toronto, ON, M5T 1G7

Emp Here 50   *Sales* 1,992,377
SIC 5461 Retail bakeries

D-U-N-S 20-644-4130   (BR)
MCDONALD'S RESTAURANTS OF CANADA LIMITED
MCDONALD'S 8623
(*Suby of* McDonald's Corporation)
344 Bathurst St, Toronto, ON, M5T 2S3
(416) 362-5499
Emp Here 55
SIC 5812 Eating places

D-U-N-S 25-810-6194   (BR)
MCDONALD'S RESTAURANTS OF CANADA LIMITED
MCDONALD'S
(*Suby of* McDonald's Corporation)
160 Spadina Ave, Toronto, ON, M5T 2C2
(416) 703-7401
Emp Here 70
SIC 5812 Eating places

D-U-N-S 20-535-1849   (HQ)
PIGEON BRANDS INC
PIGEON BRANDING + DESIGN
(*Suby of* Pigeon Canada Inc)
179 John St 2nd Fl, Toronto, ON, M5T 1X4
(416) 532-9950
Emp Here 60   *Emp Total* 3
Sales 6,930,008
SIC 7336 Commercial art and graphic design
 Thomas Pigeon
 Vince Antonacci
 Dir Fin Chris Chau
 Genl Mgr Mariane Bergeron

D-U-N-S 25-106-2758   (SL)
POINTS.COM INC
171 John St Suite 500, Toronto, ON, M5T 1X3
(416) 595-0000
Emp Here 125   *Sales* 20,731,238
SIC 7371 Custom computer programming ser-vices
 Dir Robert Maclean
 Pr Pr Christopher Barnard
 Anthony Lam

D-U-N-S 25-479-1627   (SL)
SCADDING COURT COMMUNITY CENTRE INC
707 Dundas St W, Toronto, ON, M5T 2W6
(416) 392-0335
Emp Here 50   *Sales* 1,969,939
SIC 8322 Individual and family services

D-U-N-S 25-529-3532   (BR)
SING TAO (CANADA) LIMITED
SING TAO DAILY
417 Dundas St W, Toronto, ON, M5T 1G6
(416) 596-8140
Emp Here 130
SIC 2711 Newspapers

D-U-N-S 20-506-1422   (BR)
STARBUCKS COFFEE CANADA, INC
(*Suby of* Starbucks Corporation)
205 College St, Toronto, ON, M5T 1P9
(416) 341-0101
Emp Here 21
SIC 5812 Eating places

D-U-N-S 20-569-7175   (BR)
TELEFILM CANADA
474 Bathurst St Suite 100, Toronto, ON, M5T 2S6

(416) 973-6436
Emp Here 28
SIC 7929 Entertainers and entertainment groups

D-U-N-S 20-698-7211   (BR)
TORONTO DISTRICT SCHOOL BOARD
ORDE STREET PUBLIC SCHOOL
18 Orde St, Toronto, ON, M5T 1N7
(416) 393-1900
Emp Here 25
SIC 8211 Elementary and secondary schools

D-U-N-S 20-700-2382   (BR)
TORONTO DISTRICT SCHOOL BOARD
RYERSON COMMUNITY SCHOOL
96 Denison Ave, Toronto, ON, M5T 1E4
(416) 393-1340
Emp Here 64
SIC 8211 Elementary and secondary schools

D-U-N-S 20-025-3727   (BR)
TORONTO DISTRICT SCHOOL BOARD
HEYDON PARK SECONDARY SCHOOL
70 D'Arcy St, Toronto, ON, M5T 1K1
(416) 393-1710
Emp Here 43
SIC 8211 Elementary and secondary schools

D-U-N-S 20-024-9964   (BR)
TORONTO DISTRICT SCHOOL BOARD
BEVERLEY SCHOOL
64 Baldwin St, Toronto, ON, M5T 1L4
(416) 397-2750
Emp Here 50
SIC 8211 Elementary and secondary schools

D-U-N-S 25-418-3775   (BR)
UNIVERSITY HEALTH NETWORK
222 Saint Patrick St, Toronto, ON, M5T 1V4
(416) 340-5898
Emp Here 40
SIC 8071 Medical laboratories

Toronto, ON M5V
York County

D-U-N-S 20-343-9898   (SL)
3119696 CANADA INC
QMS COURIER
269 Richmond St W Suite 201, Toronto, ON, M5V 1X1
(416) 368-1623
Emp Here 50   *Sales* 3,118,504
SIC 7389 Business services, nec

D-U-N-S 20-174-3429   (BR)
3627730 CANADA INC
FREEMAN AUDIO VISUAL
255 Front St W, Toronto, ON, M5V 2W6
(416) 585-8144
Emp Here 24
SIC 7359 Equipment rental and leasing, nec

D-U-N-S 24-794-1136   (BR)
918962 ONTARIO INC
JACK ASTOR'S BAR & GRILL
(*Suby of* 918962 Ontario Inc)
133 John St, Toronto, ON, M5V 2E4
(416) 595-9100
Emp Here 49
SIC 5812 Eating places

D-U-N-S 24-255-4710   (SL)
ACCELERATED CONNECTIONS INC
155 Wellington St W Suite 3740, Toronto, ON, M5V 3H1
(416) 637-3432
Emp Here 46   *Sales* 5,717,257
SIC 8748 Business consulting, nec

D-U-N-S 25-696-0980   (HQ)
AMATO PIZZA INC
(*Suby of* Amato Pizza Inc)
534 Queen St W, Toronto, ON, M5V 2B5

(416) 703-8989
Emp Here 30   *Emp Total* 100
Sales 2,991,389
SIC 5812 Eating places

D-U-N-S 25-504-7441   (HQ)
AMERICA ONLINE CANADA INC
AOL CANADA
(*Suby of* Verizon Communications Inc.)
99 Spadina Ave Suite 200, Toronto, ON, M5V 3P8
(416) 263-8100
Emp Here 100   *Emp Total* 166,070
Sales 94,232,900
SIC 7319 Advertising, nec
Pr Jonathan Lister
Pers/VP John Hamovitch
Dir George Haman

D-U-N-S 20-281-4943   (HQ)
ASSOCIATED FOREIGN EXCHANGE, ULC
AFEX
200 Front St W Suite 2203, Toronto, ON, M5V 3K2
(416) 360-2136
Emp Here 30   *Emp Total* 250
Sales 78,432,753
SIC 6081 Foreign bank and branches and agencies
Genl Mgr Christian Spaltenstein
Pr Fred Kunik

D-U-N-S 25-793-7151   (BR)
ASTLEY-GILBERT LIMITED
AGR
(*Suby of* Astley Gilbert Limited)
485 Wellington St W, Toronto, ON, M5V 1E9
(416) 348-0002
Emp Here 30
SIC 3861 Photographic equipment and supplies

D-U-N-S 20-010-4839   (SL)
AXYZ EDIT INC
AXYZ ANIMATION
477 Richmond St W Suite 405, Toronto, ON, M5V 3E7
(416) 504-0425
Emp Here 28   *Sales* 1,819,127
SIC 7819 Services allied to motion pictures

D-U-N-S 24-646-0505   (SL)
BCI LENO INC
366 Adelaide St W Suite 500, Toronto, ON, M5V 1R9
(416) 408-2300
Emp Here 130   *Sales* 12,760,800
SIC 2721 Periodicals
Pr Pr James Shenkman
Dir Stanley Shenkman
Dir Michael Shulman
Dir Gregorey Matus
Dir Donald Loeb

D-U-N-S 25-296-4242   (BR)
BANK OF NOVA SCOTIA, THE
SCOTIABANK
222 Queen St W, Toronto, ON, M5V 1Z3
(416) 866-6591
Emp Here 35
SIC 6021 National commercial banks

D-U-N-S 25-019-4065   (BR)
BANQUE TORONTO-DOMINION, LA
TD BANK
(*Suby of* Toronto-Dominion Bank, The)
443 Queen St W, Toronto, ON, M5V 2B1
(416) 982-2535
Emp Here 40
SIC 6021 National commercial banks

D-U-N-S 20-652-4386   (BR)
BELL MEDIA INC
GLOBE AND MAIL
444 Front St W, Toronto, ON, M5V 2S9
(416) 585-5000
Emp Here 800
SIC 5192 Books, periodicals, and newspapers

D-U-N-S 20-114-1483   (BR)
BELL MEDIA INC
REPORT ON BUSINESS TELEVISION
720 King St W Suite 1000, Toronto, ON, M5V 2T3
Emp Here 95
SIC 7922 Theatrical producers and services

D-U-N-S 20-811-5506   (BR)
BLAKE, CASSELS & GRAYDON LLP
199 Bay St Suite 4000, Toronto, ON, M5V 1V3
(416) 863-2400
Emp Here 999
SIC 8111 Legal services

D-U-N-S 20-514-7338   (BR)
BLAST RADIUS INC
99 Spadina Ave Suite 200, Toronto, ON, M5V 3P8
(416) 214-4220
Emp Here 160
SIC 7374 Data processing and preparation

D-U-N-S 25-285-5874   (SL)
BUZZBUZZHOME CORPORATION
333 Adelaide St W Suite 600, Toronto, ON, M5V 1R5
(416) 944-2899
Emp Here 50   *Sales* 5,399,092
SIC 4813 Telephone communication, except radio
Pr Pr Cliff Tefkin

D-U-N-S 24-052-8125   (HQ)
CSI GLOBAL EDUCATION INC
CSI
(*Suby of* Moody's Corporation)
200 Wellington St W Suite 1200, Toronto, ON, M5V 3G2
(416) 364-9130
Emp Here 110   *Emp Total* 10,600
Sales 8,171,598
SIC 8299 Schools and educational services, nec
Pr Pr Roberta Wilton
Dir Fin Jerry Fahrer
VP Fin Steve Rosen

D-U-N-S 20-919-4369   (BR)
CABINET DE RELATIONS PUBLIQUES NATIONAL INC, LE
AXON CLINICAL RESEARCH
(*Suby of* Groupe Conseil RES Publica Inc)
310 Front St W Suite 500, Toronto, ON, M5V 3B5
(416) 586-0180
Emp Here 100
SIC 8743 Public relations services

D-U-N-S 25-483-6133   (BR)
CADILLAC FAIRVIEW CORPORATION LIMITED, THE
SIMCOE PLACE
200 Front St W Suite 2207, Toronto, ON, M5V 3K2
(416) 340-6615
Emp Here 20
SIC 6512 Nonresidential building operators

D-U-N-S 20-073-3801   (BR)
CANADA LANDS COMPANY CLC LIMITED
CN TOWER
301 Front St W, Toronto, ON, M5V 2T6
(416) 868-6937
Emp Here 250
SIC 6531 Real estate agents and managers

D-U-N-S 20-004-2963   (BR)
CANADIAN BROADCASTING CORPORATION
TV NEWS
205 Wellington St W, Toronto, ON, M5V 3G7
Emp Here 3,000
SIC 4833 Television broadcasting stations

D-U-N-S 20-879-4651   (BR)

CANADIAN BROADCASTING CORPORATION
CBC
250 Front St W, Toronto, ON, M5V 3G5
(416) 205-3311
Emp Here 3,000
SIC 4832 Radio broadcasting stations

D-U-N-S 25-992-4124   (BR)
CANADIAN BROADCASTING CORPORATION
CBC
205 Wellington St W Unit 9a211, Toronto, ON, M5V 3G7
(416) 205-3072
Emp Here 400
SIC 4833 Television broadcasting stations

D-U-N-S 20-361-4966   (BR)
CARA OPERATIONS LIMITED
MILESTONE'S GRILL AND BAR
(*Suby of* Cara Holdings Limited)
132 John St, Toronto, ON, M5V 2E3
(416) 595-1990
Emp Here 100
SIC 5812 Eating places

D-U-N-S 20-259-4453   (BR)
CINEFLIX MEDIA INC
(*Suby of* Cineflix Media Inc)
110 Spadina Ave Suite 400, Toronto, ON, M5V 2K4
(416) 504-7317
Emp Here 200
SIC 7929 Entertainers and entertainment groups

D-U-N-S 20-085-6198   (BR)
CINEPLEX ODEON CORPORATION
SCOTIABANK THEATER TORONTO
259 Richmond St W, Toronto, ON, M5V 3M6
(416) 368-5600
Emp Here 200
SIC 7832 Motion picture theaters, except drive-in

D-U-N-S 24-000-4908   (BR)
CINTAS CANADA LIMITED
SALLY FOURMY & ASSOCIATES
(*Suby of* Cintas Corporation)
543 Richmond St W Suite 107, Toronto, ON, M5V 1Y6
(416) 593-4676
Emp Here 50
SIC 7218 Industrial launderers

D-U-N-S 20-313-5389   (BR)
CINTAS CANADA LIMITED
FOURMY SALLY & ASSOCIATES
(*Suby of* Cintas Corporation)
543 Richmond St W Suite 107, Toronto, ON, M5V 1Y6
(800) 268-1474
Emp Here 50
SIC 7218 Industrial launderers

D-U-N-S 25-321-4969   (BR)
CLUB MONACO CORP
CLUB MONACO
(*Suby of* Ralph Lauren Corporation)
403 Queen St W, Toronto, ON, M5V 2A5
(416) 979-5633
Emp Here 20
SIC 5651 Family clothing stores

D-U-N-S 25-362-8390   (BR)
COMPAGNIE DE TELEPHONE BELL DU CANADA OU BELL CANADA, LA
21 Canniff St, Toronto, ON, M5V 3G1

Emp Here 200
SIC 4813 Telephone communication, except radio

D-U-N-S 20-818-2170   (BR)
COMPAGNIE DES CHEMINS DE FER NATIONAUX DU CANADA
277 Front St W, Toronto, ON, M5V 2X4

Emp Here 50
SIC 8741 Management services

D-U-N-S 20-287-6132   (SL)
CONNECTED LAB INC
CONNECTED LAB
370 King St W Suite 300, Toronto, ON, M5V 1J9
(647) 478-7493
Emp Here 65   *Sales* 3,173,583
SIC 7371 Custom computer programming services

D-U-N-S 20-341-8611   (SL)
CONTINENTAL GOLD INC
155 Wellington St W Suite 2920, Toronto, ON, M5V 3H1
(416) 583-5610
Emp Here 372   *Sales* 40,420,228
SIC 1041 Gold ores
Ari Sussman
Pr Pr Mateo Restrepo
VP Mauricio Castaeda
VP Julian Gonzlez
VP Guillermo Salgado
VP Omar Ossma
VP Opers Jon Graham
Paul Begin
Donald Gray
Leon Teicher

D-U-N-S 20-215-4407   (HQ)
CORBY SPIRIT AND WINE LIMITED
225 King St W Suite 1100, Toronto, ON, M5V 3M2
(416) 479-2400
Emp Here 50   *Emp Total* 373
Sales 109,231,520
SIC 2085 Distilled and blended liquors
Pr Pr R. Patrick O'driscoll
Antonio Sanchez Villarreal
VP Sls Stephane Cote
Pers/VP Paul Holub
Maxime Kouchnir
VP Prd Jim Stanski
VP VP Marc Valencia
Robert Llewellyn
Donald Lussier
George Mccarthy

D-U-N-S 20-079-5248   (BR)
CORPORATION OF THE CITY OF TORONTO
FORT YORK HISTORIC SITE
100 Garrison Rd, Toronto, ON, M5V 3K9
(416) 392-6907
Emp Here 20
SIC 7999 Amusement and recreation, nec

D-U-N-S 24-247-7193   (BR)
CORPORATION OF THE CITY OF TORONTO
FORT YORK RESIDENCE
38 Bathurst St, Toronto, ON, M5V 3W3
(416) 338-8800
Emp Here 20
SIC 8361 Residential care

D-U-N-S 24-322-0519   (BR)
CRITICAL MASS INC
425 Adelaide St W, Toronto, ON, M5V 3C1
(416) 673-5275
Emp Here 80
SIC 7374 Data processing and preparation

D-U-N-S 20-534-7102   (SL)
CRUSH INC
439 Wellington St W Suite 300, Toronto, ON, M5V 1E7
(416) 345-1936
Emp Here 26   *Sales* 3,724,879
SIC 7311 Advertising agencies

D-U-N-S 24-555-4449   (HQ)
CUNDARI GROUP LTD
CUNDARI
26 Duncan St, Toronto, ON, M5V 2B9

(416) 510-1771
Emp Here 110　　*Emp Total* 630
Sales 19,230,772
SIC 7311 Advertising agencies
　Aldo Cundari
　Maria Orsini
Pr Jennifer Steinmann

D-U-N-S 20-286-9129　　(HQ)
DENTSUBOS INC
360I CANADA
276 King St W Suite 100, Toronto, ON, M5V 1J2
(416) 929-9700
Emp Here 100　　*Emp Total* 55,843
Sales 15,548,429
SIC 7311 Advertising agencies
Ch Bd Michel Ostiguy
Pr Claude Carrier
　Annie Rizen
Dir Nicholas Rey
Dir Bryan Wiener
Dir Timothy Andree
Dir Yushin Soga
Dir James Cran

D-U-N-S 24-309-8154　　(HQ)
DOME PRODUCTIONS INC
(*Suby of* Dome Productions Inc)
1 Blue Jays Way Suite 3400, Toronto, ON, M5V 1J3
(416) 341-2001
Emp Here 45　　*Emp Total* 65
Sales 3,939,878
SIC 8741 Management services

D-U-N-S 24-817-0359　　(SL)
DOWN-TOWN DUVETS & LINENS LTD
530 Adelaide St W, Toronto, ON, M5V 1T5
(416) 703-3777
Emp Here 35　　*Sales* 5,275,400
SIC 2221 Broadwoven fabric mills, manmade
Pr Freddy Faust
Treas Barbara Grnak

D-U-N-S 24-166-4023　　(SL)
E C S RECOVERY SYSTEMS INC
555 Richmond St W, Toronto, ON, M5V 3B1
(416) 628-5653
Emp Here 40　　*Sales* 31,661,120
SIC 6141 Personal credit institutions
Pr Jack Bryan

D-U-N-S 24-409-7077　　(SL)
ELECTRONICS WORKBENCH CORPORATION
(*Suby of* National Instruments Corporation)
111 Peter St Suite 801, Toronto, ON, M5V 2H1
(416) 977-5550
Emp Here 45　　*Sales* 1,751,057
SIC 7629 Electrical repair shops

D-U-N-S 25-115-6279　　(SL)
ELOQUA CORPORATION
(*Suby of* Oracle Corporation)
553 Richmond St W Suite 214, Toronto, ON, M5V 1Y6
(416) 864-0440
Emp Here 150　　*Sales* 27,068,420
SIC 7372 Prepackaged software
　Joseph Payne
　Steve Woods
Dir Ralph Riekers
Sr VP Paul Teshima
　Abe Wagner
VP Sls Alex Shootman

D-U-N-S 20-955-8472　　(SL)
EVANDTEC INC
355 Adelaide St W Suite 500, Toronto, ON, M5V 1S2

Emp Here 27　　*Sales* 5,782,650
SIC 3443 Fabricated plate work (boiler shop)
Pr Pr Paul Wickberg
CEO David Martin
CFO Graham Matthews
VP VP Steve Siverns

VP VP Aaron Nelson
VP VP Shelley Cornforth
VP VP Don Toporowski

D-U-N-S 20-809-8116　　(SL)
FGX CANADA CORP
AAI OF CANADA
555 Richmond St W Suite 1005, Toronto, ON, M5V 3B1
(416) 504-5533
Emp Here 30　　*Sales* 3,648,035
SIC 3851 Ophthalmic goods

D-U-N-S 24-773-3426　　(SL)
FOREST HILL GROUP INC
116 Spadina Ave Ste 407, Toronto, ON, M5V 2K6
(416) 785-0010
Emp Here 50　　*Sales* 1,532,175
SIC 7381 Detective and armored car services

D-U-N-S 24-388-4025　　(SL)
FRESH AND WILD GOURMET FOOD MARKET
69 Spadina Ave, Toronto, ON, M5V 3P8
(416) 979-8155
Emp Here 45　　*Sales* 5,472,053
SIC 5411 Grocery stores
Owner Peter Papadopoulos

D-U-N-S 24-143-2632　　(BR)
FUJITSU CONSEIL (CANADA) INC
FUJITSU CONSULTING
200 Front St W Suite 2300, Toronto, ON, M5V 3K2
(416) 363-8661
Emp Here 150
SIC 7379 Computer related services, nec

D-U-N-S 25-304-7583　　(BR)
GAP (CANADA) INC
GAP
(*Suby of* The Gap Inc)
375 Queen St W, Toronto, ON, M5V 2A5
(416) 591-3517
Emp Here 43
SIC 5651 Family clothing stores

D-U-N-S 24-685-0445　　(SL)
GLAM MEDIA CANADA INC
675 King St W Suite 303, Toronto, ON, M5V 1M9
(416) 368-6800
Emp Here 50　　*Sales* 7,103,258
SIC 7311 Advertising agencies
Dir Brian J. Fields
Dir Christine C. Mcnicholas
Dir Jack J. Rotolo Jr
Dir Roxanne E. Brady

D-U-N-S 24-318-4368　　(BR)
GOODMAN & COMPANY, INVESTMENT COUNSEL LTD
DYNAMIC FUNDS MATERIALS ORDER DESK
379 Adelaide St W, Toronto, ON, M5V 1S5

Emp Here 50
SIC 6282 Investment advice

D-U-N-S 20-220-6298　　(HQ)
GREY ADVERTISING ULC
GREY CANADA
46 Spadina Ave Suite 500, Toronto, ON, M5V 2H8
(416) 486-0700
Emp Here 75　　*Emp Total* 124,930
Sales 40,201,346
SIC 7311 Advertising agencies
Pr Pr Stephanie Nerlich
Dir Fin Leah Power

D-U-N-S 24-318-0705　　(BR)
GROUPE GERMAIN INC
HOTEL LE GERMAIN IN TORONTO
(*Suby of* Gestion Famiger Inc)
30 Mercer St, Toronto, ON, M5V 1H3
(416) 345-9500
Emp Here 20

SIC 7011 Hotels and motels

D-U-N-S 24-247-3622　　(HQ)
GUESTLOGIX INC
(*Suby of* GuestLogix Inc)
111 Peter St Suite 407, Toronto, ON, M5V 2H1
(416) 642-0349
Emp Here 120　　*Emp Total* 173
Sales 13,132,926
SIC 3577 Computer peripheral equipment, nec
Pr Pr Michael Abramsky
Sr VP Anthony Ashe
Sr VP Mike 03
Sr VP Jamie Dinsmore
　Robin Hopper
Sr VP Jim O'brien
VP Fin Kevin Dam
VP Blair Mcgibbon
　Brian Reddy
　Jason Chapnik

D-U-N-S 24-429-4146　　(HQ)
HACHETTE DISTRIBUTION SERVICES (CANADA) INC
LS TRAVEL RETAIL NORTH AMERICA
370 King St W Suite 600, Toronto, ON, M5V 1J9
(416) 863-6400
Emp Here 100　　*Emp Total* 9
Sales 106,012,013
SIC 5947 Gift, novelty, and souvenir shop
Pr Pr Gerald Savaria
　Dirk Van Den Haute

D-U-N-S 20-170-8716　　(HQ)
HERMAN MILLER CANADA, INC
(*Suby of* Herman Miller, Inc.)
462 Wellington St W Suite 200, Toronto, ON, M5V 1E3
(416) 366-3300
Emp Here 60　　*Emp Total* 7,607
Sales 38,634,795
SIC 5021 Furniture
VP VP Corrado Fermo
　W. Bruce Clark
　Brian Walker

D-U-N-S 24-356-0617　　(BR)
HIGH ROAD COMMUNICATIONS CORP
(*Suby of* Omnicom Group Inc.)
360 Adelaide St W Suite 400, Toronto, ON, M5V 1R7
(416) 368-8348
Emp Here 50
SIC 8743 Public relations services

D-U-N-S 24-385-4460　　(HQ)
HOGG ROBINSON CANADA INC
HRG NORTH AMERICA
(*Suby of* HOGG ROBINSON GROUP PLC)
370 King St W Suite 700, Toronto, ON, M5V 1J9
(416) 593-8866
Emp Here 70　　*Emp Total* 4,893
Sales 127,779,812
SIC 8742 Management consulting services
Pr Greg Treasure
　Randy Nanek
Pers/VP Michal Grey

D-U-N-S 25-997-3816　　(BR)
HOMES FIRST SOCIETY
STRACHAN HOUSE
805 Wellington St W, Toronto, ON, M5V 1G8
(416) 395-0928
Emp Here 22
SIC 8699 Membership organizations, nec

D-U-N-S 24-421-4446　　(SL)
HOTEL 550 WELLINGTON GP LTD
THOMPSON TORONTO
550 Wellington St W, Toronto, ON, M5V 2V4
(416) 640-7778
Emp Here 99　　*Sales* 4,304,681
SIC 7011 Hotels and motels

D-U-N-S 25-091-0049　　(SL)

INC RESEARCH TORONTO, INC
INC RESEARCH
(*Suby of* Inc Research Holdings, Inc.)
720 King St W 7th Fl, Toronto, ON, M5V 2T3
(416) 963-9338
Emp Here 200　　*Sales* 24,879,599
SIC 8733 Noncommercial research organizations
VP VP Pierre Geoffroy

D-U-N-S 20-131-8040　　(BR)
INDIGO BOOKS & MUSIC INC
INDIGO.CHAPTERS.CA
(*Suby of* Indigo Books & Music Inc)
82 Peter St Suite 300, Toronto, ON, M5V 2G5
(416) 598-8000
Emp Here 100
SIC 5942 Book stores

D-U-N-S 25-087-6455　　(BR)
INDIGO BOOKS & MUSIC INC
CHAPTERS
(*Suby of* Indigo Books & Music Inc)
142 John St, Toronto, ON, M5V 2E3

Emp Here 49
SIC 5942 Book stores

D-U-N-S 20-162-2495　　(HQ)
INDIGO BOOKS & MUSIC INC
CHAPTERS
(*Suby of* Indigo Books & Music Inc)
468 King St W Suite 500, Toronto, ON, M5V 1L8
(416) 646-8945
Emp Here 200　　*Emp Total* 6,500
Sales 765,706,765
SIC 5942 Book stores
　Heather Reisman
Ex VP Kirsten Chapman
Pers/VP Gil Dennis
Ex VP Ex VP Kathleen Flynn
Ex VP Tod Morehead
Ex VP Krishna Nikhil
Ex VP Bo Parizadeh
　Craig Loudon
　Frank Clegg
　Jonathan Deitcher

D-U-N-S 20-012-6493　　(SL)
INFUSION DEVELOPMENT CORP
INFUSION DEVELOPMENT CANADA
276 King St W, Toronto, ON, M5V 1J2
(416) 593-6595
Emp Here 115　　*Sales* 10,836,784
SIC 7379 Computer related services, nec
　Greg Brill
　Sheldon Fernandez
Pr Pr Alim Somani
　William(Bill) Baldasti

D-U-N-S 20-984-0672　　(SL)
INGLE INTERNATIONAL INC.
460 Richmond St W Suite 100, Toronto, ON, M5V 1Y1
(416) 730-8488
Emp Here 51
SIC 6141 Personal credit institutions

D-U-N-S 24-804-6273　　(SL)
INTERTAINTECH CORPORATION
VIRGIN GAMING
720 King St W Suite 820, Toronto, ON, M5V 2T3
(416) 800-4263
Emp Here 57　　*Sales* 9,333,400
SIC 4813 Telephone communication, except radio
　Harp Gahunia

D-U-N-S 20-878-7622　　(SL)
ISLAND YACHT CLUB TORONTO
57 Spadina Ave Suite 206, Toronto, ON, M5V 2J2
(416) 203-2582
Emp Here 70　　*Sales* 2,845,467
SIC 7997 Membership sports and recreation

clubs

D-U-N-S 24-856-5405 (SL)
JACKMAN, JOE BRAND INC
477 Richmond St W Suite 210, Toronto, ON,
M5V 3E7
(416) 304-9944
Emp Here 40   *Sales* 5,526,400
SIC 8741 Management services
Pr Joseph Jackman
Dir David Saffer
Opers Mgr Paul Clark

D-U-N-S 20-360-0283 (BR)
JAM FILLED ENTERTAINMENT INC
364 Richmond St W Suite 100, Toronto, ON,
M5V 1X6
(613) 366-2550
Emp Here 250
SIC 7812 Motion picture and video production

D-U-N-S 25-819-7495 (BR)
KEG RESTAURANTS LTD
KEG STEAKHOUSE & BAR, THE
560 King St W, Toronto, ON, M5V 0L5
(416) 364-7227
Emp Here 85
SIC 5812 Eating places

D-U-N-S 20-070-9975 (BR)
KONICA MINOLTA BUSINESS SOLUTIONS (CANADA) LTD
KONICA MINOLTA
200 Wellington St W Suite 310, Toronto, ON,
M5V 3C7
(416) 777-2679
Emp Here 20
SIC 5999 Miscellaneous retail stores, nec

D-U-N-S 25-087-7354 (BR)
LARCO INVESTMENTS LTD
RENAISSANCE HOTEL
(*Suby of* Larco Investments Ltd)
1 Blue Jays Way Suite 1, Toronto, ON, M5V
1J4
(416) 341-7100
Emp Here 200
SIC 7011 Hotels and motels

D-U-N-S 25-050-1905 (SL)
LAST BEST PLACE CORP, THE
MONTANA
145 John St, Toronto, ON, M5V 2E4

Emp Here 90   *Sales* 2,699,546
SIC 5812 Eating places

D-U-N-S 20-915-8349 (BR)
LULULEMON ATHLETICA CANADA INC
318 Queen St W, Toronto, ON, M5V 2A2
(416) 703-1399
Emp Here 20
SIC 2339 Women's and misses' outerwear,
nec

D-U-N-S 25-869-8141 (BR)
LUSH HANDMADE COSMETICS LTD
LUSH COSMETICS
312 Queen St W, Toronto, ON, M5V 2A2
(416) 599-5874
Emp Here 20
SIC 5999 Miscellaneous retail stores, nec

D-U-N-S 20-280-4381 (SL)
MPT UTILITIES EUROPE LTD
155 Wellington St W, Toronto, ON, M5V 3H1
(416) 649-1300
Emp Here 550   *Sales* 365,727,250
SIC 4911 Electric services
CEO Michael Bernstein
Ex VP Michael Smerdon
Stuart Miller
Sr VP Jack Bittan
Sr VP Roberto Roberti
VP Fin Jens Ehlers
Sr VP Sarah Borg-Olivier
Ch Bd James Sardo
Dir Patrick Lavelle

Dir Francois Roy

D-U-N-S 20-307-1514 (SL)
MZ CANADA LTD
366 Adelaide St W Suite 500, Toronto, ON,
M5V 1R9

Emp Here 80   *Sales* 12,662,640
SIC 7371 Custom computer programming services
James Cook

D-U-N-S 20-819-6220 (HQ)
MACKENZIE FINANCIAL CORPORATION
MACKENZIE MAXXUM DIVIDEND GROWTH FUND
180 Queen St W Suite 1600, Toronto, ON,
M5V 3K1
(416) 355-2537
Emp Here 1,100   *Emp Total* 31,126
Sales 459,459,530
SIC 6722 Management investment, open-end
Pr Pr Charles Sims
VP Fin Edward Merchand
Sr VP Frederick Sturm
Philip F Cunningham

D-U-N-S 20-300-1425 (SL)
MACKENZIE INTERNATIONAL GROWTH CLASS
180 Queen St W Suite 1600, Toronto, ON,
M5V 3K1
(416) 922-5322
Emp Here 40   *Sales* 15,359,963
SIC 6722 Management investment, open-end
Genl Mgr Jeff Carney

D-U-N-S 25-560-2039 (BR)
MAGASIN DE MUSIQUE STEVE INC
STEVE'S MUSIC STORE
415 Queen St W, Toronto, ON, M5V 2A5
(416) 593-8888
Emp Here 60
SIC 7359 Equipment rental and leasing, nec

D-U-N-S 20-170-3741 (HQ)
MCCANN WORLDGROUP CANADA INC
MACLAREN MCCANN INTERACTIVE
(*Suby of* The Interpublic Group of Companies
Inc)
200 Wellington St W Suite 1300, Toronto, ON,
M5V 0N6
(416) 594-6000
Emp Here 650   *Emp Total* 49,800
Sales 84,050,726
SIC 7311 Advertising agencies
Pr Doug Turney
Erwin Buck
John Macfarland
Dir George Recine

D-U-N-S 20-213-3398 (BR)
MCDONALD'S RESTAURANTS OF CANADA LIMITED
MCDONALD'S
(*Suby of* McDonald's Corporation)
710 King St W, Toronto, ON, M5V 2Y6
(416) 504-7268
Emp Here 55
SIC 5812 Eating places

D-U-N-S 24-680-2511 (SL)
MERCATUS TECHNOLOGIES INC
545 King St W Suite 500, Toronto, ON, M5V
1M1
(416) 603-3406
Emp Here 70   *Sales* 7,952,716
SIC 7371 Custom computer programming services
Pr Pr Sylvain Perrier
Ch Bd Bernie Nisker
VP Tony Shuparsky
Dave Conte
Bohdan Zabawskyj
Kevin Kidd
Brandon Eady
Djen Choo
Tim Zimmerman

Andrew Chang

D-U-N-S 24-771-2177 (HQ)
METROPOLITAN TORONTO WATERWORKS SYSTEM
55 John St, Toronto, ON, M5V 3C6
(416) 392-8211
Emp Here 30   *Emp Total* 39,000
Sales 63,603,840
SIC 4971 Irrigation systems
Barry Gutteridge

D-U-N-S 25-281-9883 (HQ)
MING PAO NEWSPAPERS (CANADA) LIMITED
MING PAO DAILY NEWS
23 Spadina Ave, Toronto, ON, M5V 3M5
(416) 321-0088
Emp Here 230   *Emp Total* 4,554
Sales 29,403,162
SIC 2711 Newspapers
Ka Ming Lui
Pr Pr Kiew Chiong Tiong
Sec Mary Chan
Dewitt Liew
Ngiik Siong Tiong Liew

D-U-N-S 25-402-8699 (BR)
MIRVISH, ED ENTERPRISES LIMITED
TICKET KING
284 King St W Suite 300, Toronto, ON, M5V
1J2
(416) 351-1229
Emp Here 60
SIC 7922 Theatrical producers and services

D-U-N-S 24-976-5236 (SL)
MOODY'S ANALYTICS GLOBAL EDUCATION (CANADA), INC
(*Suby of* Moody's Corporation)
200 Wellington St W, Toronto, ON, M5V 3C7
(416) 364-9130
Emp Here 100   *Sales* 5,472,053
SIC 8299 Schools and educational services,
nec
Dir Mark Almeida
Dir Simon Parmar

D-U-N-S 24-708-9717 (BR)
MOUNTAIN EQUIPMENT CO-OPERATIVE
MOUNTAIN EQUIPMENT CO-OPERATIVE
400 King St W, Toronto, ON, M5V 1K2
(416) 340-2667
Emp Here 80
SIC 5941 Sporting goods and bicycle shops

D-U-N-S 25-302-6918 (SL)
NATIONWIDE SPORTSWEAR CORPORATION
720 King St W Suite 301, Toronto, ON, M5V
2T3
(416) 603-0021
Emp Here 55   *Sales* 3,429,153
SIC 2339 Women's and misses' outerwear,
nec

D-U-N-S 20-026-3122 (BR)
NEWAD MEDIA INC
NEWAD
99 Spadina Ave Suite 100, Toronto, ON, M5V
3P8
(416) 361-3393
Emp Here 22
SIC 7312 Outdoor advertising services

D-U-N-S 20-425-5707 (HQ)
NIKE CANADA CORP
(*Suby of* Nike, Inc.)
200 Wellington St W Suite 500, Toronto, ON,
M5V 3C7
(416) 581-1585
Emp Here 150   *Emp Total* 70,700
Sales 80,821,218
SIC 5091 Sporting and recreation goods
Pr Pr Maria Montano
Sec John Coburn
Treas Robert Woodruff
Dir Bernard Pliska

Dir Hilary Krane
Dir Charles Reagh

D-U-N-S 25-398-3845 (BR)
OMNICOM CANADA CORP
PHD CANADA
(*Suby of* Omnicom Group Inc.)
96 Spadina Ave 7th Floor, Toronto, ON, M5V
2J6
(416) 922-0217
Emp Here 135
SIC 7319 Advertising, nec

D-U-N-S 20-172-3673 (SL)
OUTDOOR OUTFITS LIMITED
372 Richmond St W Suite 400, Toronto, ON,
M5V 1X6
(416) 598-4111
Emp Here 40   *Sales* 7,296,070
SIC 5136 Men's and boy's clothing
Pr Pr Sheldon Switzer

D-U-N-S 20-174-1902 (BR)
OXFORD PROPERTIES GROUP INC
315 Front St W Suite 1, Toronto, ON, M5V 3A4
(416) 408-5551
Emp Here 20
SIC 6512 Nonresidential building operators

D-U-N-S 24-227-0234 (HQ)
PVH CANADA, INC
555 Richmond St W Suite 1106, Toronto, ON,
M5V 3B1
(416) 309-7200
Emp Here 100   *Emp Total* 34,500
Sales 91,200,875
SIC 5136 Men's and boy's clothing
Pr Emanuel Chirico
Ex VP Michael A. Shaffer
Mark D. Fischer
Richard Deck

D-U-N-S 20-329-3394 (HQ)
PENGUIN RANDOM HOUSE CANADA LIMITED
320 Front St W Suite 1400, Toronto, ON, M5V
3B6
(416) 364-4449
Emp Here 100   *Emp Total* 116,434
Sales 8,828,245
SIC 2731 Book publishing
Pr Pr Bradley Martin
Douglas Foot

D-U-N-S 20-992-2553 (SL)
PLANIT SEARCH INC
PLANIT
13 Clarence Sq, Toronto, ON, M5V 1H1
(416) 260-9996
Emp Here 25   *Sales* 7,245,563
SIC 7361 Employment agencies
Pr Pr Joseph Zitek

D-U-N-S 24-101-2827 (HQ)
PORTER AIRLINES INC
(*Suby of* Porter Aviation Holdings Inc)
4-1 Island Airport, Toronto, ON, M5V 1A1
(416) 203-8100
Emp Here 1,500   *Emp Total* 21
Sales 234,057,926
SIC 4581 Airports, flying fields, and services
Pr Pr Robert Deluce
Donald J Carty

D-U-N-S 20-228-1783 (SL)
PREMIERE CONFERENCING (CANADA) LIMITED
(*Suby of* Siris Capital Group, LLC)
225 King St W Suite 900, Toronto, ON, M5V
3M2
(416) 516-0777
Emp Here 75   *Sales* 10,068,577
SIC 4899 Communication services, nec
Pr Frank Cianciulli
Ch Bd Tony Lacavera

D-U-N-S 24-857-2500 (SL)
RBC GLOBAL ASSET MANAGEMENT

(U.S.) INC.
(*Suby of* Royal Bank Of Canada)
155 Wellington St W 22 Flr, Toronto, ON, M5V 3K7
(416) 974-5008
Emp Here 1,000   *Sales* 145,921,400
SIC 6282 Investment advice
Daniel Chornous

D-U-N-S 24-121-0462   (HQ)
RBC INVESTOR SERVICES TRUST
(*Suby of* Royal Bank Of Canada)
155 Wellington St W 7 Fl, Toronto, ON, M5V 3H1
(416) 955-6251
Emp Here 100   *Emp Total* 79,000
Sales 56,826,066
SIC 6282 Investment advice
Dir Jose Placido
Robert B Bennett
Opers Mgr James M Daigle
Mark Hoffman
Martin J Lippert
Shawn L Murphy
Dir Michel F Malpas
Dir George A Cohon
Dir Victor L Young
Dir Morten N Fris

D-U-N-S 20-985-4483   (BR)
RABBA, J. COMPANY LIMITED, THE
RABBA MARCHE
361 Front St W, Toronto, ON, M5V 3R5
(416) 205-9600
Emp Here 20
SIC 5411 Grocery stores

D-U-N-S 24-703-6189   (SL)
RODNEY'S OYSTER HOUSE CORP
469 King St W Suite Lower, Toronto, ON, M5V 3M4
(416) 363-8105
Emp Here 66   *Sales* 1,969,939
SIC 5812 Eating places

D-U-N-S 24-358-1464   (BR)
ROGERS MEDIA INC
CITYTV
(*Suby of* Rogers Communications Inc)
299 Queen St W, Toronto, ON, M5V 2Z5
(416) 591-5757
Emp Here 50
SIC 4833 Television broadcasting stations

D-U-N-S 24-505-4465   (SL)
ROUIE INDUSTRIES LTD
134 Peter St, Toronto, ON, M5V 2H2
(416) 598-1932
Emp Here 50   *Sales* 7,811,650
SIC 2335 Women's, junior's, and misses' dresses
Pr Paul Kan
Ester Kan

D-U-N-S 20-588-1894   (BR)
ROYAL BANK OF CANADA
RBC
(*Suby of* Royal Bank Of Canada)
320 Front St W Suite 1400, Toronto, ON, M5V 3B6
(416) 955-8527
Emp Here 20
SIC 6021 National commercial banks

D-U-N-S 20-536-6516   (BR)
ROYAL   TRUST   CORPORATION   OF CANADA
(*Suby of* Royal Bank Of Canada)
155 Wellington St W Suite 1000, Toronto, ON, M5V 3K7
(416) 955-5254
Emp Here 20
SIC 6021 National commercial banks

D-U-N-S 24-144-2040   (BR)
SIR CORP
PARLOR FOODS
333 King St W, Toronto, ON, M5V 1J5

Emp Here 20
SIC 5812 Eating places

D-U-N-S 20-011-4176   (BR)
SNC-LAVALIN OPERATIONS & MAINTE-NANCE INC
250 Front St W, Toronto, ON, M5V 3G5

Emp Here 30
SIC 8741 Management services

D-U-N-S 20-532-8052   (SL)
SCHOOL EDITING INC
PUBLIC ASSEMBLY, THE
379 Adelaide St W Suite 200, Toronto, ON, M5V 1S5
(416) 907-9070
Emp Here 20   *Sales* 2,338,878
SIC 7338 Secretarial and court reporting

D-U-N-S 20-278-1787   (SL)
SCORE MEDIA VENTURES INC
500 King St W, Toronto, ON, M5V 1L9
(416) 479-8812
Emp Here 120   *Sales* 9,130,500
SIC 7374 Data processing and preparation
Dir John Levy

D-U-N-S 25-365-6425   (HQ)
SENTINELLE MEDICAL INC
130 Spadina Ave, Toronto, ON, M5V 2L4
(866) 243-2533
Emp Here 24   *Emp Total* 5,290
Sales 2,115,860
SIC 3841 Surgical and medical instruments

D-U-N-S 20-860-3238   (BR)
SOURCE (BELL) ELECTRONICS INC, THE
SOURCE, THE
200 Wellington St W Suite 1200, Toronto, ON, M5V 3G2

Emp Here 25
SIC 5999 Miscellaneous retail stores, nec

D-U-N-S 25-486-9498   (SL)
SOUTHERN ONTARIO LIBRARY SERVICE
SOLS
111 Peter St Suite 902, Toronto, ON, M5V 2H1
(416) 961-1669
Emp Here 33   *Sales* 7,786,394
SIC 8231 Libraries
Dir Laurey Gillies
Dir Opers Daryl Novak
Dir Barbra Franchetto
Dir Lynne Baxter
Dir Lorraine Bourdeau
Dir Ian Brebner
Dir Brenda Corrigan
Dir Bob Coryell
Dir Virginia Dilauro
Dir Bob Ernest

D-U-N-S 20-337-8765   (BR)
STANTEC CONSULTING LTD
49 Bathurst St Suite 300, Toronto, ON, M5V 2P2
(416) 364-8401
Emp Here 37
SIC 8711 Engineering services

D-U-N-S 24-745-6593   (SL)
STRATICOM PLANNING ASSOCIATES INC
366 Adelaide St W, Toronto, ON, M5V 1R9
(416) 362-7407
Emp Here 40   *Sales* 2,115,860
SIC 7389 Business services, nec

D-U-N-S 24-946-8273   (HQ)
SWATCH GROUP (CANADA) LTD, THE
555 Richmond St W Suite 1105, Toronto, ON, M5V 3B1
(416) 703-1667
Emp Here 34   *Emp Total* 35,705
Sales 8,480,961
SIC 5094 Jewelry and precious stones
Pr Pr John Maraston

D-U-N-S 24-763-3113   (BR)
SYMCOR INC
320 Front St W Suite 17, Toronto, ON, M5V 3B6
(416) 673-8600
Emp Here 50
SIC 7374 Data processing and preparation

D-U-N-S 24-126-6548   (BR)
SYMCOR INC
325 Front St W, Toronto, ON, M5V 2Y1

Emp Here 20
SIC 7374 Data processing and preparation

D-U-N-S 24-523-3874   (HQ)
TICKETMASTER CANADA LP
TICKETMASTER
1 Blue Jays Way Suite 3900, Toronto, ON, M5V 1J3
(416) 345-9200
Emp Here 100   *Emp Total* 8,300
Sales 47,730,430
SIC 7999 Amusement and recreation, nec
Thomas Worrall

D-U-N-S 20-796-1694   (SL)
TIP TOP LOFTS DEVELOPMENT INC
637 Lake Shore Blvd W Suite 1009, Toronto, ON, M5V 3J6
(416) 863-0202
Emp Here 24   *Sales* 7,660,874
SIC 6552 Subdividers and developers, nec
Pr Howard Cohen

D-U-N-S 25-356-9834   (BR)
TOMMY HILFIGER CANADA INC
555 Richmond St W Suite 1202, Toronto, ON, M5V 3B1
(416) 703-3700
Emp Here 25
SIC 5136 Men's and boy's clothing

D-U-N-S 24-385-2378   (BR)
TORSTAR CORPORATION
TORSTAR
590 King St W Suite 400, Toronto, ON, M5V 1M3
(416) 687-5700
Emp Here 200
SIC 2752 Commercial printing, lithographic

D-U-N-S 20-560-1821   (SL)
ULTRA SUPPER CLUB INC
ULTRA
314 Queen St W, Toronto, ON, M5V 2A2
(416) 263-0330
Emp Here 60   *Sales* 1,824,018
SIC 5812 Eating places

D-U-N-S 24-120-6544   (BR)
UNITED PARCEL SERVICE CANADA LTD
UPS
12 Mercer St, Toronto, ON, M5V 1H3

Emp Here 80
SIC 4513 Air courier services

D-U-N-S 20-650-1772   (HQ)
VIRGIN MOBILE CANADA
720 King St W Suite 905, Toronto, ON, M5V 2T3
(416) 607-8500
Emp Here 75   *Emp Total* 48,090
Sales 7,077,188
SIC 4812 Radiotelephone communication
Andrew Bridge

D-U-N-S 20-281-5429   (BR)
VIZEUM CANADA INC
317 Adelaide St W Suite 700, Toronto, ON, M5V 1P9
(416) 967-7282
Emp Here 70
SIC 7311 Advertising agencies

D-U-N-S 20-163-6099   (HQ)
WALT DISNEY COMPANY (CANADA) LTD, THE

BUENA VISTA TELEVISION DISTRIBUTION
200 Front St W Suite 2900, Toronto, ON, M5V 3L4
(416) 695-2918
Emp Here 20   *Emp Total* 80
Sales 16,112,269
SIC 6794 Patent owners and lessors
Dir Susan Patterson
Peter Noonan

D-U-N-S 24-330-8983   (SL)
WELLINGTON WINDSOR HOLDINGS LTD
RESIDENCE   INN   TORONTO   DOWN-TOWN/ENTERTAINMENT DISTRICT
255 Wellington St W, Toronto, ON, M5V 3P9
(416) 581-1800
Emp Here 75   *Sales* 3,283,232
SIC 7011 Hotels and motels

D-U-N-S 20-949-1583   (BR)
WINNERS MERCHANTS INTERNATIONAL L.P.
WINNERS
(*Suby of* The TJX Companies Inc)
57 Spadina Ave Suite 201, Toronto, ON, M5V 2J2
(416) 585-2052
Emp Here 35
SIC 5651 Family clothing stores

D-U-N-S 24-752-9456   (HQ)
YOUNG & RUBICAM GROUP OF COMPA-NIES ULC, THE
495 Wellington St W Suite 102, Toronto, ON, M5V 1E9
(416) 961-5111
Emp Here 145   *Emp Total* 124,930
Sales 21,396,400
SIC 7311 Advertising agencies
Pr Chris Jordan

D-U-N-S 20-771-1607   (HQ)
ZEIDLER PARTNERSHIP ARCHITECTS
(*Suby of* Zeidler Partnership Architects)
315 Queen St W Unit 200, Toronto, ON, M5V 2X2
(416) 596-8300
Emp Here 95   *Emp Total* 180
Sales 20,356,035
SIC 8712 Architectural services
Pt Vaidila Banelis
Pt Eberhard H Zeidler
Pt Alan Munn
Pt Tarek Elkhatib
Pt Francise Kwok
Pt Gerald Stein
Pt Jurgen Henze
Pt Donald (Don) Vetere
Pt Ronald(Ron) Nemeth
Pt Andrea Richardson

D-U-N-S 25-716-8369   (BR)
ACT3 M.H.S. INC
MEDIA EXPERTS M.H.S. INC
(*Suby of* 157341 Canada Inc)
495 Wellington St W Suite 250, Toronto, ON, M5V 1E9
(416) 597-0707
Emp Here 30
SIC 7319 Advertising, nec

Toronto, ON M5W
York County

D-U-N-S 20-074-5912   (BR)
SEARS CANADA INC
SEARS CARPET AND UPHOLSTERY CARE
1970 Ellesmere Rd, Toronto, ON, M5W 2G9
(416) 750-9533
Emp Here 50
SIC 7217 Carpet and upholstery cleaning

▲ Public Company   ■ Public Company Family Member   **HQ** Headquarters   **BR** Branch   **SL** Single Location

Toronto, ON M5X
York County

D-U-N-S 20-321-5918   (BR)
AIMIA INC
130 King St W Suite 1600, Toronto, ON, M5X 2A2
(905) 214-8699
Emp Here 200
SIC 8743 Public relations services

D-U-N-S 24-685-8042   (HQ)
AIMIA PROPRIETARY LOYALTY CANADA INC
130 King St W Suite 1600, Toronto, ON, M5X 2A2
(905) 214-8699
Emp Here 250   *Emp Total* 3,800
Sales 121,621,640
SIC 8732 Commercial nonphysical research
Ch Bd Robert Brown
Pr Pr Rupert Duchesne
   David Adams

D-U-N-S 20-294-5101   (SL)
ALIGNVEST CAPITAL MANAGEMENT INC
100 King St W Suite 7050, Toronto, ON, M5X 1C7
(416) 775-1009
Emp Here 25   *Sales* 10,347,900
SIC 6722 Management investment, open-end
Pt Reza Satchu

D-U-N-S 24-761-6159   (SL)
ALMONTY INDUSTRIES INC
100 King S: W Suite 5700, Toronto, ON, M5X 1C7
(647) 438-9766
Emp Here 135   *Sales* 28,953,903
SIC 1061 Ferroalloy ores, except vanadium
Pr Pr Lewis Black
   Daniel D'amato
   Mark Trachuk
   Thomas Gutschlag

D-U-N-S 20-896-8979   (SL)
ATTICUS CANADA INC
ATTICUS INTERIM MANAGEMENT
100 King St W Suite 3700, Toronto, ON, M5X 2A1
(416) 644-8795
Emp Here 43   *Sales* 5,987,760
SIC 8741 Management services
Pr Pr Gregory Petkovich

D-U-N-S 24-828-1800   (HQ)
BMO INVESTORLINE INC
100 King St W Suite 1, Toronto, ON, M5X 2A1
(416) 867-6300
Emp Here 150   *Emp Total* 46,000
Sales 43,776,420
SIC 6211 Security brokers and dealers
   Connie Stefankiewicz
   Susan Payne
Dir Viki Lazaris
Dir Robertson Lucas Seabrook
Dir Jennifer Marks
Dir Silvio Stroescu

D-U-N-S 20-002-6545   (BR)
BMO NESBITT BURNS INC
100 King St W Fl 44, Toronto, ON, M5X 1A1
(416) 365-6000
Emp Here 80
SIC 6211 Security brokers and dealers

D-U-N-S 24-311-4126   (BR)
BMO NESBITT BURNS INC
BANK OF MONTREAL SECURITIES CANADA
1 First Canadian Pl 21st Fl, Toronto, ON, M5X 1H3
(416) 359-4000
Emp Here 3,300
SIC 6211 Security brokers and dealers

D-U-N-S 25-845-2150   (BR)
BMO NESBITT BURNS INC
1 First Canadian Place 38th Fl, Toronto, ON,

M5X 1H3
(416) 359-4440
Emp Here 20
SIC 6211 Security brokers and dealers

D-U-N-S 20-518-1204   (BR)
BANK OF MONTREAL
BMO
302 Bay St, Toronto, ON, M5X 1A1
(416) 867-6404
Emp Here 40
SIC 6021 National commercial banks

D-U-N-S 20-588-9848   (BR)
BANK OF MONTREAL
BMO
100 King St W Suite 2100, Toronto, ON, M5X 2A1
(416) 867-5050
Emp Here 20
SIC 6021 National commercial banks

D-U-N-S 20-153-0156   (BR)
BANQUE NATIONALE DU CANADA
NATIONAL BANK CORRESPONDENT NETWORK
130 King St Suite 3000, Toronto, ON, M5X 1J9
(416) 542-2383
Emp Here 110
SIC 7389 Business services, nec

D-U-N-S 20-708-7342   (BR)
BANQUE NATIONALE DU CANADA
130 King St W Suite 3200, Toronto, ON, M5X 2A2
(416) 864-7759
Emp Here 100
SIC 6021 National commercial banks

D-U-N-S 24-511-5436   (BR)
BENNETT JONES LLP
100 King St W Suite 3400, Toronto, ON, M5X 2A1
(416) 863-1200
Emp Here 400
SIC 8111 Legal services

D-U-N-S 25-214-5891   (SL)
CHAIR RESOURCES INC
100 King St W Suite 7080, Toronto, ON, M5X 2A1
(416) 863-0447
Emp Here 20   *Sales* 22,478,640
SIC 1382 Oil and gas exploration services
Pr Pr Louis Strauss
VP VP Alan Butler

D-U-N-S 24-852-5805   (SL)
CINRO RESOURCES INC
100 King St W, Toronto, ON, M5X 2A1

Emp Here 700   *Sales* 454,971,600
SIC 3341 Secondary nonferrous Metals
   Roy Singh

D-U-N-S 24-425-4178   (SL)
CLEARESULT CANADA INC
100 King St W Suite 5800, Toronto, ON, M5X 2A1
(416) 504-3400
Emp Here 35   *Sales* 3,210,271
SIC 8711 Engineering services

D-U-N-S 20-195-2632   (HQ)
CREDIT SUISSE SECURITIES (CANADA) INC
1 First Canadian Pl Suite 2900, Toronto, ON, M5X 1C9
(416) 352-4500
Emp Here 150   *Emp Total* 47,170
Sales 25,987,530
SIC 6211 Security brokers and dealers
Ch Bd Ronald Lloyd
   Andrew Stewart

D-U-N-S 25-829-1061   (BR)
DAVIS LLP
100 King St W Suite 367, Toronto, ON, M5X 2A1

(416) 365-3414
Emp Here 40
SIC 8111 Legal services

D-U-N-S 24-119-6356   (BR)
DAVIS MANAGEMENT LTD
100 King St W Unit 60, Toronto, ON, M5X 2A1
(416) 365-3500
Emp Here 130
SIC 8111 Legal services

D-U-N-S 24-971-8839   (SL)
DEEPAK INTERNATIONAL LTD
1 First Canadian Pl Unit 6000, Toronto, ON, M5X 1B5

Emp Here 37   *Sales* 101,862,619
SIC 3915 Jewelers' materials and lapidary work
Pr Pr Deepak Kumar

D-U-N-S 20-052-5694   (SL)
EDGESTONE CAPITAL EQUITY PARTNERS INC
(*Suby of* Edgestone Capital GP Holdco Inc)
130 King St W Suite 600, Toronto, ON, M5X 2A2
(416) 860-3740
Emp Here 29   *Sales* 13,564,800
SIC 6722 Management investment, open-end
Pr Pr Samuel L. Duboc
Dir Gilbert S. Palter
Dir Bryan Kerdman

D-U-N-S 20-652-1804   (BR)
FAIRWEATHER LTD
100 King St W, Toronto, ON, M5X 2A1

Emp Here 20
SIC 5621 Women's clothing stores

D-U-N-S 20-015-6003   (BR)
GOWLING WLG (CANADA) LLP
100 King St W Suite 1600, Toronto, ON, M5X 1G5
(416) 862-7525
Emp Here 524
SIC 8111 Legal services

D-U-N-S 20-140-2257   (SL)
ITG CANADA CORP
130 King St W Suite 1040, Toronto, ON, M5X 2A2
(416) 874-0900
Emp Here 80   *Sales* 16,232,000
SIC 6211 Security brokers and dealers
Pr Pr Robert Gasser
   Nicholas Thadaney
CFO Steven Vigliotti

D-U-N-S 20-295-9136   (SL)
JIFFY TELECOMMUNICATIONS INC
JIFFY
100 King St W Suite 5600, Toronto, ON, M5X 2A1

Emp Here 1,300   *Sales* 332,857,450
SIC 4899 Communication services, nec
Dir Adam-Joshua Noel-Steeves
Dir Andrew Winston
Dir Matthew Sullivan
Dir Derrick Matthias
Dir Leslie Michael
Dir Jason Harwood

D-U-N-S 20-301-9526   (SL)
JIFFY TELECOMMUNICATIONS INC
HARMONY SYSTEMS
100 King St W, Toronto, ON, M5X 2A1
(888) 979-7560
Emp Here 375   *Sales* 92,116,600
SIC 4899 Communication services, nec
   Matthew Sullivan

D-U-N-S 25-869-2284   (BR)
MCI MEDICAL CLINICS INC
FIRST CANADIAN MEDICAL CENTRE
(*Suby of* MCI Medical Clinics Inc)
100 King St W Suite 1600, Toronto, ON, M5X

2A1
(416) 368-6787
Emp Here 40
SIC 8062 General medical and surgical hospitals

D-U-N-S 25-926-3739   (BR)
MCI MEDICAL CLINICS INC
ACHES & PAINS TORONTO'S PREMIER MEDICINE & THERAPY
(*Suby of* MCI Medical Clinics Inc)
100 King St W Suite 119, Toronto, ON, M5X 2A1
(416) 368-1926
Emp Here 45
SIC 8049 Offices of health practitioner

D-U-N-S 24-131-9685   (SL)
MAVRIX GLOBAL FUND INC
MATRIX
130 King St W Suite 2200, Toronto, ON, M5X 2A2
(416) 362-3077
Emp Here 24   *Sales* 9,517,760
SIC 6722 Management investment, open-end
Pr David Levi

D-U-N-S 20-309-7647   (SL)
NEWS MARKETING CANADA CORP
(*Suby of* News Corporation)
100 King St W Suite 7000, Toronto, ON, M5X 1A4
(416) 775-3000
Emp Here 50   *Sales* 5,399,092
SIC 8743 Public relations services
Sr VP Omar El Kady
Pr Pr William Vanderburg
Dir Chris Mixson
Dir Adam North

D-U-N-S 25-735-4878   (BR)
PHARMA PLUS DRUGMARTS LTD
100 King St W, Toronto, ON, M5X 2A1
(416) 362-6406
Emp Here 20
SIC 5912 Drug stores and proprietary stores

D-U-N-S 24-688-6089   (SL)
RUSSELL INVESTMENTS CANADA LIMITED
(*Suby of* Northwestern Mutual Life International, Inc.)
100 King St W Suite 5900, Toronto, ON, M5X 2A1
(416) 362-8411
Emp Here 70   *Sales* 8,104,029
SIC 6411 Insurance agents, brokers, and service
Pr David Feather
   David Steele

D-U-N-S 25-137-4229   (BR)
SIR CORP
RED VINE HEAVEN
77 Adelaide St W, Toronto, ON, M5X 1B1
(416) 862-7337
Emp Here 50
SIC 5812 Eating places

D-U-N-S 20-294-2652   (SL)
SKYPOWER SERVICES ULC
(*Suby of* Cim Group, L.P.)
100 King St W Fl 52, Toronto, ON, M5X 1C9
(416) 979-4625
Emp Here 50   *Sales* 2,699,546
SIC 8731 Commercial physical research

D-U-N-S 25-198-6472   (BR)
SOBEYS CAPITAL INCORPORATED
FRESHCO
100 King St W Suite 3900, Toronto, ON, M5X 2A1
(613) 447-7472
Emp Here 20
SIC 5411 Grocery stores

D-U-N-S 20-452-8801   (HQ)
SPEKTRA DRILLING CANADA INC
100 King St W Suite 5600, Toronto, ON, M5X

1C9
(416) 644-5096
Emp Here 35   *Emp Total* 650
Sales 7,796,259
SIC 1381 Drilling oil and gas wells
Pr Pr Levent Okay
Kerem Usenmez

D-U-N-S 24-361-7763   (BR)
STATE STREET TRUST COMPANY CANADA
(*Suby of* State Street Corporation)
100 King St W Suite 2800, Toronto, ON, M5X 2A1
(416) 214-4846
Emp Here 30
SIC 6719 Holding companies, nec

D-U-N-S 20-313-6353   (SL)
TGR RAIL CANADA INC
130 King St W Suite 1800, Toronto, ON, M5X 2A2
(519) 574-3357
Emp Here 40   *Sales* 15,321,747
SIC 4011 Railroads, line-haul operating
Kevin Street

D-U-N-S 24-425-4160   (SL)
WYZDOM TECHNOLOGIES INC
100 King St W Suite 3700, Toronto, ON, M5X 2A1
(416) 642-3064
Emp Here 500   *Sales* 49,080,000
SIC 7379 Computer related services, nec
Dir Yuliya Karassev
Pr Daniel Tobok

D-U-N-S 25-681-4096   (HQ)
WILLIS CANADA INC
WILLIS TOWERS WATSON
100 King St W Suite 4700, Toronto, ON, M5X 1K7
(416) 368-9641
Emp Here 100   *Emp Total* 120
Sales 10,798,184
SIC 6411 Insurance agents, brokers, and ser-vice
Pr Richard T Hynes
VP Opers Sarah Flint
Sec Daniel Beaudry
Eric Brooks
Derek Smyth

D-U-N-S 20-771-4551   (HQ)
ZURICH INSURANCE COMPANY LTD
100 King St W Suite 5500, Toronto, ON, M5X 2A1
(416) 586-3000
Emp Here 50   *Emp Total* 5,000
Sales 21,396,400
SIC 6411 Insurance agents, brokers, and ser-vice
Pr Alister Campbell
Sr VP Gordon E Thompson
Nigel Ayers

Toronto, ON M6A
York County

D-U-N-S 20-595-3701   (BR)
ASSOCIATED HEBREW SCHOOLS OF TORONTO
POSLUNS SCHOOL
18 Neptune Dr, Toronto, ON, M6A 1X1
(416) 787-1872
Emp Here 50
SIC 8211 Elementary and secondary schools

D-U-N-S 25-511-2666   (BR)
CASCADES CANADA ULC
NORAMPAC NORTH YORK
1280 Caledonia Rd, Toronto, ON, M6A 3B9
(416) 784-2866
Emp Here 23
SIC 2621 Paper mills

D-U-N-S 20-352-1026   (SL)
ECOHOME FINANCIAL INC
(*Suby of* Dealnet Capital Corp)
700 Lawrence Ave W Suite 325, Toronto, ON, M6A 3B4
(905) 695-8557
Emp Here 50   *Sales* 5,399,092
SIC 8742 Management consulting services
CEO Michael Hilmer
Paul Leonard
Sec Christopher Alexander

D-U-N-S 25-079-2694   (BR)
FOOT LOCKER CANADA CO.
FOOT LOCKER
3401 Dufferin St Unit 193, Toronto, ON, M6A 2T9
(416) 785-5260
Emp Here 50
SIC 5661 Shoe stores

D-U-N-S 24-109-2654   (BR)
OLD NAVY (CANADA) INC
(*Suby of* The Gap Inc)
1 Yorkdale Rd, Toronto, ON, M6A 3A1
(416) 787-9384
Emp Here 120
SIC 5651 Family clothing stores

D-U-N-S 20-283-3752   (BR)
RIOCAN REAL ESTATE INVESTMENT TRUST
RIOCAN MANAGEMENT
700 Lawrence Ave W Suite 310, Toronto, ON, M6A 3B4
(416) 866-3033
Emp Here 25
SIC 6531 Real estate agents and managers

D-U-N-S 20-025-5193   (BR)
TORONTO DISTRICT SCHOOL BOARD
SIR SANDFORD FLEMING ACADEMY
50 Ameer Ave, Toronto, ON, M6A 2L3
(416) 395-3300
Emp Here 50
SIC 8211 Elementary and secondary schools

D-U-N-S 25-000-6590   (BR)
TORONTO DISTRICT SCHOOL BOARD
LAWRENCE HEIGHTS MIDDLE SCHOOL
50 Highland Hill, Toronto, ON, M6A 2R1
(416) 395-2620
Emp Here 34
SIC 8211 Elementary and secondary schools

D-U-N-S 24-666-2980   (SL)
WEG ELECTRIC MOTORS
64 Samor Rd, Toronto, ON, M6A 1J6
(416) 781-4617
Emp Here 49   *Sales* 9,849,695
SIC 5063 Electrical apparatus and equipment
Owner Victor Pamansky

Toronto, ON M6B
York County

D-U-N-S 25-709-3666   (HQ)
DARREN MASON & ASSOCIATES LTD
ANDREWS DEPARTMENT STORE
(*Suby of* Darren Mason & Associates Ltd)
89 Tycos Dr Unit 101, Toronto, ON, M6B 1W3
(416) 969-9875
Emp Here 42   *Emp Total* 50
Sales 3,064,349
SIC 5621 Women's clothing stores

D-U-N-S 24-370-0312   (BR)
ELTE CARPETS LIMITED
ELTE WAREHOUSE
100 Miranda Ave Suite 6, Toronto, ON, M6B 3W7
(416) 785-7885
Emp Here 25
SIC 4225 General warehousing and storage

D-U-N-S 24-181-6693   (SL)
FYBON INDUSTRIES LIMITED
202 Fairbank Ave, Toronto, ON, M6B 4C5

Emp Here 70
SIC 2297 Nonwoven fabrics

D-U-N-S 25-213-0851   (HQ)
HOLLANDER SLEEP PRODUCTS CANADA LIMITED
724 Caledonia Rd, Toronto, ON, M6B 3X7
(416) 780-0168
Emp Here 50   *Emp Total* 2,124
Sales 10,395,012
SIC 2515 Mattresses and bedsprings
Pr Pr Jeff Hollander

D-U-N-S 24-918-7394   (HQ)
KITCHEN STUFF PLUS INC
125 Tycos Dr, Toronto, ON, M6B 1W6
(416) 944-2847
Emp Here 25   *Emp Total* 250
Sales 27,460,157
SIC 5719 Miscellaneous homefurnishings
Pr Pr Mark Halpern

D-U-N-S 25-246-7519   (BR)
PRISMATIQUE DESIGNS LTD
97 Wingold Ave, Toronto, ON, M6B 1P8
(416) 961-7333
Emp Here 50
SIC 2521 Wood office furniture

D-U-N-S 20-718-7233   (BR)
SOBEYS CAPITAL INCORPORATED
I G A
145 Marlee Ave, Toronto, ON, M6B 3H3
(416) 781-0145
Emp Here 35
SIC 5141 Groceries, general line

D-U-N-S 20-192-8020   (BR)
SPORT MASKA INC
ROGER EDWARDS SPORT
2811 Dufferin St, Toronto, ON, M6B 3R9
(905) 266-4321
Emp Here 24
SIC 2329 Men's and boy's clothing, nec

D-U-N-S 20-711-1001   (BR)
TORONTO CATHOLIC DISTRICT SCHOOL BOARD
OUR LADY OF THE ASSUMPTION CATHOLIC SCHOOL
125 Glenmount Ave, Toronto, ON, M6B 3C2
(416) 393-5265
Emp Here 40
SIC 8211 Elementary and secondary schools

D-U-N-S 20-698-6643   (BR)
TORONTO CATHOLIC DISTRICT SCHOOL BOARD
STS. COSMAS AND DAMIAN CATHOLIC SCHOOL
111 Danesbury Ave, Toronto, ON, M6B 3L3
(416) 393-5398
Emp Here 50
SIC 8211 Elementary and secondary schools

Toronto, ON M6C
York County

D-U-N-S 25-342-3693   (SL)
AISH HATORAH
THE VILLAGE SHUL
1072 Eglinton Ave W, Toronto, ON, M6C 2E2
(416) 785-1107
Emp Here 40   *Sales* 3,283,232
SIC 8661 Religious organizations

D-U-N-S 24-118-0517   (BR)
BANQUE TORONTO-DOMINION, LA
TORONTO-DOMINION BANK, THE
(*Suby of* Toronto-Dominion Bank, The)
687 St Clair Ave W, Toronto, ON, M6C 1B2

(416) 653-1130
Emp Here 25
SIC 6021 National commercial banks

D-U-N-S 20-583-0396   (BR)
CANADA POST CORPORATION
509 St Clair Ave W, Toronto, ON, M6C 1A1

Emp Here 20
SIC 4311 U.s. postal service

D-U-N-S 24-148-4000   (BR)
REVERA INC
1035 Eglinton Ave W Suite 302, Toronto, ON, M6C 2C8
(416) 787-5626
Emp Here 50
SIC 6513 Apartment building operators

D-U-N-S 20-711-1019   (BR)
TORONTO CATHOLIC DISTRICT SCHOOL BOARD
ST. ALPHONSUS CATHOLIC SCHOOL
60 Atlas Ave, Toronto, ON, M6C 3N9
(416) 393-5326
Emp Here 30
SIC 8211 Elementary and secondary schools

D-U-N-S 20-938-8300   (BR)
TORONTO DISTRICT SCHOOL BOARD
ARLINGTON MIDDLE SCHOOL
501 Arlington Ave, Toronto, ON, M6C 3A4
(416) 787-9899
Emp Here 20
SIC 8211 Elementary and secondary schools

D-U-N-S 25-300-9237   (BR)
TORONTO DISTRICT SCHOOL BOARD
CEDARVALE COMMUNITY SCHOOL
145 Ava Rd, Toronto, ON, M6C 1W4
(416) 394-2244
Emp Here 24
SIC 8211 Elementary and secondary schools

D-U-N-S 25-294-5035   (BR)
TORONTO DISTRICT SCHOOL BOARD
HUMEWOOD COMMUNITY SCHOOL
15 Cherrywood Ave, Toronto, ON, M6C 2X4
(416) 394-2383
Emp Here 50
SIC 8211 Elementary and secondary schools

D-U-N-S 25-294-4996   (BR)
TORONTO DISTRICT SCHOOL BOARD
J R WILCOX COMMUNITY SCHOOL
231 Ava Rd, Toronto, ON, M6C 1X3
(416) 394-2388
Emp Here 35
SIC 8211 Elementary and secondary schools

D-U-N-S 20-067-8857   (BR)
TORONTO DISTRICT SCHOOL BOARD
VAUGHAN ROAD ACADEMY
529 Vaughan Rd, Toronto, ON, M6C 2R1
(416) 394-3222
Emp Here 65
SIC 8211 Elementary and secondary schools

D-U-N-S 25-226-7836   (BR)
TORONTO DISTRICT SCHOOL BOARD
WEST PREPARATORY PUBLIC SCHOOL
70 Ridge Hill Dr, Toronto, ON, M6C 2J6
(416) 393-1633
Emp Here 35
SIC 8211 Elementary and secondary schools

Toronto, ON M6E
York County

D-U-N-S 24-987-4173   (BR)
BANK OF MONTREAL
BMO
1226 St Clair Ave W, Toronto, ON, M6E 1B4
(416) 652-3444
Emp Here 21
SIC 6021 National commercial banks

D-U-N-S 20-580-2171   (BR)
CANADA POST CORPORATION
1773 Eglinton Ave W, Toronto, ON, M6E 2H7

Emp Here 20
SIC 4311 U.s. postal service

D-U-N-S 25-302-9615   (BR)
CANADIAN IMPERIAL BANK OF COM-MERCE
CIBC
1164 St Clair Ave W, Toronto, ON, M6E 1B3
(416) 652-1152
Emp Here 20
SIC 6021 National commercial banks

D-U-N-S 20-042-8956   (BR)
CORPORATION OF THE CITY OF TORONTO
HORIZONS FOR YOUTH
422 Gilbert Ave W, Toronto, ON, M6E 4X3
(416) 781-9898
Emp Here 25
SIC 8322 Individual and family services

D-U-N-S 25-475-7792   (BR)
LOBLAW COMPANIES LIMITED
NO FRILLS PANCH'S
1951 Eglinton Ave W, Toronto, ON, M6E 2J7
(416) 256-1686
Emp Here 48
SIC 5411 Grocery stores

D-U-N-S 25-478-3434   (SL)
LYCEE FRANCAIS DE TORONTO
2327 Dufferin St, Toronto, ON, M6E 3S5
(416) 924-1789
Emp Here 60   Sales 4,012,839
SIC 8211 Elementary and secondary schools

D-U-N-S 25-344-2651   (BR)
MORIAH FOOD SERVICES LTD
MCDONALD'S
(Suby of Moriah Food Services Ltd)
1168 St Clair Ave W, Toronto, ON, M6E 1B4
(416) 652-9536
Emp Here 29
SIC 5812 Eating places

D-U-N-S 20-067-8865   (BR)
RE/MAX 2000 REALTY INC
1221 St Clair Ave W, Toronto, ON, M6E 1B5
(416) 656-3500
Emp Here 55
SIC 6531 Real estate agents and managers

D-U-N-S 20-651-3157   (BR)
SODEXO CANADA LTD
2339 Dufferin St, Toronto, ON, M6E 4Z5
(416) 781-1178
Emp Here 60
SIC 5812 Eating places

D-U-N-S 24-023-3379   (SL)
ST. HILDA'S TOWERS, INC
2339 Dufferin St, Toronto, ON, M6E 4Z5
(416) 781-6621
Emp Here 100   Sales 3,648,035
SIC 8361 Residential care

D-U-N-S 20-923-5134   (SL)
SUTTON GROUP-SECURITY REAL ESTATE INC
1239 St Clair Ave W, Toronto, ON, M6E 1B5
(416) 654-1010
Emp Here 50   Sales 4,742,446
SIC 6531 Real estate agents and managers

D-U-N-S 20-082-2240   (BR)
TORONTO CATHOLIC DISTRICT SCHOOL BOARD
ST. JOHN BOSCO CATHOLIC ELEMENTARY SCHOOL
75 Holmesdale Rd, Toronto, ON, M6E 1Y2
(416) 393-5305
Emp Here 26
SIC 8211 Elementary and secondary schools

D-U-N-S 20-700-2119   (BR)

TORONTO CATHOLIC DISTRICT SCHOOL BOARD
ST. NICHOLAS OF BARI CATHOLIC SCHOOL
363 Rogers Rd, Toronto, ON, M6E 1R6
(416) 393-5355
Emp Here 50
SIC 8211 Elementary and secondary schools

D-U-N-S 20-700-1921   (BR)
TORONTO CATHOLIC DISTRICT SCHOOL BOARD
ST. THOMAS AQUINAS ELEMENTARY
636 Glenholme Ave, Toronto, ON, M6E 3G9
(416) 393-5236
Emp Here 70
SIC 8211 Elementary and secondary schools

D-U-N-S 20-519-7473   (BR)
TORONTO CATHOLIC DISTRICT SCHOOL BOARD
STELLA MARIS CATHOLIC SCHOOL
31 Ascot Ave, Toronto, ON, M6E 1E6
(416) 393-5371
Emp Here 45
SIC 8211 Elementary and secondary schools

D-U-N-S 20-698-6726   (BR)
TORONTO CATHOLIC DISTRICT SCHOOL BOARD
D'ARCY MCGEE CATHOLIC SCHOOL
20 Bansley Ave, Toronto, ON, M6E 2A2
(416) 393-5318
Emp Here 45
SIC 8211 Elementary and secondary schools

D-U-N-S 20-698-6528   (BR)
TORONTO CATHOLIC DISTRICT SCHOOL BOARD
ST CLARE CATHOLIC SCHOOL
124 Northcliffe Blvd, Toronto, ON, M6E 3K4
(416) 393-5214
Emp Here 50
SIC 8211 Elementary and secondary schools

D-U-N-S 25-294-4715   (BR)
TORONTO DISTRICT SCHOOL BOARD
FRED H. MILLER JUNIOR PUBLIC SCHOOL
300 Caledonia Rd, Toronto, ON, M6E 4T5
(416) 394-2336
Emp Here 20
SIC 8211 Elementary and secondary schools

D-U-N-S 25-265-1385   (BR)
TORONTO DISTRICT SCHOOL BOARD
FAIRBANK PUBLIC SCHOOL
2335 Dufferin St, Toronto, ON, M6E 3S5
(416) 394-2323
Emp Here 28
SIC 8211 Elementary and secondary schools

D-U-N-S 25-294-4632   (BR)
TORONTO DISTRICT SCHOOL BOARD
FAIRBANK MEMORIAL COMMUNITY SCHOOL
555 Harvie Ave, Toronto, ON, M6E 4M2
(416) 394-2333
Emp Here 50
SIC 8211 Elementary and secondary schools

D-U-N-S 25-294-4798   (BR)
TORONTO DISTRICT SCHOOL BOARD
RAWLINSON COMMUNITY SCHOOL
231 Glenholme Ave, Toronto, ON, M6E 3C7
(416) 394-3080
Emp Here 60
SIC 8211 Elementary and secondary schools

D-U-N-S 20-290-9326   (BR)
TORONTO DISTRICT SCHOOL BOARD
OAKWOOD COLLEGIATE INSTITUTE
991 St Clair Ave W, Toronto, ON, M6E 1A3
(416) 393-1780
Emp Here 75
SIC 8211 Elementary and secondary schools

D-U-N-S 24-823-5582   (BR)
TORONTO PUBLIC LIBRARY BOARD

MARIA A. SHCHUKA BRANCH
1745 Eglinton Ave W, Toronto, ON, M6E 2H4
(416) 394-1000
Emp Here 62
SIC 8231 Libraries

D-U-N-S 25-684-5223   (BR)
TORONTO-DOMINION BANK, THE
TD CANADA TRUST
(Suby of Toronto-Dominion Bank, The)
1886 Eglinton Ave W, Toronto, ON, M6E 2J6
(416) 785-7742
Emp Here 25
SIC 6021 National commercial banks

D-U-N-S 24-021-8656   (BR)
YOUNG WOMEN'S CHRISTIAN ASSOCIA-TION OF GREATER TORONTO
YWCA
177 Caledonia Rd, Toronto, ON, M6E 4S8
(416) 652-0077
Emp Here 27
SIC 8322 Individual and family services

Toronto, ON M6G
York County

D-U-N-S 25-995-4790   (HQ)
1100833 ONTARIO LIMITED
FAEMA
(Suby of 1100833 Ontario Limited)
672 Dupont St Suite 201, Toronto, ON, M6G 1Z6
(416) 535-1555
Emp Here 43   Emp Total 50
Sales 3,648,035
SIC 5722 Household appliance stores

D-U-N-S 20-968-0487   (SL)
848357 ONTARIO INC
O'NEILL CENTER, THE
33 Christie St, Toronto, ON, M6G 3B1
(416) 536-1117
Emp Here 120   Sales 7,608,750
SIC 8051 Skilled nursing care facilities
Pr Pr C. William Dillane

D-U-N-S 24-121-0884   (BR)
BANK OF NOVA SCOTIA, THE
SCOTIABANK
643 College St, Toronto, ON, M6G 1B7
(416) 537-2191
Emp Here 20
SIC 6021 National commercial banks

D-U-N-S 24-011-4343   (BR)
CANADA TORONTO EAST MISSION
CHURCH OF JESUS CHRIST OF LATTER DAY SAINTS, THE
(Suby of Corporation of The President of The Church of Jesus Christ of Latter-Day Saints)
851 Ossington Ave, Toronto, ON, M6G 3V2
(416) 531-0535
Emp Here 100
SIC 8661 Religious organizations

D-U-N-S 25-669-0769   (BR)
CARA OPERATIONS LIMITED
SWISS CHALET ROTISSERIE & GRILL # 1751
(Suby of Cara Holdings Limited)
570 Bloor St W, Toronto, ON, M6G 1K1
(416) 538-3100
Emp Here 35
SIC 5812 Eating places

D-U-N-S 20-939-8874   (SL)
CHEN, J PHARMACY INC
SHOPPERS DRUG MART
725 College St Suite 813, Toronto, ON, M6G 1C5
(416) 534-2375
Emp Here 80   Sales 15,724,750
SIC 5912 Drug stores and proprietary stores
Pr Pr Jean Chen

D-U-N-S 25-319-9699   (SL)
CHRISTIE GARDENS APARTMENTS AND CARE INC
600 Melita Cres, Toronto, ON, M6G 3Z4
(416) 530-1330
Emp Here 100   Sales 4,523,563
SIC 8051 Skilled nursing care facilities

D-U-N-S 20-041-1218   (BR)
CORPORATION OF THE CITY OF TORONTO
BOB ABATE COMMUNITY CENTRE
485 Montrose Ave, Toronto, ON, M6G 3H2
(416) 392-0745
Emp Here 50
SIC 8322 Individual and family services

D-U-N-S 20-984-0375   (BR)
DENTSUBOS INC
DENTSUBOS INC
559 College St Suite 401, Toronto, ON, M6G 1A9
(416) 343-0010
Emp Here 40
SIC 7311 Advertising agencies

D-U-N-S 24-991-5554   (SL)
HELLENIC HOME FOR THE AGE INC
33 Winona Dr, Toronto, ON, M6G 3Z7
(416) 654-7700
Emp Here 90   Sales 3,283,232
SIC 8361 Residential care

D-U-N-S 25-374-9220   (BR)
LOBLAWS SUPERMARKETS LIMITED
LOBLAWS
650 Dupont St Suite 1029, Toronto, ON, M6G 4B1
(416) 588-3756
Emp Here 400
SIC 5141 Groceries, general line

D-U-N-S 20-799-9553   (BR)
MEDICAL PHARMACIES GROUP LIMITED
METRO MEDICAL PHARMACY
351 Christie St, Toronto, ON, M6G 3C3
(416) 530-1055
Emp Here 20
SIC 5912 Drug stores and proprietary stores

D-U-N-S 25-300-3248   (BR)
METRO ONTARIO INC
DOMINION SAVER CENTER
735 College St, Toronto, ON, M6G 1C5
(416) 533-2515
Emp Here 200
SIC 5411 Grocery stores

D-U-N-S 24-744-1686   (HQ)
RADIO 1540 LIMITED
CHIN RADIO/TV INTERNATIONAL
(Suby of Radio 1540 Limited)
622 College St Suite 2, Toronto, ON, M6G 1B6
(416) 531-9991
Emp Here 70   Emp Total 75
Sales 4,742,446
SIC 4832 Radio broadcasting stations

D-U-N-S 25-805-4154   (BR)
RE/MAX WEST REALTY INC
570 Bloor St W, Toronto, ON, M6G 1K1
(416) 588-6777
Emp Here 35
SIC 6531 Real estate agents and managers

D-U-N-S 24-763-3766   (SL)
SNAKES & LATTES INC
600 Bloor St W Suite 3, Toronto, ON, M6G 1K4
(647) 342-9229
Emp Here 70   Sales 2,115,860
SIC 5812 Eating places

D-U-N-S 25-360-6578   (BR)
SOBEYS CAPITAL INCORPORATED
SOBEYS ONTARIO
840 Dupont St, Toronto, ON, M6G 1Z8
(416) 534-3588
Emp Here 90

SIC 5411 Grocery stores

D-U-N-S 20-653-3478   (BR)
TORONTO CATHOLIC DISTRICT SCHOOL BOARD
MONSIGNOR FRASER COLLEGE - ANNEX CAMPUS
700 Markham St, Toronto, ON, M6G 2M3
(416) 393-5557
Emp Here 25
SIC 8211 Elementary and secondary schools

D-U-N-S 20-653-4898   (BR)
TORONTO CATHOLIC DISTRICT SCHOOL BOARD
ST. RAYMOND SEPARATE SCHOOL
270 Barton Ave, Toronto, ON, M6G 1R4
(416) 393-5293
Emp Here 250
SIC 8211 Elementary and secondary schools

D-U-N-S 20-711-1563   (BR)
TORONTO CATHOLIC DISTRICT SCHOOL BOARD
ST. BRUNO CATHOLIC SCHOOL
402 Melita Cres, Toronto, ON, M6G 3X6
(416) 393-5376
Emp Here 20
SIC 8211 Elementary and secondary schools

D-U-N-S 20-711-2561   (BR)
TORONTO DISTRICT SCHOOL BOARD
WINONA DRIVE SENIOR SCHOOL
101 Winona Dr, Toronto, ON, M6G 3S8
(416) 393-1680
Emp Here 50
SIC 8211 Elementary and secondary schools

D-U-N-S 20-698-7724   (BR)
TORONTO DISTRICT SCHOOL BOARD
MONTROSE JUNIOR PUBLIC SCHOOL
301 Montrose Ave, Toronto, ON, M6G 3G9
(416) 259-7823
Emp Here 20
SIC 8211 Elementary and secondary schools

D-U-N-S 20-025-2604   (BR)
TORONTO DISTRICT SCHOOL BOARD
HARBORD COLLEGIATE INSTITUTE
286 Harbord St, Toronto, ON, M6G 1G5
(416) 393-1650
Emp Here 90
SIC 8211 Elementary and secondary schools

D-U-N-S 20-711-2496   (BR)
TORONTO DISTRICT SCHOOL BOARD
MCMURRICH JUNIOR PUBLIC SCHOOL
115 Winona Dr, Toronto, ON, M6G 3S8
(416) 393-1770
Emp Here 60
SIC 8211 Elementary and secondary schools

D-U-N-S 20-711-2389   (BR)
TORONTO DISTRICT SCHOOL BOARD
CLINTON STREET JUNIOR SCHOOL
460 Manning Ave, Toronto, ON, M6G 2V7
(416) 393-9155
Emp Here 50
SIC 8211 Elementary and secondary schools

D-U-N-S 25-214-3870   (BR)
TORONTO DISTRICT SCHOOL BOARD
CENTRAL TORONTO ACADEMY
570 Shaw St, Toronto, ON, M6G 3L6
(416) 393-0030
Emp Here 86
SIC 8211 Elementary and secondary schools

D-U-N-S 25-684-4911   (BR)
TORONTO-DOMINION BANK, THE
TD CANADA TRUST
(*Suby of* Toronto-Dominion Bank, The)
574 Bloor St W, Toronto, ON, M6G 1K1
(416) 534-9211
Emp Here 25
SIC 6021 National commercial banks

Toronto, ON M6H
York County

D-U-N-S 25-231-7235   (BR)
BRICK WAREHOUSE LP, THE
1352 Dufferin St, Toronto, ON, M6H 4G4
(416) 535-3000
Emp Here 40
SIC 5712 Furniture stores

D-U-N-S 20-540-9241   (BR)
CANADA POST CORPORATION
TORONTO STN E
772 Dovercourt Rd, Toronto, ON, M6H 0A2

Emp Here 50
SIC 4311 U.s. postal service

D-U-N-S 25-342-8601   (BR)
CATHOLIC CHILDREN'S AID SOCIETY OF TORONTO, THE
900 Dufferin St Suite 219, Toronto, ON, M6H 4B1
(416) 395-1690
Emp Here 180
SIC 8322 Individual and family services

D-U-N-S 20-985-4913   (BR)
CHILDREN'S PLACE (CANADA) LP, THE
CHILDREN'S PLACE, THE
900 Dufferin St Suite 10, Toronto, ON, M6H 4A9
(416) 535-8935
Emp Here 25
SIC 5311 Department stores

D-U-N-S 20-707-8309   (BR)
CHRISTIE OSSINGTON NEIGHBOURHOOD CENTRE
CHRISTIE OSSINGTON MEN'S HOSTEL
(*Suby of* Christie Ossington Neighbourhood Centre)
973 Lansdowne Ave, Toronto, ON, M6H 3Z5
(416) 516-8642
Emp Here 20
SIC 8322 Individual and family services

D-U-N-S 20-038-2120   (BR)
CORPORATION OF THE CITY OF TORONTO
WALLACE EMMERSON COMMUNITY CENTER
1260 Dufferin St, Toronto, ON, M6H 4C3
(416) 392-0039
Emp Here 50
SIC 8322 Individual and family services

D-U-N-S 20-130-2028   (BR)
DOLLARAMA S.E.C.
DOLLARAMA
900 Dufferin St Suite 9000, Toronto, ON, M6H 4A9
(416) 538-2558
Emp Here 41
SIC 5399 Miscellaneous general merchandise

D-U-N-S 24-005-8131   (SL)
DOVERCOURT BAPTIST FOUNDATION
NEW HORIZONS TOWER
1140 Bloor St W, Toronto, ON, M6H 4E6
(416) 536-6111
Emp Here 90   *Sales* 3,283,232
SIC 8361 Residential care

D-U-N-S 25-054-7130   (BR)
FOOT LOCKER CANADA CO.
FOOTLOCKER
900 Dufferin St Unit 10, Toronto, ON, M6H 4A9
(416) 534-0076
Emp Here 25
SIC 5651 Family clothing stores

D-U-N-S 24-978-0230   (BR)
GENERAL ELECTRIC CANADA COMPANY
GE CANADA
(*Suby of* General Electric Company)
1025 Lansdowne Ave, Toronto, ON, M6H 3Z6

---

(416) 583-4200
Emp Here 50
SIC 3625 Relays and industrial controls

D-U-N-S 20-702-0652   (SL)
H.A.S. NOVELTIES LIMITED
H A S MARKETING
300 Geary Ave, Toronto, ON, M6H 2C5
(416) 593-1101
Emp Here 50   *Sales* 3,064,349
SIC 3993 Signs and advertising specialties

D-U-N-S 25-321-7442   (BR)
LONG & MCQUADE LIMITED
LONG & MCQUADE
925 Bloor St W, Toronto, ON, M6H 1L5
(416) 588-7886
Emp Here 120
SIC 5736 Musical instrument stores

D-U-N-S 25-310-8880   (BR)
MCDONALD'S   RESTAURANTS   OF CANADA LIMITED
MCDONALD'S
(*Suby of* McDonald's Corporation)
1185 Dupont St, Toronto, ON, M6H 2A5
(416) 536-4188
Emp Here 90
SIC 5812 Eating places

D-U-N-S 25-318-1812   (BR)
MCDONALD'S   RESTAURANTS   OF CANADA LIMITED
MCDONALD'S #8350
(*Suby of* McDonald's Corporation)
900 Dufferin St Unit 200, Toronto, ON, M6H 4B1
(416) 537-0934
Emp Here 50
SIC 5812 Eating places

D-U-N-S 24-849-6325   (SL)
NITTA GELATIN CANADA, INC
60 Paton Rd, Toronto, ON, M6H 1R8
(416) 532-5111
Emp Here 42   *Sales* 7,276,508
SIC 2899 Chemical preparations, nec
Pr Pr Raymond Merz
  Noryuki Tsuji
Ch Bd Noromichi Soga
  Jurgen Gallert

D-U-N-S 20-859-9550   (BR)
PACIFIC LINK COMMUNICATIONS INC
BELL WORLD
900 Dufferin St, Toronto, ON, M6H 4B1
(416) 535-3403
Emp Here 25
SIC 5999 Miscellaneous retail stores, nec

D-U-N-S 20-967-6431   (SL)
PRODUCTIVE SECURITY INC
940 Lansdowne Ave, Toronto, ON, M6H 3Z4
(416) 535-9341
Emp Here 60   *Sales* 1,896,978
SIC 7381 Detective and armored car services

D-U-N-S 20-975-9021   (BR)
SOBEYS CAPITAL INCORPORATED
FRESHCO
1245 Dupont St, Toronto, ON, M6H 2A6
(416) 537-2670
Emp Here 25
SIC 5411 Grocery stores

D-U-N-S 20-041-1259   (BR)
TORONTO CATHOLIC DISTRICT SCHOOL BOARD
ST. ANTHONY ELEMENTARY SCHOOL
130 Shanly St, Toronto, ON, M6H 1L9
(416) 393-5210
Emp Here 50
SIC 8211 Elementary and secondary schools

D-U-N-S 20-711-1241   (BR)
TORONTO CATHOLIC DISTRICT SCHOOL BOARD
ST. HELEN ELEMENTARY SCHOOL
1196 College St, Toronto, ON, M6H 1B8

---

(416) 393-5208
Emp Here 50
SIC 8211 Elementary and secondary schools

D-U-N-S 20-700-1871   (BR)
TORONTO CATHOLIC DISTRICT SCHOOL BOARD
ST. MARY OF ANGELS CATHOLIC SCHOOL
1477 Dufferin St, Toronto, ON, M6H 4C7
(416) 393-5228
Emp Here 25
SIC 8211 Elementary and secondary schools

D-U-N-S 20-025-1622   (BR)
TORONTO DISTRICT SCHOOL BOARD
BLOOR COLLEGIATE INSTITUTE
1141 Bloor St W, Toronto, ON, M6H 1M9
(416) 393-1420
Emp Here 50
SIC 8211 Elementary and secondary schools

D-U-N-S 20-067-9004   (BR)
TORONTO DISTRICT SCHOOL BOARD
DOVERCOURT PUBLIC SCHOOL
228 Bartlett Ave, Toronto, ON, M6H 3G4
(416) 393-9220
Emp Here 40
SIC 8211 Elementary and secondary schools

D-U-N-S 20-700-3315   (BR)
TORONTO DISTRICT SCHOOL BOARD
DEWSON STREET JUNIOR SCHOOL
65 Concord Ave, Toronto, ON, M6H 2N9
(416) 393-9120
Emp Here 40
SIC 8211 Elementary and secondary schools

D-U-N-S 25-373-7241   (BR)
TOYS 'R' US (CANADA) LTD
TOYS 'R' US
(*Suby of* Toys "r" Us, Inc.)
900 Dufferin St Unit 200, Toronto, ON, M6H 4B1
(416) 532-8697
Emp Here 40
SIC 5945 Hobby, toy, and game shops

D-U-N-S 25-213-6692   (BR)
VALUE VILLAGE STORES, INC
VALUE VILLAGE
(*Suby of* Savers, Inc.)
1319 Bloor St W, Toronto, ON, M6H 1P3
(416) 539-0585
Emp Here 52
SIC 5399 Miscellaneous general merchandise

D-U-N-S 25-294-8989   (BR)
WAL-MART CANADA CORP
900 Dufferin St Suite 3106, Toronto, ON, M6H 4B1
(416) 537-2561
Emp Here 100
SIC 5311 Department stores

D-U-N-S 20-106-2887   (BR)
WINNERS MERCHANTS INTERNATIONAL L.P.
WINNERS
(*Suby of* The TJX Companies Inc)
900 Dufferin St, Toronto, ON, M6H 4B1
(416) 534-9774
Emp Here 45
SIC 5651 Family clothing stores

D-U-N-S 25-375-0699   (BR)
YM INC. (SALES)
SIRENS
900 Dufferin St, Toronto, ON, M6H 4B1
(416) 536-5248
Emp Here 20
SIC 5621 Women's clothing stores

D-U-N-S 24-248-0148   (BR)
YMCA OF GREATER TORONTO
YMCA WEST END
931 College St, Toronto, ON, M6H 1A1
(416) 536-9622
Emp Here 20
SIC 8322 Individual and family services

Toronto, ON M6J
York County

D-U-N-S 20-772-3792   (SL)
341822 ONTARIO INC
MAYNARD NURSING HOME
28 Halton St, Toronto, ON, M6J 1R3
(416) 533-5198
Emp Here 84   *Sales 3,793,956*
SIC 8051 Skilled nursing care facilities

D-U-N-S 25-119-1656   (BR)
CANADA POST CORPORATION
CANADA POST STATION C
1117 Queen St W Suite 156, Toronto, ON,
M6J 3X7
(416) 532-1234
Emp Here 50
SIC 4311 U.s. postal service

D-U-N-S 20-582-6980   (BR)
CONSEIL SCOLAIRE VIAMONDE
ECOLE ELEMENTAIRE PIERRE-ELLIOTT-TRUDEAU
65 Grace St, Toronto, ON, M6J 2S4
(416) 397-2097
Emp Here 25
SIC 8211 Elementary and secondary schools

D-U-N-S 25-708-6223   (SL)
CROSS-TORONTO COMMUNITY DEVEL-OPMENT CORPORATION
FRESH START CLEANING AND MAINTE-NANCE
761 Queen St W Suite 207, Toronto, ON, M6J
1G1
(416) 504-4262
Emp Here 70   *Sales 2,425,503*
SIC 7349 Building maintenance services, nec

D-U-N-S 25-317-8016   (BR)
LIQUOR CONTROL BOARD OF ONTARIO, THE
L.C.B.O. #3
1230 Dundas St W, Toronto, ON, M6J 1X5
(416) 536-4634
Emp Here 45
SIC 5921 Liquor stores

D-U-N-S 20-133-6588   (BR)
TORONTO CATHOLIC DISTRICT SCHOOL BOARD
ST LUKE'S CATHOLIC ELEMENTARY SCHOOL
319 Ossington Ave, Toronto, ON, M6J 3A6
(416) 393-5347
Emp Here 40
SIC 8211 Elementary and secondary schools

D-U-N-S 20-078-8987   (BR)
TORONTO CATHOLIC DISTRICT SCHOOL BOARD
ST MARY ELEMENTARY SCHOOL
20 Portugal Sq, Toronto, ON, M6J 3P2
(416) 393-5205
Emp Here 25
SIC 8211 Elementary and secondary schools

D-U-N-S 20-711-2330   (BR)
TORONTO DISTRICT SCHOOL BOARD
ALEXANDER MUIR & GLADSTONE AVE SCHOOL
108 Gladstone Ave, Toronto, ON, M6J 3L2
(416) 534-8454
Emp Here 50
SIC 8211 Elementary and secondary schools

D-U-N-S 25-181-2889   (BR)
TORONTO DISTRICT SCHOOL BOARD
NIAGARA STREET PUBLIC SCHOOL
222 Niagara St, Toronto, ON, M6J 2L3
(416) 393-1371
Emp Here 25
SIC 8211 Elementary and secondary schools

D-U-N-S 20-026-0789   (BR)

TORONTO DISTRICT SCHOOL BOARD
CHARLES G FRASER JUNIOR PUBLIC SCHOOL
79 Manning Ave, Toronto, ON, M6J 2K6
(416) 393-1830
Emp Here 40
SIC 8211 Elementary and secondary schools

D-U-N-S 20-698-7252   (BR)
TORONTO DISTRICT SCHOOL BOARD
OSSINGTON OLD ORCHARD JR PUBLIC SCHOOL
380 Ossington Ave, Toronto, ON, M6J 3A5
(416) 393-0710
Emp Here 25
SIC 8211 Elementary and secondary schools

D-U-N-S 20-702-6662   (BR)
UNIVERSITY HEALTH NETWORK
WOMAN'S OWN WITHDRAWAL MANAGE-MENT CENTRE
892 Dundas St W Suite 2, Toronto, ON, M6J
1W1
(416) 603-1462
Emp Here 20
SIC 8069 Specialty hospitals, except psychi-atric

Toronto, ON M6K
York County

D-U-N-S 25-249-4174   (SL)
ACADEMY OF SPHERICAL ARTS LTD, THE
1 Snooker St, Toronto, ON, M6K 1G1
(416) 532-3075
Emp Here 50   *Sales 1,819,127*
SIC 5812 Eating places

D-U-N-S 25-988-4088   (BR)
ARCTURUS REALTY CORPORATION
100 Princes Blvd, Toronto, ON, M6K 3C3
(416) 263-3034
Emp Here 60
SIC 6512 Nonresidential building operators

D-U-N-S 25-321-5149   (BR)
BMO NESBITT BURNS INC
1360 King St W, Toronto, ON, M6K 1H3
(416) 365-6008
Emp Here 60
SIC 6211 Security brokers and dealers

D-U-N-S 20-818-4556   (SL)
BOULEVARD CLUB LIMITED, THE
1491 Lake Shore Blvd W, Toronto, ON, M6K
3C2
(416) 532-3341
Emp Here 100   *Sales 4,012,839*
SIC 7997 Membership sports and recreation
clubs

D-U-N-S 24-802-8698   (BR)
CANADA BREAD COMPANY, LIMITED
DEMPSTER BREAD
2 Fraser Ave, Toronto, ON, M6K 1Y6

Emp Here 214
SIC 2051 Bread, cake, and related products

D-U-N-S 20-823-5010   (SL)
CANADIAN NATIONAL EXHIBITION ASSO-CIATION
CNEA
210 Princes Blvd, Toronto, ON, M6K 3C3
(416) 263-3600
Emp Here 1,500   *Sales 57,055,267*
SIC 7996 Amusement parks
Pr Jim Mcmillen

D-U-N-S 25-465-2287   (BR)
CARA OPERATIONS LIMITED
HARVEY'S
(Suby of Cara Holdings Limited)
75 Hanna Ave Suite 3, Toronto, ON, M6K 3N7

(416) 535-2662
Emp Here 20
SIC 5812 Eating places

D-U-N-S 25-104-0846   (BR)
CHARTWELL RETIREMENT RESIDENCES
CHARTWELL SENIORS HOUSING REAL ESTATE INVESTMENT TRUST
138 Dowling Ave, Toronto, ON, M6K 3A6
(416) 533-7935
Emp Here 60
SIC 8051 Skilled nursing care facilities

D-U-N-S 24-342-2370   (BR)
CINEPLEX ODEON CORPORATION
CINEPLEX MEDIA CENTRAL SALES OF-FICE
102 Atlantic Ave Suite 100, Toronto, ON, M6K
1X9
(416) 695-7206
Emp Here 30
SIC 7832 Motion picture theaters, except
drive-in

D-U-N-S 20-983-1770   (SL)
COOLER SOLUTIONS INC
BRIDGEABLE
1179 King St W Suite 101, Toronto, ON, M6K
3C5
(416) 531-2665
Emp Here 50   *Sales 4,331,255*
SIC 7336 Commercial art and graphic design

D-U-N-S 24-353-5874   (BR)
CORUS ENTERTAINMENT INC
32 Atlantic Ave, Toronto, ON, M6K 1X8
(416) 479-6214
Emp Here 300
SIC 7922 Theatrical producers and services

D-U-N-S 20-699-6329   (BR)
EXTENDICARE INC
PINES LONG-TERM CARE CENTRE
150 Dunn Ave, Toronto, ON, M6K 2R6
(705) 645-4488
Emp Here 25
SIC 8051 Skilled nursing care facilities

D-U-N-S 20-364-1188   (SL)
FORTY CREEK DISTILLERY LTD
GRUPPO CAMPARI
1 Pardee Ave Suite 102, Toronto, ON, M6K
3H1
(905) 945-9225
Emp Here 100   *Sales 59,025,206*
SIC 2085 Distilled and blended liquors

D-U-N-S 24-992-2451   (SL)
GALLOP LOGISTICS CORPORATION
74 Fraser Ave Suite 100, Toronto, ON, M6K
3E1
(416) 252-1002
Emp Here 23   *Sales 5,803,882*
SIC 4731 Freight transportation arrangement
Pr Pr Tyler Ellison
  Rodger Mullen
VP VP Robert C Larose
VP Dave Shatto
Sec John Hove

D-U-N-S 20-316-9560   (SL)
GJONAJ TRANSPORT LTD
90 Tyndall Ave Suite 101, Toronto, ON, M6K
2E6
(416) 530-1014
Emp Here 117   *Sales 12,760,960*
SIC 4212 Local trucking, without storage
  Yan Zhang

D-U-N-S 24-358-2892   (BR)
MARK ANTHONY GROUP INC
249 Dufferin Ave Suite 202, Toronto, ON, M6K
1Z5
(647) 428-3123
Emp Here 20
SIC 5921 Liquor stores

D-U-N-S 25-173-6948   (SL)
MARKETING   STORE   WORLDWIDE

(CANADA) L.P., THE
MARKETING STORE, THE
1209 King St W, Toronto, ON, M6K 1G2
(416) 583-3931
Emp Here 80   *Sales 9,703,773*
SIC 8743 Public relations services
Pr John Hilbrich
Sr VP Mark Eden
Sr VP Paul Hains

D-U-N-S 20-552-8743   (BR)
METRO ONTARIO INC
METRO
100 Lynn Williams St Suite 572, Toronto, ON,
M6K 3N6
(416) 588-1300
Emp Here 250
SIC 5411 Grocery stores

D-U-N-S 24-364-1417   (SL)
MORGAN SOLAR INC
30 Ordnance St, Toronto, ON, M6K 1A2
(416) 203-1655
Emp Here 51   *Sales 3,580,850*
SIC 8731 Commercial physical research

D-U-N-S 24-461-8559   (SL)
MOVEABLE INC
67 Mowat Ave Suite 500, Toronto, ON, M6K
3E3
(416) 532-5690
Emp Here 50   *Sales 2,480,664*
SIC 2759 Commercial printing, nec

D-U-N-S 24-075-0315   (SL)
ONTARIO PLACE CORPORATION
955 Lake Shore Blvd W, Toronto, ON, M6K
3B9
(416) 314-9900
Emp Here 60   *Sales 2,699,546*
SIC 7999 Amusement and recreation, nec

D-U-N-S 25-300-6399   (BR)
REDBERRY FRANCHISING CORP
BURGER KING
1194 King St W, Toronto, ON, M6K 1E6
(416) 588-4955
Emp Here 30
SIC 5812 Eating places

D-U-N-S 20-179-7276   (BR)
REED ELSEVIER CANADA LTD
ELSEVIER CANADA
905 King St W Suite 400, Toronto, ON, M6K
3G9
(416) 253-3640
Emp Here 60
SIC 2731 Book publishing

D-U-N-S 24-886-4415   (HQ)
SOFTCHOICE CORPORATION
173 Dufferin St Suite 200, Toronto, ON, M6K
3H7
(416) 588-9002
Emp Here 600   Emp Total 35
Sales 196,118,362
SIC 7371 Custom computer programming ser-vices
Pr Pr David Macdonald
VP Fin Simon Parmar
Sr VP Kevin Wright
Sr VP Anna Filipopoulos
VP Fin Linda Millage

D-U-N-S 24-035-2885   (SL)
SOHO VFX INC
99 Atlantic Ave Suite 303, Toronto, ON, M6K
3J8
(416) 516-7863
Emp Here 50   *Sales 2,772,507*
SIC 7819 Services allied to motion pictures

D-U-N-S 20-289-9048   (BR)
TORONTO CATHOLIC DISTRICT SCHOOL BOARD
HOLY FAMILY CATHOLIC SCHOOL
141 Close Ave, Toronto, ON, M6K 2V6
(416) 393-5212
Emp Here 40

SIC 8211 Elementary and secondary schools

D-U-N-S 25-238-1009   (BR)
TORONTO DISTRICT SCHOOL BOARD
PARKDALE COLLEGIATE INSTITUTE
209 Jameson Ave, Toronto, ON, M6K 2Y3
(416) 393-9000
Emp Here 75
SIC 8211 Elementary and secondary schools

D-U-N-S 20-700-2069   (BR)
TORONTO DISTRICT SCHOOL BOARD
SHIRLEY STREET PUBLIC SCHOOL
38 Shirley St, Toronto, ON, M6K 1S9
(416) 393-9270
Emp Here 29
SIC 8211 Elementary and secondary schools

D-U-N-S 20-698-7492   (BR)
TORONTO DISTRICT SCHOOL BOARD
QUEEN VICTORIA PUBLIC SCHOOL
100 Close Ave, Toronto, ON, M6K 2V3
(416) 530-0683
Emp Here 100
SIC 8211 Elementary and secondary schools

D-U-N-S 24-745-3343   (SL)
VISION TV: CANADA'S FAITH NET-WORK/RESEAU RELIGIEUX CANADIEN
ONE: THE BODY MIND & SPIRIT CHANNEL
171 East Liberty St Suite 230, Toronto, ON,
M6K 3P6
(416) 368-3194
Emp Here 48   *Sales* 8,441,760
SIC 7922 Theatrical producers and services
Pr William Roberts
 Mark Prasuhn
 Jane Macnaughton
 Paul Mitchell

D-U-N-S 25-101-6853   (SL)
WEB KREW INC
107 Atlantic Ave, Toronto, ON, M6K 1Y2

Emp Here 70   *Sales* 4,591,130
SIC 7374 Data processing and preparation

Toronto, ON M6L
York County

D-U-N-S 24-335-0472   (BR)
METRO ONTARIO INC
METRO
1411 Lawrence Ave W, Toronto, ON, M6L 1A4
(416) 248-5846
Emp Here 150
SIC 5411 Grocery stores

D-U-N-S 25-294-8948   (BR)
WAL-MART CANADA CORP
1305 Lawrence Ave W, Toronto, ON, M6L 1A5
(416) 244-1171
Emp Here 260
SIC 5311 Department stores

Toronto, ON M6M
York County

D-U-N-S 24-952-9074   (HQ)
COMMISSO BROS. & RACCO ITALIAN BAKERY INC
(*Suby of* Commisso Bros. & Racco Italian
Bakery Inc)
8 Kincort St, Toronto, ON, M6M 3E1
(416) 651-7671
Emp Here 47   *Emp Total* 60
Sales 4,320,640
SIC 2051 Bread, cake, and related products

D-U-N-S 20-311-9284   (BR)
IRVING CONSUMER PRODUCTS LIMITED
JD IRVING

1551 Weston Rd, Toronto, ON, M6M 4Y4
(416) 246-6666
Emp Here 400
SIC 2676 Sanitary paper products

D-U-N-S 25-936-9635   (BR)
IRVING CONSUMER PRODUCTS LIMITED
IRVING, J D
1551 Weston Rd, Toronto, ON, M6M 4Y4
(416) 246-6600
Emp Here 400
SIC 2676 Sanitary paper products

D-U-N-S 24-526-1821   (HQ)
LEARNING ENRICHMENT FOUNDATION, THE
LEF
(*Suby of* Learning Enrichment Foundation,
The)
116 Industry St, Toronto, ON, M6M 4L8
(416) 769-0830
Emp Here 100   *Emp Total* 300
Sales 12,459,520
SIC 8351 Child day care services
Ex Dir Peter Frampton
Pr Pr Ed Lamoureux
VP VP Grace Nalbandian
VP VP Louise Mahood
 Kathleen Macdonald

D-U-N-S 24-033-9775   (BR)
LOBLAW PROPERTIES LIMITED
LOBLAWS INC
605 Rogers Rd Suite 208, Toronto, ON, M6M
1B9
(416) 653-1951
Emp Here 80
SIC 5411 Grocery stores

D-U-N-S 20-079-0249   (BR)
NUCLEUS INDEPENDENT LIVING
30 Denarda St Suite 309, Toronto, ON, M6M
5C3
(416) 244-1234
Emp Here 150
SIC 8361 Residential care

D-U-N-S 24-631-5766   (BR)
REVERA INC
HAROLD & GRACE BAKER CENTRE
1 Northwestern Ave, Toronto, ON, M6M 2J7
(416) 654-2889
Emp Here 200
SIC 8051 Skilled nursing care facilities

D-U-N-S 20-698-6551   (BR)
TORONTO CATHOLIC DISTRICT SCHOOL BOARD
ST BERNARD CATHOLIC SCHOOL
12 Duckworth St, Toronto, ON, M6M 4W4
(416) 393-5261
Emp Here 45
SIC 8211 Elementary and secondary schools

D-U-N-S 20-281-1873   (BR)
TORONTO DISTRICT SCHOOL BOARD
GEORGE HARVEY COLLEGIATE INSTI-TUTE
1700 Keele St, Toronto, ON, M6M 3W5
(416) 394-3180
Emp Here 50
SIC 8211 Elementary and secondary schools

D-U-N-S 24-937-1980   (BR)
TORONTO DISTRICT SCHOOL BOARD
YORK MEMORIAL COLLEGIATE INSTITUTE
2690 Eglinton Ave W, Toronto, ON, M6M 1T9
(416) 394-3000
Emp Here 150
SIC 8211 Elementary and secondary schools

D-U-N-S 20-079-2757   (BR)
TORONTO DISTRICT SCHOOL BOARD
PORTAGE TRAIL COMMUNITY SCHOOL
100 Sidney Belsey Cres, Toronto, ON, M6M
5H6
(416) 394-4260
Emp Here 50

SIC 8211 Elementary and secondary schools

D-U-N-S 20-700-2564   (BR)
TORONTO DISTRICT SCHOOL BOARD
BROOKHAVEN PUBLIC SCHOOL
70 Brookhaven Dr, Toronto, ON, M6M 4N8
(416) 395-2110
Emp Here 60
SIC 8211 Elementary and secondary schools

D-U-N-S 25-294-4913   (BR)
TORONTO DISTRICT SCHOOL BOARD
KEELESDALE JUNIOR PUBLIC SCHOOL
200 Bicknell Ave, Toronto, ON, M6M 4G9
(416) 394-3050
Emp Here 24
SIC 8211 Elementary and secondary schools

D-U-N-S 20-700-2721   (BR)
TORONTO DISTRICT SCHOOL BOARD
CHARLES E. WEBSTER PUBLIC SCHOOL
1900 Keele St, Toronto, ON, M6M 3X7
(416) 394-2250
Emp Here 50
SIC 8211 Elementary and secondary schools

D-U-N-S 25-300-9153   (BR)
TORONTO DISTRICT SCHOOL BOARD
YORK HUMBER HIGH SCHOOL
100 Emmett Ave, Toronto, ON, M6M 2E6
(416) 394-3280
Emp Here 75
SIC 8211 Elementary and secondary schools

D-U-N-S 25-294-4475   (BR)
TORONTO DISTRICT SCHOOL BOARD
BALA AVENUE JUNIOR SCHOOL
6 Bala Ave, Toronto, ON, M6M 2E1
(416) 394-2210
Emp Here 42
SIC 8211 Elementary and secondary schools

D-U-N-S 25-802-1351   (BR)
VALUE VILLAGE STORES, INC
SAVERS
(*Suby of* Savers, Inc.)
605 Rogers Rd, Toronto, ON, M6M 1B9
(416) 247-7372
Emp Here 25
SIC 5399 Miscellaneous general merchandise

Toronto, ON M6N
York County

D-U-N-S 24-333-8845   (SL)
A.C.D. WHOLESALE MEATS LTD
140 Ryding Ave, Toronto, ON, M6N 1H2
(416) 766-2200
Emp Here 30   *Sales* 7,660,874
SIC 5147 Meats and meat products
Pr Pr Albert Domingues

D-U-N-S 24-844-0661   (SL)
BENNY STARK LIMITED
200 Union St, Toronto, ON, M6N 3M9
(416) 654-3464
Emp Here 55   *Sales* 13,351,808
SIC 5093 Scrap and waste materials
Pt Stephen Stark
 Martin Gollan

D-U-N-S 24-363-0915   (BR)
BEST BUY CANADA LTD
FUTURE SHOP
(*Suby of* Best Buy Co., Inc.)
10 Old Stock Yards Rd, Toronto, ON, M6N 5G8
(416) 766-1577
Emp Here 50
SIC 5731 Radio, television, and electronic
stores

D-U-N-S 20-042-1308   (BR)
CANADA BREAD COMPANY, LIMITED
CENTRAL BAKERY DEMPSTER
130 Cawthra Ave, Toronto, ON, M6N 3C2

(416) 626-4382
Emp Here 100
SIC 2051 Bread, cake, and related products

D-U-N-S 20-580-4664   (BR)
CANADA POST CORPORATION
JAN PARK POST OFFICE
873 Jane St, Toronto, ON, M6N 4C4
(416) 763-1311
Emp Here 20
SIC 4311 U.s. postal service

D-U-N-S 20-015-6839   (BR)
CANADIAN PACIFIC RAILWAY COMPANY
750 Runnymede Rd, Toronto, ON, M6N 3V4
(416) 761-5405
Emp Here 25
SIC 4011 Railroads, line-haul operating

D-U-N-S 25-088-6645   (BR)
CARA OPERATIONS LIMITED
SWISS CHALET
(*Suby of* Cara Holdings Limited)
590 Keele St, Toronto, ON, M6N 3E2
(416) 760-7893
Emp Here 100
SIC 5812 Eating places

D-U-N-S 25-794-1500   (SL)
CONTINENTAL MAINTENANCE CORP
1565 Keele St, Toronto, ON, M6N 3G1
(416) 604-3435
Emp Here 66   *Sales* 1,896,978
SIC 7349 Building maintenance services, nec

D-U-N-S 25-344-4053   (SL)
DAVENPORT/PERTH   NEIGHBORHOOD CENTER
1900 Davenport Rd, Toronto, ON, M6N 1B7
(416) 656-8025
Emp Here 50   *Sales* 1,969,939
SIC 8322 Individual and family services

D-U-N-S 25-754-2944   (BR)
HOME DEPOT OF CANADA INC
HOME DEPOT
(*Suby of* The Home Depot Inc)
2121 St Clair Ave W, Toronto, ON, M6N 5A8
(416) 766-2800
Emp Here 300
SIC 5251 Hardware stores

D-U-N-S 20-629-2740   (BR)
ICS UNIVERSAL DRUM RECONDITIONING LIMITED PARTNERSHIP
110 Glen Scarlett Rd, Toronto, ON, M6N 1P4
(416) 763-1102
Emp Here 40
SIC 5085 Industrial supplies

D-U-N-S 20-784-7997   (SL)
LAMBTON GOLF AND COUNTRY CLUB LIMITED, THE
100 Scarlett Rd, Toronto, ON, M6N 4K2
(416) 767-2175
Emp Here 60   *Sales* 2,407,703
SIC 7997 Membership sports and recreation
clubs

D-U-N-S 24-344-5108   (BR)
MAPLE LEAF FOODS INC
100 Ethel Ave, Toronto, ON, M6N 4Z7
(416) 767-5151
Emp Here 700
SIC 2015 Poultry slaughtering and processing

D-U-N-S 24-173-8231   (BR)
MCDONALD'S   RESTAURANTS   OF CANADA LIMITED
MCDONALD'S
(*Suby of* McDonald's Corporation)
630 Keele St, Toronto, ON, M6N 3E2
(416) 604-1496
Emp Here 100
SIC 5812 Eating places

D-U-N-S 24-324-0020   (BR)
NATIONAL   RUBBER   TECHNOLOGIES CORP

---

394 Symington Ave, Toronto, ON, M6N 2W3
(416) 657-1111
Emp Here 130
SIC 2822 Synthetic rubber

D-U-N-S 20-176-4479 (HQ)
PHANTOM INDUSTRIES INC
207 Weston Rd, Toronto, ON, M6N 4Z3
(416) 762-7177
Emp Here 475 *Emp Total* 450
Sales 49,943,437
SIC 2251 Women's hosiery, except socks
Treas Alex Strasser
Pr Pr Ronnie Strasser
VP Prd Franca Rossini
VP Fin Frank Marascio

D-U-N-S 24-228-3252 (BR)
ROGERS COMMUNICATIONS INC
ROGERS TELEPHONE ANSWERING SVC
(*Suby of* Rogers Communications Inc)
35 Scarlett Rd, Toronto, ON, M6N 4J9
(416) 769-6123
Emp Here 50
SIC 4899 Communication services, nec

D-U-N-S 20-860-3287 (BR)
SOURCE (BELL) ELECTRONICS INC, THE
SOURCE, THE
2151 St Clair Ave W Unit 103, Toronto, ON, M6N 1K5
(416) 604-3224
Emp Here 25
SIC 5999 Miscellaneous retail stores, nec

D-U-N-S 25-791-5728 (BR)
STAPLES CANADA INC
STAPLES THE BUSINESS DEPOT
(*Suby of* Staples, Inc.)
542 Keele St, Toronto, ON, M6N 3E2
(416) 762-2816
Emp Here 40
SIC 5943 Stationery stores

D-U-N-S 20-700-1913 (BR)
TORONTO CATHOLIC DISTRICT SCHOOL BOARD
ST MATTHEW'S ELEMENTARY SCHOOL
18 Lavender Rd, Toronto, ON, M6N 2B5
(416) 393-5240
Emp Here 60
SIC 8211 Elementary and secondary schools

D-U-N-S 20-700-2390 (BR)
TORONTO CATHOLIC DISTRICT SCHOOL BOARD
BLESSED POPE PAUL VI ELEMENTARY SCHOOL
270 Laughton Ave, Toronto, ON, M6N 2X8
(416) 393-5374
Emp Here 30
SIC Elementary and secondary schools

D-U-N-S 20-067-9228 (BR)
TORONTO CATHOLIC DISTRICT SCHOOL BOARD
ARCHBISHOP ROMERO CATHOLIC SEC-ONDARY SCHOOL
99 Humber Blvd, Toronto, ON, M6N 2H4
(416) 393-5555
Emp Here 100
SIC 8211 Elementary and secondary schools

D-U-N-S 20-711-1027 (BR)
TORONTO CATHOLIC DISTRICT SCHOOL BOARD
SANTA MARIA CATHOLIC SCHOOL
25 Avon Ave, Toronto, ON, M6N 4X8
(416) 393-5368
Emp Here 25
SIC 8211 Elementary and secondary schools

D-U-N-S 20-700-2275 (BR)
TORONTO CATHOLIC DISTRICT SCHOOL BOARD
OUR LADY OF VICTORY CATHOLIC SCHOOL
70 Guestville Ave, Toronto, ON, M6N 4N3

(416) 393-5247
Emp Here 100
SIC 8211 Elementary and secondary schools

D-U-N-S 20-081-7034 (BR)
TORONTO DISTRICT SCHOOL BOARD
GENERAL MERCER JUNIOR PUBLIC SCHOOL
30 Turnberry Ave, Toronto, ON, M6N 1P8
(416) 393-1414
Emp Here 45
SIC 8211 Elementary and secondary schools

D-U-N-S 25-294-5191 (BR)
TORONTO DISTRICT SCHOOL BOARD
GEORGE SYME COMMUNITY SCHOOL
69 Pritchard Ave, Toronto, ON, M6N 1T6
(416) 394-2340
Emp Here 90
SIC 8211 Elementary and secondary schools

D-U-N-S 20-025-2638 (BR)
TORONTO DISTRICT SCHOOL BOARD
CARLETON VILLAGE JUNIOR AND SENIOR SPORTS AND WELLNESS ACADEMY
315 Osler St, Toronto, ON, M6N 2Z4
(416) 393-1600
Emp Here 50
SIC 8211 Elementary and secondary schools

D-U-N-S 25-294-4830 (BR)
TORONTO DISTRICT SCHOOL BOARD
LAMBTON PARK COMMUNITY SCHOOL
50 Bernice Cres, Toronto, ON, M6N 1W9
(416) 394-3070
Emp Here 30
SIC 8211 Elementary and secondary schools

D-U-N-S 25-294-4590 (BR)
TORONTO DISTRICT SCHOOL BOARD
DENNIS AVENUE COMMUNITY SCHOOL
17 Dennis Ave, Toronto, ON, M6N 2T7
(416) 394-2311
Emp Here 30
SIC 8211 Elementary and secondary schools

D-U-N-S 24-174-4437 (BR)
TORONTO DISTRICT SCHOOL BOARD
FACILITIES SERVICES
401 Alliance Ave, Toronto, ON, M6N 2J1
(416) 394-3411
Emp Here 40
SIC 7349 Building maintenance services, nec

D-U-N-S 25-294-4756 (BR)
TORONTO DISTRICT SCHOOL BOARD
ROCKCLIFFE MIDDLE SCHOOL
400 Rockcliffe Blvd, Toronto, ON, M6N 4R8
(416) 394-3100
Emp Here 45
SIC 8211 Elementary and secondary schools

D-U-N-S 25-300-8957 (BR)
TORONTO DISTRICT SCHOOL BOARD
FRANK OKE SECONDARY SCHOOL
500 Alliance Ave, Toronto, ON, M6N 2H8
(416) 394-3158
Emp Here 25
SIC 8211 Elementary and secondary schools

D-U-N-S 25-294-5159 (BR)
TORONTO DISTRICT SCHOOL BOARD
HARWOOD JUNIOR MIDDLE SCHOOL
50 Leigh St, Toronto, ON, M6N 3X3
(416) 394-2350
Emp Here 25
SIC 8211 Elementary and secondary schools

D-U-N-S 25-294-4400 (BR)
TORONTO DISTRICT SCHOOL BOARD
CORDELLA JUNIOR SCHOOL
175 Cordella Ave, Toronto, ON, M6N 2K1
(416) 394-2258
Emp Here 34
SIC 8211 Elementary and secondary schools

D-U-N-S 25-300-8791 (BR)
TORONTO DISTRICT SCHOOL BOARD
ROSELANDS JUNIOR PUBLIC SCHOOL

990 Jane St, Toronto, ON, M6N 4E2
(416) 394-3110
Emp Here 40
SIC 8211 Elementary and secondary schools

D-U-N-S 24-319-1090 (BR)
WAL-MART CANADA CORP
WAL-MART
2525 St Clair Ave W, Toronto, ON, M6N 4Z5
(416) 763-7325
Emp Here 120
SIC 5311 Department stores

Toronto, ON M6P
York County

D-U-N-S 20-563-8385 (BR)
CANADIAN RED CROSS SOCIETY, THE
21 Randolph Ave, Toronto, ON, M6P 4G4
(416) 480-2500
Emp Here 45
SIC 8399 Social services, nec

D-U-N-S 20-067-9277 (BR)
CORPORATION OF THE CITY OF TORONTO
KEELE RECREATION CENTRE
181 Glenlake Ave, Toronto, ON, M6P 4B6
(416) 392-0695
Emp Here 30
SIC 8322 Individual and family services

D-U-N-S 25-462-2947 (SL)
CULTURELINK SETTLEMENT SERVICES OF METROPOLITAN TORONTO
2340 Dundas St W Suite 301, Toronto, ON, M6P 4A9
(416) 588-6288
Emp Here 52 *Sales* 2,042,900
SIC 8322 Individual and family services

D-U-N-S 25-794-2375 (SL)
DOMINION JANITORIAL SERVICES LTD
23 Humberside Ave, Toronto, ON, M6P 1J6
(416) 766-1082
Emp Here 50 *Sales* 1,459,214
SIC 7349 Building maintenance services, nec

D-U-N-S 25-925-8960 (BR)
GOVERNING COUNCIL OF THE SALVA-TION ARMY IN CANADA, THE
GOVERNING COUNCIL OF THE SALVATION ARMY IN CANADA, THE
2808 Dundas St W, Toronto, ON, M6P 1Y5
(416) 762-9636
Emp Here 30
SIC 8322 Individual and family services

D-U-N-S 25-310-8922 (BR)
MCDONALD'S RESTAURANTS OF CANADA LIMITED
MCDONALD'S #8325
(*Suby of* McDonald's Corporation)
2365 Dundas St W, Toronto, ON, M6P 1W7
(416) 536-3715
Emp Here 40
SIC 5812 Eating places

D-U-N-S 20-081-0450 (BR)
TORONTO CATHOLIC DISTRICT SCHOOL BOARD
ST. CECILIA CATHOLIC SCHOOL
355 Annette St, Toronto, ON, M6P 1R3
(416) 393-5218
Emp Here 31
SIC 8211 Elementary and secondary schools

D-U-N-S 20-711-1324 (BR)
TORONTO CATHOLIC DISTRICT SCHOOL BOARD
ST. LUIGI CATHOLIC SCHOOL
2 Ruskin Ave, Toronto, ON, M6P 3P8
(416) 393-5370
Emp Here 50
SIC 8211 Elementary and secondary schools

D-U-N-S 20-711-1456 (BR)
TORONTO CATHOLIC DISTRICT SCHOOL BOARD
ST. RITA CATHOLIC SCHOOL
178 Edwin Ave, Toronto, ON, M6P 3Z9
(416) 393-5216
Emp Here 50
SIC 8211 Elementary and secondary schools

D-U-N-S 20-711-1290 (BR)
TORONTO CATHOLIC DISTRICT SCHOOL BOARD
THOMAS MERTON CATHOLIC SEC-ONDARY SCHOOL
1515 Bloor St W, Toronto, ON, M6P 1A3
(416) 393-5545
Emp Here 50
SIC 8211 Elementary and secondary schools

D-U-N-S 20-698-7674 (BR)
TORONTO DISTRICT SCHOOL BOARD
KEELE ST JR PS
99 Mountview Ave, Toronto, ON, M6P 2L5
(416) 393-9035
Emp Here 40
SIC 8211 Elementary and secondary schools

D-U-N-S 20-592-0932 (BR)
TORONTO DISTRICT SCHOOL BOARD
ANNETTE STREET PUBLIC SCHOOL
265 Annette St, Toronto, ON, M6P 1R3
(416) 393-9040
Emp Here 20
SIC 8211 Elementary and secondary schools

D-U-N-S 20-025-0004 (BR)
TORONTO DISTRICT SCHOOL BOARD
LUCY MCCORMICK SCHOOL
2717 Dundas St W, Toronto, ON, M6P 1Y1
(416) 397-2713
Emp Here 61
SIC 8211 Elementary and secondary schools

D-U-N-S 20-025-3255 (BR)
TORONTO DISTRICT SCHOOL BOARD
URSULA FRANKLIN ACADEMY
146 Glendonwynne Rd, Toronto, ON, M6P 3J7
(416) 393-0430
Emp Here 41
SIC 8211 Elementary and secondary schools

D-U-N-S 20-025-0020 (BR)
TORONTO DISTRICT SCHOOL BOARD
PERTH AVENUE JUNIOR PUBLIC SCHOOL
14 Ruskin Ave, Toronto, ON, M6P 3P8
(416) 393-1410
Emp Here 38
SIC 8211 Elementary and secondary schools

Toronto, ON M6R
York County

D-U-N-S 20-983-8726 (SL)
AUTHENTIC CONCIERGE AND SECURITY SERVICES INC
PILLAR SECURITY
2333 Dundas St W Suite 206, Toronto, ON, M6R 3A6
(416) 777-1812
Emp Here 55 *Sales* 1,678,096
SIC 7381 Detective and armored car services

D-U-N-S 25-794-1948 (SL)
DAFINA HOLDINGS LIMITED
128 Sterling Rd, Toronto, ON, M6R 2B7
(416) 364-8128
Emp Here 60 *Sales* 13,695,750
SIC 2399 Fabricated textile products, nec
Pr Farooque Dawood

D-U-N-S 20-641-3663 (BR)
LUCAS & MARCO INC
MCDONALD'S
10 The Queensway, Toronto, ON, M6R 1B4

(416) 538-2444
Emp Here 50
SIC 5812 Eating places

D-U-N-S 24-803-1122   (BR)
NESTLE CANADA INC
72 Sterling Rd, Toronto, ON, M6R 2B6
(416) 535-2181
Emp Here 505
SIC 2064 Candy and other confectionery products

D-U-N-S 20-714-7658   (SL)
ONTARIO FAMILY GROUP HOMES INC
146 Westminster Ave, Toronto, ON, M6R 1N7
(416) 532-6234
Emp Here 75   *Sales* 3,291,754
SIC 8361 Residential care

D-U-N-S 24-568-5651   (SL)
PARKDALE COMMUNITY FOOD BANK
1499 Queen St W, Toronto, ON, M6R 1A3
(416) 532-2375
Emp Here 49   *Sales* 9,193,048
SIC 8399 Social services, nec
Nancy Leblanc
Emmanuelle Fontaine
Kristy Smith
Benjamin Trister
David White
Jack Martino
Jeannette Body
Brian Mcguire

D-U-N-S 24-620-2753   (BR)
SOBEYS CAPITAL INCORPORATED
SOBEYS
199 Roncesvalles Ave, Toronto, ON, M6R 2L5
(416) 588-3363
Emp Here 30
SIC 5411 Grocery stores

D-U-N-S 20-081-0443   (BR)
TORONTO CATHOLIC DISTRICT SCHOOL BOARD
ST. VINCENT DE PAUL ELEMENTARY SCHOOL
116 Fermanagh Ave, Toronto, ON, M6R 1M2
(416) 393-5227
Emp Here 24
SIC 8211 Elementary and secondary schools

D-U-N-S 20-711-2447   (BR)
TORONTO DISTRICT SCHOOL BOARD
FERN AVENUE PUBLIC SCHOOL
128 Fern Ave, Toronto, ON, M6R 1K3
(416) 393-9130
Emp Here 50
SIC 8211 Elementary and secondary schools

D-U-N-S 20-698-7740   (BR)
TORONTO DISTRICT SCHOOL BOARD
GARDEN AVENUE PUBLIC SCHOOL
225 Garden Ave, Toronto, ON, M6R 1H9
(416) 393-9165
Emp Here 30
SIC 8211 Elementary and secondary schools

D-U-N-S 20-698-7393   (BR)
TORONTO DISTRICT SCHOOL BOARD
HOWARD JR PUBLIC SCHOOL
30 Marmaduke St, Toronto, ON, M6R 1T2
(416) 393-9255
Emp Here 38
SIC 8211 Elementary and secondary schools

D-U-N-S 25-692-6890   (BR)
TURNER & PORTER FUNERAL DIRECTORS LIMITED
TURNER & PORTER RONCESVALLES CHAPEL
436 Roncesvalles Ave, Toronto, ON, M6R 2N2

Emp Here 20
SIC 7261 Funeral service and crematories

Toronto, ON M6S
York County

D-U-N-S 25-296-8888   (BR)
BANK OF NOVA SCOTIA, THE
SCOTIABANK
2295 Bloor St W, Toronto, ON, M6S 1P1
(416) 760-2330
Emp Here 30
SIC 6021 National commercial banks

D-U-N-S 25-721-2142   (BR)
BANK OF MONTREAL
BMO
2330 Bloor St W, Toronto, ON, M6S 1P3
(416) 769-4151
Emp Here 20
SIC 6021 National commercial banks

D-U-N-S 20-588-2181   (BR)
BANQUE TORONTO-DOMINION, LA
TD CANADA TRUST
(*Suby of* Toronto-Dominion Bank, The)
3422 Dundas St W, Toronto, ON, M6S 2S1

Emp Here 20
SIC 6021 National commercial banks

D-U-N-S 25-295-1918   (BR)
BREWERS RETAIL INC
BEER STORE, THE
3524 Dundas St W, Toronto, ON, M6S 2S1
(416) 767-0441
Emp Here 20
SIC 5921 Liquor stores

D-U-N-S 24-346-5502   (BR)
CHAUHAN FOOD SERVICES INC
TIM HORTONS
3487 Dundas St W, Toronto, ON, M6S 2S5
(416) 763-3113
Emp Here 20
SIC 5812 Eating places

D-U-N-S 24-847-2870   (HQ)
CINTAS CANADA LIMITED
SALLY FOURMY & ASSOCIATES
(*Suby of* Cintas Corporation)
3370 Dundas St W Suite 882, Toronto, ON, M6S 2S1
(416) 763-4400
Emp Here 200   *Emp Total* 35,000
Sales 57,493,032
SIC 7218 Industrial launderers
Dir Richard Scott
Anna Costa

D-U-N-S 20-164-7500   (SL)
CORONA JEWELLERY COMPANY LTD
CORONA COMPANY
16 Ripley Ave, Toronto, ON, M6S 3P1
(416) 762-2222
Emp Here 60   *Sales* 5,197,506
SIC 3911 Jewelry, precious Metal
Pr Pr Albert Minister
Carl Morawetz
John Minister

D-U-N-S 20-067-9293   (BR)
LIQUOR CONTROL BOARD OF ONTARIO, THE
THE LIQUOR STORE
3520 Dundas St W, Toronto, ON, M6S 2S1
(416) 762-8215
Emp Here 22
SIC 5921 Liquor stores

D-U-N-S 20-940-4610   (BR)
LOBLAWS SUPERMARKETS LIMITED
LOBLAWS
3671 Dundas St W, Toronto, ON, M6S 2T3
(416) 769-7171
Emp Here 50
SIC 5411 Grocery stores

D-U-N-S 20-092-2701   (BR)
MORIAH FOOD SERVICES LTD
MCDONALD'S

2218 Bloor St W, Toronto, ON, M6S 1N4
(416) 762-9949
Emp Here 40
SIC 5812 Eating places

D-U-N-S 25-193-2513   (BR)
NORTHERN REFLECTIONS LTD
2198 Bloor St W, Toronto, ON, M6S 1N4
(416) 769-8378
Emp Here 108
SIC 5621 Women's clothing stores

D-U-N-S 25-805-4733   (BR)
ROYAL LEPAGE LIMITED
ROYAL LEPAGE REAL ESTATE SERVICES
2320 Bloor St W, Toronto, ON, M6S 1P2
(416) 762-8255
Emp Here 60
SIC 6531 Real estate agents and managers

D-U-N-S 24-860-8507   (SL)
SCANFIELD HOLDINGS LIMITED
2 Jane St Suite 211, Toronto, ON, M6S 4W8
(416) 763-4531
Emp Here 2,191   *Sales* 60,464,200
SIC 6553 Cemetery subdividers and developers
David Scanlan

D-U-N-S 20-735-0067   (SL)
SMARDANKA RESTAURANTS LIMITED
FAN SPORTS CAFE, THE
2448 Bloor St W, Toronto, ON, M6S 1R2

Emp Here 60   *Sales* 1,824,018
SIC 5812 Eating places

D-U-N-S 25-341-8446   (BR)
SOBEYS CAPITAL INCORPORATED
FRESHCO
3400 Dundas St W, Toronto, ON, M6S 2S1
(416) 767-1510
Emp Here 50
SIC 5411 Grocery stores

D-U-N-S 25-874-7179   (BR)
SUTTON GROUP REALTY SYSTEMS INC
SUTTON GROUP REALTY
2186 Bloor St W, Toronto, ON, M6S 1N3
(416) 762-4200
Emp Here 60
SIC 6531 Real estate agents and managers

D-U-N-S 20-700-2473   (BR)
TORONTO CATHOLIC DISTRICT SCHOOL BOARD
ST. PIUS X ELEMENTARY SCHOOL
71 Jane St, Toronto, ON, M6S 3Y3
(416) 393-5237
Emp Here 30
SIC 8211 Elementary and secondary schools

D-U-N-S 25-265-4108   (BR)
TORONTO CATHOLIC DISTRICT SCHOOL BOARD
JAMES CULNAN CATHOLIC SCHOOL
605 Willard Ave, Toronto, ON, M6S 3S1
(416) 393-5325
Emp Here 50
SIC 8211 Elementary and secondary schools

D-U-N-S 20-520-3818   (BR)
TORONTO CATHOLIC DISTRICT SCHOOL BOARD
ST. JAMES ELEMENTARY SCHOOL
230 Humbercrest Blvd, Toronto, ON, M6S 4L3
(416) 393-5275
Emp Here 20
SIC 8211 Elementary and secondary schools

D-U-N-S 20-711-2512   (BR)
TORONTO DISTRICT SCHOOL BOARD
RUNNYMEDE JUNIOR AND SENIOR PUBLIC SCHOOL
357 Runnymede Rd, Toronto, ON, M6S 2Y7
(416) 393-9055
Emp Here 70
SIC 8211 Elementary and secondary schools

D-U-N-S 20-084-0937   (BR)
TORONTO DISTRICT SCHOOL BOARD
HUMBERCREST PUBLIC SCHOOL
14 Saint Marks Rd, Toronto, ON, M6S 2H7
(416) 394-2370
Emp Here 52
SIC 8211 Elementary and secondary schools

D-U-N-S 25-281-3605   (BR)
TORONTO DISTRICT SCHOOL BOARD
SWANSEA PUBLIC SCHOOL
207 Windermere Ave, Toronto, ON, M6S 3J9
(416) 763-1908
Emp Here 60
SIC 8211 Elementary and secondary schools

D-U-N-S 25-214-7509   (BR)
TORONTO DISTRICT SCHOOL BOARD
RUNNYMEDE COLLEGIATE INSTITUTE
569 Jane St, Toronto, ON, M6S 4A3
(416) 394-3200
Emp Here 50
SIC 8211 Elementary and secondary schools

D-U-N-S 25-294-4871   (BR)
TORONTO DISTRICT SCHOOL BOARD
KING GEORGE JUNIOR PUBLIC SCHOOL
25 Rexford Rd, Toronto, ON, M6S 2M2
(416) 394-3060
Emp Here 20
SIC 8211 Elementary and secondary schools

D-U-N-S 24-308-4464   (HQ)
TRILLIUM FUNERAL SERVICE CORPORATION
DODSWORTH & BROWN FUNERAL HOME
2 Jane St Suite 211, Toronto, ON, M6S 4W8
(416) 763-4531
Emp Here 100   *Emp Total* 4,055
Sales 58,896,000
SIC 7261 Funeral service and crematories
Pr Pr Jeffrey Scott
VP VP Jack Doney
Terry Eccles
Laurel Ancheta

Toronto, ON M7A
York County

D-U-N-S 20-868-3974   (BR)
BMO NESBITT BURNS INC
95 Grosvenor St Suite 600, Toronto, ON, M7A 1Z1
(416) 325-0755
Emp Here 25
SIC 6211 Security brokers and dealers

D-U-N-S 24-330-8702   (BR)
GOVERNMENT OF ONTARIO
MINISTRY OF THE ATTORNEY GENERAL
720 Bay St Suite 204, Toronto, ON, M7A 2S9
(416) 326-4525
Emp Here 20
SIC 8111 Legal services

D-U-N-S 20-868-4733   (BR)
GOVERNMENT OF ONTARIO
INTERGOVERNMENTAL AFFAIRS
77 Wellesley St W 12th Fl, Toronto, ON, M7A 1N3

Emp Here 30
SIC 8111 Legal services

D-U-N-S 20-868-1911   (BR)
GOVERNMENT OF ONTARIO
CENTRAL REGION
33 Bloor St E Suite 100, Toronto, ON, M7A 2S2
(416) 326-5855
Emp Here 300
SIC 8741 Management services

D-U-N-S 20-914-9447   (BR)
GOVERNMENT OF ONTARIO

MINISTRY OF HEALTH & LONG TERM CARE LEGAL SERVICE BRANCH
56 Wellesley St W Suite 1200, Toronto, ON, M7A 2B7
(416) 327-8613
Emp Here 65
SIC 8111 Legal services

D-U-N-S 24-336-1040   (BR)
GOVERNMENT OF ONTARIO
ONTARIO MINISTRY OF LABOUR
400 University Ave 14th Flr, Toronto, ON, M7A 1T7
(416) 326-7600
Emp Here 500
SIC 8111 Legal services

D-U-N-S 20-891-6341   (BR)
GOVERNMENT OF ONTARIO
FREEDOM OF INFORMATION AND PRIVACY OFFICE
5630-99 Wellesley St W, Toronto, ON, M7A 1W1
(416) 327-0690
Emp Here 25
SIC 8399 Social services, nec

D-U-N-S 20-868-3461   (BR)
GOVERNMENT OF ONTARIO
OFFICE OF THE CHIEF INFORMATION OFFICER
900 Bay St Suite 200, Toronto, ON, M7A 1L2
(416) 325-4598
Emp Here 250
SIC 7299 Miscellaneous personal service

D-U-N-S 25-867-8390   (BR)
KITCHEN TABLE INCORPORATED, THE
KITCHEN TABLE, THE
595 Bay St, Toronto, ON, M7A 2B4
(416) 977-2225
Emp Here 38
SIC 5411 Grocery stores

Toronto, ON M8V
York County

D-U-N-S 24-693-2313   (BR)
CANPAR TRANSPORT L.P.
(Suby of Canpar Transport L.P.)
205 New Toronto St, Toronto, ON, M8V 0A1
(416) 869-1332
Emp Here 600
SIC 4213 Trucking, except local

D-U-N-S 24-760-1540   (SL)
ELVINS OIL LTD
3000 Lake Shore Blvd W Suite 11, Toronto, ON, M8V 4B9
(416) 949-2115
Emp Here 285   Sales 104,638,560
SIC 1381 Drilling oil and gas wells
Pr Pr Harry Elvins

D-U-N-S 20-153-1253   (BR)
GOVERNING COUNCIL OF THE UNIVERSITY OF TORONTO
FACULTY OF LAW
84 Queens Ave, Toronto, ON, M8V 2N3
(416) 978-8789
Emp Here 100
SIC 8221 Colleges and universities

D-U-N-S 20-153-1097   (BR)
GOVERNING COUNCIL OF THE UNIVERSITY OF TORONTO
MUSIC DEPARTMENT
80 Queens Ave, Toronto, ON, M8V 2N3
(416) 978-0414
Emp Here 80
SIC 8299 Schools and educational services, nec

D-U-N-S 24-463-7724   (BR)
LANTIC INC

LANTIC SUGAR
198 New Toronto St, Toronto, ON, M8V 2E8
(416) 252-9435
Emp Here 25
SIC 2062 Cane sugar refining

Toronto, ON M8W
York County

D-U-N-S 20-037-8896   (BR)
CORPORATION OF THE CITY OF TORONTO
JAMES S BELL COMMUNITY SCHOOL
90 Thirty First St, Toronto, ON, M8W 3E9
(416) 394-8707
Emp Here 30
SIC 7999 Amusement and recreation, nec

D-U-N-S 25-294-5456   (HQ)
FREEMAN EXPOSITIONS, LTD
FREEMAN
61 Browns Line, Toronto, ON, M8W 3S2
(416) 252-3361
Emp Here 38   Emp Total 30,129
Sales 5,465,508
SIC 7389 Business services, nec
 Barbara Baird
Pr Joe Popolo

D-U-N-S 20-711-1282   (BR)
TORONTO CATHOLIC DISTRICT SCHOOL BOARD
ST. JOSAPHAT ELEMENTARY SCHOOL
85 Forty First St, Toronto, ON, M8W 3P1
(416) 393-5291
Emp Here 27
SIC 8211 Elementary and secondary schools

D-U-N-S 20-711-1084   (BR)
TORONTO CATHOLIC DISTRICT SCHOOL BOARD
ST. AMBROSE CATHOLIC SCHOOL
20 Coules Crt, Toronto, ON, M8W 2N9
(416) 393-5259
Emp Here 50
SIC 8211 Elementary and secondary schools

D-U-N-S 20-698-7914   (BR)
TORONTO DISTRICT SCHOOL BOARD
JAMES S BELL JUNIOR MIDDLE SCHOOL
90 Thirty First St, Toronto, ON, M8W 3E9
(416) 394-7680
Emp Here 35
SIC 8211 Elementary and secondary schools

Toronto, ON M8X
York County

D-U-N-S 20-504-7066   (BR)
GOODLIFE FITNESS CENTRES INC
3300 Bloor St W, Toronto, ON, M8X 2W8
(416) 231-3300
Emp Here 49
SIC 7999 Amusement and recreation, nec

D-U-N-S 25-352-0878   (BR)
GROUPE SANTE MEDISYS INC
MEDISYS HEALTH GROUP
3300 Bloor St. W Suite 2802, Toronto, ON, M8X 2X2
(416) 926-2698
Emp Here 50
SIC 8093 Specialty outpatient clinics, nec

D-U-N-S 25-805-0202   (BR)
MASTERMIND LP
MASTERMIND EDUCTIONAL
4242 Dundas St W Suite 12, Toronto, ON, M8X 1Y6
(416) 239-1600
Emp Here 20
SIC 5947 Gift, novelty, and souvenir shop

D-U-N-S 25-510-4028   (SL)
REAL ESTATE COUNCIL OF ONTARIO
RECO
3300 Bloor St W Suite 1200 West Tower, Toronto, ON, M8X 2X2
(416) 207-4800
Emp Here 119   Sales 10,135,137
SIC 8641 Civic and social associations
CEO Kate Murray

Toronto, ON M8Y
York County

D-U-N-S 20-806-2617   (BR)
SOBEYS CAPITAL INCORPORATED
SOBEYS STORE 7383
125 The Queensway, Toronto, ON, M8Y 1H6
(416) 259-1758
Emp Here 100
SIC 5411 Grocery stores

D-U-N-S 20-112-2616   (BR)
TORONTO DISTRICT SCHOOL BOARD
SUNNYLEA JS
35 Glenroy Ave, Toronto, ON, M8Y 2M2
(416) 394-3850
Emp Here 50
SIC 8211 Elementary and secondary schools

Toronto, ON M8Z
York County

D-U-N-S 20-078-4051   (BR)
CANOPTEC INC
CLUB STOCK
349 Evans Ave, Toronto, ON, M8Z 1K2
(416) 521-9969
Emp Here 35
SIC 5048 Ophthalmic goods

D-U-N-S 24-253-3771   (BR)
KELSEY'S RESTAURANTS INC
KELSEY'S
(Suby of Cara Holdings Limited)
1011 The Queensway, Toronto, ON, M8Z 6C7
(416) 646-1856
Emp Here 65
SIC 5812 Eating places

D-U-N-S 20-087-4860   (BR)
NOCO CANADA INC
NOCO LUBRICANTS
2 Bradpenn Rd, Toronto, ON, M8Z 5S9
(416) 201-9900
Emp Here 50
SIC 5172 Petroleum products, nec

D-U-N-S 20-190-8568   (BR)
SOBEYS CAPITAL INCORPORATED
SOBEYS
1255 The Queensway, Toronto, ON, M8Z 1S1
(416) 252-5845
Emp Here 160
SIC 5411 Grocery stores

D-U-N-S 20-860-3204   (BR)
SOURCE (BELL) ELECTRONICS INC, THE
SOURCE, THE
1255 The Queensway, Toronto, ON, M8Z 1S1

Emp Here 25
SIC 5999 Miscellaneous retail stores, nec

D-U-N-S 20-067-9376   (BR)
TORONTO DISTRICT SCHOOL BOARD
NORSEMAN JUNIOR MIDDLE SCHOOL
105 Norseman St, Toronto, ON, M8Z 2R1
(416) 394-7880
Emp Here 25
SIC 8211 Elementary and secondary schools

D-U-N-S 20-106-3166   (BR)

WINNERS MERCHANTS INTERNATIONAL L.P.
WINNERS
(Suby of The TJX Companies Inc)
1255 The Queensway, Toronto, ON, M8Z 1S1
(416) 251-9871
Emp Here 40
SIC 5651 Family clothing stores

Toronto, ON M9A
York County

D-U-N-S 20-700-2424   (BR)
TORONTO DISTRICT SCHOOL BOARD
ROSETHORN JUNIOR SCHOOL
2 Remington Dr, Toronto, ON, M9A 2J1
(416) 394-6360
Emp Here 30
SIC 8211 Elementary and secondary schools

D-U-N-S 20-700-1780   (BR)
TORONTO DISTRICT SCHOOL BOARD
ST GEORGE'S JUNIOR PUBLIC SCHOOL
70 Princess Anne Cres, Toronto, ON, M9A 2P7
(416) 394-7990
Emp Here 20
SIC 8211 Elementary and secondary schools

D-U-N-S 20-698-7435   (BR)
TORONTO DISTRICT SCHOOL BOARD
HUMBER VALLEY VILLAGE J M S
65 Hartfield Rd, Toronto, ON, M9A 3E1
(416) 394-7860
Emp Here 40
SIC 8211 Elementary and secondary schools

D-U-N-S 25-684-5348   (BR)
TORONTO-DOMINION BANK, THE
TD CANADA TRUST
(Suby of Toronto-Dominion Bank, The)
1498 Islington Ave, Toronto, ON, M9A 3L7
(416) 239-4352
Emp Here 25
SIC 6021 National commercial banks

Toronto, ON M9B
York County

D-U-N-S 24-335-0498   (BR)
METRO ONTARIO INC
METRO
25 Vickers Rd, Toronto, ON, M9B 1C1
(416) 234-6590
Emp Here 400
SIC 5141 Groceries, general line

D-U-N-S 20-252-2306   (SL)
STRATEGIC SECURITY GROUP LTD
225 The East Mall Suite 1681, Toronto, ON, M9B 6J1
(416) 602-9188
Emp Here 65   Sales 2,638,521
SIC 7381 Detective and armored car services

D-U-N-S 24-344-0810   (BR)
SUPERIOR PLUS LP
ERCO WORLDWIDE
302 The East Mall Suite 200, Toronto, ON, M9B 6C7
(416) 239-7111
Emp Here 95
SIC 2819 Industrial inorganic chemicals, nec

D-U-N-S 20-026-2181   (BR)
TORONTO CATHOLIC DISTRICT SCHOOL BOARD
ST. ELIZABETH ELEMENTARY SCHOOL
5 Redcar Ave, Toronto, ON, M9B 1J8
(416) 393-5278
Emp Here 30
SIC 8211 Elementary and secondary schools

D-U-N-S 20-025-0996   (BR)
TORONTO CATHOLIC DISTRICT SCHOOL BOARD
OUR LADY OF PEACE CATHOLIC SCHOOL
70 Mattice Ave, Toronto, ON, M9B 1T6
(416) 393-5253
Emp Here 35
SIC 8211 Elementary and secondary schools

D-U-N-S 20-711-2819   (BR)
TORONTO DISTRICT SCHOOL BOARD
WEST GLEN SCHOOL
47 Cowley Ave, Toronto, ON, M9B 2E4
(416) 394-7160
Emp Here 37
SIC 8211 Elementary and secondary schools

D-U-N-S 20-698-7799   (BR)
TORONTO DISTRICT SCHOOL BOARD
JOHN G ALTHOUSE MS
130 Lloyd Manor Rd, Toronto, ON, M9B 5K1
(416) 394-7580
Emp Here 45
SIC 8211 Elementary and secondary schools

D-U-N-S 20-698-7484   (BR)
TORONTO DISTRICT SCHOOL BOARD
MARTINGROVE COLLEGIATE INSTITUTE
50 Winterton Dr, Toronto, ON, M9B 3G7
(416) 394-7110
Emp Here 100
SIC 8211 Elementary and secondary schools

Toronto, ON M9C
York County

D-U-N-S 20-183-5290   (BR)
CLARIANT (CANADA) INC
MASTERBATCHES DIVISION
2 Lone Oak Crt, Toronto, ON, M9C 5R9
(416) 847-7000
Emp Here 60
SIC 5169 Chemicals and allied products, nec

D-U-N-S 20-411-9036   (HQ)
DIAGEO CANADA INC
(*Suby of* DIAGEO PLC)
401 The West Mall Suite 800, Toronto, ON, M9C 5P8
(416) 626-2000
Emp Here 70   *Emp Total* 32,078
Sales 826,644,731
SIC 2085 Distilled and blended liquors
 Paul Walsh
Ch Bd Franz Humer
 Deirdre Mahlan
Dir Peggy Bruzelius
Dir Laurence Danon
Dir Betsy Holden
Dir Philip Scott
Dir Todd Stitzer
Dir Paul Tunnacliffe

D-U-N-S 20-824-0119   (HQ)
G4S SECURE SOLUTIONS (CANADA) LTD
G4S CANADA
703 Evans Ave Suite 103, Toronto, ON, M9C 5E9
(416) 620-0762
Emp Here 50   *Emp Total* 592,897
Sales 332,813,634
SIC 7381 Detective and armored car services
Pr Peter Panaripis
CFO Brian Hinton
Dir Paul Rivenbark

D-U-N-S 24-021-4606   (SL)
PERSONALTOURS INC
1750 The Queensway Suite 1300, Toronto, ON, M9C 5H5

Emp Here 20   *Sales* 6,125,139
SIC 4725 Tour operators
Dir John Anderson

D-U-N-S 24-170-2088   (BR)
SIR CORP
JACK ASTOR'S BAR AND GRILL
1900 The Queensway, Toronto, ON, M9C 5H5
(416) 626-2700
Emp Here 100
SIC 5813 Drinking places

D-U-N-S 20-096-4166   (BR)
TORONTO CATHOLIC DISTRICT SCHOOL BOARD
MOTHER CABRINI SCHOOL
720 Renforth Dr, Toronto, ON, M9C 2N9
(416) 393-5340
Emp Here 23
SIC 8211 Elementary and secondary schools

D-U-N-S 20-698-7229   (BR)
TORONTO DISTRICT SCHOOL BOARD
EATONVILLE JUNIOR SCHOOL
15 Rossburn Dr, Toronto, ON, M9C 2P7
(416) 394-7040
Emp Here 20
SIC 8211 Elementary and secondary schools

D-U-N-S 20-024-9816   (BR)
TORONTO DISTRICT SCHOOL BOARD
BROADACRES ELEMENTARY SCHOOL
45 Crendon Dr, Toronto, ON, M9C 3G6
(416) 394-7030
Emp Here 20
SIC 8211 Elementary and secondary schools

D-U-N-S 25-293-9137   (BR)
TOYS 'R' US (CANADA) LTD
TOYS 'R' US
(*Suby of* Toys "r" Us, Inc.)
690 Evans Ave, Toronto, ON, M9C 1A1
(416) 621-8697
Emp Here 20
SIC 5945 Hobby, toy, and game shops

D-U-N-S 25-535-8103   (BR)
TRILLIUM HEALTH PARTNERS
QUEENSWAY HEALTH CENTRE
150 Sherway Dr, Toronto, ON, M9C 1A5
(416) 259-6671
Emp Here 400
SIC 8062 General medical and surgical hospitals

Toronto, ON M9L
York County

D-U-N-S 20-341-0808   (SL)
2355294 ONTARIO INC
REVOLUTION RECYCLING
94 Fenmar Dr, Toronto, ON, M9L 1M5
(416) 222-1773
Emp Here 25   *Sales* 3,898,130
SIC 4953 Refuse systems

D-U-N-S 24-196-1598   (BR)
CROWN METAL PACKAGING CANADA LP
(*Suby of* Crown Holdings Inc.)
21 Fenmar Dr, Toronto, ON, M9L 2Y9
(416) 741-6003
Emp Here 200
SIC 3411 Metal cans

D-U-N-S 20-547-8717   (HQ)
CROWN METAL PACKAGING CANADA LP
(*Suby of* Crown Holdings Inc.)
21 Fenmar Dr, Toronto, ON, M9L 2Y9
(416) 741-6002
Emp Here 25   *Emp Total* 24,000
SIC 3411 Metal cans

D-U-N-S 25-747-6119   (BR)
GRANDE CHEESE COMPANY LIMITED
175 Milvan Dr, Toronto, ON, M9L 1Z8
(416) 740-8847
Emp Here 50
SIC 2022 Cheese; natural and processed

D-U-N-S 24-353-2046   (SL)
MAD ENGINE LLC
(*Suby of* Mad Engine, LLC)
5145 Steeles Ave W Unit 100, Toronto, ON, M9L 1R5
(416) 745-4698
Emp Here 21   *Sales* 14,792,900
SIC 2329 Men's and boy's clothing, nec
Ex VP Angelina Yagudayev
 Danish Gajiani
 Faizan Bakali

D-U-N-S 24-344-5538   (HQ)
PROGISTIX-SOLUTIONS INC
(*Suby of* Canada Post Corporation)
99 Signet Dr Suite 300, Toronto, ON, M9L 0A2
(416) 401-7000
Emp Here 388   *Emp Total* 63,000
Sales 75,092,400
SIC 8742 Management consulting services
Pr James H Eckler
Dir Cal Hart

D-U-N-S 24-801-4750   (HQ)
SDI SUPPLIES LTD
4935 Steeles Ave W, Toronto, ON, M9L 1R4
(416) 745-8665
Emp Here 25   *Emp Total* 1
Sales 7,891,855
SIC 5085 Industrial supplies
Pr Pr Peter Cetnarski
 Robert Todd

D-U-N-S 20-700-1962   (BR)
TORONTO CATHOLIC DISTRICT SCHOOL BOARD
VEN JOHN MERLINI (ELEMENTARY)
123 Whitfield Ave, Toronto, ON, M9L 1G9
(416) 393-5397
Emp Here 40
SIC 8211 Elementary and secondary schools

D-U-N-S 20-082-2265   (BR)
TORONTO CATHOLIC DISTRICT SCHOOL BOARD
ST. ROCH ELEMENTARY SCHOOL
174 Duncanwoods Dr, Toronto, ON, M9L 2E3
(416) 393-5320
Emp Here 52
SIC 8211 Elementary and secondary schools

D-U-N-S 25-237-7999   (BR)
TORONTO DISTRICT SCHOOL BOARD
GRACEDALE PUBLIC SCHOOL
186 Gracedale Blvd, Toronto, ON, M9L 2C1
(416) 395-2480
Emp Here 60
SIC 8211 Elementary and secondary schools

D-U-N-S 20-294-6141   (HQ)
TRIUMPH GEAR SYSTEMS-TORONTO ULC
TGST
9 Fenmar Dr, Toronto, ON, M9L 1L5
(416) 743-4417
Emp Here 120   *Emp Total* 14,602
Sales 31,970,778
SIC 3728 Aircraft parts and equipment, nec
Pr Bruce Van Nus

Toronto, ON M9M
York County

D-U-N-S 24-360-1130   (SL)
EILEEN ROOFING INC
1825 Wilson Ave, Toronto, ON, M9M 1A2
(416) 762-1819
Emp Here 50   *Sales* 4,961,328
SIC 1761 Roofing, siding, and sheetMetal work

Toronto, ON M9N
York County

D-U-N-S 20-716-3952   (BR)
2063414 ONTARIO LIMITED
WESTON TERRACE CARE COMMUNITY
(*Suby of* 2063414 Ontario Limited)
2005 Lawrence Ave W Suite 323, Toronto, ON, M9N 3V4
(416) 243-8879
Emp Here 220
SIC 8051 Skilled nursing care facilities

D-U-N-S 24-335-2481   (SL)
ANNETTE'S DONUTS LIMITED
1965 Lawrence Ave W, Toronto, ON, M9N 1H5
(416) 656-3444
Emp Here 84   *Sales* 4,377,642
SIC 2051 Bread, cake, and related products

D-U-N-S 24-437-7367   (BR)
BANQUE TORONTO-DOMINION, LA
TORONTO-DOMINION BANK, THE
(*Suby of* Toronto-Dominion Bank, The)
1746 Jane St, Toronto, ON, M9N 2S9
(416) 244-1121
Emp Here 20
SIC 6021 National commercial banks

D-U-N-S 25-293-9228   (BR)
CIBC WORLD MARKETS INC
CIBC WOOD GUNDY
25 King St, Toronto, ON, M9N 1K8
(416) 594-7897
Emp Here 22
SIC 6211 Security brokers and dealers

D-U-N-S 20-299-6398   (BR)
CANADA POST CORPORATION
2050 Weston Rd, Toronto, ON, M9N 1X4

Emp Here 100
SIC 4311 U.s. postal service

D-U-N-S 24-365-9179   (HQ)
DALKIA CANADA INC
130 King St Suite 1800, Toronto, ON, M9N 1L5
(416) 860-6232
Emp Here 20   *Emp Total* 1,019
Sales 1,824,018
SIC 8741 Management services

D-U-N-S 20-109-0151   (BR)
FINANCIERE BANQUE NATIONALE INC
130 King St Suite 3200, Toronto, ON, M9N 1L5
(416) 869-3707
Emp Here 39
SIC 6211 Security brokers and dealers

D-U-N-S 24-216-4812   (SL)
FINISHED WOODFLOOR LTD
8 Oak St, Toronto, ON, M9N 1R8
(416) 241-8631
Emp Here 50   *Sales* 7,255,933
SIC 2426 Hardwood dimension and flooring mills
Pr Pr Nicholas Stern
 David Hofstedter

D-U-N-S 20-087-8838   (BR)
GDI SERVICES (CANADA) LP
130 King St, Toronto, ON, M9N 1L5
(416) 364-0643
Emp Here 20
SIC 1799 Special trade contractors, nec

D-U-N-S 25-221-2089   (BR)
LEON'S FURNITURE LIMITED
LEON'S FURNITURE
10 Suntract Rd, Toronto, ON, M9N 3N9
(416) 243-8300
Emp Here 160
SIC 5712 Furniture stores

D-U-N-S 24-359-1604   (BR)
LOBLAWS INC
REAL CANADIAN SUPERSTORE WESTON
2549 Weston Rd, Toronto, ON, M9N 2A7
(416) 246-1906
Emp Here 100

▲ Public Company   ■ Public Company Family Member   **HQ** Headquarters   **BR** Branch   **SL** Single Location

SIC 5411 Grocery stores

D-U-N-S 20-997-6922   (BR)
NUCLEUS INDEPENDENT LIVING
2100 Weston Rd Suite 1007, Toronto, ON,
M9N 3W6
(416) 242-4433
Emp Here 25
SIC 8361 Residential care

D-U-N-S 24-227-9524   (BR)
**ONTARIO PUBLIC SERVICE EMPLOYEES
UNION PENSION PLAN TRUST FUND**
OPTRUST PRIVATE MARKETS GROUP
130 King St Suite 700, Toronto, ON, M9N 1L5
(416) 681-3016
Emp Here 20
SIC 6541 Title abstract offices

D-U-N-S 25-826-3797   (BR)
SOBEYS CAPITAL INCORPORATED
FRESHCO
1731 Weston Rd, Toronto, ON, M9N 1V5

Emp Here 45
SIC 5411 Grocery stores

D-U-N-S 25-294-5118   (BR)
TORONTO DISTRICT SCHOOL BOARD
H J ALEXANDER COMMUNITY SCHOOL
30 King St, Toronto, ON, M9N 1K9
(416) 394-2359
Emp Here 45
SIC 8211 Elementary and secondary schools

D-U-N-S 25-300-8916   (BR)
TORONTO DISTRICT SCHOOL BOARD
WESTON MEMORIAL JUNIOR PUBLIC
SCHOOL
200 John St, Toronto, ON, M9N 1K2
(416) 394-3150
Emp Here 28
SIC 8211 Elementary and secondary schools

D-U-N-S 20-008-7687   (BR)
TORONTO DISTRICT SCHOOL BOARD
WESTON COLLEGIATE INSTITUTE
100 Pine St, Toronto, ON, M9N 2Y9
(416) 394-3250
Emp Here 130
SIC 8211 Elementary and secondary schools

D-U-N-S 25-294-4293   (BR)
TORONTO DISTRICT SCHOOL BOARD
C R MARCHANT MIDDLE SCHOOL
1 Ralph St, Toronto, ON, M9N 3A8
(416) 394-2268
Emp Here 37
SIC 8211 Elementary and secondary schools

D-U-N-S 20-813-3350   (SL)
Y FIRM MANAGEMENT INC
130 King St Suite 2700, Toronto, ON, M9N 1L5
(416) 860-8370
Emp Here 50   Sales 5,399,092
SIC 8741 Management services
Dir Cindy Davies

Toronto, ON M9P
York County

D-U-N-S 20-129-0054   (SL)
**JENSEN HUGHES CONSULTING CANADA
LTD**
2150 Islington Ave Suite 100, Toronto, ON,
M9P 3V4
(647) 559-1251
Emp Here 49   Sales 5,253,170
SIC 8748 Business consulting, nec
Prin Peter Senez

D-U-N-S 20-711-1183   (BR)
**TORONTO CATHOLIC DISTRICT SCHOOL
BOARD**
ST. EUGENE CATHOLIC ELEMENTARY

SCHOOL
30 Westroyal Rd, Toronto, ON, M9P 2C3
(416) 393-5337
Emp Here 50
SIC 8211 Elementary and secondary schools

D-U-N-S 20-698-6882   (BR)
**TORONTO CATHOLIC DISTRICT SCHOOL
BOARD**
FATHER SERRA ELEMENTARY SCHOOL
111 Sun Row Dr, Toronto, ON, M9P 3J3
(416) 393-5391
Emp Here 40
SIC 8211 Elementary and secondary schools

D-U-N-S 20-025-0988   (BR)
TORONTO DISTRICT SCHOOL BOARD
VALLEYFIELD JR SCHOOL
35 Saskatoon Dr, Toronto, ON, M9P 2E8
(416) 394-7590
Emp Here 29
SIC 8211 Elementary and secondary schools

D-U-N-S 25-684-5546   (BR)
TORONTO-DOMINION BANK, THE
TD CANADA TRUST
(Suby of Toronto-Dominion Bank, The)
1440 Royal York Rd, Toronto, ON, M9P 3B1
(416) 243-0855
Emp Here 30
SIC 6021 National commercial banks

Toronto, ON M9R
York County

D-U-N-S 20-025-1127   (BR)
CONSEIL SCOLAIRE VIAMONDE
ECOLE FELIX-LECLERC
50 Celestine Dr, Toronto, ON, M9R 3N3
(416) 397-2075
Emp Here 35
SIC 8211 Elementary and secondary schools

D-U-N-S 25-092-4326   (BR)
MOE'S TRANSPORT TRUCKING INC
MOE'S TRANSPORTATION
416 The Westway Suite 511, Toronto, ON,
M9R 1H7
(519) 253-8442
Emp Here 175
SIC 4213 Trucking, except local

D-U-N-S 20-698-6759   (BR)
**TORONTO CATHOLIC DISTRICT SCHOOL
BOARD**
DON BOSCO CATHOLIC SCHOOL
2 St Andrews Blvd, Toronto, ON, M9R 1V8
(416) 393-5525
Emp Here 20
SIC 8211 Elementary and secondary schools

D-U-N-S 20-711-1340   (BR)
**TORONTO CATHOLIC DISTRICT SCHOOL
BOARD**
ST. MARCELLUS CATHOLIC SCHOOL
15 Denfield St, Toronto, ON, M9R 3H2
(416) 393-5311
Emp Here 40
SIC 8211 Elementary and secondary schools

D-U-N-S 20-079-2708   (BR)
TORONTO DISTRICT SCHOOL BOARD
PARKFIELD JUNIOR SCHOOL
31 Redgrave Dr, Toronto, ON, M9R 3T9
(416) 394-7960
Emp Here 35
SIC 8211 Elementary and secondary schools

D-U-N-S 20-025-3735   (BR)
TORONTO DISTRICT SCHOOL BOARD
DIXON GROVE JUNIOR MIDDLE SCHOOL
315 The Westway, Toronto, ON, M9R 1H1
(416) 394-7940
Emp Here 66
SIC 8211 Elementary and secondary schools

Toronto, ON M9V
York County

D-U-N-S 20-708-9280   (BR)
**CORPORATION OF THE CITY OF
TORONTO**
ELMBANK COMMUNITY CENTRE
10 Rampart Rd, Toronto, ON, M9V 4L9
(416) 394-8670
Emp Here 25
SIC 8322 Individual and family services

D-U-N-S 20-025-9989   (BR)
TORONTO DISTRICT SCHOOL BOARD
ALBION HEIGHTS JUNIOR MIDDLE
SCHOOL
45 Lynmont Rd, Toronto, ON, M9V 3W9
(416) 394-7520
Emp Here 40
SIC 8211 Elementary and secondary schools

D-U-N-S 20-698-7344   (BR)
TORONTO DISTRICT SCHOOL BOARD
ELMBANK JMA
10 Pittsboro Dr, Toronto, ON, M9V 3R4
(416) 394-7560
Emp Here 40
SIC 8211 Elementary and secondary schools

D-U-N-S 20-025-3867   (BR)
TORONTO DISTRICT SCHOOL BOARD
GREENHOLME JUNIOR MIDDLE SCHOOL
10 Jamestown Cres, Toronto, ON, M9V 3M5
(416) 394-7700
Emp Here 64
SIC 8211 Elementary and secondary schools

D-U-N-S 20-025-0962   (BR)
TORONTO DISTRICT SCHOOL BOARD
HIGHFIELD JUNIOR SCHOOL
85 Mount Olive Dr, Toronto, ON, M9V 2C9
(416) 394-7510
Emp Here 50
SIC 8211 Elementary and secondary schools

Toronto, ON M9W
York County

D-U-N-S 20-152-7574   (BR)
2063414 ONTARIO LIMITED
LEISUREWORLD CAREGIVING CENTRES
(Suby of 2063414 Ontario Limited)
70 Humberline Dr, Toronto, ON, M9W 7H3
(416) 213-7300
Emp Here 170
SIC 8051 Skilled nursing care facilities

D-U-N-S 20-282-5527   (HQ)
AEC INTERNATIONAL INC
(Suby of AEC International Inc)
10 Carlson Crt Suite 640, Toronto, ON, M9W
6L2
(416) 224-5115
Emp Here 25   Emp Total 75
Sales 14,723,205
SIC 8741 Management services
Pr Pr Gary Newell
VP VP Robert Gagne
VP VP Robert Langlois
  Charles Johnstone

D-U-N-S 20-300-7794   (SL)
ABCOR FILTERS INC
(Suby of Cerberus Capital Management, L.P.)
41 City View Dr, Toronto, ON, M9W 5A5
(416) 245-6886
Emp Here 25   Sales 3,939,878
SIC 3714 Motor vehicle parts and accessories

D-U-N-S 25-190-9776   (BR)
BBA INC
(Suby of Groupe BBA Inc)
10 Carlson Crt Suite 420, Toronto, ON, M9W

6L2
(416) 585-2115
Emp Here 700
SIC 8711 Engineering services

D-U-N-S 24-909-6025   (BR)
CBRE LIMITED
87 Skyway Ave Suite 100, Toronto, ON, M9W
6R3
(416) 674-7900
Emp Here 60
SIC 6531 Real estate agents and managers

D-U-N-S 24-340-0822   (BR)
FGL SPORTS LTD
SPORT CHEK WOODBINE
500 Rexdale Blvd Unit A22a, Toronto, ON,
M9W 6K5
(416) 746-5073
Emp Here 20
SIC 5941 Sporting goods and bicycle shops

D-U-N-S 24-333-8233   (BR)
FRANKLIN EMPIRE INC
350 Carlingview Dr, Toronto, ON, M9W 5G6
(416) 248-0176
Emp Here 50
SIC 5085 Industrial supplies

D-U-N-S 25-511-5107   (SL)
FRESENIUS KABI CANADA LTD
165 Galaxy Blvd Suite 100, Toronto, ON, M9W
0C8
(905) 770-3711
Emp Here 95   Sales 11,746,673
SIC 5122 Drugs, proprietaries, and sundries
Pr John Ducker
CEO Matthew Rotenburg

D-U-N-S 24-687-5090   (SL)
GEOFF & KRISTA SIMS ENTERPRISES INC
WILKINSON CHUTES CANADA
23 Racine Rd, Toronto, ON, M9W 2Z4
(416) 746-5547
Emp Here 25   Sales 3,866,917
SIC 3443 Fabricated plate work (boiler shop)

D-U-N-S 24-920-3019   (BR)
GUARDIAN INDUSTRIES CANADA CORP
(Suby of Koch Industries, Inc.)
355 Attwell Dr, Toronto, ON, M9W 5C2
(416) 674-6945
Emp Here 100
SIC 3211 Flat glass

D-U-N-S 24-505-3665   (BR)
HOLT, RENFREW & CIE, LIMITEE
HOLT RENFREW
396 Humberline Dr, Toronto, ON, M9W 6J7
(416) 675-9200
Emp Here 100
SIC 5632 Women's accessory and specialty
stores

D-U-N-S 20-278-9111   (SL)
IPS OF CANADA, U.L.C.
INTELISPEND
170 Attwell Dr Suite 550, Toronto, ON, M9W
5Z5
(800) 293-1136
Emp Here 51   Sales 33,681,400
SIC 6153 Short-term business credit institu-
tions, except agricultural
W. Stephen Maritz
Holly Francois
Chris Carril
Richard T. Ramos
Steven M. Gallant
Jeffrey R. Blucher

D-U-N-S 25-272-8738   (BR)
KEG RESTAURANTS LTD
KEG STEAK HOUSE & BAR, THE
927 Dixon Rd, Toronto, ON, M9W 1J8
(416) 675-2311
Emp Here 100
SIC 5812 Eating places

D-U-N-S 20-364-3374   (SL)

LAPORTE ENGINEERING INC
89 Skyway Ave Suite 100, Toronto, ON, M9W 6R4
(416) 675-6761
Emp Here 50   *Sales* 4,961,328
SIC 8711 Engineering services

D-U-N-S 20-271-5025   (SL)
LOVSUNS TUNNELING CANADA LIMITED
441 Carlingview Dr, Toronto, ON, M9W 5G7
(647) 255-0018
Emp Here 75   *Sales* 17,145,765
SIC 3531 Construction machinery
VP Harry Tian
 Hongyu Xue
Ch Bd Ch Bd Shuangzhong Liu
Sec Yan Dong

D-U-N-S 20-306-3581   (SL)
M. BLOCK CANADA, ULC
M. BLOCK & SONS
134 Bethridge Rd, Toronto, ON, M9W 1N3
(705) 252-6471
Emp Here 20   *Sales* 2,188,821
SIC 5023 Homefurnishings

D-U-N-S 24-094-7697   (BR)
MAGNA POWERTRAIN INC
ROTO-FORM, DIV OF
175 Claireville Dr, Toronto, ON, M9W 6K9
(416) 798-3880
Emp Here 184
SIC 3714 Motor vehicle parts and accessories

D-U-N-S 24-645-7741   (BR)
NESTLE CANADA INC
NESTLE FOOD SERVICES, DIV OF
65 Carrier Dr, Toronto, ON, M9W 5V9
(416) 675-1300
Emp Here 100
SIC 5149 Groceries and related products, nec

D-U-N-S 24-344-8862   (BR)
ONTARIO LOTTERY AND GAMING CORPO-RATION
SLOTS AT WOODBINE RACETRACK
555 Rexdale Blvd, Toronto, ON, M9W 5L1
(416) 675-1101
Emp Here 50
SIC 7999 Amusement and recreation, nec

D-U-N-S 24-363-7998   (SL)
PREMIUM BEER COMPANY INC, THE
NIAGARA BREWING COMPANY
275 Belfield Rd, Toronto, ON, M9W 7H9
(905) 855-7743
Emp Here 45   *Sales* 3,898,130
SIC 5181 Beer and ale

D-U-N-S 20-145-7645   (HQ)
S & C ELECTRIC CANADA LTD
(*Suby of* S & C Electric Company)
90 Belfield Rd, Toronto, ON, M9W 1G4
(416) 249-9171
Emp Here 295   *Emp Total* 2,500
Sales 35,167,057
SIC 3613 Switchgear and switchboard appara-tus
Pr Pr Grant Buchanan
Dir Marcello Lagrotta
 John Estey
Sec Clare Webb

D-U-N-S 24-253-3383   (BR)
SIR CORP
JACK ASTOR'S BAR AND GRILL
25 Carlson Crt, Toronto, ON, M9W 6A2
(416) 213-1688
Emp Here 80
SIC 5812 Eating places

D-U-N-S 24-319-4441   (BR)
SNC-LAVALIN INC
345 Carlingview Dr, Toronto, ON, M9W 6N9

Emp Here 200
SIC 8711 Engineering services

D-U-N-S 20-711-2827   (BR)
TORONTO DISTRICT SCHOOL BOARD
WEST HUMBER JUNIOR MIDDLE
15 Delsing Dr, Toronto, ON, M9W 4S7
(416) 394-7760
Emp Here 50
SIC 8211 Elementary and secondary schools

D-U-N-S 20-025-4287   (BR)
TORONTO DISTRICT SCHOOL BOARD
RIVERCREST JUNIOR SCHOOL
30 Harefield Dr, Toronto, ON, M9W 4C9
(416) 394-7920
Emp Here 25
SIC 8211 Elementary and secondary schools

D-U-N-S 20-026-0094   (BR)
TORONTO DISTRICT SCHOOL BOARD
THISTLETOWN COLLEGIATE INSTITUTE
20 Fordwich Cres, Toronto, ON, M9W 2T4
(416) 394-7710
Emp Here 70
SIC 8211 Elementary and secondary schools

D-U-N-S 20-818-6445   (HQ)
WOODBINE ENTERTAINMENT GROUP
WOODBINE RACETRACK
(*Suby of* Woodbine Entertainment Group)
555 Rexdale Blvd, Toronto, ON, M9W 5L2
(416) 675-7223
Emp Here 1,000   *Emp Total* 2,700
Sales 325,565
SIC 7948 Racing, including track operation

Toronto, ON N8Z
York County

D-U-N-S 24-780-2536   (BR)
ARAMARK CANADA LTD.
105 East Mall, Toronto, ON, N8Z 5X9
(800) 263-6344
Emp Here 20
SIC 5812 Eating places

Torrance, ON P0C
Muskoka County

D-U-N-S 20-780-9497   (BR)
YMCA OF GREATER TORONTO
YMCA CAMP PINE CREST
1090 Gullwing Lake Rd Rr 1, Torrance, ON, P0C 1M0
(705) 762-3377
Emp Here 174
SIC 7032 Sporting and recreational camps

Tottenham, ON L0G
Simcoe County

D-U-N-S 24-663-2277   (HQ)
F&P MFG., INC
1 Nolan Rd, Tottenham, ON, L0G 1W0
(905) 936-3435
Emp Here 630   *Emp Total* 6,632
Sales 400,325,663
SIC 3714 Motor vehicle parts and accessories
Pr Pr Kazuhiao Ojawa
 Kenneth Bradley
 Kiyoshi Horiuchi
Treas Stuart Fraser
Dir Yasuyuki Ikezawa
Dir Geoff Smith
 Andrew Kochanek

D-U-N-S 25-292-4899   (BR)
SIMCOE COUNTY DISTRICT SCHOOL BOARD, THE
TOTTENHAM PUBLIC SCHOOL
(*Suby of* Simcoe County District School

Board, The)
21 Rogers Rd, Tottenham, ON, L0G 1W0
(905) 936-4951
Emp Here 40
SIC 8211 Elementary and secondary schools

D-U-N-S 20-711-2017   (BR)
SIMCOE COUNTY DISTRICT SCHOOL BOARD, THE
TECUMSETH SOUTH CENTRAL PUBLIC SCHOOL
(*Suby of* Simcoe County District School Board, The)
2124 5 Rd 10, Tottenham, ON, L0G 1W0
(905) 936-3711
Emp Here 25
SIC 8211 Elementary and secondary schools

D-U-N-S 25-293-5507   (BR)
SIMCOE MUSKOKA CATHOLIC DISTRICT SCHOOL BOARD
FATHER F X O'REILLY SCHOOL
(*Suby of* Simcoe Muskoka Catholic District School Board)
235 Queen St N, Tottenham, ON, L0G 1W0
(905) 936-3364
Emp Here 31
SIC 8211 Elementary and secondary schools

D-U-N-S 25-224-8729   (BR)
SIMCOE MUSKOKA CATHOLIC DISTRICT SCHOOL BOARD
ST. THOMAS AQUINAS HIGH SCHOOL
(*Suby of* Simcoe Muskoka Catholic District School Board)
2 Nolan Rd, Tottenham, ON, L0G 1W0
(905) 936-4743
Emp Here 80
SIC 8211 Elementary and secondary schools

D-U-N-S 24-189-3937   (BR)
SOBEYS CAPITAL INCORPORATED
TOTTENHAM FOODLAND STORE
260 Queen St N, Tottenham, ON, L0G 1W0
(905) 936-1077
Emp Here 120
SIC 5411 Grocery stores

D-U-N-S 24-280-0241   (BR)
VENTRA GROUP CO
VMA TOTTENHAM, DIV OF
65 Industrial Rd, Tottenham, ON, L0G 1W0
(905) 936-4245
Emp Here 250
SIC 3465 Automotive stampings

Townsend, ON N0A
Norfolk County

D-U-N-S 24-032-1633   (SL)
COMMUNITY ADDICTION & MENTAL HEALTH SERVICES OF HALDIMAN & NORFOLK
ADULT MENTAL HEALTH SERVICES
101 Nanticoke Creek Pky, Townsend, ON, N0A 1S0
(519) 587-4658
Emp Here 50   *Sales* 3,283,232
SIC 8093 Specialty outpatient clinics, nec

Trenton, ON K8V
Hastings County

D-U-N-S 25-950-2813   (BR)
1036028 ONTARIO LIMITED
WENDY'S
Highway 401, Trenton, ON, K8V 6B4
(613) 392-4603
Emp Here 35
SIC 5812 Eating places

D-U-N-S 25-745-2805   (BR)

ALGONQUIN & LAKESHORE CATHOLIC DISTRICT SCHOOL BOARD
ST MARY'S CATHOLIC SCHOOL
85 Campbell St, Trenton, ON, K8V 3A2
(613) 392-3538
Emp Here 45
SIC 8211 Elementary and secondary schools

D-U-N-S 20-025-0582   (BR)
ALGONQUIN & LAKESHORE CATHOLIC DISTRICT SCHOOL BOARD
ST PETER'S CATHOLIC SCHOOL
15 A Tripp Blvd, Trenton, ON, K8V 6M2
(613) 392-6577
Emp Here 53
SIC 8211 Elementary and secondary schools

D-U-N-S 20-590-6980   (BR)
ALGONQUIN & LAKESHORE CATHOLIC DISTRICT SCHOOL BOARD
ST PAUL CATHOLIC SECONDARY SCHOOL
15 Tripp Blvd, Trenton, ON, K8V 6M2
(613) 394-4843
Emp Here 50
SIC 8211 Elementary and secondary schools

D-U-N-S 25-296-3863   (BR)
BANK OF NOVA SCOTIA, THE
SCOTIABANK
68 Dundas St W, Trenton, ON, K8V 3P3
(613) 392-2531
Emp Here 25
SIC 6021 National commercial banks

D-U-N-S 24-470-4987   (BR)
BOLDRICK BUS SERVICE LIMITED
BOLDRICK TRUCK & AUTO CENTRE
(*Suby of* Boldrick Bus Service Limited)
1029 County Rd 40, Trenton, ON, K8V 5P4

Emp Here 24
SIC 4151 School buses

D-U-N-S 25-369-9441   (BR)
CANADA POST CORPORATION
CANADA POST TRENTON
70 Front St, Trenton, ON, K8V 4N4
(613) 392-4402
Emp Here 35
SIC 4311 U.s. postal service

D-U-N-S 25-021-1927   (BR)
CANADIAN IMPERIAL BANK OF COM-MERCE
CIBC
91 Dundas St W, Trenton, ON, K8V 3P4
(613) 394-3364
Emp Here 26
SIC 6021 National commercial banks

D-U-N-S 25-585-9878   (BR)
CARA OPERATIONS LIMITED
HARVEY'S SERVING SWISS CHALET
(*Suby of* Cara Holdings Limited)
283 Dundas St E, Trenton, ON, K8V 1M1
(613) 394-5780
Emp Here 30
SIC 5812 Eating places

D-U-N-S 25-503-9133   (BR)
CASCADES CANADA ULC
CASCADES CONTAINER BOARD PACKAG-ING
300 Marmora St, Trenton, ON, K8V 5R8
(613) 392-6505
Emp Here 140
SIC 2679 Converted paper products, nec

D-U-N-S 25-585-9647   (BR)
CENTURY 21 LANTHORN REAL ESTATE LTD
441 Front St, Trenton, ON, K8V 6C1
(613) 392-2511
Emp Here 20
SIC 6531 Real estate agents and managers

D-U-N-S 25-237-9987   (BR)
CONSEIL DES ECOLES PUBLIQUES DE

L'EST DE L'ONTARIO
ECOLE SECONDAIRE MARC-GARNEAU
11 Fullerton Ave, Trenton, ON, K8V 1E4
(613) 392-6961
Emp Here 20
SIC 8211 Elementary and secondary schools

D-U-N-S 25-833-4135   (BR)
CONSEIL DES ECOLES PUBLIQUES DE L'EST DE L'ONTARIO
ECOLE CIT -JEUNESSE
30 Fullerton Ave, Trenton, ON, K8V 1E4
(613) 392-6961
Emp Here 25
SIC 8211 Elementary and secondary schools

D-U-N-S 24-346-5429   (BR)
CRANE PLUMBING CANADA CORP
(*Suby of* Crane Plumbing Canada Corp)
420 Sidney St, Trenton, ON, K8V 2V2

Emp Here 20
SIC 3431 Metal sanitary ware

D-U-N-S 25-542-2669   (BR)
CRAWFORD METAL CORPORATION
(*Suby of* Crawford Metal Corporation)
300 West St, Trenton, ON, K8V 2N3
(613) 394-1994
Emp Here 40
SIC 5051 Metals service centers and offices

D-U-N-S 25-321-8614   (BR)
ERB TRANSPORT LIMITED
ERB TRANSPORT LIMITED
4 Riverside Dr, Trenton, ON, K8V 5P8

Emp Here 170
SIC 4212 Local trucking, without storage

D-U-N-S 25-831-1158   (BR)
HASTINGS AND PRINCE EDWARD DISTRICT SCHOOL BOARD
TRENTON HIGH SCHOOL
15 Fourth Ave, Trenton, ON, K8V 5N4
(613) 392-1227
Emp Here 75
SIC 8211 Elementary and secondary schools

D-U-N-S 20-087-9844   (BR)
HASTINGS AND PRINCE EDWARD DISTRICT SCHOOL BOARD
COLLEGE STREET SCHOOL
20 South St, Trenton, ON, K8V 1P8
(613) 392-4524
Emp Here 30
SIC 8211 Elementary and secondary schools

D-U-N-S 25-237-7817   (BR)
HASTINGS AND PRINCE EDWARD DISTRICT SCHOOL BOARD
PRINCE CHARLES SCHOOL
138 Dufferin Ave, Trenton, ON, K8V 5E1
(613) 392-5461
Emp Here 38
SIC 8211 Elementary and secondary schools

D-U-N-S 25-237-7841   (BR)
HASTINGS AND PRINCE EDWARD DISTRICT SCHOOL BOARD
QUEEN ELIZABETH PUBLIC SCHOOL
16 Sillers Ave, Trenton, ON, K8V 1X6

Emp Here 30
SIC 8211 Elementary and secondary schools

D-U-N-S 25-238-0159   (BR)
KAWARTHA PINE RIDGE DISTRICT SCHOOL BOARD
MURRAY CENTENNIAL ELEMENTARY SCHOOL
654 County Rd 40, Trenton, ON, K8V 5P4
(613) 392-9238
Emp Here 30
SIC 8211 Elementary and secondary schools

D-U-N-S 24-832-3516   (SL)
KILMARNOCK ENTERPRISE

166 North Murray St, Trenton, ON, K8V 6R8
(613) 394-4422
Emp Here 81   *Sales* 11,694,389
SIC 8742 Management consulting services

D-U-N-S 20-190-0946   (BR)
L-3 COMMUNICATIONS MAS (CANADA) INC
(*Suby of* L3 Technologies, Inc.)
374 Sidney St, Trenton, ON, K8V 2V2
(613) 965-3207
Emp Here 100
SIC 4581 Airports, flying fields, and services

D-U-N-S 25-300-0517   (BR)
METRO ONTARIO INC
53 Quinte St, Trenton, ON, K8V 3S8
(613) 394-2525
Emp Here 110
SIC 5411 Grocery stores

D-U-N-S 20-536-7907   (BR)
MOORE CANADA CORPORATION
R.R. DONNELLEY
(*Suby of* R. R. Donnelley & Sons Company)
8 Douglas Rd, Trenton, ON, K8V 5R4
(613) 392-1205
Emp Here 135
SIC 2761 Manifold business forms

D-U-N-S 20-879-9429   (BR)
NESTLE CANADA INC
1 Douglas Rd, Trenton, ON, K8V 5S7
(613) 394-3328
Emp Here 200
SIC 2037 Frozen fruits and vegetables

D-U-N-S 20-974-6767   (SL)
PARKER BROTHERS TEXTILE MILLS LIMITED
(*Suby of* 133672 Canada Inc)
52 Film St, Trenton, ON, K8V 5J8
(613) 392-1217
Emp Here 30
SIC 2231 Broadwoven fabric mills, wool

D-U-N-S 24-006-3008   (BR)
PEPSICO CANADA ULC
FRITO LAY CANADA
(*Suby of* Pepsico, Inc.)
19 Alberta St, Trenton, ON, K8V 4E7
(613) 392-1496
Emp Here 40
SIC 2041 Flour and other grain mill products

D-U-N-S 20-179-0797   (BR)
PEPSICO CANADA ULC
PET FOOD, DIV OF
(*Suby of* Pepsico, Inc.)
106 Dufferin Ave, Trenton, ON, K8V 5E1

Emp Here 150
SIC 2047 Dog and cat food

D-U-N-S 24-386-9906   (SL)
PERFECT EQUIPMENT CANADA LTD
19 Frankford Cres Unit 3, Trenton, ON, K8V 6H8
(613) 394-8710
Emp Here 25   *Sales* 1,896,978
SIC 3369 Nonferrous foundries, nec

D-U-N-S 25-628-8762   (BR)
QUINTE HEALTHCARE CORPORATION
TRENTON MEMORIAL HOSPITAL
242 King St, Trenton, ON, K8V 5S6
(613) 392-2541
Emp Here 375
SIC 8062 General medical and surgical hospitals

D-U-N-S 25-586-0355   (BR)
ROYAL LEPAGE LIMITED
ROYAL LEPAGE PRO ALLIANCE REALTY
253 Dundas St E, Trenton, ON, K8V 1M1
(613) 243-0909
Emp Here 25
SIC 6531 Real estate agents and managers

D-U-N-S 25-690-5076   (BR)
SAPUTO INC
SAPUTO DAIRY PRODUCTS CANADA G.P.
7 Riverside Drive, Trenton, ON, K8V 5R7
(613) 392-6762
Emp Here 150
SIC 2022 Cheese; natural and processed

D-U-N-S 20-799-9132   (SL)
SCHMIDT, KEN RESTAURANT INC
MACDONALD'S
18 Monogram Pl, Trenton, ON, K8V 5P8
(613) 394-4533
Emp Here 40   *Sales* 1,824,018
SIC 5812 Eating places

D-U-N-S 20-733-9503   (BR)
SOBEYS CAPITAL INCORPORATED
PRICE CHOPPER
30 Ontario St, Trenton, ON, K8V 5S9
(613) 394-2791
Emp Here 85
SIC 5411 Grocery stores

D-U-N-S 24-506-4019   (BR)
SONOCO CANADA CORPORATION
(*Suby of* Sonoco Products Company)
5 Bernard Long Rd, Trenton, ON, K8V 5P6
(613) 394-6903
Emp Here 130
SIC 2631 Paperboard mills

D-U-N-S 20-860-3386   (BR)
SOURCE (BELL) ELECTRONICS INC, THE
SOURCE, THE
266 Dundas St E, Trenton, ON, K8V 5Z9
(613) 394-4253
Emp Here 25
SIC 5999 Miscellaneous retail stores, nec

D-U-N-S 20-278-8501   (BR)
TCS LOGISTICS INCORPORATED
178 Stockdale Rd, Trenton, ON, K8V 5P6
(613) 394-3317
Emp Here 50
SIC 4222 Refrigerated warehousing and storage

D-U-N-S 24-028-4786   (SL)
TRENT VALLEY LODGE NURSING HOME
195 Bay St Suite 363, Trenton, ON, K8V 1H9
(613) 392-9235
Emp Here 70   *Sales* 2,553,625
SIC 8361 Residential care

D-U-N-S 25-527-9119   (BR)
TRENTON COLD STORAGE INC
TRI COUNTY APPLE GROWERS
178 Stockdale Rd, Trenton, ON, K8V 5P6
(613) 392-2498
Emp Here 35
SIC 4222 Refrigerated warehousing and storage

D-U-N-S 20-259-6649   (BR)
TRENTON COLD STORAGE INC
FRASER GLENBURNIE
17489 Telephone Rd, Trenton, ON, K8V 5P4
(613) 394-3317
Emp Here 100
SIC 4225 General warehousing and storage

D-U-N-S 20-651-2035   (BR)
VICTORIAN ORDER OF NURSES FOR CANADA
VON HASTINGS-NORTHUMBERLAND-PE DISTRICT
80 Division St Suite 14, Trenton, ON, K8V 5S5
(613) 392-4181
Emp Here 350
SIC 8082 Home health care services

D-U-N-S 24-318-0820   (BR)
WAL-MART CANADA CORP
WALMART
Hwy 2 At 2nd Dughill Rd, Trenton, ON, K8V 5P7
(613) 394-2191
Emp Here 150

SIC 5311 Department stores

D-U-N-S 24-534-8052   (BR)
WASTE MANAGEMENT OF CANADA CORPORATION
(*Suby of* Waste Management, Inc.)
270 West St, Trenton, ON, K8V 2N3

Emp Here 40
SIC 5093 Scrap and waste materials

D-U-N-S 20-939-8908   (HQ)
WHITLEY, DOUG INSURANCE BROKER LIMITED
WHITLEY FINANCIAL SERVICES
41 Dundas St W, Trenton, ON, K8V 3N9
(613) 392-1283
Emp Here 20   *Emp Total* 165
Sales 3,137,310
SIC 6411 Insurance agents, brokers, and service

D-U-N-S 24-121-1309   (HQ)
WILKINSON & COMPANY LLP
(*Suby of* Wilkinson & Company LLP)
71 Dundas St W, Trenton, ON, K8V 3P4
(888) 713-7283
Emp Here 25   *Emp Total* 55
Sales 2,407,703
SIC 8721 Accounting, auditing, and bookkeeping

Trout Creek, ON P0H
Parry Sound County

D-U-N-S 24-026-4077   (SL)
LADY ISABELLE NURSING HOME LTD
102 Corkery St, Trout Creek, ON, P0H 2L0
(705) 723-5232
Emp Here 75   *Sales* 3,429,153
SIC 8051 Skilled nursing care facilities

D-U-N-S 20-710-4345   (BR)
NEAR NORTH DISTRICT SCHOOL BOARD
TROUT CREEK PUBLIC SCHOOL
121 Mccarthy St S, Trout Creek, ON, P0H 2L0
(705) 723-5351
Emp Here 50
SIC 8211 Elementary and secondary schools

Troy, ON L0R

D-U-N-S 20-054-6596   (SL)
ARCHIE MCCOY (HAMILTON) LIMITED
MCCOY FOUNDRY
1890 Highway 5 W, Troy, ON, L0R 2B0
(519) 647-3411
Emp Here 65
SIC 3321 Gray and ductile iron foundries

D-U-N-S 20-653-3791   (BR)
HAMILTON-WENTWORTH DISTRICT SCHOOL BOARD, THE
BEVERLY CENTRAL SCHOOL
1346 Concession 4 W, Troy, ON, L0R 2B0
(905) 628-9444
Emp Here 20
SIC 8211 Elementary and secondary schools

D-U-N-S 24-143-4455   (BR)
KANEFF PROPERTIES LIMITED
CENTURY PINES GOLF CLUB
592 Westover Rd Suite 2, Troy, ON, L0R 2B0
(905) 628-2877
Emp Here 20
SIC 7992 Public golf courses

Tunis, ON P0N
Cochrane County

D-U-N-S 24-165-5369 (BR)
TRANSCANADA CORPORATION
T C P L
Gd, Tunis, ON, P0N 1J0
(705) 232-5208
Emp Here 20
SIC 4922 Natural gas transmission

Tweed, ON K0K
Hastings County

D-U-N-S 20-711-5002 (BR)
ALGONQUIN & LAKESHORE CATHOLIC DISTRICT SCHOOL BOARD
ST CARTHAGH CATHOLIC SCHOOL
114 Hunderford Rd, Tweed, ON, K0K 3J0
(613) 478-2601
Emp Here 24
SIC 8211 Elementary and secondary schools

D-U-N-S 20-606-4537 (HQ)
BOLDRICK BUS SERVICE LIMITED
BOLDRICK TRUCK & AUTO CENTRE
(*Suby of* Boldrick Bus Service Limited)
341 Victoria N, Tweed, ON, K0K 3J0
(613) 478-3322
Emp Here 46   *Emp Total* 85
Sales 2,407,703
SIC 4151 School buses

D-U-N-S 20-258-1935 (BR)
GOVERNING COUNCIL OF THE SALVATION ARMY IN CANADA, THE
SALVATION ARMY COMMUNITY AND FAMILY SERVICES
253 Victoria St, Tweed, ON, K0K 3J0
(613) 478-3375
Emp Here 20
SIC 5812 Eating places

D-U-N-S 25-265-4272 (BR)
HASTINGS AND PRINCE EDWARD DISTRICT SCHOOL BOARD
TWEED ELEMENTARY SCHOOL
52 Mcclellan St, Tweed, ON, K0K 3J0
(613) 478-2714
Emp Here 26
SIC 8211 Elementary and secondary schools

D-U-N-S 25-265-4397 (BR)
HASTINGS AND PRINCE EDWARD DISTRICT SCHOOL BOARD
S H CONNOR PUBLIC SCHOOL
165 Pomeroy St, Tweed, ON, K0K 3J0
(613) 478-2714
Emp Here 22
SIC 8211 Elementary and secondary schools

Unionville, ON L3P
York County

D-U-N-S 25-056-2865 (SL)
MARKHAM CENTENNIAL CENTRE
8600 Mccowan Rd, Unionville, ON, L3P 3M2
(905) 294-6111
Emp Here 115   *Sales* 4,523,563
SIC 8322 Individual and family services

D-U-N-S 25-092-6102 (BR)
TORONTO-DOMINION BANK, THE
TD CANADA TRUST
(*Suby of* Toronto-Dominion Bank, The)
8545 Mccowan Rd Suite 7, Unionville, ON, L3P 1W9
(905) 471-4200
Emp Here 25
SIC 6021 National commercial banks

D-U-N-S 20-711-4120 (BR)
YORK REGION DISTRICT SCHOOL BOARD
CENTRAL PARK PUBLIC SCHOOL

(*Suby of* York Region District School Board)
100 Central Park Dr, Unionville, ON, L3P 7G2
(905) 940-1444
Emp Here 50
SIC 8211 Elementary and secondary schools

D-U-N-S 20-711-4187 (BR)
YORK REGION DISTRICT SCHOOL BOARD
MARKVILLE SECONDARY SCHOOL
(*Suby of* York Region District School Board)
1000 Carlton Rd, Unionville, ON, L3P 7P5
(905) 940-8840
Emp Here 110
SIC 8211 Elementary and secondary schools

Unionville, ON L3R
York County

D-U-N-S 24-437-5734 (BR)
BANQUE TORONTO-DOMINION, LA
TORONTO-DOMINION BANK, THE
(*Suby of* Toronto-Dominion Bank, The)
4630 Highway 7, Unionville, ON, L3R 1M5
(905) 475-9960
Emp Here 22
SIC 6021 National commercial banks

D-U-N-S 24-995-8752 (BR)
BEST BUY CANADA LTD
FUTURE SHOP
(*Suby of* Best Buy Co., Inc.)
8601 Warden Ave Suite 1, Unionville, ON, L3R 0B5

Emp Here 105
SIC 5731 Radio, television, and electronic stores

D-U-N-S 25-303-4748 (BR)
CANADIAN IMPERIAL BANK OF COMMERCE
CIBC
4360 Highway 7 E, Unionville, ON, L3R 1L9
(905) 477-2540
Emp Here 20
SIC 6021 National commercial banks

D-U-N-S 24-345-9414 (BR)
CARA OPERATIONS LIMITED
MILESTONES GRILL & BAR
(*Suby of* Cara Holdings Limited)
3760 Highway 7, Unionville, ON, L3R 0N2

Emp Here 150
SIC 5812 Eating places

D-U-N-S 24-251-2023 (BR)
CARA OPERATIONS LIMITED
SWISS CHALET
(*Suby of* Cara Holdings Limited)
5070 Highway 7 E, Unionville, ON, L3R 5R9
(905) 305-1809
Emp Here 45
SIC 5812 Eating places

D-U-N-S 24-322-3778 (BR)
MCDONALD'S RESTAURANTS OF CANADA LIMITED
MCDONALD'S
(*Suby of* McDonald's Corporation)
3760 Highway 7, Unionville, ON, L3R 0N2
(905) 513-8978
Emp Here 65
SIC 5812 Eating places

D-U-N-S 20-641-9108 (BR)
MCDONALD'S RESTAURANTS OF CANADA LIMITED
MCDONALD'S RESTAURANTS
(*Suby of* McDonald's Corporation)
5225 Highway 7 E, Unionville, ON, L3R 1N3
(905) 477-2891
Emp Here 90
SIC 5812 Eating places

D-U-N-S 20-038-0561 (BR)
MERCEDES-BENZ CANADA INC
8350 Kennedy Rd, Unionville, ON, L3R 0W4
(905) 305-1088
Emp Here 70
SIC 5511 New and used car dealers

D-U-N-S 24-855-5109 (SL)
RFI CANADA PARTNERSHIP
178 Main St, Unionville, ON, L3R 2G9
(905) 534-1044
Emp Here 100   *Sales* 14,373,258
SIC 5149 Groceries and related products, nec
Dir Grant Smith

D-U-N-S 25-711-0031 (BR)
STARBUCKS COFFEE CANADA, INC
(*Suby of* Starbucks Corporation)
201 Main St, Unionville, ON, L3R 2G8
(905) 944-0703
Emp Here 20
SIC 5812 Eating places

D-U-N-S 20-209-9052 (SL)
SUNRISE OF MARKHAM LIMITED
SUNRISE ASSISTED LIVING UNIONVILLE
38 Swansea Rd, Unionville, ON, L3R 5K2
(905) 947-4566
Emp Here 84   *Sales* 3,793,956
SIC 8051 Skilled nursing care facilities

D-U-N-S 20-754-5708 (SL)
UNIONVILLE MOTORS (1973) LIMITED
4630 Highway 7, Unionville, ON, L3R 1M5

Emp Here 60   *Sales* 30,435,000
SIC 5511 New and used car dealers
Genl Mgr Kelly Jamieson
Treas Dennis Hext
Pr Pr John Jamieson

D-U-N-S 25-151-0319 (BR)
YORK CATHOLIC DISTRICT SCHOOL BOARD
ST MATTHEW CATHOLIC ELEMENTARY SCHOOL
75 Waterbridge Lane, Unionville, ON, L3R 4G3
(905) 475-0517
Emp Here 30
SIC 8211 Elementary and secondary schools

D-U-N-S 25-297-9000 (BR)
YORK REGION DISTRICT SCHOOL BOARD
PARKVIEW PUBLIC SCHOOL
(*Suby of* York Region District School Board)
22 Fonthill Blvd, Unionville, ON, L3R 1V6
(905) 477-2172
Emp Here 35
SIC 8211 Elementary and secondary schools

D-U-N-S 25-297-9554 (BR)
YORK REGION DISTRICT SCHOOL BOARD
WILLIAM BERCZY PUBLIC SCHOOL
(*Suby of* York Region District School Board)
120 Carlton Rd, Unionville, ON, L3R 1Z9
(905) 477-2047
Emp Here 50
SIC 8211 Elementary and secondary schools

D-U-N-S 20-591-2533 (BR)
YORK REGION DISTRICT SCHOOL BOARD
UNIONVILLE PUBLIC SCHOOL
(*Suby of* York Region District School Board)
300 Main St, Unionville, ON, L3R 2H2
(905) 477-1824
Emp Here 25
SIC 8211 Elementary and secondary schools

Unionville, ON L6G
York County

D-U-N-S 20-703-3630 (HQ)
MOTOROLA SOLUTIONS CANADA INC
COMMERCIAL GOVERNMENT AND INDUS-

TRIAL SOLUTIONS SECTOR DIV
(*Suby of* Motorola Solutions, Inc.)
8133 Warden Ave, Unionville, ON, L6G 1B3
(905) 948-5200
Emp Here 60   *Emp Total* 14,000
Sales 51,922,328
SIC 5065 Electronic parts and equipment, nec
Jahangir Chandani
George Krausz

D-U-N-S 24-817-6174 (BR)
WORLEYPARSONS CANADA SERVICES LTD
8133 Warden Ave, Unionville, ON, L6G 1B3
(905) 940-4774
Emp Here 75
SIC 8711 Engineering services

D-U-N-S 24-319-8574 (BR)
YMCA OF GREATER TORONTO
YMCA MARKHAM
101 Ymca Blvd, Unionville, ON, L6G 0A1
(905) 513-0884
Emp Here 50
SIC 8699 Membership organizations, nec

Utopia, ON L0M
Simcoe County

D-U-N-S 25-686-2087 (SL)
1084130 ONTARIO LIMITED
STRATEGIC SERVICES GROUP
5691 Sideroad 20, Utopia, ON, L0M 1T0

Emp Here 60   *Sales* 2,261,590
SIC 7349 Building maintenance services, nec

D-U-N-S 20-042-4311 (BR)
UPI INC
8894 County Road 56, Utopia, ON, L0M 1T0
(705) 726-8915
Emp Here 20
SIC 5541 Gasoline service stations

Utterson, ON P0B
Muskoka County

D-U-N-S 25-263-6592 (BR)
TRILLIUM LAKELANDS DISTRICT SCHOOL BOARD
GREER, V K MEMORIAL PUBLIC SCHOOL
130 Muskoka 10 Rd, Utterson, ON, P0B 1M0
(705) 385-2200
Emp Here 30
SIC 8211 Elementary and secondary schools

Uxbridge, ON L9P

D-U-N-S 25-758-2171 (BR)
ALEX WILLIAMSON MOTOR SALES LIMITED
WILLIAMSON BUICK PONTIAC, DIV
1 Banff Rd, Uxbridge, ON, L9P 1S9
(905) 852-3357
Emp Here 52
SIC 5511 New and used car dealers

D-U-N-S 25-707-0953 (BR)
CORPORATION OF THE TOWNSHIP OF UXBRIDGE, THE
UXBRIDGE & AREA SWIMMING POOL
1 Parkside Dr, Uxbridge, ON, L9P 1K7
(905) 852-7831
Emp Here 35
SIC 7999 Amusement and recreation, nec

D-U-N-S 25-265-2151 (BR)
DURHAM CATHOLIC DISTRICT SCHOOL BOARD

ST JOSEPH CATHOLIC SCHOOL
25 Quaker Village Dr, Uxbridge, ON, L9P 1A1
(905) 852-6242
Emp Here 35
SIC 8211 Elementary and secondary schools

D-U-N-S 25-263-7657   (BR)
DURHAM DISTRICT SCHOOL BOARD
JOSEPH GOULD PUBLIC SCHOOL
144 Planks Lane, Uxbridge, ON, L9P 1K6
(905) 852-7631
Emp Here 40
SIC 8211 Elementary and secondary schools

D-U-N-S 25-301-7198   (BR)
DURHAM DISTRICT SCHOOL BOARD
UXBRIDGE PUBLIC SCHOOL
64 Victoria Dr, Uxbridge, ON, L9P 1H2
(905) 852-9101
Emp Here 30
SIC 8211 Elementary and secondary schools

D-U-N-S 24-318-8369   (BR)
EXCO TECHNOLOGIES LIMITED
CASTOOL TOOLING SYSTEMS
2 Parratt Rd, Uxbridge, ON, L9P 1R1
(905) 852-0121
Emp Here 101
SIC 3545 Machine tool accessories

D-U-N-S 24-411-2694   (SL)
FITZPATRICK ELECTRICAL CONTRACTOR INC
(*Suby of* FE Capital Inc)
41 Maple St, Uxbridge, ON, L9P 1C8
(905) 686-1661
Emp Here 40   *Sales* 16,121,626
SIC 1731 Electrical work
Pr Pr Robert J. Somers
VP VP John H. Somers

D-U-N-S 24-802-6937   (BR)
MARKHAM STOUFFVILLE HOSPITAL
UXBRIDGE COTTAGE HOSPITAL
4 Campbell Dr, Uxbridge, ON, L9P 1S4
(905) 852-9771
Emp Here 100
SIC 8062 General medical and surgical hospitals

D-U-N-S 25-028-5350   (BR)
REVERA LONG TERM CARE INC
REACHVIEW VILLAGE
130 Reach St Suite 25, Uxbridge, ON, L9P 1L3
(905) 852-5191
Emp Here 85
SIC 8051 Skilled nursing care facilities

D-U-N-S 24-985-3698   (SL)
ROYAL EDITION INC, THE
TIM HORTONS
325 Toronto St S, Uxbridge, ON, L9P 1Z7
(905) 852-6680
Emp Here 120   *Sales* 5,072,500
SIC 5812 Eating places
Pr Jan King
Dir Rodney King
Dir Heather King
Dir Margaret King

D-U-N-S 24-330-6268   (BR)
STAPLES CANADA INC
STAPLES THE BUSINESS DEPOT
(*Suby of* Staples, Inc.)
4 Banff Rd Unit 101, Uxbridge, ON, L9P 1S9
(905) 862-2614
Emp Here 20
SIC 5943 Stationery stores

D-U-N-S 25-322-1352   (BR)
TORONTO-DOMINION BANK, THE
TD BANK
(*Suby of* Toronto-Dominion Bank, The)
1 Brock St W, Uxbridge, ON, L9P 1P6
(905) 852-3324
Emp Here 20

SIC 6021 National commercial banks

D-U-N-S 24-317-2025   (BR)
WAL-MART CANADA CORP
WALMART
6 Welwood Dr, Uxbridge, ON, L9P 1Z7
(905) 862-0721
Emp Here 150
SIC 5311 Department stores

Val Caron, ON P3N
Sudbury County

D-U-N-S 20-058-0459   (SL)
1011191 ONTARIO INC
METRO VAL-EAST
3140 Old Hwy 69 N Suite 28, Val Caron, ON, P3N 1G3
(705) 897-4958
Emp Here 100   *Sales* 13,424,769
SIC 5411 Grocery stores
Pr Pr Lionel Dutrisac
Gilles Dutrisac

D-U-N-S 20-715-5805   (BR)
COMSTOCK CANADA LTD
2736 Belisle Dr, Val Caron, ON, P3N 1N4

Emp Here 25
SIC 1711 Plumbing, heating, air-conditioning

D-U-N-S 20-655-9366   (BR)
CONSEIL SCOLAIRE DE DISTRICT CATHOLIQUE DU NOUVEL-ONTARIO, LE
NOTRE DAMES DE L'ESPERANCE
2965 Hope St, Val Caron, ON, P3N 1R8
(705) 897-3741
Emp Here 20
SIC 8211 Elementary and secondary schools

D-U-N-S 20-710-4105   (BR)
CONSEIL SCOLAIRE DE DISTRICT CATHOLIQUE DU NOUVEL-ONTARIO, LE
ECOLE SECONDAIRE CATHOLIQUE L'HORIZON
1650 Valleyview Rd, Val Caron, ON, P3N 1K7
(705) 897-2503
Emp Here 50
SIC 8211 Elementary and secondary schools

D-U-N-S 20-276-5095   (BR)
FNX MINING COMPANY INC
DMC MINING SERVICES
2650 White St, Val Caron, ON, P3N 0A7
(705) 897-8461
Emp Here 25
SIC 1081 Metal mining services

D-U-N-S 20-179-1345   (BR)
JARLETTE LTD
VALLEY EAST LONG TERM CARE
2100 Main St, Val Caron, ON, P3N 1S7
(705) 897-7695
Emp Here 150
SIC 8059 Nursing and personal care, nec

D-U-N-S 25-197-7302   (HQ)
NICKEL CENTRE PHARMACY INC
VAL EST PHARMACY
(*Suby of* Nickel Centre Pharmacy Inc)
3140 Old Hwy 69 N Suite 17, Val Caron, ON, P3N 1G3
(705) 897-1867
Emp Here 20   *Emp Total* 50
Sales 2,772,507
SIC 5947 Gift, novelty, and souvenir shop

D-U-N-S 20-710-4006   (BR)
RAINBOW DISTRICT SCHOOL BOARD
CONFEDERATION SECONDARY SCHOOL
1918 Main St, Val Caron, ON, P3N 1R8
(705) 671-5948
Emp Here 50

SIC 8211 Elementary and secondary schools

D-U-N-S 20-710-3990   (BR)
RAINBOW DISTRICT SCHOOL BOARD
VALLEYVIEW PUBLIC SCHOOL
1840 Valleyview Rd, Val Caron, ON, P3N 1S1
(705) 671-5956
Emp Here 20
SIC 8211 Elementary and secondary schools

D-U-N-S 20-081-4155   (BR)
SUDBURY CATHOLIC DISTRICT SCHOOL BOARD
IMMACULATE CONCEPTION SCHOOL
1748 Pierre St, Val Caron, ON, P3N 1C5
(705) 897-4483
Emp Here 20
SIC 8211 Elementary and secondary schools

Val Rita, ON P0L
Cochrane County

D-U-N-S 20-581-4465   (BR)
CANADA POST CORPORATION
Gd, Val Rita, ON, P0L 2G0
(705) 335-3026
Emp Here 20
SIC 4311 U.s. postal service

Vanier, ON K1K
Carleton County

D-U-N-S 24-595-7840   (SL)
1070481 ONTARIO INC
EDGEWOOD CARE CENTRE
9 Stevens Ave Suite 502, Vanier, ON, K1K 1K4
(613) 748-7000
Emp Here 110   *Sales* 5,579,750
SIC 8361 Residential care
Pr Pr Thomas Howcraft

Vanier, ON K1L
Carleton County

D-U-N-S 24-229-3079   (SL)
1799795 ONTARIO LIMITED
LABOUR GROUP
171 Montreal Rd, Vanier, ON, K1L 6E4
(613) 745-5720
Emp Here 50   *Sales* 4,331,255
SIC 7361 Employment agencies

D-U-N-S 20-362-1651   (BR)
CANADIAN ADDICTION TREATMENT PHARMACY LP
311 Mcarthur Ave Suite 105, Vanier, ON, K1L 6P1
(613) 749-2324
Emp Here 20
SIC 5122 Drugs, proprietaries, and sundries

D-U-N-S 25-307-2011   (BR)
CANADIAN DIABETES ASSOCIATION
EASTERN ONTARIO REGIONAL LEADERSHIP CENTRE (OTTAWA)
45 Montreal Rd, Vanier, ON, K1L 6E8
(613) 521-1902
Emp Here 25
SIC 8699 Membership organizations, nec

D-U-N-S 25-238-2817   (BR)
CHIGNECTO CENTRAL REGIONAL SCHOOL BOARD
ECOLE LE TRILLIUM
(*Suby of* Chignecto Central Regional School Board)
307 Montgomery St, Vanier, ON, K1L 7W8
(613) 744-8523
Emp Here 30

SIC 8211 Elementary and secondary schools

D-U-N-S 25-263-4654   (BR)
CONSEIL DES ECOLES CATHOLIQUES DE LANGUE FRANCAISE DU CENTRE-EST
ECOLE VISION JEUNESSE
235 Mcarthur Ave, Vanier, ON, K1L 6P3
(613) 749-5307
Emp Here 22
SIC 8211 Elementary and secondary schools

D-U-N-S 24-342-8260   (BR)
GOODLIFE FITNESS CENTRES INC
GOOD LIFE FITNESS CLUB
100 Mcarthur Ave, Vanier, ON, K1L 8H5
(613) 842-8797
Emp Here 20
SIC 7991 Physical fitness facilities

D-U-N-S 25-773-7619   (BR)
LOBLAWS INC
LOBLAWS
100 Mcarthur Ave, Vanier, ON, K1L 8H5
(613) 744-0705
Emp Here 260
SIC 5411 Grocery stores

D-U-N-S 24-344-5074   (BR)
METRO ONTARIO INC
METRO
50 Beechwood Ave, Vanier, ON, K1L 8B3
(613) 744-6676
Emp Here 100
SIC 5411 Grocery stores

D-U-N-S 25-238-1678   (BR)
OTTAWA CATHOLIC DISTRICT SCHOOL BOARD
ASSUMPTION SCHOOL
(*Suby of* Ottawa Catholic District School Board)
236 Levis Ave, Vanier, ON, K1L 6H8
(613) 746-4822
Emp Here 25
SIC 8211 Elementary and secondary schools

D-U-N-S 20-033-9989   (BR)
OTTAWA CATHOLIC DISTRICT SCHOOL BOARD
JEAN VANIER CATHOLIC INTERMEDIATE SCHOOL
(*Suby of* Ottawa Catholic District School Board)
320 Lajoie St, Vanier, ON, K1L 7H4
(613) ?
Emp Here 30
SIC 8211 Elementary and secondary schools

D-U-N-S 25-131-8002   (BR)
OTTAWA CATHOLIC DISTRICT SCHOOL BOARD
SAINT JOSEPH ADULT SCHOOL
(*Suby of* Ottawa Catholic District School Board)
330 Lajoie St, Vanier, ON, K1L 7H4
(613) 741-6808
Emp Here 22
SIC 8299 Schools and educational services, nec

D-U-N-S 24-179-2030   (BR)
S.L. DEVISON PHARMACIES INC
SHOPPERS DRUG MART
150 Montreal Rd, Vanier, ON, K1L 8H2
(613) 842-7544
Emp Here 25
SIC 5912 Drug stores and proprietary stores

Vankleek Hill, ON K0B
Prescott County

D-U-N-S 20-590-7301   (BR)
CATHOLIC DISTRICT SCHOOL BOARD OF EASTERN ONTARIO
ST JUDES CATHOLIC ELEMENTARY

Gd, Vankleek Hill, ON, K0B 1R0
(613) 678-5455
Emp Here 25
SIC 8211 Elementary and secondary schools

D-U-N-S 20-575-2806   (BR)
CONSEIL DES ECOLES PUBLIQUES DE L'EST DE L'ONTARIO
ECOLE SECONDAIRE PUBLIQUE DE VAN-KLEEK HILL
5814 Rte 34, Vankleek Hill, ON, K0B 1R0
(613) 678-8786
Emp Here 25
SIC 8211 Elementary and secondary schools

D-U-N-S 25-673-9004   (BR)
REVERA INC
VANKLEEK HILL HERITAGE LODGE
48 Wall St, Vankleek Hill, ON, K0B 1R0
(613) 678-2690
Emp Here 24
SIC 8361 Residential care

D-U-N-S 25-238-1298   (BR)
UPPER CANADA DISTRICT SCHOOL BOARD, THE
PLEASANT CORNERS PUBLIC SCHOOL
(*Suby of* Upper Canada District School Board, The)
4099 Highway 34, Vankleek Hill, ON, K0B 1R0
(613) 678-2030
Emp Here 55
SIC 8211 Elementary and secondary schools

D-U-N-S 25-238-1280   (BR)
UPPER CANADA DISTRICT SCHOOL BOARD, THE
VAN KLEEK HILL COLLEGIATE INSTITUTE
(*Suby of* Upper Canada District School Board, The)
5814 34 Hwy, Vankleek Hill, ON, K0B 1R0
(613) 678-2023
Emp Here 48
SIC 8211 Elementary and secondary schools

Varna, ON N0M
Huron County

D-U-N-S 25-174-1104   (SL)
VARNA GRAIN LIMITED
38839 Mill Rd Rr 1, Varna, ON, N0M 2R0
(519) 233-7908
Emp Here 20   *Sales* 68,123,040
SIC 4221 Farm product warehousing and storage
Pr Beverley Hill

Vars, ON K0A
Carleton County

D-U-N-S 20-294-2975   (BR)
ADESA AUCTIONS CANADA CORPORATION
ADESA OTTAWA
1717 Ch Burton Ss 4, Vars, ON, K0A 3H0
(613) 443-4400
Emp Here 150
SIC 5012 Automobiles and other motor vehicles

D-U-N-S 24-595-6263   (SL)
AUTOBUS BERGERON BUS LINES INC
1801 Russland Rd Ss 4, Vars, ON, K0A 3H0

Emp Here 60   *Sales* 1,992,377
SIC 4151 School buses

D-U-N-S 20-328-3338   (HQ)
GROUPE TIF GROUP INC
(*Suby of* Groupe TIF Group Inc)
112 Rue Clement Ss 4, Vars, ON, K0A 3H0

(613) 656-7978
Emp Here 50   *Emp Total* 50
Sales 4,617,412
SIC 7532 Top and body repair and paint shops

D-U-N-S 20-542-6950   (BR)
TOMLINSON, R. W. LIMITED
ONTARIO TRAP ROCK, DIV OF
(*Suby of* Tomlinson, R. W. Limited)
8125 Russell Rd, Vars, ON, K0A 3H0
(613) 835-3395
Emp Here 75
SIC 5211 Lumber and other building materials

Vaughan, ON L4K
York County

D-U-N-S 20-335-2534   (SL)
2298679 ONTARIO INC
GOLD STANDARD DEVELOPMENT
201 Millway Ave Unit 18, Vaughan, ON, L4K 5K8
(905) 695-1670
Emp Here 50   *Sales* 1,126,126
SIC 7349 Building maintenance services, nec

D-U-N-S 20-342-4478   (BR)
CHAMPION PRODUCTS CORP
10 Ronrose Dr, Vaughan, ON, L4K 4R3
(289) 695-3900
Emp Here 35
SIC 5113 Industrial and personal service paper

D-U-N-S 25-091-6710   (BR)
COLABOR LIMITED PARTNERSHIP
SUMMIT FOOD SERVICE, DIV OF
(*Suby of* Groupe Colabor Inc)
10 Ronrose Dr, Vaughan, ON, L4K 4R3
(800) 265-9267
Emp Here 73
SIC 5141 Groceries, general line

D-U-N-S 25-347-7038   (BR)
COMPAGNIE DES CHEMINS DE FER NATIONAUX DU CANADA
MACMILLAN YARD
1 Administration Rd, Vaughan, ON, L4K 1B9
(905) 669-3128
Emp Here 1,000
SIC 4011 Railroads, line-haul operating

D-U-N-S 20-294-5759   (SL)
CONCORD VAUGHAN LTD PARTNERSHIP
COURTYARD MARRIOTT HOTEL
150 Interchange Way, Vaughan, ON, L4K 5P7
(905) 660-9938
Emp Here 50   *Sales* 2,188,821
SIC 7011 Hotels and motels

D-U-N-S 20-321-7070   (BR)
FRESHPOINT VANCOUVER, LTD
(*Suby of* Sysco Corporation)
1400 Creditstone Rd Unit A, Vaughan, ON, L4K 0E2
(416) 251-6112
Emp Here 100
SIC 5148 Fresh fruits and vegetables

D-U-N-S 20-338-3138   (BR)
GROUPE TOUCHETTE INC
DT TIRE DISTRIBUTION
370 Caldari Rd, Vaughan, ON, L4K 4J4
(905) 761-2023
Emp Here 40
SIC 5014 Tires and tubes

D-U-N-S 24-342-6868   (BR)
KRISTOFOAM INDUSTRIES INC
120 Planchet Rd, Vaughan, ON, L4K 2C7
(905) 669-6616
Emp Here 75
SIC 3086 Plastics foam products

D-U-N-S 20-112-2319   (HQ)
MARTINREA AUTOMOTIVE INC

ATLAS FLUID SYSTEM, DIV OF
3210 Langstaff Rd, Vaughan, ON, L4K 5B2
(289) 982-3000
Emp Here 400   *Emp Total* 14,000
Sales 328,323,150
SIC 3499 Fabricated Metal products, nec
Pr Pr Nick Orlando
Ch Bd Robert Wildeboer

D-U-N-S 25-202-7883   (HQ)
MARTINREA INTERNATIONAL INC
HYDROFORM SOLUTIONS, DIV OF
(*Suby of* Martinrea International Inc)
3210 Langstaff Rd, Vaughan, ON, L4K 5B2
(289) 982-3000
Emp Here 100   *Emp Total* 14,000
Sales 3,152,834,061
SIC 3499 Fabricated Metal products, nec
Pr Pat D'eramo
Fred Di Tosto
Robert P Wildeboer
Dir Scott Balfour
Dir Roman Doroniuk
Dir Terry Lyons
Dir Frank Macher
Dir Fred Olson
Dir Sandra Pupatello

D-U-N-S 24-978-0669   (HQ)
MARTINREA METALLIC CANADA INC
3210 Langstaff Rd, Vaughan, ON, L4K 5B2
(416) 749-0314
Emp Here 250   *Emp Total* 14,000
Sales 21,450,446
SIC 3465 Automotive stampings
Pr Pr Nick Orlando
Fred Jaekel

D-U-N-S 24-910-9471   (HQ)
MIRCOM TECHNOLOGIES LTD
25 Interchange Way Suite 1, Vaughan, ON, L4K 5W3
(905) 660-4655
Emp Here 100   *Emp Total* 400
Sales 57,274,150
SIC 3669 Communications equipment, nec
Pr Pr Tony Falbo
Mark Falbo

D-U-N-S 24-485-5979   (BR)
PUMPCRETE CORPORATION
161 Caldari Rd, Vaughan, ON, L4K 3Z9
(905) 669-2017
Emp Here 20
SIC 7353 Heavy construction equipment rental

D-U-N-S 24-852-7207   (SL)
SKYREACH L&S EXTRUSIONS CORP
55 Freshway Dr, Vaughan, ON, L4K 1S1
(416) 663-1888
Emp Here 65   *Sales* 19,553,468
SIC 5031 Lumber, plywood, and millwork
Sec Ping Huang
Georgia Leung
Dir Wai-Tao Lai

D-U-N-S 20-291-5799   (BR)
SUPERIOR SEATING HOSPITALITY INC
(*Suby of* Superior Seating Hospitality Inc)
9000 Keele St Unit 11, Vaughan, ON, L4K 0B3
(905) 738-7900
Emp Here 100
SIC 2599 Furniture and fixtures, nec

D-U-N-S 20-285-9179   (BR)
THERMO DESIGN INSULATION LTD
8301 Jane St Unit 10, Vaughan, ON, L4K 5P3
(905) 761-0100
Emp Here 30
SIC 1742 Plastering, drywall, and insulation

D-U-N-S 20-288-3588   (BR)
YORK REGION DISTRICT SCHOOL BOARD
FOREST RUN PUBLIC SCHOOL
(*Suby of* York Region District School Board)
200 Forest Run Blvd, Vaughan, ON, L4K 5H3

(905) 417-9227
Emp Here 40
SIC 8211 Elementary and secondary schools

Vaughan, ON L4L
York County

D-U-N-S 25-991-7979   (BR)
GROUPE ALDO INC, LE
GLOBO SHOES
3900 Highway 7, Vaughan, ON, L4L 9C3
(905) 264-4562
Emp Here 30
SIC 5661 Shoe stores

D-U-N-S 20-699-1122   (BR)
KGHM INTERNATIONAL LTD
DMC MINING SERVICES, DIV OF
191 Creditview Rd Suite 400, Vaughan, ON, L4L 9T1
(905) 780-1980
Emp Here 40
SIC 1081 Metal mining services

D-U-N-S 20-512-6134   (SL)
WINDOW CITY INDUSTRIES INC
5690 Steeles Ave W, Vaughan, ON, L4L 9T4
(905) 265-9975
Emp Here 50   *Sales* 4,596,524
SIC 3231 Products of purchased glass

Vaughan, ON L6A
York County

D-U-N-S 24-329-1924   (SL)
CANADA'S WONDERLAND COMPANY
9580 Jane St, Vaughan, ON, L6A 1S6
(905) 832-7000
Emp Here 100   *Sales* 4,504,505
SIC 7996 Amusement parks

D-U-N-S 24-329-6857   (BR)
LOBLAWS INC
FORTINOS
2911 Major Mackenzie Dr Suite 80, Vaughan, ON, L6A 3N9
(905) 417-0490
Emp Here 250
SIC 5411 Grocery stores

D-U-N-S 20-590-4654   (BR)
YORK CATHOLIC DISTRICT SCHOOL BOARD
ST. DAVID CATHOLIC ELEMENTARY SCHOOL
240 Killian Rd, Vaughan, ON, L6A 1A8
(905) 832-1887
Emp Here 25
SIC 8211 Elementary and secondary schools

D-U-N-S 20-711-4278   (BR)
YORK REGION DISTRICT SCHOOL BOARD
MICHAEL CRANNY ELEMENTARY SCHOOL
(*Suby of* York Region District School Board)
155 Melville Ave, Vaughan, ON, L6A 1Y9
(905) 832-4922
Emp Here 50
SIC 8211 Elementary and secondary schools

Verner, ON P0H
Nipissing County

D-U-N-S 25-132-9447   (BR)
CONSEIL SCOLAIRE CATHOLIQUE DU DISTRICT FRANCO-NORD
?COLE STE MARGUERITE D'YOUVILLE
(*Suby of* Conseil Scolaire Catholique Du District Franco-Nord)
73 Principal St, Verner, ON, P0H 2M0

(705) 594-2385
Emp Here 26
SIC 8211 Elementary and secondary schools

Verona, ON K0H

D-U-N-S 25-305-5164   (BR)
LIMESTONE DISTRICT SCHOOL BOARD
PRINCE CHARLES PUBLIC SCHOOL
6875 38 Hwy, Verona, ON, K0H 2W0
(613) 374-2003
Emp Here 28
SIC 8211 Elementary and secondary schools

D-U-N-S 20-179-6026   (SL)
REVELL MOTORS SALES LIMITED
REVELL FORD LINCOLN MERCURY
6628 38 Hwy, Verona, ON, K0H 2W0
(613) 374-2133
Emp Here 38   *Sales* 13,862,533
SIC 5511 New and used car dealers
Pr Pr Harry Revell
Allan Revell
Larry Revell

Victoria Harbour, ON L0K
Simcoe County

D-U-N-S 25-297-6048   (BR)
SIMCOE COUNTY DISTRICT SCHOOL BOARD, THE
VICTORIA HARBOUR ELEMENTARY SCHOOL
(*Suby of* Simcoe County District School Board, The)
1 Mackenzie Cres, Victoria Harbour, ON, L0K 2A0
(705) 534-3101
Emp Here 30
SIC 8211 Elementary and secondary schools

D-U-N-S 24-971-3223   (BR)
SIMCOE MUSKOKA CATHOLIC DISTRICT SCHOOL BOARD
ST ANTOINE DANIEL SCHOOL
(*Suby of* Simcoe Muskoka Catholic District School Board)
460 Park St, Victoria Harbour, ON, L0K 2A0
(705) 534-3391
Emp Here 28
SIC 8211 Elementary and secondary schools

Vineland, ON L0R

D-U-N-S 24-488-9507   (SL)
984379 ONTARIO INC
VINELAND ESTATES WINERY
3620 Moyer Rd, Vineland, ON, L0R 2C0
(905) 562-7088
Emp Here 50   *Sales* 1,459,214
SIC 2084 Wines, brandy, and brandy spirits

D-U-N-S 25-350-3296   (BR)
BETHESDA HOME FOR THE MENTALLY HANDICAPPED INC
BETHESDA PROGRAMS
3950 Fly Rd Rr 1, Vineland, ON, L0R 2C0
(905) 562-4134
Emp Here 100
SIC 8399 Social services, nec

D-U-N-S 25-872-0994   (BR)
CORPORATION OF THE TOWN OF LINCOLN
LINCOLN PUBLIC LIBRARY
(*Suby of* Corporation Of The Town Of Lincoln)
4080 John Charles Blvd, Vineland, ON, L0R 2C0

(905) 562-5711
Emp Here 20
SIC 8231 Libraries

D-U-N-S 25-913-2702   (BR)
DISTRICT SCHOOL BOARD OF NIAGARA
VINELAND/MAPLE GROVE PUBLIC SCHOOL
4057 Victoria Ave, Vineland, ON, L0R 2C0
(905) 562-5211
Emp Here 45
SIC 8211 Elementary and secondary schools

Virgil, ON L0S

D-U-N-S 20-710-8478   (BR)
DISTRICT SCHOOL BOARD OF NIAGARA
CROSSROADS PUBLIC SCHOOL
1359 Stone Rd, Virgil, ON, L0S 1J0
(905) 468-7793
Emp Here 30
SIC 8211 Elementary and secondary schools

D-U-N-S 20-133-5085   (SL)
HERITAGE PLACE CARE FACILITY
Gd, Virgil, ON, L0S 1T0
(905) 468-1111
Emp Here 80   *Sales* 3,793,956
SIC 8059 Nursing and personal care, nec

D-U-N-S 25-010-4791   (BR)
MERIDIAN CREDIT UNION LIMITED
Gd, Virgil, ON, L0S 1T0
(905) 468-2131
Emp Here 30
SIC 6062 State credit unions

Wainfleet, ON L0S
Welland County

D-U-N-S 24-487-1893   (SL)
K.A.M. TRUCKING INC
54028 Wellandport Rd Suite 1, Wainfleet, ON, L0S 1V0
(905) 899-3399
Emp Here 60   *Sales* 7,369,031
SIC 4213 Trucking, except local
Pr Pr Mark Zavitz
Karl Zavitz

Walkerton, ON N0G
Bruce County

D-U-N-S 20-278-4690   (BR)
ARMTEC LP
ARMTEC
857 Conc 14, Walkerton, ON, N0G 2V0
(519) 392-6929
Emp Here 25
SIC 3312 Blast furnaces and steel mills

D-U-N-S 24-974-5803   (BR)
BDO CANADA LLP
121 Jackson St, Walkerton, ON, N0G 2V0
(519) 881-1211
Emp Here 20
SIC 8721 Accounting, auditing, and bookkeeping

D-U-N-S 25-903-6549   (BR)
BLUEWATER DISTRICT SCHOOL BOARD
WALKERTON PUBLIC SCHOOL
400 Colborne St S Rr 4, Walkerton, ON, N0G 2V0

Emp Here 33
SIC 8211 Elementary and secondary schools

D-U-N-S 25-228-0920   (BR)
BLUEWATER DISTRICT SCHOOL BOARD

BRANT TOWNSHIP CENTRAL PUBLIC SCHOOL
595 Warden St, Walkerton, ON, N0G 2V0

Emp Here 20
SIC 8211 Elementary and secondary schools

D-U-N-S 25-238-9689   (BR)
BRUCE-GREY CATHOLIC DISTRICT SCHOOL BOARD
SACRED HEART HIGH SCHOOL
450 Robinson St, Walkerton, ON, N0G 2V0
(519) 881-1900
Emp Here 80
SIC 8211 Elementary and secondary schools

D-U-N-S 24-122-4732   (SL)
BRUCELEA HAVEN HOME FOR THE AGED
41 Mcgivern St, Walkerton, ON, N0G 2V0
(519) 881-1570
Emp Here 125   *Sales* 6,184,080
SIC 8361 Residential care
Eleanor Macewen

D-U-N-S 20-717-8083   (BR)
CANPAR TRANSPORT L.P.
(*Suby of* Canpar Transport L.P.)
18 Industrial Rd, Walkerton, ON, N0G 2V0
(519) 881-2770
Emp Here 120
SIC 4731 Freight transportation arrangement

D-U-N-S 20-179-0768   (BR)
CORPORATION OF THE COUNTY OF BRUCE, THE
ONTARIO WORK'S PROGRAM
30 Park St, Walkerton, ON, N0G 2V0
(519) 881-0431
Emp Here 30
SIC 8399 Social services, nec

D-U-N-S 20-059-0169   (BR)
ENERGIZER CANADA INC
(*Suby of* Edgewell Personal Care Company)
165 Kincardine Hwy, Walkerton, ON, N0G 2V0
(519) 881-3310
Emp Here 80
SIC 3691 Storage batteries

D-U-N-S 20-708-1493   (BR)
HYDRO ONE NETWORKS INC
Gd, Walkerton, ON, N0G 2V0
(519) 423-6253
Emp Here 30
SIC 4911 Electric services

Wallaceburg, ON N8A

D-U-N-S 20-343-6126   (BR)
1528593 ONTARIO INC
SELECT FINISHING
(*Suby of* 1528593 Ontario Inc)
6950 Base Line, Wallaceburg, ON, N8A 1A1

Emp Here 35
SIC 3479 Metal coating and allied services

D-U-N-S 20-547-7222   (HQ)
1528593 ONTARIO INC
SELECT FINISHING
(*Suby of* 1528593 Ontario Inc)
6941 Base Line, Wallaceburg, ON, N8A 4L3
(519) 627-7885
Emp Here 35   *Emp Total* 70
Sales 3,387,573
SIC 3479 Metal coating and allied services

D-U-N-S 25-525-2611   (BR)
ACTIVE INDUSTRIAL SOLUTIONS INC
WALLACEBURG LIGHTING DIV
(*Suby of* Active Industrial Solutions Inc)
980 Old Glass Rd, Wallaceburg, ON, N8A 3T2

Emp Here 42
SIC 3089 Plastics products, nec

D-U-N-S 25-296-3947   (BR)
BANK OF NOVA SCOTIA, THE
SCOTIABANK
541 James St, Wallaceburg, ON, N8A 2P1
(519) 627-2268
Emp Here 23
SIC 6021 National commercial banks

D-U-N-S 20-520-0855   (BR)
CANADA POST CORPORATION
WALLACEBURG POST OFFICE
620 Wellington St, Wallaceburg, ON, N8A 2Y5
(519) 627-4771
Emp Here 23
SIC 4311 U.s. postal service

D-U-N-S 20-051-8137   (SL)
ECR INTERNATIONAL LTD
(*Suby of* ECR International, Inc.)
6800 Base Line, Wallaceburg, ON, N8A 2K6
(519) 627-0791
Emp Here 70   *Sales* 8,901,205
SIC 3585 Refrigeration and heating equipment
Pr Michael Paparone
Genl Mgr Brian Brown

D-U-N-S 24-773-0778   (BR)
FIRSTCANADA ULC
LAIDLAW EDUCATION SERVICES SUBSIDIARY
304 Arnold St, Wallaceburg, ON, N8A 3P5
(519) 352-1040
Emp Here 22
SIC 4142 Bus charter service, except local

D-U-N-S 25-652-6351   (SL)
GIL AND SONS LIMITED
GSL GROUP
304 Arnold St, Wallaceburg, ON, N8A 3P5
(519) 627-5924
Emp Here 45   *Sales* 5,478,300
SIC 1731 Electrical work
Pr Pr Stephen Bilodeau

D-U-N-S 25-852-7209   (BR)
GOVERNMENT OF ONTARIO
WALPOLE ISLAND FIRST NATION NATIVE FAMILY SERVICES
150 Tecumseh Rd, Wallaceburg, ON, N8A 4K9
(519) 627-3907
Emp Here 22
SIC 8399 Social services, nec

D-U-N-S 20-710-4840   (BR)
LAMBTON KENT DISTRICT SCHOOL BOARD
D A GORDON
430 King St, Wallaceburg, ON, N8A 1J1

Emp Here 30
SIC 8211 Elementary and secondary schools

D-U-N-S 20-710-4824   (BR)
LAMBTON KENT DISTRICT SCHOOL BOARD
A A WRIGHT PUBLIC SCHOOL
55 Elm Dr S, Wallaceburg, ON, N8A 3M7
(519) 627-2581
Emp Here 20
SIC 8211 Elementary and secondary schools

D-U-N-S 20-025-2646   (BR)
LAMBTON KENT DISTRICT SCHOOL BOARD
WALLACEBURG DISTRICT SECONDARY SCHOOL
920 Elgin St, Wallaceburg, ON, N8A 3E1
(519) 627-3368
Emp Here 90
SIC 8211 Elementary and secondary schools

D-U-N-S 20-710-4865   (BR)
LAMBTON KENT DISTRICT SCHOOL BOARD
H.W. BURGESS PUBLIC SCHOOL
140 Lawrence Ave, Wallaceburg, ON, N8A

2B3
(519) 627-3822
Emp Here 50
SIC 8211 Elementary and secondary schools

D-U-N-S 24-417-6590   (SL)
OAK'S INN (WALLACEBURG) INC
ACORN DINNER THEATRE
80 Mcnaughton Ave, Wallaceburg, ON, N8A 1R9

Emp Here 65   *Sales* 2,845,467
SIC 7011 Hotels and motels

D-U-N-S 24-055-1507   (SL)
PRECISMECA LIMITED
75 Mason St, Wallaceburg, ON, N8A 4L7
(519) 627-2277
Emp Here 49   *Sales* 8,952,126
SIC 3535 Conveyors and conveying equipment
Pr Philip Hartney

D-U-N-S 25-278-6371   (BR)
PRISZM LP
PIZZA HUT
78 Mcnaughton Ave, Wallaceburg, ON, N8A 1R9
(519) 627-9663
Emp Here 25
SIC 5812 Eating places

D-U-N-S 20-995-0273   (BR)
SOBEYS CAPITAL INCORPORATED
SOBEYS
62 Mcnaughton Ave, Wallaceburg, ON, N8A 1R9

Emp Here 50
SIC 5411 Grocery stores

D-U-N-S 20-860-3410   (BR)
SOURCE (BELL) ELECTRONICS INC, THE
SOURCE, THE
30 Mcnaughton Ave, Wallaceburg, ON, N8A 1R9
(519) 628-5963
Emp Here 25
SIC 5999 Miscellaneous retail stores, nec

D-U-N-S 20-513-0193   (BR)
SOUTH WEST AG PARTNERS INC
1504 Lambton Line, Wallaceburg, ON, N8A 4L2
(519) 627-1491
Emp Here 20
SIC 5191 Farm supplies

D-U-N-S 20-653-7925   (BR)
ST. CLAIR CATHOLIC DISTRICT SCHOOL BOARD
ST ELIZABETH CATHOLIC SCHOOL
1350 Bertha Ave, Wallaceburg, ON, N8A 3K4

Emp Here 20
SIC 8211 Elementary and secondary schools

D-U-N-S 25-249-3317   (BR)
ST. CLAIR CATHOLIC DISTRICT SCHOOL BOARD
HOLY FAMILY CATHOLIC SCHOOL
(*Suby of* St. Clair Catholic District School Board)
649 Murray St, Wallaceburg, ON, N8A 1W1
(519) 627-6003
Emp Here 25
SIC 8211 Elementary and secondary schools

D-U-N-S 24-412-8369   (BR)
TRAVELERS TRANSPORTATION SERVICES INC
735 Gillard St, Wallaceburg, ON, N8A 5G7
(519) 627-5848
Emp Here 85
SIC 4213 Trucking, except local

D-U-N-S 20-700-1319   (BR)
WABTEC CANADA INC
WABTEC FOUNDRY

40 Mason St, Wallaceburg, ON, N8A 4M1
(519) 627-1244
Emp Here 180
SIC 3321 Gray and ductile iron foundries

D-U-N-S 24-609-0661   (BR)
WAL-MART CANADA CORP
WALMART
60 Mcnaughton Ave Unit 16, Wallaceburg, ON, N8A 1R9
(519) 627-8840
Emp Here 176
SIC 5311 Department stores

Walsingham, ON N0E
Norfolk County

D-U-N-S 24-761-0525   (BR)
CORPORATION OF NORFOLK COUNTY
SOUTH WALSINGHAM WASTE AND RECYCLING
1180 3rd Concession Rd, Walsingham, ON, N0E 1X0
(519) 586-7011
Emp Here 20
SIC 4953 Refuse systems

Wardsville, ON N0L

D-U-N-S 20-934-6931   (SL)
BABCOCK COMMUNITY CARE CENTRE
196 Wellington St, Wardsville, ON, N0L 2N0

Emp Here 65   *Sales* 2,991,389
SIC 8051 Skilled nursing care facilities

D-U-N-S 25-593-1966   (BR)
LANGS BUS LINES LIMITED
MCNAUGHTON BUS LINES
1733 Longwoods Dr Rr 2, Wardsville, ON, N0L 2N0
(519) 693-4416
Emp Here 25
SIC 4111 Local and suburban transit

Warkworth, ON K0K

D-U-N-S 25-237-9755   (BR)
KAWARTHA PINE RIDGE DISTRICT SCHOOL BOARD
PERCY CENTENNIAL PUBLIC SCHOOL
129 Church St, Warkworth, ON, K0K 3K0
(705) 924-2202
Emp Here 20
SIC 8211 Elementary and secondary schools

Warren, ON P0H
Sudbury County

D-U-N-S 20-536-3141   (BR)
MANITOULIN-SUDBURY DISTRICT SERVICES BOARD
5 Dyke St, Warren, ON, P0H 2N0
(705) 967-0639
Emp Here 20
SIC 8399 Social services, nec

Wasaga Beach, ON L9Z
Simcoe County

D-U-N-S 24-121-1528   (BR)
BANK OF NOVA SCOTIA, THE
SCOTIABANK

1263 Mosley St Unit 1, Wasaga Beach, ON, L9Z 2Y7
(705) 429-0977
Emp Here 20
SIC 6021 National commercial banks

D-U-N-S 20-994-8343   (BR)
LOBLAWS INC
REAL CANADIAN SUPERSTORE
25 45th St S, Wasaga Beach, ON, L9Z 1A7
(705) 429-4315
Emp Here 200
SIC 5411 Grocery stores

D-U-N-S 20-101-9580   (BR)
ONTARIO CLEAN WATER AGENCY
O W C A
30 Woodland Dr, Wasaga Beach, ON, L9Z 2V5
(705) 429-2525
Emp Here 24
SIC 8734 Testing laboratories

D-U-N-S 20-956-3373   (BR)
PARKBRIDGE LIFESTYLE COMMUNITIES INC
690 River Rd W Suite 1, Wasaga Beach, ON, L9Z 2P1
(705) 429-8559
Emp Here 23
SIC 6719 Holding companies, nec

D-U-N-S 25-297-6642   (BR)
SIMCOE COUNTY DISTRICT SCHOOL BOARD, THE
BIRCHVIEW DUNES ELEMENTARY SCHOOL
(*Suby of* Simcoe County District School Board, The)
1315 River Rd W Suite B, Wasaga Beach, ON, L9Z 2W6
(705) 429-2551
Emp Here 40
SIC 8211 Elementary and secondary schools

D-U-N-S 25-292-4584   (BR)
SIMCOE COUNTY DISTRICT SCHOOL BOARD, THE
WORSLEY ELEMENTARY SCHOOL
(*Suby of* Simcoe County District School Board, The)
31 40th St S, Wasaga Beach, ON, L9Z 1Z9
(705) 429-2552
Emp Here 36
SIC 8211 Elementary and secondary schools

D-U-N-S 20-591-9819   (BR)
SIMCOE MUSKOKA CATHOLIC DISTRICT SCHOOL BOARD
ST NOEL CHABENEL CATHOLIC SCHOOL
(*Suby of* Simcoe Muskoka Catholic District School Board)
425 Ramblewood Dr, Wasaga Beach, ON, L9Z 1P3
(705) 429-1081
Emp Here 30
SIC 8211 Elementary and secondary schools

D-U-N-S 24-606-1894   (BR)
WAL-MART CANADA CORP
100 Stonebridge Blvd, Wasaga Beach, ON, L9Z 0C1
(705) 422-7100
Emp Here 40
SIC 5311 Department stores

Washago, ON L0K
Simcoe County

D-U-N-S 24-120-9894   (BR)
COMPAGNIE DES CHEMINS DE FER NATIONAUX DU CANADA
CN RAIL
303 Quettron St, Washago, ON, L0K 2B0

(705) 689-8199
Emp Here 55
SIC 4789 Transportation services, nec

D-U-N-S 25-297-6709   (BR)
SIMCOE COUNTY DISTRICT SCHOOL BOARD, THE
RAMA CENTRAL PUBLIC SHCOOL
(*Suby of* Simcoe County District School Board, The)
7269 County Rd 169, Washago, ON, L0K 2B0
(705) 689-2031
Emp Here 25
SIC 8211 Elementary and secondary schools

Waterdown, ON L0R
Wentworth County

D-U-N-S 20-574-0389   (BR)
ATTRIDGE TRANSPORTATION INCORPORATED
27 Mill St S, Waterdown, ON, L0R 2H0
(905) 690-2632
Emp Here 650
SIC 4141 Local bus charter service

D-U-N-S 25-303-4961   (BR)
CANADIAN IMPERIAL BANK OF COMMERCE
CIBC
9 Hamilton St N, Waterdown, ON, L0R 2H0
(905) 689-6685
Emp Here 20
SIC 6021 National commercial banks

D-U-N-S 25-952-4106   (BR)
CITY OF HAMILTON, THE
NORTH WENTWORTH COMMUNITY CENTRE
27 Hwy 5, Waterdown, ON, L0R 2H0
(905) 690-3966
Emp Here 20
SIC 8322 Individual and family services

D-U-N-S 20-291-3369   (BR)
HAMILTON-WENTWORTH DISTRICT SCHOOL BOARD, THE
MARY HOPKINS SCHOOL
211 Mill St N, Waterdown, ON, L0R 2H0
(905) 689-7905
Emp Here 30
SIC 8211 Elementary and secondary schools

D-U-N-S 20-179-5627   (BR)
JARLETTE LTD
ALEXANDER PLACE LONG TERM CARE
329 Parkside Dr E, Waterdown, ON, L0R 2H0
(905) 689-2662
Emp Here 120
SIC 8051 Skilled nursing care facilities

D-U-N-S 20-180-3525   (HQ)
SUN-CANADIAN PIPE LINE COMPANY LIMITED
830 Highway 6 N, Waterdown, ON, L0R 2H0
(905) 689-6641
Emp Here 28   *Emp Total* 12,837
SIC 4613 Refined petroleum pipelines

Waterdown, ON L8B
Wentworth County

D-U-N-S 20-537-9253   (BR)
CANADA POST CORPORATION
WATERDOWN PO
17 Main St N, Waterdown, ON, L8B 1R4
(905) 689-8364
Emp Here 22
SIC 4311 U.s. postal service

D-U-N-S 25-293-9608   (BR)
HAMILTON-WENTWORTH CATHOLIC

SCHOOL BOARD
ST THOMAS CATHOLIC ELEMENTARY SCHOOL
170 Skinner Rd, Waterdown, ON, L8B 1C7
(905) 523-2328
Emp Here 25
SIC 8211 Elementary and secondary schools

    D-U-N-S 20-590-5461   (BR)
HAMILTON-WENTWORTH   DISTRICT SCHOOL BOARD, THE
WATERDOWN DISTRICT HIGH SCHOOL
215 Parkside Dr, Waterdown, ON, L8B 1B9
(905) 689-6692
Emp Here 100
SIC 8211 Elementary and secondary schools

    D-U-N-S 20-291-1215   (BR)
HAMILTON-WENTWORTH   DISTRICT SCHOOL BOARD, THE
ALLAN A GREENLEAF SCHOOL
211 Parkside Dr, Waterdown, ON, L8B 1B9
(905) 690-6813
Emp Here 40
SIC 8211 Elementary and secondary schools

    D-U-N-S 25-000-3134   (BR)
HAMILTON-WENTWORTH   DISTRICT SCHOOL BOARD, THE
GUY BROWN PUBLIC SCHOOL
55 Braeheid Ave, Waterdown, ON, L8B 0C5
(905) 689-8254
Emp Here 60
SIC 8211 Elementary and secondary schools

    D-U-N-S 20-109-0193   (BR)
YMCA   OF   HAMILTON/BURLINGTON/BRANTFORD
YMCA
207 Parkside Dr, Waterdown, ON, L8B 1B9
(905) 690-3555
Emp Here 75
SIC 7997 Membership sports and recreation clubs

Waterdown, ON L9H
Wentworth County

    D-U-N-S 24-606-1910   (BR)
WAL-MART CANADA CORP
90 Dundas St E Suite 1107, Waterdown, ON, L9H 0C2
(905) 690-7090
Emp Here 40
SIC 5311 Department stores

Waterford, ON N0E
Norfolk County

    D-U-N-S 25-833-3525   (BR)
BRANT HALDIMAND NORFOLK CATHOLIC DISTRICT SCHOOL BOARD
ST. BERNARD'S OF CLAIRVILLE
250 Washington St, Waterford, ON, N0E 1Y0
(519) 443-8607
Emp Here 20
SIC 8211 Elementary and secondary schools

    D-U-N-S 20-710-6274   (BR)
GRAND ERIE DISTRICT SCHOOL BOARD
ADA B MASSECAR CAMPUS WATERFORD PUBLIC SCHOOL
(*Suby of* Grand Erie District School Board)
100 Church St E, Waterford, ON, N0E 1Y0
(519) 443-8942
Emp Here 50
SIC 8211 Elementary and secondary schools

    D-U-N-S 20-851-9116   (SL)
NORFOLK DISPOSAL SERVICES LIMITED
811 Old Highway 24, Waterford, ON, N0E 1Y0

(519) 443-8022
Emp Here 51   *Sales* 4,012,839
SIC 4212 Local trucking, without storage

    D-U-N-S 20-793-0749   (BR)
SOBEYS CAPITAL INCORPORATED
792 Old Highway 24, Waterford, ON, N0E 1Y0
(519) 443-8609
Emp Here 40
SIC 5411 Grocery stores

Waterloo, ON N2J
Waterloo County

    D-U-N-S 25-842-3227   (BR)
1260848 ONTARIO INC
TIM HORTONS
109 King St N Unit D, Waterloo, ON, N2J 2X5
(519) 884-6774
Emp Here 28
SIC 5812 Eating places

    D-U-N-S 20-850-2229   (SL)
ADLYS HOTELS INC
HUETHER HOTEL
59 King St N, Waterloo, ON, N2J 2X2
(519) 886-3350
Emp Here 100   *Sales* 2,991,389
SIC 5812 Eating places

    D-U-N-S 25-296-4069   (BR)
BANK OF NOVA SCOTIA, THE
SCOTIABANK
115 King St S, Waterloo, ON, N2J 5A3
(519) 886-2500
Emp Here 20
SIC 6021 National commercial banks

    D-U-N-S 25-607-9013   (BR)
BANK OF MONTREAL
BANK OF MONTREAL
3 King St S, Waterloo, ON, N2J 1N9
(519) 885-9250
Emp Here 23
SIC 6021 National commercial banks

    D-U-N-S 25-010-2365   (BR)
BELL MEDIA INC
CKKW AND CFCA
255 King St N Suite 207, Waterloo, ON, N2J 4V2

Emp Here 40
SIC 4832 Radio broadcasting stations

    D-U-N-S 24-778-7088   (SL)
BOUCHER & JONES INC
BOUCHER & JONES FUELS
155 Roger St Suite 1, Waterloo, ON, N2J 1B1
(519) 653-3501
Emp Here 30   *Sales* 8,098,638
SIC 5171 Petroleum bulk stations and terminals
Pr Pr Gregory Cusimano

    D-U-N-S 20-945-2320   (BR)
CIBC WORLD MARKETS INC
CIBC WOOD GUNDY
255 King St N Suite 400, Waterloo, ON, N2J 4V2
(519) 888-6688
Emp Here 50
SIC 6211 Security brokers and dealers

    D-U-N-S 20-580-4417   (BR)
CANADA POST CORPORATION
CANADA WATERLOO POST OFFICE
70 King St N, Waterloo, ON, N2J 2X1
(519) 886-1330
Emp Here 80
SIC 4311 U.s. postal service

    D-U-N-S 24-046-3281   (SL)
CHANTENAY HOLDINGS LIMITED
GLENBRIAR HOME HARDWARE
262 Weber St N, Waterloo, ON, N2J 3H6

(519) 886-2950
Emp Here 45   *Sales* 5,928,320
SIC 5251 Hardware stores
Pr Pr Scott Uffelman
VP VP William Uffelman
  James Uffelman
Off Mgr Ilse Kropf
Mgr Wayne Thomas

    D-U-N-S 20-711-7578   (BR)
CONSEIL   SCOLAIRE   DE   DISTRICT CATHOLIQUE CENTRE-SUD
MERE ELISABETH BROYERE
280 Glenridge Dr, Waterloo, ON, N2J 3W4
(519) 880-9859
Emp Here 20
SIC 8211 Elementary and secondary schools

    D-U-N-S 20-711-7255   (BR)
CONSEIL SCOLAIRE VIAMONDE
ECOLE L HARMONIE
158 Bridgeport Rd E, Waterloo, ON, N2J 2K4
(519) 746-7224
Emp Here 27
SIC 8211 Elementary and secondary schools

    D-U-N-S 24-212-0629   (BR)
CRAWFORD & COMPANY (CANADA) INC
CRAWFORD CLASS ACTION SERVICES
(*Suby of* Crawford & Company)
180 King St S Ste 610, Waterloo, ON, N2J 1P8
(519) 578-4053
Emp Here 120
SIC 6411 Insurance agents, brokers, and service

    D-U-N-S 25-971-3303   (SL)
EAST SIDE MARIO'S
450 King St N Suite Side, Waterloo, ON, N2J 2Z6
(226) 647-2587
Emp Here 90   *Sales* 2,699,546
SIC 5812 Eating places

    D-U-N-S 24-337-2922   (BR)
FGL SPORTS LTD
NATIONAL SPORTS
24 Forwell Creek Rd, Waterloo, ON, N2J 3Z3
(519) 886-1433
Emp Here 20
SIC 5941 Sporting goods and bicycle shops

    D-U-N-S 20-283-1582   (BR)
GOODLIFE FITNESS CENTRES INC
GOODLIFE FITNESS CENTRES INC
289 Marsland Dr, Waterloo, ON, N2J 3Z2
(519) 662-6806
Emp Here 50
SIC 7991 Physical fitness facilities

    D-U-N-S 25-560-7657   (BR)
HGC MANAGEMENT INC
H G C
925 Erb St W, Waterloo, ON, N2J 3Z4

Emp Here 20
SIC 4953 Refuse systems

    D-U-N-S 20-302-3432   (BR)
HAUSER INDUSTRIES INC
HAUSER COMPANY STORE
330 Weber St N, Waterloo, ON, N2J 3H6
(519) 747-3818
Emp Here 235
SIC 5712 Furniture stores

    D-U-N-S 24-543-4626   (HQ)
HAUSER INDUSTRIES INC
330 Weber St N, Waterloo, ON, N2J 3H6
(519) 747-1138
Emp Here 70   *Emp Total* 75
Sales 8,952,126
SIC 2514 Metal household furniture
Pr Pr Ernie Hauser
  Eric Hauser
S&M/Dir Christopher Hauser
Sls Dir Jason Hauser
Sls Dir Stephanie Hauser

Sls Dir Holly Hauser
Fin Mgr Donald Pickett

    D-U-N-S 25-292-7413   (BR)
INDIGO BOOKS & MUSIC INC
CHAPTERS
(*Suby of* Indigo Books & Music Inc)
428 King St N, Waterloo, ON, N2J 2Z6
(519) 886-4015
Emp Here 45
SIC 5942 Book stores

    D-U-N-S 25-315-7796   (BR)
INVESTORS GROUP FINANCIAL SERVICES INC
INVESTORS GROUP
80 King St S Suite 201, Waterloo, ON, N2J 1P5
(519) 886-2360
Emp Here 30
SIC 8742 Management consulting services

    D-U-N-S 24-829-9950   (BR)
KPMG LLP
(*Suby of* KPMG LLP)
115 King St S Suite 201, Waterloo, ON, N2J 5A3
(519) 747-8800
Emp Here 170
SIC 8721 Accounting, auditing, and bookkeeping

    D-U-N-S 20-358-2291   (SL)
KOGNITIV CORPORATION
187 King St S, Waterloo, ON, N2J 1R1
(226) 476-1124
Emp Here 100   *Sales* 12,403,319
SIC 7372 Prepackaged software
  Peter Schwartz
  Kamal Pastakia
  Don Tapscott
  John Bowey
  Mark Rider
  Ken Teslia
  Rick Nathan
  Mark Lerohi

    D-U-N-S 24-092-5979   (BR)
LOBLAWS SUPERMARKETS LIMITED
REAL CANADIAN WHOLESALE CLUB, THE
24 Forwell Creek Rd, Waterloo, ON, N2J 3Z3
(519) 880-0355
Emp Here 65
SIC 5141 Groceries, general line

    D-U-N-S 20-279-4673   (BR)
MANUFACTURERS   LIFE   INSURANCE COMPANY, THE
MANULIFE
500 King St N, Waterloo, ON, N2J 4C6
(519) 747-7000
Emp Here 3,000
SIC 6311 Life insurance

    D-U-N-S 24-363-2770   (SL)
OB GOLF MANAGEMENT LP
75 King St S, Waterloo, ON, N2J 1P2
(519) 749-8893
Emp Here 60   *Sales* 2,407,703
SIC 7997 Membership sports and recreation clubs

    D-U-N-S 20-180-6791   (SL)
ORNAMENTAL MOULDINGS COMPANY
289 Marsland Dr, Waterloo, ON, N2J 3Z2
(519) 884-4080
Emp Here 45   *Sales* 8,854,200
SIC 2431 Millwork
Sls Mgr Susan Reid

    D-U-N-S 24-333-7045   (SL)
PAIVA, J FOODS LTD
SWISS CHALET
267 Weber St N, Waterloo, ON, N2J 3H8
(519) 884-9410
Emp Here 66   *Sales* 1,969,939
SIC 5812 Eating places

D-U-N-S 24-859-4749 (BR)
PRICEWATERHOUSECOOPERS LLP
95 King St W Ste 201, Waterloo, ON, N2J 5A2
(519) 570-5700
Emp Here 60
SIC 8721 Accounting, auditing, and book-keeping

D-U-N-S 24-010-5403 (HQ)
QLO MANAGEMENT INC
JIFFY LUBE
130 Dearborn Pl, Waterloo, ON, N2J 4N5
(519) 886-0561
Emp Here 20   *Emp Total* 2
Sales 14,167,680
SIC 7549 Automotive services, nec
Pr Pr Peter Walsh
   George Walsh

D-U-N-S 25-293-7503 (BR)
RBC DOMINION SECURITIES INC
(*Suby of* Royal Bank Of Canada)
95 King St S Suite 202, Waterloo, ON, N2J 5A2
(519) 747-8007
Emp Here 30
SIC 6211 Security brokers and dealers

D-U-N-S 25-300-4758 (BR)
REDBERRY FRANCHISING CORP
BURGER KING
396 King St N, Waterloo, ON, N2J 2Z3

Emp Here 45
SIC 5812 Eating places

D-U-N-S 25-608-0789 (BR)
SOBEYS CAPITAL INCORPORATED
SOBEY'S 649
94 Bridgeport Rd E, Waterloo, ON, N2J 2J9
(519) 885-4170
Emp Here 100
SIC 5411 Grocery stores

D-U-N-S 24-175-5383 (BR)
STARBUCKS COFFEE CANADA, INC
(*Suby of* Starbucks Corporation)
247 King St N, Waterloo, ON, N2J 2Y8
(519) 886-0101
Emp Here 20
SIC 5812 Eating places

D-U-N-S 25-102-0087 (BR)
SUN LIFE ASSURANCE COMPANY OF CANADA
227 King St S Suite 3010, Waterloo, ON, N2J 1R2
(519) 888-2076
Emp Here 100
SIC 6282 Investment advice

D-U-N-S 20-710-7223 (BR)
WATERLOO CATHOLIC DISTRICT SCHOOL BOARD
ST. AGNES CATHOLIC ELEMENTARY SCHOOL
254 Neilson Ave, Waterloo, ON, N2J 2M3
(519) 885-3180
Emp Here 50
SIC 8211 Elementary and secondary schools

D-U-N-S 25-228-1464 (BR)
WATERLOO REGION DISTRICT SCHOOL BOARD
BLUEVALE COLLEGIATE INSTITUTE
80 Bluevale St N, Waterloo, ON, N2J 3R5
(519) 885-4620
Emp Here 130
SIC 8211 Elementary and secondary schools

D-U-N-S 25-237-8856 (BR)
WATERLOO REGION DISTRICT SCHOOL BOARD
ELIZABETH ZIEGLER PUBLIC SCHOOL
90 Moore Ave S, Waterloo, ON, N2J 1X2
(519) 742-4402
Emp Here 55
SIC 8211 Elementary and secondary schools

D-U-N-S 25-137-3924 (BR)
WATERLOO REGION DISTRICT SCHOOL BOARD
LINCOLN HEIGHTS PUBLIC SCHOOL
270 Quickfall Dr, Waterloo, ON, N2J 3S9
(519) 884-4010
Emp Here 40
SIC 8211 Elementary and secondary schools

D-U-N-S 20-710-7082 (BR)
WATERLOO REGION DISTRICT SCHOOL BOARD
ALTERNATIVE AND CONTINUING EDUCATION CENTRE
151 Weber St S, Waterloo, ON, N2J 2A9
(519) 885-0800
Emp Here 50
SIC 8211 Elementary and secondary schools

D-U-N-S 25-523-9212 (BR)
WENDCORP HOLDINGS INC
WENDY'S
221 Weber St N, Waterloo, ON, N2J 3H5
(519) 746-2728
Emp Here 48
SIC 5812 Eating places

D-U-N-S 25-221-2600 (BR)
WINNERS MERCHANTS INTERNATIONAL L.P.
WINNERS
(*Suby of* The TJX Companies Inc)
663a Erb St W, Waterloo, ON, N2J 3Z4
(519) 576-3699
Emp Here 40
SIC 5651 Family clothing stores

D-U-N-S 25-297-8721 (BR)
ZEHRMART INC
ZEHRS MARKETS
315 Lincoln Rd Suite 1, Waterloo, ON, N2J 4H7
(519) 885-1360
Emp Here 165
SIC 5411 Grocery stores

Waterloo, ON N2K
Waterloo County

D-U-N-S 24-375-2867 (BR)
BLACKBERRY LIMITED
2240 University Ave E, Waterloo, ON, N2K 0A9
(519) 888-7465
Emp Here 1,000
SIC 3663 Radio and t.v. communications equipment

D-U-N-S 20-068-0382 (BR)
CORPORATION OF THE CITY OF WATERLOO, THE
CITY OF WATERLOO SERVICE CENTER
(*Suby of* Corporation Of The City Of Waterloo, The)
265 Lexington Crt, Waterloo, ON, N2K 1W9
(519) 886-2310
Emp Here 100
SIC 7389 Business services, nec

D-U-N-S 20-210-3177 (BR)
PHARMA PLUS DRUGMARTS LTD
425 University Ave E, Waterloo, ON, N2K 4C9
(519) 743-5738
Emp Here 22
SIC 5912 Drug stores and proprietary stores

D-U-N-S 20-102-6304 (BR)
QUALIDEC CORPORATION
MCDONALD'S
55 Northfield Dr E, Waterloo, ON, N2K 3T6
(519) 884-5503
Emp Here 75
SIC 5812 Eating places

D-U-N-S 24-357-1085 (BR)

REGIONAL MUNICIPALITY OF WATERLOO, THE
RIM PARK
2001 University Ave E Suite 104, Waterloo, ON, N2K 4K4
(519) 746-6563
Emp Here 90
SIC 7999 Amusement and recreation, nec

D-U-N-S 20-710-7488 (BR)
WATERLOO CATHOLIC DISTRICT SCHOOL BOARD
ST MATTHEW CATHOLIC ELEMENTARY SCHOOL
405 Pastern Trail, Waterloo, ON, N2K 3V6
(519) 886-9311
Emp Here 40
SIC 8211 Elementary and secondary schools

D-U-N-S 20-710-7520 (BR)
WATERLOO CATHOLIC DISTRICT SCHOOL BOARD
ST LUKE CATHOLIC SCHOOL
550 Chesapeake Dr, Waterloo, ON, N2K 4G5
(519) 884-4912
Emp Here 50
SIC 8211 Elementary and secondary schools

D-U-N-S 25-228-1605 (BR)
WATERLOO REGION DISTRICT SCHOOL BOARD
SANDOWNE ELEMENTARY SCHOOL
265 Sandowne Dr, Waterloo, ON, N2K 2C1
(519) 884-4800
Emp Here 40
SIC 8211 Elementary and secondary schools

D-U-N-S 20-026-1886 (BR)
WATERLOO REGION DISTRICT SCHOOL BOARD
LEXINGTON PUBLIC SCHOOL
431 Forestlawn Rd, Waterloo, ON, N2K 2J5
(519) 747-3314
Emp Here 33
SIC 8211 Elementary and secondary schools

D-U-N-S 20-653-3023 (BR)
WATERLOO REGION DISTRICT SCHOOL BOARD
LESTER B PEARSON PUBLIC SCHOOL
520 Chesapeake Dr, Waterloo, ON, N2K 4G5
(519) 880-0300
Emp Here 75
SIC 8211 Elementary and secondary schools

Waterloo, ON N2L
Waterloo County

D-U-N-S 20-780-4415 (BR)
A & W FOOD SERVICES OF CANADA INC
A & W RESTAURANT
550 King St N Suite F12, Waterloo, ON, N2L 5W6
(519) 747-9394
Emp Here 20
SIC 5812 Eating places

D-U-N-S 24-918-0852 (BR)
ATC-FROST MAGNETICS INC
(*Suby of* Standex International Corporation)
550 Parkside Dr Unit D6, Waterloo, ON, N2L 5V4
(905) 844-6681
Emp Here 130
SIC 3677 Electronic coils and transformers

D-U-N-S 20-552-0336 (BR)
AGFA HEALTHCARE INC
375 Hagey Blvd, Waterloo, ON, N2L 6R5
(519) 746-2900
Emp Here 250
SIC 7371 Custom computer programming services

D-U-N-S 20-180-4432 (HQ)

ANGIE'S KITCHEN LIMITED
ANGIE'S KITCHEN
(*Suby of* Angie's Kitchen Limited)
47 Erb St W, Waterloo, ON, N2L 1S8
(519) 886-2540
Emp Here 20   *Emp Total* 60
Sales 1,824,018
SIC 5812 Eating places

D-U-N-S 24-622-4179 (BR)
BDO CANADA LLP
KITCHENER & WATERLOO ACCOUNTING
150 Caroline St S Suite 201, Waterloo, ON, N2L 0A5
(519) 576-5220
Emp Here 29
SIC 8721 Accounting, auditing, and book-keeping

D-U-N-S 20-301-0017 (BR)
BMO NESBITT BURNS INC
20 Erb St W Suite 601, Waterloo, ON, N2L 1T2
(519) 886-3100
Emp Here 30
SIC 6211 Security brokers and dealers

D-U-N-S 24-036-6950 (BR)
BEST BUY CANADA LTD
FUTURE SHOP
(*Suby of* Best Buy Co., Inc.)
580 King St N Unit B, Waterloo, ON, N2L 6L3
(519) 886-1073
Emp Here 20
SIC 5999 Miscellaneous retail stores, nec

D-U-N-S 24-368-1397 (BR)
BLACKBERRY LIMITED
RESEARCH IN MOTION
450 Phillip St, Waterloo, ON, N2L 5J2
(519) 888-7465
Emp Here 20
SIC 3663 Radio and t.v. communications equipment

D-U-N-S 25-303-4920 (BR)
CANADIAN IMPERIAL BANK OF COMMERCE
CIBC
550 King St N, Waterloo, ON, N2L 5W6
(519) 884-9230
Emp Here 20
SIC 6021 National commercial banks

D-U-N-S 25-542-5357 (BR)
CENTRA INDUSTRIES INC
103 Bauer Pl, Waterloo, ON, N2L 6B5
(519) 650-2828
Emp Here 20
SIC 3599 Industrial machinery, nec

D-U-N-S 20-779-3618 (BR)
CINEPLEX ODEON CORPORATION
GALAXY CINEMAS WATERLOO
550 King St N, Waterloo, ON, N2L 5W6
(519) 883-8843
Emp Here 20
SIC 7832 Motion picture theaters, except drive-in

D-U-N-S 24-366-3432 (HQ)
COLLINS BARROW REGION OF WATERLOO
COLLINS BARROWS
(*Suby of* Collins Barrow Region of Waterloo)
554 Weber St N, Waterloo, ON, N2L 5C6
(519) 725-7700
Emp Here 35   *Emp Total* 50
Sales 2,188,821
SIC 8721 Accounting, auditing, and book-keeping

D-U-N-S 25-775-7781 (BR)
CORPORATION OF THE CITY OF WATERLOO, THE
WATERLOO MEMORIAL RECREATION COMPLEX
(*Suby of* Corporation Of The City Of Waterloo, The)

---

101 Father David Bauer Dr, Waterloo, ON,
N2L 0B4
(519) 886-1177
Emp Here 80
SIC 7299 Miscellaneous personal service

D-U-N-S 25-293-3106   (BR)
**DATA COMMUNICATIONS MANAGEMENT
CORP**
465 Phillip St Suite 202, Waterloo, ON, N2L
6C7
(519) 885-2440
Emp Here 22
SIC 5112 Stationery and office supplies

D-U-N-S 20-994-8046   (HQ)
ECLIPSE SCIENTIFIC PRODUCTS INC
ECLIPSE SCIENTIFIC
(*Suby of* Rockwood Service Corporation)
440 Phillip St Suite 100, Waterloo, ON, N2L
5R9
(800) 490-1072
Emp Here 29   *Emp Total* 3,009
Sales 4,012,839
SIC 3569 General industrial machinery, nec

D-U-N-S 24-340-2554   (BR)
FGL SPORTS LTD
550 King St N, Waterloo, ON, N2L 5W6
(519) 886-6336
Emp Here 49
SIC 5941 Sporting goods and bicycle shops

D-U-N-S 25-483-1506   (BR)
FEDEX OFFICE CANADA LIMITED
FEDEX OFFICE PRINT & SHIP CENTRE
(*Suby of* Fedex Corporation)
170 University Ave W, Waterloo, ON, N2L 3E9
(519) 746-3363
Emp Here 20
SIC 7334 Photocopying and duplicating ser-
vices

D-U-N-S 20-124-8221   (SL)
FIRST UNITED CHURCH
16 William St W, Waterloo, ON, N2L 1J3
(519) 745-8487
Emp Here 395   *Sales* 34,944,960
SIC 8661 Religious organizations
 Kellie Mccomb
 Bill Steadman

D-U-N-S 20-004-0595   (BR)
GAP (CANADA) INC
GAP
(*Suby of* The Gap Inc)
550 King St N, Waterloo, ON, N2L 5W6
(519) 746-8874
Emp Here 40
SIC 5651 Family clothing stores

D-U-N-S 20-918-3347   (BR)
GOODLIFE FITNESS CENTRES INC
140 Columbia St W, Waterloo, ON, N2L 3K8

Emp Here 25
SIC 7991 Physical fitness facilities

D-U-N-S 25-486-6312   (BR)
**HAMMOND MANUFACTURING COMPANY
LIMITED**
ELECTONICS GROUP
485 Conestogo Rd, Waterloo, ON, N2L 4C9

Emp Here 50
SIC 3469 Metal stampings, nec

D-U-N-S 20-327-8762   (BR)
HOERBIGER FINESTAMPING INC
145 Northfield Dr W, Waterloo, ON, N2L 5J3
(519) 772-0951
Emp Here 120
SIC 3469 Metal stampings, nec

D-U-N-S 20-549-1777   (SL)
**IANYWHERE SOLUTIONS CANADA LIM-
ITED**
415 Phillip St, Waterloo, ON, N2L 3X2

(519) 883-6488
Emp Here 200   *Sales* 37,637,950
SIC 7371 Custom computer programming ser-
vices
Pr Pr Terrence Stepien

D-U-N-S 25-971-2545   (SL)
JB MONGOLIAN GRILL INC
170 University Ave W, Waterloo, ON, N2L 3E9
(519) 747-4400
Emp Here 50   *Sales* 1,532,175
SIC 5812 Eating places

D-U-N-S 25-220-3062   (SL)
KASSIK INVESTMENTS INC
B K MOTORS
527 King St N, Waterloo, ON, N2L 5Z6
(519) 885-5091
Emp Here 40   *Sales* 35,507,500
SIC 5511 New and used car dealers
Pr Pr Helmut Kassik

D-U-N-S 20-738-7239   (SL)
KEG STEAKHOUSE & BAR, THE
42 Northfield Dr E, Waterloo, ON, N2L 6A1
(519) 725-4444
Emp Here 85   *Sales* 2,553,625
SIC 5812 Eating places

D-U-N-S 20-270-1249   (HQ)
KIK INTERACTIVE INC.
KIK
(*Suby of* Kik Interactive Inc.)
420 Weber St N Suite I, Waterloo, ON, N2L
4E7
(226) 868-0056
Emp Here 96   *Emp Total* 125
Sales 19,057,522
SIC 7371 Custom computer programming ser-
vices
Pr Ted Livingston
 Christopher Best
 Peter Heinke

D-U-N-S 25-092-2486   (SL)
KRAUS CARPET LP
KRAUS FLOORS WITHMORE
65 Northfield Dr W, Waterloo, ON, N2L 0A8
(519) 884-2310
Emp Here 350
SIC 2273 Carpets and rugs

D-U-N-S 24-343-0977   (BR)
LATEM INDUSTRIES LIMITED
475 Conestogo Rd Suite Side, Waterloo, ON,
N2L 4C9
(519) 886-6290
Emp Here 30
SIC 3471 Plating and polishing

D-U-N-S 25-317-5533   (BR)
**LIQUOR CONTROL BOARD OF ONTARIO,
THE**
L.C.B.O.
571 King St N, Waterloo, ON, N2L 5Z7
(519) 884-8140
Emp Here 20
SIC 5921 Liquor stores

D-U-N-S 25-526-2057   (HQ)
LUBRICOR INC
(*Suby of* Quaker Chemical Corporation)
475 Conestogo Rd, Waterloo, ON, N2L 4C9
(519) 884-8455
Emp Here 22   *Emp Total* 2,040
Sales 10,741,512
SIC 5172 Petroleum products, nec
 Jorma Braks

D-U-N-S 25-965-6536   (HQ)
LUTHERWOOD
(*Suby of* Lutherwood)
139 Father David Bauer Dr Suite 1, Waterloo,
ON, N2L 6L1
(519) 884-7755
Emp Here 67   *Emp Total* 350
Sales 21,804,160
SIC 8399 Social services, nec

 John Colangeli
 Kelly Enair

D-U-N-S 25-555-0469   (BR)
**MCG. RESTAURANTS (WONDERLAND)
INC**
MCGINNIS FRONT ROW RESTAURANT
160 University Ave W, Waterloo, ON, N2L 3E9
(519) 886-6490
Emp Here 55
SIC 5812 Eating places

D-U-N-S 20-278-9181   (BR)
MILLER THOMSON LLP
295 Hagey Blvd Suite 300, Waterloo, ON, N2L
6R5
(519) 579-3660
Emp Here 100
SIC 8111 Legal services

D-U-N-S 24-340-9427   (SL)
NAVTECH INC
(*Suby of* Cambridge Information Group, Inc.)
295 Hagey Blvd Suite 200, Waterloo, ON, N2L
6R5
(519) 747-1170
Emp Here 80   *Sales* 32,571,038
SIC 8711 Engineering services
Pr Mike Hulley
VP Fin Sean Doherty

D-U-N-S 20-180-6767   (SL)
**ONTARIO GLOVE MANUFACTURING COM-
PANY LIMITED, THE**
(*Suby of* Kennor Inc)
500 Dotzert Crt, Waterloo, ON, N2L 6A7
(800) 332-1810
Emp Here 60   *Sales* 14,724,000
SIC 5136 Men's and boy's clothing
Dir Randall More
 John Mccarthy
Dir Mary Jane More

D-U-N-S 20-808-5048   (BR)
PEAK REALTY LTD
410 Conestogo Rd Suite 210, Waterloo, ON,
N2L 4E2
(519) 747-0231
Emp Here 75
SIC 6411 Insurance agents, brokers, and ser-
vice

D-U-N-S 25-690-4418   (HQ)
PRECEPT GROUP INC, THE
(*Suby of* Aligned Insurance Inc)
375 Hagey Blvd Suite 302, Waterloo, ON, N2L
6R5
(519) 747-5210
Emp Here 30   *Emp Total* 5
Sales 5,371,275
SIC 6411 Insurance agents, brokers, and ser-
vice
Pr Pr James Mcgregor

D-U-N-S 20-180-7047   (BR)
RAYTHEON CANADA LIMITED
(*Suby of* Raytheon Company)
400 Phillip St, Waterloo, ON, N2L 6R7
(519) 885-0110
Emp Here 400
SIC 3669 Communications equipment, nec

D-U-N-S 25-609-7130   (BR)
RE/MAX TWIN CITY REALTY INC
83 Erb St W, Waterloo, ON, N2L 6C2
(519) 744-2653
Emp Here 120
SIC 6531 Real estate agents and managers

D-U-N-S 24-024-8885   (SL)
RIVERSIDE DOOR & TRIM INC
520 Conestogo Rd, Waterloo, ON, N2L 4E2
(519) 578-3265
Emp Here 50   *Sales* 4,331,255
SIC 1751 Carpentry work

D-U-N-S 25-965-6890   (BR)
ROYAL BANK OF CANADA
RBC

(*Suby of* Royal Bank Of Canada)
50 Westmount Rd N, Waterloo, ON, N2L 2R5
(519) 747-8300
Emp Here 30
SIC 6021 National commercial banks

D-U-N-S 25-495-4993   (BR)
SAP CANADA INC
SAP SYBASE OFFICES
445 Wes Graham Way, Waterloo, ON, N2L
6R2
(519) 886-3700
Emp Here 250
SIC 7371 Custom computer programming services

D-U-N-S 20-056-6904   (HQ)
SANDVINE INCORPORATED ULC
408 Albert St, Waterloo, ON, N2L 3V3
(519) 880-2600
Emp Here 170   *Emp Total* 521
Sales 76,681,696
SIC 3825 Instruments to measure electricity
Pr Pr David Caputo
 Tom Donnelly
 Scott Hamilton
 Brad Siim
VP Sls Angelo Compagnoni
 Don Bowman

D-U-N-S 25-084-6284   (SL)
SOLE RESTAURANT AND WINE BAR
83 Erb St W Unit 2, Waterloo, ON, N2L 6C2
(519) 747-5622
Emp Here 50   *Sales* 1,532,175
SIC 5812 Eating places

D-U-N-S 25-399-1459   (BR)
STANTEC CONSULTING LTD
300 Hagey Boulevard Suite 100, Waterloo,
ON, N2L 0A4
(519) 579-4410
Emp Here 325
SIC 8711 Engineering services

D-U-N-S 20-300-7232   (BR)
STANTEC GEOMATICS LTD
300 Hagey Boulevard Suite 100, Waterloo,
ON, N2L 0A4
(519) 579-4410
Emp Here 340
SIC 8713 Surveying services

D-U-N-S 25-967-3051   (BR)
UTC FIRE & SECURITY CANADA
*EDWARDS PART OF GE SECURITY
CANADA*
(*Suby of* United Technologies Corporation)
560 Parkside Dr Unit 401, Waterloo, ON, N2L
5Z4
(519) 746-4667
Emp Here 21
SIC 3669 Communications equipment, nec

D-U-N-S 20-347-9779   (BR)
UNIVERSITY OF WATERLOO
EARTH AND ENVIRONMENTAL SCIENCES
(*Suby of* University of Waterloo)
200 University Ave W Eit 2036, Waterloo, ON,
N2L 3G1
(519) 888-4567
Emp Here 50
SIC 8221 Colleges and universities

D-U-N-S 24-558-4060   (BR)
UNIVERSITY OF WATERLOO
UNIVERSITY OF WATERLOO, THE
(*Suby of* University of Waterloo)
200 University Ave W Suite 103, Waterloo,
ON, N2L 3G1
(519) 888-4700
Emp Here 30
SIC 5812 Eating places

D-U-N-S 20-788-3609   (BR)
UNIVERSITY OF WATERLOO
UNIVERSITY OF WATERLOO, THE
(*Suby of* University of Waterloo)

200 University Ave W Suite 103, Waterloo, ON, N2L 3G1
(519) 888-4567
Emp Here 200
SIC 8042 Offices and clinics of optometrists

D-U-N-S 24-992-2188   (SL)
VIA PERSONNEL SERVICES LTD
105 Bauer Pl, Waterloo, ON, N2L 6B5

Emp Here 50   Sales 3,648,035
SIC 7361 Employment agencies

D-U-N-S 20-710-7272   (BR)
WATERLOO   CATHOLIC   DISTRICT SCHOOL BOARD
ST DAVID CATHOLIC SECONDARY
4 High St, Waterloo, ON, N2L 3X5
(519) 885-1340
Emp Here 40
SIC 8211 Elementary and secondary schools

D-U-N-S 20-710-7207   (BR)
WATERLOO   CATHOLIC   DISTRICT SCHOOL BOARD
SIR EDGARD BAUER SCHOOL
660 Glen Forrest Blvd, Waterloo, ON, N2L 4K2
(519) 884-8480
Emp Here 33
SIC 8211 Elementary and secondary schools

D-U-N-S 25-228-1373   (BR)
WATERLOO REGION DISTRICT SCHOOL BOARD
CENTENNIAL SENIOR PUBLIC SCHOOL
141 Amos Ave, Waterloo, ON, N2L 2W8
(519) 885-5660
Emp Here 40
SIC 8211 Elementary and secondary schools

D-U-N-S 25-237-9045   (BR)
WATERLOO REGION DISTRICT SCHOOL BOARD
MACGREGOR SENIOR PUBLIC SCHOOL
32 Central St, Waterloo, ON, N2L 3A6
(519) 885-6200
Emp Here 34
SIC 8211 Elementary and secondary schools

D-U-N-S 25-228-0961   (BR)
WATERLOO REGION DISTRICT SCHOOL BOARD
WINSTON CHURCHILL PUBLIC SCHOOL
100 Milford Ave, Waterloo, ON, N2L 3Z3
(519) 884-3722
Emp Here 25
SIC 8211 Elementary and secondary schools

D-U-N-S 25-137-3858   (BR)
WATERLOO REGION DISTRICT SCHOOL BOARD
N. A. MACEACHERN SCHOOL
580 Rolling Hills Dr, Waterloo, ON, N2L 4Z9
(519) 885-1731
Emp Here 30
SIC 8211 Elementary and secondary schools

D-U-N-S 25-237-9052   (BR)
WATERLOO REGION DISTRICT SCHOOL BOARD
EMPIRE PUBLIC SCHOOL
83 Empire St, Waterloo, ON, N2L 2M1
(519) 742-8375
Emp Here 35
SIC 8211 Elementary and secondary schools

D-U-N-S 25-174-0692   (BR)
WATERLOO REGION DISTRICT SCHOOL BOARD
WATERLOO COLLEGIATE INSTITUTE
300 Hazel St, Waterloo, ON, N2L 3P2
(519) 884-9590
Emp Here 250
SIC 8211 Elementary and secondary schools

D-U-N-S 25-228-1365   (BR)
WATERLOO REGION DISTRICT SCHOOL BOARD

CEDARBRAE PUBLIC SCHOOL
230 Cedarbrae Ave, Waterloo, ON, N2L 4S7
(519) 884-4940
Emp Here 25
SIC 8211 Elementary and secondary schools

D-U-N-S 25-228-1654   (BR)
WATERLOO REGION DISTRICT SCHOOL BOARD
KEATSWAY ELEMENTARY SCHOOL
323 Keats Way, Waterloo, ON, N2L 5V9
(519) 886-1650
Emp Here 30
SIC 8211 Elementary and secondary schools

D-U-N-S 20-106-3604   (BR)
WINNERS MERCHANTS INTERNATIONAL L.P.
WINNERS
(Suby of The TJX Companies Inc)
550 King St N, Waterloo, ON, N2L 5W6
(519) 747-1919
Emp Here 50
SIC 5651 Family clothing stores

D-U-N-S 20-184-3229   (BR)
WINNERS MERCHANTS INTERNATIONAL L.P.
HOMESENSE
(Suby of The TJX Companies Inc)
578 King St N, Waterloo, ON, N2L 6L3
(519) 885-2782
Emp Here 40
SIC 5651 Family clothing stores

Waterloo, ON N2T
Waterloo County

D-U-N-S 20-003-3855   (BR)
BANQUE TORONTO-DOMINION, LA
TORONTO-DOMINION BANK, THE
(Suby of Toronto-Dominion Bank, The)
460 Erb St W, Waterloo, ON, N2T 1N5
(519) 885-8586
Emp Here 25
SIC 6021 National commercial banks

D-U-N-S 20-321-8334   (BR)
CARA OPERATIONS LIMITED
MILESTONE'S GRILL & BAR
(Suby of Cara Holdings Limited)
410 The Boardwalk, Waterloo, ON, N2T 0A6
(519) 579-4949
Emp Here 40
SIC 5812 Eating places

D-U-N-S 20-566-5958   (SL)
GPS PRODUCTS INC
622 Frieburg Dr, Waterloo, ON, N2T 2Y4
(519) 885-7235
Emp Here 100   Sales 12,184,437
SIC 5015 Motor vehicle parts, used
Pr David Godwin

D-U-N-S 20-300-5124   (BR)
SOBEYS CAPITAL INCORPORATED
SOBEYS
450 Columbia St W, Waterloo, ON, N2T 2W1
(519) 880-9143
Emp Here 100
SIC 5411 Grocery stores

D-U-N-S 25-453-5839   (BR)
STARBUCKS COFFEE CANADA, INC
(Suby of Starbucks Corporation)
650 Erb St W, Waterloo, ON, N2T 2Z7
(519) 886-5237
Emp Here 30
SIC 5812 Eating places

D-U-N-S 20-710-7413   (BR)
WATERLOO   CATHOLIC   DISTRICT SCHOOL BOARD
HOLY ROSARY SCHOOL
485 Thorndale Dr, Waterloo, ON, N2T 1W5

(519) 747-9005
Emp Here 35
SIC 8211 Elementary and secondary schools

D-U-N-S 20-591-4653   (BR)
WATERLOO REGION DISTRICT SCHOOL BOARD
LAURELWOOD PUBLIC SCHOOL
460 Brentcliffe Dr, Waterloo, ON, N2T 2R5
(519) 884-9999
Emp Here 25
SIC 8211 Elementary and secondary schools

D-U-N-S 20-710-7124   (BR)
WATERLOO REGION DISTRICT SCHOOL BOARD
MARY JOHNSTON PUBLIC SCHOOL
475 Brynhurst Blvd, Waterloo, ON, N2T 2C6
(519) 747-1620
Emp Here 50
SIC 8211 Elementary and secondary schools

D-U-N-S 24-253-8432   (BR)
WATERLOO REGION DISTRICT SCHOOL BOARD
STAEBLER, EDNA PUBLIC SCHOOL
450 Bernay Dr, Waterloo, ON, N2T 3A3
(519) 880-2646
Emp Here 50
SIC 8211 Elementary and secondary schools

D-U-N-S 25-137-9822   (BR)
WATERLOO REGION DISTRICT SCHOOL BOARD
WESTVALE PUBLIC SCHOOL
265 Westvale Dr, Waterloo, ON, N2T 2B2
(519) 746-8104
Emp Here 50
SIC 8211 Elementary and secondary schools

D-U-N-S 25-297-8689   (BR)
ZEHRMART INC
ZEHRS MARKET
450 Erb St W, Waterloo, ON, N2T 1H4
(519) 886-4900
Emp Here 350
SIC 5411 Grocery stores

Waterloo, ON N2V
Waterloo County

D-U-N-S 20-291-4847   (BR)
1003694 ONTARIO INC
CARE PARTNERS
(Suby of 1003694 Ontario Inc)
151 Frobisher Dr Suite B207, Waterloo, ON, N2V 2C9
(519) 725-4999
Emp Here 50
SIC 8082 Home health care services

D-U-N-S 20-278-2652   (BR)
A & W FOOD SERVICES OF CANADA INC
A & W
335 Farmer'S Market Rd Unit 201, Waterloo, ON, N2V 0A4
(519) 746-0550
Emp Here 25
SIC 5812 Eating places

D-U-N-S 20-056-6730   (BR)
ALS CANADA LTD
ENVIRO-TEST LABORATORIES
60 Northland Rd Unit 1, Waterloo, ON, N2V 2B8
(519) 886-6910
Emp Here 60
SIC 8731 Commercial physical research

D-U-N-S 20-808-7309   (BR)
AMJ CAMPBELL INC
AMJ CAMPBELL
275 Frobisher Dr Unit 2, Waterloo, ON, N2V 2G4
(519) 833-1200
Emp Here 55

SIC 4214 Local trucking with storage

D-U-N-S 25-824-6016   (BR)
AIRWAYS TRANSIT SERVICE LIMITED
99 Northland Rd Unit A, Waterloo, ON, N2V 1Y8
(519) 658-5521
Emp Here 160
SIC 4131 Intercity and rural bus transportation

D-U-N-S 24-194-2247   (SL)
BOSTON PIZZA
597 King St N, Waterloo, ON, N2V 2N3
(519) 880-1828
Emp Here 50   Sales 1,532,175
SIC 5812 Eating places

D-U-N-S 20-342-5913   (BR)
DEMATIC LIMITED
609 Kumpf Dr Unit 201, Waterloo, ON, N2V 1K8
(226) 772-7300
Emp Here 39
SIC 7371 Custom computer programming services

D-U-N-S 20-607-9790   (HQ)
DONALD CHOI CANADA LIMITED
(Suby of Donald Choi Canada Limited)
147 Bathurst Drive, Waterloo, ON, N2V 1Z4
(519) 886-5010
Emp Here 29   Emp Total 35
Sales 10,529,782
SIC 5072 Hardware
Pr Pr Donald Choi
VP VP Bo Choi

D-U-N-S 20-017-1705   (SL)
DSPFACTORY LTD
(Suby of On Semiconductor Corporation)
611 Kumpf Dr Unit 200, Waterloo, ON, N2V 1K8
(519) 884-9696
Emp Here 45   Sales 9,030,720
SIC 3651 Household audio and video equipment
Pr Pr Robert Tong

D-U-N-S 20-123-3983   (HQ)
GLOBAL BEVERAGE GROUP INC
GBG
120 Randall Dr Suite E, Waterloo, ON, N2V 1C6

Emp Here 100   Emp Total 771
Sales 27,068,420
SIC 7371 Custom computer programming services
Ted Hastings
VP Fin Jeff Collins
Bruce Mcintyre
VP VP Greg Pogue
VP Opers Chris Varney
VP Sls Vince Schneider

D-U-N-S 24-357-1192   (BR)
GRAND & TOY LIMITED
(Suby of Office Depot, Inc.)
588 Colby Dr Suite 1, Waterloo, ON, N2V 1A2
(519) 888-9605
Emp Here 25
SIC 5712 Furniture stores

D-U-N-S 25-033-7235   (BR)
GROTE INDUSTRIES CO.
GROTE ELECTRONICS, DIV. OF
95 Bathurst Dr, Waterloo, ON, N2V 1N2
(519) 884-4991
Emp Here 100
SIC 2821 Plastics materials and resins

D-U-N-S 25-220-6602   (BR)
HAMMOND MANUFACTURING COMPANY LIMITED
ELECTRONICS GROUP, DIV OF
52 Rankin St, Waterloo, ON, N2V 1V9

Emp Here 60

SIC 3677 Electronic coils and transformers

D-U-N-S 20-998-1265 (SL)
HANDTMANN-PIEREDER MACHINERY LTD
654 Colby Dr, Waterloo, ON, N2V 1A2
(519) 888-7300
Emp Here 26 *Sales* 3,617,280
SIC 3556 Food products machinery

D-U-N-S 24-359-5134 (SL)
HIGHJUMP SOFTWARE CANADA INC
60 Bathurst Dr Unit 9, Waterloo, ON, N2V 2A9
(519) 746-3736
Emp Here 20 *Sales* 1,459,214
SIC 7371 Custom computer programming services

D-U-N-S 25-671-4353 (BR)
HOME DEPOT OF CANADA INC
HOME DEPOT
(*Suby of* The Home Depot Inc)
600 King St N, Waterloo, ON, N2V 2J5
(519) 883-0580
Emp Here 250
SIC 5211 Lumber and other building materials

D-U-N-S 24-371-7035 (SL)
LANGGUTH AMERICA LTD
109 Randall Dr Suite 7, Waterloo, ON, N2V 1C5
(519) 888-0099
Emp Here 21 *Sales* 4,343,718
SIC 3565 Packaging machinery

D-U-N-S 25-995-8585 (HQ)
MENNONITE ECONOMIC DEVELOPMENT ASSOCIATES OF CANADA
MEDA
(*Suby of* Mennonite Economic Development Associates of Canada)
155 Frobisher Dr Suite I-106, Waterloo, ON, N2V 2E1
(519) 725-1633
Emp Here 45 *Emp Total* 47
Sales 21,843,883
SIC 8699 Membership organizations, nec
Pr Pr Allan Sauder
Ch Bd Albert Friesen
Gary Leis
Zachary Bishop

D-U-N-S 25-974-1163 (BR)
MOLEX CANADA LTD
WOODHEAD SOFTWARE & ELECTRONIC, DIV OF
(*Suby of* Koch Industries, Inc.)
50 Northland Rd, Waterloo, ON, N2V 1N3
(519) 725-5136
Emp Here 61
SIC 3695 Magnetic and optical recording media

D-U-N-S 20-171-4730 (HQ)
NCR CANADA CORP
FINANCIAL SOLUTION, DIV OF
(*Suby of* NCR Corporation)
50 Northland Rd, Waterloo, ON, N2V 1N3
(905) 826-9000
Emp Here 200 *Emp Total* 33,500
Sales 194,906,475
SIC 5044 Office equipment
Pr William Nuti
Dir Nicholas Hames
Dir Luc Villeneuve

D-U-N-S 24-198-7692 (HQ)
NORTHERN DIGITAL INC
NDI
(*Suby of* Roper Technologies, Inc.)
103 Randall Dr, Waterloo, ON, N2V 1C5
(519) 884-5142
Emp Here 120 *Emp Total* 14,205
Sales 72,960,700
SIC 3841 Surgical and medical instruments
Pr Pr David Rath
VP Dave Hoover
Gary Barfoot

D-U-N-S 20-811-3998 (BR)
ORION SECURITY INCORPORATED
ORION SECURITY & INVESTIGATION SERVICES
(*Suby of* Orion Security Incorporated)
119 White Pine Cres, Waterloo, ON, N2V 1B3

Emp Here 20
SIC 7389 Business services, nec

D-U-N-S 24-784-5175 (SL)
RESEARCH DEVELOPMENT & MANUFACTURING CORPORATION
(*Suby of* Deluxe Corporation)
619a Kumpf Dr, Waterloo, ON, N2V 1K8
(519) 746-8483
Emp Here 100 *Sales* 16,019,593
SIC 7371 Custom computer programming services
Pr Randy Fowlie
Ch Bd Jean Noelting
Rui Mulhinha

D-U-N-S 20-592-3316 (BR)
REVERA INC
COLUMBIA FOREST LONG TERM SERVICES
650 Mountain Maple Ave Suite 3117, Waterloo, ON, N2V 2P7

Emp Here 50
SIC 8051 Skilled nursing care facilities

D-U-N-S 25-600-2932 (BR)
ROYAL BANK OF CANADA
RBC
(*Suby of* Royal Bank Of Canada)
585 Weber St N, Waterloo, ON, N2V 1V8
(519) 747-8360
Emp Here 20
SIC 6021 National commercial banks

D-U-N-S 24-816-6928 (SL)
SIRSIDYNIX (CANADA) INC
611 Kumpf Dr Unit 300, Waterloo, ON, N2V 1K8

Emp Here 30 *Sales* 5,496,960
SIC 5045 Computers, peripherals, and software
Pr Pr Patrick Sommers
Dean Mccausland
Stephen Abram

D-U-N-S 25-689-5269 (BR)
STAPLES CANADA INC
STAPLES THE BUSINESS DEPOT
(*Suby of* Staples, Inc.)
620 King St N, Waterloo, ON, N2V 2J5
(519) 888-1716
Emp Here 55
SIC 5943 Stationery stores

D-U-N-S 20-124-8812 (BR)
ULTRA MANUFACTURING LIMITED
MITCHELL PLASTIC DIV
640 Conrad Pl, Waterloo, ON, N2V 1C4
(519) 884-0448
Emp Here 50
SIC 3089 Plastics products, nec

D-U-N-S 24-312-0701 (BR)
UNION GAS LIMITED
603 Kumpf Dr, Waterloo, ON, N2V 1K3
(519) 885-7400
Emp Here 50
SIC 4922 Natural gas transmission

D-U-N-S 24-198-3964 (HQ)
VIESSMANN MANUFACTURING COMPANY INC
750 Mcmurray Rd, Waterloo, ON, N2V 2G5
(519) 885-6300
Emp Here 60 *Emp Total* 11,600
Sales 6,420,542
SIC 3433 Heating equipment, except electric
Martin Viessmann

Pr Harald Prell
Fin Ex Michele Scherrer

D-U-N-S 24-599-1711 (BR)
WAL-MART CANADA CORP
335 Farmer'S Market Rd Suite 3156, Waterloo, ON, N2V 0A4
(519) 746-6700
Emp Here 40
SIC 5311 Department stores

D-U-N-S 24-587-3377 (BR)
WASTE MANAGEMENT OF CANADA CORPORATION
WASTE MANAGEMENT
(*Suby of* Waste Management, Inc.)
645 Conrad Pl, Waterloo, ON, N2V 1C4
(519) 886-6932
Emp Here 100
SIC 4953 Refuse systems

D-U-N-S 20-710-7546 (BR)
WATERLOO CATHOLIC DISTRICT SCHOOL BOARD
ST NICHOLAS CATHOLIC ELEMENTAY SCHOOL
525 Laurelwood Dr, Waterloo, ON, N2V 2N1
(519) 884-9198
Emp Here 50
SIC 8211 Elementary and secondary schools

D-U-N-S 25-137-3890 (BR)
WATERLOO REGION DISTRICT SCHOOL BOARD
NORTHLAKE WOODS PUBLIC SCHOOL
500 Northlake Dr, Waterloo, ON, N2V 2A4
(519) 885-1115
Emp Here 50
SIC 8211 Elementary and secondary schools

D-U-N-S 20-059-9673 (BR)
WISMER DEVELOPMENTS INC
PILLER SAUSAGES
250 Frobisher Dr, Waterloo, ON, N2V 2L8
(519) 743-1412
Emp Here 60
SIC 2013 Sausages and other prepared meats

D-U-N-S 24-347-6038 (SL)
ESOLUTIONSGROUP LIMITED
651 Colby Dr, Waterloo, ON, N2V 1C2
(519) 884-3352
Emp Here 45 *Sales* 2,553,625
SIC 7374 Data processing and preparation

Watford, ON N0M
Lambton County

D-U-N-S 25-997-2586 (BR)
AUTOTUBE LIMITED
7963 Confederation Line, Watford, ON, N0M 2S0
(519) 849-6318
Emp Here 38
SIC 3312 Blast furnaces and steel mills

D-U-N-S 25-249-3721 (BR)
LAMBTON KENT DISTRICT SCHOOL BOARD
EAST LAMBTON ELEMENTARY SCHOOL
139 Centennial Ave, Watford, ON, N0M 2S0
(519) 876-2610
Emp Here 25
SIC 8211 Elementary and secondary schools

D-U-N-S 24-142-1700 (SL)
QCC CORP
WATFORD QUALITY CARE CENTRE
344 Victoria St Ss 1, Watford, ON, N0M 2S0

Emp Here 65 *Sales* 2,991,389
SIC 8051 Skilled nursing care facilities

D-U-N-S 25-854-5995 (BR)

Pr Harald Prell
Fin Ex Michele Scherrer

ST. CLAIR CATHOLIC DISTRICT SCHOOL BOARD
ST PETER CANISIUS
(*Suby of* St. Clair Catholic District School Board)
424 Victoria St, Watford, ON, N0M 2S0
(519) 876-3018
Emp Here 30
SIC 8211 Elementary and secondary schools

Wawa, ON P0S
Algoma County

D-U-N-S 20-992-5507 (BR)
768812 ONTARIO INC
VIANET
53 Broadway, Wawa, ON, P0S 1K0
(705) 856-7007
Emp Here 45
SIC 4813 Telephone communication, except radio

D-U-N-S 24-030-5800 (BR)
CONSEIL SCOLAIRE DE DISTRICT DU GRAND NORD DE L'ONTARIO
CONSEIL SCOLAIRE DE DISTRICT DU GRAND NORD DE L'ON
52 Winston Rd, Wawa, ON, P0S 1K0
(705) 856-0123
Emp Here 25
SIC 8211 Elementary and secondary schools

D-U-N-S 20-844-5952 (BR)
PEPSICO CANADA ULC
FRITO LAY CANADA
(*Suby of* Pepsico, Inc.)
30 Pinewood Dr, Wawa, ON, P0S 1K0
(705) 856-4553
Emp Here 20
SIC 2096 Potato chips and similar snacks

Welland, ON L3B
Welland County

D-U-N-S 20-699-3961 (SL)
ATLAS TUBE CANADA ULC
ENERGEX TUBE
160 Dain Ave, Welland, ON, L3B 5Y6
(905) 735-7473
Emp Here 480
SIC 3317 Steel pipe and tubes

D-U-N-S 20-180-9951 (HQ)
BOSCH REXROTH CANADA CORP
490 Prince Charles Dr S, Welland, ON, L3B 5X7
(905) 735-0510
Emp Here 200 *Emp Total* 2,428
Sales 122,556,440
SIC 5084 Industrial machinery and equipment
John Mataya
Ch Bd Paul Cooke

D-U-N-S 20-333-4206 (BR)
CANADA FORGINGS INC
CANFORGE
166 Major St, Welland, ON, L3B 3T4
(905) 735-1220
Emp Here 20
SIC 3462 Iron and steel forgings

D-U-N-S 20-739-7493 (BR)
CANADA POST CORPORATION
26 Division St, Welland, ON, L3B 3Z6
(905) 734-4211
Emp Here 52
SIC 4311 U.s. postal service

D-U-N-S 20-246-1310 (BR)
CANADIAN PACIFIC RAILWAY COMPANY
CPR
60749 Reilly Rd W, Welland, ON, L3B 5N6

(905) 735-0154
Emp Here 50
SIC 4011 Railroads, line-haul operating

D-U-N-S 20-648-6198   (BR)
CANADIAN TIRE SERVICES LIMITED
CTFS
1000 East Main St, Welland, ON, L3B 3Z3
(905) 735-3131
Emp Here 1,000
SIC 6153 Short-term business credit institutions, except agricultural

D-U-N-S 20-026-7255   (BR)
CONSEIL SCOLAIRE DE DISTRICT CATHOLIQUE CENTRE-SUD
ECOLE SECONDAIRE CATHOLIQUE JEAN VANIER
620 River Rd, Welland, ON, L3B 5N4
(905) 714-7882
Emp Here 50
SIC 8211 Elementary and secondary schools

D-U-N-S 20-711-7453   (BR)
CONSEIL SCOLAIRE DE DISTRICT CATHOLIQUE CENTRE-SUD
ECOLE ST FRANCOIS D'ASSISE
58 Empress Ave, Welland, ON, L3B 1K9
(905) 735-0837
Emp Here 30
SIC 8211 Elementary and secondary schools

D-U-N-S 20-582-5545   (BR)
CONSEIL SCOLAIRE DE DISTRICT CATHOLIQUE CENTRE-SUD
ECOLE SECONDAIRE CONFEDERATION
670 Tanguay Ave, Welland, ON, L3B 4G2
(905) 732-1361
Emp Here 50
SIC 8211 Elementary and secondary schools

D-U-N-S 20-913-7178   (BR)
CONSEIL SCOLAIRE VIAMONDE
ECOLE CHAMPLAIN
101 Afton Ave, Welland, ON, L3B 1W1
(905) 732-3113
Emp Here 20
SIC 8211 Elementary and secondary schools

D-U-N-S 20-710-8700   (BR)
DISTRICT SCHOOL BOARD OF NIAGARA
PLYMOUTH SCHOOL
111 First St, Welland, ON, L3B 4S1
(905) 732-4110
Emp Here 50
SIC 8211 Elementary and secondary schools

D-U-N-S 20-710-8668   (BR)
DISTRICT SCHOOL BOARD OF NIAGARA
MATTHEWS SCHOOL
315 Southworth St S, Welland, ON, L3B 1Z8
(905) 734-3208
Emp Here 50
SIC 8211 Elementary and secondary schools

D-U-N-S 20-286-9272   (BR)
DISTRICT SCHOOL BOARD OF NIAGARA
EASTDALE SECONDARY SCHOOL
170 Wellington St, Welland, ON, L3B 1B3
(905) 734-7458
Emp Here 60
SIC 8211 Elementary and secondary schools

D-U-N-S 20-710-8569   (BR)
DISTRICT SCHOOL BOARD OF NIAGARA
CROWLAND CENTRAL ELEMENTARY SCHOOL
738 Lyons Creek Rd, Welland, ON, L3B 5N4
(905) 735-0310
Emp Here 20
SIC 8211 Elementary and secondary schools

D-U-N-S 25-178-9004   (BR)
DURWARD JONES BARKWELL & COMPANY LLP
(*Suby of* Durward Jones Barkwell & Company LLP)
171 Division St, Welland, ON, L3B 4A1

(905) 735-2140
Emp Here 22
SIC 8721 Accounting, auditing, and bookkeeping

D-U-N-S 25-624-2801   (SL)
FOYER RICHELIEU WELLAND
655 Tanguay Ave, Welland, ON, L3B 6A1
(905) 734-1400
Emp Here 96   *Sales* 3,502,114
SIC 8361 Residential care

D-U-N-S 25-654-6482   (BR)
GILLESPIE PONTIAC BUICK CADILLAC LIMITED
Gd, Welland, ON, L3B 5N3
(905) 735-7151
Emp Here 60
SIC 7538 General automotive repair shops

D-U-N-S 24-023-5734   (BR)
GOVERNING COUNCIL OF THE SALVATION ARMY IN CANADA, THE
GOVERNING COUNCIL OF THE SALVATION ARMY IN CANADA, THE
129 Hagar St, Welland, ON, L3B 5V9
(905) 735-0551
Emp Here 25
SIC 8399 Social services, nec

D-U-N-S 24-353-3630   (SL)
HENNIGES AUTOMOTIVE SEALING SYSTEMS CANADA INC
HENNIGES AUTOMOTIVE
100 Kennedy St, Welland, ON, L3B 0B4

Emp Here 800   *Sales* 167,600,640
SIC 3069 Fabricated rubber products, nec
Dir Steve Smith
Fin Ex Tim Mauro

D-U-N-S 20-770-8475   (BR)
LOBLAWS SUPERMARKETS LIMITED
NO FRILLS
390 Lincoln St, Welland, ON, L3B 4N4
(905) 732-3367
Emp Here 50
SIC 5411 Grocery stores

D-U-N-S 20-710-8924   (BR)
NIAGARA CATHOLIC DISTRICT SCHOOL BOARD
ST ANDREW ELEMENTARY SCHOOL
16 St Andrews Ave, Welland, ON, L3B 1E1
(905) 732-5663
Emp Here 35
SIC 8211 Elementary and secondary schools

D-U-N-S 20-024-9790   (BR)
NIAGARA CATHOLIC DISTRICT SCHOOL BOARD
ST MARY'S CATHOLIC SCHOOL
120 Plymouth Rd, Welland, ON, L3B 3C7
(905) 734-7326
Emp Here 41
SIC 8211 Elementary and secondary schools

D-U-N-S 25-623-4857   (BR)
NIAGARA CHILD AND YOUTH SERVICES
(*Suby of* Niagara Child and Youth Services)
1604 Merrittville Hwy, Welland, ON, L3B 5N5
(905) 384-9551
Emp Here 30
SIC 8322 Individual and family services

D-U-N-S 24-794-7369   (HQ)
PANABRASIVE INC
650 Rusholme Rd, Welland, ON, L3B 5N7
(905) 735-4691
Emp Here 56   *Emp Total* 10
Sales 5,284,131
SIC 3291 Abrasive products
VP Fin Jean-Charles Peluchon
Dir William Koshub
Dir Jeff Glaser

D-U-N-S 20-992-7081   (BR)
PENSAFE INC

HAUN DROP FORGE
300 Major St, Welland, ON, L3B 0B9

Emp Here 27
SIC 3443 Fabricated plate work (boiler shop)

D-U-N-S 25-178-7446   (SL)
PENINSULA SECURITY SERVICES LTD
50 Division St, Welland, ON, L3B 3Z6
(905) 732-2337
Emp Here 125   *Sales* 3,866,917
SIC 7381 Detective and armored car services

D-U-N-S 20-641-4364   (BR)
REGIONAL MUNICIPALITY OF NIAGARA, THE
D.H. RAPELJE LODGE
277 Plymouth Rd, Welland, ON, L3B 6E3
(905) 714-7428
Emp Here 200
SIC 8361 Residential care

D-U-N-S 20-256-4977   (BR)
REVERA INC
PLYMOUTH CORDAGE RETIREMENT COMMUNITY
110 First St, Welland, ON, L3B 4S2
(905) 735-3322
Emp Here 30
SIC 6513 Apartment building operators

D-U-N-S 24-327-4508   (BR)
WAL-MART CANADA CORP
102 Primeway Dr, Welland, ON, L3B 0A1
(905) 735-3500
Emp Here 250
SIC 5311 Department stores

D-U-N-S 20-181-5008   (HQ)
WHITING EQUIPMENT CANADA INC
350 Alexander St, Welland, ON, L3B 2R3
(905) 732-7585
Emp Here 65   *Emp Total* 320
SIC 3559 Special industry machinery, nec

Welland, ON L3C
Welland County

D-U-N-S 20-937-3075   (SL)
626394 ONTARIO INC
VERMEER'S GREENHOUSES
684 South Pelham Rd, Welland, ON, L3C 3C8
(905) 735-5744
Emp Here 50   *Sales* 2,626,585
SIC 5992 Florists

D-U-N-S 24-663-0974   (SL)
954559 ONTARIO INC
HARVEYS-SWISS CHALET
830 Niagara St, Welland, ON, L3C 1M3
(905) 735-4040
Emp Here 55   *Sales* 1,678,096
SIC 5812 Eating places

D-U-N-S 24-151-7197   (BR)
CHARTWELL RETIREMENT RESIDENCES
CHARTWELL SENIORS HOUSING REAL ESTATE INVESTMENT TRUST
163 First Ave, Welland, ON, L3C 0A3
(905) 735-5333
Emp Here 70
SIC 6513 Apartment building operators

D-U-N-S 24-187-8953   (BR)
COMARK INC
CLEO
(*Suby of* Comark Inc)
800 Niagara St, Welland, ON, L3C 5Z4
(905) 788-9271
Emp Here 20
SIC 5137 Women's and children's clothing

D-U-N-S 20-025-9732   (BR)
CONSEIL SCOLAIRE DE DISTRICT CATHOLIQUE CENTRE-SUD

ECOLE DU SACRE-COEUR
310 Fitch St, Welland, ON, L3C 4W5
(905) 734-8133
Emp Here 30
SIC 8211 Elementary and secondary schools

D-U-N-S 20-710-8601   (BR)
DISTRICT SCHOOL BOARD OF NIAGARA
FITCH STREET PUBLIC SCHOOL
164 Fitch St, Welland, ON, L3C 4V5
(905) 732-3683
Emp Here 50
SIC 8211 Elementary and secondary schools

D-U-N-S 20-286-9280   (BR)
DISTRICT SCHOOL BOARD OF NIAGARA
WELLAND CENTENNIAL SECONDARY SCHOOL
240 Thorold Rd, Welland, ON, L3C 3W2
(905) 735-0700
Emp Here 70
SIC 8211 Elementary and secondary schools

D-U-N-S 20-292-1206   (BR)
DISTRICT SCHOOL BOARD OF NIAGARA
GORDON ELEMENTARY SCHOOL
468 Thorold Rd, Welland, ON, L3C 3W6
(905) 734-3730
Emp Here 25
SIC 8211 Elementary and secondary schools

D-U-N-S 20-288-4578   (BR)
DISTRICT SCHOOL BOARD OF NIAGARA
QUAKER ROAD PUBLIC SCHOOL
333 Quaker Rd, Welland, ON, L3C 3G7
(905) 732-5412
Emp Here 30
SIC 8211 Elementary and secondary schools

D-U-N-S 20-710-8775   (BR)
DISTRICT SCHOOL BOARD OF NIAGARA
ROSS PUBLIC SCHOOL
358 Niagara St, Welland, ON, L3C 1K9
(905) 734-4273
Emp Here 20
SIC 8211 Elementary and secondary schools

D-U-N-S 25-272-1209   (BR)
FGL SPORTS LTD
SPORT CHEK
800 Niagara St Suite 1, Welland, ON, L3C 5Z4
(905) 732-9715
Emp Here 40
SIC 5941 Sporting goods and bicycle shops

D-U-N-S 20-844-4042   (BR)
FIRSTCANADA ULC
LAIDLAW EDUCATIONAL SERVICES
1049 Niagara St, Welland, ON, L3C 1M5
(905) 735-5944
Emp Here 130
SIC 4151 School buses

D-U-N-S 20-818-2766   (SL)
HILL-BOLES AUTO ELECTRIC LTD
HILL-BOLES AUTOMOTIVE
26 Thorold Rd, Welland, ON, L3C 3T4
(905) 734-7454
Emp Here 32   *Sales* 5,376,850
SIC 5013 Motor vehicle supplies and new parts
Pr Pr Daniel Mckenzie

D-U-N-S 20-181-2369   (BR)
LEON'S FURNITURE LIMITED
LEON'S FURNITURE
803 Niagara St, Welland, ON, L3C 1M4
(905) 735-2880
Emp Here 40
SIC 5712 Furniture stores

D-U-N-S 24-037-5043   (BR)
LOBLAWS SUPERMARKETS LIMITED
ZEHRS FOOD PLUS
821 Niagara St, Welland, ON, L3C 1M4
(905) 732-9010
Emp Here 150
SIC 5411 Grocery stores

D-U-N-S 25-300-0509   (BR)
METRO ONTARIO INC
FOOD BASICS
325 Thorold Rd, Welland, ON, L3C 3W4
(905) 735-4320
Emp Here 70
SIC 5411 Grocery stores

D-U-N-S 20-710-8981   (BR)
NIAGARA CATHOLIC DISTRICT SCHOOL BOARD
ST KEVIN CATHOLIC SCHOOL
182 Aqueduct St, Welland, ON, L3C 1C4
(905) 734-7709
Emp Here 32
SIC 8211 Elementary and secondary schools

D-U-N-S 20-591-6179   (BR)
NIAGARA CATHOLIC DISTRICT SCHOOL BOARD
NOTRE DAME HIGH SCHOOL
64 Smith St, Welland, ON, L3C 4H4
(905) 788-3060
Emp Here 120
SIC 8211 Elementary and secondary schools

D-U-N-S 25-934-3366   (BR)
NIAGARA CATHOLIC DISTRICT SCHOOL BOARD
ALEXANDER KUSKA KSG CATHOLIC SCHOOL
333 Rice Rd, Welland, ON, L3C 2V9
(905) 735-4471
Emp Here 30
SIC 8211 Elementary and secondary schools

D-U-N-S 20-710-9096   (BR)
NIAGARA CATHOLIC DISTRICT SCHOOL BOARD
CATHOLIC EDUCATION CENTRE
427 Rice Rd Suite 1, Welland, ON, L3C 7C1
(905) 735-0240
Emp Here 50
SIC 8211 Elementary and secondary schools

D-U-N-S 20-591-5965   (BR)
NIAGARA CATHOLIC DISTRICT SCHOOL BOARD
HOLY NAME CATHOLIC SCHOOL
290 Fitch St, Welland, ON, L3C 4W5
(905) 732-4992
Emp Here 30
SIC 8211 Elementary and secondary schools

D-U-N-S 20-710-8957   (BR)
NIAGARA CATHOLIC DISTRICT SCHOOL BOARD
ST AUGUSTINE SCHOOL
300 Santone Ave, Welland, ON, L3C 2J8
(905) 734-4659
Emp Here 30
SIC 8211 Elementary and secondary schools

D-U-N-S 20-859-8685   (BR)
PACIFIC LINK COMMUNICATIONS INC
BELL WORLD
800 Niagara St, Welland, ON, L3C 5Z4
(905) 788-2355
Emp Here 25
SIC 5999 Miscellaneous retail stores, nec

D-U-N-S 20-292-0273   (BR)
ROYAL LEPAGE NIAGARA REAL ESTATE CENTRE
637 Niagara St Unit 2, Welland, ON, L3C 1L9
(905) 734-4545
Emp Here 25
SIC 6531 Real estate agents and managers

D-U-N-S 25-138-3055   (BR)
SOBEYS CAPITAL INCORPORATED
609 South Pelham Rd, Welland, ON, L3C 3C7
(905) 735-7467
Emp Here 50
SIC 5411 Grocery stores

D-U-N-S 25-498-9841   (BR)
STAPLES CANADA INC

STAPLES THE BUSINESS DEPOT
(*Suby of* Staples, Inc.)
800 Niagara St Suite 102, Welland, ON, L3C 5Z4
(905) 714-7607
Emp Here 30
SIC 5943 Stationery stores

D-U-N-S 24-972-7777   (BR)
TORONTO-DOMINION BANK, THE
TD BANK
(*Suby of* Toronto-Dominion Bank, The)
845 Niagara St, Welland, ON, L3C 1M4
(905) 732-2461
Emp Here 25
SIC 6021 National commercial banks

D-U-N-S 25-640-2405   (BR)
TWINCORP INC
TACO BELL
800 Niagara St, Welland, ON, L3C 5Z4

Emp Here 20
SIC 5812 Eating places

D-U-N-S 25-644-3599   (BR)
WATCH TOWER BIBLE AND TRACT SOCIETY OF CANADA
KINGDOM HALL JEHOVAH'S WITNESS
390 Clare Ave, Welland, ON, L3C 5R2

Emp Here 92
SIC 8661 Religious organizations

D-U-N-S 25-638-5014   (BR)
WENDCORP HOLDINGS INC
WENDY'S OLD FASHIONED HAMBURGER
530 Niagara St, Welland, ON, L3C 1L8
(905) 788-0930
Emp Here 40
SIC 5812 Eating places

D-U-N-S 24-357-2604   (BR)
WINNERS MERCHANTS INTERNATIONAL L.P.
WINNERS
(*Suby of* The TJX Companies Inc)
800 Niagara St N, Welland, ON, L3C 5Z6
(905) 788-3914
Emp Here 30
SIC 5651 Family clothing stores

D-U-N-S 20-117-9053   (BR)
YMCA OF NIAGARA
YMCA
310 Woodland Rd, Welland, ON, L3C 7N3
(905) 735-9622
Emp Here 250
SIC 8641 Civic and social associations

D-U-N-S 20-789-4689   (BR)
ZEHRMART INC
ZEHRS MARKETS
821 Niagara St, Welland, ON, L3C 1M4
(905) 732-9380
Emp Here 130
SIC 5411 Grocery stores

Wellandport, ON L0R

D-U-N-S 24-317-9009   (SL)
CREATIVE CENTRE FOR LEARNING & DEVELOPMENT LIMITED
ROBERT LAND ACADEMY
6727 South Chippawa Rd, Wellandport, ON, L0R 2J0
(905) 386-6203
Emp Here 65   *Sales* 3,575,074
SIC 8299 Schools and educational services, nec

Wellesley, ON N0B
Waterloo County

D-U-N-S 25-228-1399   (BR)
WATERLOO REGION DISTRICT SCHOOL BOARD
WELLESLEY PUBLIC SCHOOL
1059 Queens Bush Rd, Wellesley, ON, N0B 2T0
(519) 656-2830
Emp Here 54
SIC 8211 Elementary and secondary schools

Wellington, ON K0K
Prince Edward County

D-U-N-S 20-025-0640   (BR)
HASTINGS AND PRINCE EDWARD DISTRICT SCHOOL BOARD
C M L SNIDER SCHOOL
240 Wellington Main St, Wellington, ON, K0K 3L0
(613) 399-3474
Emp Here 30
SIC 8211 Elementary and secondary schools

West Lorne, ON N0L
Elgin County

D-U-N-S 24-805-6389   (BR)
BADDER BUS SERVICE LIMITED
(*Suby of* Badder Bus Service Limited)
290 Finney St, West Lorne, ON, N0L 2P0
(519) 768-2820
Emp Here 25
SIC 4142 Bus charter service, except local

D-U-N-S 25-238-8095   (BR)
THAMES VALLEY DISTRICT SCHOOL BOARD
WEST ELGIN SECONDARY SCHOOL
139 Graham St, West Lorne, ON, N0L 2P0
(519) 768-1350
Emp Here 60
SIC 8211 Elementary and secondary schools

D-U-N-S 20-697-7782   (SL)
WEST LORNE BIOOIL CO-GENERATION LIMITED PARTNERSHIP
191 Jane St, West Lorne, ON, N0L 2P0

Emp Here 100   *Sales* 125,760,000
SIC 2911 Petroleum refining
Dir Nathan Numer

Westport, ON K0G
Leeds County

D-U-N-S 25-857-9226   (BR)
ROYAL CANADIAN LEGION, THE
ROYAL CANADIAN LEGION UPPER RIDEAU BRANCH 542
(*Suby of* Royal Canadian Legion, The)
10099 Perth Rd, Westport, ON, K0G 1X0
(613) 273-3615
Emp Here 25
SIC 8641 Civic and social associations

Wheatley, ON N0P

D-U-N-S 24-522-1481   (SL)
BOLTHOUSE FARMS CANADA INC
303 Milo Rd, Wheatley, ON, N0P 2P0
(519) 825-3412
Emp Here 100   *Sales* 8,536,402
SIC 5431 Fruit and vegetable markets

Dir Phil Kooy
Dir Scott Laporta
Dir Lyndon Richardson
Dir Tracy Marchant Saiki

D-U-N-S 25-249-2111   (BR)
GREATER ESSEX COUNTY DISTRICT SCHOOL BOARD
EAST MERSEA PUBLIC SCHOOL
547 Mersea Road 21, Wheatley, ON, N0P 2P0
(519) 825-4596
Emp Here 20
SIC 8211 Elementary and secondary schools

D-U-N-S 20-699-1627   (BR)
OMSTEAD FOODS LIMITED
20887 Erie St S, Wheatley, ON, N0P 2P0
(416) 226-7524
Emp Here 50
SIC 2037 Frozen fruits and vegetables

D-U-N-S 24-374-3981   (BR)
OMSTEAD FOODS LIMITED
1 Erie St S, Wheatley, ON, N0P 2P0
(519) 825-4611
Emp Here 50
SIC 2092 Fresh or frozen packaged fish

D-U-N-S 24-043-6704   (BR)
PRESTEVE FOODS LIMITED
20954 Erie St S, Wheatley, ON, N0P 2P0
(519) 825-4677
Emp Here 200
SIC 5146 Fish and seafoods

Whitby, ON L1M

D-U-N-S 20-703-1712   (BR)
ARMTEC LP
BROOKLIN CONCRETE, DIV OF
6760 Baldwin St N, Whitby, ON, L1M 1X8
(905) 655-3311
Emp Here 70
SIC 3272 Concrete products, nec

D-U-N-S 25-932-9100   (SL)
CONSUMER PERCEPTIONS INC
40 Croxall Blvd, Whitby, ON, L1M 2E4
(905) 655-6874
Emp Here 50   *Sales* 1,678,096
SIC 7299 Miscellaneous personal service

D-U-N-S 24-213-9652   (BR)
DURHAM CATHOLIC DISTRICT SCHOOL BOARD
ST BRIDGET CATHOLIC SCHOOL
200 Carnwith Dr W, Whitby, ON, L1M 2J8
(905) 655-1875
Emp Here 25
SIC 8211 Elementary and secondary schools

D-U-N-S 24-676-3085   (BR)
DURHAM CATHOLIC DISTRICT SCHOOL BOARD
BLAIR RIDGE PUBLIC SCHOOL
100 Blackfriar Ave, Whitby, ON, L1M 0E8
(905) 620-0600
Emp Here 25
SIC 8211 Elementary and secondary schools

D-U-N-S 25-265-1922   (BR)
DURHAM CATHOLIC DISTRICT SCHOOL BOARD
ST LEO SCHOOL
120 Watford St, Whitby, ON, L1M 1H2
(905) 655-3852
Emp Here 22
SIC 8211 Elementary and secondary schools

D-U-N-S 24-154-9810   (BR)
DURHAM DISTRICT SCHOOL BOARD
BROOKLIN VILLAGE PUBLIC SCHOOL
25 Selkirk Dr, Whitby, ON, L1M 2L5
(905) 655-8959
Emp Here 45

▲ Public Company   ■ Public Company Family Member   **HQ** Headquarters   **BR** Branch   **SL** Single Location

SIC 8211 Elementary and secondary schools

D-U-N-S 20-206-5343   (BR)
DURHAM DISTRICT SCHOOL BOARD
WINCHESTER PUBLIC SCHOOL
70 Watford St, Whitby, ON, L1M 1E8
(905) 655-7328
Emp Here 50
SIC 8211 Elementary and secondary schools

D-U-N-S 25-300-7983   (BR)
DURHAM DISTRICT SCHOOL BOARD
MEADOWCREST PUBLIC SCHOOL
20 Vipond Rd, Whitby, ON, L1M 1B3
(905) 655-3731
Emp Here 27
SIC 8211 Elementary and secondary schools

D-U-N-S 20-774-3712   (SL)
HANLEY HOSPITALITY INC
TIM HORTONS
5939 Baldwin St S, Whitby, ON, L1M 2J7
(905) 655-6693
Emp Here 60   *Sales* 2,165,628
SIC 5812 Eating places

Whitby, ON L1N

D-U-N-S 20-597-6082   (SL)
1413249 ONTARIO INC
DENNY'S RESTAURANT
75 Consumers Dr Suite 17, Whitby, ON, L1N 9S2
(905) 665-6575
Emp Here 95   *Sales* 3,956,550
SIC 5812 Eating places

D-U-N-S 24-394-4035   (SL)
ASCS CANADIAN SIGNAL CORPORATION
606 Beech St W, Whitby, ON, L1N 7T8
(905) 665-4300
Emp Here 70   *Sales* 9,095,636
SIC 3679 Electronic components, nec
Pr Pr Keith Buckley
VP Fin Troy Depuma
Mgr Alex Condie

D-U-N-S 24-387-8142   (BR)
AECOM CANADA LTD
300 Water St Suite 1, Whitby, ON, L1N 9J2
(905) 668-9363
Emp Here 300
SIC 8711 Engineering services

D-U-N-S 20-571-8526   (BR)
ARBOR MEMORIAL SERVICES INC
MOUNT   LAWN   FUNERAL   HOME CEMETARY
21 Garrard Rd, Whitby, ON, L1N 3K4
(905) 665-0600
Emp Here 20
SIC 7261 Funeral service and crematories

D-U-N-S 24-312-0974   (BR)
ATLANTIC PACKAGING PRODUCTS LTD
ATLANTIC NEWSPRINT COMPANY, DIV
1900 Thickson Rd S, Whitby, ON, L1N 9E1
(905) 686-5944
Emp Here 100
SIC 2621 Paper mills

D-U-N-S 24-372-2795   (HQ)
BALL PACKAGING PRODUCTS CANADA CORP
METAL BEVERAGE PACKAGING, DIV OF
1506 Wentworth St, Whitby, ON, L1N 7C1
(905) 666-3600
Emp Here 142   *Emp Total* 18,450
SIC 3411 Metal cans

D-U-N-S 24-685-5501   (BR)
BANQUE TORONTO-DOMINION, LA
TORONTO-DOMINION BANK, THE
(*Suby of* Toronto-Dominion Bank, The)
80 Thickson Rd S Suite 2, Whitby, ON, L1N

7T2
(905) 666-9933
Emp Here 22
SIC 6021 National commercial banks

D-U-N-S 20-207-1077   (BR)
BANQUE TORONTO-DOMINION, LA
TORONTO-DOMINION BANK, THE
(*Suby of* Toronto-Dominion Bank, The)
209 Dundas St E Suite 500, Whitby, ON, L1N 7H8
(905) 665-8016
Emp Here 23
SIC 6021 National commercial banks

D-U-N-S 24-363-2119   (BR)
BEST BUY CANADA LTD
BEST BUY
(*Suby of* Best Buy Co., Inc.)
1751 Victoria St E, Whitby, ON, L1N 9W4
(905) 666-3453
Emp Here 20
SIC 5731 Radio, television, and electronic stores

D-U-N-S 25-303-4342   (BR)
CANADIAN IMPERIAL BANK OF COMMERCE
CIBC
80 Thickson Rd S, Whitby, ON, L1N 7T2
(905) 430-1801
Emp Here 30
SIC 6021 National commercial banks

D-U-N-S 25-303-4425   (BR)
CANADIAN IMPERIAL BANK OF COMMERCE
CIBC
101 Brock St N, Whitby, ON, L1N 4H3
(905) 668-3352
Emp Here 22
SIC 6021 National commercial banks

D-U-N-S 20-809-7845   (BR)
CARA OPERATIONS LIMITED
KELSEY'S RESTAURANT
(*Suby of* Cara Holdings Limited)
195 Consumers Dr, Whitby, ON, L1N 1C4
(905) 665-0605
Emp Here 35
SIC 5812 Eating places

D-U-N-S 24-342-7957   (BR)
CARA OPERATIONS LIMITED
SWISS CHALET ROTISSERIE & GRILL
(*Suby of* Cara Holdings Limited)
175 Consumers Dr, Whitby, ON, L1N 1C4
(905) 666-1411
Emp Here 75
SIC 5812 Eating places

D-U-N-S 24-015-5486   (BR)
CAREPARTNERS INC
206 Gilbert St W, Whitby, ON, L1N 1R8
(905) 668-7161
Emp Here 60
SIC 8082 Home health care services

D-U-N-S 24-002-1985   (BR)
CAREMED SERVICES INC
WE CARE HOME HEALTH SERVICES
1450 Hopkins St Suite 205, Whitby, ON, L1N 2C3
(905) 666-6656
Emp Here 80
SIC 8059 Nursing and personal care, nec

D-U-N-S 24-385-3624   (BR)
CASCADES CANADA ULC
CASCADES TISSUE GROUP
1900 Thickson Rd S, Whitby, ON, L1N 9E1
(416) 329-5200
Emp Here 65
SIC 2621 Paper mills

D-U-N-S 25-405-3887   (BR)
CHARTWELL SENIORS HOUSING REAL ESTATE INVESTMENT TRUST

COLONIAL, THE
101 Manning Rd Suite 101, Whitby, ON, L1N 9M2
(905) 665-9560
Emp Here 30
SIC 8361 Residential care

D-U-N-S 24-525-4177   (BR)
CONSEIL SCOLAIRE DE DISTRICT CATHOLIQUE CENTRE-SUD
EEC JEAN-PAUL II
1001 Hutchison Ave, Whitby, ON, L1N 2A3
(905) 665-5393
Emp Here 25
SIC 8211 Elementary and secondary schools

D-U-N-S 25-658-0507   (BR)
CORPORATION OF THE TOWN OF WHITBY, THE
IROQUOIS PARK SPORTS CENTRE, THE
500 Victoria St W, Whitby, ON, L1N 9G4
(905) 668-7765
Emp Here 100
SIC 7999 Amusement and recreation, nec

D-U-N-S 25-721-3843   (BR)
CORPORATION OF THE REGIONAL MUNICIPALITY OF DURHAM, THE
FAIRVIEW LODGE HOME FOR AGED
632 Dundas St W, Whitby, ON, L1N 5S3
(905) 668-5851
Emp Here 200
SIC 8361 Residential care

D-U-N-S 24-976-8896   (BR)
CORPORATION OF THE REGIONAL MUNICIPALITY OF DURHAM, THE
REGION OF DURHAM WORKS DEPARTMENT
105 Consumers Dr, Whitby, ON, L1N 6A3
(905) 668-7721
Emp Here 200
SIC 4941 Water supply

D-U-N-S 24-381-1762   (SL)
CREATIVE VISTAS ACQUISITION CORP
2100 Forbes St, Whitby, ON, L1N 9T3
(905) 666-8676
Emp Here 1,100   *Sales* 124,387,428
SIC 1731 Electrical work
Pr Dominic Burns

D-U-N-S 25-265-2276   (BR)
DURHAM CATHOLIC DISTRICT SCHOOL BOARD
ST PAUL CATHOLIC SCHOOL
200 Garrard Rd, Whitby, ON, L1N 3K6
(905) 728-7011
Emp Here 35
SIC 8211 Elementary and secondary schools

D-U-N-S 25-265-2110   (BR)
DURHAM CATHOLIC DISTRICT SCHOOL BOARD
ST JOHN EVANGELIST CATHOLIC SCHOOL
1103 Giffard St, Whitby, ON, L1N 2S3
(905) 668-4011
Emp Here 30
SIC 8211 Elementary and secondary schools

D-U-N-S 20-105-9388   (BR)
DURHAM COLLEGE OF APPLIED ARTS AND TECHNOLOGY
GM PRO
1610 Champlain Ave Suite 155, Whitby, ON, L1N 6A7
(905) 721-3311
Emp Here 20
SIC 8222 Junior colleges

D-U-N-S 20-087-0215   (BR)
DURHAM DISTRICT SCHOOL BOARD
LESLIE   MCFARLANE   ELEMENTARY SCHOOL
300 Garden St, Whitby, ON, L1N 3W4
(905) 668-2225
Emp Here 30
SIC 8211 Elementary and secondary schools

D-U-N-S 20-087-0207   (BR)
DURHAM DISTRICT SCHOOL BOARD
ANDERSON COLLEGIATE VOCATIONAL INSTITUTE
400 Anderson St, Whitby, ON, L1N 3V6
(905) 668-5809
Emp Here 93
SIC 8211 Elementary and secondary schools

D-U-N-S 25-300-7777   (BR)
DURHAM DISTRICT SCHOOL BOARD
DR ROBERT THORNTON PUBLIC SCHOOL
101 Hazelwood Dr, Whitby, ON, L1N 3L4
(905) 723-9912
Emp Here 40
SIC 8211 Elementary and secondary schools

D-U-N-S 20-086-7245   (BR)
DURHAM DISTRICT SCHOOL BOARD
C E BROUGHTON PUBLIC SCHOOL
80 Crawforth St, Whitby, ON, L1N 9L6
(905) 665-8229
Emp Here 36
SIC 8211 Elementary and secondary schools

D-U-N-S 25-300-7876   (BR)
DURHAM DISTRICT SCHOOL BOARD
PRINGLE CREEK PUBLIC SCHOOL
80 Ribblesdale Dr, Whitby, ON, L1N 8M1
(905) 430-2488
Emp Here 33
SIC 8211 Elementary and secondary schools

D-U-N-S 25-301-7107   (BR)
DURHAM DISTRICT SCHOOL BOARD
WEST LYNDE PUBLIC SCHOOL
270 Michael Blvd, Whitby, ON, L1N 6B1
(905) 668-3354
Emp Here 32
SIC 8211 Elementary and secondary schools

D-U-N-S 25-300-8288   (BR)
DURHAM DISTRICT SCHOOL BOARD
HENRY STREET HIGH SCHOOL
600 Henry St, Whitby, ON, L1N 5C7
(905) 666-5500
Emp Here 120
SIC 8211 Elementary and secondary schools

D-U-N-S 25-300-7827   (BR)
DURHAM DISTRICT SCHOOL BOARD
R. A. SENNETT PUBLIC SCHOOL
300 King St, Whitby, ON, L1N 4Z4

Emp Here 26
SIC 8211 Elementary and secondary schools

D-U-N-S 25-091-9359   (BR)
EMPIRE THEATRES LIMITED
EMPIRE THEATERS WHITBY
75 Consumers Dr, Whitby, ON, L1N 9S2
(905) 665-7210
Emp Here 30
SIC 7832 Motion picture theaters, except drive-in

D-U-N-S 20-554-6737   (SL)
EWING INTERNATIONAL INC
1445 Hopkins St, Whitby, ON, L1N 2C2
(416) 291-1675
Emp Here 50   *Sales* 2,480,664
SIC 3463 Nonferrous forgings

D-U-N-S 24-340-0798   (BR)
FGL SPORTS LTD
NATIONAL SPORTS
1650 Victoria St E Suite 1, Whitby, ON, L1N 9L4
(905) 571-4500
Emp Here 20
SIC 5941 Sporting goods and bicycle shops

D-U-N-S 24-736-0837   (BR)
FISHER SCIENTIFIC COMPANY
(*Suby of* Thermo Fisher Scientific Inc.)
111 Scotia Crt, Whitby, ON, L1N 6J6
(905) 725-7341
Emp Here 90

SIC 5049 Professional equipment, nec

D-U-N-S 20-852-4892   (HQ)
GERDAU AMERISTEEL CORPORATION
GERDAU AMERISTEEL METALS RECY-CLING
1801 Hopkins St, Whitby, ON, L1N 5T1
(905) 668-3535
Emp Here 500   *Emp Total* 4,800
Sales 525,317,040
SIC 3312 Blast furnaces and steel mills
Pr Pr Mario Longhi
 Phillip E Casey
Dir Joseph J Heffernan
VP VP Andre Gerdau Johannpeter
Dir Jorge Gerdau Johannpeter
Dir J Spencer Lanthier
Dir Arthur Scace
Dir Frederico C Gerdau Johannpeter
Dir Richard Mccoy
Dir Claudio Gerdau Johannpeter

D-U-N-S 24-885-9423   (BR)
GLASVAN TRAILERS INC
1025 Hopkins St, Whitby, L1N 2C2
(905) 430-1262
Emp Here 20
SIC 7539 Automotive repair shops, nec

D-U-N-S 24-889-6623   (BR)
GOLDER ASSOCIATES LTD
2001 Thickson Rd S, Whitby, L1N 6J3
(905) 723-2727
Emp Here 50
SIC 8741 Management services

D-U-N-S 20-999-4800   (BR)
GOLF TOWN LIMITED
GOLF TOWN
1635 Victoria St E Unit A14, Whitby, ON, L1N 9W4
(905) 579-7486
Emp Here 20
SIC 5941 Sporting goods and bicycle shops

D-U-N-S 24-348-5377   (BR)
GOVERNMENT OF ONTARIO
BYRON STREET ACADEMY
142 Byron St N, Whitby, ON, L1N 4M9
(905) 430-0818
Emp Here 20
SIC 8351 Child day care services

D-U-N-S 24-374-4252   (BR)
GROUND EFFECTS LTD
920 Champlain Crt Suite 7, Whitby, ON, L1N 6K9

Emp Here 20
SIC 3714 Motor vehicle parts and accessories

D-U-N-S 20-353-2007   (BR)
GROUND EFFECTS LTD
300 Water St, Whitby, ON, L1N 9B6
(519) 919-1751
Emp Here 50
SIC 3714 Motor vehicle parts and accessories

D-U-N-S 25-664-2109   (BR)
HOME DEPOT OF CANADA INC
HOME DEPOT
(*Suby of* The Home Depot Inc)
1700 Victoria St E, Whitby, ON, L1N 9K6
(905) 571-5900
Emp Here 225
SIC 5251 Hardware stores

D-U-N-S 20-698-6379   (BR)
HUDSON'S BAY COMPANY
HOME OUTFITTERS
1650 Victoria St E, Whitby, ON, L1N 9L4

Emp Here 30
SIC 5311 Department stores

D-U-N-S 24-874-8824   (BR)
INNVEST PROPERTIES CORP
QUALITY SUITES

(*Suby of* Innvest Properties Corp)
1700 Champlain Ave, Whitby, ON, L1N 6A7
(905) 432-8800
Emp Here 30
SIC 7011 Hotels and motels

D-U-N-S 24-421-4982   (SL)
INTEVA PRODUCTS CANADA, ULC
INTEVA OSHAWA PLANT
(*Suby of* The Renco Group Inc)
1555 Wentworth St, Whitby, L1N 9T6
(905) 666-4600
Emp Here 120   *Sales* 10,221,762
SIC 7532 Top and body repair and paint shops
Manager Robert Cooper

D-U-N-S 25-315-8877   (BR)
INVESTORS GROUP FINANCIAL SER-VICES INC
1614 Dundas St E Unit 111, Whitby, ON, L1N 8Y8
(905) 434-8400
Emp Here 129
SIC 8741 Management services

D-U-N-S 20-170-5100   (SL)
J. H. MCNAIRN LIMITED
MCNAIRN PACKAGING
(*Suby of* McNairn Packaging, Inc.)
125 Consumers Dr, Whitby, ON, L1N 1C4
(905) 668-7533
Emp Here 180   *Sales* 35,689,541
SIC 2671 Paper; coated and laminated pack-aging
Pr Pr Kenneth W A Miller
Sr VP Dennis E Czosnek

D-U-N-S 24-381-2216   (SL)
JCIM WHITBY
185 William Smith Dr, Whitby, L1N 0A3
(905) 665-3902
Emp Here 200   *Sales* 18,469,648
SIC 3465 Automotive stampings
Fin Ex Catherine Walker

D-U-N-S 24-762-4872   (BR)
JOHNSON INC
500 Brock St S, Whitby, L1N 4K7
(905) 668-6025
Emp Here 32
SIC 6411 Insurance agents, brokers, and ser-vice

D-U-N-S 24-872-4981   (SL)
KEYSCAN INC
901 Burns St E, Whitby, L1N 0E6
(905) 430-7226
Emp Here 55   *Sales* 4,231,721
SIC 3625 Relays and industrial controls

D-U-N-S 25-709-7915   (SL)
LAARK ENTERPRISES LIMITED
TIM HORTONS
516 Brock St N, Whitby, ON, L1N 4J2
(905) 430-3703
Emp Here 50   *Sales* 1,678,096
SIC 5461 Retail bakeries

D-U-N-S 20-920-8263   (BR)
LAKERIDGE HEALTH
LAKERIDGE HEALTH WHITBY
(*Suby of* Lakeridge Health)
300 Gordon St Suite 779, Whitby, ON, L1N 5T2
(905) 668-6831
Emp Here 250
SIC 8069 Specialty hospitals, except psychi-atric

D-U-N-S 20-999-7860   (BR)
LEON'S FURNITURE LIMITED
1500 Victoria St E, Whitby, ON, L1N 9M3
(905) 430-9050
Emp Here 20
SIC 5712 Furniture stores

D-U-N-S 25-317-6150   (BR)
LIQUOR CONTROL BOARD OF ONTARIO,

THE
LCBO
2000 Boundary Rd, Whitby, ON, L1N 7G4
(905) 723-3417
Emp Here 300
SIC 5921 Liquor stores

D-U-N-S 20-774-4447   (BR)
LOBLAWS INC
REAL CANADIAN WHOLESALE CLUB
400 Glen Hill Dr Suite 211, Whitby, ON, L1N 7R6
(905) 668-2514
Emp Here 55
SIC 5141 Groceries, general line

D-U-N-S 20-106-4073   (BR)
LOBLAWS SUPERMARKETS LIMITED
NO FRILLS
303 Brock St S, Whitby, ON, L1N 4K3
(905) 668-5940
Emp Here 23
SIC 5411 Grocery stores

D-U-N-S 24-967-3125   (BR)
LONE STAR GROUP OF COMPANIES LIM-ITED
75 Consumers Dr, Whitby, ON, L1N 9S2
(905) 665-3077
Emp Here 65
SIC 5812 Eating places

D-U-N-S 20-848-6084   (HQ)
MAKITA CANADA INC
1950 Forbes St, Whitby, ON, L1N 7B7
(905) 571-2200
Emp Here 98   *Emp Total* 15,261
Sales 40,973,672
SIC 5072 Hardware
Pr Pr Hideyuki Terajima
 Shiro Hori

D-U-N-S 24-333-1670   (BR)
METRO ONTARIO INC
METRO
70 Thickson Rd S, Whitby, L1N 7T2
(905) 668-5334
Emp Here 100
SIC 5411 Grocery stores

D-U-N-S 24-187-8987   (BR)
METRO ONTARIO INC
FOOD BASICS
601 Dundas St W, Whitby, ON, L1N 2N3

Emp Here 50
SIC 5411 Grocery stores

D-U-N-S 25-214-7996   (SL)
MULTI-PLASTICS CANADA CO
55 Moore Crt, Whitby, ON, L1N 9Z8
(905) 430-7511
Emp Here 39   *Sales* 12,861,440
SIC 5162 Plastics materials and basic shapes
Pr Pr John Parsio
Genl Mgr Doug Caillier
Off Mgr Lynn Begley

D-U-N-S 25-404-0181   (BR)
ONTARIO POWER GENERATION INC
O P G
1549 Victoria St E, Whitby, ON, L1N 9E3
(905) 430-2215
Emp Here 65
SIC 4911 Electric services

D-U-N-S 20-547-5333   (BR)
PATHEON INC
111 Consumers Dr, Whitby, ON, L1N 5Z5
(905) 668-3368
Emp Here 500
SIC 2834 Pharmaceutical preparations

D-U-N-S 25-574-1597   (BR)
PETERBILT OF ONTARIO INC
1311 Hopkins St, Whitby, ON, L1N 2C2
(905) 665-8888
Emp Here 29

SIC 5511 New and used car dealers

D-U-N-S 25-174-0874   (BR)
PIONEER FAST FOODS INC
WENDY'S RESTAURANTS
(*Suby of* Pioneer Fast Foods Inc)
1601 Champlain Ave, Whitby, ON, L1N 9M1
(905) 432-9866
Emp Here 35
SIC 5812 Eating places

D-U-N-S 25-707-5812   (BR)
PIONEER FOOD SERVICES LIMITED
TIM HORTONS
(*Suby of* Pioneer Food Services Limited)
1 Paisley Crt Suite 1076, Whitby, ON, L1N 9L2
(905) 665-1206
Emp Here 42
SIC 5461 Retail bakeries

D-U-N-S 20-122-7449   (BR)
PRINCESS AUTO LTD
1550 Victoria St E, Whitby, ON, L1N 9W7
(905) 665-8581
Emp Here 40
SIC 5085 Industrial supplies

D-U-N-S 24-719-2529   (SL)
PRINGLES, MELANIE RESTAURANT LTD
80 Thickson Rd S, Whitby, ON, L1N 7T2
(905) 430-1959
Emp Here 60   *Sales* 1,824,018
SIC 5812 Eating places

D-U-N-S 24-611-3765   (SL)
PROMOTIONAL PRODUCTS FULFILL-MENT & DISTRIBUTION LTD
PPFD
80 William Smith Dr, Whitby, ON, L1N 9W1
(905) 668-5060
Emp Here 60   *Sales* 3,064,349
SIC 7389 Business services, nec

D-U-N-S 25-634-3260   (BR)
R M R REAL ESTATE LIMITED
COLDWELL BANKER
10 Sunray St Suite 23, Whitby, ON, L1N 9B5
(905) 430-6655
Emp Here 30
SIC 6531 Real estate agents and managers

D-U-N-S 25-192-2910   (BR)
RPM CANADA
STONCOR GROUP
(*Suby of* RPM International Inc.)
95 Sunray St, Whitby, ON, L1N 9C9
(905) 430-3333
Emp Here 40
SIC 5023 Homefurnishings

D-U-N-S 24-387-2087   (HQ)
RPM CANADA COMPANY
RPM CANADA
(*Suby of* RPM International Inc.)
95 Sunray St, Whitby, ON, L1N 9C9
(905) 430-3333
Emp Here 450   *Emp Total* 14,318
Sales 136,001,407
SIC 2851 Paints and allied products
Rgnl Mgr Tim Stover
 Frank C. Sullivan
 Keith R. Smiley
 P. Kelly Tomkins

D-U-N-S 25-882-8292   (BR)
REDBERRY FRANCHISING CORP
BURGER KING
1650 Victoria St E, Whitby, ON, L1N 9L4
(905) 436-6556
Emp Here 30
SIC 5812 Eating places

D-U-N-S 25-527-7410   (SL)
ROGERS, JOHN C. SHEET METAL LTD
2300 Forbes St, Whitby, ON, L1N 8M3
(905) 571-2422
Emp Here 50   *Sales* 4,377,642
SIC 1711 Plumbing, heating, air-conditioning

▲ Public Company   ■ Public Company Family Member   **HQ** Headquarters   **BR** Branch   **SL** Single Location

D-U-N-S 25-695-3316   (BR)
ROYAL BANK OF CANADA
RBC
(*Suby of* Royal Bank Of Canada)
307 Brock St S, Whitby, ON, L1N 4K3
(905) 665-7200
Emp Here 25
SIC 6021 National commercial banks

D-U-N-S 24-364-5269   (BR)
SIR CORP
JACK ASTOR'S BAR AND GRILL
75 Consumers Dr Unit E1, Whitby, ON, L1N 9S2
(905) 666-9429
Emp Here 50
SIC 5812 Eating places

D-U-N-S 25-634-3963   (BR)
SAINT ELIZABETH HEALTH CARE
420 Green St Suite 202, Whitby, ON, L1N 8R1
(905) 430-6997
Emp Here 150
SIC 8361 Residential care

D-U-N-S 24-607-0838   (BR)
SOBEYS CAPITAL INCORPORATED
SOBEYS
1615 Dundas St E, Whitby, ON, L1N 2L1
(905) 435-0780
Emp Here 100
SIC 5411 Grocery stores

D-U-N-S 25-693-2146   (BR)
SOBEYS CAPITAL INCORPORATED
FRESHCO
350 Brock St S, Whitby, ON, L1N 4K4
(905) 666-1691
Emp Here 55
SIC 5411 Grocery stores

D-U-N-S 20-179-7425   (BR)
SOBEYS CAPITAL INCORPORATED
SOBEYS WHITBY
100 Nordeagle Ave, Whitby, ON, L1N 9S1
(905) 665-9318
Emp Here 600
SIC 4225 General warehousing and storage

D-U-N-S 24-744-2734   (BR)
SONY OF CANADA LTD
1602 Tricont Ave, Whitby, ON, L1N 7C3

Emp Here 130
SIC 5065 Electronic parts and equipment, nec

D-U-N-S 24-212-7017   (BR)
SWISH MAINTENANCE LIMITED
500 Hopkins St, Whitby, ON, L1N 2B9
(905) 666-1224
Emp Here 45
SIC 5087 Service establishment equipment

D-U-N-S 25-528-8771   (BR)
TST SOLUTIONS L.P.
TST AUTOMOTIVE SERVICES
1601 Tricont Ave, Whitby, ON, L1N 7N5

Emp Here 150
SIC 4225 General warehousing and storage

D-U-N-S 24-805-5589   (BR)
THE PIC GROUP LTD
202 South Blair St Unit 12, Whitby, ON, L1N 8X9
(416) 676-5659
Emp Here 140
SIC 4225 General warehousing and storage

D-U-N-S 20-641-3965   (SL)
THICKSON ROAD INVESTMENTS LIMITED
718 Centre St N, Whitby, ON, L1N 9A9

Emp Here 250   *Sales* 10,449,350
SIC 5812 Eating places
Pr Pr Raymond J Gilchrist

D-U-N-S 25-297-8036   (BR)

TOYS 'R' US (CANADA) LTD
TOYS 'R' US
(*Suby of* Toys "r" Us, Inc.)
50 Thickson Rd S, Whitby, ON, L1N 7T2
(905) 668-2090
Emp Here 50
SIC 5945 Hobby, toy, and game shops

D-U-N-S 20-769-8226   (SL)
TRAFALGAR CASTLE SCHOOL
401 Reynolds St, Whitby, ON, L1N 3W9
(905) 668-3358
Emp Here 53   *Sales* 3,575,074
SIC 8211 Elementary and secondary schools

D-U-N-S 25-174-3993   (BR)
VALUE VILLAGE STORES, INC
VVS
(*Suby of* Savers, Inc.)
1801 Dundas St E, Whitby, ON, L1N 7C5
(905) 571-4977
Emp Here 39
SIC 5399 Miscellaneous general merchandise

D-U-N-S 24-826-9602   (BR)
VENTRA GROUP CO
VENTRA OSHAWA SPD, DIV OF
200 Montecorte St, Whitby, ON, L1N 9V8

Emp Here 80
SIC 3714 Motor vehicle parts and accessories

D-U-N-S 20-106-3414   (BR)
WINNERS MERCHANTS INTERNATIONAL L.P.
WINNERS
(*Suby of* The TJX Companies Inc)
1650 Victoria St E Unit 7, Whitby, ON, L1N 9L4
(905) 432-7732
Emp Here 35
SIC 5651 Family clothing stores

D-U-N-S 20-860-4418   (BR)
WINNERS MERCHANTS INTERNATIONAL L.P.
HOMESENSE
(*Suby of* The TJX Companies Inc)
1650 Victoria St E Unit 3, Whitby, ON, L1N 9L4
(905) 433-4588
Emp Here 25
SIC 5651 Family clothing stores

D-U-N-S 24-720-2609   (BR)
WOODBRIDGE FOAM CORPORATION
WOODBRIDGE GROUP, THE
1999 Forbes St, Whitby, ON, L1N 7V4
(905) 434-8473
Emp Here 150
SIC 3086 Plastics foam products

Whitby, ON L1P

D-U-N-S 25-641-1877   (SL)
COMMUNITY ADVANTAGE REHABILITATION INC
C A R
965 Dundas St W Suite 201a, Whitby, ON, L1P 1G8
(905) 666-2540
Emp Here 49   *Sales* 1,824,018
SIC 8361 Residential care

D-U-N-S 24-031-0586   (BR)
DURHAM CATHOLIC DISTRICT SCHOOL BOARD
ST. LUKE THE EVANGELIST CATHOLIC SCHOOL
55 Twin Streams Rd, Whitby, ON, L1P 1N9
(905) 665-5828
Emp Here 50
SIC 8211 Elementary and secondary schools

D-U-N-S 20-711-3817   (BR)
DURHAM CATHOLIC DISTRICT SCHOOL BOARD

ALL SAINT CATHOLIC SECONDARY SCHOOL
3001 Country Lane, Whitby, ON, L1P 1M1
(905) 666-7753
Emp Here 135
SIC 8211 Elementary and secondary schools

D-U-N-S 20-646-5804   (BR)
DURHAM DISTRICT SCHOOL BOARD
DONALD A WILSON SECONDARY SCHOOL
681 Rossland Rd W, Whitby, ON, L1P 1Y1
(905) 665-5057
Emp Here 120
SIC 8211 Elementary and secondary schools

D-U-N-S 20-591-0180   (BR)
DURHAM DISTRICT SCHOOL BOARD
CAPTAIN MICHAEL VANDENBOS PUBLIC SCHOOL
3121 Country Lane, Whitby, ON, L1P 1N3
(905) 665-2001
Emp Here 60
SIC 8211 Elementary and secondary schools

D-U-N-S 20-711-3528   (BR)
DURHAM DISTRICT SCHOOL BOARD
COLONEL J.E. FAREWELL PUBLIC SCHOOL
810 Mcquay Blvd, Whitby, ON, L1P 1J1
(905) 666-3901
Emp Here 50
SIC 8211 Elementary and secondary schools

D-U-N-S 24-029-9003   (BR)
DURHAM DISTRICT SCHOOL BOARD
WILLIAMSBURG PUBLIC SCHOOL
20 Kirkland Pl, Whitby, ON, L1P 1W7
(905) 668-6613
Emp Here 28
SIC 8211 Elementary and secondary schools

D-U-N-S 24-000-7810   (BR)
SHERIDAN NURSERIES LIMITED
SHERIDAN NURSERIES
410 Taunton Rd W, Whitby, ON, L1P 2A9
(905) 686-0844
Emp Here 20
SIC 5261 Retail nurseries and garden stores

Whitby, ON L1R

D-U-N-S 24-002-4971   (SL)
1608296 ONTARIO LIMITED
EAST SIDE MARIO'S
4170 Baldwin St S, Whitby, ON, L1R 3H8
(905) 655-2075
Emp Here 50   *Sales* 1,532,175
SIC 5812 Eating places

D-U-N-S 20-010-7717   (SL)
AINSWORTH MANAGEMENT SERVICES INC
SERVICEMASTER OF DURHAM CONTRACT SERVICES
56 Carlinds Dr, Whitby, ON, L1R 3B9
(905) 666-9156
Emp Here 100   *Sales* 3,769,316
SIC 7349 Building maintenance services, nec

D-U-N-S 20-536-9791   (BR)
BANK OF MONTREAL
BMO
3960 Brock St N, Whitby, ON, L1R 3E1
(905) 665-2740
Emp Here 20
SIC 6021 National commercial banks

D-U-N-S 20-711-7545   (BR)
CONSEIL SCOLAIRE DE DISTRICT CATHOLIQUE CENTRE-SUD
ST CHARLES GARNIER SCHOOL
4101 Baldwin St S, Whitby, ON, L1R 2W6
(905) 655-5635
Emp Here 50

SIC 8211 Elementary and secondary schools

D-U-N-S 20-086-9399   (BR)
CORPORATION OF THE REGIONAL MUNICIPALITY OF DURHAM, THE
MAINTENANCE DEPOT
825 Conlin Rd, Whitby, ON, L1R 3K3
(905) 655-5344
Emp Here 100
SIC 1611 Highway and street construction

D-U-N-S 20-015-4982   (BR)
DURHAM CATHOLIC DISTRICT SCHOOL BOARD
FATHER LEO J AUSTIN
1020 Dryden Blvd, Whitby, ON, L1R 2A2
(905) 666-2010
Emp Here 200
SIC 8211 Elementary and secondary schools

D-U-N-S 25-938-0764   (BR)
DURHAM CATHOLIC DISTRICT SCHOOL BOARD
ST MATTHEW EVANGELIST CATHOLIC SCHOOL
60 Willowbrook Dr, Whitby, ON, L1R 2A8
(905) 430-8597
Emp Here 40
SIC 8211 Elementary and secondary schools

D-U-N-S 20-711-3718   (BR)
DURHAM CATHOLIC DISTRICT SCHOOL BOARD
ST. BERNARD CATHOLIC SCHOOL
1000 Dryden Blvd, Whitby, ON, L1R 2A2
(905) 668-3772
Emp Here 38
SIC 8211 Elementary and secondary schools

D-U-N-S 25-300-7520   (BR)
DURHAM DISTRICT SCHOOL BOARD
GLEN DHU PUBLIC SCHOOL
29 Fallingbrook St, Whitby, ON, L1R 1M7
(905) 668-8779
Emp Here 40
SIC 8211 Elementary and secondary schools

D-U-N-S 20-711-3577   (BR)
DURHAM DISTRICT SCHOOL BOARD
JACK MINER PUBLIC SCHOOL
144 Whitburn St, Whitby, ON, L1R 2N1
(905) 668-3249
Emp Here 50
SIC 8211 Elementary and secondary schools

D-U-N-S 25-300-7959   (BR)
DURHAM DISTRICT SCHOOL BOARD
ORMISTON PUBLIC SCHOOL
20 Forest Heights St, Whitby, ON, L1R 1T5
(905) 430-8755
Emp Here 27
SIC 8211 Elementary and secondary schools

D-U-N-S 25-300-8270   (BR)
DURHAM DISTRICT SCHOOL BOARD
JOHN DRYDEN PUBLIC SCHOOL
40 Rolling Acres Dr, Whitby, ON, L1R 2A1
(905) 434-7400
Emp Here 65
SIC 8211 Elementary and secondary schools

D-U-N-S 25-265-1971   (BR)
DURHAM DISTRICT SCHOOL BOARD
UXBRIDGE SECONDARY SCHOOL
400 Taunton Rd E, Whitby, ON, L1R 2K6
(905) 666-5500
Emp Here 60
SIC 8211 Elementary and secondary schools

D-U-N-S 20-653-8014   (BR)
DURHAM DISTRICT SCHOOL BOARD
55 Bakerville St, Whitby, ON, L1R 2S6
(905) 723-2944
Emp Here 40
SIC 8211 Elementary and secondary schools

D-U-N-S 20-591-0172   (BR)
DURHAM DISTRICT SCHOOL BOARD

FALLING BROOK PUBLIC SCHOOL
155 Fallingbrook St, Whitby, ON, L1R 2G2
(905) 668-5211
Emp Here 25
SIC 8211 Elementary and secondary schools

D-U-N-S 24-977-2042   (BR)
FGL SPORTS LTD
SPORT CHEK WHITBY
320 Taunton Rd E, Whitby, ON, L1R 0H4
(905) 655-9195
Emp Here 20
SIC 5941 Sporting goods and bicycle shops

D-U-N-S 24-251-2072   (BR)
H&R DEVELOPMENTS
TAUNTON WOODS ESTATES
(Suby of H&R Developments)
26 Puttingedge Dr, Whitby, ON, L1R 0H7

Emp Here 20
SIC 1522 Residential construction, nec

D-U-N-S 24-175-6217   (BR)
HOME DEPOT OF CANADA INC
(Suby of The Home Depot Inc)
4200 Garden St, Whitby, ON, L1R 3K5
(905) 655-2900
Emp Here 50
SIC 5251 Hardware stores

D-U-N-S 24-794-2589   (BR)
KUMON CANADA INC
KUMON NORTH WHITBY
3500 Brock St N Unit 5b, Whitby, ON, L1R 3J4
(905) 430-2006
Emp Here 20
SIC 8299 Schools and educational services, nec

D-U-N-S 24-383-8807   (BR)
LOBLAWS INC
REAL CANADIAN SUPERSTORE
200 Taunton Rd W Suite 1058, Whitby, ON, L1R 3H8
(905) 665-1164
Emp Here 150
SIC 5411 Grocery stores

D-U-N-S 25-709-4417   (BR)
LOBLAWS SUPERMARKETS LIMITED
LA ROSA'S NOFRILLS
3100 Garden St Unit 2, Whitby, ON, L1R 2G8
(866) 987-6453
Emp Here 220
SIC 5411 Grocery stores

D-U-N-S 24-858-2780   (BR)
LOWE'S COMPANIES CANADA, ULC
4005 Garrard Rd, Whitby, ON, L1R 0J1
(905) 433-2870
Emp Here 150
SIC 5211 Lumber and other building materials

D-U-N-S 24-335-0464   (BR)
METRO ONTARIO INC
METRO
4111 Thickson Rd N, Whitby, ON, L1R 2X3
(905) 655-1553
Emp Here 200
SIC 5411 Grocery stores

D-U-N-S 25-116-7706   (BR)
MILLER PAVING LIMITED
4615 Thickson Rd N, Whitby, ON, L1R 2X2
(905) 655-3889
Emp Here 60
SIC 1611 Highway and street construction

D-U-N-S 24-329-6980   (BR)
WAL-MART CANADA CORP
4100 Baldwin St S, Whitby, ON, L1R 3H8
(905) 655-0206
Emp Here 200
SIC 5311 Department stores

White River, ON P0M
Algoma County

D-U-N-S 24-162-2468   (BR)
ROYAL CANADIAN LEGION, THE
(Suby of Royal Canadian Legion, The)
108 Winnipeg St N, White River, ON, P0M 3G0
(807) 822-2480
Emp Here 40
SIC 7389 Business services, nec

Whitefish, ON P0M
Sudbury County

D-U-N-S 20-411-9481   (HQ)
DUHAMEL AND DEWAR INC
LEGEND BOATS
(Suby of Duhamel and Dewar Inc)
4805 Regional Road 55 Rr 1, Whitefish, ON, P0M 3E0
(705) 866-2821
Emp Here 40   Emp Total 50
Sales 3,957,782
SIC 3732 Boatbuilding and repairing

Whitney, ON K0J
Nipissing County

D-U-N-S 20-719-1529   (SL)
COUPLES RESORT INC
BEAR TRAIL
Gd, Whitney, ON, K0J 2M0
(613) 637-1179
Emp Here 75   Sales 3,283,232
SIC 7011 Hotels and motels

D-U-N-S 20-571-0275   (BR)
GOVERNMENT OF ONTARIO
ALGONQUIS PARK
Gd, Whitney, ON, K0J 2M0
(613) 637-2780
Emp Here 20
SIC 7033 Trailer parks and campsites

D-U-N-S 20-183-3746   (SL)
MCRAE LUMBER COMPANY LIMITED
MCRAE MILLS
160 Haycreek Rd, Whitney, ON, K0J 2M0
(613) 637-2190
Emp Here 70   Sales 9,840,650
SIC 2411 Logging
John Mcrae
Robert Mcrae

D-U-N-S 24-525-7394   (BR)
RENFREW COUNTY DISTRICT SCHOOL BOARD
WHITNEY PUBLIC SCHOOL
60 Hwy, Whitney, ON, K0J 2M0
(613) 637-2171
Emp Here 25
SIC 8211 Elementary and secondary schools

D-U-N-S 25-228-0508   (BR)
RENFREW COUNTY DISTRICT SCHOOL BOARD
MADAWASKA PUBLIC SCHOOL
25272 60 Hwy, Whitney, ON, K0J 2C0

Emp Here 50
SIC 8211 Elementary and secondary schools

Wiarton, ON N0H
Bruce County

D-U-N-S 25-350-0672   (BR)
CORPORATION OF THE COUNTY OF

BRUCE, THE
GATEWAY HAVEN
671 Frank St, Wiarton, ON, N0H 2T0
(519) 534-1113
Emp Here 95
SIC 8051 Skilled nursing care facilities

D-U-N-S 20-039-7482   (BR)
GREY BRUCE HEALTH SERVICES
WIARTON SITE
369 Mary St Suite 202, Wiarton, ON, N0H 2T0
(519) 534-1260
Emp Here 50
SIC 8062 General medical and surgical hospitals

Wikwemikong, ON P0P
Manitoulin County

D-U-N-S 20-939-3891   (SL)
WIKWEMIKONG NURSING HOME LTD
2281 Wikwemikong Way, Wikwemikong, ON, P0P 2J0
(705) 859-3361
Emp Here 60   Sales 2,699,546
SIC 8051 Skilled nursing care facilities

Williamstown, ON K0C
Glengarry County

D-U-N-S 25-225-0501   (BR)
CATHOLIC DISTRICT SCHOOL BOARD OF EASTERN ONTARIO
IONA ACADEMY CATHOLIC SCHOOL
(Suby of Catholic District School Board of Eastern Ontario)
20019 Kings Rd, Williamstown, ON, K0C 2J0
(613) 347-3518
Emp Here 20
SIC 8211 Elementary and secondary schools

D-U-N-S 20-590-6295   (BR)
UPPER CANADA DISTRICT SCHOOL BOARD, THE
WILLIAMSTOWN PUBLIC SCHOOL
19754 County Rd 17 Rr 1, Williamstown, ON, K0C 2J0
(613) 347-3461
Emp Here 35
SIC 8211 Elementary and secondary schools

D-U-N-S 20-125-9467   (BR)
UPPER CANADA DISTRICT SCHOOL BOARD, THE
CHAR-LAN DISTRICT HIGH SCHOOL
19743 John St, Williamstown, ON, K0C 2J0
(613) 347-2441
Emp Here 40
SIC 8211 Elementary and secondary schools

Winchester, ON K0C
Dundas County

D-U-N-S 24-104-1540   (SL)
DUNDAS MANOR LTD
533 Clarence St Suite 970, Winchester, ON, K0C 2K0
(613) 774-2293
Emp Here 104   Sales 4,742,446
SIC 8051 Skilled nursing care facilities

D-U-N-S 20-799-6740   (BR)
HYDRO ONE INC
636 St Lawrence St, Winchester, ON, K0C 2K0
(613) 774-4120
Emp Here 20
SIC 4911 Electric services

D-U-N-S 24-002-6265   (BR)
IDEAL PIPE
ADS CANNADA
691 St Lawrence, Winchester, ON, K0C 2K0
(613) 774-2662
Emp Here 20
SIC 3498 Fabricated pipe and fittings

D-U-N-S 24-966-1539   (SL)
WINCHESTER DISTRICT MEMORIAL HOSPITAL
566 Louise St Rr 4, Winchester, ON, K0C 2K0
(613) 774-2420
Emp Here 280   Sales 26,208,720
SIC 8062 General medical and surgical hospitals
Trudy Reid
Michelle Blouin
Lynn Hall
Peter Sorby

Windermere, ON P0B
Muskoka County

D-U-N-S 24-035-8585   (SL)
1090769 ONTARIO INC
2508 Windermere Rd, Windermere, ON, P0B 1P0
(705) 769-3611
Emp Here 107   Sales 4,669,485
SIC 7011 Hotels and motels

Windsor, ON N0R
Essex County

D-U-N-S 20-186-7769   (SL)
WINDSOR PALLET LIMITED
2890 N Talbot, Windsor, ON, N0R 1K0
(519) 737-1406
Emp Here 38   Sales 7,369,031
SIC 5085 Industrial supplies
Pr Pr Louis Calsavara Jr

Windsor, ON N8N
Essex County

D-U-N-S 25-638-0205   (SL)
1109131 ONTARIO INC
CLASSIC BINGO III
13300 Desro Dr, Windsor, ON, N8N 2L9
(519) 979-7999
Emp Here 160   Sales 12,072,550
SIC 7999 Amusement and recreation, nec
Pr Pr Michael Duval

D-U-N-S 20-750-6668   (SL)
1230839 ONTARIO LIMITED
BROUILLETTE MANOR
11900 Brouillette Crt, Windsor, ON, N8N 4X8
(519) 735-9810
Emp Here 60   Sales 2,699,546
SIC 8051 Skilled nursing care facilities

D-U-N-S 25-189-8149   (BR)
AMEC FOSTER WHEELER INC
11865 County Rd 42, Windsor, ON, N8N 2M1
(519) 735-2499
Emp Here 30
SIC 8741 Management services

D-U-N-S 20-002-8004   (BR)
BANQUE TORONTO-DOMINION, LA
TORONTO-DOMINION BANK, THE
(Suby of Toronto-Dominion Bank, The)
13300 Tecumseh Rd E, Windsor, ON, N8N 4R8
(519) 735-0010
Emp Here 35
SIC 6021 National commercial banks

D-U-N-S 20-849-3189   (SL)
BEACH GROVE GOLF AND COUNTRY CLUB LIMITED
BEACH GROVE GOLF AND COUNTRY CLUB
14134 Riverside Dr E, Windsor, ON, N8N 1B6
(519) 979-8134
Emp Here 70   *Sales* 2,845,467
SIC 7997 Membership sports and recreation clubs

D-U-N-S 25-361-7773   (BR)
CAN ART ALUMINUM EXTRUSION INC
428 Jutras Dr S, Windsor, ON, N8N 5C5
(519) 272-4399
Emp Here 70
SIC 3354 Aluminum extruded products

D-U-N-S 20-583-0362   (BR)
CANADA POST CORPORATION
TECUMSEH POST OFFICE
11910 Tecumseh Rd E, Windsor, ON, N8N 0B9
(519) 735-9808
Emp Here 45
SIC 4311 U.s. postal service

D-U-N-S 20-180-8941   (SL)
COCO DEVELOPMENTS LTD
6725 South Service Rd E, Windsor, ON, N8N 2M1
(519) 948-7133
Emp Here 300   *Sales* 61,795,200
SIC 1521 Single-family housing construction
VP VP Jenny Coco
Mgr Phil Hong

D-U-N-S 24-034-6085   (BR)
COMMUNITY LIVING ESSEX COUNTY
ESSEX COUNTY ASSOCIATION FOR COMMUNITY LIVING
13158 Tecumseh Rd E, Windsor, ON, N8N 3T6
(519) 979-0057
Emp Here 600
SIC 8322 Individual and family services

D-U-N-S 24-745-4952   (HQ)
CONCORDE PRECISION MACHINING INC
CONCORD MACHINE TOOL, DIV OF
469 Silver Creek Industrial Dr, Windsor, ON, N8N 4W2
(519) 727-3287
Emp Here 50   *Emp Total* 280
Sales 13,570,690
SIC 3544 Special dies, tools, jigs, and fixtures
  Diane Reko

D-U-N-S 24-425-8492   (BR)
CONCORDE PRECISION MACHINING INC
CONCORDE MACHINE TOOL
481 Silver Creek Industrial Dr, Windsor, ON, N8N 4W2
(519) 727-5100
Emp Here 20
SIC 3599 Industrial machinery, nec

D-U-N-S 20-299-5820   (BR)
CONSEIL SCOLAIRE DE DISTRICT DES ECOLES CATHOLIQUES DU SUD-OUEST
STE MARGARET D'YOUVILLE
13025 St. Thomas St, Windsor, ON, N8N 3P3
(519) 735-5766
Emp Here 24
SIC 8211 Elementary and secondary schools

D-U-N-S 24-486-4542   (SL)
DIEFFENBACHER NORTH AMERICA INC
9495 Twin Oaks Dr, Windsor, ON, N8N 5B8
(519) 979-6937
Emp Here 60   *Sales* 7,796,259
SIC 3542 Machine tools, Metal forming type
Genl Mgr Colin Folco
Opers Mgr Heiko Heitlinger
Pr Pr Wolf-Gerd Dieffenbacher
  Peter Lynch

D-U-N-S 24-337-2963   (BR)

FGL SPORTS LTD
NATIONAL SPORTS
13580 Tecumseh Rd E, Windsor, ON, N8N 3N7
(519) 979-4855
Emp Here 20
SIC 5941 Sporting goods and bicycle shops

D-U-N-S 20-290-8054   (BR)
FOREST CITY FIRE PROTECTION LTD
13455 Sylvestre Dr, Windsor, ON, N8N 2L9
(519) 944-4774
Emp Here 23
SIC 1711 Plumbing, heating, air-conditioning

D-U-N-S 20-822-9559   (BR)
G&K SERVICES CANADA INC
(*Suby of* Cintas Corporation)
9085 Twin Oaks Dr, Windsor, ON, N8N 5B8
(519) 979-5913
Emp Here 115
SIC 7213 Linen supply

D-U-N-S 20-037-0265   (BR)
GREATER ESSEX COUNTY DISTRICT SCHOOL BOARD
VICTORIA PUBLIC ELEMENTARY SCHOOL
12433 Dillon Dr, Windsor, ON, N8N 1C1
(519) 735-4051
Emp Here 20
SIC 8211 Elementary and secondary schools

D-U-N-S 25-137-3270   (BR)
GREATER ESSEX COUNTY DISTRICT SCHOOL BOARD
A V GRAHAM SCHOOL
815 Brenda Cres, Windsor, ON, N8N 2G5
(519) 735-6260
Emp Here 40
SIC 8211 Elementary and secondary schools

D-U-N-S 20-286-5650   (BR)
HELIGEAR CANADA ACQUISITION CORPORATION
NORTHSTAR AEROSPACE (CANADA)
(*Suby of* Heligear Acquisition Co.)
204 East Pike Creek Rd, Windsor, ON, N8N 2L9
(519) 979-9400
Emp Here 70
SIC 3728 Aircraft parts and equipment, nec

D-U-N-S 24-383-8831   (BR)
HIRAM WALKER & SONS LIMITED
156 East Pike Creek Rd, Windsor, ON, N8N 2L9
(519) 735-9486
Emp Here 20
SIC 5182 Wine and distilled beverages

D-U-N-S 20-957-6672   (BR)
JAMIESON LABORATORIES LTD
9650 Twin Oaks Dr, Windsor, ON, N8N 5E7
(519) 979-5420
Emp Here 30
SIC 5122 Drugs, proprietaries, and sundries

D-U-N-S 25-829-5989   (HQ)
LATCH KEY DAYCARE & LEARNING CENTRE INC
(*Suby of* Latch Key Daycare & Learning Centre Inc)
13163 Tecumseh Rd E, Windsor, ON, N8N 3T4
(519) 979-4309
Emp Here 35   *Emp Total* 70
Sales 2,115,860
SIC 8351 Child day care services

D-U-N-S 20-113-4918   (BR)
LINAMAR CORPORATION
EXKOR MANUFACTURING
3590 Valtec Crt, Windsor, ON, N8N 5E6
(519) 739-3465
Emp Here 200
SIC 3714 Motor vehicle parts and accessories

D-U-N-S 20-186-1051   (SL)
MERCURY PRODUCTS CO.

(*Suby of* Mercury Products Corp.)
439 Jutras Dr S, Windsor, ON, N8N 5C4
(519) 727-4050
Emp Here 28   *Sales* 3,724,879
SIC 3469 Metal stampings, nec

D-U-N-S 24-333-1639   (BR)
METRO ONTARIO INC
METRO
11729 Tecumseh Rd E, Windsor, ON, N8N 1L8
(519) 979-9366
Emp Here 100
SIC 5411 Grocery stores

D-U-N-S 20-702-4675   (BR)
PALLET MANAGEMENT GROUP INC
5155 Rhodes Dr, Windsor, ON, N8N 2M1
(519) 974-6163
Emp Here 50
SIC 2448 Wood pallets and skids

D-U-N-S 24-989-6460   (SL)
POLYTECH CANADA INC
5505 Rhodes Dr, Windsor, ON, N8N 2M1

Emp Here 40   *Sales* 13,391,400
SIC 5169 Chemicals and allied products, nec
Pr Don Goodman

D-U-N-S 24-744-9788   (HQ)
RIVERVIEW STEEL CO. LTD
(*Suby of* Anobile Enterprises Corp)
8165 Anchor Dr, Windsor, ON, N8N 5B7
(519) 979-8255
Emp Here 40   *Emp Total* 1
Sales 16,926,882
SIC 5051 Metals service centers and offices
Pr Pr Michael Anobile
  Cheryl Anobile

D-U-N-S 24-557-4137   (BR)
SUN LIFE FINANCIAL TRUST INC
SUN LIFE WINDSOR ESSEX
8255 Anchor Dr, Windsor, ON, N8N 5G1
(519) 739-7777
Emp Here 40
SIC 6411 Insurance agents, brokers, and service

D-U-N-S 24-314-9635   (HQ)
TRW CANADA LIMITED
TRW AUTOMOTIVE
3355 Munich Crt, Windsor, ON, N8N 5G2
(519) 739-9861
Emp Here 50   *Emp Total* 3
Sales 12,184,437
SIC 5013 Motor vehicle supplies and new parts
Fin Ex Luke Razny
Pr Pr John C. Plant

D-U-N-S 20-793-2927   (BR)
UNITED PARCEL SERVICE CANADA LTD
UPS
5325 Rhodes Dr, Windsor, ON, N8N 2M1
(519) 251-7050
Emp Here 100
SIC 7389 Business services, nec

D-U-N-S 25-095-8154   (BR)
VALIANT MACHINE & TOOL INC
VALIANT TOOL & GAGE
9355 Anchor Dr, Windsor, ON, N8N 5A8
(519) 974-5200
Emp Here 75
SIC 3541 Machine tools, Metal cutting type

D-U-N-S 25-249-1758   (BR)
WINDSOR-ESSEX CATHOLIC DISTRICT SCHOOL BOARD, THE
ST GREGORY ELEMENTARY SCHOOL
13765 St. Gregory'S Rd, Windsor, ON, N8N 1K3
(519) 735-4583
Emp Here 40
SIC 8211 Elementary and secondary schools

Windsor, ON N8P
Essex County

D-U-N-S 20-642-2987   (SL)
SNR NURSING HOMES LTD
HERON TERRACE
11550 Mcnorton St, Windsor, ON, N8P 1T9
(519) 979-6730
Emp Here 180   *Sales* 6,566,463
SIC 8361 Residential care
Dir John Scotland

Windsor, ON N8R
Essex County

D-U-N-S 25-874-9902   (BR)
ASSOCIATION FOR PERSONS WITH PHYSICAL DISABILITIES WINDSOR ESSEX
A P P D
3185 Forest Glade Dr, Windsor, ON, N8R 1W7
(519) 979-1641
Emp Here 32
SIC 8322 Individual and family services

D-U-N-S 20-089-3134   (BR)
CORPORATION OF THE CITY OF WINDSOR
FOREST GLADE ARENA
(*Suby of* Corporation of the City of Windsor)
3205 Forest Glade Dr, Windsor, ON, N8R 1W7
(519) 735-7121
Emp Here 30
SIC 7999 Amusement and recreation, nec

D-U-N-S 25-669-4050   (SL)
EASTWAY SALES & LEASING INC
EASTWAY TOYOTA & LEXUS OF WINDSOR
9375 Tecumseh Rd E, Windsor, ON, N8R 1A1
(519) 979-1900
Emp Here 40   *Sales* 14,592,140
SIC 5511 New and used car dealers
Pr Pr Talal (Terry) Rafih

D-U-N-S 20-710-5730   (BR)
GREATER ESSEX COUNTY DISTRICT SCHOOL BOARD
FORTH LANE PUBLIC SCHOOL
9485 Esplanade Dr, Windsor, ON, N8R 1J5
(519) 735-3113
Emp Here 60
SIC 8211 Elementary and secondary schools

D-U-N-S 25-249-1147   (BR)
GREATER ESSEX COUNTY DISTRICT SCHOOL BOARD
EASTWOOD ELEMENTARY SCHOOL
3555 Forest Glade Dr, Windsor, ON, N8R 1X8
(519) 735-6087
Emp Here 31
SIC 8211 Elementary and secondary schools

D-U-N-S 25-249-0859   (BR)
GREATER ESSEX COUNTY DISTRICT SCHOOL BOARD
PARKVIEW ELEMENTARY SCHOOL
3070 Stillmeadow Rd, Windsor, ON, N8R 1N3
(519) 735-4445
Emp Here 22
SIC 8211 Elementary and secondary schools

D-U-N-S 25-300-4873   (BR)
REDBERRY FRANCHISING CORP
BURGER KING
7955 Tecumseh Rd E, Windsor, ON, N8R 1A1
(519) 945-7922
Emp Here 50
SIC 5812 Eating places

D-U-N-S 24-816-1127   (BR)
SECURITAS CANADA LIMITED
PINKERTON'S OF CANADA
11210 Tecumseh Rd E, Windsor, ON, N8R

1A8
(519) 979-1317
Emp Here 160
SIC 7381 Detective and armored car services

D-U-N-S 25-635-7245   (SL)
TOKHASEPYAN FAMILY ENTERPRISES LIMITED
BASKIN-ROBBINS
9945 Tecumseh Rd E, Windsor, ON, N8R 1A5
(519) 735-8445
Emp Here 74   *Sales* 2,261,782
SIC 5812 Eating places

D-U-N-S 25-467-8980   (BR)
TOYOTA CANADA INC
EASTWAY TOYOTA LEXUS OF WINDSOR
9375 Tecumseh Rd E, Windsor, ON, N8R 1A1
(519) 979-1900
Emp Here 25
SIC 5511 New and used car dealers

D-U-N-S 20-710-5854   (BR)
WINDSOR-ESSEX CATHOLIC DISTRICT SCHOOL BOARD, THE
L. A. DESMARAIS CATHOLIC ELEMENTARY SCHOOL
10715 Eastcourt Dr, Windsor, ON, N8R 1E9
(519) 735-2892
Emp Here 50
SIC 8211 Elementary and secondary schools

D-U-N-S 20-034-2769   (BR)
WINDSOR-ESSEX CATHOLIC DISTRICT SCHOOL BOARD, THE
H J LASSALINE CATHOLIC SCHOOL
3145 Wildwood Dr, Windsor, ON, N8R 1Y1
(519) 735-9474
Emp Here 20
SIC 8211 Elementary and secondary schools

Windsor, ON N8S
Essex County

D-U-N-S 25-636-8523   (BR)
ABC DAY NURSERY OF WINDSOR
(*Suby of* ABC Day Nursery Of Windsor)
1225 Lauzon Rd, Windsor, ON, N8S 3M9
(519) 945-1110
Emp Here 26
SIC 8351 Child day care services

D-U-N-S 20-003-3749   (BR)
CANADA TRUST COMPANY, THE
(*Suby of* Toronto-Dominion Bank, The)
5790 Wyandotte St E, Windsor, ON, N8S 1M5
(519) 944-4355
Emp Here 20
SIC 6021 National commercial banks

D-U-N-S 25-249-3887   (BR)
CONSEIL SCOLAIRE DE DISTRICT DES ECOLES CATHOLIQUES DU SUD-OUEST
ECOLE GEORGES P VANIER
6200 Edgar St, Windsor, ON, N8S 2A6
(519) 948-9481
Emp Here 25
SIC 8211 Elementary and secondary schools

D-U-N-S 25-635-8698   (BR)
CORPORATION OF THE CITY OF WIND-SOR
PARKS AND RECREATION DEPARTMENT
(*Suby of* Corporation of the City of Windsor)
1150 Edward Ave, Windsor, ON, N8S 3A1

Emp Here 30
SIC 8322 Individual and family services

D-U-N-S 24-180-3121   (SL)
EVERYDAY STYLE LTD
7675 Tranby Ave, Windsor, ON, N8S 2B7
(519) 258-7905
Emp Here 50   *Sales* 3,648,035
SIC 5963 Direct selling establishments

D-U-N-S 25-249-1121   (BR)
GREATER ESSEX COUNTY DISTRICT SCHOOL BOARD
M.S. HETHERINGTON SCHOOL
8800 Menard St, Windsor, ON, N8S 1W4
(519) 948-0951
Emp Here 32
SIC 8211 Elementary and secondary schools

D-U-N-S 25-249-1006   (BR)
GREATER ESSEX COUNTY DISTRICT SCHOOL BOARD
PRINCESS ANNE ELEMENTARY SCHOOL
6320 Raymond Ave, Windsor, ON, N8S 1Z9
(519) 987-6020
Emp Here 24
SIC 8211 Elementary and secondary schools

D-U-N-S 25-249-1014   (BR)
GREATER ESSEX COUNTY DISTRICT SCHOOL BOARD
RIVERSIDE SECONDARY SCHOOL
8465 Jerome St, Windsor, ON, N8S 1W8
(519) 948-4116
Emp Here 80
SIC 8211 Elementary and secondary schools

D-U-N-S 20-025-0848   (BR)
GREATER ESSEX COUNTY DISTRICT SCHOOL BOARD
CONCORD PUBLIC SCHOOL
6700 Raymond Ave, Windsor, ON, N8S 2A1

Emp Here 28
SIC 8211 Elementary and secondary schools

D-U-N-S 25-300-0004   (BR)
METRO ONTARIO INC
A & P STORES
6740 Wyandotte St E, Windsor, ON, N8S 1P6
(519) 948-5676
Emp Here 100
SIC 5411 Grocery stores

D-U-N-S 24-497-5483   (SL)
RIVERSIDE PRICE CHOPPER
8100 Wyandotte St E, Windsor, ON, N8S 1T3
(519) 251-8875
Emp Here 40   *Sales* 5,449,600
SIC 5411 Grocery stores

D-U-N-S 20-328-3171   (BR)
TDL GROUP CORP, THE
TIM HORTONS
5720 Wyandotte St E, Windsor, ON, N8S 1M5
(519) 944-5549
Emp Here 25
SIC 5812 Eating places

D-U-N-S 24-009-8095   (SL)
WINDSOR YACHT CLUB
9000 Riverside Dr E, Windsor, ON, N8S 1H1
(519) 945-1748
Emp Here 55   *Sales* 2,188,821
SIC 7997 Membership sports and recreation clubs

D-U-N-S 25-249-0610   (BR)
WINDSOR-ESSEX CATHOLIC DISTRICT SCHOOL BOARD, THE
ST MARIA GORETTI ELEMENTARY SCHOOL
1166 Eastlawn Ave, Windsor, ON, N8S 0A7
(519) 948-1111
Emp Here 20
SIC 8211 Elementary and secondary schools

D-U-N-S 20-710-5961   (BR)
WINDSOR-ESSEX CATHOLIC DISTRICT SCHOOL BOARD, THE
ST. ROSE CATHOLIC ELEMENTARY SCHOOL
871 St Rose Ave, Windsor, ON, N8S 1X4
(519) 945-7501
Emp Here 50
SIC 8211 Elementary and secondary schools

D-U-N-S 25-249-0693   (BR)

WINDSOR-ESSEX CATHOLIC DISTRICT SCHOOL BOARD, THE
ST JOHN VIANNEY ELEMENTARY SCHOOL
8405 Cedarview St, Windsor, ON, N8S 1K9
(519) 948-8817
Emp Here 40
SIC 8211 Elementary and secondary schools

Windsor, ON N8T
Essex County

D-U-N-S 20-597-6769   (SL)
1287788 ONTARIO LTD
EAST SIDE MARIOS
7780 Tecumseh Rd E, Windsor, ON, N8T 1E9
(519) 945-1800
Emp Here 70   *Sales* 2,115,860
SIC 5812 Eating places

D-U-N-S 24-408-1428   (BR)
AUTO WAREHOUSING COMPANY CANADA LIMITED
AWC
(*Suby of* Auto Warehousing Co., Inc.)
5500 North Service Rd E, Windsor, ON, N8T 3P3
(519) 948-7877
Emp Here 25
SIC 4789 Transportation services, nec

D-U-N-S 25-296-5553   (BR)
BANK OF NOVA SCOTIA, THE
SCOTIABANK
7041 Tecumseh Rd E, Windsor, ON, N8T 3K7
(519) 974-4530
Emp Here 20
SIC 6021 National commercial banks

D-U-N-S 24-437-7508   (BR)
BANQUE TORONTO-DOMINION, LA
TORONTO-DOMINION BANK, THE
(*Suby of* Toronto-Dominion Bank, The)
7404 Tecumseh Rd E, Windsor, ON, N8T 1E9
(519) 944-8822
Emp Here 30
SIC 6021 National commercial banks

D-U-N-S 20-536-3091   (BR)
CANADIAN IMPERIAL BANK OF COMMERCE
CIBC
6800 Tecumseh Rd E, Windsor, ON, N8T 1E6
(519) 948-5295
Emp Here 20
SIC 6021 National commercial banks

D-U-N-S 20-651-9758   (BR)
CARA OPERATIONS LIMITED
HARVEY'S RESTAURANTS 2440
(*Suby of* Cara Holdings Limited)
7011 Tecumseh Rd E, Windsor, ON, N8T 3K7
(519) 945-6585
Emp Here 20
SIC 5812 Eating places

D-U-N-S 25-156-1593   (SL)
CENTRE COMMUNAUTAIRE FRANCO-PHONE WINDSOR-ESSEX-KENT INC
PLACE CONCORDE
7515 Forest Glade Dr, Windsor, ON, N8T 3P5
(519) 948-5545
Emp Here 100   *Sales* 3,283,232
SIC 7299 Miscellaneous personal service

D-U-N-S 25-249-3952   (BR)
CONSEIL SCOLAIRE DE DISTRICT DES ECOLES CATHOLIQUES DU SUD-OUEST
ECOLE STE THERESE
5305 Tecumseh Rd E, Windsor, ON, N8T 1C5
(519) 945-2628
Emp Here 35
SIC 8211 Elementary and secondary schools

D-U-N-S 24-336-9134   (BR)
CORPORATION OF THE CITY OF WIND-

SOR
FIELD ENGINEERING
(*Suby of* Corporation of the City of Windsor)
2545 Pillette Rd, Windsor, ON, N8T 1P9

Emp Here 20
SIC 8711 Engineering services

D-U-N-S 20-937-2254   (SL)
DIRTY JERSEY SPORTS GRILL
6675 Tecumseh Rd E, Windsor, ON, N8T 1E7
(519) 944-9990
Emp Here 50   *Sales* 1,532,175
SIC 5812 Eating places

D-U-N-S 25-301-4229   (BR)
FABRICLAND DISTRIBUTORS INC
7683 Tecumseh Rd E, Windsor, ON, N8T 3H1
(519) 974-1090
Emp Here 21
SIC 5949 Sewing, needlework, and piece goods

D-U-N-S 24-909-6611   (BR)
FORD MOTOR COMPANY OF CANADA, LIMITED
ESSEX ALUMINUM PLANT
(*Suby of* Ford Motor Company)
6500 Cantelon Dr, Windsor, ON, N8T 0A6
(519) 251-4401
Emp Here 700
SIC 3711 Motor vehicles and car bodies

D-U-N-S 25-811-8835   (BR)
GOVERNING COUNCIL OF THE SALVATION ARMY IN CANADA, THE
SALVATION ARMY, THE
3199 Lauzon Rd, Windsor, ON, N8T 2Z7
(519) 944-4922
Emp Here 25
SIC 8351 Child day care services

D-U-N-S 25-249-1030   (BR)
GREATER ESSEX COUNTY DISTRICT SCHOOL BOARD
DAVIS, WILLIAM G SCHOOL
2855 Rivard Ave, Windsor, ON, N8T 2H9
(519) 945-1147
Emp Here 30
SIC 8211 Elementary and secondary schools

D-U-N-S 20-590-6055   (BR)
GREATER ESSEX COUNTY DISTRICT SCHOOL BOARD
ROSEVILLE PUBLIC SCHOOL
6265 Roseville Garden Dr, Windsor, ON, N8T 3B9
(519) 944-3611
Emp Here 25
SIC 8211 Elementary and secondary schools

D-U-N-S 25-249-0446   (BR)
GREATER ESSEX COUNTY DISTRICT SCHOOL BOARD
CORONATION ELEMENTARY SCHOOL
5400 Coronation Ave, Windsor, ON, N8T 1B1
(519) 945-2346
Emp Here 35
SIC 8211 Elementary and secondary schools

D-U-N-S 24-024-1179   (BR)
HOME DEPOT OF CANADA INC
HOME DEPOT
(*Suby of* The Home Depot Inc)
6570 Tecumseh Rd E, Windsor, ON, N8T 1E6
(519) 974-5420
Emp Here 150
SIC 5251 Hardware stores

D-U-N-S 25-637-1733   (BR)
LAUGHTON, JAMES ENTERPRISES INC
ARBY'S RESTAURANTS
(*Suby of* Laughton, James Enterprises Inc)
6807 Tecumseh Rd E, Windsor, ON, N8T 3K7
(519) 945-9191
Emp Here 35
SIC 5812 Eating places

D-U-N-S 25-310-9573   (BR)
MCDONALD'S RESTAURANTS OF CANADA LIMITED
MCDONALD'S
(*Suby of* McDonald's Corporation)
7777 Tecumseh Rd E, Windsor, ON, N8T 1G3
(519) 945-4751
Emp Here 100
SIC 5812 Eating places

D-U-N-S 24-369-2386   (BR)
METRO ONTARIO INC
FOOD BASICS
2090 Lauzon Rd, Windsor, ON, N8T 2Z3
(519) 944-7335
Emp Here 120
SIC 5411 Grocery stores

D-U-N-S 24-015-2749   (BR)
NORTHERN REFLECTIONS LTD
7654 Tecumseh Rd E, Windsor, ON, N8T 1E9
(519) 974-8067
Emp Here 20
SIC 5621 Women's clothing stores

D-U-N-S 24-318-2628   (BR)
PRINCESS AUTO LTD
3575 Forest Glade Dr, Windsor, ON, N8T 0A3
(519) 974-1261
Emp Here 51
SIC 5531 Auto and home supply stores

D-U-N-S 25-925-5404   (BR)
RED LOBSTER HOSPITALITY LLC
RED LOBSTER RESTAURANTS
(*Suby of* Red Lobster Seafood Co., LLC)
6575 Tecumseh Rd E, Windsor, ON, N8T 1E7
(519) 948-7677
Emp Here 90
SIC 5812 Eating places

D-U-N-S 25-028-5368   (BR)
REVERA LONG TERM CARE INC
RIVERSIDE HEALTH CARE CENTRE
3181 Meadowbrook Lane, Windsor, ON, N8T 0A4
(519) 974-0148
Emp Here 25
SIC 8051 Skilled nursing care facilities

D-U-N-S 20-232-0094   (BR)
SOBEYS CAPITAL INCORPORATED
SOBEY'S
7676 Tecumseh Rd E, Windsor, ON, N8T 1E9

Emp Here 50
SIC 5411 Grocery stores

D-U-N-S 25-498-9916   (BR)
STAPLES CANADA INC
STAPLES THE BUSINESS DEPOT
(*Suby of* Staples, Inc.)
7126 Tecumseh Rd E, Windsor, ON, N8T 1E6
(519) 948-1283
Emp Here 30
SIC 5943 Stationery stores

D-U-N-S 20-260-9707   (BR)
THK RHYTHM AUTOMOTIVE CANADA LIMITED
TRW AUTOMOTIVE
6365 Hawthorne Dr, Windsor, ON, N8T 3G6
(519) 739-4222
Emp Here 226
SIC 3674 Semiconductors and related devices

D-U-N-S 24-215-6263   (BR)
TRADER CORPORATION
AUTO TRADER
5960 Tecumseh Rd E, Windsor, ON, N8T 1E3

Emp Here 30
SIC 2721 Periodicals

D-U-N-S 24-098-5940   (BR)
VALUE VILLAGE STORES, INC
(*Suby of* Savers, Inc.)
6711 Tecumseh Rd E, Windsor, ON, N8T 3K7

(519) 944-1372
Emp Here 30
SIC 5399 Miscellaneous general merchandise

D-U-N-S 25-504-1683   (BR)
VENTRA GROUP CO
VENTRA PLASTICS DIVISIONS
2800 Kew Dr, Windsor, ON, N8T 3C6
(519) 944-1102
Emp Here 250
SIC 3089 Plastics products, nec

D-U-N-S 24-512-0472   (BR)
WAL-MART CANADA CORP
7100 Tecumseh Rd E Suite 3115, Windsor, ON, N8T 1E6
(519) 945-3065
Emp Here 150
SIC 5311 Department stores

D-U-N-S 25-249-3986   (BR)
WINDSOR-ESSEX CATHOLIC DISTRICT SCHOOL BOARD, THE
W. J. LANGLOIS SCHOOL
3110 Rivard Ave, Windsor, ON, N8T 2J2
(519) 948-9122
Emp Here 32
SIC 8211 Elementary and secondary schools

D-U-N-S 25-249-3226   (BR)
WINDSOR-ESSEX CATHOLIC DISTRICT SCHOOL BOARD, THE
ST ALEXANDER ELEMENTARY SCHOOL
5305 Adstoll Ave, Windsor, ON, N8T 1G9
(519) 945-5021
Emp Here 25
SIC 8211 Elementary and secondary schools

D-U-N-S 25-249-0651   (BR)
WINDSOR-ESSEX CATHOLIC DISTRICT SCHOOL BOARD, THE
ST. JULES CATHOLIC ELEMENTARY SCHOOL
1982 Norman Rd, Windsor, ON, N8T 1S2
(519) 945-2611
Emp Here 25
SIC 8211 Elementary and secondary schools

D-U-N-S 25-221-3251   (BR)
WINNERS MERCHANTS INTERNATIONAL L.P.
WINNERS
(*Suby of* The TJX Companies Inc)
7201 Tecumseh Rd E Suite 1, Windsor, ON, N8T 3K4
(519) 974-8519
Emp Here 40
SIC 5651 Family clothing stores

Windsor, ON N8W
Essex County

D-U-N-S 25-321-4324   (BR)
ALLIED SYSTEMS (CANADA) COMPANY
1790 Provincial Rd, Windsor, ON, N8W 5W3

Emp Here 100
SIC 4213 Trucking, except local

D-U-N-S 20-850-5081   (SL)
ARLEN TOOL CO. LTD
3305 Deziel Dr, Windsor, ON, N8W 5A5
(519) 944-4444
Emp Here 50   *Sales* 4,085,799
SIC 3544 Special dies, tools, jigs, and fixtures

D-U-N-S 25-843-6542   (BR)
BDO CANADA LLP
WINDSOR INSOLVENCY
3630 Rhodes Dr Suite 200, Windsor, ON, N8W 5A4
(519) 944-6993
Emp Here 20
SIC 8721 Accounting, auditing, and bookkeeping

D-U-N-S 25-296-5595   (BR)
BANK OF NOVA SCOTIA, THE
SCOTIA BANK
3751 Tecumseh Rd E, Windsor, ON, N8W 1H8
(519) 974-4500
Emp Here 26
SIC 6021 National commercial banks

D-U-N-S 20-571-9581   (BR)
BANK OF MONTREAL
BMO
1435 Tecumseh Rd E, Windsor, ON, N8W 1C2

Emp Here 20
SIC 6021 National commercial banks

D-U-N-S 24-015-4927   (BR)
BEST BUY CANADA LTD
BEST BUY
(*Suby of* Best Buy Co., Inc.)
4379 Walker Rd, Windsor, ON, N8W 3T6
(519) 967-2070
Emp Here 50
SIC 5731 Radio, television, and electronic stores

D-U-N-S 25-231-7706   (BR)
BRICK WAREHOUSE LP, THE
BRICK, THE
4001 Legacy Park Dr Suite B, Windsor, ON, N8W 5S6
(519) 969-1585
Emp Here 50
SIC 5712 Furniture stores

D-U-N-S 24-462-4615   (BR)
BRINK'S CANADA LIMITED
(*Suby of* The Brink's Company)
3275 Electricity Dr, Windsor, ON, N8W 5J1
(519) 944-5556
Emp Here 60
SIC 7381 Detective and armored car services

D-U-N-S 25-921-6315   (BR)
CAW LEGAL SERVICES PLAN
2345 Central Ave, Windsor, ON, N8W 4J1
(519) 944-5866
Emp Here 20
SIC 8111 Legal services

D-U-N-S 20-794-5465   (BR)
CANADA POST CORPORATION
1430 Grand Marais W, Windsor, ON, N8W 1W2
(519) 966-4231
Emp Here 50
SIC 4311 U.s. postal service

D-U-N-S 25-649-9724   (BR)
CANADIAN LINEN AND UNIFORM SERVICE CO
(*Suby of* Ameripride Services, Inc.)
2975 St Etienne Blvd, Windsor, ON, N8W 5B1
(519) 944-5811
Emp Here 20
SIC 7213 Linen supply

D-U-N-S 20-568-3241   (BR)
CANADIAN RED CROSS SOCIETY, THE
CANADIAN RED CROSS COMMUNITY HEALTH SERVICES
3909 Grand Marais Rd E Suite 400, Windsor, ON, N8W 1W9
(519) 944-8144
Emp Here 55
SIC 8099 Health and allied services, nec

D-U-N-S 25-635-7773   (BR)
CANADIAN UNION OF POSTAL WORKERS
LOCAL 630
3719 Walker Rd, Windsor, ON, N8W 3S9
(519) 944-4102
Emp Here 60
SIC 8631 Labor organizations

D-U-N-S 24-372-1169   (BR)
CARA OPERATIONS LIMITED
MONTANA'S COOKHOUSE

(*Suby of* Cara Holdings Limited)
5011 Legacy Park Dr, Windsor, ON, N8W 5S6

Emp Here 42
SIC 5812 Eating places

D-U-N-S 24-776-3449   (BR)
CENTRELINE EQUIPMENT RENTALS LTD
VOLVO RENTS
3950 Rhodes Dr, Windsor, ON, N8W 5C2
(519) 944-4500
Emp Here 22
SIC 7359 Equipment rental and leasing, nec

D-U-N-S 20-921-1551   (BR)
CHARTWELL RETIREMENT RESIDENCES
CHARTWELL SENIORS HOUSING REAL ESTATE INVESTMENT TRUST
1750 North Service Rd E, Windsor, ON, N8W 1Y3
(519) 972-3330
Emp Here 60
SIC 6719 Holding companies, nec

D-U-N-S 24-964-5516   (SL)
COLONIAL TOOL GROUP INC
COLONIAL
1691 Walker Rd, Windsor, ON, N8W 3P1
(519) 253-2461
Emp Here 55   *Sales* 9,988,687
SIC 3541 Machine tools, Metal cutting type
Pr Pr Paul Thrasher
  Brett Froats
Dir Thomas Alterman

D-U-N-S 24-449-5094   (BR)
COMMUNITY LIVING WINDSOR
(*Suby of* Community Living Windsor)
2840 Temple Dr, Windsor, ON, N8W 5J5
(519) 944-2464
Emp Here 80
SIC 8322 Individual and family services

D-U-N-S 20-523-5968   (BR)
CORPORATION OF THE CITY OF WINDSOR
ENVIRONMENTAL SERVICES DIVISION OF PUBLIC WORKS DEPARTMENT
(*Suby of* Corporation of the City of Windsor)
3540 North Service Rd E, Windsor, ON, N8W 5X2
(519) 974-2277
Emp Here 120
SIC 4959 Sanitary services, nec

D-U-N-S 25-529-3060   (BR)
COSTCO WHOLESALE CANADA LTD
COSTCO
(*Suby of* Costco Wholesale Corporation)
4411 Walker Rd Suite 534, Windsor, ON, N8W 3T6
(519) 972-1899
Emp Here 200
SIC 5399 Miscellaneous general merchandise

D-U-N-S 25-541-6380   (SL)
CURTIS - J K PRINTING LIMITED
1555 Kildare Rd, Windsor, ON, N8W 2W2
(519) 977-9990
Emp Here 50   *Sales* 3,793,956
SIC 2752 Commercial printing, lithographic

D-U-N-S 25-487-2369   (BR)
DILLON CONSULTING LIMITED
(*Suby of* Dillon Consulting Inc)
3200 Deziel Dr Suite 608, Windsor, ON, N8W 5K8
(519) 948-5000
Emp Here 72
SIC 8711 Engineering services

D-U-N-S 25-787-2507   (HQ)
F & J CHEETHAM (WINDSOR) LIMITED
TIM HORTONS
(*Suby of* F & J Cheetham (Windsor) Limited)
3410 Walker Rd, Windsor, ON, N8W 3S3
(519) 967-9090
Emp Here 45   *Emp Total* 70
Sales 2,732,754

SIC 5812 Eating places

D-U-N-S 24-337-2898　(BR)
FGL SPORTS LTD
NATIONAL SPORTS
3051 Legacy Park Dr, Windsor, ON, N8W 5S6
(519) 969-2526
Emp Here 20
SIC 5941 Sporting goods and bicycle shops

D-U-N-S 25-281-4926　(BR)
G4S SECURE SOLUTIONS (CANADA) LTD
3372 Manrheim Way, Windsor, ON, N8W 5J9
(519) 255-1441
Emp Here 300
SIC 7381 Detective and armored car services

D-U-N-S 24-598-2819　(BR)
GOLDER ASSOCIATES LTD
1825 Provincial Rd, Windsor, ON, N8W 5V7
(519) 250-3733
Emp Here 25
SIC 8711 Engineering services

D-U-N-S 24-140-0779　(BR)
GRAYBAR CANADA LIMITED
GRAYBAR ELECTRIC ONTARIO
(*Suby of* Graybar Electric Company, Inc.)
2760 Deziel Dr, Windsor, ON, N8W 5H8
(519) 944-4414
Emp Here 20
SIC 5063 Electrical apparatus and equipment

D-U-N-S 20-590-6030　(BR)
GREATER ESSEX COUNTY DISTRICT SCHOOL BOARD
HUGH BEATON PUBLIC ELEMENTARY SCHOOLS
2229 Chilver Rd, Windsor, ON, N8W 2V4
(519) 254-2579
Emp Here 25
SIC 8211 Elementary and secondary schools

D-U-N-S 25-249-0727　(BR)
GREATER ESSEX COUNTY DISTRICT SCHOOL BOARD
J A MC WILLIAM ELEMENTARY SCHOOL
1901 E C Row Ave E, Windsor, ON, N8W 1Y6
(519) 969-9080
Emp Here 35
SIC 8211 Elementary and secondary schools

D-U-N-S 25-249-1154　(BR)
GREATER ESSEX COUNTY DISTRICT SCHOOL BOARD
JOHN CAMPBELL ELEMENTARY SCHOOL
1255 Tecumseh Rd E, Windsor, ON, N8W 1B7
(519) 254-6411
Emp Here 45
SIC 8211 Elementary and secondary schools

D-U-N-S 25-249-0933　(BR)
GREATER ESSEX COUNTY DISTRICT SCHOOL BOARD
WF HERMAN SCHOOL
1930 Rossini Blvd, Windsor, ON, N8W 4P5
(519) 944-4700
Emp Here 80
SIC 8211 Elementary and secondary schools

D-U-N-S 20-555-1182　(BR)
GROUND EFFECTS LTD
INTERNATIONAL SEATING & DECOR
2875 St Etienne Blvd, Windsor, ON, N8W 5B1
(519) 944-5730
Emp Here 21
SIC 2431 Millwork

D-U-N-S 20-175-8815　(BR)
GROUND EFFECTS LTD
3940 North Service Rd E, Windsor, ON, N8W 5X2
(519) 944-9065
Emp Here 25
SIC 5531 Auto and home supply stores

D-U-N-S 25-362-8358　(BR)
GROUND EFFECTS LTD
HYDRAGRAPHICS

2875 St Etienne, Windsor, ON, N8W 5B1
(519) 944-3800
Emp Here 30
SIC 4783 Packing and crating

D-U-N-S 20-307-3416　(BR)
GROUND EFFECTS LTD
INTERNATIONAL SEATING & DECOR
2775 St Etienne Blvd, Windsor, ON, N8W 5B1
(519) 944-3800
Emp Here 100
SIC 3714 Motor vehicle parts and accessories

D-U-N-S 24-335-5984　(SL)
HBPO CANADA INC
2570 Central Ave, Windsor, ON, N8W 4J5
(519) 251-4300
Emp Here 115　　*Sales* 28,846,158
SIC 3711 Motor vehicles and car bodies
Pr Emmanuel Boudon
Dir Richard Ling
Dir John Bulger
Dir Jen Keller
Dir Martin Schueler

D-U-N-S 24-361-7326　(BR)
HOME DEPOT OF CANADA INC
HOME DEPOT
(*Suby of* The Home Depot Inc)
1925 Division Rd, Windsor, ON, N8W 1Z7
(519) 967-3700
Emp Here 100
SIC 5251 Hardware stores

D-U-N-S 25-938-3776　(BR)
IGM FINANCIAL INC
INVESTORS GROUP FINANCIAL SERVICES
3100 Temple Dr Suite 600, Windsor, ON, N8W 5J6
(519) 969-7526
Emp Here 35
SIC 8742 Management consulting services

D-U-N-S 25-073-0017　(BR)
JAMIESON LABORATORIES LTD
4025 Rhodes Dr, Windsor, ON, N8W 5B5
(519) 974-8482
Emp Here 45
SIC 2833 Medicinals and botanicals

D-U-N-S 25-487-2427　(SL)
JORDAN MORTGAGE SERVICES (WINDSOR) INC.
3200 Deziel Dr Suite 212, Windsor, ON, N8W 5K8

Emp Here 22　　*Sales* 5,182,810
SIC 6163 Loan brokers
Dir Richard Ord
Pr Robert Ord

D-U-N-S 24-827-8137　(BR)
KPMG LLP
(*Suby of* KPMG LLP)
3200 Deziel Dr Suite 618, Windsor, ON, N8W 5K8

Emp Here 60
SIC 8721 Accounting, auditing, and bookkeeping

D-U-N-S 25-973-6304　(SL)
KOOLINI ITALIAN CUISINI LIMITED
KOOLINI EATERY
1520 Tecumseh Rd E, Windsor, ON, N8W 1C4
(519) 254-5665
Emp Here 150　　*Sales* 4,523,563
SIC 5812 Eating places

D-U-N-S 20-891-5392　(BR)
LEON'S FURNITURE LIMITED
700 Division Rd, Windsor, ON, N8W 5R9
(519) 969-7403
Emp Here 30
SIC 5712 Furniture stores

D-U-N-S 20-997-8233　(BR)
LOBLAWS INC

REAL CANADIAN SUPERSTORE
4371 Walker Rd Suite 567, Windsor, ON, N8W 3T6
(519) 972-3904
Emp Here 330
SIC 5411 Grocery stores

D-U-N-S 24-799-2592　(BR)
LOWE'S COMPANIES CANADA, ULC
1848 Provincial Rd, Windsor, ON, N8W 5W3
(519) 967-3560
Emp Here 180
SIC 5211 Lumber and other building materials

D-U-N-S 25-457-6457　(SL)
MANOR WINDSOR REALTY LTD
3276 Walker Rd, Windsor, ON, N8W 3R8
(519) 250-8800
Emp Here 60　　*Sales* 7,478,240
SIC 6531 Real estate agents and managers
Pr Steve Mustac

D-U-N-S 25-318-1739　(BR)
MCDONALD'S RESTAURANTS OF CANADA LIMITED
MCDONALD'S 8046
(*Suby of* McDonald's Corporation)
2780 Tecumseh Rd E, Windsor, ON, N8W 1G3
(519) 945-3634
Emp Here 85
SIC 5812 Eating places

D-U-N-S 20-785-1598　(BR)
MEDICAL PHARMACIES GROUP LIMITED
FIRST MEDICAL PHARMACY
2425 Tecumseh Rd E Suite 100, Windsor, ON, N8W 1E6
(519) 252-3700
Emp Here 50
SIC 5912 Drug stores and proprietary stores

D-U-N-S 25-635-5876　(SL)
PATTISON'S, NANCY DANCE WORLD INC
3900 Walker Rd, Windsor, ON, N8W 3T3
(519) 966-2259
Emp Here 60　　*Sales* 1,299,377
SIC 7911 Dance studios, schools, and halls

D-U-N-S 24-794-4515　(BR)
PENETANG-MIDLAND COACH LINES LTD
CHATHAM COACH LINES
3951 Walker Rd, Windsor, ON, N8W 3T4
(519) 966-2821
Emp Here 35
SIC 4142 Bus charter service, except local

D-U-N-S 20-641-1709　(BR)
PUROLATOR INC.
PUROLATOR INC
4520 North Service Rd E, Windsor, ON, N8W 5X2
(519) 945-1363
Emp Here 75
SIC 7389 Business services, nec

D-U-N-S 25-032-1494　(BR)
REDBERRY FRANCHISING CORP
BURGER KING 552
2850 Tecumseh Rd E, Windsor, ON, N8W 1G4
(519) 948-3161
Emp Here 35
SIC 5812 Eating places

D-U-N-S 24-977-5854　(BR)
RELIANCE COMFORT LIMITED PARTNERSHIP
RELIANCE HOME COMFORT
1825 Provincial Rd, Windsor, ON, N8W 5V7
(519) 250-7878
Emp Here 20
SIC 1711 Plumbing, heating, air-conditioning

D-U-N-S 20-911-5406　(BR)
RINK PARTNERS CORPORATION
WINDSOR ICE PARK
(*Suby of* Rink Partners Corporation)
3400 Grand Marais Rd E, Windsor, ON, N8W 1W7

Emp Here 35
SIC 7999 Amusement and recreation, nec

D-U-N-S 20-186-2778　(BR)
RYDER MATERIAL HANDLING ULC
RYDER LIFT TRUCK
(*Suby of* Crown Equipment Corporation)
2970 Walker Rd, Windsor, ON, N8W 3R3
(519) 966-2450
Emp Here 20
SIC 7699 Repair services, nec

D-U-N-S 20-999-5203　(BR)
SCIEMETRIC INSTRUMENTS INC
4570 Rhodes Dr Suite 200, Windsor, ON, N8W 5C2
(519) 972-8446
Emp Here 20
SIC 3829 Measuring and controlling devices, nec

D-U-N-S 25-295-3633　(BR)
SHOPPERS DRUG MART CORPORATION
4451 Tecumseh Rd E, Windsor, ON, N8W 1K6
(519) 948-8108
Emp Here 25
SIC 5912 Drug stores and proprietary stores

D-U-N-S 25-498-9791　(BR)
STAPLES CANADA INC
STAPLES THE BUSINESS DEPOT
(*Suby of* Staples, Inc.)
4511 Walker Rd, Windsor, ON, N8W 3T6
(519) 972-5127
Emp Here 40
SIC 5943 Stationery stores

D-U-N-S 20-186-4782　(SL)
TAMAR BUILDING PRODUCTS (1981) LTD
3957 Walker Rd, Windsor, ON, N8W 3T4
(519) 969-7060
Emp Here 20　　*Sales* 18,123,000
SIC 5039 Construction materials, nec
Pr Pr Gary Gascoigne
Fin Ex Dorene M. Brown

D-U-N-S 24-849-5541　(BR)
TYCO INTEGRATED FIRE & SECURITY CANADA, INC
TYCO INTEGRATED FIRE AND SECURITY
(*Suby of* Johnson Controls, Inc.)
4525 Rhodes Dr Unit 700, Windsor, ON, N8W 5R8
(519) 966-1910
Emp Here 25
SIC 7389 Business services, nec

D-U-N-S 20-057-4866　(SL)
ULTIMATE MANUFACTURED SYSTEMS INC
2855 Deziel Dr, Windsor, ON, N8W 5A5
(519) 250-5954
Emp Here 34　　*Sales* 3,720,996
SIC 3542 Machine tools, Metal forming type

D-U-N-S 25-481-3793　(BR)
UNIFOR
C A W CDA WINDSOR AREA OFFICE
2345 Central Ave, Windsor, ON, N8W 4J1
(519) 944-5866
Emp Here 30
SIC 8631 Labor organizations

D-U-N-S 20-520-0194　(BR)
UNION GAS LIMITED
3840 Rhodes Dr, Windsor, ON, N8W 5C2
(519) 250-2200
Emp Here 200
SIC 4923 Gas transmission and distribution

D-U-N-S 24-252-9621　(BR)
VALUE VILLAGE STORES, INC
VALUE VILLAGE
(*Suby of* Savers, Inc.)
4322 Walker Rd, Windsor, ON, N8W 3T5
(519) 250-0199
Emp Here 100
SIC 5399 Miscellaneous general merchandise

▲ Public Company　　■ Public Company Family Member　　**HQ** Headquarters　　**BR** Branch　　**SL** Single Location

D-U-N-S 25-934-1774 (BR)
VICTORIAN ORDER OF NURSES FOR CANADA
VON WINDSOR-ESSEX DISTRICT
4520 Rhodes Dr Suite 400, Windsor, ON, N8W 5C2
(519) 254-4866
Emp Here 60
SIC 8082 Home health care services

D-U-N-S 20-933-6499 (SL)
WALKER TOWNE PIZZA INC
BOSTON PIZZA
4450 Walker Rd, Windsor, ON, N8W 3T5
(519) 250-7670
Emp Here 60   *Sales* 1,824,018
SIC 5812 Eating places

D-U-N-S 25-407-3133 (SL)
WINDSOR DISPOSAL SERVICES LIMITED
2700 Deziel Dr, Windsor, ON, N8W 5H8
(519) 944-8009
Emp Here 56   *Sales* 4,450,603
SIC 4212 Local trucking, without storage

D-U-N-S 20-710-5904 (BR)
WINDSOR-ESSEX CATHOLIC DISTRICT SCHOOL BOARD, THE
ST. BERNARD CATHOLIC ELEMENTARY SCHOOL
1847 Meldrum Rd, Windsor, ON, N8W 4E1
(519) 945-6948
Emp Here 35
SIC 8211 Elementary and secondary schools

D-U-N-S 20-913-6543 (BR)
WINDSOR-ESSEX CATHOLIC DISTRICT SCHOOL BOARD, THE
ST CHRISTOPHER ELEMENTARY SCHOOL
3355 Woodward Blvd, Windsor, ON, N8W 2Y7
(519) 734-7671
Emp Here 50
SIC 8211 Elementary and secondary schools

D-U-N-S 20-710-5995 (BR)
WINDSOR-ESSEX CATHOLIC DISTRICT SCHOOL BOARD, THE
ST CHRISTOPHER CATHOLIC SCHOOL
1213c E C Row Ave E, Windsor, ON, N8W 1Y6
(519) 972-5106
Emp Here 50
SIC 8211 Elementary and secondary schools

D-U-N-S 24-313-5907 (BR)
WINNERS MERCHANTS INTERNATIONAL L.P.
HOMESENSE
(*Suby of* The TJX Companies Inc)
4324 Walker Rd, Windsor, ON, N8W 3T5
(519) 966-0260
Emp Here 30
SIC 5651 Family clothing stores

D-U-N-S 20-190-9566 (SL)
WIRELESS RONIN TECHNOLOGIES (CANADA), INC.
(*Suby of* Creative Realities, Inc.)
4510 Rhodes Dr Unit 800, Windsor, ON, N8W 5K5
(519) 974-2363
Emp Here 30   *Sales* 2,261,782
SIC 7371 Custom computer programming services

Windsor, ON N8X
Essex County

D-U-N-S 25-203-9933 (BR)
1313256 ONTARIO INC
FACTORY DIRECT
2491 Dougall Ave, Windsor, ON, N8X 1T3
(519) 946-0283
Emp Here 20
SIC 5932 Used merchandise stores

D-U-N-S 20-901-2285 (BR)
A.G. SIMPSON AUTOMOTIVE INC
A G S AUTOMOTIVE
275 Eugenie St E, Windsor, ON, N8X 2X9
(519) 969-5193
Emp Here 35
SIC 3462 Iron and steel forgings

D-U-N-S 20-774-4004 (HQ)
ABC DAY NURSERY OF WINDSOR
(*Suby of* ABC Day Nursery Of Windsor)
888 Hanna St E, Windsor, ON, N8X 2N9
(519) 256-5141
Emp Here 23   *Emp Total* 60
Sales 1,824,018
SIC 8351 Child day care services

D-U-N-S 24-002-5994 (SL)
ADEO BEAUTY INC
2855 Howard Ave, Windsor, ON, N8X 3Y4
(519) 250-5073
Emp Here 68   *Sales* 1,313,293
SIC 7231 Beauty shops

D-U-N-S 25-641-2925 (BR)
AFFINITY FOOD GROUP INC
WENDY'S RESTAURANT
1411 Ouellette Ave, Windsor, ON, N8X 1K1
(519) 254-2440
Emp Here 25
SIC 5812 Eating places

D-U-N-S 25-274-1640 (HQ)
ANGLIN ENTERPRISES INC
(*Suby of* Anglin Enterprises Inc)
220 Tecumseh Rd W, Windsor, ON, N8X 1G1
(519) 727-4398
Emp Here 70   *Emp Total* 70
Sales 12,957,120
SIC 6712 Bank holding companies
Pr Pr Loris Boschin

D-U-N-S 20-588-2694 (BR)
BANQUE TORONTO-DOMINION, LA
TD CANADA TRUST
(*Suby of* Toronto-Dominion Bank, The)
1407 Ottawa St, Windsor, ON, N8X 2G1
(519) 256-6363
Emp Here 20
SIC 6021 National commercial banks

D-U-N-S 20-588-2785 (BR)
BANQUE TORONTO-DOMINION, LA
TD CANADA TRUST
(*Suby of* Toronto-Dominion Bank, The)
3100 Howard Ave, Windsor, ON, N8X 3Y8
(519) 969-0181
Emp Here 20
SIC 6021 National commercial banks

D-U-N-S 24-384-0696 (BR)
BRENTWOOD LANES CANADA LTD
LOGAN'S GRILL HOUSE
2482 Dougall Ave, Windsor, ON, N8X 1T2
(519) 966-2724
Emp Here 20
SIC 5812 Eating places

D-U-N-S 25-832-8244 (BR)
CML HEALTHCARE INC
DIAGNOSTICARE
700 Tecumseh Rd E Ste 1, Windsor, ON, N8X 4T2
(519) 258-4515
Emp Here 25
SIC 8071 Medical laboratories

D-U-N-S 25-303-4334 (BR)
CANADIAN IMPERIAL BANK OF COMMERCE
CIBC
3100 Howard Ave, Windsor, ON, N8X 3Y8
(519) 969-5932
Emp Here 26
SIC 6021 National commercial banks

D-U-N-S 25-303-4011 (BR)
CANADIAN IMPERIAL BANK OF COM-

MERCE
CIBC
1395 Ottawa St, Windsor, ON, N8X 2E9
(519) 256-3441
Emp Here 20
SIC 6021 National commercial banks

D-U-N-S 20-290-1133 (SL)
CANARX SERVICES INC
235 Eugenie St W Suite 105d, Windsor, ON, N8X 2X7
(519) 973-3040
Emp Here 60   *Sales* 7,369,031
SIC 5122 Drugs, proprietaries, and sundries
Pr Pr G. Anthony Howard

D-U-N-S 25-653-5170 (BR)
CINEPLEX ODEON CORPORATION
CINEPLEX CINEMAS DEVONSHIRE MALL
3100 Howard Ave, Windsor, ON, N8X 3Y8
(519) 967-0197
Emp Here 20
SIC 7832 Motion picture theaters, except drive-in

D-U-N-S 24-764-0873 (BR)
CINTAS CANADA LIMITED
SALLY FOURMY & ASSOCIATES
(*Suby of* Cintas Corporation)
1550 Elsmere Ave, Windsor, ON, N8X 4H3
(519) 254-3213
Emp Here 22
SIC 5699 Miscellaneous apparel and accessory stores

D-U-N-S 25-311-0084 (BR)
CLUB MONACO CORP
(*Suby of* Ralph Lauren Corporation)
3100 Howard Ave, Windsor, ON, N8X 3Y8

Emp Here 20
SIC 5137 Women's and children's clothing

D-U-N-S 20-347-2394 (BR)
COGECO COMMUNICATIONS INC
COGECO TV
2525 Dougall Ave, Windsor, ON, N8X 5A7
(519) 972-6677
Emp Here 70
SIC 4833 Television broadcasting stations

D-U-N-S 25-711-7325 (BR)
COMCARE (CANADA) LIMITED
COMCARE HEALTH SERVICES
(*Suby of* Comcare (Canada) Limited)
880 North Service Rd E Suite 301, Windsor, ON, N8X 3J5
(519) 966-5200
Emp Here 300
SIC 8059 Nursing and personal care, nec

D-U-N-S 25-280-2335 (BR)
COMMUNITY GAMING & ENTERTAINMENT GROUP LP
BIG D BINGO
(*Suby of* Community Gaming & Entertainment Group LP)
2515 Dougall Ave, Windsor, ON, N8X 1T3
(519) 948-7500
Emp Here 45
SIC 7999 Amusement and recreation, nec

D-U-N-S 25-528-1347 (BR)
COMPAGNIE DES CHEMINS DE FER NATIONAUX DU CANADA
2597 Dougall Ave, Windsor, ON, N8X 1T5
(519) 250-3205
Emp Here 40
SIC 4011 Railroads, line-haul operating

D-U-N-S 24-410-0850 (BR)
DOLLARAMA S.E.C.
3214 Dougall Ave Unit B, Windsor, ON, N8X 1S6
(519) 972-4661
Emp Here 22
SIC 5311 Department stores

D-U-N-S 25-319-5044 (BR)
DON MICHAEL HOLDINGS INC
ROOTS
3100 Howard Ave, Windsor, ON, N8X 3Y8
(519) 966-3994
Emp Here 20
SIC 5651 Family clothing stores

D-U-N-S 20-106-0931 (BR)
EXPEDITORS CANADA INC
2485 Ouellette Ave Suite 100, Windsor, ON, N8X 1L5
(519) 967-0975
Emp Here 20
SIC 4731 Freight transportation arrangement

D-U-N-S 24-337-3102 (BR)
FGL SPORTS LTD
SORZANI
3100 Howard Ave, Windsor, ON, N8X 3Y8
(519) 972-8379
Emp Here 60
SIC 5941 Sporting goods and bicycle shops

D-U-N-S 20-185-2738 (SL)
FREED STORAGE LIMITED
FREED'S OF WINDSOR
1526 Ottawa St, Windsor, ON, N8X 2G5
(519) 258-6532
Emp Here 65   *Sales* 4,742,446
SIC 5611 Men's and boys' clothing stores

D-U-N-S 25-193-4670 (BR)
GFL ENVIRONMENTAL INC
905 Tecumseh Rd W, Windsor, ON, N8X 2A9
(519) 948-8126
Emp Here 40
SIC 4953 Refuse systems

D-U-N-S 25-079-4849 (BR)
GAP (CANADA) INC
BABYGAP
(*Suby of* The Gap Inc)
3100 Howard Ave, Windsor, ON, N8X 3Y8

Emp Here 30
SIC 5651 Family clothing stores

D-U-N-S 25-819-9983 (BR)
GOODLIFE FITNESS CENTRES INC
GOOD LIFE FITNESS CLUBS
3100 Howard Ave, Windsor, ON, N8X 3Y8
(519) 966-6005
Emp Here 35
SIC 7991 Physical fitness facilities

D-U-N-S 20-590-6048 (BR)
GREATER ESSEX COUNTY DISTRICT SCHOOL BOARD
W C KENNEDY COLLEGIATE INSTITUTE
245 Tecumseh Rd E, Windsor, ON, N8X 2R2
(519) 254-6475
Emp Here 80
SIC 8211 Elementary and secondary schools

D-U-N-S 25-833-1719 (BR)
GREATER ESSEX COUNTY DISTRICT SCHOOL BOARD
QUEEN VICTORIA ELEMENTARY SCHOOL
1376 Victoria Ave, Windsor, ON, N8X 1P1
(519) 252-5727
Emp Here 40
SIC 8211 Elementary and secondary schools

D-U-N-S 20-175-1539 (BR)
GREATER ESSEX COUNTY DISTRICT SCHOOL BOARD
ASSESSMENT CENTER
1410 Ouellette Ave, Windsor, ON, N8X 5B2
(519) 971-9698
Emp Here 25
SIC 7361 Employment agencies

D-U-N-S 25-650-3863 (BR)
HOME DEPOT OF CANADA INC
HOME DEPOT
(*Suby of* The Home Depot Inc)
655 Sydney Ave, Windsor, ON, N8X 5C4

---

(519) 967-3706
Emp Here 350
SIC 5251 Hardware stores

D-U-N-S 20-184-6441   (BR)
HONEYWELL LIMITED
(*Suby of* Honeywell International Inc.)
3096 Devon Dr Suite 1, Windsor, ON, N8X 4L2
(519) 250-2000
Emp Here 30
SIC 3822 Environmental controls

D-U-N-S 20-184-7209   (BR)
HUDSON'S BAY COMPANY
THE BAY
3030 Howard Ave, Windsor, ON, N8X 4T3
(519) 966-4666
Emp Here 300
SIC 5311 Department stores

D-U-N-S 24-952-5635   (BR)
IBM CANADA LIMITED
(*Suby of* International Business Machines Corporation)
2480 Ouellette Ave, Windsor, ON, N8X 1L4
(519) 972-0208
Emp Here 20
SIC 3578 Calculating and accounting equipment

D-U-N-S 25-638-1310   (SL)
JOSE'S NOODLE FACTORY
2731 Howard Ave, Windsor, ON, N8X 3X4
(519) 972-1760
Emp Here 60   *Sales* 1,824,018
SIC 5812 Eating places

D-U-N-S 20-787-8104   (BR)
LIQUOR CONTROL BOARD OF ONTARIO, THE
LCBO
3155 Howard Ave, Windsor, ON, N8X 4Y8
(519) 972-1772
Emp Here 27
SIC 5921 Liquor stores

D-U-N-S 20-106-7159   (BR)
LONDON LIFE INSURANCE COMPANY
FREEDOM 55 FINANCIAL
140 Ouellette Pl Suite 200, Windsor, ON, N8X 1L9
(519) 967-1180
Emp Here 90
SIC 6311 Life insurance

D-U-N-S 20-798-4431   (BR)
MAGASIN LAURA (P.V.) INC
LAURA CANADA
3100 Howard Ave, Windsor, ON, N8X 3Y8
(519) 250-0953
Emp Here 20
SIC 5621 Women's clothing stores

D-U-N-S 25-641-2602   (BR)
MCDONALD'S RESTAURANTS OF CANADA LIMITED
MCDONALD'S
(*Suby of* McDonald's Corporation)
3195 Howard Ave, Windsor, ON, N8X 3Y9
(519) 966-0131
Emp Here 60
SIC 5812 Eating places

D-U-N-S 24-977-1908   (SL)
MID SOUTH CONTRACTORS ULC
(*Suby of* Motor City Electric Co.)
3110 Devon Dr, Windsor, ON, N8X 4L2
(519) 966-6163
Emp Here 120   *Sales* 10,506,341
SIC 1731 Electrical work
Pr Pr Dale Wieczorek
VP Fin Denise Hodgins

D-U-N-S 20-527-6079   (SL)
MOXIE'S CLASSIC GRILL
3100 Howard Ave Unit 20, Windsor, ON, N8X 3Y8
(519) 250-3390
Emp Here 150   *Sales* 4,523,563

SIC 5812 Eating places

D-U-N-S 20-657-9521   (BR)
OLD NAVY (CANADA) INC
(*Suby of* The Gap Inc)
3100 Howard Ave, Windsor, ON, N8X 3Y8
(519) 250-8112
Emp Here 50
SIC 5651 Family clothing stores

D-U-N-S 20-859-9519   (BR)
PACIFIC LINK COMMUNICATIONS INC
BELL WORLD
3100 Howard Ave, Windsor, ON, N8X 3Y8
(519) 966-5606
Emp Here 25
SIC 5999 Miscellaneous retail stores, nec

D-U-N-S 24-317-4849   (BR)
RESIDENCES ALLEGRO, S.E.C., LES
ROYAL MARQUIS
(*Suby of* Residences Allegro, S.E.C., Les)
590 Grand Marais Rd E, Windsor, ON, N8X 3H4
(519) 969-0330
Emp Here 50
SIC 6513 Apartment building operators

D-U-N-S 24-002-1449   (BR)
ROMA RIBS LTD
TONY ROMA'S A PLACE FOR RIBS
(*Suby of* Roma Ribs Ltd)
3100 Howard Ave Unit D10, Windsor, ON, N8X 3Y8
(519) 250-1067
Emp Here 35
SIC 5812 Eating places

D-U-N-S 25-309-8982   (BR)
ROYAL BANK OF CANADA
ROYAL BANK FINANCIAL GROUP
(*Suby of* Royal Bank Of Canada)
2669 Howard Ave, Windsor, ON, N8X 4Z3
(519) 966-1410
Emp Here 22
SIC 6021 National commercial banks

D-U-N-S 24-330-0170   (BR)
SCM INSURANCE SERVICES INC
CLAIMSPRO
3155 Howard Ave Suite 202, Windsor, ON, N8X 4Y8
(519) 258-3555
Emp Here 20
SIC 6411 Insurance agents, brokers, and service

D-U-N-S 24-891-1299   (BR)
SEARS CANADA INC
SEARS DEVONSHIRE WINDSOR
3050 Howard Ave, Windsor, ON, N8X 3Y7
(519) 966-2822
Emp Here 500
SIC 5311 Department stores

D-U-N-S 24-873-1424   (BR)
SHOPPERS HOME HEALTH CARE (CANADA) INC
SHOPPERS HOME HEALTH CARE, DIV. OF
1624 Howard Ave, Windsor, ON, N8X 3T7
(519) 252-2715
Emp Here 30
SIC 5047 Medical and hospital equipment

D-U-N-S 25-163-5223   (BR)
STANTEC CONSULTING LTD
140 Ouellette Pl Suite 100, Windsor, ON, N8X 1L9
(519) 966-2250
Emp Here 44
SIC 8711 Engineering services

D-U-N-S 25-213-7450   (BR)
STAPLES CANADA INC
STAPLES THE BUSINESS DEPOT
(*Suby of* Staples, Inc.)
2550 Ouellette Ave, Windsor, ON, N8X 1L7
(519) 966-9495
Emp Here 40

SIC 5943 Stationery stores

D-U-N-S 20-995-1305   (BR)
THE PIC GROUP LTD
1303 Mcdougall St, Windsor, ON, N8X 3M6
(519) 252-1611
Emp Here 75
SIC 7549 Automotive services, nec

D-U-N-S 25-367-8056   (HQ)
THYSSENKRUPP INDUSTRIAL SERVICES CANADA, INC
2491 Ouellette Ave, Windsor, ON, N8X 1L5
(519) 967-0567
Emp Here 50   *Emp Total* 155,584
Sales 6,639,424
SIC 4225 General warehousing and storage
Pr Brian Diephuis

D-U-N-S 20-793-1069   (BR)
TWINCORP INC
TACO BELL
300 Tecumseh Rd E Suite 500, Windsor, ON, N8X 5E8
(519) 971-7268
Emp Here 20
SIC 5812 Eating places

D-U-N-S 20-564-4524   (BR)
VENTRA GROUP CO
VELTRI HOWARD DIV
1425 Howard Ave, Windsor, ON, N8X 5C9
(519) 253-3509
Emp Here 189
SIC 3465 Automotive stampings

D-U-N-S 24-758-1929   (SL)
W M TOOL INC
3280 Devon Dr, Windsor, ON, N8X 4L4
(519) 966-3860
Emp Here 50   *Sales* 4,085,799
SIC 3544 Special dies, tools, jigs, and fixtures

D-U-N-S 25-636-3458   (BR)
WATSON, T.J. ENTERPRISES INC
TIM HORTONS
275 Tecumseh Rd W, Windsor, ON, N8X 1G2
(519) 252-7574
Emp Here 29
SIC 5812 Eating places

D-U-N-S 25-929-8933   (SL)
WINDSOR ESSEX COMMUNITY HEALTH CENTRE
1585 Ouellette Ave, Windsor, ON, N8X 1K5
(519) 253-8481
Emp Here 125   *Sales* 4,888,367
SIC 8322 Individual and family services

D-U-N-S 20-186-7868   (SL)
WINDSOR TEXTILES LIMITED
635 Tecumseh Rd W, Windsor, ON, N8X 1H4
(519) 258-8418
Emp Here 60   *Sales* 3,429,153
SIC 7218 Industrial launderers

D-U-N-S 20-654-4095   (BR)
WINDSOR-ESSEX CATHOLIC DISTRICT SCHOOL BOARD, THE
CATHOLIC CENTRAL SECONDARY SCHOOL
441 Tecumseh Rd E, Windsor, ON, N8X 2R7
(519) 256-3171
Emp Here 100
SIC 8211 Elementary and secondary schools

D-U-N-S 25-249-3143   (BR)
WINDSOR-ESSEX CATHOLIC DISTRICT SCHOOL BOARD, THE
OUR LADY PERPETUAL HELP SCHOOL, OLPH
775 Capitol St, Windsor, ON, N8X 5E3
(519) 966-1293
Emp Here 36
SIC 8211 Elementary and secondary schools

D-U-N-S 20-710-5870   (BR)
WINDSOR-ESSEX CATHOLIC DISTRICT SCHOOL BOARD, THE

SIC 8211 Elementary and secondary schools

ST ANGELO'S SCHOOL
816 Ellis St E, Windsor, ON, N8X 2H7
(519) 254-7240
Emp Here 39
SIC 8211 Elementary and secondary schools

D-U-N-S 25-300-6829   (BR)
WORKPLACE SAFETY & INSURANCE BOARD, THE
WSIB
2485 Ouellette Ave, Windsor, ON, N8X 1L5

Emp Here 150
SIC 6331 Fire, marine, and casualty insurance

D-U-N-S 24-151-5530   (BR)
YM INC. (SALES)
URBAN PLANET
3100 Howard Ave Unit 24, Windsor, ON, N8X 3Y8
(519) 966-1897
Emp Here 22
SIC 5621 Women's clothing stores

Windsor, ON N8Y
Essex County

D-U-N-S 25-638-9693   (SL)
AMBASSADOR BUILDING MAINTENANCE LIMITED
628 Monmouth Rd, Windsor, ON, N8Y 3L1
(519) 255-1107
Emp Here 170   *Sales* 4,961,328
SIC 7349 Building maintenance services, nec

D-U-N-S 24-765-3236   (SL)
AMICA AT WINDSOR
4909 Riverside Dr E Suite 207, Windsor, ON, N8Y 0A4
(519) 948-5500
Emp Here 80   *Sales* 7,004,227
SIC 6513 Apartment building operators
Genl Mgr Lisa Rufo

D-U-N-S 20-071-8307   (BR)
BAYSHORE HEALTHCARE LTD.
BAYSHORE HOME HEALTH
1275 Walker Rd Suite 10, Windsor, ON, N8Y 4X9
(519) 973-5411
Emp Here 225
SIC 8082 Home health care services

D-U-N-S 24-700-7474   (BR)
BLACKBURN RADIO INC
2090 Wyandotte St E, Windsor, ON, N8Y 5B2
(519) 944-4400
Emp Here 37
SIC 4832 Radio broadcasting stations

D-U-N-S 24-852-2323   (BR)
CASCADES CANADA ULC
CASCADES CONTAINERBOARD PACKAGING-BIRD DIV
2470 Wyandotte St E, Windsor, ON, N8Y 4X2
(519) 254-7513
Emp Here 30
SIC 2653 Corrugated and solid fiber boxes

D-U-N-S 20-568-4959   (BR)
CONSEIL SCOLAIRE VIAMONDE
ECOLE ELEMENTAIRE L' ENVOLEE
1799 Ottawa St, Windsor, ON, N8Y 1R4
(519) 259-4860
Emp Here 25
SIC 8211 Elementary and secondary schools

D-U-N-S 25-635-9274   (BR)
CORPORATION OF THE CITY OF WINDSOR
GINO A MARCUS COMMUNITY COMPLEX
(*Suby of* Corporation of the City of Windsor)
1168 Drouillard Rd, Windsor, ON, N8Y 2R1
(519) 253-7028
Emp Here 65

SIC 8322 Individual and family services

D-U-N-S 20-185-1987   (SL)
ESSEX TERMINAL RAILWAY COMPANY, THE
1601 Lincoln Rd, Windsor, ON, N8Y 2J3
(519) 973-8222
Emp Here 81   *Sales* 8,901,205
SIC 4013 Switching and terminal services
 Murray Elder
Pr Pr Brian Mckeown
Prin Terry Berthiaume
Dir Chuck Girard
Dir William Muzzatti
Dir Yves Poirier

D-U-N-S 25-636-3466   (BR)
F & J CHEETHAM (WINDSOR) LIMITED
TIM HORTONS
(*Suby of* F & J Cheetham (Windsor) Limited)
2220 Wyandotte St E, Windsor, ON, N8Y 1E7
(519) 258-4797
Emp Here 25
SIC 5812 Eating places

D-U-N-S 25-249-0800   (BR)
GREATER ESSEX COUNTY DISTRICT SCHOOL BOARD
GORDON MCGREGOR ELEMENTARY SCHOOL
1646 Alexis Rd, Windsor, ON, N8Y 4P4
(519) 944-6300
Emp Here 53
SIC 8211 Elementary and secondary schools

D-U-N-S 25-249-1089   (BR)
GREATER ESSEX COUNTY DISTRICT SCHOOL BOARD
MCCALLUM, PERCY P SCHOOL
4195 Milloy St, Windsor, ON, N8Y 2C2
(519) 945-5808
Emp Here 30
SIC 8211 Elementary and secondary schools

D-U-N-S 25-249-0875   (BR)
GREATER ESSEX COUNTY DISTRICT SCHOOL BOARD
KING EDWARD ELEMENTARY SCHOOL
853 Chilver Rd, Windsor, ON, N8Y 2K5
(519) 256-4999
Emp Here 30
SIC 8211 Elementary and secondary schools

D-U-N-S 25-249-0487   (BR)
GREATER ESSEX COUNTY DISTRICT SCHOOL BOARD
DAVID MAXWELL ELEMENTARY SCHOOL
1648 Francois Rd, Windsor, ON, N8Y 4L9
(519) 945-1421
Emp Here 30
SIC 8211 Elementary and secondary schools

D-U-N-S 20-710-5771   (BR)
GREATER ESSEX COUNTY DISTRICT SCHOOL BOARD
WALKER VILLE SECONDARY SCHOOL
2100 Richmond St, Windsor, ON, N8Y 1L4
(519) 252-6514
Emp Here 80
SIC 8211 Elementary and secondary schools

D-U-N-S 20-186-6373   (HQ)
HIRAM WALKER & SONS LIMITED
2072 Riverside Dr E, Windsor, ON, N8Y 4S5
(519) 254-5171
Emp Here 350   *Emp Total* 373
Sales 295,198,992
SIC 2085 Distilled and blended liquors
Pr Roland P Driscoll
VP Thierry R J Pourchette
Treas Garry Quick
Sec Marc Valencia
Sec Sharon Mayers
Dir Frederick Villain
Dir Katherine Anne Mcleod
Dir Philippe A X Dreano

Paul G Holub

D-U-N-S 20-702-6258   (SL)
KLINEC ELECTRIC SERVICES AND MANU-FACTURING LIMITED
KLINEC MANUFACTURING
1585 St Luke Rd, Windsor, ON, N8Y 3N4
(519) 944-7766
Emp Here 44   *Sales* 5,325,440
SIC 1731 Electrical work
Pr Pr Paul Klinec

D-U-N-S 25-127-3470   (SL)
QUANTOFILL INC
1215 Walker Rd Unit 11, Windsor, ON, N8Y 2N9
(519) 252-5501
Emp Here 25   *Sales* 1,459,214
SIC 7389 Business services, nec

D-U-N-S 25-297-3151   (BR)
RBC DOMINION SECURITIES INC
RBC WEALTH MANAGEMENT
(*Suby of* Royal Bank Of Canada)
1922 Wyandotte St E Suite 200, Windsor, ON, N8Y 1E4
(519) 252-3663
Emp Here 22
SIC 6282 Investment advice

D-U-N-S 25-321-4175   (BR)
REVERA INC
CENTRAL PARK LODGES
3387 Riverside Dr E, Windsor, ON, N8Y 1A8

Emp Here 70
SIC 8059 Nursing and personal care, nec

D-U-N-S 20-814-7723   (BR)
SUNRISE NORTH SENIOR LIVING LTD
(*Suby of* Welltower Inc.)
5065 Riverside Dr E Suite 203, Windsor, ON, N8Y 5B3
(519) 974-5858
Emp Here 85
SIC 8059 Nursing and personal care, nec

D-U-N-S 20-769-4501   (SL)
WINDSOR UTILITIES
3665 Wyandotte St E, Windsor, ON, N8Y 1G4
(519) 251-7300
Emp Here 40   *Sales* 7,004,227
SIC 1623 Water, sewer, and utility lines

D-U-N-S 20-710-5888   (BR)
WINDSOR-ESSEX CATHOLIC DISTRICT SCHOOL BOARD, THE
ST ANNE ELEMENTARY SCHOOL
1140 Monmouth Rd, Windsor, ON, N8Y 3L8
(519) 256-1911
Emp Here 25
SIC 8211 Elementary and secondary schools

D-U-N-S 25-249-3382   (BR)
WINDSOR-ESSEX CATHOLIC DISTRICT SCHOOL BOARD, THE
F J BRENNAN CATHOLIC HIGH SCHOOL
910 Raymo Rd, Windsor, ON, N8Y 4A6
(519) 945-2351
Emp Here 60
SIC 8211 Elementary and secondary schools

D-U-N-S 25-249-3572   (BR)
WINDSOR-ESSEX CATHOLIC DISTRICT SCHOOL BOARD, THE
OUR LADY LOURDES CATHOLIC SCHOOL
4130 Franklin St, Windsor, ON, N8Y 2E2
(519) 948-3072
Emp Here 22
SIC 8211 Elementary and secondary schools

Windsor, ON N9A
Essex County

D-U-N-S 25-050-1269   (SL)
1307761 ONTARIO LTD

LEOPARDS LOUNGE & BROIL
1190 Wyandotte St W, Windsor, ON, N9A 5Y5
(519) 254-6107
Emp Here 50   *Sales* 1,532,175
SIC 5812 Eating places

D-U-N-S 25-639-5781   (SL)
882976 ONTARIO INC
IMANET
1090 University Ave W Suite 200, Windsor, ON, N9A 5S4
(519) 977-7334
Emp Here 24   *Sales* 1,751,057
SIC 7371 Custom computer programming services

D-U-N-S 20-552-7539   (BR)
A.P. PLASMAN INC.
WINDSOR PLANT 1
5250 Outer Dr Suite 1, Windsor, ON, N9A 6J3
(519) 737-1633
Emp Here 400
SIC 3089 Plastics products, nec

D-U-N-S 25-362-8226   (BR)
A.P. PLASMAN INC.
5265 Outer Dr Suite 2, Windsor, ON, N9A 6J3
(519) 737-9602
Emp Here 250
SIC 3089 Plastics products, nec

D-U-N-S 20-190-1324   (HQ)
A.P. PLASMAN INC.
BUILD-A-MOLD, DIV OF
5245 Burke St Suite 1, Windsor, ON, N9A 6J3
(519) 737-6984
Emp Here 100   *Emp Total* 900
Sales 190,938,152
SIC 3089 Plastics products, nec
Pr David Wiskel
VP Tony Romanello
VP Engg Jeff Rose
Pers/VP Mila Lucio
 Jason Keys
 Tim Berezowski

D-U-N-S 25-393-9334   (HQ)
ACTIVE INDUSTRIAL SOLUTIONS INC
ACTIVE BURGESS MOULD & DESIGN
(*Suby of* Active Industrial Solutions Inc)
2155 North Talbot Rd Suite 3, Windsor, ON, N9A 6J3
(519) 737-1341
Emp Here 250   *Emp Total* 350
Sales 28,819,477
SIC 3544 Special dies, tools, jigs, and fixtures
Pr Pr Michael Bragagnolo
 Donald Jackson
 Randy Levine
 Catherine Herring

D-U-N-S 20-117-7578   (BR)
ACTIVE INDUSTRIAL SOLUTIONS INC
5250 Pulleyblank St, Windsor, ON, N9A 6J3
(519) 737-2921
Emp Here 175
SIC 3544 Special dies, tools, jigs, and fixtures

D-U-N-S 25-675-0076   (SL)
AUTOMOTIVE GAUGE & FIXTURE LIMITED
5270 Burke St, Windsor, ON, N9A 6J3
(519) 737-7148
Emp Here 26   *Sales* 2,115,860
SIC 3544 Special dies, tools, jigs, and fixtures

D-U-N-S 24-215-9499   (BR)
BASF CANADA INC
845 Wyandotte St W, Windsor, ON, N9A 5Y1
(519) 256-3155
Emp Here 100
SIC 2851 Paints and allied products

D-U-N-S 24-128-8260   (BR)
BMO NESBITT BURNS INC
100 Ouellette Ave Suite 1100, Windsor, ON, N9A 6T3
(519) 977-6697
Emp Here 25

SIC 6211 Security brokers and dealers

D-U-N-S 20-580-0860   (BR)
BANK OF NOVA SCOTIA, THE
SCOTIABANK
388 Ouellette Ave, Windsor, ON, N9A 1A6
(519) 973-5300
Emp Here 20
SIC 6021 National commercial banks

D-U-N-S 24-136-8088   (SL)
BREAKAWAY GAMING CENTRE
655 Crawford Ave, Windsor, ON, N9A 5C7
(519) 256-0001
Emp Here 75   *Sales* 4,085,799
SIC 7999 Amusement and recreation, nec

D-U-N-S 20-573-2105   (BR)
CANADIAN BROADCASTING CORPORATION
825 Riverside Dr W, Windsor, ON, N9A 5K9
(519) 255-3497
Emp Here 20
SIC 4833 Television broadcasting stations

D-U-N-S 24-079-5997   (BR)
CANADIAN IMPERIAL BANK OF COMMERCE
CIBC BANKING CENTRE
100 Ouellette Ave Suite 203, Windsor, ON, N9A 6T3
(519) 977-7000
Emp Here 35
SIC 6021 National commercial banks

D-U-N-S 20-100-6652   (BR)
CASH MONEY CHEQUE CASHING INC
CASH MONEY
596 Wyandotte St W, Windsor, ON, N9A 5X6
(519) 258-3559
Emp Here 45
SIC 6099 Functions related to deposit banking

D-U-N-S 25-097-7238   (HQ)
CHRYSLER FINANCIAL SERVICES CANADA INC
(*Suby of* Cerberus Capital Management, L.P.)
1 Riverside Dr W, Windsor, ON, N9A 5K3
(519) 973-2000
Emp Here 30   *Emp Total* 143,502
Sales 163,211,383
SIC 6153 Short-term business credit institutions, except agricultural
Genl Mgr Brian Chillman
 Michael J Dodge
 Gilman Thomas F

D-U-N-S 24-174-1094   (BR)
COMMUNITY GAMING & ENTERTAINMENT GROUP LP
CLASSIC BINGO V
(*Suby of* Community Gaming & Entertainment Group LP)
655 Crawford Ave, Windsor, ON, N9A 5C7
(519) 256-0001
Emp Here 70
SIC 7999 Amusement and recreation, nec

D-U-N-S 24-006-3032   (HQ)
CORPORATION OF THE CITY OF WINDSOR PUBLIC LIBRARY BOARD, THE
(*Suby of* Corporation of The City Of Windsor Public Library Board, The)
850 Ouellette Ave, Windsor, ON, N9A 4M9
(519) 255-6770
Emp Here 20   *Emp Total* 93
Sales 4,304,681
SIC 8231 Libraries

D-U-N-S 20-086-8748   (BR)
CORPORATION OF THE CITY OF WINDSOR
SOUTH WINDSOR RECREATIONAL COMPLEX
(*Suby of* Corporation of the City of Windsor)
2555 Pulford Rd, Windsor, ON, N9A 6J3
(519) 966-6040
Emp Here 25

SIC 7999 Amusement and recreation, nec

D-U-N-S 24-337-1650 (BR)
CORPORATION OF THE CITY OF WINDSOR
WINDSOR FIRE & RESCUE SERVICES
(Suby of Corporation of the City of Windsor)
815 Goyeau St, Windsor, ON, N9A 1H7
(519) 253-6573
Emp Here 270
SIC 7389 Business services, nec

D-U-N-S 25-051-8693 (SL)
DETROIT & CANADA TUNNEL
555 Goyeau St, Windsor, ON, N9A 1H1
(519) 258-7424
Emp Here 100   Sales 3,502,114
SIC 4111 Local and suburban transit

D-U-N-S 25-978-8099 (HQ)
ENWIN UTILITIES LTD
787 Ouellette Ave Suite 517, Windsor, ON, N9A 4J4
(519) 255-2727
Emp Here 339   Emp Total 641
Sales 198,717,979
SIC 4911 Electric services
Pr Maxwell Zalev
VP Fin Victoria Zuber
VP John Stuart
VP John Wladarski

D-U-N-S 20-646-4666 (BR)
FORD MOTOR COMPANY OF CANADA, LIMITED
FORD (WINDSOR) ENGINE PLANT
(Suby of Ford Motor Company)
1000 Henry Ford, Windsor, ON, N9A 7E8
(519) 257-2020
Emp Here 500
SIC 3519 Internal combustion engines, nec

D-U-N-S 24-120-8029 (BR)
FORD MOTOR COMPANY OF CANADA, LIMITED
(Suby of Ford Motor Company)
3223 Lauzon Pky, Windsor, ON, N9A 6X3
(519) 944-8784
Emp Here 1,000
SIC 5521 Used car dealers

D-U-N-S 25-195-3261 (BR)
FORD MOTOR COMPANY OF CANADA, LIMITED
(Suby of Ford Motor Company)
2900 Trenton St, Windsor, ON, N9A 7B2
(519) 257-2000
Emp Here 1,000
SIC 3322 Malleable iron foundries

D-U-N-S 25-368-5960 (BR)
FORD MOTOR COMPANY OF CANADA, LIMITED
(Suby of Ford Motor Company)
1 Quality Way, Windsor, ON, N9A 6X3
(519) 944-8658
Emp Here 1,000
SIC 3714 Motor vehicle parts and accessories

D-U-N-S 24-023-6088 (BR)
GOVERNING COUNCIL OF THE SALVATION ARMY IN CANADA, THE
GOVERNING COUNCIL OF THE SALVATION ARMY IN CANADA, THE
355 Church St, Windsor, ON, N9A 7G9
(519) 253-7473
Emp Here 50
SIC 8399 Social services, nec

D-U-N-S 24-041-5294 (BR)
GREATER ESSEX COUNTY DISTRICT SCHOOL BOARD
PRINCE ANDREW ELEMENTARY SCHOOL
1950 Kelly Rd, Windsor, ON, N9A 6Z6
(519) 734-8393
Emp Here 40
SIC 8211 Elementary and secondary schools

D-U-N-S 25-249-0917 (BR)
GREATER ESSEX COUNTY DISTRICT SCHOOL BOARD
FRANK BEGLEY PUBLIC SCHOOL
1093 Assumption St, Windsor, ON, N9A 3C5
(519) 254-3217
Emp Here 50
SIC 8211 Elementary and secondary schools

D-U-N-S 25-249-1048 (BR)
GREATER ESSEX COUNTY DISTRICT SCHOOL BOARD
PRINCE EDWARD ELEMENTARY SCHOOL
949 Giles Blvd E, Windsor, ON, N9A 4G2
(519) 253-1119
Emp Here 70
SIC 8211 Elementary and secondary schools

D-U-N-S 25-249-0529 (BR)
GREATER ESSEX COUNTY DISTRICT SCHOOL BOARD
DOUGALL AVENUE PUBLIC SCHOOL
811 Dougall Ave, Windsor, ON, N9A 4R2
(519) 254-4389
Emp Here 25
SIC 8211 Elementary and secondary schools

D-U-N-S 25-124-3135 (SL)
HIATUS HOUSE
250 Louis Ave, Windsor, ON, N9A 1W2
(519) 252-7781
Emp Here 49   Sales 11,873,345
SIC 8399 Social services, nec
Dir Thomas Rolse

D-U-N-S 25-305-1783 (BR)
INNVEST PROPERTIES CORP
QUALITY SUITES
(Suby of Innvest Properties Corp)
250 Dougall Ave, Windsor, ON, N9A 7C6
(519) 977-9707
Emp Here 25
SIC 7011 Hotels and motels

D-U-N-S 24-910-5438 (BR)
INNVEST PROPERTIES CORP
WATERFRONT HOTEL - DOWNTOWN WINDSOR
(Suby of Innvest Properties Corp)
277 Riverside Dr W, Windsor, ON, N9A 5K4
(519) 973-5555
Emp Here 150
SIC 7011 Hotels and motels

D-U-N-S 20-269-7934 (SL)
INTERNATIONAL INDUSTRIAL CONTRACTING CORPORATION
251 Goyeau St Suite 1600, Windsor, ON, N9A 6V4

Emp Here 63   Sales 8,386,728
SIC 1796 Installing building equipment
Pr Pr Douglas Jardine

D-U-N-S 24-987-1906 (SL)
LAGILL ENTERPRISES INC
TIM HORTONS
525 University Ave W, Windsor, ON, N9A 5R4
(519) 253-0012
Emp Here 68   Sales 2,042,900
SIC 5812 Eating places

D-U-N-S 25-310-9532 (BR)
MCDONALD'S RESTAURANTS OF CANADA LIMITED
MCDONALD'S
(Suby of McDonald's Corporation)
77 Wyandotte St E, Windsor, ON, N9A 3H1
(519) 258-7428
Emp Here 50
SIC 5812 Eating places

D-U-N-S 24-077-2483 (SL)
MCTAGUE LAW FIRM LLP
455 Pelissier St, Windsor, ON, N9A 6Z9
(519) 255-4300
Emp Here 55   Sales 4,742,446
SIC 8111 Legal services

D-U-N-S 25-300-0632 (BR)
METRO ONTARIO INC
FOOD BASICS
880 Goyeau St, Windsor, ON, N9A 1H8
(519) 258-3064
Emp Here 110
SIC 5411 Grocery stores

D-U-N-S 25-458-2315 (SL)
MULTICULTURAL COUNCIL OF WINDSOR & ESSEX COUNTY
245 Janette Ave, Windsor, ON, N9A 4Z2
(519) 255-1127
Emp Here 65   Sales 13,188,500
SIC 8399 Social services, nec
Pr Jillian Authier

D-U-N-S 20-700-2127 (BR)
POSTMEDIA NETWORK INC
WINDSOR STAR, THE
167 Ferry St, Windsor, ON, N9A 0C5
(519) 255-5720
Emp Here 300
SIC 2711 Newspapers

D-U-N-S 20-357-9391 (BR)
PRESTRESSED SYSTEMS INCORPORATED
INTERNATIONAL PRECAST SOLUTIONS, DIVISION OF
4955 Walker Rd, Windsor, ON, N9A 6J3
(519) 737-1216
Emp Here 100
SIC 3272 Concrete products, nec

D-U-N-S 20-922-6919 (BR)
PRICEWATERHOUSECOOPERS LLP
245 Ouellette Ave 3rd Fl, Windsor, ON, N9A 7J2
(519) 985-8900
Emp Here 50
SIC 8721 Accounting, auditing, and bookkeeping

D-U-N-S 25-923-1892 (BR)
QUALITY MODELS LIMITED
QM FINISHING
5295 Pulleyblank St, Windsor, ON, N9A 6J3
(519) 737-1431
Emp Here 30
SIC 1721 Painting and paper hanging

D-U-N-S 25-300-5946 (BR)
REDBERRY FRANCHISING CORP
BURGER KING
570 Goyeau St, Windsor, ON, N9A 1H2

Emp Here 30
SIC 5812 Eating places

D-U-N-S 25-308-4487 (BR)
ROYAL BANK OF CANADA
ROYAL BANK FINANCIAL COMMERCIAL SERVICES
(Suby of Royal Bank Of Canada)
245 Ouellette Ave, Windsor, ON, N9A 7J2
(519) 255-8637
Emp Here 30
SIC 6021 National commercial banks

D-U-N-S 25-639-3588 (SL)
RYANS, PATRICK O. LTD
RYANS, PATRICK IRISH PUB
25 Pitt St E, Windsor, ON, N9A 2V3

Emp Here 50   Sales 1,978,891
SIC 5812 Eating places

D-U-N-S 24-002-3809 (BR)
SOBEYS CAPITAL INCORPORATED
FRESHCO
799 Crawford Ave, Windsor, ON, N9A 5C7
(519) 252-4777
Emp Here 50
SIC 5411 Grocery stores

D-U-N-S 24-455-4221 (BR)
ST. JOSEPH'S HEALTH CARE, LONDON

ESSEX ACT TEAM
875 Ouellette Ave 2nd Fl, Windsor, ON, N9A 4J6
(519) 254-3486
Emp Here 59
SIC 8361 Residential care

D-U-N-S 24-154-5578 (HQ)
SUTHERLAND GLOBAL SERVICES CANADA ULC
(Suby of Sutherland Global Services Inc.)
500 Ouellette Ave, Windsor, ON, N9A 1B3
(800) 591-9395
Emp Here 20   Emp Total 13,215
Sales 92,515,607
SIC 7361 Employment agencies
Dilip Vellodi
Sec Satish Raman

D-U-N-S 25-330-5817 (BR)
TIPPET-RICHARDSON LIMITED
211 Shepherd St E Suite 201, Windsor, ON, N9A 6P4
(519) 254-5111
Emp Here 25
SIC 4214 Local trucking with storage

D-U-N-S 25-637-2442 (SL)
TOTAL HOSPITALITY SERVICES INC
BAD HARE SALOON, THE
670 Ouellette Ave, Windsor, ON, N9A 1B9
(519) 977-9116
Emp Here 50   Sales 1,824,018
SIC 5813 Drinking places

D-U-N-S 25-838-0716 (BR)
UNITED CHURCH OF CANADA, THE
DOWNTOWN MISSION (WINDSOR)
664 Victoria Ave, Windsor, ON, N9A 4N2
(519) 973-5573
Emp Here 29
SIC 8661 Religious organizations

D-U-N-S 24-015-3663 (BR)
UNIVERSAL PROTECTION SERVICE OF CANADA CO
LEGACY UNIVERSAL PROTECTION SERVICE
(Suby of Universal Protection Gp, LLC)
251 Goyeau St Suite 505, Windsor, ON, N9A 6V2

Emp Here 51
SIC 7381 Detective and armored car services

D-U-N-S 24-964-8734 (BR)
VAN-ROB INC
1000 University Ave W, Windsor, ON, N9A 5S4

Emp Here 21
SIC 3469 Metal stampings, nec

D-U-N-S 20-186-6175 (HQ)
VIKING PUMP OF CANADA INC
(Suby of Idex Corporation)
661 Grove Ave, Windsor, ON, N9A 6G7
(519) 256-5438
Emp Here 31   Emp Total 7,158
Sales 12,403,319
SIC 5084 Industrial machinery and equipment
Pr John D'alessandro
S&M/VP Mike Toy
Larry Tremblay
VP Opers Gurinder Singh

D-U-N-S 25-636-9331 (BR)
WW CANADA (ONE) NOMINEE CORP
TRAVELODGE
(Suby of Westmont Hospitality Management Limited)
33 Riverside Dr E, Windsor, ON, N9A 2S4
(519) 258-7774
Emp Here 24
SIC 7011 Hotels and motels

D-U-N-S 24-991-7295 (SL)
WINDSOR CASINO LIMITED

CAESARS WINDSOR
377 Riverside Dr E, Windsor, ON, N9A 7H7
(519) 258-7878
Emp Here 3,000   Sales 131,329,260
SIC 7011 Hotels and motels
Pr Pr Kevin Laforet
Terry Black
Wallace Barr

D-U-N-S 24-798-7964   (SL)
WINDSOR URBAN DESIGN COMMUNITY
400 City Hall Sq E Suite 400, Windsor, ON,
N9A 7K6
(519) 255-6543
Emp Here 30   Sales 7,369,031
SIC 8399 Social services, nec
Owner Thom Hunt

D-U-N-S 25-403-7625   (BR)
WINDSOR-ESSEX CATHOLIC DISTRICT
SCHOOL BOARD, THE
ST. THOMAS OF VILLANOVA SECONDARY
SCHOOL
2800 North Town Line Rd, Windsor, ON, N9A
6Z6
(519) 734-6444
Emp Here 150
SIC 8211 Elementary and secondary schools

D-U-N-S 25-249-0263   (BR)
WINDSOR-ESSEX CATHOLIC DISTRICT
SCHOOL BOARD, THE
IMMACULATE CONCEPTION ELEMENTARY
SCHOOL
735 Tuscarora St, Windsor, ON, N9A 3M7
(519) 256-9156
Emp Here 44
SIC 8211 Elementary and secondary schools

D-U-N-S 20-581-3012   (HQ)
WINDSOR-ESSEX COUNTY HOUSING
CORPORATION
(Suby of Corporation of the City of Windsor)
945 Mcdougall St, Windsor, ON, N9A 1L9
(519) 254-1681
Emp Here 20   Emp Total 2,575
Sales 4,742,446
SIC 6531 Real estate agents and managers

D-U-N-S 25-354-3995   (BR)
YMCA OF GREATER TORONTO
WINDSOR ESSEX COUNTY FAMILY YMCA
500 Victoria Ave, Windsor, ON, N9A 4M8
(519) 258-9622
Emp Here 70
SIC 8641 Civic and social associations

Windsor, ON N9B
Essex County

D-U-N-S 25-283-8503   (SL)
AMBASSADOR DUTY FREE MANAGE-
MENT SERVICES LIMITED
AMBASSADOR DUTY FREE STORE, THE
707 Patricia Rd, Windsor, ON, N9B 0B5
(519) 977-9100
Emp Here 50   Sales 4,085,799
SIC 5399 Miscellaneous general merchandise

D-U-N-S 25-249-0537   (BR)
CONSEIL SCOLAIRE DE DISTRICT DES
ECOLES CATHOLIQUES DU SUD-OUEST
ECOLE SAINT-EDMOND
1880 Totten St, Windsor, ON, N9B 1X3
(519) 945-0924
Emp Here 20
SIC 8211 Elementary and secondary schools

D-U-N-S 25-249-0990   (BR)
GREATER ESSEX COUNTY DISTRICT
SCHOOL BOARD
DR H D TAYLOR ELEMENTARY SCHOOL
1275 Campbell Ave, Windsor, ON, N9B 3M7
(519) 252-7729
Emp Here 30

SIC 8211 Elementary and secondary schools

D-U-N-S 25-249-0685   (BR)
GREATER ESSEX COUNTY DISTRICT
SCHOOL BOARD
J E BENSON ELEMENTARY SCHOOL
1556 Wyandotte St W, Windsor, ON, N9B 1H5

Emp Here 35
SIC 8211 Elementary and secondary schools

D-U-N-S 20-710-5821   (BR)
GREATER ESSEX COUNTY DISTRICT
SCHOOL BOARD
TURNING POINT
284 Cameron Ave, Windsor, ON, N9B 1Y6

Emp Here 50
SIC 8211 Elementary and secondary schools

D-U-N-S 25-249-0891   (BR)
GREATER ESSEX COUNTY DISTRICT
SCHOOL BOARD
CENTURY SECONDARY SCHOOL
1375 California Ave, Windsor, ON, N9B 2Z8
(519) 254-6451
Emp Here 75
SIC 8211 Elementary and secondary schools

D-U-N-S 20-069-8509   (BR)
GREATER ESSEX COUNTY DISTRICT
SCHOOL BOARD
ADULT LEARNING CENTRE
284 Cameron Ave, Windsor, ON, N9B 1Y6
(519) 253-5006
Emp Here 30
SIC 8211 Elementary and secondary schools

D-U-N-S 25-652-6245   (BR)
METRO ONTARIO INC
METRO
2750 Tecumseh Rd W, Windsor, ON, N9B 3P9
(519) 256-1891
Emp Here 125
SIC 5411 Grocery stores

D-U-N-S 25-300-4667   (BR)
REDBERRY FRANCHISING CORP
BURGER KING
2530 Tecumseh Rd W, Windsor, ON, N9B 3R2
(519) 258-3423
Emp Here 52
SIC 5812 Eating places

D-U-N-S 25-295-3757   (BR)
SHOPPERS DRUG MART CORPORATION
2670 Tecumseh Rd W Suite 762, Windsor,
ON, N9B 3P9
(519) 252-5779
Emp Here 45
SIC 5912 Drug stores and proprietary stores

D-U-N-S 20-572-8913   (BR)
UNIVERSITY OF WINDSOR
UNIVERSITY OF WINDSOR BOOK STORE
401 Sunset Ave Suite G07, Windsor, ON, N9B
3P4
(519) 973-7018
Emp Here 24
SIC 5192 Books, periodicals, and newspapers

D-U-N-S 20-106-7126   (BR)
UNIVERSITY OF WINDSOR
GREAT LAKES INSTITUTE
401 Sunset Ave Suite G07, Windsor, ON, N9B
3P4
(519) 253-3000
Emp Here 32
SIC 8221 Colleges and universities

D-U-N-S 25-249-0735   (BR)
WINDSOR-ESSEX CATHOLIC DISTRICT
SCHOOL BOARD, THE
ST JOHN ELEMENTARY SCHOOL
1920 Grove Ave, Windsor, ON, N9B 1P6
(519) 256-4092
Emp Here 20
SIC 8211 Elementary and secondary schools

Windsor, ON N9C
Essex County

D-U-N-S 20-281-5619   (BR)
A.P. PLASMAN INC.
635 Sprucewood Ave, Windsor, ON, N9C 0B3
(519) 791-9119
Emp Here 200
SIC 3089 Plastics products, nec

D-U-N-S 24-252-3850   (BR)
APPLESHORE RESTAURANTS INC
DINE APPLE
(Suby of Appleshore Restaurants Inc)
2187 Huron Church Rd Unit 240, Windsor,
ON, N9C 2L8
(519) 972-3000
Emp Here 30
SIC 8741 Management services

D-U-N-S 25-645-0776   (BR)
CARA OPERATIONS LIMITED
SWISS CHALET ROTISSERIE & GRILL
(Suby of Cara Holdings Limited)
1690 Huron Church Rd, Windsor, ON, N9C
0A9
(519) 973-4686
Emp Here 40
SIC 5812 Eating places

D-U-N-S 24-693-5506   (SL)
CASEY'S GRILL HOUSE & BEVERAGE
CO.,
1760 Huron Church Rd, Windsor, ON, N9C
2L4

Emp Here 55   Sales 1,678,096
SIC 5812 Eating places

D-U-N-S 25-644-8358   (BR)
COLUMBIA SPORTSWEAR CANADA LIM-
ITED
COLUMBIA   SPORTSWEAR   OUTLET
STORE
(Suby of Columbia Sportswear Company)
1650 Huron Church Rd, Windsor, ON, N9C
2L1

Emp Here 23
SIC 5699 Miscellaneous apparel and accessory stores

D-U-N-S 20-058-9492   (BR)
CON-WAY FREIGHT-CANADA INC
CONWAY FREIGHT CANADA
698 Sprucewood Ave, Windsor, ON, N9C 0B2
(519) 967-9243
Emp Here 21
SIC 4213 Trucking, except local

D-U-N-S 24-911-3036   (SL)
DNN GALVANIZING LIMITED PARTNER-
SHIP
300 Sprucewood Ave, Windsor, ON, N9C 0B7

Emp Here 100   Sales 9,423,360
SIC 3479 Metal coating and allied services
Come Belisle

D-U-N-S 24-324-3933   (HQ)
FARROW GROUP INC
(Suby of Farrow Group Inc)
2001 Huron Church Rd, Windsor, ON, N9C
2L6
(519) 252-4415
Emp Here 75   Emp Total 460
Sales 113,826,900
SIC 6712 Bank holding companies
Ch Bd Richard Farrow
V Ch Bd John Farrow
Ex VP Randy Motley
Ex VP Romeo Girardi
Ex VP Brian Wikston

D-U-N-S 25-636-3565   (BR)
FEDEX TRADE NETWORKS TRANSPORT

& BROKERAGE (CANADA), INC
FEDEX TRADE NETWORKS
(Suby of Fedex Corporation)
3950 Malden Rd, Windsor, ON, N9C 2G4
(800) 463-3339
Emp Here 21
SIC 4731 Freight transportation arrangement

D-U-N-S 25-185-5581   (BR)
FORD MOTOR COMPANY OF CANADA,
LIMITED
WINDSOR ALUMINUM PLANT
(Suby of Ford Motor Company)
4600 G N Booth Dr, Windsor, ON, N9C 4G8
(519) 250-2500
Emp Here 350
SIC 3089 Plastics products, nec

D-U-N-S 25-249-1162   (BR)
GREATER ESSEX COUNTY DISTRICT
SCHOOL BOARD
MARLBOROUGH ELEMENTARY SCHOOL
3557 Melbourne Rd, Windsor, ON, N9C 1Y6
(519) 254-1420
Emp Here 43
SIC 8211 Elementary and secondary schools

D-U-N-S 25-249-0883   (BR)
GREATER ESSEX COUNTY DISTRICT
SCHOOL BOARD
GENERAL BROCK ELEMENTARY SCHOOL
3312 Sandwich St, Windsor, ON, N9C 1B1
(519) 254-2571
Emp Here 40
SIC 8211 Elementary and secondary schools

D-U-N-S 20-710-5763   (BR)
GREATER ESSEX COUNTY DISTRICT
SCHOOL BOARD
J L FORSTER PUBLIC SECONDARY
SCHOOL
749 Felix Ave, Windsor, ON, N9C 3K9

Emp Here 50
SIC 8211 Elementary and secondary schools

D-U-N-S 25-180-9281   (BR)
K+S SEL WINDSOR LTEE
30 Prospect Ave, Windsor, ON, N9C 3G3
(519) 255-5400
Emp Here 110
SIC 2899 Chemical preparations, nec

D-U-N-S 20-104-8159   (BR)
MAGNA SEATING INC
INNOVATECH SEATING SYSTEMS, DIV OF
621 Sprucewood Ave, Windsor, ON, N9C 0B3

Emp Here 165
SIC 2531 Public building and related furniture

D-U-N-S 25-318-1564   (BR)
MCDONALD'S   RESTAURANTS   OF
CANADA LIMITED
MCDONALD'S RESTAURANTS OF CANADA
LIMITED
(Suby of McDonald's Corporation)
883 Huron Church Rd, Windsor, ON, N9C 2K3
(519) 258-3531
Emp Here 101
SIC 5812 Eating places

D-U-N-S 24-347-9511   (BR)
MCDONALD'S   RESTAURANTS   OF
CANADA LIMITED
MCDONALD'S RESTAURANT
(Suby of McDonald's Corporation)
5631 Ojibway Pky, Windsor, ON, N9C 4J5
(519) 250-5311
Emp Here 102
SIC 5812 Eating places

D-U-N-S 25-479-2336   (BR)
MERITAS CARE CORPORATION
CHATEAU PARK NURSING HOME
2990 Riverside Dr W Suite B, Windsor, ON,
N9C 1A2

(519) 254-4341
Emp Here 74
SIC 8741 Management services

D-U-N-S 20-177-3988   (BR)
NEMAK OF CANADA CORPORATION
4600 G N Booth Dr, Windsor, ON, N9C 4G8
(519) 250-2545
Emp Here 400
SIC 3714 Motor vehicle parts and accessories

D-U-N-S 25-010-7190   (BR)
PRISZM LP
KFC
1797 Huron Church Rd, Windsor, ON, N9C
2L3

Emp Here 20
SIC 5812 Eating places

D-U-N-S 20-580-5943   (BR)
ROYAL BANK OF CANADA
RBC
(*Suby of* Royal Bank Of Canada)
1600 Huron Church Rd, Windsor, ON, N9C
2L1
(519) 256-3485
Emp Here 20
SIC 6021 National commercial banks

D-U-N-S 24-550-6217   (BR)
TST SOLUTIONS L.P.
TST OVERLAND EXPRESS
1855 Brunet Dr, Windsor, ON, N9C 3S2
(519) 966-0500
Emp Here 60
SIC 4213 Trucking, except local

D-U-N-S 25-098-6197   (BR)
TST SOLUTIONS L.P.
TST EXPEDITED SERVICES
710 Sprucewood Ave, Windsor, ON, N9C 0B2
(519) 972-8111
Emp Here 55
SIC 4731 Freight transportation arrangement

D-U-N-S 25-636-9984   (BR)
TWINCORP INC
TACO BELL
1790 Huron Church Rd, Windsor, ON, N9C
2L4
(519) 977-0662
Emp Here 20
SIC 5812 Eating places

D-U-N-S 25-298-0693   (BR)
UPS SCS, INC
UPS SUPPLY CHAIN SOLUTION
2970 College Ave Suite 200, Windsor, ON,
N9C 1S5
(519) 972-9800
Emp Here 40
SIC 4731 Freight transportation arrangement

D-U-N-S 25-636-3474   (BR)
WATSON, T.J. ENTERPRISES INC
TIM HORTONS
1420 Huron Church Rd, Windsor, ON, N9C
2L1
(519) 252-4343
Emp Here 30
SIC 5812 Eating places

D-U-N-S 20-770-9361   (SL)
WINDSOR RACEWAY INC
5555 Ojibway Pky, Windsor, ON, N9C 4J5

Emp Here 500
SIC 7948 Racing, including track operation

D-U-N-S 25-636-4035   (BR)
WINDSOR REGIONAL HOSPITAL
WINDSOR REGIONAL CHILDREN CENTRE
3901 Connaught Ave, Windsor, ON, N9C 4H4
(519) 257-5215
Emp Here 75
SIC 8093 Specialty outpatient clinics, nec

D-U-N-S 20-710-5946   (BR)
WINDSOR-ESSEX CATHOLIC DISTRICT

SCHOOL BOARD, THE
ST JAMES CATHOLIC SCHOOL
1601 St James St, Windsor, ON, N9C 3P6
(519) 252-9960
Emp Here 30
SIC 8211 Elementary and secondary schools

D-U-N-S 25-249-4026   (BR)
WINDSOR-ESSEX CATHOLIC DISTRICT
SCHOOL BOARD, THE
*ASSUMPTION COLLEGE CATHOLIC HIGH
SCHOOL*
1100 Huron Church Rd, Windsor, ON, N9C
2K7
(519) 256-7801
Emp Here 90
SIC 8211 Elementary and secondary schools

D-U-N-S 20-710-5920   (BR)
WINDSOR-ESSEX CATHOLIC DISTRICT
SCHOOL BOARD, THE
*ST. FRANCIS CATHOLIC ELEMENTARY
SCHOOL*
477 Detroit St, Windsor, ON, N9C 2P6
(519) 946-3761
Emp Here 30
SIC 8211 Elementary and secondary schools

Windsor, ON N9E
Essex County

D-U-N-S 20-003-7641   (BR)
BANQUE TORONTO-DOMINION, LA
TORONTO-DOMINION BANK, THE
(*Suby of* Toronto-Dominion Bank, The)
1550 Grand Marais Rd W, Windsor, ON, N9E
4L1
(519) 972-1990
Emp Here 30
SIC 6021 National commercial banks

D-U-N-S 25-303-4136   (BR)
**CANADIAN IMPERIAL BANK OF COM-
MERCE**
CIBC
3168 Dougall Ave, Windsor, ON, N9E 1S6
(519) 969-8720
Emp Here 20
SIC 6021 National commercial banks

D-U-N-S 20-629-8338   (BR)
CARA OPERATIONS LIMITED
HARVEY'S RESTAURANTS
(*Suby of* Cara Holdings Limited)
3095 Dougall Ave, Windsor, ON, N9E 1S3
(519) 972-4826
Emp Here 30
SIC 5812 Eating places

D-U-N-S 20-889-2393   (SL)
CHILDREN'S HOUSE MONTESSORI, THE
2611 Labelle St, Windsor, ON, N9E 4G4
(519) 969-5278
Emp Here 100   *Sales* 2,991,389
SIC 8351 Child day care services

D-U-N-S 20-995-1388   (BR)
CHRISTIAN HORIZONS
(*Suby of* Christian Horizons)
3635 Dougall Ave, Windsor, ON, N9E 1T5
(519) 255-7483
Emp Here 25
SIC 8361 Residential care

D-U-N-S 20-289-9550   (BR)
**CONSEIL SCOLAIRE DE DISTRICT DES
ECOLES CATHOLIQUES DU SUD-OUEST**
ECOLE MONSENIOR JEAN NOELE
3225 California Ave, Windsor, ON, N9E 3K5
(519) 966-6670
Emp Here 25
SIC 8211 Elementary and secondary schools

D-U-N-S 20-029-8540   (BR)
CONSEIL SCOLAIRE DE DISTRICT DES

ECOLES CATHOLIQUES DU SUD-OUEST
ECOLE SECONDAIRE E J LAJEUNESSE
600 E C Row Ave W, Windsor, ON, N9E 1A5
(519) 972-0071
Emp Here 40
SIC 8211 Elementary and secondary schools

D-U-N-S 25-889-9368   (BR)
**DYNACARE-GAMMA LABORATORY PART-
NERSHIP**
DYNACARE
3176 Dougall Ave Suite 22, Windsor, ON, N9E
1S6
(519) 252-3457
Emp Here 35
SIC 8071 Medical laboratories

D-U-N-S 20-026-0540   (BR)
**GREATER ESSEX COUNTY DISTRICT
SCHOOL BOARD**
VINCENT MASSEY SECONDARY SCHOOL
1800 Liberty St, Windsor, ON, N9E 1J2
(519) 969-2530
Emp Here 100
SIC 8211 Elementary and secondary schools

D-U-N-S 25-249-1113   (BR)
**GREATER ESSEX COUNTY DISTRICT
SCHOOL BOARD**
NORTHWOOD ELEMENTARY SCHOOL
1100 Northwood St, Windsor, ON, N9E 1A3
(519) 969-7610
Emp Here 60
SIC 8211 Elementary and secondary schools

D-U-N-S 20-710-5722   (BR)
**GREATER ESSEX COUNTY DISTRICT
SCHOOL BOARD**
CENTRAL PUBLIC SCHOOL
700 Norfolk St, Windsor, ON, N9E 1H4
(519) 969-3530
Emp Here 30
SIC 8211 Elementary and secondary schools

D-U-N-S 25-249-0842   (BR)
**GREATER ESSEX COUNTY DISTRICT
SCHOOL BOARD**
GLENWOOD ELEMENTARY SCHOOL
1601 Norfolk St, Windsor, ON, N9E 1H6
(519) 969-3990
Emp Here 35
SIC 8211 Elementary and secondary schools

D-U-N-S 25-840-4016   (BR)
INNVEST PROPERTIES CORP
*COMFORT INN & SUITES AMBASSADOR
BRIDGE*
(*Suby of* Innvest Properties Corp)
2330 Huron Church Rd, Windsor, ON, N9E
3S6
(519) 972-1100
Emp Here 35
SIC 7011 Hotels and motels

D-U-N-S 25-305-1825   (BR)
INNVEST PROPERTIES CORP
COMFORT INN
(*Suby of* Innvest Properties Corp)
2955 Dougall Ave, Windsor, ON, N9E 1S1
(519) 966-7800
Emp Here 20
SIC 7011 Hotels and motels

D-U-N-S 24-308-0715   (BR)
LOBLAWS INC
REAL CANADIAN SUPERSTORE
2950 Dougall Ave Suite 18, Windsor, ON, N9E
1S2
(519) 969-3087
Emp Here 100
SIC 2051 Bread, cake, and related products

D-U-N-S 24-688-8630   (BR)
**MCDONALD'S RESTAURANTS OF
CANADA LIMITED**
MANNAH FOODS
(*Suby of* McDonald's Corporation)
3354 Dougall Ave, Windsor, ON, N9E 1S6

(519) 966-0454
Emp Here 115
SIC 5812 Eating places

D-U-N-S 25-636-8853   (BR)
MOORES THE SUIT PEOPLE INC
MOORES CLOTHING FOR MEN
(*Suby of* Tailored Brands, Inc.)
3164 Dougall Ave, Windsor, ON, N9E 1S6
(519) 972-7707
Emp Here 20
SIC 5611 Men's and boys' clothing stores

D-U-N-S 24-793-4599   (SL)
P.S.I. REPAIR SERVICES INC
1909 Spring Garden Rd, Windsor, ON, N9E
3P7
(519) 948-2288
Emp Here 200   *Sales* 10,699,440
SIC 7629 Electrical repair shops
William Phillips

D-U-N-S 24-469-1846   (BR)
PRISZM LP
KFC
3006 Dougall Ave, Windsor, ON, N9E 1S4
(519) 969-7290
Emp Here 21
SIC 5812 Eating places

D-U-N-S 20-555-7841   (BR)
**REVOLUTION ENVIRONMENTAL SOLU-
TIONS LP**
TERRAPURE ENVIRONMENTAL
(*Suby of* Revolution Environmental Solutions
LP)
4505 Fourth St, Windsor, ON, N9E 4A5

Emp Here 40
SIC 4953 Refuse systems

D-U-N-S 25-638-9578   (BR)
ROYCO HOTELS & RESORTS LTD
TRAVELODGE WINDSOR
2330 Huron Church Rd, Windsor, ON, N9E
3S6
(519) 972-1100
Emp Here 32
SIC 7011 Hotels and motels

D-U-N-S 25-652-6435   (BR)
WAL-MART CANADA CORP
3120 Dougall Ave, Windsor, ON, N9E 1S7
(519) 969-8121
Emp Here 280
SIC 5311 Department stores

D-U-N-S 25-249-0578   (BR)
**WINDSOR-ESSEX CATHOLIC DISTRICT
SCHOOL BOARD, THE**
CHRIST THE KING ELEMENTARY SCHOOL
1200 Grand Marais Rd W, Windsor, ON, N9E
1C9
(519) 969-2299
Emp Here 28
SIC 8211 Elementary and secondary schools

D-U-N-S 20-710-5862   (BR)
**WINDSOR-ESSEX CATHOLIC DISTRICT
SCHOOL BOARD, THE**
NOTRE DAME ELEMENTARY SCHOOL
2751 Partington Ave, Windsor, ON, N9E 3A9
(519) 969-7040
Emp Here 38
SIC 8211 Elementary and secondary schools

D-U-N-S 25-225-1624   (BR)
**WINDSOR-ESSEX CATHOLIC DISTRICT
SCHOOL BOARD, THE**
HOLY NAMES HIGH SCHOOL
1400 Northwood St, Windsor, ON, N9E 1A4
(519) 966-2504
Emp Here 120
SIC 8211 Elementary and secondary schools

D-U-N-S 20-710-5938   (BR)
**WINDSOR-ESSEX CATHOLIC DISTRICT
SCHOOL BOARD, THE**
ST GABRIEL ELEMENTARY SCHOOL

1400 Roselawn Dr, Windsor, ON, N9E 1L8
(519) 969-3230
Emp Here 50
SIC 8211 Elementary and secondary schools

Windsor, ON N9G
Essex County

D-U-N-S 25-296-5397   (BR)
BANK OF NOVA SCOTIA, THE
SCOTIABANK
3889 Dougall Ave, Windsor, ON, N9G 1X3
(519) 969-0251
Emp Here 23
SIC 6021 National commercial banks

D-U-N-S 25-811-7027   (BR)
CORPORATION OF THE CITY OF WINDSOR
ROSELAND GOLF & CURLING CLUB
(*Suby of* Corporation of the City of Windsor)
455 Kennedy Dr W, Windsor, ON, N9G 1S8
(519) 969-5112
Emp Here 25
SIC 7997 Membership sports and recreation clubs

D-U-N-S 25-570-6988   (BR)
CORPORATION OF THE CITY OF WINDSOR
HURON LODGE HOME FOR THE AGED
(*Suby of* Corporation of the City of Windsor)
1881 Cabana Rd W, Windsor, ON, N9G 1C7
(519) 253-6060
Emp Here 250
SIC 8361 Residential care

D-U-N-S 25-733-8608   (BR)
CORPORATION OF THE CITY OF WINDSOR
OAKWOOD COMMUNITY CENTRE
(*Suby of* Corporation of the City of Windsor)
2520 Cabana Rd W, Windsor, ON, N9G 1E5
(519) 966-6065
Emp Here 65
SIC 8322 Individual and family services

D-U-N-S 20-213-2028   (BR)
EXTENDICARE INC
EXTENDICARE SOUTHWOOD LAKES
1255 North Talbot Rd, Windsor, ON, N9G 3A4
(519) 945-7249
Emp Here 160
SIC 8051 Skilled nursing care facilities

D-U-N-S 25-249-1105   (BR)
GREATER ESSEX COUNTY DISTRICT SCHOOL BOARD
OAKWOOD SCHOOL
2520 Cabana Rd W, Windsor, ON, N9G 1E5
(519) 972-0971
Emp Here 25
SIC 8211 Elementary and secondary schools

D-U-N-S 25-249-1063   (BR)
GREATER ESSEX COUNTY DISTRICT SCHOOL BOARD
SOUTHWOOD SCHOOL
1355 Cabana Rd W, Windsor, ON, N9G 1C3
(519) 969-3470
Emp Here 45
SIC 8211 Elementary and secondary schools

D-U-N-S 25-249-0925   (BR)
GREATER ESSEX COUNTY DISTRICT SCHOOL BOARD
ROSELAND ELEMENTARY SCHOOL
620 Cabana Rd E, Windsor, ON, N9G 1A4
(519) 969-3250
Emp Here 40
SIC 8211 Elementary and secondary schools

D-U-N-S 24-676-3101   (BR)
GREATER ESSEX COUNTY DISTRICT SCHOOL BOARD

TALBOT TRAIL PUBLIC SCHOOL
4000 Ducharme St, Windsor, ON, N9G 0A1
(519) 969-9748
Emp Here 50
SIC 8211 Elementary and secondary schools

D-U-N-S 25-636-8788   (BR)
ROYAL BANK OF CANADA
RBC
(*Suby of* Royal Bank Of Canada)
3854 Dougall Ave, Windsor, ON, N9G 1X2
(519) 972-3373
Emp Here 20
SIC 6021 National commercial banks

Windsor, ON N9H
Essex County

D-U-N-S 24-203-0950   (SL)
AB AUTOMATION LTD
2155 Talbot Rd, Windsor, ON, N9H 1A7
(519) 737-1900
Emp Here 25   *Sales* 2,772,003
SIC 8742 Management consulting services

D-U-N-S 24-426-1991   (SL)
CSH OAK PARK LASALLE INC
CHARTWELL CLASSIC OAK PARK LASALLE
3955 Thirteenth St Suite 722, Windsor, ON, N9H 2S7
(519) 968-2000
Emp Here 20   *Sales* 729,607
SIC 8361 Residential care

D-U-N-S 25-303-4052   (BR)
CANADIAN IMPERIAL BANK OF COMMERCE
CIBC
5870 Malden Rd, Windsor, ON, N9H 1S4
(519) 969-3712
Emp Here 25
SIC 6021 National commercial banks

D-U-N-S 24-984-9399   (BR)
GREATER ESSEX COUNTY DISTRICT SCHOOL BOARD
SANDWICH WEST PUBLIC SCHOOL
2055 Wyoming Ave, Windsor, ON, N9H 1P6
(519) 969-1750
Emp Here 50
SIC 8211 Elementary and secondary schools

D-U-N-S 20-708-8662   (BR)
NIKE CANADA CORP
(*Suby of* Nike, Inc.)
1555 Talbot Rd, Windsor, ON, N9H 2N2

Emp Here 35
SIC 5699 Miscellaneous apparel and accessory stores

D-U-N-S 25-683-4649   (BR)
TOMMY HILFIGER CANADA INC
1555 Talbot Rd Suite 180, Windsor, ON, N9H 2N2
(519) 250-7922
Emp Here 20
SIC 5651 Family clothing stores

D-U-N-S 24-560-7549   (BR)
WINDSOR-ESSEX CATHOLIC DISTRICT SCHOOL BOARD, THE
HOLY CROSS ELEMENTARY SCHOOL
2555 Sandwich West Pkwy, Windsor, ON, N9H 2P7
(519) 972-6050
Emp Here 80
SIC 8211 Elementary and secondary schools

D-U-N-S 25-033-3986   (BR)
ZEHRMART INC
ZEHRS MARKETS
5890 Malden Rd, Windsor, ON, N9H 1S4
(519) 966-6030
Emp Here 400

SIC 5411 Grocery stores

Windsor, ON N9J
Essex County

D-U-N-S 24-977-6766   (BR)
CENTERLINE (WINDSOR) LIMITED
595 Morton Dr, Windsor, ON, N9J 3T8
(519) 734-6886
Emp Here 100
SIC 3548 Welding apparatus

D-U-N-S 25-357-4594   (BR)
CENTERLINE (WINDSOR) LIMITED
655 Morton Dr, Windsor, ON, N9J 3T9
(519) 734-8330
Emp Here 150
SIC 3548 Welding apparatus

D-U-N-S 20-802-2769   (BR)
COMPAGNIE DE TELEPHONE BELL DU CANADA OU BELL CANADA, LA
BELL CANADA
935 Laurier Dr, Windsor, ON, N9J 1M9
(519) 978-0569
Emp Here 20
SIC 4899 Communication services, nec

D-U-N-S 25-249-1899   (BR)
CONSEIL SCOLAIRE DE DISTRICT DES ECOLES CATHOLIQUES DU SUD-OUEST
ECOLE ELEMENTAIRE CATHOLIQUE MONSEIGNEUR AUGUSTIN
8200 Matchette Rd, Windsor, ON, N9J 3P1
(519) 734-1380
Emp Here 40
SIC 8211 Elementary and secondary schools

D-U-N-S 20-186-2869   (SL)
E.R. ST. DENIS INC
6185 Morton Industrial Pky, Windsor, ON, N9J 3W2
(519) 734-7222
Emp Here 25   *Sales* 2,772,507
SIC 3542 Machine tools, Metal forming type

D-U-N-S 25-249-1766   (BR)
GREATER ESSEX COUNTY DISTRICT SCHOOL BOARD
SANDWICH SECONDARY SCHOOL
7050 Malden Rd, Windsor, ON, N9J 2T5
(519) 734-1237
Emp Here 65
SIC 8211 Elementary and secondary schools

D-U-N-S 20-093-2924   (BR)
GREATER ESSEX COUNTY DISTRICT SCHOOL BOARD
LASALLE PUBLIC SCHOOL
1600 Mayfair Ave, Windsor, ON, N9J 3T3
(519) 978-1823
Emp Here 45
SIC 8211 Elementary and secondary schools

D-U-N-S 24-595-4149   (BR)
K+S SEL WINDSOR LTEE
200 Morton Dr, Windsor, ON, N9J 3W9
(519) 972-2201
Emp Here 300
SIC 1479 Chemical and fertilizer mining

D-U-N-S 20-555-0085   (BR)
PAPP PLASTICS AND DISTRIBUTING LIMITED
6110 Morton Industrial Pky, Windsor, ON, N9J 3W3
(519) 734-0700
Emp Here 75
SIC 3089 Plastics products, nec

D-U-N-S 25-249-1683   (BR)
WINDSOR-ESSEX CATHOLIC DISTRICT SCHOOL BOARD, THE
ST JOSEPH CATHOLIC SCHOOL
9381 Town Line Rd, Windsor, ON, N9J 2W6

(519) 734-1219
Emp Here 60
SIC 8211 Elementary and secondary schools

Windsor, ON N9K
Essex County

D-U-N-S 20-303-3485   (BR)
CARA OPERATIONS LIMITED
KELSEY'S
(*Suby of* Cara Holdings Limited)
9 Amy Croft Dr, Windsor, ON, N9K 1C7
(519) 735-3390
Emp Here 20
SIC 5812 Eating places

D-U-N-S 20-245-9124   (BR)
SOBEYS CAPITAL INCORPORATED
19 Amy Croft Dr, Windsor, ON, N9K 1C7
(519) 735-4110
Emp Here 193
SIC 5411 Grocery stores

D-U-N-S 20-657-0579   (BR)
WENDY'S RESTAURANTS OF CANADA INC
WENDY'S
(*Suby of* The Wendy's Company)
5 Amy Croft Dr, Windsor, ON, N9K 1C7
(519) 735-3331
Emp Here 20
SIC 5812 Eating places

Wingham, ON N0G
Huron County

D-U-N-S 25-804-4817   (BR)
AVON MAITLAND DISTRICT SCHOOL BOARD
MADILL, F E SECONDARY SCHOOL
231 Madill Dr E, Wingham, ON, N0G 2W0
(519) 357-1800
Emp Here 100
SIC 8211 Elementary and secondary schools

D-U-N-S 20-710-7009   (BR)
AVON MAITLAND DISTRICT SCHOOL BOARD
WINGHAM PUBLIC SCHOOL
131 John St E, Wingham, ON, N0G 2W0

Emp Here 25
SIC 8211 Elementary and secondary schools

D-U-N-S 24-205-9827   (BR)
BLACKBURN RADIO INC
CKNX AM FM RADIO
215 Carling Terr, Wingham, ON, N0G 2W0
(519) 357-1310
Emp Here 50
SIC 4832 Radio broadcasting stations

D-U-N-S 20-580-3013   (BR)
CANADA POST CORPORATION
303 Josephine St, Wingham, ON, N0G 2W0
(519) 357-2680
Emp Here 20
SIC 4311 U.s. postal service

D-U-N-S 25-981-4069   (SL)
COMMUNITY LIVING WINGHAM & DISTRICT
153 John St W, Wingham, ON, N0G 2W0
(519) 357-3562
Emp Here 60   *Sales* 2,334,742
SIC 8322 Individual and family services

D-U-N-S 20-591-9256   (BR)
HURON PERTH CATHOLIC DISTRICT SCHOOL BOARD
SACRED HEART SEPARATE SCHOOL
225 Cornyn St, Wingham, ON, N0G 2W0

(519) 357-1090
Emp Here 25
SIC 8211 Elementary and secondary schools

D-U-N-S 20-786-6070   (SL)
MACGOWAN NURSING HOMES LTD
BRAEMAR RETIREMENT CENTRE
719 Josephine St, Wingham, ON, N0G 2W0
(519) 357-3430
Emp Here 70   *Sales* 3,210,271
SIC 8051 Skilled nursing care facilities

D-U-N-S 24-848-9283   (BR)
MASTERFEEDS INC
90540 London Rd Rr 2, Wingham, ON, N0G 2W0
(519) 357-3411
Emp Here 20
SIC 2048 Prepared feeds, nec

D-U-N-S 20-035-1653   (BR)
PHARMA PLUS DRUGMARTS LTD
VANCE'S PHARMA PLUS
55 Josephine St, Wingham, ON, N0G 2W0
(519) 357-2170
Emp Here 20
SIC 5912 Drug stores and proprietary stores

D-U-N-S 20-302-0011   (BR)
WESCAST INDUSTRIES INC
WESCAST INDUSTRIES MACHINING WINGHAM
100 Water St, Wingham, ON, N0G 2W0
(519) 357-4447
Emp Here 75
SIC 3714 Motor vehicle parts and accessories

D-U-N-S 25-371-6419   (BR)
WESCAST INDUSTRIES INC
WINGHAM CASTINGS
200 Water St, Wingham, ON, N0G 2W0
(519) 357-3450
Emp Here 400
SIC 3714 Motor vehicle parts and accessories

Woodbridge, ON L4H
York County

D-U-N-S 24-330-0303   (BR)
ADIDAS CANADA LIMITED
ADIDAS GROUP
8100 27 Hwy Suite 1, Woodbridge, ON, L4H 3N2
(905) 266-4200
Emp Here 280
SIC 5139 Footwear

D-U-N-S 20-158-3531   (HQ)
ADIDAS CANADA LIMITED
ROCKPORT CANADA
8100 27 Hwy Suite 1, Woodbridge, ON, L4H 3N2
(905) 266-4200
Emp Here 150   *Emp Total* 60,617
Sales 79,454,202
SIC 5091 Sporting and recreation goods
Pr Pr Steven Ralph
Dir Natalie Knight
Dir Robert Adam
Dir Daniel Gervais

D-U-N-S 24-121-1312   (BR)
BANK OF NOVA SCOTIA, THE
SCOTIABANK
9333 Weston Rd Unit 1, Woodbridge, ON, L4H 3G8
(905) 303-5990
Emp Here 25
SIC 6021 National commercial banks

D-U-N-S 20-296-0779   (HQ)
CERTAINTEED CANADA, INC
DECOUSTICS
61 Royal Group Cres, Woodbridge, ON, L4H 1X9

(905) 652-5200
Emp Here 93   *Emp Total* 205
Sales 8,662,510
SIC 3296 Mineral wool
Eric Marceau
John Crow

D-U-N-S 20-172-7047   (HQ)
COATS CANADA INC
COATS BELL
10 Roybridge Gate Suite 200, Woodbridge, ON, L4H 3M8
(905) 850-9200
Emp Here 20   *Emp Total* 21,751
Sales 4,319,040
SIC 5092 Toys and hobby goods and supplies

D-U-N-S 25-500-8328   (SL)
D & V ELECTRONICS LTD
130 Zenway Blvd, Woodbridge, ON, L4H 2Y7
(905) 264-7646
Emp Here 70   *Sales* 11,159,055
SIC 3694 Engine electrical equipment
CEO Scott Matrenec
Ex Dir Kalina Loukanov

D-U-N-S 25-977-6792   (HQ)
ENERGI FENESTRATION SOLUTIONS, LTD
30 Royal Group Cres, Woodbridge, ON, L4H 1X9
(905) 851-6637
Emp Here 100   *Sales* 82,726,971
SIC 3442 Metal doors, sash, and trim
Dir Jesse Hawthorne

D-U-N-S 25-366-1698   (BR)
FLYNN CANADA LTD
141 Royal Group Cres, Woodbridge, ON, L4H 1X9
(905) 671-3971
Emp Here 250
SIC 1761 Roofing, siding, and sheetMetal work

D-U-N-S 20-294-3932   (BR)
HOME DEPOT OF CANADA INC
HOME DEPOT RDC 7275
(*Suby of* The Home Depot Inc)
8966 Huntington Rd, Woodbridge, ON, L4H 3V1
(905) 265-4400
Emp Here 400
SIC 4225 General warehousing and storage

D-U-N-S 24-976-4809   (SL)
LAYER 3 SOLUTIONS INC
400 Zenway Blvd Suite 4, Woodbridge, ON, L4H 0S7
(416) 232-2552
Emp Here 50   *Sales* 5,034,288
SIC 7372 Prepackaged software
Pr Waheed Noor

D-U-N-S 20-797-6643   (BR)
MCDONALD'S RESTAURANTS OF CANADA LIMITED
MCDONALD'S
(*Suby of* McDonald's Corporation)
9600 Islington Ave Suite C1, Woodbridge, ON, L4H 2T1
(905) 893-3909
Emp Here 20
SIC 5812 Eating places

D-U-N-S 20-737-7859   (SL)
MCDONALDS RESTAURANT OF CANADA INC
9200 Weston Rd Unit E, Woodbridge, ON, L4H 2P8
(905) 832-0424
Emp Here 120   *Sales* 4,331,255
SIC 5812 Eating places

D-U-N-S 24-335-0514   (BR)
METRO ONTARIO INC
9600 Islington Ave, Woodbridge, ON, L4H 2T1

Emp Here 300
SIC 5411 Grocery stores

D-U-N-S 20-281-0693   (SL)
PACIFIC LINKS CANADA SERVICES INC
331 Cityview Blvd Suite 200, Woodbridge, ON, L4H 3M3
(866) 822-1818
Emp Here 50   *Sales* 2,425,503
SIC 7997 Membership sports and recreation clubs

D-U-N-S 20-647-6454   (BR)
ROYAL GROUP, INC
CROWN PLASTICS EXTUSSION CO
111 Royal Group Cres, Woodbridge, ON, L4H 1X9
(905) 264-0701
Emp Here 150
SIC 3089 Plastics products, nec

D-U-N-S 20-512-9906   (BR)
ROYAL GROUP, INC
ROYAL OUTDOOR PRODUCTS, DIV OF
100 Royal Group Cres Unit B, Woodbridge, ON, L4H 1X9
(905) 264-2989
Emp Here 400
SIC 3448 Prefabricated Metal buildings and components

D-U-N-S 24-340-7439   (BR)
ROYAL GROUP, INC
ROYAL WINDOW & DOOR PROFILES PLANT 2
71 Royal Group Cres Suite 2, Woodbridge, ON, L4H 1X9
(905) 264-5500
Emp Here 178
SIC 5039 Construction materials, nec

D-U-N-S 24-963-9584   (HQ)
RYCOM INC
6201 7 Hwy Unit 8, Woodbridge, ON, L4H 0K7
(905) 264-4800
Emp Here 45   *Emp Total* 1
Sales 16,739,250
SIC 5065 Electronic parts and equipment, nec
Pr Pr Casey Witkowicz
   Pat Mancuso

D-U-N-S 25-832-1132   (BR)
S.L.H. TRANSPORT INC
9601 Highway 50, Woodbridge, ON, L4H 2B9
(905) 893-4318
Emp Here 200
SIC 4213 Trucking, except local

D-U-N-S 24-826-9966   (BR)
SAPUTO PRODUITS LAITIERS CANADA S.E.N.C.
(*Suby of* Saputo Produits Laitiers Canada S.E.N.C.)
101 Royal Group Cres, Woodbridge, ON, L4H 1X9
(905) 266-8800
Emp Here 50
SIC 2022 Cheese; natural and processed

D-U-N-S 20-059-1647   (BR)
SEARS CANADA INC
9501 Highway 50, Woodbridge, ON, L4H 2B9
(905) 893-5284
Emp Here 700
SIC 4225 General warehousing and storage

D-U-N-S 24-188-9471   (BR)
SOBEYS CAPITAL INCORPORATED
PRICE CHOPPER
3737 Major Mackenzie Dr, Woodbridge, ON, L4H 0A2
(905) 303-3144
Emp Here 50
SIC 5411 Grocery stores

D-U-N-S 25-306-3981   (BR)
STARBUCKS COFFEE CANADA, INC
(*Suby of* Starbucks Corporation)
3737 Major Mackenzie Dr Suite 101, Woodbridge, ON, L4H 0A2

(905) 303-7097
Emp Here 20
SIC 5812 Eating places

D-U-N-S 20-705-1855   (SL)
STERLING TILE & CARPET
505 Cityview Blvd Unit 1, Woodbridge, ON, L4H 0L8
(905) 585-4800
Emp Here 100   *Sales* 9,776,734
SIC 1743 Terrazzo, tile, marble and mossaic work
Pt Al Silver
Pt Mark Silver

D-U-N-S 20-606-6417   (BR)
TRANSCANADA PIPELINES LIMITED
TRANSCANADA PIPELINES
11200 Weston Rd, Woodbridge, ON, L4H 3V8
(905) 832-2221
Emp Here 50
SIC 4922 Natural gas transmission

D-U-N-S 20-017-3131   (BR)
TRANSCONTINENTAL PRINTING INC
100b Royal Group Cres, Woodbridge, ON, L4H 1X9
(905) 663-1216
Emp Here 110
SIC 2711 Newspapers

D-U-N-S 24-685-7614   (HQ)
TRULITE GLASS & ALUMINUM SOLUTIONS CANADA, ULC
20 Royal Group Cres, Woodbridge, ON, L4H 1X9
(905) 605-7040
Emp Here 140   *Emp Total* 145
Sales 24,341,653
SIC 3211 Flat glass
Pr Pr Paul Schmitz
   Dave Mccallen
   Kevin Barrett

D-U-N-S 24-606-1746   (BR)
WAL-MART CANADA CORP
8300 27 Hwy, Woodbridge, ON, L4H 0R9
(905) 851-4648
Emp Here 40
SIC 5311 Department stores

D-U-N-S 20-295-7452   (SL)
WEBER-STEPHEN (CANADA) COMPANY
(*Suby of* Weber-Stephen Products LLC)
1 Roybridge Gate, Woodbridge, ON, L4H 4E6
(905) 850-8999
Emp Here 25   *Sales* 3,291,754
SIC 5023 Homefurnishings

D-U-N-S 20-336-7693   (BR)
WHEELS MSM CANADA INC.
9701 Hwy 50, Woodbridge, ON, L4H 2G4
(905) 951-6800
Emp Here 25
SIC 4213 Trucking, except local

D-U-N-S 25-151-0459   (BR)
YORK CATHOLIC DISTRICT SCHOOL BOARD
ST ANGELA MERECI
8881 Martin Grove Rd, Woodbridge, ON, L4H 1C3
(905) 856-4996
Emp Here 40
SIC 8211 Elementary and secondary schools

D-U-N-S 24-676-2749   (BR)
YORK CATHOLIC DISTRICT SCHOOL BOARD
ST PADRE PIO CATHOLIC ELEMENTARY SCHOOL
770 Napa Valley Ave, Woodbridge, ON, L4H 1W9
(905) 893-7082
Emp Here 50
SIC 8211 Elementary and secondary schools

D-U-N-S 20-711-4682   (BR)
YORK CATHOLIC DISTRICT SCHOOL

BOARD
ST AGNES OF ASSISI ELEMENTARY SCHOOL
120 La Rocca Ave, Woodbridge, ON, L4H 2A9
(905) 303-4646
Emp Here 80
SIC 8211 Elementary and secondary schools

D-U-N-S 24-525-4292　(BR)
YORK CATHOLIC DISTRICT SCHOOL BOARD
ST VERONICA CATHOLIC ELEMENTARY SCHOOL
171 Maria Antonia Rd, Woodbridge, ON, L4H 2S8
(905) 653-5920
Emp Here 25
SIC 8211 Elementary and secondary schools

D-U-N-S 20-711-4658　(BR)
YORK CATHOLIC DISTRICT SCHOOL BOARD
ST ANDREW
151 Forest Fountain Dr, Woodbridge, ON, L4H 1S4
(905) 893-1968
Emp Here 50
SIC 8211 Elementary and secondary schools

D-U-N-S 20-711-4690　(BR)
YORK CATHOLIC DISTRICT SCHOOL BOARD
ST STEPHEN CATHOLIC SCHOOL
451 Napa Valley Ave, Woodbridge, ON, L4H 1Y8
(905) 893-7557
Emp Here 50
SIC 8211 Elementary and secondary schools

D-U-N-S 20-711-4708　(BR)
YORK CATHOLIC DISTRICT SCHOOL BOARD
ST EMILY CATHOLIC SCHOOL
60 Vellore Woods Blvd, Woodbridge, ON, L4H 2K8
(905) 303-4554
Emp Here 60
SIC 8211 Elementary and secondary schools

D-U-N-S 24-676-3416　(BR)
YORK REGION DISTRICT SCHOOL BOARD
GLENN GOULD PUBLIC SCHOOL
(*Suby of* York Region District School Board)
675 Av Vellore Park, Woodbridge, ON, L4H 0G5
(905) 417-4517
Emp Here 30
SIC 8211 Elementary and secondary schools

D-U-N-S 20-568-0072　(BR)
YORK REGION DISTRICT SCHOOL BOARD
FOSSIL HILL PUBLIC SCHOOL
(*Suby of* York Region District School Board)
2 Firenza Rd, Woodbridge, ON, L4H 2P5
(905) 653-8055
Emp Here 38
SIC 8211 Elementary and secondary schools

D-U-N-S 20-711-4393　(BR)
YORK REGION DISTRICT SCHOOL BOARD
EMILY CARR SECONDARY SCHOOL
(*Suby of* York Region District School Board)
4901 Rutherford Rd, Woodbridge, ON, L4H 3C2
(905) 850-5012
Emp Here 100
SIC 8211 Elementary and secondary schools

D-U-N-S 24-676-5155　(BR)
YORK REGION DISTRICT SCHOOL BOARD
ELDER'S MILLS PUBLIC SCHOOL
(*Suby of* York Region District School Board)
120 Napa Valley Ave, Woodbridge, ON, L4H 1L1
(905) 893-1631
Emp Here 25
SIC 8211 Elementary and secondary schools

D-U-N-S 24-364-7336　(SL)
ZSEMBA APRON & UPHOLSTERY LTD
81 Royal Group Cres, Woodbridge, ON, L4H 1X9

Emp Here 175　　*Sales* 32,981,515
SIC 2515 Mattresses and bedsprings
Pr Pr Ann Zsemba
VP VP Zsold Zsemba
George Zsemba

Woodbridge, ON L4L
York County

D-U-N-S 25-369-5258　(BR)
1010360 ONTARIO INC
G-TEL
200 Hanlan Rd, Woodbridge, ON, L4L 3P6
(905) 856-1162
Emp Here 200
SIC 8748 Business consulting, nec

D-U-N-S 20-515-3047　(SL)
1428309 ONTARIO LTD
ALTA INFINITI
5585 Highway 7, Woodbridge, ON, L4L 1T5

Emp Here 25　　*Sales* 9,120,088
SIC 5511 New and used car dealers
Pr Joe Zanchin

D-U-N-S 20-643-1491　(SL)
2010665 ONTARIO LTD
TIM HORTONS
25 Woodstream Blvd Suite 1, Woodbridge, ON, L4L 7Y8
(905) 265-7843
Emp Here 65　　*Sales* 1,969,939
SIC 5812 Eating places

D-U-N-S 20-972-9784　(BR)
2063414 ONTARIO LIMITED
LEISUREWORLD CAREGIVING CENTRE
(*Suby of* 2063414 Ontario Limited)
5400 Steeles Ave W, Woodbridge, ON, L4L 9S1
(905) 856-7200
Emp Here 200
SIC 8051 Skilled nursing care facilities

D-U-N-S 24-338-6401　(BR)
446987 ONTARIO INC
BOMBAY COMPANY, THE
(*Suby of* Benix & Co. Inc)
16 Famous Ave Suite 145, Woodbridge, ON, L4L 9M3
(905) 264-1211
Emp Here 50
SIC 5712 Furniture stores

D-U-N-S 25-458-7124　(SL)
706017 ONTARIO CORP
NU TREND CONSTRUCTION CO
101 Caster Ave, Woodbridge, ON, L4L 5Z2
(905) 851-3189
Emp Here 120　　*Sales* 17,948,332
SIC 1521 Single-family housing construction
Pr Pr John Gabriele
Frank Gabriele

D-U-N-S 24-963-8255　(SL)
902316 ONTARIO LIMITED
MERCHANDISING CONSULTING ASSOCIATES
200 Hanlan Rd Suite A, Woodbridge, ON, L4L 3P6
(905) 850-5544
Emp Here 700　　*Sales* 32,981,515
SIC 2789 Bookbinding and related work
Pr Steve Kindree

D-U-N-S 20-322-4654　(SL)
ABC GROUP
ABC GROUP TRANSPORTATION
100 Hanlan Rd Suite 3, Woodbridge, ON, L4L 4V8

(905) 392-0485
Emp Here 450　　*Sales* 6,058,200
SIC 6712 Bank holding companies
Prin William Baker
Prin Jensen Linonale
Prin Mark Baker

D-U-N-S 25-504-3077　(SL)
ATS TEST INC
(*Suby of* ATS Automation Tooling Systems Inc)
600 Chrislea Rd, Woodbridge, ON, L4L 8K9
(905) 850-8600
Emp Here 50　　*Sales* 11,347,888
SIC 3823 Process control instruments
Pr Maria Perrella

D-U-N-S 20-112-3739　(HQ)
ACOSTA CANADA CORPORATION
ACOSTA CANADA
(*Suby of* Acosta Inc.)
250 Rowntree Dairy Rd, Woodbridge, ON, L4L 9J7
(905) 264-0466
Emp Here 150　　*Emp Total* 39,000
Sales 142,844,790
SIC 5141 Groceries, general line
Pr Shaun Mckenna

D-U-N-S 20-066-9708　(SL)
ALLCARE MAINTENANCE SERVICES INC
410 Chrislea Rd Unit 20, Woodbridge, ON, L4L 8B5
(905) 856-8558
Emp Here 60　　*Sales* 1,751,057
SIC 7349 Building maintenance services, nec

D-U-N-S 25-296-4093　(BR)
BANK OF NOVA SCOTIA, THE
SCOTIABANK
7600 Weston Rd Suite 3, Woodbridge, ON, L4L 8B7
(905) 850-1805
Emp Here 50
SIC 6021 National commercial banks

D-U-N-S 20-743-4767　(BR)
BEST BUY CANADA LTD
BEST BUY
(*Suby of* Best Buy Co., Inc.)
7850 Weston Rd Suite 1, Woodbridge, ON, L4L 9N8
(905) 264-3191
Emp Here 145
SIC 5731 Radio, television, and electronic stores

D-U-N-S 20-242-8806　(BR)
BONNIE TOGS CHILDREN'S LIMITED
(*Suby of* Bonnie Togs Children's Limited)
200 Windflower Gate, Woodbridge, ON, L4L 9L3
(905) 264-8411
Emp Here 20
SIC 5641 Children's and infants' wear stores

D-U-N-S 20-016-2837　(BR)
BRICK WAREHOUSE LP, THE
137 Chrislea Rd, Woodbridge, ON, L4L 8N6
(905) 850-5300
Emp Here 130
SIC 5712 Furniture stores

D-U-N-S 25-279-6180　(SL)
BROOKLIN ESTATES GENERAL PARTNER INC.
3700 Steeles Ave W Suite 800, Woodbridge, ON, L4L 8M9
(905) 850-8508
Emp Here 92　　*Sales* 40,292,480
SIC 6553 Cemetery subdividers and developers
Pr Pr Joseph Sorbara
Edward Sorbara

D-U-N-S 24-752-4572　(SL)
C.M.L. FOODS LTD
SWISS CHALET
205 Marycroft Ave Unit 14, Woodbridge, ON,

L4L 5X8
(905) 856-2948
Emp Here 50　　*Sales* 1,532,175
SIC 5812 Eating places

D-U-N-S 20-344-8308　(BR)
CIBC WORLD MARKETS INC
CIBC WOOD GUNDY
7050 Weston Rd Suite 600, Woodbridge, ON, L4L 8G7
(905) 856-9336
Emp Here 20
SIC 6211 Security brokers and dealers

D-U-N-S 24-426-2940　(SL)
CSH PINE GROVE LODGE INC
8403 Islington Ave, Woodbridge, ON, L4L 1X3
(905) 850-3605
Emp Here 20　　*Sales* 942,329
SIC 8361 Residential care

D-U-N-S 24-096-4841　(HQ)
CAMIONS INDUSTRIELS YALE INC
340 Hanlan Rd, Woodbridge, ON, L4L 3P6
(905) 851-6620
Emp Here 58　　*Emp Total* 4
Sales 32,917,538
SIC 5084 Industrial machinery and equipment
Dir Mark Barrett

D-U-N-S 24-488-2080　(SL)
CAMPIO FURNITURE LIMITED
CAMPIO GROUP
5770 Highway 7 Unit 1, Woodbridge, ON, L4L 1T8
(905) 850-6636
Emp Here 90　　*Sales* 8,025,677
SIC 2512 Upholstered household furniture
Vito Servello

D-U-N-S 20-582-5644　(BR)
CANADA POST CORPORATION
21 Haist Ave Suite 1, Woodbridge, ON, L4L 5V5
(905) 851-1237
Emp Here 80
SIC 4311 U.s. postal service

D-U-N-S 20-714-6965　(BR)
CANADIAN IMPERIAL BANK OF COMMERCE
CIBC
8535 27 Hwy, Woodbridge, ON, L4L 1A7
(905) 264-6184
Emp Here 20
SIC 6021 National commercial banks

D-U-N-S 25-303-5604　(BR)
CANADIAN IMPERIAL BANK OF COMMERCE
CIBC
7850 Weston Rd Suite 2, Woodbridge, ON, L4L 9N8
(905) 851-7003
Emp Here 24
SIC 6021 National commercial banks

D-U-N-S 24-394-9935　(BR)
CARA OPERATIONS LIMITED
MILESTONES BAR & GRILL
(*Suby of* Cara Holdings Limited)
3900 Highway 7, Woodbridge, ON, L4L 9C3
(905) 850-1580
Emp Here 30
SIC 5812 Eating places

D-U-N-S 25-369-7114　(BR)
CARA OPERATIONS LIMITED
(*Suby of* Cara Holdings Limited)
3737 Rutherford Rd, Woodbridge, ON, L4L 1A6
(905) 264-4017
Emp Here 50
SIC 5812 Eating places

D-U-N-S 20-638-9876　(HQ)
CARPENTER CANADA CO
500 Hanlan Rd, Woodbridge, ON, L4L 3P6

(416) 743-5689
Emp Here 105 *Emp Total* 5,000
Sales 11,694,389
SIC 1751 Carpentry work
Dir Dave Lemire
Genl Mgr Carlo Fazzarlari
 Stanley Pauley
 Mark Willard

D-U-N-S 20-913-3086 (SL)
CARPENTERS LOCAL UNION 27 JOINT APPRENTICESHIP AND TRAINING TRUST FUND INC
222 Rowntree Dairy Rd, Woodbridge, ON, L4L 9T2
(905) 652-5507
Emp Here 75 *Sales* 3,502,114
SIC 8331 Job training and related services

D-U-N-S 25-710-3374 (BR)
CATHOLIC CEMETERIES-ARCHDIOCESE OF TORONTO
QUEEN OF HEAVEN CEMETERY
7300 27 Hwy, Woodbridge, ON, L4L 1A5
(905) 851-5822
Emp Here 20
SIC 6531 Real estate agents and managers

D-U-N-S 25-691-5687 (BR)
CINEPLEX ODEON CORPORATION
CINEPLEX CINEMAS VAUGHAN
3555 Highway 7, Woodbridge, ON, L4L 9H4
(905) 851-1001
Emp Here 20
SIC 7832 Motion picture theaters, except drive-in

D-U-N-S 24-408-1832 (HQ)
COMPACT MOULD LIMITED
120 Haist Ave, Woodbridge, ON, L4L 5V4
(905) 851-7724
Emp Here 60 *Emp Total* 60
Sales 4,961,328
SIC 3544 Special dies, tools, jigs, and fixtures

D-U-N-S 24-665-7522 (SL)
CONCORD STEEL CENTRE LIMITED
147 Ashbridge Cir, Woodbridge, ON, L4L 3R5
(905) 856-1717
Emp Here 80 *Sales* 32,248,629
SIC 5051 Metals service centers and offices
 Bruno Bellisario
Pr Pr Marco Bellisario

D-U-N-S 24-876-9804 (HQ)
CORNERSTONE INSURANCE BROKERS LTD
8001 Weston Rd Suite 300, Woodbridge, ON, L4L 9C8
(905) 856-1981
Emp Here 25 *Emp Total* 11,000
Sales 9,095,636
SIC 6411 Insurance agents, brokers, and service
CEO Wendy De Silva
Pr Peter De Silva

D-U-N-S 20-113-2342 (BR)
CORPORATION OF THE CITY OF VAUGHAN, THE
AL PALLADINI COMMUNITY CENTRE
9201 Islington Ave, Woodbridge, ON, L4L 1A6
(905) 832-8564
Emp Here 100
SIC 8322 Individual and family services

D-U-N-S 24-336-9084 (BR)
CORPORATION OF THE CITY OF VAUGHAN, THE
CHANCELLOR COMMUNITY CENTRE
350 Ansley Grove Rd, Woodbridge, ON, L4L 3W4
(905) 832-8620
Emp Here 50
SIC 8322 Individual and family services

D-U-N-S 25-529-3227 (BR)
COSTCO WHOLESALE CANADA LTD

COSTCO
(*Suby of* Costco Wholesale Corporation)
71 Colossus Dr Suite 547, Woodbridge, ON, L4L 9J8
(905) 264-8337
Emp Here 200
SIC 5199 Nondurable goods, nec

D-U-N-S 25-167-8611 (SL)
CRAFTER'S PRIDE INC
288 Velmar Dr, Woodbridge, ON, L4L 8K3
(416) 727-5790
Emp Here 75 *Sales* 2,188,821
SIC 2396 Automotive and apparel trimmings

D-U-N-S 25-128-7074 (HQ)
DBA ENGINEERING LTD
401 Hanlan Rd, Woodbridge, ON, L4L 3T1
(905) 851-0090
Emp Here 23 *Emp Total* 33,000
Sales 2,598,753
SIC 8711 Engineering services

D-U-N-S 24-318-3688 (SL)
DA VINCI BANQUET HALL
5732 Highway 7 Suite 33, Woodbridge, ON, L4L 3A2
(905) 851-2768
Emp Here 70 *Sales* 2,334,742
SIC 7299 Miscellaneous personal service

D-U-N-S 20-714-7427 (BR)
DIRECT ENERGY MARKETING LIMITED
DIRECT ENERGY ESSENTIAL HOME SERVICE
301 Chrislea Rd, Woodbridge, ON, L4L 8N4
(905) 264-3030
Emp Here 50
SIC 1311 Crude petroleum and natural gas

D-U-N-S 20-994-8269 (BR)
DOLLARAMA S.E.C.
7600 Weston Rd Unit 27, Woodbridge, ON, L4L 8B7
(780) 723-4754
Emp Here 30
SIC 5399 Miscellaneous general merchandise

D-U-N-S 20-696-6520 (SL)
DURADRIVE SYSTEMS INTERNATIONAL INC
250 Rowntree Dairy Rd, Woodbridge, ON, L4L 9J7
(866) 774-9272
Emp Here 30 *Sales* 5,107,249
SIC 3496 Miscellaneous fabricated wire products
Pr Pr Domenic Degiorgio

D-U-N-S 24-867-1075 (HQ)
EDDIE BAUER OF CANADA INC
EDDIE BAUER SPORTSWEAR
(*Suby of* Golden Gate Capital LP)
201 Aviva Park Dr, Woodbridge, ON, L4L 9C1
(800) 426-8020
Emp Here 50 *Emp Total* 28,860
Sales 47,470,555
SIC 5699 Miscellaneous apparel and accessory stores
Pr Fabian Mansson
 Ron Gaston

D-U-N-S 24-337-3318 (BR)
FGL SPORTS LTD
SPORT-CHEK WOODBRIDGE
7850 Weston Rd, Woodbridge, ON, L4L 9N8
(905) 264-2848
Emp Here 50
SIC 5941 Sporting goods and bicycle shops

D-U-N-S 20-902-3985 (SL)
FAMEE FURLANE TORONTO
7065 Islington Ave, Woodbridge, ON, L4L 1V9
(905) 851-1166
Emp Here 50 *Sales* 3,575,074
SIC 8641 Civic and social associations

D-U-N-S 20-212-0312 (BR)

FLOWSERVE CANADA CORP
(*Suby of* Flowserve Corporation)
120 Vinyl Crt, Woodbridge, ON, L4L 4A3
(905) 856-1140
Emp Here 35
SIC 5251 Hardware stores

D-U-N-S 20-940-4560 (BR)
FORTINOS SUPERMARKET LTD
3940 Highway 7, Woodbridge, ON, L4L 9C3
(905) 851-5642
Emp Here 50
SIC 5411 Grocery stores

D-U-N-S 24-936-9919 (SL)
FOSS, ROY CHEVROLET LTD
2 Auto Park Cir, Woodbridge, ON, L4L 8R1
(905) 850-1000
Emp Here 65 *Sales* 31,902,000
SIC 5511 New and used car dealers
Pr Pr Roy Foss
Treas Paul Hartley
 Karen Foss-Ricci

D-U-N-S 24-383-8922 (BR)
GANZ CANADA
(*Suby of* Ganz)
200 Hanlan Rd Suite A, Woodbridge, ON, L4L 3P6
(905) 850-8302
Emp Here 100
SIC 4225 General warehousing and storage

D-U-N-S 20-165-6543 (HQ)
GANZ
(*Suby of* Ganz)
1 Pearce Rd, Woodbridge, ON, L4L 3T2
(905) 851-6661
Emp Here 550 *Emp Total* 750
Sales 90,033,504
SIC 5199 Nondurable goods, nec
Pt Howard Ganz
Pt Owen Rogers

D-U-N-S 20-346-9221 (SL)
GEMSTAR SECURITY SERVICE LTD
4000 Steeles Ave W Unit 29, Woodbridge, ON, L4L 4V9
(905) 850-8517
Emp Here 100 *Sales* 3,137,310
SIC 7381 Detective and armored car services

D-U-N-S 20-644-3942 (BR)
GOLF TOWN LIMITED
GOLF TOWN
55 Colossus Dr Unit 122, Woodbridge, ON, L4L 9J8
(905) 264-8809
Emp Here 30
SIC 5941 Sporting goods and bicycle shops

D-U-N-S 24-253-2286 (BR)
GOODLIFE FITNESS CENTRES INC
57 Northview Blvd, Woodbridge, ON, L4L 8X9
(905) 265-1188
Emp Here 30
SIC 7999 Amusement and recreation, nec

D-U-N-S 24-817-0664 (SL)
GRACIOUS LIVING CORPORATION
7200 Martin Grove Rd, Woodbridge, ON, L4L 9J3
(905) 264-5660
Emp Here 400 *Sales* 70,188,193
SIC 3089 Plastics products, nec
Pr Pr Enzo Macri
 Vito Galloro
 Lou Farrace

D-U-N-S 25-115-1759 (BR)
GRAND & TOY LIMITED
(*Suby of* Office Depot, Inc.)
200 Aviva Park Dr, Woodbridge, ON, L4L 9C7
(416) 401-6300
Emp Here 500
SIC 5112 Stationery and office supplies

D-U-N-S 20-166-4026 (SL)

GRIFFITHS, H. COMPANY LIMITED
140 Regina Rd Suite 15, Woodbridge, ON, L4L 8N1
(905) 850-7070
Emp Here 50 *Sales* 4,377,642
SIC 1711 Plumbing, heating, air-conditioning

D-U-N-S 20-328-0958 (HQ)
HDS CANADA, INC
HD SUPPLY CONSTRUCTION & INDUSTRIAL - BRAFASCO
100 Galcat Dr, Woodbridge, ON, L4L 0B9
(905) 850-8085
Emp Here 120 *Emp Total* 15,000
Sales 97,279,987
SIC 5072 Hardware
Pr Pr Vasken Altounian
VP VP Joseph Deangelo
 Dan Mcdevitt
VP VP Evan Levitt
VP VP Jeffrey R. Monday
 Alan W. Sollenberger
VP VP William P. Stengel
 Marc A. Gonzalez
VP James F. Brumsey
VP VP Malinda A. Miller

D-U-N-S 25-250-4931 (BR)
HOME DEPOT OF CANADA INC
HOME DEPOT
(*Suby of* The Home Depot Inc)
140 Northview Blvd, Woodbridge, ON, L4L 8T2
(905) 851-1800
Emp Here 200
SIC 5251 Hardware stores

D-U-N-S 20-290-8419 (HQ)
HUB FINANCIAL INC
3700 Steeles Ave W Unit 1001, Woodbridge, ON, L4L 8K8
(905) 264-1634
Emp Here 56 *Emp Total* 113
Sales 10,141,537
SIC 6411 Insurance agents, brokers, and service
Pr Terri Diflorio

D-U-N-S 25-155-0547 (SL)
INDEX COMPANY LIMITED
235 Trowers Rd Suite 1, Woodbridge, ON, L4L 5Z8
(905) 850-7440
Emp Here 55 *Sales* 3,429,153
SIC 2339 Women's and misses' outerwear, nec

D-U-N-S 20-207-0434 (BR)
INDIGO BOOKS & MUSIC INC
CHAPTERS
(*Suby of* Indigo Books & Music Inc)
3900 Highway 7 Unit 1, Woodbridge, ON, L4L 9C3
(905) 264-6401
Emp Here 50
SIC 5942 Book stores

D-U-N-S 20-172-3772 (HQ)
JAN K. OVERWEEL LIMITED
(*Suby of* JKO Holdings Inc)
3700 Steeles Ave W Suite 702, Woodbridge, ON, L4L 8K8
(905) 850-9010
Emp Here 45 *Emp Total* 5
Sales 14,373,258
SIC 5141 Groceries, general line
Pr Pr Arthur Pelliccione
VP VP Patrick Pelliccione
 Art Pelliccione
 Teresa Pelliccione

D-U-N-S 25-136-0962 (SL)
JARDIN BANQUET & CONFERENCE CENTRE INC, LE
8440 27 Hwy, Woodbridge, ON, L4L 1A5
(905) 851-2200
Emp Here 150 *Sales* 4,961,328

SIC 7299 Miscellaneous personal service

D-U-N-S 25-360-1041   (BR)
KNOLL NORTH AMERICA CORP
600 Rowntree Dairy Rd, Woodbridge, ON, L4L 5T8
(416) 741-5453
Emp Here 200
SIC 2514 Metal household furniture

D-U-N-S 25-193-5610   (BR)
KUMON CANADA INC
4561 Langstaff Rd, Woodbridge, ON, L4L 2B2
(905) 264-7009
Emp Here 30
SIC 8299 Schools and educational services, nec

D-U-N-S 20-647-6269   (BR)
LTP SPORTS GROUP INC
321 Hanlan Rd, Woodbridge, ON, L4L 3R7
(905) 851-1133
Emp Here 25
SIC 5941 Sporting goods and bicycle shops

D-U-N-S 25-317-8305   (BR)
LIQUOR CONTROL BOARD OF ONTARIO, THE
L.C.B.O. #346
7850 Weston Rd, Woodbridge, ON, L4L 9N8
(905) 851-2500
Emp Here 21
SIC 5921 Liquor stores

D-U-N-S 20-699-9596   (BR)
LONGO BROTHERS FRUIT MARKETS INC
LONGO'S FRUIT MARKET
8401 Weston Rd, Woodbridge, ON, L4L 1A6
(905) 850-6161
Emp Here 120
SIC 5411 Grocery stores

D-U-N-S 20-999-3695   (BR)
MAGASIN LAURA (P.V.) INC
LAURA CANADA
200 Windflower Gate Unit 300, Woodbridge, ON, L4L 9L3
(905) 264-2934
Emp Here 30
SIC 5621 Women's clothing stores

D-U-N-S 25-279-6578   (BR)
MAGNA INTERNATIONAL INC
MYTOX MANUFACTURING
251 Aviva Park Dr, Woodbridge, ON, L4L 9C1
(905) 851-6666
Emp Here 300
SIC 3429 Hardware, nec

D-U-N-S 20-042-6716   (BR)
MAGNA POWERTRAIN INC
M S M
390 Hanlan Rd, Woodbridge, ON, L4L 3P6
(905) 851-6791
Emp Here 380
SIC 3566 Speed changers, drives, and gears

D-U-N-S 24-141-2154   (HQ)
MAGNOTTA WINERY CORPORATION
(*Suby of* Magnotta Winery Corporation)
271 Chrislea Rd, Woodbridge, ON, L4L 8N6
(905) 850-5577
Emp Here 75   *Emp Total* 107
Sales 3,724,879
SIC 2084 Wines, brandy, and brandy spirits

D-U-N-S 24-822-2952   (SL)
MALFAR MECHANICAL INC
144 Woodstream Blvd Suite 7, Woodbridge, ON, L4L 7Y3
(905) 850-1242
Emp Here 55   *Sales* 4,815,406
SIC 1711 Plumbing, heating, air-conditioning

D-U-N-S 20-158-7284   (SL)
MARCH ALUMINUM LTD
172 Trowers Rd Unit 13, Woodbridge, ON, L4L 8A7

(905) 851-7183
Emp Here 30   *Sales* 6,028,800
SIC 5049 Professional equipment, nec
Bjorn Ramsvik
Genl Mgr Jeremy Carvalho

D-U-N-S 25-975-9215   (SL)
MARKHAM LABEL HOLDINGS INC
LABEL DEPOT, THE
(*Suby of* Groupe Lelys Inc)
609 Hanlan Rd, Woodbridge, ON, L4L 4R8
(905) 264-6654
Emp Here 45   *Sales* 3,793,956
SIC 2759 Commercial printing, nec

D-U-N-S 25-981-0612   (BR)
MAZDA CANADA INC
PRIMA MAZDA
7635 Martin Grove Rd, Woodbridge, ON, L4L 2C5
(905) 850-8111
Emp Here 20
SIC 5511 New and used car dealers

D-U-N-S 20-690-9678   (HQ)
NPL CANADA LTD
(*Suby of* Southwest Gas Holdings, Inc.)
1 Royal Gate Blvd Suite E, Woodbridge, ON, L4L 8Z7
(905) 265-7400
Emp Here 40   *Emp Total* 2,247
Sales 8,316,010
SIC 1623 Water, sewer, and utility lines
Pr Rick Delaney

D-U-N-S 24-777-4847   (SL)
NATIONAL E.A.S. LOSS PREVENTION SYSTEMS LTD
NATIONAL E A S
910 Rowntree Dairy Rd Unit 30, Woodbridge, ON, L4L 5W6
(905) 850-9299
Emp Here 70   *Sales* 13,447,920
SIC 3812 Search and navigation equipment
Pr Pr Jim Grant
VP VP Arcadius Kuchna

D-U-N-S 20-935-4323   (SL)
NUMBER 7 HONDA SALES LIMITED
NUMBER 7 HONDA
5555 Highway 7, Woodbridge, ON, L4L 1T5
(905) 851-2258
Emp Here 60   *Sales* 4,377,642
SIC 7538 General automotive repair shops

D-U-N-S 20-145-6563   (HQ)
O'NEIL, EARL ELECTRIC SUPPLY LIMITED
O'NEIL ELECTRIC SUPPLY
150 Creditview Rd, Woodbridge, ON, L4L 9N4
(416) 798-7722
Emp Here 30   *Emp Total* 50
Sales 11,954,264
SIC 5063 Electrical apparatus and equipment
Dir Earl O'neil
Pr Pr Michael O'neil

D-U-N-S 20-176-5703   (BR)
PFAFF MOTORS INC
PFAFF PORSCHE
101 Auto Park Cir, Woodbridge, ON, L4L 8R1
(905) 851-0852
Emp Here 30
SIC 5511 New and used car dealers

D-U-N-S 20-274-2008   (BR)
PRICE INDUSTRIES LIMITED
571 Chrislea Rd Unit 3, Woodbridge, ON, L4L 8A2
(905) 669-8988
Emp Here 20
SIC 3564 Blowers and fans

D-U-N-S 20-080-1350   (BR)
ROYAL BANK OF CANADA
RBC - WOODBRIDGE
(*Suby of* Royal Bank Of Canada)
131 Woodbridge Ave, Woodbridge, ON, L4L 2S6

(905) 851-2284
Emp Here 32
SIC 6021 National commercial banks

D-U-N-S 24-946-8562   (BR)
ROYAL GROUP, INC
ROYAL PIPE SYSTEMS
131 Regalcrest Crt, Woodbridge, ON, L4L 8P3
(905) 652-0461
Emp Here 150
SIC 3084 Plastics pipe

D-U-N-S 25-359-6779   (BR)
ROYAL GROUP, INC
ROYAL GROUP RESOURCES
131 Regalcrest Crt,, Woodbridge, ON, L4L 8P3
(905) 856-7550
Emp Here 50
SIC 4953 Refuse systems

D-U-N-S 24-389-4925   (BR)
ROYAL GROUP, INC
ROYAL FLEX
101 Regalcrest Crt, Woodbridge, ON, L4L 8P3
(905) 856-7550
Emp Here 38
SIC 3084 Plastics pipe

D-U-N-S 20-091-0235   (SL)
ROYAL LE PAGE MAXIMUM REALTY
7694 Islington Ave, Woodbridge, ON, L4L 1W3
(416) 324-2626
Emp Here 70   *Sales* 6,566,463
SIC 6531 Real estate agents and managers
Owner Mar Cello

D-U-N-S 20-090-7124   (BR)
SIR CORP
JACK ASTOR'S BAR AND GRILL
10 Colossus Dr Suite 128, Woodbridge, ON, L4L 9J5
(905) 264-3790
Emp Here 50
SIC 7389 Business services, nec

D-U-N-S 24-364-5129   (BR)
SIR CORP
ALICE FAZOOLI'S
20 Colossus Dr, Woodbridge, ON, L4L 9J5
(905) 850-3565
Emp Here 50
SIC 5812 Eating places

D-U-N-S 25-849-3139   (SL)
SAN ANTONIO FISH MARKET INC
130 Creditview Rd, Woodbridge, ON, L4L 9N4
(905) 850-4088
Emp Here 55   *Sales* 25,914,048
SIC 5146 Fish and seafoods
Pr Pr Felice Lionetti
Recvr Allan David Nackan

D-U-N-S 24-322-1251   (BR)
SILGAN PLASTICS CANADA INC
COUSINS CURRIE DIVISION OF SILGAN PLASTICS CANADA
400 Rowntree Dairy Rd, Woodbridge, ON, L4L 8H2
(905) 856-1324
Emp Here 155
SIC 3089 Plastics products, nec

D-U-N-S 24-140-9945   (SL)
SPECTRA ANODIZING LTD
201 Hanlan Rd, Woodbridge, ON, L4L 3R7
(905) 851-1141
Emp Here 60   *Sales* 4,012,839
SIC 3471 Plating and polishing

D-U-N-S 24-652-2585   (BR)
SPICERS CANADA ULC
SPICERS
(*Suby of* CNG Canada Holding Inc.)
200 Galcat Dr, Woodbridge, ON, L4L 0B9
(905) 850-1170
Emp Here 200
SIC 5111 Printing and writing paper

D-U-N-S 20-268-1847   (HQ)
SPICERS CANADA ULC
(*Suby of* CNG Canada Holding Inc.)
200 Galcat Dr, Woodbridge, ON, L4L 0B9
(905) 265-5000
Emp Here 200   *Emp Total* 73
Sales 173,281,663
SIC 5111 Printing and writing paper
Pr Cory James Turner
Meherab Chothia
Howard Herman

D-U-N-S 25-213-7492   (BR)
STAPLES CANADA INC
STAPLES THE BUSINESS DEPOT
(*Suby of* Staples, Inc.)
57 Northview Blvd Ste 4, Woodbridge, ON, L4L 8X9
(905) 856-6588
Emp Here 55
SIC 5943 Stationery stores

D-U-N-S 20-348-5966   (SL)
STINSON EQUIPMENT LIMITED
STINSON OWL LITE
50 Roysun Rd, Woodbridge, ON, L4L 8L8
(905) 669-2360
Emp Here 55   *Sales* 11,954,264
SIC 5084 Industrial machinery and equipment

D-U-N-S 24-668-6542   (SL)
STRADA SURVEY INC
41 Gaudaur Rd Suite A1, Woodbridge, ON, L4L 3R8
(905) 850-5088
Emp Here 40   *Sales* 5,579,750
SIC 8732 Commercial nonphysical research
Pr Adolfo Estrada

D-U-N-S 24-025-5463   (SL)
TOPPITS FOODS LTD
TOPPITS
301 Chrislea Rd, Woodbridge, ON, L4L 8N4
(905) 850-8900
Emp Here 55   *Sales* 22,617,817
SIC 5146 Fish and seafoods
Pr Pr Brian Xiao
Brandon Gremont
VP Sls Eleni Mauro

D-U-N-S 20-190-5689   (BR)
TORONTO STAR NEWSPAPERS LIMITED
VAUGHAN PRESS CENTRE
1 Century Pl, Woodbridge, ON, L4L 8R2

Emp Here 500
SIC 2711 Newspapers

D-U-N-S 25-322-1022   (BR)
TORONTO-DOMINION BANK, THE
TD CANADA TRUST
(*Suby of* Toronto-Dominion Bank, The)
7766 Martin Grove Rd Suite 1, Woodbridge, ON, L4L 2C7
(905) 851-3975
Emp Here 20
SIC 6021 National commercial banks

D-U-N-S 20-860-5407   (BR)
TOWN SHOES LIMITED
SHOE COMPANY, THE
7575 Weston Rd Unit 255, Woodbridge, ON, L4L 9K5
(905) 850-8081
Emp Here 25
SIC 5661 Shoe stores

D-U-N-S 20-122-7456   (BR)
TOYS 'R' US (CANADA) LTD
TOYS 'R' US
(*Suby of* Toys "r" Us, Inc.)
200 Windflower Gate, Woodbridge, ON, L4L 9L3
(905) 265-8697
Emp Here 40
SIC 5945 Hobby, toy, and game shops

D-U-N-S 24-369-3178   (BR)

UNITED FOOD AND COMMERCIAL WORK-ERS CANADA UNION
UFCW LOCAL 1000A
(*Suby of* United Food and Commercial Work-ers International Union)
70 Creditview Rd, Woodbridge, ON, L4L 9N4
(905) 850-0096
Emp Here 30
SIC 8631 Labor organizations

D-U-N-S 25-087-8543   (SL)
UNITED THERMO GROUP LTD
DIRECT ENERGY
261 Trowers Rd, Woodbridge, ON, L4L 5Z8
(905) 851-0500
Emp Here 50   *Sales* 4,377,642
SIC 1711 Plumbing, heating, air-conditioning

D-U-N-S 24-481-2954   (HQ)
VCI CONTROLS INC
1 Royal Gate Blvd Suite D, Woodbridge, ON,
L4L 8Z7
(905) 850-4464
Emp Here 31   *Emp Total* 70
Sales 9,429,516
SIC 3822 Environmental controls
Pr Pr Nicholas Price
Heather Carnduff

D-U-N-S 24-924-4294   (SL)
WATER MATRIX INC
555 Hanlan Rd Suite 1, Woodbridge, ON, L4L
4R8
(905) 850-8080
Emp Here 35   *Sales* 12,215,600
SIC 8748 Business consulting, nec
Trevor Dixon

D-U-N-S 20-139-6236   (BR)
WENDY'S RESTAURANTS OF CANADA INC
WENDY'S
(*Suby of* The Wendy's Company)
4100 Steeles Ave W, Woodbridge, ON, L4L
3S8
(905) 265-8212
Emp Here 30
SIC 5812 Eating places

D-U-N-S 20-184-1819   (BR)
WINNERS MERCHANTS INTERNATIONAL L.P.
HOMESENSE
(*Suby of* The TJX Companies Inc)
7575 Weston Rd Unit 112, Woodbridge, ON,
L4L 9K5
(905) 850-8131
Emp Here 40
SIC 5651 Family clothing stores

D-U-N-S 25-192-2126   (BR)
WINNERS MERCHANTS INTERNATIONAL L.P.
MARSHALLS
(*Suby of* The TJX Companies Inc)
7601 Weston Rd Suite 129, Woodbridge, ON,
L4L 9J9
(905) 851-3361
Emp Here 42
SIC 5651 Family clothing stores

D-U-N-S 20-106-3240   (BR)
WINNERS MERCHANTS INTERNATIONAL L.P.
WINNERS
(*Suby of* The TJX Companies Inc)
200 Windflower Gate, Woodbridge, ON, L4L
9L3
(905) 850-9830
Emp Here 40
SIC 5651 Family clothing stores

D-U-N-S 24-058-5588   (BR)
WOODBRIDGE FOAM CORPORATION
P3T LABORATORY
8214 Kipling Ave, Woodbridge, ON, L4L 2A4
(905) 851-9237
Emp Here 300
SIC 8734 Testing laboratories

D-U-N-S 25-151-0483   (BR)
YORK CATHOLIC DISTRICT SCHOOL BOARD
ST FRANCIS OF ASSISI
200 Aberdeen Ave, Woodbridge, ON, L4L 1C4
(905) 851-2859
Emp Here 35
SIC 8211 Elementary and secondary schools

D-U-N-S 20-711-4500   (BR)
YORK CATHOLIC DISTRICT SCHOOL BOARD
ST PETER SCHOOL
120 Andrew Pk, Woodbridge, ON, L4L 1G2
(905) 851-2871
Emp Here 50
SIC 8211 Elementary and secondary schools

D-U-N-S 25-151-0400   (BR)
YORK CATHOLIC DISTRICT SCHOOL BOARD
OUR LADY OF FATIMA
191 Crofters Rd, Woodbridge, ON, L4L 7G3
(905) 856-1666
Emp Here 60
SIC 8211 Elementary and secondary schools

D-U-N-S 25-151-0426   (BR)
YORK CATHOLIC DISTRICT SCHOOL BOARD
ST GABRIEL THE ARCHANGEL CATHOLIC SCHOOL
91 Fiori Dr, Woodbridge, ON, L4L 5S4
(905) 856-4155
Emp Here 42
SIC 8211 Elementary and secondary schools

D-U-N-S 20-711-4559   (BR)
YORK CATHOLIC DISTRICT SCHOOL BOARD
ST. CLARE CATHOLIC ELEMENTARY SCHOOL
391 Velmar Dr, Woodbridge, ON, L4L 8J5
(905) 856-6643
Emp Here 50
SIC 8211 Elementary and secondary schools

D-U-N-S 25-151-0111   (BR)
YORK CATHOLIC DISTRICT SCHOOL BOARD
ST JOHN BOSCO
199 Belview Ave, Woodbridge, ON, L4L 5N9
(905) 850-3280
Emp Here 30
SIC 8211 Elementary and secondary schools

D-U-N-S 25-151-0145   (BR)
YORK CATHOLIC DISTRICT SCHOOL BOARD
ST MARGARET MARY SCHOOL
30 Margaret Mary Rd, Woodbridge, ON, L4L
2W8
(905) 851-3935
Emp Here 50
SIC 8211 Elementary and secondary schools

D-U-N-S 25-151-0350   (BR)
YORK CATHOLIC DISTRICT SCHOOL BOARD
IMMACULATE CONCEPTION
500 Aberdeen Ave, Woodbridge, ON, L4L 5J4
(905) 851-9528
Emp Here 32
SIC 8211 Elementary and secondary schools

D-U-N-S 25-151-0418   (BR)
YORK CATHOLIC DISTRICT SCHOOL BOARD
SAN MARCO CATHOLIC SCHOOL
250 Coronation St, Woodbridge, ON, L4L 6H3
(905) 850-2230
Emp Here 35
SIC 8211 Elementary and secondary schools

D-U-N-S 20-711-4518   (BR)
YORK CATHOLIC DISTRICT SCHOOL BOARD
ST CLEMENTS CATHOLIC SCHOOL

40 Bainbridge Ave, Woodbridge, ON, L4L 3Y1
(905) 851-5910
Emp Here 35
SIC 8211 Elementary and secondary schools

D-U-N-S 25-151-0384   (BR)
YORK CATHOLIC DISTRICT SCHOOL BOARD
HOLY CROSS CATHOLIC ACADEMY
7501 Martin Grove Rd, Woodbridge, ON, L4L
1A5
(905) 851-6699
Emp Here 200
SIC 8211 Elementary and secondary schools

D-U-N-S 25-151-0046   (BR)
YORK CATHOLIC DISTRICT SCHOOL BOARD
ST GREGORY THE GREAT ACADEMY
140 Greenpark Blvd, Woodbridge, ON, L4L
6Z6
(905) 856-0955
Emp Here 35
SIC 8211 Elementary and secondary schools

D-U-N-S 25-100-4537   (BR)
YORK CATHOLIC DISTRICT SCHOOL BOARD
FATHER BRESSANI CATHOLIC HIGH SCHOOL
250 Ansley Grove Rd, Woodbridge, ON, L4L
3W4
(905) 851-6643
Emp Here 110
SIC 8211 Elementary and secondary schools

D-U-N-S 25-151-0467   (BR)
YORK CATHOLIC DISTRICT SCHOOL BOARD
ST CATHARINE OF SIENA
80 Terra Rd, Woodbridge, ON, L4L 3J5
(905) 851-8162
Emp Here 35
SIC 8211 Elementary and secondary schools

D-U-N-S 24-505-4569   (BR)
YORK REGION DISTRICT SCHOOL BOARD
WOODBRIDGE PUBLIC SCHOOL
(*Suby of* York Region District School Board)
60 Burwick Ave, Woodbridge, ON, L4L 1J7
(905) 851-0102
Emp Here 25
SIC 8211 Elementary and secondary schools

D-U-N-S 25-297-9737   (BR)
YORK REGION DISTRICT SCHOOL BOARD
PINE GROVE PUBLIC SCHOOL
(*Suby of* York Region District School Board)
86 Gamble St, Woodbridge, ON, L4L 1R2
(905) 850-0672
Emp Here 45
SIC 8211 Elementary and secondary schools

D-U-N-S 20-711-4195   (BR)
YORK REGION DISTRICT SCHOOL BOARD
WOODBRIDGE COLLEGE
(*Suby of* York Region District School Board)
71 Bruce St, Woodbridge, ON, L4L 1J3
(905) 851-2843
Emp Here 50
SIC 8211 Elementary and secondary schools

D-U-N-S 20-711-4286   (BR)
YORK REGION DISTRICT SCHOOL BOARD
BLUE WILLOW PUBLIC SCHOOL
(*Suby of* York Region District School Board)
250 Blue Willow Dr, Woodbridge, ON, L4L 9E1
(905) 851-0043
Emp Here 50
SIC 8211 Elementary and secondary schools

D-U-N-S 24-602-4376   (SL)
Z.M.C. METAL COATING INC
Z.M.C. WINDOW COVERINGS SUPPLIES
40 Gaudaur Rd Suite 3, Woodbridge, ON, L4L
4S6
(905) 856-3838
Emp Here 50   *Sales* 3,502,114

SIC 3479 Metal coating and allied services

Woodlawn, ON K0A
Carleton County

D-U-N-S 20-026-3833   (BR)
OTTAWA-CARLETON DISTRICT SCHOOL BOARD
STONECREST ELEMENTARY SCHOOL
3791 Stonecrest Rd, Woodlawn, ON, K0A
3M0
(613) 832-5527
Emp Here 36
SIC 8211 Elementary and secondary schools

Woodstock, ON N4S
Oxford County

D-U-N-S 20-995-1719   (BR)
591182 ONTARIO LIMITED
WOLVERINE FREIGHT SYSTEM
645 Athlone Ave, Woodstock, ON, N4S 7V8

Emp Here 25
SIC 4214 Local trucking with storage

D-U-N-S 20-561-3821   (BR)
ARCELORMITTAL TUBULAR PRODUCTS CANADA G.P.
(*Suby of* ArcelorMittal Tubular Products
Canada G.P.)
193 Givins St, Woodstock, ON, N4S 5Y8
(519) 537-6671
Emp Here 485
SIC 3714 Motor vehicle parts and accessories

D-U-N-S 24-321-4306   (HQ)
ARCELORMITTAL TUBULAR PRODUCTS CANADA G.P.
(*Suby of* ArcelorMittal Tubular Products
Canada G.P.)
193 Givins St, Woodstock, ON, N4S 5Y8
(519) 537-6671
Emp Here 450   *Emp Total* 750
Sales 118,925,941
SIC 3714 Motor vehicle parts and accessories
Pr William Chisholm
VP Rick Legate
Marcus Gonzalez

D-U-N-S 25-860-7647   (BR)
BDO CANADA LLP
WOODSTOCK ACCOUNTING
94 Graham St Suite 757, Woodstock, ON,
N4S 6J7
(519) 539-0500
Emp Here 35
SIC 8721 Accounting, auditing, and book-keeping

D-U-N-S 24-121-3227   (BR)
BANK OF NOVA SCOTIA, THE
SCOTIABANK
485 Dundas St, Woodstock, ON, N4S 1C3
(519) 421-5295
Emp Here 20
SIC 6021 National commercial banks

D-U-N-S 20-572-2148   (BR)
BANK OF MONTREAL
BANK OF MONTREAL
534 Dundas St, Woodstock, ON, N4S 1C5
(519) 539-2057
Emp Here 20
SIC 6021 National commercial banks

D-U-N-S 25-016-7061   (BR)
BANQUE TORONTO-DOMINION, LA
TD BANK
(*Suby of* Toronto-Dominion Bank, The)
539 Dundas St, Woodstock, ON, N4S 1C6

---

(519) 539-2002
Emp Here 31
SIC 6021 National commercial banks

D-U-N-S 24-138-6650 (SL)
BOSTON PIZZA
431 Norwich Ave, Woodstock, ON, N4S 3W4
(519) 536-7800
Emp Here 60 *Sales* 1,824,018
SIC 5812 Eating places

D-U-N-S 20-187-2223 (BR)
BRIDGESTONE CANADA INC
FIRESTONE TEXTILES
1200 Dundas St, Woodstock, ON, N4S 7V9
(519) 537-6231
Emp Here 250
SIC 2296 Tire cord and fabrics

D-U-N-S 20-624-7418 (BR)
CANCLEAN FINANCIAL CORP
MR HANDYMAN
(*Suby of* CanClean Financial Corp)
304 Athlone Ave, Woodstock, ON, N4S 7V8
(519) 539-4822
Emp Here 25
SIC 7542 Carwashes

D-U-N-S 20-580-2304 (BR)
CANADA POST CORPORATION
433 Norwich Ave, Woodstock, ON, N4S 3W4
(519) 537-3131
Emp Here 20
SIC 4311 U.s. postal service

D-U-N-S 20-809-7985 (BR)
CARA OPERATIONS LIMITED
MONTANA'S COOKHOUSE SALOON
(*Suby of* Cara Holdings Limited)
511 Norwich Ave, Woodstock, ON, N4S 9A2
(519) 537-3117
Emp Here 45
SIC 5812 Eating places

D-U-N-S 25-278-6066 (BR)
CARA OPERATIONS LIMITED
SWISS CHALET
(*Suby of* Cara Holdings Limited)
623 Dundas St, Woodstock, ON, N4S 1E1
(519) 539-9881
Emp Here 50
SIC 5812 Eating places

D-U-N-S 20-994-7717 (BR)
CAREPARTNERS INC
485015 Sweaburg Rd, Woodstock, ON, N4S 7V6
(519) 539-1222
Emp Here 50
SIC 8082 Home health care services

D-U-N-S 20-179-7540 (BR)
CARESSANT-CARE NURSING AND RE-TIREMENT HOMES LIMITED
81 Fyfe Ave, Woodstock, ON, N4S 8Y2
(519) 539-6461
Emp Here 200
SIC 8051 Skilled nursing care facilities

D-U-N-S 20-327-4899 (BR)
CARGILL LIMITED
AGRIBRANDS PURINA CANADA
404 Main St, Woodstock, ON, N4S 7X5
(519) 539-8561
Emp Here 75
SIC 2048 Prepared feeds, nec

D-U-N-S 20-407-0221 (HQ)
CARRIER TRUCK CENTER INC
CARRIER EMERGENCY
(*Suby of* Royalex Incorporated)
645 Athlone Ave, Woodstock, ON, N4S 7V8
(519) 539-9837
Emp Here 45 *Emp Total* 8
Sales 36,480,350
SIC 5531 Auto and home supply stores
Pr Pr Robert R. Long
  Betty Long
  Marvin Long

CFO Michael Paquette

D-U-N-S 25-918-2392 (BR)
CHESHIRE HOMES OF LONDON INC
OXFORD OUTREACH ATTENDANT SER-VICE
742 Pavey St App 125, Woodstock, ON, N4S 2L9

Emp Here 30
SIC 8322 Individual and family services

D-U-N-S 25-483-3403 (HQ)
CHILDREN'S AID SOCIETY OF OXFORD COUNTY
(*Suby of* Children's Aid Society Of Oxford County)
712 Peel St, Woodstock, ON, N4S 0B4
(519) 539-6176
Emp Here 85 *Emp Total* 90
Sales 3,502,114
SIC 8322 Individual and family services

D-U-N-S 20-071-6152 (BR)
CHRISTIAN HORIZONS
HORIZON HOUSE OXFORD 2
(*Suby of* Christian Horizons)
289 Graham St, Woodstock, ON, N4S 6K8
(519) 539-3051
Emp Here 23
SIC 8361 Residential care

D-U-N-S 20-934-5763 (BR)
CONSEIL SCOLAIRE DE DISTRICT DES ECOLES CATHOLIQUES DU SUD-OUEST
ECOLE SAINTE-MARGUERITE BOUR-GEOYS
345 Huron St, Woodstock, ON, N4S 7A5
(519) 539-2911
Emp Here 25
SIC 8211 Elementary and secondary schools

D-U-N-S 24-325-2843 (BR)
COUNTY OF OXFORD
(*Suby of* County of Oxford)
377 Mill St, Woodstock, ON, N4S 7V6
(519) 536-9389
Emp Here 20
SIC 4119 Local passenger transportation, nec

D-U-N-S 24-963-2282 (BR)
ECONOMICAL MUTUAL INSURANCE COM-PANY
WESTERN GENERAL
959 Dundas St Suite 200, Woodstock, ON, N4S 1H2
(519) 539-9883
Emp Here 30
SIC 6331 Fire, marine, and casualty insurance

D-U-N-S 20-972-9594 (BR)
ELGIE BUS LINES LIMITED
813 Alice St, Woodstock, ON, N4S 2J2
(519) 539-0306
Emp Here 30
SIC 4151 School buses

D-U-N-S 20-995-9683 (HQ)
FEDERAL WHITE CEMENT LTD
(*Suby of* Federal White Cement Ltd)
Gd Lcd Main, Woodstock, ON, N4S 7W4
(519) 485-5410
Emp Here 90 *Emp Total* 100
SIC 3241 Cement, hydraulic

D-U-N-S 24-184-2764 (BR)
GUARANTEE COMPANY OF NORTH AMERICA, THE
THE GUARANTEE
954 Dundas St, Woodstock, ON, N4S 7Z9
(519) 539-9868
Emp Here 100
SIC 6411 Insurance agents, brokers, and ser-vice

D-U-N-S 25-842-0439 (SL)
HOAM LTD
KELSEY'S RESTAURANT

525 Norwich Ave, Woodstock, ON, N4S 9A2
(519) 421-7300
Emp Here 78 *Sales* 2,334,742
SIC 5812 Eating places

D-U-N-S 20-923-8476 (SL)
KINSDALE CARRIERS LIMITED
(*Suby of* Karicin Construction (Woodstock) Limited)
Gd Lcd Main, Woodstock, ON, N4S 7W4
(519) 421-0600
Emp Here 45 *Sales* 7,165,680
SIC 4213 Trucking, except local
  David Lowes

D-U-N-S 25-249-1451 (BR)
LONDON DISTRICT CATHOLIC SCHOOL BOARD
ST MICHAELS CATHOLIC ELEMENTARY SCHOOL
1085 Devonshire Ave, Woodstock, ON, N4S 5S1
(519) 675-4425
Emp Here 27
SIC 8211 Elementary and secondary schools

D-U-N-S 25-908-7013 (BR)
MACDONALD STEEL LIMITED
TIGER CAT INDUSTRY
1403 Dundas St, Woodstock, ON, N4S 7V9
(519) 537-3000
Emp Here 150
SIC 3499 Fabricated Metal products, nec

D-U-N-S 20-556-1322 (BR)
MAGNA SEATING INC
ONTEGRA-WOODSTOCK
460 Industrial Ave, Woodstock, ON, N4S 7L1

Emp Here 40
SIC 5531 Auto and home supply stores

D-U-N-S 24-358-8360 (BR)
MAPLE AUTOMOTIVE CORPORATION
180 Beards Lane, Woodstock, ON, N4S 7W3
(519) 537-2179
Emp Here 25
SIC 3465 Automotive stampings

D-U-N-S 20-288-8707 (BR)
MARWOOD METAL FABRICATION LIMITED
(*Suby of* 1058347 Ontario Limited)
460 Industrial Dr Unit 4, Woodstock, ON, N4S 7L1
(519) 688-1144
Emp Here 40
SIC 3714 Motor vehicle parts and accessories

D-U-N-S 20-783-6250 (BR)
METRO ONTARIO INC
FOOD BASICS
868 Dundas St, Woodstock, ON, N4S 1G7
(519) 537-7021
Emp Here 125
SIC 5411 Grocery stores

D-U-N-S 20-301-8478 (SL)
OTTAWAY MOTOR EXPRESS (2010) INC
520 Beards Lane Unit B, Woodstock, ON, N4S 7W3
(519) 602-3026
Emp Here 60 *Sales* 4,742,446
SIC 4212 Local trucking, without storage

D-U-N-S 20-273-1873 (SL)
OTTAWAY MOTOR EXPRESS LIMITED
714880 Oxford County Road 4, Woodstock, ON, N4S 7V7
(519) 539-8434
Emp Here 50 *Sales* 5,088,577
SIC 4212 Local trucking, without storage
Mgr Diane Ross

D-U-N-S 20-859-8800 (BR)
PACIFIC LINK COMMUNICATIONS INC
BELL WORLD
1147 Dundas St Suite 4, Woodstock, ON, N4S 8W3

(905) 305-8100
Emp Here 25
SIC 5999 Miscellaneous retail stores, nec

D-U-N-S 24-345-4019 (BR)
PETERBILT OF ONTARIO INC
240 Universal Rd, Woodstock, ON, N4S 7W3
(519) 539-2000
Emp Here 20
SIC 7532 Top and body repair and paint shops

D-U-N-S 24-200-0888 (BR)
PIONEER HI-BRED PRODUCTION LTD
(*Suby of* E. I. Du Pont De Nemours and Com-pany)
596779 County Rd Hwy Suite 59, Woodstock, ON, N4S 7W8
(519) 462-2732
Emp Here 25
SIC 8731 Commercial physical research

D-U-N-S 24-421-4565 (BR)
PRE-CON INC
1000 Dundas St, Woodstock, ON, N4S 0A3
(519) 537-6280
Emp Here 30
SIC 3272 Concrete products, nec

D-U-N-S 25-182-1885 (BR)
PREMIER EQUIPMENT LTD.
(*Suby of* Premier Equipment Ltd.)
537098 Oxford Road 34, Woodstock, ON, N4S 7W1
(519) 655-2200
Emp Here 27
SIC 5999 Miscellaneous retail stores, nec

D-U-N-S 25-362-0231 (BR)
REIMER EXPRESS LINES LTD
FAST AS FLITE
(*Suby of* Yrc Worldwide Inc.)
1187 Welford Pl, Woodstock, ON, N4S 7W3
(519) 539-8384
Emp Here 52
SIC 4214 Local trucking with storage

D-U-N-S 20-122-7928 (BR)
REITMANS (CANADA) LIMITEE
REITMANS
493 Norwich Ave, Woodstock, ON, N4S 9A2
(519) 539-3518
Emp Here 20
SIC 5621 Women's clothing stores

D-U-N-S 20-573-8441 (BR)
ROYAL BANK OF CANADA
RBC
(*Suby of* Royal Bank Of Canada)
452 Dundas St, Woodstock, ON, N4S 1C1
(519) 537-5574
Emp Here 20
SIC 6021 National commercial banks

D-U-N-S 20-187-2694 (HQ)
SAF-HOLLAND CANADA LIMITED
595 Athlone Ave, Woodstock, ON, N4S 7V8
(519) 537-2366
Emp Here 185 *Emp Total* 1
Sales 47,990,305
SIC 3714 Motor vehicle parts and accessories
Pr Pr Kim Baechler
Treas Joseph Fransen

D-U-N-S 20-526-3754 (BR)
SAINT ELIZABETH HEALTH CARE
65 Springbank Ave N Suite 1, Woodstock, ON, N4S 8V8
(519) 539-9807
Emp Here 30
SIC 8082 Home health care services

D-U-N-S 20-526-4075 (BR)
STAPLES CANADA INC
STAPLES
(*Suby of* Staples, Inc.)
497 Norwich Ave, Woodstock, ON, N4S 9A2
(519) 421-3202
Emp Here 30
SIC 5943 Stationery stores

D-U-N-S 25-249-1287   (BR)
THAMES VALLEY DISTRICT SCHOOL BOARD
OLIVER STEPHENS PUBLIC SCHOOL
164 Fyfe Ave, Woodstock, ON, N4S 3S6
(519) 539-2068
Emp Here 35
SIC 8211 Elementary and secondary schools

D-U-N-S 20-913-6832   (BR)
THAMES VALLEY DISTRICT SCHOOL BOARD
WINCHESTER STREET PUBLIC SCHOOL
110 Winchester St, Woodstock, ON, N4S 7K5
(519) 537-3543
Emp Here 30
SIC 8211 Elementary and secondary schools

D-U-N-S 25-000-3167   (BR)
THAMES VALLEY DISTRICT SCHOOL BOARD
CENTRAL PUBLIC SCHOOL
410 Hunter St, Woodstock, ON, N4S 4G4
(519) 537-5362
Emp Here 32
SIC 8211 Elementary and secondary schools

D-U-N-S 20-655-0548   (BR)
THAMES VALLEY DISTRICT SCHOOL BOARD
NORTHDALE ELEMENTARY SCHOOL
290 Victoria St N, Woodstock, ON, N4S 6W5
(519) 537-5761
Emp Here 40
SIC 8211 Elementary and secondary schools

D-U-N-S 20-938-3210   (BR)
THAMES VALLEY DISTRICT SCHOOL BOARD
HURON PARK SECONDARY SCHOOL
900 Cromwell St, Woodstock, ON, N4S 5B5
(519) 537-2347
Emp Here 80
SIC 8211 Elementary and secondary schools

D-U-N-S 20-710-5615   (BR)
THAMES VALLEY DISTRICT SCHOOL BOARD
WOODSTOCK COLLEGIATE INSTITUTE
35 Riddell St, Woodstock, ON, N4S 6L9
(519) 537-1050
Emp Here 50
SIC 8211 Elementary and secondary schools

D-U-N-S 20-938-3202   (BR)
THAMES VALLEY DISTRICT SCHOOL BOARD
COLLEGE AVENUE SECONDARY SCHOOL
700 College Ave, Woodstock, ON, N4S 2C8
(519) 539-0020
Emp Here 80
SIC 8211 Elementary and secondary schools

D-U-N-S 25-237-8328   (BR)
THAMES VALLEY DISTRICT SCHOOL BOARD
EASTDALE PUBLIC SCHOOL
65 Aileen Dr, Woodstock, ON, N4S 4A2
(519) 537-2652
Emp Here 47
SIC 8211 Elementary and secondary schools

D-U-N-S 25-249-1329   (BR)
THAMES VALLEY DISTRICT SCHOOL BOARD
SPRINGBANK PUBLIC SCHOOL
1060 Sprucedale Rd, Woodstock, ON, N4S 4Z9
(519) 539-7140
Emp Here 25
SIC 8211 Elementary and secondary schools

D-U-N-S 25-237-8286   (BR)
THAMES VALLEY DISTRICT SCHOOL BOARD
ROCH CARRIER FRENCH IMMERSION PUBLIC SCHOOL
840 Sloane St, Woodstock, ON, N4S 7V3

(519) 537-7321
Emp Here 20
SIC 8211 Elementary and secondary schools

D-U-N-S 20-557-6718   (BR)
THE PIC GROUP LTD
80 Norwich Ave Suite 5, Woodstock, ON, N4S 8Y6
(519) 421-3791
Emp Here 40
SIC 7549 Automotive services, nec

D-U-N-S 24-370-4876   (BR)
TOYOTA MOTOR MANUFACTURING CANADA INC
TOYOTA MOTOR MANUFACTURING
1717 Dundas St, Woodstock, ON, N4S 0A4
(519) 653-1111
Emp Here 250
SIC 3711 Motor vehicles and car bodies

D-U-N-S 24-362-1492   (BR)
TOYOTA MOTOR MANUFACTURING CANADA INC
715106 Oxford Rd Suite 4, Woodstock, ON, N4S 7V9

Emp Here 260
SIC 3711 Motor vehicles and car bodies

D-U-N-S 24-364-4304   (BR)
TOYOTA TSUSHO CANADA INC
WOODSTOCK SERVICE CENTRE
270 Beards Lane, Woodstock, ON, N4S 7W3
(519) 533-5570
Emp Here 100
SIC 5013 Motor vehicle supplies and new parts

D-U-N-S 20-175-6496   (SL)
TRAVEL CENTRE CANADA INC, THE
WOODSTOCK 230 TRAVEL CENTRE
535 Mill St, Woodstock, ON, N4S 7V6
(519) 421-3144
Emp Here 120   *Sales* 36,115,547
SIC 5172 Petroleum products, nec
Genl Mgr Michelle Argoso

D-U-N-S 25-310-4079   (BR)
TWINCORP INC
KFC
670 Dundas St, Woodstock, ON, N4S 1E6
(519) 539-9801
Emp Here 23
SIC 5812 Eating places

D-U-N-S 24-335-5641   (HQ)
UVALUX INTERNATIONAL INC
ADVANCED UVALUX SUN TANNING EQUIPMENT
(*Suby of* Ranheaven Holdings Inc)
470 Industrial Ave, Woodstock, ON, N4S 7L1
(519) 421-1212
Emp Here 50   *Emp Total* 46
Sales 21,596,367
SIC 5064 Electrical appliances, television and radio
Pr Pr William Van Haeren
Antonia Van Haeren

D-U-N-S 25-003-3305   (BR)
VICTORIAN ORDER OF NURSES FOR CANADA
VON OXFORD DISTRICT
570 Ingersoll Ave, Woodstock, ON, N4S 4Y2
(519) 539-1231
Emp Here 25
SIC 8082 Home health care services

D-U-N-S 20-341-5674   (BR)
VUTEQ CANADA INC
80 Norwich Ave, Woodstock, ON, N4S 8Y6
(519) 421-0011
Emp Here 20
SIC 4225 General warehousing and storage

D-U-N-S 25-294-8492   (BR)
WAL-MART CANADA CORP
499 Norwich Ave, Woodstock, ON, N4S 9A2

(519) 539-5120
Emp Here 250
SIC 5311 Department stores

D-U-N-S 24-627-9124   (BR)
YMCA OF WESTERN ONTARIO
WOODSTOCK YMCA
808 Dundas St, Woodstock, ON, N4S 1G4
(519) 539-6181
Emp Here 40
SIC 7999 Amusement and recreation, nec

Woodstock, ON N4T
Oxford County

D-U-N-S 25-075-8133   (BR)
SCHOLASTIC CANADA LTD
SCHOLASTIC BOOK FAIRS
(*Suby of* Scholastic Corporation)
225 Bysham Park Dr Suite 15, Woodstock, ON, N4T 1P1
(519) 421-3232
Emp Here 25
SIC 5942 Book stores

D-U-N-S 25-032-1601   (BR)
SOBEYS CAPITAL INCORPORATED
SOBEY'S READY TO SERVE 640
379 Springbank Ave N, Woodstock, ON, N4T 1R3
(519) 421-3340
Emp Here 150
SIC 5411 Grocery stores

D-U-N-S 20-134-3824   (BR)
THAMES VALLEY DISTRICT SCHOOL BOARD
ALGONQUIN PUBLIC SCHOOL
59 Algonquin Rd, Woodstock, ON, N4T 1R8
(519) 421-2219
Emp Here 48
SIC 8211 Elementary and secondary schools

D-U-N-S 24-410-4840   (SL)
WOODSTOCK AND DISTRICT DEVELOPMENTAL SERVICES
ARC INDUSTRIES
212 Bysham Park Dr, Woodstock, ON, N4T 1R2
(519) 539-7447
Emp Here 160   *Sales* 16,130,550
SIC 8322 Individual and family services
Pr Pr Mal Coubrough
Nancy Springstead
Garry Honcoop
Ex Dir John Bedell

Woodstock, ON N4V
Oxford County

D-U-N-S 24-544-0979   (SL)
552653 ONTARIO INC
ALTADORE QUALITY HOTEL & SUITES
580 Bruin Blvd, Woodstock, ON, N4V 1E5
(519) 537-5586
Emp Here 100   *Sales* 4,377,642
SIC 7011 Hotels and motels

D-U-N-S 25-807-1794   (SL)
911587 ONTARIO LTD
WENDY'S RESTAURANT
570 Norwich Ave, Woodstock, ON, N4V 1C6
(519) 539-1337
Emp Here 55   *Sales* 1,678,096
SIC 5812 Eating places

D-U-N-S 25-332-7852   (BR)
ARMTEC LP
ARMTEC
901 Pattulo Ave E, Woodstock, ON, N4V 1C8
(519) 421-1102
Emp Here 30

SIC 3312 Blast furnaces and steel mills

D-U-N-S 24-829-4894   (SL)
CANADA MOLD TECHNOLOGY INC
1075 Ridgeway Rd, Woodstock, ON, N4V 1E3
(519) 421-0711
Emp Here 51   *Sales* 7,189,883
SIC 3089 Plastics products, nec
Pr Pr Yutaka Fukuta
Ian Wick
Dir Fumio Iwatsuki
Dir Yoshitaka Kuno

D-U-N-S 24-338-1451   (SL)
CONTRANS HOLDING II LP
1179 Ridgeway Rd, Woodstock, ON, N4V 1E3
(519) 421-4600
Emp Here 400   *Sales* 97,365,120
SIC 6712 Bank holding companies
Stanley George Dunford

D-U-N-S 24-925-0002   (BR)
DBG CANADA LIMITED
980 Juliana Dr, Woodstock, ON, N4V 1B9

Emp Here 90
SIC 3469 Metal stampings, nec

D-U-N-S 24-846-1071   (BR)
FANSHAWE COLLEGE OF APPLIED ARTS AND TECHNOLOGY, T
369 Finkle St, Woodstock, ON, N4V 1A3
(519) 421-0144
Emp Here 25
SIC 8222 Junior colleges

D-U-N-S 20-248-5637   (HQ)
GNI MANAGEMENT GROUP INC
(*Suby of* GNI Management Group Inc)
935 Keyes Dr, Woodstock, ON, N4V 1C3
(519) 537-5873
Emp Here 20   *Emp Total* 50
Sales 4,231,721
SIC 1742 Plastering, drywall, and insulation

D-U-N-S 24-101-1951   (BR)
HINO MOTORS CANADA, LTD
1000 Ridgeway Rd, Woodstock, ON, N4V 1E2
(519) 421-0500
Emp Here 48
SIC 3711 Motor vehicles and car bodies

D-U-N-S 25-365-8587   (BR)
HOME DEPOT OF CANADA INC
HOME DEPOT
(*Suby of* The Home Depot Inc)
901 Juliana Dr, Woodstock, ON, N4V 1B9
(519) 421-5500
Emp Here 126
SIC 5251 Hardware stores

D-U-N-S 24-966-3261   (HQ)
KERRY (CANADA) INC
AGRINOVE
615 Jack Ross Ave, Woodstock, ON, N4V 1B7
(519) 537-3461
Emp Here 65   *Emp Total* 500
Sales 52,093,940
SIC 2099 Food preparations, nec
Pr Pr Gerard Behan
Sec Lanny Schimmel
Gary S. Fogler

D-U-N-S 25-263-4811   (BR)
LONDON DISTRICT CATHOLIC SCHOOL BOARD
ST MARY'S HIGH SCHOOL
431 Juliana Dr, Woodstock, ON, N4V 1E8
(519) 675-4435
Emp Here 65
SIC 8211 Elementary and secondary schools

D-U-N-S 20-187-4088   (SL)
POW LABORATORIES INC
63 Ridgeway Cir, Woodstock, ON, N4V 1C9
(519) 539-2065
Emp Here 60   *Sales* 3,502,114
SIC 8072 Dental laboratories

D-U-N-S 24-924-9012 (BR)
VARI-FORM INC
TI GROUP AUTOMOTIVE
62 Ridgeway Cir, Woodstock, ON, N4V 1C9

Emp Here 35
SIC 8731 Commercial physical research

D-U-N-S 24-764-1970 (HQ)
VUTEQ CANADA INC
920 Keyes Dr, Woodstock, ON, N4V 1C2
(519) 421-0011
Emp Here 750   *Emp Total* 2,000
Sales 218,045,200
SIC 3089 Plastics products, nec
Pr Pr Ezio Andreola
Zaitsu Tatsuo
Dir Christopher Spence
Acct Mgr Nancy Olenio

D-U-N-S 20-315-3762 (BR)
VUTEQ CANADA INC
885 Keyes Dr, Woodstock, ON, N4V 1C3
(519) 421-0011
Emp Here 350
SIC 3465 Automotive stampings

Woodville, ON K0M
Prince Edward County

D-U-N-S 20-025-0525 (BR)
**TRILLIUM   LAKELANDS   DISTRICT
SCHOOL BOARD**
WOODVILLE ELEMENTARY SCHOOL
109 Nappadale St, Woodville, ON, K0M 2T0
(705) 439-2427
Emp Here 25
SIC 8211 Elementary and secondary schools

Wroxeter, ON N0G
Huron County

D-U-N-S 20-783-7527 (HQ)
HYNDMAN TRANSPORT (1972) LIMITED
HYNDMAN TRANSPORT
1001 Belmore Line, Wroxeter, ON, N0G 2X0
(519) 335-3575
Emp Here 174   *Emp Total* 252
Sales 38,635,489
SIC 4213 Trucking, except local
Pr Pr Mike Campbell
George Kerr
Norm Maclennan
Clare Newell

Wyoming, ON N0N
Lambton County

D-U-N-S 24-991-2213 (SL)
HURONWEB OFFSET PRINTING INC
HURONWEB PRINTING
395 Broadway St, Wyoming, ON, N0N 1T0
(519) 845-0821
Emp Here 63   *Sales* 4,742,446
SIC 2752 Commercial printing, lithographic

D-U-N-S 20-710-4774 (BR)
**LAMBTON   KENT   DISTRICT   SCHOOL
BOARD**
*SOUTH   PLYMPTON/WYOMING   PUBLIC
SCHOOL*
606 Thames St, Wyoming, ON, N0N 1T0
(519) 845-3241
Emp Here 50
SIC 8211 Elementary and secondary schools

D-U-N-S 25-249-3648 (BR)
LAMBTON   KENT   DISTRICT   SCHOOL

BOARD
WYOMING CAMPUS
606 Thames St, Wyoming, ON, N0N 1T0
(519) 845-3241
Emp Here 23
SIC 8211 Elementary and secondary schools

D-U-N-S 24-419-5392 (BR)
PARRISH & HEIMBECKER, LIMITED
NEW-LIFE MILLS - WYOMING FEED MILL
(*Suby of* Parrish & Heimbecker, Limited)
520 Main St, Wyoming, ON, N0N 1T0
(519) 845-3318
Emp Here 20
SIC 5153 Grain and field beans

Zurich, ON N0M
Huron County

D-U-N-S 20-823-8238 (SL)
BLUE WATER REST HOME
37792 Zurich-Hensall Rd Rr 3, Zurich, ON,
N0M 2T0
(519) 236-4373
Emp Here 64   *Sales* 2,918,428
SIC 8051 Skilled nursing care facilities

D-U-N-S 25-228-1712 (BR)
**HURON   PERTH   CATHOLIC   DISTRICT
SCHOOL BOARD**
ST BONIFACE ELEMENTARY SCHOOL
24 Mary St, Zurich, ON, N0M 2T0
(519) 236-4335
Emp Here 20
SIC 8211 Elementary and secondary schools

Alberton, PE C0B
Prince County

D-U-N-S 25-646-0502   (BR)
ATLANTIC WHOLESALERS LTD
BRAY'S INDEPEDENT
499 Main St, Alberton, PE, C0B 1B0
(902) 853-2220
Emp Here 20
SIC 5411 Grocery stores

D-U-N-S 20-023-8033   (BR)
WESTERN HOSPITAL
MAPLEWOOD MANOR
397 Church St, Alberton, PE, C0B 1B0

Emp Here 70
SIC 8361 Residential care

Belfast, PE C0A

D-U-N-S 24-955-9782   (SL)
SELKIRK ENTERPRISES LTD
DR JOHN GILLIS MEMORIAL LODGE
3134 Garfield Rd, Belfast, PE, C0A 1A0
(902) 659-2337
Emp Here 60   *Sales* 2,699,546
SIC 8051 Skilled nursing care facilities

Belle River, PE C0A

D-U-N-S 24-605-8101   (SL)
BELLE RIVER ENTERPRISES LTD
Gd, Belle River, PE, C0A 1B0
(902) 962-2248
Emp Here 60   *Sales* 9,995,616
SIC 2092 Fresh or frozen packaged fish
Pr Pr Howard Hancock
 Dean Hancock
 Frances Hancock
Dir Glen Hancock

D-U-N-S 20-711-7719   (BR)
EASTERN SCHOOL DISTRICT
BELFAST CONSOLIDATED SCHOOL
Gd, Belle River, PE, C0A 1B0
(902) 659-7200
Emp Here 50
SIC 8211 Elementary and secondary schools

Bloomfield Station, PE C0B
Prince County

D-U-N-S 20-554-8220   (BR)
SOBEYS CAPITAL INCORPORATED
PRICE SHOPPER
2238 Ohalloran Rd, Bloomfield Station, PE, C0B 1E0
(902) 859-1981
Emp Here 22
SIC 5411 Grocery stores

Borden-Carleton, PE C0B
Prince County

D-U-N-S 25-060-9914   (BR)
MASTER PACKAGING INC
23784 Trans Canada Highway, Borden-Carleton, PE, C0B 1X0
(902) 437-3737
Emp Here 100
SIC 3554 Paper industries machinery

D-U-N-S 20-023-8108   (BR)

PUBLIC SCHOOLS BRANCH
AMHERST COVE CONSOLIDATED SCHOOL
(*Suby of* Public Schools Branch)
300 Carleton St, Borden-Carleton, PE, C0B 1X0
(902) 437-8525
Emp Here 23
SIC 8211 Elementary and secondary schools

Cardigan, PE C0A
Kings County

D-U-N-S 20-711-7727   (BR)
EASTERN SCHOOL DISTRICT
CARDIGAN CONSOLIDATED SCHOOL
1614 Georgetown Rd, Cardigan, PE, C0A 1G0
(902) 583-8575
Emp Here 50
SIC 8211 Elementary and secondary schools

Central Bedeque, PE C0B
Prince County

D-U-N-S 24-421-5252   (SL)
P.E.I. BAG CO. LTD
982 Callbeck St Po Box 3990, Central Bedeque, PE, C0B 1G0
(902) 436-2261
Emp Here 60   *Sales* 2,553,625
SIC 2393 Textile bags

Charlottetown, PE C1A

D-U-N-S 20-605-6983   (BR)
AL-PACK ENTERPRISES LTD
5 Macmillan Cres, Charlottetown, PE, C1A 8G3
(902) 628-6637
Emp Here 50
SIC 5084 Industrial machinery and equipment

D-U-N-S 20-084-6538   (BR)
AMALGAMATED DAIRIES LIMITED
PERFECTION FOODS
215 Fitzroy St, Charlottetown, PE, C1A 1S6
(902) 566-5515
Emp Here 20
SIC 3556 Food products machinery

D-U-N-S 25-527-7444   (SL)
ANDREWS HOCKEY GROWTH PROGRAMS INC
ANDREW'S SPORT CENTRE
550 University Ave, Charlottetown, PE, C1A 4P3
(902) 894-9600
Emp Here 50   *Sales* 2,699,546
SIC 7999 Amusement and recreation, nec

D-U-N-S 25-631-1341   (BR)
ATLANTIC WHOLESALERS LTD
CHARLOTTETOWN SUPER STORE
465 University Ave, Charlottetown, PE, C1A 4N9
(902) 569-2850
Emp Here 270
SIC 5411 Grocery stores

D-U-N-S 25-646-0536   (BR)
BANK OF NOVA SCOTIA, THE
SCOTIABANK
Gd, Charlottetown, PE, C1A 7L4
(902) 566-5004
Emp Here 40
SIC 6021 National commercial banks

D-U-N-S 20-002-8723   (BR)
BANK OF NOVA SCOTIA, THE

SCOTIABANK
135 St. Peters Rd, Charlottetown, PE, C1A 5P3
(902) 894-5013
Emp Here 20
SIC 6021 National commercial banks

D-U-N-S 25-631-1440   (BR)
BANK OF MONTREAL
BMO
105 Grafton St Suite 100, Charlottetown, PE, C1A 7L2
(902) 892-2437
Emp Here 25
SIC 6021 National commercial banks

D-U-N-S 20-589-5605   (BR)
BANQUE TORONTO-DOMINION, LA
TD CANADA TRUST
(*Suby of* Toronto-Dominion Bank, The)
192 Queen St, Charlottetown, PE, C1A 4B5
(902) 629-2265
Emp Here 28
SIC 6021 National commercial banks

D-U-N-S 25-410-6867   (HQ)
BAY FERRIES LIMITED
(*Suby of* NFL Holdings Ltd)
94 Water St, Charlottetown, PE, C1A 1A6
(902) 566-3838
Emp Here 30   *Emp Total* 580
Sales 45,600,438
SIC 4449 Water transportation of freight
Pr Mark Macdonald
VP VP Gordon Macrae
 Donald Cormier
 Danny Bartlett
 Gerald Stevenson

D-U-N-S 24-334-6496   (BR)
BELL ALIANT REGIONAL COMMUNICATIONS INC
ALIANT TELECOM
69 Belvedere Ave, Charlottetown, PE, C1A 9K5
(902) 566-0131
Emp Here 70
SIC 4899 Communication services, nec

D-U-N-S 24-263-5639   (BR)
CANADIAN BROADCASTING CORPORATION
CBC
430 University Ave, Charlottetown, PE, C1A 4N6
(902) 629-6400
Emp Here 40
SIC 4832 Radio broadcasting stations

D-U-N-S 25-311-5323   (BR)
CANADIAN IMPERIAL BANK OF COMMERCE
CIBC
465 University Ave, Charlottetown, PE, C1A 4N9
(902) 892-3477
Emp Here 20
SIC 6021 National commercial banks

D-U-N-S 20-755-8243   (BR)
CANMARC REIT
DUNDEE ARMS INN
200 Pownal St, Charlottetown, PE, C1A 3W8
(902) 892-2496
Emp Here 30
SIC 7011 Hotels and motels

D-U-N-S 24-128-8950   (SL)
CITY CAB INC
168 Prince St, Charlottetown, PE, C1A 4R6
(902) 892-6567
Emp Here 80   *Sales* 2,407,703
SIC 4121 Taxicabs

D-U-N-S 20-028-6198   (BR)
COX & PALMER
97 Queen St Suite 600, Charlottetown, PE, C1A 4A9

(902) 628-1033
Emp Here 30
SIC 8111 Legal services

D-U-N-S 20-023-8256   (BR)
DAY & ROSS INC
SAMEDAY WORLDWIDE
Gd Stn Central, Charlottetown, PE, C1A 7K1
(902) 894-5354
Emp Here 40
SIC 7389 Business services, nec

D-U-N-S 24-754-5627   (BR)
DELTA HOTELS LIMITED
DELTA PRINCE EDWARD HOTEL
18 Queen St, Charlottetown, PE, C1A 4A1
(902) 566-2222
Emp Here 140
SIC 8741 Management services

D-U-N-S 20-206-2175   (BR)
EASTERN SCHOOL DISTRICT
SPRING PARK ELEMENTARY SCHOOL
30 Dunkirk St, Charlottetown, PE, C1A 3Z8
(902) 368-6400
Emp Here 42
SIC 8211 Elementary and secondary schools

D-U-N-S 20-711-7826   (BR)
EASTERN SCHOOL DISTRICT
DONAGH REGIONAL SCHOOL
928 Bethel Rd, Charlottetown, PE, C1A 7J8
(902) 569-7720
Emp Here 28
SIC 8211 Elementary and secondary schools

D-U-N-S 20-711-7842   (BR)
EASTERN SCHOOL DISTRICT
WEST KENT ELEMENTARY SCHOOL
27 Viceroy Ave, Charlottetown, PE, C1A 2E4
(902) 368-6065
Emp Here 25
SIC 8211 Elementary and secondary schools

D-U-N-S 20-023-8132   (BR)
EASTERN SCHOOL DISTRICT
COLONEL GRAY SENIOR HIGH SCHOOL
175 Spring Park Rd, Charlottetown, PE, C1A 3Y8
(902) 368-6860
Emp Here 75
SIC 8211 Elementary and secondary schools

D-U-N-S 20-028-5950   (BR)
EASTERN SCHOOL DISTRICT
PARKDALE ELEMENTARY SCHOOL
49 Confederation St, Charlottetown, PE, C1A 5V5
(902) 368-6945
Emp Here 20
SIC 8211 Elementary and secondary schools

D-U-N-S 20-023-8157   (BR)
EASTERN SCHOOL DISTRICT
PRINCE STREET ELEMENTARY
60 Upper Prince St, Charlottetown, PE, C1A 4S3
(902) 368-6950
Emp Here 50
SIC 8211 Elementary and secondary schools

D-U-N-S 20-103-8259   (BR)
EASTERN SCHOOL DISTRICT
SHERWOOD ELEMENTARY SCHOOL
64 Maple Ave, Charlottetown, PE, C1A 6E7
(902) 368-6780
Emp Here 60
SIC 8211 Elementary and secondary schools

D-U-N-S 20-023-2812   (BR)
EASTERN SCHOOL DISTRICT
STONEPARK INTERMEDIATE
50 Pope Ave, Charlottetown, PE, C1A 7P5
(902) 368-6085
Emp Here 60
SIC 8211 Elementary and secondary schools

D-U-N-S 20-032-1904   (BR)
EASTERN SCHOOL DISTRICT

ST JEAN ELEMENTARY SCHOOL
335 Queen St, Charlottetown, PE, C1A 4C5
(902) 368-6985
Emp Here 20
SIC 8211 Elementary and secondary schools

D-U-N-S 20-605-7999 (SL)
ENTIRE MECHANICAL CONTRACTORS LTD
228 Mason Rd, Charlottetown, PE, C1A 7N9
(902) 569-1650
Emp Here 54   *Sales* 4,742,446
SIC 1711 Plumbing, heating, air-conditioning

D-U-N-S 24-755-4082 (SL)
F.T.C. ENTERPRISES LIMITED
PEI FOOD TECHNOLOGY CENTRE
101 Belvedere Ave, Charlottetown, PE, C1A 7N8
(902) 368-5548
Emp Here 33   *Sales* 1,824,018
SIC 8731 Commercial physical research

D-U-N-S 25-815-7887 (BR)
FORMER RESTORATION L.P.
249 Brackley Point Rd, Charlottetown, PE, C1A 6Z2
(902) 566-4331
Emp Here 25
SIC 1799 Special trade contractors, nec

D-U-N-S 24-382-1076 (BR)
FORT CHICAGO DISTRICT ENERGY LTD
PEI ENERGY SYSTEMS, DIV OF
40 Riverside Dr, Charlottetown, PE, C1A 9M2
(902) 629-3960
Emp Here 40
SIC 4911 Electric services

D-U-N-S 20-780-0897 (SL)
GARDEN HOME (1986) INCORPORATED
310 North River Rd, Charlottetown, PE, C1A 3M4
(902) 892-4131
Emp Here 90   *Sales* 4,085,799
SIC 8051 Skilled nursing care facilities

D-U-N-S 20-075-9475 (BR)
GRANT THORNTON LLP
CAPSERVCO
98 Fitzroy St Suite 710, Charlottetown, PE, C1A 1R7
(902) 892-6547
Emp Here 30
SIC 8721 Accounting, auditing, and book-keeping

D-U-N-S 24-660-3216 (BR)
HOLLAND COLLEGE
140 Weymouth St, Charlottetown, PE, C1A 4Z1
(902) 629-4260
Emp Here 49
SIC 8211 Elementary and secondary schools

D-U-N-S 20-273-2892 (BR)
HOLLAND COLLEGE
ADMISSION OFFICE
4 Sydney St, Charlottetown, PE, C1A 1E9
(902) 894-6805
Emp Here 80
SIC 8221 Colleges and universities

D-U-N-S 20-298-5011 (BR)
INDIGO BOOKS & MUSIC INC
INDIGO 937
(*Suby of* Indigo Books & Music Inc)
465 University Ave Unit 1, Charlottetown, PE, C1A 4N9
(902) 569-9213
Emp Here 25
SIC 5942 Book stores

D-U-N-S 25-315-7887 (BR)
INVESTORS GROUP FINANCIAL SERVICES INC
18 Queen St Suite 106, Charlottetown, PE, C1A 4A1

(902) 566-4661
Emp Here 30
SIC 8741 Management services

D-U-N-S 24-362-5337 (HQ)
ISLANDSAND HOLDINGS INC
SUBWAY
(*Suby of* Islandsand Holdings Inc)
150 Queen St, Charlottetown, PE, C1A 4B5
(902) 368-1728
Emp Here 100   *Emp Total* 100
Sales 2,991,389
SIC 5812 Eating places

D-U-N-S 20-226-3083 (HQ)
MARITIME ELECTRIC COMPANY, LIMITED
180 Kent St, Charlottetown, PE, C1A 1N9
(800) 670-1012
Emp Here 85   *Emp Total* 8,000
Sales 99,358,990
SIC 4911 Electric services
Pr Pr John Gaudet
VP Fin Steven D. Loggie
James D. Bradley
Earl Ludlow
D Blair Maclauchlan
Brian Thompson
Jacqueline Macintyre
Robert Sear
Gary Smith
Keith O'neill

D-U-N-S 25-146-8302 (BR)
MEDIAS TRANSCONTINENTAL INC
MEDIAS TRANSCONTINENTAL INC
165 Prince St, Charlottetown, PE, C1A 4R7
(902) 629-6000
Emp Here 75
SIC 2711 Newspapers

D-U-N-S 24-262-2835 (HQ)
METRO CREDIT UNION LTD
(*Suby of* Metro Credit Union Ltd)
281 University Ave, Charlottetown, PE, C1A 4M3
(902) 892-4100
Emp Here 36   *Emp Total* 41
Sales 7,763,494
SIC 6062 State credit unions
Genl Mgr Bernard Gillis
Pr Pr Bernard Keefe

D-U-N-S 20-443-4609 (SL)
MITTON, V CO LTD
DAIRY QUEEN BRAZIER STORE
365 University Ave, Charlottetown, PE, C1A 4N2
(902) 892-1892
Emp Here 80   *Sales* 2,407,703
SIC 5812 Eating places

D-U-N-S 25-656-5839 (BR)
MURPHY INVESTMENTS LTD
PIZZA DELIGHT
113 Longworth Ave, Charlottetown, PE, C1A 5B1
(902) 566-4466
Emp Here 20
SIC 5812 Eating places

D-U-N-S 20-001-5878 (BR)
MURPHY INVESTMENTS LTD
GAHAN HOUSE PUB BREWERY & MERCANTILE
126 Sydney St, Charlottetown, PE, C1A 1G4
(902) 626-2337
Emp Here 20
SIC 5813 Drinking places

D-U-N-S 24-349-5467 (BR)
MURPHY'S PHARMACIES INC
PARKDALE PHARMACY
24 St. Peters Rd, Charlottetown, PE, C1A 5N4
(902) 894-8553
Emp Here 40
SIC 5912 Drug stores and proprietary stores

D-U-N-S 25-632-9574 (BR)
MURPHY, D.P. INC

TIM HORTONS
375 Grafton St E, Charlottetown, PE, C1A 1M1
(902) 892-0078
Emp Here 60
SIC 5812 Eating places

D-U-N-S 25-632-9582 (BR)
MURPHY, D.P. INC
TIM HORTONS
435 University Ave, Charlottetown, PE, C1A 4N7
(902) 892-8925
Emp Here 40
SIC 5461 Retail bakeries

D-U-N-S 25-656-5375 (BR)
MURPHY, D.P. INC
TIM HORTONS
20 Mount Edward Rd, Charlottetown, PE, C1A 5R8
(902) 892-3222
Emp Here 30
SIC 5812 Eating places

D-U-N-S 25-632-9566 (BR)
MURPHY, D.P. INC
TIM HORTONS
125 Kent St, Charlottetown, PE, C1A 1N3
(902) 892-3322
Emp Here 25
SIC 5461 Retail bakeries

D-U-N-S 25-666-4657 (BR)
MURPHY, D.P. INC
TIM HORTONS
147 St. Peters Rd, Charlottetown, PE, C1A 5P6
(902) 892-2711
Emp Here 50
SIC 5812 Eating places

D-U-N-S 24-341-0854 (BR)
NEWCAP INC
HOT 1055
90 University Ave Suite 320, Charlottetown, PE, C1A 4K9
(902) 569-1003
Emp Here 35
SIC 4832 Radio broadcasting stations

D-U-N-S 20-009-0160 (BR)
PROVINCE OF PEI
INNOVATION PEI
94 Euston St, Charlottetown, PE, C1A 1W4
(902) 368-6300
Emp Here 75
SIC 6111 Federal and federally sponsored credit agencies

D-U-N-S 20-795-6017 (BR)
PROVINCE OF PEI
PROVINCIAL ADDICTION TREATMENT FACILTY
2814 Rte 215 Mount Herbert, Charlottetown, PE, C1A 7N8
(902) 368-4120
Emp Here 60
SIC 8069 Specialty hospitals, except psychiatric

D-U-N-S 20-191-9755 (BR)
PROVINCE OF PEI
HILLSBOROUGH HOSPITAL
115 Dacon Grove Lane, Charlottetown, PE, C1A 7N5
(902) 368-5400
Emp Here 350
SIC 8063 Psychiatric hospitals

D-U-N-S 20-706-2626 (BR)
PROVINCE OF PEI
QUEEN ELIZABETH HOSPITAL
60 Riverside Dr, Charlottetown, PE, C1A 8T5
(902) 894-2111
Emp Here 2,000
SIC 8062 General medical and surgical hospitals

D-U-N-S 20-299-9368 (BR)
PROVINCE OF PEI
SPEECH, PATHOLOGY AND AUDIOLOGY
161 St. Peters Rd, Charlottetown, PE, C1A 7N8
(902) 368-5807
Emp Here 20
SIC 8049 Offices of health practitioner

D-U-N-S 20-084-6686 (SL)
QUEENS COUNTY RESIDENTIAL SERVICES INC
94 Mount Edward Rd Suite 200, Charlottetown, PE, C1A 5S6
(902) 566-4470
Emp Here 45   *Sales* 12,579,800
SIC 8399 Social services, nec
Prin Wade Durling

D-U-N-S 25-656-8858 (BR)
RBC DOMINION SECURITIES INC
(*Suby of* Royal Bank Of Canada)
134 Kent St Suite 602, Charlottetown, PE, C1A 8R8
(902) 566-5544
Emp Here 20
SIC 6211 Security brokers and dealers

D-U-N-S 24-993-6030 (SL)
SHERWOOD HARDWARE LTD
HOME HARDWARE CHARLOTTETOWN
115 St. Peters Rd, Charlottetown, PE, C1A 5P3
(902) 892-8509
Emp Here 50   *Sales* 4,815,406
SIC 5251 Hardware stores

D-U-N-S 24-806-2658 (BR)
SOBEYS CAPITAL INCORPORATED
SOBEYS STORE# 870
400 University Ave Suite 870, Charlottetown, PE, C1A 4N6
(902) 626-3334
Emp Here 25
SIC 5411 Grocery stores

D-U-N-S 24-943-4663 (BR)
SOEURS DE LA CONGREGATION DE NOTRE-DAME, LES
NOTRE DAME CONVENT
246 Sydney St, Charlottetown, PE, C1A 1H1
(902) 892-4181
Emp Here 24
SIC 8661 Religious organizations

D-U-N-S 25-139-4227 (BR)
VALUE VILLAGE STORES, INC
SAVERS
(*Suby of* Savers, Inc.)
339 University Ave Unit 5, Charlottetown, PE, C1A 4M8
(902) 566-4084
Emp Here 25
SIC 5399 Miscellaneous general merchandise

D-U-N-S 24-804-3150 (HQ)
VOGUE OPTICAL GROUP INC
VOGUE OPTICAL
5 Brackley Point Rd, Charlottetown, PE, C1A 6X8
(902) 566-3326
Emp Here 30   *Emp Total* 415
Sales 23,128,542
SIC 5995 Optical goods stores
Pr John Macleod
Dir W. John Bennett
Dir Antoine Amiel
Dir Martial Gagne
Dir C. Emmett Pearson
Dir Richard Cherney

D-U-N-S 25-632-9962 (BR)
WE CARE HEALTH SERVICES INC
WE CARE HOME HEALTH SERVICES
161 St. Peters Rd, Charlottetown, PE, C1A 5P7
(902) 894-3025
Emp Here 32

SIC 8093 Specialty outpatient clinics, nec

D-U-N-S 24-629-5471   (HQ)
WILBUR, DAVID PRODUCTS LTD
RALSTON FUELS
155 Belvedere Ave, Charlottetown, PE, C1A 2Y9
(902) 566-5011
Emp Here 40   *Emp Total* 2,300
Sales 27,068,420
SIC 5172 Petroleum products, nec
Pr Pr Blair Maclauchlan
VP VP Wade Maclauchlan
Dir Donna Maclauchlan
Dir Roger Maclauchlan

Charlottetown, PE C1C

D-U-N-S 20-711-7875   (BR)
COMISSION SCOLAIRE DE LANGUE FRANCAISE, LA
ECOLE FRANCOIS BUOTE
5 Acadian Dr, Charlottetown, PE, C1C 1M2
(902) 566-1715
Emp Here 50
SIC 8211 Elementary and secondary schools

D-U-N-S 20-657-1114   (BR)
EASTERN SCHOOL DISTRICT
LM MONTGOMERY ELEMENTARY
69 Macwilliams Rd, Charlottetown, PE, C1C 1L4
(902) 368-4150
Emp Here 25
SIC 8211 Elementary and secondary schools

Charlottetown, PE C1E

D-U-N-S 24-362-4199   (SL)
100496 P.E.I. INC
420 Mount Edward Rd, Charlottetown, PE, C1E 2A1
(902) 368-3442
Emp Here 27   *Sales* 7,558,320
SIC 5032 Brick, stone, and related material
Pr Pr Ron Martin
    Allan Martin

D-U-N-S 25-654-1541   (BR)
AMALGAMATED DAIRIES LIMITED
A.D.L.
50 Fourth St, Charlottetown, PE, C1E 2B5
(902) 566-5411
Emp Here 30
SIC 2026 Fluid milk

D-U-N-S 24-675-1346   (BR)
AMALGAMATED DAIRIES LIMITED
PERFECTION FOODS
50 Fourth St, Charlottetown, PE, C1E 2B5
(902) 628-8115
Emp Here 30
SIC 2026 Fluid milk

D-U-N-S 20-084-6785   (BR)
ATLANTIC TRACTORS & EQUIPMENT LIMITED
CATERPILLAR
130 Sherwood Rd, Charlottetown, PE, C1E 0E4
(902) 894-7329
Emp Here 35
SIC 5082 Construction and mining machinery

D-U-N-S 25-684-6718   (BR)
ATLANTIC WHOLESALERS LTD
WEST ROYALTY SUPERSTORE
680 University Ave, Charlottetown, PE, C1E 1E3
(902) 368-8163
Emp Here 74
SIC 5411 Grocery stores

D-U-N-S 20-004-0538   (BR)
BEST BUY CANADA LTD
FUTURE SHOP 660
(*Suby of* Best Buy Co., Inc.)
191 Buchanan Dr, Charlottetown, PE, C1E 2E4
(902) 626-2081
Emp Here 43
SIC 5999 Miscellaneous retail stores, nec

D-U-N-S 24-391-5043   (BR)
BIOVECTRA INC
29 Mccarville St, Charlottetown, PE, C1E 2A7
(902) 566-9116
Emp Here 200
SIC 2834 Pharmaceutical preparations

D-U-N-S 24-363-9783   (BR)
BIOVECTRA INC
17 Hillstrom Ave, Charlottetown, PE, C1E 2C2
(902) 566-9116
Emp Here 60
SIC 3841 Surgical and medical instruments

D-U-N-S 20-021-6203   (BR)
COCA-COLA REFRESHMENTS CANADA COMPANY
ALTANTIC COCA-COLA BOTTLING
(*Suby of* The Coca-Cola Company)
2 Aviation Ave, Charlottetown, PE, C1E 2M1

Emp Here 20
SIC 5149 Groceries and related products, nec

D-U-N-S 25-355-4463   (HQ)
COWS INC
(*Suby of* Cows Prince Edward Island Inc)
397 Capital Dr, Charlottetown, PE, C1E 2E2
(902) 566-5558
Emp Here 20   *Emp Total* 70
Sales 1,532,175
SIC 5651 Family clothing stores

D-U-N-S 20-711-7859   (BR)
EASTERN SCHOOL DISTRICT
WEST ROYALTY ELEMENTARY SCHOOL
80 Commonwealth Ave, Charlottetown, PE, C1E 2E9
(902) 368-6790
Emp Here 53
SIC 8211 Elementary and secondary schools

D-U-N-S 20-023-8249   (BR)
EASTERN SCHOOL DISTRICT
CHARLOTTETOWN RURAL HIGH SCHOOL
100 Raider Rd, Charlottetown, PE, C1E 1K6
(902) 368-6905
Emp Here 70
SIC 8211 Elementary and secondary schools

D-U-N-S 24-804-3101   (BR)
EMPIRE THEATRES LIMITED
CHARLOTTETOWN CINEMAS
670 University Ave, Charlottetown, PE, C1E 1H6
(902) 368-1922
Emp Here 45
SIC 7832 Motion picture theaters, except drive-in

D-U-N-S 24-337-3250   (BR)
FGL SPORTS LTD
SPORT-CHEK CHARLOTTETOWN MALL
670 University Ave Unit 1, Charlottetown, PE, C1E 1H6
(902) 628-6088
Emp Here 40
SIC 5941 Sporting goods and bicycle shops

D-U-N-S 20-735-3595   (BR)
FRESHSTONE BRANDS INC
KEYBRAND FOODS
23 Fourth St, Charlottetown, PE, C1E 2B4
(902) 629-1300
Emp Here 20
SIC 2099 Food preparations, nec

D-U-N-S 20-009-0624   (SL)
GREEN ISLE ENVIRONMENTAL INC

7 Superior Cres, Charlottetown, PE, C1E 2A1
(902) 894-9363
Emp Here 50   *Sales* 8,834,400
SIC 4953 Refuse systems
Pr Pr John Edward Clark
    John David Clark

D-U-N-S 25-672-7801   (HQ)
HGS CANADA INC
82 Hillstrom Ave, Charlottetown, PE, C1E 2C6
(902) 370-3200
Emp Here 25   *Emp Total* 23,891
Sales 207,312,380
SIC 7379 Computer related services, nec
Pr Pr Ross Beattie
VP John Hooper
VP Fin Tracy Laughlin

D-U-N-S 20-774-8695   (SL)
INNER CITY COURIERS
MACGINNIS EXPRESS
2 Macaleer Dr, Charlottetown, PE, C1E 2A1
(902) 892-5005
Emp Here 50   *Sales* 2,626,585
SIC 7389 Business services, nec

D-U-N-S 24-913-5948   (BR)
MARITIME STEEL AND FOUNDRIES LIMITED
CHARLOTTETOWN METAL PRODUCTS
2744 North York River Rd, Charlottetown, PE, C1E 1Z2
(902) 566-3000
Emp Here 32
SIC 3556 Food products machinery

D-U-N-S 25-284-3115   (SL)
MATHESON & MACMILLAN (1993) LIMITED
(*Suby of* Island Construction Limited, The)
355 Sherwood Rd, Charlottetown, PE, C1E 0E5
(902) 892-1057
Emp Here 20   *Sales* 5,024,000
SIC 2951 Asphalt paving mixtures and blocks
Pr Pr Steve Matheson

D-U-N-S 25-632-7511   (BR)
MCKENNCO INC
MCDONALDS RESTAURANTS
(*Suby of* McKennco Inc)
124 Capital Dr, Charlottetown, PE, C1E 1E7
(902) 566-6704
Emp Here 25
SIC 5812 Eating places

D-U-N-S 25-694-2103   (BR)
MURPHY, D.P. INC
TIM HORTONS
625 North River Rd, Charlottetown, PE, C1E 1J8
(902) 894-5133
Emp Here 35
SIC 5812 Eating places

D-U-N-S 20-729-4141   (SL)
MURPHY, K.W. LTD
HOLIDAY INN EXPRESS HOTEL & SUITES
200 Trans Canada Hwy, Charlottetown, PE, C1E 2E8

Emp Here 35   *Sales* 1,819,127
SIC 7011 Hotels and motels

D-U-N-S 24-130-9475   (HQ)
PADINOX INC
PADERNO COOKWEAR
489 Brackley Point Rd, Charlottetown, PE, C1E 1Z3
(902) 629-1500
Emp Here 85   *Emp Total* 150
Sales 15,248,786
SIC 3631 Household cooking equipment
    James Casey
Pr Pr Tim Casey
    Curtis Macmillan
Dir Ernest Brennan
Dir Fred Hyndman
Dir Joan Casey

Dir Doug Wright

D-U-N-S 25-631-2406   (HQ)
PARKER REALTY LTD
COLDWELL BANKER
(*Suby of* Parker Realty Ltd)
535 North River Rd Suite 1, Charlottetown, PE, C1E 1J6
(902) 566-4663
Emp Here 50   *Emp Total* 50
Sales 4,742,446
SIC 6531 Real estate agents and managers

D-U-N-S 25-068-8785   (BR)
PRINCE EDWARD ISLAND LIQUOR CONTROL COMMISSION
193 Malpeque Rd, Charlottetown, PE, C1E 0C4
(902) 368-4299
Emp Here 20
SIC 5921 Liquor stores

D-U-N-S 20-037-4978   (BR)
PROVINCE OF PEI
QUEEN REGION HOME CARE
165 John Yeo Dr, Charlottetown, PE, C1E 3J3
(902) 368-4790
Emp Here 100
SIC 8059 Nursing and personal care, nec

D-U-N-S 24-966-7945   (BR)
PROVINCE OF PEI
BEACH GROVE NURSING HOME
200 Beach Grove Rd, Charlottetown, PE, C1E 1L3
(902) 368-6750
Emp Here 200
SIC 8051 Skilled nursing care facilities

D-U-N-S 25-357-5971   (BR)
RESOLVE CORPORATION
(*Suby of* 2206997 Ontario Inc)
50 Watts Ave, Charlottetown, PE, C1E 2B8
(902) 629-3000
Emp Here 400
SIC 7389 Business services, nec

D-U-N-S 24-943-6460   (BR)
SOBEYS CAPITAL INCORPORATED
SOBEYS
679 University Ave, Charlottetown, PE, C1E 1E5
(902) 566-3218
Emp Here 135
SIC 5411 Grocery stores

D-U-N-S 25-498-9957   (BR)
STAPLES CANADA INC
STAPLES THE BUSINESS DEPOT
(*Suby of* Staples, Inc.)
655 University Ave, Charlottetown, PE, C1E 1E5
(902) 894-5011
Emp Here 30
SIC 5943 Stationery stores

D-U-N-S 25-859-3185   (BR)
SUN LIFE ASSURANCE COMPANY OF CANADA
SUN LIFE FINANCIAL
184 Buchanan Dr, Charlottetown, PE, C1E 2H8
(902) 894-8513
Emp Here 25
SIC 6311 Life insurance

D-U-N-S 20-063-8356   (BR)
TUBE-FAB LTD
36 Fourth St, Charlottetown, PE, C1E 2B3
(902) 436-3229
Emp Here 45
SIC 3671 Electron tubes

D-U-N-S 20-646-1340   (SL)
VISION RESEARCH INC
94 Watts Ave, Charlottetown, PE, C1E 2C1
(902) 569-7300
Emp Here 60   *Sales* 3,064,349
SIC 7389 Business services, nec

▲ Public Company   ■ Public Company Family Member   **HQ** Headquarters   **BR** Branch   **SL** Single Location

D-U-N-S 24-329-8721   (BR)
WAL-MART CANADA CORP
80 Buchanan Dr, Charlottetown, PE, C1E 2E5
(902) 628-4600
Emp Here 200
SIC 5311 Department stores

D-U-N-S 20-199-2984   (BR)
**WINNERS MERCHANTS INTERNATIONAL
L.P.**
WINNERS
(*Suby of* The TJX Companies Inc)
670 University Ave, Charlottetown, PE, C1E
1H6
(902) 894-5511
Emp Here 25
SIC 5651 Family clothing stores

Coleman, PE C0B
Prince County

D-U-N-S 20-199-7066   (BR)
**ANNAPOLIS VALLEY PEAT MOSS COM-
PANY LIMITED**
GOLF ISLAND PEAT MOSS
747 Canadian Rd Rr 2, Coleman, PE, C0B
1H0
(902) 831-2669
Emp Here 25
SIC 1499 Miscellaneous nonMetallic minerals,
except fuels

Cornwall, PE C0A

D-U-N-S 20-039-3457   (BR)
EASTERN SCHOOL DISTRICT
WESTWOOD PRIMARY SCHOOL
80 Meadowbank Rd, Cornwall, PE, C0A 1H0
(902) 368-6855
Emp Here 50
SIC 8211 Elementary and secondary schools

D-U-N-S 20-023-2820   (BR)
EASTERN SCHOOL DISTRICT
ELIOT RIVER ELEMENTARY SCHOOL
79 Hilltop Dr, Cornwall, PE, C0A 1H0
(902) 368-4270
Emp Here 40
SIC 8211 Elementary and secondary schools

D-U-N-S 20-711-7818   (BR)
EASTERN SCHOOL DISTRICT
EAST WILTSHIRE INTERMEDIATE SCHOOL
100 Kingston Rd, Cornwall, PE, C0A 1H8
(902) 368-4130
Emp Here 50
SIC 8211 Elementary and secondary schools

D-U-N-S 20-170-3803   (BR)
ISLAND COASTAL SERVICES LTD
15418 Trans Canada Hwy, Cornwall, PE, C0A
1H0
(902) 675-2704
Emp Here 60
SIC 1794 Excavation work

D-U-N-S 25-866-8888   (BR)
LOBLAWS SUPERMARKETS LIMITED
CORNWALL SAVE EASY
25 Meadowbank Rd Unit 17, Cornwall, PE,
C0A 1H0
(902) 628-6787
Emp Here 20
SIC 5411 Grocery stores

D-U-N-S 25-656-5367   (BR)
MURPHY, D.P. INC
TIM HORTONS
25 Meadow Bank Rd, Cornwall, PE, C0A 1H0
(902) 626-3112
Emp Here 35
SIC 5812 Eating places

Crapaud, PE C0A

D-U-N-S 20-020-8051   (BR)
EASTERN SCHOOL DISTRICT
ENGLEWOOD SCHOOL
20280 Trans Canada Hwy - Rte 1, Crapaud,
PE, C0A 1J0
(902) 658-7850
Emp Here 25
SIC 8211 Elementary and secondary schools

Ellerslie, PE C0B
Prince County

D-U-N-S 25-241-4024   (BR)
PUBLIC SCHOOLS BRANCH
ELLERSLIE ELEMENTARY SCHOOL
(*Suby of* Public Schools Branch)
Gd, Ellerslie, PE, C0B 1J0
(902) 831-7920
Emp Here 25
SIC 8211 Elementary and secondary schools

Elmsdale, PE C0B
Prince County

D-U-N-S 20-349-2400   (BR)
PUBLIC SCHOOLS BRANCH
WESTISLE COMPOSITE HIGH SCHOOL
(*Suby of* Public Schools Branch)
39570 Western Rd, Elmsdale, PE, C0B 1K0
(902) 853-8626
Emp Here 56
SIC 8211 Elementary and secondary schools

Georgetown, PE C0A
Kings County

D-U-N-S 20-023-7936   (BR)
EASTERN SCHOOL DISTRICT
GEORGETOWN ELEMENTARY SCHOOL
47 Kent St, Georgetown, PE, C0A 1L0
(902) 652-8970
Emp Here 25
SIC 8211 Elementary and secondary schools

D-U-N-S 25-895-4593   (BR)
IRVING SHIPBUILDING INC
EAST ISLE SHIPYARD
115 Water St, Georgetown, PE, C0A 1L0

Emp Here 100
SIC 3731 Shipbuilding and repairing

D-U-N-S 20-170-6632   (BR)
PROVINCE OF PEI
PROVINCE OF PEI
283 Brudenell Island, Georgetown, PE, C0A
1L0
(902) 652-8950
Emp Here 25
SIC 7033 Trailer parks and campsites

Hunter River, PE C0A

D-U-N-S 24-175-0848   (BR)
EASTERN SCHOOL DISTRICT
*CENTRAL   QUEENS   ELEMENTARY
SCHOOL*
19821 Rte 2, Hunter River, PE, C0A 1N0
(902) 964-7950
Emp Here 23
SIC 8211 Elementary and secondary schools

D-U-N-S 20-780-6340   (SL)
**NEW GLASGOW RECREATION CENTRE
(1980) INC**
NEW GLASGOW LOBSTER SUPPERS
604 Rte 258 Rr 3, Hunter River, PE, C0A 1N0
(902) 964-2870
Emp Here 110   *Sales* 3,283,232
SIC 5812 Eating places

Kensington, PE C0B
Prince County

D-U-N-S 25-823-8948   (BR)
ATLANTIC WHOLESALERS LTD
KENSINGTON SAVE-EASY
Broadway St Suite 31, Kensington, PE, C0B
1M0
(902) 836-4709
Emp Here 21
SIC 5411 Grocery stores

D-U-N-S 24-248-9909   (BR)
CAVENDISH FARMS CORPORATION
(*Suby of* J. D. Irving, Limited)
Gd, Kensington, PE, C0B 1M0
(902) 836-5555
Emp Here 1,000
SIC 5142 Packaged frozen goods

D-U-N-S 20-654-7924   (BR)
PUBLIC SCHOOLS BRANCH
QUEEN ELIZABETH ELEMENTARY
(*Suby of* Public Schools Branch)
2 Andrews Dr, Kensington, PE, C0B 1M0
(902) 836-8900
Emp Here 40
SIC 8211 Elementary and secondary schools

D-U-N-S 20-038-0132   (BR)
PUBLIC SCHOOLS BRANCH
*KENSINGTON   INTERMEDIATE   SR   HIGH
SCHOOL*
(*Suby of* Public Schools Branch)
19 Victoria St E, Kensington, PE, C0B 1M0
(902) 836-8901
Emp Here 50
SIC 8211 Elementary and secondary schools

D-U-N-S 25-856-3493   (SL)
STANLEY BRIDGE COUNTRY RESORT INC
Gd, Kensington, PE, C0B 1M0
(902) 886-2882
Emp Here 50   *Sales* 2,188,821
SIC 7011 Hotels and motels

Kinkora, PE C0B
Prince County

D-U-N-S 20-654-7916   (BR)
PUBLIC SCHOOLS BRANCH
SOMERSET ELEMENTARY SCHOOL
(*Suby of* Public Schools Branch)
30 Somerset St, Kinkora, PE, C0B 1N0
(902) 887-2505
Emp Here 20
SIC 8211 Elementary and secondary schools

Lennox Island, PE C0B
Prince County

D-U-N-S 20-366-0469   (SL)
MINIGOO FISHERIES INC
195 Eagle Feather Trail, Lennox Island, PE,
C0B 1P0
(902) 831-3325
Emp Here 20   *Sales* 7,296,070
SIC 5146 Fish and seafoods
Genl Mgr Heather Pothier

Dir Chief Matilda Ramjattan
Dir Mary Moore-Phillips
Dir Janet Banks
Dir Corrine Dyment
Dir Gerry Thomas

Miscouche, PE C0B
Prince County

D-U-N-S 20-023-8090   (BR)
PUBLIC SCHOOLS BRANCH
MISCOUCHE CONSOLIDATED SCHOOL
(*Suby of* Public Schools Branch)
19 High School St, Miscouche, PE, C0B 1T0
(902) 888-8495
Emp Here 35
SIC 8211 Elementary and secondary schools

D-U-N-S 20-345-8518   (BR)
ROYAL CANADIAN LEGION, THE
MISCOUCHE LEGION BRANCH 18
(*Suby of* Royal Canadian Legion, The)
94 Main Dr, Miscouche, PE, C0B 1T0
(902) 436-2672
Emp Here 28
SIC 8641 Civic and social associations

Montague, PE C0A
Kings County

D-U-N-S 20-004-0637   (BR)
ATLANTIC WHOLESALERS LTD
REAL ATLANTIC SUPERSTORE, THE
509 Main St, Montague, PE, C0A 1R0
(902) 838-5421
Emp Here 105
SIC 5411 Grocery stores

D-U-N-S 20-029-1537   (BR)
EASTERN SCHOOL DISTRICT
MONTAGUE REGIONAL HIGH SCHOOL
274 Valleyfield Rd, Montague, PE, C0A 1R0
(902) 838-0835
Emp Here 80
SIC 8211 Elementary and secondary schools

D-U-N-S 20-711-7768   (BR)
EASTERN SCHOOL DISTRICT
SOUTHERN KINGS CONSOLIDATED
2294 Peters Rd-Rte 324, Montague, PE, C0A
1R0
(902) 962-7400
Emp Here 50
SIC 8211 Elementary and secondary schools

D-U-N-S 20-039-3465   (BR)
EASTERN SCHOOL DISTRICT
MONTAGUE INTERMEDIATE
221 Kennedy St, Montague, PE, C0A 1R0
(902) 838-0860
Emp Here 30
SIC 8211 Elementary and secondary schools

D-U-N-S 20-037-7062   (BR)
EASTERN SCHOOL DISTRICT
MONTAGUE CONSOLIDATED SCHOOL
622 Princes Dr, Montague, PE, C0A 1R0
(902) 838-0820
Emp Here 50
SIC 8211 Elementary and secondary schools

D-U-N-S 24-629-5765   (BR)
J. D. IRVING, LIMITED
KENT BUILDING SUPPLIES
(*Suby of* J. D. Irving, Limited)
139 Sackville St, Montague, PE, C0A 1R0
(902) 838-4291
Emp Here 23
SIC 5039 Construction materials, nec

D-U-N-S 20-349-3338   (BR)
MURPHY, D.P. INC

WENDY'S
95 Main St N, Montague, PE, C0A 1R0
(902) 838-4553
Emp Here 24
SIC 5812 Eating places

D-U-N-S 20-806-2666   (BR)
SOBEYS CAPITAL INCORPORATED
SOBEYS STORE
531 Main St, Montague, PE, C0A 1R0
(902) 838-3370
Emp Here 25
SIC 5411 Grocery stores

D-U-N-S 24-943-6346   (BR)
SOBEYS CAPITAL INCORPORATED
WESTERN UNION (SOBEYS INC #721)
Gd, Montague, PE, C0A 1R0
(902) 838-3388
Emp Here 30
SIC 6099 Functions related to deposit banking

Morell, PE C0A
Kings County

D-U-N-S 20-086-3467   (BR)
EASTERN SCHOOL DISTRICT
MORELL CONSOLIDATED SCHOOL
Gd, Morell, PE, C0A 1S0
(902) 961-7340
Emp Here 30
SIC 8211 Elementary and secondary schools

North Rustico, PE C0A

D-U-N-S 20-023-8009   (BR)
EASTERN SCHOOL DISTRICT
GULF SHORE CONSOLIDATED SCHOOL
185 Hilltop Ave, North Rustico, PE, C0A 1N0
(902) 963-7810
Emp Here 40
SIC 8211 Elementary and secondary schools

O'Leary, PE C0B
Prince County

D-U-N-S 20-358-7753   (SL)
9711864 CANADA INC
MILL RIVER EXPERIENCE
180 Mill River Resort Rd, O'Leary, PE, C0B 1V0
(902) 859-3555
Emp Here 60   *Sales* 2,626,585
SIC 7011 Hotels and motels

D-U-N-S 24-629-6024   (SL)
COMMUNITY HOSPITAL O'LEARY
COMMUNITY HOSPITAL
14 Mckinnon Dr, O'Leary, PE, C0B 1V0
(902) 859-8700
Emp Here 70   *Sales* 4,888,367
SIC 8062 General medical and surgical hospitals

D-U-N-S 24-123-4041   (BR)
ISLAND HOLDINGS LTD
CAVENDISH PRODUCE
(*Suby of* J. D. Irving, Limited)
37288 Hwy 2, O'Leary, PE, C0B 1V0

Emp Here 42
SIC 5148 Fresh fruits and vegetables

D-U-N-S 20-018-0065   (HQ)
O'LEARY FARMERS' CO-OPERATIVE AS-SOCIATION LTD
(*Suby of* O'Leary Farmers' Co-Operative Association Ltd)
500 Main St, O'Leary, PE, C0B 1V0

(902) 859-2550
Emp Here 50   *Emp Total* 52
Sales 4,231,721
SIC 5399 Miscellaneous general merchandise

D-U-N-S 25-999-4259   (SL)
O'LEARY POTATO PACKERS LTD
85 Ellis Ave, O'Leary, PE, C0B 1V0

Emp Here 30   *Sales* 8,662,510
SIC 5148 Fresh fruits and vegetables

D-U-N-S 20-568-0973   (BR)
PROVINCE OF PEI
HOME CARE & PUBLIC HEALTH
14 Mackinnon Dr, O'Leary, PE, C0B 1V0
(902) 859-8730
Emp Here 40
SIC 8399 Social services, nec

D-U-N-S 20-706-4200   (BR)
PUBLIC SCHOOLS BRANCH
HERNEWOOD JUNIOR HIGH SCHOOL
(*Suby of* Public Schools Branch)
Gd, O'Leary, PE, C0B 1V0
(902) 859-8710
Emp Here 20
SIC 8211 Elementary and secondary schools

D-U-N-S 25-241-3984   (BR)
PUBLIC SCHOOLS BRANCH
O'LEARY SCHOOL
(*Suby of* Public Schools Branch)
25 Barclay Rd, O'Leary, PE, C0B 1V0
(902) 859-8713
Emp Here 21
SIC 8211 Elementary and secondary schools

Slemon Park, PE C0B
Prince County

D-U-N-S 20-153-8324   (BR)
FIBER CONNECTIONS INC
30 Aerospace Blvd, Slemon Park, PE, C0B 2A0
(902) 436-1727
Emp Here 45
SIC 2298 Cordage and twine

D-U-N-S 20-292-0661   (BR)
HOLLAND COLLEGE
POLICE ACADEMY
66 Argus Ave, Slemon Park, PE, C0B 2A0
(902) 888-6745
Emp Here 20
SIC 8221 Colleges and universities

D-U-N-S 20-107-8602   (BR)
HOLLAND COLLEGE
HOLLAND COLLEGE AEROSPACE & IN-DUSTRIAL TECHNOLOGY CENTRE
40 Parkway Dr, Slemon Park, PE, C0B 2A0

Emp Here 20
SIC 8211 Elementary and secondary schools

D-U-N-S 20-566-2500   (HQ)
MDS COATING TECHNOLOGIES CORPO-RATION
(*Suby of* MDS Aerospace Corporation)
60 Aerospace Blvd, Slemon Park, PE, C0B 2A0
(902) 888-3900
Emp Here 68   *Emp Total* 5
Sales 5,253,170
SIC 3479 Metal coating and allied services
Hans Odoerfer
Pr Pr Phil Rodger
VP Fin Kerry Butler

D-U-N-S 25-861-9832   (BR)
SLEMON PARK CORPORATION
LADY SLIPPER RESTAURANT AND LOUNGE
(*Suby of* Slemon Park Corporation)

12 Redwood Ave, Slemon Park, PE, C0B 2A0
(902) 432-1774
Emp Here 30
SIC 5812 Eating places

Souris, PE C0A
Kings County

D-U-N-S 20-086-5413   (BR)
EASTERN SCHOOL DISTRICT
SOURIS HIGH SCHOOL
15 Longworth St, Souris, PE, C0A 2B0
(902) 687-7130
Emp Here 22
SIC 8211 Elementary and secondary schools

D-U-N-S 24-877-9894   (SL)
INN AT BAY FORTUNE, THE
758 310 Rte Rr 4, Souris, PE, C0A 2B0
(902) 687-3745
Emp Here 50   *Sales* 2,188,821
SIC 7011 Hotels and motels

D-U-N-S 20-084-6264   (BR)
PROVINCE OF PEI
COLVILLE MANOR
20 Macphee Ave, Souris, PE, C0A 2B0
(902) 687-7090
Emp Here 75
SIC 8051 Skilled nursing care facilities

St-Louis, PE C0B
Prince County

D-U-N-S 20-651-1474   (BR)
PUBLIC SCHOOLS BRANCH
ST LOUIS ELEMENTARY
(*Suby of* Public Schools Branch)
3807 Union Rd, St-Louis, PE, C0B 1Z0
(902) 882-7358
Emp Here 24
SIC 8211 Elementary and secondary schools

St-Peters Bay, PE C0A
Kings County

D-U-N-S 20-711-7776   (BR)
EASTERN SCHOOL DISTRICT
Gd, St-Peters Bay, PE, C0A 2A0

Emp Here 50
SIC 8211 Elementary and secondary schools

Stratford, PE C1A

D-U-N-S 20-711-7834   (BR)
EASTERN SCHOOL DISTRICT
GLEN STEWART SCHOOL
34 Glen Stewart Dr, Stratford, PE, C1A 8B5
(902) 569-0550
Emp Here 50
SIC 8211 Elementary and secondary schools

Stratford, PE C1B

D-U-N-S 20-262-6255   (BR)
ASPIN KEMP & ASSOCIATES INC
9 Myrtle St, Stratford, PE, C1B 1P4
(902) 620-4882
Emp Here 48
SIC 8742 Management consulting services

D-U-N-S 24-347-3191   (BR)

HOME HARDWARE STORES LIMITED
14 Kinlock Rd, Stratford, PE, C1B 1R1

Emp Here 75
SIC 5211 Lumber and other building materials

D-U-N-S 25-665-7537   (BR)
MURPHY'S PHARMACIES INC
MURPHY'S STRATFORD PHARMACY
13 Stratford Rd, Stratford, PE, C1B 1T4
(902) 569-2259
Emp Here 25
SIC 5912 Drug stores and proprietary stores

D-U-N-S 25-364-3944   (BR)
SOBEYS CAPITAL INCORPORATED
9 Kinlock Rd Suite 621, Stratford, PE, C1B 1P8
(902) 894-3800
Emp Here 100
SIC 5411 Grocery stores

Summerside, PE C1N
Prince County

D-U-N-S 24-472-2625   (BR)
AMALGAMATED DAIRIES LIMITED
A D L FOODS
400 Read Dr, Summerside, PE, C1N 5A9
(902) 888-5000
Emp Here 6
SIC 5451 Dairy products stores

D-U-N-S 20-608-6469   (BR)
AMALGAMATED DAIRIES LIMITED
JOHNSTON'S TIRE & AUTOMOTIVE
30 Greenwood Dr, Summerside, PE, C1N 3Y1
(902) 436-4284
Emp Here 24
SIC 7538 General automotive repair shops

D-U-N-S 25-656-5698   (BR)
ATLANTIC WHOLESALERS LTD
REAL ATLANTIC SUPERSTORE, THE
535 Granville St, Summerside, PE, C1N 6N4
(902) 888-1581
Emp Here 250
SIC 5411 Grocery stores

D-U-N-S 25-838-3004   (BR)
BDO CANADA LLP
SUMMERSIDE ACCOUNTING
107 Walker Ave, Summerside, PE, C1N 0C9
(902) 436-2171
Emp Here 22
SIC 8721 Accounting, auditing, and book-keeping

D-U-N-S 25-716-8740   (BR)
BANK OF NOVA SCOTIA, THE
SCOTIABANK
274 Water St, Summerside, PE, C1N 1B8
(902) 436-2204
Emp Here 20
SIC 6021 National commercial banks

D-U-N-S 20-527-4017   (BR)
CANADA POST CORPORATION
SUMMERSIDE PO
454 Granville St, Summerside, PE, C1N 4K7
(902) 436-5652
Emp Here 20
SIC 4311 U.s. postal service

D-U-N-S 24-186-7845   (BR)
CAVENDISH AGRI SERVICES LIMITED
CAVENDISH FARMS - NEW ANNEN
(*Suby of* J. D. Irving, Limited)
25532 Main Hwy Suite 2, Summerside, PE, C1N 4J9
(902) 836-5555
Emp Here 750
SIC 2037 Frozen fruits and vegetables

D-U-N-S 20-169-0224   (BR)
EMPIRE THEATRES LIMITED

STUDIO 5
130 Ryan St, Summerside, PE, C1N 6G2
(902) 888-3831
Emp Here 25
SIC 7832 Motion picture theaters, except drive-in

D-U-N-S 20-727-1859　　　(BR)
FAST FOODS (P.E.I.) LTD
KFC
62 Water St, Summerside, PE, C1N 1A5
(902) 436-5717
Emp Here 22
SIC 5812 Eating places

D-U-N-S 20-018-1576　　　(SL)
GARDEN OF THE GULF COURT AND MOTEL INCORPORATED
QUALITY INN SUMMERSIDE
618 Water St E, Summerside, PE, C1N 4H7
(902) 436-2295
Emp Here 50　　　*Sales* 2,188,821
SIC 7011 Hotels and motels

D-U-N-S 25-018-3928　　　(BR)
GRAND FOREST HOLDINGS INCORPORATED
CAVENDISH FARMS, DIV OF
(*Suby of* J. D. Irving, Limited)
Gd, Summerside, PE, C1N 4J9
(902) 836-5555
Emp Here 750
SIC 5142 Packaged frozen goods

D-U-N-S 25-297-2302　　　(BR)
GRANT THORNTON LLP
220 Water St, Summerside, PE, C1N 1B3
(902) 436-9155
Emp Here 25
SIC 8721 Accounting, auditing, and bookkeeping

D-U-N-S 25-305-1684　　　(BR)
INNVEST PROPERTIES CORP
QUALITY INN & GARDEN OF THE GULF
(*Suby of* Innvest Properties Corp)
618 Water St E, Summerside, PE, C1N 4H7
(902) 436-2295
Emp Here 45
SIC 7011 Hotels and motels

D-U-N-S 24-419-6577　　　(BR)
ISLAND HOLDINGS LTD
(*Suby of* J. D. Irving, Limited)
281 Old Station Rd, Summerside, PE, C1N 4J9
(902) 836-7238
Emp Here 50
SIC 2037 Frozen fruits and vegetables

D-U-N-S 20-595-9013　　　(BR)
J. D. IRVING, LIMITED
KENT BUILDING SUPPLIES
(*Suby of* J. D. Irving, Limited)
19 Eustane St, Summerside, PE, C1N 2V4
(902) 436-4291
Emp Here 43
SIC 5211 Lumber and other building materials

D-U-N-S 20-755-7831　　　(BR)
MCCAIN PRODUCE INC
245 Macewen Rd, Summerside, PE, C1N 5V2
(902) 888-5566
Emp Here 40
SIC 5148 Fresh fruits and vegetables

D-U-N-S 20-801-1879　　　(BR)
MCKENNCO INC
MCDONALD'S
481 Granville St, Summerside, PE, C1N 4P7
(902) 436-5462
Emp Here 100
SIC 5812 Eating places

D-U-N-S 25-632-9608　　　(BR)
MURPHY, D.P. INC
TIM HORTONS
81 Water St, Summerside, PE, C1N 6A3

(902) 436-2851
Emp Here 40
SIC 5812 Eating places

D-U-N-S 25-632-9590　　　(BR)
MURPHY, D.P. INC
TIM HORTONS
466 Granville St, Summerside, PE, C1N 4K6
(902) 888-2324
Emp Here 60
SIC 5461 Retail bakeries

D-U-N-S 25-380-7259　　　(BR)
OLD DUTCH FOODS LTD
HUMPTY DUMPTY OLD DUTCH FOODS
(*Suby of* Old Dutch Foods Ltd)
4 Slemon Park Dr, Summerside, PE, C1N 4K4
(902) 888-5160
Emp Here 100
SIC 2096 Potato chips and similar snacks

D-U-N-S 20-719-9808　　　(BR)
PROVINCE OF PEI
HOME CARE
310 Brophy Ave, Summerside, PE, C1N 5N4
(902) 888-8440
Emp Here 50
SIC 8399 Social services, nec

D-U-N-S 25-656-5201　　　(BR)
PROVINCE OF PEI
SUMMERSET MANOR
15 Frank Mellish St, Summerside, PE, C1N 0H3
(902) 888-8310
Emp Here 100
SIC 8052 Intermediate care facilities

D-U-N-S 24-336-7245　　　(BR)
PROVINCE OF PEI
DEPARTMENT OF COMMUNITY SERVICES SENIORS AND LABOUR
290 Water St, Summerside, PE, C1N 1B8
(902) 888-8100
Emp Here 33
SIC 8399 Social services, nec

D-U-N-S 20-919-3510　　　(BR)
PROVINCE OF PEI
COMMUNITY MENTAL HEALTH AND ADDICTION SERVICES
65 Roy Boates Ave, Summerside, PE, C1N 6M8
(902) 888-8380
Emp Here 40
SIC 8069 Specialty hospitals, except psychiatric

D-U-N-S 20-651-1482　　　(BR)
PUBLIC SCHOOLS BRANCH
SUMMERSIDE INTERMEDIATE SCHOOL
(*Suby of* Public Schools Branch)
247 Central St, Summerside, PE, C1N 3M5
(902) 888-8470
Emp Here 50
SIC 8211 Elementary and secondary schools

D-U-N-S 20-711-7669　　　(BR)
PUBLIC SCHOOLS BRANCH
ELM ST SCHOOL
(*Suby of* Public Schools Branch)
256 Elm St, Summerside, PE, C1N 3V5
(902) 888-8490
Emp Here 50
SIC 8211 Elementary and secondary schools

D-U-N-S 20-711-7677　　　(BR)
PUBLIC SCHOOLS BRANCH
THREE OAKS SENIOR HIGH SCHOOL
(*Suby of* Public Schools Branch)
10 Kenmoore Ave, Summerside, PE, C1N 4V9
(902) 888-8460
Emp Here 50
SIC 8211 Elementary and secondary schools

D-U-N-S 20-038-6279　　　(BR)
PUBLIC SCHOOLS BRANCH
ATHENA CONSOLIDATED SCHOOL
(*Suby of* Public Schools Branch)

150 Ryan St, Summerside, PE, C1N 6G2
(902) 888-8486
Emp Here 40
SIC 8211 Elementary and secondary schools

D-U-N-S 20-037-7039　　　(BR)
PUBLIC SCHOOLS BRANCH
PARKSIDE ELEMENTARY SCHOOL
(*Suby of* Public Schools Branch)
195 Summer St, Summerside, PE, C1N 3J8
(902) 888-8472
Emp Here 26
SIC 8211 Elementary and secondary schools

D-U-N-S 20-038-5453　　　(BR)
PUBLIC SCHOOLS BRANCH
GREENFIELD ELEMENTARY
(*Suby of* Public Schools Branch)
100 Darby Dr, Summerside, PE, C1N 4V8
(902) 888-8492
Emp Here 37
SIC 8211 Elementary and secondary schools

D-U-N-S 20-554-7719　　　(BR)
RESOLVE CORPORATION
(*Suby of* 2206997 Ontario Inc)
150 Industrial Cres, Summerside, PE, C1N 5N6

Emp Here 350
SIC 7389 Business services, nec

D-U-N-S 20-084-7155　　　(BR)
ROYAL CANADIAN LEGION, THE
(*Suby of* Royal Canadian Legion, The)
340 Notre Dame St, Summerside, PE, C1N 1S5
(902) 436-2091
Emp Here 20
SIC 8641 Civic and social associations

D-U-N-S 24-943-6064　　　(BR)
SOBEYS CAPITAL INCORPORATED
SOBEYS #425
868-475 Granville St, Summerside, PE, C1N 3N9
(902) 436-5795
Emp Here 100
SIC 5411 Grocery stores

D-U-N-S 20-084-7114　　　(BR)
SOBEYS CAPITAL INCORPORATED
PRICE CHOPPER
98 Water St, Summerside, PE, C1N 4N6
(902) 436-4640
Emp Here 100
SIC 5411 Grocery stores

D-U-N-S 25-370-2310　　　(BR)
STAPLES CANADA INC
STAPLES THE BUSINESS DEPOT
(*Suby of* Staples, Inc.)
57 Water St, Summerside, PE, C1N 1A4
(902) 432-3838
Emp Here 30
SIC 5943 Stationery stores

D-U-N-S 24-955-7992　　　(HQ)
VECTOR AEROSPACE ENGINE SERVICES-ATLANTIC INC
800 Aerospace Blvd, Summerside, PE, C1N 4P6
(902) 436-1333
Emp Here 400　　　*Emp Total* 11,080
Sales 68,364,176
SIC 4581 Airports, flying fields, and services
Pr Jeff Poirier
VP Fin Mark O'keefe
VP Fin Darren Smith

D-U-N-S 20-085-0381　　　(BR)
WSP CANADA INC
DELCOM ENGINEERING
195 Macewen Rd, Summerside, PE, C1N 5Y4
(902) 436-2669
Emp Here 20
SIC 8711 Engineering services

D-U-N-S 24-120-9464　　　(BR)

WAL-MART CANADA CORP
511 Granville St, Summerside, PE, C1N 5J4
(902) 432-3570
Emp Here 200
SIC 5311 Department stores

D-U-N-S 20-722-8433　　　(BR)
WENDY'S RESTAURANTS OF CANADA INC
WENDY'S
(*Suby of* The Wendy's Company)
56 Water St, Summerside, PE, C1N 4T8
(902) 436-5075
Emp Here 24
SIC 5812 Eating places

Tignish, PE C0B
Prince County

D-U-N-S 20-651-1466　　　(BR)
PUBLIC SCHOOLS BRANCH
TIGNISH ELEMENTARY
(*Suby of* Public Schools Branch)
322 Church St, Tignish, PE, C0B 2B0
(902) 882-7357
Emp Here 40
SIC 8211 Elementary and secondary schools

D-U-N-S 20-018-2582　　　(SL)
TIGNISH CO-OPERATIVE ASSOCIATION LIMITED
283 Business St, Tignish, PE, C0B 2B0
(902) 882-2080
Emp Here 50　　　*Sales* 4,085,799
SIC 5399 Miscellaneous general merchandise

Tyne Valley, PE C0B
Prince County

D-U-N-S 20-788-4805　　　(BR)
PROVINCE OF PEI
TIME VALLEY OF CHILD AND YOUTH DEVELOPMENTAL HEALTH CENTER, THE
152 Bideford Rd, Tyne Valley, PE, C0B 2C0
(902) 831-7905
Emp Here 24
SIC 8322 Individual and family services

D-U-N-S 24-629-7956　　　(SL)
STEWART MEMORIAL HOSPITAL
6926 Tyne Valley Rd, Tyne Valley, PE, C0B 2C0
(902) 831-7900
Emp Here 50　　　*Sales* 3,502,114
SIC 8062 General medical and surgical hospitals

Wellington Station, PE C0B
Prince County

D-U-N-S 20-812-2148　　　(BR)
PROVINCE OF PEI
ECOLE EVANGELINE
1596 124 Rte, Wellington Station, PE, C0B 2E0
(902) 854-2491
Emp Here 20
SIC 8211 Elementary and secondary schools

Winsloe, PE C1E

D-U-N-S 20-524-4080　　　(SL)
DIAMOND'S TRANSFER LTD
Gd, Winsloe, PE, C1E 1Z2
(902) 368-1400
Emp Here 33　　　*Sales* 9,914,160

SIC 4213 Trucking, except local
Pr Pr Patricia Armour
VP VP Ronny Diamond
 Larry Tower

York, PE C0A

D-U-N-S 20-929-4255   (SL)
STANHOPE BEACH INN LTD
DALVAY BY THE SEA HOTEL
16 Cottage Cres., York, PE, C0A 1P0
(902) 672-2048
Emp Here 70   *Sales* 3,064,349
SIC 7011 Hotels and motels

Acton Vale, QC J0H
Bagot County

D-U-N-S 20-703-4849   (SL)
139673 CANADA INC
PLANTE INTERNATIONAL
1190 Rue Lemay, Acton Vale, QC, J0H 1A0
(450) 546-0101
Emp Here 22   *Sales* 3,486,617
SIC 5122 Drugs, proprietaries, and sundries

D-U-N-S 24-082-9069   (SL)
CLUB DE GOLF ACTON VALE INC
1000 Rte 116, Acton Vale, QC, J0H 1A0
(450) 549-5885
Emp Here 75   *Sales* 3,210,271
SIC 7992 Public golf courses

D-U-N-S 24-086-1885   (BR)
COMMISSION SCOLAIRE DE SAINT-HYACINTHE, LA
POLYVALENTE ROBERT OUIMET
1450 3e Av, Acton Vale, QC, J0H 1A0
(450) 546-5575
Emp Here 100
SIC 8211 Elementary and secondary schools

D-U-N-S 25-233-4719   (BR)
COMMISSION SCOLAIRE DE SAINT-HYACINTHE, LA
ECOLE SAINT ANDRE
1277 Rue Belair, Acton Vale, QC, J0H 1A0
(450) 546-2785
Emp Here 35
SIC 8211 Elementary and secondary schools

D-U-N-S 25-391-9310   (SL)
EQUIPEMENTS PIERRE CHAMPIGNY LTEE
PRODUIT MOBICAB CANADA
280 Rue Bonin Rr 4, Acton Vale, QC, J0H 1A0
(450) 546-0999
Emp Here 25   *Sales* 6,576,720
SIC 5599 Automotive dealers, nec
Pr Pr Pierre Champigny

D-U-N-S 24-893-5335   (SL)
LIFE SCIENCE NUTRITIONALS INC
PLANTE INTERNATIONAL
1190 Rue Lemay, Acton Vale, QC, J0H 1A0
(450) 546-0101
Emp Here 82   *Sales* 4,331,255
SIC 2833 Medicinals and botanicals

D-U-N-S 20-317-5807   (HQ)
PRODUITS MOBILICAB CANADA INC
CHAMPION GOLF CAR OF CANADA
(*Suby of* Produits Mobilicab Canada Inc)
280 Rue Bonin, Acton Vale, QC, J0H 1A0
(450) 546-0999
Emp Here 25   *Emp Total* 30
Sales 14,484,360
SIC 5088 Transportation equipment and supplies
Pierre Champigny
Dir Noiseux Yannick
Dir Roy Sylvain
Dir Daniel Vincelette

D-U-N-S 25-946-7566   (SL)
REALISATIONS NEWTECH INC, LES
725 Rue Desautels, Acton Vale, QC, J0H 1A0
(450) 546-2401
Emp Here 50   *Sales* 3,648,035
SIC 1751 Carpentry work

D-U-N-S 20-979-9837   (BR)
TRANSFREIGHT INC
575 Rue De Roxton, Acton Vale, QC, J0H 1A0
(450) 546-3254
Emp Here 40
SIC 4731 Freight transportation arrangement

Adstock, QC G0N

D-U-N-S 24-941-8898   (SL)
3099-8488 QUEBEC INC
STN PLEIN AIR MONT ADSTOCK
120 Rte Du Mont-Adstock, Adstock, QC, G0N 1S0
(418) 422-2242
Emp Here 50   *Sales* 2,188,821
SIC 7011 Hotels and motels

D-U-N-S 20-255-5496   (HQ)
BOULANGERIE ST-METHODE INC
14 Rue Principale E, Adstock, QC, G0N 1S0
(418) 422-2246
Emp Here 180   *Emp Total* 4
Sales 10,481,637
SIC 5461 Retail bakeries
Benoit Faucher
Sec Carl Pouliot

D-U-N-S 24-368-8467   (BR)
CAISSE DESJARDINS DE LA REGION DE THETFORD
CENTRE DE SERVICES SAINT-METHODE
37 Rue Principale O, Adstock, QC, G0N 1S0
(418) 422-2083
Emp Here 31
SIC 6062 State credit unions

D-U-N-S 25-918-8241   (SL)
NATURO PAIN INC
BOULANGERIE SAINT METHODE
14 Rue Principale E Rr 1, Adstock, QC, G0N 1S0
(418) 422-2246
Emp Here 200   *Sales* 9,128,880
SIC 5461 Retail bakeries
Pr Robert Faucher

Akulivik, QC J0M
Nouveau-Quebec County

D-U-N-S 20-716-8076   (BR)
COMMISSION SCOLAIRE KATIVIK
TUKISINIARVIK SCHOOL.
Gd, Akulivik, QC, J0M 1V0
(819) 496-2021
Emp Here 50
SIC 8211 Elementary and secondary schools

Albanel, QC G8M

D-U-N-S 25-232-6822   (BR)
COMMISSION SCOLAIRE DU PAYS-DES-BLEUETS
ECOLE SAINTE LUCIE
(*Suby of* Commission Scolaire du Pays-des-Bleuets)
327 Rue De L'Eglise, Albanel, QC, G8M 3E9
(418) 276-7605
Emp Here 20
SIC 8211 Elementary and secondary schools

Alma, QC G8B
Lac-St-Jean-Est County

D-U-N-S 24-942-4011   (SL)
3098-6145 QUEBEC INC
HOTEL MOTEL UNIVERSEL
1000 Boul Des Cascades, Alma, QC, G8B 3G4
(418) 668-7419
Emp Here 50   *Sales* 2,188,821
SIC 7011 Hotels and motels

D-U-N-S 24-890-8113   (SL)
9124-4269 QUEBEC INC
TIM HORTONS
1049 Av Du Pont S, Alma, QC, G8B 0E8

(418) 662-1178
Emp Here 100   *Sales* 3,551,629
SIC 5812 Eating places

D-U-N-S 24-464-2096   (HQ)
BETONS PREFABRIQUES DU LAC INC
(*Suby of* 9131-9046 Quebec Inc)
890 Rue Des Pins O, Alma, QC, G8B 7R3
(418) 668-6161
Emp Here 100   *Emp Total* 130
Sales 85,280,775
SIC 3272 Concrete products, nec
Pr Robert Bouchard
VP Christine Bouchard
VP Guy Bouchard
Sec Gaetan Bouchard
Treas Joan Bergeron

D-U-N-S 20-572-6370   (BR)
CANADA POST CORPORATION
BUREAU DE POSTE ALMA
160 Rue Saint-Joseph, Alma, QC, G8B 0E7
(418) 662-3106
Emp Here 35
SIC 4311 U.s. postal service

D-U-N-S 24-207-1538   (SL)
CENTRE DU COMPTOIR SAG-LAC INC
1500 Boul Saint-Jude, Alma, QC, G8B 3L4
(418) 662-6653
Emp Here 25   *Sales* 1,459,214
SIC 2434 Wood kitchen cabinets

D-U-N-S 24-011-6447   (BR)
COMMISSION SCOLAIRE DU LAC-ST-JEAN
CENTRE DE FORMATION PROFESSION-NELLE PAVILLON BEGIN
(*Suby of* Commission Scolaire du Lac-St-Jean)
850 Av Begin, Alma, QC, G8B 2X6
(418) 669-6063
Emp Here 150
SIC 8211 Elementary and secondary schools

D-U-N-S 20-711-8808   (BR)
COMMISSION SCOLAIRE DU LAC-ST-JEAN
PAVILLON DE FORMATION EN EMPLOYA-BILITE
(*Suby of* Commission Scolaire du Lac-St-Jean)
775 Boul Saint-Luc, Alma, QC, G8B 2K8
(418) 669-6044
Emp Here 60
SIC 8211 Elementary and secondary schools

D-U-N-S 25-023-7476   (BR)
COMMISSION SCOLAIRE DU LAC-ST-JEAN
ECOLE ARC EN CIEL
(*Suby of* Commission Scolaire du Lac-St-Jean)
685 Rue Gauthier O, Alma, QC, G8B 2H9
(418) 669-6012
Emp Here 25
SIC 8211 Elementary and secondary schools

D-U-N-S 25-463-1179   (SL)
CORPORATION REGIONALE DE DEVELOPPEMENT DE LA RECUPERATION ET DU RECYCLAGE REGION 02
GROUPE-CODERR
1000 Boul Saint-Jude, Alma, QC, G8B 3L1
(418) 668-8502
Emp Here 20   *Sales* 4,377,642
SIC 5932 Used merchandise stores

D-U-N-S 25-299-6889   (BR)
DOLLARAMA S.E.C.
DOLLARAMA 92
705 Av Du Pont N, Alma, QC, G8B 6T5
(418) 480-3149
Emp Here 20
SIC 5331 Variety stores

D-U-N-S 24-378-8767   (SL)
DUCHESNE AUTO LIMITEE

DUCHESNE CHEVROLET OLDSMOBILE
520 Boul De Quen, Alma, QC, G8B 5P8
(418) 669-9000
Emp Here 21   *Sales* 10,550,400
SIC 5511 New and used car dealers
Pr Pr Miville Duchesne
VP VP Michel Duchesne
VP Jean-Marie Duchesne

D-U-N-S 25-298-6278   (SL)
GESTION ALAIN LAFOREST INC
MARCHAND CANADIAN TIRE DE STE-FOY
50 Boul Saint-Luc, Alma, QC, G8B 6K1
(418) 662-6618
Emp Here 66   *Sales* 4,742,446
SIC 5311 Department stores

D-U-N-S 25-309-6986   (BR)
INDUSTRIELLE ALLIANCE, ASSURANCE ET SERVICES FINANCIERS INC
100 Rue Saint-Joseph Bureau 202, Alma, QC, G8B 7A6
(418) 668-0177
Emp Here 20
SIC 6411 Insurance agents, brokers, and service

D-U-N-S 20-187-9681   (SL)
LAVAL FORTIN LTEE
(*Suby of* 9102-4976 Quebec Inc)
130 Rue Notre-Dame O, Alma, QC, G8B 2K1
(418) 668-3321
Emp Here 50   *Sales* 13,349,760
SIC 1541 Industrial buildings and warehouses
VP VP Charles Deslauriers
Lynda Noel
Dir Robin Larouche
Pr Pr Yvon Fortin
Dir Gaston Munger

D-U-N-S 25-359-5144   (BR)
MALLETTE S.E.N.C.R.L.
505 Rue Sacre-Coeur O, Alma, QC, G8B 1M4
(418) 668-2324
Emp Here 60
SIC 8721 Accounting, auditing, and book-keeping

D-U-N-S 24-370-4801   (BR)
NUTRINOR COOPERATIVE
NUTRINOR PRODUITS LAITIERS
1545 Boul Saint-Jude, Alma, QC, G8B 3L3
(418) 668-3051
Emp Here 40
SIC 5143 Dairy products, except dried or canned

D-U-N-S 20-188-0978   (BR)
PF RESOLU CANADA INC
PRODUITS FORESTIERS RESOLU USINE ALMA
1100 Rue Melancon O, Alma, QC, G8B 7G2
(418) 668-9400
Emp Here 338
SIC 2621 Paper mills

D-U-N-S 24-339-8125   (BR)
PAPIERS SOLIDERR INC, LES
COLLECTES CODERR
Gd, Alma, QC, G8B 5V6
(418) 668-1234
Emp Here 130
SIC 4212 Local trucking, without storage

D-U-N-S 25-850-0545   (BR)
PROMUTUEL DU LAC AU FJORD
790 Av Du Pont S, Alma, QC, G8B 2V4
(418) 662-6595
Emp Here 80
SIC 6411 Insurance agents, brokers, and service

D-U-N-S 25-857-5877   (BR)
PROVIGO DISTRIBUTION INC
MAXI
845 Av Du Pont N, Alma, QC, G8B 6W6
(418) 668-5215
Emp Here 45

SIC 5411 Grocery stores

D-U-N-S 20-003-0976   (BR)
PROVIGO DISTRIBUTION INC
MAXI
1055 Av Du Pont S Bureau 1, Alma, QC, G8B 2V7
(418) 668-2205
Emp Here 70
SIC 5411 Grocery stores

D-U-N-S 20-016-2431   (BR)
RIO TINTO ALCAN INC
(*Suby of* RIO TINTO PLC)
3000 Rue Des Pins O, Alma, QC, G8B 5W2
(418) 480-6000
Emp Here 1,000
SIC 3399 Primary Metal products

D-U-N-S 25-019-0998   (BR)
ROYAL BANK OF CANADA
ROYAL BANK OF CANADA
(*Suby of* Royal Bank Of Canada)
510 Rue Sacre-Coeur O, Alma, QC, G8B 1L9
(418) 662-8510
Emp Here 24
SIC 6021 National commercial banks

D-U-N-S 25-294-5936   (BR)
SEARS CANADA INC
705 Av Du Pont N Bureau 45, Alma, QC, G8B 6T5
(418) 662-2222
Emp Here 68
SIC 5311 Department stores

D-U-N-S 25-307-6194   (BR)
SOCIETE DES ALCOOLS DU QUEBEC
SAQ CARREFOUR D'ALMA 33632
555 Av Du Pont N, Alma, QC, G8B 7W9
(418) 668-4657
Emp Here 20
SIC 5921 Liquor stores

D-U-N-S 20-058-2802   (HQ)
SYNDICAT DES PROFESSIONNELLES EN SOINS DE SANTE LAC ST-JEAN EST
(*Suby of* Syndicat des Professionnelles en Soins de Sante Lac St-Jean Est)
300 Boul Champlain, Alma, QC, G8B 3N8
(418) 662-1424
Emp Here 800   *Emp Total* 1,300
Sales 226,436,400
SIC 6371 Pension, health, and welfare funds
Pr Audrey Blackburn
VP David Potvin
VP Helene Cote
VP Marie-Pier Harvey
VP Sabrina Laforge
VP Louise Fortin
VP Jerome Savard
Treas Julie Boivin
Dir Karine Plourde

D-U-N-S 20-286-2624   (BR)
TETRA TECH INDUSTRIES INC
(*Suby of* Tetra Tech, Inc.)
100 Rue Saint-Joseph Bureau 111, Alma, QC, G8B 7A6
(418) 668-8307
Emp Here 20
SIC 8711 Engineering services

D-U-N-S 24-207-4255   (BR)
WAL-MART CANADA CORP
WALMART
1755 Av Du Pont S Bureau 5795, Alma, QC, G8B 7W7
(418) 480-3887
Emp Here 100
SIC 5311 Department stores

Alma, QC G8C
Lac-St-Jean-Est County

D-U-N-S 24-637-4607   (SL)
109470 CANADA INC
TRANSPORT MG
1620 Av De L'Energie, Alma, QC, G8C 1M6
(418) 668-6656
Emp Here 100   *Sales* 10,956,600
SIC 4212 Local trucking, without storage
Pr Pr Robin Desmeules

D-U-N-S 20-711-8824   (BR)
COMMISSION SCOLAIRE DU LAC-ST-JEAN
CENTRE D'ENSEIGNEMENT ET DE FORMATION PROFESSIONEL ALLMA
(*Suby of* Commission Scolaire du Lac-St-Jean)
1550 Boul Auger O, Alma, QC, G8C 1H8
(418) 669-6042
Emp Here 50
SIC 8211 Elementary and secondary schools

Alma, QC G8E
Lac-St-Jean-Est County

D-U-N-S 20-195-5796   (SL)
CHARCUTERIE L. FORTIN LIMITEE
ALIMENTS PHILIPS
5371 Av Du Pont N, Alma, QC, G8E 1T9
(418) 347-3365
Emp Here 85   *Sales* 3,720,996
SIC 2013 Sausages and other prepared meats

D-U-N-S 25-019-9643   (BR)
COMMISSION SCOLAIRE DU LAC-ST-JEAN
ECOLE JEAN GAUTHIER
(*Suby of* Commission Scolaire du Lac-St-Jean)
441 Rue Joseph-W.-Fleury, Alma, QC, G8E 2L1
(418) 669-6069
Emp Here 70
SIC 8211 Elementary and secondary schools

D-U-N-S 24-758-6019   (SL)
LOCATION A.L.R. INC
211 Rue Du Mistral, Alma, QC, G8E 2E2
(418) 347-4665
Emp Here 70   *Sales* 10,554,085
SIC 1611 Highway and street construction
Pr Pr Richard Fleury
Levis Savard
Aurelien Tremblay

D-U-N-S 24-896-5501   (SL)
PAVILLON ISIDORE GAUTHIER
5731 Av Du Pont N, Alma, QC, G8E 1W8
(418) 347-3394
Emp Here 50   *Sales* 1,824,018
SIC 8361 Residential care

Amos, QC J9T
Abitibi County

D-U-N-S 20-799-3606   (HQ)
6173306 CANADA INC
MCDONALD'S
(*Suby of* 6173306 Canada Inc)
12 1re Av E Bureau 49, Amos, QC, J9T 1H3
(819) 727-9441
Emp Here 55   *Emp Total* 110
Sales 3,283,232
SIC 5812 Eating places

D-U-N-S 25-010-1573   (BR)
BANQUE NATIONALE DU CANADA
101 1re Av O, Amos, QC, J9T 1V1
(819) 727-9391
Emp Here 21
SIC 6021 National commercial banks

D-U-N-S 24-419-2303   (BR)
BOIS TURCOTTE LTEE
RONA
(*Suby of* Bois Turcotte Ltee)
21 Rue Principale S, Amos, QC, J9T 2J4
(819) 732-6407
Emp Here 40
SIC 5211 Lumber and other building materials

D-U-N-S 24-107-3899   (HQ)
BOUTIQUE DU BUREAU GYVA INC
221 Rue Principale S, Amos, QC, J9T 2J8
(819) 732-5531
Emp Here 28   *Emp Total* 50
Sales 4,012,839
SIC 7359 Equipment rental and leasing, nec

D-U-N-S 20-581-6460   (BR)
CANADA POST CORPORATION
32 1re Av O, Amos, QC, J9T 1T8
(819) 732-5853
Emp Here 23
SIC 4311 U.s. postal service

D-U-N-S 25-357-0121   (BR)
CENTRE JEUNESSE DE L'ABITIBI TEMIS-CAMINGUE
341 Rue Principale N, Amos, QC, J9T 2L8
(819) 732-3244
Emp Here 31
SIC 8322 Individual and family services

D-U-N-S 24-509-0659   (HQ)
CENTRE NORMAND
(*Suby of* Centre Normand)
621 Rue De L'Harricana, Amos, QC, J9T 2P9
(819) 732-8241
Emp Here 20   *Emp Total* 50
Sales 3,283,232
SIC 8093 Specialty outpatient clinics, nec

D-U-N-S 24-346-7375   (BR)
CENTRE DE SANTE ET DE SERVICE SOCI-AUX LES ESKERS DE L'ABITIBI
CLSC LES ESKERS
632 1re Rue O, Amos, QC, J9T 2N2
(819) 732-3271
Emp Here 800
SIC 8062 General medical and surgical hospitals

D-U-N-S 25-259-9725   (BR)
CLAIR FOYER INC
CENTRE READAPTATION EN DEFICIENCE INTELLECTUELLE CLAIR FOYER
841 3e Rue O Bureau 100, Amos, QC, J9T 2T4
(819) 732-3710
Emp Here 30
SIC 8322 Individual and family services

D-U-N-S 25-379-1164   (BR)
COLLEGE D'ENSEIGNEMENT GENERAL & PROFESSIONEL DE L'ABITIBI-TEMISCAMINGUE
CEGEP DE L'ABITIBI TEMISCAMINGUE
(*Suby of* College d'Enseignement General & Professionel de l'Abitibi-Temiscamingue)
341 Rue Principale N, Amos, QC, J9T 2L8
(819) 732-5218
Emp Here 33
SIC 8221 Colleges and universities

D-U-N-S 25-240-2326   (BR)
COMMISSION SCOLAIRE HARRICANA
ECOLE DE FORESTIERS
751 4e Av E, Amos, QC, J9T 3Z4
(819) 732-1717
Emp Here 20
SIC 8211 Elementary and secondary schools

D-U-N-S 25-240-1211   (BR)
COMMISSION SCOLAIRE HARRICANA
ECOLE SAINTE THERESE
562 1re Rue E, Amos, QC, J9T 2H4
(819) 732-2675
Emp Here 50
SIC 8211 Elementary and secondary schools

D-U-N-S 25-375-9559   (BR)
COMMISSION SCOLAIRE HARRICANA
ECOLE INSTITUIONELLE SACRE COEUR SAINT VIATEUR
662 1re Rue E, Amos, QC, J9T 2H6
(819) 732-8983
Emp Here 40
SIC 8211 Elementary and secondary schools

D-U-N-S 25-337-1009   (BR)
COMMISSION SCOLAIRE HARRICANA
POLYVALENTE DE LA FORET
850 1re Rue E, Amos, QC, J9T 2H8
(819) 732-3221
Emp Here 106
SIC 8211 Elementary and secondary schools

D-U-N-S 25-240-1138   (BR)
COMMISSION SCOLAIRE HARRICANA
ECOLE INSTITUTIONNELLE SACRE COEUR ST VIATEUR
712 1re Rue E, Amos, QC, J9T 2H8
(819) 732-5582
Emp Here 30
SIC 8211 Elementary and secondary schools

D-U-N-S 20-712-6017   (BR)
COMMISSION SCOLAIRE HARRICANA
CENTRE DE FORMATION HARRICANA
850 1re Rue E, Amos, QC, J9T 2H8
(819) 732-3223
Emp Here 50
SIC 8211 Elementary and secondary schools

D-U-N-S 25-233-5690   (BR)
COMMISSION SCOLAIRE HARRICANA
ECOLE SECONDAIRE LA CALYPSO
800 1re Rue E, Amos, QC, J9T 2H8
(819) 732-3221
Emp Here 75
SIC 8211 Elementary and secondary schools

D-U-N-S 25-233-8587   (BR)
CONSEIL DE LA PREMIERE NATION ABITIBIWINNI
CONSEIL DE LA PREMIERE NATION ABITIBIWINNI
70 Rue Migwan, Amos, QC, J9T 3A3
(819) 732-6591
Emp Here 25
SIC 8211 Elementary and secondary schools

D-U-N-S 24-650-9780   (SL)
DISTRIBUTIONS NORYVE INC
JEAN COUTU 108
76 1re Av O Bureau 108, Amos, QC, J9T 1T8
(819) 732-3306
Emp Here 54   *Sales* 7,660,874
SIC 5912 Drug stores and proprietary stores
Pr Pr Alexandre Roy

D-U-N-S 24-084-0538   (SL)
FORAGES M. ROUILLIER INC
824 Av Des Forestiers Bureau 57, Amos, QC, J9T 4L4
(819) 727-9269
Emp Here 35   *Sales* 3,638,254
SIC 1799 Special trade contractors, nec

D-U-N-S 25-625-1695   (SL)
GESTION ANOCINQ LTEE
132 1re Av O, Amos, QC, J9T 1V2
(819) 732-7712
Emp Here 50   *Sales* 2,188,821
SIC 7011 Hotels and motels

D-U-N-S 20-994-4813   (BR)
GROUPE STAVIBEL INC
762 Av De L'Industrie, Amos, QC, J9T 4L9
(819) 732-8355
Emp Here 20
SIC 8711 Engineering services

D-U-N-S 24-669-2826   (SL)
HOTEL DES ESKERS INC
RESTO-BAR LE CHAT-O, LE
201 Av Authier, Amos, QC, J9T 1W1
(819) 732-5386
Emp Here 60   *Sales* 2,626,585

SIC 7011 Hotels and motels

D-U-N-S 25-337-1421   (BR)
L'AEROPORT MAGNY AMOS
GARAGE MUNICIPAL
(Suby of L'Aeroport Magny Amos)
1242 Rte 111 E, Amos, QC, J9T 3A1
(819) 732-2770
Emp Here 52
SIC 1611 Highway and street construction

D-U-N-S 24-614-6419   (BR)
MATERIAUX BLANCHET INC
2771 Rte De L'Aeroport, Amos, QC, J9T 3A8
(819) 732-6581
Emp Here 165
SIC 2421 Sawmills and planing mills, general

D-U-N-S 25-097-1108   (BR)
PF RESOLU CANADA INC
801 Rue Des Papetiers, Amos, QC, J9T 3X5
(819) 727-9311
Emp Here 97
SIC 2621 Paper mills

D-U-N-S 24-125-5236   (BR)
PROVIGO DISTRIBUTION INC
MAXI #8621
472 4e Rue E, Amos, QC, J9T 1Y4
(819) 732-2115
Emp Here 40
SIC 5411 Grocery stores

D-U-N-S 20-543-8133   (BR)
PROVIGO INC
82 1re Av E, Amos, QC, J9T 4B2
(819) 727-9433
Emp Here 30
SIC 5411 Grocery stores

D-U-N-S 24-178-1160   (BR)
RAYMOND CHABOT GRANT THORNTON S.E.N.C.R.L.
66 1re Av O, Amos, QC, J9T 1T8
(819) 732-3208
Emp Here 22
SIC 8721 Accounting, auditing, and bookkeeping

D-U-N-S 20-188-6053   (BR)
RUSSEL METALS INC
ACIER LEROUX
1675 Rte De L'Aeroport, Amos, QC, J9T 3A2
(819) 732-8381
Emp Here 25
SIC 5051 Metals service centers and offices

D-U-N-S 25-595-0560   (SL)
SYLVICULTURE LA VERENDRYE INC
162 Rue De L'Energie, Amos, QC, J9T 4M3
(819) 727-9127
Emp Here 25   Sales 2,553,625
SIC 2411 Logging

D-U-N-S 25-502-4242   (BR)
TELE-MOBILE COMPANY
TELUS MOBILITY
641 Av Du Parc, Amos, QC, J9T 4M1
(819) 732-8206
Emp Here 20
SIC 4899 Communication services, nec

D-U-N-S 20-281-5213   (BR)
TRANSPORT TFI 23 S.E.C.
BERGERON MAYBOIS, DIV OF
200 Rue Des Routiers, Amos, QC, J9T 3A6
(819) 727-1304
Emp Here 100
SIC 4212 Local trucking, without storage

D-U-N-S 24-851-3405   (BR)
WSP CANADA INC
GENIVAR
3 Rue Principale N Bureau 200, Amos, QC,
J9T 2K5
(819) 732-0457
Emp Here 30
SIC 8711 Engineering services

Amqui, QC G5J
Matapedia County

D-U-N-S 20-857-8005   (HQ)
9204-9170 QUEBEC INC
(Suby of 9204-9170 Quebec Inc)
135 Boul Saint-Benoit E, Amqui, QC, G5J 2C2
(418) 629-4616
Emp Here 20   Emp Total 75
Sales 10,208,640
SIC 2411 Logging
Pr Pr Joseph Lefrancois
VP VP Steve Lefrancois
Gaetane Lefrancois

D-U-N-S 24-843-2429   (BR)
AGROPUR COOPERATIVE
AGROPUR DIV. NATREL
466 132 Rte O Bureau 1320, Amqui, QC, G5J
2G7
(418) 629-3133
Emp Here 80
SIC 2026 Fluid milk

D-U-N-S 20-087-0033   (HQ)
AIDE-MAISON VALLEE DE LA MATAPEDIA
(Suby of Aide-Maison Vallee de la Matapedia)
78 Rue Des Forges, Amqui, QC, G5J 3A6
(418) 629-5812
Emp Here 111   Emp Total 123
Sales 4,815,406
SIC 8322 Individual and family services

D-U-N-S 25-363-1642   (HQ)
CAISSE DESJARDINS VALLEE DE LA MATAPEDIA
CENTRE DE SERVICE DE D'ALBERTVILLE
(Suby of Caisse Desjardins Vallee de la Matapedia)
15 Rue Du Pont, Amqui, QC, G5J 2P4
(418) 629-2271
Emp Here 40   Emp Total 85
Sales 18,768,250
SIC 6062 State credit unions
Genl Mgr Andre Thibault
Dir Jessica Rivard
Dir Jacques Parent
Dir Marc-Andre Imbeault
Dir Francois Roussel
Pr Pierre D'amours
VP VP Roger Beaulieu
Sec Huguette Blanchette
Dir Lise Bergeron
Dir Luc Chamberland

D-U-N-S 25-360-7956   (BR)
COMMISSION SCOLAIRE DES MONTS-ET-MAREES
ECOLE SAINTE URSULE
23 Rue Desbiens, Amqui, QC, G5J 3P9
(418) 629-2248
Emp Here 45
SIC 8211 Elementary and secondary schools

D-U-N-S 20-086-4093   (BR)
COMMISSION SCOLAIRE DES MONTS-ET-MAREES
ECOLE POLYVALENTE ARMAND ST-ONGE
95 Av Du Parc, Amqui, QC, G5J 2L8
(418) 629-2201
Emp Here 90
SIC 8211 Elementary and secondary schools

D-U-N-S 20-711-8436   (BR)
COMMISSION SCOLAIRE DES MONTS-ET-MAREES
CENTRE EDUCATION ADULTES
123 Rue Desbiens Bureau 102, Amqui, QC,
G5J 3P9
(418) 629-5404
Emp Here 30
SIC 8211 Elementary and secondary schools

D-U-N-S 25-309-6747   (BR)
INDUSTRIELLE ALLIANCE, ASSURANCE

ET SERVICES FINANCIERS INC
8 Boul Saint-Benoit O Unite 2, Amqui, QC,
G5J 2C6
(418) 629-4653
Emp Here 30
SIC 6411 Insurance agents, brokers, and service

D-U-N-S 20-295-7051   (BR)
MALLETTE S.E.N.C.R.L.
30 Boul Saint-Benoit E Bureau 101, Amqui,
QC, G5J 2B7
(418) 629-2255
Emp Here 25
SIC 8721 Accounting, auditing, and bookkeeping

D-U-N-S 25-484-9466   (BR)
PROVIGO DISTRIBUTION INC
MAXI
33 Boul Saint-Benoit E, Amqui, QC, G5J 2B8
(418) 629-4444
Emp Here 50
SIC 5411 Grocery stores

D-U-N-S 20-720-4947   (BR)
RESTAURANTS MICHEL DESCHENES INC, LES
MCDONALD'S
(Suby of Restaurants Michel Deschenes Inc, Les)
330 Boul Saint-Benoit O, Amqui, QC, G5J 2G2
(418) 629-6633
Emp Here 43
SIC 5812 Eating places

D-U-N-S 25-517-3627   (SL)
SELECTOTEL
RESTAURANTS PASTALI
340 Boul Saint-Benoit O, Amqui, QC, G5J 2G2
(418) 629-2241
Emp Here 50   Sales 1,532,175
SIC 5812 Eating places

D-U-N-S 20-869-8753   (BR)
SUPERMARCHES GP INC, LES
METRO G P
(Suby of Supermarches GP Inc, Les)
30 Boul Saint-Benoit E Bureau 12, Amqui, QC,
G5J 2B7
(418) 629-3560
Emp Here 60
SIC 5411 Grocery stores

Ange-Gardien, QC J0E

D-U-N-S 25-888-2679   (BR)
A & W FOOD SERVICES OF CANADA INC
RESTAURANT A & W
99 235 Rte, Ange-Gardien, QC, J0E 1E0
(450) 293-0029
Emp Here 22
SIC 5812 Eating places

D-U-N-S 24-677-8849   (HQ)
AGROMEX INC
AGROMEX VIANDES, DIV OF
251 235 Rte, Ange-Gardien, QC, J0E 1E0
(450) 293-3694
Emp Here 150   Emp Total 800
Sales 259,875,300
SIC 2011 Meat packing plants
Pr Pr Luc Menard
Yvon Paquette
Dir Francois Menard
Dir Pierre Menard

D-U-N-S 25-240-6343   (BR)
COMMISSION SCOLAIRE DES HAUTES-RIVIERES
ECOLE JEAN XXIII
273 Rue Saint-Joseph, Ange-Gardien, QC,
J0E 1E0
(450) 293-8106
Emp Here 25

SIC 8211 Elementary and secondary schools

Anjou, QC H1E

D-U-N-S 20-860-6595   (BR)
6202683 CANADA INC
MAZDA PRESIDENT
(Suby of 6202683 Canada Inc)
7050 Boul Henri-Bourassa E, Anjou, QC, H1E
7K7
(514) 328-7777
Emp Here 34
SIC 5511 New and used car dealers

Anjou, QC H1J

D-U-N-S 25-245-9474   (BR)
AIR LIQUIDE CANADA INC
CENTRE CLIENTELE DE MONTREAL
11201 Boul Ray-Lawson Bureau 6, Anjou, QC,
H1J 1M6
(450) 641-6222
Emp Here 50
SIC 2813 Industrial gases

D-U-N-S 25-091-7924   (SL)
ALIMENTS TRADITION INC, LES
9000 Boul Des Sciences, Anjou, QC, H1J 3A9
(514) 355-1131
Emp Here 50   Sales 12,061,811
SIC 8099 Health and allied services, nec
Pr Jean Filion
Sec Jacques Foisy
Dir Francois Chaurette
Dir Stephane Blanchet
Dir Michel Alain

D-U-N-S 24-340-4832   (BR)
AQUATERRA CORPORATION
LABRADOR LAURENTIENNE
9021 Boul Metropolitain E, Anjou, QC, H1J
3C4
(514) 956-2600
Emp Here 50
SIC 2899 Chemical preparations, nec

D-U-N-S 24-600-7314   (SL)
ATELIER ABACO INC
ABACO PHARMA
9100 Rue Claveau, Anjou, QC, H1J 1Z4
(514) 355-6182
Emp Here 91   Sales 4,523,563
SIC 7389 Business services, nec

D-U-N-S 24-870-1609   (BR)
AV-TECH INC
LOGIC-CONTROLE
(Suby of 3102-4284 Quebec Inc)
8002 Rue Jarry, Anjou, QC, H1J 1H5
(514) 493-1162
Emp Here 20
SIC 7349 Building maintenance services, nec

D-U-N-S 20-580-5778   (BR)
BANQUE LAURENTIENNE DU CANADA
BANQUE LAURENTIENNE
7050 Rue Jarry, Anjou, QC, H1J 1G4
(514) 351-1279
Emp Here 20
SIC 6021 National commercial banks

D-U-N-S 25-198-5248   (BR)
CAMIONS LAGUE INC
(Suby of Gestion Camions Lague Inc)
9651 Boul Louis-H.-Lafontaine, Anjou, QC,
H1J 2A3
(514) 493-6940
Emp Here 50
SIC 7513 Truck rental and leasing, no drivers

D-U-N-S 25-298-2863   (BR)
CARPENTER CANADA CO

9500 Rue De L'Innovation, Anjou, QC, H1J 2X9
(514) 351-3221
Emp Here 25
SIC 3069 Fabricated rubber products, nec

D-U-N-S 24-870-6756   (SL)
CHAUSSURES RALLYE INC
10001 Boul Ray-Lawson, Anjou, QC, H1J 1L6
(514) 353-5888
Emp Here 90
SIC 3021 Rubber and plastics footwear

D-U-N-S 25-974-6113   (HQ)
COBRA INTERNATIONAL SYSTEMES DE FIXATIONS CIE LTEE
(*Suby of* Cobra International Systemes De Fixations Cie Ltee)
8051 Boul Metropolitain E, Anjou, QC, H1J 1J8
(514) 354-2240
Emp Here 65   *Emp Total* 275
Sales 64,000,320
SIC 6712 Bank holding companies
Pr Pr Pierre Mcduff
  Richard Labelle
  Jocelyne Mousseau Mcduff

D-U-N-S 25-240-4462   (BR)
COMMISSION SCOLAIRE DE LA POINTE-DE-L'ILE
ECOLE JACQUES ROUSSEAU
7455 Rue Jarry, Anjou, QC, H1J 1G8
(514) 353-8570
Emp Here 60
SIC 8211 Elementary and secondary schools

D-U-N-S 20-712-3923   (BR)
COMMISSION SCOLAIRE DE LA POINTE-DE-L'ILE
CENTRE DE FORMATION DE METIERS DE L'ACIER
9200 Rue De L'Innovation, Anjou, QC, H1J 2X9
(514) 353-0801
Emp Here 20
SIC 8211 Elementary and secondary schools

D-U-N-S 25-222-9851   (SL)
CONFORT EXPERT INC
9771 Boul Metropolitain E, Anjou, QC, H1J 0A4
(514) 640-7711
Emp Here 60   *Sales* 7,067,520
SIC 1711 Plumbing, heating, air-conditioning
Pr Pr Pierre Boule
VP VP Jean-Claude Pettigrew
  Alain Pouliot
VP VP Pierre Dupuis
Dir Gilbert Boule
Dir Claude Simoneau

D-U-N-S 20-192-1538   (BR)
COSTCO WHOLESALE CANADA LTD
(*Suby of* Costco Wholesale Corporation)
7373 Rue Bombardier, Anjou, QC, H1J 2V2
(514) 493-4814
Emp Here 200
SIC 5099 Durable goods, nec

D-U-N-S 25-363-1576   (BR)
CRYOPAK INDUSTRIES (2007) ULC
CRYOPAK INDUSTRIES
11000 Boul Parkway, Anjou, QC, H1J 1R6
(514) 324-4720
Emp Here 30
SIC 2097 Manufactured ice

D-U-N-S 20-965-2952   (SL)
DECO SIGNALISATION INC
9225 Rue Du Parcours, Anjou, QC, H1J 3A8
(514) 494-1004
Emp Here 60   *Sales* 3,648,035
SIC 3993 Signs and advertising specialties

D-U-N-S 20-646-0193   (BR)
DESCHAMPS IMPRESSION INC
9660 Boul Du Golf, Anjou, QC, H1J 2Y7

(514) 353-2442
Emp Here 30
SIC 2759 Commercial printing, nec

D-U-N-S 20-330-0967   (SL)
ECHANTILLON DOMINION LTEE
8301 Rue J.-Rene-Ouimet, Anjou, QC, H1J 2H7
(514) 374-9010
Emp Here 50   *Sales* 3,551,629
SIC 2782 Blankbooks and looseleaf binders

D-U-N-S 24-319-7295   (BR)
ENTREPRISES MICROTEC INC, LES
ALARM CAP
8125 Boul Du Golf, Anjou, QC, H1J 0B2
(514) 388-8177
Emp Here 92
SIC 5063 Electrical apparatus and equipment

D-U-N-S 20-357-0031   (SL)
ENVIRO INDUSTRIES INC
7887 Rue Grenache Bureau 106, Anjou, QC, H1J 1C4
(514) 352-0003
Emp Here 50   *Sales* 1,459,214
SIC 7349 Building maintenance services, nec

D-U-N-S 20-215-1601   (HQ)
ETIQUETTE & RUBAN ADHESIF COMMERCE INC
SERIGRAPHIE GEMSCREEN
(*Suby of* Placements J B Inc, Les)
9700 Boul Parkway, Anjou, QC, H1J 1P2
(514) 353-6111
Emp Here 40   *Emp Total* 41
Sales 9,227,040
SIC 2672 Paper; coated and laminated, nec
Pr Pr Jean Brazeau
  Roger Brideau
Prd Dir Michel Gaudet

D-U-N-S 20-229-5754   (SL)
EXCAVATIONS PAYETTE LTEE, LES
CIMAX LA BELLECHASSOISE
7900 Rue Bombardier, Anjou, QC, H1J 1A4
(514) 322-4800
Emp Here 50   *Sales* 3,648,035
SIC 1794 Excavation work

D-U-N-S 24-226-5432   (BR)
GS1 CANADA
9200 Boul Du Golf, Anjou, QC, H1J 3A1
(514) 355-8929
Emp Here 30
SIC 8611 Business associations

D-U-N-S 20-715-4407   (BR)
GAZ METRO INC
BUREAU D'AFFAIRE D'ANJOU
11401 Av L.-J.-Forget, Anjou, QC, H1J 2Z8

Emp Here 85
SIC 4924 Natural gas distribution

D-U-N-S 24-852-6027   (BR)
GROUPE COLABOR INC
VIANDES DECARIE
(*Suby of* Groupe Colabor Inc)
9595 Boul Metropolitain E, Anjou, QC, H1J 3C1
(514) 744-6641
Emp Here 50
SIC 5147 Meats and meat products

D-U-N-S 20-240-6505   (BR)
GROUPE QUALINET INC
(*Suby of* Groupe Qualinet Inc)
8375 Rue Bombardier, Anjou, QC, H1J 1A5
(514) 344-7337
Emp Here 50
SIC 7699 Repair services, nec

D-U-N-S 24-050-7541   (BR)
GUAY INC
10801 Rue Colbert, Anjou, QC, H1J 2G5
(514) 354-7344
Emp Here 100
SIC 7353 Heavy construction equipment

rental

GUILLEVIN INTERNATIONAL CIE
10301 Rue Renaude-Lapointe, Anjou, QC, H1J 2T4
(514) 355-7582
Emp Here 20
SIC 5065 Electronic parts and equipment, nec

D-U-N-S 25-496-9397   (SL)
H-E-E-L CANADA INC
HEEL CANADA
11025 Boul Louis-H.-Lafontaine, Anjou, QC, H1J 3A3
(514) 353-4335
Emp Here 40   *Sales* 4,961,328
SIC 5122 Drugs, proprietaries, and sundries

D-U-N-S 20-234-7261   (BR)
HARMAC TRANSPORTATION INC
SEABOARD HARMAC TRANSPORTATION GROUP
8155 Rue Grenache, Anjou, QC, H1J 1C4
(514) 354-7141
Emp Here 20
SIC 4212 Local trucking, without storage

D-U-N-S 25-962-8758   (BR)
HERTZ EQUIPMENT RENTAL CORPORATION
HERTZ EQUIPMENT RENTAL (8211)
9300 Rue Edison, Anjou, QC, H1J 1T1
(514) 354-8891
Emp Here 30
SIC 7359 Equipment rental and leasing, nec

D-U-N-S 20-107-1227   (BR)
HOME DEPOT OF CANADA INC
HOME DEPOT
(*Suby of* The Home Depot Inc)
11300 Rue Renaude-Lapointe, Anjou, QC, H1J 2V7
(514) 356-3650
Emp Here 130
SIC 5251 Hardware stores

D-U-N-S 20-700-2820   (BR)
HUDSON'S BAY COMPANY
DECO DECOUVERTE
7550 Rue Beclard, Anjou, QC, H1J 2X7

Emp Here 35
SIC 5311 Department stores

D-U-N-S 20-302-0222   (BR)
HYDRO-QUEBEC
7800 Rue Jarry, Anjou, QC, H1J 1H2
(450) 565-2210
Emp Here 60
SIC 7299 Miscellaneous personal service

D-U-N-S 25-323-6475   (SL)
IMPACT DETAIL INC
7887 Rue Grenache Bureau 201, Anjou, QC, H1J 1C4
(514) 767-1555
Emp Here 300   *Sales* 53,430,054
SIC 8743 Public relations services
Pr Richard Boulay

D-U-N-S 24-852-1853   (SL)
INDUSTRIES BECO LTEE, LES
10900 Rue Colbert, Anjou, QC, H1J 2H8
(514) 353-9060
Emp Here 65   *Sales* 7,879,756
SIC 2392 Household furnishings, nec
  Richard Pinchuk
VP VP Larry Zev Rinzler

D-U-N-S 20-271-0174   (SL)
INDUSTRIES COVER INC
VITRERIE BAIE ST-PAUL
(*Suby of* Koch Industries, Inc.)
9300 Boul Ray-Lawson, Anjou, QC, H1J 1Y6
(514) 353-3880
Emp Here 250   *Sales* 10,141,537
SIC 2241 Narrow fabric mills

Pr James Boudreault
Dir Jeffrey A Knight
Dir Richard Zoulek

D-U-N-S 24-807-4929   (SL)
INTERMARK TRANSPORT INC
7887 Rue Grenache Bureau 101, Anjou, QC, H1J 1C4

Emp Here 50   *Sales* 7,963,840
SIC 4213 Trucking, except local
Pr Marek Buczkiewicz

D-U-N-S 20-297-0401   (BR)
K+S SEL WINDSOR LTEE
SEL WINDSOR, LE
10701 Boul Parkway, Anjou, QC, H1J 1S1
(514) 352-7490
Emp Here 20
SIC 5149 Groceries and related products, nec

D-U-N-S 24-500-2910   (HQ)
KARLO CORPORATION SUPPLY & SERVICES
DISTRIBUTION DU PHARE
10801 Boul Ray-Lawson Bureau 100, Anjou, QC, H1J 1M5
(514) 255-5017
Emp Here 27   *Sales* 7,103,258
SIC 5088 Transportation equipment and supplies
Pr Julian S. Jr. Hillery
Sec Sanda Hiliuta
Dir Stephen Boyd
Dir Soren Jorgensen
Dir Robert Steen Kledal

D-U-N-S 20-985-7528   (BR)
KELLOGG CANADA INC
ALIMENTS KELLOGG CANADA
(*Suby of* Kellogg Company)
9440 Boul Du Golf, Anjou, QC, H1J 3A1
(514) 351-5220
Emp Here 50
SIC 2043 Cereal breakfast foods

D-U-N-S 24-340-8023   (BR)
KOHL & FRISCH LIMITED
(*Suby of* Kohl & Frisch Limited)
10600 Boul Du Golf Bureau 247, Anjou, QC, H1J 2Y7
(514) 325-0622
Emp Here 50
SIC 5122 Drugs, proprietaries, and sundries

D-U-N-S 25-196-0852   (SL)
LE GROUPE LAVERGNE INC
(*Suby of* 6187820 Canada Inc)
8800 1er Croissant, Anjou, QC, H1J 1C8
(514) 354-5757
Emp Here 100   *Sales* 14,665,101
SIC 3087 Custom compound purchased resins
  Jean-Luc Lavergne
Pr Pr Germain Archambault

D-U-N-S 20-795-7098   (BR)
LEON'S FURNITURE LIMITED
AMEUBLEMENT LEON
11201 Rue Renaude-Lapointe, Anjou, QC, H1J 2T4
(514) 353-7506
Emp Here 60
SIC 5712 Furniture stores

D-U-N-S 25-784-4282   (BR)
LOGIC-CONTROLE INC
(*Suby of* 3102-4284 Quebec Inc)
8002 Rue Jarry E, Anjou, QC, H1J 1H5
(514) 493-1162
Emp Here 150
SIC 7521 Automobile parking

D-U-N-S 25-243-6811   (SL)
MARFOGLIA EBENISTERIE INC
(*Suby of* 159519 Canada Inc)
9031 Boul Parkway, Anjou, QC, H1J 1N4

(514) 325-8700
Emp Here 40   *Sales* 2,699,546
SIC 2521 Wood office furniture

D-U-N-S 25-728-3739   (BR)
MATERIAUX DE CONSTRUCTION OLD-CASTLE CANADA INC, LES
PERMACON, DIV DE
8140 Rue Bombardier, Anjou, QC, H1J 1A4
(514) 351-2120
Emp Here 50
SIC 3272 Concrete products, nec

D-U-N-S 25-093-3848   (HQ)
MATERIAUX DE CONSTRUCTION OLD-CASTLE CANADA INC, LES
GROUPE PERMACON
8145 Rue Bombardier, Anjou, QC, H1J 1A5
(514) 640-5355
Emp Here 100   *Emp Total* 86,778
Sales 52,093,940
SIC 5039 Construction materials, nec
Sec Michael O'driscoll
Dir Keith A. Haas
Genl Mgr George Heusel

D-U-N-S 20-024-6655   (BR)
MAXIM TRANSPORTATION SERVICES INC
CAMION REMORQUES MAXIME
11300 Rue Colbert, Anjou, QC, H1J 2S4
(514) 354-9140
Emp Here 33
SIC 7513 Truck rental and leasing, no drivers

D-U-N-S 24-713-2582   (SL)
METALFORM INC
8485 Rue Jules-Leger, Anjou, QC, H1J 1A8

Emp Here 25   *Sales* 3,392,384
SIC 3444 Sheet Metalwork

D-U-N-S 24-901-3251   (BR)
METTLER-TOLEDO INC
(*Suby of* Mettler-Toledo International Inc.)
9280 Rue Du Parcours, Anjou, QC, H1J 2Z1

Emp Here 22
SIC 5046 Commercial equipment, nec

D-U-N-S 25-356-8851   (HQ)
MODE LE GRENIER INC
LE GRENIER
(*Suby of* Investissements Sylpama Ltee)
8501 Boul Ray-Lawson, Anjou, QC, H1J 1K6
(514) 354-0650
Emp Here 83   *Emp Total* 1
Sales 19,626,428
SIC 5621 Women's clothing stores
  Real Lafrance

D-U-N-S 20-227-5129   (HQ)
MONDOU, J. E. LTEE
VET DIET
10400 Rue Renaude-Lapointe, Anjou, QC, H1J 2V7
(514) 322-8645
Emp Here 50   *Emp Total* 207
Sales 19,480,507
SIC 5999 Miscellaneous retail stores, nec
  Jules Legault
VP VP Philippe Legault

D-U-N-S 24-508-8208   (HQ)
MONIDEX DISTRIBUTION INTERNATIONAL INC
10700 Rue Colbert, Anjou, QC, H1J 2H8
(514) 323-9932
Emp Here 70   *Emp Total* 78
Sales 9,484,891
SIC 5013 Motor vehicle supplies and new parts
Pr Pr Salvatore Polletta
Dir Richard Sforzin

D-U-N-S 24-017-7196   (SL)
MONTAGE ET DECOUPAGE PROMAG INC
PROMAG DISPLAY-CORR
11150 Av L.-J.-Forget, Anjou, QC, H1J 2K9

(514) 352-9511
Emp Here 138   *Sales* 35,000,250
SIC 7319 Advertising, nec
  Raffaele Pagnotta
  Francois Cadieux
  Francesco Perrone

D-U-N-S 20-563-3410   (BR)
MOORE CANADA CORPORATION
TOPS PRODUCTS CANADA
(*Suby of* R. R. Donnelley & Sons Company)
11150 Av L.-J.-Forget, Anjou, QC, H1J 2K9
(514) 353-9090
Emp Here 120
SIC 2782 Blankbooks and looseleaf binders

D-U-N-S 20-185-0521   (BR)
NATIONAL ENERGY EQUIPMENT INC
EQUIPEMENT NATIONAL ENERGIE
10801 Boul Ray-Lawson Bureau 300, Anjou, QC, H1J 1M5
(514) 355-2366
Emp Here 30
SIC 5084 Industrial machinery and equipment

D-U-N-S 24-636-4202   (HQ)
OLDHAM BATTERIES CANADA INC
(*Suby of* 2434-0309 Quebec Inc)
9650 Rue Colbert, Anjou, QC, H1J 2N2
(514) 355-5110
Emp Here 24   *Emp Total* 15
Sales 8,974,166
SIC 3692 Primary batteries, dry and wet
Dir Robert Mcdonald Sr
  Robert Mcdonald Jr

D-U-N-S 25-729-5121   (BR)
OLYMEL S.E.C.
FLAMINGO
7770 Rue Grenache, Anjou, QC, H1J 1C3
(514) 353-2830
Emp Here 240
SIC 2011 Meat packing plants

D-U-N-S 20-195-4620   (BR)
ORTHOFAB INC
10370 Boul Louis-H.-Lafontaine, Anjou, QC, H1J 2T3
(514) 356-0777
Emp Here 20
SIC 3842 Surgical appliances and supplies

D-U-N-S 20-706-9675   (SL)
OUIMET-TOMASSO INC
8383 Rue J.-Rene-Ouimet, Anjou, QC, H1J 2P8

Emp Here 150   *Sales* 17,374,320
SIC 2032 Canned specialties
  J. Robert Ouimet
Pr Pr Robert Mckenzie
VP VP Emile Mallette
Dir Robert Belisle

D-U-N-S 20-229-4047   (SL)
PASTENE ENTERPRISES ULC
LES ENTREPRISES PASTENE
9101 Rue De L'Innovation, Anjou, QC, H1J 2X9
(514) 353-7997
Emp Here 23   *Sales* 5,982,777
SIC 5141 Groceries, general line
Pr Pr John Franciosa
VP Vincent Tangredi

D-U-N-S 25-247-5942   (BR)
POWER BATTERY SALES LTD
BATTERIES PUISSANTES, LES
7711 Rue Larrey, Anjou, QC, H1J 2T7
(514) 355-1212
Emp Here 20
SIC 5013 Motor vehicle supplies and new parts

D-U-N-S 24-336-6783   (BR)
POWRMATIC DU CANADA LTEE
9500 Boul Ray-Lawson, Anjou, QC, H1J 1L1
(514) 493-6400
Emp Here 50

SIC 5531 Auto and home supply stores

D-U-N-S 24-226-4690   (BR)
PRAXAIR CANADA INC
(*Suby of* Praxair, Inc.)
8151 Boul Metropolitain E, Anjou, QC, H1J 1X6
(514) 353-3340
Emp Here 101
SIC 5169 Chemicals and allied products, nec

D-U-N-S 24-109-2824   (SL)
PUBLI CALEN-ART LTEE
P.C.A. IMPRIMEUR LITHOGRAPHE
8075 Rue Larrey, Anjou, QC, H1J 2L4

Emp Here 50   *Sales* 3,793,956
SIC 2752 Commercial printing, lithographic

D-U-N-S 20-183-6975   (SL)
RBC BEARINGS CANADA, INC
AEROSPATIALE SARGENT CANADA
8121 Rue Jarry, Anjou, QC, H1J 1H6
(514) 352-9425
Emp Here 100
SIC 3724 Aircraft engines and engine parts

D-U-N-S 24-110-0676   (BR)
REYNOLDS AND REYNOLDS (CANADA) LIMITED
11075 Boul Louis-H.-Lafontaine, Anjou, QC, H1J 3A3
(514) 355-7550
Emp Here 80
SIC 5045 Computers, peripherals, and software

D-U-N-S 20-331-0172   (BR)
ROPACK INC
ROPACK PHARMA SOLUTIONS MC
10351 Rue Mirabeau, Anjou, QC, H1J 1T7
(514) 353-7000
Emp Here 20
SIC 4225 General warehousing and storage

D-U-N-S 24-365-9898   (BR)
ROTISSERIES ST-HUBERT LTEE, LES
MEILLEURES MARQUES
(*Suby of* Cara Holdings Limited)
9050 Imp De L'Invention, Anjou, QC, H1J 3A7
(514) 324-5400
Emp Here 154
SIC 5145 Confectionery

D-U-N-S 25-212-0738   (BR)
ROYAL GROUP, INC
PRODUITS DE BATIMENTS RESIDENTIELS
10401 Boul Ray-Lawson, Anjou, QC, H1J 1M3
(514) 354-6891
Emp Here 30
SIC 5039 Construction materials, nec

D-U-N-S 24-254-7284   (BR)
RYDER TRUCK RENTAL CANADA LTD
(*Suby of* Ryder System, Inc.)
8650 Rue Jarry, Anjou, QC, H1J 1X7
(514) 353-7070
Emp Here 25
SIC 7513 Truck rental and leasing, no drivers

D-U-N-S 24-447-7886   (SL)
SERTI PLACEMENT TI INC
10975 Boul Louis-H.-Lafontaine Bureau 201, Anjou, QC, H1J 2E8
(514) 493-1909
Emp Here 50   *Sales* 4,331,255
SIC 7361 Employment agencies

D-U-N-S 25-167-9114   (BR)
SHERWIN-WILLIAMS CANADA INC
SHERWIN WILLIAMS AUTOMOTIVE
(*Suby of* The Sherwin-Williams Company)
7875 Rue Jarry, Anjou, QC, H1J 2C3
(514) 353-2420
Emp Here 20
SIC 5013 Motor vehicle supplies and new parts

D-U-N-S 20-852-6751   (BR)
SOCIETE DE TRANSPORT DE MONTREAL
8150 Rue Larrey, Anjou, QC, H1J 2J5
(514) 280-5913
Emp Here 560
SIC 4111 Local and suburban transit

D-U-N-S 24-311-1379   (BR)
SPICERS CANADA ULC
SPICERS
(*Suby of* CNG Canada Holding Inc.)
10000 Boul Ray-Lawson, Anjou, QC, H1J 1L8
(514) 351-3520
Emp Here 60
SIC 5111 Printing and writing paper

D-U-N-S 20-989-1501   (BR)
STAPLES CANADA INC
BUREAU EN GROS
(*Suby of* Staples, Inc.)
11250 Rue Renaude-Lapointe, Anjou, QC, H1J 2V7
(514) 354-6052
Emp Here 30
SIC 5943 Stationery stores

D-U-N-S 24-580-7631   (HQ)
STEAMATIC METROPOLITAIN INC
S.M.I. QUEBEC CONSTRUCTION
8351 Boul Louis-H.-Lafontaine, Anjou, QC, H1J 3B4
(514) 351-7500
Emp Here 30   *Emp Total* 13,000
Sales 5,253,170
SIC 1799 Special trade contractors, nec
Pr Serge Lavoie
VP VP Alexandre Ashby
Sec Claire Castonguay
Dir Claude Bigras
Dir Andrew Fortier
Dir Catherine Chevalier

D-U-N-S 20-219-9154   (BR)
SUN CHEMICAL LIMITED
10501 Boul Parkway, Anjou, QC, H1J 1R4
(514) 355-7000
Emp Here 24
SIC 2893 Printing ink

D-U-N-S 24-394-6303   (HQ)
TECHNOLOGIES METAFORE INC
METAFORE
9393 Boul Louis-H.-Lafontaine, Anjou, QC, H1J 1Y8
(514) 354-3810
Emp Here 1,000   *Emp Total* 1,700
Sales 186,863,841
SIC 7371 Custom computer programming services
Pr Hary Hart
Treas Michael Lemieux
Dir Jeffrey Hart
Dir Frank Fuser

D-U-N-S 20-633-5432   (SL)
THERMOGRAPHIE TRANS CANADA LTEE
9001 Boul Parkway, Anjou, QC, H1J 1N4
(514) 351-4411
Emp Here 50   *Sales* 2,480,664
SIC 2759 Commercial printing, nec

D-U-N-S 20-420-5603   (BR)
TOROMONT INDUSTRIES LTD
CIMCO REFRIGERATION, DIVISION OF TOROMONT
9001 Rue De L'Innovation Bureau 110, Anjou, QC, H1J 2X9
(514) 331-5360
Emp Here 40
SIC 1711 Plumbing, heating, air-conditioning

D-U-N-S 25-072-7864   (BR)
TRANSCONTINENTAL PRINTING INC
TRANSMAG, DIV DE
10807 Rue Mirabeau, Anjou, QC, H1J 1T7
(514) 355-4134
Emp Here 180
SIC 2711 Newspapers

▲ Public Company   ■ Public Company Family Member   **HQ** Headquarters   **BR** Branch   **SL** Single Location

D-U-N-S 25-501-2957   (SL)
TRANSPORT BRETON-SAVARD INC
7481 Av Herisson, Anjou, QC, H1J 2G7
(514) 254-1447
Emp Here 50   *Sales* 5,088,577
SIC 4212 Local trucking, without storage

D-U-N-S 20-302-2343   (BR)
UTC FIRE & SECURITY CANADA
(*Suby of* United Technologies Corporation)
8205 Boul Du Golf, Anjou, QC, H1J 0B2
(514) 321-9961
Emp Here 80
SIC 5999 Miscellaneous retail stores, nec

D-U-N-S 20-517-3177   (BR)
UNILEVER CANADA INC
GOOD HUMOR
9600 Boul Du Golf, Anjou, QC, H1J 2Y7
(514) 353-4043
Emp Here 40
SIC 2099 Food preparations, nec

D-U-N-S 25-127-6143   (BR)
WESTOWER COMMUNICATIONS LTD
8700 Rue De L'Innovation, Anjou, QC, H1J 2X9
(514) 356-0911
Emp Here 50
SIC 1623 Water, sewer, and utility lines

Anjou, QC H1K

D-U-N-S 25-242-7026   (SL)
ASSOCIATION DE PARENTS DU CENTRE GABRIELLE MAJOR
APCGM
8150 Boul Metropolitain E, Anjou, QC, H1K 1A1

Emp Here 600   *Sales* 31,705,680
SIC 8322 Individual and family services
Pr Antoine Chase
Treas Claudine Millot
VP Danielle Gaudet
Genl Mgr Helene Duval
  Marie Bedard
  Helene Pellerin
  Lise Longpre
  Jean-Claude Gaudreau
  Gerard Dumesnil
  Richard Laplante

D-U-N-S 25-939-1147   (BR)
AUTOBUS TRANSCO (1988) INC
TRANSCO-ANJOU
7880 Boul Metropolitain E, Anjou, QC, H1K 1A1
(514) 352-2330
Emp Here 49
SIC 4151 School buses

D-U-N-S 25-298-6211   (BR)
COMMISSION SCOLAIRE ENGLISH-MONTREAL
DALKEITH SCHOOL
7951 Av De Dalkeith, Anjou, QC, H1K 3X6
(514) 352-6730
Emp Here 40
SIC 8211 Elementary and secondary schools

D-U-N-S 20-712-3915   (BR)
COMMISSION SCOLAIRE DE LA POINTE-DE-L'ILE
CENTRES SERVICES AUX ENTREPRISES
7741 Av Du Ronceray, Anjou, QC, H1K 3W7
(514) 352-7645
Emp Here 50
SIC 8211 Elementary and secondary schools

D-U-N-S 25-240-4504   (BR)
COMMISSION SCOLAIRE DE LA POINTE-DE-L'ILE
ECOLE SAINT JOSEPH
7725 Av Des Ormeaux, Anjou, QC, H1K 2Y2

Emp Here 30
SIC 8211 Elementary and secondary schools

D-U-N-S 20-355-3487   (BR)
COMMISSION SCOLAIRE DE LA POINTE-DE-L'ILE
C. S. E. CENTRE DE L'ILE
7741 Av Du Ronceray, Anjou, QC, H1K 3W7
(514) 352-7645
Emp Here 50
SIC 8211 Elementary and secondary schools

D-U-N-S 20-517-9505   (BR)
COMMISSION SCOLAIRE DE LA POINTE-DE-L'ILE
CENTRE REGIONALE DE FORMATION A DISTANCE DU GRAND MONTREAL
7741 Av Du Ronceray, Anjou, QC, H1K 3W7
(514) 353-3355
Emp Here 30
SIC 8249 Vocational schools, nec

D-U-N-S 25-240-4421   (BR)
COMMISSION SCOLAIRE DE LA POINTE-DE-L'ILE
ECOLE CHENIER
5800 Av Saint-Donat, Anjou, QC, H1K 3P4
(514) 352-4550
Emp Here 20
SIC 8211 Elementary and secondary schools

D-U-N-S 20-574-8200   (BR)
COMMISSION SCOLAIRE DE LA POINTE-DE-L'ILE
CENTRE ANJOU
5515 Av De L'Arena, Anjou, QC, H1K 4C9
(514) 354-0120
Emp Here 45
SIC 8211 Elementary and secondary schools

D-U-N-S 20-715-4126   (BR)
COMMISSION SCOLAIRE DE LA POINTE-DE-L'ILE
ANNEXE SAINT JOSEPH
7755 Av Des Ormeaux, Anjou, QC, H1K 2Y2
(514) 352-4136
Emp Here 40
SIC 8211 Elementary and secondary schools

D-U-N-S 20-422-8639   (SL)
COQ D'ANJOU INC, AU
6531 Av Baldwin, Anjou, QC, H1K 3C4
(514) 351-7160
Emp Here 50   *Sales* 1,532,175
SIC 5812 Eating places

D-U-N-S 24-125-4841   (BR)
FEDERATION DES CAISSES DESJARDINS DU QUEBEC
DOMAINE L'HYPOTHEQUE
7755 Boul Louis-H.-Lafontaine Bureau 30711, Anjou, QC, H1K 4M6
(514) 376-4420
Emp Here 200
SIC 6162 Mortgage bankers and loan correspondents

D-U-N-S 24-207-5492   (BR)
GRAND & TOY LIMITED
BUREAU-SPEC
(*Suby of* Office Depot, Inc.)
7751 Boul Louis-H.-Lafontaine, Anjou, QC, H1K 4E4
(514) 353-2000
Emp Here 60
SIC 5021 Furniture

D-U-N-S 25-747-6762   (BR)
METRO INC
METRO
6500 Boul Joseph-Renaud, Anjou, QC, H1K 3V4
(514) 354-0282
Emp Here 75
SIC 5411 Grocery stores

D-U-N-S 25-390-4155   (SL)
SERVICES PROFESSIONNELS DES AS-

SUREURS PLUS INC
S P A PLUS
8290 Boul Metropolitain E, Anjou, QC, H1K 1A2

Emp Here 50   *Sales* 2,626,585
SIC 7389 Business services, nec

D-U-N-S 25-232-1278   (BR)
VILLE DE MONTREAL ARRONDISSEMENT D'ANJOU
BIBLIOTHEQUE   ARRONDISSEMENT D'ANJOU
7500 Av Goncourt, Anjou, QC, H1K 3X9
(514) 493-8260
Emp Here 25
SIC 8231 Libraries

Anjou, QC H1M

D-U-N-S 25-986-6291   (SL)
9059-5307 QUEBEC INC
RESTAURANT BATON ROUGE
7999 Boul Des Galeries D'Anjou, Anjou, QC, H1M 1W9
(514) 355-7330
Emp Here 65   *Sales* 1,969,939
SIC 5812 Eating places

D-U-N-S 20-657-2625   (BR)
ALLSTATE INSURANCE COMPANY OF CANADA
ALLSTATE
7100 Rue Jean-Talon E Bureau 120, Anjou, QC, H1M 3S3
(514) 356-4780
Emp Here 50
SIC 6331 Fire, marine, and casualty insurance

D-U-N-S 24-363-5112   (BR)
BEST BUY CANADA LTD
BEST BUY
(*Suby of* Best Buy Co., Inc.)
7200 Boul Des Roseraies, Anjou, QC, H1M 2T5

Emp Here 50
SIC 5731 Radio, television, and electronic stores

D-U-N-S 25-216-9024   (BR)
BEST BUY CANADA LTD
FUTURE SHOP
(*Suby of* Best Buy Co., Inc.)
7400 Boul Des Roseraies, Anjou, QC, H1M 3X8
(514) 356-2168
Emp Here 50
SIC 5731 Radio, television, and electronic stores

D-U-N-S 24-222-9933   (BR)
BOSTON PIZZA INTERNATIONAL INC
BOSTON PIZZA
7300 Boul Des Roseraies, Anjou, QC, H1M 2T5
(514) 788-4848
Emp Here 90
SIC 5812 Eating places

D-U-N-S 25-540-4980   (BR)
CADILLAC FAIRVIEW CORPORATION LIMITED, THE
7999 Boul Des Galeries D'Anjou Bureau 2220, Anjou, QC, H1M 1W6
(514) 353-4411
Emp Here 37
SIC 6512 Nonresidential building operators

D-U-N-S 24-256-4474   (BR)
CAMPBELL COMPANY OF CANADA
COMPAGNIE CAMPBELL DU CANADA
(*Suby of* Campbell Soup Company)
7151 Rue Jean-Talon E Bureau 708, Anjou, QC, H1M 3N8

Emp Here 20
SIC 5149 Groceries and related products, nec

D-U-N-S 20-303-2867   (BR)
CARA OPERATIONS LIMITED
KELSEY'S
(*Suby of* Cara Holdings Limited)
7265 Boul Des Galeries D'Anjou, Anjou, QC, H1M 2W2
(514) 352-7655
Emp Here 30
SIC 5812 Eating places

D-U-N-S 20-791-4792   (BR)
CHILDREN'S PLACE (CANADA) LP, THE
CHILDREN'S PLACE, THE
7999 Boul Des Galeries D'Anjou, Anjou, QC, H1M 1W9
(514) 351-9109
Emp Here 20
SIC 5641 Children's and infants' wear stores

D-U-N-S 20-712-3808   (BR)
COMMISSION SCOLAIRE DE LA POINTE-DE-L'ILE
ECOLE PRIMAIRE DES ROSERAIES
6440 Boul Des Galeries D'Anjou, Anjou, QC, H1M 1W2
(514) 353-3130
Emp Here 50
SIC 8211 Elementary and secondary schools

D-U-N-S 20-764-9336   (HQ)
COMPAGNIE D'ASSURANCE BELAIR INC, LA
BELAIR DIRECT
7101 Rue Jean-Talon E Bureau 300, Anjou, QC, H1M 3T6
(514) 270-1700
Emp Here 450   *Emp Total* 11,000
Sales 444,403,624
SIC 6331 Fire, marine, and casualty insurance
Pr Louis Gagnon
Sec Francoise Guenette
Dir Charles Brindamour
Dir Carol Stephenson
Dir Eileen Mercier
Dir Louise Roy
Dir Claude Dussault
Dir Yves Brouillette
Dir Stephen Snyder
Dir Janet De Silva

D-U-N-S 20-126-7114   (BR)
CONSUMER IMPACT MARKETING LTD
CIM
7171 Rue Jean-Talon E Bureau 401, Anjou, QC, H1M 3N2

Emp Here 150
SIC 8743 Public relations services

D-U-N-S 20-137-2534   (BR)
CRAWFORD & COMPANY (CANADA) INC
CRAWFORD EXPERTISES CANADA
(*Suby of* Crawford & Company)
7171 Rue Jean-Talon E Bureau 500, Anjou, QC, H1M 3N2
(514) 748-7300
Emp Here 60
SIC 6411 Insurance agents, brokers, and service

D-U-N-S 20-284-6739   (BR)
DAVIDSTEA INC
DAVIDSTEA
7999 Boul Des Galeries D'Anjou, Anjou, QC, H1M 1W9
(514) 353-0571
Emp Here 25
SIC 5499 Miscellaneous food stores

D-U-N-S 24-520-4362   (BR)
DOLLARAMA S.E.C.
DOLLARAMA
7500 Boul Des Galeries D'Anjou Bureau 16, Anjou, QC, H1M 3M4

---

(514) 353-2823
Emp Here 25
SIC 5999 Miscellaneous retail stores, nec

D-U-N-S 20-545-0336   (BR)
FEDERATION DES CAISSES DESJARDINS DU QUEBEC
CENTRE FINANCIER AUX ENTREPRISES DE L'EST DE L'ISLE DE MONTREAL
7450 Boul Des Galeries D'Anjou Unite 300, Anjou, QC, H1M 3M3
(514) 253-7227
Emp Here 31
SIC 8742 Management consulting services

D-U-N-S 24-214-7804   (BR)
GROUPE ARCHAMBAULT INC
ARCHAMBAULT ANJOU
7500 Boul Des Galeries D'Anjou Bureau 50, Anjou, QC, H1M 3M4
(514) 351-2230
Emp Here 50
SIC 5736 Musical instrument stores

D-U-N-S 20-432-1509   (HQ)
GROUPE BELL NORDIQ INC
7151 Rue Jean-Talon E Bureau 700, Anjou, QC, H1M 3N8
(514) 493-5300
Emp Here 140   *Emp Total* 48,090
Sales 220,693,452
SIC 4899 Communication services, nec
  Frederick Crooks

D-U-N-S 25-309-7216   (BR)
INDUSTRIELLE ALLIANCE, ASSURANCE ET SERVICES FINANCIERS INC
INDUSTRIELLE ALLIANCE ASSURANCE ET SERVICES FINANCIERS
7100 Rue Jean-Talon E Bureau 805, Anjou, QC, H1M 3S3
(514) 353-5420
Emp Here 40
SIC 6351 Surety insurance

D-U-N-S 24-813-9719   (BR)
INTACT INSURANCE COMPANY
INTACT ASSURANCE
7101 Rue Jean-Talon E Bureau 1000, Anjou, QC, H1M 0A5
(514) 388-5466
Emp Here 350
SIC 6331 Fire, marine, and casualty insurance

D-U-N-S 20-707-7579   (BR)
KIMBERLY-CLARK INC
(*Suby of* Kimberly-Clark Corporation)
7400 Boul Des Galeries D'Anjou, Anjou, QC, H1M 3M2

Emp Here 28
SIC 5169 Chemicals and allied products, nec

D-U-N-S 24-431-9281   (BR)
LONDON LIFE INSURANCE COMPANY
FINANCIERE LIBERTE 55
7151 Rue Jean-Talon E Bureau 204, Anjou, QC, H1M 3N8

Emp Here 25
SIC 6311 Life insurance

D-U-N-S 24-522-9161   (BR)
METRO INC
ALEXANDRE GAUDET
7151 Rue Jean-Talon E, Anjou, QC, H1M 3N8
(514) 356-5800
Emp Here 200
SIC 5141 Groceries, general line

D-U-N-S 24-059-7091   (BR)
MURPHY, D.P. INC
7295 Boul Des Galeries D'Anjou, Anjou, QC, H1M 2W2
(514) 355-3230
Emp Here 30
SIC 5812 Eating places

D-U-N-S 20-716-0479   (SL)

QUALITE HABITATION
7400 Boul Les Galeries D'Anjou Bureau 205, Anjou, QC, H1M 3M2
(514) 354-7526
Emp Here 40   *Sales* 5,438,720
SIC 6351 Surety insurance
Owner Richard Di Muro

D-U-N-S 25-294-5696   (BR)
SEARS CANADA INC
SEARS ANJOU
7451 Boul Des Galeries D'Anjou, Anjou, QC, H1M 3A3
(514) 353-7770
Emp Here 270
SIC 5311 Department stores

D-U-N-S 25-308-8298   (BR)
SOCIETE DES ALCOOLS DU QUEBEC
SOCIETE DES ALCOOLS DU QUEBEC
7500 Boul Des Galeries D'Anjou Bureau 56, Anjou, QC, H1M 3M4
(514) 353-3068
Emp Here 20
SIC 5182 Wine and distilled beverages

D-U-N-S 25-830-6760   (BR)
SUN LIFE ASSURANCE COMPANY OF CANADA
SUN LIFE FINANCIAL
7101 Rue Jean-Talon E Bureau 812, Anjou, QC, H1M 3N7
(514) 353-3177
Emp Here 60
SIC 6411 Insurance agents, brokers, and service

Armagh, QC G0R
Bellechasse County

D-U-N-S 25-232-7143   (BR)
COMMISSION SCOLAIRE DE LA COTE-DU-SUD, LA
ECOLE BELLE-VUE
100 Rue Du College, Armagh, QC, G0R 1A0
(418) 466-2191
Emp Here 22
SIC 8211 Elementary and secondary schools

Asbestos, QC J1T

D-U-N-S 25-010-1425   (BR)
BANQUE NATIONALE DU CANADA
277 1re Av, Asbestos, QC, J1T 1Y6
(819) 879-5471
Emp Here 20
SIC 6021 National commercial banks

D-U-N-S 20-574-7400   (SL)
CENTRE DE SANTE ET SERVICES SOCI-AUX DES SOURCES
475 3e Av, Asbestos, QC, J1T 1X6
(819) 879-7151
Emp Here 320   *Sales* 20,319,120
SIC 8059 Nursing and personal care, nec
Genl Mgr Mario Morand
  Denis Desilets

D-U-N-S 20-712-1133   (BR)
COMMISSION SCOLAIRE DES SOMMETS
ECOLE DE LA TOURELLE
180 Rue Genest, Asbestos, QC, J1T 1A9
(819) 879-6303
Emp Here 50
SIC 8211 Elementary and secondary schools

D-U-N-S 25-233-2820   (BR)
COMMISSION SCOLAIRE DES SOMMETS
ECOLE SECONDAIRE DE L'ESCALE
(*Suby of* Commission Scolaire des Sommets)
430 5e Av, Asbestos, QC, J1T 1X2

(819) 879-5413
Emp Here 80
SIC 8211 Elementary and secondary schools

D-U-N-S 20-712-1141   (BR)
COMMISSION SCOLAIRE DES SOMMETS
ECOLES PRIMAIRE DE LA PASSERELLE
410 1re Av, Asbestos, QC, J1T 1Z2
(819) 879-6926
Emp Here 50
SIC 8211 Elementary and secondary schools

D-U-N-S 20-712-1216   (BR)
COMMISSION SCOLAIRE DES SOMMETS
CENTRES DE FORMATION PROFESSION-NELLE DE L'ABESTERI
340 Boul Morin, Asbestos, QC, J1T 3C2
(819) 879-0769
Emp Here 50
SIC 8211 Elementary and secondary schools

D-U-N-S 25-372-1906   (BR)
COOPERATIVE AGRICOLE DU PRE-VERT
COOPERATIVE AGRICOLE DU PRE-VERT
(*Suby of* Cooperative Agricole du Pre-Vert)
444 Rue Binette, Asbestos, QC, J1T 3Z1
(819) 879-4950
Emp Here 20
SIC 5251 Hardware stores

D-U-N-S 20-884-0066   (SL)
FONDATION DU CENTRE DE SANTE DE LA MRC D'ASBESTOS, LE
475 3e Av, Asbestos, QC, J1T 1X6
(819) 879-7151
Emp Here 320   *Sales* 19,600,443
SIC 8399 Social services, nec
Ch Bd Nicole Forgues
VP Marie Paule Drouin
Sec Mario Morand
Treas Erik Ducharme
Dir Claire Berube
Dir Jean Houle
Dir Pauline Lescault
Dir Normand Pellerin
Dir Collette Lessard

D-U-N-S 24-250-3662   (SL)
MAXIMA CONFECTION INC
(*Suby of* Gestion Luc Boisvert Inc)
262 Boul Coakley, Asbestos, QC, J1T 1A6
(514) 299-6754
Emp Here 35   *Sales* 5,088,577
SIC 2335 Women's, junior's, and misses' dresses
Pr Pr Luc Boisvert

D-U-N-S 25-074-0545   (SL)
MECANIQUE INDUSTRIELLE A.L. TECH INC
240 Rue Manville O, Asbestos, QC, J1T 1G7
(819) 879-6777
Emp Here 50   *Sales* 4,961,328
SIC 8711 Engineering services

D-U-N-S 20-143-3893   (SL)
MINE JEFFREY INC
111 Boul St-Luc, Asbestos, QC, J1T 3N2
(819) 879-6000
Emp Here 285   *Sales* 22,773,120
SIC 1499 Miscellaneous nonMetallic minerals, except fuels
  Bernard Coulombe
  Denis Roy

D-U-N-S 24-125-4023   (BR)
PROVIGO DISTRIBUTION INC
MAXI
205 1re Av, Asbestos, QC, J1T 1Y3
(819) 879-5457
Emp Here 38
SIC 5411 Grocery stores

Ayer'S Cliff, QC J0B
Stanstead County

D-U-N-S 20-712-1380   (BR)
COMMISSION SCOLAIRE EASTERN TOWNSHIPS
AYER'S CLIFF ELEMENTARY SCHOOL
(*Suby of* Commission Scolaire Eastern Townships)
952 Rue Sanborn, Ayer'S Cliff, QC, J0B 1C0
(819) 838-4983
Emp Here 21
SIC 8211 Elementary and secondary schools

Baie-Comeau, QC G4Z
Saguenay County

D-U-N-S 25-519-3526   (BR)
2159-2993 QUEBEC INC
HOTEL LE MANOIR, L'
8 Av Cabot, Baie-Comeau, QC, G4Z 1L8
(418) 296-3391
Emp Here 50
SIC 7011 Hotels and motels

D-U-N-S 24-759-1423   (SL)
2630-6241 QUEBEC INC
HAMILTON & BOURASSA (1988) ENR
305 Boul La Salle, Baie-Comeau, QC, G4Z 2L5
(418) 296-9191
Emp Here 40   *Sales* 9,996,000
SIC 5571 Motorcycle dealers
Pr Pr Germain Deschenes

D-U-N-S 20-702-8965   (BR)
ALCOA CANADA CIE
ALUMINERIE DE BAIE COMEAU
100 Rte Maritime, Baie-Comeau, QC, G4Z 2L6
(418) 296-3311
Emp Here 700
SIC 3354 Aluminum extruded products

D-U-N-S 20-267-3315   (BR)
APPLIED INDUSTRIAL TECHNOLOGIES, LP
(*Suby of* Applied Industrial Technologies, Inc.)
5 Av Narcisse-Blais, Baie-Comeau, QC, G4Z 1T3
(418) 296-5575
Emp Here 23
SIC 5084 Industrial machinery and equipment

D-U-N-S 24-377-6002   (SL)
AUTOBUS MANIC INC
41 Av William-Dobell, Baie-Comeau, QC, G4Z 1T8
(418) 296-6462
Emp Here 50   *Sales* 1,386,253
SIC 4151 School buses

D-U-N-S 20-189-3047   (BR)
CARGILL LIMITED
14 Rte Maritime, Baie-Comeau, QC, G4Z 2L6
(418) 296-2233
Emp Here 55
SIC 5153 Grain and field beans

D-U-N-S 25-240-0759   (BR)
COMMISSION SCOLAIRE DE L'ESTUAIRE
ECOLE BOISVERT
(*Suby of* Commission Scolaire de l'Estuaire)
105 Av Le Gardeur, Baie-Comeau, QC, G4Z 1E8
(418) 296-6523
Emp Here 25
SIC 8211 Elementary and secondary schools

D-U-N-S 24-436-1833   (BR)
DOLLARAMA S.E.C.
300 Boul La Salle Bureau 23, Baie-Comeau, QC, G4Z 2K2
(418) 294-4426
Emp Here 23
SIC 5399 Miscellaneous general merchandise

D-U-N-S 20-643-4631   (HQ)

GROUPE CONSEIL TDA INC
(*Suby of* Gestion TDA Inc)
26 Boul Comeau, Baie-Comeau, QC, G4Z
3A8
(418) 296-6711
Emp Here 88   *Emp Total* 50
Sales 9,703,773
SIC 8711 Engineering services
Pr Pr Jean-Claude Tremblay
Etienne Chapados

D-U-N-S 20-021-2413   (BR)
LOGISTEC CORPORATION
32 Av William-Dobell, Baie-Comeau, QC, G4Z
1T7
(514) 844-9381
Emp Here 60
SIC 4491 Marine cargo handling

D-U-N-S 25-001-1350   (BR)
MALLETTE S.E.N.C.R.L.
229 Boul La Salle, Baie-Comeau, QC, G4Z
1S7
(418) 296-9651
Emp Here 23
SIC 8721 Accounting, auditing, and book-keeping

D-U-N-S 24-126-2000   (BR)
MAZDA CANADA INC
BAIE COMEAU MAZDA
25 Boul Comeau, Baie-Comeau, QC, G4Z
3A7
(418) 296-2328
Emp Here 20
SIC 7539 Automotive repair shops, nec

D-U-N-S 25-389-8159   (BR)
PF RESOLU CANADA INC
ABITIBI-CONSOLIDATED, DIVISION BAIE-COMEAU
20 Av Marquette, Baie-Comeau, QC, G4Z 1K6
(418) 296-3371
Emp Here 290
SIC 2679 Converted paper products, nec

D-U-N-S 20-318-3611   (BR)
SNC-LAVALIN GEM QUEBEC INC
GROUPE QUALITAS
50 Av William-Dobell, Baie-Comeau, QC, G4Z
1T7
(418) 296-6788
Emp Here 50
SIC 8742 Management consulting services

D-U-N-S 20-290-1518   (SL)
SANTERRE ELECTRIQUE (2013) INC
311 Boul La Salle, Baie-Comeau, QC, G4Z
2L5
(418) 296-4466
Emp Here 35   *Sales* 3,957,782
SIC 1731 Electrical work

D-U-N-S 20-580-1707   (SL)
TRANSPORT SAVARD LTEE
136 Boul Comeau Bureau 51, Baie-Comeau,
QC, G4Z 3A8
(418) 296-6633
Emp Here 50   *Sales* 3,939,878
SIC 4212 Local trucking, without storage

D-U-N-S 25-361-0943   (BR)
VEOLIA ES CANADA SERVICES INDUS-TRIELS INC
51 Boul Comeau, Baie-Comeau, QC, G4Z
3A7
(418) 296-3967
Emp Here 20
SIC 7699 Repair services, nec

Baie-Comeau, QC G5C
Saguenay County

D-U-N-S 24-864-1607   (SL)
AMBULANCES COTE-NORD INC
2726 Boul Lafleche, Baie-Comeau, QC, G5C

1E4
(418) 589-3564
Emp Here 27   *Sales* 2,626,585
SIC 4119 Local passenger transportation, nec

D-U-N-S 20-176-7238   (BR)
CENTRE DE PROTECTION ET DE READAP-TATION DE LA COTE-NORD
CENTRE JEUNESSE COTE NORD
(*Suby of* Centre de Protection et de Readap-tation de la Cote-Nord)
835 Boul Jolliet, Baie-Comeau, QC, G5C 1P5
(418) 589-9927
Emp Here 650
SIC 8361 Residential care

D-U-N-S 20-871-6936   (HQ)
CENTRE DE PROTECTION ET DE READAP-TATION DE LA COTE-NORD
(*Suby of* Centre de Protection et de Readap-tation de la Cote-Nord)
1250 Rue Le Strat, Baie-Comeau, QC, G5C
1T8
(418) 589-2038
Emp Here 95   *Emp Total* 540
Sales 25,442,883
SIC 8361 Residential care
Dir Pierre Boulianne
Dir Caroline Tremblay
Pr Pr Renee Gagne

D-U-N-S 20-006-5048   (BR)
COMMISSION SCOLAIRE DE L'ESTUAIRE
CREA
600 Rue Jalbert, Baie-Comeau, QC, G5C 1Z9
(418) 589-0867
Emp Here 23
SIC 8211 Elementary and secondary schools

D-U-N-S 25-239-9985   (BR)
COMMISSION SCOLAIRE DE L'ESTUAIRE
ECOLE ST-COEUR-DE-MARIE
(*Suby of* Commission Scolaire de l'Estuaire)
711 Boul Jolliet, Baie-Comeau, QC, G5C 1P3
(418) 589-0861
Emp Here 40
SIC 8211 Elementary and secondary schools

D-U-N-S 25-240-0874   (BR)
COMMISSION SCOLAIRE DE L'ESTUAIRE
ECOLE MGR BELANGER
(*Suby of* Commission Scolaire de l'Estuaire)
920 Boul Rene-Belanger, Baie-Comeau, QC, G5C 2N9
(418) 589-5191
Emp Here 20
SIC 8211 Elementary and secondary schools

D-U-N-S 25-240-0916   (BR)
COMMISSION SCOLAIRE DE L'ESTUAIRE
ECOLE BOIS DU NORD
(*Suby of* Commission Scolaire de l'Estuaire)
2398 Rue Napoleon, Baie-Comeau, QC, G5C 1A5
(418) 295-3763
Emp Here 25
SIC 8351 Child day care services

D-U-N-S 25-240-0023   (BR)
COMMISSION SCOLAIRE DE L'ESTUAIRE
ECOLE TRUDEL
(*Suby of* Commission Scolaire de l'Estuaire)
680 Rue Marguerite, Baie-Comeau, QC, G5C 1H3
(418) 589-3279
Emp Here 20
SIC 8211 Elementary and secondary schools

D-U-N-S 24-466-0221   (SL)
GROUPE DE LA COTE INC
VETEMENTS NORFIL, LES
332 Rue De Puyjalon, Baie-Comeau, QC, G5C 1M5
(418) 589-8397
Emp Here 75   *Sales* 10,956,600
SIC 2326 Men's and boy's work clothing
Genl Mgr Claude Belzile

D-U-N-S 25-365-7167   (BR)

HYDRO-QUEBEC
TRANSENERGIE ET PRODUCTION, DIVI-SIONS DE
1161 Rue Mccormick, Baie-Comeau, QC, G5C 2S7
(418) 295-1507
Emp Here 100
SIC 4911 Electric services

D-U-N-S 25-305-1940   (BR)
INNVEST PROPERTIES CORP
COMFORT INN
(*Suby of* Innvest Properties Corp)
745 Boul Lafleche, Baie-Comeau, QC, G5C 1C7
(418) 589-8252
Emp Here 20
SIC 7011 Hotels and motels

D-U-N-S 20-003-4911   (BR)
PF RESOLU CANADA INC
PRODUITS FORESTIERS RESOLUT SCI-ERIE OUTARDES
1 Ch De La Scierie, Baie-Comeau, QC, G5C 2S9
(418) 589-9229
Emp Here 136
SIC 5099 Durable goods, nec

D-U-N-S 20-030-4439   (BR)
PROVIGO DISTRIBUTION INC
MAXI BAIE-COMEAU
570 Boul Lafleche, Baie-Comeau, QC, G5C 1C3
(418) 589-9020
Emp Here 84
SIC 5411 Grocery stores

D-U-N-S 24-327-0977   (BR)
R. CROTEAU RIMOUSKI INC
AUBAINERIE, L
(*Suby of* Gestion Alain Hebert Inc)
625 Boul Lafleche, Baie-Comeau, QC, G5C 1C5
(418) 589-7267
Emp Here 22
SIC 5651 Family clothing stores

D-U-N-S 20-284-3137   (BR)
SOCIETE DE PROTECTION DES FORETS CONTRE LE FEU (SOPFEU)
SOPFEU
251 Rte De L'Aeroport, Baie-Comeau, QC, G5C 2S6
(418) 295-2300
Emp Here 20
SIC 7389 Business services, nec

D-U-N-S 25-308-2606   (BR)
TRANSPORT THIBODEAU INC
TRANSPORT SAGUELAC
(*Suby of* Groupe Thibodeau Inc)
1331 Boul Industriel, Baie-Comeau, QC, G5C 1B8
(418) 589-6322
Emp Here 20
SIC 4213 Trucking, except local

D-U-N-S 24-634-8424   (BR)
VALEURS MOBILIERES DESJARDINS INC
990 Boul Lafleche 2e Etage, Baie-Comeau, QC, G5C 2W9
(418) 280-1204
Emp Here 30
SIC 6211 Security brokers and dealers

D-U-N-S 25-991-6005   (BR)
WAL-MART CANADA CORP
WALMART BAIE COMEAU
630 Boul Lafleche Bureau 3002, Baie-Comeau, QC, G5C 2Y3
(418) 589-9971
Emp Here 120
SIC 5311 Department stores

Baie-D'Urfe, QC H9X
Hochelaga County

D-U-N-S 20-917-9428   (BR)
ATLAS POLAR COMPANY LIMITED
HIAB QUEBEC
18980 Aut Transcanadienne, Baie-D'Urfe, QC, H9X 3R1
(514) 457-1288
Emp Here 50
SIC 3537 Industrial trucks and tractors

D-U-N-S 20-541-7892   (SL)
CAMIONNAGE C.P. INC
DISTRIBUTION T.M.T.
19501 Av Clark-Graham, Baie-D'Urfe, QC, H9X 3T1
(514) 457-2550
Emp Here 50   *Sales* 4,677,755
SIC 4212 Local trucking, without storage

D-U-N-S 20-792-4812   (HQ)
ENTREPRISES RAILQUIP INC, LES
(*Suby of* Entreprises Railquip Inc, Les)
325 Av Lee, Baie-D'Urfe, QC, H9X 3S3
(514) 457-4760
Emp Here 85   *Emp Total* 95
Sales 19,141,200
SIC 6712 Bank holding companies
Pr Pr John Natale
VP Stephen Miller
VP Nestor Lewyckyj
VP Fin Jess Fagnani
Claude Demers
Pierre A Baril

D-U-N-S 25-167-6961   (SL)
G PRODUCTION INC
G.P.C.I.
19400 Aut Transcanadienne, Baie-D'Urfe, QC, H9X 3S4
(514) 457-3366
Emp Here 190   *Sales* 21,829,525
SIC 2834 Pharmaceutical preparations
Pr Cecile Dussart
VP Stuart Raetzman
VP Stevens Murray

D-U-N-S 24-821-3407   (HQ)
GUITABEC INC
GUITARES GODIN
(*Suby of* Lasido Inc)
19420 Av Clark-Graham, Baie-D'Urfe, QC, H9X 3R8
(514) 457-7977
Emp Here 25   *Emp Total* 450
Sales 16,545,394
SIC 3931 Musical instruments
Pr Patrick Godin
VP Robert Godin
Sec Daniel Roy

D-U-N-S 20-231-7103   (HQ)
INDUSTRIES REHAU INC
FIRST PIPE
625 Av Lee, Baie-D'Urfe, QC, H9X 3S3
(514) 905-0345
Emp Here 100   *Emp Total* 823
Sales 122,502,770
SIC 3089 Plastics products, nec
Pr Pr Christian Fabian
Sec Mark Mullins

D-U-N-S 25-200-9105   (SL)
INTERNATIONAL SUPPLIERS AND CON-TRACTORS INC
ALTON
19201 Av Clark-Graham, Baie-D'Urfe, QC, H9X 3P5
(514) 457-5362
Emp Here 32   *Sales* 23,281,080
SIC 5169 Chemicals and allied products, nec
Pr Pr Jean Banna
Genl Mgr Aurelio Ferrazzano

D-U-N-S 25-526-2610   (SL)
LABORATOIRES DE RECHERCHE DE LAN WIREWERKS INC, LES

19144 Av Cruickshank, Baie-D'Urfe, QC, H9X 3P1
(514) 635-1103
Emp Here 50   *Sales* 5,545,013
SIC 3661 Telephone and telegraph apparatus
Jais Cohen

D-U-N-S 24-698-9446   (BR)
LANTHIER BAKERY LTD
725 Av Lee, Baie-D'Urfe, QC, H9X 3S3
(514) 457-9370
Emp Here 50
SIC 2051 Bread, cake, and related products

D-U-N-S 24-689-6807   (HQ)
MERIAL CANADA INC
20000 Av Clark-Graham, Baie-D'Urfe, QC, H9X 4B6
(514) 457-1555
Emp Here 30   *Emp Total* 45,692
Sales 6,493,502
SIC 2834 Pharmaceutical preparations
Sec Ghislain Lavigne
Pr Guillermo Lopez
Dir Christian Schwerd
Dir Doug Jones

D-U-N-S 24-059-0914   (BR)
O.K. TIRE STORES INC
OK PNEUS
19101 Av Clark-Graham, Baie-D'Urfe, QC, H9X 3P5
(514) 457-5275
Emp Here 20
SIC 5014 Tires and tubes

D-U-N-S 25-198-5677   (BR)
PLAZACORP RETAIL PROPERTIES LTD
GROUPE PLAZA
90 Rue Morgan Bureau 200, Baie-D'Urfe, QC, H9X 3A8
(514) 457-7007
Emp Here 25
SIC 6512 Nonresidential building operators

D-U-N-S 24-608-4136   (BR)
PROVIGO INC
PROVIGO #8850 (TROPIC)
90 Rue Morgan, Baie-D'Urfe, QC, H9X 3A8
(514) 457-2321
Emp Here 40
SIC 6719 Holding companies, nec

D-U-N-S 20-112-9488   (SL)
ROS-MAR INC
19500 Av Clark-Graham, Baie-D'Urfe, QC, H9X 3R8
(514) 694-2178
Emp Here 160   *Sales* 15,642,661
SIC 2752 Commercial printing, lithographic
Pr Pr Frank Carbone

D-U-N-S 20-013-1642   (BR)
SAMUEL, SON & CO., LIMITED
METAUX AERONAUTIQUE SAMUEL
21525 Av Clark-Graham, Baie-D'Urfe, QC, H9X 3T5
(514) 457-3399
Emp Here 198
SIC 5051 Metals service centers and offices

D-U-N-S 24-990-3931   (HQ)
SCHOLLE IPN CANADA LTD
AUTOFILL PRODUCTS
22000 Av Clark-Graham, Baie-D'Urfe, QC, H9X 4B6
(514) 457-1569
Emp Here 94   *Emp Total* 2,100
Sales 17,325,020
SIC 2673 Bags: plastic, laminated, and coated
Treas Claude Gelinas
Pr Tom Bickford
Sec Alec Marketos
Dir Fin Jerry Trousdale
Jay Goffin

D-U-N-S 25-472-1298   (SL)
SHOEI CANADA CORPORATION

CEPC
19900 Av Clark-Graham, Baie-D'Urfe, QC, H9X 3R8
(514) 336-2888
Emp Here 40   *Sales* 4,888,367
SIC 3399 Primary Metal products

D-U-N-S 20-595-1460   (SL)
SOLIGNUM INC
19500 Aut Transcanadienne, Baie-D'Urfe, QC, H9X 3S4
(514) 457-1512
Emp Here 100   *Sales* 20,908,080
SIC 5198 Paints, varnishes, and supplies
Pr Pr Zoltan Jakabovits
Thomas Jakabovits

D-U-N-S 24-848-5562   (SL)
TOMRA CANADA INC
LES SYSTEMES TOMRA
20500 Av Clark-Graham, Baie-D'Urfe, QC, H9X 4B6
(514) 457-4177
Emp Here 55   *Sales* 11,954,264
SIC 5084 Industrial machinery and equipment
Pr Alain Nault
Sec Walter F Garigliano
Dir Stefan Ranstand
Dir Espen Gundersen

Baie-Du-Febvre, QC J0G
Yamaska County

D-U-N-S 24-369-8920   (BR)
CAISSE DESJARDINS DE NICOLET
CENTRE DE SERVICES BAIE-DU-FEBVRE
324 Rte Marie-Victorin, Baie-Du-Febvre, QC, J0G 1A0
(819) 293-8570
Emp Here 40
SIC 6062 State credit unions

D-U-N-S 25-666-1372   (HQ)
COVILAC COOPERATIVE AGRICOLE
(*Suby of* Covilac Cooperative Agricole)
40 Rue De L'+Glise, Baie-Du-Febvre, QC, J0G 1A0
(450) 783-6188
Emp Here 35   *Emp Total* 50
Sales 7,896,840
SIC 7389 Business services, nec
Jean Roy
Pr Jacques Cote
Genl Mgr Richard Laroche

D-U-N-S 24-405-0357   (SL)
SOGETEL
37 Rue Verville, Baie-Du-Febvre, QC, J0G 1A0
(450) 783-1005
Emp Here 165   *Sales* 21,502,720
SIC 4813 Telephone communication, except radio
Pr Pr Jean-Philippe Saia
VP VP Maurice Proulx
Yvon Brunelle

D-U-N-S 24-570-7815   (SL)
USINE ROTEC INC
ROTEC INTERNATIONAL
125 Rue De L'Eglise, Baie-Du-Febvre, QC, J0G 1A0
(450) 783-6444
Emp Here 55   *Sales* 4,012,839
SIC 2514 Metal household furniture

Baie-Saint-Paul, QC G3Z

D-U-N-S 25-700-8177   (BR)
BOUVIDARD LTEE
CAFE DES ARTISTES
25 Rue Saint-Jean-Baptiste, Baie-Saint-Paul,

QC, G3Z 1M2
(418) 435-5585
Emp Here 30
SIC 5812 Eating places

D-U-N-S 24-169-5118   (BR)
CLUB SOCIAL DES EMPLOYES-ES DU CENTRE DE SANTE ET DE SERVICES SOCIAUX DE CHARLEVOIX, LE
CLUB SOCIAL DES EMPLOYES-ES DU CENTRE DE SANTE ET DE SERVICES SOCIAUX DE CHARLEVOIX, LE
284 Rang De Saint-Placide S, Baie-Saint-Paul, QC, G3Z 3A9
(418) 435-5093
Emp Here 40
SIC 8399 Social services, nec

D-U-N-S 24-890-8212   (BR)
CLUB SOCIAL DES EMPLOYES-ES DU CENTRE DE SANTE ET DE SERVICES SOCIAUX DE CHARLEVOIX, LE
CLUB SOCIAL DES EMPLOYES-ES DU CENTRE DE SANTE ET DE SERVICES SOCIAUX DE CHARLEVOIX, LE
10 Rue Boivin, Baie-Saint-Paul, QC, G3Z 1S8
(418) 435-5150
Emp Here 80
SIC 8361 Residential care

D-U-N-S 25-232-3597   (BR)
COMMISSION SCOLAIRE DE CHARLEVOIX, LA
ECOLES ET CENTRES EDUCATIF SAINT AUBIN
200 Rue Saint-Aubin Unite 102, Baie-Saint-Paul, QC, G3Z 2R2
(418) 435-6802
Emp Here 80
SIC 8211 Elementary and secondary schools

D-U-N-S 20-711-9202   (BR)
COMMISSION SCOLAIRE DE CHARLEVOIX, LA
ECOLE THOMAS TREMBLAY
27 Rue Ambroise-Fafard, Baie-Saint-Paul, QC, G3Z 2J2
(418) 435-2546
Emp Here 50
SIC 8211 Elementary and secondary schools

D-U-N-S 25-232-3258   (BR)
COMMISSION SCOLAIRE DE CHARLEVOIX, LA
ECOLE SIR RODOLPHE FORGET
7 Rue Forget, Baie-Saint-Paul, QC, G3Z 1T4
(418) 435-2828
Emp Here 28
SIC 8211 Elementary and secondary schools

D-U-N-S 24-749-5971   (SL)
FERME AMBROISE-FAFARD INC
HOTEL LA FERME
(*Suby of* Groupe le Massif Inc)
50 Rue De La Ferme, Baie-Saint-Paul, QC, G3Z 0G2
(418) 240-2055
Emp Here 50   *Sales* 5,718,096
SIC 7011 Hotels and motels
Pr Pr Claude Choquette

D-U-N-S 24-170-1429   (BR)
PROVIGO DISTRIBUTION INC
30 Rue Racine, Baie-Saint-Paul, QC, G3Z 2R1
(418) 240-3510
Emp Here 30
SIC 5411 Grocery stores

D-U-N-S 20-987-5637   (BR)
SIMARD SUSPENSIONS INC
707 Ch Saint-Laurent, Baie-Saint-Paul, QC, G3Z 2L6
(418) 240-2743
Emp Here 22
SIC 3711 Motor vehicles and car bodies

D-U-N-S 20-189-5182   (HQ)

SIMARD SUSPENSIONS INC
1064 Boul Monseigneur-De Laval, Baie-Saint-Paul, QC, G3Z 2W9
(418) 435-5347
Emp Here 75   *Emp Total* 115
Sales 18,240,175
SIC 3714 Motor vehicle parts and accessories
David Tremblay

Barraute, QC J0Y
Abitibi County

D-U-N-S 25-233-5575   (BR)
COMMISSION SCOLAIRE HARRICANA
ECOLE SECONDAIRE NATAGAN
570 Rue Principale N, Barraute, QC, J0Y 1A0

Emp Here 30
SIC 8211 Elementary and secondary schools

Beaconsfield, QC H9W
Hochelaga County

D-U-N-S 25-846-0278   (SL)
9038-5477 QUEBEC INC
HEALTH ACCESS
482 Boul Beaconsfield Bureau 204, Beaconsfield, QC, H9W 4C4
(514) 695-3131
Emp Here 100   *Sales* 4,742,446
SIC 8059 Nursing and personal care, nec

D-U-N-S 25-240-4595   (BR)
COMMISSION SCOLAIRE MARGUERITE-BOURGEOYS
ECOLE PRIMAIRE ST-REMI
16 Av Neveu, Beaconsfield, QC, H9W 5B4
(514) 855-4206
Emp Here 50
SIC 8351 Child day care services

D-U-N-S 24-167-8929   (SL)
KEVJAS INC
MCDONALDS RESTAURANT
44 Boul Saint-Charles, Beaconsfield, QC, H9W 5Z6
(514) 694-3427
Emp Here 125   *Sales* 5,224,960
SIC 5812 Eating places
Pr Pr George Bolanis

D-U-N-S 20-712-3626   (BR)
LESTER B. PEARSON SCHOOL BOARD
SAINT PAUL SCHOOL
230 Rue Sherbrooke, Beaconsfield, QC, H9W 1P5
(514) 697-7830
Emp Here 50
SIC 8211 Elementary and secondary schools

D-U-N-S 20-531-3625   (BR)
LESTER B. PEARSON SCHOOL BOARD
BEACONSFIELD HIGH SCHOOL
250 Beaurepaire Dr, Beaconsfield, QC, H9W 5G7
(514) 697-7220
Emp Here 100
SIC 8211 Elementary and secondary schools

D-U-N-S 25-240-6111   (BR)
LESTER B. PEARSON SCHOOL BOARD
ECOLE CHRISTMAS PARK
422 Boul Beaconsfield, Beaconsfield, QC, H9W 4B7
(514) 695-0651
Emp Here 38
SIC 8211 Elementary and secondary schools

D-U-N-S 20-712-3618   (BR)
LESTER B. PEARSON SCHOOL BOARD
ECOLE ST EDMUND
115 Boul Beaconsfield, Beaconsfield, QC,

H9W 3Z8
(514) 697-7621
Emp Here 40
SIC 8211 Elementary and secondary schools

D-U-N-S 25-794-3423   (BR)
METRO RICHELIEU INC
METRO PLUS BEACONSFIELD
50 Boul Saint-Charles Bureau 17, Beaconsfield, QC, H9W 2X3
(514) 695-5811
Emp Here 85
SIC 5411 Grocery stores

D-U-N-S 25-307-6830   (BR)
SOCIETE DES ALCOOLS DU QUEBEC
SAQ BEACONSFIELD
110 Beaurepaire Dr, Beaconsfield, QC, H9W 0A1
(514) 694-4195
Emp Here 20
SIC 5921 Liquor stores

D-U-N-S 24-367-9292   (BR)
SUNRISE NORTH SENIOR LIVING LTD
MAISON DE VIE SUNRISE OF BEACONSFIELD
(*Suby of* Welltower Inc.)
505 Av Elm, Beaconsfield, QC, H9W 2E5
(514) 693-1616
Emp Here 45
SIC 8361 Residential care

Bearn, QC J0Z
Temiscaninque County

D-U-N-S 24-706-2235   (BR)
TEMBEC INC
67 Rue Principale S, Bearn, QC, J0Z 1G0
(819) 726-3551
Emp Here 150
SIC 2421 Sawmills and planing mills, general

Beauceville, QC G5X
Beauce County

D-U-N-S 20-213-9429   (BR)
AGROPUR COOPERATIVE
AGROPUR DIVISION FROMAGE ET PRODUITS FONCTIONNELS
75 Av Lambert, Beauceville, QC, G5X 3N5
(418) 774-9848
Emp Here 125
SIC 2022 Cheese; natural and processed

D-U-N-S 25-245-1299   (BR)
AQUATECH SOCIETE DE GESTION DE L'EAU INC
AQUATECH STATION D'EPURATION
407 Boul Renault, Beauceville, QC, G5X 1N7

Emp Here 30
SIC 4941 Water supply

D-U-N-S 24-907-9963   (SL)
BOIS OUVRE DE BEAUCEVILLE (1992) INC
(*Suby of* Gestion Sylvie et Jacques Inc)
201 134e Rue, Beauceville, QC, G5X 3H9
(418) 774-3606
Emp Here 60   *Sales* 4,888,367
SIC 2431 Millwork

D-U-N-S 20-711-9269   (BR)
COMMISSION SCOLAIRE DE LA BEAUCE-ETCHEMIN
POLYVALENTE SAINT FRANCOIS
228 Av Lambert, Beauceville, QC, G5X 3N9
(418) 228-5541
Emp Here 60
SIC 8211 Elementary and secondary schools

D-U-N-S 25-232-3175   (BR)

COMMISSION SCOLAIRE DE LA BEAUCE-ETCHEMIN
ECOLE DE LERY-MONSEIGNEUR-DE-LAVAL
99 125e Rue, Beauceville, QC, G5X 2R2
(418) 774-9857
Emp Here 65
SIC 8211 Elementary and secondary schools

D-U-N-S 25-244-3270   (BR)
CORPORATION AMBULANCIERE DE BEAUCE INC
C.AM.B.I.
(*Suby of* Corporation Ambulanciere de Beauce Inc)
485 Boul Renault, Beauceville, QC, G5X 3P5
(418) 774-5199
Emp Here 160
SIC 4119 Local passenger transportation, nec

D-U-N-S 24-438-6491   (SL)
PROMUTUEL BEAUCE-ETCHEMINS, SOCIETE MUTUELLE D'ASSURANCE GENERALE
PROMUTUEL ASSURANCE
650 Boul Renault, Beauceville, QC, G5X 3P2
(418) 397-4147
Emp Here 50   *Sales* 4,523,563
SIC 6411 Insurance agents, brokers, and service

D-U-N-S 24-377-7778   (SL)
SECHOIRS A BOIS RENE BERNARD LTEE, LES
88 Av Lambert, Beauceville, QC, G5X 3N4
(418) 774-3382
Emp Here 50   *Sales* 4,742,446
SIC 2421 Sawmills and planing mills, general

D-U-N-S 25-916-1560   (BR)
SERVICES MATREC INC
139 181e Rue, Beauceville, QC, G5X 2S9
(418) 774-5275
Emp Here 20
SIC 4953 Refuse systems

D-U-N-S 25-077-5678   (BR)
TRANSCONTINENTAL PRINTING INC
150 181e Rue, Beauceville, QC, G5X 3P3
(418) 774-3367
Emp Here 500
SIC 2752 Commercial printing, lithographic

Beauharnois, QC J6N
Beauharnois County

D-U-N-S 20-530-0374   (BR)
CANADA POST CORPORATION
BEAUHARNOIS BDP
37 Rue Saint-Laurent, Beauharnois, QC, J6N 1V1
(450) 225-1065
Emp Here 25
SIC 4311 U.s. postal service

D-U-N-S 20-712-3360   (BR)
COMMISSION SCOLAIRE DE LA VALLEE-DES-TISSERANDS, LA
ECOLES SECONDAIRES PATRIOTES DE BEAUHARNOIS
250 Rue Gagnon, Beauharnois, QC, J6N 2W8
(450) 225-2260
Emp Here 75
SIC 8211 Elementary and secondary schools

D-U-N-S 20-972-4603   (BR)
COMMISSION SCOLAIRE DE LA VALLEE-DES-TISSERANDS, LA
CENTRE DE FORMATION PROFESSIONNELLE DES MOISSONS
260 Rue Gagnon, Beauharnois, QC, J6N 2W8
(450) 225-1084
Emp Here 20
SIC 8211 Elementary and secondary schools

D-U-N-S 24-294-7885   (SL)
CONSTRUCTION & EXPERTISE PG INC
LES IMMEUBLES BEAUHARNOIS
500 Rue Robert-Mckenzie, Beauharnois, QC, J6N 0N9
(450) 429-5000
Emp Here 50   *Sales* 4,961,328
SIC 8711 Engineering services

D-U-N-S 25-231-3031   (SL)
FAVREAU, GENDRON ASSURANCE ET SERVICES FINANCIERS INC
MAILLOUX, ROCHON ASSURANCE ET SERVICES FINANCIERS
505 Rue Des E?Rables, Beauharnois, QC, J6N 1T3
(450) 429-3755
Emp Here 26   *Sales* 25,828,088
SIC 6311 Life insurance

D-U-N-S 24-851-2597   (BR)
FEDERATION DES CAISSES DESJARDINS DU QUEBEC
CAISSES DESJARDINS
555 Rue Ellice, Beauharnois, QC, J6N 1X8
(450) 225-0335
Emp Here 42
SIC 6062 State credit unions

D-U-N-S 20-189-7675   (BR)
RIO TINTO ALCAN INC
(*Suby of* RIO TINTO PLC)
40 Rue De L'Aluminerie, Beauharnois, QC, J6N 0C2
(450) 225-6044
Emp Here 30
SIC 3365 Aluminum foundries

D-U-N-S 20-534-1691   (BR)
UNIPRIX INC
PHARMACIE MENARD BELANGER LAMBERT RIOPEL
330 Rue Ellice, Beauharnois, QC, J6N 1X3
(450) 429-3004
Emp Here 50
SIC 5912 Drug stores and proprietary stores

Beaumont, QC G0R
Bellechasse County

D-U-N-S 24-369-9001   (BR)
CAISSE DESJARDINS DES SEIGNEURIES DE BELLECHASE
CENTRE DE SERVICES BEAUMONT
310 Rte Du Fleuve, Beaumont, QC, G0R 1C0
(418) 887-3337
Emp Here 70
SIC 6062 State credit unions

D-U-N-S 20-712-0010   (BR)
COMMISSION SCOLAIRE DE LA COTE-DU-SUD, LA
ECOLE LA MARELLE
116 Ch Du Domaine, Beaumont, QC, G0R 1C0
(418) 838-8516
Emp Here 30
SIC 8211 Elementary and secondary schools

Beaupre, QC G0A

D-U-N-S 20-554-6703   (SL)
161251 CANADA INC
355 Rue Dupont, Beaupre, QC, G0A 1E0
(418) 827-8347
Emp Here 50   *Sales* 8,217,450
SIC 6712 Bank holding companies
Pr Jean-Guy Larouche

D-U-N-S 24-345-5602   (BR)
CENTRE DE SANTE ET DE SERVICES SOCIAUX DE QUEBEC-NORD

CLSC ORLEANS
11000 Rue Des Montagnards, Beaupre, QC, G0A 1E0
(418) 827-3726
Emp Here 350
SIC 8062 General medical and surgical hospitals

D-U-N-S 24-884-9341   (SL)
CHATEAU MONT-SAINTE-ANNE INC
HOTEL CHATEAU MONT-SAINTE-ANNE
(*Suby of* Corporation Financiere Quebecoise Inc)
500 Boul Du Beau-Pre, Beaupre, QC, G0A 1E0
(418) 827-1862
Emp Here 240   *Sales* 14,469,120
SIC 7011 Hotels and motels
Genl Mgr Sebastien Roy

D-U-N-S 25-232-7002   (BR)
COMMISSION SCOLAIRE DES PREMIERES-SEIGNEURIES
ECOLE SECONDAIRE DU MONT SAINTE ANNE
(*Suby of* Commission Scolaire Des Premieres-Seigneuries)
10975 Boul Sainte-Anne, Beaupre, QC, G0A 1E0
(418) 821-8053
Emp Here 100
SIC 8211 Elementary and secondary schools

D-U-N-S 25-232-6764   (BR)
COMMISSION SCOLAIRE DES PREMIERES-SEIGNEURIES
COMMISSION SCOLAIRE DES PREMIERES-SEIGNEURIES
(*Suby of* Commission Scolaire Des Premieres-Seigneuries)
2 Rue De Fatima E, Beaupre, QC, G0A 1E0
(418) 821-8078
Emp Here 30
SIC 8211 Elementary and secondary schools

D-U-N-S 24-890-7974   (BR)
GOUVERNEMENT DE LA PROVINCE DE QUEBEC
GOUVERNEMENT DE LA PROVINCE DE QUEBEC
11000 Rue Des Montagnards Rr 1, Beaupre, QC, G0A 1E0
(418) 661-5666
Emp Here 500
SIC 8361 Residential care

D-U-N-S 25-857-1553   (SL)
GROUPE LARO ALTA INC
CLUB VACANCES TOUTES SAISONS
355 Rue Dupont Bureau 827, Beaupre, QC, G0A 1E0
(418) 827-8347
Emp Here 50   *Sales* 2,188,821
SIC 7011 Hotels and motels

Becancour, QC G9H
Nicolet County

D-U-N-S 25-376-9368   (BR)
ALCOA CANADA CIE
USINE DE TIGE BECANCOUR
6900 Boul Raoul-Duchesne, Becancour, QC, G9H 2V2
(819) 294-2900
Emp Here 66
SIC 3334 Primary aluminum

D-U-N-S 24-678-2952   (SL)
ALUMINERIE DE BECANCOUR INC
5555 Rue Pierre-Thibault Bureau 217, Becancour, QC, G9H 2T7
(819) 294-6101
Emp Here 1,000
SIC 3463 Nonferrous forgings

D-U-N-S 24-630-6406   (BR)
AMERISPA INC
CLINIQUE DE PHYSIOTHERAPIE
(*Suby of* Amerispa Inc)
17575 Boul Becancour, Becancour, QC, G9H 1A5
(819) 233-4664
Emp Here 25
SIC 8049 Offices of health practitioner

D-U-N-S 20-314-0553   (SL)
AUTOCAR HELIE INC.
GROUPE HELIE
3505 Boul De Port-Royal, Becancour, QC, G9H 1Y2
(819) 371-1177
Emp Here 100   *Sales* 2,845,467
SIC 4151 School buses

D-U-N-S 20-502-8988   (SL)
BOUVET, ANDRE LTEE
16090 Boul Des Acadiens, Becancour, QC, G9H 1K9
(819) 233-2357
Emp Here 50   *Sales* 3,648,035
SIC 1794 Excavation work

D-U-N-S 20-261-8257   (BR)
CRDI TED NCQ IU
CENTRE DE SERVICES EN DEFICIENCE INTELLECTUELLE MA
(*Suby of* CRDI TED NCQ IU)
1582 Boul De Port-Royal Bureau 221, Becancour, QC, G9H 1X6
(819) 233-2111
Emp Here 30
SIC 8361 Residential care

D-U-N-S 25-363-0727   (HQ)
CAISSE DESJARDINS GODEFROY
CENTRE DE SERVICES BECANCOUR
(*Suby of* Caisse Desjardins Godefroy)
4265 Boul De Port-Royal, Becancour, QC, G9H 1Z3
(819) 233-2333
Emp Here 25   *Emp Total* 51
Sales 14,326,924
SIC 6062 State credit unions
Genl Mgr Dominique Raiche
Pr Pr Christian Savard
VP VP Leo Courchesne
Sec Katia St-Onge
Dir Jean Pinard
Dir Raymond Arseneault
Dir Claude Comeau
Dir Josiane Grenier
Dir Francine Pare Lampron
Dir Nancy Trottier

D-U-N-S 25-232-7812   (BR)
COMMISSION SCOLAIRE DE LA RIVERAINE
ECOLE HARFANG DES NEIGES
(*Suby of* Commission Scolaire de la Riveraine)
1875 Boul Becancour, Becancour, QC, G9H 3V4
(819) 298-2182
Emp Here 20
SIC 8211 Elementary and secondary schools

D-U-N-S 25-232-8059   (BR)
COMMISSION SCOLAIRE DE LA RIVERAINE
ECOLE BEAUSEJOUR
(*Suby of* Commission Scolaire de la Riveraine)
18000 Rue Beliveau, Becancour, QC, G9H 1H4
(819) 233-2390
Emp Here 40
SIC 8211 Elementary and secondary schools

D-U-N-S 25-376-6729   (BR)
FEDERATION DES CAISSES DESJARDINS DU QUEBEC
CAISSE POPULAIRE DESJARDINS DE GENTILLY

1780 Av Des Hirondelles, Becancour, QC, G9H 4L7
(819) 298-2844
Emp Here 30
SIC 6062 State credit unions

D-U-N-S 24-522-6431   (BR)
JOHNSTON-VERMETTE GROUPE CONSEIL INC
JOHNSTON-VERMETTE
1095 Av Des Oiselets, Becancour, QC, G9H 4P7
(819) 298-4470
Emp Here 25
SIC 8711 Engineering services

D-U-N-S 24-005-5850   (SL)
LIGNCO SIGMA INC
DURA-LIGNES
1645 Av Le Neuf Bureau 14, Becancour, QC, G9H 2E5
(819) 233-3435
Emp Here 20   *Sales* 1,751,057
SIC 1799 Special trade contractors, nec

D-U-N-S 24-370-5782   (BR)
OLIN CANADA ULC
OLIN PRODUITS CHLORALCALIS
675 Boul Alphonse-Deshaies, Becancour, QC, G9H 2Y8
(819) 294-6633
Emp Here 175
SIC 2819 Industrial inorganic chemicals, nec

D-U-N-S 25-376-6133   (BR)
PROVIGO DISTRIBUTION INC
L'INTER MARCHE
1305 Boul Becancour, Becancour, QC, G9H 3V1
(819) 298-2444
Emp Here 23
SIC 5411 Grocery stores

D-U-N-S 24-863-7506   (SL)
SOCIETE EN COMMANDITE AUBERGE GODEFROY
17575 Boul Becancour, Becancour, QC, G9H 1A5
(819) 233-2200
Emp Here 80   *Sales* 3,502,114
SIC 7011 Hotels and motels

D-U-N-S 25-370-3425   (BR)
TELEBEC, SOCIETE EN COMMANDITE
TELEBEC
625 Av Godefroy, Becancour, QC, G9H 1S3
(514) 493-5504
Emp Here 250
SIC 4813 Telephone communication, except radio

Bedford, QC J0J
Missisquoi County

D-U-N-S 24-346-5577   (BR)
CENTRE DE SANTE ET DE SERVICES SOCIAUX LA POMMERAIE
CSSS DE BEDFORD
(*Suby of* Centre de Sante et de Services Sociaux la Pommeraie)
34 Rue Saint-Joseph, Bedford, QC, J0J 1A0
(450) 248-4304
Emp Here 400
SIC 8621 Professional organizations

D-U-N-S 25-222-6006   (BR)
COMMISSION SCOLAIRE DU VAL-DES-CERFS
ECOLE MGR DESRANLEAU
12 Rue Marziali, Bedford, QC, J0J 1A0
(450) 248-3385
Emp Here 35
SIC 8211 Elementary and secondary schools

D-U-N-S 20-101-8061   (BR)
COMMISSION SCOLAIRE DU VAL-DES-

CERFS
ECOLE DU PREMIER ENVOL
6 Rue De L'Eglise, Bedford, QC, J0J 1A0
(450) 248-3364
Emp Here 30
SIC 8211 Elementary and secondary schools

D-U-N-S 25-184-1669   (BR)
DESSERCOM INC
37 Rue Campbell, Bedford, QC, J0J 1A0
(450) 248-4342
Emp Here 30
SIC 4119 Local passenger transportation, nec

D-U-N-S 20-190-2244   (HQ)
LAMOTHE ENERGIE INC
31 Rue Victoria S, Bedford, QC, J0J 1A0
(450) 248-2442
Emp Here 45   *Emp Total* 2
Sales 10,944,105
SIC 5983 Fuel oil dealers
Pr Pr Michel Lamothe
Treas Huguette Boucher

Begin, QC G0V
Chicoutimi County

D-U-N-S 20-642-1609   (BR)
COMMISSION SCOLAIRE DE LA JONQUIERE
ECOLE SAINT JEAN
(*Suby of* Commission Scolaire de la Jonquiere)
108 Rue Tremblay, Begin, QC, G0V 1B0
(418) 672-4704
Emp Here 20
SIC 8211 Elementary and secondary schools

Belleterre, QC J0Z
Temiscaninque County

D-U-N-S 20-712-5886   (BR)
COMMISSION SCOLAIRE DU LAC-TEMISCAMINGUE
L'ECOLE SAINT-ANDRE DE BELLETERRE
255 3e Av, Belleterre, QC, J0Z 1L0

Emp Here 50
SIC 8211 Elementary and secondary schools

Beloeil, QC J3G
Vercheres County

D-U-N-S 24-834-3626   (SL)
2747-6043 QUEBEC INC
ARPENTS VERTS FRUITS LEGUMES
245 Rue Duvernay, Beloeil, QC, J3G 2M3
(450) 467-2140
Emp Here 50   *Sales* 5,985,550
SIC 5431 Fruit and vegetable markets
Pr Real Riendeau

D-U-N-S 24-373-4535   (SL)
9197-4220 QUEBEC INC
SERVICES ENVIRONNEMENTAUX DES MASKOUTAINS
1205 Rue Louis-Marchand, Beloeil, QC, J3G 6S4
(450) 464-8121
Emp Here 100   *Sales* 17,668,800
SIC 4953 Refuse systems
Pr Pr Vincent Boulay
VP VP Donald Fontaine

D-U-N-S 20-569-2416   (BR)
BANQUE NATIONALE DU CANADA
NATIONAL BANK OF CANADA
180 Boul Sir-Wilfrid-Laurier, Beloeil, QC, J3G

4G7
(450) 467-0231
Emp Here 23
SIC 6021 National commercial banks

D-U-N-S 20-337-8752   (BR)
BUROPRO CITATION INC
CITATION
600 Boul Sir-Wilfrid-Laurier, Beloeil, QC, J3G 4J2
(450) 464-6464
Emp Here 66
SIC 5112 Stationery and office supplies

D-U-N-S 20-514-6272   (BR)
CRDITED MONTEREGIE EST
(*Suby of* CRDITED Monteregie Est)
255 Rue Choquette, Beloeil, QC, J3G 4V6
(450) 446-7477
Emp Here 55
SIC 8361 Residential care

D-U-N-S 20-981-5575   (BR)
CSSS RICHELIEU-YAMASKA CH DE LA MRC D'ACTON
CLSC DES PATRIOTES
300 Boul Serge-Pepin, Beloeil, QC, J3G 0B8
(450) 536-2572
Emp Here 60
SIC 8322 Individual and family services

D-U-N-S 20-580-4201   (BR)
CANADA POST CORPORATION
BUREAU DE POSTES DE BELOEIL
595 Boul Sir-Wilfrid-Laurier, Beloeil, QC, J3G 4J1

Emp Here 75
SIC 4311 U.s. postal service

D-U-N-S 20-712-3022   (BR)
COMMISSION SCOLAIRE DES PATRIOTES
ECOLE LE TOURNESOL
201 Rue Du Buisson, Beloeil, QC, J3G 5V5
(450) 467-5032
Emp Here 60
SIC 8211 Elementary and secondary schools

D-U-N-S 25-240-5477   (BR)
COMMISSION SCOLAIRE DES PATRIOTES
COMMISSION SCOLAIRE DES PATRIOTES
725 Rue De Levis, Beloeil, QC, J3G 2M1
(450) 467-0262
Emp Here 200
SIC 8211 Elementary and secondary schools

D-U-N-S 25-240-5154   (BR)
COMMISSION SCOLAIRE DES PATRIOTES
COMMISSION SCOLAIRE DES PATRIOTES
225 Rue Hubert, Beloeil, QC, J3G 2S8
(450) 467-9309
Emp Here 80
SIC 8211 Elementary and secondary schools

D-U-N-S 25-523-6697   (BR)
COMMISSION SCOLAIRE DES PATRIOTES
COMMISSION SCOLAIRE DES PATRIOTES
300 Rue Hertel, Beloeil, QC, J3G 3N3
(450) 467-6681
Emp Here 20
SIC 8211 Elementary and secondary schools

D-U-N-S 25-686-7946   (BR)
GENERAL ELECTRIC CANADA COMPANY
GE CANADA BELOEIL
(*Suby of* General Electric Company)
1691 Rue De L'Industrie, Beloeil, QC, J3G 0S5
(450) 464-9472
Emp Here 30
SIC 3625 Relays and industrial controls

D-U-N-S 24-157-0899   (BR)
GOODYEAR CANADA INC
(*Suby of* The Goodyear Tire & Rubber Company)
1655 Rue Louis-Marchand, Beloeil, QC, J3G 6S4
(450) 446-2662
Emp Here 35

SIC 7534 Tire retreading and repair shops

D-U-N-S 25-626-3088   (BR)
GROUPE PROMUTUEL FEDERATION DE SOCIETE MUTUELLES D'ASSURANCES GENERALES
GROUPE PROMUTUEL FEDERATION DE SOCIETE MUTUELLES D'ASSURANCES GENERALES
756 Rue Laurier, Beloeil, QC, J3G 4J9
(450) 446-7777
Emp Here 30
SIC 6331 Fire, marine, and casualty insurance

D-U-N-S 20-997-5010   (HQ)
INDUSTRIES BONNEVILLE LTEE, LES
ECONO-FAB
(Suby of Groupe Bonneville Inc, Le)
601 Rue De L'Industrie, Beloeil, QC, J3G 0S5
(450) 464-1001
Emp Here 200   Emp Total 2
Sales 32,832,315
SIC 2452 Prefabricated wood buildings
Pr Andre Bonneville
VP Normand Bonneville
Dir Dany Bonneville
Dir Eric Bonneville

D-U-N-S 24-685-6376   (HQ)
LES INDUSTRIES FIBROBEC INC
FIBROBEC
219 Rue Saint-Georges, Beloeil, QC, J3G 4N4
(450) 467-8611
Emp Here 45   Emp Total 1
Sales 8,217,675
SIC 3713 Truck and bus bodies
Frederic Albert
VP VP Frederic Chabanne

D-U-N-S 20-689-6495   (SL)
LES PORTES ISOLEX INC
1200 Rue Bernard-Pilon, Beloeil, QC, J3G 1V1
(450) 536-3063
Emp Here 20   Sales 8,239,360
SIC 5031 Lumber, plywood, and millwork
Pr Thierry Parisot

D-U-N-S 20-190-4133   (SL)
MARCHES PEPIN INC, LES
IGA PEPIN
865 Boul Yvon-L'Heureux N, Beloeil, QC, J3G 6P5
(450) 467-3512
Emp Here 450   Sales 85,988,160
SIC 5411 Grocery stores
Pr Pr Bernard Pepin

D-U-N-S 20-714-6288   (BR)
METRO RICHELIEU INC
SUPER C
600 Boul Sir-Wilfrid-Laurier, Beloeil, QC, J3G 4J2
(450) 467-1878
Emp Here 50
SIC 5411 Grocery stores

D-U-N-S 25-699-5861   (SL)
NATURE-ACTION QUEBEC INC
120 Rue Ledoux, Beloeil, QC, J3G 0A4
(450) 536-0422
Emp Here 50   Sales 3,575,074
SIC 8641 Civic and social associations

D-U-N-S 20-501-5159   (SL)
OUTILLAGE PLACIDE MATHIEU INC
670 Rue Picard, Beloeil, QC, J3G 5X9
(450) 467-3565
Emp Here 30   Sales 7,536,000
SIC 5084 Industrial machinery and equipment
Pr Christian Mathieu
Sec Sylvie Mathieu
Sec Solange Mathieu

D-U-N-S 25-821-1713   (BR)
PROVIGO INC
MAXI
175 Boul Sir-Wilfrid-Laurier, Beloeil, QC, J3G

4G8
(450) 464-3514
Emp Here 60
SIC 5411 Grocery stores

Berthierville, QC J0K
Berthier County

D-U-N-S 20-572-9606   (BR)
CANADA POST CORPORATION
580 Av Gilles-Villeneuve, Berthierville, QC, J0K 1A0
Emp Here 20
SIC 4311 U.s. postal service

D-U-N-S 20-190-5189   (SL)
EBI ENERGIE INC
FBI ENERGY
61 Rue De Montcalm, Berthierville, QC, J0K 1A0
(450) 836-8111
Emp Here 50   Sales 3,648,035
SIC 1794 Excavation work

D-U-N-S 24-252-3363   (BR)
GROUPE CHAMPLAIN INC
CHSLD LE CHATEAU
(Suby of Groupe Sante Sedna Inc)
1231 Rue Dr Olivier-M.-Gendron Pr, Berthierville, QC, J0K 1A0
(450) 836-6241
Emp Here 100
SIC 8361 Residential care

D-U-N-S 20-120-7276   (BR)
OLYMEL S.E.C.
OLYMEL/FLAMINGO
580 Rue Laferriere, Berthierville, QC, J0K 1A0
(450) 836-1651
Emp Here 490
SIC 2011 Meat packing plants

D-U-N-S 25-308-8645   (BR)
SOCIETE DES ALCOOLS DU QUEBEC
S.A.Q.
788 Av Gilles-Villeneuve, Berthierville, QC, J0K 1A0
(450) 836-4414
Emp Here 20
SIC 5921 Liquor stores

Blainville, QC J7B

D-U-N-S 20-249-3318   (SL)
AUTOMOBILES ST-EUSTACHE INC
16 Rue De Braine, Blainville, QC, J7B 1Z1
(514) 927-8977
Emp Here 45   Sales 22,826,250
SIC 5511 New and used car dealers
Pr Pr Gilles Pilon

D-U-N-S 20-706-6973   (BR)
CLUBLINK CORPORATION ULC
CLUB DE GOLF FONTAINEBLEAU
1 Boul De Fontainebleau, Blainville, QC, J7B 1L4
(450) 434-7569
Emp Here 80
SIC 7992 Public golf courses

D-U-N-S 25-976-1278   (BR)
COMMISSION SCOLAIRE DE LA SEIGNEURIE-DES-MILLE-ILES
COMMISSION SCOLAIRE DE LA SEIGNEURIE-DES-MILLE-ILES
(Suby of Commission Scolaire de la Seigneurie-Des-Mille-Iles)
370 Boul D'Annecy, Blainville, QC, J7B 1J7
(450) 433-5375
Emp Here 60
SIC 8211 Elementary and secondary schools

D-U-N-S 24-349-5939   (BR)
SUNRISE NORTH SENIOR LIVING LTD
MAISON DE VIE SUNRISE DE FONTAINEBLEAU
(Suby of Welltower Inc.)
50 Boul Des Chateaux, Blainville, QC, J7B 0A3
(450) 420-2727
Emp Here 80
SIC 8361 Residential care

Blainville, QC J7C

D-U-N-S 20-549-8889   (SL)
9071-3686 QUEBEC INC
ASTRA COFFRAGE
(Suby of Placements Malex Ltee)
41 Rue Gaston-Dumoulin, Blainville, QC, J7C 6B4
(450) 435-8449
Emp Here 30   Sales 3,392,384
SIC 1799 Special trade contractors, nec

D-U-N-S 24-681-3187   (HQ)
9104-4974 QUEBEC INC
TIM HORTONS
(Suby of 9104-4974 Quebec Inc)
1135 Boul Du Cure-Labelle, Blainville, QC, J7C 2N2
(450) 420-5083
Emp Here 20   Emp Total 50
Sales 1,532,175
SIC 5812 Eating places

D-U-N-S 20-323-6047   (HQ)
ALIMENTS TRIUMPH INC
ALIMENTS BILOPAGE
1020 Boul Michele-Bohec, Blainville, QC, J7C 5E2
(450) 979-0001
Emp Here 200   Emp Total 1
Sales 15,592,518
SIC 2013 Sausages and other prepared meats
Max Latifi

D-U-N-S 20-289-4754   (BR)
BANK OF MONTREAL
BMO
1099 Boul Du Cure-Labelle, Blainville, QC, J7C 2M2
(450) 434-1855
Emp Here 22
SIC 6021 National commercial banks

D-U-N-S 24-016-9750   (SL)
BERLINES TRANSIT INC
ENTRETIEN MECANIQUE BT
719 Boul Industriel Bureau 102b, Blainville, QC, J7C 3V3
(450) 437-3589
Emp Here 100   Sales 2,845,467
SIC 4151 School buses

D-U-N-S 24-126-2364   (BR)
CAISSE POPULAIRE DESJARDINS DE L'ENVOLEE
1070 Boul Du Cure-Labelle, Blainville, QC, J7C 2M7
(450) 430-4603
Emp Here 75
SIC 6062 State credit unions

D-U-N-S 24-851-2639   (BR)
CANWEL BUILDING MATERIALS LTD
CANWEL
651 Boul Industriel, Blainville, QC, J7C 3V3
(450) 435-6911
Emp Here 50
SIC 5032 Brick, stone, and related material

D-U-N-S 20-988-0249   (SL)
CENTRE DE LA PETITE ENFANCE LES CROQUIGNOLES INC
10 Rue Bibiane-Nantel, Blainville, QC, J7C

5Y4
(450) 433-3733
Emp Here 50   Sales 1,532,175
SIC 8351 Child day care services

D-U-N-S 20-721-5211   (HQ)
CHARCUTERIE LA TOUR EIFFEL INC
CHARCUTERIE DE BRETAGE
1020 Boul Michele-Bohec, Blainville, QC, J7C 5E2
(450) 979-0001
Emp Here 100   Emp Total 40,000
Sales 23,274,463
SIC 2011 Meat packing plants
Pr Pr Ken Carrier
Darryl Rowe
Jillian Moffat
Michael J Campbell

D-U-N-S 24-890-1696   (SL)
CLUB DE GOLF LE BLAINVILLIER INC
200 Rue Du Blainvillier, Blainville, QC, J7C 4X6
(450) 433-1444
Emp Here 110   Sales 4,450,603
SIC 7997 Membership sports and recreation clubs

D-U-N-S 25-240-1328   (BR)
COMMISSION SCOLAIRE DE LA SEIGNEURIE-DES-MILLE-ILES
COMMISSION SCOLAIRE DE LA SEIGNEURIE-DES-MILLE-ILES
(Suby of Commission Scolaire de la Seigneurie-Des-Mille-Iles)
40 84e Av E, Blainville, QC, J7C 3R5
(450) 433-5360
Emp Here 45
SIC 8211 Elementary and secondary schools

D-U-N-S 25-240-1369   (BR)
COMMISSION SCOLAIRE DE LA SEIGNEURIE-DES-MILLE-ILES
COMMISSION SCOLAIRE DE LA SEIGNEURIE-DES-MILLE-ILES
(Suby of Commission Scolaire de la Seigneurie-Des-Mille-Iles)
425 Boul Du Cure-Labelle, Blainville, QC, J7C 2H4
(450) 433-5350
Emp Here 45
SIC 8211 Elementary and secondary schools

D-U-N-S 25-976-1229   (BR)
COMMISSION SCOLAIRE DE LA SEIGNEURIE-DES-MILLE-ILES
COMMISSION SCOLAIRE DE LA SEIGNEURIE-DES-MILLE-ILES
(Suby of Commission Scolaire de la Seigneurie-Des-Mille-Iles)
1030 Rue Gilles-Vigneault, Blainville, QC, J7C 5N4
(450) 433-5415
Emp Here 35
SIC 8211 Elementary and secondary schools

D-U-N-S 25-976-1393   (BR)
COMMISSION SCOLAIRE DE LA SEIGNEURIE-DES-MILLE-ILES
COMMISSION SCOLAIRE DE LA SEIGNEURIE-DES-MILLE-ILES
(Suby of Commission Scolaire de la Seigneurie-Des-Mille-Iles)
60 Rue Des Grives, Blainville, QC, J7C 5J9
(450) 433-5385
Emp Here 40
SIC 8211 Elementary and secondary schools

D-U-N-S 25-976-1351   (BR)
COMMISSION SCOLAIRE DE LA SEIGNEURIE-DES-MILLE-ILES
COMMISSION SCOLAIRE DE LA SEIGNEURIE-DES-MILLE-ILES
(Suby of Commission Scolaire de la Seigneurie-Des-Mille-Iles)
1430 Rue Maurice-Cullen, Blainville, QC, J7C 5Y1

---

(450) 433-5470
Emp Here 30
SIC 8211 Elementary and secondary schools

D-U-N-S 20-712-1620   (BR)
COMMISSION SCOLAIRE DE LA SEIGNEURIE-DES-MILLE-ILES
COMMISSION SCOLAIRE DE LA SEIGNEURIE-DES-MILLE-ILES
1027 Boul Du Cure-Labelle, Blainville, QC, J7C 2M2
(450) 433-5540
Emp Here 50
SIC 8211 Elementary and secondary schools

D-U-N-S 20-712-1562   (BR)
COMMISSION SCOLAIRE DE LA SEIGNEURIE-DES-MILLE-ILES
COMMISSION SCOLAIRE DE LA SEIGNEURIE-DES-MILLE-ILES
930 Rue De La Mairie, Blainville, QC, J7C 3B4
(450) 433-5365
Emp Here 50
SIC 8211 Elementary and secondary schools

D-U-N-S 24-369-7732   (BR)
COMMISSION SCOLAIRE DE LA SEIGNEURIE-DES-MILLE-ILES
COMMISSION SCOLAIRE DE LA SEIGNEURIE-DES-MILLE-ILES
1275 Boul Celoron, Blainville, QC, J7C 5A8
(450) 430-2251
Emp Here 20
SIC 8211 Elementary and secondary schools

D-U-N-S 25-356-6590   (SL)
D.L.G.L. IMMOBILIERE LTEE
850 Boul Michele-Bohec, Blainville, QC, J7C 5E2
(450) 979-4646
Emp Here 95   *Sales* 15,077,264
SIC 7371 Custom computer programming services
Pr Jacques Guenette

D-U-N-S 24-349-7653   (SL)
D.L.G.L. TECHNOLOGIES CORPORATION
D.L.G.L. BUREAU D'AFFAIRES
850 Boul Michele Bohec, Blainville, QC, J7C 5E2
(450) 979-4646
Emp Here 50   *Sales* 2,772,507
SIC 7376 Computer facilities management

D-U-N-S 25-073-4050   (SL)
ENTREPRISES D'INSERTION GODEFROY-LAVIOLETTE, LES
PALETTES FGL
16 Rue Rolland-Briere, Blainville, QC, J7C 5N2
(450) 437-1146
Emp Here 50   *Sales* 2,334,742
SIC 8331 Job training and related services

D-U-N-S 20-715-4019   (BR)
GAZ METRO INC
1230 Boul Michele-Bohec, Blainville, QC, J7C 5S4
(514) 598-3339
Emp Here 50
SIC 4924 Natural gas distribution

D-U-N-S 20-056-3315   (HQ)
GROUPE J.S.V. INC, LE
ACIER METOSTEEL
28 Boul De La Seigneurie E, Blainville, QC, J7C 3V5
(450) 435-0717
Emp Here 45   *Emp Total* 70
Sales 9,703,773
SIC 5085 Industrial supplies
Pr Pr Marc Viau

D-U-N-S 20-573-6668   (BR)
HYDRO-QUEBEC
1000 Boul Michele-Bohec, Blainville, QC, J7C 5L6
(450) 430-5180
Emp Here 20

SIC 4911 Electric services

D-U-N-S 20-625-1642   (SL)
INVENTAIRES LAPARE INC
65 Boul De La Seigneurie E Bureau 101, Blainville, QC, J7C 4M9
(450) 435-2997
Emp Here 100   *Sales* 4,961,328
SIC 7389 Business services, nec

D-U-N-S 20-972-3329   (SL)
LABORATOIRE RIVA INC
(*Suby of* Investissements Andre St-Denis Inc, Les)
660 Boul Industriel, Blainville, QC, J7C 3V4
(450) 434-7482
Emp Here 100   *Sales* 9,703,773
SIC 2834 Pharmaceutical preparations
Pr Olivier St-Denis
VP Kaled Kadri
    Andre St-Denis
VP Opers Michel Grant
VP Fin Francois Jette
    Christian Derome

D-U-N-S 24-414-2456   (SL)
MANUFACTURE EXM LTEE
870 Boul Michele-Bohec, Blainville, QC, J7C 5E2
(450) 979-4373
Emp Here 50   *Sales* 17,656,489
SIC 3699 Electrical equipment and supplies, nec

D-U-N-S 25-311-1116   (BR)
MCDONALD'S RESTAURANTS OF CANADA LIMITED
RESTAURANTS MCDONALD'S
(*Suby of* McDonald's Corporation)
797 Boul Du Cure-Labelle, Blainville, QC, J7C 3P5
(450) 979-7131
Emp Here 75
SIC 5812 Eating places

D-U-N-S 20-571-9839   (BR)
METRO RICHELIEU INC
SUPER C
259 Boul De La Seigneurie O, Blainville, QC, J7C 4N3
(450) 435-2882
Emp Here 60
SIC 5141 Groceries, general line

D-U-N-S 24-175-7228   (SL)
MOULURES M. WARNET INC
MOULURES WARNET
100 Rue Marius-Warnet, Blainville, QC, J7C 5P9
(450) 437-1209
Emp Here 50   *Sales* 7,369,031
SIC 5211 Lumber and other building materials
    Gilles Warnet

D-U-N-S 20-262-2101   (BR)
NAUTILUS PLUS INC
775 Boul Du Cure-Labelle, Blainville, QC, J7C 2K4
(450) 433-3355
Emp Here 29
SIC 7999 Amusement and recreation, nec

D-U-N-S 20-986-2759   (BR)
ORICA CANADA INC
380 Montee Saint-Isidore, Blainville, QC, J7C 0W8
(450) 435-6934
Emp Here 20
SIC 2892 Explosives

D-U-N-S 25-896-3735   (SL)
PMG TECHNOLOGIES INC
100 Rue Du Landais, Blainville, QC, J7C 5C9
(450) 430-7981
Emp Here 50   *Sales* 3,720,996
SIC 8734 Testing laboratories

D-U-N-S 24-352-8929   (SL)
PETITE BRETONNE INC, LA

CROISSANTERIE BLANVILLE
1210 Boul Michele-Bohec, Blainville, QC, J7C 5S4
(450) 435-3381
Emp Here 50   *Sales* 2,626,585
SIC 2051 Bread, cake, and related products

D-U-N-S 24-423-6712   (BR)
PHARMETICS (2011) INC
PHARMETICS
865a Boul Michele-Bohec, Blainville, QC, J7C 5J6
(450) 682-8580
Emp Here 60
SIC 2834 Pharmaceutical preparations

D-U-N-S 24-526-9543   (SL)
PRODUITS M.G.D. INC, LES
680 Boul Industriel, Blainville, QC, J7C 3V4
(450) 437-1414
Emp Here 26   *Sales* 5,110,881
SIC 5113 Industrial and personal service paper

D-U-N-S 24-169-4454   (BR)
PROVIGO INC
MAXI
1083 Boul Du Cure-Labelle Bureau 101, Blainville, QC, J7C 3M9
(450) 435-2489
Emp Here 55
SIC 5411 Grocery stores

D-U-N-S 25-903-9527   (BR)
RE/MAX TMS INC
TMS BLAINVILLE
926 Boul Du Cure-Labelle, Blainville, QC, J7C 2L7
(450) 433-1151
Emp Here 20
SIC 6531 Real estate agents and managers

D-U-N-S 24-346-0230   (BR)
ROTISSERIES ST-HUBERT LTEE, LES
PRODUITS ALIMENTAIRES ST-HUBERT
(*Suby of* Cara Holdings Limited)
860 Boul Michele-Bohec, Blainville, QC, J7C 5E2
(450) 979-3377
Emp Here 46
SIC 5812 Eating places

D-U-N-S 20-323-8287   (HQ)
SPI SANTE SECURITE INC
EQUIPEMENTS DE SECURITE ET PREMIERS SOINS GLOBAL
60 Rue Gaston-Dumoulin, Blainville, QC, J7C 0A3
(450) 420-2012
Emp Here 40   *Emp Total* 1
Sales 16,891,895
SIC 5999 Miscellaneous retail stores, nec
Pr Martin Tremblay
Sec Marc Duchesne

D-U-N-S 20-296-3521   (BR)
SERVICES MATREC INC
750 Boul Industriel, Blainville, QC, J7C 3V4
(450) 434-2499
Emp Here 20
SIC 4212 Local trucking, without storage

D-U-N-S 24-309-5457   (HQ)
SERVICES DE CONSULTATION SUPERIEURES AEROSPATIALES (ASCS) INC
890 Boul Michele-Bohec, Blainville, QC, J7C 5E2
(450) 435-9210
Emp Here 91   *Emp Total* 130
Sales 20,809,920
SIC 8741 Management services
Pr Mario Lepine
    Michel Dussault
Fin Ex Christianne Proulx
Dir Warren Merson

D-U-N-S 20-712-2594   (BR)
SIR WILFRID LAURIER SCHOOL BOARD

ECOLES PRIMAIRES PIERRE ELLIOTT TRUDEAU
1455 Rue Jean-Paul-Riopelle, Blainville, QC, J7C 5V4
(450) 621-7606
Emp Here 50
SIC 8211 Elementary and secondary schools

D-U-N-S 25-308-8637   (BR)
SOCIETE DES ALCOOLS DU QUEBEC
SOCIETE DES ALCOOLS DU QUEBEC
259 Boul De La Seigneurie O, Blainville, QC, J7C 4N3
(450) 434-9164
Emp Here 60
SIC 5921 Liquor stores

D-U-N-S 24-788-5429   (SL)
SYSCOMAX INC
(*Suby of* Groupe Syscomax Inc, Le)
1060 Boul Michele-Bohec Bureau 106, Blainville, QC, J7C 5E2
(450) 434-0008
Emp Here 40   *Sales* 11,058,050
SIC 1541 Industrial buildings and warehouses
Pr Pr Sylvain Robitaille

D-U-N-S 25-139-3385   (BR)
UNITED PARCEL SERVICE CANADA LTD
UPS
71 Rue Omer-Deserres, Blainville, QC, J7C 5N3
(450) 979-9390
Emp Here 100
SIC 4212 Local trucking, without storage

D-U-N-S 25-232-3100   (BR)
VILLE DE BLAINVILLE
BIBLIOTHEQUE MUNICIPALE DE BLAINVILLE
1000 Ch Du Plan-Bouchard, Blainville, QC, J7C 3S9
(450) 434-5370
Emp Here 20
SIC 8231 Libraries

D-U-N-S 24-345-9208   (BR)
VILLE DE BLAINVILLE
ECO-CENTRE DE LA SEIGNEURIE
60 Boul De La Seigneurie E, Blainville, QC, J7C 4N1
(450) 434-5348
Emp Here 60
SIC 4959 Sanitary services, nec

Bois-Des-Filion, QC J6Z

D-U-N-S 25-243-2620   (HQ)
AIREAU QUALITE CONTROLE INC
AQC
(*Suby of* Aireau Qualite Controle Inc)
660 Rue De La Sabliere, Bois-Des-Filion, QC, J6Z 4T7
(450) 621-6661
Emp Here 27   *Emp Total* 30
Sales 9,995,616
SIC 5075 Warm air heating and air conditioning
Pr Pr Martin Brisebois
Dir Francois Charest

D-U-N-S 24-741-0814   (SL)
ALIMENTATION FRANCOIS GERMAIN INC
METRO RICHELIEU
425 Boul Adolphe-Chapleau, Bois-Des-Filion, QC, J6Z 1H9

Emp Here 40   *Sales* 6,125,139
SIC 5411 Grocery stores
Pr Francois Germain

D-U-N-S 25-976-1302   (BR)
COMMISSION SCOLAIRE DE LA SEIGNEURIE-DES-MILLE-ILES
COMMISSION SCOLAIRE DE LA

SEIGNEURIE-DES-MILLE-ILES
(Suby of Commission Scolaire de la Seigneurie-Des-Mille-Iles)
60 35e Av, Bois-Des-Filion, QC, J6Z 2E8
(450) 621-7760
Emp Here 20
SIC 8351 Child day care services

D-U-N-S 25-976-0171 (BR)
COMMISSION SCOLAIRE DE LA SEIGNEURIE-DES-MILLE-ILES
COMMISSION SCOLAIRE DE LA SEIGNEURIE-DES-MILLE-ILES
(Suby of Commission Scolaire de la Seigneurie-Des-Mille-Iles)
100 33e Av, Bois-Des-Filion, QC, J6Z 2C4
(450) 621-1750
Emp Here 30
SIC 8211 Elementary and secondary schools

D-U-N-S 20-230-4226 (HQ)
PLAD EQUIPEMENT LTEE
680 Rue De La Sabliere, Bois-Des-Filion, QC, J6Z 4T7
(450) 965-0224
Emp Here 40   Emp Total 61
Sales 1,884,658
SIC 3561 Pumps and pumping equipment

Bois-Franc, QC J9E
Gatineau County

D-U-N-S 25-365-3265 (BR)
LOUISIANA-PACIFIC CANADA LTD
(Suby of Louisiana-Pacific Corporation)
1012 Ch Du Parc-Industriel, Bois-Franc, QC, J9E 3A9
(819) 449-7030
Emp Here 180
SIC 2431 Millwork

Boisbriand, QC J7E

D-U-N-S 20-277-0160 (SL)
PAVAGE DION INC
ENTREPRISE DE PAVAGE DION
20855 Ch De La Cote N, Boisbriand, QC, J7E 4H5
(450) 435-0333
Emp Here 50   Sales 3,648,035
SIC 1794 Excavation work

D-U-N-S 24-165-5310 (BR)
SUNCOR ENERGY INC
PETRO CANADA
20905 Ch De La Cote N, Boisbriand, QC, J7E 4H5
(450) 435-5998
Emp Here 25
SIC 5541 Gasoline service stations

Boisbriand, QC J7G

D-U-N-S 24-000-2084 (SL)
9136-8910 QUEBEC INC
TIM HORTONS
355 Montee Sanche Bureau 2600, Boisbriand, QC, J7G 2E7
(450) 434-2223
Emp Here 65   Sales 1,969,939
SIC 5812 Eating places

D-U-N-S 25-211-4137 (BR)
9353-0251 QUEBEC INC
SOLARIS QUEBEC INC
(Suby of 2421-9974 Quebec Inc)
770 Boul Du Cure-Boivin, Boisbriand, QC, J7G 2A7

(450) 434-6223
Emp Here 20
SIC 5211 Lumber and other building materials

D-U-N-S 20-886-0908 (BR)
BOUCHERIE COTE INC
BOUCHERS ASSOCIES DE BOISBRIAND SENC, LES
387 Ch De La Grande-Cote, Boisbriand, QC, J7G 1A9
(450) 437-6877
Emp Here 25
SIC 5421 Meat and fish markets

D-U-N-S 25-976-1344 (BR)
COMMISSION SCOLAIRE DE LA SEIGNEURIE-DES-MILLE-ILES
COMMISSION SCOLAIRE DE LA SEIGNEURIE-DES-MILLE-ILES
(Suby of Commission Scolaire de la Seigneurie-Des-Mille-Iles)
500 Rue Marie-C.-Daveluy, Boisbriand, QC, J7G 3G7
(450) 433-5380
Emp Here 50
SIC 8211 Elementary and secondary schools

D-U-N-S 20-712-1653 (BR)
COMMISSION SCOLAIRE DE LA SEIGNEURIE-DES-MILLE-ILES
COMMISSION SCOLAIRE DE LA SEIGNEURIE-DES-MILLE-ILES
1650 Av Alexandre-Le-Grand, Boisbriand, QC, J7G 3K1
(450) 433-5514
Emp Here 50
SIC 8211 Elementary and secondary schools

D-U-N-S 25-233-2887 (BR)
COMMISSION SCOLAIRE DE LA SEIGNEURIE-DES-MILLE-ILES
COMMISSION SCOLAIRE DE LA SEIGNEURIE-DES-MILLE-ILES
(Suby of Commission Scolaire de la Seigneurie-Des-Mille-Iles)
1025 Rue Castelneau, Boisbriand, QC, J7G 1V7
(450) 433-5520
Emp Here 40
SIC 8211 Elementary and secondary schools

D-U-N-S 25-603-7540 (BR)
GOUVERNEMENT DE LA PROVINCE DE QUEBEC
GOUVERNEMENT DE LA PROVINCE DE QUEBEC
520 Av Adrien-Chartrand, Boisbriand, QC, J7G 2M2
(450) 435-7567
Emp Here 30
SIC 8351 Child day care services

D-U-N-S 25-244-6273 (BR)
GROUPE LYRAS INC
(Suby of Gestion Lyras Inc)
1400 Boul De La Grande-Allee Bureau, Boisbriand, QC, J7G 2Z8

Emp Here 20
SIC 6411 Insurance agents, brokers, and service

D-U-N-S 25-794-6657 (SL)
L'ECOLE DE HOCKEY CO-JEAN INC
90 Rue Champlain, Boisbriand, QC, J7G 1J8

Emp Here 50   Sales 3,486,617
SIC 7999 Amusement and recreation, nec

D-U-N-S 24-680-0143 (BR)
PHILIPS LIGHTING CANADA LTD
640 Boul Du Cure Boivin, Boisbriand, QC, J7G 2A7
(450) 430-7040
Emp Here 300
SIC 3646 Commercial lighting fixtures

D-U-N-S 24-768-7861 (BR)
PROVIGO DISTRIBUTION INC

PROVIGO
392 Ch De La Grande-Cote, Boisbriand, QC, J7G 1B1

Emp Here 34
SIC 5141 Groceries, general line

D-U-N-S 20-562-1097 (HQ)
REEL COH INC
COH
801 Boul Du Cure-Boivin, Boisbriand, QC, J7G 2J2
(450) 430-6500
Emp Here 150   Emp Total 8
Sales 55,085,329
SIC 3531 Construction machinery
Pr Philippe Frantz
Ex VP Sebastien Darveau
Sec Marie-Andree Gravel
Dir Etienne Gauthier
Dir Jean-Luc Duconseil

D-U-N-S 24-489-5108 (SL)
REVETEMENTS POLYVAL INC, LES
POLYFLEX
(Suby of 2704722 Canada Inc)
520 Boul Du Cure-Boivin, Boisbriand, QC, J7G 2A7
(450) 430-6780
Emp Here 26   Sales 3,720,996
SIC 2851 Paints and allied products

D-U-N-S 25-673-7677 (SL)
SERVICE ALIMENTAIRE DESCO INC
97 Rue Prevost, Boisbriand, QC, J7G 3A1
(450) 437-7182
Emp Here 160   Sales 30,205,730
SIC 2015 Poultry slaughtering and processing
Pr Pr Guy Chevalier

D-U-N-S 25-458-9872 (SL)
SUPERMARCHES JACQUES DAIGLE INC
IGA
(Suby of Placements Jacques Daigle Inc)
25 Boul Des Entreprises, Boisbriand, QC, J7G 3K6
(450) 430-1396
Emp Here 120   Sales 89,992,420
SIC 5411 Grocery stores
Pr Pr Luc Daigle
Robert Daigle

Boisbriand, QC J7H

D-U-N-S 24-858-4047 (HQ)
2755-4609 QUEBEC INC
AUTOCAR MTL EXPRESS
(Suby of Veolia Transdev Canada Inc)
4243 Rue Marcel-Lacasse, Boisbriand, QC, J7H 1N4
(450) 970-2045
Emp Here 20   Emp Total 26
Sales 24,638,160
SIC 4131 Intercity and rural bus transportation
Pr Mark Joseph
Sec Alan Moldawer
Dir Jean-Claude Levesque
Dir Jan Horstmann

D-U-N-S 20-317-6912 (BR)
9218-7384 QUEBEC INC
EMPIRE SPORTS QUEBEC
3330 Av Des Grandes Tourelles, Boisbriand, QC, J7H 0A2
(450) 419-4677
Emp Here 20
SIC 5941 Sporting goods and bicycle shops

D-U-N-S 20-292-5574 (SL)
AP&C REVETEMENTS & POUDRES AVANCEES INC
3765 Rue La Verendrye Bureau 110, Boisbriand, QC, J7H 1R8
(450) 434-1004
Emp Here 26   Sales 2,165,628

SIC 3479 Metal coating and allied services

D-U-N-S 20-563-3113 (BR)
ACOSTA CANADA CORPORATION
(Suby of Acosta Inc.)
1700 Boul Lionel-Bertrand Bureau 100, Boisbriand, QC, J7H 1N7
(450) 435-1000
Emp Here 70
SIC 5141 Groceries, general line

D-U-N-S 24-699-1434 (SL)
ACTIVE CANADA INC
(Suby of Jht Holdings, Inc.)
4065 Rue Marcel-Lacasse, Boisbriand, QC, J7H 1N4
(450) 430-7105
Emp Here 25   Sales 2,845,467
SIC 4213 Trucking, except local

D-U-N-S 24-843-6540 (BR)
ADIDAS CANADA LIMITED
ADIDAS ENTREPOT
3414 Av Des Grandes Tourelles, Boisbriand, QC, J7H 0A2
(450) 420-3434
Emp Here 20
SIC 5941 Sporting goods and bicycle shops

D-U-N-S 20-304-0977 (BR)
BRICK WAREHOUSE LP, THE
BRICK, THE
3400 Av Des Grandes Tourelles, Boisbriand, QC, J7H 0A2
(450) 420-4224
Emp Here 30
SIC 5712 Furniture stores

D-U-N-S 24-581-1708 (HQ)
BUSCH VACUUM TECHNICS INC
BUSCH TECHNIQUE DU VIDE
1740 Boul Lionel-Bertrand, Boisbriand, QC, J7H 1N7
(450) 435-6899
Emp Here 20   Emp Total 3,000
Sales 16,458,769
SIC 3563 Air and gas compressors
Ayhan Busch
Pr Pr Paul Wieser

D-U-N-S 20-584-8281 (BR)
CANADA POST CORPORATION
POSTE CANADA
4570 Rue Ambroise-Lafortune, Boisbriand, QC, J7H 0E5
(450) 435-4527
Emp Here 100
SIC 4311 U.s. postal service

D-U-N-S 25-976-1195 (BR)
COMMISSION SCOLAIRE DE LA SEIGNEURIE-DES-MILLE-ILES
COMMISSION SCOLAIRE DE LA SEIGNEURIE-DES-MILLE-ILES
(Suby of Commission Scolaire de la Seigneurie-Des-Mille-Iles)
3599 Rue Charlotte-Boisjoli, Boisbriand, QC, J7H 1L5
(450) 433-5475
Emp Here 50
SIC 8211 Elementary and secondary schools

D-U-N-S 20-712-1570 (BR)
COMMISSION SCOLAIRE DE LA SEIGNEURIE-DES-MILLE-ILES
COMMISSION SCOLAIRE DE LA SEIGNEURIE-DES-MILLE-ILES
2700 Rue Jean-Charles-Bonenfant, Boisbriand, QC, J7H 1P1
(450) 433-5455
Emp Here 149
SIC 8211 Elementary and secondary schools

D-U-N-S 20-827-2521 (SL)
CONSTRUCTION KIEWIT CIE
(Suby of Peter Kiewit Sons', Inc.)
4333 Boul De La Grande-Allee, Boisbriand, QC, J7H 1M7

---

(450) 435-5756
Emp Here 276   *Sales* 40,991,312
SIC 8711 Engineering services
Pr Christopher A. Loeffler
Dir Scott L. Cassels
Sec Michael F. Norton

D-U-N-S 24-354-4421   (BR)
COSTCO WHOLESALE CANADA LTD
COSTCO
(*Suby of* Costco Wholesale Corporation)
3600 Av Des Grandes Tourelles, Boisbriand,
QC, J7H 0A1
(450) 420-4500
Emp Here 200
SIC 5099 Durable goods, nec

D-U-N-S 24-409-2115   (SL)
DESSINS CADMAX INC
4965 Rue Ambroise-Lafortune Bureau 200,
Boisbriand, QC, J7H 0A4
(450) 621-5557
Emp Here 30   *Sales* 4,240,481
SIC 1791 Structural steel erection

D-U-N-S 24-769-1736   (SL)
DIMENSIONS PORTES ET FENETRES INC
DIMENSION DOORS
4065 Rue Alfred-Laliberte, Boisbriand, QC,
J7H 1P7
(450) 430-4486
Emp Here 130   *Sales* 50,414,602
SIC 5031 Lumber, plywood, and millwork
Pr Pr Francois Audette
 Remy Audette
 Mathieu Audette
 Micheline Pesant

D-U-N-S 24-677-0296   (BR)
DYNO NOBEL CANADA INC
3665 Boul De La Grande-Allee, Boisbriand,
QC, J7H 1H5
(450) 437-1441
Emp Here 40
SIC 2892 Explosives

D-U-N-S 24-391-5589   (BR)
**GOLF TOWN OPERATING LIMITED PART-
NERSHIP**
GOLF TOWN
3410 Av Des Grandes Tourelles, Boisbriand,
QC, J7H 0A2
(450) 420-5418
Emp Here 30
SIC 5941 Sporting goods and bicycle shops

D-U-N-S 24-643-1469   (BR)
GROUPE SPORTSCENE INC
CAGES AUX SPORTS BOISBRIAND
2555 Rue D'Annemasse, Boisbriand, QC, J7H
0A3
(450) 437-2011
Emp Here 20
SIC 5812 Eating places

D-U-N-S 24-346-4521   (BR)
HOME DEPOT OF CANADA INC
(*Suby of* The Home Depot Inc)
2400 Boul Du Faubourg, Boisbriand, QC, J7H
1S3
(450) 971-6061
Emp Here 140
SIC 5251 Hardware stores

D-U-N-S 24-374-0805   (BR)
HUDSON'S BAY COMPANY
DECO DECOUVERTE
3100 Av Des Grandes Tourelles, Boisbriand,
QC, J7H 0A2
(450) 420-9872
Emp Here 30
SIC 5023 Homefurnishings

D-U-N-S 20-253-5274   (SL)
KPH TURCOT, UN PARTENARIAT S.E.N.C
4333 Boul De La Grande-Allee, Boisbriand,
QC, J7H 1M7
(450) 435-5756
Emp Here 750   *Sales* 106,157,819

SIC 8742 Management consulting services
Mgr Huguette Emond

D-U-N-S 25-674-3386   (SL)
KIEWIT ENGINEERING CANADA CO.
(*Suby of* Peter Kiewit Sons', Inc.)
4333 Boul De La Grande-Allee, Boisbriand,
QC, J7H 1M7
(450) 435-5756
Emp Here 50   *Sales* 6,858,306
SIC 1629 Heavy construction, nec
Pr Pr Ernie M. Elko
 Bruce W. Ballai
Sec Gregory D. Brokke
Treas Anne E. Begley
Dir Richard W. Colf

D-U-N-S 24-000-5657   (SL)
**KIEWIT-NUVUMIUT, SOCIETE EN COPAR-
TICIPATION**
4333 Boul De La Grande-Allee, Boisbriand,
QC, J7H 1M7
(450) 435-5756
Emp Here 50   *Sales* 4,231,721
SIC 1081 Metal mining services

D-U-N-S 24-422-3306   (SL)
KINOVA INC
BRAS ROBOTISE
6110 Rue Doris-Lussier, Boisbriand, QC, J7H
0E8
(514) 277-3777
Emp Here 135   *Sales* 8,091,273
SIC 3549 Metalworking machinery, nec
 Charles Deguire
 Louis-Joseph Caron L'ecuyer

D-U-N-S 25-323-6186   (HQ)
PLAISIRS GASTRONOMIQUES INC
CROQUE-MOI
3740 Rue La Verendrye, Boisbriand, QC, J7H
1R5
(450) 433-1970
Emp Here 300   *Emp Total* 330
Sales 40,800,422
SIC 2099 Food preparations, nec
Pr Pr Christophe Beauvais
 Olivier Beauvais
Dir Jean-Philippe Beauvais

D-U-N-S 24-351-2790   (BR)
PLAISIRS GASTRONOMIQUES INC
ALIMENTS NOREL
3735 Rue La Verendrye, Boisbriand, QC, J7H
1R8
(450) 433-3600
Emp Here 30
SIC 2099 Food preparations, nec

D-U-N-S 25-359-3081   (HQ)
PROTECTION INCENDIE VIKING INC
PYROSPEC
1935 Boul Lionel-Bertrand, Boisbriand, QC,
J7H 1N8
(450) 430-7516
Emp Here 60   *Emp Total* 650
Sales 107,328,499
SIC 5063 Electrical apparatus and equipment
Pr Pr Jean-Pierre Asselin
 Marc Gagnon
 Alain Rousseau
Dir Rene Belanger
Dir Maurice Lareau
Dir Kenneth W Graham
 Robert Lapierre
Dir Aleksandar Hoffman

D-U-N-S 20-003-4218   (BR)
PROTECTION INCENDIE VIKING INC
SECURITE POLYGON
1935 Boul Lionel-Bertrand, Boisbriand, QC,
J7H 1N8
(450) 430-7516
Emp Here 80
SIC 7389 Business services, nec

D-U-N-S 25-307-6954   (BR)
SOCIETE DES ALCOOLS DU QUEBEC

S.A.Q. #23202
2735 Rue D'Annemasse, Boisbriand, QC, J7H
0A5
(450) 437-4772
Emp Here 30
SIC 5921 Liquor stores

D-U-N-S 24-354-7267   (BR)
SPECIALITES LASSONDE INC
MONDIV, DIV DE SPECIALITES LASSONDE
(*Suby of* 3346625 Canada Inc)
3810 Rue Alfred-Laliberte, Boisbriand, QC,
J7H 1P8
(450) 979-0717
Emp Here 75
SIC 2033 Canned fruits and specialties

D-U-N-S 24-329-9588   (BR)
STAPLES CANADA INC
BUREAU EN GROS
(*Suby of* Staples, Inc.)
3420 Av Des Grandes Tourelles, Boisbriand,
QC, J7H 0A2
(450) 420-3537
Emp Here 30
SIC 5943 Stationery stores

D-U-N-S 25-024-2179   (SL)
SYSTEMES FIREFLEX INC
1935 Boul Lionel-Bertrand, Boisbriand, QC,
J7H 1N8
(450) 437-3473
Emp Here 25   *Sales* 3,118,504
SIC 3569 General industrial machinery, nec

D-U-N-S 24-656-5043   (BR)
TOYS 'R' US (CANADA) LTD
TOYS 'R' US
(*Suby of* Toys "r" Us, Inc.)
3450 Av Des Grandes Tourelles, Boisbriand,
QC, J7H 0A2
(450) 435-7588
Emp Here 50
SIC 5945 Hobby, toy, and game shops

D-U-N-S 25-674-3303   (SL)
V. K. MASON CONSTRUCTION CO.
(*Suby of* Peter Kiewit Sons', Inc.)
4333 Boul De La Grande-Allee, Boisbriand,
QC, J7H 1M7
(450) 435-5756
Emp Here 50   *Sales* 13,349,760
SIC 1541 Industrial buildings and warehouses
Pr Pr Louie Chapdelaine
Sec Claude Letourneau
VP Randall Zuke
Treas Gregory Brokke
 Bruce Grewcock

D-U-N-S 20-170-2503   (HQ)
V.K. MASON CONSTRUCTION LTD
(*Suby of* V.K. Mason Construction Ltd)
4333 Boul De La Grande-Allee, Boisbriand,
QC, J7H 1M7
(450) 435-5756
Emp Here 45   *Emp Total* 205
Sales 52,487,725
SIC 1541 Industrial buildings and warehouses
Pr Louis Chapdelaine
VP VP John Pretty
VP VP Randall Zuke
Treas Gregory Brokke
 Bruce Grewcock

D-U-N-S 20-857-1471   (BR)
VETEMENTS S & F (CANADA) LTEE
VETEMENTS S F CANADA, LES
3720 Rue La Verendrye, Boisbriand, QC, J7H
1R5

Emp Here 300
SIC 2311 Men's and boy's suits and coats

D-U-N-S 25-868-5858   (SL)
VITRERIE VERTECH (2000) INC
VERTECH FENEXPERT
4275 Boul De La Grande-Allee, Boisbriand,
QC, J7H 1M7

(450) 430-6161
Emp Here 50   *Sales* 3,648,035
SIC 1751 Carpentry work

D-U-N-S 20-569-5534   (BR)
WASTE CONNECTIONS OF CANADA INC
ENVIRO CONNEXIONS
4141 Boul De La Grande-Allee, Boisbriand,
QC, J7H 1M7
(450) 435-2627
Emp Here 200
SIC 4953 Refuse systems

D-U-N-S 24-353-3788   (BR)
**WINNERS MERCHANTS INTERNATIONAL
L.P.**
HOMESENSE
(*Suby of* The TJX Companies Inc)
3430 Av Des Grandes Tourelles, Boisbriand,
QC, J7H 0A2
(450) 420-5215
Emp Here 30
SIC 5651 Family clothing stores

Boischatel, QC G0A

D-U-N-S 25-232-7044   (BR)
**COMMISSION SCOLAIRE DES
PREMIERES-SEIGNEURIES**
ECOLE DU BOCAGE ET DU BOIS JOLI
(*Suby of* Commission Scolaire Des
Premieres-Seigneuries)
25 Cote De L'Eglise, Boischatel, QC, G0A 1H0
(418) 821-8060
Emp Here 35
SIC 8211 Elementary and secondary schools

D-U-N-S 20-711-9848   (BR)
**COMMISSION SCOLAIRE DES
PREMIERES-SEIGNEURIES**
*COMMISSION SCOLAIRE DES
PREMIERES-SEIGNEURIES*
51 Rue Tardif, Boischatel, QC, G0A 1H0
(418) 821-8060
Emp Here 40
SIC 8211 Elementary and secondary schools

Bon-Conseil, QC J0C
Drummomd County

D-U-N-S 20-714-5819   (BR)
AGROPUR COOPERATIVE
NARTEL
81 Rue Saint-Felix, Bon-Conseil, QC, J0C 1A0
(819) 336-2727
Emp Here 180
SIC 5143 Dairy products, except dried or
canned

D-U-N-S 24-337-2773   (BR)
CASCADES CANADA ULC
PLASTIQUES CASCADES - REPLAST
1350 Ch Quatre-Saisons, Bon-Conseil, QC,
J0C 1A0
(819) 336-2440
Emp Here 55
SIC 2899 Chemical preparations, nec

D-U-N-S 20-033-5268   (BR)
**CENTRE DE SANTE & DE SERVICES SOCI-
AUX DRUMMOND**
L'ACCUEIL BON CONSEIL
91 Rue Saint-Thomas, Bon-Conseil, QC, J0C
1A0

Emp Here 75
SIC 8051 Skilled nursing care facilities

D-U-N-S 25-240-1765   (BR)
COMMISSION SCOLAIRE DES CHENES
ECOLE NOTRE DAME DU BON CONSEIL
(*Suby of* Commission Scolaire des Chenes)

500 Rue Saint-Bruno, Bon-Conseil, QC, J0C 1A0
(819) 850-1622
Emp Here 30
SIC 8211 Elementary and secondary schools

D-U-N-S 20-419-8113   (SL)
PIERCON INC
387 Rue Notre-Dame, Bon-Conseil, QC, J0C 1A0
(819) 336-3777
Emp Here 50   *Sales* 3,210,271
SIC 3281 Cut stone and stone products

D-U-N-S 24-405-6438   (BR)
SINTRA INC
CENTRE DU QUEBEC
911 Rue Matthieu, Bon-Conseil, QC, J0C 1A0
(819) 336-2666
Emp Here 30
SIC 1611 Highway and street construction

D-U-N-S 24-395-3259   (SL)
SIXPRO INC
1576 10e Rang De Simpson, Bon-Conseil, QC, J0C 1A0
(819) 336-2117
Emp Here 180   *Sales* 11,307,948
SIC 3479 Metal coating and allied services
  Richard Bourbeau
Dir Claude Fournier
Dir Sylvain Parenteau
Dir Nathalie Joyal
Dir Denis Valois
Dir Marc Paquin

Bonaventure, QC G0C
Bonaventure County

D-U-N-S 25-359-9823   (BR)
COMMISSION SCOLAIRE RENE-LEVESQUE
ECOLE FRANCOIS-THIBAULT
111 Av De Grand-Pre, Bonaventure, QC, G0C 1E0
(418) 534-2990
Emp Here 35
SIC 8211 Elementary and secondary schools

D-U-N-S 25-232-3506   (BR)
COMMISSION SCOLAIRE RENE-LEVESQUE
ECOLE AUX QUATRES VENTS
143 Av De Louisbourg Bureau 4, Bonaventure, QC, G0C 1E0
(418) 534-2211
Emp Here 60
SIC 8211 Elementary and secondary schools

D-U-N-S 25-231-9116   (BR)
EASTERN SHORES SCHOOL BOARD
BONAVENTURE POLYVALENTE SCHOOL
(*Suby of* Eastern Shores School Board)
143 Av De Louisbourg, Bonaventure, QC, G0C 1E0
(418) 534-3446
Emp Here 20
SIC 8211 Elementary and secondary schools

Boucherville, QC J4B
Chambly County

D-U-N-S 25-307-2946   (BR)
123273 CANADA INC
PHARMACIE JEAN COUTU
1001 Boul De Montarville Bureau 49, Boucherville, QC, J4B 6P5
(450) 641-1151
Emp Here 65
SIC 5912 Drug stores and proprietary stores

D-U-N-S 24-736-8553   (SL)

2278988 ONTARIO INC
(*Suby of* Groupe Colabor Inc)
1620 Boul De Montarville, Boucherville, QC, J4B 8P4
(450) 449-4911
Emp Here 400   *Sales* 140,761,440
SIC 5141 Groceries, general line
Pr Pr Gilles C. Lachance
  Michel Loignon
  Claude Picard
  Robert Panet-Raymond
  Donlad Dube
  Claude Gariepy
  Jacques Landreville

D-U-N-S 25-210-6000   (SL)
2639-6564 QUEBEC INC
CAGE AUX SPORTS
1150a Rue Volta, Boucherville, QC, J4B 7A2
(450) 641-2243
Emp Here 57   *Sales* 1,751,057
SIC 5812 Eating places

D-U-N-S 25-202-4211   (SL)
2953-6778 QUEBEC INC
S.R.M. PLOMBERIE & CHAUFFAGE
549 Rue De Verrazano Bureau 3000, Boucherville, QC, J4B 7W2
(450) 449-1516
Emp Here 525   *Sales* 61,840,800
SIC 1711 Plumbing, heating, air-conditioning
Pr Pr Eddy Savoie
  Carmelle Savoie Ouellette
  Nathalie Savoie
  Regis Leblanc

D-U-N-S 24-870-9628   (SL)
9124-5704 QUEBEC INC
DUVAL TOYOTA
1175 Rue Ampere, Boucherville, QC, J4B 7M6
(450) 655-2350
Emp Here 50   *Sales* 25,362,500
SIC 5511 New and used car dealers
  Luc Duval
VP VP Bernard Duval

D-U-N-S 24-368-2486   (SL)
9164-2033 QUEBEC INC
HOTEL MORTAGNE
(*Suby of* 9138-4438 Quebec Inc)
1228 Rue Nobel, Boucherville, QC, J4B 5H1
(450) 655-9966
Emp Here 90   *Sales* 3,939,878
SIC 7011 Hotels and motels

D-U-N-S 20-317-6938   (BR)
9218-7384 QUEBEC INC
EMPIRE SPORTS QUEBEC
1155 Place Nobel Bureau C, Boucherville, QC, J4B 7L3
(450) 645-9998
Emp Here 26
SIC 5941 Sporting goods and bicycle shops

D-U-N-S 20-716-0495   (BR)
A D P DEALER SERVICES LTD
A D P SERVICES AUX CONCESSIONNAIRES
(*Suby of* Automatic Data Processing, Inc.)
204 Boul De Montarville, Boucherville, QC, J4B 6S2
(450) 641-7200
Emp Here 50
SIC 7371 Custom computer programming services

D-U-N-S 24-858-9269   (BR)
ADP CANADA CO
DEALER SERVICES GROUP
(*Suby of* Automatic Data Processing, Inc.)
204 Boul De Montarville, Boucherville, QC, J4B 6S2
(450) 641-7200
Emp Here 110
SIC 7374 Data processing and preparation

D-U-N-S 25-093-3350   (HQ)
AGRI-MONDO INC

(*Suby of* 3914828 Canada Inc)
165 Rue J.-A.-Bombardier, Boucherville, QC, J4B 8P1
(450) 449-9899
Emp Here 49   *Emp Total* 70
Sales 4,377,642
SIC 5431 Fruit and vegetable markets

D-U-N-S 20-554-0565   (SL)
ART DE VIVRE FABRICATION INC
240 Boul Industriel, Boucherville, QC, J4B 2X4
(450) 449-4430
Emp Here 20   *Sales* 1,386,253
SIC 2844 Toilet preparations

D-U-N-S 24-364-8073   (HQ)
AZELIS CANADA INC
ADDITIFS DE PERFORMANCE ELITE
1570 Rue Ampere Bureau 106, Boucherville, QC, J4B 7L4
(450) 449-6363
Emp Here 50   *Sales* 14,373,258
SIC 5169 Chemicals and allied products, nec
Pr Frank Bergonzi
  Jean-Pierre Pelchat
Sec Bernard Vinet
  Terence Moriarty

D-U-N-S 24-357-2950   (BR)
BPR INC
(*Suby of* Tetra Tech, Inc.)
1205 Rue Ampere Bureau 310, Boucherville, QC, J4B 7M6
(450) 655-8440
Emp Here 50
SIC 8711 Engineering services

D-U-N-S 20-699-9752   (BR)
BANQUE DE DEVELOPPEMENT DU CANADA
BDC
1570 Rue Ampere Bureau 300, Boucherville, QC, J4B 7L4
(888) 463-6232
Emp Here 40
SIC 6141 Personal credit institutions

D-U-N-S 25-344-4970   (HQ)
BELL TECHNICAL SOLUTIONS INC
75 Rue J.-A.-Bombardier Suite 200, Boucherville, QC, J4B 8P1
(450) 449-1120
Emp Here 90   *Emp Total* 48,090
Sales 282,698,700
SIC 1731 Electrical work
Dir Declan Brady
Sec Michel Lalande

D-U-N-S 20-860-3092   (SL)
BELLEMONT POWELL LTEE
1570 Ampere St Bureau 508, Boucherville, QC, J4B 7L4
(450) 641-2661
Emp Here 22   *Sales* 7,754,640
SIC 5141 Groceries, general line
Pr Pr Michel Levac
VP Emile Bonneville

D-U-N-S 24-760-9568   (BR)
BOUTIN, V. EXPRESS INC
50 Ch Du Tremblay, Boucherville, QC, J4B 6Z5
(450) 449-7373
Emp Here 50
SIC 4213 Trucking, except local

D-U-N-S 20-175-3253   (BR)
CHEP CANADA INC
331 Ch Du Tremblay, Boucherville, QC, J4B 7M1
(450) 449-2374
Emp Here 37
SIC 7359 Equipment rental and leasing, nec

D-U-N-S 24-368-7873   (BR)
CAISSE DESJARDINS DE BOUCHERVILLE
CENTRE DE SERVICES FORT SAINT-LOUIS

500 Boul Du Fort-Saint-Louis, Boucherville, QC, J4B 1S4
(450) 655-9041
Emp Here 55
SIC 6062 State credit unions

D-U-N-S 24-741-6738   (BR)
CARQUEST CANADA LTD
CARQUEST DISTRIBUTION CENTER
(*Suby of* Advance Auto Parts, Inc.)
1670 Rue Eiffel Bureau 100, Boucherville, QC, J4B 7W1
(450) 641-5700
Emp Here 150
SIC 5531 Auto and home supply stores

D-U-N-S 20-357-2458   (BR)
CASCADES CS+ INC
131 Rue Jacques-Menard, Boucherville, QC, J4B 0K5
(819) 363-5100
Emp Here 35
SIC 8711 Engineering services

D-U-N-S 24-890-8139   (SL)
CENTRE D'ACCEUIL JEANNE CREVIER
151 Rue De Muy, Boucherville, QC, J4B 4W7

Emp Here 80   *Sales* 2,918,428
SIC 8361 Residential care

D-U-N-S 25-258-3224   (BR)
CENTRE DE SANTE ET DE SERVICES SOCIAUX PIERRE-BOUCHER
C L S C DES SEIGNEURIES
160 Boul De Montarville Bureau 201, Boucherville, QC, J4B 6S2
(450) 468-3530
Emp Here 30
SIC 8621 Professional organizations

D-U-N-S 25-523-8594   (HQ)
CENTRE DE LA PETITE ENFANCE SES AMIS
GARDERIE SES AMIS
(*Suby of* Centre de la Petite Enfance Ses Amis)
238 Rue Dupernay, Boucherville, QC, J4B 1G6
(450) 655-1357
Emp Here 45   *Emp Total* 99
Sales 2,991,389
SIC 8351 Child day care services

D-U-N-S 25-359-5581   (BR)
CINTAS CANADA LIMITED
SALLY FOURMY & ASSOCIATES
(*Suby of* Cintas Corporation)
1470 Rue Nobel, Boucherville, QC, J4B 5H3
(450) 449-4747
Emp Here 85
SIC 7218 Industrial launderers

D-U-N-S 25-233-9890   (BR)
COMMISSION SCOLAIRE DES PATRIOTES
CENTRE DES SERVICES ALTERNATIFS
544 Rue Saint-Sacrement, Boucherville, QC, J4B 3K9
(450) 655-4521
Emp Here 38
SIC 8211 Elementary and secondary schools

D-U-N-S 25-234-2068   (BR)
COMMISSION SCOLAIRE DES PATRIOTES
COMMISSION SCOLAIRE DES PATRIOTES
900 Boul Du Fort-Saint-Louis, Boucherville, QC, J4B 1T6
(450) 655-9901
Emp Here 50
SIC 8211 Elementary and secondary schools

D-U-N-S 25-240-0080   (BR)
COMMISSION SCOLAIRE DES PATRIOTES
COMMISSION SCOLAIRE DES PATRIOTES
850 Rue Etienne-Brule, Boucherville, QC, J4B 6T2
(450) 655-7892
Emp Here 40

SIC 8211 Elementary and secondary schools

D-U-N-S 24-012-1991   (BR)
COMMISSION SCOLAIRE DES PATRIOTES
COMMISSION SCOLAIRE DES PATRIOTES
225 Rue Joseph-Martel, Boucherville, QC,
J4B 1L1
(450) 655-8088
Emp Here 30
SIC 8211 Elementary and secondary schools

D-U-N-S 25-233-2176   (BR)
COMMISSION SCOLAIRE DES PATRIOTES
COMMISSION SCOLAIRE DES PATRIOTES
666 Rue Le Laboureur, Boucherville, QC, J4B
3R7
(450) 655-8930
Emp Here 40
SIC 8211 Elementary and secondary schools

D-U-N-S 25-234-1987   (BR)
COMMISSION SCOLAIRE DES PATRIOTES
ECOLE ANTOINE GIROUARD
650 Rue Antoine-Girouard, Boucherville, QC,
J4B 3E5
(450) 655-5991
Emp Here 35
SIC 8211 Elementary and secondary schools

D-U-N-S 20-765-0565   (BR)
**COMPAGNIE   COMMONWEALTH   PLY-
WOOD LTEE, LA**
100 Rue De Vaudreuil, Boucherville, QC, J4B
5G4
(514) 527-4581
Emp Here 51
SIC 5031 Lumber, plywood, and millwork

D-U-N-S 20-109-6406   (BR)
COOP FEDEREE, LA
OLYMEL
1580 Rue Eiffel, Boucherville, QC, J4B 5Y1
(450) 449-6344
Emp Here 200
SIC 5191 Farm supplies

D-U-N-S 24-340-5474   (BR)
COSTCO WHOLESALE CANADA LTD
COSTCO WHOLESALE
(*Suby of* Costco Wholesale Corporation)
635 Ch De Touraine, Boucherville, QC, J4B
5E4
(450) 645-2631
Emp Here 200
SIC 5099 Durable goods, nec

D-U-N-S 20-237-6513   (HQ)
DANONE INC
DANONE CANADA
100 Rue De Lauzon, Boucherville, QC, J4B
1E6
(450) 655-7331
Emp Here 400   *Emp Total* 844
Sales 72,595,897
SIC 2026 Fluid milk
Pr Pedro Silveira
 Isabelle Rayle-Doiron
VP Fin Clemence Delcourt

D-U-N-S 24-935-4382   (HQ)
DANS UN JARDIN CANADA INC
PARFUMERIES DANS UN JARDIN CANADA
240 Boul Industriel, Boucherville, QC, J4B
2X4
(450) 449-2121
Emp Here 40   *Emp Total* 65
Sales 1,021,450
SIC 5999 Miscellaneous retail stores, nec

D-U-N-S 20-707-3466   (BR)
**DATA COMMUNICATIONS MANAGEMENT
CORP**
LES GROUPE DE DATA
1570 Rue Ampere Bureau 3000, Boucherville,
QC, J4B 7L4

Emp Here 70
SIC 2752 Commercial printing, lithographic

D-U-N-S 24-696-2307   (SL)
**DISTRIBUTIONS ALIMENTAIRES LE MAR-
QUIS INC**
MARQUIS
1630 Rue Eiffel Bureau 1, Boucherville, QC,
J4B 7W1
(450) 645-1999
Emp Here 100   *Sales* 4,961,328
SIC 7389 Business services, nec

D-U-N-S 24-864-9527   (HQ)
EMBALLAGES CARROUSEL INC, LES
CAVALIER ET DESSIN
(*Suby of* Emballages Carrousel Inc, Les)
1401 Rue Ampere, Boucherville, QC, J4B 6C5
(450) 655-2025
Emp Here 100   *Emp Total* 250
Sales 41,076,874
SIC 5113 Industrial and personal service pa-
per
Pr Brigitte Jalbert
S&M/VP Martin Boily

D-U-N-S 24-024-9933   (BR)
EMPIRE SPORTS INC
1155c Place Nobel, Boucherville, QC, J4B
7L3
(450) 645-9998
Emp Here 80
SIC 5941 Sporting goods and bicycle shops

D-U-N-S 24-885-1722   (BR)
ENGLOBE CORP
LVM DIVISION OF
85 Rue J.-A.-Bombardier Bureau 100,
Boucherville, QC, J4B 8P1
(450) 641-1740
Emp Here 50
SIC 8742 Management consulting services

D-U-N-S 24-760-3165   (BR)
ENTREPRISES CD VARIN INC, LES
PETRO CANADA
181 Boul De Mortagne, Boucherville, QC, J4B
1A9
(450) 641-9536
Emp Here 20
SIC 5541 Gasoline service stations

D-U-N-S 25-201-3263   (SL)
**ENTREPRISES PATES ET CROUTES L.B.
INC, LES**
ALIMENTS NOVALI
14 Rue De Montgolfier, Boucherville, QC, J4B
7Y4
(450) 655-7790
Emp Here 50   *Sales* 4,450,603
SIC 2045 Prepared flour mixes and doughs

D-U-N-S 20-006-4322   (BR)
ESAB GROUP CANADA INC
ESAB WELDING & CUTTING PRODUCTS
(*Suby of* Colfax Corporation)
25 Rue De Lauzon Bureau B, Boucherville,
QC, J4B 1E7
(450) 655-4318
Emp Here 50
SIC 5084 Industrial machinery and equipment

D-U-N-S 20-265-6013   (HQ)
EUROVIA QUEBEC CONSTRUCTION INC
EUROVIA QC CONSTRUCTION
(*Suby of* Eurovia Quebec Construction Inc)
1550 Rue Ampere Bureau 200, Boucherville,
QC, J4B 7L4
(450) 641-8000
Emp Here 150   *Emp Total* 250
Sales 29,184,280
SIC 1611 Highway and street construction
Pr Patrick Sulliot
Treas Xavier Lansade
Dir Xavier Neuschwander
Dir Gabriel Duchesne

D-U-N-S 20-716-0487   (BR)
EXCELDOR COOPERATIVE
1205 Rue Ampere Bureau 201, Boucherville,
QC, J4B 7M6

Emp Here 24
SIC 5499 Miscellaneous food stores

D-U-N-S 25-646-4942   (SL)
FLEXTOR INC
61 Ch Du Tremblay, Boucherville, QC, J4B 7L6
(450) 449-9882
Emp Here 40   *Sales* 2,480,664
SIC 3822 Environmental controls

D-U-N-S 24-005-1529   (SL)
FONDATION SOURCE BLEU
*MAISON DE SOINS PALLIATIFS SOURCE
BLEUE*
1130 Rue De Montbrun, Boucherville, QC,
J4B 8W6
(450) 641-3165
Emp Here 49   *Sales* 5,982,777
SIC 8699 Membership organizations, nec
Pr Annie Moisan

D-U-N-S 24-022-8994   (BR)
FORMATRAD INC
FORMATRAD
(*Suby of* Formatrad Inc)
131 Rue Monseigneur-Tache, Boucherville,
QC, J4B 2K4
(514) 328-6819
Emp Here 50
SIC 8742 Management consulting services

D-U-N-S 24-509-8439   (SL)
FREEMAN-ALIMENTEL INC
1250 Rue Nobel Bureau 190, Boucherville,
QC, J4B 5H1

Emp Here 125   *Sales* 45,449,600
SIC 5141 Groceries, general line
Pr Pierre Lafond
VP Rene Parent

D-U-N-S 25-524-4949   (SL)
FUJI SEMEC INC
230 Rue J.-A.-Bombardier Bureau 1,
Boucherville, QC, J4B 8V6
(450) 641-4811
Emp Here 20   *Sales* 952,876
SIC 7629 Electrical repair shops

D-U-N-S 20-292-3736   (BR)
G.C.M. CONSULTANTS INC
GCM CONSULTANTS
1310 Rue Nobel, Boucherville, QC, J4B 5H3
(514) 351-8350
Emp Here 20
SIC 8711 Engineering services

D-U-N-S 24-205-4000   (SL)
GAZ METRO PLUS INC
GMP
1250 Rue Nobel Bureau 250, Boucherville,
QC, J4B 5H1
(450) 641-6300
Emp Here 57   *Sales* 3,429,153
SIC 7699 Repair services, nec

D-U-N-S 20-013-0974   (SL)
GESTION MICHEL JULIEN INC
115 Rue De Lauzon, Boucherville, QC, J4B
1E7
(450) 641-3150
Emp Here 110   *Sales* 21,956,266
SIC 6712 Bank holding companies
Pr Pr Julien Michel

D-U-N-S 24-012-3997   (BR)
GORDON FOOD SERVICE CANADA LTD
550 Rue Louis-Pasteur, Boucherville, QC, J4B
7Z1
(450) 655-4400
Emp Here 50
SIC 5141 Groceries, general line

D-U-N-S 24-814-1079   (HQ)
GRAYMONT (QC) INC
AGSTONE
25 Rue De Lauzon Bureau 206, Boucherville,
QC, J4B 1E7

(450) 449-2262
Emp Here 20   *Emp Total* 1,500
SIC 1422 Crushed and broken limestone

D-U-N-S 24-119-1431   (BR)
GROUPE ARCHAMBAULT INC
584 Ch De Touraine Bureau 104, Boucherville,
QC, J4B 8S5
(450) 552-8080
Emp Here 40
SIC 5736 Musical instrument stores

D-U-N-S 20-194-6050   (HQ)
GROUPE BMR INC
BMR AGRIZONE
(*Suby of* Gestion BMR Inc)
1501 Rue Ampere Bureau 200, Boucherville,
QC, J4B 5Z5
(450) 655-2441
Emp Here 70   *Emp Total* 1
Sales 41,660,560
SIC 5039 Construction materials, nec
Pr Ghislain Gervais
VP Luc Forget
VP Murial Dubois
Sec Jean-Francois Harel
Genl Mgr Martin Juneau

D-U-N-S 25-088-5787   (BR)
GROUPE BOUTIN INC
128 Ch Du Tremblay, Boucherville, QC, J4B
6Z6
(450) 449-7373
Emp Here 500
SIC 4213 Trucking, except local

D-U-N-S 20-139-2375   (BR)
GROUPE CANAM INC
MUROX
270 Ch Du Tremblay, Boucherville, QC, J4B
5X9
(450) 641-4000
Emp Here 150
SIC 3441 Fabricated structural Metal

D-U-N-S 25-542-5340   (BR)
GROUPE CANAM INC
CANAM HAMBRO
270 Ch Du Tremblay, Boucherville, QC, J4B
5X9
(450) 641-4000
Emp Here 35
SIC 3312 Blast furnaces and steel mills

D-U-N-S 25-883-1684   (BR)
GROUPE CANAM INC
200 Boul Industriel, Boucherville, QC, J4B
2X4
(450) 641-8770
Emp Here 80
SIC 3441 Fabricated structural Metal

D-U-N-S 24-942-4482   (BR)
GROUPE CANAM INC
INDUSTRIES TANGUAY
270 Ch Du Tremblay, Boucherville, QC, J4B
5X9
(418) 251-3152
Emp Here 140
SIC 3531 Construction machinery

D-U-N-S 20-330-7947   (BR)
GROUPE DCM INC
SINTERS AMERICA USINAGE EXPRESS
95 Ch Du Tremblay Bureau 3, Boucherville,
QC, J4B 7K4
(450) 449-1698
Emp Here 50
SIC 3357 Nonferrous wiredrawing and insulat-
ing

D-U-N-S 24-994-1873   (BR)
**GROUPE DES MEDIAS TRANSCONTINEN-
TAL DE LA NOUVELLE-ECOSSE INC**
*IMPRIMERIE   TRANSCONTINENTAL
BOUCHERVILLE*
(*Suby of* Groupe Des Medias Transcontinental
de la Nouvelle-Ecosse Inc)
1485 Rue De Coulomb, Boucherville, QC, J4B

7L8
(450) 641-9000
Emp Here 325
SIC 2721 Periodicals

D-U-N-S 24-357-7751   (BR)
GROUPE HAMELIN INC
ENTREPRISES HAMELIN, DIVISION DE
150 Boul Industriel, Boucherville, QC, J4B
2X3
(450) 655-4110
Emp Here 70
SIC 2821 Plastics materials and resins

D-U-N-S 20-980-1315   (HQ)
GROUPE MASTER INC, LE
(*Suby of* Gestion Groupe Master Inc)
1675 Boul De Montarville, Boucherville, QC,
J4B 7W4
(514) 527-2301
Emp Here 150   *Emp Total* 1
Sales 233,839,044
SIC 5075 Warm air heating and air condition-
ing
Treas Michel Ringuet
Ch Bd Jacques Foisy
Pr Louis St-Laurent
VP Alain Fournier
Sec Jean-Francois Routhier
Dir Marc Paiement

D-U-N-S 20-514-4723   (BR)
GROUPE ROBERT INC
CENTRE DE DISTRIBUTION ROBERT
65 Rue De Vaudreuil, Boucherville, QC, J4B
1K7
(450) 641-1727
Emp Here 200
SIC 4225 General warehousing and storage

D-U-N-S 25-865-1660   (BR)
GROUPE ROBERT INC
ROBERT TRANSPORT
20 Boul Marie-Victorin, Boucherville, QC, J4B
1V5
(514) 521-1011
Emp Here 100
SIC 4213 Trucking, except local

D-U-N-S 24-870-0155   (BR)
GROUPE ROBERT INC
TRANSPORT ROBERT
20 Boul Marie-Victorin, Boucherville, QC, J4B
1V5
(514) 521-1011
Emp Here 500
SIC 4212 Local trucking, without storage

D-U-N-S 20-963-2470   (SL)
GROUPE DE RADIOLOGIE RIVE-SUD INC
600 Boul Du Fort-Saint-Louis Bureau,
Boucherville, QC, J4B 1S7
(450) 655-2430
Emp Here 80   *Sales* 6,695,700
SIC 8011 Offices and clinics of medical doc-
tors
Pr Pr Maurice Dufresne
Sec Jean-Marc Dumas

D-U-N-S 24-870-0692   (BR)
HMI CONSTRUCTION INC
1451 Rue Graham-Bell, Boucherville, QC, J4B
6A1
(450) 449-3999
Emp Here 50
SIC 1711 Plumbing, heating, air-conditioning

D-U-N-S 20-760-8662   (HQ)
HALL CHEM MFG INC
(*Suby of* Chemarketing Industries Inc)
1270 Rue Nobel, Boucherville, QC, J4B 5H1
(450) 645-0296
Emp Here 38   *Emp Total* 15
Sales 5,836,856
SIC 2899 Chemical preparations, nec
Pr Pr James Robert Fell

D-U-N-S 20-104-0206   (BR)
HONDA CANADA FINANCE INC

ACURA SERVICES FINANCIER
1750 Rue Eiffel, Boucherville, QC, J4B 7W1
(450) 641-9062
Emp Here 40
SIC 6141 Personal credit institutions

D-U-N-S 20-726-4722   (BR)
HONDA CANADA INC
ACURA
1750 Rue Eiffel, Boucherville, QC, J4B 7W1
(450) 655-6161
Emp Here 115
SIC 5012 Automobiles and other motor vehi-
cles

D-U-N-S 20-646-9392   (BR)
IKEA CANADA LIMITED PARTNERSHIP
IKEA CANADA LIMITED PARTNERSHIP
586 Ch De Touraine, Boucherville, QC, J4B
5E4

Emp Here 300
SIC 5712 Furniture stores

D-U-N-S 20-016-8271   (HQ)
IMAGIX IMAGERIE MEDICALE INC
SOUTH SHORE RADIOLOGISTS
(*Suby of* Imagix Imagerie Medicale Inc)
600 Boul Du Fort-Saint-Louis Unite 202,
Boucherville, QC, J4B 1S7
(450) 655-2430
Emp Here 50   *Emp Total* 75
Sales 4,523,563
SIC 8011 Offices and clinics of medical doc-
tors

D-U-N-S 20-221-8814   (SL)
**INDUSTRIES D'ACIER INOXYDABLE LIMI-
TEE**
(*Suby of* Gestion L.P.B. Inc)
1440 Rue Graham-Bell, Boucherville, QC, J4B
6H5
(450) 449-4000
Emp Here 110   *Sales* 12,038,516
SIC 3312 Blast furnaces and steel mills
Pr Real Bourret
VP Alain Bourret
  Guy Bourret

D-U-N-S 25-305-2344   (BR)
INNVEST PROPERTIES CORP
COMFORT INN
(*Suby of* Innvest Properties Corp)
96 Boul De Mortagne, Boucherville, QC, J4B
5M7
(450) 641-2880
Emp Here 22
SIC 7011 Hotels and motels

D-U-N-S 25-857-3591   (SL)
INSTALLATION FOCUS INC
1310 Rue Nobel, Boucherville, QC, J4B 5H3
(514) 644-5551
Emp Here 50   *Sales* 5,889,600
SIC 1799 Special trade contractors, nec
Pr Pr Jean-Francois Houde
Dir Robert Lacoste
Dir Stephane Lemieux

D-U-N-S 24-164-4835   (BR)
JOHNVINCE FOODS
ALIM JONHVINCE
(*Suby of* Johnvince Foods)
1630 Rue Eiffel Bureau 1, Boucherville, QC,
J4B 7W1
(450) 645-1999
Emp Here 100
SIC 4783 Packing and crating

D-U-N-S 24-676-8782   (SL)
LABORATOIRE DU-VAR INC
1460 Rue Graham-Bell, Boucherville, QC, J4B
6H5
(450) 641-4740
Emp Here 60   *Sales* 4,937,631
SIC 2844 Toilet preparations

D-U-N-S 25-523-0443   (BR)

LES EDITIONS QUEBEC-AMERIQUE INC
1380 Rue De Coulomb, Boucherville, QC, J4B
7J4
(450) 655-5163
Emp Here 50
SIC 4226 Special warehousing and storage,
nec

D-U-N-S 24-825-8761   (BR)
MANUGYPSE INC
DISTRIBUTION ACADIA
1289 Rue Newton, Boucherville, QC, J4B 5H2
(450) 655-5100
Emp Here 30
SIC 5211 Lumber and other building materials

D-U-N-S 25-201-4071   (BR)
MARMON/KEYSTONE CANADA INC
(*Suby of* Berkshire Hathaway Inc.)
290 Ch Du Tremblay, Boucherville, QC, J4B
5X9
(514) 527-9153
Emp Here 40
SIC 5051 Metals service centers and offices

D-U-N-S 25-097-8012   (BR)
MEGA GROUP INC
MEGA GROUP
1070 Rue Lionel-Daunais Bureau 200,
Boucherville, QC, J4B 8R6
(450) 449-9007
Emp Here 21
SIC 5021 Furniture

D-U-N-S 20-715-4530   (BR)
METRO RICHELIEU INC
SUPER C
575 Ch De Touraine Bureau 300, Boucherville,
QC, J4B 5E4
(450) 655-8111
Emp Here 70
SIC 5411 Grocery stores

D-U-N-S 24-224-3780   (SL)
MODERCO INC
115 Rue De Lauzon, Boucherville, QC, J4B
1E7
(450) 641-3150
Emp Here 110   *Sales* 11,025,249
SIC 2542 Partitions and fixtures, except wood
  Stephan Julien

D-U-N-S 24-253-5243   (HQ)
MOTOVAN CORPORATION
*ACCESSOIRES DE VEHICULES TOUT TER-
RAIN*
1391 Rue Gay-Lussac Bureau 100,
Boucherville, QC, J4B 7K1
(450) 449-3903
Emp Here 130   *Emp Total* 135
Sales 21,656,275
SIC 5013 Motor vehicle supplies and new
parts
  James Paladino
VP Michael Paladino
  Carlo Paladino

D-U-N-S 25-167-3083   (BR)
NEWLY WEDS FOODS CO.
ALIMENTS NEWLY WEDS, LES
1381 Rue Ampere, Boucherville, QC, J4B 5Z5
(450) 641-2200
Emp Here 1,000
SIC 2099 Food preparations, nec

D-U-N-S 20-059-9145   (BR)
OLYMEL S.E.C.
OLYMEL
1580 Rue Eiffel, Boucherville, QC, J4B 5Y1
(450) 449-6344
Emp Here 300
SIC 5147 Meats and meat products

D-U-N-S 25-173-7888   (BR)
OLYMEL S.E.C.
1580 Rue Eiffel, Boucherville, QC, J4B 5Y1
(514) 858-9000
Emp Here 200

SIC 2011 Meat packing plants

D-U-N-S 20-563-3274   (HQ)
PLB INTERNATIONAL INC
1361 Rue Graham-Bell, Boucherville, QC, J4B
6A1
(450) 655-3155
Emp Here 25   *Emp Total* 100
Sales 10,221,762
SIC 2047 Dog and cat food
Pr Pr Jocelyn Brasseur
  Jacinthe Brasseur
  Jean Brasseur

D-U-N-S 20-323-6013   (SL)
PENIGUEL MARIE-JOSEE
CENTRE MINCEUR DE BOUCHERVILLE
1015 Rue Lionel-Daunais Bureau 104,
Boucherville, QC, J4B 0B1
(450) 552-4552
Emp Here 50   *Sales* 1,969,939
SIC 8322 Individual and family services

D-U-N-S 24-121-1973   (BR)
PEPSICO CANADA ULC
FRITO LAY CANADA
(*Suby of* Pepsico, Inc.)
1405 Rue Graham-Bell Bureau 103,
Boucherville, QC, J4B 6A1

Emp Here 20
SIC 2099 Food preparations, nec

D-U-N-S 20-050-5357   (HQ)
PLASTIPAK INDUSTRIES INC
150 Boul Industriel, Boucherville, QC, J4B
2X3
(450) 650-2200
Emp Here 21   *Emp Total* 125
Sales 49,905,119
SIC 3089 Plastics products, nec
  Nadine Hamelin

D-U-N-S 20-996-0868   (BR)
PRIME RESTAURANTS INC
CASEY'S RESTO BAR
(*Suby of* Cara Holdings Limited)
1165 Rue Volta, Boucherville, QC, J4B 7M7
(450) 641-4800
Emp Here 45
SIC 5812 Eating places

D-U-N-S 20-191-0676   (HQ)
PRODUITS CHIMIQUES MAGNUS LIMITEE
(*Suby of* Gestion Magnus Inc)
1271 Rue Ampere, Boucherville, QC, J4B 5Z5
(450) 655-1344
Emp Here 75   *Emp Total* 1
Sales 18,846,580
SIC 2899 Chemical preparations, nec
  Denis Pichet

D-U-N-S 24-211-7476   (BR)
PROVIGO DISTRIBUTION INC
MAXI
520 Boul Du Fort-Saint-Louis, Boucherville,
QC, J4B 1S5
(450) 641-4985
Emp Here 50
SIC 5411 Grocery stores

D-U-N-S 25-827-6310   (BR)
PROVIGO DISTRIBUTION INC
MAXI
1235 Rue Nobel, Boucherville, QC, J4B 8E4

Emp Here 90
SIC 5411 Grocery stores

D-U-N-S 24-813-6228   (BR)
PROVIGO DISTRIBUTION INC
*CENTRE DISTRIBUTION FRUITS ET
LEGUMES*
180 Ch Du Tremblay, Boucherville, QC, J4B
7W3
(450) 449-8000
Emp Here 700
SIC 5148 Fresh fruits and vegetables

D-U-N-S 25-323-7747   (BR)
PROVIGO INC
PROVIGO BOUCHERVILLE
1001 Boul De Montarville Bureau 1, Boucherville, QC, J4B 6P5
(450) 449-0081
Emp Here 75
SIC 5411 Grocery stores

D-U-N-S 24-515-6492   (BR)
PUROLATOR INC.
PUROLATOR INC
1330 Rue Graham-Bell, Boucherville, QC, J4B 6H5
(450) 641-2430
Emp Here 298
SIC 4731 Freight transportation arrangement

D-U-N-S 20-500-8410   (BR)
RHI CANADA INC
1465 Rue Graham-Bell, Boucherville, QC, J4B 6A1
(450) 641-1730
Emp Here 35
SIC 5023 Homefurnishings

D-U-N-S 24-676-4757   (BR)
RPM CANADA
TREMCO
(*Suby of* RPM International Inc.)
1445 Rue De Coulomb, Boucherville, QC, J4B 7L8
(450) 449-4487
Emp Here 20
SIC 3531 Construction machinery

D-U-N-S 25-684-9928   (HQ)
RTQ INC
RESERVOIRS TRANS-QUEBEC
(*Suby of* Clayton, Dubilier & Rice, Inc.)
31 Rue De Montgolfier, Boucherville, QC, J4B 8C4
(450) 449-6440
Emp Here 38   *Emp Total* 33,045
Sales 17,336,040
SIC 1389 Oil and gas field services, nec
Pr Pr Peter Schaefer
 Guy Trepanier
Dir Mike Cherpash

D-U-N-S 20-005-8431   (BR)
RIVERSIDE SCHOOL BOARD
BOUCHERVILLE ELEMENTARY SCHOOL
800 Rue Du Pere-Le Jeune, Boucherville, QC, J4B 3K1
(450) 550-2512
Emp Here 30
SIC 8211 Elementary and secondary schools

D-U-N-S 20-181-4972   (BR)
ROTISSERIES ST-HUBERT LTEE, LES
LA ROTISSERIE ST HUBERT BOUCHERVILLE 087
(*Suby of* Cara Holdings Limited)
500 Rue Albanel, Boucherville, QC, J4B 2Z6
(450) 449-9366
Emp Here 75
SIC 5812 Eating places

D-U-N-S 25-323-5196   (BR)
RUSSEL METALS INC
ACIER LEROUX
1331 Rue Graham-Bell Bureau 1, Boucherville, QC, J4B 6A1
(450) 641-1130
Emp Here 70
SIC 5051 Metals service centers and offices

D-U-N-S 24-406-2071   (HQ)
SANDOZ CANADA INC
SABEX
145 Rue Jules-Leger, Boucherville, QC, J4B 7K8
(450) 641-4903
Emp Here 50   *Emp Total* 13,000
Sales 86,278,600
SIC 2834 Pharmaceutical preparations
Pr Michel Robidoux

Pr Tristan Imbert
 Christian Danis

D-U-N-S 25-501-1512   (HQ)
SERVICES MATREC INC
BERGERON
4 Ch Du Tremblay Bureau 625, Boucherville, QC, J4B 6Z5
(450) 641-3070
Emp Here 80   *Emp Total* 3,500
Sales 181,818,064
SIC 6712 Bank holding companies
Pr Patrick Dovigi
Sec E. Joy Grahek
Treas Luke Pelosi

D-U-N-S 20-177-8615   (BR)
SOBEYS QUEBEC INC
1500 Boul De Montarville, Boucherville, QC, J4B 5Y3
(514) 324-1010
Emp Here 100
SIC 5141 Groceries, general line

D-U-N-S 20-577-5591   (BR)
SOCIETE DES ETABLISSEMENTS DE PLEIN AIR DU QUEBEC
PARC NATIONAL DES ILES-DE-BOUCHERVILLE
55 Ile-Sainte-Marguerite, Boucherville, QC, J4B 5J6
(450) 928-5089
Emp Here 100
SIC 7996 Amusement parks

D-U-N-S 20-248-7737   (SL)
SOLUTION DIGITALE INC
DIGITAL SOLUTION
1730 Rue Eiffel, Boucherville, QC, J4B 7W1
(450) 656-9150
Emp Here 26   *Sales* 1,319,261
SIC 7629 Electrical repair shops

D-U-N-S 24-338-7227   (SL)
SOLUTIONS BLEUES CANADA INC
BATHIUM
1600 Rue De Coulomb, Boucherville, QC, J4B 7Z7
(450) 655-6621
Emp Here 50   *Sales* 4,596,524
SIC 3694 Engine electrical equipment

D-U-N-S 20-798-8044   (BR)
STAPLES CANADA INC
BUREAU EN GROS
(*Suby of* Staples, Inc.)
582 Ch De Touraine Bureau 301, Boucherville, QC, J4B 5E4
(450) 655-0505
Emp Here 30
SIC 5943 Stationery stores

D-U-N-S 20-276-1391   (BR)
STRONGCO ENGINEERED SYSTEMS INC
72 Ch Du Tremblay, Boucherville, QC, J4B 6Z6
(450) 449-4666
Emp Here 30
SIC 3541 Machine tools, Metal cutting type

D-U-N-S 24-404-2495   (SL)
SYSTEMES NORBEC INC
EXSPACE
(*Suby of* Groupe Norbec Inc)
97 Rue De Vaudreuil, Boucherville, QC, J4B 1K7
(450) 449-1499
Emp Here 50   *Sales* 12,695,162
SIC 3585 Refrigeration and heating equipment
 Real Menard
VP Jean-Pierre Gingras
Dir Dominique Majeau
Dir Gaetan Desrosiers
Dir Jan Lembregts

D-U-N-S 24-340-7298   (BR)
TRANSCONTINENTAL PRINTING INC

1603 Boul De Montarville, Boucherville, QC, J4B 5Y2
(450) 655-2801
Emp Here 500
SIC 2752 Commercial printing, lithographic

D-U-N-S 24-395-2178   (BR)
TRANSPORT ROBERT (1973) LTEE
65 Rue De Vaudreuil, Boucherville, QC, J4B 1K7
(514) 521-1416
Emp Here 250
SIC 4213 Trucking, except local

D-U-N-S 20-187-5536   (BR)
VAC AERO INTERNATIONAL INC
1365 Rue Newton, Boucherville, QC, J4B 5H2
(450) 449-4612
Emp Here 25
SIC 7699 Repair services, nec

D-U-N-S 24-985-0900   (BR)
VILLE DE LONGUEUIL
VILLE DE LONGUEUIL
501 Ch Du Lac, Boucherville, QC, J4B 6V6
(450) 449-8650
Emp Here 25
SIC 8231 Libraries

D-U-N-S 20-860-4426   (BR)
WINNERS MERCHANTS INTERNATIONAL L.P.
HOMESENSE
(*Suby of* The TJX Companies Inc)
1405 Ch De Touraine Bureau 582, Boucherville, QC, J4B 5E4
(450) 650-0145
Emp Here 50
SIC 5651 Family clothing stores

Brigham, QC J2K

D-U-N-S 20-514-6314   (BR)
CRDITED MONTEREGIE EST
(*Suby of* CRDITED Monteregie Est)
278 Av Des Erables, Brigham, QC, J2K 4C9
(450) 263-3545
Emp Here 20
SIC 8361 Residential care

Bromont, QC J2L
Brome County

D-U-N-S 25-330-9090   (SL)
CARREFOUR 78 (1993) INC
ROTISSERIE ST-HUBERT
100 Boul De Bromont Unite 8, Bromont, QC, J2L 2K6
(450) 534-0223
Emp Here 50   *Sales* 1,532,175
SIC 5812 Eating places

D-U-N-S 25-871-4906   (BR)
CHATEAU BROMONT INC
AUBERGE DU CHATEAU BROMONT
(*Suby of* Chateau Bromont Inc)
95 Rue De Montmorency, Bromont, QC, J2L 2J1
(450) 534-3133
Emp Here 50
SIC 7011 Hotels and motels

D-U-N-S 25-247-3525   (HQ)
CHATEAU BROMONT INC
AUBERGE BROMONT
(*Suby of* Chateau Bromont Inc)
90 Rue De Stanstead, Bromont, QC, J2L 1K6
(450) 534-3433
Emp Here 100   *Emp Total* 100
Sales 4,377,642
SIC 7011 Hotels and motels

D-U-N-S 20-712-2875   (BR)
COMMISSION SCOLAIRE DU VAL-DES-CERFS
ECOLE DE LA CHANTIGNOLE
35 Ch De Gaspe, Bromont, QC, J2L 2N7
(450) 534-3310
Emp Here 50
SIC 8211 Elementary and secondary schools

D-U-N-S 20-267-4255   (SL)
CONCEPT ET CREATION MORDICUS INC
21 Rue Des Mouettes, Bromont, QC, J2L 1Y6
(450) 263-4891
Emp Here 40   *Sales* 5,936,673
SIC 7922 Theatrical producers and services
Pr Pr Martin Chalifoux

D-U-N-S 24-713-7706   (BR)
CONSTRUCTION DJL INC
2 Ch Des Carrieres, Bromont, QC, J2L 1S3
(450) 534-2224
Emp Here 40
SIC 1611 Highway and street construction

D-U-N-S 24-401-1367   (BR)
GENERAL ELECTRIC CANADA COMPANY
GE AIRCRAFT ENGINES
(*Suby of* General Electric Company)
2 Boul De L'Aeroport, Bromont, QC, J2L 1S6
(450) 534-0917
Emp Here 1,000
SIC 3625 Relays and industrial controls

D-U-N-S 25-706-5573   (BR)
GROUPE DAGENAIS M.D.C. INC
MOBILIER DAGENAIS, PHILIPPE
117 Boul De Bromont, Bromont, QC, J2L 2K7

Emp Here 100
SIC 5712 Furniture stores

D-U-N-S 20-634-1331   (BR)
IBM CANADA LIMITED
IBM CANADA - USINE DE BROMONT
(*Suby of* International Business Machines Corporation)
23 Boul De L'Aeroport, Bromont, QC, J2L 1A3
(450) 534-6000
Emp Here 1,500
SIC 3674 Semiconductors and related devices

D-U-N-S 25-738-2135   (SL)
IMMOBILIER SKI BROMONT INC
IMMOBILIER SKI BROMONT.COM
150 Rue Champlain, Bromont, QC, J2L 1A2
(450) 534-2200
Emp Here 80   *Sales* 2,918,428
SIC 5813 Drinking places

D-U-N-S 20-188-4744   (SL)
QUALI-T-GROUP ULC
QUALI-T-FAB
22 Boul De L'Aeroport, Bromont, QC, J2L 1S6
(450) 534-2032
Emp Here 50   *Sales* 4,377,642
SIC 3446 Architectural Metalwork

D-U-N-S 20-213-6029   (BR)
REDBERRY FRANCHISING CORP
BURGER KING
8 Boul De Bromont Bureau 102, Bromont, QC, J2L 2K1
(450) 534-2565
Emp Here 20
SIC 5812 Eating places

D-U-N-S 24-005-1669   (SL)
RESTAURANT E.S.M. INC
RESTAURANT EAST SIDE MARIO'S
2 Rue Saint-Martin, Bromont, QC, J2L 3L2
(450) 534-0947
Emp Here 50   *Sales* 1,532,175
SIC 5812 Eating places

D-U-N-S 25-974-3193   (SL)
SKI BROMONT.COM, SOCIETE EN COMMANDITE
CENTRE DE SKI BROMONT

---

150 Rue Champlain, Bromont, QC, J2L 1A2
(450) 534-2200
Emp Here 80   *Sales* 2,918,428
SIC 5813 Drinking places

D-U-N-S 24-944-8267   (SL)
SPORTS ODESSA CANADA INC
ODESSA CANADA
36 Rue Unifix, Bromont, QC, J2L 1N6
(450) 534-4534
Emp Here 22   *Sales* 10,245,000
SIC 5085 Industrial supplies
Pr Pr Robert Perrault
VP VP Danielle Gagnon

D-U-N-S 24-226-8923   (BR)
TOMMY HILFIGER CANADA INC
500 Place Champetre, Bromont, QC, J2L 0A1
(450) 534-2389
Emp Here 25
SIC 5651 Family clothing stores

Brossard, QC J4W

D-U-N-S 20-925-4320   (SL)
9139-4874 QUEBEC INC
RESTAURANT L'ACADEMIE-RIVE-SUD
2151 Boul Lapiniere, Brossard, QC, J4W 2T5
(450) 766-0404
Emp Here 50   *Sales* 1,532,175
SIC 5812 Eating places

D-U-N-S 25-242-8255   (BR)
A & W FOOD SERVICES OF CANADA INC
A & W
2151 Boul Lapiniere, Brossard, QC, J4W 2T5
(450) 672-1966
Emp Here 20
SIC 5812 Eating places

D-U-N-S 25-961-2208   (BR)
BMO NESBITT BURNS INC
NBSL
1850 Rue Panama Bureau 400, Brossard, QC, J4W 3C6
(450) 466-5500
Emp Here 25
SIC 6211 Security brokers and dealers

D-U-N-S 20-002-8491   (BR)
BANK OF NOVA SCOTIA, THE
BANK OF NOVA SCOTIA, THE
2151 Boul Lapiniere Bureau A27, Brossard, QC, J4W 2T5
(450) 672-4570
Emp Here 20
SIC 6021 National commercial banks

D-U-N-S 25-635-3640   (BR)
BOUTIQUE LINEN CHEST (PHASE II) INC
LINEN CHEST
(*Suby of* Boutique Linen Chest (Phase II) Inc)
7350 Boul Taschereau Bureau 49, Brossard, QC, J4W 1M9
(450) 671-2202
Emp Here 40
SIC 5719 Miscellaneous homefurnishings

D-U-N-S 25-311-5471   (BR)
CANADIAN IMPERIAL BANK OF COMMERCE
CIBC
7250 Boul Taschereau Bureau 1, Brossard, QC, J4W 1M9
(450) 672-5880
Emp Here 50
SIC 6021 National commercial banks

D-U-N-S 25-560-8911   (BR)
CANLAN ICE SPORTS CORP
4 GLACES, LES
5880 Boul Taschereau, Brossard, QC, J4W 1M6
(450) 462-2113
Emp Here 90

SIC 7999 Amusement and recreation, nec

D-U-N-S 25-233-7878   (BR)
COMMISSION SCOLAIRE MARIE-VICTORIN
ECOLE SAMUEL DE CHAMPLAIN
7600 Rue Tunisie, Brossard, QC, J4W 2J4
(450) 672-7950
Emp Here 50
SIC 8211 Elementary and secondary schools

D-U-N-S 20-284-6630   (BR)
DAVIDSTEA INC
DAVIDSTEA
2151 Boul Lapiniere, Brossard, QC, J4W 2T5
(450) 671-4848
Emp Here 20
SIC 5499 Miscellaneous food stores

D-U-N-S 25-789-6340   (BR)
DESJARDINS SECURITE FINANCIERE, COMPAGNIE D'ASSURANCE VIE
PARTENAIRES DE DESJARDINS SECURITE FINANCIERE, COMPAGNIE D'ASSURANCE VIE
7305 Boul Marie-Victorin, Brossard, QC, J4W 1A6
(450) 672-1758
Emp Here 45
SIC 6411 Insurance agents, brokers, and service

D-U-N-S 25-299-5972   (BR)
DOLLARAMA S.E.C.
DOLLARAMA # 103
7250 Boul Taschereau Bureau 30, Brossard, QC, J4W 1M9
(450) 672-1840
Emp Here 23
SIC 5331 Variety stores

D-U-N-S 24-103-8681   (BR)
FEDERATION DES CAISSES DESJARDINS DU QUEBEC
1850 Rue Panama Bureau 300, Brossard, QC, J4W 3C6
(450) 465-8555
Emp Here 20
SIC 6062 State credit unions

D-U-N-S 24-084-6550   (SL)
GESTION H. LEVESQUE LTEE
2180 Boul Lapiniere, Brossard, QC, J4W 1M2
(450) 462-2116
Emp Here 42   *Sales* 11,768,200
SIC 5063 Electrical apparatus and equipment
Pr Pr Hermel Levesque
    Gilles Levesque
    Lise Levesque

D-U-N-S 24-987-8638   (SL)
GESTIONS J.L. FRECHETTE INC
TIM HORTONS
1155 Boul De Rome Bureau 112, Brossard, QC, J4W 3J1
(450) 671-8686
Emp Here 50   *Sales* 1,532,175
SIC 5812 Eating places

D-U-N-S 20-254-5216   (SL)
GRAVEL CHEVROLET GEO OLDSMOBILE LTEE
5900 Boul Marie-Victorin, Brossard, QC, J4W 1A4
(450) 466-2233
Emp Here 90   *Sales* 44,172,000
SIC 5511 New and used car dealers
Pr Pr Jean-Claude Gravel

D-U-N-S 20-616-0934   (BR)
GROUPE ARCHAMBAULT INC
ARCHAMBAULT
2151 Boul Lapiniere Bureau G30, Brossard, QC, J4W 2T5
(450) 671-0801
Emp Here 30
SIC 5736 Musical instrument stores

D-U-N-S 20-700-3422   (BR)

HUDSON'S BAY COMPANY
BAIE, LA
2151 Boul Lapiniere, Brossard, QC, J4W 2T5
(450) 466-3220
Emp Here 25
SIC 5311 Department stores

D-U-N-S 25-523-7380   (BR)
IGM FINANCIAL INC
INVESTORS GROUP
1850 Rue Panama Bureau 600, Brossard, QC, J4W 3C6
(450) 443-6496
Emp Here 60
SIC 6722 Management investment, open-end

D-U-N-S 25-309-7596   (BR)
INDUSTRIELLE ALLIANCE, ASSURANCE ET SERVICES FINANCIERS INC
2 Rue De La Place-Du-Commerce Bureau 200, Brossard, QC, J4W 2T8
(450) 672-6410
Emp Here 80
SIC 6411 Insurance agents, brokers, and service

D-U-N-S 20-913-3508   (BR)
LOBLAW COMPANIES LIMITED
LOBLAWS
1575 Rue Panama, Brossard, QC, J4W 2S8
(450) 466-2828
Emp Here 20
SIC 5411 Grocery stores

D-U-N-S 25-623-2273   (BR)
NAUTILUS PLUS INC
1870 Rue Panama, Brossard, QC, J4W 3C6

Emp Here 40
SIC 7991 Physical fitness facilities

D-U-N-S 24-569-1183   (BR)
PROVIGO DISTRIBUTION INC
MAXI
7200 Boul Taschereau, Brossard, QC, J4W 1N1
(450) 672-3201
Emp Here 70
SIC 5411 Grocery stores

D-U-N-S 24-228-6094   (SL)
QUATRE GLACES (1994) INC, LES
CANLAN ICE SPORTS
5880 Boul Taschereau, Brossard, QC, J4W 1M6
(450) 462-2113
Emp Here 90   *Sales* 4,888,367
SIC 7999 Amusement and recreation, nec

D-U-N-S 25-959-7490   (BR)
ROYAL BANK OF CANADA
BANQUE ROYALE
(*Suby of* Royal Bank Of Canada)
7250 Boul Taschereau Bureau 2, Brossard, QC, J4W 1M9
(450) 923-5130
Emp Here 60
SIC 6021 National commercial banks

D-U-N-S 25-294-5654   (BR)
SEARS CANADA INC
SEARS BROSSARD
2151 Boul Lapiniere, Brossard, QC, J4W 2T5
(450) 465-1000
Emp Here 200
SIC 5311 Department stores

D-U-N-S 20-715-9497   (BR)
SUPER MARCHE COLLIN INC
METRO PLUS
2004 Boul De Rome, Brossard, QC, J4W 3M7
(450) 671-8885
Emp Here 100
SIC 5411 Grocery stores

D-U-N-S 20-165-8536   (SL)
TRILOGIE GROUPE CONSEIL INC
TRILOGIE GROUPE CONSEIL
7305 Boul Marie-Victorin Bureau 300,

Brossard, QC, J4W 1A6
(450) 671-1515
Emp Here 60   *Sales* 4,377,642
SIC 7379 Computer related services, nec

D-U-N-S 20-184-7865   (HQ)
WESTWAY HOLDINGS CANADA INC
6 Rue De La Place-Du-Commerce Bureau 202, Brossard, QC, J4W 3J9
(450) 465-1715
Emp Here 40   *Emp Total* 8
Sales 10,433,380
SIC 5191 Farm supplies
VP VP Gilbert Dagenais
Treas Marie-Josee Theriault
Fin Ex Francine Brunet
Pr Arthur W Huguley Iv
Genl Mgr Anthony Raymond Watts

D-U-N-S 24-903-5304   (BR)
YAK COMMUNICATIONS (CANADA) CORP
YAK POUR ENTREPRISES
1 Rue De La Place-Du-Commerce Bureau 340, Brossard, QC, J4W 2Z7
(514) 737-4377
Emp Here 30
SIC 5999 Miscellaneous retail stores, nec

D-U-N-S 25-360-9382   (BR)
YOPLAIT LIBERTE CANADA CIE
PRODUITS DE MARQUE LIBERTE, LES
1423 Boul Provencher, Brossard, QC, J4W 1Z3
(514) 875-3992
Emp Here 150
SIC 2026 Fluid milk

Brossard, QC J4X

D-U-N-S 24-437-4315   (BR)
BANQUE NATIONALE DU CANADA
TRUST GENERAL
8200 Boul Taschereau Bureau 1400, Brossard, QC, J4X 2S6
(450) 923-1000
Emp Here 32
SIC 6021 National commercial banks

D-U-N-S 25-198-5644   (BR)
CLS-LEXI TECH LTD.
(*Suby of* LBT Acquisition, Inc.)
7900e Boul Taschereau Bureau 204, Brossard, QC, J4X 1C2
(450) 923-5650
Emp Here 60
SIC 7389 Business services, nec

D-U-N-S 25-233-7951   (BR)
COMMISSION SCOLAIRE MARIE-VICTORIN
ECOLE SECONDAIRE PIERRE BROSSEAU
8350 Boul Pelletier, Brossard, QC, J4X 1M8
(450) 465-6290
Emp Here 80
SIC 8211 Elementary and secondary schools

D-U-N-S 25-097-1991   (BR)
COSTCO WHOLESALE CANADA LTD
COSTCO BROSSARD
(*Suby of* Costco Wholesale Corporation)
9430 Boul Taschereau, Brossard, QC, J4X 2W2
(450) 444-4466
Emp Here 50
SIC 5141 Groceries, general line

D-U-N-S 25-325-0815   (BR)
GROUPE BMTC INC
BRAULT & MARTINEAU
9500 Boul Taschereau, Brossard, QC, J4X 2W2
(450) 619-6777
Emp Here 60
SIC 5712 Furniture stores

D-U-N-S 25-191-9614   (BR)
GROUPE BMTC INC
ECONOMAX
8220 Boul Taschereau, Brossard, QC, J4X
1C2
(450) 465-3339
Emp Here 20
SIC 5712 Furniture stores

D-U-N-S 24-126-1655   (SL)
LIONBRIDGE (CANADA) INC
(*Suby of* LBT Acquisition, Inc.)
7900 Boul Taschereau O Bureau E204,
Brossard, QC, J4X 1C2
(514) 288-2243
Emp Here 53   *Sales* 2,772,507
SIC 7389 Business services, nec

D-U-N-S 20-702-7785   (BR)
**ST. LAWRENCE SEAWAY MANAGEMENT
CORPORATION, THE**
9200 Boul Marie-Victorin, Brossard, QC, J4X
1A3
(450) 672-4115
Emp Here 75
SIC 4449 Water transportation of freight

D-U-N-S 25-544-1560   (BR)
THOMAS & BETTS, LIMITEE
7900 Boul Taschereau, Brossard, QC, J4X
1C2
(450) 466-1102
Emp Here 26
SIC 5063 Electrical apparatus and equipment

Brossard, QC J4Y

D-U-N-S 20-317-4693   (BR)
9020-5758 QUEBEC INC
AVRIL SUPERMARCHE SANTE
8600 Boul Leduc, Brossard, QC, J4Y 0G6
(450) 443-4127
Emp Here 50
SIC 5499 Miscellaneous food stores

D-U-N-S 24-522-6381   (SL)
9066-7213 QUEBEC INC
I.T. & HI-FI SOLUTIONS
3820 Rue Isabelle, Brossard, QC, J4Y 2R3

Emp Here 37   *Sales* 15,411,120
SIC 5045 Computers, peripherals, and soft-
ware
Pr Pr Jamil Chaar

D-U-N-S 20-289-8243   (BR)
9218-7384 QUEBEC INC
EMPIRE SPORTS
9850 Boul Leduc Bureau 10, Brossard, QC,
J4Y 0B4
(450) 812-7413
Emp Here 20
SIC 5941 Sporting goods and bicycle shops

D-U-N-S 24-935-3731   (SL)
AUTOMATIC SYSTEMES AMERIQUE INC
4005 Boul Matte Bureau D, Brossard, QC, J4Y
2P4
(450) 659-0737
Emp Here 47   *Sales* 4,851,006
SIC 1731 Electrical work

D-U-N-S 24-815-0559   (SL)
**BELL   FLAVORS   &   FRAGRANCES
(CANADA) CO**
ESSENCES & FRAGRANCES BELL
3800 Rue Isabelle Bureau H, Brossard, QC,
J4Y 2R3
(450) 444-3819
Emp Here 50   *Sales* 2,115,860
SIC 2087 Flavoring extracts and syrups, nec

D-U-N-S 25-877-3118   (BR)
CRDITED MONTEREGIE EST
COMPLEXE MULTI BROSSARD
(*Suby of* CRDITED Monteregie Est)

3530 Rue Isabelle, Brossard, QC, J4Y 2R3
(450) 444-5588
Emp Here 40
SIC 8322 Individual and family services

D-U-N-S 20-703-5283   (BR)
CASCADES CS+ INC
9500 Av Illinois, Brossard, QC, J4Y 3B7
(450) 923-3300
Emp Here 103
SIC 8711 Engineering services

D-U-N-S 25-174-9297   (BR)
CASCADES INC
*GROUPE CORPORATIF DES ACHATS DE
FIBRES RECYCLEES*
9500 Av Illinois, Brossard, QC, J4Y 3B7
(450) 923-3120
Emp Here 32
SIC 4225 General warehousing and storage

D-U-N-S 24-389-5617   (BR)
**CENTRE DE SANTE ET DE SERVICES SO-
CIAUX CHAMPLAIN**
CENTRE D'HEBERGEMENT CHAMPLAIN
(*Suby of* Centre de sante et de services soci-
aux Champlain)
5050 Place Nogent, Brossard, QC, J4Y 2K3
(450) 672-3320
Emp Here 50
SIC 8062 General medical and surgical hospi-
tals

D-U-N-S 20-276-6650   (BR)
**CENTRE DE SANTE ET DE SERVICES SO-
CIAUX CHAMPLAIN**
CENTRE D'HEBERGEMENT CHAMPLAIN
(*Suby of* Centre de sante et de services soci-
aux Champlain)
5050 Place Nogent, Brossard, QC, J4Y 2K3
(450) 672-3328
Emp Here 80
SIC 8322 Individual and family services

D-U-N-S 24-164-4355   (BR)
CINEPLEX ODEON CORPORATION
CINEMA CINEPLEX BROSSARD & VIP
9350 Boul Leduc, Brossard, QC, J4Y 0B3
(450) 678-5542
Emp Here 100
SIC 7832 Motion picture theaters, except
drive-in

D-U-N-S 25-026-9636   (BR)
**COMMISSION   SCOLAIRE   MARIE-
VICTORIN**
*ECOLE   SECONDAIRE   ANTOINE
BROSSARD*
3055 Boul De Rome, Brossard, QC, J4Y 1S9
(450) 443-0010
Emp Here 150
SIC 8211 Elementary and secondary schools

D-U-N-S 25-980-4078   (BR)
**COMMISSION   SCOLAIRE   MARIE-
VICTORIN**
ECOLE CHARLES BRUNEAU
3010 Boul Napoleon, Brossard, QC, J4Y 2A3
(450) 676-9285
Emp Here 55
SIC 8211 Elementary and secondary schools

D-U-N-S 25-240-5543   (BR)
**COMMISSION   SCOLAIRE   MARIE-
VICTORIN**
ECOLE GUILLAUME VIGNAL
7465 Rue Malherbe, Brossard, QC, J4Y 1E6
(450) 676-5946
Emp Here 70
SIC 8211 Elementary and secondary schools

D-U-N-S 24-339-6954   (BR)
COOP FEDEREE, LA
SONIC PROPANE
4050 Boul Matte, Brossard, QC, J4Y 2Z2
(450) 444-1211
Emp Here 20
SIC 5172 Petroleum products, nec

D-U-N-S 24-361-1428   (SL)
CORPORATION DU THEATRE L'ETOILE
ETOILE, L'
6000 Boul De Rome Bureau 240, Brossard,
QC, J4Y 0B6
(450) 676-1030
Emp Here 50   *Sales* 4,596,524
SIC 6512 Nonresidential building operators

D-U-N-S 20-545-6200   (BR)
**DATA COMMUNICATIONS MANAGEMENT
CORP**
DATA IMAGENET
9005 Boul Du Quartier Bureau C, Brossard,
QC, J4Y 0A8

Emp Here 23
SIC 2759 Commercial printing, nec

D-U-N-S 24-189-9793   (BR)
DE LA FONTAINE & ASSOCIES INC
INTERNAT
7503 Boul Taschereau Bureau B, Brossard,
QC, J4Y 1A2
(450) 676-8335
Emp Here 90
SIC 5072 Hardware

D-U-N-S 24-836-0596   (BR)
EBC INC
HYDROTECH MARINE
3900 Rue Isabelle, Brossard, QC, J4Y 2R3
(450) 444-9333
Emp Here 45
SIC 1541 Industrial buildings and warehouses

D-U-N-S 25-141-3837   (HQ)
FRUITS & PASSION BOUTIQUES INC
FRUITS & PASSION
9180 Boul Leduc Bureau 280, Brossard, QC,
J4Y 0N7
(450) 678-9620
Emp Here 50   *Emp Total* 4,569
Sales 25,467,779
SIC 5122 Drugs, proprietaries, and sundries
Pr Pr Kyung Wha Rhee
Dir Kelly-Ann Mcintosh
Dir Jeong Tae Bae
Dir Lee Wukyeong

D-U-N-S 25-610-9786   (BR)
**GOUVERNEMENT DE LA PROVINCE DE
QUEBEC**
*GOUVERNEMENT DE LA PROVINCE DE
QUEBEC*
3530 Rue Isabelle, Brossard, QC, J4Y 2R3
(450) 444-5588
Emp Here 30
SIC 8361 Residential care

D-U-N-S 24-989-5137   (HQ)
GRIF & GRAF INC
9205 Boul Taschereau, Brossard, QC, J4Y
3B8
(450) 659-6999
Emp Here 200   *Emp Total* 250
Sales 15,102,865
SIC 7699 Repair services, nec
Pr Pr Pierre Gamache

D-U-N-S 24-643-1451   (BR)
GROUPE SPORTSCENE INC
CAGE AUX SPORTS BROSSARD
9300 Boul Leduc, Brossard, QC, J4Y 0B3
(450) 656-4011
Emp Here 45
SIC 5812 Eating places

D-U-N-S 25-305-2260   (BR)
INNVEST PROPERTIES CORP
COMFORT INN BROSSARD
(*Suby of* Innvest Properties Corp)
7863 Boul Taschereau, Brossard, QC, J4Y
1A4
(450) 678-9350
Emp Here 20
SIC 7011 Hotels and motels

D-U-N-S 25-974-9661   (BR)
NORTRAX CANADA INC
(*Suby of* Deere & Company)
3855 Boul Matte, Brossard, QC, J4Y 2P4
(450) 444-1030
Emp Here 40
SIC 5082 Construction and mining machinery

D-U-N-S 20-793-3979   (SL)
SANTE NATURELLE A.G. LTEE
3555 Boul Matte Porte C, Brossard, QC, J4Y
2P4
(450) 659-7723
Emp Here 80   *Sales* 4,158,005
SIC 2833 Medicinals and botanicals

D-U-N-S 20-519-1484   (BR)
SEARS CANADA INC
8505 Boul Taschereau, Brossard, QC, J4Y
1A4

Emp Here 30
SIC 5311 Department stores

D-U-N-S 24-063-9026   (BR)
SOCIETE DE GESTION COGIR S.E.N.C.
L'EMERITE DE BROSSARD
2455 Boul De Rome Bureau 20, Brossard,
QC, J4Y 2W9
(450) 678-1882
Emp Here 45
SIC 8361 Residential care

D-U-N-S 24-798-1280   (SL)
SPORTS DIX 30 INC
9550 Boul Leduc Bureau 15, Brossard, QC,
J4Y 0B3
(450) 926-2000
Emp Here 55   *Sales* 4,677,755
SIC 5311 Department stores

D-U-N-S 24-393-7914   (SL)
STATION SKYSPA INC
6000 Boul De Rome Bureau 400, Brossard,
QC, J4Y 0B6
(450) 462-9111
Emp Here 100   *Sales* 3,283,232
SIC 7991 Physical fitness facilities

D-U-N-S 25-064-0745   (BR)
UNITED PARCEL SERVICE CANADA LTD
UPS
3850 Boul Matte, Brossard, QC, J4Y 2Z2
(450) 444-9544
Emp Here 108
SIC 7389 Business services, nec

D-U-N-S 20-572-9010   (BR)
VALEURS MOBILIERES DESJARDINS INC
DESJARDINS SECURITIES
9120 Boul Leduc Bureau 205, Brossard, QC,
J4Y 0L3
(450) 671-6788
Emp Here 24
SIC 6211 Security brokers and dealers

D-U-N-S 25-297-7103   (BR)
WAL-MART CANADA CORP
WALMART SUPERCENTRE
9000 Boul Leduc Unite 102, Brossard, QC,
J4Y 0E6
(450) 672-5000
Emp Here 250
SIC 5311 Department stores

D-U-N-S 24-354-3860   (BR)
**WINNERS MERCHANTS INTERNATIONAL
L.P.**
WINNERS
(*Suby of* The TJX Companies Inc)
9650 Boul Leduc Bureau 15, Brossard, QC,
J4Y 0B3
(450) 443-5546
Emp Here 60
SIC 5651 Family clothing stores

Brossard, QC J4Z

D-U-N-S 20-355-9463 (SL)
9291-5487 QUEBEC INC
LAUCANDRIQUE TREMBLANT
4305 Boul Lapiniere Bureau 100, Brossard, QC, J4Z 3H8
(450) 677-0007
Emp Here 50   *Sales* 4,742,446
SIC 6531 Real estate agents and managers

D-U-N-S 20-536-4743 (BR)
BERLITZ CANADA INC
CENTRE DE LANGUES BERLITZ
6300 Av Auteuil Bureau 230, Brossard, QC, J4Z 3P2

Emp Here 20
SIC 8299 Schools and educational services, nec

D-U-N-S 20-313-9563 (BR)
BUNGE CANADA
4605 Boul Lapiniere Bureau 160, Brossard, QC, J4Z 3T5
(450) 462-6100
Emp Here 20
SIC 5153 Grain and field beans

D-U-N-S 20-297-8706 (BR)
CEGERTEC INC
CEGERTEC WORLEYPARSONS INC
(*Suby of* Ceger Inc)
4805 Boul Lapiniere Bureau 4300, Brossard, QC, J4Z 0G2
(450) 656-3356
Emp Here 300
SIC 8621 Professional organizations

D-U-N-S 24-389-5609 (BR)
CENTRE DE SANTE ET DE SERVICES SO-CIAUX CHAMPLAIN
CLSC SAMUEL-DE-CHAMPLAIN
(*Suby of* Centre de sante et de services sociaux Champlain)
5811 Boul Taschereau Bureau 100, Brossard, QC, J4Z 1A5
(450) 445-4452
Emp Here 50
SIC 8062 General medical and surgical hospitals

D-U-N-S 20-712-2792 (BR)
COMMISSION SCOLAIRE MARIE-VICTORIN
ECOLE GEORGES-P.-VANIER
3400 Rue Boisclair, Brossard, QC, J4Z 2C2
(450) 678-0490
Emp Here 24
SIC 8211 Elementary and secondary schools

D-U-N-S 20-007-7696 (BR)
DELOITTE & TOUCHE INC
(*Suby of* Deloitte LLP)
4605 Boul Lapiniere Bureau 200, Brossard, QC, J4Z 3T5
(450) 618-4270
Emp Here 60
SIC 8721 Accounting, auditing, and book-keeping

D-U-N-S 20-571-8708 (BR)
DESJARDINS SECURITE FINANCIERE, COMPAGNIE D'ASSURANCE VIE
CENTRE FINANCIER IBERVILLE CHAM-PLAIN
6400 Av Auteuil Bureau 300, Brossard, QC, J4Z 3P5
(450) 462-9231
Emp Here 30
SIC 6311 Life insurance

D-U-N-S 24-812-8154 (BR)
GHD CONSULTANTS LTEE
INSPEC-SOL
9955 Rue De Chateauneuf Unite 220, Brossard, QC, J4Z 3V5

(450) 678-3951
Emp Here 30
SIC 8621 Professional organizations

D-U-N-S 24-567-9303 (BR)
GAZ METRO INC
4305 Boul Lapiniere, Brossard, QC, J4Z 3H8
(450) 443-7000
Emp Here 60
SIC 4924 Natural gas distribution

D-U-N-S 20-266-9875 (BR)
GESTION I-TECH SOLUTIONS INC
7005 Boul Taschereau Bureau 330, Brossard, QC, J4Z 1A7
(418) 628-2100
Emp Here 20
SIC 7378 Computer maintenance and repair

D-U-N-S 20-852-8906 (BR)
INDUSTRIELLE ALLIANCE, ASSURANCE ET SERVICES FINANCIERS INC
4255 Boul Lapiniere Bureau 120, Brossard, QC, J4Z 0C7
(450) 465-0630
Emp Here 25
SIC 6331 Fire, marine, and casualty insurance

D-U-N-S 25-610-3961 (BR)
LIBRAIRIE RENAUD-BRAY INC
6925 Boul Taschereau, Brossard, QC, J4Z 1A7
(450) 443-5350
Emp Here 50
SIC 5942 Book stores

D-U-N-S 25-996-0180 (BR)
PLACEMENTS SERGAKIS INC
STATION DES SPORTS
5773 Boul Taschereau, Brossard, QC, J4Z 1A5
(450) 462-4587
Emp Here 60
SIC 5812 Eating places

D-U-N-S 25-298-1907 (BR)
RAYMOND CHABOT GRANT THORNTON S.E.N.C.R.L.
4805 Boul Lapiniere Bureau 2100, Brossard, QC, J4Z 0G2
(450) 445-6226
Emp Here 50
SIC 8721 Accounting, auditing, and book-keeping

D-U-N-S 24-388-9347 (BR)
REVOLUTION ENVIRONMENTAL SOLU-TIONS LP
TERRAPURE ENVIRONMENTAL
(*Suby of* Revolution Environmental Solutions LP)
9955 Rue De Chateauneuf Unite 245, Brossard, QC, J4Z 3V5

Emp Here 200
SIC 4953 Refuse systems

D-U-N-S 25-024-2286 (BR)
RIVERSIDE SCHOOL BOARD
GOOD SHEPHERD SCHOOL
5770 Rue Aline, Brossard, QC, J4Z 1R3
(450) 676-8166
Emp Here 40
SIC 8211 Elementary and secondary schools

D-U-N-S 25-240-3803 (BR)
RIVERSIDE SCHOOL BOARD
ECOLE HAROLD NAPPER
6375 Av Baffin, Brossard, QC, J4Z 2H9
(450) 676-2651
Emp Here 40
SIC 8211 Elementary and secondary schools

D-U-N-S 20-535-2524 (BR)
ROTISSERIES ST-HUBERT LTEE, LES
(*Suby of* Cara Holdings Limited)
6325 Boul Taschereau, Brossard, QC, J4Z 1A6

(514) 385-5555
Emp Here 80
SIC 5812 Eating places

D-U-N-S 24-570-1792 (HQ)
SANEXEN SERVICES ENVIRONNEMEN-TAUX INC
9935 Rue De Ch2teauneuf Unit9 200, Brossard, QC, J4Z 3V4
(450) 466-2123
Emp Here 120   *Emp Total* 1,250
Sales 20,210,114
SIC 4959 Sanitary services, nec
Pr Alain Sauriol
 Jean Paquin
 Ingrid Stefancic
Dir Nicole Paquin
Dir Madeleine Paquin
Dir Jean-Claude Dugas
Dir Stephane Blanchette
Genl Mgr Rejean Loiselle

D-U-N-S 25-213-7252 (BR)
STAPLES CANADA INC
BUREAU EN GROS
(*Suby of* Staples, Inc.)
6555 Boul Taschereau, Brossard, QC, J4Z 1A7
(450) 445-2229
Emp Here 20
SIC 5943 Stationery stores

D-U-N-S 25-293-9459 (BR)
TOYS 'R' US (CANADA) LTD
TOYS 'R' US
(*Suby of* Toys "r" Us, Inc.)
6855 Boul Taschereau, Brossard, QC, J4Z 1A7
(450) 445-1889
Emp Here 30
SIC 5945 Hobby, toy, and game shops

D-U-N-S 24-495-8315 (BR)
TYCO SAFETY PRODUCTS CANADA LTD
SYSTEMES KANTECH
9995 Rue De Chateauneuf Unite L, Brossard, QC, J4Z 3V7
(450) 444-2040
Emp Here 90
SIC 3699 Electrical equipment and supplies, nec

D-U-N-S 25-324-8728 (BR)
VIGI SANTE LTEE
CHSLD VIGI BROSSARD
(*Suby of* Vigi Sante Ltee)
5955 Grande-Allee, Brossard, QC, J4Z 3S3
(450) 656-8500
Emp Here 150
SIC 8361 Residential care

D-U-N-S 20-015-4487 (HQ)
VOITH HYDRO INC
9955 Rue De Chateauneuf Bureau 160, Brossard, QC, J4Z 3V5
(450) 766-2100
Emp Here 150   *Emp Total* 36,771
Sales 25,987,530
SIC 1731 Electrical work
Pr Pr William Malus
 Ronald Munch
VP VP Francois Trudeau
Dir Stefan Schroeder
 Rene Habets

D-U-N-S 20-197-5497 (SL)
WOLTERS KLUWER QUEBEC LTEE
7005 Boul Taschereau Bureau 190, Brossard, QC, J4Z 1A7
(450) 678-4443
Emp Here 26   *Sales* 2,252,253
SIC 2721 Periodicals

Brownsburg-Chatham, QC J8G
Argenteuil County

D-U-N-S 24-920-4413 (BR)
ORICA CANADA INC
342 Rue Mcmaster, Brownsburg-Chatham, QC, J8G 3A8
(450) 533-4201
Emp Here 400
SIC 2892 Explosives

D-U-N-S 25-527-7956 (HQ)
ORICA CANADA INC
SOUTENEMENT DU SOL MINOVA CANADA
301 Rue De L'Hotel-De-Ville, Brownsburg-Chatham, QC, J8G 3B5
(450) 533-4201
Emp Here 550   *Emp Total* 12,000
Sales 1,505,544,045
SIC 2892 Explosives
Pr James K. Bonnor
VP Charles Major
Sec Suzanne R. Thigpen
Treas Patricia Jacobs

Candiac, QC J5R
Laprairie County

D-U-N-S 20-856-2686 (BR)
ADM AGRI-INDUSTRIES COMPANY
COMPAGNIE ARCHER-DANIELS-MIDLAND DU CANADA
(*Suby of* Archer-Daniels-Midland Company)
155 Av D'Iberia, Candiac, QC, J5R 3H1
(450) 659-1911
Emp Here 100
SIC 2046 Wet corn milling

D-U-N-S 25-623-5664 (SL)
BISTHRAM CLUB DE GOLF CANDIAC INC
CANDIAC GOLF CLUB
45 Ch D'Auteuil, Candiac, QC, J5R 2C8
(450) 659-9163
Emp Here 50   *Sales* 2,188,821
SIC 7992 Public golf courses

D-U-N-S 24-337-2732 (BR)
CASCADES CANADA ULC
CASCADES TISSUE GROUP - CANDIAC
77 Boul Marie-Victorin, Candiac, QC, J5R 1C2
(450) 444-6400
Emp Here 210
SIC 2676 Sanitary paper products

D-U-N-S 24-126-3313 (BR)
CASCADES CANADA ULC
CASCADES GROUPE TISSU-CANDIAC
75 Boul Marie-Victorin, Candiac, QC, J5R 1C2
(450) 444-6500
Emp Here 225
SIC 2621 Paper mills

D-U-N-S 20-191-5964 (HQ)
CHANEL INC
55 Boul Marie-Victorin, Candiac, QC, J5R 1B6
(450) 659-1981
Emp Here 60   *Emp Total* 14,000
Sales 19,057,522
SIC 5122 Drugs, proprietaries, and sundries
 Sylvain Gagnon
Dir Olivier Nicolay
Dir Michael Rena

D-U-N-S 25-240-2201 (BR)
COMMISSION SCOLAIRE DES GRANDES-SEIGNEURIES
ECOLE JEAN LEMAN
4 Av De Champagne, Candiac, QC, J5R 4W3
(514) 380-8899
Emp Here 80
SIC 8211 Elementary and secondary schools

D-U-N-S 25-502-8870 (SL)
CORRUPAL INC
225 Av Liberte, Candiac, QC, J5R 3X8
(450) 638-4222
Emp Here 25   *Sales* 5,173,950

SIC 2657 Folding paperboard boxes
Pr Pr Yvan Quirion

D-U-N-S 24-354-8877   (BR)
COSTCO WHOLESALE CANADA LTD
COSTCO
(*Suby of* Costco Wholesale Corporation)
60 Rue Strasbourg, Candiac, QC, J5R 0B4
(450) 444-3453
Emp Here 200
SIC 5099 Durable goods, nec

D-U-N-S 20-806-7376   (BR)
COUCHE-TARD INC
87b Boul Marie-Victorin, Candiac, QC, J5R
1C3
(450) 444-0110
Emp Here 25
SIC 5411 Grocery stores

D-U-N-S 25-745-9487   (BR)
DIVERSEY CANADA, INC
(*Suby of* Sealed Air Corporation)
110 Boul Montcalm N, Candiac, QC, J5R 3L9
(450) 444-8000
Emp Here 20
SIC 2869 Industrial organic chemicals, nec

D-U-N-S 20-281-4427   (BR)
ENTREPOTS P C G INC, LES
85 Boul Montcalm N, Candiac, QC, J5R 3L6
(450) 444-0702
Emp Here 20
SIC 4225 General warehousing and storage

D-U-N-S 20-715-4118   (BR)
ENTREPRISES JMC (1973) LTEE, LES
MCDONALD'S CANDIAC
(*Suby of* Entreprises JMC (1973) Ltee, Les)
101 Ch Saint-Francois-Xavier, Candiac, QC,
J5R 4V4
(450) 632-4723
Emp Here 100
SIC 5812 Eating places

D-U-N-S 24-337-8051   (SL)
GESTION JEAN & GUY HURTEAU INC
21 Rue Paul-Gauguin, Candiac, QC, J5R 3X8
(450) 638-2212
Emp Here 550   *Sales* 135,648,000
SIC 6712 Bank holding companies
Pr Pr Jean Hurteau
VP VP Guy Hurteau

D-U-N-S 24-391-5654   (BR)
GOLF TOWN OPERATING LIMITED PART-NERSHIP
GOLF TOWN
30 Rue Strasbourg, Candiac, QC, J5R 0B4
(450) 659-6929
Emp Here 20
SIC 5941 Sporting goods and bicycle shops

D-U-N-S 20-271-3244   (SL)
JOHNSON MATTHEY MATERIAUX POUR BATTERIES LTEE
280 Av Liberte, Candiac, QC, J5R 6X1
(514) 906-1396
Emp Here 50   *Sales* 3,638,254
SIC 7699 Repair services, nec

D-U-N-S 24-921-6854   (HQ)
LE GROUPE F&P SRI
FRUITS & PASSION
21 Rue Paul-Gauguin Bureau 103, Candiac,
QC, J5R 3X8
(450) 638-2212
Emp Here 450   *Sales* 77,304,900
SIC 5999 Miscellaneous retail stores, nec
Pr Pr Grise Isabelle
Dir Kenneth G. Kumer
Dir Jay E. Gueldner

D-U-N-S 20-120-2772   (BR)
MATERIAUX DE CONSTRUCTION OLD-CASTLE CANADA INC, LES
PRODUITS MOULES SYNERTECH
2 Av D'Inverness, Candiac, QC, J5R 4W5

(450) 444-5214
Emp Here 80
SIC 2822 Synthetic rubber

D-U-N-S 20-438-8276   (BR)
MATERIAUX DE CONSTRUCTION OLD-CASTLE CANADA INC, LES
GROUPE PERMACON
2 Av D'Inverness, Candiac, QC, J5R 4W5
(450) 444-5214
Emp Here 80
SIC 5039 Construction materials, nec

D-U-N-S 20-277-3867   (SL)
NEOLECT INC
104 Boul Montcalm N, Candiac, QC, J5R 3L8
(450) 659-5457
Emp Here 50   *Sales* 1,969,939
SIC 3643 Current-carrying wiring devices

D-U-N-S 20-191-5816   (BR)
OC CANADA HOLDINGS COMPANY
USINE DE CANDIAC
131 Boul Montcalm N, Candiac, QC, J5R 3L6
(450) 619-2000
Emp Here 100
SIC 3296 Mineral wool

D-U-N-S 20-265-7094   (BR)
PHARMASCIENCE INC
100 Boul De L'Industrie, Candiac, QC, J5R 1J1
(450) 444-9989
Emp Here 120
SIC 2834 Pharmaceutical preparations

D-U-N-S 20-707-5243   (SL)
PRECIMOLD INC
PRECIMOULE
9 Boul Marie-Victorin, Candiac, QC, J5R 4S8
(450) 659-2921
Emp Here 60   *Sales* 11,600,751
SIC 5085 Industrial supplies
John Alvin Mcdonald

D-U-N-S 20-589-2099   (BR)
ROYAL BANK OF CANADA
RBC BANQUE ROYALE
(*Suby of* Royal Bank Of Canada)
201 Boul De L'Industrie, Candiac, QC, J5R
6A6
(450) 659-9681
Emp Here 20
SIC 6021 National commercial banks

D-U-N-S 20-314-1601   (BR)
STAPLES CANADA INC
BUREAU EN GROS
(*Suby of* Staples, Inc.)
40 Rue Strasbourg, Candiac, QC, J5R 0B4
(450) 659-1012
Emp Here 20
SIC 5943 Stationery stores

D-U-N-S 24-376-6503   (SL)
UPGI PHARMA INC
100 Boul De L'Industrie, Candiac, QC, J5R 1J1
(514) 998-9059
Emp Here 50   *Sales* 4,815,406
SIC 2834 Pharmaceutical preparations

Canton Bedford, QC J0J
St-Jean County

D-U-N-S 25-730-6217   (BR)
GRAYMONT (QC) INC
1015 Ch De La Carriere, Canton Bedford, QC,
J0J 1A0
(450) 248-3307
Emp Here 70
SIC 3274 Lime

Canton Tremblay, QC G7H
Chicoutimi County

D-U-N-S 24-378-2059   (SL)
EQUIPMENT COMACT (CHICOUTIMI) INC
850 Rte De Tadoussac, Canton Tremblay, QC,
G7H 5A8
(418) 628-0791
Emp Here 80   *Sales* 10,601,280
SIC 3553 Woodworking machinery
Pr Pierre Morency

Canton-De-Hatley, QC J0B
Stanstead County

D-U-N-S 24-547-3921   (SL)
MANOIR HOVEY (1985) INC
575 Ch Hovey, Canton-De-Hatley, QC, J0B
2C0
(819) 842-2421
Emp Here 80   *Sales* 3,502,114
SIC 7011 Hotels and motels

D-U-N-S 20-859-7906   (BR)
SINTRA INC
ESTRIE, DIV DE
3600 Ch Dunant, Canton-De-Hatley, QC, J0B
2C0
(819) 569-6333
Emp Here 160
SIC 1611 Highway and street construction

D-U-N-S 25-080-5892   (BR)
SODEM INC
CENTRE RECREOTOURISTIQUE MON-TJOYE
4765 Ch De Capelton, Canton-De-Hatley, QC,
J0B 2C0
(819) 842-2447
Emp Here 100
SIC 7299 Miscellaneous personal service

Cap-Aux-Meules, QC G4T

D-U-N-S 24-863-6763   (SL)
C.T.M.A. TRAVERSIER LTEE
LE MADELEINE
(*Suby of* Cooperative De Transport Maritime
Aerien Association Cooperative)
435 Ch Avila-Arseneau, Cap-Aux-Meules, QC,
G4T 1J3
(418) 986-6600
Emp Here 120   *Sales* 35,054,639
SIC 4424 Deep sea domestic transportation of
freight
Pr Edee Chevarie
VP VP Jean-Paul Richard
Sec Paul Delaney
Dir Fin Johanne Turbide
Dir Louis Hebert
Dir Jean-Yves Miousse
Dir Paul Duclos
Dir Sylvain Miousse
Genl Mgr Emmanuel Aucoin

D-U-N-S 24-731-2643   (BR)
FRUITS & PASSION BOUTIQUES INC
310 Ch Principal, Cap-Aux-Meules, QC, G4T
1C9
(418) 986-3133
Emp Here 50
SIC 5122 Drugs, proprietaries, and sundries

D-U-N-S 24-791-8246   (HQ)
GESTION C.T.M.A. INC
(*Suby of* Cooperative De Transport Maritime
Aerien Association Cooperative)
435 Ch Avila-Arseneau, Cap-Aux-Meules, QC,
G4T 1J3
(418) 986-6600
Emp Here 150   *Emp Total* 500
Sales 116,058,800
SIC 6712 Bank holding companies
Pr Pr Edee Chevarie

VP VP Jacques Chevarie
Claude Boudreau
Dir Jean-Paul Richard
Dir Louis Hebert
Dir Jean Miousse
Dir Paul Delaney

D-U-N-S 25-376-4278   (BR)
MUNICIPALITE DE ILES-DE-LA-MADELEINE, LA
*CENTRE DE GESTION DES MATIERES
RESIDUELLES DE LA MUNICIPALITE DES
ILES-DE-LA-MADELEINE*
460 Principal, Cap-Aux-Meules, QC, G4T 1A1
(418) 969-4615
Emp Here 20
SIC 4953 Refuse systems

Cap-Chat, QC G0J
Gaspe-Ouest County

D-U-N-S 25-232-1096   (BR)
COMMISSION SCOLAIRE DES CHIC-CHOCS
ECOLE ST-NORBERT
1 Rue Des Ecoliers, Cap-Chat, QC, G0J 1E0
(418) 786-5668
Emp Here 20
SIC 8211 Elementary and secondary schools

D-U-N-S 25-517-3577   (BR)
GROUPE LEBEL INC
Gd, Cap-Chat, QC, G0J 1E0
(418) 786-5522
Emp Here 50
SIC 2421 Sawmills and planing mills, general

Cap-D'Espoir, QC G0C
Gaspe-Est County

D-U-N-S 20-244-2104   (SL)
FUMOIRS GASPE CURED INC, LES
65 Rue De La Station, Cap-D'Espoir, QC, G0C
1G0
(418) 782-5920
Emp Here 94   *Sales* 14,368,640
SIC 2091 Canned and cured fish and
seafoods
Pr Pr Real Nicolas
VP Roch Lelievre

Cap-Saint-Ignace, QC G0R
Montmagny County

D-U-N-S 20-008-1086   (BR)
CENTRE DE SANTE ET SERVICES SOCI-AUX DE MONTMAGNY - L'ISLET
CENTRE D'HEBERGEMENT DE CAP-SAINT-IGNACE
146 Rue Du Manoir E, Cap-Saint-Ignace, QC,
G0R 1H0
(418) 246-5644
Emp Here 50
SIC 8361 Residential care

D-U-N-S 24-379-7800   (SL)
PABER ALUMINIUM INC
TECHNOLOGIES DE MOULAGE
296 Ch Vincelotte, Cap-Saint-Ignace, QC,
G0R 1H0
(418) 246-5626
Emp Here 70   *Sales* 7,806,795
SIC 3365 Aluminum foundries
Pr Pr Luc Paris
VP VP Bryan Paris
VP VP Genevieve Paris
Diane Collin

Cap-Sante, QC G0A
Portneuf County

D-U-N-S 20-192-2259   (SL)
PLAMONDON AUTOS INC
(*Suby of* Gestion Plamondon Ltee)
125 138 Rte, Cap-Sante, QC, G0A 1L0
(418) 285-3311
Emp Here 25   *Sales* 12,681,250
SIC 5511 New and used car dealers
Pr Rejean Plamondon
VP VP Rene Plamondon

Carignan, QC J3L
Chambly County

D-U-N-S 20-281-0243   (BR)
CONSTRUCTION DJL INC
MONCTON CONSTRUCTION
1463 Ch De Chambly, Carignan, QC, J3L 0J6
(450) 658-7527
Emp Here 50
SIC 1611 Highway and street construction

Carleton, QC G0C
Bonaventure County

D-U-N-S 24-960-5262   (BR)
AQUA-MER INC
CENTRE DE THALASSOTHERAPIE
868 Boul Perron, Carleton, QC, G0C 1J0
(418) 364-7055
Emp Here 50
SIC 7991 Physical fitness facilities

D-U-N-S 24-097-5875   (BR)
COMMISSION   SCOLAIRE   RENE-LEVESQUE
C F P L'ENVOLE
15 Rue Comeau, Carleton, QC, G0C 1J0
(418) 364-7510
Emp Here 38
SIC 8331 Job training and related services

D-U-N-S 20-573-6700   (BR)
HYDRO-QUEBEC
1021 Boul Perron, Carleton, QC, G0C 1J0
(418) 364-5300
Emp Here 40
SIC 4911 Electric services

Causapscal, QC G0J
Matapedia County

D-U-N-S 20-212-7077   (BR)
BOIS D'OEUVRE CEDRICO INC
USINE CAUSAP
562 Rte 132 E, Causapscal, QC, G0J 1J0
(418) 756-5727
Emp Here 100
SIC 5099 Durable goods, nec

D-U-N-S 25-232-1005   (BR)
COMMISSION SCOLAIRE DE MONTS-ET-MAREES
POLYVALENTE FORIMONT
(*Suby of* Commission Scolaire De Monts-Et-Marees)
145 Rue Saint-Luc, Causapscal, QC, G0J 1J0
(418) 756-3481
Emp Here 40
SIC 8211 Elementary and secondary schools

D-U-N-S 20-711-8444   (BR)
COMMISSION SCOLAIRE DES MONTS-ET-MAREES

CENTRE DE FORMATION ET D'EXTENSION EN FORESTERIE
165 Rue Saint-Luc, Causapscal, QC, G0J 1J0
(418) 756-6115
Emp Here 40
SIC 8211 Elementary and secondary schools

D-U-N-S 25-240-6392   (BR)
COMMISSION SCOLAIRE DES MONTS-ET-MAREES
ECOLE SAINT-ROSAIRE
1 Place De L'Eglise, Causapscal, QC, G0J 1J0
(418) 756-3817
Emp Here 33
SIC 8211 Elementary and secondary schools

Chambly, QC J3L
Chambly County

D-U-N-S 25-010-1219   (BR)
BANQUE NATIONALE DU CANADA
1117 Boul De Perigny, Chambly, QC, J3L 1W7
(450) 658-4374
Emp Here 20
SIC 6021 National commercial banks

D-U-N-S 20-537-2068   (BR)
CANADA POST CORPORATION
CHAMBLY SUCC BUREAU-CHEF
1223 Boul De Perigny, Chambly, QC, J3L 1W7
(450) 658-0232
Emp Here 40
SIC 4311 U.s. postal service

D-U-N-S 24-314-2523   (BR)
CARGILL LIMITED
CARGILL FOODS
7901 Rue Samuel-Hatt, Chambly, QC, J3L 6V7
(450) 447-4600
Emp Here 700
SIC 5153 Grain and field beans

D-U-N-S 25-233-4826   (BR)
COMMISSION SCOLAIRE DES PATRIOTES
ECOLE PRIMAIRE DE SALABERRY
1371 Rue Hertel, Chambly, QC, J3L 2M5
(450) 461-5905
Emp Here 25
SIC 8211 Elementary and secondary schools

D-U-N-S 25-233-4263   (BR)
COMMISSION SCOLAIRE DES PATRIOTES
COMMISSION SCOLAIRE DES PATRIOTES
1111 Rue Denault, Chambly, QC, J3L 2L7
(450) 461-5907
Emp Here 40
SIC 8211 Elementary and secondary schools

D-U-N-S 25-233-4305   (BR)
COMMISSION SCOLAIRE DES PATRIOTES
ECOLE JACQUES-DE-CHAMBLY
5 Rue Des Voltigeurs, Chambly, QC, J3L 3H3
(450) 461-5902
Emp Here 25
SIC 8211 Elementary and secondary schools

D-U-N-S 25-233-0915   (BR)
COMMISSION SCOLAIRE DES PATRIOTES
ECOLE CHAMBLY DE BOURGOGNE
1415 Av Bourgogne, Chambly, QC, J3L 1Y4
(450) 461-5901
Emp Here 70
SIC 8211 Elementary and secondary schools

D-U-N-S 20-026-3619   (BR)
COMMISSION SCOLAIRE DES PATRIOTES
COMMISSION SCOLAIRE DES PATRIOTES
535 Boul Brassard, Chambly, QC, J3L 6H3
(450) 461-5908
Emp Here 100
SIC 8211 Elementary and secondary schools

D-U-N-S 20-712-3154   (BR)
COMMISSION SCOLAIRE DES PATRIOTES

ECOLE SECONDAIRE LE TREMPLIN
1501 Av De Salaberry, Chambly, QC, J3L 4V8
(450) 461-5909
Emp Here 50
SIC 8211 Elementary and secondary schools

D-U-N-S 24-991-2432   (SL)
CONTINENTAL   BUILDING   PRODUCTS CANADA INC
MATERIAUX DE CONSTRUCTION CANADA CONTINENTAL
(*Suby of* Continental Building Products, Inc.)
8802 Boul Industriel, Chambly, QC, J3L 4X3
(450) 447-3206
Emp Here 250
SIC 1499 Miscellaneous nonMetallic minerals, except fuels

D-U-N-S 24-815-1326   (SL)
FORAGES CABO INC
DIV. FORDEM INTERNATIONAL
3000 Boul Industriel, Chambly, QC, J3L 4X3
(450) 572-1400
Emp Here 20   *Sales* 2,188,821
SIC 1781 Water well drilling

D-U-N-S 24-890-8878   (BR)
INTEGRATED   DISTRIBUTION   SYSTEMS LIMITED PARTNERSHIP
WAJAX EQUIPMENT
1970 Rue John-Yule, Chambly, QC, J3L 6W3
(905) 212-3300
Emp Here 30
SIC 5084 Industrial machinery and equipment

D-U-N-S 24-328-9175   (SL)
MACONNERIE PRO-CONSEIL INC
CONSTRUCTION M.B.
2825 Boul Industriel, Chambly, QC, J3L 4W3
(450) 447-6363
Emp Here 20   *Sales* 3,648,035
SIC 1741 Masonry and other stonework

D-U-N-S 24-474-5691   (SL)
MANOIR SOLEIL INC
125 Rue Daigneault, Chambly, QC, J3L 1G7
(450) 658-4441
Emp Here 50   *Sales* 1,969,939
SIC 8322 Individual and family services

D-U-N-S 24-390-0789   (BR)
MARCHE LAMBERT ET FRERES INC
(*Suby of* Investissements B.I.L. Inc)
3500 Boul Frechette, Chambly, QC, J3L 6Z6
(450) 447-1983
Emp Here 50
SIC 5411 Grocery stores

D-U-N-S 24-050-8127   (BR)
REINHART FOODS LIMITED
2050 Boul Industriel, Chambly, QC, J3L 4V2
(450) 658-7501
Emp Here 22
SIC 2099 Food preparations, nec

D-U-N-S 20-581-1602   (BR)
REMTEC INC
(*Suby of* 128707 Canada Inc)
2055 Boul Industriel, Chambly, QC, J3L 4C5
(450) 658-0588
Emp Here 55
SIC 3715 Truck trailers

D-U-N-S 25-257-0122   (SL)
RESIDENCE ST-JOSEPH DE CHAMBLY
CENTRE DE SOINS LONGUE DUREE SAINT JOSEPH DE CHAMBLY
100 Rue Martel, Chambly, QC, J3L 1V3
(450) 658-6271
Emp Here 50   *Sales* 1,824,018
SIC 8361 Residential care

D-U-N-S 20-317-5851   (BR)
TECHO-BLOC INC
PIERRES STONEDGE, LES
7800 Rue Samuel-Hatt, Chambly, QC, J3L 6W4

(450) 447-4780
Emp Here 50
SIC 2679 Converted paper products, nec

D-U-N-S 24-835-0613   (BR)
THOMAS, LARGE & SINGER INC
2050 Boul Industriel, Chambly, QC, J3L 4V2
(450) 658-7501
Emp Here 32
SIC 5141 Groceries, general line

D-U-N-S 20-651-8081   (BR)
UAP INC
MTC SUSPENSION
(*Suby of* Genuine Parts Company)
950 Av Simard, Chambly, QC, J3L 4X2
(450) 658-3893
Emp Here 55
SIC 5531 Auto and home supply stores

Chambord, QC G0W

D-U-N-S 20-192-5930   (SL)
COOPERATIVE   D'APPROVISIONNEMENT DE CHAMBORD
COOP CHAMBORD
1945 169 Rte, Chambord, QC, G0W 1G0
(418) 342-6495
Emp Here 60   *Sales* 10,306,800
SIC 5411 Grocery stores
Genl Mgr Claude Berube
Pr Pr Jean-Paul Boily

D-U-N-S 24-531-3887   (SL)
FERICAR INC
112 Rte 155, Chambord, QC, G0W 1G0
(418) 342-6221
Emp Here 70   *Sales* 9,557,852
SIC 3715 Truck trailers
Pr Pr Sabin Jean
Daniel Jean

D-U-N-S 20-698-0901   (BR)
LOUISIANA-PACIFIC CANADA LTD
LOUISIANA-PACIFIQUE   CANADA   LTEE-DIVISON QUEBEC CHAMBORD OSB
(*Suby of* Louisiana-Pacific Corporation)
572 155 Rte, Chambord, QC, G0W 1G0
(418) 342-6212
Emp Here 200
SIC 2611 Pulp mills

Champlain, QC G0X
Champlain County

D-U-N-S 25-232-7168   (BR)
COMMISSION SCOLAIRE DU CHEMIN-DU-ROY
ECOLE CHAMPS & MAREES-CHAMPLAIN
963 Rue Notre-Dame, Champlain, QC, G0X 1C0
(819) 840-4317
Emp Here 20
SIC 8211 Elementary and secondary schools

Chandler, QC G0C
Gaspe-Est County

D-U-N-S 20-029-1693   (BR)
CENTRE READAPTATION DE GASPESIE
(*Suby of* Centre Readaptation De Gaspesie)
328 Boul Rene-Levesque Bureau 102, Chandler, QC, G0C 1K0
(418) 689-4286
Emp Here 26
SIC 8361 Residential care

D-U-N-S 20-711-8055   (BR)
COMMISSION   SCOLAIRE   RENE-

LEVESQUE
ECOLE POLYVALENTE MGR SEVIGNY
155 Rue Monseigneur-Ross O, Chandler, QC,
G0C 1K0
(418) 689-2233
Emp Here 50
SIC 8211 Elementary and secondary schools

D-U-N-S 20-711-7990   (BR)
COMMISSION SCOLAIRE RENE-LEVESQUE
ECOLE POLYVALENTE MGR SEVIGNY
155 Rue Monseigneur-Ross O, Chandler, QC,
G0C 1K0
(418) 689-2233
Emp Here 50
SIC 8211 Elementary and secondary schools

D-U-N-S 20-711-8709   (BR)
EASTERN SHORES SCHOOL BOARD
ECOLE POLYVALENTE MGR SEVIGNY
155 Rue Monseigneur-Ross O, Chandler, QC,
G0C 1K0
(418) 689-2233
Emp Here 50
SIC 8211 Elementary and secondary schools

D-U-N-S 20-801-1416   (BR)
LEALIN LTD
MCDONALD'S RESTAURANT
(*Suby* of Lealin Ltd)
550 Av Daigneault, Chandler, QC, G0C 1K0

Emp Here 40
SIC 5812 Eating places

Chapais, QC G0W
Abitibi County

D-U-N-S 25-728-0107   (BR)
CENTRE REGIONAL DE SANTE ET DE SERVICE SOCIAUX DE LA BAIE-JAMES
CENTRE REGIONALE DE SANTE & DE SERVICE SOCIAUX DE LA BAIE-JAMES
32 3e Rue Bureau 238, Chapais, QC, G0W 1H0
(418) 748-7658
Emp Here 60
SIC 8093 Specialty outpatient clinics, nec

Charette, QC G0X
St-Maurice County

D-U-N-S 25-233-1137   (BR)
COMMISSION SCOLAIRE DE L'ENERGIE
ECOLE NOTRE DAME DES NEIGES
351 Rue De L'Eglise, Charette, QC, G0X 1E0
(819) 221-2820
Emp Here 50
SIC 8211 Elementary and secondary schools

Charlemagne, QC J5Z
L'Assomption County

D-U-N-S 25-081-1395   (SL)
DIVERTISSEMENT DIRECT INC
GROUPE EN FETE, LE
60 Rue Saint-Paul, Charlemagne, QC, J5Z 1G3
(450) 654-5064
Emp Here 50   *Sales* 1,678,096
SIC 7299 Miscellaneous personal service

D-U-N-S 20-101-2924   (SL)
ROTISSERIES LANAUDIERE INC, LES
ROTISSERIE ST-HUBERT B.B.Q.
99 Rue Emile-Despins, Charlemagne, QC,
J5Z 3L6

---

(450) 581-0645
Emp Here 50   *Sales* 1,819,127
SIC 5812 Eating places

Chateau-Richer, QC G0A

D-U-N-S 25-232-6921   (BR)
COMMISSION SCOLAIRE DES PREMIERES-SEIGNEURIES
COMMISSION SCOLAIRE DES PREMIERES-SEIGNEURIES
(*Suby of* Commission Scolaire Des Premieres-Seigneuries)
273 Rue Du Couvent, Chateau-Richer, QC, G0A 1N0
(418) 821-8077
Emp Here 26
SIC 8211 Elementary and secondary schools

D-U-N-S 20-193-3389   (SL)
GIGUERE PORTES ET FENETRES INC
7068 Boul Sainte-Anne, Chateau-Richer, QC, G0A 1N0
(418) 824-4379
Emp Here 60   *Sales* 4,888,367
SIC 2431 Millwork

D-U-N-S 24-622-8928   (BR)
PF RESOLU CANADA INC
CHATEAU RICHER MILL
7499 Boul Sainte-Anne, Chateau-Richer, QC, G0A 1N0
(418) 824-4233
Emp Here 108
SIC 2421 Sawmills and planing mills, general

Chateauguay, QC J6J
Chateauguay County

D-U-N-S 20-707-7942   (SL)
141517 CANADA LTEE
CLERMONT
(*Suby* of Les Gestions Prismes C.M. Inc)
1155 Boul Ford, Chateauguay, QC, J6J 4Z2
(450) 692-5527
Emp Here 125   *Sales* 12,330,358
SIC 1761 Roofing, siding, and sheetMetal work
Pr Pr Mario Levesque
Treas Carole Dube

D-U-N-S 20-234-7881   (SL)
3722007 CANADA INC
1241 Rue Des Cascades Bureau 1, Chateauguay, QC, J6J 4Z2
(450) 691-5510
Emp Here 50   *Sales* 7,913,100
SIC 3469 Metal stampings, nec
Pr Pr Steve Zimmerman
Treas John Zimmermann
Dir Martha Zimmermann
Dir Hans Zimmermann
Dir Daniel Zimmermann

D-U-N-S 24-853-9442   (SL)
9205-2976 QUEBEC INC
1200 Rue Des Cascades, Chateauguay, QC, J6J 4Z2
(450) 699-9300
Emp Here 50   *Sales* 4,244,630
SIC 3465 Automotive stampings

D-U-N-S 20-571-1059   (BR)
BANQUE NATIONALE DU CANADA
99 Boul D'Anjou, Chateauguay, QC, J6J 2R2
(450) 692-1990
Emp Here 30
SIC 6021 National commercial banks

D-U-N-S 24-799-6465   (BR)
CARBON STEEL PROFILES LIMITED
1175 Boul Ford, Chateauguay, QC, J6J 4Z2

---

(450) 692-5600
Emp Here 28
SIC 3541 Machine tools, Metal cutting type

D-U-N-S 25-232-3035   (BR)
CHATEAUGUAY, VILLE DE
BIBLIOTHEQUE MUNICIPALE DE CHATEAUGUAY
25 Boul Maple, Chateauguay, QC, J6J 3P7
(450) 698-3080
Emp Here 20
SIC 8231 Libraries

D-U-N-S 25-240-5758   (BR)
COMMISSION SCOLAIRE NEW FRONTIER
ST WILLIBRORD SCHOOL
300 Rue Mcleod, Chateauguay, QC, J6J 2H6
(450) 691-4550
Emp Here 50
SIC 8211 Elementary and secondary schools

D-U-N-S 20-712-3477   (BR)
COMMISSION SCOLAIRE NEW FRONTIER
EDUCATION AUX ADULTES ET FORMA-TION PROFESSIONNELLE
70 Boul Maple, Chateauguay, QC, J6J 3P8
(450) 691-2540
Emp Here 30
SIC 8211 Elementary and secondary schools

D-U-N-S 20-712-3444   (BR)
COMMISSION SCOLAIRE NEW FRONTIER
ECOLE HOWARD S BELINGS
210 Rue Mcleod, Chateauguay, QC, J6J 2H4
(450) 691-3230
Emp Here 105
SIC 8211 Elementary and secondary schools

D-U-N-S 25-240-5790   (BR)
COMMISSION SCOLAIRE NEW FRONTIER
ECOLE PRIMAIRE CENTENNIAL PARK
85 Rue Jeffries, Chateauguay, QC, J6J 4A4
(450) 692-8251
Emp Here 30
SIC 8211 Elementary and secondary schools

D-U-N-S 25-885-8497   (BR)
COMMISSION SCOLAIRE DES GRANDES-SEIGNEURIES
ECOLE LABERGE
315 Rue Rideau, Chateauguay, QC, J6J 1S1
(514) 380-8899
Emp Here 61
SIC 8211 Elementary and secondary schools

D-U-N-S 20-806-8200   (BR)
COUCHE-TARD INC
125 Boul Maple, Chateauguay, QC, J6J 5C3
(450) 691-1162
Emp Here 25
SIC 5411 Grocery stores

D-U-N-S 25-196-2239   (SL)
DEJUMP INC
GROUPE DEJUMP
255 Boul D'Anjou Bureau 207, Chateauguay, QC, J6J 2R4

Emp Here 50   *Sales* 2,626,585
SIC 7389 Business services, nec

D-U-N-S 24-859-8570   (SL)
EMBALLAGES SALERNO CANADA INC
SALERNO PACKAGING
2275 Boul Ford, Chateauguay, QC, J6J 4Z2
(450) 692-8642
Emp Here 100   *Sales* 15,238,762
SIC 2673 Bags: plastic, laminated, and coated
Dir Joe Chen
Pr Pr Kurt Strater
  Joseph Wang
  Robert H. Wang
Dir John Ding-E Young
Dir Ben Tseng
Dir Benjamin Tsao
Prd Dir Tony Incollingo

D-U-N-S 24-711-8979   (SL)
GICLEURS ALERTE INC
1250 Rue Des Cascades, Chateauguay, QC, J6J 4Z2
(450) 692-9098
Emp Here 50   *Sales* 4,377,642
SIC 1711 Plumbing, heating, air-conditioning

D-U-N-S 25-685-0082   (SL)
MACLEAN POWER COMPANY (CANADA)
MACLEAN POWER SYSTEMS
(*Suby of* Mac Lean-Fogg Company)
225 Boul Ford, Chateauguay, QC, J6J 4Z2
(450) 698-0520
Emp Here 30   *Sales* 2,480,664
SIC 3621 Motors and generators

D-U-N-S 20-016-4705   (BR)
NAUTILUS PLUS INC
47 Boul Saint-Jean-Baptiste, Chateauguay, QC, J6J 3H5
(514) 666-0668
Emp Here 20
SIC 5941 Sporting goods and bicycle shops

D-U-N-S 25-299-9602   (BR)
PRISZM LP
PFK ET TACOBELL
129 Boul D'Anjou, Chateauguay, QC, J6J 2R3

Emp Here 23
SIC 5812 Eating places

D-U-N-S 24-053-9114   (HQ)
PYRO-AIR LTEE
(*Suby of* Pyro-Air Ltee)
2575 Boul Ford, Chateauguay, QC, J6J 4Z2
(450) 691-3460
Emp Here 45   *Emp Total* 53
Sales 4,669,485
SIC 1711 Plumbing, heating, air-conditioning

D-U-N-S 25-190-1443   (SL)
ROCHE LTEE
301 Boul Industriel, Chateauguay, QC, J6J 4Z2
(450) 691-1858
Emp Here 49   *Sales* 6,797,150
SIC 8711 Engineering services
Pr Alex Brisson

D-U-N-S 20-233-4884   (SL)
SALERNO PELLICULE ET SACS DE PLAS-TIQUE (CANADA) INC
2275 Boul Ford, Chateauguay, QC, J6J 4Z2
(450) 692-8642
Emp Here 140   *Sales* 26,385,212
SIC 2673 Bags: plastic, laminated, and coated
Pr Kurt Strater
VP Roger Sullivan
Sec Marco Ferraresi

D-U-N-S 24-778-4874   (SL)
SALERNO SACS TRANSPARENTS LTEE
2275 Boul Ford, Chateauguay, QC, J6J 4Z2
(450) 692-8642
Emp Here 55
SIC 2673 Bags: plastic, laminated, and coated

D-U-N-S 24-541-3463   (SL)
TEXTILES WIN-SIR INC, LES
295 Boul Industriel Bureau A, Chateauguay, QC, J6J 4Z2
(514) 384-3072
Emp Here 100   *Sales* 1,824,018
SIC 2322 Men's and boy's underwear and nightwear

D-U-N-S 25-174-9289   (BR)
WENDY'S RESTAURANTS OF CANADA INC
WENDY'S RESTAURANTS OF CANADA INC
(*Suby of* The Wendy's Company)
251 Boul D'Anjou, Chateauguay, QC, J6J 2R4
(450) 692-1733
Emp Here 30
SIC 5812 Eating places

Chateauguay, QC J6K
Chateauguay County

D-U-N-S 24-541-9390 (BR)
ALIMENTS SAVEURS DU MONDE INC, LES
AKI SUSHI BAR
105 Rue Principale, Chateauguay, QC, J6K 1G2
(450) 699-0819
Emp Here 48
SIC 5812 Eating places

D-U-N-S 20-988-0066 (SL)
AUBAINERIE CONCEPT MODE, L
80 Boul D'Anjou, Chateauguay, QC, J6K 1C3
(450) 699-0444
Emp Here 60   *Sales* 3,648,035
SIC 5651 Family clothing stores

D-U-N-S 20-801-9633 (BR)
CENTRE INTEGRE DE SANTE ET DE SERVICES SOCIAUX DE LA MONTEREGIE-OUEST
CENTRE D'HEBERGEMENT DE CHATEAUGUAY
(*Suby of* Centre Integre de Sante et de Services Sociaux de la Monteregie-Ouest)
95 Ch De La Haute-Riviere, Chateauguay, QC, J6K 3P1
(450) 692-8231
Emp Here 205
SIC 8322 Individual and family services

D-U-N-S 25-240-5832 (BR)
COMMISSION SCOLAIRE NEW FRONTIER
ECOLE MARY GARDNER
42 Rue Saint-Hubert, Chateauguay, QC, J6K 3K8
(450) 691-2600
Emp Here 40
SIC 8211 Elementary and secondary schools

D-U-N-S 25-126-0816 (BR)
COMMISSION SCOLAIRE NEW FRONTIER
HARMONY SCHOOL
280 Av Brahms, Chateauguay, QC, J6K 5G1
(450) 691-9099
Emp Here 25
SIC 8211 Elementary and secondary schools

D-U-N-S 25-232-9727 (BR)
COMMISSION SCOLAIRE DES GRANDES-SEIGNEURIES
ECOLE DE FORMATION PROFESSIONELLE CHATEAUGUAY
225 Boul Brisebois, Chateauguay, QC, J6K 3X4
(514) 380-8899
Emp Here 65
SIC 8211 Elementary and secondary schools

D-U-N-S 24-205-5981 (SL)
CONCEPT MODE CHATEAUGUAY INC
80 Boul D'Anjou Bureau 450, Chateauguay, QC, J6K 1C3
(450) 699-0444
Emp Here 60   *Sales* 3,648,035
SIC 5651 Family clothing stores

D-U-N-S 20-724-3189 (SL)
DESJARDINS CHEVROLET INC
190 Boul Saint-Jean-Baptiste, Chateauguay, QC, J6K 3B6
(514) 990-9899
Emp Here 35   *Sales* 17,584,000
SIC 5511 New and used car dealers
Pr Pr Andre Desjardins

D-U-N-S 20-002-1277 (BR)
FEDERATION DES CAISSES DESJARDINS DU QUEBEC
CAISSES DESJARDINS
235 Ch De La Haute-Riviere, Chateauguay, QC, J6K 5B1
(450) 692-1000
Emp Here 75

SIC 6062 State credit unions

D-U-N-S 24-251-8470 (SL)
GESTION CARBO LTEE
117 Boul Saint-Jean-Baptiste, Chateauguay, QC, J6K 3B1
(450) 691-4130
Emp Here 48   *Sales* 24,115,200
SIC 5511 New and used car dealers
Pr Robert Leblanc

D-U-N-S 25-879-7232 (BR)
GOUVERNEMENT DE LA PROVINCE DE QUEBEC
CENTRE JEUNESSE DE LA MONTEREGIE
278 Boul Saint-Jean-Baptiste Bureau 200, Chateauguay, QC, J6K 3C2
(450) 692-6741
Emp Here 50
SIC 8322 Individual and family services

D-U-N-S 20-526-8274 (BR)
GROUPE LALIBERTE SPORTS INC
SPORTS EXPERTS
298 Boul D'Anjou, Chateauguay, QC, J6K 1C6
(450) 699-3939
Emp Here 20
SIC 5941 Sporting goods and bicycle shops

D-U-N-S 20-224-6943 (BR)
GROUPE SPORTSCENE INC
CAGE AUX SPORTS, LA
72 Boul Saint-Jean-Baptiste Bureau 120, Chateauguay, QC, J6K 4Y7

Emp Here 30
SIC 5812 Eating places

D-U-N-S 25-174-7101 (BR)
METRO RICHELIEU INC
SUPER C
200 Boul D'Anjou Bureau 626, Chateauguay, QC, J6K 1C5
(450) 691-2880
Emp Here 105
SIC 5411 Grocery stores

D-U-N-S 20-646-1019 (BR)
SOBEYS CAPITAL INCORPORATED
SOBEYS # 439
90 Boul D'Anjou, Chateauguay, QC, J6K 1C3
(450) 692-3446
Emp Here 200
SIC 5411 Grocery stores

Chelsea, QC J9B
Gatineau County

D-U-N-S 24-347-1872 (SL)
AUBERGE & SPA LE NORDIK INC
LE NORDIK-SPA EN NATURE
16 Ch Nordik, Chelsea, QC, J9B 2P7
(819) 827-1111
Emp Here 140   *Sales* 4,669,485
SIC 7991 Physical fitness facilities

D-U-N-S 25-233-8223 (BR)
COMMISSION SCOLAIRE WESTERN QUEBEC
CHELSEA ELEMENTARY SCHOOL
(*Suby of* Commission Scolaire Western Quebec)
74 Ch D'Old Chelsea, Chelsea, QC, J9B 1K9
(819) 827-0245
Emp Here 35
SIC 8211 Elementary and secondary schools

D-U-N-S 20-086-9100 (BR)
FONDATION DE LA COMMISSION SCOLAIRE DES PORTAGES-DE-L'OUTAOUAIS
FONDATION DE LA COMMISSION SCOLAIRE DES PORTAGES-D
135 Ch Scott, Chelsea, QC, J9B 1R6
(819) 827-4581
Emp Here 55

SIC 8211 Elementary and secondary schools

D-U-N-S 20-544-9767 (BR)
HYDRO-QUEBEC
128 Ch Mill, Chelsea, QC, J9B 1K8
(819) 827-7137
Emp Here 100
SIC 4911 Electric services

Chibougamau, QC G8P
Abitibi County

D-U-N-S 24-907-2430 (SL)
156307 CANADA INC
HOTEL CHIBOUGAMAU 1993 ENR
473 3e Rue, Chibougamau, QC, G8P 1N6
(418) 748-2669
Emp Here 50   *Sales* 2,188,821
SIC 7011 Hotels and motels

D-U-N-S 25-447-8647 (SL)
9003-3416 QUEBEC INC
PHARMACIE BOURGET & TREMBLAY
503 3e Rue, Chibougamau, QC, G8P 1N8
(418) 748-2606
Emp Here 35   *Sales* 7,837,440
SIC 5912 Drug stores and proprietary stores
Pr Pr Francis Bourget
    Robin Tremblay

D-U-N-S 24-592-2450 (SL)
9170-7570 QUEBEC INC
BIRON
949 3e Rue, Chibougamau, QC, G8P 1R4
(418) 748-2691
Emp Here 50   *Sales* 4,377,642
SIC 1711 Plumbing, heating, air-conditioning

D-U-N-S 25-257-4082 (HQ)
CAISSE DESJARDINS DE CHIBOUGAMAU
CENTRE DE SERVICE DE CHAPAIS
(*Suby of* Caisse Desjardins de Chibougamau)
519 3e Rue, Chibougamau, QC, G8P 1N8
(418) 748-6461
Emp Here 28   *Emp Total* 51
Sales 6,328,026
SIC 6062 State credit unions

D-U-N-S 25-376-2637 (BR)
CEGEP DE SAINT-FELICIEN
CENTRE D'ETUDES COLLEGIALES A CHIBOUGAMAU
(*Suby of* Cegep de Saint-Felicien)
110 Rue Obalski, Chibougamau, QC, G8P 2E9
(418) 748-7637
Emp Here 35
SIC 8221 Colleges and universities

D-U-N-S 25-093-3707 (BR)
CENTRE REGIONAL DE SANTE ET DE SERVICE SOCIAUX DE LA BAIE-JAMES
CENTRE REGIONALE DE SANTE & DE SERVICE SOCIAUX DE LA BAIE-JAMES
51 3e Rue, Chibougamau, QC, G8P 1N1
(418) 748-3662
Emp Here 60
SIC 8093 Specialty outpatient clinics, nec

D-U-N-S 25-232-1112 (BR)
COMMISSION SCOLAIRE CENTRAL QUEBEC
MACLEAN MEMORIAL SCHOOL
(*Suby of* Commission Scolaire Central Quebec)
159 5e Av, Chibougamau, QC, G8P 2E6
(418) 748-2038
Emp Here 24
SIC 8211 Elementary and secondary schools

D-U-N-S 25-337-0654 (BR)
COMMISSION SCOLAIRE DE LA BAIE JAMES
ECOLE VATICAN II
(*Suby of* Commission Scolaire de la Baie

James)
291 Rue Wilson, Chibougamau, QC, G8P 1J4
(418) 748-2089
Emp Here 32
SIC 8211 Elementary and secondary schools

D-U-N-S 20-712-6090 (BR)
COMMISSION SCOLAIRE DE LA BAIE JAMES
COMPLEXE VIGNETTE
(*Suby of* Commission Scolaire de la Baie James)
596 4e Rue, Chibougamau, QC, G8P 1S3
(418) 748-7621
Emp Here 50
SIC 8211 Elementary and secondary schools

D-U-N-S 25-233-5658 (BR)
COMMISSION SCOLAIRE DE LA BAIE JAMES
ECOLE NOTRE DAME DU ROSAIRE
(*Suby of* Commission Scolaire de la Baie James)
585 Rue Wilson, Chibougamau, QC, G8P 1K2
(418) 748-2307
Emp Here 25
SIC 8211 Elementary and secondary schools

D-U-N-S 25-024-8903 (BR)
FERLAC INC
(*Suby of* 9072-4725 Quebec Inc)
935 3e Rue, Chibougamau, QC, G8P 1R4
(418) 748-7664
Emp Here 30
SIC 5251 Hardware stores

D-U-N-S 25-336-7064 (BR)
GOUVERNEMENT DE LA PROVINCE DE QUEBEC
GOUVERNEMENT DE LA PROVINCE DE QUEBEC
1240 Rte 113, Chibougamau, QC, G8P 2K5
(418) 748-7608
Emp Here 51
SIC 1611 Highway and street construction

D-U-N-S 20-567-5643 (BR)
HEALTH CANADA
CENTRES DE RESSOURCES HUMAINES
623 3e Rue, Chibougamau, QC, G8P 3A2

Emp Here 20
SIC 6321 Accident and health insurance

D-U-N-S 25-690-0796 (BR)
SOCIETE DES ETABLISSEMENTS DE PLEIN AIR DU QUEBEC
RESERVE FAUNIQUE ASSINICA ET DES LACS ALBANEL, MISTASSINI ET WACONICHI
1584 Rte 167, Chibougamau, QC, G8P 2K5
(418) 748-7748
Emp Here 20
SIC 7999 Amusement and recreation, nec

Chicoutimi, QC G7G
Chicoutimi County

D-U-N-S 20-649-1412 (SL)
9095-9133 QUEBEC INC
IGA ROBERT MARTIN
625 Boul Sainte-Genevieve, Chicoutimi, QC, G7G 2E5
(418) 545-7680
Emp Here 100   *Sales* 18,168,160
SIC 5411 Grocery stores
Pr Robert Martin

D-U-N-S 24-333-0656 (HQ)
CAISSE DESJARDINS DE LA RIVE-NORD DU SAGUENAY
CENTRE DE SERVICE BEGIN
(*Suby of* Caisse Desjardins de la Rive-Nord du Saguenay)

2212 Rue Roussel, Chicoutimi, QC, G7G 1W7
(418) 549-4273
Emp Here 25   *Emp Total* 100
Sales 22,319,000
SIC 6062 State credit unions
Genl Mgr Robin St-Pierre
Dir Guy Poulin
Pr Andre Lessard
VP VP Serge Lavoie
Sec Serge Therreault
Dir Gaetan Tremblay
Dir Raynald Turcotte
Dir Jean-Marie Savard
Dir Marjolaine Maltais
Dir Claude Gaudreault

D-U-N-S 25-797-2406   (HQ)
CENTRE DE LA PETITE ENFANCE LES PE-TITS CAILLOUX
(*Suby of* Centre de la petite enfance les Petits Cailloux)
210 Rue Mezy, Chicoutimi, QC, G7G 1J5
(418) 698-4663
Emp Here 27   *Emp Total* 67
Sales 2,042,900
SIC 8351 Child day care services

D-U-N-S 25-022-6941   (BR)
COMMISSION SCOLAIRE DES RIVES-DU-SAGUENAY
ECOLE SAINTE-CLAIRE
(*Suby of* Commission Scolaire des Rives-du-Saguenay)
136 Rue Des Saules, Chicoutimi, QC, G7G 4C3
(418) 543-3680
Emp Here 25

D-U-N-S 25-234-0765   (BR)
COMMISSION SCOLAIRE DES RIVES-DU-SAGUENAY
ECOLE PRIMAIRE LA CARRIERE
(*Suby of* Commission Scolaire des Rives-du-Saguenay)
245 Rue Des Epervieres, Chicoutimi, QC, G7G 4Y8
(418) 549-3480
Emp Here 30
SIC 8211 Elementary and secondary schools

D-U-N-S 24-237-9522   (BR)
COMMISSION SCOLAIRE DES RIVES-DU-SAGUENAY
ECOLE SECONDAIRE CHARLES GRAVEL
350 Rue Saint-Gerard, Chicoutimi, QC, G7G 1J2
(418) 541-4343
Emp Here 180
SIC 8211 Elementary and secondary schools

D-U-N-S 20-711-9061   (BR)
COMMISSION SCOLAIRE DES RIVES-DU-SAGUENAY
ECOLE PRIMAIRE LE ROSEAU
41 Rue Saint-Benoit, Chicoutimi, QC, G7G 2R4
(418) 543-2213
Emp Here 50
SIC 8211 Elementary and secondary schools

D-U-N-S 20-720-6116   (BR)
ENTREPRISES MACBAIE INC, LES
MCDONALD
717 Boul Sainte-Genevieve, Chicoutimi, QC, G7G 4Z4
(418) 696-5017
Emp Here 40
SIC 5812 Eating places

D-U-N-S 25-211-9615   (BR)
PROVIGO DISTRIBUTION INC
PROVIGO CHICOUTIMI NORD # 8406
2120 Rue Roussel, Chicoutimi, QC, G7G 1W3
(418) 543-9113
Emp Here 50
SIC 5411 Grocery stores

D-U-N-S 20-988-0462   (BR)
UNIPRIX INC
PHARMACIENS GAUDREAULT GIRARD & PERRON, LES
711 Boul Sainte-Genevieve, Chicoutimi, QC, G7G 4Z4
(418) 549-9544
Emp Here 30
SIC 5122 Drugs, proprietaries, and sundries

Chicoutimi, QC G7H
Chicoutimi County

D-U-N-S 24-568-3693   (SL)
2318-7081 QUEBEC INC
1080 Boul Talbot, Chicoutimi, QC, G7H 4B6
(418) 543-1521
Emp Here 140   *Sales* 8,521,800
SIC 7011 Hotels and motels
Jean-Marc Couture

D-U-N-S 25-984-9545   (SL)
2538-1245 QUEBEC INC
PUB AVENUE
381 Rue Racine E, Chicoutimi, QC, G7H 1S8
(418) 543-9025
Emp Here 50   *Sales* 1,824,018
SIC 5813 Drinking places

D-U-N-S 25-135-4353   (SL)
2852-7414 QUEBEC INC
COQ ROTI PIZZA DELIGHT
805 Boul Talbot, Chicoutimi, QC, G7H 4B3
(418) 698-8877
Emp Here 50   *Sales* 1,532,175
SIC 5812 Eating places

D-U-N-S 25-488-3630   (SL)
3111326 CANADA INC
CAGE AUX SPORTS, LA
1611 Boul Talbot, Chicoutimi, QC, G7H 4C3
(418) 698-8611
Emp Here 75   *Sales* 2,261,782
SIC 5812 Eating places

D-U-N-S 20-024-6762   (HQ)
9067-7022 QUEBEC INC
TIM HORTONS
(*Suby of* 9067-7022 Quebec Inc)
1494 Boul Talbot, Chicoutimi, QC, G7H 4C2
(418) 696-3158
Emp Here 32   *Emp Total* 57
Sales 1,751,057
SIC 5812 Eating places

D-U-N-S 24-159-3263   (SL)
9129-4710 QUEBEC INC
SAGUENAY INFORMATIQUE
1740 Boul Du Royaume O, Chicoutimi, QC, G7H 5B1
(418) 698-6668
Emp Here 55   *Sales* 4,012,839
SIC 7378 Computer maintenance and repair

D-U-N-S 20-362-5678   (SL)
9216-3146 QUEBEC INC
MICRO BREWERY OF SAGUENAY
224 Rue Des Laurentides, Chicoutimi, QC, G7H 7X8
(418) 615-1414
Emp Here 40   *Sales* 5,180,210
SIC 2082 Malt beverages
Pr Pr Daniel Giguere
Guillaume St-Gelais

D-U-N-S 25-844-5386   (BR)
AMEUBLEMENTS TANGUAY INC
1990 Boul Talbot, Chicoutimi, QC, G7H 7Y3
(418) 698-4411
Emp Here 120
SIC 5712 Furniture stores

D-U-N-S 25-597-8116   (BR)
ASTRAL MEDIA RADIO INC
ROCK DETENTE

(*Suby of* Astral Media Radio Inc)
267 Racine St E, Chicoutimi, QC, G7H 1S5
(418) 543-9797
Emp Here 30
SIC 4832 Radio broadcasting stations

D-U-N-S 25-257-2888   (BR)
ASTRAL MEDIA RADIO INC
CKRS CJAB FM, DIV DE
(*Suby of* Astral Media Radio Inc)
121 Rue Racine E, Chicoutimi, QC, G7H 1R6
(418) 545-2577
Emp Here 25
SIC 4832 Radio broadcasting stations

D-U-N-S 25-010-1342   (BR)
BANQUE NATIONALE DU CANADA
1180 Boul Talbot Bureau 201, Chicoutimi, QC, G7H 4B6
(418) 545-1655
Emp Here 35
SIC 6021 National commercial banks

D-U-N-S 20-588-2421   (BR)
BANQUE TORONTO-DOMINION, LA
TD CANADA TRUST
(*Suby of* Toronto-Dominion Bank, The)
255 Rue Racine E Bureau 100, Chicoutimi, QC, G7H 7L2
(418) 549-0412
Emp Here 20
SIC 6021 National commercial banks

D-U-N-S 24-362-5634   (BR)
BEST BUY CANADA LTD
FUTURE SHOP
(*Suby of* Best Buy Co., Inc.)
1401 Boul Talbot, Chicoutimi, QC, G7H 5N6
(418) 698-6701
Emp Here 100
SIC 5731 Radio, television, and electronic stores

D-U-N-S 20-265-9041   (BR)
BIBLIOTHEQUE ET ARCHIVES NA-TIONALES DU QUEBEC
BANQ
930 Rue Jacques-Cartier E Bureau C-103, Chicoutimi, QC, G7H 7K9
(418) 698-3516
Emp Here 30
SIC 8231 Libraries

D-U-N-S 24-759-5184   (SL)
BLACKBURN SERVICE D'INVENTAIRE INC
125 Rue Dube, Chicoutimi, QC, G7H 2V3
(418) 543-4567
Emp Here 50   *Sales* 2,626,585
SIC 7389 Business services, nec

D-U-N-S 20-792-2423   (BR)
BOUTIQUE LA VIE EN ROSE INC
BOUTIQUE LA VIE EN ROSE INC
1401 Boul Talbot, Chicoutimi, QC, G7H 5N6
(418) 690-2537
Emp Here 22
SIC 5632 Women's accessory and specialty stores

D-U-N-S 20-873-8401   (SL)
CSSS DE CHICOUTIMI
305 Rue Saint-Vallier, Chicoutimi, QC, G7H 5H6
(418) 541-1000
Emp Here 1,900   *Sales* 183,827,400
SIC 8062 General medical and surgical hospitals
Genl Mgr Richard Lemieux
Yves Fortin

D-U-N-S 24-821-6855   (HQ)
CAIN LAMARRE CASGRAIN WELLS, S.E.N.C.R.L.
CAIN LAMARRE CASGRAIN WELLS
(*Suby of* Cain Lamarre Casgrain Wells, S.E.N.C.R.L.)
255 Rue Racine E Bureau 600, Chicoutimi, QC, G7H 7L2

(418) 545-4580
Emp Here 60   *Emp Total* 360
Sales 42,913,350
SIC 8111 Legal services
Pt Pierre Tremblay
Pt Guy Wells
Pt Francois Bouchard
Pt Richard Bergeron
Pt Yvan Bujold
Pt Jean Dauphinais
Pt Alain Letourneau
Pt J. Lucie Perron
Pt Francois G. Tremblay
Pt Gina Doucet

D-U-N-S 20-002-5893   (BR)
CAISSE DESJARDINS DE CHICOUTIMI
CENTRE FINANCIER
1685 Boul Talbot Bureau 700, Chicoutimi, QC, G7H 7Y4
(418) 543-1700
Emp Here 45
SIC 6062 State credit unions

D-U-N-S 24-213-5098   (BR)
CANAC-MARQUIS GRENIER LTEE
2061 Boul Talbot, Chicoutimi, QC, G7H 8B2
(418) 698-2992
Emp Here 60
SIC 5211 Lumber and other building materials

D-U-N-S 20-538-1101   (BR)
CANADA POST CORPORATION
1939 Rue Des Sapins Unite 1, Chicoutimi, QC, G7H 0H7
(418) 690-0350
Emp Here 125
SIC 4311 U.s. postal service

D-U-N-S 25-026-3928   (BR)
CANADIAN BROADCASTING CORPORA-TION
SOCIETE RADIO CANADA
500 Rue Des Sagueneens, Chicoutimi, QC, G7H 6N4
(418) 696-6600
Emp Here 30
SIC 4832 Radio broadcasting stations

D-U-N-S 20-308-9412   (HQ)
CEGERTEC INC
CEGERTEC
(*Suby of* Ceger Inc)
255 Rue Racine E Bureau 150, Chicoutimi, QC, G7H 7L2
(418) 549-6680
Emp Here 150   *Emp Total* 650
Sales 27,360,263
SIC 8621 Professional organizations
Treas Andre Salesse
Dir Jean-Philippe Harvey
Dir Eloise Harvey
Dir Melanie St-Pierre
Genl Mgr Serge Savard

D-U-N-S 25-849-3626   (BR)
CENTRE DE READAPTATION EN DEFI-CIENCE INTELLECTUELLE DU SAGUENAY LAC-ST-JEAN
(*Suby of* Centre De Readaptation En De-ficience Intellectuelle Du Saguenay Lac-St-Jean)
766 Rue Du Cenacle, Chicoutimi, QC, G7H 2J2
(418) 549-4003
Emp Here 60
SIC 8361 Residential care

D-U-N-S 20-030-4678   (BR)
CENTRE DE SANTE ET DE SERVICES SO-CIAUX DE CHICOUTIMI
CENTRE MGR VICTOR TREMBLAY
1236 Rue D'Angouleme, Chicoutimi, QC, G7H 6P9
(418) 698-3907
Emp Here 100
SIC 8361 Residential care

D-U-N-S 25-047-8526   (HQ)

CENTRE DE SANTE ET DE SERVICES SO-CIAUX DE CHICOUTIMI
CSSSC
305 Rue Saint-Vallier, Chicoutimi, QC, G7H 5H6
(418) 541-1046
Emp Here 2,200   *Emp Total* 40,000
Sales 260,320,365
SIC 8011 Offices and clinics of medical doctors
Genl Mgr Richard Lemieux

     D-U-N-S 24-908-2181   (SL)
CENTRE LOCAL DES SERVICES COMMU-NAUTAIRES DU GRAND CHICOUTIMI
C.L.S.C. DU GRAND CHICOUTIMI
411 Rue De L'Hotel-Dieu, Chicoutimi, QC, G7H 7Z5
(418) 543-2221
Emp Here 300   *Sales* 19,035,046
SIC 8399 Social services, nec
Dir Marcel Giguere

     D-U-N-S 24-240-1318   (SL)
CERADYNE CANADA ULC
CERADYNE CANADA
(*Suby of* 3M Company)
2702 Boul Talbot, Chicoutimi, QC, G7H 5B1
(418) 693-0227
Emp Here 30   *Sales* 5,987,760
SIC 3334 Primary aluminum
Pr David P Reed
Treas Jerrold J Pellizzon
   Joel P Moskowitz

     D-U-N-S 20-581-0765   (SL)
CHARPENTERIE INC, LA
1651 Boul Du Royaume O Bureau 4, Chicoutimi, QC, G7H 5B1
(418) 549-7731
Emp Here 50   *Sales* 5,690,935
SIC 2439 Structural wood members, nec
   Richard Letourneau
Sec Sonia Morneau

     D-U-N-S 24-592-4519   (SL)
CLUB DE GOLF DE CHICOUTIMI INC
2743 Boul Talbot, Chicoutimi, QC, G7H 5B1
(418) 549-6608
Emp Here 50   *Sales* 2,042,900
SIC 7997 Membership sports and recreation clubs

     D-U-N-S 24-803-2075   (BR)
COMMISSION SCOLAIRE DES RIVES-DU-SAGUENAY
CENTRE DE FORMATION PROFESSION-NELLE EN METALLURGIE ET MULTISER-VICES
847 Rue Georges-Vanier, Chicoutimi, QC, G7H 4M1
(418) 615-0083
Emp Here 30
SIC 8211 Elementary and secondary schools

     D-U-N-S 20-711-9087   (BR)
COMMISSION SCOLAIRE DES RIVES-DU-SAGUENAY
CENTRE DE FORMATION EN EQUIPEMENT MOTORISE
980 Rue Georges-Vanier, Chicoutimi, QC, G7H 4M3
(418) 698-5199
Emp Here 50
SIC 8211 Elementary and secondary schools

     D-U-N-S 25-232-1963   (HQ)
COMMISSION SCOLAIRE DES RIVES-DU-SAGUENAY
(*Suby of* Commission Scolaire des Rives-du-Saguenay)
36 Rue Jacques-Cartier E, Chicoutimi, QC, G7H 1W2
(418) 698-5000
Emp Here 100   *Emp Total* 2,000
Sales 172,634,673
SIC 8211 Elementary and secondary schools
Genl Mgr Christine Tremblay

Genl Mgr Gilles Routhier

     D-U-N-S 25-233-6862   (BR)
COMMISSION SCOLAIRE DES RIVES-DU-SAGUENAY
ECOLE L'ODYSEE DOMINIQUE RACINE
(*Suby of* Commission Scolaire des Rives-du-Saguenay)
985 Rue Begin, Chicoutimi, QC, G7H 4P1
(418) 698-5185
Emp Here 140
SIC 8211 Elementary and secondary schools

     D-U-N-S 20-867-4171   (BR)
COMMISSION SCOLAIRE DES RIVES-DU-SAGUENAY
CEA LAURE CONON
847 Rue Georges-Vanier, Chicoutimi, QC, G7H 4M1
(418) 698-5170
Emp Here 100
SIC 8211 Elementary and secondary schools

     D-U-N-S 25-240-5808   (BR)
COMMISSION SCOLAIRE DES RIVES-DU-SAGUENAY
ECOLE SAINT ISIDORE
(*Suby of* Commission Scolaire des Rives-du-Saguenay)
97 Rue Arthur-Hamel, Chicoutimi, QC, G7H 3M9
(418) 698-5148
Emp Here 23
SIC 8211 Elementary and secondary schools

     D-U-N-S 20-178-0314   (BR)
COMMISSION SCOLAIRE DES RIVES-DU-SAGUENAY
SERVICE DE L'INFORMATIQUE
475 Rue La Fontaine Bureau 13, Chicoutimi, QC, G7H 4V2
(418) 541-7799
Emp Here 25
SIC 7376 Computer facilities management

     D-U-N-S 25-232-2284   (BR)
COMMISSION SCOLAIRE DES RIVES-DU-SAGUENAY
ECOLE ANDRE GAGNON
(*Suby of* Commission Scolaire des Rives-du-Saguenay)
128 Rue Louis-Francoeur, Chicoutimi, QC, G7H 3A8
(418) 698-5142
Emp Here 20
SIC 8211 Elementary and secondary schools

     D-U-N-S 20-711-9012   (BR)
COMMISSION SCOLAIRE DES RIVES-DU-SAGUENAY
CENTRE L'OASIS
624 Rue La Fontaine, Chicoutimi, QC, G7H 4V4
(418) 698-5012
Emp Here 50
SIC 8211 Elementary and secondary schools

     D-U-N-S 25-526-5688   (BR)
COMPAGNIE DE TELEPHONE BELL DU CANADA OU BELL CANADA, LA
BELL ALIANT
483 Rue Begin, Chicoutimi, QC, G7H 4N3
(418) 696-5445
Emp Here 49
SIC 4813 Telephone communication, except radio

     D-U-N-S 20-030-4629   (BR)
CONFEDERATION DES SYNDICATS NA-TIONAUX (C.S.N.)
73 Rue Arthur-Hamel, Chicoutimi, QC, G7H 3M9
(418) 549-7702
Emp Here 25
SIC 8631 Labor organizations

     D-U-N-S 25-919-1492   (BR)
CONSEILLERS EN GESTION ET INFORMA-

TIQUE CGI INC
CGI
930 Rue Jacques-Cartier E 3rd Floor, Chicoutimi, QC, G7H 7K9
(418) 696-6789
Emp Here 425
SIC 7379 Computer related services, nec

     D-U-N-S 20-276-5785   (BR)
COOPERATIVE FUNERAIRE DE CHICOUTIMI
ALLIANCE FUNERAIRE DU ROYAUME
(*Suby of* Cooperative Funeraire de Chicoutimi)
520 Boul Du Saguenay E, Chicoutimi, QC, G7H 1L2
(418) 543-5200
Emp Here 30
SIC 7261 Funeral service and crematories

     D-U-N-S 20-801-2638   (BR)
COSTCO WHOLESALE CANADA LTD
(*Suby of* Costco Wholesale Corporation)
2500 Boul Talbot, Chicoutimi, QC, G7H 5B1
(418) 696-1112
Emp Here 200
SIC 5199 Nondurable goods, nec

     D-U-N-S 24-418-4649   (BR)
DELOITTE LLP
901 Boul Talbot Bureau 400, Chicoutimi, QC, G7H 0A1
(418) 549-6650
Emp Here 80
SIC 6733 Trusts, nec

     D-U-N-S 25-173-1519   (HQ)
DIOCESE DE CHICOUTIMI
(*Suby of* Diocese De Chicoutimi)
602 Rue Racine E, Chicoutimi, QC, G7H 1V1
(418) 543-0783
Emp Here 26   *Emp Total* 60
Sales 3,939,878
SIC 8661 Religious organizations

     D-U-N-S 20-738-5985   (BR)
DOLLARAMA S.E.C.
392 Rue Des Sagueneens, Chicoutimi, QC, G7H 5S5
(418) 543-4092
Emp Here 25
SIC 5331 Variety stores

     D-U-N-S 24-681-8988   (BR)
ENTREPRISES MACBAIE INC, LES
RESTAURANT MC DONALD'S
1451 Boul Talbot, Chicoutimi, QC, G7H 5N8
(418) 693-4753
Emp Here 50
SIC 5812 Eating places

     D-U-N-S 24-681-7436   (BR)
ENTREPRISES MACBAIE INC, LES
MCDONALD'S
1401 Boul Talbot Bureau 1, Chicoutimi, QC, G7H 5N6
(418) 545-3593
Emp Here 100
SIC 5812 Eating places

     D-U-N-S 20-723-6910   (BR)
FINANCIERE BANQUE NATIONALE INC
1180 Boul Talbot Bureau 201, Chicoutimi, QC, G7H 4B6
(418) 549-8888
Emp Here 29
SIC 6211 Security brokers and dealers

     D-U-N-S 25-181-1980   (SL)
FOYER ST-FRANCOIS INC
912 Rue Jacques-Cartier E, Chicoutimi, QC, G7H 2A9
(418) 549-3727
Emp Here 86   *Sales* 3,137,310
SIC 8361 Residential care

     D-U-N-S 20-193-7141   (SL)
GESTION GEORGES ABRAHAM INC
RESTAURANT CHEZ GEORGES

433 Rue Racine E, Chicoutimi, QC, G7H 1T5
(418) 543-2875
Emp Here 80   *Sales* 2,407,703
SIC 5812 Eating places

     D-U-N-S 24-388-5824   (BR)
GROUPE ARCHAMBAULT INC
ARCHAMBAULT CHICOUTIMI
1120 Boul Talbot, Chicoutimi, QC, G7H 7R2
(418) 698-1586
Emp Here 30
SIC 5736 Musical instrument stores

     D-U-N-S 24-863-1723   (HQ)
GROUPE GAGNON FRERES INC
GALERIE DU SOMMEIL
1460 Boul Talbot, Chicoutimi, QC, G7H 4C2
(418) 690-3366
Emp Here 27   *Emp Total* 1
Sales 22,690,778
SIC 5712 Furniture stores
Pr Pr Frederic Gagnon
   Lise Mercier
   Richard Dionne

     D-U-N-S 24-126-3008   (BR)
GROUPE JEAN COUTU (PJC) INC, LE
JEAN COUTU #21
(*Suby of* 3958230 Canada Inc)
413 Rue Racine E, Chicoutimi, QC, G7H 1S8
(418) 543-7921
Emp Here 20
SIC 5912 Drug stores and proprietary stores

     D-U-N-S 25-309-6861   (BR)
INDUSTRIELLE ALLIANCE, ASSURANCE ET SERVICES FINANCIERS INC
INDUSTRIELLE ALLIANCE
345 Rue Des Sagueneens Bureau 120, Chicoutimi, QC, G7H 6K9
(418) 549-6914
Emp Here 50
SIC 6411 Insurance agents, brokers, and service

     D-U-N-S 25-364-8430   (BR)
INTER-CITE CONSTRUCTION LTEE
209 Boul Du Royaume O, Chicoutimi, QC, G7H 5C2
(418) 549-0532
Emp Here 250
SIC 1611 Highway and street construction

     D-U-N-S 20-777-3487   (BR)
INVENTAIRES DE L'EST INC
INVENTAIRES DE L'EST INC
(*Suby of* Inventaires De L'Est Inc)
672 Rue Des Hospitalieres Bureau 60, Chicoutimi, QC, G7H 4C8
(418) 698-0275
Emp Here 20
SIC 7389 Business services, nec

     D-U-N-S 25-315-7804   (BR)
INVESTORS GROUP FINANCIAL SER-VICES INC
GROUP INVESTORS
901 Boul Talbot Bureau 101, Chicoutimi, QC, G7H 6N7
(418) 696-1331
Emp Here 35
SIC 8742 Management consulting services

     D-U-N-S 25-019-6557   (BR)
LONDON LIFE INSURANCE COMPANY
FINANCIERE LIBERTE 55
901 Boul Talbot Bureau 102, Chicoutimi, QC, G7H 6N7
(418) 543-4471
Emp Here 25
SIC 6311 Life insurance

     D-U-N-S 20-795-2925   (BR)
METRO RICHELIEU INC
299 Rue Des Sagueneens, Chicoutimi, QC, G7H 3A5
(418) 696-4114
Emp Here 80

SIC 5411 Grocery stores

D-U-N-S 25-484-9177   (BR)
PROVIGO DISTRIBUTION INC
MAXI
180 Boul Barrette, Chicoutimi, QC, G7H 7W8
(418) 549-9357
Emp Here 30
SIC 5411 Grocery stores

D-U-N-S 24-635-0813   (BR)
RAYMOND CHABOT GRANT THORNTON S.E.N.C.R.L.
255 Rue Racine E Bureau 800, Chicoutimi, QC, G7H 7L2
(418) 549-4142
Emp Here 53
SIC 8721 Accounting, auditing, and book-keeping

D-U-N-S 20-991-5201   (BR)
REGIE REGIONALE DE LA SANTE ET DES SERVICES SOCIAUX SAGUENAY LAC-SAINT-JEAN
CSSS DE CHICOUTIMI
305 Rue Saint-Vallier Bureau 2250, Chicoutimi, QC, G7H 5H6
(418) 541-1000
Emp Here 50
SIC 8399 Social services, nec

D-U-N-S 24-985-6928   (BR)
REVOLUTION ENVIRONMENTAL SOLU-TIONS LP
TERRAPURE ENVIRONMENTAL
(*Suby of* Revolution Environmental Solutions LP)
100 Rue Des Routiers, Chicoutimi, QC, G7H 5B1
(866) 546-1150
Emp Here 30
SIC 4959 Sanitary services, nec

D-U-N-S 20-188-6178   (BR)
RUSSEL METALS INC
ACIER LEROUX
2149 Rue De La Fonderie, Chicoutimi, QC, G7H 8C1
(418) 545-8881
Emp Here 45
SIC 5051 Metals service centers and offices

D-U-N-S 24-254-7292   (BR)
SMS EQUIPMENT INC
CONECO EQUIPMENT
205 Rue Clement-Gilbert, Chicoutimi, QC, G7H 5B1
(418) 549-0022
Emp Here 30
SIC 5083 Farm and garden machinery

D-U-N-S 24-591-6796   (HQ)
SABLIERE DRAPEAU (1986) INC
205 Boul Du Royaume E, Chicoutimi, QC, G7H 5H2
(418) 549-0532
Emp Here 20   *Emp Total* 250
Sales 10,742,551
SIC 5032 Brick, stone, and related material
Pr Real Riverin
Sec Nicolas Riverin

D-U-N-S 24-374-8956   (SL)
SEFAR BDH INC
BDH TECH
200 Rue Clement-Gilbert, Chicoutimi, QC, G7H 5B1
(418) 690-0888
Emp Here 30   *Sales* 3,210,271
SIC 3569 General industrial machinery, nec

D-U-N-S 20-300-7815   (SL)
SEMINAIRE DE CHICOUTIMI SERVICE ED-UCATIF
679 Rue Chabanel, Chicoutimi, QC, G7H 1Z7
(418) 549-0190
Emp Here 59   *Sales* 3,939,878
SIC 8211 Elementary and secondary schools

D-U-N-S 25-115-3953   (BR)
SERVICES MATREC INC
3199 Boul Talbot, Chicoutimi, QC, G7H 5B1
(418) 549-8074
Emp Here 50
SIC 4959 Sanitary services, nec

D-U-N-S 25-484-8880   (BR)
SOBEYS QUEBEC INC
IGA YVON HACHE
1324 Boul Talbot, Chicoutimi, QC, G7H 4B8
(418) 549-9751
Emp Here 122
SIC 5411 Grocery stores

D-U-N-S 20-745-0151   (BR)
SOCIETE DES ALCOOLS DU QUEBEC
SAQ CLASSIQUE
1075 Boul Talbot, Chicoutimi, QC, G7H 4B5
(418) 543-4011
Emp Here 25
SIC 5921 Liquor stores

D-U-N-S 20-291-0212   (BR)
SOLOTECH QUEBEC INC
758 Rue D'Alma, Chicoutimi, QC, G7H 4E6
(418) 602-3545
Emp Here 20
SIC 5099 Durable goods, nec

D-U-N-S 25-985-3364   (BR)
STAPLES CANADA INC
BUREAU EN GROS
(*Suby of* Staples, Inc.)
1470 Boulevard Talbot, Chicoutimi, QC, G7H 4C2
(418) 543-3477
Emp Here 27
SIC 5943 Stationery stores

D-U-N-S 25-304-1917   (BR)
SUN LIFE ASSURANCE COMPANY OF CANADA
FINANCIERE SUN LIFE
255 Rue Racine E Bureau 200, Chicoutimi, QC, G7H 7L2
(418) 549-5161
Emp Here 20
SIC 6311 Life insurance

D-U-N-S 24-841-5585   (BR)
TOMMY HILFIGER CANADA INC
1401 Boul Talbot, Chicoutimi, QC, G7H 5N6
(418) 698-3408
Emp Here 20
SIC 5621 Women's clothing stores

D-U-N-S 24-970-7209   (SL)
VILLA DU SAGUENAY INC
1901 Rue Des Roitelets Bureau 302, Chicoutimi, QC, G7H 7L7
(418) 693-1212
Emp Here 21   *Sales* 802,568
SIC 8322 Individual and family services

D-U-N-S 24-346-0271   (BR)
VILLE DE SAGUENAY
SERVICE DE GENIE
216 Rue Racine E, Chicoutimi, QC, G7H 1R9
(418) 698-3130
Emp Here 30
SIC 8711 Engineering services

D-U-N-S 20-126-9458   (BR)
VILLE DE SAGUENAY
CENTRE GEORGES VEZINA
643 Rue Begin, Chicoutimi, QC, G7H 4N7
(418) 698-3071
Emp Here 40
SIC 2321 Men's and boy's furnishings

D-U-N-S 25-297-7301   (BR)
WAL-MART CANADA CORP
3017-1451 Boul Talbot, Chicoutimi, QC, G7H 5N8
(418) 693-1500
Emp Here 240
SIC 5311 Department stores

D-U-N-S 20-184-2858   (BR)
WINNERS MERCHANTS INTERNATIONAL L.P.
WINNERS
(*Suby of* The TJX Companies Inc)
1401 Boul Talbot Bureau D1, Chicoutimi, QC, G7H 5N6
(418) 690-0303
Emp Here 40
SIC 5651 Family clothing stores

D-U-N-S 24-250-6645   (BR)
YM INC. (SALES)
URBAN PLANET
1401 Boul Talbot, Chicoutimi, QC, G7H 5N6
(418) 549-9982
Emp Here 26
SIC 5621 Women's clothing stores

Chicoutimi, QC G7J
Chicoutimi County

D-U-N-S 25-835-7110   (BR)
ADT CANADA INC
RELIANCE PROTECTRON
58 Boul De L'Universite O, Chicoutimi, QC, G7J 1T3
(418) 690-5000
Emp Here 20
SIC 1731 Electrical work

D-U-N-S 20-711-9079   (BR)
COMMISSION SCOLAIRE DES RIVES-DU-SAGUENAY
CARREFOUR ENVIRONNEMENT SAGUE-NAY
216 Rue Des Oblats O, Chicoutimi, QC, G7J 2B1
(418) 698-5160
Emp Here 50
SIC 8211 Elementary and secondary schools

D-U-N-S 25-240-6475   (BR)
COMMISSION SCOLAIRE DES RIVES-DU-SAGUENAY
ECOLE ST COEUR DE MARIE
(*Suby of* Commission Scolaire des Rives-du-Saguenay)
465 Ch De La Reserve, Chicoutimi, QC, G7J 3N7
(418) 698-5120
Emp Here 20
SIC 8211 Elementary and secondary schools

D-U-N-S 25-232-2045   (BR)
COMMISSION SCOLAIRE DES RIVES-DU-SAGUENAY
ECOLE DE LA PULPERIE
(*Suby of* Commission Scolaire des Rives-du-Saguenay)
906 Rue Comeau, Chicoutimi, QC, G7J 3J3
(418) 698-5126
Emp Here 54
SIC 8211 Elementary and secondary schools

D-U-N-S 24-843-2747   (BR)
ENGLOBE CORP
LVM DIVISION OF
1309 Boul Saint-Paul, Chicoutimi, QC, G7J 3Y2
(418) 698-6827
Emp Here 30
SIC 8742 Management consulting services

D-U-N-S 24-380-7091   (SL)
FILTRAR TECH INC
1251 Rue Des Societaires, Chicoutimi, QC, G7J 0K6
(418) 549-2727
Emp Here 60   *Sales* 3,064,349
SIC 7389 Business services, nec

D-U-N-S 24-532-9003   (BR)
GHD CONSULTANTS LTEE
INSPEC-SOL

1600 Boul Saint-Paul Bureau 150, Chicoutimi, QC, G7J 4N1
(418) 698-4018
Emp Here 40
SIC 8621 Professional organizations

D-U-N-S 20-013-6948   (SL)
IOS SERVICES GEOSCIENTIFIQUES INC
1319 Boul Saint-Paul, Chicoutimi, QC, G7J 3Y2
(418) 698-4498
Emp Here 50   *Sales* 2,772,507
SIC 1481 NonMetallic mineral services

D-U-N-S 24-851-2951   (SL)
K.L.S (2009) INC
1615 Rue Saint-Paul, Chicoutimi, QC, G7J 3Y3
(418) 543-1515
Emp Here 150   *Sales* 32,510,351
SIC 3354 Aluminum extruded products
Pr Remi Roy
Dir Clement Tremblay
Dir Mike Breed
Dir Leslie Hammond

D-U-N-S 25-144-1101   (BR)
RIO TINTO ALCAN INC
USINE DUBUC
(*Suby of* RIO TINTO PLC)
2040 Ch De La Reserve, Chicoutimi, QC, G7J 0E1
(418) 699-6305
Emp Here 53
SIC 3355 Aluminum rolling and drawing, nec

Chicoutimi, QC G7K
Chicoutimi County

D-U-N-S 25-323-8018   (SL)
9015-7009 QUEBEC INC
1235 Rue Bersimis, Chicoutimi, QC, G7K 1A4
(418) 549-0744
Emp Here 400   *Sales* 91,311,680
SIC 6719 Holding companies, nec
Pr Jacques Grimard
Jean Grimard
Gilbert Grimard

D-U-N-S 24-344-2162   (SL)
9165-8021 QUEBEC INC
TRANSPORT R.C.I.
1690 Rue De La Manic, Chicoutimi, QC, G7K 1J1
(418) 543-5111
Emp Here 60   *Sales* 2,991,389
SIC 7549 Automotive services, nec

D-U-N-S 24-358-3122   (HQ)
CEGER INC
(*Suby of* Ceger Inc)
1180 Rue Bersimis, Chicoutimi, QC, G7K 1A5
(418) 543-4938
Emp Here 50   *Emp Total* 650
Sales 161,169,920
SIC 6712 Bank holding companies
Pr Pr Jeannot Harvey
Sec Eloise Harvey
Andre Salesse

D-U-N-S 20-547-5150   (HQ)
CEGERCO INC
DEMOTEC
(*Suby of* 9123-6794 Quebec Inc)
1180 Rue Bersimis, Chicoutimi, QC, G7K 1A5
(418) 543-6159
Emp Here 50   *Emp Total* 3
Sales 40,857,992
SIC 1611 Highway and street construction
Pr Pr Jeannot Harvey
Christiane Carmel
Dir Andre St-Cyr
Dir Eloise Harvey
Dir Andre Salesse
Dir Pierre Halle

Dir Jean-Philippe Harvey

D-U-N-S 24-706-9990   (HQ)
GROUPE GIROUX MACONNEX INC
BRIQUE ET PAVE CHICOINE
(*Suby of* 2846-3065 Quebec Inc)
2223 Boul Saint-Paul, Chicoutimi, QC, G7K
1E5
(418) 549-7345
Emp Here 42   *Emp Total* 10
Sales 41,660,560
SIC 5032 Brick, stone, and related material
Pr Martin Vandry
   Gerald Tremblay

D-U-N-S 20-309-5831   (SL)
GROUPE PGS 2009 INC
1371 Rue De La Manic, Chicoutimi, QC, G7K
1G7
(418) 696-1212
Emp Here 93   *Sales* 9,795,000
SIC 1711 Plumbing, heating, air-conditioning
Pr Pr Serge Blackburn
VP VP Remi Pageau
VP VP Keiven Tremblay
   Andre Barriault
   Maxime Parent

D-U-N-S 20-949-7999   (BR)
HEWITT EQUIPEMENT LIMITEE
CATERPILLAR
1466 Rue Bersimis, Chicoutimi, QC, G7K 1H9
(418) 545-1560
Emp Here 60
SIC 5084 Industrial machinery and equipment

D-U-N-S 20-874-1058   (HQ)
INDUSTRIES DODEC INC
(*Suby of* Groupe Rosbon Inc, Le)
1275 Rue Bersimis, Chicoutimi, QC, G7K 1A4
(418) 549-5027
Emp Here 60   *Emp Total* 91
Sales 6,596,303
SIC 3599 Industrial machinery, nec
Pr Pr Rosaire Bonneau

D-U-N-S 25-502-3905   (SL)
**PRODUITS ALIMENTAIRES ALLARD (1998)
LTEE, LES**
ALLARD SIGNATURE
1216 Rue De La Manic, Chicoutimi, QC, G7K
1A2
(418) 543-6659
Emp Here 40   *Sales* 2,512,128
SIC 2051 Bread, cake, and related products

D-U-N-S 25-024-0108   (BR)
**PRODUITS INDUSTRIELS DE HAUTE TEM-
PERATURE PYROTEK INC, LES**
PYROTEK
(*Suby of* Pyrotek Incorporated)
1623 Rue De La Manic, Chicoutimi, QC, G7K
1G8
(418) 545-8093
Emp Here 50
SIC 3569 General industrial machinery, nec

D-U-N-S 25-175-0139   (BR)
RADIO-ONDE INC
SYSTEME DE RADIOCOMMUNICATION
1265 Rue Bersimis, Chicoutimi, QC, G7K 1A4
(418) 545-9215
Emp Here 26
SIC 5999 Miscellaneous retail stores, nec

D-U-N-S 25-290-6342   (BR)
**WAJAX INDUSTRIAL COMPONENTS LIM-
ITED PARTNERSHIP**
WAJAX INDUSTRIAL COMPONENTS
1006 Rue De La Rupert, Chicoutimi, QC, G7K
0A1
(418) 690-1447
Emp Here 20
SIC 5084 Industrial machinery and equipment

Chisasibi, QC J0M
Abitibi County

D-U-N-S 20-043-8980   (SL)
**COMPAGNIE DE CONSTRUCTION ET DE
DEVELOPPEMENT CRIE LTEE, LA**
(*Suby of* Cree Regional Economic Enterprises
Company (Cree Co) Inc)
3 Rue Aahppisaach, Chisasibi, QC, J0M 1E0
(819) 855-1700
Emp Here 250   *Sales* 29,184,280
SIC 1611 Highway and street construction
Pr Robert Baribeau
Treas Tanya Pash
Dir Emily Whiskeychan
Dir Raymond Blackned
Dir Randy Bosum
Dir Jackie Blacksmith
Dir Emily Whiskeychan Gilpin
Dir James Bobbish
Dir Clarence Sr. Joly
Dir Louie-Rene Kanatewat

D-U-N-S 20-712-6603   (BR)
CREE SCHOOL BOARD
JAMES BAY EEYOU SCHOOL
(*Suby of* Cree School Board)
11 Maamuu, Chisasibi, QC, J0M 1E0
(819) 855-2833
Emp Here 80
SIC 8211 Elementary and secondary schools

D-U-N-S 20-340-7499   (BR)
NORTH WEST COMPANY LP, THE
Gd, Chisasibi, QC, J0M 1E0
(819) 855-2810
Emp Here 40
SIC 5411 Grocery stores

Clarenceville, QC J0J
Missisquoi County

D-U-N-S 25-232-9479   (BR)
**COMMISSION SCOLAIRE DES HAUTES-
RIVIERES**
*COMMISSION SCOLAIRE DES HAUTES-
RIVIERES*
1132 Rue Front S, Clarenceville, QC, J0J 1B0
(450) 515-8047
Emp Here 30
SIC 8211 Elementary and secondary schools

Clermont, QC G4A
Charlevoix-Est County

D-U-N-S 24-706-2508   (SL)
ATELIER DU MARTIN-PECHEUR INC
192 Boul Notre-Dame, Clermont, QC, G4A
1E9
(418) 439-3941
Emp Here 60   *Sales* 1,751,057
SIC 7349 Building maintenance services, nec

D-U-N-S 25-022-6776   (BR)
**COMMISSION SCOLAIRE DE
CHARLEVOIX, LA**
ECOLE LAURE GAUDREAULT
19 Rue Saint-Philippe, Clermont, QC, G4A
1K3
(418) 439-3862
Emp Here 30
SIC 8351 Child day care services

D-U-N-S 20-194-7504   (BR)
PF RESOLU CANADA INC
100 Rue De La Donohue, Clermont, QC, G4A
1A7
(418) 439-5300
Emp Here 213
SIC 2621 Paper mills

D-U-N-S 20-525-7913   (BR)

**SOCIETE DES ETABLISSEMENTS DE
PLEIN AIR DU QUEBEC**
*PARC NATIONAL DES GRANDS JARDINS
ET LE PARC NATIONAL HAUTES GORGES
DE LA RIVIERE MALBAIE*
25 Boul Notre-Dame, Clermont, QC, G4A 1C2
(418) 439-1227
Emp Here 140
SIC 7999 Amusement and recreation, nec

Coaticook, QC J1A
Stanstead County

D-U-N-S 24-630-6935   (BR)
9099-9012 QUEBEC INC
CODET
(*Suby of* 9099-9012 Quebec Inc)
709 Rue Merrill, Coaticook, QC, J1A 2S2

Emp Here 90
SIC 5699 Miscellaneous apparel and accessory stores

D-U-N-S 20-013-5932   (HQ)
ANSUL CANADA LIMITEE
LIFELINE
675 Rue Merrill, Coaticook, QC, J1A 2S2
(819) 849-2751
Emp Here 150   *Emp Total* 190
Sales 40,639,110
SIC 3052 Rubber and plastics hose and belt-
ings
Pr Pr David Grinstead
VP VP William Bower

D-U-N-S 24-352-3438   (BR)
**COMMISSION SCOLAIRE DE LA BEAUCE-
ETCHEMIN**
SOUTH SHORE INDUSTRIES
323 Rue De L'Union, Coaticook, QC, J1A 1Z5
(819) 849-4844
Emp Here 150
SIC 2511 Wood household furniture

D-U-N-S 20-712-1018   (BR)
**COMMISSION SCOLAIRE DES HAUTS-
CANTONS**
ECOLE SECONDAIRE LA FRONTALIERE
311 Rue Saint-Paul E, Coaticook, QC, J1A
1G1
(819) 849-4825
Emp Here 120
SIC 8211 Elementary and secondary schools

D-U-N-S 25-232-7499   (BR)
**COMMISSION SCOLAIRE DES HAUTS-
CANTONS**
ECOLE GENDREAU
(*Suby of* Commission Scolaire des Hauts-
Cantons)
102 Rue Cutting, Coaticook, QC, J1A 2G4
(819) 849-7075
Emp Here 23
SIC 8211 Elementary and secondary schools

D-U-N-S 24-352-2294   (BR)
**COMMISSION SCOLAIRE DES HAUTS-
CANTONS**
DEPARTEMENT DE FINANCE
249 Rue Saint-Jean-Baptiste, Coaticook, QC,
J1A 2J4
(819) 849-7051
Emp Here 20
SIC 8211 Elementary and secondary schools

D-U-N-S 20-712-0994   (BR)
**COMMISSION SCOLAIRE DES HAUTS-
CANTONS**
ECOLE PIMAIRE MGR DURAND
367 Rue Saint-Paul E, Coaticook, QC, J1A
1G1
(819) 849-7084
Emp Here 50
SIC 8211 Elementary and secondary schools

D-U-N-S 20-712-0978   (BR)
**COMMISSION SCOLAIRE DES HAUTS-
CANTONS**
CRIFA-CS DES HAUTS-CANTONS
125 Ch Morgan, Coaticook, QC, J1A 1V6
(819) 849-9588
Emp Here 25
SIC 8221 Colleges and universities

D-U-N-S 25-233-2309   (BR)
**COMMISSION SCOLAIRE DES HAUTS-
CANTONS**
ECOLE SACRE- COEUR
(*Suby of* Commission Scolaire des Hauts-
Cantons)
211 Rue Saint-Jean-Baptiste, Coaticook, QC,
J1A 2J4
(819) 849-2749
Emp Here 40
SIC 8211 Elementary and secondary schools

D-U-N-S 25-487-7939   (SL)
EQUIPEMENTS VEILLEUX INC, LES
544 Rue Main E, Coaticook, QC, J1A 1N9
(819) 849-0300
Emp Here 30   *Sales* 7,709,634
SIC 5083 Farm and garden machinery

D-U-N-S 24-050-0298   (SL)
GANTERIE BEST LTEE
GANTERIE BEST
253 Rue Michaud, Coaticook, QC, J1A 1A9
(819) 849-6381
Emp Here 25   *Sales* 6,785,345
SIC 2381 Fabric dress and work gloves
Pr Shuji Kondo
   William A. Alico
Genl Mgr Jackie Bernais

D-U-N-S 25-355-9942   (SL)
GEO. SHEARD FABRICS LTD
84 Rue Merrill, Coaticook, QC, J1A 1X4
(819) 849-6311
Emp Here 103   *Sales* 4,504,505
SIC 5949 Sewing, needlework, and piece
goods

D-U-N-S 24-842-5712   (SL)
GUAY, DENIS
93 Ch Menard, Coaticook, QC, J1A 2S5
(819) 849-3788
Emp Here 50   *Sales* 6,150,382
SIC 2099 Food preparations, nec

D-U-N-S 24-747-5106   (SL)
MEUBLES GOBER INC
GOBER
80 Av De La Graviere, Coaticook, QC, J1A
3E6
(819) 849-7066
Emp Here 50   *Sales* 2,918,428
SIC 2434 Wood kitchen cabinets

D-U-N-S 25-314-0032   (SL)
NIEDNER INC
675 Rue Merrill, Coaticook, QC, J1A 2S2
(819) 849-2751
Emp Here 100   *Sales* 10,579,302
SIC 3569 General industrial machinery, nec
Pr Pr Alain Souriol
Sec Rejean Loiselle

D-U-N-S 24-821-0551   (SL)
**SOCIETE DE DEVELOPPEMENT DE LA
GORGE DE COATICOOK INC**
PARC GORGE COATICOOK
135 Rue Michaud, Coaticook, QC, J1A 1A9
(819) 849-2331
Emp Here 50   *Sales* 2,699,546
SIC 7999 Amusement and recreation, nec

D-U-N-S 25-685-4100   (BR)
WATERVILLE TG INC
500 Rue Dionne, Coaticook, QC, J1A 2E8
(819) 849-7031
Emp Here 250
SIC 3069 Fabricated rubber products, nec

Compton, QC J0B
Sherbrooke County

D-U-N-S 25-966-9299   (BR)
COMMISSION SCOLAIRE DES HAUTS-CANTONS
ECOLE LOUIS-SAINT-LAURENT
(*Suby of* Commission Scolaire des Hauts-Cantons)
6835 Rte Louis-S.-Saint-Laurent, Compton, QC, J0B 1L0
(819) 849-7803
Emp Here 25
SIC 8211 Elementary and secondary schools

D-U-N-S 24-463-4775   (BR)
REGROUPEMENT DES ARCHIVES DU SEMINAIRE DE SHERBROOKE ET DE L'ARCHIDIOCESE DE SHERBROOKE
REGROUPEMENT DES ARCHIVES DU SEMINAIRE DE SHERBROO
6747 Rte Louis-S.-Saint-Laurent, Compton, QC, J0B 1L0
(819) 835-5474
Emp Here 26
SIC 8661 Religious organizations

Contrecoeur, QC J0L
Vercheres County

D-U-N-S 20-253-6413   (BR)
ARCELORMITTAL PRODUITS LONGS CANADA S.E.N.C.
3900 Rte Des Acieries, Contrecoeur, QC, J0L 1C0
(450) 392-3226
Emp Here 700
SIC 3312 Blast furnaces and steel mills

D-U-N-S 20-323-5379   (BR)
ARCELORMITTAL PRODUITS LONGS CANADA S.E.N.C.
2050 Rte Des Acieries, Contrecoeur, QC, J0L 1C0
(450) 587-2012
Emp Here 379
SIC 3312 Blast furnaces and steel mills

D-U-N-S 25-376-4716   (BR)
CENTRE DE SANTE ET DE SERVICES SOCIAUX PIERRE-BOUCHER
CENTRE D'HEBERGEMENT DE CONTRECOEUR
4700 Rte Marie-Victorin, Contrecoeur, QC, J0L 1C0
(450) 468-8410
Emp Here 75
SIC 8361 Residential care

D-U-N-S 25-233-1814   (BR)
COMMISSION SCOLAIRE DES PATRIOTES
ECOLE MERE MARIE ROSE
351 Rue Chabot, Contrecoeur, QC, J0L 1C0
(450) 645-2342
Emp Here 35
SIC 8211 Elementary and secondary schools

D-U-N-S 20-195-0284   (BR)
GENFOOT INC
KAMIK
4945 Rue Legendre, Contrecoeur, QC, J0L 1C0
(450) 587-2051
Emp Here 250
SIC 3143 Men's footwear, except athletic

D-U-N-S 24-101-2553   (BR)
SYNAGRI S.E.C.
PEDIGRAIN
4075 Rue Industrielle, Contrecoeur, QC, J0L 1C0
(450) 587-5222
Emp Here 40

SIC 2875 Fertilizers, mixing only

D-U-N-S 20-793-8390   (SL)
TRANSPORT JACLIN INC
2050 Rue Saint-Antoine, Contrecoeur, QC, J0L 1C0
(450) 587-2743
Emp Here 26   *Sales* 2,918,428
SIC 4213 Trucking, except local

Cookshire-Eaton, QC J0B
Compton County

D-U-N-S 24-353-0222   (BR)
ARMOIRES FABRITEC LTEE
BOISERIE IMPERIAL WOODCRAFT
705 Rue Pope, Cookshire-Eaton, QC, J0B 1M0

Emp Here 40
SIC 2434 Wood kitchen cabinets

D-U-N-S 25-233-3471   (BR)
COMMISSION SCOLAIRE DES HAUTS-CANTONS
ECOLE ST CAMILLE
(*Suby of* Commission Scolaire des Hauts-Cantons)
150 Rue Bibeau, Cookshire-Eaton, QC, J0B 1M0
(819) 875-5556
Emp Here 40
SIC 8211 Elementary and secondary schools

D-U-N-S 20-050-7536   (BR)
PLASTIPAK INDUSTRIES INC
PLASTIPAK INDUSTRIES
345 Rue Bibeau, Cookshire-Eaton, QC, J0B 1M0
(819) 875-3355
Emp Here 140
SIC 3089 Plastics products, nec

D-U-N-S 25-468-5183   (BR)
SOBEYS QUEBEC INC
I G A COOKSHIRE
35 Rue Principale E, Cookshire-Eaton, QC, J0B 1M0
(819) 875-5455
Emp Here 65
SIC 5411 Grocery stores

Cote Saint-Luc, QC H3X
Hochelaga County

D-U-N-S 20-106-3174   (BR)
WINNERS MERCHANTS INTERNATIONAL L.P.
WINNERS
(*Suby of* The TJX Companies Inc)
6900 Boul Decarie Bureau 3550, Cote Saint-Luc, QC, H3X 2T8
(514) 733-4200
Emp Here 100
SIC 5651 Family clothing stores

Cote Saint-Luc, QC H4V
Hochelaga County

D-U-N-S 25-298-5726   (BR)
COMMISSION SCOLAIRE ENGLISH-MONTREAL
MERTON SCHOOL
5554 Av Robinson, Cote Saint-Luc, QC, H4V 2P8
(514) 481-7425
Emp Here 25
SIC 8211 Elementary and secondary schools

D-U-N-S 20-700-6714   (BR)

REITMANS (CANADA) LIMITEE
REITMANS
7021 Ch De La Cote-Saint-Luc, Cote Saint-Luc, QC, H4V 1J2

Emp Here 25
SIC 5621 Women's clothing stores

Cote Saint-Luc, QC H4W
Hochelaga County

D-U-N-S 25-874-7500   (BR)
ALLIED SYSTEMS (CANADA) COMPANY
5901 Av Westminster, Cote Saint-Luc, QC, H4W 2J9

Emp Here 175
SIC 4213 Trucking, except local

D-U-N-S 24-128-0572   (SL)
CSH CASTEL ROYAL INC
CASTLE ROYALE
5740 Boul Cavendish Bureau 2006, Cote Saint-Luc, QC, H4W 2T8
(514) 487-5664
Emp Here 80   *Sales* 2,918,428
SIC 8361 Residential care

D-U-N-S 20-296-0758   (BR)
CANADIAN PACIFIC RAILWAY COMPANY
CPR
5901 Av Westminster, Cote Saint-Luc, QC, H4W 2J9
(514) 483-7102
Emp Here 200
SIC 4011 Railroads, line-haul operating

D-U-N-S 24-345-8556   (BR)
COMMISSION SCOLAIRE ENGLISH-MONTREAL
CENTRE DES ADULTES MARYMOUNT
5785 Av Parkhaven, Cote Saint-Luc, QC, H4W 1X8
(514) 488-8203
Emp Here 60
SIC 8211 Elementary and secondary schools

D-U-N-S 24-451-2260   (BR)
COMMISSION SCOLAIRE ENGLISH-MONTREAL
JOHN GRANT HIGH ECOLE
5785 Av Parkhaven, Cote Saint-Luc, QC, H4W 1X8
(514) 484-4161
Emp Here 20
SIC 8211 Elementary and secondary schools

D-U-N-S 20-714-2303   (BR)
ECOLE MAIMONIDE
5615 Av Parkhaven, Cote Saint-Luc, QC, H4W 1X3
(514) 488-9224
Emp Here 50
SIC 8211 Elementary and secondary schools

D-U-N-S 20-024-0344   (BR)
JEWISH PEOPLE'S SCHOOLS AND PERETZ SCHOOLS INC
BIALIK HIGH SCHOOL
(*Suby of* Jewish People's Schools and Peretz Schools Inc)
6500 Ch Kildare, Cote Saint-Luc, QC, H4W 3B8
(514) 731-3841
Emp Here 75
SIC 8211 Elementary and secondary schools

D-U-N-S 24-338-8225   (BR)
REVERA INC
MANOIR MONTEFIORE
5885 Boul Cavendish Bureau 202, Cote Saint-Luc, QC, H4W 3H4
(514) 485-5994
Emp Here 150
SIC 8051 Skilled nursing care facilities

D-U-N-S 25-309-8750   (BR)
ROYAL BANK OF CANADA
RBC
(*Suby of* Royal Bank Of Canada)
5755 Boul Cavendish, Cote Saint-Luc, QC, H4W 2X8
(514) 874-2226
Emp Here 20
SIC 6021 National commercial banks

D-U-N-S 20-655-6859   (BR)
TORONTO-DOMINION BANK, THE
TD CANADA TRUST BRANCH & ATM
(*Suby of* Toronto-Dominion Bank, The)
5800 Boul Cavendish, Cote Saint-Luc, QC, H4W 2T5
(514) 369-2622
Emp Here 20
SIC 6021 National commercial banks

D-U-N-S 24-175-5172   (BR)
UNITED CHURCH OF CANADA, THE
GRIFFITH-MCCONNELL RESIDENCE
5790 Av Parkhaven, Cote Saint-Luc, QC, H4W 1X9

Emp Here 200
SIC 8051 Skilled nursing care facilities

Cote Saint-Luc, QC H7G
Hochelaga County

D-U-N-S 25-419-1992   (HQ)
9061-9552 QUEBEC INC
TIM HORTONS
(*Suby of* 9061-9552 Quebec Inc)
489 Boul Des Laurentides Bureau 133, Cote Saint-Luc, QC, H7G 2V2
(450) 669-9009
Emp Here 25   *Emp Total* 50
Sales 1,532,175
SIC 5812 Eating places

D-U-N-S 20-716-7904   (BR)
COMMISSION SCOLAIRE DE LAVAL
ECOLE PRIMAIRE J.-JEAN-JOUBERT
1775 Rue Rochefort, Cote Saint-Luc, QC, H7G 2P8
(450) 662-7000
Emp Here 50
SIC 8211 Elementary and secondary schools

D-U-N-S 20-716-7755   (BR)
COMMISSION SCOLAIRE DE LAVAL
ECOLE PRIMAIRE ST-JULIEN
525 Av De La Sorbonne, Cote Saint-Luc, QC, H7G 3R9
(450) 662-7000
Emp Here 50
SIC 8211 Elementary and secondary schools

D-U-N-S 24-426-7352   (BR)
CONNORS BROS. CLOVER LEAF SEAFOODS COMPANY
CLOVER LEAF SEAFOODS
1600 Boul Rue Martin E, Cote Saint-Luc, QC, H7G 4R8
(450) 667-2574
Emp Here 20
SIC 5146 Fish and seafoods

D-U-N-S 20-059-1662   (SL)
GROUPE MARKETING INTERNATIONAL INC
37 Boul Des Laurentides, Cote Saint-Luc, QC, H7G 2S3
(450) 972-1540
Emp Here 75   *Sales* 3,793,956
SIC 7389 Business services, nec

D-U-N-S 24-253-2521   (HQ)
LESPERANCE, FRANCOIS INC
RONA LESPERANCE
164 Boul Des Laurentides, Cote Saint-Luc, QC, H7G 4P6

---

(450) 667-0255
Emp Here 25   *Emp Total* 3
Sales 36,699,232
SIC 5211 Lumber and other building materials
Pr Pr Claude Guevin
   Claude Bernier
Sec France Charlebois

   D-U-N-S 20-357-0395   (BR)
METRO INC
1600 Boul Saint-Martin E Bureau A, Cote
Saint-Luc, QC, H7G 4S7
(514) 643-1000
Emp Here 100
SIC 5141 Groceries, general line

   D-U-N-S 25-210-7206   (BR)
METRO RICHELIEU INC
DIVISION INFORMATIQUE
1600b Boul Saint-Martin E Bureau 300, Cote
Saint-Luc, QC, H7G 4S7
(450) 662-3300
Emp Here 300
SIC 7374 Data processing and preparation

   D-U-N-S 20-712-2537   (BR)
SIR WILFRID LAURIER SCHOOL BOARD
ECOLE ALTERNATIVE PHONIX
1105 Rue Victor-Morin, Cote Saint-Luc, QC,
H7G 4B8
(450) 680-3036
Emp Here 20
SIC 8211 Elementary and secondary schools

Cote Saint-Luc, QC H7L
Hochelaga County

   D-U-N-S 24-323-5343   (BR)
WOLSELEY CANADA INC
(*Suby of* WOLSELEY PLC)
4133 Boul Industriel, Cote Saint-Luc, QC, H7L
6G9
(450) 624-2110
Emp Here 20
SIC 5074 Plumbing and heating equipment
and supplies (hydronics)

Cote Saint-Luc, QC H7M
Hochelaga County

   D-U-N-S 25-778-8786   (BR)
**ASSURANCES ROLAND GROULX INC,
LES**
ASSURANCES GROULX
666 Boul Saint-Martin O Bureau 120, Cote
Saint-Luc, QC, H7M 5G4

Emp Here 40
SIC 6411 Insurance agents, brokers, and service

   D-U-N-S 20-573-7401   (BR)
BANQUE LAURENTIENNE DU CANADA
1899 Boul Rene-Laennec, Cote Saint-Luc,
QC, H7M 5E2
(450) 629-1459
Emp Here 20
SIC 6021 National commercial banks

   D-U-N-S 24-018-8888   (HQ)
**CENTRE DE SANTE ET DE SERVICES SO-
CIAUX DE LAVAL**
1755 Boul Rene-Laennec, Cote Saint-Luc,
QC, H7M 3L9
(450) 668-1010
Emp Here 2,815   *Emp Total* 40,000
Sales 619,149,350
SIC 8062 General medical and surgical hospitals
Pr Pr Jean-Francois Caron
VP VP Celine Marchand
VP VP Louise Paquette

   Robert Ouellet
Dir Fin Jean Maher

   D-U-N-S 25-259-1631   (BR)
CIMENT QUEBEC INC
UNIBETON
(*Suby of* Groupe Ciment Quebec Inc)
300 Rue Saulnier, Cote Saint-Luc, QC, H7M
3T3
(450) 629-0100
Emp Here 40
SIC 3273 Ready-mixed concrete

   D-U-N-S 25-093-1425   (SL)
SYSTEMES INTERTRADE INC
INTERTRADE CATALOGUE
666 Boul Saint-Martin O Bureau 300, Cote
Saint-Luc, QC, H7M 5G4
(450) 786-1666
Emp Here 30   *Sales* 2,685,378
SIC 7373 Computer integrated systems design

Cote Saint-Luc, QC H7N
Hochelaga County

   D-U-N-S 20-271-3012   (SL)
AGENCE DE PLACEMENT TRESOR INC
AGENCE DE PLACEMENT TRESOR
2a Rue Grenon O, Cote Saint-Luc, QC, H7N
2G6
(450) 933-7090
Emp Here 50   *Sales* 3,648,035
SIC 7361 Employment agencies

   D-U-N-S 25-782-6321   (SL)
**ARPENTEURS-GEOMETRES GENDRON,
LEFEBVRE & ASSOCIES, LES**
1 Place Laval Bureau 200, Cote Saint-Luc,
QC, H7N 1A1
(450) 967-1260
Emp Here 75   *Sales* 10,699,440
SIC 8713 Surveying services
Pt Marc Gendron
Pt Andre Larouche
Pt Claude Lefebvre
Pt Martin Themens

   D-U-N-S 20-569-2481   (BR)
BANQUE NATIONALE DU CANADA
3 Place Laval Bureau 60, Cote Saint-Luc, QC,
H7N 1A2
(450) 442-9091
Emp Here 20
SIC 6021 National commercial banks

   D-U-N-S 25-286-3097   (SL)
CRDI NORMAND-LARAMEE
RESIDENCE LOUISE-VACHON
304 Boul Cartier O, Cote Saint-Luc, QC, H7N
2J2
(450) 972-2099
Emp Here 450   *Sales* 39,754,800
SIC 8011 Offices and clinics of medical doctors
Pr Jean-Louis Bedard
VP Jean-Marie Bouchard
Sec Suzanne Daigneault
Treas Robert Pilon
Genl Mgr Claude Belley

   D-U-N-S 24-368-9226   (BR)
**CAISSE DESJARDINS DES GRANDS
BOULEVARDS DE LAVAL**
CENTRE DE SERVICES LAURIER
(*Suby of* Caisse Desjardins des Grands boulevards de Laval)
387 Rue Laurier, Cote Saint-Luc, QC, H7N
2P3
(450) 663-6020
Emp Here 20
SIC 6062 State credit unions

   D-U-N-S 25-975-9199   (BR)
COMMISSION SCOLAIRE DE LAVAL

ECOLE DE LA MOSAIQUE
310 Boul Cartier O, Cote Saint-Luc, QC, H7N
2J2
(450) 975-4060
Emp Here 40
SIC 8211 Elementary and secondary schools

   D-U-N-S 24-404-2466   (BR)
CONSULTANTS AECOM INC
AECOM TECSULT
1 Place Laval Bureau 200, Cote Saint-Luc,
QC, H7N 1A1
(450) 967-1260
Emp Here 75
SIC 8711 Engineering services

   D-U-N-S 20-719-9493   (BR)
GOLF TOWN LIMITED
GOLF TOWN
920 Boul Le Corbusier, Cote Saint-Luc, QC,
H7N 0A8
(450) 687-0648
Emp Here 30
SIC 5941 Sporting goods and bicycle shops

   D-U-N-S 20-002-2312   (BR)
**GOUVERNEMENT DE LA PROVINCE DE
QUEBEC**
*GOUVERNEMENT DE LA PROVINCE DE
QUEBEC*
308 Boul Cartier O, Cote Saint-Luc, QC, H7N
2J2
(450) 975-4150
Emp Here 200
SIC 8322 Individual and family services

   D-U-N-S 24-069-5374   (HQ)
GROUPECHO CANADA INC
RAPPORTS PRE-EMPLOI GROUPECHO
(*Suby of* Groupecho Canada Inc)
1 Place Laval Bureau 400, Cote Saint-Luc,
QC, H7N 1A1
(514) 335-3246
Emp Here 147   *Emp Total* 194
Sales 9,922,655
SIC 7323 Credit reporting services
   Louis Senecal
Dir Gilles Senecal

   D-U-N-S 20-127-2221   (BR)
SEARS CANADA INC
SEARS DECOR
690 Boul Le Corbusier, Cote Saint-Luc, QC,
H7N 0A9
(450) 682-0495
Emp Here 20
SIC 5712 Furniture stores

   D-U-N-S 25-224-2086   (BR)
**VANCOUVER CAREER COLLEGE (BURN-
ABY) INC**
COLLEGE CDI
(*Suby of* Chung Family Holdings Inc)
3 Place Laval Bureau 400, Cote Saint-Luc,
QC, H7N 1A2
(450) 662-9090
Emp Here 60
SIC 8211 Elementary and secondary schools

Cote Saint-Luc, QC H7R
Hochelaga County

   D-U-N-S 25-233-3703   (BR)
COMMISSION SCOLAIRE DE LAVAL
ECOLE RAYMOND
6145 27e Av, Cote Saint-Luc, QC, H7R 3K7
(450) 662-7000
Emp Here 40
SIC 8211 Elementary and secondary schools

Cote Saint-Luc, QC H7S
Hochelaga County

   D-U-N-S 24-901-1149   (SL)
2393689 CANADA INC
ORTHO CONCEPT INTERNATIONAL
1850 Boul Le Corbusier Bureau 200, Cote
Saint-Luc, QC, H7S 2K1
(450) 973-6700
Emp Here 40   *Sales* 5,376,850
SIC 3842 Surgical appliances and supplies
Pr Pr Andre Blain

   D-U-N-S 24-990-9821   (BR)
ARI FINANCIAL SERVICES INC
(*Suby of* Holman Enterprises Inc.)
2570 Boul Le Corbusier, Cote Saint-Luc, QC,
H7S 2K8
(450) 978-7070
Emp Here 28
SIC 5511 New and used car dealers

   D-U-N-S 20-420-3673   (SL)
BEDCO DIVISION DE GERODON INC
2305 Av Francis-Hughes, Cote Saint-Luc, QC,
H7S 1N5
(514) 384-2820
Emp Here 115   *Sales* 12,622,201
SIC 3499 Fabricated Metal products, nec
Pr Ronald Bedard
Sec Alexandre Bedard
Dir Louis Potvin
Dir Gilles Genest
Dir Benoit Duplessis
Dir Marie-Claude Gevry

   D-U-N-S 25-145-3775   (BR)
BOEHRINGER INGELHEIM (CANADA) LTD
2100 Rue Cunard, Cote Saint-Luc, QC, H7S
2G5

Emp Here 200
SIC 8731 Commercial physical research

   D-U-N-S 20-652-1051   (BR)
CARA OPERATIONS LIMITED
HARVEY'S
(*Suby of* Cara Holdings Limited)
1925 Boul Saint-Martin O, Cote Saint-Luc,
QC, H7S 1N2
(450) 687-6575
Emp Here 25
SIC 5812 Eating places

   D-U-N-S 24-527-8049   (BR)
COMARK INC
COMARK DISTRIBUTION CENTRE
(*Suby of* Comark Inc)
930 Boul Saint-Martin O, Cote Saint-Luc, QC,
H7S 2K9
(450) 967-9467
Emp Here 40
SIC 5621 Women's clothing stores

   D-U-N-S 20-716-7417   (BR)
COMMISSION SCOLAIRE DE LAVAL
ECOLE PRIMAIRE ALFRED-PELLAN
955 Boul Saint-Martin O Bureau 144, Cote
Saint-Luc, QC, H7S 1M5
(450) 662-7000
Emp Here 50
SIC 8211 Elementary and secondary schools

   D-U-N-S 20-032-7554   (BR)
COMMISSION SCOLAIRE DE LAVAL
ECOLE SOCRATES-DEMOSTHENE
1565 Boul Saint-Martin O, Cote Saint-Luc,
QC, H7S 1N1
(450) 972-1800
Emp Here 25
SIC 8211 Elementary and secondary schools

   D-U-N-S 20-716-7763   (BR)
COMMISSION SCOLAIRE DE LAVAL
ECOLE PRIMAIRE SIMON-VANIER
1755 Av Dumouchel, Cote Saint-Luc, QC, H7S
1J7
(450) 662-7000
Emp Here 50
SIC 8211 Elementary and secondary schools

D-U-N-S 24-357-2513   (HQ)
FD ALPHA CANADA ACQUISITION INC
FORT DEARBORN
2277 Des Laurentides (A-15) E, Cote Saint-Luc, QC, H7S 1Z6
(450) 680-5000
Emp Here 100   *Emp Total* 300
Sales 30,643,494
SIC 2679 Converted paper products, nec
Pr Jeffrey L. Brezek
Dir Chris Lumbard

D-U-N-S 20-289-1214   (SL)
GENPAK, LP
1890 Boul Fortin, Cote Saint-Luc, QC, H7S 1N8
(450) 662-1030
Emp Here 50
SIC 2656 Sanitary food containers

D-U-N-S 20-284-0190   (BR)
GOUVERNEMENT DE LA PROVINCE DE QUEBEC
REGIE DU BATIMENT DU QUEBEC
1760 Boul Le Corbusier, Cote Saint-Luc, H7S 2K1

Emp Here 60
SIC 7389 Business services, nec

D-U-N-S 20-860-9680   (BR)
GREAT PACIFIC ENTERPRISES INC
GENPAK DIV
1890 Boul Fortin, Cote Saint-Luc, QC, H7S 1N8
(450) 662-1030
Emp Here 100
SIC 3081 Unsupported plastics film and sheet

D-U-N-S 20-166-4158   (SL)
GROLIER LIMITEE
GROLIER ENTERPRISES
(*Suby* of Scholastic Corporation)
1700 Boul Laval Bureau 580, Cote Saint-Luc, QC, H7S 2J2
(450) 667-1510
Emp Here 48   *Sales* 2,699,546
SIC 2731 Book publishing

D-U-N-S 20-543-9560   (BR)
GROUPE ARCHAMBAULT INC
ARCHAMBAULT LAVAL
1545 Boul Le Corbusier, Cote Saint-Luc, QC, H7S 2K6
(450) 978-7275
Emp Here 65
SIC 5736 Musical instrument stores

D-U-N-S 25-325-1433   (BR)
GROUPE HOTELIER GRAND CHATEAU INC
HILTON MONTREAL LAVAL
(*Suby* of Groupe Hotelier Grand Chateau Inc)
2225 Des Laurentides (A-15) E, Cote Saint-Luc, QC, H7S 1Z6
(450) 682-2225
Emp Here 105
SIC 7011 Hotels and motels

D-U-N-S 24-583-4184   (SL)
HAYES COMMUNICATIONS INC
HAYES SIGNALISATION
2075 Boul Fortin, Cote Saint-Luc, QC, H7S 1P4
(514) 382-1550
Emp Here 20   *Sales* 1,696,192
SIC 4899 Communication services, nec

D-U-N-S 25-305-2385   (BR)
INNVEST PROPERTIES CORP
QUALITY SUITES
(*Suby* of Innvest Properties Corp)
2035 Des Laurentides (A-15) E, Cote Saint-Luc, QC, H7S 1Z6
(450) 686-6777
Emp Here 30
SIC 7011 Hotels and motels

D-U-N-S 25-526-2024   (HQ)
INSTECH TELECOMMUNICATION INC
2075 Boul Fortin, Cote Saint-Luc, QC, H7S 1P4
(514) 388-4337
Emp Here 56   *Emp Total* 1,300
Sales 13,569,538
SIC 1623 Water, sewer, and utility lines
Pr Edith Poudrier
 Michel Matte
Dir Stephane Gauthier

D-U-N-S 24-051-4823   (BR)
MEP TECHNOLOGIES INC
(*Suby* of Double A Corp Inc)
1690 Rue Cunard, Cote Saint-Luc, QC, H7S 2B2
(450) 978-9214
Emp Here 40
SIC 8731 Commercial physical research

D-U-N-S 25-687-6178   (BR)
MAPLE LEAF FOODS INC
2525 Av Fran Is-Hughes, Cote Saint-Luc, QC, H7S 2H7
(450) 967-1130
Emp Here 70
SIC 2011 Meat packing plants

D-U-N-S 25-310-9961   (BR)
MCDONALD'S   RESTAURANTS   OF CANADA LIMITED
MCDONALD'S
(*Suby* of McDonald's Corporation)
2005 Boul Saint-Martin O, Cote Saint-Luc, QC, H7S 1N3
(450) 688-8531
Emp Here 20
SIC 5812 Eating places

D-U-N-S 24-379-0248   (BR)
PARKER HANNIFIN CANADA
MICRO THERMO TECHNOLOGIES, DIV OF
2584 Boul Le Corbusier, Cote Saint-Luc, QC, H7S 2K8
(450) 668-3033
Emp Here 50
SIC 5075 Warm air heating and air conditioning

D-U-N-S 20-115-9949   (SL)
PLACEMENTS ORBI CONSTRUCTION INC
2225 Boul Industriel, Cote Saint-Luc, QC, H7S 1P8

Emp Here 75   *Sales* 13,938,720
SIC 3441 Fabricated structural Metal
Pr Pr Carlos Mario Stella
 Nestor Emir Stella

D-U-N-S 24-933-8757   (SL)
PLACEMENTS SAMUEL S SEGAL INC
2205 Av Francis-Hughes, Cote Saint-Luc, QC, H7S 1N5

Emp Here 115   *Sales* 24,718,080
SIC 6712 Bank holding companies
 Jerrick Segal
 Stanley Segal

D-U-N-S 25-513-4512   (HQ)
RETOUCHES DE FIL EN AIGUILLE INC, LES
(*Suby* of Retouches De Fil en Aiguille Inc, Les)
1600 Boul Le Corbusier Bureau 110, Cote Saint-Luc, QC, H7S 1Y9

Emp Here 20   *Emp Total* 60
Sales 1,896,978
SIC 7219 Laundry and garment services, nec

D-U-N-S 24-050-8866   (SL)
REVETEMENTS SCELL-TECH INC, LES
SCELLTECH
1478 Rue Cunard, Cote Saint-Luc, QC, H7S 2B7
(514) 990-7886
Emp Here 65   *Sales* 4,158,760

SIC 1721 Painting and paper hanging

D-U-N-S 20-503-3608   (BR)
SAMUEL, SON & CO., LIMITED
2225 Av Francis-Hughes, Cote Saint-Luc, QC, H7S 1N5
(514) 384-5220
Emp Here 200
SIC 5051 Metals service centers and offices

D-U-N-S 20-553-3651   (BR)
STAPLES CANADA INC
STAPLES
(*Suby* of Staples, Inc.)
1600 Boul Le Corbusier Bureau 99, Cote Saint-Luc, QC, H7S 1Y9
(450) 973-1070
Emp Here 40
SIC 5943 Stationery stores

D-U-N-S 20-056-9338   (HQ)
TRANSELEC/COMMON INC
2075 Boul Fortin, Cote Saint-Luc, QC, H7S 1P4
(514) 382-1550
Emp Here 200   *Emp Total* 1,300
Sales 210,126,816
SIC 1623 Water, sewer, and utility lines
 Claude Gauthier
Pr Pr Stephane Gauthier
 Michel Matte
Dir Fin Richard Lafrance

D-U-N-S 25-297-6352   (BR)
WAL-MART CANADA CORP
WALMART
1660 Boul Le Corbusier, Cote Saint-Luc, QC, H7S 1Z2
(450) 681-1126
Emp Here 313
SIC 5311 Department stores

Cote Saint-Luc, QC H7T
Hochelaga County

D-U-N-S 24-178-3740   (BR)
3819299 CANADA INC
TIM HORTONS
(*Suby* of 3819299 Canada Inc)
2600 Boul Daniel-Johnson, Cote Saint-Luc, QC, H7T 2K1
(450) 973-3804
Emp Here 21
SIC 5499 Miscellaneous food stores

D-U-N-S 24-383-6959   (BR)
APPLE CANADA INC
(*Suby* of Apple Inc.)
3035 Boul Le Carrefour Bureau C14b, Cote Saint-Luc, QC, H7T 1C8
(450) 902-4400
Emp Here 60
SIC 5045 Computers, peripherals, and software

D-U-N-S 25-896-5235   (BR)
AUTOMOBILE ET TOURING CLUB DU QUEBEC (A.T.C.Q.)
CAA QUEBEC
3131 Boul Saint-Martin O Bureau 100, Cote Saint-Luc, QC, H7T 2Z5
(450) 682-8100
Emp Here 25
SIC 8699 Membership organizations, nec

D-U-N-S 20-699-9950   (BR)
BANQUE DE DEVELOPPEMENT DU CANADA
BDC
2525 Boul Daniel-Johnson Bureau 100, Cote Saint-Luc, QC, H7T 1S9
(450) 973-3727
Emp Here 35
SIC 6141 Personal credit institutions

D-U-N-S 24-312-6955   (BR)
BOSTON PIZZA INTERNATIONAL INC
BOSTON PIZZA
3030 Boul Le Carrefour Bureau 802, Cote Saint-Luc, QC, H7T 2P5
(450) 687-2004
Emp Here 25
SIC 6794 Patent owners and lessors

D-U-N-S 24-337-9398   (BR)
BOSTON PIZZA INTERNATIONAL INC
450 Prom Du Centropolis, Cote Saint-Luc, QC, H7T 3C2
(450) 688-2229
Emp Here 80
SIC 5812 Eating places

D-U-N-S 24-644-0080   (BR)
BOUCLAIR INC
2585 Boul Daniel-Johnson, Cote Saint-Luc, QC, H7T 1S8
(450) 682-5541
Emp Here 25
SIC 5947 Gift, novelty, and souvenir shop

D-U-N-S 25-787-7969   (BR)
BOUTIQUE JACOB INC
JACOB
(*Suby* of Boutique Jacob Inc)
3035 Boul Le Carrefour, Cote Saint-Luc, QC, H7T 1C8
(450) 681-5231
Emp Here 30
SIC 5621 Women's clothing stores

D-U-N-S 25-794-7184   (BR)
BOUTIQUE TRISTAN & ISEUT INC
3035 Boul Le Carrefour, Cote Saint-Luc, QC, H7T 1C8
(450) 687-6382
Emp Here 20
SIC 5651 Family clothing stores

D-U-N-S 20-519-0767   (BR)
CIBC WORLD MARKETS INC
CIBC WOOD GUNDY
2540 Boul Daniel-Johnson Bureau 800, Cote Saint-Luc, QC, H7T 2S3
(450) 688-1004
Emp Here 30
SIC 6211 Security brokers and dealers

D-U-N-S 25-257-3217   (SL)
CAMP SPATIAL CANADA
COSMODOME
2150 Des Laurentides A-15 O, Cote Saint-Luc, QC, H7T 2T8
(450) 978-3600
Emp Here 52   *Sales* 4,450,603
SIC 7032 Sporting and recreational camps

D-U-N-S 25-257-3217   (SL)
CENTRE D'HEBERGEMENT ET DE SANTE DE LONGUE DUREE ST-JUDE INC
4410 Boul Saint-Martin O, Cote Saint-Luc, QC, H7T 1C3
(450) 687-7714
Emp Here 300   *Sales* 17,621,552
SIC 8051 Skilled nursing care facilities
Pr Pr Daniel Leclerc

D-U-N-S 24-319-1595   (BR)
CENTRE DE SERVICES DE PAIE CGI INC
NETHRIS PAYROLL SERVICES
3206 Sud Laval (A-440) O, Cote Saint-Luc, QC, H7T 2H6
(514) 850-6291
Emp Here 40
SIC 8721 Accounting, auditing, and bookkeeping

D-U-N-S 20-791-4511   (BR)
CHILDREN'S PLACE (CANADA) LP, THE
CHILDREN PLACE, THE
3035 Boul Le Carrefour, Cote Saint-Luc, QC, H7T 1C8
(450) 973-5208
Emp Here 40

SIC 5641 Children's and infants' wear stores

D-U-N-S 24-576-3540   (BR)
CINEPLEX ODEON CORPORATION
CINEMA CINEPLEX LAVAL
2800 Av Du Cosmodome, Cote Saint-Luc, QC,
H7T 2X1
(450) 978-0212
Emp Here 100
SIC 7832 Motion picture theaters, except
drive-in

D-U-N-S 25-243-3982   (SL)
COMPLEXE AUTO 440 DE LAVAL INC
LOCATION D'AUTO 440, DIV DE
3670 Sud Laval A-440 O, Cote Saint-Luc, QC,
H7T 2H6
(450) 682-3670
Emp Here 65   *Sales* 30,625,693
SIC 5511 New and used car dealers
 Jean-Paul Lalonde

D-U-N-S 20-511-7380   (BR)
CORDEE PLEIN AIR INC, LA
2777 Boul Saint-Martin O, Cote Saint-Luc,
QC, H7T 2Y7
(514) 524-1326
Emp Here 75
SIC 5941 Sporting goods and bicycle shops

D-U-N-S 20-284-6655   (BR)
DAVIDSTEA INC
DAVIDSTEA
3035 Boul Le Carrefour, Cote Saint-Luc, QC,
H7T 1C8
(450) 681-0776
Emp Here 50
SIC 5499 Miscellaneous food stores

D-U-N-S 20-108-8536   (BR)
DELOITTE & TOUCHE INC
GESTION DELOITTE
(*Suby of* Deloitte LLP)
2540 Boul Daniel-Johnson Bureau 210, Cote
Saint-Luc, QC, H7T 2S3
(450) 978-3500
Emp Here 100
SIC 8721 Accounting, auditing, and book-
keeping

D-U-N-S 25-510-3921   (BR)
FEDERATED INSURANCE COMPANY OF
CANADA
3100 Boul Le Carrefour Bureau 660, Cote
Saint-Luc, QC, H7T 2K7
(450) 687-8650
Emp Here 20
SIC 6331 Fire, marine, and casualty insurance

D-U-N-S 25-063-6008   (BR)
FOOT LOCKER CANADA CO.
3035 Boul Le Carrefour, Cote Saint-Luc, QC,
H7T 1C8
(450) 682-3733
Emp Here 25
SIC 5661 Shoe stores

D-U-N-S 24-522-6282   (BR)
GPL ASSURANCE INC
GPL PROULX ASSURANCE
(*Suby of* GPL Assurance Inc)
3131 Boul Saint-Martin O Bureau 600, Cote
Saint-Luc, QC, H7T 2Z5
(450) 978-5599
Emp Here 49
SIC 6411 Insurance agents, brokers, and ser-
vice

D-U-N-S 25-780-9517   (BR)
GAP (CANADA) INC
GAP
(*Suby of* The Gap Inc)
3035 Boul Le Carrefour, Cote Saint-Luc, QC,
H7T 1C8
(450) 686-4027
Emp Here 30
SIC 5651 Family clothing stores

D-U-N-S 20-703-3700   (SL)

GESTION CENTRIA COMMERCE INC
3131 Boul Saint-Martin O, Cote Saint-Luc,
QC, H7T 2Z5
(514) 874-0122
Emp Here 65   *Sales* 11,681,040
SIC 6712 Bank holding companies
 Levis Doucet
 Jean-Pierre Lambert

D-U-N-S 20-308-8703   (HQ)
GROUPE ADONIS INC
ADONIS
2425 Boul Cure-Labelle, Cote Saint-Luc, QC,
H7T 1R3
(450) 978-2333
Emp Here 80   *Emp Total* 65,000
Sales 107,179,268
SIC 5411 Grocery stores
 Pr Pr Jamil Cheaib
 VP VP Georges Ghrayeb
 Sec Simon Rivet
 Francois Thibault
 Dir Christian Bourbonniere
 Dir Elie Cheaib

D-U-N-S 25-359-3735   (BR)
GROUPE HOTELIER GRAND CHATEAU
INC
HOTEL SHERATON LAVAL
(*Suby of* Groupe Hotelier Grand Chateau Inc)
2440 Des Laurentides (A-15) O, Cote Saint-
Luc, QC, H7T 1X5
(450) 687-2440
Emp Here 200
SIC 7011 Hotels and motels

D-U-N-S 25-924-0885   (BR)
H.B. GROUP INSURANCE MANAGEMENT
LTD
H B GESTION ASSURANCE COLLECTIVE
3080 Boul Le Carrefour Bureau 700, Cote
Saint-Luc, QC, H7T 2R5
(450) 681-4950
Emp Here 52
SIC 6411 Insurance agents, brokers, and ser-
vice

D-U-N-S 25-778-7267   (BR)
HSBC BANK CANADA
3030 Boul Le Carrefour Bureau 100, Cote
Saint-Luc, QC, H7T 2P5
(450) 687-6920
Emp Here 26
SIC 6021 National commercial banks

D-U-N-S 25-857-3385   (SL)
HUBERT, GUY & ASSOCIES INC
4150 Boul Saint-Martin O, Cote Saint-Luc,
QC, H7T 1C1
(450) 688-3252
Emp Here 53   *Sales* 1,605,135
SIC 5812 Eating places

D-U-N-S 25-301-2983   (BR)
HUDSON'S BAY COMPANY
3045 Boul Le Carrefour, Cote Saint-Luc, QC,
H7T 1C7
(450) 687-1540
Emp Here 200
SIC 5311 Department stores

D-U-N-S 25-309-7349   (BR)
INDUSTRIELLE ALLIANCE, ASSURANCE
ET SERVICES FINANCIERS INC
AGENCE ST MARTIN
3030 Boul Le Carrefour Bureau 702, Cote
Saint-Luc, QC, H7T 2P5
(450) 681-1614
Emp Here 30
SIC 6411 Insurance agents, brokers, and ser-
vice

D-U-N-S 20-237-1456   (BR)
INTEGRATED DISTRIBUTION SYSTEMS
LIMITED PARTNERSHIP
WAJAX EQUIPMENT
2000 Rue John-Molson, Cote Saint-Luc, QC,

H7T 0H4
(450) 682-3737
Emp Here 130
SIC 5084 Industrial machinery and equipment

D-U-N-S 25-873-9676   (BR)
INTEGRATED DISTRIBUTION SYSTEMS
LIMITED PARTNERSHIP
EQUIPEMENT WAJAX
(*Suby of* Integrated Distribution Systems Lim-
ited Partnership)
2000 Rue John-Molson, Cote Saint-Luc, QC,
H7T 0H4
(450) 682-3737
Emp Here 100
SIC 5084 Industrial machinery and equipment

D-U-N-S 25-061-9905   (BR)
LE CHATEAU INC
(*Suby of* Le Chateau Inc)
3003 Boul Le Carrefour, Cote Saint-Luc, QC,
H7T 1C7
(450) 688-4142
Emp Here 20
SIC 5651 Family clothing stores

D-U-N-S 20-765-7834   (BR)
LEON'S FURNITURE LIMITED
LEON AMEUBLEMENT
2000 Boul Daniel-Johnson, Cote Saint-Luc,
QC, H7T 1A3
(450) 688-3851
Emp Here 80
SIC 5712 Furniture stores

D-U-N-S 25-325-1714   (BR)
LIBRAIRIE RENAUD-BRAY INC
3035 Boul Le Carrefour, Cote Saint-Luc, QC,
H7T 1C8
(450) 681-3032
Emp Here 30
SIC 5942 Book stores

D-U-N-S 25-303-9275   (BR)
LONDON LIFE INSURANCE COMPANY
FINANCIERE LIBERTE 55
3090 Boul Le Carrefour Bureau 400, Cote
Saint-Luc, QC, H7T 2J7
(450) 687-3971
Emp Here 60
SIC 6311 Life insurance

D-U-N-S 20-297-7778   (BR)
MAISON SIMONS INC, LA
3025 Boul Le Carrefour Bureau Y008, Cote
Saint-Luc, QC, H7T 1C7
(514) 282-1840
Emp Here 50
SIC 5311 Department stores

D-U-N-S 20-305-3624   (HQ)
MASON GRAPHITE INC
(*Suby of* Mason Graphite Inc)
3030 Boul Le Carrefour Bureau 600, Cote
Saint-Luc, QC, H7T 2P5
(514) 289-3580
Emp Here 20   *Emp Total* 75
Sales 4,450,603
SIC 1499 Miscellaneous nonMetallic minerals,
except fuels

D-U-N-S 20-227-0906   (HQ)
MICHELIN AMERIQUE DU NORD
(CANADA) INC
2500 Boul Daniel-Johnson Bureau 500, Cote
Saint-Luc, QC, H7T 2P6
(450) 978-4700
Emp Here 150   *Emp Total* 6
Sales 1,559,251,800
SIC 5014 Tires and tubes
 Ch Bd Clyde A. Selleck
 Pr R. Jeff Maclean
 VP VP Joan E. Martin
 Sec Catherine Mckean

D-U-N-S 24-769-9549   (BR)
NATIONAL BANK TRUST INC
BANQUE NATIONALE

2500 Boul Daniel-Johnson Bureau 115, Cote
Saint-Luc, QC, H7T 2P6
(450) 682-3200
Emp Here 25
SIC 8742 Management consulting services

D-U-N-S 25-775-8615   (BR)
NAUTILUS PLUS INC
NAUTILUS CHOMEDY
3216 Boul Saint-Martin O, Cote Saint-Luc,
QC, H7T 1A1
(450) 688-0850
Emp Here 50
SIC 7991 Physical fitness facilities

D-U-N-S 20-657-9513   (BR)
OLD NAVY (CANADA) INC
OLD NAVY
(*Suby of* The Gap Inc)
3035 Boul Le Carrefour, Cote Saint-Luc, QC,
H7T 1C8
(450) 682-9410
Emp Here 40
SIC 5651 Family clothing stores

D-U-N-S 20-511-9089   (BR)
PRIMMUM INSURANCE COMPANY
(*Suby of* Toronto-Dominion Bank, The)
2990 Av Pierre-Peladeau Bureau 200, Cote
Saint-Luc, QC, H7T 0B1
(514) 874-1686
Emp Here 75
SIC 6331 Fire, marine, and casualty insurance

D-U-N-S 24-208-6085   (BR)
PROVIGO INC
MAXI & CIE
3500 Boul Saint-Martin O, Cote Saint-Luc,
QC, H7T 2W4
(450) 688-2969
Emp Here 145
SIC 5421 Meat and fish markets

D-U-N-S 20-714-6684   (BR)
RBC DOMINION SECURITIES INC
(*Suby of* Royal Bank Of Canada)
545 Prom Du Centropolis Bureau 200, Cote
Saint-Luc, QC, H7T 0A3
(450) 686-3434
Emp Here 50
SIC 6282 Investment advice

D-U-N-S 20-127-1033   (BR)
RAYMOND CHABOT GRANT THORNTON
S.E.N.C.R.L.
2500 Boul Daniel-Johnson Bureau 300, Cote
Saint-Luc, QC, H7T 2P6
(514) 382-0270
Emp Here 70
SIC 8721 Accounting, auditing, and book-
keeping

D-U-N-S 20-240-3259   (HQ)
ROTISSERIES ST-HUBERT LTEE, LES
ST-HUBERT EXPRESS
(*Suby of* Cara Holdings Limited)
2500 Boul Daniel-Johnson Bureau 700, Cote
Saint-Luc, QC, H7T 2P6
(450) 435-0674
Emp Here 135   *Emp Total* 14,038
Sales 127,462,343
SIC 6794 Patent owners and lessors
 Ch Bd Kenneth J. Grondin
 Pr Richard Scofield
 VP Fin Diane Bouchard
 VP Dave Lantz
 Sec Sophie Gagne

D-U-N-S 25-364-3589   (BR)
SCOTIA CAPITAL INC
SCOTIA MCLEOD
3090 Boul Le Carrefour Bureau 125, Cote
Saint-Luc, QC, H7T 2J7
(450) 680-3100
Emp Here 20
SIC 6211 Security brokers and dealers

D-U-N-S 25-294-6785   (BR)

SEARS CANADA INC
SEARS LAVAL
3005 Boul Le Carrefour Bureau Y005, Cote
Saint-Luc, QC, H7T 1C7
(450) 682-1200
Emp Here 320
SIC 5311 Department stores

D-U-N-S 25-232-8240   (BR)
SIR WILFRID LAURIER SCHOOL BOARD
LAURIER SENIOR HIGH SCHOOL
(*Suby of* Sir Wilfrid Laurier School Board)
2323 Boul Daniel-Johnson, Cote Saint-Luc,
QC, H7T 1H8
(450) 686-6300
Emp Here 75
SIC 8211 Elementary and secondary schools

D-U-N-S 24-212-9265   (BR)
SOCIETE DES ALCOOLS DU QUEBEC
S.A.Q.
250 Prom Du Centropolis, Cote Saint-Luc,
QC, H7T 2Z6
(450) 978-3189
Emp Here 50
SIC 5921 Liquor stores

D-U-N-S 20-700-4453   (BR)
TOMMY HILFIGER CANADA INC
TOMMY HILFIGER OUTLET
2400 Boul Chomedey, Cote Saint-Luc, QC,
H7T 2W3
(450) 689-0039
Emp Here 20
SIC 5651 Family clothing stores

D-U-N-S 20-700-4651   (BR)
TOMMY HILFIGER CANADA INC
TOMMY HILFIGER STORE
3035 Boul Le Carrefour, Cote Saint-Luc, QC,
H7T 1C8

Emp Here 20
SIC 5136 Men's and boy's clothing

D-U-N-S 25-293-9210   (BR)
TOYS 'R' US (CANADA) LTD
TOYS 'R' US
(*Suby of* Toys "r" Us, Inc.)
2600 Boul Daniel-Johnson, Cote Saint-Luc,
QC, H7T 2K1
(450) 682-6194
Emp Here 45
SIC 5945 Hobby, toy, and game shops

D-U-N-S 24-352-6571   (BR)
**TYCO INTEGRATED FIRE & SECURITY
CANADA, INC**
SIMPLEX GRINNELL, DIV. OF
(*Suby of* Johnson Controls, Inc.)
3300 Sud Laval (A-440) O, Cote Saint-Luc,
QC, H7T 2H6

Emp Here 60
SIC 1731 Electrical work

D-U-N-S 20-519-4553   (BR)
VALEURS MOBILIERES DESJARDINS INC
2550 Boul Daniel-Johnson Bureau 140, Cote
Saint-Luc, QC, H7T 2L1
(450) 682-5858
Emp Here 30
SIC 6211 Security brokers and dealers

D-U-N-S 24-346-3143   (BR)
WSP CANADA INC
GENIVAR
2525 Boul Daniel-Johnson Bureau 525, Cote
Saint-Luc, QC, H7T 1S9
(450) 686-0980
Emp Here 200
SIC 8711 Engineering services

Cote Saint-Luc, QC H7V
Hochelaga County

D-U-N-S 20-716-7458   (BR)
COMMISSION SCOLAIRE DE LAVAL
*ECOLE   SECONDAIRE   ALPHONSE-
DESJARDINS*
3680 Boul Levesque O, Cote Saint-Luc, QC,
H7V 1E8
(450) 662-7000
Emp Here 50
SIC 8211 Elementary and secondary schools

D-U-N-S 24-179-8255   (BR)
DUNTON RAINVILLE SENC
3333 Boul Du Souvenir Bureau 200, Cote
Saint-Luc, QC, H7V 1X1
(450) 686-8683
Emp Here 40
SIC 8111 Legal services

D-U-N-S 20-715-3292   (BR)
GESTOLEX, SOCIETE EN COMMANDITE
(*Suby of* Gestolex, Societe en Commandite)
3333 Boul Du Souvenir Bureau 200, Cote
Saint-Luc, QC, H7V 1X1
(450) 686-8683
Emp Here 40
SIC 8111 Legal services

D-U-N-S 24-294-3132   (SL)
MANOIR ST-PATRICE INC
3615 Boul Perron, Cote Saint-Luc, QC, H7V
1P4
(450) 681-1621
Emp Here 125   *Sales* 4,596,524
SIC 8361 Residential care

D-U-N-S 20-270-8491   (BR)
UNIVERSITE DU QUEBEC
*INSTITUT NATIONALDE LA RECHERCHE
SCIENTIFIQUE (INR*
531 Boul Des Prairies, Cote Saint-Luc, QC,
H7V 1B7
(450) 687-5010
Emp Here 100
SIC 8221 Colleges and universities

D-U-N-S 25-308-1228   (BR)
VILLE DE LAVAL
ENVIRONNEMENT USINE POTABLE
3810 Boul Levesque O, Cote Saint-Luc, QC,
H7V 1E8
(450) 978-8936
Emp Here 30
SIC 2899 Chemical preparations, nec

Coteau-Du-Lac, QC J0P
Soulanges County

D-U-N-S 24-858-2736   (SL)
ARCELORMITTAL COTEAU-DU-LAC INC
25 Rue De L'Acier, Coteau-Du-Lac, QC, J0P
1B0
(450) 763-0915
Emp Here 66   *Sales* 4,669,485
SIC 3479 Metal coating and allied services

D-U-N-S 25-240-4884   (BR)
**COMMISSION SCOLAIRE DES TROIS-
LACS**
ECOLE ST IGNACE
1 Rue Du Parc, Coteau-Du-Lac, QC, J0P 1B0
(450) 267-3458
Emp Here 25
SIC 8211 Elementary and secondary schools

D-U-N-S 20-195-0987   (BR)
COMPAGNIE MELOCHE INC, LA
105 338 Rte, Coteau-Du-Lac, QC, J0P 1B0
(450) 267-3333
Emp Here 45
SIC 1429 Crushed and broken stone, nec

D-U-N-S 24-387-0214   (BR)
**FEDEX SUPPLY CHAIN DISTRIBUTION
SYSTEM OF CANADA, INC**
SYSTEME   DE   DISTRIBUTION   DE   LA

*CHAINE D'APPROVISIONNEMENT FEDEX
DU CANADA*
(*Suby of* Fedex Corporation)
50 Boul Dupont, Coteau-Du-Lac, QC, J0P 1B0
(800) 463-3339
Emp Here 350
SIC 4731 Freight transportation arrangement

D-U-N-S 20-577-5930   (SL)
SOREVCO AND COMPANY LIMITED
SOREVCO SOCIETE EN COMMANDITE
25 Rue De L'Acier, Coteau-Du-Lac, QC, J0P
1B0
(450) 763-0915
Emp Here 69   *Sales* 4,815,406
SIC 3479 Metal coating and allied services

Courcelette, QC G0A
Portneuf County

D-U-N-S 20-711-8576   (BR)
**COMMISSION SCOLAIRE CENTRAL QUE-
BEC**
DOLLARD DES ORMEAUX SCHOOL
18 Rue Ladas, Courcelette, QC, G0A 1R1
(418) 844-1457
Emp Here 60
SIC 8211 Elementary and secondary schools

Cowansville, QC J2K
Missisquoi County

D-U-N-S 25-209-8579   (SL)
A.P.M. DIESEL (1992) INC.
A.P.M. DIESEL
135 Rue Miner, Cowansville, QC, J2K 3Y5
(450) 260-1999
Emp Here 55   *Sales* 4,012,839
SIC 3519 Internal combustion engines, nec

D-U-N-S 24-835-3872   (SL)
ANSELL CANADA INC
105 Rue Lauder, Cowansville, QC, J2K 2K8
(450) 266-1850
Emp Here 35   *Sales* 4,304,681
SIC 5122 Drugs, proprietaries, and sundries

D-U-N-S 25-475-4625   (BR)
ARAMARK QUEBEC INC
222 Rue Mercier, Cowansville, QC, J2K 3R9
(450) 263-6660
Emp Here 60
SIC 5812 Eating places

D-U-N-S 25-182-3100   (SL)
CLSC ET CHSLD DE LA POMMERAIE
SOUTIEN A DOMICILE
133 Rue Larouche, Cowansville, QC, J2K 1T2
(450) 266-4342
Emp Here 75   *Sales* 4,617,412
SIC 8059 Nursing and personal care, nec

D-U-N-S 20-715-8010   (SL)
CRDI MONTEREGIE EST
159 Rue Des Textiles, Cowansville, QC, J2K
3P8
(450) 263-8383
Emp Here 35   *Sales* 11,877,360
SIC 8322 Individual and family services
  Denise Gagnon

D-U-N-S 20-584-8802   (BR)
CANADA POST CORPORATION
224 Rue Du Sud, Cowansville, QC, J2K 2X4
(450) 266-2101
Emp Here 20
SIC 4311 U.s. postal service

D-U-N-S 20-857-5472   (SL)
CLUB DE GOLF DE COWANSVILLE INC
RESTAURANT L'HERBE LONGUE
225 Ch Du Golf, Cowansville, QC, J2K 3G6

(450) 263-3131
Emp Here 50   *Sales* 1,532,175
SIC 5812 Eating places

D-U-N-S 25-232-9230   (BR)
**COMMISSION   SCOLAIRE   EASTERN
TOWNSHIPS**
ECOLE PRIMAIRE HEROES MEMORIAL
(*Suby of* Commission Scolaire Eastern Town-
ships)
317 Rue Du Sud, Cowansville, QC, J2K 2X6
(450) 263-1612
Emp Here 30
SIC 8211 Elementary and secondary schools

D-U-N-S 20-576-4140   (BR)
**COMMISSION   SCOLAIRE   EASTERN
TOWNSHIPS**
MASSEY VANIER HIGH SCHOOL
(*Suby of* Commission Scolaire Eastern Town-
ships)
224 Rue Mercier, Cowansville, QC, J2K 5C3
(450) 263-3772
Emp Here 83
SIC 8211 Elementary and secondary schools

D-U-N-S 25-240-6137   (BR)
**COMMISSION SCOLAIRE DU VAL-DES-
CERFS**
ECOLE STE THERESE
201 Boul Saint-Joseph, Cowansville, QC, J2K
1R9
(450) 263-5841
Emp Here 25
SIC 8211 Elementary and secondary schools

D-U-N-S 25-240-6053   (BR)
**COMMISSION SCOLAIRE DU VAL-DES-
CERFS**
ECOLE SECONDAIRE MASSEY VANIER
222 Rue Mercier, Cowansville, QC, J2K 3R9
(450) 263-6660
Emp Here 125
SIC 8211 Elementary and secondary schools

D-U-N-S 25-240-6095   (BR)
**COMMISSION SCOLAIRE DU VAL-DES-
CERFS**
ECOLE ST LEON
201 Boul Davignon, Cowansville, QC, J2K
1N7
(450) 263-5923
Emp Here 25
SIC 8211 Elementary and secondary schools

D-U-N-S 24-800-8872   (BR)
EDITIONS YVON BLAIS INC, LES
137 Rue John, Cowansville, QC, J2K 1W9

Emp Here 25
SIC 2731 Book publishing

D-U-N-S 24-107-2511   (SL)
**ENTREPRISES COMMERCIALES PAUL A
MEUNIER INC, LES**
UNIPRIX
101 Rue Albert Bureau 106, Cowansville, QC,
J2K 2W4
(450) 263-2666
Emp Here 39   *Sales* 7,710,200
SIC 5912 Drug stores and proprietary stores
Pr Laurier Lavoie
VP VP Marcel Tremblay
Treas Rene-Claude Gagnon

D-U-N-S 20-195-3106   (HQ)
INDUSTRIES PEPIN LIMITEE
(*Suby of* Industries Pepin Limitee)
536 Rue De La Riviere, Cowansville, QC, J2K
3G6
(450) 263-1848
Emp Here 30   *Emp Total* 30
Sales 5,559,741
SIC 2851 Paints and allied products
Pr Paul Pepin
VP VP David Pepin
Treas Jocelyne Pepin

D-U-N-S 24-125-4411   (BR)

LOBLAW COMPANIES LIMITED
LOBLAWS # 8312
1122 Rue Du Sud, Cowansville, QC, J2K 2Y3

Emp Here 110
SIC 5411 Grocery stores

   D-U-N-S 20-715-8044   (BR)
METRO RICHELIEU INC
SUTER-C
1775 Rue Du Sud, Cowansville, QC, J2K 3G8
(450) 263-2955
Emp Here 40
SIC 5411 Grocery stores

   D-U-N-S 25-299-9594   (BR)
PRISZM LP
PFK/PIZZA HUT
1533 Rue Du Sud, Cowansville, QC, J2K 2Z4

Emp Here 20
SIC 5812 Eating places

   D-U-N-S 25-298-2491   (BR)
RAYMOND CHABOT GRANT THORNTON S.E.N.C.R.L.
112 Rue Du Sud Bureau 100, Cowansville, QC, J2K 2X2
(450) 263-2010
Emp Here 20
SIC 8721 Accounting, auditing, and bookkeeping

   D-U-N-S 25-063-8756   (BR)
SERVICE CORPORATION INTERNATIONAL (CANADA) LIMITED
MAISON FUNERAIRE DESOURDY-WILSON, LA
104 Rue Buzzell, Cowansville, QC, J2K 2N5
(450) 263-1212
Emp Here 23
SIC 7261 Funeral service and crematories

   D-U-N-S 24-500-9402   (SL)
SUPERMARCHE A R G INC
PROVIGO GAGNON
175 Rue Principale, Cowansville, QC, J2K 3L9
(450) 263-3310
Emp Here 120   *Sales* 16,343,197
SIC 5411 Grocery stores
Pr Pr Richard Gagnon
 Andre Gagnon

   D-U-N-S 25-361-2931   (SL)
TORA COWANSVILLE LIMITEE
TIGRE GEANT
(*Suby of* Giant Tiger Stores Limited)
179 Rue Principale, Cowansville, QC, J2K 1J3
(450) 266-3369
Emp Here 50   *Sales* 4,085,799
SIC 5399 Miscellaneous general merchandise

   D-U-N-S 24-207-4248   (BR)
WAL-MART CANADA CORP
WALMART
1770 Rue Du S, Cowansville, QC, J2K 3G8
(450) 263-8981
Emp Here 100
SIC 5311 Department stores

Crabtree, QC J0K

   D-U-N-S 20-540-2126   (BR)
KRUGER PRODUCTS L.P.
100 1e Av, Crabtree, QC, J0K 1B0
(450) 754-2855
Emp Here 662
SIC 2676 Sanitary paper products

Danville, QC J0A

   D-U-N-S 25-233-2705   (BR)

COMMISSION SCOLAIRE DES SOMMETS
ECOLE MASSON
(*Suby of* Commission Scolaire des Sommets)
30 Rue Du College, Danville, QC, J0A 1A0
(819) 839-2930
Emp Here 35
SIC 8211 Elementary and secondary schools

Daveluyville, QC G0Z
Arthabaska County

   D-U-N-S 20-712-0721   (BR)
COMMISSION SCOLAIRE DES BOIS-FRANCS
ECOLE SAINTE-ANNE
111 7e Av, Daveluyville, QC, G0Z 1C0
(819) 367-2980
Emp Here 40
SIC 8211 Elementary and secondary schools

   D-U-N-S 24-235-2909   (BR)
COMMISSION SCOLAIRE DES BOIS-FRANCS
ECOLE PRIMAIRE NOTRE DAME DE L'ASSOMPTION
414 Rue Principale, Daveluyville, QC, G0Z 1C0
(819) 367-2241
Emp Here 20
SIC 8211 Elementary and secondary schools

Degelis, QC G5T
Temiscouata County

   D-U-N-S 24-024-6566   (BR)
CENTRE DE SANTE ET DE SERVICE SOCI-AUX DU TEMISCOUATA
CENTRE HOSPITALIER NOTRE-DAME-DU-LAC
(*Suby of* Centre de Sante et de Service Sociaux du Temiscouata)
103 7e Rue E, Degelis, QC, G5T 1Y6
(418) 853-2572
Emp Here 25
SIC 8062 General medical and surgical hospitals

   D-U-N-S 25-232-3415   (BR)
COMMISSION SCOLAIRE DU FLEUVE ET DES LACS
ECOLE SECONDAIRE DE DEGELIS
385 Av Principale, Degelis, QC, G5T 1L3
(418) 854-3421
Emp Here 60
SIC 8211 Elementary and secondary schools

   D-U-N-S 20-711-9632   (BR)
COMMISSION SCOLAIRE DU FLEUVE ET DES LACS
ECOLE SAINT PIERRE
666 6e Rue O Bureau 6, Degelis, QC, G5T 1Y4
(418) 853-3438
Emp Here 50
SIC 8211 Elementary and secondary schools

   D-U-N-S 25-233-0386   (BR)
COMMISSION SCOLAIRE DU FLEUVE ET DES LACS
ECOLE PRIMAIRE DE DEGELIS
383 Av Principale, Degelis, QC, G5T 1L3
(418) 853-3921
Emp Here 40
SIC 8211 Elementary and secondary schools

   D-U-N-S 25-872-8112   (SL)
G.D.S. VALORIBOIS INC
(*Suby of* Gestion G et S Deschenes Inc)
1208 185 Rte S, Degelis, QC, G5T 1P8

Emp Here 43   *Sales* 4,851,006

SIC 2421 Sawmills and planing mills, general

   D-U-N-S 24-524-1562   (SL)
REGIE INTERMUNICIPALE DES DECHETS DE TEMISCOUATA
RIDT
369 Rue Principale Bureau 100, Degelis, QC, G5T 2G3
(418) 853-2220
Emp Here 34   *Sales* 6,188,450
SIC 4953 Refuse systems
Mng Dir Maxime Groleau
Pr Claude Lavoie
VP VP Andre Chouinard

Delson, QC J5B
Laprairie County

   D-U-N-S 25-388-7509   (SL)
BOIS GOODFELLOW (MARITIMES) LTEE
225 Rue Goodfellow, Delson, QC, J5B 1V5
(450) 635-6511
Emp Here 250   *Sales* 101,006,640
SIC 5031 Lumber, plywood, and millwork
Pr Pr Richard Goodfellow
 Keith R. Rattray

   D-U-N-S 25-888-8858   (BR)
CINEPLEX ODEON CORPORATION
CINEMA CINEPLEX ODEON DELSON
47 Boul Georges-Gagne S, Delson, QC, J5B 2E5

Emp Here 20
SIC 7832 Motion picture theaters, except drive-in

   D-U-N-S 25-240-5345   (BR)
COMMISSION SCOLAIRE DES GRANDES-SEIGNEURIES
ECOLE ALTERNATIVE DES CHEMINOTS
35 Rue Boardman, Delson, QC, J5B 2C3
(514) 380-8899
Emp Here 270
SIC 8211 Elementary and secondary schools

   D-U-N-S 24-423-8536   (BR)
NII NORTHERN INTERNATIONAL INC
10 Rue Industrielle, Delson, QC, J5B 1V8
(450) 638-4644
Emp Here 25
SIC 5063 Electrical apparatus and equipment

   D-U-N-S 24-871-4339   (SL)
PNR COYLE INC
100 Rue Goodfellow, Delson, QC, J5B 1V4
(450) 632-6241
Emp Here 25   *Sales* 2,845,467
SIC 4789 Transportation services, nec

   D-U-N-S 25-841-0497   (BR)
PROVIGO DISTRIBUTION INC
LOBLAWS
31 Boul Georges-Gagne S, Delson, QC, J5B 2E4
(450) 638-5041
Emp Here 93
SIC 5411 Grocery stores

   D-U-N-S 20-715-3128   (BR)
SSAB SWEDISH STEEL LTD
SWEDISH STEEL
220 Rue Industrielle, Delson, QC, J5B 1W4
(514) 364-1752
Emp Here 20
SIC 5051 Metals service centers and offices

   D-U-N-S 24-150-7198   (BR)
TOWER SCAFFOLD SERVICES INC
161 Rue Brossard, Delson, QC, J5B 1W9
(450) 638-7111
Emp Here 40
SIC 1541 Industrial buildings and warehouses

   D-U-N-S 20-014-7135   (SL)
TRANSPORT ALAIN GIROUX ET FILS INC

---

115 Rue Goodfellow, Delson, QC, J5B 1V3
(450) 638-5254
Emp Here 60   *Sales* 9,914,160
SIC 4213 Trucking, except local
Pr Pr Alain Giroux

   D-U-N-S 25-335-5713   (SL)
VISION CHEVROLET BUICK GMC INC
30 Rte 132, Delson, QC, J5B 1H3
(450) 659-5471
Emp Here 45   *Sales* 16,416,158
SIC 5511 New and used car dealers
Pr Pr Gabriel Dallaire

Denholm, QC J8N
Abitibi County

   D-U-N-S 25-372-9487   (BR)
COMPAGNIE COMMONWEALTH PLYWOOD LTEE, LA
SCIERIE PRO FOLIA
118 Ch Des Voyageurs, Denholm, QC, J8N 9C1
(819) 457-2815
Emp Here 50
SIC 2421 Sawmills and planing mills, general

Deschaillons-Sur-Saint-Laurent, QC G0S
Lotbiniere County

   D-U-N-S 20-195-6885   (HQ)
COTE-RECO INC
CENTRE DU TRAVAIL
100 12e Av, Deschaillons-Sur-Saint-Laurent, QC, G0S 1G0
(819) 292-2323
Emp Here 100   *Emp Total* 6
Sales 24,514,795
SIC 5139 Footwear
Pr Michel Cote
Sec Pierre Cote
Treas Andre Cote

Deschambault, QC G0A
Portneuf County

   D-U-N-S 24-907-9310   (SL)
2852-7885 QUEBEC INC
RESTAURANT MOTEL LE CHAVIGNY
11 Rue Des Pins, Deschambault, QC, G0A 1S0
(418) 286-4959
Emp Here 55   *Sales* 2,407,703
SIC 7011 Hotels and motels

   D-U-N-S 20-714-9225   (BR)
ALCOA CANADA CIE
ALUMINERIE DE BAIE-COMEAU
1 Boul Des Sources, Deschambault, QC, G0A 1S0
(418) 286-5287
Emp Here 100
SIC 3334 Primary aluminum

   D-U-N-S 25-063-7857   (BR)
RESTAURANT NORMANDIN INC
139 2e Rang, Deschambault, QC, G0A 1S0
(418) 286-6733
Emp Here 48
SIC 5812 Eating places

Deux-Montagnes, QC J7R
Deux-Montagnes County

   D-U-N-S 24-460-5184   (SL)
CENTRE HOSPITALIER DEUX-

MONTAGNES INC
2700 Ch D'Oka, Deux-Montagnes, QC, J7R 1P2
(450) 473-5111
Emp Here 60   *Sales* 6,219,371
SIC 8069 Specialty hospitals, except psychiatric
Pr Pr Madeleine Fournier
Robert Fournier
Louis H Fournier

D-U-N-S 20-545-6101   (BR)
COMMISSION SCOLAIRE DE LA SEIGNEURIE-DES-MILLE-ILES
COMMISSION SCOLAIRE DE LA SEIGNEURIE-DES-MILLE-ILES
1415 Ch De L'Avenir, Deux-Montagnes, QC, J7R 7B4
(450) 623-3079
Emp Here 30
SIC 8299 Schools and educational services, nec

D-U-N-S 25-233-9569   (BR)
COMMISSION SCOLAIRE DE LA SEIGNEURIE-DES-MILLE-ILES
COMMISSION SCOLAIRE DE LA SEIGNEURIE-DES-MILLE-ILES
(*Suby of* Commission Scolaire de la Seigneurie-Des-Mille-Iles)
203 14e Av, Deux-Montagnes, QC, J7R 3W1
(450) 491-5756
Emp Here 40
SIC 8211 Elementary and secondary schools

D-U-N-S 25-233-2564   (BR)
COMMISSION SCOLAIRE DE LA SEIGNEURIE-DES-MILLE-ILES
COMMISSION SCOLAIRE DE LA SEIGNEURIE-DES-MILLE-ILES
(*Suby of* Commission Scolaire de la Seigneurie-Des-Mille-Iles)
1400 Ch De L'Avenir, Deux-Montagnes, QC, J7R 6A6
(450) 472-2670
Emp Here 58
SIC 8211 Elementary and secondary schools

D-U-N-S 25-976-1260   (BR)
COMMISSION SCOLAIRE DE LA SEIGNEURIE-DES-MILLE-ILES
COMMISSION SCOLAIRE DE LA SEIGNEURIE-DES-MILLE-ILES
(*Suby of* Commission Scolaire de la Seigneurie-Des-Mille-Iles)
600 28e Av, Deux-Montagnes, QC, J7R 6L2
(450) 491-5454
Emp Here 50
SIC 8211 Elementary and secondary schools

D-U-N-S 25-233-3786   (BR)
COMMISSION SCOLAIRE DE LA SEIGNEURIE-DES-MILLE-ILES
COMMISSION SCOLAIRE DE LA SEIGNEURIE-DES-MILLE-ILES
(*Suby of* Commission Scolaire de la Seigneurie-Des-Mille-Iles)
500 Ch Des Anciens, Deux-Montagnes, QC, J7R 6A7
(450) 472-3070
Emp Here 180
SIC 8211 Elementary and secondary schools

D-U-N-S 25-877-3183   (BR)
GOUVERNEMENT DE LA PROVINCE DE QUEBEC
GOUVERNEMENT DE LA PROVINCE DE QUEBEC
333 Rue Antonin-Campeau Bureau 101, Deux-Montagnes, QC, J7R 0A2
(450) 491-5656
Emp Here 40
SIC 8322 Individual and family services

D-U-N-S 25-240-5881   (BR)
SIR WILFRID LAURIER SCHOOL BOARD
MOUNTAIN VIEW

(*Suby of* Sir Wilfrid Laurier School Board)
2001 Rue Guy, Deux-Montagnes, QC, J7R 1W6

Emp Here 25
SIC 8211 Elementary and secondary schools

D-U-N-S 20-025-5748   (BR)
SIR WILFRID LAURIER SCHOOL BOARD
LAKE OF TWO MOUNTAINS HIGH SCHOOL
2105 Rue Guy, Deux-Montagnes, QC, J7R 1W6
(450) 621-7830
Emp Here 50
SIC 8211 Elementary and secondary schools

D-U-N-S 20-867-3819   (BR)
SOBEYS QUEBEC INC
IGA
850 Ch D'Oka, Deux-Montagnes, QC, J7R 1L7
(450) 473-6280
Emp Here 90
SIC 5411 Grocery stores

Disraeli, QC G0N
Wolfe County

D-U-N-S 20-037-5389   (BR)
CENTRE DE SANTE ET DE SERVICE SOCIAUX DE LA REGION DE THETFORD
HEBERGEMENT RENE LAVOIE
260 Av Champlain, Disraeli, QC, G0N 1E0
(418) 449-2020
Emp Here 65
SIC 8361 Residential care

D-U-N-S 20-995-9696   (BR)
CENTRE DE LA PETITE ENFANCE PARC-EN-CIEL
888 Rue Saint-Antoine, Disraeli, QC, G0N 1E0
(418) 449-3004
Emp Here 75
SIC 8351 Child day care services

D-U-N-S 25-232-6582   (BR)
COMMISSION SCOLAIRE DES APPALACHES
ECOLE SAINTE LUCE
(*Suby of* Commission Scolaire des Appalaches)
290 Rue Montcalm, Disraeli, QC, G0N 1E0
(418) 449-2591
Emp Here 45
SIC 8211 Elementary and secondary schools

Dolbeau-Mistassini, QC G8L

D-U-N-S 25-257-7879   (BR)
CENTRE DE READAPTATION EN DEFICIENCE INTELLECTUELLE DU SAGUENAY LAC-ST-JEAN
CEDAP
(*Suby of* Centre De Readaptation En Deficience Intellectuelle Du Saguenay Lac-St-Jean)
364 8e Av Bureau 8e, Dolbeau-Mistassini, QC, G8L 3E5
(418) 276-7491
Emp Here 25
SIC 8322 Individual and family services

D-U-N-S 24-200-5064   (HQ)
CENTRE DE SANTE SERVICES SOCIAUX MARIA CHAPDELAINE
CSSS MARIA CHAPDELAINE
2000 Boul Du Sacre-Coeur, Dolbeau-Mistassini, QC, G8L 2R5
(418) 276-1234
Emp Here 600   *Emp Total* 40,000
Sales 52,166,901
SIC 8062 General medical and surgical hospi-

tals
Pr Andre Perron
VP Rejean Lavoie
Sec Nathalie Villeneuve
Dir Marc Audet
Dir Sandra Grenier
Dir Marc-Andre Servant
Dir Jean-Pierre Boivin
Dir Isabelle Gagnon
Dir Nathalie Maltais
Dir Pascal Cloutier

D-U-N-S 25-233-6888   (BR)
COMMISSION SCOLAIRE DU PAYS-DES-BLEUETS
POLYVALENTE JEAN DOLBEAU
(*Suby of* Commission Scolaire du Pays-des-Bleuets)
300 Av Jean-Dolbeau, Dolbeau-Mistassini, QC, G8L 2T7
(418) 276-0984
Emp Here 80
SIC 8211 Elementary and secondary schools

D-U-N-S 20-006-4686   (BR)
COMMISSION SCOLAIRE DU PAYS-DES-BLEUETS
CENTRE DE FORMATION PROFESSION-NEL
400 2e Av, Dolbeau-Mistassini, QC, G8L 3C6
(418) 276-8654
Emp Here 20
SIC 8211 Elementary and secondary schools

D-U-N-S 25-877-4777   (BR)
COMMISSION SCOLAIRE DU PAYS-DES-BLEUETS
ECOLE ST THERESE
(*Suby of* Commission Scolaire du Pays-des-Bleuets)
242 3e Av, Dolbeau-Mistassini, QC, G8L 2V4
(418) 276-5101
Emp Here 30
SIC 8211 Elementary and secondary schools

D-U-N-S 25-232-2375   (BR)
COMMISSION SCOLAIRE DU PAYS-DES-BLEUETS
ECOLE BON PASTEUR STE JEANNE D'ARC
(*Suby of* Commission Scolaire du Pays-des-Bleuets)
1950 Boul Sacre-C Ur, Dolbeau-Mistassini, QC, G8L 2R3
(418) 276-2012
Emp Here 20
SIC 8211 Elementary and secondary schools

D-U-N-S 25-232-2052   (BR)
COMMISSION SCOLAIRE DU PAYS-DES-BLEUETS
ECOLE NOTRE-DAME-DES-ANGES
(*Suby of* Commission Scolaire du Pays-des-Bleuets)
68 Rue Savard, Dolbeau-Mistassini, QC, G8L 4L3
(418) 276-2763
Emp Here 50
SIC 8211 Elementary and secondary schools

D-U-N-S 25-023-9977   (BR)
DOLLARAMA S.E.C.
DOLLARAMA
1271 Boul Wallberg, Dolbeau-Mistassini, QC, G8L 1H3
(418) 276-9400
Emp Here 20
SIC 5331 Variety stores

D-U-N-S 24-499-9397   (SL)
ENTREPRISE DE CONSTRUCTION GASTON MORIN LTEE
310 Rue De Quen, Dolbeau-Mistassini, QC, G8L 5N1
(418) 276-4166
Emp Here 45   *Sales* 4,596,524
SIC 6512 Nonresidential building operators

D-U-N-S 25-279-7469   (BR)

FERLAC INC
(*Suby of* 9072-4725 Quebec Inc)
388 8e Av, Dolbeau-Mistassini, QC, G8L 3E5
(418) 276-3918
Emp Here 50
SIC 5211 Lumber and other building materials

D-U-N-S 20-721-2341   (SL)
GILBRO INC
1230 Boul Wallberg, Dolbeau-Mistassini, QC, G8L 1H2
(418) 276-0392
Emp Here 50   *Sales* 6,596,303
SIC 2411 Logging
Pr Rejean Pare
Sec Roger Tremblay

D-U-N-S 24-863-1244   (BR)
GOUVERNEMENT DE LA PROVINCE DE QUEBEC
CENTRE JEUNESSE DU SAGUENAY LAC SAINT JEAN
201 Boul Des Peres, Dolbeau-Mistassini, QC, G8L 5K6
(418) 276-4628
Emp Here 20
SIC 8399 Social services, nec

D-U-N-S 20-547-8089   (BR)
MALLETTE S.E.N.C.R.L.
1264 Boul Wallberg, Dolbeau-Mistassini, QC, G8L 1H1
(418) 276-1152
Emp Here 35
SIC 8721 Accounting, auditing, and bookkeeping

D-U-N-S 25-008-6238   (BR)
PF RESOLU CANADA INC
1 4e Av, Dolbeau-Mistassini, QC, G8L 2R4
(418) 239-2350
Emp Here 149
SIC 2621 Paper mills

D-U-N-S 20-869-2707   (BR)
PRODUITS ALBA INC
USINE PRODUITS ALBA
331 7e Av, Dolbeau-Mistassini, QC, G8L 1Y8

Emp Here 60
SIC 3251 Brick and structural clay tile

D-U-N-S 20-717-3902   (BR)
PROVIGO DISTRIBUTION INC
ALIMENTATION YVON LAMONTAGNE
224 Boul Saint-Michel, Dolbeau-Mistassini, QC, G8L 4P5

Emp Here 50
SIC 5411 Grocery stores

D-U-N-S 24-464-2971   (SL)
TRANSPORT DOUCET & FILS MISTASSINI INC
124 Rue Lavoie, Dolbeau-Mistassini, QC, G8L 4M8
(418) 276-7395
Emp Here 100   *Sales* 17,652,300
SIC 4213 Trucking, except local
Pr Pr Ghislain Doucet

Dollard-Des-Ormeaux, QC H8Y

D-U-N-S 20-002-8707   (BR)
ROYAL BANK OF CANADA
RBC
(*Suby of* Royal Bank Of Canada)
4400 Boul Des Sources, Dollard-Des-Ormeaux, QC, H8Y 3B7
(514) 684-8110
Emp Here 20
SIC 6021 National commercial banks

Dollard-Des-Ormeaux, QC H9A

D-U-N-S 24-527-0392   (SL)
CONGREGATION BETH TIKVAH AHAVAT SHALOM NUSACH HOARI
136 Boul Westpark, Dollard-Des-Ormeaux, QC, H9A 2K2
(514) 683-5610
Emp Here 70   *Sales* 4,596,524
SIC 8661 Religious organizations

Dollard-Des-Ormeaux, QC H9B

D-U-N-S 24-714-4157   (SL)
156861 CANADA INC
ADVANCED TECHNOLOGY & ASSEMBLY
64 Boul Brunswick, Dollard-Des-Ormeaux, QC, H9B 2L3
(514) 421-4445
Emp Here 50   *Sales* 3,866,917
SIC 3625 Relays and industrial controls

D-U-N-S 20-059-1753   (BR)
2320-3755 QUEBEC INC
MAZDA 2-20
(*Suby of* Alliance Ford Inc)
3800 Boul Des Sources, Dollard-Des-Ormeaux, QC, H9B 1Z9
(514) 685-5555
Emp Here 42
SIC 5511 New and used car dealers

D-U-N-S 24-958-5456   (SL)
2758792 CANADA INC
BOUTIQUE ELECTRONIQUE, LA
3352 Boul Des Sources, Dollard-Des-Ormeaux, QC, H9B 1Z9
(514) 684-6846
Emp Here 42   *Sales* 4,523,563
SIC 5999 Miscellaneous retail stores, nec

D-U-N-S 20-363-9224   (SL)
9213-9674 QUEBEC INC
DK TRANSPORT
218 Rue Andras, Dollard-Des-Ormeaux, QC, H9B 1R6
(514) 501-9273
Emp Here 50   *Sales* 10,944,105
SIC 4731 Freight transportation arrangement
   Paul Feher

D-U-N-S 20-562-8048   (BR)
ATLAS COPCO CANADA INC
ATLAS COPCO COMPRESSORS CANADA
30 Rue Montrose, Dollard-Des-Ormeaux, QC, H9B 3J9
(514) 421-4121
Emp Here 50
SIC 5084 Industrial machinery and equipment

D-U-N-S 20-298-1051   (BR)
BANQUE NATIONALE DU CANADA
3550 Boul Des Sources, Dollard-Des-Ormeaux, QC, H9B 1Z9
(514) 684-5670
Emp Here 30
SIC 6021 National commercial banks

D-U-N-S 20-589-4731   (BR)
BANQUE TORONTO-DOMINION, LA
TD CANADA TRUST
(*Suby of* Toronto-Dominion Bank, The)
3720 Boul Des Sources, Dollard-Des-Ormeaux, QC, H9B 1Z9
(514) 683-0391
Emp Here 20
SIC 6021 National commercial banks

D-U-N-S 24-815-1920   (SL)
BIOFORCE CANADA INC
AROMAFORCE
66 Boul Brunswick, Dollard-Des-Ormeaux, QC, H9B 2L3

---

(514) 421-3441
Emp Here 40   *Sales* 6,843,383
SIC 5149 Groceries and related products, nec
Pr Pr Immacolata (Mackie) Vadcchino
   Robert Baldinger
   Hermann Geider

D-U-N-S 20-539-2678   (BR)
CANADA POST CORPORATION
CENTENNIAL PLAZA P.O.
3347 Boul Des Sources, Dollard-Des-Ormeaux, QC, H9B 1Z8
(514) 683-5460
Emp Here 65
SIC 4311 U.s. postal service

D-U-N-S 24-385-1933   (BR)
DISCOVERY AIR DEFENCE SERVICES INC
79b Boul Brunswick, Dollard-Des-Ormeaux, QC, H9B 2J5
(514) 694-5565
Emp Here 130
SIC 8299 Schools and educational services, nec

D-U-N-S 24-387-0339   (SL)
GLOAPSO INC
154 Rue Spring Garden, Dollard-Des-Ormeaux, QC, H9B 2C6
(514) 817-7047
Emp Here 20   *Sales* 5,072,500
SIC 5136 Men's and boy's clothing
Pr Pr Sukhvir Basram

D-U-N-S 25-357-0840   (SL)
IMMOBILIER JACK ASTOR'S (DORVAL) INC
RESTAURANT JACK ASTOR'S BAR & GRILL
3051 Boul Des Sources, Dollard-Des-Ormeaux, QC, H9B 1Z6
(514) 685-5225
Emp Here 80   *Sales* 2,918,428
SIC 5813 Drinking places

D-U-N-S 20-181-8838   (HQ)
INVENSYS SYSTEMS CANADA INC
FOXBORO
4 Rue Lake, Dollard-Des-Ormeaux, QC, H9B 3H9
(514) 421-4210
Emp Here 200   *Emp Total* 1
Sales 28,406,000
SIC 3556 Food products machinery
Pr Chris Relton
Dir William G Vanderburgh
Dir Jay S. Ehle
Dir Daniel Peloquin
Dir Linda Cleroux

D-U-N-S 24-836-4184   (HQ)
LABORATOIRES DELON (1990) INC
(*Suby of* Laboratoires Delon (1990) Inc)
69 Boul Brunswick, Dollard-Des-Ormeaux, QC, H9B 2N4
(514) 685-9966
Emp Here 20   *Emp Total* 100
Sales 6,931,267
SIC 2844 Toilet preparations
Pr Pr Pascale Sasson
VP VP Selim Sasson
   Joseph Sasson

D-U-N-S 25-233-7118   (BR)
LESTER B. PEARSON SCHOOL BOARD
SPRINGDALE ELEMENTARY SCHOOL
150 Rue Hyman, Dollard-Des-Ormeaux, QC, H9B 1L6
(514) 798-0767
Emp Here 55
SIC 8211 Elementary and secondary schools

D-U-N-S 20-737-2731   (BR)
MEMORIAL GARDENS CANADA LIMITED
CEMETERY & PRE-PLANNING
4239 Boul Des Sources, Dollard-Des-Ormeaux, QC, H9B 2A6
(514) 683-6700
Emp Here 25

SIC 6531 Real estate agents and managers

D-U-N-S 24-226-7628   (BR)
METRO RICHELIEU INC
SUPER C
3291 Boul Des Sources, Dollard-Des-Ormeaux, QC, H9B 1Z6
(514) 685-0071
Emp Here 50
SIC 5411 Grocery stores

D-U-N-S 20-699-7509   (BR)
NORDION INC
MDS DIAGNOSTIC SERVICES
3400 Rue Du Marche Bureau 106, Dollard-Des-Ormeaux, QC, H9B 2Y1
(450) 698-0563
Emp Here 25
SIC 8071 Medical laboratories

D-U-N-S 20-553-3255   (BR)
PEPINIERE CRAMER INC
3000 Rue Du Marche, Dollard-Des-Ormeaux, QC, H9B 2Y3

Emp Here 30
SIC 7389 Business services, nec

D-U-N-S 25-356-0692   (SL)
PRODUITS DE BEAUTE IRIS INC
69 Boul Brunswick, Dollard-Des-Ormeaux, QC, H9B 2N4
(514) 685-9966
Emp Here 50   *Sales* 4,158,005
SIC 2844 Toilet preparations

D-U-N-S 24-150-8758   (BR)
VALUE VILLAGE STORES, INC
VILLAGE DES VALEURS
(*Suby of* Savers, Inc.)
3399 Boul Des Sources, Dollard-Des-Ormeaux, QC, H9B 1Z8
(514) 684-1326
Emp Here 25
SIC 5399 Miscellaneous general merchandise

D-U-N-S 20-761-7341   (HQ)
VIGI SANTE LTEE
C.H.S.L.D.
(*Suby of* Vigi Sante Ltee)
197 Rue Thornhill, Dollard-Des-Ormeaux, QC, H9B 3H8
(514) 684-0930
Emp Here 60   *Emp Total* 1,700
Sales 106,609,280
SIC 8051 Skilled nursing care facilities
Pr Pr Giovanni Simonetta
   Vincent Simonetta

D-U-N-S 24-562-5777   (BR)
WENDY'S RESTAURANTS OF CANADA INC
WENDY'S
(*Suby of* The Wendy's Company)
3600 Boul Des Sources, Dollard-Des-Ormeaux, QC, H9B 1Z9
(514) 683-6263
Emp Here 40
SIC 5812 Eating places

Dollard-Des-Ormeaux, QC H9G

D-U-N-S 20-277-4535   (HQ)
3105822 CANADA INC
AMRO TRAVEL
(*Suby of* 3105822 Canada Inc)
3883 Boul Saint-Jean Bureau 300, Dollard-Des-Ormeaux, QC, H9G 3B9
(514) 624-4244
Emp Here 25   *Emp Total* 30
Sales 9,234,824
SIC 4724 Travel agencies
Pr Mohamed Amro
VP VP Tarek Amro

D-U-N-S 25-475-4336   (SL)

D-U-N-S 9025-5159 QUEBEC INC
9025-5159 QUEBEC INC
RESTAURANT BATON ROUGE
3839 Boul Saint-Jean, Dollard-Des-Ormeaux, QC, H9G 1X2
(514) 626-6440
Emp Here 50   *Sales* 1,532,175
SIC 5812 Eating places

D-U-N-S 20-927-6880   (SL)
CHENOY'S DELICATESSEN & STEAK HOUSE INC
3616 Boul Saint-Jean, Dollard-Des-Ormeaux, QC, H9G 1X1
(514) 620-2584
Emp Here 75   *Sales* 2,261,782
SIC 5812 Eating places

D-U-N-S 25-233-7274   (BR)
LESTER B. PEARSON SCHOOL BOARD
WILDER PENFIELD SCHOOL
551 Av Westminster, Dollard-Des-Ormeaux, QC, H9G 1E8
(514) 626-0670
Emp Here 40
SIC 8211 Elementary and secondary schools

D-U-N-S 24-770-1147   (SL)
MAITRE D'AUTO STEVE INC
LAVE AUTO STEVE
4216 Boul Saint-Jean, Dollard-Des-Ormeaux, QC, H9G 1X5
(514) 696-9274
Emp Here 50   *Sales* 1,992,377
SIC 7542 Carwashes

D-U-N-S 20-213-6532   (BR)
UNIPRIX INC
UNIPRIX ZAKRZEWSKI-JAKUBIAK ET MELKI (PHARMACIE AFFILIEE)
3708 Boul Saint-Jean, Dollard-Des-Ormeaux, QC, H9G 1X1
(514) 620-9160
Emp Here 45
SIC 5912 Drug stores and proprietary stores

Dollard-Des-Ormeaux, QC H9H

D-U-N-S 20-806-9208   (BR)
COUCHE-TARD INC
4500 Boul Saint-Jean, Dollard-Des-Ormeaux, QC, H9H 2A6
(514) 624-8264
Emp Here 25
SIC 5411 Grocery stores

D-U-N-S 20-720-5753   (BR)
MERCEDES-BENZ CANADA INC
MERCEDES BENZ WEST ISLAND
4525 Boul Saint-Jean, Dollard-Des-Ormeaux, QC, H9H 2A7
(514) 620-5900
Emp Here 30
SIC 5511 New and used car dealers

D-U-N-S 24-367-9284   (BR)
SUNRISE NORTH SENIOR LIVING LTD
MAISON DE VIE SUNRISE OF DOLLARD DES ORMEAUX
(*Suby of* Welltower Inc.)
4377 Boul Saint-Jean Bureau 207, Dollard-Des-Ormeaux, QC, H9H 2A4
(514) 620-4556
Emp Here 70
SIC 8361 Residential care

Donnacona, QC G3M
Portneuf County

D-U-N-S 24-481-6450   (BR)
9229-3786 QUEBEC INC
DONNACONA CHRYSLER FIAT
160 Rue Commerciale, Donnacona, QC, G3M

1W1

Emp Here 40
SIC 5511 New and used car dealers

D-U-N-S 20-029-1594   (BR)
**CENTRE DE SANTE ET DE SERVICES SO-
CIAUX DE PORTNEUF**
*CENTRE HERBERGEMENT DE DONNA-
CONA*
250 Boul Gaudreau Bureau 370, Donnacona,
QC, G3M 1L7
(418) 285-3025
Emp Here 115
SIC 8361 Residential care

D-U-N-S 24-543-3537   (HQ)
COMMISSION SCOLAIRE DE PORTNEUF
(*Suby of* Commission Scolaire de Portneuf)
310 Rue De L'Eglise, Donnacona, QC, G3M
1Z8
(418) 285-2600
Emp Here 40   *Emp Total* 1,000
Sales 86,317,336
SIC 8211 Elementary and secondary schools
Pr Serge Tremblay
Genl Mgr Jean-Pierre Soucy

D-U-N-S 20-712-0093   (BR)
COMMISSION SCOLAIRE DE PORTNEUF
COMMISSION SCOLAIRE DE PORTNEUF
(*Suby of* Commission Scolaire de Portneuf)
451 Av Jacques-Cartier, Donnacona, QC,
G3M 2C1
(418) 285-2666
Emp Here 50
SIC 8211 Elementary and secondary schools

D-U-N-S 20-712-0101   (BR)
COMMISSION SCOLAIRE DE PORTNEUF
COMMISSION SCOLAIRE DE PORTNEUF
(*Suby of* Commission Scolaire de Portneuf)
320 Rue De L'Eglise, Donnacona, QC, G3M
2A1
(418) 285-2612
Emp Here 50
SIC 8211 Elementary and secondary schools

D-U-N-S 20-712-0135   (BR)
COMMISSION SCOLAIRE DE PORTNEUF
COMMISSION SCOLAIRE DE PORTNEUF
(*Suby of* Commission Scolaire de Portneuf)
250 Av Cote, Donnacona, QC, G3M 2V7
(418) 285-5026
Emp Here 25
SIC 8211 Elementary and secondary schools

D-U-N-S 24-119-5572   (BR)
PROVIGO DISTRIBUTION INC
PROVIGO MAXI # 8955
482 138 Rte, Donnacona, QC, G3M 1C2
(418) 285-5101
Emp Here 40
SIC 5411 Grocery stores

D-U-N-S 24-884-4722   (HQ)
RESTAURANTS RENE BOISVERT INC, LES
MCDONALD'S
(*Suby of* Restaurants Rene Boisvert Inc, Les)
325 138 Rte, Donnacona, QC, G3M 1C4
(418) 285-0404
Emp Here 50   *Emp Total* 100
Sales 2,991,389
SIC 5812 Eating places

D-U-N-S 25-010-5582   (BR)
TELUS COMMUNICATIONS (QUEBEC) INC
149 Rue Saint-Jules, Donnacona, QC, G3M
2K8

Emp Here 20
SIC 4899 Communication services, nec

Dorval, QC H4S
Hochelaga County

D-U-N-S 25-331-8505   (BR)
BOMBARDIER INC
BOMBARDIER AERONAUTIQUE
400 Ch De La Cote-Vertu, Dorval, QC, H4S
1Y9
(514) 855-5000
Emp Here 3,500
SIC 3721 Aircraft

D-U-N-S 25-999-6981   (BR)
BOMBARDIER INC
BOMBARDIER AERONAUTIQUE
200 Ch De La Cote-Vertu Bureau 1110, Dor-
val, QC, H4S 2A3
(514) 420-4000
Emp Here 1,800
SIC 3721 Aircraft

D-U-N-S 20-996-0942   (BR)
CARA OPERATIONS LIMITED
TIM HORTONS
(*Suby of* Cara Holdings Limited)
730 Ch De La Cote-Vertu, Dorval, QC, H4S
1Y9
(514) 422-7031
Emp Here 20
SIC 5812 Eating places

D-U-N-S 24-321-1294   (BR)
JAZZ AVIATION LP
AIR CANADA JAZZ - REGIONAL OFFICE
740 Ch De La Cote-Vertu, Dorval, QC, H4S
1Y9
(514) 422-6101
Emp Here 30
SIC 4512 Air transportation, scheduled

D-U-N-S 25-999-3145   (BR)
SODEXO QUEBEC LIMITEE
730 Ch De La Cote-Vertu Bureau 1007, Dorval, QC, H4S 1Y9
(514) 633-8167
Emp Here 40
SIC 5812 Eating places

Dorval, QC H4Y
Hochelaga County

D-U-N-S 24-890-4203   (BR)
AEROPORTS DE MONTREAL
AEROPORTS DE MONTREAL
580 Boul Stuart-Graham S, Dorval, QC, H4Y
1G4
(514) 633-2811
Emp Here 500
SIC 4581 Airports, flying fields, and services

D-U-N-S 25-318-2240   (BR)
AVISCAR INC
AVIS
(*Suby of* Avis Budget Group, Inc.)
975 Boul Romeo-Vachon N Bureau 317, Dor-
val, QC, H4Y 1H2
(514) 636-1902
Emp Here 100
SIC 7514 Passenger car rental

D-U-N-S 25-093-2394   (BR)
BOMBARDIER INC
CENTRE DE FINITION MONTREAL
595 Boul Stuart-Graham N, Dorval, QC, H4Y
1E2
(514) 420-4000
Emp Here 45
SIC 5599 Automotive dealers, nec

D-U-N-S 20-417-0823   (HQ)
BUDGETAUTO INC
(*Suby of* Avis Budget Group, Inc.)
575 Boul Albert-De Niverville, Dorval, QC,
H4Y 1J3
(514) 636-0743
Emp Here 30   *Emp Total* 30,000
Sales 5,107,249
SIC 7514 Passenger car rental

Pr David B. Wyshner
Dir Jon Zuber
Dir Larry De Shon

D-U-N-S 24-800-9912   (BR)
CARA OPERATIONS LIMITED
ENTREPRISES CARA DU QUEBEC, LES
(*Suby of* Cara Holdings Limited)
1185 Rue Rodolphe-Page Bureau 1, Dorval,
QC, H4Y 1H3
(514) 636-5824
Emp Here 650
SIC 5812 Eating places

D-U-N-S 25-857-0977   (SL)
CARGOLUTION INC
(*Suby of* 9149-2280 Quebec Inc)
800 Boul Stuart-Graham S Bureau 360, Dor-
val, QC, H4Y 1J6
(514) 636-2576
Emp Here 55   *Sales* 13,860,016
SIC 4731 Freight transportation arrangement
Pr Pr Daniel Soucy
Treas Carole St-Cyr

D-U-N-S 24-787-1465   (BR)
ENGIE SERVICES INC
ENGIE SERVICES INC
975 Boul Romeo-Vachon N Bureau 317, Dor-
val, QC, H4Y 1H2
(514) 631-7020
Emp Here 60
SIC 6531 Real estate agents and managers

D-U-N-S 20-576-6475   (BR)
**ENTERPRISE RENT-A-CAR CANADA COM-
PANY**
(*Suby of* The Crawford Group Inc)
600 Rue Arthur-Fecteau, Dorval, QC, H4Y
1K5
(514) 422-1100
Emp Here 200
SIC 7514 Passenger car rental

D-U-N-S 24-606-1951   (BR)
**LUXURY HOTELS INTERNATIONAL OF
CANADA, ULC**
MARRIOTT MONTREAL AIRPORT
(*Suby of* Marriott International, Inc.)
800 Place Leigh-Capreol, Dorval, QC, H4Y
0A5
(514) 636-6700
Emp Here 200
SIC 7011 Hotels and motels

D-U-N-S 25-297-9869   (BR)
UPS SCS, INC
UPS SUPPLY CHAIN SOLUTION
800 Boul Stuart-Graham S Bureau 351, Dorval, QC, H4Y 1J6

Emp Here 100
SIC 4731 Freight transportation arrangement

Dorval, QC H7V
Hochelaga County

D-U-N-S 24-357-2612   (BR)
**CENTRE DE SANTE ET DE SERVICES SO-
CIAUX DE LAVAL**
1515 Boul Chomedey, Dorval, QC, H7V 3Y7
(450) 978-8300
Emp Here 350
SIC 8062 General medical and surgical hospi-
tals

D-U-N-S 24-252-8610   (BR)
HOFFMANN-LA ROCHE LIMITED
ROCHE DIAGNOSTICS
201 Boul Armand-Frappier, Dorval, QC, H7V
4A2
(450) 686-7050
Emp Here 400
SIC 5122 Drugs, proprietaries, and sundries

Dorval, QC H9P
Hochelaga County

D-U-N-S 24-958-9946   (SL)
132405 CANADA INC
GIBBONS MAINTENANCE
1484 Boul Hymus, Dorval, QC, H9P 1J6
(514) 685-1425
Emp Here 100   *Sales* 2,918,428
SIC 7349 Building maintenance services, nec

D-U-N-S 24-890-3452   (SL)
167986 CANADA INC
KARMIN GROUP
(*Suby of* 4269853 Canada Inc)
1901 Rte Transcanadienne, Dorval, QC, H9P
1J1
(514) 685-2202
Emp Here 100   *Sales* 10,360,419
SIC 5099 Durable goods, nec
Pr Pr Lee Karls
Johnny Karls

D-U-N-S 24-059-7737   (HQ)
3857387 CANADA INC
VOLKSWAGEN DES SOURCES
(*Suby of* 3406032 Canada Inc)
2311 Place Transcanadienne, Dorval, QC,
H9P 2X7
(514) 683-2030
Emp Here 56   *Emp Total* 1
Sales 29,448,000
SIC 5511 New and used car dealers
Pr Pr Charles Hammer

D-U-N-S 20-883-8284   (HQ)
4211677 CANADA INC
10315 Ch Cote-De-Liesse, Dorval, QC, H9P
1A6
(514) 636-8033
Emp Here 150   *Emp Total* 900
Sales 91,877,078
SIC 4212 Local trucking, without storage
Pr Pierre Poliquin
Sec Peter L. Overing

D-U-N-S 24-381-0343   (SL)
9207-4616 QUEBEC INC
SHERATON MONTREAL AIRPORT HOTEL
555 Boul Mcmillan, Dorval, QC, H9P 1B7
(514) 631-2411
Emp Here 100   *Sales* 4,377,642
SIC 7011 Hotels and motels

D-U-N-S 25-356-7044   (BR)
ABCO INTERNATIONAL FREIGHT INC
670 Av Orly Bureau 201, Dorval, QC, H9P 1E9
(514) 636-2226
Emp Here 40
SIC 4731 Freight transportation arrangement

D-U-N-S 24-225-8254   (BR)
**AMEC FOSTER WHEELER AMERICAS LIM-
ITED**
AMEC EARTH & ENVIRONMENTAL DIV OF
1425 Rte Transcanadienne Bureau 400, Dor-
val, QC, H9P 2W9
(514) 684-5555
Emp Here 150
SIC 8748 Business consulting, nec

D-U-N-S 24-835-0423   (SL)
ABRASIVE TECHNOLOGY NA INC
(*Suby of* Abrasive Technology, Inc.)
2250 Boul Hymus, Dorval, QC, H9P 1J9
(514) 421-7396
Emp Here 30   *Sales* 5,836,856
SIC 5085 Industrial supplies
Pr Pr Loyal M. Jr Peterman
VP VP Shahla Amiri

D-U-N-S 24-788-3184   (SL)
ACIER ARGO LTEE
2175 Boul Hymus, Dorval, QC, H9P 1J8
(514) 634-8066
Emp Here 20   *Sales* 21,693,360

SIC 5051 Metals service centers and offices
VP VP Bryan D. Jones
Gaetane Michaud

D-U-N-S 20-554-7636   (BR)
ACUITY HOLDINGS, INC
ZEP MANUFACTURING OF CANADA
(*Suby of* NM Z Parent Inc.)
660 Av Lepine, Dorval, QC, H9P 1G2
(514) 631-9041
Emp Here 50
SIC 5999 Miscellaneous retail stores, nec

D-U-N-S 24-353-3572   (BR)
ADVANTECH SANS FIL INC
ADVANCED MICROWAVE TECHNOLOGY
657 Av Orly, Dorval, QC, H9P 1G1
(514) 420-0045
Emp Here 250
SIC 3679 Electronic components, nec

D-U-N-S 25-245-5530   (BR)
AIR CREEBEC INC
(*Suby of* Cree Regional Economic Enterprises
Company (Cree Co) Inc)
9475 Av Ryan, Dorval, QC, H9P 1A2
(514) 636-8501
Emp Here 50
SIC 4512 Air transportation, scheduled

D-U-N-S 20-508-9191   (BR)
AKZO NOBEL COATINGS LTD
*INTERNATIONAL PAINT (PEINTURE INTER-
NATIONALE)*
1405 55e Av, Dorval, QC, H9P 2W3
(514) 631-8686
Emp Here 20
SIC 5231 Paint, glass, and wallpaper stores

D-U-N-S 25-194-5044   (SL)
AVIONAIR INC
9025 Av Ryan, Dorval, QC, H9P 1A2
(514) 631-7500
Emp Here 44   *Sales* 4,742,446
SIC 4522 Air transportation, nonscheduled

D-U-N-S 25-293-3692   (BR)
BAILEY METAL PRODUCTS LIMITED
PRODUITS METALLIQUES BAILEY, LES
(*Suby of* Bailey-Hunt Limited)
525 Av Edward Vii, Dorval, QC, H9P 1E7
(514) 735-3455
Emp Here 50
SIC 3312 Blast furnaces and steel mills

D-U-N-S 24-175-5933   (SL)
BARRY-ROBERT ENTREPRISES LTD
ROSCO GROUP
290 Av Guthrie, Dorval, QC, H9P 2V2
(514) 931-7789
Emp Here 55   *Sales* 2,188,821
SIC 8322 Individual and family services

D-U-N-S 25-093-2451   (BR)
BOMBARDIER INC
BOMBARDIER AERONAUTIQUE
9501 Av Ryan, Dorval, QC, H9P 1A2
(514) 855-5000
Emp Here 1 200
SIC 8711 Engineering services

D-U-N-S 24-890-4005   (BR)
CHALLENGER MOTOR FREIGHT INC
2770 Av Ancre, Dorval, QC, H9P 1K6
(514) 684-2025
Emp Here 300
SIC 4213 Trucking, except local

D-U-N-S 25-316-1194   (BR)
COLE INTERNATIONAL INC
QUEBEC COURTIERS EN DOUANES
670 Av Orly Bureau 201, Dorval, QC, H9P 1E9
(514) 631-2653
Emp Here 50
SIC 4731 Freight transportation arrangement

D-U-N-S 24-362-9412   (SL)
CONVATEC CANADA LTEE

1425 Rte Transcanadienne Bureau 250, Dor-
val, QC, H9P 2W9
(514) 822-5985
Emp Here 75   *Sales* 10,944,105
SIC 5047 Medical and hospital equipment
Pr Pr Sylvain Chiasson
   Mario Gosselin
   Nathalie Theoret
   Fabien Paquette
   Luc Massicotte
   Michael John Langford
   Bradford Carlton Barton
   Rita Guirguis

D-U-N-S 25-501-5075   (HQ)
COTY CANADA INC
COSMETIQUES LANCASTER
1255 Rte Transcanadienne Bureau 200, Dor-
val, QC, H9P 2V4
(514) 421-5050
Emp Here 120   *Emp Total* 9
Sales 29,622,044
SIC 5122 Drugs, proprietaries, and sundries
Sec Stuart S. Aronovitch
Mgr Amaury De Vallois

D-U-N-S 20-270-7543   (BR)
CUISINES DE L'AIR CULIN-AIR INC, LES
(*Suby of* Cuisines de l'Air Culin-Air Inc, Les)
9553 Ch Cote-De-Liesse, Dorval, QC, H9P 1A3
(514) 441-4277
Emp Here 40
SIC 5812 Eating places

D-U-N-S 24-128-4632   (BR)
DICOM TRANSPORTATION GROUP CANADA, INC
DICOM TRANSPORTATION GROUP CANADA INC
10755 Ch Cote-De-Liesse, Dorval, QC, H9P 1A7
(514) 631-1242
Emp Here 800
SIC 4212 Local trucking, without storage

D-U-N-S 20-725-4129   (BR)
DIESEL EQUIPMENT LIMITED
DEL EQUIPMENT
1655 Boul Hymus, Dorval, QC, H9P 1J5
(514) 684-1760
Emp Here 25
SIC 3713 Truck and bus bodies

D-U-N-S 24-349-5392   (HQ)
DISCOVERY AIR DEFENCE SERVICES INC
SERVICES DE DEFENSE DISCOVERY AIR
1675 Rte Transcanadienne Bureau 201, Dor-
val, QC, H9P 1J1
(514) 694-5565
Emp Here 140   *Emp Total* 319
Sales 9,193,048
SIC 8299 Schools and educational services, nec
Pr Pr Paul Bouchard
Sec David Kleiman
Dir Didier Toussaint

D-U-N-S 25-812-8289   (BR)
DOLLAR THRIFTY AUTOMOTIVE GROUP CANADA INC
(*Suby of* Hertz Global Holdings, Inc.)
2005 55e Av, Dorval, QC, H9P 2Y6

Emp Here 35
SIC 7514 Passenger car rental

D-U-N-S 25-368-7453   (BR)
DOLLARAMA S.E.C.
DOLLARAMA
11250 Ch Cote-De-Liesse, Dorval, QC, H9P 1A9
(514) 631-9319
Emp Here 20
SIC 5399 Miscellaneous general merchandise

D-U-N-S 24-522-9153   (BR)
ELECTROLUX CANADA CORP

1789 Av Cardinal, Dorval, QC, H9P 1Y5
(514) 636-4600
Emp Here 20
SIC 5722 Household appliance stores

D-U-N-S 25-368-9822   (BR)
FEDEX FREIGHT CANADA, CORP
FEDEX FREIGHT
(*Suby of* Fedex Corporation)
10765 Ch Cote-De-Liesse Bureau 232, Dor-
val, QC, H9P 2R9
(800) 463-3339
Emp Here 50
SIC 4212 Local trucking, without storage

D-U-N-S 24-353-3684   (HQ)
FLIGHTSAFETY CANADA LTD
FLIGHTSAFETY INTERNATIONAL
(*Suby of* Berkshire Hathaway Inc.)
9555 Av Ryan, Dorval, QC, H9P 1A2
(514) 631-2084
Emp Here 50   *Emp Total* 331,000
Sales 9,095,636
SIC 8299 Schools and educational services, nec
Pr Pr Bruce Whitman
   Kenneth E W Motschwiller
Genl Mgr Doug Ware

D-U-N-S 20-107-3710   (HQ)
FORMATION INFO-TECHNIQUE S.B. INC
COLLEGE INFO-TECHNIQUE
(*Suby of* Formation Info-Technique S.B. Inc)
1805 Rte Transcanadienne, Dorval, QC, H9P 1J1

Emp Here 45   *Emp Total* 59
Sales 5,024,000
SIC 8249 Vocational schools, nec
Genl Mgr Sylvie Bourassa
Fin Mgr Dianne Deslandes

D-U-N-S 24-849-2238   (BR)
FORMER RESTORATION L.P.
290 Av Guthrie, Dorval, QC, H9P 2V2
(514) 931-7789
Emp Here 70
SIC 1799 Special trade contractors, nec

D-U-N-S 24-834-4798   (SL)
GESTION CANADADIRECT INC
CANADA DIRECT
743 Av Renaud, Dorval, QC, H9P 2N1
(514) 422-8557
Emp Here 700   *Sales* 133,104,960
SIC 8732 Commercial nonphysical research
Pr Pr Alain Harari
   Tom Taylor

D-U-N-S 24-509-6169   (SL)
GOLF DORVAL
2000 Av Reverchon, Dorval, QC, H9P 2S7
(514) 631-4653
Emp Here 60   *Sales* 2,553,625
SIC 7992 Public golf courses

D-U-N-S 20-714-6759   (BR)
**HEIDELBERG CANADA GRAPHIC EQUIP-
MENT LIMITED**
703 Av Meloche, Dorval, QC, H9P 2S4
(514) 631-6270
Emp Here 20
SIC 2621 Paper mills

D-U-N-S 20-112-6419   (BR)
I.M.P. GROUP LIMITED
EXECAIRE
10225 Av Ryan, Dorval, QC, H9P 1A2
(514) 636-7070
Emp Here 700
SIC 4581 Airports, flying fields, and services

D-U-N-S 20-314-3573   (BR)
INFOR (CANADA), LTD
GROUPE LAURIER CIM, LE
(*Suby of* Infor Lux Bond Company)
1255 Rte Transcanadienne Bureau 100, Dor-
val, QC, H9P 2V4

(514) 763-0400
Emp Here 33
SIC 7372 Prepackaged software

D-U-N-S 25-526-9524   (BR)
**INFORMATION COMMUNICATION SER-
VICES (ICS) INC**
ICS SERVICE DE COURIER
81 Av Lindsay, Dorval, QC, H9P 2S6
(514) 636-9744
Emp Here 200
SIC 4212 Local trucking, without storage

D-U-N-S 25-305-2468   (BR)
INNVEST PROPERTIES CORP
COMFORT INN AEROPORT
(*Suby of* Innvest Properties Corp)
340 Av Michel-Jasmin, Dorval, QC, H9P 1C1
(514) 636-3391
Emp Here 20
SIC 7011 Hotels and motels

D-U-N-S 24-989-3363   (BR)
**INTEGRATED DISTRIBUTION SYSTEMS
LIMITED PARTNERSHIP**
WAJAX POWER SYSTEMS
10955 Ch Cote-De-Liesse, Dorval, QC, H9P 1A7
(514) 636-0680
Emp Here 62
SIC 5084 Industrial machinery and equipment

D-U-N-S 20-852-6868   (BR)
KONECRANES CANADA INC
1875 Ch Saint-Francois, Dorval, QC, H9P 1K3
(514) 421-3030
Emp Here 30
SIC 7353 Heavy construction equipment
rental

D-U-N-S 24-227-6061   (BR)
L.V. LOMAS LIMITED
1660 Boul Hymus, Dorval, QC, H9P 2N6
(514) 683-0660
Emp Here 45
SIC 5169 Chemicals and allied products, nec

D-U-N-S 20-996-0397   (BR)
LEON'S FURNITURE LIMITED
AMMEUBLEMENT LEON
2020 Rte Transcanadienne, Dorval, QC, H9P 2N4
(514) 684-6116
Emp Here 30
SIC 5712 Furniture stores

D-U-N-S 20-857-1042   (HQ)
LOCATION BROSSARD INC
(*Suby of* 2313-5338 Quebec Inc)
2190 Boul Hymus, Dorval, QC, H9P 1J7
(514) 367-1343
Emp Here 100   *Emp Total* 190
Sales 12,038,516
SIC 7513 Truck rental and leasing, no drivers
Pr Pr Guy Brossard
   Yves Carmel

D-U-N-S 20-330-1593   (HQ)
LOGISTIQUE KERRY (CANADA) INC
*PARTENAIRE TOTAL LOGISTIQUES (TLP)
AIR EXPRESS*
1425 Rte Transcanadienne Bureau 150, Dor-
val, QC, H9P 2W9
(514) 420-0282
Emp Here 23   *Sales* 7,660,874
SIC 4731 Freight transportation arrangement
Sec Peter Sancho
Dir Fuk Yuen Kenneth Ko
Pr Alan Kam Sang Yip

D-U-N-S 24-834-5530   (BR)
**MARITIME-ONTARIO FREIGHT LINES LIM-
ITED**
2800 Av Andre, Dorval, QC, H9P 1K6
(514) 684-5458
Emp Here 20
SIC 4213 Trucking, except local

D-U-N-S 20-883-8292   (HQ)

MCCANN EQUIPMENT LTD
ETALONNAGE TECHNIQUE
(Suby of McCann, James A Holdings Ltd)
10255 Ch Cote-De-Liesse, Dorval, QC, H9P
1A3
(514) 636-6344
Emp Here 25   *Emp Total* 56
Sales 12,127,514
SIC 5084 Industrial machinery and equipment
Pr Pr James A Mccann
 Daniel Mccann
VP Fin James A Jr Mccann
 Patricia Mccann
Dir Kathleen Quart
Dir Robert Mccann

D-U-N-S 24-226-4653   (HQ)
MICRO-ONDES APOLLO LTEE
APOLLO MICROWAVES
(Suby of 147780 Canada Inc)
1650 Rte Transcanadienne, Dorval, QC, H9P
1H7
(514) 421-2211
Emp Here 125   *Emp Total* 1
Sales 21,450,446
SIC 3663 Radio and t.v. communications
equipment
 Nickolaos Vouloumanos

D-U-N-S 24-509-9593   (BR)
MIDLAND TRANSPORT LIMITED
(Suby of J. D. Irving, Limited)
1560 Boul Hymus, Dorval, QC, H9P 1J6
(514) 421-5500
Emp Here 100
SIC 4212 Local trucking, without storage

D-U-N-S 20-212-1450   (BR)
MUELLER CANADA LTD
MUELLER FLOW CONTROL
(Suby of Mueller Water Products, Inc.)
1820 Ch Saint-Francois, Dorval, QC, H9P 2P6
(514) 342-2100
Emp Here 30
SIC 5074 Plumbing and heating equipment
and supplies (hydronics)

D-U-N-S 24-710-8111   (HQ)
MULTIBOND INC
DURAL, DIV OF
(Suby of CFS Group Inc)
550 Av Marshall, Dorval, QC, H9P 1C9
(514) 636-6230
Emp Here 90   *Emp Total* 300
Sales 7,796,259
SIC 2891 Adhesives and sealants
Pr Serge Berube
Sec Domenic Scozzafava
Dir Patrick Donahue

D-U-N-S 20-652-0228   (BR)
NAV CANADA
1750 Ch Saint-Francois, Dorval, QC, H9P 2P6
(514) 633-3393
Emp Here 400
SIC 4522 Air transportation, nonscheduled

D-U-N-S 20-324-5662   (SL)
NETTOYEURS ZRO INC
SINISCO
2365 Ch Saint-Francois, Dorval, QC, H9P 1K3
(514) 335-5907
Emp Here 50   *Sales* 4,377,642
SIC 1799 Special trade contractors, nec

D-U-N-S 24-548-5370   (BR)
PARKER HANNIFIN CANADA
FLUID CONNECTOR GROUP
2001 Rue De L'Aviation, Dorval, QC, H9P 2X6
(514) 684-3000
Emp Here 45
SIC 3593 Fluid power cylinders and actuators

D-U-N-S 24-896-5373   (BR)
PUROLATOR INC.
PUROLATOR INC
10525 Ch Cote-De-Liesse Bureau 201, Dorval, QC, H9P 1A7

(514) 631-4958
Emp Here 40
SIC 7389 Business services, nec

D-U-N-S 24-959-7618   (BR)
RPM CANADA
STONHARD
(Suby of RPM International Inc.)
3170 Av Miller, Dorval, QC, H9P 1K5
(514) 874-9191
Emp Here 20
SIC 1752 Floor laying and floor work, nec

D-U-N-S 20-424-0642   (BR)
REIMER EXPRESS LINES LTD
REIMER EXPRESS
(Suby of Yrc Worldwide Inc.)
1725 Ch Saint-Francois, Dorval, QC, H9P 2S1
(514) 684-9970
Emp Here 100
SIC 4231 Trucking terminal facilities

D-U-N-S 20-356-9132   (BR)
ROBINSON, C.H. COMPANY (CANADA) LTD
FRAIS ROBINSON
2200 Av Reverchon Bureau 260, Dorval, QC, H9P 2S7
(514) 636-8694
Emp Here 44
SIC 4731 Freight transportation arrangement

D-U-N-S 20-715-2146   (BR)
ROLLS-ROYCE CANADA LIMITEE
9545 Ch Cote-De-Liesse Bureau 100, Dorval, QC, H9P 1A5
(514) 636-0964
Emp Here 150
SIC 4581 Airports, flying fields, and services

D-U-N-S 24-710-3393   (BR)
ROSEDALE TRANSPORT LIMITED
510 Av Orly, Dorval, QC, H9P 1E9
(514) 636-6606
Emp Here 35
SIC 4212 Local trucking, without storage

D-U-N-S 25-337-8343   (SL)
SDP TELECOM ULC
TELECOM SDP
1725 Rte Transcanadienne, Dorval, QC, H9P 1J1
(514) 421-5959
Emp Here 280   *Sales* 40,055,424
SIC 3663 Radio and t.v. communications
equipment
Pr Yash Gupta
Ch Bd Ghanshyam Gupta
Sec Sophie Gupta
Genl Mgr Michael Clayton
Pr Pr Michael Miskin
 Robert J. Zeitler
Dir Keith Travis George
Dir Deirdre Logel
Dir Liam Mccarthy
Dir Martin P. Slark

D-U-N-S 20-502-7709   (BR)
SKF CANADA LIMITED
S K F
101 Av Lindsay, Dorval, QC, H9P 2S6
(514) 636-5230
Emp Here 20
SIC 5085 Industrial supplies

D-U-N-S 20-297-9295   (BR)
SMS CONSTRUCTION AND MINING SYSTEMS INC
LOCATION KOMATSU
1965 55e Av, Dorval, QC, H9P 1G9
(514) 636-8515
Emp Here 20
SIC 7353 Heavy construction equipment
rental

D-U-N-S 24-676-6799   (BR)
SMS EQUIPMENT INC
EQUIPEMENT FEDERAL QUEBEC

1945 55e Av, Dorval, QC, H9P 1G9
(514) 636-4950
Emp Here 50
SIC 5084 Industrial machinery and equipment

D-U-N-S 20-059-2975   (SL)
SERVICES ADMINISTRATIFS F.G.B. INC, LES
(Suby of 2313-5338 Quebec Inc)
2190 Boul Hymus, Dorval, QC, H9P 1J7
(514) 367-1343
Emp Here 60   *Sales* 9,445,120
SIC 8742 Management consulting services
Pr Guy Brossard
Fin Ex Sylvie Belanger

D-U-N-S 20-536-6784   (HQ)
SERVICES AIRBASE INC, LES
(Suby of Airbase Canada Holdings Inc)
81 Av Lindsay, Dorval, QC, H9P 2S6
(514) 735-5260
Emp Here 70   *Emp Total* 131
Sales 24,500,554
SIC 6211 Security brokers and dealers
Pr Pr Tom Mckeown
 Lloyd Anderson

D-U-N-S 20-164-9469   (SL)
SERVICES INTERNATIONAL SKYPORT INC
(Suby of Capital Draco Inc)
400 Av Michel-Jasmin Bureau 200, Dorval, QC, H9P 1C1
(514) 631-1155
Emp Here 85   *Sales* 3,866,917
SIC 4111 Local and suburban transit

D-U-N-S 20-651-9550   (BR)
SIEMENS CANADA LIMITED
1425 Rte Trans-Canada Bureau 400, Dorval, QC, H9P 2W9

Emp Here 125
SIC 3625 Relays and industrial controls

D-U-N-S 24-852-9419   (BR)
SKY SERVICE F.B.O. INC.
9785 Av Ryan, Dorval, QC, H9P 1A2
(514) 636-3300
Emp Here 200
SIC 4512 Air transportation, scheduled

D-U-N-S 24-344-3798   (BR)
SKYSERVICE BUSINESS AVIATION INC
9785 Av Ryan, Dorval, QC, H9P 1A2
(514) 636-3300
Emp Here 500
SIC 4522 Air transportation, nonscheduled

D-U-N-S 24-214-7499   (BR)
SOCIETE BRISTOL-MYERS SQUIBB CANADA, LA
(Suby of Bristol-Myers Squibb Company)
11215 Ch Cote-De-Liesse, Dorval, QC, H9P 1B1
(514) 636-4711
Emp Here 20
SIC 2834 Pharmaceutical preparations

D-U-N-S 20-857-6991   (HQ)
SOCIETE INDUSTRIELLE JASON (CANADA) LTEE
JASON INDUSTRIAL CANADA
9135 Ch Cote-De-Liesse, Dorval, QC, H9P 2N9
(514) 631-6781
Emp Here 20   *Emp Total* 215
Sales 7,369,031
SIC 5085 Industrial supplies
Pr Pr Philip Cohenca
Dir Marco Tadolini
Dir Georgio Tadolini

D-U-N-S 20-011-8938   (SL)
STANPRO LIGHTING SYSTEMS INC
SYSTEMES D'ECLAIRAGE STANPRO
2233 Rue De L'Aviation, Dorval, QC, H9P 2X6
(514) 739-9984
Emp Here 60   *Sales* 12,038,516

SIC 5063 Electrical apparatus and equipment
Pr Victoria Nathaniel
VP David Nathaniel
Sec Katy Shebath

D-U-N-S 20-114-2960   (SL)
SYSTEMES LUMINESCENT CANADA INC
ASTRONICS LSI CANADA
(Suby of Astronics Corporation)
55 Av Lindsay, Dorval, QC, H9P 2S6
(514) 636-9921
Emp Here 90   *Sales* 11,381,869
SIC 4213 Trucking, except local
Pr James S. Cramer
 David Burney
Dir Stephen Weinstein

D-U-N-S 25-243-5193   (HQ)
SYSTEMES WESTCON CANADA (WCSI) INC, LES
2100 Rte Transcanadienne, Dorval, QC, H9P 2N4
(514) 420-5400
Emp Here 31   *Emp Total* 8,500
Sales 8,316,010
SIC 5065 Electronic parts and equipment, nec
Sec Ilia Khankine
Dir Lynn Smurthwaite-Murphy
Pr Dean Douglas
Dir Melissa Davis
Dir Cathy Jessup

D-U-N-S 20-918-7033   (HQ)
TECHNOLOGIES SURFACE PRAXAIR MONTREAL S.E.C.
PRAXAIR TECHNOLOGIES DE SURFACE
(Suby of Technologies Surface Praxair Montreal S.E.C.)
10300 Av Ryan, Dorval, QC, H9P 2T7
(514) 631-2240
Emp Here 26   *Emp Total* 50
Sales 3,502,114
SIC 3479 Metal coating and allied services

D-U-N-S 24-241-1218   (SL)
TRAVAILLEURS CANADIEN DE L'AUTOMOBILE SECTION LOCALE 62
TCA SECTION LOCALE 62
9045 Ch Cote-De-Liesse Bureau 203, Dorval, QC, H9P 2M9
(514) 636-8080
Emp Here 1,044   *Sales* 148,614,240
SIC 8631 Labor organizations
Pr Adam Lamoureux

D-U-N-S 20-716-7250   (BR)
UNIVAR CANADA LTD
2200 Ch Saint-Francois, Dorval, QC, H9P 1K2
(514) 421-0303
Emp Here 125
SIC 5169 Chemicals and allied products, nec

D-U-N-S 20-337-8539   (HQ)
VICTORIA'S SECRET (CANADA) CORP.
VICTORIA'S SECRET
1608 Boul Saint-Regis, Dorval, QC, H9P 1H6
(514) 684-7700
Emp Here 25   *Sales* 14,466,392
SIC 5632 Women's accessory and specialty
stores
 Pamela Edwards
Sr VP Sr VP Timothy J Faber

Dorval, QC H9S
Hochelaga County

D-U-N-S 20-187-4257   (BR)
ADACEL INC
ADECEL TECHNOLOGIES
455 Boul Fenelon Bureau 208, Dorval, QC, H9S 5T8
(514) 636-6365
Emp Here 48
SIC 3812 Search and navigation equipment

D-U-N-S 25-851-9222   (BR)
BELL EXPRESSVU INC
200 Boul Bouchard Bureau 72, Dorval, QC,
H9S 1A8
(514) 828-6600
Emp Here 350
SIC 4833 Television broadcasting stations

D-U-N-S 25-060-5037   (BR)
BELL MOBILITE INC
*BELL DISTRIBUTION BUREAU DE MON-
TREAL*
200 Boul Bouchard Bureau 500, Dorval, QC,
H9S 5X5
(514) 420-7700
Emp Here 2,000
SIC 5999 Miscellaneous retail stores, nec

D-U-N-S 20-294-3952   (BR)
**CHSLD LACHINE, NAZAIRE PICHE ET
FOYER DORVAL, LES**
CENTRE D'HERBEGREMNT DE DORVAL
(*Suby of* CHSLD Lachine, Nazaire Piche et
Foyer Dorval, Les)
225 Av De La Presentation, Dorval, QC, H9S
3L7
(514) 631-9094
Emp Here 200
SIC 8361 Residential care

D-U-N-S 25-232-1344   (BR)
CITE DE DORVAL
BIBLIOTHEQUE DE DORVAL
1401 Ch Du Bord-Du-Lac Lakeshore, Dorval,
QC, H9S 2E5
(514) 633-4170
Emp Here 24
SIC 8231 Libraries

D-U-N-S 25-234-0377   (BR)
**COMMISSION SCOLAIRE MARGUERITE-
BOURGEOYS**
ECOLE PRIMAIRE GENTILLY
355 Boul Fenelon, Dorval, QC, H9S 5T8
(514) 855-4229
Emp Here 70
SIC 8211 Elementary and secondary schools

D-U-N-S 25-152-1118   (BR)
DOLLARAMA S.E.C.
DOLLARAMA
352 Av Dorval, Dorval, QC, H9S 3H8
(514) 556-3032
Emp Here 20
SIC 5331 Variety stores

D-U-N-S 25-905-4690   (SL)
GROUPE ALLOS INC
ROTISSERIE SCORES DORVAL
444 Av Dorval Bureau 115, Dorval, QC, H9S
3H7
(514) 636-6060
Emp Here 65   *Sales* 1,969,939
SIC 5812 Eating places

D-U-N-S 25-301-2314   (BR)
HUDSON'S BAY COMPANY
BAIE, LA
386 Av Dorval, Dorval, QC, H9S 3H7
(514) 631-6741
Emp Here 50
SIC 5311 Department stores

D-U-N-S 20-024-0625   (BR)
**LES CENTRES DE LA JEUNESSE ET DE LA
FAMILLE BATSHAW**
*CENTRES DE LA JEUNESSE ET DE LA
FAMILLE BATSHAW*
(*Suby of* Les Centres de la Jeunesse et de la
Famille Batshaw)
825 Av Dawson, Dorval, QC, H9S 1X4
(514) 636-0910
Emp Here 50
SIC 8322 Individual and family services

D-U-N-S 25-240-3951   (BR)
LESTER B. PEARSON SCHOOL BOARD
BISHOP WHELAN SCHOOL

244 Av De La Presentation, Dorval, QC, H9S
3L6
Emp Here 40
SIC 8211 Elementary and secondary schools

D-U-N-S 25-240-6350   (BR)
LESTER B. PEARSON SCHOOL BOARD
DORVAL ELEMENTARY SCHOOL
1750 Av Carson, Dorval, QC, H9S 1N3
(514) 798-0738
Emp Here 30
SIC 8211 Elementary and secondary schools

D-U-N-S 20-518-8183   (BR)
MEDIAS TRANSCONTINENTAL INC
MEDIAS TRANSCONTINENTAL INC
455 Boul Fenelon Bureau 303, Dorval, QC,
H9S 5T8
(514) 636-7314
Emp Here 20
SIC 2711 Newspapers

D-U-N-S 20-309-3620   (SL)
PERSONNEL UNIQUE CANADA INC
ECOLE DU ROUTIER FUTUR-CAM
455 Boul Fenelon Bureau 210, Dorval, QC,
H9S 5T8
(514) 633-6220
Emp Here 750   *Sales* 147,609,750
SIC 8741 Management services
  Michael Cote Gagnon

D-U-N-S 20-294-3440   (BR)
PROVIGO DISTRIBUTION INC
960 Ch Herron, Dorval, QC, H9S 1B3
Emp Here 55
SIC 5411 Grocery stores

D-U-N-S 25-306-6757   (BR)
**ROYAL   TRUST   CORPORATION   OF
CANADA**
ROYAL BANK OF CANADA
(*Suby of* Royal Bank Of Canada)
316 Av Dorval, Dorval, QC, H9S 3H7
(514) 636-4740
Emp Here 34
SIC 6021 National commercial banks

D-U-N-S 24-698-4884   (BR)
**SOEURS   DE   LA   CONGREGATION   DE
NOTRE-DAME, LES**
CONGREGATION DE NOTRE DAME
12 Av Dahlia, Dorval, QC, H9S 3N2
(514) 631-3422
Emp Here 40
SIC 8661 Religious organizations

D-U-N-S 20-644-9949   (BR)
TORONTO-DOMINION BANK, THE
TD CANADA TRUST
(*Suby of* Toronto-Dominion Bank, The)
890 Ch Herron, Dorval, QC, H9S 1B3
(514) 631-6754
Emp Here 25
SIC 6021 National commercial banks

Drummondville, QC J2A
Drummomd County

D-U-N-S 25-756-2967   (BR)
2310-3393 QUEBEC INC
GROUPE JEAN COUTU
4534 Boul Saint-Joseph Bureau 289, Drummondville, QC, J2A 1B5
(819) 472-7442
Emp Here 25
SIC 5912 Drug stores and proprietary stores

D-U-N-S 24-855-4789   (BR)
2946-6380 QUEBEC INC
PRODUCTION P.H.
2550b 139 Rte, Drummondville, QC, J2A 2K3
(819) 478-2023
Emp Here 50

SIC 2448 Wood pallets and skids

D-U-N-S 20-194-3334   (BR)
COMMISSION SCOLAIRE DES CHENES
ECOLE SAINT NECIPHORE
(*Suby of* Commission Scolaire des Chenes)
2065 139 Rte, Drummondville, QC, J2A 2G2
(819) 474-0716
Emp Here 40
SIC 8211 Elementary and secondary schools

D-U-N-S 20-289-5488   (BR)
EMBALLAGES CARROUSEL INC, LES
(*Suby of* Emballages Carrousel Inc, Les)
2540 Rte 139, Drummondville, QC, J2A 2P9
(819) 478-4967
Emp Here 60
SIC 5113 Industrial and personal service pa-
per

D-U-N-S 20-196-4079   (SL)
EMBALLAGES J.C. LTEE, LES
2540 139 Rte, Drummondville, QC, J2A 2P9
(819) 478-4967
Emp Here 48   *Sales* 10,851,840
SIC 5113 Industrial and personal service pa-
per
Pr Pr Denis Jalbert
  Brigitte Jalbert

D-U-N-S 20-289-9308   (BR)
POLYNT COMPOSITES CANADA INC
2650 Rue Therese-Casgrain, Drummondville,
QC, J2A 4J5
(819) 477-4516
Emp Here 33
SIC 3087 Custom compound purchased
resins

D-U-N-S 24-485-7764   (BR)
**WASTE MANAGEMENT OF CANADA COR-
PORATION**
WASTE MANAGEMENT
(*Suby of* Waste Management, Inc.)
25 Rue Gagnon, Drummondville, QC, J2A
3H3
(819) 477-6609
Emp Here 20
SIC 4953 Refuse systems

Drummondville, QC J2B
Drummomd County

D-U-N-S 24-864-6424   (HQ)
ABZAC CANADA INC
ABZAC AMERIQUE
2945 Boul Lemire, Drummondville, QC, J2B
6Y8
(514) 866-3488
Emp Here 100   *Emp Total* 6
Sales 9,140,591
SIC 2655 Fiber cans, drums, and similar prod-
ucts
Pr Pr Jean-Louis D'anglade
  Maryse Poire
Dir Pierre-Michel D'anglade
Dir Luc Langevin
Dir Eric Phaneuf

D-U-N-S 25-010-1433   (BR)
BANQUE NATIONALE DU CANADA
1950 Boul Saint-Joseph, Drummondville, QC,
J2B 1R2
(819) 477-9494
Emp Here 22
SIC 6021 National commercial banks

D-U-N-S 24-342-0093   (BR)
CASCADES CANADA ULC
CASCADES INOPAK
500 Rue Lauzon, Drummondville, QC, J2B
2Z3
(819) 472-5757
Emp Here 40
SIC 3089 Plastics products, nec

D-U-N-S 24-359-5795   (BR)
**CENTRE JEUNESSE DE LA MAURICIE ET
DU CENTRE-DU-QUEBEC, LE**
*CENTRE JEUNESSE DE LA MAURICIE ET
DU CENTRE-DU-QUEBEC, LE*
(*Suby of* Centre Jeunesse de la Mauricie et du
Centre-du-Quebec, Le)
3100 Boul Lemire, Drummondville, QC, J2B
7R2
(819) 477-5115
Emp Here 120
SIC 8361 Residential care

D-U-N-S 24-901-5959   (SL)
CENTRE DU CAMION BEAUDOIN INC
(*Suby of* Placements Claude Halle Inc, Les)
5360 Rue Saint-Roch S, Drummondville, QC,
J2B 6V4
(819) 478-8186
Emp Here 100   *Sales* 49,080,000
SIC 5511 New and used car dealers
Pr Pr Claude Halle
Dir Bernard Thibeault
  Dominique Beauregard

D-U-N-S 24-769-5844   (HQ)
CHEZ LOUIS POULET ET PIZZA INC
(*Suby of* Chez Louis Poulet et Pizza Inc)
2815 Boul Lemire, Drummondville, QC, J2B
8E7
(819) 474-3494
Emp Here 50   *Emp Total* 90
Sales 3,486,617
SIC 5812 Eating places

D-U-N-S 25-240-2805   (BR)
COMMISSION SCOLAIRE DES CHENES
ECOLE L'AQUARELLE
(*Suby of* Commission Scolaire des Chenes)
1140 Rue Saint-Edgar, Drummondville, QC,
J2B 2V9
(819) 474-0727
Emp Here 29
SIC 8211 Elementary and secondary schools

D-U-N-S 20-712-0911   (BR)
COMMISSION SCOLAIRE DES CHENES
ECOLES PRIMAIRES SAINT JOSEPH
(*Suby of* Commission Scolaire des Chenes)
180 Rue Saint-Albert, Drummondville, QC,
J2B 2A9
(819) 474-0714
Emp Here 60
SIC 8211 Elementary and secondary schools

D-U-N-S 24-011-5746   (BR)
COMMISSION SCOLAIRE DES CHENES
NOTRE DAME DU ROSAIRE
(*Suby of* Commission Scolaire des Chenes)
154 18e Av, Drummondville, QC, J2B 3T3
(819) 474-0710
Emp Here 35
SIC 8211 Elementary and secondary schools

D-U-N-S 24-224-5470   (HQ)
COMMISSION SCOLAIRE DES CHENES
(*Suby of* Commission Scolaire des Chenes)
457 Rue Des Ecoles Bureau 846, Drum-
mondville, QC, J2B 1J3
(819) 478-6700
Emp Here 100   *Emp Total* 1,500
Sales 139,392,300
SIC 8211 Elementary and secondary schools
Pr Jeanne-Mance Paul
Genl Mgr Christiane Desbiens

D-U-N-S 24-011-5779   (BR)
COMMISSION SCOLAIRE DES CHENES
ECOLE DUVERNAY
(*Suby of* Commission Scolaire des Chenes)
1355 Rue Duvernay, Drummondville, QC, J2B
2R8
(819) 474-0704
Emp Here 20
SIC 8211 Elementary and secondary schools

D-U-N-S 24-011-5803   (BR)
COMMISSION SCOLAIRE DES CHENES

ECOLE PRIMAIRE SAINTE MARIE
(Suby of Commission Scolaire des Chenes)
100 13e Av, Drummondville, QC, J2B 2Z9
(819) 474-0711
Emp Here 30
SIC 8211 Elementary and secondary schools

D-U-N-S 24-011-5753   (BR)
COMMISSION SCOLAIRE DES CHENES
ECOLE ST SIMON
(Suby of Commission Scolaire des Chenes)
1180 Rue Saint-Thomas, Drummondville, QC,
J2B 3A9
(819) 474-0720
Emp Here 20
SIC 8211 Elementary and secondary schools

D-U-N-S 25-232-8158   (BR)
COMMISSION SCOLAIRE DES CHENES
ECOLE SECONDAIRE ST-FREDERIC
(Suby of Commission Scolaire des Chenes)
457 Rue Des Ecoles Bureau 846, Drum-
mondville, QC, J2B 1J3
(819) 474-0756
Emp Here 70
SIC 8211 Elementary and secondary schools

D-U-N-S 25-240-7783   (SL)
EXPEDIBUS
330 Rue Heriot, Drummondville, QC, J2B 1A8
(819) 477-2111
Emp Here 49   Sales 6,930,008
SIC 4213 Trucking, except local

D-U-N-S 24-871-2028   (SL)
FESTIVAL MONDIAL DE FOLKLORE
(DRUMMOND)
MONDIALE DES CULTURES DE DRUM-
MONDVILLE
226 Rue Saint-Marcel, Drummondville, QC,
J2B 2E4
(819) 472-1184
Emp Here 90   Sales 4,888,367
SIC 7999 Amusement and recreation, nec

D-U-N-S 25-904-4378   (BR)
FONDATION DU CENTRE DE READAPTA-
TION INTERVALE
CENTRE DE READAPTATION INTERVAL
(Suby of Fondation du Centre de Readapta-
tion Intervale)
570 Rue Heriot, Drummondville, QC, J2B 1C1
(819) 477-9010
Emp Here 25
SIC 8361 Residential care

D-U-N-S 24-760-3488   (HQ)
GROUPE TYT INC
B R LOGISTIQUE INTERNATIONAL
675 Boul Lemire O, Drummondville, QC, J2B
8A9
(819) 474-4884
Emp Here 75   Emp Total 85
Sales 33,735,378
SIC 4213 Trucking, except local
Pr Pr Patrick Turcotte
Mickael Turcotte
VP Jean-Marc Turcotte
VP Fin Francois Raiche

D-U-N-S 25-872-7262   (BR)
OPTO-PLUS INC
GESTION MARIE JOSSE PEPIN
50 Rue Dunkin, Drummondville, QC, J2B 8B1
(819) 479-2020
Emp Here 20
SIC 8042 Offices and clinics of optometrists

D-U-N-S 20-856-5051   (SL)
OUTILLEURS ARPEX INC, LES
565 Rue Des Ecoles, Drummondville, QC, J2B
1J6
(819) 474-5585
Emp Here 40   Sales 2,918,428
SIC 3599 Industrial machinery, nec

D-U-N-S 24-253-3727   (HQ)
PRODUITS INDUSTRIELS DE HAUTE TEM-

PERATURE PYROTEK INC, LES
ISOMAG
(Suby of Pyrotek Incorporated)
2400 Boul Lemire, Drummondville, QC, J2B
6X9
(819) 477-0734
Emp Here 60   Emp Total 2,437
Sales 11,162,987
SIC 3569 General industrial machinery, nec
Pr Pr Rejean Dault
VP Don Zel Tong

D-U-N-S 25-485-1868   (BR)
PROVIGO INC
MAXI #8689
1850 Boul Saint-Joseph, Drummondville, QC,
J2B 1R3
(819) 472-1197
Emp Here 200
SIC 5411 Grocery stores

D-U-N-S 24-336-8276   (BR)
RAD TECHNOLOGIES INC
PULVERISATEUR M S
4300 Rue Vachon, Drummondville, QC, J2B
6V4
(819) 474-1910
Emp Here 65
SIC 3523 Farm machinery and equipment

D-U-N-S 24-582-0089   (SL)
RECUPERACTION CENTRE DU QUEBEC
INC
5620 Rue Saint-Roch S, Drummondville, QC,
J2B 6V4
(819) 477-1312
Emp Here 105   Sales 19,174,050
SIC 4953 Refuse systems
Pr Pr Jean-Pierre Henri
Genl Mgr Daniel Lemay

D-U-N-S 20-792-9063   (BR)
ROTISSERIES ST-HUBERT LTEE, LES
ROTISSERIE ST HUBERT
(Suby of Cara Holdings Limited)
2875 Boul Saint-Joseph Bureau 230, Drum-
mondville, QC, J2B 7P5
(819) 475-8888
Emp Here 35
SIC 5812 Eating places

D-U-N-S 25-536-0893   (BR)
SEALED AIR (CANADA) CO./CIE
CRYVAC
(Suby of Sealed Air Corporation)
2350 Boul Lemire, Drummondville, QC, J2B
6X9

Emp Here 40
SIC 3086 Plastics foam products

D-U-N-S 20-565-5699   (SL)
SOUCY BELGEN INC
4475 Boul Saint-Joseph, Drummondville, QC,
J2B 1T8
(819) 477-2434
Emp Here 72
SIC 3321 Gray and ductile iron foundries

D-U-N-S 24-444-9422   (SL)
VIDEO DU DOLLARD DRUMMONDVILLE
INC
350 Rue Saint-Jean, Drummondville, QC, J2B
5L4
(819) 475-1957
Emp Here 50   Sales 4,596,524
SIC 7812 Motion picture and video production

D-U-N-S 25-853-9949   (BR)
VILLE DE DRUMMONDVILLE, LA
BIBLIOTHEQUE MUNICIPALE
545 Rue Des Ecoles, Drummondville, QC, J2B
1J6
(819) 478-6573
Emp Here 24
SIC 8231 Libraries

Drummondville, QC J2C
Drummomd County

D-U-N-S 25-758-5232   (SL)
141081 CANADA INC
LA CASA DU SPAGHETTI
570 Boul Saint-Joseph, Drummondville, QC,
J2C 2B9
(819) 477-3334
Emp Here 70   Sales 2,115,860
SIC 5812 Eating places

D-U-N-S 25-484-8807   (SL)
2316-7240 QUEBEC INC
HOTEL LE DAUPHIN
600 Boul Saint-Joseph, Drummondville, QC,
J2C 2C1
(819) 478-4141
Emp Here 90   Sales 3,939,878
SIC 7011 Hotels and motels

D-U-N-S 24-352-5768   (SL)
2535-0356 QUEBEC INC
1015 Boul Saint-Joseph, Drummondville, QC,
J2C 2C4
(819) 477-0442
Emp Here 50   Sales 5,465,508
SIC 5941 Sporting goods and bicycle shops
Pr Pr Eric Lamoureux
Michel Pelletier

D-U-N-S 25-742-5249   (BR)
4211677 CANADA INC
GO GIT
330 Rue Rocheleau, Drummondville, QC, J2C
7S7
(819) 477-9005
Emp Here 30
SIC 4212 Local trucking, without storage

D-U-N-S 20-013-0107   (SL)
9021-2200 QUEBEC INC
1275 Rue Janelle, Drummondville, QC, J2C
3E4

Emp Here 350   Sales 83,926,800
SIC 2531 Public building and related furniture
Pr Michel Nadeau
Benoit Nadeau
Dir Gerard Nadeau

D-U-N-S 25-074-5551   (SL)
9029-5015 QUEBEC INC
915 Rue Hains, Drummondville, QC, J2C 3A1
(819) 478-4971
Emp Here 49   Sales 5,763,895
SIC 6712 Bank holding companies
Pr Lise Lagueux

D-U-N-S 25-904-4949   (SL)
9045-4604 QUEBEC INC
DRUMONDVILLE NISSAN
1200 Boul Rene-Levesque, Drummondville,
QC, J2C 5W4
(819) 474-3930
Emp Here 35   Sales 16,996,000
SIC 5511 New and used car dealers
Pr Daniel Beaucage

D-U-N-S 24-374-8493   (HQ)
9122-1994 QUEBEC INC
(Suby of 9122-1994 Quebec Inc)
350 Rue Rocheleau, Drummondville, QC, J2C
7S7
(819) 477-6891
Emp Here 40   Emp Total 40
Sales 5,626,880
SIC 6712 Bank holding companies
Nathalie Prince
Pr Alexandre Prince
VP Guylain Prince
VP Bernard Malo

D-U-N-S 20-879-4417   (BR)
AIREX INDUSTRIES INC
3025 Rue Kunz, Drummondville, QC, J2C 6Y4
(819) 477-3030
Emp Here 40

SIC 3999 Manufacturing industries, nec

D-U-N-S 24-349-2175   (BR)
ALIMENTS PRINCE, S.E.C.
OLYMEL
255 Rue Rocheleau, Drummondville, QC, J2C
7G2
(819) 475-3030
Emp Here 570
SIC 2013 Sausages and other prepared
meats

D-U-N-S 24-406-0968   (SL)
ARMOTEC 2008 INC
2250 Rue Sigouin, Drummondville, QC, J2C
5Z4
(819) 478-4024
Emp Here 50   Sales 2,918,428
SIC 2434 Wood kitchen cabinets

D-U-N-S 24-204-6266   (SL)
AUTOBUS THOMAS INC
2275 Rue Canadien, Drummondville, QC, J2C
7V9
(819) 474-2700
Emp Here 55   Sales 1,532,175
SIC 4151 School buses

D-U-N-S 24-650-4799   (SL)
AUTOBUS VOLTIGEURS INC
1600 Boul Lemire, Drummondville, QC, J2C
5A4
(819) 474-4181
Emp Here 63   Sales 2,991,389
SIC 4142 Bus charter service, except local

D-U-N-S 24-907-2794   (BR)
BUROPRO CITATION INC
1050 Boul Rene-Levesque, Drummondville,
QC, J2C 5W4
(819) 478-7878
Emp Here 65
SIC 5112 Stationery and office supplies

D-U-N-S 24-600-5748   (SL)
CEGEP DE DRUMMONDVILLE
960 Rue Saint-Georges, Drummondville, QC,
J2C 6A2
(819) 850-2093
Emp Here 400   Sales 55,951,200
SIC 8221 Colleges and universities
Mng Dir Normand W. Bernier

D-U-N-S 20-799-6443   (BR)
CRDI TED NCQ IU
CENTRE DE SERVICES EN DEFICIENCE
INTELLECTUELLE
(Suby of CRDI TED NCQ IU)
440 Rue Saint-Georges, Drummondville, QC,
J2C 4H4
(819) 477-5687
Emp Here 50
SIC 8093 Specialty outpatient clinics, nec

D-U-N-S 24-368-9770   (BR)
CAISSE DESJARDINS DE DRUM-
MONDVILLE
CAISSE DESJARDINS DE DRUM-
MONDVILLE
905 Rue Gauthier, Drummondville, QC, J2C
0A1
(819) 474-2524
Emp Here 43
SIC 6159 Miscellaneous business credit insti-
tutions

D-U-N-S 20-518-9512   (BR)
CAISSE DESJARDINS DE DRUM-
MONDVILLE
CAISSE SAINT JEAN BAPTIST
460 Boul Saint-Joseph, Drummondville, QC,
J2C 2A8
(819) 474-2524
Emp Here 200
SIC 6062 State credit unions

D-U-N-S 20-002-9887   (BR)
CAISSE DESJARDINS DE DRUM-
MONDVILLE

CENTRE DE SERVICES BOULEVARD
460 Boul Saint-Joseph, Drummondville, QC, J2C 2A8
(819) 474-2524
Emp Here 250
SIC 6062 State credit unions

D-U-N-S 24-403-9921   (HQ)
CANIMEX INC
285 Rue Saint-Georges, Drummondville, QC, J2C 4H3
(819) 477-1335
Emp Here 400   Emp Total 420
Sales 43,338,656
SIC 3429 Hardware, nec
Pr Pr Roger Dubois
  Daniel Dubois

D-U-N-S 20-555-1224   (BR)
CASCADES CANADA ULC
CASCADES MULTI-PRO
495 Rue Haggerty, Drummondville, QC, J2C 3G5
(819) 478-5983
Emp Here 50
SIC 2671 Paper; coated and laminated packaging

D-U-N-S 24-405-0738   (BR)
CENTRE JEUNESSE DE LA MAURICIE ET DU CENTRE-DU-QUEBEC, LE
CENTRE JEUNESSE DE LA MAURICIE ET DU CENTRE-DU-QUEBEC, LE
(Suby of Centre Jeunesse de la Mauricie et du Centre-du-Quebec, Le)
787 Rue Saint-Pierre, Drummondville, QC, J2C 3X2
(819) 478-8123
Emp Here 45
SIC 8322 Individual and family services

D-U-N-S 24-855-3070   (BR)
CHEZ LOUIS POULET ET PIZZA INC
(Suby of Chez Louis Poulet et Pizza Inc)
150 Rue Saint-Georges, Drummondville, QC, J2C 4H1
(819) 474-5158
Emp Here 27
SIC 5812 Eating places

D-U-N-S 24-011-5720   (BR)
COMMISSION SCOLAIRE DES CHENES
IMMACULATE CONCEPTION
(Suby of Commission Scolaire des Chenes)
155 Rue Saint-Felix, Drummondville, QC, J2C 1N1
(819) 474-0706
Emp Here 30
SIC 8211 Elementary and secondary schools

D-U-N-S 20-033-9047   (BR)
COMMISSION SCOLAIRE DES CHENES
ECOLE ST CHARLES
(Suby of Commission Scolaire des Chenes)
650 Rue Victorin, Drummondville, QC, J2C 1B8
(819) 474-0702
Emp Here 35
SIC 8211 Elementary and secondary schools

D-U-N-S 25-232-8273   (BR)
COMMISSION SCOLAIRE DES CHENES
ECOLE SAINT-PIERRE
(Suby of Commission Scolaire des Chenes)
690 Rue Saint-Pierre, Drummondville, QC, J2C 3W5
(819) 474-0719
Emp Here 30
SIC 8211 Elementary and secondary schools

D-U-N-S 20-712-0879   (BR)
COMMISSION SCOLAIRE DES CHENES
ECOLE SECONDAIRE JEAN RAIMBAULT
(Suby of Commission Scolaire des Chenes)
175 Rue Pelletier, Drummondville, QC, J2C 2W1
(819) 474-0750
Emp Here 112
SIC 8211 Elementary and secondary schools

D-U-N-S 24-011-5696   (BR)
COMMISSION SCOLAIRE DES CHENES
ECOLE BRUYERE
(Suby of Commission Scolaire des Chenes)
850 Rue Florette-Lavigne, Drummondville, QC, J2C 4X1
(819) 474-0701
Emp Here 30
SIC 8211 Elementary and secondary schools

D-U-N-S 20-033-6332   (BR)
COMMISSION SCOLAIRE DES CHENES
(Suby of Commission Scolaire des Chenes)
125 Rue Ringuet, Drummondville, QC, J2C 2P7
(819) 474-0751
Emp Here 55
SIC 8331 Job training and related services

D-U-N-S 24-011-5761   (BR)
COMMISSION SCOLAIRE DES CHENES
ECOLES PRIMAIRES SAINT PIE X
(Suby of Commission Scolaire des Chenes)
227 Rue Bruno, Drummondville, QC, J2C 4M6
(819) 474-8341
Emp Here 40
SIC 8211 Elementary and secondary schools

D-U-N-S 25-232-8125   (BR)
COMMISSION SCOLAIRE DES CHENES
CENTRE ST-LOUIS-DE-GONZAGUE
(Suby of Commission Scolaire des Chenes)
269 Rue Ringuet, Drummondville, QC, J2C 2R1
(819) 474-0715
Emp Here 60
SIC 8211 Elementary and secondary schools

D-U-N-S 25-232-8232   (BR)
COMMISSION SCOLAIRE DES CHENES
ECOLE POLYVALENTE MARIE RIVIER
(Suby of Commission Scolaire des Chenes)
265 Rue Saint-Felix, Drummondville, QC, J2C 5M1
(819) 478-6600
Emp Here 100
SIC 8211 Elementary and secondary schools

D-U-N-S 24-934-0654   (BR)
DATA COMMUNICATIONS MANAGEMENT CORP
DATA GROUP OF COMPANIES
1750 Rue Jean-Berchmans-Michaud, Drummondville, QC, J2C 7S2
(819) 472-1111
Emp Here 316
SIC 2761 Manifold business forms

D-U-N-S 24-012-3583   (BR)
DAY & ROSS INC
FASTRAX TRANSPORTATION
1855 Rue Power, Drummondville, QC, J2C 5X4
(819) 471-5198
Emp Here 20
SIC 4213 Trucking, except local

D-U-N-S 25-161-7155   (BR)
DESJARDINS SECURITE FINANCIERE, COMPAGNIE D'ASSURANCE VIE
SERVICES FINANCIERS SFF
235 Rue Heriot Bureau 435, Drummondville, QC, J2C 6X5
(819) 477-5300
Emp Here 20
SIC 6411 Insurance agents, brokers, and service

D-U-N-S 25-103-8055   (BR)
EMBALLAGES MITCHEL-LINCOLN LTEE
MITCHPAK
925 Rue Rocheleau, Drummondville, QC, J2C 6L8
(819) 477-9700
Emp Here 250
SIC 2653 Corrugated and solid fiber boxes

D-U-N-S 24-744-3893   (BR)

ENGLOBE CORP
LVM DIVISION N-GLOBE CORT
1430 Boul Lemire, Drummondville, QC, J2C 5A4
(819) 475-6688
Emp Here 20
SIC 8711 Engineering services

D-U-N-S 25-356-2201   (SL)
FEMPRO CONSUMER PRODUCTS ULC
FEMPRO
(Suby of First Quality International, Inc.)
1330 Rue Jean-Berchmans-Michaud, Drummondville, QC, J2C 2Z5
(819) 475-8900
Emp Here 100   Sales 18,240,175
SIC 2676 Sanitary paper products
Pr James Dodge
  Moshe Oppenheim
Treas Thomas Lucarelli

D-U-N-S 24-175-1577   (HQ)
FORESBEC INC
FORESBEC FORESFLOOR
1750 Rue Haggerty, Drummondville, QC, J2C 5P8
(819) 477-8787
Emp Here 100   Emp Total 150
Sales 25,171,442
SIC 2426 Hardwood dimension and flooring mills
  Edward Heidt Jr
  Carl Gade

D-U-N-S 24-959-2718   (SL)
GESTION J.L.T. UNIVERSELLE INC
BEST WESTERN HOTEL UNIVERSEL
915 Rue Hains, Drummondville, QC, J2C 3A1
(819) 472-2942
Emp Here 90   Sales 3,939,878
SIC 7011 Hotels and motels

D-U-N-S 24-862-8104   (BR)
GOODFELLOW INC
1750 Rue Haggerty, Drummondville, QC, J2C 5P8
(819) 477-6898
Emp Here 100
SIC 2426 Hardwood dimension and flooring mills

D-U-N-S 24-388-5717   (BR)
GROUPE AGRITEX INC, LES
AGRITEX DRUMMONDVILLE
(Suby of Groupe Agritex Inc, Le)
150 Rue Robert-Bernard, Drummondville, QC, J2C 8N1
(819) 474-0002
Emp Here 20
SIC 5999 Miscellaneous retail stores, nec

D-U-N-S 24-254-5846   (BR)
GROUPE MASKA INC
GROUPE MASKA PIECES AUTO
(Suby of Gestion M. A. E. Inc)
1348 Rue Hebert, Drummondville, QC, J2C 1Z8
(819) 478-2549
Emp Here 22
SIC 5013 Motor vehicle supplies and new parts

D-U-N-S 20-319-5768   (BR)
GROUPE PROMUTUEL FEDERATION DE SOCIETE MUTUELLES D'ASSURANCES GENERALES
PROMUTUEL
1500 Boul Lemire, Drummondville, QC, J2C 5A4
(819) 477-8844
Emp Here 20
SIC 8742 Management consulting services

D-U-N-S 25-258-3828   (BR)
GROUPE SPORTSCENE INC
CAGE AUX SPORTS DRUMMONDVILLE
400 Boul Saint-Joseph, Drummondville, QC, J2C 2A8

(819) 474-6373
Emp Here 44
SIC 5812 Eating places

D-U-N-S 25-672-9138   (SL)
IMMEUBLES J.C. MILOT INC, LES
HOTEL & SUITES LE DAUPHIN
600 Boul Saint-Joseph, Drummondville, QC, J2C 2C1
(819) 478-4141
Emp Here 90   Sales 3,939,878
SIC 7011 Hotels and motels

D-U-N-S 25-309-7158   (BR)
INDUSTRIELLE ALLIANCE, ASSURANCE ET SERVICES FINANCIERS INC
INDUSTRIEL ALLIANCE ASSURANCE ET SERVICES FINANCIERS
333 Rue Janelle, Drummondville, QC, J2C 3E2
(819) 478-4159
Emp Here 50
SIC 6311 Life insurance

D-U-N-S 25-305-2021   (BR)
INNVEST PROPERTIES CORP
COMFORT INN
(Suby of Innvest Properties Corp)
1055 Rue Hains, Drummondville, QC, J2C 6G6
(819) 477-4000
Emp Here 20
SIC 7011 Hotels and motels

D-U-N-S 24-003-2537   (BR)
MARCHE VEGETARIEN INC, LE
1100 Boul Saint-Joseph, Drummondville, QC, J2C 2C7

Emp Here 35
SIC 5431 Fruit and vegetable markets

D-U-N-S 20-196-3113   (HQ)
MATECH B.T.A. INC
1570 Boul Saint-Charles, Drummondville, QC, J2C 4Z5
(819) 478-4015
Emp Here 64   Emp Total 3
Sales 9,338,970
SIC 5013 Motor vehicle supplies and new parts
Pr Serge Valois
VP Rene Valois
Sec Martin Valois

D-U-N-S 20-765-2777   (BR)
MEDIAS TRANSCONTINENTAL INC
MEDIAS TRANSCONTINENTAL INC
1050 Rue Cormier, Drummondville, QC, J2C 2N6
(819) 478-8171
Emp Here 52
SIC 2711 Newspapers

D-U-N-S 25-808-7774   (BR)
METRO RICHELIEU INC
SUPER C
565 Boul Saint-Joseph Bureau 4, Drummondville, QC, J2C 2B6
(819) 474-2702
Emp Here 120
SIC 5411 Grocery stores

D-U-N-S 20-252-4021   (BR)
OLYMEL S.E.C.
OLYMEL DRUMMONDVILLE
255 Rue Rocheleau, Drummondville, QC, J2C 7G2
(819) 475-3030
Emp Here 450
SIC 2011 Meat packing plants

D-U-N-S 24-522-5789   (BR)
PPD FOAM SOLUTION INC
1275 Rue Janelle, Drummondville, QC, J2C 3E4
(819) 850-0159
Emp Here 120
SIC 2531 Public building and related furniture

D-U-N-S 24-569-6737   (SL)
PRODUIT FREDERIC INC
880 Rue Cormier, Drummondville, QC, J2C
2N6
(819) 472-4569
Emp Here 50   *Sales* 1,532,175
SIC 5812 Eating places

D-U-N-S 24-682-0323   (SL)
PRODUITS DISQUE AMERIC INC
2525 Rue Canadien, Drummondville, QC, J2C
7W2

Emp Here 50   *Sales* 7,754,640
SIC 3652 Prerecorded records and tapes
Pr Louis-Roch Langlois

D-U-N-S 24-125-7158   (BR)
PROVIGO DISTRIBUTION INC
LOBLAWS DRUMMONDVILLE
325 Boul Saint-Joseph, Drummondville, QC,
J2C 8P7

Emp Here 100
SIC 5411 Grocery stores

D-U-N-S 24-542-2910   (BR)
REDBERRY FRANCHISING CORP
RESTAURANT BURGER KING
350 Boul Saint-Joseph, Drummondville, QC,
J2C 2A8
(819) 477-0245
Emp Here 40
SIC 5812 Eating places

D-U-N-S 20-700-6722   (BR)
REITMANS (CANADA) LIMITEE
REITMANS
1025 Boul Rene-Levesque Bureau 2, Drum-
mondville, QC, J2C 7V4
(819) 478-3915
Emp Here 25
SIC 5621 Women's clothing stores

D-U-N-S 25-156-2430   (SL)
**RESEAU AQUATIQUE DRUMMONDVILLE
INC**
1380 Rue Montplaisir, Drummondville, QC,
J2C 0M6
(819) 477-1063
Emp Here 49   *Sales* 22,617,817
SIC 2451 Mobile homes
Pr Jean Fournier

D-U-N-S 24-150-0391   (BR)
RESTAURANT NORMANDIN INC
130 Boul Saint-Joseph, Drummondville, QC,
J2C 2A8
(819) 472-7522
Emp Here 63
SIC 5812 Eating places

D-U-N-S 24-855-0373   (SL)
RESTO DU FAUBOURG DRUMMOND INC.
BOSTON PIZZA
161 Boul Saint-Joseph, Drummondville, QC,
J2C 2A7
(819) 475-6222
Emp Here 50   *Sales* 1,532,175
SIC 5812 Eating places

D-U-N-S 25-294-5977   (BR)
SEARS CANADA INC
SEARS
755 Boul Rene-Levesque, Drummondville,
QC, J2C 6Y7
(819) 478-1381
Emp Here 100
SIC 5311 Department stores

D-U-N-S 24-354-0127   (BR)
SINTRA INC
CENTRE ST-CHARLES
1340 Boul Foucault, Drummondville, QC, J2C
1B1
(819) 472-4852
Emp Here 30
SIC 2951 Asphalt paving mixtures and blocks

D-U-N-S 25-307-6863   (BR)
SOCIETE DES ALCOOLS DU QUEBEC
SOCIETE DES ALCOOLS DU QUEBEC
695 Boul Saint-Joseph, Drummondville, QC,
J2C 2B6
(819) 478-8184
Emp Here 20
SIC 5921 Liquor stores

D-U-N-S 20-512-6068   (BR)
**SOCIETE EN COMMANDITE SERVICES
PLUS**
SERVITECH ENERGIE SEC
1170 Rue Bergeron, Drummondville, QC, J2C
7G3
(819) 477-2000
Emp Here 21
SIC 1711 Plumbing, heating, air-conditioning

D-U-N-S 24-827-6110   (HQ)
SOPREMA INC
ACOUSTIBOARD
1688 Rue Jean-Berchmans-Michaud, Drum-
mondville, QC, J2C 8E9
(819) 478-8163
Emp Here 100   *Emp Total* 1
Sales 82,080,788
SIC 2952 Asphalt felts and coatings
Pr Pr Pierre-Etienne Bindschedler
   Richard Voyer
Dir Raymond Gauthier
Dir Monique Dupuis

D-U-N-S 25-687-2441   (BR)
STAPLES CANADA INC
BUREAU EN GROS
(*Suby of* Staples, Inc.)
565 Boul Saint-Joseph, Drummondville, QC,
J2C 2B6
(819) 474-3147
Emp Here 35
SIC 5943 Stationery stores

D-U-N-S 25-062-9375   (BR)
STEAMATIC METROPOLITAIN INC
STEAMATIC
2375 Rue Canadien, Drummondville, QC, J2C
7W1
(819) 474-5050
Emp Here 23
SIC 7349 Building maintenance services, nec

D-U-N-S 20-561-9567   (BR)
TAPIS VENTURE INC
VENTURE CARPETS
1600 Rue Janelle, Drummondville, QC, J2C
3E5
(819) 477-4117
Emp Here 65
SIC 2273 Carpets and rugs

D-U-N-S 20-799-4901   (BR)
UNITED PARCEL SERVICE CANADA LTD
UPS
1777 Rue Sigouin, Drummondville, QC, J2C
5R7
(819) 472-3977
Emp Here 20
SIC 4215 Courier services, except by air

D-U-N-S 25-919-0395   (SL)
VIDEO DU DOLLAR DRUMMONDVILLE INC
565 Boul Saint-Joseph Bureau 16, Drummondville, QC, J2C 2B6
(819) 474-4124
Emp Here 60   *Sales* 3,043,500
SIC 7841 Video tape rental

D-U-N-S 25-481-4270   (BR)
WAL-MART CANADA CORP
1205 Boul Rene-Levesque, Drummondville,
QC, J2C 7V4
(819) 472-7446
Emp Here 100
SIC 5311 Department stores

D-U-N-S 24-943-4325   (BR)
ZCL COMPOSITES INC
(*Suby of* ZCL Composites Inc)

250 Rue Rocheleau, Drummondville, QC, J2C
6Z7
(819) 474-4114
Emp Here 40
SIC 3299 NonMetallic mineral products,

Drummondville, QC J2E
Drummomd County

D-U-N-S 20-630-8392   (BR)
A & W FOOD SERVICES OF CANADA INC
RESTAURANT A & W
5000 Rue Girardin, Drummondville, QC, J2E
1A1
(819) 474-7255
Emp Here 20
SIC 5812 Eating places

D-U-N-S 24-600-2059   (SL)
**ASSURANCES JEAN-CLAUDE LECLERC
INC**
*LECLERC ASSURANCES ET SERVICES FI-
NANCIERS*
230 Boul Saint-Joseph O, Drummondville,
QC, J2E 0G3
(819) 477-3156
Emp Here 50   *Sales* 4,523,563
SIC 6411 Insurance agents, brokers, and ser-
vice

D-U-N-S 20-249-7145   (SL)
GIRARDIN, A. INC
(*Suby of* Groupe Autobus Girardin Ltee)
4000 Rue Girardin, Drummondville, QC, J2E
0A1
(819) 477-3222
Emp Here 80   *Sales* 2,261,782
SIC 4151 School buses

D-U-N-S 25-976-2599   (SL)
LA FINANCIERE AGRICOLE DU QUEBEC
380 Boul Saint-Joseph O, Drummondville,
QC, J2E 1C6

Emp Here 49   *Sales* 6,784,769
SIC 8748 Business consulting, nec
Dir Annie Lafrance

D-U-N-S 25-078-9955   (SL)
MARIO VINCENT
RESTAURANT BLANCHET
225 Boul Saint-Joseph O, Drummondville,
QC, J2E 1A9
(819) 477-0222
Emp Here 50   *Sales* 1,532,175
SIC 5812 Eating places

Duhamel, QC J0V

D-U-N-S 20-103-4910   (BR)
**SOCIETE DES ETABLISSEMENTS DE
PLEIN AIR DU QUEBEC**
SEPAQ
1216 Rue Principale, Duhamel, QC, J0V 1G0
(819) 428-7931
Emp Here 30
SIC 7033 Trailer parks and campsites

Duhamel-Ouest, QC J9V

D-U-N-S 24-501-7959   (SL)
TRANSPORT L.R.L. INC
252 101 Rte S, Duhamel-Ouest, QC, J9V 2E5

Emp Here 120   *Sales* 13,062,400
SIC 4212 Local trucking, without storage
Pr Pr Andre Bergeron
   Claudine Bellehumeur
   Henri Bergeron

Monic Bergeron

Dunham, QC J0E
Missisquoi County

D-U-N-S 25-916-0695   (SL)
ATHENA CONSTRUCTION INC
2311 Rue Principale, Dunham, QC, J0E 1M0
(450) 263-0445
Emp Here 25   *Sales* 6,898,600
SIC 1541 Industrial buildings and warehouses
Pr Pr Benoit Desgens
Treas Nathalie Dion

D-U-N-S 25-240-6210   (BR)
**COMMISSION SCOLAIRE DU VAL-DES-
CERFS**
*ECOLE DE LA CLE DES CHAMPUBLIC
SCHOOL*
3858 Rue Principale, Dunham, QC, J0E 1M0
(450) 295-2722
Emp Here 20
SIC 8211 Elementary and secondary schools

Dupuy, QC J0Z
Abitibi County

D-U-N-S 24-001-2307   (SL)
3158764 CANADA INC
METAUX GILLES PARE
512 111 Rte, Dupuy, QC, J0Z 1X0

Emp Here 20   *Sales* 6,576,720
SIC 5093 Scrap and waste materials
Pr Pr Gilles Pare

East Angus, QC J0B
Compton County

D-U-N-S 20-712-0945   (BR)
**COMMISSION SCOLAIRE DES HAUTS-
CANTONS**
ECOLE DU PARCHEMIN
96 Rue Saint-Jacques, East Angus, QC, J0B
1R0
(819) 832-2484
Emp Here 35
SIC 8211 Elementary and secondary schools

D-U-N-S 25-233-4107   (BR)
**COMMISSION SCOLAIRE DES HAUTS-
CANTONS**
ECOLE DU PARCHEMIN COTE COUVENT
(*Suby of* Commission Scolaire des Hauts-
Cantons)
162 Rue Saint-Jean E, East Angus, QC, J0B
1R0
(819) 832-2477
Emp Here 30
SIC 8211 Elementary and secondary schools

D-U-N-S 25-911-9253   (SL)
**DANIEL DESRUISSEAUX, GERARD LALIB-
ERTE, NATHALIE CHOUINARD, PHARMA-
CIENS S.E.N.C.**
150 Rue Angus S Bureau 1, East Angus, QC,
J0B 1R0
(819) 832-4343
Emp Here 20   *Sales* 5,253,170
SIC 5912 Drug stores and proprietary stores
Pt Daniel Desruisseaux
Pt Nathalie Chouinard
Pt Gerard Laliberte

D-U-N-S 24-863-4065   (BR)
HOOD PACKAGING CORPORATION
SOCIETE EMBALLAGES HOOD
(*Suby of* Hood Packaging Corporation)
15 Rue David-Swan, East Angus, QC, J0B

1R0
(819) 832-4971
Emp Here '00
SIC 2674 Bags: uncoated paper and multiwall

D-U-N-S 20-197-2650   (SL)
PHARMACIE ANGUS INC
D. DESUISSEAUX G. LALIBERTE
150 Rue Argus S Bureau 1, East Angus, QC,
J0B 1R0
(819) 832-4343
Emp Here 30   *Sales* 5,884,100
SIC 5912 Drug stores and proprietary stores
Pr Pr Daniel Desruisseaux
Dir Gerard Laliberte
    Nathalie Chouinard

D-U-N-S 25-999-9894   (BR)
TEXTILES MERCEDES LIMITEE, LES
MERCEDES TEXTILES LIMITED
287 Rue Saint-Jean O, East Angus, QC, J0B
1R0
(819) 832-4219
Emp Here 35
SIC 3561 Pumps and pumping equipment

East Broughton, QC G0N
Beauce County

D-U-N-S 25-223-9595   (BR)
COMMISSION SCOLAIRE DES AP-PALACHES
ECOLES PRIMAIRES PAUL VI
(*Suby of* Commission Scolaire des Ap-palaches)
372 Av Du College, East Broughton, QC, G0N
1G0
(418) 427-2606
Emp Here 22
SIC 8211 Elementary and secondary schools

East Farnham, QC J2K

D-U-N-S 25-685-2948   (BR)
URGEL CHARETTE TRANSPORT LIMITEE
TRANSPORTS URGEL CHARETTE LTEE
(*Suby of* Gestion Robert Goyette Inc)
131 Rue Maple Dale, East Farnham, QC, J2K
4M7
(450) 263-2631
Emp Here 100
SIC 4212 Local trucking, without storage

Eastmain, QC J0M
Abitibi County

D-U-N-S 25-240-0114   (BR)
CREE SCHOOL BOARD
WABANNUTAO EYOU SCHOOL
(*Suby of* Cree School Board)
142 Shabow Eastmain, QC, J0M 1W0
(819) 977-0244
Emp Here 30
SIC 8211 Elementary and secondary schools

Eastman, QC J0E
Brome County

D-U-N-S 20-913-7061   (BR)
COMMISSION SCOLAIRE DES SOMMETS
ECOLE VAL DE GRACE
500 Rue Principale, Eastman, QC, J0E 1P0
(450) 297-2190
Emp Here 30
SIC 8211 Elementary and secondary schools

Egan, QC J9E
Gatineau County

D-U-N-S 20-614-8389   (SL)
ENTREPRISES FREMAKI INC, LES
MARTEL & FILS
(*Suby of* Placements Fremaki Ltee, Les)
120 105 Rte, Egan, QC, J9E 3A9
(819) 449-1590
Emp Here 25   *Sales* 5,072,500
SIC 5211 Lumber and other building materials
Pr Pr Luc Martel

D-U-N-S 20-121-1658   (SL)
GESTION LOUIS-ARTHUR BRANCHAUD INC
52 105 Rte, Egan, QC, J9E 3A9
(819) 449-2610
Emp Here 60   *Sales* 8,763,660
SIC 5712 Furniture stores
Pr Louis-Arthur Branchaud

Fabreville, QC H7L

D-U-N-S 25-779-0964   (HQ)
3100-7669 QUEBEC INC
PRO KONTROL
(*Suby of* Groupe Techno Design BM Ltee, Le)
1989 Rue Michelin, Fabreville, QC, H7L 5B7
(450) 973-7765
Emp Here 20   *Emp Total* 11
Sales 11,684,880
SIC 5063 Electrical apparatus and equipment
Pr Pierre Martin
    Marc Bergeron
Dir Richard Caouette

D-U-N-S 25-412-6295   (SL)
BACHMANN DAMPJOINT INC
(*Suby of* Canerector Inc)
1460 Rue Michelin, Fabreville, QC, H7L 4R3
(450) 786-8686
Emp Here 33   *Sales* 2,042,900
SIC 3822 Environmental controls

D-U-N-S 24-368-9283   (BR)
CAISSE DESJARDINS DU NORD DE LAVAL
CENTRE DE SERVICES DOMAINE DES FORGES
(*Suby of* Caisse Desjardins du Nord de Laval)
269 Boul Sainte-Rose Bureau 318, Fabreville,
QC, H7L 0A2
(450) 625-5558
Emp Here 25
SIC 6062 State credit unions

D-U-N-S 24-946-6335   (HQ)
CAPELLA TELECOMMUNICATIONS INC
(*Suby of* 6456669 Canada Inc)
2065 Rue Michelin, Fabreville, QC, H7L 5B7
(450) 686-0033
Emp Here 25   *Emp Total* 27
Sales 8,171,598
SIC 4899 Communication services, nec
Pr Pr Wayne Rabey
    Jeffrey Minicola
    Roger Gilodo

D-U-N-S 25-907-1553   (SL)
ECO-NATURE
PARC DE LA RIVIERE DES MILLE-ILES
345 Boul Sainte-Rose, Fabreville, QC, H7L
1M7
(450) 622-1020
Emp Here 50   *Sales* 2,699,546
SIC 7999 Amusement and recreation, nec

D-U-N-S 24-362-4470   (BR)
ROYAL GROUP, INC
PROFILES POUR PORTES ET FENETRES ROYAL
3035 Boul Le Corbusier Bureau 7, Fabreville,

QC, H7L 4C3
(450) 687-5115
Emp Here 160
SIC 3431 Metal sanitary ware

Fabreville, QC H7P

D-U-N-S 24-815-0765   (HQ)
RESTAURANTS DUMAS LTEE, LES
RESTAURANT MCDONALDS
410 Boul Cure-Labelle, Fabreville, QC, H7P
2P1
(450) 628-0171
Emp Here 20   *Emp Total* 200
Sales 10,349,440
SIC 5812 Eating places
Pr Pr Paul Dumas

Fabreville, QC H7W

D-U-N-S 25-286-8666   (BR)
COMMUNAUTE HELLENIQUE DE MON-TREAL
ECOLE SOCRATES DE LAVAL
931 Rue Emerson, Fabreville, QC, H7W 3Y5
(450) 681-5142
Emp Here 35
SIC 8211 Elementary and secondary schools

Falardeau, QC G0V
Chicoutimi County

D-U-N-S 24-369-7724   (BR)
CAISSE DESJARDINS DE LA RIVE-NORD DU SAGUENAY
CENTRE DE SERVICE FALARDEAU
(*Suby of* Caisse Desjardins de la Rive-Nord du Saguenay)
122 Boul Saint-David, Falardeau, QC, G0V
1C0
(418) 549-4273
Emp Here 60
SIC 6062 State credit unions

Farnham, QC J2N
Missisquoi County

D-U-N-S 24-225-8903   (HQ)
ALPHA-VICO INC
(*Suby of* 9028-2658 Quebec Inc)
1035 Boul Magenta E, Farnham, QC, J2N 1B9
(450) 293-5354
Emp Here 55   *Emp Total* 1
Sales 14,429,520
SIC 2531 Public building and related furniture
Pr Pr Gilles Berthiaume

D-U-N-S 24-337-2401   (BR)
CENTRE DE SANTE ET DE SERVICES SO-CIAUX LA POMMERAIE
FOYER FARNHAM
(*Suby of* Centre de Sante et de Services So-ciaux la Pommeraie)
800 Rue Saint-Paul, Farnham, QC, J2N 2K6
(450) 293-3167
Emp Here 90
SIC 8361 Residential care

D-U-N-S 20-978-8710   (SL)
CLUB DE GOLF FARNHAM INC
55 Ch Du Golf, Farnham, QC, J2N 2P9
(450) 293-3171
Emp Here 55   *Sales* 2,334,742
SIC 7992 Public golf courses

D-U-N-S 25-233-4701   (BR)

COMMISSION SCOLAIRE EASTERN TOWNSHIPS
FARNHAM ELEMENTARY SCHOOL
(*Suby of* Commission Scolaire Eastern Town-ships)
425 Rue Saint-Joseph, Farnham, QC, J2N
1P4
(450) 293-6087
Emp Here 40
SIC 8211 Elementary and secondary schools

D-U-N-S 25-234-2019   (BR)
COMMISSION SCOLAIRE DU VAL-DES-CERFS
ECOLE ST JACQUES
250 Rue Aikman, Farnham, QC, J2N 1T2
(450) 293-6929
Emp Here 21
SIC 8211 Elementary and secondary schools

D-U-N-S 24-102-8864   (BR)
COMMISSION SCOLAIRE DU VAL-DES-CERFS
ECOLE MONSEIGNEUR DOUVILLE
260 Rue Saint-Romuald, Farnham, QC, J2N
2P2
(450) 293-4280
Emp Here 25
SIC 8211 Elementary and secondary schools

D-U-N-S 24-210-8582   (BR)
COMMISSION SCOLAIRE DU VAL-DES-CERFS
ECOLE SECONDAIRE JEAN JACQUES BERTRAND
255 Rue Saint-Andre S, Farnham, QC, J2N
2B8
(450) 293-3181
Emp Here 70
SIC 8211 Elementary and secondary schools

D-U-N-S 24-651-0804   (SL)
CONFECTION 2001 INC
1525 Rue Saint-Paul, Farnham, QC, J2N 2L3
(450) 293-6426
Emp Here 75   *Sales* 5,224,960
SIC 7389 Business services, nec
Pr Pr Jean Fortin
Dir Claudette Delorme Brodeur

D-U-N-S 24-511-4959   (BR)
ELECTROGROUPE PIONEER CANADA INC
TRANSFORMATEUR BEMAG
33 Rue Racine, Farnham, QC, J2N 3A3
(450) 293-8998
Emp Here 60
SIC 3612 Transformers, except electric

D-U-N-S 24-005-1891   (BR)
KAYCAN LTEE
VINYLE KAYTEC
(*Suby of* Administration F.L.T. Ltee)
1120 Boul Industriel, Farnham, QC, J2N 3B5
(450) 293-2463
Emp Here 24
SIC 3089 Plastics products, nec

D-U-N-S 24-458-5972   (BR)
SUPER MARCHE LAPLANTE INC
I G A
999 Rue Principale E, Farnham, QC, J2N 1M9
(450) 293-4210
Emp Here 50
SIC 5411 Grocery stores

D-U-N-S 24-590-5716   (SL)
SUPER MARCHE LARIVE INC
MARCHE LAPLANTE
999 Rue Principale E, Farnham, QC, J2N 1M9
(450) 293-4210
Emp Here 45   *Sales* 7,536,000
SIC 5411 Grocery stores
Pr Pr Germain Laplante
VP VP Michel Gazaille

D-U-N-S 20-547-5473   (HQ)
TARKETT INC
FIELDTURF TARKETT DIV OF

1001 Rue Yamaska E, Farnham, QC, J2N 1J7
(450) 293-3173
Emp Here 230   *Emp Total* 3
Sales 343,717,858
SIC 2851 Paints and allied products
Pr Glen Morrison
Sec Souha Azar
Dir Fin Nicolas Carre
Dir Michel Serge Giannuzzi
Dir Raphael Bauer

Fatima, QC G4T

D-U-N-S 25-232-0890   (BR)
COMMISSION SCOLAIRE DES ILES
ECOLE STELLA-MARIS
730 Ch Des Caps, Fatima, QC, G4T 2T3
(418) 986-2686
Emp Here 30
SIC 8211 Elementary and secondary schools

Ferme-Neuve, QC J0W
Labelle County

D-U-N-S 20-643-2598   (BR)
COMMISSION SCOLAIRE PIERRE-NEVEU, LA
ECOLE DE LA FERME NEUVE
148 12e Rue, Ferme-Neuve, QC, J0W 1C0
(819) 587-3321
Emp Here 20
SIC 8211 Elementary and secondary schools

Fermont, QC G0G
Saguenay County

D-U-N-S 20-712-6496   (BR)
COMMISSION SCOLAIRE DU FER
ECOLE POLYVALENTE HORIZON BLANC
130 Le Carrefour, Fermont, QC, G0G 1J0
(418) 287-5496
Emp Here 50
SIC 8211 Elementary and secondary schools

Forestville, QC G0T
Saguenay County

D-U-N-S 20-029-2220   (BR)
CENTRE DE SANTE ET DES SERVICES SOCIAUX DE LA HAUTE-COTE-NORD
(*Suby of* Centre de Sante et des Services Sociaux de la Haute-Cote-Nord)
2 7e Rue, Forestville, QC, G0T 1E0
(418) 587-2212
Emp Here 50
SIC 8093 Specialty outpatient clinics, nec

D-U-N-S 25-240-7168   (BR)
COMMISSION SCOLAIRE DE L'ESTUAIRE
ECOLE POLYVALENTE DE L'ESTUAIRE
(*Suby of* Commission Scolaire de l'Estuaire)
16 5e Av Bureau 190, Forestville, QC, G0T 1E0
(418) 587-4491
Emp Here 55
SIC 8211 Elementary and secondary schools

D-U-N-S 20-712-6322   (BR)
COMMISSION SCOLAIRE DE L'ESTUAIRE
CENTRE DE FORMATION PROFESSIONELLE DE FORESTVILLE
34 Rue 11 Rr 1, Forestville, QC, G0T 1E0
(418) 587-4735
Emp Here 50
SIC 8211 Elementary and secondary schools

D-U-N-S 24-706-9735   (SL)
COQUILLAGE NORDIQUE INC
10 Rte Maritime, Forestville, QC, G0T 1E0

Emp Here 65   *Sales* 14,871,040
SIC 2092 Fresh or frozen packaged fish
 Gerald Mills
Pr Pr Steven Mills
Genl Mgr Patrice Jean

D-U-N-S 20-573-7203   (BR)
HYDRO-QUEBEC
73 138 Rte O, Forestville, QC, G0T 1E0
(418) 587-6422
Emp Here 20
SIC 4911 Electric services

D-U-N-S 25-484-9490   (BR)
PROVIGO DISTRIBUTION INC
PROVIGO FORESTVILLE #4843116
25 138 Rte E Bureau 100, Forestville, QC, G0T 1E0
(418) 587-2202
Emp Here 50
SIC 5411 Grocery stores

Fort-Coulonge, QC J0X
Pontiac County

D-U-N-S 20-103-6253   (BR)
GOUVERNEMENT DE LA PROVINCE DE QUEBEC
MINISTERE DES RESSOURCES NATURELLES ET DE LA FAUNE
163 Ch De La Chute, Fort-Coulonge, QC, J0X 1V0
(819) 683-2626
Emp Here 20
SIC 8999 Services, nec

Frelighsburg, QC J0J
Missisquoi County

D-U-N-S 24-619-7131   (SL)
MAISON DE LA POMME DE FRELIGHSBURG INC
32 237 Rte N, Frelighsburg, QC, J0J 1C0
(450) 298-5275
Emp Here 50   *Sales* 4,304,681
SIC 5431 Fruit and vegetable markets

Gaspe, QC G4X
Gaspe-Est County

D-U-N-S 20-266-1419   (BR)
BIBLIOTHEQUE ET ARCHIVES NATIONALES DU QUEBEC
BANQ
80 Boul De Gaspe, Gaspe, QC, G4X 1A9
(418) 727-3500
Emp Here 25
SIC 8231 Libraries

D-U-N-S 25-514-4867   (BR)
BIOREX INC
198 Boul De Gaspe Bureau 102, Gaspe, QC, G4X 1B1
(418) 368-5597
Emp Here 50
SIC 8748 Business consulting, nec

D-U-N-S 20-530-0143   (BR)
CANADA POST CORPORATION
POSTES CANADA
52 Rue Fontenelle, Gaspe, QC, G4X 6R2
(418) 368-4325
Emp Here 20
SIC 4311 U.s. postal service

D-U-N-S 20-002-2155   (BR)
CANADIAN TIRE CORPORATION, LIMITED
CANADIAN TIRE CORPORATION, LTD
39 Montee De Sandy Beach, Gaspe, QC, G4X 2A9
(418) 368-6868
Emp Here 49
SIC 5531 Auto and home supply stores

D-U-N-S 24-097-6501   (BR)
CENTRE READAPTATION DE GASPESIE
CENTRE READAPTATION DE GASPESIE
(*Suby of* Centre Readaptation De Gaspesie)
150 Rue Mgr-Ross Bureau 550, Gaspe, QC, G4X 2R8
(418) 368-2306
Emp Here 200
SIC 8093 Specialty outpatient clinics, nec

D-U-N-S 25-091-5071   (BR)
CENTRE DE SANTE ET DE SERVICES SOCIAUX DE LA COTE-DE-GASPE
CLSC MER ET MONTAGNES
(*Suby of* Centre de sante et de services sociaux de la Cote-De-Gaspe)
154 Boul Renard E, Gaspe, QC, G4X 5R5
(418) 269-2572
Emp Here 30
SIC 8062 General medical and surgical hospitals

D-U-N-S 20-759-5351   (BR)
CENTRE DE SANTE ET DE SERVICES SOCIAUX DE LA COTE-DE-GASPE
CENTRE D'HEBERGEMENT MGR ROSS
(*Suby of* Centre de sante et de services sociaux de la Cote-De-Gaspe)
150 Rue Monseigneur-Ross, Gaspe, QC, G4X 2S7

Emp Here 50
SIC 8322 Individual and family services

D-U-N-S 20-711-8493   (BR)
COMMISSION SCOLAIRE DES CHIC-CHOCS
ECOLE C E POULIOT
85 Boul De Gaspe Bureau Rc, Gaspe, QC, G4X 2T8
(418) 368-6117
Emp Here 50
SIC 8211 Elementary and secondary schools

D-U-N-S 25-232-0916   (BR)
COMMISSION SCOLAIRE DES CHIC-CHOCS
ECOLE ANTOINE ROY
110 Boul Renard E, Gaspe, QC, G4X 5H8
(418) 269-3301
Emp Here 25
SIC 8211 Elementary and secondary schools

D-U-N-S 25-233-9007   (BR)
COMMISSION SCOLAIRE DES CHIC-CHOCS
ECOLE SAINT JOSPHE ALBAN
615 Boul Du Griffon, Gaspe, QC, G4X 6A5
(418) 892-5311
Emp Here 20
SIC 8211 Elementary and secondary schools

D-U-N-S 25-232-0791   (BR)
COMMISSION SCOLAIRE DES CHIC-CHOCS
ECOLE PRIMAIRES SAINT ROSAIRE
151 Rue Jacques-Cartier, Gaspe, QC, G4X 2P7
(418) 368-2237
Emp Here 60
SIC 8211 Elementary and secondary schools

D-U-N-S 20-573-5157   (BR)
DESJARDINS SECURITE FINANCIERE, COMPAGNIE D'ASSURANCE VIE
PETER SAMS
110 Rue De La Reine, Gaspe, QC, G4X 1T3
(418) 368-2625
Emp Here 20

SIC 6311 Life insurance

D-U-N-S 24-532-0478   (SL)
ENTREPRISES AGRICOLES & FORESTIERES DE LA PENINSULE INC
54 Rue Eden, Gaspe, QC, G4X 1Z2
(418) 368-5646
Emp Here 50   *Sales* 5,107,249
SIC 2411 Logging
Genl Mgr Michel Joncas

D-U-N-S 20-137-4084   (BR)
MCDONALD'S RESTAURANTS OF CANADA LIMITED
MCDONALD'S
(*Suby of* McDonald's Corporation)
180 Rue De Gaspe, Gaspe, QC, G4X 1B1
(418) 368-7070
Emp Here 26
SIC 5812 Eating places

D-U-N-S 20-197-9432   (SL)
MOTEL ADAMS INC
RESTAURANT ADAMS
20 Rue Adams, Gaspe, QC, G4X 1E4
(418) 368-6666
Emp Here 55   *Sales* 2,407,703
SIC 7011 Hotels and motels

D-U-N-S 25-514-4818   (SL)
RES-MAR
478 Montee De Wakeham, Gaspe, QC, G4X 1Y6
(418) 368-5373
Emp Here 63   *Sales* 3,210,271
SIC 7389 Business services, nec

D-U-N-S 25-010-5632   (BR)
TELUS COMMUNICATIONS (QUEBEC) INC
11 Rue Adams, Gaspe, QC, G4X 1E5
(418) 368-3532
Emp Here 20
SIC 4899 Communication services, nec

Gatineau, QC J8L
Hull County

D-U-N-S 24-481-9116   (SL)
AUTOBUS DU VILLAGE INC, LES
65 Rue Thibault, Gatineau, QC, J8L 3Z1
(819) 281-9235
Emp Here 80   *Sales* 2,261,782
SIC 4151 School buses

D-U-N-S 25-182-8844   (SL)
CH-CHSLD DE PAPINEAU
500 Rue Belanger, Gatineau, QC, J8L 2M4
(819) 986-3341
Emp Here 500   *Sales* 25,816,080
SIC 8399 Social services, nec
Dir Jacques Prud'homme
Dir Fin Daniel Labelle

D-U-N-S 24-975-7915   (BR)
COMMISSION SCOLAIRE WESTERN QUEBEC
ECOLE PRIMAIRE DE BUCKINGHAM
(*Suby of* Commission Scolaire Western Quebec)
615 Rue Georges, Gatineau, QC, J8L 2E1
(819) 986-3191
Emp Here 23
SIC 8211 Elementary and secondary schools

D-U-N-S 20-712-5555   (BR)
COMMISSION SCOLAIRE AU COEUR DES VALLEES
ECOLE MGR CHARBONNEAU
661 Rue Allaire, Gatineau, QC, J8L 2B8
(819) 281-5333
Emp Here 20
SIC 8211 Elementary and secondary schools

D-U-N-S 25-233-5377   (BR)
COMMISSION SCOLAIRE AU COEUR DES

▲ Public Company   ■ Public Company Family Member   **HQ** Headquarters   **BR** Branch   **SL** Single Location

VALLEES
ECOLE ST LAURENT
402 Rue Belanger, Gatineau, QC, J8L 2M2
(819) 281-0233
Emp Here 30
SIC 8211 Elementary and secondary schools

D-U-N-S 25-240-5824   (BR)
COMMISSION SCOLAIRE AU COEUR DES VALLEES
ECOLE ST-MICHEL
146 Rue Maclaren E Bureau B, Gatineau, QC, J8L 1K1
(819) 986-8676
Emp Here 40
SIC 8211 Elementary and secondary schools

D-U-N-S 20-025-7223   (BR)
COMMISSION SCOLAIRE AU COEUR DES VALLEES
CENTRE DE FORMATION PROFESSION-NELLE RELAIS DE LA LIEVRE
584 Rue Maclaren E, Gatineau, QC, J8L 2W1
(819) 986-8514
Emp Here 40
SIC 8249 Vocational schools, nec

D-U-N-S 25-310-0721   (BR)
ENTREPRISES P. BONHOMME LTEE, LES
BONHOMMES, LES
700 Rue Dollard, Gatineau, QC, J8L 3H3
(819) 986-7155
Emp Here 20
SIC 5039 Construction materials, nec

D-U-N-S 24-518-6585   (SL)
LES PROFESSIONNELLES EN SOINS DE SANTE UNIS DE PAPINEAU
CSSS PAPINEAU
578 Rue Maclaren E, Gatineau, QC, J8L 2W1
(819) 986-3359
Emp Here 250   *Sales* 23,362,080
SIC 8062 General medical and surgical hospitals
Pr Helene Lagace
VP Marlene Croussette
VP Lise St-Denis
Sec Julie Mageau

D-U-N-S 25-183-8397   (BR)
MAGASINS HART INC
HART DEPARTMENT STORES
999 Rue Dollard Bureau 19, Gatineau, QC, J8L 3E6
(819) 986-7223
Emp Here 40
SIC 5311 Department stores

D-U-N-S 25-247-1651   (BR)
MATERIAUX BONHOMME INC
ENTREPRISES P BONHOMME
700 Rue Dollard, Gatineau, QC, J8L 3H3
(819) 986-7155
Emp Here 20
SIC 5211 Lumber and other building materials

D-U-N-S 20-555-0739   (BR)
PAVILLON DU PARC
(*Suby of* Pavillon du Parc)
895 Rue Dollard, Gatineau, QC, J8L 3T4
(819) 986-3018
Emp Here 20
SIC 8399 Social services, nec

D-U-N-S 24-728-5161   (BR)
PROVIGO DISTRIBUTION INC
PROVIGO
130 Av Lepine, Gatineau, QC, J8L 4M4
(819) 281-5232
Emp Here 90
SIC 5411 Grocery stores

D-U-N-S 20-290-7994   (BR)
SUPERIOR GENERAL PARTNER INC
101 Ch Donaldson, Gatineau, QC, J8L 3X3
(819) 986-1135
Emp Here 90
SIC 5169 Chemicals and allied products, nec

D-U-N-S 24-344-0471   (BR)
SUPERIOR PLUS LP
101 Ch Donaldson, Gatineau, QC, J8L 3X3
(819) 986-1135
Emp Here 75
SIC 2819 Industrial inorganic chemicals, nec

Gatineau, QC J8M
Hull County

D-U-N-S 20-712-5605   (BR)
COMMISSION SCOLAIRE AU COEUR DES VALLEES
ECOLE AUX QUATRE VENTS
1115 Rue De Neuville Bureau 1, Gatineau, QC, J8M 2C7
(819) 281-6225
Emp Here 40
SIC 8211 Elementary and secondary schools

D-U-N-S 25-233-5450   (BR)
COMMISSION SCOLAIRE AU COEUR DES VALLEES
ECOLE DU SACRE-COEUR
420 Rue Du Progres, Gatineau, QC, J8M 1T3
(819) 986-8296
Emp Here 35
SIC 8211 Elementary and secondary schools

D-U-N-S 25-233-5492   (BR)
COMMISSION SCOLAIRE AU COEUR DES VALLEES
ECOLE ST-JEAN-DE-BREBEUF
32 Ch De Montreal E, Gatineau, QC, J8M 1E9
(819) 986-5100
Emp Here 28
SIC 8211 Elementary and secondary schools

D-U-N-S 25-233-5252   (BR)
COMMISSION SCOLAIRE AU COEUR DES VALLEES
EDUCATION DES ADULTES CENTRE LA CITE
50 Rue Des Servantes, Gatineau, QC, J8M 1C2
(819) 281-2054
Emp Here 30
SIC 8211 Elementary and secondary schools

D-U-N-S 20-170-0379   (BR)
COMMISSION SCOLAIRE AU COEUR DES VALLEES
ECOLE DU RUISSEAU
175 Rue Des Samares, Gatineau, QC, J8M 2B7
(819) 281-4846
Emp Here 30
SIC 8211 Elementary and secondary schools

D-U-N-S 20-188-6264   (HQ)
THEO MINEAULT INC
(*Suby of* Theo Mineault Inc)
2135 Ch De Montreal O, Gatineau, QC, J8M 1P3
(819) 986-3190
Emp Here 55   *Emp Total* 60
Sales 4,888,367
SIC 2431 Millwork

Gatineau, QC J8P
Hull County

D-U-N-S 24-959-0969   (SL)
153926 CANADA INC
PHARMACIES JEAN-COUTU
381 Boul Maloney E Bureau 15, Gatineau, QC, J8P 1E3
(819) 663-4164
Emp Here 115   *Sales* 22,623,350
SIC 5912 Drug stores and proprietary stores
Pr Pr Gilles Lalonde

D-U-N-S 25-256-3572   (SL)
3373738 CANADA INC
ATTACHE-REMORQUES GATINEAU
655 Boul Maloney E, Gatineau, QC, J8P 1G2
(819) 669-6111
Emp Here 20   *Sales* 5,465,508
SIC 5599 Automotive dealers, nec

D-U-N-S 25-893-7945   (BR)
CENTRES JEUNESSE DE L'OUTAOUAIS, LES
MAISON BERGERON
(*Suby of* Centres Jeunesse de l'Outaouais, Les)
621 Rue Notre-Dame, Gatineau, QC, J8P 1N1
(819) 663-3344
Emp Here 22
SIC 8322 Individual and family services

D-U-N-S 20-192-1009   (BR)
CIMA+ S.E.N.C.
420 Boul Maloney E Bureau 201, Gatineau, QC, J8P 7N8
(819) 663-9294
Emp Here 160
SIC 8711 Engineering services

D-U-N-S 25-240-1856   (BR)
COMMISSION SCOLAIRE DES DRAVEURS
ECOLE LA SABLONNIERE
143 Rue Des Sables, Gatineau, QC, J8P 7G6
(819) 643-1882
Emp Here 55
SIC 8211 Elementary and secondary schools

D-U-N-S 25-233-5443   (BR)
COMMISSION SCOLAIRE DES DRAVEURS
POLYVALENTE NICHOLAS GATINEAU
360 Boul La Verendrye E, Gatineau, QC, J8P 6K7
(819) 663-9241
Emp Here 200
SIC 8211 Elementary and secondary schools

D-U-N-S 20-712-5407   (BR)
COMMISSION SCOLAIRE DES DRAVEURS
ECOLE LA TRAVERSEE EDIFICE LAVIGNE
257 Rue Luck, Gatineau, QC, J8P 3S4
(819) 663-5326
Emp Here 50
SIC 8211 Elementary and secondary schools

D-U-N-S 20-712-5431   (BR)
COMMISSION SCOLAIRE DES DRAVEURS
ECOLE DE L'ODYSSEE
179 Boul Saint-Rene O, Gatineau, QC, J8P 2V5
(819) 643-5242
Emp Here 30
SIC 8211 Elementary and secondary schools

D-U-N-S 20-708-0040   (BR)
COMMISSION SCOLAIRE DES DRAVEURS
CENTRE ADMINISTRATION COMMERCE ET SECRETARIAT
183 Rue Broadway O Bureau 103, Gatineau, QC, J8P 3T6
(819) 643-4640
Emp Here 40
SIC 8211 Elementary and secondary schools

D-U-N-S 25-233-5203   (BR)
COMMISSION SCOLAIRE DES DRAVEURS
ECOLE BELLE RIVE
23 Rue Forget, Gatineau, QC, J8P 2H7
(819) 663-3360
Emp Here 45
SIC 8211 Elementary and secondary schools

D-U-N-S 20-712-5514   (BR)
COMMISSION SCOLAIRE DES DRAVEURS
SECONDARYTEUR ADULTES CENTRES DE FORMATION PROFESS
361 Boul Maloney O, Gatineau, QC, J8P 7E9
(819) 643-2000
Emp Here 40
SIC 8211 Elementary and secondary schools

D-U-N-S 25-240-0486   (BR)
COMMISSION SCOLAIRE DES DRAVEURS
ECOLE DE LA TRAVERSEE EDIFICE STE MARIA GORETTI
563 Rue Clement Bureau 103, Gatineau, QC, J8P 3Y9
(819) 663-5983
Emp Here 30
SIC 8211 Elementary and secondary schools

D-U-N-S 25-233-5369   (BR)
COMMISSION SCOLAIRE DES DRAVEURS
ECOLE CARLE
306 Rue Jacques-Buteux Bureau 102, Gatineau, QC, J8P 6A2
(819) 643-3422
Emp Here 35
SIC 8211 Elementary and secondary schools

D-U-N-S 25-233-6359   (BR)
COMMISSION SCOLAIRE DES DRAVEURS
ECOLE DE L'ODYSSEE
180 Rue Magnus O, Gatineau, QC, J8P 2R2
(819) 663-9226
Emp Here 50
SIC 8211 Elementary and secondary schools

D-U-N-S 25-233-6755   (BR)
COMMISSION SCOLAIRE DES DRAVEURS
ECOLE DE LA MONTEE
500 Rue Joseph-Demontigny, Gatineau, QC, J8P 7C4
(819) 663-6000
Emp Here 30
SIC 8211 Elementary and secondary schools

D-U-N-S 20-573-5645   (BR)
FEDERATION DES CAISSES DESJARDINS DU QUEBEC
420 Boul Maloney E Bureau 107, Gatineau, QC, J8P 7N8
(819) 669-3508
Emp Here 20
SIC 6062 State credit unions

D-U-N-S 25-171-5645   (BR)
HOME DEPOT OF CANADA INC
HOME DEPOT
(*Suby of* The Home Depot Inc)
243 Montee Paiement, Gatineau, QC, J8P 6M7
(819) 246-4060
Emp Here 150
SIC 5231 Paint, glass, and wallpaper stores

D-U-N-S 24-347-7598   (BR)
MARCHE LEBLANC MONTEE PAIEMENT INC
METRO PLUS
(*Suby of* Marche Leblanc Montee Paiement Inc)
435 Montee Paiement, Gatineau, QC, J8P 0B1
(819) 561-5478
Emp Here 150
SIC 5411 Grocery stores

D-U-N-S 24-105-7173   (SL)
MARCHE METRO LEBLANC MALONEY INC
METRO PLUS
910 Boul Maloney E, Gatineau, QC, J8P 1H5
(819) 643-2353
Emp Here 150   *Sales* 28,710,350
SIC 5411 Grocery stores
Pr Pierre Leblanc
VP VP Andre Leblanc
Dir Pascal St-Pierre

D-U-N-S 25-784-4647   (SL)
MONT-BLEU FORD INC
GEORGE PETRIC AUTOMOBILE
375 Boul Maloney O, Gatineau, QC, J8P 3W1
(819) 669-0111
Emp Here 55   *Sales* 26,994,000
SIC 5511 New and used car dealers
Pr Pr George Petric

D-U-N-S 24-254-6062   (BR)
PF RESOLU CANADA INC
79 Rue Main, Gatineau, QC, J8P 4X6
(819) 643-7500
Emp Here 113
SIC 4911 Electric services

D-U-N-S 25-299-9412   (BR)
PRISZM LP
POULET FRIT KENTUCKY
258 Rue Notre-Dame, Gatineau, QC, J8P 1K4
(819) 663-8686
Emp Here 21
SIC 5812 Eating places

D-U-N-S 20-117-2579   (BR)
PROVIGO INC
381 Boul Maloney E, Gatineau, QC, J8P 1E3
(819) 663-5374
Emp Here 20
SIC 5411 Grocery stores

D-U-N-S 24-420-8133   (BR)
SCM INSURANCE SERVICES INC
CLAIMSPRO
510 Boul Maloney E Bureau 104, Gatineau, QC, J8P 1E7
(819) 663-6068
Emp Here 20
SIC 6411 Insurance agents, brokers, and service

D-U-N-S 24-853-1407   (BR)
SNC-LAVALIN GEM QUEBEC INC
GROUPE QUALITAS
420 Boul Maloney E Bureau 6, Gatineau, QC, J8P 7N8
(819) 669-1225
Emp Here 36
SIC 8742 Management consulting services

D-U-N-S 25-213-7625   (BR)
STAPLES CANADA INC
BUREAU EN GROS
(*Suby of* Staples, Inc.)
235 Montee Paiement, Gatineau, QC, J8P 6M7
(819) 246-9470
Emp Here 40
SIC 5943 Stationery stores

D-U-N-S 25-806-7446   (BR)
TRANSPORT GUILBAULT INC
899 Boul Maloney E, Gatineau, QC, J8P 1H6
(819) 663-7717
Emp Here 30
SIC 4213 Trucking, except local

D-U-N-S 20-747-2960   (SL)
TRANSPORT THOM LTEE
592 Boul Saint-Rene E, Gatineau, QC, J8P 8A9
(819) 663-7253
Emp Here 50   *Sales* 2,334,742
SIC 4142 Bus charter service, except local

D-U-N-S 25-070-2537   (BR)
VALUE VILLAGE STORES, INC
VILLAGE DES VALEURS
(*Suby of* Savers, Inc.)
361 Boul Maloney O, Gatineau, QC, J8P 7E9
(819) 663-4343
Emp Here 30
SIC 5399 Miscellaneous general merchandise

D-U-N-S 20-034-1746   (BR)
VILLE DE GATINEAU
USINE D'EPURATION DES EAUX SECTOR GATINEAU
858a Rue Notre-Dame, Gatineau, QC, J8P 1N9
(819) 663-5585
Emp Here 65
SIC 7389 Business services, nec

Gatineau, QC J8R
Hull County

D-U-N-S 24-813-5667   (BR)
ALIMENTS MARTEL INC
ALI-PRET
212 Boul De L'Aeroport, Gatineau, QC, J8R 3X3
(819) 663-0835
Emp Here 200
SIC 5963 Direct selling establishments

D-U-N-S 20-642-0585   (BR)
COMMISSION SCOLAIRE DES DRAVEURS
ECOLE DE L 'ESCALADE
605 Rue Davidson E, Gatineau, QC, J8R 2V9
(819) 663-5558
Emp Here 70
SIC 8211 Elementary and secondary schools

D-U-N-S 20-034-1761   (BR)
COMMISSION SCOLAIRE DES DRAVEURS
ECOLE DU BOIS JOLI
1165 Boul Saint-Rene E, Gatineau, QC, J8R 1N1
(819) 669-1207
Emp Here 40
SIC 8211 Elementary and secondary schools

D-U-N-S 20-712-5530   (BR)
COMMISSION SCOLAIRE DES DRAVEURS
ECOLES DES CEPAGES
445 Rue Nobert, Gatineau, QC, J8R 3P2
(819) 663-1973
Emp Here 50
SIC 8211 Elementary and secondary schools

D-U-N-S 20-716-0958   (BR)
EXCAVATION LOISELLE INC
1679 Rue Jean-Louis-Malette, Gatineau, QC, J8R 0C1

Emp Here 150
SIC 1794 Excavation work

D-U-N-S 24-324-3206   (SL)
GESTION DELTA SIGMA INC
PHARMACIE JOHANNE GIGUERE
710 Montee Paiement Bureau 110, Gatineau, QC, J8R 4A3
(819) 669-1734
Emp Here 60   *Sales* 11,768,200
SIC 5912 Drug stores and proprietary stores
Johanne Giguere
VP VP Danny Seguin

D-U-N-S 20-017-1200   (BR)
J.Y. MOREAU ELECTRIQUE INC
MOREAU ELECTRIQUE
(*Suby of* J.Y. Moreau Electrique Inc)
295 Ch Industriel, Gatineau, QC, J8R 0C6
(819) 777-5287
Emp Here 20
SIC 1731 Electrical work

D-U-N-S 24-366-7839   (BR)
LABATT BREWING COMPANY LIMITED
1675 Rue Atmec, Gatineau, QC, J8R 3Y2
(800) 361-5252
Emp Here 70
SIC 5181 Beer and ale

D-U-N-S 24-920-6152   (BR)
MOLSON CANADA 2005
MOLSON CANADA
(*Suby of* Molson Coors Brewing Company)
1655 Rue Atmec, Gatineau, QC, J8R 3Y2
(819) 669-1786
Emp Here 40
SIC 5181 Beer and ale

D-U-N-S 20-225-6173   (BR)
MULTI-MARQUES INC
BOULANGERIE MULTI-MARQUES
1731 Boul Maloney E, Gatineau, QC, J8R 1B4
(819) 669-8155
Emp Here 20
SIC 5149 Groceries and related products, nec

D-U-N-S 20-184-4292   (BR)
WESTON BAKERIES LIMITED
MOISSON DOREE
255 Ch Industriel, Gatineau, QC, J8R 3V8
(819) 669-7246
Emp Here 81
SIC 5461 Retail bakeries

Gatineau, QC J8T
Hull County

D-U-N-S 24-483-3232   (SL)
128374 CANADA LTD
RESTAURANT DU BARRY
343 Boul Greber, Gatineau, QC, J8T 5R3

Emp Here 50   *Sales* 1,532,175
SIC 5812 Eating places

D-U-N-S 25-672-7314   (SL)
173569 CANADA INC
LA CAGE AUX SPORTS
325 Boul Greber Bureau C, Gatineau, QC, J8T 8J3
(819) 246-2243
Emp Here 50   *Sales* 1,532,175
SIC 5812 Eating places

D-U-N-S 25-773-3949   (SL)
3193560 CANADA INC
DELI CHENOY'S
120 Boul De L'Hopital Bureau 105, Gatineau, QC, J8T 8M2
(819) 561-3354
Emp Here 60   *Sales* 1,824,018
SIC 5812 Eating places

D-U-N-S 24-256-0733   (SL)
9095-1302 QUEBEC INC
CITE-JARDIN
60 Rue De La Futaie Bureau 512, Gatineau, QC, J8T 8P5
(819) 568-2355
Emp Here 45   *Sales* 4,677,755
SIC 6513 Apartment building operators

D-U-N-S 20-526-7243   (SL)
9107-1696 QUEBEC INC
SCORES ROTISSERIE BBQ & RIBS (GATINEAU)
1000 Boul Maloney O, Gatineau, QC, J8T 3R6
(819) 243-8080
Emp Here 70   *Sales* 2,115,860
SIC 5812 Eating places

D-U-N-S 24-958-9920   (SL)
964211 ONTARIO LTD
MARCHE FRAIS DE GATINEAU
215 Rue Bellehumeur, Gatineau, QC, J8T 8H3

Emp Here 50   *Sales* 4,304,681
SIC 5431 Fruit and vegetable markets

D-U-N-S 24-154-5404   (BR)
ALL SENIORS CARE LIVING CENTRES LTD
RESIDENCES DE LA GAPPE
(*Suby of* All Seniors Care Holdings Inc)
465 Boul De La Gappe Bureau 214, Gatineau, QC, J8T 0A2
(819) 246-5050
Emp Here 35
SIC 8361 Residential care

D-U-N-S 25-080-4820   (BR)
BENSON GROUP INC
BENSON AUTO PARTS
(*Suby of* Benapac Inc)
95 Boul Greber, Gatineau, QC, J8T 3P9
(819) 669-6555
Emp Here 80
SIC 5013 Motor vehicle supplies and new parts

D-U-N-S 24-240-1433   (BR)

BEST BUY CANADA LTD
BEST BUY
(*Suby of* Best Buy Co., Inc.)
920 Boul Maloney O, Gatineau, QC, J8T 3R6
(819) 966-2222
Emp Here 50
SIC 5731 Radio, television, and electronic stores

D-U-N-S 24-760-3934   (BR)
BIBLIOTHEQUE ET ARCHIVES NATIONALES DU QUEBEC
BANQ
855 Boul De La Gappe, Gatineau, QC, J8T 8H9
(819) 568-8798
Emp Here 25
SIC 8231 Libraries

D-U-N-S 24-979-5266   (BR)
BRICK WAREHOUSE LP, THE
BRICK, THE
920 Boul Maloney O, Gatineau, QC, J8T 3R6
(819) 568-5115
Emp Here 39
SIC 5712 Furniture stores

D-U-N-S 25-990-9513   (SL)
BROOKFIELD ENERGY MARKETING INC
480 Boul De La Cite Bureau 200, Gatineau, QC, J8T 8R3
(819) 561-2722
Emp Here 90   *Sales* 59,283,200
SIC 4911 Electric services
Pr Pr Richard Legault
Donald Tremblay
VP Opers Laurent Cusson
Ex VP Colin Clark
VP Fin Gilles Larocque
Ed Kress
Ch Bd Harry Goldgut

D-U-N-S 24-342-2156   (BR)
CARA OPERATIONS LIMITED
HARVEY'S RESTAURANT
(*Suby of* Cara Holdings Limited)
180 Boul Greber, Gatineau, QC, J8T 6K2
(819) 243-3024
Emp Here 24
SIC 5812 Eating places

D-U-N-S 25-070-2586   (BR)
COMMISSION SCOLAIRE DES DRAVEURS
CENTRE L'ESCALE
85 Rue Du Barry Bureau 141, Gatineau, QC, J8T 3N5
(819) 243-2151
Emp Here 50
SIC 8211 Elementary and secondary schools

D-U-N-S 25-233-5526   (BR)
COMMISSION SCOLAIRE DES DRAVEURS
ECOLE RIVIERA
59 Rue De Provence, Gatineau, QC, J8T 4V2
(819) 568-4331
Emp Here 30
SIC 8211 Elementary and secondary schools

D-U-N-S 25-233-5484   (BR)
COMMISSION SCOLAIRE DES DRAVEURS
ECOLE DU NOUVEAU MONDE
9 Rue Sainte-Yvonne Bureau 253, Gatineau, QC, J8T 1X6
(819) 568-0233
Emp Here 90
SIC 8211 Elementary and secondary schools

D-U-N-S 25-240-1229   (BR)
COMMISSION SCOLAIRE DES DRAVEURS
ECOLE LE PETIT PRINCE
44 Rue De Juan-Les-Pins Bureau 102, Gatineau, QC, J8T 6H2
(819) 568-3777
Emp Here 50
SIC 8211 Elementary and secondary schools

D-U-N-S 25-240-1427   (BR)
COMMISSION SCOLAIRE DES DRAVEURS

ECOLE L' OISEAU BLEU
184 Rue Nelligan, Gatineau, QC, J8T 6J9
(819) 568-2101
Emp Here 50
SIC 8211 Elementary and secondary schools

D-U-N-S 20-025-6340   (BR)
COMMISSION SCOLAIRE DES DRAVEURS
POLYVALENTE LE CARREFOUR
50 Ch De La Savane, Gatineau, QC, J8T 3N2
(819) 568-9012
Emp Here 40
SIC 8211 Elementary and secondary schools

D-U-N-S 24-975-7352   (BR)
COMMISSION SCOLAIRE DES DRAVEURS
ECOLE DU NOUVEAU MONDE
25 Rue Saint-Arthur, Gatineau, QC, J8T 3C2
(819) 568-0844
Emp Here 51
SIC 8211 Elementary and secondary schools

D-U-N-S 25-240-1260   (BR)
COMMISSION SCOLAIRE DES DRAVEURS
ECOLE LA SOURCE
22 Rue De L'Acadie, Gatineau, QC, J8T 6G8
(819) 568-7861
Emp Here 35
SIC 8211 Elementary and secondary schools

D-U-N-S 24-354-8885   (BR)
COSTCO WHOLESALE CANADA LTD
COSTCO WHOLESALE
(*Suby of* Costco Wholesale Corporation)
1100 Boul Maloney O Bureau 542, Gatineau,
QC, J8T 6G3
(819) 246-4005
Emp Here 400
SIC 5099 Durable goods, nec

D-U-N-S 24-391-5621   (BR)
GOLF TOWN OPERATING LIMITED PART-NERSHIP
GOLF TOWN
91 Boul De La Gappe Bureau B4, Gatineau,
QC, J8T 0B5
(819) 246-6601
Emp Here 25
SIC 5941 Sporting goods and bicycle shops

D-U-N-S 20-509-8226   (BR)
GOUVERNEMENT DE LA PROVINCE DE QUEBEC
AGENCE DE REVENUE DU CANADA
1100 Boul Maloney O Bureau 1600, Gatineau,
QC, J8T 6G3
(819) 994-7739
Emp Here 110
SIC 7389 Business services, nec

D-U-N-S 24-871-4396   (BR)
GROUPE BMTC INC
BRAULT & MARTINEAU
500 Boul De La Gappe, Gatineau, QC, J8T
8A8
(819) 561-5007
Emp Here 80
SIC 5712 Furniture stores

D-U-N-S 20-103-8069   (BR)
GROUPE RESTAURANTS IMVESCOR INC
RESTAURANT MIKES
370 Boul Greber Unite 200, Gatineau, QC,
J8T 5R6
(819) 561-8000
Emp Here 45
SIC 5812 Eating places

D-U-N-S 24-192-0284   (BR)
GROUPE YELLOW INC
CHAUSSURES YELLOW
(*Suby of* Les Placements Yellow Inc)
680 Boul Maloney O, Gatineau, QC, J8T 8K7

Emp Here 21
SIC 5661 Shoe stores

D-U-N-S 25-773-8526   (BR)

HUDSON'S BAY COMPANY
1100 Boul Maloney O, Gatineau, QC, J8T 6G3
(819) 243-7036
SIC 5311 Department stores

D-U-N-S 25-026-2672   (SL)
LOEB CLUB PLUS GILLES DIONNE INC
900 Boul Maloney O, Gatineau, QC, J8T 3R6
(514) 243-5231
Emp Here 145   *Sales* 52,754,000
SIC 5141 Groceries, general line
Genl Mgr Guy Raymond

D-U-N-S 20-249-4329   (BR)
MAGASIN LAURA (P.V.) INC
LAURA - LAURA PETITES - LAURA PLUS
1076 Boul Maloney O, Gatineau, QC, J8T 3R6
(819) 561-8071
Emp Here 150
SIC 5651 Family clothing stores

D-U-N-S 25-310-9912   (BR)
**MCDONALD'S   RESTAURANTS   OF
CANADA LIMITED**
MCDONALD'S # 8114
(*Suby of* McDonald's Corporation)
80 Boul Greber, Gatineau, QC, J8T 3P8
(819) 561-1436
Emp Here 120
SIC 5812 Eating places

D-U-N-S 25-311-0506   (BR)
**MCDONALD'S   RESTAURANTS   OF
CANADA LIMITED**
MCDONALD'S #8486
(*Suby of* McDonald's Corporation)
640 Boul Maloney O, Gatineau, QC, J8T 8K7
(819) 246-8202
Emp Here 50
SIC 5812 Eating places

D-U-N-S 25-812-5582   (BR)
METRO RICHELIEU INC
SUPER C
720 Boul Maloney O, Gatineau, QC, J8T 8K7
(819) 243-5117
Emp Here 100
SIC 5411 Grocery stores

D-U-N-S 24-003-4418   (BR)
NAUTILUS PLUS INC
NAUTILUS PLUS GATINEAU
920 Boul Maloney O, Gatineau, QC, J8T 3R6
(819) 561-6555
Emp Here 20
SIC 7997 Membership sports and recreation
clubs

D-U-N-S 24-798-3971   (BR)
PVH CANADA, INC
75 Boul De La Gappe, Gatineau, QC, J8T 0B5
(819) 561-0630
Emp Here 25
SIC 5136 Men's and boy's clothing

D-U-N-S 25-836-3258   (BR)
PAGEAU, MOREL & ASSOCIES INC
365 Boul Greber Bureau 302, Gatineau, QC,
J8T 5R3
(819) 776-4665
Emp Here 20
SIC 8711 Engineering services

D-U-N-S 24-270-1555   (BR)
PRISZM LP
PFK GREBER
164 Boul Greber, Gatineau, QC, J8T 6K2
(819) 561-2663
Emp Here 30
SIC 5812 Eating places

D-U-N-S 24-104-0153   (SL)
PROMENADES DE L'OUTAOUAIS LTD, LES
1100 Boul Maloney O, Gatineau, QC, J8T 6G3
(819) 205-1340
Emp Here 50   *Sales* 4,596,524
SIC 6512 Nonresidential building operators

D-U-N-S 20-288-1827   (BR)
PROVIGO DISTRIBUTION INC
MAXI & CIE
800 Boul Maloney O, Gatineau, QC, J8T 3R6
(819) 561-9244
Emp Here 100
SIC 5499 Miscellaneous food stores

D-U-N-S 24-701-1971   (BR)
PROVIGO DISTRIBUTION INC
PROVIGO
25 Ch De La Savane, Gatineau, QC, J8T 8A4
(819) 243-3149
Emp Here 27
SIC 5411 Grocery stores

D-U-N-S 25-827-6377   (BR)
PROVIGO DISTRIBUTION INC
LOBLAW'S
800 Boul Maloney O, Gatineau, QC, J8T 3R6
(819) 561-9244
Emp Here 150
SIC 5411 Grocery stores

D-U-N-S 25-300-6027   (BR)
REDBERRY FRANCHISING CORP
BURGER KING
104 Boul Greber, Gatineau, QC, J8T 3P8
(819) 568-5159
Emp Here 30
SIC 5812 Eating places

D-U-N-S 25-784-6436   (BR)
TOMMY & LEFEBVRE INC
530 Boul De La Gappe, Gatineau, QC, J8T
8A8

Emp Here 20
SIC 5941 Sporting goods and bicycle shops

D-U-N-S 20-518-6278   (BR)
**TURQUOISE, CABINET EN ASSURANCE
DE DOMMAGES INC, LA**
LA TURQUOISE
500 Boul Greber Bureau 103, Gatineau, QC,
J8T 7W3
(819) 243-3211
Emp Here 40
SIC 6411 Insurance agents, brokers, and ser-
vice

D-U-N-S 25-886-0154   (BR)
WSP CANADA INC
GENIVAR
500 Greber Blvd, Gatineau, QC, J8T 7W3
(819) 243-2827
Emp Here 20
SIC 8711 Engineering services

D-U-N-S 20-555-7916   (BR)
WAL-MART CANADA CORP
WALMART
640 Boul Maloney O, Gatineau, QC, J8T 8K7
(819) 246-8808
Emp Here 350
SIC 5311 Department stores

D-U-N-S 24-606-2082   (BR)
WAL-MART CANADA CORP
51 Boul De La Gappe Bureau 1086, Gatineau,
QC, J8T 0B5
(819) 246-4633
Emp Here 40
SIC 5311 Department stores

Gatineau, QC J8V
Hull County

D-U-N-S 20-276-6239   (SL)
3130606 CANADA INC
SERVICES A DOMICILE DE L'OUTAOUAIS
203-492 Boul De L'Hopital, Gatineau, QC, J8V
2P4
(819) 561-0911
Emp Here 50   *Sales* 2,334,742

SIC 8059 Nursing and personal care, nec

D-U-N-S 20-712-5464   (BR)
COMMISSION SCOLAIRE DES DRAVEURS
POLYVALENTE DE L'ERABLIERE
500 Rue De Cannes Bureau 542, Gatineau,
QC, J8V 1J6
(819) 561-2320
Emp Here 50
SIC 8211 Elementary and secondary schools

D-U-N-S 20-712-5498   (BR)
COMMISSION SCOLAIRE DES DRAVEURS
ECOLE DE L'ENVOLEE
299 Rue Ernest-Gaboury, Gatineau, QC, J8V
2P8
(819) 568-5764
Emp Here 50
SIC 8211 Elementary and secondary schools

D-U-N-S 20-712-5506   (BR)
COMMISSION SCOLAIRE DES DRAVEURS
ECOLE DU VALLON
88 Rue De Cannes, Gatineau, QC, J8V 2M4
(819) 246-1992
Emp Here 32
SIC 8211 Elementary and secondary schools

D-U-N-S 25-233-5609   (BR)
COMMISSION SCOLAIRE DES DRAVEURS
ECOLE MASSE
1 Rue Saint-Alexandre, Gatineau, QC, J8V
1A8
(819) 561-3313
Emp Here 60
SIC 8211 Elementary and secondary schools

D-U-N-S 20-806-9844   (BR)
COUCHE-TARD INC
730 Boul Du Mont-Royal, Gatineau, QC, J8V
2S3
(819) 243-7686
Emp Here 25
SIC 5411 Grocery stores

D-U-N-S 24-946-1393   (SL)
LASANTE CONSEIL INC
430 Boul De L'Hopital Bureau 102, Gatineau,
QC, J8V 1T7
(819) 776-9107
Emp Here 50   *Sales* 9,746,560
SIC 5912 Drug stores and proprietary stores
Pr Pr Jean Dumont

D-U-N-S 25-886-2614   (BR)
**MCDONALD'S   RESTAURANTS   OF
CANADA LIMITED**
RESTAURANT MCDONALD'S
(*Suby of* McDonald's Corporation)
2335 Rue Saint-Louis Bureau 3, Gatineau,
QC, J8V 1J2
(819) 246-3221
Emp Here 45
SIC 5812 Eating places

D-U-N-S 24-818-8570   (BR)
RELANCE OUTAOUAIS INC, LA
(*Suby of* Relance Outaouais Inc, La)
700 Boul Greber, Gatineau, QC, J8V 3P8
(819) 243-5237
Emp Here 30
SIC 8399 Social services, nec

Gatineau, QC J8X
Hull County

D-U-N-S 24-308-7223   (SL)
9132-1554 QUEBEC INC
PLAZA LACHAUDIERE
2 Rue Montcalm, Gatineau, QC, J8X 4B4
(819) 778-3880
Emp Here 70   *Sales* 2,115,860
SIC 5812 Eating places

D-U-N-S 20-291-1749   (BR)
CAISSE DESJARDINS DE HULL-AYLMER

CENTRE DE SERVICES ILE DE HULL
30 Rue Victoria Bureau 100, Gatineau, QC,
J8X 0A8
(819) 776-3000
Emp Here 20
SIC 6062 State credit unions

D-U-N-S 24-334-6553   (BR)
CENTRE DE SANTE ET DE SERVICES SO-
CIAUX DE GATINEAU
CENTRE D'HEBERGEMENT LA PIETA
273 Rue Laurier, Gatineau, QC, J8X 3W8
(819) 966-6420
Emp Here 300
SIC 8062 General medical and surgical hospi-
tals

D-U-N-S 24-011-7353   (BR)
FONDATION DE LA COMMISSION SCO-
LAIRE DES PORTAGES-DE-L'OUTAOUAIS
FONDATION DE LA COMMISSION SCO-
LAIRE DES PORTAGES-D
39 Rue Saint-Florent, Gatineau, QC, J8X 2Z8
(819) 771-8478
Emp Here 65
SIC 8211 Elementary and secondary schools

D-U-N-S 25-240-1500   (BR)
FONDATION DE LA COMMISSION SCO-
LAIRE DES PORTAGES-DE-L'OUTAOUAIS
FONDATION DE LA COMMISSION SCO-
LAIRE DES PORTAGES-D
255 Rue Saint-Redempteur, Gatineau, QC,
J8X 2T4
(819) 771-6126
Emp Here 130
SIC 8211 Elementary and secondary schools

D-U-N-S 25-234-0856   (BR)
FONDATION DE LA COMMISSION SCO-
LAIRE DES PORTAGES-DE-L'OUTAOUAIS
FONDATION DE LA COMMISSION SCO-
LAIRE DES PORTAGES-D
170 Rue Papineau, Gatineau, QC, J8X 1V9
(819) 777-2818
Emp Here 35
SIC 8211 Elementary and secondary schools

D-U-N-S 24-437-0649   (BR)
GOUVERNEMENT DE LA PROVINCE DE
QUEBEC
GOUVERNEMENT DE LA PROVINCE DE
QUEBEC
105 Boul Sacre-Coeur Bureau 1, Gatineau,
QC, J8X 1C5
(819) 771-6631
Emp Here 465
SIC 8322 Individual and family services

D-U-N-S 24-049-2822   (BR)
GOUVERNEMENT DE LA PROVINCE DE
QUEBEC
CENTRE D'EMPLOIE LOCAL DE HULL
170 Rue De L'Hotel-De-Ville, Gatineau, QC,
J8X 4C2

Emp Here 40
SIC 8322 Individual and family services

D-U-N-S 20-584-3738   (BR)
GOUVERNEMENT DE LA PROVINCE DE
QUEBEC
MINISTERE DE LA JUSTICE
17 Rue Laurier Bureau 1460, Gatineau, QC,
J8X 4C1
(819) 776-8110
Emp Here 60
SIC 7338 Secretarial and court reporting

D-U-N-S 25-305-3052   (BR)
INNVEST PROPERTIES CORP
BEST WESTERN
(Suby of Innvest Properties Corp)
131 Rue Laurier, Gatineau, QC, J8X 3W3
(819) 770-8550
Emp Here 50
SIC 7011 Hotels and motels

D-U-N-S 20-861-2460   (BR)
KSD ENTERPRISES LTD
FOUR POINTS BY SHERATON HOTEL &
CONFERENCE CENTER
(Suby of KSD Enterprises Ltd)
35 Rue Laurier, Gatineau, QC, J8X 4E9
(819) 778-6111
Emp Here 65
SIC 7011 Hotels and motels

D-U-N-S 24-378-4233   (BR)
KRUGER PRODUCTS L.P.
20 Rue Laurier, Gatineau, QC, J8X 4H3
(819) 595-5302
Emp Here 480
SIC 2621 Paper mills

D-U-N-S 24-226-9913   (BR)
PUBLIC SERVICES AND PROCUREMENT
CANADA
SERVICE CANADA
140 Prom Du Portage Bureau 4, Gatineau,
QC, J8X 4B6

Emp Here 50
SIC 8111 Legal services

D-U-N-S 24-356-8180   (BR)
RELANCE OUTAOUAIS INC, LA
(Suby of Relance Outaouais Inc, La)
45 Boul Sacre-Coeur, Gatineau, QC, J8X 1C6
(819) 776-5870
Emp Here 150
SIC 8399 Social services, nec

D-U-N-S 24-072-7607   (BR)
SOCIETE DES ALCOOLS DU QUEBEC
S A Q DEPOT
210 Rue Champlain, Gatineau, QC, J8X 3R5
(819) 777-1955
Emp Here 40
SIC 5921 Liquor stores

D-U-N-S 20-585-1384   (BR)
VILLE DE GATINEAU
CENTRE ROBERT GUERTIN
125 Rue De Carillon, Gatineau, QC, J8X 2P8
(819) 595-7700
Emp Here 60
SIC 7999 Amusement and recreation, nec

Gatineau, QC J8Y
Hull County

D-U-N-S 20-103-7186   (BR)
2786591 CANADA INC
MULTI PRETS HYPOTHEQUES
251 Boul Saint-Joseph Bureau 2, Gatineau,
QC, J8Y 3X5
(819) 775-2590
Emp Here 25
SIC 6162 Mortgage bankers and loan correspondents

D-U-N-S 25-103-8618   (SL)
3243753 CANADA INC
PROVANCE
490 Boul Saint-Joseph Bureau 203, Gatineau,
QC, J8Y 3Y7
(819) 568-8787
Emp Here 40   Sales 3,648,035
SIC 7379 Computer related services, nec

D-U-N-S 24-001-3776   (BR)
AGENCE DE PLACEMENT HELENE ROY
LTEE
266 Boul Saint-Joseph Bureau 200, Gatineau,
QC, J8Y 3X9
(819) 771-7333
Emp Here 50
SIC 7361 Employment agencies

D-U-N-S 20-252-9038   (SL)
ASCENTIUM INC
SMITH

(Suby of Ascentium Corporation)
490 Boul Saint-Joseph Bureau 300, Gatineau,
QC, J8Y 3Y7
(819) 778-0313
Emp Here 50   Sales 5,399,092
SIC 4899 Communication services, nec
Pr Anthony Steel
Sec Fabrizio Dicarlantonio
Treas Colleen Mc Cann - Lillie

D-U-N-S 20-646-9731   (BR)
ASTRAL MEDIA RADIO INC
ENERGIE 14.1
(Suby of Astral Media Radio Inc)
15 Rue Taschereau, Gatineau, QC, J8Y 2V6
(819) 243-5555
Emp Here 43
SIC 6794 Patent owners and lessors

D-U-N-S 25-281-9842   (BR)
BANK OF MONTREAL
SUCCURSALE LES GALERIES DE HULL
320 Boul Saint-Joseph Bureau 348, Gatineau,
QC, J8Y 3Y8
(819) 775-7930
Emp Here 20
SIC 6021 National commercial banks

D-U-N-S 20-589-4749   (BR)
BANQUE TORONTO-DOMINION, LA
TD CANADA TRUST
(Suby of Toronto-Dominion Bank, The)
349 Boul Saint-Joseph, Gatineau, QC, J8Y
3Z4
(819) 770-5672
Emp Here 20
SIC 6021 National commercial banks

D-U-N-S 20-563-3311   (BR)
BELLAI BROTHERS CONSTRUCTION LTD
BELLAI CANADA
30 Rue Adrien-Robert, Gatineau, QC, J8Y
3S2
(819) 771-7704
Emp Here 30
SIC 1771 Concrete work

D-U-N-S 20-323-4455   (BR)
CAISSE DESJARDINS DE HULL-AYLMER
CENTRE FINANCIER AUX ENTREPRISES
DE L'OUTAOUAIS
880 Boul De La Carriere Bureau 100,
Gatineau, QC, J8Y 6T5
(819) 778-1400
Emp Here 62
SIC 6062 State credit unions

D-U-N-S 20-715-9117   (BR)
COCA-COLA REFRESHMENTS CANADA
COMPANY
(Suby of The Coca-Cola Company)
885 Boul De La Carriere Bureau 1, Gatineau,
QC, J8Y 6S6
(819) 770-8877
Emp Here 50
SIC 5149 Groceries and related products, nec

D-U-N-S 20-127-3385   (HQ)
COLLEGE PREUNIVERSITAIRE NOU-
VELLES FRONTIERES
SECTION COLLEGIALE
(Suby of College Preuniversitaire Nouvelles
Frontieres)
250 Rue Gamelin, Gatineau, QC, J8Y 1W9
(819) 561-8922
Emp Here 45   Emp Total 50
Sales 3,356,192
SIC 8211 Elementary and secondary schools

D-U-N-S 20-126-7452   (BR)
COMMISSION SCOLAIRE WESTERN QUE-
BEC
EDUCATION ADULT CENTRE HULL
(Suby of Commission Scolaire Western Que-
bec)
185 Rue Archambault, Gatineau, QC, J8Y 5E3
(819) 595-1226
Emp Here 35

SIC 8211 Elementary and secondary schools

D-U-N-S 25-023-9944   (BR)
CONSTRUCTION DJL INC
20 Rue Emile-Bond, Gatineau, QC, J8Y 3M7
(819) 770-2300
Emp Here 75
SIC 1611 Highway and street construction

D-U-N-S 24-103-5427   (BR)
CONSULTANTS AECOM INC
AECOM TECSULT
228 Boul Saint-Joseph Bureau 303, Gatineau,
QC, J8Y 3X4
(819) 777-1630
Emp Here 20
SIC 8711 Engineering services

D-U-N-S 24-634-0418   (SL)
DENIS CROTEAU INC
L'AUBAINERIE
9 Boul Montclair Bureau 19, Gatineau, QC,
J8Y 2E2
(819) 770-6886
Emp Here 60   Sales 3,648,035
SIC 5651 Family clothing stores

D-U-N-S 20-712-5332   (BR)
FONDATION DE LA COMMISSION SCO-
LAIRE DES PORTAGES-DE-L'OUTAOUAIS
FONDATION DE LA COMMISSION SCO-
LAIRE DES PORTAGES-D
249 Boul De La Cite-Des-Jeunes, Gatineau,
QC, J8Y 6L2
(819) 771-0863
Emp Here 50
SIC 8211 Elementary and secondary schools

D-U-N-S 20-797-7724   (BR)
FONDATION DE LA COMMISSION SCO-
LAIRE DES PORTAGES-DE-L'OUTAOUAIS
FONDATION DE LA COMMISSION SCO-
LAIRE DES PORTAGES-D
35 Rue Davies, Gatineau, QC, J8Y 4S8
(819) 771-2503
Emp Here 35
SIC 8211 Elementary and secondary schools

D-U-N-S 24-011-7361   (BR)
FONDATION DE LA COMMISSION SCO-
LAIRE DES PORTAGES-DE-L'OUTAOUAIS
FONDATION DE LA COMMISSION SCO-
LAIRE DES PORTAGES-D
15 Rue Doucet, Gatineau, QC, J8Y 5N4
(819) 771-8531
Emp Here 25
SIC 8211 Elementary and secondary schools

D-U-N-S 25-240-1310   (BR)
FONDATION DE LA COMMISSION SCO-
LAIRE DES PORTAGES-DE-L'OUTAOUAIS
FONDATION DE LA COMMISSION SCO-
LAIRE DES PORTAGES-D
4 Rue Camille-Gay, Gatineau, QC, J8Y 2K5
(819) 777-6889
Emp Here 50
SIC 8231 Libraries

D-U-N-S 20-712-5308   (BR)
FONDATION DE LA COMMISSION SCO-
LAIRE DES PORTAGES-DE-L'OUTAOUAIS
FONDATION DE LA COMMISSION SCO-
LAIRE DES PORTAGES-D
71 Rue Saint-Jean-Bosco, Gatineau, QC, J8Y
3G5
(819) 777-8662
Emp Here 50
SIC 8211 Elementary and secondary schools

D-U-N-S 20-712-5290   (BR)
FONDATION DE LA COMMISSION SCO-
LAIRE DES PORTAGES-DE-L'OUTAOUAIS
FONDATION DE LA COMMISSION SCO-
LAIRE DES PORTAGES-D
30 Boul Saint-Raymond, Gatineau, QC, J8Y
1R6

Emp Here 50

SIC 8299 Schools and educational services, nec

D-U-N-S 25-234-0930   (BR)
FONDATION DE LA COMMISSION SCO-LAIRE DES PORTAGES-DE-L'OUTAOUAIS
FONDATION DE LA COMMISSION SCO-LAIRE DES PORTAGES-D
45 Rue Boucher, Gatineau, QC, J8Y 6G2
(819) 777-5921
Emp Here 50
SIC 8211 Elementary and secondary schools

D-U-N-S 25-845-7894   (SL)
GAGNE, ISABELLE, PATRY, LAFLAMME & ASSOCIES NOTAIRES INC
188 Rue Montcalm Bureau 300, Gatineau, QC, J8Y 3E5
(819) 771-3231
Emp Here 50   *Sales* 2,626,585
SIC 7389 Business services, nec

D-U-N-S 20-102-7740   (BR)
GOUVERNEMENT DE LA PROVINCE DE QUEBEC
COMISSION DE LA SANTE ET DE LA SECU-RITE
15 Rue Garnelin, Gatineau, QC, J8Y 6N5
(819) 778-8600
Emp Here 75
SIC 6331 Fire, marine, and casualty insurance

D-U-N-S 20-914-7870   (BR)
GOUVERNEMENT DE LA PROVINCE DE QUEBEC
CSSSG
116 Boul Lionel-Emond, Gatineau, QC, J8Y 1W7

Emp Here 2,000
SIC 8062 General medical and surgical hospitals

D-U-N-S 24-348-1830   (BR)
GOUVERNEMENT DE LA PROVINCE DE QUEBEC
QUEBEC AIDE JURIDIQUE
768 Boul Saint-Joseph Unite 210, Gatineau, QC, J8Y 4B8
(819) 772-3013
Emp Here 20
SIC 8111 Legal services

D-U-N-S 24-653-2394   (BR)
GOUVERNEMENT DE LA PROVINCE DE QUEBEC
CENTRE READAPTATION LA RESSOURSE
135 Boul Saint-Raymond, Gatineau, QC, J8Y 6X7
(819) 777-6261
Emp Here 300
SIC 8011 Offices and clinics of medical doctors

D-U-N-S 25-876-5957   (BR)
GOUVERNEMENT DE LA PROVINCE DE QUEBEC
COOPERATIVE   FUNERAIRE   DE L'OUTAOUAIS
95 Boul De La Cite-Des-Jeunes, Gatineau, QC, J8Y 6X3
(819) 778-2425
Emp Here 30
SIC 7261 Funeral service and crematories

D-U-N-S 25-801-0933   (BR)
INVESTORS GROUP FINANCIAL SER-VICES INC
INVESTORS GROUP FINANCIAL SER-VICES
228 Boul Saint-Joseph Bureau 400, Gatineau, QC, J8Y 3X4
(819) 243-6497
Emp Here 35
SIC 6282 Investment advice

D-U-N-S 25-448-3803   (BR)
MEDIAS TRANSCONTINENTAL INC

MEDIAS TRANSCONTINENTAL INC
130 Rue Adrien-Robert, Gatineau, QC, J8Y 3S2
(819) 777-6045
Emp Here 50
SIC 7389 Business services, nec

D-U-N-S 25-812-5574   (BR)
METRO RICHELIEU INC
SUPER C
725a Boul De La Carriere, Gatineau, QC, J8Y 6T9
(819) 595-1344
Emp Here 125
SIC 5411 Grocery stores

D-U-N-S 20-262-2119   (BR)
NAUTILUS PLUS INC
425 Boul Saint-Joseph Bureau 64, Gatineau, QC, J8Y 3Z8
(819) 420-4646
Emp Here 40
SIC 5941 Sporting goods and bicycle shops

D-U-N-S 24-589-0876   (BR)
PCI GEOMATICS ENTERPRISES INC
490 Boul Saint-Joseph Unite 400, Gatineau, QC, J8Y 3Y7
(819) 770-0022
Emp Here 40
SIC 7371 Custom computer programming services

D-U-N-S 25-025-8563   (BR)
PROVIGO DISTRIBUTION INC
PROVIGO MONT BLEU
775 Boul Saint-Joseph, Gatineau, QC, J8Y 4C1
(819) 771-7701
Emp Here 75
SIC 5411 Grocery stores

D-U-N-S 24-270-0615   (BR)
RAYMOND CHABOT GRANT THORNTON S.E.N.C.R.L.
15 Rue Gamelin Bureau 400, Gatineau, QC, J8Y 6N5
(819) 770-9833
Emp Here 30
SIC 8721 Accounting, auditing, and book-keeping

D-U-N-S 20-913-9083   (BR)
REDBERRY FRANCHISING CORP
BURGER KING
650 Boul Saint-Joseph, Gatineau, QC, J8Y 4A8

Emp Here 20
SIC 5812 Eating places

D-U-N-S 25-447-9322   (BR)
REVERA INC
MANOIR GATINEAU
100 Boul De La Cite-Des-Jeunes Bureau 218, Gatineau, QC, J8Y 6T6
(819) 778-6070
Emp Here 20
SIC 8361 Residential care

D-U-N-S 24-016-3209   (BR)
ROTISSERIE NOJO INC
BENNY & CO
(*Suby of* Rotisserie Nojo Inc)
531 Boul Saint-Joseph, Gatineau, QC, J8Y 4A1
(819) 778-0880
Emp Here 27
SIC 5812 Eating places

D-U-N-S 25-118-1835   (BR)
SEARS CANADA INC
320 Boul Saint-Joseph Bureau 1, Gatineau, QC, J8Y 3Y9
(819) 776-4187
Emp Here 150
SIC 5311 Department stores

D-U-N-S 24-676-4971   (HQ)

SERVICE DE PNEUS LAVOIE OUTAOUAIS INC
G.O. EQUIPEMENT / VENTES & SERVICE
(*Suby of* 6809421 Canada Inc)
27 Rue Mangin, Gatineau, QC, J8Y 3L8
(819) 568-2161
Emp Here 20   *Emp Total* 78
Sales 43,312,550
SIC 5014 Tires and tubes
Pr Normand Lavoie
VP Pierre Tremblay

D-U-N-S 24-470-8371   (BR)
SOCIETE DES CASINOS DU QUEBEC INC, LA
RESTAURANT AROME
3 Boul Du Casino, Gatineau, QC, J8Y 6X4
(819) 790-6410
Emp Here 20
SIC 5812 Eating places

D-U-N-S 20-291-0204   (BR)
SOLOTECH QUEBEC INC
79 Rue Cremazie, Gatineau, QC, J8Y 3P1
(819) 777-3681
Emp Here 25
SIC 5099 Durable goods, nec

D-U-N-S 25-316-7811   (BR)
SUN LIFE ASSURANCE COMPANY OF CANADA
15 Rue Gamelin Bureau 601, Gatineau, QC, J8Y 6N5
(819) 771-6208
Emp Here 20
SIC 6311 Life insurance

D-U-N-S 25-002-2308   (BR)
UNIVERSITE DU QUEBEC
UNIVERSITE DU QUEBEC EN OUTOUAIS
101 Rue Saint-Jean-Bosco Bureau B0150, Gatineau, QC, J8Y 3G5
(819) 595-3900
Emp Here 40
SIC 8221 Colleges and universities

Gatineau, QC J8Z
Hull County

D-U-N-S 20-211-6880   (BR)
ALSTOM CANADA INC
(*Suby of* General Electric Company)
60 Rue Jean-Proulx, Gatineau, QC, J8Z 1W1

Emp Here 50
SIC 3443 Fabricated plate work (boiler shop)

D-U-N-S 24-104-4478   (HQ)
CENTRE DE TRAVAIL LARO INC
(*Suby of* Centre De Travail Laro Inc)
179 Rue Deveault, Gatineau, QC, J8Z 1S7
(819) 770-6434
Emp Here 20   *Emp Total* 80
Sales 3,793,956
SIC 8331 Job training and related services

D-U-N-S 25-893-7937   (BR)
CENTRES JEUNESSE DE L'OUTAOUAIS, LES
COMPLEXE HERITAGE
(*Suby of* Centres Jeunesse de l'Outaouais, Les)
155 Ch Freeman, Gatineau, QC, J8Z 2A7
(819) 778-2099
Emp Here 50
SIC 8322 Individual and family services

D-U-N-S 25-773-3717   (BR)
CLUBLINK CORPORATION ULC
CLUB DE GOLF HAUTES PLAINES
(*Suby of* TWC Enterprises Limited)
75 Av De La Citadelle, Gatineau, QC, J8Z 3L1
(819) 772-9219
Emp Here 50
SIC 7992 Public golf courses

D-U-N-S 25-240-4009   (BR)
COMMISSION SCOLAIRE WESTERN QUE-BEC
PHILEMON WRIGHT HIGH SCHOOL
(*Suby of* Commission Scolaire Western Quebec)
80 Rue Daniel-Johnson, Gatineau, QC, J8Z 1S3
(819) 776-3158
Emp Here 60
SIC 8211 Elementary and secondary schools

D-U-N-S 24-885-0468   (BR)
EXP SERVICES INC
170 Rue Deveault Bureau 100, Gatineau, QC, J8Z 1S6
(819) 777-0332
Emp Here 35
SIC 8711 Engineering services

D-U-N-S 25-295-2635   (BR)
ENBRIDGE ENERGY DISTRIBUTION INC
71a Rue Jean-Proulx, Gatineau, QC, J8Z 1W2
(819) 771-8321
Emp Here 50
SIC 4924 Natural gas distribution

D-U-N-S 25-365-5385   (BR)
FONDATION DE LA COMMISSION SCO-LAIRE DES PORTAGES-DE-L'OUTAOUAIS
FONDATION DE LA COMMISSION SCO-LAIRE DES PORTAGES-D
389 Boul De La Cite-Des-Jeunes Bureau 3, Gatineau, QC, J8Z 1W6
(819) 771-7131
Emp Here 120
SIC 8211 Elementary and secondary schools

D-U-N-S 25-233-8348   (BR)
FONDATION DE LA COMMISSION SCO-LAIRE DES PORTAGES-DE-L'OUTAOUAIS
FONDATION DE LA COMMISSION SCO-LAIRE DES PORTAGES-D
40 Rue Du Dome, Gatineau, QC, J8Z 3J4
(819) 595-5125
Emp Here 40
SIC 8211 Elementary and secondary schools

D-U-N-S 24-383-0767   (BR)
GROUPE ROBERT INC
TRANSPORT ROBERT
1040 Boul Saint-Joseph, Gatineau, QC, J8Z 1T3
(819) 771-8311
Emp Here 20
SIC 4213 Trucking, except local

D-U-N-S 20-787-9693   (BR)
HEWITT EQUIPEMENT LIMITEE
CATERPILLAR
61 Rue Jean-Proulx, Gatineau, QC, J8Z 1W2
(819) 770-1601
Emp Here 29
SIC 6159 Miscellaneous business credit institutions

D-U-N-S 25-309-6978   (BR)
INDUSTRIELLE ALLIANCE, ASSURANCE ET SERVICES FINANCIERS INC
NATIONAL LIFE ASSURANCE COMPANY
1160 Boul Saint-Joseph Unite 101, Gatineau, QC, J8Z 1T3
(819) 771-6645
Emp Here 30
SIC 6411 Insurance agents, brokers, and service

D-U-N-S 24-373-7363   (SL)
INFOVISTA CANADA INC
71 Rue Jean-Proulx, Gatineau, QC, J8Z 1W2
(819) 483-7000
Emp Here 50   *Sales* 3,648,035
SIC 7361 Employment agencies

D-U-N-S 25-497-3548   (BR)
MATERIAUX BONHOMME INC
921 Boul Saint-Joseph, Gatineau, QC, J8Z 1S8

(819) 595-2772
Emp Here 25
SIC 5211 Lumber and other building materials

D-U-N-S 24-270-4716 (BR)
RNC MEDIA INC
CHOTV CFGSTV
171a Rue Jean-Proulx Bureau 5, Gatineau, QC, J8Z 1W5
(819) 503-9711
Emp Here 80
SIC 4833 Television broadcasting stations

D-U-N-S 24-269-3679 (SL)
SPORTHEQUE DE HULL INC
72 Rue Jean-Proulx, Gatineau, QC, J8Z 1W1

Emp Here 70 Sales 2,845,467
SIC 7991 Physical fitness facilities

D-U-N-S 25-010-9659 (BR)
WELCH LLP
LEVESQUE, MARCHAND WELCH & COMPANY
975 Boul Saint-Joseph Bureau 201, Gatineau, QC, J8Z 1W8
(819) 771-7381
Emp Here 23
SIC 8721 Accounting, auditing, and bookkeeping

D-U-N-S 24-799-6622 (SL)
WILFRID POIRIER LTEE
PIECES D'AUTO EXPERT
(Suby of Advance Auto Parts, Inc.)
165 Rue Jean-Proulx Bureau 1, Gatineau, QC, J8Z 1T4

Emp Here 26 Sales 3,137,310
SIC 5013 Motor vehicle supplies and new parts

Gatineau, QC J9A
Hull County

D-U-N-S 20-309-6557 (SL)
6861083 CANADA INC
S3
53 Rue Du Blizzard, Gatineau, QC, J9A 0C8
(819) 777-2222
Emp Here 50 Sales 5,690,935
SIC 5091 Sporting and recreation goods
Pr Pierre Champagne
VP Roch Carpentier

D-U-N-S 20-291-1731 (BR)
CAISSE DESJARDINS DE HULL-AYLMER
CENTRE DE SERVICES DU PLATEAU
219 Boul Du Plateau, Gatineau, QC, J9A 0N4
(819) 776-3000
Emp Here 225
SIC 6062 State credit unions

D-U-N-S 25-893-7911 (BR)
CENTRES JEUNESSE DE L'OUTAOUAIS, LES
MAISON DE L'APPRENTI
(Suby of Centres Jeunesse de l'Outaouais, Les)
452 Boul Alexandre-Tache, Gatineau, QC, J9A 1M7
(819) 778-1813
Emp Here 50
SIC 8322 Individual and family services

D-U-N-S 20-166-0920 (BR)
FONDATION DE LA COMMISSION SCOLAIRE DES PORTAGES-DE-L'OUTAOUAIS
FONDATION DE LA COMMISSION SCOLAIRE DES PORTAGES-D
145 Rue De L'Atmosphere, Gatineau, QC, J9A 3G3
(819) 772-2694
Emp Here 40
SIC 8211 Elementary and secondary schools

D-U-N-S 25-234-0898 (BR)
FONDATION DE LA COMMISSION SCOLAIRE DES PORTAGES-DE-L'OUTAOUAIS
FONDATION DE LA COMMISSION SCOLAIRE DES PORTAGES-D
360 Ch De Lucerne, Gatineau, QC, J9A 1A7
(819) 777-9353
Emp Here 40
SIC 8211 Elementary and secondary schools

D-U-N-S 20-709-4694 (SL)
GESTION VALMIRA INC
MCDONALD'S
25 Rue De L'Embellie, Gatineau, QC, J9A 3K3
(819) 595-4989
Emp Here 100 Sales 2,991,389
SIC 5812 Eating places

D-U-N-S 20-704-8567 (BR)
METRO RICHELIEU INC
SUPER C
65 Boul Du Plateau, Gatineau, QC, J9A 3G1
(819) 772-2230
Emp Here 55
SIC 5411 Grocery stores

D-U-N-S 20-548-3584 (BR)
PROVIGO DISTRIBUTION INC
LOBLAWS
1 Boul Du Plateau, Gatineau, QC, J9A 3G1
(819) 777-2747
Emp Here 170
SIC 5411 Grocery stores

D-U-N-S 25-498-9395 (BR)
STAPLES CANADA INC
BUREAU EN GROS
(Suby of Staples, Inc.)
55a Boul Du Plateau, Gatineau, QC, J9A 3G1
(819) 770-2332
Emp Here 45
SIC 5943 Stationery stores

D-U-N-S 24-267-8373 (BR)
UNIVERSITE DU QUEBEC
PAVILLON ALEXANDRE TACHE
283 Boul Alexandre-Tache, Gatineau, QC, J9A 1L8
(819) 595-3900
Emp Here 300
SIC 8221 Colleges and universities

D-U-N-S 20-003-4770 (BR)
WAL-MART CANADA CORP
WALMART
35 Boul Du Plateau, Gatineau, QC, J9A 3G1
(819) 772-1911
Emp Here 150
SIC 5311 Department stores

D-U-N-S 24-312-4323 (BR)
WINNERS MERCHANTS INTERNATIONAL L.P.
WINNERS
(Suby of The TJX Companies Inc)
129 Boul Du Plateau, Gatineau, QC, J9A 3G1
(819) 966-0120
Emp Here 30
SIC 5651 Family clothing stores

Gatineau, QC J9H
Hull County

D-U-N-S 20-589-4665 (BR)
BANQUE TORONTO-DOMINION, LA
TD CANADA TRUST
(Suby of Toronto-Dominion Bank, The)
181 Rue Principale Bureau A7, Gatineau, QC, J9H 6A6
(819) 682-5375
Emp Here 20
SIC 6021 National commercial banks

D-U-N-S 20-788-0626 (SL)
CLUB DE GOLF ROYAL OTTAWA, LE

1405 Ch D'Aylmer, Gatineau, QC, J9H 7L2
(819) 777-3866
Emp Here 50 Sales 2,042,900
SIC 7997 Membership sports and recreation clubs

D-U-N-S 20-103-6287 (BR)
COMMISSION SCOLAIRE WESTERN QUEBEC
WESTERN QUEBEC CAREER CENTRE
(Suby of Commission Scolaire Western Quebec)
100 Av Frank-Robinson, Gatineau, QC, J9H 4A6
(819) 684-1770
Emp Here 30
SIC 8211 Elementary and secondary schools

D-U-N-S 20-101-0266 (BR)
COMMISSION SCOLAIRE WESTERN QUEBEC
AYLMER, LORD SENIOR CAMPUS
(Suby of Commission Scolaire Western Quebec)
116 Av Frank-Robinson, Gatineau, QC, J9H 4A6
(819) 684-6801
Emp Here 40
SIC 8211 Elementary and secondary schools

D-U-N-S 24-339-4074 (BR)
FONDATION DE LA COMMISSION SCOLAIRE DES PORTAGES-DE-L'OUTAOUAIS
ECOLE INTERNATIONALE DU VILLAGE
45 Ch Eardley, Gatineau, QC, J9H 4J9
(819) 685-2611
Emp Here 50
SIC 8211 Elementary and secondary schools

D-U-N-S 20-938-8425 (BR)
FONDATION DE LA COMMISSION SCOLAIRE DES PORTAGES-DE-L'OUTAOUAIS
FONDATION DE LA COMMISSION SCOLAIRE DES PORTAGES-D
100 Rue Broad, Gatineau, QC, J9H 6A9
(819) 682-2557
Emp Here 182
SIC 8211 Elementary and secondary schools

D-U-N-S 20-712-5365 (BR)
FONDATION DE LA COMMISSION SCOLAIRE DES PORTAGES-DE-L'OUTAOUAIS
FONDATION DE LA COMMISSION SCOLAIRE DES PORTAGES-D
113 Ch Vanier, Gatineau, QC, J9H 1Z2
(819) 685-2635
Emp Here 50
SIC 8211 Elementary and secondary schools

D-U-N-S 25-233-8264 (BR)
FONDATION DE LA COMMISSION SCOLAIRE DES PORTAGES-DE-L'OUTAOUAIS
ECOLE DES TROIS PORTAGES
120 Rue Broad, Gatineau, QC, J9H 6W3
(819) 682-2742
Emp Here 30
SIC 8211 Elementary and secondary schools

D-U-N-S 20-712-5324 (BR)
FONDATION DE LA COMMISSION SCOLAIRE DES PORTAGES-DE-L'OUTAOUAIS
FONDATION DE LA COMMISSION SCOLAIRE DES PORTAGES-D
450 Rue Leguerrier, Gatineau, QC, J9H 7J1
(819) 684-0409
Emp Here 20
SIC 8211 Elementary and secondary schools

D-U-N-S 25-233-6193 (BR)
FONDATION DE LA COMMISSION SCOLAIRE DES PORTAGES-DE-L'OUTAOUAIS
FONDATION DE LA COMMISSION SCOLAIRE DES PORTAGES-D
550 Boul Wilfrid-Lavigne, Gatineau, QC, J9H 6L5
(819) 684-0222
Emp Here 44
SIC 8211 Elementary and secondary schools

D-U-N-S 20-555-0531 (BR)
GOUVERNEMENT DE LA PROVINCE DE QUEBEC
GOUVERNEMENT DE LA PROVINCE DE QUEBEC
200 Rue Robert-Wright, Gatineau, QC, J9H 5L1
(819) 684-1022
Emp Here 20
SIC 8399 Social services, nec

D-U-N-S 24-097-6550 (BR)
GOUVERNEMENT DE LA PROVINCE DE QUEBEC
GOUVERNEMENT DE LA PROVINCE DE QUEBEC
200 Rue Robert-Wright, Gatineau, QC, J9H 5L1
(819) 685-1313
Emp Here 20
SIC 8322 Individual and family services

D-U-N-S 25-356-9784 (BR)
GROUPE JEAN COUTU (PJC) INC, LE
PHARMACIE JEAN COUTU
(Suby of 3958230 Canada Inc)
181 Rue Principale, Gatineau, QC, J9H 6A6
(819) 684-0006
Emp Here 45
SIC 5912 Drug stores and proprietary stores

D-U-N-S 20-189-1645 (BR)
LAFLAMME, HENRI INC
MARCHE LAFLAMME
126 Rue Principale, Gatineau, QC, J9H 3M4
(819) 684-4156
Emp Here 53
SIC 5411 Grocery stores

D-U-N-S 25-448-3795 (BR)
METRO RICHELIEU INC
SUPER C
181 Rue Principale, Gatineau, QC, J9H 6A6
(819) 684-2010
Emp Here 70
SIC 5141 Groceries, general line

D-U-N-S 25-474-8650 (BR)
PROVIGO INC
PROVIGO
375 Ch D'Aylmer Bureau 5, Gatineau, QC, J9H 1A5
(819) 682-4433
Emp Here 165
SIC 5411 Grocery stores

D-U-N-S 25-840-5422 (BR)
UNIPRIX INC
PHARMACIE ASSOCIEE A UNIPRIX
210 Ch D'Aylmer, Gatineau, QC, J9H 1A2
(819) 684-6594
Emp Here 30
SIC 5912 Drug stores and proprietary stores

Gatineau, QC J9J
Hull County

D-U-N-S 20-217-3154 (BR)
AUTOBUS LA QUEBECOISE INC
AUTOBUS OUTAOUAIS
(Suby of Autobus la Quebecoise Inc)
545 Rue De Vernon, Gatineau, QC, J9J 3K4
(819) 770-1070
Emp Here 80
SIC 4151 School buses

D-U-N-S 20-103-6337 (BR)
COMMISSION SCOLAIRE WESTERN QUEBEC
SYMNES JUNIOR HIGH SCHOOL
(Suby of Commission Scolaire Western Quebec)
701 Boul Du Plateau, Gatineau, QC, J9J 3G2
(819) 684-7472
Emp Here 30

▲ Public Company ■ Public Company Family Member **HQ** Headquarters **BR** Branch **SL** Single Location

SIC 8211 Elementary and secondary schools

D-U-N-S 24-270-2363   (HQ)
COMMISSION SCOLAIRE WESTERN QUE-BEC
(*Suby of* Commission Scolaire Western Quebec)
15 Rue Katimavik Bureau 1, Gatineau, QC, J9J 0E9
(819) 684-2336
Emp Here 50   *Emp Total* 1,200
Sales 110,427,520
SIC 8211 Elementary and secondary schools
Mike Dawson
Dir Colin Oshea

D-U-N-S 20-892-5255   (SL)
CONSTRUCTION LARIVIERE LTEE
640 Rue Auguste-Mondoux, Gatineau, QC, J9J 3K3
(819) 770-2280
Emp Here 60   *Sales* 4,377,642
SIC 1794 Excavation work

D-U-N-S 25-480-5880   (BR)
ENTREPRISES P. BONHOMME LTEE, LES
BOIS BYTOWN
455 Ch Mcconnell, Gatineau, QC, J9J 3M3
(819) 684-9859
Emp Here 29
SIC 5211 Lumber and other building materials

D-U-N-S 25-150-7216   (SL)
SIMBOL TEST SYSTEMS INC
ASSET RELAY
616 Rue Auguste-Mondoux, Gatineau, QC, J9J 3K3
(819) 770-7771
Emp Here 35   *Sales* 8,316,010
SIC 5065 Electronic parts and equipment, nec

D-U-N-S 24-221-0289   (SL)
TIM HORTONS
405 Ch Varier, Gatineau, QC, J9J 3H9
(819) 682-4949
Emp Here 60   *Sales* 1,824,018
SIC 5812 Eating places

Gatineau, QC K1A
Hull County

D-U-N-S 24-813-5188   (BR)
GOUVERNEMENT DE LA PROVINCE DE QUEBEC
GOUVERNEMENT DE LA PROVINCE DE QUEBEC
100 Rue Laurier, Gatineau, QC, K1A 0M8
(819) 776-7000
Emp Here 500
SIC 8412 Museums and art galleries

Girardville, QC G0W

D-U-N-S 20-198-3228   (SL)
BOUCHER. J.C. & FILS LTEE
1400 Rue Principale Rr 1, Girardville, QC, G0W 1R0
(418) 258-3261
Emp Here 110   *Sales* 15,373,440
SIC 2411 Logging
Pr Pr Jean-Charles Boucher
VP VP Martin Boucher
Treas Gaetan Boucher
Marlene Boucher
Jimmy Boucher
Maryse Boucher
Sec Josee Boucher

D-U-N-S 20-279-1146   (BR)
PF RESOLU CANADA INC
2250 Rang Saint-Joseph Nord, Girardville, QC, G0W 1R0

(418) 630-3433
Emp Here 112
SIC 2421 Sawmills and planing mills, general

Gracefield, QC J0X
Gatineau County

D-U-N-S 20-574-5743   (BR)
CENTRE HOSPITALIER DES FORESTIERS
(*Suby of* Centre Hospitalier Des Forestiers)
1 Rue Du Foyer, Gracefield, QC, J0X 1W0
(819) 463-2100
Emp Here 45
SIC 8361 Residential care

Granby, QC J2G
Shefford County

D-U-N-S 25-307-2821   (BR)
123273 CANADA INC
PHARMACIE JEAN COUTU
751 Rue Principale Bureau 121, Granby, QC, J2G 2Y6
(450) 375-5596
Emp Here 60
SIC 5912 Drug stores and proprietary stores

D-U-N-S 24-580-9132   (SL)
2420-5064 QUEBEC INC
RESTAURANT CASA DU SPAGHETTI
604 Rue Principale, Granby, QC, J2G 2X7
(450) 372-3848
Emp Here 50   *Sales* 1,819,127
SIC 5812 Eating places

D-U-N-S 25-088-6124   (SL)
2746-2993 QUEBEC INC
DEMENAGEMENT SERGE LAPALME ENR
140 Rue Martin, Granby, QC, J2G 8B4
(450) 361-3790
Emp Here 30   *Sales* 3,898,130
SIC 4213 Trucking, except local

D-U-N-S 24-297-3873   (SL)
9054-2747 QUEBEC INC
ST-AMBROISE, LE
791 Rue Principale, Granby, QC, J2G 2Y6
(450) 777-3511
Emp Here 70   *Sales* 2,512,128
SIC 5812 Eating places

D-U-N-S 20-309-3844   (SL)
9101-5925 QUEBEC INC
GESTION DUMONT
603 Rue Principale, Granby, QC, J2G 2X9
(450) 777-3030
Emp Here 55   *Sales* 1,678,096
SIC 5812 Eating places

D-U-N-S 20-332-4439   (SL)
9267-8010 QUEBEC INC
UNIPRIX ISABELLE DUPONT
338 Rue Saint-Jacques, Granby, QC, J2G 3N2
(450) 372-4447
Emp Here 50   *Sales* 4,304,681
SIC 5961 Catalog and mail-order houses

D-U-N-S 25-201-7074   (HQ)
ACCESSORIES BY/PAR RAE INC
395 Rue Saint-Vallier, Granby, QC, J2G 7Y1
(450) 378-5600
Emp Here 36   *Emp Total* 6
Sales 5,545,013
SIC 2387 Apparel belts
Pr Pr Udo Scherff
Dagmar Scherff
Steven Macphail

D-U-N-S 20-792-6457   (BR)
ACKLANDS - GRAINGER INC
AGI
(*Suby of* W.W. Grainger, Inc.)

415 Rue Robinson S, Granby, QC, J2G 7N2
(450) 375-1771
Emp Here 50
SIC 5085 Industrial supplies

D-U-N-S 24-382-9590   (BR)
AGROPUR COOPERATIVE
NARTEL
510 Rue Principale, Granby, QC, J2G 2X2
(450) 375-1991
Emp Here 650
SIC 2022 Cheese; natural and processed

D-U-N-S 24-890-6943   (SL)
AIR-TERRE EQUIPEMENT INCORPOREE
(*Suby of* Coradin Inc)
420 Rue Edouard, Granby, QC, J2G 3Z3
(450) 378-8107
Emp Here 60   *Sales* 16,679,223
SIC 3728 Aircraft parts and equipment, nec
Pr Pr Camil Poulin
Dir Benoit Vezina

D-U-N-S 20-198-7583   (SL)
ARMSTRONG-HUNT INC
ARMSTRONG HEAT TRANSFER GROUP
648 Rue Moeller, Granby, QC, J2G 8N1
(450) 378-2655
Emp Here 30   *Sales* 6,030,906
SIC 3443 Fabricated plate work (boiler shop)
Pr Pr Claude A Levesque

D-U-N-S 20-171-7803   (BR)
BPR-INFRASTRUCTURE INC
(*Suby of* Tetra Tech, Inc.)
155 Rue Saint-Jacques Bureau 404, Granby, QC, J2G 9A7
(450) 378-3779
Emp Here 25
SIC 8711 Engineering services

D-U-N-S 24-475-6946   (BR)
BANK OF MONTREAL
BMO BANK OF MONTREAL
399 Rue Principale, Granby, QC, J2G 2W7
(450) 375-6748
Emp Here 24
SIC 6021 National commercial banks

D-U-N-S 20-002-8533   (BR)
BANQUE LAURENTIENNE DU CANADA
BANK LAURENTIAN DU CANADA
40 Rue Evangeline, Granby, QC, J2G 8K1
(450) 378-7942
Emp Here 30
SIC 6021 National commercial banks

D-U-N-S 25-010-1441   (BR)
BANQUE NATIONALE DU CANADA
193 Rue Principale, Granby, QC, J2G 2V5
(450) 372-5859
Emp Here 30
SIC 6021 National commercial banks

D-U-N-S 24-334-6900   (BR)
BOW GROUPE DE PLOMBERIE INC
DIV DE BOW PLASTIQUES
15 Rue Vittie, Granby, QC, J2G 6N8
(450) 372-5481
Emp Here 200
SIC 3089 Plastics products, nec

D-U-N-S 24-545-6764   (SL)
CRDITED MONTEREGIE EST
CRDITED MONTEREGIE EST
(*Suby of* CRDITED Monteregie Est)
290 Rue Saint-Hubert, Granby, QC, J2G 5N3
(450) 375-0437
Emp Here 60
SIC 8361 Residential care

D-U-N-S 24-362-5121   (BR)
CAISSE DESJARDINS DE GRANBY-HAUTE-YAMASKA
CENTRE DE SERVICE DERAGON
190 Rue Deragon, Granby, QC, J2G 5H9
(450) 777-5353
Emp Here 91

SIC 6062 State credit unions

D-U-N-S 25-628-2229   (SL)
CAMP LE RANCH MASSAWIPPI INC
1695 8e Rang E, Granby, QC, J2G 8C7
(450) 777-4511
Emp Here 50   *Sales* 4,231,721
SIC 7032 Sporting and recreational camps

D-U-N-S 25-409-9518   (BR)
CANADA POST CORPORATION
297 Rue Principale, Granby, QC, J2G 2W1
(450) 372-3987
Emp Here 70
SIC 4311 U.s. postal service

D-U-N-S 24-697-7771   (SL)
CHEVALIER DE COLOMB (CONSEIL NO 1093)
170 Rue Saint-Antoine N, Granby, QC, J2G 5G8
(450) 375-1093
Emp Here 500   *Sales* 48,392,880
SIC 8641 Civic and social associations
Pr Denis Bonneau
VP Marcel Guertin
Treas Andre Charpentier

D-U-N-S 20-712-1455   (BR)
COMMISSION SCOLAIRE EASTERN TOWNSHIPS
PARKVIEW SCHOOL
(*Suby of* Commission Scolaire Eastern Townships)
50 Rue Lorne, Granby, QC, J2G 4W2
(450) 372-6058
Emp Here 40
SIC 8211 Elementary and secondary schools

D-U-N-S 25-222-5990   (BR)
COMMISSION SCOLAIRE DU VAL-DES-CERFS
ECOLE DE LA MOISSON-D'OR
309 Rue Principale, Granby, QC, J2G 2W3
(450) 375-4701
Emp Here 35
SIC 8211 Elementary and secondary schools

D-U-N-S 25-240-6624   (BR)
COMMISSION SCOLAIRE DU VAL-DES-CERFS
ECOLE SAINT BERNARD
74 Rue Glen, Granby, QC, J2G 4K4
(450) 372-5655
Emp Here 40
SIC 8211 Elementary and secondary schools

D-U-N-S 25-722-8148   (BR)
COMMISSION SCOLAIRE DU VAL-DES-CERFS
ECOLE ST JOSEPH
254 Rue Laurier, Granby, QC, J2G 5K8
(450) 372-7767
Emp Here 48
SIC 8351 Child day care services

D-U-N-S 25-240-6103   (BR)
COMMISSION SCOLAIRE DU VAL-DES-CERFS
ECOLE SAINT JEAN
52 Boul Leclerc E, Granby, QC, J2G 1S6
(450) 372-7290
Emp Here 50
SIC 8211 Elementary and secondary schools

D-U-N-S 25-240-6186   (BR)
COMMISSION SCOLAIRE DU VAL-DES-CERFS
ECOLE SAINT LUC
250 Rue Desjardins N, Granby, QC, J2G 6J1
(450) 378-4260
Emp Here 35
SIC 8211 Elementary and secondary schools

D-U-N-S 25-240-6301   (BR)
COMMISSION SCOLAIRE DU VAL-DES-CERFS
ECOLE STE FAMILLE

---

100 Rue Dufferin, Granby, QC, J2G 4W9
(450) 378-9330
Emp Here 45
SIC 8211 Elementary and secondary schools

D-U-N-S 25-240-6384 (BR)
COMMISSION SCOLAIRE DU VAL-DES-CERFS
ECOLE JOSEPH-HERMAS-LECLERC
1111 Rue Simonds S, Granby, QC, J2G 9H7
(450) 378-9981
Emp Here 180
SIC 8211 Elementary and secondary schools

D-U-N-S 24-012-2130 (BR)
COMMISSION SCOLAIRE DU VAL-DES-CERFS
ECOLE SAINTE MARIE
90 Rue Laval S, Granby, QC, J2G 7G7
(450) 375-1113
Emp Here 25
SIC 8211 Elementary and secondary schools

D-U-N-S 25-023-9928 (BR)
COMMISSION SCOLAIRE DU VAL-DES-CERFS
ECOLE SAINT-ANDRE
415 Rue Calixa-Lavallee, Granby, QC, J2G 1C4
(450) 378-8419
Emp Here 45
SIC 8211 Elementary and secondary schools

D-U-N-S 20-918-5482 (BR)
COMMISSION SCOLAIRE DU VAL-DES-CERFS
ECOLE DE LA HAUTE-VILLE
150 Rue Lansdowne, Granby, QC, J2G 4P4
(450) 372-5454
Emp Here 25
SIC 8211 Elementary and secondary schools

D-U-N-S 25-240-6228 (BR)
COMMISSION SCOLAIRE DU VAL-DES-CERFS
PAVILLION SAINT MARC
673 Rue Cabana, Granby, QC, J2G 1R3
(450) 378-5343
Emp Here 25
SIC 8211 Elementary and secondary schools

D-U-N-S 25-024-1122 (BR)
COMMISSION SCOLAIRE DU VAL-DES-CERFS
ECOLE SAINT EUGENE
460 Rue Notre-Dame, Granby, QC, J2G 3L8
(450) 375-1155
Emp Here 40
SIC 8211 Elementary and secondary schools

D-U-N-S 24-012-2122 (BR)
COMMISSION SCOLAIRE DU VAL-DES-CERFS
CEA CENTRE REGIONAL INTEGRE DE FORMATION
700 Rue Denison O, Granby, QC, J2G 4G3
(450) 378-8544
Emp Here 125
SIC 8249 Vocational schools, nec

D-U-N-S 25-409-9476 (BR)
DELOITTE & TOUCHE INC
(*Suby of* Deloitte LLP)
190 Rue Deragon, Granby, QC, J2G 5H9
(450) 372-3347
Emp Here 40
SIC 8721 Accounting, auditing, and book-keeping

D-U-N-S 20-571-8625 (BR)
DESJARDINS SECURITE FINANCIERE, COMPAGNIE D'ASSURANCE VIE
SERVICES FINANCIERS SSL
66 Rue Court Bureau 210, Granby, QC, J2G 4Y5
(450) 378-0088
Emp Here 20
SIC 6311 Life insurance

D-U-N-S 24-935-8268 (SL)
ENGRENAX HYDRAULIX (2005) INC
(*Suby of* Gestrudo Inc)
476 Rue Edouard, Granby, QC, J2G 3Z3
(450) 777-4555
Emp Here 30 *Sales* 656,646
SIC 3561 Pumps and pumping equipment

D-U-N-S 24-611-8624 (SL)
FABRIQUE ST-JOSEPH DE GRANBY
270 Rue Deragon, Granby, QC, J2G 5J5
(450) 372-0811
Emp Here 50 *Sales* 4,240,481
SIC 8661 Religious organizations

D-U-N-S 24-174-8409 (SL)
GESTION RESTO GRANBY INC
ROTISSERIE ST-HUBERT
940 Rue Principale, Granby, QC, J2G 2Z4
(450) 378-4656
Emp Here 85 *Sales* 2,553,625
SIC 5812 Eating places

D-U-N-S 25-309-7638 (BR)
INDUSTRIELLE ALLIANCE, ASSURANCE ET SERVICES FINANCIERS INC
AGENCE GRANBY, L'
615 Rue Principale, Granby, QC, J2G 2Y1
(450) 372-4054
Emp Here 30
SIC 6411 Insurance agents, brokers, and service

D-U-N-S 24-234-5724 (SL)
INDUSTRIES CRESSWELL INC
CRESSWELL INDUSTRIES INC
424 Rue Saint-Vallier, Granby, QC, J2G 7Y4
(450) 378-4611
Emp Here 49 *Sales* 5,982,777
SIC 3399 Primary Metal products
Pr Bryan Jones

D-U-N-S 24-390-7107 (HQ)
INDUSTRIES CRESSWELL INC
(*Suby of* 3195538 Canada Inc)
553 Rue Leon-Harmel, Granby, QC, J2G 3G5
(450) 378-4611
Emp Here 42 *Emp Total* 1
Sales 12,993,765
SIC 3499 Fabricated Metal products, nec
Pr Pr Bryan D. Jones
Scott B. Jones
Dir Lawrence P. Cannon

D-U-N-S 24-837-2310 (SL)
INDUSTRIES DE MOULAGE POLYCELL INC, LES
(*Suby of* Plastiques Cellulaires Polyform Inc)
454 Rue Edouard, Granby, QC, J2G 3Z3
(450) 378-9093
Emp Here 60 *Sales* 8,834,400
SIC 2821 Plastics materials and resins
Pr Pr Jean-Louis Beliveau
VP VP Charles Beliveau

D-U-N-S 20-017-0954 (SL)
INDUSTRIES DE MOULAGE POLYTECH INC
454 Rue Edouard, Granby, QC, J2G 3Z3
(450) 378-9093
Emp Here 75 *Sales* 14,304,450
SIC 3081 Unsupported plastics film and sheet
Pr Pr Jean-Louis Beliveau
Danielle Beliveau

D-U-N-S 24-871-8348 (SL)
L. DAVIS TEXTILES (1991) INC
231 Rue Saint-Charles S, Granby, QC, J2G 9M6
(450) 375-1665
Emp Here 100 *Sales* 20,188,550
SIC 5137 Women's and children's clothing
Pr Yvon Ranger
Sec Robert Ranger
Daniel Ranger
Philippe Ranger

D-U-N-S 20-790-6454 (HQ)

LANDES CANADA INC
ACCESSORIES BY/PAR RAE
400 Rue Saint-Vallier, Granby, QC, J2G 7Y4
(450) 378-9853
Emp Here 120 *Emp Total* 29,341
Sales 43,659,050
SIC 3199 Leather goods, nec
Pr Pr Gilles Beaudoin
Dir Christian Ockenfub
Dir Klaus Hilgert

D-U-N-S 20-566-0483 (SL)
LEVEILLE, J.A. & FILS (1990) INC
(*Suby of* Affimex Inc)
250 Rue Saint-Urbain, Granby, QC, J2G 8M8
(450) 378-8474
Emp Here 20 *Sales* 6,674,880
SIC 4731 Freight transportation arrangement
Pr Pr Gilles Remillard
Genl Mgr Jean Dufour
VP VP Daniel Menard

D-U-N-S 24-836-6874 (SL)
LUBECKI TECHNICAL HOLDINGS INC
PLASTAIR
435 Rue Saint-Vallier, Granby, QC, J2G 8Y4
(450) 375-9129
Emp Here 40 *Sales* 5,559,741
SIC 3089 Plastics products, nec
Thomas Ashcroft
Dir Maria Lubecki

D-U-N-S 20-694-4493 (SL)
PRODUITS BELT-TECH INC
386 Rue Dorchester, Granby, QC, J2G 3Z7
(450) 372-5826
Emp Here 120 *Sales* 19,699,389
SIC 2399 Fabricated textile products, nec
Pr Robert J. Belanger
VP Sylvie Nerbonne
Sec Hugo Boisclair
Dir Guy Ouimet

D-U-N-S 25-483-1191 (BR)
PROVIGO DISTRIBUTION INC
320 Boul Leclerc O, Granby, QC, J2G 1V3
(450) 378-0014
Emp Here 50
SIC 5411 Grocery stores

D-U-N-S 20-102-0315 (BR)
PUROLATOR INC.
PUROLATOR INC
732 Boul Industriel, Granby, QC, J2G 9J5
(450) 375-1091
Emp Here 30
SIC 7389 Business services, nec

D-U-N-S 25-257-8463 (BR)
REDBERRY FRANCHISING CORP
BURGER KING
855 Rue Principale, Granby, QC, J2G 2Y9
(450) 375-9412
Emp Here 35
SIC 5812 Eating places

D-U-N-S 25-294-6058 (BR)
SEARS CANADA INC
60 Rue Evangeline, Granby, QC, J2G 8K3
(450) 777-0476
Emp Here 165
SIC 5311 Department stores

D-U-N-S 20-010-0126 (SL)
SERVICE D'ECHANGE RAPIDGAZ INC
RAPIDGAZ
241 Rue Saint-Charles S, Granby, QC, J2G 7A7
(450) 375-6644
Emp Here 20 *Sales* 7,727,098
SIC 5172 Petroleum products, nec
VP VP Francois Rainville
Pr Andre Rainville
Richard Rainville
Dir Raymond Beaudoin

D-U-N-S 25-370-1569 (BR)
STAPLES CANADA INC

BUREAU EN GROS
(*Suby of* Staples, Inc.)
921 Rue Principale, Granby, QC, J2G 2Z5
(450) 776-7555
Emp Here 20
SIC 5943 Stationery stores

D-U-N-S 20-198-4994 (SL)
SUPER MARCHE G BRETON INC
METRO
65 Rue Principale, Granby, QC, J2G 2T7
(450) 378-9926
Emp Here 80 *Sales* 14,569,600
SIC 5411 Grocery stores
Pr Marc Breton
Normand Desloges

D-U-N-S 25-409-9559 (SL)
TAXI 3000 INC
12 Rue Du Centre, Granby, QC, J2G 5B3
(450) 372-3000
Emp Here 50 *Sales* 1,532,175
SIC 4121 Taxicabs

D-U-N-S 20-820-8467 (BR)
TEKNIKA HBA INC
30 Rue Dufferin, Granby, QC, J2G 4W6
(450) 378-3322
Emp Here 60
SIC 1521 Single-family housing construction

D-U-N-S 24-696-8663 (HQ)
VITRERIE CLAUDE LTEE
PLOMBERIE TETREAULT
110 Rue Court, Granby, QC, J2G 4Y9
(450) 372-3019
Emp Here 24 *Emp Total* 25
Sales 5,180,004
SIC 5211 Lumber and other building materials
Pr Pr Richard Tetreault

D-U-N-S 24-353-5536 (BR)
WESTCLIFF MANAGEMENT LTD
GALERIES DE GRANBY
40 Rue Evangeline, Granby, QC, J2G 8K1
(450) 378-5598
Emp Here 23
SIC 6512 Nonresidential building operators

Granby, QC J2H
Shefford County

D-U-N-S 24-177-4413 (SL)
131289 CANADA INC
JARDIN DU MONT ENR
252 Rue Denison E, Granby, QC, J2H 2R6
(450) 375-3941
Emp Here 50 *Sales* 10,306,800
SIC 5431 Fruit and vegetable markets
Pr Pr Bruno Ouellette
Suzette Ouellette

D-U-N-S 25-361-0588 (BR)
COMMISSION SCOLAIRE DU VAL-DES-CERFS
ECOLE JOSEPH POITEVIN
831 Rue Saint-Hubert, Granby, QC, J2H 2K7
(450) 777-3804
Emp Here 25
SIC 8211 Elementary and secondary schools

D-U-N-S 20-642-2706 (HQ)
MEUBLES GEMO INC
CENTRE DE LIQUIDATION GEMO
633 Rue Dufferin, Granby, QC, J2H 0Y7
(450) 372-3988
Emp Here 44 *Emp Total* 1
Sales 5,690,935
SIC 5712 Furniture stores
Pr Benoit Morin
Sec Jean-Guy Racine

Granby, QC J2J
Shefford County

D-U-N-S 20-708-7990   (SL)
9248-1464 QUEBEC INC
BUANDERIES PIERRE R DEXTRAZE
599 Rue Simonds S, Granby, QC, J2J 1C1
(450) 378-3187
Emp Here 60   *Sales* 1,896,978
SIC 7219 Laundry and garment services, nec

D-U-N-S 25-307-3548   (BR)
AGROPUR COOPERATIVE
FROMAGERIE DE GRANDBY
1100 Rue Omer-Deslauriers, Granby, QC, J2J
0S7
(450) 777-5300
Emp Here 280
SIC 2022 Cheese; natural and processed

D-U-N-S 24-310-6460   (BR)
ALLAN CANDY COMPANY LIMITED, THE
(*Suby of* Hershey Company)
850 Boul Industriel, Granby, QC, J2J 1B8
(450) 372-1080
Emp Here 400
SIC 2064 Candy and other confectionery
products

D-U-N-S 20-541-6720   (HQ)
AMADA CANADA LTD
885 Rue Georges-Cros, Granby, QC, J2J 1E8
(514) 866-2012
Emp Here 30   *Emp Total* 8,005
Sales 8,974,166
SIC 5084 Industrial machinery and equipment
Pr Pr Katsumi Karimura
Dir Louis L Gascon
   Koji Yamamoto

D-U-N-S 24-954-2820   (HQ)
ARTOPEX INC
(*Suby of* Groupe Pro-Plus Inc)
800 Rue Vadnais, Granby, QC, J2J 1A7
(450) 378-0189
Emp Here 60   *Emp Total* 1
Sales 16,632,019
SIC 2522 Office furniture, except wood
Pr Daniel Pelletier
Sec Martin Pelletier

D-U-N-S 25-023-9175   (SL)
AUTOS R. CHAGNON DE GRANBY INC
CHAGNON HONDA
1711 Rue Principale, Granby, QC, J2J 0M9
(450) 378-9963
Emp Here 40   *Sales* 20,096,000
SIC 5511 New and used car dealers
Pr Pr Real Chagnon
   Sylvain Chagnon
   Manon Chagnon
Fin Ex Annie Chagnon

D-U-N-S 24-363-5757   (BR)
BEST BUY CANADA LTD
FUTURE SHOP
(*Suby of* Best Buy Co., Inc.)
90 Rue Simonds N, Granby, QC, J2J 2L1
(450) 372-0883
Emp Here 50
SIC 5731 Radio, television, and electronic
stores

D-U-N-S 25-147-6610   (SL)
CFA, SOCIETE EN COMMANDITE
CIRCUIT FCIL AMERICA
625 Rue Du Luxembourg, Granby, QC, J2J
2S9
(450) 770-8558
Emp Here 70   *Sales* 14,724,000
SIC 3497 Metal foil and leaf
Genl Mgr Kurt Acx
Plant Mgr Damien Michel

D-U-N-S 25-845-7183   (BR)
CANPAR TRANSPORT L.P.
(*Suby of* Canpar Transport L.P.)
1065 Boul Industriel, Granby, QC, J2J 2B8

(450) 378-6405
Emp Here 23
SIC 7389 Business services, nec

D-U-N-S 24-946-9339   (BR)
**COCA-COLA REFRESHMENTS CANADA
COMPANY**
*COMPAGNIE D'EMBOUTEILLAGE COCA-
COLA*
(*Suby of* The Coca-Cola Company)
940 Rue Andre-Line, Granby, QC, J2J 1E2
(450) 375-2429
Emp Here 45
SIC 5149 Groceries and related products, nec

D-U-N-S 20-033-9070   (BR)
**COMMISSION SCOLAIRE DU VAL-DES-
CERFS**
ECOLE SECONDAIRE L'ENVOLEE
549 Rue Fournier, Granby, QC, J2J 2K5
(450) 777-7536
Emp Here 75
SIC 8211 Elementary and secondary schools

D-U-N-S 20-806-8358   (BR)
COUCHE-TARD INC
825 Rue Maisonneuve, Granby, QC, J2J 1S5
(450) 777-8025
Emp Here 25
SIC 5411 Grocery stores

D-U-N-S 24-339-6590   (BR)
**DATA COMMUNICATIONS MANAGEMENT
CORP**
DATA GROUP OF COMPANIES
855 Boul Industriel, Granby, QC, J2J 1A6
(450) 378-4601
Emp Here 125
SIC 2761 Manifold business forms

D-U-N-S 20-689-3435   (SL)
DE BALL INC
835 Boul Industriel, Granby, QC, J2J 1A5
(514) 934-3454
Emp Here 50   *Sales* 4,742,446
SIC 2221 Broadwoven fabric mills, manmade

D-U-N-S 25-337-9234   (SL)
FORMULES D'AFFAIRES SUPRATECH INC
960 Rue Andre-Line, Granby, QC, J2J 1E2
(450) 777-1041
Emp Here 62   *Sales* 6,030,906
SIC 2752 Commercial printing, lithographic
Pr Pr Marcel Guertin
   Paul Gagnon
   Michel Labonte

D-U-N-S 24-422-0682   (BR)
GREAT PACIFIC ENTERPRISES INC
COROPLAST DIV
700 Rue Vadnais, Granby, QC, J2J 1A7
(450) 378-3995
Emp Here 75
SIC 3081 Unsupported plastics film and sheet

D-U-N-S 24-461-6538   (SL)
**GROUPE ALLAIREGINCE INFRASTRUC-
TURES INC**
LES TERRASSEMENTS ALLAIRE & GINCE
70 Rue De Gatineau, Granby, QC, J2J 0P1
(450) 378-1623
Emp Here 50   *Sales* 3,648,035
SIC 1794 Excavation work

D-U-N-S 24-779-6316   (BR)
GROUPE BMTC INC
BRAULT ET MARTINEAU
50 Rue Simonds N, Granby, QC, J2J 2L1
(450) 372-5656
Emp Here 20
SIC 5712 Furniture stores

D-U-N-S 20-870-2022   (BR)
HOME DEPOT OF CANADA INC
HOME DEPOT
(*Suby of* The Home Depot Inc)
165 Rue Simonds N, Granby, QC, J2J 0R7
(450) 375-5544
Emp Here 100

SIC 5251 Hardware stores

D-U-N-S 20-266-8059   (SL)
INDUSTRIES SPECTAL INC
GROUPE SPECTAL
(*Suby of* LCI Industries)
850 Rue Moeller, Granby, QC, J2J 1K7
(450) 378-6722
Emp Here 100   *Sales* 21,673,567
SIC 3354 Aluminum extruded products
Pr Jason Lippert

D-U-N-S 24-641-8235   (BR)
LOBLAWS INC
LOBLAWS GRANBY
80 Rue Saint-Jude N, Granby, QC, J2J 2T7
(450) 777-2875
Emp Here 60
SIC 5141 Groceries, general line

D-U-N-S 25-183-9494   (SL)
MICHEL THIBAUDEAU INC
CANADIAN TIRE 138
70 Rue Simonds N, Granby, QC, J2J 2L1
(450) 378-9884
Emp Here 50   *Sales* 4,815,406
SIC 5251 Hardware stores

D-U-N-S 20-002-8368   (BR)
PEPSICO CANADA ULC
FRITO LAY CANADA
(*Suby of* Pepsico, Inc.)
855 Rue J.-A.-Bombardier, Granby, QC, J2J
1E9
(450) 375-5555
Emp Here 125
SIC 2086 Bottled and canned soft drinks

D-U-N-S 24-347-5352   (BR)
POLYFORM A.G.P. INC
INDUSTRIES DE MOULAGE POLYMAX, LES
870 Boul Industriel, Granby, QC, J2J 1A4
(450) 378-9093
Emp Here 100
SIC 3081 Unsupported plastics film and sheet

D-U-N-S 20-199-0272   (BR)
SONOCO CANADA CORPORATION
(*Suby of* Sonoco Products Company)
875 Boul Industriel, Granby, QC, J2J 1A6
(514) 861-0097
Emp Here 60
SIC 2655 Fiber cans, drums, and similar prod-
ucts

D-U-N-S 20-908-7196   (BR)
VELAN INC
1010 Rue Cowie, Granby, QC, J2J 1E7
(450) 378-2305
Emp Here 108
SIC 3494 Valves and pipe fittings, nec

D-U-N-S 25-297-7863   (BR)
WAL-MART CANADA CORP
WAL MART GRANBY STORE- #3035
75 Rue Simonds N, Granby, QC, J2J 2S3
(450) 777-8863
Emp Here 300
SIC 5311 Department stores

D-U-N-S 20-303-5100   (BR)
**WINNERS MERCHANTS INTERNATIONAL
L.P.**
WINNERS
(*Suby of* The TJX Companies Inc)
140 Rue Saint-Jude N, Granby, QC, J2J 2L5
(450) 378-8300
Emp Here 25
SIC 5651 Family clothing stores

Grand-Mere, QC G9T
Champlain County

D-U-N-S 24-941-5241   (SL)
2857-4077 QUEBEC INC

ALIMENTATION GAUTHIER & FRERES ENR
850 7e Av, Grand-Mere, QC, G9T 2B8
(819) 533-4553
Emp Here 110   *Sales* 14,883,983
SIC 5411 Grocery stores
Pr Pr Claude Gauthier
   Jean Gauthier
   Gaston Gauthier
   Lise Gauthier

D-U-N-S 25-363-6708   (BR)
CANADA POST CORPORATION
696 5e Av, Grand-Mere, QC, G9T 2M6
(819) 538-1651
Emp Here 22
SIC 4311 U.s. postal service

D-U-N-S 20-716-8977   (BR)
COMMISSION SCOLAIRE DE L'ENERGIE
ECOLE DE SAINT FLORE
3351 33e Rue, Grand-Mere, QC, G9T 3N9
(819) 536-0706
Emp Here 50
SIC 8211 Elementary and secondary schools

D-U-N-S 20-030-4975   (BR)
COMMISSION SCOLAIRE DE L'ENERGIE
ECOLE LAFLECHE
1321 5e Av, Grand-Mere, QC, G9T 2N6
(819) 536-7836
Emp Here 32
SIC 8211 Elementary and secondary schools

D-U-N-S 20-871-3057   (SL)
**ENTREPRISES ROBERT ROUSSEAU INC,
LES**
CLUB DE GOLF GRAND MERE
1 Ch Du Golf, Grand-Mere, QC, G9T 5K8
(819) 538-3560
Emp Here 50   *Sales* 2,188,821
SIC 7992 Public golf courses

D-U-N-S 25-358-5822   (SL)
GESTION GRATIEN PAQUIN INC
1173 6e Av, Grand-Mere, QC, G9T 2J4
(819) 538-1707
Emp Here 60   *Sales* 9,717,840
SIC 4899 Communication services, nec
Pr Pr Gratien Paquin

D-U-N-S 20-212-2235   (SL)
INDUSTRIES STEMA-PRO INC., LES
2699 5e Av Bureau 26, Grand-Mere, QC, G9T
2P7
(819) 533-4756
Emp Here 75   *Sales* 4,377,642
SIC 2511 Wood household furniture

D-U-N-S 24-729-9258   (HQ)
KONGSBERG INC
90 28e Rue, Grand-Mere, QC, G9T 5K7
(819) 533-3201
Emp Here 60   *Emp Total* 1
Sales 43,849,381
SIC 3679 Electronic components, nec
Pr Scott Paquette
VP Robert Cowans
Sec Rachel Baxter
Dir Reeve Jonathan

D-U-N-S 24-841-9236   (BR)
PMA ASSURANCES INC
632 6e Av, Grand-Mere, QC, G9T 2H5
(819) 538-8626
Emp Here 102
SIC 6411 Insurance agents, brokers, and service

D-U-N-S 25-308-9064   (BR)
SOCIETE DES ALCOOLS DU QUEBEC
SOCIETE DES ALCOOLS DU QUEBEC
910 7e Av, Grand-Mere, QC, G9T 2B8
(819) 538-4466
Emp Here 20
SIC 5921 Liquor stores

D-U-N-S 20-199-3763   (SL)
ST-ONGE FORD INC

1870 6e Ave, Grand-Mere, QC, G9T 2K7
(819) 538-3357
Emp Here 38   *Sales* 27,484,800
SIC 5511 New and used car dealers
Pr Pr Claude Mondou
VP VP Ruthe Mondou

D-U-N-S 20-872-7644   (SL)
VALLEE DU PARC DE SHAWINIGAN INC
VALLEE DU PARC
10000 Ch Vallee-Du-Parc, Grand-Mere, QC,
G9T 5K5
(819) 538-1639
Emp Here 85   *Sales* 4,596,524
SIC 7999 Amusement and recreation, nec

Grande-Riviere, QC G0C
Gaspe-Est County

D-U-N-S 20-913-7038   (BR)
COMMISSION SCOLAIRE RENE-LEVESQUE
ECOLE BON PASTEUR
113 Rue Du Carrefour, Grande-Riviere, QC,
G0C 1V0
(418) 385-2133
Emp Here 30
SIC 8211 Elementary and secondary schools

D-U-N-S 25-309-1474   (BR)
SOBEYS CAPITAL INCORPORATED
IGA
143 Grande Allee O, Grande-Riviere, QC,
G0C 1V0
(418) 385-3494
Emp Here 35
SIC 5411 Grocery stores

Grande-Vallee, QC G0E
Gaspe-Est County

D-U-N-S 24-907-7751   (SL)
BOIS GRANVAL G.D.S. INC
(*Suby of* Gestion G et S Deschenes Inc)
10 Rue Industrielle Bureau 280, Grande-Vallee, QC, G0E 1K0
(418) 393-2244
Emp Here 38   *Sales* 3,575,074
SIC 2421 Sawmills and planing mills, general

Grandes-Bergeronnes, QC G0T
Saguenay County

D-U-N-S 24-069-4724   (SL)
BERSACO INC
717 Rue De La Montagne, Grandes-Bergeronnes, QC, G0T 1G0
(418) 232-1100
Emp Here 70   *Sales* 9,227,040
SIC 2448 Wood pallets and skids
Pr Marc Gilbert
Genl Mgr Karl Gauthier

D-U-N-S 25-233-6839   (BR)
COMMISSION SCOLAIRE DE L'ESTUAIRE
ECOLE DOMINIQUE-SAVIO
(*Suby of* Commission Scolaire de l'Estuaire)
433b Rue De La Mer, Grandes-Bergeronnes,
QC, G0T 1G0
(418) 232-6687
Emp Here 45
SIC 8211 Elementary and secondary schools

Greenfield Park, QC J4V
Chambly County

D-U-N-S 20-323-4468   (SL)
ALIMENTS OLYMPUS (CANADA), LES
3201 Boul Taschereau, Greenfield Park, QC,
J4V 2H4

Emp Here 1,000   *Sales* 38,918,188
SIC 5812 Eating places
Pr Emmanuel Jalandoni
VP VP Dhinno Francis Tiu
   Mamuel Eduardo Carlos
   Joseph Lawrence Tanlu
Genl Mgr Manolo P. Tingzon

D-U-N-S 25-217-0006   (BR)
BEST BUY CANADA LTD
(*Suby of* Best Buy Co., Inc.)
1800 Av Auguste, Greenfield Park, QC, J4V
3R4
(450) 443-3817
Emp Here 70
SIC 5731 Radio, television, and electronic
stores

D-U-N-S 24-363-5070   (BR)
BEST BUY CANADA LTD
BEST BUY
(*Suby of* Best Buy Co., Inc.)
1000 Av Auguste, Greenfield Park, QC, J4V
3R4
(450) 766-2300
Emp Here 100
SIC 5731 Radio, television, and electronic
stores

D-U-N-S 20-712-2677   (BR)
COMMISSION SCOLAIRE MARIE-VICTORIN
CENTRE DES 16 18 ANS
274 Rue Hubert, Greenfield Park, QC, J4V
1S1
(450) 443-0017
Emp Here 30
SIC 8211 Elementary and secondary schools

D-U-N-S 25-001-8983   (BR)
COMMISSION SCOLAIRE MARIE-VICTORIN
ECOLE PIERRE LAPORTE
1005 Rue Du Centenaire, Greenfield Park,
QC, J4V 1B7
(450) 678-7858
Emp Here 40
SIC 8211 Elementary and secondary schools

D-U-N-S 24-049-7862   (BR)
COMMISSION SCOLAIRE MARIE-VICTORIN
*ECOLE SECONDAIRE PARTICIPATIVE
L'AGORA*
482 Rue De Springfield, Greenfield Park, QC,
J4V 1Y1
(450) 671-7209
Emp Here 50
SIC 8211 Elementary and secondary schools

D-U-N-S 20-642-2557   (BR)
COMMISSION SCOLAIRE MARIE-VICTORIN
ECOLE INTERNATIONALE SAINT EMOND
346 Rue Hubert, Greenfield Park, QC, J4V
1S2
(450) 671-6339
Emp Here 45
SIC 8211 Elementary and secondary schools

D-U-N-S 24-394-7871   (SL)
GESTION DENIS M. ROSSIGNOL INC
CANADIAN TIRE
4909 Boul Taschereau Bureau 190, Greenfield
Park, QC, J4V 3K3
(450) 676-1818
Emp Here 49   *Sales* 7,963,840
SIC 5531 Auto and home supply stores
Pr Denis Rossignol

D-U-N-S 24-656-2644   (BR)
GROUPE JEAN COUTU (PJC) INC, LE
(*Suby of* 3958230 Canada Inc)

3216 Boul Taschereau, Greenfield Park, QC,
J4V 2H3
(450) 465-5225
Emp Here 60
SIC 5122 Drugs, proprietaries, and sundries

D-U-N-S 20-175-9797   (BR)
HOME DEPOT OF CANADA INC
HOME DEPOT
(*Suby of* The Home Depot Inc)
500 Av Auguste, Greenfield Park, QC, J4V
3R4
(450) 462-5020
Emp Here 130
SIC 5251 Hardware stores

D-U-N-S 20-882-5414   (SL)
HOPITAL CHARLES LEMOYNE
3120 Boul Taschereau, Greenfield Park, QC,
J4V 2H1
(450) 466-5000
Emp Here 2,500   *Sales* 241,856,800
SIC 8062 General medical and surgical hospi-
tals
Pr Pr Marc Duclos
VP VP Colin J. Coole
   Daniel Castonguay
Dir Regent Beaudet
Dir Elizabeth Chittim
Dir Pierre Cossette
Dir Jean-Denis Cote
Dir Alain Deslauriers
Dir Katy Godbout
Dir Josee Livernoche

D-U-N-S 25-309-6770   (BR)
**INDUSTRIELLE ALLIANCE, ASSURANCE
ET SERVICES FINANCIERS INC**
2120 Av Victoria Bureau 10, Greenfield Park,
QC, J4V 1M9
(450) 672-3510
Emp Here 60
SIC 6411 Insurance agents, brokers, and ser-
vice

D-U-N-S 24-715-0944   (BR)
MARK'S WORK WEARHOUSE LTD
L'EQUIPEUR
3388 Boul Taschereau Bureau 794, Greenfield
Park, QC, J4V 2H7
(450) 671-3750
Emp Here 30
SIC 5611 Men's and boys' clothing stores

D-U-N-S 25-360-0712   (BR)
MERCEDES-BENZ CANADA INC
MERCEDES BENZ RIVE SUD
4844 Boul Taschereau, Greenfield Park, QC,
J4V 2J2
(450) 672-2720
Emp Here 70
SIC 5511 New and used car dealers

D-U-N-S 24-509-9296   (BR)
METRO RICHELIEU INC
SUPER C
5012 Boul Taschereau, Greenfield Park, QC,
J4V 2J2
(450) 672-8966
Emp Here 75
SIC 5411 Grocery stores

D-U-N-S 20-002-2387   (BR)
PROVIGO DISTRIBUTION INC
MAXI
3398 Boul Taschereau, Greenfield Park, QC,
J4V 2H7
(450) 671-8183
Emp Here 65
SIC 5411 Grocery stores

D-U-N-S 25-233-5054   (BR)
RIVERSIDE SCHOOL BOARD
SAINT JUDE SCHOOL
781 Rue Miller, Greenfield Park, QC, J4V 1W8
(450) 672-2090
Emp Here 40
SIC 8211 Elementary and secondary schools

D-U-N-S 20-712-3741   (BR)
RIVERSIDE SCHOOL BOARD
*GREENFIELD PARK PRIMARY INTERNA-
TIONAL SCHOOL*
776 Rue Campbell, Greenfield Park, QC, J4V
1Y7
(450) 672-0042
Emp Here 88
SIC 8211 Elementary and secondary schools

D-U-N-S 24-254-2686   (BR)
RIVERSIDE SCHOOL BOARD
CENTENNIAL REGIONAL HIGH SCHOOL
880 Rue Hudson, Greenfield Park, QC, J4V
1H1
(450) 656-6100
Emp Here 200
SIC 8211 Elementary and secondary schools

D-U-N-S 25-628-0207   (BR)
SIR CORP
JACK ASTOR'S BAR AND GRILL
3500 Boul Taschereau, Greenfield Park, QC,
J4V 2H7
(450) 671-4444
Emp Here 60
SIC 5812 Eating places

D-U-N-S 20-050-9953   (BR)
SAIL PLEIN AIR INC
(*Suby of* Sail Plein Air Inc)
3680 Boul Taschereau, Greenfield Park, QC,
J4V 2H8

Emp Here 50
SIC 5941 Sporting goods and bicycle shops

D-U-N-S 25-486-5678   (BR)
STAPLES CANADA INC
BUREAU EN GROS
(*Suby of* Staples, Inc.)
3344 Boul Taschereau Bureau C, Greenfield
Park, QC, J4V 2H7
(450) 466-7772
Emp Here 30
SIC 5943 Stationery stores

D-U-N-S 25-628-3060   (BR)
VALUE VILLAGE STORES, INC
VILLAGE DES VALEURS
(*Suby of* Savers, Inc.)
3860 Boul Taschereau, Greenfield Park, QC,
J4V 2H9
(450) 923-4767
Emp Here 45
SIC 5399 Miscellaneous general merchandise

D-U-N-S 24-311-1023   (BR)
**WINNERS MERCHANTS INTERNATIONAL
L.P.**
TJX CANADA
(*Suby of* The TJX Companies Inc)
3390 Boul Taschereau, Greenfield Park, QC,
J4V 2H7
(450) 923-2540
Emp Here 46
SIC 5651 Family clothing stores

Grenville-Sur-La-Rouge, QC J0V

D-U-N-S 24-352-0053   (SL)
**EXPEDITIONS EN RIVIERE DU NOUVEAU
MONDE LTEE, LES**
NOUVEAU MONDE EXPEDITIONS RIVIERE
100 Rue De La Riviere Rouge, Grenville-Sur-
La-Rouge, QC, J0V 1B0
(819) 242-7238
Emp Here 100   *Sales* 32,098,320
SIC 4725 Tour operators
Pr Pr Chris Phelan

Grosse-Ile, QC G4T

D-U-N-S 24-747-0412   (BR)
K+S SEL WINDSOR LTEE
MINES SELEINE
50 Ch Principal, Grosse-Ile, QC, G4T 6A6
(418) 985-2931
Emp Here 162
SIC 1479 Chemical and fertilizer mining

Ham-Nord, QC G0P
Wolfe County

D-U-N-S 20-454-2794   (SL)
DESPERADO LEGEND INC.
280 Rang Des Chutes, Ham-Nord, QC, G0P
1A0
(819) 352-9074
Emp Here 55
SIC 2621 Paper mills

Harrington Harbour, QC G0G

D-U-N-S 20-029-1800   (BR)
**CENTRE DE LA SANTE ET DU SERVICES
SOCIAUX DE LA BASSE COTE-NORD**
PAVILLON D.G. HODD
Gd, Harrington Harbour, QC, G0G 1N0

Emp Here 34
SIC 8059 Nursing and personal care, nec

Havelock, QC J0S
Huntingdon County

D-U-N-S 20-542-3510   (SL)
CARRIERES DUCHARME INC, LES
564 Ch De Covey Hill, Havelock, QC, J0S 2C0
(450) 247-2787
Emp Here 60   *Sales* 3,866,917
SIC 3281 Cut stone and stone products

Havre-Aubert, QC G4T

D-U-N-S 24-369-1347   (BR)
**CAISSE POPULAIRE DESJARDINS DES
RAMEES**
*CENTRE DE SERVICE DE L'ILE DU HAVRE-
AUBERT*
(*Suby of* Caisse Populaire Desjardins des
Ramees)
142 Rte 199, Havre-Aubert, QC, G4T 9B6
(418) 937-2361
Emp Here 50
SIC 6062 State credit unions

Havre-Aux-Maisons, QC G4T

D-U-N-S 25-232-0817   (BR)
COMMISSION SCOLAIRE DES ILES
ECOLE CENTRALE
51 Ch Central, Havre-Aux-Maisons, QC, G4T
5H1
(418) 986-5511
Emp Here 28
SIC 8211 Elementary and secondary schools

Havre-Saint-Pierre, QC G0G
Saguenay County

D-U-N-S 20-172-0559   (BR)
**GOUVERNEMENT DE LA PROVINCE DE
QUEBEC**
*COMMISSION SCOLAIRE DE LA
MOYENNE-COTE-NORD*
1235 Rue De La Digue, Havre-Saint-Pierre,
QC, G0G 1P0
(418) 538-2662
Emp Here 200
SIC 8211 Elementary and secondary schools

Hebertville, QC G8N

D-U-N-S 25-019-9502   (BR)
**COMMISSION SCOLAIRE DU LAC-ST-
JEAN**
ECOLE SAINT JOSEPH D'HEBERTVILLE
(*Suby of* Commission Scolaire du Lac-St-
Jean)
236 Rue Hebert, Hebertville, QC, G8N 1P4
(418) 669-6032
Emp Here 20
SIC 8211 Elementary and secondary schools

D-U-N-S 20-711-8741   (BR)
**COMMISSION SCOLAIRE DU LAC-ST-
JEAN**
ECOLE SECONDAIRE CURE HEBERT
(*Suby of* Commission Scolaire du Lac-St-
Jean)
250 Rue Turgeon, Hebertville, QC, G8N 1S1
(418) 669-6064
Emp Here 50
SIC 8211 Elementary and secondary schools

D-U-N-S 20-323-5374   (BR)
**COOPERATIVE DE SOLIDARITE DU MONT
LAC-VERT**
STATION TOURISTIQUE MONT LAC VERT
(*Suby of* Cooperative de Solidarite du Mont
Lac-Vert)
173 Ch Du Vallon, Hebertville, QC, G8N 1M5
(418) 344-4000
Emp Here 55
SIC 7011 Hotels and motels

Hebertville-Station, QC G0W
Lac-St-Jean-Est County

D-U-N-S 25-372-1765   (BR)
GROUPE GOYETTE INC
ENTREPOSAGE MASKA
7 Rue Industrielle, Hebertville-Station, QC,
G0W 1T0

Emp Here 20
SIC 4213 Trucking, except local

D-U-N-S 24-356-8214   (BR)
SYSTEMES ADEX INC, LES
(*Suby of* 9171-6803 Quebec Inc)
67 Rue Saint-Paul, Hebertville-Station, QC,
G0W 1T0
(418) 343-2640
Emp Here 30
SIC 3446 Architectural Metalwork

D-U-N-S 25-052-8965   (HQ)
SYSTEMES ADEX INC, LES
ADEXMAT
(*Suby of* 9171-6803 Quebec Inc)
67 Rue Saint-Paul Rr 1, Hebertville-Station,
QC, G0W 1T0
(418) 343-2640
Emp Here 30   *Emp Total* 65
Sales 4,908,000
SIC 3299 NonMetallic mineral products,

Hemmingford, QC J0L
Huntingdon County

D-U-N-S 20-997-6786   (SL)
**CLUB SPORTIF & CHAMPETRE DE HEM-
MINGFORD**
CLUB DE GOLF HEMMINGFORD
313 219 Rte S Bureau 2, Hemmingford, QC,
J0L 1H0
(514) 866-6004
Emp Here 50   *Sales* 2,042,900
SIC 7997 Membership sports and recreation
clubs

Hope, QC G0C
Gaspe-Est County

D-U-N-S 20-797-5447   (SL)
MAGASIN JEAN DUMAS INC
CANADIAN TIRE
Boul Pr, Hope, QC, G0C 2K0
(418) 752-5050
Emp Here 45   *Sales* 7,362,000
SIC 5531 Auto and home supply stores
Pr Jean Dumas
Mgr Sonia Delarosbil

Huberdeau, QC J0T
Argenteuil County

D-U-N-S 25-233-5468   (BR)
**COMMISSION SCOLAIRE DES LAUREN-
TIDES**
ECOLE L'ARC EN CIEL
(*Suby of* Commission Scolaire Des Lauren-
tides)
200 Rue Principale, Huberdeau, QC, J0T 1G0
(819) 429-4101
Emp Here 20
SIC 8211 Elementary and secondary schools

D-U-N-S 24-083-0831   (BR)
**YOUNG MEN'S & YOUNG WOMEN'S HE-
BREW ASSOCIATION OF MONTREAL**
HARRY BRONFMAN Y COUNTRY CAMP
(*Suby of* Young Men's & Young Women's He-
brew Association Of Montreal)
130 Ch Du Lac-Blanc, Huberdeau, QC, J0T
1G0

Emp Here 50
SIC 7032 Sporting and recreational camps

Hudson, QC J0P
Vaudreuil County

D-U-N-S 20-572-2080   (BR)
BANK OF MONTREAL
BMO HUDSON BRANCH
54 Rue Cameron, Hudson, QC, J0P 1H0
(450) 458-5316
Emp Here 20
SIC 6021 National commercial banks

D-U-N-S 24-342-8013   (BR)
CARA OPERATIONS LIMITED
HARVEY'S
(*Suby of* Cara Holdings Limited)
95 Montee Lavigne, Hudson, QC, J0P 1H0
(450) 458-1999
Emp Here 20
SIC 5812 Eating places

D-U-N-S 24-159-8130   (SL)
FOUNDATION WEREDALE
CAMP WEREDALE
608 Ch Du Golf, Hudson, QC, J0P 1H0
(450) 563-3145
Emp Here 70   *Sales* 5,982,777

SIC 7032 Sporting and recreational camps
Sec Howard Martin

D-U-N-S 25-105-4557   (BR)
ROYAL LEPAGE LIMITED
ROYALE LEPAGE CAVAGNAL
472b Rue Main, Hudson, QC, J0P 1H0

Emp Here 31
SIC 6531 Real estate agents and managers

Hudson Heights, QC J0P
Vaudreuil County

D-U-N-S 25-240-4694   (BR)
LESTER B. PEARSON SCHOOL BOARD
WESTWOOD HIGH SCHOOL
69 Cote Saint-Charles, Hudson Heights, QC,
J0P 1J0
(514) 798-4900
Emp Here 46
SIC 8211 Elementary and secondary schools

Huntingdon, QC J0S
Huntingdon County

D-U-N-S 20-777-8130   (BR)
**BARRIE MEMORIAL HOSPITAL FOUNDA-
TION**
C L S C HUNTINGDON
(*Suby of* Barrie Memorial Hospital Founda-
tion)
10 Rue King Bureau 200, Huntingdon, QC,
J0S 1H0
(450) 829-3877
Emp Here 90
SIC 8322 Individual and family services

D-U-N-S 25-240-8745   (BR)
COMMISSION SCOLAIRE NEW FRONTIER
ECOLE ST JOSEPH
24 Rue York, Huntingdon, QC, J0S 1H0
(450) 264-9276
Emp Here 20
SIC 8211 Elementary and secondary schools

D-U-N-S 24-110-6475   (SL)
SYSTEME HUNTINGDON INC
FOLIA INDUSTRIES
110 Rue Wellington, Huntingdon, QC, J0S
1H0
(450) 264-6122
Emp Here 50   *Sales* 1,824,018
SIC 2789 Bookbinding and related work

Ile-Aux-Noix, QC J0J
St-Jean County

D-U-N-S 20-845-2453   (SL)
GAMEX INC
(*Suby of* 9177-3572 Quebec Inc)
609 Rue Principale, Ile-Aux-Noix, QC, J0J
1G0
(450) 246-3881
Emp Here 29   *Sales* 3,502,114
SIC 5531 Auto and home supply stores

Inukjuak, QC J0M
Nouveau-Quebec County

D-U-N-S 24-116-5229   (BR)
CENTRE DE SANTE INUULITSIVIK
CENTRE DE SANTE INUULITSIVIK
Gd, Inukjuak, QC, J0M 1M0
(819) 254-9090
Emp Here 40

SIC 7991 Physical fitness facilities

D-U-N-S 20-716-8209   (BR)
COMMISSION SCOLAIRE KATIVIK
NUNAVIMMI PIGIURSAVIK CENTRE DE FORMATION
Pr, Inukjuak, QC, J0M 1M0
(819) 254-8686
Emp Here 46
SIC 8211 Elementary and secondary schools

D-U-N-S 25-240-6905   (BR)
COMMISSION SCOLAIRE KATIVIK
INNALIK SCHOOL
Pr, Inukjuak, QC, J0M 1M0
(819) 254-8211
Emp Here 80
SIC 8211 Elementary and secondary schools

D-U-N-S 20-029-4853   (BR)
FEDERATION DES COOPERATIVES DU NOUVEAU-QUEBEC, LA
FEDERATION DES COOPERATIVES DU NOUVEAU-QUEBEC, LA
Gd, Inukjuak, QC, J0M 1M0
(819) 254-8969
Emp Here 20
SIC 5999 Miscellaneous retail stores, nec

Isle-Aux-Coudres, QC G0A

D-U-N-S 20-029-1602   (BR)
COMMISSION   SCOLAIRE   DE CHARLEVOIX, LA
ECOLE DE LA ROSE DES VENTS PAVILLON SAINT PIERRE
1955 Ch Des Coudriers, Isle-Aux-Coudres, QC, G0A 1X0
(418) 760-5003
Emp Here 20
SIC 8211 Elementary and secondary schools

Ivujivik, QC J0M
Nouveau-Quebec County

D-U-N-S 25-232-9982   (BR)
COMMISSION SCOLAIRE KATIVIK
ECOLE NUVVITI
Gd, Ivujivik, QC, J0M 1H0
(819) 922-9917
Emp Here 20
SIC 8211 Elementary and secondary schools

Joliette, QC J6E
Joliette County

D-U-N-S 20-309-6102   (SL)
8561567 CANADA INC
GAMME SIGNATURE PASSION
585 Rue Saint-Pierre S, Joliette, QC, J6E 8R8
(450) 759-6361
Emp Here 52   *Sales* 3,793,956
SIC 2053 Frozen bakery products, except bread

D-U-N-S 25-200-7927   (SL)
9064-4048 QUEBEC INC
DISTINCTION, LA
1505 Boul Base-De-Roc, Joliette, QC, J6E 0L1
(450) 759-6900
Emp Here 75   *Sales* 2,261,782
SIC 5812 Eating places

D-U-N-S 20-590-9070   (SL)
9185-2335 QUEBEC INC
CHATEAU JOLIETTE
450 Rue Saint-Thomas, Joliette, QC, J6E 3R1

(450) 752-2525
Emp Here 61   *Sales* 2,699,546
SIC 7011 Hotels and motels

D-U-N-S 25-233-0196   (SL)
ACADEMIE ANTOINE-MANSEAU
20 Rue Saint-Charles-Borromee S, Joliette, QC, J6E 4T1
(450) 753-4271
Emp Here 58   *Sales* 3,866,917
SIC 8211 Elementary and secondary schools

D-U-N-S 24-901-6791   (SL)
AMBULANCES JOLIETTE INC
AMBULANCE LANAUDIERE
(*Suby of* Ambulance Richelieu Inc)
751 Rue Samuel-Racine, Joliette, QC, J6E 0E8
(450) 759-6106
Emp Here 100   *Sales* 6,690,536
SIC 4119 Local passenger transportation, nec
Pr Pr Dave Hebert
VP VP Kevin Hebert

D-U-N-S 20-569-2606   (BR)
BANQUE LAURENTIENNE DU CANADA
373 Rue Notre-Dame, Joliette, QC, J6E 3H5
(450) 759-3132
Emp Here 20
SIC 6021 National commercial banks

D-U-N-S 24-434-2135   (SL)
BELLEMARE COUVERTURES LTEE
1044 Rue Raoul-Charette, Joliette, QC, J6E 8S6
(450) 759-4933
Emp Here 50   *Sales* 4,961,328
SIC 1761 Roofing, siding, and sheetMetal work

D-U-N-S 24-870-4595   (BR)
BRIDGESTONE CANADA INC
1200 Boul Firestone, Joliette, QC, J6E 2W5
(450) 756-1061
Emp Here 1,300
SIC 3011 Tires and inner tubes

D-U-N-S 24-434-3448   (BR)
CRH CANADA GROUP INC
CIMENT ST-LAURENT
966 Ch Des Prairies, Joliette, QC, J6E 0L4
(450) 756-1076
Emp Here 250
SIC 3241 Cement, hydraulic

D-U-N-S 25-812-2563   (BR)
CANADA POST CORPORATION
POSTE CANADA
877 Rue Papineau, Joliette, QC, J6E 2L6
(450) 752-6612
Emp Here 60
SIC 4311 U.s. postal service

D-U-N-S 20-171-7480   (BR)
CANADIAN IMPERIAL BANK OF COMMERCE
CIBC
95 Place Bourget N Bureau 204, Joliette, QC, J6E 5E6
(450) 756-4521
Emp Here 30
SIC 6021 National commercial banks

D-U-N-S 24-125-7000   (SL)
CENTRE CHAMPAGNEUR
LES CLERCS DU ST VIATEUR
132 Rue Saint-Charles-Borromee S, Joliette, QC, J6E 4T3
(450) 756-4568
Emp Here 50   *Sales* 1,824,018
SIC 8361 Residential care

D-U-N-S 20-332-3613   (BR)
CENTRE INTEGRE DE SANTE ET DE SERVICES SOCIAUX DE LANAUDIERE
CISSS DE LANAUDIERE - LE BOUCLIER
1075 Boul Firestone Bureau 100, Joliette, QC, J6E 6X6
(450) 755-2929
Emp Here 30

SIC 8011 Offices and clinics of medical doctors

D-U-N-S 20-261-8604   (BR)
CENTRES JEUNESSE DE LANAUDIERE, LES
(*Suby of* Centres Jeunesse de Lanaudiere, Les)
1170 Rue Ladouceur, Joliette, QC, J6E 3W7
(450) 759-0755
Emp Here 650
SIC 8641 Civic and social associations

D-U-N-S 25-371-5833   (BR)
CIE MATERIAUX DE CONSTRUCTION BP CANADA, LA
ROOFING MANUFACTURING PLANT
(*Suby of* 3077578 Nova Scotia Corp)
351 Rue Alice, Joliette, QC, J6E 8P2
(450) 682-4428
Emp Here 200
SIC 2429 Special product sawmills, nec

D-U-N-S 24-460-9145   (BR)
CLERCS DU SAINT-VIATEUR DU CANADA
132 Rue Saint-Charles-Borromee S, Joliette, QC, J6E 4T3
(450) 756-4568
Emp Here 25
SIC 8661 Religious organizations

D-U-N-S 25-232-9008   (BR)
COMMISSION SCOLAIRE DES SAMARES
ECOLE SAINTE THERESE
305 Rue Calixa-Lavallee, Joliette, QC, J6E 4K3
(450) 758-3718
Emp Here 25
SIC 8211 Elementary and secondary schools

D-U-N-S 20-712-2164   (BR)
COMMISSION SCOLAIRE DES SAMARES
ECOLE SECONDAIRE ESPACE JEUNESSE
810 Rue De Lanaudiere, Joliette, QC, J6E 3N3
(450) 758-3556
Emp Here 70
SIC 8211 Elementary and secondary schools

D-U-N-S 25-240-2045   (BR)
COMMISSION SCOLAIRE DES SAMARES
ECOLE INTEGREE DE SAINT-PIERRE
940 Rue De Lanaudiere, Joliette, QC, J6E 3N6
(450) 758-3721
Emp Here 40
SIC 8211 Elementary and secondary schools

D-U-N-S 25-233-2614   (BR)
COMMISSION SCOLAIRE DES SAMARES
ECOLE MARIE-CHARLOTTE
981 Rue Notre-Dame, Joliette, QC, J6E 3K1
(450) 758-3723
Emp Here 50
SIC 8211 Elementary and secondary schools

D-U-N-S 20-712-2214   (BR)
COMMISSION SCOLAIRE DES SAMARES
CENTRE MULTI SERVICE DES SAMARES PAVILLON DE FORMATION PROFESSIONNELLE DE L'ARGILE
918 Rue Ladouceur, Joliette, QC, J6E 3W7
(450) 758-3630
Emp Here 50
SIC 8211 Elementary and secondary schools

D-U-N-S 25-240-2003   (BR)
COMMISSION SCOLAIRE DES SAMARES
ECOLE MGR J. PAPINEAU
485 Rue Laval, Joliette, QC, J6E 5H1
(450) 758-3716
Emp Here 30
SIC 8211 Elementary and secondary schools

D-U-N-S 24-836-1230   (BR)
COOP FEDEREE, LA
MEUNERIE JOLIETTE
845 Rue Papineau, Joliette, QC, J6E 2L6

(450) 759-2536
Emp Here 30
SIC 5191 Farm supplies

D-U-N-S 25-163-0786   (BR)
DOLLARAMA S.E.C.
DOLLARAMA
44 Place Bourget S, Joliette, QC, J6E 5E7
(450) 759-9588
Emp Here 22
SIC 5411 Grocery stores

D-U-N-S 20-602-8763   (SL)
EQUIPEMENTS INDUSTRIELS JOLIETTE INC
1295 Rue De Lanaudiere, Joliette, QC, J6E 3N9
(450) 756-0564
Emp Here 30   *Sales* 6,784,769
SIC 5072 Hardware
Pr Pr Louis Desrochers

D-U-N-S 25-240-5360   (SL)
FONDATION DE L'ECOLE LES MELEZES
393 Rue De Lanaudiere, Joliette, QC, J6E 3L9
(450) 752-4433
Emp Here 60   *Sales* 4,012,839
SIC 8211 Elementary and secondary schools

D-U-N-S 24-211-3731   (BR)
GARAGE VILLEMAIRE & FILS INC
CENTRE DU PNEU VILLEMAIRE ENR
980 Ch Des Prairies, Joliette, QC, J6E 0L4
(450) 752-1000
Emp Here 20
SIC 5531 Auto and home supply stores

D-U-N-S 20-570-2454   (BR)
GOUVERNEMENT DE LA PROVINCE DE QUEBEC
MINISTERE DES TRANSPORTS
1163 Boul Manseau, Joliette, QC, J6E 3G9
(450) 759-5661
Emp Here 25
SIC 1611 Highway and street construction

D-U-N-S 24-378-2542   (BR)
GOUVERNEMENT DE LA PROVINCE DE QUEBEC
CENTRE DE READAPTATION EN DEFICIENCE PHYSIQUE LE BOUCLIER
1075 Boul Firestone Bureau 1000, Joliette, QC, J6E 6X6
(450) 755-2741
Emp Here 100
SIC 8011 Offices and clinics of medical doctors

D-U-N-S 25-412-4894   (BR)
GOUVERNEMENT DE LA PROVINCE DE QUEBEC
CENTRE LOCAL DE SANTE COMMUNAUTAIRE DE JOLIETTE
380 Boul Base-De-Roc, Joliette, QC, J6E 9J6
(450) 755-2111
Emp Here 150
SIC 8399 Social services, nec

D-U-N-S 24-346-2228   (BR)
GOUVERNEMENT DE LA PROVINCE DE QUEBEC
CENTRE INTEGRE DE SANTE ET DE SERVICES SOCIAUX DE LANAUDIERE
245 Rue Du Cure-Majeau, Joliette, QC, J6E 8S8
(450) 759-1157
Emp Here 200
SIC 8399 Social services, nec

D-U-N-S 24-562-7849   (BR)
GRAYMONT (QC) INC
1300 Rue Notre-Dame, Joliette, QC, J6E 3Z9
(450) 759-8195
Emp Here 100
SIC 1422 Crushed and broken limestone

D-U-N-S 25-309-6853   (BR)
INDUSTRIELLE ALLIANCE, ASSURANCE ET SERVICES FINANCIERS INC

INDUSTRIELLE ALLIANCE
40 Rue Gauthier S Bureau 2100, Joliette, QC,
J6E 4J4
(450) 756-2189
Emp Here 30
SIC 6411 Insurance agents, brokers, and service

D-U-N-S 24-812-3853   (SL)
JOLIETTE DODGE CHRYSLER LTEE
305 Rue Du Cure-Majeau, Joliette, QC, J6E
8S9
(450) 586-6002
Emp Here 50   *Sales* 24,540,000
SIC 5511 New and used car dealers
Pr Pr Christian Le Roux
  Serge Le Roux

D-U-N-S 24-003-5654   (BR)
**LES BENEVOLES DU CENTRE HOSPITAL-
IER REGIONAL DE LANAUDIERE CHRDL**
*LES BENEVOLES DU CENTRE HOSPITAL-
IER REGIONAL DE LA*
256 Rue Lavaltrie S, Joliette, QC, J6E 5X7
(450) 755-6655
Emp Here 50
SIC 8062 General medical and surgical hospitals

D-U-N-S 24-988-0709   (SL)
LIARD INDUSTRIES INC
ATELIERS D'USINAGE MDM, LES
(*Suby of* Gestion Dave-Li Inc)
1707 Rue Lepine, Joliette, QC, J6E 4B7
(450) 759-5884
Emp Here 35   *Sales* 2,553,625
SIC 3599 Industrial machinery, nec

D-U-N-S 20-201-9287   (SL)
MALO, A. COMPAGNIE LIMITEE
171 Rue Saint-Barthelemy S, Joliette, QC,
J6E 5N9
(450) 756-1612
Emp Here 50   *Sales* 4,331,255
SIC 3599 Industrial machinery, nec

D-U-N-S 20-201-9386   (SL)
MARCHE BEL AIR INC
METRO-RICHELIEU 0198
180 Rue Beaudry N, Joliette, QC, J6E 6A6
(450) 759-8731
Emp Here 135   *Sales* 24,834,480
SIC 5411 Grocery stores
Pr Pr Andre Belair
  Bernard Belair

D-U-N-S 25-291-6267   (BR)
MEDIAS TRANSCONTINENTAL INC
MEDIAS TRANSCONTINENTAL INC
342 Rue Beaudry N, Joliette, QC, J6E 6A6
(450) 759-3664
Emp Here 25
SIC 2721 Periodicals

D-U-N-S 24-115-1401   (BR)
METRO RICHELIEU INC
SUPER C
1445 Boul Firestone, Joliette, QC, J6E 9E5
(450) 752-0088
Emp Here 60
SIC 5411 Grocery stores

D-U-N-S 24-945-4737   (SL)
PLASTREC INC
1461 Rue Lepine, Joliette, QC, J6E 4B7
(450) 760-3830
Emp Here 100   *Sales* 16,961,922
SIC 4953 Refuse systems
Pr Pr Jean Roy
  Louis Robitaille

D-U-N-S 20-703-6901   (BR)
PREMIER TECH TECHNOLOGIES LIMITEE
595 Rue Frenette, Joliette, QC, J6E 9B2
(450) 752-5111
Emp Here 40
SIC 3589 Service industry machinery, nec

D-U-N-S 25-849-3204   (BR)
PROVIGO DISTRIBUTION INC
MAXI JOLIETTE
909 Boul Firestone, Joliette, QC, J6E 2W4
(450) 755-2781
Emp Here 120
SIC 5411 Grocery stores

D-U-N-S 20-584-3977   (BR)
SEARS CANADA INC
SEARS DEPARTMENT STORE # 6398
1195 Boul Firestone, Joliette, QC, J6E 2W4
(450) 759-5858
Emp Here 175
SIC 5311 Department stores

D-U-N-S 25-222-6014   (BR)
SIR WILFRID LAURIER SCHOOL BOARD
JOLIETTE HIGH SCHOOL
(*Suby of* Sir Wilfrid Laurier School Board)
107 Rue Delorimier, Joliette, QC, J6E 6E8
(450) 755-1556
Emp Here 30
SIC 8211 Elementary and secondary schools

D-U-N-S 25-308-8413   (BR)
SOCIETE DES ALCOOLS DU QUEBEC
SOCIETE DES ALCOOLS DU QUEBEC
975 Boul Firestone, Joliette, QC, J6E 2W4

Emp Here 20
SIC 5921 Liquor stores

D-U-N-S 24-943-5405   (BR)
**SOEURS DE LA CONGREGATION DE
NOTRE-DAME, LES**
*RESIDENCE   NOTRE-DAME-DE-LA-
PROTECTION*
393 Rue De Lanaudiere, Joliette, QC, J6E 3L9
(450) 752-1481
Emp Here 200
SIC 8661 Religious organizations

D-U-N-S 20-553-3669   (BR)
STAPLES CANADA INC
BUREAU EN GROS
(*Suby of* Staples, Inc.)
845 Boul Firestone, Joliette, QC, J6E 2W4
(450) 752-5515
Emp Here 35
SIC 5943 Stationery stores

D-U-N-S 24-378-9992   (SL)
**SYSTEMES D'ECRAN STRONG/MDI INC,
LES**
(*Suby of* Ballantyne Strong, Inc.)
1440 Rue Raoul-Charette, Joliette, QC, J6E
8S7
(450) 755-3795
Emp Here 35   *Sales* 2,165,628
SIC 3861 Photographic equipment and supplies

D-U-N-S 24-851-3520   (BR)
WSP CANADA INC
138 Rue Saint-Paul, Joliette, QC, J6E 5G3
(450) 756-0617
Emp Here 40
SIC 8711 Engineering services

D-U-N-S 25-297-6071   (BR)
WAL-MART CANADA CORP
WALMART
1505 Boul Firestone Bureau 521, Joliette, QC,
J6E 9E5
(450) 752-8210
Emp Here 160
SIC 5311 Department stores

Jonquiere, QC G7S
Chicoutimi County

D-U-N-S 20-124-9732   (SL)
9020-4983 QUEBEC INC
INSTITUT D' ECHAFAUDAGE-QUEBEC

2035 Rue Deschenes, Jonquiere, QC, G7S
5E3
(418) 548-5000
Emp Here 60   *Sales* 4,815,406
SIC 7353 Heavy construction equipment
rental

D-U-N-S 24-290-6704   (SL)
9190-0738 QUEBEC INC
SST 2006 (SERVICES SERGE TURCOTTE)
2694 Rue De La Salle Bureau 101, Jonquiere,
QC, G7S 2A7
(418) 699-7777
Emp Here 50   *Sales* 2,699,546
SIC 7999 Amusement and recreation, nec

D-U-N-S 20-715-5917   (BR)
BANK OF MONTREAL
BMO BANK OF MONTREAL
2840 Place Davis, Jonquiere, QC, G7S 2C5
(418) 548-7133
Emp Here 28
SIC 6021 National commercial banks

D-U-N-S 20-949-0614   (SL)
CLUB SAGUENAY D'ARVIDA INC
2680 Boul Du Saguenay, Jonquiere, QC, G7S
0L3
(418) 548-4235
Emp Here 50   *Sales* 2,042,900
SIC 7997 Membership sports and recreation
clubs

D-U-N-S 20-000-9947   (BR)
**COMMISSION SCOLAIRE CENTRAL QUE-
BEC**
RIVERSIDE REGIONAL HIGH SCHOOL
1770 Rue Joule, Jonquiere, QC, G7S 3B1
(418) 548-3181
Emp Here 21
SIC 8211 Elementary and secondary schools

D-U-N-S 20-006-9917   (BR)
**COMMISSION SCOLAIRE CENTRAL QUE-
BEC**
ECOLE PRIMAIRE RIVERSIDE
1782 Rue Neilson, Jonquiere, QC, G7S 3A2
(418) 548-8296
Emp Here 30
SIC 8211 Elementary and secondary schools

D-U-N-S 20-031-3562   (BR)
**COMMISSION SCOLAIRE DE LA JON-
QUIERE**
*CENTRE DE FORMATION JONQUIERE EDI-
FICE MELLON HOTELERIE*
(*Suby of* Commission Scolaire de la Jonquiere)
2215 Boul Mellon Bureau 101, Jonquiere, QC,
G7S 3G4
(418) 548-4689
Emp Here 40
SIC 8211 Elementary and secondary schools

D-U-N-S 20-711-8832   (BR)
**COMMISSION SCOLAIRE DE LA JON-
QUIERE**
E+COLE POLYVALENTE ARVIDA
(*Suby of* Commission Scolaire de la Jonquiere)
2215 Boul Mellon Bureau 101, Jonquiere, QC,
G7S 3G4
(418) 548-3113
Emp Here 135
SIC 8211 Elementary and secondary schools

D-U-N-S 25-231-9439   (BR)
**COMMISSION SCOLAIRE DE LA JON-
QUIERE**
ECOLE NOTRE DAME DE L'ASSOMPTION
(*Suby of* Commission Scolaire de la Jonquiere)
2075 Rue Hudson, Jonquiere, QC, G7S 3R4
(418) 548-7158
Emp Here 40
SIC 8211 Elementary and secondary schools

D-U-N-S 25-231-9751   (BR)

**COMMISSION SCOLAIRE DE LA JON-
QUIERE**
ECOLE STE LUCIE
(*Suby of* Commission Scolaire de la Jonquiere)
2330 Rue Levesque, Jonquiere, QC, G7S 3T3
(418) 548-8238
Emp Here 30
SIC 8211 Elementary and secondary schools

D-U-N-S 20-711-8840   (BR)
**COMMISSION SCOLAIRE DE LA JON-
QUIERE**
ECOLE POLYVALENTE JONQUIERE
(*Suby of* Commission Scolaire de la Jonquiere)
3450 Boul Du Royaume, Jonquiere, QC, G7S
5T2
(418) 547-5781
Emp Here 120
SIC 8211 Elementary and secondary schools

D-U-N-S 20-801-8668   (BR)
**COMMISSION SCOLAIRE DE LA JON-
QUIERE**
*CENTRE DES SERVICES AUX EN-
TREPRISES*
(*Suby of* Commission Scolaire de la Jonquiere)
2875 Boul Du Saguenay, Jonquiere, QC, G7S
2H2
(418) 548-7373
Emp Here 25
SIC 8741 Management services

D-U-N-S 25-231-9397   (BR)
**COMMISSION SCOLAIRE DE LA JON-
QUIERE**
ECOLE NOTRE DAME DU SOURIRE
(*Suby of* Commission Scolaire de la Jonquiere)
1796 Rue Neilson, Jonquiere, QC, G7S 3A2
(418) 548-8205
Emp Here 30
SIC 8211 Elementary and secondary schools

D-U-N-S 20-030-4694   (BR)
**COMMISSION SCOLAIRE DE LA JON-
QUIERE**
ATELIERS DE REPARATION
(*Suby of* Commission Scolaire de la Jonquiere)
2195 Boul Mellon, Jonquiere, QC, G7S 3G4
(418) 548-7185
Emp Here 20
SIC 7349 Building maintenance services, nec

D-U-N-S 20-873-9011   (BR)
GUAY INC
GUAY SERVICE DE GRUE
2474 Rue Dubose, Jonquiere, QC, G7S 1B4
(418) 548-3192
Emp Here 25
SIC 7353 Heavy construction equipment
rental

D-U-N-S 25-104-4855   (SL)
LIGNES DU FJORD INC, LES
(*Suby of* Prowatt Inc)
2361 Rue Bauman, Jonquiere, QC, G7S 5A9
(418) 548-0048
Emp Here 26   *Sales* 4,523,563
SIC 1623 Water, sewer, and utility lines

D-U-N-S 24-415-8858   (BR)
MOTEURS ELECTRIQUES LAVAL LTEE
2050 Rue Deschenes, Jonquiere, QC, G7S
2A9
(418) 548-3134
Emp Here 28
SIC 7694 Armature rewinding shops

D-U-N-S 20-795-5787   (BR)
NOVELIS INC
2040 Rue Fay, Jonquiere, QC, G7S 2N4
(418) 699-5213
Emp Here 60
SIC 3365 Aluminum foundries

D-U-N-S 24-568-6571   (SL)
PLACEMENTS GILLES ARNOLD INC
2595 Rue Godbout, Jonquiere, QC, G7S 5S9
(418) 548-0821
Emp Here 55   *Sales* 25,914,048
SIC 5511 New and used car dealers
Pr Pr Gilles Arnold Tremblay

D-U-N-S 24-864-3009   (BR)
RIO TINTO ALCAN INC
ENERGIE ELECTRIQUE, DIV OF
(*Suby of* RIO TINTO PLC)
1954 Rue Davis, Jonquiere, QC, G7S 3B6
(418) 699-2131
Emp Here 650
SIC 4911 Electric services

D-U-N-S 20-190-8956   (BR)
RIO TINTO ALCAN INC
(*Suby of* RIO TINTO PLC)
1955 Boul Mellon, Jonquiere, QC, G7S 0L4
(418) 699-2002
Emp Here 600
SIC 3334 Primary aluminum

D-U-N-S 24-058-3968   (BR)
**SERVICE CORPORATION INTERNATIONAL
(CANADA) LIMITED**
MAISON FUNERAIRE NAULT & CARON
2770 Rue De La Salle, Jonquiere, QC, G7S
2A4
(418) 548-8831
Emp Here 20
SIC 7261 Funeral service and crematories

D-U-N-S 24-848-2072   (SL)
**SOCIETE EN COMMANDITE LE SAGUE-
NAY**
*DELTA SAGUENAY HOTEL ET CENTRE DES
CONGRES*
2675 Boul Du Royaume, Jonquiere, QC, G7S
5B8
(418) 548-3124
Emp Here 50   *Sales* 2,188,821
SIC 7011 Hotels and motels

D-U-N-S 20-526-9405   (BR)
STAPLES CANADA INC
BUREAU EN GROS
(*Suby of* Staples, Inc.)
2380 Boul Rene-Levesque, Jonquiere, QC,
G7S 5Y5
(418) 542-1646
Emp Here 20
SIC 5943 Stationery stores

D-U-N-S 20-526-4067   (SL)
SUPER MARCHE MELLON INC
SUPER MARCHE MELLON I G A
2085 Boul Mellon, Jonquiere, QC, G7S 3G4
(418) 548-7557
Emp Here 130   *Sales* 23,993,820
SIC 5411 Grocery stores
Pt Rejeanne St-Pierre

D-U-N-S 25-919-3423   (BR)
**VEOLIA ES CANADA SERVICES INDUS-
TRIELS INC**
1995 Rue Fay, Jonquiere, QC, G7S 2N5
(418) 548-8247
Emp Here 30
SIC 1799 Special trade contractors, nec

Jonquiere, QC G7T
Chicoutimi County

D-U-N-S 20-581-3608   (BR)
CANADA POST CORPORATION
BDP JONQUIERE
3219 Boul Saint-Francois, Jonquiere, QC,
G7T 0A6
(418) 548-0588
Emp Here 55
SIC 4311 U.s. postal service

Jonquiere, QC G7X
Chicoutimi County

D-U-N-S 20-319-6030   (BR)
9065-0805 QUEBEC INC
SUTTON GROUP
2395 Rue Saint-Dominique, Jonquiere, QC,
G7X 6L1
(418) 542-7587
Emp Here 24
SIC 6531 Real estate agents and managers

D-U-N-S 24-737-9550   (SL)
9111-3829 QUEBEC INC
1180 Bellevue St, Jonquiere, QC, G7X 1A5
(418) 543-1632
Emp Here 90   *Sales* 17,963,280
SIC 6712 Bank holding companies
Pr Pr Eloise Harvey

D-U-N-S 24-137-7865   (SL)
9214-6489 QUEBEC INC
PLANCHERS EN GROS 2009
162 Rue Joseph-Gagne N, Jonquiere, QC,
G7X 9H3
(418) 695-1793
Emp Here 100   *Sales* 20,391,450
SIC 5211 Lumber and other building materials
Pr Robert Millette
   Gerard Leclerc

D-U-N-S 20-801-4121   (SL)
AUTOCARS JASMIN INC
2249 Rue Saint-Hubert, Jonquiere, QC, G7X
5P1
(418) 547-2167
Emp Here 400   *Sales* 18,186,950
SIC 4111 Local and suburban transit
Pr Jasmin Gilbert

D-U-N-S 20-202-1333   (SL)
BARILLET JONQUIERE INC, LE
2523 Rue Saint-Dominique, Jonquiere, QC,
G7X 6K1
(418) 547-2668
Emp Here 50   *Sales* 1,532,175
SIC 5812 Eating places

D-U-N-S 24-545-7945   (BR)
CHAINE DE TRAVAIL ADAPTE C.T.A. INC
CHAINE DE TRAVAIL ADAPTE
(*Suby of* Chaine de Travail Adapte C.T.A. Inc)
2440 Rue Cantin Bureau 102, Jonquiere, QC,
G7X 8S6
(418) 543-6758
Emp Here 40
SIC 7349 Building maintenance services, nec

D-U-N-S 24-501-9369   (HQ)
**COLLEGE D'ENSEIGNEMENT GENERAL
ET PROFESSIONNEL DE JONQUIERE**
CEGEP DE JONQUIERE
(*Suby of* College d'Enseignement General et
Professionnel de Jonquiere)
2505 Rue Saint-Hubert, Jonquiere, QC, G7X
7W2
(418) 547-2191
Emp Here 532   *Emp Total* 550
Sales 79,536,800
SIC 8221 Colleges and universities
Pr Denis Chayer
Treas Simon Belley
Dir Michel Gravel
Dir David Marchand
Dir Guylaine Lapierre
Dir Fanny Labelle
Dir Emile Gagnon

D-U-N-S 24-568-2042   (SL)
COMETAL S. L. INC
2361 Rue De La Metallurgie, Jonquiere, QC,
G7X 9V8
(418) 547-3322
Emp Here 40   *Sales* 23,009,920
SIC 5075 Warm air heating and air condition-
ing

VP Remi Bouchard
Pr Pr Alain Pouliot
   Stephane Moreau

D-U-N-S 25-231-9553   (BR)
**COMMISSION SCOLAIRE DE LA JON-
QUIERE**
ECOLE SACRE COEUR
(*Suby of* Commission Scolaire de la Jon-
quiere)
1930 Rue De Frontenac, Jonquiere, QC, G7X
4W3
(418) 542-4555
Emp Here 30
SIC 8211 Elementary and secondary schools

D-U-N-S 25-232-2441   (BR)
**COMMISSION SCOLAIRE DE LA JON-
QUIERE**
EDIFICE NOTRE-DAME-DU-ROSAIRE
(*Suby of* Commission Scolaire de la Jon-
quiere)
2390 Rue Pelletier, Jonquiere, QC, G7X 6B9
(418) 547-2681
Emp Here 30
SIC 8211 Elementary and secondary schools

D-U-N-S 25-231-9595   (BR)
**COMMISSION SCOLAIRE DE LA JON-
QUIERE**
ECOLE IMMACULEE CONCEPTION
(*Suby of* Commission Scolaire de la Jon-
quiere)
3795 Rue Saint-Laurent, Jonquiere, QC, G7X
2P5
(418) 547-4708
Emp Here 30
SIC 8211 Elementary and secondary schools

D-U-N-S 25-002-1664   (BR)
**COMMISSION SCOLAIRE DE LA JON-
QUIERE**
ECOLE SECONDAIRE KENOGAMI
(*Suby of* Commission Scolaire de la Jon-
quiere)
1954 Rue Des Etudiants, Jonquiere, QC, G7X
4B1
(418) 542-3571
Emp Here 120
SIC 8211 Elementary and secondary schools

D-U-N-S 20-711-8865   (BR)
**COMMISSION SCOLAIRE DE LA JON-
QUIERE**
*CENTRE DE FORMATION GENERALE DES
ADULTES DE LA JONQUIERE*
(*Suby of* Commission Scolaire de la Jon-
quiere)
3842 Boul Harvey, Jonquiere, QC, G7X 2Z4
(418) 547-4702
Emp Here 80
SIC 8211 Elementary and secondary schools

D-U-N-S 25-232-2524   (BR)
**COMMISSION SCOLAIRE DE LA JON-
QUIERE**
ECOLE SAINT LUC
(*Suby of* Commission Scolaire de la Jon-
quiere)
3950 Rue De La Bretagne, Jonquiere, QC,
G7X 3W3
(418) 547-2619
Emp Here 20
SIC 8211 Elementary and secondary schools

D-U-N-S 25-231-9678   (BR)
**COMMISSION SCOLAIRE DE LA JON-
QUIERE**
ECOLE STE CECILE
(*Suby of* Commission Scolaire de la Jon-
quiere)
1769 Rue Saint-Francois-Xavier, Jonquiere,
QC, G7X 4N8
(418) 542-4549
Emp Here 30
SIC 8211 Elementary and secondary schools

D-U-N-S 20-711-8881   (BR)

**COMMISSION SCOLAIRE DE LA JON-
QUIERE**
*CENTRE DE FORMATION PROFES-
SIONELLE JONQUIERE EDIFICE SAINT-
GERMAIN*
(*Suby of* Commission Scolaire de la Jon-
quiere)
3829 Rue Saint-Germain, Jonquiere, QC,
G7X 2W1
(418) 542-8760
Emp Here 22
SIC 8211 Elementary and secondary schools

D-U-N-S 20-430-8704   (HQ)
CORNEAU & CANTIN LTEE
(*Suby of* Corneau & Cantin Ltee)
3650 Rue Du Roi-Georges, Jonquiere, QC,
G7X 1V1
(418) 542-9556
Emp Here 75   *Emp Total* 150
Sales 27,779,280
SIC 5411 Grocery stores
Pr Pr Jean-Marie Cantin
   Pierre Cantin

D-U-N-S 20-806-8572   (BR)
COUCHE-TARD INC
3754 Boul Du Royaume, Jonquiere, QC, G7X
1Y3
(418) 547-9292
Emp Here 25
SIC 5411 Grocery stores

D-U-N-S 25-299-6210   (BR)
DOLLARAMA S.E.C.
DOLLARAMA
3880 Boul Harvey, Jonquiere, QC, G7X 8R6
(418) 547-8617
Emp Here 20
SIC 5331 Variety stores

D-U-N-S 25-309-6945   (BR)
**INDUSTRIELLE ALLIANCE, ASSURANCE
ET SERVICES FINANCIERS INC**
3639 Boul Harvey Bureau 100, Jonquiere, QC,
G7X 3B2
(418) 542-9004
Emp Here 40
SIC 6411 Insurance agents, brokers, and ser-
vice

D-U-N-S 20-294-2111   (BR)
**LE CENTRE JEUNESSE DU SAGUENAY-
LAC-SAINT-JEAN**
CENTRES JEUNESSE JONQUIERE
3639 Boul Harvey Bureau 203, Jonquiere, QC,
G7X 3B2
(418) 547-5773
Emp Here 45
SIC 8322 Individual and family services

D-U-N-S 20-004-8812   (BR)
METRO RICHELIEU INC
SUPER C GALERIES JONQUIERE
3460 Boul Saint-Francois, Jonquiere, QC,
G7X 8L3
(418) 547-9356
Emp Here 70
SIC 5411 Grocery stores

D-U-N-S 24-325-4021   (BR)
PF RESOLU CANADA INC
3750 Rue De Champlain, Jonquiere, QC, G7X
1M1
(418) 695-9100
Emp Here 199
SIC 2621 Paper mills

D-U-N-S 20-314-4431   (SL)
PATRO DE JONQUIERE INC, LE
2565 Rue Saint-Dominique, Jonquiere, QC,
G7X 6J6
(418) 542-7536
Emp Here 50   *Sales* 2,699,546
SIC 7999 Amusement and recreation, nec

D-U-N-S 24-943-1495   (SL)
POLY-TOITURE INC
3459 Rue De L'Energie, Jonquiere, QC, G7X

0C1
(418) 695-1315
Emp Here 46   *Sales* 6,289,900
SIC 1761 Roofing, siding, and sheetMetal
work
Pr Pr Normand Bilodeau
  Jean-Clauce Gaudreault

D-U-N-S 20-171-7894   (BR)
PROVIGO DISTRIBUTION INC
ENTREPOTS PRESTO, LES
2460 Rue Cantin, Jonquiere, QC, G7X 8S6
(418) 547-3675
Emp Here 25
SIC 5141 Groceries, general line

D-U-N-S 24-742-5978   (BR)
PUROLATOR INC.
PUROLATCR INC
3479 Rue De L'Energie, Jonquiere, QC, G7X
0C1
(418) 695-1235
Emp Here 80
SIC 7389 Business services, nec

D-U-N-S 24-058-3943   (BR)
SGS CANADA INC
2345 Rue De La Metallurgie, Jonquiere, QC,
G7X 0B8
(418) 547-6631
Emp Here 20
SIC 4785 Inspection and fixed facilities

D-U-N-S 20-287-9912   (BR)
SNC-LAVALIN GEM QUEBEC INC
GROUPE QUALITAS
3306 Boul Saint-Francois, Jonquiere, QC,
G7X 2W9
(418) 547-5716
Emp Here 100
SIC 8742 Management consulting services

D-U-N-S 25-307-6970   (BR)
SOCIETE DES ALCOOLS DU QUEBEC
SOCIETE DES ALCOOLS DU QUEBEC
3821 Boul Harvey, Jonquiere, QC, G7X 2Z8
(418) 542-6301
Emp Here 20
SIC 5921 Liquor stores

D-U-N-S 24-610-3910   (SL)
UNIPRIX PHARMACY
2095 Rue Sainte-Famille, Jonquiere, QC, G7X
4W8
(418) 547-3689
Emp Here 45   *Sales* 6,347,581
SIC 5912 Drug stores and proprietary stores
Pr Suzanne Beauchard

D-U-N-S 25-841-1040   (BR)
VILLE DE SAGUENAY
PALAIS DES SPORTS
2315 Rue Pelletier, Jonquiere, QC, G7X 6C2
(418) 698-3200
Emp Here 20
SIC 7941 Sports clubs, managers, and pro-
moters

Jonquiere, QC G7Z
Chicoutimi County

D-U-N-S 20-703-2272   (BR)
CASCADES CANADA ULC
NORAMPAC-JONQUIERE
4010 Ch Saint-Andre, Jonquiere, QC, G7Z
0A5
(418) 542-9544
Emp Here 145
SIC 2631 Paperboard mills

Jonquiere, QC G8A
Chicoutimi County

D-U-N-S 25-232-2482   (BR)
**COMMISSION SCOLAIRE DE LA JON-
QUIERE**
ECOLE ST JEAN BAPTISTE
(*Suby of* Commission Scolaire de la Jon-
quiere)
2176 Rue Saint-Edmond, Jonquiere, QC, G8A
1Y9
(418) 547-2631
Emp Here 35
SIC 8211 Elementary and secondary schools

D-U-N-S 25-231-9637   (BR)
**COMMISSION SCOLAIRE DE LA JON-
QUIERE**
ECOLE MARGUERITE BELLEY
(*Suby of* Commission Scolaire de la Jon-
quiere)
4080 Boul Harvey, Jonquiere, QC, G8A 1K3
(418) 547-2611
Emp Here 20
SIC 8211 Elementary and secondary schools

Kahnawake, QC J0L
Laprairie County

D-U-N-S 24-107-9920   (SL)
KANAWAKI GOLF CLUB INC
Gd, Kahnawake, QC, J0L 1B0
(450) 632-7200
Emp Here 65   *Sales* 2,626,585
SIC 7997 Membership sports and recreation
clubs

D-U-N-S 20-037-3434   (BR)
KAHNAWAKE EDUCATION CENTRE
KAHNAWAKE SURVIVAL SCHOOL
1 Boul Industrial Bureau 132, Kahnawake,
QC, J0L 1B0
(450) 632-8831
Emp Here 55
SIC 8211 Elementary and secondary schools

D-U-N-S 20-024-0641   (BR)
KAHNAWAKE EDUCATION CENTRE
KATERI SCHOOL
Gd, Kahnawake, QC, J0L 1B0
(450) 632-3350
Emp Here 90
SIC 8211 Elementary and secondary schools

D-U-N-S 20-877-1654   (BR)
KAHNAWAKE EDUCATION CENTRE
KAHNAWAKE EDUCATION CENTRE
Gd, Kahnawake, QC, J0L 1B0
(450) 638-1435
Emp Here 46
SIC 8211 Elementary and secondary schools

Kangiqsualujjuaq, QC J0M
Nouveau-Quebec County

D-U-N-S 25-325-1565   (BR)
COMMISSION SCOLAIRE KATIVIK
ULLURIAQ SCHOOL
Gd, Kangiqsualujjuaq, QC, J0M 1N0
(819) 337-5250
Emp Here 30
SIC 8211 Elementary and secondary schools

Kangiqsujuaq, QC J0M
Nouveau-Quebec County

D-U-N-S 25-240-6780   (BR)
COMMISSION SCOLAIRE KATIVIK
ECOLE ARSANIQ
Gd, Kangiqsujuaq, QC, J0M 1K0
(819) 338-3332
Emp Here 30

SIC 8211 Elementary and secondary schools

Kangirsuk, QC J0M
Nouveau-Quebec County

D-U-N-S 25-325-1482   (BR)
COMMISSION SCOLAIRE KATIVIK
SAUTJUIT SCHOOL
Gd, Kangirsuk, QC, J0M 1A0
(819) 935-4318
Emp Here 35
SIC 8211 Elementary and secondary schools

Kegaska, QC G0G
Saguenay County

D-U-N-S 20-213-5955   (BR)
COMMISSION SCOLAIRE DU LITTORAL
KEGASKA SCHOOL
(*Suby of* Commission Scolaire du Littoral)
Gd, Kegaska, QC, G0G 1S0
(418) 726-3283
Emp Here 30
SIC 8211 Elementary and secondary schools

Kingsey Falls, QC J0A
Drummomd County

D-U-N-S 20-327-4956   (BR)
CASCADES CS+ INC
CASCADES GIE
15 Rue Lamontagne, Kingsey Falls, QC, J0A
1B0
(819) 363-5971
Emp Here 21
SIC 8711 Engineering services

D-U-N-S 24-337-2724   (BR)
CASCADES CANADA ULC
CASCADES GROUPE TISSU
467 Boul Marie-Victorin, Kingsey Falls, QC,
J0A 1B0
(819) 363-5600
Emp Here 167
SIC 2676 Sanitary paper products

D-U-N-S 20-803-4574   (BR)
CASCADES CANADA ULC
NORAMPAC-KINGSEY FALLS
398 Boul Marie-Victorin, Kingsey Falls, QC,
J0A 1B0
(819) 363-5000
Emp Here 60
SIC 2631 Paperboard mills

D-U-N-S 24-337-2765   (BR)
CASCADES CANADA ULC
CASCADES FORMA-PAK
406 Boul Marie-Victorin, Kingsey Falls, QC,
J0A 1B0
(819) 363-5060
Emp Here 35
SIC 2631 Paperboard mills

D-U-N-S 24-395-3291   (BR)
CASCADES INC
CASCADES PAPIER KINGSEY FALLS
408 Boul Marie-Victorin, Kingsey Falls, QC,
J0A 1B0
(819) 363-5200
Emp Here 70
SIC 2631 Paperboard mills

D-U-N-S 25-978-4080   (BR)
CASCADES INC
*CENTRE DE RECHERCHE ET DEVEL-
OPPEMENT, DIV. OF*
471 Boul Marie-Victorin, Kingsey Falls, QC,
J0A 1B0

(819) 363-5700
Emp Here 30
SIC 8731 Commercial physical research

D-U-N-S 20-689-4607   (BR)
CASCADES INC
CASCADES PLASTIQUES DIV DE
455 Boul Marie-Victorin, Kingsey Falls, QC,
J0A 1B0
(819) 363-5300
Emp Here 180
SIC 3081 Unsupported plastics film and sheet

D-U-N-S 24-821-8430   (SL)
CASCADES SONOCO INC
CASCADE SONOCO DIV KINGSEY FALLS
457 Boul Marie-Victorin, Kingsey Falls, QC,
J0A 1B0
(819) 363-5400
Emp Here 90   *Sales* 9,193,048
SIC 2679 Converted paper products, nec
Pr Luc Langevin
Sec Jerome Nadeau
Dir Rodger D. Fuller
Dir Douglas Schwartz
Dir Emilie Allen

D-U-N-S 24-051-1118   (BR)
**COMMISSION SCOLAIRE DES BOIS-
FRANCS**
ECOLE CASCATELLE
2 Rue Lajeunesse, Kingsey Falls, QC, J0A
1B0
(819) 363-2213
Emp Here 20
SIC 8211 Elementary and secondary schools

Kirkland, QC H9H
Hochelaga County

D-U-N-S 25-330-8464   (BR)
1207273 ALBERTA ULC
INVACARE CANADA
16767 Boul Hymus, Kirkland, QC, H9H 3L4
(514) 630-6080
Emp Here 40
SIC 3842 Surgical appliances and supplies

D-U-N-S 24-935-4259   (SL)
ACADEMIE KUPER INC
2 Rue Aesop, Kirkland, QC, H9H 5G5
(514) 426-3007
Emp Here 60   *Sales* 4,012,839
SIC 8211 Elementary and secondary schools

D-U-N-S 24-426-2999   (SL)
CSH MANOIR KIRKLAND INC
2 Rue Canvin, Kirkland, QC, H9H 4B5
(514) 695-1253
Emp Here 20   *Sales* 729,607
SIC 8361 Residential care

D-U-N-S 20-712-4046   (BR)
**COMMISSION SCOLAIRE MARGUERITE-
BOURGEOYS**
CFPOM
3501 Boul Saint-Charles, Kirkland, QC, H9H
4S3
(514) 333-8886
Emp Here 50
SIC 8211 Elementary and secondary schools

D-U-N-S 20-212-8666   (SL)
CONSTRUCTION BROCCOLINI INC
16766 Rte Trans-Canada Bureau 500, Kirk-
land, QC, H9H 4M7
(514) 737-0076
Emp Here 115   *Sales* 27,516,007
SIC 1542 Nonresidential construction, nec
Pr Pr John Broccolini
  Joseph Broccolini
VP VP Paul Broccolini

D-U-N-S 25-412-8291   (BR)
DISTRIBUTION DENIS JALBERT INC
(*Suby of* Distribution Denis Jalbert Inc)

16710 Rte Transcanadienne, Kirkland, QC, H9H 4M7
(514) 695-6662
Emp Here 20
SIC 5511 New and used car dealers

D-U-N-S 24-633-2410   (BR)
DOLLARAMA S.E.C.
2989 Boul Saint-Charles, Kirkland, QC, H9H 3B5
(514) 428-5895
Emp Here 20
SIC 5331 Variety stores

D-U-N-S 20-802-0490   (BR)
GROUPE BMTC INC
BRAULT & MARTINEAU
16975 Rte Transcanadienne, Kirkland, QC, H9H 5J1
(514) 697-9228
Emp Here 60
SIC 5021 Furniture

D-U-N-S 24-222-8018   (BR)
GROUPE RESTAURANTS IMVESCOR INC
RESTAURANT MIKES
2945 Boul Saint-Charles, Kirkland, QC, H9H 3B5
(514) 695-8720
Emp Here 30
SIC 5812 Eating places

D-U-N-S 24-343-3989   (BR)
ITW CANADA INVESTMENTS LIMITED PARTNERSHIP
MULLER MFG
(*Suby of* Illinois Tool Works Inc.)
16715 Boul Hymus, Kirkland, QC, H9H 5M8
(514) 426-9248
Emp Here 60
SIC 6159 Miscellaneous business credit institutions

D-U-N-S 24-655-0623   (BR)
LOBLAWS INC
PROVIGO LE MARCHE
16900 Rte Transcanadienne, Kirkland, QC, H9H 4M7
(514) 426-3005
Emp Here 20
SIC 5411 Grocery stores

D-U-N-S 20-233-7986   (HQ)
SCHERING-PLOUGH CANADA INC
MERCK
(*Suby of* Merck & Co., Inc.)
16750 Rte Transcanadienne, Kirkland, QC, H9H 4M7
(514) 426-7300
Emp Here 1,078   *Emp Total* 68,000
Sales 106,595,583
SIC 2834 Pharmaceutical preparations
Pr Pr Simard Daniel
VP VP Kirk Duguid
Bernard Houde

D-U-N-S 25-308-9429   (BR)
SOCIETE DES ALCOOLS DU QUEBEC
SOCIETE DES ALCOOLS DU QUEBEC
2955 Boul Saint-Charles, Kirkland, QC, H9H 3B5
(514) 694-2042
Emp Here 55
SIC 5921 Liquor stores

D-U-N-S 24-904-2961   (HQ)
TRAFFIC TECH INC
TRAFFIC TECH
(*Suby of* 2809664 Canada Inc)
16711 Rte Transcanadienne, Kirkland, QC, H9H 3L1
(514) 343-0044
Emp Here 139   *Emp Total* 321
Sales 86,604,351
SIC 4731 Freight transportation arrangement
Brian Arnott
Pr Mark Schiele
Sr VP Neil Arnott

Sec Lori Posluns
Dir Keith Winrow
Fin Mgr David Valela

Kirkland, QC H9J
Hochelaga County

D-U-N-S 20-165-6183   (SL)
ACADEMIE MARIE-CLAIRE
18190 Boul Elkas, Kirkland, QC, H9J 3Y4
(514) 697-9995
Emp Here 50   *Sales* 3,356,192
SIC 8211 Elementary and secondary schools

D-U-N-S 24-115-1484   (BR)
BOUTIQUE LA VIE EN ROSE INC
BOUTIQUE LA VIE EN ROSE INC
3204 Rue Jean-Yves, Kirkland, QC, H9J 2R6
(514) 630-9288
Emp Here 20
SIC 5632 Women's accessory and specialty stores

D-U-N-S 20-643-9189   (SL)
CARA FOODS
MONTANA'S COOKHOUSE SALOON
3100 Rue Jean-Yves, Kirkland, QC, H9J 2R6

Emp Here 65   *Sales* 1,969,939
SIC 5812 Eating places

D-U-N-S 25-232-9735   (BR)
COMMISSION SCOLAIRE MARGUERITE-BOURGEOYS
ECOLE EMILE NELLIGAN
101 Rue Charlevoix, Kirkland, QC, H9J 3E2
(514) 855-4235
Emp Here 60
SIC 8211 Elementary and secondary schools

D-U-N-S 20-725-6710   (HQ)
CONTROLES LAURENTIDE LTEE
ATLANTIC CONTROLS DIV OF
(*Suby of* 3224635 Canada Inc)
18000 Rte Trans-Canada, Kirkland, QC, H9J 4A1
(514) 697-9230
Emp Here 120   *Emp Total* 1
Sales 39,154,545
SIC 5085 Industrial supplies
Pr Stephen Dustin
Sec Dean Whitelaw

D-U-N-S 20-857-6496   (BR)
ESIT CANADA ENTERPRISE SERVICES CO
ESIT CANADA ENTERPRISE SERVICES CO
(*Suby of* Dxc Technology Company)
17500 Rte Transcanadienne, Kirkland, QC, H9J 2X8

Emp Here 389
SIC 5084 Industrial machinery and equipment

D-U-N-S 24-486-6922   (SL)
JOURNEY AIR FREIGHT INTERNATIONAL INC
18100 Rte Transcanadienne, Kirkland, QC, H9J 4A1
(514) 733-2277
Emp Here 49   *Sales* 5,836,856
SIC 4213 Trucking, except local

D-U-N-S 25-115-0975   (SL)
MAISON ENCHANTEE DE MARIE-CLAIRE INC, LA
18122 Boul Elkas Bureau A, Kirkland, QC, H9J 3Y4
(514) 697-0001
Emp Here 50   *Sales* 1,978,891
SIC 8351 Child day care services

D-U-N-S 20-703-9822   (BR)
MEUBLES JCPERREAULT INC
LA-Z-BOY FURNITURE GALLERIES
17850 Rte Transcanadienne, Kirkland, QC,

H9J 4A1
(514) 695-2311
Emp Here 50
SIC 5712 Furniture stores

D-U-N-S 20-229-8782   (HQ)
PFIZER CANADA INC
DIVISION MONDIALE DE RECHERCHE ET DEVELOPPEMENT DE PFIZER
(*Suby of* Pfizer Inc.)
17300 Rte Transcanadienne, Kirkland, QC, H9J 2M5
(514) 695-0500
Emp Here 100   *Emp Total* 96,500
Sales 96,891,810
SIC 2834 Pharmaceutical preparations
Pr Pr John Helou
VP Fin Serge Roussel
Sec Jonathan Cullen

D-U-N-S 25-356-1609   (BR)
SSH BEDDING CANADA CO.
SIMMONS CANADA, DIV OF
(*Suby of* SSH Bedding Canada Co.)
17400 Rte Transcanadienne, Kirkland, QC, H9J 2M5
(514) 694-3030
Emp Here 110
SIC 2394 Canvas and related products

D-U-N-S 20-105-0122   (BR)
STAPLES CANADA INC
BUREAU EN GROS
(*Suby of* Staples, Inc.)
3330 Rue Jean-Yves, Kirkland, QC, H9J 2R6

Emp Here 55
SIC 5943 Stationery stores

D-U-N-S 20-726-4839   (BR)
TOSHIBA OF CANADA LIMITED
TOSHIBA OF CANADA
18050 Rte Transcanadienne, Kirkland, QC, H9J 4A1
(514) 390-7766
Emp Here 25
SIC 5065 Electronic parts and equipment, nec

D-U-N-S 25-222-3524   (SL)
TRESORS DE MARIE-CLAIRE INC, LES
18122 Boul Elkas, Kirkland, QC, H9J 3Y4
(514) 697-0001
Emp Here 50   *Sales* 1,532,175
SIC 8351 Child day care services

D-U-N-S 25-297-6238   (BR)
WAL-MART CANADA CORP
17000 Rte Transcanadienne, Kirkland, QC, H9J 2M5
(514) 695-3040
Emp Here 200
SIC 5311 Department stores

D-U-N-S 20-106-3257   (BR)
WINNERS MERCHANTS INTERNATIONAL L.P.
WINNERS
(*Suby of* The TJX Companies Inc)
3200 Rue Jean-Yves, Kirkland, QC, H9J 2R6
(514) 428-0633
Emp Here 40
SIC 5651 Family clothing stores

Knowlton, QC J0E
Brome County

D-U-N-S 24-990-3899   (SL)
2936950 CANADA INC
(*Suby of* Corporation Developpement Knowlton Inc)
315 Ch De Knowlton, Knowlton, QC, J0E 1V0
(450) 243-6161
Emp Here 500   *Sales* 46,724,160
SIC 2844 Toilet preparations
Pr Pr Michel Cote

VP Fin Pierre Prud'homme

D-U-N-S 20-267-1418   (BR)
9128-3820 QUEBEC INC
IGA KNOWLTON
461 Ch De Knowlton, Knowlton, QC, J0E 1V0
(450) 243-6692
Emp Here 60
SIC 5411 Grocery stores

D-U-N-S 20-712-1430   (BR)
COMMISSION SCOLAIRE EASTERN TOWNSHIPS
KNOWLTON ACADEMY
(*Suby of* Commission Scolaire Eastern Townships)
81 Rue Victoria Bureau 180, Knowlton, QC, J0E 1V0
(450) 243-6187
Emp Here 20
SIC 8211 Elementary and secondary schools

D-U-N-S 20-790-7619   (SL)
KNOWLTON GOLF CLUB
CLUB DE GOLF KNOWLTON
264 Ch Lakeside, Knowlton, QC, J0E 1V0
(450) 243-6622
Emp Here 50   *Sales* 2,042,900
SIC 7997 Membership sports and recreation clubs

Kuujjuaq, QC J0M
Nouveau-Quebec County

D-U-N-S 25-245-6702   (BR)
AIR INUIT LTEE
(*Suby of* Societe Makivik)
Gd, Kuujjuaq, QC, J0M 1C0
(819) 964-2935
Emp Here 20
SIC 4512 Air transportation, scheduled

D-U-N-S 24-321-8880   (SL)
CENTRE DE SANTE TULATTAVIK DE L'UNGAVA
UNGAVA HOSPITAL
Gd, Kuujjuaq, QC, J0M 1C0
(819) 964-2905
Emp Here 300   *Sales* 18,355,920
SIC 8051 Skilled nursing care facilities
Madge Pomerleau

D-U-N-S 20-791-7894   (SL)
CENTRE DE LA PETITE ENFANCE IQITAU-VIK
C.P.E. TUMIAPIIT
Gd, Kuujjuaq, QC, J0M 1C0
(819) 964-2389
Emp Here 50   *Sales* 1,532,175
SIC 8351 Child day care services

D-U-N-S 20-296-6748   (BR)
COMMISSION SCOLAIRE KATIVIK
KATIVIK SCHOOLBOARD
828 Rue Kaivvivik, Kuujjuaq, QC, J0M 1C0
(819) 964-2912
Emp Here 76
SIC 8211 Elementary and secondary schools

D-U-N-S 24-180-1773   (BR)
GOUVERNEMENT DE LA PROVINCE DE QUEBEC
CS TUTATTAVIK DE L'UNGAVA
Gd, Kuujjuaq, QC, J0M 1C0
(819) 964-2905
Emp Here 100
SIC 8011 Offices and clinics of medical doctors

D-U-N-S 24-915-5086   (BR)
NORTH WEST COMPANY LP, THE
NORTHERN STORES
Gd, Kuujjuaq, QC, J0M 1C0
(819) 964-2877
Emp Here 20

SIC 5411 Grocery stores

D-U-N-S 24-529-2800   (BR)
SOCIETE MAKIVIK
(*Suby of* Societe Makivik)
Pr, Kuujjuaq, QC, J0M 1C0
(819) 964-2925
Emp Here 30
SIC 7389 Business services, nec

Kuujjuarapik, QC J0M
Nouveau-Quebec County

D-U-N-S 20-716-8118   (BR)
COMMISSION SCOLAIRE KATIVIK
ECOLE ASIMAUTAQ
Pr, Kuujjuarapik, QC, J0M 1G0
(819) 929-3409
Emp Here 50
SIC 8211 Elementary and secondary schools

D-U-N-S 20-028-6610   (BR)
CREE SCHOOL BOARD
BADAVIN EEYOU SCHOOL
(*Suby of* Cree School Board)
Pr, Kuujjuarapik, QC, J0M 1G0
(819) 929-3257
Emp Here 32
SIC 8211 Elementary and secondary schools

L'Ancienne-Lorette, QC G2E
Quebec County

D-U-N-S 24-820-2301   (SL)
163048 CANADA INC
CAGE AUX SPORTS, LA
6476 Boul Wilfrid-Hamel, L'Ancienne-Lorette,
QC, G2E 2J1
(418) 872-3000
Emp Here 50   *Sales* 1,532,175
SIC 5812 Eating places

D-U-N-S 25-363-1139   (HQ)
CAISSE POPULAIRE DESJARDINS DU PIEMONT LAURENTIEN
CENTRE DE SERVICES VAL-BELAIR
(*Suby of* Caisse Populaire Desjardins du Piemont Laurentien)
1638 Rue Notre-Dame, L'Ancienne-Lorette,
QC, G2E 336
(418) 872-1445
Emp Here 50   *Emp Total* 95
Sales 16,394,971
SIC 6062 State credit unions
Genl Mgr Renaud Audet
Pr Claude Lefebvre
VP Gervais Morisette
Sec Amelie Beauchesne
Dir Marie-Eve Fradette
Dir Jocelyn Ouellet
Dir Melanie Argouin
Dir Catherine Aubert
Dir Francis Helie
Dir Annie Fare

D-U-N-S 24-206-1687   (HQ)
CANAC IMMOBILIER INC
6245 Boul Wilfrid-Hamel Bureau 400,
L'Ancienne-Lorette, QC, G2E 5W2
(418) 667-1313
Emp Here 75   *Emp Total* 13,000
Sales 234,787,533
SIC 5211 Lumber and other building materials
Pr Pr Jean Laberge
VP VP Pierre Laberge
Gilles Laberge

D-U-N-S 20-363-5214   (HQ)
CANAC-MARQUIS GRENIER LTEE
CANAC
6245 Boul Wilfrid-Hamel, L'Ancienne-Lorette,

QC, G2E 5W2
(418) 667-1313
Emp Here 100   *Emp Total* 13,000
Sales 181,818,064
SIC 6719 Holding companies, nec
Pr Jean Laberge
VP Pierre Laberge
Sec Gilles Laberge

D-U-N-S 24-359-0051   (BR)
CANAC-MARQUIS GRENIER LTEE
6235 Boul Wilfrid-Hamel, L'Ancienne-Lorette,
QC, G2E 5W2
(418) 872-2874
Emp Here 150
SIC 5211 Lumber and other building materials

D-U-N-S 20-797-5371   (BR)
CANADA POST CORPORATION
DEPOT DE FACTEUR DE L'ANCIENNE LORETTE
1697 Rue Notre-Dame, L'Ancienne-Lorette,
QC, G2E 3B9

Emp Here 48
SIC 4311 U.s. postal service

D-U-N-S 24-690-3256   (HQ)
CENTRE JARDIN HAMEL INC
(*Suby of* Centre Jardin Hamel Inc)
6029 Boul Wilfrid-Hamel, L'Ancienne-Lorette,
QC, G2E 2H3
(418) 872-9705
Emp Here 40   *Emp Total* 80
Sales 17,885,440
SIC 5261 Retail nurseries and garden stores
Dir Fin Christian Drouin
Pr Michel Cauvel De Beauville
   Philippe Poullain

D-U-N-S 20-712-0481   (BR)
COMMISSION SCOLAIRE DES DECOUVREURS
ECOLE SECONDAIRE POLYVALENTE L'ANCIENNE LORETTE
(*Suby of* Commission Scolaire des Decouvreurs)
1801 Rue Notre-Dame, L'Ancienne-Lorette,
QC, G2E 3C6
(418) 872-9836
Emp Here 50
SIC 8211 Elementary and secondary schools

D-U-N-S 20-712-0499   (BR)
COMMISSION SCOLAIRE DES DECOUVREURS
ECOLE DES HAUTS PLACES
(*Suby of* Commission Scolaire des Decouvreurs)
1591 Rue Notre-Dame, L'Ancienne-Lorette,
QC, G2E 3B4
(418) 871-6412
Emp Here 50
SIC 8211 Elementary and secondary schools

D-U-N-S 20-712-0465   (BR)
COMMISSION SCOLAIRE DES DECOUVREURS
HAUTS-CLOCHERS PAVILLON SAINT-CHARLES
(*Suby of* Commission Scolaire des Decouvreurs)
1350 Rue Saint-Charles, L'Ancienne-Lorette,
QC, G2E 1V4
(418) 871-6409
Emp Here 50
SIC 8211 Elementary and secondary schools

D-U-N-S 20-363-5313   (SL)
EDT GCV CIVIL S.E.P.
1095 Rue Valets, L'Ancienne-Lorette, QC,
G2E 4M7
(418) 872-0600
Emp Here 100   *Sales* 12,622,201
SIC 8742 Management consulting services
Genl Mgr Jean-Francois Racine

D-U-N-S 20-579-9653   (SL)

G.L.R. INC
GLR
1095 Rue Valets, L'Ancienne-Lorette, QC,
G2E 4M7
(418) 872-3365
Emp Here 100   *Sales* 17,510,568
SIC 1623 Water, sewer, and utility lines
   Martin Chagnon

D-U-N-S 25-765-9185   (HQ)
GESTION LABERGE INC
(*Suby of* Gestion Laberge Inc)
6245 Boul Wilfrid-Hamel, L'Ancienne-Lorette,
QC, G2E 5W2
(418) 667-1313
Emp Here 75   *Emp Total* 13,000
Sales 2,403,690,262
SIC 6712 Bank holding companies
Pr Jean Laberge
VP VP Pierre Laberge
Sec Gilles Laberge

D-U-N-S 24-316-6712   (SL)
GLR - THIRO S.E.N.C.
1095 Rue Valets, L'Ancienne-Lorette, QC,
G2E 4M7
(418) 872-7420
Emp Here 200   *Sales* 45,231,792
SIC 1623 Water, sewer, and utility lines
Pr Pr Louis-Andre Royer

D-U-N-S 25-765-7213   (BR)
NAUTILUS PLUS INC
TENNISPORT
6280 Boul Wilfrid-Hamel, L'Ancienne-Lorette,
QC, G2E 2H8
(418) 872-1230
Emp Here 45
SIC 7997 Membership sports and recreation clubs

D-U-N-S 25-477-2023   (SL)
POSIMAGE INC
6285 Boul Wilfrid-Hamel, L'Ancienne-Lorette,
QC, G2E 5W2
(418) 877-2775
Emp Here 60   *Sales* 3,648,035
SIC 3993 Signs and advertising specialties

D-U-N-S 20-354-0070   (HQ)
RESTAURANTS RENE BOISVERT INC, LES
RESTAURANT MC DONALD'S
(*Suby of* Restaurants Rene Boisvert Inc, Les)
6565 Boul Wilfrid-Hamel, L'Ancienne-Lorette,
QC, G2E 5W3
(418) 871-5866
Emp Here 20   *Emp Total* 80
Sales 2,858,628
SIC 5812 Eating places

D-U-N-S 20-059-3965   (BR)
SERVICES MATREC INC
6205 Boul Wilfrid-Hamel, L'Ancienne-Lorette,
QC, G2E 5G8
(418) 628-8666
Emp Here 50
SIC 7389 Business services, nec

D-U-N-S 20-240-5577   (HQ)
TRANSPORT THIBODEAU INC
(*Suby of* Groupe Thibodeau Inc)
6205 Boul Wilfrid-Hamel, L'Ancienne-Lorette,
QC, G2E 5G8

Emp Here 50   *Emp Total* 800
Sales 53,202,720
SIC 4213 Trucking, except local
Pr Pierre Thibodeau
Sec Josiane-Melanie Langlois
Pr Pr Alain Bedard

D-U-N-S 20-544-2499   (BR)
UNIPRIX INC
1372 Rue Saint-Jacques, L'Ancienne-Lorette,
QC, G2E 2X1
(418) 872-2857
Emp Here 35
SIC 5912 Drug stores and proprietary stores

L'Ancienne-Lorette, QC G2G
Quebec County

D-U-N-S 25-305-2351   (BR)
INNVEST PROPERTIES CORP
COMFORT INN
(*Suby of* Innvest Properties Corp)
1255 Aut Duplessis, L'Ancienne-Lorette, QC,
G2G 2B4
(418) 872-5900
Emp Here 25
SIC 7011 Hotels and motels

D-U-N-S 24-119-5531   (BR)
PROVIGO DISTRIBUTION INC
LOBLAWS
1201 Aut Duplessis, L'Ancienne-Lorette, QC,
G2G 2B4
(418) 872-2400
Emp Here 130
SIC 5411 Grocery stores

L'Ange Gardien, QC G0A

D-U-N-S 20-711-9871   (BR)
COMMISSION SCOLAIRE DES PREMIERES-SEIGNEURIES
ECOLE PRIMAIRE PETIT PRINCE
20 Rue Du Couvent E, L'Ange Gardien, QC,
G0A 2K0
(418) 821-8062
Emp Here 20
SIC 8211 Elementary and secondary schools

D-U-N-S 24-370-4397   (HQ)
GAMMA MURS ET FENETRES INTERNATIONAL INC
GAMMA INDUSTRIES
(*Suby of* Gamma Usa, Inc.)
6130 Boul Sainte-Anne Rr 4, L'Ange Gardien,
QC, G0A 2K0
(418) 822-1448
Emp Here 30   *Emp Total* 175
Sales 29,330,201
SIC 5211 Lumber and other building materials
VP VP Hai Wang
VP VP Jidong Qin
Sec Pierre Belanger

D-U-N-S 24-424-3742   (SL)
SOLARIS INTERNATIONAL INC
(*Suby of* 2421-9974 Quebec Inc)
6150 Boul Sainte-Anne Rr 4, L'Ange Gardien,
QC, G0A 2K0
(418) 822-0643
Emp Here 200   *Sales* 40,392,960
SIC 5211 Lumber and other building materials
Pr Nicolas Chalifour
VP Serge Chalifour

L'Ange-Gardien, QC J8L

D-U-N-S 24-651-5923   (BR)
LAFARGE PAVING & CONSTRUCTION (EASTERN) LIMITED
545 Ch Deschenes, L'Ange-Gardien, QC, J8L
4A1
(819) 281-8542
Emp Here 20
SIC 1611 Highway and street construction

L'Anse-Saint-Jean, QC G0V
Chicoutimi County

D-U-N-S 25-001-8777   (BR)
COMMISSION SCOLAIRE DES RIVES-DU-

SAGUENAY
ECOLE PRIMAIRE ET SECONDAIRE FRECHETTE
(*Suby of* Commission Scolaire des Rives-du-Saguenay)
37 Rue Saint-Jean-Baptiste, L'Anse-Saint-Jean, QC, G0V 1J0
(418) 615-0090
Emp Here 30
SIC 8211 Elementary and secondary schools

L'Ascension, QC J0T
Labelle County

D-U-N-S 25-383-4261 (BR)
PRODUITS FORESTIERS ARBEC S.E.N.C.
SCIERIE PERIBONKA, DIV DE
5005 Rte Aniforet, L'Ascension, QC, J0T 1W0
(418) 347-4900
Emp Here 215
SIC 2421 Sawmills and planing mills, general

L'Ascension-De-Notre-Seigneur, QC G0W
Lac-St-Jean-Est County

D-U-N-S 25-685-2146 (BR)
PRODUITS FORESTIERS ARBEC S.E.N.C.
5005 Rte Uniforet, L'Ascension-De-Notre-Seigneur, QC, G0W 1Y0
(418) 347-4900
Emp Here 200
SIC 2421 Sawmills and planing mills, general

L'Assomption, QC J5W
L'Assomption County

D-U-N-S 20-015-5021 (BR)
COMMISSION SCOLAIRE DES AFFLU-ENTS
ECOLE SECONDAIRE DE L'AMITIE
1600 Boul De L'Ange-Gardien N, L'Assomption, QC, J5W 5H1
(450) 492-3588
Emp Here 50
SIC 8211 Elementary and secondary schools

D-U-N-S 25-233-3307 (BR)
COMMISSION SCOLAIRE DES AFFLU-ENTS
ECOLE SAINT LOUIS
(*Suby of* Commission Scolaire des Affluents)
761 Rue Du Pont, L'Assomption, QC, J5W 3E6
(450) 492-3508
Emp Here 41
SIC 8211 Elementary and secondary schools

D-U-N-S 20-712-2347 (BR)
COMMISSION SCOLAIRE DES AFFLU-ENTS
ECOLE PRIMAIRE GAREAU
2600 Boul De L'Ange-Gardien N, L'Assomption, QC, J5W 4R5
(450) 492-3565
Emp Here 50
SIC 8211 Elementary and secondary schools

D-U-N-S 20-806-7723 (BR)
COUCHE-TARD INC
711 Rue Saint-Etienne, L'Assomption, QC, J5W 1Y9
(450) 589-7536
Emp Here 25
SIC 5411 Grocery stores

D-U-N-S 25-475-1266 (SL)
CUISISTOCK INC
901 Rang Du Bas-De-L'Assomption S, L'Assomption, QC, J5W 2A3

(450) 589-2121
Emp Here 50 *Sales* 2,918,428
SIC 2434 Wood kitchen cabinets

D-U-N-S 24-515-6039 (SL)
EBENISTERIE A. BEAUCAGE INC
FIRST CHOICE CABINET
188 Ch Des Commissaires, L'Assomption, QC, J5W 2T7
(450) 589-6412
Emp Here 65 *Sales* 3,793,956
SIC 2434 Wood kitchen cabinets

D-U-N-S 24-337-0215 (BR)
ELECTROLUX CANADA CORP
ELECTROLUX HOME PRODUCTS
802 Boul De L'Ange-Gardien, L'Assomption, QC, J5W 1T6
(450) 589-5701
Emp Here 1,000
SIC 3634 Electric housewares and fans

D-U-N-S 24-214-7473 (BR)
FONDATION DU CEGEP REGIONAL DE LANAUDIERE
COLLEGE CONSTITUANT DE L'ASSOMPTION
180 Rue Dorval, L'Assomption, QC, J5W 6C1
(450) 470-0922
Emp Here 50
SIC 8221 Colleges and universities

D-U-N-S 24-540-9016 (SL)
SUPERMARCHE CREVIER L'ASSOMPTION INC
860 Boul De L'Ange-Gardien N, L'Assomption, QC, J5W 1P1
(450) 589-5738
Emp Here 135 *Sales* 25,421,440
SIC 5411 Grocery stores
Pr Pr Jean-Claude Crevier
Micheline Papin

D-U-N-S 20-204-5068 (BR)
UNIPRIX INC
330 Boul De L'Ange-Gardien, L'Assomption, QC, J5W 1S3
(450) 589-4741
Emp Here 30
SIC 5912 Drug stores and proprietary stores

L'Epiphanie, QC J5X
L'Assomption County

D-U-N-S 20-577-4354 (BR)
COMMISSION SCOLAIRE DES AFFLU-ENTS
ECOLE ST-GUILLAUME
81 Rue Des Sulpiciens, L'Epiphanie, QC, J5X 2Y2
(450) 492-3592
Emp Here 40
SIC 8211 Elementary and secondary schools

D-U-N-S 20-712-2396 (BR)
COMMISSION SCOLAIRE DES AFFLU-ENTS
ECOLE MGR MONGEAU
119 Rue Amireault, L'Epiphanie, QC, J5X 2T2
(450) 492-3595
Emp Here 50
SIC 8211 Elementary and secondary schools

D-U-N-S 25-651-8754 (BR)
MASKIMO CONSTRUCTION INC
861 Rang De L'Achigan S, L'Epiphanie, QC, J5X 3M9
(450) 588-2591
Emp Here 60
SIC 2911 Petroleum refining

L'Etang-Du-Nord, QC G4T

D-U-N-S 20-000-1147 (BR)
ATLANTIC RETAIL CO-OPERATIVES FED-ERATION
CO-OP ATLANTIC
1069 Ch Du Gros-Cap, L'Etang-Du-Nord, QC, G4T 3M9
(418) 986-2219
Emp Here 48
SIC 5411 Grocery stores

D-U-N-S 20-585-1475 (HQ)
CAISSE POPULAIRE DESJARDINS DES RAMEES
CENTRE DE SERVICE DE CAP-AUX-MEULES
(*Suby of* Caisse Populaire Desjardins des Ramees)
1278 Ch De La Verniere, L'Etang-Du-Nord, QC, G4T 3E6
(418) 986-2319
Emp Here 29 *Emp Total* 100
Sales 10,711,539
SIC 6062 State credit unions
Genl Mgr Lucien Presseault
Pr Maryse Lapierre
VP Charles-Claude Dion
Sec Jean-Pierre Miousse
Dir Christian Arsenault
Dir Jules Arseneau
Dir Pascale Boudreau
Dir Martine Bourgeois
Dir Marc-Olivier Corbeil
Dir Michel Leblanc

D-U-N-S 25-061-8378 (BR)
COLLEGE D'ENSEIGNEMENT GENERALE & PROFESSIONNEL DE LA GASPESIE & DES ILES
CAMPUS DES ILES
(*Suby of* College d'Enseignement Generale & Professionnel de La Gaspesie & des Iles)
15 Ch De La Piscine, L'Etang-Du-Nord, QC, G4T 3X4
(418) 986-5187
Emp Here 40
SIC 8221 Colleges and universities

D-U-N-S 25-019-8629 (BR)
COMMISSION SCOLAIRE DES ILES
ECOLE SAINT-PIERRE
1332 Ch De La Verniere, L'Etang-Du-Nord, QC, G4T 3G3
(418) 986-5511
Emp Here 40
SIC 8211 Elementary and secondary schools

L'Ile-Bizard, QC H9C
Hochelaga County

D-U-N-S 25-232-9719 (BR)
COMMISSION SCOLAIRE MARGUERITE-BOURGEOYS
ECOLE JONATHAN WILSON
3243 Boul Chevremont, L'Ile-Bizard, QC, H9C 2L8
(514) 855-4242
Emp Here 70
SIC 8351 Child day care services

L'Ile-Perrot, QC J7V
Abitibi County

D-U-N-S 20-234-8392 (BR)
BANQUE NATIONALE DU CANADA
60 Boul Don-Quichotte, L'Ile-Perrot, QC, J7V 6L7
(514) 453-7142
Emp Here 20
SIC 6021 National commercial banks

D-U-N-S 25-233-8173 (BR)

COMMISSION SCOLAIRE DES TROIS-LACS
ECOLE VIRGINIE ROY
476 Boul Grand, L'Ile-Perrot, QC, J7V 4X5
(514) 453-5441
Emp Here 25
SIC 8211 Elementary and secondary schools

D-U-N-S 25-001-8942 (BR)
COMMISSION SCOLAIRE DES TROIS-LACS
ECOLE FRANCOIS PERROT
300 Boul Grand, L'Ile-Perrot, QC, J7V 4X2
(514) 453-4011
Emp Here 30
SIC 8211 Elementary and secondary schools

D-U-N-S 20-712-2933 (BR)
COMMISSION SCOLAIRE DES TROIS-LACS
ECOLE NOTRE-DAME-DE-LA-GARDE
2254 Boul Perrot, L'Ile-Perrot, QC, J7V 8P4
(514) 453-2576
Emp Here 20
SIC 8211 Elementary and secondary schools

D-U-N-S 25-899-8129 (BR)
WSP CANADA INC
GENIVAR
89 Boul Don-Quichotte Bureau 9, L'Ile-Perrot, QC, J7V 6X2
(514) 453-1621
Emp Here 20
SIC 8711 Engineering services

L'Isle-Aux-Grues, QC G0R
Montmagny County

D-U-N-S 24-389-5724 (BR)
CENTRE DE SANTE ET SERVICES SOCI-AUX DE MONTMAGNY - L'ISLET
CLSC DE L'ISLE-AUX-GRUES
101 Ch De La Voli Re, L'Isle-Aux-Grues, QC, G0R 1P0
(418) 248-4651
Emp Here 50
SIC 8062 General medical and surgical hospitals

L'Islet, QC G0R
L'Islet County

D-U-N-S 24-247-6401 (BR)
CENTRE DE SANTE ET SERVICES SOCI-AUX DE MONTMAGNY - L'ISLET
MAISONS D'HEBERGEMENT DE SAINT-EUGENE
2 Rue De La Madone, L'Islet, QC, G0R 1X0
(418) 247-3927
Emp Here 50
SIC 8361 Residential care

D-U-N-S 20-712-0085 (BR)
COMMISSION SCOLAIRE DE LA COTE-DU-SUD, LA
ECOLE SECONDAIRE BON PASTEUR
166 Ch Des Pionniers O, L'Islet, QC, G0R 2B0
(418) 247-3957
Emp Here 50
SIC 8211 Elementary and secondary schools

D-U-N-S 25-233-7696 (BR)
COMMISSION SCOLAIRE DE LA COTE-DU-SUD, LA
COMMISSION SCOLAIRE DE LA COTE-DU-SUD, LA
25 Ch Des Pionniers O, L'Islet, QC, G0R 2B0
(418) 247-3147
Emp Here 25
SIC 8211 Elementary and secondary schools

La Baie, QC G7B
Chicoutimi County

D-U-N-S 20-183-3733 (HQ)
2737-2895 QUEBEC INC
DISTRIBUTION FROMAGERIE BOIVIN
(*Suby of* 2737-2895 Quebec Inc)
2152 Ch Saint-Joseph, La Baie, QC, G7B 3N9
(418) 544-2622
Emp Here 40   *Emp Total* 80
Sales 24,736,320
SIC 5143 Dairy products, except dried or canned
Pr Pr Pierre Boivin
VP VP Jean-Marc Boivin
Michel Boivin

D-U-N-S 24-682-3186 (SL)
9172-2785 QUEBEC INC
TIM HORTONS
1000 Rue Bagot, La Baie, QC, G7B 2N9
(418) 544-2224
Emp Here 20   *Sales* 605,574
SIC 5812 Eating places

D-U-N-S 20-642-2383 (SL)
AEROGARE DE BAGOTVILLE, L'
7000 Ch De L'Aeroport, La Baie, QC, G7B 0E4
(418) 677-2651
Emp Here 49   *Sales* 31,956,750
SIC 4581 Airports, flying fields, and services
Pr Jean-Marc Dufour

D-U-N-S 24-778-7497 (BR)
AIR CANADA
7000 Ch De L'Aeroport, La Baie, QC, G7B 0E4
(418) 677-3424
Emp Here 20
SIC 4512 Air transportation, scheduled

D-U-N-S 20-273-6059 (HQ)
ASSOCIATION DES AUXILIAIRES BENEVOLES DU CSSS DE CLEOPHAS-CLAVEAU, L'
(*Suby of* Association des Auxiliaires Benevoles du CSSS de Cleophas-Claveau, L')
1000 Rue Du Docteur-Desgagne, La Baie, QC, G7B 2Y6
(418) 544-3381
Emp Here 300   *Emp Total* 502
Sales 46,645,286
SIC 8641 Civic and social associations
Pr Louise Boudreault
VP Monique Simard
Sec Marcelle Savard
Treas Linda Larouche
Dir Rejeanne Hottote

D-U-N-S 24-368-8558 (BR)
CAISSE DESJARDINS DE LA BAIE
CENTRE DE SERVICE 6E AVENUE
1262 6e Av, La Baie, QC, G7B 1R4
(418) 544-7365
Emp Here 50
SIC 6062 State credit unions

D-U-N-S 24-394-9596 (BR)
CHARL-POL INC
(*Suby of* 8132992 Canada Inc)
805 Rue De L'Innovation, La Baie, QC, G7B 3N8
(418) 677-1518
Emp Here 80
SIC 3569 General industrial machinery, nec

D-U-N-S 24-128-4442 (BR)
COMMISSION SCOLAIRE DES RIVES-DU-SAGUENAY
CENTRE DE SERVICE DE LA BAIE
3111 Rue Monseigneur-Dufour, La Baie, QC, G7B 4H5
(418) 698-5000
Emp Here 30
SIC 8211 Elementary and secondary schools

D-U-N-S 25-232-1807 (BR)

COMMISSION SCOLAIRE DES RIVES-DU-SAGUENAY
ECOLE ST-JOSEPH
(*Suby of* Commission Scolaire des Rives-du-Saguenay)
3300 Rue Prince-Albert, La Baie, QC, G7B 3R6
(418) 544-6822
Emp Here 31
SIC 8211 Elementary and secondary schools

D-U-N-S 25-126-0758 (BR)
COMMISSION SCOLAIRE DES RIVES-DU-SAGUENAY
ECOLE MEDERIC GRAVEL
(*Suby of* Commission Scolaire des Rives-du-Saguenay)
1351 6e Av, La Baie, QC, G7B 1R5
(418) 544-0327
Emp Here 46
SIC 8211 Elementary and secondary schools

D-U-N-S 25-233-6706 (BR)
COMMISSION SCOLAIRE DES RIVES-DU-SAGUENAY
ECOLE SECONDAIRE DES GRANDES-MAREES
(*Suby of* Commission Scolaire des Rives-du-Saguenay)
1802 Av John-Kane, La Baie, QC, G7B 1K2
(418) 544-2843
Emp Here 115
SIC 8211 Elementary and secondary schools

D-U-N-S 25-877-4736 (BR)
COMMISSION SCOLAIRE DES RIVES-DU-SAGUENAY
CENTRE DUROCHER
(*Suby of* Commission Scolaire des Rives-du-Saguenay)
2511 Rue Monseigneur-Dufour, La Baie, QC, G7B 1E2
(418) 544-2324
Emp Here 30
SIC 8211 Elementary and secondary schools

D-U-N-S 25-232-2672 (BR)
COMMISSION SCOLAIRE DES RIVES-DU-SAGUENAY
ECOLE STE THERESE
(*Suby of* Commission Scolaire des Rives-du-Saguenay)
737 Rue Victoria, La Baie, QC, G7B 3M8
(418) 544-3223
Emp Here 25
SIC 8211 Elementary and secondary schools

D-U-N-S 20-432-4883 (HQ)
DERY TELECOM INC
(*Suby of* Dery Telecom Inc)
1013 Rue Bagot, La Baie, QC, G7B 2N6
(418) 544-3358
Emp Here 75   *Emp Total* 95
Sales 17,810,018
SIC 4841 Cable and other pay television services
Remi Tremblay
Julien Cote

D-U-N-S 20-720-4905 (BR)
ENTREPRISES MACBAIE INC, LES
MCDONALD
1082 Rue Aime-Gravel, La Baie, QC, G7B 2M5
(418) 545-3593
Emp Here 75
SIC 5812 Eating places

D-U-N-S 24-135-6042 (SL)
MACWILL INC
RESTAURANT MCDONALD'S
1082 Rue Aime-Gravel, La Baie, QC, G7B 2M5
(418) 544-3369
Emp Here 60   *Sales* 1,824,018
SIC 5812 Eating places

D-U-N-S 20-512-5011 (BR)

POTVIN & BOUCHARD INC
2880 Av Du Port, La Baie, QC, G7B 3P6
(418) 544-3000
Emp Here 40
SIC 5251 Hardware stores

D-U-N-S 24-593-0979 (BR)
RIO TINTO ALCAN INC
USINE GRANDE BAIE
(*Suby of* RIO TINTO PLC)
6000 6e Av, La Baie, QC, G7B 4G9
(418) 697-9540
Emp Here 600
SIC 3365 Aluminum foundries

D-U-N-S 20-013-9843 (BR)
RIO TINTO ALCAN INC
(*Suby of* RIO TINTO PLC)
5000 Rte Du Petit Parc, La Baie, QC, G7B 4G9
(418) 697-9600
Emp Here 800
SIC 3334 Primary aluminum

D-U-N-S 24-109-7414 (BR)
RIO TINTO ALCAN INC
(*Suby of* RIO TINTO PLC)
262 1re Rue, La Baie, QC, G7B 3R1
(418) 544-9660
Emp Here 150
SIC 4512 Air transportation, scheduled

La Dore, QC G8J
Abitibi County

D-U-N-S 20-511-8768 (BR)
PF RESOLU CANADA INC
PRODUIT FORESTIERS RESOLU SECTEUR LA DORE
5850 Av Des Jardins, La Dore, QC, G8J 1B4
(418) 256-3816
Emp Here 233
SIC 2421 Sawmills and planing mills, general

La Guadeloupe, QC G0M
Frontenac County

D-U-N-S 24-074-3935 (BR)
CITADELLE COOPERATIVE DE PRODUCTEURS DE SIROP D'ERABLE
(*Suby of* Citadelle Cooperative de Producteurs de Sirop d'Erable)
786 8e Rue E, La Guadeloupe, QC, G0M 1G0

Emp Here 20
SIC 2099 Food preparations, nec

D-U-N-S 25-379-9506 (BR)
COMMISSION SCOLAIRE DE LA BEAUCE-ETCHEMIN
ECOLE ROY
427 11e Rue O, La Guadeloupe, QC, G0M 1G0
(418) 228-5541
Emp Here 20
SIC 8211 Elementary and secondary schools

D-U-N-S 20-302-6398 (SL)
STRUCTURES ROYAL INC
266 22e Av, La Guadeloupe, QC, G0M 1G0
(418) 459-3733
Emp Here 50   *Sales* 4,888,367
SIC 2448 Wood pallets and skids

D-U-N-S 24-884-3864 (SL)
UNIFORMES F.O.B. (1991) LTEE
645 14e Av, La Guadeloupe, QC, G0M 1G0

Emp Here 65   *Sales* 2,991,389
SIC 2311 Men's and boy's suits and coats

La Malbaie, QC G5A
Charlevoix-Est County

D-U-N-S 24-942-4714 (BR)
(T.P.Q.) TERMINAUX PORTUAIRES DU QUEBEC INC
500 Ch Du Havre, La Malbaie, QC, G5A 2Y9
(418) 665-4485
Emp Here 20
SIC 4491 Marine cargo handling

D-U-N-S 25-391-6506 (HQ)
CAISSE POPULAIRE DESJARDINS DE LA MALBAIE
CENTRE DE SERVICE CAP-A-L'AIGLE
(*Suby of* Caisse Populaire Desjardins de la Malbaie)
130 Rue John-Nairne, La Malbaie, QC, G5A 1Y1
(418) 665-4443
Emp Here 25   *Emp Total* 61
Sales 6,711,932
SIC 6062 State credit unions

D-U-N-S 20-793-5649 (BR)
CENTRE INTEGRE UNIVERSITAIRE DE SANTE ET DE SERVICES SOCIAUX DE LA CAPITALE-NATIONALE, LE
CENTRE D'HEBERGEMENT BELLERIVE
555 Boul De Comporte Bureau 1, La Malbaie, QC, G5A 1W3
(418) 665-1727
Emp Here 49
SIC 8361 Residential care

D-U-N-S 24-340-5599 (BR)
CLUB SOCIAL DES EMPLOYES-ES DU CENTRE DE SANTE ET DE SERVICES SOCIAUX DE CHARLEVOIX, LE
CLUB SOCIAL DES EMPLOYES-ES DU CENTRE DE SANTE ET DE SERVICES SOCIAUX DE CHARLEVOIX, LE
303 Rue Saint-Etienne, La Malbaie, QC, G5A 1T1
(418) 665-1700
Emp Here 300
SIC 8062 General medical and surgical hospitals

D-U-N-S 20-711-9152 (BR)
COMMISSION SCOLAIRE DE CHARLEVOIX, LA
ECOLE MARGUERITE D'YOUVILLE
309 Rue Saint-Etienne, La Malbaie, QC, G5A 1T1
(418) 665-6494
Emp Here 25
SIC 8211 Elementary and secondary schools

D-U-N-S 25-232-3639 (BR)
COMMISSION SCOLAIRE DE CHARLEVOIX, LA
ECOLE FELIX ANTOINE SAVARD
250 Rue Saint-Etienne, La Malbaie, QC, G5A 1T2
(418) 665-3796
Emp Here 25
SIC 8211 Elementary and secondary schools

D-U-N-S 20-711-9210 (BR)
COMMISSION SCOLAIRE DE CHARLEVOIX, LA
EDUCATION DES ADULTES ET FORMATION PROFESSIONNELLE DE CHARLEVOIX
88 Rue Des Cimes, La Malbaie, QC, G5A 1T3
(418) 665-4487
Emp Here 50
SIC 8211 Elementary and secondary schools

D-U-N-S 25-232-7507 (BR)
COMMISSION SCOLAIRE DE CHARLEVOIX, LA
ECOLE SECONDAIRE DU PLATEAU
88 Rue Des Cimes, La Malbaie, QC, G5A 1T3
(418) 665-3791
Emp Here 150

SIC 8211 Elementary and secondary schools

D-U-N-S 24-687-8842   (BR)
COOP FEDEREE, LA
SONIC
2190 Boul De Comporte, La Malbaie, QC,
G5A 1N2
(418) 439-3991
Emp Here 40
SIC 5251 Hardware stores

D-U-N-S 20-699-9018   (BR)
FAIRMONT HOTELS & RESORTS INC
FAIRMONT LE MANOIR RICHELIEU
181 Rue Richelieu Bureau 200, La Malbaie,
QC, G5A 1X7
(418) 665-3703
Emp Here 600
SIC 7011 Hotels and motels

D-U-N-S 20-102-0521   (BR)
FAIRMONT HOTELS & RESORTS INC
CLUB DE GOLF DU MANOIR RICHELIEU
595 Cote Bellevue, La Malbaie, QC, G5A 3B2
(418) 665-2526
Emp Here 40
SIC 7992 Public golf courses

D-U-N-S 24-381-5131   (SL)
RESTOTEL CONSULTANTS INC
AUBERGE DES FALAISES
250 Ch Des Falaises, La Malbaie, QC, G5A
2V2
(418) 665-3731
Emp Here 52   *Sales* 2,261,782
SIC 7011 Hotels and motels

D-U-N-S 20-609-4943   (BR)
**SOCIETE DES CASINOS DU QUEBEC INC,
LA**
CASINO DE CHARLEVOIX, LE
183 Rue Richelieu, La Malbaie, QC, G5A 1X8
(418) 665-5300
Emp Here 375
SIC 7032 Sporting and recreational camps

D-U-N-S 24-942-4045   (SL)
**SOCIETE EN COMMANDITE MANOIR
RICHELIEU**
FAIRMOUNT MANOIR RICHELIEU
181 Rue Richelieu Bureau 200, La Malbaie,
QC, G5A 1X7
(418) 665-3703
Emp Here 570   *Sales* 24,952,559
SIC 7011 Hotels and motels
Genl Mgr Louise Champagne

La Patrie, QC J0B
Compton County

D-U-N-S 24-368-1603   (BR)
GUITABEC INC
(*Suby of* Lasido Inc)
42 Rue Principale S Bureau 600, La Patrie,
QC, J0B 1Y0
(819) 888-2255
Emp Here 40
SIC 3931 Musical instruments

La Pocatiere, QC G0R
Kamouraska County

D-U-N-S 24-827-1731   (BR)
**BOMBARDIER   TRANSPORTATION
CANADA INC**
BOMBARDIER TRANSPORT
230 Rte O Bureau 130, La Pocatiere, QC, G0R
1Z0
(418) 856-1232
Emp Here 500
SIC 5088 Transportation equipment and sup-
plies

D-U-N-S 24-568-9211   (HQ)
**COLLEGE D'ENSEIGNEMENT GENERAL &
PROFESSIONEL DE LA POCATIERE**
CEGEP DE LA POCATIERE
(*Suby of* College D'Enseignement General &
Professionel De La Pocatiere)
140 4e Av, La Pocatiere, QC, G0R 1Z0
(418) 856-1525
Emp Here 210   *Emp Total* 250
Sales 34,944,960
SIC 8221 Colleges and universities
Dir Fin Didier Rioux
Genl Mgr Claude Harvey

D-U-N-S 25-232-6996   (BR)
**COMMISSION   SCOLAIRE   DE
KAMOURASKA RIVIERE-DU-LOUP**
ECOLE SACRE COEUR
1005 6e Av, La Pocatiere, QC, G0R 1Z0
(418) 856-2823
Emp Here 42
SIC 8211 Elementary and secondary schools

D-U-N-S 20-252-9541   (HQ)
GROUPE COOPERATIF DYNACO
CENTRE DE MACHINERIE DYNACO
(*Suby of* Groupe Cooperatif Dynaco)
205 Av Industrielle Bureau 200, La Pocatiere,
QC, G0R 1Z0
(418) 856-3807
Emp Here 25   *Emp Total* 451
Sales 192,071,250
SIC 5251 Hardware stores
Pr Pr Denis Levesque
VP Jean Francois Pelletier
Sec Stephane Dufour
Treas Michel Robichaud
Dir Bertrand Caron
Dir Simon Beaulieu
Dir Stephane April
Dir Roland Morneau
Dir Hugo Berube
Dir Sophie Gendron

D-U-N-S 20-642-8547   (BR)
GROUPE COOPERATIF DYNACO
DYNACO MACHINERIE
(*Suby of* Groupe Cooperatif Dynaco)
87 Rte 132 O, La Pocatiere, QC, G0R 1Z0
(418) 856-1765
Emp Here 22
SIC 5083 Farm and garden machinery

D-U-N-S 25-298-2582   (BR)
**RAYMOND CHABOT GRANT THORNTON
S.E.N.C.R.L.**
901 5e Rue Rouleau Unite 400, La Pocatiere,
QC, G0R 1Z0
(418) 856-2547
Emp Here 20
SIC 8721 Accounting, auditing, and book-
keeping

D-U-N-S 20-543-5659   (BR)
UNIPRIX INC
UNIPRIX ARSENAULT & COUILLARD
611 1re Rue Poire, La Pocatiere, QC, G0R
1Z0
(418) 856-3094
Emp Here 40
SIC 5912 Drug stores and proprietary stores

D-U-N-S 25-224-1807   (BR)
VILLE DE LA POCATIERE
*BIBLIOTHEQUE   MUNICIPALE   LA
POCATIERE*
(*Suby of* Ville De La Pocatiere)
900 6e Av Bureau 4, La Pocatiere, QC, G0R
1Z0
(418) 856-3394
Emp Here 60
SIC 8231 Libraries

La Prairie, QC J5R
Laprairie County

D-U-N-S 24-163-4521   (BR)
ARAMARK QUEBEC INC
870 Ch De Saint-Jean, La Prairie, QC, J5R
2L5
(450) 444-2793
Emp Here 25
SIC 5812 Eating places

D-U-N-S 20-237-8998   (HQ)
BOULANGERIE GADOUA LTEE
170 Boul Tascherau Bureau 220, La Prairie,
QC, J5R 5H6
(450) 245-3326
Emp Here 40   *Emp Total* 138,000
Sales 39,325,817
SIC 2051 Bread, cake, and related products
Pr Pascal Gadoua
 Robert A. Balcom
 Ralph A. Robinson

D-U-N-S 24-368-8947   (BR)
CAISSE POPULAIRE DE LA PRAIRIE
CENTRE DE SERVICES DE LA COMMUNE
1600 Ch De Saint-Jean, La Prairie, QC, J5R
0J1
(450) 659-5431
Emp Here 46
SIC 6062 State credit unions

D-U-N-S 25-363-8381   (BR)
CANADA POST CORPORATION
BDP LA PRAIRIE
550 Boul Tascherau, La Prairie, QC, J5R 1V1
(450) 659-1183
Emp Here 30
SIC 4311 U.s. postal service

D-U-N-S 25-258-8355   (BR)
**CENTRE INTEGRE DE SANTE ET DE SER-
VICES SOCIAUX DE LA MONTEREGIE-
OUEST**
CSSS JARDIN ROUSSILLON
(*Suby of* Centre Integre de Sante et de Ser-
vices Sociaux de la Monteregie-Ouest)
500 Av De Balmoral, La Prairie, QC, J5R 4N5
(450) 659-9148
Emp Here 200
SIC 8361 Residential care

D-U-N-S 20-102-5512   (BR)
CIMENT QUEBEC INC
UNIBETON
(*Suby of* Groupe Ciment Quebec Inc)
1250 Ch Saint-Jose, La Prairie, QC, J5R 6A9
(450) 444-7942
Emp Here 170
SIC 3273 Ready-mixed concrete

D-U-N-S 20-024-0708   (BR)
**COMMISSION SCOLAIRE DES GRANDES-
SEIGNEURIES**
ECOLE ST-FRANTOIS-XAVIER
500 Boul Tascherau, La Prairie, QC, J5R 1V1
(514) 380-8899
Emp Here 35
SIC 8211 Elementary and secondary schools

D-U-N-S 25-240-0122   (BR)
**COMMISSION SCOLAIRE DES GRANDES-
SEIGNEURIES**
ECOLE DES BOURLINGUEURS
50 Boul Tascherau Bureau 310, La Prairie,
QC, J5R 4V3
(514) 380-8899
Emp Here 30
SIC 8211 Elementary and secondary schools

D-U-N-S 25-233-6573   (BR)
**COMMISSION SCOLAIRE DES GRANDES-
SEIGNEURIES**
ECOLE DE LA MAGDELEINE
1100 Boul Tascherau, La Prairie, QC, J5R
1W8
(514) 380-8899
Emp Here 200

SIC 8211 Elementary and secondary schools

D-U-N-S 20-295-0213   (BR)
**COMMISSION SCOLAIRE DES GRANDES-
SEIGNEURIES**
*CENTRE DE FORMATION COMPETENCE
RIVE SUD*
399 Rue Conrad-Pelletier, La Prairie, QC, J5R
4V1
(514) 380-8899
Emp Here 60
SIC 8249 Vocational schools, nec

D-U-N-S 25-240-5303   (BR)
**COMMISSION SCOLAIRE DES GRANDES-
SEIGNEURIES**
ECOLE SAINT-MARC
50 Boul Tascherau Bureau 310, La Prairie,
QC, J5R 4V3
(514) 380-8899
Emp Here 50
SIC 8211 Elementary and secondary schools

D-U-N-S 20-024-6481   (BR)
**GROUPE PROMUTUEL FEDERATION DE
SOCIETE MUTUELLES D'ASSURANCES
GENERALES**
*PROMUTUEL ASSURANCE VALLEE DU ST-
LAURENT*
48 Boul Tascherau, La Prairie, QC, J5R 6C1
(450) 444-0988
Emp Here 35
SIC 6311 Life insurance

D-U-N-S 20-514-4061   (BR)
MERIDIAN BRICK CANADA LTD
BRIQUES MERIDIAN CANADA LTEE
955 Ch Saint-Jose, La Prairie, QC, J5R 3Y1
(450) 659-1944
Emp Here 50
SIC 3271 Concrete block and brick

D-U-N-S 24-858-7412   (SL)
PIZZERIA COMO LTEE
577 Boul Tascherau, La Prairie, QC, J5R 1V4
(450) 659-5497
Emp Here 50   *Sales* 1,532,175
SIC 5812 Eating places

D-U-N-S 24-944-2690   (SL)
RAPIDE INVESTIGATION CANADA LTEE
114 Rue Saint-Georges, La Prairie, QC, J5R
2L9
(514) 879-1199
Emp Here 60   *Sales* 3,064,349
SIC 7323 Credit reporting services

D-U-N-S 25-248-2070   (SL)
**TRANSPORT EN COMMUN LA QUEBE-
COISE INC**
300 Rue Des Conseillers, La Prairie, QC, J5R
2E6
(450) 659-8598
Emp Here 100   *Sales* 3,502,114
SIC 4111 Local and suburban transit

La Presentation, QC J0H
St Hyacinthe County

D-U-N-S 20-604-6062   (SL)
AUBIN & ST-PIERRE INC
KUBOTA
350 Rue Raygo Rr 1, La Presentation, QC,
J0H 1B0
(450) 796-2966
Emp Here 20   *Sales* 11,995,200
SIC 5083 Farm and garden machinery
VP VP Pierre Rathe
Pr Pr Jacques Rathe
 Nicole Rathe

La Sarre, QC J9Z
Abitibi County

D-U-N-S 25-379-9803   (BR)
6173306 CANADA INC
RESTAURANT MCDONALD'S
(*Suby of* 6173306 Canada Inc)
616 2e Rue E, La Sarre, QC, J9Z 2S5
(819) 339-5619
Emp Here 65
SIC 5812 Eating places

D-U-N-S 20-211-5510   (SL)
9088-6615 QUEBEC INC
NORMEX METAL
11 Boul Industriel, La Sarre, QC, J9Z 2X2
(819) 333-1200
Emp Here 30   *Sales* 3,283,232
SIC 3312 Blast furnaces and steel mills

D-U-N-S 20-023-1590   (BR)
**CENTRE DE SANTE ET DE SERVICES SO-
CIAUX DES AURORES BOREALES**
*CENTRE DE SANTE ET DE SERVICES SO-
CIAUX DES AURORES BOREALES*
22 1re Av E, La Sarre, QC, J9Z 1C4
(819) 333-5525
Emp Here 35
SIC 8361 Residential care

D-U-N-S 24-637-0787   (HQ)
CLUB DE GOLF BEATTIE LA SARRE INC
(*Suby of* Club De Golf Beattie La Sarre Inc)
18 Ch Du Golf, La Sarre, QC, J9Z 2X5
(819) 333-9944
Emp Here 47   *Emp Total* 60
Sales 2,407,703
SIC 7997 Membership sports and recreation
clubs

D-U-N-S 25-240-0932   (BR)
COMMISSION SCOLAIRE ABITIBI
ECOLE DE L' ENVOL
(*Suby of* Commission Scolaire Abitibi)
24 5e Av E, La Sarre, QC, J9Z 1K8
(819) 333-5591
Emp Here 85
SIC 8211 Elementary and secondary schools

D-U-N-S 20-963-8261   (HQ)
COMMISSION SCOLAIRE ABITIBI
(*Suby of* Commission Scolaire Abitibi)
500 Rue Principale, La Sarre, QC, J9Z 2A2
(819) 333-5411
Emp Here 20   *Emp Total* 50
Sales 3,356,192
SIC 8211 Elementary and secondary schools

D-U-N-S 25-298-1675   (BR)
COMMISSION SCOLAIRE ABITIBI
*ECOLE DE L'ENVOL PAVILLON VICTOR
CORMIER*
(*Suby of* Commission Scolaire Abitibi)
54 111 Rte E, La Sarre, QC, J9Z 1S1
(819) 333-5548
Emp Here 33
SIC 8211 Elementary and secondary schools

D-U-N-S 20-712-6132   (BR)
COMMISSION SCOLAIRE ABITIBI
*CENTRE DE FORMATION PROFESSION-
NELLE LAC ABITIBI*
(*Suby of* Commission Scolaire Abitibi)
500 Rue Principale, La Sarre, QC, J9Z 2A2
(819) 333-2387
Emp Here 60
SIC 8249 Vocational schools, nec

D-U-N-S 24-384-6479   (SL)
COOP VAL-NORD, LA
357 2e Rue E, La Sarre, QC, J9Z 2H6
(819) 333-2307
Emp Here 77   *Sales* 10,246,450
SIC 5251 Hardware stores
  Francoise Mongrain
Mng Dir Michel Therrien
Pr Guy Beauregard

D-U-N-S 24-661-2225   (BR)
DELOITTE & TOUCHE INC

(*Suby of* Deloitte LLP)
226 2e Rue E, La Sarre, QC, J9Z 2G9
(819) 333-2392
Emp Here 20
SIC 8721 Accounting, auditing, and book-
keeping

D-U-N-S 20-726-5364   (SL)
MOTEL VILLA MON REPOS INC
32 111 Rte E, La Sarre, QC, J9Z 1R7
(819) 333-2224
Emp Here 50   *Sales* 2,188,821
SIC 7011 Hotels and motels

D-U-N-S 25-380-2557   (BR)
NORBORD INDUSTRIES INC
210 9e Av E, La Sarre, QC, J9Z 2L2
(819) 333-5464
Emp Here 180
SIC 2499 Wood products, nec

D-U-N-S 20-546-3578   (BR)
UNIVERSITE DU QUEBEC
CENTRE DE LA SARRE
500 Rue Principale Bureau Ar60, La Sarre,
QC, J9Z 2A2
(819) 333-2624
Emp Here 100
SIC 8221 Colleges and universities

D-U-N-S 24-737-5020   (SL)
VARIETES LNJF INC
JEAN COUTU
84 5e Av E Bureau 73, La Sarre, QC, J9Z 1K9
(819) 333-5458
Emp Here 98   *Sales* 3,939,878
SIC 6519 Real property lessors, nec

La Tuque, QC G9X
Champlain County

D-U-N-S 20-363-6063   (SL)
ARBEC, BOIS D'OEUVRE INC
1053 Boul Ducharme, La Tuque, QC, G9X
3C3
(514) 327-2733
Emp Here 750   *Sales* 71,136,683
SIC 2421 Sawmills and planing mills, general
Pr Serge Mercier
Sec Roger Tremblay
Dir Opers Rejean Pare
Dir Pierre Moreau
Dir Joey Saputo
Dir Eric Bouchard

D-U-N-S 25-232-1153   (BR)
**COMMISSION SCOLAIRE CENTRAL QUE-
BEC**
ECOLE SECONDAIRE DE LA TUQUE
(*Suby of* Commission Scolaire Central Que-
bec)
531 Rue Du Saint-Maurice, La Tuque, QC,
G9X 3E9
(819) 523-2515
Emp Here 25
SIC 8211 Elementary and secondary schools

D-U-N-S 25-233-2242   (BR)
COMMISSION SCOLAIRE DE L'ENERGIE
ECOLE SECONDAIRE CHAMPAGNAT
600 Rue Desbiens, La Tuque, QC, G9X 2K1
(819) 523-4505
Emp Here 60
SIC 8211 Elementary and secondary schools

D-U-N-S 20-716-9009   (BR)
COMMISSION SCOLAIRE DE L'ENERGIE
ECOLE PRIMAIRE JACQUES BUTEUX
380 Rue Jacques-Buteux, La Tuque, QC, G9X
2C6
(819) 523-9519
Emp Here 50
SIC 8211 Elementary and secondary schools

D-U-N-S 20-030-5014   (BR)

COMMISSION SCOLAIRE DE L'ENERGIE
ECOLE FORESTIERE DE LA TUQUE
461 Rue Saint-Francois, La Tuque, QC, G9X
1T8
(819) 676-3006
Emp Here 50
SIC 8331 Job training and related services

D-U-N-S 20-204-6298   (SL)
DUMAIS, G. AUTOMOBILES LTEE
1608 Boul Ducharme, La Tuque, QC, G9X
4R9
(819) 523-4541
Emp Here 24   *Sales* 11,779,200
SIC 5511 New and used car dealers
Pr Pr Paul Girard
VP VP Louis Girard
  Dany Girard

D-U-N-S 20-580-4073   (BR)
GROUPE MARINEAU LTEE
MOTEL DES 9
3250 Boul Ducharme, La Tuque, QC, G9X 4T3
(819) 523-4551
Emp Here 30
SIC 7011 Hotels and motels

D-U-N-S 25-002-2647   (BR)
HYDRO-QUEBEC
90 Rue Beaumont, La Tuque, QC, G9X 3P7

Emp Here 150
SIC 4911 Electric services

D-U-N-S 20-643-2437   (SL)
MORISSETTE, CHARLES INC
150 Ch Des Hamelin, La Tuque, QC, G9X 3N6
(819) 523-3366
Emp Here 50   *Sales* 6,674,880
SIC 8711 Engineering services
Pr Pr Gilles Morissette

D-U-N-S 25-374-3306   (BR)
PROVIGO INC
MAXI
1200 Boul Ducharme Bureau 1, La Tuque, QC,
G9X 3Z9
(819) 523-8125
Emp Here 40
SIC 5411 Grocery stores

D-U-N-S 25-334-5334   (BR)
**SOCIETE DE PROTECTION DES FORETS
CONTRE LE FEU (SOPFEU)**
SOPFEU
(*Suby of* Societe de Protection des Forets
contre le feu (SOPFEU))
3000 Boul Ducharme, La Tuque, QC, G9X 4S9
(819) 523-4564
Emp Here 30
SIC 7389 Business services, nec

D-U-N-S 20-330-2401   (SL)
USINE ARBEC DOLBEAU INC
1053 Boul Ducharme, La Tuque, QC, G9X
3C3
(418) 347-4900
Emp Here 26   *Sales* 3,378,379
SIC 2429 Special product sawmills, nec

D-U-N-S 25-258-9411   (BR)
WESTROCK COMPANY OF CANADA INC
ROCKTENN
(*Suby of* Westrock Company)
1000 Ch De L'Usine Bureau 2632, La Tuque,
QC, G9X 3P8
(819) 676-8100
Emp Here 475
SIC 2657 Folding paperboard boxes

Labelle, QC J0T
Labelle County

D-U-N-S 20-631-5959   (BR)
CENTRE DE LA PETITE ENFANCE

L'ANTRE-TEMPS
61 Rue De L'Eglise, Labelle, QC, J0T 1H0
(819) 686-9469
Emp Here 20
SIC 8351 Child day care services

D-U-N-S 25-232-7895   (BR)
**COMMISSION SCOLAIRE DES LAUREN-
TIDES**
*COMMISSION SCOLAIRE DES LAUREN-
TIDES*
(*Suby of* Commission Scolaire Des Lauren-
tides)
155 Rue Du College, Labelle, QC, J0T 1H0
(819) 429-4103
Emp Here 40
SIC 8211 Elementary and secondary schools

Labrecque, QC G0W
Lac-St-Jean-Est County

D-U-N-S 20-917-9485   (BR)
**CAISSE   POPULAIRE   DESJARDINS
D'ALMA**
CENTRE DE SERVICES LABRECQUE
1350 Rue Principale, Labrecque, QC, G0W
2S0
(418) 669-1414
Emp Here 20
SIC 6062 State credit unions

Lac Des Loups, QC J0X
Pontiac County

D-U-N-S 20-195-2392   (BR)
**FONDATION DE LA COMMISSION SCO-
LAIRE DES PORTAGES-DE-L'OUTAOUAIS**
*FONDATION DE LA COMMISSION SCO-
LAIRE DES PORTAGES-D*
1 Ch Lionel Beausoleil, Lac Des Loups, QC,
J0X 3K0
(819) 456-3694
Emp Here 30
SIC 8211 Elementary and secondary schools

Lac-Au-Saumon, QC G0J
Matapedia County

D-U-N-S 20-711-8345   (BR)
**COMMISSION SCOLAIRE DES MONTS-ET-
MAREES**
ECOLE LAC-AU-SAUMON
81 Rue Du Rosaire, Lac-Au-Saumon, QC,
G0J 1M0
(418) 778-3363
Emp Here 50
SIC 8211 Elementary and secondary schools

D-U-N-S 20-799-5916   (BR)
GROUPE CEDRICO INC
BOIS D' OEUVRE CEDRICO
(*Suby of* Investissements Gilles Berube)
50 Rang Didier, Lac-Au-Saumon, QC, G0J
1M0

Emp Here 80
SIC 2491 Wood preserving

D-U-N-S 25-481-3694   (HQ)
**SERVANTES DE NOTRE-DAME REINE DU
CLERGE**
(*Suby of* Servantes De Notre-Dame Reine Du
Clerge)
13 Rue Du Foyer Bureau 310, Lac-Au-
Saumon, QC, G0J 1M0
(418) 778-5836
Emp Here 30   *Emp Total* 60
Sales 3,939,878

SIC 8661 Religious organizations

Lac-Aux-Sables, QC G0X
Portneuf County

D-U-N-S 20-234-8665   (BR)
COMPAGNIE COMMONWEALTH PLY-WOOD LTEE, LA
419 Ch Sainte-Marie, Lac-Aux-Sables, QC, G0X 1M0
(819) 722-4006
Emp Here 28
SIC 2435 Hardwood veneer and plywood

Lac-Beauport, QC G3B
Quebec County

D-U-N-S 24-145-5096   (SL)
CENTRE DE SKI LE RELAIS (1988) INC.
CENTRE DE SKI LE RELAIS
1084 Boul Du Lac, Lac-Beauport, QC, G3B 0X5
(418) 849-1851
Emp Here 50   *Sales* 2,188,821
SIC 7011 Hotels and motels

D-U-N-S 20-711-9806   (BR)
COMMISSION SCOLAIRE DES PREMIERES-SEIGNEURIES
COMMISSION SCOLAIRE DES PREMIERES-SEIGNEURIES
570 Ch Du Tour-Du-Lac, Lac-Beauport, QC, G3B 0W1
(418) 634-5542
Emp Here 65
SIC 8211 Elementary and secondary schools

Lac-Delage, QC G3C
Quebec County

D-U-N-S 25-674-1505   (SL)
MANOIR DU LAC DELAGE INC
MANOIR DU LAC DELAGE, LE
40 Av Du Lac, Lac-Delage, QC, G3C 5C4
(418) 848-0691
Emp Here 90   *Sales* 3,939,878
SIC 7011 Hotels and motels

Lac-Des-Ecorces, QC J0W
Labelle County

D-U-N-S 20-712-5191   (BR)
COMMISSION SCOLAIRE PIERRE-NEVEU, LA
ECOLE AUX QUATRE VENTS
576 Boul Saint-Francois, Lac-Des-Ecorces, QC, J0W 1H0
(819) 585-2976
Emp Here 50
SIC 8211 Elementary and secondary schools

D-U-N-S 24-294-0195   (HQ)
SERVICES FORESTIERS DE MONT-LAURIER LTEE
EQUIPMENT LAURENTIEN
327 Ch Du Golf Rr 1, Lac-Des-Ecorces, QC, J0W 1H0
(819) 623-3143
Emp Here 21   *Emp Total* 2
Sales 5,690,935
SIC 5084 Industrial machinery and equipment
  Jean-Luc Lemieux
  Denis Leduc

Lac-Drolet, QC G0Y
Frontenac County

D-U-N-S 24-202-3752   (SL)
ATTRACTION INC
672 Rue Du Parc, Lac-Drolet, QC, G0Y 1C0
(819) 549-2477
Emp Here 76   *Sales* 19,275,500
SIC 5136 Men's and boy's clothing
Pr Pr Jean-Marc Gagnon
  Simon Gagnon

D-U-N-S 25-389-8050   (SL)
SCIERIE TECH INC
126 Rue Du Moulin Bureau 99, Lac-Drolet, QC, G0Y 1C0
(819) 549-2533
Emp Here 50   *Sales* 4,742,446
SIC 2421 Sawmills and planing mills, general

Lac-Etchemin, QC G0R
Dorchester County

D-U-N-S 20-776-6114   (HQ)
CENTRE DE SANTE DES ETCHEMIN
(*Suby of* Centre De Sante Des Etchemin)
331 Rue Du Sanatorium Rr 1, Lac-Etchemin, QC, G0R 1S0
(418) 625-3101
Emp Here 590   *Emp Total* 600
Sales 59,484,160
SIC 8063 Psychiatric hospitals
Pr Pr Germain Roy
VP Sylvain Dion

D-U-N-S 25-232-7622   (BR)
COMMISSION SCOLAIRE DE LA BEAUCE-ETCHEMIN
ECOLE NOTRE-DAME DE LAC ETCHEMIN
1468 Rte 277, Lac-Etchemin, QC, G0R 1S0
(418) 625-5631
Emp Here 40
SIC 8211 Elementary and secondary schools

D-U-N-S 20-202-9724   (SL)
DUPONT, B. AUTO INC
1404 277 Rte, Lac-Etchemin, QC, G0R 1S0
(418) 625-6701
Emp Here 25   *Sales* 12,681,250
SIC 5511 New and used car dealers
Pr Pr Serge Dupont
VP VP Bertrand Dupont

D-U-N-S 20-777-7491   (SL)
MANOIR DU LAC ETCHEMIN INC
1415 Rte 227, Lac-Etchemin, QC, G0R 1S0
(418) 625-2101
Emp Here 50   *Sales* 2,188,821
SIC 7011 Hotels and motels

D-U-N-S 24-149-5290   (BR)
SOGETEL INC
(*Suby of* Gestion Michel Biron Inc)
1601 277 Rte, Lac-Etchemin, QC, G0R 1S0
(418) 625-4271
Emp Here 22
SIC 4813 Telephone communication, except radio

Lac-Megantic, QC G6B
Frontenac County

D-U-N-S 24-061-2718   (BR)
CEGEP BEAUCE-APPALACHES
CENTRE D'ETUDES COLLEGIALES DE LAC MEGANTIC - CEGEP
3800 Rue Cousineau, Lac-Megantic, QC, G6B 2A3
(819) 583-5432
Emp Here 32
SIC 8221 Colleges and universities

D-U-N-S 20-023-9957   (BR)
COMMISSION SCOLAIRE DES HAUTS-CANTONS
ECOLE NOTRE DAME DE FATIMA
6381 Rue Notre-Dame, Lac-Megantic, QC, G6B 2M9
(819) 583-1086
Emp Here 50
SIC 8211 Elementary and secondary schools

D-U-N-S 20-297-5053   (BR)
COMMISSION SCOLAIRE DES HAUTS-CANTONS
LES EQUIPES D'ANIMATION DE PASSE-PARTOUT
4730 Rue Dollard, Lac-Megantic, QC, G6B 1G6
(819) 583-2351
Emp Here 28
SIC 8741 Management services

D-U-N-S 20-252-7677   (BR)
COMMISSION SCOLAIRE DES HAUTS-CANTONS
COMMISSION SCOLAIRE DES HAUTS-CANTONS
3409 Rue Laval, Lac-Megantic, QC, G6B 1A5
(819) 583-3023
Emp Here 145
SIC 8211 Elementary and secondary schools

D-U-N-S 25-233-2952   (BR)
COMMISSION SCOLAIRE DES HAUTS-CANTONS
ECOLE SACRE COEUR
(*Suby of* Commission Scolaire des Hauts-Cantons)
4747 Rue Champlain, Lac-Megantic, QC, G6B 1X5
(819) 583-1144
Emp Here 55
SIC 8211 Elementary and secondary schools

D-U-N-S 20-277-0731   (SL)
LES PETROLES R. TURMEL INC
TRANSPORT RT
4575 Rue Latulippe Bureau 1, Lac-Megantic, QC, G6B 3H1
(819) 583-3838
Emp Here 40   *Sales* 13,391,400
SIC 5169 Chemicals and allied products, nec
Pr Robert Turmel
VP Fin Real Turmel
VP Denis Turmel

D-U-N-S 20-208-2368   (BR)
MASONITE INTERNATIONAL CORPORA-TION
INDUSTRIES MANUFACTURIERES MEGANTIC DIV.
(*Suby of* Masonite International Corporation)
6184 Rue Notre-Dame, Lac-Megantic, QC, G6B 3B5
(819) 583-1550
Emp Here 250
SIC 2435 Hardwood veneer and plywood

D-U-N-S 25-212-0779   (BR)
MASONITE INTERNATIONAL CORPORA-TION
(*Suby of* Masonite International Corporation)
4180 Rue Villeneuve, Lac-Megantic, QC, G6B 2C3
(819) 583-5885
Emp Here 200
SIC 2431 Millwork

D-U-N-S 24-023-5676   (BR)
PROVIGO DISTRIBUTION INC
MAXI #8630
3560 Rue Laval, Lac-Megantic, QC, G6B 2X4
(819) 583-4001
Emp Here 80
SIC 5141 Groceries, general line

D-U-N-S 24-864-3900   (SL)
TAFISA CANADA INC
4660 Rue Villeneuve, Lac-Megantic, QC, G6B 2C3
(819) 583-2930
Emp Here 330   *Sales* 32,102,708
SIC 2499 Wood products, nec
  George Christopher Lawrie
  Louis Brassard
VP VP Eric Dedekam
  Robert Torralbo

D-U-N-S 20-633-8415   (BR)
TRANSPORT ROBERT (1973) LTEE
4075 Rue Villeneuve, Lac-Megantic, QC, G6B 2C2
(819) 583-2230
Emp Here 80
SIC 4213 Trucking, except local

D-U-N-S 20-581-3546   (SL)
VARIETES CHARRON & LECLERC, SENC
PHARMACIE JEAN COUTU
6240 Rue Salaberry, Lac-Megantic, QC, G6B 1H8
(819) 583-2123
Emp Here 40   *Sales* 5,690,935
SIC 5912 Drug stores and proprietary stores
Pt Claude Charron
Pt Antoine Leclerc

D-U-N-S 24-319-5133   (BR)
WAL-MART CANADA CORP
WAL-MART
3130 Rue Laval, Lac-Megantic, QC, G6B 1A4
(819) 583-2882
Emp Here 120
SIC 5311 Department stores

Lac-Simon, QC J0Y
Papineau County

D-U-N-S 24-100-6902   (BR)
CENTRE JEUNESSE DE L'ABITIBI TEMIS-CAMINGUE
1020 Av Amikwiche, Lac-Simon, QC, J0Y 3N0
(819) 736-7466
Emp Here 20
SIC 8399 Social services, nec

Lachine, QC H8R
Hochelaga County

D-U-N-S 24-827-1384   (HQ)
ANACHEMIA CANADA CO
ANACHEMIA SCIENCE
(*Suby of* VWR Corporation)
255 Rue Norman, Lachine, QC, H8R 1A3
(514) 489-5711
Emp Here 100   *Emp Total* 9,426
Sales 36,480,350
SIC 5049 Professional equipment, nec
Pr Pr Stephen Harsh
  Gregory Blakely
Sec Thomas Salus
VP VP Theresa Balog
VP VP Theodore Pulkownik
Dir Martin Goldman
VP VP James Kalinovich

D-U-N-S 25-240-3225   (BR)
COMMISSION SCOLAIRE MARGUERITE-BOURGEOYS
ECOLE MARTIN BELANGER
29 Av Ouellette, Lachine, QC, H8R 1L4
(514) 595-2057
Emp Here 30
SIC 8211 Elementary and secondary schools

D-U-N-S 25-359-6886   (BR)
NORTHGATE INDUSTRIES LTD
USINES INDUSTRIES NORTHGATE, LES
(*Suby of* Northgate Equipment & Supply Ltd)
187 Rue Richer, Lachine, QC, H8R 1R4

(514) 482-0696
Emp Here 20
SIC 2452 Prefabricated wood buildings

D-U-N-S 24-698-1542 (SL)
REFENDOIRS C. R. LTEE, LES
300 Rue De La Berge-Du-Canal Bureau 4, Lachine, QC, H8R 1H3
(514) 366-2222
Emp Here 50 *Sales* 2,626,585
SIC 7389 Business services, nec

Lachine, QC H8S
Hochelaga County

D-U-N-S 20-699-1668 (SL)
3401987 CANADA INC.
900 Rue Du Pacifique, Lachine, QC, H8S 1C4
(514) 367-3001
Emp Here 60 *Sales* 9,988,687
SIC 6712 Bank holding companies
Noella Clouatre
Clifford Herer

D-U-N-S 25-361-8029 (BR)
ALIMENTS MARTEL INC
2387 Rue Remembrance, Lachine, QC, H8S 1X4

Emp Here 200
SIC 2099 Food preparations, nec

D-U-N-S 24-378-8721 (BR)
ANDRITZ HYDRO CANADA INC
390 Rue Sherbrooke, Lachine, QC, H8S 1G4
(514) 428-6843
Emp Here 40
SIC 8711 Engineering services

D-U-N-S 24-378-8713 (BR)
ANDRITZ HYDRO CANADA INC
895 Av George-V, Lachine, QC, H8S 2R9
(514) 428-6320
Emp Here 20
SIC 8711 Engineering services

D-U-N-S 24-308-4584 (BR)
CARLSTAR GROUP ULC, THE
DYN AIR
2100 Rue Remembrance, Lachine, QC, H8S 1X3
(514) 639-1616
Emp Here 20
SIC 3429 Hardware, nec

D-U-N-S 20-652-2109 (BR)
CASCADES CANADA ULC
CASCADES RECUPERATION +
63 Boul Saint-Joseph, Lachine, QC, H8S 2K9
(514) 363-9118
Emp Here 75
SIC 4953 Refuse systems

D-U-N-S 24-637-0118 (SL)
CENTRE D'HEBERGEMENT SOIN DE LONGUE DUREE BUSSEY (QUEBEC) INC
C.H.S.L.D.
2069 Boul Saint-Joseph, Lachine, QC, H8S 4B7
(514) 637-1127
Emp Here 56 *Sales* 2,626,585
SIC 8051 Skilled nursing care facilities

D-U-N-S 24-678-5521 (SL)
CENTRE DE VISION
1087 Rue Notre-Dame, Lachine, QC, H8S 2C3
(514) 634-5952
Emp Here 58 *Sales* 11,768,200
SIC 5049 Professional equipment, nec
Pr Jean Cohen

D-U-N-S 24-352-5354 (BR)
CENTRE DE SANTE ET DE SERVICES SOCIAUX DE DORVAL-LACHINE-LASALLE
CLSC DE DORVAL-LACHINE

1900 Rue Notre-Dame Bureau 262, Lachine, QC, H8S 2G2
(514) 639-0650
Emp Here 200
SIC 7991 Physical fitness facilities

D-U-N-S 24-382-9608 (BR)
CENTRE DE SANTE ET DE SERVICES SOCIAUX DE DORVAL-LACHINE-LASALLE
CENTRE D'HEBERGEMENT DE LACHINE
650 Place D'Accueil, Lachine, QC, H8S 3Z5
(514) 634-7161
Emp Here 250
SIC 8361 Residential care

D-U-N-S 25-233-6631 (BR)
COMMISSION SCOLAIRE MARGUERITE-BOURGEOYS
ECOLE TRES SAINT SACREMENT
704 5e Av, Lachine, QC, H8S 2W4
(514) 855-4234
Emp Here 35
SIC 8211 Elementary and secondary schools

D-U-N-S 24-475-0514 (BR)
COMMISSION SCOLAIRE MARGUERITE-BOURGEOYS
CEA DE LA SALLE PAVILLON
1625 Rue Saint-Antoine, Lachine, QC, H8S 1T8
(514) 855-4197
Emp Here 25
SIC 8211 Elementary and secondary schools

D-U-N-S 25-240-3746 (BR)
COMMISSION SCOLAIRE MARGUERITE-BOURGEOYS
ECOLE PHILIPPE-MORIN
1825 Rue Provost, Lachine, QC, H8S 1P5
(514) 855-4233
Emp Here 40
SIC 8211 Elementary and secondary schools

D-U-N-S 25-240-2862 (BR)
COMMISSION SCOLAIRE MARGUERITE-BOURGEOYS
ECOLE JARDIN DES SAINTS ANGES
1225 Rue Saint-Louis, Lachine, QC, H8S 2K6
(514) 855-4200
Emp Here 35
SIC 8211 Elementary and secondary schools

D-U-N-S 24-348-4602 (BR)
COMMISSION SCOLAIRE MARGUERITE-BOURGEOYS
CFPL PAVILLON DALBE VIAU
750 Rue Esther-Blondin, Lachine, QC, H8S 4C4
(514) 855-4185
Emp Here 50
SIC 8211 Elementary and secondary schools

D-U-N-S 25-498-1558 (SL)
CORPORATION FERROVIAIRE PROGRESS CANADA
125h Boul Saint-Joseph, Lachine, QC, H8S 2K9
(514) 639-1785
Emp Here 20 *Sales* 707,719
SIC 4111 Local and suburban transit

D-U-N-S 20-333-1769 (SL)
EMBALLAGES SXP INC
DURABOX
(*Suby of* Supremex Inc)
845 Rue Du Pacifique, Lachine, QC, H8S 2R1
(514) 364-3269
Emp Here 50 *Sales* 5,472,053
SIC 2631 Paperboard mills
Pr Emerson Stewart
Sec Lyne Begin

D-U-N-S 20-873-0460 (SL)
ENCHERES AUTOMOBILES ST-PIERRE (ESP LTEE) LES
ESP
1600 Rue Norman, Lachine, QC, H8S 1A9
(514) 489-3131
Emp Here 45 *Sales* 27,873,440

SIC 5012 Automobiles and other motor vehicles
Genl Mgr Alain Joyal

D-U-N-S 24-340-2760 (BR)
GLENCORE CANADA CORPORATION
GENERAL SMELTING COMPANY OF CANADA
1400 Rue Norman, Lachine, QC, H8S 1A8
(514) 637-3591
Emp Here 40
SIC 1021 Copper ores

D-U-N-S 20-216-9074 (BR)
METSO MINERALS CANADA INC
795 Av George-V, Lachine, QC, H8S 2R9
(514) 485-4000
Emp Here 40
SIC 3532 Mining machinery

D-U-N-S 20-025-7777 (BR)
POLYMER DISTRIBUTION INC
1111 12e Av, Lachine, QC, H8S 4K9
(514) 634-3338
Emp Here 35
SIC 4213 Trucking, except local

D-U-N-S 25-827-6336 (BR)
PROVIGO DISTRIBUTION INC
MAXI
3150 Rue Remembrance, Lachine, QC, H8S 1X8
(514) 637-4606
Emp Here 70
SIC 5141 Groceries, general line

D-U-N-S 20-232-8035 (SL)
ROSS AND ANGLIN LIMITEE
45 Boul Saint-Joseph, Lachine, QC, H8S 2K9
(514) 364-4220
Emp Here 35 *Sales* 9,637,750
SIC 1522 Residential construction, nec
Sec Mark Thompson
Treas Michael Thompson
Dir Peter Thompson

D-U-N-S 20-555-0036 (SL)
SERVICES PARTAGES METSO LTEE
795 Av George-V, Lachine, QC, H8S 2R9
(877) 677-2005
Emp Here 85 *Sales* 4,231,721
SIC 7389 Business services, nec

Lachine, QC H8T
Hochelaga County

D-U-N-S 20-279-3209 (BR)
3627730 CANADA INC
FREEMAN AUDIO VISUAL
2056 32e Av, Lachine, QC, H8T 3H7
(514) 631-1821
Emp Here 90
SIC 7812 Motion picture and video production

D-U-N-S 20-513-9947 (HQ)
3627730 CANADA INC
FREEMAN AUDIO VISUAL
1930 Rue Onesime-Gagnon, Lachine, QC, H8T 3M6
(514) 631-0710
Emp Here 70 *Emp Total* 1
Sales 56,398,621
SIC 7359 Equipment rental and leasing, nec
Ch Bd Joseph V. Popolo, Jr.
David Campbell
Sec Victoria Prince
Dir Carrie Freeman Parsons

D-U-N-S 25-502-3710 (SL)
5U SERVICES INC
10220 Ch De La Cote-De-Liesse, Lachine, QC, H8T 1A3
(514) 635-1103
Emp Here 50 *Sales* 4,377,642
SIC 1731 Electrical work

D-U-N-S 20-290-6657 (SL)
8843848 CANADA INC
MAISON FAMEUSE
2100 52e Av Bureau 100, Lachine, QC, H8T 2Y5
(514) 556-3088
Emp Here 50 *Sales* 4,815,406
SIC 5251 Hardware stores

D-U-N-S 24-524-1604 (SL)
9205-6126 QUEBEC INC
AMJ CAMPBELL VAN LINES MONTREAL
1255 32e Av, Lachine, QC, H8T 3H2
(514) 631-5223
Emp Here 50 *Sales* 2,845,467
SIC 4214 Local trucking with storage

D-U-N-S 24-244-9887 (BR)
ABB INC
2117 32e Av, Lachine, QC, H8T 3J1

Emp Here 100
SIC 5211 Lumber and other building materials

D-U-N-S 20-260-6059 (HQ)
ANDRITZ LTEE
2260 32e Av, Lachine, QC, H8T 3H4
(514) 631-7700
Emp Here 115 *Emp Total* 25,056
Sales 36,480,350
SIC 5084 Industrial machinery and equipment
Pr Scott Ross
Sec Jeffrey Wise
Dir Humbert Koefler
Dir Thimothy J. Ryan
Dir Carl Luhrmann

D-U-N-S 25-095-4492 (BR)
ANIXTER CANADA INC
3000 Rue Louis-A.-Amos, Lachine, QC, H8T 3P8
(514) 636-3636
Emp Here 110
SIC 5063 Electrical apparatus and equipment

D-U-N-S 20-254-0985 (BR)
ASIA PULP & PAPER (CANADA) LTD
APP CANADA
1820 46e Av, Lachine, QC, H8T 2P2
(514) 631-2300
Emp Here 20
SIC 5113 Industrial and personal service paper

D-U-N-S 24-335-6172 (SL)
BOULART INC
BAGUETTECO
1355 32e Av, Lachine, QC, H8T 3H2
(514) 631-4040
Emp Here 60 *Sales* 3,724,879
SIC 2051 Bread, cake, and related products

D-U-N-S 20-015-9122 (BR)
BRENNTAG CANADA INC
2900 Boul Jean-Baptiste-Deschamps, Lachine, QC, H8T 1C8
(514) 636-9230
Emp Here 50
SIC 5169 Chemicals and allied products, nec

D-U-N-S 20-014-3472 (HQ)
CBCI TELECOM CANADA INC
CBCI TELECOM
(*Suby of* 1357000 Alberta ULC)
2260 46e Av, Lachine, QC, H8T 2P3
(514) 422-9333
Emp Here 40 *Emp Total* 80
Sales 9,338,970
SIC 4899 Communication services, nec
Pr Denis Dumouchel
Amelie Cote

D-U-N-S 24-525-7378 (BR)
CANADA DRAYAGE INC
4415 Rue Fairway, Lachine, QC, H8T 1B5
(514) 639-7878
Emp Here 100
SIC 4212 Local trucking, without storage

▲ Public Company ■ Public Company Family Member **HQ** Headquarters **BR** Branch **SL** Single Location

D-U-N-S 20-265-7433 (BR)
COCA-COLA REFRESHMENTS CANADA COMPANY
(Suby of The Coca-Cola Company)
1515 46e Av, Lachine, QC, H8T 2N8
(514) 636-4791
Emp Here 150
SIC 2086 Bottled and canned soft drinks

D-U-N-S 24-590-7019 (BR)
COMMISSION SCOLAIRE MARGUERITE-BOURGEOYS
ECOLE SECONDAIRES REGROUPEMENT SUD COLLEGE SAINT LOUIS
50 34e Av, Lachine, QC, H8T 1Z2
(514) 748-4662
Emp Here 80
SIC 8211 Elementary and secondary schools

D-U-N-S 24-590-7019 (BR)
CONSOLIDATED FASTFRATE INC
FASTFRATE
4415 Rue Fairway, Lachine, QC, H8T 1B5
(514) 639-7747
Emp Here 100
SIC 4731 Freight transportation arrangement

D-U-N-S 24-354-7309 (HQ)
CORPORATION D'ETIQUETTE MULTI-COLOR CANADA
CAMEO CRAFTS
1925 32e Av, Lachine, QC, H8T 3J1
(514) 341-4850
Emp Here 82   Emp Total 8
Sales 11,967,578
SIC 2752 Commercial printing, lithographic
Pr Pr Nigel A Vinecombe
  Mary T Fetch
  Sharon E Birkett
Dir Nicolas Blin

D-U-N-S 20-806-9257 (BR)
COUCHE-TARD INC
COUCHE-TARD
685 32e Av, Lachine, QC, H8T 3G6
(514) 634-1708
Emp Here 25
SIC 5411 Grocery stores

D-U-N-S 24-516-9321 (SL)
COURTIER DOUANES INTERNATIONAL SKYWAY LTEE
CALTEX TRANSPORT
9230 Ch De La Cote-De-Liesse, Lachine, QC, H8T 1A1
(514) 636-0250
Emp Here 40   Sales 12,815,674
SIC 4731 Freight transportation arrangement
Pr Pr Joseph Brown Zatylny
  Karen B Zatylny

D-U-N-S 24-743-1893 (SL)
DIVERSITECH EQUIPMENT AND SALES 1984 LTD
DIVERSITECH
2500 Rue Alphonse-Gariepy, Lachine, QC, H8T 3M2
(514) 631-7300
Emp Here 50   Sales 9,161,700
SIC 3564 Blowers and fans
  Jared Simms
Dir Marvin Simms
Dir Andrew Simms

D-U-N-S 24-313-7960 (BR)
DUNDEE SECURITIES CORPORATION
HOLLISWEALTH
10340 Ch De La Cote-De-Liesse Unite 150, Lachine, QC, H8T 1A3
(514) 227-2700
Emp Here 20
SIC 6211 Security brokers and dealers

D-U-N-S 20-651-1128 (BR)
ENERGIZER CANADA INC
ENERGIZER HOLDINGS
(Suby of Edgewell Personal Care Company)
9970 Ch De La Cote-De-Liesse Bureau 100,

Lachine, QC, H8T 1A1

Emp Here 30
SIC 5063 Electrical apparatus and equipment

D-U-N-S 20-032-7919 (BR)
FRESENIUS MEDICAL CARE CANADA INC
1660 32e Av, Lachine, QC, H8T 3R1
(514) 633-0013
Emp Here 65
SIC 5047 Medical and hospital equipment

D-U-N-S 20-219-8917 (HQ)
GENFOOT INC
KAMIK
1940 55e Av, Lachine, QC, H8T 3H3
(514) 341-3950
Emp Here 90   Emp Total 500
Sales 18,104,646
SIC 5661 Shoe stores
Pr Pr Richard Cook
  Norman Cook
  Stephen Cook
VP VP Catherine Cook
Dir Gordon Cook

D-U-N-S 25-283-9980 (BR)
GRAND & TOY LIMITED
GRAND & TOY
(Suby of Office Depot, Inc.)
2275 52e Av, Lachine, QC, H8T 2Y8
(514) 636-7733
Emp Here 123
SIC 5943 Stationery stores

D-U-N-S 20-230-9647 (HQ)
GROUPE MARCELLE INC
COSMETIQUES LISE WATIER
(Suby of Investissements M.B.V.H. Inc, Les)
9200 Ch De La Cote-De-Liesse, Lachine, QC, H8T 1A1
(514) 631-7710
Emp Here 190   Emp Total 1
Sales 16,458,769
SIC 2844 Toilet preparations
Treas Michael Cape
  David Cape
Dir David Petrie

D-U-N-S 25-149-6428 (SL)
HELIX UNIFORME LTEE
(Suby of Preformed Line Products Company)
1600 46e Av, Lachine, QC, H8T 3J9
(514) 828-0057
Emp Here 40   Sales 8,402,635
SIC 3644 Noncurrent-carrying wiring devices
Pr Pr Philip S. Jones
VP Dennis F. Mckenna
Sec Caroline S. Vaccariello
Dir Robert G. Ruhlman

D-U-N-S 24-857-7751 (BR)
HIGH LINER FOODS INCORPORATED
LES ALIMENTS HIGH LINER
9960 Ch De La Cote-De-Liesse Bureau 200, Lachine, QC, H8T 1A1
(514) 636-5114
Emp Here 20
SIC 2092 Fresh or frozen packaged fish

D-U-N-S 25-295-2353 (BR)
HONEYWELL LIMITED
(Suby of Honeywell International Inc.)
2100 52e Av, Lachine, QC, H8T 2Y5
(514) 422-3400
Emp Here 190
SIC 3822 Environmental controls

D-U-N-S 20-221-5133 (SL)
HUBSCHER RIBBON CORPORATION LTD
(Suby of Hubscher Label Industries (1986) Inc)
2325 52e Av, Lachine, QC, H8T 3C3
(514) 636-6610
Emp Here 50
SIC 2269 Finishing plants, nec

D-U-N-S 25-524-6472 (BR)

HUDSON'S BAY COMPANY
LOGISTIQUE HBC
2105 23e Av, Lachine, QC, H8T 1X3

Emp Here 300
SIC 8742 Management consulting services

D-U-N-S 24-431-9372 (BR)
ITW CANADA INVESTMENTS LIMITED PARTNERSHIP
HORBART FOOD EQUIPMENT GROUP CANADA
(Suby of Illinois Tool Works Inc.)
3195 Rue Louis-A.-Amos, Lachine, QC, H8T 1C4
(514) 631-0073
Emp Here 36
SIC 1799 Special trade contractors, nec

D-U-N-S 20-888-4916 (HQ)
JEAN BLEU INC, LE
MEGA BLUES
1895 46e Av, Lachine, QC, H8T 2N9
(514) 631-3300
Emp Here 20   Emp Total 216
Sales 18,711,022
SIC 5611 Men's and boys' clothing stores
Pr Pr Allan Berlach

D-U-N-S 24-973-8600 (BR)
LESTER B. PEARSON SCHOOL BOARD
LAKESIDE ACADEMY
5050 Rue Sherbrooke, Lachine, QC, H8T 1H8
(514) 637-2505
Emp Here 75
SIC 8211 Elementary and secondary schools

D-U-N-S 20-165-5524 (BR)
LIFTOW LIMITED
1936 32e Av, Lachine, QC, H8T 3J7
(514) 633-9360
Emp Here 100
SIC 5084 Industrial machinery and equipment

D-U-N-S 20-175-7486 (SL)
MACHINES A PAPIER ANDRITZ LIMITEE
2260 32e Av, Lachine, QC, H8T 3H4
(514) 631-7700
Emp Here 28   Sales 2,626,585
SIC 8748 Business consulting, nec

D-U-N-S 20-177-4267 (BR)
MEDIAS TRANSCONTINENTAL INC
MEDIAS TRANSCONTINENTAL INC
1865 32e Av, Lachine, QC, H8T 3J1
(514) 636-5559
Emp Here 30
SIC 7319 Advertising, nec

D-U-N-S 20-124-5383 (BR)
MORBERN INC
INTERNATIONAL KNITTING MILLS
1967 46e Av, Lachine, QC, H8T 2P1
(514) 631-2990
Emp Here 65
SIC 2295 Coated fabrics, not rubberized

D-U-N-S 20-508-9803 (BR)
PANASONIC CANADA INC
3075 Rue Louis-A.-Amos, Lachine, QC, H8T 1C4

Emp Here 50
SIC 5045 Computers, peripherals, and software

D-U-N-S 24-516-9800 (BR)
PERMICOM PERMITS SERVICES INC
10340 Ch De La Cote-De-Liesse Bureau 150, Lachine, QC, H8T 1A3
(514) 828-1118
Emp Here 25
SIC 4731 Freight transportation arrangement

D-U-N-S 24-419-1305 (BR)
PHILIPS LIGHTING CANADA LTD
CANLYTE, DIV OF
3015 Rue Louis-A.-Amos, Lachine, QC, H8T 1C4

(514) 636-0670
Emp Here 250
SIC 3646 Commercial lighting fixtures

D-U-N-S 24-126-3883 (BR)
R.O.E. LOGISTICS INC
10340 Ch De La Cote-De-Liesse Bureau 210, Lachine, QC, H8T 1A3

Emp Here 22
SIC 4212 Local trucking, without storage

D-U-N-S 24-100-4949 (BR)
REGULVAR INC
1600 55e Av, Lachine, QC, H8T 3J5
(514) 636-2878
Emp Here 20
SIC 5084 Industrial machinery and equipment

D-U-N-S 24-812-0719 (BR)
RICHARDS PACKAGING INC
EMBALLAGES RICHARD, LES
1939 Rue Onesime-Gagnon, Lachine, QC, H8T 3M5
(514) 422-8690
Emp Here 35
SIC 5099 Durable goods, nec

D-U-N-S 20-220-4111 (HQ)
ROLLS-ROYCE CANADA LIMITEE
9500 Ch De La Cote-De-Liesse, Lachine, QC, H8T 1A2
(514) 631-3541
Emp Here 1,400   Emp Total 50,500
Sales 228,002,188
SIC 4581 Airports, flying fields, and services
Pr Denis Giangi
VP Vincent Morello
Sec Daniel Majeau
Dir Diana Hargrave

D-U-N-S 25-307-3282 (BR)
ROTISSERIES ST-HUBERT LTEE, LES
ROTISSERIES ST-HUBERT
(Suby of Cara Holdings Limited)
665 32e Av, Lachine, QC, H8T 3G6
(514) 637-4417
Emp Here 55
SIC 5812 Eating places

D-U-N-S 20-421-9802 (BR)
SAMUEL, SON & CO., LIMITED
SAMUEL PACKAGING SYSTEMS GROUP
3289 Boul Jean-Baptiste-Deschamps, Lachine, QC, H8T 3E4
(514) 631-5551
Emp Here 30
SIC 5051 Metals service centers and offices

D-U-N-S 24-000-9956 (SL)
SCHWAN'S CANADA CORPORATION
2900 Rue Louis-A.-Amos, Lachine, QC, H8T 3K6
(514) 631-9275
Emp Here 110   Sales 23,411,840
SIC 6712 Bank holding companies
Genl Mgr Michael Aucoin
Pr Greg Flack

D-U-N-S 24-921-8439 (HQ)
SERVICES D'ESSAIS INTERTEK AN LTEE
CONTRLE TECHNIQUE APPLIQUE
1829 32e Av, Lachine, QC, H8T 3J1
(514) 631-3100
Emp Here 40   Emp Total 30,521
Sales 11,590,647
SIC 8734 Testing laboratories
Pr Gregg Tiemman
VP VP Richard Adams
VP VP Nimer Al-Hafi

D-U-N-S 25-298-9900 (SL)
SYSTEMES JOINER INC
(Suby of US Joiner Holding Company)
1925 52e Av, Lachine, QC, H8T 3C3
(514) 636-5555
Emp Here 26   Sales 2,261,782
SIC 8711 Engineering services

D-U-N-S 24-392-8426   (BR)
TECHNOLOGIES METAFORE INC
METAFORE FINANCIAL SERVICES
9900 Ch De La Cote-De-Liesse, Lachine, QC,
H8T 1A1
(514) 636-5127
Emp Here 21
SIC 5045 Computers, peripherals, and software

D-U-N-S 24-516-8281   (SL)
TENSOR MACHINERY LTD
1570 52e Av, Lachine, QC, H8T 2X9
(514) 636-3121
Emp Here 21   *Sales* 1,386,253
SIC 4899 Communication services, nec

D-U-N-S 24-359-0960   (BR)
UNITED PARCEL SERVICE CANADA LTD
UPS
1221 32e Av Bureau 209, Lachine, QC, H8T
3H2
(514) 633-0010
Emp Here 100
SIC 7389 Business services, nec

D-U-N-S 25-125-1781   (SL)
VCS INVESTIGATION INC
SPEQ
10500 Ch De La Cote-De-Liesse Bureau 200,
Lachine, QC, H8T 1A4
(514) 737-1911
Emp Here 100   *Sales* 4,961,328
SIC 7389 Business services, nec

D-U-N-S 24-313-6202   (BR)
VPC GROUP INC
FABRICATION ULTRA
(*Suby of* VPC Group Inc)
2350 Rue Louis-A.-Amos, Lachine, QC, H8T
3K6
(514) 631-0691
Emp Here 30
SIC 3069 Fabricated rubber products, nec

D-U-N-S 24-062-5918   (BR)
VITRAN EXPRESS CANADA INC
3333 Rue Joseph-Dubreuil, Lachine, QC, H8T
3P7
(514) 932-6588
Emp Here 45
SIC 4213 Trucking, except local

D-U-N-S 24-372-1482   (BR)
WABTEC CANADA INC
WABCO FREIGHT CAR PRODUCTS
2610 Boul Jean-Baptiste-Deschamps, Lachine, QC, H8T 1C9
(514) 636-3115
Emp Here 25
SIC 4789 Transportation services, nec

D-U-N-S 25-298-3689   (BR)
WAJAX INDUSTRIAL COMPONENTS LIMITED PARTNERSHIP
WAJAX INDUSTRIAL COMPONENTS
2202 52e Av, Lachine, QC, H8T 2Y3
(514) 636-7366
Emp Here 155
SIC 5084 Industrial machinery and equipment

Lachute, QC J8H
Argenteuil County

D-U-N-S 24-337-2708   (BR)
CASCADES CANADA ULC
CASCADES GROUPE TISSU LACHUTE
115 Rue De La Princesse, Lachute, QC, J8H
4M3
(450) 562-8585
Emp Here 150
SIC 2676 Sanitary paper products

D-U-N-S 25-232-8802   (BR)
COMMISSION SCOLAIRE DE LA RIVIERE-DU-NORD

ECOLE ST JULIEN
(*Suby of* Commission Scolaire de la Riviere-du-Nord)
218 Rue Wilson, Lachute, QC, J8H 3J3
(450) 562-8521
Emp Here 40
SIC 8211 Elementary and secondary schools

D-U-N-S 25-232-8729   (BR)
COMMISSION SCOLAIRE DE LA RIVIERE-DU-NORD
ECOLE POLYVALENTE LAVIGNE
(*Suby of* Commission Scolaire de la Riviere-du-Nord)
452 Av D'Argenteuil Bureau 103, Lachute,
QC, J8H 1W9
(450) 562-8841
Emp Here 120
SIC 8211 Elementary and secondary schools

D-U-N-S 20-712-1810   (BR)
COMMISSION SCOLAIRE DE LA RIVIERE-DU-NORD
CENTRE DE FORMATION PROFESSION-NEL PERFORMANCE PLUS
(*Suby of* Commission Scolaire de la Riviere-du-Nord)
462 Av D'Argenteuil, Lachute, QC, J8H 1W9
(450) 566-7587
Emp Here 60
SIC 8211 Elementary and secondary schools

D-U-N-S 20-712-1760   (BR)
COMMISSION SCOLAIRE DE LA RIVIERE-DU-NORD
CENTRE DE FORMATION GENERALE LE PARALLELE
(*Suby of* Commission Scolaire de la Riviere-du-Nord)
190 Rue Mary, Lachute, QC, J8H 2C4
(450) 566-0088
Emp Here 50
SIC 8211 Elementary and secondary schools

D-U-N-S 20-712-1778   (BR)
GOUVERNEMENT DE LA PROVINCE DE QUEBEC
ECOLES PRIMAIRES L'OASIS
80 Rue Hammond, Lachute, QC, J8H 2V3
(450) 562-2223
Emp Here 50
SIC 8211 Elementary and secondary schools

D-U-N-S 24-328-6981   (BR)
PROVIGO INC
355 Rue Principale, Lachute, QC, J8H 2Z7
(450) 566-0761
Emp Here 70
SIC 5411 Grocery stores

D-U-N-S 20-858-6768   (SL)
RESIDENCE DE LACHUTE INC, LA
377 Rue Principale, Lachute, QC, J8H 1Y1
(450) 562-5203
Emp Here 60   *Sales* 2,188,821
SIC 8361 Residential care

D-U-N-S 24-742-2207   (HQ)
RESTAURANT LOUJAC INC
RESTAURANT MACDONALDS
(*Suby of* Restaurant Loujac Inc)
237 Av Bethany, Lachute, QC, J8H 2M9
(450) 562-8569
Emp Here 50   *Emp Total* 275
Sales 10,742,551
SIC 5812 Eating places
Pr Jacques Giguere

D-U-N-S 20-792-1412   (SL)
SCIERIE CARRIERE LTEE
(*Suby of* Caslumber Inc)
525 Boul De L'Aeroparc, Lachute, QC, J8H
3R8
(450) 562-8578
Emp Here 38   *Sales* 3,575,074
SIC 2421 Sawmills and planing mills, general

D-U-N-S 25-234-2530   (BR)

ECOLE ST JULIEN
(*Suby of* Commission Scolaire de la Riviere-du-Nord)

SIR WILFRID LAURIER SCHOOL BOARD
LAURENTIAN ELEMENTARY SCHOOL
(*Suby of* Sir Wilfrid Laurier School Board)
455 Rue Court, Lachute, QC, J8H 1T2
(450) 562-2401
Emp Here 40
SIC 8211 Elementary and secondary schools

D-U-N-S 24-973-8188   (BR)
SIR WILFRID LAURIER SCHOOL BOARD
LAURENTIAN REGIONAL HIGH SCHOOL
448 Av D'Argenteuil, Lachute, QC, J8H 1W9
(450) 562-8571
Emp Here 80
SIC 8211 Elementary and secondary schools

D-U-N-S 25-294-8856   (BR)
WAL-MART CANADA CORP
480 Av Bethany, Lachute, QC, J8H 4H5
(450) 562-0258
Emp Here 150
SIC 5311 Department stores

Lacolle, QC J0J
St-Jean County

D-U-N-S 24-800-2776   (SL)
ARNEG CANADA INC
18 Rue Richelieu, Lacolle, QC, J0J 1J0
(450) 246-3837
Emp Here 140   *Sales* 21,049,899
SIC 3585 Refrigeration and heating equipment
Pr Rejean Lalumiere
Sec Michel Beaudry
Dir Daniele Marzaro

D-U-N-S 25-651-4527   (BR)
ENTREPRISE ROBERT THIBERT INC
16 Rue Richelieu, Lacolle, QC, J0J 1J0
(450) 246-2460
Emp Here 30
SIC 5013 Motor vehicle supplies and new parts

D-U-N-S 20-737-3739   (SL)
MARCHE H. DAUPHINAIS INC
IGA
60 202 Rte, Lacolle, QC, J0J 1J0
(450) 246-3037
Emp Here 50   *Sales* 8,343,600
SIC 5411 Grocery stores
Pr Henri Dauphinais
  Robert Dauphinais

Lambton, QC G0M
Frontenac County

D-U-N-S 20-837-1877   (BR)
GOUVERNEMENT DE LA PROVINCE DE QUEBEC
GOUVERNEMENT DE LA PROVINCE DE QUEBEC
310 Rue Principale, Lambton, QC, G0M 1H0
(418) 486-7417
Emp Here 45
SIC 8322 Individual and family services

D-U-N-S 24-377-7893   (BR)
SOCIETE COOPERATIVE AGRICOLE DE LAC MEGANTIC-LAMBTON
SOCIETE COOPERATIVE AGRICOLE DE LAC MEGANTIC-LAMBT
136 Rue Principale, Lambton, QC, G0M 1H0
(418) 486-7474
Emp Here 20
SIC 5211 Lumber and other building materials

Landrienne, QC J0Y
Abitibi County

D-U-N-S 20-203-8279   (SL)
SCIERIE LANDRIENNE INC
389 Ch Du Moulin, Landrienne, QC, J0Y 1V0
(819) 732-6404
Emp Here 200   *Sales* 25,521,600
SIC 2421 Sawmills and planing mills, general
Pr Pr Gilbert Gonthier
VP VP Rejean Boisvert
  Luc Dufour
VP VP Benoit Cote
  Yvon Lafontaine
Dir Daniel Tardif
  Eric Bisson

Lanoraie, QC J0K
Berthier County

D-U-N-S 20-267-0550   (BR)
INTEPLAST BAGS AND FILMS CORPORATION
VIAMFILMS
1 Rue Vifan, Lanoraie, QC, J0K 1E0
(450) 887-7711
Emp Here 100
SIC 3081 Unsupported plastics film and sheet

D-U-N-S 24-433-0445   (HQ)
PRODUITS D'ACIER HASON INC, LES
(*Suby of* Hason Management Corporation)
7 Rue Pinat, Lanoraie, QC, J0K 1E0
(450) 887-0800
Emp Here 170   *Emp Total* 1
Sales 31,008,298
SIC 3443 Fabricated plate work (boiler shop)
  Denis Blain
VP Dang-Loc Nguyen

Lasalle, QC H8N

D-U-N-S 24-251-0626   (SL)
9246-4759 QUEBEC INC
CHEVROLET BUICK GMC DE LASALLE
8000 Boul Newman, Lasalle, QC, H8N 1X9
(514) 595-5666
Emp Here 49   *Sales* 23,087,061
SIC 5511 New and used car dealers
Pr Pierre Couture

D-U-N-S 20-715-2591   (HQ)
ACIER NOVA INC
(*Suby of* 3195538 Canada Inc)
6001 Rue Irwin, Lasalle, QC, H8N 1A1
(514) 789-0511
Emp Here 77   *Emp Total* 1
Sales 105,249,497
SIC 5051 Metals service centers and offices
Pr D.Bryan Jones
  Scott B. Jones
VP Lawrence P. Cannon

D-U-N-S 25-309-9154   (BR)
ADDENDA CAPITAL INC
RBC
2101 Av Dollard Bureau 38, Lasalle, QC, H8N
1S2
(514) 368-5610
Emp Here 24
SIC 6282 Investment advice

D-U-N-S 24-349-7281   (SL)
ALIMENTS LEVITTS INC, LES
LEVITTS MC
7070 Rue Saint-Patrick, Lasalle, QC, H8N 1V2
(514) 367-1654
Emp Here 20   *Sales* 2,772,003
SIC 2011 Meat packing plants

D-U-N-S 25-331-0825   (BR)
ALSCO CANADA CORPORATION

UNIFORMS & LINGE D'HOTELERIE ALSCO
2500 Rue Senkus, Lasalle, QC, H8N 2X9
(514) 595-7381
Emp Here 125
SIC 7218 Industrial launderers

D-U-N-S 24-936-2302   (HQ)
AUTOBUS TRANSCO (1988) INC
FIRST STUDENT CANADA
8201 Rue Elmslie, Lasalle, QC, H8N 2W6
(514) 363-4315
Emp Here 175   *Emp Total* 120,475
Sales 12,721,442
SIC 4151 School buses
Genl Mgr Michel Larocque
  Jim Switzer

D-U-N-S 24-052-0700   (SL)
AUTOMOBILES AUTOHAUS LTEE, LES
(*Suby of* Gestion Herwolf Ltee)
1855 Av Dollard, Lasalle, QC, H8N 1T9

Emp Here 27   *Sales* 13,251,600
SIC 5511 New and used car dealers
Pr Gabriel Azouz

D-U-N-S 20-299-1126   (BR)
BANQUE NATIONALE DU CANADA
8449 Boul Newman, Lasalle, QC, H8N 2Y7
(514) 367-0112
Emp Here 20
SIC 6021 National commercial banks

D-U-N-S 25-060-5193   (BR)
BEST BUY CANADA LTD
GEEK SQUAD
(*Suby of* Best Buy Co., Inc.)
7077 Boul Newman, Lasalle, QC, H8N 1X1
(514) 368-6570
Emp Here 100
SIC 5731 Radio, television, and electronic stores

D-U-N-S 20-609-9447   (BR)
BRICK WAREHOUSE LP, THE
6867 Boul Newman, Lasalle, QC, H8N 3E4
(514) 595-9900
Emp Here 50
SIC 5712 Furniture stores

D-U-N-S 25-311-3773   (BR)
CANADIAN IMPERIAL BANK OF COMMERCE
CIBC
7077 Boul Newman, Lasalle, QC, H8N 1X1
(514) 365-0592
Emp Here 28
SIC 6021 National commercial banks

D-U-N-S 20-213-0162   (BR)
CIE MATERIAUX DE CONSTRUCTION BP CANADA, LA
BP CANADA
(*Suby of* 3077578 Nova Scotia Corp)
2850 Av Dollard, Lasalle, QC, H8N 2V2
(514) 364-0161
Emp Here 400
SIC 5199 Nondurable goods, nec

D-U-N-S 20-046-1643   (BR)
COMMISSION SCOLAIRE MARGUERITE-BOURGEOYS
ECOLE TERRE DES JEUNES
2311 Rue Menard, Lasalle, QC, H8N 1J4
(514) 595-2056
Emp Here 50
SIC 8211 Elementary and secondary schools

D-U-N-S 20-712-4236   (BR)
COMMISSION SCOLAIRE MARGUERITE-BOURGEOYS
CENTRE INTREGRE DE MECANIQUE
1100 Rue Ducas, Lasalle, QC, H8N 3E6
(514) 364-5300
Emp Here 50
SIC 8211 Elementary and secondary schools

D-U-N-S 25-240-4439   (BR)

COMMISSION SCOLAIRE MARGUERITE-BOURGEOYS
ECOLE LAURENDEAU DUNTON
1515 Rue Rancourt, Lasalle, QC, H8N 1R7
(514) 595-2049
Emp Here 30
SIC 8211 Elementary and secondary schools

D-U-N-S 24-869-9225   (SL)
CONCIERGERIE SPEICO INC
7651 Rue Cordner, Lasalle, QC, H8N 2X2
(514) 364-0777
Emp Here 120   *Sales* 3,502,114
SIC 7349 Building maintenance services, nec

D-U-N-S 20-887-0501   (SL)
CORPORATION DE CEGEP ANDRE-LAURENDEAU
1111 Rue Lapierre Bureau 300, Lasalle, QC, H8N 2J4
(514) 364-3320
Emp Here 500   *Sales* 69,988,080
SIC 8221 Colleges and universities
Genl Mgr Herve Pilon

D-U-N-S 24-959-6693   (BR)
CRANE CANADA CO.
CRANE DISTRIBUTION
(*Suby of* Crane Co.)
7800 Rue Elmslie, Lasalle, QC, H8N 3E5
(514) 766-8541
Emp Here 22
SIC 5074 Plumbing and heating equipment and supplies (hydronics)

D-U-N-S 20-105-4959   (SL)
E.D.M. LASALLE INC
AUBAINERIE CONCEPT MODE, L'
7427 Boul Newman Bureau 36, Lasalle, QC, H8N 1X3
(514) 365-6633
Emp Here 60   *Sales* 4,304,681
SIC 5311 Department stores

D-U-N-S 20-108-5672   (BR)
FEDERATION DES CAISSES DESJARDINS DU QUEBEC
CENTRE FINANCIER AUX ENTREPRISES DU SUD OUEST DE MONTREAL
2140 Av Dollard, Lasalle, QC, H8N 1S6

Emp Here 22
SIC 6211 Security brokers and dealers

D-U-N-S 20-106-9825   (BR)
GAP (CANADA) INC
GAP
(*Suby of* The Gap Inc)
7077 Boul Newman Bureau 111, Lasalle, QC, H8N 1X1
(514) 367-1114
Emp Here 20
SIC 5651 Family clothing stores

D-U-N-S 20-715-0074   (BR)
GAZ METRO INC
2200 Rue De Cannes-Brulees, Lasalle, QC, H8N 2Z2
(514) 367-2525
Emp Here 75
SIC 4924 Natural gas distribution

D-U-N-S 20-290-7663   (BR)
GROUPE LALIBERTE SPORTS INC
SPORTS EXPERTS
7077 Boul Newman Bureau 500, Lasalle, QC, H8N 1X1
(514) 419-4105
Emp Here 20
SIC 5941 Sporting goods and bicycle shops

D-U-N-S 25-199-4703   (BR)
GROUPE SPORTSCENE INC
CAGE AUX SPORTS, LA
7077 Boul Newman Bureau 150, Lasalle, QC, H8N 1X1
(514) 363-1403
Emp Here 40
SIC 5812 Eating places

D-U-N-S 25-818-0355   (BR)
HOPITAL DOUGLAS
CLINIQUE EXTERNE LASALLE 8560
(*Suby of* Hopital Douglas)
8550 Boul Newman, Lasalle, QC, H8N 1Y5
(514) 366-0980
Emp Here 20
SIC 8093 Specialty outpatient clinics, nec

D-U-N-S 20-179-6393   (BR)
INTRIA ITEMS INC
8301 Rue Elmslie, Lasalle, QC, H8N 3H9
(514) 368-5222
Emp Here 800
SIC 7374 Data processing and preparation

D-U-N-S 25-503-4159   (BR)
IMMEUBLES CARREFOUR RICHELIEU LTEE, LES
CARREFOUR ANGRIGNON
7077 Boul Newman Bureau 1, Lasalle, QC, H8N 1X1
(514) 363-9413
Emp Here 60
SIC 6512 Nonresidential building operators

D-U-N-S 25-309-7174   (BR)
INDUSTRIELLE ALLIANCE, ASSURANCE ET SERVICES FINANCIERS INC
INDUSTRIA ALLIANCE LIFE INSURANCE
7655 Boul Newman Bureau 207, Lasalle, QC, H8N 1X7
(514) 364-0179
Emp Here 40
SIC 6411 Insurance agents, brokers, and service

D-U-N-S 24-669-2586   (BR)
KRUGER INC
PACKAGING DIVISION
7474 Rue Cordner, Lasalle, QC, H8N 2W3
(514) 366-8050
Emp Here 190
SIC 2653 Corrugated and solid fiber boxes

D-U-N-S 24-125-4783   (BR)
LABATT BREWING COMPANY LIMITED
BRASSERIE LABATT
2505 Rue Senkus, Lasalle, QC, H8N 2X8
(514) 595-2505
Emp Here 250
SIC 5813 Drinking places

D-U-N-S 24-959-8269   (SL)
LES ELEMENTS CHAUFFANTS TEMPORA INC
ELEMENTS CHAUFFANTS TEMPORA
2501 Av Dollard, Lasalle, QC, H8N 1S2
(514) 933-1649
Emp Here 120   *Sales* 17,291,686
SIC 3567 Industrial furnaces and ovens
Pr Claire Ebrahim

D-U-N-S 25-240-4397   (BR)
LESTER B. PEARSON SCHOOL BOARD
CHILDREN'S WORLD ACADEMY (CWA)
2241 Rue Menard, Lasalle, QC, H8N 1J4
(514) 595-2043
Emp Here 100
SIC 8211 Elementary and secondary schools

D-U-N-S 20-592-0317   (SL)
MAGASINS D'ESCOMPTE PLUS MART, LES
PEARSON, DONALD PHARMACIEN
2101 Av Dollard Unite 12, Lasalle, QC, H8N 1S2
(514) 363-4402
Emp Here 55   *Sales* 10,855,150
SIC 5912 Drug stores and proprietary stores
Pr Pr Donald H J Pearson

D-U-N-S 20-858-3971   (SL)
MANYAN INC
2611 Rue Leger, Lasalle, QC, H8N 2V9
(514) 364-2420
Emp Here 50   *Sales* 2,115,860
SIC 2393 Textile bags

D-U-N-S 20-549-5851   (BR)
METRO RICHELIEU INC
SUPER C
7401 Boul Newman, Lasalle, QC, H8N 1X3
(514) 366-9512
Emp Here 70
SIC 5411 Grocery stores

D-U-N-S 20-317-7282   (BR)
PRODUITS DE PISCINE TRENDIUM INC
(*Suby of* Compagnie de Gestion Trendium)
2673 Boul Angrignon, Lasalle, QC, H8N 3J3
(514) 363-7001
Emp Here 75
SIC 3949 Sporting and athletic goods, nec

D-U-N-S 20-013-5650   (SL)
RAPIDE SNACK INC
MAXI SNACK
7232 Rue Cordner, Lasalle, QC, H8N 2W8
(514) 364-0258
Emp Here 56   *Sales* 4,851,006
SIC 2064 Candy and other confectionery products

D-U-N-S 25-300-6274   (BR)
REDBERRY FRANCHISING CORP
BURGER KING
7077 Boul Newman, Lasalle, QC, H8N 1X1
(514) 365-5532
Emp Here 25
SIC 5812 Eating places

D-U-N-S 24-347-4256   (BR)
REVERA INC
RESIDENCE LASALLE
1070 Boul Shevchenko, Lasalle, QC, H8N 1N6
(514) 368-0000
Emp Here 25
SIC 8361 Residential care

D-U-N-S 20-124-2562   (BR)
RIOCAN REAL ESTATE INVESTMENT TRUST
CENTRE CARNAVAL
7475 Boul Newman Bureau 500, Lasalle, QC, H8N 1X3
(514) 363-4151
Emp Here 20
SIC 6531 Real estate agents and managers

D-U-N-S 20-232-4380   (HQ)
ROBCO INC
ANCHOR PACKING
7200 Rue Saint-Patrick, Lasalle, QC, H8N 2W7
(514) 367-2252
Emp Here 70   *Emp Total* 160
Sales 41,839,408
SIC 3053 Gaskets; packing and sealing devices
  Barry J. Macdonald
Pr John C. Macdonald
Sec Pierre Mercier

D-U-N-S 25-025-3838   (BR)
ROYAL BANK OF CANADA
RBC
(*Suby of* Royal Bank Of Canada)
7191 Boul Newman, Lasalle, QC, H8N 2K3
(514) 368-0996
Emp Here 23
SIC 6021 National commercial banks

D-U-N-S 20-532-5108   (BR)
SEARS CANADA INC
SEARS FURNITURE AND APPLIANCE
7101 Boul Newman, Lasalle, QC, H8N 1X1

Emp Here 30
SIC 5311 Department stores

D-U-N-S 20-705-8863   (BR)
SOCIETE DE TRANSPORT DE MONTREAL
SOCIETE DE TRANSPORT DE MONTREAL
7770 Rue Saint-Patrick, Lasalle, QC, H8N 1V1
(514) 280-6382
Emp Here 600

SIC 4111 Local and suburban transit

D-U-N-S 25-307-6590   (BR)
SOCIETE DES ALCOOLS DU QUEBEC
SOCIETE DES ALCOOLS DU QUEBEC
2500 Boul Angrignon, Lasalle, QC, H8N 0C1
(514) 364-4343
Emp Here 40
SIC 5921 Liquor stores

D-U-N-S 20-105-0023   (BR)
STAPLES CANADA INC
STAPLES THE BUSINESS DEPOT
(*Suby of* Staples, Inc.)
7097 Boul Newman, Lasalle, QC, H8N 1X1
(514) 364-3872
Emp Here 60
SIC 5943 Stationery stores

D-U-N-S 24-319-8389   (HQ)
SUPREMEX INC
(*Suby of* Supremex Inc)
7213 Rue Cordner, Lasalle, QC, H8N 2J7
(514) 595-0555
Emp Here 150   *Emp Total* 500
Sales 118,765,059
SIC 2677 Envelopes
Pr Emerson Stewart
  Bertrand Jolicoeur
VP VP Benoit Crowe
Dir Mathieu Gauvin
  Georges Kobrynsky
  Dany Paradis
Dir Robert B. Johnston
Dir Warren J. White

D-U-N-S 20-514-9250   (HQ)
TRANSPORTS FUEL INC, LES
(*Suby of* Administration Robert Piccioni Inc)
2480 Rue Senkus, Lasalle, QC, H8N 2X9
(514) 948-2225
Emp Here 44   *Emp Total* 50
Sales 12,330,358
SIC 4731 Freight transportation arrangement
  Robert Piccioni

D-U-N-S 20-793-4543   (BR)
UAP INC
CMAX LASALLE
(*Suby of* Genuine Parts Company)
7214 Boul Newman, Lasalle, QC, H8N 1X2
(514) 365-2651
Emp Here 21
SIC 7532 Top and body repair and paint shops

D-U-N-S 25-232-1468   (BR)
VILLE DE MONTREAL ARRONDISSEMENT LASALLE
OCTOGONE BIBLIOTHEQUE MUNICIPALE DE LASALLE
1080 Av Dollard, Lasalle, QC, H8N 2T9
(514) 367-6384
Emp Here 40
SIC 8231 Libraries

D-U-N-S 25-297-6311   (BR)
WAL-MART CANADA CORP
WALMART SUPERCENTRE
6797 Boul Newman, Lasalle, QC, H8N 3E4
(514) 368-2248
Emp Here 250
SIC 5311 Department stores

D-U-N-S 24-329-0652   (BR)
WEIR CANADA, INC
8600 Rue Saint-Patrick, Lasalle, QC, H8N 1V1
(514) 366-5900
Emp Here 70
SIC 7699 Repair services, nec

D-U-N-S 25-906-0606   (BR)
WESTCLIFF MANAGEMENT LTD
CARREFOUR ANGRIGNON
7077 Boul Newman, Lasalle, QC, H8N 1X1
(514) 363-9413
Emp Here 55
SIC 6512 Nonresidential building operators

D-U-N-S 25-294-0879   (BR)
WINNERS MERCHANTS INTERNATIONAL L.P.
WINNERS
(*Suby of* The TJX Companies Inc)
2101 Av Dollard, Lasalle, QC, H8N 1S2
(514) 595-5545
Emp Here 30
SIC 5651 Family clothing stores

Lasalle, QC H8P

D-U-N-S 20-573-7708   (BR)
BANQUE LAURENTIENNE DU CANADA
8262 Boul Champlain, Lasalle, QC, H8P 1B5
(514) 367-1411
Emp Here 20
SIC 6021 National commercial banks

D-U-N-S 24-368-8210   (BR)
CAISSE DESJARDINS DE LASALLE
CENTRE DE SERVICES CHAMPLAIN
8180 Boul Champlain, Lasalle, QC, H8P 1B4
(514) 366-6231
Emp Here 20
SIC 6062 State credit unions

D-U-N-S 24-355-0279   (BR)
CENTRE DE SANTE ET DE SERVICES SOCIAUX DE DORVAL-LACHINE-LASALLE
CENTRE HOSPITALIER DE LACHINE DU CUSM
650 16e Av, Lasalle, QC, H8P 2S3
(514) 637-2351
Emp Here 685
SIC 8062 General medical and surgical hospitals

D-U-N-S 25-305-1528   (BR)
CINEPLEX ODEON CORPORATION
CINEMA CINEPLEX PLACE LA SALLE
7816 Boul Champlain Bureau 62, Lasalle, QC, H8P 1B3

Emp Here 30
SIC 7832 Motion picture theaters, except drive-in

D-U-N-S 25-240-4355   (BR)
COMMISSION SCOLAIRE MARGUERITE-BOURGEOYS
ECOLE SAINTE-GENEVIEVE
7520 Rue Edouard, Lasalle, QC, H8P 1S2
(514) 595-2055
Emp Here 30
SIC 8211 Elementary and secondary schools

D-U-N-S 25-240-4157   (BR)
COMMISSION SCOLAIRE MARGUERITE-BOURGEOYS
CENTRE D'EDUCATION DES ADULTES DE LASALLE
8825 Rue Centrale, Lasalle, QC, H8P 1P3
(514) 595-2047
Emp Here 40
SIC 8322 Individual and family services

D-U-N-S 25-240-4231   (BR)
COMMISSION SCOLAIRE MARGUERITE-BOURGEOYS
ECOLE NOTRE DAME DES RAPIDES
8585 Rue George, Lasalle, QC, H8P 1G5
(514) 595-2052
Emp Here 140
SIC 8211 Elementary and secondary schools

D-U-N-S 25-233-6649   (BR)
COMMISSION SCOLAIRE MARGUERITE-BOURGEOYS
ECOLE DES RAPIDES DE LACHINE
695 35e Av, Lasalle, QC, H8P 2Y9
(514) 366-0028
Emp Here 40
SIC 8211 Elementary and secondary schools

D-U-N-S 25-233-0212   (BR)
COMMISSION SCOLAIRE MARGUERITE-BOURGEOYS
ECOLE DU GRAND HERON
7676 Rue Centrale, Lasalle, QC, H8P 1L5
(514) 365-9337
Emp Here 30
SIC 8211 Elementary and secondary schools

D-U-N-S 25-871-3213   (BR)
ENTREPRISES MICHEL MARCHAND INC, LES
MCDONALD'S
8100 Boul Champlain, Lasalle, QC, H8P 1B3
(514) 364-4313
Emp Here 50
SIC 5812 Eating places

D-U-N-S 24-049-1360   (BR)
GESTION IMMOBILIERE LUC MAURICE INC
LES CAVALIER DE LA SALLE
(*Suby of* Gestion Immobiliere Luc Maurice Inc)
800 Rue Gagne, Lasalle, QC, H8P 3W3
(514) 364-0004
Emp Here 29
SIC 8361 Residential care

D-U-N-S 25-240-4116   (BR)
LESTER B. PEARSON SCHOOL BOARD
ECOLE ALLION SCHOOL
140 9e Av, Lasalle, QC, H8P 2N9
(514) 595-2040
Emp Here 25
SIC 8211 Elementary and secondary schools

D-U-N-S 20-712-3642   (BR)
LESTER B. PEARSON SCHOOL BOARD
LASALLE COMMUNITY COMPREHENSIVE HIGH SCHOOLS
140 9e Av, Lasalle, QC, H8P 2N9
(514) 595-2050
Emp Here 50
SIC 8211 Elementary and secondary schools

D-U-N-S 20-712-3659   (BR)
LESTER B. PEARSON SCHOOL BOARD
FORMATION PROFESSIONNELLE
8310 Rue George, Lasalle, QC, H8P 1E5
(514) 363-6213
Emp Here 150
SIC 8211 Elementary and secondary schools

D-U-N-S 24-354-1146   (SL)
RESIDENCE FLORALIES LASALLE INC
8200 Rue George, Lasalle, QC, H8P 3T6
(514) 363-8200
Emp Here 50   *Sales* 5,889,600
SIC 6513 Apartment building operators
Pr Manuel Folla
  Luc Bourdeau

D-U-N-S 20-852-8237   (BR)
SOBEYS QUEBEC INC
IGA
8130 Boul Champlain, Lasalle, QC, H8P 1B4
(514) 364-4777
Emp Here 100
SIC 5411 Grocery stores

Lasalle, QC H8R

D-U-N-S 20-126-7072   (SL)
3510000 CANADA INC
NATIONAL GRAPHICS
9216 Rue Boivin, Lasalle, QC, H8R 2E7
(514) 367-1025
Emp Here 50   *Sales* 3,648,035
SIC 7336 Commercial art and graphic design

D-U-N-S 20-254-9291   (SL)
4489161 CANADA INC
PAVILLONS LASALLE, LES
400 Rue Louis-Fortier Bureau 100a, Lasalle,

QC, H8R 0A8
(514) 370-8000
Emp Here 100   *Sales* 3,648,035
SIC 8361 Residential care

D-U-N-S 24-713-3093   (SL)
9270-5425 QUEBEC INC
ELECTRICITE KINGSTON
9100 Rue Elmslie Bureau 200, Lasalle, QC, H8R 1V6
(514) 365-1642
Emp Here 50   *Sales* 4,377,642
SIC 1731 Electrical work

D-U-N-S 24-652-6859   (HQ)
AB MAURI (CANADA) LIMITEE
LEVURE FLEISCHMANN, DIV OF
31 Rue Airlie, Lasalle, QC, H8R 1Z8
(514) 366-1053
Emp Here 115   *Emp Total* 8,000
Sales 14,592,140
SIC 2099 Food preparations, nec
Pr Mark A. Prendergast
Sec Carmen Sciackitano
Sec Kathy Hayek
Dir Daniel Kucera
Dir Frederic Elias

D-U-N-S 20-573-7732   (BR)
BANQUE LAURENTIENNE DU CANADA
8787 Boul Newman, Lasalle, QC, H8R 1Y9
(514) 363-0113
Emp Here 20
SIC 6021 National commercial banks

D-U-N-S 20-527-6681   (BR)
CANADA POST CORPORATION
SOCIETE CANADIENNE DES POSTES
9566 Rue Jean-Milot, Lasalle, QC, H8R 1X7

Emp Here 55
SIC 4311 U.s. postal service

D-U-N-S 20-297-4924   (HQ)
CIE MATERIAUX DE CONSTRUCTION BP CANADA, LA
(*Suby of* 3077578 Nova Scotia Corp)
9510 Rue Saint-Patrick, Lasalle, QC, H8R 1R9
(514) 364-0161
Emp Here 300   *Emp Total* 3,000
Sales 144,462,186
SIC 2493 Reconstituted wood products
Pr Yves Gosselin
Sec Mark F. Whitley
Treas Allain Marcouiller
Dir Keith W. Colburn

D-U-N-S 24-943-6668   (BR)
CIE MATERIAUX DE CONSTRUCTION BP CANADA, LA
(*Suby of* 3077578 Nova Scotia Corp)
9500 Rue Saint-Patrick, Lasalle, QC, H8R 1R8
(514) 364-0161
Emp Here 280
SIC 2429 Special product sawmills, nec

D-U-N-S 25-240-4272   (BR)
COMMISSION SCOLAIRE MARGUERITE-BOURGEOYS
ECOLE SECONDAIRE CAVELIER DE LASALLE
9199 Rue Centrale, Lasalle, QC, H8R 2J9
(514) 595-2044
Emp Here 50
SIC 8211 Elementary and secondary schools

D-U-N-S 25-240-4314   (BR)
COMMISSION SCOLAIRE MARGUERITE-BOURGEOYS
ECOLE SAINTE CATHERINE LABOURE
441 Rue Trudeau, Lasalle, QC, H8R 3C3
(514) 595-2054
Emp Here 40
SIC 8211 Elementary and secondary schools

D-U-N-S 25-240-4033   (BR)
COMMISSION SCOLAIRE MARGUERITE-BOURGEOYS

ECOLE PIERRE REMY
360 80e Av, Lasalle, QC, H8R 2T3
(514) 595-2067
Emp Here 50
SIC 8211 Elementary and secondary schools

D-U-N-S 24-636-9289   (BR)
COMMISSION SCOLAIRE MARGUERITE-BOURGEOYS
EDIFICE CLEMENT
9569 Rue Jean-Milot, Lasalle, QC, H8R 1X8
(514) 595-2041
Emp Here 34
SIC 8211 Elementary and secondary schools

D-U-N-S 20-712-4152   (BR)
COMMISSION SCOLAIRE MARGUERITE-BOURGEOYS
CENTRE DE FORMATION POUR ADULTES CEA CLEMENT
9569 Rue Jean-Milot, Lasalle, QC, H8R 1X8
(514) 595-2041
Emp Here 50
SIC 8211 Elementary and secondary schools

D-U-N-S 25-240-4199   (BR)
COMMISSION SCOLAIRE MARGUERITE-BOURGEOYS
ECOLE HENRI-FOREST
100 Av Du Tresor-Cache, Lasalle, QC, H8R 3K3
(514) 595-2046
Emp Here 30
SIC 8211 Elementary and secondary schools

D-U-N-S 20-229-6117   (HQ)
COMPAGNIE D'APPAREILS ELECTRIQUES PEERLESS LTEE
(*Suby* of 102835 Canada Inc)
9145 Rue Boivin, Lasalle, QC, H8R 2E5
(514) 595-1671
Emp Here 110   *Emp Total* 110
Sales 15,592,518
SIC 1731 Electrical work
Dir Rosa Samuels
Pr Pr Barry Fagen
  Francine Samuels

D-U-N-S 24-865-7629   (SL)
CORPORATION TRIBOSPEC, LA
(*Suby* of 9188-0187 Quebec Inc)
220 Av Lafleur, Lasalle, QC, H8R 4C9
(514) 595-7579
Emp Here 50   *Sales* 8,138,880
SIC 6712 Bank holding companies
Pr Pr Guiliano Cininni

D-U-N-S 25-939-3841   (SL)
CORPORATION L'ESPOIR DU DEFICIENT
ESPOIR DU DEFICIENT, L
55 Av Dupras Bureau 511, Lasalle, QC, H8R 4A8
(514) 367-3757
Emp Here 22   *Sales* 6,674,880
SIC 8322 Individual and family services
Brnch Mgr Huguette Giroux

D-U-N-S 20-632-1812   (BR)
GCP CANADA INC
GRACE CANADA, INC
(*Suby* of W. R. Grace & Co.)
255 Av Lafleur, Lasalle, QC, H8R 3H4
(514) 366-3362
Emp Here 100
SIC 2819 Industrial inorganic chemicals, nec

D-U-N-S 20-298-2773   (SL)
GDI SERVICES TECHNIQUES S.E.C.
695 90e Av, Lasalle, QC, H8R 3A4
(514) 368-1500
Emp Here 100   *Sales* 2,918,428
SIC 7349 Building maintenance services, nec

D-U-N-S 24-083-2357   (BR)
GROUPE ROBERT INC
ROBERTS WAREHOUSING & STORAGE
1001 90e Av, Lasalle, QC, H8R 3A4

(514) 368-8772
Emp Here 30
SIC 4225 General warehousing and storage

D-U-N-S 25-672-5045   (BR)
ITW CANADA INVESTMENTS LIMITED PARTNERSHIP
DIV DE ITW CANADA; ARBORITE
(*Suby* of Illinois Tool Works Inc.)
385 Av Lafleur, Lasalle, QC, H8R 3H7
(514) 366-2710
Emp Here 200
SIC 2821 Plastics materials and resins

D-U-N-S 20-591-9400   (HQ)
KINGSTON BYERS INC
HAUTS BOISES DU CHATEAUGUAY, LES
9100 Rue Elmslie, Lasalle, QC, H8R 1V6
(514) 365-1642
Emp Here 100   *Emp Total* 250
Sales 23,562,027
SIC 1541 Industrial buildings and warehouses
  Edmund W Colton
VP Karianne Colton
Dir Giuliano Sanviti

D-U-N-S 25-004-2850   (BR)
LABATT BREWING COMPANY LIMITED
BRASSERIE LABATT
50 Av Labatt Bureau 42, Lasalle, QC, H8R 3E7
(514) 366-5050
Emp Here 1,070
SIC 2082 Malt beverages

D-U-N-S 25-298-6054   (BR)
LESTER B. PEARSON SCHOOL BOARD
ORCHARD ELEMENTARY
400 80e Av, Lasalle, QC, H8R 2T3

Emp Here 25
SIC 8211 Elementary and secondary schools

D-U-N-S 20-544-6065   (SL)
MONTCALM SERVICES TECHNIQUES INC
695 90e Av, Lasalle, QC, H8R 3A4

Emp Here 600   *Sales* 23,558,400
SIC 7349 Building maintenance services, nec
  Claude Bigras

D-U-N-S 25-997-7069   (BR)
NATIONAL DEFENCE AND THE CANADIAN ARMED FORCES
NAVAL ENGINEERING TEST ESTABLISHMENT
9401 Rue Wanklyn, Lasalle, QC, H8R 1Z2
(514) 366-4310
Emp Here 100
SIC 7389 Business services, nec

D-U-N-S 20-704-7973   (SL)
RESTAURANT D. LAFLEUR INC
RESTAURANTS LAFLEUR, LES
99 Av Lafleur, Lasalle, QC, H8R 3G8

Emp Here 339   *Sales* 14,067,200
SIC 5812 Eating places
Pr Pr Denis Vinet
VP Pierre Prud'homme
Treas Mariette Pitre

D-U-N-S 20-876-4337   (BR)
SISCA SOLUTIONS D'AFFAIRES CANADA INC
SISCA SOLUTIONS D'AFFAIRES CANADA INC
790 Rue D'Upton, Lasalle, QC, H8R 2T9
(514) 363-5511
Emp Here 30
SIC 2741 Miscellaneous publishing

D-U-N-S 24-361-3614   (SL)
TOTAL CANADA INC
TOTAL RM CANADA
220 Av Lafleur, Lasalle, QC, H8R 4C9
(514) 595-7579
Emp Here 75   *Sales* 106,012,013

SIC 2911 Petroleum refining
  Franck Bagouet
Dir Jean-Sebastien Desroches
Dir Pierre-Yves Sachet
Dir Pascal Boutier
Ch Bd Jean-Philippe Torres

D-U-N-S 20-719-3371   (BR)
TRANSCONTINENTAL PRINTING INC
TRANSCONTINENTAL ROSS-ELLIS
999 90e Av, Lasalle, QC, H8R 3A4
(514) 861-2411
Emp Here 100
SIC 2752 Commercial printing, lithographic

D-U-N-S 24-109-6031   (BR)
UNIFIRST CANADA LTD
UNIFORME PREMIER CHOIX
(*Suby* of Unifirst Corporation)
8951 Rue Salley, Lasalle, QC, H8R 2C8
(514) 365-8301
Emp Here 100
SIC 7218 Industrial launderers

D-U-N-S 24-680-4058   (BR)
WEIR CANADA, INC
MARINE ENGINEERING, DIV OF
9401 Rue Wanklyn, Lasalle, QC, H8R 1Z2
(514) 366-4310
Emp Here 100
SIC 5084 Industrial machinery and equipment

Laterriere, QC G7N
Chicoutimi County

D-U-N-S 25-232-2326   (BR)
COMMISSION SCOLAIRE DES RIVES-DU-SAGUENAY
ECOLE NOTRE DAME
(*Suby* of Commission Scolaire des Rives-du-Saguenay)
860 Rue Gauthier, Laterriere, QC, G7N 1G8

Emp Here 25
SIC 8211 Elementary and secondary schools

D-U-N-S 24-841-8535   (SL)
SCP 89 INC
PEDNO
3641 Rue Des Forges, Laterriere, QC, G7N 1N4
(418) 678-1506
Emp Here 75   *Sales* 17,079,840
SIC 3496 Miscellaneous fabricated wire products
Pr Pr Maurice Dupere
VP VP Denis Simard

D-U-N-S 20-356-7144   (SL)
TRANSPORT ST-MICHEL INC
TRANSPORT JULES SAVARD
4710 Boul Talbot, Laterriere, QC, G7N 1V2
(418) 548-7187
Emp Here 50   *Sales* 3,939,878
SIC 4212 Local trucking, without storage

Latulipe, QC J0Z
Temiscaninque County

D-U-N-S 25-240-1617   (BR)
COMMISSION SCOLAIRE DU LAC-TEMISCAMINGUE
ECOLE DU CARREFOUR
(*Suby* of Commission Scolaire du Lac-Temiscamingue)
5 Rue Du Carrefour N Rr 4, Latulipe, QC, J0Z 2N0
(819) 747-4521
Emp Here 20
SIC 8211 Elementary and secondary schools

Laurier-Station, QC G0S
Lotbiniere County

D-U-N-S 20-574-3672   (BR)
CAISSE DESJARDINS DU CENTRE DE LOTBINIERE
CENTRE DE SERVICES DE LAURIER STATION
377 Rue Saint-Joseph, Laurier-Station, QC, G0S 1N0
(418) 728-9222
Emp Here 20
SIC 6062 State credit unions

D-U-N-S 24-689-9934   (SL)
CETAL
179 Boul Laurier, Laurier-Station, QC, G0S 1N0
(418) 728-3119
Emp Here 62   *Sales* 8,420,350
SIC 2448 Wood pallets and skids
Mng Dir Stephane Levac
Ch Bd Rene Blais
VP VP Gino Demers

D-U-N-S 24-346-3044   (BR)
COMMISSION SCOLAIRE DES NAVIGATEURS
ECOLE DE LA SOURCE
139 Rue De La Station, Laurier-Station, QC, G0S 1N0
(418) 888-0504
Emp Here 40
SIC 8211 Elementary and secondary schools

D-U-N-S 24-205-4732   (SL)
LOCATION V.A. INC
156 Boul Laurier Rr 1, Laurier-Station, QC, G0S 1N0
(418) 728-2140
Emp Here 100   *Sales* 12,466,320
SIC 7513 Truck rental and leasing, no drivers
Pr Jean-Francois Audet

D-U-N-S 24-888-4772   (SL)
TEKNION LS INC
359 Rue Saint-Joseth, Laurier-Station, QC, G0S 1N0
(418) 830-0855
Emp Here 100   *Sales* 10,068,577
SIC 2211 Broadwoven fabric mills, cotton
Pr Jacques Alain
Dir Scott Bond
Dir David Feldberg
Dir Jeffrey Wilson

Laval, QC H7A

D-U-N-S 24-369-1958   (BR)
CAISSE POPULAIRE DESJARDINS DES MILLE-ILES
CENTRE DE SERVICE ST-NOEL CHABANEL
(*Suby* of Caisse populaire Desjardins des Mille-Iles)
600 Montee Du Moulin Bureau 6, Laval, QC, H7A 1Z6
(450) 661-7274
Emp Here 20
SIC 6062 State credit unions

D-U-N-S 24-328-6486   (BR)
PROVIGO DISTRIBUTION INC
MAXI
8475 Rue Francois-Chartrand, Laval, QC, H7A 4J3
(450) 665-7361
Emp Here 70
SIC 5411 Grocery stores

Laval, QC H7E

D-U-N-S 20-580-3617   (BR)
CANADA POST CORPORATION
850 Rue Montrose, Laval, QC, H7E 0H1
(514) 345-7503
Emp Here 20
SIC 4311 U.s. postal service

D-U-N-S 20-024-4791   (BR)
SIR WILFRID LAURIER SCHOOL BOARD
ST PAUL ANNEX SCHOOL
1305 Rue L'Assomption, Laval, QC, H7E 4C5
(450) 663-5833
Emp Here 60
SIC 8211 Elementary and secondary schools

Laval, QC H7G

D-U-N-S 20-960-3844   (SL)
CLAUDETTE CROTEAU INC
70 Boul Des Laurentides, Laval, QC, H7G 2T3
(450) 669-5415
Emp Here 60   *Sales* 5,072,500
SIC 5651 Family clothing stores
Pr Pr Emile Rene

D-U-N-S 20-007-5050   (SL)
MESURE D'URGENCE
80 Rue Saint-Hubert, Laval, QC, H7G 2X9
(450) 680-2800
Emp Here 49   *Sales* 5,110,881
SIC 1799 Special trade contractors, nec

Laval, QC H7K
Hochelaga County

D-U-N-S 20-500-5713   (SL)
BOIS PELADEAU INC
137 Boul Be lerose O, Laval, QC, H7K 3B5
(450) 667-6950
Emp Here 35   *Sales* 22,636,725
SIC 2426 Hardwood dimension and flooring mills
Pr Pr Gregory Patenaude
VP VP Christian Clavel
  Chantal Labonte
Dir Edward J. Patenaude

D-U-N-S 20-712-2578   (BR)
SIR WILFRID LAURIER SCHOOL BOARD
TERRY FOX SCHOOL
900 Av Des Lacasse, Laval, QC, H7K 3V9
(450) 680-3040
Emp Here 50
SIC 8211 Elementary and secondary schools

Laval, QC H7L
Hochelaga County

D-U-N-S 24-475-2168   (HQ)
ENTREPRISES DE REFRIGERATION L.S. INC, LES
(*Suby of* 9081-5432 Quebec Inc)
1610 Rue Guillet, Laval, QC, H7L 5B2
(450) 682-8105
Emp Here 50   *Emp Total* 100
Sales 29,059,064
SIC 1711 Plumbing, heating, air-conditioning
Pr Pr Sylvain Sergerie
  Maurice Peladeau

D-U-N-S 24-336-7997   (SL)
4131185 CANADA INC
LABORATOIRES D'ANALYSES ET DE DI-AGONOSTICS NORCIENCE
(*Suby of* Neopharm Labs Inc)
3885 Boul Industriel, Laval, QC, H7L 4S3
(450) 663-6724
Emp Here 50   *Sales* 4,417,880

SIC 8734 Testing laboratories

D-U-N-S 20-620-0763   (BR)
BENTO NOUVEAU LTD
1487 Rue Berlier, Laval, QC, H7L 3Z1

Emp Here 20
SIC 5141 Groceries, general line

D-U-N-S 25-973-8102   (BR)
COMMISSION SCOLAIRE DE LAVAL
ECOLE DEMERS
155 Rue Deslauriers, Laval, QC, H7L 2S2
(450) 662-7000
Emp Here 30
SIC 8211 Elementary and secondary schools

D-U-N-S 20-716-7383   (BR)
COMMISSION SCOLAIRE DE LAVAL
ECOLE PRIMAIRE DES CARDINAUX
6060 Rue Des Cardinaux, Laval, QC, H7L 6B7
(450) 662-7000
Emp Here 50
SIC 8211 Elementary and secondary schools

D-U-N-S 20-716-7896   (BR)
COMMISSION SCOLAIRE DE LAVAL
CENTRE   LE   TREMPLIN-ROLLAND-GRATTON
2475 Rue Honore-Mercier, Laval, QC, H7L 2S9
(450) 662-7000
Emp Here 50
SIC 8211 Elementary and secondary schools

D-U-N-S 25-359-0301   (BR)
MULTI-MARQUES INC
3443 Av Francis-Hughes Bureau 1, Laval, QC, H7L 5A6
(450) 629-9444
Emp Here 700
SIC 5149 Groceries and related products, nec

D-U-N-S 25-355-2350   (SL)
SMITHS DETECTION MONTREAL INC
SMITHS DETECTION CANADA
3225 Av Francis-Hughes Bureau 100, Laval, QC, H7L 5A5

Emp Here 25   *Sales* 32,589,120
SIC 5099 Durable goods, nec
  Shaun Doherty
Dir Karen Elizabeth Jacques

D-U-N-S 20-715-2542   (BR)
WHOLESOME HARVEST BAKING LTD.
MAISON COUSIN
4000 Boul Industriel, Laval, QC, H7L 4R9

Emp Here 65
SIC 5142 Packaged frozen goods

Laval, QC H7M

D-U-N-S 24-213-3135   (BR)
INTERNATIONAL GRAPHICS ULC
(*Suby of* Taylor Corporation)
2135a Boul Des Laurentides, Laval, QC, H7M 4M2
(450) 625-5092
Emp Here 90
SIC 2678 Stationery products

Laval, QC H7N

D-U-N-S 25-234-2761   (BR)
COMMISSION SCOLAIRE DE LAVAL
ECOLE   PRIMAIRE   MARCEL   VAILLAN-COURT
150 Av Legrand, Laval, QC, H7N 3T3
(450) 662-7000
Emp Here 60

SIC 8211 Elementary and secondary schools

D-U-N-S 20-716-7672   (BR)
COMMISSION SCOLAIRE DE LAVAL
ECOLE LEON-GUILBAULT
133 Boul Cartier O, Laval, QC, H7N 2H7
(450) 662-7000
Emp Here 50
SIC 8211 Elementary and secondary schools

D-U-N-S 20-575-2822   (BR)
ECOLE VANGUARD QUEBEC LIMITEE
ECOLE VANGUARD SECONDAIRE
83 Boul Des Prairies, Laval, QC, H7N 2T3

Emp Here 30
SIC 8211 Elementary and secondary schools

D-U-N-S 24-391-5662   (BR)
GOLF TOWN OPERATING LIMITED PART-NERSHIP
GOLF TOWN
920 Boul Le Corbusier, Laval, QC, H7N 0A8
(450) 687-0648
Emp Here 20
SIC 5941 Sporting goods and bicycle shops

Laval, QC H7P

D-U-N-S 24-683-3540   (SL)
9207-1869 QUEBEC INC
IMPORT EXPORT RV
2785 Boul Saint-Elzear O, Laval, QC, H7P 4J8

Emp Here 26   *Sales* 6,502,070
SIC 5561 Recreational vehicle dealers
Pr Pr Bernard Beauregard
Dir Noella Arsenault

D-U-N-S 20-311-2222   (BR)
CONNEX ONTARIO INC
CONNEX SOCIETE DE TELECOMMUNICA-TIONS
4616 Rue Louis-B.-Mayer, Laval, QC, H7P 6E4
(450) 680-2255
Emp Here 30
SIC 4899 Communication services, nec

Laval, QC H7R

D-U-N-S 24-815-3462   (SL)
AUTOBUS UNCLE HARRY INC
(*Suby of* Autobus Gerald Seguin Inc, Les)
4010 Boul Dagenais O, Laval, QC, H7R 1L2
(450) 625-0506
Emp Here 70   *Sales* 2,338,878
SIC 4151 School buses

D-U-N-S 24-368-8061   (BR)
CAISSE DESJARDINS DE L'OUEST DE LAVAL
CENTRE DE SERVICES SAINT-LEOPOLD
4791 Boul Dagenais O, Laval, QC, H7R 1L7
(450) 962-1800
Emp Here 20
SIC 6062 State credit unions

Laval, QC H7S

D-U-N-S 24-051-8105   (BR)
144503 CANADA INC
CENTRE D'ANIMAUX NATURE
(*Suby of* Investissements Hohag Inc)
1600 Boul Le Corbusier Bureau 502, Laval, QC, H7S 1Y9
(450) 687-5710
Emp Here 26
SIC 5999 Miscellaneous retail stores, nec

D-U-N-S 24-362-9644   (BR)
BEST BUY CANADA LTD
GEEK SQUAD
(*Suby of* Best Buy Co., Inc.)
1560 Boul Le Corbusier, Laval, QC, H7S 1Y8
(450) 781-2030
Emp Here 50
SIC 5999 Miscellaneous retail stores, nec

D-U-N-S 20-716-7540   (BR)
COMMISSION SCOLAIRE DE LAVAL
955 Boul Saint-Martin O Bureau 144, Laval, QC, H7S 1M5
(450) 662-7000
Emp Here 50
SIC 8211 Elementary and secondary schools

D-U-N-S 24-092-8031   (BR)
ELECTRO SAGUENAY LTEE
1555 Boul De L'Avenir Bureau 306, Laval, QC, H7S 2N5

Emp Here 75
SIC 4899 Communication services, nec

D-U-N-S 25-300-4790   (BR)
REDBERRY FRANCHISING CORP
RESTAURANT BURGER KING
1505 Boul Saint-Martin O, Laval, QC, H7S 1N1
(450) 669-1736
Emp Here 30
SIC 5812 Eating places

D-U-N-S 24-115-1815   (BR)
SOROC TECHNOLOGY INC
1800 Boul Le Corbusier Bureau 132, Laval, QC, H7S 2K1
(450) 682-5029
Emp Here 200
SIC 7378 Computer maintenance and repair

Laval, QC H7T

D-U-N-S 20-913-9620   (BR)
AGENCE DE VOYAGES D'AUTOMOBILE ET TOURING CLUB DU QUEBEC INC
AGENCE DE VOYAGES D'AUTOMOBILE ET TOURING CLUB DU
3131 Boul Saint-Martin O Bureau 100, Laval, QC, H7T 2Z5
(450) 682-8100
Emp Here 20
SIC 4724 Travel agencies

D-U-N-S 25-780-4633   (BR)
BANQUE NATIONALE DU CANADA
2500 Boul Daniel-Johnson Bureau 100, Laval, QC, H7T 2P6
(450) 686-7030
Emp Here 25
SIC 6021 National commercial banks

D-U-N-S 20-715-0900   (BR)
CAPITALE GESTION FINANCIERE INC, LA
3080 Boul Le Carrefour Bureau 520, Laval, QC, H7T 2R5
(514) 873-9364
Emp Here 55
SIC 8742 Management consulting services

D-U-N-S 24-814-5146   (BR)
FINANCIERE BANQUE NATIONALE INC
FINANCIERE BANQUE NATIONALE
2500 Boul Daniel-Johnson Bureau 610, Laval, QC, H7T 2P6
(450) 686-5700
Emp Here 50
SIC 6211 Security brokers and dealers

D-U-N-S 24-126-2885   (BR)
GREAT-WEST LIFE ASSURANCE COM-PANY, THE
2500 Boul Daniel-Johnson Bureau 1004, Laval, QC, H7T 2P6

---

(450) 978-6134
Emp Here 20
SIC 6311 Life insurance

D-U-N-S 20-332-4785   (SL)
MADESSA PROFESSIONNEL INC
3055 Boul Saint-Martin O 5e Etage, Laval,
QC, H7T 0J3
(450) 902-2669
Emp Here 160   *Sales* 560,538
SIC 7361 Employment agencies

D-U-N-S 20-989-9520   (BR)
PACKALL PACKAGING INC
3470 Boul De Chenonceau, Laval, QC, H7T
3B6

Emp Here 150
SIC 3089 Plastics products, nec

D-U-N-S 20-562-7115   (BR)
RBC LIFE INSURANCE COMPANY
ASSURANCES RBC
(*Suby of* Royal Bank Of Canada)
3100 Boul Le Carrefour Bureau 115, Laval,
QC, H7T 2K7

Emp Here 30
SIC 6311 Life insurance

D-U-N-S 20-580-6198   (BR)
SUN LIFE ASSURANCE COMPANY OF CANADA
FINANCIERE SUNLIFE, LA
3100 Boul Le Carrefour Bureau 770, Laval,
QC, H7T 2K7
(450) 682-6550
Emp Here 50
SIC 6311 Life insurance

Laval, QC H7V

D-U-N-S 20-716-7854   (BR)
COMMISSION SCOLAIRE DE LAVAL
ECOLE PRIMAIRE MONSEIGNEUR-LAVAL
3690 Ch Du Souvenir, Laval, QC, H7V 1X8
(450) 662-7000
Emp Here 50
SIC 8211 Elementary and secondary schools

D-U-N-S 25-308-0832   (BR)
VILLE DE LAVAL
SERVICE DE LA VIE COMMUNAUTAIRE DE LA CULTURE ET DES COMMUNICATIONS
1333 Boul De Chomedy Bureau 302, Laval,
QC, H7V 3Z4
(450) 662-4343
Emp Here 30
SIC 1731 Electrical work

Laval, QC H7W

D-U-N-S 25-618-7951   (BR)
2757-5158 QUEBEC INC
ARMOIRES CUISINES ACTION
4589 Aut 440 O Bureau 103, Laval, QC, H7W
0J7
(450) 688-9050
Emp Here 300
SIC 5211 Lumber and other building materials

D-U-N-S 25-234-2753   (BR)
SIR WILFRID LAURIER SCHOOL BOARD
ECOLE PRIMAIRE CRESTVIEW
(*Suby of* Sir Wilfrid Laurier School Board)
750 Av Du Devonshire, Laval, QC, H7W 4C7
(450) 681-6703
Emp Here 40
SIC 8211 Elementary and secondary schools

Laval, QC H7X

D-U-N-S 24-353-2694   (SL)
JOSE & GEORGES INC
654 Ch Du Bord-De-L'Eau, Laval, QC, H7X
1V3
(450) 689-6007
Emp Here 80   *Sales* 3,315,840
SIC 5812 Eating places

Laval, QC H7Y

D-U-N-S 20-716-7649   (BR)
COMMISSION SCOLAIRE DE LAVAL
ECOLE PRIMAIRE LES TROIS-SOLEILS
1295 Ch Du Bord-De-L'Eau, Laval, QC, H7Y
1B9
(450) 662-7000
Emp Here 50
SIC 8211 Elementary and secondary schools

Laval-Ouest, QC H7E
Ile-Jesus County

D-U-N-S 20-716-7474   (BR)
COMMISSION SCOLAIRE DE LAVAL
CENTRE L'IMPULTION
3995 Boul Levesque E Bureau 1, Laval-Ouest,
QC, H7E 2R3
(450) 662-7000
Emp Here 31
SIC 8211 Elementary and secondary schools

D-U-N-S 20-032-7323   (BR)
COMMISSION SCOLAIRE DE LAVAL
ECOLE POLYMECANIQUE DE LAVAL
4095 Boul Levesque E Bureau 57, Laval-Ouest, QC, H7E 2R3
(450) 662-7000
Emp Here 40
SIC 8211 Elementary and secondary schools

Laval-Ouest, QC H7L
Ile-Jesus County

D-U-N-S 20-708-6380   (SL)
ARTHUR ROGER & ASSOCIES INC
2010 Boul Dagenais O, Laval-Ouest, QC, H7L
5W2
(450) 963-5080
Emp Here 20   *Sales* 5,253,170
SIC 5141 Groceries, general line
Pr Benoit Guglia
Treas Daniel Parent
Dir Roger Guglia

D-U-N-S 20-224-7284   (HQ)
BOUTIQUE LINEN CHEST (PHASE II) INC
BOUTIQUE ET MAGASIN A RAYONS LINEN CHEST
(*Suby of* Boutique Linen Chest (Phase II) Inc)
4455 Des Laurentides (A-15) E, Laval-Ouest,
QC, H7L 5X8
(514) 331-5260
Emp Here 100   *Emp Total* 700
Sales 53,990,918
SIC 5719 Miscellaneous homefurnishings
 Sheldon Leibner
Pr Pr Stanley Leibner

D-U-N-S 20-719-1219   (BR)
FOURNITURES DE BUREAU DENIS INC
DENIS OFFICE SUPPLIES
(*Suby of* Placements Denis Latulippe Inc, Les)
2725 Rue Michelin, Laval-Ouest, QC, H7L
5X6
(450) 681-5300
Emp Here 80

SIC 5712 Furniture stores

D-U-N-S 24-980-8481   (SL)
LOUISBOURG SBC, SOCIETE EN COMMANDITE
4125 Des Laurentides (A-15) E, Laval-Ouest,
QC, H7L 5W5

Emp Here 250   *Sales* 51,975,060
SIC 1623 Water, sewer, and utility lines
Pr Frank Minicucci

D-U-N-S 24-864-5855   (BR)
NWD SYSTEMS (MONTREAL) INC
MICROAGE
4209 Des Laurentides (A-15) E, Laval-Ouest,
QC, H7L 5W5
(514) 483-6040
Emp Here 45
SIC 5045 Computers, peripherals, and software

D-U-N-S 24-426-6776   (HQ)
NUERA ENTREPRISES CANADA INC
BANDES M.W.E.
(*Suby of* Nuera Inc)
1980 Boul Dagenais O, Laval-Ouest, QC, H7L
5W2
(450) 625-0219
Emp Here 40   *Emp Total* 32
Sales 8,056,134
SIC 3496 Miscellaneous fabricated wire products
Pr Pr Frederic Paquette
Sec Susan Lecouffe
Dir Peter W Webster
Dir Thomas Gillespie
Dir Walter Markham

D-U-N-S 20-954-5990   (HQ)
NUERA INC
(*Suby of* Nuera Inc)
1980 Boul Dagenais O, Laval-Ouest, QC, H7L
5W2
(514) 955-1024
Emp Here 27   *Emp Total* 32
Sales 8,009,797
SIC 5085 Industrial supplies
Pr Tom Gillespie
VP Howard Davidson
Sec Susan Lecouffe
Dir Jellinek Gabor
Dir Peter Webster
Dir M.Walter Markham

Laval-Ouest, QC H7R
Ile-Jesus County

D-U-N-S 25-823-0655   (SL)
VINCAR LTEE
PJC CLINIQUE
3366 Boul Sainte-Rose, Laval-Ouest, QC,
H7R 1T8
(450) 627-7777
Emp Here 48   *Sales* 9,434,850
SIC 5912 Drug stores and proprietary stores
Pr Pr Pierre Carbonneau

Lavaltrie, QC J5T
Berthier County

D-U-N-S 20-286-4497   (BR)
COMMISSION SCOLAIRE DE LA POINTE-DE-L'ILE
CENTRE DANIEL JOHNSON
1100 Rue Du Tricentenaire, Lavaltrie, QC, J5T
2S5
(514) 642-0245
Emp Here 60
SIC 8211 Elementary and secondary schools

D-U-N-S 25-233-6961   (BR)

COMMISSION SCOLAIRE DES SAMARES
ECOLES PRIMAIRES DE LA SOURCE
1020 Rue Du Tricentenaire, Lavaltrie, QC, J5T
2S4
(450) 758-3592
Emp Here 42
SIC 8211 Elementary and secondary schools

D-U-N-S 24-684-5973   (BR)
FCM RECYCLING INC
91 Ch Boisjoly, Lavaltrie, QC, J5T 3L7
(450) 586-5185
Emp Here 35
SIC 4953 Refuse systems

Lawrenceville, QC J0E
Shefford County

D-U-N-S 20-205-3559   (SL)
MILLETTE & FILS LTEE
2105 Rue De L'Eglise, Lawrenceville, QC, J0E
1W0
(450) 535-6305
Emp Here 100   *Sales* 8,974,166
SIC 2441 Nailed wood boxes and shook
Pr Stephane Millette
VP Pierre J. Tessier
Sec Dominique Millette
Treas Joanne Morissette
Dir Marcelle Lemay-Millette
Dir Robert Carignan

Lebel-Sur-Quevillon, QC J0Y
Abitibi County

D-U-N-S 25-847-2372   (BR)
BLAIS & LANGLOIS INC
1137 Boul Industriel Gd, Lebel-Sur-Quevillon,
QC, J0Y 1X0
(819) 755-3220
Emp Here 20
SIC 1531 Operative builders

D-U-N-S 25-093-3665   (BR)
CENTRE REGIONAL DE SANTE ET DE SERVICE SOCIAUX DE LA BAIE-JAMES
CENTRE REGIONALE DE SANTE & DE SERVICE SOCIAUX DE LA BAIE-JAMES
950 Boul Quevillon, Lebel-Sur-Quevillon, QC,
J0Y 1X0
(819) 755-4881
Emp Here 60
SIC 8093 Specialty outpatient clinics, nec

D-U-N-S 25-240-1013   (BR)
COMMISSION SCOLAIRE DE LA BAIE JAMES
ECOLE BOREALE
(*Suby of* Commission Scolaire de la Baie James)
221 Place Quevillon, Lebel-Sur-Quevillon,
QC, J0Y 1X0
(819) 755-4833
Emp Here 30
SIC 8211 Elementary and secondary schools

D-U-N-S 25-240-1815   (BR)
COMMISSION SCOLAIRE DE LA BAIE JAMES
ECOLE SECONDAIRE LA TAIGA
(*Suby of* Commission Scolaire de la Baie James)
140 Rue Principale N, Lebel-Sur-Quevillon,
QC, J0Y 1X0
(819) 755-4136
Emp Here 36
SIC 8211 Elementary and secondary schools

D-U-N-S 25-370-5438   (BR)
PF RESOLU CANADA INC
RESOLUTE FOREST PRODUCTS
2050 Rte 805 N, Lebel-Sur-Quevillon, QC,

J0Y 1X0
(819) 755-2500
Emp Here 83
SIC 2439 Structural wood members, nec

D-U-N-S 24-845-6068   (BR)
REVOLUTION ENVIRONMENTAL SOLUTIONS LP
TERRAPURE ENVIRONMENTAL
(*Suby of* Revolution Environmental Solutions LP)
1114 Boul Industriel, Lebel-Sur-Quevillon, QC, J0Y 1X0
(450) 633-4400
Emp Here 23
SIC 1731 Electrical work

Lemoyne, QC J4R
Chambly County

D-U-N-S 25-233-4388   (BR)
COMMISSION SCOLAIRE MARIE-VICTORIN
ECOLE LAJEUNESSE
160 Rue Rene-Philippe, Lemoyne, QC, J4R 2K1
(450) 671-7293
Emp Here 30
SIC 8211 Elementary and secondary schools

Lery, QC J6N
Beauharnois County

D-U-N-S 20-790-3980   (SL)
CLUB DE GOLF DE BELLE VUE (1984) INC
CLUB DE GOLF CHATEAUGUAY
880 Boul De Lery, Lery, QC, J6N 1B7
(450) 692-6793
Emp Here 100   *Sales* 4,012,839
SIC 7997 Membership sports and recreation clubs

Les Cedres, QC J7T

D-U-N-S 24-351-5640   (SL)
PLASTICON CANADA INC
A.C. PLASTICS CANADA
1395 Montee Chenier, Les Cedres, QC, J7T 1L9
(450) 452-1104
Emp Here 50   *Sales* 4,331,255
SIC 3299 NonMetallic mineral products,

D-U-N-S 25-834-4993   (BR)
ROCH GAUTHIER ET FILS INC
1655 Boul De La Cite-Des-Jeunes, Les Cedres, QC, J7T 1K9
(450) 452-4764
Emp Here 25
SIC 5251 Hardware stores

Les Coteaux, QC J7X
Soulanges County

D-U-N-S 20-582-6436   (BR)
COMPAGNIE DES CHEMINS DE FER NATIONAUX DU CANADA
53 Rue Daoust, Les Coteaux, QC, J7X 1J7
(450) 267-2459
Emp Here 53
SIC 4011 Railroads, line-haul operating

Les Escoumins, QC G0T
Saguenay County

D-U-N-S 20-213-1509   (BR)
COMMISSION SCOLAIRE DE L'ESTUAIRE
ECOLE MARIE IMACULE
297 138 Rte, Les Escoumins, QC, G0T 1K0
(418) 233-2815
Emp Here 21
SIC 8211 Elementary and secondary schools

D-U-N-S 24-804-7933   (BR)
GROUPE NAMESH, S.E.C.
PECHERIE MANICOUAGAN
(*Suby of* Groupe Namesh, S.E.C.)
152 Rue Saint-Marcellin O, Les Escoumins, QC, G0T 1K0
(418) 233-3122
Emp Here 40
SIC 5812 Eating places

Les Mechins, QC G0J
Matane County

D-U-N-S 20-719-1011   (BR)
BOIS BSL INC
BOIS BSL GASPESIE
239 Rte Bellevue O, Les Mechins, QC, G0J 1T0
(418) 729-3728
Emp Here 30
SIC 2426 Hardwood dimension and flooring mills

Levis, QC G6C
Levis County

D-U-N-S 20-712-0317   (BR)
COMMISSION SCOLAIRE DES NAVIGATEURS
ECOLE DES MOUSSAILLONS
807 Ch Pintendre, Levis, QC, G6C 1C6
(418) 838-8557
Emp Here 50
SIC 8211 Elementary and secondary schools

D-U-N-S 24-864-5053   (SL)
DISTRIBUTION MADICO INC
707 Rte Du President-Kennedy, Levis, QC, G6C 1E1
(418) 835-0825
Emp Here 50   *Sales* 4,304,681
SIC 3429 Hardware, nec

Levis, QC G6K
Levis County

D-U-N-S 25-231-9801   (BR)
COMMISSION SCOLAIRE DES NAVIGATEURS
ECOLE DU TOURNESOL
2435 Rte Des Rivieres, Levis, QC, G6K 1E9
(418) 834-2481
Emp Here 30
SIC 8211 Elementary and secondary schools

D-U-N-S 25-240-5782   (BR)
COMMISSION SCOLAIRE DES NAVIGATEURS
ECOLE ET FORMATION ECOLE DE LA RUCHIE
1000 Rue Du Bourgeois, Levis, QC, G6K 1P1
(418) 831-0086
Emp Here 30
SIC 8211 Elementary and secondary schools

Levis, QC G6V
Levis County

D-U-N-S 24-049-0230   (BR)
9074-1190 QUEBEC INC
SEIGNEURIE DE LEVY
(*Suby of* 9074-1190 Quebec Inc)
790 Boul Alphonse-Desjardins Bureau 27, Levis, QC, G6V 7J5
(418) 833-3407
Emp Here 35
SIC 8361 Residential care

D-U-N-S 24-682-7971   (SL)
9192-2732 QUEBEC INC
TIM HORTON
5865 Rue Des Arpents, Levis, QC, G6V 6Y1
(418) 837-4774
Emp Here 43   *Sales* 1,313,293
SIC 5812 Eating places

D-U-N-S 24-746-4910   (BR)
AMEUBLEMENTS TANGUAY INC
1600 Boul Alphonse-Desjardins, Levis, QC, G6V 0G9
(418) 833-4511
Emp Here 55
SIC 5712 Furniture stores

D-U-N-S 24-637-6875   (BR)
BANQUE NATIONALE DU CANADA
NBC
49b Rte Du President-Kennedy Bureau 200, Levis, QC, G6V 6C3
(418) 833-8020
Emp Here 30
SIC 6021 National commercial banks

D-U-N-S 25-023-9233   (SL)
C.L.S.C. C.H. S. L. D MAC DE DESJARDINS
15 Rue De L'Arsenal, Levis, QC, G6V 4P6
(418) 835-3400
Emp Here 300   *Sales* 19,828,320
SIC 8399 Social services, nec
Mng Dir Renee Lachance-Auger

D-U-N-S 25-117-7650   (BR)
CAISSE DESJARDINS DE LEVIS
LES GALERIES CHAGNON SERVICE CENTRE
(*Suby of* Caisse Desjardins de Levis)
1200 Boul Alphonse-Desjardins, Levis, QC, G6V 6Y8
(418) 833-5515
Emp Here 30
SIC 6062 State credit unions

D-U-N-S 25-761-5369   (BR)
CANAC-MARQUIS GRENIER LTEE
(*Suby of* Gestion Laberge Inc)
1805 Boul Alphonse-Desjardins, Levis, QC, G6V 9K5
(418) 833-6667
Emp Here 50
SIC 5211 Lumber and other building materials

D-U-N-S 25-488-8886   (HQ)
CENTRE DE READAPTATION EN DEFICIENCE INTELLECTUELLE ET TED
CRDITED DE CHAUDIERE-APPALACHES
(*Suby of* Centre de Readaptation en Deficience Intellectuelle et TED)
55 Rue Du Mont-Marie, Levis, QC, G6V 0B8
(418) 833-3218
Emp Here 60   *Emp Total* 800
Sales 40,580,000
SIC 8361 Residential care
Pr Corriveau Roger
VP Julien Andre
Genl Mgr Dominique Paquette

D-U-N-S 25-776-3995   (HQ)
CENTRES JEUNESSE CHAUDIERE-APPALACHES, LES
(*Suby of* Centres Jeunesse Chaudiere-Appalaches, Les)
100 Rte Monseigneur-Bourget Bureau 300, Levis, QC, G6V 2Y9

(418) 837-9331
Emp Here 80   *Emp Total* 550
Sales 27,892,938
SIC 8322 Individual and family services
Mng Dir Pierre Morin

D-U-N-S 24-012-0597   (BR)
CENTRES JEUNESSE CHAUDIERE-APPALACHES, LES
25 Rue Vincent-Chagnon, Levis, QC, G6V 4V6
(418) 835-9659
Emp Here 25
SIC 8322 Individual and family services

D-U-N-S 20-776-7658   (SL)
CLUB DE GOLF LEVIS INC
6100 Boul Guillaume-Couture, Levis, QC, G6V 8Z7
(418) 837-3618
Emp Here 70   *Sales* 2,845,467
SIC 7997 Membership sports and recreation clubs

D-U-N-S 25-688-8579   (BR)
COMMISSION SCOLAIRE DES NAVIGATEURS
ECOLE SAINT JOSEPH
295 Rue Saint-Joseph, Levis, QC, G6V 1G3
(418) 838-8562
Emp Here 45
SIC 8211 Elementary and secondary schools

D-U-N-S 20-712-0259   (BR)
COMMISSION SCOLAIRE DES NAVIGATEURS
CENTRE DE FORMATION PROFESSIONNEL DE LEVIS
30 Rue Vincent-Chagnon, Levis, QC, G6V 4V6
(418) 838-8400
Emp Here 120
SIC 8221 Colleges and universities

D-U-N-S 25-688-2770   (BR)
COMMISSION SCOLAIRE DES NAVIGATEURS
ECOLE NOTRE DAME
6045 Rue Saint-Georges, Levis, QC, G6V 4K6
(418) 838-8548
Emp Here 250
SIC 8211 Elementary and secondary schools

D-U-N-S 25-231-8738   (BR)
COMMISSION SCOLAIRE DES NAVIGATEURS
ECOLE SECONDAIRE CHAMPAGNAT
30 Rue Champagnat, Levis, QC, G6V 2A5
(418) 838-8500
Emp Here 40
SIC 8211 Elementary and secondary schools

D-U-N-S 25-233-1285   (BR)
COMMISSION SCOLAIRE DES NAVIGATEURS
ECOLE GUILLAUME COUTURE
70 Rue Philippe-Boucher, Levis, QC, G6V 1M5
(418) 838-8550
Emp Here 50
SIC 8211 Elementary and secondary schools

D-U-N-S 25-689-8875   (BR)
COMMISSION SCOLAIRE DES NAVIGATEURS
CENTRE EDUCATION ADULTES DES BATELIERS SECTEUR LEVIS
23 Rue Pie-X, Levis, QC, G6V 4W5
(418) 838-8566
Emp Here 30
SIC 8211 Elementary and secondary schools

D-U-N-S 25-688-2614   (BR)
COMMISSION SCOLAIRE DES NAVIGATEURS
ECOLE DU RUISSEAU
688 Rue Saint-Joseph, Levis, QC, G6V 1J4
(418) 838-8560
Emp Here 35

SIC 8211 Elementary and secondary schools

D-U-N-S 25-688-8611   (BR)
COMMISSION SCOLAIRE DES NAVIGA-TEURS
ECOLE SAINTE-MARIE
15 Rue Letourneau, Levis, QC, G6V 3J8
(418) 838-8565
Emp Here 25
SIC 8211 Elementary and secondary schools

D-U-N-S 25-231-8696   (BR)
COMMISSION SCOLAIRE DES NAVIGA-TEURS
ECOLE POINTE LEVIS
55 Rue Des Commandeurs, Levis, QC, G6V 6P5
(418) 838-8402
Emp Here 150
SIC 8211 Elementary and secondary schools

D-U-N-S 24-852-6035   (BR)
COMPAGNIE AMERICAINE DE FER & METAUX INC, LA
AIM LEVIS
251 Ch Des Iles, Levis, QC, G6V 7M5
(418) 838-1008
Emp Here 30
SIC 3341 Secondary nonferrous Metals

D-U-N-S 25-870-9294   (SL)
COOPERATIVE DE SERVICES RIVE-SUD
37 Rte Du President-Kennedy, Levis, QC, G6V 6C3
(418) 838-4019
Emp Here 300   *Sales* 15,901,920
SIC 8322 Individual and family services
Genl Mgr Reginald Samson
Mng Dir Andre Morin

D-U-N-S 20-558-4118   (HQ)
CREAFORM INC
CREAFORME
(*Suby of* Ametek, Inc.)
5825 Rue Saint-Georges, Levis, QC, G6V 4L2
(418) 833-4446
Emp Here 258   *Emp Total* 15,700
Sales 51,364,333
SIC 7373 Computer integrated systems design
Pr Pr Martin Lamontagne
Sec Bernard G. Boulet

D-U-N-S 24-884-5299   (HQ)
DESJARDINS ASSURANCES GENERALES INC
DESJARDINS ASSURANCES
6300 Boul De La Rive-Sud, Levis, QC, G6V 6P9
(418) 835-4850
Emp Here 625   *Emp Total* 15,000
Sales 668,976,658
SIC 6331 Fire, marine, and casualty insurance
Pr Pr Guy Cormier
VP VP Marcel Lauzon
 Stephanie Lee
 Jean Royer
Dir Clermont Tremblay
Dir Robert J. Boucher
Dir Alex Johnston
Dir Aldea Landry
Dir Andre Lord
Dir Sonia Gauthier

D-U-N-S 20-571-8658   (BR)
DESJARDINS SECURITE FINANCIERE, COMPAGNIE D'ASSURANCE VIE
150 Rue Des Commandeurs, Levis, QC, G6V 6P8
(418) 838-7800
Emp Here 20
SIC 6311 Life insurance

D-U-N-S 20-697-3351   (BR)
DESJARDINS SECURITE FINANCIERE, COMPAGNIE D'ASSURANCE VIE
5790 Boul Etienne-Dallaire Bureau 3950, Levis, QC, G6V 8V6

(418) 838-3940
Emp Here 30
SIC 6311 Life insurance

D-U-N-S 20-580-5489   (BR)
DESJARDINS SECURITE FINANCIERE, COMPAGNIE D'ASSURANCE VIE
95 Rue Des Commandeurs, Levis, QC, G6V 6P6
(418) 838-7800
Emp Here 582
SIC 6311 Life insurance

D-U-N-S 24-707-3794   (SL)
E G AUTOMOBILES INC
LEVY HONDA
5035 Rue Louis-H.-La Fontaine, Levis, QC, G6V 8X4
(418) 833-2135
Emp Here 30   *Sales* 15,072,000
SIC 5511 New and used car dealers
Pr Pr Michel Caron
 Jean-Marc Caron

D-U-N-S 25-240-5246   (SL)
ECOLE MARCELLE-MALLET
51 Rue Deziel, Levis, QC, G6V 3T7
(418) 833-7691
Emp Here 60   *Sales* 4,012,839
SIC 8211 Elementary and secondary schools

D-U-N-S 25-164-6592   (BR)
ENERGIE VALERO INC
UTRAMAR RAFFINERIE JEAN GAULIN
165 Ch Des Iles, Levis, QC, G6V 7M5
(418) 837-3641
Emp Here 500
SIC 2911 Petroleum refining

D-U-N-S 25-541-5742   (BR)
FARM CREDIT CANADA
1655 Boul Alphonse-Desjardins Bureau 180, Levis, QC, G6V 0B7
(418) 837-5184
Emp Here 25
SIC 6159 Miscellaneous business credit institutions

D-U-N-S 20-573-5736   (BR)
FEDERATION DES CAISSES DESJARDINS DU QUEBEC
95 Rue Des Commandeurs, Levis, QC, G6V 6P6
(418) 835-8444
Emp Here 20
SIC 6062 State credit unions

D-U-N-S 24-942-7873   (SL)
GESTION DANIEL DUBE INC
PHARMACIE BRUNET
6700 Rue Saint-Georges Bureau 105, Levis, QC, G6V 4H3
(418) 837-9363
Emp Here 46   *Sales* 9,029,050
SIC 5912 Drug stores and proprietary stores
Pr Pr Daniel Dube
 Michel Cadrin

D-U-N-S 24-391-2180   (SL)
GESTION MECNOV INC
864 Rue Archimede, Levis, QC, G6V 7M5
(418) 837-7475
Emp Here 40   *Sales* 5,465,508
SIC 3569 General industrial machinery, nec
Pr Pr Kennedy Gagnon
Treas Guy Labrie
VP VP Erick Pelletier

D-U-N-S 20-265-5064   (HQ)
GESTION N. AUGER INC
MCDONALD
(*Suby of* Gestion N. Auger Inc)
5480 Rue Saint-Georges, Levis, QC, G6V 4M6
(418) 833-3241
Emp Here 100   *Emp Total* 100
Sales 2,991,389
SIC 5812 Eating places

D-U-N-S 20-353-9817   (BR)
GESTION N. AUGER INC
RESTAURANT MCDONALD'S
(*Suby of* Gestion N. Auger Inc)
44d Rte Du President-Kennedy, Levis, QC, G6V 6C5
(418) 833-3241
Emp Here 25
SIC 5812 Eating places

D-U-N-S 24-345-9224   (BR)
GROUPE SPORTSCENE INC
CAGE AUX SPORTS, LA
5500 Boul Guillaume-Couture, Levis, QC, G6V 4Z2
(418) 835-6000
Emp Here 45
SIC 5812 Eating places

D-U-N-S 24-051-2017   (BR)
INDUSTRO-TECH INC
165 Ch Des Iles, Levis, QC, G6V 7M5

Emp Here 30
SIC 1541 Industrial buildings and warehouses

D-U-N-S 25-305-2278   (BR)
INNVEST PROPERTIES CORP
COMFORT INN LEVIS
(*Suby of* Innvest Properties Corp)
10 Rue Du Terroir, Levis, QC, G6V 9J3
(418) 835-5605
Emp Here 25
SIC 7011 Hotels and motels

D-U-N-S 20-521-3031   (BR)
LANGLOIS KRONSTROM DESJARDINS S.E.N.C.
5790 Boul Etienne-Dallaire Bureau 205, Levis, QC, G6V 8V6
(418) 838-5505
Emp Here 40
SIC 8111 Legal services

D-U-N-S 20-107-0427   (HQ)
LEMIEUX NOLET COMPTABLES AGREES S.E.N.C.R.L.
(*Suby of* Lemieux Nolet Comptables Agrees S.E.N.C.R.L.)
5020 Boul Guillaume-Couture, Levis, QC, G6V 4Z6
(418) 833-2114
Emp Here 60   *Emp Total* 100
Sales 4,377,642
SIC 8721 Accounting, auditing, and bookkeeping

D-U-N-S 24-395-1360   (SL)
LEVIS SUZUKI
1925 Boul Alphonse-Desjardins, Levis, QC, G6V 9K5
(418) 835-5050
Emp Here 20   *Sales* 9,816,000
SIC 5511 New and used car dealers
Genl Mgr Ghislain Pelletier

D-U-N-S 25-224-0833   (BR)
LEVIS, VILLE DE
7 Rue Monseigneur-Gosselin, Levis, QC, G6V 5J9
(418) 838-4122
Emp Here 25
SIC 8231 Libraries

D-U-N-S 20-704-9144   (BR)
LOBLAWS INC
MAXI
50 Rte Du President-Kennedy Bureau 190, Levis, QC, G6V 6W8
(418) 837-9505
Emp Here 70
SIC 5411 Grocery stores

D-U-N-S 24-909-1976   (BR)
METRO RICHELIEU INC
44 Rte Du President-Kennedy, Levis, QC, G6V 6C5
(418) 835-6313
Emp Here 50

SIC 5411 Grocery stores

D-U-N-S 25-361-7195   (BR)
MODE CHOC (ALMA) LTEE
MODE CHOC
5475 Rue Wilfrid-Halle Bureau 1004, Levis, QC, G6V 9J1
(418) 838-2846
Emp Here 60
SIC 5651 Family clothing stores

D-U-N-S 20-281-5879   (BR)
NAUTILUS PLUS INC
50 Rte Du President-Kennedy Bureau 260, Levis, QC, G6V 6W8
(418) 838-1505
Emp Here 25
SIC 7991 Physical fitness facilities

D-U-N-S 24-623-0635   (SL)
PAVILLON BELLEVUE INC
CENTRE D'ACCUEIL BELLEVUE
99 Rte Monseigneur-Bourget, Levis, QC, G6V 9V2
(418) 833-3490
Emp Here 50   *Sales* 1,824,018
SIC 8361 Residential care

D-U-N-S 20-579-6873   (BR)
PEPSICO CANADA ULC
FRITO-LAY CANADA
(*Suby of* Pepsico, Inc.)
8450 Boul Guillaume-Couture, Levis, QC, G6V 7L7
(418) 833-2121
Emp Here 450
SIC 2096 Potato chips and similar snacks

D-U-N-S 25-767-0703   (BR)
PRISZM LP
PFK
140 Rte Du President-Kennedy, Levis, QC, G6V 6C9
(418) 833-4486
Emp Here 20
SIC 5812 Eating places

D-U-N-S 25-973-7005   (BR)
PROVIGO DISTRIBUTION INC
PROVIGO
6700 Rue Saint-Georges, Levis, QC, G6V 4H3
(418) 833-3404
Emp Here 40
SIC 5141 Groceries, general line

D-U-N-S 20-003-0042   (BR)
PROVIGO DISTRIBUTION INC
PROVIGO
7777 Boul Guillaume-Couture, Levis, QC, G6V 6Z1
(418) 837-5496
Emp Here 55
SIC 5411 Grocery stores

D-U-N-S 25-298-1865   (BR)
RAYMOND CHABOT GRANT THORNTON S.E.N.C.R.L.
5700 Rue J.-B.-Michaud Bureau 400, Levis, QC, G6V 0B1
(418) 835-3965
Emp Here 30
SIC 8721 Accounting, auditing, and bookkeeping

D-U-N-S 25-300-5821   (BR)
REDBERRY FRANCHISING CORP
BURGER KING
94 Rte Du President-Kennedy, Levis, QC, G6V 6C9
(418) 833-9371
Emp Here 40
SIC 5812 Eating places

D-U-N-S 20-577-2267   (BR)
RESTAURANT NORMANDIN INC
7405 Boul Guillaume-Couture, Levis, QC, G6V 7A3
(418) 835-1177
Emp Here 45

SIC 5812 Eating places

D-U-N-S 20-205-9671   (SL)
SCIES MERCIER INC, LES
GARANT MACHINERIE
8860 Boul Guillaume-Couture, Levis, QC,
G6V 9H1
(418) 837-5832
Emp Here 36   *Sales* 8,633,340
SIC 3425 Saw blades and handsaws
Pr Gilles Garant
  Yves Garant
Sec Gisele Garant
  Patrick Garant

D-U-N-S 20-874-3211   (BR)
SEARS CANADA INC
1200 Boul Alphonse-Desjardins, Levis, QC,
G6V 6Y8
(418) 833-4711
Emp Here 150
SIC 5311 Department stores

D-U-N-S 24-466-1492   (HQ)
SOCIETE PETROLIERE P.L.C. INC
(*Suby of* Societe Petroliere P.L.C. Inc)
4 Rue Du Vallon E, Levis, QC, G6V 9J3
(418) 833-9602
Emp Here 40   *Emp Total* 40
Sales 16,579,200
SIC 5172 Petroleum products, nec
Pr Pr Jacques Paquet

D-U-N-S 25-307-6475   (BR)
SOCIETE DES ALCOOLS DU QUEBEC
S.A.Q # 33615
50 Rte Du President-Kennedy, Levis, QC, G6V
6W8
(418) 835-0946
Emp Here 40
SIC 5921 Liquor stores

D-U-N-S 25-788-6192   (BR)
STAPLES CANADA INC
BUREAU EN GROS
(*Suby of* Staples, Inc.)
80 Rte Du President-Kennedy, Levis, QC, G6V
6C9
(418) 833-7547
Emp Here 40
SIC 5943 Stationery stores

D-U-N-S 24-689-7029   (HQ)
TRANSPORT JACQUES AUGER INC
QUEENSWAY TANK LINE
860 Rue Archimede, Levis, QC, G6V 7M5
(418) 835-9266
Emp Here 250   *Emp Total* 301
Sales 23,475,402
SIC 4212 Local trucking, without storage
  Jacques Auger

D-U-N-S 24-180-7655   (BR)
UNIPRIX INC
40 Rte Du President-Kennedy Bureau 101,
Levis, QC, G6V 6C4
(418) 835-3300
Emp Here 20
SIC 5912 Drug stores and proprietary stores

D-U-N-S 20-583-1709   (BR)
UNIVERSITE DU QUEBEC
CAMPUS DE LEVIS
1595 Boul Alphonse-Desjardins, Levis, QC,
G6V 0A6
(418) 833-8800
Emp Here 100
SIC 8221 Colleges and universities

D-U-N-S 25-498-2580   (BR)
WAL-MART CANADA CORP
WALMART DE LEVIS
5303 Rue Louis-H.-La Fontaine, Levis, QC,
G6V 8X4
(418) 833-8555
Emp Here 150
SIC 5311 Department stores

D-U-N-S 20-106-2853   (BR)

WINNERS MERCHANTS INTERNATIONAL L.P.
WINNERS
(*Suby of* The TJX Companies Inc)
82 Rte Du President-Kennedy, Levis, QC, G6V
6C9
(418) 833-0031
Emp Here 30
SIC 5651 Family clothing stores

Levis, QC G6W
Levis County

D-U-N-S 25-140-1092   (BR)
9020-5758 QUEBEC INC
AVRIL SUPERMARCHE SANTE
1218 Rue De La Concorde, Levis, QC, G6W
0M7
(418) 903-5454
Emp Here 25
SIC 5499 Miscellaneous food stores

D-U-N-S 20-550-6723   (SL)
9119-6832 QUEBEC INC
PAQUET MITSUBISHI
1 Ch Des Iles, Levis, QC, G6W 8B6
(418) 835-6161
Emp Here 30   *Sales* 15,072,000
SIC 5511 New and used car dealers
Pr Pr Yolande Paquet
  Stephane Paquet
VP VP Gratien Paquet

D-U-N-S 20-257-1089   (SL)
ARMOIRES DE CUISINE BERNIER INC
1955 3e Rue Bureau 70, Levis, QC, G6W 5M6
(418) 839-8142
Emp Here 75   *Sales* 4,377,642
SIC 2434 Wood kitchen cabinets

D-U-N-S 20-295-2789   (SL)
CHSLD CHANOINE-AUDET INC
2155 Ch Du Sault, Levis, QC, G6W 2K7
(418) 834-5322
Emp Here 100   *Sales* 6,418,100
SIC 8051 Skilled nursing care facilities
Genl Mgr Sophie Barsetti

D-U-N-S 24-530-4175   (BR)
CANAC-MARQUIS GRENIER LTEE
CANAC
376 Av Taniata, Levis, QC, G6W 5M6
(418) 839-0621
Emp Here 30
SIC 5251 Hardware stores

D-U-N-S 20-030-0270   (BR)
CARGILL LIMITED
CARGILL ANIMAL NUTRITION DIV
1875 2e Rue, Levis, QC, G6W 5M6
(418) 839-8884
Emp Here 50
SIC 2048 Prepared feeds, nec

D-U-N-S 20-295-6160   (BR)
CENTRES JEUNESSE CHAUDIERE-APPALACHES, LES
BUREAU DE ST ROMUALD
1120 Boul Guillaume-Couture, Levis, QC,
G6W 5M6
(418) 839-6888
Emp Here 50
SIC 8322 Individual and family services

D-U-N-S 20-712-0218   (BR)
COMMISSION SCOLAIRE DES NAVIGA-TEURS
ECOLE SECONDAIRE DE L'AUBIER
1020 Ch Du Sault, Levis, QC, G6W 5M6
(418) 839-9468
Emp Here 50
SIC 8211 Elementary and secondary schools

D-U-N-S 20-712-0283   (BR)
COMMISSION SCOLAIRE DES NAVIGA-TEURS

ECOLE DESJARDINS
3700 Rue De La Fabrique, Levis, QC, G6W
1J5
(418) 838-8555
Emp Here 35
SIC 8211 Elementary and secondary schools

D-U-N-S 20-712-0176   (BR)
COMMISSION SCOLAIRE DES NAVIGA-TEURS
ECOLE DU GRAND FLEUVE
2111 Ch Du Sault, Levis, QC, G6W 2K7
(418) 839-8851
Emp Here 50
SIC 8211 Elementary and secondary schools

D-U-N-S 25-233-7936   (BR)
COMMISSION SCOLAIRE DES NAVIGA-TEURS
ECOLE DE L'AUBERIVIERE
350 Rue De L'Eglise, Levis, QC, G6W 1T8
(418) 838-8553
Emp Here 20
SIC 8211 Elementary and secondary schools

D-U-N-S 20-712-0267   (BR)
COMMISSION SCOLAIRE DES NAVIGA-TEURS
CENTRE DE FORMATION EN MECANIQUE DE VEHICULES LOURD
2775 Rue De L'Etchemin, Levis, QC, G6W
7X5
(418) 838-8542
Emp Here 20
SIC 8249 Vocational schools, nec

D-U-N-S 25-240-2524   (BR)
COMMISSION SCOLAIRE DES NAVIGA-TEURS
ECOLE NOTRE-DAME D'ETCHEMIN
2233 Rue Dollard, Levis, QC, G6W 2H8
(418) 839-8839
Emp Here 30
SIC 8211 Elementary and secondary schools

D-U-N-S 24-942-0514   (SL)
CONTROLES A.C. INC, LES
2185 5e Rue, Levis, QC, G6W 5M6
(418) 834-2777
Emp Here 50   *Sales* 6,028,800
SIC 1711 Plumbing, heating, air-conditioning
Pr Pr Real Audet
VP VP Pierre Guillmette
  Michel Tremblay

D-U-N-S 24-746-0272   (SL)
COURTIERS EN TRANSPORT G.M.R. INC, LES
G.M.R. FREIGHT BROKERS
2111 4e Rue Bureau 100, Levis, QC, G6W
5M6
(418) 839-5768
Emp Here 22   *Sales* 5,472,053
SIC 4731 Freight transportation arrangement
  Martin Tremblay

D-U-N-S 20-248-7112   (HQ)
COUVRE-PLANCHERS PELLETIER INC
COUVRE PLANCHERS MAURICE PEL-LETIER
4600 Boul Guillaume-Couture, Levis, QC,
G6W 5N6
(418) 837-3681
Emp Here 30   *Emp Total* 70
Sales 8,244,559
SIC 5713 Floor covering stores
Pr Pr Yvan Pelletier
  Sabrina Pelletier

D-U-N-S 24-161-2600   (SL)
CUT TECHNOLOGIES
460 3e Av Bureau 100, Levis, QC, G6W 5M6
(418) 834-7772
Emp Here 100   *Sales* 18,240,175
SIC 5084 Industrial machinery and equipment
Owner Mike Cloutier

D-U-N-S 20-993-4541   (HQ)
DISTRIBUTION BRUNET INC
DBI
(*Suby of* 7956576 Canada Inc)
777 Rue Perreault Bureau 100, Levis, QC,
G6W 7Z9
(418) 830-1208
Emp Here 23   *Emp Total* 1
Sales 18,159,550
SIC 4941 Water supply
Pr Pr Bernard Brunet

D-U-N-S 25-384-1035   (HQ)
EVIMBEC LTEE
ROCHE, GROUPE-CONSEIL
(*Suby of* Corporoche Ltee)
1175 Boul Guillaume-Couture Bureau 200,
Levis, QC, G6W 5M6
(418) 834-7000
Emp Here 30   *Emp Total* 1
Sales 5,399,092
SIC 8742 Management consulting services
Pr Pr Serge Dussault
Dir Alex Brisson
Dir Jean-Pierre Caron
Dir Pierre-Luc Dussault
Dir Mathieu Demers

D-U-N-S 20-292-3579   (BR)
G.C.M. CONSULTANTS INC
GCM CONSULTANTS
4000 Boul Guillaume-Couture Unite 200,
Levis, QC, G6W 1H7
(418) 834-0014
Emp Here 60
SIC 8711 Engineering services

D-U-N-S 20-284-5587   (BR)
GHD CONSULTANTS LTEE
INSPEC-SOL
2181 4e Rue, Levis, QC, G6W 5M6
(418) 839-0041
Emp Here 30
SIC 8731 Commercial physical research

D-U-N-S 25-355-3127   (SL)
GESTION R.M.L. RODRIGUE INC
1890 1re Rue, Levis, QC, G6W 5M6
(418) 839-0671
Emp Here 120   *Sales* 20,919,704
SIC 3564 Blowers and fans
Pr Claude Rodrigue

D-U-N-S 25-370-1999   (BR)
GOUVERNEMENT DE LA PROVINCE DE QUEBEC
FINANCIERE AGRICOLE DU QUEBEC
1400 Boul Guillaume-Couture Unite Rc, Levis,
QC, G6W 8K7
(418) 838-5615
Emp Here 125
SIC 8748 Business consulting, nec

D-U-N-S 20-430-2392   (SL)
HAMEL INC
436 Av Taniata, Levis, QC, G6W 5M6
(418) 839-4193
Emp Here 50   *Sales* 3,648,035
SIC 2038 Frozen specialties, nec

D-U-N-S 24-358-4187   (BR)
HOME DEPOT OF CANADA INC
HOME DEPOT STORE # 7189
(*Suby of* The Home Depot Inc)
500 Rue De La Concorde, Levis, QC, G6W
8A8
(418) 834-7050
Emp Here 125
SIC 5251 Hardware stores

D-U-N-S 20-714-2014   (SL)
JUVENAT NOTRE-DAME DU SAINT-LAURENT (F.I.C.)
30 Rue Du Juvenat, Levis, QC, G6W 7X2
(418) 839-9592
Emp Here 50   *Sales* 3,356,192
SIC 8211 Elementary and secondary schools

D-U-N-S 20-621-2503   (BR)
MALLETTE S.E.N.C.R.L.
1200 Boul Guillaume-Couture Unite 501,
Levis, QC, G6W 5M6
(418) 839-7531
Emp Here 20
SIC 8721 Accounting, auditing, and book-
keeping

D-U-N-S 20-555-7296   (BR)
**MASONITE INTERNATIONAL CORPORA-
TION**
CELCO
(*Suby of* Masonite International Corporation)
445 1re Av, Levis, QC, G6W 5M6
(418) 839-0062
Emp Here 110
SIC 2431 Millwork

D-U-N-S 20-291-2366   (HQ)
MISTRAS SERVICES INC
MISTRAS METALTEC
765 Rue De Saint-Romuald, Levis, QC, G6W
5M6
(418) 837-4664
Emp Here 63   *Emp Total* 250
Sales 22,089,401
SIC 8734 Testing laboratories
Genl Mgr Dennis Bertolotti
Ch Bd Sotirios J. Vahaviolos
V Ch Bd Michael J. Lange
Pr Pr Yves Richer
  Valerie Goulet

D-U-N-S 24-530-2971   (BR)
MORIN & ROULEAU INC
RESTAURANT RYNA PIZZA
(*Suby of* Morin & Rouleau Inc)
4300 Boul Guillaume-Couture, Levis, QC,
G6W 6N1
(418) 833-8677
Emp Here 40
SIC 5812 Eating places

D-U-N-S 24-567-8883   (HQ)
MORIN & ROULEAU INC
RESTAURANT RYNA
(*Suby of* Morin & Rouleau Inc)
4300 Boul Guillaume-Couture, Levis, QC,
G6W 6N1
(418) 833-8677
Emp Here 30   *Emp Total* 60
Sales 1,824,018
SIC 5812 Eating places

D-U-N-S 25-767-0372   (BR)
RESTAURANT NORMANDIN INC
*RESTAURANT NORMANDIN SAINT-
ROMUALD*
2080 Boul Guillaume-Couture, Levis, QC,
G6W 2S6
(418) 839-5861
Emp Here 30
SIC 5812 Eating places

D-U-N-S 25-767-0364   (BR)
**RESTAURANT LES TROIS MOUSSAIL-
LONS INC**
MCDONALD'S
(*Suby of* Restaurant les Trois Moussaillons
Inc)
481 Av Taniata, Levis, QC, G6W 5M6
(418) 834-1265
Emp Here 60
SIC 5812 Eating places

D-U-N-S 20-265-9355   (HQ)
RODRIGUE METAL LTEE
ROD-AIR DIV. DE RODRIGUE METAL LTEE
(*Suby of* Canerector Inc)
1890 1re Rue, Levis, QC, G6W 5M6
(418) 839-0400
Emp Here 70   *Emp Total* 3,000
Sales 12,695,162
SIC 3569 General industrial machinery, nec
Pr Daniel Beaupre
Sec Tim Buckland
Dir William Nickel

Dir Amanda Hawkins
Dir Pierre Desormeaux

D-U-N-S 20-871-7509   (BR)
SOBEYS QUEBEC INC
IGA EXTRA
1060 Boul Guillaume-Couture, Levis, QC,
G6W 5M6
(418) 834-3811
Emp Here 150
SIC 5411 Grocery stores

D-U-N-S 24-378-2851   (SL)
STRUCTURES C.D.L. INC, LES
2045 4e Rue, Levis, QC, G6W 5M6
(418) 839-1421
Emp Here 40   *Sales* 7,636,480
SIC 3441 Fabricated structural Metal
Pr Pr Gilles Brisson
VP VP Laurent Halle
  Louise Dion

D-U-N-S 25-304-1875   (BR)
**SUN LIFE ASSURANCE COMPANY OF
CANADA**
FINANCIERE SUN LIFE
994 Rue De La Concorde, Levis, QC, G6W
5M6
(418) 839-4909
Emp Here 45
SIC 6311 Life insurance

D-U-N-S 24-344-0257   (BR)
SUPERIOR PLUS LP
485 2e Av, Levis, QC, G6W 5M6
(418) 839-9434
Emp Here 25
SIC 5984 Liquefied petroleum gas dealers

D-U-N-S 25-001-1830   (BR)
SUPERMARCHES GP INC, LES
METRO
(*Suby of* Supermarches GP Inc, Les)
2150 Boul Guillaume-Couture, Levis, QC,
G6W 2S6
(418) 839-6003
Emp Here 40
SIC 5411 Grocery stores

D-U-N-S 20-317-7704   (SL)
SUPERMETAL QUEBEC INC
(*Suby of* Gestion Releve SMS Inc)
1955 5e Rue, Levis, QC, G6W 5M6
(418) 834-1955
Emp Here 50   *Sales* 7,362,000
SIC 1791 Structural steel erection
  Jean-Francois Blouin

D-U-N-S 20-290-9826   (BR)
TRANSPORT TFI 6 S.E.C.
BESNER
1950 3e Rue, Levis, QC, G6W 5M6
(418) 834-9891
Emp Here 120
SIC 4212 Local trucking, without storage

D-U-N-S 24-319-5075   (BR)
WAL-MART CANADA CORP
WALMART
700 Rue De La Concorde, Levis, QC, G6W
8A8
(418) 834-5115
Emp Here 120
SIC 5311 Department stores

Levis, QC G6X
Levis County

D-U-N-S 20-319-4571   (SL)
9059-2114 QUEBEC INC
DUPROPRIO.COM
8389 Av Sous-Le-Vent Bureau 300, Levis, QC,
G6X 1K7
(418) 832-2222
Emp Here 220   *Sales* 27,877,440
SIC 6531 Real estate agents and managers

Dir Nicolas Bouchard
Pr Pr Lisette Beaulieu
Treas Marie-Elise Bouchard
VP Samuel Bouchard

D-U-N-S 25-321-4365   (BR)
ALLIED SYSTEMS (CANADA) COMPANY
2709 Av De La Rotonde, Levis, QC, G6X 2M2
(418) 832-8707
Emp Here 46
SIC 4213 Trucking, except local

D-U-N-S 24-908-1118   (SL)
AUTOBUS FLEUR DE LYS INC
2591 Av De La Rotonde, Levis, QC, G6X 2M2
(418) 832-7788
Emp Here 60   *Sales* 2,845,467
SIC 4142 Bus charter service, except local

D-U-N-S 24-079-0555   (BR)
BPR INC
(*Suby of* Tetra Tech, Inc.)
8165 Rue Du Mistral Bureau 201, Levis, QC,
G6X 3R8
(418) 835-2366
Emp Here 50
SIC 8711 Engineering services

D-U-N-S 25-822-0383   (BR)
**BLANCHETTE VACHON ET ASSOCIES CA
SENCRL**
8149 Rue Du Mistral Bureau 202, Levis, QC,
G6X 1G5
(418) 387-3636
Emp Here 100
SIC 8721 Accounting, auditing, and book-
keeping

D-U-N-S 25-752-5642   (SL)
**CENTRE DE SERVICE SANTE ET SOCIAUX
DU GRAND LITTORAL**
CENTRE DE SANTE PAUL-GILBERT
9330 Boul Du Centre-Hospitalier, Levis, QC,
G6X 1L6
(418) 380-8993
Emp Here 500   *Sales* 76,666,240
SIC 8062 General medical and surgical hospi-
tals
Dir Fin Luc Adam
Dir Michelle Collard
  Jacques Fortin

D-U-N-S 20-712-0192   (BR)
**COMMISSION SCOLAIRE DES NAVIGA-
TEURS**
ECOLE DES PETITS CHEMINOTS
6200 Av Des Belles-Amours, Levis, QC, G6X
1R2
(418) 834-2469
Emp Here 40
SIC 8211 Elementary and secondary schools

D-U-N-S 25-234-0526   (BR)
**COMMISSION SCOLAIRE DES NAVIGA-
TEURS**
ECOLE SECONDAIRE LES ETCHEMINS
3724 Av Des Eglises, Levis, QC, G6X 1X4
(418) 839-0500
Emp Here 190
SIC 8211 Elementary and secondary schools

D-U-N-S 20-580-5018   (BR)
**COMPAGNIE DES CHEMINS DE FER NA-
TIONAUX DU CANADA**
CANADIEN NATIONAL
2600 Av De La Rotonde, Levis, QC, G6X 2M1

Emp Here 250
SIC 4011 Railroads, line-haul operating

D-U-N-S 20-799-3465   (BR)
GROUPE JEAN COUTU (PJC) INC, LE
JEAN COUTU
(*Suby of* 3958230 Canada Inc)
3535 Av Des Eglises, Levis, QC, G6X 1W8
(418) 832-4449
Emp Here 35
SIC 5912 Drug stores and proprietary stores

D-U-N-S 24-496-1160   (BR)
QUALIFAB INC
2256 Av De La Rotonde, Levis, QC, G6X 2L8
(418) 832-9193
Emp Here 100
SIC 3498 Fabricated pipe and fittings

D-U-N-S 25-788-6432   (BR)
**RESTAURANT LES TROIS MOUSSAIL-
LONS INC**
RESTAURANT MCDONALD'S
(*Suby of* Restaurant les Trois Moussaillons
Inc)
8000 Av Des Eglises, Levis, QC, G6X 1X4
(418) 832-2962
Emp Here 30
SIC 5812 Eating places

Levis, QC G6Y
Levis County

D-U-N-S 24-500-1680   (SL)
**EQUIPEMENTS RECREATIFS JAMBETTE
INC**
JAMBETTE
700 Rue Des Calfats, Levis, QC, G6Y 9E6
(418) 837-8246
Emp Here 60   *Sales* 4,961,328
SIC 3949 Sporting and athletic goods, nec

D-U-N-S 24-568-8072   (BR)
MULTI-MARQUES INC
LEVIS DISTRIBUTION CENTRE
845 Rue Jean-Marchand, Levis, QC, G6Y 9G4
(418) 837-3611
Emp Here 80
SIC 5461 Retail bakeries

D-U-N-S 20-582-1960   (SL)
STURO METAL INC
600 Rue Jean-Marchand, Levis, QC, G6Y 9G6
(418) 833-2107
Emp Here 50   *Sales* 8,952,126
SIC 3441 Fabricated structural Metal
Pr Francis Lacasse
VP Vicky Lacassa
VP Harry Lacasse
Sec Carole Lacasse

D-U-N-S 25-190-3522   (BR)
TEKNION LIMITED
TEKNION CONCEPT
975 Rue Des Calfats Bureau 45, Levis, QC,
G6Y 9E8
(418) 833-0047
Emp Here 230
SIC 2522 Office furniture, except wood

Levis, QC G6Z
Levis County

D-U-N-S 25-784-9703   (BR)
**ASSURANCES FONTAINE LEMAY & ASS
INC, LES**
AFL GROUPE FINANCIER
(*Suby of* Assurances Fontaine Lemay & Ass
Inc, Les)
893 Av Taniata, Levis, QC, G6Z 2E3
(418) 839-5951
Emp Here 30
SIC 6411 Insurance agents, brokers, and ser-
vice

D-U-N-S 25-522-3315   (BR)
AUTOBUS LA QUEBECOISE INC
(*Suby of* Autobus la Quebecoise Inc)
1043 Rue Du Parc-Industriel, Levis, QC, G6Z
1C5
(418) 834-3133
Emp Here 32
SIC 4111 Local and suburban transit

D-U-N-S 24-369-1818   (BR)
CAISSE DESJARDINS DES RIVIERES CHAUDIERE ET ETCHEMIN
CENTRE DE SERVICE SAINT-JEAN-CHRYSOSTOME
(*Suby of* Caisse Desjardins des Rivieres Chaudiere et Etchemin)
730 Av Taniata Unite 100, Levis, QC, G6Z 2C5
(418) 839-8819
Emp Here 30
SIC 6062 State credit unions

D-U-N-S 25-233-1178   (BR)
COMMISSION SCOLAIRE DES NAVIGATEURS
ECOLE DE LA ROSE DES VENTS
50 Rue Arlette-Fortin, Levis, QC, G6Z 3B9
(418) 839-0098
Emp Here 42
SIC 8211 Elementary and secondary schools

D-U-N-S 25-232-1450   (BR)
COMMISSION SCOLAIRE DES NAVIGATEURS
ECOLE DE LA NACELLE
1110 Rue Des Pres, Levis, QC, G6Z 1W4
(418) 839-3131
Emp Here 45
SIC 8211 Elementary and secondary schools

D-U-N-S 25-688-8470   (BR)
COMMISSION SCOLAIRE DES NAVIGATEURS
200 Rue Arlette-Fortin, Levis, QC, G6Z 3B9
(418) 834-2320
Emp Here 40
SIC 8211 Elementary and secondary schools

D-U-N-S 20-712-0358   (BR)
COMMISSION SCOLAIRE DES NAVIGATEURS
ECOLE DE L'ALIZE & MOUSSERONS
851 Rue Des Herons, Levis, QC, G6Z 3L3
(418) 839-7877
Emp Here 35
SIC 8211 Elementary and secondary schools

D-U-N-S 24-115-8737   (BR)
COMMISSION SCOLAIRE DES NAVIGATEURS
ECOLE DE TANIATA
1002 Rue Des Ecoliers, Levis, QC, G6Z 0C4
(418) 839-4188
Emp Here 40
SIC 8231 Libraries

D-U-N-S 25-532-0277   (SL)
DISTRIBUTIONS ICE INC, LES
1006 Rue Renault, Levis, QC, G6Z 2Y8
(418) 839-0928
Emp Here 54   *Sales* 1,605,135
SIC 7349 Building maintenance services, nec

D-U-N-S 25-246-2411   (BR)
ENTREPRISES ROLLAND INC, LES
FIBRES BREAKEY
3805 Av Saint-Augustin, Levis, QC, G6Z 8J4
(418) 832-6115
Emp Here 60
SIC 1455 Kaolin and ball clay

D-U-N-S 24-611-2739   (BR)
RESTAURANT NORMANDIN INC
679 Av Taniata, Levis, QC, G6Z 2C1
(418) 834-8343
Emp Here 60
SIC 5812 Eating places

D-U-N-S 24-146-7406   (BR)
SINTRA INC
CONSTRUCTION B M L, DIV.DE SINTRA
678 Av Taniata Unite 839, Levis, QC, G6Z 2C2
(418) 839-4175
Emp Here 150
SIC 1611 Highway and street construction

Levis, QC G7A
Levis County

D-U-N-S 20-819-6332   (SL)
9124-4905 QUEBEC INC
CONSTRUCTION COUTURE & TANGUAY
1019 Ch Industriel, Levis, QC, G7A 1B3
(418) 831-1019
Emp Here 30   *Sales* 5,545,013
SIC 1542 Nonresidential construction, nec
Henri Tanguay

D-U-N-S 20-267-4701   (SL)
9252-6698 QUEBEC INC
MERCEDES-BENZ ST-NICOLAS
510 Rue De Bernieres, Levis, QC, G7A 1E1
(418) 830-1234
Emp Here 30   *Sales* 40,437,527
SIC 5812 Eating places
Pr Benoit Theetge
Sec Donald Theetge

D-U-N-S 24-767-9165   (BR)
BAINS ULTRA INC
(*Suby of* Bains Ultra Inc)
1200 Ch Industriel Bureau 4, Levis, QC, G7A 1B1
(418) 831-7132
Emp Here 100
SIC 5999 Miscellaneous retail stores, nec

D-U-N-S 24-146-1045   (HQ)
BAINS ULTRA INC
BAINULTRA
(*Suby of* Bains Ultra Inc)
956 Ch Olivier, Levis, QC, G7A 2N1
(418) 831-4344
Emp Here 123   *Emp Total* 135
Sales 28,073,760
SIC 3089 Plastics products, nec
Pr Pr Henri Brunelle
Treas Jean Fortin
Serge Lauzon

D-U-N-S 24-223-1525   (BR)
BOSTON PIZZA INTERNATIONAL INC
1432 Rte Des Rivieres, Levis, QC, G7A 2N9
(418) 831-1999
Emp Here 40
SIC 5812 Eating places

D-U-N-S 20-712-0143   (BR)
COMMISSION SCOLAIRE DES NAVIGATEURS
ECOLE DU GRAND VOILIER DES HIRONDELLES
1438 Rue Des Pionniers, Levis, QC, G7A 4L6
(418) 834-2479
Emp Here 50
SIC 8211 Elementary and secondary schools

D-U-N-S 25-688-8231   (BR)
COMMISSION SCOLAIRE DES NAVIGATEURS
ECOLE DE L'ODYSSEE
885 Rue Des Melezes, Levis, QC, G7A 4B1
(418) 834-2474
Emp Here 50
SIC 8211 Elementary and secondary schools

D-U-N-S 25-688-8116   (BR)
COMMISSION SCOLAIRE DES NAVIGATEURS
ECOLE LA MARTINIERE
520 Rue De La Sorbonne, Levis, QC, G7A 1Y5
(418) 834-2482
Emp Here 30
SIC 8211 Elementary and secondary schools

D-U-N-S 20-348-8486   (BR)
ENERGIE VALERO INC
DEPANNEUR DU COIN
1505 Rte Des Rivieres, Levis, QC, G7A 2N9
(418) 831-0464
Emp Here 20
SIC 5541 Gasoline service stations

D-U-N-S 20-577-0311   (BR)
GROUPE VOLVO CANADA INC
PREVOST CAR
850 Ch Olivier, Levis, QC, G7A 2N1
(418) 831-2046
Emp Here 30
SIC 7699 Repair services, nec

D-U-N-S 25-412-8705   (SL)
KENWORTH QUEBEC INC
KENWORTH BEAUCE
(*Suby of* Groupe Michel Cadrin Inc)
800 Ch Olivier, Levis, QC, G7A 2N1
(418) 831-2061
Emp Here 26   *Sales* 3,137,310
SIC 5013 Motor vehicle supplies and new parts

D-U-N-S 20-618-4892   (BR)
MARTIN DESSERT INC
ST-HUBERT RESTAURANTS
500 Rue De Bernieres, Levis, QC, G7A 1E1
(418) 836-1234
Emp Here 100
SIC 5812 Eating places

D-U-N-S 20-954-2679   (SL)
MATERIAUX BOMAT INC
BOKIT MC
(*Suby of* Entreprises Grandbois Ltee)
1212 Ch Industriel, Levis, QC, G7A 1B1
(418) 831-4848
Emp Here 75   *Sales* 2,662,722
SIC 5039 Construction materials, nec

D-U-N-S 20-251-4352   (HQ)
NORMAND, J.R. INC
NORMAND MACHINERY
(*Suby of* Groupe Normand Inc)
752 Rue J.-Ambroise-Craig, Levis, QC, G7A 2N2
(418) 831-3226
Emp Here 40   *Emp Total* 40
Sales 14,134,935
SIC 5084 Industrial machinery and equipment
Pr Andre Normand
VP Gaston Bilodeau
Sec Jean-Pierre Normand

D-U-N-S 24-680-0028   (BR)
ORGILL CANADA HARDLINES ULC
(*Suby of* Orgill, Inc.)
1181 Ch Industriel, Levis, QC, G7A 1B2
(418) 836-1055
Emp Here 30
SIC 5211 Lumber and other building materials

D-U-N-S 24-907-9500   (SL)
VIANDES DROLET INC
(*Suby of* Groupe Colabor Inc)
816 Rue Alphonse-Desrochers, Levis, QC, G7A 5H9
(418) 831-8200
Emp Here 20   *Sales* 5,107,249
SIC 5147 Meats and meat products
Genl Mgr Marcel Emond
Pr Gilles Lachance
Sec Michel Loignon

Longueuil, QC J4G

D-U-N-S 25-165-8936   (HQ)
162069 CANADA INC
EXTRA MULTI-RESSOURCES
1800 Boul Marie-Victorin Bureau 203, Longueuil, QC, J4G 1Y9
(450) 670-1110
Emp Here 425   *Emp Total* 500
Sales 50,240,000
SIC 7361 Employment agencies
Pr Pr Gilles Fournier

D-U-N-S 25-097-7089   (SL)
9064-3792 QUEBEC INC
2025 Rue De La Metropole, Longueuil, QC,

J4G 1S9
(450) 676-9141
Emp Here 100   *Sales* 20,417,280
SIC 6712 Bank holding companies
Pr Pr Jean Tremblay
VP VP Yves Tremblay

D-U-N-S 24-921-5245   (SL)
A.R.C. RESINS CORPORATION
2525 Rue Jean-Desy, Longueuil, QC, J4G 1G6
(450) 928-3688
Emp Here 40   *Sales* 4,377,642
SIC 2821 Plastics materials and resins

D-U-N-S 25-857-7667   (BR)
AFA FOREST PRODUCTS INC
2085 Rue De La Metropole, Longueuil, QC, J4G 1S9
(514) 598-7735
Emp Here 30
SIC 5211 Lumber and other building materials

D-U-N-S 20-219-8586   (SL)
ACIER GENDRON LTEE
2270 Rue Garneau, Longueuil, QC, J4G 1E7
(450) 442-9494
Emp Here 800   *Sales* 448,104,650
SIC 5051 Metals service centers and offices
Pr Pr Serge Gendron

D-U-N-S 20-532-7518   (BR)
AQUATECH SOCIETE DE GESTION DE L'EAU INC
AQUATECH SOCIETE DE GESTION DE L'EAU INC
2999 Rue De L'Ile-Charron, Longueuil, QC, J4G 1R6
(450) 442-1480
Emp Here 25
SIC 4952 Sewerage systems

D-U-N-S 24-799-7232   (BR)
BOSCH REXROTH CANADA CORP
REXROTH BOSCH GROUPE
725 Rue Delage, Longueuil, QC, J4G 2P8
(450) 928-1111
Emp Here 25
SIC 5084 Industrial machinery and equipment

D-U-N-S 20-188-0775   (BR)
CRH CANADA GROUP INC
DEMIX CONSTRUCTION
435 Rue Jean-Neveu, Longueuil, QC, J4G 2P9
(450) 651-1117
Emp Here 1,200
SIC 3241 Cement, hydraulic

D-U-N-S 20-738-0577   (BR)
CRH CANADA GROUP INC
DEMIX BETON
435 Rue Jean-Neveu, Longueuil, QC, J4G 2P9
(450) 651-1117
Emp Here 250
SIC 3273 Ready-mixed concrete

D-U-N-S 20-979-3199   (SL)
CENTRE D'INFORMATION RX LTEE
(*Suby of* 3958230 Canada Inc)
2165 Rue De La Province, Longueuil, QC, J4G 1Y6
(450) 646-9760
Emp Here 70   *Sales* 4,994,344
SIC 7376 Computer facilities management

D-U-N-S 25-611-1709   (BR)
CENTRE DE JEUNESSE DE MONTEREGIE
(*Suby of* Centre de Jeunesse de Monteregie)
2010 Rue Limoges, Longueuil, QC, J4G 1C3
(450) 677-8991
Emp Here 40
SIC 8322 Individual and family services

D-U-N-S 24-011-0655   (BR)
CENTRE DE LA PETITE ENFANCE SES AMIS
GARDERIE SES AMIS

625 Rue Adoncour, Longueuil, QC, J4G 2M6
(450) 651-6349
Emp Here 54
SIC 8351 Child day care services

D-U-N-S 20-286-1766   (BR)
CIMA+ S.E.N.C.
2147 Rue De La Province, Longueuil, QC, J4G 1Y6
(514) 337-2462
Emp Here 45
SIC 8711 Engineering services

D-U-N-S 25-233-1806   (BR)
COMMISSION SCOLAIRE MARIE-VICTORIN
ECOLE MARIE VICTORIN PAVILLON LE JARDIN
2190 Rue Limoges, Longueuil, QC, J4G 1E3
(450) 674-1388
Emp Here 50
SIC 8211 Elementary and secondary schools

D-U-N-S 25-624-5606   (BR)
COOP FEDEREE, LA
LABORATOIRE AGROALIMENTAIRE
604 Rue Jean-Neveu, Longueuil, QC, J4G 1P1
(450) 674-5271
Emp Here 35
SIC 8731 Commercial physical research

D-U-N-S 24-668-7107   (BR)
COOP FEDEREE, LA
CENTRE DE DISTRIBUTION LONGUEUIL
2405 Rue De La Province, Longueuil, QC, J4G 1G3
(450) 670-2231
Emp Here 20
SIC 8699 Membership organizations, nec

D-U-N-S 25-359-0160   (BR)
CRAWFORD METAL CORPORATION
ACIER C M C, DIV DE LONGUEUIL
(Suby of Crawford Metal Corporation)
2290 Rue De La Metropole, Longueuil, QC, J4G 1E6
(450) 646-6000
Emp Here 50
SIC 5051 Metals service centers and offices

D-U-N-S 24-340-5425   (BR)
DH CORPORATION
DAVIS HENDERSON INTERCHEQUES
830 Rue Delage, Longueuil, QC, J4G 2V4
(450) 463-6372
Emp Here 200
SIC 6211 Security brokers and dealers

D-U-N-S 24-933-5878   (HQ)
DANACA TRANSPORT MONTREAL LTEE
(Suby of Gestion Real Grondin Inc)
2555 Rue Jean-Desy, Longueuil, QC, J4G 1G6
(450) 463-0020
Emp Here 54   Emp Total 60
Sales 5,630,632
SIC 4212 Local trucking, without storage
Pr Pr Real Grondin
Dir Tommy St-Arnaud

D-U-N-S 20-715-9356   (BR)
DESSAU INC
883 Rue Beriault, Longueuil, QC, J4G 1X7

Emp Here 20
SIC 1761 Roofing, siding, and sheetMetal work

D-U-N-S 20-221-1376   (BR)
EXIDE TECHNOLOGIES CANADA CORPORATION
EXIDE TECHNOLOGIES
(Suby of Exide Technologies)
2109 Boul Fernand-Lafontaine, Longueuil, QC, J4G 2J4
(450) 655-1616
Emp Here 20

SIC 5013 Motor vehicle supplies and new parts

D-U-N-S 25-503-1916   (SL)
FORCETEK INC
(Suby of 3543838 Canada Inc)
430 Boul Guimond, Longueuil, QC, J4G 1P8
(450) 463-3344
Emp Here 76   Sales 13,852,236
SIC 6712 Bank holding companies
Pr Michel Hemond
 Mario Bouthillier

D-U-N-S 25-172-2427   (HQ)
FORTIN, JEAN & ASSOCIES SYNDICS INC
(Suby of Fortin, Jean & Associes Syndics Inc)
2360 Boul Marie-Victorin, Longueuil, QC, J4G 1B5
(450) 442-3260
Emp Here 40   Emp Total 65
Sales 3,378,379
SIC 8111 Legal services

D-U-N-S 24-368-6438   (BR)
GROUPE EMBALLAGE SPECIALISE S.E.C.
IVEX PROTECTIVE PACKAGING
610 Rue Beriault, Longueuil, QC, J4G 1S8
(450) 651-8887
Emp Here 65
SIC 3086 Plastics foam products

D-U-N-S 24-305-3667   (SL)
GROUPE PANDA DETAIL INC.
667 Rue Giffard, Longueuil, QC, J4G 1Y3
(450) 646-6889
Emp Here 50   Sales 3,064,349
SIC 5661 Shoe stores

D-U-N-S 20-303-1265   (BR)
GROUPE TYT INC
454 Rue Jean-Neveu, Longueuil, QC, J4G 1N8
(819) 474-4884
Emp Here 150
SIC 4213 Trucking, except local

D-U-N-S 20-358-9320   (BR)
HASBRO CANADA CORPORATION
(Suby of Hasbro, Inc.)
2350 Rue De La Province, Longueuil, QC, J4G 1G2
(450) 670-9820
Emp Here 40
SIC 5092 Toys and hobby goods and supplies

D-U-N-S 20-309-3208   (SL)
MECANO-SOUDURE DRUMMOND INC
(Suby of Canerector Inc)
700 Rue Talon, Longueuil, QC, J4G 1P7
(514) 526-4411
Emp Here 60   Sales 7,296,070
SIC 3399 Primary Metal products
Sec Tim Buckland
Dir Amanda Hawkins
Dir William Nickel

D-U-N-S 24-634-3669   (SL)
NOUVELLE TECHNOLOGIE (TEKNO) INC
2099 Boul Fernand-Lafontaine, Longueuil, QC, J4G 2J4
(514) 457-9991
Emp Here 50   Sales 6,566,463
SIC 4971 Irrigation systems
 Jean-Pierre Azzopardi

D-U-N-S 24-392-8590   (HQ)
PPG ARCHITECTURAL COATINGS CANADA INC
BETONEL MD
(Suby of PPG Industries, Inc.)
2025 Rue De La Metropole, Longueuil, QC, J4G 1S9
(514) 527-5111
Emp Here 150   Emp Total 47,000
Sales 259,521,210
SIC 2851 Paints and allied products
Pr David J. Cole
VP Vincent Rea

VP Claude Brosseau
Sec Claude St-Pierre
Dir Daniel Archambault
Dir Michael Mcgarry

D-U-N-S 20-201-5897   (HQ)
PRATT & WHITNEY CANADA CORP
P & WC
(Suby of Pratt Aero Limited Partnership)
1000 Boul Marie-Victorin, Longueuil, QC, J4G 1A1
(450) 677-9411
Emp Here 5,000   Emp Total 1
Sales 552,677,303
SIC 3519 Internal combustion engines, nec
Pr John Saabas
VP Maria Della Posta
VP Fin Nicolas Amyot
Sec Alain C. Rondeau
Genl Mgr Patrick Bertrand

D-U-N-S 20-574-0371   (BR)
QUINCAILLERIE RICHELIEU LTEE
ATTACHES RELIABLES, LES
800 Rue Beriault, Longueuil, QC, J4G 1R8
(514) 259-3737
Emp Here 80
SIC 5072 Hardware

D-U-N-S 24-370-4827   (BR)
QUINCAILLERIE RICHELIEU LTEE
ATTACHES RELIABLES, LES
800 Rue Beriault, Longueuil, QC, J4G 1R8
(450) 674-0888
Emp Here 60,514
SIC 5072 Hardware

D-U-N-S 20-518-1220   (HQ)
RESEAU DE TRANSPORT DE LONGUEUIL
SOCIETE DE TRANSPORT DE LONGUEUIL
(Suby of Reseau de Transport de Longueuil)
1150 Boul Marie-Victorin, Longueuil, QC, J4G 2M4
(450) 442-8600
Emp Here 500   Emp Total 1,000
Sales 48,531,840
SIC 4111 Local and suburban transit
Mng Dir Pierre Del Fante

D-U-N-S 25-733-7071   (BR)
SNC-LAVALIN INC
2271 Boul Fernand-Lafontaine, Longueuil, QC, J4G 2R7
(514) 393-1000
Emp Here 70
SIC 8748 Business consulting, nec

D-U-N-S 20-642-2813   (SL)
SERVICES DE PERSONNEL QUARTZ INC
476 Rue Jean-Neveu Bureau 201, Longueuil, QC, J4G 1N8
(450) 670-1118
Emp Here 50   Sales 4,331,255
SIC 7361 Employment agencies

D-U-N-S 20-278-9363   (BR)
UAP INC
TW DISTRIBUTION CENTRE
(Suby of Genuine Parts Company)
2500 Rue De La Metropole, Longueuil, QC, J4G 1E6
(514) 251-2348
Emp Here 30
SIC 5013 Motor vehicle supplies and new parts

D-U-N-S 25-391-9930   (BR)
UAP INC
UAP PIECES VEHICULES LOURDS, DIV
(Suby of Genuine Parts Company)
400 Rue Jean-Neveu, Longueuil, QC, J4G 1N8
(450) 463-2353
Emp Here 50
SIC 5013 Motor vehicle supplies and new parts

D-U-N-S 20-191-3378   (SL)

UNICEL ARCHITECTURAL CORP
2155 Boul Fernand-Lafontaine, Longueuil, QC, J4G 2J4
(450) 670-6844
Emp Here 50   Sales 4,377,642
SIC 3446 Architectural Metalwork

D-U-N-S 24-958-8583   (SL)
VENTILATION BELLE-RIVE INC
2001 Rue De La Metropole Bureau 712, Longueuil, QC, J4G 1S9
(450) 332-9832
Emp Here 20   Sales 301,686,000
SIC 1711 Plumbing, heating, air-conditioning
Pr Pr Andre Martineau
 Robert Dupont

D-U-N-S 25-357-0089   (BR)
WSP CANADA INC
GENIVAR
816 Boul Guimond, Longueuil, QC, J4G 1T5
(450) 448-5000
Emp Here 50
SIC 8711 Engineering services

D-U-N-S 20-182-6448   (HQ)
YVES ROCHER AMERIQUE DU NORD INC
EXPERTS DE LA COSMETIQUE VEGETALE, LES
2199 Boul Fernand-Lafontaine, Longueuil, QC, J4G 2V7
(450) 442-9555
Emp Here 40   Emp Total 2,000
Sales 56,306,315
SIC 5999 Miscellaneous retail stores, nec
 Jean-David Schwartz
Dir Chantal Lavallee

Longueuil, QC J4H

D-U-N-S 25-201-3016   (SL)
9003-7755 QUEBEC INC
HOLIDAY INN MONTREAL LONGUEUIL
900 Rue Saint-Charles E, Longueuil, QC, J4H 3Y2
(450) 646-8100
Emp Here 85   Sales 3,720,996
SIC 7011 Hotels and motels

D-U-N-S 25-392-9814   (HQ)
9152-2177 QUEBEC INC
(Suby of 9152-2177 Quebec Inc)
116 Rue Guilbault, Longueuil, QC, J4H 2T2
(450) 679-2300
Emp Here 46   Emp Total 60
Sales 4,428,946
SIC 8021 Offices and clinics of dentists

D-U-N-S 25-762-2993   (BR)
ABATTEURS JACQUES ELEMENT INC, LES
RESTAURANT MCDONALD'S
(Suby of Abatteurs Jacques Element Inc, Les)
650 Boul Roland-Therrien, Longueuil, QC, J4H 3V9
(450) 928-2761
Emp Here 50
SIC 5812 Eating places

D-U-N-S 24-390-5283   (SL)
AQUATECH SERVICES TECHNIQUES DES EAUX INC
IMS EXPERTS-CONSEILS INTERNATIONAL
101 Boul Roland-Therrien Bureau 110, Longueuil, QC, J4H 4B9
(450) 646-5270
Emp Here 20   Sales 3,429,153
SIC 4941 Water supply

D-U-N-S 25-065-3565   (BR)
ATLIFIC INC
HOLIDAY INN LONGUEUIL
(Suby of 3376290 Canada Inc)
900 Rue Saint-Charles E, Longueuil, QC, J4H

3Y2
(450) 646-8100
Emp Here 75
SIC 7011 Hotels and motels

D-U-N-S 24-475-6888　　(BR)
BANK OF MONTREAL
BMO
279 Rue Saint-Charles O, Longueuil, QC, J4H
1E4
(450) 463-5008
Emp Here 20
SIC 6021 National commercial banks

D-U-N-S 20-573-7492　　(BR)
BANQUE LAURENTIENNE DU CANADA
4 Rue Saint-Charles E, Longueuil, QC, J4H
1A9
(514) 284-7309
Emp Here 20
SIC 6021 National commercial banks

D-U-N-S 20-362-2998　　(HQ)
CAISSE DESJARDINS DU VIEUX-LONGUEUIL
CENTRE DE SERVICES MONTREAL-SUD
(*Suby of* Caisse Desjardins du Vieux-Longueuil)
1 Rue Saint-Charles O, Longueuil, QC, J4H
1C4
(450) 646-9311
Emp Here 20　　*Emp Total* 50
Sales 7,077,188
SIC 6062 State credit unions
Genl Mgr Sebastien Laliberte
Pr Pierre Tardif
VP Gilles Sicotte
Sec Jocelyne Pepin
Dir Olivier Audet
Dir Rene Beaudry
Dir Gilbert R. Bertin
Dir Andre Bruneau
Dir Jocelyn Cote

D-U-N-S 24-107-3154　　(BR)
CENTRE SPORTIF PALADIUM INC
PALADIUM
475 Boul Roland-Therrien, Longueuil, QC,
J4H 4A6
(450) 646-9995
Emp Here 90
SIC 7999 Amusement and recreation, nec

D-U-N-S 25-986-0229　　(HQ)
CENTRES DENTAIRES LAPOINTE INC
(*Suby of* 9152-2177 Quebec Inc)
116 Rue Guilbault, Longueuil, QC, J4H 2T2
(450) 679-2300
Emp Here 48　　*Emp Total* 60
Sales 10,944,105
SIC 8021 Offices and clinics of dentists
Pr Pr Larry Lapointe
　Yves Lapointe

D-U-N-S 20-712-2669　　(BR)
COMMISSION SCOLAIRE MARIE-VICTORIN
CENTRE D'EDUCATION DES ADULTES LEMOYNE D'IBERVILLE
560 Rue Le Moyne O, Longueuil, QC, J4H 1X3
(450) 670-3130
Emp Here 60
SIC 8211 Elementary and secondary schools

D-U-N-S 25-234-2100　　(BR)
COMMISSION SCOLAIRE MARIE-VICTORIN
ECOLE DE NORMANDIE
450 Rue De Normandie, Longueuil, QC, J4H
3P4
(450) 679-4650
Emp Here 30
SIC 8211 Elementary and secondary schools

D-U-N-S 24-895-6880　　(BR)
COMMISSION SCOLAIRE MARIE-VICTORIN

ECOLE SECONDAIRE JACQUES ROUSSEAU
444 Rue De Gentilly E, Longueuil, QC, J4H
3X7
(450) 651-6800
Emp Here 200
SIC 8211 Elementary and secondary schools

D-U-N-S 24-346-3127　　(BR)
CONSEIL DE VIE ETUDIANTE DE L'ECOLE NATIONALE AEROTECHNIQUE COLLEGE EDOUARD-MONTPETIT INC
CENTRE SPORTIF
(*Suby of* Conseil de Vie Etudiante de l'Ecole Nationale Aerotechnique College Edouard-Montpetit Inc)
260 Rue De Gentilly E, Longueuil, QC, J4H
4A4

Emp Here 40
SIC 7999 Amusement and recreation, nec

D-U-N-S 25-466-3123　　(SL)
EGLISE NOUVELLE VIE DE LONGUEUIL INC
200 Rue Du Parc-Industriel, Longueuil, QC,
J4H 3V6
(450) 646-2150
Emp Here 50　　*Sales* 3,283,232
SIC 8661 Religious organizations

D-U-N-S 20-920-0463　　(SL)
GROUPE SUTTON ACTUEL INC
115 Rue Saint-Charles O, Longueuil, QC, J4H
1C7
(450) 651-1079
Emp Here 45　　*Sales* 5,884,100
SIC 6531 Real estate agents and managers
Mgr Nicole Cyr

D-U-N-S 25-090-5122　　(BR)
HEROUX-DEVTEK INC
LANDING GEAR DIV
755 Rue Thurber, Longueuil, QC, J4H 3N2
(450) 679-5450
Emp Here 480
SIC 3728 Aircraft parts and equipment, nec

D-U-N-S 24-161-3897　　(BR)
IMVESCOR RESTAURANT GROUP INC
RESTAURANT ROTISSERIE SCORES
999 Ch De Chambly, Longueuil, QC, J4H 3Z8
(450) 677-7373
Emp Here 40
SIC 5812 Eating places

D-U-N-S 24-591-4747　　(SL)
LABORATOIRE DENTAIRE SUMMUM INC
LABORATOIRE DENTAIRE SUMMUM
116 Rue Guilbault, Longueuil, QC, J4H 2T2
(450) 679-5525
Emp Here 50　　*Sales* 2,918,428
SIC 8072 Dental laboratories

D-U-N-S 25-499-8842　　(SL)
PATISSERIE ROLLAND INC
170 Rue Saint-Charles O, Longueuil, QC, J4H
1C9
(450) 674-4450
Emp Here 80　　*Sales* 16,029,100
SIC 5149 Groceries and related products, nec
Pr Gerard Rolland
VP VP Luc Rolland

D-U-N-S 24-461-2438　　(SL)
RE/MAX LONGUEUIL INC
50 Rue Saint-Charles O Bureau 100,
Longueuil, QC, J4H 1C6
(450) 651-8331
Emp Here 51　　*Sales* 4,815,406
SIC 6531 Real estate agents and managers

D-U-N-S 25-243-4659　　(SL)
RESSOURCES NATURAL ALBERTON INC, LES
695 Rue Saint-Charles O Unite 13, Longueuil,
QC, J4H 1H2
(514) 631-3333
Emp Here 300　　*Sales* 49,767,120

SIC 5122 Drugs, proprietaries, and sundries
Pr Ginette St-Pierre

D-U-N-S 25-026-2821　　(BR)
ROYAL BANK OF CANADA
RBC
(*Suby of* Royal Bank Of Canada)
43 Rue Saint-Charles O Bureau 101,
Longueuil, QC, J4H 1C5
(450) 442-5611
Emp Here 22
SIC 6021 National commercial banks

D-U-N-S 24-502-2702　　(HQ)
SPB PSYCHOLOGIE ORGANISATIONELLE INC
SPB DIMENSIONS
555 Boul Roland-Therrien Bureau 300,
Longueuil, QC, J4H 4E7
(450) 646-1022
Emp Here 40　　*Emp Total* 52
Sales 2,261,782
SIC 8999 Services, nec

D-U-N-S 24-077-4419　　(BR)
SOCIETE DE GESTION COGIR S.E.N.C.
SOCIETE DE GESTION COGIR S.E.N.C.
70 Rue Levis, Longueuil, QC, J4H 4C2
(450) 442-4221
Emp Here 20
SIC 6513 Apartment building operators

Longueuil, QC J4J

D-U-N-S 25-463-2557　　(SL)
CENTRE DENTAIRE LA VALLEE & ASOCIES S.E.N.C.R.L.
2066 Ch De Chambly Bureau 300, Longueuil,
QC, J4J 3Y7
(450) 463-0050
Emp Here 50　　*Sales* 2,845,467
SIC 8021 Offices and clinics of dentists

D-U-N-S 24-116-0543　　(BR)
CENTRE DE SANTE ET DE SERVICES SOCIAUX PIERRE-BOUCHER
CENTRE D'INTERVENTION DE CRISE L'ACCES
90 Boul Sainte-Foy Bureau 200, Longueuil,
QC, J4J 1W4
(450) 679-8689
Emp Here 25
SIC 8322 Individual and family services

D-U-N-S 25-233-2044　　(BR)
COMMISSION SCOLAIRE MARIE-VICTORIN
ECOLE CARILLON
1360 Rue Laurier, Longueuil, QC, J4J 4H2
(450) 674-3210
Emp Here 42
SIC 8211 Elementary and secondary schools

D-U-N-S 25-233-1525　　(BR)
COMMISSION SCOLAIRE MARIE-VICTORIN
ECOLE STE-CLAIRE
805 Rue Gardenville, Longueuil, QC, J4J 3B3
(450) 670-0211
Emp Here 25
SIC 8211 Elementary and secondary schools

D-U-N-S 25-233-1608　　(BR)
COMMISSION SCOLAIRE MARIE-VICTORIN
ECOLE SECONDAIRE HELENE CHAMPLAIN
2115 Rue Gamache, Longueuil, QC, J4J 4A3
(450) 468-3604
Emp Here 26
SIC 8211 Elementary and secondary schools

D-U-N-S 25-233-1681　　(BR)
COMMISSION SCOLAIRE MARIE-VICTORIN

ECOLE PIERRE D'IBERVILLE
897 Rue Maple, Longueuil, QC, J4J 4N3
(450) 674-3285
Emp Here 45
SIC 8211 Elementary and secondary schools

D-U-N-S 20-712-2644　　(BR)
COMMISSION SCOLAIRE MARIE-VICTORIN
ECOLE DES PETITS EXPLORATEURS
1711 Rue Bourassa, Longueuil, QC, J4J 3A5
(450) 616-8035
Emp Here 50
SIC 8211 Elementary and secondary schools

D-U-N-S 25-627-7096　　(BR)
PHARMACIE CHARLES RIVEST INC
PHARMA AMP INC
1748 Ch De Chambly, Longueuil, QC, J4J 3X5
(450) 651-2000
Emp Here 40
SIC 5912 Drug stores and proprietary stores

D-U-N-S 25-299-9677　　(BR)
PRISZM LP
PFK
140 Boul Sainte-Foy, Longueuil, QC, J4J 1W6

Emp Here 20
SIC 5812 Eating places

D-U-N-S 25-300-6225　　(BR)
REDBERRY FRANCHISING CORP
BURGER KING
1395 Ch De Chambly, Longueuil, QC, J4J 5C6

Emp Here 20
SIC 5812 Eating places

D-U-N-S 25-233-5559　　(BR)
RIVERSIDE SCHOOL BOARD
ST. MARY'S ELEMENTARY SCHOOL
1863 Rue Brebeuf, Longueuil, QC, J4J 3P3
(450) 674-0851
Emp Here 55
SIC 8211 Elementary and secondary schools

D-U-N-S 25-610-3649　　(BR)
ROYAL BANK OF CANADA
RBC
(*Suby of* Royal Bank Of Canada)
2068 Ch De Chambly, Longueuil, QC, J4J 3Y7
(450) 442-5570
Emp Here 23
SIC 6021 National commercial banks

D-U-N-S 24-353-5775　　(BR)
SERVICE CORPORATION INTERNATIONAL (CANADA) LIMITED
MAISON DARCHE SERVICES FUNERAIRES, LA
505 Boul Cure-Poirier O, Longueuil, QC, J4J
2H5
(450) 463-1900
Emp Here 20
SIC 7261 Funeral service and crematories

D-U-N-S 25-308-8801　　(BR)
SOCIETE DES ALCOOLS DU QUEBEC
SOCIETE DES ALCOOLS DU QUEBEC
1611 Boul Roland-Therrien, Longueuil, QC,
J4J 5C5
(450) 468-3811
Emp Here 40
SIC 5921 Liquor stores

D-U-N-S 25-978-8792　　(SL)
SOGEP INC
SOGEP
1895 Rue Adoncour, Longueuil, QC, J4J 5G8
(450) 468-7640
Emp Here 50　　*Sales* 7,435,520
SIC 8741 Management services
Pr Pr Richard Gareau
VP VP Mario Trudeau

D-U-N-S 25-174-4041　　(BR)
VALUE VILLAGE STORES, INC

VILLAGE DES VALEURS
(Suby of Savers, Inc.)
1401 Ch De Chambly Bureau 31a, Longueuil,
QC, J4J 3X6
(450) 677-1677
Emp Here 35
SIC 5399 Miscellaneous general merchandise

Longueuil, QC J4K

D-U-N-S 25-307-2987   (BR)
123273 CANADA INC
PHARMACIE JEAN COUTU #42
832 Rue Saint-Laurent O, Longueuil, QC, J4K
1C3
(450) 677-6311
Emp Here 40
SIC 5912 Drug stores and proprietary stores

D-U-N-S 24-688-6001   (BR)
4010205 CANADA INC
ISCANCO
1010 Rue De Serigny, Longueuil, QC, J4K
5G7
(450) 651-3702
Emp Here 50
SIC 6531 Real estate agents and managers

D-U-N-S 20-882-8343   (SL)
**AGENCE DE LA SANTE ET DES SERVICES
SOCIAUX DE LA MONTEREGIE, L'**
1255 Rue Beauregard, Longueuil, QC, J4K
2M3
(450) 679-6772
Emp Here 600   Sales 27,610,240
SIC 8399 Social services, nec
Pr Pr Richard Deschenes

D-U-N-S 20-514-6355   (BR)
CRDITED MONTEREGIE EST
(Suby of CRDITED Monteregie Est)
1219 Rue Maisonneuve, Longueuil, QC, J4K
2S7
(450) 670-3965
Emp Here 50
SIC 8322 Individual and family services

D-U-N-S 24-180-1661   (HQ)
CRDITED MONTEREGIE EST
(Suby of CRDITED Monteregie Est)
1255 Rue Beauregard Bureau 2201,
Longueuil, QC, J4K 2M3
(450) 679-6511
Emp Here 67   Emp Total 850
Sales 40,048,983
SIC 8361 Residential care
Genl Mgr Joanne Gauthier
Dir Fin Eric Methot

D-U-N-S 24-811-0629   (SL)
CENTRE BUTTERS-SAVOY ET HORIZON
1255 Rue Beauregard Bureau 2201,
Longueuil, QC, J4K 2M3
(450) 679-6511
Emp Here 800   Sales 40,192,000
SIC 8361 Residential care
Pr Michel Patenaude
VP Lauren Zakaib
VP Lucille Bargiel
Genl Mgr Jean-Pierre Hotte

D-U-N-S 20-281-6596   (HQ)
**CENTRE DE LA PETITE ENFANCE PIER-
ROT LA LUNE INC**
(Suby of Centre de la Petite Enfance Pierrot la
Lune Inc)
1080 Boul Sainte-Foy, Longueuil, QC, J4K
1W6
(450) 670-2336
Emp Here 50   Emp Total 57
Sales 1,751,057
SIC 8351 Child day care services

D-U-N-S 25-232-9990   (BR)
COLLEGE   CHARLES-LEMOYNE   DE

LONGUEUIL INC
COLLEGE   CHARLES-LEMOYNE   DE
LONGUEUIL INC
1430 Rue Patenaude, Longueuil, QC, J4K
5H4
(450) 463-1592
Emp Here 230
SIC 8211 Elementary and secondary schools

D-U-N-S 24-763-6459   (BR)
COLLEGE FRANCAIS (1965) INC
(Suby of College Francais (1965) Inc)
1340 Boul Nobert, Longueuil, QC, J4K 2P4
(450) 679-0770
Emp Here 60
SIC 8222 Junior colleges

D-U-N-S 25-233-0311   (BR)
COLLEGE FRANCAIS (1965) INC
COLLEGE FRANCAIS ANNEXE RIVE SUD
PRIMAIRE
(Suby of College Francais (1965) Inc)
1391 Rue Beauregard, Longueuil, QC, J4K
2M3
(450) 670-7391
Emp Here 150
SIC 8211 Elementary and secondary schools

D-U-N-S 24-069-4872   (BR)
**COMMISSION   SCOLAIRE   MARIE-
VICTORIN**
ECOLE JACQUES OUELLETTE
1240 Boul Nobert, Longueuil, QC, J4K 2P4
(450) 670-2951
Emp Here 68
SIC 8211 Elementary and secondary schools

D-U-N-S 25-233-1442   (BR)
**COMMISSION   SCOLAIRE   MARIE-
VICTORIN**
ECOLE ST JUDE
653 Rue Prefontaine, Longueuil, QC, J4K 3V8
(450) 670-7581
Emp Here 70
SIC 8211 Elementary and secondary schools

D-U-N-S 25-233-1483   (BR)
**COMMISSION   SCOLAIRE   MARIE-
VICTORIN**
ECOLE   SECONDAIRE   SAINT-JEAN-
BAPTISTE
700 Rue Duvernay, Longueuil, QC, J4K 4L1
(450) 679-3990
Emp Here 30
SIC 8211 Elementary and secondary schools

D-U-N-S 25-233-1889   (BR)
**COMMISSION   SCOLAIRE   MARIE-
VICTORIN**
ECOLE HUBERT PERRON
1100 Rue Beauregard, Longueuil, QC, J4K
2L1
(450) 674-7784
Emp Here 50
SIC 8211 Elementary and secondary schools

D-U-N-S 25-233-1723   (BR)
**COMMISSION   SCOLAIRE   MARIE-
VICTORIN**
ECOLE PAUL DE MARICOURT
1275 Rue Papineau, Longueuil, QC, J4K 3K9
(450) 674-1753
Emp Here 25
SIC 8211 Elementary and secondary schools

D-U-N-S 20-712-2685   (BR)
**COMMISSION   SCOLAIRE   MARIE-
VICTORIN**
ECOLE PRIMAIRES FELIX-LECLERC
1450 Rue De Wagram, Longueuil, QC, J4K
1G1
(450) 651-7768
Emp Here 50
SIC 8211 Elementary and secondary schools

D-U-N-S 20-573-3343   (BR)
**COMPAGNIE DES CHEMINS DE FER NA-
TIONAUX DU CANADA**

COMPAGNIE DES CHEMINS DE FER NA-
TIONAUX DU CANADA
1510 Boul Jacques-Cartier O, Longueuil, QC,
J4K 5K8
(450) 923-4893
Emp Here 50
SIC 4011 Railroads, line-haul operating

D-U-N-S 24-681-7733   (BR)
EQUIPE PCJ INC
MCDONALD'S
(Suby of Equipe PCJ Inc)
822 Rue Saint-Laurent O, Longueuil, QC, J4K
1C3
(450) 651-1154
Emp Here 200
SIC 5812 Eating places

D-U-N-S 24-425-9573   (SL)
FORUM DES COURTIERS INC, LE
ACTIFAX
1111 Rue Saint-Charles O, Longueuil, QC,
J4K 5G4
(450) 449-8713
Emp Here 30   Sales 2,512,128
SIC 4813 Telephone communication, except
radio

D-U-N-S 20-555-5837   (BR)
**GOUVERNEMENT DE LA PROVINCE DE
QUEBEC**
GOUVERNEMENT DE LA PROVINCE DE
QUEBEC
1255 Rue Beauregard, Longueuil, QC, J4K
2M3
(450) 928-6777
Emp Here 460
SIC 8399 Social services, nec

D-U-N-S 24-872-1409   (SL)
INNERGEX INC
1225 Rue Saint-Charles O10e Etage,
Longueuil, QC, J4K 0B9
(450) 928-2550
Emp Here 150   Sales 33,051,197
SIC 4931 Electric and other services com-
bined
Pr Pr Michel Letellier
Dir Jean Perron

D-U-N-S 24-861-1147   (SL)
**JACQUES CARTIER AND CHAMPLAIN
BRIDGES INCORPORATED, THE**
1225 Rue Saint-Charles O 5e Etage,
Longueuil, QC, J4K 0B9
(450) 651-8771
Emp Here 44   Sales 16,270,236
SIC 1622 Bridge, tunnel, and elevated high-
way construction
Pr Pr Michel Fournier
Sec Sylvie Lefebvre

D-U-N-S 20-504-3029   (HQ)
LOCATION RADIO TAXI UNION LTEE
(Suby of Location Radio Taxi Union Ltee)
1605 Rue Vercheres, Longueuil, QC, J4K 2Z6
(450) 679-6262
Emp Here 103   Emp Total 109
Sales 3,283,232
SIC 4121 Taxicabs

D-U-N-S 24-973-9335   (BR)
LONDON LIFE INSURANCE COMPANY
FINANCIERE LIBERTE 55
1111 Rue Saint-Charles O Unite 950,
Longueuil, QC, J4K 5G4
(450) 928-1321
Emp Here 65
SIC 6311 Life insurance

D-U-N-S 20-319-9781   (SL)
MAVENIR SYSTEMS NORTH AMERICA LTD
1111 Rue Saint-Charles O Bureau 850,
Longueuil, QC, J4K 5G4
(877) 248-7103
Emp Here 25   Sales 1,896,978
SIC 7371 Custom computer programming ser-
vices

D-U-N-S 20-703-9582   (BR)
**NORTHLAND PROPERTIES CORPORA-
TION**
SANDMAN   HOTEL   MONTREAL   -
LONGUEUIL
(Suby of Northland Properties Corporation)
999 Rue De Serigny, Longueuil, QC, J4K 2T1
(450) 670-3030
Emp Here 50
SIC 7011 Hotels and motels

D-U-N-S 24-562-7393   (SL)
PERM-A-TEM INC
45 Place Charles-Le Moyne Bureau 100,
Longueuil, QC, J4K 5G5

Emp Here 50   Sales 3,648,035
SIC 7361 Employment agencies

D-U-N-S 24-330-1020   (BR)
POMERLEAU INC
1111 Rue Saint-Charles O Bureau 4,
Longueuil, QC, J4K 5G4

Emp Here 50
SIC 1541 Industrial buildings and warehouses

D-U-N-S 20-795-6157   (SL)
REGIE DU BATIMENT DU QUEBEC
201 Place Charles-Le Moyne Bureau 310,
Longueuil, QC, J4K 2T5
(450) 928-7603
Emp Here 50   Sales 2,626,585
SIC 7389 Business services, nec

D-U-N-S 25-610-3821   (BR)
RESTAURANTS T.S.N.A. INC
MCDONALD'S
100 Place Charles-Le Moyne Bureau 109,
Longueuil, QC, J4K 2T4
(450) 442-2295
Emp Here 52
SIC 5812 Eating places

D-U-N-S 25-368-6695   (BR)
**SISCA SOLUTIONS D'AFFAIRES CANADA
INC**
IMPRIMERIE SISCA INTERNATIONAL
1219 Rue Maisonneuve, Longueuil, QC, J4K
2S7
(450) 670-0000
Emp Here 30
SIC 2752 Commercial printing, lithographic

D-U-N-S 24-369-5454   (SL)
SOCIETE D'INVESTISSEMENT M-S, S.E.C.
GLOBAL-VINS & SPIRITUEUX
1010 Rue De Serigny Bureau 800, Longueuil,
QC, J4K 5G7

Emp Here 300   Sales 57,575,040
SIC 7371 Custom computer programming ser-
vices
Fin Ex Jean-Michel Stam
Pr Robert Bonneau

D-U-N-S 20-087-0157   (BR)
SOCIETE DE GESTION COGIR S.E.N.C.
SOCIETE DE GESTION COGIR S.E.N.C.
100 Boul La Fayette Unite 426, Longueuil, QC,
J4K 5H6
(450) 674-8111
Emp Here 100
SIC 6513 Apartment building operators

D-U-N-S 24-725-4501   (HQ)
STORNOWAY DIAMOND CORPORATION
SOCIETE DE DIAMANT STORNOWAY
(Suby of Stornoway Diamond Corporation)
111 Rue Saint-Charles O Bureau 400,
Longueuil, QC, J4K 5G4
(450) 616-5555
Emp Here 25   Emp Total 75
Sales 4,450,603
SIC 1499 Miscellaneous nonMetallic minerals,
except fuels

D-U-N-S 25-366-2498   (BR)

TECHNOLOGIES INTERACTIVES MEDIA-GRIF INC
1010 Rue De Serigny Bureau 800, Longueuil, QC, J4K 5G7
(450) 449-0102
Emp Here 20
SIC 7372 Prepackaged software

D-U-N-S 20-705-8855   (BR)
THOMSON TREMBLAY INC
(*Suby of* R.G.F.M. Bertucci Management Corp Inc)
101 Place Charles-Le Moyne Bureau 206, Longueuil, QC, J4K 4Z1
(450) 677-9979
Emp Here 40
SIC 7361 Employment agencies

D-U-N-S 25-623-2984   (BR)
UNIPRIX INC
PHARMACIE UNIPRIX
825 Rue Saint-Laurent O, Longueuil, QC, J4K 2V1
(450) 677-2876
Emp Here 23
SIC 5912 Drug stores and proprietary stores

D-U-N-S 24-345-0793   (BR)
UNIVERSITE DE SHERBROOKE
CAMPUS LONGUEUIL
150 Place Charles-Le Moyne Bureau 200, Longueuil, QC, J4K 0A8
(450) 463-1835
Emp Here 150
SIC 8221 Colleges and universities

Longueuil, QC J4L

D-U-N-S 25-611-1691   (SL)
3116506 CANADA INC
BOULANGERIE PREMIERE MOISSON
2479 Ch De Chambly, Longueuil, QC, J4L 1M2
(450) 468-4406
Emp Here 72   *Sales* 2,480,664
SIC 5461 Retail bakeries

D-U-N-S 20-589-4707   (BR)
BANQUE TORONTO-DOMINION, LA
TD CANADA TRUST
(*Suby of* Toronto-Dominion Bank, The)
2665 Ch De Chambly, Longueuil, QC, J4L 1M3
(450) 647-5243
Emp Here 20
SIC 6021 National commercial banks

D-U-N-S 25-233-2085   (BR)
COMMISSION SCOLAIRE MARIE-VICTORIN
ECOLE CHRIST-ROI
3000 Rue Dumont, Longueuil, QC, J4L 3S9
(450) 674-7062
Emp Here 40
SIC 8211 Elementary and secondary schools

D-U-N-S 25-234-2183   (BR)
COMMISSION SCOLAIRE MARIE-VICTORIN
ECOLE GEORGE ETIENNE CARTIER
3455 Rue Soissons, Longueuil, QC, J4L 3M5
(450) 463-1406
Emp Here 30
SIC 8211 Elementary and secondary schools

D-U-N-S 25-222-6204   (BR)
COMMISSION SCOLAIRE MARIE-VICTORIN
ECOLE PRIMAIRE DU TOURNESOL
2515 Rue De Boulogne, Longueuil, QC, J4L 4A3
(450) 674-9145
Emp Here 40
SIC 8211 Elementary and secondary schools

D-U-N-S 25-233-2002   (BR)
COMMISSION SCOLAIRE MARIE-VICTORIN
ECOLE ADRIEN GAMACHE
2375 Rue Lavallee, Longueuil, QC, J4L 1R5
(450) 468-3402
Emp Here 35
SIC 8211 Elementary and secondary schools

D-U-N-S 25-233-1848   (BR)
COMMISSION SCOLAIRE MARIE-VICTORIN
ECOLE LIONEL GROULX
2725 Rue Plessis, Longueuil, QC, J4L 1S3
(450) 651-6104
Emp Here 45
SIC 8211 Elementary and secondary schools

D-U-N-S 24-509-1681   (BR)
METRO RICHELIEU INC
SUPER C, DIV DE
2901 Ch De Chambly, Longueuil, QC, J4L 1M7
(450) 651-6886
Emp Here 125
SIC 5411 Grocery stores

D-U-N-S 24-208-7455   (BR)
PROVIGO DISTRIBUTION INC
MAXI & COMPAGNIE
2655 Ch De Chambly, Longueuil, QC, J4L 1M3
(450) 448-5771
Emp Here 20
SIC 5411 Grocery stores

D-U-N-S 20-058-0301   (BR)
PROVIGO DISTRIBUTION INC
CLUB ENTREPOT PROVIGO
3708 Ch De Chambly, Longueuil, QC, J4L 1N8
(450) 679-5952
Emp Here 45
SIC 5141 Groceries, general line

D-U-N-S 20-720-6108   (BR)
RESTAURANTS T.S.N.A. INC
RESTAURANT MCDONALD
2689 Ch De Chambly, Longueuil, QC, J4L 1M3

Emp Here 50
SIC 5812 Eating places

D-U-N-S 25-498-9718   (BR)
STAPLES CANADA INC
BUREAU EN GROS
(*Suby of* Staples, Inc.)
2790 De Chambly Ch, Longueuil, QC, J4L 1M9
(450) 670-1698
Emp Here 40
SIC 5943 Stationery stores

Longueuil, QC J4M

D-U-N-S 20-033-9344   (BR)
COMMISSION SCOLAIRE MARIE-VICTORIN
ECOLE GENTILLY BOISE DES LUTINS
1280 Rue Beauharnois, Longueuil, QC, J4M 1C2
(450) 468-1267
Emp Here 50
SIC 8211 Elementary and secondary schools

D-U-N-S 24-808-0017   (BR)
UNIPRIX INC
PHARMACIE UNIPRIX
1615 Boul Jacques-Cartier E Bureau 120, Longueuil, QC, J4M 2X1
(450) 468-5040
Emp Here 51
SIC 5912 Drug stores and proprietary stores

Longueuil, QC J4N

D-U-N-S 24-167-7160   (BR)
ARCELORMITTAL PRODUITS LONGS CANADA S.E.N.C.
MITTAL CANADA
2555 Ch Du Lac, Longueuil, QC, J4N 1C1
(450) 442-7700
Emp Here 150
SIC 3316 Cold finishing of steel shapes

D-U-N-S 25-750-3607   (BR)
BANK OF NOVA SCOTIA, THE
SCOTIABANK
2235 Boul Roland-Therrien, Longueuil, QC, J4N 1P2
(450) 647-4770
Emp Here 25
SIC 6021 National commercial banks

D-U-N-S 24-103-7972   (HQ)
BOULANGERIES WESTON QUEBEC LIMITEE
2700 Boul Jacques-Cartier E, Longueuil, QC, J4N 1L5
(450) 448-7246
Emp Here 245   *Emp Total* 138,000
Sales 15,592,518
SIC 2051 Bread, cake, and related products
Pr Pr Ralph Robinson
VP VP Geoffrey H. Wilson
Sec Robert A. Balcon
Dir Brian Bidulka
Dir Darryl Rowe

D-U-N-S 20-293-7285   (BR)
CANADIAN TIRE REAL ESTATE LIMITED
INVESTISSEMENTS RAYMOND GAGNE, LES
2211 Boul Roland-Therrien Bureau 256, Longueuil, QC, J4N 1P2
(450) 448-1177
Emp Here 150
SIC 6531 Real estate agents and managers

D-U-N-S 24-828-0161   (BR)
CARA OPERATIONS LIMITED
HARVEY'S
(*Suby of* Cara Holdings Limited)
1165 Ch Du Tremblay, Longueuil, QC, J4N 1R4
(450) 647-6000
Emp Here 20
SIC 5812 Eating places

D-U-N-S 25-233-4859   (SL)
CENTRE DE FORMATION PROFESSIONNELLE PIERRE DUPUY
1150 Ch Du Tremblay, Longueuil, QC, J4N 1A2
(450) 468-4000
Emp Here 300   *Sales* 26,994,000
SIC 8211 Elementary and secondary schools
Genl Mgr Michel Lapierre
Richard Charest

D-U-N-S 25-233-1640   (BR)
COMMISSION SCOLAIRE MARIE-VICTORIN
ECOLE BEL ESSOR
1250 Ch Du Tremblay, Longueuil, QC, J4N 1A2
(450) 468-0833
Emp Here 80
SIC 8211 Elementary and secondary schools

D-U-N-S 25-233-0634   (BR)
COMMISSION SCOLAIRE MARIE-VICTORIN
ECOLE ST ROMAIN
1995 Rue Bedard, Longueuil, QC, J4N 1B4
(450) 468-1226
Emp Here 25
SIC 8211 Elementary and secondary schools

D-U-N-S 20-228-5300   (SL)

ENTREPRISES NORD CONSTRUCTION (1962) INC, LES
2604 Ch Du Lac, Longueuil, QC, J4N 1B8
(450) 670-2330
Emp Here 45   *Sales* 7,234,560
SIC 1611 Highway and street construction
Dir Roberto Alacchi
Pr Pr Vincent Alacchi

D-U-N-S 24-226-5317   (BR)
FLYING J CANADA INC
SHELL
2801 Boul Jacques-Cartier E, Longueuil, QC, J4N 1L8

Emp Here 30
SIC 5541 Gasoline service stations

D-U-N-S 20-121-0767   (SL)
GESTION ANDRE LEROUX INC
1992 Rue Jean-Paul-Riopelle, Longueuil, QC, J4N 1P6
(450) 448-6798
Emp Here 153   *Sales* 34,797,350
SIC 6712 Bank holding companies
Pr Pr Andre Leroux

D-U-N-S 24-353-1600   (BR)
IMPERIAL MANUFACTURING GROUP INC
IMPERIAL BOFLEX
2600 Boul Jacques-Cartier E, Longueuil, QC, J4N 1P8
(450) 651-3539
Emp Here 30
SIC 3444 Sheet Metalwork

D-U-N-S 20-572-0761   (BR)
METRO RICHELIEU INC
SUPER C
Super C, Longueuil, QC, J4N 1P4
(450) 448-8229
Emp Here 70
SIC 5411 Grocery stores

D-U-N-S 25-027-3349   (BR)
PROVIGO DISTRIBUTION INC
PROVIGO LE MARCHE LONGUEUIL
1150 Rue King-George, Longueuil, QC, J4N 1P3
(450) 647-1717
Emp Here 120
SIC 5411 Grocery stores

D-U-N-S 24-198-4876   (BR)
ROTISSERIES ST-HUBERT LTEE, LES
(*Suby of* Cara Holdings Limited)
1901 Boul Roland-Therrien, Longueuil, QC, J4N 1A3
(450) 448-4748
Emp Here 52
SIC 5812 Eating places

D-U-N-S 20-798-2898   (SL)
SERVIR + SOINS ET SOUTIEN A DOMICILE INC
1887 Ch Du Tremblay Bureau 200, Longueuil, QC, J4N 1A4

Emp Here 100   *Sales* 25,227,120
SIC 8099 Health and allied services, nec
Pr Normand Laurin

D-U-N-S 24-066-9122   (BR)
SOCIETE EN COMMANDITE LES PROMENADES DU PARC
SOCIETE EN COMMANDITE LES PROMENADES DU PARC
1910 Rue Adoncour Bureau 500, Longueuil, QC, J4N 1T3
(450) 448-3448
Emp Here 100
SIC 3993 Signs and advertising specialties

D-U-N-S 25-411-1495   (HQ)
WM QUEBEC INC
WASTE MANAGEMENT
(*Suby of* Waste Management, Inc.)
2457 Ch Du Lac, Longueuil, QC, J4N 1P1

---

(450) 646-7870
Emp Here 50   *Emp Total* 41,350
Sales 32,832,315
SIC 4953 Refuse systems
Pr Pr Kevin Cinq-Mars
VP VP Don Wright

D-U-N-S 20-914-0651   (BR)
WSP CANADA INC
GENIVAR
2405 Boul Fernand-Lafontaine Bureau 101,
Longueuil, QC, J4N 1N7
(450) 679-7220
Emp Here 45
SIC 8711 Engineering services

D-U-N-S 25-294-7536   (BR)
WAL-MART CANADA CORP
1999 Boul Roland-Therrien, Longueuil, QC,
J4N 1A3
(450) 448-2688
Emp Here 300
SIC 5311 Department stores

D-U-N-S 24-104-6072   (BR)
WESTON BAKERIES LIMITED
READY BAKE
2700 Boul Jacques-Cartier E Bureau 67,
Longueuil, QC, J4N 1L5
(450) 448-7259
Emp Here 325
SIC 2051 Bread, cake, and related products

Longueuil, QC J4P

D-U-N-S 25-752-5097   (BR)
**COLLEGE   CHARLES-LEMOYNE   DE
LONGUEUIL INC**
*COLLEGE   CHARLES-LEMOYNE   DE
LONGUEUIL INC*
905 Ch Tiffin, Longueuil, QC, J4P 3G6
(450) 670-1157
Emp Here 40
SIC 8221 Colleges and universities

Lorraine, QC J6Z

D-U-N-S 25-233-4297   (BR)
**COMMISSION   SCOLAIRE   DE   LA
SEIGNEURIE-DES-MILLE-ILES**
*COMMISSION   SCOLAIRE   DE   LA
SEIGNEURIE-DES-MILLE-ILES*
(*Suby of* Commission Scolaire de la
Seigneurie-des-Mille-Iles)
59 Boul De Vignory, Lorraine, QC, J6Z 3L5
(450) 621-2500
Emp Here 50
SIC 8211 Elementary and secondary schools

D-U-N-S 25-027-3844   (BR)
PROVIGO DISTRIBUTION INC
PROVIGO LORRAINE
95 Boul De Gaulle, Lorraine, QC, J6Z 3R8
(450) 621-1115
Emp Here 60
SIC 5141 Groceries, general line

Lorrainville, QC J0Z
Temiscaninque County

D-U-N-S 25-379-6783   (HQ)
**CAISSE DESJARDINS DE BEARN-FABRE-
LORRAINVILLE**
CENTRE DE SERVICES DE BEARN
(*Suby of* Caisse Desjardins De Bearn-Fabre-
Lorrainville)
1 Rue Notre-Dame O, Lorrainville, QC, J0Z
2R0

Emp Here 31   *Emp Total* 40
Sales 7,350,166
SIC 6062 State credit unions
Genl Mgr Marcelin Grenier
Pr Monique Rivest
VP VP Marie-Paule Vezina
Sec Jacques Chabot
Dir Denis Drouin
Dir France Lavergne
Dir Myriam Therrien
Dir Claudette Lapierre
Dir Karine Neveu

D-U-N-S 25-240-2896   (BR)
**COMMISSION   SCOLAIRE   DU   LAC-
TEMISCAMINGUE**
ECOLE MARCEL RAYMOND
(*Suby of* Commission Scolaire du Lac-
Temiscamingue)
45 Rue Notre-Dame E, Lorrainville, QC, J0Z
2R0
(819) 625-2444
Emp Here 50
SIC 8211 Elementary and secondary schools

Lots-Renverses, QC G0L
Temiscouata County

D-U-N-S 20-254-3815   (SL)
BEGIN & BEGIN INCORPOREE
76 295 Rte, Lots-Renverses, QC, G0L 1V0
(418) 899-6786
Emp Here 60   *Sales* 9,244,160
SIC 2426 Hardwood dimension and flooring
mills
Pr Pr Gilles Begin
VP VP Reginald Tremblay
VP Gervais Bourque
  Daniel Fauteux

Louiseville, QC J5V
Maskinonge County

D-U-N-S 24-933-5845   (SL)
120776 CANADA INC
700 Rue Canadel, Louiseville, QC, J5V 3A4
(819) 228-8471
Emp Here 950   *Sales* 239,929,250
SIC 6712 Bank holding companies
Pr Pr Guy Deveault

D-U-N-S 24-421-3216   (SL)
9107-7081 QUEBEC INC
351 Rue Notre-Dame N, Louiseville, QC, J5V
1X9
(819) 228-9497
Emp Here 75   *Sales* 14,569,600
SIC 6712 Bank holding companies
  Monia Lacasse

D-U-N-S 20-795-7759   (HQ)
**CAISSE DESJARDINS DE L'OUEST DE LA
MAURICIE**
CENTRE DE SERVICES SAINT-BARNABE
(*Suby of* Caisse Desjardins de l'Ouest de la
Mauricie)
75 Av Saint-Laurent Bureau 300, Louiseville,
QC, J5V 1J6
(819) 228-9422
Emp Here 140   *Emp Total* 140
Sales 17,094,675
SIC 6062 State credit unions
Genl Mgr Jacques Duranleau
Pr Luc Pombert
VP Johanne Beaulieu Sylvestre
VP Annie Plante
VP Rene J. Lemire
Sec Jean Boisvert
Dir Karine Arseneault
Dir Monique Bellemare

Dir Jules Berneche
Dir Michel Bournival

D-U-N-S 24-314-7498   (BR)
CANADEL INC
700 Rue Canadel, Louiseville, QC, J5V 3A4
(819) 228-8471
Emp Here 500
SIC 2511 Wood household furniture

D-U-N-S 20-206-6304   (SL)
CARON & GAGNON LTEE
RONA
171 Av Dalcourt, Louiseville, QC, J5V 1A6

Emp Here 20   *Sales* 5,595,120
SIC 5039 Construction materials, nec
Pr Pr Raymond Gagnon
VP VP Alain Gagnon
  Guylaine Gagnon

D-U-N-S 20-034-1605   (BR)
**COMMISSION SCOLAIRE DU CHEMIN-DU-
ROY**
ECOLE JEAN XXIIII
50 Av Saint-Jacques, Louiseville, QC, J5V
1C2
(819) 840-4327
Emp Here 30
SIC 8211 Elementary and secondary schools

D-U-N-S 25-232-7416   (BR)
**COMMISSION SCOLAIRE DU CHEMIN-DU-
ROY**
PAVILLON ST LOUIS
60 Av Saint-Jacques, Louiseville, QC, J5V
1C2
(819) 840-4325
Emp Here 55
SIC 8211 Elementary and secondary schools

D-U-N-S 24-120-7930   (BR)
**GOUVERNEMENT DE LA PROVINCE DE
QUEBEC**
RESIDENCE AVELLIN DALCOURT
450 2e Rue, Louiseville, QC, J5V 1V3
(819) 228-2700
Emp Here 300
SIC 8361 Residential care

D-U-N-S 24-337-3664   (BR)
**IMPRIMERIES TRANSCONTINENTAL 2005
S.E.N.C**
TRANSCONTINENTAL GAGNE
750 Rue Deveault, Louiseville, QC, J5V 3C2
(819) 228-2766
Emp Here 325
SIC 7389 Business services, nec

D-U-N-S 24-664-2102   (BR)
MARQUIS IMPRIMEUR INC
MARQUIS GAGNE
750 Rue Deveault, Louiseville, QC, J5V 3C2
(819) 228-2766
Emp Here 100
SIC 2732 Book printing

D-U-N-S 20-795-4665   (BR)
PROVIGO DISTRIBUTION INC
MAXXI
550 Boul Saint-Laurent E, Louiseville, QC, J5V
2R5
(819) 228-2715
Emp Here 20
SIC 5411 Grocery stores

Lourdes-De-Blanc-Sablon, QC G0G
Saguenay County

D-U-N-S 25-240-0098   (BR)
COMMISSION SCOLAIRE DU LITTORAL
ECOLE MGR SCHEFFER
(*Suby of* Commission Scolaire du Littoral)
20 Rue Mgr Scheffer, Lourdes-De-Blanc-
Sablon, QC, G0G 1W0

---

(418) 461-2030
Emp Here 30
SIC 8211 Elementary and secondary schools

Lourdes-De-Joliette, QC J0K
Joliette County

D-U-N-S 20-712-1950   (BR)
COMMISSION SCOLAIRE DES SAMARES
ECOLE STE BERNADETTE
3961 Rue Principale, Lourdes-De-Joliette,
QC, J0K 1K0
(450) 758-3576
Emp Here 20
SIC 8211 Elementary and secondary schools

Low, QC J0X
Gatineau County

D-U-N-S 24-204-9000   (BR)
**COMPAGNIE   COMMONWEALTH   PLY-
WOOD LTEE, LA**
ENTREPRISES ATLAS
325 105 Rte, Low, QC, J0X 2C0
(819) 422-3572
Emp Here 65
SIC 2421 Sawmills and planing mills, general

Lyster, QC G0S
Megantic County

D-U-N-S 20-024-0567   (BR)
**CENTRE   LOCAL   DES   SERVICES
COMMUNAUTAIRES-CTRE   D'HEBERG.
DE SOINS DE LONGUE DUREE DE L'ER**
FOYER DE LYSTER
(*Suby of* Centre Local des Services
Communautaires-Ctre d'Heberg. de Soins de
Longue Duree de l'Er)
2180 Rue Becancour, Lyster, QC, G0S 1V0
(819) 389-5437
Emp Here 30
SIC 8361 Residential care

D-U-N-S 25-232-9214   (BR)
**COMMISSION SCOLAIRE DES BOIS-
FRANCS**
ECOLE BON PASTEUR
(*Suby of* Commission Scolaire des Bois-
Francs)
3345 Rue King, Lyster, QC, G0S 1V0
(819) 389-5437
Emp Here 20
SIC 8351 Child day care services

Macamic, QC J0Z
Abitibi County

D-U-N-S 24-021-7646   (BR)
COMMISSION SCOLAIRE ABITIBI
*ECOLE DU ROYAL ROUSSILLON PAVILLON
TREMBLAY*
(*Suby of* Commission Scolaire Abitibi)
16 8e Av O, Macamic, QC, J0Z 2S0
(819) 782-4455
Emp Here 55
SIC 8211 Elementary and secondary schools

Magog, QC J1X
Stanstead County

D-U-N-S 24-226-4596   (SL)
98002 CANADA LTEE

PHARMACIE JEAN COUTU
325 Rue Sherbrooke Bureau 133, Magog, QC,
J1X 2R9
(819) 843-1115
Emp Here 75   *Sales* 14,811,700
SIC 5912 Drug stores and proprietary stores
Pr Pr Norman Chicoyne

D-U-N-S 24-107-1687   (HQ)
AKZO NOBEL PATE ET PERFORMANCE
CANADA INC
1900 Rue Saint-Patrice E Bureau 25, Magog,
QC, J1X 3W5
(819) 843-8942
Emp Here 65   *Emp Total* 46,100
Sales 23,181,293
SIC 2899 Chemical preparations, nec
Pr Cynthia Martin
VP VP Line Poulin
Treas Alain Letourneau

D-U-N-S 20-885-2871   (HQ)
CAMSO INC
*CAMOPLAST SOLIDEAL-CENTRE TECH-
NIQUE*
(*Suby of* Camso Inc)
2633 Rue Macpherson, Magog, QC, J1X 0E6
(819) 823-1777
Emp Here 75   *Emp Total* 7,400
Sales 785,057,132
SIC 3569 General industrial machinery, nec
 Pierre Marcouiller
Pr Thomas Bottcher
Sec Catherine Conides
Dir Alain Tremblay
Dir W.Brian Edwards
Dir Pierre Racine
Dir Philippe Danneels
Dir Pierre Pringiers
Dir Pierre Alary
Dir Fin Kent Carson

D-U-N-S 24-352-2898   (BR)
CAMSO INC
SYSTEMES DE CHENILLES CTC DIV OF
(*Suby of* Camso Inc)
2675 Rue Macpherson, Magog, QC, J1X 0E6
(819) 868-1500
Emp Here 85
SIC 8731 Commercial physical research

D-U-N-S 25-223-9256   (SL)
CENTRE DE LA PETITE ENFANCE JARDIN
DE FANFAN
431 Rue Du Moulin, Magog, QC, J1X 4A1
(819) 843-5349
Emp Here 50   *Sales* 1,532,175
SIC 8351 Child day care services

D-U-N-S 24-907-2802   (BR)
CODET INC
BIG BILL
143 Rue Pomerleau, Magog, QC, J1X 5P7
(819) 847-4045
Emp Here 20
SIC 5136 Men's and boy's clothing

D-U-N-S 24-348-4545   (BR)
COMMISSION   SCOLAIRE   EASTERN
TOWNSHIPS
JOB LINKS
(*Suby of* Commission Scolaire Eastern Town-
ships)
101 Rue Du Moulin Bureau 205, Magog, QC,
J1X 4A1
(819) 868-3100
Emp Here 1,200
SIC 8331 Job training and related services

D-U-N-S 25-234-2175   (BR)
COMMISSION   SCOLAIRE   EASTERN
TOWNSHIPS
EASTERN TOWNSHIPS SHOOL BOARD
(*Suby of* Commission Scolaire Eastern Town-
ships)
120 Rue Bellevue, Magog, QC, J1X 3H2

(819) 843-4847
Emp Here 21
SIC 8211 Elementary and secondary schools

D-U-N-S 25-240-5907   (BR)
COMMISSION SCOLAIRE DES SOMMETS
ECOLE SAINT PIE X
(*Suby of* Commission Scolaire des Sommets)
176 Rue Saint-Alphonse S, Magog, QC, J1X
3T6
(819) 843-4016
Emp Here 23
SIC 8211 Elementary and secondary schools

D-U-N-S 25-674-8617   (BR)
COMMISSION SCOLAIRE DES SOMMETS
ECOLE SAINT JEAN BOSCO
(*Suby of* Commission Scolaire des Sommets)
63 Rue Pie-Xii, Magog, QC, J1X 6A5
(819) 843-4641
Emp Here 30
SIC 8211 Elementary and secondary schools

D-U-N-S 25-674-3360   (HQ)
COMMISSION SCOLAIRE DES SOMMETS
(*Suby of* Commission Scolaire des Sommets)
449 Rue Percy, Magog, QC, J1X 1B5
(819) 847-1610
Emp Here 60   *Emp Total* 60
Sales 4,012,839
SIC 8211 Elementary and secondary schools

D-U-N-S 25-674-8575   (BR)
COMMISSION SCOLAIRE DES SOMMETS
ECOLE BRASSARD-ST-PATRICE
(*Suby of* Commission Scolaire des Sommets)
265 Rue Saint-Patrice O, Magog, QC, J1X
1W4
(819) 843-3004
Emp Here 30
SIC 8211 Elementary and secondary schools

D-U-N-S 25-674-8534   (BR)
COMMISSION SCOLAIRE DES SOMMETS
ECOLE BRASSARD-ST-PATRICE
(*Suby of* Commission Scolaire des Sommets)
360 Rue Saint-Patrice O, Magog, QC, J1X
1W6
(819) 843-4347
Emp Here 30
SIC 8211 Elementary and secondary schools

D-U-N-S 25-233-2515   (BR)
COMMISSION SCOLAIRE DES SOMMETS
*ECOLES PRIMAIRES - MRC DE MEM-
PHREMAGOG - SAINTE-MARGUERITE*
(*Suby of* Commission Scolaire des Sommets)
295 Rue Saint-David, Magog, QC, J1X 2Z8
(819) 843-9566
Emp Here 28
SIC 8211 Elementary and secondary schools

D-U-N-S 20-712-1109   (BR)
COMMISSION SCOLAIRE DES SOMMETS
*CENTRE D'EDUCATION DES ADULTES
DES SOMMETS POINT DE SERVICE DE
MAGOG*
277 Rue Saint-Patrice O, Magog, QC, J1X
1W4
(819) 843-6116
Emp Here 50
SIC 8211 Elementary and secondary schools

D-U-N-S 24-501-6717   (BR)
COMMISSION SCOLAIRE DES SOMMETS
ECOLE DES DEUX-SOLEILS
495 Rue Gerin, Magog, QC, J1X 4B1
(819) 843-5666
Emp Here 25
SIC 8211 Elementary and secondary schools

D-U-N-S 20-712-1224   (BR)
COMMISSION SCOLAIRE DES SOMMETS
*CENTRE DE FORMATION PROFESSION-
NELLE*
1255 Boul Des Etudiants, Magog, QC, J1X
3Y6
(819) 843-1343
Emp Here 50

SIC 8249 Vocational schools, nec

D-U-N-S 24-680-6066   (BR)
DIFCO, TISSUS DE PERFORMANCE INC
160 Rue Principale E, Magog, QC, J1X 4X5
(819) 868-0267
Emp Here 200
SIC 2299 Textile goods, nec

D-U-N-S 24-736-0725   (SL)
ESCAPADES MEMPHREMAGOG INC
ESCAPADES EXPRESS
2400 Rue Principale O, Magog, QC, J1X 0J1
(819) 843-7000
Emp Here 50   *Sales* 2,699,546
SIC 7999 Amusement and recreation, nec

D-U-N-S 25-259-9139   (BR)
GOUVERNEMENT DE LA PROVINCE DE
QUEBEC
*GOUVERNEMENT DE LA PROVINCE DE
QUEBEC*
50 Rue Saint-Patrice E, Magog, QC, J1X 3X3
(819) 843-2572
Emp Here 900
SIC 8062 General medical and surgical hospi-
tals

D-U-N-S 25-966-3227   (BR)
GROUPE JEAN COUTU (PJC) INC, LE
*PHARMACIE NORMAN CHICOYNE &
MARC-ANTOINE BERTRAND*
(*Suby of* 3958230 Canada Inc)
448 Rue Saint-Patrice O, Magog, QC, J1X
1W9
(819) 843-3366
Emp Here 45
SIC 5912 Drug stores and proprietary stores

D-U-N-S 20-860-4553   (SL)
HERMITAGE CLUB, THE
200 Rue De L'Hermitage Bureau 31, Magog,
QC, J1X 0M7
(819) 843-6579
Emp Here 60   *Sales* 2,407,703
SIC 7997 Membership sports and recreation
clubs

D-U-N-S 24-532-7296   (BR)
INDUSTRIELLE ALLIANCE, FIDUCIE INC
INDUSTRIELLE ALLIANCE
45 Rue Du Centre Bureau 200, Magog, QC,
J1X 5B6
(819) 847-0494
Emp Here 35
SIC 6411 Insurance agents, brokers, and ser-
vice

D-U-N-S 25-366-8883   (SL)
KANWAL INC
INDUSTRIEL RPT
(*Suby of* Groupe Kanwal Inc)
1426 Boul Industriel, Magog, QC, J1X 4V9
(819) 868-5152
Emp Here 160   *Sales* 29,972,285
SIC 3089 Plastics products, nec
 Singh Sutinderpaul Kanwal

D-U-N-S 20-207-0652   (SL)
LEFKO PRODUITS DE PLASTIQUE INC
(*Suby of* Placements Scans Inc, Les)
1700 Boul Industriel, Magog, QC, J1X 4V9
(819) 843-9237
Emp Here 60   *Sales* 8,480,961
SIC 2821 Plastics materials and resins
Pr Pr Serge Lamoureux
 Christian Lamoureux
 Normand Lamoureux
Dir Sylvain Lamoureux

D-U-N-S 24-384-8038   (BR)
LINDE CANADA LIMITED
BOC GASES
1980 Rue Saint-Patrice E, Magog, QC, J1X
3W5
(819) 847-3036
Emp Here 55
SIC 5169 Chemicals and allied products, nec

D-U-N-S 25-355-3630   (SL)
MAGOTTEAUX LTEE
601 Rue Champlain, Magog, QC, J1X 2N1
(819) 843-0443
Emp Here 100   *Sales* 16,025,644
SIC 3325 Steel foundries, nec
Ch Bd Ch Bd Sebastien Dossogne
Sec Rene Latour
Dir Jean-Marc Xhenseval
Dir Marc Babineau

D-U-N-S 24-823-4739   (BR)
MAZDA CANADA INC
2940 Rue Sherbrooke, Magog, QC, J1X 4G4
(819) 843-2424
Emp Here 20
SIC 5511 New and used car dealers

D-U-N-S 20-840-2052   (BR)
PAVAGES MASKA INC
2150 Rue Tanguay, Magog, QC, J1X 5Y5
(819) 843-6767
Emp Here 39
SIC 1611 Highway and street construction

D-U-N-S 25-956-0951   (SL)
PERSONNAIDE INC
FONDATION PERSONNAIDE
56 Rue Saint-Patrice O, Magog, QC, J1X 1V9
(819) 868-0487
Emp Here 50   *Sales* 1,969,939
SIC 8322 Individual and family services

D-U-N-S 24-404-5811   (SL)
PLACEMENTS PAUL BROUILLARD INC
CLUB DE GOLF VENISE ENR
1519 Ch De La Riviere Bureau 25, Magog,
QC, J1X 3W5
(819) 864-9891
Emp Here 71   *Sales* 2,845,467
SIC 7997 Membership sports and recreation
clubs

D-U-N-S 24-190-5657   (BR)
PROVIGO DISTRIBUTION INC
LOBLAWS
1350 Rue Sherbrooke, Magog, QC, J1X 2T3
(819) 868-8630
Emp Here 100
SIC 5411 Grocery stores

D-U-N-S 25-876-5254   (BR)
PYRO-AIR INC
(*Suby of* Pyro-Air Ltee)
2301 Rue Principale O, Magog, QC, J1X 0J4
(819) 847-2014
Emp Here 75
SIC 1711 Plumbing, heating, air-conditioning

D-U-N-S 24-132-0782   (SL)
QUALITE PERFORMANCE MAGOG INC
MAGOG HONDA
2400 Rue Sherbrooke, Magog, QC, J1X 4E6
(819) 843-0099
Emp Here 28   *Sales* 4,669,485
SIC 5088 Transportation equipment and sup-
plies

D-U-N-S 24-890-1043   (SL)
R-MAG 118 INC
ROTISSERIE ST-HUBERT
1615 Ch De La Riviere-Aux-Cerises Bureau 2,
Magog, QC, J1X 3W3
(819) 847-3366
Emp Here 80   *Sales* 2,407,703
SIC 5812 Eating places

D-U-N-S 25-308-9098   (BR)
SOCIETE DES ALCOOLS DU QUEBEC
SOCIETE DES ALCOOLS DU QUEBEC
790 Rue Principale O, Magog, QC, J1X 2B3
(819) 843-4543
Emp Here 20
SIC 5182 Wine and distilled beverages

D-U-N-S 25-361-2691   (SL)
TORA MAGOG LIMITEE
TIGRE GEANT

(*Suby of* Giant Tiger Stores Limited)
1730 Rue Sherbrooke, Magog, QC, J1X 2T3
(819) 843-3043
Emp Here 50   *Sales* 4,085,799
SIC 5399 Miscellaneous general merchandise

D-U-N-S 24-356-8131   (BR)
WAL-MART CANADA CORP
ACCES PHARMA CHEZ WALMART
1935 Rue Sherbrooke, Magog, QC, J1X 2T5
(819) 868-3895
Emp Here 80
SIC 5311 Department stores

Malartic, QC J0Y
Abitibi County

D-U-N-S 24-118-6175   (BR)
CENTRE DE SANTE ET DE SERVICES SO-CIAUX DE LA VALLEE-DE-L'OR
CLSC DE MALARTIC
691 Rue Royale, Malartic, QC, J0Y 1Z0

Emp Here 50
SIC 8062 General medical and surgical hospitals

D-U-N-S 20-574-5941   (BR)
CENTRE DE SANTE ET DE SERVICES SO-CIAUX DE LA VALLEE-DE-L'OR
HOPITAL PSYCHIATRIQUE DE MALARTIC
1141 Rue Royale, Malartic, QC, J0Y 1Z0
(819) 825-5858
Emp Here 110
SIC 8062 General medical and surgical hospitals

D-U-N-S 20-712-6199   (BR)
COMMISSION SCOLAIRE DE L'OR-ET-DES-BOIS
CENTRE DU TRAIT D'UNION
(*Suby of* Commission Scolaire de l'Or-et-des-Bois)
99 Ch Du Camping-Regional, Malartic, QC, J0Y 1Z0
(819) 757-3695
Emp Here 50
SIC 8211 Elementary and secondary schools

D-U-N-S 25-240-7085   (BR)
COMMISSION SCOLAIRE DE L'OR-ET-DES-BOIS
ECOLE SECONDAIRE DE TRAMPLAIN
(*Suby of* Commission Scolaire de l'Or-et-des-Bois)
701 Rue Des Erables, Malartic, QC, J0Y 1Z0
(819) 757-4381
Emp Here 70
SIC 8211 Elementary and secondary schools

D-U-N-S 20-712-6231   (BR)
COMMISSION SCOLAIRE DE L'OR-ET-DES-BOIS
ECOLES PRIMAIRES MALARTIC RENAUD
(*Suby of* Commission Scolaire de l'Or-et-des-Bois)
855 Av Dargis-Menard, Malartic, QC, J0Y 1Z0
(819) 757-4355
Emp Here 50
SIC 8211 Elementary and secondary schools

D-U-N-S 20-799-7193   (BR)
GOUVERNEMENT DE LA PROVINCE DE QUEBEC
691 Rue Royale, Malartic, QC, J0Y 1Z0

Emp Here 20
SIC 8399 Social services, nec

D-U-N-S 25-851-2243   (BR)
MINES RICHMONT INC
USINE CAMFLO
100 Rte 117, Malartic, QC, J0Y 1Z0
(819) 757-3674
Emp Here 25

SIC 1081 Metal mining services

D-U-N-S 24-884-5232   (BR)
ROYMICK INC
JEAN COUTU MALARTIC
600 Re Royale Bureau198, Malartic, QC, J0Y 1Z0
(819) 757-6777
Emp Here 20
SIC 5912 Drug stores and proprietary stores

D-U-N-S 24-861-1303   (SL)
USINE CAMFLO INC
100 Rte 117, Malartic, QC, J0Y 1Z0
(819) 797-2465
Emp Here 28   *Sales* 3,064,349
SIC 1041 Gold ores

Maniwaki, QC J9E
Gatineau County

D-U-N-S 25-526-0499   (SL)
3323773 CANADA INC
TRONCONNAGE GAGNON
33 Rue Du Lac, Maniwaki, QC, J9E 3K4
(819) 441-0040
Emp Here 50   *Sales* 4,742,446
SIC 2421 Sawmills and planing mills, general

D-U-N-S 25-744-6534   (SL)
9013-1194 QUEBEC INC
RESTAURANT LE WILLIAMSON
83 Rue Principale N, Maniwaki, QC, J9E 2B5
(819) 449-3600
Emp Here 58   *Sales* 1,751,057
SIC 5812 Eating places

D-U-N-S 24-569-2648   (BR)
BANQUE LAURENTIENNE DU CANADA
111 Boul Desjardins, Maniwaki, QC, J9E 2C9
(800) 252-1846
Emp Here 20
SIC 6021 National commercial banks

D-U-N-S 24-341-2470   (BR)
CENTRE DE SANTE ET DE SERVICES SO-CIAUX DE LA VALLEE-DE-LA-GATINEAU
CLSC
(*Suby of* Centre de Sante et de Services Sociaux de la Vallee-de-la-Gatineau)
177 Rue Des Oblats, Maniwaki, QC, J9E 1G5
(819) 449-2513
Emp Here 100
SIC 8361 Residential care

D-U-N-S 25-993-4461   (BR)
GOUVERNEMENT DE LA PROVINCE DE QUEBEC
RESEAU PETITS PAS
150 Rue Principale N, Maniwaki, QC, J9E 2B8
(819) 449-7659
Emp Here 20
SIC 8351 Child day care services

D-U-N-S 20-535-6012   (BR)
GROUPE RESTAURANTS IMVESCOR INC
RESTAURANT MIKES
100 Rue Principale S Bureau 24, Maniwaki, QC, J9E 3L4
(819) 441-1234
Emp Here 20
SIC 5812 Eating places

D-U-N-S 20-366-2791   (BR)
KITIGAN ZIBI ANISHINABEG
KITIGAN ZIBI HEALTH & SOCIAL SERVICES
8 Kikinamage Mikan, Maniwaki, QC, J9E 3B1
(819) 449-5593
Emp Here 20
SIC 8059 Nursing and personal care, nec

D-U-N-S 25-150-0278   (BR)
PF RESOLU CANADA INC
ABITIBIBOWATER
200 Ch De Montcerf, Maniwaki, QC, J9E 1A1

(819) 449-2100
Emp Here 98
SIC 2421 Sawmills and planing mills, general

D-U-N-S 25-835-3846   (BR)
PAVILLON DU PARC
(*Suby of* Pavillon du Parc)
160 Rue King, Maniwaki, QC, J9E 3N2
(819) 449-3235
Emp Here 20
SIC 8399 Social services, nec

Manouane, QC J0K
Champlain County

D-U-N-S 24-064-2905   (BR)
CONSEIL DES ATIKAMEKW DE MANAWAN
ECOLE PRIMAIRE SIMON P OTTAWA DE MANAOUANE
(*Suby of* Conseil Des Atikamekw de Manawan)
150 Rue Wapoc, Manouane, QC, J0K 1M0
(819) 971-8839
Emp Here 50
SIC 8211 Elementary and secondary schools

D-U-N-S 20-296-5682   (BR)
CONSEIL DES ATIKAMEKW DE MANAWAN
ECOLE SECONDAIRE OTAPI
(*Suby of* Conseil Des Atikamekw de Manawan)
120 Rue Amiskw, Manouane, QC, J0K 1M0
(819) 971-1379
Emp Here 35
SIC 8211 Elementary and secondary schools

D-U-N-S 20-367-3574   (SL)
SERVICES FORESTIERS ET TERRITORI-AUX DE MANAWAN (SFTM) INC
180 Rue Amiskw, Manouane, QC, J0K 1M0
(819) 971-1242
Emp Here 80   *Sales* 4,377,642
SIC 7999 Amusement and recreation, nec

Manseau, QC G0X
Nicolet County

D-U-N-S 24-045-1117   (BR)
RESOLUTE FOREST PRODUCTS INC
PRODUITS FORESTIERS RESOLU SECTEUR MANSEAU
490 Rue Saint-Georges, Manseau, QC, G0X 1V0
(819) 356-2200
Emp Here 50
SIC 2421 Sawmills and planing mills, general

Mansfield, QC J0X

D-U-N-S 20-197-7865   (SL)
131387 CANADA INC
METRO
231 Rue Herault Rr 1, Mansfield, QC, J0X 1R0
(819) 683-2740
Emp Here 37   *Sales* 5,628,700
SIC 5411 Grocery stores
Pr Pr Julienne Beland
VP VP Jean-Paul Beland

Mansonville, QC J0E
Brome County

D-U-N-S 20-921-0991   (BR)
CAISSE DESJARDINS DU LAC-MEMPHREMAGOG
CENTRE DE SERVICE

342 Rue Principale, Mansonville, QC, J0E 1X0
(819) 843-3328
Emp Here 111
SIC 6036 Savings institutions, except federal

D-U-N-S 20-712-1083   (BR)
COMMISSION SCOLAIRE DES SOMMETS
ECOLE DU BALUCHON
330 Rue Principale, Mansonville, QC, J0E 1X0
(450) 292-5717
Emp Here 50
SIC 8211 Elementary and secondary schools

D-U-N-S 24-515-4737   (SL)
COMPAGNIE CHIMIQUE HUNTSMAN DU CANADA, INC
24 Rue Bellevue, Mansonville, QC, J0E 1X0
(450) 292-4154
Emp Here 50   *Sales* 7,536,000
SIC 2821 Plastics materials and resins
Pr Pr John Huntsman
Manager Pierre Beaudry

D-U-N-S 20-978-1673   (SL)
DEVELOPPEMENT OWL'S HEAD INC
CENTRE SKI OWL'S HEAD
40 Ch Mont Owl'S Head, Mansonville, QC, J0E 1X0
(450) 292-3342
Emp Here 60   *Sales* 2,626,585
SIC 7011 Hotels and motels

D-U-N-S 24-365-6415   (HQ)
NEXKEMIA PETROCHIMIE INC
(*Suby of* Nexkemia Petrochimie Inc)
24 Rue Bellevue, Mansonville, QC, J0E 1X0
(450) 292-3333
Emp Here 55   *Emp Total* 60
Sales 2,338,878
SIC 2519 Household furniture, nec

Marbleton, QC J0B
Wolfe County

D-U-N-S 20-206-0018   (SL)
BRETON, L. TRANSPORT LTEE
(*Suby of* Gestion Andre Chalut Inc)
439 Rte 255 N, Marbleton, QC, J0B 2L0
(819) 887-6773
Emp Here 70   *Sales* 11,681,040
SIC 4213 Trucking, except local
Pr Alain Chalut

D-U-N-S 24-909-4079   (BR)
GRAYMONT (QC) INC
303 Rue Principale O, Marbleton, QC, J0B 2L0
(819) 887-6381
Emp Here 70
SIC 3281 Cut stone and stone products

Maria, QC G0C
Bonaventure County

D-U-N-S 24-943-0653   (SL)
SERVICES DES BENEVOLES DU CENTRE HOSPITALIER BAIE-DES-CHALEURS INC
419 Boul Perron, Maria, QC, G0C 1Y0
(418) 759-3443
Emp Here 550   *Sales* 53,261,250
SIC 8062 General medical and surgical hospitals
Pr Suzanne Dugas
VP VP Rejane Fugere
Sec Norma Leblanc
Treas Rita Savoie
Dir Gustave Garant
Dir Claudette Leblanc
Dir Carol Barter

Maricourt, QC J0E
Shefford County

D-U-N-S 25-093-2378   (BR)
BOMBARDIER INC
2042 Ch Laverdure, Maricourt, QC, J0E 2L2
(514) 861-9481
Emp Here 45
SIC 5599 Automotive dealers, nec

Marieville, QC J3M
Rouville County

D-U-N-S 20-033-9211   (BR)
COMMISSION SCOLAIRE DES HAUTES-RIVIERES
ECOLE MGR EUCLIDE THEBERGE
677 Rue Desjardins, Marieville, QC, J3M 1R1
(450) 460-4491
Emp Here 115
SIC 8211 Elementary and secondary schools

D-U-N-S 20-712-6561   (BR)
COMMISSION SCOLAIRE DES HAUTES-RIVIERES
ECOLE NCTRE DAME DE FATIMA
1800 Rue Edmond-Guillet, Marieville, QC, J3M 1G5
(450) 460-7461
Emp Here 21
SIC 8211 Elementary and secondary schools

D-U-N-S 24-425-2941   (BR)
HOME HARDWARE STORES LIMITED
CENTRE DE RENOVATION HOME HARD-WARE MARIEVILLE
100 Rue Ouellette, Marieville, QC, J3M 1A5
(450) 460-4419
Emp Here 70
SIC 5211 Lumber and other building materials

Martinville, QC J0B
Compton County

D-U-N-S 24-336-4960   (BR)
COMMISSION SCOLAIRE DE LA REGION-DE-SHERBROOKE
ECOLE NOTRE-DAME-DE-LA-PAIX
51 Ch Jordan Hill, Martinville, QC, J0B 2A0
(819) 822-5581
Emp Here 20
SIC 8211 Elementary and secondary schools

D-U-N-S 20-712-0986   (BR)
COMMISSION SCOLAIRE DES HAUTS-CANTONS
ECOLE DE SAINTE-EDWIDGE & LIGUGE
194 Rue De L'Eglise, Martinville, QC, J0B 2A0
(819) 849-4470
Emp Here 50
SIC 8211 Elementary and secondary schools

Mascouche, QC J7K
L'Assomption County

D-U-N-S 24-508-8901   (HQ)
AUTOMOBILES DELEC INC
ALBI MAZDA
(*Suby of* Automobiles Delec Inc)
3550 Av De La Gare, Mascouche, QC, J7K 3C1
(514) 722-5555
Emp Here 79   *Emp Total* 100
Sales 26,012,400
SIC 5521 Used car dealers
Pr Denis Leclerc

D-U-N-S 24-851-7117   (BR)
BANK OF NOVA SCOTIA, THE

SCOTIABANK
258 Montee Masson, Mascouche, QC, J7K 3B5
(450) 474-7575
Emp Here 20
SIC 6021 National commercial banks

D-U-N-S 20-036-4131   (SL)
BESSER PRONEQ INC
765 Rue Sicard, Mascouche, QC, J7K 3L7
(450) 966-3000
Emp Here 34   *Sales* 2,772,507
SIC 3544 Special dies, tools, jigs, and fixtures

D-U-N-S 24-818-4280   (BR)
BOSTON PIZZA INTERNATIONAL INC
BOSTON PIZZA
150 Montee Masson Bureau 622, Mascouche, QC, J7K 3B5
(450) 474-6363
Emp Here 50
SIC 5812 Eating places

D-U-N-S 20-107-0104   (BR)
CAISSE DESJARDINS DE TERREBONNE
CAISSE DESJARDINS
115 Montee Masson Unite 1, Mascouche, QC, J7K 3B4
(450) 474-1186
Emp Here 21
SIC 8741 Management services

D-U-N-S 20-538-1465   (BR)
CANADA POST CORPORATION
PHARMACIE JEAN COUTU #163
3131 Boul Mascouche, Mascouche, QC, J7K 1Y0

Emp Here 35
SIC 4311 U.s. postal service

D-U-N-S 25-965-9068   (BR)
CENTRE DE READAPTATION LA MYRI-ADE, LE
1280 Ch Saint-Henri, Mascouche, QC, J7K 2N1
(450) 474-4175
Emp Here 80
SIC 8361 Residential care

D-U-N-S 25-240-2391   (BR)
COMMISSION SCOLAIRE DES AFFLU-ENTS
ECOLE AUX 4 VENTS
(*Suby of* Commission Scolaire des Affluents)
3000 Av Bourque, Mascouche, QC, J7K 2A3
(450) 492-3639
Emp Here 50
SIC 8211 Elementary and secondary schools

D-U-N-S 20-712-2412   (BR)
COMMISSION SCOLAIRE DES AFFLU-ENTS
CENTRE DE L'AVENIR
825 Rue Bombardier Bureau 7, Mascouche, QC, J7K 3G7
(450) 492-3737
Emp Here 50
SIC 8211 Elementary and secondary schools

D-U-N-S 25-233-0204   (BR)
COMMISSION SCOLAIRE DES AFFLU-ENTS
ECOLE SECONDAIRE L'IMPACT
(*Suby of* Commission Scolaire des Affluents)
815 Rue Bombardier Bureau 16, Mascouche, QC, J7K 3E6
(450) 492-3738
Emp Here 41
SIC 8211 Elementary and secondary schools

D-U-N-S 25-201-5631   (SL)
CULASSES DU FUTUR L. R. INC, LES
1390 Av De La Gare, Mascouche, QC, J7K 2Z2
(514) 966-3450
Emp Here 60   *Sales* 12,250,277
SIC 3714 Motor vehicle parts and accessories

Pr Pr Rene Labrecque
Line Lehoux

D-U-N-S 20-357-0593   (SL)
ENTREPRISES LISE LAVOIE INC, LES
1407 Av De La Gare, Mascouche, QC, J7K 3G6
(450) 474-0404
Emp Here 30   *Sales* 6,274,620
SIC 5039 Construction materials, nec
Lise Lavoie

D-U-N-S 24-852-6076   (SL)
GESTION ALEM INC
161 Montee Masson, Mascouche, QC, J7K 3B4
(450) 474-3315
Emp Here 85   *Sales* 6,690,536
SIC 5651 Family clothing stores
Pr Pr Yanick Dessureault

D-U-N-S 20-234-1939   (SL)
HANSON TUYAUX ET PREFABRIQUES QUEBEC LTEE
1331 Av De La Gare, Mascouche, QC, J7K 3G6
(450) 474-6189
Emp Here 50   *Sales* 13,966,720
SIC 3272 Concrete products, nec
Pr Pr Antonio Accurso
Dominic Miceli
Giovanni Miceli

D-U-N-S 20-700-3265   (BR)
HUDSON'S BAY COMPANY
HOME OUTFITTERS
111 Montee Masson, Mascouche, QC, J7K 3B4
(450) 966-0002
Emp Here 24
SIC 5719 Miscellaneous homefurnishings

D-U-N-S 24-338-5023   (BR)
INDUSTRIELLE ALLIANCE, ASSURANCE ET SERVICES FINANCIERS INC
500 Montee Masson Bureau 200, Mascouche, QC, J7K 2L5
(450) 474-2225
Emp Here 50
SIC 6311 Life insurance

D-U-N-S 25-906-8625   (SL)
INDUSTRIES THINOX INC, LES
1271 Av De La Gare, Mascouche, QC, J7K 2Z3
(450) 966-0084
Emp Here 26   *Sales* 6,639,424
SIC 3317 Steel pipe and tubes

D-U-N-S 24-065-5937   (BR)
SOBEYS QUEBEC INC
I G A EXTRA MASCOUCHE
65 Montee Masson, Mascouche, QC, J7K 3B4
(450) 474-2444
Emp Here 120
SIC 5411 Grocery stores

D-U-N-S 25-687-2409   (BR)
STAPLES CANADA INC
BUREAU EN GROS
(*Suby of* Staples, Inc.)
145 Montee Masson Bureau 138, Mascouche, QC, J7K 3B4
(450) 474-6555
Emp Here 40
SIC 5943 Stationery stores

D-U-N-S 25-341-7075   (SL)
USINAGE LAURENTIDES INC
1250 Av De La Gare, Mascouche, QC, J7K 2Z2
(450) 474-4523
Emp Here 50   *Sales* 3,648,035
SIC 3599 Industrial machinery, nec

D-U-N-S 25-199-1154   (BR)
VIGI SANTE LTEE
CHSLD VIGI ET BLAIS
(*Suby of* Vigi Sante Ltee)

2893 Av Des Ancetres, Mascouche, QC, J7K 1X6
(450) 474-6991
Emp Here 150
SIC 8051 Skilled nursing care facilities

D-U-N-S 25-498-2903   (BR)
WAL-MART CANADA CORP
WAL-MART
155 Montee Masson Bureau 3149, Mascouche, QC, J7K 3B4
(450) 474-2679
Emp Here 225
SIC 5311 Department stores

D-U-N-S 20-003-9829   (BR)
WINNERS MERCHANTS INTERNATIONAL L.P.
WINNERS
(*Suby of* The TJX Companies Inc)
121 Montee Masson, Mascouche, QC, J7K 3B4
(450) 474-4423
Emp Here 30
SIC 5651 Family clothing stores

Mascouche, QC J7L
L'Assomption County

D-U-N-S 24-889-9866   (HQ)
AUTOBUS TERREMONT LTEE
(*Suby of* Societe Industrielle Laurentide Inc)
343 Ch Des Anglais, Mascouche, QC, J7L 3P8
(450) 477-1500
Emp Here 105   *Emp Total* 150
Sales 3,939,878
SIC 4151 School buses

D-U-N-S 25-240-2516   (BR)
COMMISSION SCOLAIRE DES AFFLU-ENTS
ECOLE DES HAUTS BOIS
(*Suby of* Commission Scolaire des Affluents)
99 Av Napoleon, Mascouche, QC, J7L 3B3
(450) 492-3628
Emp Here 30
SIC 8211 Elementary and secondary schools

D-U-N-S 25-240-2672   (BR)
COMMISSION SCOLAIRE DES AFFLU-ENTS
ECOLE SECONDAIRE LE COTEAU
(*Suby of* Commission Scolaire des Affluents)
2121 Rue De L'Alize, Mascouche, QC, J7L 4C9
(450) 492-9400
Emp Here 40
SIC 8211 Elementary and secondary schools

D-U-N-S 20-806-7616   (BR)
COUCHE-TARD INC
6 Av Napoleon, Mascouche, QC, J7L 3A8
(450) 477-6441
Emp Here 25
SIC 5411 Grocery stores

D-U-N-S 25-232-8489   (BR)
SIR WILFRID LAURIER SCHOOL BOARD
ECOLE PRIMAIRE PINEWOOD
(*Suby of* Sir Wilfrid Laurier School Board)
412 Ch Des Anglais, Mascouche, QC, J7L 3R1
(450) 477-5353
Emp Here 30
SIC 8211 Elementary and secondary schools

Mashteuiatsh, QC G0W

D-U-N-S 24-748-3212   (SL)
9137-1666 QUEBEC INC
CONSTRUCTION P3L

1134 Rue Ouiatchouan Rr 1, Mashteuiatsh, QC, G0W 2H0

Emp Here 20   *Sales* 5,425,920
SIC 1541 Industrial buildings and warehouses
Pr Jean Launiere

D-U-N-S 24-943-0612   (SL)
GESTION A.D.L. SENC
A.D.L. TOBACO
1665 Rue Nishk, Mashteuiatsh, QC, G0W 2H0
(418) 275-6161
Emp Here 80   *Sales* 4,742,446
SIC 2131 Chewing and smoking tobacco

Maskinonge, QC J0K
Maskinonge County

D-U-N-S 24-826-8588   (BR)
CANWEL BUILDING MATERIALS LTD
BOIS TRAITE DU QUEBEC
50 Rue Saint-Denis, Maskinonge, QC, J0K 1N0
(819) 227-4449
Emp Here 20
SIC 5039 Construction materials, nec

Massueville, QC J0G
Abitibi County

D-U-N-S 25-240-2110   (BR)
COMMISSION SCOLAIRE DE SOREL-TRACY
ECOLE CHRIST ROI
(*Suby of* Commission Scolaire de Sorel-Tracy)
270 Rue Bonsecours, Massueville, QC, J0G 1K0
(450) 788-2208
Emp Here 40
SIC 8211 Elementary and secondary schools

Matagami, QC J0Y
Abitibi County

D-U-N-S 20-289-3624   (BR)
BLAIS & LANGLOIS INC
3100 Boul Industriel, Matagami, QC, J0Y 2A0
(819) 739-2905
Emp Here 60
SIC 1542 Nonresidential construction, nec

D-U-N-S 20-712-6074   (BR)
COMMISSION SCOLAIRE DE LA BAIE JAMES
CENTRE D'EDUCATION DES ADULTES
(*Suby of* Commission Scolaire de la Baie James)
5 Rue Petite Allee, Matagami, QC, J0Y 2A0

Emp Here 50
SIC 8211 Elementary and secondary schools

D-U-N-S 25-240-1054   (BR)
COMMISSION SCOLAIRE DE LA BAIE JAMES
ECOLE GALINEE
(*Suby of* Commission Scolaire de la Baie James)
100 Rue Rupert, Matagami, QC, J0Y 2A0
(819) 739-2055
Emp Here 25
SIC 8211 Elementary and secondary schools

D-U-N-S 20-712-6082   (BR)
COMMISSION SCOLAIRE DE LA BAIE JAMES
ECOLE LE DELTA
(*Suby of* Commission Scolaire de la Baie

James)
100 Rue Rupert, Matagami, QC, J0Y 2A0
(819) 739-2303
Emp Here 20
SIC 8211 Elementary and secondary schools

D-U-N-S 25-259-0088   (BR)
EACOM TIMBER CORPORATION
EACOM TIMBER CORPORATION
2000 Boul Industriel, Matagami, QC, J0Y 2A0
(819) 739-2552
Emp Here 50
SIC 2421 Sawmills and planing mills, general

Matane, QC G4W
Matane County

D-U-N-S 24-907-6381   (SL)
134736 CANADA INC
AUBERGE GOUVERNEURS MATANE ENR
250 Av Du Phare E, Matane, QC, G4W 3N4
(418) 566-2651
Emp Here 50   *Sales* 2,188,821
SIC 7011 Hotels and motels

D-U-N-S 20-052-3525   (SL)
9029-2970 QUEBEC INC
VETEMENTS B.D.
135 Boul Dion, Matane, QC, G4W 3L8
(418) 562-3751
Emp Here 80   *Sales* 4,012,839
SIC 7389 Business services, nec

D-U-N-S 20-581-3616   (BR)
CANADA POST CORPORATION
BUREAU DE POSTES DE MATANE
200 Av Saint-Jerome, Matane, QC, G4W 0C7
(418) 562-0537
Emp Here 20
SIC 4311 U.s. postal service

D-U-N-S 24-378-8569   (BR)
CANADIAN BROADCASTING CORPORATION
SOCIETE RADIO CANADA
155 Rue Saint-Sacrement, Matane, QC, G4W 1Y9
(418) 562-0290
Emp Here 30
SIC 4832 Radio broadcasting stations

D-U-N-S 25-240-6236   (BR)
COMMISSION SCOLAIRE DE MONTS-ET-MAREES
ECOLE MARIE GUYART
(*Suby of* Commission Scolaire De Monts-Et-Marees)
611 Av Saint-Redempteur, Matane, QC, G4W 1K7
(418) 562-6148
Emp Here 40
SIC 8211 Elementary and secondary schools

D-U-N-S 20-574-8283   (BR)
COMMISSION SCOLAIRE DE MONTS-ET-MAREES
POLYVALENTE DE MATANE
(*Suby of* Commission Scolaire De Monts-Et-Marees)
455 Av Saint-Redempteur, Matane, QC, G4W 1K7
(418) 562-5429
Emp Here 80
SIC 8211 Elementary and secondary schools

D-U-N-S 25-234-1961   (BR)
COMMISSION SCOLAIRE DE MONTS-ET-MAREES
ECOLE ZENON SOUCY, L
(*Suby of* Commission Scolaire De Monts-Et-Marees)
152 Av Saint-Redempteur, Matane, QC, G4W 1K2
(418) 562-0827
Emp Here 50

SIC 8211 Elementary and secondary schools

D-U-N-S 20-954-7298   (HQ)
COMMISSION SCOLAIRE DE MONTS-ET-MAREES
(*Suby of* Commission Scolaire De Monts-Et-Marees)
530 Av Saint-Jerome, Matane, QC, G4W 3B5
(418) 566-2500
Emp Here 300   *Emp Total* 1,000
Sales 92,039,680
SIC 8211 Elementary and secondary schools
Pr Leopold Marquis
VP VP Berthe Simard

D-U-N-S 20-711-8485   (BR)
COMMISSION SCOLAIRE DES MONTS-ET-MAREES
POLYVALENTE DE MATANE
455 Av Saint-Redempteur, Matane, QC, G4W 1K7
(418) 562-5429
Emp Here 50
SIC 8211 Elementary and secondary schools

D-U-N-S 25-002-1326   (BR)
COMMISSION SCOLAIRE DES MONTS-ET-MAREES
ECOLE VICTOR COTE
505 Av Saint-Jerome, Matane, QC, G4W 3B8
(418) 562-2645
Emp Here 25
SIC 8211 Elementary and secondary schools

D-U-N-S 20-868-6956   (SL)
COMPAGNIE DE GESTION DE MATANE INC
COGEMA
1410 Rue De Matane-Sur-Mer, Matane, QC, G4W 3M6
(418) 562-5028
Emp Here 30   *Sales* 4,244,630
SIC 4482 Ferries

D-U-N-S 20-723-6472   (SL)
COULOMBE ARMOIRES DE CUISINE INC
PORTE D'ARMOIRE PARCO
20 Rue Deschenes, Matane, QC, G4W 0K2
(418) 562-0009
Emp Here 50   *Sales* 4,085,799
SIC 2431 Millwork

D-U-N-S 20-137-1155   (SL)
ENTREPRISES TOURISTIQUES RIVENVEL LTEE, LES
RESTAURANT CAFE AUX DELICES
109 Rue Saint-Jean, Matane, QC, G4W 2G8
(418) 562-0578
Emp Here 60   *Sales* 1,824,018
SIC 5812 Eating places

D-U-N-S 20-949-9060   (SL)
ENTREPRISES D'ELECTRICITE J.M.N. INC
19 Rue Durette, Matane, QC, G4W 0J5
(418) 562-4009
Emp Here 100   *Sales* 8,755,284
SIC 1731 Electrical work
VP VP Paul-Andre Dion
Pr Pr Eric Mcneil
Martin Beland

D-U-N-S 25-785-7375   (BR)
FONDATION DU CENTRE DE JEUNESSE DU BAS-SAINT-LAURENT
(*Suby of* Fondation du Centre de Jeunesse du Bas-Saint-Laurent)
568 Av Du Phare E, Matane, QC, G4W 1B1
(418) 562-0566
Emp Here 20
SIC 8322 Individual and family services

D-U-N-S 20-239-9312   (BR)
GOUVERNEMENT DE LA PROVINCE DE QUEBEC
SAPAQ RESERVE FAUNIQUE DE MATANE
257 Av Saint-Jerome, Matane, QC, G4W 3A7
(418) 562-3700
Emp Here 45
SIC 7999 Amusement and recreation, nec

D-U-N-S 24-908-0144   (BR)
GROUPE COOPERATIF DYNACO
CENTRE DE RENOVATION DYNACO BMR
(*Suby of* Groupe Cooperatif Dynaco)
515 Av Du Phare E, Matane, QC, G4W 1A5
(418) 562-1590
Emp Here 22
SIC 5211 Lumber and other building materials

D-U-N-S 25-188-6409   (BR)
PROVIGO DISTRIBUTION INC
PROVIGO
595 Av Du Phare E, Matane, QC, G4W 1A9
(418) 562-9066
Emp Here 40
SIC 5411 Grocery stores

D-U-N-S 25-244-2280   (BR)
QUESNEL, MICHEL
JEAN COUTU
550 Av Du Phare E, Matane, QC, G4W 1A7
(418) 566-2894
Emp Here 40
SIC 5912 Drug stores and proprietary stores

D-U-N-S 24-842-5050   (BR)
RAYMOND CHABOT GRANT THORNTON S.E.N.C.R.L.
305 Rue De La Gare, Matane, QC, G4W 3J2
(418) 562-0203
Emp Here 30
SIC 8721 Accounting, auditing, and book-keeping

D-U-N-S 20-207-9273   (BR)
SUPERMARCHES GP INC, LES
METRO G P
(*Suby of* Supermarches GP Inc, Les)
750 Av Du Phare O Bureau 4415, Matane, QC, G4W 3W8
(418) 562-4434
Emp Here 75
SIC 5411 Grocery stores

D-U-N-S 25-146-3394   (BR)
TEMBEC INC
400 Rue Du Port, Matane, QC, G4W 3M6
(418) 794-2001
Emp Here 148
SIC 2611 Pulp mills

D-U-N-S 24-319-5026   (BR)
WAL-MART CANADA CORP
WAL MART 1025
150 Rue Piuze, Matane, QC, G4W 4T2
(418) 566-6037
Emp Here 120
SIC 5311 Department stores

Matapedia, QC G0J
Bonaventure County

D-U-N-S 25-090-7441   (BR)
GOUVERNEMENT DE LA PROVINCE DE QUEBEC
C.L.S.C. MALAUZE
14 Boul Perron E, Matapedia, QC, G0J 1V0
(418) 865-2221
Emp Here 125
SIC 8399 Social services, nec

Mcmasterville, QC J3G
Vercheres County

D-U-N-S 20-712-3238   (BR)
COMMISSION SCOLAIRE DES PATRIOTES
COMMISSION SCOLAIRE DES PATRIOTES
720 Rue Morin, Mcmasterville, QC, J3G 1H1
(450) 467-6205
Emp Here 50
SIC 8211 Elementary and secondary schools

D-U-N-S 25-240-3217   (BR)
COMMISSION SCOLAIRE DES PATRIOTES
ECOLE LA FARANDOLE
265 3e Av, Mcmasterville, QC, J3G 1R7
(450) 467-3467
Emp Here 40
SIC 8211 Elementary and secondary schools

D-U-N-S 24-079-8830   (BR)
SOCIETE DE GESTION COGIR INC
RESIDENCES RICHELOISES, LES
701 Ch Du Richelieu Bureau 139, Mcmasterville, QC, J3G 6T5
(450) 467-7667
Emp Here 100
SIC 6513 Apartment building operators

Melocheville, QC J0S
Beauharnois County

D-U-N-S 20-715-6535   (BR)
ST. LAWRENCE SEAWAY MANAGEMENT CORPORATION, THE
85 Boul Hebert, Melocheville, QC, J0S 1J0
(450) 429-7181
Emp Here 50
SIC 4482 Ferries

Mercier, QC J6R
Chateauguay County

D-U-N-S 24-226-2298   (BR)
CLEAN HARBORS CANADA, INC
1294 Boul Sainte-Marguerite, Mercier, QC, J6R 2L1
(450) 691-9610
Emp Here 32
SIC 4953 Refuse systems

Metabetchouan-Lac-A-La-Croix, QC G8G

D-U-N-S 24-884-3690   (SL)
SERVICES EDUCATIFS DU SEMINAIRE MARIE-REINE-DU-CLERGE
SEMIGYM
1569 Rte 169, Metabetchouan-Lac-A-La-Croix, QC, G8G 1A8
(418) 349-2816
Emp Here 50   *Sales* 3,356,192
SIC 8211 Elementary and secondary schools

Mirabel, QC J7J
Deux-Montagnes County

D-U-N-S 20-309-2317   (SL)
4392230 CANADA INC
CULB DE GOLF LE DIAMANT
(*Suby of* Grcupe Beaudet Inc)
10466 Montee Clement, Mirabel, QC, J7J 1Z4
(450) 476-1922
Emp Here 45   *Sales* 1,824,018
SIC 7997 Membership sports and recreation clubs

D-U-N-S 20-563-2128   (HQ)
AGENCES KYOTO LTEE, LES
ST-JEROME TOYOTA
(*Suby of* Groupe Automobiles Kyoto Ltee)
16500 Montee Guenette, Mirabel, QC, J7J 2E2
(450) 438-1255
Emp Here 90   *Emp Total* 3
Sales 32,832,315
SIC 5511 New and used car dealers
Pr Pr Aime V alle

Jean–Louis Vialle

D-U-N-S 20-859-4093   (BR)
ASPHALTE DESJARDINS INC
CARRIERES LAURENTIENNES
17250 Cote Saint-Antoine, Mirabel, QC, J7J 2G9
(450) 432-4317
Emp Here 40
SIC 1442 Construction sand and gravel

D-U-N-S 25-836-8968   (BR)
CENTRE DU GOLF U.F.O. INC
CLUB DE GOLF GLENDALE
(*Suby of* Centre Du Golf U.F.O. Inc)
9500 Rang Sainte-Henriette, Mirabel, QC, J7J 2A1
(514) 990-8392
Emp Here 100
SIC 7997 Membership sports and recreation clubs

D-U-N-S 25-233-0139   (BR)
COMMISSION SCOLAIRE DE LA RIVIERE-DU-NORD
CENTRE FORMATION DU TRANSPORT ROUTIER
(*Suby of* Commission Scolaire de la Riviere-du-Nord)
17000 Rue Aubin, Mirabel, QC, J7J 1B1
(450) 435-0167
Emp Here 100
SIC 8299 Schools and educational services, nec

D-U-N-S 24-065-1153   (BR)
COMMISSION SCOLAIRE DE LA RIVIERE-DU-NORD
ECOLE AUX QUATRE-VENT
(*Suby of* Commission Scolaire de la Riviere-du-Nord)
13815 Rue Therrien, Mirabel, QC, J7J 1J4
(450) 569-2239
Emp Here 35
SIC 8211 Elementary and secondary schools

D-U-N-S 20-800-0542   (BR)
GROUPE JEAN COUTU (PJC) INC, LE
PHARMACIE JEAN COUTU 220
(*Suby of* 3958230 Canada Inc)
13400 Boul Du Cure-Labelle Bureau 220, Mirabel, QC, J7J 1G9
(450) 971-5145
Emp Here 30
SIC 5912 Drug stores and proprietary stores

D-U-N-S 25-092-8632   (SL)
HALO PHARMACEUTICAL CANADA INC
AUREOLE PHARMACEUTIQUE CANADA
17800 Rue Lapointe, Mirabel, QC, J7J 0W8
(450) 433-7673
Emp Here 250   *Sales* 36,982,250
SIC 2834 Pharmaceutical preparations
Dir Lee Karras
   Mohd Asif
Dir Aaron Davenport
Dir Jamshid Keynejad

D-U-N-S 24-834-3758   (SL)
INDUSTRIES WARNET INC
MOULURES ET COMPOSANTES DE BOIS ALGONQUIN
14353 Boul Du Cure-Labelle, Mirabel, QC, J7J 1M2
(450) 435-1320
Emp Here 50   *Sales* 4,851,006
SIC 2431 Millwork

D-U-N-S 20-560-5228   (SL)
INGENIA TECHNOLOGIES INC
18101 Rue J.A.Bombardier, Mirabel, QC, J7J 2H8
(450) 979-1212
Emp Here 65   *Sales* 8,244,559
SIC 3585 Refrigeration and heating equipment
   Giuseppe J Racanelli
VP Lise Daigle

D-U-N-S 20-297-8656   (HQ)
LALLEMAND SOLUTIONS SANTE INC
NICAR INTERNATIONAL
17975 Rue Des Gouverneurs, Mirabel, QC, J7J 2K7
(450) 433-9139
Emp Here 100   *Emp Total* 100
Sales 11,965,555
SIC 2836 Biological products, except diagnostic
Pr Francine Mondou
Sec Tatiana Mikhailova
Treas Francois Leblanc
Dir Jerome Panes
Dir Antoine Chagnon
Dir William Nankervis

D-U-N-S 20-689-6396   (HQ)
MAGASINS TREVI INC
PISCINES TREVI
(*Suby of* Investissements Trevi Inc)
12775 Rue Brault, Mirabel, QC, J7J 0C4
(450) 973-1249
Emp Here 180   *Emp Total* 250
Sales 28,153,158
SIC 5999 Miscellaneous retail stores, nec
Pr Pr Clement Hudon
Sec Chantal Bourdon
Dir John Leboutillier
Dir Michel Bernard
Dir Benoit Hudon

D-U-N-S 24-619-3510   (SL)
RAYMOND, J. COUVREUR & FILS INC
20550 Ch De La Cote N, Mirabel, QC, J7J 2B7
(450) 430-7900
Emp Here 50   *Sales* 4,961,328
SIC 1761 Roofing, siding, and sheetMetal work

D-U-N-S 20-925-6689   (BR)
RESTAURANT LOUJAC INC
MCDONALD'S
(*Suby of* Restaurant Loujac Inc)
17515 Ch Charles, Mirabel, QC, J7J 1P3
(450) 434-1112
Emp Here 60
SIC 5812 Eating places

D-U-N-S 24-870-7341   (BR)
SAFRAN LANDING SYSTEMS CANADA INC
13000 Rue Du Parc, Mirabel, QC, J7J 0W6
(450) 434-3400
Emp Here 200
SIC 3728 Aircraft parts and equipment, nec

D-U-N-S 24-365-2083   (SL)
TECHNILAB PHARMA INC
17800 Rue Lapointe, Mirabel, QC, J7J 1P3
(450) 433-7673
Emp Here 400   *Sales* 95,117,040
SIC 6712 Bank holding companies
Pr Jean-Guy Goulet
Sec Matthias Eschrichts
   Walter Buhl
   Gerd Lehmann
Dir Fin Joel Belanger

D-U-N-S 24-804-8097   (BR)
TEVA CANADA LIMITED
17800 Rue Lapointe Unite 123, Mirabel, QC, J7J 0W8
(450) 433-7673
Emp Here 250
SIC 2834 Pharmaceutical preparations

Mirabel, QC J7N
Deux-Montagnes County

D-U-N-S 25-093-2303   (BR)
BOMBARDIER INC
BOMBARDIER AERONAUTIQUE
10200 Rue Irenee-Vachon Bureau 450,
Mirabel, QC, J7N 3E3
(450) 476-0550
Emp Here 20
SIC 8711 Engineering services

D-U-N-S 25-369-6397   (BR)
BOMBARDIER INC
BOMDARDIER AERONAUTIQUE
13100 Boul Henri-Fabre, Mirabel, QC, J7N 3C6
(514) 855-5000
Emp Here 25
SIC 3721 Aircraft

D-U-N-S 24-678-0998   (BR)
BOMBARDIER INC
BOMBARDIER AERONAUTIQUE
13100 Boul Henri-Fabre Bureau 209, Mirabel, QC, J7N 3C6
(514) 855-5000
Emp Here 20
SIC 8711 Engineering services

D-U-N-S 24-125-0815   (BR)
CENTRE INTEGRE DE SANTE ET DE SERVICES SOCIAUX DES LAURENTIDES
CENTRE INTEGRE DE SANTE ET DE SERVICES SOCIAUX DES
9100 Rue Dumouchel, Mirabel, QC, J7N 5A1
(450) 258-2481
Emp Here 100
SIC 7041 Membership-basis organization hotels

D-U-N-S 25-240-1088   (BR)
COMMISSION SCOLAIRE DE LA RIVIERE-DU-NORD
COMMISSION SCOLAIRE DE LA RIVIERE-DU-NORD
(*Suby of* Commission Scolaire de la Riviere-du-Nord)
9984 Boul De Saint-Canut, Mirabel, QC, J7N 1K1
(450) 438-0424
Emp Here 50
SIC 8211 Elementary and secondary schools

D-U-N-S 25-976-1237   (BR)
COMMISSION SCOLAIRE DE LA SEIGNEURIE-DES-MILLE-ILES
COMMISSION SCOLAIRE DE LA SEIGNEURIE-DES-MILLE-ILES
(*Suby of* Commission Scolaire de la Seigneurie-Des-Mille-Iles)
14700 Rue Jean-Simon, Mirabel, QC, J7N 2J6
(450) 434-8143
Emp Here 50
SIC 8211 Elementary and secondary schools

D-U-N-S 25-233-2762   (BR)
COMMISSION SCOLAIRE DE LA SEIGNEURIE-DES-MILLE-ILES
COMMISSION SCOLAIRE DE LA SEIGNEURIE-DES-MILLE-ILES
(*Suby of* Commission Scolaire de la Seigneurie-Des-Mille-Iles)
15074 Rue De Saint-Augustin, Mirabel, QC, J7N 2B2
(450) 434-8656
Emp Here 25
SIC 8211 Elementary and secondary schools

D-U-N-S 20-712-1596   (BR)
COMMISSION SCOLAIRE DE LA SEIGNEURIE-DES-MILLE-ILES
COMMISSION SCOLAIRE DE LA SEIGNEURIE-DES-MILLE-ILES
9850 Rue De Belle-Riviere, Mirabel, QC, J7N 2X8
(450) 434-8150
Emp Here 25
SIC 8699 Membership organizations, nec

D-U-N-S 25-233-2606   (BR)
COMMISSION SCOLAIRE DE LA SEIGNEURIE-DES-MILLE-ILES
COMMISSION SCOLAIRE DE LA SEIGNEURIE-DES-MILLE-ILES

(*Suby of* Commission Scolaire de la Seigneurie-Des-Mille-Iles)
9030 Rue Dumouchel, Mirabel, QC, J7N 2N8
(450) 434-8612
Emp Here 20
SIC 8211 Elementary and secondary schools

D-U-N-S 25-903-4999   (SL)
DESJARDINS & MALLETTE PHARMACIENS, S.E.N.C.
UNIPRIX
13960 Rue Saint-Simon Bureau 1, Mirabel, QC, J7N 1P4
(450) 565-0529
Emp Here 50   *Sales* 9,840,650
SIC 5912 Drug stores and proprietary stores
Pt Pierre Desjardins
Pt Isabelle Mallette

D-U-N-S 20-552-9352   (BR)
HYDRO-QUEBEC
11175 Rang Saint-Etienne, Mirabel, QC, J7N 2S9
(450) 476-0444
Emp Here 20
SIC 4911 Electric services

D-U-N-S 24-094-1299   (BR)
LILYDALE INC
LILYDALE HATCHERIES DIV
9051 Rte Sir-Wilfrid-Laurier, Mirabel, QC, J7N 1L6

Emp Here 300
SIC 5144 Poultry and poultry products

D-U-N-S 24-851-7794   (BR)
MATERIAUX PONT MASSON INC
9070 Rte Sir-Wilfrid-Laurier, Mirabel, QC, J7N 0T2
(450) 371-1162
Emp Here 60
SIC 5211 Lumber and other building materials

D-U-N-S 20-277-3610   (SL)
MECACHROME TECHNOLOGIES INC
(*Suby of* Mecachrome Canada Inc)
11100 Rue Julien-Audette, Mirabel, QC, J7N 3L3
(450) 476-3939
Emp Here 170   *Sales* 14,883,983
SIC 1711 Plumbing, heating, air-conditioning
Sec Jocelyn Cote

D-U-N-S 20-183-2362   (SL)
SAFRAN MOTEURS D'HELICOPTERES CANADA INC
TURBOMECA CANADA
11800 Rue Helen-Bristol, Mirabel, QC, J7N 3G8
(450) 476-2550
Emp Here 55   *Sales* 4,764,381
SIC 7538 General automotive repair shops

D-U-N-S 24-177-8799   (BR)
SOCIETE DES ALCOOLS DU QUEBEC
SOCIETE DES ALCOOLS DU QUEBEC
13855 Ch Saint-Simon, Mirabel, QC, J7N 1P3
(450) 436-2607
Emp Here 60
SIC 5921 Liquor stores

D-U-N-S 24-864-8339   (BR)
UNIMIN CANADA LTD
11974 Rte Sir-Wilfrid-Laurier, Mirabel, QC, J7N 1P5
(450) 438-1238
Emp Here 35
SIC 1429 Crushed and broken stone, nec

D-U-N-S 24-785-4354   (SL)
VOLAILLES MIRABEL LTEE
9051 Rte Sir-Wilfrid-Laurier, Mirabel, QC, J7N 1L6
(450) 258-0444
Emp Here 20   *Sales* 14,592,140
SIC 6799 Investors, nec
Pr Elias Simitsakos
   Emmanuel Simitsakos

D-U-N-S 20-284-9196   (BR)
WORLDWIDE FLIGHT SERVICES LTD
11955 Henry-Giffard Suite 200, Mirabel, QC, J7N 1G3
(450) 476-9248
Emp Here 80
SIC 4731 Freight transportation arrangement

Mistissini, QC G0W
Lac-St-Jean-Ouest County

D-U-N-S 20-101-2213   (BR)
CREE BOARD OF HEALTH & SOCIAL SERVICES OF JAMES BAY
CLSC INLAND
302 Queen St, Mistissini, QC, G0W 1C0
(418) 923-3376
Emp Here 30
SIC 8093 Specialty outpatient clinics, nec

D-U-N-S 24-051-6294   (HQ)
CREE SCHOOL BOARD
(*Suby of* Cree School Board)
203 Main St, Mistissini, QC, G0W 1C0
(418) 923-2764
Emp Here 47   *Emp Total* 670
Sales 44,797,870
SIC 8211 Elementary and secondary schools
Ch Bd Kathleen Wootton
Sec Bella Mianscum
Genl Mgr Abraham Jolly
Dir Serge Beliveau
Dir Caroline Mark
Dir Kimberly Quinn
Dir Pierre Desjardins
Dir Jane Blacksmith
Dir Matthew Rabbitskin
Dir Natalie Petawabano

Mont-Joli, QC G5H
Rimouski County

D-U-N-S 25-001-9056   (BR)
ARMOIRES FABRITEC LTEE
ARMOIRES CAMBOARD
1230 Rue Industrielle, Mont-Joli, QC, G5H 3S2
(418) 775-7010
Emp Here 85
SIC 2434 Wood kitchen cabinets

D-U-N-S 24-341-3965   (HQ)
BOIS BSL INC
BOIS B.S.L MATANE
1081 Boul Industriel, Mont-Joli, QC, G5H 3K8
(418) 775-5360
Emp Here 145   *Emp Total* 325
Sales 27,360,263
SIC 5023 Homefurnishings
   Gino Ouellet

D-U-N-S 25-487-9315   (SL)
BOURGEONS DE LA MITIS, LES
1811 Boul Gaboury, Mont-Joli, QC, G5H 4B5
(418) 775-3077
Emp Here 50   *Sales* 1,459,214
SIC 7349 Building maintenance services, nec

D-U-N-S 20-208-6658   (BR)
BRADKEN CANADA MANUFACTURED PRODUCTS LTD
105 Av De La Fonderie, Mont-Joli, QC, G5H 1W2
(418) 775-4358
Emp Here 200
SIC 3321 Gray and ductile iron foundries

D-U-N-S 20-537-6929   (BR)
CANADA POST CORPORATION
BDP MONT JOLI SUCCURSALE BUREAU CHEF
1496 Boul Jacques-Cartier Bureau 183113,

Mont-Joli, QC, G5H 0B3
(418) 775-2271
Emp Here 28
SIC 4311 U.s. postal service

D-U-N-S 24-660-8256   (BR)
CENTRE INTEGRE DE SANTE ET DE SERVICES SOCIAUX DU BAS-SAINT-LAURENT
1526 Boul Jacques-Cartier, Mont-Joli, QC, G5H 2V8
(418) 775-9753
Emp Here 20
SIC 8399 Social services, nec

D-U-N-S 20-711-8246   (BR)
COMMISSION SCOLAIRE DES PHARES
CENTRE DE FORMATION DES ADULTES DE MONT-JOLI-MITIS
(*Suby of* Commission Scolaire des Phares)
1632 Rue Lindsay, Mont-Joli, QC, G5H 3A6
(418) 775-4466
Emp Here 20
SIC 8211 Elementary and secondary schools

D-U-N-S 20-711-8311   (BR)
COMMISSION SCOLAIRE DES PHARES
FORMATION PROFESSIONNELLE MONT JOLI MITIS
(*Suby of* Commission Scolaire des Phares)
1414 Rue Des Erables, Mont-Joli, QC, G5H 4A8
(418) 775-7577
Emp Here 50
SIC 8211 Elementary and secondary schools

D-U-N-S 25-232-3092   (BR)
COMMISSION SCOLAIRE DES PHARES
ECOLE NORJOLI
(*Suby of* Commission Scolaire des Phares)
70 Av Beaupre, Mont-Joli, QC, G5H 1C7
(418) 775-5265
Emp Here 25
SIC 8211 Elementary and secondary schools

D-U-N-S 25-232-3233   (BR)
COMMISSION SCOLAIRE DES PHARES
ECOLE DES ALIZEES
(*Suby of* Commission Scolaire des Phares)
45 Av De La Grotte, Mont-Joli, QC, G5H 1W4
(418) 775-3383
Emp Here 20
SIC 8211 Elementary and secondary schools

D-U-N-S 25-232-3316   (BR)
COMMISSION SCOLAIRE DES PHARES
ECOLE LES ALIZES PAVILLONS NOTRE DAME DE LOURDES
(*Suby of* Commission Scolaire des Phares)
1632 Rue Lindsay, Mont-Joli, QC, G5H 3A6
(418) 775-4466
Emp Here 30
SIC 8211 Elementary and secondary schools

D-U-N-S 25-169-0723   (BR)
EQUIPEMENTS SIGMA INC
(*Suby of* Deere & Company)
930 Boul Jacques-Cartier, Mont-Joli, QC, G5H 3K6
(418) 775-2941
Emp Here 20
SIC 7699 Repair services, nec

D-U-N-S 25-307-3183   (BR)
SUPERMARCHES GP INC, LES
METRO G P
(*Suby of* Supermarches GP Inc, Les)
40 Av Doucet, Mont-Joli, QC, G5H 0B8
(418) 775-8848
Emp Here 80
SIC 5411 Grocery stores

D-U-N-S 20-208-6401   (HQ)
SUPERMARCHES GP INC, LES
METRO GP , DIV DE
(*Suby of* Supermarches GP Inc, Les)
1665 Boul Benoit-Gaboury, Mont-Joli, QC, G5H 3J1

(418) 775-2214
Emp Here 30   *Emp Total* 1,600
Sales 309,204,000
SIC 5411 Grocery stores
   Russell Negus
Genl Mgr Michel Coulombe

D-U-N-S 20-529-6655   (BR)
VIA RAIL CANADA INC
48 Av De La Gare, Mont-Joli, QC, G5H 1N7
(418) 775-7853
Emp Here 20
SIC 4111 Local and suburban transit

Mont-Laurier, QC J9L
Labelle County

D-U-N-S 20-290-5634   (SL)
9144-8720 QUEBEC INC
GROUPE KTG
1092 Rue Lachapelle, Mont-Laurier, QC, J9L 3T9
(819) 623-6745
Emp Here 70   *Sales* 4,921,260
SIC 1799 Special trade contractors, nec

D-U-N-S 20-255-1198   (BR)
BEN DESHAIES INC
3900 Ch De La Lievre N, Mont-Laurier, QC, J9L 3G4
(819) 623-6244
Emp Here 36
SIC 5141 Groceries, general line

D-U-N-S 24-676-5593   (SL)
BOIS NOBLES KA'N'ENDA LTEE
701 Rue Iberville, Mont-Laurier, QC, J9L 3W7
(819) 623-2445
Emp Here 100   *Sales* 12,760,800
SIC 2421 Sawmills and planing mills, general
Pr Pierre Grand'maison

D-U-N-S 20-581-3582   (BR)
CANADA POST CORPORATION
BUREAU DE POSTE MONT LAURIER
530 Boul Packard, Mont-Laurier, QC, J9L 0A0
(819) 623-3463
Emp Here 27
SIC 4311 U.s. postal service

D-U-N-S 25-525-5259   (HQ)
CENTRE HOSPITALIER ET CENTRE DE READAPTATION ANTOINE-LABELLE
CSSS ANTOINE-LABELLE
(*Suby of* Centre Hospitalier Et Centre De Readaptation Antoine-Labelle)
757 Rue De La Madone, Mont-Laurier, QC, J9L 1T3
(819) 623-1234
Emp Here 100   *Emp Total* 1,400
Sales 135,435,750
SIC 8062 General medical and surgical hospitals
Genl Mgr Francine Laroche

D-U-N-S 24-345-6279   (BR)
CENTRE HOSPITALIER ET CENTRE DE READAPTATION ANTOINE-LABELLE
CENTRE D HEBERGEMENT SAINTE-ANNE
411 Rue De La Madone, Mont-Laurier, QC, J9L 1S1
(819) 623-5940
Emp Here 150
SIC 8361 Residential care

D-U-N-S 25-374-4833   (BR)
CENTRE JEUNESSE DES LAURENTIDES
419 Rue De La Madone, Mont-Laurier, QC, J9L 1S1
(819) 623-3884
Emp Here 30
SIC 8322 Individual and family services

D-U-N-S 25-233-5765   (BR)
COMMISSION SCOLAIRE PIERRE-NEVEU, LA

ECOLE DE LA MADONE
(Suby of Commission Scolaire Pierre-Neveu, La)
631 Rue Hebert, Mont-Laurier, QC, J9L 2X4
(819) 623-1657
Emp Here 34
SIC 8211 Elementary and secondary schools

D-U-N-S 25-233-5880 (BR)
COMMISSION SCOLAIRE PIERRE-NEVEU, LA
ECOLE DE LA CARRIERE
(Suby of Commission Scolaire Pierre-Neveu, La)
654 Rue Leonard, Mont-Laurier, QC, J9L 2Z8
(819) 623-2417
Emp Here 20
SIC 8211 Elementary and secondary schools

D-U-N-S 25-233-5963 (BR)
COMMISSION SCOLAIRE PIERRE-NEVEU, LA
ECOLE SAINT EUGENE
(Suby of Commission Scolaire Pierre-Neveu, La)
318 Rue Du Pont, Mont-Laurier, QC, J9L 2R2
(819) 623-3899
Emp Here 40
SIC 8211 Elementary and secondary schools

D-U-N-S 25-233-5849 (HQ)
COMMISSION SCOLAIRE PIERRE-NEVEU, LA
(Suby of Commission Scolaire Pierre-Neveu, La)
525 Rue De La Madone, Mont-Laurier, QC, J9L 1S4
(819) 623-4310
Emp Here 50   Emp Total 800
Sales 69,072,716
SIC 8211 Elementary and secondary schools
Dir Bernard Lajeunesse
Pr Gilles Letourneau
Ex Dir Diane Sirard

D-U-N-S 20-712-5274 (BR)
COMMISSION SCOLAIRE PIERRE-NEVEU, LA
CENTRE CHRISTE ROY
545 Rue Du Pont, Mont-Laurier, QC, J9L 2S2
(819) 623-1266
Emp Here 50
SIC 8211 Elementary and secondary schools

D-U-N-S 20-712-5183 (BR)
COMMISSION SCOLAIRE PIERRE-NEVEU, LA
ECOLE PRIMAIRE ST JEAN L'EVANGELISTE
1420 Boul Des Ruisseaux, Mont-Laurier, QC, J9L 0H6
(819) 623-3137
Emp Here 25
SIC 8211 Elementary and secondary schools

D-U-N-S 20-712-5209 (BR)
COMMISSION SCOLAIRE PIERRE-NEVEU, LA
525 Rue De La Madone, Mont-Laurier, QC, J9L 1S4
(819) 623-4310
Emp Here 25
SIC 8211 Elementary and secondary schools

D-U-N-S 20-715-4340 (BR)
COMPAGNIE COMMONWEALTH PLYWOOD LTEE, LA
3757 Ch De La Lievre N, Mont-Laurier, QC, J9L 3G4
(819) 623-3900
Emp Here 30
SIC 7389 Business services, nec

D-U-N-S 25-374-5533 (HQ)
COOPERATIVE DE SOLIDARITE DEFI-AUTONOMIE D'ANTOINE-LABELLE
C.S. DEFI-AUTONOMIE D'ANTOINE-LABELLE

(Suby of Cooperative de Solidarite Defi-Autonomie d'Antoine-Labelle)
677 Rue De La Madone, Mont-Laurier, QC, J9L 1T2
(819) 623-6681
Emp Here 70   Emp Total 79
Sales 3,137,310
SIC 8322 Individual and family services

D-U-N-S 25-299-6574 (BR)
DOLLARAMA S.E.C.
DOLLARAMA
939 Boul Albiny-Paquette, Mont-Laurier, QC, J9L 3J1
(819) 623-7001
Emp Here 20
SIC 5399 Miscellaneous general merchandise

D-U-N-S 20-961-5046 (SL)
ENTREPRISES D'HOTELLERIE DUQUETTE INC, LES
QUALITY INN
111 Boul Albiny-Paquette, Mont-Laurier, QC, J9L 1J2
(819) 623-3555
Emp Here 50   Sales 2,188,821
SIC 7011 Hotels and motels

D-U-N-S 25-383-3479 (BR)
GOUVERNEMENT DE LA PROVINCE DE QUEBEC
MINISTERE DES RESSOURCES NATURELLES ET DE LA FAUNE
142 Rue Godard, Mont-Laurier, QC, J9L 3T7
(819) 623-5781
Emp Here 41
SIC 6519 Real property lessors, nec

D-U-N-S 25-320-5231 (BR)
RESTAURANT SYLVAIN VINCENT INC, LES
RESTURANT MCDONALDS
850 Boul Albiny-Paquette, Mont-Laurier, QC, J9L 1L4
(819) 623-6811
Emp Here 35
SIC 5812 Eating places

D-U-N-S 25-374-4239 (BR)
ROTISSERIES ST-HUBERT LTEE, LES
RESTAURANT ST HUBERT
(Suby of Cara Holdings Limited)
1108 Boul Albiny-Paquette, Mont-Laurier, QC, J9L 1M1
(819) 623-4040
Emp Here 55
SIC 5812 Eating places

D-U-N-S 24-668-7255 (BR)
SAPUTO PRODUITS LAITIERS CANADA S.E.N.C.
(Suby of Saputo Produits Laitiers Canada S.E.N.C.)
1485 Boul Albiny-Paquette Bureau 3, Mont-Laurier, QC, J9L 1M8
(819) 623-4350
Emp Here 45
SIC 2022 Cheese; natural and processed

D-U-N-S 20-208-8738 (SL)
ST-PIERRE, JULES LTEE
1054 Boul Albiny-Paquette, Mont-Laurier, QC, J9L 1M1

Emp Here 35   Sales 5,034,288
SIC 5149 Groceries and related products, nec
Jacques St-Pierre

D-U-N-S 25-683-9564 (BR)
UNIBOARD CANADA INC
845 Rue Jean-Baptiste-Reid, Mont-Laurier, QC, J9L 3W3
(819) 623-7133
Emp Here 105
SIC 2493 Reconstituted wood products

D-U-N-S 24-860-4949 (BR)
WSP CANADA INC
GENIVAR
595 Boul Albiny-Paquette, Mont-Laurier, QC,

J9L 1L5
(819) 623-3302
Emp Here 20
SIC 8711 Engineering services

Mont-Louis, QC G0E
Gaspe-Ouest County

D-U-N-S 25-232-1054 (BR)
COMMISSION SCOLAIRE DES CHIC-CHOCS
ECOLE SAINT MAXIME
2 2e Av E, Mont-Louis, QC, G0E 1T0
(418) 797-2254
Emp Here 25
SIC 8211 Elementary and secondary schools

D-U-N-S 24-884-8988 (SL)
CUSIMER (1991) INC
52 1e Av O, Mont-Louis, QC, G0E 1T0
(418) 797-2728
Emp Here 40   Sales 20,096,000
SIC 5146 Fish and seafoods
Pr Pr Laurent Normand
   Helene Ouellet

Mont-Royal, QC H3P
Hochelaga County

D-U-N-S 20-234-2713 (SL)
7790643 CANADA INC
CLUB DE GOLF L'ESTEREL
(Suby of Zardev Inc)
2265 Crois Ainsley, Mont-Royal, QC, H3P 2S8
(450) 228-2571
Emp Here 160   Sales 9,046,358
SIC 7011 Hotels and motels
Pr Pr Donald Zarbatany
VP VP Shawn Zarbatany

D-U-N-S 24-012-2247 (BR)
ALTASCIENCES COMPAGNIE INC
ALGORITHME PHARMA
(Suby of Audax Group, L.P.)
1100 Av Beaumont Bureau 101, Mont-Royal, QC, H3P 3H5
(514) 341-6077
Emp Here 20
SIC 8731 Commercial physical research

D-U-N-S 20-202-4472 (BR)
ALTASCIENCES COMPAGNIE INC
ALGORITHME PHARMA
(Suby of Audax Group, L.P.)
1200 Av Beaumont, Mont-Royal, QC, H3P 3P1
(514) 858-6077
Emp Here 200
SIC 8731 Commercial physical research

D-U-N-S 25-097-8301 (BR)
BOUTIQUE LINEN CHEST (PHASE II) INC
LINEN CHEST
(Suby of Boutique Linen Chest (Phase II) Inc)
2305 Ch Rockland Bureau 500, Mont-Royal, QC, H3P 3E9
(514) 341-7810
Emp Here 79
SIC 5714 Drapery and upholstery stores

D-U-N-S 25-233-6938 (BR)
COMMISSION SCOLAIRE ENGLISH-MONTREAL
DUNRAE GARDENS SCHOOL
235 Av Dunrae, Mont-Royal, QC, H3P 1T5
(514) 735-1916
Emp Here 30
SIC 8211 Elementary and secondary schools

D-U-N-S 25-240-3621 (BR)
COMMISSION SCOLAIRE MARGUERITE-BOURGEOYS

ECOLE SECONDAIRE PIERRE LAPORTE
1101 Ch Rockland, Mont-Royal, QC, H3P 2X8
(514) 739-6311
Emp Here 125
SIC 8211 Elementary and secondary schools

D-U-N-S 20-712-4228 (BR)
COMMISSION SCOLAIRE MARGUERITE-BOURGEOYS
ACADEMIE ST-CLEMENT
1345 Ch Regent, Mont-Royal, QC, H3P 2K8
(514) 739-5070
Emp Here 50
SIC 8211 Elementary and secondary schools

D-U-N-S 20-002-9960 (BR)
GAP (CANADA) INC
GAP
(Suby of The Gap Inc)
2305 Ch Rockland Bureau 240, Mont-Royal, QC, H3P 3E9
(514) 737-2334
Emp Here 24
SIC 5651 Family clothing stores

D-U-N-S 25-821-0210 (BR)
GROUPE JEAN COUTU (PJC) INC, LE
PHARMACIE JEAN COUTU
(Suby of 3958230 Canada Inc)
1365 Av Beaumont, Mont-Royal, QC, H3P 2H7
(514) 738-2401
Emp Here 70
SIC 5912 Drug stores and proprietary stores

D-U-N-S 20-798-9570 (HQ)
GROUPE OPMEDIC INC
CENTRE DE FERTILITE PROCREA
(Suby of Groupe OPMEDIC Inc)
1361 Av Beaumont Bureau 301, Mont-Royal, QC, H3P 2W3
(514) 345-9877
Emp Here 40   Emp Total 50
Sales 3,283,232
SIC 8093 Specialty outpatient clinics, nec

D-U-N-S 25-665-0706 (BR)
HUDSON'S BAY COMPANY
BAY, THE
2435 Ch Rockland, Mont-Royal, QC, H3P 2Z3
(514) 739-5521
Emp Here 200
SIC 5331 Variety stores

D-U-N-S 24-762-3101 (BR)
NAUTILUS PLUS INC
2305 Ch Rockland Bureau 42, Mont-Royal, QC, H3P 3E9
(514) 341-1553
Emp Here 20
SIC 7991 Physical fitness facilities

D-U-N-S 25-475-2439 (SL)
RADIOLOGIE LAENNEC INC
(Suby of Imagix Imagerie Medicale Inc)
1100 Av Beaumont Bureau 104, Mont-Royal, QC, H3P 3H5
(514) 738-6866
Emp Here 35   Sales 2,115,860
SIC 8011 Offices and clinics of medical doctors

D-U-N-S 24-904-5220 (SL)
REEL ALESA LTEE
(Suby of RIO TINTO PLC)
150 Ch Rockland, Mont-Royal, QC, H3P 2V9
(514) 937-9105
Emp Here 20   Sales 3,378,379
SIC 3535 Conveyors and conveying equipment

D-U-N-S 25-309-9477 (BR)
ROYAL BANK OF CANADA
RBC
(Suby of Royal Bank Of Canada)
1427 Boul Graham, Mont-Royal, QC, H3P 3M9

(514) 340-3080
Emp Here 20
SIC 6021 National commercial banks

D-U-N-S 20-765-2251   (SL)
ROYAL LEPAGE (1598)
1301 Ch Canora, Mont-Royal, QC, H3P 2J5
(514) 735-2281
Emp Here 50   *Sales* 4,742,446
SIC 6531 Real estate agents and managers

D-U-N-S 25-308-9395   (BR)
SOCIETE DES ALCOOLS DU QUEBEC
SAQ
2305 Ch Rockland Bureau 502.1, Mont-Royal,
QC, H3P 3E9
(514) 733-6414
Emp Here 33
SIC 5921 Liquor stores

D-U-N-S 25-307-2748   (BR)
VIGI SANTE LTEE
*CENTRE D'HEBERGEMENT ET DE SOINS
DE LONGUE DUREE MONT-ROYAL*
(*Suby of* Vigi Sante Ltee)
275 Av Brittany, Mont-Royal, QC, H3P 3C2
(514) 739-5593
Emp Here 350
SIC 8361 Residential care

Mont-Royal, QC H3R
Hochelaga County

D-U-N-S 20-002-8236   (BR)
BANK OF NOVA SCOTIA, THE
BANQUE SCOTIA
2380 Ch Lucerne, Mont-Royal, QC, H3R 2J8
(514) 735-2261
Emp Here 23
SIC 6021 National commercial banks

D-U-N-S 25-233-6813   (BR)
**COMMISSION SCOLAIRE ENGLISH-
MONTREAL**
CARLYLE SCHOOL
109 Av Carlyle, Mont-Royal, QC, H3R 1S8
(514) 738-1256
Emp Here 25
SIC 8211 Elementary and secondary schools

D-U-N-S 25-298-6468   (BR)
**COMMISSION SCOLAIRE MARGUERITE-
BOURGEOYS**
ECOLE SECONDAIRE MONT-ROYAL
50 Av Montgomery, Mont-Royal, QC, H3R 2B3
(514) 731-2761
Emp Here 80
SIC 8211 Elementary and secondary schools

D-U-N-S 25-233-7050   (BR)
**COMMISSION SCOLAIRE MARGUERITE-
BOURGEOYS**
ECOLE SAINT CLEMENT PAVILLON O
555 Av Mitchell, Mont-Royal, QC, H3R 1L5
(514) 735-0400
Emp Here 25
SIC 8211 Elementary and secondary schools

D-U-N-S 24-676-6034   (SL)
PSB BOISJOLI S.E.N.R.C.L
3333 Boul Graham Bureau 400, Mont-Royal,
QC, H3R 3L5
(514) 341-5511
Emp Here 65   *Sales* 2,845,467
SIC 8721 Accounting, auditing, and book-
keeping

D-U-N-S 24-970-6136   (BR)
PROVIGO DISTRIBUTION INC
2300 Ch Lucerne, Mont-Royal, QC, H3R 2J8

Emp Here 50
SIC 5411 Grocery stores

D-U-N-S 24-394-8614   (SL)
THOMSON   REUTERS   DT   IMPOT   ET

COMPTABILITE INC
DR TAX SOFTWARE
3333 Boul Graham Bureau 222, Mont-Royal,
QC, H3R 3L5
(514) 733-8355
Emp Here 22   *Sales* 1,605,135
SIC 7372 Prepackaged software

D-U-N-S 25-232-1229   (BR)
VILLE DE MONTREAL
VILLE DE MONTREAL
1967 Boul Graham, Mont-Royal, QC, H3R
1G9
(514) 734-2967
Emp Here 20
SIC 8231 Libraries

Mont-Royal, QC H4N
Hochelaga County

D-U-N-S 20-236-4618   (HQ)
CORPORATION UTEX
UTEX
(*Suby of* Corporation Utex)
4360 Ch De La Cote-De-Liesse Bureau 200,
Mont-Royal, QC, H4N 2P7
(514) 737-4300
Emp Here 100   *Emp Total* 120
Sales 30,144,000
SIC 5136 Men's and boy's clothing
Pr Pr David Gurberg
VP VP Richard Gurberg
    Marian Gurberg
    Joan Zafran

Mont-Royal, QC H4P
Hochelaga County

D-U-N-S 24-890-3015   (SL)
85605 CANADA INC
845 Av Plymouth, Mont-Royal, QC, H4P 1B2

Emp Here 175   *Sales* 44,010,240
SIC 5136 Men's and boy's clothing
Pr Pr David Gurberg
VP Marian Gurberg
Crdt Mgr Emile Khadoury

D-U-N-S 20-424-1509   (HQ)
AMERELLA OF CANADA LTD
5703 Rue Ferrier, Mont-Royal, QC, H4P 1N3
(514) 683-9511
Emp Here 103   *Emp Total* 5
Sales 22,836,699
SIC 5136 Men's and boy's clothing
Pr Pr Carlos Schuster
    Isaac Schuster
    Leonard Osten
    Jaime Merbaum
    Albert Schuster

D-U-N-S 24-205-9611   (SL)
BASQ INTERNATIONAL INC
8515 Place Devonshire Bureau 214, Mont-
Royal, QC, H4P 2K1
(514) 733-0066
Emp Here 50   *Sales* 2,626,585
SIC 7389 Business services, nec

D-U-N-S 20-289-6676   (SL)
BENTLEY CANADA INC
BENTLEY SYSTEMS
5375-85 Rue Pare Bureau 201, Mont-Royal,
QC, H4P 1P7
(514) 341-9646
Emp Here 26   *Sales* 1,386,002
SIC 5948 Luggage and leather goods stores

D-U-N-S 25-974-7509   (BR)
DCM INTEGRATED SOLUTIONS INC
SOLUTIONS INTEGREES DCM

8315 Ch Devonshire, Mont-Royal, QC, H4P
2L1
(514) 603-8105
Emp Here 50
SIC 1629 Heavy construction, nec

D-U-N-S 25-299-6087   (BR)
DOLLARAMA S.E.C.
DOLLARAMA
5805 Av Royalmount, Mont-Royal, QC, H4P
0A1
(514) 737-1006
Emp Here 450
SIC 5331 Variety stores

D-U-N-S 24-390-5101   (SL)
DYNAMITE STORES INC.
5592 Rue Ferrier Bureau 262, Mont-Royal,
QC, H4P 1M2
(514) 733-3962
Emp Here 50   *Sales* 3,064,349
SIC 5621 Women's clothing stores

D-U-N-S 24-526-8354   (SL)
EMBALLAGES STUART INC
(*Suby of* Supremex Inc)
5454 Ch De La Cote-De-Liesse, Mont-Royal,
QC, H4P 1A5
(514) 344-5000
Emp Here 75   *Sales* 11,235,948
SIC 2657 Folding paperboard boxes
Pr Pr Stuart Goldman
VP Stewart Emerson
Treas Bertrand Jolicoeur

D-U-N-S 20-218-1491   (HQ)
ERICSSON CANADA INC
RECHERCHE ERICSSON CANADA
8400 Boul Decarie, Mont-Royal, QC, H4P 2N2
(514) 345-7900
Emp Here 200   *Emp Total* 200
Sales 305,126,130
SIC 5065 Electronic parts and equipment, nec
Pr Mark Henderson
Ch Bd Lionel Hurtubise
Dir Michel Peladeau

D-U-N-S 20-956-3365   (BR)
ERICSSON CANADA INC
8400 Boul Decarie, Mont-Royal, QC, H4P 2N2
(514) 345-7900
Emp Here 1,550
SIC 5065 Electronic parts and equipment, nec

D-U-N-S 20-059-2611   (BR)
EXCEL AUTOMOBILES MONTREAL LTEE
EXCEL HONDA
5470 Rue Pare, Mont-Royal, QC, H4P 2M1
(514) 342-6363
Emp Here 25
SIC 5521 Used car dealers

D-U-N-S 20-355-7251   (SL)
**FREEMARK APPAREL BRANDS GROUP
INC**
(*Suby of* Freemark Apparel Group Holdings
Inc)
5640 Rue Pare, Mont-Royal, QC, H4P 2M1
(514) 341-7333
Emp Here 75   *Sales* 13,716,612
SIC 5136 Men's and boy's clothing
Pr Mark Routtenberg
VP Sls Lawrence Routtenberg
Sec Michael Routtenberg
Treas Treas Howard Schnider

D-U-N-S 20-355-7608   (SL)
**FREEMARK APPAREL BRANDS RETAIL
BE INC**
(*Suby of* Freemark Apparel Group Holdings
Inc)
5640 Rue Pare, Mont-Royal, QC, H4P 2M1
(514) 341-7333
Emp Here 20   *Sales* 27,360,263
SIC 5651 Family clothing stores
Pr Mark Routtenberg
VP Lawrence Routtenberg
Sec Michael Routtenberg

Treas Howard Schnider

D-U-N-S 20-315-9835   (BR)
LEGGETT & PLATT CANADA CO.
HANES INDUSTRIES, DIV OF
5675 Av Royalmount, Mont-Royal, QC, H4P
1K3
(514) 335-2520
Emp Here 22
SIC 5131 Piece goods and notions

D-U-N-S 20-760-7235   (SL)
PENSHU INC
CHAUSSURES GABY
(*Suby of* Investissements Biscayne Inc)
5745 Rue Pare, Mont-Royal, QC, H4P 1S1
(514) 731-2112
Emp Here 90   *Sales* 4,304,681
SIC 3144 Women's footwear, except athletic

D-U-N-S 24-814-6128   (SL)
**R.S.M. PRET A PORTER INTERNATIONAL
INC**
5798 Rue Ferrier, Mont-Royal, QC, H4P 1M7

Emp Here 70   *Sales* 10,648,318
SIC 2331 Women's and misses' blouses and
shirts
Pr Pr Ram Mahtani
    Moti Mahtani
    Ramesh Sadhwani

D-U-N-S 24-158-7588   (SL)
**SERVICES   INDUSTRIELS   SYSTEMEX
(S.I.S.) INC**
8260 Ch Devonshire Unite 240, Mont-Royal,
QC, H4P 2P7
(514) 738-6323
Emp Here 50   *Sales* 4,742,446
SIC 5999 Miscellaneous retail stores, nec

D-U-N-S 20-234-9080   (HQ)
STOKES INC
ARTICLES INTERNATIONAUX
(*Suby of* Movex Inc)
5660 Rue Ferrier, Mont-Royal, QC, H4P 1M7
(514) 341-4334
Emp Here 100   *Emp Total* 1
Sales 49,175,512
SIC 5719 Miscellaneous homefurnishings
Pr Jordan Shiveck
    Morris Shiveck
Sec Stuart Shiveck

D-U-N-S 20-013-8613   (SL)
SYSTEMES DELEVANTE INC
RAYMARK
(*Suby of* Mi9 Retail Inc.)
5460 Ch De La Cote-De-Liesse, Mont-Royal,
QC, H4P 1A5
(514) 737-0941
Emp Here 25   *Sales* 6,502,070
SIC 7371 Custom computer programming ser-
vices
Pr Marc Chriqui

D-U-N-S 20-213-9387   (BR)
UNILEVER CANADA INC
UNILEVER BESTFOODS
5430 Ch De La Cote-De-Liesse, Mont-Royal,
QC, H4P 1A5
(514) 735-1141
Emp Here 80
SIC 2086 Bottled and canned soft drinks

D-U-N-S 24-489-4499   (BR)
**WAWANESA MUTUAL INSURANCE COM-
PANY, THE**
COMPAGNIE D'ASSURANCE WAWANESA
(*Suby of* Wawanesa Mutual Insurance Com-
pany, The)
8585 Boul Decarie, Mont-Royal, QC, H4P 2J4
(514) 342-2211
Emp Here 150
SIC 6331 Fire, marine, and casualty insurance

D-U-N-S 20-552-3637   (BR)
WESTROCK COMPANY OF CANADA INC

(*Suby of* Westrock Company)
5550 Av Royalmount, Mont-Royal, QC, H4P
1H7
(514) 736-6889
Emp Here 225
SIC 4225 General warehousing and storage

Mont-Royal, QC H4T
Hochelaga County

D-U-N-S 24-799-4155   (SL)
**C S G BRODERIE & SOIE INTERNA-
TIONALE INC**
8660 Ch Darnley Bureau 102, Mont-Royal,
QC, H4T 1M4

Emp Here 70   *Sales* 3,575,074
SIC 7389 Business services, nec

D-U-N-S 25-658-7536   (BR)
**ENTERPRISE RENT-A-CAR CANADA COM-
PANY**
(*Suby of* The Crawford Group Inc)
5830 Ch De La Cote-De-Liesse Bureau 200,
Mont-Royal, QC, H4T 1B1
(514) 735-3722
Emp Here 30
SIC 7514 Passenger car rental

D-U-N-S 25-368-1738   (BR)
GLASSCELL ISOFAB INC
5760 Ch De La Cote-De-Liesse, Mont-Royal,
QC, H4T 1B1
(514) 738-1916
Emp Here 30
SIC 5033 Roofing, siding, and insulation

D-U-N-S 20-032-7182   (BR)
PRGX CANADA CORP
PROFIT RECOVERY GROUP
8569 Ch Dalton, Mont-Royal, QC, H4T 1V5
(514) 341-6888
Emp Here 30
SIC 8742 Management consulting services

D-U-N-S 24-155-5098   (BR)
SCHINDLER ELEVATOR CORPORATION
8577 Ch Dalton, Mont-Royal, QC, H4T 1V5
(514) 737-5507
Emp Here 100
SIC 3534 Elevators and moving stairways

D-U-N-S 20-119-8418   (HQ)
SUPERTEK CANADA INC
PRODUITS DIVINE
(*Suby of* 9256-2669 Quebec Inc)
8605 Ch Darnley, Mont-Royal, QC, H4T 1X2
(514) 737-8354
Emp Here 46   *Emp Total* 25
Sales 5,180,210
SIC 5099 Durable goods, nec
Pr Denis Benoit
Sec Pierre Benoit

D-U-N-S 20-118-7445   (HQ)
ULTRA ELECTRONICS TCS INC
*SYSTEMES DE COMMUNICATION TAC-
TIQUES ULTRA ELECTRONICS*
5990 Ch De La Cote-De-Liesse, Mont-Royal,
QC, H4T 1V7
(514) 855-6363
Emp Here 150   *Emp Total* 4,006
Sales 26,074,155
SIC 3679 Electronic components, nec
Alan Barker
Dir Rakesh Sharma
Dir Paul Dean
Dir Mary Waldner
Pr Pr Iwan Jemczyk
Dir Carlos Santiago

D-U-N-S 25-246-1603   (BR)
VWR INTERNATIONAL CO.
VWR CANLAB
(*Suby of* VWR Corporation)

8567 Ch Dalton, Mont-Royal, QC, H4T 1V5
(514) 344-3525
Emp Here 25
SIC 5049 Professional equipment, nec

Mont-Saint-Gregoire, QC J0J
Iberville County

D-U-N-S 25-233-0436   (BR)
**COMMISSION SCOLAIRE DES HAUTES-
RIVIERES**
*COMMISSION SCOLAIRE DES HAUTES-
RIVIERES*
230 Rue Bessette, Mont-Saint-Gregoire, QC,
J0J 1K0
(450) 347-2612
Emp Here 30
SIC 8211 Elementary and secondary schools

Mont-Saint-Hilaire, QC J3H

D-U-N-S 24-712-0173   (SL)
2855-6512 QUEBEC INC
MANOIR ROUVILLE-CAMPBELL
125 Ch Des Patriotes S, Mont-Saint-Hilaire,
QC, J3H 3G5
(450) 446-6060
Emp Here 50   *Sales* 2,188,821
SIC 7011 Hotels and motels

D-U-N-S 25-523-0427   (SL)
**ARPENTS VERTS, FRUITS & LEGUMES
INC, LES**
365 Boul Sir-Wilfrid-Laurier Bureau 107, Mont-
Saint-Hilaire, QC, J3H 6A2

Emp Here 49   *Sales* 5,782,650
SIC 5431 Fruit and vegetable markets
Pr Pr Real Riendeau
Gisele Oligny

D-U-N-S 24-364-7836   (HQ)
BBA INC
TOP CONTROL
(*Suby of* Groupe BBA Inc)
375 Boul Sir-Wilfrid-Laurier, Mont-Saint-
Hilaire, QC, J3H 6C3
(450) 464-2111
Emp Here 100   *Emp Total* 508
Sales 55,093,564
SIC 8711 Engineering services
Pr Andre Allard
Sec Normand Girard
Dir Opers Martin Milot
Dir Christophe Desage
Dir Angelo Grandillo
Dir Pierre Girard
Dir Serge Benoit
Dir Guy Janneteau
Dir Stephan Landry
Dir Mathieu Riedl

D-U-N-S 25-233-4412   (BR)
COMMISSION SCOLAIRE DES PATRIOTES
ECOLE DE L'AQUARELLE
50 Rue Michel, Mont-Saint-Hilaire, QC, J3H
3R3
(450) 467-0971
Emp Here 48
SIC 8211 Elementary and secondary schools

D-U-N-S 25-240-5519   (BR)
COMMISSION SCOLAIRE DES PATRIOTES
*ECOLES SECONDAIRES - MONT-SAINT-
HILAIRE - OZIAS-LEDUC*
525 Rue Jolliet, Mont-Saint-Hilaire, QC, J3H
3N2
(450) 467-0261
Emp Here 140
SIC 8211 Elementary and secondary schools

D-U-N-S 20-712-3014   (BR)
COMMISSION SCOLAIRE DES PATRIOTES
ECOLE AU-FIL-DE-L'EAU
120 Rue Sainte-Anne, Mont-Saint-Hilaire, QC,
J3H 3A4
(450) 467-6773
Emp Here 50
SIC 8211 Elementary and secondary schools

D-U-N-S 24-110-7841   (BR)
EMERGIS INC
ENTREPRISE TELLUS, DE
505 Boul Sir-Wilfrid-Laurier, Mont-Saint-
Hilaire, QC, J3H 4X7
(800) 363-9398
Emp Here 105
SIC 7371 Custom computer programming ser-
vices

D-U-N-S 20-333-0217   (SL)
ENDOCEUTICS PHARMA (MSH) INC
ENDOCEUTICS PHARMACEUTIQUE MSH
597 Boul Sir-Wilfrid-Laurier, Mont-Saint-
Hilaire, QC, J3H 6C4
(450) 467-5138
Emp Here 35   *Sales* 3,984,755
SIC 2834 Pharmaceutical preparations

D-U-N-S 25-577-4911   (BR)
GROUPE CIMENT QUEBEC INC
UNIBETON
(*Suby of* Groupe Ciment Quebec Inc)
960 Ch Benoit, Mont-Saint-Hilaire, QC, J3H
0L9
(450) 467-2864
Emp Here 20
SIC 3531 Construction machinery

D-U-N-S 25-309-6812   (BR)
**INDUSTRIELLE ALLIANCE, ASSURANCE
ET SERVICES FINANCIERS INC**
AGENCE BELOEIL
370 Boul Sir-Wilfrid-Laurier Bureau 203, Mont-
Saint-Hilaire, QC, J3H 5V3
(450) 467-0993
Emp Here 20
SIC 6411 Insurance agents, brokers, and ser-
vice

D-U-N-S 24-712-0215   (SL)
**PROPRIETES IMMOBILIERE GRAND DUC
INC, LES**
125 Ch Des Patriotes S, Mont-Saint-Hilaire,
QC, J3H 3G5
(450) 464-5250
Emp Here 66   *Sales* 12,376,900
SIC 6712 Bank holding companies
Pr Roger Jauvin

D-U-N-S 25-665-3999   (SL)
**RITCHIE BROS. AUCTIONEERS INCORPO-
RATED**
1373 Rue Briere, Mont-Saint-Hilaire, QC, J3H
6E9
(450) 464-2888
Emp Here 25
SIC 7389 Business services, nec

Mont-Tremblant, QC J8E
Terrebonne County

D-U-N-S 24-000-2019   (BR)
2646-2937 QUEBEC INC
TIM HORTONS
(*Suby of* 2646-2937 Quebec Inc)
61 Montee Ryan Bureau 2534, Mont-
Tremblant, QC, J8E 1S3

Emp Here 25
SIC 5812 Eating places

D-U-N-S 24-941-9409   (SL)
3090-9626 QUEBEC INC
AUBERGE GRAY ROCKS
100 Ch Champagne, Mont-Tremblant, QC,

J8E 1V4
(819) 425-2772
Emp Here 400   *Sales* 22,615,896
SIC 7011 Hotels and motels
Pr Pr Phillip Robinson
VP Daniel Cordier
Dir William Robinson

D-U-N-S 24-471-4072   (BR)
AUTOBUS GALLAND LTEE
GALLANT MONT-TREMBLANT
(*Suby of* Autobus Galland Ltee)
360 Rue Magloire-Gosselin Unite 1, Mont-
Tremblant, QC, J8E 2R3
(819) 681-0871
Emp Here 50
SIC 4131 Intercity and rural bus transportation

D-U-N-S 20-792-4697   (SL)
AUTOBUS LE PROMENEUR INC
240 117 Rte, Mont-Tremblant, QC, J8E 2X1
(819) 425-3096
Emp Here 65   *Sales* 1,824,018
SIC 4151 School buses

D-U-N-S 24-729-6999   (SL)
CLUB TREMBLANT INC
121 Rue Cuttle, Mont-Tremblant, QC, J8E 1B9
(819) 425-2731
Emp Here 80   *Sales* 3,502,114
SIC 7011 Hotels and motels

D-U-N-S 25-232-8216   (BR)
**COMMISSION SCOLAIRE DES LAUREN-
TIDES**
*CAMPUS PRIMAIRE MONT TRAMBLANT
PAVILLON FLEUR SOLEIL*
(*Suby of* Commission Scolaire Des Lauren-
tides)
439 Rue Labelle, Mont-Tremblant, QC, J8E
3H2
(819) 425-3565
Emp Here 30
SIC 8211 Elementary and secondary schools

D-U-N-S 20-034-1415   (BR)
**COMMISSION SCOLAIRE DES LAUREN-
TIDES**
*CENTRE DE FORMATION GENERALE DES
MONT-TREMBLANT*
(*Suby of* Commission Scolaire Des Lauren-
tides)
700 Boul Du Docteur-Gervais, Mont-
Tremblant, QC, J8E 2T3
(819) 425-2710
Emp Here 20
SIC 8211 Elementary and secondary schools

D-U-N-S 25-541-6588   (BR)
**COMMISSION SCOLAIRE DES LAUREN-
TIDES**
ECOLE POLYVALENTE CURE MERCURE
(*Suby of* Commission Scolaire Des Lauren-
tides)
700 Boul Du Docteur-Gervais, Mont-
Tremblant, QC, J8E 2T3
(819) 425-3743
Emp Here 50
SIC 8211 Elementary and secondary schools

D-U-N-S 24-012-1942   (BR)
**COMMISSION SCOLAIRE DES LAUREN-
TIDES**
*ECOLE SECTEUR NORD CAMPUS PRI-
MAIRE MONT TREMBLANT PAVILLON
TROIS SAISONS*
(*Suby of* Commission Scolaire Des Lauren-
tides)
509 Rue Labelle, Mont-Tremblant, QC, J8E
3H2
(819) 425-3420
Emp Here 20
SIC 8211 Elementary and secondary schools

D-U-N-S 25-537-1478   (SL)
**COMPAGNIE DE VILLEGIATURE ET DE DE-
VELOPEMENT GRAND LODGE INC, LA**
GRAND LODGE DU MONT TREMBLANT, LE

2396 Rue Labelle, Mont-Tremblant, QC, J8E 1T8
(819) 425-2734
Emp Here 110   *Sales* 4,815,406
SIC 7011 Hotels and motels

D-U-N-S 24-360-3805   (SL)
COUPAL & FILS INC
GROUPE YVES GAGNON MONT-TREMBLANT
(*Suby of* 168566 Canada Inc)
349 117 Rte, Mont-Tremblant, QC, J8E 2X4
(819) 425-8771
Emp Here 70   *Sales* 14,167,680
SIC 5211 Lumber and other building materials
Pr Pr Yves Gagnon

D-U-N-S 20-959-7306   (SL)
GESTION HOTEL QUINTESSENCE INC
HOTEL QUINTESSENCE
(*Suby of* 2755866 Canada Inc)
3004 Ch De La Chapelle, Mont-Tremblant, QC, J8E 1E1
(819) 425-3400
Emp Here 50   *Sales* 2,826,987
SIC 7011 Hotels and motels

D-U-N-S 24-101-5101   (BR)
GROUPE BARBE & ROBIDOUX.SAT INC
PLANISAT
991 Rue De Saint-Jovite Bureau 201, Mont-Tremblant, QC, J8E 3J8
(819) 425-2777
Emp Here 45
SIC 8713 Surveying services

D-U-N-S 20-290-7655   (BR)
GROUPE LALIBERTE SPORTS INC
SPORTS EXPERTS
348 Rue De Saint-Jovite, Mont-Tremblant, QC, J8E 2Z9
(819) 425-3421
Emp Here 24
SIC 5941 Sporting goods and bicycle shops

D-U-N-S 20-589-8880   (BR)
HYDRO-QUEBEC
365 Rue Simeon, Mont-Tremblant, QC, J8E 2R2
(450) 565-2210
Emp Here 20
SIC 4911 Electric services

D-U-N-S 20-023-0402   (BR)
INTRAWEST RESORT CLUB GROUP
EMBARC TREMBLANT
(*Suby of* Intrawest Resorts Holdings, Inc.)
200 Ch Des Saisons, Mont-Tremblant, QC, J8E 1G1
(819) 681-3535
Emp Here 50
SIC 7011 Hotels and motels

D-U-N-S 20-630-9549   (SL)
ROTISSERIES MONT TREMBLANT INC
ST HUBERT
330 Rue De Saint-Jovite, Mont-Tremblant, QC, J8E 2Z9
(819) 425-2721
Emp Here 70   *Sales* 2,115,860
SIC 5812 Eating places

D-U-N-S 25-115-0462   (SL)
SKI LE GAP INC
CHATEAU LE GAP
220 Ch Wheeler, Mont-Tremblant, QC, J8E 1V3
(819) 429-6599
Emp Here 58   *Sales* 3,137,310
SIC 7999 Amusement and recreation, nec

D-U-N-S 20-847-3376   (BR)
SOCIETE IMMOBILIERE M.C.M. INC, LA
979 Rue De Saint-Jovite, Mont-Tremblant, QC, J8E 3J8
(819) 429-6464
Emp Here 20
SIC 6531 Real estate agents and managers

D-U-N-S 25-308-9643   (BR)
SOCIETE DES ALCOOLS DU QUEBEC
SOCIETE DES ALCOOLS DU QUEBEC
1122 Rue De Saint-Jovite, Mont-Tremblant, QC, J8E 3J9
(819) 425-6301
Emp Here 30
SIC 5921 Liquor stores

D-U-N-S 25-359-2109   (SL)
STATION MONT TREMBLANT INC
(*Suby of* Hawk Holding Company, LLC)
1000 Ch Des Voyageurs, Mont-Tremblant, QC, J8E 1T1
(819) 681-3000
Emp Here 2,000   *Sales* 87,552,840
SIC 7011 Hotels and motels
Pr Patrice Malo
VP Thierry Brossard
Sec Julie Bodden
Dir Karen Sanford

D-U-N-S 24-528-2082   (SL)
STATION MONT-TREMBLANT SOCIETE EN COMMANDITE
BAR CAPPUCINO
(*Suby of* Hawk Holding Company, LLC)
1000 Ch Des Voyageurs, Mont-Tremblant, QC, J8E 1T1
(819) 681-2000
Emp Here 2,000   *Sales* 87,552,840
SIC 7011 Hotels and motels
Pr Patrice Malo

D-U-N-S 24-885-0091   (BR)
TRANSCONTINENTAL INC
JOURNAL DE L'INFORMATION DU NORD
1107 Rue De Saint-Jovite, Mont-Tremblant, QC, J8E 3J9
(819) 425-8658
Emp Here 20
SIC 2711 Newspapers

D-U-N-S 20-354-2654   (SL)
VINCENT, SYLVAIN
MCDONALDS 22028 NA
387 117 Rte, Mont-Tremblant, QC, J8E 2X4
(819) 425-1333
Emp Here 70   *Sales* 2,115,860
SIC 5812 Eating places

D-U-N-S 24-095-4326   (BR)
WSP CANADA INC
GENIVAR
386 Rue De Saint-Jovite Bureau 1, Mont-Tremblant, QC, J8E 2Z9
(819) 425-3483
Emp Here 20
SIC 8711 Engineering services

Montcerf-Lytton, QC J0W

D-U-N-S 20-242-5414   (BR)
SOCIETE DES ETABLISSEMENTS DE PLEIN AIR DU QUEBEC
SEPAQ
Gd, Montcerf-Lytton, QC, J0W 1N0

Emp Here 50
SIC 8641 Civic and social associations

D-U-N-S 25-595-0438   (BR)
SOCIETE DES ETABLISSEMENTS DE PLEIN AIR DU QUEBEC
POURVOIRIE LE DOMAINE
1 Rte 117, Montcerf-Lytton, QC, J0W 1N0

Emp Here 50
SIC 7011 Hotels and motels

Montebello, QC J0V
Papineau County

D-U-N-S 20-712-5597   (BR)
COMMISSION SCOLAIRE AU COEUR DES VALLEES
ECOLE ST MICHEL
240 Rue Bonsecours, Montebello, QC, J0V 1L0
(819) 427-1015
Emp Here 20
SIC 8211 Elementary and secondary schools

D-U-N-S 25-292-4287   (BR)
FAIRMONT HOTELS & RESORTS INC
FAIRMONT KENAUK AT LE CHATEAU MON-TEBELLO
1000 Ch Kenauk Bureau D, Montebello, QC, J0V 1L0
(819) 423-5573
Emp Here 24
SIC 7011 Hotels and motels

D-U-N-S 24-698-8778   (BR)
FAIRMONT HOTELS & RESORTS INC
FAIRMONT LE CHATEAU MONTEBELLO
392 Rue Notre-Dame, Montebello, QC, J0V 1L0
(819) 423-6341
Emp Here 175
SIC 7011 Hotels and motels

Montmagny, QC G5V
Montmagny County

D-U-N-S 20-265-5569   (HQ)
BUREAUTIQUE COTE-SUD INC
MONBURO
(*Suby of* Bureautique Cote-Sud Inc)
49 Rue Saint-Jean-Baptiste E, Montmagny, QC, G5V 1J6
(418) 248-4949
Emp Here 25   *Emp Total* 50
Sales 3,648,035
SIC 5112 Stationery and office supplies

D-U-N-S 20-295-8513   (BR)
CENTRE DE READAPTATION EN DEFI-CIENCE INTELLECTUELLE ET TED
CRDI CHAUDIERE-APPALACHES
20 Av Cote, Montmagny, QC, G5V 1Z9
(418) 248-4970
Emp Here 150
SIC 8361 Residential care

D-U-N-S 20-002-3310   (BR)
CENTRES JEUNESSE CHAUDIERE-APPALACHES, LES
CISSS - CENTRE INTEGRE DE SANTE ET DE SERVICES SOCIAUX DE CHAUDIERE-APPALACHES
117 Av Collin, Montmagny, QC, G5V 2S7
(418) 248-3934
Emp Here 20
SIC 8322 Individual and family services

D-U-N-S 25-066-3317   (SL)
CHABOT CARROSSERIE INC
264 Ch Des Poirier, Montmagny, QC, G5V 4S5
(418) 234-1525
Emp Here 50   *Sales* 3,575,074
SIC 7532 Top and body repair and paint shops

D-U-N-S 20-574-5867   (BR)
COLLEGE D'ENSEIGNEMENT GENERAL & PROFESSIONEL DE LA POCATIERE
COLLEGE D'ENSEIGNEMENT GENERAL & PROFESSIONEL DE LA POCATIERE
(*Suby of* College D'Enseignement General & Professionel De La Pocatiere)
115 Boul Tache E, Montmagny, QC, G5V 1B9
(418) 248-7164
Emp Here 50
SIC 8221 Colleges and universities

D-U-N-S 25-233-0402   (BR)
COMMISSION SCOLAIRE DE LA COTE-DU-SUD, LA
COMMISSION SCOLAIRE DE LA COTE-DU-SUD, LA
111 7e Rue, Montmagny, QC, G5V 3H2
(418) 248-1666
Emp Here 21
SIC 8211 Elementary and secondary schools

D-U-N-S 25-240-2482   (BR)
COMMISSION SCOLAIRE DE LA COTE-DU-SUD, LA
COMMISSION SCOLAIRE DE LA COTE-DU-SUD, LA
388 Boul Tache E, Montmagny, QC, G5V 1E2
(418) 248-8198
Emp Here 20
SIC 8211 Elementary and secondary schools

D-U-N-S 25-232-6871   (BR)
COMMISSION SCOLAIRE DE LA COTE-DU-SUD, LA
ECOLE BEAUBIEN
95 Rue De L'Anse, Montmagny, QC, G5V 1G9
(418) 248-0646
Emp Here 40
SIC 8211 Elementary and secondary schools

D-U-N-S 20-711-9962   (BR)
COMMISSION SCOLAIRE DE LA COTE-DU-SUD, LA
COMMISSION SCOLAIRE DE LA COTE-DU-SUD, LA
141 Boul Tache E, Montmagny, QC, G5V 1B9
(418) 248-2370
Emp Here 112
SIC 8211 Elementary and secondary schools

D-U-N-S 25-489-2896   (BR)
GESTION N. AUGER INC
RESTAURANT MCDONALD'S
(*Suby of* Gestion N. Auger Inc)
85 Boul Tache E, Montmagny, QC, G5V 4J8
(418) 248-5911
Emp Here 25
SIC 5812 Eating places

D-U-N-S 24-791-7610   (BR)
GROUPE COOPERATIF DYNACO
CENTRE DE RENOVATION DYNACO BMR
(*Suby of* Groupe Cooperatif Dynaco)
111 Boul Tache O, Montmagny, QC, G5V 3A6
(418) 248-0845
Emp Here 27
SIC 5211 Lumber and other building materials

D-U-N-S 24-530-4910   (HQ)
GUY THIBAULT CHEVROLET BUICK GMC CADILLAC LTEE
(*Suby of* Groupe Automobile Frechette Thibault Ltee, Le)
500 Av Saint-David Bureau 224, Montmagny, QC, G5V 4P9
(418) 248-7122
Emp Here 30   *Emp Total* 1
Sales 15,321,747
SIC 5511 New and used car dealers
Pr Pr Francis Frechette
VP VP Ronald Thibault
Sec Christian Thibault

D-U-N-S 20-320-5153   (BR)
LEMIEUX NOLET COMPTABLES AGREES S.E.N.C.R.L.
(*Suby of* Lemieux Nolet Comptables Agrees S.E.N.C.R.L.)
25 Boul Tache O Bureau 205, Montmagny, QC, G5V 2Z9
(418) 248-1910
Emp Here 130
SIC 3578 Calculating and accounting equipment

D-U-N-S 24-340-7314   (BR)
MARQUIS IMPRIMEUR INC
305 Boul Tache E, Montmagny, QC, G5V 1C7
(418) 248-0737
Emp Here 30

▲ Public Company   ■ Public Company Family Member   **HQ** Headquarters   **BR** Branch   **SL** Single Location

SIC 2732 Book printing

D-U-N-S 20-209-1104 (SL)
MONTEL INC
225 4e Av, Montmagny, QC, G5V 4N9
(418) 248-0235
Emp Here 195   Sales 15,102,865
SIC 2542 Partitions and fixtures, except wood
Pr Pr Michel Doucet
 Claire Brunelle
Dir Jerome Doucet

D-U-N-S 20-642-7960 (BR)
PROVIGO INC
MAXI MONTMAGNY
101 Boul Tache O, Montmagny, QC, G5V 3T8
(418) 248-C912
Emp Here 60
SIC 5411 Grocery stores

D-U-N-S 20-519-8323 (BR)
RAYMOND CHABOT INC
5 Boul Tache E, Montmagny, QC, G5V 1B6
(418) 248-1303
Emp Here 30
SIC 8721 Accounting, auditing, and book-keeping

D-U-N-S 24-638-7054 (SL)
RESTAURANT A LA RIVE INC
153 Rue Saint-Louis, Montmagny, QC, G5V 1N4
(418) 248-3494
Emp Here 80   Sales 2,407,703
SIC 5812 Eating places

D-U-N-S 25-489-2730 (BR)
RESTAURANT NORMANDIN INC
RESTAURANT MONTMAGNY
25 Boul Tache E, Montmagny, QC, G5V 1B6
(418) 248-3667
Emp Here 40
SIC 5812 Eating places

D-U-N-S 20-113-1294 (BR)
TEKNION LIMITED
TEKNION QUEBEC
45 Ch Des Cascades, Montmagny, QC, G5V 3M6
(418) 248-5711
Emp Here 175
SIC 2522 Office furniture, except wood

Montreal, QC H1A
Hochelaga County

D-U-N-S 20-240-2389 (SL)
ABP LOCATION INC
12900 Boul Industriel, Montreal, QC, H1A 4Z6
(514) 528-5445
Emp Here 65   Sales 5,253,170
SIC 7359 Equipment rental and leasing, nec
Pr Pierre Lepine
VP Martin Houde
Sec Stephane Marin

D-U-N-S 24-368-8608 (BR)
CAISSE POPULAIRE DESJARDINS DE POINTE-AUX-TREMBLES
CAISSE POPULAIRE DESJARDINS DE POINTE-AUX-TREMBLES
13990 Rue De Montigny, Montreal, QC, H1A 1J6
(514) 640-5200
Emp Here 20
SIC 6062 State credit unions

D-U-N-S 24-368-8616 (BR)
CAISSE POPULAIRE DESJARDINS DE POINTE-AUX-TREMBLES
CENTRE DE SERVICES NOTRE-DAME E
850 Rue Notre-Dame E Bureau 15, Montreal, QC, H1A 1X6

Emp Here 20

SIC 6062 State credit unions

D-U-N-S 20-216-3614 (HQ)
DELOM SERVICES INC
DELOM SOLUTIONS
13065 Rue Jean-Grou, Montreal, QC, H1A 3N6
(514) 642-8220
Emp Here 150   Emp Total 30
Sales 16,562,079
SIC 7694 Armature rewinding shops
Pr Pr Mario Montpetit
 Marc Sarazin

Montreal, QC H1B
Hochelaga County

D-U-N-S 25-001-8934 (BR)
COMMISSION SCOLAIRE DE LA POINTE-DE-L'ILE
ECOLE FELIX LECLERC
1750 Boul Du Tricentenaire, Montreal, QC, H1B 3B1
(514) 642-9910
Emp Here 30
SIC 8211 Elementary and secondary schools

D-U-N-S 25-001-9130 (BR)
COMMISSION SCOLAIRE DE LA POINTE-DE-L'ILE
POLYVALENTE SECONDAIRE DANIEL-JOHNSON
1200 Boul Du Tricentenaire, Montreal, QC, H1B 3A8
(514) 642-0240
Emp Here 80
SIC 8211 Elementary and secondary schools

D-U-N-S 20-226-3653 (SL)
HUTCHINSON AERONAUTIQUE & INDUS-TRIE LIMITEE
MARQUEZ TRANSTECH
3650 Boul Du Tricentenaire, Montreal, QC, H1B 5M8
(514) 640-9006
Emp Here 119   Sales 18,021,293
SIC 3089 Plastics products, nec
Ch Bd Cedric Duclos
Pr Eric Faucher
Sec Patricia Fauconnier
Treas Jean-Francois Simonnet

D-U-N-S 24-419-2097 (BR)
MARK'S WORK WEARHOUSE LTD
L'EQUIPEUR
3500 Boul Du Tricentenaire, Montreal, QC, H1B 0A3
(514) 645-9882
Emp Here 20
SIC 5699 Miscellaneous apparel and accessory stores

D-U-N-S 25-358-9667 (BR)
METRO RICHELIEU INC
PECHERIES ATLANTIQUES DE MONTREAL
3785 Rue Francois-Bricault, Montreal, QC, H1B 0A2
(514) 355-7966
Emp Here 60
SIC 5146 Fish and seafoods

Montreal, QC H1C
Hochelaga County

D-U-N-S 20-357-1690 (SL)
8919470 CANADA INC
10000 Boul Henri-Bourassa E, Montreal, QC, H1C 1T1
(514) 648-6366
Emp Here 23   Sales 2,407,703
SIC 1795 Wrecking and demolition work

D-U-N-S 20-012-0850 (BR)

A. LASSONDE INC
ORANGE MAISON, DIV DE
(Suby of 3346625 Canada Inc)
11500 Boul Henri-Bourassa E, Montreal, QC, H1C 1S9
(514) 351-4010
Emp Here 20
SIC 2033 Canned fruits and specialties

D-U-N-S 20-533-3961 (SL)
ATPAC INC
10700 Boul Henri-Bourassa E, Montreal, QC, H1C 1G9
(514) 881-8888
Emp Here 70   Sales 8,536,402
SIC 5013 Motor vehicle supplies and new parts
Pr Dolores Richardson

D-U-N-S 25-360-6628 (BR)
CIMENT QUEBEC INC
UNIBETON HENRI-BOURASSA
(Suby of Groupe Ciment Quebec Inc)
10705 Boul Henri-Bourassa E, Montreal, QC, H1C 1G7
(514) 332-1901
Emp Here 44
SIC 3273 Ready-mixed concrete

D-U-N-S 20-712-5019 (BR)
COMMISSION SCOLAIRE ENGLISH-MONTREAL
12165 Boul Saint-Jean-Baptiste, Montreal, QC, H1C 1S4
(514) 881-4351
Emp Here 50
SIC 8211 Elementary and secondary schools

D-U-N-S 20-025-7918 (BR)
COMMISSION SCOLAIRE ENGLISH-MONTREAL
EAST HILL ELEMENTARY SCHOOL
10350 Boul Perras, Montreal, QC, H1C 2H1
(514) 494-3202
Emp Here 55
SIC 8211 Elementary and secondary schools

D-U-N-S 20-712-3899 (BR)
COMMISSION SCOLAIRE DE LA POINTE-DE-L'ILE
ECOLE LA PASSERELLE
12165 Boul Saint-Jean-Baptiste, Montreal, QC, H1C 1S4
(514) 881-4690
Emp Here 40
SIC 8211 Elementary and secondary schools

D-U-N-S 24-362-4397 (SL)
G.T. SERVICE DE CONTENEURS INC
G.T. ENTREPOSAGE
10000 Boul Maurice-Duplessis, Montreal, QC, H1C 2A2
(514) 648-4848
Emp Here 65   Sales 3,939,878
SIC 7692 Welding repair

D-U-N-S 20-763-8412 (SL)
INSTITUT PHILIPPE PINEL DE MONTREAL
10905 Boul Henri-Bourassa E, Montreal, QC, H1C 1H1
(514) 648-8461
Emp Here 600   Sales 58,110,720
SIC 8063 Psychiatric hospitals
Dir Fin Jacques Jodoin
 Helene-Louise Dupont-Elie
Ex Dir Jocelyn Aubut

D-U-N-S 24-852-8320 (BR)
METRO RICHELIEU INC
11555 Boul Maurice-Duplessis Bureau 1, Montreal, QC, H1C 2A1
(514) 643-1000
Emp Here 250
SIC 4225 General warehousing and storage

D-U-N-S 20-791-2551 (SL)
TRANSPORT GARIEPY (CANADA) INC
11525 Av Armand-Chaput, Montreal, QC, H1C

1S8
(514) 494-3400
Emp Here 50   Sales 3,939,878
SIC 4212 Local trucking, without storage

D-U-N-S 20-236-1259 (SL)
TRIPAR INC
TRIPAR ENOVA, DIV OF
(Suby of 122504 Canada Inc)
9750 Boul Maurice-Duplessis, Montreal, QC, H1C 1G1
(514) 648-7471
Emp Here 50   Sales 7,350,166
SIC 3469 Metal stampings, nec
Pr Pr Ben Sevack
 Lloyd Sevack

D-U-N-S 20-707-5867 (BR)
VILLE DE MONTREAL
VILLE DE MONTREAL
12001 Boul Maurice-Duplessis, Montreal, QC, H1C 1V3
(514) 280-4359
Emp Here 300
SIC 7389 Business services, nec

D-U-N-S 20-517-4977 (BR)
VILLE DE MONTREAL
VILLE DE MONTREAL
12001 Boul Maurice-Duplessis, Montreal, QC, H1C 1V3
(514) 280-4400
Emp Here 300
SIC 4971 Irrigation systems

Montreal, QC H1E
Hochelaga County

D-U-N-S 24-669-1588 (BR)
AUTOBUS TRANSCO (1988) INC
AUTOBUS TRANSCO
7975 Boul Henri-Bourassa E, Montreal, QC, H1E 1N9
(514) 648-8625
Emp Here 100
SIC 4151 School buses

D-U-N-S 20-231-5784 (HQ)
BOISERIES RAYMOND INC
BOISERIES MILLE ILES
(Suby of Gestion Andre Waechter Inc)
11880 56e Av, Montreal, QC, H1E 2L6
(514) 494-1141
Emp Here 202   Emp Total 1
Sales 20,428,996
SIC 2431 Millwork
 Raymond Waechter
Pr Pr Luc Desrosiers
Genl Mgr Dominique Santoire

D-U-N-S 25-391-5441 (HQ)
CAISSE DESJARDINS DE RIVIERE-DES-PRAIRIES
CENTRE DE SERVICES RENE-MASSON
(Suby of Caisse Desjardins de Riviere-des-Prairies)
8300 Boul Maurice-Duplessis, Montreal, QC, H1E 3A3
(514) 648-5800
Emp Here 28   Emp Total 44
Sales 8,009,797
SIC 6062 State credit unions
Genl Mgr Andre-Paul Turcot
Dir Denise Lavoie
Pr Jean-Guy Lessard
VP VP Nicole Rouillier
Sec Nicole Bourgeois
Dir Michel Minuto
Dir Cecile Paquette
Dir Jocylyne Gauthier
Dir Marc Gervais
Dir Stephane Lessard

D-U-N-S 25-233-9338 (BR)
COMMISSION SCOLAIRE ENGLISH-

MONTREAL
MICHELANGELO ELEMENTARY SCHOOL
9360 5e Rue, Montreal, QC, H1E 1K1
(514) 648-1218
Emp Here 50
SIC 8211 Elementary and secondary schools

D-U-N-S 25-240-3100   (BR)
COMMISSION SCOLAIRE DE LA POINTE-DE-L'ILE
ECOLE FERNAND GAUTHIER
12600 Av Paul-Dufault, Montreal, QC, H1E 2B6
(514) 881-7140
Emp Here 30
SIC 8211 Elementary and secondary schools

D-U-N-S 25-232-9438   (BR)
COMMISSION SCOLAIRE DE LA POINTE-DE-L'ILE
ECOLE MARC AURELE FORTIN
12230 Av Fernand-Gauthier, Montreal, QC, H1E 5N4
(514) 881-7180
Emp Here 50
SIC 8211 Elementary and secondary schools

D-U-N-S 20-169-8284   (BR)
COMMISSION SCOLAIRE DE LA POINTE-DE-L'ILE
ECOLE DENISE PELLETIER
12160 27e Av, Montreal, QC, H1E 1Z5
(514) 881-7190
Emp Here 40
SIC 8211 Elementary and secondary schools

D-U-N-S 20-712-3881   (BR)
COMMISSION SCOLAIRE DE LA POINTE-DE-L'ILE
ECOLES SECONDAIRES JEAN GROU
9030 Boul Gouin E, Montreal, QC, H1E 1C6
(514) 881-7135
Emp Here 50
SIC 8211 Elementary and secondary schools

D-U-N-S 20-228-2612   (HQ)
COMPAGNIE D'ECHANTILLONS NATIONAL LIMITEE
COMPAGNIE U.S. SAMPLE
(*Suby of* 132179 Canada Inc)
11500 Boul Armand-Bombardier, Montreal, QC, H1E 2W9
(514) 648-4000
Emp Here 250   *Emp Total* 600
Sales 49,913,400
SIC 2782 Blankbooks and looseleaf binders
Pr Pr Morton Kader
Sec Randi Kader

D-U-N-S 20-588-8444   (BR)
COMPAGNIE DES CHEMINS DE FER NATIONAUX DU CANADA
11455 26e Av, Montreal, QC, H1E 3K3
(514) 881-2053
Emp Here 50
SIC 4111 Local and suburban transit

D-U-N-S 24-334-0671   (BR)
CONGEBEC INC
7801 Boul Henri-Bourassa E, Montreal, QC, H1E 1N9
(514) 648-1712
Emp Here 20
SIC 4222 Refrigerated warehousing and storage

D-U-N-S 24-920-8802   (SL)
CONVERTISSEUR DE PAPIERS ARTEAU INC
11420 Boul Armand-Bombardier, Montreal, QC, H1E 2W9
(514) 494-2222
Emp Here 42   *Sales* 4,304,681
SIC 2679 Converted paper products, nec

D-U-N-S 24-174-1008   (SL)
ENTREPOSEURS DE FIBRES R & F LTEE
7975 Av Marco-Polo, Montreal, QC, H1E 1N8

(514) 648-8171
Emp Here 100   *Sales* 20,391,450
SIC 3081 Unsupported plastics film and sheet
Pr Hersey Friedman

D-U-N-S 20-926-8168   (SL)
FORNIRAMA INC
9100 Boul Maurice-Duplessis, Montreal, QC, H1E 7C2
(514) 494-1400
Emp Here 45   *Sales* 3,808,655
SIC 2512 Upholstered household furniture

D-U-N-S 25-257-2128   (BR)
GATX RAIL CANADA CORPORATION
CORPORATION GATX RAIL CANADA
9300 Boul Maurice-Duplessis, Montreal, QC, H1E 1M7
(514) 648-3801
Emp Here 65
SIC 4741 Rental of railroad cars

D-U-N-S 24-374-2371   (BR)
GROUPE J.S.V. INC, LE
HEXCO STAINLESS
8015 Av Marco-Polo, Montreal, QC, H1E 5Y8
(514) 881-8260
Emp Here 22
SIC 3452 Bolts, nuts, rivets, and washers

D-U-N-S 24-371-0600   (BR)
IMPRIMERIES TRANSCONTINENTAL 2005 S.E.N.C
TRANSCONTINENTAL O'KEEFE MONTREAL
8000 Av Blaise-Pascal, Montreal, QC, H1E 2S7

Emp Here 250
SIC 2752 Commercial printing, lithographic

D-U-N-S 20-419-7255   (SL)
JPMA GLOBAL INC
ENTREPRISE JPMA GLOBAL
7335 Boul Henri-Bourassa E, Montreal, QC, H1E 3T5
(514) 648-1042
Emp Here 400   *Sales* 31,008,298
SIC 2542 Partitions and fixtures, except wood
Pr Pr Guiseppe Paventi
VP Martino Paventi
VP Virginio Basile
VP Joseph Belli
VP Roberto Ciricillo
 Antonietta E Paventi
Dir Giuseppina Paventi
Dir Maria Paventi

D-U-N-S 24-592-3362   (SL)
LES ENTREPRISES REAL CARON LTEE
8455 Boul Henri-Bourassa E, Montreal, QC, H1E 1P4
(514) 352-5754
Emp Here 50   *Sales* 2,845,467
SIC 4214 Local trucking with storage

D-U-N-S 25-385-0192   (BR)
METRIE CANADA LTD
MOLDING AND MILLWORK
8801 Boul Henri-Bourassa E, Montreal, QC, H1E 1P4
(514) 955-3290
Emp Here 55
SIC 2431 Millwork

D-U-N-S 24-611-9601   (BR)
METRO RICHELIEU INC
SUPER C
8115 Boul Maurice-Duplessis, Montreal, QC, H1E 2S6
(514) 648-5077
Emp Here 36
SIC 5411 Grocery stores

D-U-N-S 24-501-3586   (HQ)
PORTES DUSCO LTEE, LES
STANLEY DOOR SYSTEMS
(*Suby of* Extrubec Plastics Inc)
11825 Av J.-J.-Joubert, Montreal, QC, H1E

7J5
(514) 355-4877
Emp Here 57   *Emp Total* 1
Sales 5,472,053
SIC 3231 Products of purchased glass
Pr Pr Harvey Dubrofsky

D-U-N-S 20-019-6447   (BR)
ROYAL BANK OF CANADA
RBC
(*Suby of* Royal Bank Of Canada)
7945 Boul Maurice-Duplessis, Montreal, QC, H1E 1M5
(514) 494-7977
Emp Here 25
SIC 6021 National commercial banks

D-U-N-S 20-101-1280   (HQ)
SERVICES ENVIRONNEMENTAUX DELSAN-A.I.M. INC, LES
AIM DELSAN
7825 Boul Henri-Bourassa E, Montreal, QC, H1E 1N9
(514) 494-9898
Emp Here 200   *Emp Total* 2,000
Sales 52,148,310
SIC 1795 Wrecking and demolition work
Pr Herbert Black
VP Ronald Black
Sec Kamila Wirpszo

D-U-N-S 24-109-6684   (BR)
SOCIETE LAURENTIDE INC
9355 Boul Henri-Bourassa E, Montreal, QC, H1E 1P4
(514) 643-1917
Emp Here 20
SIC 2899 Chemical preparations, nec

D-U-N-S 24-763-1331   (BR)
SOCIETE DES ALCOOLS DU QUEBEC
SAQ CLASSIQUE
12401 Boul Rodolphe-Forget, Montreal, QC, H1E 0A2
(514) 648-8382
Emp Here 30
SIC 5921 Liquor stores

D-U-N-S 20-214-4155   (BR)
SYSCO CANADA, INC
SYSCO QUEBEC
(*Suby of* Sysco Corporation)
11625 55e Av Bureau 864, Montreal, QC, H1E 2K2
(514) 494-5200
Emp Here 260
SIC 5141 Groceries, general line

D-U-N-S 24-113-4738   (BR)
VILLE DE MONTREAL
VILLE DE MONTREAL
9001 Boul Perras, Montreal, QC, H1E 3J7
(514) 872-9386
Emp Here 20
SIC 8231 Libraries

D-U-N-S 20-587-0699   (BR)
VILLE DE MONTREAL
VILLE DE MONTREAL
12515 Boul Rodolphe-Forget, Montreal, QC, H1E 6P6
(514) 494-9718
Emp Here 30
SIC 7999 Amusement and recreation, nec

Montreal, QC H1G
Hochelaga County

D-U-N-S 24-668-3635   (HQ)
GROUPE CHAMPLAIN INC
(*Suby of* Groupe Sante Sedna Inc)
7150 Rue Marie-Victorin, Montreal, QC, H1G 2J5
(514) 324-2044
Emp Here 25   *Emp Total* 3,000
Sales 96,887,669

SIC 8361 Residential care
Ch Bd Francois Campeau
Pr Christine Lessard
Sec Johanne Brien
Sec Corinne Ferrie
Dir Anne Beauchamp
Dir Guillaume Journel

Montreal, QC H1K
Hochelaga County

D-U-N-S 24-326-8443   (BR)
CENTRE DE SANTE ET DE SERVICES SO-CIAUX DE LA POINTE-DE-L'ILE
(*Suby of* Centre de Sante et de Services Sociaux de la Pointe-de-l'Ile)
4900 Boul Lapointe, Montreal, QC, H1K 4W9
(514) 353-1227
Emp Here 350
SIC 8361 Residential care

D-U-N-S 25-240-7507   (BR)
COMMISSION SCOLAIRE DE MONTREAL
ECOLE ST-JUSTIN
5005 Rue Mousseau, Montreal, QC, H1K 2V8
(514) 596-5040
Emp Here 54
SIC 8211 Elementary and secondary schools

D-U-N-S 25-298-5775   (BR)
COMMISSION SCOLAIRE ENGLISH-MONTREAL
ACADEMIE DUNTON
5555 Rue De Boucherville, Montreal, QC, H1K 4B6
(514) 596-2028
Emp Here 55
SIC 8211 Elementary and secondary schools

D-U-N-S 25-240-0965   (BR)
COMMISSION SCOLAIRE DE LA POINTE-DE-L'ILE
ECOLE SECONDAIRE ANJOU
8205 Rue Fonteneau, Montreal, QC, H1K 4E1
(514) 353-9970
Emp Here 150
SIC 8211 Elementary and secondary schools

D-U-N-S 20-706-9621   (BR)
SOCIETE DE TRANSPORT DE MONTREAL
L'ATTELIER BEAUGRAND
7800 Rue Chenier, Montreal, QC, H1K 4E7
(514) 280-5499
Emp Here 100
SIC 4213 Trucking, except local

Montreal, QC H1L
Hochelaga County

D-U-N-S 20-643-9262   (BR)
CAISSE DESJARDINS DE L'EDUCATION
9405 Rue Sherbrooke E Bureau 2500, Montreal, QC, H1L 6P3
(514) 351-7295
Emp Here 60
SIC 6062 State credit unions

D-U-N-S 24-810-9738   (BR)
CENTRALE DES SYNDICATS DEMOCRATIQUES
9405 Rue Sherbrooke E Bureau 200, Montreal, QC, H1L 6P3
(514) 899-1070
Emp Here 50
SIC 8631 Labor organizations

D-U-N-S 25-449-7027   (BR)
CENTRE INTEGRE UNIVERSITAIRE SANTE ET SERVICES SOCIAUX DU CENTRE-SUD-DE-L'ILE-DE-MONTREAL
CENTRE JEUNESSE DE MONTREAL MONT ST-ANTOINE

8147 Rue Sherbrooke E, Montreal, QC, H1L 1A7
(514) 356-4500
Emp Here 100
SIC 8322 Individual and family services

D-U-N-S 20-533-1239   (HQ)
CENTRE DE SANTE ET DE SERVICES SO-CIAUX DE LA POINTE-DE-L'ILE
CSSS DE LA POINTE-DE-L'ILE
(*Suby of* Centre de Sante et de Services Sociaux de la Pointe-de-l'Ile)
9503 Rue Sherbrooke E, Montreal, QC, H1L 6P2
(514) 356-2572
Emp Here 300   *Emp Total* 1,400
Sales 63,905,280
SIC 7991 Physical fitness facilities
Genl Mgr Andre Gagniere

D-U-N-S 25-240-7614   (BR)
COMMISSION SCOLAIRE DE MONTREAL
ECOLE PRIMAIRE SAINTE CLAIRE
8500 Rue Sainte-Claire, Montreal, QC, H1L 1X7
(514) 596-4944
Emp Here 30
SIC 8211 Elementary and secondary schools

D-U-N-S 25-240-6814   (BR)
COMMISSION SCOLAIRE DE MONTREAL
ECOLE PHILIPPE LABARRE
3125 Av Fletcher, Montreal, QC, H1L 4E2
(514) 596-4920
Emp Here 20
SIC 8211 Elementary and secondary schools

D-U-N-S 25-240-2540   (BR)
COMMISSION SCOLAIRE DE MONTREAL
ECOLE STE LOUISE DE MARILLAC
8100 Rue De Marseille, Montreal, QC, H1L 1P3
(514) 596-5044
Emp Here 35
SIC 8211 Elementary and secondary schools

D-U-N-S 25-240-7523   (BR)
COMMISSION SCOLAIRE DE MONTREAL
COMMISSION SCOLAIRE DE MONTREAL
2150 Rue L ebert, Montreal, QC, H1L 5R1
(514) 596-5032
Emp Here 30
SIC 8211 E ementary and secondary schools

D-U-N-S 25-240-3191   (BR)
COMMISSION SCOLAIRE DE MONTREAL
COMMISSION SCOLAIRE DE MONTREAL
2600 Av Fletcher, Montreal, QC, H1L 4C5
(514) 596-5115
Emp Here 30
SIC 8211 Elementary and secondary schools

D-U-N-S 25-240-7366   (BR)
COMMISSION SCOLAIRE DE MONTREAL
COMMISSION SCOLAIRE DE MONTREAL
2800 Boul Lapointe, Montreal, QC, H1L 5M1
(514) 596-5035
Emp Here 108
SIC 8211 Elementary and secondary schools

D-U-N-S 20-037-5447   (BR)
COMMISSION SCOLAIRE DE MONTREAL
COMMISSION SCOLAIRE DE MONTREAL
8147 Rue Sherbrooke E, Montreal, QC, H1L 1A7
(514) 356-4450
Emp Here 60
SIC 8211 Elementary and secondary schools

D-U-N-S 20-642-1062   (BR)
ROTISSERIES ST-HUBERT LTEE, LES
ST-HUBERT EXPRESS
(*Suby of* Cara Holdings Limited)
7870 Rue Sherbrooke E, Montreal, QC, H1L 1A5
(514) 385-5555
Emp Here 34
SIC 5812 Eating places

D-U-N-S 24-474-0510   (SL)
SOCIETE DE TERMINUS CAST
SOCIETE DE TERMINUS RACINE (MONTREAL)
305 Rue Curatteau, Montreal, QC, H1L 6R6
(514) 257-3047
Emp Here 33   *Sales* 7,000,050
SIC 4491 Marine cargo handling
Kevin M Doherty
Michael Fatiani

D-U-N-S 20-031-1277   (BR)
SOCIETE DES ALCOOLS DU QUEBEC
S.A.Q.
560 Av Hector, Montreal, QC, H1L 3W9
(514) 254-8686
Emp Here 100
SIC 5921 Liquor stores

Montreal, QC H1M
Hochelaga County

D-U-N-S 20-331-4125   (SL)
93168185 QUEBEC INC
7100 Rue Jean-Talon E Bureau 210, Montreal, QC, H1M 3S3
(514) 722-0024
Emp Here 20   *Sales* 1,905,752
SIC 7371 Custom computer programming services

D-U-N-S 25-240-3357   (BR)
COMMISSION SCOLAIRE DE MONTREAL
COMMISSION SCOLAIRE DE MONTREAL
6300 Av Albani, Montreal, QC, H1M 2R8
(514) 596-4871
Emp Here 30
SIC 8211 Elementary and secondary schools

D-U-N-S 25-233-7761   (BR)
COMMISSION SCOLAIRE DE MONTREAL
COMMISSION SCOLAIRE DE MONTREAL
5850 Av De Carignan, Montreal, QC, H1M 2V4
(514) 596-4134
Emp Here 140
SIC 8211 Elementary and secondary schools

D-U-N-S 25-233-5799   (BR)
COMMISSION SCOLAIRE DE LA POINTE-DE-L'ILE
ECOLE MARIE REINE DES COEURS
5200 Rue Bossuet, Montreal, QC, H1M 2M4
(514) 596-4245
Emp Here 20
SIC 8211 Elementary and secondary schools

D-U-N-S 25-309-7257   (BR)
INDUSTRIELLE ALLIANCE, ASSURANCE ET SERVICES FINANCIERS INC
BEAUGRAND AGENCY
5125 Rue Du Trianon Bureau 400, Montreal, QC, H1M 2S5
(514) 353-3230
Emp Here 30
SIC 6411 Insurance agents, brokers, and service

Montreal, QC H1N
Hochelaga County

D-U-N-S 20-703-6380   (BR)
AGROPUR COOPERATIVE
NATREL
5635 Av Pierre-De Coubertin, Montreal, QC, H1N 1R1
(514) 254-8046
Emp Here 35
SIC 5143 Dairy products, except dried or canned

D-U-N-S 24-366-2744   (BR)

BLINDS TO GO INC
3100 Boul De L'Assomption, Montreal, QC, H1N 3S4
(514) 259-9955
Emp Here 200
SIC 2591 Drapery hardware and window blinds and shades

D-U-N-S 20-572-9887   (BR)
CANADA POST CORPORATION
DEPOT K
6700 Rue Sherbrooke E, Montreal, QC, H1N 1C9
(514) 259-3233
Emp Here 80
SIC 4311 U.s. postal service

D-U-N-S 24-345-6196   (BR)
CENTRE DE SANTE ET DE SERVICES SO-CIAUX LUCILLE-TEASDALE
SITE OLIVIER GUIMOND
5810 Rue Sherbrooke E, Montreal, QC, H1N 1B2
(514) 255-2365
Emp Here 220
SIC 8322 Individual and family services

D-U-N-S 24-345-6204   (BR)
CENTRE DE SANTE ET DE SERVICES SO-CIAUX LUCILLE-TEASDALE
CENTRE HEBERGEMENT JEANNE-LEBER
7445 Rue Hochelaga, Montreal, QC, H1N 3V2
(514) 251-6000
Emp Here 200
SIC 8322 Individual and family services

D-U-N-S 20-714-5942   (BR)
CENTRES DENTAIRES LAPOINTE INC
DENTUROLOGISTE LAPOINTE THIBAULT ET WENDLANDT-DESJARDINS
5878 Rue Sherbrooke E Bureau 201, Montreal, QC, H1N 1B5
(514) 255-5801
Emp Here 20
SIC 8021 Offices and clinics of dentists

D-U-N-S 25-233-8041   (BR)
COMMISSION SCOLAIRE DE MONTREAL
COMMISSION SCOLAIRE DE MONTREAL
3155 Rue Desautels, Montreal, QC, H1N 3B8
(514) 596-5037
Emp Here 25
SIC 8211 Elementary and secondary schools

D-U-N-S 25-240-2623   (BR)
COMMISSION SCOLAIRE ENGLISH-MONTREAL
EDWARD MURPHY SCHOOL
6800 Av Pierre-De Coubertin, Montreal, QC, H1N 1T2
(514) 259-8883
Emp Here 35
SIC 8211 Elementary and secondary schools

D-U-N-S 25-232-9651   (BR)
COMMISSION SCOLAIRE DE MONTREAL
COMMISSION SCOLAIRE DE MONTREAL
6200 Av Pierre-De Coubertin, Montreal, QC, H1N 1S4
(514) 596-4140
Emp Here 100
SIC 8211 Elementary and secondary schools

D-U-N-S 25-240-7374   (BR)
COMMISSION SCOLAIRE DE MONTREAL
COMMISSION SCOLAIRE DE MONTREAL
5555 Rue Sherbrooke E, Montreal, QC, H1N 1A2
(514) 596-5100
Emp Here 100
SIC 8211 Elementary and secondary schools

D-U-N-S 25-240-7572   (BR)
COMMISSION SCOLAIRE DE MONTREAL
COMMISSION SCOLAIRE DE MONTREAL
6400 Av Pierre-De Coubertin, Montreal, QC, H1N 1S4
(514) 596-5136
Emp Here 54

SIC 8211 Elementary and secondary schools

D-U-N-S 20-712-4566   (BR)
COMMISSION SCOLAIRE DE MONTREAL
COMMISSION SCOLAIRE DE MONTREAL
5300 Rue Chauveau, Montreal, QC, H1N 3V7
(514) 596-2376
Emp Here 50
SIC 8249 Vocational schools, nec

D-U-N-S 20-997-2512   (HQ)
DUBO ELECTRIQUE LTEE
DUBO DEPOT
5780 Rue Ontario E, Montreal, QC, H1N 0A2
(514) 255-7711
Emp Here 105   *Emp Total* 3
Sales 29,799,034
SIC 5063 Electrical apparatus and equipment
Sylvie Boileau

D-U-N-S 25-990-1304   (HQ)
EXPERTECH BATISSEUR DE RESEAUX INC
EXPERTECH
(*Suby of* Expertech Batisseur de Reseaux Inc)
2555 Boul De L'Assomption, Montreal, QC, H1N 2G8
(866) 616-8459
Emp Here 200   *Emp Total* 500
Sales 56,539,740
SIC 1731 Electrical work
Pr Sylvie Couture
Sec Michel Lalande
Dir Stephen G Howe
Dir Bernard Le Duc

D-U-N-S 24-374-1449   (BR)
EXPERTECH NETWORK INSTALLATION INC
EXPERTECH
2555 Boul De L'Assomption, Montreal, QC, H1N 2G8
(514) 255-6665
Emp Here 200
SIC 1731 Electrical work

D-U-N-S 25-335-3916   (BR)
FEDERATION DES CAISSES DESJARDINS DU QUEBEC
CCPEDQ
3155 Boul De L'Assomption, Montreal, QC, H1N 3S8
(514) 253-7300
Emp Here 800
SIC 4899 Communication services, nec

D-U-N-S 20-562-9512   (SL)
FILLION, LOUIS ELECTRONIQUE INC
5690 Rue Sherbrooke E, Montreal, QC, H1N 1A1
(514) 254-6041
Emp Here 54   *Sales* 4,961,328
SIC 5731 Radio, television, and electronic stores

D-U-N-S 24-434-1012   (HQ)
FRIGOVIANDE INC
FRIGO
(*Suby of* Frigoviande Inc)
6065 Rue Hochelaga, Montreal, QC, H1N 1X7
(514) 256-0400
Emp Here 35   *Emp Total* 50
SIC 5421 Meat and fish markets

D-U-N-S 24-943-7716   (HQ)
GROUPE ARCHAMBAULT INC
ARCHAMBAULT
5655 Av Pierre-De Coubertin, Montreal, QC, H1N 1R2
(514) 272-4049
Emp Here 90   *Emp Total* 1,065
Sales 42,463,127
SIC 5736 Musical instrument stores
Blaise Renaud

D-U-N-S 24-126-3248   (BR)
GROUPE RESTAURANTS IMVESCOR INC
RESTAURANT MIKES

7275 Rue Sherbrooke E Bureau 148, Montreal, QC, H1N 1E9
(514) 355-4955
Emp Here 50
SIC 5812 Eating places

D-U-N-S 20-309-3042   (SL)
GRUES J.M. FRANCOEUR INC
6155 Rue La Fontaine, Montreal, QC, H1N 2B8
(514) 747-5700
Emp Here 60   *Sales* 3,064,349
SIC 7389 Business services, nec

D-U-N-S 20-708-9657   (SL)
INDUSTRIES BELLON INC, LES
(*Suby of* Canevas Generale (1988) Ltee)
5598 Rue Hochelaga, Montreal, QC, H1N 3L7
(514) 526-0894
Emp Here 40   *Sales* 1,751,057
SIC 2394 Canvas and related products

D-U-N-S 24-320-9475   (SL)
L J M MARKETING INC
JEAN COUTU #55
6420 Rue Sherbrooke E Bureau 55, Montreal, QC, H1N 3P6
(514) 259-6991
Emp Here 50   *Sales* 7,077,188
SIC 5912 Drug stores and proprietary stores
Louis-Phillipe Michaud
Johanne Michaud
Suzanne Michaud

D-U-N-S 24-678-1038   (BR)
LALLEMAND INC
LALLEMAND BIO-INGREDIENTS
5494 Rue Notre-Dame E, Montreal, QC, H1N 2C4
(514) 522-2133
Emp Here 80
SIC 2099 Food preparations, nec

D-U-N-S 25-990-9273   (HQ)
LIBRAIRIE RENAUD-BRAY INC
FOIRE DU LIVRE
5655 Av Pierre-De Coubertin, Montreal, QC, H1N 1R2
(514) 272-4049
Emp Here 100   *Emp Total* 1,065
Sales 35,094,097
SIC 5942 Book stores
Blaise Renauld

D-U-N-S 25-361-4432   (BR)
MAISON DES FUTAILLES, S.E.C.
2021 Rue Des Futailles, Montreal, QC, H1N 3M7
(450) 645-9777
Emp Here 200
SIC 2084 Wines, brandy, and brandy spirits

D-U-N-S 25-356-9867   (BR)
METRO RICHELIEU INC
JARDIN MERITE MONTREAL, DIV OF
5400 Av Pierre-De Coubertin, Montreal, QC, H1N 1P7

Emp Here 150
SIC 5148 Fresh fruits and vegetables

D-U-N-S 25-310-1174   (BR)
NATURISTE INC
7275 Rue Sherbrooke E Bureau 5, Montreal, QC, H1N 1E9
(514) 352-4741
Emp Here 25
SIC 5499 Miscellaneous food stores

D-U-N-S 20-703-0144   (BR)
PORTOLA PACKAGING CANADA LTD.
EMBALLAGES PORTOLA, LES
7301 Rue Tellier, Montreal, QC, H1N 3S9
(514) 254-2333
Emp Here 30
SIC 2821 Plastics materials and resins

D-U-N-S 20-805-5272   (BR)
PROVIGO DISTRIBUTION INC

LOBLAWS
7600 Rue Sherbrooke E, Montreal, QC, H1N 3W1
(514) 257-4511
Emp Here 140
SIC 5411 Grocery stores

D-U-N-S 25-745-6756   (BR)
REDBERRY FRANCHISING CORP
BURGER KING
6348 Rue Sherbrooke E Bureau 3411, Montreal, QC, H1N 3P6
(514) 252-9634
Emp Here 25
SIC 5812 Eating places

D-U-N-S 20-908-7071   (BR)
ROTISSERIES ST-HUBERT LTEE, LES
ST HUBERT CADILLAC
(*Suby of* Cara Holdings Limited)
6225 Rue Sherbrooke E, Montreal, QC, H1N 1C3
(514) 259-6939
Emp Here 80
SIC 5812 Eating places

D-U-N-S 24-323-5376   (BR)
SOCIETE DES ALCOOLS DU QUEBEC
SOCIETE DES ALCOOLS DU QUEBEC
560 Rue Hector-Barsalou, Montreal, QC, H1N 3T2
(514) 254-6000
Emp Here 300
SIC 5921 Liquor stores

D-U-N-S 24-179-6023   (BR)
SOCIETE DES ALCOOLS DU QUEBEC
SAQ EXPRESS
6360 Rue Sherbrooke E, Montreal, QC, H1N 3P6
(514) 251-4711
Emp Here 23
SIC 5921 Liquor stores

D-U-N-S 24-314-0550   (BR)
SOCIETE DES ALCOOLS DU QUEBEC
SOCIETE DES ALCOOLS DU QUEBEC
7500 Rue Tellier, Montreal, QC, H1N 3W5
(514) 254-6000
Emp Here 500
SIC 5921 Liquor stores

D-U-N-S 24-357-6845   (SL)
SOGEFI AIR & COOLING CANADA CORP
1500 Rue De Boucherville, Montreal, QC, H1N 3V3
(514) 764-8806
Emp Here 390   *Sales* 28,454,673
SIC 3599 Industrial machinery, nec
Pr Keith Drew
VP Alberto Marastoni
Genl Mgr Patrick Mertes

D-U-N-S 24-101-3551   (BR)
STAPLES CANADA INC
BUREAU EN GROS
(*Suby of* Staples, Inc.)
7275 Rue Sherbrooke E Unite 316, Montreal, QC, H1N 1E9
(514) 351-6776
Emp Here 29
SIC 5943 Stationery stores

D-U-N-S 24-796-9251   (BR)
UAP INC
NAPA PIECES D'AUTO
(*Suby of* Genuine Parts Company)
2095 Av Haig, Montreal, QC, H1N 3E2
(514) 252-1127
Emp Here 300
SIC 5013 Motor vehicle supplies and new parts

D-U-N-S 20-860-4442   (BR)
WINNERS MERCHANTS INTERNATIONAL L.P.
HOMESENSE
(*Suby of* The TJX Companies Inc)

7275 Rue Sherbrooke E Bureau 2000, Montreal, QC, H1N 1E9
(514) 798-1908
Emp Here 25
SIC 5651 Family clothing stores

D-U-N-S 24-050-0632   (BR)
WINNERS MERCHANTS INTERNATIONAL L.P.
WINNERS
(*Suby of* The TJX Companies Inc)
7275 Rue Sherbrooke E Bureau 2000, Montreal, QC, H1N 1E9
(514) 798-1908
Emp Here 100
SIC 5651 Family clothing stores

Montreal, QC H1P
Hochelaga County

D-U-N-S 20-330-9828   (HQ)
9631984 CANADA INC
EMBALLAGES C&C
6800 Boul Des Grandes-Prairies, Montreal, QC, H1P 3P3
(450) 424-0500
Emp Here 35   *Emp Total* 4,507
Sales 11,090,026
SIC 2011 Meat packing plants
Pr George Paleologou
Sec Douglas O. Goss
Treas William D. Kalutycz

D-U-N-S 25-900-3023   (SL)
URGENCES-SANTE
6700 Rue Jarry E, Montreal, QC, H1P 0A4
(514) 723-5600
Emp Here 1,426   *Sales* 93,853,709
SIC 4119 Local passenger transportation, nec
Pr Nicola D'ulisse
Dir Fin Arianne Trudeau
Dir Opers Louis Poirier
Prs Dir Claude Belisle
VP Gilles Bourgeois
VP Anie Samson

Montreal, QC H1R
Hochelaga County

D-U-N-S 20-331-1261   (SL)
TP-HOLIDAY GROUP LIMITED
GROUPE TP-HOLIDAY
(*Suby of* Travelpro Group Holdings Inc.)
4875 Boul Des Grandes-Prairies, Montreal, QC, H1R 1X4
(514) 325-0660
Emp Here 150   *Sales* 15,467,668
SIC 5099 Durable goods, nec
Pr Raymond Durocher
VP VP Daniel Penn
Genl Mgr Blake Lipham

Montreal, QC H1S
Hochelaga County

D-U-N-S 25-301-2835   (BR)
HUDSON'S BAY COMPANY
LA BAIE
4150 Rue Jean-Talon E, Montreal, QC, H1S 2V4
(514) 728-4571
Emp Here 50
SIC 5311 Department stores

Montreal, QC H1T
Hochelaga County

D-U-N-S 20-580-5802   (BR)
BANQUE LAURENTIENNE DU CANADA
4155 Rue Belanger, Montreal, QC, H1T 1A2
(514) 376-6963
Emp Here 20
SIC 6021 National commercial banks

D-U-N-S 20-421-1858   (SL)
BRUNELLE, GUY INC
4450 Rue Belanger, Montreal, QC, H1T 1B5
(514) 729-0008
Emp Here 75   *Sales* 4,815,406
SIC 1721 Painting and paper hanging

D-U-N-S 24-405-6503   (BR)
CANADIAN CANCER SOCIETY
SOCIETE CANADIENNE DE MONTREAL
5151 Boul De L'Assomption, Montreal, QC, H1T 4A9
(514) 255-5151
Emp Here 201
SIC 8399 Social services, nec

D-U-N-S 24-354-8422   (BR)
CENTRE HOSPITALIER UNIVERSITAIRE SAINTE-JUSTINE
CENTRE DE READAPTATION MARIE ENFANT DU CHU SAINTE-JUSTINE
5200 Rue Belanger, Montreal, QC, H1T 1C9
(514) 374-1710
Emp Here 450
SIC 8093 Specialty outpatient clinics, nec

D-U-N-S 20-333-1269   (BR)
CENTRE INTEGRE UNIVERSITAIRE SANTE ET SERVICES SOCIAUX DU CENTRE-SUD-DE-L'ILE-DE-MONTREAL
LE CENTRE JEUNESSE DE MONTREAL - INSTITUT UNIVERSITAIRE
4675 Rue Belanger, Montreal, QC, H1T 1C2
(514) 593-3979
Emp Here 200
SIC 8011 Offices and clinics of medical doctors

D-U-N-S 24-214-4439   (BR)
CENTRE DE READAPTATION GABRIELLE MAJOR
5695 Av Des Marronniers, Montreal, QC, H1T 2W3
(514) 252-6868
Emp Here 60
SIC 8361 Residential care

D-U-N-S 24-346-4356   (BR)
CENTRE DE SANTE ET DE SERVICES SOCIAUX LUCILLE-TEASDALE
SERESPRO
5601 Rue Belanger, Montreal, QC, H1T 1G3
(514) 256-5011
Emp Here 200
SIC 8093 Specialty outpatient clinics, nec

D-U-N-S 20-712-4285   (BR)
COMMISSION SCOLAIRE DE MONTREAL
ECOLE MARIE-ROLLET
6405 30e Av, Montreal, QC, H1T 3G3
(514) 596-4892
Emp Here 50
SIC 8211 Elementary and secondary schools

D-U-N-S 25-240-7549   (BR)
COMMISSION SCOLAIRE DE MONTREAL
ECOLE SAINT-JEAN-VIANNEY
6455 27e Av, Montreal, QC, H1T 3J8
(514) 596-5055
Emp Here 20
SIC 8211 Elementary and secondary schools

D-U-N-S 25-240-6897   (BR)
COMMISSION SCOLAIRE DE MONTREAL
ECOLE NOTRE-DAME-DU-FOYER
5955 41e Av, Montreal, QC, H1T 2T7
(514) 596-5133
Emp Here 35

▲ Public Company   ■ Public Company Family Member   **HQ** Headquarters   **BR** Branch   **SL** Single Location

SIC 8211 Elementary and secondary schools

D-U-N-S 20-553-2851   (BR)
COMMISSION SCOLAIRE ENGLISH-MONTREAL
ST BRENDAN SCHOOL
6650 39e Av, Montreal, QC, H1T 2W8
(514) 374-2828
Emp Here 35
SIC 8211 Elementary and secondary schools

D-U-N-S 25-233-9411   (BR)
COMMISSION SCOLAIRE DE MONTREAL
COMMISSION SCOLAIRE DE MONTREAL
6600 Rue Lemay, Montreal, QC, H1T 2L7
(514) 596-4868
Emp Here 35
SIC 8211 Elementary and secondary schools

D-U-N-S 20-806-9554   (BR)
COUCHE-TARD INC
4500 Rue Beaubien E, Montreal, QC, H1T
3Y1
(514) 729-5696
Emp Here 25
SIC 5411 Grocery stores

D-U-N-S 24-601-5606   (SL)
GIROSI INC
JEAN COUTU
4466 Rue Beaubien E, Montreal, QC, H1T
3Y8
(514) 728-3674
Emp Here 50   *Sales* 9,746,560
SIC 5912 Drug stores and proprietary stores
Pr Pr Robert Simard

D-U-N-S 20-289-1222   (SL)
INSTITUTE OF CIRCULATORY AND RESPI-RATORY HEALTH
ICRH
5000 Rue Belanger, Montreal, QC, H1T 1C8
(514) 593-7431
Emp Here 500   *Sales* 48,391,650
SIC 8062 General medical and surgical hospitals
Dir Jean-Lucien Rouleau
Dir Pierre Boyle
Dir Maryse Desjardins
Dir Ilana K.Gombos
Dir Jennifer Ralph

D-U-N-S 20-793-0264   (HQ)
LE CENTRES JEUNESSE DE MONTREAL INSTITUT UNIVERSITAIRE
(Suby of Le Centres Jeunesse de Montreal Institut Universitaire)
4675 Rue Belanger, Montreal, QC, H1T 1C2
(514) 593-3979
Emp Here 135   *Emp Total* 3,000
Sales 163,943,200
SIC 8322 Individual and family services
Pr Pierre Girard
VP Jean Trepanier
Sec Lise Tremblay
Genl Mgr Jean-Marc Potvin

D-U-N-S 25-233-7712   (SL)
PENSIONNAT NOTRE-DAME-DES-ANGES
5680 Boul Rosemont, Montreal, QC, H1T 2H2
(514) 254-6447
Emp Here 60   *Sales* 4,012,839
SIC 8211 Elementary and secondary schools

D-U-N-S 24-387-5866   (HQ)
PLEXO INC
(Suby of Gestion Plexo Inc)
5199 Rue Sherbrooke E Bureau 2771, Montreal, QC, H1T 3X1
(514) 251-9331
Emp Here 20   *Emp Total* 20
Sales 16,579,200
SIC 8011 Offices and clinics of medical doctors
Sandrine Leroy

D-U-N-S 20-025-7736   (BR)
UNIPRIX INC

4349 Rue Belanger, Montreal, QC, H1T 1A8
(514) 725-5273
Emp Here 20
SIC 5122 Drugs, proprietaries, and sundries

D-U-N-S 25-244-4450   (SL)
VINCENT MASSEY COLLEGIATE
5925 27e Av, Montreal, QC, H1T 3J5
(514) 374-1999
Emp Here 50   *Sales* 3,356,192
SIC 8211 Elementary and secondary schools

Montreal, QC H1V
Hochelaga County

D-U-N-S 25-243-7439   (SL)
2990181 CANADA INC
HOTEL AUBERGE UNIVERSEL MONTREAL
5000 Rue Sherbrooke E, Montreal, QC, H1V
1A1
(514) 253-3365
Emp Here 80   *Sales* 3,502,114
SIC 7011 Hotels and motels

D-U-N-S 25-856-8302   (SL)
9017-2438 QUEBEC INC
SCORES ROTISSERIE
5350 Rue Sherbrooke E, Montreal, QC, H1V
1A1

Emp Here 55   *Sales* 1,678,096
SIC 5812 Eating places

D-U-N-S 25-200-9287   (BR)
AIR LIQUIDE CANADA INC
USINE DES ELECTRODES
5030 Rue De Rouen, Montreal, QC, H1V 1J2
(514) 251-6838
Emp Here 50
SIC 3823 Process control instruments

D-U-N-S 20-056-5773   (HQ)
BOUTIQUE LA VIE EN ROSE INC
BIKINI VILLAGE
4320 Av Pierre-De Coubertin, Montreal, QC,
H1V 1A6
(514) 256-9446
Emp Here 230   *Emp Total* 1,244
Sales 126,440,893
SIC 5632 Women's accessory and specialty stores
Francois Roberge

D-U-N-S 24-125-4478   (BR)
CANADA POST CORPORATION
SURCUSALE M
4290 Rue Ontario E, Montreal, QC, H1V 1K3
(514) 259-3233
Emp Here 67
SIC 4311 U.s. postal service

D-U-N-S 25-365-0493   (BR)
CASCADES CANADA ULC
NORAMPAC-SPB
2755 Rue Viau, Montreal, QC, H1V 3J4
(514) 251-3800
Emp Here 500
SIC 2652 Setup paperboard boxes

D-U-N-S 24-658-1750   (BR)
CASCADES CANADA ULC
CASCADES EMBALLAGE CARTON-CAISSE
2755 Rue Viau, Montreal, QC, H1V 3J4
(514) 251-3800
Emp Here 250
SIC 2631 Paperboard mills

D-U-N-S 24-678-4961   (SL)
CENTRE DE SOINS PROLONGES GRACE DART
CENTRE DE SOINS PROLONGES DE MON-TREAL
5155 Rue Sainte-Catherine E, Montreal, QC,
H1V 2A5
(514) 255-2833
Emp Here 600   *Sales* 66,718,720

SIC 8069 Specialty hospitals, except psychiatric
Genl Mgr Leonard Vincent
Dir Alphonse Jiard
Dir Fin Paul Glenfield

D-U-N-S 20-025-7033   (BR)
COMMISSION SCOLAIRE DE MONTREAL
4131 Rue Adam, Montreal, QC, H1V 1S8
(514) 596-4929
Emp Here 40
SIC 8211 Elementary and secondary schools

D-U-N-S 20-712-4640   (BR)
COMMISSION SCOLAIRE DE MONTREAL
ECOLE MAISONNEUVE
1680 Av Morgan, Montreal, QC, H1V 2P9
(514) 596-5442
Emp Here 50
SIC 8211 Elementary and secondary schools

D-U-N-S 25-240-7333   (BR)
COMMISSION SCOLAIRE DE MONTREAL
ECOLE ST CLEMENT
4770 Rue La-Fontaine, Montreal, QC, H1V
1R3
(514) 596-5080
Emp Here 37
SIC 8211 Elementary and secondary schools

D-U-N-S 25-240-6731   (BR)
COMMISSION SCOLAIRE DE MONTREAL
COMMISSION SCOLAIRE DE MONTREAL
2455 Av Letourneux, Montreal, QC, H1V 2N9
(514) 596-4949
Emp Here 80
SIC 8211 Elementary and secondary schools

D-U-N-S 25-233-7597   (BR)
COMMISSION SCOLAIRE DE MONTREAL
COMMISSION SCOLAIRE DE MONTREAL
4100 Rue Hochelaga, Montreal, QC, H1V 1B6
(514) 596-4250
Emp Here 40
SIC 8211 Elementary and secondary schools

D-U-N-S 25-240-3712   (BR)
COMMISSION SCOLAIRE DE MONTREAL
COMMISSION SCOLAIRE DE MONTREAL
1860 Av Morgan, Montreal, QC, H1V 2R2
(514) 596-4844
Emp Here 87
SIC 8211 Elementary and secondary schools

D-U-N-S 24-405-3492   (SL)
FRANCE DELICES INC
SUPER FINE
(Suby of 2987953 Canada Inc)
5065 Rue Ontario E, Montreal, QC, H1V 3V2
(514) 259-2291
Emp Here 185   *Sales* 9,703,773
SIC 2051 Bread, cake, and related products
VP Colette Faletto-Durot
  Laurent Durot
VP Jacques Durot
VP Ghislaine Durot

D-U-N-S 20-327-9083   (SL)
IMPACT DE MONTREAL F.C.
CONNEXION IMPACT
4750 Rue Sherbrooke E, Montreal, QC, H1V
3S8
(514) 328-3668
Emp Here 35   *Sales* 8,390,481
SIC 7941 Sports clubs, managers, and promoters
Pr Joey Saputo
Sec Joe Marsilii

D-U-N-S 20-601-6651   (SL)
INSTITUT LINGUISTIQUE PROVINCIAL INC
4930 Rue Hochelaga, Montreal, QC, H1V 1E7
(514) 254-6011
Emp Here 50   *Sales* 2,699,546
SIC 8299 Schools and educational services, nec

D-U-N-S 20-792-5442   (BR)
METRO RICHELIEU INC
SUPER C
2050 Boul Pie-Ix, Montreal, QC, H1V 2C8
(514) 521-6799
Emp Here 41
SIC 5411 Grocery stores

D-U-N-S 25-864-7155   (BR)
MULTI-MARQUES INC
BOULANGERIE MULTI-MARQUES
3265 Rue Viau, Montreal, QC, H1V 3J5
(514) 255-9492
Emp Here 200
SIC 2051 Bread, cake, and related products

D-U-N-S 24-959-6818   (BR)
P.H. VITRES D'AUTOS INC
P.H. VITRES D'AUTOS INC
2303 Av De La Salle, Montreal, QC, H1V 2K9
(514) 323-0082
Emp Here 20
SIC 5013 Motor vehicle supplies and new parts

D-U-N-S 25-209-9031   (SL)
QUALI DESSERTS INC
5067 Rue Ontario E, Montreal, QC, H1V 3V2
(514) 259-2415
Emp Here 55   *Sales* 2,918,428
SIC 2051 Bread, cake, and related products

D-U-N-S 24-676-4518   (SL)
SOCIETE DE GESTION DU RESEAU IN-FORMATIQUE DES COMMISSIONS SCO-LAIRES
SOCIETE GRICS
5100 Rue Sherbrooke E Bureau 300, Montreal, QC, H1V 3R9
(514) 251-3700
Emp Here 324   *Sales* 23,369,759
SIC 7376 Computer facilities management
Pr Pr Eric Blackburn
VP VP Paquerette Gagnon
  Sebastien Gougeon
Dir Camil Turmel
Dir Serge Carpentier
Dir Caroline Dupre

D-U-N-S 20-976-7362   (HQ)
SOLOTECH QUEBEC INC
AXION
5200 Rue Hochelaga Bureau 100, Montreal,
QC, H1V 1G3
(514) 526-7721
Emp Here 35   *Emp Total* 150
Sales 8,142,759
SIC 5099 Durable goods, nec
Pr Normand Legault
Sec Sonia Girolamo

D-U-N-S 24-362-8752   (BR)
TETRA TECH INDUSTRIES INC
BPR
(Suby of Tetra Tech, Inc.)
5100 Rue Sherbrooke E Bureau 400, Montreal, QC, H1V 3R9
(514) 257-0707
Emp Here 175
SIC 8711 Engineering services

D-U-N-S 20-181-9930   (HQ)
TETRA TECH INDUSTRIES INC
INDUSTRIES TETRA TECH
(Suby of Tetra Tech, Inc.)
5100 Rue Sherbrooke E, Montreal, QC, H1V
3R9
(514) 257-1112
Emp Here 250   *Emp Total* 16,000
Sales 52,299,260
SIC 8711 Engineering services
Pr Pr Denis Harvie
  Francois Morin
  Dan L. Batrack
VP VP Steven Burdick

D-U-N-S 20-266-8745   (SL)
TETRA TECH QB INC

(*Suby of* Tetra Tech, Inc.)
5100 Rue Sherbrooke E Bureau 900, Montreal, QC, H1V 3R9
(514) 257-1112
Emp Here 30   *Sales* 36,939,297
SIC 8711 Engineering services
Pr Denis Harvie
VP Dan L. Batrack
VP Leslie L. Shoemaker
VP VP Steven M. Burdick
VP Richard A. Lemmon
Sec Francois Morin

D-U-N-S 20-380-9181   (HQ)
TETRA TECH QC INC
(*Suby of* Tetra Tech, Inc.)
5100 Rue Sherbrooke E Bureau 900, Montreal, QC, H1V 3R9
(514) 257-0707
Emp Here 1,300   *Emp Total* 16,000
Sales 227,949,385
SIC 8711 Engineering services
Pr Denis Harvie
Sr VP Richard Klue
Sec Francois Morin

D-U-N-S 20-329-9458   (SL)
TETRA TECH QE INC
BPR
(*Suby of* Tetra Tech, Inc.)
5100 Rue Sherbrooke E Bureau 900, Montreal, QC, H1V 3R9
(514) 257-0707
Emp Here 2,000   *Sales* 279,712,448
SIC 8711 Engineering services
Pr Pr Denis Harvie

D-U-N-S 24-081-4962   (SL)
VEZINA ASSURANCES INC
VEZINA DUFAULT
(*Suby of* Marsh & McLennan Companies, Inc.)
4374 Av Pierre-De Coubertin Bureau 220, Montreal, QC, H1V 1A6
(514) 253-5221
Emp Here 70   *Sales* 8,104,029
SIC 6411 Insurance agents, brokers, and service
Ch Bd David Eslick
Sec Patrice Vezina
Dir Peter Zaffino
Dir James Mcnasby
Dir Alan Garner

D-U-N-S 24-355-4008   (BR)
VILLE DE MONTREAL
CENTRE DE SERVICES PARTAGES-MATERIEL ROULANT ET ATELIERS, LE
2269 Rue Viau, Montreal, QC, H1V 3H8
(514) 872-4303
Emp Here 450
SIC 7538 General automotive repair shops

D-U-N-S 20-587-1028   (BR)
VILLE DE MONTREAL
ARENA MAURICE RICHARD
2800 Rue Viau, Montreal, QC, H1V 3J3
(514) 872-6666
Emp Here 20
SIC 7999 Amusement and recreation, nec

D-U-N-S 25-446-8770   (BR)
YMCA DU QUEBEC, LES
4567 Rue Hochelaga, Montreal, QC, H1V 1C8
(514) 255-4651
Emp Here 70
SIC 8399 Social services, nec

Montreal, QC H1W
Hochelaga County

D-U-N-S 24-891-2896   (BR)
ADM AGRI-INDUSTRIES COMPANY
ADM COCOA, DIV OF
(*Suby of* Archer-Daniels-Midland Company)

3800 Rue Notre-Dame E, Montreal, QC, H1W 2J8
(514) 528-3224
Emp Here 25
SIC 2079 Edible fats and oils

D-U-N-S 24-294-5590   (BR)
AGENCES W PELLETIER (1980) INC
QUINCAILLERIE J. CARRIER
3075 Rue Sainte-Catherine E Bureau 1980, Montreal, QC, H1W 3X6
(514) 598-9777
Emp Here 30
SIC 5085 Industrial supplies

D-U-N-S 20-180-9766   (SL)
AMERICAN YEAST SALES CORPORATION
CORPORATION AMERICAINE DE VENTRE DE LEVURE, LA
1620 Rue Prefontaine, Montreal, QC, H1W 2N8
(514) 529-2595
Emp Here 20   *Sales* 2,115,860
SIC 2099 Food preparations, nec

D-U-N-S 20-573-7476   (BR)
BANQUE LAURENTIENNE DU CANADA
3720 Rue Ontario E, Montreal, QC, H1W 1R9
(514) 523-1144
Emp Here 20
SIC 6021 National commercial banks

D-U-N-S 20-588-2439   (BR)
BANQUE TORONTO-DOMINION, LA
TD CANADA TRUST
(*Suby of* Toronto-Dominion Bank, The)
2959 Rue Sherbrooke E, Montreal, QC, H1W 1B2
(514) 289-0361
Emp Here 20
SIC 6021 National commercial banks

D-U-N-S 20-212-3881   (HQ)
BOULANGERIE AU PAIN DORE LTEE
(*Suby of* 1852-5402 Quebec Inc)
3075 Rue De Rouen, Montreal, QC, H1W 3Z2
(514) 528-8877
Emp Here 125   *Emp Total* 250
Sales 17,668,800
SIC 2051 Bread, cake, and related products
Pr Pr Jean-Marc Etienne

D-U-N-S 25-257-8166   (BR)
CENTRE DE SANTE ET DE SERVICES SOCIAUX LUCILLE-TEASDALE
2909 Rue Rachel E, Montreal, QC, H1W 0A9
(514) 527-2161
Emp Here 100
SIC 8361 Residential care

D-U-N-S 24-667-4626   (SL)
CHIC RESTO-POP INC, LE
1500 Av D'Orleans, Montreal, QC, H1W 3R1
(514) 521-4089
Emp Here 137   *Sales* 4,158,760
SIC 5812 Eating places

D-U-N-S 25-240-6798   (BR)
COMMISSION SCOLAIRE DE MONTREAL
ECOLE BARIL
3603 Rue Adam, Montreal, QC, H1W 1Z1
(514) 596-5070
Emp Here 50
SIC 8211 Elementary and secondary schools

D-U-N-S 20-712-4806   (BR)
COMMISSION SCOLAIRE DE MONTREAL
COMMISSION SCOLAIRE DE MONTREAL
3320 Rue Hochelaga, Montreal, QC, H1W 1H1
(514) 596-4650
Emp Here 20
SIC 8211 Elementary and secondary schools

D-U-N-S 25-240-5097   (BR)
COMMISSION SCOLAIRE DE MONTREAL
COMMISSION SCOLAIRE DE MONTREAL
3450 Rue Davidson, Montreal, QC, H1W 2Z5

(514) 596-5050
Emp Here 30
SIC 8211 Elementary and secondary schools

D-U-N-S 20-712-4293   (BR)
COMMISSION SCOLAIRE DE MONTREAL
COMMISSION SCOLAIRE DE MONTREAL
2430 Rue Darling, Montreal, QC, H1W 2X1
(514) 596-5046
Emp Here 25
SIC 8211 Elementary and secondary schools

D-U-N-S 25-173-0594   (SL)
COOPERATIVE DES TRAVAILLEUSES ET TRAVAILLEURS EN RESTAURATION LA DEMOCRATE
ROTISSERIE ST-HUBERT
2901 Rue Sherbrooke E, Montreal, QC, H1W 1B2

Emp Here 100   *Sales* 2,991,389
SIC 5812 Eating places

D-U-N-S 20-714-2402   (SL)
INSTITUT TECCART
3030 Rue Hochelaga, Montreal, QC, H1W 1G2
(514) 526-2501
Emp Here 50   *Sales* 3,356,192
SIC 8211 Elementary and secondary schools

D-U-N-S 24-365-0434   (HQ)
LANTIC INC
4026 Rue Notre-Dame E, Montreal, QC, H1W 2K3
(514) 527-8686
Emp Here 300   *Emp Total* 550
Sales 359,623,290
SIC 2062 Cane sugar refining
Pr John Holliday
Sec Manon Lacroix
Dir Michel P. Desbiens
Dir Michael A. Heskin
Dir Stuart A. Belkin
Dir Ross H. Dallas
Dir Donald G. Jewell
Dir Daniel Lafrance

D-U-N-S 20-107-8503   (BR)
LANTIC INC
3950 Rue Notre-Dame E, Montreal, QC, H1W 2K3
(514) 527-8686
Emp Here 20
SIC 4226 Special warehousing and storage, nec

D-U-N-S 20-642-1856   (BR)
LOBLAWS SUPERMARKETS LIMITED
LOBLAWS ANGUS
2925 Rue Rachel E, Montreal, QC, H1W 3Z8
(514) 522-4442
Emp Here 200
SIC 5411 Grocery stores

D-U-N-S 20-739-6185   (HQ)
LOCATION JEAN LEGARE LTEE
LEGARE LOCATION D'AUTO
(*Suby of* Location Jean Legare Ltee)
3035 Rue Hochelaga, Montreal, QC, H1W 1G1
(514) 522-6466
Emp Here 20   *Emp Total* 26
Sales 12,250,277
SIC 5511 New and used car dealers
Pr Pr Nathalie Legare
Dir Jean Legare

D-U-N-S 25-832-1512   (BR)
MONTREAL PORT AUTHORITY
3400 Rue Notre-Dame E, Montreal, QC, H1W 2J2
(514) 283-7020
Emp Here 250
SIC 4111 Local and suburban transit

D-U-N-S 20-117-2199   (SL)
TOPIGEN PHARMACEUTIQUES INC
2901 Rue Rachel E Bureau 13, Montreal, QC,

H1W 4A4
(514) 868-0077
Emp Here 36   *Sales* 3,429,153
SIC 8732 Commercial nonphysical research

Montreal, QC H1X
Hochelaga County

D-U-N-S 24-474-6855   (SL)
CLSC -CHSLD DE ROSEMONT
RESIDENCE ROBERT CLICHE
3311 Boul Saint-Joseph E, Montreal, QC, H1X 1W3
(514) 524-3541
Emp Here 600   *Sales* 28,760,880
SIC 8399 Social services, nec
Dir Suzanne Crete

D-U-N-S 24-368-8012   (BR)
CAISSE DESJARDINS DE LORIMIER-VILLERAY
CENTRE DE SERVICES MASSON
3250 Rue Masson, Montreal, QC, H1X 1R2
(514) 376-7676
Emp Here 30
SIC 6062 State credit unions

D-U-N-S 24-369-5074   (BR)
CAISSE DESJARDINS DE L'EDUCATION
CENTRE DE SERVICE CSDM
3705 Rue Sherbrooke E, Montreal, QC, H1X 1Z9
(514) 351-7295
Emp Here 60
SIC 6062 State credit unions

D-U-N-S 20-543-9495   (BR)
COMMISSION SCOLAIRE DE MONTREAL
ECOLE DE FORMATION PROFESSIONNELLE STELLA MARIS ANNEXE
6255 13e Av, Montreal, QC, H1X 2Y6
(514) 596-7712
Emp Here 20
SIC 8211 Elementary and secondary schools

D-U-N-S 25-240-4975   (BR)
COMMISSION SCOLAIRE DE MONTREAL
ECOLE STE-JEANNE-D'ARC
3700 Rue Sherbrooke E, Montreal, QC, H1X 1Z8
(514) 596-4848
Emp Here 40
SIC 8211 Elementary and secondary schools

D-U-N-S 25-240-7069   (BR)
COMMISSION SCOLAIRE DE MONTREAL
ECOLE SAINTE-BERNADETTE-SOUBIROUS
6855 16e Av, Montreal, QC, H1X 2T5
(514) 596-4166
Emp Here 80
SIC 8211 Elementary and secondary schools

D-U-N-S 25-233-6516   (BR)
COMMISSION SCOLAIRE ENGLISH-MONTREAL
ROSEMOUNT HIGH SCHOOL
3737 Rue Beaubien E, Montreal, QC, H1X 1H2
(514) 376-4720
Emp Here 70
SIC 8211 Elementary and secondary schools

D-U-N-S 24-761-5615   (BR)
COMMISSION SCOLAIRE DE MONTREAL
COMMISSION SCOLAIRE DE MONTREAL
3700 Rue Rachel E, Montreal, QC, H1X 1Y6
(514) 596-4330
Emp Here 49
SIC 4151 School buses

D-U-N-S 20-712-4335   (BR)
COMMISSION SCOLAIRE DE MONTREAL
COMMISSION SCOLAIRE DE MONTREAL
3580 Rue Dandurand, Montreal, QC, H1X 1N6

---

(514) 596-4966
Emp Here 50
SIC 8211 Elementary and secondary schools

D-U-N-S 20-301-1379   (BR)
GOUVERNEMENT DE LA PROVINCE DE QUEBEC
GOUVERNEMENT DE LA PROVINCE DE QUEBEC
3730 Rue De Bellechasse, Montreal, QC, H1X 3E5
(514) 374-8665
Emp Here 125
SIC 8361 Residential care

D-U-N-S 20-522-0481   (SL)
JARDIN BOTANIQUE DE MONTREAL
4101 Rue Sherbrooke E Bureau 255, Montreal, QC, H1X 2B2
(514) 872-1493
Emp Here 450   *Sales* 32,883,600
SIC 8422 Botanical and zoological gardens
Dir Gilles Vincent
Dir Charles Mathieu Brunelle

D-U-N-S 24-375-0655   (BR)
SGS CANADA INC
3420 Boul Saint-Joseph E, Montreal, QC, H1X 1W6
(514) 255-1679
Emp Here 60
SIC 8734 Testing laboratories

D-U-N-S 20-281-7347   (BR)
SOEURS DE SAINTE-ANNE DU QUEBEC, LES
ECOLE SAINTE ANNE, L'
6855 13e Av, Montreal, QC, H1X 2Z3
(514) 725-4179
Emp Here 30
SIC 8211 Elementary and secondary schools

D-U-N-S 24-104-6569   (BR)
VILLE DE MONTREAL
INSECTARIUM DE MONTREAL
4581 Rue Sherbrooke E, Montreal, QC, H1X 2B2
(514) 872-0663
Emp Here 25
SIC 8412 Museums and art galleries

D-U-N-S 20-587-1135   (BR)
VILLE DE MONTREAL
ARENA ETIENNE DESMARTEAU
3430 Rue De Bellechasse, Montreal, QC, H1X 3C8
(514) 872-6578
Emp Here 20
SIC 7999 Amusement and recreation, nec

Montreal, QC H1Y
Hochelaga County

D-U-N-S 20-051-6479   (HQ)
2330-2029 QUEBEC INC
MEDICUS
(*Suby of* Industries J C Bleau Ltee)
5135 10e Av, Montreal, QC, H1Y 2G5
(514) 525-3757
Emp Here 50   *Emp Total* 124
Sales 15,17¹,497
SIC 5999 Miscellaneous retail stores, nec
Pr Jacinte Bleau
Sec Brigitte Dufour
Dir Serge Larocque
Dir Michel Coutu
Dir Normanc Messier

D-U-N-S 25-680-1635   (SL)
ALIMENTATION MARC BOUGIE INC
PROVIGO MARC BOUGIE
3185 Rue Beaubien E, Montreal, QC, H1Y 1H5
(514) 721-2433
Emp Here 26   *Sales* 2,991,389
SIC 5411 Grocery stores

D-U-N-S 24-350-4789   (BR)
ARCTURUS REALTY CORPORATION
4100 Rue Molson Bureau 340, Montreal, QC, H1Y 3N1
(514) 737-8635
Emp Here 40
SIC 6531 Real estate agents and managers

D-U-N-S 20-508-9720   (BR)
CPU SERVICE D'ORDINATEUR INC
C P U DESIGN
(*Suby of* CPU Service d'Ordinateur Inc)
4803 Rue Molson, Montreal, QC, H1Y 0A2
(514) 955-9280
Emp Here 25
SIC 7378 Computer maintenance and repair

D-U-N-S 24-364-8461   (BR)
CANADA DRAYAGE INC
3000 Rue Omer-Lavallee, Montreal, QC, H1Y 3R8
(514) 931-0365
Emp Here 50
SIC 4212 Local trucking, without storage

D-U-N-S 20-858-6917   (SL)
CENTRE D'INTEGRATION SCOLAIRE INC
6361 6e Av, Montreal, QC, H1Y 2R7
(514) 374-8490
Emp Here 50   *Sales* 1,824,018
SIC 8361 Residential care

D-U-N-S 20-026-3999   (BR)
COMMISSION SCOLAIRE DE MONTREAL
COMMISSION SCOLAIRE DE MONTREAL
2870 Rue Dandurand, Montreal, QC, H1Y 1T5
(514) 596-5122
Emp Here 35
SIC 8211 Elementary and secondary schools

D-U-N-S 20-277-5508   (BR)
COMMISSION SCOLAIRE DE MONTREAL
ECOLE SAINT-MARC
6365 1re Av, Montreal, QC, H1Y 3A9
(514) 596-5022
Emp Here 50
SIC 8211 Elementary and secondary schools

D-U-N-S 20-712-4509   (BR)
COMMISSION SCOLAIRE DE MONTREAL
COMMISSION SCOLAIRE DE MONTREAL
5015 9e Av, Montreal, QC, H1Y 2J3
(514) 596-5588
Emp Here 50
SIC 8211 Elementary and secondary schools

D-U-N-S 25-240-7622   (BR)
COMMISSION SCOLAIRE DE MONTREAL
COMMISSION SCOLAIRE DE MONTREAL
3120 Av Laurier E, Montreal, QC, H1Y 1Z6
(514) 596-5007
Emp Here 50
SIC 8211 Elementary and secondary schools

D-U-N-S 20-712-4707   (BR)
COMMISSION SCOLAIRE DE MONTREAL
COMMISSION SCOLAIRE DE MONTREAL
3000 Rue Beaubien E, Montreal, QC, H1Y 1H2
(514) 596-4567
Emp Here 50
SIC 8211 Elementary and secondary schools

D-U-N-S 25-240-6988   (BR)
COMMISSION SCOLAIRE DE MONTREAL
COMMISSION SCOLAIRE DE MONTREAL
5937 9e Avenue, Montreal, QC, H1Y 2K4
(514) 596-4861
Emp Here 25
SIC 8211 Elementary and secondary schools

D-U-N-S 20-806-8879   (BR)
COUCHE-TARD INC
3000 Rue Masson, Montreal, QC, H1Y 1X6
(514) 374-2158
Emp Here 25
SIC 5411 Grocery stores

D-U-N-S 25-210-7669   (SL)

EFFIGIS GEO SOLUTIONS INC
VGI SOLUTIONS
(*Suby of* Groupe Viasat Inc)
4101 Rue Molson Bureau 400, Montreal, QC, H1Y 3L1
(514) 495-6500
Emp Here 145   *Sales* 26,124,800
SIC 7371 Custom computer programming services
Pr Denis Parrot
    Pierre Vincent
VP Magella Bouchard
VP Claude Levasseur
VP Michel Rheault

D-U-N-S 25-820-9790   (BR)
GABAPHARM INC
PHARMACIE JEAN COUTU
(*Suby of* Gabapharm Inc)
2980 Rue Belanger, Montreal, QC, H1Y 1A9
(514) 725-9338
Emp Here 50
SIC 5912 Drug stores and proprietary stores

D-U-N-S 24-636-9318   (SL)
GESTION QUADRIVIUM LTEE
RACHELLE-BERY PRODUITS NATURELS
2506 Rue Beaubien E, Montreal, QC, H1Y 1G2

Emp Here 100   *Sales* 18,061,440
SIC 5411 Grocery stores
    Jacques Van Geenhoven

D-U-N-S 24-240-0211   (BR)
GROUPE JEAN COUTU (PJC) INC, LE
SAURO, ROBERT
(*Suby of* 3958230 Canada Inc)
3245 Rue Masson, Montreal, QC, H1Y 1Y4
(514) 374-3611
Emp Here 50
SIC 5912 Drug stores and proprietary stores

D-U-N-S 20-354-0237   (BR)
MCDONALD'S RESTAURANTS OF CANADA LIMITED
MCDONALD'S
(*Suby of* McDonald's Corporation)
2530 Rue Masson, Montreal, QC, H1Y 1V8
(514) 525-1220
Emp Here 50
SIC 5812 Eating places

D-U-N-S 24-593-8449   (SL)
PROLUXON INC
5549 Boul Saint-Michel, Montreal, QC, H1Y 2C9
(514) 374-4993
Emp Here 55   *Sales* 4,815,406
SIC 1731 Electrical work

D-U-N-S 24-119-8279   (BR)
PROVIGO INC
MAXI
2535 Rue Masson, Montreal, QC, H1Y 1V7
(514) 527-2413
Emp Here 60
SIC 5411 Grocery stores

D-U-N-S 25-362-6386   (BR)
SOCIETE DES ALCOOLS DU QUEBEC
SAQ
4850 Rue Molson, Montreal, QC, H1Y 3J8
(514) 254-6000
Emp Here 50
SIC 5921 Liquor stores

D-U-N-S 25-308-9544   (BR)
SOCIETE DES ALCOOLS DU QUEBEC
SAQ CLASSIQUE
2685 Rue Masson, Montreal, QC, H1Y 1W3
(514) 721-2226
Emp Here 20
SIC 5921 Liquor stores

D-U-N-S 25-224-1088   (BR)
VILLE DE MONTREAL
VILLE DE MONTREAL

3131 Boul Rosemont, Montreal, QC, H1Y 1M4
(514) 872-4701
Emp Here 25
SIC 8231 Libraries

Montreal, QC H1Z
Hochelaga County

D-U-N-S 20-547-7495   (SL)
ALTERNATURE INC
9210 Pie-Ix Blvd, Montreal, QC, H1Z 4H7
(514) 382-7520
Emp Here 100   *Sales* 6,898,600
SIC 7389 Business services, nec
Pr Jean-Francois Laverdure

D-U-N-S 20-223-9604   (HQ)
BELRON CANADA INCORPOREE
VANFAX, DIV OF
8288 Boul Pie-Ix, Montreal, QC, H1Z 3T6
(514) 593-8000
Emp Here 250   *Emp Total* 1,354
Sales 147,262,670
SIC 7536 Automotive glass replacement shops
Pr Ralph Hosker
    Sonia Mally
Dir Gary Lubner

D-U-N-S 20-211-7651   (SL)
BERWIL LTEE
8651 9e Av Bureau 1, Montreal, QC, H1Z 3A1
(514) 376-0121
Emp Here 50   *Sales* 5,889,600
SIC 1711 Plumbing, heating, air-conditioning
Pr Brian Bergeron
VP Edouard Bergeron Jr
    Edouard Bergeron Sr

D-U-N-S 25-223-6401   (SL)
CENTRE DE LA PETITE ENFANCE POPULAIRE ST-MICHEL INC
7950 2e Av, Montreal, QC, H1Z 2S3
(514) 729-1878
Emp Here 50   *Sales* 1,532,175
SIC 8351 Child day care services

D-U-N-S 25-258-8660   (SL)
CHARTIER & PAROLIN INC
PHARMACIE JEAN COUTU
9021 Boul Saint-Michel, Montreal, QC, H1Z 3G3
(514) 955-0800
Emp Here 72   *Sales* 14,203,000
SIC 5912 Drug stores and proprietary stores
Pr Livio Parolin
VP Germain Chartier

D-U-N-S 24-970-5229   (HQ)
CIRQUE DU SOLEIL
GROUPE CIRQUE DU SOLEIL
8400 2e Av, Montreal, QC, H1Z 4M6
(514) 722-2324
Emp Here 2,560   *Emp Total* 1,000
Sales 258,056,173
SIC 7999 Amusement and recreation, nec
Pr Jocelyn Cote
Sec Anne-Marie Papineau
Dir Daniel Lamarre
Asst Tr Findlay Taylor

D-U-N-S 20-553-8429   (SL)
CITE DES ARTS DU CIRQUE
TOHU
2345 Rue Jarry E, Montreal, QC, H1Z 4P3
(514) 376-8648
Emp Here 50   *Sales* 4,244,630
SIC 8641 Civic and social associations

D-U-N-S 20-031-3836   (BR)
COMMISSION SCOLAIRE DE MONTREAL
COMMISSION SCOLAIRE DE MONTREAL
8699 Boul Saint-Michel, Montreal, QC, H1Z 3G1

---

(514) 596-4455
Emp Here 40
SIC 8211 Elementary and secondary schools

D-U-N-S 25-240-2573   (BR)
COMMISSION SCOLAIRE DE MONTREAL
COMMISSION SCOLAIRE DE MONTREAL
8901 Boul Saint-Michel, Montreal, QC, H1Z 3G3
(514) 596-5550
Emp Here 25
SIC 8211 Elementary and secondary schools

D-U-N-S 25-240-7051   (BR)
COMMISSION SCOLAIRE DE MONTREAL
ECOLE MONTCALM
8800 12e Av, Montreal, QC, H1Z 3J3
(514) 596-5330
Emp Here 50
SIC 8211 Elementary and secondary schools

D-U-N-S 20-025-4188   (BR)
COMMISSION SCOLAIRE DE MONTREAL
ECOLE BIENVILLE
9275 25e Av, Montreal, QC, H1Z 4E2
(514) 596-5181
Emp Here 46
SIC 8211 Elementary and secondary schools

D-U-N-S 25-240-7226   (BR)
COMMISSION SCOLAIRE DE MONTREAL
ECOLE SAINT-NOEL-CHABANEL PAVILLON DES BATISSEURS
8801 25e Av, Montreal, QC, H1Z 4B4
(514) 596-5494
Emp Here 50
SIC 8211 Elementary and secondary schools

D-U-N-S 25-240-4850   (BR)
COMMISSION SCOLAIRE ENGLISH-MONTREAL
ECOLE PRIMAIRES ST DOROTHY
8961 6e Av, Montreal, QC, H1Z 2T7
(514) 381-0355
Emp Here 40
SIC 8211 Elementary and secondary schools

D-U-N-S 20-024-6051   (BR)
COMMISSION SCOLAIRE DE MONTREAL
COMMISSION SCOLAIRE DE MONTREAL
7900 8e Av, Montreal, QC, H1Z 2V9
(514) 596-5020
Emp Here 40
SIC 8211 Elementary and secondary schools

D-U-N-S 20-024-6564   (BR)
COMMISSION SCOLAIRE DE MONTREAL
COMMISSION SCOLAIRE DE MONTREAL
2901 Rue De Louvain E, Montreal, QC, H1Z 1J7
(514) 596-5353
Emp Here 180
SIC 8211 Elementary and secondary schools

D-U-N-S 24-254-5085   (HQ)
DESCAIR INC
AIRCO
(*Suby of* Entreprises Mirca Inc, Les)
8335 Boul Saint-Michel, Montreal, QC, H1Z 3E6
(514) 744-6751
Emp Here 40   *Emp Total* 1,342
Sales 8,575,885
SIC 5078 Refrigeration equipment and supplies
Pr Pr Martin Deschenes
VP VP Jacques Deschenes
VP Francois Deschenes
 Marc Lapierre

D-U-N-S 25-393-0689   (BR)
DESCAIR INC
AIRCO QUEMAR ET DENDEC ET BINETTE, DIV D
(*Suby of* Entreprises Mirca Inc, Les)
8335 Boul Saint-Michel, Montreal, QC, H1Z 3E6
(514) 744-6751
Emp Here 40

SIC 5075 Warm air heating and air conditioning

D-U-N-S 20-793-4605   (HQ)
DESCHENES & FILS LTEE
BALISCUS L'ESPACE EAU ET PLOMBERIE
(*Suby of* Entreprises Mirca Inc, Les)
3901 Rue Jarry E Bureau 100, Montreal, QC, H1Z 2G1
(514) 374-3110
Emp Here 140   *Emp Total* 1,342
Sales 92,630,941
SIC 5074 Plumbing and heating equipment and supplies (hydronics)
Pr Pr Martin Deschenes
VP VP Jacques Deschenes
 Marc Lapierre
VP Francois Deschenes

D-U-N-S 24-063-3227   (BR)
DIRECT ENERGY MARKETING LIMITED
4001 Boul Robert, Montreal, QC, H1Z 4H6
(514) 333-0112
Emp Here 30
SIC 1711 Plumbing, heating, air-conditioning

D-U-N-S 24-211-7807   (BR)
FONDATION DES SERVICES DE READAPTATION L'INTEGRALE
(*Suby of* Fondation des Services De Readaptation L'Integrale)
8274 Boul Pie-Ix, Montreal, QC, H1Z 3T6
(514) 723-1583
Emp Here 20
SIC 8361 Residential care

D-U-N-S 20-309-4024   (BR)
G&K SERVICES CANADA INC
(*Suby of* Cintas Corporation)
8400 19e Av, Montreal, QC, H1Z 4J3
(514) 723-7666
Emp Here 300
SIC 7213 Linen supply

D-U-N-S 25-701-4894   (SL)
GROUPE BRT INC, LE
BRT SOLUTIONS
(*Suby of* Tristar, Inc.)
8268 Boul Pie-Ix, Montreal, QC, H1Z 3T6
(514) 727-7113
Emp Here 20   *Sales* 1,459,214
SIC 7379 Computer related services, nec

D-U-N-S 24-858-1258   (HQ)
GROUPE DESCHENES INC
(*Suby of* Entreprises Mirca Inc, Les)
3901 Rue Jarry E Bureau 250, Montreal, QC, H1Z 2G1
(514) 253-3110
Emp Here 20   *Emp Total* 1,342
Sales 244,929,070
SIC 6712 Bank holding companies
 Francois Deschenes
 Jacques Deschenes
Treas Treas Marc Lapierre
Dir Andrew T. Molson
Dir John Le Boutillier
 Gilles Leroux
Dir Richard Lord

D-U-N-S 24-814-5963   (HQ)
GUESS? CANADA CORPORATION
GUESS? CANADA DETAIL
8275 19e Av, Montreal, QC, H1Z 4K2
(514) 593-4107
Emp Here 58   *Emp Total* 43
Sales 218,882,100
SIC 5136 Men's and boy's clothing
Dir Victor Herrero
VP VP Teri Manby
Sec Jason Miller

D-U-N-S 25-361-4630   (BR)
INDUSTRIELLE ALLIANCE, ASSURANCE ET SERVICES FINANCIERS INC
FINANCIAL HORIZONS
8550 Boul Pie-Ix Bureau 200, Montreal, QC, H1Z 4G2

(514) 356-2410
Emp Here 20
SIC 8742 Management consulting services

D-U-N-S 20-222-0224   (SL)
INTO (1972) INC
8630 9e Av, Montreal, QC, H1Z 2Z8
(514) 385-4686
Emp Here 50   *Sales* 3,648,035
SIC 3599 Industrial machinery, nec

D-U-N-S 20-227-8008   (BR)
MOORE, BENJAMIN & CO., LIMITED
(*Suby of* Berkshire Hathaway Inc.)
9393 Boul Saint-Michel, Montreal, QC, H1Z 3H3
(514) 321-3330
Emp Here 25
SIC 2851 Paints and allied products

D-U-N-S 25-299-9040   (BR)
PRISZM LP
PFK
8575 Boul Pie-Ix, Montreal, QC, H1Z 3T9
(514) 729-4903
Emp Here 20
SIC 5812 Eating places

D-U-N-S 24-762-9652   (BR)
ROTHMANS, BENSON & HEDGES INC
(*Suby of* Philip Morris International Inc.)
8401 19e Av Bureau V, Montreal, QC, H1Z 4J2
(514) 593-7227
Emp Here 20
SIC 5194 Tobacco and tobacco products

D-U-N-S 20-706-9266   (BR)
SIEMENS CANADA LIMITED
SIEMENS TECHNOLOGIES DU BATIMENT
8455 19e Av, Montreal, QC, H1Z 4J2
(418) 622-2991
Emp Here 125
SIC 5999 Miscellaneous retail stores, nec

D-U-N-S 25-361-6437   (BR)
SIEMENS CANADA LIMITED
SIEMENS PROTECTION INCENDIE
8455 19e Av, Montreal, QC, H1Z 4J2
(514) 822-7311
Emp Here 130
SIC 5063 Electrical apparatus and equipment

D-U-N-S 24-346-3135   (BR)
VILLE DE MONTREAL
BIBLIOTHEQUE DE MONTREAL
3565 Rue Jarry E Bureau 400, Montreal, QC, H1Z 0A2
(514) 872-1540
Emp Here 60
SIC 8231 Libraries

Montreal, QC H2A
Hochelaga County

D-U-N-S 25-240-7382   (BR)
COMMISSION SCOLAIRE DE MONTREAL
ECOLE ST MATHIEU
7230 8e Av, Montreal, QC, H2A 3C7
(514) 596-5120
Emp Here 30
SIC 8211 Elementary and secondary schools

D-U-N-S 25-234-0492   (BR)
COMMISSION SCOLAIRE DE MONTREAL
COMMISSION SCOLAIRE DE MONTREAL
7450 Rue Francois-Perrault, Montreal, QC, H2A 1L9
(514) 596-4620
Emp Here 38
SIC 8211 Elementary and secondary schools

D-U-N-S 25-240-0452   (BR)
COMMISSION SCOLAIRE DE MONTREAL
COMMISSION SCOLAIRE DE MONTREAL
7575 19e Av, Montreal, QC, H2A 2M2
(514) 596-4924
Emp Here 30

SIC 8211 Elementary and secondary schools

D-U-N-S 24-372-5145   (BR)
GENERAL DYNAMICS INFORMATION TECHNOLOGY CANADA, LIMITED
GENERAL DYNAMICS INFORMATION TECHNOLOGY CANADA, LI
(*Suby of* General Dynamics Corporation)
7701 17e Av, Montreal, QC, H2A 2S4
(514) 729-1811
Emp Here 90
SIC 7374 Data processing and preparation

D-U-N-S 20-031-4321   (BR)
MEDIAS TRANSCONTINENTAL INC
MEDIAS TRANSCONTINENTAL INC
6965 6e Av, Montreal, QC, H2A 3E3
(514) 270-8088
Emp Here 40
SIC 5192 Books, periodicals, and newspapers

D-U-N-S 24-679-2282   (SL)
MENARD & VIDAL INC
7755 Av Leonard-De Vinci, Montreal, QC, H2A 0A1
(514) 768-3243
Emp Here 50   *Sales* 6,087,000
SIC 1711 Plumbing, heating, air-conditioning
 Carl Menard

Montreal, QC H2B
Hochelaga County

D-U-N-S 20-793-5792   (SL)
CENTRE HOSPITALIER FLEURY
2180 Rue Fleury E, Montreal, QC, H2B 1K3
(514) 383-9311
Emp Here 950   *Sales* 88,932,960
SIC 8062 General medical and surgical hospitals
Pr Paul Comtois
Genl Mgr Marc Fortin

D-U-N-S 25-240-6830   (BR)
COMMISSION SCOLAIRE DE MONTREAL
COMMISSION SCOLAIRE DE MONTREAL
10591 Rue Seguin, Montreal, QC, H2B 2B8
(514) 596-5295
Emp Here 25
SIC 8211 Elementary and secondary schools

D-U-N-S 25-240-3068   (BR)
COMMISSION SCOLAIRE DE MONTREAL
COMMISSION SCOLAIRE DE MONTREAL
10055 Rue J.-J.-Gagnier, Montreal, QC, H2B 2Z7
(514) 596-5570
Emp Here 25
SIC 8211 Elementary and secondary schools

D-U-N-S 25-240-0536   (BR)
COMMISSION SCOLAIRE DE MONTREAL
COMMISSION SCOLAIRE DE MONTREAL
10600 Av Larose, Montreal, QC, H2B 2Z3
(514) 596-5435
Emp Here 40
SIC 8211 Elementary and secondary schools

D-U-N-S 24-591-3657   (SL)
EMBALLAGES AUDACE INC
2301 Rue Fleury E, Montreal, QC, H2B 1K8

Emp Here 55
SIC 2672 Paper; coated and laminated, nec

D-U-N-S 20-003-0018   (BR)
PROVIGO DISTRIBUTION INC
PROVIGO
2323 Boul Henri-Bourassa E, Montreal, QC, H2B 1T4
(514) 381-1301
Emp Here 40
SIC 5411 Grocery stores

D-U-N-S 25-757-0812   (SL)
SERVICES DE SANTE LES RAYONS DE

SOLEIL INC
2055 Rue Sauve E Bureau 100, Montreal, QC,
H2B 1A8
(514) 383-7555
Emp Here 70   *Sales* 4,231,721
SIC 7363 Help supply services

Montreal, QC H2C
Hochelaga County

D-U-N-S 24-128-4384   (SL)
CENTRE DE SANTE ET DE SERVICES SO-CIAUX D'AHUNTSIC ET MONTREAL-NORD
CSSS AM-N
1725 Boul Gouin E, Montreal, QC, H2C 3H6
(514) 384-2000
Emp Here 150   *Sales* 88,362,950
SIC 8399 Social services, nec
Genl Mgr Diane Daigle

D-U-N-S 20-979-6879   (SL)
COLLEGE REGINA ASSUMPTA (1995)
CENTRE CULTUREL & SPORTIF REGINA ASSUMPTA
1750 Rue Sauriol E, Montreal, QC, H2C 1X4
(514) 382-9998
Emp Here 300   *Sales* 26,994,000
SIC 8211 Elementary and secondary schools
Pr Pr Jean Meloche
Dir Fin Sylvain Pilon
  Christophe Bancilhon
Mng Dir Pierre Carle

D-U-N-S 25-240-7408   (BR)
COMMISSION SCOLAIRE DE MONTREAL
ECOLE LOUIS COLLIN
10122 Boul Olympia, Montreal, QC, H2C 2V9
(514) 596-5320
Emp Here 30
SIC 8211 Elementary and secondary schools

D-U-N-S 25-240-7267   (BR)
COMMISSION SCOLAIRE DE MONTREAL
ECOLE ST PAUL DE LA CROIX
10495 Av Georges-Baril, Montreal, QC, H2C
2N1
(514) 596-5505
Emp Here 40
SIC 8211 Elementary and secondary schools

D-U-N-S 20-712-4442   (BR)
COMMISSION SCOLAIRE DE MONTREAL
COMMISSION SCOLAIRE DE MONTREAL
10050 Av Durham, Montreal, QC, H2C 2G4
(514) 596-5200
Emp Here 50
SIC 8211 Elementary and secondary schools

D-U-N-S 20-712-4756   (BR)
COMMISSION SCOLAIRE DE MONTREAL
COMMISSION SCOLAIRE DE MONTREAL
750 Boul Gouin E, Montreal, QC, H2C 1A6
(514) 596-5538
Emp Here 50
SIC 8211 Elementary and secondary schools

D-U-N-S 20-109-5952   (BR)
COMMISSION SCOLAIRE DE MONTREAL
COMMISSION SCOLAIRE DE MONTREAL
1239 Boul Gouin E, Montreal, QC, H2C 1B3
(514) 596-5535
Emp Here 58
SIC 8211 Elementary and secondary schools

D-U-N-S 25-325-1912   (BR)
LIBRAIRIE RENAUD-BRAY INC
1691 Rue Fleury E, Montreal, QC, H2C 1T1
(514) 384-9920
Emp Here 25
SIC 5942 Book stores

D-U-N-S 20-856-7529   (SL)
RESIDENCE BERTHIAUME-DU TREMBLAY
1635 Boul Gouin E, Montreal, QC, H2C 1C2
(514) 381-1841
Emp Here 310   *Sales* 19,043,040

SIC 8051 Skilled nursing care facilities
Pr Robert Belisle

Montreal, QC H2E
Hochelaga County

D-U-N-S 24-945-6930   (SL)
C.L.S.C. VILLERAY
1425 Rue Jarry E, Montreal, QC, H2E 1A7
(514) 376-4141
Emp Here 150   *Sales* 15,826,200
SIC 8399 Social services, nec
  Guy Mckenzie
Genl Mgr Nicole Clouatre
Pr Pr Gerald Leonard

D-U-N-S 20-888-3223   (HQ)
CENTRE DE SANTE ET DE SERVICES SO-CIAUX DU COEUR-DE-L'ILE
HOPITAL JEAN-TALON
1385 Rue Jean-Talon E, Montreal, QC, H2E
1S6
(514) 495-6767
Emp Here 1,300   *Emp Total* 40,000
Sales 139,136,055
SIC 8062 General medical and surgical hospitals
Pr Jean-Paul Cadieux
VP Pierre Dionne
VP Danielle Lia Deixieme

D-U-N-S 25-500-0820   (HQ)
CENTRE LA TRAVERSEE
(Suby of Centre la Traversee)
1460 Boul Cremazie E, Montreal, QC, H2E
1A2
(514) 321-4984
Emp Here 130   *Emp Total* 130
Sales 4,742,446
SIC 8361 Residential care

D-U-N-S 20-031-3901   (BR)
COMMISSION SCOLAIRE DE MONTREAL
COMMISSION SCOLAIRE DE MONTREAL
1350 Boul Cremazie E, Montreal, QC, H2E
1A1
(514) 596-4300
Emp Here 100
SIC 8211 Elementary and secondary schools

D-U-N-S 20-024-0724   (BR)
COMMISSION SCOLAIRE DE MONTREAL
COMMISSION SCOLAIRE DE MONTREAL
1370 Rue De Castelnau E, Montreal, QC, H2E
1R9
(514) 596-5523
Emp Here 40
SIC 8211 Elementary and secondary schools

D-U-N-S 25-233-8009   (BR)
COMMISSION SCOLAIRE DE MONTREAL
COMMISSION SCOLAIRE DE MONTREAL
8200 Rue Rousselot, Montreal, QC, H2E 1Z6
(514) 596-4350
Emp Here 100
SIC 8211 Elementary and secondary schools

D-U-N-S 20-712-4855   (BR)
COMMISSION SCOLAIRE DE MONTREAL
COMMISSION SCOLAIRE DE MONTREAL
7400 Rue Sagard, Montreal, QC, H2E 2S9
(514) 596-4858
Emp Here 50
SIC 8211 Elementary and secondary schools

D-U-N-S 20-655-9655   (SL)
DAMSAR INC
TIM HORTONS
8115 Av Papineau, Montreal, QC, H2E 2H7
(514) 374-0177
Emp Here 50   *Sales* 2,407,703
SIC 5499 Miscellaneous food stores

D-U-N-S 25-299-9123   (BR)
PRISZM LP

PFK
1700 Rue Jarry E, Montreal, QC, H2E 1B3
(514) 725-5527
Emp Here 30
SIC 5812 Eating places

Montreal, QC H2G
Hochelaga County

D-U-N-S 20-209-6210   (SL)
ALIX AUTOMOBILES INC
ALIX TOYOTA
(Suby of Placements Xalto Ltee, Les)
6807 Av De Lorimier, Montreal, QC, H2G 2P8
(514) 376-9191
Emp Here 42   *Sales* 20,613,600
SIC 5511 New and used car dealers
Pr Pr Pierre Alix
VP VP Denis Archambeault

D-U-N-S 25-307-4561   (BR)
BELRON CANADA INCORPOREE
LEBEAU VITRES D'AUTOS
5940 Av Papineau, Montreal, QC, H2G 2W8
(514) 273-8861
Emp Here 20
SIC 7536 Automotive glass replacement shops

D-U-N-S 20-362-3012   (HQ)
CAISSE DESJARDINS DU COEUR-DE-L'ILE
CENTRE DE SERVICES ANGUS
(Suby of Caisse Desjardins du Coeur-de-L'ile)
2050 Rue Rosemont, Montreal, QC, H2G 1T1
(514) 376-7676
Emp Here 50   *Emp Total* 100
Sales 14,154,376
SIC 6062 State credit unions
Genl Mgr Jean-Pierre Cantin
Pr Michel Richer
VP Manon Landry
Sec Lucille Ouimet
Dir Isabelle Bernard
Dir Pierre Paul Boucher
Dir Laurent Bourdon
Dir Catherine Bureau-Lavallee
Dir Nicole Clouatre
Dir Guy Cousineau

D-U-N-S 25-240-5337   (BR)
COMMISSION SCOLAIRE ENGLISH-MONTREAL
PIERRE ELIOT TRUDEAU SCHOOL
6855 Rue Cartier, Montreal, QC, H2G 2W1
(514) 374-7337
Emp Here 50
SIC 8211 Elementary and secondary schools

D-U-N-S 20-913-7137   (BR)
COMMISSION SCOLAIRE DE MONTREAL
COMMISSION SCOLAIRE DE MONTREAL
6017 Rue Cartier, Montreal, QC, H2G 2V4
(514) 596-4969
Emp Here 40
SIC 8211 Elementary and secondary schools

D-U-N-S 20-852-8807   (BR)
COMMISSION SCOLAIRE DE MONTREAL
COMMISSION SCOLAIRE DE MONTREAL
6028 Rue Marquette, Montreal, QC, H2G 2Y2
(514) 596-7919
Emp Here 40
SIC 8249 Vocational schools, nec

D-U-N-S 24-458-2805   (SL)
LAMCOM TECHNOLOGIES INC
2330 Rue Masson, Montreal, QC, H2G 2A6
(514) 271-2891
Emp Here 60   *Sales* 2,991,389
SIC 2759 Commercial printing, nec

D-U-N-S 25-263-9393   (SL)
MECANICAM AUTO
5612 Rue Cartier, Montreal, QC, H2G 2T9

(514) 271-3131
Emp Here 28   *Sales* 10,214,498
SIC 5511 New and used car dealers
Owner Mario Phenoeu

D-U-N-S 25-400-4229   (BR)
MULTI-MARQUES INC
2235 Rue Dandurand, Montreal, QC, H2G 1Z5
(514) 273-8811
Emp Here 60
SIC 2051 Bread, cake, and related products

D-U-N-S 24-320-2819   (SL)
SUCO INC
1453 Rue Beaubien E Bureau 210, Montreal,
QC, H2G 3C6
(514) 272-3019
Emp Here 37   *Sales* 6,289,900
SIC 8699 Membership organizations, nec
Pr Pr Jocelyne Lacasse
Dir Richard Kabaka
Dir Mireille Poulin
Dir Diane Turbide
Dir Andre Gobeil
Dir Denis Byrnes
Dir To-Nga Huynh
  Ginette Richard
  Denis Chabot
  Ani Mekerian

D-U-N-S 20-926-6600   (SL)
SERVICES DOCUMENTAIRES MULTIME-DIA (SDM) INC
SDM
5650 Rue D'Iberville Bureau 620, Montreal,
QC, H2G 2B3
(514) 382-0895
Emp Here 60   *Sales* 4,742,446
SIC 4226 Special warehousing and storage,
nec

Montreal, QC H2H
Hochelaga County

D-U-N-S 24-901-0877   (HQ)
143962 CANADA INC
DVDO
(Suby of 143962 Canada Inc)
4329 Av Papineau, Montreal, QC, H2H 1T3
(514) 596-3800
Emp Here 30   *Emp Total* 50
Sales 1,824,018
SIC 7841 Video tape rental

D-U-N-S 20-911-1368   (SL)
9278-3430 QUEBEC INC
GROUPE LAUZON
4670 Rue D'Iberville, Montreal, QC, H2H 2M2
(514) 527-7192
Emp Here 60   *Sales* 21,405,950
SIC 5147 Meats and meat products
  Francine Lauzon

D-U-N-S 24-675-9930   (SL)
AUTO COITEUX MONTREAL LTEE
COITEUX HYUNDAI
(Suby of 161624 Canada Inc)
5265 Av Papineau, Montreal, QC, H2H 1W1
(514) 521-3201
Emp Here 40   *Sales* 19,632,000
SIC 5511 New and used car dealers
Pr Pr Robert Coiteux

D-U-N-S 24-364-1326   (HQ)
BAYARD PRESS CANADA INC
(Suby of Bayard Press Canada Inc)
4475 Rue Frontenac, Montreal, QC, H2H 2S2
(514) 844-2111
Emp Here 20   *Emp Total* 1,500
Sales 118,696,500
SIC 2731 Book publishing
  Hubert Chicou

D-U-N-S 20-031-3976   (BR)
COMMISSION DES SERVICES ELEC-

TRIQUES DE LA VILLE DE MONTREAL
CSEM
4305 Rue Hogan, Montreal, QC, H2H 2N2
(514) 868-3111
Emp Here 100
SIC 1799 Special trade contractors, nec

D-U-N-S 20-024-6069   (BR)
COMMISSION SCOLAIRE DE MONTREAL
COMMISSION SCOLAIRE DE MONTREAL
2430 Tsse Mercure, Montreal, QC, H2H 1P2
(514) 596-5880
Emp Here 30
SIC 8211 Elementary and secondary schools

D-U-N-S 20-277-5490   (BR)
COMMISSION SCOLAIRE DE MONTREAL
ECOLE SAINT-LOUIS-DE-GONZAGUE, AN-NEXE
2175 Rue Rachel E, Montreal, QC, H2H 1R3
(514) 596-5871
Emp Here 30
SIC 8211 Elementary and secondary schools

D-U-N-S 25-240-0817   (BR)
COMMISSION SCOLAIRE DE MONTREAL
COMMISSION SCOLAIRE DE MONTREAL
2110 Boul Saint-Joseph E, Montreal, QC, H2H 1E7
(514) 596-5700
Emp Here 150
SIC 8211 Elementary and secondary schools

D-U-N-S 20-712-4426   (BR)
COMMISSION SCOLAIRE DE MONTREAL
COMMISSION SCOLAIRE DE MONTREAL
5205 Rue Parthenais, Montreal, QC, H2H 2H4
(514) 596-4590
Emp Here 50
SIC 8211 Elementary and secondary schools

D-U-N-S 20-024-6382   (BR)
COMMISSION SCOLAIRE DE MONTREAL
COMMISSION SCOLAIRE DE MONTREAL
4240 Rue De Bordeaux, Montreal, QC, H2H 1Z5
(514) 596-5815
Emp Here 60
SIC 8211 Elementary and secondary schools

D-U-N-S 24-346-5312   (BR)
CORPORATION DU CENTRE DE READAP-TATION LUCIE-BRUNEAU, LA
CENTRE DE READAPTATION LUCIE-BRUNEAU
2222 Av Laurier E, Montreal, QC, H2H 1C4
(514) 527-4527
Emp Here 200
SIC 8361 Residential care

D-U-N-S 20-574-6683   (BR)
GOUVERNEMENT DE LA PROVINCE DE QUEBEC
CHSLD DU PLATEAU MONT-ROYAL
4255 Av Papineau, Montreal, QC, H2H 2P6
(514) 526-4981
Emp Here 600
SIC 7041 Membership-basis organization hotels

D-U-N-S 20-212-2987   (BR)
GROUPE MEDICUS INC, LE
ATELIER CENTRAL DE FABRICATION DE MEDICUS
(*Suby of* Industries J C Bleau Ltee)
2740 Rue Angus, Montreal, QC, H2H 1P3
(514) 521-0855
Emp Here 29
SIC 3842 Surgical appliances and supplies

D-U-N-S 20-022-1344   (HQ)
GUIJEK INSTITUT QUEBECOIS POUR LA SANTE INTEGRALE
(*Suby of* Guijek Institut Quebecois Pour La Sante Integrale)
5445 Av De Lorimier Bureau 401, Montreal, QC, H2H 2S5

(514) 527-2666
Emp Here 67   *Emp Total* 70
Sales 3,793,956
SIC 7999 Amusement and recreation, nec

D-U-N-S 24-797-0598   (SL)
ODD 1
5000 Rue D'Iberville Bureau 322, Montreal, QC, H2H 2S6

Emp Here 42   *Sales* 5,202,480
SIC 7371 Custom computer programming services

D-U-N-S 24-901-8615   (HQ)
OPTIQUE NIKON CANADA INC
LABARATOIRES TECH-CITE
5075 Rue Fullum Bureau 100, Montreal, QC, H2H 2K3
(514) 521-6565
Emp Here 132   *Emp Total* 170
Sales 26,411,773
SIC 3851 Ophthalmic goods
Pr Pr Pierre Longerna
 Benoit Doyle
Dir Tatso Ishitoya
Dir Stephane Cabeza

D-U-N-S 24-383-7593   (SL)
PUBLICATIONS SENIOR INC
4475 Rue Frontenac, Montreal, QC, H2H 2S2
(514) 278-9325
Emp Here 20   *Sales* 1,459,214
SIC 2721 Periodicals

D-U-N-S 24-811-6071   (HQ)
SUPERCLUB VIDEOTRON LTEE, LE
ACCES JEUX
(*Suby of* Placements Peladeau Inc, Les)
4545 Rue Frontenac Bureau 101, Montreal, QC, H2H 2R7
(514) 372-5200
Emp Here 60   *Emp Total* 1
Sales 141,827,100
SIC 6794 Patent owners and lessors
Pr Donald Lizotte
Sec Marc M. Tremblay
Dir Jean-Francois Pruneau

Montreal, QC H2J
Hochelaga County

D-U-N-S 20-266-9560   (SL)
9167200 CANADA INC
KANUK MC
485 Rue Rachel E, Montreal, QC, H2J 2H1
(514) 284-4494
Emp Here 50   *Sales* 2,845,467
SIC 2295 Coated fabrics, not rubberized

D-U-N-S 24-437-9850   (SL)
CAISSE DESJARDINS - CENTREDE SERVICE
1685 Rue Rachel E, Montreal, QC, H2J 2K6
(514) 524-3551
Emp Here 49   *Sales* 5,836,856
SIC 6159 Miscellaneous business credit institutions
Dir Richard Beaulieu

D-U-N-S 25-877-1906   (SL)
CAPITALE DU MONT-ROYAL COURTIER IMMOBILIER AGREE, LA
1152 Av Du Mont-Royal E, Montreal, QC, H2J 1X8
(514) 597-2121
Emp Here 49   *Sales* 6,184,080
SIC 6531 Real estate agents and managers
Owner Nathalie Clement

D-U-N-S 20-214-5504   (SL)
CHEVREFILS, E. & FILS INC
METRO #014
1293 Av Laurier E Bureau 1290, Montreal, QC, H2J 1H2

(514) 524-8788
Emp Here 133   *Sales* 25,261,050
SIC 5411 Grocery stores
Pr Pr Gilles Chevrefils
 Jacques Chevrefils

D-U-N-S 25-240-7325   (BR)
COMMISSION SCOLAIRE DE MONTREAL
ECOLE PAUL BRUCHESI
1310 Boul Saint-Joseph E, Montreal, QC, H2J 1M2
(514) 596-5845
Emp Here 40
SIC 8211 Elementary and secondary schools

D-U-N-S 25-240-3514   (BR)
COMMISSION SCOLAIRE DE MONTREAL
COMMISSION SCOLAIRE DE MONTREAL
4300 Rue De Lanaudiere, Montreal, QC, H2J 3N9
(514) 596-5835
Emp Here 45
SIC 8211 Elementary and secondary schools

D-U-N-S 25-240-7499   (BR)
COMMISSION SCOLAIRE DE MONTREAL
COMMISSION SCOLAIRE DE MONTREAL
4245 Rue Berri, Montreal, QC, H2J 2P9
(514) 596-5737
Emp Here 40
SIC 8211 Elementary and secondary schools

D-U-N-S 25-240-2904   (BR)
COMMISSION SCOLAIRE DE MONTREAL
COMMISSION SCOLAIRE DE MONTREAL
505 Av Laurier E, Montreal, QC, H2J 1E9
(514) 596-5770
Emp Here 30
SIC 8211 Elementary and secondary schools

D-U-N-S 20-712-4269   (BR)
COMMISSION SCOLAIRE DE MONTREAL
COMMISSION SCOLAIRE DE MONTREAL
5455 Rue Saint-Denis, Montreal, QC, H2J 4B7
(514) 596-5855
Emp Here 50
SIC 8211 Elementary and secondary schools

D-U-N-S 20-797-0414   (BR)
DOLLARAMA S.E.C.
DOLLARAMA
1665 Av Du Mont-Royal E, Montreal, QC, H2J 1Z6
(514) 598-7519
Emp Here 20
SIC 5331 Variety stores

D-U-N-S 25-687-1427   (BR)
GAP (CANADA) INC
GAP
(*Suby of* The Gap Inc)
4210 Rue Saint-Denis, Montreal, QC, H2J 2K8
(514) 848-0058
Emp Here 20
SIC 5651 Family clothing stores

D-U-N-S 20-219-5681   (SL)
GROUPE CHASSE INC
CHASSE TOYOTA
(*Suby of* Placements Clomax Inc, Les)
819 Rue Rachel E, Montreal, QC, H2J 2H7
(514) 527-3411
Emp Here 60   *Sales* 30,144,000
SIC 5511 New and used car dealers
Pr Pr Claude Chasse

D-U-N-S 24-050-3185   (SL)
KANUK INC
485 Rue Rachel E, Montreal, QC, H2J 2H1
(514) 284-4494
Emp Here 100   *Sales* 4,596,524
SIC 2311 Men's and boy's suits and coats

D-U-N-S 20-534-8639   (BR)
RESTAURANTS LA PIZZAIOLLE INC, LES
(*Suby of* Restaurants la Pizzaiolle Inc, Les)
4801 Rue Saint-Denis, Montreal, QC, H2J 2L7
(514) 499-9711
Emp Here 20

SIC 5812 Eating places

D-U-N-S 25-308-9296   (BR)
SOCIETE DES ALCOOLS DU QUEBEC
SOCIETE DES ALCOOLS DU QUEBEC
1690 Av Du Mont-Royal E, Montreal, QC, H2J 1Z5
(514) 521-8230
Emp Here 20
SIC 5182 Wine and distilled beverages

Montreal, QC H2K
Hochelaga County

D-U-N-S 20-860-2714   (SL)
AGENCE DE SECURITE D'INVESTIGATION EXPO INC
2335 Rue Ontario E, Montreal, QC, H2K 1W2

Emp Here 75   *Sales* 2,772,003
SIC 7381 Detective and armored car services

D-U-N-S 20-052-9050   (BR)
BELL MEDIA INC
CTV
1205 Av Papineau, Montreal, QC, H2K 4R2
(514) 273-6311
Emp Here 130
SIC 4833 Television broadcasting stations

D-U-N-S 24-124-8520   (BR)
CAISSE D'ECONOMIE SOLIDAIRE DES-JARDINS
CAISSE D'ECONOMIE SOLIDAIRE DES-JARDINS
2175 Boul De Maisonneuve E Bureau 150, Montreal, QC, H2K 4S3
(514) 598-2122
Emp Here 30
SIC 6062 State credit unions

D-U-N-S 20-882-9028   (SL)
CENTRE DE PHYSIATRIE SHERBROOKE INC
INSTITUT DE PHYSIATRIE DU QUEBEC
2049 Rue Sherbrooke E, Montreal, QC, H2K 1C1
(514) 527-4155
Emp Here 40   *Sales* 2,407,703
SIC 8049 Offices of health practitioner

D-U-N-S 24-344-2659   (BR)
CENTRE DE SANTE ET DE SERVICES SO-CIAUX JEANNE-MANCE
CENTRE D'EBERGEMENT GAMELIN LAVERGNE
1440 Rue Dufresne, Montreal, QC, H2K 3J3
(514) 527-8921
Emp Here 50
SIC 8361 Residential care

D-U-N-S 25-223-6963   (SL)
CENTRE DE LA PETITE ENFANCE DU CARREFOUR INC
CPE DU CARREFOUR
2355 Rue Provencale, Montreal, QC, H2K 4P9
(514) 526-3241
Emp Here 50   *Sales* 1,532,175
SIC 8351 Child day care services

D-U-N-S 25-999-0588   (BR)
COGECO PEER 1 (CANADA) INC
COGECO PEER 1 MC
2600 Rue Ontario E Bureau 225, Montreal, QC, H2K 4K4
(514) 524-2224
Emp Here 25
SIC 1731 Electrical work

D-U-N-S 25-240-3316   (BR)
COMMISSION SCOLAIRE DE MONTREAL
ECOLE GARNEAU
1808 Av Papineau, Montreal, QC, H2K 4J1
(514) 596-5808
Emp Here 35

SIC 8211 Elementary and secondary schools

D-U-N-S 25-233-0121   (BR)
COMMISSION SCOLAIRE DE MONTREAL
ECOLE ELAN
3450 Av De Lorimier, Montreal, QC, H2K 3X6
(514) 596-7299
Emp Here 30
SIC 8211 Elementary and secondary schools

D-U-N-S 25-240-0619   (BR)
COMMISSION SCOLAIRE DE MONTREAL
COMMISSION SCOLAIRE DE MONTREAL
2743 Rue De Rouen, Montreal, QC, H2K 1N2
(514) 596-5820
Emp Here 50
SIC 8211 Elementary and secondary schools

D-U-N-S 20-712-4681   (BR)
COMMISSION SCOLAIRE DE MONTREAL
COMMISSION SCOLAIRE DE MONTREAL
2217 Av Papineau, Montreal, QC, H2K 4J5
(514) 596-4433
Emp Here 50
SIC 8211 Elementary and secondary schools

D-U-N-S 20-644-9865   (BR)
COMMISSION SCOLAIRE DE MONTREAL
COMMISSION SCOLAIRE DE MONTREAL
2000 Rue Parthenais, Montreal, QC, H2K 3S9
(514) 596-5711
Emp Here 40
SIC 8211 Elementary and secondary schools

D-U-N-S 25-233-5872   (BR)
COMMISSION SCOLAIRE DE MONTREAL
COMMISSION SCOLAIRE DE MONTREAL
2237 Rue Fullum, Montreal, QC, H2K 3P1
(514) 596-5830
Emp Here 40
SIC 8211 Elementary and secondary schools

D-U-N-S 20-118-8914   (HQ)
CONALJAN INC
(*Suby of* Conaljan Inc)
4045 Rue Parthenais, Montreal, QC, H2K 3T8
(514) 522-2121
Emp Here 75   *Emp Total* 79
Sales 15,724,750
SIC 6719 Holding companies, nec
Pierre Jean
Pr Pr Patric a Jean
Pierre-Albert Jean
Sebastien Jean

D-U-N-S 20-744-2554   (BR)
CONFEDERATION DES SYNDICATS NA-TIONAUX (C.S.N.)
SYNDICAT DES TRAVAILLEUSES ET DES TRAVAILLEURS DE LA CSN
1601 Av De Lorimier, Montreal, QC, H2K 4M5
(514) 529-4993
Emp Here 600
SIC 8631 Labor organizations

D-U-N-S 24-061-5539   (BR)
GOUVERNEMENT DE LA PROVINCE DE QUEBEC
TELE-QUEBEC
1000 Rue Fullum, Montreal, QC, H2K 3L7
(514) 521-2424
Emp Here 275
SIC 4833 Television broadcasting stations

D-U-N-S 20-223-5834   (SL)
HECTOR LARIVEE INC
D.G.B. FRUITERIE
1755 Rue Bercy, Montreal, QC, H2K 2T9
(514) 521-8331
Emp Here 100   *Sales* 24,222,952
SIC 5148 Fresh fruits and vegetables
Guy Larivee
Michel Larivee
Daniel Larivee

D-U-N-S 20-190-4633   (SL)
INNOVADERM RECHERCHES INC
1851 Sherbrooke E Suite 502, Montreal, QC,

H2K 4L5
(514) 521-4285
Emp Here 65   *Sales* 4,158,005
SIC 8731 Commercial physical research

D-U-N-S 24-083-6288   (BR)
JTI-MACDONALD CORP
2455 Rue Ontario E Bureau 4, Montreal, QC, H2K 1W3
(514) 598-2525
Emp Here 500
SIC 2111 Cigarettes

D-U-N-S 24-970-8355   (BR)
PELMOREX COMMUNICATIONS INC
METEO MEDIA
1755 Boul Rene-Levesque E Bureau 251, Montreal, QC, H2K 4P6
(514) 597-1700
Emp Here 133
SIC 4833 Television broadcasting stations

D-U-N-S 20-715-7137   (BR)
PELMOREX COMMUNICATIONS INC
WEATHER NETWORK
1205 Av Papineau Bureau 251, Montreal, QC, H2K 4R2
(514) 597-0232
Emp Here 120
SIC 8999 Services, nec

D-U-N-S 24-789-3241   (SL)
PUBLICATIONS GROUPE R.R. INTERNA-TIONAL INC, LES
EMS
(*Suby of* R.R. Finance Corporation Inc)
2322 Rue Sherbrooke E, Montreal, QC, H2K 1E5
(514) 521-8148
Emp Here 21   *Sales* 5,486,039
SIC 8743 Public relations services
Louis Luc Roy
VP Louis-Francois Pothier-Roy

D-U-N-S 20-518-9355   (BR)
SSQ SOCIETE D'ASSURANCE-VIE INC
SSQ GROUPE FINANCIER
1200 Av Papineau Bureau 460, Montreal, QC, H2K 4R5
(514) 521-7365
Emp Here 50
SIC 6411 Insurance agents, brokers, and service

D-U-N-S 20-714-5751   (BR)
SOCIETE QUEBECOISE DES INFRAS-TRUCTURES
600 Rue Fullum Bureau 1105, Montreal, QC, H2K 4L1
(514) 873-6504
Emp Here 20
SIC 6512 Nonresidential building operators

D-U-N-S 25-366-7141   (BR)
SOCIETE DE TRANSPORT DE MONTREAL
STM
1600 Rue Du Havre, Montreal, QC, H2K 2X5
(514) 280-5768
Emp Here 60
SIC 4111 Local and suburban transit

D-U-N-S 20-760-9058   (HQ)
SOCIETE DES ALCOOLS DU QUEBEC
S.A.Q.
905 Av De Lorimier, Montreal, QC, H2K 3V9
(514) 254-6000
Emp Here 100   *Emp Total* 40,000
Sales 2,405,791,207
SIC 5921 Liquor stores
Pr Johanne Brunet
Dir Louise Menard
Dir Jean-Marie Toulouse
Dir Celine Blanchet
Dir Alain Brunet
Dir Daniele Bergeron
Dir Nicole Diamond-Gelinas
Dir Thierry Duval
Dir Sylvain Lafrance

Dir Lucie Martel

D-U-N-S 24-601-4625   (SL)
TV5 QUEBEC CANADA
1755 Boul Rene-Levesque E Bureau 101, Montreal, QC, H2K 4P6
(514) 522-5322
Emp Here 50   *Sales* 2,918,428
SIC 4833 Television broadcasting stations

Montreal, QC H2L
Hochelaga County

D-U-N-S 25-469-5349   (SL)
3104346 CANADA INC
DAGIOVANNI RESTAURANT OUEST
576 Rue Sainte-Catherine E Bureau 111, Montreal, QC, H2L 2E1
(514) 845-3345
Emp Here 500   *Sales* 20,799,360
SIC 5812 Eating places
Pr Pr Paul Nakis
VP VP Phillip Nakis
Dir Leonard Daousis

D-U-N-S 24-582-0923   (SL)
ASSOCIATION SPORTIVE ET COMMUNAU-TAIRE DU CENTRE-SUD INC
CLUB DE BASKETBALL DU CENTRE-SUD
2093 Rue De La Visitation, Montreal, QC, H2L 3C9
(514) 522-2246
Emp Here 60   *Sales* 2,334,742
SIC 8322 Individual and family services

D-U-N-S 20-573-7765   (SL)
BANQUE LAURENTIENNE DU CANADA
936 Rue Sainte-Catherine E, Montreal, QC, H2L 2E7
(514) 842-8093
Emp Here 20
SIC 6021 National commercial banks

D-U-N-S 25-590-3478   (BR)
BELL MEDIA INC
VIRGIN RADIO
1717 Boul Rene-Levesque E, Montreal, QC, H2L 4T9
(514) 989-2523
Emp Here 100
SIC 4832 Radio broadcasting stations

D-U-N-S 20-533-4654   (BR)
BELL MEDIA INC
ENERGIE 94.3 FM
1717 Boul Rene-Levesque E Bureau 120, Montreal, QC, H2L 4T9
(514) 529-3200
Emp Here 400
SIC 4832 Radio broadcasting stations

D-U-N-S 20-265-8886   (HQ)
BIBLIOTHEQUE ET ARCHIVES NA-TIONALES DU QUEBEC
BANQ
475 Boul De Maisonneuve E, Montreal, QC, H2L 5C4
(514) 873-1100
Emp Here 75   *Emp Total* 40,000
Sales 45,137,559
SIC 8231 Libraries
Pr Christine Barbe

D-U-N-S 20-707-6394   (BR)
BON DIEU DANS LA RUE, ORGANISATION POUR JEUNES ADULTES INC, LE
DANS LA RUE
1662 Rue Ontario E, Montreal, QC, H2L 1S7
(514) 526-7677
Emp Here 80
SIC 8399 Social services, nec

D-U-N-S 25-197-5801   (SL)
CLSC DES FAUBOURG
1705 Rue De La Visitation, Montreal, QC, H2L

3C3
(514) 527-2361
Emp Here 300   *Sales* 19,828,320
SIC 8399 Social services, nec
Pr Fernand Matteau

D-U-N-S 20-213-4441   (BR)
CANADIAN BROADCASTING CORPORA-TION
CBC
1400 Boul Rene-Levesque E, Montreal, QC, H2L 2M2
(514) 597-6000
Emp Here 3,000
SIC 4833 Television broadcasting stations

D-U-N-S 20-911-3620   (SL)
CENTRE HOSPITALIER JACQUES VIGER
CENTRE D'ACCEUIL ERNEST ROUTHIER
1051 Rue Saint-Hubert, Montreal, QC, H2L 3Y5
(514) 842-7181
Emp Here 750   *Sales* 36,810,000
SIC 8361 Residential care
Pr Robet Valcourt

D-U-N-S 24-380-9071   (BR)
CENTRE HOSPITALIER DE L'UNIVERSITE DE MONTREAL
CHUM INFORMATIQUE
1595 Rue Ontario E, Montreal, QC, H2L 1S6
(514) 890-8004
Emp Here 80
SIC 7379 Computer related services, nec

D-U-N-S 25-091-0296   (BR)
CENTRE HOSPITALIER DE L'UNIVERSITE DE MONTREAL
HOPITAL NOTRE-DAME DU CHUM
1560 Rue Sherbrooke E, Montreal, QC, H2L 4M1
(514) 890-8000
Emp Here 2,000
SIC 8062 General medical and surgical hospitals

D-U-N-S 25-240-7416   (BR)
COMMISSION SCOLAIRE DE MONTREAL
ECOLE MARGUERITE BOURGEOYS
2070 Rue Plessis, Montreal, QC, H2L 2Y3
(514) 596-5810
Emp Here 20
SIC 8211 Elementary and secondary schools

D-U-N-S 25-234-0450   (BR)
COMMISSION SCOLAIRE DE MONTREAL
ECOLE LE PLATEAU
3700 Av Calixa-Lavallee, Montreal, QC, H2L 3A8
(514) 596-5950
Emp Here 50
SIC 8211 Elementary and secondary schools

D-U-N-S 20-712-4467   (BR)
COMMISSION SCOLAIRE DE MONTREAL
COMMISSION SCOLAIRE DE MONTREAL
3655 Rue Saint-Hubert, Montreal, QC, H2L 3Z9
(514) 596-4288
Emp Here 35
SIC 8211 Elementary and secondary schools

D-U-N-S 20-700-2168   (BR)
CORUS MEDIA HOLDINGS INC
SHAW MEDIA INC
1600 Boul De Maisonneuve E Bureau 900, Montreal, QC, H2L 4P2
(514) 521-4323
Emp Here 50
SIC 4833 Television broadcasting stations

D-U-N-S 24-395-2384   (SL)
ENTREPRISES JAEVARI INC, LES
RESTAURANT MC DONALD'S
850 Rue Sainte-Catherine E, Montreal, QC, H2L 2E2
(514) 847-0881
Emp Here 50   *Sales* 1,732,502
SIC 5812 Eating places

D-U-N-S 24-681-0043   (BR)
ENTREPRISES VANA INC
MCDONALD'S
(*Suby of* Entreprises Vana Inc)
1703 Rue Sainte-Catherine E, Montreal, QC,
H2L 2J5
(514) 523-2139
Emp Here 50
SIC 5812 Eating places

D-U-N-S 24-426-0506   (SL)
GESTION PFMJ (BILLETERIE) INC
505 Boul Maisonneuve Bureau 301, Montreal,
QC, H2L 1Y4
(514) 895-9821
Emp Here 40   *Sales* 12,858,960
SIC 4729 Passenger transportation arrange-
ment
Pr Pierre Belanger

D-U-N-S 24-475-6987   (BR)
**GOUVERNEMENT DE LA PROVINCE DE
QUEBEC**
*BIBLIOTHEQUE ET ARCHIVES NA-
TIONALES DU QUEBEC*
475 Boul De Maisonneuve E, Montreal, QC,
H2L 5C4
(514) 873-1100
Emp Here 600
SIC 8231 Libraries

D-U-N-S 25-019-2390   (BR)
**GOUVERNEMENT DE LA PROVINCE DE
QUEBEC**
*COLLECTIONS SPECIALES ET ARCHIVES
PRIVEES*
475 Boul De Maisonneuve E, Montreal, QC,
H2L 5C4
(514) 873-1100
Emp Here 500
SIC 8231 Libraries

D-U-N-S 24-469-3602   (BR)
**GOUVERNEMENT DE LA PROVINCE DE
QUEBEC**
*BIBILIOTHEQUES ET ARCHIVES NATIONAL
DU QUEBEC*
475 Boul De Maisonneuve E, Montreal, QC,
H2L 5C4
(514) 873-1100
Emp Here 20
SIC 8231 Libraries

D-U-N-S 25-325-1557   (BR)
GOUVERNEUR INC
HOTEL GOUVERNEUR
1415 Rue Saint-Hubert, Montreal, QC, H2L
3Y9
(514) 842-4881
Emp Here 145
SIC 7011 Hotels and motels

D-U-N-S 25-469-6321   (BR)
GROUPE ARCHAMBAULT INC
500 Rue Sainte-Catherine E, Montreal, QC,
H2L 2C6
(514) 849-6201
Emp Here 100
SIC 5735 Record and prerecorded tape stores

D-U-N-S 20-418-0871   (HQ)
GROUPE SOGIDES INC
LES EDITIONS DE L'HOMME
(*Suby of* Placements Peladeau Inc, Les)
955 Rue Amherst, Montreal, QC, H2L 3K4
(514) 523-1182
Emp Here 60   *Emp Total* 1
Sales 22,050,499
SIC 2731 Book publishing
Pr Lyne Robitaille
VP VP Jean-Francois Pruneau
Sec Marc M. Tremblay

D-U-N-S 20-573-7260   (BR)
HYDRO-QUEBEC
SOCIETE D'ENERGIE DE LA BAIE JAMES
888 Boul De Maisonneuve E, Montreal, QC,
H2L 4S8

(514) 286-2020
Emp Here 100
SIC 4911 Electric services

D-U-N-S 24-065-8091   (BR)
MISSION OLD BREWERY
PAVILLION PATRICIA MACKENZIE, LE
(*Suby of* Mission Old Brewery)
1301 Boul De Maisonneuve E, Montreal, QC,
H2L 2A4
(514) 526-6446
Emp Here 20
SIC 8361 Residential care

D-U-N-S 20-715-8093   (BR)
MOLSON CANADA 2005
MOLSON CANADA-REGION QUEBEC
(*Suby of* Molson Coors Brewing Company)
1555 Rue Notre-Dame E, Montreal, QC, H2L
2R5
(514) 521-1786
Emp Here 50
SIC 2082 Malt beverages

D-U-N-S 24-943-2824   (HQ)
OMER DESERRES INC
DESERRES OMER
1265 Rue Berri Bureau 1000, Montreal, QC,
H2L 4X4
(514) 842-6695
Emp Here 70   *Emp Total* 450
Sales 50,675,684
SIC 5999 Miscellaneous retail stores, nec
  Marc Deserres

D-U-N-S 20-736-6139   (SL)
**SOCIETE D'ENERGIE DE LA BAIE JAMES,
LA**
SEBJ
888 Boul De Maisonneuve E, Montreal, QC,
H2L 4S8
(514) 286-2020
Emp Here 300   *Sales* 55,656,720
SIC 8741 Management services
Pr Real Laporte
  Thierry Vandal
  Richard Cacchione
  Marie-Jose Nadeau

D-U-N-S 25-467-6034   (BR)
**SOCIETE DE SAINT-VINCENT DE PAUL DE
MONTREAL, LA**
ATELIER DE MEUBLES
1930 Rue De Champlain, Montreal, QC, H2L
2S8
(514) 525-2491
Emp Here 25
SIC 7641 Reupholstery and furniture repair

D-U-N-S 20-706-6478   (BR)
SOCIETE DE TRANSPORT DE MONTREAL
SOCIETE DE TRANSPORT DE MONTREAL
2000 Rue Berri, Montreal, QC, H2L 4V7
(514) 786-6876
Emp Here 200
SIC 4111 Local and suburban transit

D-U-N-S 24-341-0433   (BR)
STAPLES CANADA INC
BUREAU EN GROS
(*Suby of* Staples, Inc.)
845 Rue Sainte-Catherine E, Montreal, QC,
H2L 2E4
(514) 843-8647
Emp Here 30
SIC 5943 Stationery stores

D-U-N-S 24-020-8702   (HQ)
TVA VENTES ET MARKETING INC
TVA ACCES
(*Suby of* Placements Peladeau Inc, Les)
1600 Boul De Maisonneuve E, Montreal, QC,
H2L 4P2
(514) 526-9251
Emp Here 20   *Emp Total* 1
Sales 10,145,000
SIC 7319 Advertising, nec
Pr Pr Pierre Dion
  Edith Perreault

VP VP Denis Rozon

D-U-N-S 24-419-9761   (BR)
TRAVELBRANDS INC
TRAVELBRANDS INC
1221 Rue Saint-Hubert Bureau 200, Montreal,
QC, H2L 3Y8
(514) 286-9747
Emp Here 20
SIC 4725 Tour operators

D-U-N-S 24-904-0353   (BR)
UNIVERSITE DU QUEBEC
405 Rue Sainte-Catherine E, Montreal, QC,
H2L 2C4
(514) 987-3000
Emp Here 4,000
SIC 8221 Colleges and universities

D-U-N-S 24-870-3563   (BR)
UNIVERSITE DU QUEBEC
1200 Rue Berri, Montreal, QC, H2L 4S6
(514) 987-3000
Emp Here 5,000
SIC 8221 Colleges and universities

D-U-N-S 24-798-7147   (BR)
**WARNER   BROS   ENTERTAINMENT
CANADA INC**
800 Boul De Maisonneuve E Bureau 1000,
Montreal, QC, H2L 4L8

Emp Here 65
SIC 3944 Games, toys, and children's vehicles

Montreal, QC H2M
Hochelaga County

D-U-N-S 24-368-8749   (BR)
**CAISSE DESJARDINS CITE-DU-NORD DE
MONTREAL**
CENTRE DE SERVICE CREMAZIE
555 Boul Cremazie E, Montreal, QC, H2M 1L8
(514) 384-2530
Emp Here 30
SIC 6062 State credit unions

D-U-N-S 25-597-4545   (BR)
**CANADIAN UNION OF PUBLIC EMPLOY-
EES**
CUPE QUEBEC REGIONAL OFFICE
565 Boul Cremazie E Bureau 7100, Montreal,
QC, H2M 2V9
(514) 384-9681
Emp Here 70
SIC 8631 Labor organizations

D-U-N-S 24-084-3730   (BR)
**CENTRE DE RECHERCHE INDUSTRIELLE
DU QUEBEC**
*BUREAU DE NORMALISATION DU QUEBEC
(BNQ)*
1201 Boul Cremazie E Bureau 1 210, Mon-
treal, QC, H2M 0A6
(514) 383-1550
Emp Here 25
SIC 8732 Commercial nonphysical research

D-U-N-S 20-300-7265   (HQ)
CENTRE DE SERVICES DE PAIE CGI INC
1611 Boul Cremazie E 7th Floor, Montreal,
QC, H2M 2P2
(514) 850-6300
Emp Here 200   *Emp Total* 485
Sales 10,944,105
SIC 8721 Accounting, auditing, and book-
keeping
VP Fin Francois Boulanger
  Benoit Dube
VP VP Kevin Linder

D-U-N-S 25-240-3639   (BR)
COMMISSION SCOLAIRE DE MONTREAL
COMMISSION SCOLAIRE DE MONTREAL
525 Rue De Louvain E, Montreal, QC, H2M

1A1
(514) 596-5194
Emp Here 35
SIC 8211 Elementary and secondary schools

D-U-N-S 20-109-5754   (BR)
COMMISSION SCOLAIRE DE MONTREAL
COMMISSION SCOLAIRE DE MONTREAL
9335 Rue Saint-Hubert, Montreal, QC, H2M
1Y7
(514) 858-3999
Emp Here 20
SIC 8211 Elementary and secondary schools

D-U-N-S 25-233-8033   (BR)
COMMISSION SCOLAIRE DE MONTREAL
ECOLE SAINT-ISAAC-JOGUES
9355 Av De Galinee, Montreal, QC, H2M 2A7
(514) 596-5454
Emp Here 40
SIC 8211 Elementary and secondary schools

D-U-N-S 25-240-2425   (BR)
**COMMISSION   SCOLAIRE   ENGLISH-
MONTREAL**
ELEMENTARY SCHOOLS ST RAPHAEL
8735 Av Henri-Julien, Montreal, QC, H2M 1M5
(514) 381-0811
Emp Here 25
SIC 8211 Elementary and secondary schools

D-U-N-S 25-144-7132   (BR)
**COMMISSION DE LA CONSTRUCTION DU
QUEBEC**
(*Suby of* Commission de la Construction du
Quebec)
1201 Boul Cremazie E, Montreal, QC, H2M
0A6
(514) 593-3121
Emp Here 175
SIC 8611 Business associations

D-U-N-S 20-555-8914   (BR)
**CONSEILLERS EN GESTION ET INFORMA-
TIQUE CGI INC**
CGI
9555 Av Christophe-Colomb, Montreal, QC,
H2M 2E3
(514) 374-7777
Emp Here 150
SIC 4899 Communication services, nec

D-U-N-S 20-806-8937   (BR)
COUCHE-TARD INC
1420 Rue Legendre E Bureau 5, Montreal,
QC, H2M 1H5
(514) 388-3096
Emp Here 25
SIC 5411 Grocery stores

D-U-N-S 25-876-7524   (BR)
**FEDERATION   DES   TRAVAILLEURS   ET
TRAVAILLEUSES DU QUEBEC (FTQ)**
*FEDERATION DES TRAVAILLEURS ET TRA-
VAILLEUSES DU QUEBEC (FTQ)*
565 Boul Cremazie E Unite 12100, Montreal,
QC, H2M 2W3
(514) 383-8000
Emp Here 50
SIC 8631 Labor organizations

D-U-N-S 20-845-1570   (BR)
**FEDERATION DES CAISSES DESJARDINS
DU QUEBEC**
*FEDERATION DES CAISSES DESJARDINS
DU QUEBEC*
1611 Boul Cremazie E Bureau 300, Montreal,
QC, H2M 2P2
(514) 356-5000
Emp Here 400
SIC 8721 Accounting, auditing, and book-
keeping

D-U-N-S 25-822-5143   (BR)
**FONDS   DE   SOLIDARITE   DES   TRA-
VAILLEURS DU QUEBEC (F.T.Q.)**
*FONDS DE SOLIDARITE DES TRA-
VAILLEURS DU QUEBEC (F.T.Q.)*

▲ Public Company   ■ Public Company Family Member   **HQ** Headquarters   **BR** Branch   **SL** Single Location

8717 Rue Berri, Montreal, QC, H2M 2T9
(514) 383-3663
Emp Here 100
SIC 6722 Management investment, open-end

D-U-N-S 24-116-9338   (BR)
GOUVERNEMENT DE LA PROVINCE DE QUEBEC
GOUVERNEMENT DE LA PROVINCE DE QUEBEC
950 Rue De Louvain E, Montreal, QC, H2M 2E8
(514) 385-1232
Emp Here 403
SIC 8093 Specialty outpatient clinics, nec

D-U-N-S 20-961-9972   (SL)
ORDRE DES TRAVAILLEURS SOCIAUX ET DES THERAPEUTES CONJUGAUX ET FAMILIAUX DU QUEBEC
OTSTCFQ
255 Boul Cremazie E Bureau 520, Montreal, QC, H2M 1L5
(514) 731-3925
Emp Here 50   *Sales* 5,472,053
SIC 8621 Professional organizations
Pr Guylaine Ouimette
VP VP Sonia Cisternas
VP VP Pierre-Paul Malenfant
Treas Serge Turcotte
 Sylvio Rioux

D-U-N-S 24-352-9963   (SL)
PETRIE RAYMOND S.E.N.C.R.L
255 Boul Cremazie E Bureau 1000, Montreal, QC, H2M 1L5
(514) 342-4740
Emp Here 80   *Sales* 3,502,114
SIC 8721 Accounting, auditing, and bookkeeping

D-U-N-S 25-827-6294   (BR)
PROVIGO DISTRIBUTION INC
MAXI
8305 Av Papineau, Montreal, QC, H2M 2G2
(514) 376-6457
Emp Here 150
SIC 5411 Grocery stores

D-U-N-S 24-021-3066   (BR)
SCM INSURANCE SERVICES INC
SCM CANADA
255 Boul Cremazie E Bureau 1070, Montreal, QC, H2M 1L5
(514) 331-1030
Emp Here 150
SIC 6411 Insurance agents, brokers, and service

D-U-N-S 20-860-6223   (BR)
SOBEYS QUEBEC INC
MARCHER TRADITION LAJEUNESSE
9150 Rue Lajeunesse, Montreal, QC, H2M 1S2
(514) 381-6511
Emp Here 30
SIC 5411 Grocery stores

D-U-N-S 20-706-4929   (SL)
SPORTS MONTREAL INC
1000 Av Emile-Journault, Montreal, QC, H2M 2E7
(514) 872-7177
Emp Here 49   *Sales* 5,782,650
SIC 7032 Sporting and recreational camps
Genl Mgr Jean Guy Rochon

D-U-N-S 20-592-3720   (BR)
VILLE DE MONTREAL
VILLE DE MONTREAL
9335 Rue Saint-Hubert, Montreal, QC, H2M 1Y7
(514) 385-2893
Emp Here 300
SIC 8322 Individual and family services

D-U-N-S 20-707-6188   (BR)
VILLE DE MONTREAL

827 Boul Cremazie E Bureau 301, Montreal, QC, H2M 2T8
(514) 280-4300
Emp Here 50
SIC 7389 Business services, nec

Montreal, QC H2N
Hochelaga County

D-U-N-S 24-872-1664   (HQ)
163972 CANADA INC
JUDITH & CHARLES
(*Suby of* 3378683 Canada Inc)
9600 Rue Meilleur Bureau 730, Montreal, QC, H2N 2E3
(514) 385-3629
Emp Here 39   *Emp Total* 70
Sales 4,231,721
SIC 5621 Women's clothing stores

D-U-N-S 24-357-0665   (HQ)
6938001 CANADA INC
ZACKS
433 Rue Chabanel O Bureau 801, Montreal, QC, H2N 2J6
(514) 383-0026
Emp Here 105   *Emp Total* 243
Sales 9,266,009
SIC 5621 Women's clothing stores
 Jeffrey Fixman

D-U-N-S 20-292-2480   (SL)
9271-9756 QUEBEC INC
C BO
9310 Boul Saint-Laurent Bureau 1117b, Montreal, QC, H2N 1N4
(514) 562-5596
Emp Here 50   *Sales* 2,826,987
SIC 5641 Children's and infants' wear stores

D-U-N-S 20-764-6167   (HQ)
AGF ACCES INC
AGF DU-FOR
9601 Boul Saint-Laurent, Montreal, QC, H2N 1P6
(514) 385-1762
Emp Here 72   *Emp Total* 3,000
Sales 15,642,661
SIC 7353 Heavy construction equipment rental
Pr Pr Serge Gendron
 Diane Lemelin

D-U-N-S 25-368-2058   (BR)
AVIVA CANADA INC
AVIVA
555 Rue Chabanel O Bureau 900, Montreal, QC, H2N 2H8
(514) 850-4100
Emp Here 170
SIC 6411 Insurance agents, brokers, and service

D-U-N-S 24-502-6398   (BR)
BANK OF NOVA SCOTIA, THE
SCOTIABANK
352 Rue Chabanel O, Montreal, QC, H2N 1G6
(514) 385-2447
Emp Here 65
SIC 6021 National commercial banks

D-U-N-S 20-573-7609   (BR)
BANQUE LAURENTIENNE DU CANADA
555 Rue Chabanel O Unite 1500, Montreal, QC, H2N 2H7
(514) 284-4600
Emp Here 20
SIC 6021 National commercial banks

D-U-N-S 20-231-7467   (SL)
BONNETERIE RELIABLE INC
8785 Av Du Parc, Montreal, QC, H2N 1Y7
(514) 382-2861
Emp Here 50   *Sales* 3,648,035
SIC 2251 Women's hosiery, except socks

D-U-N-S 20-882-2619   (BR)
CANADIAN IMPERIAL BANK OF COMMERCE
CIBC
343 Rue Chabanel O, Montreal, QC, H2N 2G1
(514) 388-7900
Emp Here 20
SIC 6021 National commercial banks

D-U-N-S 24-023-1969   (HQ)
CIOT MONTREAL INC
CIOT FABBRICA
(*Suby of* Ciot Montreal Inc)
9151 Boul Saint-Laurent, Montreal, QC, H2N 1N2
(514) 317-6430
Emp Here 185   *Emp Total* 200
Sales 41,660,560
SIC 5032 Brick, stone, and related material
Pr Pr Giuseppe Panzera
 Michael Panzera
Treas Margaret Panzera

D-U-N-S 25-501-9440   (SL)
CUIRS SKOTTS INTERNATIONAL INC
SKOTTS LEATHERS WASH AND WEAR
555 Rue Chabanel O Bureau 600, Montreal, QC, H2N 2H8
(514) 381-4112
Emp Here 60   *Sales* 2,772,507
SIC 2386 Leather and sheep-lined clothing

D-U-N-S 20-761-7648   (HQ)
DECOLIN INC
(*Suby of* Novacap Industries IV, L.P.)
9150 Av Du Parc, Montreal, QC, H2N 1Z2
(514) 384-2910
Emp Here 50   *Emp Total* 1
Sales 10,944,105
SIC 5023 Homefurnishings
Pr Pr Harvey Bucovetsky
 Marc Paiement
 Jacques Foisy
Dir Mendel Leonard J.
Dir Alissa Rappaport
 Martin Lavallee

D-U-N-S 25-495-4563   (BR)
GROUPE ALGO INC
225 Rue Chabanel O, Montreal, QC, H2N 2C9
(514) 384-3551
Emp Here 75
SIC 2335 Women's, junior's, and misses' dresses

D-U-N-S 24-890-1431   (HQ)
GROUPE S.M. INTERNATIONAL INC, LE
(*Suby of* Le Groupe S.M. International S.E.C.)
433 Rue Chabanel O Bureau 1200, Montreal, QC, H2N 2J8
(514) 982-6001
Emp Here 148   *Emp Total* 40
Sales 51,583,215
SIC 8711 Engineering services
Pr Gerard Laganiere
Sec Guy Charbonneau

D-U-N-S 20-551-5286   (SL)
GROUPE STERLING INTIMITE INC, LE
9600 Rue Meilleur Bureau 930, Montreal, QC, H2N 2E3
(514) 385-0500
Emp Here 26   *Sales* 4,900,111
SIC 5137 Women's and children's clothing

D-U-N-S 20-188-1054   (BR)
ITW CANADA INC
ITW LAMINATIONS, DIV OF
(*Suby of* Illinois Tool Works Inc.)
417 Place De Louvain, Montreal, QC, H2N 1A1
(514) 381-7696
Emp Here 30
SIC 2671 Paper; coated and laminated packaging

D-U-N-S 20-017-4311   (HQ)
INTIMES NOUVELLE SEAMLESS INC

(*Suby of* Intimes Nouvelle Seamless Inc)
9500 Rue Meilleur Bureau 100, Montreal, QC, H2N 2B7
(514) 383-1951
Emp Here 158   *Emp Total* 160
Sales 30,942,250
SIC 2341 Women's and children's underwear
Pr Aron Lieberman
VP Willy Lieberman

D-U-N-S 20-234-6532   (SL)
MANUFACTURIER DE BAS DE NYLON SPLENDID INC
55 Rue De Louvain O Bureau 200, Montreal, QC, H2N 1A4
(514) 381-7687
Emp Here 200   *Sales* 39,890,560
SIC 5137 Women's and children's clothing
Pr Pr Aron Liberman
VP VP Frieda Lieberman
 Sam Lieberman

D-U-N-S 20-738-0254   (HQ)
MATADOR CONVERTISSEURS CIE LTEE
(*Suby of* Zumatador Holdings Inc)
270 Rue De Louvain O, Montreal, QC, H2N 1B6
(514) 389-8221
Emp Here 100   *Emp Total* 120
SIC 2297 Nonwoven fabrics

D-U-N-S 24-351-9977   (BR)
NOVEXCO INC
LYRECO CANADA
555 Rue Chabanel O Unite 901, Montreal, QC, H2N 2H7
(514) 385-9991
Emp Here 40
SIC 5044 Office equipment

D-U-N-S 20-349-2702   (BR)
REDBERRY FRANCHISING CORP
BURGER KING
55 Boul Cremazie O, Montreal, QC, H2N 1L3
(514) 389-9542
Emp Here 30
SIC 5812 Eating places

D-U-N-S 25-247-3640   (HQ)
RUDSAK INC
2XPOSE
9160 Boul Saint-Laurent Bureau 400, Montreal, QC, H2N 1M9
(514) 389-9661
Emp Here 75   *Emp Total* 50
Sales 16,458,769
SIC 2386 Leather and sheep-lined clothing
 Evik Asatoorian

D-U-N-S 24-353-0818   (HQ)
SCANIA INTERNATIONAL INC
NORTHPEAK
225 Rue Chabanel O Bureau 505, Montreal, QC, H2N 2C9
(514) 344-5270
Emp Here 20   *Emp Total* 5
Sales 5,653,974
SIC 5137 Women's and children's clothing
Pr Pr Ron Lubov
 Tibor Silber

Montreal, QC H2P
Hochelaga County

D-U-N-S 25-307-3100   (BR)
123273 CANADA INC
PHARMACIE JEAN COUTU
370 Rue Jarry E, Montreal, QC, H2P 1T9
(514) 382-4730
Emp Here 60
SIC 5912 Drug stores and proprietary stores

D-U-N-S 24-368-8301   (BR)
CAISSE DESJARDINS DE LORIMIER-VILLERAY

CENTRE DE SERVICES DE VILLERAY
8164 Rue Saint-Hubert, Montreal, QC, H2P
1Z2
(514) 376-7676
Emp Here 30
SIC 6062 State credit unions

D-U-N-S 25-240-3159   (BR)
COMMISSION SCOLAIRE DE MONTREAL
COMMISSION SCOLAIRE DE MONTREAL
8550 Rue Clark, Montreal, QC, H2P 2N7
(514) 596-4318
Emp Here 60
SIC 8211 Elementary and secondary schools

D-U-N-S 25-233-7555   (BR)
COMMISSION SCOLAIRE DE MONTREAL
ECOLE GADBOIS
8305 Rue Saint-Andre, Montreal, QC, H2P
1Y7
(514) 596-4246
Emp Here 50
SIC 8211 Elementary and secondary schools

D-U-N-S 20-712-4517   (BR)
COMMISSION SCOLAIRE DE MONTREAL
COMMISSION SCOLAIRE DE MONTREAL
85 Rue Jarry O, Montreal, QC, H2P 1S6
(514) 596-4381
Emp Here 60
SIC 8211 Elementary and secondary schools

D-U-N-S 25-240-7564   (BR)
COMMISSION SCOLAIRE DE MONTREAL
COMMISSION SCOLAIRE DE MONTREAL
8525 Rue Berri, Montreal, QC, H2P 2G5
(514) 596-5450
Emp Here 54
SIC 8211 Elementary and secondary schools

D-U-N-S 25-240-2789   (BR)
COMMISSION SCOLAIRE DE MONTREAL
COMMISSION SCOLAIRE DE MONTREAL
1205 Rue Jarry E, Montreal, QC, H2P 1W9
(514) 596-4160
Emp Here 125
SIC 8211 Elementary and secondary schools

D-U-N-S 24-121-5396   (BR)
COMMISSION SCOLAIRE DE MONTREAL
COMMISSION SCOLAIRE DE MONTREAL
8200 Boul Saint-Laurent, Montreal, QC, H2P
2L8
(514) 596-5400
Emp Here 250
SIC 8211 Elementary and secondary schools

D-U-N-S 25-334-2810   (SL)
FAUTEUX, BRUNO, BUSSIERE, LEEWAR-
DEN, CPA, S.E.N.C.R.L.
F.B.B.L.
1100 Boul Cremazie E Bureau 805, Montreal,
QC, H2P 2X2
(514) 729-3221
Emp Here 110   Sales 4,815,406
SIC 8721 Accounting, auditing, and book-
keeping

D-U-N-S 20-327-4571   (BR)
GENERAL CREDIT SERVICES INC
(Suby of General Credit Services Inc)
1100 Boul Cremazie E Bureau 410, Montreal,
QC, H2P 2X2
(877) 313-4274
Emp Here 20
SIC 7322 Adjustment and collection services

D-U-N-S 25-334-5565   (BR)
HYDRO-QUEBEC
140 Boul Cremazie O, Montreal, QC, H2P 1C3
(514) 858-8500
Emp Here 821
SIC 8731 Commercial physical research

D-U-N-S 20-221-6651   (SL)
IMPENCO LTEE
240 Rue Guizot O, Montreal, QC, H2P 1L5
(514) 383-1200
Emp Here 100

SIC 3172 Personal leather goods, nec

D-U-N-S 24-936-0843   (SL)
INDUSTRIES ESTED INC
8484 Av De L'Esplanade, Montreal, QC, H2P
2R7
(514) 858-9595
Emp Here 20   Sales 5,377,995
SIC 2369 Girl's and children's outerwear, nec
Edward Binet
VP Juda Deutsch

D-U-N-S 24-390-8238   (HQ)
MEDISOLUTION (2009) INC
MEDISOLUTION
110 Boul Cremazie O Bureau 1200, Montreal,
QC, H2P 1B9
(514) 850-5000
Emp Here 60   Emp Total 12,124
Sales 17,715,785
SIC 5045 Computers, peripherals, and soft-
ware
Pr Pr Jeff Bender
John Billowits
Dir Mark H Leonard

D-U-N-S 24-828-6411   (HQ)
MELOCHE MONNEX INC
(Suby of Toronto-Dominion Bank, The)
50 Boul Cremazie O Bureau 1200, Montreal,
QC, H2P 1B6
(514) 382-6060
Emp Here 700   Emp Total 81,233
Sales 126,076,090
SIC 6411 Insurance agents, brokers, and ser-
vice
Pr Kenneth W. Lalonde Lalonde
Dir Barbara Coyle
Dir Tonny Menon
Dir Raymond C.H. Chun
Dir James V. Russell
Genl Mgr Antonietta Di Girolamo

D-U-N-S 20-297-9113   (HQ)
OS4 TECHNO INC
(Suby of OS4 Techno Inc)
1100 Boul Cremazie E Bureau 600, Montreal,
QC, H2P 2X2
(514) 722-9333
Emp Here 40   Emp Total 65
Sales 6,380,400
SIC 7379 Computer related services, nec
Pr Pr Michel Caron
VP VP Danny Redmond
Kim Perron

D-U-N-S 20-790-7833   (HQ)
PAGEAU, MOREL & ASSOCIES INC
210 Boul Cremazie O Bureau 110, Montreal,
QC, H2P 1C6
(514) 382-5150
Emp Here 125   Emp Total 140
Sales 22,427,430
SIC 8711 Engineering services
Pr Pr Nicolas Lemire
Roland Charneux
Nicole Vachon
Francois Laframboise
Dir Jacques De Grace
Dir Claude Giguere

D-U-N-S 20-979-9225   (BR)
PHARMASCIENCE INC
PENDOPHARM
8580 Av De L'Esplanade, Montreal, QC, H2P
2R8
(514) 384-6516
Emp Here 250
SIC 2834 Pharmaceutical preparations

D-U-N-S 20-765-0771   (SL)
PRESTIGE SALES INC
IMPERIAL HOUSE SALES
(Suby of 136712 Canada Inc)
50 Boul Cremazie O Bureau 700, Montreal,
QC, H2P 2T4

Emp Here 20   Sales 7,234,560

SIC 5141 Groceries, general line
Pr Pr Michael Korenberg
Leonard Pedvis

D-U-N-S 24-873-7504   (HQ)
PRIMMUM INSURANCE COMPANY
(Suby of Toronto-Dominion Bank, The)
50 Boul Cremazie O Bureau 1200, Montreal,
QC, H2P 1B6
(514) 382-6060
Emp Here 260   Emp Total 81,233
Sales 191,157,034
SIC 6331 Fire, marine, and casualty insurance
Pr Kenneth W. Lalonde
Dir Riaz Ahmed
Dir Mark Chauvin
Dir Susan Anne Cummings
Dir Philip C. Moore
Dir Richard Gauthier
Dir John W. Thompson
Dir John Capozzolo
Genl Mgr Antonietta Di Girolamo

D-U-N-S 24-305-2040   (HQ)
SECURITE   NATIONALE   COMPAGNIE
D'ASSURANCE
(Suby of Toronto-Dominion Bank, The)
50 Boul Cremazie O Bureau 1200, Montreal,
QC, H2P 1B6
(514) 382-6060
Emp Here 1,500   Emp Total 81,233
Sales 153,144,509
SIC 6411 Insurance agents, brokers, and ser-
vice
Pr Kenneth Lalonde
Sec Joanne Simard
Dir Riaz Ahmed
Dir Mark Chauvin
Dir Susan Anne Cummings
Dir Philip C Moore
Dir Thomas Dyck
Dir Erik Von Schilling
Genl Mgr Antonietta Di Girolamo

D-U-N-S 20-327-5123   (BR)
UNITED FOOD AND COMMERCIAL WORK-
ERS CANADA UNION
TUAC LOCAL 500
(Suby of United Food and Commercial Work-
ers International Union)
1200 Boul Cremazie E Bureau 100, Montreal,
QC, H2P 3A7
(514) 332-5825
Emp Here 50
SIC 8631 Labor organizations

Montreal, QC H2R
Hochelaga County

D-U-N-S 25-144-7009   (BR)
168662 CANADA INC
LINGERIE LILIANNE
260 Rue Gary-Carter, Montreal, QC, H2R 2V7
(514) 384-7691
Emp Here 100
SIC 5632 Women's accessory and specialty
stores

D-U-N-S 24-922-8529   (SL)
2618-1833 QUEBEC INC
274 Rue Jean-Talon E, Montreal, QC, H2R
1S7
(514) 273-3224
Emp Here 60   Sales 10,753,700
SIC 6712 Bank holding companies
Pr Flavio Zeffiro

D-U-N-S 24-984-2118   (SL)
ASSOCIATION QUEBECOISE DES CEN-
TRES DE LA PETITE ENFANCE
7245 Rue Clark Bureau 401, Montreal, QC,
H2R 2Y4
(514) 326-8008
Emp Here 25   Sales 5,909,817

SIC 8399 Social services, nec
Pr Gina Gasparrini

D-U-N-S 25-248-3730   (SL)
ASSOCIATION DE TAXI DIAMOND DE
MONTREAL LTEE, L'
DIAMOND TAXI
(Suby of Taxelco Inc)
7294 Rue Lajeunesse Bureau A, Montreal,
QC, H2R 2H4
(514) 273-1725
Emp Here 45   Sales 1,386,253
SIC 4121 Taxicabs

D-U-N-S 20-580-5612   (BR)
BANQUE LAURENTIENNE DU CANADA
BANQUE LAURENTIENNE, LA
10 Rue Jean-Talon E, Montreal, QC, H2R 1S3
(514) 273-1585
Emp Here 20
SIC 6021 National commercial banks

D-U-N-S 25-003-9757   (BR)
BANQUE NATIONALE DU CANADA
8091 Rue Saint-Denis, Montreal, QC, H2R
2G2
(514) 381-2391
Emp Here 30
SIC 6021 National commercial banks

D-U-N-S 20-213-1744   (SL)
C & M TEXTILES INC
C & M
7500 Rue Saint-Hubert, Montreal, QC, H2R
2N6
(514) 272-0247
Emp Here 50   Sales 1,824,018
SIC 5949 Sewing, needlework, and piece
goods

D-U-N-S 24-501-0699   (BR)
CANADIAN TENNIS ASSOCIATION
TENNIS CANADA
285 Rue Gary-Carter, Montreal, QC, H2R
2W1
(514) 273-0094
Emp Here 25
SIC 7999 Amusement and recreation, nec

D-U-N-S 25-240-3399   (BR)
COMMISSION SCOLAIRE DE MONTREAL
COMMISSION SCOLAIRE DE MONTREAL
8050 Av De Gaspe, Montreal, QC, H2R 2A7
(514) 596-5275
Emp Here 45
SIC 8211 Elementary and secondary schools

D-U-N-S 20-712-4384   (BR)
COMMISSION SCOLAIRE DE MONTREAL
ECOLE STE-CECILE
7230 Av De Gaspe, Montreal, QC, H2R 1Z6
(514) 596-5530
Emp Here 60
SIC 8211 Elementary and secondary schools

D-U-N-S 20-737-8522   (SL)
CONFECTIONS DONNA LTEE
7445 Rue Du Mile End, Montreal, QC, H2R
2Z7
(514) 271-1122
Emp Here 55   Sales 9,894,455
SIC 2341 Women's and children's underwear
Pr Pr George Asfour
VP VP Joseph Asfour
VP Amal Jabbour
VP Dina Asfour

D-U-N-S 25-960-5400   (BR)
ENCAISSEMENT DE CHEQUE MONTREAL
LTEE
INSTA-CHEQUES
7166 Rue Saint-Hubert, Montreal, QC, H2R
2N1

Emp Here 20
SIC 6099 Functions related to deposit banking

D-U-N-S 20-332-9607   (HQ)
ENTREPRISES VANA INC

RESTAURANT MCDONALD'S
(Suby of Entreprises Vana Inc)
7275 Saint-Laurent, Montreal, QC, H2R 1W5
(514) 664-4545
Emp Here 50   Emp Total 100
Sales 3,551,629
SIC 5812 Eating places

D-U-N-S 24-528-3817   (HQ)
FROMAGERIES PIMAR INC, LES
FROMAGERIE HAMEL
(Suby of Fromageries Pimar Inc, Les)
220 Rue Jean-Talon E, Montreal, QC, H2R 1S7
(514) 272-1161
Emp Here 40   Emp Total 72
Sales 2,991,389
SIC 5451 Dairy products stores

D-U-N-S 25-310-9920   (BR)
MCDONALD'S RESTAURANTS OF CANADA LIMITED
RESTAURANT MCDONALD'S
(Suby of McDonald's Corporation)
7275 Boul Saint-Laurent, Montreal, QC, H2R 1W5
(514) 276-6878
Emp Here 50
SIC 5812 Eating places

D-U-N-S 25-287-0928   (SL)
PATRO LE PREVOST INC
7355 Av Christophe-Colomb, Montreal, QC, H2R 2S5
(514) 273-8535
Emp Here 83   Sales 3,283,232
SIC 8322 Individual and family services

D-U-N-S 25-263-5926   (HQ)
PROMARK-TELECON INC
7450 Rue Du Mile End, Montreal, QC, H2R 2Z6
(514) 644-2214
Emp Here 60   Emp Total 2,907
Sales 44,870,831
SIC 4899 Communication services, nec
Pr Pr Andre Heroux

D-U-N-S 25-243-0897   (HQ)
TELELANGUES INTERNATIONAL LTEE
(Suby of Telelangues International Ltee)
7977 Rue Saint-Denis, Montreal, QC, H2R 2G2
(514) 388-6998
Emp Here 25   Emp Total 50
Sales 2,699,546
SIC 8299 Schools and educational services, nec

D-U-N-S 24-382-9178   (BR)
UNIPRIX INC
340661
1275 Rue Villeray, Montreal, QC, H2R 1J9
(514) 274-1114
Emp Here 30
SIC 5912 Drug stores and proprietary stores

D-U-N-S 20-332-9631   (BR)
VILLE DE MONTREAL
CULTURE ET BIBLIOTHEQUES, DIV
800 Boul Maisonneuve E Bureau 700, Montreal, QC, H2R 4L8
(514) 868-4402
Emp Here 33
SIC 8231 Libraries

D-U-N-S 25-223-9306   (BR)
VILLE DE MONTREAL
VILLE DE MONTREAL
7355 Av Christophe-Colomb, Montreal, QC, H2R 2S5
(514) 872-1523
Emp Here 25
SIC 8231 Libraries

D-U-N-S 24-325-9769   (HQ)
ACT3 M.H.S. INC
(Suby of 157341 Canada Inc)

7236 Rue Marconi, Montreal, QC, H2R 2Z5
(514) 844-5050
Emp Here 75   Emp Total 60
Sales 22,836,699
SIC 7319 Advertising, nec
Sec Mark Sherman
Pr Penny Stevens

Montreal, QC H2S
Hochelaga County

D-U-N-S 20-270-8590   (SL)
7979134 CANADA INC
BOULANGERIE PREMIERE MOISSON
7075 Av Casgrain, Montreal, QC, H2S 3A3
(450) 477-4100
Emp Here 50   Sales 3,118,504
SIC 2051 Bread, cake, and related products

D-U-N-S 20-224-8089   (BR)
AUTOBUS TERREMONT LTEE
(Suby of Societe Industrielle Laurentide Inc)
7190 Rue Marconi, Montreal, QC, H2S 3K1
(514) 272-1779
Emp Here 40
SIC 4142 Bus charter service, except local

D-U-N-S 20-213-6425   (BR)
CENTRE COMMUNAUTAIRE JURIDIQUE DE MONTREAL
JEUNEUSSE
5800 Rue Saint-Denis Bureau 802, Montreal, QC, H2S 3L5
(514) 864-9833
Emp Here 21
SIC 8111 Legal services

D-U-N-S 20-800-1854   (BR)
CENTRE DE SANTE ET DE SERVICES SOCIAUX DU COEUR-DE-L'ILE
CENTRE D'EBERGEMENT AUCLAIRE
6910 Rue Boyer, Montreal, QC, H2S 2J7
(514) 272-3011
Emp Here 100
SIC 8322 Individual and family services

D-U-N-S 20-856-2967   (SL)
CHAMPLAIN TAXI MONTREAL (1974) LTD
5775 Rue Saint-Andre, Montreal, QC, H2S 2K2
(514) 273-2435
Emp Here 56   Sales 1,678,096
SIC 4121 Taxicabs

D-U-N-S 20-031-4305   (BR)
COMMISSION SCOLAIRE DE MONTREAL
ECOLE ST-JEAN-DE-LA-CROIX
35 Rue Saint-Zotique E, Montreal, QC, H2S 1K5
(514) 596-5485
Emp Here 30
SIC 8211 Elementary and secondary schools

D-U-N-S 24-805-2529   (BR)
COMMISSION SCOLAIRE DE MONTREAL
ECOLE ST-AMBROISE
6555 Rue De Normanville, Montreal, QC, H2S 2B8
(514) 596-4940
Emp Here 100
SIC 8211 Elementary and secondary schools

D-U-N-S 25-240-7028   (BR)
COMMISSION SCOLAIRE DE MONTREAL
ECOLE SAINT-ETIENNE
5959 Av Christophe-Colomb, Montreal, QC, H2S 2G3
(514) 596-5165
Emp Here 50
SIC 8211 Elementary and secondary schools

D-U-N-S 25-240-6970   (BR)
COMMISSION SCOLAIRE DE MONTREAL
COMMISSION SCOLAIRE DE MONTREAL
6841 Av Henri-Julien, Montreal, QC, H2S 2V3
Emp Here 40

(514) 596-5480
Emp Here 20
SIC 8211 Elementary and secondary schools

D-U-N-S 25-240-3431   (BR)
COMMISSION SCOLAIRE DE MONTREAL
ECOLE LA MENNAIS
6521 Rue Saint-Denis, Montreal, QC, H2S 2S1
(514) 596-5288
Emp Here 50
SIC 8211 Elementary and secondary schools

D-U-N-S 25-233-5831   (BR)
COMMISSION SCOLAIRE DE MONTREAL
ECOLE CHARLES BRUNEAU
5927 Rue Boyer, Montreal, QC, H2S 2H8
(514) 596-4266
Emp Here 35
SIC 8211 Elementary and secondary schools

D-U-N-S 20-032-6408   (BR)
COMMISSION SCOLAIRE DE MONTREAL
COMMISSION SCOLAIRE DE MONTREAL
6972 Av Christophe-Colomb, Montreal, QC, H2S 2H5
(514) 596-5011
Emp Here 50
SIC 8211 Elementary and secondary schools

D-U-N-S 20-259-5711   (SL)
GFP LES HOTES DE MONTREAL INC
HM SECURITE
6983 Rue De La Roche, Montreal, QC, H2S 2E6
(514) 274-6837
Emp Here 400   Sales 17,182,080
SIC 7381 Detective and armored car services
Pr Pr Pierre Touzin

D-U-N-S 20-553-4360   (BR)
HOME DEPOT OF CANADA INC
HOME DEPOT
(Suby of The Home Depot Inc)
100 Rue Jarry O, Montreal, QC, H2S 3S1
(514) 490-8030
Emp Here 175
SIC 5211 Lumber and other building materials

D-U-N-S 25-857-1264   (BR)
LES CENTRES DE LA JEUNESSE ET DE LA FAMILLE BATSHAW
BATSHAW YOUTH AND FAMILY CENTRES
(Suby of Les Centres de la Jeunesse et de la Famille Batshaw)
410 Rue De Bellechasse Bureau 2002, Montreal, QC, H2S 1X3
(514) 273-9533
Emp Here 20
SIC 8322 Individual and family services

D-U-N-S 24-768-2909   (SL)
RAMVAL INC
PHARMACIE JEAN COUTU
(Suby of Placements A. Lajeunesse Inc)
6500 Rue Saint-Hubert, Montreal, QC, H2S 2M3
(514) 272-8233
Emp Here 70   Sales 19,043,040
SIC 5912 Drug stores and proprietary stores
Pr Pr Andre Lajeunesse

D-U-N-S 20-112-2210   (SL)
RONOR INTERNATIONAL INC
90 Rue Beaubien O Bureau 500, Montreal, QC, H2S 1V6
(514) 278-5787
Emp Here 50   Sales 7,296,070
SIC 5049 Professional equipment, nec
Yves Langelier

D-U-N-S 25-307-3241   (BR)
ROTISSERIES ST-HUBERT LTEE, LES
ST HUBERT EXPRESS
(Suby of Cara Holdings Limited)
6355 Rue Saint-Hubert, Montreal, QC, H2S 2L9
(514) 274-4477
Emp Here 40

SIC 5812 Eating places

D-U-N-S 20-852-8229   (BR)
SOBEYS QUEBEC INC
IGA BARCELO
900 Rue Saint-Zotique E, Montreal, QC, H2S 1M8
(514) 270-9440
Emp Here 70
SIC 5411 Grocery stores

D-U-N-S 25-308-8512   (BR)
SOCIETE DES ALCOOLS DU QUEBEC
SOCIETE DES ALCOOLS DU QUEBEC
900 Rue Beaubien E, Montreal, QC, H2S 1T1
(514) 270-1776
Emp Here 30
SIC 5921 Liquor stores

Montreal, QC H2T
Hochelaga County

D-U-N-S 24-762-5460   (SL)
162404 CANADA INC
TYR SPORT
160 Rue Saint-Viateur E Bureau 602, Montreal, QC, H2T 1A8
(514) 276-2000
Emp Here 70   Sales 4,304,681
SIC 2339 Women's and misses' outerwear, nec

D-U-N-S 25-256-8076   (SL)
2744-4215 QUEBEC INC
FILMS MORRISON
5455 Av De Gaspe Bureau 801, Montreal, QC, H2T 3B3
(514) 844-1636
Emp Here 50   Sales 4,596,524
SIC 7812 Motion picture and video production

D-U-N-S 20-715-4431   (SL)
ATTRACTION IMAGES PRODUCTIONS INC
(Suby of Attraction Media Inc)
5455 Av De Gaspe Bureau 804, Montreal, QC, H2T 3B3
(514) 285-7001
Emp Here 1,000   Sales 114,548,299
SIC 7922 Theatrical producers and services
Pr Marleen Beaulieu
Richard Speer

D-U-N-S 20-996-8734   (HQ)
COLLEGE FRANCAIS (1965) INC
(Suby of College Francais (1965) Inc)
185 Av Fairmount O, Montreal, QC, H2T 2M6
(514) 495-2581
Emp Here 94   Emp Total 252
Sales 22,674,960
SIC 8211 Elementary and secondary schools
Pr Pr Collette Portal
VP VP Jean-Louis Portal
George Biron
Roger Goehry
Marie-Therese Goehry
Claude Bigras

D-U-N-S 20-024-5277   (BR)
COMMISSION SCOLAIRE DE MONTREAL
ECOLE LAMBERT CLOSSE
5840 Rue Saint-Urbain, Montreal, QC, H2T 2X5
(514) 596-5890
Emp Here 55
SIC 8211 Elementary and secondary schools

D-U-N-S 25-233-6730   (BR)
COMMISSION SCOLAIRE ENGLISH-MONTREAL
BANCROFT SCHOOL
4563 Rue Saint-Urbain, Montreal, QC, H2T 2V9
(514) 845-8031
Emp Here 20
SIC 8211 Elementary and secondary schools

D-U-N-S 20-712-4616   (BR)
COMMISSION SCOLAIRE DE MONTREAL
COMMISSION SCOLAIRE DE MONTREAL
6080 Av De L'Esplanade, Montreal, QC, H2T
3A3
(514) 596-4800
Emp Here 85
SIC 8211 Elementary and secondary schools

D-U-N-S 20-291-2739   (SL)
**CORPS CANADIEN DES COMMISSION-
NAIRES (DIVISION DU QUEBEC)**
201 Av Laurier E Bureau 400, Montreal, QC,
H2T 3E6
(514) 273-8578
Emp Here 100   *Sales* 43,319,150
SIC 7381 Detective and armored car services
Pr Robin Gagnon
VP Jean Gervais
Sec Guy Theriault
Dir Denis Belleau
Dir Pierre Cadotte
Dir Louis Farley
Dir Alain Forand
Dir Jean Forget
Dir Gaetan Houle
Dir Gordon Lewis

D-U-N-S 24-793-3364   (SL)
CRUDESSENCE INC
5445 Av De Gaspe Bureau 906, Montreal, QC,
H2T 3B2
(514) 271-0333
Emp Here 74   *Sales* 4,012,839
SIC 8299 Schools and educational services,
nec

D-U-N-S 20-209-4553   (SL)
ECHANTILLONNAGE A S C INC
5425 Av Casgrain Bureau 403, Montreal, QC,
H2T 1X6
(514) 277-7515
Emp Here 50   *Sales* 2,991,389
SIC 2782 Blankbooks and looseleaf binders

D-U-N-S 20-126-7379   (BR)
**GOUVERNEMENT DE LA PROVINCE DE
QUEBEC**
*GOUVERNEMENT DE LA PROVINCE DE
QUEBEC*
4750 Av Henri-Julien, Montreal, QC, H2T 3E4
(514) 873-4283
Emp Here 35
SIC 8299 Schools and educational services,
nec

D-U-N-S 20-237-6463   (HQ)
GROUPE YELLOW INC
CHAUSSURES YELLOW
(*Suby of* Les Placements Yellow Inc)
5665 Boul Saint-Laurent, Montreal, QC, H2T
1S9
(514) 273-0424
Emp Here 70   *Emp Total* 1,200
Sales 73,325,504
SIC 5661 Shoe stores
Pr Pr Douglas Avrith

D-U-N-S 24-989-1813   (SL)
INTIMODE CANADA INC
JM DESIGN
5425 Av Casgrain Bureau 502, Montreal, QC,
H2T 1X6
(514) 271-3133
Emp Here 65   *Sales* 1,167,371
SIC 2322 Men's and boy's underwear and
nightwear

D-U-N-S 25-825-4531   (BR)
KIDS HELP PHONE
JEUNESSE J ECOUTE
5605 Av De Gaspe Unite 303, Montreal, QC,
H2T 2A4
(514) 273-7007
Emp Here 35
SIC 8322 Individual and family services

D-U-N-S 24-619-6265   (HQ)

LE COLLEGE FRANCAIS PRIMAIRE INC
185 Av Fairmount O, Montreal, QC, H2T 2M6
(514) 271-2823
Emp Here 25   *Emp Total* 5
Sales 12,985,600
SIC 8211 Elementary and secondary schools
Pr Claude Bigras
Jean-Louis Portal
Treas Alexandre Bigras
Dir Lelia Farout
Dir Elise Beausoleil

D-U-N-S 20-331-8761   (BR)
MAISON DU BAGEL INC
ST-VIATEUR BAGEL MILE-END
(*Suby of* Maison Du Bagel Inc)
158 Rue Saint-Viateur O, Montreal, QC, H2T
2L3
(514) 270-2972
Emp Here 20
SIC 5461 Retail bakeries

D-U-N-S 20-236-4154   (SL)
MANUFACTURE UNIVERSELLE S.B. INC
5555 Av Casgrain Bureau 300, Montreal, QC,
H2T 1Y1
(514) 271-1177
Emp Here 100   *Sales* 19,376,950
SIC 2341 Women's and children's underwear
Pr Pr Stephen Brownstein
Harold Brownstein

D-U-N-S 20-617-1873   (SL)
MECANIQUE A VAPEUR MAURICE ENR
5445 Av De Gaspe Bureau 99, Montreal, QC,
H2T 3B2

Emp Here 540   *Sales* 53,006,400
SIC 3599 Industrial machinery, nec
Owner Maurice Cormier

D-U-N-S 20-544-9544   (BR)
**NATURE CONSERVANCY OF CANADA,
THE**
CONSERVATION DE LA NATURE
55 Av Du Mont-Royal O Bureau 1000, Mon-
treal, QC, H2T 2S6
(514) 876-1606
Emp Here 25
SIC 8999 Services, nec

D-U-N-S 20-010-7576   (SL)
**OPSIS GESTION D'INFRASTRUCTURES
INC**
4750 Av Henri-Julien, Montreal, QC, H2T 2C8
(514) 982-6774
Emp Here 80   *Sales* 6,576,720
SIC 8741 Management services
Pr Jean-Pierre Azzopardi

D-U-N-S 24-061-6420   (BR)
PATISSERIE DE GASCOGNE INC
237 Av Laurier E, Montreal, QC, H2T 1G2
(514) 490-0235
Emp Here 30
SIC 5461 Retail bakeries

D-U-N-S 20-912-2964   (BR)
RNC MEDIA INC
91.9 SPORT
200 Av Laurier O Bureau 250, Montreal, QC,
H2T 2N8
(514) 871-0919
Emp Here 20
SIC 4832 Radio broadcasting stations

D-U-N-S 24-806-2569   (SL)
TENDANCES & CONCEPT MTL INC
4823 Boul Saint-Laurent Bureau A, Montreal,
QC, H2T 1R6
(514) 504-7788
Emp Here 49   *Sales* 7,223,109
SIC 5211 Lumber and other building materials

D-U-N-S 24-374-4575   (SL)
UBISOFT ARTS NUMERIQUES INC
5505 Boul Saint-Laurent Bureau 2000, Montreal, QC, H2T 1S6

(514) 490-2000
Emp Here 100   *Sales* 10,048,000
SIC 7336 Commercial art and graphic design
Genl Mgr Yannis Mallat
Pr Pr Yves Guillemot
Sec Claude Guillemot

D-U-N-S 20-515-4110   (BR)
UNIVERSITE DU QUEBEC
*ECOLE NATIONALE D'ADMINISTRATION
PUBLIQUE*
4750 Av Henri-Julien, Montreal, QC, H2T 3E5
(514) 849-3989
Emp Here 50
SIC 8221 Colleges and universities

Montreal, QC H2V
Hochelaga County

D-U-N-S 20-277-9138   (SL)
8003149 CANADA INC
DEMENAGEMENT LA CAPITALE
6674 Av De L'Esplanade, Montreal, QC, H2V
4L5
(514) 273-3300
Emp Here 50   *Sales* 2,845,467
SIC 4214 Local trucking with storage

D-U-N-S 20-534-3655   (BR)
CSG SECURITY CORPORATION
SYSTEMES DE SECURITE CHUBB
(*Suby of* United Technologies Corporation)
6680 Av Du Parc, Montreal, QC, H2V 4H9
(514) 272-7700
Emp Here 220
SIC 1731 Electrical work

D-U-N-S 24-793-2978   (SL)
CONSTRUCTION STEEVE GAGNON INC
6250 Hutchison St Suite 301, Montreal, QC,
H2V 4C5

Emp Here 25   *Sales* 6,492,800
SIC 1542 Nonresidential construction, nec
Pr Steeve Gagnon

D-U-N-S 20-555-5142   (BR)
LIBRAIRIE RENAUD-BRAY INC
5117 Av Du Parc, Montreal, QC, H2V 4G3
(514) 276-7651
Emp Here 55
SIC 5942 Book stores

D-U-N-S 20-210-9039   (HQ)
MAISON DU BAGEL INC
ST-VIATEUR BAGEL
(*Suby of* Maison Du Bagel Inc)
263 Rue Saint-Viateur O, Montreal, QC, H2V
1Y1
(514) 276-8044
Emp Here 50   *Emp Total* 50
Sales 1,678,096
SIC 5461 Retail bakeries

D-U-N-S 24-804-8048   (SL)
STUDIOS MOMENT FACTORY INC, LES
MOMENT FACTORY
6250 Av Du Parc, Montreal, QC, H2V 4H8
(514) 843-8433
Emp Here 53   *Sales* 3,866,917
SIC 7336 Commercial art and graphic design

D-U-N-S 24-071-6907   (BR)
UNIPRIX INC
PHARMACIE DU PARC
5647 Av Du Parc, Montreal, QC, H2V 4H2
(514) 276-9353
Emp Here 38
SIC 5912 Drug stores and proprietary stores

D-U-N-S 25-446-8788   (BR)
YMCA DU QUEBEC, LES
CENTRE Y DU PARC, LE
5550 Av Du Parc, Montreal, QC, H2V 4H1
(514) 271-9622
Emp Here 130

SIC 7991 Physical fitness facilities

Montreal, QC H2W
Hochelaga County

D-U-N-S 24-432-4620   (SL)
95781 CANADA INC
L'EXPRESS
3927 Rue Saint-Denis, Montreal, QC, H2W
2M4
(514) 845-5333
Emp Here 50   *Sales* 1,532,175
SIC 5812 Eating places

D-U-N-S 20-337-2537   (BR)
ALLIED INTERNATIONAL CREDIT CORP
4200 Boul Saint-Laurent Suite 600, Montreal,
QC, H2W 2R2
(866) 259-4317
Emp Here 45
SIC 4899 Communication services, nec

D-U-N-S 25-248-2989   (SL)
**ASSOCIATION D'ENTRAIDE LE CHAINON
INC, L'**
LE CHAINON
4373 Av De L'Esplanade, Montreal, QC, H2W
1T2
(514) 845-0151
Emp Here 105   *Sales* 4,158,760
SIC 8322 Individual and family services

D-U-N-S 25-366-6945   (BR)
CARAT CANADA INC
4446 Boul Saint-Laurent Bureau 500, Montreal, QC, H2W 1Z5
(514) 287-2555
Emp Here 75
SIC 7311 Advertising agencies

D-U-N-S 20-714-2444   (SL)
COLLEGE RACHEL
310 Rue Rachel E, Montreal, QC, H2W 0A1
(514) 287-1944
Emp Here 50   *Sales* 3,356,192
SIC 8211 Elementary and secondary schools

D-U-N-S 25-240-7465   (BR)
COMMISSION SCOLAIRE DE MONTREAL
COMMISSION SCOLAIRE DE MONTREAL
4285 Rue Drolet, Montreal, QC, H2W 2L7
(514) 596-5800
Emp Here 30
SIC 8211 Elementary and secondary schools

D-U-N-S 20-712-4343   (BR)
COMMISSION SCOLAIRE DE MONTREAL
COMMISSION SCOLAIRE DE MONTREAL
4265 Av Laval, Montreal, QC, H2W 2J6
(514) 350-8860
Emp Here 50
SIC 8211 Elementary and secondary schools

D-U-N-S 20-574-8226   (BR)
COMMISSION SCOLAIRE DE MONTREAL
COMMISSION SCOLAIRE DE MONTREAL
311 Av Des Pins E, Montreal, QC, H2W 1P5
(514) 350-8840
Emp Here 40
SIC 8211 Elementary and secondary schools

D-U-N-S 24-827-1335   (BR)
**EDELMAN PUBLIC RELATIONS WORLD-
WIDE CANADA INC**
4446 Boul Saint-Laurent Bureau 501, Mon-
treal, QC, H2W 1Z5
(514) 844-6665
Emp Here 35
SIC 8743 Public relations services

D-U-N-S 20-764-0848   (SL)
**FONDATION DE L'INSTITUT DE
RECHERCHES CLINIQUE DE MONTREAL**
110 Av Des Pins O, Montreal, QC, H2W 1R7
(514) 987-5500
Emp Here 450   *Sales* 32,981,760

SIC 8731 Commercial physical research
Pr Alain Mayrand
Sec Stephane Letourneau
Benoit Papineau

D-U-N-S 20-714-6635   (SL)
MAKWA AVENTURES INC, LES
CAMP USA-MONDE
4079 Rue Saint-Denis, Montreal, QC, H2W
2M7
(514) 285-2583
Emp Here 88   *Sales* 4,377,642
SIC 7389 Business services, nec

D-U-N-S 20-332-9644   (BR)
RELIGIEUSES HOSPITALIERES DE SAINT-JOSEPH
SOEURS HOSPITALIERES DE ST JOSEPH
(*Suby of* Religieuses Hospitalieres de Saint-Joseph)
251 Av Des Pins O, Montreal, QC, H2W 1R6
(514) 844-3961
Emp Here 50
SIC 8661 Religious organizations

D-U-N-S 24-355-6409   (BR)
SPAFAX CANADA INC
4200 Boul Saint-Laurent Bureau 707, Montreal, QC, H2W 2R2
(514) 844-2001
Emp Here 45
SIC 5199 Nondurable goods, nec

D-U-N-S 24-065-7374   (SL)
TRIBAL NOVA INC
TRIBAL NOVA KIDS
(*Suby of* Houghton Mifflin Harcourt Company)
4200 Boul Saint-Laurent Bureau 1203, Montreal, QC, H2W 2R2
(514) 598-0444
Emp Here 25   *Sales* 3,648,035
SIC 5092 Toys and hobby goods and supplies

D-U-N-S 20-106-2705   (BR)
UNIVERSITE DE MONTREAL, L'
UNITE DE SANTE INTERNATIONALE
3875 Rue Saint-Urbain, Montreal, QC, H2W
1V1
(514) 890-8156
Emp Here 20
SIC 8399 Social services, nec

Montreal, QC H2X
Hochelaga County

D-U-N-S 25-894-5484   (BR)
119859 CANADA INC
SUPER MARCHE QUATRE FRERES
(*Suby of* 119859 Canada Inc)
3701 Boul Saint-Laurent, Montreal, QC, H2X
2V7
(514) 844-1874
Emp Here 25
SIC 5411 Grocery stores

D-U-N-S 24-993-8390   (SL)
9016-1126 QUEBEC INC
RESTAURANT BATON ROUGE
180 Rue Sainte-Catherine O, Montreal, QC,
H2X 3Y2
(514) 282-7444
Emp Here 50   *Sales* 1,532,175
SIC 5812 Eating places

D-U-N-S 25-903-2477   (SL)
9212-4007 QUEBEC INC
BOUDOIR 1861
3670 Boul Saint-Laurent, Montreal, QC, H2X
2V4
(514) 670-6110
Emp Here 50   *Sales* 3,064,349
SIC 5621 Women's clothing stores

D-U-N-S 24-226-7636   (SL)
ALIMENTATION NORMAND HUDON INC
METRO

3575 Av Du Parc Bureau 5100, Montreal, QC,
H2X 3P9
(514) 843-3530
Emp Here 75   *Sales* 13,329,900
SIC 5411 Grocery stores
Pr Normand Hudon

D-U-N-S 20-716-9819   (SL)
**ASSOCIATION   INTERNATIONALE
DES   ETUDIANTS   EN   SCIENCES
ECONOMIQUES ET COMMERCIALES**
AIESEC
315 Rue Sainte-Catherine E Bureau 213,
Montreal, QC, H2X 3X2
(514) 987-3288
Emp Here 49   *Sales* 7,405,850
SIC 8621 Professional organizations
Pr Lloyd Tenj

D-U-N-S 20-051-6552   (SL)
AVID TECHNOLOGY CANADA CORP
3510 Boul Saint-Laurent Bureau 300, Montreal, QC, H2X 2V2
(514) 845-1636
Emp Here 60   *Sales* 16,687,200
SIC 7371 Custom computer programming services
Fin Ex Helene Ferland

D-U-N-S 25-210-6257   (SL)
BAR BUONANOTTE INC
RESTAURANT BUONA NOTTE
3518 Boul Saint-Laurent, Montreal, QC, H2X
2V1
(514) 848-0644
Emp Here 80   *Sales* 2,407,703
SIC 5812 Eating places

D-U-N-S 20-543-5555   (SL)
CAFE CHERRIER INC
3635 Rue Saint-Denis, Montreal, QC, H2X
3L6
(514) 843-4308
Emp Here 50   *Sales* 1,532,175
SIC 5812 Eating places

D-U-N-S 20-331-4893   (SL)
CAPRION BIOSCIENCES INC
CAPRION PROTEOME
201 Av Du President-Kennedy Bureau 3900,
Montreal, QC, H2X 3Y7
(514) 360-3600
Emp Here 50   *Sales* 4,815,406
SIC 2834 Pharmaceutical preparations

D-U-N-S 24-362-4355   (BR)
**CENTRE HOSPITALIER DE L'UNIVERSITE
DE MONTREAL**
HOPITAL SAINT-LUC
1058 Rue Saint-Denis, Montreal, QC, H2X 3J4
(514) 890-8000
Emp Here 1,000
SIC 8062 General medical and surgical hospitals

D-U-N-S 24-293-9841   (SL)
**COOPERATIVE   TRAVAILLEURS   TRA-
VAILLEUSES CAFE-CAMPUS**
CAFE CAMPUS
57 Rue Prince-Arthur E, Montreal, QC, H2X
1B4
(514) 844-1010
Emp Here 72   *Sales* 2,626,585
SIC 5813 Drinking places

D-U-N-S 24-353-7029   (BR)
**DESJARDINS   SECURITE   FINANCIERE,
COMPAGNIE D'ASSURANCE VIE**
150 Rue Sainte-Catherine O, Montreal, QC,
H2X 3Y2
(514) 350-8700
Emp Here 50
SIC 6311 Life insurance

D-U-N-S 25-525-1381   (SL)
**FESTIVAL DU NOUVEAU CINEMA DE MON-
TREAL**
FESTIVAL DU CINEMA DE MONTREAL

3536 Boul Saint-Laurent, Montreal, QC, H2X
2V1
(514) 282-0004
Emp Here 50   *Sales* 1,896,978
SIC 7832 Motion picture theaters, except
drive-in

D-U-N-S 24-190-3546   (BR)
**GOUVERNEMENT DE LA PROVINCE DE
QUEBEC**
*GOUVERNEMENT DE LA PROVINCE DE
QUEBEC*
3530 Rue Saint-Urbain, Montreal, QC, H2X
2N7
(514) 982-1232
Emp Here 30
SIC 8322 Individual and family services

D-U-N-S 24-346-4349   (BR)
**GOUVERNEMENT DE LA PROVINCE DE
QUEBEC**
*INSTITUT   DE   TOURISME   ET
D'HOTELLERIE DU QUEBEC, L'*
3535 Rue Saint-Denis, Montreal, QC, H2X
3P1
(514) 282-5111
Emp Here 200
SIC 8249 Vocational schools, nec

D-U-N-S 20-031-4503   (BR)
GREENWICH ASSOCIATES ULC
CONSUMER CONTACT RESEARCH
(*Suby of* Greenwich Associates LLC)
67 Rue Sainte-Catherine O Bureau 790, Montreal, QC, H2X 1Z7
(514) 282-6482
Emp Here 200
SIC 8732 Commercial nonphysical research

D-U-N-S 24-226-7289   (BR)
GROUPE ARCHAMBAULT INC
ARCHAMBAULT PLACE DES ARTS
175 Rue Sainte-Catherine O, Montreal, QC,
H2X 1Z8
(514) 281-0367
Emp Here 20
SIC 5736 Musical instrument stores

D-U-N-S 24-355-9510   (BR)
GROUPE LALIBERTE SPORTS INC
ATMOSPHERE
1610 Rue Saint-Denis, Montreal, QC, H2X
3K2
(514) 844-2228
Emp Here 25
SIC 5941 Sporting goods and bicycle shops

D-U-N-S 24-193-2750   (BR)
GROUPE RESTAURANTS IMVESCOR INC
RESTAURANT MIKES
150 Rue Sainte-Catherine O Bureau 5, Montreal, QC, H2X 3Y2
(514) 845-8128
Emp Here 42
SIC 5812 Eating places

D-U-N-S 24-353-6596   (HQ)
GROUPE ROY SANTE INC
CENTRE HEBERGEMENT ST-GEORGES
(*Suby of* Gestion Royal-Mig Inc)
3550 Rue Saint-Urbain, Montreal, QC, H2X
4C5
(514) 849-1357
Emp Here 230   *Emp Total* 5
Sales 17,948,332
SIC 8051 Skilled nursing care facilities
Stephane Roy
Guy Joly

D-U-N-S 25-525-0334   (SL)
IC AXON INC
3575 Boul Saint-Laurent Bureau 650, Montreal, QC, H2X 2T7
(514) 940-1142
Emp Here 65   *Sales* 7,587,913
SIC 8742 Management consulting services
Carole Gins

D-U-N-S 25-332-0329   (SL)

**INSTITUT NATIONAL DE L'IMAGE ET DU
SON (INIS)**
301 Boul De Maisonneuve E, Montreal, QC,
H2X 1K1
(514) 285-4647
Emp Here 57   *Sales* 2,699,546
SIC 8331 Job training and related services

D-U-N-S 25-394-2106   (BR)
**INSTITUT NATIONAL DE LA RECHERCHE
SCIENTIFIQUE**
385 Rue Sherbrooke E, Montreal, QC, H2X
1E3
(514) 499-4000
Emp Here 65
SIC 8733 Noncommercial research organizations

D-U-N-S 20-031-4776   (BR)
JONVIEW CANADA INC
300 Rue Leo-Pariseau Bureau 1102, Montreal, QC, H2X 4C2
(514) 861-9190
Emp Here 40
SIC 4725 Tour operators

D-U-N-S 24-502-6190   (BR)
KUEHNE + NAGEL LTD
KUEHNE + NAGEL
3510 Boul Saint-Laurent Bureau 400, Montreal, QC, H2X 2V2
(514) 397-9900
Emp Here 100
SIC 4731 Freight transportation arrangement

D-U-N-S 20-060-9086   (BR)
KUEHNE + NAGEL LTD
LOGISTIQUES KUEHNE + NAGEL
3510 Boul Saint-Laurent Unite 400, Montreal,
QC, H2X 2V2
(514) 395-2025
Emp Here 49
SIC 4731 Freight transportation arrangement

D-U-N-S 25-856-1026   (SL)
**LE CENTRE DE SANTE ET DE SERVICES
SOCIAUX JEANNE-MANCE**
*CENTRE D'HEBERGEMENT DU CENTRE
VILLE DE MONTREAL*
66 Boul Rene-Levesque E, Montreal, QC, H2X
1N3
(514) 878-2898
Emp Here 300   *Sales* 18,281,183
SIC 8051 Skilled nursing care facilities
Genl Mgr Elaine Mc Alister

D-U-N-S 20-715-9364   (BR)
MCGILL UNIVERSITY HEALTH CENTRE
MONTREAL CHEST INSTITUTE, MUHC
3650 Rue Saint-Urbain Bureau K 124, Montreal, QC, H2X 2P4
(514) 934-1934
Emp Here 20
SIC 8011 Offices and clinics of medical doctors

D-U-N-S 20-059-3056   (SL)
MEDIAVISION W.W.P. INC
300 Rue Leo-Pariseau, Montreal, QC, H2X
4B3
(514) 842-1010
Emp Here 40   *Sales* 6,631,680
SIC 7311 Advertising agencies
Pr Charles Choquette
Treas Claude Boulay
Dir Peter Clark

D-U-N-S 24-672-1802   (BR)
NATIONAL FILM BOARD OF CANADA
ONF NFB CINEROBOTHEQUE
1564 Rue Saint-Denis, Montreal, QC, H2X
3K2

Emp Here 20
SIC 7812 Motion picture and video production

D-U-N-S 20-885-1365   (SL)
NEURORX RESEARCH INC

RECHERCHE NEURORX
3575 Av Du Parc Bureau 5322, Montreal, QC,
H2X 3P9
(514) 908-0088
Emp Here 50   *Sales* 2,699,546
SIC 8731 Commercial physical research

D-U-N-S 25-689-8990   (BR)
OMER DESERRES INC
DESERRES
334 Rue Sainte-Catherine E, Montreal, QC,
H2X 1L7
(514) 842-3021
Emp Here 49
SIC 5945 Hobby, toy, and game shops

D-U-N-S 25-543-6396   (SL)
PROPERTIES TERRA INCOGNITA INC
TERRW INCONNUE
3530 Boul Saint-Laurent Bureau 500, Mon-
treal, QC, H2X 2V1
(514) 847-3536
Emp Here 50   *Sales* 4,742,446
SIC 6531 Real estate agents and managers

D-U-N-S 25-526-4772   (BR)
PROVIGO DISTRIBUTION INC
3421 Av Du Parc, Montreal, QC, H2X 2H6
(514) 281-0488
Emp Here 75
SIC 5411 Grocery stores

D-U-N-S 25-514-1301   (HQ)
PUBLICIS CANADA INC
PUBLICIS CONSULTANTS
3530 Boul Saint-Laurent Bureau 400, Mon-
treal, QC, H2X 2V1
(514) 285-1414
Emp Here 75   *Emp Total* 17
Sales 47,580,050
SIC 7311 Advertising agencies
Dir Andrew Bruce
Pr Duncan Bruce
Sec Claude Renaud
Dir Yves Gougoux
Dir Arthur Sadoun
Dir Ann Garreaud

D-U-N-S 20-763-3058   (SL)
RESIDENCE SAINT-CHARLES BARROMEE
66 Boul Rene-Levesque E, Montreal, QC, H2X
1N3
(514) 861-9331
Emp Here 650   *Sales* 70,577,040
SIC 8069 Specialty hospitals, except psychiatric
Dir Fin Pierre Lajoie

D-U-N-S 20-715-6824   (BR)
ROTISSERIES ST-HUBERT LTEE, LES
(*Suby of* Cara Holdings Limited)
100 Rue Sainte-Catherine E, Montreal, QC,
H2X 1K7
(514) 284-3440
Emp Here 20
SIC 5812 Eating places

D-U-N-S 25-306-2244   (HQ)
SNC-LAVALIN O&M SOLUTIONS INC
NEXACOR
87 Rue Ontario O Bureau 200, Montreal, QC,
H2X 0A7
(514) 840-8660
Emp Here 120   *Emp Total* 33,000
Sales 44,785,177
SIC 6531 Real estate agents and managers
Pr Dale Clarke
Sec Christina Costy

D-U-N-S 24-845-7558   (HQ)
TECSULT EDUPLUS INC
85 Rue Sainte-Catherine O, Montreal, QC,
H2X 3P4
(514) 287-8677
Emp Here 75   *Emp Total* 87,000
Sales 19,845,310
SIC 8741 Management services
 Yves Pigeon

Pr Pr Luc Benoit

D-U-N-S 20-584-4157   (SL)
TICKETPRO INC
375 Boul De Maisonneuve E, Montreal, QC,
H2X 1K1
(514) 790-1111
Emp Here 70   *Sales* 11,159,500
SIC 7922 Theatrical producers and services
Pr Serge Grimaux
VP VP Martin Enault

D-U-N-S 24-355-5922   (SL)
TRAFICTOURS CANADA INC
300 Rue Leo-Pariseau Bureau 600, Montreal,
QC, H2X 4C2
(514) 987-1660
Emp Here 25   *Sales* 2,407,703
SIC 6712 Bank holding companies

D-U-N-S 20-253-2743   (BR)
UNIVERSITE MCGILL
*RESEARCH FINANCIAL MANAGEMENT
SERVICES (RFMS)*
3465 Rue Durocher Bureau 310, Montreal,
QC, H2X 0A8
(514) 398-3884
Emp Here 40
SIC 8741 Management services

D-U-N-S 24-113-4993   (BR)
UNIVERSITE DU QUEBEC
MATHEMATIQUE
201 Av Du President-Kennedy Bureau
Pk5151, Montreal, QC, H2X 3Y7
(514) 987-3000
Emp Here 100
SIC 8221 Colleges and universities

D-U-N-S 20-581-9928   (BR)
UNIVERSITE DU QUEBEC
315 Rue Sainte-Catherine E Bureau 3570,
Montreal, QC, H2X 3X2
(514) 987-3000
Emp Here 250
SIC 8221 Colleges and universities

D-U-N-S 24-309-2744   (BR)
UNIVERSITE DU QUEBEC
UNIVERSITE DU QUEBEC A MONTREAL
1255 Rue Saint-Denis, Montreal, QC, H2X
3R9
(514) 987-3000
Emp Here 26
SIC 8221 Colleges and universities

D-U-N-S 25-211-4533   (BR)
UNIVERSITE DU QUEBEC
COMPTES A PAYER
1430 Rue Saint-Denis, Montreal, QC, H2X 3J8
(514) 987-6140
Emp Here 20
SIC 8721 Accounting, auditing, and book-
keeping

D-U-N-S 25-541-1282   (SL)
**VIDEOTRON SERVICE INFORMATIQUE
LTEE**
300 Av Viger E Bureau 6, Montreal, QC, H2X
3W4
(514) 281-1232
Emp Here 4,000   *Sales* 294,480,000
SIC 7374 Data processing and preparation
Pr Claude Chagnon

D-U-N-S 20-190-7552   (SL)
**WCC WARRANTY COMPANY OF CANADA
LTD**
WCC
(*Suby of* New Asurion Corporation)
300 Leo-Pariseau St, Montreal, QC, H2X 4B3
(514) 448-5496
Emp Here 65   *Sales* 9,143,680
SIC 6351 Surety insurance
Sr VP Tom Magger
Dir Opers Michael Manzo
CFO Randy Barkowitz

D-U-N-S 25-355-6211   (SL)

XLR8 MEDIA INC
PHD MONTREAL
(*Suby of* Omnicom Group Inc.)
3575 Boul Saint-Laurent Bureau 400, Mon-
treal, QC, H2X 2T7
(514) 286-9000
Emp Here 97   *Sales* 15,832,472
SIC 7311 Advertising agencies
Pr Pr Alain Desormiers
Treas Cam Reston
Dir Fred Forster

D-U-N-S 24-343-8756   (HQ)
ZOOM MEDIA INC
3510 Boul Saint-Laurent Bureau 200, Mon-
treal, QC, H2X 2V2
(514) 842-1155
Emp Here 40   *Emp Total* 7
Sales 16,196,400
SIC 7311 Advertising agencies
Pr Pr Andy Querin
 Francois De Gaspe Beaubien
Dir Fin Bruno Antonios

Montreal, QC H2Y
Hochelaga County

D-U-N-S 24-368-6313   (BR)
9071-3975 QUEBEC INC
ALIMENTS LUCYPORC
410 Rue Saint-Nicolas Bureau 5, Montreal,
QC, H2Y 2P5
(514) 286-1754
Emp Here 225
SIC 2011 Meat packing plants

D-U-N-S 20-721-8541   (SL)
9117-4383 QUEBEC INC
HOLDER RESTAURANT BAR
407 Rue Mcgill Bureau 101, Montreal, QC,
H2Y 2G3
(514) 849-0333
Emp Here 50   *Sales* 1,824,018
SIC 5813 Drinking places

D-U-N-S 20-332-9438   (SL)
9310-8405 QUEBEC INC
ZONE EN SECURITE
239 Rue Du Saint-Sacrement Bureau 304,
Montreal, QC, H2Y 1W9
(514) 793-1761
Emp Here 100   *Sales* 3,724,879
SIC 7381 Detective and armored car services

D-U-N-S 20-266-6269   (HQ)
AGENCE MIRUM CANADA INC
IMAGE TWIST
407 Rue Mcgill 2e Etage, Montreal, QC, H2Y
2G3
(514) 987-9992
Emp Here 45   *Sales* 12,127,514
SIC 7311 Advertising agencies
Dir Tom Lobene
Dir Kevin Farewell
 Brian Fraser
Dir Eric Gross

D-U-N-S 25-503-9232   (BR)
**AIMIA PROPRIETARY LOYALTY CANADA
INC**
CARLSON MARKETING
759 Rue Du Square-Victoria Bureau 105,
Montreal, QC, H2Y 2J7

Emp Here 120
SIC 8732 Commercial nonphysical research

D-U-N-S 24-231-4875   (SL)
**AQUILINI GROUP PROPERTIES LIMITED
PARTNERSHIP**
HOTEL EMBASSY SUITES
208 Rue Saint-Antoine O, Montreal, QC, H2Y
0A6
(514) 288-8886
Emp Here 49   *Sales* 5,748,207

SIC 6512 Nonresidential building operators
 Francesco Aquilini

D-U-N-S 25-673-9616   (SL)
ASSURANCE MARTIN & CYR INC
460 Rue Mcgill, Montreal, QC, H2Y 2H2
(514) 527-9546
Emp Here 706   *Sales* 175,438,080
SIC 6712 Bank holding companies
Pr Pr Serge Robillard
Sec Michel Poitras
VP Michel Collins

D-U-N-S 20-418-6985   (HQ)
ATLIFIC INC
ATLIFIC HOTELS
(*Suby of* 3376290 Canada Inc)
250 Rue Saint-Antoine O Bureau 400, Mon-
treal, QC, H2Y 0A3
(514) 509-5500
Emp Here 25   *Emp Total* 110
Sales 18,186,950
SIC 8741 Management services
Pr Richard Ade
Sec Bonnie Ng
Genl Mgr Christine Kennedey
Dir Robert Chartrand
Dir Raymond St-Pierre

D-U-N-S 25-095-6638   (HQ)
**AXXESS INTERNATIONAL COURTIERS EN
DOUANES INC**
(*Suby of* 6668437 Canada Inc)
360 Rue Saint-Jacques 12eme Etage, Mon-
treal, QC, H2Y 1P5
(514) 849-9377
Emp Here 65   *Emp Total* 116
Sales 37,033,530
SIC 4731 Freight transportation arrangement
Pr Pr Richard Gervais
 Anthony J. (Tony) Yakubosky

D-U-N-S 24-679-0146   (BR)
BMO LIFE ASSURANCE COMPANY
BMO
119 Rue Saint-Jacques, Montreal, QC, H2Y
1L6
(514) 877-7373
Emp Here 26
SIC 6011 Federal reserve banks

D-U-N-S 20-536-6045   (BR)
BANK OF MONTREAL
BMO
105 Rue Saint-Jacques Bureau 2, Montreal,
QC, H2Y 1L6
(514) 877-7816
Emp Here 20
SIC 6021 National commercial banks

D-U-N-S 20-715-6899   (BR)
BANQUE NATIONALE DU CANADA
500 Place D'Armes Bureau 500, Montreal,
QC, H2Y 2W3
(514) 394-6642
Emp Here 80
SIC 6021 National commercial banks

D-U-N-S 20-573-7997   (BR)
BANQUE NATIONALE DU CANADA
500 Place D'Armes Bureau 500, Montreal,
QC, H2Y 2W3
(514) 271-4166
Emp Here 30
SIC 6021 National commercial banks

D-U-N-S 20-164-5434   (BR)
BANQUE TORONTO-DOMINION, LA
TORONTO-DOMINION BANK, THE
(*Suby of* Toronto-Dominion Bank, The)
500 Rue Saint-Jacques Bureau 151, Montreal,
QC, H2Y 1S1
(514) 289-0799
Emp Here 25
SIC 6021 National commercial banks

D-U-N-S 20-858-2130   (BR)
CANADIAN PRESS, THE

215 Rue Saint-Jacques Unite 100, Montreal, QC, H2Y 1M6
(514) 849-3212
Emp Here 75
SIC 7383 News syndicates

D-U-N-S 20-324-3832   (BR)
CITADELLE COOPERATIVE DE PRODUC-TEURS DE SIROP D'ERABLE
CANADIAN MAPLE DELIGHTS
(*Suby of* Citadelle Cooperative de Produc-teurs de Sirop d'Erable)
84 Rue Saint-Paul E, Montreal, QC, H2Y 1G6
(514) 765-3456
Emp Here 20
SIC 2099 Food preparations, nec

D-U-N-S 24-800-4426   (SL)
COALISION INC
LOLE
700 Rue Saint-Antoine E Bureau 110, Mon-treal, QC, H2Y 1A6
(514) 798-3534
Emp Here 100   *Sales* 6,201,660
SIC 2339 Women's and misses' outerwear, nec
Todd Steele
Genl Mgr Bernard Mariette
Ch Bd Francois Plamondon
Sec Olaf Guerrand Hermes
Dir Eric D'anjou
Dir Pierre Servan-Schreiber
Dir Jimmy Argyropolous
Dir Stephen H. Simon
Dir Anthony Sigel

D-U-N-S 20-103-3664   (BR)
COMMUNICATION DEMO INC
407 Rue Mcgill Bureau 311, Montreal, QC, H2Y 2G3
(514) 985-2523
Emp Here 75
SIC 7389 Business services, nec

D-U-N-S 24-388-5410   (SL)
COMPAGNIE AMPLEXOR CANADA INC
152 Rue Notre-Dame E Bureau 400, Montreal, QC, H2Y 3P6
(514) 871-1409
Emp Here 25   *Sales* 2,002,150
SIC 7389 Business services, nec

D-U-N-S 20-907-8646   (SL)
CORPORATION IMAGE ENTERTAINMENT INC
417 Saint-Pierre St Suite 600, Montreal, QC, H2Y 2M4
(514) 844-1244
Emp Here 50   *Sales* 4,596,524
SIC 7812 Motion picture and video production

D-U-N-S 24-896-1419   (SL)
CORPORATION DES HOTELS INTER-CONTINENTAL (MONTREAL), LA
HOTEL INTER-CONTINENTAL (MONTREAL)
360 Rue Saint-Antoine O, Montreal, QC, H2Y 3X4
(514) 987-9900
Emp Here 300   *Sales* 13,132,926
SIC 7011 Hotels and motels
Pr Lewis N. Fader
Sec Hammer Randall S.
Dir Frank Guarascio

D-U-N-S 25-370-2070   (BR)
EXPEDIA CANADA CORP
63 Rue De Bresoles Bureau 100, Montreal, QC, H2Y 1V7
(514) 286-8180
Emp Here 80
SIC 3823 Process control instruments

D-U-N-S 24-993-9141   (SL)
FTM DISTRIBUTION INC
152 Rue Notre-Dame E Bureau 500, Montreal, QC, H2Y 3P6
(514) 954-1223
Emp Here 50   *Sales* 17,081,600

SIC 4731 Freight transportation arrangement
Pr Pr Joe Alberga
Ch Bd Pierre Tremblay

D-U-N-S 24-858-2926   (SL)
FONDATION PAUL GERIN-LAJOIE POUR LA COOPERATION INTERNATIONALE, LA
465 Rue Saint-Jean Bureau 900, Montreal, QC, H2Y 2R6
(514) 288-3888
Emp Here 20   *Sales* 6,087,000
SIC 8399 Social services, nec
Dir Paul Gerin-Lajoie
Dir Patrick Beaduin
Dir Bernard Gerin-Lajoie
Dir Sylvain Pion
Dir Yves Masson
Dir Paul Belanger
Dir Charles-Albert Poissant
Mamadou Ndoye
Michel Agnaieff
Jean-Paul Servant

D-U-N-S 25-739-4247   (SL)
GTI CANADA INC
465 Rue Mcgill Bureau 1000, Montreal, QC, H2Y 2H1
(514) 937-6122
Emp Here 50   *Sales* 3,648,035
SIC 7379 Computer related services, nec

D-U-N-S 20-760-5361   (HQ)
GESCA LTEE
(*Suby of* Gesca Ltee)
750 Boul Saint-Laurent, Montreal, QC, H2Y 2Z4
(514) 285-7000
Emp Here 20   *Emp Total* 1,000
Sales 82,883,355
SIC 2711 Newspapers
Pr Pierre-Elliott Levasseur
VP VP Guy Crevier
Patrick Buchholz
Dir Andre Desmarais
Dir Desmarais Paul Jr.
Dir Michel Plessis-Belair
Dir Jacques Parisien

D-U-N-S 24-073-2631   (SL)
GESTION 357 DE LA COMMUNE INC
357C, LE
357 Rue De La Commune O, Montreal, QC, H2Y 2E2
(514) 499-0357
Emp Here 50   *Sales* 2,626,585
SIC 7389 Business services, nec

D-U-N-S 24-345-6212   (BR)
GEXEL TELECOM INTERNATIONAL INC
507 Place D'Armes Bureau 1503, Montreal, QC, H2Y 2W8
(514) 935-9300
Emp Here 200
SIC 8732 Commercial nonphysical research

D-U-N-S 25-026-8810   (BR)
GOUVERNEMENT DE LA PROVINCE DE QUEBEC
COMMISSION QUEBECOISE DES LIBERA-TIONS CONDITIONNELLES
1 Rue Notre-Dame E Bureau 1140, Montreal, QC, H2Y 1B6
(514) 873-2230
Emp Here 30
SIC 8322 Individual and family services

D-U-N-S 24-345-5149   (BR)
GOUVERNEMENT DE LA PROVINCE DE QUEBEC
REGIE DU CINEMA QUEBEC
390 Rue Notre-Dame O Bureau 100, Mon-treal, QC, H2Y 1T9
(514) 873-2371
Emp Here 50
SIC 6794 Patent owners and lessors

D-U-N-S 20-798-9752   (BR)
GOUVERNEMENT DE LA PROVINCE DE

QUEBEC
GOUVERNEMENT DE LA PROVINCE DE QUEBEC
276 Rue Saint-Jacques, Montreal, QC, H2Y 1N3
(514) 725-5221
Emp Here 85
SIC 8331 Job training and related services

D-U-N-S 20-124-3545   (BR)
GOUVERNEMENT DE LA PROVINCE DE QUEBEC
DIRECTEUR DE POURSUITES CRIM-INELLES ET PENALES
1 Rue Notre-Dame E Bureau 4.100, Montreal, QC, H2Y 1B6
(514) 393-2703
Emp Here 150
SIC 8111 Legal services

D-U-N-S 20-518-8019   (BR)
GOUVERNEMENT DE LA PROVINCE DE QUEBEC
DIRECTION DES REGISTRES ET DE LA CERTIFICATION DU MINISTERE DE LA JUSTICE
1 Rue Notre-Dame E Bureau 735, Montreal, QC, H2Y 1B6
(514) 864-4949
Emp Here 100
SIC 8111 Legal services

D-U-N-S 24-501-3438   (BR)
GROUPE SPORTSCENE INC
CAGE AUX SPORTS, LA
114 Rue Saint-Paul E, Montreal, QC, H2Y 1G6
(514) 288-1115
Emp Here 20
SIC 5812 Eating places

D-U-N-S 20-965-9304   (SL)
HOTEL PLACE D'ARMES (MONTREAL) INC
HOTEL PLACE D'ARMES
55 Rue Saint-Jacques Unite 300, Montreal, QC, H2Y 1K9
(514) 842-1887
Emp Here 50   *Sales* 2,188,821
SIC 7011 Hotels and motels

D-U-N-S 20-295-3126   (SL)
HOTEL ST-PAUL DE MONTREAL INC
(*Suby of* 150000 Canada Inc)
355 Rue Mcgill, Montreal, QC, H2Y 2E8
(514) 380-2220
Emp Here 50   *Sales* 2,188,821
SIC 7011 Hotels and motels

D-U-N-S 24-163-5411   (SL)
ICL INTERNATIONAL INC
209 Rue Saint-Paul O, Montreal, QC, H2Y 2A1

Emp Here 50   *Sales* 10,208,640
SIC 4581 Airports, flying fields, and services
Pr Jean Laferriere

D-U-N-S 20-293-9257   (BR)
ILSC (VANCOUVER) INC
ILSC MONTREAL
410 Rue Saint-Nicolas Bureau 300, Montreal, QC, H2Y 2P5
(514) 876-4572
Emp Here 25
SIC 8299 Schools and educational services, nec

D-U-N-S 24-742-8782   (BR)
INVESTISSEMENT QUEBEC
413 Rue Saint-Jacques Bureau 500, Montreal, QC, H2Y 1N9
(514) 873-4375
Emp Here 100
SIC 8748 Business consulting, nec

D-U-N-S 25-894-8264   (BR)
IVANHOE CAMBRIDGE INC
IVANHOE CAMBRIDGE INC
747 Rue Du Square-Victoria Bureau 247, Montreal, QC, H2Y 3Y9

(514) 982-9888
Emp Here 20
SIC 6531 Real estate agents and managers

D-U-N-S 20-221-4318   (SL)
JARDINS NELSON INC
407 Place Jacques-Cartier, Montreal, QC, H2Y 3B1
(514) 861-5731
Emp Here 100   *Sales* 2,991,389
SIC 5812 Eating places

D-U-N-S 20-107-9642   (SL)
LEGAULT JOLY THIFFAULT S.E.N.C.R.L.
380 Rue Saint-Antoine O Bureau 7100, Mon-treal, QC, H2Y 3X7
(514) 842-8891
Emp Here 55   *Sales* 4,742,446
SIC 8111 Legal services

D-U-N-S 24-920-9404   (HQ)
LEGER MARKETING INC
LEGER ANALYTICS
(*Suby of* Leger Marketing Inc)
507 Place D'Armes Bureau 700, Montreal, QC, H2Y 2W8
(514) 845-5660
Emp Here 425   *Emp Total* 800
Sales 152,540,640
SIC 8732 Commercial nonphysical research
Pr Pr Jean-Marc Leger
Dir Anne-Marie Marois

D-U-N-S 20-329-4546   (BR)
LEXISNEXIS CANADA INC
215 Rue Saint-Jacques Bureau 1111, Mon-treal, QC, H2Y 1M6
(514) 287-0339
Emp Here 20
SIC 2731 Book publishing

D-U-N-S 20-192-6594   (HQ)
LOUISIANA-PACIFIC CANADA LTD
(*Suby of* Louisiana-Pacific Corporation)
507 Place D'Armes Bureau 400, Montreal, QC, H2Y 2W8
(514) 861-4724
Emp Here 22   *Emp Total* 4,800
Sales 29,106,034
SIC 2431 Millwork
Curtis M Stevens
Mark A Fuchs
Dir Peter H Finley
Dir John S Mckercher

D-U-N-S 24-361-6146   (SL)
LUDIA INC
410 Rue Saint-Nicolas Bureau 400, Montreal, QC, H2Y 2P5
(514) 313-3370
Emp Here 70   *Sales* 13,192,606
SIC 5092 Toys and hobby goods and supplies
Jean-Francois Marcoux
Pr Pr Alexandre Thabet
Dir Robert Bradley Martin

D-U-N-S 25-311-0464   (BR)
MCDONALD'S RESTAURANTS OF CANADA LIMITED
MCDONALD'S
(*Suby of* McDonald's Corporation)
1 Rue Notre-Dame E, Montreal, QC, H2Y 1B6
(514) 285-8720
Emp Here 75
SIC 5812 Eating places

D-U-N-S 24-392-8095   (BR)
MONSTER WORLDWIDE CANADA INC
276 Rue Saint-Jacques, Montreal, QC, H2Y 1N3
(514) 288-9004
Emp Here 20
SIC 7311 Advertising agencies

D-U-N-S 20-227-7554   (HQ)
MONTSHIP INC
(*Suby of* Trealmont Transport Inc)
360 Rue Saint-Jacques Bureau 1000, Mon-treal, QC, H2Y 1R2

(514) 286-4646
Emp Here 44   *Emp Total* 188
Sales 42,827,931
SIC 4731 Freight transportation arrangement
Pr Pr D. Brian Mcdonald
  Domenic Bravi
  Brent M. Coulthard
  Robert Rabnett
  Scott Pichette
Sec Gracinda Pires

D-U-N-S 20-303-1133   (SL)
NVENTIVE INC
AGENCE MEDIA EQUATION HUMAINE
215 Rue Saint-Jacques Bureau 500, Montreal,
QC, H2Y 1M6
(514) 312-4969
Emp Here 80   *Sales* 11,174,638
SIC 7371 Custom computer programming services
  Francois Tanguay

D-U-N-S 24-084-9117   (SL)
OGILVY MONTREAL INC
COMMUNICATION ID EST
215 Rue Saint-Jacques Bureau 333, Montreal,
QC, H2Y 1M6
(514) 861-1811
Emp Here 50   *Sales* 5,982,777
SIC 7311 Advertising agencies
Pr Pr Daniel Demers
Sec Martin Gosselin
Dir Steven Goldstein
Dir Tro Piliguian
Dir Andy Watson
Dir Denis Piquette
Dir John Seifert
Dir David Aubert

D-U-N-S 20-962-0095   (SL)
ORDRE DES PHARMACIENS DU QUEBEC
266 Rue Notre-Dame O Bureau 301, Montreal, QC, H2Y 1T6
(514) 284-9588
Emp Here 38   *Sales* 5,782,650
SIC 8621 Professional organizations
  Manon Lambert
Pr Claude Gagnon

D-U-N-S 20-914-6054   (BR)
POMERLEAU INC
500 Rue Saint-Jacques, Montreal, QC, H2Y
0A2
(514) 789-2728
Emp Here 40
SIC 1522 Residential construction, nec

D-U-N-S 24-773-1693   (SL)
PRAIRIE INTERNATIONAL CONTAINER INC
(*Suby of* Trealmont Transport Inc)
360 Rue Saint-Jacques Bureau 1000, Montreal, QC, H2Y 1R2
(514) 286-4646
Emp Here 20   *Sales* 1,605,135
SIC 4212 Local trucking, without storage

D-U-N-S 20-215-2138   (HQ)
PRESSE, LTEE, LA
AUTO LOISIRS
(*Suby of* Gesca Ltee)
750 Boul Saint-Laurent, Montreal, QC, H2Y
2Z4
(514) 285-7000
Emp Here 900   *Emp Total* 1,000
Sales 74,638,796
SIC 2711 Newspapers
Pr Pr Pierre-Elliott Levasseur
VP VP Guy Crevier
  Patrick Buchholz
Dir Andre Desmarais
Dir Paul Desmarais Jr.
Dir Michel Plessis-Belair
Dir Jacques Parisien

D-U-N-S 20-793-7061   (SL)
PRETRES DE SAINT-SULPICE DE MONTREAL, LES

SEMINAIRE DE SAINT-SULPICE
116 Rue Notre-Dame O, Montreal, QC, H2Y
1T2
(514) 849-6561
Emp Here 50   *Sales* 3,283,232
SIC 8661 Religious organizations

D-U-N-S 24-761-2745   (SL)
PRODUCTIONS LA PRESSE TELE LTEE, LES
ETOILES.TV
750 Boul Saint-Laurent, Montreal, QC, H2Y
2Z4
(514) 285-7000
Emp Here 35   *Sales* 5,526,400
SIC 7922 Theatrical producers and services
Pr Marleen Beaulieu
Pr Pr Andre Provencher
VP VP Robert Bourque
  Guy Crevier

D-U-N-S 20-791-8780   (SL)
PROMANAC SERVICES IMMOBILIERS (1992) LTEE
500 Place D'Armes Bureau 2300, Montreal,
QC, H2Y 2W2
(514) 282-7654
Emp Here 200   *Sales* 25,120,000
SIC 6512 Nonresidential building operators
Pr Pr Jean-Jacques Laurans
VP VP Jean-Luc Binette

D-U-N-S 20-727-5814   (BR)
RE/MAX SIGNATURE INC
510 Rue Mcgill, Montreal, QC, H2Y 2H6
(514) 788-4444
Emp Here 20
SIC 6531 Real estate agents and managers

D-U-N-S 24-214-7796   (HQ)
RESIDENCES ALLEGRO, S.E.C., LES
(*Suby of* Residences Allegro, S.E.C., Les)
485 Rue Mcgill Bureau 300, Montreal, QC,
H2Y 2H4
(514) 878-1374
Emp Here 100   *Emp Total* 125
Sales 4,596,524
SIC 8361 Residential care

D-U-N-S 24-787-8267   (SL)
RESSOURCES PROFESSIONELLES INFORMATIQUES R P I INC
485 Rue Mcgill Bureau 920, Montreal, QC,
H2Y 2H4
(514) 341-7760
Emp Here 50   *Sales* 3,648,035
SIC 7379 Computer related services, nec

D-U-N-S 20-924-8371   (SL)
RESTAURANT AIX INC
BAR SUITE 701
711 Cote De La Place-D'Armes, Montreal,
QC, H2Y 2X6
(514) 904-1201
Emp Here 100   *Sales* 2,991,389
SIC 5812 Eating places

D-U-N-S 24-515-2582   (SL)
RESTAURANT DU VIEUX PORT INC
39 Rue Saint-Paul E, Montreal, QC, H2Y 1G2
(514) 866-3175
Emp Here 80   *Sales* 2,858,628
SIC 5812 Eating places

D-U-N-S 24-474-5634   (SL)
RESTO CARTOON INC
420 Place Jacques-Cartier, Montreal, QC,
H2Y 3B3

Emp Here 50   *Sales* 1,532,175
SIC 5812 Eating places

D-U-N-S 25-324-1202   (BR)
SAP CANADA INC
380 Rue Saint-Antoine O Bureau 2000, Montreal, QC, H2Y 3X7
(514) 350-7300
Emp Here 90

SIC 7372 Prepackaged software

D-U-N-S 20-296-9650   (SL)
SAULNIER ROBILLARD LORTIE, S.E.N.C.
SRL HUISSIERS DE JUSTICE
407 Boul Saint-Laurent Bureau 700, Montreal,
QC, H2Y 2Y5
(514) 878-4721
Emp Here 50   *Sales* 2,626,585
SIC 7381 Detective and armored car services

D-U-N-S 20-211-9264   (SL)
SERVICES CONSEILS ARBITREX INC, LES
ARBITRIX
500 Place D'Armes Bureau 2500, Montreal,
QC, H2Y 2W2
(514) 845-3533
Emp Here 30
SIC 8111 Legal services

D-U-N-S 25-108-1022   (HQ)
SERVICES FINANCIERS PENSON CANADA INC
360 Rue Saint-Jacques Bureau 1201, Montreal, QC, H2Y 1P5

Emp Here 140   *Emp Total* 180
Sales 51,195,434
SIC 6289 Security and commodity service
Pr Pr Richard Ness
  Liam Cheung
  Francois Gervais

D-U-N-S 20-702-9286   (BR)
SOCIETE QUEBECOISE DES INFRASTRUCTURES
445 Rue Saint-Gabriel, Montreal, QC, H2Y
3A2
(514) 873-5485
Emp Here 50
SIC 6512 Nonresidential building operators

D-U-N-S 25-588-3894   (BR)
SOCIETE QUEBECOISE DES INFRASTRUCTURES
DIRECTION IMMOBILIERE VILLE DE MONTREAL
1 Rue Notre-Dame E Bureau 1165, Montreal,
QC, H2Y 1B6
(514) 873-6316
Emp Here 36
SIC 6512 Nonresidential building operators

D-U-N-S 24-801-0548   (SL)
SOCIETE DU DROITS DE REPRODUCTIONS DES AUTEURS, COMPOSITEURS ET EDITEURS AU CANADA INC
759 Rue Du Square-Victoria Bureau 420,
Montreal, QC, H2Y 2J7
(514) 845-3268
Emp Here 30   *Sales* 9,676,520
SIC 6289 Security and commodity service
Pr Paul Baillargeon
VP Diane Juster

D-U-N-S 20-890-3729   (BR)
SOCIETE DU MUSEE D'ARCHEOLOGIE ET D'HISTOIRE DE MONTREAL POINTE-A-CALLIERE
SOCIETE DU MUSEE D'ARCHEOLOGIE ET D'HISTOIRE DE MO
173 Place D'Youville, Montreal, QC, H2Y 2B2
(514) 872-9150
Emp Here 20
SIC 8412 Museums and art galleries

D-U-N-S 25-259-9170   (BR)
SOCIETE DU VIEUX-PORT DE MONTREAL INC
IMAX TELUS CENTRE DES SCIENCES DE MONTREAL
2 Rue De La Commune O, Montreal, QC, H2Y
4B2
(514) 496-4629
Emp Here 30
SIC 7832 Motion picture theaters, except drive-in

D-U-N-S 20-121-0130   (BR)
TD WATERHOUSE CANADA INC
TD WATERHOUSE
(*Suby of* Toronto-Dominion Bank, The)
500 Rue Saint-Jacques Unite 6, Montreal, QC,
H2Y 0A2
(514) 289-8439
Emp Here 60
SIC 6211 Security brokers and dealers

D-U-N-S 24-173-6776   (SL)
TOURS CHANTECLERC INC
152 Rue Notre-Dame E, Montreal, QC, H2Y
3P6
(514) 398-9535
Emp Here 50   *Sales* 16,378,240
SIC 4725 Tour operators
Pr Pr Bernard Beauchamp
  Claude St-Pierre

D-U-N-S 24-763-6590   (SL)
TRADUCTIONS SERGE BELAIR INC
276 Rue Saint-Jacques Bureau 900, Montreal,
QC, H2Y 1N3
(514) 844-4682
Emp Here 65   *Sales* 3,283,232
SIC 7389 Business services, nec

D-U-N-S 20-933-4676   (BR)
YVES ROCHER AMERIQUE DU NORD INC
465 Rue Mcgill, Montreal, QC, H2Y 2H1
(514) 523-4144
Emp Here 60
SIC 5999 Miscellaneous retail stores, nec

Montreal, QC H2Z
Hochelaga County

D-U-N-S 24-085-8589   (SL)
115768 CANADA INC
RESTAURANT LE LATINI
1130 Rue Jeanne-Mance, Montreal, QC, H2Z
1L7
(514) 861-3166
Emp Here 40   *Sales* 1,532,175
SIC 5812 Eating places

D-U-N-S 24-630-4930   (HQ)
9130-1093 QUEBEC INC
CARREFOUR SAINT-GEORGES
1001 Rue Du Square-Victoria Bureau 500,
Montreal, QC, H2Z 2B5
(514) 841-7600
Emp Here 26   *Emp Total* 95
Sales 27,360,263
SIC 6512 Nonresidential building operators
Pr Pr Michel Dallaire
  Manon Deslauriers

D-U-N-S 25-093-3228   (HQ)
9130-1168 QUEBEC INC
CENTRE COMMERCIAL RIVIERE-DU-LOUP
1001 Rue Du Square-Victoria Bureau 500,
Montreal, QC, H2Z 2B5
(514) 841-7600
Emp Here 20   *Emp Total* 95
Sales 2,626,585
SIC 6512 Nonresidential building operators

D-U-N-S 24-376-8145   (HQ)
9132-4285 QUEBEC INC
QA COURIER
(*Suby of* 9132-4285 Quebec Inc)
1100 Cote Du Beaver Hall, Montreal, QC, H2Z
1S8
(514) 875-1515
Emp Here 42   *Emp Total* 70
Sales 3,575,074
SIC 7389 Business services, nec

D-U-N-S 20-715-3185   (BR)
ALSTOM CANADA INC
ALSTOM TELECITE MONTREAL
(*Suby of* General Electric Company)
1050 Cote Du Beaver Hall, Montreal, QC, H2Z

0A5
(514) 333-0888
Emp Here 100
SIC 7311 Advertising agencies

D-U-N-S 20-292-1441   (BR)
AUSENCO ENGINEERING CANADA INC
555 Boul Rene-Levesque O Bureau 200, Montreal, QC, H2Z 1B1
(514) 866-1221
Emp Here 40
SIC 8711 Engineering services

D-U-N-S 24-988-1020   (SL)
CAPITAL TRAITEUR MONTREAL INC
201 Av Viger O, Montreal, QC, H2Z 1X7
(514) 871-3111
Emp Here 98   *Sales* 2,991,389
SIC 5812 Eating places

D-U-N-S 24-241-3255   (SL)
CAPITAL TRAITEUR MONTREAL INC
CAPITAL TRAITEUR
159 Rue Saint-Antoine O Bureau 400, Montreal, QC, H2Z 2A7
(514) 875-1897
Emp Here 150   *Sales* 4,523,563
SIC 5812 Eating places

D-U-N-S 20-582-6030   (BR)
COMMONWEALTH HOSPITALITY LTD
HOLIDAY   INN   SELECT   MONTREAL CENTRE-ViLLE
(*Suby of* WXI/WWH Parallel Amalco (Ontario) Ltd)
99 Av Viger O, Montreal, QC, H2Z 1E9
(514) 878-9888
Emp Here 30
SIC 7011 Hotels and motels

D-U-N-S 20-806-9737   (BR)
COUCHE-TARD INC
159 Rue Saint-Antoine O Bureau 161, Montreal, QC, H2Z 2A7
(514) 866-0675
Emp Here 25
SIC 5411 Grocery stores

D-U-N-S 25-107-7301   (SL)
FIME INC
1080 Cote Du Beaver Hall Bureau 1400, Montreal, QC, H2Z 1S8
(514) 935-1331
Emp Here 25   *Sales* 1,824,018
SIC 7379 Computer related services, nec

D-U-N-S 25-672-1812   (BR)
FEDERATION DES CAISSES DESJARDINS DU QUEBEC
SERVICES DE CARTES DESJARDINS
425 Av Viger O Bureau 900, Montreal, QC, H2Z 1W5
(514) 397-4789
Emp Here 300
SIC 6062 State credit unions

D-U-N-S 20-176-6172   (BR)
GOUVERNEMENT DE LA PROVINCE DE QUEBEC
GOUVERNEMENT DE LA PROVINCE DE QUEBEC
159 Rue Saint-Antoine O Bureau 900, Montreal, QC, H2Z 1H2
(514) 871-8122
Emp Here 125
SIC 7389 Business services, nec

D-U-N-S 25-362-0371   (BR)
GOUVERNEMENT DE LA PROVINCE DE QUEBEC
GOUVERNEMENT DE LA PROVINCE DE QUEBEC
159 Rue Saint-Antoine O Bureau 900, Montreal, QC, H2Z 1H2
(514) 871-8122
Emp Here 222
SIC 7389 Business services, nec

D-U-N-S 20-137-2757   (BR)
GOUVERNEMENT DE LA PROVINCE DE QUEBEC
PROTECTEUR DU CITOYEN
1080 Cote Du Beaver Hall Bureau 1000, Montreal, QC, H2Z 1S8
(514) 873-2032
Emp Here 132
SIC 8322 Individual and family services

D-U-N-S 24-167-6154   (HQ)
HYDRO-QUEBEC INTERNATIONAL INC
75 Boul Rene-Levesque O Bureau 101, Montreal, QC, H2Z 1A4
(514) 289-2211
Emp Here 100   *Emp Total* 40,000
Sales 24,587,756
SIC 6719 Holding companies, nec
Ch Bd Eric Martel
Steve Demers
Sec Pierre-Luc Desgagne
Treas Jean-Hugues Lafleur
Dir Lise Croteau
Dir Real Laporte
Dir Elie Saheb

D-U-N-S 24-346-8860   (BR)
KBS+P CANADA INC
555 Boul Rene-Levesque O Bureau 1700, Montreal, QC, H2Z 1B1
(514) 875-7430
Emp Here 59
SIC 7311 Advertising agencies

D-U-N-S 24-323-1073   (HQ)
L.P.S. LANGUES PRODUCTIONS SERVICES LTEE
(*Suby of* L.P.S. Langues Productions Services Ltee)
505 Boul Rene-Levesque O Bureau 1101, Montreal, QC, H2Z 1Y7
(514) 878-2821
Emp Here 20   *Emp Total* 70
Sales 3,793,956
SIC 8299 Schools and educational services, nec

D-U-N-S 20-764-0905   (SL)
MET-CHEM CANADA INC
MET-CHAM
555 Boul Rene-Levesque O Bureau 300, Montreal, QC, H2Z 1B1
(514) 288-5211
Emp Here 50   *Sales* 5,890,507
SIC 8711 Engineering services
Pr Pr Subbiah Srinivasan

D-U-N-S 20-329-9466   (HQ)
SNC-LAVALIN GEM QUEBEC INC
GROUPE QUALITAS
455 Boul Rene-Levesque O, Montreal, QC, H2Z 1Z3
(514) 393-8000
Emp Here 100   *Emp Total* 33,000
Sales 83,333,346
SIC 8742 Management consulting services
Pr Robert Landry
Sec Arden R. Furlotte
Dir Sebastien Guerard
Genl Mgr Louise Pelletier

D-U-N-S 24-935-0083   (HQ)
SNC-LAVALIN INTERNATIONAL INC
455 Boul Rene-Levesque O 21e Etage, Montreal, QC, H2Z 1Z3
(514) 393-1000
Emp Here 39   *Emp Total* 33,000
Sales 3,648,035
SIC 8711 Engineering services

D-U-N-S 20-713-6545   (SL)
SOCIETE EN COMMANDITE 901 SQUARE VICTORIA
HOTEL W MONTREAL
901 Rue Du Square-Victoria Bureau 1471, Montreal, QC, H2Z 1R1
(514) 395-3100
Emp Here 80   *Sales* 3,502,114

SIC 7011 Hotels and motels

D-U-N-S 24-327-0217   (BR)
TORONTO-DOMINION BANK, THE
TD VISA
(*Suby of* Toronto-Dominion Bank, The)
525 Av Viger O Bureau 100, Montreal, QC, H2Z 0B2
(514) 289-0799
Emp Here 120
SIC 6021 National commercial banks

D-U-N-S 24-600-3917   (BR)
VERREAULT INC
1080 Cote Du Beaver Hall Bureau 800, Montreal, QC, H2Z 1S8
(514) 845-4104
Emp Here 76
SIC 1541 Industrial buildings and warehouses

D-U-N-S 25-446-8796   (BR)
YMCA DU QUEBEC, LES
YMCA GUY FAVREAU
200 Boul Rene-Levesque O, Montreal, QC, H2Z 1X4
(514) 845-4277
Emp Here 27
SIC 7999 Amusement and recreation, nec

Montreal, QC H3A
Hochelaga County

D-U-N-S 20-105-5923   (SL)
3025235 NOVA SCOTIA ULC
HOTEL OMNI MONT-ROYAL
1050 Rue Sherbrooke O, Montreal, QC, H3A 2R6
(514) 985-6225
Emp Here 200   *Sales* 8,755,284
SIC 7011 Hotels and motels
Pr Pr James Caldwell
Genl Mgr Joy Pappas
Fin Ex Joanne Blanchard
Genl Mgr Dominique Lapointe

D-U-N-S 25-382-7745   (SL)
3056309 CANADA INC
BEST WESTERN VILLE-MARIE HOTELS & SUITES
3407 Rue Peel, Montreal, QC, H3A 1W7
(514) 288-4141
Emp Here 50   *Sales* 2,188,821
SIC 7011 Hotels and motels

D-U-N-S 20-014-4322   (BR)
3794873 CANADA LTD
SHERATON
475 Rue Sherbrooke O, Montreal, QC, H3A 2L9

Emp Here 100
SIC 7011 Hotels and motels

D-U-N-S 20-550-9438   (HQ)
4207602 CANADA INC
CAMEO KNITTING
2024 Rue Peel Bureau 400, Montreal, QC, H3A 1W5
(514) 281-2525
Emp Here 20   *Emp Total* 75
Sales 11,954,264
SIC 5136 Men's and boy's clothing
William Cleman

D-U-N-S 25-332-2648   (SL)
9027-7757 QUEBEC INC
COURTYARD MARRIOTT MONTREAL
410 Rue Sherbrooke O, Montreal, QC, H3A 1B3
(514) 844-8844
Emp Here 60   *Sales* 2,626,585
SIC 7011 Hotels and motels

D-U-N-S 25-981-6809   (SL)
9041-1273 QUEBEC INC
MARRIOTT RESIDENCE INN - MONTREAL

(*Suby of* Marriott International, Inc.)
2045 Rue Peel, Montreal, QC, H3A 1T6
(514) 982-6064
Emp Here 20   *Sales* 875,528
SIC 7011 Hotels and motels

D-U-N-S 20-363-7103   (SL)
9235078 CANADA INC
ACTION MEDIA
2000 Rue Peel Bureau 400, Montreal, QC, H3A 2W5
(514) 316-9277
Emp Here 26   *Sales* 3,137,310
SIC 7311 Advertising agencies

D-U-N-S 20-355-9034   (SL)
9235078 CANADA INC
ACTION MEDIA
2000 Rue Peel Bureau 400, Montreal, QC, H3A 2W5
(514) 384-1570
Emp Here 26   *Sales* 3,137,310
SIC 7311 Advertising agencies

D-U-N-S 20-856-6349   (BR)
AIG INSURANCE COMPANY OF CANADA
CHARTIS
(*Suby of* American International Group, Inc.)
2000 Av Mcgill College Bureau 1200, Montreal, QC, H3A 3H3
(514) 842-0603
Emp Here 100
SIC 6411 Insurance agents, brokers, and service

D-U-N-S 24-685-1294   (SL)
AXA ASSISTANCE CANADA INC
2001 Boul Robert-Bourassa Bureau 1850, Montreal, QC, H3A 2L8
(514) 285-9053
Emp Here 50   *Sales* 5,842,440
SIC 6411 Insurance agents, brokers, and service
Pr Bernard Ferrand
VP VP Fabien Navet
Sec Mathieu Labouree
Dir Serge Morelli
Dir Franz Regimbeau

D-U-N-S 25-671-5582   (BR)
ALCATEL-LUCENT CANADA INC
ALCATEL NETWORKS
600 Boul De Maisonneuve O Bureau 75, Montreal, QC, H3A 3J2
(514) 484-1616
Emp Here 40
SIC 4899 Communication services, nec

D-U-N-S 24-762-4943   (HQ)
ANDRE FILION & ASSOCIES INC
(*Suby of* Andre Filion & Associes Inc)
1801 Av Mcgill College Bureau 910, Montreal, QC, H3A 2N4
(514) 844-9160
Emp Here 36   *Emp Total* 50
Sales 2,261,782
SIC 8999 Services, nec

D-U-N-S 24-103-3260   (BR)
BMO INVESTORLINE INC
BMO LIGNE D'ACTION
2015 Rue Peel Unite 200, Montreal, QC, H3A 1T8
(888) 776-6886
Emp Here 30
SIC 6211 Security brokers and dealers

D-U-N-S 24-356-2865   (BR)
BMO NESBITT BURNS INC
1501 Av Mcgill College Bureau 3000, Montreal, QC, H3A 3M8
(514) 282-5800
Emp Here 45
SIC 6211 Security brokers and dealers

D-U-N-S 20-763-3413   (HQ)
BNP PARIBAS (CANADA)
1981 Av Mcgill College Bureau 515, Montreal,

QC, H3A 2W8
(514) 285-6000
Emp Here 200   *Emp Total* 10,000
Sales 74,757,461
SIC 6021 National commercial banks
Dir David R. Peterson
Pr Jacques H. Wahl
Sec Marise Chenier Jette
Dir Jean Lavoie
Dir John Rae
Dir Leonard Waverman
Dir Monique Vialatou
Dir Bruno D'illiers

D-U-N-S 20-657-2997   (BR)
BANCTEC (CANADA), INC
BANCTEC
400 Boul De Maisonneuve O Bureau 1120,
Montreal, QC, H3A 1L4
(514) 392-4900
Emp Here 60
SIC 7371 Custom computer programming services

D-U-N-S 20-580-0662   (BR)
BANK OF NOVA SCOTIA, THE
CENTRE DE SERVICES AU ENTREPRISES
1800 Av Mcgill College Bureau 1600, Montreal, QC, H3A 3K9
(514) 281-8811
Emp Here 40
SIC 6021 National commercial banks

D-U-N-S 24-365-1713   (BR)
BANK OF NOVA SCOTIA, THE
SCOTIAMCLEOD
1002 Rue Sherbrooke O Bureau 600, Montreal, QC, H3A 3L6
(514) 287-3600
Emp Here 200
SIC 6021 National commercial banks

D-U-N-S 25-295-9069   (BR)
BANK OF NOVA SCOTIA, THE
BANQUE SCOTIA
1900 Av Mcgill College, Montreal, QC, H3A
3L2

Emp Here 40
SIC 6021 National commercial banks

D-U-N-S 24-104-6437   (BR)
BANK OF NOVA SCOTIA, THE
SCOTIABANK
1002 Rue Sherbrooke O Bureau 200, Montreal, QC, H3A 3L6
(514) 499-5432
Emp Here 90
SIC 6021 National commercial banks

D-U-N-S 20-300-3681   (BR)
BANQUE NATIONALE DU CANADA
955 Boul De Maisonneuve O, Montreal, QC,
H3A 1M4
(514) 281-9620
Emp Here 20
SIC 6021 National commercial banks

D-U-N-S 20-858-2940   (SL)
BECHTEL QUEBEC LIMITEE
(*Suby of* Bechtel Group, Inc.)
1500 Boul Robert-Bourassa Bureau 910,
Montreal, QC, H3A 3S7
(514) 871-1711
Emp Here 200   *Sales* 26,940,406
SIC 8711 Engineering services
Pr Pr Andrew C. Greig
Victor Tom
Dir Russell J. Barretta

D-U-N-S 25-864-3121   (BR)
BERLITZ CANADA INC
CENTRE DE LANGUE
2001 Av Mcgill College, Montreal, QC, H3A
1G1
(514) 288-3111
Emp Here 70
SIC 8299 Schools and educational services,

nec

D-U-N-S 25-501-7592   (BR)
BORALEX INC
772 Rue Sherbrooke O Bureau 200, Montreal,
QC, H3A 1G1
(514) 284-9890
Emp Here 25
SIC 4911 Electric services

D-U-N-S 20-852-9995   (BR)
BURGUNDY ASSET MANAGEMENT LTD
GESTION D' ACTIF BURGUNDY
1501 Av Mcgill College Bureau 2090, Montreal, QC, H3A 3M8
(514) 844-8091
Emp Here 80
SIC 8741 Management services

D-U-N-S 20-025-7553   (BR)
CIBC MELLON TRUST COMPANY
COMPANIE TRUST CIBC MELLON
2001 Boul Robert-Bourassa Unite 1600, Montreal, QC, H3A 2A6
(514) 285-3600
Emp Here 24
SIC 6289 Security and commodity service

D-U-N-S 20-591-0847   (BR)
CIBC WORLD MARKETS INC
CIBC WOOD GUNDY
600 Boul De Maisonneuve O Bureau 3050,
Montreal, QC, H3A 3J2
(514) 847-6300
Emp Here 200
SIC 6211 Security brokers and dealers

D-U-N-S 20-715-9331   (BR)
CNA CANADA
(*Suby of* Loews Corporation)
1800 Av Mcgill College Bureau 520, Montreal,
QC, H3A 3J6
(514) 398-9572
Emp Here 20
SIC 6411 Insurance agents, brokers, and service

D-U-N-S 20-700-6979   (BR)
CANADIAN IMPERIAL BANK OF COMMERCE
CANADIAN IMPERIAL BANK OF COMMERCE
2001 Boul Robert-Bourassa Unite 1600, Montreal, QC, H3A 2A6
(514) 285-3600
Emp Here 22
SIC 6289 Security and commodity service

D-U-N-S 24-101-8725   (SL)
CANADIAN TEST CASE 158
505 Boul De Maisonneuve O Bureau 906,
Montreal, QC, H3A 3C2
(514) 904-1496
Emp Here 158   *Sales* 9,894,455
SIC 5499 Miscellaneous food stores
Owner Donna Copelli

D-U-N-S 25-392-9400   (SL)
CANSOLV TECHNOLOGIES INC
400 Boul De Maisonneuve O Bureau 200,
Montreal, QC, H3A 1L4
(514) 382-4411
Emp Here 40   *Sales* 4,504,505
SIC 8711 Engineering services

D-U-N-S 24-524-2016   (BR)
CARAT CANADA INC
400 Boul De Maisonneuve O Bureau 250,
Montreal, QC, H3A 1L4
(514) 284-4446
Emp Here 74
SIC 7311 Advertising agencies

D-U-N-S 20-366-5984   (BR)
CENTRE DE SANTE D'EASTMAN INC
CENTRE DE SANTE D'EASTMAN INC
(*Suby of* Centre de Sante d'Eastman Inc)
666 Rue Sherbrooke O Bureau 1601, Mon-

treal, QC, H3A 1E7
(514) 845-8455
Emp Here 25
SIC 7299 Miscellaneous personal service

D-U-N-S 25-200-9402   (BR)
CISCO SYSTEMS CANADA CO
SYSTEMS CISCO CANADA
(*Suby of* Cisco Systems, Inc.)
1800 Av Mcgill College Bureau 700, Montreal,
QC, H3A 3J6
(514) 847-6800
Emp Here 80
SIC 5999 Miscellaneous retail stores, nec

D-U-N-S 20-763-0260   (SL)
CLUB MAA INC
2070 Rue Peel, Montreal, QC, H3A 1W6
(514) 845-2233
Emp Here 100   *Sales* 4,012,839
SIC 7997 Membership sports and recreation
clubs

D-U-N-S 25-321-4233   (BR)
CLUB MONACO CORP
CLUB MONACO
(*Suby of* Ralph Lauren Corporation)
1455 Rue Peel Bureau 226, Montreal, QC,
H3A 1T5

Emp Here 30
SIC 5621 Women's clothing stores

D-U-N-S 25-298-6021   (BR)
COMMISSION SCOLAIRE ENGLISH-MONTREAL
ECOLE SECONDAIRE F A C E
3449 Rue University, Montreal, QC, H3A 2A8
(514) 350-8899
Emp Here 70
SIC 8299 Schools and educational services,
nec

D-U-N-S 24-375-0119   (BR)
COMPUTERSHARE TRUST COMPANY OF CANADA
COMPUTERSHARE
1500 Boul Robert-Bourassa Bureau 700,
Montreal, QC, H3A 3S8
(514) 982-7888
Emp Here 450
SIC 6733 Trusts, nec

D-U-N-S 25-675-8525   (SL)
CONNEXIM, SOCIETE EN COMMANDITE
505 Boul De Maisonneuve O, Montreal, QC,
H3A 3C2

Emp Here 700   *Sales* 174,935,680
SIC 4899 Communication services, nec
Pr Pr Scott Garvey

D-U-N-S 24-620-0240   (SL)
CORPORATION D'EXPLOITATION CANDEREL LTEE
2000 Rue Peel Bureau 900, Montreal, QC,
H3A 2W5
(514) 842-8636
Emp Here 150   *Sales* 19,681,300
SIC 6531 Real estate agents and managers
Jonathan Wener

D-U-N-S 25-195-6504   (SL)
COVERDELL CANADA CORPORATION
1801 Av Mcgill College Bureau 800, Montreal,
QC, H3A 2N4
(514) 847-7800
Emp Here 241   *Sales* 22,184,160
SIC 7389 Business services, nec
Gary A Johnson
Pr Vince Di Bennedetto

D-U-N-S 25-195-5928   (BR)
DAVIES WARD PHILLIPS & VINEBERG LLP
DAVIES
1501 Av Mcgill College Bureau 2600, Montreal, QC, H3A 3N9
(514) 841-6400
Emp Here 200

SIC 8111 Legal services

D-U-N-S 24-535-9570   (BR)
DAVIS LLP
1501 Av Mcgill College Bureau 1400, Montreal, QC, H3A 3M8
(514) 392-1991
Emp Here 30
SIC 8111 Legal services

D-U-N-S 24-959-1298   (HQ)
DEVOIR INC, LE
JOURNAL LE DEVOIR
2050 Rue De Bleury, Montreal, QC, H3A 2J5
(514) 985-3333
Emp Here 114   *Emp Total* 120
Sales 9,922,655
SIC 2711 Newspapers
Pr Pr Jean Lamarre
Dir Pierre Poirier
Dir Denis Sirois
Dir Francine Harel Giasson
Dir Fares Khoury
Dir Sylvain Lafrance
Dir Patrick Pierra
Dir Andre Ryan
Dir Eric Desrosiers
Sec Michel Rioux

D-U-N-S 25-541-1159   (HQ)
DIFCO, TISSUS DE PERFORMANCE INC
DIFCO
1411 Rue Peel Bureau 505, Montreal, QC,
H3A 1S5
(819) 434-2159
Emp Here 100   *Emp Total* 21,000
Sales 42,970,202
SIC 2299 Textile goods, nec
Dir Fin Ioannis Pananis
Dir Dennis Norman
Dir Eric Henderson

D-U-N-S 20-657-1783   (BR)
ESI CANADA
(*Suby of* Express Scripts Holding Company)
625 Av Du President-Kennedy Bureau 1600,
Montreal, QC, H3A 1K2
(514) 844-4420
Emp Here 40
SIC 5941 Sporting goods and bicycle shops

D-U-N-S 24-522-5037   (SL)
EVO MERCHANT SERVICES CORP. CANADA
EVO CANADA
505 Boul De Maisonneuve O Bureau 150,
Montreal, QC, H3A 3C2

Emp Here 100   *Sales* 13,716,612
SIC 5046 Commercial equipment, nec
Pr Pr Mark Lachance
Alon Kindler
Ayman Ibrahim
Kevin Lambrix
Dir Kevin Lavigne

D-U-N-S 24-851-8073   (BR)
EXP SERVICES INC
EXP GLOBAL
1001 Boul De Maisonneuve O Bureau 800b,
Montreal, QC, H3A 3C8
(514) 788-6158
Emp Here 100
SIC 8711 Engineering services

D-U-N-S 20-302-8790   (BR)
EMBASSY OF MEXICO
EMBASSY OF MEXICO
2055 Rue Peel Bureau 100, Montreal, QC,
H3A 1V4
(514) 288-2502
Emp Here 25
SIC 5963 Direct selling establishments

D-U-N-S 25-294-7858   (BR)
EMPIRE LIFE INSURANCE COMPANY, THE
EMPIRE VIE
600 Boul De Maisonneuve O Bureau 1600,

Montreal, QC, H3A 3J2
(514) 842-0003
Emp Here 20
SIC 6311 Life insurance

D-U-N-S 20-409-2654   (HQ)
ENERGIE VALERO INC
ULTRAMAR
1801 Av Mcgill College Bureau 1300, Montreal, QC, H3A 2N4
(514) 982-8200
Emp Here 425   *Emp Total* 9,996
Sales 1,053,260,665
SIC 5172 Petroleum products, nec
VP Martine Peloquin
Sec Julie Normand
Treas Bruce Macdonald
Dir Michael S. Ciskowski

D-U-N-S 24-312-6989   (BR)
ENERGIE VALERO INC
ULTRACONFORT
2200 Av Mcgill College Unite 400, Montreal, QC, H3A 3P8
(514) 493-5201
Emp Here 100
SIC 5983 Fuel oil dealers

D-U-N-S 24-343-8715   (HQ)
ENTREPRISES CANDEREL INC
(*Suby* of Entreprises Canderel Inc)
2000 Rue Peel Bureau 900, Montreal, QC, H3A 2W5
(514) 842-8636
Emp Here 85   *Emp Total* 100
Sales 20,859,840
SIC 6712 Bank holding companies
  Jonathan Wener
Pr Luc Sicotte
  Douglas Pascal
Genl Mgr David Hawrysh

D-U-N-S 20-852-9730   (BR)
F. D. L. COMPAGNIE LTEE
L'APPARTEMENT HOTEL
(*Suby* of F. D. L. Compagnie Ltee)
455 Rue Sherbrooke O, Montreal, QC, H3A 1B7
(514) 284-3634
Emp Here 40
SIC 6513 Apartment building operators

D-U-N-S 20-025-6738   (SL)
FM RESTO DESIGN INC
CAFE FERREIRA
1446 Rue Peel, Montreal, QC, H3A 1S8
(514) 848-0988
Emp Here 60   *Sales* 1,824,018
SIC 5812 Eating places

D-U-N-S 24-711-0554   (HQ)
FEDERATION INTERPROFESSIONNELLE DE LA SANTE DU QUEBEC-FIQ
(*Suby* of Federation Interprofessionnelle de la sante du Quebec-FIQ)
2050 Rue De Bleury, Montreal, QC, H3A 2J5
(514) 987-1141
Emp Here 100   *Emp Total* 220
Sales 30,060,295
SIC 8631 Labor organizations
Pr Lina Bonamie
VP VP Daniel Gilbert
VP VP Sylvie Savard
VP VP Michele Boisclair
VP VP Birgitte Fauteux
VP VP Monique Leroux
VP VP Elaine Trottier
  Suzanne Lavoie
Treas Lise Martel

D-U-N-S 24-448-6663   (SL)
FESTIVAL INTERNATIONAL DE JAZZ DE MONTREAL INC, LE
BLUES CAMP
400 Boul De Maisonneuve O Bureau 800, Montreal, QC, H3A 1L4
(514) 871-1881
Emp Here 50   *Sales* 2,699,546

SIC 7999 Amusement and recreation, nec

D-U-N-S 20-319-3966   (BR)
FIRST NATIONAL FINANCIAL CORPORATION
2000 Rue Peel Bureau 200, Montreal, QC, H3A 2W5
(514) 499-7918
Emp Here 70
SIC 6798 Real estate investment trusts

D-U-N-S 20-737-7086   (HQ)
FUJITSU CONSEIL (CANADA) INC
DMR
1000 Rue Sherbrooke O Bureau 1400, Montreal, QC, H3A 3G4
(514) 877-3301
Emp Here 350   *Emp Total* 156,515
Sales 94,232,900
SIC 7379 Computer related services, nec
Pr Pr David Shearer
Sec Jeremy Barry
Treas Perry Tenser
  Robert Pryor

D-U-N-S 25-866-4788   (BR)
GWL REALTY ADVISORS INC
2001 Boul Robert-Bourassa, Montreal, QC, H3A 2A6
(514) 350-7940
Emp Here 20
SIC 6531 Real estate agents and managers

D-U-N-S 24-158-2209   (BR)
GENWORTH FINANCIAL MORTGAGE INSURANCE COMPANY CANADA
999 Boul De Maisonneuve O Bureau 1800, Montreal, QC, H3A 3L4
(514) 215-3166
Emp Here 40
SIC 6351 Surety insurance

D-U-N-S 24-569-3122   (HQ)
GESTION CANDEREL INC
(*Suby* of Entreprises Canderel Inc)
2000 Rue Peel Bureau 900, Montreal, QC, H3A 2W5
(514) 842-8636
Emp Here 30   *Emp Total* 100
Sales 37,768,544
SIC 6553 Cemetery subdividers and developers
Pr Pr Jonathan Wener
Sec David Hawrysh

D-U-N-S 24-850-1900   (HQ)
GESTION D'ACTIFS MANUVIE ACCORD (2015) INC
1001 Boul De Maisonneuve O Bureau 700, Montreal, QC, H3A 3C8
(514) 499-6844
Emp Here 50   *Emp Total* 34,000
Sales 14,206,516
SIC 6282 Investment advice
  Roger Renaud
Sec Karen Shaw
Dir Charles Guay
Dir Barry Evans
Dir Paul Lorentz
  Michael Evans

D-U-N-S 24-062-7625   (BR)
GLOBAL CREDIT & COLLECTION INC
2055 Rue Peel Bureau 100, Montreal, QC, H3A 1V4
(514) 284-5533
Emp Here 200
SIC 7322 Adjustment and collection services

D-U-N-S 25-365-2713   (HQ)
GLOBALEX GESTION DE RISQUES INC
(*Suby* of Globalex Gestion De Risques Inc)
2001 Av Mcgill College Bureau 600, Montreal, QC, H3A 1G1
(514) 382-9625
Emp Here 50   *Emp Total* 50
Sales 6,085,920
SIC 6411 Insurance agents, brokers, and ser-

vice
Pr Jacques L Brouillette
  Claude Boivin
  Michele Boutet
  Bertin Castonguay
  Valier Boivin
Genl Mgr Hang Le Hong

D-U-N-S 24-458-5238   (SL)
GOUDREAU GAGE DUBUC S.E.N.C.R.L
2000 Av Mcgill College Bureau 2200, Montreal, QC, H3A 3H3
(514) 397-7602
Emp Here 50   *Sales* 4,304,681
SIC 8111 Legal services

D-U-N-S 24-097-6782   (BR)
GOUVERNEMENT DE LA PROVINCE DE QUEBEC
GOUVERNEMENT DE LA PROVINCE DE QUEBEC
2050 Rue De Bleury Bureau 1.20, Montreal, QC, H3A 2J5
(514) 873-0001
Emp Here 35
SIC 8742 Management consulting services

D-U-N-S 20-212-9305   (BR)
GREAT-WEST LIFE ASSURANCE COMPANY, THE
GREAT WEST MARKETING & PENSION DEPARTMENT
2001 Boul Robert-Bourassa Unite 1000, Montreal, QC, H3A 2A6
(514) 350-7975
Emp Here 400
SIC 6411 Insurance agents, brokers, and service

D-U-N-S 24-366-3395   (BR)
GREAT-WEST LIFE ASSURANCE COMPANY, THE
1800 Av Mcgill College Bureau 2010, Montreal, QC, H3A 3J6
(514) 878-6182
Emp Here 50
SIC 6311 Life insurance

D-U-N-S 24-960-5684   (SL)
GROUPE AXOR INC
(*Suby* of 158473 Canada Inc)
1555 Rue Peel Bureau 1100, Montreal, QC, H3A 3L8
(514) 846-4000
Emp Here 150   *Sales* 36,185,434
SIC 1542 Nonresidential construction, nec
Pr Pr Yvan Dupont
Sec Maurice Choquette

D-U-N-S 24-020-7712   (HQ)
GROUPE CONSEIL RES PUBLICA INC
RES PUBLICA
(*Suby* of Groupe Conseil RES Publica Inc)
2001 Av Mcgill College Bureau 800, Montreal, QC, H3A 1G1
(514) 843-7171
Emp Here 100   *Emp Total* 250
Sales 55,503,178
SIC 6712 Bank holding companies
  Luc Beauregard
Pr Pr James Crossland
  Robert Mccoy
  Jean-Pierre Vasseur

D-U-N-S 25-167-9379   (BR)
GROUPE GERMAIN INC
HOTEL LE GERMAIN
(*Suby* of Gestion Famiger Inc)
2050 Rue Mansfield, Montreal, QC, H3A 1Y9
(514) 849-2050
Emp Here 60
SIC 7011 Hotels and motels

D-U-N-S 25-147-0969   (BR)
HSBC BANK CANADA
BANQUE HSBC CANADA
2001 Av Mcgill College Bureau 160, Montreal, QC, H3A 1G1

(514) 288-8858
Emp Here 27
SIC 6021 National commercial banks

D-U-N-S 25-095-0508   (BR)
HSBC SECURITIES (CANADA) INC
VALEURS MOBILIERES HSBC
2001 Av Mcgill College Bureau 300, Montreal, QC, H3A 1G1
(514) 393-6071
Emp Here 30
SIC 6211 Security brokers and dealers

D-U-N-S 20-007-9676   (BR)
HITACHI DATA SYSTEMS INC
625 Av Du President-Kennedy Bureau 1700, Montreal, QC, H3A 1K2
(514) 982-0707
Emp Here 20
SIC 7379 Computer related services, nec

D-U-N-S 20-234-3757   (BR)
HOGG ROBINSON CANADA INC
HRG AMERIQUE DU NORD
(*Suby* of HOGG ROBINSON GROUP PLC)
1550 Rue Metcalfe Bureau 700, Montreal, QC, H3A 1X6
(514) 286-6300
Emp Here 200
SIC 4725 Tour operators

D-U-N-S 24-128-1612   (HQ)
INDUSTRIELLE ALLIANCE VALEURS MOBILIERES INC
IA VALEURS MOBILIERES
2200 Av Mcgill College Bureau 350, Montreal, QC, H3A 3P8
(514) 499-1066
Emp Here 40   *Emp Total* 5,350
Sales 7,296,070
SIC 6211 Security brokers and dealers
Pr Richard Legault
Sec Caroline Labrecque
Dir Mark Arthur
Dir I. David Bird
Dir Lise Douville
Dir Andre Dubuc
Dir Marc-Andre Elie
Dir Donald Mcfarlane
Dir Normand Pepin

D-U-N-S 25-372-5295   (HQ)
ITERGY INTERNATIONAL INC
(*Suby* of Itergy International Inc)
2075 Boul Robert-Bourassa Bureau 700, Montreal, QC, H3A 2L1
(514) 845-5881
Emp Here 30   *Emp Total* 54
Sales 4,677,755
SIC 7379 Computer related services, nec

D-U-N-S 25-544-1347   (BR)
IVANHOE CAMBRIDGE INC
SITQ IMMOBILIER
770 Rue Sherbrooke O Bureau 540, Montreal, QC, H3A 1G1
(514) 861-9393
Emp Here 20
SIC 6512 Nonresidential building operators

D-U-N-S 25-010-8388   (BR)
IVARI CANADA ULC
TRANSAMERICA VIE CANADA
(*Suby* of Wilton RE Ltd)
2001 Av Mcgill Coll Ge Bureau 410, Montreal, QC, H3A 1G1
(514) 846-9844
Emp Here 40
SIC 6311 Life insurance

D-U-N-S 24-581-8828   (HQ)
JPDL MULTI MANAGEMENT INC
JPDL
(*Suby* of JPDL Multi Management Inc)
1555 Rue Peel Bureau 500, Montreal, QC, H3A 3L8
(514) 287-1070
Emp Here 24   *Emp Total* 53
Sales 2,772,507

SIC 7389 Business services, nec

D-U-N-S 20-294-3721   (BR)
JOLI-COEUR LACASSE S.E.N.C.R.L
2001 Av Mcgill College Bureau 900, Montreal,
QC, H3A 1G1
(514) 871-2800
Emp Here 70
SIC 8111 Legal services

D-U-N-S 20-882-2981   (BR)
KPMG LLP
(*Suby of* KPMG LLP)
600 Boul De Maisonneuve O Unite 1500, Montreal, QC, H3A 0A3
(514) 840-2100
Emp Here 750
SIC 8721 Accounting, auditing, and book-
keeping

D-U-N-S 25-308-6136   (SL)
LES INVESTISSEMENTS RAMAN 'S.E.N.C.'
LE CATLIE SUITES HOTEL
1110 Rue Sherbrooke O Bureau 301, Mon-
treal, QC, H3A 1G8
(514) 844-3951
Emp Here 100   *Sales* 4,377,642
SIC 7011 Hotels and motels

D-U-N-S 25-212-6214   (SL)
LETKO BROSSEAU & ASSOCIES INC
1800 Av Mcgill College Bureau 2510, Mon-
treal, QC, H3A 3J6
(514) 499-1200
Emp Here 50   *Sales* 10,145,000
SIC 6211 Security brokers and dealers
Pr Pr Daniel Brosseau
 Peter Letko

D-U-N-S 24-121-4527   (BR)
LONDON LIFE INSURANCE COMPANY
*LONDON LIFE GREAT WEST LIFE AND
CANADA LIFE*
2001 Boul Robert-Bourassa Unite 800, Mon-
treal, QC, H3A 2A6
(514) 350-5500
Emp Here 400
SIC 6411 Insurance agents, brokers, and ser-
vice

D-U-N-S 20-165-9054   (BR)
LONDON LIFE INSURANCE COMPANY
FINANCIERE LIBERTE 55
1800 Av Mcgill College Unite 1100, Montreal,
QC, H3A 3J6
(514) 931-4242
Emp Here 100
SIC 6311 Life insurance

D-U-N-S 25-532-0079   (BR)
LOYALTYONE, CO
GROUPE LOYALTY
625 Av Du President-Kennedy Bureau 600,
Montreal, QC, H3A 1K2
(514) 843-7164
Emp Here 35
SIC 7299 Miscellaneous personal service

D-U-N-S 24-119-7917   (BR)
LUSSIER DALE PARIZEAU INC
1001 Boul De Maisonneuve O Bureau 310,
Montreal, QC, H3A 3C8
(514) 840-9918
Emp Here 25
SIC 6531 Real estate agents and managers

D-U-N-S 25-466-4998   (SL)
MALAGA INC
MINES D'OR DYNACOR
2000 Av Mcgill College Bureau 510, Montreal,
QC, H3A 3H3
(514) 288-3224
Emp Here 100   *Sales* 11,768,200
SIC 1081 Metal mining services
 Jean Martineau
 Pierre Monet
 Luc Filiatreault
 Gilles Masson

Martin Wong
Renald Marchant
Daniel Danis
Rene Branchaud

D-U-N-S 24-109-6155   (BR)
**MANUFACTURERS LIFE INSURANCE
COMPANY, THE**
FINANCIERE MANUVIE
2000 Rue Mansfield Unite 200, Montreal, QC,
H3A 2Z4
(514) 845-2122
Emp Here 50
SIC 6411 Insurance agents, brokers, and ser-
vice

D-U-N-S 24-354-5993   (BR)
**MANUFACTURERS LIFE INSURANCE
COMPANY, THE**
FINANCIERE MANUVIE
2000 Rue Mansfield Unite 300, Montreal, QC,
H3A 2Z4
(514) 288-6268
Emp Here 800
SIC 6311 Life insurance

D-U-N-S 20-914-8514   (BR)
MANULIFE CANADA LTD
MANULIFE FINANCIAL 1182
2000 Rue Mansfield Unite 200, Montreal, QC,
H3A 2Z4
(514) 845-1612
Emp Here 750
SIC 8742 Management consulting services

D-U-N-S 20-553-6688   (BR)
MARSH CANADA LIMITED
(*Suby of* Marsh & McLennan Companies, Inc.)
1981 Av Mcgill College Bureau 820, Montreal,
QC, H3A 3T4
(514) 285-5800
Emp Here 250
SIC 6411 Insurance agents, brokers, and ser-
vice

D-U-N-S 25-039-9102   (BR)
MCGILL UNIVERSITY HEALTH CENTRE
*MCGILL HOPITAL NEUROLOGIQUE DE
MONTREAL*
3801 Rue University Bureau 548, Montreal,
QC, H3A 2B4
(514) 398-6644
Emp Here 2,000
SIC 8062 General medical and surgical hospi-
tals

D-U-N-S 24-346-5361   (BR)
MCGILL UNIVERSITY HEALTH CENTRE
853 Rue Sherbrooke O Bureau 115, Montreal,
QC, H3A 0G5

Emp Here 20
SIC 8299 Schools and educational services,
nec

D-U-N-S 24-342-6454   (BR)
MCGILL UNIVERSITY HEALTH CENTRE
ROYAL VICTORIA HOSPITAL
687 Av Des Pins O Bureau 1408, Montreal,
QC, H3A 1A1
(514) 934-1934
Emp Here 3,000
SIC 8062 General medical and surgical hospi-
tals

D-U-N-S 24-425-1364   (BR)
MCMILLAN LLP
1000 Rue Sherbrooke O Bureau 2700, Montreal, QC, H3A 3G4
(514) 987-5000
Emp Here 100
SIC 8111 Legal services

D-U-N-S 20-308-9073   (BR)
MEDAVIE INC
CROIX BLEUE MEDAVIE
550 Rue Sherbrooke O Bureau 1200, Montreal, QC, H3A 1B9

(514) 286-7778
Emp Here 300
SIC 6321 Accident and health insurance

D-U-N-S 25-903-1243   (BR)
MEDIA BUYING SERVICES ULC
GROUPE TMC, LE
(*Suby of* Media Buying Services ULC)
999 Boul De Maisonneuve O Bureau 600,
Montreal, QC, H3A 3L4

Emp Here 25
SIC 7311 Advertising agencies

D-U-N-S 24-371-7563   (BR)
MEDIA BUYING SERVICES ULC
PUBLICITE MBS
(*Suby of* Media Buying Services ULC)
2000 Rue Mansfield Bureau 910, Montreal,
QC, H3A 2Z6
(514) 282-9320
Emp Here 20
SIC 7319 Advertising, nec

D-U-N-S 24-337-7947   (SL)
MEDISYS HOLDING LP
500 Rue Sherbrooke O Bureau 1100, Mon-
treal, QC, H3A 3C6
(514) 845-1211
Emp Here 700   *Sales* 173,930,880
SIC 6712 Bank holding companies
 Bryant Tse

D-U-N-S 24-460-7578   (BR)
MERCER (CANADA) LIMITED
MERCER INVESTMENT CONSULTING
(*Suby of* Marsh & McLennan Companies, Inc.)
1981 Av Mcgill College Bureau 800, Montreal,
QC, H3A 3T5
(514) 285-1802
Emp Here 500
SIC 8999 Services, nec

D-U-N-S 20-518-6120   (SL)
MERCER CONSULTATION (QUEBEC) LTEE
(*Suby of* Marsh & McLennan Companies, Inc.)
600 Boul De Maisonneuve O Unite 1100, Montreal, QC, H3A 3J2
(514) 282-7282
Emp Here 35   *Sales* 3,137,310
SIC 6411 Insurance agents, brokers, and service

D-U-N-S 20-117-6737   (BR)
MICROSOFT CANADA INC
MICROSOFT
(*Suby of* Microsoft Corporation)
2000 Av Mcgill College Bureau 450, Montreal,
QC, H3A 3H3
(514) 846-5800
Emp Here 50
SIC 5045 Computers, peripherals, and soft-
ware

D-U-N-S 24-051-7198   (BR)
**MULTIPLE SCLEROSIS SOCIETY OF
CANADA**
550 Rue Sherbrooke O Bureau 1010, Mon-
treal, QC, H3A 1B9
(514) 849-7591
Emp Here 36
SIC 8399 Social services, nec

D-U-N-S 24-351-2600   (BR)
OMYA CANADA INC
OMYA ST-ARMAND
2020 Boul Robert-Bourassa Unite 1720, Montreal, QC, H3A 2A5

Emp Here 28
SIC 1481 NonMetallic mineral services

D-U-N-S 20-534-1162   (BR)
OPINION SEARCH INC
NIELSEN
(*Suby of* Decima Inc)
1080 Rue Beaverhall Bureau 400, Montreal,
QC, H3A 1E4

(514) 288-0199
Emp Here 460
SIC 8732 Commercial nonphysical research

D-U-N-S 24-713-7755   (BR)
ORACLE CANADA ULC
(*Suby of* Oracle Corporation)
600 Boul De Maisonneuve O Bureau 1900,
Montreal, QC, H3A 3J2
(514) 843-6762
Emp Here 200
SIC 7372 Prepackaged software

D-U-N-S 24-892-6870   (SL)
ORDRE DES DENTISTES DU QUEBEC
*FONDS D'ASSURANCE-RESPONSABILITE
PROFESSIONNELLE DE L'ORDRE DES
DENTISTES DU QUEBEC*
2020 Boul Robert-Bourassa Bureau 2160,
Montreal, QC, H3A 2A5
(514) 281-0300
Emp Here 49   *Sales* 117,028,963
SIC 6324 Hospital and medical service plans
Pr Barry Dolman

D-U-N-S 20-215-5537   (HQ)
OREAL CANADA INC, L'
BIOTHERM CANADA
1500 Boul Robert-Bourassa Bureau 600,
Montreal, QC, H3A 3S7
(514) 287-4800
Emp Here 250   *Emp Total* 6,653
Sales 83,394,080
SIC 2844 Toilet preparations
 Frank Kollmar
 Frederic Roze
Dir Philippe Dalle
Dir Serge L. Bordeur

D-U-N-S 20-002-2395   (BR)
RBC DOMINION SECURITIES INC
(*Suby of* Royal Bank Of Canada)
1501 Av Mcgill College Bureau 2150, Mon-
treal, QC, H3A 3M8
(514) 840-7644
Emp Here 50
SIC 6211 Security brokers and dealers

D-U-N-S 24-342-1349   (BR)
**RGA LIFE REINSURANCE COMPANY OF
CANADA**
1981 Av Mcgill College Unite 1300, Montreal,
QC, H3A 3A8
(514) 985-5260
Emp Here 130
SIC 6311 Life insurance

D-U-N-S 20-255-7091   (BR)
RANDSTAD INTERIM INC
810 Boul De Maisonneuve O, Montreal, QC,
H3A 3E6
(514) 350-0033
Emp Here 25
SIC 7361 Employment agencies

D-U-N-S 25-194-0805   (BR)
RANDSTAD INTERIM INC
1001 Boul De Maisonneuve O Bureau 1510,
Montreal, QC, H3A 3C8
(514) 845-5775
Emp Here 23
SIC 7379 Computer related services, nec

D-U-N-S 24-367-2123   (SL)
RENEWPLAST INC
PLACEMENT RENEWPLAST
(*Suby of* Gestion Industriel Capvest Inc)
2000 Rue Peel Bureau 900, Montreal, QC,
H3A 2W5
(514) 842-8636
Emp Here 65   *Sales* 12,072,550
SIC 6712 Bank holding companies
Pr Pr David Hawrysh

D-U-N-S 24-889-9916   (BR)
**ROYAL & SUN ALLIANCE INSURANCE
COMPANY OF CANADA**
RSA
2000 Av Mcgill College Bureau 800, Montreal,

QC, H3A 3H3
(514) 847-8000
Emp Here 70
SIC 6331 Fire, marine, and casualty insurance

D-U-N-S 20-716-0040   (BR)
ROYAL & SUN ALLIANCE INSURANCE COMPANY OF CANADA
1001 Boul De Maisonneuve O Bureau 1004, Montreal, QC, H3A 3C8
(514) 844-1116
Emp Here 80
SIC 6411 Insurance agents, brokers, and service

D-U-N-S 20-025-7009   (BR)
SAS INSTITUTE (CANADA) INC
(*Suby of* Sas Institute Inc.)
1000 Rue Sherbrooke O Bureau 2100, Montreal, QC, H3A 3G4
(514) 395-8922
Emp Here 22
SIC 7372 Prepackaged software

D-U-N-S 24-125-5202   (BR)
SCDA (2015) INC
COMPAGNIE D'ASSURANCE STANDARD LIFE DU CANADA
2045 Rue Stanley Bureau 1200, Montreal, QC, H3A 2V4
(514) 284-6924
Emp Here 22
SIC 6411 Insurance agents, brokers, and service

D-U-N-S 24-373-2588   (BR)
SNC-LAVALIN INC
SNC-LAVALIN ET HATCH
1801 Av Mcgill College Unite 1200, Montreal, QC, H3A 2N4
(514) 393-8000
Emp Here 50
SIC 8711 Engineering services

D-U-N-S 25-624-3817   (BR)
SCOTIA CAPITAL INC
SCOTIA MCLEOD
1002 Rue Sherbrooke O Bureau 1210, Montreal, QC, H3A 3L6

Emp Here 40
SIC 6211 Security brokers and dealers

D-U-N-S 20-564-0725   (BR)
SCOTIA CAPITAL INC
SCOTIAMCLEOD
1002 Rue Sherbrooke O Bureau 600, Montreal, QC, H3A 3L6
(514) 287-3600
Emp Here 180
SIC 6211 Security brokers and dealers

D-U-N-S 20-861-3583   (BR)
SCOTIA CAPITAL INC
1002 Rue Sherbrooke O Bureau 840, Montreal, QC, H3A 3L6
(514) 287-3600
Emp Here 180
SIC 6211 Security brokers and dealers

D-U-N-S 24-923-0657   (SL)
SERVICE DE GESTION REALMINT LTEE
CARLOS & PEPE'S
1420 Rue Peel Bureau 1420, Montreal, QC, H3A 1S8
(514) 288-3090
Emp Here 50   *Sales* 1,532,175
SIC 5812 Eating places

D-U-N-S 25-370-0660   (SL)
SERVICES DE GROSSISTE EN PHARMACIE PROFESSIONNELS INC
PHARMACY WHOLESALE SERVICES
666 Rue Sherbrooke O Bureau 4e, Montreal, QC, H3A 1E7
(514) 286-0660
Emp Here 224   *Sales* 38,348,100
SIC 5122 Drugs, proprietaries, and sundries

Pr Douglas Parker Rudderham

D-U-N-S 20-882-8855   (HQ)
SOCIETE GENERALE (CANADA)
SOCIETE GENERALE CORPORATE INVESTMENT
1501 Av Mcgill College Bureau 1800, Montreal, QC, H3A 3M8
(514) 841-6000
Emp Here 115   *Emp Total* 10,000
Sales 235,298,258
SIC 6081 Foreign bank and branches and agencies
Sec Diletta Prando
Dir Alain Lellouche
Dir Didier Varlet
Dir Pierre Matuszewski
Dir Jean-Louis Mongrain
Dir Maria Patsios
Dir Emilio Imbriglio

D-U-N-S 24-942-2437   (HQ)
SOCIETE DES CASINOS DU QUEBEC INC, LA
CASINO DE MONTREAL
500 Rue Sherbrooke O Bureau 1500, Montreal, QC, H3A 3C6
(514) 282-8000
Emp Here 769   *Emp Total* 40,000
Sales 291,186,154
SIC 7999 Amusement and recreation, nec
Pr Pr Claude Poisson
   Lynne Roiter
Dir Alain Cousineau

D-U-N-S 25-287-1835   (SL)
SOCIETE DES ETABLISSEMENTS DE JEUX DU QUEBEC INC
LOTO-QUEBEC
500 Rue Sherbrooke O Bureau 1600, Montreal, QC, H3A 3C6
(514) 282-8000
Emp Here 40   *Sales* 2,188,821
SIC 7999 Amusement and recreation, nec

D-U-N-S 20-102-0133   (BR)
SOCIETY OF COMPOSERS, AUTHORS AND MUSIC PUBLISHERS OF CANADA
SOCAN
600 Boul De Maisonneuve O Bureau 500, Montreal, QC, H3A 3J2
(514) 844-8377
Emp Here 31
SIC 6794 Patent owners and lessors

D-U-N-S 20-553-9294   (HQ)
SOLUTIONS VICTRIX INC, LES
(*Suby of* Solutions Victrix Inc, les)
630 Rue Sherbrooke O Bureau 1100, Montreal, QC, H3A 1E4
(514) 879-1919
Emp Here 125   *Emp Total* 200
Sales 20,096,000
SIC 7379 Computer related services, nec
Pr Pr Marc-Andre Poulin
   Xavier Jiraud
   Jean Mathieu
VP Fin Christian Breton
VP Stephan Gariepy
VP Simon Martel

D-U-N-S 20-565-2592   (SL)
SOURCE EVOLUTION INC
2000 Rue Peel, Montreal, QC, H3A 2W5
(514) 354-6565
Emp Here 80   *Sales* 8,116,000
SIC 7379 Computer related services, nec
Pr Pr Yves Perron

D-U-N-S 20-290-9115   (BR)
STERICYCLE COMMUNICATION SOLUTIONS, ULC
(*Suby of* Stericycle Communication Solutions, ULC)
550 Rue Sherbrooke O Bureau 1650, Montreal, QC, H3A 1B9

---

(514) 843-4313
Emp Here 30
SIC 4899 Communication services, nec

D-U-N-S 20-847-1763   (HQ)
SYNERGIE HUNT INTERNATIONAL INC
HUNT PERSONNEL
666 Rue Sherbrooke O Bureau 1801, Montreal, QC, H3A 1E7
(514) 842-4691
Emp Here 35   *Sales* 42,517,422
SIC 7361 Employment agencies
Pr Daniel Augereau
Sec Yvon Drouet
Genl Mgr Jacqueline Pourreaux

D-U-N-S 20-825-3828   (BR)
T.E. FINANCIAL CONSULTANTS LTD
T E MIRADOR T E WEALTH
2020 Boul Robert-Bourassa Unite 2100, Montreal, QC, H3A 2A5
(514) 845-3200
Emp Here 25
SIC 8742 Management consulting services

D-U-N-S 20-852-6876   (BR)
TAXI CANADA LTD.
TAXI L'AGENCE DE PUBLICITE
1435 Rue Saint-Alexandre Bureau 620, Montreal, QC, H3A 2G4
(514) 842-8294
Emp Here 80
SIC 7311 Advertising agencies

D-U-N-S 24-811-9109   (SL)
TECSULT QUEBEC LTEE
2001 Rue University, Montreal, QC, H3A 2A6
(514) 287-8500
Emp Here 400   *Sales* 76,867,200
SIC 8741 Management services
Pr Luc Benoit

D-U-N-S 20-800-9683   (BR)
THE ROYAL INSTITUTE FOR THE ADVANCEMENT OF LEARNING MCGILL UNIVERSITY
ROYAL INSTITUTION FOR THE ADVANCEMENT OF LEARNING / MCGILL UNIVERSITY
817 Rue Sherbrooke O Bureau 382, Montreal, QC, H3A 0C3
(514) 398-7251
Emp Here 150
SIC 8221 Colleges and universities

D-U-N-S 20-570-9384   (BR)
THE ROYAL INSTITUTE FOR THE ADVANCEMENT OF LEARNING MCGILL UNIVERSITY
ROYAL INSTITUTION FOR THE ADVANCEMENT OF LEARNING / MCGILL UNIVERSITY
817 Rue Sherbrooke O Bureau 492, Montreal, QC, H3A 0C3
(514) 398-6860
Emp Here 20
SIC 8711 Engineering services

D-U-N-S 20-961-2191   (HQ)
THOMSON TREMBLAY INC
(*Suby of* R.G.F.M. Bertucci Management Corp Inc)
2040 Rue Peel Bureau 200, Montreal, QC, H3A 1W5
(514) 861-9971
Emp Here 45   *Emp Total* 3,500
Sales 355,075,000
SIC 7361 Employment agencies
Pr Pr Giuseppe Bertucci
VP Fin George Gawrych

D-U-N-S 25-756-9509   (BR)
TRANSCONTINENTAL INC
MEDIAS TRANSCONTINENTAL
2001 Boul Robert-Bourassa Unite 900, Montreal, QC, H3A 2A6
(514) 499-0491
Emp Here 110

SIC 2721 Periodicals

D-U-N-S 20-309-2887   (BR)
TRIOVEST REALTY ADVISORS INC
999 Boul De Maisonneuve O Bureau 800, Montreal, QC, H3A 3L4
(514) 879-1597
Emp Here 20
SIC 6512 Nonresidential building operators

D-U-N-S 20-112-2806   (HQ)
VALEURS MOBILIERES BANQUE LAURENTIENNE INC
COURTAGE ESCOMPTE BANQUE LAURENTIENNE
1981 Av Mcgill College Bureau 1900, Montreal, QC, H3A 3K3
(514) 350-2800
Emp Here 20   *Emp Total* 2,640
Sales 5,982,777
SIC 6211 Security brokers and dealers
Ch Bd Michel C. Trudeau
Pr Francois Desjardins
VP Yves Ruest
Dir Susan Kudzman
Dir Francois Laurin

D-U-N-S 24-679-3306   (SL)
VALTECH CANADA INC
6657443 CANADA
400 Boul De Maisonneuve O Bureau 700, Montreal, QC, H3A 1L4
(514) 448-4035
Emp Here 50   *Sales* 2,772,507
SIC 7374 Data processing and preparation

D-U-N-S 20-253-1922   (BR)
VANCOUVER CAREER COLLEGE (BURNABY) INC
COLLEGE CDI
(*Suby of* Chung Family Holdings Inc)
416 Boul De Maisonneuve O Bureau 700, Montreal, QC, H3A 1L2
(514) 849-1234
Emp Here 20
SIC 8211 Elementary and secondary schools

D-U-N-S 20-857-5100   (HQ)
WESTCLIFF DEVELOPMENT LTD
600 Boul De Maisonneuve O Bureau 2600, Montreal, QC, H3A 3J2
(514) 499-8300
Emp Here 20   *Emp Total* 2
Sales 6,933,120
SIC 6512 Nonresidential building operators
   William Penser Sr
   Bernard Caron Sr

D-U-N-S 20-184-3294   (BR)
WINNERS MERCHANTS INTERNATIONAL L.P.
WINNERS
(*Suby of* The TJX Companies Inc)
1500 Av Mcgill College, Montreal, QC, H3A 3J5
(514) 788-4949
Emp Here 120
SIC 5651 Family clothing stores

D-U-N-S 25-287-0720   (BR)
YMCA DU QUEBEC, LES
YMCA DU QUEBEC, LES
1440 Rue Stanley Bureau 6, Montreal, QC, H3A 1P7
(514) 849-8393
Emp Here 46
SIC 7999 Amusement and recreation, nec

D-U-N-S 25-995-0199   (SL)
ZENITH MERCHANT SERVICES INC
(*Suby of* Evo Payments International, LLC)
2075 Boul Robert-Bourassa Bureau 1500, Montreal, QC, H3A 2L1
(514) 228-1235
Emp Here 26   *Sales* 12,330,358
SIC 6153 Short-term business credit institutions, except agricultural
Pr Diego Vazquez

Montreal, QC H3B
Hochelaga County

D-U-N-S 24-106-7797   (SL)
123179 CANADA INC
RESTER MANAGEMENT HERMES EDIFICE
1117 Rue Sainte-Catherine O Bureau 303,
Montreal, QC, H3B 1H9
(514) 844-2612
Emp Here 100   *Sales* 4,012,839
SIC 6519 Real property lessors, nec

D-U-N-S 24-872-0351   (SL)
138440 CANADA INC
CONCESSIONS QUEBEC
Gd, Montreal, QC, H3B 4B5
(514) 876-1376
Emp Here 300   *Sales* 21,889,680
SIC 7999 Amusement and recreation, nec
Pr Pr Tewfik Saleh

D-U-N-S 20-284-3223   (SL)
2295822 CANADA INC.
800 Boul Rene-Levesque O Bureau 2200,
Montreal, QC, H3B 1X9

Emp Here 100   *Sales* 6,898,600
SIC 7389 Business services, nec
Pr Paul H Benjamin

D-U-N-S 25-413-0446   (SL)
3169693 CANADA INC
BOULANG PREMIERE MOISSON GARS
895 Rue De La Gauchetiere O Bureau 401,
Montreal, QC, H3B 4G1
(514) 393-1247
Emp Here 50   *Sales* 1,678,096
SIC 5461 Retail bakeries

D-U-N-S 20-184-3336   (SL)
4078187 CANADA INC
600 Rue De La Gaucheti Re Bureau 1900,
Montreal, QC, H3B 4L8

Emp Here 20   *Sales* 5,748,207
SIC 3357 Nonferrous wiredrawing and insulating
Pr Pr Eric Geoffrion
  Mohammed Saad

D-U-N-S 20-297-8557   (SL)
9280-4475 QUEBEC INC
IREPARATION MTL
1184 Rue Sainte-Catherine O Bureau 101,
Montreal, QC, H3B 1K1
(514) 508-9139
Emp Here 50   *Sales* 3,064,349
SIC 7629 Electrical repair shops

D-U-N-S 24-848-9366   (BR)
A.S.A.P. SECURED INC
1255 Rue Peel Bureau 1101, Montreal, QC,
H3B 2T9
(514) 868-0202
Emp Here 200
SIC 7381 Detective and armored car services

D-U-N-S 25-245-6827   (BR)
AGF MANAGEMENT LIMITED
1 Place Ville-Marie Unite 1630, Montreal, QC,
H3B 2B6
(514) 982-0070
Emp Here 22
SIC 6282 Investment advice

D-U-N-S 24-870-3944   (BR)
AON CANADA INC
700 Rue De La Gauchetiere O Unite 1800,
Montreal, QC, H3B 0A5
(514) 842-5000
Emp Here 225
SIC 6411 Insurance agents, brokers, and service

D-U-N-S 20-563-2990   (BR)
AON CONSULTING INC

GROUPE CONSEIL AON
700 Rue De La Gauchetiere O Bureau 1900,
Montreal, QC, H3B 0A7
(514) 845-6231
Emp Here 500
SIC 8999 Services, nec

D-U-N-S 25-496-6245   (HQ)
AON PARIZEAU INC
700 Rue De La Gauchetiere O Bureau 1600,
Montreal, QC, H3B 0A4
(514) 842-5000
Emp Here 200   *Emp Total* 67,562
Sales 18,532,018
SIC 6411 Insurance agents, brokers, and service
Pr Joanne Lepine
Treas Daniel Green
Dir Christine Lithgow
Dir Robert Parizeau

D-U-N-S 24-449-5771   (BR)
AON REED STENHOUSE INC
700 De La Gauchetiere O Bureau 1800, Montreal, QC, H3B 0A4
(514) 842-5000
Emp Here 650
SIC 6411 Insurance agents, brokers, and service

D-U-N-S 20-024-0450   (HQ)
ADDENDA CAPITAL INC
800 Boul Rene-Levesque O Bureau 2750,
Montreal, QC, H3B 1X9
(514) 287-0223
Emp Here 25   *Emp Total* 4,567
Sales 12,858,960
SIC 6282 Investment advice
Pr Pr Michael White
Ch Bd Carmand Normand
  Kathy Bardswick
  Daniel Burns
  Ann Marshal
  Roland Courtois
  Michel Therien
  Bruce West

D-U-N-S 20-286-4430   (BR)
AECOM CANADA LTD
1010 Rue De La Gauchetiere O Bureau 1400,
Montreal, QC, H3B 2N2
(514) 940-6862
Emp Here 50
SIC 8711 Engineering services

D-U-N-S 20-503-8771   (HQ)
ALCOA CANADA CIE
ALUMINERIE DE BAIE-COMEAU
1 Place Ville-Marie Bureau 2310, Montreal,
QC, H3B 3M5
(514) 904-5030
Emp Here 100   *Emp Total* 90
Sales 334,087,045
SIC 3334 Primary aluminum
Pr Jean-Francois Cyr
VP Amelie Moreault
VP Agnello Borim
VP Alain Taillefer
VP Louis Langlois
Sec Nicklaus A. Oliver
Genl Mgr Nicolas Dalmau

D-U-N-S 24-814-5336   (SL)
ALES GROUPE CANADA INC
1255 Rue University Bureau 1600, Montreal,
QC, H3B 3X4
(514) 932-3636
Emp Here 25   *Sales* 5,630,632
SIC 5131 Piece goods and notions
  Gerard Chantrot
  Rachid Yousri
Sec Lise Arsenault
Dir Raphael Desrues

D-U-N-S 20-317-5575   (BR)
ALTUS GROUP LIMITED
1100 Boul Rene-Levesque O Bureau 1600,

Montreal, QC, H3B 4N4
(514) 392-7700
Emp Here 100
SIC 6531 Real estate agents and managers

D-U-N-S 24-509-9783   (BR)
AVISCAR INC
(*Suby of* Avis Budget Group, Inc.)
1225 Rue Metcalfe, Montreal, QC, H3B 2V5
(514) 866-2847
Emp Here 20
SIC 7515 Passenger car leasing

D-U-N-S 24-206-6756   (BR)
AVIVA CANADA INC
AVIVA TRADERS
630 Boul Rene-Levesque O Bureau 900, Montreal, QC, H3B 1S6
(514) 876-5029
Emp Here 300
SIC 6331 Fire, marine, and casualty insurance

D-U-N-S 24-168-3804   (BR)
AVIVA INSURANCE COMPANY OF CANADA
AVIVA COMPAGNIE D'ASSURANCE DU CANADA
630 Boul Rene-Levesque O Bureau 700, Montreal, QC, H3B 1S6
(514) 399-1200
Emp Here 300
SIC 6331 Fire, marine, and casualty insurance

D-U-N-S 24-375-7528   (BR)
BBA INC
(*Suby of* Groupe BBA Inc)
630 Boul Rene-Levesque O Bureau 2500,
Montreal, QC, H3B 1S6
(514) 866-2111
Emp Here 100
SIC 8711 Engineering services

D-U-N-S 20-291-1236   (BR)
BCBG MAX AZRIA CANADA INC
960 Rue Sainte-Catherine O, Montreal, QC,
H3B 1E3
(514) 868-9561
Emp Here 25
SIC 5137 Women's and children's clothing

D-U-N-S 20-517-6782   (BR)
BDO CANADA LLP
MONTREAL ACCOUNTING
1000 Rue De La Gauchetiere O Bureau 200,
Montreal, QC, H3B 4W5
(514) 931-0841
Emp Here 125
SIC 8721 Accounting, auditing, and bookkeeping

D-U-N-S 25-021-1190   (BR)
BANK OF NOVA SCOTIA, THE
SCOTIABANK
1111 Rue Sainte-Catherine O, Montreal, QC,
H3B 1J4

Emp Here 25
SIC 6021 National commercial banks

D-U-N-S 20-567-8415   (BR)
BANK OF MONTREAL
BMO
670 Rue Sainte-Catherine O, Montreal, QC,
H3B 1C1
(514) 877-8010
Emp Here 30
SIC 6021 National commercial banks

D-U-N-S 20-535-7788   (BR)
BANK OF MONTREAL
BMO
1205 Rue Sainte-Catherine O Bureau 2118,
Montreal, QC, H3B 1K7
(514) 877-6850
Emp Here 30
SIC 6021 National commercial banks

D-U-N-S 20-573-7310   (BR)
BANQUE LAURENTIENNE DU CANADA

BANQUE LAURENTIENNE
1100 Boul Rene-Levesque O, Montreal, QC,
H3B 4N4
(514) 874-0750
Emp Here 20
SIC 6021 National commercial banks

D-U-N-S 24-350-4755   (BR)
BANQUE NATIONALE DU CANADA
NATIONAL BANK OF CANADA-FACTORING GROUP
28e Etage 600, Rue De La Gauchetiere O,
Montreal, QC, H3B 4L2
(514) 394-4385
Emp Here 40
SIC 6153 Short-term business credit institutions, except agricultural

D-U-N-S 24-365-1689   (BR)
BANQUE NATIONALE DU CANADA
ASSURANCE VIE BANQUE NATIONALE
1100 Boul Robert-Bourassa Unite 12e, Montreal, QC, H3B 3A5
(514) 871-7500
Emp Here 50
SIC 6311 Life insurance

D-U-N-S 20-837-2453   (BR)
BANQUE NATIONALE DU CANADA
ALTANIRA SECURITIES
1100 Boul Robert-Bourassa Bureau 12e,
Montreal, QC, H3B 3A5
(514) 394-5000
Emp Here 180
SIC 6531 Real estate agents and managers

D-U-N-S 20-882-6339   (HQ)
BANQUE DE DEVELOPPEMENT DU CANADA
BDC VENTURE CAPITAL
5 Place Ville-Marie Bureau 400, Montreal, QC,
H3B 5E7
(514) 283-5904
Emp Here 750   *Emp Total* 570,000
Sales 777,423,156
SIC 6141 Personal credit institutions
Pr Pr Jean-Rene Halde
  Paul Buron
Ex VP Pierre Dubreuil
Ex VP Paul Kirkconnell
Sr VP Jerome Nycz
Sr VP Chantal Belzie
  Michel Bergeron
  Louise Paradis
  Thomas R. Spencer
Dir Eric Boyko

D-U-N-S 20-827-2455   (BR)
BANQUE DE DEVELOPPEMENT DU CANADA
BDC
5 Place Ville-Marie Bureau 12525, Montreal,
QC, H3B 2G2
(514) 496-7946
Emp Here 35
SIC 6141 Personal credit institutions

D-U-N-S 20-847-6114   (BR)
BENTALL KENNEDY (CANADA) LIMITED PARTNERSHIP
SERVICES IMMOBILIERS BENTALL
1155 Rue Metcalfe Bureau 55, Montreal, QC,
H3B 2V6
(514) 393-8820
Emp Here 50
SIC 6531 Real estate agents and managers

D-U-N-S 24-101-7354   (SL)
BESSEMER & LAKE ERIE RAILROAD
935 Rue De La Gauchetiere O Bureau 11,
Montreal, QC, H3B 2M9
(514) 399-4536
Emp Here 502   *Sales* 258,553,440
SIC 4011 Railroads, line-haul operating
  Hans Burkhard

D-U-N-S 25-358-8586   (BR)
BEST BUY CANADA LTD

FUTURE SHOP
(*Suby of* Best Buy Co., Inc.)
470 Rue Sainte-Catherine O, Montreal, QC,
H3B 1A6
(514) 393-2600
Emp Here 70
SIC 5731 Radio, television, and electronic stores

D-U-N-S 20-549-7329   (BR)
BLAKE, CASSELS & GRAYDON LLP
1 Place Ville-Marie Bureau 3000, Montreal,
QC, H3B 4N8
(514) 982-4000
Emp Here 120
SIC 8111 Legal services

D-U-N-S 24-355-1405   (BR)
BOILER INSPECTION AND INSURANCE COMPANY OF CANADA, THE
B I & I
800 Boul Rene-Levesque O Bureau 1735,
Montreal, QC, H3B 1X9
(514) 861-8261
Emp Here 35
SIC 6411 Insurance agents, brokers, and service

D-U-N-S 25-498-7142   (BR)
BORDEN LADNER GERVAIS LLP
BLG
(*Suby of* Borden Ladner Gervais LLP)
1000 Rue De La Gauchetiere O Bureau 900,
Montreal, QC, H3B 5H4
(514) 879-1212
Emp Here 300
SIC 8111 Legal services

D-U-N-S 25-978-1425   (BR)
BOUTIQUE LINEN CHEST (PHASE II) INC
LINEN CHEST
(*Suby of* Boutique Linen Chest (Phase II) Inc)
625 Rue Sainte-Catherine O Bureau 222,
Montreal, QC, H3B 1B7
(514) 282-9525
Emp Here 30
SIC 5719 Miscellaneous homefurnishings

D-U-N-S 25-905-9608   (BR)
BOUTIQUE TRISTAN & ISEUT INC
TRISTAN & AMERICA
1001 Rue Sainte-Catherine O, Montreal, QC,
H3B 1H2
(514) 271-7787
Emp Here 20
SIC 5651 Family clothing stores

D-U-N-S 24-101-7396   (SL)
BULUTH MISSABE & IRON RANGE RAILROAD
935 Rue De La Gauchetiere O Bureau 4eme,
Montreal, QC, H3B 2M9
(514) 399-4536
Emp Here 502   *Sales* 258,553,440
SIC 4011 Railroads, line-haul operating
Hans Burkhard

D-U-N-S 20-714-3681   (BR)
CIBC INVESTOR SERVICES INC
CIBC INVESTORS EDGE
1155 Boul Rene-Levesque O Bureau 1501,
Montreal, QC, H3B 2J6
(514) 876-3343
Emp Here 85
SIC 6282 Investment advice

D-U-N-S 25-293-8881   (BR)
CIBC WORLD MARKETS INC
CIBC WOOD GUNDY
1 Place Ville-Marie Bureau 4125, Montreal,
QC, H3B 3P9
(514) 392-7500
Emp Here 80
SIC 6211 Security brokers and dealers

D-U-N-S 24-378-6709   (HQ)
CN WORLDWIDE AMERIQUE DU NORD (CANADA) INC

CN WORLDWIDE
935 Rue De La Gauchetiere O, Montreal, QC,
H3B 2M9
(514) 399-5430
Emp Here 100   *Emp Total* 23,172
Sales 136,347,907
SIC 4011 Railroads, line-haul operating
Pr Keith Reardon

D-U-N-S 20-052-4267   (BR)
CAIN LAMARRE CASGRAIN WELLS, S.E.N.C.R.L.
(*Suby of* Cain Lamarre Casgrain Wells, S.E.N.C.R.L.)
630 Boul Rene-Levesque O Bureau 2780,
Montreal, QC, H3B 1S6
(514) 393-4580
Emp Here 50
SIC 8111 Legal services

D-U-N-S 20-715-6741   (BR)
CALIAN LTD
SED SYSTEMS ENGINEER, A DIV OF
700 Rue De La Gauchetiere O Bureau 26e,
Montreal, QC, H3B 5M2

Emp Here 300
SIC 7361 Employment agencies

D-U-N-S 25-108-4034   (BR)
CANACCORD GENUITY CORP
(*Suby of* Canaccord Genuity Group Inc)
1250 Boul Rene-Levesque O Bureau 2000,
Montreal, QC, H3B 4W8
(514) 844-5443
Emp Here 100
SIC 6211 Security brokers and dealers

D-U-N-S 20-572-9879   (BR)
CANADA POST CORPORATION
1100 Boul Rene-Levesque O, Montreal, QC,
H3B 4N4

Emp Here 20
SIC 4311 U.s. postal service

D-U-N-S 20-588-9061   (BR)
CANADIAN PACIFIC RAILWAY COMPANY
CPR
1100 Av Des Canadiens-De-Montreal Unite
215, Montreal, QC, H3B 2S2

Emp Here 40
SIC 4011 Railroads, line-haul operating

D-U-N-S 25-992-2375   (HQ)
CANADIAN ROYALTIES INC
NUNAVIK NICKEL PROJECT
800 Boul Rene-Levesque O Bureau 410, Montreal, QC, H3B 1X9
(514) 879-1688
Emp Here 65   *Emp Total* 4,468
Sales 21,158,603
SIC 1081 Metal mining services
Parviz Farsangi
Sec Marc-Andre De Seve
Dir James Xiang
Dir Tao Li
Dir Shu Zhang
Dir Wu Shu
Dir Ruobing Wang

D-U-N-S 20-178-1833   (BR)
CARTHOS SERVICES LP
OSLER HOSKIN & HARCOURT
1000 Rue De La Gauchetiere O Bureau 2100,
Montreal, QC, H3B 4W5
(514) 904-8100
Emp Here 150
SIC 8111 Legal services

D-U-N-S 24-096-9449   (SL)
CARTONS ST-LAURENT INC
SMURFIT STONE
630 Boul Rene-Levesque O Bureau 3000,
Montreal, QC, H3B 1S6
(514) 744-6461
Emp Here 1,000   *Sales* 202,111,440

SIC 2657 Folding paperboard boxes
Pr Pr Joseph J. Gurandiano
VP VP Craig A Hunt
    Marion Allaire
Dir Alain Dubuc
Dir Joseph H Wright

D-U-N-S 20-503-9589   (SL)
CASGRAIN & COMPAGNIE LIMITEE
1200 Av Mcgill College, Montreal, QC, H3B 4G7
(514) 871-8080
Emp Here 32   *Sales* 6,430,720
SIC 6211 Security brokers and dealers
Pr Guy R Casgrain
Ex VP Roger Casgrain
Sec Pierre Casgrain

D-U-N-S 24-707-2593   (BR)
CEGERTEC INC
CEGERTEC WORLEYPARSONS INC
(*Suby of* Ceger Inc)
630 Boul Rene-Levesque O Bureau 2940,
Montreal, QC, H3B 1S6
(514) 871-8196
Emp Here 20
SIC 8621 Professional organizations

D-U-N-S 20-127-2551   (BR)
CHAUSSURES BROWNS INC
BROWNS SHOES
(*Suby of* 90401 Canada Ltee)
1191 Rue Sainte-Catherine O, Montreal, QC,
H3B 1K4
(514) 987-1206
Emp Here 20
SIC 5661 Shoe stores

D-U-N-S 24-101-7552   (SL)
CHICAGO, CENTRAL & PACIFIC RAILROAD COMPANY (INC)
935 Rue De La Gauchetiere O, Montreal, QC,
H3B 2M9
(514) 399-4536
Emp Here 3,218   *Sales* 1,657,726,080
SIC 4011 Railroads, line-haul operating
Hans Burkhard

D-U-N-S 20-107-3496   (BR)
CINEPLEX ODEON CORPORATION
CINEMA BANQUE SCOTIA MONTREAL
977 Rue Sainte-Catherine O, Montreal, QC,
H3B 4W3
(514) 842-0549
Emp Here 200
SIC 7832 Motion picture theaters, except drive-in

D-U-N-S 25-371-3739   (BR)
CLUB DE BADMINTON & SQUASH ATWATER INC, LE
MANSFIELD CLUB ATHLETIQUE
(*Suby of* Club de Badminton & Squash Atwater Inc, Le)
1230 Rue Mansfield, Montreal, QC, H3B 2Y3
(514) 390-1230
Emp Here 70
SIC 7991 Physical fitness facilities

D-U-N-S 25-759-5579   (SL)
COFOMO INC
1000 Rue De La Gauchetiere O Bureau 1500,
Montreal, QC, H3B 4X5
(514) 866-0039
Emp Here 450   *Sales* 42,404,805
SIC 7379 Computer related services, nec
Regis Desjardins

D-U-N-S 20-884-2245   (SL)
COLLEGE RABBINIQUE DE MONTREAL OIR HACHAIM D'TASH
SEMINAIRE RABBINIQUE TASH MONTREAL
1250 Boul Rene-Levesque O, Montreal, QC,
H3B 4W8
(450) 430-6380
Emp Here 250   *Sales* 33,546,912
SIC 8221 Colleges and universities

Pr Pr Ference Lowy

D-U-N-S 24-251-5476   (SL)
COLLINS BARROW MONTREAL
625 Boul Rene-Levesque O Bureau 1100,
Montreal, QC, H3B 1R2
(514) 866-8553
Emp Here 60   *Sales* 2,626,585
SIC 8721 Accounting, auditing, and book-keeping

D-U-N-S 20-317-5356   (HQ)
COLOGIX CANADA INC
COLOGIX MONTREAL
1250 Boul Rene-Levesque O Bureau 3932,
Montreal, QC, H3B 4W8
(514) 908-0083
Emp Here 20   *Emp Total* 50
Sales 7,263,840
SIC 4899 Communication services, nec
Dir Grant Van Rooyen
Pr Sean Maskell
    Heidi Diemar
    Todd Coleman

D-U-N-S 20-762-2382   (HQ)
COMPAGNIE TRUST ROYAL, LA
(*Suby of* Royal Bank Of Canada)
1 Place Ville-Marie Bureau 600, Montreal, QC,
H3B 1Z5

Emp Here 50   *Emp Total* 79,000
Sales 459,781,440
SIC 6021 National commercial banks
Pr Gordon Nixon

D-U-N-S 20-883-5231   (HQ)
COMPAGNIE D'ASSURANCE SONNET
5 Place Ville-Marie Bureau 1400, Montreal,
QC, H3B 0A8
(514) 875-5790
Emp Here 210   *Emp Total* 2,000
Sales 148,110,221
SIC 6331 Fire, marine, and casualty insurance
Pr Rowan Saunders
Sec Michael Padfield
Dir Fin Philip Mather
Dir Gerard A. Hooper
Dir Michael P. Stramaglia
Dir John H. Bowey
Dir Richard M. Freebrough
Dir W. David Wilson
Dir Elizabeth Delbianco
Dir Barbara Fraser

D-U-N-S 20-180-0419   (BR)
COMPAGNIE DE TELEPHONE BELL DU CANADA OU BELL CANADA, LA
BCE I MC
1000 Rue De La Gauchetiere O Bureau 4100,
Montreal, QC, H3B 4W5
(514) 870-8777
Emp Here 50
SIC 8111 Legal services

D-U-N-S 20-580-5000   (BR)
COMPAGNIE DES CHEMINS DE FER NATIONAUX DU CANADA
935 Rue De La Gauchetiere O, Montreal, QC,
H3B 2M9
(514) 399-5430
Emp Here 20
SIC 4011 Railroads, line-haul operating

D-U-N-S 20-581-4861   (BR)
COMPAGNIE DES CHEMINS DE FER NATIONAUX DU CANADA
COMPAGNIE DES CHEMINS DE FER NATIONAUX DU CANADA
5 Place Ville-Marie Bureau 1100, Montreal,
QC, H3B 2G2
(514) 399-4811
Emp Here 75
SIC 4011 Railroads, line-haul operating

D-U-N-S 24-900-9374   (SL)
CONSULTANTS CANARAIL INC
CANARAIL

1100 Boul Rene-Levesque O Etage 10e, Montreal, QC, H3B 4N4
(514) 985-0930
Emp Here 100　　*Sales* 10,871,144
SIC 8711 Engineering services
Pr Pr Miguel Valero
Ex VP Harry Aghjayan
　Donald Gillstrom
VP Guillaume Genin
Pers/VP Gisele Ghossein
VP Fin Linda Belanger
Ch Bd Pierre Verzat
Dir Olivier Dezorme
Dir Arnaud Valranges

　　D-U-N-S 24-226-7180　　(BR)
DENTONS CANADA LLP
SERVICES FMC
(*Suby of* Dentons Canada LLP)
1 Place Ville-Marie Bureau 3900, Montreal,
QC, H3B 4M7
(514) 878-8800
Emp Here 300
SIC 8111 Legal services

　　D-U-N-S 25-801-0842　　(BR)
DESSAU INC
1060 Boul Robert-Bourassa Unite 600, Montreal, QC, H3B 4V3
(514) 281-1033
Emp Here 800
SIC 8711 Engineering services

　　D-U-N-S 20-535-8521　　(BR)
DUNDEE SECURITIES CORPORATION
DUNDEEWEALTH
1000 Rue De La Gauchetiere O Bureau 1100,
Montreal, QC, H3B 4W5
(514) 396-0333
Emp Here 40
SIC 6211 Security brokers and dealers

　　D-U-N-S 24-356-9386　　(BR)
ECONOMICAL MUTUAL INSURANCE COMPANY
*COMPAGNIE D'ASSURANCE MISSISQUOI,
LA*
5 Place Ville-Marie Unite 1400, Montreal, QC,
H3B 2G2
(514) 875-5790
Emp Here 300
SIC 6331 Fire, marine, and casualty insurance

　　D-U-N-S 24-205-8415　　(BR)
ELECTRONIC ARTS (CANADA) INC
EA SPORTS
(*Suby of* Electronic Arts Inc.)
3 Place Ville-Marie Bureau 12350, Montreal,
QC, H3B 0E7
(514) 448-8800
Emp Here 500
SIC 7371 Custom computer programming services

　　D-U-N-S 24-346-8514　　(SL)
ELFIQ INC
ELFIQ NETWORKS
(*Suby of* Solutions Victrix Inc, les)
1155 Boul Robert-Bourassa Suite 712, Montreal, QC, H3B 3A7
(514) 667-0611
Emp Here 23　　*Sales* 3,898,130
SIC 3669 Communications equipment, nec

　　D-U-N-S 20-182-7966　　(SL)
ELITE GROUP INC
1175 Place Du Frere-Andre, Montreal, QC,
H3B 3X9
(514) 383-4720
Emp Here 50　　*Sales* 15,467,668
SIC 5064 Electrical appliances, television and
radio
Pr Pr Danny Lavy
Sec Marie-Michele Normandeau
Treas Marla Ruttenberg

　　D-U-N-S 20-925-3590　　(BR)
ENTERPRISE RENT-A-CAR CANADA COM-

PANY
(*Suby of* The Crawford Group Inc)
1200 Rue Stanley, Montreal, QC, H3B 2S8
(514) 878-2771
Emp Here 60
SIC 7514 Passenger car rental

　　D-U-N-S 25-297-1593　　(BR)
ERNST & YOUNG INC
800 Boul Rene-Levesque O Bureau 1900,
Montreal, QC, H3B 1X9
(514) 875-6060
Emp Here 700
SIC 8721 Accounting, auditing, and bookkeeping

　　D-U-N-S 25-258-6318　　(BR)
ERNST & YOUNG LLP
(*Suby of* Ernst & Young LLP)
800 Boul Rene-Levesque O Bureau 1900,
Montreal, QC, H3B 1X9
(514) 875-6060
Emp Here 800
SIC 8721 Accounting, auditing, and bookkeeping

　　D-U-N-S 24-174-2662　　(BR)
ERNST & YOUNG LLP
(*Suby of* Ernst & Young LLP)
1 Place Ville-Marie Bureau 2400, Montreal,
QC, H3B 3M9
(514) 875-6060
Emp Here 700
SIC 8721 Accounting, auditing, and bookkeeping

　　D-U-N-S 24-890-4237　　(BR)
FAIRMONT HOTELS & RESORTS INC
FAIRMONT HOTEL LE REINE ELIZABETH
900 Boul Rene-Levesque O, Montreal, QC,
H3B 4A5
(514) 861-3511
Emp Here 700
SIC 7011 Hotels and motels

　　D-U-N-S 20-234-4672　　(BR)
FAIRMONT HOTELS INC
FAIRMONT THE QUEEN ELIZABETH
900 Boul Rene-Levesque O, Montreal, QC,
H3B 4A5
(514) 861-3511
Emp Here 800
SIC 7011 Hotels and motels

　　D-U-N-S 20-760-6526　　(SL)
FEDERAL LEASING CORPORATION LTD
CANPRO INVESTMENT
1010 Rue Sainte-Catherine O Bureau 1200,
Montreal, QC, H3B 3S3
(514) 282-1155
Emp Here 120　　*Sales* 14,724,000
SIC 6512 Nonresidential building operators
Pr Pr David J Azrieli

　　D-U-N-S 24-338-0115　　(BR)
**FEDERATION DES CAISSES DESJARDINS
DU QUEBEC**
*FEDERATION DES CAISSES DESJARDINS
DU QUEBEC*
1241 Rue Peel, Montreal, QC, H3B 5L4
(514) 875-4266
Emp Here 30
SIC 6062 State credit unions

　　D-U-N-S 24-970-6052　　(HQ)
FEDNAV INTERNATIONAL LTEE
*FEDERAL ATLANTIC LAKES LINE (FALL
LINE)*
1000 Rue De La Gauchetiere O Bureau 3500,
Montreal, QC, H3B 4W5
(514) 878-6500
Emp Here 55　　*Emp Total* 60
Sales 31,358,286
SIC 4412 Deep sea foreign transportation of
freight
Pr Pr Mark L Pathy
Dir John Grey Wilkinson
Dir Barry L.V. Gale

Dir Peter N. Boos

　　D-U-N-S 20-218-5476　　(HQ)
FEDNAV LIMITEE
CANARCTIC
1000 Rue De La Gauchetiere O Bureau 3500,
Montreal, QC, H3B 4W5
(514) 878-6500
Emp Here 125　　*Emp Total* 5
Sales 125,346,520
SIC 4412 Deep sea foreign transportation of
freight
　Laurence G. Pathy
Pr Pr Paul M. Pathy
Dir Brian Levitt
Dir J. John Peacock
Dir Georges H. Robichon
Dir John Weale
Dir John Paul Setlakwe
Dir Christopher D. De Caires

　　D-U-N-S 24-502-6505　　(BR)
FETHERSTONHAUGH & CO.
FETHERSTONHAUGH SMART & BIGGAR
1000 Rue De La Gauchetiere O Bureau 3300,
Montreal, QC, H3B 5J1
(514) 954-1500
Emp Here 55
SIC 8111 Legal services

　　D-U-N-S 25-324-2481　　(BR)
FIDELITY INVESTMENTS CANADA ULC
(*Suby of* Fmr LLC)
1000 Rue De La Gauchetiere O Bureau 1400,
Montreal, QC, H3B 4W5
(514) 866-7360
Emp Here 40
SIC 6726 Investment offices, nec

　　D-U-N-S 24-342-9888　　(BR)
FINANCIERE BANQUE NATIONALE INC
1155 Rue Metcalfe Bureau 1438, Montreal,
QC, H3B 4S9
(514) 843-3088
Emp Here 40
SIC 6062 State credit unions

　　D-U-N-S 24-465-9319　　(BR)
FINANCIERE BANQUE NATIONALE INC
NATIONAL BANK FINANCIAL
1 Place Ville-Marie Bureau 1805, Montreal,
QC, H3B 4A9
(514) 879-5200
Emp Here 48
SIC 6021 National commercial banks

　　D-U-N-S 24-141-4486　　(SL)
FULLER LANDAU SENCRL
1010 Rue De La Gauchetiere O Bureau 200,
Montreal, QC, H3B 2S1
(514) 875-2865
Emp Here 70　　*Sales* 3,064,349
SIC 8721 Accounting, auditing, and bookkeeping

　　D-U-N-S 20-879-1082　　(BR)
GDI SERVICES AUX IMMEUBLES INC
INDUSTRIES DE MAINTENANCE EMPIRE
705 Rue Sainte-Catherine O, Montreal, QC,
H3B 4G5
(514) 288-9994
Emp Here 25
SIC 7349 Building maintenance services, nec

　　D-U-N-S 24-336-2485　　(SL)
GP CANADA CO
(*Suby of* GP Strategies Corporation)
1100 Av Des Canadiens-De-Montreal Bureau
253, Montreal, QC, H3B 2S2
(514) 392-9143
Emp Here 88　　*Sales* 14,625,840
SIC 8741 Management services
　Daniel Miller

　　D-U-N-S 24-686-8975　　(BR)
GAP (CANADA) INC
BANANA REPUBLIC
(*Suby of* The Gap Inc)

777 Rue Sainte-Catherine O, Montreal, QC,
H3B 1C8
(514) 842-3509
Emp Here 50
SIC 5651 Family clothing stores

　　D-U-N-S 20-796-5406　　(BR)
GAP (CANADA) INC
GAP
(*Suby of* The Gap Inc)
705 Rue Sainte-Catherine O, Montreal, QC,
H3B 4G5
(514) 281-5033
Emp Here 30
SIC 5651 Family clothing stores

　　D-U-N-S 20-057-0450　　(BR)
GOWLING WLG (CANADA) LLP
1 Place Ville-Marie Bureau 3700, Montreal,
QC, H3B 3P4
(514) 878-9641
Emp Here 200
SIC 8111 Legal services

　　D-U-N-S 20-912-5678　　(BR)
GOWLINGS CANADA INC
(*Suby of* Gowlings Canada Inc)
1 Place Ville-Marie Bureau 3700, Montreal,
QC, H3B 3P4
(514) 878-9641
Emp Here 150
SIC 8111 Legal services

　　D-U-N-S 20-548-4020　　(HQ)
GROUPE DES MEDIAS TRANSCONTINENTAL DE LA NOUVELLE-ECOSSE INC
TRURO DAILY NEW, DIV OF
(*Suby of* Groupe Des Medias Transcontinental
de la Nouvelle-Ecosse Inc)
1 Place Ville-Marie Bureau 3315, Montreal,
QC, H3B 3N2
(514) 954-4000
Emp Here 25　　*Emp Total* 377
Sales 42,012,480
SIC 2711 Newspapers
Pr Pr Natalie Lariviere
　Francois Olivier
Sec Christine Desaulniers
Genl Mgr Benoit Huard

　　D-U-N-S 25-286-0630　　(HQ)
**GROUPE FACILITE INFORMATIQUE (GFI)
INC**
(*Suby of* 3330559 Canada Inc)
5 Place Ville-Marie Bureau 1045, Montreal,
QC, H3B 2G2
(514) 284-5636
Emp Here 100　　*Emp Total* 1
Sales 34,960,406
SIC 7371 Custom computer programming services
　Gary Butler

　　D-U-N-S 24-138-1123　　(BR)
GROUPE SANTE MEDISYS INC
1255 Rue University Bureau 900, Montreal,
QC, H3B 3X4

Emp Here 50
SIC 8099 Health and allied services, nec

　　D-U-N-S 20-714-6346　　(BR)
GROUPE SPORTSCENE INC
CAGE AU SPORT, LA
1212 Rue De La Gauchetiere O, Montreal,
QC, H3B 2S2
(514) 925-2255
Emp Here 80
SIC 5812 Eating places

　　D-U-N-S 24-810-7315　　(SL)
GROUPE D'ANALYSE LTEE
(*Suby of* Analysis Group, Inc.)
1000 Rue De La Gauchetiere O Bureau 1200,
Montreal, QC, H3B 4W5
(514) 394-4460
Emp Here 20　　*Sales* 1,824,018
SIC 8748 Business consulting, nec

D-U-N-S 24-422-5905   (BR)
GUARANTEE COMPANY OF NORTH AMERICA, THE
GUARANTEE COMPANY OF NORTH AMER-ICA, THE
1010 Rue De La Gauchetiere O Bureau 1560, Montreal, QC, H3B 2R4
(514) 866-6351
Emp Here 70
SIC 6411 Insurance agents, brokers, and service

D-U-N-S 25-200-4890   (BR)
HALF, ROBERT CANADA INC
ACCOUNTEMPS
(*Suby of* Robert Half International Inc.)
1 Place Ville-Marie Bureau 2330, Montreal, QC, H3B 3M5
(514) 875-8585
Emp Here 30
SIC 7361 Employment agencies

D-U-N-S 20-323-4448   (SL)
HANDS IN THE MIDDLE PRODUCTIONS INC
PRODUCTIONS MAINS AU MILIEU
1 Place Ville-Marie Bureau 3900, Montreal, QC, H3B 4M7
(514) 447-2141
Emp Here 50   *Sales* 3,866,917
SIC 7812 Motion picture and video production

D-U-N-S 25-393-1471   (BR)
HATCH CORPORATION
5 Place Ville-Marie Bureau 1400, Montreal, QC, H3B 2G2
(514) 861-0583
Emp Here 600
SIC 8711 Engineering services

D-U-N-S 20-193-6601   (BR)
HATCH LTD
5 Place Ville-Marie Bureau 1400, Montreal, QC, H3B 2G2
(514) 861-0583
Emp Here 600
SIC 8711 Engineering services

D-U-N-S 20-573-7195   (BR)
HYDRO-QUEBEC
700 Rue De La Gauchetiere O Bureau C01, Montreal, QC, H3B 4L1
(514) 397-3939
Emp Here 20
SIC 4911 Electric services

D-U-N-S 24-101-7511   (SL)
ILLINOIS CENTRAL RAILROAD
935 Rue De La Gauchetiere O Bureau 11, Montreal, QC, H3B 2M9
(514) 399-4536
Emp Here 3,218   *Sales* 1,713,287,600
SIC 4011 Railroads, line-haul operating
Dir Hans Burkhard

D-U-N-S 25-319-1894   (BR)
INDIGO BOOKS & MUSIC INC
CHAPTERS
(*Suby of* Indigo Books & Music Inc)
1171 Rue Sainte-Catherine O Bureau 777, Montreal, QC, H3B 1K4

Emp Here 100
SIC 5942 Book stores

D-U-N-S 24-324-8999   (HQ)
INFRA-PSP CANADA INC
1250 Boul Rene-Levesque O Bureau 900, Montreal, QC, H3B 4W8
(514) 937-2772
Emp Here 65   *Emp Total* 570,000
Sales 95,797,399
SIC 6282 Investment advice
Pr Andre Bourbonnais
VP Guthrie Stewart
VP Nathalie Bernier
Sec Alison Breen
Genl Mgr Jean-Francois Ratte

D-U-N-S 24-052-8240   (BR)
INVESTMENT INDUSTRY REGULATORY ORGANIZATION OF CANADA
ASSOCIATION CANADIENNE DES COURTIERS EN VALEURS MOBILIERES
5 Place Ville-Marie Bureau 1550, Montreal, QC, H3B 2G2
(514) 878-2854
Emp Here 50
SIC 8621 Professional organizations

D-U-N-S 20-118-8310   (BR)
IVANHOE CAMBRIDGE INC
IVANHOE CAMBRIDGE INC
1000 Rue De La Gauchetiere O Bureau 610, Montreal, QC, H3B 4W5
(514) 395-1000
Emp Here 25
SIC 6512 Nonresidential building operators

D-U-N-S 24-522-6449   (BR)
JOHNSTON-VERMETTE GROUPE CON-SEIL INC
JONHSTON-VERMETTE
625 Boul Rene-Levesque O Bureau 801, Montreal, QC, H3B 1R2
(514) 396-3550
Emp Here 25
SIC 8711 Engineering services

D-U-N-S 20-716-5007   (BR)
JONES LANG LASALLE REAL ESTATE SERVICES, INC
(*Suby of* Jones Lang Lasalle Incorporated)
1 Place Ville-Marie Bureau 2121, Montreal, QC, H3B 2C6
(514) 849-8849
Emp Here 20
SIC 6531 Real estate agents and managers

D-U-N-S 24-365-0426   (BR)
LENOVO (CANADA) INC
630 Boul Rene Levesque O Bureau 2330, Montreal, QC, H3B 1S6
(514) 390-5020
Emp Here 25
SIC 5734 Computer and software stores

D-U-N-S 20-276-7802   (BR)
MNP LLP
MNP S.E.N.C.R.L., S.R.L.
1155 Boul Rene-Levesque O Bureau 2300, Montreal, QC, H3B 2K2
(514) 932-4115
Emp Here 225
SIC 8721 Accounting, auditing, and bookkeeping

D-U-N-S 25-392-3346   (SL)
MACOGEP INC
1255 Boul Robert-Bourassa Bureau 700, Montreal, QC, H3B 3W1
(514) 223-9001
Emp Here 50   *Sales* 5,890,507
SIC 8711 Engineering services

D-U-N-S 20-576-4322   (BR)
MCCARTHY TETRAULT LLP
1000 Rue De La Gauchetiere O Bureau 2500, Montreal, QC, H3B 0A2
(514) 397-4100
Emp Here 200
SIC 8111 Legal services

D-U-N-S 25-357-8686   (BR)
MEDIAS TRANSCONTINENTAL INC
MEDIAS TRANSCONTINENTAL INC
1155 Boul Rene-Levesque O Bureau 100, Montreal, QC, H3B 4P7
(514) 287-1717
Emp Here 400
SIC 7389 Business services, nec

D-U-N-S 25-315-8489   (BR)
MERRILL LYNCH CANADA INC
(*Suby of* Bank of America Corporation)
1250 Boul Rene-Levesque O Bureau 3100, Montreal, QC, H3B 4W8

(514) 846-3500
Emp Here 100
SIC 6211 Security brokers and dealers

D-U-N-S 24-058-7407   (BR)
METROMEDIA CMR PLUS INC
METROVISION
1253 Av Mcgill College Bureau 450, Montreal, QC, H3B 2Y5

Emp Here 50
SIC 7311 Advertising agencies

D-U-N-S 20-698-5587   (BR)
MILLER THOMSON LLP
1000 Rue De La Gauchetiere O Bureau 3700, Montreal, QC, H3B 4W5
(514) 875-5210
Emp Here 100
SIC 8111 Legal services

D-U-N-S 24-059-0120   (BR)
MODIS CANADA INC
MODIS
1155 Boul Robert-Bourassa Unite 1410, Montreal, QC, H3B 3A7
(514) 875-9520
Emp Here 37
SIC 4899 Communication services, nec

D-U-N-S 25-056-3541   (BR)
MOORES THE SUIT PEOPLE INC
MOORES CLOTHING FOR MEN
(*Suby of* Tailored Brands, Inc.)
966 Rue Sainte-Catherine O, Montreal, QC, H3B 1E3
(514) 845-1548
Emp Here 20
SIC 5611 Men's and boys' clothing stores

D-U-N-S 20-015-8587   (HQ)
NAKISA INC
(*Suby of* 4538081 Canada Inc)
733 Rue Cathcart, Montreal, QC, H3B 1M6
(514) 228-2000
Emp Here 113   *Emp Total* 1
Sales 19,923,773
SIC 7371 Custom computer programming services
  Babak Varjavandi

D-U-N-S 24-127-3676   (SL)
NATIONAL BANK CORPORATE CASH MANAGEMENT FUND
1100 Boul Robert-Bourassa Unite 12e, Montreal, QC, H3B 3A5

Emp Here 20   *Sales* 8,049,120
SIC 6722 Management investment, open-end

D-U-N-S 25-102-0194   (SL)
NATIONAL BANK LIFE INSURANCE COMPANY INC
1100 Boul Robert-Bourassa Unite 12, Montreal, QC, H3B 3A5
(514) 871-7500
Emp Here 30   *Sales* 2,699,546
SIC 6411 Insurance agents, brokers, and service

D-U-N-S 25-869-4652   (SL)
NICHOLL PASKELL-MEDE INC
630 Boul Rene-Levesque O Bureau 1700, Montreal, QC, H3B 1S6
(514) 843-3777
Emp Here 50   *Sales* 4,304,681
SIC 8111 Legal services

D-U-N-S 24-489-7203   (BR)
NORTHBRIDGE FINANCIAL CORPORATION
1000 Rue De La Gauchetiere O, Montreal, QC, H3B 4W5
(514) 843-1111
Emp Here 120
SIC 6411 Insurance agents, brokers, and service

D-U-N-S 24-796-1514   (SL)

NORTON ROSE CANADA S.E.N.C.R.L., S.R.L.
A LIFE CHOICE (MARQUE DE COMMERCE)
1 Place Ville-Marie Bureau 2500, Montreal, QC, H3B 4S2
(514) 847-4747
Emp Here 500   *Sales* 59,551,150
SIC 8111 Legal services
Pt Norman Steinberg

D-U-N-S 24-677-5857   (BR)
OCEANEX INC
630 Boul Rene-Levesque O Bureau 2550, Montreal, QC, H3B 1S6
(514) 875-8558
Emp Here 100
SIC 4424 Deep sea domestic transportation of freight

D-U-N-S 20-212-4132   (SL)
ODESIA SOLUTIONS INC
1 Place Ville-Marie, Montreal, QC, H3B 4E7
(514) 876-1155
Emp Here 60   *Sales* 4,377,642
SIC 7379 Computer related services, nec

D-U-N-S 24-668-4013   (SL)
OFFICE DES CONGRES ET DU TOURISME DU GRAND MONTREAL INC, L'
ASSOCIATION TOURISTIQUE REGIONALE DE MONTREAL, L'
800 Boul Rene-Levesque O Bureau 2450, Montreal, QC, H3B 1X9
(514) 844-5400
Emp Here 69   *Sales* 876,117
SIC 8743 Public relations services

D-U-N-S 24-394-6022   (SL)
ORCKESTRA INC
ORCKESTRA
1100 Av Des Canadiens-De-Montreal Bureau 540, Montreal, QC, H3B 2S2
(514) 398-0999
Emp Here 150   *Sales* 10,944,105
SIC 7379 Computer related services, nec
Pr Louis Fournier

D-U-N-S 24-075-8552   (SL)
OSISOFT CANADA ULC
(*Suby of* Osisoft, LLC)
1155 Boul Robert-Bourassa Unite 612, Montreal, QC, H3B 3A7
(514) 493-0663
Emp Here 26   *Sales* 1,969,939
SIC 7372 Prepackaged software

D-U-N-S 24-680-6033   (BR)
OSLER, HOSKIN & HARCOURT LLP
1000 Rue De La Gauchetiere O Bureau 2100, Montreal, QC, H3B 4W5
(514) 904-8100
Emp Here 100
SIC 8111 Legal services

D-U-N-S 20-860-7085   (BR)
OXFORD PROPERTIES GROUP INC
1250 Boul Rene-Levesque O Bureau 410, Montreal, QC, H3B 4W8
(514) 939-7229
Emp Here 20
SIC 6512 Nonresidential building operators

D-U-N-S 25-840-9358   (BR)
PANTORAMA INDUSTRIES INC, LES
AUTHENTIQUE MAGASIN LEVI'S, L'
705 Rue Sainte-Catherine O, Montreal, QC, H3B 4G5
(514) 286-1574
Emp Here 30
SIC 5651 Family clothing stores

D-U-N-S 24-600-9146   (SL)
PINSONNAULT TORRALBO HUDON
630 Boul Rene-Levesque O Bureau 2700, Montreal, QC, H3B 1S6

Emp Here 50   *Sales* 4,304,681
SIC 8111 Legal services

D-U-N-S 24-168-0859   (BR)
POLARIS REALTY (CANADA) LIMITED
POLARIS IMMOBILIER
(*Suby of* Polaris Realty (Canada) Limited)
800 Boul Rene-Levesque O Bureau 1125, Montreal, QC, H3B 1X9
(514) 861-5501
Emp Here 20
SIC 6512 Nonresidential building operators

D-U-N-S 25-534-1166   (BR)
POSTMEDIA NETWORK INC
LA GAZETTE
1010 Rue Sainte-Catherine O Unite 200, Montreal, QC, H3B 5L1
(514) 284-0040
Emp Here 100
SIC 2711 Newspapers

D-U-N-S 20-309-5716   (BR)
PRICEWATERHOUSECOOPERS LLP
1250 Boul Rene-Levesque O Bureau 2800, Montreal, QC, H3B 4W8
(514) 205-5000
Emp Here 750
SIC 8721 Accounting, auditing, and bookkeeping

D-U-N-S 20-333-0733   (SL)
PRO2P SERVICES CONSEILS INC
GROUPE ALITHYA
700 Rue De La Gauchetiere O Bureau 2400, Montreal, QC, H3B 5M2
(514) 285-5552
Emp Here 22   *Sales* 1,459,214
SIC 7374 Data processing and preparation

D-U-N-S 24-915-7855   (SL)
QUEBEC STATISQUES
1200 Av Mcgill College Bur.1905, Montreal, QC, H3B 4J7
(514) 864-8686
Emp Here 48   *Sales* 5,626,880
SIC 8111 Legal services
Dir Stephane Mercier

D-U-N-S 20-356-6336   (BR)
QUEBECOR MEDIA INC
QUEBECOR NUMERIQUE
1100 Boul Rene-Levesque O 20e Etage, Montreal, QC, H3B 4N4
(514) 380-1999
Emp Here 75
SIC 7311 Advertising agencies

D-U-N-S 20-595-5706   (BR)
RBC DOMINION SECURITIES INC
RBC DOMINION VALEURS MOBILIERES
(*Suby of* Royal Bank Of Canada)
1 Place Ville-Marie Bureau 300, Montreal, QC, H3B 4R8
(514) 878-7000
Emp Here 200
SIC 8742 Management consulting services

D-U-N-S 25-404-0058   (BR)
RBC DOMINION SECURITIES INC
RBC DOMINION VALEURS MOBILIERES
(*Suby of* Royal Bank Of Canada)
1000 Rue De La Gauchetiere O Bureau 4000, Montreal, QC, H3B 4W5
(514) 878-5000
Emp Here 70
SIC 6211 Security brokers and dealers

D-U-N-S 20-584-9065   (BR)
RBC GENERAL INSURANCE COMPANY
RBC INSURANCES
(*Suby of* Royal Bank Of Canada)
1100 Boul Rene-Levesque O Bureau 710, Montreal, QC, H3B 4N4
(514) 954-1205
Emp Here 35
SIC 6399 Insurance carriers, nec

D-U-N-S 25-361-3194   (BR)
RGA LIFE REINSURANCE COMPANY OF CANADA

1255 Rue Peel Bureau 1000, Montreal, QC, H3B 2T9
(514) 985-5502
Emp Here 78
SIC 6311 Life insurance

D-U-N-S 24-667-6258   (HQ)
RAYMOND CHABOT INC
600 Rue De La Gauchetiere O Bureau 2000, Montreal, QC, H3B 4L8
(514) 879-1385
Emp Here 25   *Emp Total* 2,516
Sales 7,304,400
SIC 8111 Legal services
Pr Pr Jean Gagnon

D-U-N-S 25-257-8067   (BR)
REDBERRY FRANCHISING CORP
BURGER KING
500 Rue Sainte-Catherine O, Montreal, QC, H3B 1A6
(514) 861-3455
Emp Here 35
SIC 5812 Eating places

D-U-N-S 25-309-2480   (BR)
REITMANS (CANADA) LIMITEE
ADDITION-ELLE
724 Rue Sainte-Catherine O, Montreal, QC, H3B 1B9
(514) 954-0087
Emp Here 35
SIC 5621 Women's clothing stores

D-U-N-S 25-360-8574   (SL)
RESSOURCES MSV INC
1155 Boul Robert-Bourassa Unite 1405, Montreal, QC, H3B 3A7
(418) 748-7691
Emp Here 75   *Sales* 2,991,389
SIC 6519 Real property lessors, nec

D-U-N-S 24-346-3093   (BR)
ROTISSERIES ST-HUBERT LTEE, LES
(*Suby of* Cara Holdings Limited)
1180 Av Des Canadiens-De-Montreal, Montreal, QC, H3B 2S2
(514) 866-0500
Emp Here 90
SIC 5812 Eating places

D-U-N-S 25-309-9394   (BR)
ROYAL BANK OF CANADA
RBC
(*Suby of* Royal Bank Of Canada)
1140 Rue Sainte-Catherine O Bureau 7, Montreal, QC, H3B 1H7
(514) 874-3043
Emp Here 24
SIC 6021 National commercial banks

D-U-N-S 25-018-9131   (BR)
ROYAL BANK OF CANADA
ROYAL DIRECT MONTREAL CALL CENTRE
(*Suby of* Royal Bank Of Canada)
630 Boul Rene-Levesque O Bureau 1384, Montreal, QC, H3B 1S6
(877) 244-2100
Emp Here 60
SIC 7389 Business services, nec

D-U-N-S 20-852-1661   (BR)
S & E SERVICES LIMITED PARTNERSHIP
(*Suby of* S & E Services Limited Partnership)
1155 Boul Rene-Levesque O Unite 4000, Montreal, QC, H3B 3V2
(514) 397-3196
Emp Here 49
SIC 8741 Management services

D-U-N-S 24-353-1209   (SL)
SDL INTERNATIONAL (CANADA) INC
ALPNET CANADA
1155 Rue Metcalfe Bureau 1200, Montreal, QC, H3B 2V6
(514) 844-2577
Emp Here 200   *Sales* 9,703,773
SIC 7389 Business services, nec

Pr Pr Frank Raco
Sec Frank Tortorici
Dir Nadya Lynne Bentley
Dir Dominic Lavelle

D-U-N-S 24-309-6307   (SL)
SNC-SNAM, S.E.N.C.
620 Boul Rene-Levesque O Bureau 3e, Montreal, QC, H3B 1N7
(514) 393-8000
Emp Here 50   *Sales* 10,753,700
SIC 3443 Fabricated plate work (boiler shop)
 Andrew Sharp
Mgr Kamal Naser

D-U-N-S 24-870-4983   (SL)
SAJELEX INC
1 Place Ville-Marie Bureau 1900, Montreal, QC, H3B 2C3

Emp Here 60   *Sales* 9,536,300
SIC 8741 Management services
Pr Pr Francis Meager

D-U-N-S 25-502-6684   (SL)
SERVICES CONSEILS INTELLISOFT INC
1 Place Ville-Marie Bureau 2821, Montreal, QC, H3B 4R4
(514) 393-3009
Emp Here 60   *Sales* 4,377,642
SIC 7379 Computer related services, nec

D-U-N-S 25-978-5657   (SL)
SHAWA ENTERPRISES CORP
SHAWA ENTERPRISES CANADA
1250 Rue University Bureau 921, Montreal, QC, H3B 3B8

Emp Here 55   *Sales* 6,773,040
SIC 6512 Nonresidential building operators
Pr Pr Hasan Shawa
VP Hazem Shawa

D-U-N-S 24-182-8693   (SL)
SIGMA ASSISTEL INC
1100 Boul Rene-Levesque O Bureau 514, Montreal, QC, H3B 4N4
(514) 875-9170
Emp Here 60   *Sales* 3,064,349
SIC 7389 Business services, nec

D-U-N-S 20-295-8356   (BR)
SOCIETE DES ALCOOLS DU QUEBEC
SOCIETE DES ALCOOLS DU QUEBEC
677 Rue Sainte-Catherine O Unite M-31, Montreal, QC, H3B 5K4
(514) 282-9445
Emp Here 20
SIC 5921 Liquor stores

D-U-N-S 24-370-4785   (BR)
STANTEC CONSULTING LTD
1060 Boul Robert-Bourassa Bureau 600, Montreal, QC, H3B 4V3
(514) 281-1010
Emp Here 30
SIC 8711 Engineering services

D-U-N-S 20-589-6561   (BR)
STAPLES CANADA INC
BUREAU EN GROS
(*Suby of* Staples, Inc.)
895 Rue De La Gauchetiere O Bureau 240, Montreal, QC, H3B 4G1
(514) 879-1515
Emp Here 50
SIC 5943 Stationery stores

D-U-N-S 20-183-0416   (BR)
STARWOOD HOTELS & RESORTS, INC
SHERATON MONTREAL, LE
(*Suby of* Marriott International, Inc.)
1201 Boul Rene-Levesque O Bureau 217, Montreal, QC, H3B 2L7
(514) 878-2046
Emp Here 375
SIC 7011 Hotels and motels

D-U-N-S 24-358-3866   (BR)
STIKEMAN ELLIOTT LLP
1155 Boul Rene-Levesque O Unite B01, Montreal, QC, H3B 4P9
(514) 397-3000
Emp Here 501
SIC 8111 Legal services

D-U-N-S 24-799-1297   (BR)
STRAUSS, LEVI & CO. (CANADA) INC
LEVI STRAUSS & CO
705 Rue Sainte-Catherine O, Montreal, QC, H3B 4G5
(514) 286-1318
Emp Here 25
SIC 5651 Family clothing stores

D-U-N-S 24-865-9633   (HQ)
STUDIOS DESIGN GHA INC
GHA DESIGN
(*Suby of* Studios Design GHA Inc)
1100 Av Des Canadiens-De-Montreal Bureau 130, Montreal, QC, H3B 2S2
(514) 843-5812
Emp Here 25   *Emp Total* 50
Sales 3,118,504
SIC 7389 Business services, nec

D-U-N-S 24-974-0150   (BR)
SUN LIFE ASSURANCE COMPANY OF CANADA
SUN LIFE ASSURANCE COMPANY OF CANADA
1001 Rue Du Square-Dorchester Bureau 600, Montreal, QC, H3B 1N1
(514) 731-7961
Emp Here 100
SIC 6311 Life insurance

D-U-N-S 24-108-3161   (BR)
SUN LIFE ASSURANCE COMPANY OF CANADA
1155 Rue Metcalfe Bureau 20, Montreal, QC, H3B 2V9
(514) 866-6411
Emp Here 2,500
SIC 6311 Life insurance

D-U-N-S 20-577-6961   (SL)
SUN LIFE ASSURANCES (CANADA) LIMITEE
SUN LIFE FINANCIAL
1155 Rue Metcalfe Bureau 1024, Montreal, QC, H3B 2V9
(514) 866-6411
Emp Here 50   *Sales* 4,523,563
SIC 6411 Insurance agents, brokers, and service

D-U-N-S 20-113-8695   (HQ)
SYSTEMES MEDICAUX INTELERAD INCORPOREE, LES
INTELERAD
(*Suby of* Systemes Medicaux Intelerad Incorporee, Les)
895 Rue De La Gauchetiere O Bureau 400, Montreal, QC, H3B 4G1
(514) 931-6222
Emp Here 250   *Emp Total* 280
Sales 24,806,638
SIC 7371 Custom computer programming services
Pr Pr Randall Oka
Eng/Dir Richard Rubin
Sec Francois Laflamme
Dir Pascal Tremblay
Dir David Brassard

D-U-N-S 20-323-4435   (BR)
TD WATERHOUSE CANADA INC
TD WATERHOUSE PRIVATE INVESTMENT ADVICE
(*Suby of* Toronto-Dominion Bank, The)
1000 Rue De La Gauchetiere O Bureau 2600, Montreal, QC, H3B 4W5
(514) 289-8400
Emp Here 60

SIC 6282 Investment advice

D-U-N-S 20-844-8212   (BR)
TD WATERHOUSE CANADA INC
CONSEILS DE PLACEMENTS PRIVES GESTION DE PATRIMOINE TD
(*Suby of* Toronto-Dominion Bank, The)
1000 Rue De La Gauchetiere O Bureau 2600, Montreal, QC, H3B 4W5
(514) 842-0707
Emp Here 33
SIC 6211 Security brokers and dealers

D-U-N-S 20-555-8856   (BR)
TELUS COMMUNICATIONS (QUEBEC) INC
630 Boul Rene-Levesque O Bureau 2200, Montreal, QC, H3B 1S6
(514) 242-8870
Emp Here 200
SIC 4899 Communication services, nec

D-U-N-S 24-423-0517   (HQ)
TELUS SOLUTIONS EN SANTE INC
TELUS HEALTH WOLF EMR
22e Etage 630, Boul Rene-Levesque O, Montreal, QC, H3B 1S6
(514) 665-3050
Emp Here 50   *Emp Total* 51,250
Sales 276,420,694
SIC 7372 Prepackaged software
Pr Pr Paul Lepage
Ex VP Josh Blair
Sec Monique Mercier

D-U-N-S 20-763-4510   (HQ)
TRANSCONTINENTAL PRINTING INC
ABONNEMENT QUEBEC & DESSIN
1 Place Ville-Marie Bureau 3240, Montreal, QC, H3B 3N2
(514) 954-4000
Emp Here 160   *Emp Total* 8,000
Sales 296,804,128
SIC 2752 Commercial printing, lithographic
Pr Brian Reid
Sec Christine Desaulniers
Dir Francois Olivier
Dir Donald Lecavalier

D-U-N-S 25-848-0953   (BR)
TRAVELERS INSURANCE COMPANY OF CANADA
THE DOMINION OF CANADA GENERAL INSURANCE COMPANY
1010 Rue De La Gauchetiere O Bureau 1100, Montreal, QC, H3B 2N2
(514) 875-0600
Emp Here 55
SIC 6351 Surety insurance

D-U-N-S 20-577-8363   (HQ)
V INTERACTIONS INC
ACTION TQS
(*Suby of* Groupe V Media Inc)
355 Rue Sainte-Catherine O, Montreal, QC, H3B 1A5
(514) 390-6100
Emp Here 120   *Emp Total* 1
Sales 15,171,497
SIC 4833 Television broadcasting stations
Pr Pr Maxime Remillard
Sec Tony Porrello

D-U-N-S 20-743-9089   (BR)
VALEURS MOBILIERES DESJARDINS INC
1 Place Ville-Marie Bureau 3401, Montreal, QC, H3B 3N6
(514) 876-1441
Emp Here 40
SIC 6211 Security brokers and dealers

D-U-N-S 20-323-3890   (BR)
VALEURS MOBILIERES DESJARDINS INC
DISNAT
1170 Rue Peel Bureau 105, Montreal, QC, H3B 4P2
(514) 842-2685
Emp Here 30
SIC 6211 Security brokers and dealers

D-U-N-S 24-019-7160   (HQ)
VIA RAIL CANADA INC
3 Place Ville-Marie Bureau 500, Montreal, QC, H3B 2C9
(514) 871-6000
Emp Here 270   *Emp Total* 570,000
Sales 102,144,980
SIC 4111 Local and suburban transit
Pr Pr Yves Desjardins-Siciliano
Ch Bd Paul G Smith
Pr Steve Del Bosco
 Jean Tierney
Dir David Hoff
Dir Denis Durand
Dir Stephen Mallory
Dir Ramona Rosanne Materi
Dir Jane Mowat
Dir William M Wheatley

D-U-N-S 20-179-5148   (BR)
VIA RAIL CANADA INC
895 Rue De La Gauchetiere O Bureau 429, Montreal, QC, H3B 4G1
(514) 989-2626
Emp Here 100
SIC 4111 Local and suburban transit

D-U-N-S 20-010-8525   (HQ)
VINCI PARK SERVICES (CANADA) INC
1 Place Ville-Marie Bureau 2131, Montreal, QC, H3B 2C6
(514) 874-1208
Emp Here 40   *Emp Total* 1
Sales 12,061,811
SIC 7521 Automobile parking
Pr Jean-Pierre Bonnet
Sec Louis Jacob
Dir Serge Clemente

D-U-N-S 24-342-2339   (BR)
VOLT CANADA INC
VMC GAME LABS
1155 Rue Metcalfe Bureau 2002, Montreal, QC, H3B 2V6
(514) 787-3175
Emp Here 200
SIC 8734 Testing laboratories

D-U-N-S 25-645-6476   (BR)
YVES ROCHER AMERIQUE DU NORD INC
INSTITUT DE BEAUTE YVES ROCHER
705 Rue Sainte-Catherine O, Montreal, QC, H3B 4G5
(514) 844-6223
Emp Here 20
SIC 7231 Beauty shops

D-U-N-S 20-908-8517   (HQ)
ZIM CIE DE SERVICES DE NAVIGATION INTEGREE (CANADA) LTEE
1155 Boul Rene-Levesque O Bureau 400, Montreal, QC, H3B 4R1
(514) 875-2335
Emp Here 35   *Emp Total* 4,050
Sales 14,466,392
SIC 4491 Marine cargo handling
Pr Volker Kluge
VP VP Asad Amath
Dir Rafael Ben Ari

D-U-N-S 20-717-1708   (BR)
ZURICH CANADIAN HOLDINGS LIMITED
ZURICH CANADA
1100 Boul Rene-Levesque O Bureau 1840, Montreal, QC, H3B 4N4
(514) 393-7222
Emp Here 30
SIC 6411 Insurance agents, brokers, and service

Montreal, QC H3C
Hochelaga County

D-U-N-S 24-365-7876   (SL)

4441028 CANADA INC
740 Rue Notre-Dame O Bureau 1120, Montreal, QC, H3C 3X6
(514) 871-1033
Emp Here 57   *Sales* 20,122,800
SIC 6712 Bank holding companies
Pr Pr Christopher Gillespie
Dir Karen Shanahan
Dir Maurice Vezina
VP VP Garry Mooney
Dir Jeremy P Bolger

D-U-N-S 24-424-4385   (BR)
ADM AGRI-INDUSTRIES COMPANY
ADM LYSAC, DIV
(*Suby of* Archer-Daniels-Midland Company)
995 Rue Mill, Montreal, QC, H3C 1Y5
(514) 937-9937
Emp Here 25
SIC 2079 Edible fats and oils

D-U-N-S 24-837-1023   (HQ)
AUTOCARS ORLEANS EXPRESS INC
740 Rue Notre-Dame O Bureau 1000, Montreal, QC, H3C 3X6
(514) 395-4000
Emp Here 35   *Sales* 13,059,965
SIC 4131 Intercity and rural bus transportation
Pr Pr Sylvain Langis
Treas Michel Masson
Dir Patrick Jeantet

D-U-N-S 24-901-5827   (HQ)
AUTODESK CANADA CIE
(*Suby of* Autodesk, Inc.)
10 Rue Duke, Montreal, QC, H3C 2L7
(514) 393-1616
Emp Here 325   *Emp Total* 9,000
Sales 114,171,882
SIC 7371 Custom computer programming services
 Deborah Lynn Clifford
Genl Mgr Susan Marie Pirri
Dir Kristen Marie Nordlof

D-U-N-S 20-573-7369   (BR)
BANQUE LAURENTIENNE DU CANADA
LBC
1390 Rue Barre, Montreal, QC, H3C 5X9
(514) 989-1487
Emp Here 35
SIC 6021 National commercial banks

D-U-N-S 24-327-8350   (SL)
CF CABLE TV INC
(*Suby of* Placements Peladeau Inc, Les)
612 Rue Saint-Jacques, Montreal, QC, H3C 4M8
(514) 380-1999
Emp Here 50   *Sales* 7,435,520
SIC 4841 Cable and other pay television services
Pr Pr Robert Depatie
VP Louis Morin
Sec Claudine Tremblay
 Pierre Karl Peladeau

D-U-N-S 20-553-5219   (HQ)
CMA CGM (CANADA) INC
DELMAS
740 Rue Notre-Dame O Bureau 1330, Montreal, QC, H3C 3X6
(514) 908-7001
Emp Here 78   *Emp Total* 90
Sales 40,055,424
SIC 4412 Deep sea foreign transportation of freight
Pr Rodolphe Saade
 Remi Samad
Dir Jean-Philippe Thenoz
Dir Olivier Nivoix

D-U-N-S 25-526-2354   (HQ)
CNIM CANADA INC
1499 Rue William, Montreal, QC, H3C 1R4
(514) 932-1220
Emp Here 51   *Sales* 7,915,564

SIC 3534 Elevators and moving stairways
Dir Jacques Rompre
Pr Philipe Demigne
Sec Didier Rauld
Genl Mgr Bernard Dabezies

D-U-N-S 20-417-1508   (SL)
CAMEO OPTICAL LTD
ASPEX GROUP
600 Rue Peel Bureau 302, Montreal, QC, H3C 2H1
(514) 938-3000
Emp Here 48   *Sales* 9,739,200
SIC 5049 Professional equipment, nec
Pr Pr Nonu Ifergan

D-U-N-S 20-255-1255   (BR)
CANADA MALTING CO. LIMITED
CANADA MALTAGE
205 Rue Riverside, Montreal, QC, H3C 2H9
(514) 935-1133
Emp Here 35
SIC 2083 Malt

D-U-N-S 24-459-6847   (BR)
CANADIAN IMPERIAL BANK OF COMMERCE
CIBC
610 Rue Saint-Jacques, Montreal, QC, H3C 1C7
(514) 845-2119
Emp Here 25
SIC 6011 Federal reserve banks

D-U-N-S 24-896-7234   (BR)
CANADIAN PACIFIC RAILWAY COMPANY
CPR
1100 Rue De La Gauchetiere, Montreal, QC, H3C 3E4
(514) 395-5151
Emp Here 500
SIC 4111 Local and suburban transit

D-U-N-S 20-519-1179   (BR)
CIMA+ S.E.N.C.
6740 Rue Notre-Dame O Bureau 900, Montreal, QC, H3C 3X6
(514) 337-2462
Emp Here 200
SIC 8711 Engineering services

D-U-N-S 24-351-9704   (SL)
ENTREPRISE DE COMMUNICATIONS TANK INC
55 Rue Prince, Montreal, QC, H3C 2M7
(514) 373-3333
Emp Here 40   *Sales* 4,815,406
SIC 7311 Advertising agencies

D-U-N-S 24-425-8914   (SL)
FRESCHE SOLUTIONS INC
EXCELSYSTEMS DEVELOPPEMENT DE LOGICIELS
995 Rue Wellington Unit9 200, Montreal, QC, H3C 1V3
(514) 747-7007
Emp Here 50   *Sales* 5,909,817
SIC 6712 Bank holding companies
Pr Andy Kulakowski
Sec Patrick Thibault
Dir Stephan Morency
Dir Irwin Kramer
Dir Stephane Marois
Dir Leonidas Lymberopoulos
Dir Martial Vincent
Dir Natalie Lariviere

D-U-N-S 24-636-7619   (SL)
GESTION ACCEO INC
75 Rue Queen Bureau 4700, Montreal, QC, H3C 2N6
(514) 288-7161
Emp Here 140   *Sales* 13,192,606
SIC 7379 Computer related services, nec
Pr Pr Gilles Letourneau
Dir Gisele Desrochers
Dir Robert Cloutier
Dir Andre Thompson

Dir Robert G. Beauchemin
Dir Rene Vachon
Dir Nathalie Le Prohon

D-U-N-S 20-501-6413   (HQ)
GILLESPIE-MUNRO INC
NAVIGATION GILLSHIP
740 Rue Notre-Dame O Bureau 1120, Montreal, QC, H3C 3X6
(514) 871-1033
Emp Here 57   *Emp Total* 2
Sales 21,085,642
SIC 4731 Freight transportation arrangement
 Christopher J Gillespie
VP VP Maurice Vezina
Dir Karen Shanahan
VP Gary Stephen
Dir P. Jeremy Bolger

D-U-N-S 20-031-4859   (BR)
GLOBAL UPHOLSTERY CO. INC
GLOBAL LE GROUPE
980 Rue Saint-Antoine O Bureau 200, Montreal, QC, H3C 1A8
(514) 866-4331
Emp Here 36
SIC 5021 Furniture

D-U-N-S 20-117-1126   (HQ)
GROUPE CAFE VIENNE 1998 INC, LE
CAFE VIENNE
1422 Rue Notre-Dame O, Montreal, QC, H3C 1K9
(514) 935-5553
Emp Here 56   *Emp Total* 60
Sales 13,742,400
SIC 6794 Patent owners and lessors
 Marcel Hachem

D-U-N-S 20-314-0272   (BR)
GROUPE GERMAIN INC
GROUPE GERMAIN HOTELS
(*Suby of* Gestion Famiger Inc)
120 Rue Peel Bureau 5, Montreal, QC, H3C 0L8
(514) 954-4414
Emp Here 20
SIC 7011 Hotels and motels

D-U-N-S 25-244-9285   (HQ)
GROUPE ORLEANS EXPRESS INC
740 Rue Notre-Dame O Bureau 1000, Montreal, QC, H3C 3X6
(514) 395-4000
Emp Here 42   *Sales* 17,985,920
SIC 4131 Intercity and rural bus transportation
Pr Pr Sylvain Langis
 Anne Lambusson

D-U-N-S 24-993-8937   (SL)
IMAGINA SOLUTIONS TECHNOLOGIQUES INC
75 Rue Queen Bureau 4700, Montreal, QC, H3C 2N6

Emp Here 100   *Sales* 10,145,000
SIC 7379 Computer related services, nec
Pr Pr Enzo Blasi

D-U-N-S 24-433-8505   (HQ)
LOGIBEC INC
LOGIBES GROUPE INFORMATIQUE
700 Rue Wellington Bureau 1500, Montreal, QC, H3C 3S4
(514) 766-0134
Emp Here 80   *Emp Total* 1
Sales 32,978,236
SIC 7372 Prepackaged software
Pr Marc Brunet
Sec David Smolen
Dir Howard Park
Dir Dave Kreter
Dir Travis Pearson
Dir Patrick Hampson

D-U-N-S 24-402-3735   (SL)
MARQUE D'OR INC
651 Rue Notre-Dame O, Montreal, QC, H3C

1H9
(514) 393-9900
Emp Here 50   *Sales* 4,304,681
SIC 8111 Legal services

D-U-N-S 25-685-4431   (HQ)
NSTEIN TECHNOLOGIES INC
75 Rue Queen Bureau 4400, Montreal, QC, H3C 2N6
(514) 908-5406
Emp Here 75   *Emp Total* 8,500
Sales 37,637,950
SIC 7371 Custom computer programming services
Pr Luc Filiatriault
VP Jean-Michel Texier
 Michel Lozeau
 Michel Lavigne
 Pierre Donaldson
 Rainer Busch
 Bruno Martel
 Andre Courtemanche

D-U-N-S 24-592-1309   (HQ)
NURUN INC
NURUN SERVICES CONSEILS
740 Rue Notre-Dame O Bureau 600, Montreal, QC, H3C 3X6
(514) 392-1900
Emp Here 120   *Emp Total* 17
Sales 136,867,658
SIC 7371 Custom computer programming services
VP Sylvio Rancourt
Sec Claude Renaud
Dir Ducan Bruce
Dir Ariel Marciano

D-U-N-S 20-004-5867   (BR)
OPEN TEXT CORPORATION
75 Rue Queen O Bureau 4400, Montreal, QC, H3C 2N6
(514) 281-5551
Emp Here 20
SIC 7371 Custom computer programming services

D-U-N-S 20-585-2838   (SL)
RESEAU QUEBECOR MEDIA INC
ALEX MEDIA SERVICES
612 Rue Saint-Jacques, Montreal, QC, H3C 4M8

Emp Here 26   *Sales* 4,742,446
SIC 7319 Advertising, nec

D-U-N-S 20-852-4806   (BR)
ROYAL BANK OF CANADA
EASTERN VISA CENTRE
(*Suby of* Royal Bank Of Canada)
Cp 11444 Succ Centre Ville, Montreal, QC, H3C 5J4

Emp Here 20
SIC 6021 National commercial banks

D-U-N-S 24-206-6699   (BR)
SAP CANADA INC
SAP LABS CANADA DIV OF
111 Rue Duke Bureau 2100, Montreal, QC, H3C 2M1
(514) 940-3840
Emp Here 25
SIC 7372 Prepackaged software

D-U-N-S 24-340-7231   (BR)
SAIL PLEIN AIR INC
BARON SPORTS
(*Suby of* Sail Plein Air Inc)
932 Rue Notre-Dame O, Montreal, QC, H3C 1J9

Emp Here 30
SIC 5941 Sporting goods and bicycle shops

D-U-N-S 20-760-5015   (SL)
SOCIETE D'HYPOTHEQUE DE LA BANQUE ROYALE

(*Suby of* Royal Bank Of Canada)
1 Place Ville-Marie, Montreal, QC, H3C 3A9
(514) 874-7222
Emp Here 700   *Sales* 184,740,450
SIC 6162 Mortgage bankers and loan correspondents
Pr Darren D. Walker
Sec Jessica Clinton
Dir Anthony Maiorino
Dir Douglas Gunton
Dir Wayne E. Bossert
Dir Andrea E. Bolger
Dir Ashif N. Ratanshi
Dir E. Gay Mitchell
Dir David John Agnew

D-U-N-S 20-651-6929   (HQ)
SODEXO QUEBEC LIMITEE
A VOTRE SANTE
930 Rue Wellington Bureau 100, Montreal, QC, H3C 1T8
(514) 866-5561
Emp Here 30   *Emp Total* 337
Sales 1,149,422,868
SIC 8741 Management services
Pr Barry Telford
VP Thomas R. Morse
Sec Michel J Lanctot

D-U-N-S 25-213-7781   (BR)
STAPLES CANADA INC
BUREAU EN GROS
(*Suby of* Staples, Inc.)
770 Rue Notre-Dame O, Montreal, QC, H3C 1J5
(514) 875-0977
Emp Here 60
SIC 5943 Stationery stores

D-U-N-S 24-835-2494   (SL)
STATIONNEMENT & DEVELOPPEMENT INTERNATIONAL INC
PARCOBEC
544 Rue De L'Inspecteur Bureau 200, Montreal, QC, H3C 2K9
(514) 396-6421
Emp Here 75   *Sales* 1,021,450
SIC 7521 Automobile parking

D-U-N-S 24-125-6879   (BR)
TELUS COMMUNICATIONS INC
TELUS SOLUTIONS D'AFFAIRES
111 Rue Duke Bureau 4200, Montreal, QC, H3C 2M1
(514) 392-0373
Emp Here 90
SIC 4899 Communication services, nec

D-U-N-S 24-933-5423   (SL)
TAMEC INC
L'ANNUAIRE DU TELECOPIEUR
980 Rue Saint-Antoine O Bureau 400, Montreal, QC, H3C 1A8

Emp Here 80   *Sales* 4,669,485
SIC 2741 Miscellaneous publishing

D-U-N-S 20-189-7886   (HQ)
TATA COMMUNICATIONS (CANADA) LTD
1555 Rue Carrie-Derick, Montreal, QC, H3C 6W2
(514) 868-7272
Emp Here 400   *Emp Total* 800
Sales 670,337,265
SIC 4899 Communication services, nec
Sec John Randall Freeman
Dir Ilangovan Gnanaprakasam
VP Sls David M. Ryan

D-U-N-S 25-623-5581   (BR)
THOMSON REUTERS CANADA LIMITED
EDITION YVON BLAIS CARSWELL
75 Rue Queen Bureau 4700, Montreal, QC, H3C 2N6
(514) 842-3937
Emp Here 65
SIC 2731 Book publishing

D-U-N-S 24-101-1399   (BR)
THOMSON REUTERS CANADA LIMITED
THOMSON COMPUMARK
75 Rue Queen Bureau 4700, Montreal, QC, H3C 2N6
(514) 393-9911
Emp Here 20
SIC 8732 Commercial nonphysical research

D-U-N-S 24-813-8745   (SL)
TRANSPORT NANUK INC
2100 Av Pierre-Dupuy Bureau 2060, Montreal, QC, H3C 3R5
(514) 597-0186
Emp Here 20   *Sales* 6,229,760
SIC 4424 Deep sea domestic transportation of freight
 Suzanne Paquin
VP Fin Michel Couture

D-U-N-S 20-534-4091   (BR)
UNIVERSITE DU QUEBEC
UNIVERSITE DU QUEBEC A MONTREAL
1440 Rue Saint-Denis, Montreal, QC, H3C 3P8
(514) 987-3092
Emp Here 3,500
SIC 8221 Colleges and universities

D-U-N-S 24-098-8902   (BR)
VILLE DE MONTREAL
VILLE DE MONTREAL
801 Rue Brennan Bureau 1200, Montreal, QC, H3C 0G4
(514) 872-2706
Emp Here 90
SIC 2741 Miscellaneous publishing

Montreal, QC H3G
Hochelaga County

D-U-N-S 25-212-2270   (SL)
3090-0872 QUEBEC INC
HURLEY'S IRISH PUB
1225 Rue Crescent, Montreal, QC, H3G 2B1
(514) 861-4111
Emp Here 60   *Sales* 1,824,018
SIC 5812 Eating places

D-U-N-S 20-717-4116   (BR)
4010205 CANADA INC
ISCANCO
1425 Boul Rene-Levesque O Bureau 406, Montreal, QC, H3G 1T7

Emp Here 20
SIC 6512 Nonresidential building operators

D-U-N-S 20-796-0167   (SL)
8649545 CANADA INC
ROSALIE
1232 Rue De La Montagne, Montreal, QC, H3G 1Z1
(514) 392-1970
Emp Here 70   *Sales* 2,115,860
SIC 5812 Eating places

D-U-N-S 20-180-1813   (SL)
9010-5826 QUEBEC INC
SIR WINSTON CHURCHILL PUB
1459 Rue Crescent, Montreal, QC, H3G 2B2
(514) 288-3814
Emp Here 100   *Sales* 2,991,389
SIC 5812 Eating places

D-U-N-S 25-847-7389   (BR)
BOUTIQUE JACOB INC
JACOB
(*Suby of* Boutique Jacob Inc)
1220 Rue Sainte-Catherine O, Montreal, QC, H3G 1P1
(514) 228-7986
Emp Here 20
SIC 5621 Women's clothing stores

D-U-N-S 20-790-8310   (SL)

COLLEGE O'SULLIVAN DE MONTREAL INC
1191 Rue De La Montagne, Montreal, QC, H3G 1Z2
(514) 866-4622
Emp Here 70   *Sales* 4,231,721
SIC 8244 Business and secretarial schools

D-U-N-S 20-010-3310   (BR)
COMPUTER SCIENCES CANADA INC
C S C
(*Suby of* Dxc Technology Company)
1360 Boul Rene-Levesque O Bureau 300, Montreal, QC, H3G 2W7

Emp Here 700
SIC 7379 Computer related services, nec

D-U-N-S 20-806-9703   (BR)
COUCHE-TARD INC
1287 Boul De Maisonneuve O, Montreal, QC, H3G 1M3
(514) 843-4458
Emp Here 25
SIC 5411 Grocery stores

D-U-N-S 25-327-7834   (HQ)
DUNDEE 360 REAL ESTATE CORPORATION
IMMOBILIERE DUNDEE 360
(*Suby of* Dundee Corporation)
1430 Rue Sherbrooke O, Montreal, QC, H3G 1K4
(514) 987-6452
Emp Here 20   *Emp Total* 490
Sales 2,334,742
SIC 8742 Management consulting services

D-U-N-S 20-593-7522   (SL)
FINANCE ELKAY (QUEBEC) INC
BEST WESTERN HOTEL EUROPA
1240 Rue Drummond, Montreal, QC, H3G 1V7
(514) 866-6492
Emp Here 65   *Sales* 2,845,467
SIC 7011 Hotels and motels

D-U-N-S 20-211-7565   (BR)
GROUPE ALITHYA INC
C.I.A
1350 Boul Rene-Levesque O Bureau 200, Montreal, QC, H3G 1T4
(514) 285-5552
Emp Here 131
SIC 7379 Computer related services, nec

D-U-N-S 25-307-3662   (BR)
GROUPE SPORTSCENE INC
CAGE AUX SPORTS RENE LEVESQUE, LA
1437 Boul Rene-Levesque O, Montreal, QC, H3G 1T7

Emp Here 30
SIC 5812 Eating places

D-U-N-S 25-825-9977   (BR)
HRC CANADA INC
HARD ROCK CAFE MONTREAL
(*Suby of* Hard Rock Heals Foundation, Inc.)
1458 Rue Crescent, Montreal, QC, H3G 2B6

Emp Here 80
SIC 5812 Eating places

D-U-N-S 24-669-1679   (BR)
HOLT, RENFREW & CIE, LIMITEE
HOLT RENFREW
1300 Rue Sherbrooke O, Montreal, QC, H3G 1H9
(514) 842-5111
Emp Here 200
SIC 5651 Family clothing stores

D-U-N-S 24-402-0301   (SL)
HOTEL EUROPA INC
1240 Rue Drummond, Montreal, QC, H3G 1V7
(514) 866-6492
Emp Here 80   *Sales* 3,502,114

SIC 7011 Hotels and motels

D-U-N-S 24-385-4622   (BR)
IBM CANADA LIMITED
(*Suby of* International Business Machines Corporation)
1360 Boul Rene-Levesque O Bureau 400, Montreal, QC, H3G 2W6
(888) 245-5572
Emp Here 150
SIC 7372 Prepackaged software

D-U-N-S 20-286-3499   (BR)
LES SERVICES EXP INC
GROUPE TEKNIKA (MC)
1441 Boul Rene-Levesque O Bureau 200, Montreal, QC, H3G 1T7
(514) 931-1080
Emp Here 100
SIC 8711 Engineering services

D-U-N-S 25-115-5396   (SL)
MAISON OGILVY INC, LA
OGILVY
(*Suby of* Edgefund Equities Inc)
1307 Rue Sainte-Catherine O, Montreal, QC, H3G 1P7
(514) 842-7711
Emp Here 50   *Sales* 4,742,446
SIC 6531 Real estate agents and managers

D-U-N-S 25-311-1066   (BR)
MCDONALD'S RESTAURANTS OF CANADA LIMITED
MCDONALD'S
(*Suby of* McDonald's Corporation)
1472 Rue Sainte-Catherine O, Montreal, QC, H3G 1S8
(514) 935-5159
Emp Here 70
SIC 5812 Eating places

D-U-N-S 24-248-5865   (BR)
MCGILL UNIVERSITY HEALTH CENTRE
1650 Av Cedar Bureau 111, Montreal, QC, H3G 1A4
(514) 934-1934
Emp Here 20
SIC 8062 General medical and surgical hospitals

D-U-N-S 25-371-0768   (HQ)
MICHAEL KORS (CANADA) HOLDINGS LTD
GESTION MICHAEL KORS (CANADA)
3424 Rue Simpson, Montreal, QC, H3G 2J3
(514) 737-5677
Emp Here 100   *Emp Total* 600
Sales 29,184,280
SIC 5632 Women's accessory and specialty stores
Dir John D Idol
Pr Pr Debra Margles
Sec Lee S Sporon
VP Fin Rosina Silla
Joseph B Parsons

D-U-N-S 20-588-6984   (BR)
MUSEE DES BEAUX-ARTS DE MONTREAL
1379 Rue Sherbrooke O, Montreal, QC, H3G 1J5
(514) 285-1600
Emp Here 200
SIC 8412 Museums and art galleries

D-U-N-S 20-288-0902   (BR)
NESTLE CANADA INC
NESPRESSO CANADA
2060 Rue De La Montagne Bureau 304, Montreal, QC, H3G 1Z7
(514) 350-5754
Emp Here 100
SIC 3634 Electric housewares and fans

D-U-N-S 20-760-3911   (SL)
RESTAURANT & BAR THURSDAY INC
HOTEL DE LA MONTAGNE THURSDAY'S
1430 Rue De La Montagne, Montreal, QC,

H3G 1Z5
(514) 288-5656
Emp Here 350   *Sales* 21,100,800
SIC 7011 Hotels and motels
Pr Pr Bernard Ragueneau

D-U-N-S 25-194-3080   (SL)
RESTAURANT NEWTOWN INC
NEWTOWN
1476 Rue Crescent, Montreal, QC, H3G 2B6
(514) 284-6555
Emp Here 100   *Sales* 2,991,389
SIC 5812 Eating places

D-U-N-S 20-502-9655   (HQ)
RONSCO INC
(*Suby of* Investissements Donnelgan Inc)
1440 Rue Sainte-Catherine O Bureau 712, Montreal, QC, H3G 1R8
(514) 866-1033
Emp Here 24   *Emp Total* 45
Sales 8,922,385
SIC 5088 Transportation equipment and supplies
Pr Pr Donald G Regan
VP Domenica Francescangeli
VP Kent Montgomery
Sec Mimma Francescangeli

D-U-N-S 20-762-3190   (HQ)
SCDA (2015) INC
1245 Rue Sherbrooke O Bureau 2100, Montreal, QC, H3G 1G3
(514) 499-8855
Emp Here 1,600   *Emp Total* 34,000
Sales 2,359,494,474
SIC 6311 Life insurance
Pr Charles Guay
Sec Penny J. Westman
Dir Bill Dawson
Dir Wayne Zuk
Dir Hung Ko

D-U-N-S 24-315-5277   (SL)
SAMORAIS LTEE
NOVOTEL MONTREAL
1180 Rue De La Montagne, Montreal, QC, H3G 1Z1
(514) 861-6000
Emp Here 55   *Sales* 2,407,703
SIC 7011 Hotels and motels

D-U-N-S 24-178-5666   (HQ)
SOCIETE CONSEIL GROUPE LGS
SERVICES-CONSEILS EN AFFAIRES IBM
(*Suby of* International Business Machines Corporation)
1360 Boul Rene-Levesque O Bureau 400, Montreal, QC, H3G 2W6
(514) 964-0939
Emp Here 300   *Emp Total* 380,300
Sales 134,615,405
SIC 8741 Management services
Pr Claude Guay
Sec Matthew R. Snell
Genl Mgr Daniel Renaud

D-U-N-S 24-345-5313   (BR)
UNIVERSITE CONCORDIA
CENTRE FOR CONTINUING EDUCATION
1600 Rue Sainte-Catherine O 1er Etage Fb-117, Montreal, QC, H3G 1M8
(514) 848-3600
Emp Here 175
SIC 8221 Colleges and universities

D-U-N-S 20-254-8400   (BR)
UNIVERSITE CONCORDIA
OFFICE OF RESEARCH
1455 Boul De Maisonneuve O Bureau Gm 900, Montreal, QC, H3G 1M8
(514) 848-2424
Emp Here 25
SIC 8732 Commercial nonphysical research

Montreal, QC H3H
Hochelaga County

D-U-N-S 24-935-9563   (SL)
3096-0876 QUEBEC INC
NOUVEL HOTEL, LE
1740 Boul Rene-Levesque O, Montreal, QC, H3H 1R3
(514) 931-8916
Emp Here 50   *Sales* 2,188,821
SIC 7011 Hotels and motels

D-U-N-S 20-703-6620   (BR)
3855155 CANADA INC
SUPERMARCHE P.A.
1420 Rue Du Fort, Montreal, QC, H3H 2C4
(514) 274-8008
Emp Here 100
SIC 5411 Grocery stores

D-U-N-S 24-312-4133   (SL)
9145-1971 QUEBEC INC
MERIDIEN VERSAILLES- MONTREAL, LE
1808 Rue Sherbrooke O, Montreal, QC, H3H 1E5
(514) 933-8111
Emp Here 100   *Sales* 4,377,642
SIC 7011 Hotels and motels

D-U-N-S 20-298-0736   (SL)
9284-3473 QUEBEC INC
RESTAURANT LA QUEUE DE CHEVAL, LE
1980 Rue Sherbrooke O Bureau 29, Montreal, QC, H3H 1E8
(514) 935-9993
Emp Here 50   *Sales* 1,532,175
SIC 5812 Eating places

D-U-N-S 25-975-4794   (SL)
9828-3573 QUEBEC INC
DAYS INN METRO-CENTRE
1005 Rue Guy, Montreal, QC, H3H 2K4
(514) 938-0810
Emp Here 70   *Sales* 3,064,349
SIC 7011 Hotels and motels

D-U-N-S 24-204-9406   (BR)
ASTRAL BROADCASTING GROUP INC
CHAINES TELE ASTRAL
(*Suby of* Astral Broadcasting Group Inc)
1616 Boul Rene-Levesque O Bureau 300, Montreal, QC, H3H 1P8
(514) 939-3150
Emp Here 100
SIC 4833 Television broadcasting stations

D-U-N-S 24-000-7497   (HQ)
ASTRAL MEDIA RADIO INC
ENERGIE
(*Suby of* Astral Media Radio Inc)
2100 Rue Sainte-Catherine O Bureau 1000, Montreal, QC, H3H 2T3
(514) 529-3200
Emp Here 50   *Emp Total* 782
Sales 68,884,550
SIC 4832 Radio broadcasting stations
Pr Pr Jacques Parisien
Claude Gagnon
Ian Greenberg
Andre Bureau

D-U-N-S 20-178-0363   (BR)
BANK OF NOVA SCOTIA, THE
SCOTIABANK
1922 Rue Sainte-Catherine O Bureau 300, Montreal, QC, H3H 1M4
(514) 846-8017
Emp Here 100
SIC 6021 National commercial banks

D-U-N-S 24-176-6542   (SL)
BELLEVUE PATHE HOLDINGS LTD
2100 Rue Sainte-Catherine O Bureau 1000, Montreal, QC, H3H 2T3
(514) 939-5000
Emp Here 600   *Sales* 65,130,900
SIC 7812 Motion picture and video production
Pr Pr Ian Greenberg

▲ Public Company   ■ Public Company Family Member   **HQ** Headquarters   **BR** Branch   **SL** Single Location

D-U-N-S 24-061-5943 (BR)
BEST BUY CANADA LTD
FUTURE SHOP
(*Suby of* Best Buy Co., Inc.)
2313 Rue Sainte-Catherine O Bureau 108,
Montreal, QC, H3H 1N2

Emp Here 100
SIC 5731 Radio, television, and electronic
stores

D-U-N-S 24-250-2409 (SL)
**CLINIQUE DE MEDECINE INDUSTRIELLE
& PREVENTIVE DU QUEBEC INC**
2155 Rue Guy Bureau 880, Montreal, QC,
H3H 2R9
(514) 931-0801
Emp Here 68　*Sales* 4,450,603
SIC 8093 Specialty outpatient clinics, nec

D-U-N-S 25-371-3697 (HQ)
**CLUB DE BADMINTON & SQUASH ATWA-
TER INC, LE**
MANSFIELD CLUB ATHLETIQUE
(*Suby of* Club de Badminton & Squash Atwa-
ter Inc, Le)
3505 Av Atwater, Montreal, QC, H3H 1Y2
(514) 935-2431
Emp Here 50　*Emp Total* 120
Sales 4,815,406
SIC 7991 Physical fitness facilities

D-U-N-S 20-277-5334 (BR)
COMMISSION SCOLAIRE DE MONTREAL
COMMISSION SCOLAIRE DE MONTREAL
1822 Boul De Maisonneuve O, Montreal, QC,
H3H 1J8
(514) 350-8049
Emp Here 30
SIC 8221 Colleges and universities

D-U-N-S 25-201-4204 (SL)
CONCUPISCO INC
CLARION HOTEL & SUITES CENTRE-VILLE
2100 Boul De Maisonneuve O, Montreal, QC,
H3H 1K6

Emp Here 50　*Sales* 2,188,821
SIC 7011 Hotels and motels

D-U-N-S 24-528-2736 (BR)
CUNNINGHAM LINDSEY CANADA LIMITED
1250 Rue Guy Bureau 1000, Montreal, QC,
H3H 2T4
(514) 938-5400
Emp Here 30
SIC 6411 Insurance agents, brokers, and ser-
vice

D-U-N-S 24-773-3186 (BR)
DOLLARAMA S.E.C.
DOLLARAMA
1616 Rue Sainte-Catherine O Unite 300, Mon-
treal, QC, H3H 1L7
(514) 904-2814
Emp Here 22
SIC 5331 Variety stores

D-U-N-S 24-817-9806 (BR)
ECOLE DE LANGUES DE L'ESTRIE INC
1819 Boul Rene-Levesque O Bureau 200,
Montreal, QC, H3H 2P5

Emp Here 30
SIC 8299 Schools and educational services,
nec

D-U-N-S 24-509-6714 (SL)
FULFORD RESIDENCE
1221 Rue Guy Bureau 27, Montreal, QC, H3H
2K8
(514) 933-7975
Emp Here 50　*Sales* 1,824,018
SIC 8361 Residential care

D-U-N-S 25-542-0580 (SL)
IMMEUBLES OCEANIE INC
MERIDIEN VERSAILLES

1808 Rue Sherbrooke O, Montreal, QC, H3H
1E5
(514) 933-3611
Emp Here 61　*Sales* 2,699,546
SIC 7011 Hotels and motels

D-U-N-S 25-880-3477 (BR)
INSTITUT HERZING DE MONTREAL INC
HERZING COLLEGE
1616 Boul Rene-Levesque O, Montreal, QC,
H3H 1P8
(514) 935-7494
Emp Here 26
SIC 8243 Data processing schools

D-U-N-S 20-764-0632 (HQ)
INSTITUT HERZING DE MONTREAL INC
COLLEGE HERZING
1616 Boul Rene-Levesque O, Montreal, QC,
H3H 1P8
(514) 935-7494
Emp Here 30　*Emp Total* 475
Sales 2,553,625
SIC 8249 Vocational schools, nec

D-U-N-S 25-747-4114 (SL)
L'ECOLE SACRE-COEUR DE MONTREAL
*THE SACRED HEART SCHOOL OF MON-
TREAL*
3635 Av Atwater, Montreal, QC, H3H 1Y4
(514) 937-7972
Emp Here 50　*Sales* 3,356,192
SIC 8211 Elementary and secondary schools

D-U-N-S 24-345-2880 (BR)
MCGILL UNIVERSITY HEALTH CENTRE
*HOPITAL DE MONTREAL POUR ENFANTS,
L'*
2300 Rue Tupper Bureau F372, Montreal, QC,
H3H 1P3
(514) 412-4307
Emp Here 2,000
SIC 8069 Specialty hospitals, except psychi-
atric

D-U-N-S 20-547-4369 (BR)
MCGILL UNIVERSITY HEALTH CENTRE
HOPITAL DE MONTREAL POUR ENFANTS
2300 Rue Tupper, Montreal, QC, H3H 1P3
(514) 934-1934
Emp Here 25
SIC 8069 Specialty hospitals, except psychi-
atric

D-U-N-S 25-458-2620 (SL)
RECHERCHE HEAD INC, LA
HEAD RESEARCH
1610 Rue Sainte-Catherine O Bureau 410,
Montreal, QC, H3H 2S2
(514) 938-4323
Emp Here 60　*Sales* 10,347,900
SIC 8733 Noncommercial research organiza-
tions
Pr Pr Melinda Head
VP VP Mirella Vendramin

D-U-N-S 25-299-2847 (BR)
SCDA (2015) INC
1600 Boul Rene-Levesque O, Montreal, QC,
H3H 1P9

Emp Here 30
SIC 6531 Real estate agents and managers

D-U-N-S 24-570-5397 (SL)
SAINE MARKETING INC
1600 Boul Rene-Levesque O Bureau 1800,
Montreal, QC, H3H 1P9
(514) 931-8236
Emp Here 900　*Sales* 165,001,808
SIC 8732 Commercial nonphysical research
Pr Pr Jean Saine
　Yves Masson
　Maurice Guertin

D-U-N-S 20-032-6994 (BR)
SECURITAS CANADA LIMITED
1980 Rue Sherbrooke O Bureau 300, Mon-

treal, QC, H3H 1E8
(514) 935-2533
Emp Here 1,500
SIC 7381 Detective and armored car services

D-U-N-S 24-256-7402 (HQ)
**SOCIETE POUR LES ENFANTS HANDI-
CAPES DU QUEBEC**
SEHQ
(*Suby of* Societe pour les Enfants Handicapes
du Quebec)
2300 Boul Rene-Levesque O, Montreal, QC,
H3H 2R5
(514) 937-6171
Emp Here 40　*Emp Total* 50
Sales 1,969,939
SIC 8322 Individual and family services

D-U-N-S 20-101-0662 (SL)
SOEURS GRISES DE MONTREAL, LES
*MAISON MERE DES SOEURS GRISES DE
MONTREAL*
1190 Rue Guy, Montreal, QC, H3H 2L4

Emp Here 130　*Sales* 8,536,402
SIC 8661 Religious organizations
VP VP Elizabeth Bagen

D-U-N-S 20-112-2392 (HQ)
TECHNICOLOR CANADA, INC
MPC CANADA
2101 Rue Sainte-Catherine O Bureau 300,
Montreal, QC, H3H 1M6
(514) 939-5060
Emp Here 100　*Emp Total* 156
Sales 27,200,281
SIC 7334 Photocopying and duplicating ser-
vices
Pr Louis Major
Sec Meggan Ehret
Dir Luc Thibaudeau
　Eric Belanger

D-U-N-S 24-813-6939 (HQ)
**TECHNICOLOR SERVICES CREATIFS
CANADA INC**
2101 Rue Sainte-Catherine O Bureau 300,
Montreal, QC, H3H 1M6
(514) 939-5060
Emp Here 600　*Emp Total* 156
Sales 55,613,314
SIC 7812 Motion picture and video production
Pr Pr Claude Gagnon
VP Alain Baccanale
VP Sls Nicolas Savoie
Dir Marc Gaudette
Dir Philippe Pelletier

D-U-N-S 24-383-8690 (BR)
TRADER CORPORATION
1600 Boul Rene-Levesque O Bureau 140,
Montreal, QC, H3H 1P9
(514) 764-4000
Emp Here 200
SIC 2721 Periodicals

D-U-N-S 20-736-0439 (BR)
TRAVELBRANDS INC
TRAVELBRANDS INC
2155 Rue Guy Bureau 1190, Montreal, QC,
H3H 2R9
(514) 935-8435
Emp Here 60
SIC 4725 Tour operators

Montreal, QC H3J
Hochelaga County

D-U-N-S 20-545-4437 (SL)
9123-2017 QUEBEC INC
CENTURY 21 IMMO PLUS
1982 Rue Notre-Dame O Bureau 2, Montreal,
QC, H3J 1M8

Emp Here 45　*Sales* 5,726,920

SIC 6531 Real estate agents and managers
Pr Mohamad Al Hajj

D-U-N-S 20-266-3431 (SL)
9264-7387 QUEBEC INC
VIANDE ET VIN GRINDER
1708 Rue Notre-Dame O, Montreal, QC, H3J
1M3
(514) 439-1130
Emp Here 50　*Sales* 1,532,175
SIC 5812 Eating places

D-U-N-S 25-234-0575 (BR)
COMMISSION SCOLAIRE DE MONTREAL
COMMISSION SCOLAIRE DE MONTREAL
555 Rue Des Seigneurs, Montreal, QC, H3J
1Y1
(514) 596-5730
Emp Here 45
SIC 8211 Elementary and secondary schools

D-U-N-S 25-780-9863 (SL)
GESTION COLIMAT INC
1600 Rue Notre-Dame O Bureau 213, Mon-
treal, QC, H3J 1M1
(514) 934-1515
Emp Here 400　*Sales* 39,264,000
SIC 7361 Employment agencies
Pr Pr Claude Laflamme
　Josee Veilleux

D-U-N-S 24-669-1463 (BR)
**GOVERNING COUNCIL OF THE SALVA-
TION ARMY IN CANADA, THE**
*GOVERNING COUNCIL OF THE SALVATION
ARMY IN CANADA, THE*
880 Rue Guy, Montreal, QC, H3J 1T4
(514) 932-2214
Emp Here 40
SIC 8699 Membership organizations, nec

D-U-N-S 24-333-6646 (BR)
**GOVERNING COUNCIL OF THE SALVA-
TION ARMY IN CANADA, THE**
*GOVERNING COUNCIL OF THE SALVATION
ARMY IN CANADA, THE*
2000 Rue Notre-Dame O, Montreal, QC, H3J
1M8
(514) 934-5615
Emp Here 30
SIC 8322 Individual and family services

D-U-N-S 20-180-9709 (BR)
METRO RICHELIEU INC
SUPER C
147 Av Atwater, Montreal, QC, H3J 2J4
(514) 939-3542
Emp Here 70
SIC 5411 Grocery stores

D-U-N-S 25-357-7340 (SL)
**NATABEC RECHERCHES ET TECHNOLO-
GIES INC**
MATIERES REFRACTAIRES PEGASE
1744 Rue William Bureau 200, Montreal, QC,
H3J 1R4
(514) 937-0002
Emp Here 50　*Sales* 4,523,179
SIC 3479 Metal coating and allied services

D-U-N-S 25-628-3581 (HQ)
PROGRAM DE PORTAGE INC, LE
PORTAGE CENTRE DE READAPTATION
(*Suby of* Program de Portage Inc, Le)
865 Place Richmond, Montreal, QC, H3J 1V8
(514) 939-0202
Emp Here 20　*Emp Total* 330
Sales 30,130,650
SIC 8093 Specialty outpatient clinics, nec
Pr Peter Howlett

D-U-N-S 24-208-5616 (BR)
PROGRAM DE PORTAGE INC, LE
*PROGRAM FOR MENTALLY ILL CHEMICAL
ABUSERS (MICA)*
2455 Av Lionel-Groulx, Montreal, QC, H3J 1J6
(514) 935-3431
Emp Here 300

SIC 8322 Individual and family services

D-U-N-S 24-245-8623   (SL)
VOLAILLES DES GRANDES-PRAIRIES INC, LES
(*Suby of* 3818641 Canada Inc)
370 Rue Des Seigneurs, Montreal, QC, H3J 2M9
(514) 939-2615
Emp Here 20   *Sales* 6,380,400
SIC 5144 Poultry and poultry products
Pr Pr Stanley Cons
 Michael Cons
VP VP Ronald Cons

Montreal, QC H3K
Hochelaga County

D-U-N-S 20-689-6602   (SL)
9143-1874 QUEBEC INC.
LES PENCHANTS
1751 Rue Richardson Bureau 1000, Montreal, QC, H3K 1G6

Emp Here 120   *Sales* 13,330,560
SIC 2015 Poultry slaughtering and processing
Pr Claude Mignon

D-U-N-S 20-210-5094   (HQ)
9273-9127 QUEBEC INC
383 Rue Bridge, Montreal, QC, H3K 2C7
(514) 935-5446
Emp Here 45   *Emp Total* 75
Sales 22,782,401
SIC 5147 Meats and meat products
Pr Pr Clauce Chatel
VP VP Gilles Chatel
VP VP Laurence Letourneau

D-U-N-S 20-223-8408   (HQ)
9278-3455 QUEBEC INC
GROUPE LAUZON
2715 Rue De Reading, Montreal, QC, H3K 1P7
(514) 937-8571
Emp Here 125   *Emp Total* 150
Sales 69,006,480
SIC 5147 Meats and meat products
VP Fin Ghislain Marcil
Pr Francine Lauzon

D-U-N-S 20-309-1079   (BR)
ARCTIC GLACIER INC
2760 Rue De Reading, Montreal, QC, H3K 1P5
(514) 935-7413
Emp Here 50
SIC 2097 Manufactured ice

D-U-N-S 20-762-7811   (HQ)
BOUTIQUE TRISTAN & ISEUT INC
TRISTAN
20 Rue Des Seigneurs, Montreal, QC, H3K 3K3
(514) 937-4601
Emp Here 150   *Emp Total* 75
Sales 50,589,058
SIC 5621 Women's clothing stores
 Gilles R. Fortin

D-U-N-S 20-213-3716   (HQ)
CANFAB PACKAGING INC
(*Suby of* Canfab Packaging Inc)
2740 Rue Saint-Patrick, Montreal, QC, H3K 1B8
(514) 935-5265
Emp Here 53   *Emp Total* 65
Sales 4,071,380
SIC 2655 Fiber cans, drums, and similar products

D-U-N-S 25-240-3027   (BR)
COMMISSION SCOLAIRE DE MONTREAL
COMMISSION SCOLAIRE DE MONTREAL
2120 Rue Favard, Montreal, QC, H3K 1Z7

(514) 596-5788
Emp Here 40
SIC 8211 Elementary and secondary schools

D-U-N-S 25-240-2748   (BR)
COMMISSION SCOLAIRE DE MONTREAL
COMMISSION SCOLAIRE DE MONTREAL
2001 Rue Mullins, Montreal, QC, H3K 1N9
(514) 596-5684
Emp Here 70
SIC 8211 Elementary and secondary schools

D-U-N-S 25-365-5666   (BR)
CONEX BUSINESS SYSTEMS INC
TOSHIBA SOLUTIONS D'AFFAIRES
1467 Rue Wellington, Montreal, QC, H3K 1V6
(514) 527-2381
Emp Here 62
SIC 5999 Miscellaneous retail stores, nec

D-U-N-S 25-832-1876   (BR)
COSTCO WHOLESALE CANADA LTD
COSTCO MONTREAL
(*Suby of* Costco Wholesale Corporation)
300 Rue Bridge, Montreal, QC, H3K 2C3
(514) 938-5170
Emp Here 150
SIC 5399 Miscellaneous general merchandise

D-U-N-S 24-365-2943   (HQ)
ECLAIRAGE LUMENPULSE INC
LUMENPULSE
(*Suby of* Lumenpulse Inc)
1751 Rue Richardson Bureau 1505, Montreal, QC, H3K 1G6
(514) 937-3003
Emp Here 150   *Emp Total* 587
Sales 32,484,413
SIC 3646 Commercial lighting fixtures

D-U-N-S 24-177-8880   (SL)
ENTREPRISES AMILIA INC, LES
AMILIA
1751 Rue Richardson Bureau 3.105, Montreal, QC, H3K 1G6
(514) 343-0004
Emp Here 52   *Sales* 5,326,131
SIC 7372 Prepackaged software
 Francois Gaouette
Dir Yves Lepine

D-U-N-S 25-646-3027   (BR)
FIBRES J. C. INC, LES
(*Suby of* 3667120 Canada Inc)
1305 Rue De Montmorency, Montreal, QC, H3K 2G3

Emp Here 30
SIC 5093 Scrap and waste materials

D-U-N-S 20-419-4799   (SL)
GESTION YVES MAGNAN INC.
2602 Rue Saint-Patrick, Montreal, QC, H3K 1B8
(514) 935-9647
Emp Here 105   *Sales* 4,052,015
SIC 5812 Eating places

D-U-N-S 20-919-0003   (BR)
GOVERNING COUNCIL OF THE SALVATION ARMY IN CANADA, THE
GOVERNING COUNCIL OF THE SALVATION ARMY IN CANADA, THE
1655 Rue Richardson, Montreal, QC, H3K 3J7
(514) 288-2848
Emp Here 30
SIC 8399 Social services, nec

D-U-N-S 20-363-7793   (SL)
GROUPE LUMENPULSE INC
LUMENPULSE
1751 Rue Richardson Bureau 1505, Montreal, QC, H3K 1G6
(514) 937-3003
Emp Here 587   *Sales* 64,278,377
SIC 3646 Commercial lighting fixtures
Pr Francois-Xavier Souvay
Ch Bd Pierre Larochelle

VP Fin Peter Timothaetos
Sec Marilyn Mauricio
Dir Leslie Raenden
Dir Olivier Desmarais
Dir Nicolas Belanger
Dir Michel Ringuet

D-U-N-S 20-289-1669   (BR)
INTERPUBLIC GROUP OF COMPANIES CANADA, INC, THE
FCB MONTREAL
(*Suby of* The Interpublic Group of Companies Inc)
1751 Rue Richardson Bureau 6.200, Montreal, QC, H3K 1G6
(514) 938-4141
Emp Here 46
SIC 7336 Commercial art and graphic design

D-U-N-S 20-289-0398   (HQ)
LUMENPULSE INC
LUMENPULSE GROUP
(*Suby of* Lumenpulse Inc)
1751 Rue Richardson Bureau 1505, Montreal, QC, H3K 1G6
(514) 937-3003
Emp Here 250   *Emp Total* 587
Sales 108,621,365
SIC 6712 Bank holding companies

D-U-N-S 20-651-0427   (BR)
MOORE CANADA CORPORATION
R.R. DONNELLEY
(*Suby of* R. R. Donnelley & Sons Company)
1500 Rue Saint-Patrick, Montreal, QC, H3K 0A3
(514) 415-7300
Emp Here 100
SIC 2759 Commercial printing, nec

D-U-N-S 25-412-4233   (BR)
QUINCAILLERIE NOTRE-DAME DE ST-HENRI INC
RONA
2400 Rue Saint-Patrick, Montreal, QC, H3K 1B7
(514) 931-2561
Emp Here 20
SIC 5251 Hardware stores

D-U-N-S 24-363-0329   (BR)
RAY-MONT LOGISTIQUES CANADA INC
1600 Rue Wellington, Montreal, QC, H3K 1V4
(514) 933-2957
Emp Here 70
SIC 4783 Packing and crating

D-U-N-S 20-416-5054   (SL)
RESTAURANT BAR-B INC
RESTAURANT BAR-B BARN
675 Rue Butler, Montreal, QC, H3K 3B3
(514) 937-2811
Emp Here 75   *Sales* 2,685,378
SIC 5812 Eating places

D-U-N-S 24-296-3304   (HQ)
RESTAURANT LES BON GARS INC
BAR-B-BARN
(*Suby of* Restaurant les Bon Gars Inc)
675 Rue Butler, Montreal, QC, H3K 3B3
(514) 937-2811
Emp Here 40   *Emp Total* 80
Sales 3,109,686
SIC 5812 Eating places

D-U-N-S 20-567-8969   (BR)
SOCIETE DES CASINOS DU QUEBEC INC, LA
325 Rue Bridge Bureau 1178, Montreal, QC, H3K 2C7
(514) 409-3111
Emp Here 350
SIC 7311 Advertising agencies

D-U-N-S 24-098-7896   (BR)
SYMCOR INC
650 Rue Bridge, Montreal, QC, H3K 3K9

(514) 787-4325
Emp Here 400
SIC 2621 Paper mills

D-U-N-S 25-446-8812   (BR)
YMCA DU QUEBEC, LES
YMCA DE POINTE ST CHARLES
255 Av Ash, Montreal, QC, H3K 2R1
(514) 935-4711
Emp Here 50
SIC 8399 Social services, nec

Montreal, QC H3L
Hochelaga County

D-U-N-S 20-544-3380   (SL)
3097-0230 QUEBEC INC
PHARMACIE BRUNET
148 Rue Fleury O, Montreal, QC, H3L 1T4
(514) 387-6436
Emp Here 30   *Sales* 5,024,256
SIC 5912 Drug stores and proprietary stores

D-U-N-S 25-849-4087   (SL)
9031-7520 QUEBEC INC
PLACEMENT R.H. QUEVILLON
500 Boul Gouin E Bureau 201, Montreal, QC, H3L 3R9
(514) 858-1883
Emp Here 450   *Sales* 45,216,000
SIC 7361 Employment agencies
Pr Pr Line Regis

D-U-N-S 24-129-3278   (BR)
AIR CANADA
Gd, Montreal, QC, H3L 3N6
(514) 422-7445
Emp Here 30
SIC 4581 Airports, flying fields, and services

D-U-N-S 20-298-7926   (BR)
BANQUE NATIONALE DU CANADA
451 Boul Henri-Bourassa E, Montreal, QC, H3L 1C5
(514) 387-6291
Emp Here 20
SIC 6021 National commercial banks

D-U-N-S 25-240-0650   (BR)
COMMISSION SCOLAIRE DE MONTREAL
ECOLE ST ANDRE APOTRE
215 Rue Prieur O, Montreal, QC, H3L 1R7
(514) 596-5366
Emp Here 30
SIC 8211 Elementary and secondary schools

D-U-N-S 25-298-5817   (BR)
COMMISSION SCOLAIRE DE MONTREAL
ECOLE PRIMAIRE AHUNTSIC
10615 Boul Saint-Laurent, Montreal, QC, H3L 2P5
(514) 596-5167
Emp Here 50
SIC 8211 Elementary and secondary schools

D-U-N-S 20-712-4251   (BR)
COMMISSION SCOLAIRE DE MONTREAL
COMMISSION SCOLAIRE DE MONTREAL
100 Rue Sauve E, Montreal, QC, H3L 1H1
(514) 596-5460
Emp Here 65
SIC 8211 Elementary and secondary schools

D-U-N-S 20-222-1388   (HQ)
COMPAGNIE MANUFACTURIERE JACK SPRATT INC
(*Suby of* Compagnie Manufacturiere Jack Spratt Inc)
9880 Av De L'Esplanade, Montreal, QC, H3L 2X5
(514) 382-1490
Emp Here 40   *Emp Total* 500
Sales 42,704,000
SIC 2339 Women's and misses' outerwear, nec
Pr Pr Stan Kivenko

VP VP Jack Kivenko

D-U-N-S 20-806-8952   (BR)
COUCHE-TARD INC
500 Rue Fleury E, Montreal, QC, H3L 1G5
(514) 389-0357
Emp Here 25
SIC 5411 Grocery stores

D-U-N-S 25-362-0702   (BR)
DOUBLETEX
9785 Rue Jeanne-Mance, Montreal, QC, H3L 3B6
(514) 382-1770
Emp Here 175
SIC 2211 Broadwoven fabric mills, cotton

D-U-N-S 20-856-7677   (SL)
ECOLE SECONDAIRE DUVAL INC
260 Boul Henri-Bourassa E, Montreal, QC, H3L 1B8
(514) 382-6070
Emp Here 60   *Sales* 4,012,839
SIC 8211 Elementary and secondary schools

D-U-N-S 24-053-7019   (HQ)
FONDATION DES SERVICES DE READAP-TATION L'INTEGRALE
(*Suby of* Fondation des Services De Readaptation L'Integrale)
75 Rue De Port-Royal E Bureau 110, Montreal, QC, H3L 3T1
(514) 387-1234
Emp Here 40   *Emp Total* 400
Sales 20,290,000
SIC 8361 Residential care
Pr Pr Joseph-Charles Giguere
VP Pierre Gabriele
Treas Pierre Major
Mng Dir Louis-Marie Marsan

D-U-N-S 24-327-1389   (BR)
GOUVERNEMENT DE LA PROVINCE DE QUEBEC
GOUVERNEMENT DE LA PROVINCE DE QUEBEC
35 Rue De Port-Royal E, Montreal, QC, H3L 3T1
(514) 873-1923
Emp Here 21
SIC 8748 Business consulting, nec

D-U-N-S 24-125-0286   (BR)
GROUPE RESTAURANTS IMVESCOR INC
10490 Rue Lajeunesse, Montreal, QC, H3L 2E5
(514) 385-0123
Emp Here 35
SIC 5812 Eating places

D-U-N-S 20-792-0315   (SL)
LE CENTRE DE SANTE ET DE SERVICES SOCIAUX DE BORDEAUX-CARTIERVILLE-SAINT-LAURENT
LE CSSS BORDEAUX-CARTIERVILLE-SAINT-LAURENT
555 Boul Gouin O, Montreal, QC, H3L 1K5
(514) 331-3020
Emp Here 2,003   *Sales* 193,769,500
SIC 8062 General medical and surgical hospitals
Genl Mgr Daniel Corbeil
Pr Genevieve Hotte
Sec Josee Desroche

D-U-N-S 24-046-0159   (BR)
LONDON LIFE INSURANCE COMPANY
COACHING FINANCIER TREK
560 Boul Henri-Bourassa O Bureau 209, Montreal, QC, H3L 1P4
(514) 334-8701
Emp Here 25
SIC 8742 Management consulting services

D-U-N-S 25-122-3306   (SL)
MAISON MERCER INC, LA
9875 Rue Meilleur, Montreal, QC, H3L 3J6
(514) 388-3551
Emp Here 20   *Sales* 3,648,035

SIC 5136 Men's and boy's clothing

D-U-N-S 25-485-2684   (BR)
PROVIGO INC
10455 Boul Saint-Laurent, Montreal, QC, H3L 2P1
(514) 387-7183
Emp Here 65
SIC 5411 Grocery stores

D-U-N-S 20-688-4335   (BR)
REITMANS (CANADA) LIMITEE
REITMANS
250 Rue Sauve O, Montreal, QC, H3L 1Z2
(514) 384-1140
Emp Here 200
SIC 5621 Women's clothing stores

D-U-N-S 20-289-7810   (SL)
SERVICE A LA CLIENTELE ALORICA LTEE
APAC SOLUTIONS GLOBALES
(*Suby of* Alorica Inc.)
75 Rue De Port-Royal E Bureau 240, Montreal, QC, H3L 3T1
(514) 385-4444
Emp Here 1,400   *Sales* 132,715,513
SIC 4813 Telephone communication, except radio
Pr Pr Pasquale (Pat) Di Franco
VP Fin Maria A. Albino
Dir Irving Shapiro

D-U-N-S 20-849-6729   (HQ)
SERVICES FINANCIERS NCO, INC
AGENCE DE RECOUVREMENT NCO
(*Suby of* Egs Shell Company, Inc.)
75 Rue De Port-Royal E Bureau 240, Montreal, QC, H3L 3T1
(514) 385-4444
Emp Here 1,000   *Emp Total* 162
Sales 153,217,470
SIC 7322 Adjustment and collection services
Pr Pr Pasquale Di Franco
   Maria A. Albino
Dir Irving Shapiro

D-U-N-S 25-308-9858   (BR)
SOCIETE DES ALCOOLS DU QUEBEC
SAQ
450 Boul Henri-Bourassa O, Montreal, QC, H3L 0A2
(514) 336-4266
Emp Here 20
SIC 5921 Liquor stores

D-U-N-S 24-958-5969   (SL)
THEODORE AZUELOS CONSULTANTS EN TECHNOLOGIE (TACT) INC
LE GROUPE TACT
9855 Rue Meilleur Bureau 200, Montreal, QC, H3L 3J6
(514) 877-0373
Emp Here 50   *Sales* 4,377,642
SIC 7379 Computer related services, nec

D-U-N-S 20-587-0632   (BR)
VILLE DE MONTREAL
BIBLIOTHEQUE AHUNTSIC
10300 Rue Lajeunesse, Montreal, QC, H3L 2E5
(514) 872-4025
Emp Here 30
SIC 8231 Libraries

Montreal, QC H3M
Hochelaga County

D-U-N-S 20-012-3656   (SL)
176441 CANADA INC
11177 Rue Hamon, Montreal, QC, H3M 3E4
(514) 335-0310
Emp Here 125   *Sales* 25,537,116
SIC 6712 Bank holding companies
Pr Pr Francois Angers
   Jean E. Clerk

Kamilia Mekhailm

D-U-N-S 20-573-7435   (BR)
BANQUE LAURENTIENNE DU CANADA
2490 Rue De Salaberry, Montreal, QC, H3M 1K9
(514) 334-7481
Emp Here 20
SIC 6021 National commercial banks

D-U-N-S 24-102-0390   (BR)
BIRON LABORATOIRE MEDICAL INC
APNAIR
1575 Boul Henri-Bourassa O, Montreal, QC, H3M 3A9
(514) 331-9279
Emp Here 250
SIC 8071 Medical laboratories

D-U-N-S 25-380-7879   (SL)
CENTRE D'URGENCE DE SALABERRY
2758 Rue De Salaberry, Montreal, QC, H3M 1L3
(514) 337-4772
Emp Here 50   *Sales* 3,283,232
SIC 8093 Specialty outpatient clinics, nec

D-U-N-S 20-033-8833   (BR)
COMMISSION SCOLAIRE DE MONTREAL
ECOLE FRANCOIS DE LAVAL
12050 Av Du Bois-De-Boulogne, Montreal, QC, H3M 2X9
(514) 596-5540
Emp Here 50
SIC 8211 Elementary and secondary schools

D-U-N-S 20-712-4632   (BR)
COMMISSION SCOLAIRE DE MONTREAL
COMMISSION SCOLAIRE DE MONTREAL
11400 Av De Poutrincourt, Montreal, QC, H3M 1Z7
(514) 596-5298
Emp Here 44
SIC 8211 Elementary and secondary schools

D-U-N-S 25-240-2417   (BR)
COMMISSION SCOLAIRE DE MONTREAL
COMMISSION SCOLAIRE DE MONTREAL
11600 Boul De L'Acadie, Montreal, QC, H3M 2T2
(514) 596-5285
Emp Here 20
SIC 8211 Elementary and secondary schools

D-U-N-S 25-240-6699   (BR)
COMMISSION SCOLAIRE DE MONTREAL
COMMISSION SCOLAIRE DE MONTREAL
11845 Boul De L'Acadie Bureau 281, Montreal, QC, H3M 2T4
(514) 596-5280
Emp Here 100
SIC 8211 Elementary and secondary schools

D-U-N-S 20-228-8346   (HQ)
LABORATOIRES OMEGA LIMITEE
11177 Rue Hamon, Montreal, QC, H3M 3E4
(514) 335-0310
Emp Here 100   *Emp Total* 1,142
Sales 9,703,773
SIC 2834 Pharmaceutical preparations
Ch Bd Yuichi Tamura
Pr Bruce W. Levins
Dir Fin Jonathon Singer
Dir Kenji Matsuyama
Dir Peter Kaemmerer

D-U-N-S 24-073-0601   (BR)
NAUTILUS PLUS INC
2676 Rue De Salaberry, Montreal, QC, H3M 1L3
(514) 337-9456
Emp Here 20
SIC 7999 Amusement and recreation, nec

D-U-N-S 20-591-3577   (HQ)
PATTERSON DENTAIRE CANADA INC
DEPOT DENTAIRE
1205 Boul Henri-Bourassa O, Montreal, QC, H3M 3E6

(514) 745-4040
Emp Here 200   *Emp Total* 7,000
Sales 76,316,892
SIC 5047 Medical and hospital equipment
Ch Bd Paul Guggenheim
Pr Pr Andre Desjardins
 R Stephen Armstrong
Dir Scott P Anderson

Montreal, QC H3N
Hochelaga County

D-U-N-S 24-600-2646   (SL)
138984 CANADA LTEE
KILO GATEAUX
6744 Rue Hutchison, Montreal, QC, H3N 1Y4
(514) 270-3024
Emp Here 60   *Sales* 3,137,310
SIC 2051 Bread, cake, and related products

D-U-N-S 24-562-3103   (SL)
CENTRE DE RECHERCHE INFORMATIQUE DE MONTREAL INC
COMPUTER RESEARCH INSTITUTE OF MONTREAL
405 Av Ogilvy Bureau 101, Montreal, QC, H3N 1M3
(514) 840-1234
Emp Here 60   *Sales* 3,283,232
SIC 8731 Commercial physical research

D-U-N-S 25-240-3233   (BR)
COMMISSION SCOLAIRE DE MONTREAL
COMMISSION SCOLAIRE DE MONTREAL
8000 Av De L'Epee, Montreal, QC, H3N 2E9
(514) 596-5175
Emp Here 30
SIC 8351 Child day care services

D-U-N-S 20-712-4574   (BR)
COMMISSION SCOLAIRE DE MONTREAL
COMMISSION SCOLAIRE DE MONTREAL
7700 Av D'Outremont, Montreal, QC, H3N 2L9
(514) 596-3410
Emp Here 50
SIC 8211 Elementary and secondary schools

D-U-N-S 20-712-4533   (BR)
COMMISSION SCOLAIRE DE MONTREAL
COMMISSION SCOLAIRE DE MONTREAL
415 Rue Saint-Roch, Montreal, QC, H3N 1K2
(514) 596-4572
Emp Here 50
SIC 8211 Elementary and secondary schools

D-U-N-S 25-233-5781   (BR)
COMMISSION SCOLAIRE ENGLISH-MONTREAL
SINCLAIR LAIRD SCHOOL
8380 Av Wiseman, Montreal, QC, H3N 2P6
(514) 279-9026
Emp Here 35
SIC 8211 Elementary and secondary schools

D-U-N-S 25-233-5302   (BR)
COMMISSION SCOLAIRE DE MONTREAL
COMMISSION SCOLAIRE DE MONTREAL
7941 Av Wiseman, Montreal, QC, H3N 2P2
(514) 596-4533
Emp Here 50
SIC 8211 Elementary and secondary schools

D-U-N-S 20-363-7947   (SL)
ENTRETIEN P.E.A.C.E. PLUS INC
ECOLIGHTING SOLUTIONS
950 Av Ogilvy Bureau 200, Montreal, QC, H3N 1P4
(514) 273-9764
Emp Here 100   *Sales* 2,918,428
SIC 7349 Building maintenance services, nec

D-U-N-S 25-488-3705   (BR)
GROUPE JEAN COUTU (PJC) INC, LE
(*Suby of* 3958230 Canada Inc)
930 Rue Jean-Talon O, Montreal, QC, H3N 1S8

---

(514) 276-3155
Emp Here 40
SIC 5912 Drug stores and proprietary stores

D-U-N-S 24-063-3664   (SL)
PHARMACIE SPYRIDON KOUTSOURIS
375 Rue Jean-Talon O, Montreal, QC, H3N 2Y8
(514) 272-5565
Emp Here 30   *Sales* 5,465,508
SIC 5912 Drug stores and proprietary stores
Owner Spyridon Koutsouris

D-U-N-S 24-177-5902   (BR)
PROVIGO DISTRIBUTION INC
LOBLAWS
375 Rue Jean-Talon O, Montreal, QC, H3N 2Y8
(514) 948-2600
Emp Here 350
SIC 5411 Grocery stores

D-U-N-S 20-233-4470   (SL)
SALAISON LEVESQUE INC
500 Av Beaumont, Montreal, QC, H3N 1T7
(514) 273-1702
Emp Here 30   *Sales* 10,652,250
SIC 5147 Meats and meat products
Pr Pr Regis Levesque
VP VP Annie Levesque

D-U-N-S 20-318-7778   (SL)
UNIFORMES LOFT INC, LES
ATELIER LOFT
6744 Rue Hutchison, Montreal, QC, H3N 1Y4
(514) 270-6044
Emp Here 50   *Sales* 2,845,467
SIC 5699 Miscellaneous apparel and accessory stores

Montreal, QC H3R
Hochelaga County

D-U-N-S 20-764-5318   (HQ)
COMMISSION DE LA CONSTRUCTION DU QUEBEC
CCQ
(*Suby of* Commission de la Construction du Quebec)
3530 Rue Jean-Talon O, Montreal, QC, H3R 2G3
(514) 341-7740
Emp Here 400   *Emp Total* 1,000
Sales 141,475,840
SIC 8611 Business associations
Pr Pr Andre Menard
Sec Michel Mclaughlin

Montreal, QC H3S
Hochelaga County

D-U-N-S 24-253-5920   (SL)
100979 CANADA INC
PARAMOUNT CONSTRUCTION & RENOVATION
2550 Ch Bates Bureau 110, Montreal, QC, H3S 1A7

Emp Here 40   *Sales* 10,248,960
SIC 1542 Nonresidential construction, nec
Pr Pr Antonio Baldassarre
Pasquale Buono

D-U-N-S 25-543-0340   (SL)
9074-8898 QUEBEC INC
GILTEX
3195 Ch De Bedford, Montreal, QC, H3S 1G3
(514) 376-6240
Emp Here 500   *Sales* 205,984,000
SIC 2342 Bras, girdles, and allied garments
Pr Kenneth Stewart

D-U-N-S 20-002-5745   (BR)

CANADIAN TIRE CORPORATION, LIMITED
CANADIAN TIRE CORPORATION, LTD
6700 Ch De La Cote-Des-Neiges Bureau 240, Montreal, QC, H3S 2B2
(514) 737-2954
Emp Here 49
SIC 5999 Miscellaneous retail stores, nec

D-U-N-S 24-815-2225   (SL)
CENTRE D'ACCUEIL FATHER DOWD
6565 Ch Hudson Bureau 217, Montreal, QC, H3S 2T7
(514) 341-1007
Emp Here 77   *Sales* 2,845,467
SIC 8361 Residential care

D-U-N-S 20-535-0585   (BR)
CENTRE DE SANTE ET DE SERVICES SOCIAUX DE LA MONTAGNE
CENTRE DE SANTE ET DE SERVICES SOCIAUX DE LA MONTAGNE
6560 Ch De La Cote-Des-Neiges, Montreal, QC, H3S 2A7
(514) 736-2323
Emp Here 25
SIC 8742 Management consulting services

D-U-N-S 25-298-5973   (BR)
COMMISSION SCOLAIRE DE MONTREAL
ECOLE BEDFORD
3131 Rue Goyer, Montreal, QC, H3S 1H7
(514) 736-3505
Emp Here 20
SIC 8211 Elementary and secondary schools

D-U-N-S 20-712-4368   (BR)
COMMISSION SCOLAIRE DE MONTREAL
ECOLE SAINT-PASCAL-BAYLON
6320 Ch De La Cote-Des-Neiges, Montreal, QC, H3S 2A4
(514) 736-8100
Emp Here 30
SIC 8211 Elementary and secondary schools

D-U-N-S 25-233-9536   (BR)
COMMISSION SCOLAIRE DE LA POINTE-DE-L'ILE
ECOLE FELIX LECLERC
6055 Av De Darlington, Montreal, QC, H3S 2H9
(514) 736-8130
Emp Here 58
SIC 8211 Elementary and secondary schools

D-U-N-S 20-302-6778   (SL)
GESTIONS MILLER CARMICHAEL INC
3822 Av De Courtrai, Montreal, QC, H3S 1C1
(514) 735-4361
Emp Here 540   *Sales* 130,062,000
SIC 6712 Bank holding companies
Miller Carmichael

D-U-N-S 25-687-6640   (HQ)
INGENIERIE CARMICHAEL LTEE
(*Suby of* Ingenierie Carmichael Ltee)
3822 Av De Courtrai, Montreal, QC, H3S 1C1
(514) 735-4361
Emp Here 36   *Emp Total* 540
Sales 62,965,084
SIC 8711 Engineering services
Miller Carmichael

D-U-N-S 20-885-0453   (SL)
L'HOPITAL DE READAPTION LINDSAY
6363 Ch Hudson, Montreal, QC, H3S 1M9
(514) 737-3661
Emp Here 330   *Sales* 37,029,250
SIC 8069 Specialty hospitals, except psychiatric
Pr Geraldine Gahan
Sec Catherine Duff-Caron
Treas Caroline Emblem
Dir Doreen Kane
Dir Judith Shea-Hamelin
Dir Rita Gallagher
Dir Jeanne Gagnon
Dir K Hutchings

D-U-N-S 24-687-1586   (BR)
L'INSTITUT DE READAPTATION GINGRAS-LINDSAY-DE-MONTREAL
L'INSTITUT DE READAPTATION GINGRAS-LINDSAY-DE-MONTREAL
6363 Ch Hudson, Montreal, QC, H3S 1M9
(514) 737-3661
Emp Here 100
SIC 8069 Specialty hospitals, except psychiatric

D-U-N-S 25-308-8249   (BR)
SOCIETE DES ALCOOLS DU QUEBEC
SOCIETE DES ALCOOLS DU QUEBEC
5252 Ch De La Cote-Des-Neiges Local 112, Montreal, QC, H3S 2A9
(514) 738-6375
Emp Here 47
SIC 5921 Liquor stores

D-U-N-S 20-791-4656   (SL)
YESHIVA GEDOLAH L'ECOLE D'ETUDES SUPERIEURES DE MONTREAL
CENTRE D'ETUDES KOLEL BOKER
6155 Ch Deacon, Montreal, QC, H3S 2P4
(514) 735-6961
Emp Here 70   *Sales* 4,669,485
SIC 8211 Elementary and secondary schools

Montreal, QC H3T
Hochelaga County

D-U-N-S 20-794-1345   (SL)
ASSOCIATION DES GESTIONNAIRES DE L'HOPITAL SAINTE-JUSTINE
3175 Ch De La Cote-Sainte-Catherine, Montreal, QC, H3T 1C5
(514) 345-4931
Emp Here 3,500   *Sales* 392,712,950
SIC 8069 Specialty hospitals, except psychiatric
Pr Franceen Alovisi
VP Monique Blandin
Sec Gratien Roussel
Treas Marchel Cusson

D-U-N-S 20-567-8332   (BR)
BANK OF MONTREAL
SUCCURSALE COTE DES NEIGE ET QUEEN MARY
5145 Ch De La Cote-Des-Neiges, Montreal, QC, H3T 1X9
(514) 341-2240
Emp Here 20
SIC 6021 National commercial banks

D-U-N-S 25-298-8126   (BR)
BANQUE NATIONALE DU CANADA
5355 Ch De La Cote-Des-Neiges, Montreal, QC, H3T 1Y4
(514) 340-9550
Emp Here 35
SIC 6021 National commercial banks

D-U-N-S 20-795-3253   (BR)
BOULANGERIE AU PAIN DORE LTEE
(*Suby of* 1852-5402 Quebec Inc)
5214 Ch De La Cote-Des-Neiges, Montreal, QC, H3T 1X8
(514) 342-8995
Emp Here 20
SIC 2051 Bread, cake, and related products

D-U-N-S 20-355-5347   (SL)
CENTRE COMMUNAUTAIRE DE LOISIR DE LA COTE-DES-NEIGES
5347 Ch De La Cote-Des-Neiges, Montreal, QC, H3T 1Y4
(514) 733-1478
Emp Here 100   *Sales* 3,939,878
SIC 8322 Individual and family services

D-U-N-S 20-026-1266   (BR)
COMMISSION SCOLAIRE DE MONTREAL
COMMISSION SCOLAIRE DE MONTREAL

3850 Av Dupuis, Montreal, QC, H3T 1E6
(514) 736-8140
Emp Here 50
SIC 8211 Elementary and secondary schools

D-U-N-S 20-178-7988   (BR)
COOPERATIVE DE L'ECOLE DES HAUTES ETUDES COMMERCIALES
COOPERATIVE DE L'ECOLE DES HAUTES ETUDES COMMERCIALES
5255 Av Decelles Bureau 2340, Montreal, QC, H3T 2B1
(514) 340-6396
Emp Here 100
SIC 8249 Vocational schools, nec

D-U-N-S 20-858-3054   (SL)
CORPORATION DE L'ECOLE DES HAUTES ETUDES COMMERCIALES DE MONTREAL, LA
HSC MONTREAL
3000 Ch De La Cote-Sainte-Catherine, Montreal, QC, H3T 2A7
(514) 340-6000
Emp Here 650   *Sales* 90,994,320
SIC 8221 Colleges and universities
Dir Fin Moreno Dumont
Genl Mgr Michel Patry
Pr Helene Desmarais
Sec Jacques Nantel
Hugues Boisvert
Guy Frechette
Monique F Leroux
Alexandre Bedard
Claude Seguin
Louis Hebert

D-U-N-S 20-857-4053   (HQ)
CORPORATION DU COLLEGE JEAN-DE-BREBEUF, LA
(*Suby of* Corporation Du College Jean-de-Brebeuf, La)
3200 Ch De La Cote-Sainte-Catherine, Montreal, QC, H3T 1C1
(514) 342-9342
Emp Here 375   *Emp Total* 389
Sales 56,168,320
SIC 8222 Junior colleges
Pr Pr Bernard Amyot
Luc Vinet
Bernard Dugas
Louis Bourgeois
Pierre Charette
Sylvie Beaulieu
Adrien Veres
VP VP Francois Morrison
Michelle Jones
Michel April

D-U-N-S 20-806-9612   (BR)
COUCHE-TARD INC
5405 Ch De La Cote-Des-Neiges, Montreal, QC, H3T 1Y7
(514) 739-8444
Emp Here 25
SIC 5411 Grocery stores

D-U-N-S 20-003-0141   (BR)
ROYAL BANK OF CANADA
ROYAL BANK OF CANADA
(*Suby of* Royal Bank Of Canada)
5700 Ch De La Cote-Des-Neiges, Montreal, QC, H3T 2A6
(514) 340-3130
Emp Here 22
SIC 6021 National commercial banks

D-U-N-S 25-354-0165   (BR)
UNIVERSITE DE MONTREAL, L'
BUREAU DE DEVELOPMENT DE MONTREAL
3744 Rue Jean-Brillant Bureau 480, Montreal, QC, H3T 1P1
(514) 343-6812
Emp Here 49
SIC 7389 Business services, nec

D-U-N-S 25-764-7792   (BR)
UNIVERSITE DE MONTREAL, L'
FACULTE L'EDUCATION PERMANENTE
3744 Rue Jean-Brillant, Montreal, QC, H3T 1P1
(514) 343-6090
Emp Here 125
SIC 8221 Colleges and universities

D-U-N-S 25-223-9587   (BR)
VILLE DE MONTREAL
VILLE DE MONTREAL
5290 Ch De La Cote-Des-Neiges, Montreal, QC, H3T 1Y2
(514) 872-6603
Emp Here 30
SIC 8231 Libraries

Montreal, QC H3V
Hochelaga County

D-U-N-S 24-570-0646   (SL)
COLLEGE NOTRE-DAME DU SACRE-COEUR
3791 Ch Queen-Mary, Montreal, QC, H3V 1A8
(514) 739-3371
Emp Here 200   *Sales* 17,963,280
SIC 8211 Elementary and secondary schools
Pr Benoit Durand
VP Jean Laporte
Treas Francois Dussault
Sec Michele Moisan
Jean-Francois Brault
Pierre G. Hebert
Louis Trempe

D-U-N-S 24-107-4756   (SL)
PLACEMENTS ROCKHILL LTEE, LES
ROCKHILL APARTMENTS
4858 Ch De La Cote-Des-Neiges Bureau 503, Montreal, QC, H3V 1G8
(514) 738-4704
Emp Here 45   *Sales* 3,939,878
SIC 6513 Apartment building operators

D-U-N-S 20-057-5145   (BR)
SERVICE CORPORATION INTERNATIONAL (CANADA) LIMITED
CENTRE FUNERAIRE COTE DES NEIGES
4525 Ch De La Cote-Des-Neiges, Montreal, QC, H3V 1E7
(514) 342-8000
Emp Here 30
SIC 7261 Funeral service and crematories

D-U-N-S 24-377-4416   (HQ)
SYSTEMES CANADIEN KRONOS INC
(*Suby of* Kronos Parent Corporation)
3535 Ch Queen-Mary Bureau 500, Montreal, QC, H3V 1H8
(514) 345-0580
Emp Here 182   *Emp Total* 4,128
Sales 44,352,051
SIC 7371 Custom computer programming services
Pr Pr Aron J. Ain
Spiros Paleologos
Dir Fin Mark V. Julien

Montreal, QC H3W
Hochelaga County

D-U-N-S 24-945-3184   (SL)
2739-9708 QUEBEC INC
EXO-FRUITS
5192 Ch De La Cote-Saint-Luc, Montreal, QC, H3W 2G9
(514) 738-1384
Emp Here 50   *Sales* 4,304,681
SIC 5431 Fruit and vegetable markets

D-U-N-S 20-517-9752   (SL)

BRONFMAN JEWISH EDUCATION CENTRE
1 Car Cummings Bureau 502, Montreal, QC, H3W 1M6
(514) 345-2610
Emp Here 45   *Sales* 7,608,750
SIC 8699 Membership organizations, nec
Helene Kaufman
Dir Shlomo Shimon
Pr Susan Laxer
VP Michael Frankel
VP Eta Blitzer
VP Paul Levine
Dale Boidman

D-U-N-S 20-547-2009   (SL)
CHSLD JUIFS DE MONTREAL
JEWISH ELDERCARE CENTRE
5725 Av Victoria Bureau 131, Montreal, QC, H3W 3H6
(514) 738-4500
Emp Here 550   *Sales* 59,681,280
SIC 8069 Specialty hospitals, except psychiatric
Ex Dir Barbra Gold

D-U-N-S 20-928-8133   (SL)
COLLEGE RABBINIQUE DU CANADA
TOMCHE TMIMIM LUBAZITCH
6405 Av De Westbury, Montreal, QC, H3W 2X5
(514) 735-2201
Emp Here 60   *Sales* 4,012,839
SIC 8211 Elementary and secondary schools

D-U-N-S 20-712-4699   (BR)
COMMISSION SCOLAIRE DE MONTREAL
ECOLE DU PETIT CHAPITEAU
4890 Av Carlton, Montreal, QC, H3W 1G6
(514) 736-8192
Emp Here 50
SIC 8211 Elementary and secondary schools

D-U-N-S 24-189-8951   (BR)
COMMISSION SCOLAIRE DE MONTREAL
COMMISSION SCOLAIRE DE MONTREAL
5000 Av Iona, Montreal, QC, H3W 2A2
(514) 736-3535
Emp Here 20
SIC 8211 Elementary and secondary schools

D-U-N-S 20-712-4871   (BR)
COMMISSION SCOLAIRE ENGLISH-MONTREAL
CORONATION SCHOOL
4810 Av Van Horne, Montreal, QC, H3W 1J3
(514) 733-7790
Emp Here 50
SIC 8211 Elementary and secondary schools

D-U-N-S 25-240-2706   (BR)
COMMISSION SCOLAIRE ENGLISH-MONTREAL
MARYMOUNT ACADEMY
5100 Ch De La Cote-Saint-Luc, Montreal, QC, H3W 2G9
(514) 488-8144
Emp Here 65
SIC 8211 Elementary and secondary schools

D-U-N-S 20-644-8248   (BR)
COMMISSION SCOLAIRE DE MONTREAL
COMMISSION SCOLAIRE DE MONTREAL
4860 Rue Vezina, Montreal, QC, H3W 1C1
(514) 736-1537
Emp Here 50
SIC 8211 Elementary and secondary schools

D-U-N-S 20-764-9823   (SL)
FEDERATION CJA
FEDERATION DES SERVICES COMMUNAUTAIRES
5151 Ch De La Cote-Sainte-Catherine, Montreal, QC, H3W 1M6
(514) 735-3541
Emp Here 100   *Sales* 4,677,755
SIC 8322 Individual and family services

D-U-N-S 20-211-5507   (SL)

LOCATION BENCH & TABLE INC
PARTY TIME RENTS, DIV OF
6999 Av Victoria, Montreal, QC, H3W 3E9
(514) 738-4755
Emp Here 50   *Sales* 4,012,839
SIC 7359 Equipment rental and leasing, nec

D-U-N-S 25-183-8884   (BR)
ROYAL BANK OF CANADA
RBC
(*Suby of* Royal Bank Of Canada)
4851 Av Van-Horne, Montreal, QC, H3W 1J2
(514) 340-3050
Emp Here 27
SIC 6021 National commercial banks

D-U-N-S 24-833-2348   (BR)
SOBEYS QUEBEC INC
4885 Av Van-Horne, Montreal, QC, H3W 1J2
(514) 731-8336
Emp Here 80
SIC 5141 Groceries, general line

D-U-N-S 20-714-2170   (BR)
TALMUD TORAHS UNIS DE MONTREAL INC
TALMUD TORAH ELEMENTARY SCHOOL
4850 Av Saint-Kevin, Montreal, QC, H3W 1P2
(514) 739-2297
Emp Here 50
SIC 8211 Elementary and secondary schools

D-U-N-S 24-044-3346   (BR)
WORLD FINANCIAL GROUP INSURANCE AGENCY OF CANADA INC
4721 Av Van Horne, Montreal, QC, H3W 1H8
(514) 731-2300
Emp Here 20
SIC 8742 Management consulting services

D-U-N-S 20-512-4931   (BR)
YOUNG MEN'S & YOUNG WOMEN'S HEBREW ASSOCIATION OF MONTREAL
CENTRE DES ARTS SAIDYE BRONFMAN
(*Suby of* Young Men's & Young Women's Hebrew Association Of Montreal)
5170 Ch De La Cote-Sainte-Catherine, Montreal, QC, H3W 1M7
(514) 739-2301
Emp Here 25
SIC 8322 Individual and family services

Montreal, QC H3X
Hochelaga County

D-U-N-S 20-003-0125   (BR)
BANK OF MONTREAL
BMO
5353 Ch Queen-Mary, Montreal, QC, H3X 1V2
(514) 877-8186
Emp Here 20
SIC 6021 National commercial banks

D-U-N-S 20-540-2360   (BR)
CANADA POST CORPORATION
5345 Ch Queen-Mary, Montreal, QC, H3X 1T9
(514) 489-7207
Emp Here 45
SIC 4311 U.s. postal service

D-U-N-S 20-584-0064   (BR)
CANADA POST CORPORATION
POSTE CANADA
4944 Boul Decarie, Montreal, QC, H3X 2H7
(514) 369-4813
Emp Here 30
SIC 4311 U.s. postal service

D-U-N-S 20-024-5285   (BR)
COMMISSION SCOLAIRE DE MONTREAL
COMMISSION SCOLAIRE DE MONTREAL
5530 Av Dupuis, Montreal, QC, H3X 1N8
(514) 596-5287
Emp Here 20
SIC 7011 Hotels and motels

D-U-N-S 20-712-4319   (BR)
COMMISSION SCOLAIRE DE MONTREAL
COMMISSION SCOLAIRE DE MONTREAL
5325 Av Macdonald, Montreal, QC, H3X 2W6
(514) 596-5688
Emp Here 50
SIC 8211 Elementary and secondary schools

D-U-N-S 20-109-5911   (BR)
COMMISSION SCOLAIRE DE MONTREAL
COMMISSION SCOLAIRE DE MONTREAL
6300 Ch De La Cote-Saint-Luc, Montreal, QC, H3X 2H4
(514) 596-5920
Emp Here 150
SIC 8211 Elementary and secondary schools

D-U-N-S 24-126-4600   (SL)
LEVY PILOTTE S.E.N.C.R.L.
DSK
5250 Boul Decarie Bureau 700, Montreal, QC, H3X 3Z6
(514) 487-1566
Emp Here 50   *Sales* 2,188,821
SIC 8721 Accounting, auditing, and bookkeeping

D-U-N-S 24-354-6772   (SL)
RESIDENCE SEPHARADE SALOMON (COMMUNAUTE SEPHARADE UNIFIEE DU QUEBEC)
5900 Boul Decarie, Montreal, QC, H3X 2J7
(514) 733-2157
Emp Here 100   *Sales* 3,648,035
SIC 8361 Residential care

D-U-N-S 25-198-6105   (BR)
SERRUMAX INC
SERRURIER SNOWDOWN
4650 Boul Decarie, Montreal, QC, H3X 2H5
(514) 489-2688
Emp Here 5
SIC 7699 Repair services, nec

D-U-N-S 20-793-5896   (BR)
WENDY'S RESTAURANTS OF CANADA INC
WENDY'S
(*Suby of* The Wendy's Company)
5180 Boul Decarie, Montreal, QC, H3X 2H9
(514) 481-4060
Emp Here 51
SIC 5812 Eating places

Montreal, QC H3Y
Hochelaga County

D-U-N-S 20-738-6350   (HQ)
MULTIPAK LTEE
(*Suby of* Acer McLernon Canada Inc)
4048 Ch Gage, Montreal, QC, H3Y 1R5
(514) 726-5527
Emp Here 140   *Emp Total* 1
Sales 16,545,394
SIC 2759 Commercial printing, nec
Pr Pr David H Mclernon
Dir Robert Mclernon

D-U-N-S 20-314-0918   (SL)
SPIVO CANADA INC
3150 Place De Ramezay Bureau 202, Montreal, QC, H3Y 0A3
(514) 501-4256
Emp Here 50   *Sales* 4,937,631
SIC 3949 Sporting and athletic goods, nec

Montreal, QC H3Z
Hochelaga County

D-U-N-S 25-380-7606   (HQ)
HAPAG-LLOYD (CANADA) INC
3400 Boul De Maisonneuve O Bureau 1200, Montreal, QC, H3Z 3E7

---

(514) 934-5133
Emp Here 250   *Emp Total* 9,384
Sales 81,643,023
SIC 4731 Freight transportation arrangement
Pr Wolfgang Freese
Treas Tim Whittaker
 Wolfgang Schoch

D-U-N-S 24-356-7968   (BR)
HOMBURG REALTY FUNDS INCORPORATED
(*Suby of* Homburg Realty Funds Incorporated)
3400 Boul De Maisonneuve O Bureau 1010, Montreal, QC, H3Z 3B8
(514) 931-C374
Emp Here 50
SIC 6799 Investors, nec

D-U-N-S 24-359-5878   (SL)
NAVIGATION CP LIMITEE
3400 Boul De Maisonneuve O Bureau 1200, Montreal, QC, H3Z 3E7
(514) 934-5133
Emp Here 130   *Sales* 32,175,669
SIC 4731 Freight transportation arrangement
Pr Deiter Brettshneider
Sec Tim Whittaker
Treas Wilfred Rau
Dir Holger G. Oetjen

D-U-N-S 24-354-3852   (BR)
WINNERS MERCHANTS INTERNATIONAL L.P.
WINNERS
(*Suby of* The TJX Companies Inc)
1500 Av Atwater Bureau F48, Montreal, QC, H3Z 1X5
(514) 939-3327
Emp Here 40
SIC 5651 Family clothing stores

D-U-N-S 24-527-8205   (BR)
XEROX CANADA LTD
(*Suby of* Xerox Corporation)
3400 Boul De Maisonneuve O Bureau 900, Montreal, QC, H3Z 3G1
(514) 939-3769
Emp Here 150
SIC 5044 Office equipment

Montreal, QC H4A
Hochelaga County

D-U-N-S 20-172-0989   (BR)
BANK OF MONTREAL
BMO MONKLAND & GIROUARD BRANCH
5501 Av De Monkland, Montreal, QC, H4A 1C8
(514) 877-9028
Emp Here 20
SIC 6021 National commercial banks

D-U-N-S 20-883-6874   (SL)
CENTENNIAL ACADEMY
3641 Av Prud'Homme, Montreal, QC, H4A 3H6
(514) 486-5533
Emp Here 70   *Sales* 4,669,485
SIC 8211 Elementary and secondary schools

D-U-N-S 24-099-2524   (BR)
COMMISSION SCOLAIRE DE MONTREAL
ECOLE DES METIERS DES FAUBOURGS-DE-MONTREAL, ANNEXE 1
2055 Av D'Oxford, Montreal, QC, H4A 2X6
(514) 596-5227
Emp Here 60
SIC 8211 Elementary and secondary schools

D-U-N-S 25-233-5427   (BR)
COMMISSION SCOLAIRE ENGLISH-MONTREAL
WILLINGDON SCHOOL
5870 Rue De Terrebonne, Montreal, QC, H4A

1B5
(514) 484-2881
Emp Here 50
SIC 8299 Schools and educational services, nec

D-U-N-S 25-232-9560   (BR)
COMMISSION SCOLAIRE ENGLISH-MONTREAL
SHADD BUSINESS CENTRE
1000 Av Old Orchard, Montreal, QC, H4A 3A4
(514) 484-0485
Emp Here 50
SIC 8244 Business and secretarial schools

D-U-N-S 20-023-9981   (BR)
COMMISSION SCOLAIRE DE MONTREAL
COMMISSION SCOLAIRE DE MONTREAL
5435 Av Notre-Dame-De-Grace, Montreal, QC, H4A 1L2
(514) 596-5676
Emp Here 45
SIC 8211 Elementary and secondary schools

D-U-N-S 20-712-4525   (BR)
COMMISSION SCOLAIRE DE MONTREAL
COMMISSION SCOLAIRE DE MONTREAL
5619 Ch De La Cote-Saint-Antoine, Montreal, QC, H4A 1R5
(514) 596-5682
Emp Here 50
SIC 8211 Elementary and secondary schools

D-U-N-S 24-076-7751   (SL)
ENSEMBLE AMATIE
4011 Av Grey, Montreal, QC, H4A 3N9
(514) 482-0964
Emp Here 65   *Sales* 4,158,760
SIC 7929 Entertainers and entertainment groups

D-U-N-S 25-998-2916   (SL)
INTER.NET CANADA LTEE
INTER.NET
(*Suby of* Uniserve Communications Corporation)
5252 Boul De Maisonneuve O Bureau 200, Montreal, QC, H4A 3S5
(514) 481-2585
Emp Here 100   *Sales* 19,828,320
SIC 4813 Telephone communication, except radio
Pr Pr Stephane Goyette
VP Fin Sophie Leger

D-U-N-S 20-633-0383   (BR)
OTIS CANADA, INC
(*Suby of* United Technologies Corporation)
5311 Boul De Maisonneuve O, Montreal, QC, H4A 1Z5
(514) 489-9781
Emp Here 80
SIC 7699 Repair services, nec

D-U-N-S 24-872-0252   (SL)
PREMIER COIFFURE INC, AU
PREMIER EXPERT CHEVEUX, AU
5487 Av De Monkland, Montreal, QC, H4A 1C6
(514) 489-8872
Emp Here 63   *Sales* 1,240,332
SIC 7231 Beauty shops

D-U-N-S 25-198-2336   (BR)
PROVIGO DISTRIBUTION INC
PROVIGO
5595 Av De Monkland, Montreal, QC, H4A 1E1
(514) 482-7273
Emp Here 64
SIC 5411 Grocery stores

D-U-N-S 20-214-1818   (SL)
RESTAURANT LE CHALET BAR-B-Q INC
5456 Rue Sherbrooke O, Montreal, QC, H4A 1V9
(514) 489-7235
Emp Here 60   *Sales* 1,824,018

SIC 5812 Eating places

D-U-N-S 24-711-6379   (SL)
SERVICES DE SANTE ALTERNACARE INC
2100 Av De Marlowe Bureau 449, Montreal, QC, H4A 3L5
(514) 485-5050
Emp Here 300   *Sales* 75,583,200
SIC 8082 Home health care services
Pr Lyon Gould
VP Cynthia Feigin

D-U-N-S 25-868-0768   (SL)
SOCIETE DE SANTE ET BIEN-ETRE DE LA COMMUNAUTE CENTRE-OUEST
QUEEN ELIZABETH HEALTH COMPLEX
2100 Av De Marlowe Bureau 115, Montreal, QC, H4A 3L5
(514) 485-5013
Emp Here 50   *Sales* 3,898,130
SIC 8011 Offices and clinics of medical doctors

D-U-N-S 24-943-5694   (BR)
SOEURS DE LA CONGREGATION DE NOTRE-DAME, LES
INFIRMERIE NOTRE DAME DE BON SECOURS
5015 Av Notre-Dame-De-Grace, Montreal, QC, H4A 1K2
(514) 485-1461
Emp Here 150
SIC 8661 Religious organizations

D-U-N-S 24-870-3662   (BR)
VIGI SANTE LTEE
CHSLD VIGI REINE ELIZABETH
(*Suby of* Vigi Sante Ltee)
2055 Av Northcliffe Bureau 412, Montreal, QC, H4A 3K6
(514) 788-2085
Emp Here 200
SIC 8361 Residential care

D-U-N-S 24-683-2039   (BR)
VILLE DE MONTREAL
VILLE DE MONTREAL
5600 Ch Upper-Lachine, Montreal, QC, H4A 2A7
(514) 872-1765
Emp Here 25
SIC 8631 Labor organizations

D-U-N-S 25-446-8820   (BR)
YMCA DU QUEBEC, LES
NOTRE DAME DE GRACE YMCA
4335 Av De Hampton, Montreal, QC, H4A 2L3
(514) 486-7315
Emp Here 20
SIC 7991 Physical fitness facilities

Montreal, QC H4B
Hochelaga County

D-U-N-S 20-715-1031   (BR)
COMMISSION SCOLAIRE ENGLISH-MONTREAL
GREAVES ADVENTIST ACADEMY
2330 Av West Hill, Montreal, QC, H4B 2S4
(514) 486-5092
Emp Here 20
SIC 8211 Elementary and secondary schools

D-U-N-S 25-684-4648   (SL)
DI-TECH INC
2125 Rue Lily-Simon, Montreal, QC, H4B 3A1

Emp Here 85
SIC 2269 Finishing plants, nec

D-U-N-S 24-634-2588   (BR)
GENERAL ELECTRIC CANADA COMPANY
GE POWER CENTER
(*Suby of* General Electric Company)
7420 Rue Saint-Jacques, Montreal, QC, H4B

1W3
(514) 485-7400
Emp Here 50
SIC 3625 Relays and industrial controls

D-U-N-S 25-746-1855   (BR)
GOUVERNEMENT DE LA PROVINCE DE QUEBEC
GOUVERNEMENT DE LA PROVINCE DE QUEBEC
7005 Boul De Maisonneuve O Bureau 620, Montreal, QC, H4B 1T3
(514) 487-1770
Emp Here 205
SIC 7352 Medical equipment rental

D-U-N-S 24-083-1370   (BR)
GOVERNING COUNCIL OF THE SALVATION ARMY IN CANADA, THE
HOPITAL CATHERINE BOOTH
4375 Av Montclair, Montreal, QC, H4B 2J5
(514) 481-0431
Emp Here 20
SIC 8661 Religious organizations

D-U-N-S 20-512-3693   (SL)
MOTO LOCATION M.T.L. INTERNATIONAL INC
6695 Rue Saint-Jacques, Montreal, QC, H4B 1V3
(514) 483-6686
Emp Here 50   *Sales* 3,205,129
SIC 7999 Amusement and recreation, nec

D-U-N-S 20-361-9502   (BR)
PLACEMENTS SERGAKIS INC
CABARET LES AMAZONES
6820 Rue Saint-Jacques, Montreal, QC, H4B 1V8
(514) 484-8695
Emp Here 20
SIC 5813 Drinking places

D-U-N-S 24-709-7066   (SL)
PROTEC INVESTIGATION SECURITY INC
3333 Boul Cavendish Bureau 200, Montreal, QC, H4B 2M5
(514) 485-3255
Emp Here 150   *Sales* 4,669,485
SIC 7381 Detective and armored car services

D-U-N-S 20-571-3956   (BR)
PROVIGO DISTRIBUTION INC
6485 Rue Sherbrooke O, Montreal, QC, H4B 1N3
(514) 488-5521
Emp Here 70
SIC 5141 Groceries, general line

D-U-N-S 25-456-9122   (BR)
PROVIGO DISTRIBUTION INC
MAXI
7455 Rue Sherbrooke O, Montreal, QC, H4B 1S3
(514) 353-7930
Emp Here 70
SIC 5141 Groceries, general line

Montreal, QC H4C
Hochelaga County

D-U-N-S 20-252-5556   (BR)
6894658 CANADA INC
ZOHAR PLASTIQUES
4035 Rue Saint-Ambroise, Montreal, QC, H4C 2E1
(514) 932-8054
Emp Here 50
SIC 2673 Bags: plastic, laminated, and coated

D-U-N-S 20-115-8313   (SL)
9015-9492 QUEBEC INC
BOULANGERIE PREMIERE MOISSON
3025 Rue Saint-Ambroise, Montreal, QC, H4C 2C2

(514) 932-0328
Emp Here 75 *Sales* 2,553,625
SIC 5461 Retail bakeries

D-U-N-S 24-773-2998 (SL)
9189-8957 QUEBEC INC
LEMAY ASSOCIES ARCHITECTURE & DE-SIGN
780 Av Brewster, Montreal, QC, H4C 2K1
(514) 932-5101
Emp Here 49 *Sales* 6,313,604
SIC 8712 Architectural services
 Louis-T Lemay

D-U-N-S 20-217-6376 (SL)
ATELIER DE COUPAGE ECONOMIE LTEE
6200 Rue Notre-Dame O, Montreal, QC, H4C 1V4
(514) 767-6767
Emp Here 50 *Sales* 4,085,799
SIC 3544 Special dies, tools, jigs, and fixtures

D-U-N-S 24-050-2406 (BR)
ATELIER LA FLECHE DE FER INC
CUISINE CENTRALE
(*Suby of* Atelier la Fleche de Fer Inc)
4750 Rue Dagenais, Montreal, QC, H4C 1L7

Emp Here 38
SIC 2099 Food preparations, nec

D-U-N-S 20-573-7518 (BR)
BANQUE LAURENTIENNE DU CANADA
BANQUE LAURENTIENNE
4080 Rue Saint-Jacques, Montreal, QC, H4C 1J2
(514) 935-9624
Emp Here 20
SIC 6021 National commercial banks

D-U-N-S 25-483-0631 (BR)
COMMISSION SCOLAIRE DE MONTREAL
CENTRE ST-PAUL
4976 Rue Notre-Dame O, Montreal, QC, H4C 1S8
(514) 596-4544
Emp Here 60
SIC 8211 Elementary and secondary schools

D-U-N-S 25-240-7531 (BR)
COMMISSION SCOLAIRE DE MONTREAL
ECOLE LUDGER DUVERNAY
770 Rue Du Couvent, Montreal, QC, H4C 2R6
(514) 596-5666
Emp Here 50
SIC 8211 Elementary and secondary schools

D-U-N-S 25-240-2664 (BR)
COMMISSION SCOLAIRE ENGLISH-MONTREAL
JAMES LYNG HIGH SCHOOL
5440 Rue Notre-Dame O, Montreal, QC, H4C 1T9
(514) 846-8814
Emp Here 20
SIC 8211 Elementary and secondary schools

D-U-N-S 20-574-8242 (BR)
COMMISSION SCOLAIRE DE MONTREAL
COMMISSION SCOLAIRE DE MONTREAL
4115 Rue Saint-Jacques, Montreal, QC, H4C 1J3
(514) 596-5970
Emp Here 40
SIC 8211 Elementary and secondary schools

D-U-N-S 20-852-8799 (BR)
COMMISSION SCOLAIRE DE MONTREAL
ECOLE DES METIERS DU SUD OUEST DE MONTREAL
717 Rue Saint-Ferdinand, Montreal, QC, H4C 2T3
(514) 596-5960
Emp Here 85
SIC 8211 Elementary and secondary schools

D-U-N-S 20-289-6734 (BR)
DENTSUBOS INC
DENTSUBOS INC

3970 Rue Saint-Ambroise, Montreal, QC, H4C 2C7
(514) 848-0010
Emp Here 100
SIC 7311 Advertising agencies

D-U-N-S 24-369-4499 (SL)
GROUPE CANTIN GEOFFRION SERVICES CONSEILS INC
4030 Rue Saint-Ambroise Bureau 110, Montreal, QC, H4C 2C7
(514) 935-2453
Emp Here 30 *Sales* 948,489
SIC 7381 Detective and armored car services

D-U-N-S 25-408-1813 (SL)
H.C. VIDAL LTEE
5700 Rue Philippe-Turcot, Montreal, QC, H4C 1V6
(514) 937-6187
Emp Here 70 *Sales* 4,231,721
SIC 7699 Repair services, nec

D-U-N-S 20-553-4527 (BR)
HOME DEPOT OF CANADA INC
HOME DEPOT
(*Suby of* The Home Depot Inc)
4625 Rue Saint-Antoine O, Montreal, QC, H4C 1E2
(514) 846-4770
Emp Here 200
SIC 5039 Construction materials, nec

D-U-N-S 24-027-7603 (BR)
IRON MOUNTAIN CANADA OPERATIONS ULC
ARCHIVES IRON MOUNTAIN
4005 Rue De Richelieu, Montreal, QC, H4C 1A1
(800) 327-8345
Emp Here 20
SIC 7389 Business services, nec

D-U-N-S 24-339-1419 (SL)
JEKYLL PRODUCTIONS (MUSE) INC
706 Av Brewster, Montreal, QC, H4C 2K1
(514) 932-2580
Emp Here 100 *Sales* 12,560,000
SIC 7812 Motion picture and video production
Pr Pr Michael Prupas
VP VP Irene Litinsky
 Alexander (Sandy) Jesion

D-U-N-S 25-631-9500 (SL)
KLB GROUP CANADA INC
1001 Rue Lenoir Suite A417-B, Montreal, QC, H4C 2Z6
(438) 387-4404
Emp Here 20 *Sales* 1,824,018
SIC 8748 Business consulting, nec

D-U-N-S 20-703-2520 (BR)
KRUGER INC
KRUGER RECYCLAGE
5820 Place Turcot, Montreal, QC, H4C 1W3
(514) 595-7447
Emp Here 38
SIC 4953 Refuse systems

D-U-N-S 25-217-4206 (BR)
KRUGER INC
5845 Place Turcot, Montreal, QC, H4C 1V9
(514) 934-0600
Emp Here 140
SIC 2631 Paperboard mills

D-U-N-S 20-266-2128 (BR)
KRUGER INC
TURCAL
5770 Rue Notre-Dame O, Montreal, QC, H4C 1V2
(514) 937-4255
Emp Here 34
SIC 4953 Refuse systems

D-U-N-S 25-467-2421 (HQ)
MISSION BON ACCEUIL
(*Suby of* Mission Bon Acceuil)
606 Rue De Courcelle, Montreal, QC, H4C

3L5
(514) 523-5288
Emp Here 50 *Emp Total* 100
Sales 3,648,035
SIC 8361 Residential care

D-U-N-S 20-228-7587 (SL)
O'CONNELL, THOMAS INC
5700 Rue Notre-Dame O, Montreal, QC, H4C 1V1
(514) 932-2145
Emp Here 50 *Sales* 4,377,642
SIC 1711 Plumbing, heating, air-conditioning

D-U-N-S 20-707-0673 (SL)
TRANSFORMATEURS RAPIDES LTEE, LES
937 Rue Du College Bureau 26, Montreal, QC, H4C 2S3
(514) 935-3543
Emp Here 30 *Sales* 8,480,961
SIC 3612 Transformers, except electric
 Barry Marcus
 Karys Figarella

Montreal, QC H4E
Hochelaga County

D-U-N-S 24-490-0411 (SL)
132087 CANADA INC
SUPER MARCHE CLAUDE ST-PIERRE IGA
(*Suby of* Breuvages Claude St-Pierre inc)
6675 Boul Monk, Montreal, QC, H4E 3J2
(514) 767-5323
Emp Here 52 *Sales* 8,942,720
SIC 5411 Grocery stores
Pr Claude St Pierre

D-U-N-S 20-566-9617 (SL)
ALLIED TEXTILES & REFUSE INC
(*Suby of* 118584 Canada Inc)
3700 Rue Saint-Patrick Bureau 200, Montreal, QC, H4E 1A2
(514) 932-5962
Emp Here 46 *Sales* 15,373,440
SIC 5093 Scrap and waste materials
Pr Pr Mark Kaufman

D-U-N-S 25-331-0338 (BR)
ARCELORMITTAL PRODUITS LONGS CANADA S.E.N.C.
5900 Rue Saint-Patrick, Montreal, QC, H4E 1B3
(514) 762-5260
Emp Here 140
SIC 3312 Blast furnaces and steel mills

D-U-N-S 20-537-2092 (BR)
CANADA POST CORPORATION
SUCC SD3
5820 Boul Monkland, Montreal, QC, H4E 3H6

Emp Here 25
SIC 4311 U.s. postal service

D-U-N-S 24-346-5585 (HQ)
CENTRE DE SANTE ET DE SERVICES SOCIAUX DU SUD-QUEST-VERDUN
HOPITAL DE VERDUN
6161 Rue Laurendeau, Montreal, QC, H4E 3X6
(514) 762-2777
Emp Here 20 *Emp Total* 40,000
Sales 341,500,030
SIC 8062 General medical and surgical hospitals
Pr Lorraine Duchesne-Noiseux
VP Gilles Beaudry
Sec Sonia Belanger
Dir Pascale Bedard
Dir Andreia Bittencourt
Dir Patrice Catoir
Dir Bernard Circe
Dir Gaetan Couture
Dir Jennifer De Combe
Dir Robert Degray

D-U-N-S 25-233-7803 (BR)
COMMISSION SCOLAIRE DE MONTREAL
ECOLE SECONDAIRE HONORE MERCIER
1935 Boul Desmarchais, Montreal, QC, H4E 2B9
(514) 732-1400
Emp Here 40
SIC 8211 Elementary and secondary schools

D-U-N-S 25-240-7580 (BR)
COMMISSION SCOLAIRE DE MONTREAL
ECOLE ST JEAN DE MATHA
6970 Rue Dumas, Montreal, QC, H4E 3A3
(514) 732-1460
Emp Here 45
SIC 8211 Elementary and secondary schools

D-U-N-S 25-233-6524 (BR)
COMMISSION SCOLAIRE ENGLISH-MONTREAL
OPTIONS II HIGH SCHOOL
1741 Rue De Biencourt, Montreal, QC, H4E 1T4
(514) 769-5282
Emp Here 20
SIC 8211 Elementary and secondary schools

D-U-N-S 25-090-6229 (BR)
COMMISSION SCOLAIRE DE MONTREAL
COMMISSION SCOLAIRE DE MONTREAL
6025 Rue Beaulieu, Montreal, QC, H4E 3E7
(514) 766-1239
Emp Here 30
SIC 8211 Elementary and secondary schools

D-U-N-S 25-099-1965 (BR)
CONSTRUCTION DJL INC
6200 Rue Saint-Patrick, Montreal, QC, H4E 1B3
(514) 766-8256
Emp Here 100
SIC 1611 Highway and street construction

D-U-N-S 25-335-9202 (SL)
CONSTRUCTIONS QUORUM INC
5200 Rue Saint-Patrick Bureau 200, Montreal, QC, H4E 4N9
(514) 822-2882
Emp Here 51 *Sales* 10,141,537
SIC 1522 Residential construction, nec
Pr Peter Cosentini
Sec Guy Laporte

D-U-N-S 20-265-6203 (BR)
EUROVIA QUEBEC CONSTRUCTION INC
(*Suby of* Eurovia Quebec Construction Inc)
6200 Rue Saint-Patrick, Montreal, QC, H4E 1B3
(514) 766-8256
Emp Here 100
SIC 1611 Highway and street construction

D-U-N-S 20-883-5827 (SL)
INVESTIGATIONS RK INC
2100 Av De L'Eglise, Montreal, QC, H4E 1H4
(514) 761-7121
Emp Here 100 *Sales* 3,137,310
SIC 7381 Detective and armored car services

D-U-N-S 25-637-8618 (SL)
L'ANCIEN PENSIONNAT COTE-SAINT-PAUL INC
1734 Av De L'Eglise, Montreal, QC, H4E 1G5
(514) 903-1734
Emp Here 49 *Sales* 5,559,741
SIC 6513 Apartment building operators
Pr Luc Bourdeau

D-U-N-S 20-715-7962 (BR)
MOTOR COACH INDUSTRIES LIMITED
3500 Rue Saint-Patrick, Montreal, QC, H4E 1A2
(514) 938-4510
Emp Here 20
SIC 3711 Motor vehicles and car bodies

D-U-N-S 24-607-9573 (BR)
PROVIGO INC
6000 Rue Laurendeau, Montreal, QC, H4E

3X4
(514) 766-7367
Emp Here 40
SIC 6719 Holding companies, nec

D-U-N-S 20-910-8000   (SL)
TEXTILES ABERTON LTEE
3700 Rue Saint-Patrick, Montreal, QC, H4E
1A2
(514) 932-3711
Emp Here 30   *Sales* 7,263,840
SIC 5131 Piece goods and notions
Pr Pr Mark Kaufman
VP VP Anne Kaufman
VP VP Melanie Kaufman
Dir Howard Kaufman

Montreal, QC H4J
Hochelaga County

D-U-N-S 24-812-2467   (SL)
159211 CANADA INC
PORT D'ELEGANCE
11870 Boul Saint-Germain, Montreal, QC,
H4J 2A2

Emp Here 60   *Sales* 8,803,200
SIC 5137 Women's and children's clothing
Pr Pr Adam Karawi

D-U-N-S 20-027-1893   (BR)
COMMISSION SCOLAIRE DE MONTREAL
ECOLE ALICE PARIZEAU
11715 Rue Filion, Montreal, QC, H4J 1T2
(514) 596-7330
Emp Here 70
SIC 8211 Elementary and secondary schools

D-U-N-S 25-240-2581   (BR)
COMMISSION SCOLAIRE DE MONTREAL
ECOLE STE-ODILE
12055 Rue Depatie, Montreal, QC, H4J 1W9
(514) 596-5565
Emp Here 75
SIC 8211 Elementary and secondary schools

D-U-N-S 20-712-4780   (BR)
COMMISSION SCOLAIRE DE MONTREAL
COMMISSION SCOLAIRE DE MONTREAL
12330 Rue Lavigne, Montreal, QC, H4J 1Y4
(514) 596-5586
Emp Here 50
SIC 8211 Elementary and secondary schools

D-U-N-S 20-234-6771   (HQ)
SALLE DE QUILLES SPOT LIMITEE
SALLE DE QUILLES LASALLE
12255 Rue Grenet Bureau 1, Montreal, QC,
H4J 2J9
(514) 334-7881
Emp Here 20   *Emp Total* 105
Sales 584,244
SIC 7933 Bowling centers

Montreal, QC H4K
Hochelaga County

D-U-N-S 24-345-5933   (BR)
FONDATION LE PILIER
MAISON ST DENIS BOURGET, LA
23 Av Du Ruisseau, Montreal, QC, H4K 2C8
(450) 624-9922
Emp Here 150
SIC 8361 Residential care

Montreal, QC H4N
Hochelaga County

D-U-N-S 25-467-7149   (SL)

9050-6347 QUEBEC INC
SIRENE DE LA MER
1805 Rue Sauve O Unite 202, Montreal, QC,
H4N 3B8
(514) 332-2255
Emp Here 50   *Sales* 1,532,175
SIC 5812 Eating places

D-U-N-S 20-567-8449   (BR)
BANK OF MONTREAL
BMO
9150 Boul De L'Acadie Bureau 10, Montreal,
QC, H4N 2T2
(514) 382-8060
Emp Here 25
SIC 6021 National commercial banks

D-U-N-S 20-569-2523   (BR)
BANQUE LAURENTIENNE DU CANADA
1805 Rue Sauve O Bureau 105, Montreal, QC,
H4N 3B8
(514) 748-6150
Emp Here 20
SIC 6021 National commercial banks

D-U-N-S 20-267-4024   (SL)
BELLA HOSIERY MILLS INC
SUPERFIT
1401 Rue Legendre O Bureau 200, Montreal,
QC, H4N 2R9
(514) 274-6500
Emp Here 50   *Sales* 4,815,406
SIC 3842 Surgical appliances and supplies

D-U-N-S 24-011-8625   (BR)
BEST BUY CANADA LTD
BEST BUY
(*Suby of* Best Buy Co., Inc.)
8871 Boul De L'Acadie, Montreal, QC, H4N
3K1
(514) 905-4269
Emp Here 50
SIC 5731 Radio, television, and electronic
stores

D-U-N-S 24-760-9592   (BR)
BONNETERIE BELLA INC.
SUPER FIX
1401 Rue Legendre O, Montreal, QC, H4N
2R9
(514) 381-8519
Emp Here 120
SIC 2251 Women's hosiery, except socks

D-U-N-S 24-125-4809   (BR)
BRICK WAREHOUSE LP, THE
8701 Boul De L'Acadie, Montreal, QC, H4N
3K1
(514) 381-1313
Emp Here 20
SIC 5722 Household appliance stores

D-U-N-S 24-740-8263   (HQ)
CELLULAR ONE INC
(*Suby of* Cellular One Inc)
9280 Boul De L'Acadie, Montreal, QC, H4N
3C5
(514) 385-0770
Emp Here 20   *Emp Total* 90
Sales 15,875,840
SIC 5065 Electronic parts and equipment, nec
Pr Pr Peter Laschuck
Crdt Mgr Michael Vacca

D-U-N-S 25-502-3269   (HQ)
CHEMINS DE FER QUEBEC-GATINEAU INC
(*Suby of* Genesee & Wyoming Inc.)
9001 Boul De L'Acadie Bureau 600, Montreal,
QC, H4N 3H5
(514) 948-6999
Emp Here 20   *Emp Total* 7,516
Sales 4,961,328
SIC 4111 Local and suburban transit

D-U-N-S 20-884-6121   (SL)
COLLEGE DE BOIS-DE-BOULOGNE
10555 Av Du Bois-De-Boulogne, Montreal,
QC, H4N 1L4

(514) 332-3000
Emp Here 550   *Sales* 76,957,440
SIC 8221 Colleges and universities
Michelle Patenaude
Mng Dir Maurice Piche

D-U-N-S 20-318-8511   (SL)
CONSTRUCTION DI PAOLO INC
AMENAGEMENT DI PAOLO
255 Rue Benjamin-Hudon, Montreal, QC, H4N
1J3
(450) 661-4745
Emp Here 26   *Sales* 5,180,210
SIC 1522 Residential construction, nec
Pr Pr Emilio Di Paolo
Treas Johanne Papineau

D-U-N-S 24-369-9746   (BR)
COSTCO WHOLESALE CANADA LTD
COSTCO
(*Suby of* Costco Wholesale Corporation)
1015 Rue Du Marche-Central, Montreal, QC,
H4N 3J8
(514) 381-1251
Emp Here 150
SIC 5399 Miscellaneous general merchandise

D-U-N-S 20-362-2451   (SL)
DISTRIBUTION MFG INC
DISTRIBUTEUR H. MIRON
387 Rue Deslauriers, Montreal, QC, H4N 1W2
(514) 344-5558
Emp Here 26   *Sales* 5,982,777
SIC 5143 Dairy products, except dried or
canned
Pr Maria Skotidakis
VP George Michopoulos
VP Constantinos Mastrantonis
Sec Charalambos Nikolidakis
Treas Dimitrios Nikolidakis

D-U-N-S 20-958-2886   (BR)
DOLLARAMA S.E.C.
1033 Rue Du Marche-Central, Montreal, QC,
H4N 1J8
(514) 387-3910
Emp Here 20
SIC 5399 Miscellaneous general merchandise

D-U-N-S 24-802-8685   (SL)
FRESCADEL INTERNATIONAL INC
(*Suby of* 3123472 Canada Inc)
1370 Rue De Beauharnois O, Montreal, QC,
H4N 1J5
(514) 382-3232
Emp Here 49   *Sales* 15,359,963
SIC 5148 Fresh fruits and vegetables
Pr George Pitsikoulis
VP VP Michael Pitsikoulis
Treas Nick Pitsiloulis

D-U-N-S 25-973-5033   (SL)
GESTION GUY GERVAIS INC
1370 Rue Chabanel O, Montreal, QC, H4N
1H4
(514) 384-5590
Emp Here 100   *Sales* 29,014,700
SIC 5032 Brick, stone, and related material
Pr Guy Gervais
Dir Fin Sylvain Albert

D-U-N-S 24-357-7629   (BR)
GOLDER ASSOCIATES LTD
GOLDER ASSOCIES
9200 Boul De L'Acadie Bureau 10, Montreal,
QC, H4N 2T2
(514) 383-0990
Emp Here 200
SIC 8748 Business consulting, nec

D-U-N-S 20-593-4800   (BR)
GOLF TOWN LIMITED
GOLF TOWN
1001 Rue Du Marche-Central, Montreal, QC,
H4N 1J8
(514) 382-4666
Emp Here 25
SIC 5941 Sporting goods and bicycle shops

D-U-N-S 20-031-4206   (BR)
HSBC BANK CANADA
8999 Boul De L'Acadie, Montreal, QC, H4N
3K1
(514) 381-8566
Emp Here 30
SIC 6021 National commercial banks

D-U-N-S 20-514-1794   (BR)
HOME DEPOT OF CANADA INC
HOME DEPOT 7146 L'ACADIE
(*Suby of* The Home Depot Inc)
1000 Rue Sauve O Bureau 1000, Montreal,
QC, H4N 3L5
(514) 333-6868
Emp Here 117
SIC 5251 Hardware stores

D-U-N-S 20-700-3224   (BR)
HUDSON'S BAY COMPANY
DECO DECOUVERTE
1001 Rue Du Marche-Central, Montreal, QC,
H4N 1J8
(514) 383-8939
Emp Here 30
SIC 5311 Department stores

D-U-N-S 24-256-2643   (SL)
**IMPORTATIONS-EXPORTATIONS BENISTI
INC**
POINT ZERO
1650 Chabanel St West, Montreal, QC, H4N
3M8
(514) 384-0140
Emp Here 100   *Sales* 18,240,175
SIC 5136 Men's and boy's clothing
Maurice Benisti

D-U-N-S 25-309-7463   (BR)
**INDUSTRIELLE ALLIANCE, ASSURANCE
ET SERVICES FINANCIERS INC**
9001 Boul De L'Acadie Bureau 404, Montreal,
QC, H4N 3H5
(514) 381-4411
Emp Here 40
SIC 6311 Life insurance

D-U-N-S 25-674-7882   (SL)
INDUSTRIES CANZIP (2000) INC, LES
1615 Rue Chabanel O, Montreal, QC, H4N
2T7
(514) 934-0331
Emp Here 75
SIC 3965 Fasteners, buttons, needles, and
pins

D-U-N-S 24-328-4275   (SL)
MAGASIN MYRLANIE INC
*MARCHAND CANADIAN TIRE DE MON-
TREAL*
9050 Boul De L'Acadie, Montreal, QC, H4N
2S5
(514) 388-6464
Emp Here 50   *Sales* 4,377,642
SIC 5531 Auto and home supply stores

D-U-N-S 24-475-7415   (HQ)
**MARCHANDS EN GROS DE FRUITS
CANADAWIDE INC, LES**
(*Suby of* 3123472 Canada Inc)
1370 Rue De Beauharnois O Bureau 200,
Montreal, QC, H4N 1J5
(514) 382-3232
Emp Here 145   *Emp Total* 150
Sales 36,334,429
SIC 5148 Fresh fruits and vegetables
Pr George Pitsikoulis
VP Michael Pitsikoulis
Nick Pitsikoulis

D-U-N-S 20-017-4857   (HQ)
MONTRES BIG TIME INC
(*Suby of* Montres Big Time Inc)
9250 Boul De L'Acadie Bureau 340, Montreal,
QC, H4N 3C5
(514) 384-6464
Emp Here 47   *Emp Total* 50
Sales 2,772,507

SIC 5944 Jewelry stores

D-U-N-S 20-545-5129 (BR)
MOUNTAIN EQUIPMENT CO-OPERATIVE
8989 Boul De L'Acadie, Montreal, QC, H4N 3K1
(514) 788-5878
Emp Here 70
SIC 5941 Sporting goods and bicycle shops

D-U-N-S 20-512-5987 (BR)
OMER DESERRES INC
DESERRES, OMER MARCHE CENTRAL
1001 Rue Du Marche-Central, Montreal, QC, H4N 1J8
(514) 908-0505
Emp Here 26
SIC 5999 Miscellaneous retail stores, nec

D-U-N-S 24-810-9167 (SL)
POINT ZERO GIRLS CLUB INC
POINT ZERO
1650 Chabanel St West, Montreal, QC, H4N 3M8
(514) 384-0140
Emp Here 94   *Sales* 5.763,895
SIC 5137 Women's and children's clothing
 Nicole Benisti

D-U-N-S 20-688-5290 (BR)
REITMANS (CANADA) LIMITEE
REITMANS
1007 Rue Du Marche-Central Bureau B, Montreal, QC, H4N 1J8
(514) 388-1925
Emp Here 23
SIC 5621 Women's clothing stores

D-U-N-S 24-215-7084 (BR)
RESIDENCES ALLEGRO, S.E.C., LES
MANOIR BOIS DE BOULOGNE
(*Suby of* Residences Allegro, S.E.C., Les)
10005 Av Du Bois-De-Boulogne Bureau 622, Montreal, QC, H4N 3B2
(866) 396-4483
Emp Here 38
SIC 8361 Residential care

D-U-N-S 25-368-5077 (BR)
ROBINSON, C.H. COMPANY (CANADA) LTD
FRAIS ROBINSON
9001 Boul De L'Acadie Bureau 901, Montreal, QC, H4N 3H5
(514) 389-8233
Emp Here 22
SIC 4731 Freight transportation arrangement

D-U-N-S 20-104-9884 (BR)
STAPLES CANADA INC
PUROLATOR
(*Suby of* Staples, Inc.)
1041 Rue Du Marche-Central Bureau 49, Montreal, QC, H4N 1J8
(514) 383-6323
Emp Here 70
SIC 5943 Stationery stores

D-U-N-S 24-240-5251 (BR)
TRYLON TSF INC
9455 Rue Charles-De La Tour, Montreal, QC, H4N 1M5

Emp Here 28
SIC 4899 Communication services, nec

Montreal, QC H4P
Hochelaga County

D-U-N-S 25-412-7327 (SL)
2930862 CANADA INC
6111 Av Royalmount Bureau 100, Montreal, QC, H4P 2T4
(514) 340-1114
Emp Here 26   *Sales* 1,400,148

SIC 8731 Commercial physical research

D-U-N-S 20-560-3785 (SL)
6091636 CANADA INC
MARKET ENGINES
4700 Rue De La Savane Bureau 310, Montreal, QC, H4P 1T7
(514) 448-6931
Emp Here 90   *Sales* 4,523,563
SIC 7389 Business services, nec

D-U-N-S 24-418-0548 (SL)
9209-5256 QUEBEC INC
LINKNOW MEDIA
4700 Rue De La Savane Bureau 210, Montreal, QC, H4P 1T7
(514) 906-4713
Emp Here 60   *Sales* 3,283,232
SIC 7374 Data processing and preparation

D-U-N-S 20-002-8517 (BR)
BANK OF NOVA SCOTIA, THE
SCOTIABANK
7885 Boul Decarie, Montreal, QC, H4P 2H2
(514) 731-6844
Emp Here 25
SIC 6021 National commercial banks

D-U-N-S 20-332-2425 (SL)
BONBONS OINK OINK INC, LES
SQUISH CANDIES
4810 Rue Jean-Talon O, Montreal, QC, H4P 2N5
(514) 731-4555
Emp Here 250   *Sales* 2,165,628
SIC 2064 Candy and other confectionery products

D-U-N-S 20-556-1314 (SL)
CLINIQUE OVO INC
8000 Boul Decarie Bureau 100, Montreal, QC, H4P 2S4
(514) 798-2000
Emp Here 50   *Sales* 3,283,232
SIC 8093 Specialty outpatient clinics, nec

D-U-N-S 24-351-0286 (HQ)
COLLECTIONS DE STYLE R.D. INTERNATIONALES LTEE, LES
R.D. INTERNATIONAL
(*Suby of* 6479987 Canada Inc)
5275 Rue Ferrier Bureau 200, Montreal, QC, H4P 1L7
(514) 342-1222
Emp Here 20   *Emp Total* 11
Sales 9,411,930
SIC 5137 Women's and children's clothing
 Kenneth Hollinger

D-U-N-S 20-927-4653 (BR)
EMCO CORPORATION
BATIMAT
4790 Rue Jean-Talon O, Montreal, QC, H4P 1W9
(514) 735-5747
Emp Here 25
SIC 5074 Plumbing and heating equipment and supplies (hydronics)

D-U-N-S 25-837-6763 (BR)
ENTREPRISES MARCHAND LTEE, LES
4865 Rue Jean-Talon O Bureau 101, Montreal, QC, H4P 1W7
(514) 343-3335
Emp Here 100
SIC 2431 Millwork

D-U-N-S 20-417-5046 (HQ)
GROUPE RESTAURANTS IMVESCOR INC
BATON ROUGE
8250 Boul Decarie Bureau 310, Montreal, QC, H4P 2P5
(514) 341-5544
Emp Here 30   *Emp Total* 800
Sales 878,062,162
SIC 6794 Patent owners and lessors
Pr Frank Hennessey
Dir Arnaud Ajdler

William R. Lane
Dir Francois-Xavier Seigneur
Dir Gary O'connor
Dir Roland Boudreau
Dir Pierre A. Raymond
Dir Michael Forsayeth
Dir Patrick H. Sugrue
 Anne-Marie Laberge

D-U-N-S 25-945-6171 (BR)
GROUPE SPORTSCENE INC
CAGE AUX SPORTS, LA
5485 Rue Des Jockeys, Montreal, QC, H4P 2T7
(514) 731-2020
Emp Here 100
SIC 5812 Eating places

D-U-N-S 24-890-7123 (SL)
HOTEL RUBY FOO'S INC
7655 Boul Decarie, Montreal, QC, H4P 2H2
(514) 731-7701
Emp Here 70   *Sales* 3,064,349
SIC 7011 Hotels and motels

D-U-N-S 25-871-1522 (HQ)
INTERPRO CONSULTANTS INC
(*Suby of* Interpro Consultants Inc)
7777 Boul Decarie Bureau 501, Montreal, QC, H4P 2H2
(514) 321-4505
Emp Here 49   *Emp Total* 50
Sales 3,648,035
SIC 7379 Computer related services, nec

D-U-N-S 24-320-6120 (BR)
INVESTORS GROUP FINANCIAL SERVICES INC
8250 Boul Decarie Bureau 200, Montreal, QC, H4P 2P5
(514) 733-3950
Emp Here 80
SIC 8742 Management consulting services

D-U-N-S 20-187-0800 (SL)
JANIN-BOT (ENTREPRISE CONJOINTE)
8200 Decarie Blvd, Montreal, QC, H4P 2P5
(514) 739-3291
Emp Here 100   *Sales* 23,935,157
SIC 1542 Nonresidential construction, nec
Pr Pr Jean-Yves Tassini

D-U-N-S 24-890-3312 (HQ)
MULTI RESTAURANTS INC
PIK NIK
(*Suby of* Cleman Ludmer Steinberg Inc)
5000 Rue Jean-Talon O Bureau 240, Montreal, QC, H4P 1W9
(514) 739-7939
Emp Here 25   *Emp Total* 4
Sales 20,799,360
SIC 5812 Eating places
Pr Pr Derek Patterson

D-U-N-S 24-763-2417 (SL)
NEXIA FRIEDMAN S.E.N.C.R.L.
8000 Boul Decarie Bureau 500, Montreal, QC, H4P 2S4
(514) 731-7901
Emp Here 75   *Sales* 3,283,232
SIC 8721 Accounting, auditing, and bookkeeping

D-U-N-S 24-459-6946 (HQ)
PHARMASCIENCE INC
ROYALMOUNT PHARMACEUTICALS
6111 Av Royalmount Bureau 100, Montreal, QC, H4P 2T4
(514) 340-1114
Emp Here 650   *Emp Total* 1,000
Sales 145,337,714
SIC 2834 Pharmaceutical preparations
Pr David Goodman
 Morris Goodman
Treas Murielle Lortie
Dir Laurence Macgirr
 Jean-Guy Goulet

D-U-N-S 20-330-3243 (HQ)
POSITRON ACCESS SOLUTIONS CORPORATION
5101 Rue Buchan Bureau 220, Montreal, QC, H4P 2R9
(514) 345-2220
Emp Here 20   *Emp Total* 150
Sales 2,115,860
SIC 4899 Communication services, nec

D-U-N-S 24-362-9479 (BR)
RGIS CANADA ULC
RGIS SPECIALISTES EN INVENTAIRE
8300 Rue Bougainville, Montreal, QC, H4P 2G1
(514) 521-5258
Emp Here 150
SIC 7389 Business services, nec

D-U-N-S 24-403-2140 (SL)
RESTAURANT MACGEORGES INC
HARVEY'S
7475 Boul Decarie, Montreal, QC, H4P 2G9
(514) 738-3588
Emp Here 75   *Sales* 2,261,782
SIC 5812 Eating places

D-U-N-S 20-557-6619 (SL)
SNC-LAVALIN PHARMA INC
8000 Boul Decarie, Montreal, QC, H4P 2S4
(514) 735-5651
Emp Here 160   *Sales* 24,245,520
SIC 8711 Engineering services
 Rejean Goulet
 Jean Nehme
 Gilles Laramee

D-U-N-S 20-793-5743 (HQ)
SINTRA INC
EMULSIONS & BITUMES S.T.E.B.
4984 Place De La Savane, Montreal, QC, H4P 2M9
(514) 341-5331
Emp Here 25   *Emp Total* 169
Sales 198,307,183
SIC 1611 Highway and street construction
Pr Francois Vachon
VP VP Germain Perron
Dir Louis R Gabanna
Dir Jean-Yves Llenas
Dir Frederic Roussel

D-U-N-S 25-370-0991 (BR)
STAPLES CANADA INC
BUREAU EN GROS
(*Suby of* Staples, Inc.)
4205 Rue Jean-Talon O, Montreal, QC, H4P 2T6
(514) 344-3044
Emp Here 40
SIC 5943 Stationery stores

D-U-N-S 24-108-8350 (HQ)
SYSTEMES SYNTAX LTEE
SYNTAX.NET
(*Suby of* Systemes Syntax Ltee)
8000 Boul Decarie Bureau 300, Montreal, QC, H4P 2S4
(514) 733-7777
Emp Here 43   *Emp Total* 68
Sales 7,660,874
SIC 7371 Custom computer programming services
Pr Pr Kenneth Etinson
Pr Pr Ryan Etinson
 Michael Etinson
Dir David Lewin
Dir Stephane Tremblay
Dir Kristian Valenta

D-U-N-S 25-355-4737 (HQ)
TECHNOLOGIE SILANIS INC
ESIGNLIVE
(*Suby of* Vasco Data Security International, Inc.)
8200 Decarie Blvd Suite 300, Montreal, QC, H4P 2P5

---

(514) 337-5255
Emp Here 93   *Emp Total* 613
Sales 19,057,522
SIC 7371 Custom computer programming services
Pr Pr Tommy Petrogiannis
Sec Michael Laurie
Dir Justin Lafayette
    Matthew Lane

D-U-N-S 25-489-1450   (BR)
VALUE VILLAGE STORES, INC
VILLAGE DES VALEURS
(Suby of Savers, Inc.)
4906 Rue Jean-Talon O, Montreal, QC, H4P 1W9
(514) 739-1962
Emp Here 45
SIC 5399 Miscellaneous general merchandise

D-U-N-S 20-572-9168   (BR)
WAL-MART CANADA CORP
WALMART
5400 Rue Jean-Talon O, Montreal, QC, H4P 2T5
(514) 735-5295
Emp Here 250
SIC 5311 Department stores

Montreal, QC H4T
Hochelaga County

D-U-N-S 20-338-4532   (SL)
HOTELS COTE-DE-LIESSE INC
HOLIDAY INN MONTREAL AEROPORT
6500 Ch De La Cote-De-Liesse, Montreal, QC, H4T 1E3
(514) 739-6440
Emp Here 200   *Sales* 8,755,284
SIC 7011 Hotels and motels
Pr Pr Michael Rosenberg
VP VP Martin Rosenberg
Dir Herman Luger
Dir Chanie Rosenberg

D-U-N-S 24-431-0095   (SL)
MARTINI-VISPAK INC
ACHOO TISSU
174 Rue Merizzi, Montreal, QC, H4T 1S4
(514) 344-1551
Emp Here 49   *Sales* 5,909,817
SIC 7311 Advertising agencies
Pr David Futerman

Montreal, QC H4V
Hochelaga County

D-U-N-S 20-580-5760   (BR)
BANQUE LAURENTIENNE DU CANADA
6640 Av Somerled, Montreal, QC, H4V 1T2
(514) 481-2728
Emp Here 20
SIC 6021 National commercial banks

D-U-N-S 25-240-6707   (BR)
COMMISSION SCOLAIRE DE MONTREAL
ECOLE STE CATHERINE DE SIENNE
7065 Av Somerled, Montreal, QC, H4V 1V8
(514) 596-5691
Emp Here 30
SIC 8211 Elementary and secondary schools

D-U-N-S 25-240-1799   (BR)
COMMISSION SCOLAIRE DE MONTREAL
ECOLE LES ENFANTS DU MONDE
5350 Av Rosedale, Montreal, QC, H4V 2H9
(514) 596-5745
Emp Here 25
SIC 8211 Elementary and secondary schools

D-U-N-S 25-198-6022   (SL)
INSTITUT CANADIEN POUR DEVELOPPE-MENT NEURO-INTEGRATIF, L

GIANT STEP SCHOOL
5460 Av Connaught, Montreal, QC, H4V 1X7
(514) 935-1911
Emp Here 110   *Sales* 7,369,031
SIC 8211 Elementary and secondary schools
Genl Mgr Jocelyne Lecompte

Montreal, QC H4Y
Hochelaga County

D-U-N-S 20-698-8490   (BR)
AIR CANADA
AIR CANADA CARGO
735 Stuart Graham N, Montreal, QC, H4Y 1C3

Emp Here 125
SIC 4512 Air transportation, scheduled

Montreal, QC H4Z
Hochelaga County

D-U-N-S 20-827-3271   (SL)
EDITIONS JOBBOOM INC, LES
JOBBOOM
800 Rue Du Square-Victoria Bureau 5, Montreal, QC, H4Z 1A1

Emp Here 300   *Sales* 22,969,440
SIC 2731 Book publishing
VP Prd Julie Thaneuf

D-U-N-S 24-052-8703   (BR)
EXPORT DEVELOPMENT CANADA
EDC
800 Rue Du Square-Victoria Bureau 4520, Montreal, QC, H4Z 1A1
(514) 215-7200
Emp Here 25
SIC 6111 Federal and federally sponsored credit agencies

D-U-N-S 24-590-5203   (BR)
FASKEN MARTINEAU DUMOULIN LLP
800 Rue Du Square-Victoria Bureau 3700, Montreal, QC, H4Z 1A1
(514) 397-7400
Emp Here 175
SIC 8111 Legal services

D-U-N-S 20-554-2884   (BR)
GOUVERNEMENT DE LA PROVINCE DE QUEBEC
GOUVERNEMENT DE LA PROVINCE DE QUEBEC
800 Sq Victoria 22e Etage, Montreal, QC, H4Z 1G3
(514) 395-0337
Emp Here 520
SIC 8741 Management services

D-U-N-S 24-081-4707   (SL)
GROUPEMENT DES ASSUREURS AUTO-MOBILES
800 Place-Victoria 2410, Montreal, QC, H4Z 0A2
(514) 288-1537
Emp Here 55   *Sales* 4,961,328
SIC 6411 Insurance agents, brokers, and service

D-U-N-S 24-125-0534   (BR)
INSURANCE BUREAU OF CANADA
GROUPEMENT DES ASSUREURS AUTO-MOBILES (GAA)
(Suby of Insurance Bureau of Canada)
800 Rue Du Square-Victoria Bureau 2410, Montreal, QC, H4Z 0A2
(514) 288-4321
Emp Here 75
SIC 6411 Insurance agents, brokers, and service

D-U-N-S 24-903-6948   (HQ)
MAGIL LAURENTIENNE GESTION IMMO-BILIERE INC
MAGIL LAURENTIENNE GESTION IMMO-BILLIERE/TERRAINS ST-JACQUES
(Suby of Magil Laurentienne Gestion Immo-biliere Inc)
800 Rue Du Square-Victoria Bureau 4120, Montreal, QC, H4Z 1A1
(514) 875-6010
Emp Here 47   *Emp Total* 50
Sales 4,596,524
SIC 6512 Nonresidential building operators

D-U-N-S 24-194-3497   (BR)
MORNEAU SHEPELL INC
(Suby of Morneau Shepell Inc)
800 Rue Du Square-Victoria, Montreal, QC, H4Z 1A1
(514) 878-9090
Emp Here 20
SIC 6722 Management investment, open-end

D-U-N-S 25-528-6064   (BR)
MORNEAU SHEPELL LTD
SHEPPELL FGI DIV OF
(Suby of Morneau Shepell Inc)
800 Square Victoria Bureau 4000, Montreal, QC, H4Z 0A4
(514) 878-9090
Emp Here 1,000
SIC 8999 Services, nec

D-U-N-S 24-067-0146   (BR)
NAUTILUS PLUS INC
800 Rue Du Square-Victoria, Montreal, QC, H4Z 1A1
(514) 871-9544
Emp Here 22
SIC 7997 Membership sports and recreation clubs

Montreal, QC H5A
Hochelaga County

D-U-N-S 24-246-2799   (BR)
CORUS ENTERTAINMENT INC
800 Rue De La Gauchetiere O Bureau 1100, Montreal, QC, H5A 1M1
(514) 767-9250
Emp Here 500
SIC 7922 Theatrical producers and services

D-U-N-S 25-094-8296   (HQ)
FIDO SOLUTIONS INC
FIDO
(Suby of Rogers Communications Inc)
800 Rue De La Gauchetiere O Bureau 4000, Montreal, QC, H5A 1K3
(514) 937-2121
Emp Here 300   *Emp Total* 25,200
Sales 439,795,633
SIC 4899 Communication services, nec
Sr VP Graeme H. Mcphail
Sec David P. Miller
    Anthony Staffieri

D-U-N-S 24-246-5826   (BR)
SILVERBIRCH HOTELS AND RESORTS LIMITED PARTNERSHIP
HILTON MONTREAL BONAVENTURE
900 Rue De La Gauchetiere O Bureau 10750, Montreal, QC, H5A 1E4
(514) 878-2332
Emp Here 20
SIC 7011 Hotels and motels

Montreal, QC H5B
Hochelaga County

D-U-N-S 20-585-4727   (BR)
BANQUE NATIONALE DU CANADA

---

2 Complexe Desjardins, Montreal, QC, H5B 1B4
(514) 281-9650
Emp Here 20
SIC 6021 National commercial banks

D-U-N-S 24-082-3914   (BR)
DESJARDINS GROUPE D'ASSURANCES GENERALES INC
1 Complexe Desjardins Bureau 1, Montreal, QC, H5B 1B1
(514) 350-8300
Emp Here 200
SIC 6411 Insurance agents, brokers, and service

D-U-N-S 24-987-7804   (HQ)
DESJARDINS HOLDING FINANCIER INC
1 Rue Complexe Desjardins S 40e Etage, Montreal, QC, H5B 1J1
(418) 838-7870
Emp Here 100   *Emp Total* 15,000
Sales 687,216,833
SIC 6411 Insurance agents, brokers, and service
Sec Renaud Coulombe
Dir Real Bellemare

D-U-N-S 20-571-8609   (BR)
DESJARDINS SECURITE FINANCIERE, COMPAGNIE D'ASSURANCE VIE
1 Complex Desjardins, Montreal, QC, H5B 1E2
(514) 285-7700
Emp Here 500
SIC 6311 Life insurance

D-U-N-S 25-108-9967   (BR)
DESJARDINS SECURITE FINANCIERE, COMPAGNIE D'ASSURANCE VIE
2 Complexe Desjardins Tour E, Montreal, QC, H5B 1E2
(514) 350-8700
Emp Here 500
SIC 6311 Life insurance

D-U-N-S 25-190-7978   (BR)
DESJARDINS SECURITE FINANCIERE, COMPAGNIE D'ASSURANCE VIE
DESJARDINS FINANCIAL SECURITIES, LIFE INSURANCE COMPANY
1 Complexe Desjardins, Montreal, QC, H5B 1E2
(514) 285-3000
Emp Here 500
SIC 6311 Life insurance

D-U-N-S 25-334-5227   (BR)
FEDERATION DES CAISSES DESJARDINS DU QUEBEC
1 Complex Desjardins, Montreal, QC, H5B 1B2
(514) 281-7000
Emp Here 500
SIC 6062 State credit unions

D-U-N-S 20-857-0440   (HQ)
FIDUCIE DESJARDINS INC
DESJARDINS
1 Complexe Desjardins Tour S, Montreal, QC, H5B 1E4
(514) 286-9441
Emp Here 700   *Emp Total* 15,000
Sales 151,174,570
SIC 6733 Trusts, nec
Pr Guy Cormier
VP Yvon Vinet
Sec Renaud Coulombe
Dir Serge Tourangeau
Dir Carole Chevalier
Dir Annie P. Belanger
Dir Sylvain Dessureault
Dir Yves Genest
Dir Jean-Robert Laporte
Dir Neil Hawthorn

D-U-N-S 24-240-4585   (BR)
FIDUCIE DESJARDINS INC

DESJARDINS TRUST
2 Complexe Desjardinstour E, Montreal, QC, H5B 1C1
(514) 499-8440
Emp Here 20
SIC 6733 Trusts, nec

D-U-N-S 20-332-4280   (SL)
GROUPE IMMOBILIER DESJARDINS INC
GID
1 Complexe Desjardins S 25e Etage, Montreal, QC, H5B 1B3
(514) 281-7000
Emp Here 26   *Sales* 2,480,664
SIC 6531 Real estate agents and managers

D-U-N-S 25-142-8033   (BR)
VALEURS MOBILIERES DESJARDINS INC
DESJARDINS SECURITIES
2 Complexe Desjardins Tour E 15 +Tage, Montreal, QC, H5B 1J2
(514) 286-3180
Emp Here 1,200
SIC 6211 Security brokers and dealers

Montreal, QC H7A
Hochelaga County

D-U-N-S 20-716-7409   (BR)
COMMISSION SCOLAIRE DE LAVAL
ECOLE PRIMAIRE FLEUR-SOLEIL
8585 Rue De L'Eglise, Montreal, QC, H7A 1L1
(450) 662-7000
Emp Here 50
SIC 8211 Elementary and secondary schools

D-U-N-S 20-716-7680   (BR)
COMMISSION SCOLAIRE DE LAVAL
ECOLE PRIMAIRE NOTRE-DAME-DU-SOURIRE
240 Rue Des Sapins, Montreal, QC, H7A 2W7
(450) 662-7000
Emp Here 50
SIC 8211 Elementary and secondary schools

D-U-N-S 20-806-8002   (BR)
COUCHE-TARD INC
8050 Av Marcel-Villeneuve, Montreal, QC, H7A 4C5
(450) 665-4367
Emp Here 25
SIC 5411 Grocery stores

Montreal, QC H7B
Hochelaga County

D-U-N-S 24-678-8079   (SL)
CENTRE D'HEBERGEMENT ST-FRANCOIS INC
4105 Montee Masson, Montreal, QC, H7B 1B6
(450) 666-6541
Emp Here 60   *Sales* 2,845,467
SIC 8059 Nursing and personal care, nec

D-U-N-S 20-716-7425   (BR)
COMMISSION SCOLAIRE DE LAVAL
ECOLE PRIMAIRE HEBERT
50 Rue Pare, Montreal, QC, H7B 1B3
(450) 662-7000
Emp Here 50
SIC 8211 Elementary and secondary schools

D-U-N-S 25-791-6817   (SL)
PLACEMENTS M.G.O INC
RESIDENCE DU BOHNEUR, LA
5855 Rue Boulard, Montreal, QC, H7B 1A3
(450) 666-1567
Emp Here 50   *Sales* 2,261,782
SIC 8051 Skilled nursing care facilities

Montreal, QC H7C
Hochelaga County

D-U-N-S 24-902-8598   (SL)
2321-1998 QUEBEC INC
MONTREAL BRIQUE ET PIERRE
1070 Montee Masson, Montreal, QC, H7C 2R2
(450) 661-1515
Emp Here 60   *Sales* 9,988,687
SIC 6712 Bank holding companies
Pr Pr Guy Lucas

D-U-N-S 24-855-2841   (BR)
4207602 CANADA INC
TRICOTS CAMEO, LES
875 Montee Saint-Francois, Montreal, QC, H7C 2S8
(514) 881-2525
Emp Here 35
SIC 4225 General warehousing and storage

D-U-N-S 20-055-7374   (SL)
ALGON ISOLATIONS (2000) INC
4800 Rue Bernard-Lefebvre, Montreal, QC, H7C 0A5
(450) 661-3472
Emp Here 50   *Sales* 4,231,721
SIC 1742 Plastering, drywall, and insulation

D-U-N-S 20-190-8451   (HQ)
CAISSE POPULAIRE DESJARDINS DES MILLE-ILES
CENTRE DE SERVICE DUVERNAY
(*Suby of* Caisse populaire Desjardins des Mille-Iles)
4433 Boul De La Concorde E, Montreal, QC, H7C 1M4
(450) 661-7274
Emp Here 40   *Emp Total* 100
Sales 16,184,912
SIC 6062 State credit unions
Genl Mgr Sylvain Filion
Pr Normand De Montigny
VP Martine Lafrance
Sec Guy Villeneuve
Dir Anne-Catherine Farley
Dir Marie-Helene Forget
Dir Michel Gingras
Dir Bilal Khoder
Dir Chilandre Patry
Dir Jessica Pilon

D-U-N-S 24-358-2363   (BR)
CANARM LTD
2555 Rue Bernard-Lefebvre, Montreal, QC, H7C 0A5
(450) 665-2535
Emp Here 40
SIC 5063 Electrical apparatus and equipment

D-U-N-S 25-783-3590   (SL)
CENTRE DE CONDITIONEMENT PHYSIQUE ATLANTIS INC
ATLANTIS
4745 Av Des Industries, Montreal, QC, H7C 1A1
(450) 664-2285
Emp Here 55   *Sales* 4,596,524
SIC 3949 Sporting and athletic goods, nec

D-U-N-S 24-346-3358   (BR)
CENTRE DE SANTE ET DE SERVICES SOCIAUX DE LAVAL
CENTRE D'HEBERGEMENT DE LA PINIERE
4895 Rue Saint-Joseph, Montreal, QC, H7C 1H6
(450) 661-3305
Emp Here 100
SIC 8361 Residential care

D-U-N-S 20-215-6303   (HQ)
GEORGE COUREY INC
COURTEX
6620 Rue Ernest-Cormier, Montreal, QC, H7C 2T5

(450) 661-6620
Emp Here 78   *Emp Total* 90
Sales 9,849,695
SIC 5023 Homefurnishings
Pr Pr Ronald Courey
  Micheal Courey
VP VP Gerald Courey

D-U-N-S 24-557-8062   (BR)
GRIMARD.CA INC
TELECOMMUNICATIONS GRIMARD, DIV
1855 Rue Bernard-Lefebvre Bureau 100, Montreal, QC, H7C 0A5
(450) 665-5553
Emp Here 20
SIC 3625 Relays and industrial controls

D-U-N-S 24-515-3648   (HQ)
MAGASINS HART INC
BARGAIN GIANT STORES
900 Place Paul-Kane, Montreal, QC, H7C 2T2
(450) 661-4155
Emp Here 170   *Emp Total* 100
Sales 57,055,267
SIC 5311 Department stores
Pr Paul Nassar

D-U-N-S 24-562-0927   (BR)
METRO RICHELIEU INC
SUPER C
4400 Boul De La Concorde E, Montreal, QC, H7C 2R4
(450) 661-4525
Emp Here 60
SIC 5411 Grocery stores

D-U-N-S 20-181-1275   (BR)
PEPSICO CANADA ULC
FRITO-LAY CANADA
(*Suby of* Pepsico, Inc.)
6755 Rue Ernest-Cormier, Montreal, QC, H7C 2T4
(450) 664-5800
Emp Here 250
SIC 2096 Potato chips and similar snacks

D-U-N-S 24-683-7673   (SL)
SYSTEMES INTERIEURS BERNARD MNJ & ASSOCIES INC
5000 Rue Bernard-Lefebvre, Montreal, QC, H7C 0A5
(450) 665-1335
Emp Here 250   *Sales* 21,304,524
SIC 1742 Plastering, drywall, and insulation
Pr Pr Hugo Bernard
  Nick Bernard
Genl Mgr Daniel Courchesne
Fin Ex Jean-Luc Villette

D-U-N-S 24-343-9515   (BR)
UNIBOARD CANADA INC
UNIBOARD SURFACES
5555 Rue Ernest-Cormier, Montreal, QC, H7C 2S9
(450) 661-7122
Emp Here 100
SIC 2426 Hardwood dimension and flooring mills

Montreal, QC H7E
Hochelaga County

D-U-N-S 20-300-9399   (BR)
BANQUE NATIONALE DU CANADA
3131 Boul De La Concorde E Bureau A, Montreal, QC, H7E 4W4
(450) 661-4132
Emp Here 25
SIC 6021 National commercial banks

D-U-N-S 24-426-3005   (SL)
CSH VILLA VAL DES ARBRES INC
LOGGIAS ET LA VILLA VAL-DES-ARBRES, LES
3245 Boul Saint-Martin E Bureau 3241, Montreal, QC, H7E 4T6

(450) 661-0911
Emp Here 20   *Sales* 729,607
SIC 8361 Residential care

D-U-N-S 25-847-3818   (BR)
CHARTWELL QUEBEC (MEL) HOLDINGS INC
LOGGIAS VILLA VAL DES ARBRES, LES
3245 Boul Saint-Martin E, Montreal, QC, H7E 4T6
(450) 661-0911
Emp Here 149
SIC 8361 Residential care

D-U-N-S 20-716-7813   (BR)
COMMISSION SCOLAIRE DE LAVAL
ECOLE PRIMAIRE VAL-DES-ARBRES
3145 Av Du Saguenay, Montreal, QC, H7E 1H6
(450) 662-7000
Emp Here 50
SIC 8211 Elementary and secondary schools

D-U-N-S 24-893-3483   (BR)
COMMISSION SCOLAIRE DE LAVAL
INSTITUT DE PROTECTION CONTRE LES INCENDIES DU QUEBEC (IPIQ), L'
1740 Montee Masson, Montreal, QC, H7E 4P2
(450) 662-7000
Emp Here 75
SIC 8331 Job training and related services

D-U-N-S 24-052-6814   (HQ)
COMPAGNIE DE CONSTRUCTION ET DE DEVELOPPEMENT CRIE LTEE, LA
(*Suby of* Cree Regional Economic Enterprises Company (Cree Co) Inc)
3983 Boul Lite, Montreal, QC, H7E 1A3
(450) 661-1102
Emp Here 35   *Emp Total* 300
Sales 69,677,469
SIC 1522 Residential construction, nec
Pr Robert Baribeau
Sec Tanya Pash
Dir Randy Bosum
Dir Jackie Blacksmith
Dir Emily Whiskeychan Gilpin
Dir James Bobbish
Dir Clarence Sr. Joly
Dir Rusty Cheezo
Dir Derrick Neeposh
Dir George Sandy

D-U-N-S 24-768-9623   (SL)
CONSTRUCTION SAVITE INC
1200 Place Verner, Montreal, QC, H7E 4P2
(450) 661-3977
Emp Here 40   *Sales* 4,908,000
SIC 1741 Masonry and other stonework

D-U-N-S 24-049-6237   (BR)
CORPORATION ARCHIEPISCOPALE CATHOLIQUE ROMAINE DE MONTREAL
PAROISE SAINT-SYLVAIN
(*Suby of* Corporation Archiepiscopale Catholique Romaine de Montreal)
750 Boul Saint-Sylvain, Montreal, QC, H7E 2X3
(450) 661-1532
Emp Here 25
SIC 8661 Religious organizations

D-U-N-S 24-520-4222   (BR)
DOLLARAMA S.E.C.
DOLLARAMA
5845 Boul Robert-Bourassa, Montreal, QC, H7E 0A4
(450) 661-4038
Emp Here 20
SIC 5999 Miscellaneous retail stores, nec

D-U-N-S 24-650-5606   (SL)
DONCAR CONSTRUCTION INC
4085 Rang Saint-Elzear E, Montreal, QC, H7E 4P2

Emp Here 70   *Sales* 12,257,398
SIC 1623 Water, sewer, and utility lines
Pr Pr Jocelyn Giguere

Eric Giguere
Joseph Giguere

D-U-N-S 25-527-9770   (SL)
ENTREPRISES D'ELECTRICITE OMEGA INC, LES
3751 Boul Lite, Montreal, QC, H7E 4X8
(514) 328-1893
Emp Here 50   *Sales* 4,377,642
SIC 1731 Electrical work

D-U-N-S 25-335-2702   (SL)
J-H QUALITY FOOD INC
1700 Montee Masson, Montreal, QC, H7E 4P2
(819) 469-7945
Emp Here 50   *Sales* 18,159,550
SIC 5141 Groceries, general line
Pr Guy Nantais

D-U-N-S 24-085-8451   (SL)
LES ENTREPRISES UNI VAL INC
1195 Montee Masson, Montreal, QC, H7E 4P2
(450) 661-8444
Emp Here 20   *Sales* 5,526,400
SIC 1522 Residential construction, nec
Pr Pr Frank Mentone
VP VP Luciano Mentone

D-U-N-S 25-200-7547   (SL)
NABASHOU CONSTRUCTION INC
(*Suby of* Cree Regional Economic Enterprises Company (Cree Co) Inc)
3983 Boul Lite, Montreal, QC, H7E 1A3
(450) 661-1102
Emp Here 20   *Sales* 3,246,400
SIC 1611 Highway and street construction

D-U-N-S 24-354-2144   (BR)
SIMARD-BEAUDRY CONSTRUCTION INC
4297 Rang Saint-Elzear E, Montreal, QC, H7E 4P2

Emp Here 60
SIC 1429 Crushed and broken stone, nec

Montreal, QC H7J
Hochelaga County

D-U-N-S 25-780-0979   (SL)
CLUB DE GOLF ST-FRANCOIS LTEE
3000 Boul Des Mille-Iles, Montreal, QC, H7J 1G1
(450) 666-4958
Emp Here 65   *Sales* 2,626,585
SIC 7997 Membership sports and recreation clubs

D-U-N-S 24-710-7675   (SL)
TRANSPORT SCOLAIRE DUVERNAY INC
6990 Av Des Perron, Montreal, QC, H7J 1G6
(450) 625-1887
Emp Here 30   *Sales* 875,528
SIC 4151 School buses

Montreal, QC H7K
Hochelaga County

D-U-N-S 20-716-7797   (BR)
COMMISSION SCOLAIRE DE LAVAL
ECOLE PRIMAIRE STE-BEATRICE
5409 Rue De Prince-Rupert, Montreal, QC, H7K 2L7
(450) 662-7000
Emp Here 50
SIC 8211 Elementary and secondary schools

D-U-N-S 20-716-7870   (BR)
COMMISSION SCOLAIRE DE LAVAL
ECOLE PRIMAIRE LA SOURCE
2255 Boul Prudentiel, Montreal, QC, H7K 2C1
(450) 662-7000
Emp Here 50
SIC 8211 Elementary and secondary schools

D-U-N-S 20-716-7490   (BR)
COMMISSION SCOLAIRE DE LAVAL
ECOLE PRIMAIRE CHARLES-BRUNEAU
3001 Rue D'Amay, Montreal, QC, H7K 3P9
(450) 662-7000
Emp Here 50
SIC 8211 Elementary and secondary schools

D-U-N-S 20-716-7516   (BR)
COMMISSION SCOLAIRE DE LAVAL
ECOLE SECONDAIRE L'ODYSSEE-DES-JEUNES
4600 Rue Cyrille-Delage, Montreal, QC, H7K 2S4
(450) 662-7000
Emp Here 50
SIC 8211 Elementary and secondary schools

Montreal, QC H7L
Hochelaga County

D-U-N-S 25-674-4442   (SL)
2525-7577 QUEBEC INC.
3050 Boul Industriel, Montreal, QC, H7L 4P7

Emp Here 150   *Sales* 21,202,403
SIC 2821 Plastics materials and resins
Pr Pr Guy David
James Quinn
Richard Maille

D-U-N-S 25-242-7315   (HQ)
2982897 CANADA INC
EPM MECANIC
(*Suby of* 2982897 Canada Inc)
2425 Rue Michelin, Montreal, QC, H7L 5B9
(514) 332-4830
Emp Here 50   *Emp Total* 50
Sales 4,377,642
SIC 1711 Plumbing, heating, air-conditioning

D-U-N-S 25-257-9339   (SL)
3093-6975 QUEBEC INC
CIE D'ENSIGNES MONTREAL NEON
1780 Place Martenot Bureau 17, Montreal, QC, H7L 5B5
(450) 668-4888
Emp Here 50   *Sales* 3,064,349
SIC 3993 Signs and advertising specialties

D-U-N-S 24-365-3990   (SL)
9183-0943 QUEBEC INC
2130 Boul Dagenais O, Montreal, QC, H7L 5X9
(450) 963-9558
Emp Here 380   *Sales* 92,341,120
SIC 6712 Bank holding companies
Pr Pr Marc Mercier
VP VP Jean-Guy Dumoulin
Jacques Dumoulin
Gerald Dumoulin
Richard Desautels

D-U-N-S 24-335-6560   (BR)
ALCOA CANADA CIE
DIV HOWMET LAVAL CASTING
4001 Des Laurentides (A-15) E, Montreal, QC, H7L 3H7
(450) 680-2500
Emp Here 273
SIC 3334 Primary aluminum

D-U-N-S 20-257-2731   (HQ)
ALIMENTS WHYTE'S INC, LES
MRS. WHYTE'S PRODUCTS
1540 Rue Des Patriotes, Montreal, QC, H7L 2N6
(450) 625-1976
Emp Here 25   *Emp Total* 20
Sales 31,011,786
SIC 5141 Groceries, general line
Ch Bd Paul Kawaja
Pr Elisabeth Kawaja
Sec Andrew Anderson

D-U-N-S 20-210-7827   (SL)
AVMOR LTEE
ECOPURE
950 Rue Michelin, Montreal, QC, H7L 5C1
(450) 629-8074
Emp Here 100   *Sales* 9,703,773
SIC 2842 Polishes and sanitation goods
Avrum Morrow
Mattie Chinks
Dir Juli Morrow

D-U-N-S 25-307-3159   (SL)
CLSC-CHSLD STE-ROSE-DE-LAVAL
280 Boul Du Roi-Du-Nord, Montreal, QC, H7L 4L2
(450) 622-5110
Emp Here 450   *Sales* 27,582,960
SIC 8051 Skilled nursing care facilities
Genl Mgr Marie Beauchamp
France Ferron

D-U-N-S 20-738-0809   (HQ)
CAMFIL CANADA INC
ENTREPRISE CAMFIL FARR POWER SYSTEMS N A
2785 Av Francis-Hughes, Montreal, QC, H7L 3J6
(450) 629-3030
Emp Here 50   *Emp Total* 50
Sales 24,222,952
SIC 5085 Industrial supplies
Pr Pr Armando Brunetti
Darrell Cain
Dir Carl Larochelle
Dir Per Carlsson

D-U-N-S 25-247-4866   (SL)
CATHELLE INC
3465 Boul Industriel, Montreal, QC, H7L 4S3

Emp Here 25   *Sales* 6,502,070
SIC 5063 Electrical apparatus and equipment

D-U-N-S 20-261-9867   (SL)
CENTRE DE READAPTATION DEFICIENCE INTELECTUELLE NORMAND-LARAMEE, LE
CRDI
261 Boul Sainte-Rose, Montreal, QC, H7L 1M1
(450) 622-4376
Emp Here 36   *Sales* 5,889,600
SIC 8699 Membership organizations, nec
Francois Ducharme

D-U-N-S 25-780-6380   (SL)
CIRION BIOPHARMA RECHERCHE INC
(*Suby of* Cirion Services d'Essais Cliniques Inc)
3150 Rue Delaunay, Montreal, QC, H7L 5E1
(450) 688-6445
Emp Here 80   *Sales* 4,377,642
SIC 8731 Commercial physical research

D-U-N-S 20-716-7532   (BR)
COMMISSION SCOLAIRE DE LAVAL
ECOLE SECONDAIRE PAVILLON LATOUR
234 Boul Sainte-Rose, Montreal, QC, H7L 1L6
(450) 662-7000
Emp Here 50
SIC 8211 Elementary and secondary schools

D-U-N-S 20-716-7466   (BR)
COMMISSION SCOLAIRE DE LAVAL
ECOLE SECONDAIRE CURE-ANTOINE-LABELLE
216 Boul Marc-Aurele-Fortin, Montreal, QC, H7L 1Z5
(450) 662-7000
Emp Here 50
SIC 8211 Elementary and secondary schools

D-U-N-S 20-716-7839   (BR)
COMMISSION SCOLAIRE DE LAVAL
ECOLE PRIMAIRE VILLEMAIRE
211 Boul Sainte-Rose, Montreal, QC, H7L 1L7
(450) 662-7000
Emp Here 50

SIC 8211 Elementary and secondary schools

D-U-N-S 20-806-7756   (BR)
COUCHE-TARD INC
258 Boul Sainte-Rose, Montreal, QC, H7L 1M2
(450) 625-3260
Emp Here 25
SIC 5411 Grocery stores

D-U-N-S 25-357-6409   (BR)
DEVTEK AEROSPACE INC.
AEROSPATIALE HOCHELAGA DIV OF
3675 Boul Industriel, Montreal, QC, H7L 4S3
(450) 629-3454
Emp Here 180
SIC 3599 Industrial machinery, nec

D-U-N-S 20-533-7350   (SL)
ENSEIGNES MONTREAL NEON INC
CIE D'ENSEIGNES MONTREAL NEON
1780 Place Martenot, Montreal, QC, H7L 5B5
(514) 955-3333
Emp Here 50   *Sales* 3,957,782
SIC 3993 Signs and advertising specialties

D-U-N-S 25-110-1150   (BR)
GENERAL ELECTRIC CANADA COMPANY
GE
(*Suby of* General Electric Company)
3060 Rue Peugeot, Montreal, QC, H7L 5C5
(450) 688-9690
Emp Here 50
SIC 3625 Relays and industrial controls

D-U-N-S 20-309-4859   (SL)
GROUPE DIJON INC
2117 Rue Berlier, Montreal, QC, H7L 3M9
(450) 622-5522
Emp Here 50   *Sales* 1,969,939
SIC 8322 Individual and family services

D-U-N-S 24-763-5337   (HQ)
GROUPE F.G.B. 2000 INC, LE
(*Suby of* Groupe F.G.B. 2000 Inc, Le)
1225 Rue Bergar, Montreal, QC, H7L 4Z7
(450) 967-0076
Emp Here 80   *Emp Total* 172
Sales 58,141,699
SIC 5141 Groceries, general line
Pr Pr Sylva Belanger

D-U-N-S 25-863-1704   (BR)
GROUPE LD INC
DISTRIBUTION D.M.C.
1865 Boul Dagenais O, Montreal, QC, H7L 5A3
(450) 622-3220
Emp Here 20
SIC 5084 Industrial machinery and equipment

D-U-N-S 20-298-1197   (BR)
IMPORTATIONS DE-RO-MA (1983) LTEE
GLUTINO
3750 Av Francis-Hughes, Montreal, QC, H7L 5A9
(450) 667-6549
Emp Here 100
SIC 6111 Federal and federally sponsored credit agencies

D-U-N-S 20-999-6289   (SL)
INSTALLATIONS ELECTRIQUES PICHETTE INC, LES
3080 Rue Peugeot, Montreal, QC, H7L 5C5
(450) 682-4411
Emp Here 50   *Sales* 4,377,642
SIC 1731 Electrical work

D-U-N-S 20-222-8763   (HQ)
KOLOSTAT INC
KOLOFIS
2005 Rue Le Chatelier, Montreal, QC, H7L 5B3
(514) 333-7333
Emp Here 195   *Emp Total* 2
Sales 17,510,568
SIC 1711 Plumbing, heating, air-conditioning
Pr Pr Stanley H. Segal

▲ Public Company   ■ Public Company Family Member   **HQ** Headquarters   **BR** Branch   **SL** Single Location

John P. Billick
VP Fin Peter Murray
Sr VP Eric Hintermueller
Sr VP Jacques Destrempes

D-U-N-S 20-332-5001   (BR)
LIFTOW LIMITED
1445 Rue Bergar, Montreal, QC, H7L 4Z7
(450) 901-3500
Emp Here 20
SIC 5084 Industrial machinery and equipment

D-U-N-S 20-226-9254   (HQ)
MEP TECHNOLOGIES INC
(*Suby of* Double A Corp Inc)
3100 Rue Peugeot, Montreal, QC, H7L 5C6
(450) 682-0804
Emp Here 164   *Emp Total* 250
Sales 36,772,193
SIC 3444 Sheet Metalwork
Armand Afilalo
Dir Joseph Sassano
Dir Kathy Afilalo

D-U-N-S 20-300-7711   (BR)
PARKER HANNIFIN CANADA
PARKER FILTERATION CANADA DIV OF
2785 Av Francis-Hughes, Montreal, QC, H7L 3J6
(450) 629-3030
Emp Here 90
SIC 3569 General industrial machinery, nec

D-U-N-S 20-715-2948   (BR)
PERI FORMWORK SYSTEMS INC
PERI SYSTEME DE COFFRAGE
3981 Boul Industriel, Montreal, QC, H7L 4S3
(450) 662-0057
Emp Here 30
SIC 1799 Special trade contractors, nec

D-U-N-S 24-401-3751   (SL)
PLOMBERIE DANIEL COTE INC
3000 Montee Saint-Aubin, Montreal, QC, H7L 3N8
(450) 973-2545
Emp Here 133   *Sales* 11,673,712
SIC 1711 Plumbing, heating, air-conditioning
Pr Pr Daniel Cote
Benoit Malouin
Sec Marie-Claude Lebeuf
Dir Cote Jeremie

D-U-N-S 20-725-9482   (SL)
PNEUS EXPRESS INC, LES
DISTRIBUTION PNEUS GLOBAL
1333 Nord Laval A-440 O, Montreal, QC, H7L 3W3
(450) 668-0463
Emp Here 30   *Sales* 15,072,000
SIC 5014 Tires and tubes
Pr Pr Daniel Guenette

D-U-N-S 20-107-2407   (HQ)
PRODUITS INTEGRES AVIOR INC
(*Suby of* Produits Integres Avior Inc)
1001 Nord Laval (A-440) O Bureau 200, Montreal, QC, H7L 3W3
(450) 629-6200
Emp Here 250   *Emp Total* 250
Sales 53,772,036
SIC 3728 Aircraft parts and equipment, nec
Pr Stephen Kearns
Sec Karanjit S. Dulat
Dir Alexander Smirnow
Dir Pierre Racine
Dir Cynthia Z Brighton
Dir Howard L. Romanow
Dir Guy Boutin

D-U-N-S 24-860-1671   (SL)
R.E.A.L. BAGEL EN GROS INC.
VENTE EN GROS R.E.A.L. BAGEL
1585 Boul Dagenais O, Montreal, QC, H7L 5A3

Emp Here 24   *Sales* 6,594,250
SIC 1541 Industrial buildings and warehouses

Lennie Ryer
Samuel J. Frishman
Opers Mgr Mitchell Litwin

D-U-N-S 20-257-3192   (SL)
S & L TRANSPORT INC
30 Rue Jacques-Cartier, Montreal, QC, H7L 1B2
(450) 622-7985
Emp Here 50   *Sales* 1,386,253
SIC 4151 School buses

D-U-N-S 20-535-2334   (BR)
WOLSELEY CANADA INC
WOLSELEY GROUPE CVACR, DIV OF
(*Suby of* WOLSELEY PLC)
4075 Boul Industriel Bureau 624, Montreal, QC, H7L 6E3
(450) 628-5777
Emp Here 30
SIC 5074 Plumbing and heating equipment and supplies (hydronics)

D-U-N-S 20-115-0294   (BR)
WOLSELEY CANADA INC
REFAC CLIMAREF DIV
(*Suby of* WOLSELEY PLC)
4075 Boul Industriel Bureau 624, Montreal, QC, H7L 6E3
(450) 628-6053
Emp Here 50
SIC 3822 Environmental controls

Montreal, QC H7M
Hochelaga County

D-U-N-S 20-716-7714   (BR)
COMMISSION SCOLAIRE DE LAVAL
ECOLE PRIMAIRE PAUL-COMTOIS
1701 Rue De Lucerne, Montreal, QC, H7M 2E9
(450) 662-7000
Emp Here 50
SIC 8211 Elementary and secondary schools

D-U-N-S 20-215-8820   (HQ)
CYRS LTEE
(*Suby of* Cyrs Ltee)
1789 Boul Des Laurentides, Montreal, QC, H7M 2P7
(450) 669-5644
Emp Here 50   *Emp Total* 70
Sales 4,231,721
SIC 5621 Women's clothing stores

D-U-N-S 25-779-5203   (SL)
D B D AUTO INC
DESMEULES HUYNDAI
1215 Boul Des Laurentides, Montreal, QC, H7M 2Y1
(450) 668-6393
Emp Here 26   *Sales* 11,261,263
SIC 5511 New and used car dealers
Pr Pr Claude Desmeules

D-U-N-S 20-573-5272   (BR)
DESJARDINS SECURITE FINANCIERE, COMPAGNIE D'ASSURANCE VIE
500 Boul Saint-Martin O Bureau 220, Montreal, QC, H7M 3Y2
(450) 629-0342
Emp Here 20
SIC 6311 Life insurance

D-U-N-S 24-351-7104   (SL)
DISTRIBUTION G.V.A. (CANADA) INC
(*Suby of* Distribution G.V.A. Inc)
1950 Boul Des Laurentides, Montreal, QC, H7M 2Y5
(450) 629-6660
Emp Here 50   *Sales* 21,108,170
SIC 5194 Tobacco and tobacco products
Pr Pr Vincent Albanese

D-U-N-S 25-325-0930   (BR)
GROUPE BMTC INC

CENTRE DE LIQUIDATION BRAULT & MARTINEAU
1770 Boul Des Laurentides, Montreal, QC, H7M 2Y4
(450) 667-3211
Emp Here 30
SIC 5712 Furniture stores

D-U-N-S 25-617-7168   (BR)
GROUPE BMTC INC
ECONOMAX
1770 Boul Des Laurentides, Montreal, QC, H7M 2Y4
(450) 667-8333
Emp Here 20
SIC 5712 Furniture stores

D-U-N-S 25-778-6434   (BR)
NAUTILUS PLUS INC
1780 Boul Des Laurentides, Montreal, QC, H7M 2Y4
(450) 668-2686
Emp Here 50
SIC 7999 Amusement and recreation, nec

D-U-N-S 20-852-8765   (BR)
SIR WILFRID LAURIER SCHOOL BOARD
VIMONT COMPETENCY DEVELOPMENT CENTRE
2100 Boul Des Laurentides, Montreal, QC, H7M 2Y6
(450) 688-2933
Emp Here 25
SIC 8211 Elementary and secondary schools

Montreal, QC H7N
Hochelaga County

D-U-N-S 24-409-8757   (BR)
ASM CANADA, INC
ADVANTAGE SALES AND MARKETING CANADA
(*Suby of* Advantage Sales & Marketing Inc.)
2 Place Laval Unite 460, Montreal, QC, H7N 5N6
(450) 975-2525
Emp Here 30
SIC 5141 Groceries, general line

D-U-N-S 25-963-6470   (BR)
BANK OF MONTREAL
BMO CENTRE DE FINANCEMENT DE VEHICULE
2 Place Laval Bureau 270, Montreal, QC, H7N 5N6
(450) 975-2884
Emp Here 40
SIC 6159 Miscellaneous business credit institutions

D-U-N-S 24-018-1495   (SL)
COLLEGE ENSEIGNANT GENERAL ET PROFESSIONNEL MONTMORENCY
CEGEP MONTMORENCY
475 Boul De L'Avenir, Montreal, QC, H7N 5H9
(450) 975-6100
Emp Here 600   *Sales* 80,569,130
SIC 8221 Colleges and universities
Genl Mgr Francois Allard

D-U-N-S 20-003-8862   (BR)
HOME DEPOT OF CANADA INC
HOME DEPOT
(*Suby of* The Home Depot Inc)
1400 Boul Le Corbusier, Montreal, QC, H7N 6J5
(450) 680-2225
Emp Here 100
SIC 5251 Hardware stores

Montreal, QC H7P
Hochelaga County

D-U-N-S 24-853-4831   (SL)
3609022 CANADA INC
4155 Chomedey A-13 E, Montreal, QC, H7P 0A8
(450) 628-4488
Emp Here 75   *Sales* 22,521,663
SIC 5021 Furniture
Pr Pr David Berger
Dir Ronald Leader

D-U-N-S 24-256-1020   (SL)
9016-8063 QUEBEC INC
FUNTROPOLIS
3925 Boul Cure-Labelle, Montreal, QC, H7P 0A5
(450) 688-9222
Emp Here 70   *Sales* 2,699,546
SIC 7996 Amusement parks

D-U-N-S 20-152-3656   (BR)
AIA AUTOMATION INC
2886 Boul Daniel-Johnson, Montreal, QC, H7P 5Z7
(450) 680-1846
Emp Here 30
SIC 3569 General industrial machinery, nec

D-U-N-S 20-197-4839   (SL)
C.A. SPENCER INC
(*Suby of* Caslumber Inc)
2930 Boul Dagenais O, Montreal, QC, H7P 1T1
(450) 622-2420
Emp Here 125   *Sales* 48,529,944
SIC 5031 Lumber, plywood, and millwork
Pr Pr Claude Cadrin
Remi Cadrin
Michel Ferron

D-U-N-S 24-021-0583   (SL)
CENTRE SPORTIF CARREFOUR 1992 LTEE
CARREFOUR MULTISPORT
3095 Nord Laval (A-440) O, Montreal, QC, H7P 4W5
(450) 687-1857
Emp Here 60   *Sales* 2,407,703
SIC 7997 Membership sports and recreation clubs

D-U-N-S 24-330-8082   (BR)
CHEVRONS LAVALLOIS INC, LES
(*Suby of* GDTM Inc)
2907 Boul Dagenais O, Montreal, QC, H7P 1T2
(450) 622-4990
Emp Here 20
SIC 2439 Structural wood members, nec

D-U-N-S 24-020-4867   (SL)
CIMENTS LAVALLEE LTEE
4300 Boul Saint-Elzear O, Montreal, QC, H7P 4J4
(450) 622-5448
Emp Here 425   *Sales* 68,225,920
SIC 1611 Highway and street construction
Pr Pr Lyan Lavallee

D-U-N-S 24-570-4655   (BR)
COINAMATIC CANADA INC
COINAMATIC LAUNDRY
4479 Nord Laval (A-440) O, Montreal, QC, H7P 4W6
(450) 688-4808
Emp Here 50
SIC 7359 Equipment rental and leasing, nec

D-U-N-S 25-973-8185   (BR)
COMMISSION SCOLAIRE DE LAVAL
ECOLE DES CEDRES
3785 Boul Sainte-Rose, Montreal, QC, H7P 1C6
(450) 662-7000
Emp Here 64
SIC 8211 Elementary and secondary schools

D-U-N-S 20-032-7513   (BR)
COMMISSION SCOLAIRE DE LAVAL
ECOLE COEUR SOLEIL

3516 Rue Edgar, Montreal, QC, H7P 2E5
(450) 662-7000
Emp Here 30
SIC 8211 Elementary and secondary schools

D-U-N-S 20-716-7664   (BR)
COMMISSION SCOLAIRE DE LAVAL
ECOLE PRIMAIRE MARC-AURELE-FORTIN
3225 Rue Christiane, Montreal, QC, H7P 1K2
(450) 662-7000
Emp Here 50
SIC 8211 Elementary and secondary schools

D-U-N-S 20-716-7615   (BR)
COMMISSION SCOLAIRE DE LAVAL
ECOLE PRIMAIRE LE PETIT-PRINCE
700 Rue Fleury, Montreal, QC, H7P 3B8
(450) 662-7000
Emp Here 50
SIC 8211 Elementary and secondary schools

D-U-N-S 20-716-7482   (BR)
COMMISSION SCOLAIRE DE LAVAL
ECOLE SECONDAIRE JEAN-PIAGET
3150 Boul Dagenais, Montreal, QC, H7P 1V1
(450) 662-7000
Emp Here 50
SIC 8211 Elementary and secondary schools

D-U-N-S 24-126-4089   (BR)
CONNEX TELECOMMUNICATIONS INC
CONNEX SEE SERVICE INC
4616 Rue Louis-B Mayer, Montreal, QC, H7P 6E4
(450) 680-2255
Emp Here 30
SIC 4899 Communication services, nec

D-U-N-S 20-533-1775   (BR)
COSTCO WHOLESALE CANADA LTD
(*Suby of* Costco Wholesale Corporation)
2999 Nord Laval A-440 O, Montreal, QC, H7P 5P4
(450) 686-7420
Emp Here 150
SIC 5099 Durable goods, nec

D-U-N-S 25-274-2655   (BR)
EMCO CORPORATION
3700 Des Laurentides (A-15) O, Montreal, QC, H7P 6A9
(450) 978-0314
Emp Here 40
SIC 5074 Plumbing and heating equipment and supplies (hydronics)

D-U-N-S 24-226-2165   (BR)
ENERGIE VALERO INC
4575 Nord Laval (A-440) O, Montreal, QC, H7P 4W6
(450) 973-9916
Emp Here 20
SIC 5541 Gasoline service stations

D-U-N-S 24-373-2422   (BR)
FGL SPORTS LTD
4855 Rue Louis-B.-Mayer, Montreal, QC, H7P 6C8
(450) 687-5200
Emp Here 137
SIC 5941 Sporting goods and bicycle shops

D-U-N-S 24-250-3030   (SL)
GESKO CONSTRUCTION INC
563 Rue Lindbergh Bureau 200, Montreal, QC, H7P 2N8

Emp Here 25   *Sales* 6,714,320
SIC 1522 Residential construction, nec
Pr Serge Tremblay
VP Josee Otis

D-U-N-S 20-891-0419   (BR)
INDUSTRIELLE ALLIANCE, ASSURANCE ET SERVICES FINANCIERS INC
INDUSTRIELLE ALLIANCE ASSURANCE ET SERVICES FINANCIERS
4455 Nord Laval (A-440) O Unite 200, Montreal, QC, H7P 4W6

(450) 781-1328
Emp Here 25
SIC 6351 Surety insurance

D-U-N-S 25-837-1269   (BR)
INDUSTRO-TECH INC
2886 Boul Daniel-Johnson, Montreal, QC, H7P 5Z7
(450) 682-4498
Emp Here 50
SIC 3613 Switchgear and switchboard apparatus

D-U-N-S 25-779-9684   (BR)
INFORMATIQUE COTE, COULOMBE INC
ICC TECHNOLOGIES
4885 Nord Laval (A-440) O, Montreal, QC, H7P 5P9
(450) 682-7200
Emp Here 25
SIC 7371 Custom computer programming services

D-U-N-S 20-572-0068   (BR)
METRO RICHELIEU INC
SUPER C
3850 Boul Dagenais O, Montreal, QC, H7P 1W1
(450) 628-8143
Emp Here 60
SIC 5141 Groceries, general line

D-U-N-S 25-686-7995   (HQ)
NORDIA INC
3020 Av Jacques-Bureau 2e, Montreal, QC, H7P 6G2
(514) 415-7088
Emp Here 35   *Emp Total* 2,200
Sales 124,653,519
SIC 7389 Business services, nec
Pr Pr John Di Nardo
Sec Stacey Hoisak
Dir Paul R. Henry

D-U-N-S 24-426-0894   (BR)
QUINCAILLERIE RICHELIEU LTEE
SIMTAB NEOS
4855 Nord Laval (A-440) O, Montreal, QC, H7P 5P9
(450) 687-5716
Emp Here 78
SIC 5072 Hardware

D-U-N-S 20-544-0795   (HQ)
SAIL PLEIN AIR INC
BARON SPORTS
(*Suby of* Sail Plein Air Inc)
2850 Av Jacques-Bureau, Montreal, QC, H7P 0B7
(450) 688-6264
Emp Here 100   *Emp Total* 1,400
Sales 119,144,823
SIC 5941 Sporting goods and bicycle shops
Pr Norman Decarie
Sec Daniel Desmrais
  Dale Tschritter
Dir Michel Saucier
Dir Claude Lemieux
Dir Martin Fafard

D-U-N-S 25-428-7654   (SL)
SERVICES EXP INC, LES
4500 Rue Louis-B.-Mayer, Montreal, QC, H7P 6E4
(450) 682-8013
Emp Here 49   *Sales* 3,648,035
SIC 8734 Testing laboratories

D-U-N-S 24-359-2248   (BR)
STAPLES CANADA INC
BUREAU EN GROS
(*Suby of* Staples, Inc.)
4141 Nord Laval (A-440) O, Montreal, QC, H7P 4W6
(450) 680-4200
Emp Here 30
SIC 5943 Stationery stores

D-U-N-S 20-577-8108   (BR)

STRUCTURES BARRETTE INC
(*Suby of* GDTM Inc)
2907 Boul Dagenais O, Montreal, QC, H7P 1T2
(450) 622-4900
Emp Here 20
SIC 2439 Structural wood members, nec

D-U-N-S 24-051-7305   (BR)
TOITURE MAURICIENNE (1982) INC
(*Suby of* GDTM Inc)
2907 Boul Dagenais O, Montreal, QC, H7P 1T2
(450) 328-1612
Emp Here 100
SIC 1761 Roofing, siding, and sheetMetal work

D-U-N-S 25-146-5720   (BR)
TOTAL CREDIT RECOVERY LIMITED
AGENCE DE RECOUVREMENT TCR
4455 Nord Laval (A-440) O, Montreal, QC, H7P 4W6
(450) 680-1800
Emp Here 72
SIC 7322 Adjustment and collection services

D-U-N-S 20-915-3175   (BR)
WOLSELEY CANADA INC
(*Suby of* WOLSELEY PLC)
4200 Rue Louis-B.-Mayer, Montreal, QC, H7P 0G1
(450) 680-4040
Emp Here 220
SIC 5075 Warm air heating and air conditioning

Montreal, QC H7R
Hochelaga County

D-U-N-S 25-284-5508   (SL)
CLUB LAVAL-SUR-LE-LAC, LE
150 Rue Les Peupliers, Montreal, QC, H7R 1G4
(450) 627-2643
Emp Here 100   *Sales* 4,304,681
SIC 7992 Public golf courses

D-U-N-S 20-716-7631   (BR)
COMMISSION SCOLAIRE DE LAVAL
ECOLE PRIMAIRE L'OREE-DES-BOIS
4185 Rue Seguin, Montreal, QC, H7R 2V2
(450) 662-7000
Emp Here 50
SIC 8211 Elementary and secondary schools

Montreal, QC H7S
Hochelaga County

D-U-N-S 25-673-8717   (BR)
AFFILIATED AGENTS EN DOUANES LIMITEE
AFFILIATED INTL TRANSPORT
1616 Sud Laval (A-440) O, Montreal, QC, H7S 2E7
(450) 681-4555
Emp Here 50
SIC 4731 Freight transportation arrangement

D-U-N-S 20-009-5243   (BR)
BOUTIQUE LINEN CHEST (PHASE II) INC
A-1 LINEN CHEST
(*Suby of* Boutique Linen Chest (Phase II) Inc)
1655 Boul Le Corbusier, Montreal, QC, H7S 1Z3
(450) 681-9090
Emp Here 30
SIC 5023 Homefurnishings

D-U-N-S 24-337-2716   (BR)
CASCADES CANADA ULC
CASCADES GROUPE TISSUS LAVAL
2345 Des Laurentides (A-15) E, Montreal, QC,

H7S 1Z7
(450) 688-1152
Emp Here 75
SIC 2676 Sanitary paper products

D-U-N-S 24-892-8595   (SL)
CONCEPT MODE 47 INC
CONCEPT 47 GALERIES LAVAL
1605 Boul Le Corbusier, Montreal, QC, H7S 1Z3
(450) 681-3317
Emp Here 50   *Sales* 3,064,349
SIC 5651 Family clothing stores

D-U-N-S 20-504-5933   (SL)
DIECO EMPORTE-PIECES INC
2577 Boul Le Corbusier, Montreal, QC, H7S 2E8
(450) 682-3129
Emp Here 60   *Sales* 4,961,328
SIC 3544 Special dies, tools, jigs, and fixtures

D-U-N-S 24-676-0375   (BR)
G2MC INC
LA MAISON DU MEUBLE CORBEIL
2323 Des Laurentides (A-15) E, Montreal, QC, H7S 1Z7
(450) 682-3022
Emp Here 100
SIC 5712 Furniture stores

D-U-N-S 24-340-2828   (BR)
GLENCORE CANADA CORPORATION
MINE RAGLAN - LAVAL
1950 Rue Maurice-Gauvin Bureau 300, Montreal, QC, H7S 1Z5
(450) 668-2112
Emp Here 20
SIC 1021 Copper ores

D-U-N-S 24-421-8041   (BR)
GROUPE CANAM INC
GOODCO Z-TECH
807 Rue Marshall Unite 100, Montreal, QC, H7S 1J9
(450) 786-1300
Emp Here 40
SIC 3568 Power transmission equipment, nec

D-U-N-S 24-835-0084   (BR)
GROUPE D'ALIMENTATION MTY INC
GIORGIO
2121 Boul Le Carrefour, Montreal, QC, H7S 2J7
(450) 688-6371
Emp Here 30
SIC 5812 Eating places

D-U-N-S 20-914-9835   (BR)
HILLMAN GROUP CANADA ULC, THE
H. PAULIN & CO., DIV OF
2591 Rue Debray, Montreal, QC, H7S 2J4
(450) 688-4292
Emp Here 30
SIC 5085 Industrial supplies

D-U-N-S 24-274-5615   (HQ)
LABORATOIRE VICTHOM INC
CLINIQUE DU PIED EQUILIBRE
2101 Boul Le Carrefour Bureau 102, Montreal, QC, H7S 2J7
(450) 239-6162
Emp Here 50   *Emp Total* 10
Sales 8,098,638
SIC 8069 Specialty hospitals, except psychiatric
Pr Sylvain Boucher
VP Danielle Boucher
Dir Gilles Laporte

D-U-N-S 20-926-8325   (SL)
MANUFACTURIER TECHCRAFT INC
2025 Rue Cunard, Montreal, QC, H7S 2N1
(450) 767-2020
Emp Here 50
SIC 2517 Wood television and radio cabinets

D-U-N-S 24-762-9975   (BR)
PROVIGO DISTRIBUTION INC

2700 Av Francis-Hughes Bureau 2172, Montreal, QC, H7S 2B9
(514) 383-8800
Emp Here 350
SIC 4225 General warehousing and storage

D-U-N-S 24-363-0907   (BR)
RGIS CANADA ULC
1882 Boul Saint-Martin O Bureau 200, Montreal, QC, H7S 1M9

Emp Here 100
SIC 7389 Business services, nec

D-U-N-S 20-709-6918   (SL)
SOCIETE DE TRANSPORT DE LAVAL
STL
2250 Av Francis-Hughes, Montreal, QC, H7S 2C3
(450) 662-5400
Emp Here 707   *Sales* 33,472,560
SIC 4111 Local and suburban transit
Pr Pr Jean Jacques Beldie
Sec Pierre Cote
Genl Mgr Pierre Giard
VP Sylvie Clermont

D-U-N-S 20-033-6665   (SL)
TRIMAX SECURITE INC
1965 Boul Industriel Bureau 200, Montreal, QC, H7S 1P6
(450) 934-5200
Emp Here 70   *Sales* 2,626,585
SIC 7389 Business services, nec

D-U-N-S 20-243-5244   (HQ)
VERREAULT INC
CONSORTIUM POMERLEAU VERREAULT ACCIONA
1200 Boul Saint-Martin O Bureau 300, Montreal, QC, H7S 2E4
(514) 845-4104
Emp Here 70   *Emp Total* 6,000
Sales 34,960,406
SIC 1542 Nonresidential construction, nec
Pr Pr Marc Verreault
Luc Belanger

D-U-N-S 25-308-0519   (BR)
VILLE DE LAVAL
TRAVAUX PUBLICS
2550 Boul Industriel, Montreal, QC, H7S 2G7
(450) 662-4600
Emp Here 300
SIC 4953 Refuse systems

Montreal, QC H7W
Hochelaga County

D-U-N-S 20-327-9521   (BR)
CENTRE DE SANTE ET DE SERVICES SOCIAUX DE LAVAL
CLSC CHSLD DU RUISSEAU PAPINEAU
1665 Rue Du Couvent, Montreal, QC, H7W 3A8
(450) 687-5690
Emp Here 60
SIC 8093 Specialty outpatient clinics, nec

D-U-N-S 20-716-7789   (BR)
COMMISSION SCOLAIRE DE LAVAL
ECOLE PRIMAIRE SAINT-PAUL
280 92e Av, Montreal, QC, H7W 3N3
(450) 662-7000
Emp Here 50
SIC 8211 Elementary and secondary schools

D-U-N-S 20-716-7573   (BR)
COMMISSION SCOLAIRE DE LAVAL
ECOLE PRIMAIRE LE TANDEM - PAVILLON 1
1640 Rue Gratton, Montreal, QC, H7W 2X8
(450) 662-7000
Emp Here 50
SIC 8211 Elementary and secondary schools

D-U-N-S 25-794-7291   (SL)
CORPORATION DU CENTRE DU SABLON INC
CENTRE DU SABLON
755 Ch Du Sablon, Montreal, QC, H7W 4H5
(450) 688-8961
Emp Here 75   *Sales* 2,918,428
SIC 8322 Individual and family services

D-U-N-S 24-697-4364   (HQ)
GLORY GLOBAL SOLUTIONS (CANADA) INC
GLORY SOLUTIONS GLOBALES CANADA
1111 Chomedey (A-13) E Unit9 200, Montreal, QC, H7W 5J8
(450) 686-8800
Emp Here 40   *Emp Total* 8,440
Sales 10,141,537
SIC 5044 Office equipment
Chris Reagan
Dir Michael R. Henry

D-U-N-S 24-851-7703   (SL)
SIDEL ETK INC
1045 Chomedey A-13 E, Montreal, QC, H7W 4V3
(450) 973-3337
Emp Here 250   *Sales* 47,125,120
SIC 8748 Business consulting, nec
Pr Marc Aury

D-U-N-S 24-736-8023   (BR)
SIR WILFRID LAURIER SCHOOL BOARD
ECOLE PRIMAIRE SOUVENIR
4885 Ch Du Souvenir, Montreal, QC, H7W 1E1
(450) 688-1944
Emp Here 45
SIC 8211 Elementary and secondary schools

D-U-N-S 20-534-3150   (BR)
SIR WILFRID LAURIER SCHOOL BOARD
HILLCREST ACADEMY
265 Rue Bladen, Montreal, QC, H7W 4J8
(450) 688-3002
Emp Here 55
SIC 8211 Elementary and secondary schools

D-U-N-S 24-176-2392   (SL)
TENNIS 13 INC
1013 Chomedey (A-13) E, Montreal, QC, H7W 4V3
(450) 687-9913
Emp Here 60   *Sales* 2,407,703
SIC 7997 Membership sports and recreation clubs

Montreal, QC H7X
Hochelaga County

D-U-N-S 25-780-4658   (BR)
BANQUE NATIONALE DU CANADA
47 Boul Samson, Montreal, QC, H7X 3R8
(450) 689-2120
Emp Here 24
SIC 6021 National commercial banks

D-U-N-S 24-389-5252   (BR)
CENTRE DE SANTE ET DE SERVICES SOCIAUX DE LAVAL
CENTRE D'HEBERGEMENT STE-DOROTHEE
350 Boul Samson, Montreal, QC, H7X 1J4
(450) 689-0933
Emp Here 300
SIC 8361 Residential care

D-U-N-S 25-975-9272   (BR)
COMMISSION SCOLAIRE DE LAVAL
ECOLE SAINT-FRANCOIS
530 Rue Huberdeau, Montreal, QC, H7X 1P7
(450) 662-7000
Emp Here 25
SIC 8211 Elementary and secondary schools

D-U-N-S 24-254-2355   (BR)
FRERES DES ECOLES CHRETIENNES DU CANADA FRANCOPHONE, LES
RESIDENCE DE LA SALLE
(*Suby of* Freres des Ecoles chretiennes du Canada francophone, Les)
300 Ch Du Bord-De-L'Eau Bureau 159, Montreal, QC, H7X 1S9
(450) 689-4151
Emp Here 50
SIC 8361 Residential care

D-U-N-S 20-649-1644   (SL)
GESTION WALTER VANIER
300 Ch Du Bord-De-L'Eau, Montreal, QC, H7X 1S9
(450) 689-4151
Emp Here 65   *Sales* 2,407,703
SIC 8361 Residential care

Montreal, QC H8T
Hochelaga County

D-U-N-S 20-333-0386   (SL)
FABE CUSTOM DOWNSTREAM SYSTEMS INC
CDS
1930 52e Av, Montreal, QC, H8T 2Y3
(514) 633-5933
Emp Here 50   *Sales* 3,638,254
SIC 7699 Repair services, nec

Montreal, QC M5G
Hochelaga County

D-U-N-S 24-630-9665   (BR)
FIDELITY INVESTMENTS CANADA ULC
(*Suby of* Fmr LLC)
100 Rue De La Gauchetiere O Bureau 1400, Montreal, QC, M5G 2N7
(514) 866-7360
Emp Here 50
SIC 6722 Management investment, open-end

Montreal-Est, QC H1B

D-U-N-S 20-420-9225   (SL)
3323501 CANADA INC
GALVAN METAL
8201 Place Marien, Montreal-Est, QC, H1B 5W6
(514) 322-9120
Emp Here 50   *Sales* 3,502,114
SIC 3479 Metal coating and allied services

D-U-N-S 25-625-1331   (SL)
CARDINAL METAL INC
10305 Boul Metropolitain E, Montreal-Est, QC, H1B 1A1
(450) 659-1572
Emp Here 26   *Sales* 2,261,782
SIC 5932 Used merchandise stores

D-U-N-S 20-563-5907   (BR)
ENTREPRISES DOMINION BLUELINE INC, LES
8681 Place Marien, Montreal-Est, QC, H1B 5W6
(514) 323-8982
Emp Here 20
SIC 5112 Stationery and office supplies

D-U-N-S 24-827-8868   (BR)
FEDERAL EXPRESS CANADA CORPORATION
FEDERAL EXPRESS CANADA LTD
(*Suby of* Fedex Corporation)
8481 Place Marien, Montreal-Est, QC, H1B 5W6

(800) 463-3339
Emp Here 50
SIC 7389 Business services, nec

D-U-N-S 24-366-6083   (HQ)
GESTION P & F LALONDE INC
(*Suby of* Gestion P & F Lalonde Inc)
485 Av Marien, Montreal-Est, QC, H1B 4V8
(514) 645-9233
Emp Here 20   *Emp Total* 20
Sales 5,425,920
SIC 1541 Industrial buildings and warehouses
Patrick Lalonde

D-U-N-S 20-219-0294   (BR)
GUAY INC
FORTIER TRANSFERT
11225 Boul Metropolitain E, Montreal-Est, QC, H1B 1A3
(514) 259-1535
Emp Here 25
SIC 7353 Heavy construction equipment rental

D-U-N-S 24-328-1503   (BR)
K+S SEL WINDSOR LTEE
LE SEL DE LA TERRE TM
199 Boul Joseph-Versailles, Montreal-Est, QC, H1B 5J1
(514) 640-4655
Emp Here 20
SIC 2899 Chemical preparations, nec

D-U-N-S 20-922-6260   (BR)
LAFARGE CANADA INC
9990 Boul Metropolitain E, Montreal-Est, QC, H1B 1A2
(514) 640-6130
Emp Here 50
SIC 3273 Ready-mixed concrete

D-U-N-S 20-213-6185   (BR)
NEXEO SOLUTIONS CANADA CORP
(*Suby of* Nexeo Solutions, Inc.)
10515 Rue Notre-Dame E, Montreal-Est, QC, H1B 2V1
(514) 650-3865
Emp Here 60
SIC 5169 Chemicals and allied products, nec

D-U-N-S 24-325-3440   (BR)
PRAXAIR CANADA INC
(*Suby of* Praxair, Inc.)
10449 Boul Metropolitain E, Montreal-Est, QC, H1B 1A1
(514) 645-5020
Emp Here 20
SIC 5169 Chemicals and allied products, nec

D-U-N-S 24-251-8983   (BR)
SGS CANADA INC
SOCIETE GENERALE DE SURVEILLANCE
11000 Rue Sherbrooke E Suite 33a, Montreal-Est, QC, H1B 5W1
(514) 645-8754
Emp Here 30
SIC 7389 Business services, nec

D-U-N-S 20-737-2251   (BR)
SHELL CANADA LIMITED
PRODUITS SHELL CANADA
10501 Rue Sherbrooke E, Montreal-Est, QC, H1B 1B3
(514) 645-1661
Emp Here 450
SIC 2911 Petroleum refining

D-U-N-S 25-080-5850   (BR)
SODEM INC
CENTRE RECREATIF EDOUARD RIVET
11111 Rue Notre-Dame E, Montreal-Est, QC, H1B 2V7
(514) 640-2737
Emp Here 75
SIC 7999 Amusement and recreation, nec

Montreal-Est, QC H1L

D-U-N-S 24-580-4885   (HQ)
GROUPE PETROLIER OLCO ULC
GROUPE PETROLIER OLCO, LE
2775 Av Georges-V, Montreal-Est, QC, H1L 6J7
(514) 645-6526
Emp Here 85   *Emp Total* 246
Sales 74,055,111
SIC 5172 Petroleum products, nec
Pr Jack Trykoski
  Richard Pouliot
  Georges Karawani
  Kamil Khan
Sec Erik B Carlson
  Randall O'connor

D-U-N-S 24-970-9528   (SL)
TRANSPORT LYON INC
A AB ACTION ADMINISTRATION
9999 Rue Notre-Dame E, Montreal-Est, QC, H1L 3R5
(514) 322-4422
Emp Here 80   *Sales* 4,523,563
SIC 4214 Local trucking with storage

Montreal-Nord, QC H1G

D-U-N-S 25-002-4569   (BR)
BANQUE NATIONALE DU CANADA
BANQUE NATIONAL DU CANADA
6425 Boul Leger, Montreal-Nord, QC, H1G 6J7
(514) 327-1611
Emp Here 20
SIC 6021 National commercial banks

D-U-N-S 24-368-8129   (BR)
CAISSE DESJARDINS DE SAULT-AU-RECOLLET-MONTREAL-NORD
SAINTE-COLETTE SERVICE CENTRE
5640 Boul Leger, Montreal-Nord, QC, H1G 1K5
(514) 322-9310
Emp Here 30
SIC 6062 State credit unions

D-U-N-S 20-913-7186   (BR)
COMMISSION SCOLAIRE ENGLISH-MONTREAL
LESTER B PEARSON HIGH SCHOOL
11575 Av P.-M.-Favier, Montreal-Nord, QC, H1G 6E5
(514) 328-4442
Emp Here 150
SIC 8211 Elementary and secondary schools

D-U-N-S 25-240-2656   (BR)
COMMISSION SCOLAIRE ENGLISH-MONTREAL
MCSHANE, GERALD SCHOOL
6111 Boul Maurice-Duplessis, Montreal-Nord, QC, H1G 1Y6
(514) 321-1100
Emp Here 50
SIC 8211 Elementary and secondary schools

D-U-N-S 25-240-2342   (BR)
COMMISSION SCOLAIRE DE LA POINTE-DE-L'ILE
ECOLE SECONDAIRE HENRI BOURASSA
6051 Boul Maurice-Duplessis, Montreal-Nord, QC, H1G 1Y6
(514) 328-3200
Emp Here 200
SIC 8211 Elementary and secondary schools

D-U-N-S 25-240-2532   (BR)
COMMISSION SCOLAIRE DE LA POINTE-DE-L'ILE
ECOLE STE GERTRUDE
11813 Boul Sainte-Gertrude, Montreal-Nord, QC, H1G 5P8

(514) 328-3566
Emp Here 60
SIC 8211 Elementary and secondary schools

D-U-N-S 20-712-3865   (BR)
COMMISSION SCOLAIRE DE LA POINTE-DE-L'ILE
ECOLE ADELARD DESROSIERS
12600 Av Fortin, Montreal-Nord, QC, H1G 4A1
(514) 328-3555
Emp Here 50
SIC 8211 Elementary and secondary schools

D-U-N-S 25-242-8909   (BR)
COMMISSION SCOLAIRE DE LA POINTE-DE-L'ILE
CENTRE LOUIS FRECHETTE
5009 Rue Des Ardennes, Montreal-Nord, QC, H1G 2H7
(514) 328-3588
Emp Here 50
SIC 8211 Elementary and secondary schools

D-U-N-S 25-240-3555   (BR)
COMMISSION SCOLAIRE DE LA POINTE-DE-L'ILE
ECOLE LE CARIGNAN
11480 Boul Rolland, Montreal-Nord, QC, H1G 3T9
(514) 328-3570
Emp Here 85
SIC 8211 Elementary and secondary schools

D-U-N-S 25-240-6996   (BR)
COMMISSION SCOLAIRE DE LA POINTE-DE-L'ILE
ECOLE JEAN NICOLET
11235 Av Salk, Montreal-Nord, QC, H1G 4Y3
(514) 328-3560
Emp Here 50
SIC 8211 Elementary and secondary schools

D-U-N-S 20-913-5362   (BR)
COMMISSION SCOLAIRE DE LA POINTE-DE-L'ILE
ECOLE MARC LAFLAMME
11960 Boul Sainte-Colette, Montreal-Nord, QC, H1G 4V1
(514) 328-3575
Emp Here 40
SIC 8211 Elementary and secondary schools

D-U-N-S 20-712-3949   (BR)
COMMISSION SCOLAIRE DE LA POINTE-DE-L'ILE
ECOLE SECONDAIRE LE PRELUDE AU TRAVAIL
4975 Rue D'Amos, Montreal-Nord, QC, H1G 2X2
(514) 326-0660
Emp Here 50
SIC 8211 Elementary and secondary schools

D-U-N-S 20-806-8549   (BR)
COUCHE-TARD INC
6331 Boul Henri-Bourassa E, Montreal-Nord, QC, H1G 2V4
(514) 321-7680
Emp Here 25
SIC 5411 Grocery stores

D-U-N-S 24-083-7034   (BR)
DOLLARAMA S.E.C.
5610 Boul Henri-Bourassa E, Montreal-Nord, QC, H1G 2T2
(514) 323-7511
Emp Here 25
SIC 5331 Variety stores

D-U-N-S 25-685-0793   (BR)
DOREL INDUSTRIES INC
DOREL HOME PRODUCTS
12345 Boul Albert-Hudon Bureau 100, Montreal-Nord, QC, H1G 3L1
(514) 323-1247
Emp Here 325
SIC 2511 Wood household furniture

D-U-N-S 25-869-9656   (SL)
FONDATION DU CENTRE DE SANTE ET DE SERVICES SOCIAUX D'AHUNTSIC ET MONTREAL-NORD
6500 Boul Henri-Bourassa E, Montreal-Nord, QC, H1G 5W9
(514) 384-2000
Emp Here 55   *Sales* 13,286,839
SIC 8099 Health and allied services, nec
Pr Eric Thibaudeau
Dir Lionel Rodgers
VP VP Gervais Edouard
VP VP Denis Cloutier
Sec Denis Lagarde
Sec Michel Hamel
Dir Pierre Corriveau
Dir Diane Daine
Dir Gilles Desaulniers
Dir Vincent Dorais

D-U-N-S 20-363-9427   (SL)
GABRIEL MONTREAL-NORD, S.E.C.
GABRIEL KIA
6464 Boul Henri-Bourassa E, Montreal-Nord, QC, H1G 5W9
(514) 323-7777
Emp Here 25   *Sales* 9,120,088
SIC 5511 New and used car dealers
Genl Mgr Roch Sinclair

D-U-N-S 24-529-2289   (SL)
IMMEUBLES GABRIEL AZOUZ INC
MAIL CARNAVAL
7000 Boul Henri-Bourassa E, Montreal-Nord, QC, H1G 6C4
(514) 327-7777
Emp Here 50   *Sales* 8,138,880
SIC 6719 Holding companies, nec
Pr Gabriel Azouz

D-U-N-S 20-763-2886   (SL)
INDUSTRIES POLTEC LTEE, LES
(Suby of 120280 Canada Inc)
10440 Av Henault, Montreal-Nord, QC, H1G 5R4

Emp Here 20   *Sales* 5,526,400
SIC 5063 Electrical apparatus and equipment
Pr Pr Giacomo Grimaudo

D-U-N-S 20-925-6838   (BR)
MCDONALD'S RESTAURANTS OF CANADA LIMITED
MCDONALD'S
(Suby of McDonald's Corporation)
6140 Boul Henri-Bourassa E, Montreal-Nord, QC, H1G 5X3
(514) 321-0467
Emp Here 27
SIC 5812 Eating places

D-U-N-S 20-709-3944   (BR)
METRO RICHELIEU INC
SUPER C
6000 Boul Henri-Bourassa E, Montreal-Nord, QC, H1G 2T6
(514) 323-4370
Emp Here 98
SIC 5411 Grocery stores

D-U-N-S 20-230-9365   (HQ)
PRODUITS BEL INC
6868 Boul Maurice-Duplessis, Montreal-Nord, QC, H1G 1Z6
(514) 327-2800
Emp Here 61   *Emp Total* 70
Sales 13,686,766
SIC 3644 Noncurrent-carrying wiring devices
Pr Pr Real Belanger
VP VP Catherine Belanger
  Denis Belanger
  Eric Belanger

D-U-N-S 20-002-5026   (BR)
PROVIGO DISTRIBUTION INC
PROVIGO
6475 Boul Leger, Montreal-Nord, QC, H1G

1L4
(514) 321-0503
Emp Here 48
SIC 5411 Grocery stores

D-U-N-S 24-787-9823   (SL)
RITEPRO CORPORATION
CHECKRITE
12200 Boul Albert-Hudon, Montreal-Nord, QC, H1G 3K7
(514) 324-8900
Emp Here 26   *Sales* 3,429,153
SIC 3492 Fluid power valves and hose fittings

D-U-N-S 20-715-8069   (BR)
SIMARD-BEAUDRY CONSTRUCTION INC
5250 Rue D'Amiens, Montreal-Nord, QC, H1G 3G5
(514) 324-0055
Emp Here 60
SIC 1611 Highway and street construction

D-U-N-S 25-525-5903   (BR)
SOBEYS CAPITAL INCORPORATED
DISTRIBUTION BONISOIR
11281 Boul Albert-Hudon, Montreal-Nord, QC, H1G 3J5
(514) 324-1010
Emp Here 150
SIC 5141 Groceries, general line

D-U-N-S 20-251-8254   (BR)
SOBEYS CAPITAL INCORPORATED
SOBEYS
11281 Boul Albert-Hudon, Montreal-Nord, QC, H1G 3J5
(514) 324-5700
Emp Here 800
SIC 5141 Groceries, general line

D-U-N-S 20-651-3629   (BR)
SOBEYS QUEBEC INC
SOBEYS
11281 Boul Albert-Hudon, Montreal-Nord, QC, H1G 3J5
(514) 324-1010
Emp Here 150
SIC 5411 Grocery stores

D-U-N-S 20-544-5737   (HQ)
SOBEYS QUEBEC INC
ACHILLE DE LA CHEVROTIERE
11281 Boul Albert-Hudon, Montreal-Nord, QC, H1G 3J5
(514) 324-1010
Emp Here 800   *Emp Total* 125,000
Sales 1,046,183,477
SIC 5141 Groceries, general line
Pr Michael Medline
VP Pierre St-Laurent
  Karin Mccaskill
Dir Fin Michael Vels

D-U-N-S 24-525-3823   (BR)
TELECON INC
6789 Boul Leger, Montreal-Nord, QC, H1G 6H8
(514) 852-3322
Emp Here 120
SIC 4899 Communication services, nec

D-U-N-S 24-067-1094   (BR)
VALUE VILLAGE STORES, INC
VILLAGE DES VALEURS
(Suby of Savers, Inc.)
5630 Boul Henri-Bourassa E, Montreal-Nord, QC, H1G 2T2
(514) 327-7447
Emp Here 50
SIC 5399 Miscellaneous general merchandise

D-U-N-S 20-416-9452   (SL)
W. LAFRAMBOISE LTEE
(Suby of Gestion Jean Laframboise Inc)
11450 Boul Albert-Hudon, Montreal-Nord, QC, H1G 3J9
(514) 352-8228
Emp Here 35   *Sales* 3,648,035

SIC 2326 Men's and boy's work clothing

D-U-N-S 24-319-5224   (BR)
WAL-MART CANADA CORP
WALMART
6140 Boul Henri-Bourassa E, Montreal-Nord, QC, H1G 5X3
(514) 324-7853
Emp Here 200
SIC 5311 Department stores

D-U-N-S 24-313-5758   (BR)
WINNERS MERCHANTS INTERNATIONAL L.P.
WINNERS
(*Suby of* The TJX Companies Inc)
6136 Boul Henri-Bourassa E, Montreal-Nord, QC, H1G 5X3
(514) 798-2129
Emp Here 30
SIC 5651 Family clothing stores

Montreal-Nord, QC H1H

D-U-N-S 20-165-6704   (SL)
2969-9899 QUEBEC INC
S.I.R.C.O.
3905 Boul Industriel, Montreal-Nord, QC, H1H 2Z2
(514) 744-1010
Emp Here 60   *Sales* 1,896,978
SIC 7381 Detective and armored car services

D-U-N-S 20-999-4540   (SL)
CHSLD MARIE-CLARET INC
3345 Boul Henri-Bourassa E, Montreal-Nord, QC, H1H 1H6
(514) 322-4380
Emp Here 100   *Sales* 3,648,035
SIC 8361 Residential care

D-U-N-S 20-033-4915   (BR)
COMMISSION SCOLAIRE ENGLISH-MONTREAL
GALILEO ADULT CENTRE
10921 Av Gariepy, Montreal-Nord, QC, H1H 4C6
(514) 483-7575
Emp Here 40
SIC 8211 Elementary and secondary schools

D-U-N-S 25-240-7143   (BR)
COMMISSION SCOLAIRE DE LA POINTE-DE-L'ILE
ECOLE ST REMI
10152 Av De Rome, Montreal-Nord, QC, H1H 4N6
(514) 328-3590
Emp Here 51
SIC 8211 Elementary and secondary schools

D-U-N-S 25-240-6772   (BR)
COMMISSION SCOLAIRE DE LA POINTE-DE-L'ILE
ECOLE RENE GUENETTE
11070 Av De Rome, Montreal-Nord, QC, H1H 4P6
(514) 328-3083
Emp Here 60
SIC 8211 Elementary and secondary schools

D-U-N-S 25-233-5955   (BR)
COMMISSION SCOLAIRE DE LA POINTE-DE-L'ILE
ECOLE PIERRE DE COUBERTIN
4660 Rue De Charleroi, Montreal-Nord, QC, H1H 1T7
(514) 328-3580
Emp Here 25
SIC 8211 Elementary and secondary schools

D-U-N-S 20-910-6251   (BR)
COMMISSION SCOLAIRE DE LA POINTE-DE-L'ILE
ECOLE SECONDAIRE CALIXA LAVALEE

11411 Av Pelletier, Montreal-Nord, QC, H1H 3S3
(514) 328-3250
Emp Here 220
SIC 8211 Elementary and secondary schools

D-U-N-S 20-216-4620   (SL)
ENTREPRISES DERO INC
9960 Av Plaza, Montreal-Nord, QC, H1H 4L6
(514) 327-1108
Emp Here 65   *Sales* 11,025,249
SIC 3089 Plastics products, nec
Pr Pr Damiano Di Liello
Joseph Paventi

D-U-N-S 24-815-1995   (SL)
HOPITAL MARIE-CLARAC SOEURS CHARITE DE SAINTE-MARIE (1995) INC
3530 Boul Gouin E, Montreal-Nord, QC, H1H 1B7
(514) 321-8800
Emp Here 300   *Sales* 31,285,323
SIC 8069 Specialty hospitals, except psychiatric
Louise Beaulac
Pr Pr Soeur Anne-Marie Marolo

D-U-N-S 20-058-2885   (BR)
HUBBELL CANADA LP
4700 Rue D'Amiens, Montreal-Nord, QC, H1H 2H8
(514) 322-3543
Emp Here 30
SIC 3644 Noncurrent-carrying wiring devices

D-U-N-S 24-322-1327   (BR)
PRODUITS ALIMENTAIRES VIAU INC, LES
PRODUITS ALIMENTAIRES VIAU, LES
10035 Av Plaza, Montreal-Nord, QC, H1H 4L5
(514) 321-8260
Emp Here 230
SIC 5147 Meats and meat products

D-U-N-S 20-642-7671   (BR)
PROVIGO INC
MAXI
10200 Boul Pie-Ix, Montreal-Nord, QC, H1H 3Z1
(514) 321-3111
Emp Here 120
SIC 5411 Grocery stores

D-U-N-S 25-628-2112   (SL)
SERVICE D'ENTRETIEN CARLOS INC
10465 Av Balzac, Montreal-Nord, QC, H1H 3L6
(514) 727-3415
Emp Here 50   *Sales* 1,459,214
SIC 7349 Building maintenance services, nec

D-U-N-S 20-503-2048   (HQ)
SERVICE DE PNEUS SALOIS INC
UNIPNEU
9970 Av Des Recollets, Montreal-Nord, QC, H1H 4E5
(514) 321-7511
Emp Here 33   *Emp Total* 36
Sales 18,086,400
SIC 5014 Tires and tubes
Pr Pr Georges Morel
VP Annick Morel

D-U-N-S 20-104-9926   (BR)
STAPLES CANADA INC
BUREAU EN GROS
(*Suby of* Staples, Inc.)
10651 Boul Pie-Ix, Montreal-Nord, QC, H1H 4A3

Emp Here 60
SIC 5943 Stationery stores

Montreal-Ouest, QC H4X
Hochelaga County

D-U-N-S 25-233-7191   (BR)

COMMISSION SCOLAIRE ENGLISH-MONTREAL
ROYAL WEST ACADEMY
189 Av Easton, Montreal-Ouest, QC, H4X 1L4
(514) 489-8454
Emp Here 40
SIC 8211 Elementary and secondary schools

D-U-N-S 25-298-6377   (BR)
COMMISSION SCOLAIRE ENGLISH-MONTREAL
ECOLE ELIZABETH BALLANTYNE
314 Rue Northview, Montreal-Ouest, QC, H4X 1E2
(514) 484-1006
Emp Here 25
SIC 8211 Elementary and secondary schools

D-U-N-S 25-233-5666   (BR)
COMMISSION SCOLAIRE ENGLISH-MONTREAL
EDINBURGH SCHOOL
500 Av Hudson, Montreal-Ouest, QC, H4X 1X1
(514) 486-0981
Emp Here 20
SIC 8211 Elementary and secondary schools

Montreal-Ouest, QC H7H
Hochelaga County

D-U-N-S 25-125-6368   (BR)
COMMISSION SCOLAIRE DE LAVAL
CENTRE FORMATION MITALURGIE DE LAVAL
155 Boul Sainte-Rose E, Montreal-Ouest, QC, H7H 1P2
(450) 662-7000
Emp Here 21
SIC 8331 Job training and related services

Montreal-Ouest, QC H7N
Hochelaga County

D-U-N-S 20-716-7524   (BR)
COMMISSION SCOLAIRE DE LAVAL
ECOLE SECONDAIRE MONT-DE-LA SALLE
125 Boul Des Prairies, Montreal-Ouest, QC, H7N 2T6
(450) 662-7000
Emp Here 50
SIC 8211 Elementary and secondary schools

D-U-N-S 25-234-0989   (BR)
COMMISSION SCOLAIRE DE LAVAL
ECOLE PRIMAIRE SAINTE-MARGUERITE
40 Av Dussault, Montreal-Ouest, QC, H7N 3K1
(450) 662-7000
Emp Here 50
SIC 8211 Elementary and secondary schools

D-U-N-S 20-240-3010   (SL)
COQ PONT VIAU INC, AU
30 Rue Du Pont-Viau, Montreal-Ouest, QC, H7N 2X9
(450) 667-9550
Emp Here 45   *Sales* 1,790,425
SIC 5812 Eating places

D-U-N-S 25-362-6683   (BR)
IRON MOUNTAIN CANADA OPERATIONS ULC
ARCHIVE IRON MOUNTAIN
1655 Rue Fleetwood, Montreal-Ouest, QC, H7N 4B2
(450) 667-5960
Emp Here 100
SIC 4226 Special warehousing and storage, nec

Montreal-Ouest, QC H7V
Hochelaga County

D-U-N-S 24-801-0290   (SL)
2955-7196 QUEBEC INC
PHARMAPRIX 26
965 Boul Cure-Labelle, Montreal-Ouest, QC, H7V 2V7
(450) 681-1683
Emp Here 40   *Sales* 7,350,166
SIC 5912 Drug stores and proprietary stores
Pr Pr Katerina Karaindros

D-U-N-S 25-393-0465   (HQ)
3091-0418 QUEBEC INC
BUFFET MAISON KIRIN , LE
(*Suby of* 3091-0418 Quebec Inc)
545 Boul Cure-Labelle, Montreal-Ouest, QC, H7V 2T3
(450) 681-0600
Emp Here 40   *Emp Total* 150
Sales 4,523,563
SIC 5812 Eating places

D-U-N-S 25-051-4213   (SL)
3459128 CANADA INC
MARCHE ADONIS
705 Boul Cure-Labelle, Montreal-Ouest, QC, H7V 2T8
(450) 978-2333
Emp Here 300   *Sales* 58,278,400
SIC 5411 Grocery stores
Pr Pr Jamil Cheaib
VP VP Georges Ghorayeb
Elie Cheaib

D-U-N-S 24-385-2501   (SL)
6423264 CANADA INC
BOISE NOTRE DAME, LES RESIDENCES
3055 Boul Notre-Dame Bureau 1700, Montreal-Ouest, QC, H7V 4C6
(450) 681-3055
Emp Here 100   *Sales* 3,648,035
SIC 8361 Residential care

D-U-N-S 24-373-4709   (HQ)
ALTASCIENCES COMPAGNIE INC
ALGORITHME PHARMA
(*Suby of* Audax Group, L.P.)
575 Boul Armand-Frappier, Montreal-Ouest, QC, H7V 4B3
(450) 973-6077
Emp Here 200   *Emp Total* 4,114
Sales 24,514,795
SIC 8731 Commercial physical research
Pr Douglas Peel
Sec William Blackburn
Dir Marc Lefebvre
Dir Pierre Lapalme
Dir Francois Bourret
Genl Mgr Christopher Perkin

D-U-N-S 20-033-5102   (BR)
CENTRE DE SANTE ET DE SERVICES SO-CIAUX DE LAVAL
CLSC-CHSLD DU RUISSEAU-PAPINEAU
800 Boul Chomedey Bureau 200, Montreal-Ouest, QC, H7V 3Y4
(450) 682-2952
Emp Here 600
SIC 8399 Social services, nec

D-U-N-S 24-737-0864   (SL)
CITOXLAB AMERIQUE DU NORD INC
445 Boul Armand-Frappier, Montreal-Ouest, QC, H7V 4B3
(450) 973-2240
Emp Here 340   *Sales* 23,935,157
SIC 8731 Commercial physical research
Pr Pr Jean-Francois Georges Le Bigot
Patrick Spies
Dir Roy Forster
Dir Andrew Graham
Dir Raffi Mikaelian

D-U-N-S 20-716-7623   (BR)
COMMISSION SCOLAIRE DE LAVAL

QUATRE-VENTS MONSEIGNEUR LAVAL, LES
740 75e Av, Montreal-Ouest, QC, H7V 2Y6
(450) 662-7000
Emp Here 50
SIC 8211 Elementary and secondary schools

     D-U-N-S 25-293-0516   (BR)
MICHAEL ROSSY LTEE
ROSSY
965 Boul Cure-Labelle, Montreal-Ouest, QC, H7V 2V7

Emp Here 20
SIC 5311 Department stores

     D-U-N-S 20-266-0718   (BR)
NORDION INC
CENTRE D'EXCELLENCE EN IRRADIATION GAMMA
535 Boul Cartier O, Montreal-Ouest, QC, H7V 3S8
(450) 687-5165
Emp Here 20
SIC 8731 Commercial physical research

     D-U-N-S 20-703-6703   (BR)
PROMETIC SCIENCES DE LA VIE INC
500 Boul Cartier O Bureau 150, Montreal-Ouest, QC, H7V 5B7
(450) 781-1394
Emp Here 30
SIC 2834 Pharmaceutical preparations

     D-U-N-S 20-002-2346   (BR)
PROVIGO DISTRIBUTION INC
CLUB ENTREPOT PROVIGO
1005 Boul Cure-Labelle, Montreal-Ouest, QC, H7V 2V6
(450) 681-3014
Emp Here 70
SIC 5141 Groceries, general line

     D-U-N-S 25-778-9347   (BR)
ROYAL BANK OF CANADA
RBC
(Suby of Royal Bank Of Canada)
965 Boul Cure-Labelle, Montreal-Ouest, QC, H7V 2V7
(450) 686-3446
Emp Here 25
SIC 6021 National commercial banks

     D-U-N-S 24-619-7123   (SL)
SILVER STAR MANUFACTURING CO INC
MANUFACTURE DE BIJOUX ETOILES D'ARGENT
750 Boul Cure-Labelle Bureau 205, Montreal-Ouest, QC, H7V 2T9
(450) 682-3381
Emp Here 60   *Sales* 4,377,642
SIC 3911 Jewelry, precious Metal

     D-U-N-S 20-798-8069   (BR)
STAPLES CANADA INC
BUREAU EN GROS
(Suby of Staples, Inc.)
1000 Boul Chomedey, Montreal-Ouest, QC, H7V 3X8
(450) 689-6763
Emp Here 40
SIC 5943 Stationery stores

     D-U-N-S 25-982-4563   (BR)
VALUE VILLAGE STORES, INC
VILLAGE DES VALEURS
(Suby of Savers, Inc.)
875 Boul Cure-Labelle, Montreal-Ouest, QC, H7V 2V2
(450) 978-4191
Emp Here 30
SIC 5399 Miscellaneous general merchandise

Morin-Heights, QC J0R

     D-U-N-S 24-855-1074   (SL)

9181-8153 QUEBEC INC
IGA MARCHE MORIN-HEIGHTS
680 Ch Du Village Rr 2, Morin-Heights, QC, J0R 1H0
(450) 226-5769
Emp Here 70   *Sales* 12,560,000
SIC 5411 Grocery stores
Pr Pierre Desmanches

     D-U-N-S 24-502-3288   (SL)
CONCEPT GOURMET DU VILLAGE INC
GOURMET DU VILLAGE
(Suby of 3522920 Canada Inc)
539 Ch Du Village, Morin-Heights, QC, J0R 1H0
(450) 226-2314
Emp Here 26   *Sales* 2,685,378
SIC 2032 Canned specialties

     D-U-N-S 25-234-2571   (BR)
SIR WILFRID LAURIER SCHOOL BOARD
ECOLE MORIN HEIGHTS SCHOOL
(Suby of Sir Wilfrid Laurier School Board)
647 Ch Du Village, Morin-Heights, QC, J0R 1H0
(450) 226-2017
Emp Here 25
SIC 8211 Elementary and secondary schools

Murdochville, QC G0E
Gaspe-Ouest County

     D-U-N-S 20-029-1750   (BR)
CENTRE DE SANTE ET DE SERVICES SOCIAUX DE LA COTE-DE-GASPE
CENTRE DE SANTE ET DE SERVICES SOCIAUX DE LA COTE-DE-GASPE
(Suby of Centre de sante et de services sociaux de la Cote-De-Gaspe)
600 Av William-May, Murdochville, QC, G0E 1W0
(418) 784-2572
Emp Here 40
SIC 8062 General medical and surgical hospitals

     D-U-N-S 25-231-9652   (BR)
COMMISSION SCOLAIRE DES CHIC-CHOCS
ECOLE DES PROSPECTEURS
530 Av William-May, Murdochville, QC, G0E 1W0
(418) 784-2487
Emp Here 20
SIC 8211 Elementary and secondary schools

Napierville, QC J0J
Napierville County

     D-U-N-S 20-423-1476   (SL)
MARCHE CORRIVEAU INC
METRO-RICHELIEU
370 Rue Saint-Jacques, Napierville, QC, J0J 1L0
(450) 245-3316
Emp Here 98   *Sales* 17,668,800
SIC 5411 Grocery stores
Pr Pr Jean-Pierre Corriveau
Genl Mgr Marie-Eve Corriveau

     D-U-N-S 25-211-5092   (SL)
NAPIERVILLE REFINERIES INC
175 Rue De L'Eglise, Napierville, QC, J0J 1L0
(450) 245-0040
Emp Here 25   *Sales* 3,580,850
SIC 3312 Blast furnaces and steel mills

     D-U-N-S 20-267-3943   (BR)
RECOCHEM INC.
NAPIERVILLE REFINERIE
175 Rue De Leglise, Napierville, QC, J0J 1L0

(450) 245-0040
Emp Here 24
SIC 2865 Cyclic crudes and intermediates

     D-U-N-S 20-252-3247   (BR)
WESTON BAKERIES LIMITED
BOULANGERIES WESTON
150 Boul Industriel, Napierville, QC, J0J 1L0
(450) 245-7542
Emp Here 200
SIC 2051 Bread, cake, and related products

Natashquan, QC G0G
Saguenay County

     D-U-N-S 20-029-1834   (BR)
COMMISSION SCOLAIRE DE LA MOYENNE-COTE-NORD, LA
ECOLE NOTRE-DAME-DES-ANGES
14 Allee Des Pere Udiste, Natashquan, QC, G0G 2E0
(418) 726-3378
Emp Here 26
SIC 8211 Elementary and secondary schools

Nemiscau, QC J0Y
Nouveau-Quebec County

     D-U-N-S 25-240-3241   (BR)
CREE SCHOOL BOARD
LUKE METTAWESKUM SCHOOL
(Suby of Cree School Board)
9 Rue Lake Shore, Nemiscau, QC, J0Y 3B0
(819) 673-2536
Emp Here 50
SIC 8211 Elementary and secondary schools

Neuville, QC G0A
Portneuf County

     D-U-N-S 25-234-2191   (BR)
COMMISSION SCOLAIRE DE PORTNEUF
COMMISSION SCOLAIRE DE PORTNEUF
(Suby of Commission Scolaire de Portneuf)
619 Rue Des Erables, Neuville, QC, G0A 2R0
(418) 876-2102
Emp Here 20
SIC 8211 Elementary and secondary schools

New Carlisle, QC G0C
Bonaventure County

     D-U-N-S 20-711-8683   (BR)
EASTERN SHORES SCHOOL BOARD
NEW CARLISLE HIGH SCHOOL
177 Boul Gerard-D.-Levesque, New Carlisle, QC, G0C 1Z0
(418) 752-3316
Emp Here 50
SIC 8211 Elementary and secondary schools

     D-U-N-S 20-529-6606   (BR)
VIA RAIL CANADA INC
6 Rue De Vimy, New Carlisle, QC, G0C 1Z0

Emp Here 20
SIC 4111 Local and suburban transit

New Richmond, QC G0C
Bonaventure County

     D-U-N-S 25-232-3449   (BR)
COMMISSION SCOLAIRE RENE-

LEVESQUE
ECOLE LE BOIS VIVANT
121 Av Terry-Fox Gd, New Richmond, QC, G0C 2B0
(418) 392-4350
Emp Here 35
SIC 8211 Elementary and secondary schools

     D-U-N-S 24-388-5451   (BR)
COMPAGNIE DES CHEMINS DE FER NATIONAUX DU CANADA
SOCIETE DU CHEMIN DE FER DE LA GASPESIE
180 Ch St Edgar, New Richmond, QC, G0C 2B0
(418) 392-5746
Emp Here 25
SIC 4011 Railroads, line-haul operating

     D-U-N-S 24-365-8742   (BR)
CONSTRUCTION DJL INC
PAVAGES BEAU BASSIN DIV DE
136 Boul Perron O, New Richmond, QC, G0C 2B0
(418) 392-5055
Emp Here 30
SIC 1611 Highway and street construction

     D-U-N-S 25-231-9249   (BR)
EASTERN SHORES SCHOOL BOARD
NEW RICHMOND HIGH SCHOOL
(Suby of Eastern Shores School Board)
163 Boul Perron O, New Richmond, QC, G0C 2B0
(418) 392-4441
Emp Here 30
SIC 8211 Elementary and secondary schools

     D-U-N-S 20-005-4570   (BR)
REXFORET INC
190 Rue Armand-Lelievre Bureau 114, New Richmond, QC, G0C 2B0
(418) 392-5076
Emp Here 60
SIC 2411 Logging

     D-U-N-S 25-309-1631   (BR)
SOBEYS CAPITAL INCORPORATED
I G A
120 Boul Perron O, New Richmond, QC, G0C 2B0
(418) 392-4237
Emp Here 60
SIC 5411 Grocery stores

Newport, QC G0C
Gaspe-Est County

     D-U-N-S 20-252-3288   (SL)
3886298 CANADA INC
USINE DE CONGELATION DE NEWPORT
24 Rte Germain, Newport, QC, G0C 2A0
(418) 343-2206
Emp Here 75   *Sales* 40,048,983
SIC 5142 Packaged frozen goods
Pr Pr Gilles Dery

Nicolet, QC J3T
Nicolet County

     D-U-N-S 24-362-4603   (HQ)
CENTRE DE SANTE ET DE SERVICES SOCIAUX DE BECANCOUR-NICOLET-YAMASKA
CENTRE CHRIST-ROI
(Suby of Centre de Sante et de Services Sociaux de Becancour-Nicolet-Yamaska)
675 Rue Saint-Jean-Baptiste, Nicolet, QC, J3T 1S4
(819) 293-2071
Emp Here 800   *Emp Total* 1,000
Sales 112,203,700

SIC 8069 Specialty hospitals, except psychiatric
Genl Mgr Danielle Gamelin
Pr Pr Herve Dion

D-U-N-S 25-324-0964   (SL)
COLLEGE   NOTRE-DAME-DE-L'ASSOMPTION
225 Rue Saint-Jean-Baptiste, Nicolet, QC, J3T 0A2
(819) 293-4500
Emp Here 70   *Sales* 4,669,485
SIC 8211 Elementary and secondary schools

D-U-N-S 25-233-2168   (BR)
COMMISSION   SCOLAIRE   DE   LA RIVERAINE
ECOLE SECONDAIRE JEAN NICOLET
(*Suby of* Commission Scolaire de la Riveraine)
497 Rue De Monseigneur-Brunault, Nicolet, QC, J3T 1Y6
(819) 293-5821
Emp Here 20
SIC 8211 Elementary and secondary schools

D-U-N-S 25-019-3117   (BR)
COMMISSION   SCOLAIRE   DE   LA RIVERAINE
ECOLE CURE BRASSARD
(*Suby of* Commission Scolaire de la Riveraine)
1150 Boul Louis-Frechette, Nicolet, QC, J3T 1V5
(819) 293-2185
Emp Here 50
SIC 8211 Elementary and secondary schools

D-U-N-S 20-712-0846   (BR)
COMMISSION   SCOLAIRE   DE   LA RIVERAINE
FORMATION PROFESSIONNELLE ECOLE D'AGRICULTURE
(*Suby of* Commission Scolaire de la Riveraine)
375 Rue De Monseigneur-Brunault, Nicolet, QC, J3T 1Y6
(819) 293-5821
Emp Here 50
SIC 8211 Elementary and secondary schools

D-U-N-S 24-940-7669   (HQ)
GESTION MICHEL BIRON INC
(*Suby of* Gestion Michel Biron Inc)
111 Rue Du 12-Novembre, Nicolet, QC, J3T 1S3
(819) 293-6125
Emp Here 81   *Emp Total* 83
Sales 16,579,200
SIC 6712 Bank holding companies
Pr Pr Michel Biron

D-U-N-S 24-419-7641   (BR)
H. MATTEAU ET FILS (1987) INC
RONA
2145 Boul Louis-Frechette, Nicolet, QC, J3T 1M9
(819) 293-5586
Emp Here 30
SIC 5211 Lumber and other building materials

D-U-N-S 24-403-6505   (SL)
NITEK LASER INC
305 Rte Du Port, Nicolet, QC, J3T 1R7
(819) 293-4887
Emp Here 50   *Sales* 2,334,742
SIC 3398 Metal heat treating

D-U-N-S 20-281-7305   (BR)
SOEURS   DE   L'ASSOMPTION   DE   LA SAINTE VIERGE, LES
SOEURS DE L'ASSOMPTION DE LA SAINTE VIERGE, LES
(*Suby of* Soeurs De L'Assomption De La Sainte Vierge, Les)
160 Rue Du Carmel, Nicolet, QC, J3T 1Z8
(819) 293-4559
Emp Here 30

SIC 8661 Religious organizations

D-U-N-S 20-238-1935   (HQ)
SOGETEL INC
DIMENSION HUMAINE
(*Suby of* Gestion Michel Biron Inc)
111 Rue Du 12-Novembre, Nicolet, QC, J3T 1S3
(819) 293-6125
Emp Here 80   *Emp Total* 83
Sales 9,484,891
SIC 4813 Telephone communication, except radio
Pr Pr Michel Biron
VP Isabelle Biron
VP Georges Biron
Sec Louise Begin
Dir Sylvain Bellerive
Treas Sophie Houde
Dir Helene Biron
Dir Alain Duhaime
Dir Yves Duval
Dir Jean-Philippe Saia

Nominingue, QC J0W
Labelle County

D-U-N-S 24-103-1777   (BR)
CAISSE DESJARDINS DE LA ROUGE
(*Suby of* Caisse Desjardins de la Rouge)
2260 Ch Du Tour-Du-Lac, Nominingue, QC, J0W 1R0
(819) 278-0520
Emp Here 22
SIC 6021 National commercial banks

Normandin, QC G8M

D-U-N-S 20-238-4228   (HQ)
CO-OP DES DEUX RIVES
(*Suby of* Co-Op Des Deux Rives)
1455 Av Du Rocher Bureau 102, Normandin, QC, G8M 3X5
(418) 274-2910
Emp Here 20   *Emp Total* 45
Sales 6,639,424
SIC 5211 Lumber and other building materials
Genl Mgr Gervais Laprise

D-U-N-S 20-213-5732   (BR)
COMMISSION SCOLAIRE DU PAYS-DES-BLEUETS
ECOLE STE MARIE
1017 Rue Du Centre-Sportif, Normandin, QC, G8M 4L7
(418) 276-5883
Emp Here 25
SIC 8211 Elementary and secondary schools

D-U-N-S 20-211-6658   (BR)
PF RESOLU CANADA INC
RESOLUTE FOREST PRODUCTS
1165 Rue Industrielle, Normandin, QC, G8M 4S9
(418) 274-2424
Emp Here 70
SIC 2431 Millwork

Normetal, QC J0Z
Abitibi County

D-U-N-S 25-298-2939   (BR)
COMMISSION SCOLAIRE ABITIBI
ECOLE ABANA
(*Suby of* Commission Scolaire Abitibi)
36 Rue Principale, Normetal, QC, J0Z 3A0
(819) 788-2505
Emp Here 20

SIC 8211 Elementary and secondary schools

North Hatley, QC J0B
Stanstead County

D-U-N-S 24-206-4033   (BR)
COMMUNAUTES DE RETRAITES MASSAWIPPI, LES
FOYER DES RETRAITES CHRETIENNE MASSAWIPPI
77 Rue Main, North Hatley, QC, J0B 2C0
(819) 842-2164
Emp Here 30
SIC 8059 Nursing and personal care, nec

D-U-N-S 24-056-8485   (SL)
MAISON BLANCHE DE NORTH HATLEY INC, LA
977 Rue Massawippi, North Hatley, QC, J0B 2C0
(450) 666-1567
Emp Here 82   *Sales* 2,991,389
SIC 7021 Rooming and boarding houses

Notre-Dame-De-L'Ile-Perrot, QC J7V

D-U-N-S 20-631-8883   (SL)
KELLY SANI-VAC INC
100 Rue Huot, Notre-Dame-De-L'Ile-Perrot, QC, J7V 7Z8
(514) 453-2279
Emp Here 71   *Sales* 4,304,681
SIC 7699 Repair services, nec

D-U-N-S 20-534-0297   (BR)
METRO RICHELIEU INC
METRO PLUS FAMILLE LEMAY
450 Boul Don-Quichotte, Notre-Dame-De-L'Ile-Perrot, QC, J7V 0J9
(514) 425-6111
Emp Here 20
SIC 5411 Grocery stores

D-U-N-S 24-580-7698   (SL)
TECHNOLOGIES K.K. INC, LES
64 Rue Huot, Notre-Dame-De-L'Ile-Perrot, QC, J7V 7Z8
(514) 453-6732
Emp Here 57   *Sales* 4,158,760
SIC 3599 Industrial machinery, nec

Notre-Dame-De-La-Salette, QC J0X
Papineau County

D-U-N-S 25-233-5419   (BR)
COMMISSION SCOLAIRE AU COEUR DES VALLEES
ECOLE DE LA MONTAGNE
68 Rue Des Saules, Notre-Dame-De-La-Salette, QC, J0X 2L0
(819) 866-2645
Emp Here 20
SIC 8211 Elementary and secondary schools

Notre-Dame-Des-Pins, QC G0M
Beauce County

D-U-N-S 20-952-2630   (SL)
CONFECTIONS RAYJO INC
(*Suby of* Placements Charlesco Inc, Les)
200 34e Rue Bureau 1, Notre-Dame-Des-Pins, QC, G0M 1K0
(418) 774-9897
Emp Here 50   *Sales* 1,969,939
SIC 2329 Men's and boy's clothing, nec

D-U-N-S 25-393-0549   (SL)
GESTION L. FECTEAU LTEE
3150 Ch Royal, Notre-Dame-Des-Pins, QC, G0M 1K0
(418) 774-3324
Emp Here 80   *Sales* 11,454,830
SIC 6712 Bank holding companies
Pr Pr Marc Fecteau

D-U-N-S 24-498-9703   (HQ)
MENUISERIE DES PINS LTEE
QUINCAILLERIE FUTURA, DIVISION DE MENUISERIE DES PINS
3150 Ch Royal, Notre-Dame-Des-Pins, QC, G0M 1K0
(418) 774-3324
Emp Here 80   *Emp Total* 1,900
Sales 8,952,126
SIC 2431 Millwork
Pr Richard Lord
VP Fin Antoine Auclair
Dir Marc Fecteau
Dir Serge Labbe

Notre-Dame-Des-Prairies, QC J6E
Joliette County

D-U-N-S 20-250-5772   (SL)
AUTOMOBILES LAFRENIERE INC
525 131 Rte, Notre-Dame-Des-Prairies, QC, J6E 0M1
(450) 752-2002
Emp Here 40   *Sales* 20,096,000
SIC 5511 New and used car dealers
Pr Pr Jean Lafreniere
VP VP Guy Lafreniere

Notre-Dame-Du-Laus, QC J0X
Labelle County

D-U-N-S 24-369-8912   (BR)
CAISSE DESJARDINS DU COEUR DES HAUTES-LAURENTIDES
CENTRE DE SERVICES DE NOTRE-DAME-DU-LAUS
104 Rue Principale, Notre-Dame-Du-Laus, QC, J0X 2M0
(819) 623-4400
Emp Here 50
SIC 6062 State credit unions

Notre-Dame-Du-Nord, QC J0Z
Temiscaninque County

D-U-N-S 25-233-5898   (BR)
COMMISSION   SCOLAIRE   DU   LAC-TEMISCAMINGUE
ECOLE RIVIERE DES QUINZE
(*Suby of* Commission Scolaire du Lac-Temiscamingue)
15 Rue Desjardins, Notre-Dame-Du-Nord, QC, J0Z 3B0
(819) 723-2408
Emp Here 40
SIC 8211 Elementary and secondary schools

D-U-N-S 20-415-7739   (SL)
TEMISKO (1983) INC
TEMISKO
91 Rue Ontario, Notre-Dame-Du-Nord, QC, J0Z 3B0
(819) 723-2416
Emp Here 90   *Sales* 12,257,398
SIC 3715 Truck trailers
Pr Pr Nelson Pouliot
Sec Richard Cyrenne
Dir Dany Roy
Dir Frederic Dumont

Dir Clude De Lachevrotiere

Notre-Dame-Du-Portage, QC G0L
Riviere-Du-Loup County

D-U-N-S 20-579-6543   (SL)
AUBERGE DU PORTAGE LTEE
671 Rte Du Fleuve, Notre-Dame-Du-Portage,
QC, G0L 1Y0
(418) 862-3601
Emp Here 100   *Sales* 4,377,642
SIC 7011 Hotels and motels

Nouvelle, QC G0C
Bonaventure County

D-U-N-S 25-991-7131   (BR)
**GOUVERNEMENT DE LA PROVINCE DE
QUEBEC**
QUEBEC TRANSPORTS
356 Rue Maguire, Nouvelle, QC, G0C 2E0
(418) 794-2242
Emp Here 25
SIC 4213 Trucking, except local

Oka, QC J0N
Deux-Montagnes County

D-U-N-S 20-252-3429   (BR)
AGROPUR COOPERATIVE
FROMAGE D'OKA
1400 Ch D'Oka, Oka, QC, J0N 1E0
(450) 479-6396
Emp Here 175
SIC 2022 Cheese; natural and processed

D-U-N-S 25-293-2256   (BR)
**COMMISSION   SCOLAIRE   DE   LA
SEIGNEURIE-DES-MILLE-ILES**
*COMMISSION   SCOLAIRE   DE   LA
SEIGNEURIE-DES-MILLE-ILES*
(*Suby of* Commission Scolaire de la
Seigneurie-Des-Mille-Iles)
25 Rue Des Pins, Oka, QC, J0N 1E0
(450) 491-8400
Emp Here 40
SIC 8211 Elementary and secondary schools

D-U-N-S 25-485-2122   (BR)
**GOUVERNEMENT DE LA PROVINCE DE
QUEBEC**
*GOUVERNEMENT DE LA PROVINCE DE
QUEBEC*
2020 Ch D'Oka, Oka, QC, J0N 1E0
(450) 479-8365
Emp Here 200
SIC 7996 Amusement parks

D-U-N-S 20-238-8906   (SL)
INDUSTRIES OKAPLY LTEE
1372 Ch D'Oka, Oka, QC, J0N 1E0
(450) 479-8341
Emp Here 50   *Sales* 5,653,974
SIC 2436 Softwood veneer and plywood

D-U-N-S 25-909-5131   (BR)
**SOCIETE DES ETABLISSEMENTS DE
PLEIN AIR DU QUEBEC**
PARC NATIONAL D'OKA SEPAQ
2020 Ch D'Oka, Oka, QC, J0N 1E0
(450) 479-8337
Emp Here 40
SIC 7033 Trailer parks and campsites

Orford, QC J1X
Stanstead County

D-U-N-S 24-884-4300   (SL)
2850-1799 QUEBEC INC
AUBERGE ESTRIMONT
44 Av De L'Auberge, Orford, QC, J1X 6J3
(819) 843-1616
Emp Here 65   *Sales* 2,845,467
SIC 7011 Hotels and motels

D-U-N-S 24-365-4725   (BR)
GESTION SOROMA (MONT ORFORD) INC
(*Suby of* Gestion Soroma (Mont Orford) Inc)
4380 Ch Du Parc, Orford, QC, J1X 7N9
(514) 527-9546
Emp Here 100
SIC 8742 Management consulting services

D-U-N-S 20-052-5702   (SL)
MONT-ORFORD INC
CLUB DE GOLF MONT-ORFORD
4380 Ch Du Parc, Orford, QC, J1X 7N9
(819) 843-6548
Emp Here 100   *Sales* 4,377,642
SIC 7011 Hotels and motels

D-U-N-S 24-851-2779   (BR)
WAL-MART CANADA CORP
44 Av De L'Auberge, Orford, QC, J1X 6J3

Emp Here 75
SIC 5311 Department stores

Ormstown, QC J0S
Chateauguay County

D-U-N-S 20-171-8926   (SL)
**CENTRE D'ACCUEIL DU HAUT-ST LAU-
RENT (CHSLD)**
65 Rue Hector, Ormstown, QC, J0S 1K0
(450) 829-2346
Emp Here 120   *Sales* 4,377,642
SIC 8361 Residential care

D-U-N-S 20-024-5723   (BR)
COMMISSION SCOLAIRE NEW FRONTIER
*CHATEAUGUAY VALLEY REGIONAL HIGH
SCHOOL*
1597 138a Rte, Ormstown, QC, J0S 1K0
(450) 829-2381
Emp Here 60
SIC 8211 Elementary and secondary schools

D-U-N-S 20-712-3469   (BR)
COMMISSION SCOLAIRE NEW FRONTIER
CHATEAUGUAY VALLEY CAREER CENTER
54 Rue Roy, Ormstown, QC, J0S 1K0
(450) 829-2396
Emp Here 30
SIC 8211 Elementary and secondary schools

D-U-N-S 25-240-6376   (BR)
COMMISSION SCOLAIRE NEW FRONTIER
ORMSTOWN ELEMENTARY SCHOOL
7 Rue Georges, Ormstown, QC, J0S 1K0
(450) 829-2641
Emp Here 20
SIC 8211 Elementary and secondary schools

D-U-N-S 25-240-6459   (BR)
**COMMISSION SCOLAIRE DE LA VALLEE-
DES-TISSERANDS, LA**
ECOLE NOTRE DAME DU ROSAIRE
8 Rue Bridge, Ormstown, QC, J0S 1K0
(450) 377-6063
Emp Here 30
SIC 8211 Elementary and secondary schools

D-U-N-S 20-126-9672   (BR)
DYNO NOBEL CANADA INC
2730 Montee Du Rocher, Ormstown, QC, J0S
1K0
(450) 825-2236
Emp Here 40
SIC 2892 Explosives

D-U-N-S 24-541-5441   (SL)
MARCHES PILON MCKINNON INC, LES
IGA
4 Rue Bridge, Ormstown, QC, J0S 1K0
(450) 829-2252
Emp Here 100   *Sales* 18,666,800
SIC 5411 Grocery stores
Pr Pr Robert Pilon
 Steve Mckinnon
 Dave Mckinnon
 Line Pilon
 Michel Pilon

Otterburn Park, QC J3H

D-U-N-S 25-240-5279   (BR)
COMMISSION SCOLAIRE DES PATRIOTES
COMMISSION SCOLAIRE DES PATRIOTES
306 Rue Du Prince-Albert, Otterburn Park,
QC, J3H 1L6
(450) 467-7511
Emp Here 60
SIC 8211 Elementary and secondary schools

D-U-N-S 20-712-3733   (BR)
RIVERSIDE SCHOOL BOARD
ECOLE MOUNTAINVIEW SCHOOL
444 Rue Mountainview, Otterburn Park, QC,
J3H 2K2
(450) 467-9347
Emp Here 30
SIC 8211 Elementary and secondary schools

Ouje-Bougoumou, QC G0W
Nouveau-Quebec County

D-U-N-S 24-206-3357   (BR)
CREE SCHOOL BOARD
WAAPIHTIIWEWAN SCHOOL
(*Suby of* Cree School Board)
220 Opemiska Meskino, Ouje-Bougoumou,
QC, G0W 3C0
(418) 745-2542
Emp Here 44
SIC 8211 Elementary and secondary schools

Outremont, QC H2V

D-U-N-S 20-573-7377   (BR)
BANQUE LAURENTIENNE DU CANADA
1447 Av Van Horne, Outremont, QC, H2V 1K9
(514) 274-7792
Emp Here 20
SIC 6021 National commercial banks

D-U-N-S 24-871-2382   (HQ)
CEDROM-SNI INC.
CEDROM-SNI
(*Suby of* Cedrom-Sni Inc.)
825 Av Querbes Bureau 200, Outremont, QC,
H2V 3X1
(514) 278-6060
Emp Here 60   *Emp Total* 90
Sales 17,276,160
SIC 4899 Communication services, nec
Pr Pr Francois Aird
 Philippe Gelinas
VP Mauricio Fernandez

D-U-N-S 20-714-2493   (BR)
CENTRE FRANCOIS MICHELLE
5210 Av Durocher, Outremont, QC, H2V 3Y1
(514) 948-6434
Emp Here 30
SIC 8211 Elementary and secondary schools

D-U-N-S 25-298-6492   (BR)
COMMISSION   SCOLAIRE   ENGLISH-

MONTREAL
ECOLE GUY DRUMMOND
1475 Av Lajoie, Outremont, QC, H2V 1P9
(514) 270-4866
Emp Here 25
SIC 8211 Elementary and secondary schools

D-U-N-S 25-240-3662   (BR)
**COMMISSION SCOLAIRE MARGUERITE-
BOURGEOYS**
*ECOLE SECONDAIRE PAUL GERIN LAJOIE
OUTREMONT*
475 Av Bloomfield, Outremont, QC, H2V 3R9
(514) 276-3746
Emp Here 70
SIC 8211 Elementary and secondary schools

D-U-N-S 20-712-3998   (BR)
**COMMISSION SCOLAIRE MARGUERITE-
BOURGEOYS**
ECOLE LAJOIE
1276 Av Lajoie, Outremont, QC, H2V 1P3
(514) 272-5723
Emp Here 50
SIC 8211 Elementary and secondary schools

D-U-N-S 20-712-4004   (BR)
**COMMISSION SCOLAIRE MARGUERITE-
BOURGEOYS**
*ECOLE   PRIMAIRE   ST   GERMAIN
D'OUTREMONT*
46 Av Vincent-D'Indy, Outremont, QC, H2V
2S9
(514) 735-6691
Emp Here 50
SIC 8211 Elementary and secondary schools

D-U-N-S 25-233-0352   (SL)
**ECOLE BUISSONNIERE, CENTRE DE FOR-
MATION ARTISTIQUE INC**
215 Av De L'Epee, Outremont, QC, H2V 3T3
(514) 272-4739
Emp Here 55   *Sales* 3,648,035
SIC 8211 Elementary and secondary schools

D-U-N-S 20-714-2253   (SL)
ECOLE COMMUNAUTAIRE BELZ
HASSIDIC COMMUNITY SCHOOL
1495 Av Ducharme, Outremont, QC, H2V 1E8
(514) 271-0611
Emp Here 65   *Sales* 4,377,642
SIC 8211 Elementary and secondary schools

D-U-N-S 24-508-7416   (SL)
ECOLE DE MUSIQUE VINCENT-D'INDY
628 Ch De La Cote-Sainte-Catherine, Outremont, QC, H2V 2C5
(514) 735-5261
Emp Here 50   *Sales* 2,699,546
SIC 8299 Schools and educational services,
nec

D-U-N-S 24-433-1612   (BR)
METRO RICHELIEU INC
5 SAISONS, LES
1180 Av Bernard, Outremont, QC, H2V 1V3
(514) 276-1244
Emp Here 49
SIC 5199 Nondurable goods, nec

D-U-N-S 20-714-2154   (SL)
PENSIONNAT DU ST NOM DE MARIE
628 Ch De La Cote-Sainte-Catherine, Outremont, QC, H2V 2C5
(514) 735-5261
Emp Here 50   *Sales* 3,356,192
SIC 8211 Elementary and secondary schools

D-U-N-S 24-343-1850   (BR)
ROYAL BANK OF CANADA
RBC
(*Suby of* Royal Bank Of Canada)
1307 Av Van Horne, Outremont, QC, H2V 1K7
(514) 495-5904
Emp Here 500
SIC 6021 National commercial banks

D-U-N-S 24-713-1816   (HQ)

TVA PUBLICATIONS INC
LE GUIDE DES DEBUTANTS
(*Suby of* Placements Peladeau Inc, Les)
7 Ch Bates, Outremont, QC, H2V 4V7
(514) 848-7000
Emp Here 230   *Emp Total* 1
Sales 20,356,035
SIC 2759 Commercial printing, nec
Pr Pr Jocelyn Poirier
 Denis Rozon
 Pierre Dion

D-U-N-S 25-757-7312   (BR)
TILLEY ENDURABLES, INC
1050 Av Laurier O, Outremont, QC, H2V 2K8
(514) 272-7791
Emp Here 20
SIC 5651 Family clothing stores

Outremont, QC H3T

D-U-N-S 24-426-2932   (SL)
CSH VINCENT D'INDY INC
60 Av Willowdale, Outremont, QC, H3T 2A3
(514) 739-1707
Emp Here 20   *Sales* 942,329
SIC 8361 Residential care

Padoue, QC G0J
Matapedia County

D-U-N-S 20-711-8287   (BR)
COMMISSION SCOLAIRE DES PHARES
ECOLES PRIMAIRES LES CHEMINOTS PAVILLON DU SOMMET
(*Suby of* Commission Scolaire des Phares)
217 Rue Beaulieu, Padoue, QC, G0J 1X0
(418) 775-5829
Emp Here 50
SIC 8211 Elementary and secondary schools

Palmarolle, QC J0Z
Abitibi County

D-U-N-S 25-378-6453   (BR)
CENTRE DE SANTE ET DE SERVICES SO-CIAUX DES AURORES-BOREALES, LE
FOYER MGR HALDE
136 Rue Principale, Palmarolle, QC, J0Z 3C0
(819) 787-2612
Emp Here 30
SIC 8361 Residential care

D-U-N-S 20-712-6116   (BR)
COMMISSION SCOLAIRE ABITIBI
ECOLE DAGENAIS
(*Suby of* Commission Scolaire Abitibi)
141 Rue Principale, Palmarolle, QC, J0Z 3C0
(819) 787-2326
Emp Here 25
SIC 8211 Elementary and secondary schools

Papineauville, QC J0V
Papineau County

D-U-N-S 25-190-9990   (BR)
CAISSE DESJARDINS DE LA PETITE-NATION
CENTRE DE SERVICE PAPINEAUVILLE
276 Rue Papineau, Papineauville, QC, J0V 1R0
(819) 983-7313
Emp Here 30
SIC 6062 State credit unions

D-U-N-S 24-589-0512   (HQ)

LAUZON - PLANCHERS DE BOIS EX-CLUSIFS INC
LAUZON (THURSO) FOREST RESOURCES
2101 Cote Des Cascades, Papineauville, QC, J0V 1R0
(819) 427-5144
Emp Here 250   *Emp Total* 570
Sales 135,789,609
SIC 5031 Lumber, plywood, and millwork
 David Lauzon

Parent, QC G0X
Champlain County

D-U-N-S 24-827-7134   (SL)
INDUSTRIES PARENT INC
201 Ch Du Moulin, Parent, QC, G0X 3P0
(819) 667-2711
Emp Here 49   *Sales* 11,768,200
SIC 2421 Sawmills and planing mills, general
Pr Pr Claude Perron
Sec Janet Shulist
 Alexandre Patte
 David Chamberlain
 Michel Perron

Paspebiac, QC G0C
Bonaventure County

D-U-N-S 20-309-3281   (BR)
CENTRE DE SANTE ET DE SERVICES SO-CIAUX DE LA BAIE-DES-CHALEURS
CENTRE DE SANTE ET DE SERVICES SO-CIAUX DE LA BAIE-DES-CHALEURS
(*Suby of* Centre de sante et de services sociaux de la Baie-des-Chaleurs)
273 Boul Gerard-D.-Levesque O, Paspebiac, QC, G0C 2K0
(418) 752-2572
Emp Here 50
SIC 8062 General medical and surgical hospitals

D-U-N-S 20-711-8048   (BR)
COMMISSION SCOLAIRE RENE-LEVESQUE
ECOLE POLYVALANTE DE PASPEDIAC
158 9e Rue, Paspebiac, QC, G0C 2K0
(418) 752-3395
Emp Here 50
SIC 8211 Elementary and secondary schools

Perce, QC G0C
Gaspe-Est County

D-U-N-S 20-322-8957   (BR)
VIA RAIL CANADA INC
44 132 Rte O Bureau Lb1, Perce, QC, G0C 2L0
(418) 782-2747
Emp Here 200
SIC 4111 Local and suburban transit

Petit-Saguenay, QC G0V
Chicoutimi County

D-U-N-S 24-746-2328   (SL)
SOCIETE DE GESTION V. V. F. DE ST-ETIENNE INC
VILLAGE-VACANCES PETIT-SAGUENAY
99 Ch Saint-Etienne, Petit-Saguenay, QC, G0V 1N0
(418) 272-3193
Emp Here 55   *Sales* 2,407,703
SIC 7011 Hotels and motels

Philipsburg, QC J0J
Missisquoi County

D-U-N-S 24-180-8109   (BR)
COURTAGE BGL LTEE
39 Rte 133, Philipsburg, QC, J0J 1N0
(450) 248-7768
Emp Here 417
SIC 4731 Freight transportation arrangement

Pierrefonds, QC H8Y
Hochelaga County

D-U-N-S 24-864-6671   (HQ)
175246 CANADA INC
RESTAURANT MCDONALD'S
(*Suby of* 175246 Canada Inc)
4928 Boul Des Sources Bureau 2545, Pierrefonds, QC, H8Y 3C9
(514) 684-0779
Emp Here 250   *Emp Total* 300
Sales 11,684,880
SIC 5812 Eating places
Pr Pr Frederic Cassir

D-U-N-S 25-298-5924   (BR)
COMMISSION SCOLAIRE MARGUERITE-BOURGEOYS
ECOLE PERCE NEIGE
4770 Boul Lalande, Pierrefonds, QC, H8Y 1V2
(514) 855-4239
Emp Here 60
SIC 8211 Elementary and secondary schools

D-U-N-S 25-298-5650   (BR)
LESTER B. PEARSON SCHOOL BOARD
RIVERDALE HIGH SCHOOL
5060 Boul Des Sources, Pierrefonds, QC, H8Y 3E4
(514) 684-2337
Emp Here 80
SIC 8211 Elementary and secondary schools

Pierrefonds, QC H8Z
Hochelaga County

D-U-N-S 25-240-4751   (BR)
COMMISSION SCOLAIRE MARGUERITE-BOURGEOYS
ECOLE MURIELLE DUMONT
5005 Rue Valois, Pierrefonds, QC, H8Z 2G8
(514) 855-4211
Emp Here 40
SIC 8211 Elementary and secondary schools

D-U-N-S 25-240-3977   (BR)
LESTER B. PEARSON SCHOOL BOARD
TERRY FOX SCHOOL
13280 Rue Huntington, Pierrefonds, QC, H8Z 1G2
(514) 626-6253
Emp Here 50
SIC 8211 Elementary and secondary schools

Pierrefonds, QC H9A
Hochelaga County

D-U-N-S 24-548-0371   (SL)
BIBLIOTHEQUE INTERMUNICIPALE PIER-REFONDS/DOLLARD DES ORMEAUX
13555 Boul De Pierrefonds, Pierrefonds, QC, H9A 1A6
(514) 620-4181
Emp Here 92   *Sales* 5,884,100
SIC 8231 Libraries
Dir Michele Dupuis

D-U-N-S 20-649-3996   (BR)
LESTER B. PEARSON SCHOOL BOARD
WEST ISLAND CAREER CENTRE
13700 Boul De Pierrefonds, Pierrefonds, QC, H9A 1A7
(514) 620-0707
Emp Here 35
SIC 8249 Vocational schools, nec

D-U-N-S 25-233-6201   (BR)
LESTER B. PEARSON SCHOOL BOARD
BEECHWOOD SCHOOL
13155 Rue Shelborne, Pierrefonds, QC, H9A 1L4
(514) 626-3484
Emp Here 25
SIC 8211 Elementary and secondary schools

D-U-N-S 20-587-0723   (BR)
VILLE DE MONTREAL
BIBLIOTHEQUE PUBLIQUE PIERREFONDS
13555 Boul De Pierrefonds, Pierrefonds, QC, H9A 1A6
(514) 620-4181
Emp Here 40
SIC 8231 Libraries

Pierrefonds, QC H9H
Hochelaga County

D-U-N-S 25-874-5132   (BR)
BANQUE NATIONALE DU CANADA
14965 Boul De Pierrefonds, Pierrefonds, QC, H9H 4M5
(514) 626-7330
Emp Here 20
SIC 6021 National commercial banks

D-U-N-S 25-240-3829   (BR)
COMMISSION SCOLAIRE MARGUERITE-BOURGEOYS
ECOLE ST-GERARD
14385 Boul De Pierrefonds, Pierrefonds, QC, H9H 1Z2
(514) 855-4243
Emp Here 30
SIC 8211 Elementary and secondary schools

D-U-N-S 20-860-6330   (SL)
GESTION SFTP
PHARMAPRIX
4955 Rue Saint-Pierre, Pierrefonds, QC, H9H 5M9
(514) 624-8838
Emp Here 130   *Sales* 25,565,400
SIC 5912 Drug stores and proprietary stores
Dir Suzanne Fradet

D-U-N-S 25-240-4652   (BR)
LESTER B. PEARSON SCHOOL BOARD
THORNDALE ELEMENTARY SCHOOL
4348 Rue Thorndale, Pierrefonds, QC, H9H 1X1
(514) 626-3924
Emp Here 50
SIC 8211 Elementary and secondary schools

D-U-N-S 20-712-3600   (BR)
LESTER B. PEARSON SCHOOL BOARD
ECOLE ST CHARLES
4331 Rue Sainte-Anne, Pierrefonds, QC, H9H 4G7
(514) 626-0480
Emp Here 50
SIC 8211 Elementary and secondary schools

D-U-N-S 25-240-7598   (BR)
LESTER B. PEARSON SCHOOL BOARD
GREENDALE ELEMENTARY SCHOOL
4381 Rue King, Pierrefonds, QC, H9H 2E8
(514) 626-7880
Emp Here 35
SIC 8211 Elementary and secondary schools

D-U-N-S 20-003-0067   (BR)
PROVIGO DISTRIBUTION INC

PROVIGO PIERREFONDS
14875 Boul De Pierrefonds, Pierrefonds, QC, H9H 4M5
(514) 626-8687
Emp Here 30
SIC 5411 Grocery stores

D-U-N-S 25-258-8454   (BR)
VIGI SANTE LTEE
CENTRE D'HEBERGEMENT ET DE SOINS DE LONGUE DUREE PIERREFONDS
(*Suby of* Vigi Sante Ltee)
14775 Boul De Pierrefonds Bureau 229, Pierrefonds, QC, H9H 4Y1
(514) 620-1220
Emp Here 80
SIC 8361 Residential care

Pierrefonds, QC H9J
Hochelaga County

D-U-N-S 24-679-1677   (SL)
9060-1048 QUEBEC INC
WEST ISLAND MANOR
17725 Bou De Pierrefonds, Pierrefonds, QC, H9J 3L1
(514) 620-9850
Emp Here 52   *Sales* 2,772,003
SIC 8051 Skilled nursing care facilities

D-U-N-S 20-712-3576   (BR)
LESTER B. PEARSON SCHOOL BOARD
17750 Rue Meloche, Pierrefonds, QC, H9J 3P9
(514) 624-6614
Emp Here 30
SIC 8211 Elementary and secondary schools

Pierrefonds, QC H9K
Hochelaga County

D-U-N-S 24-736-4388   (BR)
VILLE DE MONTREAL
PIERREFONDS USINE DE FILTRATION
18025 Boul Gouin O, Pierrefonds, QC, H9K 1A1
(514) 624-1079
Emp Here 20
SIC 1446 Industrial sand

Pincourt, QC J7W
Vaudreuil County

D-U-N-S 24-600-0236   (SL)
148200 CANADA INC
PHARMAPRIX BANLIEUE OUEST FAUBOURG DE L'ILE
101 Boul Cardinal-Leger Unite 11, Pincourt, QC, J7W 3Y3
(514) 425-5885
Emp Here 120   *Sales* 23,637,850
SIC 5912 Drug stores and proprietary stores
Pr Pr Suzanne Fradet

D-U-N-S 24-713-9256   (HQ)
AQUA DATA INC
95 5e Av, Pincourt, QC, J7W 5K8
(514) 425-1010
Emp Here 100   *Emp Total* 33,000
Sales 13,862,533
SIC 7373 Computer integrated systems design
Gilles Laramee
Rejean Goulet
Yves Cadotte

D-U-N-S 25-240-6657   (BR)
COMMISSION SCOLAIRE DES TROIS-LACS

ECOLE NOTRE DAME DE LORETTE
70 Av Lussier, Pincourt, QC, J7W 5B2
(514) 453-8581
Emp Here 32
SIC 8211 Elementary and secondary schools

D-U-N-S 25-240-3720   (BR)
LESTER B. PEARSON SCHOOL BOARD
ST PATRICK ELEMENTARY SCHOOL
261 Rue Shamrock, Pincourt, QC, J7W 3W5
(514) 453-6351
Emp Here 40
SIC 8211 Elementary and secondary schools

D-U-N-S 20-642-8323   (BR)
MAGASINS HART INC
101 Boul Cardinal-Leger, Pincourt, QC, J7W 3Y3
(514) 320-6395
Emp Here 25
SIC 5999 Miscellaneous retail stores, nec

D-U-N-S 25-018-8836   (BR)
ROYAL BANK OF CANADA
RBC
(*Suby of* Royal Bank Of Canada)
101 Boul Cardinal-Leger, Pincourt, QC, J7W 3Y3
(514) 453-2294
Emp Here 20
SIC 6021 National commercial banks

Plessisville, QC G6L
Megantic County

D-U-N-S 24-200-7037   (BR)
AGROPUR COOPERATIVE
AGROPUR
2400 Rue De La Cooperative, Plessisville, QC, G6L 3G8
(819) 362-7338
Emp Here 85
SIC 2023 Dry, condensed and evaporated dairy products

D-U-N-S 20-239-6560   (HQ)
BOUTIN, V. EXPRESS INC
1397 Rue Savoie, Plessisville, QC, G6L 1J8
(819) 362-7333
Emp Here 70   *Emp Total* 500
Sales 33,735,378
SIC 4213 Trucking, except local
Pr Pr Bernard Boutin
Dir Fin Marc Binette

D-U-N-S 25-363-1550   (HQ)
CAISSE DESJARDINS DE L'ERABLE
CENTRE DE SERVICE DE LOURDES
(*Suby of* Caisse Desjardins de l'Erable)
1658 Rue Saint-Calixte, Plessisville, QC, G6L 1P9
(819) 362-3236
Emp Here 54   *Emp Total* 80
Sales 19,322,486
SIC 6062 State credit unions
Genl Mgr Paul Gagne
Pr Andre Grenier
VP Yvon Jr Fiset
Sec Valerye Bedard
Dir Danis Beauvillier
Dir Jean-Philippe Boutin
Dir Richard Cote
Dir Edith Laliberte
Dir Noel Lemieux
Dir Genevieve Manseau

D-U-N-S 20-205-9341   (HQ)
CITADELLE COOPERATIVE DE PRODUCTEURS DE SIROP D'ERABLE
SHADY MAPLE FARMS PRODUCTION
(*Suby of* Citadelle Cooperative de Producteurs de Sirop d'Erable)
2100 Av Saint-Laurent, Plessisville, QC, G6L 2R3

(819) 362-3241
Emp Here 70   *Emp Total* 100
Sales 10,433,380
SIC 2099 Food preparations, nec
Pr Michel Labbe
VP Laurent Cloutier
Sec Jean-Marie Chouinard
Dir Cecile B Pichette
Dir Simon Deschenes
Dir Paul Beauregard
Dir Michel Belanger
Dir Laurier Gauthier
Dir Jean-Claude Brochu
Dir Denis Pellerin

D-U-N-S 25-234-2654   (BR)
COMMISSION SCOLAIRE DES BOIS-FRANCS
ECOLES PRIMAIRES NOTRE DAME
(*Suby of* Commission Scolaire des Bois-Francs)
2050 Boul Des Sucreries, Plessisville, QC, G6L 1W6
(819) 362-2374
Emp Here 30
SIC 8211 Elementary and secondary schools

D-U-N-S 25-156-8317   (BR)
COMMISSION SCOLAIRE DES BOIS-FRANCS
ECOLE JEAN RIVARD
(*Suby of* Commission Scolaire des Bois-Francs)
1850 Av Rousseau, Plessisville, QC, G6L 2V3
(819) 362-3191
Emp Here 20
SIC 8211 Elementary and secondary schools

D-U-N-S 20-798-9372   (BR)
COMMISSION SCOLAIRE DES BOIS-FRANCS
CENTRE D'EDUCATION DES ADULTES ANDRE MORRISSETE
1650 Av Vallee, Plessisville, QC, G6L 2W5
(819) 362-7348
Emp Here 50
SIC 8748 Business consulting, nec

D-U-N-S 25-232-8547   (BR)
COMMISSION SCOLAIRE DES BOIS-FRANCS
ECOLE POLYVALENTE LA SAMARE
(*Suby of* Commission Scolaire des Bois-Francs)
1159 Rue Saint-Jean, Plessisville, QC, G6L 1E1
(819) 362-3226
Emp Here 130
SIC 8211 Elementary and secondary schools

D-U-N-S 20-239-7477   (HQ)
COMPAGNIE MOTOPARTS INC
1124 Rue Saint-Calixte, Plessisville, QC, G6L 1N8
(819) 362-7373
Emp Here 57   *Emp Total* 60
Sales 16,130,550
SIC 5085 Industrial supplies
Jean-Guy Cote

D-U-N-S 24-706-9578   (SL)
FONDERIE FONDALCO INC
(*Suby of* 9163-0186 Quebec Inc)
2485 Av Vallee, Plessisville, QC, G6L 3S6
(819) 362-3443
Emp Here 40   *Sales* 5,987,760
SIC 3365 Aluminum foundries
Pr Pr Marc Grenier
Guy Grenier

D-U-N-S 20-870-0591   (SL)
FOYER DES BOIS FRANCS
1450 Av Trudelle, Plessisville, QC, G6L 3K4

Emp Here 57   *Sales* 2,115,860
SIC 8361 Residential care

D-U-N-S 20-190-9652   (SL)

FRONTENAC EXPRESS INC
1397 Rue Savoie, Plessisville, QC, G6L 1J8
(819) 362-7333
Emp Here 50   *Sales* 8,239,360
SIC 4213 Trucking, except local
Pr Pr Bernard Boutin
Marc Binette

D-U-N-S 20-297-9159   (SL)
GALVANISATION QUEBEC INC
340 Rte 116 O, Plessisville, QC, G6L 2Y2
(819) 362-2095
Emp Here 50   *Sales* 3,502,114
SIC 3479 Metal coating and allied services

D-U-N-S 24-426-8723   (SL)
GESTION M.E.W. INC
(*Suby of* 9187-3612 Quebec Inc)
2255 Av Vallee, Plessisville, QC, G6L 3P8
(819) 362-6315
Emp Here 60   *Sales* 5,653,974
SIC 3599 Industrial machinery, nec
Dir Jennifer Poire
Dir Allen Poire

D-U-N-S 24-940-6893   (SL)
L.S. FINITION INDUSTRIELLE INC
(*Suby of* Groupe Machinex Inc)
2140 Rue Olivier, Plessisville, QC, G6L 3T1
(819) 362-9145
Emp Here 26   *Sales* 2,261,782
SIC 1799 Special trade contractors, nec

D-U-N-S 24-202-9312   (SL)
PLESSITECH INC
2250 Av Vallee, Plessisville, QC, G6L 3N2
(819) 362-6315
Emp Here 50   *Sales* 3,064,349
SIC 7692 Welding repair

D-U-N-S 25-485-2718   (BR)
PROVIGO DISTRIBUTION INC
MAXI PLESSISVILLE #8645
1877 Rue Bilodeau, Plessisville, QC, G6L 5N2
(819) 362-7370
Emp Here 38
SIC 5411 Grocery stores

D-U-N-S 24-102-8567   (BR)
SAPUTO PRODUITS LAITIERS CANADA S.E.N.C.
(*Suby of* Saputo Produits Laitiers Canada S.E.N.C.)
1245 Av Forand, Plessisville, QC, G6L 1X5
(819) 362-6378
Emp Here 140
SIC 2022 Cheese; natural and processed

D-U-N-S 24-378-8536   (BR)
SOCIETE COOPERATIVE AGRICOLE DES APPALACHES
CENTRE DE RENOVATION COOP A PLESSISVILLE
1850 Av Saint-Laurent, Plessisville, QC, G6L 2R2
(819) 362-8144
Emp Here 20
SIC 5211 Lumber and other building materials

D-U-N-S 24-568-1879   (HQ)
TRANSNAT EXPRESS INC
TRANSNAT LOGISTIQUE
1397 Rue Savoie, Plessisville, QC, G6L 1J8
(819) 362-7333
Emp Here 50   *Emp Total* 500
Sales 66,394,237
SIC 4213 Trucking, except local
Pr Bernard Boutin

D-U-N-S 20-575-7193   (BR)
TRANSPORT TFI 15 S.E.C.
TRANSPORT GREGOIRE
Transport Gregoire, Plessisville, QC, G6L 0A3
(819) 362-8813
Emp Here 50
SIC 4213 Trucking, except local

D-U-N-S 20-017-1283   (SL)

USNR/KOCKUMS CANCAR COMPANY
U.S.N.R.
(*Suby of* Usnr, LLC)
1600 Rue Saint-Paul, Plessisville, QC, G6L 1C1
(819) 362-7362
Emp Here 80   *Sales* 7,879,756
SIC 3553 Woodworking machinery
Pr Pr George Van Hoomissen
Dir Richard H Ward
Dir Ronald W Giesbers

Pohenegamook, QC G0L
Kamouraska County

D-U-N-S 20-711-9574   (BR)
COMMISSION SCOLAIRE DU FLEUVE ET DES LACS
ECOLE SECONDAIRE DU TRANSCONTINENTAL
685 Rang Notre-Dame-Des-Champs, Pohenegamook, QC, G0L 1J0
(418) 863-7711
Emp Here 49
SIC 8211 Elementary and secondary schools

D-U-N-S 20-201-9241   (BR)
J. D. IRVING, LIMITED
(*Suby of* J. D. Irving, Limited)
1274 Rue De La Frontiere Rr 1, Pohenegamook, QC, G0L 1J0
(418) 859-2173
Emp Here 70
SIC 2421 Sawmills and planing mills, general

Pointe-A-La-Croix, QC G0C
Bonaventure County

D-U-N-S 24-884-6693   (SL)
INDUSTRIES G. D. S. INC
(*Suby of* Gestion G et S Deschenes Inc)
6 Ch Qospem, Pointe-A-La-Croix, QC, G0C 1L0
(418) 853-2566
Emp Here 40   *Sales* 4,504,505
SIC 2421 Sawmills and planing mills, general

D-U-N-S 25-740-4905   (BR)
LISTUGUJ FIRST NATION
LISTUGUJ COMMUNITY HEALTH SERVICES
(*Suby of* Listuguj First Nation)
6 Rue Pacific, Pointe-A-La-Croix, QC, G0C 1L0
(418) 788-2155
Emp Here 55
SIC 8059 Nursing and personal care, nec

D-U-N-S 25-484-9706   (BR)
PROVIGO DISTRIBUTION INC
PROVIGO 8050
20 Rue De La Mer, Pointe-A-La-Croix, QC, G0C 1L0
(418) 788-5111
Emp Here 25
SIC 5411 Grocery stores

Pointe-A-La-Garde, QC G0C
Bonaventure County

D-U-N-S 20-721-2275   (SL)
GASTON CELLARD INC
1 Rue Cellard, Pointe-A-La-Garde, QC, G0C 2M0
(418) 788-5202
Emp Here 50   *Sales* 4,742,446
SIC 2421 Sawmills and planing mills, general

Pointe-Au-Pere, QC G5M
Rimouski County

D-U-N-S 25-209-9700   (SL)
9003-4406 QUEBEC INC
FORMULE MAZDA
(*Suby of* 9003-4414 Quebec Inc)
169 Boul Sainte-Anne, Pointe-Au-Pere, QC, G5M 1C3
(418) 725-0911
Emp Here 25   *Sales* 11,779,113
SIC 5511 New and used car dealers
Pr Andre Simard
VP Diane Defoy

Pointe-Aux-Outardes, QC G0H
Saguenay County

D-U-N-S 20-561-1044   (HQ)
SANI-MANIC COTE-NORD INC
(*Suby of* Sani-Manic Cote-Nord Inc)
37 Ch De La Scierie, Pointe-Aux-Outardes, QC. G0H 1M0
(418) 589-2376
Emp Here 35   *Emp Total* 50
Sales 3,064,349
SIC 7699 Repair services, nec

Pointe-Aux-Trembles, QC H1A

D-U-N-S 20-016-8768   (HQ)
BEACON ROOFING SUPPLY CANADA COMPANY
GROUPE BEDARD
(*Suby of* Beacon Roofing Supply, Inc.)
13145 Rue Prince-Arthur, Pointe-Aux-Trembles, QC, H1A 1A9
(514) 642-8691
Emp Here 45   *Emp Total* 3,440
Sales 25,025,520
SIC 5039 Construction materials, nec
Ex VP John C. Smith Jr.
Sec Cooper Ross D.
Dir Buck Robert R.

D-U-N-S 20-330-0801   (BR)
BEAUDOIN HURENS INC
13200 Boul Metropolitain E, Pointe-Aux-Trembles, QC, H1A 5K8
(514) 642-8422
Emp Here 40
SIC 8711 Engineering services

D-U-N-S 24-020-8645   (SL)
C.A.-C.L.S.C. J. OCTAVE ROUSSIN
CENTRE D'ACCUEIL FRANCOIS SAGUENOT
13926 Rue Notre-Dame E, Pointe-Aux-Trembles, QC, H1A 1T5
(514) 642-4050
Emp Here 220   *Sales* 10,797,600
SIC 8361 Residential care
Genl Mgr Monique Corbeil
Pr Jacques Savard

D-U-N-S 25-391-5839   (HQ)
CAISSE POPULAIRE DESJARDINS DE POINTE-AUX-TREMBLES
CENTRE DE SERVICE 2
(*Suby of* Caisse Populaire Desjardins de Pointe-Aux-Trembles)
13120 Rue Sherbrooke E, Pointe-Aux-Trembles, QC, H1A 3W2
(514) 640-5200
Emp Here 30   *Emp Total* 121
Sales 23,840,750
SIC 6062 State credit unions
Genl Mgr Alain Bastarache
Dir Guy Tremblay

Pr Jacques Baril
VP VP Judy Contant
Sec Suzanne Desrochers
Dir Gilles Denis
Dir Jean-Claude Blanchard
Dir Lucie Landreville
Dir Jacques Morin
Dir Francine St-Onge

D-U-N-S 20-712-3840   (BR)
COMMISSION SCOLAIRE DE LA POINTE-DE-L'ILE
ECOLE MONTMARTRE
1855 59e Av, Pointe-Aux-Trembles, QC, H1A 2P2
(514) 642-9343
Emp Here 50
SIC 8211 Elementary and secondary schools

D-U-N-S 20-580-7998   (BR)
COMMISSION SCOLAIRE DE LA POINTE-DE-L'ILE
ECOLE NOTRE DAME
14425 Rue Notre-Dame E, Pointe-Aux-Trembles, QC, H1A 1V6
(514) 642-3950
Emp Here 50
SIC 8211 Elementary and secondary schools

D-U-N-S 25-233-7183   (BR)
COMMISSION SCOLAIRE DE LA POINTE-DE-L'ILE
ECOLE STE-GERMAINE COUSIN
1880 48e Av, Pointe-Aux-Trembles, QC, H1A 2Y6
(514) 642-0881
Emp Here 35
SIC 8211 Elementary and secondary schools

D-U-N-S 25-233-7308   (BR)
COMMISSION SCOLAIRE DE LA POINTE-DE-L'ILE
ECOLE RENE PELLETIER
16360 Rue Bureau, Pointe-Aux-Trembles, QC, H1A 1Z5
(514) 642-7337
Emp Here 25
SIC 8211 Elementary and secondary schools

D-U-N-S 25-233-7142   (BR)
COMMISSION SCOLAIRE DE LA POINTE-DE-L'ILE
ECOLES SPECIALISEES LE TOURNESOL PRIMAIRE ET SECONDAIRE
15150 Rue Sherbrooke E, Pointe-Aux-Trembles, QC, H1A 3P9
(514) 642-0341
Emp Here 60
SIC 8211 Elementary and secondary schools

D-U-N-S 25-233-9049   (BR)
COMMISSION SCOLAIRE DE LA POINTE-DE-L'ILE
ECOLE STE-MARIA-GORETTI
15700 Rue Notre-Dame E, Pointe-Aux-Trembles, QC, H1A 1X4
(514) 642-6461
Emp Here 25
SIC 8211 Elementary and secondary schools

D-U-N-S 25-827-6351   (BR)
PROVIGO DISTRIBUTION INC
MAXI
12780 Rue Sherbrooke E, Pointe-Aux-Trembles, QC, H1A 4Y3
(514) 498-2675
Emp Here 100
SIC 5411 Grocery stores

D-U-N-S 20-022-1526   (SL)
RE/MAX DE LA POINTE INC
RE/MAX DE LA POINTE
13150 Rue Sherbrooke E Bureau 201, Pointe-Aux-Trembles, QC, H1A 4B1
(514) 644-0000
Emp Here 60   *Sales* 5,617,974
SIC 6531 Real estate agents and managers
Pr Pr Andre Theoret

D-U-N-S 20-266-3191   (HQ)
WESTROCK COMPANY OF CANADA INC
PRESENTOIRES ROCKTENN
(*Suby of* Westrock Company)
15400 Rue Sherbrooke E Bureau A-15, Pointe-Aux-Trembles, QC, H1A 3S2
(514) 642-9251
Emp Here 300   *Emp Total* 39,000
Sales 142,671,540
SIC 2657 Folding paperboard boxes
Pr Pr Steven C Voorhees
VP Ward H Dickson
Sec Robert B Mcintosh

Pointe-Aux-Trembles, QC H1B

D-U-N-S 25-370-4878   (SL)
9057-6455 QUEBEC INC
ROTISSERIE ST HUBERT
12575 Rue Sherbrooke E Bureau 205, Pointe-Aux-Trembles, QC, H1B 1C8
(514) 645-2771
Emp Here 50   *Sales* 1,532,175
SIC 5812 Eating places

D-U-N-S 24-786-9444   (BR)
AMNOR INDUSTRIES INC
(*Suby of* Amnor Industries Inc)
12480 Rue April Bureau 103, Pointe-Aux-Trembles, QC, H1B 5N5
(514) 494-4242
Emp Here 20
SIC 7699 Repair services, nec

D-U-N-S 20-739-4057   (SL)
CHRISTIN AUTOMOBILE INC
(*Suby of* Gestion Raymond Christin Inc)
12011 Rue Sherbrooke E, Pointe-Aux-Trembles, QC, H1B 1C6
(514) 640-1050
Emp Here 75   *Sales* 36,810,000
SIC 5511 New and used car dealers
Pr Pr Raymond Christin
Sec Claude Christin
Marco France

D-U-N-S 20-712-3824   (BR)
COMMISSION SCOLAIRE DE LA POINTE-DE-L'ILE
ECOLE SAINT MARCEL
1470 16e Av, Pointe-Aux-Trembles, QC, H1B 3N6
(514) 645-8531
Emp Here 30
SIC 8211 Elementary and secondary schools

D-U-N-S 25-233-8694   (BR)
COMMISSION SCOLAIRE DE LA POINTE-DE-L'ILE
ECOLE MARC-LAFLAMME / LE PRELUDE
555 19e Av, Pointe-Aux-Trembles, QC, H1B 3E3
(514) 395-9101
Emp Here 50
SIC 8211 Elementary and secondary schools

D-U-N-S 25-233-7225   (BR)
COMMISSION SCOLAIRE DE LA POINTE-DE-L'ILE
ECOLE FRANCOIS LA BERNARDE
950 Rue Pierre-Lacroix, Pointe-Aux-Trembles, QC, H1B 3C8
(514) 645-9134
Emp Here 30
SIC 8211 Elementary and secondary schools

D-U-N-S 25-233-5161   (BR)
COMMISSION SCOLAIRE DE LA POINTE-DE-L'ILE
ECOLE STE MARGUERITE BOURGEOIS
11625 Rue De La Gauchetiere, Pointe-Aux-Trembles, QC, H1B 2H8
(514) 645-5515
Emp Here 20

SIC 8211 Elementary and secondary schools

D-U-N-S 20-215-6634   (SL)
COUVREUR VERDUN INC
12168 Rue April, Pointe-Aux-Trembles, QC, H1B 5N5
(514) 640-8787
Emp Here 50   *Sales* 4,961,328
SIC 1761 Roofing, siding, and sheetMetal work

D-U-N-S 25-975-2400   (SL)
EMBALLAGES STARFLEX INC
12325 Rue April, Pointe-Aux-Trembles, QC, H1B 5L8
(514) 640-0674
Emp Here 60   *Sales* 4,377,642
SIC 7336 Commercial art and graphic design

D-U-N-S 25-654-0154   (BR)
GANOTEC INC
MUGA FAB
3777 Rue Dollard-Desjardins, Pointe-Aux-Trembles, QC, H1B 5W9

Emp Here 50
SIC 1629 Heavy construction, nec

D-U-N-S 20-801-8627   (BR)
GROUPE BMTC INC
CENTRE DE LIQUIDATION BRAULT & MARTINEAU
12605 Rue Sherbrooke E, Pointe-Aux-Trembles, QC, H1B 1C8
(514) 645-3332
Emp Here 30
SIC 5712 Furniture stores

D-U-N-S 24-424-8469   (BR)
MAMMOET CRANE INC
12400 Boul Industriel, Pointe-Aux-Trembles, QC, H1B 5M5
(514) 645-4333
Emp Here 50
SIC 4212 Local trucking, without storage

D-U-N-S 20-797-6684   (BR)
METRO RICHELIEU INC
ALIMENTATION YVES UB
1400 Boul Saint-Jean-Baptiste, Pointe-Aux-Trembles, QC, H1B 4A5
(514) 640-5167
Emp Here 70
SIC 5411 Grocery stores

D-U-N-S 24-226-5663   (BR)
METRO RICHELIEU INC
MCMAHON DISTRIBUTEUR PHARMACEUTIQUE
12225 Boul Industriel Bureau 100, Pointe-Aux-Trembles, QC, H1B 5M7
(514) 355-8350
Emp Here 200
SIC 5122 Drugs, proprietaries, and sundries

D-U-N-S 20-323-7672   (BR)
MULTIVER LTEE
LAMIVER
3805 Rue Dollard-Desjardins, Pointe-Aux-Trembles, QC, H1B 5W9
(514) 640-6490
Emp Here 40
SIC 3231 Products of purchased glass

D-U-N-S 20-715-0314   (BR)
PRESSE, LTEE, LA
LA PRESSE, LTEE
(*Suby of* Gesca Ltee)
12300 Boul Metropolitain E, Pointe-Aux-Trembles, QC, H1B 5Y2
(514) 640-1840
Emp Here 300
SIC 7319 Advertising, nec

D-U-N-S 25-193-4675   (BR)
REDBERRY FRANCHISING CORP
BURGER KING
12595 Rue Sherbrooke E, Pointe-Aux-

Trembles, QC, H1B 1C8
(514) 640-7779
Emp Here 25
SIC 5812 Eating places

D-U-N-S 25-198-4183   (BR)
SPEEDY TRANSPORT GROUP INC
SPEEDY TRANSPORT GROUP
12625 Boul Metropolitain E, Pointe-Aux-Trembles, QC, H1B 5R3
(514) 278-3337
Emp Here 60
SIC 4731 Freight transportation arrangement

D-U-N-S 24-896-3654   (BR)
SUNCOR ENERGY INC
11701 Rue Sherbrooke E, Pointe-Aux-Trembles, QC, H1B 1C3
(514) 640-8000
Emp Here 600
SIC 2911 Petroleum refining

D-U-N-S 25-837-5286   (BR)
TRANSPORT JACQUES AUGER INC
12305 Boul Metropolitain E, Pointe-Aux-Trembles, QC, H1B 5R3
(514) 493-3835
Emp Here 150
SIC 4212 Local trucking, without storage

D-U-N-S 20-649-1904   (BR)
TRANSPORT THIBODEAU INC
(*Suby of* Groupe Thibodeau Inc)
12321 Boul Metropolitain E, Pointe-Aux-Trembles, QC, H1B 5R3
(514) 645-7184
Emp Here 100
SIC 4213 Trucking, except local

D-U-N-S 24-835-4367   (HQ)
VEOLIA ES CANADA SERVICES INDUSTRIELS INC
DRAINAMAR
1705 3e Av, Pointe-Aux-Trembles, QC, H1B 5M9
(514) 645-1621
Emp Here 200   *Emp Total* 1,019
Sales 85,364,019
SIC 4953 Refuse systems
Pr Pr Bruno Lebaron
VP VP William Dicroce
Jason Salgo
VP VP Mireille Dufresne

D-U-N-S 20-645-1648   (BR)
VEOLIA ES CANADA SERVICES INDUSTRIELS INC
VEOLIA
1705 3e Av, Pointe-Aux-Trembles, QC, H1B 5M9
(514) 645-1621
Emp Here 60
SIC 4953 Refuse systems

Pointe-Calumet, QC J0N
Deux-Montagnes County

D-U-N-S 20-184-0589   (SL)
9101-6394 QUEBEC INC
BEACH CLUB
701 38e Rue, Pointe-Calumet, QC, J0N 1G2
(450) 473-1000
Emp Here 60   *Sales* 2,261,782
SIC 7999 Amusement and recreation, nec

D-U-N-S 25-292-8932   (BR)
COMMISSION SCOLAIRE DE LA SEIGNEURIE-DES-MILLE-ILES
COMMISSION SCOLAIRE DE LA SEIGNEURIE-DES-MILLE-ILES
(*Suby of* Commission Scolaire de la Seigneurie-Des-Mille-Iles)
784 Boul De La Chapelle, Pointe-Calumet, QC, J0N 1G1

(450) 473-2823
Emp Here 30
SIC 8211 Elementary and secondary schools

D-U-N-S 25-976-1104   (BR)
COMMISSION SCOLAIRE DE LA SEIGNEURIE-DES-MILLE-ILES
ECOLE DES PERSEIDES
(*Suby of* Commission Scolaire de la Seigneurie-Des-Mille-Iles)
1020 Rue Simonne, Pointe-Calumet, QC, J0N 1G5
(450) 623-9494
Emp Here 60
SIC 8211 Elementary and secondary schools

Pointe-Claire, QC H7X
Hochelaga County

D-U-N-S 24-210-3922   (BR)
BOUTIQUE LA VIE EN ROSE INC
BOUTIQUE LA VIE EN ROSE INC
2430 Chomedey (A-13) O, Pointe-Claire, QC, H7X 4G8
(450) 689-7779
Emp Here 20
SIC 5632 Women's accessory and specialty stores

D-U-N-S 25-761-7444   (BR)
CARA OPERATIONS LIMITED
HARVEY'S
(*Suby of* Cara Holdings Limited)
1130 Chomedey (A-13) O, Pointe-Claire, QC, H7X 4C9
(450) 689-9990
Emp Here 25
SIC 5812 Eating places

D-U-N-S 20-690-1063   (SL)
CONCEPT MODE LAVAL INC
2330 Chomedey (A-13) 0 Bureau 13, Pointe-Claire, QC, H7X 4G8
(450) 689-4442
Emp Here 50   *Sales* 3,575,074
SIC 5311 Department stores

D-U-N-S 20-860-4434   (BR)
WINNERS MERCHANTS INTERNATIONAL L.P.
HOMESENSE
(*Suby of* The TJX Companies Inc)
1050 Desste Chomedey (A-13) O, Pointe-Claire, QC, H7X 4C9
(450) 969-2007
Emp Here 105
SIC 5651 Family clothing stores

Pointe-Claire, QC H7Y
Hochelaga County

D-U-N-S 24-364-2357   (BR)
CLUBLINK CORPORATION ULC
CLUB DE GOLF ISLESMERE
1199 Ch Du Bord-De-L'Eau, Pointe-Claire, QC, H7Y 1A9
(450) 689-4130
Emp Here 120
SIC 7992 Public golf courses

Pointe-Claire, QC H9P
Hochelaga County

D-U-N-S 24-356-8032   (BR)
CON-WAY FREIGHT-CANADA INC
151 Av Reverchon, Pointe-Claire, QC, H9P 1K1

Emp Here 20

SIC 4213 Trucking, except local

D-U-N-S 25-291-9014   (SL)
GLOBOCAM (MONTREAL) INC
(*Suby of* 3093-5894 Quebec Inc)
155 Av Reverchon, Pointe-Claire, QC, H9P 1K1
(514) 344-4000
Emp Here 125   *Sales* 58,895,563
SIC 5511 New and used car dealers
Serge Boyer

D-U-N-S 25-977-4636   (BR)
TRIMAC TRANSPORTATION SERVICES LIMITED PARTNERSHIP
TRANSPORT TRIMAC LOCAL
151 Av Reverchon Bureau 200, Pointe-Claire, QC, H9P 1K1
(514) 636-5122
Emp Here 35
SIC 4213 Trucking, except local

Pointe-Claire, QC H9R
Hochelaga County

D-U-N-S 20-288-4607   (SL)
9121-1128 QUEBEC INC
188 Av Oneida, Pointe-Claire, QC, H9R 1A8
(514) 694-3439
Emp Here 57   *Sales* 9,329,057
SIC 6712 Bank holding companies
Pr Pr Daniel Lachapelle

D-U-N-S 24-206-6871   (BR)
9141-0720 QUEBEC INC
MANARAS OPERA
136 Av Oneida, Pointe-Claire, QC, H9R 1A8
(514) 426-1332
Emp Here 51
SIC 3699 Electrical equipment and supplies, nec

D-U-N-S 24-458-0973   (SL)
9159-9159 QUEBEC INC
PHARMAPRIX
6815 Rte Transcanadienne Unit9 28c, Pointe-Claire, QC, H9R 5J1
(514) 695-4211
Emp Here 40   *Sales* 5,690,935
SIC 5912 Drug stores and proprietary stores
Nora Al-Khoury

D-U-N-S 24-340-4782   (BR)
A. M. CASTLE & CO. (CANADA) INC
METAUX CASTLE
(*Suby of* A. M. Castle & Co.)
835 Av Selkirk, Pointe-Claire, QC, H9R 3S2
(514) 694-9575
Emp Here 20
SIC 5051 Metals service centers and offices

D-U-N-S 25-400-5945   (BR)
ABB INC
ABB BOMEM
123 Av Labrosse, Pointe-Claire, QC, H9R 1A3

Emp Here 25
SIC 7629 Electrical repair shops

D-U-N-S 25-393-9615   (SL)
ADD CANADA COMPANY
52 Boul Hymus Bureau 102, Pointe-Claire, QC, H9R 1C9
(514) 428-9020
Emp Here 28   *Sales* 2,115,860
SIC 7371 Custom computer programming services

D-U-N-S 20-217-8786   (HQ)
AMEUBLEMENTS EL RAN LTEE
ACCENT
2751 Aut Transcanadienne, Pointe-Claire, QC, H9R 1B4
(514) 630-5656
Emp Here 460   *Emp Total* 425
Sales 49,029,807

SIC 2512 Upholstered household furniture
Pr Pr Sheldon Lubin
  Eric Abecassis

D-U-N-S 24-086-9540   (SL)
ANODIZING & PAINT T.N.M INC
21 Ch De L'Aviation, Pointe-Claire, QC, H9R 4Z2
(514) 429-7777
Emp Here 50   Sales 3,356,192
SIC 3471 Plating and polishing

D-U-N-S 24-811-0249   (BR)
APOTEX INC
755 Boul Saint-Jean Bureau 607, Pointe-Claire, QC, H9R 5M9
(514) 630-3335
Emp Here 25
SIC 2834 Pharmaceutical preparations

D-U-N-S 20-571-8583   (BR)
ARBOR MEMORIAL SERVICES INC
JARDINS COMMERATIFS LAKEVIEW, LES
701 Av Donegani, Pointe-Claire, QC, H9R 5G6
(514) 694-9294
Emp Here 20
SIC 6531 Real estate agents and managers

D-U-N-S 20-292-5533   (SL)
ASHFIELD HEALTHCARE CANADA INC
SANTE ASHFIELD CANADA
263 Av Labrosse, Pointe-Claire, QC, H9R 1A3
(514) 630-7484
Emp Here 150   Sales 9,517,523
SIC 7389 Business services, nec
Dir Jason Erickson
  Mary-Anne Greenberg
  Joel Erickson
Dir Claire Bates

D-U-N-S 24-429-5093   (SL)
ASSURANCES H. BRALEY LTEE, LES
BRALEY WINTON FINANCIAL GROUP
1868 Boul Des Sources, Suite 400, Pointe-Claire, QC, H9R 5R2
(514) 620-0051
Emp Here 32   Sales 44,232,200
SIC 6311 Life insurance
Pr Pr Herbert Braley
Treas Rita Peloquin

D-U-N-S 24-319-5992   (HQ)
AVIAT NETWORKS CANADA ULC
RESEAUX AVIAT CANADA
6500 Aut Transcanadienne Bureau 400, Pointe-Claire, QC, H9R 0A5
(514) 800-1410
Emp Here 145   Emp Total 740
Sales 46,551,053
SIC 4899 Communication services, nec
Pr Pr John Madigan
Sec Kevin Holwell
Dir Daniel P.E. Fournier

D-U-N-S 25-295-9028   (BR)
BANK OF NOVA SCOTIA, THE
SCOTIABANK
6815 Aut Transcanadienne Bureau 21, Pointe-Claire, QC, H9R 1C4
(514) 695-5230
Emp Here 20
SIC 6021 National commercial banks

D-U-N-S 20-589-4699   (BR)
BANQUE TORONTO-DOMINION, LA
TD CANADA TRUST
(Suby of Toronto-Dominion Bank, The)
265 Boul Saint-Jean Bureau A, Pointe-Claire, QC, H9R 3J1
(514) 695-2590
Emp Here 20
SIC 6021 National commercial banks

D-U-N-S 20-709-3332   (BR)
BAYER INC
7600 Rte Transcanadienne, Pointe-Claire, QC, H9R 1C8

(514) 697-5550
Emp Here 600
SIC 2834 Pharmaceutical preparations

D-U-N-S 24-363-5104   (BR)
BEST BUY CANADA LTD
BEST BUY
(Suby of Best Buy Co., Inc.)
6815 Rte Transcanadienne, Pointe-Claire, QC, H9R 1C4
(514) 782-2400
Emp Here 50
SIC 5731 Radio, television, and electronic stores

D-U-N-S 20-172-0625   (BR)
BEST BUY CANADA LTD
GEEK SQUAD
(Suby of Best Buy Co., Inc.)
6321 Aut Transcanadienne Bureau 121, Pointe-Claire, QC, H9R 5A5
(514) 428-1999
Emp Here 10
SIC 5999 Miscellaneous retail stores, nec

D-U-N-S 20-927-3291   (SL)
BIRD CIVIL ET MINES LTEE
1870 Boul Des Sources Bureau 200, Pointe-Claire, QC, H9R 5N4
(514) 426-1333
Emp Here 26   Sales 3,575,074
SIC 1629 Heavy construction, nec

D-U-N-S 20-590-7587   (HQ)
BOUCLAIR INC
BOUCLAIR HOME
152 Av Alston, Pointe-Claire, QC, H9R 6B4
(514) 426-0115
Emp Here 90   Emp Total 1,000
Sales 109,927,252
SIC 5719 Miscellaneous homefurnishings
Pr Pr Peter Goldberg
Ch Bd Kerrigan Turner
Sec Lionel Trombert
Dir Real Plourde
Dir Jeff York
Dir Eric Boyko
Dir Frederic Vitre
Dir Bertrand Cesvet

D-U-N-S 24-896-4215   (SL)
BOZANTO INC
1999 Boul Des Sources, Pointe-Claire, QC, H9R 5Z4
(514) 630-3320
Emp Here 50   Sales 1,678,096
SIC 2519 Household furniture, nec

D-U-N-S 25-311-4714   (BR)
CANADIAN IMPERIAL BANK OF COMMERCE
CIBC
6341 Aut Transcanadienne Bureau 120, Pointe-Claire, QC, H9R 5A5
(514) 697-1227
Emp Here 40
SIC 6021 National commercial banks

D-U-N-S 24-226-2405   (BR)
CARDINAL HEALTH CANADA INC
(Suby of Cardinal Health, Inc.)
6800 Aut Transcanadienne, Pointe-Claire, QC, H9R 5L4

Emp Here 60
SIC 5149 Groceries and related products, nec

D-U-N-S 20-720-0085   (HQ)
CHANDELLES ET CREATIONS ROBIN INC
ARTIZAN
(Suby of Chandelles et Creations Robin Inc)
151 Av Alston, Pointe-Claire, QC, H9R 5V9
(514) 426-5999
Emp Here 36   Emp Total 42
Sales 8,420,350
SIC 5137 Women's and children's clothing
Dir Robin Valliear Barre
Pr Guy Barre

D-U-N-S 24-433-7978   (SL)
CIRCUITS CMR LTEE
CIRCUITS CMR
(Suby of Groupe Circuits C.M.R. Inc)
850 Av Selkirk, Pointe-Claire, QC, H9R 3S3
(514) 426-5525
Emp Here 40   Sales 3,652,830
SIC 3672 Printed circuit boards

D-U-N-S 20-762-4271   (SL)
CLAIREBEC INC
BRASSERIE LE MANOIR
600 Boul Saint-Jean, Pointe-Claire, QC, H9R 3J9
(514) 695-2071
Emp Here 51   Sales 1,896,978
SIC 5813 Drinking places

D-U-N-S 25-240-3878   (BR)
COMMISSION SCOLAIRE MARGUERITE-BOURGEOYS
ECOLE FELIX LECLERC
311 Av Inglewood, Pointe-Claire, QC, H9R 2Z8
(514) 855-4225
Emp Here 120
SIC 8211 Elementary and secondary schools

D-U-N-S 25-240-7473   (BR)
COMMISSION SCOLAIRE MARGUERITE-BOURGEOYS
ECOLE POINTE CLAIRE
93 Av Douglas-Shand, Pointe-Claire, QC, H9R 2A7
(514) 855-4245
Emp Here 50
SIC 8211 Elementary and secondary schools

D-U-N-S 20-884-6501   (SL)
COMPAGNIE DIVERSIFIEE DE L'EST LTEE
EDCO DU CANADA
131 Boul Hymus, Pointe-Claire, QC, H9R 1E7
(514) 694-5353
Emp Here 100
SIC 3497 Metal foil and leaf

D-U-N-S 24-813-0429   (SL)
COPAP INC
755 Boul Saint-Jean Bureau 305, Pointe-Claire, QC, H9R 5M9
(514) 693-9150
Emp Here 21   Sales 66,568,050
SIC 5084 Industrial machinery and equipment
Pr Pr David Sela
  Laurent Barbe
  Denys Lamarre

D-U-N-S 24-354-8893   (BR)
COSTCO WHOLESALE CANADA LTD
COSTCO
(Suby of Costco Wholesale Corporation)
5701 Aut Transcanadienne, Pointe-Claire, QC, H9R 1B7
(514) 426-5052
Emp Here 100
SIC 5099 Durable goods, nec

D-U-N-S 25-257-8646   (BR)
COTT CORPORATION
COTT BEVERAGE, DIV OF
333 Av Avro, Pointe-Claire, QC, H9R 5W3
(514) 428-1000
Emp Here 50
SIC 2086 Bottled and canned soft drinks

D-U-N-S 20-806-6634   (BR)
COUTTS, WILLIAM E. COMPANY, LIMITED
HALLMARK CARDS
(Suby of Hallmark Cards, Incorporated)
6801 Aut Transcanadienne, Pointe-Claire, QC, H9R 5J2
(514) 695-5325
Emp Here 25
SIC 5947 Gift, novelty, and souvenir shop

D-U-N-S 24-686-2200   (BR)
DUPONT REALTY INC
(Suby of E. I. Du Pont De Nemours and Company)

6000 Aut Transcanadienne, Pointe-Claire, QC, H9R 1B9
(514) 697-8840
Emp Here 30
SIC 6512 Nonresidential building operators

D-U-N-S 25-194-8493   (BR)
EXOVA CANADA INC
(Suby of Exova, Inc.)
121 Boul Hymus, Pointe-Claire, QC, H9R 1E6
(514) 697-3273
Emp Here 135
SIC 8734 Testing laboratories

D-U-N-S 20-706-6866   (BR)
EXPERTECH NETWORK INSTALLATION INC
BATISSEURS DE RESEAUX
133 Boul Hymus, Pointe-Claire, QC, H9R 1E7
(514) 697-0230
Emp Here 40
SIC 4899 Communication services, nec

D-U-N-S 24-346-6179   (BR)
FPINNOVATIONS
PAPRICAN
570 Boul Saint-Jean, Pointe-Claire, QC, H9R 3J9
(514) 630-4100
Emp Here 280
SIC 8733 Noncommercial research organizations

D-U-N-S 20-323-3957   (BR)
FINANCIERE BANQUE NATIONALE INC
1 Av Holiday Bureau 145, Pointe-Claire, QC, H9R 5N3
(514) 426-2522
Emp Here 20
SIC 6211 Security brokers and dealers

D-U-N-S 20-523-4953   (SL)
FONDATION DE L'HOPITAL GENERAL DU LAKESHORE
160 Av Stillview Bureau 5209, Pointe-Claire, QC, H9R 2Y2
(514) 630-2081
Emp Here 23   Sales 6,784,769
SIC 8399 Social services, nec
Genl Mgr Silvana Orrino

D-U-N-S 20-249-4485   (BR)
GAP (CANADA) INC
GAP
(Suby of The Gap Inc)
6801 Aut Transcanadienne Bureau E7a, Pointe-Claire, QC, H9R 5J2
(514) 426-8281
Emp Here 25
SIC 5651 Family clothing stores

D-U-N-S 20-123-1144   (BR)
GENERAL ELECTRIC CANADA COMPANY
GE CANADA
(Suby of General Electric Company)
179 Boul Brunswick, Pointe-Claire, QC, H9R 5N2

Emp Here 65
SIC 3625 Relays and industrial controls

D-U-N-S 20-747-8319   (BR)
GOLF TOWN LIMITED
GOLF TOWN
2315 Aut Transcanadienne Bureau A, Pointe-Claire, QC, H9R 5Z5
(514) 693-0055
Emp Here 30
SIC 5941 Sporting goods and bicycle shops

D-U-N-S 24-935-9142   (SL)
GROUPE LEGERLITE INC, LE
(Suby of 126018 Canada Inc)
5901 Aut Transcanadienne, Pointe-Claire, QC, H9R 1B7
(514) 694-2493
Emp Here 55   Sales 8,669,427

SIC 3086 Plastics foam products
Pr Pr Marc L'Ecuyer
Patrick L'Ecuyer
Albert L'Ecuyer

D-U-N-S 20-224-6950   (BR)
GROUPE SPORTSCENE INC
CAGE AUX SPORTS, LA
6321 Aut Transcanadienne Bureau 148,
Pointe-Claire, QC, H9R 5A5
(514) 694-4915
Emp Here 40
SIC 5812 Eating places

D-U-N-S 25-246-8798   (BR)
HSBC BANK CANADA
1000 Boul Saint-Jean Bureau 110, Pointe-
Claire, QC, H9R 5P1
(514) 697-8831
Emp Here 22
SIC 6021 National commercial banks

D-U-N-S 24-248-7408   (BR)
HERCULES SLR INC
3800 Aut Transcanadienne, Pointe-Claire, QC,
H9R 1B1
(514) 428-5511
Emp Here 60
SIC 3496 Miscellaneous fabricated wire prod-
ucts

D-U-N-S 24-944-8218   (BR)
HEWITT EQUIPEMENT LIMITEE
CATERPILLAR
4000 Aut Transcanadienne, Pointe-Claire, QC,
H9R 1B2
(514) 426-6700
Emp Here 120
SIC 5082 Construction and mining machinery

D-U-N-S 24-361-7276   (BR)
HOME DEPOT OF CANADA INC
HOME DEPOT
(*Suby of* The Home Depot Inc)
185 Boul Hymus, Pointe-Claire, QC, H9R 1E9
(514) 630-8631
Emp Here 100
SIC 5251 Hardware stores

D-U-N-S 20-700-3141   (BR)
HUDSON'S BAY COMPANY
DECO DECOUVERTE
6815 Rte Transcanadienne Unite Y005,
Pointe-Claire, QC, H9R 1C4
(514) 426-9031
Emp Here 42
SIC 5311 Department stores

D-U-N-S 25-301-3023   (BR)
HUDSON'S BAY COMPANY
BAY, THE
6790 Aut Transcanadienne, Pointe-Claire, QC,
H9R 1C5
(514) 697-4870
Emp Here 300
SIC 5311 Department stores

D-U-N-S 20-213-6008   (SL)
INDUSTRIES C.P.S. INC, LES
30 Ch De L'Aviation, Pointe-Claire, QC, H9R
5M6
(514) 695-7742
Emp Here 100   *Sales* 27,798,706
SIC 3728 Aircraft parts and equipment, nec
Pr Pr Herman Schaubhut
Peter Wiedemann

D-U-N-S 25-305-2500   (BR)
INNVEST PROPERTIES CORP
QUALITY SUITES MONTREAL AEROPORT
(*Suby of* Innvest Properties Corp)
6300 Aut Transcanadienne, Pointe-Claire, QC,
H9R 1B9
(514) 426-5060
Emp Here 45
SIC 7011 Hotels and motels

D-U-N-S 25-305-2476   (BR)
INNVEST PROPERTIES CORP

COMFORT INN MONTREAL AEROPORT
(*Suby of* Innvest Properties Corp)
700 Boul Saint-Jean, Pointe-Claire, QC, H9R
3K2
(514) 697-6210
Emp Here 30
SIC 7011 Hotels and motels

D-U-N-S 25-315-8794   (BR)
**INVESTORS GROUP FINANCIAL SER-
VICES INC**
*INVESTORS SALES & SERVICES WEST IS-
LAND*
6500 Aut Transcanadienne Bureau 600,
Pointe-Claire, QC, H9R 0A5
(514) 426-0886
Emp Here 160
SIC 8741 Management services

D-U-N-S 20-213-6149   (HQ)
K+S SEL WINDSOR LTEE
WINDSOR SALT
755 Boul Saint-Jean Bureau 700, Pointe-
Claire, QC, H9R 5M9
(514) 630-0900
Emp Here 35   *Emp Total* 14,446
SIC 1479 Chemical and fertilizer mining

D-U-N-S 20-192-3005   (BR)
KAYCAN LTEE
(*Suby of* Administration F.L.T. Ltee)
160 Av Oneida, Pointe-Claire, QC, H9R 1A8
(514) 694-7200
Emp Here 100
SIC 5039 Construction materials, nec

D-U-N-S 25-678-3965   (SL)
**L.B. FOSTER TECHNOLOGIES FERROVI-
AIRES CANADA LTEE**
(*Suby of* L. B. Foster Company)
172 Boul Brunswick, Pointe-Claire, QC, H9R
5P9
(514) 695-8500
Emp Here 50   *Sales* 1,751,057
SIC 4111 Local and suburban transit

D-U-N-S 25-365-5377   (BR)
LAFARGE CANADA INC
334 Av Avro, Pointe-Claire, QC, H9R 5W5
(514) 428-7150
Emp Here 150
SIC 1522 Residential construction, nec

D-U-N-S 25-241-0253   (BR)
LESTER B. PEARSON SCHOOL BOARD
LINDSAY PLACE HIGH SCHOOL
111 Av Broadview, Pointe-Claire, QC, H9R
3Z3
(514) 694-2760
Emp Here 120
SIC 8211 Elementary and secondary schools

D-U-N-S 25-240-4132   (BR)
LESTER B. PEARSON SCHOOL BOARD
SAINT JOHN FISHER SENIOR SCHOOL
121 Av Summerhill, Pointe-Claire, QC, H9R
2L8
(514) 695-1112
Emp Here 60
SIC 8211 Elementary and secondary schools

D-U-N-S 25-240-3985   (BR)
LESTER B. PEARSON SCHOOL BOARD
ST THOMAS HIGH SCHOOL
120 Av Ambassador, Pointe-Claire, QC, H9R
1S8
(514) 694-3770
Emp Here 90
SIC 8211 Elementary and secondary schools

D-U-N-S 20-712-3501   (BR)
LESTER B. PEARSON SCHOOL BOARD
NORTHVIEW ELEMENTARY SCHOOL
90 Av De Jubilee Square, Pointe-Claire, QC,
H9R 1M3
(514) 798-0758
Emp Here 50
SIC 8211 Elementary and secondary schools

D-U-N-S 20-712-3527   (BR)
LESTER B. PEARSON SCHOOL BOARD
ST JOHN FISHER JUNIOR SCHOOL
87 Av Belmont, Pointe-Claire, QC, H9R 2N7
(514) 798-0746
Emp Here 40
SIC 8211 Elementary and secondary schools

D-U-N-S 25-240-8711   (BR)
LESTER B. PEARSON SCHOOL BOARD
JOHN RENNIE HIGH SCHOOL
501 Boul Saint-Jean, Pointe-Claire, QC, H9R
3J5
(514) 697-3210
Emp Here 100
SIC 8211 Elementary and secondary schools

D-U-N-S 24-631-2628   (BR)
LIBRAIRIE RENAUD-BRAY INC
6815 Rte Transcanadienne, Pointe-Claire, QC,
H9R 1C4
(514) 782-1222
Emp Here 30
SIC 5942 Book stores

D-U-N-S 24-178-9028   (BR)
LULULEMON ATHLETICA CANADA INC
LULULEMON
6815 Aut Transcanadienne Local G013c,
Pointe-Claire, QC, H9R 5J1
(514) 695-3613
Emp Here 30
SIC 2339 Women's and misses' outerwear,
nec

D-U-N-S 24-353-9657   (SL)
MHD - ROCKLAND INC
AEROSPATIAL ROCKLAND
205 Boul Brunswick Bureau 100, Pointe-
Claire, QC, H9R 1A5
(514) 453-1632
Emp Here 50   *Sales* 10,742,551
SIC 5088 Transportation equipment and sup-
plies
Pr Pr Bryan Dollimore

D-U-N-S 25-195-8773   (SL)
MPB COMMUNICATIONS INC
147 Hymus Blvd, Pointe-Claire, QC, H9R 1E9
(514) 694-8751
Emp Here 120   *Sales* 6,566,463
SIC 8731 Commercial physical research
Pr Jane Bachynski
Dir Fin Nathalie Toupin
Dir Wallace Clements
Dir Opers Beata Klopotowska
Dir Wes Jamroz

D-U-N-S 24-668-7446   (BR)
MANITOULIN TRANSPORT INC
MEM MOTOR EXPRESS MONTREAL
1890 Boul Des Sources, Pointe-Claire, QC,
H9R 5B1
(514) 694-5111
Emp Here 30
SIC 4213 Trucking, except local

D-U-N-S 20-224-5114   (HQ)
**MANUFACTURE LEVITON DU CANADA
LTEE**
(*Suby of* Leviton Manufacturing Co., Inc.)
165 Boul Hymus, Pointe-Claire, QC, H9R 1E9
(514) 954-1840
Emp Here 145   *Emp Total* 6,095
Sales 31,300,140
SIC 5063 Electrical apparatus and equipment
Pr Pr Jean Belhumeur
Sec David Shaanan
Treas Mark Baydarian
Dir Stephan Sokolow
Dir Donald J Hendler
Genl Mgr Bruce Brown

D-U-N-S 24-251-4664   (BR)
MASTERPIECE INC
15 Place De La Triade, Pointe-Claire, QC, H9R
0A3

(514) 695-6695
Emp Here 20
SIC 8361 Residential care

D-U-N-S 20-955-0156   (HQ)
MATERIAUX DE CONSTRUCTION KP LTEE
(*Suby of* Administration F.L.T. Ltee)
3075 Aut Transcanadienne, Pointe-Claire, QC,
H9R 1B4
(514) 694-5855
Emp Here 50   *Emp Total* 900
Sales 33,923,844
SIC 3444 Sheet Metalwork
Pr Lionel Dubrofsky
Sec Tami Dubrofsky

D-U-N-S 20-024-6325   (BR)
METRO RICHELIEU INC
METRO POINTE CLAIRE
325 Boul Saint-Jean, Pointe-Claire, QC, H9R
3J1
(514) 697-6520
Emp Here 100
SIC 5411 Grocery stores

D-U-N-S 24-327-7329   (SL)
NISHAN TRANSPORT INC
160 Av Labrosse, Pointe-Claire, QC, H9R 1A1
(514) 695-4200
Emp Here 70   *Sales* 12,827,282
SIC 4213 Trucking, except local
Pr Pr Rajwinder Singh

D-U-N-S 20-657-9661   (BR)
OLD NAVY (CANADA) INC
(*Suby of* The Gap Inc)
6801 Aut Transcanadienne, Pointe-Claire, QC,
H9R 5J2
(514) 630-7771
Emp Here 50
SIC 5651 Family clothing stores

D-U-N-S 20-999-4771   (HQ)
PACE INVESTCO LTD
GESTION PACE INVESTCO
(*Suby of* WOLSELEY PLC)
193 Boul Brunswick, Pointe-Claire, QC, H9R
5N2
(514) 630-6820
Emp Here 20   *Emp Total* 48,226
Sales 9,182,261
SIC 5085 Industrial supplies
Pr Pr Cosmo Pace
VP VP Brian Pace
Sec Susan Pace
Nancy Pace

D-U-N-S 25-360-8277   (BR)
PATTISON, JIM INDUSTRIES LTD
1868 Boul Des Sources Bureau 200, Pointe-
Claire, QC, H9R 5R2
(514) 856-7756
Emp Here 35
SIC 3993 Signs and advertising specialties

D-U-N-S 25-392-5358   (SL)
PIIDEA CANADA, LTD
PIIDEA CANADA
1 Av Holiday Bureau 701, Pointe-Claire, QC,
H9R 5N3
(514) 426-8100
Emp Here 24   *Sales* 2,991,389
SIC 5122 Drugs, proprietaries, and sundries

D-U-N-S 25-476-5787   (SL)
PLACEMENT POTENTIEL INC
111 Av Donegani, Pointe-Claire, QC, H9R
2W3
(514) 694-0315
Emp Here 100   *Sales* 861,721
SIC 7361 Employment agencies

D-U-N-S 20-727-0331   (HQ)
PORTEC, PRODUITS FERROVIAIRES LTEE
(*Suby of* L. B. Foster Company)
172 Boul Brunswick, Pointe-Claire, QC, H9R
5P9

(514) 695-8500
Emp Here 21   *Emp Total* 1,241
Sales 8,171,598
SIC 5088 Transportation equipment and supplies
  Kostas Papazoglou

D-U-N-S 24-056-9822   (SL)
PYRAMID PRODUITS SPECIALISES LTEE
(*Suby of* Consolidated Glass Holdings, Inc.)
17 Ch De L'Aviation, Pointe-Claire, QC, H9R 4Z2
(514) 694-6788
Emp Here 45   *Sales* 5,681,200
SIC 3231 Products of purchased glass
Sls Mgr David Smith
Pr Paul Cody
Sec Jeff Vincent
Treas Neal Apgar

D-U-N-S 24-458-2235   (HQ)
R.O.E. LOGISTICS INC
195 Rue Voyageur, Pointe-Claire, QC, H9R 6B2
(514) 396-0000
Emp Here 90   *Emp Total* 75
Sales 32,175,669
SIC 4731 Freight transportation arrangement
Pr Pr Alan J. Barbner

D-U-N-S 20-688-6751   (BR)
REITMANS (CANADA) LIMITEE
REITMANS
755 Boul Saint-Jean, Pointe-Claire, QC, H9R 5M9
(514) 693-9701
Emp Here 20
SIC 5621 Women's clothing stores

D-U-N-S 20-002-8392   (BR)
ROYAL BANK OF CANADA
RBC
(*Suby of* Royal Bank Of Canada)
321 Boul Saint-Jean, Pointe-Claire, QC, H9R 3J1

Emp Here 30
SIC 6021 National commercial banks

D-U-N-S 25-817-3715   (BR)
SAIL PLEIN AIR INC
BARON SPORTS
(*Suby of* Sail Plein Air Inc)
187a Boul Hymus, Pointe-Claire, QC, H9R 1E9
(514) 694-4259
Emp Here 20
SIC 5941 Sporting goods and bicycle shops

D-U-N-S 24-385-0448   (SL)
SAPA CANADA INC
SAPA EXTRUSION AMERIQUE DU NORD
325 Av Avro, Pointe-Claire, QC, H9R 5W3
(514) 697-5120
Emp Here 200   *Sales* 33,561,922
SIC 3354 Aluminum extruded products
  Charles J. Straface
  Jacquelyne Belcastro
  Robert Kavanaugh
VP VP Rick Worst
Dir Paul Amirault

D-U-N-S 24-654-5136   (SL)
SCIES ACME LTEE
210 Boul Brunswick, Pointe-Claire, QC, H9R 1A6
(514) 685-6266
Emp Here 33   *Sales* 8,842,240
SIC 5085 Industrial supplies
Pr Michel Kannage

D-U-N-S 20-108-9658   (BR)
SCOTIA CAPITAL INC
SCOTIA MCLEOD
620 Boul Saint-Jean Bureau 102, Pointe-Claire, QC, H9R 3K2
(514) 428-8400
Emp Here 30
SIC 6211 Security brokers and dealers

D-U-N-S 25-294-5811   (BR)
SEARS CANADA INC
SEARS
6701 Aut Transcanadienne, Pointe-Claire, QC, H9R 5J2
(514) 694-8815
Emp Here 250
SIC 5311 Department stores

D-U-N-S 20-535-0288   (SL)
SERVICES DE GARDE DE LA POINTE, LES
85 Av De La Baie-De-Valois, Pointe-Claire, QC, H9R 4B7
(514) 695-6447
Emp Here 50   *Sales* 1,532,175
SIC 8351 Child day care services

D-U-N-S 24-737-9568   (BR)
SLEEP COUNTRY CANADA INC
DORMEZ-VOUS SLEEP CENTERS
59 Boul Hymus, Pointe-Claire, QC, H9R 1E2
(514) 695-6376
Emp Here 50
SIC 5712 Furniture stores

D-U-N-S 20-567-4281   (SL)
SOURCES 40 WESTT INC
2305 Aut Transcanadienne, Pointe-Claire, QC, H9R 5Z5
(514) 428-9378
Emp Here 80   *Sales* 2,407,703
SIC 5812 Eating places

D-U-N-S 24-798-0910   (BR)
SOUTHERN GRAPHIC SYSTEMS-CANADA LTD
(*Suby of* Logo Holdings I Corporation)
165 Av Oneida, Pointe-Claire, QC, H9R 1A9
(514) 426-5608
Emp Here 50
SIC 2796 Platemaking services

D-U-N-S 25-213-7013   (BR)
STAPLES CANADA INC
BUREAU EN GROS
(*Suby of* Staples, Inc.)
365 Boul Brunswick, Pointe-Claire, QC, H9R 4S1
(514) 694-5578
Emp Here 50
SIC 5943 Stationery stores

D-U-N-S 20-304-6292   (BR)
SUN LIFE ASSURANCE COMPANY OF CANADA
SUN LIFE FINANCIAL
1 Av Holiday Bureau 255, Pointe-Claire, QC, H9R 5N3
(514) 426-1788
Emp Here 45
SIC 6311 Life insurance

D-U-N-S 24-425-1349   (BR)
SYMPHONY SENIOR LIVING INC
15 Place De La Triade Bureau 1012, Pointe-Claire, QC, H9R 0A3
(514) 695-6695
Emp Here 25
SIC 8741 Management services

D-U-N-S 24-709-9257   (BR)
THOMAS & BETTS, LIMITEE
T & B COMMANDER
4025 Aut Transcanadienne, Pointe-Claire, QC, H9R 1B4
(514) 694-6800
Emp Here 75
SIC 3699 Electrical equipment and supplies, nec

D-U-N-S 24-051-6539   (BR)
TOMMY HILFIGER CANADA INC
TOMMY HILFIGER
6801 Aut Transcanadienne, Pointe-Claire, QC, H9R 5J2

Emp Here 21
SIC 5651 Family clothing stores

D-U-N-S 25-232-1187   (BR)
VILLE DE MONTREAL
VILLE DE MONTREAL
100 Av Douglas-Shand, Pointe-Claire, QC, H9R 4V1
(514) 630-1218
Emp Here 30
SIC 8231 Libraries

D-U-N-S 20-563-7184   (BR)
WAINBEE LIMITED
215 Boul Brunswick, Pointe-Claire, QC, H9R 4R7
(514) 697-8810
Emp Here 50
SIC 5084 Industrial machinery and equipment

D-U-N-S 20-237-1878   (HQ)
WALTER SURFACE TECHNOLOGIES INC
WALTER TECHNOLOGIES POUR SURFACES
(*Suby of* Walter Financial Inc)
5977 Rte Transcanadienne, Pointe-Claire, QC, H9R 1C1
(514) 630-2800
Emp Here 50   *Emp Total* 1
Sales 33,926,726
SIC 5085 Industrial supplies
Pr Pr Pierre Somers
  Haisook Somers
  Franco Vitale

D-U-N-S 24-050-4162   (BR)
WINNERS MERCHANTS INTERNATIONAL L.P.
WINNERS
(*Suby of* The TJX Companies Inc)
6801 Aut Transcanadienne, Pointe-Claire, QC, H9R 5J2
(514) 782-1308
Emp Here 30
SIC 5651 Family clothing stores

D-U-N-S 20-025-4212   (BR)
YMCA DU QUEBEC, LES
YMCA POINTE CLAIRE
230 Boul Brunswick, Pointe-Claire, QC, H9R 5N5
(514) 630-9622
Emp Here 135
SIC 8399 Social services, nec

Pointe-Claire, QC H9S
Hochelaga County

D-U-N-S 25-240-4025   (BR)
COMMISSION SCOLAIRE MARGUERITE-BOURGEOYS
ECOLE MARGUERITE BOURGEOYS
3 Av Sainte-Anne, Pointe-Claire, QC, H9S 4P6
(514) 855-4236
Emp Here 80
SIC 8211 Elementary and secondary schools

D-U-N-S 20-712-3519   (BR)
LESTER B. PEARSON SCHOOL BOARD
CLEARPOINT ELEMENTARY SCHOOL
17 Av Cedar, Pointe-Claire, QC, H9S 4X9
(514) 798-0792
Emp Here 45
SIC 8211 Elementary and secondary schools

D-U-N-S 20-026-3890   (SL)
PANIER & CADEAU INC, LE
BEAU CADEAU & PANIER PANACHE
274 Ch Du Bord-Du-Lac Lakeshore, Pointe-Claire, QC, H9S 4K9
(514) 695-7038
Emp Here 87   *Sales* 4,742,446
SIC 5947 Gift, novelty, and souvenir shop

D-U-N-S 20-707-4928   (BR)
POINTE-CLAIRE, VILLE DE
GALERIE D'ART STEWART HALL
176 Ch Du Bord-Du-Lac Lakeshore, Pointe-

Claire, QC, H9S 4J7
(514) 630-1220
Emp Here 20
SIC 7999 Amusement and recreation, nec

Pointe-Lebel, QC G0H
Saguenay County

D-U-N-S 20-712-6272   (BR)
COMMISSION SCOLAIRE DE L'ESTUAIRE
ECOLE LA MAREE
380 Rue Granier, Pointe-Lebel, QC, G0H 1N0
(418) 589-2325
Emp Here 25
SIC 8211 Elementary and secondary schools

D-U-N-S 25-488-6989   (BR)
PREMIER HORTICULTURE LTEE
480 Rue Granier, Pointe-Lebel, QC, G0H 1N0
(418) 589-6161
Emp Here 35
SIC 5159 Farm-product raw materials, nec

Pont-Rouge, QC G3H
Portneuf County

D-U-N-S 25-001-8827   (BR)
COMMISSION SCOLAIRE DE PORTNEUF
COMMISSION SCOLAIRE DE PORTNEUF
(*Suby of* Commission Scolaire de Portneuf)
37 Rue Du College, Pont-Rouge, QC, G3H 3A2
(418) 873-2193
Emp Here 30
SIC 8211 Elementary and secondary schools

D-U-N-S 25-233-0808   (BR)
COMMISSION SCOLAIRE DE PORTNEUF
COMMISSION SCOLAIRE DE PORTNEUF
(*Suby of* Commission Scolaire de Portneuf)
20 Rue De La Fabrique, Pont-Rouge, QC, G3H 3J6
(418) 873-2151
Emp Here 65
SIC 8211 Elementary and secondary schools

D-U-N-S 20-240-0545   (SL)
FONDERIE LAROCHE LTEE
19 Rue De Chantal, Pont-Rouge, QC, G3H 3M4
(418) 873-2516
Emp Here 70
SIC 3321 Gray and ductile iron foundries

D-U-N-S 25-489-1294   (SL)
GOLF DU GRAND PORTNEUF INC, LE
BOUTIQUE DE GOLF LE GRAND PORTNEUF
2 Rte 365, Pont-Rouge, QC, G3H 3R4
(418) 329-2238
Emp Here 80   *Sales* 3,429,153
SIC 7992 Public golf courses

D-U-N-S 24-895-2207   (HQ)
LA COOP UNIVERT
LA COOP - MARQUE DE COMMERCE
(*Suby of* La Coop Univert)
229 Rue Dupont, Pont-Rouge, QC, G3H 1P3
(418) 873-2535
Emp Here 50   *Emp Total* 100
Sales 12,111,476
SIC 8699 Membership organizations, nec
Pr Jean-Nil Laganiere
VP Cathy Fraser
VP Rene Matte
Sec Valerie Ouellet
Dir Benoit Massicotte
Dir Guy Boivin
Dir Conrad Robitaille
Dir Stephane Leclerc
Dir Christine Marcotte
Dir Jocelyn Cossette

▲ Public Company   ■ Public Company Family Member   **HQ** Headquarters   **BR** Branch   **SL** Single Location

D-U-N-S 24-203-9287   (BR)
SUPERMARCHE B.M. INC
METRO PONT-ROUGE
(*Suby of* Gestion D. Marquis Inc)
149 Rue Du College, Pont-Rouge, QC, G3H
3B3
(418) 873-2015
Emp Here 20
SIC 5411 Grocery stores

Port-Cartier, QC G5B
Saguenay County

D-U-N-S 24-941-0432   (SL)
**CLSC - CENTRE DE SANTE DES SEPT RIV-
IERES**
CLSC SEPT-RIVIERES
103 Rue Des Rochelois, Port-Cartier, QC,
G5B 1K5
(418) 766-2572
Emp Here 210   *Sales* 11,092,080
SIC 8322 Individual and family services
Genl Mgr Francois Therrien
   Pauline St-Gelais

D-U-N-S 25-003-4022   (HQ)
CAISSE DESJARDINS DE PORT-CARTIER
CENTRE DE SERVICES BAIE-TRINITE
(*Suby of* Caisse Desjardins de Port-Cartier)
8 Boul Des Iles Bureau 7, Port-Cartier, QC,
G5B 2J4
(418) 766-3032
Emp Here 22   *Emp Total* 35
Sales 6,893,600
SIC 6062 State credit unions
Genl Mgr Michele Gosselin
Pr Clermont Tremblay
VP VP Yvon-Robert Bouchard
VP VP Jean Langlois
Sec Sylvie Gagne
Dir Laurencia Bond
Dir Andre Dumont
Dir Sylvain Dubuc
Dir Brigitte St-Laurent

D-U-N-S 25-240-0346   (BR)
COMMISSION SCOLAIRE DU FER
ECOLE ST-ALEXANDRE
27 Rue Audubon, Port-Cartier, QC, G5B 1M2
(418) 766-2237
Emp Here 35
SIC 8211 Elementary and secondary schools

D-U-N-S 25-233-7480   (BR)
COMMISSION SCOLAIRE DU FER
CENTRE EDUCATIF L'ABRI
18 Boul Des Iles, Port-Cartier, QC, G5B 2N4
(418) 766-5335
Emp Here 65
SIC 8211 Elementary and secondary schools

D-U-N-S 25-240-0387   (BR)
COMMISSION SCOLAIRE DU FER
ECOLE MERE D'YOUVILLE
12 Av Boisvert, Port-Cartier, QC, G5B 1W7
(418) 766-8565
Emp Here 35
SIC 8211 Elementary and secondary schools

D-U-N-S 20-580-8306   (BR)
LOUIS DREYFUS COMPANY CANADA ULC
SILOS PORT CARTIER, LES
188 Rue Portage Des Mousses, Port-Cartier,
QC, G5B 2G9
(418) 766-2515
Emp Here 35
SIC 4221 Farm product warehousing and stor-
age

D-U-N-S 25-212-3583   (BR)
PRODUITS FORESTIERS ARBEC S.E.N.C.
175 Boul Portage Des Mousses, Port-Cartier,
QC, G5B 2V9
(418) 766-2299
Emp Here 450

SIC 2421 Sawmills and planing mills, general

D-U-N-S 25-211-8773   (BR)
PROVIGO DISTRIBUTION INC
ALIMENTATION PROVIGO PORT CARTIER
8 Boul Des Iles, Port-Cartier, QC, G5B 2J4
(418) 766-6121
Emp Here 50
SIC 5411 Grocery stores

Portneuf, QC G0A
Portneuf County

D-U-N-S 25-170-3310   (BR)
AGC FLAT GLASS NORTH AMERICA LTD
AFG GLASS
250 Rue De Copenhague, Portneuf, QC, G0A
2Y0

Emp Here 250
SIC 3211 Flat glass

D-U-N-S 24-394-8861   (BR)
CHARL-POL INC
(*Suby of* 8132992 Canada Inc)
440 Rue Lucien-Thibodeau, Portneuf, QC,
G0A 2Y0
(418) 286-4881
Emp Here 80
SIC 3569 General industrial machinery, nec

D-U-N-S 24-884-8640   (SL)
EQUIPEMENTS HARDY INC, LES
100 Rue Saint-Arthur, Portneuf, QC, G0A 2Y0
(418) 286-6621
Emp Here 40   *Sales* 6,478,560
SIC 3523 Farm machinery and equipment
Pr Rejean Pronovost

D-U-N-S 24-907-4493   (SL)
SELECTION DU PATISSIER INC
PASTRY SELECTIONS
450 2e Av, Portneuf, QC, G0A 2Y0
(418) 286-3400
Emp Here 100   *Sales* 10,995,600
SIC 2052 Cookies and crackers
Pr Mario Audet
VP Yvon Hardy
Sec Michel Baribeau
Dir Rejean Proulx

D-U-N-S 24-466-1419   (SL)
**TRANSPORT THIBODEAU SAGUELAC
MARCAN INC**
(*Suby of* Groupe Thibodeau Inc)
128 2e Av, Portneuf, QC, G0A 2Y0

Emp Here 750   *Sales* 152,344,320
SIC 4213 Trucking, except local
Pr Pr Pierre Thibodeau

Poularies, QC J0Z
Abitibi County

D-U-N-S 20-712-6140   (BR)
COMMISSION SCOLAIRE ABITIBI
*ECOLE BELLEFEUILLE PAVILLON DE
POULARIES*
(*Suby of* Commission Scolaire Abitibi)
800 Rue Drouin, Poularies, QC, J0Z 3E0
(819) 782-5150
Emp Here 50
SIC 8211 Elementary and secondary schools

Prevost, QC J0R
Terrebonne County

D-U-N-S 20-712-1836   (BR)
COMMISSION SCOLAIRE DE LA RIVIERE-

DU-NORD
ECOLE PRIMAIRE DU CHAMP-FLEURI
(*Suby of* Commission Scolaire de la Riviere-
du-Nord)
1135 Rue Du Clos-Toumalin Rr 4, Prevost,
QC, J0R 1T0
(450) 431-3327
Emp Here 90
SIC 8211 Elementary and secondary schools

D-U-N-S 25-857-1231   (BR)
**LES CENTRES DE LA JEUNESSE ET DE LA
FAMILLE BATSHAW**
CAMPUS DE PREVOST
(*Suby of* Les Centres de la Jeunesse et de la
Famille Batshaw)
3065 Boul Du Cure-Labelle, Prevost, QC, J0R
1T0
(450) 224-8234
Emp Here 150
SIC 8322 Individual and family services

D-U-N-S 25-858-3434   (BR)
**PROGRAMME DE PORTAGE RELATIF A LA
DEPENDENCE DE LA DROGUE INC, LE**
PORTAGE CENTRE DE READAPTATION
(*Suby of* Programme de Portage Relatif a la
Dependence de la Drogue Inc, Le)
1790 Ch Du Lac-Echo, Prevost, QC, J0R 1T0
(450) 224-2944
Emp Here 39
SIC 8093 Specialty outpatient clinics, nec

D-U-N-S 20-712-2560   (BR)
SIR WILFRID LAURIER SCHOOL BOARD
MOUNTAINVIEW HIGH SCHOOL
3065 Boul Du Cure-Labelle, Prevost, QC, J0R
1T0
(514) 932-7722
Emp Here 50
SIC 8211 Elementary and secondary schools

D-U-N-S 20-033-5938   (BR)
SIR WILFRID LAURIER SCHOOL BOARD
ECOLE SECONDAIRE MOUNTAINVIEW
3065 Boul Du Cure-Labelle, Prevost, QC, J0R
1T0
(450) 224-8234
Emp Here 20
SIC 8211 Elementary and secondary schools

Price, QC G0J
Matane County

D-U-N-S 24-842-9995   (HQ)
GROUPE CEDRICO INC
(*Suby of* Investissements Gilles Berube)
39 Rue Saint-Jean-Baptiste Bureau 1, Price,
QC, G0J 1Z0
(418) 775-7516
Emp Here 45   *Emp Total* 400
Sales 97,365,120
SIC 6712 Bank holding companies
Pr Pr Gilles Berube
   Camilla Malenfant

Princeville, QC G6L

D-U-N-S 20-778-2822   (SL)
BATEAUX PRINCECRAFT INC
725 Rue Saint-Henri, Princeville, QC, G6L
5C2
(819) 364-5581
Emp Here 310   *Sales* 18,823,861
SIC 3732 Boatbuilding and repairing
Pr Pr Steve Langlais
VP VP Judith P. Zelisko
   Christopher F. Dekker
Genl Mgr Claude Lebel

D-U-N-S 25-232-8463   (BR)
COMMISSION SCOLAIRE DES BOIS-

FRANCS
*COMMISSION SCOLAIRE DES BOIS-
FRANCS*
(*Suby of* Commission Scolaire des Bois-
Francs)
48 Rue Saint-Charles, Princeville, QC, G6L
4W4
(819) 364-2143
Emp Here 60
SIC 8211 Elementary and secondary schools

D-U-N-S 20-126-2487   (BR)
**COMMISSION SCOLAIRE DES BOIS-
FRANCS**
ECOLE SECONDAIRE SAINTE MARIE
75 Rue Monseigneur-Poirier, Princeville, QC,
G6L 4S7
(819) 364-2155
Emp Here 50
SIC 8211 Elementary and secondary schools

D-U-N-S 20-707-6014   (BR)
**COMPAGNIE COMMONWEALTH PLY-
WOOD LTEE, LA**
540 Rue Saint-Henri, Princeville, QC, G6L
5C1
(819) 364-5514
Emp Here 28
SIC 2421 Sawmills and planing mills, general

D-U-N-S 25-010-4882   (BR)
OLYMEL S.E.C.
FLAMINGO
155 Rue Saint-Jean-Baptiste N, Princeville,
QC, G6L 5C9
(819) 364-5501
Emp Here 350
SIC 2011 Meat packing plants

D-U-N-S 24-066-0469   (SL)
REMBOURRAGE ANP INC
105 Rue Beaudet, Princeville, QC, G6L 4L3
(819) 364-2645
Emp Here 60   *Sales* 3,648,035
SIC 3732 Boatbuilding and repairing

D-U-N-S 20-951-8067   (SL)
**SOCIETE COOPERATIVE AGRICOLE DE
PRINCEVILLE**
SCA
170 Rue Monseigneur-Poirier, Princeville, QC,
G6L 4S5
(819) 364-5331
Emp Here 40   *Sales* 5,376,850
SIC 5251 Hardware stores
Pr Martin Breton

D-U-N-S 20-240-6633   (SL)
TRICOTS DUVAL & RAYMOND LTEE, LES
DURAY
11 Rue Saint-Jacques O, Princeville, QC, G6L
5E6
(819) 364-2927
Emp Here 85   *Sales* 3,551,629
SIC 2252 Hosiery, nec

Puvirnituq, QC J0M
Nouveau-Quebec County

D-U-N-S 24-600-3131   (SL)
**CENTRE HOSPITALIER DE LA BAIE
D'HUDSON**
Gd, Puvirnituq, QC, J0M 1P0
(819) 988-2957
Emp Here 275   *Sales* 26,325,760
SIC 8062 General medical and surgical hospi-
tals
Genl Mgr Gerald Garneau

D-U-N-S 25-325-1367   (BR)
COMMISSION SCOLAIRE KATIVIK
ECOLE IGUARSIVIK
Gd, Puvirnituq, QC, J0M 1P0
(819) 988-2960
Emp Here 90

SIC 8211 Elementary and secondary schools

D-U-N-S 20-716-8159   (BR)
COMMISSION SCOLAIRE KATIVIK
POVUNGNITUK SCHOOL
Gd, Puvirnituq, QC, J0M 1P0
(819) 988-2960
Emp Here 60
SIC 8211 Elementary and secondary schools

Quaqtaq, QC J0M
Nouveau-Quebec County

D-U-N-S 20-716-8142   (BR)
COMMISSION SCOLAIRE KATIVIK
ECOLE ISUMMASAQVIK
Pr, Quaqtaq, QC, J0M 1J0
(819) 492-9955
Emp Here 50
SIC 8211 Elementary and secondary schools

Quebec, QC G1A
Quebec County

D-U-N-S 20-795-7635   (BR)
GOUVERNEMENT DE LA PROVINCE DE QUEBEC
HOTEL DU PARLEMENT A QUEBEC
1045 Rue Des Parlementaires, Quebec, QC, G1A 1A4
(418) 643-4408
Emp Here 65
SIC 8231 Libraries

Quebec, QC G1B
Quebec County

D-U-N-S 20-030-4223   (BR)
COMMISSION SCOLAIRE DES PREMIERES-SEIGNEURIES
COMMISSION SCOLAIRE DES PREMIERES-SEIGNEURIES
250 Rue Cambert, Quebec, QC, G1B 3R8
(418) 666-6091
Emp Here 50
SIC 8211 Elementary and secondary schools

D-U-N-S 25-232-7317   (BR)
COMMISSION SCOLAIRE DES PREMIERES-SEIGNEURIES
COMMISSION SCOLAIRE DES PREMIERES-SEIGNEURIES
(*Suby of* Commission Scolaire Des Premieres-Seigneuries)
139 Rue Bertrand, Quebec, QC, G1B 1H8
(418) 666-4595
Emp Here 25
SIC 8211 Elementary and secondary schools

D-U-N-S 25-233-4966   (BR)
COMMISSION SCOLAIRE DES PREMIERES-SEIGNEURIES
ECOLE DU SOUS BOIS
(*Suby of* Commission Scolaire Des Premieres-Seigneuries)
143 Rue Des Feux-Follets, Quebec, QC, G1B 1K8
(418) 666-6212
Emp Here 45
SIC 8211 Elementary and secondary schools

D-U-N-S 20-029-9589   (BR)
COURTIERS INTER-QUEBEC INC, LES
900 Boul Raymond, Quebec, QC, G1B 3G3

Emp Here 150
SIC 6531 Real estate agents and managers

D-U-N-S 24-023-5668   (BR)

PROVIGO DISTRIBUTION INC
491 Rue Seigneuriale, Quebec, QC, G1B 3A6
(418) 661-6111
Emp Here 45
SIC 5141 Groceries, general line

Quebec, QC G1C
Quebec County

D-U-N-S 20-526-7052   (SL)
9118-8706 QUEBEC INC.
BEAUPORT MAZDA
585 Rue Clemenceau, Quebec, QC, G1C 7Z9
(418) 667-3131
Emp Here 49   *Sales* 24,617,600
SIC 5511 New and used car dealers
Pr Paul Daigle

D-U-N-S 20-716-3622   (BR)
AMEUBLEMENTS TANGUAY INC
777 Rue Clemenceau, Quebec, QC, G1C 7T9
(418) 666-4411
Emp Here 64
SIC 5021 Furniture

D-U-N-S 20-204-9383   (SL)
AUTOBUS LAVAL LTEE
(*Suby of* Placements Giroux Inc)
445 Rue Des Alleghanys Bureau 201, Quebec, QC, G1C 4N4
(418) 667-3265
Emp Here 175   *Sales* 6,832,640
SIC 4151 School buses
Pr Pr Charlotte St Cyr Giroux
  Louise Giroux
Mng Dir Denis Giroux

D-U-N-S 25-761-1723   (BR)
BANQUE NATIONALE DU CANADA
945 Av Nordique, Quebec, QC, G1C 7S8
(418) 661-8772
Emp Here 20
SIC 6021 National commercial banks

D-U-N-S 24-363-5740   (BR)
BEST BUY CANADA LTD
FUTURE SHOP
(*Suby of* Best Buy Co., Inc.)
847 Rue Clemenceau, Quebec, QC, G1C 2K6

Emp Here 50
SIC 5731 Radio, television, and electronic stores

D-U-N-S 25-689-9444   (SL)
CAISSE DESJARDINS DU VIEUX-MOULIN (BEAUPORT)
PLACE D'AFFAIRE PROMENADE BEAUPORT
3341 Rue Du Carrefour, Quebec, QC, G1C 8J9
(418) 667-4440
Emp Here 26   *Sales* 11,198,225
SIC 6062 State credit unions
Genl Mgr Madeleine Arsenault
Pr Catherine Ratte
VP Jean Beaupre
Sec Frederick Desjardins
Dir Cimon Boily
Dir Jolle Boisvert
Dir Gilles Fortin
Dir Daniel Morin
Dir Nathalie Paquin
Dir Claude Pare

D-U-N-S 20-919-1290   (HQ)
CENTRE DE SANTE ET DE SERVICES SOCIAUX DE QUEBEC-NORD
LE CSSS DE QUEBEC-NORD
4e Etage 2915, Av Du Bourg-Royal, Quebec, QC, G1C 3S2
(418) 661-5666
Emp Here 100   *Emp Total* 40,000
Sales 169,087,503

SIC 8011 Offices and clinics of medical doctors
Pr Pierre Leveille
VP Christine Verner
Sec Lucie Lacroix
Treas Jean-Louis Lapointe

D-U-N-S 25-257-4546   (BR)
CENTRE DE SANTE ET DE SERVICES SOCIAUX DU PONTIAC
CENTRE ST-AUGUSTIN
2135 Rue De La Terrasse-Cadieux, Quebec, QC, G1C 1Z2
(418) 667-3910
Emp Here 500
SIC 8051 Skilled nursing care facilities

D-U-N-S 20-024-6143   (BR)
COMMISSION SCOLAIRE DES PREMIERES-SEIGNEURIES
ECOLE DE LA PRIMEROSE
155 Rue Bessette, Quebec, QC, G1C 7A7
(418) 666-4562
Emp Here 40
SIC 8211 Elementary and secondary schools

D-U-N-S 20-596-9798   (BR)
COMMISSION SCOLAIRE DES PREMIERES-SEIGNEURIES
COMMISSION SCOLAIRE DES PREMIERES-SEIGNEURIES
453 Rue Seigneuriale, Quebec, QC, G1C 3R2
(418) 666-4495
Emp Here 30
SIC 8211 Elementary and secondary schools

D-U-N-S 20-101-0241   (BR)
COMMISSION SCOLAIRE DES PREMIERES-SEIGNEURIES
COMMISSION SCOLAIRE DES PREMIERES-SEIGNEURIES
2267 Av Royale, Quebec, QC, G1C 1P5
(418) 821-0220
Emp Here 45
SIC 8211 Elementary and secondary schools

D-U-N-S 25-234-0047   (BR)
COMMISSION SCOLAIRE DES PREMIERES-SEIGNEURIES
SERVICES EDUCATIFS ET LES RESOURCES TECHNOLOGIQUES
(*Suby of* Commission Scolaire Des Premieres-Seigneuries)
2233 Av Royale, Quebec, QC, G1C 1P3
(418) 821-8988
Emp Here 130
SIC 8211 Elementary and secondary schools

D-U-N-S 20-711-9905   (BR)
COMMISSION SCOLAIRE DES PREMIERES-SEIGNEURIES
ECOLE DE COURVILLOISE
2265 Av Larue, Quebec, QC, G1C 1J9
(418) 821-4220
Emp Here 120
SIC 8211 Elementary and secondary schools

D-U-N-S 25-232-6640   (BR)
COMMISSION SCOLAIRE DES PREMIERES-SEIGNEURIES
COMMISSION SCOLAIRE DES PREMIERES-SEIGNEURIES
(*Suby of* Commission Scolaire Des Premieres-Seigneuries)
2970 Av Gaspard, Quebec, QC, G1C 3V7
(418) 626-4559
Emp Here 40
SIC 8211 Elementary and secondary schools

D-U-N-S 20-711-9731   (BR)
COMMISSION SCOLAIRE DES PREMIERES-SEIGNEURIES
COMMISSION SCOLAIRE DES PREMIERES-SEIGNEURIES
500 Rue Anick, Quebec, QC, G1C 4X5
(418) 666-4455
Emp Here 50

SIC 8211 Elementary and secondary schools

D-U-N-S 20-297-6015   (SL)
CONSTRUCTION PAVETON INC.
2671 Boul Louis-Xiv, Quebec, QC, G1C 1C7
(418) 520-7054
Emp Here 26   *Sales* 5,376,850
SIC 1521 Single-family housing construction
Pr Sandro Valcourt

D-U-N-S 25-286-0747   (SL)
CONSTRUCTIONS HAMEL & VANEAU INC, LES
325 Rue Fichet, Quebec, QC, G1C 6Y1
(418) 580-9155
Emp Here 50   *Sales* 12,174,000
SIC 1623 Water, sewer, and utility lines
Pr Pr Louis M Rompre
  Yvon Hamel
  Jean Foley
  Michel Hamel
  Guy Hamel
  Gilles Lachance

D-U-N-S 20-807-1246   (BR)
COUCHE-TARD INC
1375 Boul Des Chutes, Quebec, QC, G1C 1W3
(418) 661-8609
Emp Here 25
SIC 5411 Grocery stores

D-U-N-S 20-807-0586   (BR)
COUCHE-TARD INC
COUCHE-TARD
2438 Boul Louis-Xiv, Quebec, QC, G1C 1B3
(418) 663-3537
Emp Here 25
SIC 5411 Grocery stores

D-U-N-S 20-993-3113   (BR)
DESCIMCO INC
415 Rue Adanac, Quebec, QC, G1C 6B9
(418) 664-1077
Emp Here 23
SIC 7389 Business services, nec

D-U-N-S 25-299-6632   (BR)
DOLLARAMA S.E.C.
DOLLARAMA
3333 Rue Du Carrefour, Quebec, QC, G1C 5R9
(418) 667-8690
Emp Here 22
SIC 5331 Variety stores

D-U-N-S 24-263-3407   (BR)
DOLLARAMA S.E.C.
DOLLARAMA
749 Rue Clemenceau, Quebec, QC, G1C 7T9
(418) 661-6722
Emp Here 25
SIC 5331 Variety stores

D-U-N-S 25-046-4802   (BR)
ECLAIRAGE LUMENPULSE INC
LUMENPULSE
(*Suby of* Lumenpulse Inc)
515 Rue Adanac, Quebec, QC, G1C 6B9
(418) 664-0900
Emp Here 25
SIC 3646 Commercial lighting fixtures

D-U-N-S 24-096-9225   (BR)
FEDERATION DES CAISSES DESJARDINS DU QUEBEC
FEDERATION DES CAISSES DESJARDINS DU QUEBEC
3333 Rue Du Carrefour Bureau 280, Quebec, QC, G1C 5R9
(418) 660-2229
Emp Here 136
SIC 6159 Miscellaneous business credit institutions

D-U-N-S 25-776-4860   (BR)
FONDATION DES SOURDS DU QUEBEC (F.S.Q.) INC, LA

MAGASIN SURPLUS QUEBEC
400 Des Rocheuses, Quebec, QC, G1C 4N2
(418) 660-6300
Emp Here 43
SIC 7219 Laundry and garment services, nec

D-U-N-S 24-377-8065   (SL)
GESTION LAVOIE PERRAULT INC
UNIPRIX
1100 Av Larue, Quebec, QC, G1C 6H4
(418) 667-5499
Emp Here 30   *Sales* 5,693,280
SIC 5912 Drug stores and proprietary stores
Pr Pr Laurier Lavoie
VP VP Pierre Perrault

D-U-N-S 24-941-1281   (HQ)
GROUPE QUALINET INC
(*Suby of* Groupe Qualinet Inc)
434 Rue Des Monteregiennes, Quebec, QC,
G1C 7H3
(418) 387-4000
Emp Here 65   *Emp Total* 150
Sales 4,377,642
SIC 7349 Building maintenance services, nec

D-U-N-S 25-295-5406   (BR)
LEON'S FURNITURE LIMITED
3333 Rue Du Carrefour Bureau H, Quebec,
QC, G1C 5R9
(418) 667-4040
Emp Here 20
SIC 5712 Furniture stores

D-U-N-S 24-465-5379   (HQ)
ONDEL INC
415 Rue Adanac, Quebec, QC, G1C 6B9
(418) 664-1066
Emp Here 45   *Emp Total* 134
Sales 5,653,974
SIC 1731 Electrical work
 Berthier Thibeault
Pr Pr Donald Pelletier

D-U-N-S 25-484-9169   (BR)
PROVIGO INC
MAXI BEAUPORT
699 Rue Clemenceau, Quebec, QC, G1C 4N6
(418) 666-0155
Emp Here 90
SIC 5411 Grocery stores

D-U-N-S 20-298-1556   (BR)
SOBEYS CAPITAL INCORPORATED
BANIERE IGA EXTRA, LA
969 Av Nordique Bureau 458, Quebec, QC,
G1C 7S8
(418) 667-5700
Emp Here 150
SIC 5411 Grocery stores

D-U-N-S 25-953-5722   (BR)
**SOCIETE DES ETABLISSEMENTS DE
PLEIN AIR DU QUEBEC**
MANOIR MONTMORENCY
2490 Av Royale, Quebec, QC, G1C 1S1
(418) 663-3330
Emp Here 30
SIC 5812 Eating places

D-U-N-S 20-105-0064   (BR)
STAPLES CANADA INC
BUREAU EN GROS
(*Suby of* Staples, Inc.)
843 Rue Clemenceau, Quebec, QC, G1C 2K6
(418) 660-5222
Emp Here 60
SIC 5943 Stationery stores

D-U-N-S 24-763-8914   (SL)
**TECHNOLOGIES DE L'INFORMATION
CIVIS INC**
373 Rue De Miranda, Quebec, QC, G1C 7X2
(418) 661-4289
Emp Here 40   *Sales* 5,182,810
SIC 8742 Management consulting services
Pr Santiago Forteza
 Marcel Frigon

D-U-N-S 20-059-2942   (SL)
TRANSPORT LAVOIE LTEE
4568 Boul Sainte-Anne, Quebec, QC, G1C
2H9
(418) 661-6981
Emp Here 50   *Sales* 3,939,878
SIC 4212 Local trucking, without storage

D-U-N-S 20-642-1666   (BR)
WAL-MART CANADA CORP
WALMART
224 Av Joseph-Casavant, Quebec, QC, G1C
7Z3
(418) 660-4943
Emp Here 50
SIC 5311 Department stores

D-U-N-S 20-184-3047   (BR)
**WINNERS MERCHANTS INTERNATIONAL
L.P.**
WINNERS
(*Suby of* The TJX Companies Inc)
3333 Rue Du Carrefour Bureau 211, Quebec,
QC, G1C 5R9
(418) 666-6522
Emp Here 40
SIC 5651 Family clothing stores

Quebec, QC G1E
Quebec County

D-U-N-S 20-198-2154   (SL)
**ALIMENTS ORIGINAL, DIVISION CANTIN
INC**
1910 Av Du Sanctuaire, Quebec, QC, G1E
3L2
(418) 663-3523
Emp Here 65   *Sales* 3,638,254
SIC 2033 Canned fruits and specialties

D-U-N-S 24-195-9555   (SL)
BEAUPORT STE-ANNE INC, LE
RESTAURANT NORMANDIN
220 Boul Sainte-Anne, Quebec, QC, G1E 3L7
(418) 666-9444
Emp Here 26   *Sales* 802,568
SIC 5812 Eating places

D-U-N-S 24-101-3452   (BR)
CANAC-MARQUIS GRENIER LTEE
947 Av Royale, Quebec, QC, G1E 1Z9
(418) 667-1729
Emp Here 1,000
SIC 5039 Construction materials, nec

D-U-N-S 24-776-2557   (BR)
CANADA BREAD COMPANY, LIMITED
BOULANGERIE MULTI-MARQUES
553 Av Royale, Quebec, QC, G1E 1Y4
(418) 661-4400
Emp Here 24
SIC 2051 Bread, cake, and related products

D-U-N-S 20-003-5397   (BR)
**CENTRE INTEGRE UNIVERSITAIRE DE
SANTE ET DE SERVICES SOCIAUX DE LA
CAPITALE-NATIONALE, LE**
CENTRE D'HEBERGEMENT DU FARGY
700 Boul Des Chutes, Quebec, QC, G1E 2B7
(418) 663-9934
Emp Here 88
SIC 8361 Residential care

D-U-N-S 24-336-4259   (BR)
**CENTRE DE SANTE ET DE SERVICES SO-
CIAUX DE QUEBEC-NORD**
*CENTRE D'HEBERGEMENT YVONNE-
SYLVAIN*
3365 Rue Guimont, Quebec, QC, G1E 2H1
(418) 663-8171
Emp Here 250
SIC 8361 Residential care

D-U-N-S 24-908-0896   (BR)
CIMENT QUEBEC INC

UNIBETON
(*Suby of* Groupe Ciment Quebec Inc)
3725 Rue Saint-Henri, Quebec, QC, G1E 2T4
(418) 667-2060
Emp Here 40
SIC 3273 Ready-mixed concrete

D-U-N-S 25-232-6608   (BR)
**COMMISSION SCOLAIRE DES
PREMIERES-SEIGNEURIES**
*COMMISSION SCOLAIRE DES
PREMIERES-SEIGNEURIES*
(*Suby of* Commission Scolaire Des
Premieres-Seigneuries)
769 Av De L'Education, Quebec, QC, G1E 1J2
(418) 666-4490
Emp Here 20
SIC 8211 Elementary and secondary schools

D-U-N-S 20-006-8208   (BR)
**COMMISSION SCOLAIRE DES
PREMIERES-SEIGNEURIES**
ECOLE AUX QUATRE-VENTS I
41 Rue Tanguay, Quebec, QC, G1E 6A3
(418) 821-4883
Emp Here 45
SIC 8211 Elementary and secondary schools

D-U-N-S 20-024-5608   (BR)
**COMMISSION SCOLAIRE DES
PREMIERES-SEIGNEURIES**
CENTRE DU NOUVEL HORIZON
3255 Boul Monseigneur-Gauthier, Quebec,
QC, G1E 2W3
(418) 666-4485
Emp Here 55
SIC 8211 Elementary and secondary schools

D-U-N-S 25-232-6566   (BR)
**COMMISSION SCOLAIRE DES
PREMIERES-SEIGNEURIES**
*COMMISSION SCOLAIRE DES
PREMIERES-SEIGNEURIES*
(*Suby of* Commission Scolaire Des
Premieres-Seigneuries)
15 Rue Saint-Edmond, Quebec, QC, G1E 5C8
(418) 666-4480
Emp Here 45
SIC 8211 Elementary and secondary schools

D-U-N-S 25-232-7077   (HQ)
**COMMISSION SCOLAIRE DES
PREMIERES-SEIGNEURIES**
POLYVALENTE LA SEIGNEURIE
(*Suby of* Commission Scolaire Des
Premieres-Seigneuries)
643 Av Du Cenacle, Quebec, QC, G1E 1B3
(418) 666-4666
Emp Here 150   *Emp Total* 2,786
Sales 240,388,128
SIC 8211 Elementary and secondary schools
Pr Clement Turcotte
VP Marie-France Painchaud
Sec Jean-Francois Parent
Treas Paule Pouliot
Dir Louis Dandurand
 Serge Pelletier

D-U-N-S 20-711-9756   (BR)
**COMMISSION SCOLAIRE DES
PREMIERES-SEIGNEURIES**
ECOLE SECONDAIRE DE LA SEIGNEURIE
645 Av Du Cenacle, Quebec, QC, G1E 1B3
(418) 666-4400
Emp Here 100
SIC 8211 Elementary and secondary schools

D-U-N-S 25-232-7275   (BR)
**COMMISSION SCOLAIRE DES
PREMIERES-SEIGNEURIES**
ECOLE OPTIONNELLE YVES PREVOST
(*Suby of* Commission Scolaire Des
Premieres-Seigneuries)
945 Boul Des Chutes, Quebec, QC, G1E 2C8
(418) 666-4580
Emp Here 30
SIC 8211 Elementary and secondary schools

D-U-N-S 20-711-9749   (BR)
**COMMISSION SCOLAIRE DES
PREMIERES-SEIGNEURIES**
ECOLE DE LA RELANCE
3510 Rue Cambronne, Quebec, QC, G1E 7H2
(418) 666-6240
Emp Here 20
SIC 8211 Elementary and secondary schools

D-U-N-S 25-232-7358   (BR)
**COMMISSION SCOLAIRE DES
PREMIERES-SEIGNEURIES**
*COMMISSION SCOLAIRE DES
PREMIERES-SEIGNEURIES*
(*Suby of* Commission Scolaire Des
Premieres-Seigneuries)
2740 Av Saint-David, Quebec, QC, G1E 4K7
(418) 666-4500
Emp Here 155
SIC 8211 Elementary and secondary schools

D-U-N-S 20-807-0578   (BR)
COUCHE-TARD INC
3190 Rue Alexandra, Quebec, QC, G1E 6W2
(418) 663-3024
Emp Here 25
SIC 5411 Grocery stores

D-U-N-S 20-202-2104   (SL)
**DISTRIBUTIONS NORCAP INTERNA-
TIONAL INC, LES**
54 Rue Deschamps, Quebec, QC, G1E 3E5
(418) 661-5747
Emp Here 20   *Sales* 6,797,150
SIC 6221 Commodity contracts brokers, deal-
ers
Pr Pr Fernand Doyon

D-U-N-S 20-596-0805   (BR)
**GOUVERNEMENT DE LA PROVINCE DE
QUEBEC**
*CENTRE JEUNESSE DE QUEBEC SERVICE
D'URGENCE SOCIALE*
3510 Rue Cambronne, Quebec, QC, G1E 7H2
(418) 661-3700
Emp Here 1,200
SIC 8399 Social services, nec

D-U-N-S 24-432-9756   (BR)
METRO RICHELIEU INC
600 Rue Cambronne, Quebec, QC, G1E 6X1
(418) 663-1554
Emp Here 30
SIC 5411 Grocery stores

D-U-N-S 20-803-4988   (BR)
METRO RICHELIEU INC
2968 Boul Sainte-Anne, Quebec, QC, G1E
3J3

Emp Here 125
SIC 5431 Fruit and vegetable markets

D-U-N-S 24-201-8661   (BR)
MULTI-MARQUES INC
USINE GAILURON
553 Av Royale, Quebec, QC, G1E 1Y4
(418) 661-4400
Emp Here 130
SIC 2051 Bread, cake, and related products

D-U-N-S 25-896-6837   (BR)
**PLACEMENTS ASHTON LEBLOND INC,
LES**
CHEZ ASHTON
(*Suby of* Placements Ashton LeBlond Inc,
Les)
505 Boul Sainte-Anne, Quebec, QC, G1E 3L5

Emp Here 32
SIC 5812 Eating places

D-U-N-S 25-767-0729   (BR)
PRISZM LP
PFK
315 Boul Sainte-Anne, Quebec, QC, G1E 3L4

Emp Here 20

SIC 5812 Eating places

D-U-N-S 24-146-7257   (BR)
RESTAURANT NORMANDIN INC
875 Av Royale, Quebec, QC, G1E 1Z9
(418) 663-1722
Emp Here 30
SIC 5812 Eating places

Quebec, QC G1G
Quebec County

D-U-N-S 25-745-5550   (BR)
BANQUE NATIONALE DU CANADA
8500 Boul Henri-Bourassa Bureau 213, Quebec, QC, G1G 5X1
(418) 628-8565
Emp Here 20
SIC 6021 National commercial banks

D-U-N-S 25-761-2838   (BR)
BINGO SAINTE-FOY INC
BINGO JEAN TALON
(*Suby of* Bingo Sainte-Foy Inc)
1750 Rue Du Perigord, Quebec, QC, G1G 5X3
(418) 623-6979
Emp Here 30
SIC 7999 Amusement and recreation, nec

D-U-N-S 20-874-2163   (SL)
BRASSERIE LE GRAND BOURG INC
8500 Boul Henri-Bourassa Bureau 8, Quebec, QC, G1G 5X1
(418) 623-5757
Emp Here 50   *Sales* 1,824,018
SIC 5813 Drinking places

D-U-N-S 24-368-7881   (BR)
CAISSE POPULAIRE DESJARDINS DE CHARLESBOURG
ORSAINVILLE SERVICE CENTRE
14070 Boul Henri-Bourassa, Quebec, QC, G1G 5S9
(418) 626-1146
Emp Here 30
SIC 6062 State credit unions

D-U-N-S 25-240-5964   (BR)
COMMISSION   SCOLAIRE   DES PREMIERES-SEIGNEURIES
ECOLE GUILLAUME MATHIEU
(*Suby of* Commission Scolaire Des Premieres-Seigneuries)
615 Av Helene-Paradis, Quebec, QC, G1G 5G1
(418) 622-7887
Emp Here 30
SIC 8211 Elementary and secondary schools

D-U-N-S 20-030-4249   (BR)
COMMISSION   SCOLAIRE   DES PREMIERES-SEIGNEURIES
COMMISSION   SCOLAIRE   DES PREMIERES-SEIGNEURIES
1550 Rue Du Perigord, Quebec, QC, G1G 5T8
(418) 624-3755
Emp Here 20
SIC 8211 Elementary and secondary schools

D-U-N-S 20-127-1520   (BR)
COMMISSION   SCOLAIRE   DES PREMIERES-SEIGNEURIES
ECOLE DU CAP-SOLEIL ET DES LOUTRES
7240 Rue Des Loutres, Quebec, QC, G1G 1B1
(418) 624-3753
Emp Here 20
SIC 8211 Elementary and secondary schools

D-U-N-S 25-233-0394   (BR)
COMMISSION   SCOLAIRE   DES PREMIERES-SEIGNEURIES
ECOLE DE L'ESCALE ET DU PLATEAU
(*Suby of* Commission Scolaire Des Premieres-Seigneuries)

8805 Av De Laval, Quebec, QC, G1G 4X6
(418) 622-7891
Emp Here 30
SIC 8211 Elementary and secondary schools

D-U-N-S 25-764-8410   (BR)
DYNO NOBEL CANADA INC
8255 Boul Henri-Bourassa Bureau 210, Quebec, QC, G1G 4C8
(418) 628-4555
Emp Here 20
SIC 2892 Explosives

D-U-N-S 24-201-9222   (SL)
ENTREPRISES C LEMAY INC, LES
1349 D'Oleron Car, Quebec, QC, G1G 4W1
(418) 626-2427
Emp Here 45   *Sales* 8,147,280
SIC 5541 Gasoline service stations
Pr Pr Claude Lemay

D-U-N-S 24-206-9474   (SL)
FOND BENEFICE PERSONNES INCARCEREES CENTRE DETENTION DE QUEBEC
ATELIERS ETABLISSEMENT DETENTION QUEBEC, LES
500 Rue De La Faune, Quebec, QC, G1G 0G9
(418) 622-7100
Emp Here 60   *Sales* 1,824,018
SIC 7211 Power laundries, family and commercial

D-U-N-S 20-717-1963   (BR)
GOUVERNEMENT DE LA PROVINCE DE QUEBEC
CRDI DE QUEBEC
7843 Rue Des Santolines,, Quebec, QC, G1G 0G3
(418) 683-2511
Emp Here 741
SIC 8361 Residential care

D-U-N-S 20-224-6281   (BR)
GROUPE SPORTSCENE INC
CAGE AUX SPORTS
8000 Boul Henri-Bourassa, Quebec, QC, G1G 4C7

Emp Here 25
SIC 5812 Eating places

D-U-N-S 20-959-6787   (SL)
HOTEL & GOLF MARIGOT INC
FOUR POINTS BY SHERATON
7900 Rue Du Marigot, Quebec, QC, G1G 6T8
(418) 627-8008
Emp Here 100   *Sales* 4,377,642
SIC 7011 Hotels and motels

D-U-N-S 20-777-3896   (BR)
RESTAURANT NORMANDIN INC
NORMANDIN BDJ
15021 Boul Henri-Bourassa, Quebec, QC, G1G 3Z2
(418) 626-7216
Emp Here 78
SIC 5812 Eating places

D-U-N-S 24-710-9200   (BR)
SUPERMARCHES GP INC, LES
METRO G P
(*Suby of* Supermarches GP Inc, Les)
8500 Boul Henri-Bourassa Bureau 122, Quebec, QC, G1G 5X1
(418) 626-1056
Emp Here 27
SIC 5411 Grocery stores

Quebec, QC G1H
Quebec County

D-U-N-S 25-198-5339   (SL)
3065359 CANADA INC
(*Suby of* Entreprises Fernando Begin Ltee,

Les)
7777 Boul Henri-Bourassa, Quebec, QC, G1H 3G1
(418) 626-7777
Emp Here 50   *Sales* 24,540,000
SIC 5511 New and used car dealers
Pr Marie-Josee Begin
VP Pierre Begin

D-U-N-S 20-295-8596   (SL)
9081-3239 QUEBEC INC
CENTURY 21 PRESTIGE
7100 Boul Henri-Bourassa, Quebec, QC, G1H 3E4
(418) 627-5517
Emp Here 40   *Sales* 5,134,480
SIC 6531 Real estate agents and managers
Ghislaine Brindamour

D-U-N-S 25-896-6282   (BR)
A & W FOOD SERVICES OF CANADA INC
A & W
4685 1re Av, Quebec, QC, G1H 2T1
(418) 623-2336
Emp Here 32
SIC 5812 Eating places

D-U-N-S 25-244-7693   (BR)
ASHTON CASSE-CROUTE INC
ASHTON LOUIS XIV
(*Suby of* Placements Ashton LeBlond Inc, Les)
520 Boul Louis-Xiv, Quebec, QC, G1H 4N8
(418) 628-7352
Emp Here 20
SIC 5812 Eating places

D-U-N-S 25-748-8197   (SL)
ATELIER SIGNES D'ESPOIR
4155 4e Av O, Quebec, QC, G1H 7A6
(418) 624-4752
Emp Here 60   *Sales* 3,210,271
SIC 2732 Book printing

D-U-N-S 24-637-6958   (BR)
BANQUE NATIONALE DU CANADA
4605 1re Av, Quebec, QC, G1H 2T1
(418) 628-1331
Emp Here 20
SIC 6021 National commercial banks

D-U-N-S 24-890-1670   (SL)
BRASSELER CANADA INC
4500 Boul Henri-Bourassa Bureau 230, Quebec, QC, G1H 3A5
(418) 622-1195
Emp Here 23   *Sales* 3,356,192
SIC 5047 Medical and hospital equipment

D-U-N-S 20-644-5087   (BR)
CANAC-MARQUIS GRENIER LTEE
4250 Boul Henri-Bourassa, Quebec, QC, G1H 3A5
(418) 626-1144
Emp Here 30
SIC 5251 Hardware stores

D-U-N-S 20-273-6372   (BR)
CAPITALE IMMOBILIERE MFQ INC, LA
HOSTELLERIE AU COEUR DU BOURG
7500 Av Thomas-Baillairge, Quebec, QC, G1H 7M4
(418) 628-8968
Emp Here 20
SIC 8361 Residential care

D-U-N-S 24-346-4364   (BR)
CENTRE DE SANTE ET DE SERVICES SOCIAUX DE QUEBEC-NORD
CLSC LA SOURCE
190 76e Rue E, Quebec, QC, G1H 7K4
(418) 628-6808
Emp Here 3,000
SIC 8011 Offices and clinics of medical doctors

D-U-N-S 25-746-2812   (BR)
CERAMIQUE DECORS M.S.F. INC
4220 3e Av O, Quebec, QC, G1H 6T1

(418) 627-0123
Emp Here 40
SIC 5945 Hobby, toy, and game shops

D-U-N-S 25-233-0824   (BR)
COMMISSION   SCOLAIRE   DES PREMIERES-SEIGNEURIES
ECOLE DU RUCHER
(*Suby of* Commission Scolaire Des Premieres-Seigneuries)
1075 60e Rue E, Quebec, QC, G1H 2E3
(418) 622-7890
Emp Here 20
SIC 8211 Elementary and secondary schools

D-U-N-S 20-913-7046   (BR)
COMMISSION   SCOLAIRE   DES PREMIERES-SEIGNEURIES
ECOLE MARIE AGATHE
7220 Av Trudelle, Quebec, QC, G1H 5S3
(418) 622-7886
Emp Here 30
SIC 8211 Elementary and secondary schools

D-U-N-S 25-233-1350   (BR)
COMMISSION   SCOLAIRE   DES PREMIERES-SEIGNEURIES
ECOLE DE L'ENVOL
(*Suby of* Commission Scolaire Des Premieres-Seigneuries)
120 47e Rue E, Quebec, QC, G1H 2M2
(418) 622-7883
Emp Here 70
SIC 8211 Elementary and secondary schools

D-U-N-S 20-711-9921   (BR)
COMMISSION   SCOLAIRE   DES PREMIERES-SEIGNEURIES
ECOLE LA FOURMILIERE
5125 2e Av O, Quebec, QC, G1H 6L2
(418) 622-7893
Emp Here 50
SIC 8211 Elementary and secondary schools

D-U-N-S 24-326-2164   (BR)
COMMISSION   SCOLAIRE   DES PREMIERES-SEIGNEURIES
COMMISSION   SCOLAIRE   DES PREMIERES-SEIGNEURIES
800 Rue De La Sorbonne, Quebec, QC, G1H 1H1
(418) 622-7821
Emp Here 200
SIC 8331 Job training and related services

D-U-N-S 25-233-1830   (BR)
COMMISSION   SCOLAIRE   DES PREMIERES-SEIGNEURIES
MAISON DES ADULTES
(*Suby of* Commission Scolaire Des Premieres-Seigneuries)
480 67e Rue E, Quebec, QC, G1H 1V5
(418) 622-7825
Emp Here 30
SIC 8211 Elementary and secondary schools

D-U-N-S 20-234-5604   (BR)
COMMISSION   SCOLAIRE   DES PREMIERES-SEIGNEURIES
CENTRE ODILON GAUTHIER
742 Boul Louis-Xiv, Quebec, QC, G1H 4M7
(418) 622-7882
Emp Here 38
SIC 8211 Elementary and secondary schools

D-U-N-S 20-574-8341   (BR)
COMMISSION   SCOLAIRE   DES PREMIERES-SEIGNEURIES
ECOLE PARC ORLEANS
7550 10e Av E, Quebec, QC, G1H 4C4
(418) 622-7892
Emp Here 35
SIC 8211 Elementary and secondary schools

D-U-N-S 24-895-7219   (SL)
FOYER DE CHARLESBOURG INC
7150 Boul Cloutier, Quebec, QC, G1H 5V5
(418) 628-0456
Emp Here 125   *Sales* 4,596,524

SIC 8361 Residential care

D-U-N-S 25-470-1055 (BR)
GESTION MENARD PLANTE INC
MANOIR DU SPAGHETTI
7685 1re Av, Quebec, QC, G1H 2Y1
(418) 627-0161
Emp Here 40
SIC 5812 Eating places

D-U-N-S 24-109-7281 (BR)
GOUVERNEMENT DE LA PROVINCE DE QUEBEC
FOYER DE GROUPE
260 49e Rue O, Quebec, QC, G1H 5E4

Emp Here 40
SIC 8361 Residential care

D-U-N-S 20-300-1362 (BR)
GROUPE RESTAURANTS IMVESCOR INC
7900 Boul Henri-Bourassa, Quebec, QC, G1H 3G3
(418) 628-5887
Emp Here 40
SIC 5812 Eating places

D-U-N-S 20-300-8532 (BR)
INDUSTRIELLE ALLIANCE, ASSURANCE ET SERVICES FINANCIERS INC
4635 1re Av Bureau 200, Quebec, QC, G1H 2T1
(418) 627-3550
Emp Here 50
SIC 6311 Life insurance

D-U-N-S 25-743-5081 (SL)
MANOIR ET COURS DE L'ATRIUM INC
545 Rue Francis-Byrne, Quebec, QC, G1H 7L3
(418) 626-6060
Emp Here 90   *Sales* 3,283,232
SIC 8361 Residential care

D-U-N-S 20-003-2568 (SL)
PATRO DE CHARLESBOURG INC
7700 3e Av E, Quebec, QC, G1H 7J2
(418) 626-0161
Emp Here 250   *Sales* 1,905,752
SIC 8322 Individual and family services

D-U-N-S 25-905-9723 (BR)
PLACEMENTS ASHTON LEBLOND INC, LES
CHEZ ASHTON
(*Suby of* Placements Ashton LeBlond Inc, Les)
570 80e Rue O, Quebec, QC, G1H 4N8
(418) 628-7352
Emp Here 23
SIC 5812 Eating places

D-U-N-S 24-381-0967 (BR)
PROVIGO DISTRIBUTION INC
PRESTO CHARLESBOURG
4260 Boul Henri-Bourassa, Quebec, QC, G1H 3A5
(418) 623-1501
Emp Here 20
SIC 5141 Groceries, general line

D-U-N-S 20-913-6006 (BR)
PROVIGO INC
MAXI LOUIS XIV
1160 Boul Louis-Xiv, Quebec, QC, G1H 6V6
(418) 628-7672
Emp Here 55
SIC 5411 Grocery stores

D-U-N-S 24-568-4022 (SL)
QUE-BOURG AUTO (1984) LTEE
(*Suby of* Entreprises Fernando Begin Ltee, Les)
7777 Boul Henri-Bourassa, Quebec, QC, G1H 3G1
(418) 626-7777
Emp Here 30   *Sales* 14,724,000
SIC 5511 New and used car dealers
Pr Pr Fernando Begin

D-U-N-S 25-745-1013 (BR)
RESTAURANT NORMANDIN INC
4960 3e Av O, Quebec, QC, G1H 6G4
(418) 627-1420
Emp Here 50
SIC 5812 Eating places

D-U-N-S 25-886-2606 (BR)
RESTAURANTS MIKA INC, LES
MCDONALD'S RESTAURANTS
4100 1re Av, Quebec, QC, G1H 2S4
(418) 627-1641
Emp Here 30
SIC 5812 Eating places

Quebec, QC G1J
Quebec County

D-U-N-S 20-591-0664 (SL)
3098524 CANADA INC
OPTION SUBARU
2505 Boul Henri-Bourassa, Quebec, QC, G1J 3X2
(418) 648-9518
Emp Here 30   *Sales* 15,217,500
SIC 5511 New and used car dealers
Pr Pr Rene Martineau
   Alexandre Saillant

D-U-N-S 20-030-4256 (BR)
CENTRE DE SANTE ET DE SERVICES SO-CIAUX DE QUEBEC-NORD
UNITE MEDECINE FAMILIALE MAIZERETS
2480 Ch De La Canardiere, Quebec, QC, G1J 2G1
(418) 661-1413
Emp Here 50
SIC 8011 Offices and clinics of medical doctors

D-U-N-S 24-375-6595 (BR)
CENTRE DE SANTE ET DE SERVICES SO-CIAUX DE LA VIEILLE-CAPITALE
CENTRE DE SANTE ET DE SERVICES SO-CIAUX DE LA VIEILLE-CAPITALE
1401 Ch De La Canardiere, Quebec, QC, G1J 0A6
(418) 529-6571
Emp Here 100
SIC 8051 Skilled nursing care facilities

D-U-N-S 25-020-8204 (SL)
COLLEGE D'ENSEIGNEMENT GENERAL ET PROFESSIONNEL LIMOILOU
CEGEP LIMOILOU
1300 8e Av Bureau 1400, Quebec, QC, G1J 5L5
(418) 647-6600
Emp Here 600   *Sales* 86,739,750
SIC 8221 Colleges and universities
Pr Pierre Malouin
Dir Nicole Laflamme
Dir Russell Pierson
Dir Nicole Rousseau
Dir Anne Fillion
Dir Daniel Smith
Dir Louis Grou

D-U-N-S 25-232-8935 (BR)
COMMISSION SCOLAIRE DE LA CAPI-TALE, LA
COMMISSION SCOLAIRE DE LA CAPITALE, LA
2352 8e Av, Quebec, QC, G1J 3P2
(418) 686-4040
Emp Here 30
SIC 8211 Elementary and secondary schools

D-U-N-S 25-240-2649 (BR)
COMMISSION SCOLAIRE DE LA CAPI-TALE, LA
COMMISSION SCOLAIRE DE LA CAPITALE, LA
2490 Av Champfleury, Quebec, QC, G1J 4N9

(418) 686-4040
Emp Here 32
SIC 8211 Elementary and secondary schools

D-U-N-S 25-232-8653 (BR)
COMMISSION SCOLAIRE DE LA CAPI-TALE, LA
ECOLE PRIMAIRE DOMINIQUE SAVIO
2050 Rue De La Trinite, Quebec, QC, G1J 2M4
(418) 686-4040
Emp Here 26
SIC 8211 Elementary and secondary schools

D-U-N-S 25-232-0692 (BR)
COMMISSION SCOLAIRE DE LA CAPI-TALE, LA
ECOLE SECONDAIRE JEAN DE BREBEUF
1640 8e Av, Quebec, QC, G1J 3N5
(418) 686-4040
Emp Here 82
SIC 8211 Elementary and secondary schools

D-U-N-S 20-712-0507 (BR)
COMMISSION SCOLAIRE DE LA CAPI-TALE, LA
COMMISSION SCOLAIRE DE LA CAPITALE, LA
2050 8e Av, Quebec, QC, G1J 3P1
(418) 686-4040
Emp Here 50
SIC 8331 Job training and related services

D-U-N-S 25-371-3119 (BR)
COMPAGNIE AMERICAINE DE FER & METAUX INC, LA
A I M QUEBEC
999 Boul Montmorency, Quebec, QC, G1J 3W1
(418) 649-1000
Emp Here 155
SIC 3341 Secondary nonferrous Metals

D-U-N-S 25-762-4817 (BR)
GOUVERNEMENT DE LA PROVINCE DE QUEBEC
GOUVERNEMENT DE LA PROVINCE DE QUEBEC
2525 Ch De La Canardiere, Quebec, QC, G1J 2G2
(418) 663-5008
Emp Here 80
SIC 8361 Residential care

D-U-N-S 20-555-5175 (BR)
GOUVERNEMENT DE LA PROVINCE DE QUEBEC
DIRECTION DE LA MAINTENANCE DES AERONEFS DU SERVICE AERIEN
700 7e Rue, Quebec, QC, G1J 2S1
(418) 528-8350
Emp Here 185
SIC 4581 Airports, flying fields, and services

D-U-N-S 25-245-0853 (BR)
GOVERNING COUNCIL OF THE SALVA-TION ARMY IN CANADA, THE
GOVERNING COUNCIL OF THE SALVATION ARMY IN CANADA, THE
1125 Ch De La Canardiere, Quebec, QC, G1J 2C3
(418) 641-0050
Emp Here 20
SIC 8322 Individual and family services

D-U-N-S 25-310-8070 (BR)
HOOPER-HOLMES CANADA LIMITED
PORTAMEDIC
1900 Av Mailloux Bureau 270, Quebec, QC, G1J 5B9
(418) 661-7776
Emp Here 25
SIC 6411 Insurance agents, brokers, and service

D-U-N-S 20-104-1634 (BR)
QUEBEC STEVEDORING LTD
ARRIMAGE DU ST LAURENT
500 Rue Du Ressac, Quebec, QC, G1J 5L7

(418) 661-8477
Emp Here 30
SIC 4491 Marine cargo handling

D-U-N-S 25-746-9536 (BR)
VALUE VILLAGE STORES, INC
VILLAGE DES VALEURS
(*Suby of* Savers, Inc.)
2555 Boul Montmorency, Quebec, QC, G1J 5J3
(418) 660-5840
Emp Here 35
SIC 5399 Miscellaneous general merchandise

Quebec, QC G1K
Quebec County

D-U-N-S 24-940-5150 (SL)
2971-0886 QUEBEC INC
PREMIER MAZDA
Pr Succ B, Quebec, QC, G1K 6Z9

Emp Here 37   *Sales* 18,588,800
SIC 5511 New and used car dealers
Pr Paul Daigle

D-U-N-S 20-322-8655 (SL)
4355768 CANADA INC
CRAKMEDIA NETWORK
410 Boul Charest E Bureau 500, Quebec, QC, G1K 8G3
(418) 977-3169
Emp Here 50   *Sales* 3,064,349
SIC 3993 Signs and advertising specialties

D-U-N-S 20-566-5289 (SL)
6143580 CANADA INC.
RESTAURANT PANACHE
10 Rue Saint-Antoine, Quebec, QC, G1K 4C9
(418) 692-1022
Emp Here 100   *Sales* 2,991,389
SIC 5812 Eating places

D-U-N-S 25-019-3372 (SL)
ASSOCIATION DES PERSONNES RE-TRAITEES DE LA TELE-UNIVERSITE
TELE-UNIVERSITE
455 Rue Du Parvis, Quebec, QC, G1K 9H6
(418) 657-2262
Emp Here 275   *Sales* 25,537,116
SIC 8641 Civic and social associations
Pr Celine Lebel
VP VP Jeannine Laurent
Sec Clement Marquis
Treas Elise Fournier
Genl Mgr Ginette Legault

D-U-N-S 25-247-0737 (SL)
AUBERGE SAINT-ANTOINE INC
10 Rue Saint-Antoine, Quebec, QC, G1K 4C9
(418) 692-2211
Emp Here 100   *Sales* 4,377,642
SIC 7011 Hotels and motels

D-U-N-S 20-699-9000 (SL)
BEENOX INC
(*Suby of* Activision Blizzard, Inc.)
305 Boul Charest E Bureau 700, Quebec, QC, G1K 3H3
(418) 522-2468
Emp Here 260   *Sales* 46,362,587
SIC 7371 Custom computer programming services
Pr Eric Hirshberg
Sec Jeffrey A. Brown
   Denis Durkin
Dir Chris B. Walther
Dir Robert A. Kotick

D-U-N-S 24-352-0728 (BR)
BENJO INC
(*Suby of* Benjo Inc)
550 Boul Charest E, Quebec, QC, G1K 3J3
(418) 640-0001
Emp Here 46

SIC 5945 Hobby, toy, and game shops

D-U-N-S 20-512-4188   (HQ)
BENJO INC
BEDONDAINE
(*Suby of* Benjo Inc)
520 Boul Charest E Bureau 233, Quebec, QC,
G1K 3J3
(418) 692-7470
Emp Here 30   *Emp Total* 60
Sales 4,450,603
SIC 5945 Hobby, toy, and game shops

D-U-N-S 20-429-9689   (SL)
BUNGE DU CANADA LTEE
300 Rue Dalhousie, Quebec, QC, G1K 8M8
(418) 692-3761
Emp Here 50   *Sales* 8,420,350
SIC 3523 Farm machinery and equipment
Pr Todd A. Bastean
VP Gregory Thebeau
VP John E. Sabourin
VP Karl J. Gerrand
VP Gino Becerra
VP W.D. Mooney
VP Georges P. Ii Allard
VP Matthew K. Gibson
VP Susan T. Annis
VP Geralyn F. Hayes

D-U-N-S 24-126-3032   (BR)
**CAISSE DESJARDINS DU CENTRE-VILLE
DE QUEBEC**
CENTRE DE SERVICE QUEBEC-EST
510 Rue Saint-Francois E, Quebec, QC, G1K
2Z4
(418) 687-2810
Emp Here 40
SIC 6062 State credit unions

D-U-N-S 20-917-9477   (BR)
**CAISSE DESJARDINS DU CENTRE-VILLE
DE QUEBEC**
135 Rue Saint-Vallier O, Quebec, QC, G1K
1J9
(418) 687-2810
Emp Here 150
SIC 6062 State credit unions

D-U-N-S 24-350-0589   (BR)
**CAISSE DESJARDINS DU CENTRE-VILLE
DE QUEBEC**
*CENTRE FINANCIER AUX ENTREPRISES
DESJARDINS DE QUEBEC*
390 Boul Charest E Bureau 200, Quebec, QC,
G1K 3H4
(418) 529-8585
Emp Here 35
SIC 6062 State credit unions

D-U-N-S 25-391-4998   (HQ)
**CAISSE D'ECONOMIE SOLIDAIRE DES-
JARDINS**
CENTRE DE SERVICES QUEBEC
(*Suby of* Caisse d'Economie Solidaire Des-
jardins)
155 Boul Charest E Bureau 500, Quebec, QC,
G1K 3G6
(418) 647-1527
Emp Here 53   *Emp Total* 100
Sales 16,051,354
SIC 6062 State credit unions
Genl Mgr Paul Ouellet
Pr Gerald Larose
VP Dario Corsi
Sec Brigitte Duchesneau
Dir Jean-Claude Boucher
Dir Christianne Fradette
Dir Denise Boucher
Dir Therese Chaput
Dir Hubert Fortin
Dir Luc Bruneau

D-U-N-S 24-098-7862   (BR)
CANON CANADA INC
DES SOLUTIONS D'AFFAIRES
300 Rue Saint-Paul Bureau 410, Quebec, QC,
G1K 7R1

(418) 687-5630
Emp Here 30
SIC 5044 Office equipment

D-U-N-S 24-639-2880   (BR)
**CENTRALE DES SYNDICATS DU QUEBEC
(CSQ), LA**
CSQ
320 Rue Saint-Joseph E Bureau 100, Quebec,
QC, G1K 9E7
(418) 649-8888
Emp Here 90
SIC 8631 Labor organizations

D-U-N-S 24-346-5551   (BR)
**CENTRE DE SANTE ET DE SERVICES SO-
CIAUX DE LA VIEILLE-CAPITALE**
*CENTRE DE SANTE ET DE SERVICES SO-
CIAUX DE LA VIEILLE-CAPITALE*
105 Rue Hermine, Quebec, QC, G1K 1Y5
(418) 529-2501
Emp Here 350
SIC 8322 Individual and family services

D-U-N-S 25-291-4692   (BR)
**CENTRE DE SANTE ET DE SERVICES SO-
CIAUX DE LA VIEILLE-CAPITALE**
CLSC BASSE-VILLE LIMOILOU VANIER
50 Rue Saint-Joseph E, Quebec, QC, G1K
3A5
(418) 529-2572
Emp Here 1,300
SIC 8322 Individual and family services

D-U-N-S 20-872-5846   (BR)
CHURCH OF SCIENTOLOGY OF TORONTO
EGLISE DE SCIENTOLOGIE DE QUEBEC
(*Suby of* Church Of Scientology Of Toronto)
665 Rue Saint-Joseph E, Quebec, QC, G1K
3C1
(418) 524-4615
Emp Here 48
SIC 8661 Religious organizations

D-U-N-S 20-288-6107   (SL)
CITOYEN OPTIMUM S.E.C.
CITIZEN RELATIONS
300 Rue Saint-Paul Bureau 300, Quebec, QC,
G1K 7R1
(418) 647-2727
Emp Here 200   *Sales* 33,488,961
SIC 4899 Communication services, nec
Genl Mgr Daryl Mccullough

D-U-N-S 25-232-0452   (BR)
**COMMISSION SCOLAIRE DE LA CAPI-
TALE, LA**
ECOLE SACRE COEUR
240 Rue De Jumonville, Quebec, QC, G1K
1G4
(418) 686-4040
Emp Here 42
SIC 8211 Elementary and secondary schools

D-U-N-S 20-712-0622   (BR)
**COMMISSION SCOLAIRE DE LA CAPI-
TALE, LA**
ECOLE HOTELIERE DE LA CAPITALE
7 Rue Robert-Rumilly, Quebec, QC, G1K 2K5
(418) 686-4040
Emp Here 70
SIC 8331 Job training and related services

D-U-N-S 25-240-4686   (BR)
**COMMISSION SCOLAIRE DE LA CAPI-
TALE, LA**
ECOLE SECONDAIRE CARDINAL ROY
50 Rue Du Cardinal-Maurice-Roy, Quebec,
QC, G1K 8S9
(418) 686-4040
Emp Here 80
SIC 8211 Elementary and secondary schools

D-U-N-S 24-746-9208   (BR)
**COMMISSION SCOLAIRE DE LA CAPI-
TALE, LA**
*CENTRE DE FORMATION PROFES-
SIONELLE DE WILBROD BHERER*
5 Rue Robert-Rumilly, Quebec, QC, G1K 2K5

(418) 686-4040
Emp Here 60
SIC 8249 Vocational schools, nec

D-U-N-S 20-574-8150   (BR)
**COMMISSION SCOLAIRE DE LA CAPI-
TALE, LA**
*SERVICES DES RESSOURCES MA-
TERIELLES*
125 Rue Des Commissaires O Bureau 210,
Quebec, QC, G1K 1M7
(418) 686-4040
Emp Here 80
SIC 5049 Professional equipment, nec

D-U-N-S 25-232-8570   (BR)
**COMMISSION SCOLAIRE DE LA CAPI-
TALE, LA**
*COMMISSION SCOLAIRE DE LA CAPITALE,
LA*
325 Av Des Oblats, Quebec, QC, G1K 1R9
(418) 686-4040
Emp Here 50
SIC 8211 Elementary and secondary schools

D-U-N-S 20-363-5263   (HQ)
**COMMISSION DES NORMES, DE LEQUITE,
DE LA SANTE ET DE LA SECURITE DU
TRAVAIL, LA**
CNESST
(*Suby of* Commission des Normes, de
Lequite, de la Sante et de la Securite du Tra-
vail, La)
524 Rue Bourdages Bureau 370, Quebec,
QC, G1K 7E2
(877) 639-0744
Emp Here 1,000   *Emp Total* 3,000
Sales 1,433,604,794
SIC 6331 Fire, marine, and casualty insurance
Ch Bd Manuelle Oudar
VP Martine Begin
VP Michel Beaudoin
VP Opers Josee Dupont
VP Claude Sicard
VP Bruno Labrecque
VP Fin Carl Gauthier

D-U-N-S 25-081-3607   (BR)
COMMUNICATIONS VOIR INC
(*Suby of* Communications Voir Inc)
470 Rue De La Couronne, Quebec, QC, G1K
6G2
(418) 522-7777
Emp Here 20
SIC 2721 Periodicals

D-U-N-S 24-592-8833   (BR)
**CONSEILLERS EN GESTION ET INFORMA-
TIQUE CGI INC**
CGI
410 Boul Charest E Bureau 700, Quebec, QC,
G1K 8G3
(418) 623-0101
Emp Here 1,200
SIC 7379 Computer related services, nec

D-U-N-S 24-530-8770   (SL)
COPIES DE LA CAPITALE INC, LES
235 Boul Charest E, Quebec, QC, G1K 3G8
(418) 648-1911
Emp Here 100   *Sales* 10,449,350
SIC 2752 Commercial printing, lithographic
Michel Lavoie
Pr Pr Marie-Eve Lavoie

D-U-N-S 24-863-4891   (SL)
**CORPORATION DES PILOTES DU BAS
SAINT-LAURENT INC**
240 Rue Dalhousie, Quebec, QC, G1K 8M8
(418) 692-0444
Emp Here 80
SIC 4499 Water transportation services,

D-U-N-S 25-116-0511   (HQ)
COSSETTE COMMUNICATION INC
COSSETTE
(*Suby of* Vision 7 International Inc)
300 Rue Saint-Paul Bureau 300, Quebec, QC,

G1K 7R1
(418) 647-2727
Emp Here 78   *Emp Total* 2,174
Sales 82,153,748
SIC 4899 Communication services, nec
Pr Pr Brett Marchand
Sandra Giguere
Michael Girard

D-U-N-S 20-288-5877   (SL)
COSSETTE DIGITAL INC
(*Suby of* Vision 7 International Inc)
300 Rue Saint-Paul Bureau 300, Quebec, QC,
G1K 7R1
(418) 647-2727
Emp Here 200   *Sales* 33,488,961
SIC 4899 Communication services, nec
Pr Pr Brett Marchand
Sandra Giguere
Michael Girard

D-U-N-S 20-776-5926   (SL)
CRIBTEC INC
975 Boul Champlain, Quebec, QC, G1K 4J9
(418) 622-5992
Emp Here 25   *Sales* 2,826,987
SIC 1731 Electrical work

D-U-N-S 20-355-5180   (SL)
CROISIERES AML INC
CROISIERES DU PORT DE MONTREAL
(*Suby of* Groupe AML Inc)
124 Rue Saint-Pierre, Quebec, QC, G1K 4A7
(866) 856-6668
Emp Here 50   *Sales* 97,475,495
SIC 4424 Deep sea domestic transportation of
freight
Yan Hamel

D-U-N-S 24-207-6891   (HQ)
FINANCIERE MICADCO INC
(*Suby of* Groupe Michel Cadrin Inc)
600 Boul Charest E Bureau 3036, Quebec,
QC, G1K 3J4
(418) 529-6121
Emp Here 50   *Emp Total* 1,200
Sales 301,440,000
SIC 6712 Bank holding companies
Pr Pr Michel Cadrin

D-U-N-S 24-164-4991   (SL)
FRIMA STUDIO INC
HUMAGADE
395 Rue Victor-Revillon, Quebec, QC, G1K
3M8
(418) 529-9697
Emp Here 100   *Sales* 9,423,290
SIC 7336 Commercial art and graphic design
Pr Pr Steve Couture
Christian Diagle
Begin Phillipe
Dir Jacques Topping

D-U-N-S 20-127-2892   (BR)
G3 CANADA LIMITED
300 Rue Dalhousie, Quebec, QC, G1K 8M8
(418) 692-3761
Emp Here 50
SIC 4221 Farm product warehousing and storage

D-U-N-S 20-553-8486   (HQ)
GESTION JALMEC INC
(*Suby of* Gestion Jalmec Inc)
320 Rue Abraham-Martin Bureau 105, Que-
bec, QC, G1K 8N2
(418) 525-3013
Emp Here 50   *Emp Total* 55
Sales 8,245,440
SIC 8741 Management services
Pr Pr Louis Gagne

D-U-N-S 25-687-1484   (BR)
**GOUVERNEMENT DE LA PROVINCE DE
QUEBEC**
*COMMISSION QUEBECOISE DES LIBERA-
TIONS CONDITIONNELLES*
300 Boul Jean-Lesage Bureau 1.32a, Que-

bec, QC, G1K 8K6
(418) 646-8300
Emp Here 40
SIC 8322 Individual and family services

D-U-N-S 24-345-8630   (BR)
GOUVERNEMENT DE LA PROVINCE DE QUEBEC
CENTRE D'HEBERGEMENT NOTRE DAME DE LOURDES & SAINT CHARLES
105 Rue Hermine, Quebec, QC, G1K 1Y5
(418) 529-2501
Emp Here 350
SIC 8051 Skilled nursing care facilities

D-U-N-S 25-335-3825   (BR)
GOUVERNEMENT DE LA PROVINCE DE QUEBEC
SOCIETE DE L'ASSURANCE AUTOMOBILE DU QUEBEC
333 Boul Jean-Lesage, Quebec, QC, G1K 8Z2
(418) 528-4338
Emp Here 2,654
SIC 6411 Insurance agents, brokers, and service

D-U-N-S 24-864-4122   (SL)
GRANILAC INC
(*Suby of* Gestion Polycor Inc)
70 Rue Saint-Paul, Quebec, QC, G1K 3V9
(418) 692-4419
Emp Here 70   *Sales* 34,464,640
SIC 5032 Brick, stone, and related material
Pr Yvan Grise
Genl Mgr Paul Bird

D-U-N-S 25-501-8152   (SL)
GROUPE BGJLR INC, LE
420 Boul Charest E Bureau 400, Quebec, QC, G1K 8M4
(418) 522-0060
Emp Here 45   *Sales* 6,087,000
SIC 8713 Surveying services
Pr Pr Jean-Luc Leger
  Daniel Jodoin

D-U-N-S 24-352-2229   (BR)
GROUPE COTE REGIS INC
115 Rue Abraham-Martin Bureau 500, Quebec, QC, G1K 8N1
(418) 692-4617
Emp Here 20
SIC 8712 Architectural services

D-U-N-S 25-944-8678   (BR)
GROUPE GERMAIN INC
GERMAIN DOMINION
(*Suby of* Gestion Famiger Inc)
126 Rue Saint-Pierre, Quebec, QC, G1K 4A8
(418) 692-2224
Emp Here 40
SIC 7011 Hotels and motels

D-U-N-S 24-842-9102   (SL)
GROUPE JURISER ENR
FLYNN RIVARD AVOCATS
70 Rue Dalhousie Bureau 500, Quebec, QC, G1K 4B2

Emp Here 50   *Sales* 6,973,235
SIC 8741 Management services

D-U-N-S 25-762-8594   (BR)
GROUPE RESTOS PLAISIRS INC, LE
COCHON DINGUE, LE
(*Suby of* Groupe Restos Plaisirs Inc, Le)
46 Boul Champlain, Quebec, QC, G1K 4H7
(418) 694-0303
Emp Here 100
SIC 5812 Eating places

D-U-N-S 20-194-2872   (BR)
GROUPE RESTOS PLAISIRS INC, LE
CAFE DU MONDE
(*Suby of* Groupe Restos Plaisirs Inc, Le)
84 Rue Dalhousie Bureau 140, Quebec, QC, G1K 8M5

---

(418) 692-4455
Emp Here 80
SIC 5812 Eating places

D-U-N-S 24-204-5474   (SL)
IDEE PRO INC
54 Rue De La Pointe-Aux-Lievres Bureau 6, Quebec, QC, G1K 5Y3
(418) 522-4455
Emp Here 85   *Sales* 5,884,100
SIC 2759 Commercial printing, nec
Pr Pr Raymond Robichaud
  Benoit Robichaud

D-U-N-S 24-821-2144   (HQ)
IMPACT RESEARCH INC
(*Suby of* Vision 7 International Inc)
300 Rue Saint-Paul Bureau 300, Quebec, QC, G1K 7R1
(418) 647-2727
Emp Here 45   *Emp Total* 2,174
Sales 24,149,992
SIC 8732 Commercial nonphysical research
Pr Pr Joseph Leon
  Sandra Giguere
  Michael Girard

D-U-N-S 24-051-6943   (BR)
INDUSTRIES GRC INC, LES
(*Suby of* Industries GRC Inc, Les)
10c Cote De La Canoterie Bureau 7, Quebec, QC, G1K 3X4
(418) 692-1112
Emp Here 125
SIC 3444 Sheet Metalwork

D-U-N-S 20-029-9670   (BR)
INFOR (CANADA), LTD
(*Suby of* Infor Lux Bond Company)
330 Rue De Saint-Vallier E Bureau 230, Quebec, QC, G1K 9C5

Emp Here 70
SIC 7371 Custom computer programming services

D-U-N-S 24-820-4588   (SL)
L'AVIATIC CLUB INC
LE CHARBON
450 Rue De La Gare-Du-Palais Bureau 104, Quebec, QC, G1K 3X2
(418) 522-0133
Emp Here 85   *Sales* 2,553,625
SIC 5812 Eating places

D-U-N-S 20-655-9812   (BR)
LABARRE GAUTHIER INC
LG2
585 Boul Charest E Bureau 700b, Quebec, QC, G1K 9H4
(418) 263-8901
Emp Here 31
SIC 7311 Advertising agencies

D-U-N-S 20-126-3600   (BR)
PROGRAMME DE PORTAGE RELATIF A LA DEPENDENCE DE LA DROGUE INC, LE
CENTRE DE READAPTATION LE PORTAGE
(*Suby of* Programme de Portage Relatif a la Dependence de la Drogue Inc, Le)
150 Rue Saint-Joseph E, Quebec, QC, G1K 3A7
(418) 524-6038
Emp Here 23
SIC 8093 Specialty outpatient clinics, nec

D-U-N-S 25-501-4680   (SL)
SERVICES DE QUAI FAGEN INC
TERMINAL MARITIME SOREL-TRACY
961 Boul Champlain, Quebec, QC, G1K 4J9
(418) 522-4701
Emp Here 25   *Sales* 5,275,400
SIC 4491 Marine cargo handling
Pr Pr Denis Dupuis
VP VP Alphonse Belanger
  Yvon Dupuis

D-U-N-S 20-289-3335   (BR)
SERVICES INTEGRES LEMAY ET ASSO-

CIES INC
LEMAY ET ASSOCIES
734 Rue Saint-Joseph E Bureau 4, Quebec, QC, G1K 3C3
(418) 647-1037
Emp Here 20
SIC 8712 Architectural services

D-U-N-S 20-318-4718   (SL)
SERVICES MARITIMES DESGAGNES INC
21 Rue Du Marche-Champlain Bureau 100, Quebec, QC, G1K 8Z8
(418) 692-1000
Emp Here 50   *Sales* 4,377,642
SIC 3731 Shipbuilding and repairing

D-U-N-S 20-073-8552   (SL)
SOCIETE D'EXPLORATION MINIERE VIO
116 Rue Saint-Pierre Bureau 200, Quebec, QC, G1K 4A7
(418) 692-2678
Emp Here 180   *Sales* 15,248,786
SIC 1081 Metal mining services
Pr Hugues Belzile

D-U-N-S 24-226-2140   (BR)
SOCIETE DES TRAVERSIERS DU QUEBEC
251 Rue De L'Estuaire, Quebec, QC, G1K 8S8
(418) 643-1806
Emp Here 20
SIC 8631 Labor organizations

D-U-N-S 20-873-6900   (HQ)
SOCIETE DES TRAVERSIERS DU QUEBEC
STQ
250 Rue Saint-Paul, Quebec, QC, G1K 9K9
(418) 643-2019
Emp Here 320   *Emp Total* 40,000
Sales 77,630,185
SIC 4482 Ferries
Dir Jocelyn Fortier
Dir Lise Breton
Dir Danielle Amyot
Dir Julie Coulombe-Godbout
Dir Fabienne Desrochers
Dir Annie Fournier
Dir Richard Michaud

D-U-N-S 20-322-1564   (SL)
SOUTIEN A LA PERSONNE HANDICAPEE EN ROUTE VERS L'EMPLOI AU QUEBEC (SPHERE-QUEBEC)
210 Boul Charest E, Quebec, QC, G1K 3H1
(418) 522-4747
Emp Here 25   *Sales* 8,217,450
SIC 8322 Individual and family services
Pr Martin Trepanier
Treas Louis Adam

D-U-N-S 24-678-3786   (BR)
TRANSPORT CANADA
MARINA DU PORT-QUEBEC
155 Rue Abraham-Martin, Quebec, QC, G1K 8N1
(418) 648-2233
Emp Here 25
SIC 8049 Offices of health practitioner

D-U-N-S 24-500-0468   (HQ)
UNIQUE ASSURANCES GENERALES INC, L'
MULTI-CHOIX
625 Rue Saint Amable, Quebec, QC, G1K 0E1
(418) 683-2711
Emp Here 105   *Emp Total* 1
Sales 141,285,538
SIC 6331 Fire, marine, and casualty insurance
Pr Jean St-Gelais
VP Dominique Dubuc
Dir Rene Rouleau
Dir Francois Jutras
Dir Jean-Paul Beaulieu
Dir Richard Fiset
Dir Marie-Josee Linteau

D-U-N-S 24-853-4799   (BR)
UNIVERSITE DU QUEBEC
TELUQ

---

455 Rue Du Parvis Bureau 2140, Quebec, QC, G1K 9H6
(418) 657-2262
Emp Here 200
SIC 8221 Colleges and universities

D-U-N-S 20-293-6519   (BR)
UNIVERSITE DU QUEBEC
INRS ETE INSTITUT NATIONALE DE LA RECHECHE SCIENTIFIQUE
490 Rue De La Couronne, Quebec, QC, G1K 9A9
(418) 654-2665
Emp Here 350
SIC 8732 Commercial nonphysical research

D-U-N-S 24-309-5150   (BR)
UNIVERSITE DU QUEBEC
INSTITUT NATIONALE DE LA RECHERCHE SCIENTIFIQUE (INRS)
490 Rue De La Couronne, Quebec, QC, G1K 9A9
(418) 687-6400
Emp Here 350
SIC 8221 Colleges and universities

D-U-N-S 24-888-3840   (BR)
UNIVERSITE DU QUEBEC
CENTRE UBANISATION CULTURE ET SOCIETE
490 Rue De La Couronne, Quebec, QC, G1K 9A9
(418) 687-6400
Emp Here 175
SIC 8221 Colleges and universities

D-U-N-S 20-720-3766   (BR)
UNIVERSITE DU QUEBEC
490 Rue De La Couronne, Quebec, QC, G1K 9A9
(418) 654-4677
Emp Here 500
SIC 8221 Colleges and universities

D-U-N-S 20-713-7337   (BR)
UNIVERSITE DU QUEBEC
INRS CENTRE EAU TERRE ET ENVIRONNEMENT
490 Rue De La Couronne, Quebec, QC, G1K 9A9
(418) 654-2524
Emp Here 200
SIC 8731 Commercial physical research

D-U-N-S 20-297-9543   (BR)
VALEURS MOBILIERES DESJARDINS INC
VALEURS MOBILIERES DESJARDINS, LES
70 Rue Dalhousie Bureau 500, Quebec, QC, G1K 4B2
(418) 692-3668
Emp Here 25
SIC 6211 Security brokers and dealers

D-U-N-S 24-335-6578   (BR)
VILLE DE QUEBEC
OFFICE DU TOURISME DE QUEBEC, L
399 Rue Saint-Joseph E, Quebec, QC, G1K 8E2
(418) 641-6654
Emp Here 70
SIC 4724 Travel agencies

D-U-N-S 24-522-6407   (HQ)
VISION 7 COMMUNICATIONS INC
SIMPLESTRATUS
(*Suby of* Vision 7 International Inc)
300 Rue Saint-Paul Bureau 300, Quebec, QC, G1K 7R1
(418) 647-2727
Emp Here 27   *Emp Total* 2,174
Sales 399,022,068
SIC 6712 Bank holding companies
Pr Pr Brett Marchand
  Sandra Giguere
  Michael Girard

Quebec, QC G1L
Quebec County

D-U-N-S 24-863-0493   (BR)
AGROPUR COOPERATIVE
AGROPUR DIVISION NATREL
2465 1re Av, Quebec, QC, G1L 3M9
(418) 641-0857
Emp Here 215
SIC 2026 Fluid milk

D-U-N-S 20-521-5010   (HQ)
CAISSE DESJARDINS DE LIMOILOU
CENTRE CONSEIL SERVICES DE GESTION DES AVOIRS
(*Suby of* Caisse Desjardins de Limoilou)
800 3e Av, Quebec, QC, G1L 2W9
(418) 628-0155
Emp Here 80   *Emp Total* 130
Sales 28,011,096
SIC 6062 State credit unions
Genl Mgr Robert Desrosiers
Pr Samuel Proulx-Lemire
VP Patrick Ellyson
Sr VP Remi Vaillancourt
Jean-Eudes Boudreau
Dir Christine Labbe
Dir Gilles Blouin
Dir Jean-Francois Darche
Dir Audrey Huot Arsenault
Dir Alain Oneil

D-U-N-S 24-145-2093   (SL)
CENTRE HOSPITALIER ST-FRANCOIS INC
1604 1re Av, Quebec, QC, G1L 3L6
(418) 524-6033
Emp Here 50   *Sales* 2,261,782
SIC 8051 Skilled nursing care facilities

D-U-N-S 25-042-7663   (BR)
CENTRE HOSPITALIER UNIVERSITAIRE DE QUEBEC
HOPITAL SAINT FRANCOIS D'ASSISE
10 Rue De L'Espinay Bureau 520, Quebec, QC, G1L 3L5
(418) 525-4444
Emp Here 8,964
SIC 8062 General medical and surgical hospitals

D-U-N-S 20-712-0515   (BR)
COMMISSION SCOLAIRE DE LA CAPITALE, LA
ECOLE SECONDAIRE NOTRE DAME DE ROC AMADOUR
1625 Boul Benoit-Xv, Quebec, QC, G1L 2Z3
(418) 686-4040
Emp Here 80
SIC 8211 Elementary and secondary schools

D-U-N-S 20-712-0523   (BR)
COMMISSION SCOLAIRE DE LA CAPITALE, LA
ECOLE REGIONALE DES QUATRES-SAISONS
215 Rue Des Peupliers O, Quebec, QC, G1L 1H8
(418) 686-4040
Emp Here 30
SIC 8211 Elementary and secondary schools

D-U-N-S 25-232-9115   (BR)
COMMISSION SCOLAIRE DE LA CAPITALE, LA
COMMISSION SCOLAIRE DE LA CAPITALE, LA
301 Rue Des Peupliers E, Quebec, QC, G1L 1S6
(418) 686-4040
Emp Here 20
SIC 8211 Elementary and secondary schools

D-U-N-S 25-298-6120   (BR)
COMMISSION SCOLAIRE DE LA CAPITALE, LA
ECOLE DE LA GRANDE ERMINE
1355 2e Av, Quebec, QC, G1L 0A6

(418) 686-4040
Emp Here 30
SIC 8211 Elementary and secondary schools

D-U-N-S 20-914-4851   (BR)
COMMISSION SCOLAIRE DE LA CAPITALE, LA
CENTRE LOUIS-JOLLIET
1201 Rue De La Pointe-Aux-Lievres, Quebec, QC, G1L 4M1
(418) 686-4040
Emp Here 100
SIC 8211 Elementary and secondary schools

D-U-N-S 20-806-9984   (BR)
COUCHE-TARD INC
3240 1re Av, Quebec, QC, G1L 3P9
(418) 623-3152
Emp Here 25
SIC 5411 Grocery stores

D-U-N-S 25-776-5560   (SL)
ECOLE DE CIRQUE DE QUEBEC
CLUB DE MONOCYCLE DE L'ECOLE DE CIRQUE DE QUEBEC (CMECQ)
750 2e Av, Quebec, QC, G1L 3B7
(418) 525-0101
Emp Here 70   *Sales* 3,793,956
SIC 7999 Amusement and recreation, nec

D-U-N-S 20-974-1839   (SL)
ECOLE DE HOCKEY DE LA CAPITALE INC
21 Rue Jacques-Cartier App 2, Quebec, QC, G1L 3R6

Emp Here 100   *Sales* 33,174,150
SIC 7941 Sports clubs, managers, and promoters
Dir Louis Simard

D-U-N-S 20-515-1350   (BR)
FOR-NET INC
GROUPE FORTIN, LE
1875 Av De La Normandie, Quebec, QC, G1L 3Y8
(418) 529-6103
Emp Here 100
SIC 7349 Building maintenance services, nec

D-U-N-S 20-949-1109   (SL)
FORTIN INVESTIGATION ET SECURITE DU QUEBEC INC
1875 Av De La Normandie, Quebec, QC, G1L 3Y8
(418) 529-9391
Emp Here 50   *Sales* 1,532,175
SIC 7381 Detective and armored car services

D-U-N-S 20-713-7162   (BR)
GOUVERNEMENT DE LA PROVINCE DE QUEBEC
CENTRE DE SANTE ET DE SERVICES SOCIAUX DE QUEBEC NORD
2305 Boul Benoit-Xv Bureau 16, Quebec, QC, G1L 3A4
(418) 524-9725
Emp Here 60
SIC 8322 Individual and family services

D-U-N-S 24-835-2445   (SL)
IMTT-QUEBEC INC
(*Suby of* Macquarie Infrastructure Corporation)
Gd, Quebec, QC, G1L 4W4
(418) 667-8641
Emp Here 35   *Sales* 2,772,507
SIC 4226 Special warehousing and storage, nec

D-U-N-S 24-010-6901   (HQ)
LE PATRO ROC -AMADOUR (1978) INC.
(*Suby of* Le Patro Roc -Amadour (1978) Inc.)
2301 1re Av, Quebec, QC, G1L 3M9
(418) 529-4996
Emp Here 25   *Emp Total* 50
Sales 4,231,721
SIC 7032 Sporting and recreational camps

D-U-N-S 24-373-2521   (BR)

VIANDEX INC
195 Rue Joly, Quebec, QC, G1L 1N7
(418) 681-2482
Emp Here 70
SIC 5141 Groceries, general line

Quebec, QC G1M
Quebec County

D-U-N-S 25-786-7663   (BR)
2772981 CANADA INC
GROUPECHO COLLECTION
455 Rue Du Marais Bureau 235, Quebec, QC, G1M 3A2
(418) 681-1545
Emp Here 50
SIC 7323 Credit reporting services

D-U-N-S 25-541-0524   (SL)
9022-1672 QUEBEC INC
PALACE CABARET
955 Boul Pierre-Bertrand, Quebec, QC, G1M 2E8

Emp Here 70   *Sales* 2,553,625
SIC 5813 Drinking places

D-U-N-S 20-579-4977   (HQ)
9254-7983 QUEBEC INC
IDEE CADRE
(*Suby of* 9254-7983 Quebec Inc)
560 Boul Wilfrid-Hamel, Quebec, QC, G1M 2S9
(418) 529-6261
Emp Here 25   *Emp Total* 85
Sales 8,834,400
SIC 5719 Miscellaneous homefurnishings
Dir Jean-Bertin Gingras
Pr Pr Roger Viau
Jean-Francois Deschesnes

D-U-N-S 20-432-1772   (BR)
AIR LIQUIDE CANADA INC
225 Rue Fortin, Quebec, QC, G1M 3M2
(418) 683-1917
Emp Here 30
SIC 5169 Chemicals and allied products, nec

D-U-N-S 20-215-6795   (BR)
ASHTON CASSE-CROUTE INC
(*Suby of* Placements Ashton LeBlond Inc, Les)
600 Rue Du Marais, Quebec, QC, G1M 3R1
(418) 682-6565
Emp Here 50
SIC 5812 Eating places

D-U-N-S 25-853-7125   (BR)
ASHTON CASSE-CROUTE INC
CHEZ ASHTON
(*Suby of* Placements Ashton LeBlond Inc, Les)
550 Boul Wilfrid-Hamel, Quebec, QC, G1M 2S6
(418) 648-0895
Emp Here 20
SIC 5812 Eating places

D-U-N-S 24-206-1190   (SL)
ATELIER DE MECANIQUE PREMONT INC
MOTO ROUTE 66
1071 Boul Pierre-Bertrand, Quebec, QC, G1M 2E8
(418) 683-1340
Emp Here 50   *Sales* 3,064,349
SIC 7699 Repair services, nec

D-U-N-S 24-758-9773   (SL)
AUTOMOBILES ACADIA INC
ACADIA SUZUKI SUBARU
(*Suby of* Gestion LU-DI Inc)
999 Av Galibois, Quebec, QC, G1M 3S4
(418) 681-6000
Emp Here 30   *Sales* 15,217,500
SIC 5511 New and used car dealers

Pr Pr Luc Dion
Dir Carole Dion
VP VP Gaetan Demers
Dir Jean Dion
Dir Brigitte Dion
Dir Denis Dion
Dir Chantal Dion

D-U-N-S 24-593-2371   (BR)
BUDGETAUTO INC
BUDGET AUTO INC
(*Suby of* Avis Budget Group, Inc.)
380 Boul Wilfrid-Hamel, Quebec, QC, G1M 2S4
(418) 687-4220
Emp Here 20
SIC 7514 Passenger car rental

D-U-N-S 24-530-9547   (BR)
CANAC-MARQUIS GRENIER LTEE
475 Boul Pierre-Bertrand, Quebec, QC, G1M 3T8
(418) 687-2960
Emp Here 60
SIC 5211 Lumber and other building materials

D-U-N-S 25-883-2914   (BR)
CARON & GUAY INC
615 Boul Pierre-Bertrand, Quebec, QC, G1M 3J3
(418) 683-7534
Emp Here 200
SIC 5211 Lumber and other building materials

D-U-N-S 20-912-1925   (BR)
CENTRE DE SANTE ET DE SERVICES SOCIAUX DE LA VIEILLE-CAPITALE
RESIDENCE ST ANTOINE
1451 Boul Pere-Lelievre Bureau 363, Quebec, QC, G1M 1N8
(418) 683-2516
Emp Here 200
SIC 8361 Residential care

D-U-N-S 24-192-1787   (BR)
CHARCUTERIE LA TOUR EIFFEL INC
485 Rue Des Entrepreneurs, Quebec, QC, G1M 2V2
(418) 687-2840
Emp Here 100
SIC 5147 Meats and meat products

D-U-N-S 25-182-5360   (BR)
CHOQUETTE - CKS INC
900 Boul Pierre-Bertrand Bureau 220, Quebec, QC, G1M 3K2
(418) 681-3944
Emp Here 20
SIC 7699 Repair services, nec

D-U-N-S 24-498-3680   (BR)
COCA-COLA REFRESHMENTS CANADA COMPANY
EMBOUTEILLAGE COCA COLA
(*Suby of* The Coca-Cola Company)
990 Av Godin, Quebec, QC, G1M 2X9
(418) 686-4884
Emp Here 80
SIC 5149 Groceries and related products, nec

D-U-N-S 25-232-9099   (BR)
COMMISSION SCOLAIRE DE LA CAPITALE, LA
COMMISSION SCOLAIRE DE LA CAPITALE, LA
700 Boul Wilfrid-Hamel, Quebec, QC, G1M 2P9
(418) 686-4040
Emp Here 55
SIC 8211 Elementary and secondary schools

D-U-N-S 25-233-7134   (BR)
COMMISSION SCOLAIRE DE LA CAPITALE, LA
COMMISSION SCOLAIRE DE LA CAPITALE, LA
136 Rue Beaucage, Quebec, QC, G1M 1G6
(418) 686-4040
Emp Here 30

SIC 8211 Elementary and secondary schools

D-U-N-S 25-232-8695 (BR)
COMMISSION SCOLAIRE DE LA CAPITALE, LA
CENTRE DE FORMATION PROFESSIONEL DU QUEBEC
1925 Rue Monseigneur-Plessis, Quebec, QC, G1M 1A4
(418) 686-4040
Emp Here 50
SIC 8331 Job training and related services

D-U-N-S 25-232-8539 (BR)
COMMISSION SCOLAIRE DE LA CAPITALE, LA
ECOLE NOTRE DAME DU CANADA
383 Rue Chabot, Quebec, QC, G1M 1L4
(418) 686-4040
Emp Here 40
SIC 8211 Elementary and secondary schools

D-U-N-S 25-233-8322 (BR)
COMMISSION SCOLAIRE DE LA CAPITALE, LA
ECOLE DU DOMAINE
1630 Rue Des Balsamines, Quebec, QC, G1M 2K9
(418) 686-4040
Emp Here 30
SIC 8211 Elementary and secondary schools

D-U-N-S 24-077-4559 (BR)
DOLLARAMA S.E.C.
DOLLARAMA
245 Rue Soumande Bureau 1, Quebec, QC, G1M 3H6
(418) 263-0170
Emp Here 20
SIC 5331 Variety stores

D-U-N-S 24-226-5614 (BR)
EXFO INC
EXFO 2 PRODUCTION
436 Rue Nolin, Quebec, QC, G1M 1E7
(418) 683-0211
Emp Here 200
SIC 3827 Optical instruments and lenses

D-U-N-S 25-879-9204 (BR)
EXCELLENT GESTION INC
ECOLE DE CONDUITE TECNIC
(*Suby of* Excellente Gestion Inc)
550 Boul Pere-Lelievre Bureau 100, Quebec, QC, G1M 3R2
(418) 529-3868
Emp Here 20
SIC 8299 Schools and educational services, nec

D-U-N-S 20-254-4813 (SL)
FONDS DES RESSOURCES INFORMATIONNELLES DU SECTEUR DE LA SANTE ET DES SERVICES SOCIAUX
FRISSSS
555 Boul Wilfrid-Hamel, Quebec, QC, G1M 3X7
(418) 527-5211
Emp Here 50   *Sales* 3,580,850
SIC 7376 Computer facilities management

D-U-N-S 25-155-7062 (BR)
FRANKLIN EMPIRE INC
ELECTRO MECANIK PLAYFORD
215 Rue Fortin, Quebec, QC, G1M 3M2
(418) 683-1724
Emp Here 98
SIC 1531 Operative builders

D-U-N-S 20-743-2720 (BR)
FRANKLIN EMPIRE INC
ELECTRO MEKANIC
215 Rue Fortin, Quebec, QC, G1M 3M2
(418) 683-1725
Emp Here 50
SIC 5063 Electrical apparatus and equipment

D-U-N-S 25-247-6411 (BR)
G4S CASH SOLUTIONS (CANADA) LTD

G4S QUEBEC
538 Rue Maurice-Bois, Quebec, QC, G1M 3G3
(418) 527-5636
Emp Here 50
SIC 7381 Detective and armored car services

D-U-N-S 25-361-5108 (BR)
GOUVERNEMENT DE LA PROVINCE DE QUEBEC
INSTITUT DE READAPTATION EN DEFICIENCE PHYSIQUE DU QUEBEC (IRDPQ)
525 Boul Wilfrid-Hamel, Quebec, QC, G1M 2S8
(418) 529-9141
Emp Here 1,300
SIC 8011 Offices and clinics of medical doctors

D-U-N-S 20-713-7048 (BR)
GOUVERNEMENT DE LA PROVINCE DE QUEBEC
GOUVERNEMENT DE LA PROVINCE DE QUEBEC
525 Boul Wilfrid-Hamel, Quebec, QC, G1M 2S8
(418) 649-3700
Emp Here 1,300
SIC 8093 Specialty outpatient clinics, nec

D-U-N-S 20-363-4576 (SL)
GROUPE EDGENDA INC
AFI
1751 Rue Du Marais Bureau 300, Quebec, QC, G1M 0A2
(418) 953-1323
Emp Here 50   *Sales* 5,034,288
SIC 8243 Data processing schools
  Marie-Pier St-Hilaire
Dir Patrick St-Hilaire

D-U-N-S 20-300-8490 (BR)
GROUPECHO CANADA INC
GROUPECHO COLLECTION
(*Suby of* Groupecho Canada Inc)
455 Rue Du Marais Bureau 235, Quebec, QC, G1M 3A2
(418) 681-1545
Emp Here 45
SIC 6111 Federal and federally sponsored credit agencies

D-U-N-S 20-303-1450 (BR)
HUDSON'S BAY COMPANY
LA BAIE FLEUR DE LYS
550 Boul Wilfrid-Hamel, Quebec, QC, G1M 2S6
(418) 627-3416
Emp Here 50
SIC 5311 Department stores

D-U-N-S 25-309-6796 (BR)
INDUSTRIELLE ALLIANCE, ASSURANCE ET SERVICES FINANCIERS INC
455 Rue Du Marais Bureau 295, Quebec, QC, G1M 3A2
(418) 687-9449
Emp Here 40
SIC 6311 Life insurance

D-U-N-S 20-870-2654 (SL)
LA-BIL INC
ARMAND GENEST & FILS
895 Av Godin, Quebec, QC, G1M 2X5
(418) 687-5410
Emp Here 50   *Sales* 4,377,642
SIC 1711 Plumbing, heating, air-conditioning

D-U-N-S 24-330-9502 (BR)
LINDE CANADA LIMITED
EQUIPEMENT DE SECURITE DU QUEBEC
850 Rue Fernand-Dufour, Quebec, QC, G1M 3B1
(418) 780-3838
Emp Here 30
SIC 5099 Durable goods, nec

D-U-N-S 20-556-0837 (BR)
LINDE CANADA LIMITED

BOC CANADA
579 Av Godin, Quebec, QC, G1M 3G7
(418) 688-0150
Emp Here 30
SIC 5169 Chemicals and allied products, nec

D-U-N-S 20-241-1989 (SL)
NADOR INC
ALIMENTS LE CHIEN D'OR, LES
625 Rue Du Marais, Quebec, QC, G1M 2Y2
(418) 681-0696
Emp Here 50   *Sales* 1,507,200
SIC 2095 Roasted coffee

D-U-N-S 24-390-8220 (SL)
NUTRIART INC
550 Av Godin, Quebec, QC, G1M 2K2
(418) 687-5320
Emp Here 60   *Sales* 262,659
SIC 2066 Chocolate and cocoa products

D-U-N-S 24-633-2873 (BR)
OLD DUTCH FOODS LTD
HUMPTY DUMPTY SNACK FOODS
(*Suby of* Old Dutch Foods Ltd)
669 Av Godin, Quebec, QC, G1M 3E6
(418) 683-0453
Emp Here 40
SIC 2096 Potato chips and similar snacks

D-U-N-S 25-775-6395 (SL)
ORICOM INTERNET INC
400 Rue Nolin Bureau 150, Quebec, QC, G1M 1E7
(418) 683-4557
Emp Here 52   *Sales* 7,444,399
SIC 4813 Telephone communication, except radio
Pr Pr Bernard Lepine
  Sylvie Beaupre
  Alain Bergeron

D-U-N-S 25-779-6987 (BR)
PATTERSON DENTAIRE CANADA INC
255 Rue Fortin Bureau 160, Quebec, QC, G1M 3M2
(418) 688-6546
Emp Here 38
SIC 5047 Medical and hospital equipment

D-U-N-S 24-464-4365 (BR)
PEPSICO CANADA ULC
FRITO LAY CANADA
(*Suby of* Pepsico, Inc.)
235 Rue Fortin, Quebec, QC, G1M 3M2
(418) 681-6216
Emp Here 55
SIC 5145 Confectionery

D-U-N-S 20-984-4294 (BR)
PISCINES PRO ET PATIOS N.V. INC
945 Av Godin, Quebec, QC, G1M 2X5
(418) 687-1988
Emp Here 125
SIC 7999 Amusement and recreation, nec

D-U-N-S 25-896-6878 (BR)
PLACEMENTS ASHTON LEBLOND INC, LES
ASHTON, CHEZ
(*Suby of* Placements Ashton LeBlond Inc, Les)
550 Boul Wilfrid-Hamel, Quebec, QC, G1M 2S6
(418) 682-2288
Emp Here 21
SIC 5812 Eating places

D-U-N-S 20-645-1283 (BR)
PROVIGO DISTRIBUTION INC
MAXI FLEUR DE LYS
552 Boul Wilfrid-Hamel, Quebec, QC, G1M 3E5
(418) 640-1700
Emp Here 100
SIC 5411 Grocery stores

D-U-N-S 20-915-3274 (BR)
RANDSTAD INTERIM INC

RANDSTAD
3 Rue Marie-De-L'Incarnation, Quebec, QC, G1M 3J4
(418) 525-6766
Emp Here 22
SIC 7361 Employment agencies

D-U-N-S 25-293-8956 (BR)
RYDER TRUCK RENTAL CANADA LTD
(*Suby of* Ryder System, Inc.)
615c Boul Pierre-Bertrand, Quebec, QC, G1M 3J3
(418) 687-2483
Emp Here 30
SIC 7513 Truck rental and leasing, no drivers

D-U-N-S 20-243-2324 (BR)
SEARS CANADA INC
SEARS FLEURS DE LYS
500 Boul Wilfrid-Hamel, Quebec, QC, G1M 2S5
(418) 529-9861
Emp Here 30
SIC 5311 Department stores

D-U-N-S 24-758-6241 (BR)
SECURITE KOLOSSAL INC
325 Rue Du Marais Bureau 220, Quebec, QC, G1M 3R3
(418) 683-1713
Emp Here 3,500
SIC 7381 Detective and armored car services

D-U-N-S 25-476-0671 (BR)
SERVICE DE PNEUS AUCLAIR INC
AUTOPNEU AUCLAIR
385 Rue Des Entrepreneurs, Quebec, QC, G1M 1B4
(418) 683-1010
Emp Here 30
SIC 5531 Auto and home supply stores

D-U-N-S 24-368-7212 (BR)
SOLOTECH QUEBEC INC
465 Av Godin, Quebec, QC, G1M 3G7
(418) 682-4155
Emp Here 20
SIC 5099 Durable goods, nec

Quebec, QC G1N
Quebec County

D-U-N-S 25-469-4086 (HQ)
2972-6924 QUEBEC INC
PORTES ET CADRES METALEC
2150 Rue Leon-Harmel, Quebec, QC, G1N 4L2
(418) 683-2431
Emp Here 30   *Emp Total* 175
Sales 10,836,784
SIC 3442 Metal doors, sash, and trim
Pr Pr Paul Lacasse
  Francis Lacasse

D-U-N-S 24-942-6537 (SL)
3019969 CANADA INC
400 Rue Morse, Quebec, QC, G1N 4L4
(418) 683-2201
Emp Here 20   *Sales* 3,648,035
SIC 5136 Men's and boy's clothing

D-U-N-S 24-908-0763 (BR)
3627730 CANADA INC
FREEMAN AUDIO VISUAL
2025 Rue Lavoisier Bureau 100, Quebec, QC, G1N 4L6
(418) 687-9055
Emp Here 30
SIC 7359 Equipment rental and leasing, nec

D-U-N-S 20-356-5312 (SL)
9333-2161 QUEBEC INC
SONECPRO
2189 Rue Leon-Harmel, Quebec, QC, G1N 4N5

(418) 681-1160
Emp Here 50   Sales 3,210,271
SIC 7929 Entertainers and entertainment groups

D-U-N-S 24-381-5032   (HQ)
ALEX COULOMBE LTEE
JULES ST-PIERRE
(Suby of Entreprises Courem (1988) Ltee)
2300 Rue Cyrille-Duquet, Quebec, QC, G1N 2G5
(418) 687-2700
Emp Here 259   Emp Total 2
Sales 61,417,196
SIC 5149 Groceries and related products, nec
Marc Coulombe

D-U-N-S 24-324-7421   (BR)
ALSCO CANADA CORPORATION
UNIFORMES & LINGE D'HOTELERIE ALSCO
1150 Rue Des Ardennes, Quebec, QC, G1N 4J3
(418) 681-6185
Emp Here 70
SIC 7213 Linen supply

D-U-N-S 24-105-9935   (BR)
ALTUS GEOMATICS LIMITED PARTNERSHIP
ALTUS GROUP
1265 Boul Charest O Bureau 1200, Quebec, QC, G1N 2C9
(418) 628-6019
Emp Here 60
SIC 8713 Surveying services

D-U-N-S 20-722-3470   (HQ)
ATLANTIS POMPE STE-FOY INC
(Suby of Gro-Mec Inc)
1844 Boul Wilfrid-Hamel, Quebec, QC, G1N 3Z2
(418) 681-7301
Emp Here 40   Emp Total 23
Sales 9,849,695
SIC 5084 Industrial machinery and equipment
Pr Pr Claude Jacques
Fin Ex Josee Godbout

D-U-N-S 24-206-6330   (HQ)
AV-TECH INC
(Suby of 3102-4284 Quebec Inc)
2300 Rue Leon-Harmel Bureau 101, Quebec, QC, G1N 4L2
(418) 686-2300
Emp Here 125   Emp Total 252
Sales 20,013,336
SIC 1711 Plumbing, heating, air-conditioning
Pr Pr Gilles Shooner

D-U-N-S 24-940-9616   (BR)
BRIDGESTONE CANADA INC
GCR CENTRES DE PNEUS
120 Av Saint-Sacrement, Quebec, QC, G1N 3X6
(418) 681-0511
Emp Here 30
SIC 5014 Tires and tubes

D-U-N-S 20-515-9056   (SL)
BUANDRY PARANET INC
PARATEX, DIV DE
1105 Rue Vincent-Massey, Quebec, QC, G1N 1N2
(418) 688-0889
Emp Here 85   Sales 2,699,546
SIC 7219 Laundry and garment services, nec

D-U-N-S 24-623-0460   (HQ)
CPU SERVICE D'ORDINATEUR INC
C P U DESIGN
(Suby of CPU Service d'Ordinateur Inc)
2323 Boul Du Versant-Nord Bureau 100, Quebec, QC, G1N 4P4
(418) 681-1234
Emp Here 90   Emp Total 150
Sales 14,134,935
SIC 7378 Computer maintenance and repair
Pr Pr Lotfi Ghattas

Sylvain Tremblay

D-U-N-S 24-941-2313   (BR)
CANAC-MARQUIS GRENIER LTEE
49 Rue Marie-De-L'Incarnation, Quebec, QC, G1N 3E5
(418) 681-6221
Emp Here 40
SIC 5231 Paint, glass, and wallpaper stores

D-U-N-S 20-540-6312   (BR)
CANADA POST CORPORATION
660 Rue Graham-Bell, Quebec, QC, G1N 0B2
(418) 847-2160
Emp Here 100
SIC 4311 U.s. postal service

D-U-N-S 20-113-6442   (BR)
CASCADES CANADA ULC
UNE DIVISION DE CASCADE CANADA
1450 Rue Semple, Quebec, QC, G1N 4B4

Emp Here 150
SIC 2653 Corrugated and solid fiber boxes

D-U-N-S 20-188-3852   (HQ)
CERATEC INC
414 Av Saint-Sacrement, Quebec, QC, G1N 3Y3
(418) 681-0101
Emp Here 28   Emp Total 230
Sales 31,300,140
SIC 5032 Brick, stone, and related material
Pr Paul Raiche
VP Kenneth Raiche
VP VP Curtis Raiche
Sec Christian Houle

D-U-N-S 24-402-0090   (SL)
CLIVENCO INC
1185 Rue Philippe-Paradis Bureau 200, Quebec, QC, G1N 4E2
(418) 682-6373
Emp Here 50   Sales 6,028,800
SIC 1711 Plumbing, heating, air-conditioning
Owner Michel Blanchette

D-U-N-S 25-019-6052   (BR)
COMMISSION SCOLAIRE DE LA CAPITALE, LA
COMMISSION SCOLAIRE DE LA CAPITALE, LA
1060 Rue Borne, Quebec, QC, G1N 1L9
(418) 686-4040
Emp Here 80
SIC 8331 Job training and related services

D-U-N-S 25-232-9222   (BR)
COMMISSION SCOLAIRE DE LA CAPITALE, LA
COMMISSION SCOLAIRE DE LA CAPITALE, LA
286 Rue Marie-De-L'Incarnation, Quebec, QC, G1N 3G4
(418) 686-4040
Emp Here 50
SIC 8211 Elementary and secondary schools

D-U-N-S 24-340-8189   (SL)
DISTRI-CARR LTEE
214 Av Saint-Sacrement Bureau 130, Quebec, QC, G1N 3X6

Emp Here 126   Sales 26,895,840
SIC 6712 Bank holding companies
Pr Pr Viateur Gagnon

D-U-N-S 25-803-9171   (BR)
DOVER CORPORATION (CANADA) LIMITED
ASCENSEURS THYSSEN KRUPP
(Suby of Dover Corporation)
1990 Rue Cyrille-Duquet Bureau 146, Quebec, QC, G1N 4K8
(418) 682-1214
Emp Here 26
SIC 7699 Repair services, nec

D-U-N-S 20-241-5998   (BR)

EMCO CORPORATION
380 Rue Morse, Quebec, QC, G1N 4L4
(418) 681-4671
Emp Here 50
SIC 5074 Plumbing and heating equipment and supplies (hydronics)

D-U-N-S 24-395-0917   (SL)
ENDURIDE CANADA USA INC
1880 Rue Provinciale, Quebec, QC, G1N 4A2
(418) 266-7777
Emp Here 20   Sales 2,845,467
SIC 3535 Conveyors and conveying equipment

D-U-N-S 24-377-3702   (SL)
ENTREPRISES DE NETTOYAGE MARCEL LABBE INC
ML ENTRETIEN MULTI SERVICES
340 Rue Jackson, Quebec, QC, G1N 4C5
(418) 523-9411
Emp Here 120   Sales 3,502,114
SIC 7349 Building maintenance services, nec

D-U-N-S 20-952-9346   (HQ)
ENTREPRISES DE NETTOYAGE QUEBEC METRO INC, LES
SINISCO QUEBEC
(Suby of Entreprises de Nettoyage Quebec Metro Inc, Les)
375 Av Marconi, Quebec, QC, G1N 4A5
(418) 681-2231
Emp Here 60   Emp Total 125
Sales 4,888,367
SIC 8322 Individual and family services

D-U-N-S 25-765-0432   (BR)
FOURNITURES DE BUREAU DENIS INC
DENIS OFFICE SUPPLIES
(Suby of Placements Denis Latulippe Inc, Les)
1415 Rue Frank-Carrel, Quebec, QC, G1N 4N7
(418) 682-3113
Emp Here 20
SIC 5943 Stationery stores

D-U-N-S 20-979-9332   (BR)
GARAGE DESHARNAIS & FILS LTEE
DESHARNAIS PNEUS & MICANIQUE
710 Boul Charest O, Quebec, QC, G1N 2C1
(418) 628-0203
Emp Here 50
SIC 7538 General automotive repair shops

D-U-N-S 20-241-1864   (BR)
GENERAL ELECTRIC CANADA COMPANY
GE
(Suby of General Electric Company)
1130 Boul Charest O, Quebec, QC, G1N 2E2
(418) 682-8500
Emp Here 125
SIC 3625 Relays and industrial controls

D-U-N-S 25-257-5030   (SL)
GENICAD INC
(Suby of Ametek, Inc.)
2260 Rue Leon-Harmel, Quebec, QC, G1N 4L2
(418) 682-3313
Emp Here 40   Sales 5,104,320
SIC 8711 Engineering services
Pr Pr Jean-Paul Cyr
Bruno Henry

D-U-N-S 25-765-1778   (SL)
GESTION TRANS-ROUTE INC
2160 Rue Lavoisier, Quebec, QC, G1N 4B3
(418) 686-1133
Emp Here 60   Sales 4,377,642
SIC 7361 Employment agencies

D-U-N-S 25-335-4039   (BR)
GOUVERNEMENT DE LA PROVINCE DE QUEBEC
DIRECTION GENERALE DES TECHNOLOGIES DE L'INFORMATIONS ET DES COMMUNICATIONS
1500e Rue Cyrille-Duquet, Quebec, QC, G1N

4T6
(418) 643-1500
Emp Here 423
SIC 4899 Communication services, nec

D-U-N-S 20-702-9633   (BR)
GROUPE CANAM INC
CANAM BRIDGES
1445 Rue Du Grand-Tronc, Quebec, QC, G1N 4G1
(418) 683-2561
Emp Here 160
SIC 3443 Fabricated plate work (boiler shop)

D-U-N-S 25-392-5630   (SL)
GROUPE TRADITION'L INC
460 Av Marconi, Quebec, QC, G1N 4A8
(418) 687-3704
Emp Here 50   Sales 2,626,585
SIC 2051 Bread, cake, and related products

D-U-N-S 20-250-1318   (BR)
HONEYWELL LIMITED
(Suby of Honeywell International Inc.)
2366 Rue Galvani Bureau 4, Quebec, QC, G1N 4G4
(418) 688-8320
Emp Here 80
SIC 3822 Environmental controls

D-U-N-S 25-352-9879   (SL)
INFODEV ELECTRONIC DESIGNERS INTERNATIONAL INC
INFODEV
1995 Rue Frank-Carrel Bureau 202, Quebec, QC, G1N 4H9
(418) 681-3539
Emp Here 60   Sales 4,596,524
SIC 3571 Electronic computers

D-U-N-S 24-852-9815   (SL)
INNOVATION NUTAQ INC
NURAN WIRELESS
2150 Rue Cyrille-Duquet Bureau 100, Quebec, QC, G1N 2G3
(418) 914-7484
Emp Here 50   Sales 5,472,053
SIC 3679 Electronic components, nec
Pr Pr Martin Bedard
Pr Pr Patrice Rainville

D-U-N-S 24-226-4484   (BR)
INTEGRATED DISTRIBUTION SYSTEMS LIMITED PARTNERSHIP
WAJAX EQUIPMENT
205 Av Saint-Sacrement, Quebec, QC, G1N 3X5
(418) 681-3555
Emp Here 28
SIC 5084 Industrial machinery and equipment

D-U-N-S 24-522-3883   (BR)
JOHNSON CONTROLS NOVA SCOTIA U.L.C.
JOHNSON CONTROLS
(Suby of Johnson Controls, Inc.)
1375 Rue Frank-Carrel Bureau 3, Quebec, QC, G1N 2E7
(418) 681-7958
Emp Here 20
SIC 1711 Plumbing, heating, air-conditioning

D-U-N-S 20-295-7457   (BR)
KONICA MINOLTA BUSINESS SOLUTIONS (CANADA) LTD
KONICA MINOLTA QUEBEC
1995 Rue Frank-Carrel Bureau 106, Quebec, QC, G1N 4H9
(418) 687-5121
Emp Here 60
SIC 5999 Miscellaneous retail stores, nec

D-U-N-S 24-204-0152   (SL)
LALLIER AUTOMOBILE (QUEBEC) INC
LALLIER SAINTE-FOY
(Suby of 2543-3533 Quebec Inc)
2000 Rue Cyrille-Duquet, Quebec, QC, G1N 2E8

(418) 687-2525
Emp Here 100   *Sales* 49,080,000
SIC 5511 New and used car dealers
Pr Pr Jean-Louis Duplessis

D-U-N-S 20-912-1933   (BR)
MULTIVER LTEE
MULTIVER DIVISION ISOVER
1950 Rue Leon-Harmel, Quebec, QC, G1N
4K3
(418) 687-0770
Emp Here 100
SIC 3211 Flat glass

D-U-N-S 25-765-8039   (BR)
OTIS CANADA, INC
(*Suby of* United Technologies Corporation)
2022 Rue Lavoisier Bureau 160, Quebec, QC,
G1N 4L5
(418) 687-4848
Emp Here 40
SIC 7699 Repair services, nec

D-U-N-S 20-582-2349   (BR)
QUEBEC LINGE CO
QUEBEC LINGE, DIV OF
1230 Rue Des Artisans, Quebec, QC, G1N
4H3
(418) 683-4408
Emp Here 60
SIC 7213 Linen supply

D-U-N-S 24-790-5979   (SL)
REVENCO (1991) INC
1755 Rue Provinciale, Quebec, QC, G1N 4S9
(418) 682-5993
Emp Here 50   *Sales* 4,377,642
SIC 1731 Electrical work

D-U-N-S 25-543-0993   (BR)
SECURITE POLYGON INC
PROTECTION INCENDIE VIKING
1885 Rue Leon-Harmel, Quebec, QC, G1N
4K4
(418) 687-4222
Emp Here 30
SIC 1711 Plumbing, heating, air-conditioning

D-U-N-S 20-279-2862   (BR)
**SERVICE & CONSTRUCTION MOBILE
LTEE**
425 Rue Volta Bureau 201, Quebec, QC, G1N
4G5
(418) 688-5751
Emp Here 28
SIC 1799 Special trade contractors, nec

D-U-N-S 25-365-8066   (BR)
SERVICES DE PNEUS DESHARNAIS INC
DESHARNAIS PNEUS & MECANIQUE
710 Boul Charest O, Quebec, QC, G1N 2C1
(418) 681-6041
Emp Here 150
SIC 5531 Auto and home supply stores

D-U-N-S 24-073-5238   (SL)
SOUTEX INC
357 Rue Jackson Bureau 7, Quebec, QC, G1N
4C4
(418) 871-2455
Emp Here 50   *Sales* 4,961,328
SIC 8711 Engineering services

D-U-N-S 20-802-2348   (BR)
STAPLES CANADA INC
BUREAU EN GROS
(*Suby of* Staples, Inc.)
1400 Rue Cyrille-Duquet, Quebec, QC, G1N
2E5
(418) 527-4114
Emp Here 35
SIC 5943 Stationery stores

D-U-N-S 25-759-7328   (BR)
**THYSSENKRUPP ELEVATOR (CANADA)
LIMITED**
THYSSENKRUPP ELEVATOR
1990 Rue Cyrille-Duquet Bureau 146, Quebec, QC, G1N 4K8

(418) 682-1214
Emp Here 30
SIC 1796 Installing building equipment

D-U-N-S 24-379-2785   (HQ)
TRANSPORT BERNIERES INC
(*Suby of* 2331-7605 Quebec Inc)
1721 Rue A.-R.-Decary, Quebec, QC, G1N
3Z7
(418) 684-2421
Emp Here 170   *Emp Total* 200
Sales 32,657,663
SIC 4213 Trucking, except local
Pr Pr Daniel Bouchard

D-U-N-S 24-941-0606   (HQ)
TRANSPORT GUILBAULT CANADA INC
435 Rue Faraday, Quebec, QC, G1N 4G6
(514) 521-9023
Emp Here 200   *Emp Total* 250
Sales 137,768,500
SIC 4213 Trucking, except local
Pr Pr Jean Guilbault
VP VP Michel Gignac

D-U-N-S 25-484-1042   (BR)
TRANSPORT MORNEAU INC
902 Rue Philippe-Paradis, Quebec, QC, G1N
4E4
(418) 681-2727
Emp Here 30
SIC 4212 Local trucking, without storage

D-U-N-S 25-540-6977   (SL)
TRANSPORT THEBERGE LIMITEE
435 Rue Faraday, Quebec, QC, G1N 4G6
(418) 681-0575
Emp Here 20   *Sales* 2,407,703
SIC 4213 Trucking, except local

D-U-N-S 20-241-5113   (BR)
**TYCO INTEGRATED FIRE & SECURITY
CANADA, INC**
SIMPLEXGRINNELL
(*Suby of* Johnson Controls, Inc.)
1990 Rue Cyrille-Duquet Bureau 165, Quebec, QC, G1N 4K8
(418) 683-4937
Emp Here 20
SIC 5065 Electronic parts and equipment, nec

D-U-N-S 20-575-4273   (BR)
WESTON BAKERIES LIMITED
GROUPE TRADITIONEL
460 Av Marconi, Quebec, QC, G1N 4A8
(418) 687-3704
Emp Here 37
SIC 2051 Bread, cake, and related products

D-U-N-S 25-543-7030   (BR)
WOLSELEY INDUSTRIAL CANADA INC
ENDRIES INTERNATIONAL CANADA
(*Suby of* WOLSELEY PLC)
2150 Rue Lavoisier, Quebec, QC, G1N 4B1
(418) 683-2581
Emp Here 25
SIC 5084 Industrial machinery and equipment

Quebec, QC G1P
Quebec County

D-U-N-S 24-381-0772   (SL)
9184-2518 QUEBEC INC
LES INDUSTRIES ROCAND
2511 Boul Du Parc-Technologique, Quebec,
QC, G1P 4S5
(418) 656-9917
Emp Here 60   *Sales* 4,961,328
SIC 3544 Special dies, tools, jigs, and fixtures

D-U-N-S 24-805-7031   (BR)
ABB INC
3400 Rue Pierre-Ardouin, Quebec, QC, G1P
0B2
(418) 877-2944
Emp Here 200

SIC 3823 Process control instruments

D-U-N-S 24-792-1646   (SL)
APN INC
2659 Boul Du Parc-Technologique, Quebec,
QC, G1P 4S5
(418) 266-1247
Emp Here 45   *Sales* 6,407,837
SIC 3089 Plastics products, nec
Pr Pr Jean Proteau
    Yves Proteau
    Stephanie Laplante

D-U-N-S 24-650-7847   (BR)
ARAMARK CANADA LTD.
2350 Av Watt, Quebec, QC, G1P 4M7
(418) 650-2929
Emp Here 20
SIC 5812 Eating places

D-U-N-S 20-286-2707   (BR)
ACIER AGF INC
ACIER ECAN
595 Av Newton, Quebec, QC, G1P 4C4
(418) 877-7715
Emp Here 100
SIC 2499 Wood products, nec

D-U-N-S 24-391-4921   (BR)
AECOM CANADA LTD
AECOM CONSULTANTS
4700 Boul Wilfrid-Hamel, Quebec, QC, G1P
2J9
(418) 871-2444
Emp Here 100
SIC 8742 Management consulting services

D-U-N-S 20-242-1293   (HQ)
ALIMENTS KRISPY KERNELS INC
CROUSTILLES YUM YUM, DIV OF
2620 Av Watt, Quebec, QC, G1P 3T5
(418) 658-4640
Emp Here 100   *Emp Total* 500
SIC 2096 Potato chips and similar snacks

D-U-N-S 20-302-5432   (BR)
AMEUBLEMENTS TANGUAY INC
4875 Boul De L'Ormiere, Quebec, QC, G1P
1K6
(418) 871-4411
Emp Here 20
SIC 5712 Furniture stores

D-U-N-S 24-884-6305   (BR)
**APPLIED INDUSTRIAL TECHNOLOGIES,
LP**
PRO HYDRAULIQUE
(*Suby of* Applied Industrial Technologies, Inc.)
2584 Av Dalton, Quebec, QC, G1P 3S4
(418) 659-3924
Emp Here 40
SIC 3561 Pumps and pumping equipment

D-U-N-S 24-208-4403   (BR)
ARAMARK QUEBEC INC
3400 Boul Neuvialle, Quebec, QC, G1P 3A8
(418) 681-1459
Emp Here 21
SIC 5812 Eating places

D-U-N-S 20-616-0090   (BR)
**ATELIER DE READAPTATION AU TRAVAIL
DE BEAUCE INC**
A R T B
(*Suby of* Atelier de Readaptation au Travail de
Beauce Inc)
2485 Boul Neuvialle, Quebec, QC, G1P 3A6
(418) 682-0782
Emp Here 70
SIC 7349 Building maintenance services, nec

D-U-N-S 24-908-6687   (BR)
ATELIER LA FLECHE DE FER INC
AFFI
(*Suby of* Atelier la Fleche de Fer Inc)
1400 Av Galilee, Quebec, QC, G1P 4E3
(418) 683-2946
Emp Here 31
SIC 7629 Electrical repair shops

D-U-N-S 24-730-7374   (SL)
AUTOBUS B. R. INC
(*Suby of* Autobus Tremblay & Paradis Inc)
2625 Av Watt, Quebec, QC, G1P 3T2
(418) 653-9199
Emp Here 20   *Sales* 561,797
SIC 4151 School buses

D-U-N-S 20-289-7518   (BR)
**AXXESS INTERNATIONAL COURTIERS EN
DOUANES INC**
(*Suby of* 6668437 Canada Inc)
360 Rue Franquet Bureau 110, Quebec, QC,
G1P 4N3
(418) 658-0390
Emp Here 20
SIC 4731 Freight transportation arrangement

D-U-N-S 25-285-7578   (HQ)
BPR INC
ASSEAU-BPR
(*Suby of* Tetra Tech, Inc.)
4655 Boul Wilfrid-Hamel, Quebec, QC, G1P
2J7
(418) 871-8151
Emp Here 300   *Emp Total* 16,000
Sales 244,629,282
SIC 8711 Engineering services
Pr Denis Harvie
VP Dan L. Batrack
    Richard A. Lemmon
Sec Francois Morin
Treas Steven M. Burdick

D-U-N-S 24-335-7071   (SL)
BIOCAD MEDICALE INC
(*Suby of* Services Nobel Biocare Procera Inc)
750 Boul Du Parc-Technologique, Quebec,
QC, G1P 4S3
(418) 683-8435
Emp Here 40   *Sales* 5,325,440
SIC 3842 Surgical appliances and supplies
    Jean Robichaud
    Alain Allard
    Serge Carey

D-U-N-S 20-722-9659   (HQ)
BRASSARD BURO INC
(*Suby of* Brassard Buro Inc)
2747 Av Watt, Quebec, QC, G1P 3X3
(418) 657-5500
Emp Here 47   *Emp Total* 50
Sales 3,648,035
SIC 5112 Stationery and office supplies

D-U-N-S 24-593-1944   (SL)
CTRL INFORMATIQUE LTEE
3650 Boul Wilfrid-Hamel, Quebec, QC, G1P
2J2
(418) 650-2875
Emp Here 41   *Sales* 5,124,480
SIC 7371 Custom computer programming services
Pr Daniel Girard
Treas Charles Gauthier
    Philippe Constant
    Isabelle Rioux
    Pierre Aubin

D-U-N-S 25-762-6705   (BR)
CAFETERIA DE LA CAPITALE INC
CAFETERIA DE LA CAPITALE INC
(*Suby of* Placements Helmic Ltee)
2590 Av Watt, Quebec, QC, G1P 4S2
(418) 653-3329
Emp Here 60
SIC 5812 Eating places

D-U-N-S 20-723-7785   (SL)
CAFETERIAS MONCHATEAU LTEE
SERVICES ALIMENTAIRES MONCHATEAU
(*Suby of* Placements Helmic Ltee)
455 Rue Braille, Quebec, QC, G1P 3V2
(418) 653-8331
Emp Here 20   *Sales* 2,991,389
SIC 5812 Eating places

D-U-N-S 24-639-3383   (SL)

CAMIONS FREIGHTLINER QUEBEC INC
2380 Av Dalton, Quebec, QC, G1P 3X1
(418) 657-2425
Emp Here 62   *Sales* 30,429,600
SIC 5511 New and used car dealers
Pr Pr Denis Jalbert
  Bernard Moisan
Genl Mgr Claude Harvey

D-U-N-S 20-777-9620   (BR)
CENTURA QUEBEC LTEE
CENTURA QUEBEC
(*Suby of* Centura Limited)
2699 Av Watt, Quebec, QC, G1P 3X3
(418) 653-5267
Emp Here 42
SIC 5023 Homefurnishings

D-U-N-S 20-711-8642   (BR)
COMMISSION SCOLAIRE CENTRAL QUE-BEC
EVEREST ELEMENTARY SCHOOL
2280 Rue Laverdiere, Quebec, QC, G1P 2T3
(418) 688-8229
Emp Here 40
SIC 8211 Elementary and secondary schools

D-U-N-S 25-232-3290   (BR)
COMMISSION SCOLAIRE DE LA CAPI-TALE, LA
ECOLE GRANDS-SAULES-ECRIVAINS
4400 Rue Jacques-Crepeault, Quebec, QC, G1P 1X5
(418) 686-4040
Emp Here 25
SIC 8211 Elementary and secondary schools

D-U-N-S 20-712-0564   (BR)
COMMISSION SCOLAIRE DE LA CAPI-TALE, LA
ECOLE SAINTE MONIQUE
4120 Rue De Musset, Quebec, QC, G1P 1P1

Emp Here 50
SIC 8211 Elementary and secondary schools

D-U-N-S 25-233-8363   (BR)
COMMISSION SCOLAIRE DE LA CAPI-TALE, LA
ECOLE JEAN XXIII
3690 Rue Antonin-Marquis, Quebec, QC, G1P 3B9
(418) 686-4040
Emp Here 25
SIC 8211 Elementary and secondary schools

D-U-N-S 25-002-1425   (BR)
COMMISSION SCOLAIRE DE LA CAPI-TALE, LA
ECOLE DU BUISSON
5385 Av Banville, Quebec, QC, G1P 1H7
(418) 686-4040
Emp Here 28
SIC 8211 Elementary and secondary schools

D-U-N-S 20-712-0549   (BR)
COMMISSION SCOLAIRE DE LA CAPI-TALE, LA
ECOLE SECONDAIRE LA CAMARADIERE
3400 Boul Neuvialle, Quebec, QC, G1P 3A8
(418) 686-4040
Emp Here 50
SIC 8211 Elementary and secondary schools

D-U-N-S 25-842-1148   (HQ)
COMMUNICATION DEMO INC
(*Suby of* Communication Demo Inc)
925 Av Newton Bureau 220, Quebec, QC, G1P 4M2
(418) 877-0704
Emp Here 30   *Emp Total* 60
Sales 3,064,349
SIC 7389 Business services, nec

D-U-N-S 24-907-4329   (SL)
CONCEPTION R. P. INC
CRP
405 Av Galilee, Quebec, QC, G1P 4M6

(418) 871-6016
Emp Here 50   *Sales* 4,888,367
SIC 3553 Woodworking machinery

D-U-N-S 20-284-6601   (BR)
CONSULTANTS AECOM INC
AECOM TECSULT
4700 Boul Wilfrid-Hamel, Quebec, QC, G1P 2J9
(418) 871-2452
Emp Here 80
SIC 8711 Engineering services

D-U-N-S 25-466-1309   (BR)
COOPERATIVE DES CONSOMMATEURS DE LORETTEVILLE
IGA COOP DUBERGER
2300 Boul Pere-Lelievre, Quebec, QC, G1P 2X5
(418) 682-4197
Emp Here 50
SIC 5411 Grocery stores

D-U-N-S 20-874-4227   (SL)
CORPS CANADIEN DES COMMISSION-NAIRES DIVISION DE QUEBEC
COMMISSIONNAIRE QUEBEC
3405 Boul Wilfrid-Hamel Bureau 330, Quebec, QC, G1P 2J3
(418) 681-0609
Emp Here 600   *Sales* 25,128,960
SIC 7381 Detective and armored car services
Pr Jean-Yves Lauzier

D-U-N-S 20-722-9352   (SL)
EDITION LE TELEPHONE ROUGE INC
GROUPE ETR
2555 Av Watt Bureau 6, Quebec, QC, G1P 3T2
(418) 658-8122
Emp Here 80   *Sales* 4,085,799
SIC 7331 Direct mail advertising services

D-U-N-S 20-644-8701   (SL)
ENVIRONNEMENT (MINIST RE DE L')
CENTRE D'EXPERTISE EN ANALYSE ENVI-RONNEMENTALE DU QUEBEC
2700 Rue Einstein, Quebec, QC, G1P 3W8
(418) 643-8225
Emp Here 49   *Sales* 5,496,960
SIC 8748 Business consulting, nec
Genl Mgr Guy Chouinard

D-U-N-S 25-222-9703   (BR)
FPINNOVATIONS
319 Rue Franquet, Quebec, QC, G1P 4R4
(418) 659-2647
Emp Here 100
SIC 8731 Commercial physical research

D-U-N-S 25-765-5407   (BR)
G&K SERVICES CANADA INC
(*Suby of* Cintas Corporation)
2665 Av Dalton Bureau 10, Quebec, QC, G1P 3S8
(418) 658-0044
Emp Here 8,000
SIC 7218 Industrial launderers

D-U-N-S 25-903-0930   (BR)
GSI ENVIRONNEMENT INC
4495 Boul Wilfrid-Hamel Bureau 100, Quebec, QC, G1P 2J7
(418) 872-4227
Emp Here 200
SIC 8748 Business consulting, nec

D-U-N-S 24-380-8045   (BR)
GAZ METRO INC
GAZ METROPOLITAIN EN COMMANDITE
2388 Rue Einstein, Quebec, QC, G1P 4T1
(418) 577-5555
Emp Here 60
SIC 4923 Gas transmission and distribution

D-U-N-S 25-543-8483   (SL)
GENEOHM SCIENCES CANADA INC
BD DIAGNOSTIC
(*Suby of* Becton, Dickinson and Company)

2555 Boul Du Parc-Technologique, Quebec, QC, G1P 4S5
(418) 780-5800
Emp Here 230   *Sales* 9,268,886
SIC 2835 Diagnostic substances
Pr A. William Kozy
Sec Gary M Defazio
Dir Richard A Carbone

D-U-N-S 24-378-2575   (BR)
GOUVERNEMENT DE LA PROVINCE DE QUEBEC
MINISTERE DE DEVELOPPEMENT DE L'ENVIRONNEMENT
2700 Rue Einstein Bureau E-2-220, Quebec, QC, G1P 3W8
(418) 643-1301
Emp Here 60
SIC 8748 Business consulting, nec

D-U-N-S 20-179-5346   (BR)
GOUVERNEMENT DE LA PROVINCE DE QUEBEC
DIRECTION DES LABORATOIRES D'EXPERTISES ET D'ANALYSES ALIMEN-TAIRES
2700 Rue Einstein Bureau C2105, Quebec, QC, G1P 3W8
(418) 643-1632
Emp Here 75
SIC 8731 Commercial physical research

D-U-N-S 20-432-2564   (SL)
HICHAUD INC
2485 Boul Neuvialle, Quebec, QC, G1P 3A6
(418) 682-0782
Emp Here 60   *Sales* 1,751,057
SIC 3149 Footwear, except rubber, nec

D-U-N-S 20-302-5499   (BR)
HUOT, REAL INC
(*Suby of* Entreprises Mirca Inc, Les)
2550 Av Dalton, Quebec, QC, G1P 3S4
(418) 651-2121
Emp Here 22
SIC 5085 Industrial supplies

D-U-N-S 24-145-0949   (HQ)
HUOT, REAL INC
(*Suby of* Entreprises Mirca Inc, Les)
2640 Av Dalton, Quebec, QC, G1P 3S4
(418) 634-5967
Emp Here 24   *Emp Total* 1,342
Sales 18,240,175
SIC 5085 Industrial supplies
Pr Pr Martin Deschenes
  Jacques Deschenes
  Marc Lapierre
VP VP Francois Deschenes

D-U-N-S 25-526-0184   (HQ)
ID BIOMEDICAL CORPORATION OF QUE-BEC
GLAXOSMITHKLINE BIOLOGICAL NORTH AMERICA
2323 Boul Du Parc-Technologique, Quebec, QC, G1P 4R8
(450) 978-4599
Emp Here 100   *Emp Total* 99,817
Sales 96,933,487
SIC 8731 Commercial physical research
Dir Loren Cooper
Dir Vahe Kalusyan

D-U-N-S 24-336-8284   (BR)
ID BIOMEDICAL CORPORATION OF QUE-BEC
GLAXOSMITHKLINE BIOLOGICALS NORTH AMERICA
2323 Boul Du Parc-Technologique, Quebec, QC, G1P 4R8
(418) 650-0010
Emp Here 20
SIC 8731 Commercial physical research

D-U-N-S 25-211-9292   (HQ)
INVENTIV HEALTH CLINIQUE INC
(*Suby of* Inc Research Holdings, Inc.)

2500 Rue Einstein, Quebec, QC, G1P 0A2
(418) 527-4000
Emp Here 500   *Emp Total* 13,512
Sales 51,715,185
SIC 8731 Commercial physical research
Pr Pr Riaz Bandali
  Jesse Moore
  Eric Green
Pr Pr Richard Shimota
Dir Michael A. Gerrior

D-U-N-S 25-685-1981   (HQ)
INSTITUT DE RECHERCHE ET DEVEL-OPPEMENT EN AGROENVIRONNEMENT INC
I.R.D.A.
(*Suby of* Institut de Recherche et Developpe-ment en Agroenvironement Inc)
2700 Rue Einstein Bureau D1110, Quebec, QC, G1P 3W8
(418) 643-2380
Emp Here 50   *Emp Total* 121
Sales 8,480,961
SIC 8731 Commercial physical research
Pr Pr Jacques Lebuis
  Guy Lessard
  Harvey Mead
  Gaetan Poire
Sec Gisele Grandbois
Treas Sylvain Boucher
  Pierre Baril
  Jean-Guy Vincent
  Guy Debailleul
  Marlene Thiboutot

D-U-N-S 24-374-9970   (BR)
KONE INC
1730 Av Newton Bureau 208, Quebec, QC, G1P 4J4
(418) 877-2183
Emp Here 70
SIC 1796 Installing building equipment

D-U-N-S 25-292-8551   (BR)
LABATT BREWING COMPANY LIMITED
375 Rue Lachance, Quebec, QC, G1P 2H3
(418) 687-5050
Emp Here 30
SIC 5921 Liquor stores

D-U-N-S 24-618-3495   (BR)
LOOMIS EXPRESS
2725 Av Dalton, Quebec, QC, G1P 3T1
(418) 659-1299
Emp Here 30
SIC 7389 Business services, nec

D-U-N-S 24-099-7333   (SL)
MYCA SANTE INC
2800 Rue Louis-Lumiere Bureau 200, Que-bec, QC, G1P 0A4
(418) 683-7878
Emp Here 50   *Sales* 2,772,507
SIC 7374 Data processing and preparation

D-U-N-S 24-531-5734   (SL)
MACK STE-FOY INC
2550 Av Watt, Quebec, QC, G1P 3T4
(418) 651-9397
Emp Here 49   *Sales* 30,625,920
SIC 5012 Automobiles and other motor vehi-cles
Pr Pr Simon Poire
VP VP Eric Poire

D-U-N-S 20-330-0900   (BR)
MATERIAUX AUDET INC
2795 Boul Pere-Lelievre, Quebec, QC, G1P 2X9
(418) 681-6261
Emp Here 50
SIC 5039 Construction materials, nec

D-U-N-S 20-198-2261   (BR)
METRO RICHELIEU INC
EPICERIE QUEBEC
635 Av Newton, Quebec, QC, G1P 4C4

(418) 871-7101
Emp Here 225
SIC 5141 Groceries, general line

D-U-N-S 20-120-9934   (BR)
PREMOULE INC
2375 Av Dalton Unite 200, Quebec, QC, G1P 3S3
(418) 652-1422
Emp Here 250
SIC 2434 Wood kitchen cabinets

D-U-N-S 25-857-5893   (BR)
PROVIGO DISTRIBUTION INC
MAXI LES SAULES
5150 Boul De L'Ormiere, Quebec, QC, G1P 4B2
(418) 872-3366
Emp Here 75
SIC 5411 Grocery stores

D-U-N-S 25-197-9878   (BR)
QUINCAILLERIE RICHELIEU LTEE
DISTRIBUTIONS 2020
4500 Boul Wilfrid-Hamel, Quebec, QC, G1P 2J9
(418) 872-5310
Emp Here 55
SIC 5251 Hardware stores

D-U-N-S 25-767-0380   (BR)
RESTAURANT NORMANDIN INC
2185 Boul Pere-Lelievre, Quebec, QC, G1P 2X2
(418) 683-4967
Emp Here 25
SIC 5812 Eating places

D-U-N-S 20-778-5395   (BR)
RODRIGUE METAL LTEE
(Suby of Canerector Inc)
2515 Av Dalton, Quebec, QC, G1P 3S5
(418) 653-9371
Emp Here 22
SIC 1791 Structural steel erection

D-U-N-S 25-362-4720   (BR)
ROYAL GROUP, INC
PRODUITS DE BATIMENT RESIDENTIEL
2395 Av Watt, Quebec, QC, G1P 3X2
(418) 653-6655
Emp Here 30
SIC 5039 Construction materials, nec

D-U-N-S 25-198-7368   (BR)
SGS CANADA INC
1300 Boul Du Parc-Technologique, Quebec, QC, G1P 4S3
(418) 683-2163
Emp Here 25
SIC 8734 Testing laboratories

D-U-N-S 20-119-2096   (HQ)
SADE CANADA INC
1564 Av Ampere, Quebec, QC, G1P 4B9
(581) 300-7233
Emp Here 20   *Emp Total* 1,019
Sales 5,370,756
SIC 1623 Water, sewer, and utility lines
Pr Philippe Voisin
Genl Mgr Stephane Bernard

D-U-N-S 24-111-7022   (BR)
SERVICES G&K (QUEBEC) INC, LES
SERVICES GK, LES
(Suby of Services G&K (Quebec) Inc, Les)
2665 Av Dalton Bureau 10, Quebec, QC, G1P 3S8
(418) 658-0044
Emp Here 30
SIC 7299 Miscellaneous personal service

D-U-N-S 24-631-2719   (BR)
SERVICES G&K (QUEBEC) INC, LES
G & K SERVICES
(Suby of Services G&K (Quebec) Inc, Les)
2665 Av Dalton Bureau 10, Quebec, QC, G1P 3S8
(418) 658-0044
Emp Here 20

SIC 7213 Linen supply

D-U-N-S 25-494-4416   (SL)
SILICYCLE INC
SILICA SERVING CHEMISTRY
2500 Boul Du Parc-Technologique, Quebec, QC, G1P 4S6
(418) 874-0054
Emp Here 50   *Sales* 10,506,341
SIC 2819 Industrial inorganic chemicals, nec
Pr Pr Hugo St-Laurent
Pr Johane Boucher-Champagne
Dir Luc Fortier
Dir Serge Olivier
Dir Emile Langlois
Dir Pierre Plante
Dir Francois Morissette
Dir Louis Laflamme

D-U-N-S 25-475-1290   (BR)
SOBEYS CAPITAL INCORPORATED
IGA EXTRA
5005 Boul De L'Ormiere Bureau 445, Quebec, QC, G1P 1K6
(418) 877-3922
Emp Here 130
SIC 5411 Grocery stores

D-U-N-S 24-821-3977   (BR)
SOBEYS QUEBEC INC
950 Av Galilee Bureau 2008, Quebec, QC, G1P 4B7
(418) 681-1922
Emp Here 400
SIC 5141 Groceries, general line

D-U-N-S 25-959-9124   (BR)
SOCIETE QUEBECOISE DES INFRAS-TRUCTURES
2700 Rue Einstein Bureau Erc130, Quebec, QC, G1P 3W8
(418) 643-7846
Emp Here 35
SIC 6512 Nonresidential building operators

D-U-N-S 25-914-1047   (BR)
SOLOTECH INC
935 Rue Lachance Bureau 200, Quebec, QC, G1P 2H3
(418) 683-5553
Emp Here 100
SIC 3645 Residential lighting fixtures

D-U-N-S 20-582-0681   (BR)
STRONGCO ENGINEERED SYSTEMS INC
2550 Av Dalton, Quebec, QC, G1P 3S4
(418) 653-2801
Emp Here 25
SIC 5084 Industrial machinery and equipment

D-U-N-S 25-690-0895   (SL)
TSO3 INC
2505 Av Dalton, Quebec, QC, G1P 3S5
(418) 651-0003
Emp Here 62   *Sales* 379,347
SIC 3842 Surgical appliances and supplies

D-U-N-S 25-803-8967   (BR)
TECSULT INTERNATIONAL LIMITEE
AECOM CONSULTANTS
4700 Boul Wilfrid-Hamel Bureau 200, Quebec, QC, G1P 2J9
(418) 871-2444
Emp Here 60
SIC 8711 Engineering services

D-U-N-S 20-628-8925   (BR)
TETRA TECH INDUSTRIES INC
(Suby of Tetra Tech, Inc.)
4655 Boul Wilfrid-Hamel, Quebec, QC, G1P 2J7
(418) 872-8151
Emp Here 120
SIC 8711 Engineering services

D-U-N-S 20-151-7666   (BR)
WAJAX INDUSTRIAL COMPONENTS LIM-ITED PARTNERSHIP
WAJX INDUSTRIAL COMPONENTS

2785 Boul Wilfrid-Hamel, Quebec, QC, G1P 2H9
(418) 687-0204
Emp Here 25
SIC 5084 Industrial machinery and equipment

Quebec, QC G1R
Quebec County

D-U-N-S 24-344-9316   (BR)
6362222 CANADA INC
GROUPE CREATECH
930 Rue D'Aiguillon, Quebec, QC, G1R 5M9
(418) 780-2080
Emp Here 29
SIC 8742 Management consulting services

D-U-N-S 20-291-0238   (SL)
8815003 CANADA INC
CONCORDE, LE
1225 Cours Du General-De Montcalm, Quebec, QC, G1R 4W6
(418) 647-2222
Emp Here 50   *Sales* 2,188,821
SIC 7011 Hotels and motels

D-U-N-S 24-170-1734   (BR)
9193-9298 QUEBEC INC
SUSHI TAXI
813 Av Cartier, Quebec, QC, G1R 2R8
(418) 529-0068
Emp Here 30
SIC 5812 Eating places

D-U-N-S 24-908-8469   (BR)
ASHTON CASSE-CROUTE INC
ASHTON
(Suby of Placements Ashton LeBlond Inc, Les)
640 Grande Allee E, Quebec, QC, G1R 2K5
(418) 522-3449
Emp Here 20
SIC 5812 Eating places

D-U-N-S 20-574-6493   (BR)
ASTRAL MEDIA AFFICHAGE, S.E.C.
ENERGIE 98.9
900 Place D'Youville, Quebec, QC, G1R 3P7
(418) 687-9900
Emp Here 50
SIC 4832 Radio broadcasting stations

D-U-N-S 20-910-9979   (BR)
BANQUE NATIONALE DU CANADA
150 Boul Rene-Levesque E, Quebec, QC, G1R 5B1
(418) 647-6100
Emp Here 30
SIC 6021 National commercial banks

D-U-N-S 20-520-2901   (BR)
BANQUE NATIONALE DU CANADA
EPARGNE PLACEMENTS QUEBEC BANQUE NATIONAL
333 Grande Allee E Bureau 400, Quebec, QC, G1R 5W3
(418) 521-6400
Emp Here 75
SIC 6021 National commercial banks

D-U-N-S 25-247-0836   (SL)
BEAUVAIS, TRUCHON & ASSOCIES
79 Boul Rene-Levesque E Bureau 200, Quebec, QC, G1R 5N5
(418) 692-4180
Emp Here 55   *Sales* 4,742,446
SIC 8111 Legal services

D-U-N-S 24-591-3033   (BR)
BERLITZ CANADA INC
900 Boul Rene-Levesque E Bureau 850, Quebec, QC, G1R 2B5

Emp Here 30
SIC 8299 Schools and educational services, nec

D-U-N-S 20-950-5973   (SL)
BOURGABEC INC
CHEZ DAGOBERT
600 Grande Allee E, Quebec, QC, G1R 2K5
(418) 522-0393
Emp Here 75   *Sales* 2,772,507
SIC 5813 Drinking places

D-U-N-S 20-954-9091   (BR)
CAIN LAMARRE CASGRAIN WELLS, S.E.N.C.R.L.
(Suby of Cain Lamarre Casgrain Wells, S.E.N.C.R.L.)
580 Grande Allee E Bureau 440, Quebec, QC, G1R 2K2
(418) 681-7200
Emp Here 60
SIC 8111 Legal services

D-U-N-S 24-369-1966   (BR)
CAISSE DESJARDINS DU PLATEAU MONT-CALM
CENTRE DE SERVICES PLACE D'AFFAIRES DE BOURLAMAQUE
1165 Av De Bourlamaque, Quebec, QC, G1R 2P9

Emp Here 25
SIC 6062 State credit unions

D-U-N-S 24-368-8640   (BR)
CAISSE POPULAIRE DESJARDINS DE QUEBEC
CENTRE DE SERVICE SAINT-JEAN
550 Rue Saint-Jean, Quebec, QC, G1R 1P6
(418) 522-6806
Emp Here 40
SIC 6062 State credit unions

D-U-N-S 20-581-6549   (BR)
CANADIAN BROADCASTING CORPORA-TION
RADIO CANADA
888 Rue Saint-Jean Unite 224, Quebec, QC, G1R 5H6
(418) 656-8206
Emp Here 250
SIC 4832 Radio broadcasting stations

D-U-N-S 20-777-7749   (HQ)
CAPITALE ASSUREUR DE L'ADMINISTRATION PUBLIQUE INC, LA
CAPITALE CARD
625 Rue Jacques-Parizeau, Quebec, QC, G1R 2G5
(418) 644-4106
Emp Here 400   *Emp Total* 3,000
Sales 2,920,397,939
SIC 6311 Life insurance
Pr Jean St-Gelais
VP Dominique Dubuc
Sec Pierre Marc Bellavance
Dir Francois Latreille
Dir Richard Fiset
Dir Danielle Chevrette
Dir Alain Briere
Dir Josee Germain
Dir Jacques Cotton
Dir Nathalie Tremblay

D-U-N-S 24-531-8985   (HQ)
CAPITALE GESTION FINANCIERE INC, LA
CARTE CAPITALE
625 Rue Saint-Amable, Quebec, QC, G1R 2G5
(418) 643-3884
Emp Here 30   *Emp Total* 3,000
Sales 3,141,120
SIC 7389 Business services, nec

D-U-N-S 25-762-6879   (SL)
CAPITOLE DE QUEBEC INC, LE
HOTEL DU CAPITOLE
972 Rue Saint-Jean, Quebec, QC, G1R 1R5
(418) 694-9930
Emp Here 275   *Sales* 11,190,240

▲ Public Company   ■ Public Company Family Member   **HQ** Headquarters   **BR** Branch   **SL** Single Location

SIC 5812 Eating places
Pr Pr Jean Pilote

D-U-N-S 20-294-1519   (BR)
CENTRE HOSPITALIER UNIVERSITAIRE DE QUEBEC
CHUQ PAVILLON HOTEL DIEU DE QUEBEC
9 Rue Mcmahon, Quebec, QC, G1R 3S3
(418) 691-5281
Emp Here 300
SIC 8732 Commercial nonphysical research

D-U-N-S 24-045-4251   (BR)
CENTRE HOSPITALIER UNIVERSITAIRE DE QUEBEC
CHUQ
11 Cote Du Palais Bureau 3431, Quebec, QC, G1R 2J6
(418) 525-4444
Emp Here 400
SIC 8062 General medical and surgical hospitals

D-U-N-S 24-080-0677   (BR)
CENTRE INTEGRE UNIVERSITAIRE DE SANTE ET DE SERVICES SOCIAUX DE LA CAPITALE-NATIONALE, LE
175 Rue Saint-Jean, Quebec, QC, G1R 1N4
(418) 648-6166
Emp Here 20
SIC 8011 Offices and clinics of medical doctors

D-U-N-S 25-433-5771   (BR)
CENTRE DE SANTE ET DE SERVICES SOCIAUX DE LA VIEILLE-CAPITALE
55 Ch Sainte-Foy, Quebec, QC, G1R 1S9
(418) 641-2572
Emp Here 95
SIC 8011 Offices and clinics of medical doctors

D-U-N-S 20-241-9909   (SL)
COGIRES INC
HOTEL CHATEAU LAURIER QUEBEC
1220 Place George-V O, Quebec, QC, G1R 5B8
(418) 522-3848
Emp Here 100   Sales 4,377,642
SIC 7011 Hotels and motels

D-U-N-S 24-170-8481   (BR)
COLLEGE O'SULLIVAN DE QUEBEC INC
COLLEGE O'SULLIVAN DE QUEBEC INC
(Suby of College O'sullivan De Quebec Inc)
600 Rue Saint-Jean, Quebec, QC, G1R 1P8
(418) 529-3355
Emp Here 20
SIC 8249 Vocational schools, nec

D-U-N-S 20-169-5314   (BR)
COMMISSION SCOLAIRE CENTRAL QUEBEC
ST PATRICK'S HIGH SCHOOL
75 Rue De Maisonneuve, Quebec, QC, G1R 2C4
(418) 525-8421
Emp Here 50
SIC 8211 Elementary and secondary schools

D-U-N-S 25-232-0775   (BR)
COMMISSION SCOLAIRE DE LA CAPITALE, LA
ECOLE JOSEPH FRANCOIS PERRAULT
140 Ch Sainte-Foy, Quebec, QC, G1R 1T2
(418) 686-4040
Emp Here 70
SIC 8211 Elementary and secondary schools

D-U-N-S 25-298-6245   (BR)
COMMISSION SCOLAIRE DE LA CAPITALE, LA
ECOLE ST JEAN BAPTISTE
370 Rue Saint-Jean, Quebec, QC, G1R 1P2
(418) 686-4040
Emp Here 40
SIC 8211 Elementary and secondary schools

D-U-N-S 20-213-1004   (BR)
CONCEPTS ZONE INC, LES
999 Av Cartier, Quebec, QC, G1R 2S2
(418) 522-7373
Emp Here 20
SIC 3999 Manufacturing industries, nec

D-U-N-S 25-456-0006   (SL)
COSMOS CAFE INC
575 Grande Allee E, Quebec, QC, G1R 2K4
(418) 640-0606
Emp Here 60   Sales 1,824,018
SIC 5812 Eating places

D-U-N-S 24-591-7190   (HQ)
ENTREPRISES J'OSE LTEE
ESCOMPTE-COIFFE
(Suby of Entreprises J'Ose Ltee)
165 Ch Sainte-Foy, Quebec, QC, G1R 1T1
(418) 648-9750
Emp Here 50   Emp Total 100
Sales 1,969,939
SIC 7231 Beauty shops

D-U-N-S 24-335-7717   (BR)
FASKEN MARTINEAU DUMOULIN LLP
140 Grande Allee E Bureau 800, Quebec, QC, G1R 5M8
(418) 640-2000
Emp Here 100
SIC 8111 Legal services

D-U-N-S 24-343-1579   (BR)
FINANCIERE BANQUE NATIONALE INC
NATIONAL BANK
500 Grande Allee E Bureau 400, Quebec, QC, G1R 2J7
(418) 649-2525
Emp Here 70
SIC 6211 Security brokers and dealers

D-U-N-S 20-925-6895   (BR)
GESTION N. AUGER INC
RESTAURANT MCDONALD'S
(Suby of Gestion N. Auger Inc)
649 Grande Allee E, Quebec, QC, G1R 2K4
(418) 524-2439
Emp Here 25
SIC 5812 Eating places

D-U-N-S 20-007-4255   (BR)
GOUVERNEMENT DE LA PROVINCE DE QUEBEC
COMMISSION D'EVALUATION DE L'ENSEIGNEMENT COLLEGIALE
800 Place D'Youville Bureau 18 1, Quebec, QC, G1R 3P4
(418) 643-9938
Emp Here 30
SIC 8748 Business consulting, nec

D-U-N-S 20-332-9672   (BR)
GOUVERNEMENT DE LA PROVINCE DE QUEBEC
MUSEE NATIONAL DES BEAUX ARTS DU QUEBEC
1 Av Wolfe-Montcalm, Quebec, QC, G1R 5H3
(418) 643-2150
Emp Here 100
SIC 8412 Museums and art galleries

D-U-N-S 20-642-0890   (BR)
GOUVERNEMENT DE LA PROVINCE DE QUEBEC
PROTECTEUR DU CITOYEN, LE
525 Boul Rene-Levesque E Bureau 125, Quebec, QC, G1R 5Y4
(418) 643-2688
Emp Here 150
SIC 8111 Legal services

D-U-N-S 24-386-8358   (BR)
GOUVERNEMENT DE LA PROVINCE DE QUEBEC
GOUVERNEMENT DE LA PROVINCE DE QUEBEC
150 Boul Rene-Levesque E, Quebec, QC, G1R 5B1

(418) 646-4646
Emp Here 450
SIC 8742 Management consulting services

D-U-N-S 20-137-5255   (BR)
GOUVERNEMENT DE LA PROVINCE DE QUEBEC
GOUVERNEMENT DE LA PROVINCE DE QUEBEC
800 Place D'Youville Bureau 300, Quebec, QC, G1R 6E2
(418) 643-4326
Emp Here 50
SIC 8732 Commercial nonphysical research

D-U-N-S 20-585-5351   (BR)
GOUVERNEMENT DE LA PROVINCE DE QUEBEC
CONSERVATOIRE DE MUSIQUE DE QUEBEC
270 Rue Jacques-Parizeau, Quebec, QC, G1R 5G1
(418) 643-2190
Emp Here 20
SIC 8299 Schools and educational services, nec

D-U-N-S 25-335-3445   (BR)
GOUVERNEMENT DE LA PROVINCE DE QUEBEC
INSTITUT DE LA STATISTIQUE DE QUEBEC
200 Ch Sainte-Foy 3e Etage Bureau 300, Quebec, QC, G1R 5T4
(418) 691-2401
Emp Here 250
SIC 2721 Periodicals

D-U-N-S 25-366-0252   (BR)
GOUVERNEMENT DE LA PROVINCE DE QUEBEC
GOUVERNEMENT DE LA PROVINCE DE QUEBEC
800 Place D'Youville Bureau 12e, Quebec, QC, G1R 5S3
(418) 643-7150
Emp Here 40
SIC 7389 Business services, nec

D-U-N-S 24-623-2037   (BR)
GOUVERNEMENT DE LA PROVINCE DE QUEBEC
REGIE DU BATIMENT DU QUEBEC DIRECTION TERRITORIAL DE L'EST DU QUEBEC
800 Place D'Youville, Quebec, QC, G1R 5S3
(418) 643-7150
Emp Here 30
SIC 7389 Business services, nec

D-U-N-S 24-340-4394   (BR)
GOUVERNEMENT DE LA PROVINCE DE QUEBEC
BIBLIOTHEQUE CECILE ROULEAU
700 Rue Jacques-Parizeau Unite 307, Quebec, QC, G1R 5E5
(418) 643-1515
Emp Here 30
SIC 8231 Libraries

D-U-N-S 25-081-9943   (SL)
GRILL VOO DOO LTEE, LE
575 Grande Allee E Suite 200, Quebec, QC, G1R 2K4
(418) 647-2000
Emp Here 60   Sales 1,824,018
SIC 5812 Eating places

D-U-N-S 25-765-7056   (BR)
GROUPE IBI/DAA INC
580 Grande Allee E Bureau 590, Quebec, QC, G1R 2K2
(418) 522-0300
Emp Here 21
SIC 8748 Business consulting, nec

D-U-N-S 25-744-7847   (BR)
GROUPE RESTOS PLAISIRS INC, LE
COCHON DINGUE, LE
(Suby of Groupe Restos Plaisirs Inc, Le)
46 Boul Rene-Levesque O, Quebec, QC, G1R

2A4
(418) 523-2013
Emp Here 50
SIC 5812 Eating places

D-U-N-S 25-405-7169   (HQ)
GROUPE VOYAGES QUEBEC INC
(Suby of 3099-0907 Quebec Inc)
174 Grande Allee O, Quebec, QC, G1R 2G9
(418) 525-4585
Emp Here 32   Emp Total 35
Sales 11,565,300
SIC 4725 Tour operators
Pr Pr Paul Plourde

D-U-N-S 20-575-8704   (HQ)
HILL AND KNOWLTON LTEE
HILL+KNOWLTON STRATEGIES
580 Grande Allee E Bureau 240, Quebec, QC, G1R 2K2
(418) 523-3352
Emp Here 20   Emp Total 124,930
Sales 4,012,839
SIC 8743 Public relations services

D-U-N-S 20-776-8805   (BR)
HILTON CANADA CO.
HILTON
1100 Boul Rene-Levesque E Bureau 1797, Quebec, QC, G1R 5V2
(418) 647-2411
Emp Here 350
SIC 7011 Hotels and motels

D-U-N-S 24-367-2206   (BR)
HOTEL PALACE ROYAL INC
775 Av Honore-Mercier, Quebec, QC, G1R 6A5
(418) 694-2000
Emp Here 90
SIC 7011 Hotels and motels

D-U-N-S 25-455-9917   (SL)
LACROIX BLEAU COMMUNICATION MARKETING INC
675 Rue Saint-Amable, Quebec, QC, G1R 2G5
(418) 529-9761
Emp Here 32   Sales 5,376,850
SIC 7311 Advertising agencies
Pr Pr Marc Lacroix
Richard Lacroix
Paul Bleau

D-U-N-S 20-954-4048   (SL)
LOISIRS MONTCALM INC, LES
265 Boul Rene-Levesque O, Quebec, QC, G1R 2A7
(418) 523-6595
Emp Here 60   Sales 2,334,742
SIC 8322 Individual and family services

D-U-N-S 25-767-4002   (BR)
MORNEAU SHEPELL LTD
SHEPPELL FGI DIV OF
(Suby of Morneau Shepell Inc)
79 Boul Rene-Levesque E Bureau 100, Quebec, QC, G1R 5N5
(418) 529-4536
Emp Here 60
SIC 8999 Services, nec

D-U-N-S 20-717-3498   (BR)
MUSEE DE LA CIVILISATION
MUSEE DE L'AMERIQUE FRANCAISE
2 Cote De La Fabrique, Quebec, QC, G1R 3V6
(418) 692-2843
Emp Here 30
SIC 8412 Museums and art galleries

D-U-N-S 25-905-9749   (BR)
PLACEMENTS ASHTON LEBLOND INC, LES
CHEZ ASHTON
(Suby of Placements Ashton LeBlond Inc, Les)
54 Cote Du Palais, Quebec, QC, G1R 4H8

(418) 692-3055
Emp Here 20
SIC 5812 Eating places

D-U-N-S 25-994-4155   (BR)
RAYMOND CHABOT INC
INSOLVABILITE, DIV DE
140 Grande Allee E Bureau 200, Quebec, QC,
G1R 5P7
(888) 549-1717
Emp Here 20
SIC 8111 Legal services

D-U-N-S 20-242-9817   (SL)
**RESTAURANT AUX ANCIENS CANADIENS
INC**
34 Rue Saint-Louis, Quebec, QC, G1R 3Z1
(418) 692-1627
Emp Here 60   *Sales* 1,824,018
SIC 5812 Eating places

D-U-N-S 20-242-9981   (SL)
RESTAURANT CONTINENTAL INC
26 Rue Saint-Louis, Quebec, QC, G1R 3Y9
(418) 694-9995
Emp Here 75   *Sales* 2,261,782
SIC 5812 Eating places

D-U-N-S 24-441-6215   (BR)
**RESTAURANT LES TROIS MOUSSAIL-
LONS INC**
MCDONALDS
(*Suby of* Festaurant les Trois Moussaillons
Inc)
1151 Rue Saint-Jean, Quebec, QC, G1R 1S3
(418) 692-4848
Emp Here 49
SIC 5812 Eating places

D-U-N-S 20-535-7549   (BR)
ROYAL BANK OF CANADA
RBC
(*Suby of* Royal Bank Of Canada)
140 Grande Allee E Bureau 100, Quebec, QC,
G1R 5M8
(418) 648-6996
Emp Here 20
SIC 6021 National commercial banks

D-U-N-S 24-758-6340   (BR)
ROYAL BANK OF CANADA
RBC ROYAL BANK
(*Suby of* Royal Bank Of Canada)
700 Rue D'Youville, Quebec, QC, G1R 3P2
(418) 692-6800
Emp Here 49
SIC 6021 National commercial banks

D-U-N-S 25-848-3817   (SL)
SALON BAR CHEZ MAURICE INC
575 Grande Allee E Bureau 300, Quebec, QC,
G1R 2K4
(418) 647-2000
Emp Here 60   *Sales* 2,826,987
SIC 5813 Drinking places

D-U-N-S 20-649-0224   (BR)
SOBEYS CAPITAL INCORPORATED
IGA
255 Ch Sainte-Foy, Quebec, QC, G1R 1T5
(418) 524-9890
Emp Here 85
SIC 5411 Grocery stores

D-U-N-S 24-075-1060   (BR)
SOCIETE PARC-AUTO DU QUEBEC
SPAQ
(*Suby of* Societe Parc-Auto du Quebec)
965 Place D'Youville, Quebec, QC, G1R 3P1
(418) 694-9662
Emp Here 220
SIC 7521 Automobile parking

D-U-N-S 24-370-4819   (BR)
**SOCIETE QUEBECOISE DES INFRAS-
TRUCTURES**
*DIRECTION IMMOBILIERE CENTRE-VILLE
DE QUEBEC*
675 Boul Rene-Levesque E Bureau 500, Que-

bec, QC, G1R 5V7
(418) 644-2040
Emp Here 50
SIC 6512 Nonresidential building operators

D-U-N-S 24-499-6989   (HQ)
**SOCIETE QUEBECOISE DES INFRAS-
TRUCTURES**
1075 Rue De L'Amerique-Francaise, Quebec,
QC, G1R 5P8
(418) 646-1766
Emp Here 344   *Emp Total* 40,000
Sales 89,483,728
SIC 6531 Real estate agents and managers
Pr Luc Meunier
Sec Jonatan Julien
VP Fin Eric Thibault
VP Daniel Primeau
VP Pierre Babineau
VP Claude Dube
VP Daniel Archambault

D-U-N-S 24-530-9976   (SL)
**SOCIETE DE GESTION CAP-AUX-PIERRES
INC**
HOTEL CLARENDON
(*Suby of* Groupe Dufour Inc)
57 Rue Sainte-Anne, Quebec, QC, G1R 3X4
(418) 692-2480
Emp Here 100   *Sales* 5,889,600
SIC 7011 Hotels and motels
Pr Robert Pilleniere
VP Fin Jean-Francois Duclos

D-U-N-S 20-574-5826   (BR)
**SOCIETE DU CENTRE DES CONGRES DE
QUEBEC**
CENTRE DES CONGRES DE QUEBEC
1000 Boul Rene-Levesque E, Quebec, QC,
G1R 5T8
(418) 644-4000
Emp Here 75
SIC 7389 Business services, nec

D-U-N-S 20-545-9477   (SL)
**SOCIETE EN COMMANDITE HOTEL PLACE
D'YOUVILLE**
COURTYARD MARRIOTT QUEBEC
850 Place D'Youville, Quebec, QC, G1R 3P6
(418) 694-4004
Emp Here 50   *Sales* 2,188,821
SIC 7011 Hotels and motels

D-U-N-S 20-913-8614   (BR)
SODEXO CANADA LTD
TIM HORTONS
1060 Rue Louis-Alexandre-Taschereau, Que-
bec, QC, G1R 5E6
(418) 648-6368
Emp Here 24
SIC 5812 Eating places

D-U-N-S 25-767-0679   (SL)
VIEILLE MAISON DU SPAGHETTI INC, LA
625 Grande Allee E, Quebec, QC, G1R 2K4
(418) 529-6697
Emp Here 60   *Sales* 1,824,018
SIC 5812 Eating places

D-U-N-S 24-684-2921   (BR)
VILLE DE QUEBEC
OFFICE DU TOURISME DE QUEBEC
835 Av Wilfrid-Laurier, Quebec, QC, G1R 2L3
(418) 641-6290
Emp Here 30
SIC 7389 Business services, nec

Quebec, QC G1S
Quebec County

D-U-N-S 24-202-4511   (BR)
BANK OF MONTREAL
BMO BANK OF MONTREAL
1375 Ch Sainte-Foy, Quebec, QC, G1S 2N2

(418) 688-5800
Emp Here 20
SIC 6021 National commercial banks

D-U-N-S 25-201-2919   (BR)
**BANQUE DE DEVELOPPEMENT DU
CANADA**
BDC
1134 Grande Allee O, Quebec, QC, G1S 1E5
(418) 648-3972
Emp Here 25
SIC 6141 Personal credit institutions

D-U-N-S 25-019-6359   (BR)
CAPITALE IMMOBILIERE MFQ INC, LA
HOSTELERIE PARC DES BRAVES
750 Ch Sainte-Foy Bureau 404, Quebec, QC,
G1S 4P1
(418) 914-8747
Emp Here 40
SIC 8051 Skilled nursing care facilities

D-U-N-S 20-058-9088   (BR)
**CENTRE DE SANTE ET DE SERVICES SO-
CIAUX DE LA VIEILLE-CAPITALE**
CENTRE ANTI POISON, LE
1270 Ch Sainte-Foy, Quebec, QC, G1S 2M4
(418) 654-2731
Emp Here 20
SIC 8731 Commercial physical research

D-U-N-S 24-149-3972   (SL)
**CENTRE DES LOISIRS ST-SACREMENT
INC**
1360 Boul De L'Entente, Quebec, QC, G1S
2T9
(418) 681-7809
Emp Here 50   *Sales* 4,231,721
SIC 7032 Sporting and recreational camps

D-U-N-S 25-761-4818   (BR)
COGECO RADIO-TELEVISION INC
CJMF FM 93.3
1305 Ch Sainte-Foy Bureau 402, Quebec, QC,
G1S 4Y5
(418) 687-9330
Emp Here 35
SIC 4833 Television broadcasting stations

D-U-N-S 25-233-8504   (BR)
COLLEGE STANISLAS INCORPORE
COLLEGE STANISLAS-SILLERY
1605 Ch Sainte-Foy, Quebec, QC, G1S 2P1
(418) 527-9998
Emp Here 25
SIC 8211 Elementary and secondary schools

D-U-N-S 25-232-0999   (BR)
**COMMISSION SCOLAIRE CENTRAL QUE-
BEC**
QUEBEC HIGH SCHOOL
(*Suby of* Commission Scolaire Central Que-
bec)
945 Av Belvedere, Quebec, QC, G1S 3G2

Emp Here 40
SIC 8211 Elementary and secondary schools

D-U-N-S 20-711-8568   (BR)
**COMMISSION SCOLAIRE CENTRAL QUE-
BEC**
HOLLAND ELEMENTARY SCHOOL
940 Av Ernest-Gagnon, Quebec, QC, G1S
3R2
(418) 681-7705
Emp Here 40
SIC 8211 Elementary and secondary schools

D-U-N-S 25-232-8778   (BR)
**COMMISSION SCOLAIRE DE LA CAPI-
TALE, LA**
*ECOLE INTERNATIONALE DE SAINT-
SACREMENT*
1430 Ch Sainte-Foy, Quebec, QC, G1S 2N8
(418) 686-4040
Emp Here 45
SIC 8211 Elementary and secondary schools

D-U-N-S 25-298-8464   (BR)

**COMMISSION SCOLAIRE DE LA CAPI-
TALE, LA**
ECOLE ANNE HEBERT
555 Ch Sainte-Foy, Quebec, QC, G1S 2J9
(418) 686-4040
Emp Here 80
SIC 8211 Elementary and secondary schools

D-U-N-S 20-704-8708   (BR)
**COMMISSION SCOLAIRE DES DECOU-
VREURS**
ECOLE SAINT MICHEL SECTEUR AUTISME
(*Suby of* Commission Scolaire des Decou-
vreurs)
1255 Av Du Chanoine-Morel, Quebec, QC,
G1S 4B1
(418) 684-0064
Emp Here 90
SIC 8211 Elementary and secondary schools

D-U-N-S 25-846-7935   (BR)
COMPUGEN INC
925 Grande Allee O Bureau 360, Quebec, QC,
G1S 1C1
(418) 527-0084
Emp Here 30
SIC 7371 Custom computer programming ser-
vices

D-U-N-S 24-592-6696   (BR)
DELOITTE & TOUCHE INC
DELOITTE
(*Suby of* Deloitte LLP)
925 Grande Allee O Bureau 400, Quebec, QC,
G1S 4Z4
(418) 624-3333
Emp Here 150
SIC 8721 Accounting, auditing, and book-
keeping

D-U-N-S 20-242-7548   (SL)
**DEMERS, LISE & JEAN PHARMACIEN ET
ASSOCIES ENR**
UNIPRIX
905 Boul Rene-Levesque O, Quebec, QC,
G1S 1T7
(418) 683-3631
Emp Here 45   *Sales* 8,826,150
SIC 5912 Drug stores and proprietary stores
Pt Lise Demers
Pt Jean Demers

D-U-N-S 20-974-1730   (BR)
ECOLE DE LANGUES DE L'ESTRIE INC
1535 Ch Sainte-Foy Bureau 305, Quebec, QC,
G1S 2P1

Emp Here 25
SIC 8299 Schools and educational services,
nec

D-U-N-S 24-058-9957   (BR)
GENEX COMMUNICATIONS INC
SUMMUM WEB MEDIA
1134 Grande Allee O Bureau 300, Quebec,
QC, G1S 1E5
(418) 266-6166
Emp Here 74
SIC 4832 Radio broadcasting stations

D-U-N-S 24-890-4427   (SL)
GESTION MARC ST-GERMAIN INC
RESTAURANT ST-GERMAIN
1525 Rue Sheppard, Quebec, QC, G1S 1K1
(418) 681-6035
Emp Here 67   *Sales* 2,042,900
SIC 5812 Eating places

D-U-N-S 20-585-1095   (BR)
**GOUVERNEMENT DE LA PROVINCE DE
QUEBEC**
*MINISTERE DES TRANSPORTS; LABORA-
TOIRE DES CHAUSEES*
930 Ch Sainte-Foy Bureau 5, Quebec, QC,
G1S 2L4
(418) 643-6618
Emp Here 300
SIC 8711 Engineering services

D-U-N-S 20-535-8943   (BR)
GOUVERNEMENT DE LA PROVINCE DE QUEBEC
CENTRE DE SERVICE DES MINES
880 Ch Sainte-Foy Bureau 1 20b, Quebec, QC, G1S 2L2
(418) 627-6278
Emp Here 20
SIC 8999 Services, nec

D-U-N-S 24-759-0615   (HQ)
GROUPE GERMAIN INC
HOTEL LE GERMAIN
(*Suby of* Gestion Famiger Inc)
1200 Rue Des Soeurs-Du-Bon-Pasteur Bureau 500, Quebec, QC, G1S 0B1
(418) 687-1123
Emp Here 40   *Emp Total* 160
Sales 7,350,166
SIC 7011 Hotels and motels
 Jean-Yves Germain
Dir Christiane Germain
Dir Claude Choquette
Dir Henrick Simard
Dir Anne Darche
Dir Michel Cyr

D-U-N-S 20-955-5747   (SL)
HOPITAL JEFFERY HALE - SAINT BRIGID'S
HOSPITAL JEFFERY HALE
1250 Ch Sainte-Foy, Quebec, QC, G1S 2M6
(418) 684-5333
Emp Here 300   *Sales* 91,305,000
SIC 8621 Professional organizations
Pr Didier M Cluat
VP Richard Walling
Sec Louis Hanranhan
Dir Edward Murphy
Dir Joanne Coleman-Robertson
Dir Christiane Dion
Dir Fred Cribb
Dir Roger Lemire
Dir Brenda Rogers
Dir Gertrude Grogan

D-U-N-S 24-821-2987   (BR)
IGM FINANCIAL INC
SERVICES FINANCIERS GROUPE IN-VESTORS
1122 Grande Allee O, Quebec, QC, G1S 4Z5
(418) 681-0990
Emp Here 70
SIC 6282 Investment advice

D-U-N-S 24-063-8051   (BR)
INDUSTRIELLE ALLIANCE VALEURS MO-BILIERES INC
1040 Av Belvedere Bureau 101, Quebec, QC, G1S 3G3
(418) 681-2442
Emp Here 25
SIC 6231 Security and commodity exchanges

D-U-N-S 24-543-7590   (BR)
INDUSTRIELLE ALLIANCE, ASSURANCE AUTO ET HABITATION INC
INDUSTRIAL ALLIANCE AUTO AND HOME INSURANCE INC
925 Grande Allee O Bureau 230, Quebec, QC, G1S 1C1
(450) 473-4490
Emp Here 49
SIC 6331 Fire, marine, and casualty insurance

D-U-N-S 24-383-6207   (BR)
INDUSTRIELLE ALLIANCE, ASSURANCE ET SERVICES FINANCIERS INC
925 Grande Allee O Bureau 200, Quebec, QC, G1S 4Z4
(418) 686-7738
Emp Here 500
SIC 6411 Insurance agents brokers, and service

D-U-N-S 25-746-1335   (BR)
LAVERY DE BILLY, SOCIETE EN NOM COL-

LECTIF A RESPONSABILITE LIMITEE
LAVERY DE BILLY
925 Grande Allee O Bureau 500, Quebec, QC, G1S 1C1
(418) 688-5000
Emp Here 51
SIC 8111 Legal services

D-U-N-S 25-835-5056   (SL)
PAVILLON SAINT-DOMINIQUE
1045 Boul Rene-Levesque O, Quebec, QC, G1S 1V3
(418) 681-3561
Emp Here 115   *Sales* 4,523,563
SIC 8322 Individual and family services

D-U-N-S 25-484-9516   (BR)
PROVIGO DISTRIBUTION INC
PROVIGO SILLERY
955 Boul Rene-Levesque O, Quebec, QC, G1S 1T7
(418) 527-3481
Emp Here 45
SIC 5411 Grocery stores

D-U-N-S 24-837-5649   (BR)
RNC MEDIA INC
1134 Grande Allee O Bureau 300, Quebec, QC, G1S 1E5
(418) 687-9810
Emp Here 50
SIC 4832 Radio broadcasting stations

D-U-N-S 24-346-3499   (BR)
RESIDENCE COTE JARDINS INC
880 Av Painchaud, Quebec, QC, G1S 0A3
(418) 688-1221
Emp Here 100
SIC 8361 Residential care

D-U-N-S 24-046-2494   (BR)
SOCIETE DE GESTION COGIR INC
650 Av Murray, Quebec, QC, G1S 4V8
(418) 527-7001
Emp Here 50
SIC 6513 Apartment building operators

Quebec, QC G1T
Quebec County

D-U-N-S 25-395-0604   (HQ)
COMMISSION SCOLAIRE CENTRAL QUE-BEC
(*Suby of* Commission Scolaire Central Quebec)
2046 Ch Saint-Louis, Quebec, QC, G1T 1P4
(418) 681-7705
Emp Here 650   *Emp Total* 700
Sales 64,407,680
SIC 8211 Elementary and secondary schools
Genl Mgr Ronald Corriveau
Ch Bd Ed Murphy
 Cathleen Scott

D-U-N-S 25-240-0361   (SL)
CORPORATION DE L' EXTERNAT ST-JEAN-BERCHMANS
2303 Ch Saint-Louis, Quebec, QC, G1T 1R5
(418) 687-5871
Emp Here 50   *Sales* 3,356,192
SIC 8211 Elementary and secondary schools

D-U-N-S 25-785-1733   (SL)
ENTREPRISES PIERRE PICARD INC, LES
1350 Av Maguire Bureau 103, Quebec, QC, G1T 1Z3
(418) 683-4492
Emp Here 75   *Sales* 2,188,821
SIC 7349 Building maintenance services, nec

D-U-N-S 25-966-9141   (BR)
GROUPE RESTOS PLAISIRS INC, LE
COCHON DINGUE, LE
(*Suby of* Groupe Restos Plaisirs Inc, Le)
1326 Av Maguire, Quebec, QC, G1T 1Z3

---

(418) 684-2013
Emp Here 40
SIC 5812 Eating places

D-U-N-S 20-340-0747   (BR)
ROYAL & SUN ALLIANCE INSURANCE COMPANY OF CANADA
RSA
2475 Boul Laurier, Quebec, QC, G1T 1C4
(418) 622-2040
Emp Here 200
SIC 6411 Insurance agents, brokers, and service

D-U-N-S 24-822-6263   (BR)
STARBUCKS COFFEE CANADA, INC
(*Suby of* Starbucks Corporation)
1363 Av Maguire Bureau 300, Quebec, QC, G1T 1Z2

Emp Here 40
SIC 5812 Eating places

Quebec, QC G1V
Quebec County

D-U-N-S 24-062-4259   (BR)
2786591 CANADA INC
MULTI PRETS PARTENAIRE
2785 Boul Laurier Bureau Rc 100, Quebec, QC, G1V 2L9
(418) 659-7738
Emp Here 26
SIC 6163 Loan brokers

D-U-N-S 25-940-7138   (SL)
2959-0411 QUEBEC INC
RESTAURANT RASCAL
2955 Boul Laurier, Quebec, QC, G1V 2M2
(418) 654-3644
Emp Here 50   *Sales* 1,532,175
SIC 5812 Eating places

D-U-N-S 25-665-7222   (SL)
3089-3242 QUEBEC INC
HOTEL PLAZA
3031 Boul Laurier, Quebec, QC, G1V 2M2
(418) 658-2727
Emp Here 100   *Sales* 4,377,642
SIC 7011 Hotels and motels

D-U-N-S 20-101-1827   (BR)
87878 CANADA LTEE
AUBERGE SIR WILFRID
3055 Boul Laurier, Quebec, QC, G1V 4X2
(418) 651-2440
Emp Here 20
SIC 7011 Hotels and motels

D-U-N-S 24-355-2978   (BR)
9023-4436 QUEBEC INC
ATMOSPHERE
2450 Boul Laurier, Quebec, QC, G1V 2L1
(418) 780-8035
Emp Here 70
SIC 5941 Sporting goods and bicycle shops

D-U-N-S 20-086-7807   (SL)
9101-8713 QUEBEC INC
HOTEL LINDBERGH
2825 Boul Laurier, Quebec, QC, G1V 2L9
(418) 653-4975
Emp Here 50   *Sales* 2,188,821
SIC 7011 Hotels and motels

D-U-N-S 25-874-3509   (SL)
9102-8001 QUEBEC INC
HOTEL CLASSIQUE
2815 Boul Laurier, Quebec, QC, G1V 4H3
(418) 658-2793
Emp Here 40   *Sales* 2,826,987
SIC 7011 Hotels and motels

D-U-N-S 25-542-7239   (BR)
AON CONSULTING INC
GROUPE CONSEIL AON

2600 Boul Laurier Bureau 750, Quebec, QC, G1V 4W2
(418) 650-1119
Emp Here 85
SIC 8999 Services, nec

D-U-N-S 25-885-3449   (BR)
AON PARIZEAU INC
AON PARIZEAU INC
2600 Boul Laurier Bureau 750, Quebec, QC, G1V 4W2
(418) 529-1234
Emp Here 25
SIC 6411 Insurance agents, brokers, and service

D-U-N-S 20-777-9638   (BR)
AXA ASSURANCES INC
2640 Boul Laurier Bureau 900, Quebec, QC, G1V 5C2
(418) 654-9918
Emp Here 150
SIC 6311 Life insurance

D-U-N-S 25-309-9931   (BR)
AGENCE DE VOYAGES D'AUTOMOBILE ET TOURING CLUB DU QUEBEC INC
AGENCE DE VOYAGES D'AUTOMOBILE ET TOURING CLUB DU
2600 Boul Laurier Bureau 133, Quebec, QC, G1V 4T3
(418) 653-9200
Emp Here 35
SIC 4724 Travel agencies

D-U-N-S 25-760-0668   (BR)
ASHTON CASSE-CROUTE INC
CHEZ ASHTON
(*Suby of* Placements Ashton LeBlond Inc, Les)
2700 Boul Laurier, Quebec, QC, G1V 2L8
(418) 656-1096
Emp Here 27
SIC 5812 Eating places

D-U-N-S 20-029-9753   (BR)
ASSOCIATION DES ETUDIANTS DU COL-LEGE REGIONAL CHAMPLAIN L'
ASSOCIATION DES ETUDIANTS DU COL-LEGE REGIONAL CHAM
790 Av Neree-Tremblay, Quebec, QC, G1V 4K2
(418) 656-6921
Emp Here 112
SIC 8211 Elementary and secondary schools

D-U-N-S 20-175-3915   (BR)
BCF S.E.N.C.R.L.
BCF
2828 Boul Laurier Bureau 1200, Quebec, QC, G1V 0B9
(418) 266-4500
Emp Here 50
SIC 8111 Legal services

D-U-N-S 25-765-7254   (BR)
BMO NESBITT BURNS INC
BMO NESBITT BURNS
2828 Boul Laurier, Quebec, QC, G1V 0B9
(418) 647-3124
Emp Here 20
SIC 6211 Security brokers and dealers

D-U-N-S 25-761-1459   (BR)
BANK OF MONTREAL
BMO
2700 Boul Laurier, Quebec, QC, G1V 2L8
(418) 577-1834
Emp Here 20
SIC 6021 National commercial banks

D-U-N-S 25-761-1756   (BR)
BANQUE LAURENTIENNE DU CANADA
2828 Boul Laurier Bureau 100, Quebec, QC, G1V 0B9
(418) 659-4955
Emp Here 20
SIC 6021 National commercial banks

D-U-N-S 20-936-4145　　(SL)
BEAUGARTE (QUEBEC INC)
2590 Boul Laurier Bureau 150, Quebec, QC,
G1V 4M6
(418) 659-2442
Emp Here 100　　*Sales* 3,551,629
SIC 5812 Eating places

D-U-N-S 25-846-7919　　(SL)
BEAUGARTE (QUEBEC) INC
2600 Boul Laurier, Quebec, QC, G1V 4W1
(418) 659-2442
Emp Here 85　　*Sales* 3,031,879
SIC 5812 Eating places

D-U-N-S 20-266-1484　　(BR)
**BIBLIOTHEQUE ET ARCHIVES NA-
TIONALES DU QUEBEC**
BANQ
1055 Av Du Seminaire, Quebec, QC, G1V 4N1
(418) 643-8904
Emp Here 30
SIC 8231 Libraries

D-U-N-S 25-331-3415　　(BR)
BOIS DAAQUAM INC
2590 Boul Laurier Bureau 740, Quebec, QC,
G1V 4M6

Emp Here 250
SIC 2421 Sawmills and planing mills, general

D-U-N-S 20-348-8742　　(BR)
BOUTIQUE LINEN CHEST (PHASE II) INC
LINEN CHEST
(*Suby of* Boutique Linen Chest (Phase II) Inc)
2700 Boul Laurier Bureau 2800, Quebec, QC,
G1V 2L8
(418) 658-5218
Emp Here 43
SIC 5719 Miscellaneous homefurnishings

D-U-N-S 24-892-9317　　(BR)
CIBC WORLD MARKETS INC
CIBC WOOD GUNDY
2954 Boul Laurier Bureau 650, Quebec, QC,
G1V 4T2
(418) 652-8011
Emp Here 20
SIC 6531 Real estate agents and managers

D-U-N-S 20-867-5020　　(BR)
CAPITALE GESTION FINANCIERE INC, LA
CAPITALE, LA
650-2875 Boul Laurier, Quebec, QC, G1V 5B1
(418) 644-0038
Emp Here 300
SIC 6411 Insurance agents, brokers, and ser-
vice

D-U-N-S 25-739-8776　　(BR)
**CENTRE HOSPITALIER UNIVERSITAIRE
DE QUEBEC**
CENTRE DE RECHERCHE DU CHUL
2705 Boul Laurier Bureau 4, Quebec, QC,
G1V 4G2
(418) 654-2244
Emp Here 800
SIC 8731 Commercial physical research

D-U-N-S 25-240-3290　　(SL)
**CENTRE PSYCHO-PEDAGOGIQUE DE
QUEBEC INC**
ECOLE ST-FRANCOIS
1000 Rue Du Joli-Bois, Quebec, QC, G1V 3Z6
(418) 650-1171
Emp Here 50　　*Sales* 3,356,192
SIC 8211 Elementary and secondary schools

D-U-N-S 25-247-7633　　(BR)
CHAUSSURES BROWNS INC
BROWN'S SHOES
(*Suby of* 90401 Canada Ltee)
2450 Boul Laurier, Quebec, QC, G1V 2L1
(418) 659-1922
Emp Here 25
SIC 5661 Shoe stores

D-U-N-S 20-791-4552　　(BR)

CHILDREN'S PLACE (CANADA) LP, THE
2700 Boul Laurier, Quebec, QC, G1V 2L8
(418) 652-3589
Emp Here 26
SIC 5641 Children's and infants' wear stores

D-U-N-S 25-768-2781　　(BR)
CLS-LEXI TECH LTD.
(*Suby of* LBT Acquisition, Inc.)
2700 Boul Laurier Bureau 6340, Quebec, QC,
G1V 4K5
(418) 650-7800
Emp Here 35
SIC 7389 Business services, nec

D-U-N-S 24-464-6857　　(SL)
**COLLEGE D'ENSEIGNEMENT GENERAL &
PROFESSIONEL STE-FOY**
CEGEP DE STE-FOY
2410 Ch Sainte-Foy, Quebec, QC, G1V 1T3
(418) 659-6600
Emp Here 1,100　　*Sales* 159,073,600
SIC 8221 Colleges and universities
Pr Philippe Montreuil
VP Myriam Arseneault
Treas Emmanuelle Cloutier
Dir Francois Drouin
Dir Louise Bedard
Dir Carol Arseneault
Dir Monethalie Pratte-Singharaj
Dir Evelyne Cormier
Dir Charles-Antoine Sirois
Dir Valerie Fortin

D-U-N-S 20-711-8634　　(BR)
**COMMISSION SCOLAIRE CENTRAL QUE-
BEC**
ECOLE SAINT VINCENT
995 Av Wolfe, Quebec, QC, G1V 3J9
(418) 652-2106
Emp Here 50
SIC 8211 Elementary and secondary schools

D-U-N-S 20-656-0018　　(BR)
**COMMISSION SCOLAIRE DES DECOU-
VREURS**
*CENTRE DE FORMATION PROFESSIONEL
DE MAURICE BARBEAU*
(*Suby of* Commission Scolaire des Decou-
vreurs)
920 Rue Noel-Carter, Quebec, QC, G1V 5B6
(418) 652-2184
Emp Here 50
SIC 8211 Elementary and secondary schools

D-U-N-S 20-955-5689　　(HQ)
**COMMISSION SCOLAIRE DES DECOU-
VREURS**
(*Suby of* Commission Scolaire des Decou-
vreurs)
945 Av Wolfe Bureau 100, Quebec, QC, G1V
4E2
(418) 652-2121
Emp Here 100　　*Emp Total* 2,500
Sales 230,099,200
SIC 8211 Elementary and secondary schools
Genl Mgr Paquerette Gagnon

D-U-N-S 20-704-8690　　(BR)
**COMMISSION SCOLAIRE DES DECOU-
VREURS**
*CENTRE D'EDUCATION DES ADULTES
DES DECOUVRERS*
(*Suby of* Commission Scolaire des Decou-
vreurs)
1094 Rte De L'Eglise, Quebec, QC, G1V 3V9
(418) 652-2158
Emp Here 65
SIC 8211 Elementary and secondary schools

D-U-N-S 25-233-4800　　(BR)
**COMMISSION SCOLAIRE DES DECOU-
VREURS**
ECOLE MADELEINE BERGERON
(*Suby of* Commission Scolaire des Decou-
vreurs)
1088 Rte De L'Eglise, Quebec, QC, G1V 3V9

(418) 652-2104
Emp Here 55
SIC 8211 Elementary and secondary schools

D-U-N-S 20-712-0416　　(BR)
**COMMISSION SCOLAIRE DES DECOU-
VREURS**
*CENTRE DE FORMATION PROFESSION-
NELLE MARIE ROLLET*
(*Suby of* Commission Scolaire des Decou-
vreurs)
3000 Boul Hochelaga, Quebec, QC, G1V 3Y4
(418) 652-2159
Emp Here 90
SIC 8211 Elementary and secondary schools

D-U-N-S 20-704-8757　　(BR)
**COMMISSION SCOLAIRE DES DECOU-
VREURS**
ECOLE FERNAND-SEGUIN
(*Suby of* Commission Scolaire des Decou-
vreurs)
2590 Rue Biencourt, Quebec, QC, G1V 1H3
(418) 652-2107
Emp Here 30
SIC 8211 Elementary and secondary schools

D-U-N-S 20-704-8716　　(BR)
**COMMISSION SCOLAIRE DES DECOU-
VREURS**
*CENTRE DE FORMATION PROFESSION-
NELLE MAURICE-BARBEAU*
(*Suby of* Commission Scolaire des Decou-
vreurs)
920 Rue Noel-Carter, Quebec, QC, G1V 5B6
(418) 652-2184
Emp Here 45
SIC 8331 Job training and related services

D-U-N-S 20-544-9460　　(BR)
**COMPAGNIE DE TELEPHONE BELL DU
CANADA OU BELL CANADA, LA**
2715 Boul Du Versant-Nord, Quebec, QC,
G1V 1A3
(418) 691-1080
Emp Here 85
SIC 4899 Communication services, nec

D-U-N-S 24-309-5093　　(HQ)
COOPERATIVE DE L'UNIVERSITE LAVAL
COOP DU CEGEP DE LIMOILOU
(*Suby of* Cooperative de l'Universite Laval)
2305 Rue De L'Universite Bureau 1100, Que-
bec, QC, G1V 0B4
(418) 656-2600
Emp Here 250　　*Emp Total* 450
Sales 79,964,927
SIC 6712 Bank holding companies
Dir Christian Djoko Kamgain
VP Laurent Aubin
Sec Delphine Talamona
Dir Jean-Francois Forgues
Dir Bernard Garnier
Dir Paul Michaud
Dir Elizabeth Coulombe
Dir Francois Godbout
Dir Yan Cimon
Dir Simon Laberge

D-U-N-S 25-810-4363　　(BR)
COURTIERS INTER-QUEBEC INC, LES
ROYAL LEPAGE INTER QUEBEC
2960 Boul Laurier Bureau 50, Quebec, QC,
G1V 4S1
(418) 653-0488
Emp Here 58
SIC 6531 Real estate agents and managers

D-U-N-S 25-285-9384　　(SL)
**DALLAIRE FOREST KIROUAC, COMPT-
ABLES PROFESSIONNELS AGRES,
S.E.N.C.R.L.**
1175 Av Lavigerie Bureau 580, Quebec, QC,
G1V 4P1
(418) 650-2266
Emp Here 50　　*Sales* 2,188,821
SIC 8721 Accounting, auditing, and book-
keeping

D-U-N-S 25-299-6491　　(BR)
DOLLARAMA S.E.C.
DOLLARAMA 27
2700 Boul Laurier Bureau 167, Quebec, QC,
G1V 2L8
(418) 659-5976
Emp Here 28
SIC 5331 Variety stores

D-U-N-S 25-746-5542　　(BR)
ENGIE SERVICES INC
2700 Boul Laurier Unite 3320, Quebec, QC,
G1V 2L8
(418) 681-2322
Emp Here 23
SIC 7349 Building maintenance services, nec

D-U-N-S 20-831-7508　　(BR)
**ECONOMICAL MUTUAL INSURANCE COM-
PANY**
FEDERATION MISSISQUOI
1175 Av Lavigerie Bureau 30, Quebec, QC,
G1V 4P1

Emp Here 23
SIC 6331 Fire, marine, and casualty insurance

D-U-N-S 25-764-9467　　(BR)
ENTREPRISES J'OSE LTEE
ESCOMPTE COIFFE
(*Suby of* Entreprises J'Ose Ltee)
826 Rte Du Vallon Bureau 25, Quebec, QC,
G1V 4T1
(418) 656-6558
Emp Here 25
SIC 7231 Beauty shops

D-U-N-S 20-716-5817　　(HQ)
EPIDERMA QUEBEC INC
(*Suby of* Corporation Epiderma Inc)
2590 Boul Laurier Bureau 330, Quebec, QC,
G1V 4M6
(418) 266-2027
Emp Here 43　　*Emp Total* 140
Sales 3,203,919
SIC 7231 Beauty shops

D-U-N-S 24-945-9546　　(BR)
ERNST & YOUNG LLP
(*Suby of* Ernst & Young LLP)
2875 Boul Laurier Unite 410, Quebec, QC,
G1V 0C7
(418) 524-5151
Emp Here 100
SIC 8721 Accounting, auditing, and book-
keeping

D-U-N-S 24-875-2649　　(BR)
FACILITE INFORMATIQUE CANADA INC
FACILITE INFORMATIQUE
1100-2875 Boul Laurier, Quebec, QC, G1V
5B1
(418) 780-3950
Emp Here 41
SIC 7379 Computer related services, nec

D-U-N-S 25-827-0495　　(BR)
**FEDERATION DES CAISSES DESJARDINS
DU QUEBEC**
*FEDERATION DES CAISSES DESJARDINS
DU QUEBEC*
2640 Boul Laurier Bureau 1400, Quebec, QC,
G1V 5C2
(418) 650-6350
Emp Here 38
SIC 6211 Security brokers and dealers

D-U-N-S 24-634-9182　　(BR)
FINANCIERE BANQUE NATIONALE INC
2600 Boul Laurier Bureau 700, Quebec, QC,
G1V 4W2
(418) 654-2323
Emp Here 52
SIC 6021 National commercial banks

D-U-N-S 24-689-6955　　(BR)
FUJITSU CONSEIL (CANADA) INC
DMR
2960 Boul Laurier Bureau 400, Quebec, QC,

G1V 4S1

Emp Here 600
SIC 7379 Computer related services, nec

   D-U-N-S 24-170-1684   (BR)
GAP (CANADA) INC
(*Suby of* The Gap Inc)
2452 Boul Laurier Bureau E04, Quebec, QC,
G1V 2L1

Emp Here 40
SIC 5651 Family clothing stores

   D-U-N-S 25-168-8057   (SL)
GESTION VINNY INC
MCDONALD'S
2950 Boul Laurier, Quebec, QC, G1V 2M4
(418) 659-4484
Emp Here 100   *Sales* 2,991,389
SIC 5812 Eating places

   D-U-N-S 20-797-7765   (BR)
GOUVERNEMENT DE LA PROVINCE DE QUEBEC
MINISTERE DE LA SECURITE PUBLIQUE
2525 Boul Laurier, Quebec, QC, G1V 4Z6
(418) 646-6777
Emp Here 30
SIC 7389 Business services, nec

   D-U-N-S 25-864-5043   (BR)
GROUPE AST (1993) INC
GROUPE AST
2700 Boul Laurier Unite 1210, Quebec, QC,
G1V 2L8
(418) 650-4490
Emp Here 30
SIC 8748 Business consulting, nec

   D-U-N-S 25-665-6984   (BR)
GROUPE PAGES JAUNES CORP
2600 Boul Laurier Bureau 128, Quebec, QC,
G1V 4Y4
(418) 656-1530
Emp Here 1,000
SIC 4899 Communication services, nec

   D-U-N-S 24-126-3545   (BR)
GROUPE PAGES JAUNES CORP
2960 Boul Laurier Bureau 006, Quebec, QC,
G1V 4S1
(418) 656-1530
Emp Here 20
SIC 2741 Miscellaneous publishing

   D-U-N-S 24-758-5862   (BR)
HEMA-QUEBEC
1070 Av Des Sciences-De-La-Vie, Quebec,
QC, G1V 5C3
(418) 780-4362
Emp Here 414
SIC 8099 Health and allied services, nec

   D-U-N-S 25-318-4675   (BR)
HOLT, RENFREW & CIE, LIMITEE
HOLT RENFREW CANADA
2452 Boul Laurier, Quebec, QC, G1V 2L1
(514) 842-5111
Emp Here 106
SIC 5611 Men's and boys' clothing stores

   D-U-N-S 25-301-2793   (BR)
HUDSON'S BAY COMPANY
BAIE, LA
2740 Boul Laurier, Quebec, QC, G1V 4P7
(418) 627-5959
Emp Here 50
SIC 5311 Department stores

   D-U-N-S 25-765-2974   (SL)
HUMATECH INC
2511 Ch Sainte-Foy Bureau 050, Quebec, QC,
G1V 1T7
(418) 658-9153
Emp Here 50   *Sales* 2,334,742
SIC 8059 Nursing and personal care, nec

   D-U-N-S 25-991-7854   (BR)

IMMEUBLES JACQUES ROBITAILLE INC, LES
AUBERGE STE-FOY
3055 Boul Laurier, Quebec, QC, G1V 4X2
(418) 651-2440
Emp Here 20
SIC 7011 Hotels and motels

   D-U-N-S 25-991-8761   (HQ)
INSTITUT NATIONALE DE SANTE PUBLIQUE DU QUEBEC
CENTRE DE TOXICOLOGIE DU QUEBEC
(*Suby of* Institut Nationale De Sante Publique
Du Quebec)
945 Av Wolfe Bureau 4, Quebec, QC, G1V
5B3
(418) 650-5115
Emp Here 150   *Emp Total* 400
Sales 28,081,404
SIC 8731 Commercial physical research
Pr Pr Luc Boileau
  Jean-Louis Coulombe

   D-U-N-S 24-394-2930   (SL)
INVESTISSEMENTS YVES GAGNE LTEE
CANADIAN TIRE
1170 Rte De L'Eglise, Quebec, QC, G1V 3W7
(418) 659-4882
Emp Here 45   *Sales* 7,067,468
SIC 5531 Auto and home supply stores
Pr Yves Gagne

   D-U-N-S 25-857-1629   (BR)
J.M. CLEMENT LTEE
2450 Boul Laurier, Quebec, QC, G1V 2L1
(418) 653-1602
Emp Here 30
SIC 5641 Children's and infants' wear stores

   D-U-N-S 24-884-3880   (SL)
LXB COMMUNICATION MARKETING INC
2590 Boul Laurier, Quebec, QC, G1V 4M6
(418) 529-9761
Emp Here 33   *Sales* 5,300,640
SIC 7311 Advertising agencies
Pr Pr Marc Lacroix
  Richard Lacroix

   D-U-N-S 20-309-0899   (SL)
LANGLOIS KRONSTROM DESJARDINS AVOCATS S.E.N.C.R.L
LANGLOIS GAUDREAU O'CONNOR
2820 Boul Laurier Bureau 1300, Quebec, QC,
G1V 0C1
(418) 650-7000
Emp Here 50   *Sales* 4,304,681
SIC 8111 Legal services

   D-U-N-S 25-526-8419   (SL)
LE PUB UNIVERSITAIRE INC
LE PUB
2325 Rue De L'Universite Bureau 1312, Que-
bec, QC, G1V 0B3
(418) 656-7075
Emp Here 80   *Sales* 2,407,703
SIC 5812 Eating places

   D-U-N-S 24-843-3872   (BR)
LIBRAIRIE RENAUD-BRAY INC
2700 Boul Laurier, Quebec, QC, G1V 2L8
(418) 659-1021
Emp Here 65
SIC 5942 Book stores

   D-U-N-S 25-281-5527   (BR)
MD MANAGEMENT LIMITED
GESTION MD
(*Suby of* Canadian Medical Association)
2600 Boul Laurier Unite 2460, Quebec, QC,
G1V 4W1
(418) 657-6601
Emp Here 25
SIC 6722 Management investment, open-end

   D-U-N-S 20-137-5388   (BR)
MD MANAGEMENT LIMITED
COMPAGNIE DE GESTION MD
(*Suby of* Canadian Medical Association)

2590 Boul Laurier Bureau 560, Quebec, QC,
G1V 4M6
(418) 657-6601
Emp Here 35
SIC 6722 Management investment, open-end

   D-U-N-S 24-126-2182   (BR)
MAISON SIMONS INC, LA
2450 Boul Laurier, Quebec, QC, G1V 2L1
(418) 692-3630
Emp Here 25
SIC 5651 Family clothing stores

   D-U-N-S 25-767-4648   (BR)
MAISONS LAPRISE INC
2700 Boul Laurier Unite 2540, Quebec, QC,
G1V 2L8
(418) 683-3343
Emp Here 200
SIC 2452 Prefabricated wood buildings

   D-U-N-S 24-379-6174   (SL)
MALENFANT DALLAIRE, COMPTABLES AGREES, S.E.N.C.R.L.
2600 Boul Laurier Bureau 872, Quebec, QC,
G1V 4W2
(418) 654-0636
Emp Here 50   *Sales* 2,188,821
SIC 8721 Accounting, auditing, and book-
keeping

   D-U-N-S 25-745-0429   (BR)
MCMAHON DISTRIBUTEUR PHARMACEU-TIQUE INC
BRUNETTE PLACE SAINTE-FOY
2450 Boul Laurier, Quebec, QC, G1V 2L1
(418) 653-9333
Emp Here 20
SIC 5912 Drug stores and proprietary stores

   D-U-N-S 24-058-2697   (BR)
METRO RICHELIEU INC
METRO INNOVATION
2360 Ch Sainte-Foy Bureau 2, Quebec, QC,
G1V 4H2
(418) 656-0728
Emp Here 33
SIC 5141 Groceries, general line

   D-U-N-S 24-821-3589   (SL)
MORENCY, SOCIETE D'AVOCATS, S.E.N.C.R.L.
2875 Boul Laurier Bureau 200, Quebec, QC,
G1V 2M2
(418) 651-9900
Emp Here 55   *Sales* 4,742,446
SIC 8111 Legal services

   D-U-N-S 24-999-9277   (HQ)
MULTIFORCE TECHNOLOGIES INC
MULTIFORCE
2954 Boul Laurier, Quebec, QC, G1V 2M4
(418) 780-8020
Emp Here 45   *Emp Total* 160
Sales 27,360,263
SIC 5045 Computers, peripherals, and soft-
ware
Pr Pr Greg Rokos
Treas Pierre Courchesne
Dir Marc Veilleux

   D-U-N-S 25-456-9064   (BR)
NORTON ROSE FULBRIGHT CANADA S.E.N.C.R.L., S.R.L.
NORTON ROSE FULBRIGHT
2828 Boul Laurier Bureau 1500, Quebec, QC,
G1V 0B9
(418) 640-5000
Emp Here 150
SIC 8111 Legal services

   D-U-N-S 24-941-5332   (BR)
PETIT COIN BRETON LTEE, AU
2600 Boul Laurier Unite 1, Quebec, QC, G1V
4W1
(418) 653-6051
Emp Here 50
SIC 5812 Eating places

   D-U-N-S 25-896-6845   (BR)
PLACEMENTS ASHTON LEBLOND INC, LES
CHEZ ASHTON
(*Suby of* Placements Ashton LeBlond Inc,
Les)
2700 Boul Laurier, Quebec, QC, G1V 2L8
(418) 656-1096
Emp Here 24
SIC 5812 Eating places

   D-U-N-S 24-206-2305   (SL)
PLACEMENTS PAMBEC INC
2846 Rue Jules-Dallaire, Quebec, QC, G1V
2J8
(418) 651-6905
Emp Here 52   *Sales* 6,380,400
SIC 6512 Nonresidential building operators
Pr Pr Michel Moreau
VP VP Claude Amyot

   D-U-N-S 24-759-0151   (BR)
POMERLEAU INC
1175 Av Lavigerie Bureau 50, Quebec, QC,
G1V 4P1
(418) 626-2314
Emp Here 32
SIC 6512 Nonresidential building operators

   D-U-N-S 24-378-8312   (BR)
PRICEWATERHOUSECOOPERS LLP
2640 Boul Laurier Bureau 1700, Quebec, QC,
G1V 5C2
(418) 522-7001
Emp Here 700
SIC 8721 Accounting, auditing, and book-
keeping

   D-U-N-S 25-766-9150   (BR)
RBC DOMINION SECURITIES LIMITED
RBC DOMINION VALEURS MOBILIERES
(*Suby of* Royal Bank Of Canada)
2828 Boul Laurier Bureau 800, Quebec, QC,
G1V 0B9
(418) 527-2008
Emp Here 40
SIC 6211 Security brokers and dealers

   D-U-N-S 25-475-4427   (BR)
RESTAURANT NORMANDIN INC
2500 Ch Sainte-Foy, Quebec, QC, G1V 1T5
(418) 653-4844
Emp Here 65
SIC 5812 Eating places

   D-U-N-S 25-309-8784   (BR)
ROYAL BANK OF CANADA
RBC BANQUE ROYALE
(*Suby of* Royal Bank Of Canada)
2450 Boul Laurier, Quebec, QC, G1V 2L1
(418) 654-2454
Emp Here 65
SIC 6021 National commercial banks

   D-U-N-S 20-720-4962   (BR)
SCM INSURANCE SERVICES INC
EXPERT EN SINISTRE S C M
2954 Boul Laurier Bureau 420, Quebec, QC,
G1V 4T2
(418) 651-3525
Emp Here 30
SIC 6411 Insurance agents, brokers, and ser-
vice

   D-U-N-S 24-706-8497   (SL)
SERVICE D'INVENTAIRE PROFESSIONNEL G.B. INC
SIP
(*Suby of* Gestion P.C.B.G. Inc)
2750 Ch Sainte-Foy Bureau 250, Quebec, QC,
G1V 1V6
(418) 659-3140
Emp Here 110   *Sales* 7,362,000
SIC 7389 Business services, nec
Pr Pr Gaston Blais
  Raymond Blais
Dir Opers Chantale Drouin

D-U-N-S 25-213-7294　　(BR)
STAPLES CANADA INC
BUREAU EN GROS
(*Suby of* Staples, Inc.)
2975 Boul Laurier, Quebec, QC, G1V 2M2
(418) 652-8300
Emp Here 50
SIC 5943 Stationery stores

D-U-N-S 24-787-5243　　(BR)
STARBUCKS COFFEE CANADA, INC
CAFE STARBUCKS
(*Suby of* Starbucks Corporation)
1200 Av De Germain-Des-Pres, Quebec, QC,
G1V 3M7
(418) 650-9444
Emp Here 20
SIC 5812 Eating places

D-U-N-S 20-872-3056　　(SL)
**SYNDICAT DES INFIRMIERES, IN-
HALOTHERAPEUTES ET INFIRMIERES
AUXILIAIRES DE LAVAL (CSQ)**
HOPITAL LAVAL
2725 Ch Sainte-Foy Bureau 656, Quebec, QC,
G1V 4G5
(418) 656-4710
Emp Here 2,100　　*Sales* 235,566,900
SIC 8069 Specialty hospitals, except psychi-
atric
Pr Isabelle Dumaine
VP VP Nathalie Meunier
Treas Pierre Coulombe
Dir Sylvie Poirier
Dir Johanne Kirouac
Dir Louise Beaulieu

D-U-N-S 25-146-5597　　(BR)
TECHNOLOGIES METAFORE INC
MICROSERV
1175 Av Lavigerie Locale 305, Quebec, QC,
G1V 4P1
(418) 688-2655
Emp Here 40
SIC 5045 Computers, peripherals, and soft-
ware

D-U-N-S 25-979-7280　　(SL)
TELDIG INC
2960 Boul Laurier Bureau 120, Quebec, QC,
G1V 4S1
(418) 948-1314
Emp Here 30　　*Sales* 2,057,770
SIC 7371 Custom computer programming ser-
vices

D-U-N-S 24-523-3908　　(BR)
TICKETMASTER CANADA LP
2505 Boul Laurier Bureau 300, Quebec, QC,
G1V 2L2
(418) 694-2300
Emp Here 100
SIC 7922 Theatrical producers and services

D-U-N-S 24-050-8312　　(BR)
TOMMY HILFIGER CANADA INC
TOMMY HILFIGER
2450 Boul Laurier, Quebec, QC, G1V 2L1
(418) 657-2960
Emp Here 25
SIC 5611 Men's and boys' clothing stores

D-U-N-S 25-768-2658　　(BR)
TOYS 'R' US (CANADA) LTD
TOYS 'R' US
(*Suby of* Toys "r" Us, Inc.)
2700 Boul Laurier, Quebec, QC, G1V 2L8
(418) 656-8697
Emp Here 30
SIC 5945 Hobby, toy, and game shops

D-U-N-S 25-999-9142　　(BR)
UNIVERSITE LAVAL
CENTRE COPL
2375 Rue De La Terrasse, Quebec, QC, G1V
0A6
(418) 656-2454
Emp Here 200

SIC 3851 Ophthalmic goods

D-U-N-S 24-685-4942　　(BR)
UNIVERSITE LAVAL
CENTRE D'ETUDES INTERAMERICAINES
1030 Av Des Sciences Humaines, Quebec,
QC, G1V 0A6
(418) 656-2131
Emp Here 4,000
SIC 8221 Colleges and universities

D-U-N-S 20-289-5645　　(BR)
VALEURS MOBILIERES DESJARDINS INC
2640 Boul Laurier Bureau 1400, Quebec, QC,
G1V 5C2
(418) 650-6350
Emp Here 24
SIC 6211 Security brokers and dealers

D-U-N-S 24-788-0474　　(BR)
VILLE DE QUEBEC
VILLE DE QUEBEC
1130 Rte De L'Eglise, Quebec, QC, G1V 4X6
(418) 641-6043
Emp Here 49
SIC 7999 Amusement and recreation, nec

Quebec, QC G1W
Quebec County

D-U-N-S 24-993-9471　　(SL)
9187-7571 QUEBEC INC
CLARION HOTEL QUEBEC
3125 Boul Hochelaga, Quebec, QC, G1W 2P9
(418) 653-7267
Emp Here 90　　*Sales* 3,939,878
SIC 7011 Hotels and motels

D-U-N-S 20-777-2810　　(BR)
**ARCHEVEQUE CATHOLIQUE ROMAIN DE
QUEBEC, L'**
PRESBYTERE SAINT YVES
2470 Rue Triquet, Quebec, QC, G1W 1E2
(418) 651-2232
Emp Here 24
SIC 8661 Religious organizations

D-U-N-S 20-538-9294　　(BR)
CANADA POST CORPORATION
HEBERT, FERLATTE, PAGE PHARMACIENS
2900 Ch Saint-Louis, Quebec, QC, G1W 4R7
(418) 651-1374
Emp Here 30
SIC 5912 Drug stores and proprietary stores

D-U-N-S 24-689-6518　　(SL)
**CENTRE D'HEBERGEMENT DU BOISE
LTEE**
(*Suby of* 2153-1090 Quebec Inc)
3690 Boul Neilson, Quebec, QC, G1W 0A9
(418) 781-0471
Emp Here 100　　*Sales* 3,648,035
SIC 8361 Residential care

D-U-N-S 25-231-8993　　(BR)
**COMMISSION SCOLAIRE CENTRAL QUE-
BEC**
STE FOY ELEMENTARY SCHOOL
(*Suby of* Commission Scolaire Central Que-
bec)
1240 Rue Julien-Green, Quebec, QC, G1W
3M1
(418) 651-4396
Emp Here 30
SIC 8211 Elementary and secondary schools

D-U-N-S 20-711-8592　　(BR)
**COMMISSION SCOLAIRE CENTRAL QUE-
BEC**
*CENTRE DE FORMATION EASTERN QUE-
BEC*
3005 Rue William-Stuart, Quebec, QC, G1W
1V4
(418) 654-0537
Emp Here 30

SIC 8211 Elementary and secondary schools

D-U-N-S 20-029-9779　　(BR)
**COMMISSION SCOLAIRE DES DECOU-
VREURS**
*CENTRE D'EDUCATION DES ADULTES DE
POINTE SAINTE FOY*
(*Suby of* Commission Scolaire des Decou-
vreurs)
965 Rue Valentin, Quebec, QC, G1W 4P8
(418) 652-2144
Emp Here 50
SIC 8211 Elementary and secondary schools

D-U-N-S 25-232-9073　　(BR)
**COMMISSION SCOLAIRE DES DECOU-
VREURS**
ECOLE ST LOUIS DE FRANCE
(*Suby of* Commission Scolaire des Decou-
vreurs)
1550 Rte De L'Eglise, Quebec, QC, G1W 3P5
(418) 652-2150
Emp Here 25
SIC 8211 Elementary and secondary schools

D-U-N-S 25-232-0577　　(BR)
**COMMISSION SCOLAIRE DES DECOU-
VREURS**
*ECOLES PRIMAIRES SAINT LOUIS DE
FRANCE ET SAINT YVES ECOLE SAINT
YVES*
(*Suby of* Commission Scolaire des Decou-
vreurs)
2475 Rue Triquet, Quebec, QC, G1W 1E3
(418) 652-2105
Emp Here 30
SIC 8211 Elementary and secondary schools

D-U-N-S 24-423-0418　　(SL)
CONCEPT MODE STE-FOY INC
999 Av De Bourgogne Bureau A1, Quebec,
QC, G1W 4S6
(418) 653-3214
Emp Here 60　　*Sales* 3,648,035
SIC 5621 Women's clothing stores

D-U-N-S 20-952-0758　　(SL)
GESTION UNIVERSITAS INC
3005 Av Maricourt Bureau 250, Quebec, QC,
G1W 4T8
(418) 651-8975
Emp Here 65　　*Sales* 26,884,250
SIC 6722 Management investment, open-end
Pr Gaston Roy
　Jean Marchand
Pers/VP Isabelle Grenier
　Josiane Rivard
Manager Sonia Dupere
VP Sls Pascal Gilbert
　Christian Lebeuf

D-U-N-S 20-103-7863　　(BR)
GROUPE RESTOS PLAISIRS INC, LE
PARIS GRILL, LE
(*Suby of* Groupe Restos Plaisirs Inc, Le)
3121 Boul Hochelaga, Quebec, QC, G1W 2P9
(418) 658-4415
Emp Here 60
SIC 5812 Eating places

D-U-N-S 25-669-8887　　(BR)
**IMMEUBLES JACQUES ROBITAILLE INC,
LES**
HOTEL QUEBEC, L
3115 Av Des Hotels, Quebec, QC, G1W 3Z6
(418) 658-5120
Emp Here 80
SIC 7011 Hotels and motels

D-U-N-S 25-315-8711　　(BR)
**INVESTORS GROUP FINANCIAL SER-
VICES INC**
*SERVICES FINANCIERS GROUPE IN-
VESTORS, LES*
3075 Ch Des Quatre-Bourgeois Bureau 104,
Quebec, QC, G1W 4Y5
(418) 654-1411
Emp Here 60

SIC 8741 Management services

D-U-N-S 25-765-6116　　(BR)
MATELAS DAUPHIN INC
999 Av De Bourgogne, Quebec, QC, G1W
4S6
(418) 652-3411
Emp Here 25
SIC 5712 Furniture stores

D-U-N-S 20-914-4299　　(BR)
NORTHERN MICRO INC
3107 Av Des Hotels Bureau 2, Quebec, QC,
G1W 4W5
(418) 654-1733
Emp Here 75
SIC 5734 Computer and software stores

D-U-N-S 20-620-2009　　(BR)
PROVIGO DISTRIBUTION INC
PROVIGO ST LOUIS
2900 Ch Saint-Louis Bureau 7, Quebec, QC,
G1W 4R7
(418) 653-6277
Emp Here 30
SIC 5141 Groceries, general line

D-U-N-S 20-002-8426　　(BR)
PROVIGO DISTRIBUTION INC
PROVIGO
3440 Ch Des Quatre-Bourgeois Bureau 8047,
Quebec, QC, G1W 4T3
(418) 653-6241
Emp Here 90
SIC 5411 Grocery stores

D-U-N-S 20-006-4215　　(BR)
**SOCIETE DES ETABLISSEMENTS DE
PLEIN AIR DU QUEBEC**
PARC AQUARIUM DU QUEBEC
1675 Av Des Hotels, Quebec, QC, G1W 4S3
(418) 659-5264
Emp Here 50
SIC 8422 Botanical and zoological gardens

Quebec, QC G1X
Quebec County

D-U-N-S 24-202-7456　　(BR)
4211677 CANADA INC
GOJIT
5150 Rue John-Molson, Quebec, QC, G1X
3X4
(514) 761-2345
Emp Here 100
SIC 7389 Business services, nec

D-U-N-S 24-341-7800　　(SL)
AXE TI INC
955 Av De Bourgogne Bureau 201, Quebec,
QC, G1X 3E5
(418) 654-0222
Emp Here 61　　*Sales* 4,450,603
SIC 7361 Employment agencies

D-U-N-S 24-480-1601　　(BR)
C.D.M.V. INC
3220 Av Watt Bureau 220, Quebec, QC, G1X
4Z6
(450) 771-2368
Emp Here 30
SIC 5047 Medical and hospital equipment

D-U-N-S 24-199-8426　　(BR)
CSG SECURITY CORPORATION
CHUBB EDWARDS
(*Suby of* United Technologies Corporation)
2800 Rue Einstein Bureau 20, Quebec, QC,
G1X 4N8
(418) 681-6045
Emp Here 50
SIC 5063 Electrical apparatus and equipment

D-U-N-S 24-129-5810　　(BR)
CAISSE DESJARDINS DE SAINTE-FOY
CENTRE DE SERVICE DE LA COLLINE

3211 Ch Sainte-Foy, Quebec, QC, G1X 1R3
(418) 653-0515
Emp Here 85
SIC 6062 State credit unions

D-U-N-S 20-644-5079   (BR)
CANAC-MARQUIS GRENIER LTEE
1230 Rue Charles-Albanel, Quebec, QC, G1X 4V1
(418) 871-7900
Emp Here 50
SIC 5211 Lumber and other building materials

D-U-N-S 20-539-2199   (BR)
CANADA POST CORPORATION
QUEBEC PDF DUPLESSIS
3291 Ch Sainte-Foy Unite 225, Quebec, QC, G1X 3V2
(418) 652-1738
Emp Here 37
SIC 4311 U.s. postal service

D-U-N-S 25-234-2308   (BR)
COMMISSION SCOLAIRE DES DECOU-VREURS
ECOLES PRIMAIRES FILTEAU
(*Suby of* Commission Scolaire des Decou-vreurs)
830 Rue De Saurel, Quebec, QC, G1X 3P6
(418) 652-2152
Emp Here 50
SIC 8211 Elementary and secondary schools

D-U-N-S 25-232-1534   (BR)
COMMISSION SCOLAIRE DES DECOU-VREURS
ECOLE COEUR VAILLANT CAMPANILE
(*Suby of* Commission Scolaire des Decou-vreurs)
3645 Ch Sainte-Foy, Quebec, QC, G1X 1T1
(418) 652-2173
Emp Here 30
SIC 8211 Elementary and secondary schools

D-U-N-S 25-918-3291   (BR)
COMMISSION SCOLAIRE DES DECOU-VREURS
ECOLE SECONDAIRE LES COMPAGNONS DE QUARTIER
(*Suby of* Commission Scolaire des Decou-vreurs)
3643 Av Des Compagnons, Quebec, QC, G1X 3Z6
(418) 652-2170
Emp Here 140
SIC 8211 Elementary and secondary schools

D-U-N-S 20-801-2612   (BR)
COSTCO WHOLESALE CANADA LTD
COSTCO
(*Suby of* Costco Wholesale Corporation)
3233 Av Watt, Quebec, QC, G1X 4W2
(418) 656-0666
Emp Here 200
SIC 5099 Durable goods, nec

D-U-N-S 20-640-5826   (SL)
EINSTEIN NISSAN INC
5250 Rue John-Molson, Quebec, QC, G1X 3X4
(418) 650-5353
Emp Here 40   *Sales* 19,632,000
SIC 5511 New and used car dealers
Pr Michel Potvin
Fin Ex Francois Gervais
  Carl Latulippe

D-U-N-S 24-218-0771   (BR)
G.N. JOHNSTON EQUIPMENT CO. LTD
3200 Av Watt Bureau 105, Quebec, QC, G1X 4P8
(418) 650-1620
Emp Here 25
SIC 5084 Industrial machinery and equipment

D-U-N-S 20-709-5154   (BR)
GENESEE & WYOMING CANADA INC
QUEBEC GATINEAU RAILWAY

(*Suby of* Genesee & Wyoming Inc.)
4800 Rue John-Molson, Quebec, QC, G1X 3X4
(514) 948-6983
Emp Here 30
SIC 4111 Local and suburban transit

D-U-N-S 25-455-0437   (BR)
GOODFELLOW INC
5100 Rue John-Molson, Quebec, QC, G1X 3X4
(418) 650-5100
Emp Here 50
SIC 5039 Construction materials, nec

D-U-N-S 20-293-7897   (BR)
GROUPE VOLVO CANADA INC
PREVOST CAR
2955a Av Watt, Quebec, QC, G1X 3W1
(418) 654-0174
Emp Here 70
SIC 4225 General warehousing and storage

D-U-N-S 25-744-9355   (BR)
GROUPE DE COURTAGE OMNI LTEE
COURTIERS EN ALIMENTATION
3200 Av Watt, Quebec, QC, G1X 4P8
(418) 871-2802
Emp Here 30
SIC 6221 Commodity contracts brokers, dealers

D-U-N-S 25-744-9462   (BR)
HYPERTEC SYSTEMES INC
HYPERTEC GROUP
2800 Rue Einstein Bureau 060, Quebec, QC, G1X 4N8
(418) 683-2192
Emp Here 20
SIC 7371 Custom computer programming services

D-U-N-S 20-715-6048   (BR)
INDUSTRIES SPECTRA PREMIUM INC, LES
2950 Av Watt Bureau 5, Quebec, QC, G1X 4A8
(418) 656-1516
Emp Here 25
SIC 3433 Heating equipment, except electric

D-U-N-S 20-764-0124   (BR)
INTEGRATED DISTRIBUTION SYSTEMS LIMITED PARTNERSHIP
WAJAX POWER SYSTEMS
2997 Av Watt, Quebec, QC, G1X 3W1
(418) 651-4236
Emp Here 85
SIC 5084 Industrial machinery and equipment

D-U-N-S 20-298-3706   (SL)
L'INDUSTRIELLE-ALLIANCE SERVICES IMMOBILIERS INC
INDUSTRIAL-ALLIANCE LIFE REAL ESTATE SERVICES
3810 Rue De Marly, Quebec, QC, G1X 4B1
(418) 651-7308
Emp Here 700   *Sales* 85,218,000
SIC 6513 Apartment building operators
Pr Michel Tremblay
Sec Jennifer Dibblee

D-U-N-S 20-205-7428   (SL)
LAURIER PONTIAC BUICK GMC CADILLAC HUMMER LTEE
(*Suby of* Investissements Saillant Ltee)
3001 Av Kepler, Quebec, QC, G1X 3V4
(418) 659-6420
Emp Here 65   *Sales* 32,656,000
SIC 5511 New and used car dealers
Pr Pr Jacques Saillant

D-U-N-S 25-484-9144   (BR)
LEON'S FURNITURE LIMITED
MEUBLES LEON
2840 Rue Einstein, Quebec, QC, G1X 5H3
(418) 683-9600
Emp Here 90

SIC 5712 Furniture stores

D-U-N-S 20-720-4574   (BR)
LOBLAWS SUPERMARKETS LIMITED
MAXI & CIE
3111 Av Watt, Quebec, QC, G1X 3W2
(418) 657-1133
Emp Here 80
SIC 5411 Grocery stores

D-U-N-S 24-792-0960   (BR)
MIDLAND TRANSPORT LIMITED
(*Suby of* J. D. Irving, Limited)
2885 Av Kepler, Quebec, QC, G1X 3V4
(418) 650-1818
Emp Here 20
SIC 4213 Trucking, except local

D-U-N-S 20-297-1904   (BR)
PENSKE TRUCK LEASING CANADA INC
LOCATION DE CAMIONS PENSKE
(*Suby of* Penske Corporation)
2824 Rue Einstein, Quebec, QC, G1X 4B3
(418) 682-0301
Emp Here 24
SIC 7513 Truck rental and leasing, no drivers

D-U-N-S 25-767-0737   (BR)
PRISZM LP
PFK
3309 Ch Sainte-Foy, Quebec, QC, G1X 1S2
(418) 656-1228
Emp Here 20
SIC 5812 Eating places

D-U-N-S 20-188-6251   (BR)
RUSSEL METALS INC
ACIER LOUBIER
5225 Rue John-Molson, Quebec, QC, G1X 3X4
(418) 656-9911
Emp Here 30
SIC 5051 Metals service centers and offices

D-U-N-S 24-464-4183   (BR)
SAPUTO PRODUITS LAITIERS CANADA S.E.N.C.
SAPUTO
(*Suby of* Saputo Produits Laitiers Canada S.E.N.C.)
3240 Av Watt Bureau 110, Quebec, QC, G1X 4X7
(418) 651-5220
Emp Here 60
SIC 5143 Dairy products, except dried or canned

D-U-N-S 25-885-7192   (BR)
SLEEMAN BREWERIES LTD
SLEEMAN UNIBROUE
2955 Av Watt Bureau B, Quebec, QC, G1X 3W1
(418) 658-1834
Emp Here 35
SIC 5813 Drinking places

D-U-N-S 25-307-6541   (BR)
SOCIETE DES ALCOOLS DU QUEBEC
SAQ DEPOT DE QUEBEC
2900 Rue Einstein, Quebec, QC, G1X 4B3
(418) 646-3604
Emp Here 74
SIC 3955 Carbon paper and inked ribbons

D-U-N-S 24-730-0288   (BR)
SUPERMARCHES GP INC, LES
METRO G P, DIV DE
(*Suby of* Supermarches GP Inc, Les)
2800 Rue Einstein Bureau 20, Quebec, QC, G1X 4N8

Emp Here 20
SIC 5411 Grocery stores

D-U-N-S 25-174-3944   (BR)
VALUE VILLAGE STORES, INC
VILLAGE DES VALEURS
(*Suby of* Savers, Inc.)
3355 Rue De La Perade, Quebec, QC, G1X

3V3
(418) 651-2772
Emp Here 70
SIC 5399 Miscellaneous general merchandise

Quebec, QC G1Y
Quebec County

D-U-N-S 25-234-2159   (BR)
COMMISSION SCOLAIRE DES DECOU-VREURS
ECOLE MARGUERITE D'YOUVILLE
(*Suby of* Commission Scolaire des Decou-vreurs)
1473 Rue Provancher, Quebec, QC, G1Y 1S2
(418) 652-2176
Emp Here 30
SIC 8211 Elementary and secondary schools

D-U-N-S 20-029-9787   (BR)
COMMISSION SCOLAIRE DES DECOU-VREURS
ECOLE PRIMAIRE SECONDAIRE DES GRANDES MAREES
(*Suby of* Commission Scolaire des Decou-vreurs)
1505 Rue Des Grandes-Marees, Quebec, QC, G1Y 2T3
(418) 652-2196
Emp Here 90
SIC 8211 Elementary and secondary schools

D-U-N-S 20-712-0408   (BR)
COMMISSION SCOLAIRE DES DECOU-VREURS
ECOLE PRIMAIRE L'ARBRISSEAU
(*Suby of* Commission Scolaire des Decou-vreurs)
4675 Rue De La Promenade-Des-Soeurs, Quebec, QC, G1Y 2W2
(418) 652-2178
Emp Here 30
SIC 8211 Elementary and secondary schools

D-U-N-S 24-690-4643   (SL)
COMPRO COMMUNICATIONS INC
1097 Boul De La Chaudiere, Quebec, QC, G1Y 3T4
(418) 652-1490
Emp Here 31   *Sales* 5,496,960
SIC 4899 Communication services, nec
Pr Pr Jean-Guy Rivard

Quebec, QC G2A
Quebec County

D-U-N-S 25-905-9491   (SL)
AIDE A LA COMMUNAUTE & SERVICES A DOMICILE
14 Rue Saint-Amand Bureau 842, Quebec, QC, G2A 2K9
(418) 842-9791
Emp Here 72   *Sales* 3,429,153
SIC 8059 Nursing and personal care, nec

D-U-N-S 25-232-3431   (BR)
COMMISSION SCOLAIRE DE LA CAPI-TALE, LA
ECOLE DE CHATEAU D'EAU
3075 Rue Du Golf, Quebec, QC, G2A 1G1
(418) 686-4040
Emp Here 33
SIC 8211 Elementary and secondary schools

D-U-N-S 24-345-6295   (BR)
COMMISSION SCOLAIRE DE LA CAPI-TALE, LA
ECOLE SECONDAIRE ROGER COMTOIS
158 Boul Des Etudiants, Quebec, QC, G2A 1N8
(418) 686-4040
Emp Here 146

SIC 8211 Elementary and secondary schools

D-U-N-S 20-807-0834   (BR)
COUCHE-TARD INC
11498 Boul Valcartier, Quebec, QC, G2A 2M6
(418) 845-1362
Emp Here 25
SIC 5411 Grocery stores

Quebec, QC G2B
Quebec County

D-U-N-S 20-292-4395   (SL)
9292-2871 QUEBEC INC
RESTAURANT NORMANDIN
2335 Boul Bastien, Quebec, QC, G2B 1B3
(418) 842-9160
Emp Here 26   *Sales* 952,876
SIC 5812 Eating places

D-U-N-S 20-292-4387   (SL)
9292-2897 QUEBEC INC
N BAR
2335 Boul Bastien, Quebec, QC, G2B 1B3
(418) 842-9160
Emp Here 26   *Sales* 952,876
SIC 5812 Eating places

D-U-N-S 20-334-6452   (BR)
ASHTON CASSE-CROUTE INC
CHEZ ASHTON CASSE CROUTE
(*Suby of* Placements Ashton LeBlond Inc, Les)
9375 Boul De L'Ormiere, Quebec, QC, G2B 3K7

Emp Here 32
SIC 5812 Eating places

D-U-N-S 24-368-9275   (BR)
CAISSE DESJARDINS DES RIVIERES DE QUEBEC
CENTRE DE SERVICES NEUFCHATEL
2240 Boul Bastien, Quebec, QC, G2B 1B6
(418) 842-1214
Emp Here 30
SIC 6062 State credit unions

D-U-N-S 20-712-0630   (BR)
COMMISSION SCOLAIRE DE LA CAPI-TALE, LA
ECOLE PRIMAIRE DE L'ESCABELLE
2120 Rue Du Cure-Lacroix, Quebec, QC, G2B 1S1
(418) 686-4040
Emp Here 40
SIC 8211 Elementary and secondary schools

D-U-N-S 20-574-8127   (BR)
COMMISSION SCOLAIRE DE LA CAPI-TALE, LA
CENTRE SAINT-LOUIS EDUCATION DES ADULTES
262 Rue Racine, Quebec, QC, G2B 1E6

Emp Here 40
SIC 8211 Elementary and secondary schools

D-U-N-S 25-233-4529   (BR)
COMMISSION SCOLAIRE DE LA CAPI-TALE, LA
ECOLE DE LA CHAUMIERE
4285 Rue Rene-Chaloult, Quebec, QC, G2B 4R7
(418) 686-4040
Emp Here 45
SIC 8211 Elementary and secondary schools

D-U-N-S 25-233-8280   (BR)
COMMISSION SCOLAIRE DE LA CAPI-TALE, LA
ECOLE ST CLAUDE
12155 Boul Saint-Claude, Quebec, QC, G2B 1H4
(418) 686-4040
Emp Here 30

SIC 8211 Elementary and secondary schools

D-U-N-S 25-233-8249   (BR)
COMMISSION SCOLAIRE DE LA CAPI-TALE, LA
ECOLE NOTRE DAME DES NEIGES
4140 Boul Gastonguay, Quebec, QC, G2B 1M7
(418) 686-4040
Emp Here 30
SIC 8211 Elementary and secondary schools

D-U-N-S 24-126-2299   (BR)
COURTIERS INTER-QUEBEC INC, LES
ROYAL LEPAGE INTER QUEBEC
9105 Boul De L'Ormiere, Quebec, QC, G2B 3K2
(418) 843-1151
Emp Here 34
SIC 6531 Real estate agents and managers

D-U-N-S 24-821-6186   (BR)
FINANCIERE MICADCO INC
(*Suby of* Groupe Michel Cadrin Inc)
9550 Boul De L'Ormiere, Quebec, QC, G2B 3Z6
(418) 842-9221
Emp Here 3,020
SIC 5912 Drug stores and proprietary stores

D-U-N-S 25-816-0779   (BR)
GESTION PIERRE BARRETTE INC
TIM HORTONS
9430 Boul De L'Ormiere, Quebec, QC, G2B 3K6
(418) 842-4143
Emp Here 50   *Sales* 1,532,175
SIC 5812 Eating places

D-U-N-S 25-240-5287   (BR)
L'ECOLE DES URSULINES DE QUEBEC
ECOLE DES URSULINES LORETTEVILLE
63 Rue Racine, Quebec, QC, G2B 1C8
(418) 842-2949
Emp Here 25
SIC 8211 Elementary and secondary schools

D-U-N-S 20-292-4403   (SL)
LE FLYS INC
RESTAURANT NORMANDIN
2335 Boul Bastien, Quebec, QC, G2B 1B3
(418) 842-9160
Emp Here 26   *Sales* 952,876
SIC 5812 Eating places

D-U-N-S 20-292-4429   (SL)
LE PORT-JOLIEN INC
RESTAURANT NORMANDIN
2335 Boul Bastien, Quebec, QC, G2B 1B3
(418) 842-9160
Emp Here 50   *Sales* 1,819,127
SIC 5812 Eating places

D-U-N-S 20-292-4411   (SL)
LE STMA INC
RESTAURANT NORMANDIN
2335 Boul Bastien, Quebec, QC, G2B 1B3
(418) 842-9160
Emp Here 50   *Sales* 1,819,127
SIC 5812 Eating places

D-U-N-S 25-647-5690   (BR)
MCMAHON DISTRIBUTEUR PHARMACEU-TIQUE INC
BRUNET PHARMACIE
9550 Boul De L'Ormiere, Quebec, QC, G2B 3Z6
(418) 842-9221
Emp Here 20
SIC 5912 Drug stores and proprietary stores

D-U-N-S 24-622-8787   (SL)
PRODUITS ALIMAISON INC, LES
2335 Boul Bastien, Quebec, QC, G2B 1B3
(418) 842-9160
Emp Here 40   *Sales* 2,918,428
SIC 2038 Frozen specialties, nec

D-U-N-S 25-458-7462   (BR)

PROVIGO INC
PROVIGO L'ORMIERE
9550 Boul De L'Ormiere, Quebec, QC, G2B 3Z6
(418) 843-1732
Emp Here 70
SIC 5411 Grocery stores

D-U-N-S 24-426-3393   (SL)
RESIDENCE STE-GENEVIEVE
4855 Rte Sainte-Genevieve Bureau 264, Quebec, QC, G2B 4W3
(418) 842-4085
Emp Here 20   *Sales* 729,607
SIC 8361 Residential care

D-U-N-S 20-292-4478   (SL)
RESTAURANT NORMANDIN (STE-FOY) INC
2335 Boul Bastien, Quebec, QC, G2B 1B3
(418) 842-9160
Emp Here 50   *Sales* 1,819,127
SIC 5812 Eating places

D-U-N-S 24-730-6095   (HQ)
RESTAURANT NORMANDIN INC
2335 Boul Bastien, Quebec, QC, G2B 1B3
(418) 842-9160
Emp Here 300   *Emp Total* 2,300
Sales 95,556,480
SIC 5812 Eating places
Pr Pr Denis Pigeon
    Reginald Perron

D-U-N-S 25-896-1580   (BR)
RESTAURANT LES TROIS MOUSSAIL-LONS INC
RESTAURANT MCDONALD
(*Suby of* Restaurant les Trois Moussaillons Inc)
9400 Boul De L'Ormiere, Quebec, QC, G2B 3K6
(418) 843-7826
Emp Here 65
SIC 5812 Eating places

D-U-N-S 25-767-3566   (SL)
SERVICE REGIONAL D'INTERPRETARIAT DE L'EST DU QUEBEC INC
SRIEQ: SERVICE D'AIDE A LA COMMUNI-CATION / BAS ST-LAURENT
9885 Boul De L'Ormiere, Quebec, QC, G2B 3K9
(418) 622-1037
Emp Here 50   *Sales* 2,626,585
SIC 7389 Business services, nec

Quebec, QC G2C
Quebec County

D-U-N-S 20-700-5849   (SL)
9075-6602 QUEBEC INC
6275 Boul De L'Ormiere, Quebec, QC, G2C 1B9
(418) 842-3232
Emp Here 50   *Sales* 12,815,674
SIC 1541 Industrial buildings and warehouses
Pr Guy J Gaudet

D-U-N-S 20-362-3538   (SL)
9230-9970 QUEBEC INC
IGA EXTRA CONVIVIO
2295 Av Chauveau Bureau 200, Quebec, QC, G2C 0G7
(418) 842-3381
Emp Here 175   *Sales* 29,403,162
SIC 5411 Grocery stores
Yanic Drouin

D-U-N-S 25-479-6543   (BR)
ADT CANADA INC
2290 Rue Jean-Perrin Bureau 100, Quebec, QC, G2C 1T9
(418) 683-9472
Emp Here 30
SIC 1731 Electrical work

D-U-N-S 20-655-9671   (BR)
ADT CANADA INC
RELIANCE
2290 Rue Jean-Perrin Bureau 100, Quebec, QC, G2C 1T9
(418) 647-1382
Emp Here 30
SIC 7382 Security systems services

D-U-N-S 20-205-7345   (HQ)
AMEUBLEMENTS TANGUAY INC
SIGNATURE MAURICE TANGUAY
7200 Rue Armand-Viau, Quebec, QC, G2C 2A7
(418) 847-4411
Emp Here 200   *Emp Total* 774
Sales 107,674,999
SIC 5712 Furniture stores
Pr Maurice Tanguay
Sec Yves Des Groseillers
Genl Mgr Jacques Tanguay

D-U-N-S 25-646-6525   (BR)
ANIMALERIE DYNO INC
8925 Boul De L'Ormiere, Quebec, QC, G2C 1C4
(418) 843-1466
Emp Here 20
SIC 5999 Miscellaneous retail stores, nec

D-U-N-S 20-357-3592   (BR)
AUTOMOBILE ET TOURING CLUB DU QUE-BEC (A.T.C.Q.)
CAA-QUEBEC
8000 Rue Armand-Viau Bureau 500, Quebec, QC, G2C 2E2
(418) 624-2424
Emp Here 60
SIC 8699 Membership organizations, nec

D-U-N-S 20-864-2046   (SL)
BUFFETS JE RECOIS INC, LES
LE GROUPE JE RECOIS
2405 Rue De Celles Bureau 3, Quebec, QC, G2C 1K7
(418) 626-1010
Emp Here 50   *Sales* 1,532,175
SIC 5812 Eating places

D-U-N-S 20-712-0614   (BR)
COMMISSION SCOLAIRE DE LA CAPI-TALE, LA
CENTRE FORMATION PROFESSIONNELLE DE NEUFCHATEL
3400 Av Chauveau, Quebec, QC, G2C 1A1
(418) 686-4040
Emp Here 90
SIC 8331 Job training and related services

D-U-N-S 24-239-8886   (BR)
COMMISSION SCOLAIRE DE LA CAPI-TALE, LA
ECOLE SECONDAIRE DE NEUFCHATEL
3600 Av Chauveau, Quebec, QC, G2C 1A1
(418) 686-4040
Emp Here 150
SIC 8211 Elementary and secondary schools

D-U-N-S 20-578-7559   (BR)
COMPAGNIE COMMONWEALTH PLY-WOOD LTEE, LA
ROBERT BURY & COMPANY (CANADA)
5300 Rue Armand-Viau, Quebec, QC, G2C 1Y7
(418) 872-2879
Emp Here 30
SIC 5031 Lumber, plywood, and millwork

D-U-N-S 20-137-5883   (SL)
ENTREPRISES QUEBECOISES D'EXCAVATION L.E.Q.E.L. (1993) LTEE, LES
L.E.Q.E.L.
4055 Rue Jean-Marchand, Quebec, QC, G2C 2J2
(418) 847-1111
Emp Here 50   *Sales* 4,377,642
SIC 1731 Electrical work

D-U-N-S 20-291-1673 (BR)
GORDON FOOD SERVICE CANADA LTD
FRIGO NATIONAL
800 Rue Armand-Viau, Quebec, QC, G2C
2E2
(418) 840-5600
Emp Here 50
SIC 5141 Groceries, general line

D-U-N-S 20-511-6937 (BR)
HYDRO-QUEBEC
*HYDRO QUEBEC HYDRODIRECT SIEGE
REGIONAL TERRITOIRE MONTMORENCY*
2625 Boul Lebourgneuf Bureau 14, Quebec,
QC, G2C 1P1
(418) 845-6600
Emp Here 2,200
SIC 4911 Electric services

D-U-N-S 24-348-0733 (BR)
MEDIAS TRANSCONTINENTAL S.E.N.C.
2850 Rue Jean-Perrin, Quebec, QC, G2C 2C8

Emp Here 165
SIC 2752 Commercial printing, lithographic

D-U-N-S 25-389-8100 (SL)
METAFAB (1996) INC
4155 Rue Jean-Marchand, Quebec, QC, G2C
2J2
(418) 840-3684
Emp Here 30   *Sales* 6,879,002
SIC 3644 Noncurrent-carrying wiring devices
 Michel Lamoureux

D-U-N-S 24-791-0367 (HQ)
ORTHOFAB INC
2160 Rue De Celles, Quebec, QC, G2C 1X8
(418) 847-5225
Emp Here 50   *Emp Total* 80
Sales 9,182,261
SIC 3842 Surgical appliances and supplies
 Richard Lapierre
Sec Jean Painchaud
Dir Pierre Simard
Dir Denis Carbonneau
Dir Daniel Belanger

D-U-N-S 24-978-2694 (SL)
**PHARMACIE DOMINIQUE BOND ET
MELISSA PILOTE S.E.N.C.**
2283 Av Chauveau, Quebec, QC, G2C 0G7
(418) 843-3191
Emp Here 50   *Sales* 2,991,389
SIC 8011 Offices and clinics of medical doctors

D-U-N-S 25-761-5716 (SL)
PROLUDIK INC
2500 Rue Jean-Perrin Bureau 103, Quebec,
QC, G2C 1X1
(418) 845-1245
Emp Here 85   *Sales* 9,536,300
SIC 7359 Equipment rental and leasing, nec
Pr Pr Andre Lachance
 Gino Vallee

D-U-N-S 24-126-1176 (BR)
PROVIGO DISTRIBUTION INC
*PROVIGO CENTRE DE DISTRIBUTION ALI-
MENTATION*
8000 Rue Armand-Viau Bureau 500, Quebec,
QC, G2C 2E2

Emp Here 500
SIC 5141 Groceries, general line

D-U-N-S 25-281-7556 (BR)
PUROLATOR INC.
PUROLATOR INC
7000 Rue Armand-Viau, Quebec, QC, G2C
2C4
(888) 744-7123
Emp Here 300
SIC 4731 Freight transportation arrangement

D-U-N-S 25-165-0602 (BR)
REGULVAR INC

2800 Rue Jean-Perrin Bureau 100, Quebec,
QC, G2C 1T3
(418) 842-5114
Emp Here 300
SIC 1796 Installing building equipment

Quebec, QC G2E
Quebec County

D-U-N-S 25-474-2877 (SL)
2973-8424 QUEBEC INC
RESTAURANT TOMAS TAM
5233 Boul Wilfrid-Hamel, Quebec, QC, G2E
2H1
(418) 871-8182
Emp Here 65   *Sales* 1,969,939
SIC 5812 Eating places

D-U-N-S 20-703-8097 (SL)
9100-9647 QUEBEC INC
NOVA PERMIS & ESCORTES ROUTIERES
2800 Av Saint-Jean-Baptiste Bureau 235,
Quebec, QC, G2E 6J5
(418) 527-7775
Emp Here 25   *Sales* 5,693,280
SIC 6794 Patent owners and lessors
Pr Pr Louis Juneau
VP VP Monique Comeau

D-U-N-S 25-321-1007 (BR)
ABF FREIGHT SYSTEM CANADA, LTD
ABF TERMINAL #225
(*Suby of* Arcbest Corporation)
445 Av Saint-Jean-Baptiste Bureau 300, Que-
bec, QC, G2E 5N7
(418) 872-8812
Emp Here 24
SIC 4213 Trucking, except local

D-U-N-S 25-864-6439 (SL)
ADELE 1994 INC
ADELE
5237 Boul Wilfrid-Hamel 190, Quebec,
QC, G2E 2H2
(418) 877-1000
Emp Here 60   *Sales* 1,751,057
SIC 7349 Building maintenance services, nec

D-U-N-S 20-868-6832 (HQ)
AUTOBUS LA QUEBECOISE INC
LIGNE D'AUTOBUS DECOUVERTE
(*Suby of* Autobus la Quebecoise Inc)
5480 Rue Rideau, Quebec, QC, G2E 5V2
(418) 872-5525
Emp Here 100   *Emp Total* 112
Sales 3,137,310
SIC 4151 School buses

D-U-N-S 24-207-6974 (BR)
CANPAR TRANSPORT L.P.
(*Suby of* Canpar Transport L.P.)
5125 Rue Rideau, Quebec, QC, G2E 5H5

Emp Here 25
SIC 4213 Trucking, except local

D-U-N-S 25-022-6792 (BR)
**COMMISSION SCOLAIRE DES DECOU-
VREURS**
ECOLE L'ETINCELLE TROIS SAISONS
(*Suby of* Commission Scolaire des Decou-
vreurs)
1400 Rue Falardeau, Quebec, QC, G2E 2Z6
(418) 871-6415
Emp Here 38
SIC 8211 Elementary and secondary schools

D-U-N-S 25-484-8633 (HQ)
ESKIMO EXPRESS INC
MORNEAU ESKIMO
5055 Rue Rideau Bureau 500, Quebec, QC,
G2E 5H5
(418) 681-1212
Emp Here 75   *Emp Total* 700
Sales 19,502,959

SIC 4213 Trucking, except local
Pr Andre Morneau
 Micheline Morneau

D-U-N-S 25-747-5848 (BR)
ESSILOR GROUPE CANADA INC
525 Rue Michel-Fragasso Bureau 101, Quebec, QC, G2E 5K6
(418) 871-5193
Emp Here 20
SIC 3827 Optical instruments and lenses

D-U-N-S 24-821-1625 (BR)
**FEDERAL EXPRESS CANADA CORPORA-
TION**
FEDERAL EXPRESS CANADA LTD
(*Suby of* Fedex Corporation)
5205 Rue Rideau, Quebec, QC, G2E 5H5
(800) 463-3339
Emp Here 51
SIC 7389 Business services, nec

D-U-N-S 24-936-0942 (HQ)
FISO TECHNOLOGIES INC
500 Av Saint-Jean-Baptiste Bureau 195, Que-
bec, QC, G2E 5R9
(418) 688-8065
Emp Here 40   *Emp Total* 100
Sales 3,502,114
SIC 3827 Optical instruments and lenses

D-U-N-S 25-198-7681 (SL)
GHD CONSULTANTS LTEE
INSPEC-SOL
445 Av Saint-Jean-Baptiste Bureau 390, Que-
bec, QC, G2E 5N7
(418) 658-0112
Emp Here 500
SIC 8621 Professional organizations

D-U-N-S 24-050-4477 (SL)
GARANTIES PRIVILEGE PLUS INC
540 Rue Michel-Fragasso, Quebec, QC, G2E
5N4
(418) 780-0111
Emp Here 20   *Sales* 22,804,480
SIC 6311 Life insurance
Pr Guylaine Boyer

D-U-N-S 20-555-0069 (BR)
GECKO ALLIANCE GROUP INC
(*Suby of* Gecko Alliance Group Inc)
450 Av Saint-Jean-Baptiste Bureau 200, Que-
bec, QC, G2E 6H5
(418) 872-4411
Emp Here 208
SIC 3625 Relays and industrial controls

D-U-N-S 20-713-7139 (BR)
**GOUVERNEMENT DE LA PROVINCE DE
QUEBEC**
*GOUVERNEMENT DE LA PROVINCE DE
QUEBEC*
1400 Av Saint-Jean-Baptiste Bureau 180,
Quebec, QC, G2E 5B7
(418) 528-2035
Emp Here 35
SIC 6331 Fire, marine, and casualty insurance

D-U-N-S 24-392-8400 (BR)
**GOUVERNEMENT DE LA PROVINCE DE
QUEBEC**
FINANCIERE AGRICOLE DU QUEBEC, LA
5055 Boul Wilfrid-Hamel Bureau 100, Quebec,
QC, G2E 2G6
(418) 838-5602
Emp Here 20
SIC 6331 Fire, marine, and casualty insurance

D-U-N-S 24-191-8197 (BR)
GROUPE D'ECLAIRAGE LUXTEC INC
(*Suby of* Lumenpulse Inc)
445 Av Saint-Jean-Baptiste Bureau 120, Que-
bec, QC, G2E 5N7
(418) 871-8039
Emp Here 300
SIC 5063 Electrical apparatus and equipment

D-U-N-S 20-007-0550 (BR)
LOCATION BROSSARD INC
(*Suby of* 2313-5338 Quebec Inc)
955 Av Saint-Jean-Baptiste Bureau 100, Que-
bec, QC, G2E 5J5
(418) 877-2400
Emp Here 25
SIC 7513 Truck rental and leasing, no drivers

D-U-N-S 20-231-6860 (BR)
LOCATION DE CAMIONS EUREKA INC
(*Suby of* Gestion Camions Lague Inc)
5055 Rue Rideau Bureau 400, Quebec, QC,
G2E 5H5
(418) 877-3074
Emp Here 24
SIC 7513 Truck rental and leasing, no drivers

D-U-N-S 25-765-8054 (BR)
PROULX, G. INC
ACOUSTI PLUS
5275 Boul Wilfrid-Hamel Bureau 180, Quebec,
QC, G2E 5M7
(418) 871-4300
Emp Here 23
SIC 5032 Brick, stone, and related material

D-U-N-S 25-297-6675 (BR)
SIEMENS CANADA LIMITED
2800 Av Saint-Jean-Baptiste Bureau 190,
Quebec, QC, G2E 6J5
(418) 687-4524
Emp Here 130
SIC 3625 Relays and industrial controls

D-U-N-S 24-465-5791 (BR)
TOROMONT INDUSTRIES LTD
CIMCO REFRIGERATION
5130 Rue Rideau Bureau 150, Quebec, QC,
G2E 5S4
(418) 872-4025
Emp Here 50
SIC 3585 Refrigeration and heating equip-
ment

D-U-N-S 25-980-3765 (BR)
UNITED PARCEL SERVICE CANADA LTD
UPS
625 Rue Des Canetons, Quebec, QC, G2E
5X6
(418) 872-2686
Emp Here 80
SIC 7389 Business services, nec

Quebec, QC G2G
Quebec County

D-U-N-S 20-526-3200 (BR)
2427-9028 QUEBEC INC
SPORTS EXPERTS
1475 Av Jules-Verne, Quebec, QC, G2G 2R8
(418) 871-5150
Emp Here 30
SIC 5941 Sporting goods and bicycle shops

D-U-N-S 20-649-1727 (BR)
ACCEO SOLUTIONS INC
7710 Boul Wilfrid-Hamel, Quebec, QC, G2G
2J5
(418) 877-0088
Emp Here 960
SIC 7372 Prepackaged software

D-U-N-S 25-401-1786 (BR)
AIR CANADA
510 Rue Principale, Quebec, QC, G2G 2T9
(514) 422-5000
Emp Here 70
SIC 4512 Air transportation, scheduled

D-U-N-S 24-348-1681 (BR)
**ALLSTATE INSURANCE COMPANY OF
CANADA**
1150 Aut Duplessis Unit 600, Quebec, QC,
G2G 2B5

(819) 569-5911
Emp Here 100
SIC 6411 Insurance agents, brokers, and service

D-U-N-S 20-712-0457   (BR)
COMMISSION SCOLAIRE DES DECOUVREURS
ECOLE JOUVENCE
(*Suby of* Commission Scolaire des Decouvreurs)
215 Rue Saint-Yves, Quebec, QC, G2G 1J8
(418) 871-6417
Emp Here 25
SIC 8211 Elementary and secondary schools

D-U-N-S 25-240-4645   (BR)
COMMISSION SCOLAIRE DES DECOUVREURS
ECOLE LES PRIMEVERES
(*Suby of* Commission Scolaire des Decouvreurs)
1465 Rue Felix-Antoine-Savard, Quebec, QC, G2G 1Z2
(418) 871-6418
Emp Here 53
SIC 8211 Elementary and secondary schools

D-U-N-S 24-477-7970   (HQ)
CUISINES DE L'AIR CULIN-AIR INC, LES
(*Suby of* Cuisines de l'Air Culin-Air Inc, Les)
604 6e Rue De L'Aeroport, Quebec, QC, G2G 2S9
(418) 871-4038
Emp Here 35   *Emp Total* 75
Sales 4,565,375
SIC 5812 Eating places

D-U-N-S 24-232-1458   (BR)
GOUVERNEMENT DE LA PROVINCE DE QUEBEC
SERVICE AERIEN GOUVERNEMENTAL
700 7e Rue De L'Aeroport, Quebec, QC, G2G 2S8
(418) 528-3686
Emp Here 190
SIC 8711 Engineering services

D-U-N-S 20-179-6120   (BR)
HOME DEPOT OF CANADA INC
(*Suby of* The Home Depot Inc)
1516 Av Jules-Verne, Quebec, QC, G2G 2R5
(418) 872-8007
Emp Here 125
SIC 5211 Lumber and other building materials

D-U-N-S 24-147-5680   (HQ)
IMMEUBLES JACQUES ROBITAILLE INC, LES
HOTEL QUEBEC INN
7175 Boul Wilfrid-Hamel, Quebec, QC, G2G 1B6
(418) 872-9831
Emp Here 500   *Emp Total* 1,000
Sales 58,896,000
SIC 7011 Hotels and motels
Pr Pr Jacques Robitaille

D-U-N-S 25-305-2310   (BR)
INNVEST PROPERTIES CORP
COMFORT INN
(*Suby of* Innvest Properties Corp)
7320 Boul Wilfrid-Hamel, Quebec, QC, G2G 1C1
(418) 872-5038
Emp Here 25
SIC 7011 Hotels and motels

D-U-N-S 25-477-1884   (BR)
LEPINE-CLOUTIER LTEE
PARC LA SOUVENANCE
301 Rang Sainte-Anne, Quebec, QC, G2G 0G9
(418) 871-2372
Emp Here 40
SIC 6531 Real estate agents and managers

D-U-N-S 20-643-9130   (BR)
METRO RICHELIEU INC

SUPER C
1480 Av Jules-Verne, Quebec, QC, G2G 2R5
(418) 864-7171
Emp Here 70
SIC 5411 Grocery stores

D-U-N-S 20-576-6590   (BR)
NAV CANADA
515 Rue Principale, Quebec, QC, G2G 2T8
(418) 871-7032
Emp Here 110
SIC 4899 Communication services, nec

D-U-N-S 20-281-7131   (BR)
PROMUTUEL PORTNEUF-CHAMPLAIN SOCIETE, MUTUAL D'ASSURANCE GENERALE
1528 Av Jules-Verne, Quebec, QC, G2G 2R5
(418) 872-2430
Emp Here 20
SIC 6411 Insurance agents, brokers, and service

D-U-N-S 24-333-1837   (BR)
SEARS CANADA INC
STE-FOY SEARS HOMETOWN STORE
1430 Av Jules-Verne, Quebec, QC, G2G 2V6
(418) 871-9595
Emp Here 34
SIC 5719 Miscellaneous homefurnishings

D-U-N-S 20-726-2986   (SL)
SIGNALISATION VER-MAC INC
PANNEX
1781 Rue Bresse, Quebec, QC, G2G 2V2
(418) 654-1303
Emp Here 175   *Sales* 25,025,520
SIC 3669 Communications equipment, nec
Pr Whitney Richardson
    Sandra-Lee Mcbain
Dir Whitney Richardson

D-U-N-S 20-105-0007   (BR)
STAPLES CANADA INC
BUREAU EN GROS
(*Suby of* Staples, Inc.)
1510 Av Jules-Verne, Quebec, QC, G2G 2R5
(418) 871-4443
Emp Here 32
SIC 5943 Stationery stores

D-U-N-S 25-498-2549   (BR)
WAL-MART CANADA CORP
WALMART
1470 Av Jules-Verne Bureau 3146, Quebec, QC, G2G 2R5
(418) 874-6068
Emp Here 160
SIC 5311 Department stores

Quebec, QC G2J
Quebec County

D-U-N-S 24-805-2057   (SL)
4317572 CANADA INC
CAGE AUX SPORTS DE LEBOURGNEUF, LA
5540 Boul Des Gradins, Quebec, QC, G2J 1R7
(418) 622-0555
Emp Here 26   *Sales* 802,568
SIC 5812 Eating places

D-U-N-S 24-406-6697   (SL)
9154-7323 QUEBEC INC.
KIA QUEBEC
5055 Boul Des Gradins, Quebec, QC, G2J 1E5
(418) 626-8600
Emp Here 20   *Sales* 9,816,000
SIC 5511 New and used car dealers
Genl Mgr Sylvain Langlois

D-U-N-S 20-309-0873   (SL)
9225-4002 QUEBEC INC

DESROCHES, GROUPE PETROLIER
(*Suby of* Placements Labrecque Inc, Les)
5150 Boul Pierre-Bertrand, Quebec, QC, G2J 1B7
(418) 621-5150
Emp Here 100   *Sales* 40,441,920
SIC 5172 Petroleum products, nec
    Daniel Labrecque

D-U-N-S 24-125-6960   (BR)
ADT CANADA INC
RELIANCE PROTECTRON
4715 Av Des Replats Bureau 265, Quebec, QC, G2J 1B8
(418) 822-2288
Emp Here 20
SIC 5063 Electrical apparatus and equipment

D-U-N-S 20-952-7498   (HQ)
AGENCE DE VOYAGES D'AUTOMOBILE ET TOURING CLUB DU QUEBEC INC
ACCES VACANCES
444 Rue Bouvier, Quebec, QC, G2J 1E3
(418) 624-8222
Emp Here 25   *Emp Total* 1,000
Sales 24,441,835
SIC 6712 Bank holding companies
Pr Richard Lachance
Sec Elisabeth Larochelle-Lachance
Treas Stephane Pare
Dir Rene Proulx
Dir Benoit Bessette

D-U-N-S 20-589-4608   (BR)
BANQUE TORONTO-DOMINION, LA
TD CANADA TRUST
(*Suby of* Toronto-Dominion Bank, The)
5685 Boul Des Gradins, Quebec, QC, G2J 1V1
(418) 624-2966
Emp Here 20
SIC 6021 National commercial banks

D-U-N-S 20-240-9454   (HQ)
BEAUTE STAR BEDARD QUEBEC INC
6500 Boul Pierre-Bertrand, Quebec, QC, G2J 1R4
(418) 627-6500
Emp Here 45   *Emp Total* 95
Sales 8,239,360
SIC 5087 Service establishment equipment
Pr Pr Gaetan Bourdon

D-U-N-S 20-530-0366   (BR)
CANADA POST CORPORATION
6700 Boul Pierre-Bertrand Bureau 200, Quebec, QC, G2J 0B6

Emp Here 100
SIC 4311 U.s. postal service

D-U-N-S 25-744-7755   (SL)
CLEF DE SOL INC, LA
840 Rue Bouvier, Quebec, QC, G2J 1A3
(418) 627-0840
Emp Here 50   *Sales* 4,742,446
SIC 5999 Miscellaneous retail stores, nec

D-U-N-S 24-760-0141   (SL)
COOPERATIVE DES TECHNICIENS AMBULANCIERS DU QUEBEC METROPOLITAIN
C.T.A.Q.M.
6000 Rue Des Tournelles, Quebec, QC, G2J 1E4
(418) 624-2766
Emp Here 275   *Sales* 19,043,040
SIC 4119 Local passenger transportation, nec
Pr Andre Roy
Genl Mgr Andre Hamel
Dir Mario Bussieres

D-U-N-S 25-832-1835   (BR)
COSTCO WHOLESALE CANADA LTD
COSTCO
(*Suby of* Costco Wholesale Corporation)
440 Rue Bouvier, Quebec, QC, G2J 1E3
(418) 627-5100
Emp Here 200

SIC 5099 Durable goods, nec

D-U-N-S 20-672-3389   (BR)
COUCHE-TARD INC
825 Boul Lebourgneuf Bureau 304, Quebec, QC, G2J 0B9
(418) 624-8255
Emp Here 20
SIC 5411 Grocery stores

D-U-N-S 25-846-2092   (BR)
COUVRE-PLANCHERS PELLETIER INC
5000 Av Des Replats, Quebec, QC, G2J 1N2
(418) 624-1290
Emp Here 40
SIC 5713 Floor covering stores

D-U-N-S 25-060-0764   (BR)
DUCKS UNLIMITED CANADA
710 Rue Bouvier Bureau 260, Quebec, QC, G2J 1C2
(418) 623-1650
Emp Here 27
SIC 8999 Services, nec

D-U-N-S 24-908-5663   (SL)
GENIVAR CONSTRUCTION INC
SOLIGER
5355 Boul Des Gradins, Quebec, QC, G2J 1C8
(418) 623-2306
Emp Here 20   *Sales* 1,824,018
SIC 8741 Management services

D-U-N-S 20-914-4869   (BR)
GREAT-WEST LIFE ASSURANCE COMPANY, THE
THE GREAT-WEST LIFE ASSURANCE COMPANY
815 Boul Lebourgneuf Unite 310, Quebec, QC, G2J 0C1
(418) 650-4200
Emp Here 35
SIC 6411 Insurance agents, brokers, and service

D-U-N-S 25-767-0406   (BR)
GROUPE NORMANDIN INC
986 Rue Bouvier, Quebec, QC, G2J 1A3
(418) 627-1265
Emp Here 120
SIC 5812 Eating places

D-U-N-S 20-179-6088   (BR)
HOME DEPOT OF CANADA INC
HOME DEPOT
(*Suby of* The Home Depot Inc)
300 Rue Bouvier, Quebec, QC, G2J 1R8
(418) 634-8880
Emp Here 130
SIC 5211 Lumber and other building materials

D-U-N-S 24-051-6810   (BR)
HYDRO-QUEBEC
SYNDICAT EMPLOYES DE METIERS HYDRO-QUEBEC
5050 Boul Des Gradins Bureau 200, Quebec, QC, G2J 1P8
(418) 624-2811
Emp Here 600
SIC 8631 Labor organizations

D-U-N-S 25-315-7671   (BR)
INVESTORS GROUP INC
815 Boul Lebourgneuf Bureau 500, Quebec, QC, G2J 0C1
(418) 626-1994
Emp Here 60
SIC 8741 Management services

D-U-N-S 20-250-0211   (HQ)
J.M. CLEMENT LTEE
BEBE CONFORT
5830 Boul Pierre-Bertrand Bureau 400, Quebec, QC, G2J 1B7
(418) 626-0006
Emp Here 85   *Emp Total* 500
Sales 27,704,473

SIC 5641 Children's and infants' wear stores
Pr Pr Charles Clement
VP France Clement
VP Caroline Clement
  Marie Clement
  Jean Clement

D-U-N-S 25-285-9665 (BR)
LEMIEUX NOLET COMPTABLES AGREES S.E.N.C.R.L.
(Suby of Lemieux Nolet Comptables Agrees S.E.N.C.R.L.)
815 Boul Lebourgneuf Unite 401, Quebec, QC, G2J 0C1
(418) 659-7374
Emp Here 20
SIC 8721 Accounting, auditing, and book-keeping

D-U-N-S 24-348-0873 (BR)
MEDIAS TRANSCONTINENTAL S.E.N.C.
710 Rue Bouvier Bureau 107, Quebec, QC, G2J 1C2
(418) 628-3155
Emp Here 40
SIC 7319 Advertising, nec

D-U-N-S 24-499-0982 (BR)
NAUTILUS PLUS INC
NAUTILUS PLUS
5155 Boul Des Gradins, Quebec, QC, G2J 1C8
(418) 628-7524
Emp Here 40
SIC 7999 Amusement and recreation, nec

D-U-N-S 25-476-7437 (BR)
P.H. VITRES D'AUTOS INC
5590 Rue Des Tenailles, Quebec, QC, G2J 1S5
(418) 681-1577
Emp Here 22
SIC 7536 Automotive glass replacement shops

D-U-N-S 25-849-1570 (BR)
PROVIGO INC
MAXI # 8649
350 Rue Bouvier, Quebec, QC, G2J 1R8
(418) 623-5475
Emp Here 90
SIC 5411 Grocery stores

D-U-N-S 25-245-6512 (BR)
PUBLIC SERVICE ALLIANCE OF CANADA
ALLIANCE DE LA FONCTION PUBLIQUE DU CANADA
5050 Boul Des Gradins Bureau 130, Quebec, QC, G2J 1P8
(418) 666-6500
Emp Here 30
SIC 8631 Labor organizations

D-U-N-S 20-234-6016 (BR)
SOBEYS QUEBEC INC
I G A EXTRA LEBOURGNEUF
5555 Boul Des Gradins, Quebec, QC, G2J 1C8
(418) 622-5262
Emp Here 140
SIC 5411 Grocery stores

D-U-N-S 25-864-7437 (BR)
STAPLES CANADA INC
BUREAU EN GROS
(Suby of Staples, Inc.)
565 Boul Lebourgneuf, Quebec, QC, G2J 1R9
(418) 622-5044
Emp Here 40
SIC 5943 Stationery stores

D-U-N-S 25-767-4994 (BR)
SYNDICAT QUEBECOIS DES EMPLOYEES & EMPLOYES DE SERVICE SECTION LOCAL 298 (FTQ)
SQEES
5000 Boul Des Gradins Bureau 130, Quebec, QC, G2J 1N3

(418) 626-3100
Emp Here 30
SIC 8631 Labor organizations

D-U-N-S 24-628-3134 (BR)
SYNDICAT QUEBECOIS DES EMPLOYEES & EMPLOYES DE SERVICE SECTION LOCAL 298 (FTQ)
FTQ CTC
5000 Boul Des Gradins Bureau 130, Quebec, QC, G2J 1N3
(418) 626-3100
Emp Here 30
SIC 8631 Labor organizations

D-U-N-S 20-776-5983 (SL)
SYNDICAT DES INSPECTEURS ET DES REPARTITEURS DU RESEAU DE TRANSPORT DE LA CAPITALE (FISA)
REPARTITEURS DU RESEAU DE TRANSPORT DE LA CAPITALE
720 Rue Des Rocailles, Quebec, QC, G2J 1A5
(418) 627-2351
Emp Here 1,200   Sales 58,739,550
SIC 4111 Local and suburban transit
Pr Eric Poirier
VP Jean Cote
Sec Luc-Andre Roy
Treas Diane Beaumont
Dir Montminy Joanne

D-U-N-S 20-860-4459 (BR)
WINNERS MERCHANTS INTERNATIONAL L.P.
WINNERS
(Suby of The TJX Companies Inc)
575 Boul Lebourgneuf, Quebec, QC, G2J 1R9
(418) 621-0621
Emp Here 25
SIC 5651 Family clothing stores

Quebec, QC G2K
Quebec County

D-U-N-S 25-244-3684 (BR)
AMEUBLEMENTS TANGUAY INC
SUPER LIQUIDA MEUBLES
5000 Boul Des Galeries, Quebec, QC, G2K 2L5
(418) 622-5051
Emp Here 50
SIC 5712 Furniture stores

D-U-N-S 25-284-5573 (BR)
ASHTON CASSE-CROUTE INC
(Suby of Placements Ashton LeBlond Inc, Les)
5401 Boul Des Galeries, Quebec, QC, G2K 1N4
(418) 622-5052
Emp Here 20
SIC 5812 Eating places

D-U-N-S 24-464-5370 (BR)
AVIVA INSURANCE COMPANY OF CANADA
1305 Boul Lebourgneuf Bureau 207, Quebec, QC, G2K 2E4
(418) 621-9393
Emp Here 40
SIC 6331 Fire, marine, and casualty insurance

D-U-N-S 25-371-9140 (BR)
BEST BUY CANADA LTD
FUTURE SHOP
(Suby of Best Buy Co., Inc.)
1475 Boul Lebourgneuf, Quebec, QC, G2K 2G3
(418) 263-1044
Emp Here 70
SIC 5731 Radio, television, and electronic stores

D-U-N-S 20-242-9098 (BR)
CRH CANADA GROUP INC

DEMIX BETON
205 Boul Louis-Xiv Bureau 102, Quebec, QC, G2K 1W6
(418) 628-0440
Emp Here 45
SIC 3531 Construction machinery

D-U-N-S 20-917-9220 (SL)
CENTRE DE TELEPHONE MOBILE (QUEBEC) INC
CTM QUEBEC
1100 Rue Bouvier Bureau 400, Quebec, QC, G2K 1L9
(418) 627-7040
Emp Here 20   Sales 4,001,280
SIC 4899 Communication services, nec

D-U-N-S 20-721-1012 (BR)
CIMA+ S.E.N.C.
1145 Boul Lebourgneuf Bureau 300, Quebec, QC, G2K 2K8
(418) 623-3373
Emp Here 80
SIC 8711 Engineering services

D-U-N-S 24-149-0853 (SL)
CLUB DE TENNIS AVANTAGE INC
MULTI-SPORTS
1080 Rue Bouvier, Quebec, QC, G2K 1L9
(418) 627-3343
Emp Here 50   Sales 2,042,900
SIC 7997 Membership sports and recreation clubs

D-U-N-S 20-712-0606 (BR)
COMMISSION SCOLAIRE DE LA CAPITALE, LA
ECOLE PRIMAIRE LES PRES VERTS SAINT BERNARD
1680 Boul La Morille, Quebec, QC, G2K 2L2
(418) 686-4040
Emp Here 50
SIC 8211 Elementary and secondary schools

D-U-N-S 25-233-8488 (BR)
COMMISSION SCOLAIRE DE LA CAPITALE, LA
ECOLE ST BERNARD
1440 Boul Bastien, Quebec, QC, G2K 1G6
(418) 686-4040
Emp Here 20
SIC 8211 Elementary and secondary schools

D-U-N-S 25-244-7446 (BR)
COMPAGNIE D'ASSURANCE BELAIR INC, LA
BELAIR DIRECT
5400 Boul Des Galeries Bureau 500, Quebec, QC, G2K 2B4
(418) 877-1199
Emp Here 110
SIC 6331 Fire, marine, and casualty insurance

D-U-N-S 20-297-7000 (BR)
CREATION STRATEGIQUE ABSOLUE INC
ABSOLU COMMUNICATION MARKETING
6655 Boul Pierre-Bertrand Bureau 245, Quebec, QC, G2K 1M1
(418) 688-8008
Emp Here 22
SIC 7311 Advertising agencies

D-U-N-S 24-820-9785 (BR)
DESCHENES & FILS LTEE
LACROIX DECOR
(Suby of Entreprises Mirca Inc, Les)
1105 Rue Des Rocailles, Quebec, QC, G2K 2K6
(418) 627-4711
Emp Here 125
SIC 5074 Plumbing and heating equipment and supplies (hydronics)

D-U-N-S 25-456-1764 (BR)
DESSAU INC
1260 Boul Lebourgneuf Bureau 250, Quebec, QC, G2K 2G2
(418) 626-1688
Emp Here 120

SIC 8711 Engineering services

D-U-N-S 20-958-3751 (BR)
DOLLARAMA S.E.C.
DOLLARAMA
5401 Boul Des Galeries Bureau 1, Quebec, QC, G2K 1N4
Emp Here 25
SIC 5399 Miscellaneous general merchandise

D-U-N-S 24-707-0063 (BR)
FEDERATION INTERPROFESSIONNELLE DE LA SANTE DU QUEBEC-FIQ
(Suby of Federation Interprofessionnelle de la sante du Quebec-FIQ)
1260 Rue Du Blizzard, Quebec, QC, G2K 0J1
(418) 626-2226
Emp Here 65
SIC 8082 Home health care services

D-U-N-S 24-851-7356 (SL)
FUJITSU
2000 Boul Lebourgneuf Bureau 300, Quebec, QC, G2K 0B8
(418) 840-5100
Emp Here 800   Sales 80,384,000
SIC 7379 Computer related services, nec
Rgnl Mgr Christine Jerome

D-U-N-S 24-226-2207 (BR)
GROUPE ARCHAMBAULT INC
ARCHAMBAULT
1580 Boul Lebourgneuf, Quebec, QC, G2K 2M4
(418) 380-8118
Emp Here 40
SIC 5736 Musical instrument stores

D-U-N-S 25-875-5966 (BR)
GROUPE CLOUTIER INC
GROUPE CLOUTIER CABINET EN SERVICES FINANCIERS
(Suby of Groupe Cloutier Inc)
1145 Boul Lebourgneuf Bureau 130, Quebec, QC, G2K 2K8
(418) 624-6690
Emp Here 20
SIC 6411 Insurance agents, brokers, and service

D-U-N-S 24-368-6420 (BR)
GROUPE OPMEDIC INC
CLINIQUES PROCREA
(Suby of Groupe OPMEDIC Inc)
5600 Boul Des Galeries Bureau 401, Quebec, QC, G2K 2H6
(418) 260-9555
Emp Here 20
SIC 8011 Offices and clinics of medical doctors

D-U-N-S 24-371-9213 (HQ)
GROUPE PPP LTEE, LE
GROUPE PPP
1165 Boul Lebourgneuf Bureau 250, Quebec, QC, G2K 2C9
(418) 623-8155
Emp Here 100   Emp Total 5,350
Sales 15,321,747
SIC 6351 Surety insurance
Pr Denis Ricard
  Amelie Cantin
VP Alnoor R. Jiwani
VP Luc Samson

D-U-N-S 25-308-1467 (BR)
GROUPE YELLOW INC
CHAUSSURES YELLOW
(Suby of Les Placements Yellow Inc)
1040 Rue Bouvier, Quebec, QC, G2K 1L9
(418) 623-0975
Emp Here 30
SIC 5661 Shoe stores

D-U-N-S 20-432-6276 (HQ)
GUAY INC
ARMAND GUAY

1160 Rue Bouvier, Quebec, QC, G2K 1L9
(418) 628-8460
Emp Here 75   *Emp Total* 450
Sales 51,356,931
SIC 7353 Heavy construction equipment rental
Pr Pr Jean-Marc Baronet

D-U-N-S 24-207-0142   (BR)
HUDSON'S BAY COMPANY
LA BAIE
5401 Boul Des Galeries, Quebec, QC, G2K 1N4
(418) 627-5922
Emp Here 150
SIC 5311 Department stores

D-U-N-S 20-700-3109   (BR)
HUDSON'S BAY COMPANY
DECO DECOUVERTE
1540 Boul Lebourgneuf, Quebec, QC, G2K 2M4
(418) 263-0288
Emp Here 35
SIC 5311 Department stores

D-U-N-S 24-802-2167   (BR)
IMVESCOR RESTAURANT GROUP INC
RESTAURANT SCORES BATON ROUGE
1875 Rue Bouvier, Quebec, QC, G2K 0B5
(418) 624-2525
Emp Here 100
SIC 5812 Eating places

D-U-N-S 25-310-0952   (BR)
J.M. CLEMENT LTEE
5401 Boul Des Galeries, Quebec, QC, G2K 1N4
(418) 627-3472
Emp Here 30
SIC 5641 Children's and infants' wear stores

D-U-N-S 20-776-7500   (SL)
LABBE, HENRI & FILS INC
1080 Boul Bastien, Quebec, QC, G2K 1E6
(418) 622-0574
Emp Here 100   *Sales* 9,816,000
SIC 1794 Excavation work
Pr Pr Charles Labbe
  Robert Labbe

D-U-N-S 24-147-2682   (SL)
LIBEO INC
SYS-TECH
5700 Boul Des Galeries Bureau 300, Quebec, QC, G2K 0H5
(418) 520-0739
Emp Here 65   *Sales* 3,575,074
SIC 7374 Data processing and preparation

D-U-N-S 25-362-7426   (BR)
LUSSIER DALE PARIZEAU INC
1170 Boul Lebourgneuf Bureau 305, Quebec, QC, G2K 2E3
(418) 627-1080
Emp Here 25
SIC 6411 Insurance agents, brokers, and service

D-U-N-S 20-639-2586   (BR)
METALIUM INC
1635 Boul Jean-Talon O, Quebec, QC, G2K 2J5
(418) 656-0668
Emp Here 20
SIC 5051 Metals service centers and offices

D-U-N-S 24-780-3096   (BR)
OMER DESERRES INC
DESERRES
1505 Boul Lebourgneuf, Quebec, QC, G2K 2G3
(418) 266-0303
Emp Here 25
SIC 5999 Miscellaneous retail stores, nec

D-U-N-S 25-301-3403   (BR)
PITNEY BOWES OF CANADA LTD
PITNEY BOWES OF CANADA LTD

(*Suby of* Pitney Bowes Inc.)
1165 Boul Lebourgneuf Unite 340, Quebec, QC, G2K 2C9
(418) 627-9065
Emp Here 25
SIC 3579 Office machines, nec

D-U-N-S 25-466-1002   (SL)
RDL LEGARE MC NICOLL INC
1305 Boul Lebourgneuf Bureau 401, Quebec, QC, G2K 2E4
(418) 622-6666
Emp Here 50   *Sales* 2,188,821
SIC 8721 Accounting, auditing, and bookkeeping

D-U-N-S 20-915-2722   (BR)
RSW INC
5600 Boul Des Galeries Bureau 500, Quebec, QC, G2K 2H6
(418) 648-9512
Emp Here 23
SIC 8711 Engineering services

D-U-N-S 24-339-9081   (BR)
SNC-LAVALIN INC
PELLEMON
5500 Boul Des Galeries Bureau 200, Quebec, QC, G2K 2E2
(418) 621-5500
Emp Here 250
SIC 8711 Engineering services

D-U-N-S 20-300-4531   (BR)
SEARS CANADA INC
5401 Boul Des Galeries Bureau 1, Quebec, QC, G2K 1N4
(418) 624-7311
Emp Here 150
SIC 5311 Department stores

D-U-N-S 20-169-8128   (BR)
SEARS CANADA INC
SEARS DECOR
1700 Rue Bouvier, Quebec, QC, G2K 1N8
(418) 260-9084
Emp Here 30
SIC 5712 Furniture stores

D-U-N-S 24-045-4327   (SL)
SINAPSE INTERVENTIONS STRATEGIQUES INC
SINAPSE
1170 Boul Lebourgneuf Bureau 320, Quebec, QC, G2K 2E3
(418) 780-3300
Emp Here 80   *Sales* 8,623,250
SIC 7379 Computer related services, nec
Pr Pr Denis Beauches
  Michel Tardiff

D-U-N-S 25-203-5597   (BR)
SUN LIFE ASSURANCE COMPANY OF CANADA
SERVICES FINANCIER CLARICA
5500 Boul Des Galeries Bureau 400, Quebec, QC, G2K 2E2
(418) 623-7250
Emp Here 55
SIC 6311 Life insurance

Quebec, QC G2L
Quebec County

D-U-N-S 24-530-9604   (BR)
CANAC-MARQUIS GRENIER LTEE
1230 Boul Louis-Xiv, Quebec, QC, G2L 1M2
(418) 628-0450
Emp Here 40
SIC 5251 Hardware stores

D-U-N-S 25-742-5611   (BR)
CENTRE D'ESCOMPTE RACINE INC
(*Suby of* Centre D'Escompte Racine Inc)
1440 Boul Louis-Xiv, Quebec, QC, G2L 1M3

(418) 626-1000
Emp Here 20
SIC 5912 Drug stores and proprietary stores

D-U-N-S 25-412-7533   (BR)
CENTRE HOSPITALIER UNIVERSITAIRE DE QUEBEC
SERVICES FINANCIERS DU CHUQ
775 Rue Saint-Viateur Unite 130a, Quebec, QC, G2L 2Z3
(418) 622-1008
Emp Here 3,000
SIC 8062 General medical and surgical hospitals

D-U-N-S 20-055-7218   (BR)
COMMISSION SCOLAIRE DES PREMIERES-SEIGNEURIES
ECOLE DU CHATELET
1495 Rue Du Vice-Roi, Quebec, QC, G2L 2E5
(418) 624-3754
Emp Here 25
SIC 8211 Elementary and secondary schools

D-U-N-S 25-233-4842   (BR)
COMMISSION SCOLAIRE DES PREMIERES-SEIGNEURIES
COMMISSION SCOLAIRE DES PREMIERES-SEIGNEURIES
(*Suby of* Commission Scolaire Des Premieres-Seigneuries)
825 Av Du Bourg-Royal, Quebec, QC, G2L 1W8
(418) 622-7895
Emp Here 21
SIC 8211 Elementary and secondary schools

D-U-N-S 25-211-8930   (SL)
EXTERNAT SAINT-JEAN-EUDES
650 Av Du Bourg-Royal, Quebec, QC, G2L 1M8
(418) 627-1550
Emp Here 50   *Sales* 3,356,192
SIC 8211 Elementary and secondary schools

D-U-N-S 20-705-8715   (BR)
GOUVERNEMENT DE LA PROVINCE DE QUEBEC
INSTITUT DE READAPTATION EN DEFICIENCE PHYSIQUE DU QUEBEC IRDPQ
775 Rue Saint-Viateur, Quebec, QC, G2L 2Z3
(418) 623-9801
Emp Here 50
SIC 8049 Offices of health practitioner

Quebec, QC G2N
Quebec County

D-U-N-S 20-711-9913   (BR)
COMMISSION SCOLAIRE DES PREMIERES-SEIGNEURIES
CENTRE DE FORMATION EN TRANSPORT DE CHARLESBOURG
700 Rue De L'Argon, Quebec, QC, G2N 2G5
(418) 634-5580
Emp Here 135
SIC 8299 Schools and educational services, nec

D-U-N-S 20-711-9772   (BR)
COMMISSION SCOLAIRE DES PREMIERES-SEIGNEURIES
L'ECOLE DU BOISE
651 Rue Jacques-Bedard, Quebec, QC, G2N 1C5
(418) 634-5538
Emp Here 50
SIC 8211 Elementary and secondary schools

D-U-N-S 20-711-9764   (BR)
COMMISSION SCOLAIRE DES PREMIERES-SEIGNEURIES
ECOLE PRIMAIRE DE L'ESCALADE
20 Rue De L'Escalade, Quebec, QC, G2N 2A8
(418) 634-5533
Emp Here 50

SIC 8211 Elementary and secondary schools

D-U-N-S 20-029-9837   (BR)
COMMISSION SCOLAIRE DES PREMIERES-SEIGNEURIES
ECOLE DE L'ESCALADE PAVILLON 2E CYCLE
365 Rue Du Bienheureux-Jean-Xxiii, Quebec, QC, G2N 1V4
(418) 634-5535
Emp Here 30
SIC 8211 Elementary and secondary schools

D-U-N-S 20-711-9780   (BR)
COMMISSION SCOLAIRE DES PREMIERES-SEIGNEURIES
COMMISSION SCOLAIRE DES PREMIERES-SEIGNEURIES
99 Rue Moise-Verret, Quebec, QC, G2N 1E8
(418) 634-5537
Emp Here 50
SIC 8211 Elementary and secondary schools

D-U-N-S 20-989-8027   (SL)
CORNEAU & CANTIN CHICOUTIMI INC
2000 Boul Talbot, Quebec, QC, G2N 0C4
(418) 698-9556
Emp Here 70   *Sales* 11,779,113
SIC 5411 Grocery stores
Pr Regis Laforest

D-U-N-S 20-582-3610   (HQ)
DEMENAGEMENTS RAPIDE INC, LES
DEMENAGEMENTS RAPIDE TRANSPORT
(*Suby of* Demenagements Rapide Inc, Les)
1630 Boul Talbot, Quebec, QC, G2N 0C5
(418) 849-0653
Emp Here 50   *Emp Total* 50
Sales 3,939,878
SIC 4212 Local trucking, without storage

D-U-N-S 25-258-7704   (BR)
GROUPE CHAMPLAIN INC
CENTRE D'HEBERGEMENT CHAMPLAIN-DES-MONTAGNES
(*Suby of* Groupe Sante Sedna Inc)
791 Rue De Sherwood, Quebec, QC, G2N 1X7
(418) 849-1891
Emp Here 100
SIC 8361 Residential care

D-U-N-S 24-954-5034   (SL)
GROUPE SINISTRE 24/7 INC
550 Rue De L'Argon Bureau 300, Quebec, QC, G2N 2E1

Emp Here 26   *Sales* 5,325,440
SIC 1521 Single-family housing construction
Pr Christian Parent

D-U-N-S 24-149-6629   (SL)
MACONNERIE DYNAMIQUE LTEE
525 Rue Du Platine Bureau 200, Quebec, QC, G2N 2E4
(418) 849-1524
Emp Here 50   *Sales* 3,648,035
SIC 1741 Masonry and other stonework

Quebec, QC G3E
Quebec County

D-U-N-S 25-232-3373   (BR)
COMMISSION SCOLAIRE DE LA CAPITALE, LA
ECOLE DE L'ACCUEIL
1587 Rue Guillaume-Bresse, Quebec, QC, G3E 1G9
(418) 686-4040
Emp Here 50
SIC 8211 Elementary and secondary schools

D-U-N-S 20-029-9886   (BR)
COMMISSION SCOLAIRE DE LA CAPITALE, LA

ECOLE DU VIGNOBLE
6300 Rue De Montrachet, Quebec, QC, G3E 2A6
(418) 686-4040
Emp Here 30
SIC 8211 Elementary and secondary schools

D-U-N-S 25-232-3332 (BR)
COMMISSION SCOLAIRE DE LA CAPI-TALE, LA
ECOLE DU BEAU SEJOUR
1644 Av Lapierre, Quebec, QC, G3E 1C1
(418) 686-4040
Emp Here 40
SIC 8211 Elementary and secondary schools

D-U-N-S 25-413-0602 (SL)
GYRO-TRAC INC
2033 Rue Des Perseides, Quebec, QC, G3E 2G3

Emp Here 50 *Sales* 8,138,880
SIC 6712 Bank holding companies
Pr Pr Daniel Gaudreault
VP Fin Steve Quirion

D-U-N-S 20-925-6929 (BR)
RESTAURANTS MIKA INC, LES
RESTAURANT MCDONALD'S
1154 Rue De La Faune, Quebec, QC, G3E 1T2
(418) 845-6323
Emp Here 150
SIC 5812 Eating places

D-U-N-S 24-380-1263 (BR)
SOCIETE EN COMMANDITE STADACONA WB
SCIERIE LEDUC,
1092 Av Lapierre Bureau 220, Quebec, QC, G3E 1Z3
(418) 842-8405
Emp Here 75
SIC 2421 Sawmills and planing mills, general

Quebec, QC G3G
Quebec County

D-U-N-S 24-149-5399 (SL)
SM CONSTRUCTION INC
MORELCO
(*Suby of* Groupe S.M. Tardif Inc)
15971 Boul De La Colline, Quebec, QC, G3G 3A7
(418) 849-7104
Emp Here 50 *Sales* 12,884,150
SIC 1542 Nonresidential construction, nec
Pr Serge Tardif
VP Genevieve Tardif
Sec Claire Renaud Tardif
Genl Mgr Claude Faucher

D-U-N-S 25-798-6026 (SL)
TARDIF METAL INC
(*Suby of* Groupe S.M. Tardif Inc)
15971 Boul De La Colline, Quebec, QC, G3G 3A7
(418) 849-6919
Emp Here 20 *Sales* 3,291,754
SIC 3441 Fabricated structural Metal

Quebec, QC G3J
Quebec County

D-U-N-S 24-057-1302 (HQ)
ARCHIBALD INC
ARCHIBALD MICROBRASSERIE
(*Suby of* Gestion Tribune Amerique Inc)
1530 Av Des Affaires, Quebec, QC, G3J 1Y8
(418) 407-6033
Emp Here 20 *Emp Total* 70
Sales 2,732,754

SIC 5812 Eating places

D-U-N-S 20-584-3639 (BR)
CANADA POST CORPORATION
1340 Boul Pie-Xi N, Quebec, QC, G3J 1X3
(418) 842-3178
Emp Here 20
SIC 4311 U.s. postal service

D-U-N-S 25-232-8422 (BR)
COMMISSION SCOLAIRE DE LA CAPI-TALE, LA
ECOLE DU VAL JOLI
1735 Boul Pie-Xi N, Quebec, QC, G3J 1L6
(418) 686-4040
Emp Here 50
SIC 8211 Elementary and secondary schools

D-U-N-S 20-554-8527 (BR)
METRO RICHELIEU INC
METRO GAGNON
1370 Boul Pie-Xi N, Quebec, QC, G3J 1W7
(418) 842-8556
Emp Here 80
SIC 5141 Groceries, general line

Quebec, QC G3K
Quebec County

D-U-N-S 24-204-1788 (SL)
AUTOBUS QUEBEC METRO 2000 INC
2050 Av Industrielle, Quebec, QC, G3K 1L7
(418) 842-0525
Emp Here 70 *Sales* 1,969,939
SIC 4151 School buses

D-U-N-S 25-761-1533 (BR)
BANQUE NATIONALE DU CANADA
1135 Boul Pie-Xi N, Quebec, QC, G3K 2P8
(418) 847-7069
Emp Here 20
SIC 6021 National commercial banks

D-U-N-S 25-232-7515 (BR)
COMMISSION SCOLAIRE DE LA CAPI-TALE, LA
ECOLE JULES EMOND
1065 Av De La Montagne E, Quebec, QC, G3K 1T4
(418) 686-4040
Emp Here 70
SIC 8211 Elementary and secondary schools

D-U-N-S 20-712-0598 (BR)
COMMISSION SCOLAIRE DE LA CAPI-TALE, LA
ECOLE SECONDAIRE L'ODYSSEE
1485 Rue De L'Innovation, Quebec, QC, G3K 2P9
(418) 847-8267
Emp Here 50
SIC 8211 Elementary and secondary schools

D-U-N-S 25-240-2409 (BR)
COMMISSION SCOLAIRE DE LA CAPI-TALE, LA
ECOLE DE LA CHANTERELLE
1070 Boul Pie-Xi N, Quebec, QC, G3K 2S6
(418) 686-4040
Emp Here 40
SIC 8211 Elementary and secondary schools

D-U-N-S 20-688-7932 (BR)
COMMISSION SCOLAIRE DE LA CAPI-TALE, LA
ECOLE A L'OREE DES BOIS
1389 Rue Des Camarades, Quebec, QC, G3K 2N5
(418) 686-4040
Emp Here 50
SIC 8211 Elementary and secondary schools

D-U-N-S 24-569-0227 (SL)
PATATES PLUS INC
PATATES PLUS
1111 Boul Pie-Xi N, Quebec, QC, G3K 2S8

(418) 842-1323
Emp Here 60 *Sales* 1,824,018
SIC 5812 Eating places

D-U-N-S 25-746-2895 (BR)
RESTAURANT NORMANDIN INC
1037 Boul Pie-Xi N, Quebec, QC, G3K 2S3
(418) 845-0373
Emp Here 40
SIC 5812 Eating places

Quebec, QC J2C
Quebec County

D-U-N-S 24-908-0953 (BR)
MEDIAS TRANSCONTINENTAL INC
MEDIAS TRANSCONTINENTAL INC
5000 Boul Saint-Joseph Porte 8, Quebec, QC, J2C 2B4
(418) 686-6400
Emp Here 84
SIC 2711 Newspapers

Quebec, QC J6Y
Quebec County

D-U-N-S 24-366-3403 (BR)
SOLARCAN PORTES ET FENETRES CORP
650 Place Trans-Canada, Quebec, QC, J6Y 1W9
(450) 641-2325
Emp Here 60
SIC 2431 Millwork

Qui Obec, QC G1V

D-U-N-S 25-767-0190 (SL)
9126-5546 QUEBEC INC
OLIO CUISINE DECOUVERTES
2815 Boul Laurier, Qui Obec, QC, G1V 4H3
(418) 658-2583
Emp Here 85 *Sales* 2,553,625
SIC 5812 Eating places

Quyon, QC J0X
Pontiac County

D-U-N-S 24-075-1300 (SL)
CAMP BNAI BRITH INC
CAMP B'NAI B'RITH
7861 Ch River, Quyon, QC, J0X 2V0
(819) 458-2660
Emp Here 46 *Sales* 5,478,300
SIC 7032 Sporting and recreational camps
Pr Clifford Herer
VP VP Joelle Berdugo-Adler
VP VP Stephen Greenberg
VP VP Bram Backler
VP VP Steven Lach
VP VP Brant Bramson
VP VP Marion Sohmer
Sec Sam Zentner
Treas Joanne Maislin
VP VP Steven Wezelman

D-U-N-S 20-024-5947 (BR)
TIM HORTON CHILDREN'S FOUNDATION, INC
60 Ch Du Canal, Quyon, QC, J0X 2V0
(819) 458-3164
Emp Here 60
SIC 7032 Sporting and recreational camps

Radisson, QC J0Y
Nouveau-Quebec County

D-U-N-S 25-595-0529 (BR)
AIR INUIT LTEE
(*Suby of* Societe Makivik)
106 Rue Iberville, Radisson, QC, J0Y 2X0
(819) 638-8163
Emp Here 50
SIC 4512 Air transportation, scheduled

D-U-N-S 25-093-3673 (BR)
CENTRE REGIONAL DE SANTE ET DE SERVICE SOCIAUX DE LA BAIE-JAMES
CENTRE REGIONALE DE SANTE & DE SERVICE SOCIAUX DE LA BAIE-JAMES
199 Rue Jolliet, Radisson, QC, J0Y 2X0
(819) 638-8991
Emp Here 60
SIC 8093 Specialty outpatient clinics, nec

D-U-N-S 25-378-7360 (BR)
SOCIETE DE DEVELOPPEMENT DE LA BAIE-JAMES
RELAIS ROUTIER KILOMETRE 381
381 Rte De La Baie James, Radisson, QC, J0Y 2X0
(819) 638-8502
Emp Here 40
SIC 5812 Eating places

Rapides-Des-Joachims, QC J0X
Pontiac County

D-U-N-S 24-601-7321 (SL)
ENTREPRISES FORESTIERES G.U.S. INC
464 Ch Du Moulin Rr 1, Rapides-Des-Joachims, QC, J0X 3M0
(819) 587-3626
Emp Here 40 *Sales* 5,496,960
SIC 2411 Logging
Ghislain Papineau
Gino Papineau
Hugo Papineau

Rawdon, QC J0K
Montcalm County

D-U-N-S 20-761-7671 (SL)
151332 CANADA INC
PHARMACIE DENISE LORD
3637 Rue Queen, Rawdon, QC, J0K 1S0
(450) 834-2523
Emp Here 28 *Sales* 5,088,577
SIC 5912 Drug stores and proprietary stores
Pr Pr Denise Lord

D-U-N-S 24-345-5750 (BR)
CENTRE DE READAPTATION LA MYRI-ADE, LE
3733 Rue Charbonneau, Rawdon, QC, J0K 1S0
(450) 834-7101
Emp Here 40
SIC 8361 Residential care

D-U-N-S 20-714-1982 (SL)
COLLEGE CHAMPAGNEUR, LE
3713 Rue Queen Bureau 40, Rawdon, QC, J0K 1S0
(450) 834-5401
Emp Here 50 *Sales* 3,356,192
SIC 8211 Elementary and secondary schools

D-U-N-S 20-171-7464 (BR)
COMMISSION SCOLAIRE DES SAMARES
ECOLE SECONDAIRE DES CHUTES
3144 18e Av Bureau 760, Rawdon, QC, J0K 1S0
(450) 758-3749
Emp Here 75
SIC 8211 Elementary and secondary schools

D-U-N-S 25-232-9198   (BR)
COMMISSION SCOLAIRE DES SAMARES
ECOLE SAINTE ANNE
3790 Ch Du Lac-Morgan, Rawdon, QC, J0K
1S0
(450) 758-3701
Emp Here 45
SIC 8211 Elementary and secondary schools

D-U-N-S 25-688-2242   (BR)
COMMISSION SCOLAIRE DES SAMARES
ECOLE SAINT LOUIS
3763 Rue Albert, Rawdon, QC, J0K 1S0
(450) 758-3704
Emp Here 30
SIC 8211 Elementary and secondary schools

D-U-N-S 20-243-6523   (SL)
ENTREPRISES NOVA INC, LES
HOME HARDWARE
3330 Ch De Kildare, Rawdon, QC, J0K 1S0
(450) 834-2555
Emp Here 27   *Sales* 5,425,920
SIC 5211 Lumber and other building materials
Pr Pr Maurice Lane
Pierre Lane

D-U-N-S 24-051-7115   (BR)
GIL-BER INC
3282 1e Av, Rawdon, QC, J0K 1S0
(450) 834-3559
Emp Here 50
SIC 4151 School buses

D-U-N-S 24-063-2278   (BR)
GROUPE SUTTON SYNERGIE INC
3618 Rue Queen, Rawdon, QC, J0K 1S0
(450) 834-8840
Emp Here 52
SIC 6531 Real estate agents and managers

D-U-N-S 20-591-2454   (BR)
PRODUITS DE SECURITE NORTH LTEE
PRODUITS DE SECURITE NORTH LTEE
3719 Rue Des Commissaires, Rawdon, QC,
J0K 1S0

Emp Here 80
SIC 3699 Electrical equipment and supplies,
nec

D-U-N-S 24-195-6254   (BR)
PROVIGO DISTRIBUTION INC
MAXI
3399 Rue Queen, Rawdon, QC, J0K 1S0
(450) 834-2644
Emp Here 35
SIC 5411 Grocery stores

D-U-N-S 25-240-2995   (BR)
SIR WILFRID LAURIER SCHOOL BOARD
RAWDON ELEMENTARY SCHOOL
(*Suby of* Sir Wilfrid Laurier School Board)
4121 Rue Queen, Rawdon, QC, J0K 1S0
(450) 834-2427
Emp Here 30
SIC 8211 Elementary and secondary schools

Repentigny, QC J5Y
L'Assomption County

D-U-N-S 25-307-2789   (BR)
123273 CANADA INC
PHARMACIE JEAN COUTU
910 Boul Iberville Bureau 171, Repentigny,
QC, J5Y 2P9
(450) 585-7725
Emp Here 40
SIC 5912 Drug stores and proprietary stores

D-U-N-S 20-714-2451   (SL)
ACADEMIE FRANCOIS-LABELLE
1227 Rue Notre-Dame, Repentigny, QC, J5Y
3H2
(450) 582-2020
Emp Here 50   *Sales* 3,356,192

SIC 8211 Elementary and secondary schools

D-U-N-S 25-233-0246   (BR)
**COMMISSION SCOLAIRE DES AFFLU-
ENTS**
ECOLE PRIMAIRE DU MOULIN
(*Suby of* Commission Scolaire des Affluents)
120 Boul Laurentien, Repentigny, QC, J5Y
2R7
(450) 492-3569
Emp Here 25
SIC 8211 Elementary and secondary schools

D-U-N-S 25-233-3216   (BR)
**COMMISSION SCOLAIRE DES AFFLU-
ENTS**
ECOLE PRIMAIRE LOUIS FRECHETTE
(*Suby of* Commission Scolaire des Affluents)
835 Rue Frechette, Repentigny, QC, J5Y 1B1
(450) 492-3519
Emp Here 23
SIC 8211 Elementary and secondary schools

D-U-N-S 20-033-9435   (BR)
**COMMISSION SCOLAIRE DES AFFLU-
ENTS**
ECOLE SECONDAIRE FELIX LECLERC
250 Boul Louis-Philippe-Picard, Repentigny,
QC, J5Y 3W9
(450) 492-3578
Emp Here 125
SIC 8211 Elementary and secondary schools

D-U-N-S 24-087-0233   (BR)
**COMMISSION SCOLAIRE DES AFFLU-
ENTS**
ECOLE JEAN BAPTISTE MEILLEUR
777 Boul Iberville, Repentigny, QC, J5Y 1A2
(450) 492-3777
Emp Here 20
SIC 8211 Elementary and secondary schools

D-U-N-S 25-233-7431   (BR)
**COMMISSION SCOLAIRE DES AFFLU-
ENTS**
ECOLE DES MOISSONS
(*Suby of* Commission Scolaire des Affluents)
945 Rue Noiseux, Repentigny, QC, J5Y 1Z3
(450) 492-3562
Emp Here 46
SIC 8211 Elementary and secondary schools

D-U-N-S 20-712-2354   (BR)
**COMMISSION SCOLAIRE DES AFFLU-
ENTS**
ECOLE PRIMAIRE LA TOURTERELLE
175 Rue Philippe-Goulet, Repentigny, QC,
J5Y 3M9
(450) 492-3580
Emp Here 50
SIC 8211 Elementary and secondary schools

D-U-N-S 20-712-2503   (BR)
**COMMISSION SCOLAIRE DES AFFLU-
ENTS**
*CENTRE DE FORMATION GENERALE DE
LA CROISEE*
777 Boul Iberville, Repentigny, QC, J5Y 1A2
(450) 492-3799
Emp Here 50
SIC 8331 Job training and related services

D-U-N-S 25-995-7306   (SL)
GROUPE GAUDREAULT INC, LE
(*Suby of* Le Groupe Gaudreault Inc)
1500 Rue Raymond-Gaudreault, Repentigny,
QC, J5Y 4E3
(450) 585-1210
Emp Here 600   *Sales* 175,136,640
SIC 6712 Bank holding companies
Pr Pr Martin Gaudreault

D-U-N-S 24-322-0019   (BR)
MEDIAS TRANSCONTINENTAL INC
MEDIAS TRANSCONTINENTAL INC
1004 Rue Notre-Dame Bureau 159, Repentigny, QC, J5Y 1S9

(450) 581-5120
Emp Here 36
SIC 2711 Newspapers

D-U-N-S 20-543-4376   (SL)
SABEM SEC
1500 Rue Raymond-Gaudreault, Repentigny,
QC, J5Y 4E3
(450) 585-1210
Emp Here 150   *Sales* 5,827,840
SIC 4151 School buses
Pr Sylvain Langis
VP Manon Gaudreault

D-U-N-S 24-073-5451   (BR)
SIR WILFRID LAURIER SCHOOL BOARD
FRANKLIN HILL ELEMENTARY SCHOOL
1111 Boul Basile-Routhier, Repentigny, QC,
J5Y 4C8
(450) 470-0755
Emp Here 40
SIC 8211 Elementary and secondary schools

Repentigny, QC J5Z
L'Assomption County

D-U-N-S 20-308-6348   (SL)
**EQUIPEMENTS DE SUPERMARCHES
CONCEPT INTERNATIONAL INC**
CSF INTERNATIONAL
429 Rue Des Industries, Repentigny, QC, J5Z
4Y8
(450) 582-3017
Emp Here 50   *Sales* 2,161,572
SIC 5078 Refrigeration equipment and sup-
plies

D-U-N-S 24-697-4182   (HQ)
**GENERAL DYNAMICS PRODUITS DE
DEFENSE ET SYSTEMES TACTIQUES-
CANADA INC**
SIMUNITION
(*Suby of* General Dynamics Corporation)
5 Montee Des Arsenaux, Repentigny, QC, J5Z
2P4
(450) 581-3080
Emp Here 790   *Emp Total* 98,800
SIC 3483 Ammunition, except for small arms,
nec

D-U-N-S 24-318-9185   (SL)
KWP INC
(*Suby of* Administration F.L.T. Ltee)
101 Rue De La Couronne, Repentigny, QC,
J5Z 0B3

Emp Here 35   *Sales* 4,622,080
SIC 2421 Sawmills and planing mills, general

D-U-N-S 25-965-9147   (SL)
PHARMACIE JEAN COUTU
155 Boul Lacombe Unite 160, Repentigny,
QC, J5Z 3C4
(450) 654-6747
Emp Here 49   *Sales* 6,931,267
SIC 5912 Drug stores and proprietary stores
Owner Marc Airoldi

D-U-N-S 25-122-0331   (SL)
TELTECH TELECOMMUNICATION INC
345d Rue Marion, Repentigny, QC, J5Z 4W8
(450) 657-2000
Emp Here 60   *Sales* 10,282,000
SIC 1731 Electrical work
Francois Tessier

Repentigny, QC J6A
L'Assomption County

D-U-N-S 24-958-9615   (BR)
123273 CANADA INC
*JEAN COUTU IAN DI MAULO & DAVID
KENNY*

100 Boul Brien, Repentigny, QC, J6A 5N4
(450) 585-7880
Emp Here 45
SIC 5912 Drug stores and proprietary stores

D-U-N-S 24-402-6274   (SL)
2437-0223 QUEBEC INC
MARINA DE REPENTIGNY, LA
364 Rue Notre-Dame, Repentigny, QC, J6A
2S5
(450) 581-7071
Emp Here 50   *Sales* 3,356,192
SIC 4493 Marinas

D-U-N-S 25-847-2422   (BR)
3091-0418 QUEBEC INC
BUFFET MAISON KIRIN REPENTIGNY
(*Suby of* 3091-0418 Quebec Inc)
358 Rue Notre-Dame, Repentigny, QC, J6A
2S5

Emp Here 40
SIC 5812 Eating places

D-U-N-S 25-135-0807   (BR)
3294269 CANADA INC
SOLUTION CELLULAIRE
100 Boul Brien Bureau 129, Repentigny, QC,
J6A 5N4

Emp Here 25
SIC 4812 Radiotelephone communication

D-U-N-S 20-105-0395   (SL)
9068-5165 QUEBEC INC
JKV SERVICE DE PERSONNEL
332 Boul Notre-Dame-Des-Champs Bureau
201, Repentigny, QC, J6A 3B7
(450) 581-0051
Emp Here 60   *Sales* 4,377,642
SIC 7361 Employment agencies

D-U-N-S 25-905-5010   (SL)
9113-9303 QUEBEC INC
FAIM PRET, LE
515 Rue Leclerc Bureau 102, Repentigny,
J6A 8G9

Emp Here 55   *Sales* 2,167,357
SIC 5812 Eating places

D-U-N-S 24-401-4072   (SL)
ARENA DE REPENTIGNY LTEE
80 Boul Brien, Repentigny, QC, J6A 5K7
(450) 581-7060
Emp Here 30   *Sales* 9,942,100
SIC 7941 Sports clubs, managers, and pro-
moters
Pr Pr Yves Doucet
Michel Doucet
Collette Doucet

D-U-N-S 24-108-1298   (HQ)
ATELIERS G. PAQUETTE INC
(*Suby of* Ateliers G. Paquette Inc)
104 Rue Laroche, Repentigny, QC, J6A 7M5
(450) 654-6744
Emp Here 37   *Emp Total* 50
Sales 1,969,939
SIC 7629 Electrical repair shops

D-U-N-S 25-604-4637   (SL)
AUTO CAMIONS MICHEL AUGER INC
SUZUKI SUBARU REPENTIGNY
575 Rue Notre-Dame, Repentigny, QC, J6A
2T6
(514) 891-9950
Emp Here 35   *Sales* 14,630,000
SIC 5511 New and used car dealers
Pr Pr Michel Auger

D-U-N-S 25-002-6887   (BR)
BANQUE NATIONALE DU CANADA
100 Boul Brien Bureau 54, Repentigny, QC,
J6A 5N4
(450) 585-8111
Emp Here 30
SIC 6021 National commercial banks

▲ Public Company   ■ Public Company Family Member   **HQ** Headquarters   **BR** Branch   **SL** Single Location

D-U-N-S 25-874-5173   (BR)
BANQUE NATIONALE DU CANADA
165 Rue Notre-Dame, Repentigny, QC, J6A
0A8
(450) 585-5900
Emp Here 22
SIC 6021 National commercial banks

D-U-N-S 20-589-4582   (BR)
BANQUE TORONTO-DOMINION, LA
TD CANADA TRUST
(*Suby of* Toronto-Dominion Bank, The)
100 Boul Brien Bureau 145, Repentigny, QC,
J6A 5N4
(450) 582-1881
Emp Here 25
SIC 6021 National commercial banks

D-U-N-S 24-796-4625   (BR)
BOUTIQUE LINEN CHEST (PHASE II) INC
LINEN CHEST
(*Suby of* Boutique Linen Chest (Phase II) Inc)
100 Boul Brien, Repentigny, QC, J6A 5N4
(450) 585-7907
Emp Here 20
SIC 5719 Miscellaneous homefurnishings

D-U-N-S 24-119-7883   (BR)
**CENTRE DE READAPTATION LA MYRI-
ADE, LE**
625 Rue Leclerc, Repentigny, QC, J6A 2E4
(450) 585-7811
Emp Here 50
SIC 8361 Residential care

D-U-N-S 24-922-3488   (SL)
**CENTRE PEDAGOGIQUE NICOLAS ET
STEPHANIE INC**
C.P.S.N.
50 Rue Thouin Bureau 230, Repentigny, QC,
J6A 4J4
(450) 585-4124
Emp Here 70   *Sales* 4,669,485
SIC 8211 Elementary and secondary schools

D-U-N-S 25-258-2788   (BR)
**CENTRES JEUNESSE DE LANAUDIERE,
LES**
*CENTRES JEUNESSE DE LANAUDIERE,
LES*
(*Suby of* Centres Jeunesse de Lanaudiere,
Les)
630 Rue De Marseille Bureau 201, Re-
pentigny, QC, J6A 7A3
(450) 585-1423
Emp Here 60
SIC 8322 Individual and family services

D-U-N-S 25-233-9163   (BR)
**COMMISSION SCOLAIRE DES AFFLU-
ENTS**
ECOLE PRIMAIRE DE LA PAIX
(*Suby of* Commission Scolaire des Affluents)
830 Boul Basile-Routhier, Repentigny, QC,
J6A 7W9
(450) 492-3576
Emp Here 42
SIC 8211 Elementary and secondary schools

D-U-N-S 25-498-1426   (HQ)
**COMMISSION SCOLAIRE DES AFFLU-
ENTS**
(*Suby of* Commission Scolaire des Affluents)
80 Rue Jean-Baptiste-Meilleur, Repentigny,
QC, J6A 6C5
(450) 492-9400
Emp Here 25   *Emp Total* 100
Sales 8,669,427
SIC 8211 Elementary and secondary schools
Pr Daniel Thiffault
Genl Mgr Thomas Duzyk
Lucette Whittom
Laurent Tanguay

D-U-N-S 25-233-3091   (BR)
**COMMISSION SCOLAIRE DES AFFLU-
ENTS**
ECOLE JEAN XXIII

(*Suby of* Commission Scolaire des Affluents)
185 Rue Du Cure-Longpre, Repentigny, QC,
J6A 1V5
(450) 492-3533
Emp Here 20
SIC 8211 Elementary and secondary schools

D-U-N-S 25-231-9686   (BR)
**COMMISSION SCOLAIRE DES AFFLU-
ENTS**
ECOLE ENTRAMIS
(*Suby of* Commission Scolaire des Affluents)
595 Boul De L'Assomption, Repentigny, QC,
J6A 6Z5
(450) 492-3567
Emp Here 40
SIC 8211 Elementary and secondary schools

D-U-N-S 25-233-3059   (BR)
**COMMISSION SCOLAIRE DES AFFLU-
ENTS**
CENTRE DE L'ALIZE
(*Suby of* Commission Scolaire des Affluents)
129 Rue Notre-Dame, Repentigny, QC, J6A
2P1
(450) 492-3529
Emp Here 25
SIC 8211 Elementary and secondary schools

D-U-N-S 20-573-7781   (BR)
FINANCIERE BANQUE NATIONALE INC
FINANCIERE BANQUE NATIONALE
534 Rue Notre-Dame Bureau 201, Re-
pentigny, QC, J6A 2T8
(450) 582-7001
Emp Here 22
SIC 6211 Security brokers and dealers

D-U-N-S 20-801-8635   (BR)
GROUPE BMTC INC
BRAULT ET MARTINEAU
145 Rue De La Fayette, Repentigny, QC, J6A
8K3
(450) 470-0815
Emp Here 60
SIC 5712 Furniture stores

D-U-N-S 25-309-7414   (BR)
**INDUSTRIELLE ALLIANCE, ASSURANCE
ET SERVICES FINANCIERS INC**
*INDUSTRIELLE ALLIANCE ASSURANCE ET
SERVICES FINANCIERS*
155 Rue Notre-Dame Bureau 60, Repentigny,
QC, J6A 5L3
(450) 582-3013
Emp Here 50
SIC 6411 Insurance agents, brokers, and ser-
vice

D-U-N-S 24-125-5004   (BR)
LOBLAWS INC
LOBLAWS
86 Boul Brien, Repentigny, QC, J6A 5K7
(450) 581-8866
Emp Here 100
SIC 5411 Grocery stores

D-U-N-S 20-765-7479   (BR)
**MCDONALD'S   RESTAURANTS   OF
CANADA LIMITED**
MCDONALD'S
(*Suby of* McDonald's Corporation)
185 Rue Notre-Dame, Repentigny, QC, J6A
2R3
(450) 581-8520
Emp Here 80
SIC 5812 Eating places

D-U-N-S 25-448-3852   (BR)
METRO RICHELIEU INC
SUPER C REPENTIGNY
85 Boul Brien Bureau 101, Repentigny, QC,
J6A 8B6
(450) 581-3072
Emp Here 120
SIC 5141 Groceries, general line

D-U-N-S 25-010-4767   (BR)

NAUTILUS PLUS INC
100 Boul Brien Bureau 10, Repentigny, QC,
J6A 5N4
(450) 582-0961
Emp Here 20
SIC 7999 Amusement and recreation, nec

D-U-N-S 25-299-9669   (BR)
PRISZM LP
POULET FRIT KENTUCKY
85 Boul Brien Bureau 13, Repentigny, QC,
J6A 8B6
(450) 582-3046
Emp Here 30
SIC 5812 Eating places

D-U-N-S 25-814-9376   (BR)
ROYAL BANK OF CANADA
ROYAL BANK BRIEN IBERVILLE
(*Suby of* Royal Bank Of Canada)
85 Boul Brien Bureau B, Repentigny, QC, J6A
8B6
(450) 581-0854
Emp Here 22
SIC 6021 National commercial banks

D-U-N-S 25-294-5852   (BR)
SEARS CANADA INC
SEARS DEPARTMENT STORE
100 Boul Brien, Repentigny, QC, J6A 5N4
(450) 582-5532
Emp Here 200
SIC 5311 Department stores

D-U-N-S 25-164-2542   (BR)
SERLAN INC
505 Rue Lanaudiere Bureau 1, Repentigny,
QC, J6A 7N1
(450) 654-9574
Emp Here 40
SIC 4783 Packing and crating

D-U-N-S 25-294-7742   (BR)
WAL-MART CANADA CORP
WAL MART
100 Boul Brien Bureau 66, Repentigny, QC,
J6A 5N4
(450) 654-8886
Emp Here 200
SIC 5311 Department stores

Richelieu, QC J3L

D-U-N-S 25-363-0925   (HQ)
**CAISSE POPULAIRE DESJARDINS DE
RICHELIEU-SAINT-MATHIAS**
*DESJARDINS ENTREPRISESVALLEE DU
RICHELIEU-YAMASKA*
(*Suby of* Caisse Populaire Desjardins de
Richelieu-Saint-Mathias)
1111 3e Rue, Richelieu, QC, J3L 3Z2
(450) 658-0649
Emp Here 70   *Emp Total* 84
Sales 11,819,527
SIC 6062 State credit unions
Genl Mgr Sylvain Lessard
Pr Joanne Desjardins
VP Simon Leblanc
Sec Louise Loiselle
Dir Lucie Desgreniers
Dir Nathalie Tremblay
Dir Raynald Cornellier
Dir Maxime Elsek Gaudreault
Dir Robert Bleau
Dir Nathalie Croteau

D-U-N-S 20-712-6553   (BR)
**COMMISSION SCOLAIRE DES HAUTES-
RIVIERES**
ECOLE DE RICHELIEU
205 8e Av, Richelieu, QC, J3L 3N5
(450) 658-8284
Emp Here 20
SIC 8211 Elementary and secondary schools

D-U-N-S 20-712-6587   (BR)
**COMMISSION SCOLAIRE DES HAUTES-
RIVIERES**
ECOLE DE RICHELIEU
120 7e Av, Richelieu, QC, J3L 3N2
(450) 658-7221
Emp Here 40
SIC 8211 Elementary and secondary schools

D-U-N-S 25-731-5846   (SL)
HICAT CORPORATION INC
640 14e Av Bureau 102, Richelieu, QC, J3L
5R5
(450) 447-3652
Emp Here 350   *Sales* 28,662,720
SIC 3732 Boatbuilding and repairing
Pr Pr Albert B. Beauchamps

D-U-N-S 25-590-2793   (BR)
**MISSIONNAIRES OBLATS DE MARIE IM-
MACULEE, LES**
RESIDENCE NOTRE DAME DE RICHELIEU
(*Suby of* Missionnaires Oblats de Marie Im-
maculee, Les)
460 1re Rue Bureau 600, Richelieu, QC, J3L
4B5
(450) 658-8761
Emp Here 50
SIC 8661 Religious organizations

Richmond, QC J0B

D-U-N-S 20-574-4985   (SL)
CSSS DU VAL SAINT-FRANCOIS
FOYER RICHMOND
980 Rue Mcgauran, Richmond, QC, J0B 2H0
(819) 826-3711
Emp Here 100   *Sales* 3,939,878
SIC 8322 Individual and family services

D-U-N-S 24-012-1371   (BR)
CODET INC
525 10e Av, Richmond, QC, J0B 2H0
(819) 826-3763
Emp Here 30
SIC 2326 Men's and boy's work clothing

D-U-N-S 25-233-1079   (BR)
**COMMISSION   SCOLAIRE   EASTERN
TOWNSHIPS**
RICHMOND REGIONAL HIGH SCHOOL
(*Suby of* Commission Scolaire Eastern Town-
ships)
375 Rue Armstrong, Richmond, QC, J0B 2H0
(819) 826-3702
Emp Here 35
SIC 8211 Elementary and secondary schools

D-U-N-S 25-233-0550   (BR)
**COMMISSION   SCOLAIRE   EASTERN
TOWNSHIPS**
ST. FRANCIS ELEMENTARY SCHOOL
(*Suby of* Commission Scolaire Eastern Town-
ships)
355 Rue Du College S, Richmond, QC, J0B
2H0
(819) 826-3737
Emp Here 59
SIC 8211 Elementary and secondary schools

D-U-N-S 24-319-8058   (BR)
EXO-S INC
425 10e Av, Richmond, QC, J0B 2H0
(819) 826-5911
Emp Here 200
SIC 3089 Plastics products, nec

D-U-N-S 24-865-0624   (HQ)
GESTRUDO INC
(*Suby of* Gestrudo Inc)
34 Rue Belmont Rr 5, Richmond, QC, J0B
2H0
(819) 826-5941
Emp Here 25   *Emp Total* 60
Sales 10,650,880

SIC 6712 Bank holding companies
Pr Pr Edmond Trudeau

D-U-N-S 20-509-6865   (BR)
GOUVERNEMENT DE LA PROVINCE DE QUEBEC
MINISTERE DU TRANSPORT
770 Rue Hayes Bureau 640, Richmond, QC,
J0B 2H0
(819) 826-6565
Emp Here 50
SIC 4959 Sanitary services, nec

D-U-N-S 24-351-2501   (BR)
GROUPE AGRITEX INC, LES
AGRITEX RICHMOND
(*Suby of* Groupe Agritex Inc, Le)
1006 Rue Craig, Richmond, QC, J0B 2H0
(819) 826-3707
Emp Here 20
SIC 5999 Miscellaneous retail stores, nec

D-U-N-S 25-683-5380   (SL)
INNOTEX INC
275 Rue Gouin Bureau 1010, Richmond, QC,
J0B 2H0
(819) 826-5971
Emp Here 75   *Sales* 3,429,153
SIC 2311 Men's and boy's suits and coats

D-U-N-S 25-371-3523   (BR)
PROVIGO DISTRIBUTION INC
MAXI
44 Rue Craig, Richmond, QC, J0B 2H0
(819) 826-2413
Emp Here 50
SIC 5411 Grocery stores

Rigaud, QC J0P
Vaudreuil County

D-U-N-S 24-714-1336   (SL)
CONSTRUCTION J.R. GAUTHIER INC
216 Ch De L'Anse, Rigaud, QC, J0P 1P0
(514) 866-4788
Emp Here 60   *Sales* 4,815,406
SIC 7353 Heavy construction equipment rental

D-U-N-S 24-363-2911   (BR)
URECON LTD./LTEE
URECON LTEE
48 Rue Seguin, Rigaud, QC, J0P 1P0
(450) 451-6781
Emp Here 20
SIC 3086 Plastics foam products

D-U-N-S 25-089-0829   (SL)
VIAVIC EXPRESS INC
30 Rue Seguin, Rigaud, QC, J0P 1P0
(450) 451-3078
Emp Here 26   *Sales* 5,055,938
SIC 4731 Freight transportation arrangement
Pr Pr Victor Cesari

Rimouski, QC G0L
Rimouski County

D-U-N-S 20-572-6032   (BR)
CANADA POST CORPORATION
139 Rue De Sainte-Cecile-Du-Bic, Rimouski,
QC, G0L 1B0
(418) 736-4988
Emp Here 20
SIC 4311 U.s. postal service

D-U-N-S 20-711-8204   (BR)
COMMISSION SCOLAIRE DES PHARES
ECOLE DU HAVRE SAINT ROSAIRE PAVIL-LION MONT SAINT LOUIS
(*Suby of* Commission Scolaire des Phares)
136 Rue De La Grotte, Rimouski, QC, G0L

1B0
(418) 736-4965
Emp Here 20
SIC 8211 Elementary and secondary schools

D-U-N-S 20-719-5418   (BR)
COOP PURDEL, LA
LA MEUNERIE
2751 132 Rte E, Rimouski, QC, G0L 1B0
(418) 736-4398
Emp Here 20
SIC 2048 Prepared feeds, nec

D-U-N-S 24-863-4560   (SL)
DISTRIBUTION ALIMENTAIRE R T LTEE
(*Suby of* 9190-9200 Quebec Inc)
2188 132 Rte E Rr 1, Rimouski, QC, G0L 1B0

Emp Here 42   *Sales* 23,362,080
SIC 5142 Packaged frozen goods
  Renaud Samuel

Rimouski, QC G5L
Rimouski County

D-U-N-S 24-146-9840   (SL)
AMH CANADA LTEE
ULTAMIG
391 Rue Saint-Jean-Baptiste E, Rimouski,
QC, G5L 1Z2
(418) 724-4105
Emp Here 60   *Sales* 20,637,005
SIC 3548 Welding apparatus
Pr Pr Ali Osmani

D-U-N-S 20-801-9211   (BR)
ASTRAL BROADCASTING GROUP INC
CIKI FM 98 7
(*Suby of* Astral Broadcasting Group Inc)
875 Boul Saint-Germain, Rimouski, QC, G5L
3T9
(418) 724-8833
Emp Here 35
SIC 4832 Radio broadcasting stations

D-U-N-S 20-183-1166   (BR)
BPR - GROUPE-CONSEIL, SENC
GROUPE-CONSEIL, SENC
464 Boul Saint-Germain, Rimouski, QC, G5L
3P1
(418) 723-8151
Emp Here 50
SIC 8711 Engineering services

D-U-N-S 20-797-6239   (BR)
BOUTIQUE LA VIE EN ROSE INC
BOUTIQUE LA VIE EN ROSE INC
419 Boul Jessop, Rimouski, QC, G5L 7Y5
(418) 723-5512
Emp Here 20
SIC 5137 Women's and children's clothing

D-U-N-S 25-016-1601   (HQ)
CAISSE DESJARDINS DE RIMOUSKI
DESJARDINS ENTREPRISESBAS-SAINT-LAURENT
(*Suby of* Caisse Desjardins de Rimouski)
100 Rue Julien-Rehel, Rimouski, QC, G5L
0G6
(418) 723-3368
Emp Here 70   *Emp Total* 140
Sales 21,292,161
SIC 6062 State credit unions
Genl Mgr Martin Desrosiers
Pr Michel Emond
VP Stephane Plante
Sec Gilles Langelier
Dir Alain Beaulieu
Dir Real Chapados
Dir Melina De Champlain
Dir Richard Gauthier
Dir Gabrielle Langlais
Dir Jean-Francois Marquis

D-U-N-S 24-200-0396   (BR)

CANADIAN BROADCASTING CORPORA-TION
SOCIETE RADIO CANADA
185 Boul Rene-Lepage E, Rimouski, QC, G5L
1P2
(418) 723-2217
Emp Here 30
SIC 4832 Radio broadcasting stations

D-U-N-S 20-304-8454   (BR)
COGECO COMMUNICATIONS HOLDINGS INC
COGECO CABLE HOLDINGS INC
384 Av De La Cathedrale, Rimouski, QC, G5L
5L1
(418) 724-5737
Emp Here 25
SIC 4841 Cable and other pay television ser-vices

D-U-N-S 20-711-8238   (BR)
COMMISSION SCOLAIRE DES PHARES
CENTRE DE FORMATION RIMOUSKI NEIGETTE
(*Suby of* Commission Scolaire des Phares)
424 Av Ross, Rimouski, QC, G5L 6J2
(418) 722-4922
Emp Here 50
SIC 8211 Elementary and secondary schools

D-U-N-S 25-232-3647   (BR)
COMMISSION SCOLAIRE DES PHARES
ECOLE PAUL-HUBERT
(*Suby of* Commission Scolaire des Phares)
250 Boul Arthur-Buies O, Rimouski, QC, G5L
7A7
(418) 724-3439
Emp Here 200
SIC 8211 Elementary and secondary schools

D-U-N-S 25-232-3118   (BR)
COMMISSION SCOLAIRE DES PHARES
ECOLE ST JEAN
(*Suby of* Commission Scolaire des Phares)
245 2e Rue O, Rimouski, QC, G5L 4Y1
(418) 724-3381
Emp Here 30
SIC 8211 Elementary and secondary schools

D-U-N-S 25-232-1369   (BR)
COMMISSION SCOLAIRE DES PHARES
COMMISSION SCOLAIRE DES PHARES
(*Suby of* Commission Scolaire des Phares)
130 Rue Cote Bureau T, Rimouski, QC, G5L
2Y2
(418) 724-3555
Emp Here 20
SIC 8211 Elementary and secondary schools

D-U-N-S 20-711-8162   (BR)
COMMISSION SCOLAIRE DES PHARES
ECOLE DU ROCHER ET D'AUTEUIL
(*Suby of* Commission Scolaire des Phares)
845 Rue Saint-Arsene, Rimouski, QC, G5L
3X4
(418) 724-3566
Emp Here 50
SIC 8211 Elementary and secondary schools

D-U-N-S 24-464-9299   (HQ)
COMMISSION SCOLAIRE DES PHARES
(*Suby of* Commission Scolaire des Phares)
435 Av Rouleau, Rimouski, QC, G5L 5W6
(418) 723-5927
Emp Here 65   *Emp Total* 2,000
Sales 179,829,120
SIC 8211 Elementary and secondary schools
Dir Fin Marc Girard
Pr Pr Raymond Tudeau

D-U-N-S 25-233-6599   (BR)
COMMISSION SCOLAIRE DES PHARES
ECOLE DES BEAUX SEJOURS
(*Suby of* Commission Scolaire des Phares)
514 Rue Tessier, Rimouski, QC, G5L 4L9
(418) 724-3564
Emp Here 30
SIC 8211 Elementary and secondary schools

D-U-N-S 25-232-3563   (BR)
COMMISSION SCOLAIRE DES PHARES
ECOLE LANGEVIN, L
(*Suby of* Commission Scolaire des Phares)
105 Rue Saint-Jean-Baptiste O, Rimouski,
QC, G5L 4J2
(418) 724-3384
Emp Here 60
SIC 8211 Elementary and secondary schools

D-U-N-S 20-711-8220   (BR)
COMMISSION SCOLAIRE DES PHARES
ECOLE L'ECHO-DES-MONTAGNES-LAVOIE - PAVILLON D'AUTEUIL
(*Suby of* Commission Scolaire des Phares)
149 Rue Du Rocher-Blanc, Rimouski, QC,
G5L 7A1
(418) 724-3567
Emp Here 50
SIC 8211 Elementary and secondary schools

D-U-N-S 20-000-1472   (BR)
CONFEDERATION DES SYNDICATS NA-TIONAUX (C.S.N.)
CONFEDERATION DES SYNDICATS NA-TIONAUX (C.S.N.)
124 Rue Sainte-Marie, Rimouski, QC, G5L
4E3
(418) 723-7811
Emp Here 20
SIC 8631 Labor organizations

D-U-N-S 25-162-3633   (BR)
DELOITTE & TOUCHE MANAGEMENT CONSULTANTS
(*Suby of* Deloitte & Touche Management Con-sultants)
287 Rue Pierre-Saindon Unite 402, Rimouski,
QC, G5L 9A7
(418) 724-4136
Emp Here 30
SIC 8721 Accounting, auditing, and book-keeping

D-U-N-S 20-244-1341   (HQ)
DICKNER INC
LOUTEC
559 Rue De Lausanne, Rimouski, QC, G5L
4A7
(418) 723-7936
Emp Here 28   *Emp Total* 38
Sales 6,420,542
SIC 5084 Industrial machinery and equipment
Pr Pr Herve Dickner
  Benoit Dickner

D-U-N-S 24-335-7659   (BR)
DISTRIBUTIONS PAUL-EMILE DUBE LTEE
385 Rue Des Chevaliers, Rimouski, QC, G5L
1X3
(418) 724-2400
Emp Here 100
SIC 5147 Meats and meat products

D-U-N-S 24-843-6698   (BR)
ENGLOBE CORP
LVM DIVISION OF
331 Rue Rivard, Rimouski, QC, G5L 7J6
(418) 723-1144
Emp Here 64
SIC 8742 Management consulting services

D-U-N-S 20-102-7088   (BR)
FONDATION DU CENTRE DE JEUNESSE DU BAS-SAINT-LAURENT
(*Suby of* Fondation du Centre de Jeunesse du Bas-Saint-Laurent)
287 Rue Pierre-Saindon, Rimouski, QC, G5L
9A7
(418) 722-1897
Emp Here 20
SIC 8641 Civic and social associations

D-U-N-S 24-630-5671   (BR)
FONDATION DU CENTRE DE JEUNESSE DU BAS-SAINT-LAURENT
CENTRE JEUNESSE DU BAS-SAINT-LAURENT

(*Suby of* Fondation du Centre de Jeunesse du Bas-Saint-Laurent)
103 Rue De L'Eveche O, Rimouski, QC, G5L 4H4
(418) 723-1250
Emp Here 30
SIC 8322 Individual and family services

D-U-N-S 24-690-0567   (SL)
FOYER DE RIMOUSKI INC
645 Boul Saint-Germain, Rimouski, QC, G5L 3S2
(418) 724-4111
Emp Here 260   *Sales* 12,250,277
SIC 8361 Residential care
Genl Mgr Gilles Gauvreau

D-U-N-S 20-006-8067   (BR)
GOUVERNEMENT DE LA PROVINCE DE QUEBEC
FINANCIERE AGRICOLE DU QUEBEC, LA
337 Rue Moreault Bureau 2.10, Rimouski, QC, G5L 1P4
(418) 727-3586
Emp Here 30
SIC 8742 Management consulting services

D-U-N-S 20-007-5880   (BR)
GOUVERNEMENT DE LA PROVINCE DE QUEBEC
MINISTERE DE L'AGRICULTURE DES PECHERIES ET DE L'ALIMENTATION DU QUEBEC
335 Rue Moreault, Rimouski, QC, G5L 9C8

Emp Here 20
SIC 8748 Business consulting, nec

D-U-N-S 25-325-1599   (BR)
GOUVERNEUR INC
HOTEL GOUVERNEUR DE RIMOUSKI
155 Boul Rene-Lepage E Bureau 72, Rimouski, QC, G5L 1P2
(418) 723-4422
Emp Here 70
SIC 7011 Hotels and motels

D-U-N-S 24-863-8371   (BR)
GROUPE COOPERATIF DYNACO
CENTRE DE RENOVATION DYNACO BMR
(*Suby of* Groupe Cooperatif Dynaco)
234 Av Leonidas S, Rimouski, QC, G5L 2T2
(418) 723-2201
Emp Here 25
SIC 5211 Lumber and other building materials

D-U-N-S 25-515-5079   (BR)
GROUPE RESTAURANTS IMVESCOR INC
RESTAURANT MIKES
117 Rue Saint-Germain O, Rimouski, QC, G5L 4B6
(418) 723-3030
Emp Here 25
SIC 5812 Eating places

D-U-N-S 25-019-5781   (BR)
INDUSTRIELLE ALLIANCE, ASSURANCE ET SERVICES FINANCIERS INC
180 Rue Des Gouverneurs Bureau 001, Rimouski, QC, G5L 8G1
(418) 723-3236
Emp Here 20
SIC 6411 Insurance agents, brokers, and service

D-U-N-S 25-305-2195   (BR)
INNVEST PROPERTIES CORP
COMFORT INN
(*Suby of* Innvest Properties Corp)
455 Boul Saint-Germain Bureau 340, Rimouski, QC, G5L 3P2
(418) 724-2500
Emp Here 22
SIC 7011 Hotels and motels

D-U-N-S 25-026-5857   (BR)
MALLETTE S.E.N.C.R.L.
188 Rue Des Gouverneurs Bureau 200, Ri-

mouski, QC, G5L 8G1
(418) 724-4414
Emp Here 40
SIC 8721 Accounting, auditing, and bookkeeping

D-U-N-S 24-378-6456   (HQ)
PG SOLUTIONS INC
217 Av Leonidas S Bureau 13, Rimouski, QC, G5L 2T5
(418) 724-5037
Emp Here 60   *Emp Total* 12,124
Sales 18,240,175
SIC 7371 Custom computer programming services
Pr Pr Jeff Bender

D-U-N-S 24-853-9152   (BR)
PMT ROY ASSURANCE ET SERVICES FINANCIERS INC
(*Suby of* PMT Roy Assurance et Services Financiers Inc)
140 Rue Saint-Germain O Bureau 100, Rimouski, QC, G5L 4B5
(418) 724-4127
Emp Here 50
SIC 6411 Insurance agents, brokers, and service

D-U-N-S 20-939-6758   (SL)
PEPSI COLA CANADA LTEE
SOCIETE DU GROUPE D'EMBOUTEILLAGE PEPSI
401 Boul De La Riviere, Rimouski, QC, G5L 7R1
(418) 722-8080
Emp Here 45   *Sales* 9,029,050
SIC 5149 Groceries and related products, nec
Pr Sean Bousada

D-U-N-S 24-125-5293   (BR)
PROVIGO DISTRIBUTION INC
MAXI
419 Boul Jessop, Rimouski, QC, G5L 7Y5
(418) 723-0506
Emp Here 51
SIC 5411 Grocery stores

D-U-N-S 25-298-2020   (BR)
RAYMOND CHABOT GRANT THORNTON S.E.N.C.R.L.
165 Av Belzile, Rimouski, QC, G5L 8Y2
(418) 722-4611
Emp Here 20
SIC 8721 Accounting, auditing, and bookkeeping

D-U-N-S 25-918-4463   (HQ)
RESSOURCES APPALACHES INC
(*Suby of* Ressources Appalaches Inc)
212 Av De La Cathedrale, Rimouski, QC, G5L 5J2
(418) 724-0901
Emp Here 50   *Emp Total* 100
Sales 10,931,016
SIC 1081 Metal mining services
  Alain Hupe
  Andre Proulx
Dir John Alan Thomas
Dir Dominique Doucet

D-U-N-S 20-332-9615   (HQ)
RESTAURANTS MICHEL DESCHENES INC, LES
MCDONALD'S
(*Suby of* Restaurants Michel Deschenes Inc, Les)
395 Boul Saint-Germain, Rimouski, QC, G5L 3N5
(418) 724-6868
Emp Here 20   *Emp Total* 50
Sales 1,532,175
SIC 5812 Eating places

D-U-N-S 24-855-2486   (BR)
RESTAURANTS MICHEL DESCHENES INC, LES
MCDONALD'S

(*Suby of* Restaurants Michel Deschenes Inc, Les)
395 Boul Saint-Germain, Rimouski, QC, G5L 3N5
(418) 724-6868
Emp Here 100
SIC 5812 Eating places

D-U-N-S 24-842-2834   (SL)
SECURITE B S L LTEE
599 Rue Des Voiliers Bureau 201, Rimouski, QC, G5L 7M9
(418) 723-0277
Emp Here 50   *Sales* 1,532,175
SIC 7381 Detective and armored car services

D-U-N-S 25-488-6716   (BR)
SERVANTES DE NOTRE-DAME REINE DU CLERGE
(*Suby of* Servantes De Notre-Dame Reine Du Clerge)
57 Rue Jules-A.-Brillant, Rimouski, QC, G5L 1X1

Emp Here 60
SIC 8661 Religious organizations

D-U-N-S 25-309-1557   (BR)
SOBEYS CAPITAL INCORPORATED
IGA EXTRA
395 Av Sirois, Rimouski, QC, G5L 8R2
(418) 724-2244
Emp Here 110
SIC 5411 Grocery stores

D-U-N-S 20-270-6255   (BR)
STANTEC CONSULTING LTD
CONSORTIUM DESSAU/CEGERTEC
287 Rue Pierre-Saindon Bureau 401, Rimouski, QC, G5L 9A7
(418) 723-4010
Emp Here 24
SIC 8711 Engineering services

D-U-N-S 25-316-8595   (BR)
SUN LIFE ASSURANCE COMPANY OF CANADA
97 Rue Saint-Germain E, Rimouski, QC, G5L 1A5
(418) 723-7831
Emp Here 25
SIC 6311 Life insurance

D-U-N-S 24-364-4502   (BR)
TELUS CORPORATION
226 Rue Saint-Germain E, Rimouski, QC, G5L 1B4
(418) 722-5444
Emp Here 50
SIC 4899 Communication services, nec

D-U-N-S 20-244-3370   (HQ)
TELUS COMMUNICATIONS (QUEBEC) INC
6 Rue Jules-A.-Brillant Bureau 20602, Rimouski, QC, G5L 1W8
(418) 723-2271
Emp Here 100   *Emp Total* 51,250
Sales 473,991,487
SIC 6712 Bank holding companies
Pr Pr Francois Cote
  Isabelle Plante
  Monique Mercier

D-U-N-S 25-019-6565   (BR)
TELUS COMMUNICATIONS (QUEBEC) INC
6 Rue Jules-A.-Brillant Bureau 20602, Rimouski, QC, G5L 1W8
(418) 722-5919
Emp Here 200
SIC 4899 Communication services, nec

D-U-N-S 25-334-3271   (BR)
UNIVERSITE DU QUEBEC
INSTITUT DES SCIENCES DE LA MER DE RIMOUSKI
310 Allee Des Ursulines, Rimouski, QC, G5L 2Z9
(418) 724-1770
Emp Here 42

SIC 8733 Noncommercial research organizations

D-U-N-S 24-758-9476   (BR)
UNIVERSITE DU QUEBEC
UNIVERSITE DU QUEBEC A RIMOUSKI
300 Allee Des Ursulines, Rimouski, QC, G5L 3A1
(418) 723-1986
Emp Here 650
SIC 8221 Colleges and universities

D-U-N-S 20-006-8059   (BR)
VILLE DE RIMOUSKI
SERVICE DE SECURITE INCENDIE
11 Rue Saint-Laurent O, Rimouski, QC, G5L 8B5
(418) 724-3265
Emp Here 70
SIC 7389 Business services, nec

Rimouski, QC G5M
Rimouski County

D-U-N-S 24-441-9136   (SL)
9059-4300 QUEBEC INC
RESTAURANT TIM HORTON
367 Montee Industrielle-Et-Commerciale, Rimouski, QC, G5M 1Y1
(418) 721-2003
Emp Here 60   *Sales* 1,824,018
SIC 5812 Eating places

D-U-N-S 20-295-7010   (BR)
AMEUBLEMENTS TANGUAY INC
375 Montee Industrielle-Et-Commerciale, Rimouski, QC, G5M 1Y1
(418) 725-4411
Emp Here 60
SIC 5712 Furniture stores

D-U-N-S 25-323-4046   (BR)
CANAC-MARQUIS GRENIER LTEE
(*Suby of* Gestion Laberge Inc)
228 Rue Des Negociants, Rimouski, QC, G5M 1B6
(418) 723-0007
Emp Here 85
SIC 5211 Lumber and other building materials

D-U-N-S 25-240-6327   (BR)
COMMISSION SCOLAIRE DES PHARES
ECOLE DE LA ROSE DES VENTS
(*Suby of* Commission Scolaire des Phares)
355 Av De La Jeunesse, Rimouski, QC, G5M 1J2
(418) 724-3563
Emp Here 45
SIC 8211 Elementary and secondary schools

D-U-N-S 20-800-2969   (BR)
ENTERPRISE RENT-A-CAR CANADA COMPANY
NATIONAL CAR RENTAL
(*Suby of* The Crawford Group Inc)
370 Montee Industrielle-Et-Commerciale, Rimouski, QC, G5M 1X1
(418) 723-9191
Emp Here 20
SIC 7514 Passenger car rental

D-U-N-S 20-007-5823   (BR)
GHD CONSULTANTS LTEE
INSPEC-SOL
491 Rue Jean-Marie-Leblanc, Rimouski, QC, G5M 1B8
(418) 724-7030
Emp Here 25
SIC 8621 Professional organizations

D-U-N-S 20-706-6668   (BR)
METRO RICHELIEU INC
SUPER C
395 Montee Industrielle-Et-Commerciale, Rimouski, QC, G5M 1Y1

---

(418) 723-9862
Emp Here 60
SIC 5411 Grocery stores

D-U-N-S 20-953-0336   (BR)
MOLSON CANADA 2005
(*Suby of* Molson Coors Brewing Company)
220 Montee Industrielle-Et-Commerciale, Ri-
mouski, QC, G5M 1A5
(418) 723-1786
Emp Here 30
SIC 5181 Beer and ale

D-U-N-S 24-119-5499   (BR)
PUROLATOR INC.
PUROLATOR INC
193 Montee Industrielle-Et-Commerciale, Ri-
mouski, QC, G5M 1A7
(418) 723-3506
Emp Here 20
SIC 7389 Business services, nec

D-U-N-S 20-188-6376   (BR)
RUSSEL METALS INC
ACIER LEROUX
221 Rue Des Negociants, Rimouski, QC, G5M
1B7
(418) 724-4937
Emp Here 35
SIC 5051 Metals service centers and offices

D-U-N-S 20-105-0247   (BR)
STAPLES CANADA INC
BUREAU EN GROS
(*Suby of* Staples, Inc.)
390 Montee Industrielle-Et-Commerciale, Ri-
mouski, QC, G5M 1X1
(418) 724-7033
Emp Here 40
SIC 5943 Stationery stores

D-U-N-S 20-052-5157   (BR)
TELUS COMMUNICATIONS (QUEBEC) INC
TELUS QUEBEC
160 Rue Des Negociants, Rimouski, QC, G5M
1B6
(418) 722-5580
Emp Here 56
SIC 4899 Communication services, nec

D-U-N-S 24-207-4206   (BR)
WAL-MART CANADA CORP
WALMART
415 Montee Industrielle-Et-Commerciale Bu-
reau 3198, Rimouski, QC, G5M 1Y1
(418) 722-1990
Emp Here 200
SIC 5311 Department stores

Rimouski, QC G5N
Rimouski County

D-U-N-S 25-232-1484   (BR)
COMMISSION SCOLAIRE DES PHARES
ECOLE DES MERISIERS
(*Suby of* Commission Scolaire des Phares)
658 Rte Des Pionniers, Rimouski, QC, G5N
5P1
(418) 735-2115
Emp Here 40
SIC 8211 Elementary and secondary schools

Riviere-Bleue, QC G0L
Temiscouata County

D-U-N-S 20-029-1958   (BR)
**CENTRE DE SANTE ET DE SERVICE SOCI-
AUX DU TEMISCOUATA**
L'ESPACE VILLA DE LA RIVIERE
(*Suby of* Centre de Sante et de Service Soci-
aux du Temiscouata)
45 Rue Du Foyer S, Riviere-Bleue, CC, G0L
2B0

(418) 893-5511
Emp Here 50
SIC 8361 Residential care

D-U-N-S 20-711-9566   (BR)
**COMMISSION SCOLAIRE DU FLEUVE ET
DES LACS**
ECOLE NOTRE DAME DE GRACE
31 Rue Des Pins E, Riviere-Bleue, QC, G0L
2B0
(418) 893-2514
Emp Here 30
SIC 8211 Elementary and secondary schools

D-U-N-S 24-103-0233   (SL)
GROUPE N B G INC
99 Rue De La Frontiere O, Riviere-Bleue, QC,
G0L 2B0
(418) 893-5575
Emp Here 50   *Sales* 4,742,446
SIC 2421 Sawmills and planing mills, general

Riviere-Du-Loup, QC G5R
Riviere-Du-Loup County

D-U-N-S 24-941-7270   (SL)
2958-3465 QUEBEC INC
AUBERGE RIVIERE-DU-LOUP
311 Boul De L'Hotel-De-Ville, Riviere-Du-
Loup, QC, G5R 5S4
(418) 862-9520
Emp Here 50   *Sales* 2,188,821
SIC 7011 Hotels and motels

D-U-N-S 25-258-8405   (BR)
9130-1168 QUEBEC INC
9130-1168 QUEBEC INC.
298 Boul Armand-Theriault Bureau 2, Riviere-
Du-Loup, QC, G5R 4C2
(418) 862-7848
Emp Here 926
SIC 6512 Nonresidential building operators

D-U-N-S 25-851-5451   (BR)
AMEUBLEMENTS TANGUAY INC
245 Boul De L'Hotel-De-Ville, Riviere-Du-
Loup, QC, G5R 5H5
(418) 867-4711
Emp Here 45
SIC 5712 Furniture stores

D-U-N-S 20-244-5995   (SL)
AUBERGE DE LA POINTE INC
RESTAURANT L'ESPADON
10 Boul Cartier, Riviere-Du-Loup, QC, G5R
6A1
(418) 862-3514
Emp Here 80   *Sales* 3,502,114
SIC 7011 Hotels and motels

D-U-N-S 24-637-6792   (BR)
BANQUE NATIONALE DU CANADA
295 Boul Armand-Theriault, Riviere-Du-Loup,
QC, G5R 5H3
(418) 862-7248
Emp Here 30
SIC 6021 National commercial banks

D-U-N-S 24-368-8715   (BR)
**CAISSE POPULAIRE DESJARDINS DE
RIVIERE-DU-LOUP**
CENTRE DE SERVICE LAFONTAINE
106 Rue Lafontaine, Riviere-Du-Loup, QC,
G5R 3A1
(418) 862-7255
Emp Here 30
SIC 6062 State credit unions

D-U-N-S 20-265-4711   (SL)
CAMILLE MAILLOUX R.D.L. INC
331 Rue Temiscouata, Riviere-Du-Loup, QC,
G5R 2Y9
(418) 862-2898
Emp Here 35   *Sales* 1,021,450
SIC 4151 School buses

D-U-N-S 20-538-2257   (BR)
CANADA POST CORPORATION
BUREAU DE POSTE DE RIVIERE DU LOUP
200 Rue Lafontaine, Riviere-Du-Loup, QC,
G5R 0J4
(418) 862-6348
Emp Here 20
SIC 4311 U.s. postal service

D-U-N-S 24-326-8476   (BR)
**CENTRE DE SANTE ET DE SERVICES SO-
CIAUX DE RIVIERE-DU-LOUP**
RESIDENCE SAINT-JOSEPH, LA
28 Rue Joly, Riviere-Du-Loup, QC, G5R 3H2
(418) 862-6385
Emp Here 155
SIC 8059 Nursing and personal care, nec

D-U-N-S 25-731-7073   (BR)
CIMA+ S.E.N.C.
CIMA PLUS ENGINEERING SOCIETY
37 Rue Delage, Riviere-Du-Loup, QC, G5R
3P2
(418) 862-8217
Emp Here 33
SIC 8711 Engineering services

D-U-N-S 25-309-1862   (BR)
CLARKE INC
TRAVERSE RIV DU LOUP ST-SIMEON, LA
199 Rue Hayward, Riviere-Du-Loup, QC, G5R
6A7
(418) 862-9545
Emp Here 50
SIC 6719 Holding companies, nec

D-U-N-S 20-714-2006   (SL)
**COLLEGE NOTRE-DAME DE RIVIERE-DU-
LOUP**
56 Rue Saint-Henri, Riviere-Du-Loup, QC,
G5R 2A1
(418) 862-8257
Emp Here 51   *Sales* 3,429,153
SIC 8211 Elementary and secondary schools

D-U-N-S 25-233-7738   (BR)
**COMMISSION   SCOLAIRE   DE
KAMOURASKA RIVIERE-DU-LOUP**
ECOLE SECONDAIRE RIVIERE DU LOUP
320 Rue Saint-Pierre, Riviere-Du-Loup, QC,
G5R 3V3
(418) 862-8203
Emp Here 160
SIC 8211 Elementary and secondary schools

D-U-N-S 25-233-9809   (BR)
**COMMISSION   SCOLAIRE   DE
KAMOURASKA RIVIERE-DU-LOUP**
ECOLE ROY
55 Rue Du Rocher, Riviere-Du-Loup, QC,
G5R 1J8
(418) 862-0562
Emp Here 20
SIC 8211 Elementary and secondary schools

D-U-N-S 25-002-1318   (BR)
**COMMISSION   SCOLAIRE   DE
KAMOURASKA RIVIERE-DU-LOUP**
*CENTRE D'EDUCATION DES ADULTES DE
KAMOURASKA RIVIERE-DU-LOUP-ECOLE
THIBAUDEAU*
30 Rue Delage, Riviere-Du-Loup, QC, G5R
3N8
(418) 862-8277
Emp Here 20
SIC 8211 Elementary and secondary schools

D-U-N-S 20-025-5268   (BR)
**COMMISSION   SCOLAIRE   DE
KAMOURASKA RIVIERE-DU-LOUP**
ECOLE LACROISEE
15 Rue Vezina Bureau 2, Riviere-Du-Loup,
QC, G5R 2H2
(418) 868-2395
Emp Here 45
SIC 8211 Elementary and secondary schools

D-U-N-S 25-233-0048   (BR)
COMMISSION   SCOLAIRE   DE

KAMOURASKA RIVIERE-DU-LOUP
ECOLE ST FRANCOIS XAVIER
8a Rue Pouliot, Riviere-Du-Loup, QC, G5R
3R8
(418) 862-6901
Emp Here 32
SIC 8211 Elementary and secondary schools

D-U-N-S 25-022-6966   (BR)
**COMMISSION   SCOLAIRE   DE
KAMOURASKA RIVIERE-DU-LOUP**
ENVOL EDUCATION DES ADULTES, L
20 Rue De Gaspe, Riviere-Du-Loup, QC, G5R
1A9
(418) 862-0336
Emp Here 45
SIC 8211 Elementary and secondary schools

D-U-N-S 25-299-6681   (BR)
DOLLARAMA S.E.C.
DOLLARAMA
298 Boul Armand-Theriault, Riviere-Du-Loup,
QC, G5R 4C2
(418) 868-0207
Emp Here 24
SIC 5331 Variety stores

D-U-N-S 24-164-3670   (BR)
**FONDATION DU CENTRE DE SANTE ET DE
SERVICES SOCIAUX DE LA MITIS**
*CENTRE   DE   READAPTATION
L'INTERACTION*
48 Rue De Chauffailles, Riviere-Du-Loup, QC,
G5R 4E1
(418) 867-5215
Emp Here 50
SIC 8093 Specialty outpatient clinics, nec

D-U-N-S 20-323-7537   (BR)
GROUPE COOPERATIF DYNACO
CENTRE DE RENOVATION DYNACO BMR
(*Suby of* Groupe Cooperatif Dynaco)
273 Boul De L'Hotel-De-Ville, Riviere-Du-
Loup, QC, G5R 6H5
(418) 862-9316
Emp Here 55
SIC 5211 Lumber and other building materials

D-U-N-S 20-719-9782   (BR)
GROUPE COOPERATIF DYNACO
DYNACO MACHINERIE
(*Suby of* Groupe Cooperatif Dynaco)
411 Rue Temiscouata, Riviere-Du-Loup, QC,
G5R 6B3
(418) 867-1062
Emp Here 20
SIC 5999 Miscellaneous retail stores, nec

D-U-N-S 25-470-1113   (BR)
HENAULT & GOSSELIN INC
409 Rue Temiscouata, Riviere-Du-Loup, QC,
G5R 6B3
(418) 862-9548
Emp Here 60
SIC 1794 Excavation work

D-U-N-S 25-309-6820   (BR)
**INDUSTRIELLE ALLIANCE, ASSURANCE
ET SERVICES FINANCIERS INC**
186 Rue Fraser Bureau 300, Riviere-Du-Loup,
QC, G5R 1C8
(418) 862-0141
Emp Here 27
SIC 6411 Insurance agents, brokers, and ser-
vice

D-U-N-S 25-305-2153   (BR)
INNVEST PROPERTIES CORP
COMFORT INN
(*Suby of* Innvest Properties Corp)
85 Boul Cartier, Riviere-Du-Loup, QC, G5R
4X4
(418) 867-4162
Emp Here 27
SIC 7011 Hotels and motels

D-U-N-S 20-925-6325   (BR)
**MCDONALD'S   RESTAURANTS   OF
CANADA LIMITED**

RESTAURANT MCDONALD'S
(*Suby of* McDonald's Corporation)
100 Rue Des Cerisiers, Riviere-Du-Loup, QC, G5R 6E8
(418) 863-4242
Emp Here 80
SIC 5812 Eating places

D-U-N-S 25-880-5670 (BR)
MOLSON CANADA 2005
MOLSON CANADA
(*Suby of* Molson Coors Brewing Company)
100 Rue Lebrun, Riviere-Du-Loup, QC, G5R 3Y6
(418) 862-2186
Emp Here 20
SIC 2082 Malt beverages

D-U-N-S 24-499-1238 (SL)
MOTEL BOULEVARD CARTIER INC
ROTISSERIE ST-HUBERT
80 Boul Cartier, Riviere-Du-Loup, QC, G5R 2M9
(418) 867-3008
Emp Here 100   *Sales* 2,991,389
SIC 5812 Eating places

D-U-N-S 24-821-0627 (HQ)
PREMIER TECH TECHNOLOGIES LIMITEE
PREMIER TECH SYSTEMS
1 Av Premier Bureau 101 Riviere-Du-Loup, QC, G5R 6C1
(418) 867-8883
Emp Here 499   *Emp Total* 50
Sales 75,537,087
SIC 3565 Packaging machinery
Ch Bd Bernard Belanger
Pr Jean Belanger
Treas Germain Ouellet
 Martin Noel

D-U-N-S 24-341-3981 (BR)
PROVIGO DISTRIBUTION INC
MAXI
215 Boul De L'Hotel-De-Ville, Riviere-Du-Loup, QC, G5R 5H4
(418) 863-4100
Emp Here 65
SIC 5411 Grocery stores

D-U-N-S 25-298-2053 (BR)
RAYMOND CHABOT GRANT THORNTON S.E.N.C.R.L.
300 Boul De L'Hotel-De-Ville, Riviere-Du-Loup, QC, G5R 5C6
(418) 862-6396
Emp Here 50
SIC 8721 Accounting, auditing, and book-keeping

D-U-N-S 20-794-3577 (BR)
RESTAURANT NORMANDIN INC
83 Boul Cartier, Riviere-Du-Loup, QC, G5R 2N1
(418) 867-1366
Emp Here 75
SIC 5812 Eating places

D-U-N-S 24-729-7336 (BR)
SINTRA INC
CONSTRUCTION BML
105 Rue Louis-Philippe-Lebrun, Riviere-Du-Loup, QC, G5R 5W5
(418) 862-0000
Emp Here 250
SIC 1611 Highway and street construction

D-U-N-S 25-309-1599 (BR)
SOBEYS CAPITAL INCORPORATED
IGA EXTRA
254 Boul De L'Hotel-De-Ville Bureau 451, Riviere-Du-Loup, QC, G5R 1M4
(418) 862-7861
Emp Here 108
SIC 5411 Grocery stores

D-U-N-S 20-000-7602 (BR)
SOCIETE VIE INTEGRATION APPRENTIS-

SAGE POUR HANDICAPES V.I.A. INC, LA
100 Rue Delage, Riviere-Du-Loup, QC, G5R 3P9
(418) 868-1729
Emp Here 28
SIC 4953 Refuse systems

D-U-N-S 25-307-6780 (BR)
SOCIETE DES ALCOOLS DU QUEBEC
S.A.Q.
235 Boul De L'Hotel-De-Ville, Riviere-Du-Loup, QC, G5R 4E5
(418) 862-0299
Emp Here 22
SIC 5921 Liquor stores

D-U-N-S 24-144-7440 (SL)
VIANDES DU BRETON INC, LES
OEUFS BRETON, LES
150 Ch Des Raymond, Riviere-Du-Loup, QC, G5R 5X8
(418) 863-6711
Emp Here 540   *Sales* 62,892,123
SIC 2011 Meat packing plants
Pr Pr Vincent Breton
VP Lucien Breton
Sec Marie-Josee Landry

D-U-N-S 24-207-4230 (BR)
WAL-MART CANADA CORP
100 Rue Des Cerisiers, Riviere-Du-Loup, QC, G5R 6E8
(418) 862-3003
Emp Here 120
SIC 5311 Department stores

Riviere-Eternite, QC G0V
Chicoutimi County

D-U-N-S 25-232-2615 (BR)
COMMISSION SCOLAIRE DES RIVES-DU-SAGUENAY
ECOLE MARIE MEDIATRICE
(*Suby of* Commission Scolaire des Rives-du-Saguenay)
404 Rue Principale, Riviere-Eternite, QC, G0V 1P0
(418) 615-0064
Emp Here 40
SIC 8211 Elementary and secondary schools

Riviere-Heva, QC J0Y
Abitibi County

D-U-N-S 24-421-8074 (BR)
AGNICO EAGLE MINES LIMITED
AGNICO EAGLE MINES, LAPA DIVISION
299 Rte Saint-Paul N, Riviere-Heva, QC, J0Y 2H0
(819) 735-2034
Emp Here 30
SIC 1041 Gold ores

Riviere-Ouelle, QC G0L
Kamouraska County

D-U-N-S 20-244-9740 (HQ)
TOURBIERES LAMBERT INC
(*Suby of* Gestion Gabert Inc)
106 Ch Lambert Bureau 347, Riviere-Ouelle, QC, G0L 2C0
(418) 852-2885
Emp Here 75   *Emp Total* 1
Sales 14,119,891
SIC 1499 Miscellaneous nonMetallic minerals, except fuels
 Gabriel Lambert
Genl Mgr Jerome Lambert

Riviere-Rouge, QC J0T
Labelle County

D-U-N-S 20-203-8493 (BR)
9168-1924 QUEBEC INC
F. DAUDELIN & FILS
400 Rue L'Annonciation S, Riviere-Rouge, QC, J0T 1T0
(819) 275-2694
Emp Here 45
SIC 5251 Hardware stores

D-U-N-S 24-126-1473 (BR)
CENTRE HOSPITALIER ET CENTRE DE READAPTATION ANTOINE-LABELLE
CSSS ANTOINE-LABELLE CENTRE DE SERVICE RIVIERE ROUGE
1525 Rue L'Annonciation N, Riviere-Rouge, QC, J0T 1T0
(819) 275-2411
Emp Here 700
SIC 8062 General medical and surgical hospitals

D-U-N-S 25-192-9915 (SL)
TORA L'ANNONCIATION LIMITEE
TIGRE GEANT
(*Suby of* Giant Tiger Stores Limited)
1620 Rue Principale N, Riviere-Rouge, QC, J0T 1T0
(819) 275-3777
Emp Here 30   *Sales* 2,480,664
SIC 5399 Miscellaneous general merchandise

Roberval, QC G8H

D-U-N-S 25-247-3947 (SL)
3092-4435 QUEBEC INC
HOTEL CHATEAU ROBERVAL
1225 Boul Marcotte, Roberval, QC, G8H 2P1
(418) 275-7511
Emp Here 55   *Sales* 2,407,703
SIC 7011 Hotels and motels

D-U-N-S 24-455-3850 (BR)
CANADIAN MENTAL HEALTH ASSOCIATION, THE
ASSOCIATION CANADIENNE SANTE MENTALE LAC-ST-JEAN PARADIS
(*Suby of* Canadian Mental Health Association, The)
962 Boul Saint-Joseph, Roberval, QC, G8H 2L9
(418) 275-2405
Emp Here 59
SIC 8011 Offices and clinics of medical doctors

D-U-N-S 25-975-6542 (HQ)
CENTRE DE READAPTATION EN DEFICIENCE INTELLECTUELLE DU SAGUENAY LAC-ST-JEAN
C.R.D.I. SAGUENAY LAC-ST-JEAN
(*Suby of* Centre De Readaptation En Deficience Intellectuelle Du Saguenay Lac-St-Jean)
835 Rue Roland, Roberval, QC, G8H 3J5
(418) 765-3003
Emp Here 200   *Emp Total* 662
Sales 33,258,880
SIC 8361 Residential care
Mng Dir Laurent Bouillon
 Jean-Robert Poulin

D-U-N-S 24-970-5716 (SL)
CENTRE JEUNESSE SAGUENAY LAC ST-JEAN INC
254 Boul Sauve, Roberval, QC, G8H 1A7
(418) 543-3006
Emp Here 300   *Sales* 15,901,920
SIC 8322 Individual and family services
Genl Mgr Michel Lemay

D-U-N-S 25-277-2368 (BR)
CENTRE DE SANTE ET DE SERVICES SOCIAUX DOMAINE-DU-ROY
CENTRE DE READAPTATION POUR ALCOOLIQUES ET AUTRES TOXICOMANES SAINT-ANTOINE
(*Suby of* Centre de Sante et de Services Sociaux Domaine-du-Roy)
400 Av Bergeron, Roberval, QC, G8H 1K8
(418) 275-8775
Emp Here 30
SIC 8069 Specialty hospitals, except psychiatric

D-U-N-S 20-938-8383 (BR)
COMMISSION SCOLAIRE DU PAYS-DES-BLEUETS
ECOLE CITE ETUDIANTE
171 Boul De La Jeunesse, Roberval, QC, G8H 2N9
(418) 275-3110
Emp Here 90
SIC 8211 Elementary and secondary schools

D-U-N-S 25-196-0902 (HQ)
COMMISSION SCOLAIRE DU PAYS-DES-BLEUETS
POLYVALENTE DES QUATRE-VENTS
(*Suby of* Commission Scolaire du Pays-des-Bleuets)
828 Boul Saint-Joseph, Roberval, QC, G8H 2L5
(418) 275-2332
Emp Here 25   *Emp Total* 1,200
Sales 110,427,520
SIC 8211 Elementary and secondary schools
Mng Dir Serge Bergeron
Dir Fin Jacques Martel
Pr Remi Rousseau

D-U-N-S 20-711-9004 (BR)
COMMISSION SCOLAIRE DU PAYS-DES-BLEUETS
CENTRE DE FORMATION PROFESSIONNELLE DE F P ROBERVAL
181 Boul De La Jeunesse, Roberval, QC, G8H 2N9
(418) 275-5546
Emp Here 50
SIC 8211 Elementary and secondary schools

D-U-N-S 20-711-8907 (BR)
COMMISSION SCOLAIRE DU PAYS-DES-BLEUETS
EDUCATION DES ADULTES CENTRE L'ENVOL
654 Boul Saint-Joseph, Roberval, QC, G8H 2L2
(418) 275-5130
Emp Here 50
SIC 8211 Elementary and secondary schools

D-U-N-S 24-855-4094 (BR)
EQUIPEMENT QUADCO INC
MACHINERIE TANGUAY
(*Suby of* 6004016 Canada Inc)
625 Rte De L'Aeroport, Roberval, QC, G8H 2M9
(418) 251-3998
Emp Here 31
SIC 3531 Construction machinery

D-U-N-S 25-392-9681 (BR)
FERLAC INC
(*Suby of* 9072-4725 Quebec Inc)
255 Boul Marcotte, Roberval, QC, G8H 1Z3
(418) 275-2356
Emp Here 50
SIC 5251 Hardware stores

D-U-N-S 24-104-5827 (BR)
GOUVERNEMENT DE LA PROVINCE DE QUEBEC
CENTRE JEUNESSE DE ROBERVAL, LE
254 Boul Sauve, Roberval, QC, G8H 1A7
(418) 275-1634
Emp Here 60
SIC 8322 Individual and family services

D-U-N-S 25-153-3204   (BR)
MODE CHOC (ALMA) LTEE
MODE CHOC ROBERVAL
879 Boul Saint-Joseph, Roberval, QC, G8H 2L8
(418) 275-2231
Emp Here 30
SIC 5651 Family clothing stores

D-U-N-S 24-169-9698   (BR)
ROTISSERIES ST-HUBERT LTEE, LES
(*Suby of* Cara Holdings Limited)
21 Boul De L'Anse, Roberval, QC, G8H 1Z1
(418) 275-5994
Emp Here 40
SIC 5812 Eating places

D-U-N-S 25-299-0197   (BR)
SOCIETE DE PROTECTION DES FORETS CONTRE LE FEU (SOPFEU)
(*Suby of* Societe de Protection des Forets contre le feu (SOPFEU))
1230 Rte De L'Aeroport, Roberval, QC, G8H 2M9
(418) 275-6400
Emp Here 100
SIC 7389 Business services, nec

D-U-N-S 20-642-1799   (SL)
STAGEM DIVISION ENTREPRISE D'INSERTION INC
150 Rte De Sainte-Hedwidge, Roberval, QC, G8H 2M9
(418) 275-7241
Emp Here 52   *Sales* 4,961,328
SIC 2421 Sawmills and planing mills, general

Rosemere, QC J7A

D-U-N-S 20-295-7291   (BR)
9120-5583 QUEBEC INC
VIA CAPITALE RIVE NORD
236 Boul Labelle, Rosemere, QC, J7A 2H4
(450) 435-2200
Emp Here 65
SIC 6211 Security brokers and dealers

D-U-N-S 24-346-3168   (BR)
ACADEMIE STE-THERESE INC, L'
(*Suby of* Academie Ste-Therese Inc, L')
1 Ch Des Ecoliers, Rosemere, QC, J7A 4Y1
(450) 434-1130
Emp Here 90
SIC 8211 Elementary and secondary schools

D-U-N-S 24-056-5056   (BR)
BEAULIEU, CLAUDE SPORT INC
ATMOSPHERE ROSEMERE # 699
401 Boul Labelle Bureau A25, Rosemere, QC, J7A 3T2
(450) 435-3820
Emp Here 30
SIC 5941 Sporting goods and bicycle shops

D-U-N-S 25-647-7951   (BR)
CLSC-CHSLD THERESE DE BLAINVILLE
CENTRE D'HEBERGEMENT HUBERT MAISON NEUVE
(*Suby of* CLSC-CHSLD Therese de Blainville)
365 Ch De La Grande-Cote, Rosemere, QC, J7A 1K4
(450) 621-3760
Emp Here 200
SIC 8361 Residential care

D-U-N-S 25-311-4425   (BR)
CANADIAN IMPERIAL BANK OF COMMERCE
CIBC
299 Boul Labelle, Rosemere, QC, J7A 2H7
(450) 437-0550
Emp Here 20
SIC 6021 National commercial banks

D-U-N-S 20-102-3277   (BR)

CARA OPERATIONS LIMITED
HARVEY'S
(*Suby of* Cara Holdings Limited)
170 Boul Labelle, Rosemere, QC, J7A 2H1
(450) 437-2840
Emp Here 25
SIC 5812 Eating places

D-U-N-S 20-971-7644   (SL)
CLUB DE GOLF DE ROSEMERE
282 Boul Labelle, Rosemere, QC, J7A 2H6
(450) 437-7555
Emp Here 80   *Sales* 3,210,271
SIC 7997 Membership sports and recreation clubs

D-U-N-S 25-240-6566   (BR)
COMMISSION SCOLAIRE DE LA SEIGNEURIE-DES-MILLE-ILES
COMMISSION SCOLAIRE DE LA SEIGNEURIE-DES-MILLE-ILES
(*Suby of* Commission Scolaire de la Seigneurie-Des-Mille-Iles)
334 Rue De L'Academie, Rosemere, QC, J7A 3R9
(450) 621-2400
Emp Here 80
SIC 8211 Elementary and secondary schools

D-U-N-S 25-233-3620   (BR)
COMMISSION SCOLAIRE DE LA SEIGNEURIE-DES-MILLE-ILES
COMMISSION SCOLAIRE DE LA SEIGNEURIE-DES-MILLE-ILES
(*Suby of* Commission Scolaire de la Seigneurie-Des-Mille-Iles)
364 Rue De L'Academie, Rosemere, QC, J7A 1Z1
(450) 621-2003
Emp Here 70
SIC 8211 Elementary and secondary schools

D-U-N-S 25-984-2321   (SL)
GAMESTOP CORP
401 Boul Labelle, Rosemere, QC, J7A 3T2

Emp Here 250   *Sales* 31,902,000
SIC 5734 Computer and software stores
CEO Daniel Dematteo

D-U-N-S 25-301-2942   (BR)
HUDSON'S BAY COMPANY
BAIE, LA
401 Boul Labelle, Rosemere, QC, J7A 3T2
(450) 433-6991
Emp Here 100
SIC 5311 Department stores

D-U-N-S 20-284-0950   (BR)
J.M. CLEMENT LTEE
401 Boul Labelle, Rosemere, QC, J7A 3T2
(450) 437-7368
Emp Here 20
SIC 5641 Children's and infants' wear stores

D-U-N-S 24-348-5245   (BR)
MCDONALD'S RESTAURANTS OF CANADA LIMITED
MCDONALD'S
(*Suby of* McDonald's Corporation)
401 Boul Labelle, Rosemere, QC, J7A 3T2
(450) 979-6633
Emp Here 20
SIC 5812 Eating places

D-U-N-S 20-024-5137   (BR)
PROVIGO DISTRIBUTION INC
MAXI
339 Boul Labelle, Rosemere, QC, J7A 2H7
(450) 437-0471
Emp Here 150
SIC 5411 Grocery stores

D-U-N-S 20-536-7688   (BR)
SEARS CANADA INC
401 Boul Labelle, Rosemere, QC, J7A 3T2
(450) 433-1001
Emp Here 200

SIC 5311 Department stores

D-U-N-S 25-222-5933   (BR)
SIR WILFRID LAURIER SCHOOL BOARD
ROSEMERE HIGH SCHOOL
(*Suby of* Sir Wilfrid Laurier School Board)
530 Rue Northcote, Rosemere, QC, J7A 1Y2
(450) 621-5900
Emp Here 110
SIC 8211 Elementary and secondary schools

D-U-N-S 25-222-6097   (BR)
SIR WILFRID LAURIER SCHOOL BOARD
MCCAIG SCHOOL
(*Suby of* Sir Wilfrid Laurier School Board)
501 Rue Northcote, Rosemere, QC, J7A 1Y1
(450) 621-6111
Emp Here 70
SIC 8211 Elementary and secondary schools

D-U-N-S 25-904-7587   (HQ)
SIR WILFRID LAURIER SCHOOL BOARD
235 Montee Lesage Bureau 1, Rosemere, QC, J7A 4Y6
(450) 621-5600
Emp Here 75   *Emp Total* 1,500
Sales 138,059,520
SIC 8211 Elementary and secondary schools
Genl Mgr Donna Abel

D-U-N-S 24-840-1098   (SL)
THYME MATERNITE
401 Boul Labelle, Rosemere, QC, J7A 3T2
(450) 420-9054
Emp Here 49   *Sales* 2,991,389
SIC 5621 Women's clothing stores

D-U-N-S 24-018-9423   (BR)
WAL-MART CANADA CORP
401 Boul Labelle Bureau 3080, Rosemere, QC, J7A 3T2
(450) 435-2982
Emp Here 200
SIC 5311 Department stores

D-U-N-S 20-106-2895   (BR)
WINNERS MERCHANTS INTERNATIONAL L.P.
(*Suby of* The TJX Companies Inc)
20c Boul Bouthillier, Rosemere, QC, J7A 4B4
(450) 437-6615
Emp Here 35
SIC 5651 Family clothing stores

Rougemont, QC J0L
Rouville County

D-U-N-S 20-245-3635   (HQ)
A. LASSONDE INC
ALIMENTS MONT-ROUGE
(*Suby of* 3346625 Canada Inc)
170 5e Av, Rougemont, QC, J0L 1M0
(450) 469-4926
Emp Here 300   *Emp Total* 1,100
Sales 61,936,947
SIC 2033 Canned fruits and specialties
Pr Pr Jean Gattuso
Sec Caroline Lemoine
Pierre-Paul Lassonde
Dir Nathalie Lassonde
Jean-Pierre Le Blanc

D-U-N-S 25-240-5857   (BR)
COMMISSION SCOLAIRE DES HAUTES-RIVIERES
ECOLE SAINT-MICHEL
915 Rue Principale Rr 4, Rougemont, QC, J0L 1M0
(450) 469-3918
Emp Here 25
SIC 8211 Elementary and secondary schools

D-U-N-S 24-857-6795   (SL)
ENTREPRISES S.M.T.R. INC

500 112 Rte, Rougemont, QC, J0L 1M0
(450) 469-3153
Emp Here 25   *Sales* 12,721,442
SIC 7538 General automotive repair shops
Pr Pr Claude Robert
Gerard Bernard
Daniel St-Germain

D-U-N-S 24-960-0024   (SL)
GANOTEC MECANIQUE INC
(*Suby of* Groupe Ganotec Inc)
378 Rang De La Montagne Rr 5, Rougemont, QC, J0L 1M0
(819) 377-5533
Emp Here 50   *Sales* 7,263,840
SIC 8741 Management services
Pr Serge Larouche
Sec Michael F. Norton
Dir Bruce Grewcock
Dir Louis Chapdelaine

D-U-N-S 24-019-5297   (SL)
IMMEUBLES RB LTEE
500 Rte 112, Rougemont, QC, J0L 1M0
(450) 469-3153
Emp Here 250   *Sales* 23,712,228
SIC 4225 General warehousing and storage
Pr Claude Robert
VP Gerard Bernard

D-U-N-S 20-515-5018   (BR)
INDUSTRIES LASSONDE INC
LASSONDE, A.
(*Suby of* 3346625 Canada Inc)
705 Rue Principale, Rougemont, QC, J0L 1M0
(450) 469-4926
Emp Here 250
SIC 2033 Canned fruits and specialties

D-U-N-S 20-245-3593   (SL)
MATERIEL INDUSTRIEL LTEE, LE
CONSTANT AIR-FLO
325 La Grande-Caroline Rr 5, Rougemont, QC, J0L 1M0
(450) 469-4934
Emp Here 90   *Sales* 10,065,000
SIC 3444 Sheet Metalwork
Pr Pr Michel Sornin

D-U-N-S 20-245-3759   (HQ)
TRANSPORT ROBERT (1973) LTEE
ROBERT MEDIA
500 Rte 112, Rougemont, QC, J0L 1M0
(450) 469-3153
Emp Here 200   *Emp Total* 2,300
Sales 32,832,315
SIC 4213 Trucking, except local
Pr Pr Claude Robert
Michel Robert

D-U-N-S 25-992-5592   (SL)
VINS ARTERRA CANADA, DIVISION QUEBEC, INC
6 DEGREES DESIGN
(*Suby of* Arterra Wines Canada, Inc)
175 Ch De Marieville, Rougemont, QC, J0L 1M0
(514) 861-2404
Emp Here 126   *Sales* 3,648,035
SIC 2084 Wines, brandy, and brandy spirits

Rouyn-Noranda, QC J0Y
Temiscaninque County

D-U-N-S 24-864-0914   (BR)
AGNICO EAGLE MINES LIMITED
AGNICO EAGLE MINES, DIVISION LARONDE
10200 Rte De Preissac, Rouyn-Noranda, QC, J0Y 1C0
(819) 759-3700
Emp Here 650
SIC 1041 Gold ores

D-U-N-S 25-106-5728   (SL)

MINES AGNICO EAGLE LIMITEE
20 Rte 395 Cadillac, Rouyn-Noranda, QC, J0Y 1C0
(819) 759-3644
Emp Here 1,000
SIC 1241 Coal mining services

Rouyn-Noranda, QC J0Z
Temiscaninque County

D-U-N-S 24-792-4780   (SL)
CHSLD MAISON PIE XII
MAISON PIE XII
512 Av Richard, Rouyn-Noranda, QC, J0Z 2X0
(819) 762-0908
Emp Here 212   *Sales* 10,650,880
SIC 8361 Residential care
Genl Mgr Daniel Bergeron
Acctg Dir Rene Roberge

D-U-N-S 20-712-5746   (BR)
COMMISSION SCOLAIRE DE ROUYN-NORANDA
ECOLE GRANADA
9725 Boul Rideau, Rouyn-Noranda, QC, J0Z 2X0

Emp Here 40
SIC 8211 Elementary and secondary schools

D-U-N-S 20-276-7745   (BR)
GOLDCORP INC
ELEONORE PROJECT MINES
853 Boul Rideau, Rouyn-Noranda, QC, J0Z 2X0
(819) 764-6400
Emp Here 500
SIC 1041 Gold ores

D-U-N-S 24-600-9922   (BR)
PROVIGO DISTRIBUTION INC
PROVIGO EVAIN
23 Rue D'Evain, Rouyn-Noranda, QC, J0Z 1Y0
(819) 768-3018
Emp Here 35
SIC 5411 Grocery stores

D-U-N-S 25-863-6620   (BR)
TRANSPORT NORD-OUEST INC
TRANSPORT NORTH-WEST
(*Suby of* Transport Nord-Ouest Inc)
3357 Rue Saguenay, Rouyn-Noranda, QC, J0Z 2X0
(819) 797-5043
Emp Here 30
SIC 4213 Trucking, except local

Rouyn-Noranda, QC J9X
Temiscaninque County

D-U-N-S 24-758-7629   (HQ)
121352 CANADA INC
MANUFACTURE TECHNOSUB
(*Suby of* Groupe Technosub Inc)
1156 Av Lariviere, Rouyn-Noranda, QC, J9X 4K8
(819) 797-3300
Emp Here 75   *Emp Total* 1
Sales 23,712,228
SIC 5084 Industrial machinery and equipment
 Yvan Blais
Pr Eric Beaupre
 Sonia Leveque
Dir Gaetan Langlois
Dir Patrick Martel
Dir Benoit Desormeaux
Dir Leandre Gervais
Dir Bryan Coates

D-U-N-S 24-842-5068   (SL)

2732-2304 QUEBEC INC
AMI HONDA, L'
1225 Av Lariviere, Rouyn-Noranda, QC, J9X 6M6
(819) 762-6565
Emp Here 25   *Sales* 17,753,750
SIC 5511 New and used car dealers
Pr Pierre Cloutier
 Jean Dion

D-U-N-S 25-243-8288   (SL)
2968-5278 QUEBEC INC
HOTEL GOUVERNEUR
41 6e Rue, Rouyn-Noranda, QC, J9X 1Y8
(819) 762-2341
Emp Here 50   *Sales* 2,188,821
SIC 7011 Hotels and motels

D-U-N-S 24-112-5595   (SL)
9130-8452 QUEBEC INC
DISTRIBUTION MGF
275 Boul Industriel, Rouyn-Noranda, QC, J9X 6P2

Emp Here 64   *Sales* 7,165,680
SIC 7822 Motion picture and tape distribution
Pr Pr Ghislain Lefebvre
VP Marcel Gourde
Sec Frank Zavodnik

D-U-N-S 20-363-9450   (SL)
9213-9286 QUEBEC INC
ACCES TOYOTA
1355 Av Lariviere, Rouyn-Noranda, QC, J9X 6M6
(819) 762-5000
Emp Here 42   *Sales* 15,321,747
SIC 5511 New and used car dealers
Pr Pr Jean Dion
VP VP Dominique Perigny
 Joel Meilleur

D-U-N-S 20-552-6499   (SL)
AGENCES DE SECURITE MIRADO 2002 INC
AGENCE DE SECURITE MIRADO 2002, LES
121 8e Rue, Rouyn-Noranda, QC, J9X 2A5
(819) 797-5184
Emp Here 200   *Sales* 6,201,660
SIC 7381 Detective and armored car services
Pr Caroline Lemire

D-U-N-S 24-629-5260   (HQ)
AMNOR INDUSTRIES INC
(*Suby of* Amnor Industries Inc)
8 Rue Doyon, Rouyn-Noranda, QC, J9X 7B4
(819) 762-9044
Emp Here 25   *Emp Total* 61
Sales 3,720,996
SIC 7699 Repair services, nec

D-U-N-S 20-266-1393   (BR)
BIBLIOTHEQUE ET ARCHIVES NA-TIONALES DU QUEBEC
BANQ
27 Rue Du Terminus O, Rouyn-Noranda, QC, J9X 2P3
(819) 763-3484
Emp Here 25
SIC 8231 Libraries

D-U-N-S 25-866-6676   (BR)
CANADA POST CORPORATION
151 Av Du Lac, Rouyn-Noranda, QC, J9X 4N6
(819) 762-5555
Emp Here 50
SIC 4311 U.s. postal service

D-U-N-S 25-696-7654   (BR)
CENTRE JEUNESSE DE L'ABITIBI TEMIS-CAMINGUE
POINT DE SERVICE DE ROUYN-NORANDA
3 9e Rue, Rouyn-Noranda, QC, J9X 2A9
(819) 762-0904
Emp Here 20
SIC 8322 Individual and family services

D-U-N-S 24-489-6817   (HQ)

CENTRE DE READAPTATION LA MAISON
ORTHAIDE
(*Suby of* Centre de Readaptation La Maison)
7 9e Rue, Rouyn-Noranda, QC, J9X 2A9
(819) 762-6592
Emp Here 120   *Emp Total* 210
Sales 13,789,572
SIC 8011 Offices and clinics of medical doctors
Pr Jason Lecours
VP VP Gisele Chretien
Sec Serge Cote

D-U-N-S 24-365-8726   (BR)
CHATEAU POULET DU QUEBEC LTEE
CHATEAU POULET DU QUEBEC LTEE
(*Suby of* Master Chef Limited)
44 Av Quebec, Rouyn-Noranda, QC, J9X 6P9
(819) 764-6741
Emp Here 20
SIC 5812 Eating places

D-U-N-S 25-259-9956   (BR)
CLAIR FOYER INC
26 Rue Monseigneur-Rheaume E Bureau 300, Rouyn-Noranda, QC, J9X 3J5
(819) 762-0964
Emp Here 25
SIC 8059 Nursing and personal care, nec

D-U-N-S 25-383-9856   (SL)
CLUB DE GOLF MUNICIPAL DALLAIRE INC
720 Av Dallaire, Rouyn-Noranda, QC, J9X 4V9
(819) 797-9444
Emp Here 50   *Sales* 2,188,821
SIC 7992 Public golf courses

D-U-N-S 25-233-5815   (BR)
COMMISSION SCOLAIRE DE ROUYN-NORANDA
COMMISSION SCOLAIRE DE ROUYN-NORANDA
275 Av Forbes, Rouyn-Noranda, QC, J9X 5C9
(819) 762-8161
Emp Here 200
SIC 8211 Elementary and secondary schools

D-U-N-S 20-712-5738   (BR)
COMMISSION SCOLAIRE DE ROUYN-NORANDA
200 19e Rue, Rouyn-Noranda, QC, J9X 2N3
(819) 762-8161
Emp Here 50
SIC 8211 Elementary and secondary schools

D-U-N-S 24-481-9566   (BR)
COMMISSION SCOLAIRE DE ROUYN-NORANDA
FORMATION PROFESSIONNELLE
15 10th Rue, Rouyn-Noranda, QC, J9X 5C9
(819) 762-8161
Emp Here 60
SIC 8621 Professional organizations

D-U-N-S 20-712-5878   (BR)
COMMISSION SCOLAIRE DE ROUYN-NORANDA
ECOLE NOTRE DAME DE L'ASSOMPTION
30 Av De L'Eglise, Rouyn-Noranda, QC, J9X 5C9
(819) 762-8161
Emp Here 20
SIC 8211 Elementary and secondary schools

D-U-N-S 20-712-5621   (BR)
COMMISSION SCOLAIRE WESTERN QUE-BEC
ECOLE NORANDA
(*Suby of* Commission Scolaire Western Quebec)
10 Av Quebec, Rouyn-Noranda, QC, J9X 1G2
(819) 762-2706
Emp Here 50
SIC 8211 Elementary and secondary schools

D-U-N-S 24-671-2421   (BR)
DOLLARAMA S.E.C.

DOLLARAMA
4 15e Rue Bureau 4, Rouyn-Noranda, QC, J9X 2J8
(819) 762-6473
Emp Here 20
SIC 5331 Variety stores

D-U-N-S 20-972-6249   (BR)
GOUVERNEMENT DE LA PROVINCE DE QUEBEC
MINISTERE DES TRANSPORT DU QUEBEC
80 Av Quebec, Rouyn-Noranda, QC, J9X 6R1
(819) 763-3237
Emp Here 100
SIC 1611 Highway and street construction

D-U-N-S 24-125-2605   (BR)
GOUVERNEMENT DE LA PROVINCE DE QUEBEC
MINISTERE DU DEVELOPPEMENT DURABLE ENVIRONNEMENT ET PARC
180 Boul Rideau Unite 1.04, Rouyn-Noranda, QC, J9X 1N9
(819) 763-3333
Emp Here 60
SIC 8641 Civic and social associations

D-U-N-S 25-746-0956   (BR)
GOUVERNEUR INC
HOTEL GOUVERNEUR LE NORANDA
41 6e Rue, Rouyn-Noranda, QC, J9X 1Y8
(819) 762-2341
Emp Here 50
SIC 7011 Hotels and motels

D-U-N-S 20-356-1147   (SL)
GROUPE PROMEC INC
1300 Rue Saguenay, Rouyn-Noranda, QC, J9X 7C3
(819) 797-7500
Emp Here 50   *Sales* 4,377,642
SIC 1731 Electrical work

D-U-N-S 20-172-2308   (BR)
GROUPE PROMUTUEL FEDERATION DE SOCIETE MUTUELLES D'ASSURANCES GENERALES
GROUPE PROMUTUEL FEDERATION DE SOCIETE MUTUELLES D'ASSURANCES GENERALES
100 Av Du Lac, Rouyn-Noranda, QC, J9X 4N4
(819) 762-8105
Emp Here 27
SIC 6411 Insurance agents, brokers, and service

D-U-N-S 20-314-3300   (BR)
GROUPE STAVIBEL INC
1375 Av Lariviere, Rouyn-Noranda, QC, J9X 6M6
(819) 764-5181
Emp Here 230
SIC 8711 Engineering services

D-U-N-S 20-284-4416   (BR)
GROUPE STAVIBEL INC
150 Rue Gamble O, Rouyn-Noranda, QC, J9X 2R7
(819) 764-5181
Emp Here 150
SIC 8711 Engineering services

D-U-N-S 20-314-3292   (BR)
GROUPE STAVIBEL INC
25 Rue Gamble E, Rouyn-Noranda, QC, J9X 3B6
(819) 764-5181
Emp Here 50
SIC 8711 Engineering services

D-U-N-S 20-327-7426   (SL)
HUSKIES DE ROUYN-NORANDA INC, LES
218 Av Murdoch, Rouyn-Noranda, QC, J9X 1E6
(819) 797-6222
Emp Here 80   *Sales* 3,210,271
SIC 7997 Membership sports and recreation clubs

▲ Public Company   ■ Public Company Family Member   **HQ** Headquarters   **BR** Branch   **SL** Single Location

D-U-N-S 24-342-8146   (BR)
HYDRO-QUEBEC
1399 Av Lariviere, Rouyn-Noranda, QC, J9X 6M6
(819) 764-5124
Emp Here 66
SIC 4911 Electric services

D-U-N-S 24-019-5495   (HQ)
J.Y. MOREAU ELECTRIQUE INC
(*Suby of* J.Y. Moreau Electrique Inc)
160 Boul Industriel, Rouyn-Noranda, QC, J9X 6T3
(819) 797-0088
Emp Here 300   *Emp Total* 300
Sales 26,265,852
SIC 1731 Electrical work
Pr Jean-Francois Moreau
VP Morton Jay White
VP Jean-Yves Moreau
Chantal Cadieux
Dir John A. Hatherly
Dir Michelle Cormier
Dir Neelan Krishna Mayenkar

D-U-N-S 24-570-5579   (SL)
MDBB EST INC
BRADLEY
(*Suby of* Major Drilling Group International Inc)
270 Boul Industriel, Rouyn-Noranda, QC, J9X 6T3
(819) 797-0755
Emp Here 60   *Sales* 6,347,581
SIC 1081 Metal mining services
Wallace Bradley

D-U-N-S 20-172-2191   (SL)
PETROLES BRADLEY INC
225 Rue Saguenay, Rouyn-Noranda, QC, J9X 5N4

Emp Here 20   *Sales* 5,653,974
SIC 5983 Fuel oil dealers
Pr Philip Bradley

D-U-N-S 24-942-8970   (SL)
ROTISSERIE ROUYN-NORANDA INC
ROTISSERIE ST-HUBERT
60 Av Quebec, Rouyn-Noranda, QC, J9X 6P9
(819) 797-2151
Emp Here 75   *Sales* 2,261,782
SIC 5812 Eating places

D-U-N-S 24-760-0237   (BR)
ROUYN-NORANDA, VILLE DE
ARENA LAPERRIERE
220 Av Dallaire, Rouyn-Noranda, QC, J9X 5C3
(819) 797-7146
Emp Here 20
SIC 7999 Amusement and recreation, nec

D-U-N-S 25-683-2403   (HQ)
SERVICES D'ENTRETIEN MINIERS INDUSTRIELS R.N. 2000 INC
(*Suby of* Services d'Entretien Miniers Industriels R.N. 2000 Inc)
155 Boul Industriel, Rouyn-Noranda, QC, J9X 6P2
(819) 797-4387
Emp Here 118   *Emp Total* 168
SIC 1241 Coal mining services

D-U-N-S 20-113-8240   (BR)
SINTRA INC
LAMOTHE, DIV DE
240 Av Marcel-Baril, Rouyn-Noranda, QC, J9X 7C1
(819) 762-6505
Emp Here 95
SIC 8711 Engineering services

D-U-N-S 24-885-0039   (BR)
SOBEYS CAPITAL INCORPORATED
SOBEYS
333 Av Montemurro, Rouyn-Noranda, QC, J9X 7C6

(819) 797-1900
Emp Here 200
SIC 5141 Groceries, general line

D-U-N-S 20-245-4963   (HQ)
THIBAULT CHEVROLET CADILLAC BUICK GMC DE ROUYN-NORANDA LTEE
CENTRE DU CAMION THIBAULT
(*Suby of* 2327-5464 Quebec Inc)
375 Boul Rideau, Rouyn-Noranda, QC, J9X 5Y7
(819) 762-1751
Emp Here 28   *Emp Total* 66
Sales 32,832,315
SIC 5511 New and used car dealers
Pr Pr Alain Thibault
Jacinthe Corriveau
Marc-Andre Thibault

D-U-N-S 25-801-0693   (BR)
TRANSCONTINENTAL INC
JOURNAL LA FRONTIERE
25 Rue Gamble E, Rouyn-Noranda, QC, J9X 3B6
(819) 762-4361
Emp Here 33
SIC 2711 Newspapers

D-U-N-S 25-376-7842   (BR)
UNIPRIX INC
UNIPRIX CLAUDE JANNETEAU & ASSOCIES
100 Rue Du Terminus O, Rouyn-Noranda, QC, J9X 6H7
(819) 797-1422
Emp Here 20
SIC 5912 Drug stores and proprietary stores

D-U-N-S 24-669-2107   (BR)
UNIVERSITE DU QUEBEC
445 Boul De L'Universite, Rouyn-Noranda, QC, J9X 5E4
(819) 762-0971
Emp Here 500
SIC 8221 Colleges and universities

D-U-N-S 24-851-3512   (BR)
WSP CANADA INC
GENIVAR
152 Av Murdoch, Rouyn-Noranda, QC, J9X 1E2
(819) 797-3222
Emp Here 40
SIC 8748 Business consulting, nec

D-U-N-S 25-498-3067   (BR)
WAL-MART CANADA CORP
WALMART
275 Boul Rideau Bureau 3136, Rouyn-Noranda, QC, J9X 5Y6
(819) 762-0619
Emp Here 200
SIC 5311 Department stores

Rouyn-Noranda, QC J9Y
Temiscaninque County

D-U-N-S 25-697-9881   (BR)
AUTOBUS MAHEUX LTEE, LES
3280 Rue Saguenay, Rouyn-Noranda, QC, J9Y 0E2
(819) 797-3200
Emp Here 50
SIC 4151 School buses

D-U-N-S 24-562-0984   (SL)
MINES D'ARGENT ECU INC, LES
1116 Av Granada, Rouyn-Noranda, QC, J9Y 1G9

Emp Here 412   *Sales* 52,613,760
SIC 1081 Metal mining services
Pr Pr Stephen Altmann

Roxboro, QC H8Y
Hochelaga County

D-U-N-S 25-233-0279   (BR)
COMMUNAUTE HELLENIQUE DE MONTREAL
ECOLE PRIMAIRE SOCRATES III
11 11e Rue, Roxboro, QC, H8Y 1K6
(514) 685-1833
Emp Here 30
SIC 8211 Elementary and secondary schools

D-U-N-S 24-570-1854   (BR)
GROUPE ADONIS INC
MARCHE ADONIS
4601 Boul Des Sources, Roxboro, QC, H8Y 3C5
(514) 685-5050
Emp Here 85
SIC 5411 Grocery stores

Roxton Falls, QC J0H
Shefford County

D-U-N-S 25-685-4928   (BR)
CAMSO INC
ROSKI
(*Suby of* Camso Inc)
130 Rue De L'Eglise, Roxton Falls, QC, J0H 1E0
(450) 548-5821
Emp Here 425
SIC 3299 NonMetallic mineral products,

Roxton Pond, QC J0E
Shefford County

D-U-N-S 25-240-6541   (BR)
COMMISSION SCOLAIRE DU VAL-DES-CERFS
ECOLE ROXTON POND
676 Rue Du Lac, Roxton Pond, QC, J0E 1Z0
(450) 372-2723
Emp Here 36
SIC 8211 Elementary and secondary schools

Sabrevois, QC J0J
Iberville County

D-U-N-S 25-240-4900   (BR)
COMMISSION SCOLAIRE DES HAUTES-RIVIERES
COMMISSION SCOLAIRE DES HAUTES-RIVIERES
1202 Rang Du Bord-De-L'Eau, Sabrevois, QC, J0J 2G0
(450) 347-1097
Emp Here 20
SIC 8211 Elementary and secondary schools

Sacre-Coeur-Saguenay, QC G0T
Saguenay County

D-U-N-S 25-240-7242   (BR)
COMMISSION SCOLAIRE DE L'ESTUAIRE
ECOLE NOTRE DAME DU SACRE COEUR
(*Suby of* Commission Scolaire de l'Estuaire)
80 Rue De L'Eglise, Sacre-Coeur-Saguenay, QC, G0T 1Y0
(418) 236-4442
Emp Here 20
SIC 8211 Elementary and secondary schools

Saint-Adelphe-De-Champlain, QC G0X

D-U-N-S 25-233-0964   (BR)
COMMISSION SCOLAIRE DE L'ENERGIE
ECOLE PRIMADEL
511 Rue Principale, Saint-Adelphe-De-Champlain, QC, G0X 2G0
(418) 365-4755
Emp Here 20
SIC 8351 Child day care services

Saint-Adolphe-D'Howard, QC J0T

D-U-N-S 24-885-2501   (SL)
9026-6511 QUEBEC INC
AVALANCHE STATION DE SKI
1657 Ch De L'Avalanche, Saint-Adolphe-D'Howard, QC, J0T 2B0
(819) 327-3232
Emp Here 50   *Sales* 2,188,821
SIC 7011 Hotels and motels

Saint-Agapit, QC G0S
Lotbiniere County

D-U-N-S 20-949-1844   (SL)
CHABOT & DESMARAIS INC
1015 Rue Bergeron Local A, Saint-Agapit, QC, G0S 1Z0
(418) 888-3290
Emp Here 35   *Sales* 3,580,850
SIC 4212 Local trucking, without storage

D-U-N-S 25-233-1517   (BR)
COMMISSION SCOLAIRE DES NAVIGATEURS
ECOLE SECONDAIRE BEAURIVAGE
1134 Rue Du Centenaire, Saint-Agapit, QC, G0S 1Z0
(418) 888-3961
Emp Here 93
SIC 8211 Elementary and secondary schools

D-U-N-S 20-574-8309   (BR)
COMMISSION SCOLAIRE DES NAVIGATEURS
ECOLE DE L' EPERVIERE
1149 Av Olivier, Saint-Agapit, QC, G0S 1Z0
(418) 888-4211
Emp Here 30
SIC 8211 Elementary and secondary schools

D-U-N-S 24-907-5896   (HQ)
PRODUITS DE BOIS ST-AGAPIT INC, LES
(*Suby of* Produits de Bois St-Agapit Inc, Les)
1269 Rue Principale, Saint-Agapit, QC, G0S 1Z0
(418) 888-4142
Emp Here 35   *Emp Total* 50
Sales 2,918,428
SIC 2434 Wood kitchen cabinets

D-U-N-S 20-716-3424   (BR)
SOCIETE COOPERATIVE AGRICOLE LA SEIGNEURIE
COOP AGRICOLE LA SEIGNEURIE
1107 Av Daigle, Saint-Agapit, QC, G0S 1Z0
(418) 888-3938
Emp Here 20
SIC 5251 Hardware stores

Saint-Alexandre-D'Iberville, QC J0J

D-U-N-S 25-240-4868   (BR)
COMMISSION SCOLAIRE DES HAUTES-RIVIERES
ECOLE ST-ALEXANDRE

501 Rue Saint-Denis, Saint-Alexandre-D'Iberville, QC, J0J 1S0
(450) 347-1376
Emp Here 35
SIC 8211 Elementary and secondary schools

Saint-Alexis-Des-Monts, QC J0K

D-U-N-S 20-234-4482   (SL)
AUBERGE DU LAC SACACOMIE INC
HOTEL SACACOMIE
4000 Ch Yvon-Plante, Saint-Alexis-Des-Monts, QC, J0K 1V0
(819) 265-4444
Emp Here 100   *Sales* 4,377,642
SIC 7011 Hotels and motels

D-U-N-S 20-803-0523   (BR)
COMMISSION SCOLAIRE DE L'ENERGIE
ECOLE DES BOISOS
21 Rue Des Colleges, Saint-Alexis-Des-Monts, QC, J0K 1V0
(819) 265-2173
Emp Here 31
SIC 8211 Elementary and secondary schools

D-U-N-S 20-281-3924   (BR)
SOCIETE DES ETABLISSEMENTS DE PLEIN AIR DU QUEBEC
RESERVE FAUNIQUE MASTIGOUCHE
830 Rue Sainte-Anne, Saint-Alexis-Des-Monts, QC, J0K 1V0
(819) 265-2091
Emp Here 50
SIC 7032 Sporting and recreational camps

Saint-Alphonse-De-Granby, QC J0E

D-U-N-S 24-325-8972   (BR)
CONTITECH CANADA, INC
127 Rang Parent, Saint-Alphonse-De-Granby, QC, J0E 2A0
(450) 375-5050
Emp Here 220
SIC 3069 Fabricated rubber products, nec

D-U-N-S 24-848-6362   (BR)
SINTRA INC
101 Rue Sintre, Saint-Alphonse-De-Granby, QC, J0E 2A0
(450) 375-4471
Emp Here 100
SIC 1611 Highway and street construction

Saint-Alphonse-Rodriguez, QC J0K
Joliette County

D-U-N-S 25-968-9586   (BR)
SOCIETE POUR LES ENFANTS HANDICAPES DU QUEBEC
CAMP PAPILLON
(*Suby of* Societe pour les Enfants Handicapes du Quebec)
210 Rue Papillon, Saint-Alphonse-Rodriguez, QC, J0K 1W0
(450) 883-5642
Emp Here 150
SIC 7032 Sporting and recreational camps

Saint-Amable, QC J0L

D-U-N-S 20-033-5698   (BR)
COMMISSION SCOLAIRE DES PATRIOTES
ECOLE DE L'ENVOLEE
440 Rue De L'Eglise S, Saint-Amable, QC, J0L

1N0
(450) 645-2348
Emp Here 35
SIC 8211 Elementary and secondary schools

Saint-Ambroise, QC G7P

D-U-N-S 20-711-8857   (BR)
COMMISSION SCOLAIRE DE LA JONQUIERE
ECOLES PRIMAIRES COLLEGE ST AMBROISE
(*Suby of* Commission Scolaire de la Jonquiere)
95 Rue Blackburn, Saint-Ambroise, QC, G7P 2K4
(418) 672-4726
Emp Here 50
SIC 8211 Elementary and secondary schools

D-U-N-S 20-644-5137   (BR)
COMMISSION SCOLAIRE DE LA JONQUIERE
ECOLE SECONDAIRE BON PASTEUR
(*Suby of* Commission Scolaire de la Jonquiere)
44 Rue Du Couvent, Saint-Ambroise, QC, G7P 2J2
(418) 672-4726
Emp Here 20
SIC 8211 Elementary and secondary schools

Saint-Ambroise-De-Kildare, QC J0K
Joliette County

D-U-N-S 25-233-2739   (BR)
COMMISSION SCOLAIRE DES SAMARES
ECOLE NOTRE DAME DE LA PAIX
961 Rue Des Commissaires, Saint-Ambroise-De-Kildare, QC, J0K 1C0
(450) 758-3726
Emp Here 30
SIC 8211 Elementary and secondary schools

Saint-Anaclet, QC G0K

D-U-N-S 25-232-1526   (BR)
COMMISSION SCOLAIRE DES PHARES
ECOLE DES SOURCES
(*Suby of* Commission Scolaire des Phares)
20 Rue Banville Bureau 400, Saint-Anaclet, QC, G0K 1H0
(418) 724-3560
Emp Here 25
SIC 8211 Elementary and secondary schools

Saint-Andre-Avellin, QC J0V
Papineau County

D-U-N-S 25-183-4503   (BR)
CAISSE DESJARDINS DE LA PETITE-NATION
CENTRE DE SERVICE CHENEVILLE
79 Rue Principale, Saint-Andre-Avellin, QC, J0V 1W0
(819) 983-7313
Emp Here 40
SIC 6062 State credit unions

D-U-N-S 24-363-8355   (BR)
CENTRE DE SANTE ET SERVICES SOCIAUX DE PAPINEAU
CENTRE DE SANTE ET SERVICES SOCIAUX DE PAPINEAU
14 Rue Saint-Andre, Saint-Andre-Avellin, QC,

J0V 1W0
(819) 983-7341
Emp Here 240
SIC 8361 Residential care

D-U-N-S 20-171-8934   (BR)
COMMISSION SCOLAIRE AU COEUR DES VALLEES
ECOLE PROVIDENCE
7 Villeneuve, Saint-Andre-Avellin, QC, J0V 1W0
(819) 427-1013
Emp Here 35
SIC 8211 Elementary and secondary schools

Saint-Anselme, QC G0R
Dorchester County

D-U-N-S 20-296-5229   (BR)
COMMISSION SCOLAIRE DE LA COTE-DU-SUD, LA
ECOLE SECONDAIRE DE SAINT ANSELME
825 Rte Begin, Saint-Anselme, QC, G0R 2N0
(418) 885-4431
Emp Here 135
SIC 8211 Elementary and secondary schools

D-U-N-S 20-030-4132   (BR)
COMMISSION SCOLAIRE DE LA COTE-DU-SUD, LA
ECOLE PROVENCHER
45 Rue Provencher, Saint-Anselme, QC, G0R 2N0
(418) 885-4276
Emp Here 30
SIC 8211 Elementary and secondary schools

D-U-N-S 24-345-5586   (BR)
EXCELDOR COOPERATIVE
PRODUITS EXCELDOR, LES
1000 Rte Begin, Saint-Anselme, QC, G0R 2N0
(418) 885-4451
Emp Here 200
SIC 2015 Poultry slaughtering and processing

D-U-N-S 25-716-6785   (SL)
GROUPE SINOX INC
SINOX CONCEPT
(*Suby of* Gestion Groupe Sinox Inc)
16 Rue Turgeon, Saint-Anselme, QC, G0R 2N0
(418) 885-8276
Emp Here 75   *Sales* 5,318,747
SIC 3556 Food products machinery
Pr Gaston Lacasse
Sec Sonia Bilodeau
Dir Remi Gagne
Dir Steve Lavoie

D-U-N-S 25-489-0494   (SL)
LE ST-ANSELME INC
RESTAURANT NORMANDIN
679 Rte Begin, Saint-Anselme, QC, G0R 2N0
(418) 885-9601
Emp Here 26   *Sales* 802,568
SIC 5812 Eating places

D-U-N-S 24-591-4858   (BR)
MAPLE LEAF FOODS INC
254 Rue Principale, Saint-Anselme, QC, G0R 2N0
(418) 885-4474
Emp Here 120
SIC 5411 Grocery stores

D-U-N-S 25-471-3407   (BR)
UNICOOP, COOPERATIVE AGRICOLE
NEW HOLLAND
954 Rte Begin, Saint-Anselme, QC, G0R 2N0
(418) 885-9637
Emp Here 20
SIC 5083 Farm and garden machinery

D-U-N-S 20-719-5541   (BR)
UNICOOP, COOPERATIVE AGRICOLE

UNICOOP MACHINERIE ST-ANSELME
954 Rte Begin, Saint-Anselme, QC, G0R 2N0
(418) 885-9637
Emp Here 20
SIC 5083 Farm and garden machinery

Saint-Antoine-Abbe, QC J0S
Huntingdon County

D-U-N-S 25-240-8786   (BR)
COMMISSION SCOLAIRE DE LA VALLEE-DES-TISSERANDS, LA
ECOLE CENTRALE ST-ANTOINE-ABBE
4110 Rue De L'Eglise, Saint-Antoine-Abbe, QC, J0S 1N0
(450) 377-6062
Emp Here 40
SIC 8211 Elementary and secondary schools

Saint-Antonin, QC G0L
Riviere-Du-Loup County

D-U-N-S 25-233-0428   (BR)
COMMISSION SCOLAIRE DE KAMOURASKA RIVIERE-DU-LOUP
ECOLE LANOUETTE
18 Rue Du Couvent Unite 370, Saint-Antonin, QC, G0L 2J0
(418) 867-1616
Emp Here 37
SIC 8211 Elementary and secondary schools

D-U-N-S 25-823-0002   (BR)
IRVING OIL LIMITED
COUCHE TARD 507
960 185 Rte, Saint-Antonin, QC, G0L 2J0
(418) 862-8108
Emp Here 20
SIC 5541 Gasoline service stations

Saint-Apollinaire, QC G0S

D-U-N-S 25-232-1377   (BR)
COMMISSION SCOLAIRE DES NAVIGATEURS
ECOLE DES QUATRE-VENTS
35 Rue Roger, Saint-Apollinaire, QC, G0S 2E0
(418) 888-0507
Emp Here 40
SIC 8211 Elementary and secondary schools

D-U-N-S 24-681-8053   (SL)
GESTION CEBA INC
MC DONALD
470 Rte 273, Saint-Apollinaire, QC, G0S 2E0
(418) 881-4444
Emp Here 60   *Sales* 3,551,629
SIC 5812 Eating places

D-U-N-S 24-345-5867   (BR)
GOUVERNEMENT DE LA PROVINCE DE QUEBEC
CENTRE D'HEBERGEMENT DE SAINT-APOLLINAIRE
12 Rue Industrielle, Saint-Apollinaire, QC, G0S 2E0
(418) 881-3982
Emp Here 20
SIC 8361 Residential care

D-U-N-S 20-016-5715   (BR)
JELD-WEN OF CANADA, LTD.
JELD WEN DONAT FLAMAND, DIV OF
90 Rue Industrielle Bureau 200, Saint-Apollinaire, QC, G0S 2E0
(418) 881-3974
Emp Here 300
SIC 2431 Millwork

D-U-N-S 20-247-1983   (SL)
LAFLAMME PORTES ET FENETRES CORP
A.B.P. & DEESIN
(*Suby of* Groupe Atis Inc)
39 Rue Industrielle, Saint-Apollinaire, QC,
G0S 2E0
(418) 881-3950
Emp Here 150   *Sales* 24,514,795
SIC 2431 Millwork
Pr Pr Robert Doyon
Sec Andre Parent
Dir Mathieu Lalonde
Genl Mgr Gabriel Belanger

Saint-Armand, QC J0J

D-U-N-S 25-999-7542   (BR)
OMYA CANADA INC
OMYA ST-ARMAND
1500 Ch Des Carrieres, Saint-Armand, QC,
J0J 1T0
(450) 248-2931
Emp Here 20
SIC 1499 Miscellaneous nonMetallic minerals,
except fuels

D-U-N-S 24-934-5281   (SL)
PRODUITS FORESTIERS ST-ARMAND INC
PFS
1435 Ch De Saint-Armand, Saint-Armand,
QC, J0J 1T0
(450) 248-4334
Emp Here 65   *Sales* 7,429,418
SIC 2421 Sawmills and planing mills, general
Pr Pr Henry Alder
   Jean David Alder

Saint-Arsene, QC G0L

D-U-N-S 20-191-4975   (HQ)
TRANSPORT MORNEAU INC
40 Rue Principale, Saint-Arsene, QC, G0L
2K0
(418) 862-1314
Emp Here 125   *Emp Total* 700
Sales 54,659,766
SIC 4213 Trucking, except local
Pr Pr Andre Morneau
   Micheline Morneau

Saint-Augustin-De-Desmaures, QC G3A
Quebec County

D-U-N-S 20-051-2411   (SL)
9099-7768 QUEBEC INC
E.B.M LASER
109 Rue Des Grands-Lacs, Saint-Augustin-
De-Desmaures, QC, G3A 1V9
(418) 878-3616
Emp Here 50   *Sales* 5,253,170
SIC 3444 Sheet Metalwork
Pr Pr Gaetan St-Jean
VP VP Rodrigue Major
Sec Michel N. Dugal
Dir Daniel Potvin

D-U-N-S 20-013-1345   (SL)
A. BEAUMONT TRANSPORT INC
(*Suby of* Groupe A. Beaumont Inc)
280 Rte De Fossambault, Saint-Augustin-
Desmaures QC, G3A 2P9
(418) 878-4388
Emp Here 120   *Sales* 21,201,280
SIC 4213 Trucking, except local
Pr Andre Beaumont
Sec Linda Laperriere
   Simon Beaumont

D-U-N-S 25-335-8386   (SL)
AMEC USINAGE INC
110 Rue Des Grands-Lacs, Saint-Augustin-
De-Desmaures, QC, G3A 2K1
(418) 878-4133
Emp Here 55   *Sales* 4,012,839
SIC 3599 Industrial machinery, nec

D-U-N-S 25-146-7150   (BR)
**ATI TELECOM INTERNATIONAL, COM-
PANY**
ALTA TELECOM
278 138 Rte Bureau 216, Saint-Augustin-De-
Desmaures, QC, G3A 2C5
(418) 878-7008
Emp Here 30
SIC 4899 Communication services, nec

D-U-N-S 24-909-5829   (BR)
AIR PRODUCTS CANADA LTD
AIR PRODUCTS
(*Suby of* Air Products and Chemicals, Inc.)
185 Rue Des Grands-Lacs, Saint-Augustin-
De-Desmaures, QC, G3A 2K8
(418) 878-1400
Emp Here 26
SIC 2813 Industrial gases

D-U-N-S 24-214-8281   (SL)
ALIMENTATION OLIVIER,GUY INC
3525 Rue De L'Hetriere, Saint-Augustin-De-
Desmaures, QC, G3A 0C1
(418) 872-4444
Emp Here 49   *Sales* 6,055,738
SIC 5411 Grocery stores
Pr Guy Olivier

D-U-N-S 24-380-5905   (BR)
ARMTEC LP
ARMTEC
85 Rue De Rotterdam, Saint-Augustin-De-
Desmaures, QC, G3A 1T1
(418) 878-3630
Emp Here 30
SIC 3312 Blast furnaces and steel mills

D-U-N-S 25-395-6999   (SL)
**ATELIER MULTI-METAL ARCHITECTURAL
INC**
121 Rue De Naples, Saint-Augustin-De-
Desmaures, QC, G3A 2W6
(418) 878-5600
Emp Here 40   *Sales* 5,478,300
SIC 3553 Woodworking machinery
Pr Pr Francois Tardif

D-U-N-S 20-581-4320   (HQ)
BISCUITS LECLERC LTEE
ALIMENTS F. LECLERC
91 Rue De Rotterdam, Saint-Augustin-De-
Desmaures, QC, G3A 1T1
(418) 878-2601
Emp Here 50   *Emp Total* 1
Sales 84,719,348
SIC 2052 Cookies and crackers
   Denis Leclerc

D-U-N-S 20-721-7100   (HQ)
BREMO INC
JOINTEMENT INTER
214 138 Rte, Saint-Augustin-De-Desmaures,
QC, G3A 2X9
(418) 878-4070
Emp Here 80   *Emp Total* 140
Sales 29,913,887
SIC 3052 Rubber and plastics hose and belt-
ings
   Andre Morin
   Marc-Andre Allard
Dir Pierre Sylvain

D-U-N-S 25-265-3683   (SL)
CAN AQUA INTERNATIONAL
3126 Rue Delisle, Saint-Augustin-De-
Desmaures, QC, G3A 2W4
(418) 872-8080
Emp Here 47   *Sales* 10,221,762
SIC 5074 Plumbing and heating equipment

and supplies (hydronics)

D-U-N-S 20-712-0440   (BR)
**COMMISSION SCOLAIRE DES DECOU-
VREURS**
ECOLE PIONNIERS, L GAUDREAULT
(*Suby of* Commission Scolaire des Decou-
vreurs)
130 Rue Jean-Juneau, Saint-Augustin-De-
Desmaures, QC, G3A 2P2
(418) 878-4551
Emp Here 50
SIC 8211 Elementary and secondary schools

D-U-N-S 20-712-0390   (BR)
**COMMISSION SCOLAIRE DES DECOU-
VREURS**
*ECOLE DES PIONNIERS - PAVILLON DE LA
SALLE*
(*Suby of* Commission Scolaire des Decou-
vreurs)
99 Rue Du College, Saint-Augustin-De-
Desmaures, QC, G3A 1H1
(418) 878-2155
Emp Here 50
SIC 8211 Elementary and secondary schools

D-U-N-S 25-233-4610   (BR)
**COMMISSION SCOLAIRE DES DECOU-
VREURS**
ECOLE LES BOCAGES
(*Suby of* Commission Scolaire des Decou-
vreurs)
4832 Rue Des Landes, Saint-Augustin-De-
Desmaures, QC, G3A 2C2
(418) 877-8003
Emp Here 45
SIC 8211 Elementary and secondary schools

D-U-N-S 20-575-2707   (BR)
**COMMISSION SCOLAIRE DES DECOU-
VREURS**
*ECOLE DES PIONIERS PAVILLON MAR-
GUERITE BOURGEOIS*
(*Suby of* Commission Scolaire des Decou-
vreurs)
315 138 Rte, Saint-Augustin-De-Desmaures,
QC, G3A 1G7
(418) 878-2950
Emp Here 40
SIC 8211 Elementary and secondary schools

D-U-N-S 25-246-3179   (SL)
ENTREPOTS E.F.C. INC, LES
COOL
50 Rue Des Grands-Lacs, Saint-Augustin-De-
Desmaures, QC, G3A 2E6
(418) 878-5660
Emp Here 35   *Sales* 6,931,267
SIC 1541 Industrial buildings and warehouses
   Mario Guerin

D-U-N-S 25-501-9176   (HQ)
ENTREPRISES MICROTEC INC, LES
ALARMCAP
4780 Rue Saint-Felix, Saint-Augustin-De-
Desmaures, QC, G3A 2J9
(418) 864-7924
Emp Here 98   *Emp Total* 54,023
Sales 30,132,769
SIC 5063 Electrical apparatus and equipment
Pr Romani Piero
VP VP Craig Argyle Douglas
VP VP Michael A. Bartone
Sec Bruce H. Beat
Dir Kara J. Dean
Dir Joe Dilio

D-U-N-S 24-907-8650   (BR)
EQUIPEMENTS SIGMA INC
(*Suby of* Deere & Company)
180 Rue De Rotterdam, Saint-Augustin-De-
Desmaures, QC, G3A 1T3
(418) 870-2885
Emp Here 30
SIC 5084 Industrial machinery and equipment

D-U-N-S 25-358-8982   (HQ)

**FABRICANT DE POELES INTERNATIONAL
INC**
SBI
250 Rue De Copenhague Bureau 1, Saint-
Augustin-De-Desmaures, QC, G3A 2H3
(418) 878-3040
Emp Here 170   *Emp Total* 3
Sales 26,479,445
SIC 3433 Heating equipment, except electric
   Gilles Cantin

D-U-N-S 24-381-3151   (HQ)
GRANICOR INC
300 Rue De Rotterdam Bureau 21, Saint-
Augustin-De-Desmaures, QC, G3A 1T4
(418) 878-3530
Emp Here 75   *Emp Total* 120
Sales 6,063,757
SIC 3281 Cut stone and stone products
Pr Pr Alain Robitaille
VP Paul Robitaille
   Georges Robitaille

D-U-N-S 25-094-1614   (SL)
GROUPE C.D.J. INC
4740 Rue Saint-Felix, Saint-Augustin-De-
Desmaures, QC, G3A 1B1

Emp Here 120   *Sales* 3,502,114
SIC 7349 Building maintenance services, nec

D-U-N-S 20-253-1059   (BR)
GROUPE COOPERATIF DYNACO
GROUPE DYNACO BMR
(*Suby of* Groupe Cooperatif Dynaco)
191 138 Rte, Saint-Augustin-De-Desmaures,
QC, G3A 0G2
(418) 878-2023
Emp Here 50
SIC 5039 Construction materials, nec

D-U-N-S 20-431-9347   (BR)
HEWITT EQUIPEMENT LIMITEE
CATERPILLAR
100 Rue De Rotterdam, Saint-Augustin-De-
Desmaures, QC, G3A 1T2
(418) 878-3000
Emp Here 190
SIC 5082 Construction and mining machinery

D-U-N-S 25-367-7314   (SL)
**LE   GROUPE   MANUFACTURIER
D'ASCENSEURS GLOBAL TARDIF INC**
120 Rue De Naples, Saint-Augustin-De-
Desmaures, QC, G3A 2Y2
(418) 878-4116
Emp Here 95   *Sales* 13,286,839
SIC 8711 Engineering services
   Francois Tardif

D-U-N-S 20-861-3604   (SL)
MECART INC
(*Suby of* Entreprises Pol R Inc)
110 Rue De Rotterdam, Saint-Augustin-De-
Desmaures, QC, G3A 1T3
(418) 880-7000
Emp Here 25   *Sales* 1,126,126
SIC 3296 Mineral wool

D-U-N-S 20-716-3416   (BR)
METRO RICHELIEU INC
JARDIN MERITE DE QUEBEC
60 Rue D'Anvers, Saint-Augustin-De-
Desmaures, QC, G3A 1S4
(418) 878-8676
Emp Here 100
SIC 5431 Fruit and vegetable markets

D-U-N-S 25-789-7546   (SL)
NETTOYEUR PELICAN INC
195 Rue Georges, Saint-Augustin-De-
Desmaures, QC, G3A 1W7
(418) 871-3999
Emp Here 60   *Sales* 1,751,057
SIC 7349 Building maintenance services, nec

D-U-N-S 24-593-7177   (SL)
NEUROSTREAM TECHNOLOGIES SENC

4780 Rue Saint-Felix Bureau 105, Saint-Augustin-De-Desmaures, QC, G3A 2J9

Emp Here 51   Sales 2,772,507
SIC 8731 Commercial physical research

D-U-N-S 20-872-1548   (SL)
PLACAGE AU CHROME STE-FOY INC
50 Rue De Rotterdam, Saint-Augustin-De-Desmaures, QC, G3A 1S9
(418) 878-3548
Emp Here 30   Sales 4,377,642
SIC 5211 Lumber and other building materials

D-U-N-S 24-842-4756   (BR)
RUSSEL METALS INC
ACIER LEROUX, A DIV OF RUSSEL METALS
167 Rue De Rotterdam, Saint-Augustin-De-Desmaures, QC, G3A 2K2
(418) 878-5737
Emp Here 50
SIC 5051 Metals service centers and offices

D-U-N-S 20-515-2478   (BR)
SMS EQUIPMENT INC
EQUIPEMENT FEDERAL
120 Rue De New York, Saint-Augustin-De-Desmaures, QC, G3A 0A8
(418) 870-1502
Emp Here 40
SIC 5082 Construction and mining machinery

D-U-N-S 24-623-4298   (BR)
SAFETY-KLEEN CANADA INC.
85 Rue De Hambourg, Saint-Augustin-De-Desmaures, QC, G3A 1S6
(418) 878-4570
Emp Here 20
SIC 4953 Refuse systems

D-U-N-S 24-419-0216   (BR)
TELECON INC
104 Rue D'Anvers, Saint-Augustin-De-Desmaures, QC, G3A 1S4
(418) 878-9595
Emp Here 125
SIC 4899 Communication services, nec

D-U-N-S 24-884-8017   (HQ)
TRANSPORT TFI 4, S.E.C.
KINGSWAY VRAC
(Suby of Transport TFI 4, S.E.C.)
140 Rue Des Grands-Lacs, Saint-Augustin-De-Desmaures, QC, G3A 2K1
(418) 870-5454
Emp Here 25   Emp Total 100
Sales 12,695,162
SIC 4213 Trucking, except local
Genl Mgr Chantal Martel

D-U-N-S 24-790-7678   (BR)
VIGI SANTE LTEE
C H S L D VIGI SAINT AUGUSTIN
(Suby of Vigi Sante Ltee)
4954 Rue Clement-Lockquell, Saint-Augustin-De-Desmaures, QC, G3A 1V5
(418) 871-1232
Emp Here 130
SIC 8361 Residential care

Saint-Basile, QC G0A
Quebec County

D-U-N-S 20-247-4029   (HQ)
CIMENT QUEBEC INC
UNIBETON
(Suby of Groupe Ciment Quebec Inc)
145 Boul Du Centenaire, Saint-Basile, QC, G0A 3G0
(418) 329-2100
Emp Here 180   Emp Total 500
SIC 3241 Cement, hydraulic

D-U-N-S 25-233-1335   (BR)

COMMISSION SCOLAIRE DE PORTNEUF
COMMISSION SCOLAIRE DE PORTNEUF
(Suby of Commission Scolaire de Portneuf)
10 Pace De L'Eglise, Saint-Basile, QC, G0A 3G0

Emp Here 25
SIC 8211 Elementary and secondary schools

Saint-Basile-Le-Grand, QC J3N

D-U-N-S 20-033-9229   (BR)
COMMISSION SCOLAIRE DES PATRIOTES
ECOLE DE LA MOSAIQUE
105 Av De Montpellier, Saint-Basile-Le-Grand, QC, J3N 1C6
(450) 441-6719
Emp Here 25
SIC 8211 Elementary and secondary schools

D-U-N-S 20-712-3113   (BR)
COMMISSION SCOLAIRE DES PATRIOTES
ECOLE DE LA CHANTERELLE
1 Rue De La Chanterelle, Saint-Basile-Le-Grand, QC, J3N 1L1
(450) 461-1425
Emp Here 45
SIC 8211 Elementary and secondary schools

D-U-N-S 24-099-8612   (BR)
COMMISSION SCOLAIRE DES PATRIOTES
ECOLES PRIMAIRES - SAINT-BASILE-LE-GRAND - JACQUES ROCHELEAU
10 Rue Prefontaine, Saint-Basile-Le-Grand, QC, J3N 1L6
(450) 653-4142
Emp Here 50
SIC 8211 Elementary and secondary schools

Saint-Benoit-Labre, QC G0M

D-U-N-S 25-089-2353   (SL)
9048-9493 QUEBEC INC
COUTURE VOIE EXPRESS
(Suby of 9094-1253 Quebec Inc)
27 Rue Industrielle, Saint-Benoit-Labre, QC, G0M 1P0
(418) 228-6979
Emp Here 70   Sales 8,682,323
SIC 4213 Trucking, except local
Pr Sylvain Couture
Vincent Couture

D-U-N-S 25-241-3604   (BR)
COMMISSION SCOLAIRE DE LA BEAUCE-ETCHEMIN
ECOLE NOTRE DAME DU ROSAIRE
56 Rue De La Fabrique, Saint-Benoit-Labre, QC, G0M 1P0
(418) 226-2677
Emp Here 20
SIC 8211 Elementary and secondary schools

D-U-N-S 24-639-2229   (HQ)
CONSTRUCTIONS BINET INC, LES
227 Rte 271, Saint-Benoit-Labre, QC, G0M 1P0
(418) 228-1578
Emp Here 25   Emp Total 25
Sales 9,266,009
SIC 1542 Nonresidential construction, nec
Pr Martin Binet
VP Nadia Binet
Sec Louis-David Poirier
Treas Francine Binet

D-U-N-S 20-247-5521   (SL)
ROMEO LAFLAMME & FILS INC
25 Rte Laflamme, Saint-Benoit-Labre, QC, G0M 1P0
(418) 228-9644
Emp Here 60   Sales 3,502,114

SIC 2511 Wood household furniture

D-U-N-S 20-517-1259   (SL)
TOITURES FECTEAU INC
320 Rte 271, Saint-Benoit-Labre, QC, G0M 1P0
(418) 228-9651
Emp Here 55   Sales 6,274,620
SIC 2439 Structural wood members, nec
Pr Pr Kathy Poulin
VP VP Jean-Paul Grondin
Steeve Grondin
Jean-Pierre Chabot

Saint-Bernard, QC G0S
Dorchester County

D-U-N-S 24-851-2704   (BR)
CAISSE DESJARDINS DU CENTRE DE LA NOUVELLE-BEAUCE
1497 Rue Saint-Georges, Saint-Bernard, QC, G0S 2G0

Emp Here 65
SIC 6062 State credit unions

D-U-N-S 25-233-7456   (BR)
COMMISSION SCOLAIRE DE LA BEAUCE-ETCHEMIN
ECOLE L'AQUARELLE ST BERNARD
1492 Rue Du Couvent, Saint-Bernard, QC, G0S 2G0
(418) 475-6668
Emp Here 20
SIC 8211 Elementary and secondary schools

Saint-Blaise-Sur-Richelieu, QC J0J
St-Jean County

D-U-N-S 20-002-5950   (BR)
CAISSE DESJARDINS DES SEIGNEURIES DE LA FRONTIERE
CENTRE DE SERVICES SAINT-BLAISE
765 Rue Principale, Saint-Blaise-Sur-Richelieu, QC, J0J 1W0
(450) 291-5100
Emp Here 67
SIC 6062 State credit unions

D-U-N-S 25-234-2829   (BR)
COMMISSION SCOLAIRE DES HAUTES-RIVIERES
ECOLE ST-BLAISE
745 Rue Principale, Saint-Blaise-Sur-Richelieu, QC, J0J 1W0
(450) 291-5500
Emp Here 25
SIC 8211 Elementary and secondary schools

Saint-Boniface-De-Shawinigan, QC G0X

D-U-N-S 20-247-6370   (SL)
PORTES MILETTE INC
100 Av Industriel, Saint-Boniface-De-Shawinigan, QC, G0X 2L0
(819) 535-5588
Emp Here 150   Sales 17,043,600
SIC 2431 Millwork
Pr Pr Gerard Millette
VP VP June Millette
Mario Millette
Plant Mgr Michel Millette

D-U-N-S 25-904-8957   (BR)
PROVIGO INC
INTER MARCHE
93 Rue Principale, Saint-Boniface-De-Shawinigan, QC, G0X 2L0

---

(819) 535-3322
Emp Here 25
SIC 5411 Grocery stores

Saint-Bruno, QC J3V

D-U-N-S 24-177-8406   (SL)
ACADEMIE DES SACRES-CURS
PENSIONNAT DES SACRES-COEURS
1575 Rang Des Vingt, Saint-Bruno, QC, J3V 4P6
(450) 653-3681
Emp Here 70   Sales 4,669,485
SIC 8211 Elementary and secondary schools

D-U-N-S 24-945-3168   (BR)
AGROPUR COOPERATIVE
NATREL
57 Ch De La Rabastaliere O, Saint-Bruno, QC, J3V 1Y7

Emp Here 60
SIC 2026 Fluid milk

D-U-N-S 24-802-2225   (BR)
AUTOMOBILES NIQUET INC, LES
AUDI
(Suby of 142320 Canada Inc)
1917 Boul Sir-Wilfrid-Laurier Bureau 116, Saint-Bruno, QC, J3V 0G8
(450) 653-1553
Emp Here 30
SIC 5511 New and used car dealers

D-U-N-S 24-108-4052   (HQ)
AUTOMOBILES NIQUET INC, LES
VOLKSWAGON
(Suby of 142320 Canada Inc)
1905 Boul Sir-Wilfrid-Laurier, Saint-Bruno, QC, J3V 0G8
(450) 653-1553
Emp Here 30   Emp Total 60
Sales 21,888,210
SIC 5511 New and used car dealers
Pr Pr Sylvie Niquet

D-U-N-S 24-362-5642   (BR)
BEST BUY CANADA LTD
GEEK SQUAD
(Suby of Best Buy Co., Inc.)
1235 Boul Des Promenades, Saint-Bruno, QC, J3V 6H1
(450) 461-1557
Emp Here 50
SIC 5731 Radio, television, and electronic stores

D-U-N-S 24-512-4024   (SL)
BOIRON CANADA INC
BOIRON DOLISOS
1300 Rue Rene-Descartes, Saint-Bruno, QC, J3V 0B7
(450) 723-2066
Emp Here 26   Sales 3,210,271
SIC 5122 Drugs, proprietaries, and sundries

D-U-N-S 20-179-0420   (BR)
BOMBARDIER INC
BOMBARDIER TRANSPORTATION
1101 Rue Parent, Saint-Bruno, QC, J3V 6E6
(514) 861-9481
Emp Here 800
SIC 4111 Local and suburban transit

D-U-N-S 24-368-4458   (HQ)
BOMBARDIER TRANSPORTATION CANADA INC
BOMBARDIER TRANSPORT
1101 Rue Parent, Saint-Bruno, QC, J3V 6E6
(450) 441-2020
Emp Here 200   Emp Total 1,378
Sales 60,776,263
SIC 7363 Help supply services
Pr Pr Benoit Brossoit
Julie Turgeon

Richard Coulombe

D-U-N-S 24-404-7650   (BR)
BOUTIQUE TRISTAN & ISEUT INC
TRISTAN AMERICA
401 Boul Des Promenades Bureau 4, Saint-Bruno, QC, J3V 6A8
(450) 653-9253
Emp Here 25
SIC 5621 Women's clothing stores

D-U-N-S 20-581-3558   (BR)
CANADA POST CORPORATION
SAINT-BRUNO BDP
50 Rue Rabastaliere O, Saint-Bruno, QC, J3V 1Y0
(450) 441-1583
Emp Here 40
SIC 4311 U.s. postal service

D-U-N-S 20-777-5417   (HQ)
CENTRE DE LA PETITE ENFANCE LES MOUSSES DU MONT INC
CPE LES MOUSSES DU MONT INSTALLA-TION ALIZE
(*Suby of* Centre de la Petite Enfance Les Mousses du Mont Inc)
775 Montee Montarville, Saint-Bruno, QC, J3V 6L6
(450) 441-4311
Emp Here 48   *Emp Total* 99
Sales 2,991,389
SIC 8351 Child day care services

D-U-N-S 20-407-7825   (SL)
COLLEGE TRINITE
SEMINAIRE SAINTE-TRINITE
1475 Rang Des Vingt, Saint-Bruno, QC, J3V 4P6
(450) 653-2409
Emp Here 50   *Sales* 3,356,192
SIC 8211 Elementary and secondary schools

D-U-N-S 25-233-7068   (BR)
COMMISSION SCOLAIRE DES PATRIOTES
COMMISSION SCOLAIRE DES PATRIOTES
221 Boul Clairevue E, Saint-Bruno, QC, J3V 5J3
(450) 653-1541
Emp Here 200
SIC 8211 Elementary and secondary schools

D-U-N-S 25-233-9932   (BR)
COMMISSION SCOLAIRE DES PATRIOTES
ECOLE ALBERT-SCHWEITZER
1139 Rue Cadieux, Saint-Bruno, QC, J3V 2Z5
(450) 653-2453
Emp Here 50
SIC 8211 Elementary and secondary schools

D-U-N-S 25-233-9858   (BR)
COMMISSION SCOLAIRE DES PATRIOTES
ECOLE DE MONTARVILLE
1725 Rue Montarville, Saint-Bruno, QC, J3V 3V2
(450) 653-2411
Emp Here 40
SIC 8211 Elementary and secondary schools

D-U-N-S 25-233-9817   (BR)
COMMISSION SCOLAIRE DES PATRIOTES
COMMISSION SCOLAIRE DES PATRIOTES
1435 Rue Chateauguay, Saint-Bruno, QC, J3V 3A9
(450) 653-7610
Emp Here 30
SIC 8211 Elementary and secondary schools

D-U-N-S 24-890-4435   (BR)
CONSTRUCTION DJL INC
580 Rang Des Vingt-Cinq E, Saint-Bruno, QC, J3V 0G6
(450) 653-2423
Emp Here 100
SIC 1422 Crushed and broken limestone

D-U-N-S 24-058-1798   (BR)
FAMILIPRIX INC
PHARMACIE DEBLOIS & MONARQUE

1556 Rue Montarville, Saint-Bruno, QC, J3V 3T7
(450) 653-1331
Emp Here 30
SIC 5912 Drug stores and proprietary stores

D-U-N-S 25-856-3535   (BR)
GAP (CANADA) INC
GAPKIDS
(*Suby of* The Gap Inc)
302 Boul Des Promenades, Saint-Bruno, QC, J3V 6A7
(450) 441-7977
Emp Here 20
SIC 5651 Family clothing stores

D-U-N-S 20-115-1854   (SL)
GESTION BI-EAU PURE INC
BI-EAU PURE
(*Suby of* Primo Water Corporation)
900 Rue Sagard, Saint-Bruno, QC, J3V 6C2
(450) 441-8353
Emp Here 25
SIC 3581 Automatic vending machines

D-U-N-S 24-195-9548   (BR)
GOUVERNEMENT DE LA PROVINCE DE QUEBEC
GOUVERNEMENT DE LA PROVINCE DE QUEBEC
330 Rang Des Vingt-Cinq E, Saint-Bruno, QC, J3V 4P6
(450) 653-7544
Emp Here 20
SIC 7011 Hotels and motels

D-U-N-S 24-190-7109   (BR)
GROUPE ALDO INC, LE
CHAUSSURES GLOBO
1195 Boul Des Promenades, Saint-Bruno, QC, J3V 6H1
(450) 441-0030
Emp Here 25
SIC 5661 Shoe stores

D-U-N-S 20-715-5610   (BR)
GROUPE SPORTSCENE INC
CAGE AUX SPORTS , LA
2250 Boul Sir-Wilfrid-Laurier, Saint-Bruno, QC, J3V 4P6
(450) 461-1115
Emp Here 47
SIC 5812 Eating places

D-U-N-S 24-383-3303   (BR)
GROUPE VISION NEW LOOK INC
105 Boul Des Promenades, Saint-Bruno, QC, J3V 5K2
(450) 441-0812
Emp Here 21
SIC 5995 Optical goods stores

D-U-N-S 20-177-5637   (BR)
HOME DEPOT OF CANADA INC
(*Suby of* The Home Depot Inc)
901 Rue De L'Etang, Saint-Bruno, QC, J3V 6N8
(450) 461-2000
Emp Here 100
SIC 5251 Hardware stores

D-U-N-S 20-700-3182   (BR)
HUDSON'S BAY COMPANY
DECO DECOUVERTE
800 Rue De L'Etang, Saint-Bruno, QC, J3V 6K8
(450) 653-6398
Emp Here 25
SIC 5311 Department stores

D-U-N-S 24-654-9641   (BR)
HUDSON'S BAY COMPANY
800 Boul Des Promenades, Saint-Bruno, QC, J3V 5J9
(450) 653-4455
Emp Here 130
SIC 5311 Department stores

D-U-N-S 24-762-5692   (SL)

INVESTISSEMENT PIERRE MARCOTTE LIMITEE, LES
CANADIAN TIRE
900 Rue De L'Etang, Saint-Bruno, QC, J3V 6K8
(450) 653-0222
Emp Here 100   *Sales* 7,150,149
SIC 5311 Department stores
Pr Pr Pierre Marcotte
Stephane Marcotte

D-U-N-S 24-608-1017   (BR)
LOBLAWS INC
PROVIGO LE MARCHE
1402 Rue Roberval, Saint-Bruno, QC, J3V 5J2
(450) 653-0433
Emp Here 25
SIC 5411 Grocery stores

D-U-N-S 20-296-8298   (BR)
MAISON SIMONS INC, LA
600 Boul Des Promenades, Saint-Bruno, QC, J3V 6L9
(514) 282-1840
Emp Here 200
SIC 5311 Department stores

D-U-N-S 20-034-1506   (BR)
MARCHE LAMBERT ET FRERES INC
IGA EXTRA
(*Suby of* Investissements B.I.L. Inc)
23 Boul Seigneurial O, Saint-Bruno, QC, J3V 2G9
(450) 653-4466
Emp Here 200
SIC 5411 Grocery stores

D-U-N-S 24-490-6954   (SL)
MECAR METAL INC
1560 Rue Marie-Victorin, Saint-Bruno, QC, J3V 6B9
(450) 653-1002
Emp Here 98   *Sales* 12,403,319
SIC 3585 Refrigeration and heating equipment
Pr Pr Michael Gallagher
VP Sean Gallagher
Sec Mireille Ouellette

D-U-N-S 24-361-3747   (BR)
MELLOR, DAVID A. CONSULTANTS INC
ROYAL LEPAGE PRIVILEGE
1503 Place De L'Hotel-De-Ville, Saint-Bruno, QC, J3V 5Y6
(450) 441-1576
Emp Here 40
SIC 6531 Real estate agents and managers

D-U-N-S 24-097-6691   (BR)
OLD NAVY (CANADA) INC
OLD NAVY
(*Suby of* The Gap Inc)
1241 Boul Des Promenades, Saint-Bruno, QC, J3V 6H1
(450) 441-6300
Emp Here 30
SIC 5651 Family clothing stores

D-U-N-S 25-240-0783   (BR)
RIVERSIDE SCHOOL BOARD
MOUNT BRUNO SCHOOL
20 Rue Des Peupliers, Saint-Bruno, QC, J3V 2L8
(450) 653-2429
Emp Here 38
SIC 8211 Elementary and secondary schools

D-U-N-S 25-699-5069   (BR)
ROYAL BANK OF CANADA
RBC BANQUE ROYALE
(*Suby of* Royal Bank Of Canada)
30 Boul Clairevue O, Saint-Bruno, QC, J3V 1P8
(450) 653-7846
Emp Here 22
SIC 6021 National commercial banks

D-U-N-S 24-580-7235   (SL)
SEMINAIRE DE LA TRES SAINTE-TRINITE

1475 Rang Des Vingt, Saint-Bruno, QC, J3V 4P6
(450) 653-2409
Emp Here 50   *Sales* 3,356,192
SIC 8211 Elementary and secondary schools

D-U-N-S 25-499-0112   (BR)
STAPLES CANADA INC
BUREAU EN GROS
(*Suby of* Staples, Inc.)
1465 Boul Saint-Bruno, Saint-Bruno, QC, J3V 6J1
(450) 441-2414
Emp Here 40
SIC 5943 Stationery stores

D-U-N-S 20-928-6582   (HQ)
SYSTEMES DE DISTRIBUTION COAST (CANADA) INC, LES
COAST CANADA
1545 Rue Marie-Victorin, Saint-Bruno, QC, J3V 6B7
(450) 441-2707
Emp Here 83   *Emp Total* 42,500
Sales 12,695,162
SIC 4213 Trucking, except local
Pr Pr Stephane Lussier
Tim Mcguire
Sandy Knell

D-U-N-S 25-297-8671   (BR)
TOYS 'R' US (CANADA) LTD
TOYS R US
(*Suby of* Toys "r" Us, Inc.)
655 Boul Des Promenades, Saint-Bruno, QC, J3V 6A8
(450) 441-8697
Emp Here 50
SIC 5945 Hobby, toy, and game shops

D-U-N-S 25-498-3331   (BR)
WAL-MART CANADA CORP
1475 Boul Saint-Bruno, Saint-Bruno, QC, J3V 6J1
(450) 653-9996
Emp Here 200
SIC 5311 Department stores

D-U-N-S 20-184-3088   (BR)
WINNERS MERCHANTS INTERNATIONAL L.P.
WINNERS
(*Suby of* The TJX Companies Inc)
1201 Boul Saint-Bruno, Saint-Bruno, QC, J3V 6P4
(450) 653-7312
Emp Here 40
SIC 5651 Family clothing stores

D-U-N-S 24-847-6686   (BR)
YM INC. (SALES)
URBAN PLANET
1011 Boul Saint-Bruno, Saint-Bruno, QC, J3V 6P4
(450) 653-5299
Emp Here 25
SIC 5621 Women's clothing stores

Saint-Bruno-De-Guigues, QC J0Z

D-U-N-S 25-240-0981   (BR)
COMMISSION SCOLAIRE DU LAC-TEMISCAMINGUE
ECOLE MARIE ASSOMPTION
(*Suby of* Commission Scolaire du Lac-Temiscamingue)
23 Rue Principale N, Saint-Bruno-De-Guigues, QC, J0Z 2G0
(819) 728-2910
Emp Here 25
SIC 8211 Elementary and secondary schools

Saint-Bruno-Lac-Saint-Jean, QC G0W
Lac-St-Jean-Est County

D-U-N-S 24-885-0539   (SL)
2732-0100 QUEBEC INC
1212 Av Saint-Alphonse Rr 2, Saint-Bruno-Lac-Saint-Jean, QC, G0W 2L0
(418) 343-2989
Emp Here 100   *Sales* 20,899,840
SIC 6712 Bank holding companies
Pr Pr Marcel Maltais
VP Marc Maltais
Treas Fleurette Maltais

D-U-N-S 24-736-9759   (SL)
7246404 CANADA INC
1210 Av Saint-Alphonse, Saint-Bruno-Lac-Saint-Jean, QC, G0W 2L0
(418) 343-2989
Emp Here 50   *Sales* 14,710,250
SIC 3711 Motor vehicles and car bodies
Pr Pr Adam Lapointe
Jean-Philippe Harvey

D-U-N-S 20-102-2311   (BR)
NUTRINOR COOPERATIVE
535 6e Rang S, Saint-Bruno-Lac-Saint-Jean, QC, G0W 2L0
(418) 343-3812
Emp Here 20
SIC 5251 Hardware stores

D-U-N-S 20-144-3038   (BR)
NUTRINOR COOPERATIVE
NUTRINOR
555 6e Rang S, Saint-Bruno-Lac-Saint-Jean, QC, G0W 2L0
(418) 343-2888
Emp Here 24
SIC 5984 Liquefied petroleum gas dealers

D-U-N-S 24-169-9581   (BR)
NUTRINOR COOPERATIVE
AGRINOR
535 6e Rang O, Saint-Bruno-Lac-Saint-Jean, QC, G0W 2L0
(418) 343-3772
Emp Here 20
SIC 5451 Dairy products stores

D-U-N-S 24-170-0447   (BR)
TRANSPORT MORNEAU INC
525 Av Industrielle, Saint-Bruno-Lac-Saint-Jean, QC, G0W 2L0
(418) 344-4747
Emp Here 47
SIC 4213 Trucking, except local

D-U-N-S 24-148-1027   (HQ)
USINE DE CONGELATION DE ST-BRUNO INC
(*Suby of* Usine de Congelation de St-Bruno Inc)
698 Rue Melancon, Saint-Bruno-Lac-Saint-Jean, QC, G0W 2L0
(418) 343-2206
Emp Here 50   *Emp Total* 600
Sales 77,872,000
SIC 4222 Refrigerated warehousing and storage
Pr Pr Gilles Dery

Saint-Celestin, QC J0C

D-U-N-S 25-383-3172   (BR)
GOUVERNEMENT DE LA PROVINCE DE QUEBEC
CENTRE D'HEBERGEMENT SAINT CELESTIN
475 Rue Houde, Saint-Celestin, QC, J0C 1G0
(819) 229-3617
Emp Here 70
SIC 8361 Residential care

D-U-N-S 20-362-2717   (HQ)

GROUPE AGRITEX INC, LE
AGRICOTECH
(*Suby of* Groupe Agritex Inc, Le)
230 Rue Marquis, Saint-Celestin, QC, J0C 1G0
(819) 229-3686
Emp Here 25   *Emp Total* 250
Sales 23,712,228
SIC 5999 Miscellaneous retail stores, nec
Pr Roy Louis
VP VP Patrick Allard
Sec Simon Gauthier

Saint-Cesaire, QC J0L

D-U-N-S 24-902-7210   (SL)
CAPSULES AMCOR FLEXIBLES CANADA INC
2301 112 Rte, Saint-Cesaire, QC, J0L 1T0
(450) 469-0777
Emp Here 130
SIC 3466 Crowns and closures

D-U-N-S 25-024-2828   (BR)
CASCADES CANADA ULC
CASCADE CANADA ULC
1850 Av De L'Union, Saint-Cesaire, QC, J0L 1T0
(450) 469-3389
Emp Here 35
SIC 2621 Paper mills

D-U-N-S 20-024-0716   (BR)
CENTRE DE SANTE ET DE SERVICES SOCIAUX HAUT-RICHELIEU-ROUVILLE
CLSC DE SAINT-CESAIRE
(*Suby of* Centre de Sante et de Services Sociaux Haut-Richelieu-Rouville)
1394 Rue Notre-Dame, Saint-Cesaire, QC, J0L 1T0
(450) 469-0269
Emp Here 40
SIC 8361 Residential care

D-U-N-S 25-702-1279   (HQ)
CENTRE DE LA PETITE ENFANCE MAMIE-POM
(*Suby of* Centre de la Petite Enfance Mamie-Pom)
1298 Av Saint-Paul, Saint-Cesaire, QC, J0L 1T0
(450) 469-4242
Emp Here 20   *Emp Total* 50
Sales 1,532,175
SIC 8351 Child day care services

D-U-N-S 20-545-9766   (BR)
COMMISSION SCOLAIRE DES HAUTES-RIVIERES
ECOLE SECONDAIRE PAUL GERMAIN OSTIGUY
1881 Av Saint-Paul, Saint-Cesaire, QC, J0L 1T0
(450) 469-3187
Emp Here 75
SIC 8211 Elementary and secondary schools

D-U-N-S 20-248-0737   (HQ)
DUCHARME & FRERE INC
RONA
(*Suby of* Ducharme & Frere Inc)
1221 Rue De Vimy, Saint-Cesaire, QC, J0L 1T0
(450) 469-3137
Emp Here 20   *Emp Total* 28
Sales 5,681,200
SIC 5211 Lumber and other building materials
Pr Denis Ducharme
Line Ducharme
Dir Real Audette
Yves Ducharmes
Mario Ducharme
Dir Sylvain Ducharme

D-U-N-S 24-671-2298   (BR)

MAGASINS KORVETTE LTEE, LES
KORVETTE
941 112 Rte, Saint-Cesaire, QC, J0L 1T0
(450) 469-2686
Emp Here 29
SIC 5311 Department stores

D-U-N-S 24-434-6995   (SL)
SEMENCES PROGRAIN INC
PROGRAIN
145 Rang Du Bas-De-La-Riviere N, Saint-Cesaire, QC, J0L 1T0
(450) 469-5744
Emp Here 55   *Sales* 4,669,485
SIC 3999 Manufacturing industries, nec

Saint-Charles-Borromee, QC J6E
Joliette County

D-U-N-S 20-202-0434   (SL)
CHEZ HENRI MAJEAU ET FILS INC
RESTAURANT CHEZ HENRI
30 Rue De La Visitation, Saint-Charles-Borromee, QC, J6E 4M8
(450) 759-1113
Emp Here 100   *Sales* 2,991,389
SIC 5812 Eating places

D-U-N-S 24-296-7404   (SL)
EBENISTERIE VISITATION INC
ARMOIRES EVI
1066 Rue De La Visitation, Saint-Charles-Borromee, QC, J6E 7Y8
(450) 752-1895
Emp Here 55   *Sales* 3,811,504
SIC 2434 Wood kitchen cabinets

D-U-N-S 25-361-2899   (SL)
TORA SAINT-CHARLES-BORROMEE LIMITEE
TIGRE GEANT
(*Suby of* Giant Tiger Stores Limited)
197 Rue De La Visitation Bureau 109, Saint-Charles-Borromee, QC, J6E 4N6
(450) 760-3568
Emp Here 50   *Sales* 3,575,074
SIC 5311 Department stores

Saint-Charles-De-Bellechasse, QC G0R

D-U-N-S 20-030-4140   (BR)
COMMISSION SCOLAIRE DE LA COTE-DU-SUD, LA
ECOLE DE L'ETINCELLE
2829 Av Royale, Saint-Charles-De-Bellechasse, QC, G0R 2T0
(418) 887-3317
Emp Here 20
SIC 8211 Elementary and secondary schools

D-U-N-S 20-248-1461   (SL)
MEUBLE IDEAL LTEE
(*Suby of* Investissements Claujean Inc)
6 Rue Saint-Thomas, Saint-Charles-De-Bellechasse, QC, G0R 2T0
(418) 887-3331
Emp Here 200   *Sales* 15,607,440
SIC 2511 Wood household furniture
Pr Pr Claude Belanger
VP VP Jean Belanger

D-U-N-S 24-593-1894   (BR)
UNICOOP, COOPERATIVE AGRICOLE
ENTREPOT ST-CHARLES
28 Rue De La Gare, Saint-Charles-De-Bellechasse, QC, G0R 2T0
(418) 887-3391
Emp Here 25
SIC 5083 Farm and garden machinery

Saint-Charles-De-Bourget, QC G0V
Chicoutimi County

D-U-N-S 20-642-1591   (BR)
COMMISSION SCOLAIRE DE LA JONQUIERE
ECOLE SAINT-CHARLES
(*Suby of* Commission Scolaire de la Jonquiere)
370 Rue Principale, Saint-Charles-De-Bourget, QC, G0V 1G0
(418) 672-2233
Emp Here 20
SIC 8211 Elementary and secondary schools

Saint-Christophe-D'Arthabask, QC G6R
Arthabaska County

D-U-N-S 20-171-8298   (BR)
GAUDREAU ENVIRONNEMENT INC
25 Rte 116, Saint-Christophe-D'Arthabask, QC, G6R 0S2
(819) 357-8666
Emp Here 30
SIC 4953 Refuse systems

D-U-N-S 24-387-4190   (HQ)
ROGER GRENIER INC
RONA
(*Suby of* Roger Grenier Inc)
378 Av Pie-X, Saint-Christophe-D'Arthabask, QC, G6R 0M2
(819) 357-8282
Emp Here 32   *Emp Total* 90
Sales 11,582,880
SIC 5251 Hardware stores
Pr Pr Bernard Hamel
Jean Ducharme

Saint-Clement, QC G0L

D-U-N-S 25-089-8368   (SL)
CREATIONS JRP (1994) INC
24 Rue Du Pont, Saint-Clement, QC, G0L 2N0
(418) 963-2364
Emp Here 30   *Sales* 2,918,428
SIC 2842 Polishes and sanitation goods

Saint-Clet, QC J0P

D-U-N-S 20-642-2490   (BR)
ARMTEC LP
ARMTEC
669 201 Rte, Saint-Clet, QC, J0P 1S0
(450) 456-3366
Emp Here 40
SIC 3312 Blast furnaces and steel mills

Saint-Colomban, QC J5K

D-U-N-S 20-712-1851   (BR)
COMMISSION SCOLAIRE DE LA RIVIERE-DU-NORD
ECOLE DE LA VOLIERE
(*Suby of* Commission Scolaire de la Riviere-du-Nord)
549 Ch De La Riviere-Du-Nord, Saint-Colomban, QC, J5K 2E5
(450) 569-3307
Emp Here 20
SIC 8211 Elementary and secondary schools

D-U-N-S 25-222-6394   (BR)
COMMISSION SCOLAIRE DE LA RIVIERE-

▲ Public Company   ■ Public Company Family Member   **HQ** Headquarters   **BR** Branch   **SL** Single Location

DU-NORD
ECOLE DES HAUTBOIS
(*Suby of* Commission Scolaire de la Riviere-du-Nord)
321 Montee De L'Eglise, Saint-Colomban, QC,
J5K 2H8
(450) 438-8836
Emp Here 35
SIC 8211 Elementary and secondary schools

D-U-N-S 20-712-1828   (BR)
COMMISSION SCOLAIRE DE LA RIVIERE-DU-NORD
ECOLE A L'OREE DES BOIS
(*Suby of* Commission Scolaire de la Riviere-du-Nord)
360 Cote Saint-Nicholas, Saint-Colomban,
QC, J5K 1M6
(450) 431-1288
Emp Here 50
SIC 8211 Elementary and secondary schools

Saint-Come, QC J0K
Beauce County

D-U-N-S 25-890-9019   (HQ)
CAMP MUSICAL PERE LINDSAY INC
AUBERGE DU LAC PRISCAULT
(*Suby of* Camp Musical Pere Lindsay Inc)
100 Rang Petit Beloeil, Saint-Come, QC, J0K
2B0
(450) 883-6024
Emp Here 40   *Emp Total* 70
Sales 3,793,956
SIC 8299 Schools and educational services,
nec

Saint-Come-Liniere, QC G0M
Beauce County

D-U-N-S 24-885-1719   (SL)
DUMAS CANADA INC
195 Rue Du Parc-Industriel Rr 1, Saint-Come-Liniere, QC, G0M 1J0
(418) 685-3633
Emp Here 40   *Sales* 7,045,500
SIC 5031 Lumber, plywood, and millwork
Pr Pr Daniel Dumas
VP VP Pierre Dumas
  Dominique Dumas

D-U-N-S 24-379-4542   (BR)
MULTI-MARQUES INC
1295 1e Av O, Saint-Come-Liniere, QC, G0M
1J0
(418) 685-3351
Emp Here 30
SIC 2051 Bread, cake, and related products

D-U-N-S 24-327-3104   (BR)
PRODUITS FORESTIERS D. G. LTEE
(*Suby of* Groupe Gesco-Star Ltee)
2518 Rte President-Kennedy, Saint-Come-Liniere, QC, G0M 1J0
(418) 685-3335
Emp Here 60
SIC 2421 Sawmills and planing mills, general

Saint-Constant, QC J5A

D-U-N-S 25-973-4291   (SL)
CALIFORNIA L.I.N.E. INC
701 Rang Saint-Pierre N Unite 1, Saint-Constant, QC, J5A 0R2
(450) 632-9000
Emp Here 60   *Sales* 4,742,446
SIC 4212 Local trucking, without storage

D-U-N-S 20-585-0949   (BR)

CANADA POST CORPORATION
BUREAU DE POSTE DE SAINT CONSTANT
171 Rue Saint-Pierre Bureau 104, Saint-Constant, QC, J5A 2G9
(450) 632-2430
Emp Here 21
SIC 4311 U.s. postal service

D-U-N-S 20-294-1808   (SL)
ENTREPRISES AUTOMOBILES INC
ST-CONSTANT HONDA
270 132 Rte, Saint-Constant, QC, J5A 2C9
(450) 632-7155
Emp Here 30   *Sales* 14,568,000
SIC 5511 New and used car dealers
Pr Tom Samatas

D-U-N-S 20-643-2721   (BR)
ENTREPRISES JMC (1973) LTEE, LES
MCDONALD'S
(*Suby of* Entreprises JMC (1973) Ltee, Les)
500 Voie De La Desserte, Saint-Constant, QC,
J5A 2S5
(450) 635-4100
Emp Here 64
SIC 5812 Eating places

D-U-N-S 24-421-3265   (BR)
GROUPE CHAMPLAIN INC
CENTRE D'HEBERGEMENT CHAMPLAIN-JEAN-LOUIS-LAPIERRE
(*Suby of* Groupe Sante Sedna Inc)
199 Rue Saint-Pierre, Saint-Constant, QC,
J5A 2N8
(450) 632-4451
Emp Here 75
SIC 8361 Residential care

D-U-N-S 20-715-5628   (BR)
GROUPE SPORTSCENE INC
CAGE AUX SPORTS DE ST CONSTANT (LA)
280 Voie De La Desserte, Saint-Constant, QC,
J5A 2C9
(450) 635-0111
Emp Here 35
SIC 5812 Eating places

D-U-N-S 25-368-1589   (BR)
HOME DEPOT OF CANADA INC
HOME DEPOT
(*Suby of* The Home Depot Inc)
490 Voie De La Desserte Bureau 132, Saint-Constant, QC, J5A 2S6
(450) 633-2030
Emp Here 100
SIC 5251 Hardware stores

D-U-N-S 20-253-7890   (HQ)
MAILLOUX BAILLARGEON INC
(*Suby of* Coradin Inc)
222 Rue Saint-Pierre, Saint-Constant, QC,
J5A 2A2
(514) 861-8417
Emp Here 59   *Emp Total* 546
Sales 5,107,249
SIC 3999 Manufacturing industries, nec
Pr Pr Raynald Ostiguy

D-U-N-S 24-346-3184   (BR)
MARCHE LAMBERT ET FRERES INC
IGA
(*Suby of* Investissements B.I.L. Inc)
400 132 Rte, Saint-Constant, QC, J5A 2J8

Emp Here 100
SIC 5411 Grocery stores

D-U-N-S 24-226-7941   (BR)
SOBEYS QUEBEC INC
MARCHES FRERES LAMBERT, LES
400 132 Rte Bureau 100, Saint-Constant, QC,
J5A 2J8

Emp Here 100
SIC 5411 Grocery stores

D-U-N-S 24-207-4214   (BR)
WAL-MART CANADA CORP

WALMART
500 Voie De La Desserte Unite 132, Saint-Constant, QC, J5A 2S5
(450) 632-2192
Emp Here 100
SIC 5311 Department stores

Saint-Cyprien, QC G0L

D-U-N-S 24-179-2659   (BR)
MALLETTE S.E.N.C.R.L.
197 Rue Principale, Saint-Cyprien, QC, G0L
2P0

Emp Here 20
SIC 8721 Accounting, auditing, and book-keeping

Saint-Cyprien-De-Napierville, QC J0J

D-U-N-S 24-224-0062   (BR)
FLYING J CANADA INC
1 Rang Saint Andre, Saint-Cyprien-De-Napierville, QC, J0J 1L0
(450) 245-3539
Emp Here 30
SIC 5541 Gasoline service stations

Saint-Cyprien-Des-Etchemins, QC G0R
L'Islet County

D-U-N-S 20-166-3205   (BR)
COMMISSION SCOLAIRE DE LA BEAUCE-ETCHEMIN
ECOLE PETITE ABEILLE
404 Rue Principale, Saint-Cyprien-Des-Etchemins, QC, G0R 1B0
(418) 228-5541
Emp Here 20
SIC 8211 Elementary and secondary schools

D-U-N-S 24-349-2100   (SL)
SCIERIE BERNARD INC
225 2e Rang E, Saint-Cyprien-Des-Etchemins, QC, G0R 1B0
(418) 383-3242
Emp Here 22   *Sales* 6,087,000
SIC 1522 Residential construction, nec
Pt Ghyslain Bernard

Saint-Cyrille-De-Wendover, QC J1Z

D-U-N-S 24-987-8026   (BR)
ABATTOIR COLBEX INC
(*Suby of* Abattoir Colbex Inc)
455 4e Rang De Simpson, Saint-Cyrille-De-Wendover, QC, J1Z 1T8

Emp Here 80
SIC 2011 Meat packing plants

D-U-N-S 20-867-4163   (BR)
CAISSE POPULAIRE DESJARDINS DE L'EST DE DRUMMOND
4155 Rue Principale, Saint-Cyrille-De-Wendover, QC, J1Z 1C7
(819) 397-4243
Emp Here 40
SIC 6062 State credit unions

D-U-N-S 25-240-2102   (BR)
COMMISSION SCOLAIRE DES CHENES
ECOLE CYRILLE BRASSARD
(*Suby of* Commission Scolaire des Chenes)
4565 Rue Principale, Saint-Cyrille-De-

Wendover, QC, J1Z 1E4
(819) 397-4229
Emp Here 60
SIC 8211 Elementary and secondary schools

D-U-N-S 25-757-0333   (SL)
SECURITE ABCO INC
1215 Rue Des Bouleaux, Saint-Cyrille-De-Wendover, QC, J1Z 1L5
(819) 477-7618
Emp Here 30   *Sales* 5,889,600
SIC 6211 Security brokers and dealers
Pr Michel Arguin

Saint-Damase, QC J0H

D-U-N-S 20-913-7111   (BR)
COMMISSION SCOLAIRE DE SAINT-HYACINTHE, LA
ECOLE ST DAMASE
18 Rue Saint-Joseph, Saint-Damase, QC, J0H
1J0
(450) 773-8355
Emp Here 20
SIC 8211 Elementary and secondary schools

D-U-N-S 20-109-6059   (BR)
COOP FEDEREE, LA
OLYMEL
249 Rue Principale, Saint-Damase, QC, J0H
1J0
(450) 797-2691
Emp Here 350
SIC 5191 Farm supplies

D-U-N-S 25-705-8826   (BR)
EXCELDOR COOPERATIVE
PRODUITS EXCELDOR, LES
125 Rue Sainte-Anne Gd, Saint-Damase, QC,
J0H 1J0
(450) 797-3331
Emp Here 250
SIC 2011 Meat packing plants

D-U-N-S 24-515-5759   (SL)
MEUBLES ST-DAMASE INC, LES
SAINT-DAMASE MOBILIER HOTELIER
246 Rue Principale Bureau 1, Saint-Damase,
QC, J0H 1J0
(450) 797-3702
Emp Here 60   *Sales* 4,146,248
SIC 2599 Furniture and fixtures, nec

D-U-N-S 20-212-1542   (BR)
OLYMEL S.E.C.
OLYMEL FLAMINGO SAINT DAMASE
249 Rue Principale, Saint-Damase, QC, J0H
1J0
(450) 797-3382
Emp Here 355
SIC 2015 Poultry slaughtering and processing

Saint-Damase-Des-Aulnaies, QC G0R

D-U-N-S 24-792-6645   (SL)
COUTURE C G H INC
12 Rue Belanger, Saint-Damase-Des-Aulnaies, QC, G0R 2X0
(418) 598-3208
Emp Here 80   *Sales* 4,961,328
SIC 2339 Women's and misses' outerwear,
nec

Saint-Damien-De-Buckland, QC G0R
Bellechasse County

D-U-N-S 25-022-6610   (BR)
COMMISSION SCOLAIRE DE LA COTE-DU-SUD, LA

ECOLE DES RAYONS DE SOLEIL
75 Rte Saint-Gerard, Saint-Damien-De-Buckland, QC, G0R 2Y0
(418) 789-2871
Emp Here 20
SIC 8211 Elementary and secondary schools

D-U-N-S 25-233-7654   (BR)
COMMISSION SCOLAIRE DE LA COTE-DU-SUD, LA
ECOLE SECONDAIRE DE SAINT-DAMIEN
70 Rte Saint-Gerard, Saint-Damien-De-Buckland, QC, G0R 2Y0
(418) 789-2437
Emp Here 75
SIC 8211 Elementary and secondary schools

Saint-Dominique, QC J0H
Bagot County

D-U-N-S 25-240-5873   (BR)
COMMISSION SCOLAIRE DE SAINT-HYACINTHE, LA
ECOLE DE LA ROCADE
1236 Rue Principale, Saint-Dominique, QC, J0H 1L0
(450) 773-7223
Emp Here 24
SIC 8211 Elementary and secondary schools

Saint-Donat-De-Montcalm, QC J0T

D-U-N-S 24-890-8253   (BR)
CENTRES JEUNESSE DE LANAUDIERE, LES
(*Suby of* Centres Jeunesse de Lanaudiere, Les)
557 329 Rte, Saint-Donat-De-Montcalm, QC, J0T 2C0

Emp Here 60
SIC 8361 Residential care

D-U-N-S 25-232-8299   (BR)
COMMISSION SCOLAIRE DES LAUREN-TIDES
ECOLE SACRE COEUR
(*Suby of* Commission Scolaire Des Lauren-tides)
429 Rue Du College, Saint-Donat-De-Montcalm, QC, J0T 2C0
(819) 324-8674
Emp Here 30
SIC 8211 Elementary and secondary schools

D-U-N-S 20-706-9332   (BR)
SUPERMARCHE BOUCHER INC
METRO BOUCHER
870 Rue Principale, Saint-Donat-De-Montcalm, QC, J0T 2C0
(819) 424-7679
Emp Here 60
SIC 5411 Grocery stores

Saint-Edouard-De-Lotbiniere, QC G0S
Lotbiniere County

D-U-N-S 25-688-8652   (BR)
COMMISSION SCOLAIRE DES NAVIGA-TEURS
ECOLE DU CHENE
105 Rue De L'Ecole, Saint-Edouard-De-Lotbiniere, QC, G0S 1Y0
(418) 796-2433
Emp Here 20
SIC 8211 Elementary and secondary schools

Saint-Edouard-De-Napierville, QC J0L

D-U-N-S 20-287-7635   (SL)
9254-7553 QUEBEC INC.
TRITERRA GREENHOUSES
516, Rang Des Sloan, Saint-Edouard-De-Napierville, QC, J0L 1Y0

Emp Here 50   *Sales* 3,652,200
SIC 7389 Business services, nec

Saint-Elie-De-Caxton, QC G0X

D-U-N-S 20-795-1463   (BR)
COMMISSION SCOLAIRE DE L'ENERGIE
ECOLE VILLA DE LA JEUNESSE
2261 Av Principale, Saint-Elie-De-Caxton, QC, G0X 2N0
(819) 221-2087
Emp Here 20
SIC 8211 Elementary and secondary schools

Saint-Elzear, QC G0S
Beauce County

D-U-N-S 20-711-9400   (BR)
COMMISSION SCOLAIRE DE LA BEAUCE-ETCHEMIN
ECOLE NOTRE-DAME DE ST-ELZEAR
668 Av Principale Ss 9, Saint-Elzear, QC, G0S 2J2
(418) 387-6273
Emp Here 25
SIC 8211 Elementary and secondary schools

D-U-N-S 20-331-7628   (HQ)
TEXEL MATERIAUX TECHNIQUES INC
TEXEL MATERIAUX TECHNIQUES
(*Suby of* Lydall, Inc.)
485 Rue Des Erables, Saint-Elzear, QC, G0S 2J0
(418) 387-5910
Emp Here 250   *Emp Total* 2,700
SIC 2297 Nonwoven fabrics

Saint-Elzear-De-Bonaventure, QC G0C
Bonaventure County

D-U-N-S 25-195-2008   (SL)
SCIERIE ST-ELZEAR INC
215 Rte De L'Eglise, Saint-Elzear-De-Bonaventure, QC, G0C 2W0
(418) 534-2596
Emp Here 200   *Sales* 26,124,800
SIC 2421 Sawmills and planing mills, general
Genl Mgr Alain Tremblay
Ch Bd Sylvain Poirier

Saint-Ephrem-De-Beauce, QC G0M
Beauce County

D-U-N-S 20-249-1692   (SL)
COOP ALLIANCE, LA
470 271 Rte S Rr 1, Saint-Ephrem-De-Beauce, QC, G0M 1R0
(418) 484-2890
Emp Here 35   *Sales* 8,638,080
SIC 2048 Prepared feeds, nec
Genl Mgr Marco Nadeau
Pr Pr Mathieu Couture

D-U-N-S 20-516-3439   (SL)
INDUSTRIES LONGCHAMPS LTEE, LES
25 Boul Saint-Joseph, Saint-Ephrem-De-Beauce, QC, G0M 1R0
(418) 484-2080
Emp Here 60   *Sales* 3,064,349
SIC 7389 Business services, nec

D-U-N-S 20-266-0700   (BR)
MASONITE INTERNATIONAL CORPORA-TION
PORTES BAILLARGEON, LES
(*Suby of* Masonite International Corporation)
430 Rte 108 O Bureau 489, Saint-Ephrem-De-Beauce, QC, G0M 1R0
(418) 484-5666
Emp Here 110
SIC 2431 Millwork

D-U-N-S 24-145-7902   (HQ)
RENE MATERIAUX COMPOSITES LTEE
55 Rte 271 S, Saint-Ephrem-De-Beauce, QC, G0M 1R0
(418) 484-5282
Emp Here 50   *Emp Total* 600
Sales 84,719,348
SIC 3714 Motor vehicle parts and accessories
Denis Bertrand

Saint-Epiphane, QC G0L
Riviere-Du-Loup County

D-U-N-S 20-137-6949   (BR)
GOUVERNEMENT DE LA PROVINCE DE QUEBEC
CENTRE DE SANTE ET DE SERVICES DE RIVIERE-DU-LOUP
211 Rue Du Couvent, Saint-Epiphane, QC, G0L 2X0
(418) 868-2572
Emp Here 20
SIC 8399 Social services, nec

Saint-Esprit, QC J0K
Montcalm County

D-U-N-S 25-233-5351   (BR)
COMMISSION SCOLAIRE DES SAMARES
ECOLE DOMINIQUE SAVIO
39 Rue Des Ecoles Bureau 51, Saint-Esprit, QC, J0K 2L0
(450) 758-3737
Emp Here 27
SIC 8211 Elementary and secondary schools

D-U-N-S 25-010-4908   (BR)
OLYMEL S.E.C.
TRANSPORT TRANSBO
57 125 Rte, Saint-Esprit, QC, J0K 2L0
(450) 839-7258
Emp Here 80
SIC 4212 Local trucking, without storage

D-U-N-S 24-125-2787   (BR)
OLYMEL S.E.C.
FLAMINGO
125 Rue Saint-Isidore, Saint-Esprit, QC, J0K 2L0
(450) 839-7258
Emp Here 700
SIC 2011 Meat packing plants

D-U-N-S 24-327-7584   (BR)
OLYMEL S.E.C.
OLYMEL SEC DE SAINT-ESPRIT
57 125 Rte, Saint-Esprit, QC, J0K 2L0
(450) 839-7258
Emp Here 700
SIC 2011 Meat packing plants

D-U-N-S 24-764-0985   (BR)
SUPRALIMENT S.E.C.
25 125 Rte E, Saint-Esprit, QC, J0K 2L0
(450) 839-7258
Emp Here 800

SIC 2011 Meat packing plants

Saint-Etienne-De-Beauharnois, QC J0S

D-U-N-S 20-573-7104   (BR)
HYDRO-QUEBEC
HYDRO QUEBEC POSTE CHATEAUGUAY
610 Rang Saint-Laurent, Saint-Etienne-De-Beauharnois, QC, J0S 1S0
(450) 225-5110
Emp Here 40
SIC 4911 Electric services

Saint-Etienne-De-Lauzon, QC G6J

D-U-N-S 20-581-7489   (SL)
ENTREPRISES LEVISIENNES INC, LES
215 Rue Principale, Saint-Etienne-De-Lauzon, QC, G6J 0B9
(418) 831-4111
Emp Here 58   *Sales* 9,128,880
SIC 1611 Highway and street construction
Pr Pr Jean-Guy Bergeron
VP VP Roger Bergeron
Claude Bergeron

Saint-Etienne-Des-Gres, QC G0X

D-U-N-S 25-888-5227   (BR)
ARRISCRAFT CANADA INC
ARRISCRAFT INTERNATIONAL LIMITED PARTNERSHIP
500 Boul De La Gabelle, Saint-Etienne-Des-Gres, QC, G0X 2P0
(819) 535-1717
Emp Here 20
SIC 3271 Concrete block and brick

D-U-N-S 24-368-8038   (BR)
CAISSE DESJARDINS DE L'OUEST DE LA MAURICIE
CENTRE DE SERVICES SAINT-ETIENNE-DES-GRES
(*Suby of* Caisse Desjardins de l'Ouest de la Mauricie)
1234 Rue Principale, Saint-Etienne-Des-Gres, QC, G0X 2P0
(819) 535-2018
Emp Here 100
SIC 6062 State credit unions

D-U-N-S 25-467-7966   (BR)
COMMISSION SCOLAIRE DU CHEMIN-DU-ROY
ECOLE AMI JOIE ET DES GRES
165 Rue Saint-Joseph Rr 2, Saint-Etienne-Des-Gres, QC, G0X 2P0
(819) 840-4322
Emp Here 40
SIC 8211 Elementary and secondary schools

D-U-N-S 20-255-0729   (SL)
CONSTRUCTION ET PAVAGE BOISVERT INC
180 Boul De La Gabelle, Saint-Etienne-Des-Gres, QC, G0X 2P0
(819) 374-7277
Emp Here 50   *Sales* 3,648,035
SIC 1794 Excavation work

D-U-N-S 25-503-4233   (BR)
WASTE MANAGEMENT OF CANADA COR-PORATION
(*Suby of* Waste Management, Inc.)
460 Boul La Gabelle, Saint-Etienne-Des-Gres, QC, G0X 2P0

Emp Here 30

SIC 4953 Refuse systems

Saint-Eugene-De-Grantham, QC J0C

D-U-N-S 24-737-1276   (BR)
BETONS PREFABRIQUES TRANS-CANADA INC
(*Suby of* 9131-9095 Quebec Inc)
454 Rang De L'Eglise, Saint-Eugene-De-Grantham, QC, J0C 1J0
(819) 396-2624
Emp Here 25
SIC 5032 Brick, stone, and related material

D-U-N-S 25-991-1329   (SL)
ENTREPRISES INTERCO INC, LES
456 Rang Brodeur, Saint-Eugene-De-Grantham, QC, J0C 1J0
(819) 396-0003
Emp Here 50   *Sales* 4,888,367
SIC 2448 Wood pallets and skids

D-U-N-S 24-074-2838   (BR)
FORESBEC INC
FORESFLOOR
484 Rang Brodeur, Saint-Eugene-De-Grantham, QC, J0C 1J0
(819) 477-8787
Emp Here 225
SIC 5031 Lumber, plywood, and millwork

Saint-Eusebe, QC G0L
Temiscouata County

D-U-N-S 20-721-5229   (SL)
BARDEAUX LAJOIE INC, LES
101 10e Rang E Rr 2, Saint-Eusebe, QC, G0L 2Y0
(418) 899-2541
Emp Here 50   *Sales* 7,536,000
SIC 2429 Special product sawmills, nec
Pr Pr Denis Lajoie

Saint-Eustache, QC J7P
Deux-Montagnes County

D-U-N-S 20-314-0389   (SL)
4417194 CANADA INC
CINEMA ST-EUSTAGE
305 Av Mathers, Saint-Eustache, QC, J7P 4C1
(450) 472-7086
Emp Here 60   *Sales* 2,334,742
SIC 7832 Motion picture theaters, except drive-in

D-U-N-S 25-701-3102   (SL)
9038-7200 QUEBEC INC
TIM HORTONS
255 25e Av Bureau 926, Saint-Eustache, QC, J7P 4Y1
(450) 974-3493
Emp Here 50   *Sales* 1,678,096
SIC 5461 Retail bakeries

D-U-N-S 20-297-9790   (SL)
9063-6465 QUEBEC INC
SAINT-EUSTACHE NISSAN
272 Rue Dubois, Saint-Eustache, QC, J7P 4W9
(514) 875-3922
Emp Here 25   *Sales* 12,140,000
SIC 5511 New and used car dealers
Pr Daniel Renaud

D-U-N-S 20-580-3567   (BR)
CANADA POST CORPORATION
405 Boul Arthur-Sauve, Saint-Eustache, QC, J7P 2B2

(450) 473-6474
Emp Here 60
SIC 4311 U.s. postal service

D-U-N-S 25-240-2318   (BR)
COMMISSION SCOLAIRE DE LA SEIGNEURIE-DES-MILLE-ILES
COMMISSION SCOLAIRE DE LA SEIGNEURIE-DES-MILLE-ILES
(*Suby of* Commission Scolaire de la Seigneurie-Des-Mille-Iles)
425 Rue Hamel, Saint-Eustache, QC, J7P 4M2
(450) 472-1440
Emp Here 60
SIC 8211 Elementary and secondary schools

D-U-N-S 25-240-2193   (BR)
COMMISSION SCOLAIRE DE LA SEIGNEURIE-DES-MILLE-ILES
COMMISSION SCOLAIRE DE LA SEIGNEURIE-DES-MILLE-ILES
(*Suby of* Commission Scolaire de la Seigneurie-Des-Mille-Iles)
99 Rue Grignon, Saint-Eustache, QC, J7P 4S4
(450) 472-6060
Emp Here 190
SIC 8211 Elementary and secondary schools

D-U-N-S 25-233-2846   (BR)
COMMISSION SCOLAIRE DE LA SEIGNEURIE-DES-MILLE-ILES
COMMISSION SCOLAIRE DE LA SEIGNEURIE-DES-MILLE-ILES
(*Suby of* Commission Scolaire de la Seigneurie-Des-Mille-Iles)
128 25e Av, Saint-Eustache, QC, J7P 2V2
(450) 473-9219
Emp Here 50
SIC 8211 Elementary and secondary schools

D-U-N-S 25-233-7399   (BR)
COMMISSION SCOLAIRE DE LA SEIGNEURIE-DES-MILLE-ILES
COMMISSION SCOLAIRE DE LA SEIGNEURIE-DES-MILLE-ILES
(*Suby of* Commission Scolaire de la Seigneurie-Des-Mille-Iles)
250 Rue Therrien, Saint-Eustache, QC, J7P 4V4
(450) 472-5240
Emp Here 45
SIC 8211 Elementary and secondary schools

D-U-N-S 20-302-4757   (SL)
GESTION MAHEL INC
HAMEL AUTO DIRECT
130 Rue Dubois, Saint-Eustache, QC, J7P 4W9
(450) 974-0440
Emp Here 78   *Sales* 2,334,742
SIC 5812 Eating places

D-U-N-S 20-961-4130   (SL)
GROUPE CYR INC
104 Rue Dubois, Saint-Eustache, QC, J7P 4W9
(450) 472-5332
Emp Here 75   *Sales* 9,344,640
SIC 6411 Insurance agents, brokers, and service
Pr Jean-Jacques Cyr
VP Edith Cyr

D-U-N-S 20-137-9398   (BR)
GROUPE PROMUTUEL FEDERATION DE SOCIETE MUTUELLES D'ASSURANCES GENERALES
PROMUTUEL DEUX MONTAGNES
200 Rue Dubois, Saint-Eustache, QC, J7P 4W9
(450) 623-5774
Emp Here 40
SIC 6411 Insurance agents, brokers, and service

D-U-N-S 25-909-1726   (SL)
GROUPE TORA INC

ROTISSERIE SCORES
413 Boul Arthur-Sauve, Saint-Eustache, QC, J7P 2B2
(450) 491-6060
Emp Here 60   *Sales* 1,824,018
SIC 5812 Eating places

D-U-N-S 24-326-1182   (SL)
LOUKIL, SAID
ESPUMA
247 Rue Isabelle, Saint-Eustache, QC, J7P 4E9

Emp Here 20   *Sales* 8,147,280
SIC 5111 Printing and writing paper
Pr Said Loukil
VP Simha Loukil
Anissalah Loukil
Treas Misie-Sandra Loukil

D-U-N-S 24-811-1478   (SL)
PAQUETTE, ROBERT AUTOBUS & FILS INC
222 25e Av, Saint-Eustache, QC, J7P 4Z8
(450) 473-4526
Emp Here 120   *Sales* 3,356,192
SIC 4151 School buses

D-U-N-S 25-462-7995   (BR)
PROVIGO DISTRIBUTION INC
MAXI
199 25e Av, Saint-Eustache, QC, J7P 2V1
(450) 491-5588
Emp Here 42
SIC 5411 Grocery stores

D-U-N-S 25-814-1183   (HQ)
SAULNIER AUTOMOBILES INC
KIA ST-EUSTACHE
(*Suby of* Saulnier Automobiles Inc)
160 Rue Dubois, Saint-Eustache, QC, J7P 4W9
(450) 623-9004
Emp Here 48   *Emp Total* 60
Sales 30,435,000
SIC 5511 New and used car dealers
Pr Pr Andre Hebert

D-U-N-S 25-294-5738   (BR)
SEARS CANADA INC
SEARS ST EUSTACHE
379 Boul Arthur-Sauve, Saint-Eustache, QC, J7P 2B1
(450) 491-5000
Emp Here 85
SIC 5311 Department stores

D-U-N-S 25-027-6771   (BR)
SOBEYS QUEBEC INC
IGA
299 Boul Arthur-Sauve, Saint-Eustache, QC, J7P 2B1
(450) 472-1558
Emp Here 75
SIC 5411 Grocery stores

D-U-N-S 25-701-0454   (BR)
UNION DES PRODUCTEURS AGRICOLE, L'
U P A OUTAOUAIS LAURENTIDES
(*Suby of* Union des Producteurs Agricole, l')
15 Ch De La Grande-Cote Bureau 2, Saint-Eustache, QC, J7P 5L3
(450) 472-0440
Emp Here 58
SIC 8631 Labor organizations

Saint-Eustache, QC J7R
Deux-Montagnes County

D-U-N-S 24-710-1728   (SL)
AUTOBUS G.D. INC, LES
10 Ch Du Petit-Chicot, Saint-Eustache, QC, J7R 4K3
(450) 473-5114
Emp Here 55   *Sales* 1,532,175
SIC 4151 School buses

D-U-N-S 24-973-7453   (BR)
BANQUE NATIONALE DU CANADA
NATIONAL BANK
761 Boul Arthur-Sauve, Saint-Eustache, QC, J7R 4K3
(450) 472-8772
Emp Here 45
SIC 6021 National commercial banks

D-U-N-S 24-324-6014   (SL)
BRULEURS COEN CANADA INC, LES
COEN CANADA
(*Suby of* Koch Industries, Inc.)
226 Rue Roy, Saint-Eustache, QC, J7R 5R6

Emp Here 34   *Sales* 3,137,310
SIC 3433 Heating equipment, except electric

D-U-N-S 20-591-7198   (SL)
CENTRE DES MOTS CROISES INC
EDITIONS BLAINVILLE DE MONTAGNE, LES
53 Rue Saint-Eustache Bureau 250, Saint-Eustache, QC, J7R 2L2
(450) 473-1700
Emp Here 50   *Sales* 4,158,760
SIC 2711 Newspapers

D-U-N-S 24-851-7844   (BR)
CENTRE INTEGRE DE SANTE ET DE SERVICES SOCIAUX DES LAURENTIDES
CENTRE INTEGRE DE SANTE ET DE SERVICES SOCIAUX DES
29 Ch D'Oka, Saint-Eustache, QC, J7R 1K6
(450) 491-1233
Emp Here 300
SIC 8062 General medical and surgical hospitals

D-U-N-S 20-634-4731   (HQ)
CHRISTIE INNOMED INC
(*Suby of* Groupe Christie Inc)
516 Rue Dufour, Saint-Eustache, QC, J7R 0C3
(450) 472-9120
Emp Here 80   *Emp Total* 1
Sales 22,617,817
SIC 5047 Medical and hospital equipment
Ch Bd Erik Grandjean
Pr Martin Roy
Dir Michel Vachon
Dir Leonard Aucoin
Dir Marcel Ostiguy
Dir Josee Morin

D-U-N-S 20-712-1489   (BR)
COMMISSION SCOLAIRE DE LA SEIGNEURIE-DES-MILLE-ILES
COMMISSION SCOLAIRE DE LA SEIGNEURIE-DES-MILLE-ILES
799 Montee Lauzon, Saint-Eustache, QC, J7R 0J1
(450) 473-5614
Emp Here 50
SIC 8211 Elementary and secondary schools

D-U-N-S 20-913-7202   (BR)
COMMISSION SCOLAIRE DE LA SEIGNEURIE-DES-MILLE-ILES
COMMISSION SCOLAIRE DE LA SEIGNEURIE-DES-MILLE-ILES
130 Boul Louis-Joseph-Rodrigue, Saint-Eustache, QC, J7R 5Y5
(450) 472-7801
Emp Here 60
SIC 8211 Elementary and secondary schools

D-U-N-S 25-976-1112   (BR)
COMMISSION SCOLAIRE DE LA SEIGNEURIE-DES-MILLE-ILES
COMMISSION SCOLAIRE DE LA SEIGNEURIE-DES-MILLE-ILES
(*Suby of* Commission Scolaire de la Seigneurie-Des-Mille-Iles)
990 Rue Des Erables, Saint-Eustache, QC, J7R 6M5
(450) 491-5065
Emp Here 28

SIC 8211 Elementary and secondary schools

D-U-N-S 25-292-9179   (BR)
COMMISSION SCOLAIRE DE LA SEIGNEURIE-DES-MILLE-ILES
COMMISSION SCOLAIRE DE LA SEIGNEURIE-DES-MILLE-ILES
(*Suby of* Commission Scolaire de la Seigneurie-Des-Mille-Iles)
151 Rue Saint-Louis, Saint-Eustache, QC, J7R 1X9
(450) 473-2933
Emp Here 50
SIC 8211 Elementary and secondary schools

D-U-N-S 25-222-5776   (BR)
COMMISSION SCOLAIRE DE LA SEIGNEURIE-DES-MILLE-ILES
COMMISSION SCOLAIRE DE LA SEIGNEURIE-DES-MILLE-ILES
(*Suby of* Commission Scolaire de la Seigneurie-Des-Mille-Iles)
16 Rue Perry, Saint-Eustache, QC, J7R 2H3
(450) 473-7422
Emp Here 35
SIC 8211 Elementary and secondary schools

D-U-N-S 25-541-4732   (HQ)
COMMISSION SCOLAIRE DE LA SEIGNEURIE-DES-MILLE-ILES
(*Suby of* Commission Scolaire de la Seigneurie-Des-Mille-Iles)
430 Boul Arthur-Sauve Bureau 3050, Saint-Eustache, QC, J7R 6V7
(450) 974-7000
Emp Here 175   *Emp Total* 3,307
Sales 285,431,454
SIC 8211 Elementary and secondary schools
Dir Fin Daniel Trempe
Genl Mgr Jean-Francois Lachance

D-U-N-S 20-330-6535   (BR)
CONCORD PREMIUM MEATS LTD
VIANDES CONCORD, LES
160 Rue Williams, Saint-Eustache, QC, J7R 0A4
(450) 623-7676
Emp Here 100
SIC 5147 Meats and meat products

D-U-N-S 20-180-0989   (HQ)
DISTRIBUTION BATH FITTER INC
BAIN MAGIQUE
(*Suby of* Bath Fitter Tennessee, Inc.)
225 Rue Roy, Saint-Eustache, QC, J7R 5R5
(450) 472-0024
Emp Here 190   *Emp Total* 190
Sales 27,893,282
SIC 5211 Lumber and other building materials
Pr Glenn Cotton
Treas Brian Cotton
Dir Raffi Apanian

D-U-N-S 24-277-3963   (BR)
FAMILIPRIX INC
380 Boul Arthur-Sauve Bureau 1781, Saint-Eustache, QC, J7R 2J4
(450) 983-3121
Emp Here 20
SIC 5912 Drug stores and proprietary stores

D-U-N-S 24-205-0057   (SL)
FIDUCIE FAMILLE VACHON INC
516 Rue Du Parc, Saint-Eustache, QC, J7R 5B2
(450) 472-9120
Emp Here 135   *Sales* 29,842,560
SIC 6712 Bank holding companies
Pr Robert M Vachon Jr
Ex VP Andre Dugas

D-U-N-S 25-674-7619   (SL)
GESTION GERALD PEPIN INC
420 Rue Du Parc, Saint-Eustache, QC, J7R 0H2
(450) 473-1889
Emp Here 21   *Sales* 5,376,850
SIC 1542 Nonresidential construction, nec

Pr Gerald Pepin

D-U-N-S 20-302-5440   (BR)
GROUPE BMTC INC
ECONOMAX
640 Boul Arthur-Sauve, Saint-Eustache, QC, J7R 5A8
(450) 473-6767
Emp Here 20
SIC 5712 Furniture stores

D-U-N-S 25-770-0948   (SL)
GROUPE NEPVEU INC, LE
75 Rue Daoust, Saint-Eustache, QC, J7R 5B7
(450) 472-5166
Emp Here 65   *Sales* 8,289,996
SIC 4212 Local trucking, without storage
VP VP Benoit Nepveu
 Martin Nepveu
VP VP Jean-Marc Nepveu

D-U-N-S 24-226-2579   (BR)
GROUPE VOLVO CANADA INC
NOVA BUS
1000 Boul Industriel Bureau 1160, Saint-Eustache, QC, J7R 5A5
(450) 472-6410
Emp Here 500
SIC 3711 Motor vehicles and car bodies

D-U-N-S 20-007-2846   (BR)
INDUSTRIELLE ALLIANCE, ASSURANCE ET SERVICES FINANCIERS INC
INDUSTRIAL ALLIANCE LIFE INSURANCE
430 Boul Arthur-Sauve Bureau 2070, Saint-Eustache, QC, J7R 6V7
(450) 473-9808
Emp Here 40
SIC 6311 Life insurance

D-U-N-S 25-833-5447   (BR)
LUSSIER, BERNARD INC
PHARMACIE JEAN COUTU
578 Boul Arthur-Sauve Bureau 231, Saint-Eustache, QC, J7R 5A8
(450) 473-2711
Emp Here 30
SIC 5912 Drug stores and proprietary stores

D-U-N-S 20-290-6772   (BR)
MATERIAUX DE CONSTRUCTION OLD-CASTLE CANADA INC, LES
TRANSPAVE INCSIEGE SOCIAL
500 Rue Saint-Eustache, Saint-Eustache, QC, J7R 7E7
(450) 491-7800
Emp Here 55
SIC 5039 Construction materials, nec

D-U-N-S 20-572-0456   (BR)
METRO RICHELIEU INC
SUPER C
580 Boul Arthur-Sauve, Saint-Eustache, QC, J7R 5A8
(450) 623-7875
Emp Here 70
SIC 5141 Groceries, general line

D-U-N-S 25-299-9388   (BR)
PRISZM LP
POULET FRIT KENTUCKY
104 Boul Arthur-Sauve, Saint-Eustache, QC, J7R 2H7
(450) 473-2474
Emp Here 20
SIC 5812 Eating places

D-U-N-S 20-280-7041   (BR)
SIMARD-BEAUDRY CONSTRUCTION INC
699 Boul Industriel, Saint-Eustache, QC, J7R 6C3

Emp Here 100
SIC 1442 Construction sand and gravel

D-U-N-S 24-313-5733   (BR)
STAPLES CANADA INC
BUREAU EN GROS
(*Suby of* Staples, Inc.)

660 Boul Arthur-Sauve, Saint-Eustache, QC, J7R 5A8
(450) 623-4543
Emp Here 30
SIC 5943 Stationery stores

D-U-N-S 25-285-8097   (SL)
TRI-TEXCO INC
BARTEX
1001 Boul Industriel, Saint-Eustache, QC, J7R 6C3
(450) 974-1001
Emp Here 100   *Sales* 19,188,664
SIC 2865 Cyclic crudes and intermediates
Ch Bd Aaron Davenport
 Natalie Laham
Dir Naim Laham
Dir Barry Penney

D-U-N-S 20-651-6739   (BR)
WAL-MART CANADA CORP
764 Boul Arthur-Sauve Bureau 3089, Saint-Eustache, QC, J7R 4K3
(450) 491-6922
Emp Here 200
SIC 5311 Department stores

Saint-Evariste-De-Forsyth, QC G0M
Frontenac County

D-U-N-S 20-056-6292   (SL)
177417 CANADA INC
102 Rue Du Parc-Industriel, Saint-Evariste-De-Forsyth, QC, G0M 1S0
(418) 459-6443
Emp Here 55   *Sales* 8,927,600
SIC 3537 Industrial trucks and tractors
Pr Pr Camil Martin

Saint-Fabien-De-Panet, QC G0R
Bellechasse County

D-U-N-S 24-389-5716   (BR)
CENTRE DE SANTE ET SERVICES SOCI-AUX DE MONTMAGNY - L'ISLET
CLSC DE SAINT-FABIEN-DE-PANET
10 Rue Alphonse, Saint-Fabien-De-Panet, QC, G0R 2J0
(418) 249-2572
Emp Here 1,000
SIC 8062 General medical and surgical hospitals

D-U-N-S 20-213-1491   (BR)
CENTRE DE SANTE ET SERVICES SOCI-AUX DE MONTMAGNY - L'ISLET
CENTRE D'HEBERGEMENT DE SAINT-FABIEN-DE-PANET
19 Rue Principale E, Saint-Fabien-De-Panet, QC, G0R 2J0
(418) 249-4051
Emp Here 50
SIC 8059 Nursing and personal care, nec

Saint-Faustin-Lac-Carre, QC J0T
Terrebonne County

D-U-N-S 24-388-6913   (SL)
CONSTRUCTION VP INC
1450 Rte 117, Saint-Faustin-Lac-Carre, QC, J0T 1J2
(819) 688-3636
Emp Here 35   *Sales* 5,253,170
SIC 1521 Single-family housing construction
 Donald Provost

D-U-N-S 24-403-9426   (SL)
MONT BLANC SOCIETE EN COMMANDITE
CENTRE DE SKI MONT-BLANC

1006 Rte 117, Saint-Faustin-Lac-Carre, QC, J0T 1J2
(819) 688-2444
Emp Here 50   *Sales* 2,188,821
SIC 7011 Hotels and motels

Saint-Felicien, QC G8K
Lac-St-Jean-Est County

D-U-N-S 20-289-0943   (BR)
CAISSE DESJARDINS DU DOMAINE-DU-ROY
CENTRE DE SERVICE DE ST-FELICIEN
1297 Boul Du Sacre-Coeur, Saint-Felicien, QC, G8K 2R1
(418) 679-1381
Emp Here 20
SIC 6062 State credit unions

D-U-N-S 24-214-7002   (BR)
CENTRE DE SANTE ET DE SERVICES SO-CIAUX DOMAINE-DU-ROY
CSSS DOMAINE-DU-ROY
(*Suby of* Centre de Sante et de Services Sociaux Domaine-du-Roy)
1229 Boul Du Sacre-Coeur, Saint-Felicien, QC, G8K 1A5
(418) 679-1585
Emp Here 80
SIC 8361 Residential care

D-U-N-S 24-381-0256   (SL)
CENTRE DE TRANSMISSION J.D.H. INC
J D H PETERBILT DU LAC ST-JEAN, DIV DE
1451 Boul Industriel, Saint-Felicien, QC, G8K 1W1
(418) 679-5885
Emp Here 31   *Sales* 2,261,782
SIC 7537 Automotive transmission repair shops

D-U-N-S 20-253-4983   (BR)
EXCAVATION MICHEL PARADIS INC
FELCO
780 Boul Hamel, Saint-Felicien, QC, G8K 1X9
(418) 679-4533
Emp Here 80
SIC 1794 Excavation work

D-U-N-S 25-201-7579   (BR)
PF RESOLU CANADA INC
900 Boul Hamel, Saint-Felicien, QC, G8K 2X4
(418) 679-0552
Emp Here 97
SIC 2421 Sawmills and planing mills, general

D-U-N-S 20-302-4641   (SL)
PREMIERE VIDEO INC
LES ECURIES DANO
1269 Boul Du Sacre-Coeur, Saint-Felicien, QC, G8K 2R2
(418) 613-1122
Emp Here 50   *Sales* 1,824,018
SIC 7841 Video tape rental

D-U-N-S 24-790-7884   (HQ)
ST-FELICIEN DIESEL (1988) INC
(*Suby of* St-Felicien Diesel (1988) Inc)
981 Boul Hamel, Saint-Felicien, QC, G8K 2E3
(418) 679-2474
Emp Here 45   *Emp Total* 60
Sales 4,711,645
SIC 7699 Repair services, nec

D-U-N-S 20-582-3362   (SL)
TRANSPORT GERARD LAROUCHE & FILS LTEE
1499 Boul Du Sacre-Coeur, Saint-Felicien, QC, G8K 1B6
(418) 679-3751
Emp Here 60   *Sales* 4,742,446
SIC 4212 Local trucking, without storage

Saint-Felix-De-Kingsey, QC J0B
Drummomd County

D-U-N-S 25-233-4958   (BR)
COMMISSION SCOLAIRE DES CHENES
ECOLE SAINT-FELIX DE KINGSEY
(*Suby of* Commission Scolaire des Chenes)
6085 Rue Principale, Saint-Felix-De-Kingsey,
QC, J0B 2T0
(819) 850-1608
Emp Here 20
SIC 8211 Elementary and secondary schools

Saint-Felix-De-Valois, QC J0K
Joliette County

D-U-N-S 25-232-9081   (BR)
COMMISSION SCOLAIRE DES SAMARES
ECOLE NCTRE DAME ST FELIX
70 Rue Sainte-Marguerite, Saint-Felix-De-
Valois, QC, J0K 2M0
(450) 758-3562
Emp Here 20
SIC 8211 Elementary and secondary schools

D-U-N-S 24-355-8285   (SL)
COUVOIR JOLIBEC (1994) INC
90 Ch De Joliette, Saint-Felix-De-Valois, QC,
J0K 2M0
(450) 889-5561
Emp Here 26   *Sales* 7,913,100
SIC 5159 Farm-product raw materials, nec
Pr Claude Boire
VP Denis Boire
Treas Clement Boire

D-U-N-S 24-489-8607   (HQ)
ENTREPRISES GILLES BENNY INC, LES
RESTAURANT BENNY
(*Suby of* Entreprises Gilles Benny Inc, Les)
1010 Ch De Joliette, Saint-Felix-De-Valois,
QC, J0K 2M0
(450) 889-7272
Emp Here 45   *Emp Total* 65
Sales 1,969,939
SIC 5812 Eating places

D-U-N-S 25-736-7599   (SL)
TECHNOBEV S.E.C.
BREUVAGES KIRI
4130 Rue Principale, Saint-Felix-De-Valois,
QC, J0K 2M0

Emp Here 70   *Sales* 12,073,680
SIC 2086 Bottled and canned soft drinks
Dir Fin Jean-Claude Roy

Saint-Ferdinand, QC G0N
Megantic County

D-U-N-S 24-132-0337   (BR)
CAISSE DESJARDINS DU CARREFOUR DES LACS
CENTRE DE SERVICE SAINT FERDINAND
385 Rue Principale, Saint-Ferdinand, QC,
G0N 1N0
(418) 428-9509
Emp Here 39
SIC 6062 State credit unions

D-U-N-S 25-232-7861   (BR)
COMMISSION SCOLAIRE DES AP-PALACHES
ECOLE NOTRE-DAME
(*Suby of* Commission Scolaire des Ap-palaches)
620 Rue Notre-Dame, Saint-Ferdinand, QC,
G0N 1N0
(418) 428-3731
Emp Here 25

SIC 8211 Elementary and secondary schools

D-U-N-S 25-078-9393   (SL)
MANOIR DU LAC WILLIAM INC
3180 Rue Principale, Saint-Ferdinand, QC,
G0N 1N0
(418) 428-9188
Emp Here 60   *Sales* 2,626,585
SIC 7011 Hotels and motels

Saint-Ferreol-Les-Neiges, QC G0A

D-U-N-S 20-711-9889   (BR)
COMMISSION SCOLAIRE DES PREMIERES-SEIGNEURIES
COMMISSION SCOLAIRE DES PREMIERES-SEIGNEURIES
3455 Av Royale Bureau 1, Saint-Ferreol-Les-
Neiges, QC, G0A 3R0
(418) 821-8055
Emp Here 50
SIC 8211 Elementary and secondary schools

Saint-Flavien, QC G0S
Lotbiniere County

D-U-N-S 25-515-6697   (BR)
CENTRE DE SANTE ET DE SERVICES SO-CIAUX (CSSS) ALPHONSE-DESJARDINS
CENTRE DE SANTE ET DE SERVICE SO-CIAUX DU GRAND LITTORAL SITE SAINT-FLAVIEN
82 Rue Principale, Saint-Flavien, QC, G0S
2M0
(418) 728-2727
Emp Here 49
SIC 8361 Residential care

Saint-Francois-Du-Lac, QC J0G
Yamaska County

D-U-N-S 25-232-8257   (BR)
COMMISSION SCOLAIRE DE LA RIVERAINE
ECOLE VINCENT LEMIRE
(*Suby of* Commission Scolaire de la Riveraine)
20 Rue Du Centre-Communautaire, Saint-
Francois-Du-Lac, QC, J0G 1M0
(450) 568-2147
Emp Here 20
SIC 8211 Elementary and secondary schools

D-U-N-S 24-943-3210   (BR)
GROUPE VOLVO CANADA INC
NOVA BUS
155 Rte Marie-Victorin, Saint-Francois-Du-
Lac, QC, J0G 1M0
(450) 568-3335
Emp Here 130
SIC 3711 Motor vehicles and car bodies

D-U-N-S 24-776-1476   (SL)
NOVABUS CORPORATION
155 Rte Marie-Victorin, Saint-Francois-Du-
Lac, QC, J0G 1M0
(450) 568-3335
Emp Here 200   *Sales* 9,484,891
SIC 4142 Bus charter service, except local

Saint-Frederic, QC G0N
Beauce County

D-U-N-S 25-484-9037   (SL)
MULTI EXCEL INC
823 Rue Du Parc, Saint-Frederic, QC, G0N

1P0
(418) 426-3046
Emp Here 50   *Sales* 2,165,628
SIC 2789 Bookbinding and related work

Saint-Gabriel-De-Brandon, QC J0K

D-U-N-S 24-054-9105   (SL)
CENTRE D'ACCEUIL DESY INC
90 Rue Maskinonge, Saint-Gabriel-De-
Brandon, QC, J0K 2N0
(450) 835-4712
Emp Here 81   *Sales* 2,991,389
SIC 8361 Residential care

D-U-N-S 20-712-2008   (BR)
COMMISSION SCOLAIRE DES SAMARES
ECOLE DES GRANDS VENTS PAVILLON SACRE COEUR
35 Rue Dequoy, Saint-Gabriel-De-Brandon,
QC, J0K 2N0
(450) 758-3740
Emp Here 20
SIC 8211 Elementary and secondary schools

D-U-N-S 25-688-1921   (BR)
COMMISSION SCOLAIRE DES SAMARES
ECOLE REINE-MARIE 1 & 2
59 Rue Champagne, Saint-Gabriel-De-
Brandon, QC, J0K 2N0
(450) 758-3691
Emp Here 30
SIC 8211 Elementary and secondary schools

D-U-N-S 20-474-0018   (BR)
COMMISSION SCOLAIRE DES SAMARES
ECOLE SECONDAIRE BERMON
1919 6e Rang, Saint-Gabriel-De-Brandon,
QC, J0K 2N0
(450) 758-3640
Emp Here 32
SIC 8211 Elementary and secondary schools

Saint-Gabriel-De-Rimouski, QC G0K
Rimouski County

D-U-N-S 25-233-5138   (BR)
COMMISSION SCOLAIRE DES PHARES
ECOLE DES HAUTS-PLATEAUX PAVILLON MARIE-ELISABETH
(*Suby of* Commission Scolaire des Phares)
105 Rue Plourde, Saint-Gabriel-De-Rimouski,
QC, G0K 1M0
(418) 798-4951
Emp Here 20
SIC 8211 Elementary and secondary schools

Saint-Gabriel-De-Valcartier, QC G0A

D-U-N-S 20-953-6366   (SL)
ECOLE SECONDAIRE MONT SAINT-SACREMENT INC
200 Boul Saint-Sacrement Rr 791, Saint-
Gabriel-De-Valcartier, QC, G0A 4S0
(418) 844-3771
Emp Here 60   *Sales* 4,012,839
SIC 8211 Elementary and secondary schools

Saint-Gedeon, QC G0W
Lac-St-Jean-Est County

D-U-N-S 25-001-1376   (SL)
9122-9831 QUEBEC INC
AUBERGE DES ILES
250 Rang Des Iles, Saint-Gedeon, QC, G0W
2P0

(418) 345-2589
Emp Here 50   *Sales* 2,188,821
SIC 7011 Hotels and motels

Saint-Gedeon-De-Beauce, QC G0M
Frontenac County

D-U-N-S 20-711-9327   (BR)
COMMISSION SCOLAIRE DE LA BEAUCE-ETCHEMIN
ECOLE PRIMAIRE DE SAINT GEDEON
119 3e Av S, Saint-Gedeon-De-Beauce, QC,
G0M 1T0
(418) 582-3955
Emp Here 25
SIC 8211 Elementary and secondary schools

D-U-N-S 24-499-9157   (BR)
GROUPE CANAM INC
CANAM
115 Boul Canam N, Saint-Gedeon-De-
Beauce, QC, G0M 1T0
(418) 582-3331
Emp Here 700
SIC 3441 Fabricated structural Metal

Saint-Georges, QC G5Y
Champlain County

D-U-N-S 20-085-7535   (SL)
9042-0654 QUEBEC INC
2030 127e Rue, Saint-Georges, QC, G5Y
2W8
(418) 227-4279
Emp Here 90   *Sales* 17,963,280
SIC 6712 Bank holding companies
Pr Pr Marco Trudel

D-U-N-S 24-240-1680   (SL)
9053-3837 QUEBEC INC
11400 1re Av, Saint-Georges, QC, G5Y 5S4
(418) 227-1515
Emp Here 42   *Sales* 5,284,131
SIC 6712 Bank holding companies

D-U-N-S 20-030-0171   (HQ)
9074-1190 QUEBEC INC
SEIGNEURIE DU JASMIN
(*Suby of* 9074-1190 Quebec Inc)
11765 1re Av Bureau 317, Saint-Georges,
QC, G5Y 8G7
(418) 228-8685
Emp Here 28   *Emp Total* 63
Sales 2,334,742
SIC 8361 Residential care

D-U-N-S 25-258-4412   (SL)
9177-1436 QUEBEC INC
(*Suby of* Alta Limitee)
11505 1re Av Bureau 500, Saint-Georges,
QC, G5Y 7X3
(418) 228-8031
Emp Here 40   *Sales* 10,699,440
SIC 1541 Industrial buildings and warehouses
Pr Pr Marcel Blouin
VP Pierre Latreille
Sec Louis Guertin
  Marcel Dutil

D-U-N-S 20-264-8387   (BR)
AMEUBLEMENTS TANGUAY INC
8955 Boul Lacroix, Saint-Georges, QC, G5Y
5E2
(418) 226-4411
Emp Here 40
SIC 5021 Furniture

D-U-N-S 24-820-5148   (SL)
AUTHENTIQUE POSE CAFE INC, L'
BIOSPHERA
9555 10e Av, Saint-Georges, QC, G5Y 8J8
(418) 228-3191
Emp Here 55   *Sales* 13,534,416

SIC 5046 Commercial equipment, nec
 Michel Blais
Dir Pierre Ouellet
Dir Francois De L'Etoile
Dir Turcot Sylvain
Pr Pascal Theriault

D-U-N-S 20-722-7075   (SL)
AUTOBUS DES ERABLES LTEE
1200 38e Rue, Saint-Georges, QC, G5Y 6Y5
(418) 227-9207
Emp Here 50   *Sales* 1,386,253
SIC 4151 School buses

D-U-N-S 24-637-6750   (BR)
BANQUE NATIONALE DU CANADA
11485 1re Av, Saint-Georges, QC, G5Y 2C7
(418) 228-8828
Emp Here 20
SIC 6021 National commercial banks

D-U-N-S 24-428-4126   (SL)
BEIGNES TIM HORTON INC
9024 Boul Lacroix, Saint-Georges, QC, G5Y
5P4
(418) 227-5989
Emp Here 50   *Sales* 1,819,127
SIC 5812 Eating places

D-U-N-S 25-983-6166   (BR)
BIZOU INTERNATIONAL INC
8585 Boul Lacroix, Saint-Georges, QC, G5Y
5L6
(418) 227-0424
Emp Here 250
SIC 5944 Jewelry stores

D-U-N-S 20-519-0031   (BR)
**BLANCHETTE VACHON ET ASSOCIES CA
SENCRL**
*BLANCHETTE & VACHON COMPTABLE
AGREE*
10665 1re Av Bureau 300, Saint-Georges,
QC, G5Y 6X8
(418) 228-9761
Emp Here 51
SIC 8721 Accounting, auditing, and book-
keeping

D-U-N-S 20-174-1951   (BR)
**CAISSE DESJARDINS DU SUD DE LA
CHAUDIERE**
*CENTRE FINANCIER AUX ENTREPRISES
DES CAISSES DESJARDINS CHAUDIERE-
SUD*
1275 Boul Dionne, Saint-Georges, QC, G5Y
0R4
(418) 227-7000
Emp Here 142
SIC 8741 Management services

D-U-N-S 24-367-9250   (BR)
CANAC-MARQUIS GRENIER LTEE
15700 1re Av, Saint-Georges, QC, G5Y 2A3
(418) 228-8999
Emp Here 60
SIC 5251 Hardware stores

D-U-N-S 20-537-6127   (BR)
CANADA POST CORPORATION
SAINT GEORGES BDP
14200 Boul Lacroix, Saint-Georges, QC, G5Y
0C3
(418) 228-1354
Emp Here 40
SIC 4311 U.s. postal service

D-U-N-S 20-296-5534   (BR)
**CENTRE DE SANTE ET DE SERVICES SO-
CIAUX DE BEAUCE**
12523 25e Av, Saint-Georges, QC, G5Y 5N6
(418) 228-2244
Emp Here 150
SIC 8399 Social services, nec

D-U-N-S 24-147-3669   (SL)
**CENTRE DE SOUS-TRAITANCE BEAUCE
(C.S.T.B.) INC**

C S T B
9050 22e Av, Saint-Georges, QC, G5Y 7R6
(418) 228-7431
Emp Here 60   *Sales* 1,751,057
SIC 7349 Building maintenance services, nec

D-U-N-S 20-030-0155   (BR)
**CENTRES JEUNESSE CHAUDIERE-
APPALACHES, LES**
12521 25e Av, Saint-Georges, QC, G5Y 5N6
(418) 228-5516
Emp Here 30
SIC 8322 Individual and family services

D-U-N-S 25-233-8561   (BR)
**COMMISSION SCOLAIRE DE LA BEAUCE-
ETCHEMIN**
ECOLE MGR-FORTIER
1545 8e Av, Saint-Georges, QC, G5Y 4B4
(418) 228-5469
Emp Here 50
SIC 8211 Elementary and secondary schools

D-U-N-S 20-530-7247   (BR)
**COMMISSION SCOLAIRE DE LA BEAUCE-
ETCHEMIN**
*CENTRE INTEGRE DE MECANIQUE IN-
DUSTRIELLE DE LA CHAUDIERE CIMIC*
11700 25e Av, Saint-Georges, QC, G5Y 8B8
(418) 228-1993
Emp Here 75
SIC 8211 Elementary and secondary schools

D-U-N-S 25-233-6268   (BR)
**COMMISSION SCOLAIRE DE LA BEAUCE-
ETCHEMIN**
ECOLE PRIMAIRE LES SITTELLES
15400 10e Av, Saint-Georges, QC, G5Y 7G1
(418) 228-5514
Emp Here 45
SIC 8211 Elementary and secondary schools

D-U-N-S 25-233-8603   (BR)
**COMMISSION SCOLAIRE DE LA BEAUCE-
ETCHEMIN**
ECOLE DIONNE
1605 Boul Dionne, Saint-Georges, QC, G5Y
3W4
(418) 226-2689
Emp Here 40
SIC 8211 Elementary and secondary schools

D-U-N-S 20-711-9434   (BR)
**COMMISSION SCOLAIRE DE LA BEAUCE-
ETCHEMIN**
*CENTRE D'EDUCATION DES ADULTES
BEAUDOIN*
1600 1re Av, Saint-Georges, QC, G5Y 3N3

Emp Here 30
SIC 8211 Elementary and secondary schools

D-U-N-S 24-355-3752   (BR)
**COMMISSION SCOLAIRE DE LA BEAUCE-
ETCHEMIN**
11780 10e Av, Saint-Georges, QC, G5Y 6Z6
(418) 228-5541
Emp Here 24
SIC 8211 Elementary and secondary schools

D-U-N-S 25-232-7598   (BR)
**COMMISSION SCOLAIRE DE LA BEAUCE-
ETCHEMIN**
ECOLE POLYVALENTE DE ST GEORGES
2121 119e Rue, Saint-Georges, QC, G5Y 5S1
(418) 228-8964
Emp Here 140
SIC 8211 Elementary and secondary schools

D-U-N-S 25-233-4933   (BR)
**COMMISSION SCOLAIRE DE LA BEAUCE-
ETCHEMIN**
ECOLE DES PETITS CASTORS
11600 Boul Lacroix, Saint-Georges, QC, G5Y
1L2
(418) 228-2194
Emp Here 35
SIC 8211 Elementary and secondary schools

D-U-N-S 20-711-9293   (BR)
**COMMISSION SCOLAIRE DE LA BEAUCE-
ETCHEMIN**
ECOLE LACROIX
11655 Boul Lacroix, Saint-Georges, QC, G5Y
1L4
(418) 226-2673
Emp Here 50
SIC 8211 Elementary and secondary schools

D-U-N-S 20-711-9244   (BR)
**COMMISSION SCOLAIRE DE LA BEAUCE-
ETCHEMIN**
ECOLE NOTRE DAME DE LA TRINITE
3300 10e Av, Saint-Georges, QC, G5Y 4G2
(418) 228-7552
Emp Here 70
SIC 8211 Elementary and secondary schools

D-U-N-S 20-804-2064   (SL)
**COOPERATIVE DE SOLIDARITE DE SER-
VICE A DOMICILE BEAUCE-SARTIGA**
2385 Boul Dionne Bureau 200, Saint-
Georges, QC, G5Y 3X6
(418) 225-9144
Emp Here 65   *Sales* 3,064,349
SIC 8059 Nursing and personal care, nec

D-U-N-S 20-289-3046   (BR)
EQUIPEMENTS COMACT INC
COMACT SAINT-GEORGES
4000 40e Rue, Saint-Georges, QC, G5Y 8G4
(418) 228-8911
Emp Here 250
SIC 3553 Woodworking machinery

D-U-N-S 24-207-3427   (HQ)
EQUIPEMENTS SIGMA INC
(*Suby of* Deere & Company)
3220 127e Rue, Saint-Georges, QC, G5Y 6M5
(418) 228-8953
Emp Here 25   *Emp Total* 56,800
Sales 38,981,295
SIC 5084 Industrial machinery and equipment
Pr Lawrence Letourneau
Sec Bastien Letourneau

D-U-N-S 24-746-4571   (SL)
GESTION R.H.B. INC
GRAND HOTEL DE ST-GEORGES
11750 1re Av, Saint-Georges, QC, G5Y 2C8
(418) 228-3141
Emp Here 70   *Sales* 3,064,349
SIC 7011 Hotels and motels

D-U-N-S 20-006-2599   (BR)
**GOUVERNEMENT DE LA PROVINCE DE
QUEBEC**
*GOUVERNEMENT DE LA PROVINCE DE
QUEBEC*
11500 1re Av Bureau 110, Saint-Georges,
QC, G5Y 2C3
(418) 226-3110
Emp Here 32
SIC 8748 Business consulting, nec

D-U-N-S 25-740-5175   (BR)
**GOUVERNEMENT DE LA PROVINCE DE
QUEBEC**
ENTREPRISES RABAUD, LES
3015 127e Rue, Saint-Georges, QC, G5Y 5G4
(418) 227-0948
Emp Here 40
SIC 8322 Individual and family services

D-U-N-S 24-908-9715   (HQ)
IMAGES TURBO INC, LES
(*Suby of* Produits Reflechissants Candle-
Power Inc, Les)
1225 107e Rue, Saint-Georges, QC, G5Y 8C3
(418) 227-8872
Emp Here 43   *Emp Total* 50
Sales 4,331,255
SIC 7532 Top and body repair and paint shops

D-U-N-S 20-520-5912   (BR)
**INDUSTRIELLE ALLIANCE, ASSURANCE
ET SERVICES FINANCIERS INC**

11535 1re Av Bureau 370, Saint-Georges,
QC, G5Y 7H5
(418) 228-7171
Emp Here 20
SIC 6311 Life insurance

D-U-N-S 24-890-2004   (SL)
L'USINE TAC TIC INC
2030 127e Rue, Saint-Georges, QC, G5Y
2W8
(418) 227-4279
Emp Here 80   *Sales* 8,577,144
SIC 7389 Business services, nec
 Marco Trudel

D-U-N-S 24-782-4910   (SL)
LVM INC
DYNATEST
540 91e Rue, Saint-Georges, QC, G5Y 3K6
(418) 227-6161
Emp Here 30   *Sales* 2,261,782
SIC 8734 Testing laboratories

D-U-N-S 24-125-4650   (BR)
LOBLAW COMPANIES LIMITED
LOBLAWS
8200 Boul Lacroix, Saint-Georges, QC, G5Y
2B5
(418) 227-9228
Emp Here 70
SIC 5411 Grocery stores

D-U-N-S 20-950-6062   (SL)
MEUBLES BEAUCERONS INC
2350 95e Rue, Saint-Georges, QC, G5Y 8J4

Emp Here 90   *Sales* 11,052,800
SIC 2512 Upholstered household furniture
Pr Pr Valere Cote

D-U-N-S 20-331-3606   (BR)
MODE CHOC (ALMA) LTEE
MODE CHOC
610 90e Rue, Saint-Georges, QC, G5Y 3L2
(418) 221-6850
Emp Here 100
SIC 5651 Family clothing stores

D-U-N-S 24-747-5593   (SL)
PLACEMENTS 11655 INC, LES
VIEUX ST-GEORGES, AU
11655 1re Av, Saint-Georges, QC, G5Y 2C7
(418) 228-3651
Emp Here 65   *Sales* 2,407,703
SIC 5813 Drinking places

D-U-N-S 25-501-9473   (SL)
POULIN, NIKOL INC
NPI GROUP
3100 Boul Dionne, Saint-Georges, QC, G5Y
3Y4
(418) 228-3267
Emp Here 37   *Sales* 9,703,773
SIC 5141 Groceries, general line
 Nikol Poulin
 Dave Poulin
Dir Karine Poulin

D-U-N-S 25-299-9057   (BR)
PRISZM LP
KFC
1550 1re Av, Saint-Georges, QC, G5Y 3N2
(418) 228-7042
Emp Here 23
SIC 5812 Eating places

D-U-N-S 24-747-4984   (BR)
**RAYMOND CHABOT GRANT THORNTON
S.E.N.C.R.L.**
11505 1re Av Bureau 300, Saint-Georges,
QC, G5Y 7X3
(418) 228-8969
Emp Here 25
SIC 8721 Accounting, auditing, and book-
keeping

D-U-N-S 24-690-5848   (SL)
REMDEL INC

4200 10e Av, Saint-Georges, QC, G5Y 7S3
(418) 228-9458
Emp Here 20   *Sales* 20,290,000
SIC 7218 Industrial launderers
Pr Pr Roger Toulouse
Michel Beaudoin
Champlain Samson

D-U-N-S 24-440-5275   (BR)
RESTAURANT NORMANDIN INC
RESTAURANT NORMANDIN
8780 Boul Lacroix, Saint-Georges, QC, G5Y 2B5
(418) 227-2027
Emp Here 41
SIC 5812 Eating places

D-U-N-S 20-716-4760   (BR)
ROYAL BANK OF CANADA
RBC ROYAL BANK
(*Suby of* Royal Bank Of Canada)
12095 1re Av, Saint-Georges, QC, G5Y 2E2
(418) 227-7901
Emp Here 20
SIC 6021 National commercial banks

D-U-N-S 25-294-6173   (BR)
SEARS CANADA INC
8585 Boul Lacroix, Saint-Georges, QC, G5Y 5L6
(418) 228-2222
Emp Here 40
SIC 5311 Department stores

D-U-N-S 25-370-1528   (BR)
STAPLES CANADA INC
BUREAU EN GROS
(*Suby of* Staples, Inc.)
8585 Boul Lacroix, Saint-Georges, QC, G5Y 5L6
(418) 222-5025
Emp Here 35
SIC 5943 Stationery stores

D-U-N-S 24-205-4351   (SL)
SUPER MARCHE ROGER RODRIGUE INC
1990 Boul Dionne, Saint-Georges, QC, G5Y 3W8
(418) 228-2375
Emp Here 35   *Sales* 5,782,650
SIC 5411 Grocery stores
Pr Pr Roger Rodrigue
Louise Rodrigue
Manon Rodrigue
Pr Anne-Marie Rodrigue

D-U-N-S 25-527-1272   (HQ)
TAPIS VENTURE INC
GESTION CLUDE THIBAUDEAU
700 120e Rue, Saint-Georges, QC, G5Y 6R6
(418) 227-5955
Emp Here 50   *Emp Total* 150
SIC 2273 Carpets and rugs

D-U-N-S 20-569-1913   (BR)
TRANSPORT GUILBAULT INC
1225 95e Rue, Saint-Georges, QC, G5Y 8J1
(418) 227-3390
Emp Here 25
SIC 4212 Local trucking, without storage

D-U-N-S 20-270-8665   (BR)
UNI-SELECT QUEBEC INC
BEAUCE AUTO ACCESSOIRES
325 107e Rue, Saint-Georges, QC, G5Y 3J8
(418) 228-8817
Emp Here 21
SIC 5531 Auto and home supply stores

D-U-N-S 20-115-7794   (SL)
USINE TAC TIC INC, L'
2030 127e Rue, Saint-Georges, QC, G5Y 2W8
(418) 227-4279
Emp Here 70   *Sales* 2,553,625
SIC 2789 Bookbinding and related work

D-U-N-S 20-298-3243   (BR)
WSP CANADA INC

11535 1re Av Bureau 200, Saint-Georges, QC, G5Y 7H5
(418) 228-8041
Emp Here 50
SIC 8711 Engineering services

D-U-N-S 24-319-5067   (BR)
WAL-MART CANADA CORP
WALMART
750 107e Rue, Saint-Georges, QC, G5Y 0A1
(418) 220-0010
Emp Here 170
SIC 5311 Department stores

Saint-Georges, QC G6A
Champlain County

D-U-N-S 24-464-8812   (HQ)
GARAGA INC
(*Suby of* Gestion 3MEI Inc)
8500 25e Av, Saint-Georges, QC, G6A 1K5
(418) 227-2828
Emp Here 125   *Emp Total* 200
Sales 33,090,788
SIC 3442 Metal doors, sash, and trim
Pr Pr Michel Gendreau

D-U-N-S 25-673-6851   (SL)
GESTION G. COUTURE INC
9200 25e Av, Saint-Georges, QC, G6A 1L6
(418) 228-4822
Emp Here 60   *Sales* 6,797,150
SIC 2431 Millwork
Pr Bruno Couture

D-U-N-S 20-722-0583   (HQ)
INDUSTRIES RAD INC
FAUCHER INDUSTRIES
9095 25e Av, Saint-Georges, QC, G6A 1A1
(418) 228-8934
Emp Here 120   *Emp Total* 100
Sales 13,192,606
SIC 7539 Automotive repair shops, nec
Pr Raymond Dutil

D-U-N-S 20-265-1121   (SL)
O.S.I. PRECISION INC
OSI PRECISION
(*Suby of* Immobilisation 2010 Inc)
2510 98e Rue, Saint-Georges, QC, G6A 1E4
(418) 228-6868
Emp Here 26   *Sales* 1,824,018
SIC 3324 Steel investment foundries

D-U-N-S 24-343-0266   (SL)
PORTES GARAGA: STANDARD + INC
8500 25e Av, Saint-Georges, QC, G6A 1K5
(418) 227-2828
Emp Here 200   *Sales* 46,869,900
SIC 6712 Bank holding companies
Pr Pr Michel Gendreau

D-U-N-S 24-117-3744   (SL)
TECHNOLOGIES N'WARE INC
2885 81e Rue, Saint-Georges, QC, G6A 0C5
(418) 227-4292
Emp Here 36   *Sales* 2,991,389
SIC 7372 Prepackaged software

D-U-N-S 24-942-0456   (HQ)
VICTOR TEXTILES INC
(*Suby of* AD Investissement Inc)
2805 90e Rue, Saint-Georges, QC, G6A 1K1
(418) 227-9897
Emp Here 140   *Emp Total* 1
Sales 18,094,254
SIC 2221 Broadwoven fabric mills, manmade
Alain Duval

Saint-Georges, QC G9T
Champlain County

D-U-N-S 24-499-0271   (SL)
CONSTRUCTION BERTHIN CLOUTIER 2002 INC
230 106e Ave (St-Georges-De-Champlain, Saint-Georges, QC, G9T 3J4
(819) 533-3750
Emp Here 25   *Sales* 5,492,820
SIC 1542 Nonresidential construction, nec
Pr Andre Riberdy

Saint-Georges-De-Champlain, QC G9T

D-U-N-S 20-259-7050   (SL)
2788331 CANADA INC
MARCHE TRADITION ST-GEORGES
701 Av Saint-Georges, Saint-Georges-De-Champlain, QC, G9T 5K4
(819) 533-5445
Emp Here 49   *Sales* 6,055,738
SIC 5411 Grocery stores
Pr Pr Paul Sills
Daniel Sills

Saint-Gerard-Des-Laurentides, QC G9R
St-Maurice County

D-U-N-S 25-240-4371   (BR)
COMMISSION SCOLAIRE DE L'ENERGIE
ECOLE INSTITUTIONEL SAINT JOSEPH
1500 Ch Principal, Saint-Gerard-Des-Laurentides, QC, G9R 1E4
(819) 539-6964
Emp Here 40
SIC 8211 Elementary and secondary schools

D-U-N-S 24-942-6024   (SL)
CONSTRUCTION CLAUDE CARON & FILS INC
319 Ch Des Erables, Saint-Gerard-Des-Laurentides, QC, G9R 1G9
(819) 539-6902
Emp Here 25   *Sales* 6,898,600
SIC 1541 Industrial buildings and warehouses
Pr Pr Claude Caron

Saint-Gerard-Majella, QC J0G

D-U-N-S 25-766-0753   (BR)
GROUPE AGRITEX INC, LES
AGRITEX YAMASKA
(*Suby of* Groupe Agritex Inc, Le)
305 Rte Marie-Victorin, Saint-Gerard-Majella, QC, J0G 1X1
(450) 789-2304
Emp Here 20
SIC 5083 Farm and garden machinery

Saint-Germain-De-Grantham, QC J0C

D-U-N-S 20-290-9784   (SL)
ADVANCE DRAINAGE SYSTEM INC
(*Suby of* Advanced Drainage Systems, Inc.)
250a Boul Industriel, Saint-Germain-De-Grantham, QC, J0C 1K0
(819) 395-4244
Emp Here 49   *Sales* 4,304,681
SIC 1711 Plumbing, heating, air-conditioning

D-U-N-S 20-640-4126   (SL)
CISOLIFT DISTRIBUTION INC
192 Rue Sylvestre Rr 2, Saint-Germain-De-Grantham, QC, J0C 1K0
(819) 395-3838
Emp Here 22   *Sales* 5,182,810
SIC 5084 Industrial machinery and equipment

Pr Pr Guy Therrien
Sec Yan Leblanc
Dir Stephane Plante

D-U-N-S 25-233-4230   (BR)
COMMISSION SCOLAIRE DES CHENES
(*Suby of* Commission Scolaire des Chenes)
303 Rue Saint-Pierre, Saint-Germain-De-Grantham, QC, J0C 1K0
(819) 850-1624
Emp Here 55
SIC 8351 Child day care services

D-U-N-S 20-321-6635   (BR)
INTEGRATED DISTRIBUTION SYSTEMS LIMITED PARTNERSHIP
WAJAX POWER SYSTEMS
243 Rue Des Artisans, Saint-Germain-De-Grantham, QC, J0C 1K0
(819) 472-4076
Emp Here 100
SIC 5084 Industrial machinery and equipment

D-U-N-S 24-414-8123   (BR)
INTEGRATED DISTRIBUTION SYSTEMS LIMITED PARTNERSHIP
GENERATRICE DRUMMOND
243 Rue Des Artisans, Saint-Germain-De-Grantham, QC, J0C 1K0
(819) 472-4076
Emp Here 105
SIC 5063 Electrical apparatus and equipment

D-U-N-S 24-976-5061   (BR)
S. SETLAKWE LTEE
SETLAKWE
190 Boul Industriel Rr 2, Saint-Germain-De-Grantham, QC, J0C 1K0
(819) 395-5464
Emp Here 60
SIC 5712 Furniture stores

Saint-Gervais, QC G0R
Bellechasse County

D-U-N-S 25-018-5733   (BR)
CSSS DU GRAND LITTORAL
FOYER ST GERVAIS
(*Suby of* CSSS du Grand Littoral)
70 Rue Saint-Etienne, Saint-Gervais, QC, G0R 3C0
(418) 887-3387
Emp Here 50
SIC 8051 Skilled nursing care facilities

D-U-N-S 25-233-1954   (BR)
COMMISSION SCOLAIRE DE LA COTE-DU-SUD, LA
ECOLE DE LA NOUVELLE CADIE
177 Rue Principale, Saint-Gervais, QC, G0R 3C0
(418) 887-3465
Emp Here 21
SIC 8211 Elementary and secondary schools

D-U-N-S 20-712-0077   (BR)
COMMISSION SCOLAIRE DE LA COTE-DU-SUD, LA
CENTRE D'EDUCATION DES ADULTES DE BELLECHASSE
189 Rue Principale, Saint-Gervais, QC, G0R 3C0
(418) 887-1308
Emp Here 20
SIC 8211 Elementary and secondary schools

Saint-Guillaume, QC J0C
Yamaska County

D-U-N-S 25-233-4354   (BR)
COMMISSION SCOLAIRE DES CHENES
ECOLE SAINT-GUILLAUME

(*Suby of* Commission Scolaire des Chenes)
126 Rue Saint-Jean-Baptiste, Saint-Guillaume, QC, J0C 1L0
(819) 850-1609
Emp Here 20
SIC 8211 Elementary and secondary schools

D-U-N-S 20-791-0118   (SL)
IMMEUBLES HOULE ET CORRIVEAU INC
(*Suby of* Houle & Corriveau Ltee)
12 122 Rte, Saint-Guillaume, QC, J0C 1L0
(819) 396-2185
Emp Here 35   *Sales* 10,550,800
SIC 5083 Farm and garden machinery
Pr Pr Leo Corriveau
 Raymond Houle

Saint-Henri-De-Levis, QC G0R
Levis County

D-U-N-S 20-761-3084   (SL)
ALLEN ENTREPRENEUR GENERAL INC
CWA MECANIQUE DE PROCEDE
118 Rue De La Gare, Saint-Henri-De-Levis, QC, G0R 3E0
(418) 882-2277
Emp Here 150   *Sales* 17,510,568
SIC 1611 Highway and street construction
 Annie Allen
VP Christian Provencal
Dir Allen Maxime

D-U-N-S 25-688-2531   (BR)
COMMISSION SCOLAIRE DES NAVIGA-TEURS
ECOLE GAGNON
117 Rue Belleau, Saint-Henri-De-Levis, QC, G0R 3E0
(418) 834-2468
Emp Here 20
SIC 8211 Elementary and secondary schools

D-U-N-S 25-688-2457   (BR)
COMMISSION SCOLAIRE DES NAVIGA-TEURS
ECOLE BELLEAU GAGNON
121 Rue Belleau, Saint-Henri-De-Levis, QC, G0R 3E0
(418) 834-2465
Emp Here 35
SIC 8211 Elementary and secondary schools

D-U-N-S 20-016-5756   (BR)
JELD-WEN OF CANADA, LTD.
JELD WEN DIV PORTE
115 Rue De La Gare, Saint-Henri-De-Levis, QC, G0R 3E0
(418) 882-2223
Emp Here 150
SIC 2431 Millwork

D-U-N-S 24-376-8699   (BR)
SUPRALIMENT S.E.C.
183 Rte Du President-Kennedy, Saint-Henri-De-Levis, QC, G0R 3E0
(418) 882-2282
Emp Here 617
SIC 2011 Meat packing plants

D-U-N-S 24-388-4116   (SL)
T.M.S. SYSTEME INC
126 Rue Commerciale, Saint-Henri-De-Levis, QC, G0R 3E0
(418) 895-6000
Emp Here 50   *Sales* 14,101,550
SIC 3272 Concrete products, nec
Pr Pr Gilbert Roy

Saint-Hilarion, QC G0A
Charlevoix-Est County

D-U-N-S 24-622-8290   (BR)

PF RESOLU CANADA INC
130 Ch Cartier, Saint-Hilarion, QC, G0A 3V0
(418) 457-3308
Emp Here 45
SIC 7389 Business services, nec

Saint-Hippolyte, QC J8A
Terrebonne County

D-U-N-S 24-589-2724   (BR)
BAU-VAL INC
SABLES L G, DIV DE
435 Ch De La Carriere, Saint-Hippolyte, QC, J8A 1E9
(450) 436-8767
Emp Here 40
SIC 1429 Crushed and broken stone, nec

Saint-Honore-De-Chicoutimi, QC G0V
Chicoutimi County

D-U-N-S 20-029-9571   (BR)
COLLEGE D'ENSEIGNEMENT GENERAL & PROFESSIONNEL DE CHICOUTIMI
CENTRE QUEBECOIS DE FORMATION AERONAUTIQUE DE CHICOUTIMIE
(*Suby of* College d'Enseignement General & Professionnel de Chicoutimi)
1 Rue De L'Aeroport, Saint-Honore-De-Chicoutimi, QC, G0V 1L0
(418) 673-3421
Emp Here 50
SIC 8221 Colleges and universities

D-U-N-S 25-240-4405   (BR)
COMMISSION SCOLAIRE DES RIVES-DU-SAGUENAY
ECOLE LA SOURCE
(*Suby of* Commission Scolaire des Rives-du-Saguenay)
200 Rue Paul-Aime-Hudon, Saint-Honore-De-Chicoutimi, QC, G0V 1L0
(418) 615-0072
Emp Here 25
SIC 8211 Elementary and secondary schools

D-U-N-S 25-232-2698   (BR)
COMMISSION SCOLAIRE DES RIVES-DU-SAGUENAY
ECOLE PRIMAIRE JEAN-FORTIN
(*Suby of* Commission Scolaire des Rives-du-Saguenay)
200 Rue Paul-Aime-Hudon, Saint-Honore-De-Chicoutimi, QC, G0V 1L0
(418) 615-0065
Emp Here 20
SIC 8211 Elementary and secondary schools

D-U-N-S 24-887-9053   (BR)
IAMGOLD CORPORATION
3400 Rte Du Columbium, Saint-Honore-De-Chicoutimi, QC, G0V 1L0
(418) 673-4694
Emp Here 400
SIC 1081 Metal mining services

D-U-N-S 20-058-9799   (BR)
NIOBEC INC
MINE NIOBEC, LA
3400 Rte Du Columbium, Saint-Honore-De-Chicoutimi, QC, G0V 1L0
(418) 673-4694
Emp Here 400
SIC 1081 Metal mining services

Saint-Honore-De-Shenley, QC G0M
Beauce County

D-U-N-S 20-873-9920   (SL)

CARRIER & BEGIN INC
484 Le Grand-Shenley, Saint-Honore-De-Shenley, QC, G0M 1V0
(418) 485-6884
Emp Here 50   *Sales* 4,742,446
SIC 2421 Sawmills and planing mills, general

D-U-N-S 25-377-3667   (BR)
COMMISSION SCOLAIRE DE LA BEAUCE-ETCHEMIN
ECOLE SAINTE THERESE
434 Rue Champagne, Saint-Honore-De-Shenley, QC, G0M 1V0

Emp Here 20
SIC 8211 Elementary and secondary schools

D-U-N-S 25-336-4970   (BR)
VETEMENTS DE SPORT R.G.R. INC
SHENLEY JEANS
472 Le Grand-Shenley, Saint-Honore-De-Shenley, QC, G0M 1V0

Emp Here 50
SIC 2211 Broadwoven fabric mills, cotton

Saint-Hubert, QC J3Y
Chambly County

D-U-N-S 20-846-4185   (SL)
9064-2166 QUEBEC INC
CLUB PISCINE SAINT-HUBERT
1415 Boul Des Promenades Bureau 111, Saint-Hubert, QC, J3Y 5K2
(450) 465-9371
Emp Here 30   *Sales* 6,391,525
SIC 5999 Miscellaneous retail stores, nec
Pr Pr Annie Thibodeau

D-U-N-S 20-417-2100   (SL)
ACIES METROPOLITAN INC
METROPOLITAN STEEL
(*Suby of* 102492 Canada Ltee)
5055 Rue Ramsay, Saint-Hubert, QC, J3Y 2S3
(450) 678-5080
Emp Here 35   *Sales* 6,184,080
SIC 4953 Refuse systems
Pr Pr Larry Leibov
 Mark Leibov
 Richard Leibov

D-U-N-S 24-071-3649   (BR)
AUTOBUS TRANSCO (1988) INC
3530 Rue Richelieu, Saint-Hubert, QC, J3Y 7B1
(450) 676-5553
Emp Here 50
SIC 4151 School buses

D-U-N-S 24-763-4215   (SL)
BAILLARGEON, YVES ET FILS CON-TRACTEUR GENERAL INC
DECO JARDIN
3185 Rue Pasteur, Saint-Hubert, QC, J3Y 3Z6
(450) 656-4735
Emp Here 20   *Sales* 6,028,800
SIC 5083 Farm and garden machinery
Pr Pr Rene Baillargeon
 Guy Baillargeon

D-U-N-S 25-698-7231   (BR)
BANK OF MONTREAL
BMO
7171 Boul Cousineau Bureau100, Saint-Hubert, QC, J3Y 8N2
(450) 926-1122
Emp Here 20
SIC 6021 National commercial banks

D-U-N-S 24-226-2082   (BR)
BELL TECHNICAL SOLUTIONS INC
BELL SOLUTIONS TECHNIQUES
6396 Grande Allee, Saint-Hubert, QC, J3Y 8J8

(450) 678-0100
Emp Here 150
SIC 4899 Communication services, nec

D-U-N-S 20-610-4262   (BR)
BRICK WAREHOUSE LP, THE
BRICK
1451 Boul Des Promenades, Saint-Hubert, QC, J3Y 5K2
(450) 926-9400
Emp Here 60
SIC 5712 Furniture stores

D-U-N-S 20-514-6439   (BR)
CRDITED MONTEREGIE EST
CRDITED MONTEREGIE EST
(*Suby of* CRDITED Monteregie Est)
5980 Ch De Chambly, Saint-Hubert, QC, J3Y 6W9
(450) 445-2431
Emp Here 20
SIC 8361 Residential care

D-U-N-S 24-369-8946   (BR)
CAISSE DESJARDINS DE SAINT-HUBERT
CENTRE DE SERVICES BERNARD-RACICOT
5040 Boul Gaetan-Boucher, Saint-Hubert, QC, J3Y 7R8
(450) 443-0047
Emp Here 67
SIC 6062 State credit unions

D-U-N-S 24-369-8953   (BR)
CAISSE DESJARDINS DE SAINT-HUBERT
CENTRE DE SERVICES HECTOR-MARTIN
5045 Boul Cousineau, Saint-Hubert, QC, J3Y 3K7
(450) 443-0047
Emp Here 67
SIC 6062 State credit unions

D-U-N-S 24-153-9548   (BR)
CARA OPERATIONS LIMITED
HARVEYS
(*Suby of* Cara Holdings Limited)
5060 Boul Cousineau Bureau 2324, Saint-Hubert, QC, J3Y 7G5
(450) 445-2247
Emp Here 20
SIC 5812 Eating places

D-U-N-S 20-231-4860   (BR)
CARGILL LIMITED
CARGILL ANIMAL NUTRITION DIV
5928 Boul Cousineau Bureau 300, Saint-Hubert, QC, J3Y 7R9
(450) 676-8607
Emp Here 200
SIC 5191 Farm supplies

D-U-N-S 24-527-9294   (SL)
CENTRE ACCEUIL HENRIETTE CERE
6435 Ch De Chambly, Saint-Hubert, QC, J3Y 3R6
(450) 678-3291
Emp Here 100   *Sales* 3,648,035
SIC 8361 Residential care

D-U-N-S 25-145-2835   (HQ)
CENTRE MONTEREGIEN DE READAPTA-TION
(*Suby of* Centre Monteregien de Readaptation)
5300 Ch De Chambly, Saint-Hubert, QC, J3Y 3N7
(450) 676-7447
Emp Here 200   *Emp Total* 400
Sales 17,150,388
SIC 7991 Physical fitness facilities
Dir Francois Blais

D-U-N-S 24-389-5591   (BR)
CENTRE DE SANTE ET DE SERVICES SO-CIAUX CHAMPLAIN
CLSC SAINT-HUBERT
(*Suby of* Centre de sante et de services sociaux Champlain)
6800 Boul Cousineau, Saint-Hubert, QC, J3Y

8Z4
(450) 443-7400
Emp Here 50
SIC 8062 General medical and surgical hospitals

D-U-N-S 24-342-7742   (BR)
CENTRE DE SANTE ET DE SERVICES SOCIAUX CHAMPLAIN
CSSS CHAMPLAIN
(*Suby of* Centre de sante et de services sociaux Champlain)
5900 Boul Cousineau Bureau 200, Saint-Hubert, QC, J3Y 7R9
(450) 462-5120
Emp Here 50
SIC 8322 Individual and family services

D-U-N-S 24-389-5625   (BR)
CENTRE DE SANTE ET DE SERVICES SOCIAUX CHAMPLAIN
CENTRE D'HEBERGEMENT HENRIETTE CERE
(*Suby of* Centre de sante et de services sociaux Champlain)
6435 Ch De Chambly, Saint-Hubert, QC, J3Y 3R6
(450) 672-3320
Emp Here 60
SIC 8059 Nursing and personal care, nec

D-U-N-S 24-254-2124   (HQ)
CENTRE DE SANTE ET DE SERVICES SOCIAUX CHAMPLAIN
CLSC SAINT-HUBERT
(*Suby of* Centre de sante et de services sociaux Champlain)
5928 Boul Cousineau Bureau 200, Saint-Hubert, QC, J3Y 7R9
(450) 462-5120
Emp Here 100   *Emp Total* 1,000
Sales 50,791,533
SIC 8322 Individual and family services
VP VP Morique Poisson
Ch Bd Helene Forest Fournier
Treas Robert Hebert

D-U-N-S 24-012-2304   (BR)
COMMISSION SCOLAIRE MARIE-VICTORIN
ECOLE PAUL CHAGNON
5295 Ch De Chambly, Saint-Hubert, QC, J3Y 3N5
(450) 678-0792
Emp Here 25
SIC 8211 Elementary and secondary schools

D-U-N-S 25-233-5096   (BR)
COMMISSION SCOLAIRE MARIE-VICTORIN
ECOLE DE LA MOSAIQUE
6905 Boul Maricourt, Saint-Hubert, QC, J3Y 1T2
(450) 676-3101
Emp Here 35
SIC 8211 Elementary and secondary schools

D-U-N-S 20-712-2735   (BR)
COMMISSION SCOLAIRE MARIE-VICTORIN
ECOLE SECONDAIRE ANDRE LAURENDEAU
7450 Boul Cousineau, Saint-Hubert, QC, J3Y 3L4
(450) 678-2080
Emp Here 200
SIC 8211 Elementary and secondary schools

D-U-N-S 25-240-0007   (BR)
COMMISSION SCOLAIRE MARIE-VICTORIN
ECOLE DU JARDIN BIENVILLE
8370 Av Gervais, Saint-Hubert, QC, J3Y 7Y9
(450) 678-0670
Emp Here 29
SIC 8211 Elementary and secondary schools

D-U-N-S 20-712-2727   (BR)

COMMISSION SCOLAIRE MARIE-VICTORIN
ECOLE LAURENT-BENOIT
5905 Av Laurent-Benoit, Saint-Hubert, QC, J3Y 6H1
(450) 656-2010
Emp Here 50
SIC 8211 Elementary and secondary schools

D-U-N-S 25-233-0790   (BR)
COMMISSION SCOLAIRE MARIE-VICTORIN
ECOLE GAETAN BOUCHER
4850 Boul Westley, Saint-Hubert, QC, J3Y 2T4
(450) 656-5521
Emp Here 45
SIC 8211 Elementary and secondary schools

D-U-N-S 25-233-1152   (BR)
COMMISSION SCOLAIRE MARIE-VICTORIN
ECOLE DE MARICOURT
3675 Rue Coderre, Saint-Hubert, QC, J3Y 4P4
(450) 678-0201
Emp Here 30
SIC 8211 Elementary and secondary schools

D-U-N-S 25-233-1111   (BR)
COMMISSION SCOLAIRE MARIE-VICTORIN
ECOLE D'IBERVILLE
5095 Rue Aurele, Saint-Hubert, QC, J3Y 2E6
(450) 678-0145
Emp Here 110
SIC 8211 Elementary and secondary schools

D-U-N-S 25-284-4519   (BR)
COSTCO WHOLESALE CANADA LTD
COSTCO
(*Suby of* Costco Wholesale Corporation)
5025 Boul Cousineau, Saint-Hubert, QC, J3Y 3K7
(450) 443-3618
Emp Here 200
SIC 5099 Durable goods, nec

D-U-N-S 20-806-8168   (BR)
COUCHE-TARD INC
4960 Montee Saint-Hubert, Saint-Hubert, QC, J3Y 1V1
(450) 678-7037
Emp Here 25
SIC 5411 Grocery stores

D-U-N-S 20-806-7947   (BR)
COUCHE-TARD INC
3990 Ch De Chambly, Saint-Hubert, QC, J3Y 3M3
(450) 656-5721
Emp Here 25
SIC 5411 Grocery stores

D-U-N-S 20-123-0443   (BR)
DOLLARAMA S.E.C.
DOLLARAMA
5950 Boul Cousineau, Saint-Hubert, QC, J3Y 7R9
(450) 443-7307
Emp Here 20
SIC 5399 Miscellaneous general merchandise

D-U-N-S 24-679-8768   (BR)
ECONO-RACK GROUP (2015) INC, THE
TECHNIRACK
5455 Rue Ramsay, Saint-Hubert, QC, J3Y 2S3
(514) 871-3811
Emp Here 20
SIC 5046 Commercial equipment, nec

D-U-N-S 24-400-1587   (BR)
ENVIRONNEMENT ROUTIER NRJ INC
4865 Boul Sir-Wilfrid-Laurier, Saint-Hubert, QC, J3Y 3X5
(450) 656-0000
Emp Here 20
SIC 1521 Single-family housing construction

D-U-N-S 20-284-3277   (BR)
EQUIPEMENTS SPORTIFS PRO HOCKEY LIFE INC, LES
SPORTS GILBERT ROUSSEAU
1701 Boul Des Promenades, Saint-Hubert, QC, J3Y 5K2
(450) 656-1701
Emp Here 22
SIC 5941 Sporting goods and bicycle shops

D-U-N-S 24-871-6631   (SL)
GESTAIR LTEE
6100 Rte De L'Aeroport, Saint-Hubert, QC, J3Y 8Y9
(450) 656-1710
Emp Here 55   *Sales* 8,857,893
SIC 6712 Bank holding companies
Pr Pr Guy Prud'homme

D-U-N-S 20-998-4827   (BR)
GOLF TOWN LIMITED
GOLF TOWN
1571 Boul Des Promenades, Saint-Hubert, QC, J3Y 5K2
(450) 926-0110
Emp Here 20
SIC 5941 Sporting goods and bicycle shops

D-U-N-S 24-907-5649   (SL)
HELI-EXCEL INC
(*Suby of* Placements B. Allard Inc)
6500 Ch De La Savane, Saint-Hubert, QC, J3Y 8Y9
(418) 962-7126
Emp Here 42   *Sales* 9,619,680
SIC 4522 Air transportation, nonscheduled
Pr Pr Benoit Allard

D-U-N-S 25-841-0166   (BR)
MARCHE BELLEMARE INC
5350 Grande Allee Bureau 1353, Saint-Hubert, QC, J3Y 1A3
(450) 676-0220
Emp Here 90
SIC 5411 Grocery stores

D-U-N-S 20-178-3045   (BR)
MATERIAUX KOTT, S.E.N.C.
MATERIAUX KOTT PLUS
3400 Boul Sir-Wilfrid-Laurier, Saint-Hubert, QC, J3Y 6T1
(450) 445-5688
Emp Here 50
SIC 5039 Construction materials, nec

D-U-N-S 24-959-7808   (BR)
MEDIAS TRANSCONTINENTAL INC
MEDIAS TRANSCONTINENTAL INC
3400 Boul Losch Bureau 15, Saint-Hubert, QC, J3Y 5T6
(450) 926-1120
Emp Here 30
SIC 7319 Advertising, nec

D-U-N-S 24-860-4725   (HQ)
METROBEC INC
ACIER METROPOLITAN
(*Suby of* 102492 Canada Ltee)
5055 Rue Ramsay, Saint-Hubert, QC, J3Y 2S3
(450) 656-6666
Emp Here 110   *Emp Total* 6
Sales 17,072,804
SIC 4953 Refuse systems
Pr Richard Leibov
  Mark Leibov

D-U-N-S 24-169-5188   (SL)
NETUR INC
USINAGE NETUR
3450 Boul Losch, Saint-Hubert, QC, J3Y 5T6
(450) 676-0113
Emp Here 50   *Sales* 3,648,035
SIC 3599 Industrial machinery, nec

D-U-N-S 24-054-9415   (BR)
PLAN GROUP INC
GTTE GROUPE TECHNOLOGIQUE ET

TELECOM ET ELECTRIQUE
5974 Grande Allee Bureau 37, Saint-Hubert, QC, J3Y 1B3
(450) 462-3522
Emp Here 60
SIC 1623 Water, sewer, and utility lines

D-U-N-S 25-163-0034   (BR)
PRISZM LP
PIZZA HUT
5925 Boul Cousineau, Saint-Hubert, QC, J3Y 7P5

Emp Here 25
SIC 5812 Eating places

D-U-N-S 20-709-4140   (BR)
RE/MAX PRIVILEGE INC
RE/MAX ST-HUBERT
(*Suby of* Re/Max Privilege Inc)
5920 Boul Cousineau, Saint-Hubert, QC, J3Y 7R9
(450) 678-3150
Emp Here 50
SIC 6531 Real estate agents and managers

D-U-N-S 25-698-9997   (BR)
REGULVAR INC
3510 1re Rue, Saint-Hubert, QC, J3Y 8Y5
(450) 443-6131
Emp Here 25
SIC 5084 Industrial machinery and equipment

D-U-N-S 20-712-3774   (BR)
RIVERSIDE SCHOOL BOARD
ECOLE SECONDAIRE MACDONALD-CARTIER, L'
7445 Ch De Chambly, Saint-Hubert, QC, J3Y 3S3
(450) 678-1070
Emp Here 100
SIC 8211 Elementary and secondary schools

D-U-N-S 25-233-7985   (BR)
RIVERSIDE SCHOOL BOARD
ROYAL CHARLES SCHOOL
5525 Boul Maricourt, Saint-Hubert, QC, J3Y 1S5
(450) 676-2011
Emp Here 20
SIC 8211 Elementary and secondary schools

D-U-N-S 24-353-5791   (BR)
SERVICE CORPORATION INTERNATIONAL (CANADA) LIMITED
MAISON DARCHE SERVICES FUNERAIRES, LA
6500 Boul Cousineau, Saint-Hubert, QC, J3Y 8Z4
(450) 926-2011
Emp Here 40
SIC 7261 Funeral service and crematories

D-U-N-S 24-082-8553   (BR)
SERVICES MATREC INC
5300 Rue Albert-Millichamp, Saint-Hubert, QC, J3Y 8X7
(450) 656-2171
Emp Here 50
SIC 4953 Refuse systems

D-U-N-S 25-188-3799   (BR)
SOBEYS QUEBEC INC
MARCHE TRADITION
5935 Boul Payer, Saint-Hubert, QC, J3Y 6W6

Emp Here 30
SIC 5411 Grocery stores

D-U-N-S 20-562-0842   (SL)
STE-MARIE, CLAUDE SPORT INC
5925 Ch De Chambly, Saint-Hubert, QC, J3Y 3R4
(450) 678-4700
Emp Here 28   *Sales* 6,576,720
SIC 5571 Motorcycle dealers
Pr Pr Claude Ste-Marie
  Ginette Ste-Marie

D-U-N-S 24-799-5301   (HQ)
SUMMUM BEAUTE INTERNATIONAL INC
SUMMUM BEAUTE INTERNATIONAL (DIS-
TRIBUTION)
(*Suby of* Societe Financiere Grenco Inc)
4400 Boul Kimber, Saint-Hubert, QC, J3Y 8L4
(450) 678-3231
Emp Here 45   *Emp Total* 5
Sales 6,128,699
SIC 5122 Drugs, proprietaries, and sundries
Pr Paul-Emile Grenier
VP Jean-Yves Grenier
Sec Stephan Grenier
Dir Renaud Grenier
Dir Diane Grenier

D-U-N-S 24-834-8013   (HQ)
TECHO-BLOC INC
PIERRES STONEDGE, LES
5255 Rue Albert-Millichamp, Saint-Hubert,
QC, J3Y 8Z8
(877) 832-4625
Emp Here 90   *Emp Total* 100
Sales 60,291,070
SIC 3272 Concrete products, nec
Pr Pr Calogero Ciccarello
Nancy Larocca

D-U-N-S 24-346-8811   (SL)
TOITURES COUTURE & ASSOCIES INC
(*Suby of* Couture, Laurent & Associes Inc)
6565 Boul Maricourt, Saint-Hubert, QC, J3Y
1S8
(450) 678-2562
Emp Here 150   *Sales* 19,129,279
SIC 1761 Roofing, siding, and sheetMetal
work
Pr Maryse Couture
VP Pierre Bernard
VP Louis Bellemare
VP Lionel Alladio
Sec Andre Couture

D-U-N-S 24-969-1932   (HQ)
VARITRON TECHNOLOGIES INC
4811 Ch De La Savane, Saint-Hubert, QC,
J3Y 9G1
(450) 926-1778
Emp Here 25   *Emp Total* 150
Sales 6,420,542
SIC 5065 Electronic parts and equipment, nec
Michel Farley
Dir John Vincent
Dir Denis Chabot
Dir Etienne Veilleux

Saint-Hubert, QC J3Z
Chambly County

D-U-N-S 24-386-2427   (BR)
AGROPUR COOPERATIVE
AGROPUR FINE CHEESE DIVISION
4700 Rue Armand-Frappier, Saint-Hubert,
QC, J3Z 1G5
(450) 443-4838
Emp Here 75
SIC 8741 Management services

D-U-N-S 24-852-5839   (HQ)
AXSUN INC
ADT
4900 Rue Armand-Frappier Bureau 450,
Saint-Hubert, QC, J3Z 1G5
(450) 445-3003
Emp Here 85   *Emp Total* 75
Sales 22,253,014
SIC 4731 Freight transportation arrangement
Steve Ramescu
Francis Longpre
Dir Bruce R Hague

D-U-N-S 25-098-1396   (SL)
CICAME ENERGIE INC
POLTEC

5400 Rue J.-A.-Bombardier, Saint-Hubert,
QC, J3Z 1G8
(450) 679-7778
Emp Here 100   *Sales* 3,939,878
SIC 3643 Current-carrying wiring devices

D-U-N-S 20-286-1261   (BR)
COMMISSION SCOLAIRE MARIE-
VICTORIN
ECOLE DES MILLE-FLEURES
1600 Rue De Monaco, Saint-Hubert, QC, J3Z
1B7
(450) 462-3844
Emp Here 75
SIC 8211 Elementary and secondary schools

D-U-N-S 24-424-8766   (BR)
FEDERAL EXPRESS CANADA CORPORA-
TION
FEDERAL EXPRESS CANADA LTD
(*Suby of* Fedex Corporation)
5005 Rue J.-A.-Bombardier Bureau A, Saint-
Hubert, QC, J3Z 1G4
(800) 463-3339
Emp Here 100
SIC 7389 Business services, nec

D-U-N-S 24-390-2579   (BR)
LIBERTE NATURAL FOODS INC
5000 Rue J.-A.-Bombardier, Saint-Hubert,
QC, J3Z 1H1
(450) 926-5222
Emp Here 20
SIC 5149 Groceries and related products, nec

D-U-N-S 24-569-3874   (SL)
MAISONS SIGNEES ERIC BEAULIEU INC,
LES
5350 Rue Armand-Frappier, Saint-Hubert,
QC, J3Z 1J2
(450) 676-4413
Emp Here 23   *Sales* 5,465,508
SIC 5084 Industrial machinery and equipment
Pr Pr Eric Beaulieu

D-U-N-S 24-392-8483   (BR)
PRODUITS ALIMENTAIRES ANCO LTEE,
LES
AGROPUR
4700 Rue Armand-Frappier, Saint-Hubert,
QC, J3Z 1G5
(450) 443-4838
Emp Here 110
SIC 5143 Dairy products, except dried or
canned

D-U-N-S 20-720-4566   (BR)
PROVIGO DISTRIBUTION INC
MAXI & CIE
7900 Boul Cousineau, Saint-Hubert, QC, J3Z
1H2
(450) 676-4144
Emp Here 30
SIC 5411 Grocery stores

Saint-Hubert, QC J4T
Chambly County

D-U-N-S 25-233-4420   (BR)
COMMISSION SCOLAIRE MARIE-
VICTORIN
ECOLE MONSEIGNEUR FORGET
1700 Rue De Gaulle, Saint-Hubert, QC, J4T
1M8
(450) 678-2404
Emp Here 20
SIC 8211 Elementary and secondary schools

D-U-N-S 25-233-1277   (BR)
COMMISSION SCOLAIRE MARIE-
VICTORIN
ECOLE ST JOSEPH
3855 Grande Allee, Saint-Hubert, QC, J4T
2V8

(450) 678-2781
Emp Here 201
SIC 8211 Elementary and secondary schools

D-U-N-S 25-233-0592   (BR)
COMMISSION SCOLAIRE MARIE-
VICTORIN
ECOLE DES QUATRE VENTS
1940 Boul Marie, Saint-Hubert, QC, J4T 2A9
(450) 671-5903
Emp Here 40
SIC 8211 Elementary and secondary schools

D-U-N-S 25-233-1194   (BR)
COMMISSION SCOLAIRE MARIE-
VICTORIN
ECOLE MAURICE L DUPLESSIS
3225 Rue Windsor, Saint-Hubert, QC, J4T
2X3
(450) 678-1575
Emp Here 50
SIC 8211 Elementary and secondary schools

D-U-N-S 20-712-2743   (BR)
COMMISSION SCOLAIRE MARIE-
VICTORIN
ECOLE MONSEIGNEUR PARENT
3875 Grande Allee, Saint-Hubert, QC, J4T
2V8
(450) 676-0261
Emp Here 228
SIC 8211 Elementary and secondary schools

D-U-N-S 20-216-8857   (SL)
CORPORATIF RENAUD INC
3475 Boul Taschereau, Saint-Hubert, QC, J4T
2G1
(450) 462-9991
Emp Here 40   *Sales* 8,887,040
SIC 5521 Used car dealers
Pr Michel Renaud

D-U-N-S 25-211-1174   (HQ)
MOMENTUM DISTRIBUTION INC
F3 DISTRIBUTION
(*Suby of* 9045-2582 Quebec Inc)
2045 Rue Francis Bureau 200, Saint-Hubert,
QC, J4T 0A6
(450) 466-5115
Emp Here 35   *Emp Total* 1
Sales 8,056,134
SIC 5091 Sporting and recreation goods
Pr Pr Claude Roy
Claude Penneton
Normand Chartrand
Dir Claude Beaulieu
Dir Bertin Castonguay
Dir Louis Fortier

D-U-N-S 25-916-4333   (BR)
OMER DESERRES INC
4055 Boul Taschereau, Saint-Hubert, QC, J4T
2G6
(450) 443-6669
Emp Here 40
SIC 5999 Miscellaneous retail stores, nec

D-U-N-S 20-996-5297   (HQ)
REFPLUS INC
2777 Grande Allee, Saint-Hubert, QC, J4T
2R4
(450) 641-2665
Emp Here 150   *Emp Total* 1
Sales 21,596,367
SIC 3585 Refrigeration and heating equip-
ment
Pr Mathieu Cardinal
Sec Francois Fauteux
Dir Gilles Cyr
Dir Michel Lecompte
Dir Eric D'anjou
Dir Ness Lakdawala
Dir Aurele Cardinal

D-U-N-S 25-233-1236   (BR)
RIVERSIDE SCHOOL BOARD
TERRY FOX SCHOOL
1648 Rue Langevin, Saint-Hubert, QC, J4T
1X7

(450) 678-2142
Emp Here 20
SIC 8211 Elementary and secondary schools

D-U-N-S 25-157-6260   (BR)
VIGI SANTE LTEE
CHSLD VIGI MONTEREGIE
(*Suby of* Vigi Sante Ltee)
2042 Boul Marie, Saint-Hubert, QC, J4T 2B4
(450) 671-5596
Emp Here 120
SIC 8051 Skilled nursing care facilities

Saint-Hyacinthe, QC J2R
St Hyacinthe County

D-U-N-S 20-331-5833   (SL)
ARMOIRES CORDEAU INC
7675 Rang De La Pointe-Du-Jour, Saint-
Hyacinthe, QC, J2R 1H7
(450) 796-6128
Emp Here 50   *Sales* 2,918,428
SIC 2434 Wood kitchen cabinets

D-U-N-S 25-108-9900   (BR)
COMAX, COOPERATIVE AGRICOLE
COMAX COOPERATIVE AGRICOLE
15100 Ch De La Cooperative, Saint-
Hyacinthe, QC, J2R 1S2
(450) 799-4505
Emp Here 20
SIC 2048 Prepared feeds, nec

D-U-N-S 25-240-4801   (BR)
COMMISSION SCOLAIRE DE SAINT-
HYACINTHE, LA
ECOLE ST-THOMAS-D'AQUIN
6525 Av Pinard, Saint-Hyacinthe, QC, J2R
1B8
(450) 773-7843
Emp Here 50
SIC 8211 Elementary and secondary schools

D-U-N-S 24-111-8413   (SL)
CONSTRUCTION G. BAZINET INC
6450 Boul Laframboise, Saint-Hyacinthe, QC,
J2R 1B3
(450) 796-5825
Emp Here 21   *Sales* 5,376,850
SIC 1542 Nonresidential construction, nec
Pr Pr Bruno Bazinet
Treas Marielle Bazinet

D-U-N-S 20-566-2018   (BR)
COOP FEDEREE, LA
OLYMEL FLAMINGO, DIV OF
3250 Boul Laurier E, Saint-Hyacinthe, QC,
J2R 2B6
(450) 773-6661
Emp Here 500
SIC 5144 Poultry and poultry products

D-U-N-S 24-108-9879   (SL)
EMBALLAGES MASKA INC
7450 Av Pion, Saint-Hyacinthe, QC, J2R 1R9
(450) 796-2040
Emp Here 42   *Sales* 8,952,126
SIC 5113 Industrial and personal service pa-
per
Luc Longpre

D-U-N-S 24-393-0596   (SL)
GESTION SYREBEC INC
8350 Av Emilien-Letarte, Saint-Hyacinthe,
QC, J2R 0A3
(450) 796-2919
Emp Here 80   *Sales* 13,765,760
SIC 4213 Trucking, except local
Pr Jean Rouillard

D-U-N-S 20-886-2425   (SL)
MAROBI INC
3410 Rue Des Seigneurs E, Saint-Hyacinthe,
QC, J2R 1Z3
(450) 799-3515
Emp Here 20   *Sales* 3,239,280

SIC 4213 Trucking, except local

D-U-N-S 24-362-3266   (BR)
OLYMEL S.E.C.
OLYMEL STE-ROSALIE
3250 Boul Laurier E, Saint-Hyacinthe, QC,
J2R 2B6
(450) 773-6661
Emp Here 20
SIC 2011 Meat packing plants

D-U-N-S 24-388-9057   (BR)
SANIMAX RCI INC
6320 Boul Laurier E, Saint-Hyacinthe, QC,
J2R 2C5
(450) 799-4494
Emp Here 34
SIC 5191 Farm supplies

D-U-N-S 25-202-4203   (BR)
SINTRA INC
S.T.E.B. DIV DE
7905 Av Duplessis, Saint-Hyacinthe, QC, J2R
1S5
(450) 796-2691
Emp Here 20
SIC 2951 Asphalt paving mixtures and blocks

D-U-N-S 25-498-9924   (BR)
STAPLES CANADA INC
BUREAU EN GROS
(*Suby* of Staples, Inc.)
5970 Rue Martineau, Saint-Hyacinthe, QC,
J2R 2H6
(450) 796-4575
Emp Here 40
SIC 5943 Stationery stores

D-U-N-S 20-292-3629   (BR)
**VEOLIA ES CANADA SERVICES INDUS-
TRIELS INC**
7950 Av Pion, Saint-Hyacinthe, QC, J2R 1R9
(450) 796-6060
Emp Here 1,000
SIC 4953 Refuse systems

D-U-N-S 25-377-6009   (BR)
WAL-MART CANADA CORP
WALMART
5950 Rue Martineau, Saint-Hyacinthe, QC,
J2R 2H6
(450) 796-4001
Emp Here 200
SIC 5311 Department stores

Saint-Hyacinthe, QC J2S
St Hyacinthe County

D-U-N-S 24-355-5901   (SL)
ABMAST INC
6935 Rue Picard, Saint-Hyacinthe, QC, J2S
1H3
(450) 774-4660
Emp Here 50   *Sales* 4,805,878
SIC 3291 Abrasive products

D-U-N-S 24-420-4744   (BR)
AGROPUR COOPERATIVE
AGROPUR, DIV FROMAGES FIN
995 Rue Johnson E, Saint-Hyacinthe, QC,
J2S 7V6
(450) 773-6493
Emp Here 150
SIC 5143 Dairy products, except dried or
canned

D-U-N-S 20-325-1322   (SL)
**ALIMENTS BROOKSIDE (QUEBEC) INC,
LES**
(*Suby of* Hershey Company)
6780 Boul Choquette, Saint-Hyacinthe, QC,
J2S 8L1
(450) 771-7177
Emp Here 50   *Sales* 3,648,035
SIC 2064 Candy and other confectionery
products

D-U-N-S 25-837-6797   (SL)
ATELIERS TRANSITION INC, LES
1255 Rue Delorme Bureau 103, Saint-
Hyacinthe, QC, J2S 2J3
(450) 771-2747
Emp Here 60   *Sales* 3,064,349
SIC 7389 Business services, nec

D-U-N-S 20-004-5818   (BR)
BANQUE NATIONALE DU CANADA
1955 Rue Des Cascades, Saint-Hyacinthe,
QC, J2S 8K9
(450) 773-6111
Emp Here 35
SIC 6021 National commercial banks

D-U-N-S 25-837-0493   (BR)
BEAUWARD SHOPPING CENTRES LTD
GALERIES ST HYACINTHE, LES
3200 Boul Laframboise Bureau 1009, Saint-
Hyacinthe, QC, J2S 4Z5
(450) 773-8282
Emp Here 1,200
SIC 6512 Nonresidential building operators

D-U-N-S 25-392-1035   (SL)
BIO BISCUIT INC
5505 Av Trudeau Bureau 15, Saint-Hyacinthe,
QC, J2S 1H5
(450) 778-1349
Emp Here 135   *Sales* 11,600,751
SIC 2047 Dog and cat food
 Royal Lemieux
Pr Pr Pierre Lemieux
VP VP David Gaucher
Dir Brigitte Lemieux
Dir Marie-Claude Lemieux
Dir Claire Lemieux

D-U-N-S 20-859-8607   (HQ)
C.D.M.V. INC
2999 Boul Choquette, Saint-Hyacinthe, QC,
J2S 6H5
(450) 771-2368
Emp Here 180   *Emp Total* 40,000
Sales 50,242,558
SIC 5047 Medical and hospital equipment
Pr Pr Denis Huard
 Mario Vinet
 Marc Paquet
Dir Ernest Desrosiers
Dir Yves Bourque
Dir Lucie Henault
Dir Sylvain Raymond
Dir Caron Martin

D-U-N-S 20-009-4907   (BR)
**CSSS RICHELIEU-YAMASKA CH DE LA
MRC D'ACTON**
*CENTRE D'EBERGEMENT ANDREE PER-
RAULT*
1955 Av Pratte, Saint-Hyacinthe, QC, J2S
7W5
(450) 771-4536
Emp Here 95
SIC 7021 Rooming and boarding houses

D-U-N-S 25-812-2548   (BR)
CANADA POST CORPORATION
2020 Rue Girouard O, Saint-Hyacinthe, QC,
J2S 3A6
(450) 771-6767
Emp Here 60
SIC 4311 U.s. postal service

D-U-N-S 20-271-0414   (SL)
CASAVANT FRERES S.E.C
900 Rue Girouard E, Saint-Hyacinthe, QC,
J2S 2Y2
(450) 773-5001
Emp Here 50   *Sales* 1,532,175
SIC 3931 Musical instruments

D-U-N-S 24-046-6198   (BR)
**CENTRE MONTEREGIEN DE READAPTA-
TION**
1800 Rue Dessaulles, Saint-Hyacinthe, QC,
J2S 2T2

(450) 774-5003
Emp Here 70
SIC 8093 Specialty outpatient clinics, nec

D-U-N-S 25-240-5634   (BR)
**COMMISSION SCOLAIRE DE SAINT-
HYACINTHE, LA**
ECOLE DOUVILLE
5355 Rue Joncaire, Saint-Hyacinthe, QC, J2S
3X1
(450) 773-3835
Emp Here 50
SIC 8211 Elementary and secondary schools

D-U-N-S 25-241-4958   (BR)
**COMMISSION SCOLAIRE DE SAINT-
HYACINTHE, LA**
ECOLE SAINT-SACREMENT
2400 Rue Bourassa, Saint-Hyacinthe, QC,
J2S 1R8
(450) 773-1230
Emp Here 60
SIC 8211 Elementary and secondary schools

D-U-N-S 20-712-3345   (BR)
**COMMISSION SCOLAIRE DE SAINT-
HYACINTHE, LA**
700 Boul Casavant E, Saint-Hyacinthe, QC,
J2S 7T2
(450) 773-8401
Emp Here 50
SIC 8211 Elementary and secondary schools

D-U-N-S 25-233-9775   (BR)
**COMMISSION SCOLAIRE DE SAINT-
HYACINTHE, LA**
ECOLE SECONDAIRE CASAVANT
2475 Boul Laframboise, Saint-Hyacinthe, QC,
J2S 4Y1
(450) 773-8401
Emp Here 60
SIC 8211 Elementary and secondary schools

D-U-N-S 25-233-9619   (BR)
**COMMISSION SCOLAIRE DE SAINT-
HYACINTHE, LA**
ECOLE LAFONTAINE
350 Av Sainte-Marie, Saint-Hyacinthe, QC,
J2S 4R3
(450) 773-7162
Emp Here 32
SIC 8211 Elementary and secondary schools

D-U-N-S 25-240-5675   (BR)
**COMMISSION SCOLAIRE DE SAINT-
HYACINTHE, LA**
POLYVALENTE HYACINTHE-DELORME
2700 Av T.-D.-Bouchard, Saint-Hyacinthe, QC,
J2S 7G2
(450) 773-8408
Emp Here 160
SIC 8211 Elementary and secondary schools

D-U-N-S 25-233-9692   (BR)
**COMMISSION SCOLAIRE DE SAINT-
HYACINTHE, LA**
ECOLE BOIS JOLI SACRE COEUR
700 Rue Millet, Saint-Hyacinthe, QC, J2S 1J5
(450) 773-4505
Emp Here 70
SIC 8211 Elementary and secondary schools

D-U-N-S 20-712-3352   (BR)
**COMMISSION SCOLAIRE DE SAINT-
HYACINTHE, LA**
*COMMISSION SCOLAIRE DE SAINT-
HYACINTHE, LA*
2350 Rue Lafontaine, Saint-Hyacinthe, QC,
J2S 2N1
(450) 771-2930
Emp Here 50
SIC 8211 Elementary and secondary schools

D-U-N-S 20-712-3337   (BR)
**COMMISSION SCOLAIRE DE SAINT-
HYACINTHE, LA**
PAVILLON D' ECOLE PROFESSIONEL
1455 Boul Casavant E, Saint-Hyacinthe, QC,
J2S 8S8

(450) 773-8401
Emp Here 50
SIC 8211 Elementary and secondary schools

D-U-N-S 25-233-7860   (BR)
**COMMISSION SCOLAIRE DE SAINT-
HYACINTHE, LA**
ECOLE RENE SAINT PIERRE
2255 Boul Laframboise, Saint-Hyacinthe, QC,
J2S 4X7
(450) 773-8408
Emp Here 50
SIC 8211 Elementary and secondary schools

D-U-N-S 20-273-8626   (SL)
CORPORATION ALLFLEX INC
4135 Av Berard, Saint-Hyacinthe, QC, J2S
8Z8
(450) 261-8008
Emp Here 20   *Sales* 2,407,703
SIC 3523 Farm machinery and equipment

D-U-N-S 20-022-0460   (BR)
DBC COMMUNICATIONS INC
PUBLI ENCARTS
3275 Boul Choquette Bureau 5, Saint-
Hyacinthe, QC, J2S 7Z8
(450) 771-2332
Emp Here 25
SIC 7319 Advertising, nec

D-U-N-S 24-167-9430   (BR)
DELOITTE LLP
2200 Av Pratte Bureau 100, Saint-Hyacinthe,
QC, J2S 4B6
(450) 774-4000
Emp Here 60
SIC 8721 Accounting, auditing, and book-
keeping

D-U-N-S 20-294-8431   (BR)
DESSERCOM INC
AMBULANCES SAINT HYACINTHE
592 Av Sainte-Marie, Saint-Hyacinthe, QC,
J2S 4R5
(450) 773-5223
Emp Here 100
SIC 4119 Local passenger transportation, nec

D-U-N-S 20-033-9104   (BR)
FARM CREDIT CANADA
FINANCEMENT AGRICOLE CANADA
3271 Boul Laframboise Bureau 200, Saint-
Hyacinthe, QC, J2S 4Z6
(450) 771-7080
Emp Here 20
SIC 6159 Miscellaneous business credit insti-
tutions

D-U-N-S 24-460-5622   (HQ)
**FEDERATION DE L'UPA DE LA MON-
TEREGIE**
(*Suby of* Federation de l'UPA de la Mon-
teregie)
3800 Boul Casavant O, Saint-Hyacinthe, QC,
J2S 8E3
(450) 774-9154
Emp Here 30   *Emp Total* 77
Sales 12,985,600
SIC 8699 Membership organizations, nec
 Robert Racine
Pr Christian St-Jacques
VP Jeremie Letellier
Asst VP Normand Teasdale
Dir Yvon Boucher
Dir Yvon Lambert
Dir Mario Dupont
Dir Rejean Racine
Dir Jerome Ostiguy
Dir Andre Mousseau

D-U-N-S 24-099-1831   (BR)
**FEDERATION DES CAISSES DESJARDINS
DU QUEBEC**
*FEDERATION DES CAISSES DESJARDINS
DU QUEBEC*
2175 Rue Girouard O, Saint-Hyacinthe, QC,
J2S 3A9

▲ Public Company   ■ Public Company Family Member   **HQ** Headquarters   **BR** Branch   **SL** Single Location

(450) 773-1842
Emp Here 100
SIC 8742 Management consulting services

D-U-N-S 25-700-1982   (BR)
FINANCIERE BANQUE NATIONALE INC
FINANCIERE BANQUE NATIONALE
1355 Rue Johnson O Bureau 4100, Saint-Hyacinthe, QC, J2S 8W7
(450) 774-5354
Emp Here 20
SIC 6211 Security brokers and dealers

D-U-N-S 24-256-0407   (SL)
GESTION RESTO ST-HYACINTHE INC
ROTISSERIE ST-HUBERT
1315 Rue Johnson O, Saint-Hyacinthe, QC, J2S 8S4
(450) 774-7770
Emp Here 80   *Sales* 2,407,703
SIC 5812 Eating places

D-U-N-S 24-810-6663   (BR)
GROUPE BMTC INC
3300 Av Cusson, Saint-Hyacinthe, QC, J2S 8N9
(450) 774-6116
Emp Here 20
SIC 5712 Furniture stores

D-U-N-S 24-475-2820   (HQ)
GROUPE GOYETTE INC
GOYTERM DIV
2825 Boul Casavant O, Saint-Hyacinthe, QC, J2S 7Y4
(450) 773-9615
Emp Here 250   *Emp Total* 110
Sales 63,704,320
SIC 4213 Trucking, except local
Pr Pr Alain Caron
 Benoit Martel

D-U-N-S 20-252-2850   (HQ)
GROUPE MASKA INC
BATTERIES ELECTRIQUES QUEBEC
(*Suby of* Gestion M. A. E. Inc)
550 Av Vaudreuil, Saint-Hyacinthe, QC, J2S 4H2
(450) 372-1676
Emp Here 110   *Emp Total* 148
Sales 32,051,287
SIC 5084 Industrial machinery and equipment
 Roger Letendre
VP Simon Letendre
VP Martin Letendre

D-U-N-S 20-309-6540   (SL)
GROUPE MASKATEL LP
970 Boul Casavant O, Saint-Hyacinthe, QC, J2S 0H4
(450) 252-2000
Emp Here 50   *Sales* 5,399,092
SIC 4899 Communication services, nec
VP VP Jacques Taillefer

D-U-N-S 20-726-5141   (SL)
IMPRIMERIE MASKA INC
5605 Av Trudeau Bureau 1, Saint-Hyacinthe, QC, J2S 1H5
(450) 773-3164
Emp Here 50   *Sales* 2,480,664
SIC 2759 Commercial printing, nec

D-U-N-S 20-176-5620   (HQ)
INDECK COMBUSTION CORPORATION
4300 Av Beaudry, Saint-Hyacinthe, QC, J2S 8A5
(450) 774-5326
Emp Here 20   *Emp Total* 93
Sales 10,395,012
SIC 1711 Plumbing, heating, air-conditioning
Pr Pr Marsha Forsythe-Fournier
Genl Mgr Thomas W Mcparlan
Genl Mgr Steven Page

D-U-N-S 25-309-7430   (BR)
INDUSTRIELLE ALLIANCE, ASSURANCE ET SERVICES FINANCIERS INC
1050 Boul Casavant O Bureau 1003, Saint-

Hyacinthe, QC, J2S 8B9
(450) 773-7493
Emp Here 25
SIC 6411 Insurance agents, brokers, and service

D-U-N-S 20-126-6421   (BR)
INSTITUT DE RECHERCHE ET DEVELOPPEMENT EN AGROENVIRONEMENT INC
3300 Rue Sicotte, Saint-Hyacinthe, QC, J2S 2M2

Emp Here 30
SIC 8731 Commercial physical research

D-U-N-S 24-044-8741   (BR)
LOBLAW COMPANIES LIMITED
LOBLAWS
2000 Boul Casavant O, Saint-Hyacinthe, QC, J2S 7K2
(450) 771-6601
Emp Here 150
SIC 5411 Grocery stores

D-U-N-S 24-061-1058   (BR)
MAGASINS UREKA INC
AUBAINERIE
2235 Boul Casavant O, Saint-Hyacinthe, QC, J2S 7E5
(450) 223-1333
Emp Here 30
SIC 5621 Women's clothing stores

D-U-N-S 20-000-5366   (BR)
METRO RICHELIEU INC
SUPER C ST HYACINTHE
3800 Av Cusson, Saint-Hyacinthe, QC, J2S 8V6
(450) 771-1651
Emp Here 90
SIC 5141 Groceries, general line

D-U-N-S 20-125-3445   (BR)
NACHURS ALPINE SOLUTIONS INC
(*Suby of* Trans-Resources, Inc.)
Gd, Saint-Hyacinthe, QC, J2S 7P5
(450) 771-1742
Emp Here 20
SIC 2874 Phosphatic fertilizers

D-U-N-S 20-016-4846   (BR)
NAUTILUS PLUS INC
KINEQUIP
3190 Av Cusson, Saint-Hyacinthe, QC, J2S 8N9
(450) 250-0999
Emp Here 20
SIC 7991 Physical fitness facilities

D-U-N-S 25-105-4284   (BR)
OLYMEL S.E.C.
1425 Av St-Jacques, Saint-Hyacinthe, QC, J2S 6M7
(450) 778-2211
Emp Here 450
SIC 7299 Miscellaneous personal service

D-U-N-S 25-878-2606   (BR)
PRISZM LP
PIZZA HUT
1220 Rue Gauvin, Saint-Hyacinthe, QC, J2S 7X5
(450) 773-6606
Emp Here 31
SIC 5812 Eating places

D-U-N-S 25-542-7080   (SL)
PRODUITS NEPTUNE INC, LES
NEPTUNE INTERNATIONAL
6835 Rue Picard, Saint-Hyacinthe, QC, J2S 1H3
(450) 773-7058
Emp Here 230
SIC 3431 Metal sanitary ware

D-U-N-S 25-298-2178   (BR)
RAYMOND CHABOT GRANT THORNTON S.E.N.C.R.L.

1355 Boul Johnson O, Saint-Hyacinthe, QC, J2S 8W7
(450) 773-2424
Emp Here 35
SIC 8721 Accounting, auditing, and bookkeeping

D-U-N-S 24-440-5101   (BR)
RESTAURANTS MAC-VIC INC, LES
MC DONALDS
3200 Boul Laframboise, Saint-Hyacinthe, QC, J2S 4Z5
(450) 261-8880
Emp Here 80
SIC 5812 Eating places

D-U-N-S 24-346-3119   (BR)
RESTAURANTS MAC-VIC INC, LES
MCDONALD' S
3005 Boul Laframboise, Saint-Hyacinthe, QC, J2S 4Z6
(450) 774-5955
Emp Here 100
SIC 5812 Eating places

D-U-N-S 24-392-4029   (BR)
SAINT-HYACINTHE, VILLE DE
SERVICE INCENDIE SAINT-HYACINTHE
935 Rue Dessaulles, Saint-Hyacinthe, QC, J2S 3C4
(450) 778-8550
Emp Here 80
SIC 7389 Business services, nec

D-U-N-S 24-541-1368   (BR)
SAPUTO PRODUITS LAITIERS CANADA S.E.N.C.
SAPUTO SAINT-HYACINTHE
(*Suby of* Saputo Produits Laitiers Canada S.E.N.C.)
1195 Rue Johnson E Bureau 117, Saint-Hyacinthe, QC, J2S 7Y6
(450) 773-1004
Emp Here 100
SIC 2023 Dry, condensed and evaporated dairy products

D-U-N-S 24-353-6070   (BR)
SERVICE CORPORATION INTERNATIONAL (CANADA) LIMITED
RESIDENCES FUNERAIRES MONGEAU
1115 Rue Girouard O, Saint-Hyacinthe, QC, J2S 2Y9
(450) 774-8000
Emp Here 20
SIC 7261 Funeral service and crematories

D-U-N-S 20-120-5858   (SL)
SPECIALITES M.B. INC
5450 Av Trudeau, Saint-Hyacinthe, QC, J2S 7Y8
(450) 771-1415
Emp Here 70   *Sales* 3,638,254
SIC 2013 Sausages and other prepared meats

D-U-N-S 24-335-0266   (SL)
TELEPHONE DRUMMOND INC
3455 Boul Choquette, Saint-Hyacinthe, QC, J2S 7Z8
(819) 445-4545
Emp Here 24   *Sales* 2,261,782
SIC 4813 Telephone communication, except radio

D-U-N-S 24-179-4700   (BR)
TRANSCONTINENTAL PRINTING INC
TRANSCONTINENTAL SAINT HYACINTHE
2700 Boul Casavant O, Saint-Hyacinthe, QC, J2S 7S4
(450) 773-0289
Emp Here 260
SIC 2752 Commercial printing, lithographic

D-U-N-S 25-700-0588   (BR)
VOLKSWAGEN GROUP CANADA INC
VOLKSWAGEN SAINT-HYACINTHE
5705 Av Trudeau, Saint-Hyacinthe, QC, J2S 1H5

(514) 875-3915
Emp Here 25
SIC 5511 New and used car dealers

D-U-N-S 25-672-5086   (SL)
WILLIAM MILLENAIRE INC
6865 Rue Picard, Saint-Hyacinthe, QC, J2S 1H3
(450) 774-1471
Emp Here 50   *Sales* 4,450,603
SIC 2512 Upholstered household furniture

Saint-Hyacinthe, QC J2T
St Hyacinthe County

D-U-N-S 24-426-3401   (SL)
CSH STE-MARTHE INC
RESIDENCE STE-MARTHE
675 Rue Saint-Pierre O Bureau 238, Saint-Hyacinthe, QC, J2T 1N7
(450) 773-1279
Emp Here 20   *Sales* 729,607
SIC 8361 Residential care

D-U-N-S 20-037-5595   (BR)
CENTRE MONTEREGIEN DE READAPTATION
POINTE DE SERVICE
730 Rue Saint-Pierre E, Saint-Hyacinthe, QC, J2T 1N2
(450) 774-4104
Emp Here 26
SIC 8361 Residential care

D-U-N-S 20-357-5626   (BR)
COMAX, COOPERATIVE AGRICOLE
COOP COMAX BMR ST-HYACINTHE, LA
16755 Av Saint-Louis, Saint-Hyacinthe, QC, J2T 3G4
(450) 773-2569
Emp Here 40
SIC 5251 Hardware stores

D-U-N-S 25-233-7704   (BR)
COMMISSION SCOLAIRE DE SAINT-HYACINTHE, LA
ECOLE ROMEO FORBES
650 Rue Desranleau E, Saint-Hyacinthe, QC, J2T 2L6
(450) 773-2823
Emp Here 51
SIC 8211 Elementary and secondary schools

D-U-N-S 25-233-7829   (BR)
COMMISSION SCOLAIRE DE SAINT-HYACINTHE, LA
ECOLE SAINT-CHARLES-GARNIER
2525 Rue Crevier, Saint-Hyacinthe, QC, J2T 1T1
(450) 774-6638
Emp Here 40
SIC 8211 Elementary and secondary schools

D-U-N-S 25-233-9650   (BR)
COMMISSION SCOLAIRE DE SAINT-HYACINTHE, LA
ECOLE ASSOMPTION
1900 Rue Bernard, Saint-Hyacinthe, QC, J2T 1G4
(450) 774-8015
Emp Here 50
SIC 8211 Elementary and secondary schools

D-U-N-S 25-233-7746   (BR)
COMMISSION SCOLAIRE DE SAINT-HYACINTHE, LA
ECOLE MAURICE JODOIN
855 Rue Saint-Pierre O, Saint-Hyacinthe, QC, J2T 1N7
(450) 774-5700
Emp Here 25
SIC 8211 Elementary and secondary schools

D-U-N-S 20-252-0060   (SL)
COMPAGNIE DE TRANSPORT MASKOUTAINE INC

1005 Rue Bernard, Saint-Hyacinthe, QC, J2T
1E2
(450) 774-4411
Emp Here 70   *Sales* 3,283,232
SIC 4142 Bus charter service, except local

D-U-N-S 24-431-4548   (SL)
ORGUES LETOURNEAU LTEE
16355 Av Savoie, Saint-Hyacinthe, QC, J2T
3N1
(450) 223-1018
Emp Here 65   *Sales* 4,742,446
SIC 5736 Musical instrument stores

D-U-N-S 25-853-4544   (BR)
PROVIGO DISTRIBUTION INC
MAXI # 8975
15000 Av Saint-Louis, Saint-Hyacinthe, QC,
J2T 3E2
(450) 771-2737
Emp Here 35
SIC 5411 Grocery stores

D-U-N-S 25-258-3620   (BR)
SPORT MASKA INC
REEBOK-CCM
15855 Av Hubert, Saint-Hyacinthe, QC, J2T
4C9
(450) 773-5258
Emp Here 160
SIC 2329 Men's and boy's clothing, nec

D-U-N-S 25-114-8599   (SL)
**SYSTEMES DE DIFFUSION SPRAYLOGIK
INC, LES**
17420 Av Centrale, Saint-Hyacinthe, QC, J2T
3L7
(450) 778-1850
Emp Here 35   *Sales* 7,033,600
SIC 5047 Medical and hospital equipment
Pr Pr Richard Garon
Johanne Lacroix
VP VP Mark Garon
Michel Garon
Ch Bd Roger Garon
Therese Morin

Saint-Ignace-De-Loyola, QC J0K

D-U-N-S 20-252-5101   (SL)
L.H PLANTE & FILS INC
674 Rang Saint-Isidore,   Saint-Ignace-De-
Loyola, QC, J0K 2P0
(514) 866-5953
Emp Here 50   *Sales* 4,888,367
SIC 2448 Wood pallets and skids

Saint-Irenee, QC G0T
Charlevoix-Est County

D-U-N-S 20-711-9160   (BR)
**COMMISSION   SCOLAIRE   DE
CHARLEVOIX, LA**
ECOLE NOTRE DAME DE LORETTE
136 Rue Principale, Saint-Irenee, QC, G0T
1V0
(418) 620-5004
Emp Here 50
SIC 8211 Elementary and secondary schools

Saint-Isidore, QC G0S
Dorchester County

D-U-N-S 25-232-7465   (BR)
**COMMISSION SCOLAIRE DE LA BEAUCE-
ETCHEMIN**
ECOLE BARABE DROUIN
161 Rue Sainte-Genevieve, Saint-Isidore, QC,
G0S 2S0

Emp Here 40
SIC 8211 Elementary and secondary schools

D-U-N-S 25-852-1210   (SL)
ROUSSEAU, R. & FILS LTEE
236 Rue Sainte-Genevieve, Saint-Isidore, QC,
G0S 2S0
(418) 882-5656
Emp Here 32   *Sales* 9,231,950
SIC 5191 Farm supplies
Dir Patrice Brochu

Saint-Isidore-De-Laprairie, QC J0L

D-U-N-S 20-500-6125   (HQ)
LANCTOT, J.C. INC
LANCTOT COUVRE-SOL DESIGN
148 Rue Boyer, Saint-Isidore-De-Laprairie,
QC, J0L 2A0
(450) 692-4655
Emp Here 44   *Emp Total* 2
Sales 5,909,817
SIC 5713 Floor covering stores
Denis Lanctot

D-U-N-S 24-022-0319   (BR)
SINTRA INC
7 Rang Saint-Regis S, Saint-Isidore-De-
Laprairie, QC, J0L 2A0
(450) 638-0172
Emp Here 100
SIC 1611 Highway and street construction

Saint-Jacques, QC J0K
Montcalm County

D-U-N-S 20-003-1024   (SL)
**CAISSE DESJARDINS DE LA NOUVELLE-
ACADIE**
CENTRE DE SERVICES ST-JACQUES
4 Rue Beaudry, Saint-Jacques, QC, J0K 2R0
(450) 839-7211
Emp Here 33   *Sales* 6,136,835
SIC 6062 State credit unions
Genl Mgr Guy Tremblay
Pr Andre Lachapelle
VP Louis Parent
Sec Dominic Theriault
Dir Nathalie Genereux
Dir Simon Chapleau
Dir Lise Desrosiers
Dir Simon Leblanc

D-U-N-S 24-073-9909   (BR)
INDUSTRIES MAILHOT INC
2721 Rang Saint-Jacques, Saint-Jacques,
QC, J0K 2R0
(450) 839-3663
Emp Here 200
SIC 3569 General industrial machinery, nec

D-U-N-S 24-509-4305   (SL)
PLACEMENTS GILLES MAILHOT INC, LES
2711 Rang Saint-Jacques Rr 1, Saint-
Jacques, QC, J0K 2R0

Emp Here 55   *Sales* 5,526,400
SIC 3593 Fluid power cylinders and actuators
Pr Pr Gilles Mailhot

D-U-N-S 24-023-5684   (BR)
PROVIGO DISTRIBUTION INC
8 Rue Saint-Jacques Bureau 8037, Saint-
Jacques, QC, J0K 2R0
(450) 839-7218
Emp Here 40
SIC 5141 Groceries, general line

Saint-Jacques-De-Leeds, QC G0N
Beauce County

D-U-N-S 20-029-2063   (BR)
**COMMISSION   SCOLAIRE   DES   AP-
PALACHES**
ECOLE DE LA PASSERELLE
435 Rue Principale, Saint-Jacques-De-Leeds,
QC, G0N 1J0
(418) 424-3777
Emp Here 24
SIC 8211 Elementary and secondary schools

Saint-Jacques-Le-Mineur, QC J0J

D-U-N-S 24-369-8987   (BR)
**CAISSE DESJARDINS DES SEIGNEURIES
DE LA FRONTIERE**
*CENTRE DE SERVICES SAINT-JACQUES-
LE-MINEUR*
20 Rue Principale, Saint-Jacques-Le-Mineur,
QC, J0J 1Z0
(450) 346-8810
Emp Here 42
SIC 6062 State credit unions

Saint-Jean-Baptiste, QC J0L
Rouville County

D-U-N-S 25-240-5196   (BR)
COMMISSION SCOLAIRE DES PATRIOTES
COMMISSION SCOLAIRE DES PATRIOTES
3065 Rue Bedard, Saint-Jean-Baptiste, QC,
J0L 2B0
(450) 467-5870
Emp Here 20
SIC 8351 Child day care services

D-U-N-S 20-109-5861   (BR)
COOP FEDEREE, LA
UNIDINDON
3380 Rue Principale Bureau 430, Saint-Jean-
Baptiste, QC, J0L 2B0
(450) 467-2875
Emp Here 450
SIC 2015 Poultry slaughtering and processing

D-U-N-S 20-527-9131   (BR)
GROUPE J.F. NADEAU INC, LE
TRANSPORT G.N.D
3380 Rue Principale, Saint-Jean-Baptiste,
QC, J0L 2B0
(450) 464-8452
Emp Here 25
SIC 4111 Local and suburban transit

D-U-N-S 25-245-9433   (BR)
OLYMEL S.E.C.
UNIDINDON
3380 Rue Principale Bureau 430, Saint-Jean-
Baptiste, QC, J0L 2B0
(450) 467-2875
Emp Here 450
SIC 2015 Poultry slaughtering and processing

Saint-Jean-Chrysostome, QC G6Z
Levis County

D-U-N-S 20-288-4714   (SL)
9158-9325 QUEBEC INC
SUPERMARCHE IGA PEPIN
1015 Rue Des Lilas, Saint-Jean-
Chrysostome, QC, G6Z 3K4
(418) 834-8077
Emp Here 100   *Sales* 17,338,854
SIC 5411 Grocery stores
Pr Jocelyn Pepin
Tony Pepin

D-U-N-S 25-391-3966   (SL)
**CAISSE POPULAIRE DESJARDINS DE
SAINT-JEAN-CHRYSOSTOME**
730 Rue Commerciale, Saint-Jean-
Chrysostome, QC, G6Z 2C5
(418) 839-8819
Emp Here 44   *Sales* 8,826,150
SIC 6062 State credit unions
Genl Mgr Claude Perreault
Pr Francois Gendron
VP VP Gilles Larouche
Sec Rejean Lafleur

D-U-N-S 25-233-0337   (BR)
**COMMISSION SCOLAIRE DES NAVIGA-
TEURS**
ECOLE DE L'AIZE & MOUSSERONS
786 Ch Vanier, Saint-Jean-Chrysostome, QC,
G6Z 1Z6

Emp Here 20
SIC 7389 Business services, nec

Saint-Jean-De-Dieu, QC G0L
Riviere-Du-Loup County

D-U-N-S 25-233-7977   (BR)
**COMMISSION SCOLAIRE DU FLEUVE ET
DES LACS**
ECOLE SAINTE MARIE
3 Rue Sainte-Marie, Saint-Jean-De-Dieu, QC,
G0L 3M0
(418) 963-3226
Emp Here 35
SIC 8211 Elementary and secondary schools

Saint-Jean-De-Matha, QC J0K
Joliette County

D-U-N-S 20-712-1976   (BR)
COMMISSION SCOLAIRE DES SAMARES
ECOLE BERNECHE
239 Rue Du College, Saint-Jean-De-Matha,
QC, J0K 2S0
(450) 758-3688
Emp Here 50
SIC 8211 Elementary and secondary schools

Saint-Jean-Port-Joli, QC G0R
L'Islet County

D-U-N-S 25-090-7656   (BR)
**CENTRE DE SANTE ET SERVICES SOCI-
AUX DE MONTMAGNY - L'ISLET**
CLSC DE SAINT-JEAN PORT-JOLI
430 Rue Jean-Leclerc, Saint-Jean-Port-Joli,
QC, G0R 3G0
(418) 598-3355
Emp Here 50
SIC 8011 Offices and clinics of medical doc-
tors

D-U-N-S 24-897-0147   (SL)
**COMMISSION TOURISTIQUE DU PORT-
JOLI INC, LA**
RESTAURANT LA BOUSTIFAILLE
547 Av De Gaspe E, Saint-Jean-Port-Joli,
G0R 3G0
(418) 598-3061
Emp Here 50   *Sales* 1,532,175
SIC 5812 Eating places

D-U-N-S 25-500-1661   (BR)
METRO RICHELIEU INC
61 2e Rang E, Saint-Jean-Port-Joli, QC, G0R
3G0
(418) 598-3371
Emp Here 80
SIC 5411 Grocery stores

Saint-Jean-Sur-Richelieu, QC J2W
St-Jean County

D-U-N-S 24-211-7948   (SL)
9161-7340 QUEBEC INC
TIM HORTONS
180 Boul Omer-Marcil Bureau 2884, Saint-Jean-Sur-Richelieu, QC, J2W 2V1
(450) 359-0169
Emp Here 60   *Sales* 1,824,018
SIC 5812 Eating places

D-U-N-S 24-369-4754   (BR)
CAISSE DESJARDINS DU HAUT-RICHELIEU
CENTRE GESTION DES AVOIRS
(*Suby of* Caisse Desjardins du Haut-Richelieu)
175 Boul Omer-Marcil, Saint-Jean-Sur-Richelieu, QC, J2W 0A3
(450) 359-5933
Emp Here 250
SIC 6062 State credit unions

D-U-N-S 20-706-9324   (BR)
CARA OPERATIONS LIMITED
HARVEY'S RESTAURANT
(*Suby of* Cara Holdings Limited)
240 Boul Omer-Marcil, Saint-Jean-Sur-Richelieu, QC, J2W 2V1
(450) 348-6422
Emp Here 30
SIC 5812 Eating places

D-U-N-S 20-712-6538   (BR)
COMMISSION SCOLAIRE DES HAUTES-RIVIERES
ECOLE AUX QUATRE VENTS
185 Rue Saint-Gerard, Saint-Jean-Sur-Richelieu, QC, J2W 2L8
(450) 348-7341
Emp Here 50
SIC 8211 Elementary and secondary schools

D-U-N-S 25-193-3768   (BR)
PROVIGO DISTRIBUTION INC
MAXI
200 Boul Omer-Marcil, Saint-Jean-Sur-Richelieu, QC, J2W 2V1
(450) 348-0998
Emp Here 135
SIC 5411 Grocery stores

D-U-N-S 24-227-0544   (SL)
ROZON BATTERIES INC
TRANS-CANADA ENERGIE
700 Ch Du Grand-Bernier N, Saint-Jean-Sur-Richelieu, QC, J2W 2H1
(450) 348-8720
Emp Here 55   *Sales* 6,712,384
SIC 5013 Motor vehicle supplies and new parts
Pr Pr Elise Rozon
    Joel Rozon
Dir Sara Rozon

D-U-N-S 24-207-4198   (BR)
WAL-MART CANADA CORP
WALMART SUPERCENTRE
100 Boul Omer-Marcil, Saint-Jean-Sur-Richelieu, QC, J2W 2X2
(450) 349-0666
Emp Here 100
SIC 5311 Department stores

Saint-Jean-Sur-Richelieu, QC J2X
St-Jean County

D-U-N-S 24-804-7974   (BR)
ARMTEC LP
ARMTEC
800 Boul Pierre-Tremblay, Saint-Jean-Sur-Richelieu, QC, J2X 4W8
(450) 346-4481
Emp Here 150
SIC 3312 Blast furnaces and steel mills

D-U-N-S 24-874-8795   (BR)
BUANDERIE BLANCHELLE INC, LA
825 Av Montrichard, Saint-Jean-Sur-Richelieu, QC, J2X 5K8
(450) 347-4390
Emp Here 120
SIC 7218 Industrial launderers

D-U-N-S 25-240-4876   (BR)
COMMISSION SCOLAIRE DES HAUTES-RIVIERES
ECOLE SACRE COEUR
375 15e Av, Saint-Jean-Sur-Richelieu, QC, J2X 4W6
(450) 346-9808
Emp Here 25
SIC 8211 Elementary and secondary schools

D-U-N-S 25-240-4827   (BR)
COMMISSION SCOLAIRE DES HAUTES-RIVIERES
COMMISSION SCOLAIRE DES HAUTES-RIVIERES
295 6e Av, Saint-Jean-Sur-Richelieu, QC, J2X 1R1
(450) 347-1687
Emp Here 50
SIC 8211 Elementary and secondary schools

D-U-N-S 25-240-5691   (BR)
COMMISSION SCOLAIRE DES HAUTES-RIVIERES
COMMISSION SCOLAIRE DES HAUTES-RIVIERES
975 Rue Samuel-De-Champlain, Saint-Jean-Sur-Richelieu, QC, J2X 3X4
(450) 347-4358
Emp Here 23
SIC 8211 Elementary and secondary schools

D-U-N-S 25-240-5659   (BR)
COMMISSION SCOLAIRE DES HAUTES-RIVIERES
ECOLE HAMEL
635 Rue Yvon, Saint-Jean-Sur-Richelieu, QC, J2X 4H4
(450) 347-1443
Emp Here 34
SIC 8211 Elementary and secondary schools

D-U-N-S 25-234-2134   (BR)
COMMISSION SCOLAIRE DES HAUTES-RIVIERES
COMMISSION SCOLAIRE DES HAUTES-RIVIERES
976 Rue Honore-Mercier, Saint-Jean-Sur-Richelieu, QC, J2X 5A5
(450) 347-1327
Emp Here 22
SIC 8211 Elementary and secondary schools

D-U-N-S 25-234-2092   (BR)
COMMISSION SCOLAIRE DES HAUTES-RIVIERES
POLYVALENTE MARCEL LANDRY
365 Av Landry, Saint-Jean-Sur-Richelieu, QC, J2X 2P6
(450) 347-1376
Emp Here 180
SIC 8211 Elementary and secondary schools

D-U-N-S 20-296-6359   (BR)
GOUVERNEMENT DE LA PROVINCE DE QUEBEC
TRANSPORT QUEBEC
90 Ch Des Patriotes E, Saint-Jean-Sur-Richelieu, QC, J2X 5P9
(450) 347-2301
Emp Here 50
SIC 1611 Highway and street construction

D-U-N-S 20-500-9087   (SL)
INDUSTRIES B. RAINVILLE INC
175 Rte 104, Saint-Jean-Sur-Richelieu, QC, J2X 5T7
(450) 347-5521
Emp Here 45   *Sales* 8,244,559
SIC 5084 Industrial machinery and equipment
    Ghislain Sabourin

D-U-N-S 24-401-8412   (BR)
LES TISSUS RENTEX INC
310 5e Av, Saint-Jean-Sur-Richelieu, QC, J2X 1T9
(450) 347-4495
Emp Here 20
SIC 2258 Lace and warp knit fabric mills

D-U-N-S 20-119-8616   (BR)
SOLENO INC
1160 Route 133 Secteur Iberville Rr 1, Saint-Jean-Sur-Richelieu, QC, J2X 4J5
(450) 347-8315
Emp Here 150
SIC 3498 Fabricated pipe and fittings

D-U-N-S 20-058-2869   (HQ)
THOMAS & BETTS FABRICATION INC
700 Av Thomas, Saint-Jean-Sur-Richelieu, QC, J2X 2M9
(450) 347-5318
Emp Here 140   *Emp Total* 400
Sales 417,872,550
SIC 3644 Noncurrent-carrying wiring devices
Pr Pr Nathalie Pilon

Saint-Jean-Sur-Richelieu, QC J2Y
St-Jean County

D-U-N-S 20-253-5647   (SL)
CARRIERE BERNIER LTEE
25 Ch Du Petit-Bernier, Saint-Jean-Sur-Richelieu, QC, J2Y 1B8
(514) 875-2841
Emp Here 200
SIC 1422 Crushed and broken limestone

D-U-N-S 20-101-0274   (BR)
COMMISSION SCOLAIRE DES HAUTES-RIVIERES
ECOLE NAPOLEON BOURASSA
535 Ch Des Vieux-Moulins, Saint-Jean-Sur-Richelieu, QC, J2Y 1A2
(450) 347-1223
Emp Here 50
SIC 8211 Elementary and secondary schools

D-U-N-S 25-872-8666   (BR)
TRANSPORTS DUCAMPRO INC
1200 Boul Saint-Luc, Saint-Jean-Sur-Richelieu, QC, J2Y 1A5
(450) 348-4400
Emp Here 100
SIC 4213 Trucking, except local

Saint-Jean-Sur-Richelieu, QC J3A
St-Jean County

D-U-N-S 25-023-9274   (SL)
2550-7856 QUEBEC INC
COMPLEXE OASIS ST-JEAN
1050 Rue Stefoni, Saint-Jean-Sur-Richelieu, QC, J3A 1T5
(450) 349-5861
Emp Here 100   *Sales* 3,648,035
SIC 8361 Residential care

D-U-N-S 25-188-2163   (BR)
2757-5158 QUEBEC INC
ARMOIRES CUISINES ACTION
1050 Boul Du Seminaire N Bureau 210, Saint-Jean-Sur-Richelieu, QC, J3A 1S7
(450) 359-7980
Emp Here 100
SIC 2434 Wood kitchen cabinets

D-U-N-S 24-111-7139   (HQ)
CENTRE DE SANTE ET DE SERVICES SO-CIAUX HAUT-RICHELIEU-ROUVILLE
CSSS
(*Suby of* Centre de Sante et de Services Sociaux Haut-Richelieu-Rouville)
978 Boul Du Seminaire N, Saint-Jean-Sur-Richelieu, QC, J3A 1E5
(450) 358-2572
Emp Here 250   *Emp Total* 3,300
Sales 308,909,520
SIC 8062 General medical and surgical hospitals
    Yvan Gendron

D-U-N-S 20-033-9120   (BR)
COMMISSION SCOLAIRE DES HAUTES-RIVIERES
ECOLE MARIE RIVIER
511 Rue Pierre-Caisse, Saint-Jean-Sur-Richelieu, QC, J3A 1N5
(450) 348-0958
Emp Here 100
SIC 8211 Elementary and secondary schools

D-U-N-S 25-233-9205   (BR)
COMMISSION SCOLAIRE DES HAUTES-RIVIERES
POLYVALENTE CHAMOINE ARMAND RACICOT
940 Boul De Normandie, Saint-Jean-Sur-Richelieu, QC, J3A 1A7
(450) 348-6134
Emp Here 100
SIC 8211 Elementary and secondary schools

D-U-N-S 20-137-7996   (BR)
COMMISSION SCOLAIRE DES HAUTES-RIVIERES
ECOLE MARIE DEROME
995 Rue Camaraire, Saint-Jean-Sur-Richelieu, QC, J3A 1X2
(450) 359-6521
Emp Here 30
SIC 8211 Elementary and secondary schools

D-U-N-S 25-448-1617   (BR)
METRO RICHELIEU INC
SUPER C
600 Rue Pierre-Caisse Bureau 2000, Saint-Jean-Sur-Richelieu, QC, J3A 1M1
(450) 348-0927
Emp Here 80
SIC 5411 Grocery stores

D-U-N-S 25-092-2051   (BR)
PROVIGO DISTRIBUTION INC
MAXI
1000 Boul Du Seminaire N Bureau 6, Saint-Jean-Sur-Richelieu, QC, J3A 1E5
(450) 348-3813
Emp Here 65
SIC 5411 Grocery stores

D-U-N-S 25-023-2741   (BR)
RAYMOND CHABOT GRANT THORNTON S.E.N.C.R.L.
745 Rue Gadbois Bureau 201, Saint-Jean-Sur-Richelieu, QC, J3A 0A1
(450) 348-6886
Emp Here 25
SIC 8721 Accounting, auditing, and bookkeeping

D-U-N-S 25-259-6507   (BR)
REDBERRY FRANCHISING CORP
BURGER KING
930 Rue Douglas, Saint-Jean-Sur-Richelieu, QC, J3A 1V1
(450) 359-7745
Emp Here 30
SIC 5812 Eating places

D-U-N-S 25-993-3786   (SL)
RESTAURANT LA CAGE AUX SPORTS INC
880 Boul Du Seminaire N, Saint-Jean-Sur-Richelieu, QC, J3A 1B5

(450) 359-6484
Emp Here 50   *Sales* 1,532,175
SIC 5812 Eating places

D-U-N-S 24-174-1792   (SL)
ROTISSERIES DU HAUT RICHELIEU LTEE, LES
ROTISSERIE ST HUBERT
960 Boul Du Seminaire N, Saint-Jean-Richelieu, QC, J3A 1L2
(450) 348-6876
Emp Here 80   *Sales* 2,407,703
SIC 5812 Eating places

D-U-N-S 20-860-1109   (BR)
SOURCE (BELL) ELECTRONICS INC, THE
SOURCE, LA
600 Rue Pierre-Caisse, Saint-Jean-Richelieu, QC, J3A 1M1
(450) 349-9389
Emp Here 25
SIC 5999 Miscellaneous retail stores, nec

D-U-N-S 25-784-7806   (BR)
STAPLES CANADA INC
BUREAU EN GROS
(*Suby of* Staples, Inc.)
1000 Boul Du Seminaire N, Saint-Jean-Richelieu, QC, J3A 1E5
(450) 359-7750
Emp Here 30
SIC 5943 Stationery stores

D-U-N-S 25-830-6745   (BR)
SUN LIFE FINANCIAL INVESTMENT SERVICES (CANADA) INC
365 Rue Normand Bureau 200, Saint-Jean-Sur-Richelieu, QC, J3A 1T6
(450) 348-9239
Emp Here 25
SIC 6311 Life insurance

D-U-N-S 24-847-8864   (BR)
VALUE VILLAGE STORES, INC
(*Suby of* Savers, Inc.)
1000 Boul Du Seminaire N Bureau 7, Saint-Jean-Sur-Fichelieu, QC, J3A 1E5
(450) 359-9661
Emp Here 40
SIC 5399 Miscellaneous general merchandise

D-U-N-S 20-184-3211   (BR)
WINNERS MERCHANTS INTERNATIONAL L.P.
WINNERS
(*Suby of* The TJX Companies Inc)
600 Rue Pierre-Caisse, Saint-Jean-Richelieu, QC, J3A 1M1
(450) 348-3588
Emp Here 40
SIC 5651 Family clothing stores

Saint-Jean-Sur-Richelieu, QC J3B
St-Jean County

D-U-N-S 24-870-8638   (SL)
2434-1281 QUEBEC INC
800 Rue Pierre-Caisse, Saint-Jean-Richelieu, QC, J3B 7Y5
(450) 348-6031
Emp Here 40   *Sales* 5,496,960
SIC 6712 Bank holding companies
  Diana Feret

D-U-N-S 24-590-2481   (SL)
ATELIER INDUSTRIEL ST-JEAN (1980) INC
277 Rue Langlois, Saint-Jean-Sur-Richelieu, QC, J3B 4S4
(450) 347-2616
Emp Here 70   *Sales* 3,283,232
SIC 8331 Job training and related services

D-U-N-S 25-762-5111   (BR)
BANQUE NATIONALE DU CANADA
400 Boul Du Seminaire N Bureau D1, Saint-Jean-Sur-Richelieu, QC, J3B 5L2

(450) 348-6131
Emp Here 30
SIC 6021 National commercial banks

D-U-N-S 25-759-8649   (BR)
BOIS EXPANSION INC
285 Rue Carreau, Saint-Jean-Sur-Richelieu, QC, J3B 7Z7
(450) 358-4008
Emp Here 40
SIC 5031 Lumber, plywood, and millwork

D-U-N-S 20-852-4632   (BR)
CAISSE POPULAIRE DESJARDINS DE SAINT-JEAN-SUR-RICHELIEU
CAISSE POPULAIRE DESJARDINS DE SAINT-JEAN-SUR-RICHELIEU
211 Rue Mayrand, Saint-Jean-Sur-Richelieu, QC, J3B 3L1
(450) 347-5553
Emp Here 30
SIC 6062 State credit unions

D-U-N-S 25-782-8137   (HQ)
CAISSE POPULAIRE DESJARDINS DE SAINT-JEAN-SUR-RICHELIEU
CENTRE DE SERVICE SAINT-EDMOND
(*Suby of* Caisse Populaire Desjardins de Saint-Jean-sur-Richelieu)
25 Rue Saint-Jacques, Saint-Jean-Richelieu, QC, J3B 2J6
(450) 347-5553
Emp Here 30   *Emp Total* 70
Sales 13,797,200
SIC 6062 State credit unions
Genl Mgr Jean-Pierre Bessette
Dir Josee Mailhot
Pr Michel Robert
VP VP Yvon Payette
Sec Luc Martel
  Francois-Luc Dallaire
  Lorenzo Godbout
  Jean Darwish
  Agathe S Mansi
Dir Jean-Christophe Durand

D-U-N-S 25-894-3877   (BR)
CANADA POST CORPORATION
BUREAU DE POSTES SAINT JEAN
246 Rue Champlain, Saint-Jean-Sur-Richelieu, QC, J3B 0J8
(450) 347-5337
Emp Here 60
SIC 4311 U.s. postal service

D-U-N-S 20-882-2049   (BR)
CENTRE INTEGRE DE SANTE ET DE SERVICES SOCIAUX DE LA MONTEREGIE-OUEST
SERVICES DE READAPTATION DU SUD-OUEST ET DU RENFORT, LES
(*Suby of* Centre Integre de Sante et de Services Sociaux de la Monteregie-Ouest)
315 Rue Macdonald Bureau 105, Saint-Jean-Sur-Richelieu, QC, J3B 8J3
(450) 348-6121
Emp Here 200
SIC 8361 Residential care

D-U-N-S 25-233-8181   (BR)
COMMISSION SCOLAIRE DES HAUTES-RIVIERES
ECOLE FELIX GABRIEL MARCHAND
90 Rue Mackenzie-King, Saint-Jean-Richelieu, QC, J3B 5N9
(450) 346-3652
Emp Here 55
SIC 8211 Elementary and secondary schools

D-U-N-S 25-240-0700   (BR)
COMMISSION SCOLAIRE DES HAUTES-RIVIERES
COMMISSION SCOLAIRE DES HAUTES-RIVIERES
300 Rue Georges-Phaneuf, Saint-Jean-Sur-Richelieu, QC, J3B 8E4
(450) 348-2303
Emp Here 30

SIC 8211 Elementary and secondary schools

D-U-N-S 25-233-9288   (BR)
COMMISSION SCOLAIRE DES HAUTES-RIVIERES
COMMISSION SCOLAIRE DES HAUTES-RIVIERES
154 Rue Saint-Charles, Saint-Jean-Richelieu, QC, J3B 2C6
(450) 347-5113
Emp Here 64
SIC 8211 Elementary and secondary schools

D-U-N-S 25-240-0460   (BR)
COMMISSION SCOLAIRE DES HAUTES-RIVIERES
COMMISSION SCOLAIRE DES HAUTES-RIVIERES
800 Rue Plaza, Saint-Jean-Sur-Richelieu, QC, J3B 7Z4
(450) 347-4220
Emp Here 50
SIC 8211 Elementary and secondary schools

D-U-N-S 25-233-9320   (BR)
COMMISSION SCOLAIRE DES HAUTES-RIVIERES
ECOLE SECONDAIRE BEAULIEU
135 Boul Du Seminaire N, Saint-Jean-Richelieu, QC, J3B 5K2
(450) 347-8344
Emp Here 65
SIC 8211 Elementary and secondary schools

D-U-N-S 25-233-8819   (BR)
COMMISSION SCOLAIRE DES HAUTES-RIVIERES
ECOLE SECONDAIRE DR ALEXIS BOUTHILLIER
105 Rue Jacques-Cartier S, Saint-Jean-Richelieu, QC, J3B 6S2
(450) 347-5515
Emp Here 60
SIC 8211 Elementary and secondary schools

D-U-N-S 25-240-0882   (BR)
COMMISSION SCOLAIRE DES HAUTES-RIVIERES
ECOLE JOSEPH AMEDEE BELANGER
151 Rue Notre-Dame, Saint-Jean-Sur-Richelieu, QC, J3B 6M9
(450) 348-4747
Emp Here 300
SIC 8211 Elementary and secondary schools

D-U-N-S 20-712-6546   (BR)
COMMISSION SCOLAIRE DES HAUTES-RIVIERES
ECOLE PROFESSIONNELLE DE METIERS
100 Rue Laurier, Saint-Jean-Sur-Richelieu, QC, J3B 2Y5
(450) 347-3797
Emp Here 40
SIC 8211 Elementary and secondary schools

D-U-N-S 25-240-0171   (BR)
COMMISSION SCOLAIRE DES HAUTES-RIVIERES
COMMISSION SCOLAIRE DES HAUTES-RIVIERES
700 Rue Dorchester, Saint-Jean-Richelieu, QC, J3B 5A8
(450) 348-5095
Emp Here 40
SIC 8211 Elementary and secondary schools

D-U-N-S 20-806-7202   (BR)
COUCHE-TARD INC
290 Ch Du Grand-Bernier N Bureau 491, Saint-Jean-Sur-Richelieu, QC, J3B 4R4
(450) 358-2233
Emp Here 25
SIC 5411 Grocery stores

D-U-N-S 25-739-2308   (SL)
DNA LANDMARKS INC
RECHERCHE ET DEVELOPPEMENT DNA LANDMARKS

84 Rue Richelieu, Saint-Jean-Sur-Richelieu, QC, J3B 6X3
(450) 358-2621
Emp Here 45   *Sales* 2,480,664
SIC 8731 Commercial physical research

D-U-N-S 24-779-1549   (SL)
ENTREPRISES DOCO INC
CONCERTO LA FENETRE TOUT PVC
285 Ch Du Grand-Bernier N, Saint-Jean-Richelieu, QC, J3B 4R3
(514) 861-1765
Emp Here 50   *Sales* 4,085,799
SIC 2431 Millwork

D-U-N-S 20-253-8252   (SL)
FABRICATION METELEC LTEE
300 Rue Carreau, Saint-Jean-Richelieu, QC, J3B 2G4
(450) 346-6363
Emp Here 51   *Sales* 5,619,947
SIC 1761 Roofing, siding, and sheetMetal work
Pr Pr Michel Paquette
VP VP Roger Huber
  Doris Huber
  Peter Huber

D-U-N-S 20-107-0021   (BR)
FEDERATION DES CAISSES DESJARDINS DU QUEBEC
CFE DU HAUT-RICHELIEU
145 Boul Saint-Joseph, Saint-Jean-Richelieu, QC, J3B 1W5
(450) 359-0038
Emp Here 30
SIC 8741 Management services

D-U-N-S 25-972-1777   (BR)
FONDATION DU CENTRE JEUNESSE DE LA MONTEREGIE
145 Boul Saint-Joseph Bureau 200, Saint-Jean-Richelieu, QC, J3B 1W5
(450) 359-7525
Emp Here 80
SIC 8322 Individual and family services

D-U-N-S 20-564-6185   (HQ)
FORMICA CANADA INC
FORMICA
25 Rue Mercier, Saint-Jean-Sur-Richelieu, QC, J3B 6E9
(450) 347-7541
Emp Here 300   *Emp Total* 20,000
Sales 59,251,568
SIC 3089 Plastics products, nec
Pr Mitchell P. Quint
Sec Raul Jr. Rosado
Treas Leigh Box
Dir Claude Sarrazin

D-U-N-S 25-671-4163   (BR)
GESTION MAISON ETHIER INC
126 Rue Jacques-Cartier N, Saint-Jean-Richelieu, QC, J3B 6S5
(450) 346-1090
Emp Here 55
SIC 5021 Furniture

D-U-N-S 20-302-8857   (SL)
GROUPE CAMBLI INC
CAMBLI INTERNATIONAL
555 Rue Saint-Louis, Saint-Jean-Richelieu, QC, J3B 8X7
(450) 358-4920
Emp Here 100   *Sales* 3,137,310
SIC 7381 Detective and armored car services

D-U-N-S 20-363-1507   (SL)
GROUPE DOMISA INC
COMPLEXE SPORT ABSOLU
15 Rue Jacques-Cartier N, Saint-Jean-Richelieu, QC, J3B 8R8
(450) 358-6604
Emp Here 40   *Sales* 3,283,232
SIC 7999 Amusement and recreation, nec

D-U-N-S 24-223-3083   (BR)

GROUPE RESTAURANTS IMVESCOR INC
RESTAURANT MIKES
419 Rue Saint-Jacques, Saint-Jean-Sur-Richelieu, QC, J3B 2M1
(450) 347-8133
Emp Here 20
SIC 5812 Eating places

D-U-N-S 25-257-9214   (SL)
HOTEL VALLEE DES FORTS INC
RELAIS GOUVERNEUR ST-JEAN, LE
725 Boul Du Seminaire N, Saint-Jean-Sur-Richelieu, QC, J3B 8H1
(450) 348-7376
Emp Here 50   *Sales* 2,188,821
SIC 7011 Hotels and motels

D-U-N-S 20-253-8120   (SL)
MARTIN INC
SUEDART
285 Rue Saint-Jacques Bureau 2, Saint-Jean-Sur-Richelieu, QC, J3B 2L1
(450) 347-2373
Emp Here 90   *Sales* 2,845,467
SIC 7219 Laundry and garment services, nec

D-U-N-S 24-959-1579   (SL)
METAL POLE-LITE INC
POLE-LITE
(*Suby of* Union Metal Corporation)
405 Rue Saint-Louis, Saint-Jean-Sur-Richelieu, QC, J3B 1Y6
(514) 312-7405
Emp Here 45   *Sales* 4,961,328
SIC 3499 Fabricated Metal products, nec

D-U-N-S 24-330-9163   (SL)
NYACK TECHNOLOGY INC
160 Rue Vanier, Saint-Jean-Sur-Richelieu, QC, J3B 3R4
(450) 245-0373
Emp Here 100   *Sales* 14,134,935
SIC 2821 Plastics materials and resins
Andree Sebbag

D-U-N-S 25-993-3380   (BR)
NAUTILUS PLUS INC
KINEQUIP
315 Rue Macdonald Bureau 120, Saint-Jean-Sur-Richelieu, QC, J3B 8J3
(450) 348-5666
Emp Here 20
SIC 7999 Amusement and recreation, nec

D-U-N-S 20-007-1012   (BR)
OLYMEL S.E.C.
FLAMINGO
770 Rue Claude, Saint-Jean-Sur-Richelieu, QC, J3B 2W5
(450) 347-2241
Emp Here 100
SIC 2011 Meat packing plants

D-U-N-S 20-200-7548   (SL)
P. BAILLARGEON LTEE
800 Rue Des Carrieres, Saint-Jean-Sur-Richelieu, QC, J3B 2P2
(514) 866-8333
Emp Here 140   *Sales* 22,724,800
SIC 1611 Highway and street construction
Pr Pr Pierre Baillargeon
Pr Pr Pascale Baillargeon
VP Phillippe Antoine Baillargeon
Sec Annik Bussieres
Dir Josee De La Durantaye

D-U-N-S 24-901-7955   (SL)
PCAS CANADA INC
ST-JEAN PHOTOCHIMIE
725 Rue Trotter, Saint-Jean-Sur-Richelieu, QC, J3B 8J8
(450) 348-0901
Emp Here 50   *Sales* 9,423,290
SIC 2899 Chemical preparations, nec
Sec Seon Kang
Pr Pierre Schreiner
Dir Christian Moretti

Dir Eric Moissenot
Dir Vincent Touraille

D-U-N-S 24-814-3380   (SL)
PATELLA INDUSTRIES INC
721 Ch Du Grand-Bernier N, Saint-Jean-Sur-Richelieu, QC, J3B 8H6
(450) 359-0040
Emp Here 50   *Sales* 4,085,799
SIC 2431 Millwork

D-U-N-S 20-177-9548   (BR)
PIECES AUTOMOBILES LECAVALIER INC
LECAVALIER AUTOPARTS
1330 Rue Jacques-Cartier S, Saint-Jean-Sur-Richelieu, QC, J3B 6Y8
(450) 346-1112
Emp Here 35
SIC 5013 Motor vehicle supplies and new parts

D-U-N-S 20-571-3907   (BR)
PROVIGO DISTRIBUTION INC
PROVIGO ST JEAN
429 Rue Saint-Jacques, Saint-Jean-Sur-Richelieu, QC, J3B 2M1
(450) 347-6811
Emp Here 52
SIC 5411 Grocery stores

D-U-N-S 25-759-9068   (BR)
RESTAURANTS MAC-VIC INC, LES
MCDONALD'S
661 Boul Du Seminaire N, Saint-Jean-Sur-Richelieu, QC, J3B 5M2
(450) 348-4664
Emp Here 49
SIC 5812 Eating places

D-U-N-S 24-175-0157   (SL)
ROTISSERIES R. J. P. INC
COQ RAPIDE
365 Boul Du Seminaire N, Saint-Jean-Sur-Richelieu, QC, J3B 8C5
(450) 348-1191
Emp Here 60   *Sales* 1,824,018
SIC 5812 Eating places

D-U-N-S 25-231-8761   (BR)
SAINT-JEAN-SUR-RICHELIEU, VILLE DE
BIBLIOTHEQUE ADELARD BERGER
180 Rue Laurier, Saint-Jean-Sur-Richelieu, QC, J3B 7J9

Emp Here 30
SIC 8231 Libraries

D-U-N-S 24-978-0409   (HQ)
SYSTEMES ET CABLES PRYSMIAN CANADA LTEE
383 Boul Du Seminaire N, Saint-Jean-Sur-Richelieu, QC, J3B 8C5
(450) 359-6721
Emp Here 150   *Emp Total* 406
Sales 35,021,136
SIC 1623 Water, sewer, and utility lines
Hakan Ozmen
Dir Valerio Battista
VP VP Daniele Mazzarella
Sec Scott A. Wood
Dir Fabio Romeo

D-U-N-S 25-211-4749   (BR)
THOMAS & BETTS, LIMITEE
100 Rue Longtin, Saint-Jean-Sur-Richelieu, QC, J3B 3G5
(450) 347-2304
Emp Here 375
SIC 3644 Noncurrent-carrying wiring devices

D-U-N-S 24-019-9661   (SL)
TRANSPORT GUY BOURASSA INC
(*Suby of* Les Placements J.D.G. Inc)
800 Rue De Dijon, Saint-Jean-Sur-Richelieu, QC, J3B 8G3
(450) 346-5313
Emp Here 350   *Sales* 37,202,640
SIC 4212 Local trucking, without storage

Pr Jean Bourassa
Daniel Bourassa
Fin Ex Sylvie Bourassa

Saint-Jerome, QC J5L
Terrebonne County

D-U-N-S 24-712-5883   (SL)
AUTOBUS BRUNET INC, LES
BRUNET ET CLOUTIER
986 Rue Des Lacs, Saint-Jerome, QC, J5L 1T4
(450) 438-8363
Emp Here 103   *Sales* 3,769,316
SIC 4151 School buses

D-U-N-S 20-285-5222   (SL)
CHALIFOUX SANI LAURENTIDES INC
2 Boul Maisonneuve, Saint-Jerome, QC, J5L 0A1
(450) 224-2855
Emp Here 50   *Sales* 3,064,349
SIC 7699 Repair services, nec

D-U-N-S 20-712-1729   (BR)
COMMISSION SCOLAIRE DE LA RIVIERE-DU-NORD
CENTRE D'ETUDES PROFESSIONELLES
(*Suby of* Commission Scolaire de la Riviere-du-Nord)
917 Montee Saint-Nicolas, Saint-Jerome, QC, J5L 2P4
(450) 565-0006
Emp Here 50
SIC 8211 Elementary and secondary schools

D-U-N-S 20-213-5757   (BR)
COMMISSION SCOLAIRE DE LA RIVIERE-DU-NORD
ECOLE DE L'ENVOLEE
(*Suby of* Commission Scolaire de la Riviere-du-Nord)
1475 Rue Normand, Saint-Jerome, QC, J5L 2B6
(450) 431-4377
Emp Here 32
SIC 8211 Elementary and secondary schools

D-U-N-S 25-240-1203   (BR)
COMMISSION SCOLAIRE DE LA RIVIERE-DU-NORD
COMMISSION SCOLAIRE DE LA RIVIERE-DU-NORD
(*Suby of* Commission Scolaire de la Riviere-du-Nord)
997 Rue Des Lacs, Saint-Jerome, QC, J5L 1T3
(450) 438-9525
Emp Here 30
SIC 8211 Elementary and secondary schools

D-U-N-S 20-712-1794   (BR)
COMMISSION SCOLAIRE DE LA RIVIERE-DU-NORD
ECOLE ST JEROME
(*Suby of* Commission Scolaire de la Riviere-du-Nord)
909 Montee Saint-Nicolas, Saint-Jerome, QC, J5L 2P4
(450) 431-2114
Emp Here 50
SIC 8211 Elementary and secondary schools

D-U-N-S 25-770-3244   (SL)
PAMA MANUFACTURING
25 Boul Maisonneuve, Saint-Jerome, QC, J5L 0A1
(450) 431-5353
Emp Here 49   *Sales* 5,107,249
SIC 2326 Men's and boy's work clothing

D-U-N-S 20-102-0539   (BR)
SIGNALISATION DE L'ESTRIE INC
SIGNALISATION LAURENTIENNE
999 Rue Lauzanne, Saint-Jerome, QC, J5L

1V8
(450) 432-5872
Emp Here 50
SIC 3714 Motor vehicle parts and accessories

D-U-N-S 24-608-0084   (BR)
SUPER-SAVE ENTERPRISES LTD
SUPER GAZ
840 Rue De Martigny O, Saint-Jerome, QC, J5L 1Z6
(450) 438-2587
Emp Here 25
SIC 5172 Petroleum products, nec

Saint-Jerome, QC J7Y
Terrebonne County

D-U-N-S 24-229-1623   (SL)
106953 CANADA LTEE
ATELIER DE BOIS 80
475 Boul De Sainte-Marcelle, Saint-Jerome, QC, J7Y 2P7
(450) 438-9992
Emp Here 60   *Sales* 3,502,114
SIC 2434 Wood kitchen cabinets

D-U-N-S 20-220-8906   (HQ)
127323 CANADA INC
INDUSTRIES J HAMELIN, LES
(*Suby of* 127323 Canada Inc)
600 Boul Roland-Godard, Saint-Jerome, QC, J7Y 4C5
(450) 431-3221
Emp Here 100   *Emp Total* 130
Sales 16,490,758
SIC 3553 Woodworking machinery
Pr Pr Harold Stotland
VP VP Benoit St-Amour

D-U-N-S 24-177-1885   (SL)
9098-2067 QUEBEC INC
TIM HORTONS
1 Rue John-F.-Kennedy, Saint-Jerome, QC, J7Y 4B4
(450) 660-6200
Emp Here 150   *Sales* 4,523,563
SIC 5812 Eating places

D-U-N-S 20-102-5504   (SL)
9098-2067 QUEBEC INC
TIM HORTONS
2001 Boul Du Cure-Labelle, Saint-Jerome, QC, J7Y 1S2
(450) 431-6411
Emp Here 150   *Sales* 4,523,563
SIC 5812 Eating places

D-U-N-S 25-766-1249   (SL)
AGENCE DE PLACEMENT SELECT INC
96 Rue De Martigny O, Saint-Jerome, QC, J7Y 2G1
(450) 431-6292
Emp Here 50   *Sales* 3,648,035
SIC 7361 Employment agencies

D-U-N-S 24-050-8692   (BR)
AGRI-MARCHE INC
AGRI-MARCHE
870 Rue Alfred-Viau, Saint-Jerome, QC, J7Y 4N8
(450) 438-1214
Emp Here 20
SIC 3556 Food products machinery

D-U-N-S 24-901-4283   (BR)
AKZO NOBEL COATINGS LTD
AKZO NOBEL PEINTURES
1001 Boul Roland-Godard, Saint-Jerome, QC, J7Y 4C2

Emp Here 100
SIC 2851 Paints and allied products

D-U-N-S 25-763-7751   (SL)
AUTOBUS TRANSCOBEC (1987) INC, LES
21 Rue John-F.-Kennedy, Saint-Jerome, QC,

J7Y 4B4
(450) 432-9748
Emp Here 150   *Sales* 4,231,721
SIC 4151 School buses

D-U-N-S 20-962-2042   (SL)
AUTOMOBILES NORD SUD INC
NORD SUD HONDA
325 Rue John-F.-Kennedy, Saint-Jerome, QC,
J7Y 4B5
(450) 438-1273
Emp Here 50   *Sales* 24,540,000
SIC 5511 New and used car dealers
Pr Pr Jean Gagne
VP VP Alexandre Gagne
 Claudie Gagne

D-U-N-S 24-969-6469   (BR)
BEAULIEU, CLAUDE SPORT INC
SPORT EXPERT
900 Boul Grignon, Saint-Jerome, QC, J7Y 3S7
(450) 432-9400
Emp Here 30
SIC 5941 Sporting goods and bicycle shops

D-U-N-S 24-363-5096   (BR)
BEST BUY CANADA LTD
FUTURE SHOP
(*Suby of* Best Buy Co., Inc.)
1125 Boul Jean-Baptiste-Rolland O, Saint-
Jerome, QC, J7Y 4Y7

Emp Here 50
SIC 5999 Miscellaneous retail stores, nec

D-U-N-S 24-209-9815   (BR)
BOUCLAIR INC
1044 Boul Du Grand-Heron, Saint-Jerome,
QC, J7Y 5K8
(450) 432-4474
Emp Here 20
SIC 5023 Homefurnishings

D-U-N-S 20-860-5076   (BR)
BOUTIQUE LA VIE EN ROSE INC
BOUTIQUE LA VIE EN ROSE INC
900 Boul Grignon, Saint-Jerome, QC, J7Y 3S7
(450) 565-2999
Emp Here 25
SIC 5632 Women's accessory and specialty
stores

D-U-N-S 24-125-0195   (BR)
CAISSE DESJARDINS DE SAINT-JEROME
*CENTRE FINANCIER AUX ENTREPRISES
DES LAURENTIDES*
296 Rue De Martigny O Bureau 200, Saint-
Jerome, QC, J7Y 4C9

Emp Here 40
SIC 8741 Management services

D-U-N-S 20-997-8436   (BR)
**CENTRE INTEGRE DE SANTE ET DE SER-
VICES SOCIAUX DES LAURENTIDES**
LE CISSS DE LAURENTIDES
66 Rue Danis, Saint-Jerome, QC, J7Y 2R3
(450) 436-3131
Emp Here 20
SIC 8011 Offices and clinics of medical doc-
tors

D-U-N-S 25-758-6859   (BR)
CENTRE JEUNESSE DES LAURENTIDES
PROTECTION DE LA JEUNESSE
358 Rue Laviolette, Saint-Jerome, QC, J7Y
2T1
(450) 432-9753
Emp Here 80
SIC 8322 Individual and family services

**COMMISSION SCOLAIRE DE LA RIVIERE-
DU-NORD**
ECOLE DE LA DURANTAYE
(*Suby of* Commission Scolaire de la Riviere-
du-Nord)
31 Rue Paul, Saint-Jerome, QC, J7Y 1Z5

(450) 432-9582
Emp Here 25
SIC 8211 Elementary and secondary schools

D-U-N-S 20-797-0190   (BR)
**COMMISSION SCOLAIRE DE LA RIVIERE-
DU-NORD**
ECOLE LA FOURMILIERE
(*Suby of* Commission Scolaire de la Riviere-
du-Nord)
175 Rue Duvernay, Saint-Jerome, QC, J7Y
2Z6
(450) 432-4506
Emp Here 25
SIC 8211 Elementary and secondary schools

D-U-N-S 25-233-5914   (BR)
**COMMISSION SCOLAIRE DE LA RIVIERE-
DU-NORD**
ECOLE LA FOURMILIERE
(*Suby of* Commission Scolaire de la Riviere-
du-Nord)
175 Rue Duvernay, Saint-Jerome, QC, J7Y
2Z6
(450) 438-1220
Emp Here 25
SIC 8211 Elementary and secondary schools

D-U-N-S 20-009-4048   (BR)
**COMMISSION SCOLAIRE DE LA RIVIERE-
DU-NORD**
*COMMISSION SCOLAIRE DE LA RIVIERE-
DU-NORD*
(*Suby of* Commission Scolaire de la Riviere-
du-Nord)
85 Rue Lauzon, Saint-Jerome, QC, J7Y 1V8
(450) 438-5603
Emp Here 50
SIC 8211 Elementary and secondary schools

D-U-N-S 24-012-1660   (BR)
**COMMISSION SCOLAIRE DE LA RIVIERE-
DU-NORD**
ECOLES PRIMAIRES SACRE COEUR
(*Suby of* Commission Scolaire de la Riviere-
du-Nord)
70 Boul Des Hauteurs, Saint-Jerome, QC, J7Y
1R4
(450) 438-1259
Emp Here 52
SIC 8211 Elementary and secondary schools

D-U-N-S 20-712-1901   (BR)
**COMMISSION SCOLAIRE DE LA RIVIERE-
DU-NORD**
*ECOLE SECONDAIRE DES HAUTS SOM-
METS*
(*Suby of* Commission Scolaire de la Riviere-
du-Nord)
1000 112e Av, Saint-Jerome, QC, J7Y 5C2
(450) 436-7414
Emp Here 50
SIC 8211 Elementary and secondary schools

D-U-N-S 24-527-1606   (SL)
COMPAGNIE DU BOIS FRANC DZD INC, LA
PLANCHERS BELLEFEUILLE
(*Suby of* 100489 Canada Inc)
450 Boul Roland-Godard, Saint-Jerome, QC,
J7Y 4G8
(450) 431-1643
Emp Here 50   *Sales* 15,029,904
SIC 5031 Lumber, plywood, and millwork
Pr Sefi Dollinger
 Guy Dollinger
Dir Heinz Leeb

D-U-N-S 24-354-8901   (BR)
COSTCO WHOLESALE CANADA LTD
(*Suby of* Costco Wholesale Corporation)
1001 Boul Jean-Baptiste-Rolland O, Saint-
Jerome, QC, J7Y 4Y7
(450) 476-9000
Emp Here 50
SIC 5099 Durable goods, nec

D-U-N-S 20-806-7293   (BR)
COUCHE-TARD INC

10 Boul De La Salette, Saint-Jerome, QC, J7Y
5C8
(450) 438-4285
Emp Here 25
SIC 5411 Grocery stores

D-U-N-S 20-806-7301   (BR)
COUCHE-TARD INC
2260 Rue Schulz, Saint-Jerome, QC, J7Y 5B3
(450) 431-8721
Emp Here 25
SIC 5411 Grocery stores

D-U-N-S 25-734-2733   (BR)
DOLLARAMA S.E.C.
DOLLARAMA
1950 Du Cure-Labelle Blvd, Saint-Jerome,
QC, J7Y 1S1
(450) 432-5624
Emp Here 20
SIC 5331 Variety stores

D-U-N-S 25-362-6451   (BR)
ENTREPRISES ROLLAND INC, LES
*CASCADES CENTRE DE TRANSFORMA-
TION*
980 Rue De L'Industrie, Saint-Jerome, QC,
J7Y 4B8
(450) 569-0040
Emp Here 130
SIC 5111 Printing and writing paper

D-U-N-S 20-366-2148   (BR)
FORTIN, JEAN & ASSOCIES SYNDICS INC
30 Rue De Martigny O Bureau 100, Saint-
Jerome, QC, J7Y 2E9
(450) 432-0207
Emp Here 40
SIC 8111 Legal services

D-U-N-S 20-704-8930   (BR)
**GOUVERNEMENT DE LA PROVINCE DE
QUEBEC**
*GOUVERNEMENT DE LA PROVINCE DE
QUEBEC*
25 Rue De Martigny O, Saint-Jerome, QC, J7Y
4Z1
(450) 431-4406
Emp Here 100
SIC 8111 Legal services

D-U-N-S 20-712-1893   (BR)
**GOUVERNEMENT DE LA PROVINCE DE
QUEBEC**
CENTRE DE JOUR
330 Rue De Martigny O, Saint-Jerome, QC,
J7Y 4C9
(450) 438-2225
Emp Here 20
SIC 8059 Nursing and personal care, nec

D-U-N-S 20-515-5620   (BR)
**GOUVERNEMENT DE LA PROVINCE DE
QUEBEC**
CSST LAURENTIDES
85 Rue De Martigny O, Saint-Jerome, QC, J7Y
3R8
(450) 431-4000
Emp Here 50
SIC 6331 Fire, marine, and casualty insurance

D-U-N-S 25-493-7167   (BR)
GROUPE BMTC INC
BRAULT & MARTINEAU
21 Rue Gauthier, Saint-Jerome, QC, J7Y 0A3
(450) 431-9338
Emp Here 20
SIC 5712 Furniture stores

D-U-N-S 25-365-4719   (BR)
HOME DEPOT OF CANADA INC
HOME DEPOT
(*Suby of* The Home Depot Inc)
1045 Boul Du Grand-Heron, Saint-Jerome,
QC, J7Y 3P2
(450) 565-6020
Emp Here 150
SIC 5251 Hardware stores

D-U-N-S 20-511-7620   (BR)
ICON DU CANADA INC
ICON DU CANADA INC
(*Suby of* Bain Capital, LP)
950 Rue De L'Industrie, Saint-Jerome, QC,
J7Y 4B8
(450) 565-2955
Emp Here 30
SIC 5091 Sporting and recreation goods

D-U-N-S 24-081-7072   (HQ)
MATERIAUX LAURENTIENS INC
MATERIO
2159 Boul Du Cure-Labelle, Saint-Jerome,
QC, J7Y 1T1
(450) 438-9780
Emp Here 25   *Emp Total* 2
Sales 36,699,232
SIC 5211 Lumber and other building materials
 Denis Warnett

D-U-N-S 20-725-9466   (BR)
MUELLER CANADA LTD
(*Suby of* Mueller Water Products, Inc.)
230 Rue Castonguay, Saint-Jerome, QC, J7Y
2J7
(450) 436-2288
Emp Here 110
SIC 5999 Miscellaneous retail stores, nec

D-U-N-S 20-858-7436   (SL)
PAVILLON STE-MARIE INC
(*Suby of* Groupe Sante Sedna Inc)
45 Rue Du Pavillon, Saint-Jerome, QC, J7Y
3R6
(450) 438-3583
Emp Here 180   *Sales* 11,386,560
SIC 8052 Intermediate care facilities
Pr Pr Francyne Jolicoeur

D-U-N-S 25-853-2654   (BR)
PROVIGO DISTRIBUTION INC
MAXI COMPAGNIE
900 Boul Grignon, Saint-Jerome, QC, J7Y 3S7
(450) 436-3824
Emp Here 110
SIC 5411 Grocery stores

D-U-N-S 24-327-1348   (BR)
PUROLATOR INC.
PUROLATOR INC
370 Boul Roland-Godard, Saint-Jerome, QC,
J7Y 4P7
(450) 431-7035
Emp Here 50
SIC 4731 Freight transportation arrangement

D-U-N-S 20-253-3543   (SL)
RAYONESE TEXTILE INC
(*Suby of* Culp, Inc.)
500 Boul Monseigneur-Dubois, Saint-Jerome,
QC, J7Y 3L8
(450) 476-1991
Emp Here 160   *Sales* 15,248,786
SIC 2221 Broadwoven fabric mills, manmade
Pr Robert G. Culp Iv
 Blair C. Barwick
Sec Eric Stevens
Genl Mgr Kenneth R. Bowling

D-U-N-S 20-926-1788   (BR)
RESTAURANT LOUJAC INC
RESTAURANTS MCDONALD'S
(*Suby of* Restaurant Loujac Inc)
2040 Boul Du Cure-Labelle, Saint-Jerome,
QC, J7Y 1S4
(450) 438-1761
Emp Here 70
SIC 5812 Eating places

D-U-N-S 20-515-0555   (BR)
SEARS CANADA INC
900 Boul Grignon Bureau 111, Saint-Jerome,
QC, J7Y 3S7
(450) 432-2110
Emp Here 200
SIC 5311 Department stores

D-U-N-S 24-003-5704   (BR)
SINTRA INC
284 Boul Roland-Godard, Saint-Jerome, QC,
J7Y 4P7

Emp Here 20
SIC 7384 Photofinish laboratories

D-U-N-S 25-498-9676   (BR)
STAPLES CANADA INC
BUREAU EN GROS
(Suby of Staples, Inc.)
1135 Boul Jean-Baptiste-Rolland O, Saint-
Jerome, QC, J7Y 4Y7
(450) 436-3708
Emp Here 30
SIC 5943 Stationery stores

D-U-N-S 24-698-4801   (SL)
TRANSCOBEC (1987) INC
AUTOBUS C MONGEAU
21 Rue John-F.-Kennedy, Saint-Jerome, QC,
J7Y 4B4
(450) 432-9748
Emp Here 120   Sales 3,984,755
SIC 4151 School buses

D-U-N-S 24-099-9909   (BR)
WAL-MART CANADA CORP
1030 Boul Du Grand-Heron, Saint-Jerome,
QC, J7Y 5K8
(450) 438-6776
Emp Here 200
SIC 5311 Department stores

D-U-N-S 25-446-8762   (BR)
WESTCLIFF MANAGEMENT LTD
*IMMEUBLES CARREFOUR RICHELIEU
CARREFOUR DU NORD*
900 Boul Grignon Bureau 4, Saint-Jerome,
QC, J7Y 3S7
(450) 431-0042
Emp Here 22
SIC 6512 Nonresidential building operators

D-U-N-S 20-003-9811   (BR)
**WINNERS MERCHANTS INTERNATIONAL
L.P.**
WINNERS
(Suby of The TJX Companies Inc)
1105 Boul Jean-Baptiste-Rolland O, Saint-
Jerome, QC, J7Y 4Y7
(450) 569-9597
Emp Here 30
SIC 5651 Family clothing stores

Saint-Jerome, QC J7Z
Terrebonne County

D-U-N-S 24-167-7418   (BR)
123273 CANADA INC
PHARMACIE JEAN COUTU
25 Rue Saint-Georges, Saint-Jerome, QC,
J7Z 4Z1
(450) 432-1120
Emp Here 40
SIC 5912 Drug stores and proprietary stores

D-U-N-S 20-927-5692   (HQ)
**ASSOCIATION GENERALE DES ETUDI-
ANTS DU C.E.G.E.P. DE ST-JEROME INC, L**
C.E.G.E.P. DE ST-JEROME
(Suby of Association generale des Etudiants
du C.E.G.E.P. de St-Jerome Inc, L)
455 Rue Fournier Bureau 450, Saint-Jerome,
QC, J7Z 4V2
(450) 435-7147
Emp Here 638   Emp Total 650
Sales 94,044,150
SIC 8221 Colleges and universities
Genl Mgr Francine Paquette
Pr Pr Jessy Letourneau
  Mikael Lavoie-Bourdages
  Claudiane Duguay
Dir Alexis Desrosiers

Dir Francis Grenier
Dir Valerie Laplante
Dir Cloe Jeannotte

D-U-N-S 24-541-1673   (BR)
BANQUE NATIONALE DU CANADA
265 Rue Saint-Georges Bureau 100, Saint-
Jerome, QC, J7Z 5A1
(450) 436-3314
Emp Here 30
SIC 6021 National commercial banks

D-U-N-S 24-328-1487   (BR)
BENSON GROUP INC
BENSON PIECES D'AUTO
(Suby of Benapac Inc)
829 Rue Saint-Georges, Saint-Jerome, QC,
J7Z 5E2
(450) 431-5355
Emp Here 20
SIC 5013 Motor vehicle supplies and new
parts

D-U-N-S 25-727-4597   (BR)
CAISSE DESJARDINS DE SAINT-JEROME
CENTRE DE SERVICE BELLEFEUILLE
100 Place Du Cure-Labelle, Saint-Jerome,
QC, J7Z 1Z6
(450) 436-5335
Emp Here 186
SIC 6062 State credit unions

D-U-N-S 25-766-1439   (BR)
**CENTRE INTEGRE DE SANTE ET DE SER-
VICES SOCIAUX DE LANAUDIERE**
CISSS DE LANAUDIERE - LE BOUCLIER
11 Rue Boyer, Saint-Jerome, QC, J7Z 2K5
(450) 432-7588
Emp Here 87
SIC 8049 Offices of health practitioner

D-U-N-S 20-844-8253   (BR)
**CENTRE DE READAPTATION EN DEFI-
CIENCE PHYSIQUE LE BOUCLIER**
CENTRE DE READAPTATION LE BOUCLIER
(Suby of Centre de Readaptation en Defi-
cience Physique le Bouclier)
225 Rue Du Palais, Saint-Jerome, QC, J7Z
1X7
(450) 560-9898
Emp Here 350
SIC 8011 Offices and clinics of medical doc-
tors

D-U-N-S 20-100-4053   (BR)
**COMMISSION SCOLAIRE DE LA RIVIERE-
DU-NORD**
ECOLE DE L'HORIZON SOLEIL
(Suby of Commission Scolaire de la Riviere-
du-Nord)
1155 Av Du Parc, Saint-Jerome, QC, J7Z 6X6
(450) 438-1296
Emp Here 110
SIC 8211 Elementary and secondary schools

D-U-N-S 24-012-1694   (BR)
**COMMISSION SCOLAIRE DE LA RIVIERE-
DU-NORD**
ECOLE PRIMAIRE SAINTE-PAULE
(Suby of Commission Scolaire de la Riviere-
du-Nord)
1030 Rue Saint-Georges, Saint-Jerome, QC,
J7Z 5E8
(450) 436-1757
Emp Here 30
SIC 8211 Elementary and secondary schools

D-U-N-S 25-234-2365   (BR)
**COMMISSION SCOLAIRE DE LA RIVIERE-
DU-NORD**
*ECOLE STE THERESE DE L'ENFANT JE-
SUS*
(Suby of Commission Scolaire de la Riviere-
du-Nord)
700 9e Rue, Saint-Jerome, QC, J7Z 2Z5
(450) 438-8828
Emp Here 50
SIC 8211 Elementary and secondary schools

D-U-N-S 25-222-6311   (BR)
**COMMISSION SCOLAIRE DE LA RIVIERE-
DU-NORD**
ECOLE SAINT JOSEPH
(Suby of Commission Scolaire de la Riviere-
du-Nord)
616 Rue Saint-Georges, Saint-Jerome, QC,
J7Z 5B9
(450) 438-3981
Emp Here 30
SIC 8211 Elementary and secondary schools

D-U-N-S 25-650-6379   (BR)
**COMMISSION SCOLAIRE DE LA RIVIERE-
DU-NORD**
CENTRE ADMINISTRATIF I
(Suby of Commission Scolaire de la Riviere-
du-Nord)
995 Rue Labelle, Saint-Jerome, QC, J7Z 5N7
(450) 438-3131
Emp Here 30
SIC 8351 Child day care services

D-U-N-S 25-232-8844   (BR)
**COMMISSION SCOLAIRE DE LA RIVIERE-
DU-NORD**
ECOLE POLYVALENTE ST JEROME
(Suby of Commission Scolaire de la Riviere-
du-Nord)
535 Rue Filion, Saint-Jerome, QC, J7Z 1J6
(450) 436-4330
Emp Here 240
SIC 8211 Elementary and secondary schools

D-U-N-S 20-712-1737   (BR)
**COMMISSION SCOLAIRE DE LA RIVIERE-
DU-NORD**
*CENTRE DE FORMATION GENERALE AUX
ADULTES DE LA RIVIERE DU NORD
L'EDIFICE MARCHAND*
(Suby of Commission Scolaire de la Riviere-
du-Nord)
471 Rue Melancon, Saint-Jerome, QC, J7Z
4K3
(450) 436-5850
Emp Here 50
SIC 8211 Elementary and secondary schools

D-U-N-S 24-012-1652   (BR)
**COMMISSION SCOLAIRE DE LA RIVIERE-
DU-NORD**
*COMMISSION SCOLAIRE DE LA RIVIERE-
DU-NORD*
(Suby of Commission Scolaire de la Riviere-
du-Nord)
600 36e Av, Saint-Jerome, QC, J7Z 5W2
(450) 436-1858
Emp Here 120
SIC 8211 Elementary and secondary schools

D-U-N-S 24-474-0742   (HQ)
**COMMISSION SCOLAIRE DE LA RIVIERE-
DU-NORD**
(Suby of Commission Scolaire de la Riviere-
du-Nord)
995 Rue Labelle Bureau 1, Saint-Jerome, QC,
J7Z 5N7
(450) 438-3131
Emp Here 100   Emp Total 3,500
Sales 325,147,250
SIC 8211 Elementary and secondary schools
Pr Jean Roy
VP Manon Villeneuve
Treas Manon Desautels
Dir Lison Girard
Dir Patrick Labelle
Dir Francois Landry
Dir Roy J Dove
Genl Mgr Lise Allaire

D-U-N-S 25-232-8885   (BR)
**COMMISSION SCOLAIRE DE LA RIVIERE-
DU-NORD**
ECOLE DUBOIS
(Suby of Commission Scolaire de la Riviere-
du-Nord)
562 Rue Du Palais, Saint-Jerome, QC, J7Z

1Y6
(450) 438-5008
Emp Here 40
SIC 8211 Elementary and secondary schools

D-U-N-S 25-284-5987   (BR)
CORUS ENTERTAINMENT INC
CIME-FM 103.9 & 101.3
120 Rue De La Gare, Saint-Jerome, QC, J7Z
2C2
(450) 431-2463
Emp Here 22
SIC 4832 Radio broadcasting stations

D-U-N-S 24-896-7135   (SL)
CUISINES NUTRI-DELI INC, LES
535 Rue Filion, Saint-Jerome, QC, J7Z 1J6
(450) 438-5278
Emp Here 100   Sales 2,991,389
SIC 5812 Eating places

D-U-N-S 25-462-7680   (SL)
DES LAURENTIDES FORD INC
(Suby of Gestion Aucar Inc)
380 Boul Des Laurentides, Saint-Jerome, QC,
J7Z 4M1
(514) 332-2264
Emp Here 48   Sales 23,558,225
SIC 5511 New and used car dealers
Pr Richard Caron
VP Marie-Josee Aube

D-U-N-S 20-290-4926   (BR)
ENTREPRISES ROLLAND INC, LES
455 Rue Rolland, Saint-Jerome, QC, J7Z 5S2
(450) 436-4140
Emp Here 50
SIC 2621 Paper mills

D-U-N-S 20-857-1484   (BR)
GAZ PROPANE RAINVILLE INC
1460 Boul Saint-Antoine, Saint-Jerome, QC,
J7Z 7M2
(450) 431-0627
Emp Here 20
SIC 5984 Liquefied petroleum gas dealers

D-U-N-S 24-311-1130   (SL)
GESTION LOUIS GIGUERE INC
MCDONALD'S ST-ANTOINE
305 Boul Des Laurentides, Saint-Jerome, QC,
J7Z 4L8
(450) 436-3595
Emp Here 50   Sales 1,978,891
SIC 5812 Eating places

D-U-N-S 25-291-4874   (BR)
**GOUVERNEMENT DE LA PROVINCE DE
QUEBEC**
*GOUVERNEMENT DE LA PROVINCE DE
QUEBEC*
430 Rue Labelle, Saint-Jerome, QC, J7Z 5L3
(450) 431-2221
Emp Here 260
SIC 8399 Social services, nec

D-U-N-S 25-701-3375   (BR)
GROUPE VEZINA & ASSOCIES LTEE, LE
446 Rue Saint-Georges, Saint-Jerome, QC,
J7Z 5B1
(450) 436-2922
Emp Here 20
SIC 6411 Insurance agents, brokers, and ser-
vice

D-U-N-S 20-590-2711   (SL)
JUTEAU & RUEL INC
C.T. COPIEUR / JUTEAU & RUEL
70 Rue Belanger, Saint-Jerome, QC, J7Z 1A1
(450) 436-3630
Emp Here 55   Sales 6,282,240
SIC 5943 Stationery stores
Jean-Luc Roy

D-U-N-S 25-758-7741   (SL)
MANOIR ST-JEROME INC
RESIDENCE MANOIR ST-JEROME
475 Rue Aubry Bureau 115, Saint-Jerome,
QC, J7Z 7H7

(450) 432-9432
Emp Here 50   *Sales* 1,824,018
SIC 8361 Residential care

D-U-N-S 20-416-1483   (HQ)
PAUL GRAND'MAISON INC
GRAND'MAISON HEATING-AIR CONDI-TIONNING
(*Suby of* Paul Grand'maison Inc)
200 Boul Lachapelle, Saint-Jerome, QC, J7Z 7L2
(450) 438-1266
Emp Here 21   *Emp Total* 26
Sales 5,690,935
SIC 5983 Fuel oil dealers
Pr Pr Marc Grand'maison
VP VP Pascal Grand'maison
Lyne Grand'maison

D-U-N-S 25-783-5389   (SL)
PRESENTOIR FILOTECH INC
234 Rue De Sainte-Paule, Saint-Jerome, QC, J7Z 1A8
(450) 432-2266
Emp Here 50   *Sales* 3,064,349
SIC 3993 Signs and advertising specialties

D-U-N-S 25-857-5927   (BR)
PROVIGO DISTRIBUTION INC
MAXI
500 Boul Des Laurentides, Saint-Jerome, QC, J7Z 4M2
(450) 431-2886
Emp Here 50
SIC 5411 Grocery stores

D-U-N-S 20-033-9898   (BR)
SUN LIFE FINANCIAL INVESTMENT SERVICES (CANADA) INC
FINANCIERE SUN LIFE
500 Boul Des Laurentides Bureau 260, Saint-Jerome, QC, J7Z 4M2

Emp Here 35
SIC 6311 Life insurance

D-U-N-S 24-901-2584   (BR)
TRANSCONTINENTAL INC
MIRABEL, LE
179 Rue Saint-Georges, Saint-Jerome, QC, J7Z 4Z8
(450) 436-3303
Emp Here 20
SIC 2711 Newspapers

D-U-N-S 24-969-6501   (SL)
VUE LOINTAINE INC
BUFFET CHINOIS MING WAH
1195 Boul Des Laurentides, Saint-Jerome, QC, J7Z 7L3
(450) 565-9020
Emp Here 50   *Sales* 1,532,175
SIC 5812 Eating places

Saint-Joachim-De-Shefford, QC J0E

D-U-N-S 25-737-1955   (BR)
SERVICES MATREC INC
278 Ch De La Grande-Ligne, Saint-Joachim-De-Shefford, QC, J0E 2G0

Emp Here 25
SIC 4212 Local trucking, without storage

Saint-Joseph-De-Beauce, QC G0S

D-U-N-S 20-006-3340   (BR)
CENTRES JEUNESSE CHAUDIERE-APPALACHES, LES
CENTRE JEUNESSE CHAUDIERE AP-PALACHES
851 Av Sainte-Therese, Saint-Joseph-De-

Beauce, QC, G0S 2V0
(418) 397-5781
Emp Here 41
SIC 8322 Individual and family services

D-U-N-S 20-711-9251   (BR)
COMMISSION SCOLAIRE DE LA BEAUCE-ETCHEMIN
ECOLE SECONDAIRE VEILLEUX
695 Av Robert-Cliche, Saint-Joseph-De-Beauce, QC, G0S 2V0
(418) 397-6841
Emp Here 102
SIC 8211 Elementary and secondary schools

D-U-N-S 25-233-8769   (BR)
COMMISSION SCOLAIRE DE LA BEAUCE-ETCHEMIN
ECOLE D'YOUVILLE
721 Av Du Palais, Saint-Joseph-De-Beauce, QC, G0S 2V0
(418) 397-6894
Emp Here 55
SIC 8211 Elementary and secondary schools

D-U-N-S 25-495-0363   (SL)
TRANSPORTS JEAN-FRANCOIS INC, LES
770 Av Guy-Poulin Rr 1, Saint-Joseph-De-Beauce, QC, G0S 2V0
(418) 397-6310
Emp Here 45   *Sales* 5,877,000
SIC 4213 Trucking, except local
Pr Richard Carrier
Jean-Guy Fluet
Dir Jimmy Carrier

Saint-Joseph-De-Coleraine, QC G0N

D-U-N-S 25-170-0613   (BR)
CAISSE DESJARDINS DU CARREFOUR DES LACS
CENTRE DE SERVICE COLERAINE
118 Av Saint-Joseph, Saint-Joseph-De-Coleraine, QC, G0N 1B0
(418) 423-7501
Emp Here 35
SIC 6062 State credit unions

Saint-Joseph-De-Sorel, QC J3R

D-U-N-S 25-233-9056   (BR)
COMMISSION SCOLAIRE DE SOREL-TRACY
ECOLE MARTEL
(*Suby of* Commission Scolaire de Sorel-Tracy)
1055 Rue Saint-Pierre, Saint-Joseph-De-Sorel, QC, J3R 1B3
(450) 743-6417
Emp Here 20
SIC 8211 Elementary and secondary schools

D-U-N-S 20-551-5260   (HQ)
FORGES DE SOREL CIE, LES
FINKL STEEL - SOREL
100 Rue Mccarthy, Saint-Joseph-De-Sorel, QC, J3R 3M8
(450) 746-4030
Emp Here 350   *Emp Total* 8,877
Sales 46,777,554
SIC 3312 Blast furnaces and steel mills
Richard Lahaye
Dir Fin Michael Lutter
Dir Mark Shirley
Genl Mgr Richard Godin

D-U-N-S 24-886-2687   (SL)
LOGISTIQUE SAINT LAURENT
320 Rue De L'Ilmenite, Saint-Joseph-De-Sorel, QC, J3R 4A2
(450) 742-1212
Emp Here 50   *Sales* 4,012,839

SIC 7359 Equipment rental and leasing, nec

D-U-N-S 24-098-8704   (HQ)
MINERAUX MART INC
(*Suby of* Minereaux Mart Inc)
201 Rue Montcalm Bureau 213, Saint-Joseph-De-Sorel, QC, J3R 1B9
(450) 746-1126
Emp Here 40   *Emp Total* 50
Sales 2,772,507
SIC 1481 NonMetallic mineral services

Saint-Joseph-Du-Lac, QC J0N

D-U-N-S 25-292-9062   (BR)
COMMISSION SCOLAIRE DE LA SEIGNEURIE-DES-MILLE-ILES
COMMISSION SCOLAIRE DE LA SEIGNEURIE-DES-MILLE-ILES
(*Suby of* Commission Scolaire de la Seigneurie-Des-Mille-Iles)
70 Montee Du Village Rr 81, Saint-Joseph-Du-Lac, QC, J0N 1M0
(450) 473-5116
Emp Here 25
SIC 8211 Elementary and secondary schools

D-U-N-S 20-374-8025   (BR)
LAFARGE CANADA INC
30 Rue Des Sables, Saint-Joseph-Du-Lac, QC, J0N 1M0
(450) 473-8616
Emp Here 20
SIC 2891 Adhesives and sealants

Saint-Jude, QC J0H
St Hyacinthe County

D-U-N-S 25-377-6405   (BR)
COMMISSION SCOLAIRE DE SAINT-HYACINTHE, LA
ECOLE AUX QUATRE-VENTS-ST_JUDE
1441 Rue Saint-Pierre, Saint-Jude, QC, J0H 1P0
(450) 792-3413
Emp Here 40
SIC 8211 Elementary and secondary schools

D-U-N-S 24-360-5057   (BR)
COOP FEDEREE, LA
FERME CHABOT
235 Rte De Michaudville, Saint-Jude, QC, J0H 1P0
(450) 792-2437
Emp Here 40
SIC 7389 Business services, nec

Saint-Lambert, QC J4P
Chambly County

D-U-N-S 20-714-2121   (BR)
COLLEGE DUROCHER SAINT-LAMBERT
PAVILLON SAINT-LAMBERT
375 Rue Riverside, Saint-Lambert, QC, J4P 1B1
(450) 671-5585
Emp Here 50
SIC 8211 Elementary and secondary schools

D-U-N-S 25-233-2010   (BR)
COMMISSION SCOLAIRE MARIE-VICTORIN
ECOLE DES SAINTS ANGES
126 Rue Logan, Saint-Lambert, QC, J4P 1H2
(450) 671-8151
Emp Here 30
SIC 8211 Elementary and secondary schools

D-U-N-S 25-176-8784   (BR)

DARE FOODS LIMITED
ALIMENTS DARE
845 Av Saint-Charles, Saint-Lambert, QC, J4P 2A2
(450) 671-6121
Emp Here 280
SIC 2051 Bread, cake, and related products

D-U-N-S 25-064-0323   (BR)
MAGASINS J.L. TAYLOR INC, LES
TAYLOR'S
556 Av Victoria, Saint-Lambert, QC, J4P 2J5
(450) 672-9722
Emp Here 100
SIC 5651 Family clothing stores

D-U-N-S 25-665-3239   (HQ)
RE/MAX PERFORMANCE INC
RE/MAX
(*Suby of* Re/Max Performance Inc)
15 Rue Du Prince-Arthur, Saint-Lambert, QC, J4P 1X1
(450) 466-4000
Emp Here 25   *Emp Total* 50
Sales 4,742,446
SIC 6531 Real estate agents and managers

D-U-N-S 25-321-4001   (BR)
REVERA INC
RESIDENCE DU PARC
33 Av Argyle, Saint-Lambert, QC, J4P 3P5
(450) 465-1401
Emp Here 100
SIC 8051 Skilled nursing care facilities

D-U-N-S 25-240-7077   (BR)
RIVERSIDE SCHOOL BOARD
REACH SCHOOL
471 Rue Green, Saint-Lambert, QC, J4P 1V2

Emp Here 25
SIC 8211 Elementary and secondary schools

D-U-N-S 25-665-5093   (BR)
ROYAL BANK OF CANADA
RBC
(*Suby of* Royal Bank Of Canada)
635 Av Victoria, Saint-Lambert, QC, J4P 3R4
(450) 923-5320
Emp Here 20
SIC 6021 National commercial banks

Saint-Lambert, QC J4R
Chambly County

D-U-N-S 25-665-2769   (BR)
CANADIAN MINI-WAREHOUSE PROPERTIES COMPANY
ENTREPOT PUBLIC
380 Boul Sir-Wilfrid-Laurier, Saint-Lambert, QC, J4R 2L2
(450) 465-9970
Emp Here 41
SIC 4225 General warehousing and storage

D-U-N-S 24-389-5633   (BR)
CENTRE DE SANTE ET DE SERVICES SOCIAUX CHAMPLAIN
CENTRE D'HEBERGEMENT SAINT-LAMBERT
(*Suby of* Centre de sante et de services sociaux Champlain)
831 Av Notre-Dame, Saint-Lambert, QC, J4R 1S1
(450) 672-3328
Emp Here 50
SIC 8059 Nursing and personal care, nec

D-U-N-S 24-012-2312   (BR)
COMMISSION SCOLAIRE MARIE-VICTORIN
ECOLE RABEAU
830 Av Notre-Dame, Saint-Lambert, QC, J4R 1R8

---

(450) 671-0178
Emp Here 30
SIC 8211 Elementary and secondary schools

D-U-N-S 24-441-6587   (BR)
MCDONALD'S RESTAURANTS OF CANADA LIMITED
MCDONALD'S
(*Suby of* McDonald's Corporation)
400 Boul Sir-Wilfrid-Laurier, Saint-Lambert, QC, J4R 2M2
(450) 466-1020
Emp Here 25
SIC 5812 Eating places

D-U-N-S 25-100-1244   (BR)
PROVIGO DISTRIBUTION INC
PROVIGO
1461 Av Victoria, Saint-Lambert, QC, J4R 1R5
(450) 671-6205
Emp Here 46
SIC 5411 Grocery stores

D-U-N-S 20-125-2736   (BR)
RIVERSIDE SCHOOL BOARD
ACCESS TO CONTINUING EDUCATION CENTRE
163 Av Cleghorn, Saint-Lambert, QC, J4R 2J4
(450) 676-1843
Emp Here 25
SIC 8211 Elementary and secondary schools

D-U-N-S 24-125-4114   (BR)
ST. LAWRENCE SEAWAY MANAGEMENT CORPORATION, THE
CORPORATION GESTION DE LA VOIE MARITME DU ST LAURENT
151 Rue De L'Ecluse, Saint-Lambert, QC, J4R 2V6
(450) 672-4115
Emp Here 40
SIC 7363 Help supply services

Saint-Lambert, QC J4S
Chambly County

D-U-N-S 20-706-6734   (BR)
COMMISSION SCOLAIRE MARIE-VICTORIN
ECOLE PREVILLE
139 Av D'Alsace, Saint-Lambert, QC, J4S 1M8
(450) 671-2662
Emp Here 40
SIC 8211 Elementary and secondary schools

D-U-N-S 20-961-9790   (SL)
COUNTRY CLUB DE MONTREAL
5 Rue Riverside, Saint-Lambert, QC, J4S 1B7
(450) 671-6181
Emp Here 75   *Sales* 2 991,389
SIC 7997 Membership sports and recreation clubs

Saint-Lambert-De-Lauzon, QC G0S
Levis County

D-U-N-S 25-717-6750   (BR)
CAISSE DESJARDINS DE LA CHAUDIERE
CENTRE DE SERVICES SAINT-LAMBERT-DE-LAUZON
1240 Rue Du Pont, Saint-Lambert-De-Lauzon, QC, G0S 2W0
(418) 831-2674
Emp Here 60
SIC 6062 State credit unions

D-U-N-S 25-233-1202   (BR)
COMMISSION SCOLAIRE DES NAVIGA-TEURS
ECOLE DU BAC
1285 Rue Des Erables, Saint-Lambert-De-

Lauzon, QC, G0S 2W0
(418) 834-2478
Emp Here 55
SIC 8211 Elementary and secondary schools

D-U-N-S 20-181-8254   (BR)
ROYAL GROUP, INC
PRODUITS DE BATIMENT RESIDENTIEL
1401 Rue Bellevue, Saint-Lambert-De-Lauzon, QC, G0S 2W0

Emp Here 130
SIC 3089 Plastics products, nec

Saint-Laurent, QC H4K

D-U-N-S 25-240-3340   (BR)
COMMISSION SCOLAIRE MARGUERITE-BOURGEOYS
ECOLE MORAND NANTEL BEAU SEJOUR
2681 Rue Baker, Saint-Laurent, QC, H4K 1K7
(514) 331-5823
Emp Here 20
SIC 8211 Elementary and secondary schools

D-U-N-S 25-240-3506   (BR)
COMMISSION SCOLAIRE MARGUERITE-BOURGEOYS
ECOLE MORAND NANTEL BEAUSEJOUR
3600 Rue Beausejour, Saint-Laurent, QC, H4K 1W7
(514) 334-7350
Emp Here 30
SIC 8211 Elementary and secondary schools

Saint-Laurent, QC H4L

D-U-N-S 24-970-8975   (SL)
2970-9177 QUEBEC INC
PHARMAPRIX
1051 Rue D9carie Unit9 52, Saint-Laurent, QC, H4L 3M8
(514) 748-7725
Emp Here 94   *Sales* 13,278,847
SIC 5912 Drug stores and proprietary stores
Pr Donald Newhook
VP VP Salvatore Coppa

D-U-N-S 24-154-1858   (SL)
ACADEMIE MAXIMUM SECURITE ET IN-VESTIGATION INC
901 Av Sainte-Croix, Saint-Laurent, QC, H4L 3Y5
(514) 747-7642
Emp Here 200   *Sales* 8,343,600
SIC 7381 Detective and armored car services
Pr Laurette Aubert
Sec Cynthia Lecavalier

D-U-N-S 25-320-5199   (SL)
ALIMENTS CARAVAN INC, LES
RESTAURANT MCDONALD'S
1565 Boul De La Cote-Vertu Bureau 2314, Saint-Laurent, QC, H4L 2A1
(514) 336-9489
Emp Here 50   *Sales* 1,532,175
SIC 5812 Eating places

D-U-N-S 20-569-2507   (BR)
BANQUE LAURENTIENNE DU CANADA
1430 Rue Poirier, Saint-Laurent, QC, H4L 1H3
(514) 252-1846
Emp Here 20
SIC 6021 National commercial banks

D-U-N-S 24-081-0150   (SL)
CENTRE D'HEBERGEMENT ST-VINCENT DE MARIE INC
1175 Boul De La Cote-Vertu, Saint-Laurent, QC, H4L 5J1
(514) 744-1175
Emp Here 105   *Sales* 4,961,328

SIC 8051 Skilled nursing care facilities

D-U-N-S 25-240-3548   (BR)
COMMISSION SCOLAIRE DE MONTREAL
ECOLE BOIS-FRANC AQUARELLE
2085 Rue De Londres, Saint-Laurent, QC, H4L 3A5
(514) 855-4227
Emp Here 35
SIC 8211 Elementary and secondary schools

D-U-N-S 25-233-6854   (BR)
COMMISSION SCOLAIRE ENGLISH-MONTREAL
ECOLE CEDARCREST
1505 Rue Muir, Saint-Laurent, QC, H4L 4T1
(514) 744-2614
Emp Here 25
SIC 8211 Elementary and secondary schools

D-U-N-S 25-233-5740   (BR)
COMMISSION SCOLAIRE ENGLISH-MONTREAL
PARKDALE ELEMENTARY SCHOOL
1475 Rue Deguire, Saint-Laurent, QC, H4L 1M4
(514) 744-6423
Emp Here 50
SIC 8211 Elementary and secondary schools

D-U-N-S 25-240-3266   (BR)
COMMISSION SCOLAIRE MARGUERITE-BOURGEOYS
ECOLE ENFANT SOLEIL
1615 Rue Tasse, Saint-Laurent, QC, H4L 1R1
(514) 747-3065
Emp Here 65
SIC 8211 Elementary and secondary schools

D-U-N-S 25-240-3381   (BR)
COMMISSION SCOLAIRE MARGUERITE-BOURGEOYS
ECOLE EDOUARD LAURIN
1085 Rue Tasse, Saint-Laurent, QC, H4L 1P7
(514) 744-1422
Emp Here 35
SIC 8211 Elementary and secondary schools

D-U-N-S 25-233-7092   (BR)
COMMISSION SCOLAIRE MARGUERITE-BOURGEOYS
ECOLE PRIMAIRE LAURENTIDE
465 Rue Cardinal, Saint-Laurent, QC, H4L 3C5
(514) 744-2101
Emp Here 35
SIC 8211 Elementary and secondary schools

D-U-N-S 20-714-2212   (SL)
ECOLE BILINGUE NOTRE DAME SION
FOUNDATION DES AMIS DE NOTRE-DAME DE SION
1775 Rue Decarie, Saint-Laurent, QC, H4L 3N5
(514) 747-3895
Emp Here 50   *Sales* 3,356,192
SIC 8211 Elementary and secondary schools

D-U-N-S 25-501-7436   (SL)
GESTION RICHARD DUGRE INC
HUNT PERSSONEL INTERIM AIDE
935 Boul Decarie Bureau 212, Saint-Laurent, QC, H4L 3M3
(514) 744-8400
Emp Here 50   *Sales* 4,331,255
SIC 7363 Help supply services

D-U-N-S 24-612-5983   (SL)
MARCHAND ENTREPRENEUR ELEC-TRICIEN LTEE
1480 Rue Barre, Saint-Laurent, QC, H4L 4M6
(514) 748-6745
Emp Here 50   *Sales* 4,377,642
SIC 1731 Electrical work

D-U-N-S 20-112-3267   (SL)
MITCHELL AEROSPACE INC
(*Suby of* Canerector Inc)
350 Boul Decarie, Saint-Laurent, QC, H4L

3K5
(514) 748-3447
Emp Here 50   *Sales* 5,545,013
SIC 3365 Aluminum foundries
Pr Milan Kavena
Sec Tim Buckland
Dir Amanda Hawkins
Dir Nickel William
Dir Pierre Desormeaux

D-U-N-S 25-537-1650   (BR)
PROVIGO INC
1115 Rue Decarie, Saint-Laurent, QC, H4L 3M8
(514) 748-6805
Emp Here 50
SIC 5411 Grocery stores

D-U-N-S 25-628-3420   (BR)
TORONTO-DOMINION BANK, THE
GROUPE BANQUE TD
(*Suby of* Toronto-Dominion Bank, The)
1825 Av O'Brien, Saint-Laurent, QC, H4L 3W6
(514) 956-0909
Emp Here 20
SIC 6021 National commercial banks

Saint-Laurent, QC H4M

D-U-N-S 24-742-8287   (SL)
155501 CANADA INC
BARER ENGINEERING COMPANY
180 Rue Authier, Saint-Laurent, QC, H4M 2C6

Emp Here 28   *Sales* 7,101,500
SIC 5084 Industrial machinery and equipment
Pr Pr David Barer

D-U-N-S 25-281-6970   (BR)
BERLITZ CANADA INC
BERLITZ LANGUAGE CENTRES OF CANADA
9900 Boul Cavendish Bureau 305, Saint-Laurent, QC, H4M 2V2
(514) 387-2566
Emp Here 20
SIC 8299 Schools and educational services, nec

D-U-N-S 24-011-8666   (BR)
BEST BUY CANADA LTD
(*Suby of* Best Buy Co., Inc.)
7075 Place Robert-Joncas Bureau M101, Saint-Laurent, QC, H4M 2Z2
(514) 905-7700
Emp Here 50
SIC 5731 Radio, television, and electronic stores

D-U-N-S 20-517-3995   (BR)
CIBC WORLD MARKETS INC
9900 Boul Cavendish Bureau 100, Saint-Laurent, QC, H4M 2V2
(514) 856-2286
Emp Here 20
SIC 6211 Security brokers and dealers

D-U-N-S 20-213-5604   (HQ)
CMC ELECTRONIQUE INC
(*Suby of* Esterline Technologies Corp)
600 Boul Dr.-Frederik-Philips, Saint-Laurent, QC, H4M 2S9
(514) 748-3148
Emp Here 800   *Emp Total* 13,290
Sales 117,320,806
SIC 8711 Engineering services
Pr Michel Potvin
VP Albert S. Yost
VP VP Robert D. George
Dir Curtis Carl Reusser
Dir Robin St-Arnaud

D-U-N-S 25-894-4008   (BR)
CAMBRIDGE MERCANTILE CORP
SOCIETE FINANCIERE CAMBRIDGE

9800 Boul Cavendish Bureau 505, Saint-Laurent, QC, H4M 2V9
(514) 956-6005
Emp Here 30
SIC 6099 Functions related to deposit banking

D-U-N-S 25-257-7598   (SL)
CATO RESEARCH CANADA INC
9900 Boul Cavendish Bureau 300, Saint-Laurent, QC, H4M 2V2
(514) 856-2286
Emp Here 30   *Sales* 2,772,507
SIC 8732 Commercial nonphysical research

D-U-N-S 20-712-4962   (BR)
COMMISSION SCOLAIRE ENGLISH-MONTREAL
LAUREN HILL JUNIOR CAMPUS
2355 Rue Decelles, Saint-Laurent, QC, H4M 1C2
(514) 331-8019
Emp Here 40
SIC 8211 Elementary and secondary schools

D-U-N-S 20-712-4921   (BR)
COMMISSION SCOLAIRE ENGLISH-MONTREAL
ECOLES PRIMAIRES HOLY CROSS
950 Rue Fraser, Saint-Laurent, QC, H4M 1Z6
(514) 334-9555
Emp Here 30
SIC 8211 Elementary and secondary schools

D-U-N-S 20-712-4954   (BR)
COMMISSION SCOLAIRE ENGLISH-MONTREAL
ST LAURENT ADULT CENTRE
2405 Place Lafortune O, Saint-Laurent, QC, H4M 1A7
(514) 337-3856
Emp Here 50
SIC 8211 Elementary and secondary schools

D-U-N-S 25-240-8836   (BR)
COMMISSION SCOLAIRE ENGLISH-MONTREAL
GARDENVIEW SCHOOL
700 Rue Brunet, Saint-Laurent, QC, H4M 1Y2
(514) 744-1401
Emp Here 50
SIC 8211 Elementary and secondary schools

D-U-N-S 20-032-6895   (BR)
COMMISSION SCOLAIRE MARGUERITE-BOURGEOYS
ECOLE CARDINAL LEGER
2000 Rue Decelles, Saint-Laurent, QC, H4M 1B3
(514) 744-0763
Emp Here 70
SIC 8211 Elementary and secondary schools

D-U-N-S 20-800-8982   (SL)
CORPORATION DE SOINS DE LA SANTE HOSPIRA
(*Suby of* Pfizer Inc.)
1111 Boul Dr.-Frederik-Philips Bureau 600, Saint-Laurent, QC, H4M 2X6
(514) 905-2600
Emp Here 450   *Sales* 90,432,000
SIC 5047 Medical and hospital equipment
VP VP Jerry Stefanatos
Sarah Joseph

D-U-N-S 24-773-7427   (BR)
FEDEX TRADE NETWORKS TRANSPORT & BROKERAGE (CANADA), INC
FEDEX TRADE NETWORKS
(*Suby of* Fedex Corporation)
9800 Cavendish Blvd 3rd Fl, Saint-Laurent, QC, H4M 2V9
(800) 463-3339
Emp Here 100
SIC 4731 Freight transportation arrangement

D-U-N-S 24-860-4444   (HQ)
GROUPE CANTREX NATIONWIDE INC
(*Suby of* Groupe Cantrex Nationwide Inc)

9900 Boul Cavendish Bureau 400, Saint-Laurent, QC, H4M 2V2
(514) 335-0260
Emp Here 66   *Emp Total* 85
Sales 5,465,508
SIC 7389 Business services, nec

D-U-N-S 24-064-1592   (BR)
INGRAM MICRO INC
7075 Place Robert-Joncas Bureau M100, Saint-Laurent, QC, H4M 2Z2
(514) 334-9785
Emp Here 30
SIC 5063 Electrical apparatus and equipment

D-U-N-S 24-296-3726   (HQ)
INTERTAPE POLYMER INC
9999 Boul Cavendish Bureau 200, Saint-Laurent, QC, H4M 2X5
(514) 731-7591
Emp Here 2,000   *Emp Total* 2,200
Sales 169,611,946
SIC 2295 Coated fabrics, not rubberized
Pr Gregory A. Yull
VP Trevor Arthurs
Sec Charmaine Martin

D-U-N-S 20-653-6059   (BR)
LE CENTRES JEUNESSE DE MONTREAL INSTITUT UNIVERSITAIRE
(*Suby of* Le Centres Jeunesse de Montreal Institut Universitaire)
750 Boul Marcel-Laurin Bureau 230, Saint-Laurent, QC, H4M 2M4
(514) 855-5470
Emp Here 22
SIC 8322 Individual and family services

D-U-N-S 20-718-0659   (BR)
MANULIFE SECURITIES INVESTMENT SERVICES INC
MANULIFE SECURITIES
9800 Boul Cavendish Bureau 200, Saint-Laurent, QC, H4M 2V9
(514) 788-4884
Emp Here 50
SIC 6722 Management investment, open-end

D-U-N-S 24-382-0102   (SL)
MARRIOTT COURTYARD MONTREAL AIRPORT
7000 Place Robert-Joncas, Saint-Laurent, QC, H4M 2Z5
(514) 339-5333
Emp Here 65   *Sales* 2,845,467
SIC 7011 Hotels and motels

D-U-N-S 20-956-4397   (BR)
MELOCHE MONNEX INC
5-YEAR REPLACEMENT COST ADVANTAGE/ SOLUTION
(*Suby of* Toronto-Dominion Bank, The)
1111 Boul Dr.-Frederik-Philips Bureau 105, Saint-Laurent, QC, H4M 2X6
(514) 335-6660
Emp Here 20
SIC 6311 Life insurance

D-U-N-S 20-884-5560   (SL)
PIRELLI PNEUS INC
1111 Boul Dr.-Frederik-Philips Bureau 506, Saint-Laurent, QC, H4M 2X6
(514) 331-4241
Emp Here 20   *Sales* 7,296,070
SIC 5014 Tires and tubes
Ch Bd Paolo Ferrari
Pr Pr Prieto Roberto
Francesco Ruffini
Alexander Rosenzweig

D-U-N-S 24-022-7496   (BR)
PROCTER & GAMBLE INC
(*Suby of* The Procter & Gamble Company)
9900 Boul Cavendish Bureau 108, Saint-Laurent, QC, H4M 2V2

Emp Here 50
SIC 2676 Sanitary paper products

D-U-N-S 20-831-7599   (BR)
ROYAL BANK OF CANADA
RBC ROYAL BANK
(*Suby of* Royal Bank Of Canada)
9900 Boul Cavendish Bureau 310, Saint-Laurent, QC, H4M 2V2

Emp Here 20
SIC 6021 National commercial banks

D-U-N-S 20-794-0610   (HQ)
SOCIETE MAKIVIK
(*Suby of* Societe Makivik)
1111 Boul Dr.-Frederik-Philips, Saint-Laurent, QC, H4M 2X6
(514) 745-8880
Emp Here 70   *Emp Total* 1,390
Sales 237,560,039
SIC 4512 Air transportation, scheduled
Pr Jobie Tukkiapik
VP Adamie Delisle Alaku
VP Andrew Moorhouse
Treas Andy Pirti
Dir Ali Novalinga
Dir Etua Kaukai
Dir Noah Tayara
Dir Rohda Kokiapik
Dir Maggie Akapahatak
Dir Louisa Tookalook

D-U-N-S 24-341-9343   (SL)
SOCIETE EN COMMANDITE HOTEL CAVENDISH
RESIDENCE INN BY MARRIOTT MONTREAL AIRPORT, THE
6500 Place Robert-Joncas, Saint-Laurent, QC, H4M 2Z5
(514) 336-9333
Emp Here 65   *Sales* 2,845,467
SIC 7011 Hotels and motels

D-U-N-S 20-327-4584   (SL)
STANTEC ARCHITECTURE QUEBEC LTD
100 Boul Alexis-Nihon Bureau 110, Saint-Laurent, QC, H4M 2N6
(514) 739-0708
Emp Here 61   *Sales* 6,274,620
SIC 8712 Architectural services
Pr Robert J Gomes

D-U-N-S 20-002-6081   (BR)
SUN LIFE ASSURANCE COMPANY OF CANADA
SUN LIFE ASSURANCE COMPANY OF CANADA
1111 Boul Dr.-Frederik-Philips Bureau 200, Saint-Laurent, QC, H4M 2X6
(514) 335-3445
Emp Here 42
SIC 6311 Life insurance

D-U-N-S 25-240-1864   (BR)
TALMUD TORAHS UNIS DE MONTREAL INC
HERZLIAH HIGH SCHOOL
805 Rue Dorais, Saint-Laurent, QC, H4M 2A2
(514) 739-2291
Emp Here 40
SIC 8211 Elementary and secondary schools

D-U-N-S 20-794-1183   (BR)
TALMUD TORAHS UNIS DE MONTREAL INC
2205 Rue De L'Eglise, Saint-Laurent, QC, H4M 1G5

Emp Here 30
SIC 8211 Elementary and secondary schools

D-U-N-S 20-555-5274   (BR)
VELAN INC
2125 Rue Ward, Saint-Laurent, QC, H4M 1T6
(514) 748-7743
Emp Here 149
SIC 3494 Valves and pipe fittings, nec

D-U-N-S 25-368-4203   (SL)
IBWAVE SOLUTIONS INC

(*Suby of* Corning Incorporated)
7075 Place Robert-Joncas Bureau 95, Saint-Laurent, QC, H4M 2Z2
(514) 397-0606
Emp Here 70   *Sales* 10,271,386
SIC 7371 Custom computer programming services
Pr Mario Bouchard
Sec Steven W. Morris
Dir Fin Patrick Bertrand
Dir Michael Bell
Dir Claudio Mazzali
Dir Mike O'day

Saint-Laurent, QC H4N

D-U-N-S 20-229-6604   (HQ)
AGENCES W PELLETIER (1980) INC
A.P.A
1400 Boul Jules-Poitras, Saint-Laurent, QC, H4N 1X7
(514) 276-6700
Emp Here 61   *Emp Total* 150
Sales 15,939,018
SIC 5087 Service establishment equipment
Pr Pr Claude Desrochers
Dir Andre Cheply

D-U-N-S 24-052-0705   (BR)
AGROPUR COOPERATIVE
NARTEL
333 Boul Lebeau, Saint-Laurent, QC, H4N 1S3
(514) 332-2220
Emp Here 400
SIC 3556 Food products machinery

D-U-N-S 24-813-9461   (SL)
ALIMENTS TOUSAIN INC
95 Rue Stinson, Saint-Laurent, QC, H4N 2E1
(514) 748-7353
Emp Here 38   *Sales* 9,922,655
SIC 5141 Groceries, general line
Dikran Markarian

D-U-N-S 25-021-2859   (BR)
CANADIAN IMPERIAL BANK OF COMMERCE
CIBC
249 Boul De La Cote-Vertu, Saint-Laurent, QC, H4N 1C8
(514) 334-3405
Emp Here 27
SIC 6021 National commercial banks

D-U-N-S 20-634-5373   (BR)
CERATEC INC
CERATEC VAUDREUIL
1620 Boul Jules-Poitras, Saint-Laurent, QC, H4N 1Z3
(514) 956-0341
Emp Here 75
SIC 5032 Brick, stone, and related material

D-U-N-S 25-240-3464   (BR)
COMMISSION SCOLAIRE MARGUERITE-BOURGEOYS
ECOLE HENRI BEAULIEU
235 Rue Bleignier, Saint-Laurent, QC, H4N 1B1
(514) 332-0742
Emp Here 75
SIC 8211 Elementary and secondary schools

D-U-N-S 20-213-6388   (HQ)
COMPAGNIE CANADIAN TECHNICAL TAPE LTEE
455 Boul De La Cote-Vertu, Saint-Laurent, QC, H4N 1E8
(514) 334-1510
Emp Here 80   *Emp Total* 2,200
Sales 50,051,040
SIC 2672 Paper; coated and laminated, nec
Howard Cohen
Paul Cohen

D-U-N-S 24-848-3773 (SL)
COMPAGNIE MEXX CANADA
MEXX
905 Rue Hodge, Saint-Laurent, QC, H4N 2B3
(514) 383-5555
Emp Here 750   *Sales* 140,312,788
SIC 5137 Women's and children's clothing
Pr Robbie Reynders
VP Kurt Hans
Sec Steve Eisner

D-U-N-S 20-050-3196 (SL)
CONSTRUCTION N.R.C. INC
160 Rue Deslauriers, Saint-Laurent, QC, H4N 1V8
(514) 331-7944
Emp Here 50   *Sales* 4,377,642
SIC 1731 Electrical work

D-U-N-S 24-426-7386 (SL)
CONTINU-GRAPH INC
409 Boul Lebeau, Saint-Laurent, QC, H4N 1S2
(514) 331-0741
Emp Here 100   *Sales* 9,705,989
SIC 2752 Commercial printing, lithographic
Pr Pr Francois Chartrand

D-U-N-S 20-309-4313 (HQ)
DEVELOPPEMENT OLYMBEC INC
333 Boul Decarie Bureau 500, Saint-Laurent, QC, H4N 3M9
(514) 344-3334
Emp Here 36   *Emp Total* 80
Sales 6,184,080
SIC 6512 Nonresidential building operators
Pr Richard Stern
Sec Stern Derek
 Brian Glasberg

D-U-N-S 25-200-4098 (HQ)
DEX BROS. CIE DE VETEMENTS LTEE
DEX
390 Rue Deslauriers, Saint-Laurent, QC, H4N 1V8
(514) 383-2474
Emp Here 60   *Emp Total* 35
Sales 18,863,650
SIC 5137 Women's and children's clothing
Pr Pr Jacky Alloul

D-U-N-S 25-365-8538 (BR)
DOREL INDUSTRIES INC
DIV OF DOREL INDUSTRIES INC; DOREL DISTRIBUTION CANADA
873 Rue Hodge, Saint-Laurent, QC, H4N 2B1
(514) 332-3737
Emp Here 60
SIC 5099 Durable goods, nec

D-U-N-S 24-053-7183 (SL)
ECOLE ARMEN–QUEBEC DE L'UNION GENERALE ARMENIENNE DE BIENFAISANCE
ECOLE ALEX MANOOGIAN-D'ARMEN QUEBEC DE L'U.G.A.B.
755 Rue Manoogian, Saint-Laurent, QC, H4N 1Z5
(514) 744-5636
Emp Here 60   *Sales* 4,012,839
SIC 8211 Elementary and secondary schools

D-U-N-S 24-634-2869 (BR)
HOSKIN SCIENTIFIC LIMITED
300 Rue Stinson, Saint-Laurent, QC, H4N 2E7
(514) 735-5267
Emp Here 20
SIC 5049 Professional equipment, nec

D-U-N-S 24-458-7028 (BR)
HUBERGROUP CANADA LIMITED
425 Rue Deslauriers, Saint-Laurent, QC, H4N 1W2
(514) 335-2197
Emp Here 30
SIC 2893 Printing ink

D-U-N-S 24-324-0319 (SL)

D-U-N-S 24-222-4176 (BR)
ITF LABORATORIES INC
ITF LABS
400 Boul Montpellier, Saint-Laurent, QC, H4N 2G7
(514) 748-4848
Emp Here 50   *Sales* 15,420,400
SIC 3357 Nonferrous wiredrawing and insulating
Pr Hassan Kassi
Treas Didier Sauvage

D-U-N-S 20-222-4176 (BR)
JOHNSON CONTROLS NOVA SCOTIA U.L.C.
SOCIETE DE CONTROLE JOHNSON
(*Suby of* Johnson Controls, Inc.)
395 Av Sainte-Croix Bureau 100, Saint-Laurent, QC, H4N 2L3
(514) 747-2580
Emp Here 135
SIC 1711 Plumbing, heating, air-conditioning

D-U-N-S 24-679-3582 (BR)
LASON CANADA COMPANY
HOV SERVICES
125 Rue Gagnon Bureau 201, Saint-Laurent, QC, H4N 1T1

Emp Here 49
SIC 7389 Business services, nec

D-U-N-S 20-762-6201 (HQ)
LE CHATEAU INC
ANABANANA & DESIGN (HORIZONTAL)
(*Suby of* Le Chateau Inc)
105 Boul Marcel-Laurin, Saint-Laurent, QC, H4N 2M3
(514) 738-7000
Emp Here 300   *Emp Total* 2,500
Sales 172,690,336
SIC 5621 Women's clothing stores
 Jane Silverstone Segal
Pr Emilia Di Raddo
 Johnny Del Ciancio
Dir Herschel H Segal
Dir David Martz
Dir Norman Daitchman
 Michael Pesner

D-U-N-S 24-990-4285 (SL)
LE GROUPE LEMUR INC
PETIT LEM
275 Rue Stinson Bureau 201, Saint-Laurent, QC, H4N 2E1
(514) 748-6234
Emp Here 60   *Sales* 34,448,820
SIC 5137 Women's and children's clothing
Pr Pr Gabriel Di Miele

D-U-N-S 20-309-0527 (SL)
LES BOIS LAURENTIEN INC
395 Rue Stinson, Saint-Laurent, QC, H4N 2E1
(514) 748-2028
Emp Here 50   *Sales* 8,690,616
SIC 2431 Millwork
Pr Pr Alain Beaudoin
 Martin Boutet
Dir Alexandre Lebeau

D-U-N-S 25-362-1007 (BR)
LIBRAIRIE RENAUD-BRAY INC
ENTREPOT
775 Boul Lebeau, Saint-Laurent, QC, H4N 1S5
(514) 335-9814
Emp Here 30
SIC 5942 Book stores

D-U-N-S 24-953-4418 (BR)
LOBLAWS INC
LOBLAWS
300 Av Sainte-Croix, Saint-Laurent, QC, H4N 3K4
(514) 747-0944
Emp Here 60
SIC 5411 Grocery stores

D-U-N-S 25-918-5551 (BR)

D-U-N-S (no value)
MEDIAS TRANSCONTINENTAL INC
MEDIAS TRANSCONTINENTAL INC
1500 Boul Jules-Poitras Bureau 200, Saint-Laurent, QC, H4N 1X7
(514) 745-5720
Emp Here 25
SIC 2711 Newspapers

D-U-N-S 20-232-8266 (HQ)
MICHAEL ROSSY LTEE
MAGAUBAINES
450 Boul Lebeau, Saint-Laurent, QC, H4N 1R7
(514) 335-6255
Emp Here 65   *Emp Total* 900
Sales 64,497,259
SIC 5311 Department stores
Pr Pr Michael Ditullio
 Douglas Khoury

D-U-N-S 25-019-5315 (SL)
MULTIBOX INC
377 Av Sainte-Croix, Saint-Laurent, QC, H4N 2L3
(514) 748-1222
Emp Here 55
SIC 2652 Setup paperboard boxes

D-U-N-S 20-764-5425 (HQ)
NATIONAL FILM BOARD OF CANADA
ONF
3155 Ch De La Cote-De-Liesse, Saint-Laurent, QC, H4N 2N4
(514) 283-9000
Emp Here 350   *Emp Total* 570,000
Sales 3,599,371
SIC 7812 Motion picture and video production

D-U-N-S 24-788-6278 (BR)
ORKIN CANADA CORPORATION
ORKIN PCO SERVICES
(*Suby of* Rollins, Inc.)
2021 Ch De La Cote-De-Liesse, Saint-Laurent, QC, H4N 2M5
(514) 333-4111
Emp Here 50
SIC 7342 Disinfecting and pest control services

D-U-N-S 24-325-0458 (SL)
PNB NATION LLC
95 Rue Gince, Saint-Laurent, QC, H4N 1J7
(514) 384-3872
Emp Here 100   *Sales* 6,055,738
SIC 5651 Family clothing stores
Pr Jonathan Burman

D-U-N-S 24-054-8057 (HQ)
PROVIGO DISTRIBUTION INC
PROVIGO
400 Av Sainte-Croix, Saint-Laurent, QC, H4N 3L4
(514) 383-3000
Emp Here 800   *Emp Total* 138,000
Sales 7,763,254,837
SIC 5141 Groceries, general line
VP Jocyanne Bourdeau
Sec Robert Balcom
Dir Pierre Dandoy

D-U-N-S 25-405-0669 (BR)
RICOH CANADA INC
DELCOM SOLUTIONS D AFFAIRES
460 Boul Montpellier, Saint-Laurent, QC, H4N 2G7
(514) 744-3610
Emp Here 50
SIC 5044 Office equipment

D-U-N-S 24-021-5087 (SL)
RUBANS D'OURLET DE MONTREAL INC
HI-VIS.COM
1440 Boul Jules-Poitras, Saint-Laurent, QC, H4N 1X7
(514) 271-2561
Emp Here 50   *Sales* 2,042,900
SIC 2241 Narrow fabric mills

D-U-N-S 25-728-3200 (BR)
SNC-LAVALIN GEM QUEBEC INC
GROUPE QUALITAS
275 Rue Benjamin-Hudon, Saint-Laurent, QC, H4N 1J1
(514) 331-6910
Emp Here 50
SIC 8742 Management consulting services

D-U-N-S 20-550-7523 (HQ)
SAPUTO PRODUITS LAITIERS CANADA S.E.N.C.
(*Suby of* Saputo Produits Laitiers Canada S.E.N.C.)
2365 Ch De La Cote-De-Liesse, Saint-Laurent, QC, H4N 2M7
(514) 328-6663
Emp Here 150   *Emp Total* 4,517
Sales 439,442,296
SIC 2022 Cheese; natural and processed
Genl Mgr Emmanuel Saputo

D-U-N-S 24-374-8675 (BR)
SAPUTO PRODUITS LAITIERS CANADA S.E.N.C.
SAPUTO DAIRY PRODUCTS CANADA GP
(*Suby of* Saputo Produits Laitiers Canada S.E.N.C.)
2365 Ch De La Cote-De-Liesse, Saint-Laurent, QC, H4N 2M7
(514) 856-0157
Emp Here 225
SIC 5143 Dairy products, except dried or canned

D-U-N-S 25-501-3468 (BR)
SAPUTO PRODUITS LAITIERS CANADA S.E.N.C.
(*Suby of* Saputo Produits Laitiers Canada S.E.N.C.)
100 Rue Stinson, Saint-Laurent, QC, H4N 2E7
(514) 328-3312
Emp Here 90
SIC 5143 Dairy products, except dried or canned

D-U-N-S 24-933-7049 (SL)
SPIKE MARKS INC
CASA CUBANA
275 Rue Stinson, Saint-Laurent, QC, H4N 2E1
(514) 737-0066
Emp Here 115   *Sales* 37,574,761
SIC 5194 Tobacco and tobacco products
Pr Pr Andre Dunn
 Gilda Estrella

D-U-N-S 24-365-9906 (BR)
SUPREMEX INC
ENVELOPPE MONTREAL
(*Suby of* Supremex Inc)
645 Rue Stinson, Saint-Laurent, QC, H4N 2E6
(514) 331-7110
Emp Here 88
SIC 2677 Envelopes

D-U-N-S 24-107-6041 (HQ)
TELIO & CIE INC
TELIO
(*Suby of* Gestion Telio Inc)
625 Rue Deslauriers, Saint-Laurent, QC, H4N 1W8
(514) 271-4607
Emp Here 50   *Emp Total* 2
Sales 12,549,240
SIC 5131 Piece goods and notions
Pr Pr Andre Telio
 Raymond Telio

D-U-N-S 25-284-8114 (SL)
TOUCHTUNES DIGITAL JUKEBOX INC
400 Av Sainte-Croix Bureau 200e, Saint-Laurent, QC, H4N 3L4
(514) 762-6244
Emp Here 100   *Sales* 3,064,349
SIC 3931 Musical instruments

D-U-N-S 20-557-5397 (SL)
TRANSPORT FLS INC

▲ Public Company   ■ Public Company Family Member   **HQ** Headquarters   **BR** Branch   **SL** Single Location

333 Boul Decarie Bureau 250, Saint-Laurent, QC, H4N 3M9
(514) 739-0939
Emp Here 25   *Sales* 2,845,467
SIC 4213 Trucking, except local

D-U-N-S 20-188-6772   (BR)
UPS SCS, INC
UPS SUPPLY CHAIN SOLUTIONS-CANADA
101 Boul Marcel-Laurin, Saint-Laurent, QC, H4N 2M3
(514) 285-1500
Emp Here 250
SIC 4731 Freight transportation arrangement

D-U-N-S 24-357-0160   (SL)
VISCOFAN CANADA INC
290 Rue Benjamin-Hudon Bureau 2, Saint-Laurent, QC, H4N 1J4
(514) 333-1700
Emp Here 20   *Sales* 2,845,467
SIC 5149 Groceries and related products, nec

D-U-N-S 24-827-8595   (SL)
VISTANCE TECHNOLOGY SOLUTIONS INC
(*Suby of* Solutions de Reconnaissance Rideau Inc)
473 Rue Deslauriers, Saint-Laurent, QC, H4N 1W2
(514) 336-9200
Emp Here 40   *Sales* 5,977,132
SIC 7371 Custom computer programming services
Pr Peter Hart
Treas Stephen Hart

D-U-N-S 24-110-4918   (SL)
VOYAGES ENCORE TRAVEL INC
GROUPE ENCORE
1285 Rue Hodge Bureau 101, Saint-Laurent, QC, H4N 2J6
(514) 738-7171
Emp Here 50   *Sales* 11,892,594
SIC 4724 Travel agencies
 Monique Mardinian

Saint-Laurent, QC H4P

D-U-N-S 20-178-9182   (SL)
BAGUE COURONNEE INC, LA
CARLEX
5565 Ch De La Cote-De-Liesse, Saint-Laurent, QC, H4P 1A1
(514) 381-1589
Emp Here 50   *Sales* 3,648,035
SIC 3911 Jewelry, precious Metal

Saint-Laurent, QC H4R

D-U-N-S 25-311-0944   (BR)
175246 CANADA INC
MCDONALD'S
(*Suby of* 175246 Canada Inc)
3330 Boul De La Cote-Vertu, Saint-Laurent, QC, H4R 1P8
(514) 331-3177
Emp Here 20
SIC 5812 Eating places

D-U-N-S 24-524-8914   (SL)
6931014 CANADA INC
ADONIS MARKET
(*Suby of* Gestion G. Ghorayeb Inc)
3100 Boul Thimens, Saint-Laurent, QC, H4R 0C9
(514) 904-6789
Emp Here 50   *Sales* 18,159,550
SIC 5141 Groceries, general line
Pr Pr Georges Ghrayeb
 Jamil Cheaib
 Elie Cheaib

D-U-N-S 20-221-5369   (BR)
ADIDAS CANADA LIMITED
SALOMON CANADA SPORTS
3545 Boul Thimens, Saint-Laurent, QC, H4R 1V5
(514) 331-4943
Emp Here 30
SIC 5091 Sporting and recreation goods

D-U-N-S 24-569-2918   (HQ)
ARGUS TELECOM INTERNATIONAL INC
(*Suby of* Entreprises Argus Telecom Inc)
2505 Rue Guenette, Saint-Laurent, QC, H4R 2E9
(514) 331-0840
Emp Here 29   *Emp Total* 85
Sales 16,051,354
SIC 5065 Electronic parts and equipment, nec
Pr Pr John Mccabe

D-U-N-S 20-519-9396   (BR)
BANQUE NATIONALE DU CANADA
1130 Boul Marcel-Laurin, Saint-Laurent, QC, H4R 1J7
(514) 332-4220
Emp Here 79
SIC 6021 National commercial banks

D-U-N-S 20-008-0575   (BR)
BANQUE TORONTO-DOMINION, LA
TORONTO-DOMINION BANK, THE
(*Suby of* Toronto-Dominion Bank, The)
3131 Boul De La Cote-Vertu, Saint-Laurent, QC, H4R 1Y8
(514) 337-2772
Emp Here 29
SIC 6021 National commercial banks

D-U-N-S 20-519-6673   (BR)
BEST BUY CANADA LTD
FUTURE SHOP #664
(*Suby of* Best Buy Co., Inc.)
3820 Boul De La C Te-Vertu, Saint-Laurent, QC, H4R 1P8
(514) 906-2500
Emp Here 50
SIC 5999 Miscellaneous retail stores, nec

D-U-N-S 25-540-9823   (BR)
BOMBARDIER INC
BOMBARDIER AERONATIQUE
1800 Boul Marcel-Laurin, Saint-Laurent, QC, H4R 1K2
(514) 855-5000
Emp Here 1,100
SIC 3812 Search and navigation equipment

D-U-N-S 20-304-1582   (BR)
CAISSE POPULAIRE DESJARDINS DE SAINT-LAURENT
CENTRE DE SERVICES SPHERETECH
3500 Boul De La Cote-Vertu Bureau 160, Saint-Laurent, QC, H4R 2X7
(514) 748-8821
Emp Here 30
SIC 6062 State credit unions

D-U-N-S 25-672-0525   (BR)
CANON CANADA INC
4767 Rue Levy, Saint-Laurent, QC, H4R 2P9
(514) 745-6363
Emp Here 23
SIC 5049 Professional equipment, nec

D-U-N-S 24-381-8494   (BR)
CANSEL SURVEY EQUIPMENT INC
CAN-NET CANADA
(*Suby of* Cansel Survey Equipment Inc)
2295 Rue Guenette, Saint-Laurent, QC, H4R 2E9
(888) 222-6735
Emp Here 20
SIC 5049 Professional equipment, nec

D-U-N-S 25-471-3423   (BR)
CARRIER ENTERPRISE CANADA, L.P.
CARRIER ENTERPRISE CANADA, L.P
5060 Rue Levy, Saint-Laurent, QC, H4R 2P1

(514) 856-1336
Emp Here 50
SIC 1711 Plumbing, heating, air-conditioning

D-U-N-S 20-212-9581   (HQ)
CHAUSSURES BROWNS INC
BROWNS
(*Suby of* 90401 Canada Ltee)
2255 Rue Cohen, Saint-Laurent, QC, H4R 2N7
(514) 334-5000
Emp Here 80   *Emp Total* 700
Sales 68,866,955
SIC 5661 Shoe stores
Pr Pr Michael Brownstein
VP VP Andre Lescarbeau
Sec Robert Laufer
Dir David Brownstein
Dir Cheryl Brownstein
Dir Janis Brownstein

D-U-N-S 20-237-6083   (HQ)
CIRCUL-AIRE INC
(*Suby of* Specified Air Solutions)
3999 Boul De La Cote-Vertu, Saint-Laurent, QC, H4R 1R2
(514) 337-3331
Emp Here 65   *Emp Total* 370
Sales 9,338,970
SIC 3564 Blowers and fans
Pr Pr Ness Lakdawala
Sec David Johnson

D-U-N-S 20-918-6639   (BR)
COMMISSION SCOLAIRE ENGLISH-MONTREAL
LAUREN HILL ACADEMY
2505 Boul De La Cote-Vertu, Saint-Laurent, QC, H4R 1P3
(514) 331-8781
Emp Here 80
SIC 8211 Elementary and secondary schools

D-U-N-S 25-240-3308   (BR)
COMMISSION SCOLAIRE MARGUERITE-BOURGEOYS
ECOLE SECONDAIRE SAINT LAURENT
2395 Boul Thimens, Saint-Laurent, QC, H4R 1T4
(514) 332-3190
Emp Here 110
SIC 8211 Elementary and secondary schools

D-U-N-S 20-271-4705   (BR)
CONFISERIES REGAL INC
CHOCOLAT JEAN-TALON
4620 Boul Thimens, Saint-Laurent, QC, H4R 2B2
(514) 333-8540
Emp Here 110
SIC 5145 Confectionery

D-U-N-S 25-688-8306   (BR)
CONGLOM INC
4600 Boul Poirier, Saint-Laurent, QC, H4R 2C5
(514) 333-6666
Emp Here 100
SIC 5122 Drugs, proprietaries, and sundries

D-U-N-S 20-115-0567   (SL)
CONSTRUCTIONS L. J. P. INC, LES
2035 Rue Lucien-Thimens, Saint-Laurent, QC, H4R 1K8

Emp Here 350   *Sales* 52,752,000
SIC 1771 Concrete work
Pr Pr Sylvain Cote
VP VP Martin Cote
 Pierre Cote

D-U-N-S 20-807-1394   (BR)
COUCHE-TARD INC
1275 Boul Alexis-Nihon, Saint-Laurent, QC, H4R 2K1
(514) 337-5980
Emp Here 25
SIC 5411 Grocery stores

D-U-N-S 20-806-8663   (BR)
COUCHE-TARD INC
PROVI-SOIR
2555 Rue Des Nations, Saint-Laurent, QC, H4R 3C8
(514) 336-2626
Emp Here 25
SIC 5411 Grocery stores

D-U-N-S 20-715-9042   (BR)
CRANE, JOHN CANADA INC
2519 Rue Cohen, Saint-Laurent, QC, H4R 2N5
(514) 335-6335
Emp Here 20
SIC 5084 Industrial machinery and equipment

D-U-N-S 20-585-9635   (BR)
DECISIONONE CORPORATION
(*Suby of* D1 Holdings, LLC)
2505 Rue Cohen, Saint-Laurent, QC, H4R 2N5
(514) 338-1927
Emp Here 80
SIC 7378 Computer maintenance and repair

D-U-N-S 20-715-6865   (BR)
DECTRON INC
(*Suby of* Specified Air Solutions)
3999 Boul De La Cote-Vertu, Saint-Laurent, QC, H4R 1R2
(514) 337-3331
Emp Here 80
SIC 3585 Refrigeration and heating equipment

D-U-N-S 24-012-3674   (BR)
DECTRON INTERNATIONALE INC
(*Suby of* Specified Air Solutions)
4001 Boul De La Cote-Vertu, Saint-Laurent, QC, H4R 1R5
(514) 333-4050
Emp Here 60
SIC 3585 Refrigeration and heating equipment

D-U-N-S 25-324-1293   (BR)
DIEBOLD COMPANY OF CANADA LIMITED, THE
(*Suby of* Diebold Nixdorf, Incorporated)
2445 Rue Cohen, Saint-Laurent, QC, H4R 2N5
(514) 332-8865
Emp Here 50
SIC 1731 Electrical work

D-U-N-S 25-299-5956   (BR)
DOLLARAMA S.E.C.
DOLLARAMA
2065 Boul Marcel-Laurin, Saint-Laurent, QC, H4R 1K4
(514) 332-7400
Emp Here 30
SIC 5411 Grocery stores

D-U-N-S 20-958-4213   (BR)
DOLLARAMA S.E.C.
DOLLARAMA
3131 Boul De La Cote-Vertu, Saint-Laurent, QC, H4R 1Y8
(514) 333-0264
Emp Here 20
SIC 5399 Miscellaneous general merchandise

D-U-N-S 25-686-2863   (BR)
FEDERATION DES CAISSES DESJARDINS DU QUEBEC
CENTRE DE FINANCEMENT AUX ENTREPRISES NORD OUEST DE MONTREAL
3500 Boul De La Cote-Vertu Bureau 165, Saint-Laurent, QC, H4R 2X7
(514) 748-2999
Emp Here 25
SIC 6062 State credit unions

D-U-N-S 25-536-1560   (SL)
FERSTEN WORLDWIDE INC
FW

4600 Boul Poirier, Saint-Laurent, QC, H4R 2C5
(514) 739-1644
Emp Here 100   *Sales* 2,553,625
SIC 2353 Hats, caps, and millinery

D-U-N-S 20-882-5984   (BR)
G.N. JOHNSTON EQUIPMENT CO. LTD
EQUIPMENTS JOHNSTON
5000 Rue Levy, Saint-Laurent, QC, H4R 2P1
(514) 956-0020
Emp Here 275
SIC 5084 Industrial machinery and equipment

D-U-N-S 24-347-8380   (BR)
GROUPE ALDO INC, LE
CENTRE DE DISTRIBUTION GROUPE ALDO
3665 Boul Poirier, Saint-Laurent, QC, H4R 3J2
(514) 747-5892
Emp Here 100
SIC 5139 Footwear

D-U-N-S 25-540-6472   (HQ)
HEMA-QUEBEC
(*Suby of* Hema-Quebec)
4045 Boul De La Cote-Vertu, Saint-Laurent, QC, H4R 2W7
(514) 832-5000
Emp Here 915   *Emp Total* 1,329
Sales 321,428,422
SIC 8099 Health and allied services, nec
Pr Martine Carre
VP Michele Beaupre Beriau
Sec Jean De Serres
Dir Serge Montplaisir
Dir Patricia Pelletier
Dir Annie Lagace
Dir Rene Carignan
Dir Christine Beaubien
Dir Lucie Letendre
Dir Jean-Marie Leclerc

D-U-N-S 20-876-7264   (BR)
IAN MARTIN LIMITED
(*Suby of* Martin, Ian Technology Staffing Limited)
3333 Boul De La Cote-Vertu Bureau 202, Saint-Laurent, QC, H4R 2N1
(514) 338-3800
Emp Here 100
SIC 7361 Employment agencies

D-U-N-S 20-649-0596   (SL)
INDUSTRIES MON-TEX LTEE
4105 Boul Thimens, Saint-Laurent, QC, H4R 2K7
(514) 933-7493
Emp Here 50   *Sales* 5,202,480
SIC 5719 Miscellaneous homefurnishings
Pr Jerry Schwartz
 Pina Schwartz
 Jya Jung Ho
Dir Stanley Ho

D-U-N-S 24-697-2251   (BR)
KRINOS FOODS CANADA LTD
5555 Boul Thimens, Saint-Laurent, QC, H4R 2H4
(514) 273-8529
Emp Here 20
SIC 5141 Groceries, general line

D-U-N-S 24-107-0945   (SL)
L D G ENTRETIEN GENERAL D'IMMEUBLES INC
5445 Boul Henri-Bourassa O, Saint-Laurent, QC, H4R 1B7
(514) 333-8123
Emp Here 75   *Sales* 2,188,821
SIC 7349 Building maintenance services, nec

D-U-N-S 25-303-9697   (BR)
LONDON LIFE INSURANCE COMPANY
FREEDOM 55 FINANCIAL A DIVISION OF LONDON LIFE INSURANCE COMPANY
3773 Boul De La Cote-Vertu Bureau 200, Saint-Laurent, QC, H4R 2M3

(514) 331-5838
Emp Here 80
SIC 6311 Life insurance

D-U-N-S 24-350-7084   (SL)
MAINTENANCE SERVIKO INC
2670 Rue Duchesne Bureau 100, Saint-Laurent, QC, H4R 1J3
(514) 332-2600
Emp Here 1,000   *Sales* 98,160,000
SIC 7361 Employment agencies
Pr Diane Monk

D-U-N-S 20-883-0968   (SL)
MENUISERIES MONT-ROYAL INC
(*Suby of* Groupe Desjardins Mont-Royal Inc)
1777 Rue Begin, Saint-Laurent, QC, H4R 2B5
(514) 747-1196
Emp Here 40   *Sales* 2,918,428
SIC 1751 Carpentry work

D-U-N-S 24-372-1490   (BR)
METSO MINERALS CANADA INC
4900 Boul Thimens, Saint-Laurent, QC, H4R 2B2
(514) 335-5426
Emp Here 80
SIC 5084 Industrial machinery and equipment

D-U-N-S 24-858-5510   (BR)
OPTUMINSIGHT (CANADA) INC
OPTUM
3333 Boul De La Cote-Vertu Bureau 200, Saint-Laurent, QC, H4R 2N1
(514) 940-0313
Emp Here 100
SIC 8748 Business consulting, nec

D-U-N-S 20-927-3820   (HQ)
PETROLES CREVIER INC
LE GROUPE DES MARCHANDS DE PETROLES DU QUEBEC
(*Suby of* Entreprises Emile Crevier Inc)
2025 Rue Lucien-Thimens, Saint-Laurent, QC, H4R 1K8
(514) 331-2951
Emp Here 45   *Emp Total* 40
Sales 22,898,595
SIC 5172 Petroleum products, nec
Pr Jean-Francois Crevier
Sec Crevier Louis Philippe
Treas Jacques Crevier

D-U-N-S 24-677-0197   (BR)
PFIZER CANADA INC
(*Suby of* Pfizer Inc.)
1025 Boul Marcel-Laurin, Saint-Laurent, QC, H4R 1J6
(514) 744-6771
Emp Here 150
SIC 2834 Pharmaceutical preparations

D-U-N-S 20-230-3566   (HQ)
PINKHAM & SONS BUILDING MAINTENANCE INC
(*Suby of* Pinkham & Sons Building Maintenance Inc)
2449 Rue Guenette, Saint-Laurent, QC, H4R 2E9
(514) 332-4522
Emp Here 130   *Emp Total* 150
Sales 4,377,642
SIC 7349 Building maintenance services, nec

D-U-N-S 24-246-5859   (SL)
PLACEMENTS VIASYSTEMS CANADA, INC
5400 Boul Thimens Bureau 200a, Saint-Laurent, QC, H4R 2K9

Emp Here 400   *Sales* 58,994,160
SIC 3672 Printed circuit boards
Pr David Sindelar

D-U-N-S 25-170-1785   (BR)
PROVIGO DISTRIBUTION INC
MAXI
1757 Boul Marcel-Laurin, Saint-Laurent, QC, H4R 1J5

(514) 747-2203
Emp Here 145
SIC 5411 Grocery stores

D-U-N-S 24-339-2565   (HQ)
PUMA CANADA INC
2315 Rue Cohen, Saint-Laurent, QC, H4R 2N7
(514) 339-2575
Emp Here 50   *Emp Total* 259
Sales 33,697,164
SIC 5091 Sporting and recreation goods
Dir Jay Piccola
Pr Michael Laemmermann
Sec Peter Mastrostefano
Sec Cyril Hottot
Genl Mgr Ritchie Benford
Dir Fin Luc Cousineau

D-U-N-S 20-882-8129   (BR)
PUROLATOR INC.
PUROLATOR INC
1305 Rue Tees, Saint-Laurent, QC, H4R 2A7
(514) 337-6710
Emp Here 250
SIC 4731 Freight transportation arrangement

D-U-N-S 25-810-2227   (HQ)
RANDSTAD INTERIM INC
GROUPE RANDSTAD
3333 Boul De La Cote-Vertu Bureau 600, Saint-Laurent, QC, H4R 2N1
(514) 332-1555
Emp Here 32   *Emp Total* 29,750
Sales 43,158,668
SIC 7361 Employment agencies
Pr Linda Smith
Dir Tom Turpin
Dir Marc-Etienne Julien

D-U-N-S 25-357-1673   (BR)
S.L.H. TRANSPORT INC
3075 Boul Thimens, Saint-Laurent, QC, H4R 1Y3
(514) 335-4990
Emp Here 100
SIC 4213 Trucking, except local

D-U-N-S 20-714-6486   (BR)
SNC-LAVALIN GEM QUEBEC INC
GROUPE QUALITAS
2299 Rue Guenette, Saint-Laurent, QC, H4R 2E9
(514) 335-0083
Emp Here 20
SIC 8742 Management consulting services

D-U-N-S 24-344-8870   (BR)
SALUMATICS INC.
5930 Boul Henri-Bourassa O, Saint-Laurent, QC, H4R 1V9
(514) 336-0077
Emp Here 20
SIC 7379 Computer related services, nec

D-U-N-S 20-595-9179   (BR)
SEARS CANADA INC
SEARS DEPARTMENT STORE
3055 Boul De La Cote-Vertu, Saint-Laurent, QC, H4R 1Y6
(514) 335-7770
Emp Here 20
SIC 5311 Department stores

D-U-N-S 24-421-1384   (BR)
SEARS CANADA INC
ENTREPOT SEARS
3075 Boul Thimens Bureau 562, Saint-Laurent, QC, H4R 1Y3
(514) 335-4980
Emp Here 200
SIC 4225 General warehousing and storage

D-U-N-S 20-688-0135   (BR)
SEARS CANADA INC
1655 Rue Beaulac, Saint-Laurent, QC, H4R 1Z1
(514) 335-5824
Emp Here 2,000

SIC 5311 Department stores

D-U-N-S 24-600-8098   (HQ)
SERVICES KAMTECH INC
CONSTRUCTION KEI
5055 Rue Levy, Saint-Laurent, QC, H4R 2N9
(418) 808-4276
Emp Here 30   *Emp Total* 1,700
Sales 133,301,280
SIC 1541 Industrial buildings and warehouses
VP Eric Akelaitis

D-U-N-S 25-168-0690   (BR)
SHRED-IT INTERNATIONAL ULC
SHRED-IT MONTREAL
5000 Boul Thimens, Saint-Laurent, QC, H4R 2B2
(514) 939-7473
Emp Here 60
SIC 7389 Business services, nec

D-U-N-S 24-769-3500   (SL)
SIGVARIS CORPORATION
4535 Rue Dobrin, Saint-Laurent, QC, H4R 2L8
(514) 336-2362
Emp Here 28   *Sales* 1,605,135
SIC 5699 Miscellaneous apparel and accessory stores

D-U-N-S 25-308-8793   (BR)
SOCIETE DES ALCOOLS DU QUEBEC
SOCIETE DES ALCOOLS DU QUEBEC
3111 Boul De La Cote-Vertu, Saint-Laurent, QC, H4R 1Y5
(514) 337-1158
Emp Here 40
SIC 5921 Liquor stores

D-U-N-S 25-673-8725   (BR)
SPORT MASKA INC
3400 Rue Raymond-Lasnier, Saint-Laurent, QC, H4R 3L3
(514) 461-8000
Emp Here 200
SIC 3949 Sporting and athletic goods, nec

D-U-N-S 20-252-1043   (HQ)
SPORT MASKA INC
REEBOK CANADA
3400 Rue Raymond-Lasnier, Saint-Laurent, QC, H4R 3L3
(514) 461-8000
Emp Here 550   *Emp Total* 60,617
Sales 78,505,713
SIC 3949 Sporting and athletic goods, nec
Pr Philippe Dube
Sec Keith Wexelblatt
Fin Ex Joanne Aucoin

D-U-N-S 25-213-7740   (BR)
STAPLES CANADA INC
STAPLES THE BUSINESS DEPOT
(*Suby of* Staples, Inc.)
3660 Boul De La Cote-Vertu, Saint-Laurent, QC, H4R 1P8
(514) 338-1036
Emp Here 40
SIC 5943 Stationery stores

D-U-N-S 24-368-5182   (SL)
STELLAR NORDIA SERVICES LLC
3100 Boul De La Cote-Vertu Bureau 280, Saint-Laurent, QC, H4R 2J8
(514) 332-5888
Emp Here 350   *Sales* 23,434,950
SIC 7389 Business services, nec
 Bernard Durocher

D-U-N-S 24-433-5477   (BR)
SYNNEX CANADA LIMITED
3300 Boul De La Cote-Vertu Bureau 310, Saint-Laurent, QC, H4R 2B7
(514) 745-1690
Emp Here 50
SIC 5045 Computers, peripherals, and software

SYSTEMES D'ENTRAINEMENT MEGGITT (QUEBEC) INC
D-U-N-S 25-501-1785 (SL)
(Suby of MEGGITT PLC)
6140 Boul Henri-Bourassa O, Saint-Laurent, QC, H4R 3A6
(514) 339-9938
Emp Here 60   Sales 8,609,363
SIC 3699 Electrical equipment and supplies, nec
Andrea Czop
Dir Tayeb Ghilanie
Dir Ron Vadas
Dir Marina Thomas

TCA QUEBEC
D-U-N-S 24-502-0727 (SL)
4868 Rue Levy, Saint-Laurent, QC, H4R 2P1
(514) 332-9346
Emp Here 40   Sales 5,197,506
SIC 8621 Professional organizations

TI TITANIUM LTEE
D-U-N-S 20-856-0870 (SL)
(Suby of Titanium Fabrication Corp)
5055 Rue Levy, Saint-Laurent, QC, H4R 2N9
(514) 334-5781
Emp Here 75   Sales 11,600,751
SIC 3443 Fabricated plate work (boiler shop)
Daniel Lefebvre
Pr Pr Brent Willey

THALES CANADA INC
D-U-N-S 20-190-1233 (BR)
THALES CANADA, LAND & JOINT SYSTEMS, OPTRONICS BUSINESS UNIT
4868 Rue Levy, Saint-Laurent, QC, H4R 2P1
(514) 337-7378
Emp Here 59
SIC 3827 Optical instruments and lenses

THALES OPTRONIQUE CANADA INC
D-U-N-S 20-302-6174 (SL)
4868 Rue Levy, Saint-Laurent, QC, H4R 2P1
(514) 337-7378
Emp Here 55   Sales 3,210,271
SIC 3827 Optical instruments and lenses

THYSSENKRUPP MATERIALS CA, LTD
D-U-N-S 20-032-7117 (BR)
VIFAB
2700 Rue Cohen, Saint-Laurent, QC, H4R 2N6
Emp Here 40
SIC 5051 Metals service centers and offices

TREE OF LIFE CANADA ULC
D-U-N-S 20-645-9021 (BR)
TREE OF LIFE GOURMET AWARD FOODS CANADA
(Suby of Kehe Distributors, LLC)
5626 Boul Thimens, Saint-Laurent, QC, H4R 2K9
(514) 333-3343
Emp Here 40
SIC 5149 Groceries and related products, nec

TYCO INTEGRATED FIRE & SECURITY CANADA, INC
D-U-N-S 20-573-6403 (BR)
SIMPLEXGRINNELL
(Suby of Johnson Controls, Inc.)
5700 Boul Henri-Bourassa O, Saint-Laurent, QC, H4R 1V9
(514) 745-3890
Emp Here 150
SIC 7382 Security systems services

TYCO INTEGRATED FIRE & SECURITY CANADA, INC
D-U-N-S 20-553-3784 (BR)
SIMPLEXGRINNELL
(Suby of Johnson Controls, Inc.)
5800 Boul Henri-Bourassa O, Saint-Laurent, QC, H4R 1V9
(514) 737-5505
Emp Here 108

SIC 7389 Business services, nec

WATERAX INC
D-U-N-S 24-760-1904 (SL)
6635 Boul Henri-Bourassa W, Saint-Laurent, QC, H4R 1E1
(514) 637-1818
Emp Here 50   Sales 1,094,411
SIC 3561 Pumps and pumping equipment

WINNERS MERCHANTS INTERNATIONAL L.P.
D-U-N-S 24-250-6751 (BR)
WINNERS 301 ST LAURENT
(Suby of The TJX Companies Inc)
3205 Boul De La Cote-Vertu, Saint-Laurent, QC, H4R 1Y5
(514) 332-7682
Emp Here 25
SIC 5651 Family clothing stores

WINNERS MERCHANTS INTERNATIONAL L.P.
D-U-N-S 20-106-3216 (BR)
WINNERS
(Suby of The TJX Companies Inc)
3205 Boul De La Cote-Vertu, Saint-Laurent, QC, H4R 1Y5
(514) 334-6222
Emp Here 40
SIC 5651 Family clothing stores

XEROX CANADA LTD
D-U-N-S 24-225-7959 (BR)
(Suby of Xerox Corporation)
4898 Rue Levy, Saint-Laurent, QC, H4R 2P1
(514) 832-7603
Emp Here 35
SIC 7699 Repair services, nec

YKK CANADA INC
D-U-N-S 20-418-3974 (HQ)
3939 Boul Thimens, Saint-Laurent, QC, H4R 1X3
(514) 332-3350
Emp Here 95   Emp Total 44,250
SIC 3965 Fasteners, buttons, needles, and pins

Saint-Laurent, QC H4S

176815 CANADA INC
D-U-N-S 24-835-0910 (SL)
6400 Rue Vanden-Abeele, Saint-Laurent, QC, H4S 1R9
(514) 333-5340
Emp Here 85   Sales 20,071,608
SIC 5074 Plumbing and heating equipment and supplies (hydronics)
Pr Pr Joseph J. Paulin

4126254 CANADA INC
D-U-N-S 24-423-7249 (SL)
TAG TRACKING
5631 Ch Saint-Francois, Saint-Laurent, QC, H4S 1W6
(514) 745-8241
Emp Here 50   Sales 1,678,096
SIC 7299 Miscellaneous personal service

ABB INC
D-U-N-S 25-242-8024 (BR)
2575 Boul Alfred-Nobel, Saint-Laurent, QC, H4S 2G1
(438) 843-6672
Emp Here 250
SIC 3612 Transformers, except electric

AGAT LABORATORIES LTD
D-U-N-S 24-322-2374 (BR)
AGAT
9770 Rte Transcanadienne, Saint-Laurent, QC, H4S 1V9
(514) 337-1000
Emp Here 60

SIC 8731 Commercial physical research

ABLOY CANADA INC
D-U-N-S 20-417-3363 (HQ)
9630 Rte Transcanadienne, Saint-Laurent, QC, H4S 1V9
(514) 335-9500
Emp Here 24   Emp Total 200
Sales 4,377,642
SIC 5072 Hardware

ACCESSOIRES POUR VELOS O G D LTEE
D-U-N-S 24-111-9148 (HQ)
OUTDOOR GEAR CANADA
10555 Boul Henri-Bourassa O Bureau 10, Saint-Laurent, QC, H4S 1A1
(514) 332-0416
Emp Here 74   Emp Total 80
Sales 29,184,280
SIC 7312 Outdoor advertising services
Pr Pr David Bowman
Jean Cloutier
Rob White

ACIER INOXYDABLE PINACLE INC
D-U-N-S 24-328-9662 (BR)
4665 Rue Cousens, Saint-Laurent, QC, H4S 1X5
(514) 745-0360
Emp Here 35
SIC 5023 Homefurnishings

ADVANTECH ALLGON TECHNOLOGIES MICRO-ONDE INC
D-U-N-S 24-355-5914 (SL)
2341 Boul Alfred-Nobel, Saint-Laurent, QC, H4S 2B8
Emp Here 21   Sales 3,551,629
SIC 3663 Radio and t.v. communications equipment

AERO-MAG 2000 (YUL) INC
D-U-N-S 24-057-8166 (SL)
(Suby of Groupe Aero Mag 2000 Inc)
8181 Rue Herve-Saint-Martin, Saint-Laurent, QC, H4S 2A5
(514) 636-1930
Emp Here 75   Sales 22,206,080
SIC 3728 Aircraft parts and equipment, nec
Mario Lepine
Dir Fin Pierre Lesperance

AIR INUIT LTEE
D-U-N-S 24-402-4733 (HQ)
(Suby of Societe Makivik)
6005 Boul De La Cote-Vertu, Saint-Laurent, QC, H4S 0B1
(514) 905-9445
Emp Here 600   Emp Total 1,390
Sales 134,658,814
SIC 4512 Air transportation, scheduled
Pr Pita Aatami
Andrew Moorhouse
VP Opers Christian Busch
Sec Andy Pirti
Dir Louisa Tookalook
Dir Adamie Delisle Alaku
Dir Noah Tayara
Dir Michael Gordon
Dir Jobie Tukkiapik
Dir Johnny May

AIR TRANSAT A.T. INC
D-U-N-S 24-676-9129 (HQ)
AIR TRANSAT CARGO
5959 Boul De La Cote-Vertu, Saint-Laurent, QC, H4S 2E6
(514) 906-0330
Emp Here 300   Emp Total 5,000
Sales 88,866,133
SIC 4512 Air transportation, scheduled
Pr Pr Jean-Francois Lemay
VP Denis Petrin
Sec Agnieszka Charysz
Dir Jean-Marc Eustache
Dir Andre De Montigny

Genl Mgr Bernard Bussieres

ALFAGOMMA CANADA INC
D-U-N-S 25-392-6356 (HQ)
AG ALFAGOMMA DESIGN
6550 Rue Abrams Bureau 6540, Saint-Laurent, QC, H4S 1Y2
(514) 333-5577
Emp Here 25   Emp Total 11
Sales 7,004,227
SIC 5085 Industrial supplies
Pr Gennasio Enrico
Sec Dino Vincent Sacchetti
Dir Massimo Eritale

ALTITUDE AEROSPACE INC
D-U-N-S 24-390-3734 (SL)
2705 Boul Pitfield Bureau 200, Saint-Laurent, QC, H4S 1T2
(514) 335-6922
Emp Here 50   Sales 4,961,328
SIC 8711 Engineering services

ALUMICOR LIMITED
D-U-N-S 25-866-5421 (BR)
(Suby of Apogee Enterprises, Inc.)
9355 Rte Transcanadienne, Saint-Laurent, QC, H4S 1V3
(514) 335-7760
Emp Here 20
SIC 2819 Industrial inorganic chemicals, nec

AMDOCS CANADIAN MANAGED SERVICES INC
D-U-N-S 20-719-2753 (BR)
200-2351 Boul Alfred-Nobel, Saint-Laurent, QC, H4S 0B2
(514) 338-3100
Emp Here 400
SIC 7371 Custom computer programming services

APTOS CANADA INC
D-U-N-S 20-253-1919 (SL)
SOLUTIONS APTOS CANADA
9300 Rte Transcanadienne Bureau 300, Saint-Laurent, QC, H4S 1K5
(514) 426-0822
Emp Here 350   Sales 74,499,456
SIC 7371 Custom computer programming services
Dir Noel Goggin
David Baum
Mark Bentler
Dir Jason Wright
Dir Umang Kajaria

BOLLORE LOGISTIQUES CANADA INC
D-U-N-S 20-270-5653 (BR)
BOLLORE LOGISTICS CANADA INC
10045 Boul Henri-Bourassa O, Saint-Laurent, QC, H4S 1A1
(514) 956-7870
Emp Here 50
SIC 4731 Freight transportation arrangement

CHEP CANADA INC
D-U-N-S 24-600-3826 (BR)
3805 Rue Sartelon, Saint-Laurent, QC, H4S 2A6
(514) 745-2437
Emp Here 50
SIC 7353 Heavy construction equipment rental

CANADA COLORS AND CHEMICALS (EASTERN) LIMITED
D-U-N-S 24-933-7551 (BR)
PRODUITS CHIMIQUES CCC
9999 Rte Transcanadienne, Saint-Laurent, QC, H4S 1V1
(514) 333-7820
Emp Here 50
SIC 5169 Chemicals and allied products, nec

CANADIAN SPECIALTY METALS ULC
D-U-N-S 24-377-3749 (BR)
MAGNA STAINLESS, DIV OF

5775 Rue Kieran, Saint-Laurent, QC, H4S 0A3
(514) 339-1211
Emp Here 48
SIC 5051 Metals service centers and offices

D-U-N-S 24-256-6966   (BR)
CANON CANADA INC
CANON
8801 Rte Transcanadienne Bureau 176, Saint-Laurent, QC, H4S 1Z6
(514) 342-8821
Emp Here 250
SIC 5044 Office equipment

D-U-N-S 20-697-3468   (BR)
CERIDIAN CANADA LTD
8777 Rte Transcanadienne, Saint-Laurent, QC, H4S 1Z6
(514) 908-3000
Emp Here 100
SIC 8721 Accounting, auditing, and bookkeeping

D-U-N-S 24-678-5422   (BR)
COMPAGNIE COMMONWEALTH PLYWOOD LTEE, LA
ROBERT BURY & COMPANY (CANADA)
3500 Boul Pitfield, Saint-Laurent, QC, H4S 1W1
(514) 745-0260
Emp Here 40
SIC 5039 Construction materials, nec

D-U-N-S 20-999-6131   (SL)
CONTROLES PROVAN ASSOCIES INC, LES
(*Suby of* 3979504 Canada Inc)
2315 Rue Halpern, Saint-Laurent, QC, H4S 1S3
(514) 376-8000
Emp Here 27   *Sales* 6,898,600
SIC 5084 Industrial machinery and equipment
Severina Nazarene
VP VP Daniel Forest

D-U-N-S 20-322-9489   (SL)
CORPORATION ABBVIE
8401 Rte Transcanadienne, Saint-Laurent, QC, H4S 1Z1
(514) 906-9700
Emp Here 400   *Sales* 38,742,132
SIC 2834 Pharmaceutical preparations
Steven G. Ramage
Dir Willaim Chase
Dir Stephane Lassignardie

D-U-N-S 24-816-7983   (HQ)
CORPORATION ADFAST
(*Suby of* David & Claude Holdings Canada Inc)
2670 Rue Paulus, Saint-Laurent, QC, H4S 1G1
(514) 337-7307
Emp Here 50   *Emp Total* 60
Sales 11,454,830
SIC 6712 Bank holding companies
Pr Yves Dandurand
Sec Lucie Gautier
Dir Claude Dandurand

D-U-N-S 25-300-8809   (BR)
CROWN METAL PACKAGING CANADA LP
(*Suby of* Crown Holdings Inc.)
5789 Rue Cypihot, Saint-Laurent, QC, H4S 1R3
(514) 956-8900
Emp Here 100
SIC 3411 Metal cans

D-U-N-S 20-216-0024   (HQ)
DANSON DECOR INC
(*Suby of* Ricmaral Inc)
3425 Rue Douglas-B.-Floreani, Saint-Laurent, QC, H4S 1Y6
(514) 335-2435
Emp Here 87   *Emp Total* 90
Sales 10,798,184
SIC 5199 Nondurable goods, nec

Pr Pr Mark Steven Aziz
Richard Aziz
Albert Aziz

D-U-N-S 25-112-8083   (SL)
DECISIONONE CORPORATION
SERVICES INFORMATIQUES DECISIONONE
5766 Rue Cypihot, Saint-Laurent, QC, H4S 1Y5
(514) 338-1798
Emp Here 50   *Sales* 3,648,035
SIC 7379 Computer related services, nec

D-U-N-S 20-608-6233   (SL)
DIAMANT BOART TRUCO LTD
SCIES TARGET CANADA
9430 Rte Transcanadienne, Saint-Laurent, QC, H4S 1R7
(514) 335-2900
Emp Here 20   *Sales* 3,648,035
SIC 5084 Industrial machinery and equipment

D-U-N-S 24-911-3689   (BR)
DYNAMEX CANADA LIMITED
6600 Ch Saint-Francois Bureau 100, Saint-Laurent, QC, H4S 1B7

Emp Here 100
SIC 4212 Local trucking, without storage

D-U-N-S 25-645-6047   (SL)
ENTRETIEN ET NETTOYAGE GENERALE D'IMMEUBLES LBG LTEE
L.D.G. MAINTENANCE PLUS
9442 Rte Transcanadienne, Saint-Laurent, QC, H4S 1R7
(514) 333-8123
Emp Here 60   *Sales* 1,751,057
SIC 7349 Building maintenance services, nec

D-U-N-S 20-227-8057   (HQ)
EQUIPEMENT MOORE LTEE
DICKIE MOORE RENTAL
(*Suby of* Placements R.J.L. Ltee, Les)
4955 Ch Saint-Francois, Saint-Laurent, QC, H4S 1P3
(514) 333-1212
Emp Here 85   *Emp Total* 1
Sales 23,712,228
SIC 5084 Industrial machinery and equipment
John R. Moore

D-U-N-S 24-351-5889   (SL)
ETIQUETTES IMS INC
9000 Boul Henri-Bourassa O, Saint-Laurent, QC, H4S 1L5
(514) 336-3213
Emp Here 60   *Sales* 7,915,564
SIC 2679 Converted paper products, nec
Pr Pr Gilles Baillargeon

D-U-N-S 24-799-7976   (SL)
G.T.C.A. MET-ALL INC
1215 Montee De Liesse, Saint-Laurent, QC, H4S 1J7
(514) 334-2801
Emp Here 53   *Sales* 7,460,160
SIC 3444 Sheet Metalwork
Pr Pr Arpad Danny Toth
VP VP Robert Rachella

D-U-N-S 25-114-9290   (BR)
GROUPE ALGO INC
GREEN JEANS
5555 Rue Cypihot, Saint-Laurent, QC, H4S 1R3
(514) 744-5559
Emp Here 20
SIC 2339 Women's and misses' outerwear, nec

D-U-N-S 20-183-1216   (BR)
GROUPE VISION NEW LOOK INC
LUNETTERIE NEW LOOK
4405 Ch Du Bois-Franc, Saint-Laurent, QC, H4S 1A8
(514) 904-5665
Emp Here 30

SIC 8731 Commercial physical research

D-U-N-S 20-052-8995   (SL)
INDUSTRIES ALGO LTEE, LES
5555 Rue Cypihot, Saint-Laurent, QC, H4S 1R3
(514) 382-1240
Emp Here 36   *Sales* 6,840,000
SIC 5137 Women's and children's clothing
Sol Chankowsky
Pr Pr Marc Kakon

D-U-N-S 20-210-4436   (SL)
INDUSTRIES HAGEN LTEE
3235 Rue Guenette, Saint-Laurent, QC, H4S 1N2
(514) 331-2818
Emp Here 50   *Sales* 12,474,014
SIC 2819 Industrial inorganic chemicals, nec
Pr Pr Rolf C Hagen
VP Edward J. Purcell
VP Mark Hagen
Thomas Hagen
Dir Rolf H. Hagen

D-U-N-S 24-907-5128   (HQ)
INDUSTRIES MIDCON INC
QUICKSTYLE INDUSTRIES
(*Suby of* Courey International (Commerce) Inc)
4505 Rue Cousens, Saint-Laurent, QC, H4S 1X5
(514) 956-9711
Emp Here 50   *Emp Total* 1
Sales 8,244,559
SIC 5023 Homefurnishings
Stephen Courey

D-U-N-S 24-190-9931   (SL)
JSS RECHERCHE MEDICALE INC
9400 Boul Henri-Bourassa O, Saint-Laurent, QC, H4S 1N8
(514) 934-6116
Emp Here 50   *Sales* 2,699,546
SIC 8731 Commercial physical research

D-U-N-S 24-860-5508   (BR)
JOSTENS CANADA LTD
MANUFACTURING PLANT
(*Suby of* Newell Brands Inc.)
6630 Rue Abrams, Saint-Laurent, QC, H4S 1Y1
(514) 687-3926
Emp Here 30
SIC 2731 Book publishing

D-U-N-S 24-085-9975   (SL)
KAYJON GRAPHIQUES INC
8150 Rte Transcanadienne Bureau 100, Saint-Laurent, QC, H4S 1M5
(514) 333-1933
Emp Here 30   *Sales* 2,685,378
SIC 2752 Commercial printing, lithographic

D-U-N-S 25-502-7062   (BR)
KONE INC
KONE QUEBEC
3330 Rue De Miniac, Saint-Laurent, QC, H4S 1Y4
(514) 284-5663
Emp Here 40
SIC 1796 Installing building equipment

D-U-N-S 20-500-1456   (BR)
KONE INC
3330 Rue De Miniac, Saint-Laurent, QC, H4S 1Y4
(514) 735-5353
Emp Here 20
SIC 5084 Industrial machinery and equipment

D-U-N-S 24-419-6403   (BR)
KONICA MINOLTA BUSINESS SOLUTIONS (CANADA) LTD
KONICA MINOLTA
8555 Rte Transcanadienne, Saint-Laurent, QC, H4S 1Z6
(514) 335-2157
Emp Here 80

SIC 5044 Office equipment

D-U-N-S 24-836-3772   (SL)
L.E.S. MECANIQUE INC
1200 Rue Saint-Amour, Saint-Laurent, QC, H4S 1J2
(514) 333-6968
Emp Here 50   *Sales* 3,648,035
SIC 7538 General automotive repair shops

D-U-N-S 20-277-9369   (SL)
LA COMPAGNIE ROBERT BURY (CANADA) LTEE
3500 Boul Pitfield, Saint-Laurent, QC, H4S 1W1
(514) 745-0260
Emp Here 50   *Sales* 10,459,852
SIC 2435 Hardwood veneer and plywood
Pr William T Caine
VP VP Mike Graham
Treas Hussein Dharsee

D-U-N-S 20-209-2896   (HQ)
LABORATOIRES ABBOTT LIMITEE
GROUPE CANALAC LABORATOIRES ABBOTT
(*Suby of* Abbott Laboratories)
8625 Rte Transcanadienne, Saint-Laurent, QC, H4S 1Z6
(514) 832-7000
Emp Here 300   *Emp Total* 94,000
Sales 145,337,714
SIC 2834 Pharmaceutical preparations
Sec Benedetta D'elia
Treas Rina Mercuri
Dir Elizabeth Onwudiwe
Dir Briyan B. Yoor
Dir Matt Harris

D-U-N-S 24-889-9130   (SL)
LES PLACEMENTS E.G.B. INC
9000 Boul Henri-Bourassa O, Saint-Laurent, QC, H4S 1L5
(514) 336-3213
Emp Here 60   *Sales* 10,753,700
SIC 6712 Bank holding companies
Pr Pr Gilles Baillargeon
Sec Lise David

D-U-N-S 24-902-7509   (HQ)
LES SYSTEMES FONEX DATA INC
(*Suby of* Technologies Corpnet Inc)
5400 Ch Saint-Francois, Saint-Laurent, QC, H4S 1P6
(514) 333-6639
Emp Here 50   *Emp Total* 1
Sales 15,548,429
SIC 5065 Electronic parts and equipment, nec
Pasquale Dipierro

D-U-N-S 20-224-5627   (SL)
LIBERTY HOME PRODUCTS CORP
1450 Rue Saint-Amour, Saint-Laurent, QC, H4S 1J3
(514) 336-2943
Emp Here 50   *Sales* 7,608,750
SIC 5023 Homefurnishings
Andy Levy
Pr Pr Ralph Levy
Eli Amber
Lisa Levy

D-U-N-S 25-107-9810   (HQ)
LOCATION HEWITT INC
CATERPILLAR
3000 Boul Pitfield, Saint-Laurent, QC, H4S 1K6
(514) 334-4125
Emp Here 25   *Emp Total* 2,075
Sales 24,149,992
SIC 7353 Heavy construction equipment rental
Pr Pr James William Hewitt
Roni Farah
Dir Suzanne Bergeron
Dir Marie Diamond

D-U-N-S 20-291-0261   (BR)

▲ Public Company   ■ Public Company Family Member   **HQ** Headquarters   **BR** Branch   **SL** Single Location

MTD PRODUCTS LIMITED
LES DISTRIBUTIONS RVI
(*Suby of* Mtd Holdings Inc.)
10655 Boul Henri-Bourassa O, Saint-Laurent,
QC, H4S 1A1
(514) 956-6500
Emp Here 20
SIC 5083 Farm and garden machinery

    D-U-N-S 25-509-7156   (SL)
MARTEL EXPRESS (MONTREAL) INC
10105 Boul Henri-Bourassa O, Saint-Laurent,
QC, H4S 1A1
(514) 331-3311
Emp Here 50   *Sales* 3,939,878
SIC 4212 Local trucking, without storage

    D-U-N-S 20-703-8386   (SL)
METRO INTERNATIONAL TRUCKS (CANADA) INC
6400 Ch Saint-Francois, Saint-Laurent, QC,
H4S 1B7
(514) 333-5133
Emp Here 100   *Sales* 6,832,640
SIC 7389 Business services, nec
  George Hasrouni

    D-U-N-S 24-056-9426   (HQ)
OPTIQUE DIRECTE INC
GREICHE & SCAFF
(*Suby of* Optique Directe Inc)
4405 Ch Du Bois-Franc Bureau 100, Saint-
Laurent, QC, H4S 1A8
(514) 336-4444
Emp Here 50   *Emp Total* 308
Sales 37,693,160
SIC 5995 Optical goods stores
Pr Ian D. Collier
Sec Gerard G. Mcgrath

    D-U-N-S 24-460-7156   (BR)
PANALPINA INC
2520 Av Marie-Curie, Saint-Laurent, QC, H4S
1N1
(514) 685-3364
Emp Here 120
SIC 4731 Freight transportation arrangement

    D-U-N-S 24-528-5069   (SL)
PARKWAY PONTIAC BUICK INC
(*Suby of* Gestion H T Hoy Ltee)
9595 Rte Transcanadienne, Saint-Laurent,
QC, H4S 1T6
(514) 333-5140
Emp Here 100   *Sales* 49,080,000
SIC 5511 New and used car dealers
Pr Diane H Hoy
VP Richard Hoy
  Harry Hoy

    D-U-N-S 20-266-6744   (HQ)
PATRIOT FREIGHT SERVICES INC
SERVICES DE FRET PATRIOTE
6800 Ch Saint-Francois, Saint-Laurent, QC,
H4S 1B7
(514) 631-2900
Emp Here 29   *Emp Total* 25,438
Sales 9,095,636
SIC 4731 Freight transportation arrangement
  Josiane-Melanie Langlois
VP Chanta Martel

    D-U-N-S 25-541-0904   (BR)
PENSKE TRUCK LEASING CANADA INC
LOCATION DE CAMIONS PENSKE
(*Suby of* Penske Corporation)
2500 Boul Pitfield, Saint-Laurent, QC, H4S
1Z7
(514) 333-4080
Emp Here 15,000
SIC 7513 Truck rental and leasing, no drivers

    D-U-N-S 20-699-3920   (BR)
PHILIPS ELECTRONICS LTD
PHILIPS MEDICAL SYSTEMS CANADA
2250 Boul Alfred-Nobel Bureau 200, Saint-
Laurent, QC, H4S 2C9

Emp Here 20
SIC 3841 Surgical and medical instruments

    D-U-N-S 24-678-9895   (HQ)
PLACEMENTS ARDEN INC, LES
ARDENE
(*Suby of* 4233964 Canada Inc)
2575 Boul Pitfield, Saint-Laurent, QC, H4S
1T2
(514) 383-4442
Emp Here 70   *Emp Total* 614
Sales 37,064,036
SIC 5621 Women's clothing stores
Pr Pr Arden Dervishian
  Mark Dervishian
Treas Jerry Dervishian
Sls Dir Dorine Dervishian

    D-U-N-S 24-362-5576   (SL)
PLACEMENTS RRJ INC, LES
5800 Rue Kieran, Saint-Laurent, QC, H4S 2B5
(514) 336-6226
Emp Here 200   *Sales* 53,806,986
SIC 5191 Farm supplies
Pr Rene Modugno

    D-U-N-S 20-234-5724   (SL)
PNEUS SOUTHWARD LTEE
5125 Boul De La Cote-Vertu, Saint-Laurent,
QC, H4S 1E3
(514) 335-2800
Emp Here 30   *Sales* 14,724,000
SIC 5014 Tires and tubes
Pr Pr Robert Snelgrove
VP VP Marc Kaufman

    D-U-N-S 24-836-3558   (BR)
PRAXAIR CANADA INC
MEDIGAS
(*Suby of* Praxair, Inc.)
3200 Boul Pitfield Bureau 100, Saint-Laurent,
QC, H4S 1K6
(514) 324-0202
Emp Here 30
SIC 5169 Chemicals and allied products, nec

    D-U-N-S 20-230-8383   (HQ)
PRESTON PHIPPS INC
(*Suby of* Preston Phipps Inc)
6400 Rue Vanden-Abeele, Saint-Laurent, QC,
H4S 1R9
(514) 333-5340
Emp Here 40   *Emp Total* 85
Sales 15,540,629
SIC 5074 Plumbing and heating equipment
and supplies (hydronics)
  Mark J. Paulin
VP VP Rino Forgione
VP VP Richard Cyr

    D-U-N-S 20-114-4057   (BR)
PRETIUM CANADA COMPANY
PRETIUM PACKAGING
2800 Rue Halpern, Saint-Laurent, QC, H4S
1R2
(514) 336-8210
Emp Here 100
SIC 3089 Plastics products, nec

    D-U-N-S 20-998-4129   (HQ)
PROTECH CHIMIE LTEE
(*Suby of* 2885425 Canada Inc)
7600 Boul Henri-Bourassa O, Saint-Laurent,
QC, H4S 1W3
(514) 745-0200
Emp Here 180   *Emp Total* 1
Sales 39,398,778
SIC 2851 Paints and allied products
Pr Pr David Ades

    D-U-N-S 24-367-6439   (BR)
PROTECTION INCENDIE VIKING INC
3005 Boul Pitfield, Saint-Laurent, QC, H4S
1H4
(514) 332-5110
Emp Here 95
SIC 5063 Electrical apparatus and equipment

    D-U-N-S 20-250-4395   (SL)
QSG INC
TECHNOLOGIES VIASCANQDATA
(*Suby of* Groupe Viascan Inc)
8102 Rte Transcanadienne, Saint-Laurent,
QC, H4S 1M5
(514) 744-1000
Emp Here 85   *Sales* 7,223,109
SIC 2759 Commercial printing, nec
Pr Gilles Gaudreault

    D-U-N-S 25-210-7974   (SL)
REMATEK INC
REMATEK-ATE
8975 Boul Henri-Bourassa O, Saint-Laurent,
QC, H4S 1P7
(514) 333-0101
Emp Here 56   *Sales* 4,596,524
SIC 3544 Special dies, tools, jigs, and fixtures

    D-U-N-S 20-059-6372   (BR)
ROLF C. HAGEN INC
2450 Av Marie-Curie, Saint-Laurent, QC, H4S
1N1

Emp Here 75
SIC 5199 Nondurable goods, nec

    D-U-N-S 24-809-3796   (BR)
SECURITAS CANADA LIMITED
2915 Rue Diab, Saint-Laurent, QC, H4S 1M1
(514) 938-3433
Emp Here 90
SIC 7381 Detective and armored car services

    D-U-N-S 24-813-7556   (HQ)
SERVICES AEROPORTUAIRE HANDLEX INC
5959 Boul De La Cote-Vertu, Saint-Laurent,
QC, H4S 2E6

Emp Here 300   *Emp Total* 1,500
Sales 516,668,160
SIC 4581 Airports, flying fields, and services
Pr Jean-Luc Paiement

    D-U-N-S 20-882-2767   (HQ)
SHAH TRADING COMPANY LIMITED
ALL SEASONS
(*Suby of* Groupe Somchand Kastur Limitee)
3401 Rue Douglas-B.-Floreani, Saint-Laurent,
QC, H4S 1Y6
(514) 336-2462
Emp Here 40   *Emp Total* 4
Sales 111,590,550
SIC 2068 Salted and roasted nuts and seeds
Pr Pr Kirit Shah
Dir Kamal Shah
Dir Sanjeev Shah

    D-U-N-S 24-710-1520   (SL)
SHIRE THERAPIES GENETIQUES HU-MAINES (CANADA) INC
SHIRE CANADA
(*Suby of* SHIRE PLC)
2250 Boul Alfred-Nobel Bureau 500, Saint-
Laurent, QC, H4S 2C9
(514) 787-2300
Emp Here 50   *Sales* 13,570,690
SIC 5122 Drugs, proprietaries, and sundries
Pr Pr Sylvie Lafrance
  William Moran
Dir Ellen Rosenberg
  Eric Tse

    D-U-N-S 20-234-4065   (HQ)
SMITH & NEPHEW INC
2250 Boul Alfred-Nobel Bureau 300, Saint-
Laurent, QC, H4S 2C9
(514) 956-1010
Emp Here 60   *Emp Total* 10,743
Sales 19,553,468
SIC 5047 Medical and hospital equipment
Sec Andrew Oldale
Dir Robin Carlstein
Dir Neil Taylor

    D-U-N-S 20-412-2998   (HQ)

SOCIETE BRISTOL-MYERS SQUIBB CANADA, LA
(*Suby of* Bristol-Myers Squibb Company)
2344 Boul Alfred-Nobel Bureau 300, Saint-
Laurent, QC, H4S 0A4
(514) 333-3200
Emp Here 250   *Emp Total* 25,000
Sales 49,943,437
SIC 2834 Pharmaceutical preparations
Pr Pr Jeffrey Galik
VP Michael Rea
VP Nawal Peacock
Sec Katherine Kelly
Sec Joanie Schwartz

    D-U-N-S 24-896-3894   (SL)
SUBLIME DESSERT INC
7777 Boul Thimens, Saint-Laurent, QC, H4S
2A2
(514) 333-0338
Emp Here 55   *Sales* 6,931,267
SIC 2024 Ice cream and frozen deserts
Pr Pr George Michael

    D-U-N-S 20-333-1228   (BR)
TFI TRANSPORT 17 L.P.
TFORCE INTEGRATED SOLUTIONS
8801 Rte Transcanadienne Bureau 500, Saint-
Laurent, QC, H4S 1Z6
(514) 331-4000
Emp Here 26
SIC 4731 Freight transportation arrangement

    D-U-N-S 25-364-7630   (BR)
TST SOLUTIONS L.P.
TST LOAD BROKERAGE SERVICES
6800 Ch Saint-Francois Bureau 878, Saint-
Laurent, QC, H4S 1B7
(514) 745-4617
Emp Here 40
SIC 4731 Freight transportation arrangement

    D-U-N-S 20-519-4306   (BR)
TELE-MOBILE COMPANY
TELUS MOBILITY
8851 Rte Transcanadienne Bureau 1, Saint-
Laurent, QC, H4S 1Z6
(514) 832-2000
Emp Here 700
SIC 4899 Communication services, nec

    D-U-N-S 24-954-4164   (SL)
TENTES FIESTA LTEE
9091 Boul Henri-Bourassa O, Saint-Laurent,
QC, H4S 1H9
(514) 336-8368
Emp Here 60   *Sales* 2,626,585
SIC 2394 Canvas and related products

    D-U-N-S 20-229-5945   (BR)
THYSSENKRUPP MATERIALS CA, LTD
VIMETAL, DIV OF
4700 Ch Du Bois-Franc, Saint-Laurent, QC,
H4S 1A7
(514) 337-0161
Emp Here 83
SIC 5093 Scrap and waste materials

    D-U-N-S 24-226-1212   (SL)
TRANSPORT ARGUS CANADA INC
ARGUS TRANSPORT
1115 Rue Saint-Amour, Saint-Laurent, QC,
H4S 1T4
(514) 956-8800
Emp Here 50   *Sales* 4,742,446
SIC 4225 General warehousing and storage

    D-U-N-S 25-362-7491   (BR)
TRANSPORT TFI 2, S.E.C.
CK LOGISTICS
6750 Ch Saint-Francois, Saint-Laurent, QC,
H4S 1B7
(514) 856-7580
Emp Here 20
SIC 4731 Freight transportation arrangement

    D-U-N-S 24-366-2561   (BR)
TRANSPORT TFI 2, S.E.C.

TLS TRAILER LEASING SERVICES
7050 Ch Saint-Francois Bureau 200, Saint-Laurent, QC, H4S 1B7
(514) 351-5050
Emp Here 30
SIC 4213 Trucking, except local

D-U-N-S 24-375-5266   (HQ)
TRANSPORT TFI 21, S.E.C.
MCARTHUR EXPRESS
(Suby of Transport TFI 21, S.E.C.)
8801 Rte Transcanadienne Bureau 500, Saint-Laurent, QC, H4S 1Z6
(514) 856-7500
Emp Here 50   Emp Total 3,500
Sales 813,438,844
SIC 5021 Furniture
Mgr Alain Bedard

D-U-N-S 25-996-0255   (BR)
UAP INC
DIVISION DES PIECES POUR VEHICULE LOURD ET FABRICATION
(Suby of Genuine Parts Company)
1080 Montee De Liesse, Saint-Laurent, QC, H4S 1J4
(514) 332-1003
Emp Here 25
SIC 5013 Motor vehicle supplies and new parts

D-U-N-S 20-171-8785   (BR)
UAP INC
TRACTION
(Suby of Genuine Parts Company)
4915 Boul De La Cote-Vertu, Saint-Laurent, QC, H4S 1E1
(514) 332-3130
Emp Here 23
SIC 5013 Motor vehicle supplies and new parts

D-U-N-S 25-658-6058   (BR)
UNITED RENTALS OF CANADA, INC
3185 Boul Pitfield, Saint-Laurent, QC, H4S 1H6
(514) 331-7550
Emp Here 30
SIC 7353 Heavy construction equipment rental

D-U-N-S 20-419-4757   (BR)
VAC AERO INTERNATIONAL INC
7450 Rue Verite, Saint-Laurent, QC, H4S 1C5
(514) 334-4240
Emp Here 23
SIC 3479 Metal coating and allied services

D-U-N-S 20-227-0518   (HQ)
VEOLIA EAU TECHNOLOGIES CANADA INC
GROUPE JMI
4105 Rue Sartelon, Saint-Laurent, QC, H4S 2B3
(514) 334-7230
Emp Here 168   Emp Total 1,019
Sales 24,660,717
SIC 1629 Heavy construction, nec
Pr Benoit Gagne
Sec Olivier Marcadet
Dir Gilles Filion
Dir Klaus Andresen
Dir John Santelli

D-U-N-S 20-253-2651   (BR)
VEOLIA EAU TECHNOLOGIES CANADA INC
3901 Rue Sartelon, Saint-Laurent, QC, H4S 2A6
(514) 334-7230
Emp Here 300
SIC 1629 Heavy construction, nec

D-U-N-S 25-223-2157   (SL)
VERSASCAN INC
6545 Rue Vanden Abeele, Saint-Laurent, QC, H4S 1S1

Emp Here 55
SIC 2657 Folding paperboard boxes

D-U-N-S 24-167-9315   (BR)
VERTIV CANADA ULC
(Suby of Vertiv Canada ULC)
3001 Rue Douglas-B.-Floreani, Saint-Laurent, QC, H4S 1Y7
(514) 333-1966
Emp Here 20
SIC 5063 Electrical apparatus and equipment

D-U-N-S 24-382-3585   (BR)
WABTEC CANADA INC
VAPOR RAIL DIV OF
10655 Boul Henri-Bourassa O, Saint-Laurent, QC, H4S 1A1
(514) 335-4200
Emp Here 275
SIC 3743 Railroad equipment

D-U-N-S 20-609-9751   (BR)
WOLSELEY INDUSTRIAL CANADA INC
MURRAY INDUSTRIAL, DIV OF
(Suby of WOLSELEY PLC)
4953 Boul De La Cote-Vertu, Saint-Laurent, QC, H4S 1E1

Emp Here 20
SIC 5085 Industrial supplies

D-U-N-S 20-531-3591   (HQ)
ZANIN CD/DVD INC
REPLICATION MEDIA DE DIVERTISSE-MENT
(Suby of Administration Sogelem Inc)
3305 Boul Pitfield, Saint-Laurent, QC, H4S 1H3
(514) 342-6396
Emp Here 25   Emp Total 35
Sales 7,937,920
SIC 3652 Prerecorded records and tapes
Pr Pr Joseph Lemme
VP Fin Charles Thibodeau

Saint-Laurent, QC H4T

D-U-N-S 24-319-1488   (SL)
3522997 CANADA INC
180 Montee De Liesse, Saint-Laurent, QC, H4T 1N7
(514) 341-6161
Emp Here 4,000   Sales 1,025,152,250
SIC 6712 Bank holding companies
Mario Levasseur
Treas Glenn R Leduc
Sec Lise Piche

D-U-N-S 20-013-9769   (BR)
3529495 CANADA INC
HOTEL RAMADA
(Suby of 3529495 Canada Inc)
7300 Ch De La Cote-De-Liesse, Saint-Laurent, QC, H4T 1E7
(514) 733-8818
Emp Here 60
SIC 7011 Hotels and motels

D-U-N-S 24-668-6463   (BR)
4513380 CANADA INC
LIVINGSTON INTERNATIONAL
6700 Ch De La Cote-De-Liesse Bureau 300, Saint-Laurent, QC, H4T 2B5
(514) 735-2000
Emp Here 60
SIC 4731 Freight transportation arrangement

D-U-N-S 25-886-8819   (SL)
9052-9975 QUEBEC INC
PLAZA VOLARE
6600 Ch De La Cote-De-Liesse, Saint-Laurent, QC, H4T 1E3
(514) 735-5150
Emp Here 80   Sales 2,626,585

SIC 7299 Miscellaneous personal service

D-U-N-S 20-288-4664   (SL)
9248-5523 QUEBEC INC
DISTRIBUTION DIRECTE
4575 Rue Hickmore, Saint-Laurent, QC, H4T 1S5
(514) 934-4545
Emp Here 50   Sales 2,626,585
SIC 7389 Business services, nec

D-U-N-S 24-328-1115   (BR)
9297-6232 QUEBEC INC
CLAIR DE LUNE
361 Rue Locke, Saint-Laurent, QC, H4T 1X7
(514) 389-5757
Emp Here 40
SIC 2911 Petroleum refining

D-U-N-S 24-650-7909   (BR)
ACKLANDS - GRAINGER INC
AGI
(Suby of W.W. Grainger, Inc.)
4475 Rue Griffith, Saint-Laurent, QC, H4T 2A2
(514) 332-6105
Emp Here 35
SIC 5099 Durable goods, nec

D-U-N-S 20-254-4680   (HQ)
ALEVA GENERATIONS INC
BOUTIQUE JACOB
(Suby of 9182-6065 Quebec Inc)
6125 Ch De La Cote-De-Liesse, Saint-Laurent, QC, H4T 1C8
(514) 228-7989
Emp Here 25   Emp Total 1
Sales 39,295,119
SIC 5621 Women's clothing stores
Pr Pr Joseph Basmaji

D-U-N-S 24-082-9200   (HQ)
ARAMARK QUEBEC INC
4900 Rue Fisher, Saint-Laurent, QC, H4T 1J6
(514) 341-7770
Emp Here 75   Emp Total 266,500
Sales 75,368,403
SIC 5812 Eating places
Pr Pr Andy Siklos
 Nicolas Seguier
Treas Doug Weatherbee

D-U-N-S 20-297-7401   (SL)
AVELIA GROUPE
AVELIA AIR
951 Rue Reverchon, Saint-Laurent, QC, H4T 4L2

Emp Here 1,700   Sales 453,204,720
SIC 1541 Industrial buildings and warehouses
Ch Bd Richard A Granier
VP Juan A Tobaruela
Dir Eric Peugeot
Dir Xiang-Rong Chen
Dir Yann Massoulier
Dir Dean Renouf
Dir Valerie Robain Jean-Marc Bize
Dir Michael Boevink
Dir A.M.M Aries
Dir Carl T Johnson

D-U-N-S 24-458-0544   (BR)
AVNET INTERNATIONAL (CANADA) LTD
AVNET CANADA
(Suby of Avnet, Inc.)
7575 Rte Transcanadienne Bureau 600, Saint-Laurent, QC, H4T 1V6
(514) 335-1000
Emp Here 25
SIC 5065 Electronic parts and equipment, nec

D-U-N-S 24-719-1661   (BR)
BASF CANADA INC
162 Rue Barr, Saint-Laurent, QC, H4T 1Y4
(514) 341-4082
Emp Here 25
SIC 2821 Plastics materials and resins

D-U-N-S 20-212-0432   (BR)
BLACK & MCDONALD LIMITED
625 Rue Gougeon, Saint-Laurent, QC, H4T 2B4
(514) 735-6671
Emp Here 25
SIC 1731 Electrical work

D-U-N-S 24-944-0843   (BR)
BOMBARDIER INC
BOMBARDIER AERONAUTIQUE
8575 Ch De La Cote-De-Liesse, Saint-Laurent, QC, H4T 1G5
(514) 344-6620
Emp Here 230
SIC 8249 Vocational schools, nec

D-U-N-S 20-261-5340   (HQ)
BOUTIQUE JACOB INC
JACOB JR
(Suby of Boutique Jacob Inc)
6125 Ch De La Cote-De-Liesse, Saint-Laurent, QC, H4T 1C8
(514) 228-7989
Emp Here 150   Emp Total 750
Sales 58,989,795
SIC 5621 Women's clothing stores

D-U-N-S 24-752-3533   (HQ)
BRAY CONTROLS CANADA LTD
377 Rue Mccaffrey, Saint-Laurent, QC, H4T 1Z7
(514) 344-2729
Emp Here 22   Emp Total 400
Sales 3,031,879
SIC 3625 Relays and industrial controls

D-U-N-S 24-467-3752   (BR)
CN WORLDWIDE DISTRIBUTION SERVICES (CANADA) INC
8050 Boul Cavendish, Saint-Laurent, QC, H4T 1T1
(514) 734-2334
Emp Here 21
SIC 4225 General warehousing and storage

D-U-N-S 20-796-8798   (BR)
CANADA POST CORPORATION
DEPARTEMENT DES COMMUNICATIONS
555 Rue Mcarthur Bureau 1506, Saint-Laurent, QC, H4T 1T4
(514) 345-4571
Emp Here 3,500
SIC 4311 U.s. postal service

D-U-N-S 24-339-0478   (SL)
CAPESPAN NORTH AMERICA LLC
6700 Ch De La Cote-De-Liesse Bureau 301, Saint-Laurent, QC, H4T 2B5
(514) 739-9181
Emp Here 30   Sales 9,816,000
SIC 5148 Fresh fruits and vegetables
Pr Pr Marc Solomon
VP VP Paul Marier
VP VP Mark Greenberg

D-U-N-S 25-528-0265   (HQ)
CIE D'HABILLEMENT SE CE LTEE, LA
SE CE DISTRIBUTION
(Suby of Placements ZZACC Inc, Les)
6445 Ch De La Cote-De-Liesse, Saint-Laurent, QC, H4T 1S9
(514) 341-4440
Emp Here 40   Emp Total 45
Sales 25,254,417
SIC 5137 Women's and children's clothing
Catherine Claman

D-U-N-S 24-342-7429   (BR)
COMPAGNIE DES CHEMINS DE FER NATIONAUX DU CANADA
CN INTERMODAL
4500 Rue Hickmore, Saint-Laurent, QC, H4T 1K2
(514) 734-2288
Emp Here 130
SIC 4013 Switching and terminal services

D-U-N-S 20-192-2866   (BR)
**COMPAGNIE DES CHEMINS DE FER NA-
TIONAUX DU CANADA**
CN CARGO FLO MONTREAL
8050 Boul Cavendish, Saint-Laurent, QC, H4T
1T1
(514) 734-2121
Emp Here 22
SIC 5169 Chemicals and allied products, nec

D-U-N-S 24-698-1963   (HQ)
CUIRS BENTLEY INC
ACCESS
(*Suby of* Corporation de Developpement Cuirs
Bentley Inc, La)
6125 Ch De La Cote-De-Liesse,   Saint-
Laurent, QC, H4T 1C8
(514) 341-9333
Emp Here 100   *Emp Total* 1,714
Sales 78,432,753
SIC 5948 Luggage and leather goods stores
Pr Pr John Gunn
Sec Jacques Foisy
Dir Frederick Perrault
Dir Antoine Casimir
 Eric Cadorette

D-U-N-S 25-756-8527   (BR)
CUSHMAN & WAKEFIELD LTD
(*Suby of* Cushman & Wakefield Holdings, Inc.)
6505 Rte Transcanadienne Bureau 600, Saint-
Laurent, QC, H4T 1S3
(514) 747-2100
Emp Here 20
SIC 6531 Real estate agents and managers

D-U-N-S 24-205-7201   (BR)
**DHL GLOBAL FORWARDING (CANADA)
INC**
555 Montee De Liesse, Saint-Laurent, QC,
H4T 1P5
(514) 344-3447
Emp Here 150
SIC 4731 Freight transportation arrangement

D-U-N-S 24-917-4558   (BR)
ENDRESS + HAUSER CANADA LTD
6800 Ch De La Cote-De-Liesse Bureau 100,
Saint-Laurent, QC, H4T 2A7
(514) 733-0254
Emp Here 20
SIC 5084 Industrial machinery and equipment

D-U-N-S 20-851-8907   (SL)
EQUIPEMENT D'INCENDIE PRIORITE INC
7528 Ch De La Cote-De-Liesse, Saint-
Laurent, QC, H4T 1E7
(514) 636-2431
Emp Here 45   *Sales* 6,030,906
SIC 5099 Durable goods, nec
Pr Pr Elias Khury
 Lisa Gregory

D-U-N-S 25-196-0498   (BR)
EXPEDITORS CANADA INC
6700 Ch De La Cote-De-Liesse Bureau 501,
Saint-Laurent, QC, H4T 2B5
(514) 340-1614
Emp Here 30
SIC 4731 Freight transportation arrangement

D-U-N-S 25-297-5594   (BR)
**FEDERAL EXPRESS CANADA CORPORA-
TION**
FEDERAL EXPRESS CANADA LTD
(*Suby of* Fedex Corporation)
4041 Rue Sere, Saint-Laurent, QC, H4T 2A3
(800) 463-3339
Emp Here 200
SIC 7389 Business services, nec

D-U-N-S 24-934-5638   (BR)
FLEXTILE LTD
*INDUSTRIES CERAMIQUES MAPLE LEAF,
LES*
555 Rue Locke, Saint-Laurent, QC, H4T 1X7
(514) 345-8666
Emp Here 60

SIC 3253 Ceramic wall and floor tile

D-U-N-S 20-115-7323   (BR)
FLINT GROUP CANADA LIMITED
(*Suby of* Flint Group US LLC)
890 Montee De Liesse, Saint-Laurent, QC,
H4T 1N8
(514) 731-9405
Emp Here 66
SIC 2893 Printing ink

D-U-N-S 20-424-0212   (BR)
**FORD MOTOR COMPANY OF CANADA,
LIMITED**
(*Suby of* Ford Motor Company)
6505 Rte Transcanadienne Bureau 200, Saint-
Laurent, QC, H4T 1S3
(514) 744-1800
Emp Here 150
SIC 5012 Automobiles and other motor vehi-
cles

D-U-N-S 24-697-2137   (HQ)
GANT PARIS DU CANADA LTEE, LE
GANTERIE AUCLAIR
255 Montee De Liesse, Saint-Laurent, QC,
H4T 1P5
(514) 345-0135
Emp Here 70   *Sales* 21,888,210
SIC 5136 Men's and boy's clothing
Ch Bd Ernest R Johnson
Pr Guy Darveau
Dir Jens I Peterson
Dir Torsten Jansson

D-U-N-S 25-407-8058   (BR)
GESCO INDUSTRIES INC
6660 Ch De La Cote-De-Liesse,   Saint-
Laurent, QC, H4T 1E3
(514) 341-6181
Emp Here 30
SIC 5713 Floor covering stores

D-U-N-S 24-335-5554   (BR)
GROUPE POLYALTO INC
4105 Rue Hickmore, Saint-Laurent, QC, H4T
1S5
(514) 738-6817
Emp Here 100
SIC 5162 Plastics materials and basic shapes

D-U-N-S 24-834-5035   (SL)
GROUPE SANTE PHYSIMED INC
CENTRE MEDICAL PHYSIMED
6363 Rte Transcanadienne Bureau 121, Saint-
Laurent, QC, H4T 1Z9
(514) 747-8888
Emp Here 100   *Sales* 7,821,331
SIC 8011 Offices and clinics of medical doc-
tors
Pr Albert Benham
VP VP Gilles Racine

D-U-N-S 20-124-3446   (SL)
GROUPE TECHNA INC
GROUPE GTECHNA
8550 Ch De La Cote-De-Liesse Bureau 100,
Saint-Laurent, QC, H4T 1H2
(514) 953-9898
Emp Here 43   *Sales* 4,012,839
SIC 7371 Custom computer programming ser-
vices

D-U-N-S 20-288-3294   (BR)
HAGGAR CANADA CO.
TRIBAL SPORTWEAR
7445 Ch De La Cote-De-Liesse Bureau 300,
Saint-Laurent, QC, H4T 1G2
(514) 322-5337
Emp Here 50
SIC 5136 Men's and boy's clothing

D-U-N-S 20-210-3081   (BR)
HENRY SCHEIN CANADA, INC
3403 Rue Griffith, Saint-Laurent, QC, H4T
1W5
(514) 337-3368
Emp Here 91

SIC 5047 Medical and hospital equipment

D-U-N-S 25-526-1380   (SL)
HOSPITALITE R.D. (AEROPORT) INC
FOUR POINTS BY SHARATON
6600 Ch De La Cote-De-Liesse,   Saint-
Laurent, QC, H4T 1E3
(514) 270-7000
Emp Here 50   *Sales* 2,188,821
SIC 7011 Hotels and motels

D-U-N-S 20-190-0870   (SL)
IHG HARILELA HOTELS LTD
HILTON GARDEN INN
7880 Ch De La Cote-De-Liesse,   Saint-
Laurent, QC, H4T 1E7
(514) 788-5120
Emp Here 85   *Sales* 5,173,950
SIC 7011 Hotels and motels
Pr Pr Daulat Dipshan
Recvr Benoit Clouatre

D-U-N-S 24-214-7713   (BR)
IKEA CANADA LIMITED PARTNERSHIP
IKEA CANADA LIMITED PARTNERSHIP
9090 Boul Cavendish, Saint-Laurent, QC, H4T
1Z8
(514) 904-8619
Emp Here 200
SIC 5712 Furniture stores

D-U-N-S 20-248-6770   (BR)
KONTRON CANADA INC
KONTRON COMMUNICATIONS
600 Rue Mccaffrey, Saint-Laurent, QC, H4T
1N1
(450) 437-4661
Emp Here 125
SIC 4899 Communication services, nec

D-U-N-S 25-969-2960   (BR)
LAFARGE CANADA INC
4000 Rue Hickmore, Saint-Laurent, QC, H4T
1K2
(514) 344-1788
Emp Here 80
SIC 5032 Brick, stone, and related material

D-U-N-S 20-223-4944   (HQ)
LANIEL (CANADA) INC
AUTOMEX
(*Suby of* Brokerhouse Distributors Inc)
7101 Rte Transcanadienne, Saint-Laurent,
QC, H4T 1A2
(514) 331-3031
Emp Here 54   *Emp Total* 50
Sales 10,648,318
SIC 5044 Office equipment
Pr Jean-Marc Laniel

D-U-N-S 20-298-0637   (SL)
LE BIFTHEQUE INC
BOUCHERIE LE BIFTHEQUE
6705 Ch De La Cote-De-Liesse,   Saint-
Laurent, QC, H4T 1E5
(514) 739-6336
Emp Here 100   *Sales* 2,991,389
SIC 5812 Eating places

D-U-N-S 24-366-0680   (BR)
**MAXXAM ANALYTICS INTERNATIONAL
CORPORATION**
MAXXAM ANALYTICS
889 Montee De Liesse, Saint-Laurent, QC,
H4T 1P5
(514) 448-9001
Emp Here 180
SIC 8748 Business consulting, nec

D-U-N-S 20-642-7853   (BR)
MIRCOM TECHNOLOGIES LTD
381 Rue Mccaffrey, Saint-Laurent, QC, H4T
1Z7
(514) 343-9644
Emp Here 20
SIC 5941 Sporting goods and bicycle shops

D-U-N-S 20-914-3598   (BR)
NAUTILUS PLUS INC

3303 Rue Griffith, Saint-Laurent, QC, H4T
1W5
(514) 739-3655
Emp Here 30
SIC 7997 Membership sports and recreation
clubs

D-U-N-S 20-421-5792   (SL)
NIVEL INC
MARKETING TANBORE
(*Suby of* Rennat Inc)
4850 Rue Bourg, Saint-Laurent, QC, H4T 1J2
(514) 735-4255
Emp Here 180   *Sales* 30,132,769
SIC 5046 Commercial equipment, nec
 Marvin Tanner
Dir Fin Munawer Chattoo
Dir Joyce Tanner

D-U-N-S 20-500-9236   (BR)
OLYMPIA TILE INTERNATIONAL INC
TILES OLYMPIA INTERNATIONAL
555 Rue Locke, Saint-Laurent, QC, H4T 1X7
(514) 345-8666
Emp Here 60
SIC 5032 Brick, stone, and related material

D-U-N-S 24-896-4371   (BR)
PACCAR OF CANADA LTD
PACCAR LEASING
(*Suby of* Paccar Inc)
7500 Rte Transcanadienne, Saint-Laurent,
QC, H4T 1A5
(514) 735-2581
Emp Here 150
SIC 5511 New and used car dealers

D-U-N-S 20-297-9902   (BR)
PVH CANADA, INC
CALVIN KLEVIN
7445 Ch De La Cote-De-Liesse,   Saint-
Laurent, QC, H4T 1G2
(514) 278-6000
Emp Here 500
SIC 5136 Men's and boy's clothing

D-U-N-S 24-194-9242   (BR)
PREMIER SCHOOL AGENDAS LTD
PREMIER AGENDAS
6800 Ch De La Cote-De-Liesse Bureau 301,
Saint-Laurent, QC, H4T 2A7
(514) 736-3940
Emp Here 20
SIC 2782 Blankbooks and looseleaf binders

D-U-N-S 25-899-9361   (BR)
PRODUITS INTEGRES AVIOR INC
(*Suby of* Produits Integres Avior Inc)
380 Montee De Liesse, Saint-Laurent, QC,
H4T 1N8
(514) 739-3193
Emp Here 70
SIC 3728 Aircraft parts and equipment, nec

D-U-N-S 24-144-2131   (BR)
PSION INC
(*Suby of* Motorola Solutions, Inc.)
7575 Rte Transcanadienne Bureau 500, Saint-
Laurent, QC, H4T 1V6

Emp Here 250
SIC 3571 Electronic computers

D-U-N-S 20-703-0151   (HQ)
REBOX CORP
CORPORATION REBOX
(*Suby of* Rebox Holdings Inc)
7500 Ch De La Cote-De-Liesse,   Saint-
Laurent, QC, H4T 1E7
(514) 335-1717
Emp Here 35   *Emp Total* 50
Sales 7,016,633
SIC 5113 Industrial and personal service pa-
per
Pr Pr Mark Young
VP VP Keith Primeau
 Brian Young

D-U-N-S 20-290-6756 (SL)
RECHERCHE CLINIQUE ICON (CANADA) INC
7405 Rte Transcanadienne Bureau 300, Saint-Laurent, QC, H4T 1Z2
(514) 332-0700
Emp Here 50 *Sales* 4,085,799
SIC 8071 Medical laboratories

D-U-N-S 24-294-5830 (HQ)
RECOCHEM INC
ENTREPRISES RECOCHEM, LES
850 Montee De Liesse, Saint-Laurent, QC, H4T 1P4
(514) 341-3550
Emp Here 225 *Emp Total* 681
Sales 316,287,715
SIC 2899 Chemical preparations, nec
Pr Pr Richard Boudreaux
VP Fin Gabrielle Daigle
Treas Alain Tanguay

D-U-N-S 24-387-8639 (BR)
ROYAL GROUP, INC
PLASTIQUES PVC MONTREAL
5055 Rue Courval Bureau 9, Saint-Laurent, QC, H4T 1X6
(514) 739-3399
Emp Here 75
SIC 3089 Plastics products, nec

D-U-N-S 20-233-0494 (BR)
RYDER MATERIAL HANDLING ULC
RYDER, J H MACHINERIE LIMITEE
(*Suby of* Crown Equipment Corporation)
3430 Rue Griffith, Saint-Laurent, QC, H4T 1A7
(514) 342-3471
Emp Here 70
SIC 5084 Industrial machinery and equipment

D-U-N-S 20-223-7400 (HQ)
SALON DE QUILLES LAURENTIEN LTEE
(*Suby of* Salon de Quilles Laurentien Ltee)
222 Montee De Liesse, Saint-Laurent, QC, H4T 1N8
(514) 341-4525
Emp Here 20 *Emp Total* 100
Sales 2,261,782
SIC 7933 Bowling centers

D-U-N-S 25-073-4241 (BR)
SAMUEL, SON & CO., LIMITED
UNALLOY IWRC, DIV DE
131 Rue Barr, Saint-Laurent, QC, H4T 1W6
(514) 735-6563
Emp Here 25
SIC 5051 Metals service centers and offices

D-U-N-S 25-308-5740 (SL)
SAVOIR FLEUR INC
935 Rue Reverchon, Saint-Laurent, QC, H4T 4L2
(514) 733-6087
Emp Here 50 *Sales* 2,626,585
SIC 5992 Florists

D-U-N-S 25-291-7125 (SL)
SERVICE D'ENTRETIEN ADVANCE INC
180 Montee De Liesse, Saint-Laurent, QC, H4T 1N7
(514) 363-3311
Emp Here 250 *Sales* 9,816,000
SIC 7349 Building maintenance services, nec
Pr Pr Avelino Conceicao
Acct Mgr Carole Malo

D-U-N-S 20-911-0204 (HQ)
SERVICES FERROVIAIRES CANAC INC
(*Suby of* Savage Companies)
6505 Rte Transcanadienne Bureau 405, Saint-Laurent, QC, H4T 1S3
(514) 734-4700
Emp Here 125 *Emp Total* 1,800
Sales 90,652,050
SIC 8741 Management services
Pr Allen B Alexander
VP VP Michel Martineau

VP VP Isaac Haboucha
VP VP Lewis Benson
Treas Curtis Dowd

D-U-N-S 24-489-5348 (HQ)
SERVICES DE PERSONNEL UNIQUE INC
(*Suby of* 170592 Canada Inc)
6380 Ch De La Cote-De-Liesse Bureau 100, Saint-Laurent, QC, H4T 1E3

Emp Here 22 *Emp Total* 875
Sales 87,920,000
SIC 7361 Employment agencies
Pr Pr Paul Christie

D-U-N-S 25-080-4978 (BR)
SODEXO CANADA LTD
8585 Ch De La Cote-De-Liesse, Saint-Laurent, QC, H4T 1G6
(514) 341-6780
Emp Here 40
SIC 1011 Iron ores

D-U-N-S 24-581-9644 (BR)
STANLEY BLACK & DECKER CANADA CORPORATION
BEST ACCESS SYSTEMS, DIV OF
160 Rue Graveline, Saint-Laurent, QC, H4T 1R7

Emp Here 60
SIC 3429 Hardware, nec

D-U-N-S 20-856-5960 (HQ)
STRUC-TUBE LTEE
6000 Rte Transcanadienne, Saint-Laurent, QC, H4T 1X9
(514) 333-9747
Emp Here 20 *Emp Total* 85
Sales 9,630,812
SIC 5712 Furniture stores
Pr Pr Marcel Knafo
Dir Eric Knafo
Dir Julien Knafo

D-U-N-S 24-330-9288 (SL)
VAN ACTION (2005) INC
VAN ACTION SAVARIA
4870 Rue Courval, Saint-Laurent, QC, H4T 1L1
(514) 342-5000
Emp Here 65
SIC 3716 Motor homes

D-U-N-S 25-258-4677 (BR)
VELAN INC
550 Rue Mcarthur, Saint-Laurent, QC, H4T 1X8
(514) 748-7743
Emp Here 230
SIC 3494 Valves and pipe fittings, nec

D-U-N-S 24-783-8709 (HQ)
VERITIV CANADA, INC
ADELCO
(*Suby of* Veritiv Corporation)
4300 Rue Hickmore, Saint-Laurent, QC, H4T 1K2
(514) 367-3111
Emp Here 69 *Emp Total* 8,700
Sales 432,875,833
SIC 5111 Printing and writing paper
 Mark W. Hianik
Sec Daniel Rowntree
Dir Erminia Shulak

D-U-N-S 20-010-8038 (BR)
WOLSELEY CANADA INC
(*Suby of* WOLSELEY PLC)
4200 Rue Hickmore, Saint-Laurent, QC, H4T 1K2
(514) 344-9378
Emp Here 100
SIC 5074 Plumbing and heating equipment and supplies (hydronics)

Saint-Laurent, QC H7C

D-U-N-S 25-494-7716 (BR)
SCI GROUP INC
SCI LOGISTICS
5860 Rue Maurice-Cullen, Saint-Laurent, QC, H7C 2V1
(450) 661-8300
Emp Here 40
SIC 4213 Trucking, except local

Saint-Laurent, QC H7L

D-U-N-S 25-973-8037 (BR)
COMMISSION SCOLAIRE DE LAVAL
ECOLE DU PARC
5 Rue Du Ruisseau, Saint-Laurent, QC, H7L 1C1
(450) 662-7000
Emp Here 20
SIC 7389 Business services, nec

Saint-Laurent, QC H7M

D-U-N-S 24-347-9263 (BR)
CRH CANADA GROUP INC
DEMIX CONSTRUCTION
26 Rue Saulnier, Saint-Laurent, QC, H7M 1S8
(450) 629-3533
Emp Here 50
SIC 1611 Highway and street construction

D-U-N-S 24-101-6430 (BR)
MULTI RECYCLAGE S.D. INC
140 Rue Saulnier, Saint-Laurent, QC, H7M 1S8
(450) 975-9952
Emp Here 104
SIC 4953 Refuse systems

Saint-Laurent, QC H7N

D-U-N-S 25-091-4736 (SL)
COOPERATIVE DES TRAVAILLEURS ET TRAVAILLEUSES PREMIER DEFI LAVAL
ROTISSERIES ST-HUBERT # 19
1111 Boul Des Laurentides, Saint-Laurent, QC, H7N 5B5
(450) 668-7085
Emp Here 115 *Sales* 3,502,114
SIC 5812 Eating places

Saint-Laurent, QC H7P

D-U-N-S 24-375-3568 (BR)
CATERPILLAR OF CANADA CORPORATION
2900 Rue Joseph-A.-Bombardier, Saint-Laurent, QC, H7P 6E3
(450) 681-0681
Emp Here 45
SIC 5082 Construction and mining machinery

D-U-N-S 20-318-5140 (BR)
HERSHEY CANADA INC
(*Suby of* Hershey Company)
2976 Rue Joseph-A.-Bombardier, Saint-Laurent, QC, H7P 6E3
(514) 955-1580
Emp Here 50
SIC 2064 Candy and other confectionery products

Saint-Laurent, QC H7R

D-U-N-S 25-909-2591 (SL)
AIDE AUX PERSONNES AGEES DE LAVAL INC
2388 35e Av, Saint-Laurent, QC, H7R 3P4
(450) 627-4641
Emp Here 60 *Sales* 2,334,742
SIC 8322 Individual and family services

D-U-N-S 20-124-1655 (SL)
BLEU TECH MONTREAL INC
BLEU TECH
4150 Chomedey (A-13) O, Saint-Laurent, QC, H7R 6E9
(450) 767-2890
Emp Here 100 *Sales* 10,871,144
SIC 8712 Architectural services
Pr John Fasanella
Sec Gregory K. Holness
Dir Daniele Crose
Genl Mgr Johannes Prinsloo

D-U-N-S 25-658-3469 (BR)
LIEBHERR-CANADA LTD
LIEBHERR-AEROSPACE CANADA
4250 Chomedey (A-13) O, Saint-Laurent, QC, H7R 6E9
(450) 963-7174
Emp Here 50
SIC 5082 Construction and mining machinery

D-U-N-S 25-138-9128 (HQ)
NORTRAX QUEBEC INC
(*Suby of* Deere & Company)
4500 Chomedey (A-13) O, Saint-Laurent, QC, H7R 6E9
(450) 625-3221
Emp Here 40 *Emp Total* 56,800
Sales 15,540,629
SIC 5084 Industrial machinery and equipment
VP James Fodi
Sec Gail E Mccombs
VP VP Michael Rugeroni
Pr Pr Tim Murphy
Dir Domenic Ruccolo
Fin Ex Wendy Stevenson

D-U-N-S 25-258-7811 (SL)
SANTE COURVILLE INC
CENTRE GERIATRIQUE DE BEL AGE
5200 80e Rue, Saint-Laurent, QC, H7R 5T6
(450) 627-7990
Emp Here 101 *Sales* 3,720,996
SIC 8361 Residential care

D-U-N-S 24-163-1592 (SL)
SUPERMARCHE PERRIER ET MARTEL INC
MARCHE METRO PERRIER ET MARTEL
6155 Boul Arthur-Sauve, Saint-Laurent, QC, H7R 3X8
(450) 627-4496
Emp Here 168 *Sales* 31,313,040
SIC 5411 Grocery stores
Pr Pr Suzanne Perrier
Dir Michel Perrier

Saint-Laurent, QC H7S

D-U-N-S 20-229-0359 (HQ)
ACIER PACIFIQUE INC
(*Suby of* Acier Pacifique Inc)
845 Av Munck, Saint-Laurent, QC, H7S 1A9
(514) 384-4690
Emp Here 39 *Emp Total* 50
Sales 20,137,153
SIC 5051 Metals service centers and offices
 Joseph Antebi
Fin Ex Anthony Andreoli

D-U-N-S 20-215-8531 (SL)
CUSTOM DIAMOND INTERNATIONAL INC
BRUTE KITCHEN EQUIPMENT

---

895 Av Munck, Saint-Laurent, QC, H7S 1A9
(450) 668-0330
Emp Here 50   *Sales* 5,690,935
SIC 3469 Metal stampings, nec
 Ronald Diamond
Genl Mgr Ron Tepper

Saint-Laurent, QC H7V

D-U-N-S 25-190-1083   (HQ)
CIMA CANADA INC
CIMA +
3400 Boul Du Souvenir Suite 600, Saint-Laurent, QC, H7V 3Z2
(514) 337-2462
Emp Here 250   *Emp Total* 2,500
Sales 49,754,971
SIC 8741 Management services
Pr Francois Plourde
VP Andre Couturier
VP Andre Desjardins
VP Jean-Pierre Normand
VP Marc Cantin
VP Andre Chaumont
VP Luc Jolicoeur

D-U-N-S 25-129-5002   (BR)
GLAXOSMITHKLINE INC
GSK
245 Boul Armand-Frappier, Saint-Laurent, QC, H7V 4A7
(450) 978-4599
Emp Here 50
SIC 2834 Pharmaceutical preparations

D-U-N-S 24-334-6314   (BR)
ID BIOMEDICAL CORPORATION OF QUEBEC
GLAXOSMITHKLINE BIOLOGICAL NORTH AMERICA
245 Boul Armand-Frappier, Saint-Laurent, QC, H7V 4A7
(450) 978-4599
Emp Here 20
SIC 5122 Drugs, proprietaries, and sundries

Saint-Lazare, QC J7T
Bellechasse County

D-U-N-S 24-230-9818   (SL)
9136-6419 QUEBEC INC
CONSTRUCTION J GRAVEL
1766 Ch Sainte-Angelique, Saint-Lazare, QC, J7T 2X8

Emp Here 40   *Sales* 5,331,960
SIC 1761 Roofing, siding, and sheetMetal work
Pr Jonathan Gravel

D-U-N-S 25-919-8638   (BR)
BIRON LABORATOIRE MEDICAL INC
LABORATOIRE MEDICAL BIRON
1811 Ch Sainte-Angelique, Saint-Lazare, QC, J7T 2X9

Emp Here 100
SIC 8071 Medical laboratories

D-U-N-S 20-804-8863   (BR)
COMMISSION SCOLAIRE DES TROIS-LACS
ECOLE AUCLAIR
1550 Rue Des Cedres, Saint-Lazare, QC, J7T 2P9
(514) 477-7002
Emp Here 40
SIC 8211 Elementary and secondary schools

D-U-N-S 25-296-2469   (BR)
ENERGIE VALERO INC
DEPANNEUR DU COIN

2662 Cote Saint-Charles, Saint-Lazare, QC, J7T 2H9
(450) 458-7666
Emp Here 35
SIC 5411 Grocery stores

D-U-N-S 24-458-9115   (SL)
HOTEL CHARTRAND & FILS INC
CHEZ MAURICE
1897 Ch Sainte-Angelique, Saint-Lazare, QC, J7T 2Y2
(450) 455-3544
Emp Here 50   *Sales* 1,824,018
SIC 5813 Drinking places

D-U-N-S 24-126-7462   (BR)
LESTER B. PEARSON SCHOOL BOARD
EVERGREEN ELEMENTARY SCHOOL
2625 Rue Du Bordelais, Saint-Lazare, QC, J7T 2Z9
(514) 798-4445
Emp Here 40
SIC 8211 Elementary and secondary schools

D-U-N-S 25-362-4332   (BR)
LESTER B. PEARSON SCHOOL BOARD
WESTWOOD HIGH SCHOOL JUNIOR CAMPUS
2800 Rue Du Bordelais, Saint-Lazare, QC, J7T 3E3
(514) 798-4500
Emp Here 25
SIC 8211 Elementary and secondary schools

D-U-N-S 24-942-2726   (BR)
POIRIER & FILS LTEE
I G A POIRIER
1869 Ch Sainte-Angelique, Saint-Lazare, QC, J7T 2X9
(450) 455-6165
Emp Here 150
SIC 5411 Grocery stores

Saint-Lazare-De-Bellechasse, QC G0R

D-U-N-S 20-309-5976   (BR)
CENTRE INTEGRE DE SANTE ET DE SERVICES SOCIAUX DE CHAUDIERE-APPALACHES
CLSC DE SAINT-LAZARE-DE-BELLECHASSE
100a Rue Monseigneur-Bilodeau, Saint-Lazare-De-Bellechasse, QC, G0R 3J0
(418) 883-2227
Emp Here 65
SIC 8322 Individual and family services

Saint-Leonard, QC H1P

D-U-N-S 25-393-8849   (SL)
3378918 CANADA INC
FIBRE ANS FIBERGLASS
6255 Boul Couture, Saint-Leonard, QC, H1P 3G7
(514) 668-3532
Emp Here 30   *Sales* 6,594,250
SIC 3714 Motor vehicle parts and accessories
Pr Marius Sebastian

D-U-N-S 24-226-7966   (SL)
9150-3979 QUEBEC INC
INTERMARCHE DE RISI
8700 Boul Langelier, Saint-Leonard, QC, H1P 3C6
(514) 323-0740
Emp Here 70   *Sales* 12,681,250
SIC 5411 Grocery stores
Pr Joseph De Risi
 Silvana De Risi
 Tony De Risi
 Lucrezia De Risi

D-U-N-S 24-126-8700   (BR)
A. LASSONDE INC
LASSONDE GROUPE DES VENTES
(*Suby of* 3346625 Canada Inc)
9430 Boul Langelier, Saint-Leonard, QC, H1P 3H8
(514) 323-8896
Emp Here 35
SIC 5149 Groceries and related products, nec

D-U-N-S 24-083-9142   (HQ)
ALIMENTS SAPUTO LIMITEE
LANDMARK
6869 Boul Metropolitain E, Saint-Leonard, QC, H1P 1X8
(514) 328-6662
Emp Here 70   *Emp Total* 10,357
Sales 189,333,017
SIC 5141 Groceries, general line
Pr Lino Anthony Jr. Saputo
VP VP Emanuele Saputo
Sec Louis-Phillipe Carriere

D-U-N-S 25-201-4113   (BR)
BANQUE NATIONALE DU CANADA
8020 Boul Langelier, Saint-Leonard, QC, H1P 3K1
(514) 327-4133
Emp Here 30
SIC 6021 National commercial banks

D-U-N-S 24-889-7738   (HQ)
BOULANGERIE VACHON INC
8770 Boul Langelier Bureau 230, Saint-Leonard, QC, H1P 3C6
(514) 326-5084
Emp Here 50   *Emp Total* 130,913
Sales 204,695,111
SIC 5149 Groceries and related products, nec
Pr Jean-Luc Breton
Dir Alejandro Pintado
Dir Darrell Miller

D-U-N-S 20-537-2175   (BR)
CANADA POST CORPORATION
BDP DE SAINT LEONARD
6105 Boul Metropolitain E, Saint-Leonard, QC, H1P 0A3
(514) 955-3148
Emp Here 60
SIC 4311 U.s. postal service

D-U-N-S 20-699-1221   (BR)
CLEAVER-BROOKS OF CANADA LIMITED
NATCOM
(*Suby of* Harbour Group Ltd.)
8515 Rue Lafrenaie, Saint-Leonard, QC, H1P 2B3
(514) 326-2571
Emp Here 50
SIC 3433 Heating equipment, except electric

D-U-N-S 20-617-7813   (BR)
COMMISSION SCOLAIRE DE LA POINTE-DE-L'ILE
COMMISSION SCOLAIRE DE LA POINTE-DE-L'ILE
8157 Rue Collerette, Saint-Leonard, QC, H1P 2V6
(514) 327-8092
Emp Here 23
SIC 8211 Elementary and secondary schools

D-U-N-S 24-479-9909   (BR)
COMMISSION SCOLAIRE DE LA POINTE-DE-L'ILE
ECOLE PRIMAIRE GABRIELLE ROY
5950 Rue Honore-Mercier, Saint-Leonard, QC, H1P 3E4
(514) 321-8475
Emp Here 100
SIC 8211 Elementary and secondary schools

D-U-N-S 25-240-3852   (BR)
COMMISSION SCOLAIRE DE LA POINTE-DE-L'ILE
ECOLE WILFRID BASTIEN
8155 Rue Collerette, Saint-Leonard, QC, H1P

2V6
(514) 323-1340
Emp Here 66
SIC 8211 Elementary and secondary schools

D-U-N-S 25-900-1014   (BR)
COMMISSION SCOLAIRE DE LA POINTE-DE-L'ILE
ECOLE GABRIELLE ROY
5950 Rue Honore-Mercier, Saint-Leonard, QC, H1P 3E4
(514) 323-9527
Emp Here 21
SIC 7299 Miscellaneous personal service

D-U-N-S 25-832-1769   (BR)
ESKIMO EXPRESS INC
GROUPE MORNEAU
8655 Rue Pascal-Gagnon, Saint-Leonard, QC, H1P 1Y5
(514) 322-1212
Emp Here 20
SIC 4213 Trucking, except local

D-U-N-S 24-020-3158   (HQ)
GAMBRO INC
(*Suby of* Baxter International Inc.)
9157 Rue Champ D'Eau, Saint-Leonard, QC, H1P 3M3
(514) 327-1635
Emp Here 40   *Emp Total* 48,000
Sales 14,592,140
SIC 5047 Medical and hospital equipment
Pr Nick Mendez
 Pierre Bourgon
 David Doerr

D-U-N-S 24-167-5990   (HQ)
GIVESCO INC
GUENETTE, DIV OF
9495 Rue Pascal-Gagnon, Saint-Leonard, QC, H1P 1Z4
(514) 327-7175
Emp Here 125   *Emp Total* 1
Sales 41,660,560
SIC 5039 Construction materials, nec
 Max Latifi

D-U-N-S 20-719-5319   (BR)
GOLF TOWN LIMITED
GOLF TOWN
6745 Boul Metropolitain E, Saint-Leonard, QC, H1P 1X8
(514) 329-2069
Emp Here 25
SIC 5941 Sporting goods and bicycle shops

D-U-N-S 20-124-4253   (SL)
GROUPE MONTECH INC
MONTECH
6250 Boul Des Grandes-Prairies, Saint-Leonard, QC, H1P 1A2
(514) 494-9744
Emp Here 50   *Sales* 3,064,349
SIC 3993 Signs and advertising specialties

D-U-N-S 24-176-0768   (HQ)
HEBDRAULIQUE INC
BOYAUX MULTIFLEX
(*Suby of* Hebdraulique Inc)
8410 Rue Champ D'Eau, Saint-Leonard, QC, H1P 1Y3
(514) 327-5966
Emp Here 20   *Emp Total* 60
Sales 7,879,756
SIC 3492 Fluid power valves and hose fittings
Pr Rene Hebert
VP Louis Tremblay
Sec Louis-Rene Hebert
Treas Alexandre Hebert

D-U-N-S 25-309-7091   (BR)
INDUSTRIELLE ALLIANCE, ASSURANCE ET SERVICES FINANCIERS INC
INDUSTRIELLE ALLIANCE ASSURANCE ET SERVICES FINANCE
6555 Boul Metropolitain E Bureau 403, Saint-Leonard, QC, H1P 3H3

(514) 324-3811
Emp Here 80
SIC 6411 Insurance agents, brokers, and service

D-U-N-S 20-707-0251   (HQ)
INDUSTRIES RAD INC
FAUCHER INDUSTRIES
6363 Boul Des Grandes-Prairies, Saint-Leonard, QC, H1P 1A5
(514) 321-6363
Emp Here 50   *Emp Total* 100
Sales 14,119,891
SIC 5072 Hardware
Pr Pr Raymond Dutil

D-U-N-S 24-509-2416   (SL)
JOVACO SOLUTIONS INC
6555 Boul Metropolitain E Bureau 302, Saint-Leonard, QC, H1P 3H3
(514) 323-3535
Emp Here 53   *Sales* 7,608,750
SIC 7371 Custom computer programming services
 Jean-Claude Coutu
 Treas Marie-Claude Frenette

D-U-N-S 24-061-0829   (HQ)
LES ENTREPRISES DORO J.C.S. INC
MCDONALD RESTAURANST OF CANADA
(*Suby of* Les Entreprises Doro J.C.S. Inc)
6050 Boul Des Grandes-Prairies Bureau 204, Saint-Leonard, QC, H1P 1A2
(514) 722-3676
Emp Here 60   *Emp Total* 250
Sales 7,514,952
SIC 5812 Eating places
 John Diiorio

D-U-N-S 20-416-4560   (HQ)
MAISON AMI-CO (1981) INC, LA
AMI-CO
(*Suby of* Gestion Oudama Ltee)
8455 Boul Langelier, Saint-Leonard, QC, H1P 2C5
(514) 351-7520
Emp Here 25   *Emp Total* 1
Sales 10,836,784
SIC 5087 Service establishment equipment
Pr Pr Gilbert Ouellette
VP Sophie Ouellette
Dir Bruno Rochette
Dir Anne-Marie Clouthier

D-U-N-S 20-603-2179   (SL)
MANUFACTURE DE MEUBLE VALENTINO INC, LA
MEUBLES DOMANI
(*Suby of* Placements D. & J. Valentino Inc)
6950 Boul Couture, Saint-Leonard, QC, H1P 3A9
(514) 325-4222
Emp Here 27   *Sales* 1,819,127
SIC 2511 Wood household furniture

D-U-N-S 25-672-0731   (BR)
MCFADDEN'S HARDWOOD & HARDWARE INC
8935 Rue Pascal-Gagnon, Saint-Leonard, QC, H1P 1Z4
(514) 343-5414
Emp Here 20
SIC 5031 Lumber, plywood, and millwork

D-U-N-S 25-834-6857   (BR)
PLACEMENTS SERGAKIS INC
CENTRE DE BILLARD INTERNATIONAL
6862 Rue Jarry E, Saint-Leonard, QC, H1P 3C1
(514) 328-5777
Emp Here 40
SIC 1542 Nonresidential construction, nec

D-U-N-S 24-080-5965   (SL)
PLASTIPRO LTEE
6855 Boul Couture, Saint-Leonard, QC, H1P 3M6
(514) 321-4368
Emp Here 40   *Sales* 5,928,320

SIC 3089 Plastics products, nec
Pr Pr Frank Carozza
VP VP Cosimo Rossi
 Paolino Rocco
 Antonio Christiano

D-U-N-S 25-835-2905   (BR)
PROVIGO INC
MAXI
5850 Boul Des Grandes-Prairies, Saint-Leonard, QC, H1P 1A2

Emp Here 70
SIC 5411 Grocery stores

D-U-N-S 25-495-3201   (SL)
ROULEAU GRAPHIC (QUEBEC) LTEE
9209 Boul Langelier, Saint-Leonard, QC, H1P 3K9
(514) 328-8111
Emp Here 25   *Sales* 5,275,400
SIC 3069 Fabricated rubber products, nec
Pr Pr Brian Venis
Mng Dir Marcel Demers

D-U-N-S 20-107-7414   (SL)
RUSTBLOCK CORROSION PRETECTION INC
5730 Boul Robert, Saint-Leonard, QC, H1P 1M4
(514) 722-1928
Emp Here 42   *Sales* 14,000,100
SIC 5169 Chemicals and allied products, nec
Pr Pr Walter Fortunato
 Gino Sazioli

D-U-N-S 25-308-3513   (BR)
SAPUTO PRODUITS LAITIERS CANADA S.E.N.C.
(*Suby of* Saputo Produits Laitiers Canada S.E.N.C.)
7750 Rue Pascal-Gagnon, Saint-Leonard, QC, H1P 3L1
(514) 328-6662
Emp Here 150
SIC 2022 Cheese; natural and processed

D-U-N-S 20-104-1378   (BR)
TRANSPORT MORNEAU INC
8575 Rue Pascal-Gagnon, Saint-Leonard, QC, H1P 1Y5
(514) 325-2727
Emp Here 125
SIC 4212 Local trucking, without storage

D-U-N-S 24-870-8448   (SL)
VETEMENTS PRESTIGIO INC, LES
(*Suby of* 3914968 Canada Inc)
6370 Boul Des Grandes-Prairies, Saint-Leonard, QC, H1P 1A2
(514) 955-7131
Emp Here 80   *Sales* 4,012,839
SIC 7389 Business services, nec

Saint-Leonard, QC H1R

D-U-N-S 24-870-8604   (SL)
173532 CANADA INC
7870 Rue Fleuricourt, Saint-Leonard, QC, H1R 2L3
(514) 274-2870
Emp Here 80   *Sales* 15,775,360
SIC 6712 Bank holding companies
Pr Alain Delisle
Sec Benoit Delisle

D-U-N-S 24-324-5391   (SL)
3812073 CANADA INC
I G P SPECIALISTES D'INVENTAIRE
4929 Rue Jarry E Bureau 208, Saint-Leonard, QC, H1R 1Y1
(514) 324-1024
Emp Here 60   *Sales* 3,064,349
SIC 7389 Business services, nec

D-U-N-S 24-256-8855   (SL)
AGENCE ANDRE BEAULNE LTEE
BEAULNE & RHEAUME
5055 Boul Metropolitain E Bureau 200, Saint-Leonard, QC, H1R 1Z7
(514) 329-3333
Emp Here 50   *Sales* 4,523,563
SIC 6411 Insurance agents, brokers, and service

D-U-N-S 25-285-8378   (SL)
ASSOCIATION DES GENS D'AFFAIRES & PROFESSIONNELS ITALO-CANADIENS INC, L'
CIBPA
8370 Boul Lacordaire Bureau 310, Saint-Leonard, QC, H1R 3Y6
(514) 254-4929
Emp Here 500   *Sales* 73,620,000
SIC 8621 Professional organizations
Pr Pr Luciano D'ijnazio

D-U-N-S 20-580-5711   (BR)
BANQUE LAURENTIENNE DU CANADA
4725 Rue Jarry E, Saint-Leonard, QC, H1R 1X7
(514) 374-0817
Emp Here 20
SIC 6021 National commercial banks

D-U-N-S 25-021-2487   (BR)
BANQUE NATIONALE DU CANADA
8730 Boul Provencher, Saint-Leonard, QC, H1R 3N7
(514) 729-1886
Emp Here 21
SIC 6021 National commercial banks

D-U-N-S 24-901-2030   (BR)
CENTENNIAL OPTICAL LIMITED
4555 Boul Des Grandes-Prairies Bureau 40, Saint-Leonard, QC, H1R 1A5
(514) 327-3891
Emp Here 20
SIC 5049 Professional equipment, nec

D-U-N-S 24-067-7976   (SL)
CENTRE COMMUNAUTAIRE LEONARDO DA VINCI
8370 Boul Lacordaire, Saint-Leonard, QC, H1R 3Y6
(514) 955-8350
Emp Here 100   *Sales* 3,939,878
SIC 8322 Individual and family services

D-U-N-S 25-201-3503   (SL)
CENTRE DE RECEPTION LE MADISON INC
MADISON, LE
8750 Boul Provencher, Saint-Leonard, QC, H1R 3N7
(514) 374-7428
Emp Here 100   *Sales* 3,283,232
SIC 7299 Miscellaneous personal service

D-U-N-S 25-240-3811   (BR)
COMMISSION SCOLAIRE ENGLISH-MONTREAL
PIERRE DE COUBERTIN SCHOOL
4700 Boul Lavoisier, Saint-Leonard, QC, H1R 1H9
(514) 323-6586
Emp Here 50
SIC 8211 Elementary and secondary schools

D-U-N-S 20-922-6484   (BR)
COMMISSION SCOLAIRE ENGLISH-MONTREAL
JOHN PAUL I HIGH SCHOOL
8455 Rue Du Pre-Laurin, Saint-Leonard, QC, H1R 3P3
(514) 328-7171
Emp Here 63
SIC 8211 Elementary and secondary schools

D-U-N-S 25-240-4173   (BR)
COMMISSION SCOLAIRE DE LA POINTE-DE-L'ILE
ECOLE VICTOR LAVIGNE
5400 Boul Couture, Saint-Leonard, QC, H1R

1C7
(514) 321-9234
Emp Here 50
SIC 8211 Elementary and secondary schools

D-U-N-S 25-240-4744   (BR)
COMMISSION SCOLAIRE DE LA POINTE-DE-L'ILE
ECOLE PIE XII
5455 Rue Dujarie, Saint-Leonard, QC, H1R 1K4
(514) 321-7570
Emp Here 25
SIC 8211 Elementary and secondary schools

D-U-N-S 20-206-8875   (BR)
FIBRES JASZTEX INC
(*Suby of* Fibres Jasztex Inc)
5375 Boul Des Grandes-Prairies, Saint-Leonard, QC, H1R 1B1
(514) 321-5452
Emp Here 20
SIC 2297 Nonwoven fabrics

D-U-N-S 24-334-0028   (BR)
HOOD PACKAGING CORPORATION
GLOPAK
(*Suby of* Hood Packaging Corporation)
4755 Boul Des Grandes-Prairies, Saint-Leonard, QC, H1R 1A6
(514) 323-4517
Emp Here 150
SIC 2673 Bags: plastic, laminated, and coated

D-U-N-S 25-309-7133   (BR)
INDUSTRIELLE ALLIANCE, ASSURANCE ET SERVICES FINANCIERS INC
4555 Boul Metropolitain E Bureau 200, Saint-Leonard, QC, H1R 1Z4
(514) 721-6220
Emp Here 40
SIC 6411 Insurance agents, brokers, and service

D-U-N-S 24-945-6211   (SL)
INTER V MEDICAL INC
5179 Boul Metropolitain E, Saint-Leonard, QC, H1R 1Z7

Emp Here 30   *Sales* 5,889,600
SIC 5047 Medical and hospital equipment
Pr Pr Genevieve Bedard
 Richard Wood
 Noel Bedard
VP Sls Jacques Lachance

D-U-N-S 20-217-1885   (HQ)
JOHN SCOTTI AUTOMOTIVE LTEE
4315 Boul Metropolitain E, Saint-Leonard, QC, H1R 1Z4
(514) 725-9394
Emp Here 50   *Emp Total* 10
Sales 28,454,673
SIC 5521 Used car dealers
 John Scotti

D-U-N-S 25-311-0621   (BR)
LES ENTREPRISES DORO J.C.S INC
MCDONALD'S RESTAURANT
(*Suby of* Les Entreprises Doro J.C.S. Inc)
9216 Boul Lacordaire, Saint-Leonard, QC, H1R 2B7
(514) 322-9143
Emp Here 60
SIC 5812 Eating places

D-U-N-S 20-590-6720   (BR)
LINDE CANADA LIMITED
BOC GASES
5555 Boul Des Grandes-Prairies, Saint-Leonard, QC, H1R 1B4
(514) 323-6410
Emp Here 70
SIC 5085 Industrial supplies

D-U-N-S 24-175-6683   (SL)
MAISON DE VETEMENTS PIACENTE LTEE, LA

4435 Boul Des Grandes-Prairies, Saint-Leonard, QC, H1R 3N4
(514) 324-1240
Emp Here 50   *Sales* 2,845,467
SIC 5699 Miscellaneous apparel and accessory stores

D-U-N-S 20-210-9427   (HQ)
PLASTIQUES BALCAN LIMITEE, LES
PLOYMAX
(*Suby* of Gestions Guilkohn Inc)
9340 Rue De Meaux, Saint-Leonard, QC, H1R 3H2
(514) 326-0200
Emp Here 190   *Emp Total* 1
Sales 32,321,590
SIC 3081 Unsupported plastics film and sheet
 Marcos Kohn

D-U-N-S 25-299-9552   (BR)
PRISZM LP
PFK
9205 Boul Lacordaire, Saint-Leonard, QC, H1R 2B6
(514) 325-3521
Emp Here 20
SIC 5812 Eating places

D-U-N-S 20-211-4583   (BR)
RUSSELL FOOD EQUIPMENT LIMITED
RUSSELL RINFRET, DIV DE
5485 Boul Des Grandes-Prairies, Saint-Leonard, QC, H1R 1B1
(514) 382-1160
Emp Here 25
SIC 5046 Commercial equipment, nec

D-U-N-S 20-008-8545   (BR)
SODEM INC
COMPLEXE AQUATIQUE DE SAINT LEONARD, LE
5115 Rue Des Galets, Saint-Leonard, QC, H1R 3W6
(514) 328-8595
Emp Here 50
SIC 7999 Amusement and recreation, nec

D-U-N-S 25-224-0924   (BR)
VILLE DE MONTREAL
BIBLIOTHEQUE DE SAINT-LEONARD
8420 Boul Lacordaire, Saint-Leonard, QC, H1R 3G5
(514) 328-8500
Emp Here 30
SIC 8231 Libraries

Saint-Leonard, QC H1S

D-U-N-S 24-728-6987   (SL)
9101-6451 QUEBEC INC
TIM HORTONS
4266 Rue Jean-Talon E Bureau 3004, Saint-Leonard, QC, H1S 1J7
(514) 376-9119
Emp Here 20   *Sales* 605,574
SIC 5812 Eating places

D-U-N-S 24-141-7885   (SL)
9288-3461 QUEBEC INC
ST-LEONARD TOYOTA
7665 Boul Lacordaire, Saint-Leonard, QC, H1S 2A7
(514) 253-8696
Emp Here 26   *Sales* 12,111,476
SIC 5012 Automobiles and other motor vehicles
Pr Gravel Jean Claude

D-U-N-S 25-298-2004   (BR)
BOUCLAIR INC
4425 Rue Jean-Talon E, Saint-Leonard, QC, H1S 1J9
(514) 725-9175
Emp Here 25
SIC 5949 Sewing, needlework, and piece goods

D-U-N-S 25-976-1062   (BR)
CAISSE DESJARDINS DU CENTRE-EST DE LA METROPOLE
4565 Rue Jean-Talon E, Saint-Leonard, QC, H1S 3H6
(514) 725-5050
Emp Here 60
SIC 6062 State credit unions

D-U-N-S 20-545-6168   (BR)
COMMISSION SCOLAIRE ENGLISH-MONTREAL
DANTI SCHOOL
6090 Rue De Lachenaie, Saint-Leonard, QC, H1S 1P1
(514) 254-5941
Emp Here 40
SIC 8211 Elementary and secondary schools

D-U-N-S 20-553-2893   (BR)
COMMISSION SCOLAIRE ENGLISH-MONTREAL
LAURIER MCDONALD VOCATIONAL CENTRE
5025 Rue Jean-Talon E, Saint-Leonard, QC, H1S 3G6
(514) 374-4278
Emp Here 40
SIC 8211 Elementary and secondary schools

D-U-N-S 25-240-4306   (BR)
COMMISSION SCOLAIRE ENGLISH-MONTREAL
LAURIER MACDONALD HIGH SCHOOL
7355 Boul Viau, Saint-Leonard, QC, H1S 3C2
(514) 374-6000
Emp Here 85
SIC 8211 Elementary and secondary schools

D-U-N-S 20-712-4970   (BR)
COMMISSION SCOLAIRE ENGLISH-MONTREAL
GENERAL VANIER SCHOOL
4555 Rue Buies, Saint-Leonard, QC, H1S 1J2
(514) 723-2229
Emp Here 40
SIC 8211 Elementary and secondary schools

D-U-N-S 20-712-3816   (BR)
COMMISSION SCOLAIRE DE LA POINTE-DE-L'ILE
ECOLE PRIMAIRE LAMBERT CLOSSE
6105 Rue La Dauversiere, Saint-Leonard, QC, H1S 1R6
(514) 255-4166
Emp Here 50
SIC 8211 Elementary and secondary schools

D-U-N-S 24-800-3592   (SL)
CROTEAU, J. A. (1989) INC
AUBAINERIE JEAN TALON
4265 Rue Jean-Talon E Bureau 2, Saint-Leonard, QC, H1S 1J9
(514) 374-4230
Emp Here 60   *Sales* 3,648,035
SIC 5651 Family clothing stores

D-U-N-S 25-325-0971   (BR)
GROUPE BMTC INC
BRAULT ET MARTINEAU
6700 Rue Jean-Talon E, Saint-Leonard, QC, H1S 1N1
(514) 254-9455
Emp Here 70
SIC 5712 Furniture stores

D-U-N-S 25-309-7547   (BR)
INDUSTRIELLE ALLIANCE, ASSURANCE ET SERVICES FINANCIERS INC
6455 Rue Jean-Talon E, Saint-Leonard, QC, H1S 3E8
(514) 729-3281
Emp Here 43
SIC 6411 Insurance agents, brokers, and service

D-U-N-S 24-869-9076   (SL)

LES PLACEMENTS ROGER POIRIER INC
7388 Boul Viau, Saint-Leonard, QC, H1S 2N9
(514) 727-2847
Emp Here 75   *Sales* 14,710,250
SIC 6712 Bank holding companies
Pr Pr Jacques Poirier
VP Nathalie Poirier
Treas Isabelle Poirier

D-U-N-S 24-138-2188   (BR)
MCDONALD'S RESTAURANTS OF CANADA LIMITED
RESTAURANTS MCDONALD'S
(*Suby* of McDonald's Corporation)
7445 Boul Langelier, Saint-Leonard, QC, H1S 1V6
(514) 252-1105
Emp Here 80
SIC 5812 Eating places

D-U-N-S 24-502-5960   (BR)
METRO RICHELIEU INC
SUPER C
6775 Rue Jean-Talon E, Saint-Leonard, QC, H1S 1N2
(514) 252-0230
Emp Here 100
SIC 5411 Grocery stores

D-U-N-S 24-314-0774   (BR)
MONTREAL AUTO PRIX INC
7200 Boul Langelier, Saint-Leonard, QC, H1S 2X6
(514) 257-8020
Emp Here 20
SIC 7538 General automotive repair shops

D-U-N-S 20-588-0672   (BR)
MOORES THE SUIT PEOPLE INC
MOORES CLOTHING FOR MEN
(*Suby* of Tailored Brands, Inc.)
6835 Rue Jean-Talon E, Saint-Leonard, QC, H1S 1N2
(514) 253-6555
Emp Here 23
SIC 5611 Men's and boys' clothing stores

D-U-N-S 24-667-9286   (BR)
NAUTILUS PLUS INC
6705 Rue Jean-Talon E, Saint-Leonard, QC, H1S 1N2
(514) 353-7860
Emp Here 20
SIC 7999 Amusement and recreation, nec

D-U-N-S 25-210-3197   (HQ)
PIECES POUR AUTOMOBILE JEAN-TALON (1993) LTEE
(*Suby* of Pieces pour Automobile Jean-Talon (1993) Ltee)
7655 Boul Viau, Saint-Leonard, QC, H1S 2P4
(514) 374-2113
Emp Here 29   *Emp Total* 60
Sales 9,423,290
SIC 5013 Motor vehicle supplies and new parts
Pr Pr Matteo Del Vasto

D-U-N-S 20-019-6249   (BR)
ROYAL BANK OF CANADA
RBC
(*Suby* of Royal Bank Of Canada)
4286 Rue Jean-Talon E, Saint-Leonard, QC, H1S 1J7
(514) 722-3568
Emp Here 33
SIC 6021 National commercial banks

D-U-N-S 20-527-4884   (BR)
SEARS CANADA INC
6875 Rue Jean-Talon E, Saint-Leonard, QC, H1S 1N2

Emp Here 30
SIC 5311 Department stores

D-U-N-S 20-323-6393   (BR)
SOBEYS QUEBEC INC
IGA EXTRA

7150 Boul Langelier, Saint-Leonard, QC, H1S 2X6
(514) 254-5454
Emp Here 150
SIC 5141 Groceries, general line

D-U-N-S 24-935-1370   (SL)
ST-LEONARD TOYOTA (1992) LTEE
7665 Boul Lacordaire, Saint-Leonard, QC, H1S 2A7
(514) 252-1373
Emp Here 37   *Sales* 18,588,800
SIC 5511 New and used car dealers
Pr Pr Claude Dubois
VP Gilles Richard
 Serge Maheux
Treas Marie-Elise Mathieu

D-U-N-S 20-574-6402   (BR)
STAPLES CANADA INC
BUREAU EN GROS
(*Suby* of Staples, Inc.)
4625 Rue Jean-Talon E, Saint-Leonard, QC, H1S 1K3
(514) 593-6813
Emp Here 30
SIC 5943 Stationery stores

D-U-N-S 20-703-8782   (BR)
TEVA CANADA LIMITED
TEVA NOVOPHARM
6455 Rue Jean-Talon E Bureau 100, Saint-Leonard, QC, H1S 3E8

Emp Here 25
SIC 5122 Drugs, proprietaries, and sundries

D-U-N-S 24-321-4587   (BR)
VALUE VILLAGE STORES, INC
VILLAGE DES VALEURS
(*Suby* of Savers, Inc.)
6779 Rue Jean-Talon E, Saint-Leonard, QC, H1S 1N2
(514) 254-0433
Emp Here 30
SIC 5399 Miscellaneous general merchandise

D-U-N-S 25-294-8500   (BR)
WAL-MART CANADA CORP
WALMART SUPERCENTRE
7445 Boul Langelier, Saint-Leonard, QC, H1S 1V6
(514) 899-1889
Emp Here 300
SIC 5311 Department stores

D-U-N-S 25-947-5952   (BR)
WINNERS MERCHANTS INTERNATIONAL L.P.
WINNERS
(*Suby* of The TJX Companies Inc)
4375 Rue Jean-Talon E, Saint-Leonard, QC, H1S 1J9
(514) 374-0880
Emp Here 30
SIC 5651 Family clothing stores

D-U-N-S 20-308-7705   (BR)
YM INC. (SALES)
URBAN PLANET
4254 Rue Jean-Talon E, Saint-Leonard, QC, H1S 1J7
(514) 725-7449
Emp Here 25
SIC 5621 Women's clothing stores

Saint-Leonard, QC H1T

D-U-N-S 25-687-8638   (BR)
PROVIGO INC
PROVIGO BELANGER
5915 Rue Belanger, Saint-Leonard, QC, H1T 1G8
(514) 259-4216
Emp Here 50

SIC 5411 Grocery stores

Saint-Leonard-D'Aston, QC J0C
Nicolet County

D-U-N-S 20-584-0338   (BR)
COMMISSION SCOLAIRE DE LA RIVERAINE
ECOLE TOURNESOL
(*Suby of* Commission Scolaire de la Riveraine)
174 Rue Des Ecoles, Saint-Leonard-D'Aston, QC, J0C 1M0
(819) 399-2668
Emp Here 35
SIC 8211 Elementary and secondary schools

D-U-N-S 25-021-5696   (BR)
COMMISSION SCOLAIRE DE LA RIVERAINE
ECOLE SECONDAIRE LA DECOUVERTE
(*Suby of* Commission Scolaire de la Riveraine)
401 Rue Germain, Saint-Leonard-D'Aston, QC, J0C 1M0
(819) 399-2122
Emp Here 86
SIC 8211 Elementary and secondary schools

D-U-N-S 20-184-2163   (BR)
NORTEK AIR SOLUTIONS CANADA, INC
200 Rue Carter, Saint-Leonard-D'Aston, QC, J0C 1M0
(819) 399-2175
Emp Here 230
SIC 1711 Plumbing, heating, air-conditioning

Saint-Liguori, QC J0K
Montcalm County

D-U-N-S 24-458-1419   (SL)
CLUB DE GOLF MONTCALM INC
1800 Ch Nadeau, Saint-Liguori, QC, J0K 2X0
(450) 834-6981
Emp Here 50   *Sales* 2,042,900
SIC 7997 Membership sports and recreation clubs

Saint-Lin-Laurentides, QC J5M
Montcalm County

D-U-N-S 20-512-9690   (BR)
BURO DESIGN INTERNATIONAL A.Q. INC
(*Suby of* Buro Design International A.Q. Inc)
125 Rue Quintal, Saint-Lin-Laurentides, QC, J5M 2S8
(450) 439-8554
Emp Here 180
SIC 2521 Wood office furniture

D-U-N-S 20-712-2057   (BR)
COMMISSION SCOLAIRE DES SAMARES
ECOLE PRIMAIRE ARC EN CIEL
263 14e Av, Saint-Lin-Laurentides, QC, J5M 2X6
(450) 439-3138
Emp Here 50
SIC 8211 Elementary and secondary schools

D-U-N-S 20-712-2099   (BR)
COMMISSION SCOLAIRE DES SAMARES
PAVILLON SIR WILFRID-LAURIER
265 16e Av, Saint-Lin-Laurentides, QC, J5M 2X8
(450) 439-7135
Emp Here 50
SIC 8211 Elementary and secondary schools

D-U-N-S 25-690-0192   (BR)

COMMISSION SCOLAIRE DES SAMARES
ECOLE L'AUBIER
250 Ch Saint-Stanislas, Saint-Lin-Laurentides, QC, J5M 2H2
(450) 439-6051
Emp Here 25
SIC 8211 Elementary and secondary schools

D-U-N-S 24-346-4505   (BR)
GOUVERNEMENT DE LA PROVINCE DE QUEBEC
CENTRE D' HEBERGEMENT ST-ANTOINE-DE-PADOUE
521 Rue Saint-Antoine, Saint-Lin-Laurentides, QC, J5M 3A3
(450) 439-2609
Emp Here 125
SIC 8361 Residential care

D-U-N-S 24-815-0625   (SL)
MAISONS USINEES COTE INC
388 Rue Saint-Isidore, Saint-Lin-Laurentides, QC, J5M 2V1
(450) 439-8737
Emp Here 85   *Sales* 15,521,850
SIC 2452 Prefabricated wood buildings
Rejean Cote

D-U-N-S 24-329-9570   (BR)
PROVIGO DISTRIBUTION INC
1095 Rue Saint-Isidore, Saint-Lin-Laurentides, QC, J5M 2V5
(450) 439-5986
Emp Here 70
SIC 5411 Grocery stores

Saint-Lucien, QC J0C
Drummomd County

D-U-N-S 25-382-8735   (BR)
COMMISSION SCOLAIRE DES CHENES
ECOLE DES 2 RIVIERES
(*Suby of* Commission Scolaire des Chenes)
5330 7e Rang, Saint-Lucien, QC, J0C 1N0
(819) 850-1612
Emp Here 20
SIC 8351 Child day care services

Saint-Ludger, QC G0M
Frontenac County

D-U-N-S 24-118-9302   (BR)
EQUIPEMENTS LAPIERRE INC, LES
CONFECTION LAPIERRE
183 Rue Boisvert, Saint-Ludger, QC, G0M 1W0
(819) 548-5395
Emp Here 45
SIC 5651 Family clothing stores

Saint-Majorique, QC J2B
Drummomd County

D-U-N-S 20-127-2239   (BR)
COMMISSION SCOLAIRE DES CHENES
ECOLE PRIMAIRE SAINT MAJORIQUE
(*Suby of* Commission Scolaire des Chenes)
770 Ch Du Sanctuaire, Saint-Majorique, QC, J2B 8A8
(819) 474-0707
Emp Here 50
SIC 8211 Elementary and secondary schools

Saint-Malo, QC J0B
Compton County

D-U-N-S 25-690-0192   (BR)

COMMISSION SCOLAIRE DES SAMARES
D-U-N-S 24-125-3413   (BR)
CAISSE DESJARDINS DES VERTS-SOMMETS DE L'ESTRIE
225 Rte 253 S, Saint-Malo, QC, J0B 2Y0
(819) 849-9822
Emp Here 50
SIC 6021 National commercial banks

Saint-Marc-Des-Carrieres, QC G0A
Portneuf County

D-U-N-S 20-029-1651   (BR)
CENTRE DE SANTE ET DE SERVICES SOCIAUX DE PORTNEUF
CENTRE D' HEBERGEMENT ST MARC DES CARRIERES
444 Rue Beauchamp, Saint-Marc-Des-Carrieres, QC, G0A 4B0
(418) 268-3511
Emp Here 95
SIC 8361 Residential care

D-U-N-S 25-479-9950   (SL)
GRAYMONT (PORTNEUF) INC
BETON ST-MARC
595 Boul Bona-Dussault, Saint-Marc-Des-Carrieres, QC, G0A 4B0
(418) 268-3501
Emp Here 80   *Sales* 4,377,642
SIC 1481 NonMetallic mineral services

D-U-N-S 20-356-2728   (SL)
MARIE-LOU INC
585 Av Principale, Saint-Marc-Des-Carrieres, QC, G0A 4B0
(418) 268-5550
Emp Here 50   *Sales* 1,313,293
SIC 2353 Hats, caps, and millinery

D-U-N-S 24-246-6261   (BR)
SERVICES MATREC INC
139 Rue Du Parc-Industriel, Saint-Marc-Des-Carrieres, QC, G0A 4B0
(418) 268-4816
Emp Here 20
SIC 4212 Local trucking, without storage

D-U-N-S 24-379-7271   (SL)
TOURNAGE DE BOIS DYNASTIE LTEE
M.S.M.
200 Rue Saint-Dominique, Saint-Marc-Des-Carrieres, QC, G0A 4B0
(418) 268-8755
Emp Here 50   *Sales* 4,888,367
SIC 2499 Wood products, nec

Saint-Marc-Sur-Richelieu, QC J0L

D-U-N-S 24-973-8329   (BR)
COMMISSION SCOLAIRE DES PATRIOTES
ECOLE DES TROIS TEMPS
103 Rue De La Fabrique, Saint-Marc-Sur-Richelieu, QC, J0L 2E0
(450) 467-1921
Emp Here 20
SIC 8211 Elementary and secondary schools

D-U-N-S 25-591-0762   (SL)
HOSTELLERIE LES TROIS TILLEULS INC
290 Rue Richelieu, Saint-Marc-Sur-Richelieu, QC, J0L 2E0
(514) 856-7787
Emp Here 60   *Sales* 1,824,018
SIC 5812 Eating places

Saint-Martin, QC G0M
Beauce County

D-U-N-S 24-808-0843   (BR)

CAISSE DESJARDINS DU SUD DE LA CHAUDIERE
140 1re Av E, Saint-Martin, QC, G0M 1B0
(418) 382-5391
Emp Here 25
SIC 6211 Security brokers and dealers

D-U-N-S 25-232-7580   (BR)
COMMISSION SCOLAIRE DE LA BEAUCE-ETCHEMIN
POLYVALENTE BELANGER
30a Ch De La Polyvalente Bureau 3033, Saint-Martin, QC, G0M 1B0
(418) 228-5541
Emp Here 85
SIC 8211 Elementary and secondary schools

Saint-Mathieu-D'Harricana, QC J0Y
Abitibi County

D-U-N-S 24-310-6338   (BR)
EAUX VIVES WATER INC
ESKA
(*Suby of* Morgan Stanley)
11 Ch Des Sabli Res Bureau 6, Saint-Mathieu-D'Harricana, QC, J0Y 1M0
(819) 727-9000
Emp Here 20
SIC 5149 Groceries and related products, nec

Saint-Mathieu-De-Beloeil, QC J3G
Vercheres County

D-U-N-S 20-254-2924   (HQ)
BEAUCHESNE, EDOUARD (1985) INC
3211 Rue De L'Industrie, Saint-Mathieu-De-Beloeil, QC, J3G 4S5
(450) 467-8776
Emp Here 100   *Emp Total* 30
Sales 28,737,280
SIC 5039 Construction materials, nec
Pr Pr Robert Leonard

D-U-N-S 24-223-6404   (SL)
CABANONS FONTAINE INC
CABANONS DIRECT
3497 Rue De L'Industrie, Saint-Mathieu-De-Beloeil, QC, J3G 0R9
(450) 536-3563
Emp Here 50   *Sales* 6,566,463
SIC 2452 Prefabricated wood buildings
Pr Pr Bernard Fontaine
Treas Mathieu Brunelle-Fontaine
Dir Andre Coulombe
Dir Pierrette Brunelle

D-U-N-S 24-740-1003   (SL)
FINES HERBES DE CHEZ NOUS INC, LES
FINES HERBES AROMATIQUES FRAICHES
116 Ch Trudeau, Saint-Mathieu-De-Beloeil, QC, J3G 0E3
(450) 464-2920
Emp Here 50   *Sales* 4,304,681
SIC 5431 Fruit and vegetable markets

D-U-N-S 20-919-0896   (BR)
GUAY INC
SERVICE DE GRUES INTERPROVINCIALE
2845 Rue De L'Industrie Bureau B, Saint-Mathieu-De-Beloeil, QC, J3G 4S5
(450) 922-8344
Emp Here 65
SIC 7389 Business services, nec

D-U-N-S 24-360-0942   (BR)
IFASTGROUPE 2004 L.P.
GALVANO
2620 Rue Bernard-Pilon, Saint-Mathieu-De-Beloeil, QC, J3G 4S5
(450) 464-0547
Emp Here 53

SIC 5085 Industrial supplies

D-U-N-S 20-615-6148 (BR)
LAIDLAW CARRIERS BULK LP
LAIDLAW CARRIERS
3135 Rue Bernard-Pilon, Saint-Mathieu-De-Beloeil, QC, J3G 4S5
(450) 536-3001
Emp Here 20
SIC 4213 Trucking, except local

D-U-N-S 25-479-8895 (SL)
MAISON VICTOR GADBOIS INC, LA
1000 Rue Chabot, Saint-Mathieu-De-Beloeil, QC, J3G 0R8
(450) 467-1710
Emp Here 58   *Sales* 2,626,585
SIC 8051 Skilled nursing care facilities

D-U-N-S 25-509-9756 (SL)
RAYONNAGE CAMRACK INC
3112 Rue Bernard-Pilon, Saint-Mathieu-De-Beloeil, QC, J3G 4S5
(450) 446-3003
Emp Here 55   *Sales* 4,231,721
SIC 2542 Partitions and fixtures, except wood

Saint-Maurice, QC G0X
Champlain County

D-U-N-S 25-232-6616 (BR)
COMMISSION SCOLAIRE DU CHEMIN-DU-ROY
ECOLES FRIMAIRES DE LA SOURCE
1380 Rue Notre-Dame, Saint-Maurice, QC, G0X 2X0

Emp Here 20
SIC 8211 Elementary and secondary schools

Saint-Michel, QC J0L
Richelieu County

D-U-N-S 25-240-7218 (BR)
COMMISSION SCOLAIRE DE MONTREAL
ECOLE MARIE RIVIER
9200 8 Av, Saint-Michel, QC, J0L 2J0
(514) 596-5340
Emp Here 60
SIC 8211 Elementary and secondary schools

Saint-Michel-De-Bellechasse, QC G0R
Bellechasse County

D-U-N-S 25-261-9577 (BR)
GOUVERNEMENT DE LA PROVINCE DE QUEBEC
QUEBEC TRANSPORT SOUS CENTER
146 132 Rte E, Saint-Michel-De-Bellechasse, QC, G0R 3S0
(418) 884-2363
Emp Here 20
SIC 4213 Trucking, except local

D-U-N-S 25-324-8561 (BR)
VIGI SANTE LTEE
C.H.S.L.D. NOTRE DAME DE LOURDES, DIV. DE
(*Suby of* Vigi Sante Ltee)
80 Rue Principale, Saint-Michel-De-Bellechasse, QC, G0R 3S0
(418) 884-2811
Emp Here 40
SIC 8361 Residential care

Saint-Michel-Des-Saints, QC J0K
Berthier County

D-U-N-S 20-712-1992 (BR)
COMMISSION SCOLAIRE DES SAMARES
ECOLE PRIMAIRE ST JEAN BAPTISTE
380 Rue Brassard, Saint-Michel-Des-Saints, QC, J0K 3B0
(450) 758-3697
Emp Here 20
SIC 8211 Elementary and secondary schools

D-U-N-S 20-712-2016 (BR)
COMMISSION SCOLAIRE DES SAMARES
ECOLE SECONDAIRE DES MONTAGNES
290 Rue Brassard, Saint-Michel-Des-Saints, QC, J0K 3B0
(450) 758-3643
Emp Here 30
SIC 8211 Elementary and secondary schools

Saint-Modeste, QC G0L
Riviere-Du-Loup County

D-U-N-S 24-326-2883 (SL)
GESTION CLAUDIN BERGER LTEE
121 Rang 1, Saint-Modeste, QC, G0L 3W0
(418) 862-4462
Emp Here 280   *Sales* 22,380,480
SIC 1499 Miscellaneous nonMetallic minerals, except fuels
Pr Claudin Berger

D-U-N-S 25-471-3076 (BR)
GOUVERNEMENT DE LA PROVINCE DE QUEBEC
GOUVERNEMENT DE LA PROVINCE DE QUEBEC
410 Rue Principale, Saint-Modeste, QC, G0L 3W0
(418) 862-5511
Emp Here 45
SIC 7389 Business services, nec

Saint-Narcisse, QC G0X
Champlain County

D-U-N-S 25-199-8126 (BR)
CENTRE DE SANTE ET DE SERVICES SOCIAUX DE LA VALLEE-DE-LA-BATISCAN
CENTRE D'ACCUEIL ST-NARCISSE
361 Rue Du College, Saint-Narcisse, QC, G0X 2Y0
(418) 328-3351
Emp Here 50
SIC 8051 Skilled nursing care facilities

D-U-N-S 25-199-8324 (BR)
PROMUTUEL   PORTNEUF-CHAMPLAIN SOCIETE, MUTUAL D'ASSURANCE GENERALE
PROMUTUEL PORTNEUF CHAMPLAIN
401 Rue Principale, Saint-Narcisse, QC, G0X 2Y0
(418) 328-8270
Emp Here 45
SIC 6411 Insurance agents, brokers, and service

D-U-N-S 20-553-0012 (BR)
SEALY CANADA LTD
GESTION CENTURION
(*Suby of* Tempur Sealy International, Inc.)
555 Rue Panneton Bureau 97, Saint-Narcisse, QC, G0X 2Y0
(418) 328-3361
Emp Here 60
SIC 2515 Mattresses and bedsprings

Saint-Narcisse-De-Rimouski, QC G0K

D-U-N-S 25-232-1294 (BR)
COMMISSION SCOLAIRE DES PHARES
ECOLE BOIJOLI SAINT NARCISSE
(*Suby of* Commission Scolaire des Phares)
37 Rue De La Montagne, Saint-Narcisse-De-Rimouski, QC, G0K 1S0
(418) 735-2149
Emp Here 25
SIC 8211 Elementary and secondary schools

D-U-N-S 20-518-7854 (BR)
SOCIETE DES ETABLISSEMENTS DE PLEIN AIR DU QUEBEC
RESERVE FAUNIQUE DE RIMOUSKI
112 Rte De La Reserve-De-Rimouski, Saint-Narcisse-De-Rimouski, QC, G0K 1S0
(418) 735-5672
Emp Here 25
SIC 8999 Services, nec

Saint-Nicolas, QC G7A
Levis County

D-U-N-S 25-941-1536 (SL)
9048-4270 QUEBEC INC
V.R. DANIEL EMOND
594 Ch Olivier, Saint-Nicolas, QC, G7A 2N6
(418) 836-5050
Emp Here 25   *Sales* 6,087,000
SIC 5571 Motorcycle dealers
Pr Pr Daniel Emond
Recvr Mark Berneier

D-U-N-S 25-233-6920 (BR)
COMMISSION SCOLAIRE DES NAVIGATEURS
ECOLE SECONDAIRE DE L'ENVOL
368 Rte Du Pont, Saint-Nicolas, QC, G7A 2V3
(418) 834-2461
Emp Here 75
SIC 8211 Elementary and secondary schools

D-U-N-S 20-517-1119 (SL)
HOTEL BERNIERES INC
535 Rue De L'Arena, Saint-Nicolas, QC, G7A 1C9
(418) 831-3119
Emp Here 90   *Sales* 3,939,878
SIC 7011 Hotels and motels

D-U-N-S 24-635-8514 (BR)
MAHEU & MAHEU INC
526 Rue De L'Arena, Saint-Nicolas, QC, G7A 1E1
(418) 831-2600
Emp Here 100
SIC 5191 Farm supplies

D-U-N-S 25-762-5897 (BR)
PLACEMENTS ASHTON LEBLOND INC, LES
CHEZ ASHTON
(*Suby of* Placements Ashton LeBlond Inc, Les)
455 Rte Du Pont, Saint-Nicolas, QC, G7A 2N9

Emp Here 55
SIC 5812 Eating places

D-U-N-S 20-716-1212 (BR)
RESTAURANT NORMANDIN INC
530 Rte Du Pont, Saint-Nicolas, QC, G7A 2N9
(418) 831-1991
Emp Here 80
SIC 5812 Eating places

Saint-Norbert, QC J0K
Berthier County

D-U-N-S 24-352-2500 (BR)

LAUZON - PLANCHERS DE BOIS EXCLUSIFS INC
1680 Rue Principale Rr 5, Saint-Norbert, QC, J0K 3C0
(450) 836-4405
Emp Here 100
SIC 2426 Hardwood dimension and flooring mills

Saint-Odilon, QC G0S
Dorchester County

D-U-N-S 25-400-3445 (BR)
COMMISSION SCOLAIRE DE LA BEAUCE-ETCHEMIN
ECOLE ARC-EN-CIEL DE SAINT-ODILON
105 Rue De L'Hotel De Ville, Saint-Odilon, QC, G0S 3A0
(418) 464-4511
Emp Here 20
SIC 8211 Elementary and secondary schools

D-U-N-S 24-820-2269 (SL)
STRUCTURES DE BEAUCE INC, LES
(*Suby of* Gestion Benoit Drouin Inc)
305 Rue Du Parc Rr 1, Saint-Odilon, QC, G0S 3A0
(418) 464-2000
Emp Here 50   *Sales* 7,362,000
SIC 1791 Structural steel erection
Pr Pr Benoit Drouin

Saint-Omer, QC G0C
Bonaventure County

D-U-N-S 20-520-1945 (BR)
CENTRE DE SANTE ET DE SERVICES SOCIAUX DE BAIE DES CHALEURS
CLSC DE SAINT-OMER
(*Suby of* Centre de Sante et de Services Sociaux de Baie des Chaleurs)
107 Route 132 O, Saint-Omer, QC, G0C 2Z0
(418) 364-7064
Emp Here 45
SIC 8322 Individual and family services

Saint-Ours, QC J0G
Richelieu County

D-U-N-S 24-970-5500 (BR)
CANADA PIPE COMPANY ULC
FONDERIE LAPERLE, DIV DE
106 Montee Basse, Saint-Ours, QC, J0G 1P0
(450) 785-2205
Emp Here 100
SIC 3322 Malleable iron foundries

Saint-Pacome, QC G0L
Kamouraska County

D-U-N-S 20-255-9662 (SL)
ROLAND & FRERES LIMITEE
22 Rue Fortier, Saint-Pacome, QC, G0L 3X0
(418) 852-2191
Emp Here 30   *Sales* 10,956,600
SIC 5141 Groceries, general line
Pr Pr Sylvain Levesque
VP VP Stephane Levesque
Gaetan Dube
Michel Martin

Saint-Pamphile, QC G0R
L'Islet County

D-U-N-S 25-233-0444   (BR)
COMMISSION SCOLAIRE DE LA COTE-DU-SUD, LA
ECOLE ST JOSEPH
58 Rue Du College, Saint-Pamphile, QC, G0R 3X0
(418) 356-3161
Emp Here 25
SIC 8211 Elementary and secondary schools

D-U-N-S 25-232-7028   (BR)
COMMISSION SCOLAIRE DE LA COTE-DU-SUD, LA
COMMISSION SCOLAIRE DE LA COTE-DU-SUD, LA
240 Rue Saint-Pierre, Saint-Pamphile, QC, G0R 3X0
(418) 356-3314
Emp Here 60
SIC 8211 Elementary and secondary schools

D-U-N-S 20-256-0199   (SL)
MAGASIN CO-OP DE ST-PAMPHILE
MAGASIN COOP DE ST-PAMPHILE
12 Rue Principale, Saint-Pamphile, QC, G0R 3X0
(418) 356-3373
Emp Here 65   *Sales* 11,666,750
SIC 5411 Grocery stores
Pr Clermont Gagnon
Genl Mgr Dominique Troie

D-U-N-S 20-578-6445   (BR)
MAIBEC INC
24 6e Rang Bureau 6, Saint-Pamphile, QC, G0R 3X0
(418) 356-3331
Emp Here 800
SIC 2421 Sawmills and planing mills, general

D-U-N-S 24-377-9576   (BR)
MATERIAUX BLANCHET INC
1030 Rue Elgin S Bureau 356, Saint-Pamphile, QC, G0R 3X0
(418) 356-3344
Emp Here 260
SIC 2421 Sawmills and planing mills, general

Saint-Pascal, QC G0L
Kamouraska County

D-U-N-S 20-256-0652   (SL)
AUTOMOBILE KAMOURASKA (1992) INC
OLIVIER KAMOURASKA CHRYSLER DODGE JEEP RAM
255 Av Patry, Saint-Pascal, QC, G0L 3Y0
(418) 492-3432
Emp Here 30   *Sales* 10,944,105
SIC 5511 New and used car dealers
Pr Jacques Jr Olivier
  Daniel Fox

D-U-N-S 24-349-5764   (SL)
CENTRE DE SANTE ET DE SERVICES SOCIAUX DE KAMOURASKA
CENTRE D'ANJOU
575 Av Martin, Saint-Pascal, QC, G0L 3Y0
(418) 856-7000
Emp Here 500   *Sales* 48,391,650
SIC 8062 General medical and surgical hospitals
Genl Mgr Marie-Claude Ouellet
Pr Pr Jean Desjardins
Dir Johanne Laplante
Dir Diane Bissonnette
Dir Annie Caron
Dir Claude Dufour
Dir Jean-Simon Belanger
Dir Ghislaine Milliard-Lavoie
Dir Mario Lebel
Dir Anne-Marie Lapointe

D-U-N-S 25-233-0741   (BR)
COMMISSION SCOLAIRE DE

KAMOURASKA RIVIERE-DU-LOUP
ECOLE MONSEIGNEUR BOUCHER
325 Av Chapleau, Saint-Pascal, QC, G0L 3Y0
(418) 856-7050
Emp Here 30
SIC 8211 Elementary and secondary schools

D-U-N-S 25-232-7770   (BR)
COMMISSION SCOLAIRE DE KAMOURASKA RIVIERE-DU-LOUP
ECOLE SECONDAIRE CHANOINE BEAUDET
525 Av De L'Eglise, Saint-Pascal, QC, G0L 3Y0
(418) 856-7030
Emp Here 75
SIC 8211 Elementary and secondary schools

D-U-N-S 24-599-0077   (BR)
EQUITRAC INC
345 Rang 2 E, Saint-Pascal, QC, G0L 3Y0
(418) 492-3068
Emp Here 20
SIC 5999 Miscellaneous retail stores, nec

D-U-N-S 24-380-1362   (BR)
GROUPE COOPERATIF DYNACO
CENTRE DE RENOVATION DYNACO BMR
(*Suby of* Groupe Cooperatif Dynaco)
230 Rue Rochette, Saint-Pascal, QC, G0L 3Y0
(418) 492-6343
Emp Here 24
SIC 5251 Hardware stores

D-U-N-S 24-144-5931   (SL)
MARCEL CHAREST ET FILS INC
997 230 Rte E, Saint-Pascal, QC, G0L 3Y0
(418) 492-5911
Emp Here 25   *Sales* 18,240,175
SIC 1542 Nonresidential construction, nec

Saint-Paul, QC J0K
Joliette County

D-U-N-S 25-233-2770   (BR)
COMMISSION SCOLAIRE DES SAMARES
ECOLE NOTRE DAME DU SACRE COEUR
33 Boul Brassard, Saint-Paul, QC, J0K 3E0
(450) 758-3728
Emp Here 28
SIC 8211 Elementary and secondary schools

D-U-N-S 24-325-1394   (SL)
VOLAILLES GILLES LAFORTUNE INC
330 Boul Brassard, Saint-Paul, QC, J0K 3E0
(450) 754-2955
Emp Here 50   *Sales* 3,939,878
SIC 4212 Local trucking, without storage

Saint-Paul-D'Abbotsford, QC J0E

D-U-N-S 25-240-5931   (BR)
COMMISSION SCOLAIRE DES HAUTES-RIVIERES
ECOLE MICHELINE BRODEUR
23 Rue Sainte-Anne, Saint-Paul-D'Abbotsford, QC, J0E 1A0
(450) 379-5674
Emp Here 32
SIC 8211 Elementary and secondary schools

D-U-N-S 20-187-6927   (HQ)
PNEUS ROBERT BERNARD LTEE, LES
765 Rue Principale E, Saint-Paul-D'Abbotsford, QC, J0E 1A0
(450) 379-5757
Emp Here 30   *Emp Total* 2
Sales 21,888,210
SIC 5014 Tires and tubes
Pr Pr Gerard Bernard
  Jocelyn Bernard

Saint-Paul-De-Montminy, QC G0R
Montmagny County

D-U-N-S 25-232-1617   (BR)
COMMISSION SCOLAIRE DE LA COTE-DU-SUD, LA
ECOLE SECONDAIRE DE ST PAUL
420 283 Rte S, Saint-Paul-De-Montminy, QC, G0R 3Y0
(418) 469-2117
Emp Here 50
SIC 8211 Elementary and secondary schools

D-U-N-S 20-100-3998   (BR)
COMMISSION SCOLAIRE DE LA COTE-DU-SUD, LA
ECOLE PRIMAIRE DE LA COLLINE
399 13e Rue, Saint-Paul-De-Montminy, QC, G0R 3Y0
(418) 469-2098
Emp Here 22
SIC 8211 Elementary and secondary schools

Saint-Paulin, QC J0K
Maskinonge County

D-U-N-S 24-841-8964   (SL)
CONCEPT ECO-PLEIN AIR LE BALUCHON INC
AUBERGE LE BALUCHON, GASTRONOMIE.SPA.PLEIN ET CULTURE
3550 Ch Des Trembles Rr 3, Saint-Paulin, QC, J0K 3G0
(819) 268-2695
Emp Here 200   *Sales* 8,339,840
SIC 5812 Eating places
  Louis Lessard
  Yves Savard
  Celine Lessard
Dir Gilles Lessard

D-U-N-S 24-477-6154   (SL)
CREATIONS VIE BOIS INC
VB2
1820 Rue Guimond, Saint-Paulin, QC, J0K 3G0
(819) 268-2206
Emp Here 50   *Sales* 2,918,428
SIC 2511 Wood household furniture

D-U-N-S 24-111-0386   (SL)
TELEPHONE MILOT INC
(*Suby of* Gestion Michel Biron Inc)
2640 Rue Lafleche, Saint-Paulin, QC, J0K 3G0
(819) 268-2050
Emp Here 20   *Sales* 1,896,978
SIC 4813 Telephone communication, except radio

Saint-Philippe-De-Neri, QC G0L
Kamouraska County

D-U-N-S 24-145-4651   (BR)
GROUPE COOPERATIF DYNACO
(*Suby of* Groupe Cooperatif Dynaco)
41 Rte 287 S, Saint-Philippe-De-Neri, QC, G0L 4A0
(418) 498-2366
Emp Here 30
SIC 8699 Membership organizations, nec

Saint-Pie, QC J0H
Bagot County

D-U-N-S 20-886-2979   (HQ)
GROUPE DUTAILIER INC

AVANTGLIDE
(*Suby of* 2694212 Canada Inc)
299 Rue Chaput, Saint-Pie, QC, J0H 1W0
(450) 772-2403
Emp Here 150   *Emp Total* 1
Sales 19,144,147
SIC 2512 Upholstered household furniture
  Fernand Fontaine

D-U-N-S 24-252-0443   (SL)
QUEFER INC
153 Rue Saint-Pierre, Saint-Pie, QC, J0H 1W0
(450) 772-6613
Emp Here 40   *Sales* 6,229,760
SIC 3469 Metal stampings, nec
Pr Pr Claude Petit

Saint-Pierre-Ile-D'Orleans, QC G0A

D-U-N-S 24-896-5824   (HQ)
2540-9392 QUEBEC INC
BUFFETS MAISON ENR, LES
(*Suby of* 2540-9392 Quebec Inc)
995 Rte Prevost Bureau 1, Saint-Pierre-Ile-D'Orleans, QC, G0A 4E0
(418) 828-2287
Emp Here 50   *Emp Total* 56
Sales 1,678,096
SIC 5812 Eating places

D-U-N-S 20-711-9863   (BR)
COMMISSION SCOLAIRE DES PREMIERES-SEIGNEURIES
COMMISSION SCOLAIRE DES PREMIERES-SEIGNEURIES
1300 Ch Royal, Saint-Pierre-Ile-D'Orleans, QC, G0A 4E0
(418) 821-8066
Emp Here 20
SIC 8211 Elementary and secondary schools

D-U-N-S 24-126-3040   (BR)
FEDERATION DES CAISSES DESJARDINS DU QUEBEC
FEDERATION DES CAISSES DESJARDINS DU QUEBEC
627 Ch Royal, Saint-Pierre-Ile-D'Orleans, QC, G0A 4E0
(418) 828-1501
Emp Here 27
SIC 6062 State credit unions

D-U-N-S 20-717-8000   (BR)
LE PATRO ROC -AMADOUR (1978) INC.
CAMP O CARREFOUR, LE
(*Suby of* Le Patro Roc -Amadour (1978) Inc.)
1503 Ch Royal, Saint-Pierre-Ile-D'Orleans, QC, G0A 4E0
(418) 828-1151
Emp Here 25
SIC 7032 Sporting and recreational camps

Saint-Pierre-Les-Becquets, QC G0X
Nicolet County

D-U-N-S 20-864-1881   (BR)
BUFFET NICO INC
(*Suby of* Buffet Nico Inc)
485 Rte Marie-Victorin Bureau 2, Saint-Pierre-Les-Becquets, QC, G0X 2Z0
(819) 376-8093
Emp Here 50
SIC 5812 Eating places

D-U-N-S 20-563-2193   (HQ)
BUFFET NICO INC
(*Suby of* Buffet Nico Inc)
14 Plage Poisson, Saint-Pierre-Les-Becquets, QC, G0X 2Z0
(819) 376-8093
Emp Here 35   *Emp Total* 60
Sales 1,824,018

SIC 5812 Eating places

D-U-N-S 20-027-6033   (BR)
COMMISSION SCOLAIRE DE LA RIVERAINE
ECOLE SECONDAIRE LES SEIGNEURIES
(*Suby* of Commission Scolaire de la Riveraine)
165 218 Rte, Saint-Pierre-Les-Becquets, QC, G0X 2Z0
(819) 263-2323
Emp Here 80
SIC 8211 Elementary and secondary schools

D-U-N-S 20-171-9536   (BR)
GROUPE ESTRIE-RICHELIEU, COMPAGNIE D'ASSURANCE, LE
414 Rte Marie-Victorin, Saint-Pierre-Becquets, QC, G0X 2Z0

Emp Here 50
SIC 6411 Insurance agents, brokers, and service

Saint-Polycarpe, QC J0P
Soulanges County

D-U-N-S 24-870-8737   (SL)
GESTION ROCH GAUTHIER INC
68 Rue Sainte-Catherine, Saint-Polycarpe, QC, J0P 1X0
(450) 265-3256
Emp Here 20   *Sales* 5,626,880
SIC 6712 Bank holding companies
Pr Pr Sylvain Gauthier
VP VP Pierre Gauthier
 Bernard Gauthier

Saint-Prime, QC G8J
Abitibi County

D-U-N-S 20-955-6757   (SL)
BOIS D'INGENIERIE ABITIBI-LP II INC
ALP II ST-PRIME
101 Rue Du Parc-Industriel, Saint-Prime, QC, G8J 1H3
(418) 251-4545
Emp Here 80   *Sales* 12,815,674
SIC 2491 Wood preserving
Pr Eric Paradis
Sec Neil Sherman
Dir Yves Laflamme
Dir Robert Fournier

D-U-N-S 24-000-7166   (BR)
BOIS D'INGENIERIE ABITIBI-LP INC
101 Rue Du Parc-Industriel, Saint-Prime, QC, G8J 1H3
(418) 251-3333
Emp Here 58
SIC 3443 Miscellaneous Metalwork

Saint-Prosper-De-Dorchester, QC G0M

D-U-N-S 25-515-1516   (BR)
CENTRE DE SANTE DES ETCHEMIN
PAVILLON DE L'HOSPITALITE DE ST PROSPER
(*Suby of* Centre De Sante Des Etchemin)
2770 20e Av, Saint-Prosper-De-Dorchester, QC, G0M 1Y0

Emp Here 40
SIC 8361 Residential care

D-U-N-S 25-232-7903   (BR)
COMMISSION SCOLAIRE DE LA BEAUCE-ETCHEMIN
ECOLE POLYVALENTE DES ABENAQUIS

2105 25e Av, Saint-Prosper-De-Dorchester, QC, G0M 1Y0
(418) 594-8231
Emp Here 90
SIC 8211 Elementary and secondary schools

D-U-N-S 25-835-8910   (BR)
FEDERATION DES CAISSES DESJARDINS DU QUEBEC
CAISSE POPULAIRE DESJARDINS DU PLATEAU D'APPALACHES
2880 25e Av, Saint-Prosper-De-Dorchester, QC, G0M 1Y0
(418) 594-8227
Emp Here 72
SIC 6062 State credit unions

D-U-N-S 25-741-0845   (SL)
SPECIALISTE DU BARDEAU DE CEDRE INC, LE
SBC
754 8e Rue, Saint-Prosper-De-Dorchester, QC, G0M 1Y0
(418) 594-6201
Emp Here 85   *Sales* 9,338,970
SIC 2429 Special product sawmills, nec
Pr Pr Rita Rancourt
 Marco Belanger
 Francis Belanger
Dir Michel Belanger

Saint-Raphael, QC G0R
Bellechasse County

D-U-N-S 25-233-1871   (BR)
COMMISSION SCOLAIRE DE LA COTE-DU-SUD, LA
COMMISSION SCOLAIRE DE BELLECHASSE
88 Rue Du Foyer, Saint-Raphael, QC, G0R 4C0
(418) 243-2999
Emp Here 20
SIC 8211 Elementary and secondary schools

Saint-Raymond, QC G3L
Portneuf County

D-U-N-S 24-324-3545   (BR)
CENTRE DE SANTE ET DE SERVICES SOCIAUX DE PORTNEUF
HOPITAL REGIONAL DE PORTNEUF
700 Rue Saint-Cyrille Bureau 850, Saint-Raymond, QC, G3L 1W1
(418) 337-4611
Emp Here 350
SIC 8062 General medical and surgical hospitals

D-U-N-S 25-233-0600   (BR)
COMMISSION SCOLAIRE DE PORTNEUF
COMMISSION SCOLAIRE DE PORTNEUF
(*Suby of* Commission Scolaire de Portneuf)
400 Boul Cloutier, Saint-Raymond, QC, G3L 3M8
(418) 337-6721
Emp Here 90
SIC 8211 Elementary and secondary schools

D-U-N-S 20-712-0119   (BR)
COMMISSION SCOLAIRE DE PORTNEUF
COMMISSION SCOLAIRE DE PORTNEUF
(*Suby of* Commission Scolaire de Portneuf)
150 Av De L'Hotel-De-Ville, Saint-Raymond, QC, G3L 3V9
(418) 337-7657
Emp Here 50
SIC 8211 Elementary and secondary schools

D-U-N-S 20-778-4844   (SL)
DION MOTO INC
SUZUKI

840 Cote Joyeuse, Saint-Raymond, QC, G3L 4B3
(418) 337-2776
Emp Here 35   *Sales* 9,344,640
SIC 5571 Motorcycle dealers
Pr Pr Mario Lirette

D-U-N-S 20-256-7434   (SL)
GARAGISTES INDEPENDANTS DE PORTNEUF INC
A G I AUTO ACCESSOIRES
131 Av Saint-Jacques, Saint-Raymond, QC, G3L 3Y4
(418) 337-2244
Emp Here 34   *Sales* 5,595,120
SIC 5013 Motor vehicle supplies and new parts
Pr Leo Leblanc
VP Michel Leblanc
Treas Luc Leblanc

D-U-N-S 24-147-4840   (SL)
INDUSTRIES LEGARE LTEE
(*Suby of* Groupe Legare Ltee)
488 Rue Saint-Pierre, Saint-Raymond, QC, G3L 1R5
(418) 337-2286
Emp Here 50   *Sales* 4,888,367
SIC 2499 Wood products, nec

D-U-N-S 20-703-2280   (BR)
PLACAGES ST-RAYMOND INC
71 Rue Delaney, Saint-Raymond, QC, G3L 2B3
(418) 337-4607
Emp Here 45
SIC 5031 Lumber, plywood, and millwork

D-U-N-S 24-345-5370   (BR)
SAINT-RAYMOND, VILLE DE
CENTRE DE SKI ST-RAYMOND
(*Suby of* Saint-Raymond, Ville de)
1226 Rang Notre-Dame, Saint-Raymond, QC, G3L 1N4
(418) 337-2866
Emp Here 31
SIC 7011 Hotels and motels

D-U-N-S 20-715-7806   (BR)
SAPUTO PRODUITS LAITIERS CANADA S.E.N.C.
(*Suby of* Saputo Produits Laitiers Canada S.E.N.C.)
71 Av Saint-Jacques, Saint-Raymond, QC, G3L 3X9
(418) 337-4287
Emp Here 80
SIC 2022 Cheese; natural and processed

Saint-Remi, QC J0L
Napierville County

D-U-N-S 25-201-6209   (SL)
BOISERIES B.G. INC
5 Rue Des Pionniers, Saint-Remi, QC, J0L 2L0
(450) 454-5755
Emp Here 50   *Sales* 4,085,799
SIC 2431 Millwork

D-U-N-S 25-857-1454   (BR)
GOUVERNEMENT DE LA PROVINCE DE QUEBEC
CHSLD TREFLE D'OR, LES CENTRE D'HEBERGEMENT DE ST REMI
110 Rue Du College, Saint-Remi, QC, J0L 2L0
(450) 454-4694
Emp Here 110
SIC 8322 Individual and family services

D-U-N-S 20-256-8572   (SL)
LECUYER & FILS LTEE
(*Suby of* 90477 Canada Ltee)
17 Rue Du Moulin, Saint-Remi, QC, J0L 2L0
(514) 861-5623
Emp Here 100   *Sales* 27,386,640

SIC 3272 Concrete products, nec
Pr Pr Maurice Lecuyer
VP VP Marcelle Lecuyer

D-U-N-S 20-961-7695   (HQ)
PAVAGES CHENAIL INC, LES
CHENAIL
104 Boul Saint-Remi, Saint-Remi, QC, J0L 2L0
(450) 454-5171
Emp Here 50   *Emp Total* 50
Sales 13,860,016
SIC 1611 Highway and street construction
Pr Emmanuel Chenail
VP Marie-Josee Chenail

D-U-N-S 25-169-6381   (BR)
PROVIGO DISTRIBUTION INC
INTERMARCHE SAINT REMI
91 Rue Lachapelle E, Saint-Remi, QC, J0L 2L0

Emp Here 35
SIC 5411 Grocery stores

D-U-N-S 24-346-7680   (BR)
THOMAS & BETTS FABRICATION INC
T & B COMMANDER
760 Rue Notre-Dame, Saint-Remi, QC, J0L 2L0
(450) 454-2452
Emp Here 20
SIC 3644 Noncurrent-carrying wiring devices

D-U-N-S 25-699-1464   (BR)
UNIPRIX INC
897 Rue Notre-Dame, Saint-Remi, QC, J0L 2L0
(450) 454-3981
Emp Here 20
SIC 5912 Drug stores and proprietary stores

D-U-N-S 20-794-5549   (BR)
VILLE DE SAINT-REMI
SAINT-REMI, VILLE DE
1104 Rue Notre-Dame, Saint-Remi, QC, J0L 2L0
(450) 454-5345
Emp Here 20
SIC 7521 Automobile parking

Saint-Remi-D'Amherst, QC J0T
Papineau County

D-U-N-S 25-232-8174   (BR)
COMMISSION SCOLAIRE DES LAURENTIDES
ECOLES SECTEUR NORD - LE CARREFOUR
(*Suby of* Commission Scolaire Des Laurentides)
259 Rue Amherst, Saint-Remi-D'Amherst, QC, J0T 2L0
(819) 429-4102
Emp Here 20
SIC 8211 Elementary and secondary schools

Saint-Roch-De-L'Achigan, QC J0K

D-U-N-S 24-370-8372   (SL)
9175-3681 QUEBEC INC
AMTECH
530 Rue J Oswald Forest Bureau 3, Saint-Roch-De-L'Achigan, QC, J0K 3H0
(450) 588-6909
Emp Here 26   *Sales* 2,638,521
SIC 2542 Partitions and fixtures, except wood

D-U-N-S 24-062-2626   (BR)
COMMISSION SCOLAIRE DES SAMARES
ECOLE NOTRE DAME
20 Rue Vezina, Saint-Roch-De-L'Achigan, QC,

J0K 3H0
(450) 588-7851
Emp Here 30
SIC 8211 Elementary and secondary schools

D-U-N-S 24-187-7138   (BR)
COMMISSION SCOLAIRE DES SAMARES
ECOLES SECONDAIRES ACHIGAN
60 Montee Remi-Henri, Saint-Roch-De-L'Achigan, QC, J0K 3H0
(450) 588-7410
Emp Here 130
SIC 8211 Elementary and secondary schools

D-U-N-S 24-330-9486   (BR)
MEUBLES JCPERREAULT INC
AMEUBLEMENTS J.C. PERREAULT, LES
5 Rue Industrielle, Saint-Roch-De-L'Achigan, QC, J0K 3H0
(450) 588-7211
Emp Here 60
SIC 5712 Furniture stores

D-U-N-S 25-485-2700   (SL)
SUPERMARCHE MALO INC
PROVIGO 8902
31 Montue Rumi-Henri, Saint-Roch-De-L'Achigan, QC, J0K 3H0
(450) 588-2811
Emp Here 33   *Sales* 5,376,850
SIC 5411 Grocery stores
Pr Michel Malo

Saint-Roch-De-Mekinac, QC G0X

D-U-N-S 25-337-2601   (BR)
COMMISSION SCOLAIRE DE L'ENERGIE
ECOLE DE LA VALLEE DE MEKINAC
1216 Rue Principale, Saint-Roch-De-Mekinac, QC, G0X 2E0
(418) 365-4789
Emp Here 20
SIC 8211 Elementary and secondary schools

Saint-Roch-Des-Aulnaies, QC G0R

D-U-N-S 24-388-8976   (BR)
CAISSE DESJARDINS DE L'ANSE DE LA POCATIERE
CENTRE DE SERVICES ST-ROCH-DES-AULNAIES
(*Suby of* Caisse Desjardins de l'Anse de la Pocatiere)
1009 Rte De La Seigneurie, Saint-Roch-Des-Aulnaies, QC, G0R 4E0
(418) 856-2340
Emp Here 25
SIC 6062 State credit unions

Saint-Romain, QC G0Y
Frontenac County

D-U-N-S 24-163-7565   (SL)
ROULOTTES R G INC, LES
200 Ch Du Parc-Industriel Rr 2, Saint-Romain, QC, G0Y 1L0
(418) 486-2626
Emp Here 30   *Sales* 18,650,400
SIC 2451 Mobile homes
Pr Pr Richard Labrecque
Mgr Ginette Lagace

Saint-Romuald, QC G6W
Levis County

D-U-N-S 20-430-6666   (HQ)
ALIMENTS MARTEL INC
ALI-PRET
670 Rue De L'Eglise, Saint-Romuald, QC, G6W 5M6
(418) 839-8841
Emp Here 200   *Emp Total* 130,913
Sales 72,435,300
SIC 2099 Food preparations, nec
Pr Raymond Martel
Sec Dianne Singer
Genl Mgr Rene Mclean
  Barry C Mclean
  Michael H Vels
  Rocco Cappuccitti
  Richard A Lan
  Gaetan Roy
Fin Mgr Steve Attridge

D-U-N-S 20-712-0226   (BR)
COMMISSION SCOLAIRE DES NAVIGA-TEURS
CENTRES D'EDUCATION DES ADULTES
1172 Boul De La Rive-Sud, Saint-Romuald, QC, G6W 5M6
(418) 839-6482
Emp Here 50
SIC 8211 Elementary and secondary schools

D-U-N-S 20-712-0234   (BR)
COMMISSION SCOLAIRE DES NAVIGA-TEURS
CENTRES DE FORMATION PROFESSION-NELLE GABRIEL ROUSSEAU
1155 Boul De La Rive-Sud, Saint-Romuald, QC, G6W 5M6
(418) 839-0508
Emp Here 60
SIC 8211 Elementary and secondary schools

D-U-N-S 25-627-9738   (SL)
QSL QUEBEC INC
MISTRAS METALTECH
765 Rue De L'Eglise Bureau 90, Saint-Romuald, QC, G6W 5M6
(418) 837-4664
Emp Here 150   *Sales* 14,959,500
SIC 8734 Testing laboratories
Dir Michale J Lange
Genl Mgr Stephan Verreault
Ch Bd Sotirios J. Vahaviolos
Sec Michael Keefe

D-U-N-S 20-513-3734   (BR)
VEOLIA ES CANADA SERVICES INDUS-TRIELS INC
857 Rue De L'Eglise, Saint-Romuald, QC, G6W 5M6
(418) 839-5500
Emp Here 40
SIC 7699 Repair services, nec

D-U-N-S 24-341-9715   (BR)
WSP CANADA INC
1300 Boul De La Rive-Sud Bureau 401, Saint-Romuald, QC, G6W 5M6
(418) 839-1733
Emp Here 60
SIC 8711 Engineering services

Saint-Rosaire, QC G0Z
Arthabaska County

D-U-N-S 24-012-1769   (BR)
COMMISSION SCOLAIRE DES BOIS-FRANCS
ECOLE DE LA CROISSE
11 Rue Saint-Pierre, Saint-Rosaire, QC, G0Z 1K0
(819) 758-1600
Emp Here 20
SIC 8211 Elementary and secondary schools

Saint-Rosaire, QC G6T
Arthabaska County

D-U-N-S 25-360-5190   (BR)
ENGLOBE CORP
ENGLOBE CORP
318 Ch De La Grande-Ligne, Saint-Rosaire, QC, G6T 0G1
(418) 653-4422
Emp Here 75
SIC 8748 Business consulting, nec

Saint-Sauveur, QC J0R
Maskinonge County

D-U-N-S 25-365-3703   (SL)
9061-3845 QUEBEC INC
RESTAURANT DELI & BAR MOE'S - ST-JOVITE
21a Av De La Gare, Saint-Sauveur, QC, J0R 1R0
(450) 227-8803
Emp Here 50   *Sales* 2,130,450
SIC 5812 Eating places

D-U-N-S 25-541-4856   (SL)
BOURASSA, S. (ST-SAUVEUR) LTEE
105b Av Guindon Rr 6, Saint-Sauveur, QC, J0R 1R6
(450) 227-4737
Emp Here 80   *Sales* 13,663,771
SIC 5411 Grocery stores
  Serge Bourassa
  Micheline Barbe
VP VP Sylvie Bourassa

D-U-N-S 25-232-8455   (BR)
COMMISSION SCOLAIRE DES LAUREN-TIDES
ECOLE DE LA VALLEE
(*Suby of* Commission Scolaire Des Lauren-tides)
167 Rue Principale, Saint-Sauveur, QC, J0R 1R6
(450) 227-2686
Emp Here 35
SIC 8211 Elementary and secondary schools

D-U-N-S 25-232-8414   (BR)
COMMISSION SCOLAIRE DES LAUREN-TIDES
ECOLE MARIE ROSE
(*Suby of* Commission Scolaire Des Lauren-tides)
35 Av Filion, Saint-Sauveur, QC, J0R 1R0
(450) 227-2660
Emp Here 40
SIC 8211 Elementary and secondary schools

D-U-N-S 25-365-7381   (BR)
GROUPE LES MANOIRS DU QUEBEC INC
MANOIR ST-SAUVEUR, LE
246 Ch Du Lac-Millette, Saint-Sauveur, QC, J0R 1R3
(800) 361-0505
Emp Here 200
SIC 7011 Hotels and motels

D-U-N-S 25-200-4007   (BR)
GROUPE LES MANOIRS DU QUEBEC INC
MANOIR ST-SAUVEUR
246 Ch Du Lac-Millette, Saint-Sauveur, QC, J0R 1R3
(450) 227-1811
Emp Here 200
SIC 7011 Hotels and motels

D-U-N-S 25-906-9110   (BR)
INDUSTRIELLE ALLIANCE, ASSURANCE ET SERVICES FINANCIERS INC
75 Av De La Gare, Saint-Sauveur, QC, J0R 1R6
Emp Here 25

SIC 6411 Insurance agents, brokers, and ser-vice

D-U-N-S 24-058-2218   (BR)
MCDONALD'S RESTAURANTS OF CANADA LIMITED
RESTAURANT MCDONALD'S
(*Suby of* McDonald's Corporation)
105 Av Guindon, Saint-Sauveur, QC, J0R 1R6
(450) 227-2331
Emp Here 50
SIC 5812 Eating places

D-U-N-S 20-003-0158   (BR)
PROVIGO DISTRIBUTION INC
LOBLA SAINT SAUVEUR
50 Av Saint-Denis, Saint-Sauveur, QC, J0R 1R4
(450) 227-2827
Emp Here 180
SIC 5411 Grocery stores

D-U-N-S 20-276-7112   (SL)
RESIDENCES DESJARDINS (ST-SAUVEUR) INC, LES
ETABLISSEMENT RESIDENCE DES-JARDIN, L
55 Av Hochar, Saint-Sauveur, QC, J0R 1R6
(450) 227-2241
Emp Here 60   *Sales* 2,188,821
SIC 8361 Residential care

D-U-N-S 25-127-6911   (SL)
RESSOURCES SANTE L M INC
21 Rue Forget, Saint-Sauveur, QC, J0R 1R0
(450) 227-6663
Emp Here 75   *Sales* 2,918,428
SIC 8322 Individual and family services

D-U-N-S 24-922-5798   (SL)
RESTAURATION MIMAR INC
ROTISSERIE ST-HUBERT
725 Ch Jean-Adam, Saint-Sauveur, QC, J0R 1R3
(450) 227-4664
Emp Here 75   *Sales* 2,261,782
SIC 5812 Eating places

D-U-N-S 25-683-6925   (BR)
TOMMY HILFIGER CANADA INC
170 Ch Du Lac-Millette, Saint-Sauveur, QC, J0R 1R6
(450) 227-4002
Emp Here 30
SIC 5651 Family clothing stores

Saint-Sebastien, QC J0J
Iberville County

D-U-N-S 20-585-0527   (BR)
CANADA POST CORPORATION
BUREAU DE POSTE DE SAINT SEBASTIEN
548 Rue Principale, Saint-Sebastien, QC, J0J 2C0
(450) 244-5593
Emp Here 27
SIC 4311 U.s. postal service

Saint-Sebastien-De-Frontenac, QC G0Y

D-U-N-S 20-257-5692   (SL)
A. LACROIX & FILS GRANIT LTEE
450 Rue Principale, Saint-Sebastien-De-Frontenac, QC, G0Y 1M0
(819) 652-2828
Emp Here 100
SIC 1411 Dimension stone

Saint-Simon-De-Bagot, QC J0H
Bagot County

▲ **Public Company**   ■ **Public Company Family Member**   **HQ** Headquarters   **BR** Branch   **SL** Single Location

D-U-N-S 20-204-1315   (HQ)
HOUDE, WILLIAM LTEE
ENGRAIS LAPRAIRIE
8 3e Rang O, Saint-Simon-De-Bagot, QC, J0H
1Y0
(450) 798-2002
Emp Here 20   *Emp Total* 100
Sales 10,287,459
SIC 2874 Phosphatic fertilizers
 Alain Fortier
Dir Marc Bouvry
Pr Jorge Boucas

Saint-Stanislas-De-Champlain, QC G0X

D-U-N-S 25-323-8562   (HQ)
ADF DIESEL MONTREAL INC
(*Suby of* Groupe Fournier Diesel Inc)
5 Ch De La Cote-Saint-Paul, Saint-Stanislas-
De-Champlain, QC, G0X 3E0
(418) 328-8713
Emp Here 60   *Emp Total* 1
Sales 49,809,433
SIC 5084 Industrial machinery and equipment
Pr Pr Andre Fournier

Saint-Stanislas-De-Kostka, QC J0S

D-U-N-S 20-033-5979   (BR)
**COMMISSION SCOLAIRE DE LA VALLEE-
DES-TISSERANDS, LA**
ECOLE NOTRE DAME DE L'ASSOMPTION
115 Rue Centrale, Saint-Stanislas-De-Kostka,
QC, J0S 1W0
(450) 377-8887
Emp Here 20
SIC 8211 Elementary and secondary schools

Saint-Sulpice, QC J5W
L'Assomption County

D-U-N-S 20-558-5206   (SL)
9217-5637 QUEBEC INC
DOMAINE DE L'ILE RONDE
734 Rue Notre-Dame, Saint-Sulpice, QC, J5W
3W7
(514) 771-7161
Emp Here 50   *Sales* 18,086,400
SIC 5921 Liquor stores
Owner Jocelyn Lafortune

Saint-Sylvere, QC G0Z

D-U-N-S 25-240-8828   (BR)
**COMMISSION SCOLAIRE DE LA
RIVERAINE**
ECOLE LE RUCHER
(*Suby of* Commission Scolaire de la
Riveraine)
260 Rte De L'Ecole, Saint-Sylvere, QC, G0Z
1H0
(819) 235-2992
Emp Here 20
SIC 8211 Elementary and secondary schools

Saint-Theophile, QC G0M

D-U-N-S 24-368-8517   (BR)
**CAISSE DESJARDINS DU SUD DE LA
BEAUCE**
CENTRE DE SERVICE DE SAINT-

THEOPHILE
(*Suby of* Caisse Desjardins du Sud de la
Beauce)
629 Rue Principale, Saint-Theophile, QC,
G0M 2A0
(418) 685-3078
Emp Here 60
SIC 6062 State credit unions

D-U-N-S 20-106-8066   (BR)
MAIBEC INC
MAIBEC DIV. SAINT THEOPHILE
340 Rte 173, Saint-Theophile, QC, G0M 2A0
(418) 597-3388
Emp Here 140
SIC 2429 Special product sawmills, nec

Saint-Thomas, QC J0K
Joliette County

D-U-N-S 20-058-2703   (SL)
BETON ADAM INC
CIMENT PERREAULT
300 Rang Brule, Saint-Thomas, QC, J0K 3L0
(450) 759-8434
Emp Here 45   *Sales* 5,917,160
SIC 3273 Ready-mixed concrete
Pr Pr Daniel Adam
VP VP Sebastien Landry
 Robert Gervais

D-U-N-S 24-527-7199   (BR)
BOULANGERIE GADOUA LTEE
BOULANGERIE ST THOMAS
561 Rue Principale, Saint-Thomas, QC, J0K
3L0

Emp Here 100
SIC 5461 Retail bakeries

D-U-N-S 20-297-9469   (BR)
SYNAGRI S.E.C.
PEDIGRAIN
80 Rue Des Erables, Saint-Thomas, QC, J0K
3L0
(450) 759-8070
Emp Here 250
SIC 2874 Phosphatic fertilizers

Saint-Thomas-Didyme, QC G0W

D-U-N-S 25-004-2496   (BR)
PF RESOLU CANADA INC
RESOLUTE FOREST PRODUCTS
300 Av Du Moulin, Saint-Thomas-Didyme,
QC, G0W 1P0
(418) 274-3340
Emp Here 111
SIC 2421 Sawmills and planing mills, general

Saint-Tite, QC G0X

D-U-N-S 20-357-2680   (HQ)
**CAISSE DESJARDINS DE MEKINAC-DES
CHENAUX**
CENTRE DE SERVICES CHAMPLAIN
(*Suby of* Caisse Desjardins De Mekinac-Des
Chenaux)
400 Rue Notre-Dame, Saint-Tite, QC, G0X
3H0
(418) 365-7591
Emp Here 24   *Emp Total* 50
Sales 7,441,991
SIC 6062 State credit unions
Pr Leo Trepanier
VP Line Veillette
Sec Jacqueline Bergeron
Dir Cynthia Chenevert

Dir Sylvain Dery
Dir Claire Desaulniers
Dir Leon Gagnon
Dir Claude Groleau

D-U-N-S 25-233-1004   (BR)
COMMISSION SCOLAIRE DE L'ENERGIE
ECOLE SECONDAIRE PAUL LE JEUNE
405 Boul Saint-Joseph Rr 1, Saint-Tite, QC,
G0X 3H0
(418) 365-5191
Emp Here 75
SIC 8211 Elementary and secondary schools

D-U-N-S 25-495-1551   (SL)
FINITION U.V. CRYSTAL INC
U.V. CRYSTAL
(*Suby of* Gestion Bayonne Inc)
115 153 Route, Saint-Tite, QC, G0X 3H0
(418) 365-7752
Emp Here 50   *Sales* 13,665,280
SIC 2491 Wood preserving
Pr Pr Pierre Sylvestre
 Claude Joly
 Rene Sylvestre

Saint-Ubalde, QC G0A
Portneuf County

D-U-N-S 25-199-6245   (SL)
BRAS DE FER GINGRAS INC, LES
367 Boul Chabot, Saint-Ubalde, QC, G0A 4L0
(418) 277-2690
Emp Here 60   *Sales* 12,250,277
SIC 3714 Motor vehicle parts and accessories
Pr Pr Claude Boivin

Saint-Urbain-De-Charlevoix, QC G0A
Charlevoix-Est County

D-U-N-S 20-178-5578   (SL)
**VIANDES BIOLOGIQUES DE CHARLEVOIX
INC, LES**
125 Rue Saint-Edouard, Saint-Urbain-De-
Charlevoix, QC, G0A 4K0
(418) 639-1111
Emp Here 32   *Sales* 6,767,208
SIC 5147 Meats and meat products
Pr Pr Damien Girard
 Natasha Mcnicoll

Saint-Urbain-Premier, QC J0S
Chateauguay County

D-U-N-S 24-769-3641   (SL)
SG CERESCO INC
MRTG LOGISTIQUE
164 Ch De La Grande-Ligne, Saint-Urbain-
Premier, QC, J0S 1Y0
(450) 427-3831
Emp Here 55   *Sales* 33,923,844
SIC 5153 Grain and field beans
 Thierry Gripon
 Mireille Raymond

Saint-Valere, QC G0P
Arthabaska County

D-U-N-S 25-240-1567   (BR)
**COMMISSION SCOLAIRE DES BOIS-
FRANCS**
ECOLE COEUR IMMACULE ST VALERE
(*Suby of* Commission Scolaire des Bois-
Francs)
1641 161 Rte, Saint-Valere, QC, G0P 1M0

(819) 353-2223
Emp Here 20
SIC 8211 Elementary and secondary schools

D-U-N-S 20-012-8036   (SL)
IDEAL CARGO INC
IDEAL TRAILER
2245 Rte 161, Saint-Valere, QC, G0P 1M0
(819) 353-3350
Emp Here 40   *Sales* 5,472,053
SIC 3715 Truck trailers
 Yves Bergeron
Dir Guillaume Bergeron
Dir Vincent Desilets

Saint-Vallier, QC G0R

D-U-N-S 24-369-9019   (BR)
**CAISSE DESJARDINS DES SEIGNEURIES
DE BELLECHASE**
CENTRE DE SERVICES SAINT-VALLIER
361 Rue Principale, Saint-Vallier, QC, G0R
4J0
(418) 887-3337
Emp Here 70
SIC 6062 State credit unions

Saint-Victor, QC G0M
Beauce County

D-U-N-S 25-233-8645   (BR)
**COMMISSION SCOLAIRE DE LA BEAUCE-
ETCHEMIN**
ECOLE LE TREMPLIN
124 Rue Des Ecoliers, Saint-Victor, QC, G0M
2B0
(418) 588-3948
Emp Here 20
SIC 8211 Elementary and secondary schools

Saint-Wenceslas, QC G0Z

D-U-N-S 25-324-7944   (SL)
HYCO CANADA LIMITED
1025 Rue Principale, Saint-Wenceslas, QC,
G0Z 1J0
(819) 224-4000
Emp Here 130   *Sales* 9,484,891
SIC 3593 Fluid power cylinders and actuators
Pr Denis Deshaies
Dir Carsten Storm

Saint-Zotique, QC J0P

D-U-N-S 24-369-1370   (BR)
**CAISSE DESJARDINS DE VAUDREUIL-
SOULANGES**
CENTRE DE SERVICE ST-ZOTIQUE
1004 Rue Principale, Saint-Zotique, QC, J0P
1Z0
(450) 763-5500
Emp Here 20
SIC 6062 State credit unions

D-U-N-S 25-240-4843   (BR)
**COMMISSION SCOLAIRE DES TROIS-
LACS**
*ECOLE DE LA RIVEREINE ET SAINT-
ZOTIQUE*
425 34e Av, Saint-Zotique, QC, J0P 1Z0
(450) 267-3290
Emp Here 30
SIC 8211 Elementary and secondary schools

D-U-N-S 20-792-4775   (BR)
RESTAURANTS LUC HARVEY INC, LES

▲ Public Company   ■ Public Company Family Member   **HQ** Headquarters   **BR** Branch   **SL** Single Location

MCDONALD'S
505 34e Av, Saint-Zotique, QC, J0P 1Z0
(450) 267-4242
Emp Here 20
SIC 5812 Eating places

Sainte-Adele, QC J8B
Terrebonne County

D-U-N-S 25-233-4990   (BR)
**COMMISSION SCOLAIRE DES LAUREN-
TIDES**
ECOLE ST JOSEPH
(*Suby of* Commission Scolaire Des Lauren-
tides)
491 Ch Pierre-Peladeau, Sainte-Adele, QC,
J8B 1Z3
(450) 240-6223
Emp Here 40
SIC 8211 Elementary and secondary schools

D-U-N-S 25-232-8448   (BR)
**COMMISSION SCOLAIRE DES LAUREN-
TIDES**
ECOLE CHANTE-AU-VENT
(*Suby of* Commission Scolaire Des Lauren-
tides)
1400 Rue Saint-Jean, Sainte-Adele, QC, J8B
1E6
(450) 240-6224
Emp Here 25
SIC 8211 Elementary and secondary schools

D-U-N-S 20-100-9524   (BR)
**COMMISSION SCOLAIRE DES LAUREN-
TIDES**
ECOLE HOTELIERE DES LAURENTIDES
(*Suby of* Commission Scolaire Des Lauren-
tides)
150 Rue Lesage, Sainte-Adele, QC, J8B 2R4
(450) 240-6227
Emp Here 20
SIC 8299 Schools and educational services,
nec

D-U-N-S 24-973-5028   (BR)
**COMMISSION SCOLAIRE DES LAUREN-
TIDES**
*ECOLE SECONDAIRE AUGUSTIN NORBET
MORIN*
(*Suby of* Commission Scolaire Des Lauren-
tides)
258 Boul De Sainte-Adele, Sainte-Adele, QC,
J8B 1A8
(450) 240-6220
Emp Here 120
SIC 8211 Elementary and secondary schools

D-U-N-S 24-432-6711   (BR)
COUCHE-TARD INC
955 Boul De Sainte-Adele, Sainte-Adele, QC,
J8B 2N4
(450) 229-4746
Emp Here 20
SIC 5411 Grocery stores

D-U-N-S 24-490-6426   (SL)
MARCHE AU CHALET (1978) INC
I G A
1300 Boul De Sainte-Adele, Sainte-Adele,
QC, J8B 2N5
(450) 229-4256
Emp Here 90   *Sales* 3,939,878
SIC 7011 Hotels and motels

D-U-N-S 25-408-4379   (SL)
ROTISSERIE STE-ADELE
ROTISSERIE ST-HUBERT
500 Boul De Sainte-Adele, Sainte-Adele, QC,
J8B 2N2
(450) 229-6655
Emp Here 60   *Sales* 1,824,018
SIC 5812 Eating places

D-U-N-S 25-307-7465   (BR)

SOCIETE DES ALCOOLS DU QUEBEC
SOCIETE DES ALCOOLS DU QUEBEC
423 Boul De Sainte-Adele, Sainte-Adele, QC,
J8B 2N1
(450) 229-7673
Emp Here 20
SIC 5921 Liquor stores

D-U-N-S 24-095-4334   (BR)
TRANSPORT SCOLAIRE SOGESCO INC
AUTOBUS LA DILIGENCE
4050 Boul De Sainte-Adele, Sainte-Adele,
QC, J8B 2N7
(450) 229-3114
Emp Here 65
SIC 4151 School buses

Sainte-Agathe-Des-Monts, QC J8C
Terrebonne County

D-U-N-S 24-601-5895   (HQ)
ALLIANCE FORD INC
(*Suby of* Alliance Ford Inc)
90 Boul Norbert-Morin, Sainte-Agathe-Des-
Monts, QC, J8C 3K8
(514) 875-1925
Emp Here 30   *Emp Total* 70
Sales 25,536,245
SIC 5511 New and used car dealers
Pr Pr Normand Mcgrail
Dir Jean-Paul Mcgrail
Dir Patrice Mcgrai

D-U-N-S 24-510-0065   (SL)
AU ROYAUME CHRYSLER DODGE JEEP
700 Rue Principale, Sainte-Agathe-Des-
Monts, QC, J8C 1L3
(819) 326-4524
Emp Here 30   *Sales* 15,072,000
SIC 5511 New and used car dealers
Pr Marcel Martin

D-U-N-S 20-572-0795   (BR)
BANK OF MONTREAL
*GROUPE FINANCIER BANQUE DE MON-
TREAL*
40 Boul Norbert-Morin Bureau 234, Sainte-
Agathe-Des-Monts, QC, J8C 2V6
(819) 326-1030
Emp Here 20
SIC 6021 National commercial banks

D-U-N-S 20-539-3981   (BR)
CANADA POST CORPORATION
*BUREAU DE POSTE SAINTE-AGATHE-DES-
MONTS*
36 Rue Principale E, Sainte-Agathe-Des-
Monts, QC, J8C 1J4
(819) 326-1096
Emp Here 20
SIC 4311 U.s. postal service

D-U-N-S 20-332-3381   (BR)
**CENTRE INTEGRE DE SANTE ET DE SER-
VICES SOCIAUX DES LAURENTIDES**
CENTRE JEUNESSE DES LAURENTIDES
125 Ch Du Tour-Du-Lac, Sainte-Agathe-Des-
Monts, QC, J8C 1B4
(819) 326-6221
Emp Here 150
SIC 8361 Residential care

D-U-N-S 24-096-9118   (SL)
**CENTRE DE SANTE ET DE SERVICES SO-
CIAUX DES SOMMETS**
PAVILLON PHILIPPE LAPOINTE
234 Rue Saint-Vincent, Sainte-Agathe-Des-
Monts, QC, J8C 2B8
(819) 324-4055
Emp Here 500   *Sales* 16,134,800
SIC 8051 Skilled nursing care facilities
Genl Mgr Yves Lachapelle

D-U-N-S 24-368-6263   (BR)
COMMISSION SCOLAIRE DES LAUREN-

TIDES
*CENTRE DE FORMATION PROFESSION-
NELLE DES SOMMETS*
(*Suby of* Commission Scolaire Des Lauren-
tides)
36 Rue Brissette, Sainte-Agathe-Des-Monts,
QC, J8C 1T4
(819) 326-8911
Emp Here 40
SIC 8211 Elementary and secondary schools

D-U-N-S 25-232-8406   (BR)
**COMMISSION SCOLAIRE DES LAUREN-
TIDES**
ECOLE NOTRE-DAME-DE-LA-SAGESSE
(*Suby of* Commission Scolaire Des Lauren-
tides)
37 Rue Larocque E, Sainte-Agathe-Des-
Monts, QC, J8C 1H8
(819) 326-2812
Emp Here 30
SIC 8211 Elementary and secondary schools

D-U-N-S 25-232-8364   (BR)
**COMMISSION SCOLAIRE DES LAUREN-
TIDES**
ECOLE FLEUR-DES-NEIGES
(*Suby of* Commission Scolaire Des Lauren-
tides)
99 Rue Sainte-Agathe, Sainte-Agathe-Des-
Monts, QC, J8C 2J9
(819) 326-3414
Emp Here 60
SIC 8211 Elementary and secondary schools

D-U-N-S 25-232-8323   (BR)
**COMMISSION SCOLAIRE DES LAUREN-
TIDES**
*ECOLE SECTEUR CENTRE LIONEL
GROULX*
(*Suby of* Commission Scolaire Des Lauren-
tides)
510 Rue Groulx, Sainte-Agathe-Des-Monts,
QC, J8C 1N6
(819) 326-2634
Emp Here 20
SIC 8211 Elementary and secondary schools

D-U-N-S 20-712-2255   (BR)
**COMMISSION SCOLAIRE DES LAUREN-
TIDES**
CENTRE DES CIMES
(*Suby of* Commission Scolaire Des Lauren-
tides)
2 Rue Saint-Joseph, Sainte-Agathe-Des-
Monts, QC, J8C 1M4
(819) 326-6663
Emp Here 50
SIC 8211 Elementary and secondary schools

D-U-N-S 20-712-2222   (BR)
**COMMISSION SCOLAIRE DES LAUREN-
TIDES**
POLYVALENTE DES MONTS
(*Suby of* Commission Scolaire Des Lauren-
tides)
101 Rue Legare, Sainte-Agathe-Des-Monts,
QC, J8C 2T6
(819) 326-3522
Emp Here 50
SIC 8211 Elementary and secondary schools

D-U-N-S 24-747-5437   (HQ)
**COMMISSION SCOLAIRE DES LAUREN-
TIDES**
(*Suby of* Commission Scolaire Des Lauren-
tides)
13 Rue Saint-Antoine, Sainte-Agathe-Des-
Monts, QC, J8C 2C3
(819) 324-8670
Emp Here 4   *Emp Total* 1,100
Sales 98,847,120
SIC 8211 Elementary and secondary schools
Genl Mgr Andre Bouchard

D-U-N-S 20-961-6960   (HQ)
FENETRES MQ INC

MQ FENETRES
(*Suby of* 126285 Canada Ltee)
50 Rue Brissette, Sainte-Agathe-Des-Monts,
QC, J8C 2Z8
(819) 326-0302
Emp Here 40   *Emp Total* 20
Sales 9,009,010
SIC 3089 Plastics products, nec
Pr Pr Gilles Morin
Pierre Morin

D-U-N-S 24-126-2547   (BR)
GESTION LYRAS INC
(*Suby of* Gestion Lyras Inc)
8 Rue Sainte-Agathe, Sainte-Agathe-Des-
Monts, QC, J8C 2J4
(819) 326-3030
Emp Here 30
SIC 6351 Surety insurance

D-U-N-S 20-246-1075   (SL)
J.L. BRISSETTE LTEE
24 Rue Brissette, Sainte-Agathe-Des-Monts,
QC, J8C 1T4
(819) 326-3263
Emp Here 70   *Sales* 10,068,577
SIC 5149 Groceries and related products, nec
Sylvain Labelle

D-U-N-S 25-734-0398   (HQ)
LE GROUPE AMYOT, GELINAS INC
(*Suby of* Le Groupe Amyot, Gelinas Inc)
124 Rue Saint-Vincent, Sainte-Agathe-Des-
Monts, QC, J8C 2B1
(819) 326-3400
Emp Here 28   *Emp Total* 50
Sales 7,507,300
SIC 8742 Management consulting services
Pr Pr Michel Amyot
Christan Gelinas
Patrice Forget

D-U-N-S 24-440-5150   (BR)
RESTAURANT SYLVAIN VINCENT INC, LES
MC DONALDS
690 Rue Principale, Sainte-Agathe-Des-
Monts, QC, J8C 1L3
(819) 326-2053
Emp Here 35
SIC 5812 Eating places

D-U-N-S 25-246-0993   (BR)
SIR WILFRID LAURIER SCHOOL BOARD
STE-AGATHE ACADEMY
(*Suby of* Sir Wilfrid Laurier School Board)
26 Rue Napoleon, Sainte-Agathe-Des-Monts,
QC, J8C 1Z3
(819) 326-2563
Emp Here 40
SIC 8211 Elementary and secondary schools

D-U-N-S 24-319-5141   (BR)
WAL-MART CANADA CORP
WALMART
400 Rue Laverdure, Sainte-Agathe-Des-
Monts, QC, J8C 0A2
(819) 326-9559
Emp Here 184
SIC 5311 Department stores

Sainte-Angele-De-Premont, QC J0K
Maskinonge County

D-U-N-S 24-370-0080   (BR)
**CAISSE DESJARDINS DE L'OUEST DE LA
MAURICIE**
*CENTRE DE SERVICES SAINTE-ANGELE-
DE-PREMONT*
(*Suby of* Caisse Desjardins de l'Ouest de la
Mauricie)
2310 Rue Paul-Lemay, Sainte-Angele-De-
Premont, QC, J0K 1R0
(819) 268-2138
Emp Here 50

▲ Public Company   ■ Public Company Family Member   **HQ** Headquarters   **BR** Branch   **SL** Single Location

SIC 6062 State credit unions

Sainte-Anne-De-Bellevue, QC H9X
Hochelaga County

D-U-N-S 20-271-1255   (SL)
COLLEGE D'ENSEIGNEMENT GENERAL ET PROFESSIONNEL JOHN ABBOTT
21275 Rue Lakeshore, Sainte-Anne-De-Bellevue, QC, H9X 3L9
(514) 457-6610
Emp Here 800   *Sales* 107,425,506
SIC 8221 Colleges and universities
Genl Mgr John Louis Halpin

D-U-N-S 24-536-7487   (HQ)
CORPORATION DE VALVES TRUELINE, LA
20675 Bcul Industriel, Sainte-Anne-De-Bellevue, CC, H9X 4B2
(514) 457-5777
Emp Here 44   *Emp Total* 48
Sales 8,755,284
SIC 5085 Industrial supplies
Pr Pr Jean-Paul Dimarzio

D-U-N-S 20-016-2787   (BR)
INSTITUT NATIONALE DE SANTE PUBLIQUE DU QUEBEC
LABORATOIRE DE SANTE PUBLIQUE DU QUEBEC
20045 Ch Sainte-Marie, Sainte-Anne-De-Bellevue, QC, H9X 3R5
(514) 457-2070
Emp Here 125
SIC 8731 Commercial physical research

D-U-N-S 25-240-1526   (BR)
LESTER B. PEARSON SCHOOL BOARD
MACDONALD HIGH SCHOOL
17 Rue Maple, Sainte-Anne-De-Bellevue, QC, H9X 2E5
(514) 457-3770
Emp Here 75
SIC 8211 Elementary and secondary schools

D-U-N-S 20-266-8034   (BR)
MACDONALD, DETTWILER AND ASSOCIATES CORPORATION
MDA
21025 Aut Transcanadienne, Sainte-Anne-De-Bellevue, QC, H9X 3R2
(514) 457-2150
Emp Here 25
SIC 3663 Radio and t.v. communications equipment

D-U-N-S 20-549-2353   (HQ)
SCN INDUSTRIEL INC
20701 Ch Sainte-Marie, Sainte-Anne-De-Bellevue, QC, H9X 5X5
(514) 457-1709
Emp Here 30   *Emp Total* 44
Sales 8,025,677
SIC 5084 Industrial machinery and equipment
Pr Shirley Reed
VP VP David Reed
Sec Glenn Watt

D-U-N-S 24-226-2470   (BR)
SODEXO CANADA LTD
21275 Rue Lakeshore Bureau 2000, Sainte-Anne-De-Bellevue, QC, H9X 3L9
(514) 457-6610
Emp Here 30
SIC 5812 Eating places

D-U-N-S 24-366-3379   (BR)
THYSSENKRUPP MATERIALS CA, LTD
TMX AEROSPACE
21025 Rue Daoust, Sainte-Anne-De-Bellevue, QC, H9X 0A3
(514) 782-9500
Emp Here 50
SIC 5051 Metals service centers and offices

D-U-N-S 25-078-3669   (SL)
VALACTA INC
VALACTA, CENTRE D'EXPERTISE EN PRODUCTION LAITERE DU QUEBEC
(*Suby of* Producteurs de Lait du Quebec, Les)
555 Boul Des Anciens-Combattants, Sainte-Anne-De-Bellevue, QC, H9X 3R4
(514) 459-3030
Emp Here 300   *Sales* 21,108,170
SIC 8731 Commercial physical research
Pr Pr Marcel Groleau

D-U-N-S 20-270-5620   (SL)
VALACTA, SOCIETE EN COMMANDITE
555 Boul Des Anciens-Combattants, Sainte-Anne-De-Bellevue, QC, H9X 3R4
(514) 459-3030
Emp Here 310   *Sales* 59,551,150
SIC 8742 Management consulting services
Genl Mgr Daniel Lefebere

Sainte-Anne-De-La-Perade, QC G0X
Champlain County

D-U-N-S 25-199-7839   (BR)
CENTRE DE SANTE ET DE SERVICES SOCIAUX DE LA VALLEE-DE-LA-BATISCAN
FOYER LA PERADE
60 Rue De La Fabrique Bureau 217, Sainte-Anne-De-La-Perade, QC, G0X 2J0
(418) 325-2313
Emp Here 80
SIC 8051 Skilled nursing care facilities

Sainte-Anne-De-Sorel, QC J3P
Richelieu County

D-U-N-S 25-234-2738   (BR)
COMMISSION SCOLAIRE DE SOREL-TRACY
ECOLE SAINTE-ANNE-LES-ILES
(*Suby of* Commission Scolaire de Sorel-Tracy)
581 Ch Du Chenal-Du-Moine, Sainte-Anne-De-Sorel, QC, J3P 1V8
(450) 746-4575
Emp Here 35
SIC 8211 Elementary and secondary schools

Sainte-Anne-Des-Monts, QC G4V
Gaspe-Est County

D-U-N-S 20-610-8461   (HQ)
CAISSE POPULAIRE DESJARDINS DE LA HAUTE-GASPESIE
CENTRE DE SERVICE DE TOURELLE
(*Suby of* Caisse Populaire Desjardins de la Haute-Gaspesie)
10 1re Av E, Sainte-Anne-Des-Monts, QC, G4V 1A3
(418) 763-2214
Emp Here 20   *Emp Total* 30
Sales 5,884,100
SIC 6062 State credit unions
Genl Mgr Real Henley
Pr Jean-Claude Levesque
VP VP Suzanne Cote
Sec Diane Lever
Dir Rene Levesque
Dir Jacques Soucy
Dir Daniel Thibault
Dir Pierre-Yves Gosselin

D-U-N-S 24-791-2686   (HQ)
CENTRE READAPTATION DE GASPESIE
(*Suby of* Centre Readaptation De Gaspesie)
230 Rte Du Parc, Sainte-Anne-Des-Monts, QC, G4V 2C4

(418) 763-3325
Emp Here 40   *Emp Total* 260
Sales 12,760,800
SIC 8361 Residential care
Genl Mgr Jacques Tremblay
  Pierre Roger

D-U-N-S 24-456-1861   (BR)
CENTRE DE SANTE ET DE SERVICES SOCIAUX DE LA HAUTE-GASPESIE
INFO-SANTE CLSC
(*Suby of* Centre de Sante et de Services Sociaux de la Haute-Gaspesie)
50 Rue Du Belvedere, Sainte-Anne-Des-Monts, QC, G4V 1X4
(418) 797-2744
Emp Here 500
SIC 8621 Professional organizations

D-U-N-S 20-711-8527   (BR)
COMMISSION SCOLAIRE DES CHIC-CHOCS
CENTRE D'EDUCATION DES ADULTES ET DE FORMATION PROFESSSIONNELLE
27 Rte Du Parc, Sainte-Anne-Des-Monts, QC, G4V 2B9
(418) 763-5323
Emp Here 50
SIC 8211 Elementary and secondary schools

D-U-N-S 25-232-1336   (BR)
COMMISSION SCOLAIRE DES CHIC-CHOCS
ECOLE DE L'ANSE
398 1re Av O Bureau 685, Sainte-Anne-Des-Monts, QC, G4V 1G9
(418) 763-2733
Emp Here 25
SIC 8211 Elementary and secondary schools

D-U-N-S 20-711-8550   (BR)
COMMISSION SCOLAIRE DES MONTS-ET-MAREES
ECOLE GABRIEL LE COURTOIS
170 Boul Sainte-Anne O, Sainte-Anne-Des-Monts, QC, G4V 1R8
(418) 763-3191
Emp Here 50
SIC 8211 Elementary and secondary schools

D-U-N-S 24-308-0251   (SL)
ENTRE-TIENS DE LA HAUTE-GASPESIE CORPORATION D'AIDE A DOMICILE
378 Boul Sainte-Anne O, Sainte-Anne-Des-Monts, QC, G4V 1S8
(418) 763-7163
Emp Here 95   *Sales* 2,772,507
SIC 7349 Building maintenance services, nec

D-U-N-S 25-309-1433   (BR)
SOBEYS QUEBEC INC
MARCHE IGA
6 Boul Sainte-Anne O, Sainte-Anne-Des-Monts, QC, G4V 1P3

Emp Here 60
SIC 5411 Grocery stores

D-U-N-S 24-980-2377   (BR)
SUPERMARCHES GP INC, LES
(*Suby of* Supermarches GP Inc, Les)
2 Boul Sainte-Anne E, Sainte-Anne-Des-Monts, QC, G4V 1M5
(418) 763-2026
Emp Here 49
SIC 5411 Grocery stores

Sainte-Anne-Des-Plaines, QC J0N
Terrebonne County

D-U-N-S 24-419-7872   (BR)
2950-4602 QUEBEC INC
RONA
2 Boul Sainte-Anne, Sainte-Anne-Des-Plaines, QC, J0N 1H0

(450) 478-1701
Emp Here 30
SIC 5251 Hardware stores

D-U-N-S 20-939-6154   (BR)
CAISSE POPULAIRE DESJARDINS DE L'ENVOLEE
SAINTE-ANNE-DES-PLAINES SERVICE CENTRE
148 Boul Sainte-Anne, Sainte-Anne-Des-Plaines, QC, J0N 1H0
(450) 430-4603
Emp Here 27
SIC 6062 State credit unions

D-U-N-S 25-976-1435   (BR)
COMMISSION SCOLAIRE DE LA SEIGNEURIE-DES-MILLE-ILES
COMMISSION SCOLAIRE DE LA SEIGNEURIE-DES-MILLE-ILES
(*Suby of* Commission Scolaire de la Seigneurie-Des-Mille-Iles)
540 Rue Des Colibris, Sainte-Anne-Des-Plaines, QC, J0N 1H0
(450) 434-8408
Emp Here 30
SIC 8211 Elementary and secondary schools

D-U-N-S 25-976-0379   (BR)
COMMISSION SCOLAIRE DE LA SEIGNEURIE-DES-MILLE-ILES
COMMISSION SCOLAIRE DE LA SEIGNEURIE-DES-MILLE-ILES
(*Suby of* Commission Scolaire de la Seigneurie-Des-Mille-Iles)
140 Rue Des Saisons, Sainte-Anne-Des-Plaines, QC, J0N 1H0
(450) 434-8570
Emp Here 65
SIC 8211 Elementary and secondary schools

D-U-N-S 25-233-2929   (BR)
COMMISSION SCOLAIRE DE LA SEIGNEURIE-DES-MILLE-ILES
COMMISSION SCOLAIRE DE LA SEIGNEURIE-DES-MILLE-ILES
(*Suby of* Commission Scolaire de la Seigneurie-Des-Mille-Iles)
1 Rue Chaumont, Sainte-Anne-Des-Plaines, QC, J0N 1H0
(450) 434-8458
Emp Here 30
SIC 8211 Elementary and secondary schools

D-U-N-S 25-369-2495   (BR)
PROVIGO DISTRIBUTION INC
PROVIGO
480 Boul Sainte-Anne, Sainte-Anne-Des-Plaines, QC, J0N 1H0
(450) 478-1864
Emp Here 100
SIC 5141 Groceries, general line

Sainte-Anne-Du-Lac, QC J0W

D-U-N-S 20-643-9338   (BR)
COMMISSION SCOLAIRE PIERRE-NEVEU, LA
ECOLE DES RIVIERES ST ANNE DU LAC
13 Rue Notre-Dame, Sainte-Anne-Du-Lac, QC, J0W 1V0
(819) 586-2411
Emp Here 30
SIC 8211 Elementary and secondary schools

Sainte-Aurelie, QC G0M
Dorchester County

D-U-N-S 20-002-7642   (BR)
PRODUITS FORESTIERS D. G. LTEE
(*Suby of* Groupe Gesco-Star Ltee)
313 Rang Saint-Joseph, Sainte-Aurelie, QC,

G0M 1M0
(418) 593-3516
Emp Here 160
SIC 2431 Millwork

Sainte-Brigide-D'Iberville, QC J0J
Iberville County

D-U-N-S 25-540-7702   (SL)
GASTRONOME ANIMAL INC, LE
NATURALIMENT
300 Rang Des Ecossais, Sainte-Brigide-D'Iberville, QC, J0J 1X0
(450) 469-0921
Emp Here 26   *Sales* 5,399,092
SIC 5191 Farm supplies
Pr Pierre Gadbois
VP Gary Leis
Sec Paul-Eric Boulanger

Sainte-Brigitte-De-Laval, QC G0A

D-U-N-S 25-232-7234   (BR)
COMMISSION   SCOLAIRE   DES PREMIERES-SEIGNEURIES
COMMISSION   SCOLAIRE   DES PREMIERES-SEIGNEURIES
(*Suby of* Commission Scolaire Des Premieres-Seigneuries)
3 Rue Du Couvent, Sainte-Brigitte-De-Laval, QC, G0A 3K0
(418) 821-8044
Emp Here 30
SIC 8211 Elementary and secondary schools

Sainte-Catherine, QC J5C
Portneuf County

D-U-N-S 20-548-5951   (SL)
9070-9734 QUEBEC INC
BURGER KING
1580 Boul Des Ecluses, Sainte-Catherine, QC, J5C 2B4
(450) 638-9018
Emp Here 110   *Sales* 3,283,232
SIC 5812 Eating places

D-U-N-S 20-277-6076   (SL)
CENTRE   D'HEBERGEMENT   ET   DE SOINS DE LONGUE DUREE DE SAINTE-CATHERINE S.E.C.
3065 Boul Marie-Victorin, Sainte-Catherine, QC, J5C 1Z3
(450) 290-7646
Emp Here 50   *Sales* 4,012,839
SIC 8069 Specialty hospitals, except psychiatric

D-U-N-S 20-918-7108   (BR)
CERTAINTEED GYPSUM CANADA, INC
700 1re Av, Sainte-Catherine, QC, J5C 1C5
(450) 632-5440
Emp Here 100
SIC 3275 Gypsum products

D-U-N-S 25-221-2352   (BR)
CLEAN HARBORS CANADA, INC
CLEAN HARBORS ENVIRONMENTAL SERVICES QUEBEC
6785 132 Rte, Sainte-Catherine, QC, J5C 1B6
(450) 632-6640
Emp Here 60
SIC 4212 Local trucking, without storage

D-U-N-S 20-252-3767   (BR)
DARLING INTERNATIONAL CANADA INC
ROTHSAY
(*Suby of* Darling Ingredients Inc.)

605 1re Av, Sainte-Catherine, QC, J5C 1C5
(450) 632-3250
Emp Here 100
SIC 4953 Refuse systems

D-U-N-S 24-049-3259   (BR)
MAPLE LEAF FOODS INC
ROTHSAY
605 1re Av, Sainte-Catherine, QC, J5C 1C5
(800) 263-0302
Emp Here 50
SIC 4953 Refuse systems

D-U-N-S 20-761-8919   (SL)
MORAND FORD LINCOLN LTEE
4105 132 Rte, Sainte-Catherine, QC, J5C 1V9
(450) 632-1340
Emp Here 39   *Sales* 19,782,750
SIC 5511 New and used car dealers
 Henry Wieczorek

D-U-N-S 20-583-9736   (BR)
TREALSHIP SERVICES INC
(*Suby of* Trealmont Transport Inc)
1980 Rue Laurier, Sainte-Catherine, QC, J5C 1B8

Emp Here 20
SIC 7623 Refrigeration service and repair

Sainte-Cecile-De-Masham, QC J0X
Gatineau County

D-U-N-S 20-712-5282   (BR)
FONDATION DE LA COMMISSION SCOLAIRE DES PORTAGES-DE-L'OUTAOUAIS
FONDATION DE LA COMMISSION SCOLAIRE DES PORTAGES-D
32 Ch Passe-Partout, Sainte-Cecile-De-Masham, QC, J0X 2W0
(819) 503-8810
Emp Here 30
SIC 8211 Elementary and secondary schools

D-U-N-S 24-206-1369   (BR)
FONDATION DE LA COMMISSION SCOLAIRE DES PORTAGES-DE-L'OUTAOUAIS
FONDATION DE LA COMMISSION SCOLAIRE DES PORTAGES-D
3 Rte Principale E, Sainte-Cecile-De-Masham, QC, J0X 2W0
(819) 503-8809
Emp Here 30
SIC 8211 Elementary and secondary schools

D-U-N-S 20-023-2184   (BR)
FONDATION DE LA COMMISSION SCOLAIRE DES PORTAGES-DE-L'OUTAOUAIS
FONDATION DE LA COMMISSION SCOLAIRE DES PORTAGES-D
3 Rte Principale E, Sainte-Cecile-De-Masham, QC, J0X 2W0

Emp Here 32
SIC 8211 Elementary and secondary schools

Sainte-Claire, QC G0R
Dorchester County

D-U-N-S 24-773-0133   (BR)
BALDOR ELECTRIC CANADA INC
DIVISION MASKA
180 Boul Gagnon, Sainte-Claire, QC, G0R 2V0
(418) 883-3322
Emp Here 150
SIC 3429 Hardware, nec

D-U-N-S 20-029-2147   (BR)
CSSS DU GRAND LITTORAL
CENTRE D'HEBERGEMENT DE SAINTE-CLAIRE

80 Boul Begin, Sainte-Claire, QC, G0R 2V0
(418) 883-3357
Emp Here 70
SIC 8361 Residential care

D-U-N-S 20-698-1065   (BR)
COMMISSION SCOLAIRE DE LA COTE-DU-SUD, LA
COMMISSION SCOLAIRE DE LA COTE-DU-SUD, LA
60 Rue De La Fabrique, Sainte-Claire, QC, G0R 2V0
(418) 883-3750
Emp Here 30
SIC 8211 Elementary and secondary schools

D-U-N-S 24-849-8839   (SL)
GROUPE C.F.R. INC
195 1e Rue O, Sainte-Claire, QC, G0R 2V0
(418) 883-2955
Emp Here 35   *Sales* 6,797,150
SIC 3541 Machine tools, Metal cutting type
Pr Pr Mario Langlois
 Etienne Audet
VP VP David Caron

D-U-N-S 24-351-2451   (HQ)
GROUPE VOLVO CANADA INC
PREVOST
35 Boul Gagnon, Sainte-Claire, QC, G0R 2V0
(418) 883-3391
Emp Here 950   *Emp Total* 200
Sales 1,395,373,388
SIC 5012 Automobiles and other motor vehicles
Pr Ralph Acs
VP Emmanuelle Toussaint
Sec Krzysztof Trembecki
Dir W. Macdonal Macintosh

D-U-N-S 20-266-2003   (SL)
IMBC BLOWMOLDING 2014 INC
21 Boul Begin, Sainte-Claire, QC, G0R 2V0
(418) 883-3333
Emp Here 26   *Sales* 2,626,585
SIC 3089 Plastics products, nec

D-U-N-S 20-314-3003   (HQ)
PREVOST CAR INC
35 Boul Gagnon, Sainte-Claire, QC, G0R 2V0
(418) 883-3391
Emp Here 25   *Emp Total* 200
Sales 7,189,883
SIC 7519 Utility trailer rental
Pr Gaetan Bolduc
Sec Rene Begin
Dir Don Macinthosh
Dir Tore Backstorm

D-U-N-S 20-356-7730   (BR)
PRODUITS VERSAPROFILES INC, LES
(*Suby of* 9244-6699 Quebec Inc)
185 1re Rue O, Sainte-Claire, QC, G0R 2V0
(418) 883-2036
Emp Here 35
SIC 3089 Plastics products, nec

Sainte-Clotilde-De-Beauce, QC G0N
Beauce County

D-U-N-S 25-365-2994   (BR)
COMMISSION   SCOLAIRE   DES   AP-PALACHES
ECOLE DU SAINT-NOM-DE-MARIE
(*Suby of* Commission Scolaire des Appalaches)
307 Rue Du Couvent, Sainte-Clotilde-De-Beauce, QC, G0N 1C0
(418) 427-2018
Emp Here 30
SIC 8211 Elementary and secondary schools

D-U-N-S 24-170-9695   (BR)
RENE MATERIAUX COMPOSITES LTEE
12 Av Du Parc Rr 1, Sainte-Clotilde-De-

Beauce, QC, G0N 1C0
(418) 427-4288
Emp Here 50
SIC 3714 Motor vehicle parts and accessories

Sainte-Croix, QC G0S
Lotbiniere County

D-U-N-S 24-908-3841   (BR)
CANADA PIPE COMPANY ULC
BIBBY STE CROIX
6200 Rue Principale, Sainte-Croix, QC, G0S 2H0
(418) 926-3262
Emp Here 300
SIC 3312 Blast furnaces and steel mills

D-U-N-S 25-688-8934   (BR)
COMMISSION SCOLAIRE DES NAVIGA-TEURS
ECOLE LA MENNAIS
105 Rue Laflamme, Sainte-Croix, QC, G0S 2H0
(418) 796-0502
Emp Here 20
SIC 8211 Elementary and secondary schools

D-U-N-S 24-346-3051   (BR)
COMMISSION SCOLAIRE DES NAVIGA-TEURS
ECOLE SECONDAIRE PANTHILE LE MAY
6380 Rue Garneau, Sainte-Croix, QC, G0S 2H0
(418) 796-0503
Emp Here 100
SIC 8211 Elementary and secondary schools

D-U-N-S 25-957-8573   (BR)
FEDERATION DES CAISSES DESJARDINS DU QUEBEC
6276 Rue Principale, Sainte-Croix, QC, G0S 2H0
(418) 926-3240
Emp Here 25
SIC 6062 State credit unions

Sainte-Dorothee, QC H7C
Ile-Jesus County

D-U-N-S 24-431-2062   (SL)
CENTRES D'ACCUEIL LAVAL INC, LES
CENTRE   D'ACCUEIL   FERNAND LAROCQUE
5436 Boul Levesque E, Sainte-Dorothee, QC, H7C 1N7
(450) 661-5440
Emp Here 420   *Sales* 24,689,020
SIC 8051 Skilled nursing care facilities
Genl Mgr Gilbert Cadieux

D-U-N-S 25-924-1081   (BR)
GOUVERNEMENT DE LA PROVINCE DE QUEBEC
CENTRE   D'HEBERGEMENT   FERNAND LAROCQUE
5436 Boul Levesque E, Sainte-Dorothee, QC, H7C 1N7
(450) 661-5440
Emp Here 100
SIC 8361 Residential care

Sainte-Dorothee, QC H7R
Ile-Jesus County

D-U-N-S 20-197-4268   (SL)
LOCATION DAGENAIS INC
LOCATION DAGENAIS
2700 Rue Etienne-Lenoir, Sainte-Dorothee, QC, H7R 0A3

---

(450) 625-2415
Emp Here 75   *Sales* 38,043,750
SIC 5511 New and used car dealers
Pr Pr Luc Paquin

Sainte-Eulalie, QC G0Z
Nicolet County

D-U-N-S 20-102-9811   (BR)
HYDRO-QUEBEC
260 Rang Des Cedres, Sainte-Eulalie, QC,
G0Z 1E0
(819) 225-7254
Emp Here 21
SIC 4911 Electric services

Sainte-Felicite, QC G0J

D-U-N-S 20-037-5355   (BR)
COMMISSION SCOLAIRE DE MONTS-ET-MAREES
ECOLE SAINTE FELICITE
(*Suby of* Commission Scolaire De Monts-Et-Marees)
207 Boul Perron, Sainte-Felicite, QC, G0J 2K0
(418) 733-4276
Emp Here 20
SIC 8211 Elementary and secondary schools

Sainte-Felicite-De-L'Islet, QC G0R
L'Islet County

D-U-N-S 20-300-7286   (BR)
COMMISSION SCOLAIRE DE LA COTE-DU-SUD, LA
ECOLE DE SAINTE FELICITE
714 Rue Principale, Sainte-Felicite-De-L'Islet,
QC, G0R 4P0
(418) 359-3043
Emp Here 40
SIC 8211 Elementary and secondary schools

Sainte-Flavie, QC G0J
Rimouski County

D-U-N-S 24-236-7279   (SL)
MOTEL LE GASPESIANA
460 Rte De La Mer, Sainte-Flavie, QC, G0J 2L0
(418) 775-7233
Emp Here 50   *Sales* 2,188,821
SIC 7011 Hotels and motels

Sainte-Genevieve, QC H9H
Hochelaga County

D-U-N-S 25-201-4915   (SL)
CHATEAU PIERREFONDS INC
RESIDENCE CHATEAU PIERREFONDS
15928 Boul Gouin O Bureau 107, Sainte-Genevieve QC, H9H 1C8
(514) 626-2300
Emp Here 50   *Sales* 1,824,018
SIC 8361 Residential care

D-U-N-S 24-800-8492   (SL)
CHATEAU SUR LE LAC STE GENEVIEVE INC
16289 Boul Gouin O, Sainte-Genevieve, QC,
H9H 1E2
(514) 620-9794
Emp Here 51   *Sales* 2,334,742
SIC 8051 Skilled nursing care facilities

Sainte-Genevieve-De-Batiscan, QC G0X
Champlain County

D-U-N-S 24-908-4096   (BR)
CENTRE DE SANTE ET DE SERVICES SOCIAUX DE LA VALLEE-DE-LA-BATISCAN
SECTEUR DES CHENAUX
90 Rang Riviere Veillette, Sainte-Genevieve-De-Batiscan, QC, G0X 2R0
(418) 362-2727
Emp Here 600
SIC 8399 Social services, nec

Sainte-Germaine-Boule, QC J0Z
Abitibi County

D-U-N-S 20-971-3296   (SL)
TRANSPORT CLEMENT BEGIN INC
3R-BUS
200 Rue Du Parc Industriel, Sainte-Germaine-Boule, QC, J0Z 1M0
(819) 787-6154
Emp Here 50   *Sales* 1,386,253
SIC 4151 School buses

Sainte-Helene-De-Bagot, QC J0H
Bagot County

D-U-N-S 25-240-5204   (BR)
COMMISSION SCOLAIRE DE SAINT-HYACINTHE, LA
ECOLE PLEIN SOLEIL
401 4e Av, Sainte-Helene-De-Bagot, QC, J0H 1M0
(450) 773-1237
Emp Here 20
SIC 8211 Elementary and secondary schools

Sainte-Helene-De-Breakeyville, QC G0S
Levis County

D-U-N-S 20-696-1356   (SL)
CLUB DE GOLF LE ROYAL CHAUDIERE INC
GOLF LA TEMPETE
151 Rue Des Trois-Manoirs Bureau 12,
Sainte-Helene-De-Breakeyville, QC, G0S 1E2
(418) 832-8111
Emp Here 50   *Sales* 2,638,521
SIC 7997 Membership sports and recreation clubs

D-U-N-S 25-688-8272   (BR)
COMMISSION SCOLAIRE DES NAVIGATEURS
ECOLE SAINTE HELENE
11 Rue Saint-Maurice, Sainte-Helene-De-Breakeyville, QC, G0S 1E1
(418) 834-2472
Emp Here 30
SIC 8211 Elementary and secondary schools

Sainte-Henedine, QC G0S
Dorchester County

D-U-N-S 25-955-3287   (BR)
UNICOOP, COOPERATIVE AGRICOLE
FERME JOS LACASSE
81 Rue Langevin, Sainte-Henedine, QC, G0S 2R0

Emp Here 50
SIC 5191 Farm supplies

Sainte-Julie, QC J3E
Vercheres County

D-U-N-S 24-293-9577   (SL)
188669 CANADA INC
ENTRETIEN MENAGER LYNA
1999 Rue Nobel Bureau 7a, Sainte-Julie, QC,
J3E 1Z7
(450) 649-9400
Emp Here 100   *Sales* 2,918,428
SIC 7349 Building maintenance services, nec

D-U-N-S 20-585-3521   (SL)
9130-4930 QUEBEC INC
RESTAURANT SCORES
1940 Rue Leonard-De Vinci, Sainte-Julie, QC,
J3E 1Y8
(450) 922-3131
Emp Here 65   *Sales* 1,969,939
SIC 5812 Eating places

D-U-N-S 25-876-6880   (BR)
BANQUE NATIONALE DU CANADA
1033 Boul Armand-Frappier, Sainte-Julie, QC,
J3E 3R5
(450) 649-1141
Emp Here 27
SIC 6021 National commercial banks

D-U-N-S 24-000-2126   (BR)
BEIGNES G.L.C. INC, LES
TIM HORTONS
1911 Ch Du Fer-A-Cheval, Sainte-Julie, QC,
J3E 2T4
(450) 649-0756
Emp Here 25
SIC 5812 Eating places

D-U-N-S 20-539-8600   (BR)
CANADA POST CORPORATION
SAINTE-JULIE SUCC BUREAU-CHEF
461 Rue Saint-Joseph, Sainte-Julie, QC, J3E 1W8
(450) 649-5471
Emp Here 30
SIC 4311 U.s. postal service

D-U-N-S 20-881-7858   (SL)
CLUB DE GOLF DE LA VALLEE DU RICHELIEU INC, LE
100 Ch Du Golf, Sainte-Julie, QC, J3E 1Y1
(450) 649-1511
Emp Here 120   *Sales* 4,815,406
SIC 7997 Membership sports and recreation clubs

D-U-N-S 25-240-6061   (BR)
COMMISSION SCOLAIRE DES PATRIOTES
COMMISSION SCOLAIRE DES PATRIOTES
450 Rue Charles-De Gaulle, Sainte-Julie, QC,
J3E 2V6
(450) 645-2346
Emp Here 70
SIC 8211 Elementary and secondary schools

D-U-N-S 24-327-1439   (BR)
COMMISSION SCOLAIRE DES PATRIOTES
ECOLE SECONDAIRE DU GRAND COTEAU
2020 Rue Borduas, Sainte-Julie, QC, J3E 2G2
(450) 645-2361
Emp Here 60
SIC 8211 Elementary and secondary schools

D-U-N-S 20-712-3220   (BR)
COMMISSION SCOLAIRE DES PATRIOTES
COMMISSION SCOLAIRE DES PATRIOTES
2121 Rue Darwin, Sainte-Julie, QC, J3E 0C9
(450) 645-2370
Emp Here 50
SIC 8331 Job training and related services

D-U-N-S 24-814-9171   (SL)
DESCHAMPS CHEVROLET PONTIAC BUICK CADILLAC GMC LTEE
DUPRE, CHEVROLET-CADILLAC
(*Suby of* Gestion P & H Des Champs Ltee)
333 Boul Armand-Frappier, Sainte-Julie, QC,

J3E 0C7
(450) 649-9333
Emp Here 88   *Sales* 43,190,400
SIC 5511 New and used car dealers
Pr Pr Eric Deschamps
VP VP Hubert Deschamps

D-U-N-S 20-328-5254   (BR)
GAS DRIVE GLOBAL LP
ENERFLEX
2091 Rue Leonard-De Vinci Unite A, Sainte-Julie, QC, J3E 1Z2
(450) 649-3174
Emp Here 100
SIC 7699 Repair services, nec

D-U-N-S 24-056-8709   (HQ)
GROUPE BIKINI VILLAGE INC
BIKINI VILLAGE
(*Suby of* Groupe Bikini Village Inc)
2101 Rue Nobel Bureau A, Sainte-Julie, QC,
J3E 1Z8
(450) 449-1310
Emp Here 40   *Emp Total* 500
Sales 32,920,625
SIC 5651 Family clothing stores
Pr Jocelyn Dumas
Pr Isabelle Grise
Dir Joe Marsilli
Dir Cedric Canu
Dir Nancy Herman
Genl Mgr Chantal Letourneau

D-U-N-S 24-419-2295   (BR)
MATERIAUX R.M. BIBEAU LTEE
RONA-BIBEAU SAINTE-JULIE
1185 Rue Principale, Sainte-Julie, QC, J3E 0C3
(450) 649-3350
Emp Here 30
SIC 5211 Lumber and other building materials

D-U-N-S 24-018-5843   (BR)
PROVIGO DISTRIBUTION INC
PROVIGO
101 Boul Des Hauts-Bois, Sainte-Julie, QC,
J3E 3J8
(450) 649-2421
Emp Here 50
SIC 5411 Grocery stores

D-U-N-S 25-880-2511   (BR)
RE/MAX SIGNATURE INC
633 Boul Armand-Frappier Bureau 102,
Sainte-Julie, QC, J3E 3R4
(450) 922-7777
Emp Here 27
SIC 6531 Real estate agents and managers

D-U-N-S 20-925-7646   (BR)
RESTAURANT NORMANDIN INC
2001 Rue Nobel, Sainte-Julie, QC, J3E 1Z8
(450) 922-9221
Emp Here 45
SIC 5812 Eating places

D-U-N-S 24-705-0839   (SL)
SPG HYDRO INTERNATIONAL INC
2161 Rue Leonard-De Vinci Bureau 101,
Sainte-Julie, QC, J3E 1Z3
(450) 922-3515
Emp Here 49   *Sales* 6,313,604
SIC 7373 Computer integrated systems design
Pr Michael L Lange

D-U-N-S 25-307-7242   (BR)
SOCIETE DES ALCOOLS DU QUEBEC
SOCIETE DES ALCOOLS DU QUEBEC
1700 Ch Du Fer-A-Cheval Unite 102, Sainte-Julie, QC, J3E 1G2
(450) 649-6564
Emp Here 25
SIC 5921 Liquor stores

D-U-N-S 24-214-7457   (SL)
SUPERMARCHE RIENDEAU INC
1700 Ch Du Fer-A-Cheval Bureau 102, Sainte-

Julie, QC, J3E 1G2

Emp Here 49   *Sales* 7,821,331
SIC 5411 Grocery stores
Owner Philippe D'avignon

Sainte-Julie, QC J3X
Vercheres County

D-U-N-S 24-160-8616   (BR)
HYDRO-QUEBEC
ELECTRIUM
2001 Rue Michael-Faraday, Sainte-Julie, QC,
J3X 1S1
(450) 652-8977
Emp Here 20
SIC 4911 Electric services

Sainte-Justine-De-Newton, QC J0P
Vaudreuil County

D-U-N-S 20-282-7924   (BR)
ASPHALTE TRUDEAU LTEE
3600 Ch Des Bedard, Sainte-Justine-De-
Newton, QC, J0P 1T0
(450) 764-3617
Emp Here 30
SIC 1499 Miscellaneous nonMetallic minerals,
except fuels

Sainte-Luce, QC G0K
Rimouski County

D-U-N-S 20-802-8006   (BR)
COMMISSION SCOLAIRE DES PHARES
ECOLE DES BOIS-ET-MAREES
(*Suby of* Commission Scolaire des Phares)
53 Rue Saint-Pierre E, Sainte-Luce, QC, G0K
1P0
(418) 739-4214
Emp Here 25
SIC 8211 Elementary and secondary schools

Sainte-Madeleine, QC J0H
St Hyacinthe County

D-U-N-S 25-125-9024   (BR)
**COMMISSION SCOLAIRE DE SAINT-
HYACINTHE, LA**
ECOLE ST-JOSEPH SPENARD
150 Rue Du Cinquantenaire, Sainte-
Madeleine, QC, J0H 1S0
(450) 773-6881
Emp Here 40
SIC 8211 Elementary and secondary schools

D-U-N-S 24-203-3525   (SL)
JARDINS M.G. S.E.N.C., LES
985 Rang Saint-Simon, Sainte-Madeleine,
QC, J0H 1S0
(450) 795-3459
Emp Here 27   *Sales* 6,566,463
SIC 5148 Fresh fruits and vegetables
Pt Sylvain Palardy
Pt Guy Palardy
Pt Micheline Palardy

D-U-N-S 20-255-0893   (HQ)
NMP GOLF CONSTRUCTION INC
2674 Ch Plamondon Bureau 201, Sainte-
Madeleine, QC, J0H 1S0
(450) 795-9878
Emp Here 20   *Emp Total* 25
Sales 9,338,970
SIC 1629 Heavy construction, nec
Pr Pr Normand Poirier

Mario Poirier

Sainte-Marie, QC G6E
Ile-Jesus County

D-U-N-S 20-519-9982   (BR)
BANQUE NATIONALE DU CANADA
160 Rue Notre-Dame N, Sainte-Marie, QC,
G6E 3Z9
(418) 387-2333
Emp Here 25
SIC 6021 National commercial banks

D-U-N-S 20-243-5095   (BR)
BOULANGERIE VACHON INC
380 Rue Notre-Dame N, Sainte-Marie, QC,
G6E 2K7
(418) 387-5421
Emp Here 600
SIC 5149 Groceries and related products, nec

D-U-N-S 20-174-1993   (SL)
**CENTRE FINANCIER AUX ENTREPRISES
DES CAISSES DESJARDIN CHAUDIERE-
NORD**
CFE CHAUDIERE NORD
1017 Boul Vachon N Bureau 300, Sainte-
Marie, QC, G6E 1M3
(418) 386-1333
Emp Here 49   *Sales* 6,992,640
SIC 8741 Management services
Genl Mgr Pierre Giroux

D-U-N-S 20-030-0197   (BR)
**COMMISSION SCOLAIRE DE LA BEAUCE-
ETCHEMIN**
ECOLE PRIMAIRE MARIBEL
62 Rue Saint-Antoine, Sainte-Marie, QC, G6E
4B8
(418) 387-6616
Emp Here 50
SIC 8211 Elementary and secondary schools

D-U-N-S 25-234-0609   (BR)
**COMMISSION SCOLAIRE DE LA BEAUCE-
ETCHEMIN**
ECOLE PRIMAIRE L'EVEIL (092)
717 Rue Etienne-Raymond, Sainte-Marie,
QC, G6E 3R1
(418) 386-5541
Emp Here 24
SIC 8211 Elementary and secondary schools

D-U-N-S 20-711-9392   (BR)
**COMMISSION SCOLAIRE DE LA BEAUCE-
ETCHEMIN**
ECOLE MONSEIGNEUR FEUILTAULT
35 Boul Vachon S, Sainte-Marie, QC, G6E
4G8
(418) 387-5837
Emp Here 40
SIC 8211 Elementary and secondary schools

D-U-N-S 20-030-4553   (BR)
**COMMISSION SCOLAIRE DE LA BEAUCE-
ETCHEMIN**
ECOLE POLYVALENTE BENOIT VACHON
919 Rte Saint-Martin, Sainte-Marie, QC, G6E
1E6
(418) 387-6636
Emp Here 40
SIC 8211 Elementary and secondary schools

D-U-N-S 20-711-9384   (BR)
**COMMISSION SCOLAIRE DE LA BEAUCE-
ETCHEMIN**
*CENTRE DE FORMATION DES BATIS-
SEURS, LE*
925 Rte Saint-Martin, Sainte-Marie, QC, G6E
1E6
(418) 386-5541
Emp Here 50
SIC 8211 Elementary and secondary schools

D-U-N-S 24-205-2405   (SL)
CONSTRUCTIONS BEAUCE-ATLAS INC,

LES
(*Suby of* Gestion Beauce-Atlas Inc)
600 1re Av Du Parc-Industriel, Sainte-Marie,
QC, G6E 1B5
(418) 387-4872
Emp Here 130   *Sales* 67,659,222
SIC 5051 Metals service centers and offices
Germain Blais

D-U-N-S 20-431-8869   (SL)
CONSTRUCTIONS EDGUY INC, LES
500 1re Av Du Parc-Industriel, Sainte-Marie,
QC, G6E 1B5
(418) 387-6270
Emp Here 28   *Sales* 2,042,900
SIC 1794 Excavation work

D-U-N-S 24-344-4754   (SL)
CONSTRUCTIONS EXCEL S.M. INC, LES
1083 Vachon N Bureau 300, Sainte-
Marie, QC, G6E 1M8
(418) 386-1442
Emp Here 35   *Sales* 9,380,300
SIC 1541 Industrial buildings and warehouses
Pr Mario Cliche

D-U-N-S 25-721-6168   (BR)
DOLLARAMA S.E.C.
DOLLARAMA
1116 Boul Vachon N Bureau 47, Sainte-Marie,
QC, G6E 1N7
(418) 387-8121
Emp Here 20
SIC 5399 Miscellaneous general merchandise

D-U-N-S 25-716-7478   (SL)
EACOM TIMBER CORPORATION
EACOM TIMBER CORPORATION
1492 Boul Vachon S, Sainte-Marie, QC, G6E
2S5
(418) 387-5670
Emp Here 60
SIC 2421 Sawmills and planing mills, general

D-U-N-S 20-050-8021   (SL)
FABRICATION BEAUCE-ATLAS INC
(*Suby of* Gestion Beauce-Atlas Inc)
600 1re Av Du Parc-Industriel, Sainte-Marie,
QC, G6E 1B5
(418) 387-4872
Emp Here 110   *Sales* 20,428,996
SIC 1542 Nonresidential construction, nec
Pr Pr Germain Blais
 Guy Fradette

D-U-N-S 25-367-5979   (SL)
GESTION AJJARO INC
MC DONALD'S
900 Boul Vachon N, Sainte-Marie, QC, G6E
1M2
(418) 387-2877
Emp Here 50   *Sales* 1,732,502
SIC 5812 Eating places

D-U-N-S 24-942-0910   (SL)
GESTION ARMELLE INC
1116 Boul Vachon N Bureau 36, Sainte-Marie,
QC, G6E 1N7
(418) 387-3120
Emp Here 125   *Sales* 25,537,116
SIC 6712 Bank holding companies
Pr Pr Armelle Labonte

D-U-N-S 20-285-8333   (SL)
INOVIA INC
AIGUISAGE INDUSTRIEL DE BEAUCHE
1291 1re Rue Du Parc-Industriel, Sainte-
Marie, QC, G6E 3T3
(418) 387-3144
Emp Here 50   *Sales* 5,326,131
SIC 3569 General industrial machinery, nec
Pr Pr Claude Bilodeau
 Lambert Champagne
 Michel Marcoux
 Serge Routhier
 Alain Jacques
 Pierre Lehoux

D-U-N-S 24-803-2067   (BR)
**PHILIPPE GOSSELIN & ASSOCIES LIMI-
TEE**
SHELL
424 2e Av Du Parc-Industriel, Sainte-Marie,
QC, G6E 1B6
(418) 387-5493
Emp Here 20
SIC 5172 Petroleum products, nec

D-U-N-S 24-942-5000   (SL)
POUTRELLES DELTA INC
1270 2e Rue Du Parc-Industriel, Sainte-Marie,
QC, G6E 1G8

Emp Here 100   *Sales* 18,990,720
SIC 3441 Fabricated structural Metal
Pr Pr Gilles Lachance
 Renald Filion
 George Michaud
 Katrine Lachance

D-U-N-S 20-006-3266   (BR)
PROVIGO DISTRIBUTION INC
MAXI
1030 Boul Vachon N, Sainte-Marie, QC, G6E
1M5
(418) 387-5779
Emp Here 70
SIC 5411 Grocery stores

D-U-N-S 25-671-4031   (BR)
TELUS COMMUNICATIONS (QUEBEC) INC
TELUS QUEBEC
555 1re Av Du Parc-Industriel, Sainte-Marie,
QC, G6E 1B4

Emp Here 50
SIC 4899 Communication services, nec

D-U-N-S 20-356-8142   (BR)
TEXEL MATERIAUX TECHNIQUES INC
TEXEL MATERIAUX TECHNIQUES
(*Suby of* Lydall, Inc.)
1300 2e Rue Du Parc-Industriel, Sainte-Marie,
QC, G6E 1G8
(418) 387-5910
Emp Here 150
SIC 2297 Nonwoven fabrics

D-U-N-S 25-685-2237   (BR)
TRANSPORT ROBERT (1973) LTEE
1199 2e Rue Du Parc-Industriel, Sainte-Marie,
QC, G6E 1G7
(514) 521-1416
Emp Here 100
SIC 4213 Trucking, except local

D-U-N-S 24-455-7419   (BR)
WESTROCK COMPANY OF CANADA INC
PRESENTOIRES ROCKTENN
(*Suby of* Westrock Company)
433 2e Av Du Parc-Industriel, Sainte-Marie,
QC, G6E 3H2
(418) 387-5438
Emp Here 150
SIC 2657 Folding paperboard boxes

Sainte-Marie-Salome, QC J0K
Montcalm County

D-U-N-S 20-276-3087   (SL)
CONSTRUCTION JULIEN DALPE INC
350 Ch Des Pres, Sainte-Marie-Salome, QC,
J0K 2Z0
(450) 754-2059
Emp Here 24   *Sales* 6,129,280
SIC 1542 Nonresidential construction, nec
Pr Julien Dalpe

Sainte-Marthe, QC J0P
Vaudreuil County

D-U-N-S 20-999-1892   (SL)
2528-6360 QUEBEC INC
AUBERGE DES GALLANT
1171 Ch Saint-Henri Bureau 1, Sainte-Marthe, QC, J0P 1W0
(450) 459-4241
Emp Here 60   *Sales* 1,824,018
SIC 5812 Eating places

Sainte-Marthe-Sur-Le-Lac, QC J0N
Deux-Montagnes County

D-U-N-S 20-978-4263   (SL)
ABBAYE STE-MARIE DES DEUX-MONTAGNES
2803 Ch D'Oka, Sainte-Marthe-Sur-Le-Lac, QC, J0N 1P0
(450) 473-7278
Emp Here 50   *Sales* 3,283,232
SIC 8661 Religious organizations

D-U-N-S 25-292-9211   (BR)
COMMISSION SCOLAIRE DE LA SEIGNEURIE-DES-MILLE-ILES
COMMISSION SCOLAIRE DE LA SEIGNEURIE-DES-MILLE-ILES
(*Suby of* Commission Scolaire de la Seigneurie-Des-Mille-Iles)
2919 Boul Des Promenades, Sainte-Marthe-Sur-Le-Lac, QC, J0N 1P0
(450) 623-4666
Emp Here 60
SIC 8211 Elementary and secondary schools

D-U-N-S 25-292-8940   (BR)
COMMISSION SCOLAIRE DE LA SEIGNEURIE-DES-MILLE-ILES
COMMISSION SCOLAIRE DE LA SEIGNEURIE-DES-MILLE-ILES
(*Suby of* Commission Scolaire de la Seigneurie-Des-Mille-Iles)
320 Rue De La Seve, Sainte-Marthe-Sur-Le-Lac, QC, J0N 1P0
(450) 472-8060
Emp Here 40
SIC 8211 Elementary and secondary schools

D-U-N-S 25-233-3711   (BR)
COMMISSION SCOLAIRE DE LA SEIGNEURIE-DES-MILLE-ILES
COMMISSION SCOLAIRE DE LA SEIGNEURIE-DES-MILLE-ILES
(*Suby of* Commission Scolaire de la Seigneurie-Des-Mille-Iles)
3099 Ch D'Oka, Sainte-Marthe-Sur-Le-Lac, QC, J0N 1P0
(450) 473-2043
Emp Here 20
SIC 8211 Elementary and secondary schools

D-U-N-S 25-485-2403   (BR)
LUSSIER, BERNARD INC
PHARMACIE JEAN COUTU
3003 Ch D'Oka, Sainte-Marthe-Sur-Le-Lac, QC, J0N 1P0
(450) 473-5480
Emp Here 50
SIC 5912 Drug stores and proprietary stores

D-U-N-S 24-125-4619   (BR)
PROVIGO DISTRIBUTION INC
MAXI
2840 Boul Des Promenades, Sainte-Marthe-Sur-Le-Lac, QC, J0N 1P0
(450) 472-3551
Emp Here 40
SIC 5411 Grocery stores

Sainte-Martine, QC J0S
Chateauguay County

D-U-N-S 25-240-3480   (BR)
COMMISSION SCOLAIRE DE LA VALLEE-DES-TISSERANDS, LA
ECOLE STE-MARTINE
5 Rue Ronaldo-Belanger, Sainte-Martine, QC, J0S 1V0
(450) 225-4972
Emp Here 25
SIC 8211 Elementary and secondary schools

D-U-N-S 20-708-0412   (BR)
DARE FOODS LIMITED
BOULANGERIE SAINTE MARTINE
15 Rang Dubuc, Sainte-Martine, QC, J0S 1V0
(450) 427-8410
Emp Here 150
SIC 2051 Bread, cake, and related products

Sainte-Melanie, QC J0K
Joliette County

D-U-N-S 24-438-0288   (BR)
CAISSE DESJARDINS DE KILDARE
21 Rue Louis-Charles-Panet, Sainte-Melanie, QC, J0K 3A0
(450) 752-0602
Emp Here 20
SIC 6021 National commercial banks

D-U-N-S 20-419-1266   (SL)
INDUSTRIES J. S. P. INC, LES
41 Rue De L'Industrie, Sainte-Melanie, QC, J0K 3A0
(450) 889-2229
Emp Here 50
SIC 2517 Wood television and radio cabinets

D-U-N-S 20-422-0198   (SL)
TRANSPORT GASTON NADEAU INC
850 Rte Principale, Sainte-Melanie, QC, J0K 3A0
(514) 861-0040
Emp Here 50   *Sales* 4,677,755
SIC 4212 Local trucking, without storage

Sainte-Monique-Lac-Saint-Jea, QC G0W
Lac-St-Jean-Est County

D-U-N-S 24-336-9894   (SL)
INDUSTRIE T.L.T. INC
144 Rue Larouche, Sainte-Monique-Lac-Saint-Jea, QC, G0W 2T0
(418) 347-3355
Emp Here 100   *Sales* 9,484,891
SIC 2421 Sawmills and planing mills, general
Pr Sergio Lifraine
   Claude Hebert

Sainte-Perpetue, QC J0C
Nicolet County

D-U-N-S 24-214-8141   (BR)
GROUPE ALIMENTAIRE NORDIQUE INC, LE
(*Suby of* Groupe Alimentaire Nordique Inc, Le)
2592 Rang Saint-Joseph, Sainte-Perpetue, QC, J0C 1R0
(819) 336-6444
Emp Here 50
SIC 5812 Eating places

Sainte-Perpetue-De-L'Islet, QC G0R
L'Islet County

D-U-N-S 25-233-0725   (BR)
COMMISSION SCOLAIRE DE LA COTE-DU-SUD, LA
ECOLE STE PERPETUE
5 Rue Du Couvent, Sainte-Perpetue-De-L'Islet, QC, G0R 3Z0
(418) 359-2969
Emp Here 30
SIC 8211 Elementary and secondary schools

Sainte-Rose, QC H7C
Ile-Jesus County

D-U-N-S 20-726-8012   (SL)
AUTOBUS LA MONTREALAISE INC, LES
1200 Av Laplace, Sainte-Rose, QC, H7C 2M4
(450) 664-0449
Emp Here 30   *Sales* 875,528
SIC 4151 School buses

D-U-N-S 24-394-5461   (BR)
OPTA MINERALS INC
MINERAUX OPTA
1320 Av De Valleyfield, Sainte-Rose, QC, H7C 2K6
(450) 664-1001
Emp Here 20
SIC 3291 Abrasive products

D-U-N-S 24-106-3221   (HQ)
PRODUITS ALIMENTAIRES VIAU INC, LES
6625 Rue Ernest-Cormier, Sainte-Rose, QC, H7C 2V2
(450) 665-6100
Emp Here 250   *Emp Total* 250
Sales 76,056,838
SIC 5147 Meats and meat products
Pr Pasquale De Marco
   Ivano Scattolin
Dir Enzo Reda
Dir Giuseppe Reda
Dir Vira Reda

Sainte-Rose, QC H7E
Ile-Jesus County

D-U-N-S 24-682-8631   (BR)
9061-9552 QUEBEC INC
TIM HORTONS
3099 Boul De La Concorde E, Sainte-Rose, QC, H7E 2C1
(450) 664-2995
Emp Here 20
SIC 5812 Eating places

D-U-N-S 24-319-5166   (BR)
WAL-MART CANADA CORP
WALMART
5205 Boul Robert-Bourassa, Sainte-Rose, QC, H7E 0A3
(450) 661-7447
Emp Here 120
SIC 5311 Department stores

Sainte-Rose, QC H7L
Ile-Jesus County

D-U-N-S 24-433-7101   (SL)
ARTICLES MENAGERS DURA INC
DURA KIT
2105 Boul Dagenais O, Sainte-Rose, QC, H7L 5W9
(450) 622-3872
Emp Here 25   *Sales* 8,116,000
SIC 5021 Furniture
   Salim Aintabi
   Saad Aintabi

D-U-N-S 25-286-9516   (BR)

BELRON CANADA INCORPOREE
TECHNICENTRE PLUS
1485 Boul Saint-Elzear O Bureau 201, Sainte-Rose, QC, H7L 3N6
(514) 327-1122
Emp Here 25
SIC 7622 Radio and television repair

D-U-N-S 20-692-9783   (HQ)
CAISSE DESJARDINS DU NORD DE LAVAL
CENTRE DE SERVICES FABREVILLE
(*Suby of* Caisse Desjardins du Nord de Laval)
396 Boul Cure-Labelle, Sainte-Rose, QC, H7L 4T7
(450) 622-8130
Emp Here 24   *Emp Total* 74
Sales 13,926,776
SIC 6062 State credit unions
Genl Mgr Guy Benoit
Pr Stephane Corbeil
VP Hubert Bernatchez
Sec Alexandre Jarry
Dir Michel Beaumont
Dir Jean Boisvert
Dir Serge Bouchard
Dir Mario Gebrayel
Dir Edith Lauzon
Dir Jean-Pierre Nadeau

D-U-N-S 24-525-6750   (BR)
CANADA BREAD COMPANY, LIMITED
3455 Av Francis-Hughes, Sainte-Rose, QC, H7L 5A5
(450) 669-2222
Emp Here 700
SIC 5461 Retail bakeries

D-U-N-S 20-180-2399   (BR)
CARRIER ENTERPRISE CANADA, L.P.
CARRIER ENTERPRISE CANADA, L.P
2025 Boul Dagenais O, Sainte-Rose, QC, H7L 5V1
(514) 324-5050
Emp Here 100
SIC 5075 Warm air heating and air conditioning

D-U-N-S 20-716-7599   (BR)
COMMISSION SCOLAIRE DE LAVAL
ECOLE PRIMAIRE L'AQUARELLE
707 Av Marc-Aurele-Fortin, Sainte-Rose, QC, H7L 5M6
(450) 662-7000
Emp Here 50
SIC 8211 Elementary and secondary schools

D-U-N-S 20-216-1782   (SL)
DILMONT INC
1485 Boul Saint-Elzear O Bureau 301, Sainte-Rose, QC, H7L 3N6
(514) 272-5741
Emp Here 25   *Sales* 2,407,703
SIC 2842 Polishes and sanitation goods

D-U-N-S 24-111-6524   (SL)
DYNE-A-PAK INC
3375 Av Francis-Hughes, Sainte-Rose, QC, H7L 5A5
(450) 667-3626
Emp Here 100   *Sales* 14,665,101
SIC 3089 Plastics products, nec
Pr Harvey Rosenbloom
VP VP Richard Rosenbloom
Treas Nicki Lang
VP VP Gerald Maldoff

D-U-N-S 24-865-7249   (HQ)
ECHAFAUDS PLUS (LAVAL) INC
2897 Av Francis-Hughes, Sainte-Rose, QC, H7L 4G8
(450) 663-1926
Emp Here 50   *Emp Total* 100
Sales 8,292,495
SIC 7359 Equipment rental and leasing, nec
Pr Pr Bruno Tasse
VP Michel Champigny
VP Jean Marc Champigny
   Hugues Poulin

VP Fin Yvan Despres

D-U-N-S 24-988-8629   (HQ)
ENTREPRISES H. PEPIN (1991) INC, LES
MOTEL IDEAL
(*Suby of* Entreprises H. Pepin (1991) Inc, Les)
379 Boul Cure-Labelle, Sainte-Rose, QC, H7L 3A3
(450) 625-0773
Emp Here 34   *Emp Total* 101
Sales 4,450,603
SIC 7011 Hotels and motels

D-U-N-S 24-433-5212   (SL)
FERCO FERRURES DE BATIMENTS INC
2000 Rue Berlier, Sainte-Rose, QC, H7L 4S4
(450) 973-1437
Emp Here 26   *Sales* 4,523,563
SIC 5072 Hardware

D-U-N-S 20-187-3499   (SL)
GESCLADO INC
1400 Boul Dagenais O, Sainte-Rose, QC, H7L 5C7
(450) 622-1600
Emp Here 70   *Sales* 12,957,120
SIC 6712 Bank holding companies
Pr Pr Normand Tremblay

D-U-N-S 24-548-9794   (SL)
GROUPE FERTEK INC
3000 Av Francis-Hughes, Sainte-Rose, QC, H7L 3J5
(450) 663-8700
Emp Here 90   *Sales* 18,565,350
SIC 6712 Bank holding companies
Pr Pr Bruno Tasse
VP Fin Yvan Despres
Sec Hugues T Poulin

D-U-N-S 24-903-9553   (BR)
GROUPE JEAN COUTU (PJC) INC, LE
PHARMACIE JEAN COUTU
(*Suby of* 3958230 Canada Inc)
580 Boul Cure-Labelle Bureau 1, Sainte-Rose, QC, H7L 4V6
(450) 963-9507
Emp Here 25
SIC 5912 Drug stores and proprietary stores

D-U-N-S 24-988-6748   (SL)
LABORATOIRES D'OPTIQUE S.D.L. INC
1450 Boul Dagenais O, Sainte-Rose, QC, H7L 5C7
(450) 622-8668
Emp Here 28   *Sales* 2,626,585
SIC 5995 Optical goods stores

D-U-N-S 24-904-5436   (HQ)
METALTECH-OMEGA INC
BOIS DE STRUCTURE LEE
1735 Boul Saint-Elzear O Bureau B, Sainte-Rose, QC, H7L 3N6
(450) 681-6440
Emp Here 89   *Emp Total* 100
Sales 8,317,520
SIC 3446 Architectural Metalwork
Pr Pr Bruno Tasse
Sec Hugues Poulin
Dir Yvan Despres

D-U-N-S 24-529-8369   (HQ)
MULTI-MARQUES INC
BON MATIN
3455 Av Francis-Hughes, Sainte-Rose, QC, H7L 5A5
(450) 669-2222
Emp Here 800   *Emp Total* 130,913
Sales 126,920,880
SIC 2051 Bread, cake, and related products
VP Jean-Luc Breton
Dir Fin Gaetan Roy

D-U-N-S 24-675-4894   (BR)
OVATION LOGISTIQUE INC
2745 Av Francis-Hughes, Sainte-Rose, QC, H7L 3S8
(450) 967-9329
Emp Here 21

SIC 4215 Courier services, except by air

D-U-N-S 20-205-0779   (SL)
PRO DOC LTEE
(*Suby of* 3958230 Canada Inc)
2925 Boul Industriel, Sainte-Rose, QC, H7L 3W9
(450) 668-9750
Emp Here 48   *Sales* 6,030,906
SIC 2834 Pharmaceutical preparations
Pr Marcel A. Raymond
Sec Brigitte Dufour
Dir Francois J. Coutu
Dir Andre Belzile

D-U-N-S 24-125-7083   (BR)
PUROLATOR INC.
PUROLATOR INC
2005 Boul Dagenais O, Sainte-Rose, QC, H7L 5V1
(450) 963-3050
Emp Here 150
SIC 7389 Business services, nec

D-U-N-S 25-361-4598   (BR)
RYERSON CANADA, INC
3399 Av Francis-Hughes, Sainte-Rose, QC, H7L 5A5
(450) 975-7171
Emp Here 110
SIC 5051 Metals service centers and offices

D-U-N-S 24-502-3887   (SL)
THOMAS MARINE
357 Boul Cure-Labelle, Sainte-Rose, QC, H7L 3A3
(450) 625-2476
Emp Here 30   *Sales* 5,977,132
SIC 5551 Boat dealers

D-U-N-S 20-428-0569   (HQ)
VALEANT CANADA LP
(*Suby of* Valeant Canada LP)
2150 Boul Saint-Elzear O, Sainte-Rose, QC, H7L 4A8
(514) 744-6792
Emp Here 260   *Emp Total* 300
Sales 36,991,075
SIC 5122 Drugs, proprietaries, and sundries
Dir Fin Martin Beaudoin

D-U-N-S 20-237-5143   (HQ)
VALEANT CANADA LIMITEE
GESTION VALEANT CANADA
2150 Boul Saint-Elzear O, Sainte-Rose, QC, H7L 4A8
(514) 744-6792
Emp Here 69   *Emp Total* 1,368
Sales 19,577,273
SIC 2834 Pharmaceutical preparations
Pr Jacques Dessureault
Ex VP Robert R Chai-Onn
Ex VP Howard B. Schiller
Sec Daniel Yelin

D-U-N-S 20-540-2241   (HQ)
VAN DE WATER-RAYMOND LTD
COURTIERS EN ALIMENTATION VAN-RAY
(*Suby of* Gestion Francois Raymond 1994 Inc)
2300 Rue Monterey, Sainte-Rose, QC, H7L 3H9
(450) 688-7580
Emp Here 105   *Emp Total* 150
Sales 46,604,304
SIC 5141 Groceries, general line
Yves Raymond
VP Stephane Raymond
Pierre Rivest
Dir Francois Raymond
Dir Maxine Raymond
Dir Sophie Raymond

Sainte-Rose, QC H7P
Ile-Jesus County

D-U-N-S 24-391-5845   (SL)
3952851 CANADA INC
2875 Rue Jules-Brillant, Sainte-Rose, QC, H7P 6B2
(450)
Emp Here 75   *Sales* 14,569,600
SIC 6712 Bank holding companies
James Ronald

D-U-N-S 24-402-3362   (HQ)
ENERTRAK INC
(*Suby of* 161576 Canada Inc)
2875 Rue Jules-Brillant, Sainte-Rose, QC, H7P 6B2
(450) 973-2000
Emp Here 20   *Emp Total* 23
Sales 9,095,636
SIC 5075 Warm air heating and air conditioning
Pr Pr Samir Trak
Ada Trak
Dir Karine Trak
Dir Tanya Trak
Dir Fin Serge Bechard

D-U-N-S 20-102-0810   (SL)
ENLEVEMENT DE DECHETS BERGERON INC
4365 Boul Saint-Elzear O, Sainte-Rose, QC, H7P 4J3
(450) 687-3838
Emp Here 50   *Sales* 3,939,878
SIC 4212 Local trucking, without storage

D-U-N-S 20-003-3327   (BR)
PROVIGO DISTRIBUTION INC
MAXI
444 Boul Cure-Labelle, Sainte-Rose, QC, H7P 4W7
(450) 625-4221
Emp Here 76
SIC 5411 Grocery stores

D-U-N-S 24-125-6341   (BR)
STRONGCO ENGINEERED SYSTEMS INC
4535 Rue Louis-B.-Mayer, Sainte-Rose, QC, H7P 6B5
(450) 686-8911
Emp Here 50
SIC 4212 Local trucking, without storage

Sainte-Rose, QC H7R
Ile-Jesus County

D-U-N-S 24-355-6131   (SL)
CLINIQUE DENTAIRE MICHEL A. LAVOIE & ASSOCIE
5585 Boul Dagenais O, Sainte-Rose, QC, H7R 1L9
(450) 627-1119
Emp Here 60   *Sales* 3,429,153
SIC 8021 Offices and clinics of dentists

Sainte-Rose, QC H7W
Ile-Jesus County

D-U-N-S 20-892-4592   (BR)
3618358 CANADA INC
ATS
655 Chomedey (A-13) E Unite 13, Sainte-Rose, QC, H7W 5N4
(450) 688-2882
Emp Here 30
SIC 4731 Freight transportation arrangement

D-U-N-S 20-175-9862   (BR)
INDUSTRIES SPECTRA PREMIUM INC, LES
1313 Chomedey (A-13) E, Sainte-Rose, QC, H7W 5L7
(450) 681-1313
Emp Here 200

SIC 3433 Heating equipment, except electric

Sainte-Rose, QC H7X
Ile-Jesus County

D-U-N-S 25-242-6473   (SL)
2173-4108 QUEBEC INC
INTERSPORT
640 Chomedey (A-13) O, Sainte-Rose, QC, H7X 3S9
(450)
Emp Here 50   *Sales* 4,231,721
SIC 5941 Sporting goods and bicycle shops

D-U-N-S 24-218-6059   (HQ)
3819299 CANADA INC
TIM HORTONS
(*Suby of* 3819299 Canada Inc)
760 Chomedey (A-13) O, Sainte-Rose, QC, H7X 3S9
(450) 969-3435
Emp Here 50   *Emp Total* 110
Sales 3,283,232
SIC 5812 Eating places

D-U-N-S 25-672-7868   (HQ)
CAISSE DESJARDINS DE L'OUEST DE LAVAL
CENTRE DE SERVICE DAGENAIS
(*Suby of* Caisse Desjardins de l'Ouest de Laval)
440 Desste Chomedey (A-13) O, Sainte-Rose, QC, H7X 3S9
(450) 962-1800
Emp Here 20   *Emp Total* 100
Sales 14,359,468
SIC 6062 State credit unions
Genl Mgr Jacinthe Godmer
Pr Pr Daniel Belanger
VP Andre Gionet
Sec Louise Durocher
Dir Audrey Duguay
Dir Nadine Sigouin
Dir Andre Dunnigan
Dir Claude Gendron
Dir Gabriel Lapierre
Dir Marie Corriveau

D-U-N-S 20-716-7847   (BR)
COMMISSION SCOLAIRE DE LAVAL
ECOLE PRIMAIRE PIERRE-LAPORTE
805 Rue Lauzon, Sainte-Rose, QC, H7X 2N4
(450) 662-7000
Emp Here 50
SIC 8211 Elementary and secondary schools

D-U-N-S 20-716-7805   (BR)
COMMISSION SCOLAIRE DE LAVAL
ECOLE PRIMAIRE SAINTE-DOROTHEE
956 Montee Gravel, Sainte-Rose, QC, H7X 2B8
(450) 662-7000
Emp Here 50
SIC 8211 Elementary and secondary schools

D-U-N-S 24-195-6189   (SL)
GESTION MICHEL SEGUIN INC
CANADIAN TIRE
500 Aut Chomedey, Sainte-Rose, QC, H7X 3S9
(450) 969-4141
Emp Here 100   *Sales* 14,001,280
SIC 5531 Auto and home supply stores
Pr Michel Sequin

D-U-N-S 20-993-4426   (BR)
GROUPE ALDO INC, LE
GLOBO
850 Chomedey (A-13) O, Sainte-Rose, QC, H7X 3S9
(450) 969-1296
Emp Here 20
SIC 5661 Shoe stores

D-U-N-S 25-190-4488   (BR)

GROUPE ARCHAMBAULT INC
ARCHAMBAULT ECOLE DE MUSIQUE
520 Chomedey (A-13) O, Sainte-Rose, QC,
H7X 3S9
(450) 689-5063
Emp Here 70
SIC 8299 Schools and educational services,
nec

　　D-U-N-S 20-191-7254　　　(BR)
HUDSON'S BAY COMPANY
DECO DECOUVERTE
880 Chomedey (A-13) O, Sainte-Rose, QC,
H7X 3S9
(450) 969-0041
Emp Here 25
SIC 5311 Department stores

　　D-U-N-S 24-226-7479　　　(BR)
WAL-MART CANADA CORP
ACCES PHARMA CHEZ WALMART
700 Chomedey (A-13) O, Sainte-Rose, QC,
H7X 3S9
(450) 969-3226
Emp Here 150
SIC 5311 Department stores

Sainte-Rose-De-Watford, QC G0R
Dorchester County

　　D-U-N-S 24-101-3494　　　(SL)
9111-2128 QUEBEC INC
237 204 Rte, Sainte-Rose-De-Watford, QC,
G0R 4G0
(418) 267-4151
Emp Here 35　　　*Sales* 5,376,850
SIC 3679 Electronic components, nec
Pr Audet Charles
　Richard Auclair

　　D-U-N-S 20-257-3572　　　(SL)
JOSEPH AUDET LTEE
237 204 Rte, Sainte-Rose-De-Watford, QC,
G0R 4G0
(418) 267-4151
Emp Here 50　　　*Sales* 4,742,446
SIC 2421 Sawmills and planing mills, general

　　D-U-N-S 25-374-1094　　　(SL)
PRECITECH INTERNATIONAL INC
237 Rte 204, Sainte-Rose-De-Watford, QC,
G0R 4G0
(418) 267-4151
Emp Here 35　　　*Sales* 5,376,850
SIC 3679 Electronic components, nec
　Charles Audet

Sainte-Sophie, QC J5J
Abitibi County

　　D-U-N-S 25-480-1889　　　(BR)
CLUBLINK CORPORATION ULC
CLUB DE GOLF VAL DES LACS
(*Suby of* TWC Enterprises Limited)
300 Rue Des Cedres, Sainte-Sophie, QC, J5J
2T6
(450) 476-9001
Emp Here 50
SIC 7992 Public golf courses

　　D-U-N-S 25-197-2550　　　(BR)
**COMMISSION SCOLAIRE DE LA RIVIERE-
DU-NORD**
ECOLE DU JOLI BOIS
(*Suby of* Commission Scolaire de la Riviere-
du-Nord)
100 Rue De Val-Des-Chenes, Sainte-Sophie,
QC, J5J 2M5
(450) 431-0640
Emp Here 50
SIC 8211 Elementary and secondary schools

　　D-U-N-S 20-170-3951　　　(BR)

DYNO NOBEL CANADA INC
DYNO NOBEL
2697 Boul Sainte-Sophie, Sainte-Sophie, QC,
J5J 2V3
(450) 438-8681
Emp Here 20
SIC 5169 Chemicals and allied products, nec

　　D-U-N-S 20-152-3219　　　(HQ)
PIECES AUTOMOBILES LECAVALIER INC
LECAVALIER
2925 Boul Sainte-Sophie, Sainte-Sophie, QC,
J5J 1L1
(450) 436-2441
Emp Here 110　　　*Emp Total* 42,500
Sales 19,699,389
SIC 4953 Refuse systems
Pr Pr Roger Fugere Jr
　Philippe Fugere

　　D-U-N-S 25-501-0142　　　(BR)
WM QUEBEC INC
CANADIAN WASTE MANAGEMENT
(*Suby of* Waste Management, Inc.)
2535 1re Rue, Sainte-Sophie, QC, J5J 2R7
(450) 438-5604
Emp Here 60
SIC 4953 Refuse systems

　　D-U-N-S 25-916-2329　　　(BR)
**WASTE MANAGEMENT OF CANADA COR-
PORATION**
(*Suby of* Waste Management, Inc.)
2535 1re Rue, Sainte-Sophie, QC, J5J 2R7
(450) 431-2313
Emp Here 75
SIC 4212 Local trucking, without storage

Sainte-Sophie-D'Halifax, QC G0P
Terrebonne County

　　D-U-N-S 24-210-3039　　　(BR)
**COMMISSION SCOLAIRE DES BOIS-
FRANCS**
ECOLE MARIE-IMMACULEE
441 Rue De L'Ecole, Sainte-Sophie-D'Halifax,
QC, G0P 1L0
(418) 362-3277
Emp Here 25
SIC 8211 Elementary and secondary schools

Sainte-Sophie-De-Levrard, QC G0X
Terrebonne County

　　D-U-N-S 25-470-1857　　　(SL)
ENTREPRISES H.M. METAL INC, LES
583 Rang Saint-Ovide, Sainte-Sophie-De-
Levrard, QC, G0X 3C0
(819) 288-5287
Emp Here 50　　　*Sales* 3,064,349
SIC 7692 Welding repair

Sainte-Thecle, QC G0X
Megantic County

　　D-U-N-S 24-388-5733　　　(BR)
**CENTRE DE SANTE ET DE SERVICES SO-
CIAUX DE LA VALLEE-DE-LA-BATISCAN**
FOYER DE SAINTE-THECLE
651 Rue Saint-Jacques, Sainte-Thecle, QC,
G0X 3G0
(418) 289-2114
Emp Here 30
SIC 8361 Residential care

Sainte-Therese, QC J7E
Champlain County

　　D-U-N-S 24-005-3780　　　(BR)
ASPHALTE DESJARDINS INC
BETONNIERES MODERNES
300 Boul Ducharme, Sainte-Therese, QC, J7E
2E9
(450) 430-7160
Emp Here 20
SIC 3273 Ready-mixed concrete

　　D-U-N-S 25-242-8727　　　(SL)
**ASSOCIATION GENERALE DES ETUDI-
ANTS ET ETUDIANTES DU COLLEGE
LIONEL-GROULX INC**
A.G.E.E.C.L.G.
100 Rue Duquet, Sainte-Therese, QC, J7E
3G6

Emp Here 3,000　　　*Sales* 299,987,650
SIC 8641 Civic and social associations
Pr Stephane Godin

　　D-U-N-S 25-701-3490　　　(BR)
BANQUE NATIONALE DU CANADA
206 Boul Du Cure-Labelle, Sainte-Therese,
QC, J7E 2X7
(450) 430-2077
Emp Here 40
SIC 6021 National commercial banks

　　D-U-N-S 20-709-3956　　　(SL)
BLAINVILLE TOYOTA INC
120 Boul Desjardins E, Sainte-Therese, QC,
J7E 1C8
(450) 435-3685
Emp Here 40　　　*Sales* 20,096,000
SIC 5511 New and used car dealers
Pr Pr Marziale Piccoli

　　D-U-N-S 20-555-0267　　　(HQ)
CLSC-CHSLD THERESE DE BLAINVILLE
(*Suby of* CLSC-CHSLD Therese de Blainville)
55 Rue Saint-Joseph, Sainte-Therese, QC,
J7E 4Y5
(450) 430-4400
Emp Here 450　　　*Emp Total* 900
Sales 58,479,360
SIC 8051 Skilled nursing care facilities
Pr Robert Dean

　　D-U-N-S 25-689-0492　　　(BR)
**CAISSE DESJARDINS THERESE-DE
BLAINVILLE**
200 Boul Du Cure-Labelle Bureau 100,
Sainte-Therese, QC, J7E 2X5
(450) 430-6550
Emp Here 30
SIC 6062 State credit unions

　　D-U-N-S 24-012-0530　　　(BR)
CENTRE JEUNESSE DES LAURENTIDES
*PARTENAIRES POUR LA REUSSITE ED-
UCATIVE DANS LES LAURENTIDES*
120 Boul Du Seminaire, Sainte-Therese, QC,
J7E 1Z2
(450) 434-7735
Emp Here 20
SIC 8322 Individual and family services

　　D-U-N-S 24-637-0386　　　(SL)
**CENTRE DE SANTE ET DE SERVICES SO-
CIAUX DE THERESE-DE-BLAINVILLE**
*CENTRE D'HEBERGEMENT DRAPEAU-
DESCHAMBAULT*
125 Rue Duquet, Sainte-Therese, QC, J7E
0A5
(450) 430-4553
Emp Here 200　　　*Sales* 10,601,280
SIC 8322 Individual and family services
Pr Joe Belanger
VP Jean-Claude Langlois
VP Yvon Fournier
Sec Andre Poirier
Genl Mgr Diane Filiatrault

　　D-U-N-S 25-701-4019　　　(BR)
CINEMAS GUZZO INC

CINEMA STE THERESE
(*Suby of* Cinemas Guzzo Inc)
300 Rue Sicard Bureau 77, Sainte-Therese,
QC, J7E 3X5
(450) 979-4444
Emp Here 20
SIC 7832 Motion picture theaters, except
drive-in

　　D-U-N-S 20-928-6244　　　(SL)
COLLEGE LIONEL-GROULX
*COLLEGE D'ENSEIGNEMENT GENERAL
ET PROFESSIONEL LIONEL-GROULX*
100 Rue Duquet, Sainte-Therese, QC, J7E
3G6
(450) 430-3120
Emp Here 650　　　*Sales* 87,353,898
SIC 8221 Colleges and universities
Genl Mgr Claude Shayer
Ch Bd Marcel Menard

　　D-U-N-S 20-712-1539　　　(BR)
**COMMISSION SCOLAIRE DE LA
SEIGNEURIE-DES-MILLE-ILES**
*COMMISSION SCOLAIRE DE LA
SEIGNEURIE-DES-MILLE-ILES*
125 Rue Beauchamp, Sainte-Therese, QC,
J7E 5A4
(450) 433-5432
Emp Here 70
SIC 8211 Elementary and secondary schools

　　D-U-N-S 20-712-1604　　　(BR)
**COMMISSION SCOLAIRE DE LA
SEIGNEURIE-DES-MILLE-ILES**
*COMMISSION SCOLAIRE DE LA
SEIGNEURIE-DES-MILLE-ILES*
301 Boul Du Domaine, Sainte-Therese, QC,
J7E 4S4
(450) 433-5435
Emp Here 25
SIC 8211 Elementary and secondary schools

　　D-U-N-S 25-234-1383　　　(BR)
**COMMISSION SCOLAIRE DE LA
SEIGNEURIE-DES-MILLE-ILES**
*COMMISSION SCOLAIRE DE LA
SEIGNEURIE-DES-MILLE-ILES*
(*Suby of* Commission Scolaire de la
Seigneurie-Des-Mille-Iles)
70 Rue Saint-Stanislas, Sainte-Therese, QC,
J7E 3M7
(450) 433-5500
Emp Here 20
SIC 8211 Elementary and secondary schools

　　D-U-N-S 25-240-1443　　　(BR)
**COMMISSION SCOLAIRE DE LA
SEIGNEURIE-DES-MILLE-ILES**
ECOLE SAINTE-THERESE
(*Suby of* Commission Scolaire de la
Seigneurie-Des-Mille-Iles)
401 Boul Du Domaine, Sainte-Therese, QC,
J7E 4S4
(450) 433-5400
Emp Here 225
SIC 8211 Elementary and secondary schools

　　D-U-N-S 20-712-1646　　　(BR)
**COMMISSION SCOLAIRE DE LA
SEIGNEURIE-DES-MILLE-ILES**
*COMMISSION SCOLAIRE DE LA
SEIGNEURIE-DES-MILLE-ILES*
75 Rue Duquet, Sainte-Therese, QC, J7E 5R8
(450) 433-5480
Emp Here 50
SIC 8221 Colleges and universities

　　D-U-N-S 25-359-5367　　　(BR)
**COMMISSION SCOLAIRE DE LA
SEIGNEURIE-DES-MILLE-ILES**
*COMMISSION SCOLAIRE DE LA
SEIGNEURIE-DES-MILLE-ILES*
(*Suby of* Commission Scolaire de la
Seigneurie-Des-Mille-Iles)
101 Rue Blanchard, Sainte-Therese, QC, J7E
4N4

(450) 433-4612
Emp Here 30
SIC 8211 Elementary and secondary schools

D-U-N-S 25-233-9965   (BR)
COMMISSION SCOLAIRE DE LA SEIGNEURIE-DES-MILLE-ILES
ECOLE ST GABRIEL
(*Suby of* Commission Scolaire de la Seigneurie-Des-Mille-Iles)
8 Rue Tasse, Sainte-Therese, QC, J7E 1V3
(450) 433-5445
Emp Here 80
SIC 8211 Elementary and secondary schools

D-U-N-S 25-233-3661   (BR)
COMMISSION SCOLAIRE DE LA SEIGNEURIE-DES-MILLE-ILES
COMMISSION SCOLAIRE DE LA SEIGNEURIE-DES-MILLE-ILES
(*Suby of* Commission Scolaire de la Seigneurie-Des-Mille-Iles)
10 Rue Belisle, Sainte-Therese, QC, J7E 3P6
(450) 433-5525
Emp Here 40
SIC 8211 Elementary and secondary schools

D-U-N-S 25-234-1581   (BR)
COMMISSION SCOLAIRE DE LA SEIGNEURIE-DES-MILLE-ILES
COMMISSION SCOLAIRE DE LA SEIGNEURIE-DES-MILLE-ILES
(*Suby of* Commission Scolaire de la Seigneurie-Des-Mille-Iles)
201 Rue Saint-Pierre, Sainte-Therese, QC, J7E 2S3
(450) 433-5545
Emp Here 40
SIC 8211 Elementary and secondary schools

D-U-N-S 25-234-1540   (BR)
COMMISSION SCOLAIRE DE LA SEIGNEURIE-DES-MILLE-ILES
COMMISSION SCOLAIRE DE LA SEIGNEURIE-DES-MILLE-ILES
(*Suby of* Commission Scolaire de la Seigneurie-Des-Mille-Iles)
800 Rue De Seve, Sainte-Therese, QC, J7E 2M6
(450) 433-5355
Emp Here 20
SIC 8211 Elementary and secondary schools

D-U-N-S 24-490-9768   (BR)
EDITIONS BLAINVILLE-DEUX-MONTAGNES INC, LES
LA VOIX DES MILLE ILES
50b Rue Turgeon Bureau 248, Sainte-Therese, QC, J7E 3H4
(450) 435-6537
Emp Here 20
SIC 2711 Newspapers

D-U-N-S 20-258-2128   (SL)
FORMES UNITED INC
COMPOSANTS J V CANADA, DIV OF
(*Suby of* Jones & Vining, Incorporated)
101 Boul Du Cure-Labelle, Sainte-Therese, QC, J7E 2X6
(450) 435-1977
Emp Here 60   *Sales* 7,587,913
SIC 3089 Plastics products, nec
Pr Pr Tom Iredale
Sven Jr Vaule

D-U-N-S 24-065-4843   (BR)
GESTION IMMOBILIERE LUC MAURICE INC
RESIDENCES DU MARCHE, LES
(*Suby of* Gestion Immobiliere Luc Maurice Inc)
25 Rue Du Marche Bureau 435, Sainte-Therese, QC, J7E 5T2
(450) 433-6544
Emp Here 30
SIC 6513 Apartment building operators

D-U-N-S 20-261-8612   (BR)

GOUVERNEMENT DE LA PROVINCE DE QUEBEC
CENTRES JEUNESSE DES LAURENTIDES, LES
6 Rue De L'Eglise Bureau 330, Sainte-Therese, QC, J7E 3L1
(450) 430-6900
Emp Here 50
SIC 8322 Individual and family services

D-U-N-S 25-787-8132   (BR)
GROUPE BMTC INC
BRAULT & MARTINEAU
125 Boul Desjardins E, Sainte-Therese, QC, J7E 1C5
(450) 430-0555
Emp Here 60
SIC 5712 Furniture stores

D-U-N-S 25-307-2904   (BR)
GROUPE JEAN COUTU (PJC) INC, LE
PHARMACIE JEAN COUTU #54
(*Suby of* 3958230 Canada Inc)
253 Boul Labelle, Sainte-Therese, QC, J7E 2X6
(450) 437-9151
Emp Here 40
SIC 5912 Drug stores and proprietary stores

D-U-N-S 25-027-5914   (BR)
GROUPE SPORTSCENE INC
CAGE AUX SPORTS
100 Place Fabien-Drapeau, Sainte-Therese, QC, J7E 5W6
(450) 434-2243
Emp Here 50
SIC 5812 Eating places

D-U-N-S 24-501-3933   (SL)
LES PLACEMENTS ANDRE SOUCY LTEE
255 Boul Du Cure-Labelle, Sainte-Therese, QC, J7E 2X6
(450) 437-4476
Emp Here 50   *Sales* 5,072,500
SIC 7533 Auto exhaust system repair shops
Pr Pr France Merrette Soucy

D-U-N-S 24-177-1534   (BR)
PACCAR OF CANADA LTD
PACCAR LEASING
(*Suby of* Paccar Inc)
10 Rue Sicard, Sainte-Therese, QC, J7E 4K9
(450) 435-6171
Emp Here 800
SIC 3711 Motor vehicles and car bodies

D-U-N-S 24-406-1552   (SL)
RESTAURANT LA STANZA INC
380 Boul Labelle, Sainte-Therese, QC, J7E 2Y1

Emp Here 50   *Sales* 2,061,360
SIC 5812 Eating places

D-U-N-S 25-701-6022   (SL)
RESTAURANT LE FRIAND'OEUF INC
190 Boul Du Cure-Labelle, Sainte-Therese, QC, J7E 2X5
(450) 437-1261
Emp Here 50   *Sales* 1,532,175
SIC 5812 Eating places

D-U-N-S 25-701-3516   (BR)
ROYAL BANK OF CANADA
ROYAL BANK OF CANADA
(*Suby of* Royal Bank Of Canada)
60 Rue Turgeon, Sainte-Therese, QC, J7E 3H4
(450) 433-2202
Emp Here 20
SIC 6021 National commercial banks

D-U-N-S 25-233-9718   (BR)
SAINTE-THERESE, VILLE DE
BIBLIOTHEQUE DE LA VILLE DE SAINTE THERESE
150 Boul Du Seminaire, Sainte-Therese, QC, J7E 1Z2

(450) 434-1440
Emp Here 20
SIC 8231 Libraries

D-U-N-S 25-498-9759   (BR)
STAPLES CANADA INC
BUREAU EN GROS
(*Suby of* Staples, Inc.)
315 Boul Du Cure-Labelle, Sainte-Therese, QC, J7E 2Y2
(450) 435-7121
Emp Here 50
SIC 5943 Stationery stores

Sainte-Victoire-De-Sorel, QC J0G
Richelieu County

D-U-N-S 25-234-1904   (BR)
COMMISSION SCOLAIRE DE SOREL-TRACY
ECOLE PRIMAIRES SAINTE VICTOIRE
(*Suby of* Commission Scolaire de Sorel-Tracy)
345 Montee Sainte-Victoire, Sainte-Victoire-De-Sorel, QC, J0G 1T0
(450) 746-3511
Emp Here 30
SIC 8211 Elementary and secondary schools

D-U-N-S 20-698-1107   (BR)
MINERAUX MART INC
(*Suby of* Mineraux Mart Inc)
206 Rang Nord, Sainte-Victoire-De-Sorel, QC, J0G 1T0
(450) 782-2233
Emp Here 30
SIC 4226 Special warehousing and storage, nec

D-U-N-S 24-548-6316   (BR)
MINERAUX MART INC
(*Suby of* Mineraux Mart Inc)
206 Rang Nord, Sainte-Victoire-De-Sorel, QC, J0G 1T0
(450) 743-9200
Emp Here 26
SIC 1481 NonMetallic mineral services

Saints-Anges, QC G0S
Beauce County

D-U-N-S 20-030-4199   (BR)
COMMISSION SCOLAIRE DE LA BEAUCE-ETCHEMIN
ECOLE PRIMAIRE DE SAINTS ANGES
320 Rue Des Erables, Saints-Anges, QC, G0S 3E0
(418) 253-6234
Emp Here 30
SIC 8211 Elementary and secondary schools

Salaberry-De-Valleyfield, QC J6S
Beauharnois County

D-U-N-S 24-164-7408   (SL)
9129-0163 QUEBEC INC
MAISON DES COTTONIERS, LA
39 Rue Buntin, Salaberry-De-Valleyfield, QC, J6S 6V9
(450) 377-9200
Emp Here 50   *Sales* 1,824,018
SIC 8361 Residential care

D-U-N-S 20-517-1882   (BR)
ASTENJOHNSON, INC
(*Suby of* Astenjohnson, Inc.)
213 Boul Du Havre, Salaberry-De-Valleyfield, QC, J6S 1R9
(450) 373-2425
Emp Here 126

SIC 2299 Textile goods, nec

D-U-N-S 20-264-5792   (SL)
AUTOBUS VENISE LTEE
50 Rue Mcarthur, Salaberry-De-Valleyfield, QC, J6S 4M5
(450) 373-4144
Emp Here 50   *Sales* 1,386,253
SIC 4151 School buses

D-U-N-S 24-676-2657   (BR)
BAU-VAL INC
CARRIERES REGIONALES
355 Boul Monseigneur-Langlois, Salaberry-De-Valleyfield, QC, J6S 0G5
(450) 377-4544
Emp Here 20
SIC 1429 Crushed and broken stone, nec

D-U-N-S 25-957-2279   (BR)
CRH CANADA GROUP INC
DEMIX BETON
189 Rue Des Betonnieres, Salaberry-De-Valleyfield, QC, J6S 0A5
(450) 373-3322
Emp Here 35
SIC 5032 Brick, stone, and related material

D-U-N-S 20-652-7702   (HQ)
CAISSE DESJARDINS DE SALABERRY-DE-VALLEYFIELD
CENTRE DE SERVICE SAINT-THOMAS
(*Suby of* Caisse Desjardins de Salaberry-de-Valleyfield)
120 Rue Alexandre, Salaberry-De-Valleyfield, QC, J6S 3K4
(450) 377-4177
Emp Here 60   *Emp Total* 100
Sales 15,890,840
SIC 6062 State credit unions
Genl Mgr Gino Napoleoni
Pr Pr Yvon Vinet
VP Jean-Francois Gagnon
Sec Marcel Gougeon
Dir Nancy Daoust
Dir Jean-Michel Montpetit
Dir Martin Pilotte
Dir Patricia Gagne Claude
Dir Jean-Luc Vincent
Dir Nicolas Julien

D-U-N-S 20-363-4329   (SL)
CENTRE DE MAINTENANCE ANDY INC, LE
4225 Boul Hebert, Salaberry-De-Valleyfield, QC, J6S 6J2
(514) 667-8500
Emp Here 26   *Sales* 6,420,542
SIC 4731 Freight transportation arrangement
Pr Ilie Crisan
Sec Andreea Crisan
Treas Golan Moryoussef

D-U-N-S 20-883-2068   (BR)
COGECO COMMUNICATIONS INC
13 Rue Saint-Urbain, Salaberry-De-Valleyfield, QC, J6S 4M6
(450) 377-1373
Emp Here 20
SIC 4841 Cable and other pay television services

D-U-N-S 25-233-8215   (BR)
COMMISSION SCOLAIRE DE LA VALLEE-DES-TISSERANDS, LA
ECOLE SACRE COEUR
285 Rue Alphonse-Desjardins, Salaberry-De-Valleyfield, QC, J6S 2P2
(450) 373-1270
Emp Here 35
SIC 8211 Elementary and secondary schools

D-U-N-S 20-712-3402   (BR)
COMMISSION SCOLAIRE DE LA VALLEE-DES-TISSERANDS, LA
CENTRE DU NOUVEL ENVOL
115 Rue Saint-Charles, Salaberry-De-Valleyfield, QC, J6S 4A2

(450) 371-2006
Emp Here 30
SIC 8211 Elementary and secondary schools

D-U-N-S 25-233-8371   (BR)
COMMISSION SCOLAIRE DE LA VALLEE-DES-TISSERANDS, LA
ECOLE SAINT EUGENE
415 Rue Dufferin, Salaberry-De-Valleyfield, QC, J6S 2A9
(450) 373-0673
Emp Here 30
SIC 8211 Elementary and secondary schools

D-U-N-S 25-233-9486   (BR)
COMMISSION SCOLAIRE DE LA VALLEE-DES-TISSERANDS, LA
ECOLE MONTPETIT
537 Rue Montpetit, Salaberry-De-Valleyfield, QC, J6S 4A7
(450) 373-2420
Emp Here 25
SIC 8211 Elementary and secondary schools

D-U-N-S 25-233-8850   (BR)
COMMISSION SCOLAIRE DE LA VALLEE-DES-TISSERANDS, LA
ECOLE ELISABETH MONETTE
10 Rue Kent, Salaberry-De-Valleyfield, QC, J6S 4T3
(450) 373-1256
Emp Here 30
SIC 8211 Elementary and secondary schools

D-U-N-S 25-233-8454   (BR)
COMMISSION SCOLAIRE DE LA VALLEE-DES-TISSERANDS, LA
ECOLE SAINTE-AGNES
269 Rue Grande-Ile, Salaberry-De-Valleyfield, QC, J6S 3N3
(450) 373-2616
Emp Here 20
SIC 8211 Elementary and secondary schools

D-U-N-S 24-072-6260   (SL)
DASSYLOI INC
575 Rue Gaetan, Salaberry-De-Valleyfield, QC, J6S 0A7
(450) 377-5204
Emp Here 30   *Sales* 6,784,769
SIC 1623 Water, sewer, and utility lines
Pr Daniel Loiselle

D-U-N-S 24-802-8453   (BR)
E-CYCLE SOLUTIONS INC
ECYCLE SOLUTIONS
35 Rue Robineault, Salaberry-De-Valleyfield, QC, J6S 5J9
(888) 945-2611
Emp Here 20
SIC 4953 Refuse systems

D-U-N-S 20-514-8930   (BR)
GCP CANADA INC
GRACE CANADA, INC
(*Suby of* W. R. Grace & Co.)
42 Rue Fabre, Salaberry-De-Valleyfield, QC, J6S 4K7
(450) 373-4224
Emp Here 120
SIC 2819 Industrial inorganic chemicals, nec

D-U-N-S 20-631-7646   (BR)
GOODYEAR CANADA INC
(*Suby of* The Goodyear Tire & Rubber Company)
2600 Boul Monseigneur-Langlois, Salaberry-De-Valleyfield, QC, J6S 5G6
(450) 377-6800
Emp Here 200
SIC 3011 Tires and inner tubes

D-U-N-S 24-900-3146   (SL)
INDUSTRIES B & X INC
(*Suby of* 7956576 Canada Inc)
501 Imp Martin, Salaberry-De-Valleyfield, QC, J6S 4C6
(450) 373-9292
Emp Here 50   *Sales* 10,404,960

SIC 3443 Fabricated plate work (boiler shop)
Pr Bernard Brunet

D-U-N-S 24-815-0724   (SL)
MAISON DES AINEES DE ST-TIMOTHEE INC
1 Rue Des Aines, Salaberry-De-Valleyfield, QC, J6S 6M8
(450) 377-3925
Emp Here 70   *Sales* 2,772,507
SIC 8322 Individual and family services

D-U-N-S 25-835-1766   (BR)
PROVIGO INC
MAXI
70 Rue Dufferin, Salaberry-De-Valleyfield, QC, J6S 1Y2
(450) 377-7670
Emp Here 57
SIC 5411 Grocery stores

D-U-N-S 25-307-6715   (BR)
SOCIETE DES ALCOOLS DU QUEBEC
SAQ
2150 Boul Monseigneur-Langlois, Salaberry-De-Valleyfield, QC, J6S 5R1
(450) 377-8332
Emp Here 35
SIC 5921 Liquor stores

D-U-N-S 25-372-8034   (BR)
STAPLES CANADA INC
BUREAU EN GROS
(*Suby of* Staples, Inc.)
1560 Boul Monseigneur-Langlois, Salaberry-De-Valleyfield, QC, J6S 1E3
(450) 373-7070
Emp Here 27
SIC 5943 Stationery stores

D-U-N-S 20-568-0077   (BR)
UNIVAR CANADA LTD
100 Rue Mcarthur, Salaberry-De-Valleyfield, QC, J6S 4M5
(450) 371-1086
Emp Here 40
SIC 4226 Special warehousing and storage, nec

D-U-N-S 24-321-3597   (SL)
VICONTE INC
CENTRE VICTOR-LEGER
26 Rue Saint-Philippe, Salaberry-De-Valleyfield, QC, J6S 5X8
(450) 371-3763
Emp Here 55   *Sales* 2,042,900
SIC 8361 Residential care

D-U-N-S 20-715-8077   (BR)
VILLE DE SALABERRY DE VALLEYFIELD
SERVICE DE L'ENVIRONNEMENT ET DES TRAVAUX PUBLICS
275 Rue Hebert, Salaberry-De-Valleyfield, QC, J6S 5Y9
(450) 370-4820
Emp Here 100
SIC 8743 Public relations services

D-U-N-S 20-330-7731   (SL)
W. R. GRACE CANADA CORP
(*Suby of* W. R. Grace & Co.)
42 Rue Fabre, Salaberry-De-Valleyfield, QC, J6S 4K7
(450) 373-4224
Emp Here 112   *Sales* 23,493,345
SIC 2819 Industrial inorganic chemicals, nec
Pr Pr Alfred E. Festa
VP Genevieve Fortier
VP Mark A. Shelnitz
Sec John A. Mcfarland
Dir Thomas E. Blaser

D-U-N-S 20-643-9619   (BR)
WAL-MART CANADA CORP
ACCES PHARMA CHEZ WALMART
2050 Boul Monseigneur-Langlois, Salaberry-De-Valleyfield, QC, J6S 5R1

(450) 371-9026
Emp Here 208
SIC 5311 Department stores

Salaberry-De-Valleyfield, QC J6T
Beauharnois County

D-U-N-S 24-896-4488   (BR)
AKZO NOBEL PATE ET PERFORMANCE CANADA INC
EKA CHIMIE
640 Boul Des Erables, Salaberry-De-Valleyfield, QC, J6T 6G4
(450) 377-1131
Emp Here 50
SIC 2899 Chemical preparations, nec

D-U-N-S 24-357-6340   (SL)
ATELIER D'USINAGE QUENNEVILLE INC
ACIER DEMERS
(*Suby of* 9092-4127 Quebec Inc)
39 Av Du Parc, Salaberry-De-Valleyfield, QC, J6T 2R1
(450) 377-5991
Emp Here 40   *Sales* 5,884,100
SIC 3569 General industrial machinery, nec
Pr Pr Renee Demers
 Jocelyn Demers

D-U-N-S 24-351-2683   (BR)
CAISSE DESJARDINS DE SALABERRY-DE-VALLEYFIELD
(*Suby of* Caisse Desjardins de Salaberry-de-Valleyfield)
15 Rue Saint-Thomas, Salaberry-De-Valleyfield, QC, J6T 4J1
(450) 377-4177
Emp Here 100
SIC 6062 State credit unions

D-U-N-S 25-868-5643   (BR)
CANADA POST CORPORATION
180 Rue Victoria, Salaberry-De-Valleyfield, QC, J6T 0B6
(450) 373-3030
Emp Here 50
SIC 4311 U.s. postal service

D-U-N-S 20-914-4497   (BR)
CENTRE DE SANTE ET DE SERVICES SO-CIAUX DU SUROIT
CLINIQUE EXTERNE EN SANTE MENTAL
181 Rue Victoria Bureau 200, Salaberry-De-Valleyfield, QC, J6T 1A7
(450) 373-6252
Emp Here 25
SIC 8011 Offices and clinics of medical doctors

D-U-N-S 20-712-3378   (BR)
COMMISSION SCOLAIRE DE LA VALLEE-DES-TISSERANDS, LA
CENTRE DE FORMATION PROFESSION-NELLE DE LA POINTE-D
445 Rue Jacques-Cartier, Salaberry-De-Valleyfield, QC, J6T 6L9
(450) 373-2009
Emp Here 65
SIC 8211 Elementary and secondary schools

D-U-N-S 20-712-3410   (BR)
COMMISSION SCOLAIRE DE LA VALLEE-DES-TISSERANDS, LA
ECOLE BAIE SAINT FRANCOIS
70 Rue Louis Vi-Major, Salaberry-De-Valleyfield, QC, J6T 3G2
(450) 371-2004
Emp Here 130
SIC 8211 Elementary and secondary schools

D-U-N-S 25-233-8256   (BR)
COMMISSION SCOLAIRE DE LA VALLEE-DES-TISSERANDS, LA
ECOLE LANGLOIS
316 Rue Saint-Jean-Baptiste, Salaberry-De-

Valleyfield, QC, J6T 2A9
(450) 373-6661
Emp Here 20
SIC 8211 Elementary and secondary schools

D-U-N-S 24-374-0938   (BR)
DIAGEO CANADA INC
(*Suby of* DIAGEO PLC)
1 Rue Salaberry, Salaberry-De-Valleyfield, QC, J6T 2G9
(450) 373-3230
Emp Here 200
SIC 5182 Wine and distilled beverages

D-U-N-S 24-745-7950   (BR)
FONDATION DU CENTRE JEUNESSE DE LA MONTEREGIE
CSRE VALLEYFIELD
30 Rue Saint-Thomas Bureau 300, Salaberry-De-Valleyfield, QC, J6T 4J2
(450) 377-0540
Emp Here 30
SIC 8322 Individual and family services

D-U-N-S 20-577-9007   (BR)
GOUVERNEMENT DE LA PROVINCE DE QUEBEC
PALAIS DE JUSTICE
180 Rue Salaberry, Salaberry-De-Valleyfield, QC, J6T 2J2
(450) 370-4004
Emp Here 50
SIC 8111 Legal services

D-U-N-S 24-005-4747   (BR)
METRO RICHELIEU INC
METRO PLUS
398 Ch Larocque, Salaberry-De-Valleyfield, QC, J6T 4C5
(450) 370-1444
Emp Here 80
SIC 5411 Grocery stores

D-U-N-S 24-348-1152   (BR)
SERVICES DE READAPTATION SUD OUEST ET DU RENFORT, LES
30 Rue Saint-Thomas Bureau 200, Salaberry-De-Valleyfield, QC, J6T 4J2
(450) 371-4816
Emp Here 600
SIC 8361 Residential care

D-U-N-S 20-704-8112   (SL)
SOCIETE EN COMMANDITE REVENUE NO-RANDA
860 Boul Gerard-Cadieux, Salaberry-De-Valleyfield, QC, J6T 6L4
(450) 373-9144
Emp Here 600
SIC 3339 Primary nonferrous Metals, nec

Salluit, QC J0M
Nouveau-Quebec County

D-U-N-S 20-716-8126   (BR)
COMMISSION SCOLAIRE KATIVIK
Gd, Salluit, QC, J0M 1S0
(819) 255-8931
Emp Here 30
SIC 8211 Elementary and secondary schools

Sayabec, QC G0J
Matapedia County

D-U-N-S 24-908-2421   (BR)
AIDE-MAISON VALLEE DE LA MATAPEDIA
VILLA GEORGES FOURNIER
(*Suby of* Aide-Maison Vallee de la Matapedia)
1 Rue Saindon, Sayabec, QC, G0J 3K0
(418) 536-5456
Emp Here 30
SIC 8361 Residential care

D-U-N-S 25-004-2694   (BR)
COMMISSION SCOLAIRE DE MONTS-ET-MAREES
POLYVALENTE DE SAYABEC
(*Suby of* Commission Scolaire De Monts-Et-Marees)
8 Rue Keable, Sayabec, QC, G0J 3K0
(418) 536-5431
Emp Here 30
SIC 8211 Elementary and secondary schools

D-U-N-S 25-022-6974   (BR)
COMMISSION SCOLAIRE DES MONTS-ET-MAREES
ECOLE SAINTE-MARIE
3 Rue De L'Eglise, Sayabec, QC, G0J 3K0
(418) 536-5481
Emp Here 26
SIC 8211 Elementary and secondary schools

D-U-N-S 24-591-4205   (BR)
UNIBOARD CANADA INC
152 Rte Pouliot, Sayabec, QC, G0J 3K0
(418) 536-5465
Emp Here 400
SIC 2493 Reconstituted wood products

Scott, QC G0S
Dorchester County

D-U-N-S 25-233-6078   (BR)
COMMISSION SCOLAIRE DE LA BEAUCE-ETCHEMIN
ECOLE L'ACCUEIL (057)
1030 Rte Du President-Kennedy, Scott, QC, G0S 3G0
(418) 386-5541
Emp Here 21
SIC 8211 Elementary and secondary schools

D-U-N-S 24-884-7055   (HQ)
IMPRIMERIE SOLISCO INC
SOLISCOM
(*Suby of* 2856-8848 Quebec Inc)
120 10e Rue, Scott, QC, G0S 3G0
(418) 387-8908
Emp Here 320   *Emp Total* 450
Sales 30,492,035
SIC 2752 Commercial printing, lithographic
Alain Jacques
Pr Andre Heroux

Senneterre, QC J0Y
Abitibi County

D-U-N-S 24-389-5583   (BR)
CENTRE DE SANTE ET DE SERVICES SOCIAUX DE LA VALLEE-DE-L'OR
CLSC DE SENNETERRE
961 Rue De La Clinique, Senneterre, QC, J0Y 2M0

Emp Here 50
SIC 8062 General medical and surgical hospitals

D-U-N-S 25-240-4207   (BR)
COMMISSION SCOLAIRE DE L'OR-ET-DES-BOIS
ECOLE CHANOINE DELISLE
(*Suby of* Commission Scolaire de l'Or-et-des-Bois)
361 4e Rue O, Senneterre, QC, J0Y 2M0
(819) 737-2321
Emp Here 40
SIC 8211 Elementary and secondary schools

D-U-N-S 20-712-6207   (BR)
COMMISSION SCOLAIRE DE L'OR-ET-DES-BOIS
ECOLE SECONDAIRE LA CONCORDE

(*Suby of* Commission Scolaire de l'Or-et-des-Bois)
40 Rte 386, Senneterre, QC, J0Y 2M0
(819) 737-2386
Emp Here 40
SIC 8211 Elementary and secondary schools

D-U-N-S 20-573-2493   (BR)
COMPAGNIE DES CHEMINS DE FER NATIONAUX DU CANADA
171 4e Rue O, Senneterre, QC, J0Y 2M0
(819) 737-8121
Emp Here 100
SIC 4111 Local and suburban transit

D-U-N-S 25-073-6415   (BR)
PF RESOLU CANADA INC
40 Ch Saint-Pierre, Senneterre, QC, J0Y 2M0
(819) 737-2300
Emp Here 140
SIC 2621 Paper mills

Senneville, QC H9X
Hochelaga County

D-U-N-S 25-234-0294   (BR)
COMMISSION SCOLAIRE MARGUERITE-BOURGEOYS
ECOLE SECONDAIRE SAINT GEORGES
300 Rue Sainte-Anne, Senneville, QC, H9X 3P7
(514) 855-4241
Emp Here 60
SIC 8211 Elementary and secondary schools

D-U-N-S 24-743-2339   (SL)
FABRICATION KLETON INC
22555 Aut Transcanadienne, Senneville, QC, H9X 3L7
(514) 457-6865
Emp Here 31   *Sales* 3,429,153
SIC 3499 Fabricated Metal products, nec

D-U-N-S 20-418-3255   (HQ)
TENAQUIP LIMITEE
ATTACHES KINGSTON
22555 Aut Transcanadienne, Senneville, QC, H9X 3L7
(514) 457-7801
Emp Here 210   *Emp Total* 280
Sales 53,334,272
SIC 5085 Industrial supplies
Pr Shirley Reed
VP David Reed
  Glenn Watt

Sept-Iles, QC G4R
Saguenay County

D-U-N-S 25-488-9769   (HQ)
116106 CANADA INC
TIM HORTON
(*Suby of* 116106 Canada Inc)
810 Boul Laure, Sept-Iles, QC, G4R 0E8
(418) 962-1254
Emp Here 65   *Emp Total* 140
Sales 4,231,721
SIC 5812 Eating places

D-U-N-S 24-689-5767   (SL)
2424-4931 QUEBEC INC
VIGNEAULT AUTOMOBILES
119 Rue Monseigneur-Blanche, Sept-Iles, QC, G4R 3G7
(418) 962-2555
Emp Here 25   *Sales* 12,560,000
SIC 5511 New and used car dealers
Pr Pr Richard Vigneault
  Louis Vigneault

D-U-N-S 20-281-4476   (BR)
2553-4330 QUEBEC INC

AEROPRO
(*Suby of* 2553-4330 Quebec Inc)
18 Aviation General E, Sept-Iles, QC, G4R 4K2
(418) 961-2808
Emp Here 250
SIC 4512 Air transportation, scheduled

D-U-N-S 20-290-0189   (BR)
ARAMARK QUEBEC INC
441 Av Brochu Bureau 101, Sept-Iles, QC, G4R 2W9
(418) 968-7537
Emp Here 35
SIC 5812 Eating places

D-U-N-S 24-329-9414   (SL)
AUTOBUS DU FER INC
126 Rue Monseigneur-Blanche, Sept-Iles, QC, G4R 3G8
(418) 968-9515
Emp Here 20   *Sales* 561,797
SIC 4151 School buses

D-U-N-S 24-530-4456   (BR)
AXOR EXPERTS-CONSEILS INC
660 Boul Laure Bureau 105, Sept-Iles, QC, G4R 1X9
(418) 968-1320
Emp Here 35
SIC 8711 Engineering services

D-U-N-S 20-266-1401   (BR)
BIBLIOTHEQUE ET ARCHIVES NATIONALES DU QUEBEC
BANQ
700 Boul Laure Bureau 190, Sept-Iles, QC, G4R 1Y1
(418) 964-8434
Emp Here 25
SIC 8231 Libraries

D-U-N-S 24-853-7487   (BR)
BIRON LABORATOIRE MEDICAL INC
BIRON SOIN DU SOMMEIL
140 Rue Du Pere-Divet, Sept-Iles, QC, G4R 3P6
(418) 960-2345
Emp Here 25
SIC 7363 Help supply services

D-U-N-S 20-540-7567   (BR)
CANADA POST CORPORATION
POSTAL OUTLETS FOR PRODUCTS AND SERVICES
203-701 Boul Laure, Sept-Iles, QC, G4R 0G6
(418) 962-7730
Emp Here 40
SIC 4311 U.s. postal service

D-U-N-S 20-532-2741   (BR)
CANADIAN BROADCASTING CORPORATION
RADIO CANADA
350 Rue Smith Bureau 30, Sept-Iles, QC, G4R 3X2
(418) 968-0720
Emp Here 22
SIC 4832 Radio broadcasting stations

D-U-N-S 20-261-8422   (BR)
CENTRE DE PROTECTION ET DE READAPTATION DE LA COTE-NORD
CENTRE JEUNESSE COTE NORD
(*Suby of* Centre de Protection et de Readaptation de la Cote-Nord)
128 Rue Regnault Bureau 206, Sept-Iles, QC, G4R 5T9
(418) 962-2578
Emp Here 50
SIC 8399 Social services, nec

D-U-N-S 25-240-0395   (BR)
COMMISSION SCOLAIRE DU FER
ECOLE GAMACHE
532 Av Gamache, Sept-Iles, QC, G4R 2J2
(418) 962-7781
Emp Here 35
SIC 8211 Elementary and secondary schools

D-U-N-S 25-233-7787   (BR)
COMMISSION SCOLAIRE DU FER
ECOLE JACQUES-CARTIER
10 Rue Johnny-Montigny, Sept-Iles, QC, G4R 1W3
(418) 962-6156
Emp Here 50
SIC 8211 Elementary and secondary schools

D-U-N-S 20-712-6454   (BR)
COMMISSION SCOLAIRE DU FER
CENTRE DE FORMATION PROFESSIONNELLE ET GENERALE A.W. GAGNE
9 Rue De La Verendrye, Sept-Iles, QC, G4R 5E3
(418) 964-2881
Emp Here 45
SIC 8221 Colleges and universities

D-U-N-S 25-240-0718   (BR)
COMMISSION SCOLAIRE DU FER
ECOLE MANIKOUTAI
40 Rue Comeau, Sept-Iles, QC, G4R 4N3
(418) 964-2760
Emp Here 50
SIC 8211 Elementary and secondary schools

D-U-N-S 25-240-0593   (BR)
COMMISSION SCOLAIRE DU FER
ECOLE MAISONNEUVE
18 Rue Maisonneuve, Sept-Iles, QC, G4R 1C7
(418) 962-6198
Emp Here 40
SIC 8211 Elementary and secondary schools

D-U-N-S 25-240-0676   (BR)
COMMISSION SCOLAIRE DU FER
COMMISSION SCOLAIRE DU FER
110 Rue Comeau, Sept-Iles, QC, G4R 1J4
(418) 964-2811
Emp Here 80
SIC 8211 Elementary and secondary schools

D-U-N-S 24-375-6587   (BR)
COMMISSION DE LA SANTE ET DE LA SECURITE DU TRAVAIL
COMMISSION DE LA SANTE ET DE LA SECURITE DU TRAVAIL
700 Boul Laure Bureau 236, Sept-Iles, QC, G4R 1Y1
(418) 964-3900
Emp Here 45
SIC 6331 Fire, marine, and casualty insurance

D-U-N-S 24-895-9202   (BR)
COMPAGNIE MINIERE IOC INC
1 Rue Retty, Sept-Iles, QC, G4R 3C7
(418) 968-7400
Emp Here 475
SIC 1011 Iron ores

D-U-N-S 24-417-2081   (SL)
COMPAGNIE DE CHEMIN DE FER ARNAUD
(*Suby of* Mines Wabush)
1505 Pointe Noire, Sept-Iles, QC, G4R 4L4
(418) 964-3101
Emp Here 440   *Sales* 19,788,909
SIC 4011 Railroads, line-haul operating
Pr D.B Blake
VP T.R. Mee
VP D.J Gallagher
Sec James D. Graham

D-U-N-S 20-644-0703   (BR)
GOUVERNEUR INC
GOUVERNEURS SEPT ILES
666 Boul Laure, Sept-Iles, QC, G4R 1X9
(418) 962-7071
Emp Here 20
SIC 7011 Hotels and motels

D-U-N-S 25-305-2039   (BR)
INNVEST PROPERTIES CORP
COMFORT INN
(*Suby of* Innvest Properties Corp)
854 Boul Laure, Sept-Iles, QC, G4R 1Y7
(418) 968-6005
Emp Here 20

SIC 7011 Hotels and motels

D-U-N-S 20-431-9354   (BR)
LOCATION HEWITT INC
400 Boul Laure, Sept-Iles, QC, G4R 1X4
(418) 962-7791
Emp Here 20
SIC 5082 Construction and mining machinery

D-U-N-S 24-893-7935   (BR)
LOGISTEC STEVEDORING INC
400 Ch De Ln Pointe-N, Sept-Iles, QC, G4R
5C7
(418) 962-7638
Emp Here 50
SIC 4491 Marine cargo handling

D-U-N-S 20-952-4529   (BR)
PRISZM LP
KFC
602 Boul Laure, Sept-Iles, QC, G4R 1X9
(418) 962-7487
Emp Here 20
SIC 5812 Eating places

D-U-N-S 25-211-8781   (BR)
PROVIGO DISTRIBUTION INC
649 Boul Laure Bureau 100, Sept-Iles, QC,
G4R 1X8
(418) 962-2240
Emp Here 65
SIC 5411 Grocery stores

D-U-N-S 20-913-8374   (BR)
PROVIGO DISTRIBUTION INC
MAXI
1005 Boul Laure, Sept-Iles, QC, G4R 4S6
(418) 968-1213
Emp Here 70
SIC 5411 Grocery stores

D-U-N-S 20-592-4970   (SL)
R. S. AUTO INC
109 Rue Monseigneur-Blanche, Sept-Iles,
QC, G4R 4Y3
(418) 962-7668
Emp Here 21   Sales 10,652,250
SIC 5511 New and used car dealers
Pr Pr Serge Paradis
Real Boily

D-U-N-S 20-793-5615   (BR)
UNIVERSITE DU QUEBEC A CHICOUTIMI
CENTRE D'ETUDES UNIVERSITAIRES DE
L'EST DE LA COTE-NORD
175 Rue De La Verendrye, Sept-Iles, QC, G4R
5B7
(418) 968-4801
Emp Here 20
SIC 8221 Colleges and universities

D-U-N-S 20-642-2797   (BR)
VEOLIA ES CANADA SERVICES INDUS-
TRIELS INC
268 Rue Des Pionniers, Sept-Iles, QC, G4R
0P5
(418) 962-0233
Emp Here 25
SIC 7699 Repair services, nec

D-U-N-S 24-426-3070   (BR)
WAINBEE LIMITED
453 Noel St, Sept-Iles, QC, G4R 1M1
(418) 962-4949
Emp Here 30
SIC 5084 Industrial machinery and equipment

D-U-N-S 20-949-7031   (BR)
WAL-MART CANADA CORP
WALMART
1005 Boul Laure Bureau 500, Sept-Iles, QC,
G4R 4S6
(418) 968-5151
Emp Here 150
SIC 5311 Department stores

Sept-Iles, QC G4S
Saguenay County

D-U-N-S 25-240-3175   (BR)
COMMISSION SCOLAIRE DU FER
ECOLE BOIS-JOLI
95 Rue Des Chanterelles, Sept-Iles, QC, G4S
2B9
(418) 960-5551
Emp Here 30
SIC 8211 Elementary and secondary schools

D-U-N-S 24-870-5738   (BR)
GESTION CHRISTIAN BASTIEN INC
JEAN COUTU
78 Rue Lemaire, Sept-Iles, QC, G4S 1A3
(418) 968-4946
Emp Here 25
SIC 5912 Drug stores and proprietary stores

D-U-N-S 24-097-6030   (BR)
GOLDER ASSOCIATES LTD
22b Rue Lemaire, Sept-Iles, QC, G4S 1S3
(418) 968-6111
Emp Here 20
SIC 8748 Business consulting, nec

Shawinigan, QC G9N
St-Maurice County

D-U-N-S 25-752-1989   (BR)
CRDI TED NCQ IU
CRDI TED NCQ IU
(Suby of CRDI TED NCQ IU)
750 Prom Du Saint-Maurice, Shawinigan,
G9N 1L6
(819) 536-7159
Emp Here 55
SIC 7389 Business services, nec

D-U-N-S 24-891-3811   (BR)
CAMSO INC
(Suby of Camso Inc)
4162 Rue Burrill, Shawinigan, QC, G9N 0C3
(819) 539-2220
Emp Here 50
SIC 3569 General industrial machinery, nec

D-U-N-S 20-171-3422   (BR)
CENTRE HOSPITALIER DU CENTRE LA
MAURICIE
CLINIQUE DE PREVENTION EN SEXU-
ALITE
(Suby of Centre Hospitalier du Centre la
Mauricie)
1265 Rue Trudel Bureau 6, Shawinigan, QC,
G9N 8T3
(819) 539-8371
Emp Here 100
SIC 7363 Help supply services

D-U-N-S 24-890-7867   (BR)
CENTRE HOSPITALIER DU CENTRE LA
MAURICIE
CSSS RESIDENCE DOCTEUR JOSEPH
GARCEAU
(Suby of Centre Hospitalier du Centre la
Mauricie)
243 1re Rue De La Pointe, Shawinigan, QC,
G9N 1K2

Emp Here 100
SIC 8361 Residential care

D-U-N-S 20-213-6383   (BR)
CENTRE JEUNESSE DE LA MAURICIE ET
DU CENTRE-DU-QUEBEC, LE
CENTRE JEUNESSE DE LA MAURICIE ET
DU CENTRE-DU-QUEBEC, LE
(Suby of Centre Jeunesse de la Mauricie et du
Centre-du-Quebec, Le)
750 Prom Du Saint-Maurice Bureau 300,
Shawinigan, QC, G9N 1L6
(819) 536-7111
Emp Here 32

SIC 8322 Individual and family services

D-U-N-S 25-854-2984   (BR)
CENTRE LAFLECHE GRAND-MERE
RESIDENCE SAINT MAURICE
(Suby of Centre Lafleche Grand-Mere)
555 Av De La Station, Shawinigan, QC, G9N
1V9
(819) 536-0071
Emp Here 200
SIC 8361 Residential care

D-U-N-S 25-233-1491   (BR)
COMMISSION SCOLAIRE DE L'ENERGIE
ECOLE ST JACQUES
2015 Rue Saint-Jacques, Shawinigan, QC,
G9N 4A9
(819) 539-9595
Emp Here 45
SIC 8211 Elementary and secondary schools

D-U-N-S 25-471-0569   (BR)
COMMISSION SCOLAIRE DE L'ENERGIE
ECOLE ST JOSEPH
1452 Rue Chateauguay, Shawinigan, QC,
G9N 5C4
(819) 539-5963
Emp Here 35
SIC 8211 Elementary and secondary schools

D-U-N-S 25-233-1459   (BR)
COMMISSION SCOLAIRE DE L'ENERGIE
ECOLE ST CHARLES GARNIER
2265 Av Lafleche, Shawinigan, QC, G9N 6H3
(819) 539-4004
Emp Here 30
SIC 8211 Elementary and secondary schools

D-U-N-S 25-240-2722   (BR)
COMMISSION SCOLAIRE DE L'ENERGIE
ECOLE IMMACULEE CONCEPTION
153 8e Rue De La Pointe, Shawinigan, QC,
G9N 1B5
(819) 537-4690
Emp Here 25
SIC 8211 Elementary and secondary schools

D-U-N-S 25-233-1418   (BR)
COMMISSION SCOLAIRE DE L'ENERGIE
ECOLE DE LA JEUNE-RELEVE
1133 Rue Notre-Dame, Shawinigan, QC, G9N
3S3
(819) 539-2203
Emp Here 29
SIC 8211 Elementary and secondary schools

D-U-N-S 25-001-8231   (BR)
COMMISSION SCOLAIRE DE L'ENERGIE
ECOLE SECONDAIRE DES CHUTES
5285 Av Albert Tessier, Shawinigan, QC, G9N
6T9
(819) 539-2285
Emp Here 100
SIC 8211 Elementary and secondary schools

D-U-N-S 25-379-9381   (BR)
COMMISSION SCOLAIRE DE L'ENERGIE
CARREFOUR FORMATION MAURICIE
5105 Av Albert-Tessier Bureau 840, Shawini-
gan, QC, G9N 7A3
(819) 539-2265
Emp Here 100
SIC 8211 Elementary and secondary schools

D-U-N-S 20-125-1506   (BR)
COMPAGNIE COMMONWEALTH PLY-
WOOD LTEE, LA
1155 Av De La Fonderie, Shawinigan, QC,
G9N 1W9
(819) 537-6621
Emp Here 80
SIC 2435 Hardwood veneer and plywood

D-U-N-S 24-855-0027   (BR)
CONSTRUCTION DJL INC
CONTINENTAL DIV DE
3200 Boul Hubert-Biermans, Shawinigan, QC,
G9N 0A4

(819) 539-2271
Emp Here 165
SIC 1611 Highway and street construction

D-U-N-S 24-341-5465   (BR)
CONSTRUCTION DJL INC
CONSTRUCTION CONTINENTAL
3200 Boul Hubert-Biermans, Shawinigan, QC,
G9N 0A4
(819) 539-2271
Emp Here 25
SIC 1611 Highway and street construction

D-U-N-S 24-209-0712   (SL)
COOP DE TRAVAIL BRASSERIE ARTI-
SANALE LE TROU DU DIABLE
MICROBRASSIE LE TROU DU DIABLE
412 Willow Ave, Shawinigan, QC, G9N 1X2
(819) 537-9151
Emp Here 50   Sales 3,575,074
SIC 8641 Civic and social associations

D-U-N-S 24-060-9748   (SL)
COUVREUR LOUIS BLAIS INC
4800 Boul Royal, Shawinigan, QC, G9N 4R6
(819) 539-8133
Emp Here 50   Sales 4,961,328
SIC 1761 Roofing, siding, and sheetMetal
work

D-U-N-S 25-150-9894   (SL)
ENTREPRISES SYLVIE DROLET INC
MARCHAND CANADIAN TIRE DE SHAWINI-
GAN
1555 Rue Trudel Bureau 131, Shawinigan,
QC, G9N 8K8
(819) 537-3888
Emp Here 49   Sales 17,875,372
SIC 5014 Tires and tubes
Pr Pr Sylvie Drolet

D-U-N-S 24-965-5817   (BR)
GENERAL PAINT CORP
(Suby of The Sherwin-Williams Company)
5230 Boul Royal, Shawinigan, QC, G9N 4R6
(819) 537-5925
Emp Here 100
SIC 2851 Paints and allied products

D-U-N-S 20-000-0722   (SL)
GESTION C.F.L.M. LTEE, LA
ROTISSERIE ST-HUBERT
1515 Rue Trudel, Shawinigan, QC, G9N 8K8
(819) 537-6671
Emp Here 50   Sales 1,532,175
SIC 5812 Eating places

D-U-N-S 25-298-7904   (BR)
H. MATTEAU ET FILS (1987) INC
RONA H MATTEAU
1650 Rue Trudel, Shawinigan, QC, G9N 0A2
(819) 539-8328
Emp Here 100
SIC 5251 Hardware stores

D-U-N-S 24-350-2668   (BR)
HYDRO-QUEBEC
600 Av De La Montagne, Shawinigan, QC,
G9N 7N5
(819) 539-1400
Emp Here 60
SIC 4911 Electric services

D-U-N-S 24-728-5591   (BR)
METRO RICHELIEU INC
SUPER C
3283 Boul Royal, Shawinigan, QC, G9N 8K7
(819) 539-7498
Emp Here 58
SIC 5411 Grocery stores

D-U-N-S 24-747-2640   (SL)
MULTI-RELIURE S.F. INC
MULTI BOOKBINDING
2112 Av De La Transmission, Shawinigan,
QC, G9N 8N8
(819) 537-6008
Emp Here 80   Sales 2,918,428
SIC 2789 Bookbinding and related work

D-U-N-S 24-222-2920   (SL)
PHABERVIN INC
PHARMACIE BERGERON ET VINCENT
2312 Av Saint-Marc, Shawinigan, QC, G9N 2J7
(819) 539-5479
Emp Here 30   *Sales* 5,693,280
SIC 5912 Drug stores and proprietary stores
Pr Andre Vincent

D-U-N-S 25-485-1892   (BR)
PROVIGO INC
MAXI
1643 Rue D'Youville, Shawinigan, QC, G9N 8M8
(819) 536-4412
Emp Here 25
SIC 5411 Grocery stores

D-U-N-S 25-356-8992   (BR)
RIO TINTO ALCAN INC
ALCAN USINE SHAWINIGAN
(*Suby of* RIO TINTO PLC)
1100 Boul Saint-Sacrement, Shawinigan, QC, G9N 6W4
(819) 539-0765
Emp Here 100
SIC 3334 Primary aluminum

D-U-N-S 24-425-9821   (BR)
ROBERT FER ET METEAUX S.E.C.
TRAITEMENT ROBERT
122 Dr Wilson, Shawinigan, QC, G9N 6T6
(819) 537-9824
Emp Here 25
SIC 1796 Installing building equipment

D-U-N-S 25-240-2961   (SL)
SEMINAIRE STE-MARIE DE SHAWINIGAN, LE
5655 Boul Des Hetres, Shawinigan, QC, G9N 4V9
(819) 539-5493
Emp Here 70   *Sales* 4,669,485
SIC 8211 Elementary and secondary schools

D-U-N-S 20-003-9845   (BR)
STAPLES CANADA INC
BUREAU EN GROS
(*Suby of* Staples, Inc.)
1 Rue La Plaza-De-Mauricie, Shawinigan, QC, G9N 7C1
(819) 539-4300
Emp Here 30
SIC 5943 Stationery stores

D-U-N-S 25-258-3802   (BR)
VIGI SANTE LTEE
CHSLD VIGI ET LES CHUTES
(*Suby of* Vigi Sante Ltee)
5000 Av Albert-Tessier, Shawinigan, QC, G9N 8P9
(819) 539-5408
Emp Here 100
SIC 8361 Residential care

D-U-N-S 20-736-2638   (BR)
WAL-MART CANADA CORP
1600 Boul Royal, Shawinigan, QC, G9N 8S8
(819) 537-0113
Emp Here 200
SIC 5311 Department stores

Shawinigan, QC G9P
St-Maurice County

D-U-N-S 25-233-0972   (BR)
COMMISSION SCOLAIRE DE L'ENERGIE
ECOLE SECONDAIRE VAL MAURICIE
1200 Rue De Val-Mauricie, Shawinigan, QC, G9P 2L9
(819) 536-5675
Emp Here 160
SIC 8211 Elementary and secondary schools

D-U-N-S 25-757-7320   (BR)

GESTION R.Y. MENARD INC
TIM HORTONS
(*Suby of* Gestion R.Y. Menard Inc)
2180 105e Av, Shawinigan, QC, G9P 1N8

Emp Here 20
SIC 5812 Eating places

Shawinigan, QC G9T
St-Maurice County

D-U-N-S 24-378-4225   (BR)
PRODUITS FORESTIERS ARBEC S.E.N.C.
775 Ch De Turcotte, Shawinigan, QC, G9T 5K7
(819) 538-0735
Emp Here 150
SIC 2421 Sawmills and planing mills, general

D-U-N-S 24-071-4522   (SL)
SYNAPSE ELECTRONIQUE INC
1010 7e Av, Shawinigan, QC, G9T 2B8
(819) 533-3553
Emp Here 65   *Sales* 4,085,799
SIC 3822 Environmental controls

D-U-N-S 24-157-5567   (BR)
TRANSPORT SCOLAIRE SOGESCO INC
AUTOBUS DE L'ENERGIE
311 Av De Saint-Georges, Shawinigan, QC, G9T 3M8
(819) 533-5663
Emp Here 33
SIC 4151 School buses

Shawinigan-Sud, QC G9N
St-Maurice County

D-U-N-S 20-259-9940   (SL)
PATISSERIE CHEVALIER INC
155 Boul Industriel, Shawinigan-Sud, QC, G9N 6T5
(819) 537-8807
Emp Here 100   *Sales* 5,253,170
SIC 2051 Bread, cake, and related products
Pr Pr Real Menard

Shawinigan-Sud, QC G9P
St-Maurice County

D-U-N-S 25-097-4391   (BR)
COMMISSION SCOLAIRE DE L'ENERGIE
ECOLE ST GEORGES
975 111e Rue, Shawinigan-Sud, QC, G9P 2T5
(819) 536-4068
Emp Here 30
SIC 8211 Elementary and secondary schools

D-U-N-S 25-233-1012   (BR)
COMMISSION SCOLAIRE DE L'ENERGIE
ECOLE DE LA SOURCE
1350 120e Rue, Shawinigan-Sud, QC, G9P 3K9
(819) 537-8937
Emp Here 28
SIC 8211 Elementary and secondary schools

D-U-N-S 24-855-0118   (BR)
SOCIETE EN COMMANDITE LES PROME-NADES DU PARC
SOCIETE EN COMMANDITE LES PROME-NADES DU PARC
200 116e Rue, Shawinigan-Sud, QC, G9P 5K7
(819) 536-5050
Emp Here 40
SIC 8361 Residential care

Shawville, QC J0X
Pontiac County

D-U-N-S 24-899-8320   (SL)
CENTRE D'ACCEUIL PONTIAC
C H S L D SHAWVILLE
290 Rue Marion, Shawville, QC, J0X 2Y0
(819) 647-5755
Emp Here 87   *Sales* 3,210,271
SIC 8361 Residential care

D-U-N-S 20-185-0786   (HQ)
CENTRE DE SANTE ET SERVICES SOCI-AUX DU PONTIAC
(*Suby of* Centre De Sante Et Services Soci-aux Du Pontiac)
200 Rue Argue, Shawville, QC, J0X 2Y0
(819) 647-2211
Emp Here 35   *Emp Total* 523
Sales 134,844,160
SIC 8099 Health and allied services, nec
 Gail Ryan
 Gaston Lacroix
 Richard Grimard
Pr Jean-Guy Patenaude

D-U-N-S 20-213-6276   (BR)
CENTRE DE SANTE ET DE SERVICES SO-CIAUX DU PONTIAC
CENTRE DE SANTE ET DE SERVICES SO-CIAUX DU PONTIAC
290 Rue Marion, Shawville, QC, J0X 2Y0
(819) 647-3553
Emp Here 35
SIC 8399 Social services, nec

D-U-N-S 20-712-5654   (BR)
COMMISSION SCOLAIRE WESTERN QUE-BEC
DR S E MCDOWELL ELEMENTARY SCHOOL
(*Suby of* Commission Scolaire Western Que-bec)
89 Rue Centre, Shawville, QC, J0X 2Y0
(819) 647-3800
Emp Here 30
SIC 8211 Elementary and secondary schools

D-U-N-S 25-240-1534   (BR)
COMMISSION SCOLAIRE WESTERN QUE-BEC
PONTIAC HIGH SCHOOL
(*Suby of* Commission Scolaire Western Que-bec)
455 Rue Maple St, Shawville, QC, J0X 2Y0
(819) 647-2244
Emp Here 55
SIC 8211 Elementary and secondary schools

D-U-N-S 25-240-1492   (BR)
COMMISSION SCOLAIRE WESTERN QUE-BEC
DR S.E. MCDOWELL ELEMENTARY SCHOOL
(*Suby of* Commission Scolaire Western Que-bec)
89 Rue Centre, Shawville, QC, J0X 2Y0
(819) 647-3800
Emp Here 30
SIC 8211 Elementary and secondary schools

D-U-N-S 20-712-5704   (BR)
COMMISSION SCOLAIRE WESTERN QUE-BEC
PONTIAC ADULT EDUCATION
(*Suby of* Commission Scolaire Western Que-bec)
89 Rue Maple, Shawville, QC, J0X 2Y0
(819) 647-5605
Emp Here 50
SIC 8211 Elementary and secondary schools

D-U-N-S 25-143-5111   (BR)
GROUPE PROMUTUEL FEDERATION DE SOCIETE MUTUELLES D'ASSURANCES

GENERALES
PROMUTUEL LA VALLEE
34 Av Victoria, Shawville, QC, J0X 2Y0
(819) 647-2953
Emp Here 20
SIC 6411 Insurance agents, brokers, and ser-vice

D-U-N-S 24-102-4640   (BR)
MAIBEC INC
PONTIAC DIVISION OF MAIBEC
245c 13e Conc, Shawville, QC, J0X 2Y0
(819) 647-5959
Emp Here 50
SIC 2429 Special product sawmills, nec

Sherbrooke, QC J1C
Sherbrooke County

D-U-N-S 20-714-1818   (SL)
ECOLE SECONDAIRE DE BROMP-TONVILLE
125 Rue Du Frere-Theode, Sherbrooke, QC, J1C 0S3
(819) 846-2738
Emp Here 50   *Sales* 3,356,192
SIC 8211 Elementary and secondary schools

D-U-N-S 20-552-6861   (BR)
ISE METAL INC
20 Rte De Windsor, Sherbrooke, QC, J1C 0E5
(819) 846-1044
Emp Here 165
SIC 3469 Metal stampings, nec

D-U-N-S 24-386-8275   (BR)
MATERIAUX DE CONSTRUCTION LE-TOURNEAU INC
550 Rue Du Parc-Industriel, Sherbrooke, QC, J1C 0J2
(888) 566-5633
Emp Here 23
SIC 5211 Lumber and other building materials

D-U-N-S 24-884-4839   (BR)
PAPIERS DE PUBLICATION KRUGER INC
220 Rte De Windsor, Sherbrooke, QC, J1C 0E6
(819) 846-2721
Emp Here 460
SIC 5093 Scrap and waste materials

Sherbrooke, QC J1E
Sherbrooke County

D-U-N-S 20-945-1355   (BR)
CENTRE DE SANTE ET DE SERVICE SOCI-AUX DU HAUT SAINT-FRANCOIS, LE
CSSS DU HAUT SAINT FRANCOIS
(*Suby of* Centre de Sante et de Service Soci-aux du Haut Saint-Francois, Le)
840 Rue Papineau, Sherbrooke, QC, J1E 1Z2
(819) 829-9772
Emp Here 30
SIC 8093 Specialty outpatient clinics, nec

D-U-N-S 24-018-4929   (SL)
CHOEUR DU CEGEP DE SHERBROOKE
475 Rue Du Cegep, Sherbrooke, QC, J1E 4K1
(819) 564-6350
Emp Here 800   *Sales* 107,425,506
SIC 8221 Colleges and universities
Pr Remi Naaman
VP VP Josee Leclair
Dir Real Jr Desautels
Dir Rejean Bergeron
Ex Dir Marie-France Belanger

D-U-N-S 24-336-4978   (BR)
COMMISSION SCOLAIRE DE LA REGION-DE-SHERBROOKE
CENTRE 24-JUIN FORMATION PROFES-

SIONNELLE
639 Rue Du 24-Juin, Sherbrooke, QC, J1E 1H1
(819) 822-5420
Emp Here 50
SIC 8211 Elementary and secondary schools

D-U-N-S 24-336-4986   (BR)
COMMISSION SCOLAIRE DE LA REGION-DE-SHERBROOKE
ECOLE PIE-X-DE L'ASSOMPTION
565 Rue Triest, Sherbrooke, QC, J1E 2M7
(819) 822-5668
Emp Here 50
SIC 8211 Elementary and secondary schools

D-U-N-S 24-334-7361   (BR)
COMMISSION SCOLAIRE DE LA REGION-DE-SHERBROOKE
ECOLE PRIMAIRE STE-FAMILLE
233 8e Av N, Sherbrooke, QC, J1E 2S6
(819) 822-5694
Emp Here 25
SIC 8211 Elementary and secondary schools

D-U-N-S 24-901-6783   (SL)
GESTION LOUMA INC
BRASSERIE FLEURIMONT
1325 12e Av N, Sherbrooke, QC, J1E 3P6
(819) 566-4844
Emp Here 80   *Sales* 2,407,703
SIC 5812 Eating places

────────────────

Sherbrooke, QC J1G
Sherbrooke County

D-U-N-S 24-018-3103   (SL)
9013-3489 QUEBEC INC
GROUPE BEIGNEBEC
1105 Rue King E, Sherbrooke, QC, J1G 1E5

Emp Here 60   *Sales* 2,638,521
SIC 5461 Retail bakeries

D-U-N-S 20-571-0895   (BR)
BANQUE NATIONALE DU CANADA
578 Rue King E, Sherbrooke, QC, J1G 1B5
(819) 346-8448
Emp Here 25
SIC 6021 National commercial banks

D-U-N-S 20-362-2972   (HQ)
CAISSE DESJARDINS DES DEUX-RIVIERES DE SHERBROOKE
CENTRE DE SERVICES D'ASCOT CORNER
(*Suby of* Caisse Desjardins des Deux-Rivieres de Sherbrooke)
1261 Rue King E, Sherbrooke, QC, J1G 1E7
(819) 565-9991
Emp Here 25   *Emp Total* 50
Sales 7,077,188
SIC 6062 State credit unions
Pr Denis Pare
VP Raymond Fillion
Sec France Boisse
Dir Nancy Bastille
Dir Lorraine Beaudoin
Dir Gina Bergeron
Dir Carole Bricault
Dir Claudia Champagne
Dir Richard Duplessis

D-U-N-S 20-799-6351   (BR)
CAISSE DESJARDINS DU NORD DE SHER-BROOKE
CENTRE DE SERVICE PLATEAUX DE SHERBROOKE
630 Rue King E, Sherbrooke, QC, J1G 1B8
(819) 566-0050
Emp Here 55
SIC 6062 State credit unions

D-U-N-S 24-834-3923   (HQ)
CENTRE DE READAPTION ESTRIE INC
(*Suby of* Centre de Readaption Estrie Inc)

300 Rue King E Bureau 200, Sherbrooke, QC, J1G 1B1
(819) 346-8411
Emp Here 275   *Emp Total* 325
Sales 16,000,080
SIC 8361 Residential care
Genl Mgr Lucie Dumas

D-U-N-S 24-330-5435   (BR)
COMMISSION SCOLAIRE DE LA REGION-DE-SHERBROOKE
ECOLE SECONDAIRE DE LA MONTEE
825 Rue Bowen S, Sherbrooke, QC, J1G 2G2
(819) 822-5444
Emp Here 93
SIC 8211 Elementary and secondary schools

D-U-N-S 24-334-7189   (BR)
COMMISSION SCOLAIRE DE LA REGION-DE-SHERBROOKE
ECOLE PRIMAIRE MARIE REINE
976 Rue De Caen, Sherbrooke, QC, J1G 2A4
(819) 822-5662
Emp Here 20
SIC 8211 Elementary and secondary schools

D-U-N-S 24-334-7320   (BR)
COMMISSION SCOLAIRE DE LA REGION-DE-SHERBROOKE
ECOLE PRIMAIRE DESRANLEAU
1970 Rue Galt E, Sherbrooke, QC, J1G 3J1
(819) 822-5684
Emp Here 25
SIC 8211 Elementary and secondary schools

D-U-N-S 24-334-7197   (BR)
COMMISSION SCOLAIRE DE LA REGION-DE-SHERBROOKE
ECOLE PRIMAIRE COEUR-IMMACULE
330 15e Av S, Sherbrooke, QC, J1G 2X5
(819) 822-5696
Emp Here 36
SIC 8211 Elementary and secondary schools

D-U-N-S 20-725-5167   (BR)
COMPAGNIE MANUFACTURIERE JACK SPRATT INC
(*Suby of* Compagnie Manufacturiere Jack Spratt Inc)
550 10e Av S, Sherbrooke, QC, J1G 2R9

Emp Here 20
SIC 2339 Women's and misses' outerwear, nec

D-U-N-S 20-807-0115   (BR)
COUCHE-TARD INC
1780 Rue King E, Sherbrooke, QC, J1G 5G6
(819) 564-0011
Emp Here 20
SIC 5411 Grocery stores

D-U-N-S 24-373-2513   (BR)
FILLES DE LA CHARITE DU SACRE-COEUR DE JESUS, LES
MAISON ROSE-GIET
60 Rue Jean-Maurice, Sherbrooke, QC, J1G 1V5

Emp Here 40
SIC 8661 Religious organizations

D-U-N-S 24-458-5980   (BR)
GOUVERNEMENT DE LA PROVINCE DE QUEBEC
AGENCE DE LA SANTE ET DES SERVICES SOCIAUX DE L'ESTRIE
300 Rue King E Bureau 300, Sherbrooke, QC, J1G 1B1
(819) 566-7861
Emp Here 150
SIC 8399 Social services, nec

D-U-N-S 20-564-0592   (SL)
LOUIS LUNCHEONETTE INC
386 Rue King E, Sherbrooke, QC, J1G 1A8
(819) 563-5581
Emp Here 100   *Sales* 2,991,389

SIC 5812 Eating places

D-U-N-S 24-226-2447   (BR)
METRO RICHELIEU INC
SUPER C FLEURIMONT
1775 Rue King E, Sherbrooke, QC, J1G 5G7
(819) 563-0110
Emp Here 70
SIC 5411 Grocery stores

D-U-N-S 24-080-9863   (SL)
PIZZERIA DEMERS INC
RESTAURANT DEMERS
936 Rue Du Conseil, Sherbrooke, QC, J1G 1L7
(819) 564-2811
Emp Here 110   *Sales* 3,283,232
SIC 5812 Eating places

D-U-N-S 25-299-8927   (BR)
PRISZM LP
PFK
665 Rue Du Conseil, Sherbrooke, QC, J1G 1K7
(819) 562-1144
Emp Here 20
SIC 5812 Eating places

D-U-N-S 20-002-8251   (BR)
PROVIGO DISTRIBUTION INC
PROVIGO
800 Rue King E, Sherbrooke, QC, J1G 1C7
(819) 562-8684
Emp Here 50
SIC 5411 Grocery stores

D-U-N-S 20-005-7169   (BR)
REDBERRY FRANCHISING CORP
BURGER KING
736 Rue King E, Sherbrooke, QC, J1G 1C4
(819) 564-3221
Emp Here 20
SIC 5812 Eating places

D-U-N-S 20-643-4946   (SL)
ROY DANIEL LTEE
CANADIAN TIRE #096
1850 Rue King E, Sherbrooke, QC, J1G 5G6
(819) 566-0303
Emp Here 100   *Sales* 15,736,894
SIC 5531 Auto and home supply stores
Pr Pr Daniel Roy
   Edith Roy

D-U-N-S 24-529-5159   (BR)
SOBEYS QUEBEC INC
IGA COUTURE
2240 Rue King E, Sherbrooke, QC, J1G 5G8
(819) 566-8282
Emp Here 100
SIC 5411 Grocery stores

D-U-N-S 20-544-6532   (BR)
UNIPRIX INC
PHARMACIE UNIPRIX CHEMIKA
610 Rue King E, Sherbrooke, QC, J1G 1B8
(819) 569-9251
Emp Here 30
SIC 5912 Drug stores and proprietary stores

────────────────

Sherbrooke, QC J1H
Sherbrooke County

D-U-N-S 25-448-3779   (BR)
AQUATECH SOCIETE DE GESTION DE L'EAU INC
2275 Rue Claude-Greffard, Sherbrooke, QC, J1H 5H1
(819) 566-0775
Emp Here 25
SIC 4941 Water supply

D-U-N-S 24-096-9878   (BR)
BIBLIOTHEQUE ET ARCHIVES NA-TIONALES DU QUEBEC

BANQ
225 Rue Frontenac Bureau 401, Sherbrooke, QC, J1H 1K1
(819) 820-3010
Emp Here 25
SIC 8231 Libraries

D-U-N-S 20-881-8260   (SL)
C.H.S.L.D. SHERMONT INC
3220 12e Av N, Sherbrooke, QC, J1H 5H3
(819) 820-8900
Emp Here 70   *Sales* 3,283,232
SIC 8051 Skilled nursing care facilities

D-U-N-S 25-021-3758   (BR)
CASCADES INC
RECUPERATION CASCADES
2180 Rue Claude-Greffard, Sherbrooke, QC, J1H 5H1
(819) 563-0011
Emp Here 30
SIC 4953 Refuse systems

D-U-N-S 25-464-8876   (HQ)
CENTRE COMMUNAUTAIRE JURIDIQUE DE L'ESTRIE
(*Suby of* Centre Communautaire Juridique de l'Estrie)
225 Rue King O Bureau 234, Sherbrooke, QC, J1H 1P8
(819) 563-6122
Emp Here 25   *Emp Total* 57
Sales 4,888,367
SIC 8111 Legal services

D-U-N-S 20-296-2036   (SL)
CENTRE JEAN-PATRICE-CHIASSON MAI-SON SAINT-GEORGES, LE
1270 Rue Galt O, Sherbrooke, QC, J1H 2A7
(819) 821-2500
Emp Here 70   *Sales* 2,553,625
SIC 8361 Residential care

D-U-N-S 20-284-3384   (BR)
CENTRE JEUNESSE DE L'ESTRIE
340 Rue Dufferin, Sherbrooke, QC, J1H 4M7

Emp Here 500
SIC 8322 Individual and family services

D-U-N-S 20-927-5882   (SL)
CENTRE DE SANTE ET DE SERVICES SOCIAUX-INSTITUT UNIVERSITAIRE DE GERIATRIE DE SHERBROOKE
1036 Rue Belvedere S, Sherbrooke, QC, J1H 4C4

Emp Here 1,100   *Sales* 69,889,920
SIC 8051 Skilled nursing care facilities
   Daniel Bergeron

D-U-N-S 25-201-2646   (SL)
CLUB DE GOLF LONGCHAMP INC
3455 Rue Du Fer-Droit, Sherbrooke, QC, J1H 0A8
(819) 563-9393
Emp Here 50   *Sales* 2,042,900
SIC 7997 Membership sports and recreation clubs

D-U-N-S 24-334-7312   (BR)
COMMISSION SCOLAIRE DE LA REGION-DE-SHERBROOKE
ECOLE PRIMAIRE LAROCQUE
910 Rue Larocque, Sherbrooke, QC, J1H 4R6
(819) 822-5688
Emp Here 45
SIC 8211 Elementary and secondary schools

D-U-N-S 24-334-7163   (BR)
COMMISSION SCOLAIRE DE LA REGION-DE-SHERBROOKE
PAVILLON MITCHELL
955 Rue De Cambridge, Sherbrooke, QC, J1H 1E2
(819) 822-5400
Emp Here 92
SIC 8211 Elementary and secondary schools

D-U-N-S 24-334-7247   (BR)
COMMISSION SCOLAIRE DE LA REGION-DE-SHERBROOKE
ECOLE PRIMAIRE SYLVESTRE
1020 Rue De Kingston, Sherbrooke, QC, J1H 3S1
(819) 822-5676
Emp Here 30
SIC 8211 Elementary and secondary schools

D-U-N-S 24-336-4994   (BR)
COMMISSION SCOLAIRE DE LA REGION-DE-SHERBROOKE
CENTRE SAINT-MICHEL FORMATION POUR ADULTS
135 Rue King O, Sherbrooke, QC, J1H 1P4
(819) 822-5520
Emp Here 100
SIC 8211 Elementary and secondary schools

D-U-N-S 24-334-7304   (BR)
COMMISSION SCOLAIRE DE LA REGION-DE-SHERBROOKE
ECOLE PRIMAIRE SACRE-COEUR
137 Rue Gillespie, Sherbrooke, QC, J1H 4W9
(819) 822-5690
Emp Here 35
SIC 8211 Elementary and secondary schools

D-U-N-S 24-336-4952   (BR)
COMMISSION SCOLAIRE DE LA REGION-DE-SHERBROOKE
ECOLE INTERNATIONALE DU PHARE
405 Rue Sara, Sherbrooke, QC, J1H 5S6
(819) 822-5455
Emp Here 140
SIC 8211 Elementary and secondary schools

D-U-N-S 24-334-7130   (BR)
COMMISSION SCOLAIRE DE LA REGION-DE-SHERBROOKE
ECOLE NOTRE DAME DU ROSAIRE
1625 Rue Du Rosaire, Sherbrooke, QC, J1H 2T6
(819) 822-5666
Emp Here 21
SIC 8211 Elementary and secondary schools

D-U-N-S 24-336-4861   (BR)
COMMISSION SCOLAIRE DE LA REGION-DE-SHERBROOKE
CENTRE FORMATION PROFESSIONNELLE PAVILLON DU VIEUX
164 Rue Wellington N, Sherbrooke, QC, J1H 5C5
(819) 822-5484
Emp Here 50
SIC 8211 Elementary and secondary schools

D-U-N-S 24-055-3990   (SL)
CORPORATION ASICS CANADA
AGENCE QUEBEC PLUS
101 Rue Des Abenaquis Bureau 201, Sherbrooke, QC, J1H 1H1
(819) 566-8866
Emp Here 25   *Sales* 4,742,446
SIC 5139 Footwear

D-U-N-S 24-125-7182   (BR)
DRUMMOND INFORMATIQUE LTEE
MICROAGE SHERBROOKE
(*Suby of* Drummond Informatique Ltee)
740 Rue Galt O Bureau 300, Sherbrooke, QC, J1H 1Z3
(819) 569-3016
Emp Here 35
SIC 7371 Custom computer programming services

D-U-N-S 25-361-8755   (BR)
ENERKEM INC
375 Rue De Courcelette Bureau 900, Sherbrooke, QC, J1H 3X4
(819) 347-1111
Emp Here 20
SIC 8731 Commercial physical research

D-U-N-S 20-101-1405   (BR)

GOUVERNEMENT DE LA PROVINCE DE QUEBEC
MINISTRE DU TRAVAIL REGIE DU BATIMENT DU QUEBEC
200 Rue Belvedere N Bureau 202, Sherbrooke, QC, J1H 4A9
(819) 820-3646
Emp Here 25
SIC 7389 Business services, nec

D-U-N-S 25-822-9319   (BR)
HEENAN BLAIKIE S.E.N.C.R.L.
HEENAN BLAIKIE, SENCRL
455 Rue King O Bureau 210, Sherbrooke, QC, J1H 6E9
(819) 346-5058
Emp Here 40
SIC 8111 Legal services

D-U-N-S 20-252-5341   (SL)
HYPERSHELL TECHNOLOGIES INC
740 Rue Galt O Bureau 401, Sherbrooke, QC, J1H 1Z3
(819) 822-3890
Emp Here 23   *Sales* 2,167,357
SIC 7371 Custom computer programming services

D-U-N-S 24-712-8168   (HQ)
INVENTAIRES DE L'EST INC
(*Suby of* Inventaires De L'Est Inc)
64 Rue Alexandre, Sherbrooke, QC, J1H 4S6
(819) 569-8065
Emp Here 344   *Emp Total* 344
Sales 22,808,960
SIC 7389 Business services, nec
Pr Pr Suzanne Veilleux
VP VP Richard Veilleux

D-U-N-S 25-447-0024   (BR)
METRO RICHELIEU INC
SUPER C
350 Rue Belvedere N, Sherbrooke, QC, J1H 4B1
(819) 564-6014
Emp Here 75
SIC 5411 Grocery stores

D-U-N-S 24-668-7057   (BR)
NESTLE CANADA INC
1212 Rue Wellington S, Sherbrooke, QC, J1H 5E7
(819) 569-3614
Emp Here 20
SIC 2023 Dry, condensed and evaporated dairy products

D-U-N-S 25-285-9087   (BR)
PPD HOLDING INC
INDUSTRIES P.P.D. INC
(*Suby of* 148220 Canada Inc)
1649 Rue Belvedere S, Sherbrooke, QC, J1H 4E4
(819) 837-2491
Emp Here 150
SIC 3089 Plastics products, nec

D-U-N-S 20-102-1388   (BR)
PROVIGO DISTRIBUTION INC
MAXI
150 Rue Des Grandes-Fourches S, Sherbrooke, QC, J1H 5G5
(819) 566-9300
Emp Here 65
SIC 5141 Groceries, general line

D-U-N-S 24-799-3793   (BR)
RBC DOMINION SECURITIES INC
RBC DOMINION VALEURS MOBILIERES
(*Suby of* Royal Bank Of Canada)
455 Rue King O Bureau 320, Sherbrooke, QC, J1H 6E9
(819) 829-5533
Emp Here 25
SIC 6211 Security brokers and dealers

D-U-N-S 24-801-0886   (BR)
RAYMOND CHABOT GRANT THORNTON S.E.N.C.R.L.

455 Rue King O Bureau 500, Sherbrooke, QC, J1H 6G4
(819) 822-4000
Emp Here 160
SIC 8721 Accounting, auditing, and bookkeeping

D-U-N-S 20-886-0148   (HQ)
SERVICE DE L'ESTRIE (VENTE & REPARATION) INC
SPECIALISTES DE L'ELECTROMENAGER, LES
(*Suby of* Service de l'Estrie (Vente & Reparation) Inc)
225 Rue Wellington S, Sherbrooke, QC, J1H 5E1
(819) 563-0563
Emp Here 50   *Emp Total* 150
Sales 10,944,105
SIC 5722 Household appliance stores
 Claude Villemaire

D-U-N-S 20-852-2370   (BR)
SOBEYS CAPITAL INCORPORATED
IGA EXTRA 514
775 Rue Galt O Bureau 514, Sherbrooke, QC, J1H 1Z1
(819) 564-8686
Emp Here 90
SIC 5411 Grocery stores

D-U-N-S 20-123-2670   (SL)
SUPERMETAL SHERBROOKE INC
(*Suby of* Gestion Releve SMS Inc)
375 Rue De Courcelette, Sherbrooke, QC, J1H 3X4
(819) 566-2965
Emp Here 97   *Sales* 13,424,769
SIC 3441 Fabricated structural Metal
 Jean-Francois Blouin

D-U-N-S 25-871-2124   (BR)
VALEURS MOBILIERES DESJARDINS INC
300 Rue Belvedere N Bureau 201, Sherbrooke, QC, J1H 4B1
(819) 820-2999
Emp Here 21
SIC 6211 Security brokers and dealers

D-U-N-S 24-804-7859   (BR)
VIGI SANTE LTEE
CHSLD VIGI SHERMONT
(*Suby of* Vigi Sante Ltee)
3220 12e Av N, Sherbrooke, QC, J1H 5H3
(819) 820-8900
Emp Here 90
SIC 8051 Skilled nursing care facilities

D-U-N-S 24-341-6802   (BR)
VILLE DE SHERBROOKE
BIBLIOTHEQUE EVA SENECAL
450 Rue Marquette, Sherbrooke, QC, J1H 1M4
(819) 821-5861
Emp Here 40
SIC 8231 Libraries

Sherbrooke, QC J1J
Sherbrooke County

D-U-N-S 20-008-5731   (BR)
AGENCE DE PLACEMENT HELENE ROY LTEE
1335 Rue King O Bureau 220, Sherbrooke, QC, J1J 2B8
(819) 822-0088
Emp Here 56
SIC 7361 Employment agencies

D-U-N-S 25-010-5756   (BR)
ASTRAL MEDIA RADIO INC
ENERGIE CIMO 106
(*Suby of* Astral Media Radio Inc)
1845 Rue King O, Sherbrooke, QC, J1J 2E4
(819) 347-1414
Emp Here 25

SIC 4832 Radio broadcasting stations

D-U-N-S 20-597-3386   (BR)
ASTRAL MEDIA RADIO INC
C I T E ROCK DETENTE F M 102.7
(*Suby of* Astral Media Radio Inc)
1840 Rue King O Bureau 200, Sherbrooke, QC, J1J 2E2
(819) 566-6655
Emp Here 40
SIC 4832 Radio broadcasting stations

D-U-N-S 24-851-2795   (BR)
CAISSE DESJARDINS DU MONT-BELLEVUE DE SHERBROOKE
1815 Rue King O Bureau 300, Sherbrooke, QC, J1J 2E3
(819) 821-2201
Emp Here 60
SIC 5999 Miscellaneous retail stores, nec

D-U-N-S 24-369-5272   (BR)
CAISSE DESJARDINS DU NORD DE SHERBROOKE
CENTRE DE SERVICES PERPETUEL
1268 Rue Prospect, Sherbrooke, QC, J1J 1J5

Emp Here 26
SIC 6062 State credit unions

D-U-N-S 20-021-3960   (BR)
CANADIAN BROADCASTING CORPORATION
CBC RADIO
1335 Rue King O Bureau 330, Sherbrooke, QC, J1J 2B8
(819) 620-0000
Emp Here 20
SIC 4832 Radio broadcasting stations

D-U-N-S 24-226-2330   (BR)
CARA OPERATIONS LIMITED
HARVEYS
(*Suby of* Cara Holdings Limited)
2360 Rue King O, Sherbrooke, QC, J1J 2E8
(819) 565-0909
Emp Here 20
SIC 5812 Eating places

D-U-N-S 20-548-3345   (SL)
CENTRE NOTRE DAME DE L'ENFANT SHERBROOKE INC
CRDITED ESTRIE
1621 Rue Prospect, Sherbrooke, QC, J1J 1K4
(819) 346-8471
Emp Here 350   *Sales* 21,300,720
SIC 8322 Individual and family services
 Louis Trudel
Pr Gaetan Duford
VP Richard Mclernon
Treas Gerald Cutting
Genl Mgr Danielle Lareau

D-U-N-S 24-890-7834   (BR)
CENTRE D'ACCEUIL DIXVILLE INC
CENTRE D'ACCEUIL NOTRE DAME DE L'ENFANT
(*Suby of* Centre d'Acceuil Dixville Inc)
1621 Rue Prospect, Sherbrooke, QC, J1J 1K4
(819) 346-8471
Emp Here 120
SIC 8361 Residential care

D-U-N-S 24-388-4769   (BR)
COMMISSION SCOLAIRE EASTERN TOWNSHIPS
ECOLE PRIMAIRE DE SHERBROOKE
(*Suby of* Commission Scolaire Eastern Townships)
242 Rue De L'Ontario, Sherbrooke, QC, J1J 3R1
(819) 562-3515
Emp Here 50
SIC 8211 Elementary and secondary schools

D-U-N-S 24-334-7346   (BR)
COMMISSION SCOLAIRE DE LA REGION-DE-SHERBROOKE

ECOLE PRIMAIRE SOLEIL LEVANT
830 Rue Buck, Sherbrooke, QC, J1J 3L5
(819) 822-5664
Emp Here 20
SIC 8211 Elementary and secondary schools

D-U-N-S 24-334-7262   (BR)
COMMISSION SCOLAIRE DE LA REGION-
DE-SHERBROOKE
ECOLE PRIMAIRE STE-ANNE
851 Rue De L'Ontario, Sherbrooke, QC, J1J
3R9
(819) 822-5674
Emp Here 40
SIC 8211 Elementary and secondary schools

D-U-N-S 24-334-7148   (BR)
COMMISSION SCOLAIRE DE LA REGION-
DE-SHERBROOKE
ECOLE HELENE BOULLE
1500 Rue Finard, Sherbrooke, QC, J1J 3E1
(819) 823-3233
Emp Here 32
SIC 8211 Elementary and secondary schools

D-U-N-S 24-336-4911   (BR)
COMMISSION SCOLAIRE DE LA REGION-
DE-SHERBROOKE
ECOLE DE CARILLON
43 Rue De Carillon, Sherbrooke, QC, J1J 2K9
(819) 822-5682
Emp Here 40
SIC 8211 Elementary and secondary schools

D-U-N-S 20-807-0149   (BR)
COUCHE-TARD INC
2525 Rue King O, Sherbrooke, QC, J1J 2G9
(819) 564-7767
Emp Here 25
SIC 5411 Grocery stores

D-U-N-S 24-509-9890   (BR)
DELOITTE LLP
1802 Rue King O Bureau 300, Sherbrooke,
QC, J1J 0A2
(819) 823-1616
Emp Here 75
SIC 8111 Legal services

D-U-N-S 25-789-6324   (BR)
DESJARDINS SECURITE FINANCIERE,
COMPAGNIE D'ASSURANCE VIE
1650 Rue King O Bureau 100, Sherbrooke,
QC, J1J 2C3
(819) 821-2131
Emp Here 30
SIC 6411 Insurance agents, brokers, and ser-
vice

D-U-N-S 20-541-3909   (SL)
EXCAVATION RENE ST-PIERRE INC
DEMOLITION ST-PIERRE
(Suby of 9105-8032 Quebec Inc)
3055 Boul Queen-Victoria, Sherbrooke, QC,
J1J 4N8
(819) 565-1494
Emp Here 40   Sales 5,782,650
SIC 1795 Wrecking and demolition work
 Bernard St-Pierre

D-U-N-S 25-293-2603   (BR)
FINANCIERE BANQUE NATIONALE INC
FINANCIERE BANQUE NATIONALE
1802 Rue King O Bureau 200, Sherbrooke,
QC, J1J 0A2
(819) 566-7212
Emp Here 20
SIC 6211 Security brokers and dealers

D-U-N-S 25-485-2130   (BR)
GOUVERNEMENT DE LA PROVINCE DE
QUEBEC
INSTITUE UNIVERSITAIRE GERIATRIE
375 Rue Argyll, Sherbrooke, QC, J1J 3H5
(819) 821-1170
Emp Here 500
SIC 8051 Skilled nursing care facilities

D-U-N-S 24-145-7410   (BR)
GROUPE JEAN COUTU (PJC) INC, LE
(Suby of 3958230 Canada Inc)
1470 Rue King O, Sherbrooke, QC, J1J 2C2
(819) 564-3111
Emp Here 50
SIC 5912 Drug stores and proprietary stores

D-U-N-S 25-913-4237   (BR)
GROUPE RESTAURANTS IMVESCOR INC
RESTAURANTS MIKES
1705 Rue King O, Sherbrooke, QC, J1J 2C8
(819) 564-1090
Emp Here 35
SIC 5812 Eating places

D-U-N-S 24-065-2151   (BR)
MARCHE VEGETARIEN INC, LE
MARCHE VEGETARIEN, LE
50 Boul Jacques-Cartier N, Sherbrooke, QC,
J1J 2Z8
(819) 823-7646
Emp Here 65
SIC 5143 Dairy products, except dried or
canned

D-U-N-S 24-814-0592   (HQ)
SERVICES DE GESTION TEKNIKA HBA
INC, LES
150 Rue De Vimy, Sherbrooke, QC, J1J 3M7
(819) 562-3871
Emp Here 60   Emp Total 2,840
Sales 116,456,320
SIC 8741 Management services
Pr Pr Wilfrid Morin

D-U-N-S 24-569-2926   (HQ)
TEKNIKA HBA INC
150 Rue De Vimy, Sherbrooke, QC, J1J 3M7
(819) 562-3871
Emp Here 150   Emp Total 2,840
Sales 120,877,440
SIC 8711 Engineering services
Pr Pr Wilfrid Morin
 Normand Brousseau

D-U-N-S 25-062-9144   (BR)
UNITED PARCEL SERVICE CANADA LTD
UPS
2389 Rue Hertel, Sherbrooke, QC, J1J 2J1

Emp Here 32
SIC 7389 Business services, nec

D-U-N-S 24-987-9305   (SL)
VOYAGES ESCAPADE 2000 INC
2624 Rue King O, Sherbrooke, QC, J1J 2H1
(819) 563-5344
Emp Here 49   Sales 16,232,000
SIC 4724 Travel agencies
Pr Pr Jacques Guay
 Diane Dupuis

D-U-N-S 24-852-5987   (BR)
EXP SERVICES INC
EXP SERVICES INC
150 Rue De Vimy, Sherbrooke, QC, J1J 3M7
(819) 562-3871
Emp Here 20
SIC 8711 Engineering services

Sherbrooke, QC J1K
Sherbrooke County

D-U-N-S 24-082-9213   (BR)
A. & R. BELLEY INC
965 Rue Cabana, Sherbrooke, QC, J1K 2M3
(819) 563-2667
Emp Here 50
SIC 5113 Industrial and personal service paper

D-U-N-S 24-000-4957   (HQ)
CABCOR INC
(Suby of Cabcor Inc)

980 Rue Panneton, Sherbrooke, QC, J1K 2B2
(819) 566-2401
Emp Here 50   Emp Total 103
Sales 20,354,306
SIC 6712 Bank holding companies
 Yves Gagnon

D-U-N-S 24-369-9282   (BR)
CAISSE DESJARDINS DU MONT-
BELLEVUE DE SHERBROOKE
CENTRE DE SERVICES ST-ESPRIT
2370 Rue Galt O Bureau 2, Sherbrooke, QC,
J1K 2W7
(819) 566-4363
Emp Here 25
SIC 6062 State credit unions

D-U-N-S 20-712-1414   (BR)
COMMISSION SCOLAIRE EASTERN
TOWNSHIPS
NEW HORIZONS ADULT EDUCATION CEN-
TRE
(Suby of Commission Scolaire Eastern Town-
ships)
2365 Rue Galt O, Sherbrooke, QC, J1K 1L1
(819) 566-0250
Emp Here 25
SIC 8211 Elementary and secondary schools

D-U-N-S 24-336-5041   (BR)
COMMISSION SCOLAIRE DE LA REGION-
DE-SHERBROOKE
CENTRE 24-JUIN PAVILLON DES TECH-
NIQUES INDUSTRIELLES
2965 Boul De L'Universite, Sherbrooke, QC,
J1K 2X6
(819) 822-5508
Emp Here 50
SIC 8249 Vocational schools, nec

D-U-N-S 24-336-5033   (BR)
COMMISSION SCOLAIRE DE LA REGION-
DE-SHERBROOKE
ECOLE SECONDAIRE DU TRIOLET
2965 Boul De L'Universite, Sherbrooke, QC,
J1K 2X6
(819) 822-5388
Emp Here 186
SIC 8211 Elementary and secondary schools

D-U-N-S 24-334-7288   (BR)
COMMISSION SCOLAIRE DE LA REGION-
DE-SHERBROOKE
ECOLE PRIMAIRE ST-ESPRIT
2425 Rue Galt O, Sherbrooke, QC, J1K 1L1
(819) 822-5670
Emp Here 20
SIC 8211 Elementary and secondary schools

D-U-N-S 25-429-2662   (BR)
EXP SERVICES INC
2605 Rue Bonin, Sherbrooke, QC, J1K 1C5
(819) 821-4373
Emp Here 28
SIC 8711 Engineering services

D-U-N-S 25-456-7787   (SL)
LENNOX ASSEMBLIES INC
1073 Rue Du Saint-Esprit, Sherbrooke, QC,
J1K 2K4
(819) 822-1328
Emp Here 22   Sales 2,480,664
SIC 3469 Metal stampings, nec

D-U-N-S 20-616-9018   (BR)
UNIVERSITE DE SHERBROOKE
SERVICES DES STAGES ET DU PLACE-
MENT
2500 Boul De L'Universite Bureau 2005, Sher-
brooke, QC, J1K 2R1
(819) 821-7747
Emp Here 43
SIC 8221 Colleges and universities

D-U-N-S 25-672-3867   (BR)
VILLE DE SHERBROOKE
HYDRO SHERBROOKE
1800 Rue Roy, Sherbrooke, QC, J1K 1B6

(819) 821-5727
Emp Here 149
SIC 4911 Electric services

D-U-N-S 25-394-3138   (BR)
WOLTERS KLUWER CANADA LIMITED
CANTAX
1120 Rue De Cherbourg, Sherbrooke, QC,
J1K 2N8
(819) 566-2000
Emp Here 160
SIC 7291 Tax return preparation services

Sherbrooke, QC J1L
Sherbrooke County

D-U-N-S 24-784-3118   (SL)
9074-0747 QUEBEC INC.
CNSP CHARLAND
4100 Rue Lesage, Sherbrooke, QC, J1L 0B6
(819) 346-1881
Emp Here 49   Sales 9,434,850
SIC 3441 Fabricated structural Metal
Pr Pierre Charland

D-U-N-S 25-010-0344   (BR)
AUTOMOBILE ET TOURING CLUB DU QUE-
BEC (A.T.C.Q.)
CAA SHERBROOKE
2990 Rue King O, Sherbrooke, QC, J1L 1Y7
(819) 566-5132
Emp Here 25
SIC 8699 Membership organizations, nec

D-U-N-S 20-261-1752   (SL)
AUTOMOBILES VAL ESTRIE INC
CARROSSIER PROCOLOR SHERBROOKE
OUEST
4141 Rue King O, Sherbrooke, QC, J1L 1P5
(819) 563-4466
Emp Here 75   Sales 35,337,338
SIC 5511 New and used car dealers
Pr Pr Michel Dionne
 Andre Dionne
Dir Rene Janelle

D-U-N-S 20-572-0944   (BR)
BANK OF MONTREAL
BMO BANQUE DE MONTREAL
2959 Rue King O, Sherbrooke, QC, J1L 1C7
(819) 822-5145
Emp Here 36
SIC 6021 National commercial banks

D-U-N-S 20-086-5462   (BR)
BANQUE NATIONALE DU CANADA
3075 Boul De Portland, Sherbrooke, QC, J1L
2Y7
(819) 563-4011
Emp Here 25
SIC 6021 National commercial banks

D-U-N-S 25-091-8906   (BR)
BIBLAIRIE G.G.C. LTEE
AGENCE DU LIVRE
3770 Boul Industriel, Sherbrooke, QC, J1L
1N6
(514) 525-4442
Emp Here 30
SIC 5192 Books, periodicals, and newspapers

D-U-N-S 24-773-0521   (BR)
BOMBARDIER PRODUITS RECREATIFS
INC
BRP
75 Rue J.-A.-Bombardier, Sherbrooke, QC,
J1L 1W3
(819) 566-3000
Emp Here 20
SIC 5599 Automotive dealers, nec

D-U-N-S 24-222-3647   (BR)
BOSTON PIZZA INTERNATIONAL INC
BOSTON PIZZA
550 Rue Jean-Paul-Perrault, Sherbrooke, QC,
J1L 3A6

---

(819) 565-0606
Emp Here 45
SIC 5812 Eating places

D-U-N-S 25-732-8930   (SL)
C-MAC MICROCIRCUITS ULC
C-MAC MICROSYSTEMS SOLUTIONS
(*Suby of* C-MAC AUTOMOTIVE HOLDING LIMITED)
3000 Boul Industriel, Sherbrooke, QC, J1L 1V8
(819) 821-4524
Emp Here 150   *Sales* 24,514,903
SIC 5411 Grocery stores
Sec Jacques Bruneau

D-U-N-S 25-311-4300   (BR)
CANADIAN IMPERIAL BANK OF COMMERCE
CIBC
3050 Boul De Portland, Sherbrooke, QC, J1L 1K1
(819) 569-9911
Emp Here 20
SIC 6021 National commercial banks

D-U-N-S 24-178-5661   (BR)
CHARTWELL QUEBEC (MEL) HOLDINGS INC
CHARTWELL SEIGNEURIES DU CARREFOUR RETIREMENT RESIDENCE
445 Rue Des Erables, Sherbrooke, QC, J1L 0C2
(819) 566-0808
Emp Here 30
SIC 8361 Residential care

D-U-N-S 20-174-6117   (BR)
CIMA+ S.E.N.C.
3385 Rue King O, Sherbrooke, QC, J1L 1P8
(819) 565-3385
Emp Here 200
SIC 8711 Engineering services

D-U-N-S 24-063-7566   (BR)
COGECO RADIO-TELEVISION INC
RYTHME FM 93.7 & 98.1
3720 Boul Industriel, Sherbrooke, QC, J1L 1N6
(819) 822-0937
Emp Here 20
SIC 4833 Television broadcasting stations

D-U-N-S 25-308-7761   (SL)
COMPOSITES B.H.S. INC
2880 Boul Industriel, Sherbrooke, QC, J1L 1V8
(819) 846-0810
Emp Here 50   *Sales* 3,414,558
SIC 2821 Plastics materials and resins

D-U-N-S 24-851-9147   (BR)
COOPER-STANDARD AUTOMOTIVE CANADA LIMITED
3870 Boul Industriel, Sherbrooke, QC, J1L 2V1
(819) 562-4440
Emp Here 100
SIC 3465 Automotive stampings

D-U-N-S 20-302-8881   (BR)
COOPER-STANDARD AUTOMOTIVE CANADA LIMITED
3995 Boul Industriel, Sherbrooke, QC, J1L 2S7
(819) 562-4440
Emp Here 342
SIC 3465 Automotive stampings

D-U-N-S 24-851-9220   (BR)
COOPER-STANDARD AUTOMOTIVE CANADA LIMITED
4045 Rue Brodeur, Sherbrooke, QC, J1L 1K4
(819) 562-4440
Emp Here 120
SIC 3465 Automotive stampings

D-U-N-S 24-109-7331   (BR)
CORUS ENTERTAINMENT INC

CHLT 107, 7 FM
4020 Boul De Portland, Sherbrooke, QC, J1L 2V6
(819) 563-6363
Emp Here 20
SIC 4832 Radio broadcasting stations

D-U-N-S 24-354-8919   (BR)
COSTCO WHOLESALE CANADA LTD
COSTCO
(*Suby of* Costco Wholesale Corporation)
3400 Rue King O, Sherbrooke, QC, J1L 1C9
(819) 822-2121
Emp Here 200
SIC 5199 Nondurable goods, nec

D-U-N-S 20-284-6796   (BR)
DAVIDSTEA INC
DAVIDSTEA
3050 Boul De Portland Bureau 14a, Sherbrooke, QC, J1L 1K1
(819) 346-4208
Emp Here 20
SIC 5499 Miscellaneous food stores

D-U-N-S 20-972-0358   (SL)
DELAFONTAINE INC
DE LA FONTAINE
4115 Rue Brodeur, Sherbrooke, QC, J1L 1K4
(819) 348-1219
Emp Here 160   *Sales* 22,325,974
SIC 3442 Metal doors, sash, and trim
 Robert De La Fontaine

D-U-N-S 24-835-0167   (BR)
DELTA HOTELS LIMITED
2685 Rue King O, Sherbrooke, QC, J1L 1C1
(819) 822-1989
Emp Here 165
SIC 8741 Management services

D-U-N-S 25-504-2269   (SL)
DELTA SHERBROOKE
2685 Rue King O, Sherbrooke, QC, J1L 1C1
(819) 822-1989
Emp Here 100   *Sales* 4,377,642
SIC 7011 Hotels and motels

D-U-N-S 25-909-4035   (BR)
DICOM TRANSPORTATION GROUP CANADA, INC
DICOM TRANSPORTATION GROUP CANADA INC
4155 Boul Industriel, Sherbrooke, QC, J1L 2S7
(819) 566-8636
Emp Here 25
SIC 7389 Business services, nec

D-U-N-S 20-260-4229   (HQ)
DOYON, G. T. V. (SHERBROOKE) INC
DUMOULIN ELECTRONIQUE
(*Suby of* Doyon, G. T. V. (Sherbrooke) Inc)
525 Rue Northrop-Frye, Sherbrooke, QC, J1L 2Y3
(819) 565-3177
Emp Here 33   *Emp Total* 51
Sales 4,669,485
SIC 5731 Radio, television, and electronic stores

D-U-N-S 20-102-1412   (SL)
FABRIDOR INC
(*Suby of* Cabcor Inc)
4445 Rue Robitaille, Sherbrooke, QC, J1L 2Y9
(819) 565-3663
Emp Here 20   *Sales* 1,386,002
SIC 2434 Wood kitchen cabinets

D-U-N-S 24-353-4104   (BR)
GARLOCK OF CANADA LTD
GARLOCK CEALING TECHNOLGY
(*Suby of* Enpro Industries, Inc.)
4100 Rue De La Garlock, Sherbrooke, QC, J1L 1W5
(819) 563-8080
Emp Here 75

SIC 2299 Textile goods, nec

D-U-N-S 25-020-8782   (BR)
GAZ METRO INC
240 Rue Leger, Sherbrooke, QC, J1L 1M1
(800) 361-4005
Emp Here 20
SIC 4924 Natural gas distribution

D-U-N-S 24-125-4338   (BR)
GOUVERNEMENT DE LA PROVINCE DE QUEBEC
GOUVERNEMENT DE LA PROVINCE DE QUEBEC
2865 Boul De Portland, Sherbrooke, QC, J1L 2S1
(819) 820-3061
Emp Here 23
SIC 7549 Automotive services, nec

D-U-N-S 25-325-0732   (BR)
GROUPE BMTC INC
3950 Boul Josaphat-Rancourt, Sherbrooke, QC, J1L 3C6
(819) 562-4242
Emp Here 35
SIC 5712 Furniture stores

D-U-N-S 24-935-4903   (SL)
GROUPE POLY-M2 INC, LE
4005a Rue De La Garlock, Sherbrooke, QC, J1L 1W9
(819) 562-2161
Emp Here 150   *Sales* 4,377,642
SIC 7349 Building maintenance services, nec

D-U-N-S 20-002-4508   (BR)
GROUPE DE COURTAGE OMNI LTEE
4056 Rue Lesage, Sherbrooke, QC, J1L 0B6
(819) 562-5505
Emp Here 50
SIC 5411 Grocery stores

D-U-N-S 20-015-4420   (BR)
GUAY INC
GRUES MARTEL
4300 Rue Hector-Brien, Sherbrooke, QC, J1L 0E2
(819) 569-2041
Emp Here 25
SIC 7353 Heavy construction equipment rental

D-U-N-S 24-161-0018   (BR)
HOME DEPOT OF CANADA INC
HOME DEPOT SHERBROOKE
(*Suby of* The Home Depot Inc)
1355 Boul Du Plateau-Saint-Joseph, Sherbrooke, QC, J1L 3E2
(819) 348-4481
Emp Here 100
SIC 5251 Hardware stores

D-U-N-S 25-309-7265   (BR)
INDUSTRIELLE ALLIANCE, ASSURANCE ET SERVICES FINANCIERS INC
2655 Rue King O Bureau 137, Sherbrooke, QC, J1L 2G4
(819) 348-9906
Emp Here 50
SIC 6411 Insurance agents, brokers, and service

D-U-N-S 25-315-7879   (BR)
INVESTORS GROUP FINANCIAL SERVICES INC
3425 Rue King O Bureau 140, Sherbrooke, QC, J1L 1P8
(819) 566-0666
Emp Here 40
SIC 8742 Management consulting services

D-U-N-S 25-646-3209   (BR)
KONE INC
4054 Rue Lesage, Sherbrooke, QC, J1L 0B6
(819) 821-2182
Emp Here 23
SIC 7699 Repair services, nec

D-U-N-S 20-922-4679   (BR)
MAISON SIMONS INC, LA
3050 Boul De Portland, Sherbrooke, QC, J1L 1K1
(819) 829-1840
Emp Here 100
SIC 5651 Family clothing stores

D-U-N-S 24-020-5211   (SL)
MESOTEC INC
(*Suby of* Gestion Convrier Inc)
4705 Boul De Portland, Sherbrooke, QC, J1L 0H3
(819) 822-2777
Emp Here 80   *Sales* 17,218,725
SIC 3728 Aircraft parts and equipment, nec
 Philippe Constancis
Dir Paul Constancis

D-U-N-S 20-653-0888   (SL)
MULTI-P E P INC
4025 Rue De La Garlock, Sherbrooke, QC, J1L 1W9

Emp Here 40   *Sales* 12,145,020
SIC 8399 Social services, nec
Pr Michel Pepin

D-U-N-S 20-571-3428   (BR)
PEPSICO CANADA ULC
FRITO LAY
(*Suby of* Pepsico, Inc.)
4130 Boul Industriel, Sherbrooke, QC, J1L 2S6
(819) 563-8544
Emp Here 25
SIC 2096 Potato chips and similar snacks

D-U-N-S 25-210-6927   (SL)
PREIMPRESSION AD HOC LE GROUPE INC
AD HOC IMEDIA
4130 Rue Lesage, Sherbrooke, QC, J1L 0B6

Emp Here 28   *Sales* 7,101,500
SIC 7319 Advertising, nec
Pr Pr Alain Beliveau
 Louis Leblanc
 Sylvain Lord
 Martin Duchaineau

D-U-N-S 20-555-8583   (BR)
PRODUITS AMERICAN BILTRITE (CANADA) LTEE
635 Rue Pepin, Sherbrooke, QC, J1L 2P8
(819) 823-3300
Emp Here 250
SIC 3069 Fabricated rubber products, nec

D-U-N-S 20-005-7177   (BR)
REDBERRY FRANCHISING CORP
BURGER KING
3005 Rue King O, Sherbrooke, QC, J1L 1C7
(819) 566-6555
Emp Here 25
SIC 5812 Eating places

D-U-N-S 20-736-9914   (BR)
REGULVAR INC
4101 Boul Industriel, Sherbrooke, QC, J1L 2S7
(819) 829-1311
Emp Here 20
SIC 5084 Industrial machinery and equipment

D-U-N-S 24-056-1261   (BR)
RESIDENCES ALLEGRO, S.E.C., LES
(*Suby of* Residences Allegro, S.E.C., Les)
3300 Rue Des Chenes, Sherbrooke, QC, J1L 2G1
(819) 823-1123
Emp Here 50
SIC 8361 Residential care

D-U-N-S 20-927-8811   (BR)
SEARS CANADA INC
SEARS DEPARTMENT STORE
3150 Boul De Portland, Sherbrooke, QC, J1L

1K3
(819) 563-9440
Emp Here 200
SIC 5311 Department stores

D-U-N-S 24-022-2950   (HQ)
SHERMAG IMPORT INC
MEUBLES DEZMO
(*Suby of* Groupe Bermex Inc)
3035 Boul Industriel, Sherbrooke, QC, J1L
2T9
(819) 566-1515
Emp Here 30   *Emp Total* 26
Sales 89,898,187
SIC 2511 Wood household furniture
Pr Alex Adimari
Sec Richard Darveau
VP Fin VP Fin Christian Roy
Dir Brenda Mariasine
Dir Laura Amelia Carlucci

D-U-N-S 20-002-4441   (BR)
SOBEYS CAPITAL INCORPORATED
IGA EXTRA
3950 Rue King O Bureau B, Sherbrooke, QC,
J1L 1P6
(819) 563-5172
Emp Here 100
SIC 5411 Grocery stores

D-U-N-S 25-213-7534   (BR)
STAPLES CANADA INC
BUREAU EN GROS
(*Suby of* Staples, Inc.)
3325 Boul De Portland, Sherbrooke, QC, J1L
2P1
(819) 562-1966
Emp Here 50
SIC 5943 Stationery stores

D-U-N-S 25-316-8132   (BR)
**SUN LIFE ASSURANCE COMPANY OF
CANADA**
MUTUELLE DU CAN CO D'ASSUR SUR
2665 Rue King O Bureau 500, Sherbrooke,
QC, J1L 2G5
(819) 569-6328
Emp Here 40
SIC 6311 Life insurance

D-U-N-S 20-191-8252   (SL)
TAUNTON ENGINEERING COMPANY INC
SHERBROOK OEM
262 Rue Pepin, Sherbrooke, QC, J1L 2V8
(819) 563-7374
Emp Here 100   *Sales* 21,656,275
SIC 5084 Industrial machinery and equipment

D-U-N-S 24-872-0443   (HQ)
TEKNA SYSTEMES PLASMA INC
TEKNA PLASMA
2935 Boul Industriel, Sherbrooke, QC, J1L
2T9
(819) 820-2204
Emp Here 100   *Emp Total* 26
Sales 13,253,640
SIC 3569 General industrial machinery, nec
Pr Luc Dionne
Dir Daniel Delage
Dir Bjorn Eldar Petersen
Dir Maher Boulos

D-U-N-S 25-297-8606   (BR)
TOYS 'R' US (CANADA) LTD
TOYS 'R' US
(*Suby of* Toys "r" Us, Inc.)
3050 Boul De Portland, Sherbrooke, QC, J1L
1K1
(819) 820-8697
Emp Here 27
SIC 5945 Hobby, toy, and game shops

D-U-N-S 20-213-4206   (BR)
TRANSCONTINENTAL PRINTING INC
*TRANSCONTINENTAL   IMPRESSION
METROLITHO*
4001 Boul De Portland, Sherbrooke, QC, J1L
1X9

(819) 563-4001
Emp Here 130
SIC 2752 Commercial printing, lithographic

D-U-N-S 24-477-1619   (BR)
WSP CANADA INC
GENIVAR
171 Rue Leger, Sherbrooke, QC, J1L 1M2
(819) 562-8888
Emp Here 31
SIC 8711 Engineering services

D-U-N-S 24-327-4524   (BR)
WAL-MART CANADA CORP
WALMART
4050 Boul Josaphat-Rancourt Bureau 3086,
Sherbrooke, QC, J1L 3C6
(819) 823-1661
Emp Here 225
SIC 5311 Department stores

D-U-N-S 24-313-6152   (BR)
**WINNERS MERCHANTS INTERNATIONAL
L.P.**
WINNERS
(*Suby of* The TJX Companies Inc)
3050 Boul De Portland, Sherbrooke, QC, J1L
1K1
(819) 780-1307
Emp Here 30
SIC 5651 Family clothing stores

D-U-N-S 20-422-7797   (BR)
WOLSELEY CANADA INC
(*Suby of* WOLSELEY PLC)
230 Rue Leger, Sherbrooke, QC, J1L 1M1
(819) 562-2662
Emp Here 20
SIC 5074 Plumbing and heating equipment
and supplies (hydronics)

Sherbrooke, QC J1M
Sherbrooke County

D-U-N-S 24-460-4369   (SL)
CENTRE DE LA PETITE ENFANCE PANDA
2600 Rue College, Sherbrooke, QC, J1M 1Z7
(819) 346-1414
Emp Here 50   *Sales* 1,532,175
SIC 8351 Child day care services

D-U-N-S 25-234-2290   (BR)
**COMMISSION   SCOLAIRE   EASTERN
TOWNSHIPS**
LENNOXVILLE ELEMETARY SCHOOL
(*Suby of* Commission Scolaire Eastern Town-
ships)
1 Rue Academy, Sherbrooke, QC, J1M 2A6
(819) 569-5103
Emp Here 40
SIC 8211 Elementary and secondary schools

D-U-N-S 24-345-6220   (BR)
**COMMISSION   SCOLAIRE   EASTERN
TOWNSHIPS**
*LENNOXVILLE   VOCATIONAL   TRAINING
CENTRE*
(*Suby of* Commission Scolaire Eastern Town-
ships)
1700 Rue College Bureau 5, Sherbrooke, QC,
J1M 0C8
(819) 563-5627
Emp Here 50
SIC 8211 Elementary and secondary schools

D-U-N-S 24-291-5507   (SL)
**FIDUCIE TECHNOLOGIES DE FIBRES
AIKAWA**
AIKAWA GROUP
72 Rue Queen, Sherbrooke, QC, J1M 2C3
(819) 562-4754
Emp Here 49   *Sales* 14,883,983
SIC 5111 Printing and writing paper
Pt Masaki Aikawa

D-U-N-S 25-737-0338   (BR)

KRUGER PRODUCTS L.P.
2888 Rue College, Sherbrooke, QC, J1M 1T4
(819) 565-8220
Emp Here 46
SIC 2676 Sanitary paper products

D-U-N-S 24-388-4710   (SL)
PRO-PAR INC
(*Suby of* TerraVest Capital Inc)
65 Rue Winder, Sherbrooke, QC, J1M 1L5
(819) 566-8211
Emp Here 80   *Sales* 16,545,394
SIC 3443 Fabricated plate work (boiler shop)
Pierre Fournier

D-U-N-S 20-707-0702   (BR)
PROVIGO DISTRIBUTION INC
PROVIGO
169 Rue Queen, Sherbrooke, QC, J1M 1K1
(819) 823-0448
Emp Here 30
SIC 5411 Grocery stores

D-U-N-S 20-285-7053   (BR)
**SOCIETE DES MISSIONAIRES D'AFRIQUE
(PERES   BLANCS)   PROVINCE   DE
L'AMERIQUE DU NORD**
100 Rue Du Cardinal-Lavigerie, Sherbrooke,
QC, J1M 0A2
(819) 346-4844
Emp Here 26
SIC 8661 Religious organizations

D-U-N-S 20-033-6282   (BR)
UNIVERSITE BISHOP'S
CLUB DE GOLF VIEUX LENNOXVILLE
19 Ch Du Golf, Sherbrooke, QC, J1M 2E6
(819) 562-4922
Emp Here 20
SIC 7992 Public golf courses

Sherbrooke, QC J1N
Sherbrooke County

D-U-N-S 20-520-5573   (BR)
9028-3409 QUEBEC INC
JEANS DEPOT
4801 Boul Bourque, Sherbrooke, QC, J1N
2G6
(819) 563-2602
Emp Here 20
SIC 5651 Family clothing stores

D-U-N-S 24-192-3734   (HQ)
9098-0145 QUEBEC INC
GROUPE GASTON COTE
(*Suby of* 9062-6284 Quebec Inc)
4701 Boul Bourque, Sherbrooke, QC, J1N
2G6
(819) 564-2257
Emp Here 40   *Emp Total* 2
Sales 12,184,437
SIC 3272 Concrete products, nec
Pr Pr Gesner Blenkhorn
Sec Stephane Cote

D-U-N-S 20-294-3911   (SL)
9101-2468 QUEBEC INC
MAZDA DE SHERBROOKE
5119 Boul Bourque, Sherbrooke, QC, J1N
2K6
(819) 564-8664
Emp Here 40   *Sales* 19,424,000
SIC 5511 New and used car dealers
Pr Pr Daniel Beaucage

D-U-N-S 24-459-6987   (BR)
CRH CANADA GROUP INC
5607 Rue Mills, Sherbrooke, QC, J1N 3B6
(819) 564-3989
Emp Here 20
SIC 3273 Ready-mixed concrete

D-U-N-S 24-377-9787   (SL)
CASTONGUAY S.E.N.C.

5939 Rue Joyal, Sherbrooke, QC, J1N 1H1
(819) 864-4201
Emp Here 300   *Sales* 55,264,080
SIC 1629 Heavy construction, nec
Genl Mgr Pierre Tellier

D-U-N-S 25-200-5046   (BR)
CENTRE JEUNESSE DE L'ESTRIE
CENTRE JEUNESSE VAL DU LAC
8475 Ch Blanchette, Sherbrooke, QC, J1N
3A3
(819) 864-4221
Emp Here 200
SIC 8361 Residential care

D-U-N-S 24-336-4853   (BR)
**COMMISSION SCOLAIRE DE LA REGION-
DE-SHERBROOKE**
ECOLE BEAULIEU
4565 Rue De Chambois, Sherbrooke, QC,
J1N 2B7
(819) 822-5642
Emp Here 30
SIC 8211 Elementary and secondary schools

D-U-N-S 24-336-4945   (BR)
**COMMISSION SCOLAIRE DE LA REGION-
DE-SHERBROOKE**
ECOLE DE LA MAISONNEE
1500 Boul Du Mi-Vallon, Sherbrooke, QC, J1N
3Y5
(819) 822-5686
Emp Here 50
SIC 8211 Elementary and secondary schools

D-U-N-S 24-336-4903   (BR)
**COMMISSION SCOLAIRE DE LA REGION-
DE-SHERBROOKE**
ECOLE NOTRE-DAME-DE-LIESSE
7409 Boul Bourque, Sherbrooke, QC, J1N
3K7
(819) 822-5514
Emp Here 35
SIC 8211 Elementary and secondary schools

D-U-N-S 24-336-4895   (BR)
**COMMISSION SCOLAIRE DE LA REGION-
DE-SHERBROOKE**
ECOLE DU TOURET
4076 Boul De L'Universite, Sherbrooke, QC,
J1N 2Y1
(819) 822-5577
Emp Here 80
SIC 8211 Elementary and secondary schools

D-U-N-S 20-807-0156   (BR)
COUCHE-TARD INC
4980 Boul Bourque, Sherbrooke, QC, J1N
2A7
(819) 564-8475
Emp Here 25
SIC 5411 Grocery stores

D-U-N-S 20-195-5317   (HQ)
LEPROHON INC
(*Suby of* Gestion J M P le Prohon Inc)
6171 Boul Bourque, Sherbrooke, QC, J1N
1H2
(819) 563-2454
Emp Here 80   *Emp Total* 3
Sales 17,510,568
SIC 1711 Plumbing, heating, air-conditioning
Pr Alain Dubois
Sec Veronique Le Prohon
Dir Guillaume Le Prohon
Dir Sebastien Dupont
Dir Yvan Laberge
Dir Jean Le Prohon

D-U-N-S 24-562-0695   (SL)
**MISSIONAIRES DE MARIANNHILL INC,
LES**
2075 Ch De Sainte-Catherine, Sherbrooke,
QC, J1N 1E7
(819) 562-4676
Emp Here 50   *Sales* 3,283,232
SIC 8661 Religious organizations

D-U-N-S 24-169-0783   (HQ)

RELAIS PNEUS FREINS ET SUSPENSIONS INC, LE
4255 Boul Bourque, Sherbrooke, QC, J1N 1S4
(819) 566-7722
Emp Here 40   *Emp Total* 1
Sales 5,472,053
SIC 5531 Auto and home supply stores
Pr Pr Yvan Desgreniers
Genl Mgr Real Arnold

Sherbrooke, QC J1R
Sherbrooke County

D-U-N-S 24-711-4820   (SL)
ANI-MAT INC
395 Rue Rodolphe-Racine, Sherbrooke, QC, J1R 0S7
(819) 821-2091
Emp Here 115
SIC 2273 Carpets and rugs

D-U-N-S 24-336-4879   (BR)
COMMISSION SCOLAIRE DE LA REGION-DE-SHERBROOKE
ECOLE ALFRED DESROCHERS
7282 Ch De Saint-Elie, Sherbrooke, QC, J1R 0K5
(819) 822-5680
Emp Here 60
SIC 8211 Elementary and secondary schools

D-U-N-S 20-354-7013   (BR)
COOPER-STANDARD   AUTOMOTIVE CANADA LIMITED
4870 Rue Robert Boyd, Sherbrooke, QC, J1R 0W8
(819) 347-5593
Emp Here 250
SIC 3465 Automotive stampings

D-U-N-S 25-233-8624   (SL)
LES PLACEMENTS J.G. BERNARD LTEE
5040 Boul Industriel, Sherbrooke, QC, J1R 0P4
(819) 564-2966
Emp Here 49   *Sales* 23,087,061
SIC 5014 Tires and tubes
Pr Gerard Bernard

D-U-N-S 24-347-0601   (SL)
TOITURES VICK & ASSOCIES INC, LES
(*Suby of* Gestion Toivick Inc)
71 Ch Godin, Sherbrooke, QC, J1R 0S6
(450) 658-4300
Emp Here 50   *Sales* 6,674,880
SIC 1761 Roofing, siding, and sheetMetal work
Pr Pr Marcel Bernier
VP VP Stephane Maurice
Steve Roy
Maxime Vachon
Paul Beauchesnes

Sherrington, QC J0L
Napierville County

D-U-N-S 25-812-2639   (BR)
COOP UNIFORCE, LA
291 Rue Saint-Patrice, Sherrington, QC, J0L 2N0
(450) 454-3986
Emp Here 65
SIC 5261 Retail nurseries and garden stores

Shipshaw, QC G7P

D-U-N-S 25-234-0807   (BR)
COMMISSION SCOLAIRE DE LA JON-

QUIERE
ECOLE BOIS-JOLI
(*Suby of* Commission Scolaire de la Jonquiere)
4411 Rue Du Bois-Joli, Shipshaw, QC, G7P 1M4
(418) 547-2656
Emp Here 30
SIC 8211 Elementary and secondary schools

Sorel-Tracy, QC J3P
Richelieu County

D-U-N-S 25-400-3536   (SL)
AUBERGE DE LA RIVE INC
165 Ch Sainte-Anne, Sorel-Tracy, QC, J3P 6J7
(450) 742-5691
Emp Here 75   *Sales* 3,283,232
SIC 7011 Hotels and motels

D-U-N-S 25-694-2798   (BR)
BANQUE NATIONALE DU CANADA
58 Rue Du Roi, Sorel-Tracy, QC, J3P 4M7
(450) 742-5684
Emp Here 22
SIC 6021 National commercial banks

D-U-N-S 25-257-7499   (SL)
C.L.S.C. DU HAVRE
30 Rue Ferland, Sorel-Tracy, QC, J3P 3C7
(450) 746-4545
Emp Here 150   *Sales* 13,695,750
SIC 8093 Specialty outpatient clinics, nec
Genl Mgr Benoit Marchessault
Lucie Pepin

D-U-N-S 24-921-7001   (SL)
CACTUS CAFE 'EL PIQUANTE' INC
RESTO BAR O CACTUS ENR
30 Rue Du Roi, Sorel-Tracy, QC, J3P 4M5
(450) 742-8208
Emp Here 55   *Sales* 1,678,096
SIC 5812 Eating places

D-U-N-S 25-648-0559   (BR)
CENTE D'HEBERGEMENT ET DE SOIN DE LONGUE DUREE DU BAS-RICHELIEU
C.H.S.L.D DU BAS-RICHELIEU
(*Suby of* Cente d'Hebergement et de Soin de Longue Duree du Bas-Richelieu)
30 Rue Ferland, Sorel-Tracy, QC, J3P 3C7
(450) 743-5569
Emp Here 55
SIC 8093 Specialty outpatient clinics, nec

D-U-N-S 25-234-2597   (BR)
COMMISSION SCOLAIRE DE SOREL-TRACY
ECOLE MARIA GORETTI
(*Suby of* Commission Scolaire de Sorel-Tracy)
172 Rue Guevremont, Sorel-Tracy, QC, J3P 3K6
(450) 743-6370
Emp Here 30
SIC 8211 Elementary and secondary schools

D-U-N-S 24-044-8204   (BR)
COMMISSION SCOLAIRE DE SOREL-TRACY
ECOLE SECONDAIRE FERNAND LEFEBVRE
(*Suby of* Commission Scolaire de Sorel-Tracy)
265 Rue De Ramezay, Sorel-Tracy, QC, J3P 4A5
(450) 742-5901
Emp Here 100
SIC 8211 Elementary and secondary schools

D-U-N-S 25-027-5005   (BR)
COMMISSION SCOLAIRE DE SOREL-TRACY
ECOLE SAINT GABRIEL LALEMANT
(*Suby of* Commission Scolaire de Sorel-Tracy)
50 Rue Brebeuf, Sorel-Tracy, QC, J3P 2X5

(450) 746-1591
Emp Here 45
SIC 8211 Elementary and secondary schools

D-U-N-S 24-865-2661   (SL)
FERME LE COMPTOIR RICHELIEU INC
RONA
(*Suby of* Comptoir Richelieu Inc)
350 Rue Du College, Sorel-Tracy, QC, J3P 6T7
(450) 742-9444
Emp Here 30   *Sales* 6,797,150
SIC 5261 Retail nurseries and garden stores
Pr Pr Jean Paquin
VP Eloise Paquin
Sec Sophie Paquin

D-U-N-S 25-648-4130   (BR)
FONDATION DU CENTRE JEUNESSE DE LA MONTEREGIE
61 Rue Morgan, Sorel-Tracy, QC, J3P 3B6
(450) 743-1201
Emp Here 33
SIC 8322 Individual and family services

D-U-N-S 20-265-8464   (BR)
GROUPE MASKA INC
(*Suby of* Gestion M. A. E. Inc)
370 Boul Fiset, Sorel-Tracy, QC, J3P 3R2
(450) 742-2703
Emp Here 20
SIC 5013 Motor vehicle supplies and new parts

D-U-N-S 20-544-9635   (BR)
HYDRO-QUEBEC
385 Boul Fiset, Sorel-Tracy, QC, J3P 3R4
(450) 746-3600
Emp Here 49
SIC 4911 Electric services

D-U-N-S 20-261-3816   (SL)
LAITERIE CHALIFOUX INC
FROMAGES RIVIERA, LES
(*Suby of* Investissements J.P.C. & Fils Inc, Les)
493 Boul Fiset, Sorel-Tracy, QC, J3P 6J9
(450) 743-4439
Emp Here 100   *Sales* 9,703,773
SIC 2022 Cheese; natural and processed
Pr Alain Chalifoux
VP Maxime Chalifoux
Treas Melanie Chalifoux

D-U-N-S 25-448-3886   (BR)
METRO RICHELIEU INC
SUPER C SOREL
250 Boul Fiset, Sorel-Tracy, QC, J3P 3P7
(450) 742-4563
Emp Here 80
SIC 5142 Packaged frozen goods

D-U-N-S 20-289-4721   (SL)
RICHARDSON INTERNATIONAL (QUEBEC) LIMITEE
JAMES RICHARDSON INTERNATIONAL (QUEBEC)
10 Rue De La Reine, Sorel-Tracy, QC, J3P 4R2
(450) 743-3893
Emp Here 26   *Sales* 5,690,935
SIC 5083 Farm and garden machinery
Pr Curt Vossen
VP VP Darwin Sobkow
Sec Jean-Marc Ruest
Dir Hartley Richardson

D-U-N-S 25-655-2456   (BR)
RICHARDSON INTERNATIONAL LIMITED
RICHARDSON PIONEER GRAIN
(*Suby of* James Richardson & Sons, Limited)
10 Rue De La Reine, Sorel-Tracy, QC, J3P 4R2
(450) 743-3893
Emp Here 35
SIC 5153 Grain and field beans

D-U-N-S 24-333-1811   (BR)

SEARS CANADA INC
H&R BLOCK
525 Rue De Ramezay, Sorel-Tracy, QC, J3P 8B4
(450) 746-2508
Emp Here 70
SIC 5311 Department stores

D-U-N-S 20-856-2017   (BR)
SINTRA INC
290 Rue Monseigneur-Desranleau, Sorel-Tracy, QC, J3P 7Y6
(450) 742-5993
Emp Here 30
SIC 1611 Highway and street construction

D-U-N-S 25-307-6798   (BR)
SOCIETE DES ALCOOLS DU QUEBEC
SOCIETE DES ALCOOLS DU QUEBEC
340 Boul Poliquin, Sorel-Tracy, QC, J3P 0G4
(450) 746-2711
Emp Here 20
SIC 5921 Liquor stores

D-U-N-S 24-216-9550   (BR)
SOCIETE DES TRAVERSIERS DU QUEBEC
9 Rue Elizabeth, Sorel-Tracy, QC, J3P 4G1
(450) 742-3313
Emp Here 250
SIC 4111 Local and suburban transit

D-U-N-S 20-104-9389   (BR)
STAPLES CANADA INC
BUREAU EN GROS
(*Suby of* Staples, Inc.)
450 Boul Poliquin Bureau 5004, Sorel-Tracy, QC, J3P 7R5
(450) 743-3888
Emp Here 60
SIC 5943 Stationery stores

Sorel-Tracy, QC J3R
Richelieu County

D-U-N-S 20-708-7685   (SL)
2970-7163 QUEBEC INC.
RESTAURANT TRACY
1115 Rte Marie-Victorin, Sorel-Tracy, QC, J3R 1L7
(450) 742-1655
Emp Here 50   *Sales* 1,532,175
SIC 5812 Eating places

D-U-N-S 24-312-5197   (BR)
ALIMENTATION TRACY INC
6950 Rte Marie-Victorin, Sorel-Tracy, QC, J3R 1S6
(450) 743-9999
Emp Here 25
SIC 5146 Fish and seafoods

D-U-N-S 20-225-8757   (BR)
ALSTOM CANADA INC
POWER ENVIRONMENT ALSTOM HYDRO CANADA
(*Suby of* General Electric Company)
1350 Ch Saint-Roch, Sorel-Tracy, QC, J3R 5P9
(450) 746-6500
Emp Here 400
SIC 4911 Electric services

D-U-N-S 20-589-4590   (BR)
BANQUE TORONTO-DOMINION, LA
TD CANADA TRUST
(*Suby of* Toronto-Dominion Bank, The)
1005 Rte Marie-Victorin Bureau 250, Sorel-Tracy, QC, J3R 1L5
(450) 742-2769
Emp Here 20
SIC 6021 National commercial banks

D-U-N-S 20-978-1392   (SL)
CLUB DE GOLF SOREL-TRACY LES DUNES INC

12000 Ch Saint-Roch, Sorel-Tracy, QC, J3R 5E8
(450) 742-4444
Emp Here 50   *Sales* 1,532,175
SIC 5812 Eating places

D-U-N-S 20-910-3977   (BR)
COMMISSION SCOLAIRE DE SOREL-TRACY
ECOLE SECONDAIRE BERNARD GARIEPY
(*Suby of* Commission Scolaire de Sorel-Tracy)
2800 Boul Des Erables, Sorel-Tracy, QC, J3R 2W4
(450) 746-3510
Emp Here 150
SIC 8211 Elementary and secondary schools

D-U-N-S 25-233-1897   (BR)
COMMISSION SCOLAIRE DE SOREL-TRACY
ECOLE ST JEAN BOSCO
(*Suby of* Commission Scolaire de Sorel-Tracy)
2425 Boul Cournoyer, Sorel-Tracy, QC, J3R 2N3
(450) 743-6334
Emp Here 45
SIC 8211 Elementary and secondary schools

D-U-N-S 25-234-0401   (BR)
COMMISSION SCOLAIRE DE SOREL-TRACY
ECOLE LAPLUME
(*Suby of* Commission Scolaire de Sorel-Tracy)
2555 Rue Cardin, Sorel-Tracy, QC, J3R 2S5
(450) 746-3515
Emp Here 27
SIC 8211 Elementary and secondary schools

D-U-N-S 25-233-1939   (BR)
COMMISSION SCOLAIRE DE SOREL-TRACY
CENTRE BERNARD GARIEPY
(*Suby of* Commission Scolaire de Sorel-Tracy)
5105 Boul Des Etudiants, Sorel-Tracy, QC, J3R 4K7
(450) 743-1284
Emp Here 60
SIC 8221 Colleges and universities

D-U-N-S 24-903-9660   (BR)
HATCH LTD
3220 Boul Saint-Louis, Sorel-Tracy, QC, J3R 5P8
(450) 743-2763
Emp Here 55
SIC 8711 Engineering services

D-U-N-S 24-426-3344   (SL)
MARQUIS DE TRACY I, LE
7075 Av Du Major-Beaudet, Sorel-Tracy, QC, J3R 5R2
(450) 742-9555
Emp Here 20   *Sales* 729,607
SIC 8361 Residential care

D-U-N-S 24-426-3369   (SL)
MARQUIS DE TRACY II
8200 Rue Industrielle, Sorel-Tracy, QC, J3R 5R3
(450) 746-9229
Emp Here 20   *Sales* 729,607
SIC 8361 Residential care

D-U-N-S 25-542-9821   (BR)
MATERIAUX R.M. BIBEAU LTEE
BIBEAU RONA
2425 Boul Saint-Louis, Sorel-Tracy, QC, J3R 4S6
(450) 743-3321
Emp Here 100
SIC 5072 Hardware

D-U-N-S 25-124-6120   (BR)
TRANSPORT ROBERT (1973) LTEE
GROUPE ROBERT TRANSPORT
2250 Rte Marie-Victorin, Sorel-Tracy, QC, J3R 1M9
(450) 743-0311
Emp Here 20

SIC 4213 Trucking, except local

Squatec, QC G0L
Temiscouata County

D-U-N-S 24-478-7461   (BR)
GROUPE LEBEL INC
4 Rue Saint-Marc, Squatec, QC, G0L 4H0
(418) 855-2951
Emp Here 30
SIC 2421 Sawmills and planing mills, general

D-U-N-S 20-261-7015   (HQ)
PELLETIER, RICHARD & FILS INC
4 Rue Saint-Marc, Squatec, QC, G0L 4H0
(418) 855-2951
Emp Here 85   *Emp Total* 24
Sales 37,574,761
SIC 5031 Lumber, plywood, and millwork
Pr Pr Lucette Pelletier
  Maurice Pelletier
  Brigitte Pelletier
Dir Fin Francis Beaulieu

St-Barnabe-Nord, QC G0X
St-Maurice County

D-U-N-S 25-365-3638   (BR)
COMMISSION SCOLAIRE DE L'ENERGIE
ECOLE NOTRE DAME DE LA JOIE
801 Rue Saint-Joseph, St-Barnabe-Nord, QC, G0X 2K0
(819) 221-2820
Emp Here 20
SIC 8211 Elementary and secondary schools

St-Francois-De-La-Riviere-Du-S, QC G0R
L'Islet County

D-U-N-S 20-237-8238   (SL)
MEUBLES MORIGEAU LTEE
25 Rue De L'Etang Rr 1, St-Francois-De-La-Riviere-Du-S, QC, G0R 3A0
(418) 259-7721
Emp Here 275   *Sales* 21,497,040
SIC 2511 Wood household furniture
Pr Pr Yves Jean
VP VP Sarto Jean
  Pierre Jean
  Ginette Jean

St-Francois-Xavier-De-Brompton, QC J0B

D-U-N-S 20-175-9904   (SL)
9049-5243 QUEBEC INC
59 Ch Labrie Rr 4, St-Francois-Xavier-De-Brompton, QC, J0B 2V0

Emp Here 126   *Sales* 14,167,680
SIC 2431 Millwork
Pr Robert Hunt

D-U-N-S 25-240-2383   (BR)
COMMISSION SCOLAIRE DES SOMMETS
ECOLE L'ARC-EN-CIEL
(*Suby of* Commission Scolaire des Sommets)
177 Rue De L'Eglise, St-Francois-Xavier-De-Brompton, QC, J0B 2V0
(819) 845-3976
Emp Here 30
SIC 8211 Elementary and secondary schools

St-Joachim-De-Montmorency, QC G0A

D-U-N-S 20-006-8257   (BR)
COMMISSION SCOLAIRE DES PREMIERES-SEIGNEURIES
COMMISSION SCOLAIRE DES PREMIERES-SEIGNEURIES
37 Ch Du Trait-Carre, St-Joachim-De-Montmorency, QC, G0A 3X0
(418) 821-8086
Emp Here 30
SIC 8211 Elementary and secondary schools

St-Octave, QC G0J
Matane County

D-U-N-S 20-711-8253   (BR)
COMMISSION SCOLAIRE DES PHARES
PAVILLON AUX QUATRE VENTS
(*Suby of* Commission Scolaire des Phares)
203 Rue De L'Eglise, St-Octave, QC, G0J 3B0
(418) 775-3531
Emp Here 55
SIC 8211 Elementary and secondary schools

St-Valerien, QC J0H
Shefford County

D-U-N-S 25-115-1692   (HQ)
TENCO INC
EQUIPEMENTS TENCO
1318 Rue Principale, St-Valerien, QC, J0H 2B0
(450) 549-2411
Emp Here 107   *Emp Total* 1
Sales 27,546,782
SIC 3711 Motor vehicles and car bodies
Pr Daniel Beaudoin
  Robert H George
  Richard J Wehrle
Dir Ronald A Robinson
Genl Mgr Robert Caron

Stanstead, QC J0B
Stanstead County

D-U-N-S 25-233-0998   (BR)
COMMISSION SCOLAIRE EASTERN TOWNSHIPS
SUNNYSIDE ELEMENTARY SCHOOL
(*Suby of* Commission Scolaire Eastern Townships)
441 Rue Dufferin, Stanstead, QC, J0B 3E2
(819) 876-2469
Emp Here 25
SIC 8211 Elementary and secondary schools

D-U-N-S 20-712-1190   (BR)
COMMISSION SCOLAIRE DES SOMMETS
ECOLES PRIMAIRES SECTEUR MEM-PHREMAGOG JARDIN DES FRONTIERES
7 Rue Park Rr 1, Stanstead, QC, J0B 3E0
(819) 876-7534
Emp Here 50
SIC 8211 Elementary and secondary schools

Ste-Catherine-De-La-J-Cartie, QC G3N

D-U-N-S 24-499-9702   (HQ)
2169-5762 QUEBEC INC
NERO BIANCO GROUP
(*Suby of* 2169-5762 Quebec Inc)
281 Rue Edward-Assh, Ste-Catherine-De-La-J-Cartie, QC, G3N 1A3

---

(418) 875-1839
Emp Here 35   *Emp Total* 250
Sales 15,248,786
SIC 5661 Shoe stores
  Jean-Luc Transon

D-U-N-S 20-309-2432   (HQ)
9264-6231 QUEBEC INC
NERO BIANCO
(*Suby of* Gestion Pelicane Inc)
281 Rue Edward-Assh, Ste-Catherine-De-La-J-Cartie, QC, G3N 1A3
(418) 875-1839
Emp Here 100   *Emp Total* 1
Sales 26,630,656
SIC 5621 Women's clothing stores
  Eric Chatila

D-U-N-S 24-791-4971   (HQ)
BOUTIQUE LE PENTAGONE INC
MODE F17
(*Suby of* Gestion Pelicane Inc)
281 Rue Edward-Assh, Ste-Catherine-De-La-J-Cartie, QC, G3N 1A3
(418) 875-1839
Emp Here 40   *Emp Total* 1
Sales 25,819,815
SIC 5621 Women's clothing stores
  Eric Chatila
Dir Jean-Luc Transon

D-U-N-S 20-712-0556   (BR)
COMMISSION SCOLAIRE DE LA CAPITALE, LA
ECOLE SAINT DENIS GARNEAU, L
10 Rue Des Etudiants, Ste-Catherine-De-La-J-Cartie, QC, G3N 0P4
(418) 686-4040
Emp Here 30
SIC 8211 Elementary and secondary schools

D-U-N-S 25-785-0701   (BR)
SOCIETE DES ETABLISSEMENTS DE PLEIN AIR DU QUEBEC
140 Montee De L'Auberge, Ste-Catherine-De-La-J-Cartie, QC, G3N 2Y6
(418) 875-2711
Emp Here 150
SIC 7032 Sporting and recreational camps

D-U-N-S 25-240-0197   (BR)
VILLE DE SAINTE-CATHERINE-DE-LA-JACQUES
VILLE DE SAINTE-CATHERINE-DE-LA-JACQUES
1 Rue Rouleau, Ste-Catherine-De-La-J-Cartie, QC, G3N 2S5

Emp Here 46
SIC 8231 Libraries

Ste-Marguerite-De-Dorchester, QC G0S
Dorchester County

D-U-N-S 24-942-5687   (SL)
C.G. AIR SYSTEMES INC
207 Rue Industrielle, Ste-Marguerite-De-Dorchester, QC, G0S 2X0
(418) 935-7075
Emp Here 50   *Sales* 4,815,406
SIC 3842 Surgical appliances and supplies

Ste-Marguerite-Du-Lac-Masson, QC J0T

D-U-N-S 25-847-8023   (BR)
C.S.S.S. DES PAYS-D'EN-HAUT
CCHSLD DES PAYS D'EN HAUT
(*Suby of* C.S.S.S. des Pays-d'En-Haut)
428 Rue Du Baron-Louis-Empain, Ste-Marguerite-Du-Lac-Masson, QC, J0T 1L0

Emp Here 120

SIC 8361 Residential care

Stoke, QC J0B

D-U-N-S 24-334-7114   (BR)
COMMISSION SCOLAIRE DE LA REGION-DE-SHERBROOKE
ECOLE NOTRE DAME DES CHAMPS
222 8e Rang E, Stoke, QC, J0B 3G0
(819) 822-5519
Emp Here 30
SIC 8211 Elementary and secondary schools

Stoneham-Et-Tewkesbury, QC G3C

D-U-N-S 20-868-8978   (SL)
CLUB DE GOLF DE STONEHAM INC
56 1re Av, Stoneham-Et-Tewkesbury, QC,
G3C 0K7
(418) 848-2414
Emp Here 50   *Sales* 2,042,900
SIC 7997 Membership sports and recreation clubs

D-U-N-S 25-233-1673   (BR)
**COMMISSION   SCOLAIRE   DES
PREMIERES-SEIGNEURIES**
ECOLE DU HARFANG DES NEIGES
(*Suby of* Commission Scolaire Des
Premieres-Seigneuries)
114 1re Av, Stoneham-Et-Tewkesbury, QC,
G3C 0L5
(418) 634-5546
Emp Here 50
SIC 8211 Elementary and secondary schools

D-U-N-S 20-777-5685   (SL)
ENTREPRISES DE STONEHAM INC, LES
SKI STONEHAM
600 Ch Du Hibou, Stoneham-Et-Tewkesbury,
QC, G3C 1T3
(418) 848-2415
Emp Here 70   *Sales* 3,064,349
SIC 7011 Hotels and motels

D-U-N-S 20-925-6606   (BR)
RESTAURANTS MIKA INC, LES
RESTAURANT MCDONALD'S
2766 Boul Talbot, Stoneham-Et-Tewkesbury,
QC, G3C 1K1
(418) 848-3838
Emp Here 54
SIC 5812 Eating places

D-U-N-S 24-111-6979   (BR)
**SOCIETE   DES   ETABLISSEMENTS   DE
PLEIN AIR DU QUEBEC**
PARC   NATIONAL   DE   LA   JACQUES-CARTIER
103 Ch Du Parc-National, Stoneham-Et-Tewkesbury, QC, G3C 2T5
(418) 848-3169
Emp Here 49
SIC 7996 Amusement parks

Sutton, QC J0E
Brome County

D-U-N-S 25-258-9064   (SL)
CENTRE DE SANTE ET DE SERVICES SO-CIAUX DE LA POMMERAIE, LE
FOYER SUTTON
50 Rue Western, Sutton, QC, J0E 2K0
(450) 538-3332
Emp Here 110   *Sales* 4,012,839
SIC 8361 Residential care

D-U-N-S 25-232-9156   (BR)
COMMISSION SCOLAIRE DU VAL-DES-

CERFS
ECOLE DE SUTTON
19 Rue Highland, Sutton, QC, J0E 2K0
(450) 538-5843
Emp Here 40
SIC 8211 Elementary and secondary schools

D-U-N-S 24-084-5511   (BR)
FILTEX INC
(*Suby of* Filtex Inc)
5 Rue Pine, Sutton, QC, J0E 2K0
(450) 538-2331
Emp Here 55
SIC 2299 Textile goods, nec

D-U-N-S 25-836-3720   (SL)
HYLAND'S HOMEOPATHIC CANADA INC
381 139 Rte N, Sutton, QC, J0E 2K0
(450) 538-6636
Emp Here 26   *Sales* 3,210,271
SIC 5122 Drugs, proprietaries, and sundries

Tadoussac, QC G0T
Saguenay County

D-U-N-S 20-290-3555   (SL)
1006823 BC LTD
HOTEL TADOUSSAC
165 Rue Du Bord-De-L'Eau, Tadoussac, QC,
G0T 2A0
(418) 235-4421
Emp Here 50   *Sales* 2,188,821
SIC 7011 Hotels and motels

D-U-N-S 20-777-1135   (BR)
**CENTRE DE SANTE ET DES SERVICES
SOCIAUX DE LA HAUTE-COTE-NORD**
(*Suby of* Centre de Sante et des Services So-ciaux de la Haute-Cote-Nord)
162 Rue Des Jesuites, Tadoussac, QC, G0T
2A0
(418) 235-4588
Emp Here 150
SIC 8062 General medical and surgical hospi-tals

Taschereau, QC J0Z
Abitibi County

D-U-N-S 25-298-1519   (BR)
COMMISSION SCOLAIRE ABITIBI
ECOLE BELLEFEUILLE
(*Suby of* Commission Scolaire Abitibi)
190 Av Privat, Taschereau, QC, J0Z 3N0
(819) 796-3321
Emp Here 25
SIC 8211 Elementary and secondary schools

Temiscaming, QC J0Z
Temiscaninque County

D-U-N-S 20-712-5696   (BR)
COMMISSION SCOLAIRE WESTERN QUE-BEC
G THEBERGE SCHOOL
(*Suby of* Commission Scolaire Western Que-bec)
38 Rue Boucher, Temiscaming, QC, J0Z 3R0

Emp Here 50
SIC 8211 Elementary and secondary schools

D-U-N-S 25-233-5930   (BR)
COMMISSION   SCOLAIRE   DU   LAC-TEMISCAMINGUE
ECOLE GILBERT THEBERGE
(*Suby of* Commission Scolaire du Lac-Temiscamingue)
40 Rue Boucher, Temiscaming, QC, J0Z 3R0

---

(819) 627-3337
Emp Here 40
SIC 8211 Elementary and secondary schools

D-U-N-S 20-195-4612   (BR)
TEMBEC INC
BOLT
10 Ch Gatineau, Temiscaming, QC, J0Z 3R0
(819) 627-4387
Emp Here 800
SIC 2611 Pulp mills

Temiscouata-Sur-Le-Lac, QC G0L

D-U-N-S 20-317-5229   (BR)
CASCADES CANADA ULC
NORAMPAC
520 Rue Commerciale N, Temiscouata-Sur-Le-Lac, QC, G0L 1E0
(418) 854-2803
Emp Here 542
SIC 2631 Paperboard mills

D-U-N-S 25-232-3134   (BR)
**COMMISSION SCOLAIRE DU FLEUVE ET
DES LACS**
ECOLE SECONDAIRE DE CABANO
120 Boul Phil-Latulippe, Temiscouata-Sur-Le-Lac, QC, G0L 1E0
(418) 854-3640
Emp Here 70
SIC 8211 Elementary and secondary schools

D-U-N-S 25-628-8312   (BR)
GROUPE COOPERATIF DYNACO
CENTRE DE RENOVATION DYNACO BMR
(*Suby of* Groupe Cooperatif Dynaco)
562 Rue Commerciale N, Temiscouata-Sur-Le-Lac, QC, G0L 1E0
(418) 854-6705
Emp Here 30
SIC 5251 Hardware stores

D-U-N-S 24-942-0225   (BR)
GROUPE LEBEL INC
200 Rue De L'Eglise, Temiscouata-Sur-Le-Lac, QC, G0L 1X0
(418) 899-6737
Emp Here 30
SIC 2421 Sawmills and planing mills, general

D-U-N-S 24-344-6577   (BR)
**PROMUTUEL   TEMISCOUTA   SOCIETE
MUTUELLE D'ASSURANCE GENERALE**
PROMUTULE DES RIBERAINS
592b Rue Commerciale N, Temiscouata-Sur-Le-Lac, QC, G0L 1E0
(418) 854-2016
Emp Here 30
SIC 6411 Insurance agents, brokers, and ser-vice

D-U-N-S 24-201-7945   (BR)
SUPERMARCHES GP INC, LES
METRO CABANO
(*Suby of* Supermarches GP Inc, Les)
633   Rue   Commerciale   N   Unite   100,
Temiscouata-Sur-Le-Lac, QC, G0L 1E0
(418) 854-2177
Emp Here 76
SIC 5411 Grocery stores

Terrebonne, QC J6V
Terrebonne County

D-U-N-S 20-343-9161   (SL)
9277-9230 QUEBEC INC
STEAK FRITES ST-PAUL & GIORGIO RIS-TORANTE TM
950 Montee Des Pionniers, Terrebonne, QC,
J6V 1S8
(450) 704-0605
Emp Here 50   *Sales* 1,532,175

SIC 5812 Eating places

D-U-N-S 24-062-5827   (BR)
BEST BUY CANADA LTD
FUTURE SHOP
(*Suby of* Best Buy Co., Inc.)
790 Montee Des Pionniers, Terrebonne, QC,
J6V 1N9
(450) 470-9636
Emp Here 56
SIC 5731 Radio, television, and electronic stores

D-U-N-S 24-325-0334   (BR)
BRICK WAREHOUSE LP, THE
BRICK, THE
274 Montee Des Pionniers, Terrebonne, QC,
J6V 1S6
(450) 657-7171
Emp Here 20
SIC 5712 Furniture stores

D-U-N-S 20-236-4600   (HQ)
BROWNING-FERRIS QUEBEC INC
(*Suby of* Browning-Ferris Quebec Inc)
3779 Ch Des Quarante-Arpents, Terrebonne,
QC, J6V 9T6
(450) 474-2423
Emp Here 45   *Emp Total* 45
Sales 8,138,880
SIC 4953 Refuse systems
Pr Yves Normandin
VP Hector Chamberland

D-U-N-S 24-347-4330   (BR)
**CAISSE   DESJARDINS   PIERRE-LE
GARDEUR**
*CAISSE   DESJARDINS   PIERRE-LE
GARDEUR*
1000 Montee Des Pionniers Unite 100, Terre-bonne, QC, J6V 1S8
(450) 581-4740
Emp Here 35
SIC 6062 State credit unions

D-U-N-S 24-227-1229   (SL)
**CENTRE   HOSPITALIER   PIERRE   LE
GARDEUR**
911 Montee Des Pionniers, Terrebonne, QC,
J6V 2H2
(450) 654-7525
Emp Here 3,700   *Sales* 346,406,640
SIC 8062 General medical and surgical hospi-tals
Genl Mgr Michel Boffard

D-U-N-S 20-712-2461   (BR)
COMMISSION SCOLAIRE DES AFFLU-ENTS
ECOLE PRIMAIRE JEAN DE LA FONTAINE
192 Rue De L'Eglise, Terrebonne, QC, J6V
1B4
(450) 492-3736
Emp Here 50
SIC 8211 Elementary and secondary schools

D-U-N-S 20-119-1728   (SL)
COMPLEXE ENVIRO CONNEXIONS LTEE
BFI USINE DE TRIAGE LACHENAIE
3779 Ch Des Quarante-Arpents, Terrebonne,
QC, J6V 9T6
(450) 474-2423
Emp Here 26   *Sales* 2,042,900
SIC 4212 Local trucking, without storage

D-U-N-S 25-188-5125   (BR)
HOME DEPOT OF CANADA INC
HOME DEPOT LACHENAIE
(*Suby of* The Home Depot Inc)
660 Montee Des Pionniers, Terrebonne, QC,
J6V 1N9
(450) 657-4400
Emp Here 160
SIC 5211 Lumber and other building materials

D-U-N-S 20-541-6910   (HQ)
KILDAIR SERVICE ULC
1000 Montee Des Pionniers Bureau 110, Ter-

---

rebonne, QC, J6V 1S8
(450) 756-8091
Emp Here 25   *Sales* 140,532,550
SIC 5172 Petroleum products, nec
Pr Daniel Morin
Ch Bd Gary Rinaldi
 Jacques Ferraro
Sec Paul A Scoff
Dir Joseph Smith

D-U-N-S 20-017-2441   (SL)
LIBRAIRIE RENAUD-BRAY INC
BISTRO OLIVIERI
3213 Ch Saint-Charles Bureau 81, Terrebonne, QC, J6V 0G8
(450) 492-1011
Emp Here 49   *Sales* 7,296,070
SIC 1521 Single-family housing construction

D-U-N-S 25-360-0746   (BR)
PROVIGO DISTRIBUTION INC
MAXI LACHENAIE 8622
390 Montee Des Pionniers, Terrebonne, QC, J6V 1S6
(450) 657-7710
Emp Here 50
SIC 5411 Grocery stores

D-U-N-S 20-847-3897   (BR)
RE-MAX DES MILLE-ILES INC
293 Montee Des Pionniers, Terrebonne, QC, J6V 1H4
(450) 582-5544
Emp Here 20
SIC 6531 Real estate agents and managers

D-U-N-S 20-003-9860   (BR)
STAPLES CANADA INC
BUREAU EN GROS
(*Suby of* Staples, Inc.)
590 Montee Des Pionniers, Terrebonne, QC, J6V 1N9
(450) 657-9600
Emp Here 30
SIC 5943 Stationery stores

D-U-N-S 20-706-5082   (BR)
WENDY'S RESTAURANTS OF CANADA INC
(*Suby of* The Wendy's Company)
400 Montee Des Pionniers, Terrebonne, QC, J6V 1S6

Emp Here 25
SIC 5812 Eating places

D-U-N-S 20-184-2973   (BR)
WINNERS MERCHANTS INTERNATIONAL L.P.
WINNERS
(*Suby of* The TJX Companies Inc)
570 Montee Des Pionniers, Terrebonne, QC, J6V 1N9
(450) 654-4634
Emp Here 40
SIC 5651 Family clothing stores

Terrebonne, QC J6W
Terrebonne County

D-U-N-S 25-651-8739   (BR)
9046-2680 QUEBEC INC
TIM HORTONS
1030 Boul Moody, Terrebonne, QC, J6W 3K9
(450) 492-5156
Emp Here 40
SIC 5812 Eating places

D-U-N-S 24-251-7811   (SL)
9230-5713 QUEBEC INC
MOON PALACE RESTAURANT
569 Boul Des Seigneurs, Terrebonne, QC, J6W 1T5
(450) 471-9912
Emp Here 60   *Sales* 1,824,018
SIC 5812 Eating places

D-U-N-S 25-410-0639   (BR)
BANQUE NATIONALE DU CANADA
1080 Boul Des Seigneurs, Terrebonne, QC, J6W 3W4
(450) 471-3768
Emp Here 30
SIC 6021 National commercial banks

D-U-N-S 24-057-0853   (SL)
CENTRE D'HEBERGEMENT DES MOULINS INC
934 Rue Saint-Sacrement, Terrebonne, QC, J6W 3G2
(450) 964-8448
Emp Here 80   *Sales* 3,465,004
SIC 8361 Residential care

D-U-N-S 24-346-3366   (BR)
CENTRE DE SANTE ET DE SERVICES SOCIAUX DU SUD DE LANAUDIERE
CENTRE DE SANTE ET DE SERVICES SOCIAUX DU SUD DE LANAUDIERE
1317 Boul Des Seigneurs, Terrebonne, QC, J6W 5B1
(450) 471-2881
Emp Here 300
SIC 8011 Offices and clinics of medical doctors

D-U-N-S 20-007-7811   (BR)
CENTRE DE SANTE ET DE SERVICES SOCIAUX DU SUD DE LANAUDIERE
CENTRE DE SANTE ET DE SERVICES SOCIAUX DU SUD DE LANAUDIERE
1355 Grande Allee Bureau 101, Terrebonne, QC, J6W 4K6

Emp Here 32
SIC 8011 Offices and clinics of medical doctors

D-U-N-S 25-210-6539   (HQ)
CINEMAS GUZZO INC
MEGA PLEX
(*Suby of* Cinemas Guzzo Inc)
1055 Ch Du Coteau, Terrebonne, QC, J6W 5Y8
(450) 961-2945
Emp Here 400   *Emp Total* 500
Sales 25,914,240
SIC 7832 Motion picture theaters, except drive-in
Pr Pr Angelo Guzzo
 Vincenzo Guzzo
Dir Rosetta Rubino-Guzzo

D-U-N-S 20-712-2479   (BR)
COMMISSION SCOLAIRE DES AFFLUENTS
ECOLES PRIMAIRES NOTRE DAME
508 Montee Masson, Terrebonne, QC, J6W 2Z3
(450) 492-3605
Emp Here 50
SIC 8211 Elementary and secondary schools

D-U-N-S 20-033-9518   (BR)
COMMISSION SCOLAIRE DES AFFLUENTS
ECOLE SECONDAIRE DES RIVES
400 Montee Dumais, Terrebonne, QC, J6W 5W9
(450) 492-3613
Emp Here 100
SIC 8211 Elementary and secondary schools

D-U-N-S 25-257-2433   (BR)
ENGLOBE CORP
ENGLOBE CORP
1140 Rue Levis, Terrebonne, QC, J6W 5S6
(450) 961-3535
Emp Here 40
SIC 8748 Business consulting, nec

D-U-N-S 24-563-9505   (HQ)
ENCRES INTERNATIONALE INX CORP
INX INTERNATIONAL INK
1247 Rue Nationale, Terrebonne, QC, J6W

6H8
(450) 477-9145
Emp Here 40   *Emp Total* 3,909
Sales 8,669,427
SIC 2899 Chemical preparations, nec
Pr Pr Richard Clendenning
 Normand Leduc
Treas Brice Kristo

D-U-N-S 24-818-3548   (SL)
GROUPE ROYAL INC
ROYALPLAST DOOR SYSTEMS CO
1085 Rue Des Cheminots, Terrebonne, QC, J6W 0A1
(450) 492-5080
Emp Here 100   *Sales* 20,866,760
SIC 5039 Construction materials, nec
Pr Andre Touchette
 Bradley K. Reynolds
VP VP Guy Prentice
Ex VP Simon Bates
Treas Christian Huot
Dir Jean-Sebastien L'Ecuyer
Genl Mgr Timothy Mann Jr.

D-U-N-S 24-648-1931   (SL)
JESCOS PHOTO INC
IMPORTATION LOREX
133 Rue Chapleau, Terrebonne, QC, J6W 2T2

Emp Here 50   *Sales* 9,536,300
SIC 5046 Commercial equipment, nec
Pr Pr Charles Lemieux

D-U-N-S 24-581-7622   (SL)
LABORATOIRES LALCO INC
DISTRIBUTION IRIS
(*Suby of* 171920 Canada Inc)
1542 Rue Nationale, Terrebonne, QC, J6W 6M1
(450) 492-6435
Emp Here 25   *Sales* 3,638,254
SIC 5122 Drugs, proprietaries, and sundries

D-U-N-S 24-801-2320   (SL)
MACONNERIE S D L INC
1159 Rue Levis, Terrebonne, QC, J6W 0A9
(450) 492-7111
Emp Here 50   *Sales* 3,648,035
SIC 1741 Masonry and other stonework

D-U-N-S 25-291-5210   (BR)
MEDIAS TRANSCONTINENTAL S.E.N.C.
TRAIT D'UNION, LE
1300 Grande Allee Suite 210, Terrebonne, QC, J6W 4M4
(450) 964-4400
Emp Here 23
SIC 2711 Newspapers

D-U-N-S 20-703-9020   (BR)
PREMIER TECH TECHNOLOGIES LIMITEE
PREMIER TECH AQUA
1153 Rue Levis, Terrebonne, QC, J6W 0A9
(450) 471-8444
Emp Here 20
SIC 3589 Service industry machinery, nec

D-U-N-S 25-299-9115   (BR)
PRISZM LP
PFK
947 Boul Des Seigneurs, Terrebonne, QC, J6W 3W5
(450) 471-1103
Emp Here 20
SIC 5812 Eating places

D-U-N-S 20-314-0181   (BR)
PRODUITS POUR TOITURES FRANSYL LTEE
671 Rue Leveille, Terrebonne, QC, J6W 1Z9
(450) 492-2392
Emp Here 81
SIC 5033 Roofing, siding, and insulation

D-U-N-S 25-827-6286   (BR)
PROVIGO DISTRIBUTION INC
MAXI

1345 Boul Moody, Terrebonne, QC, J6W 3L1
(450) 471-1009
Emp Here 120
SIC 5411 Grocery stores

D-U-N-S 25-257-0312   (BR)
REDBERRY FRANCHISING CORP
BURGER KING
1110 Boul Moody, Terrebonne, QC, J6W 3K9

Emp Here 27
SIC 5812 Eating places

D-U-N-S 24-329-2369   (BR)
ROYAL GROUP, INC
ROYAL WINDOW & DOOR PROFILES, PLANT 10
1085 Rue Des Cheminots Bureau 10, Terrebonne, QC, J6W 0A1
(450) 668-5549
Emp Here 100
SIC 5031 Lumber, plywood, and millwork

D-U-N-S 24-210-4946   (BR)
SOBEYS QUEBEC INC
IGA EXTRA THIBAULT
675 Boul Des Seigneurs, Terrebonne, QC, J6W 1T5
(450) 492-5580
Emp Here 100
SIC 5411 Grocery stores

D-U-N-S 25-308-9676   (BR)
SOCIETE DES ALCOOLS DU QUEBEC
SOCIETE DES ALCOOLS DU QUEBEC
1100 Boul Des Seigneurs, Terrebonne, QC, J6W 3W4
(450) 471-9180
Emp Here 29
SIC 5921 Liquor stores

D-U-N-S 24-698-3126   (SL)
TOILE SOLEIL INC
1500 Rue Nationale, Terrebonne, QC, J6W 6M1
(450) 964-2218
Emp Here 50   *Sales* 4,158,760
SIC 3949 Sporting and athletic goods, nec

D-U-N-S 25-412-9497   (BR)
TURQUOISE, CABINET EN ASSURANCE DE DOMMAGES ET SERVICES FINANCIERS INC, LA
GROUPE CYR & LYRAS
1190 Rue Levis, Terrebonne, QC, J6W 5S6
(450) 961-4567
Emp Here 30
SIC 6411 Insurance agents, brokers, and service

D-U-N-S 25-150-5558   (SL)
VANICO-MARONYX INC
1000 Rue Nationale, Terrebonne, QC, J6W 6B4
(450) 471-4447
Emp Here 85   *Sales* 4,961,328
SIC 2434 Wood kitchen cabinets

D-U-N-S 25-010-9451   (BR)
WESTCLIFF MANAGEMENT LTD
GALLERIES TERREBONNE
1185 Boul Moody Unite 552, Terrebonne, QC, J6W 3Z5
(450) 471-9726
Emp Here 100
SIC 6512 Nonresidential building operators

Terrebonne, QC J6X
Terrebonne County

D-U-N-S 25-256-5338   (SL)
2850401 CANADA INC
BOULANGERIE PREMIERE MOISSON
2021 Ch Gascon, Terrebonne, QC, J6X 4H2
(450) 964-9333
Emp Here 75   *Sales* 2,553,625

SIC 5461 Retail bakeries

D-U-N-S 24-189-4729   (SL)
9030-5582 QUEBEC INC
RESTAURANT MANGIAMO
1460 Ch Gascon Bureau 101, Terrebonne, QC, J6X 2Z5
(450) 492-5225
Emp Here 90   *Sales* 2,699,546
SIC 5812 Eating places

D-U-N-S 24-895-7300   (BR)
9046-2680 QUEBEC INC
TIM HORTONS
2980 Ch Gascon, Terrebonne, QC, J6X 3Z3
(450) 477-1600
Emp Here 50
SIC 5812 Eating places

D-U-N-S 24-056-1428   (SL)
9064-3032 QUEBEC INC
JR SERVICES SANITAIRES
2565 Ch Comtois, Terrebonne, QC, J6X 0H6
(514) 648-4222
Emp Here 50   *Sales* 3,939,878
SIC 4212 Local trucking, without storage

D-U-N-S 25-647-7118   (BR)
BANQUE NATIONALE DU CANADA
2135 Ch Gascon, Terrebonne, QC, J6X 4H2
(450) 964-4859
Emp Here 20
SIC 6021 National commercial banks

D-U-N-S 20-033-9526   (BR)
COMMISSION SCOLAIRE DES AFFLU-ENTS
ECOLE PRIMAIRE DE LA FABLIERE
1659 Boul Des Seigneurs, Terrebonne, QC, J6X 3E3
(450) 492-3622
Emp Here 100
SIC 8211 Elementary and secondary schools

D-U-N-S 25-026-4702   (BR)
COMMISSION SCOLAIRE DES AFFLU-ENTS
ECOLE LE CASTELET
(*Suby of* Commission Scolaire des Affluents)
4200 Rue Robert, Terrebonne, QC, J6X 2N9
(450) 492-3636
Emp Here 60
SIC 8211 Elementary and secondary schools

D-U-N-S 20-712-2438   (BR)
COMMISSION SCOLAIRE DES AFFLU-ENTS
ECOLE DE L'ETINCELLE
2225 Boul Des Seigneurs, Terrebonne, QC, J6X 4A8
(450) 492-3740
Emp Here 50
SIC 8211 Elementary and secondary schools

D-U-N-S 25-474-7561   (BR)
COMMISSION SCOLAIRE DES AFFLU-ENTS
ECOLES SECONDAIRES DES TROIS SAISONS
(*Suby of* Commission Scolaire des Affluents)
1658 Boul Des Seigneurs, Terrebonne, QC, J6X 4T1
(450) 492-3746
Emp Here 25
SIC 8211 Elementary and secondary schools

D-U-N-S 25-172-8077   (SL)
CONCEPT S.G.A. INC
DISTRIBUTION SGA
3160 Boul Des Entreprises, Terrebonne, QC, J6X 4J8
(450) 477-0526
Emp Here 50   *Sales* 4,851,006
SIC 2431 Millwork

D-U-N-S 24-214-7903   (BR)
FONDATION DU CEGEP REGIONAL DE LANAUDIERE
CEGEP REGIONAL DE LANAUDIERE A

TERREBONNE
2505 Boul Des Entreprises, Terrebonne, QC, J6X 5S5
(450) 470-0933
Emp Here 100
SIC 8221 Colleges and universities

D-U-N-S 25-916-3921   (BR)
GROUPE SPORTSCENE INC
CAGE AUX SPORTS, LE
2247 Ch Gascon Bureau 403, Terrebonne, QC, J6X 4H3
(450) 961-2243
Emp Here 40
SIC 5812 Eating places

D-U-N-S 20-252-6224   (HQ)
INDUSTRIES MAILHOT INC
MALIHOT HYDRAUTECH
3330 Boul Des Entreprises, Terrebonne, QC, J6X 4J8
(450) 477-6222
Emp Here 20   *Emp Total* 225
Sales 30,814,158
SIC 3569 General industrial machinery, nec
Pr Pr Charles Massicotte

D-U-N-S 20-714-9423   (BR)
INSURANCE BUREAU OF CANADA
BUREAU D'ASSURANCE DU CANADA SER-VICE D'ENQUETE
(*Suby of* Insurance Bureau of Canada)
4150 Sainte Catherine O, Terrebonne, QC, J6X 3P2

Emp Here 20
SIC 6411 Insurance agents, brokers, and service

D-U-N-S 24-016-8745   (BR)
NAUTILUS PLUS INC
NAUTILUS PLUS
1507 Ch Gascon, Terrebonne, QC, J6X 2Z6
(450) 964-7177
Emp Here 30
SIC 7999 Amusement and recreation, nec

D-U-N-S 20-107-8305   (SL)
RESTAURANTS SERQUA INC, LES
ST-HUBERT
1415 Boul Moody, Terrebonne, QC, J6X 4C8
(450) 471-1161
Emp Here 80   *Sales* 2,407,703
SIC 5812 Eating places

D-U-N-S 24-070-0778   (BR)
SOCIETE DES ALCOOLS DU QUEBEC
SOCIETE DES ALCOOLS DU QUEBEC
2151 Ch Gascon, Terrebonne, QC, J6X 4H2
(450) 964-9551
Emp Here 60
SIC 5921 Liquor stores

D-U-N-S 20-211-0677   (BR)
UAP INC
CENTRE DE CULASSE, LE
(*Suby of* Genuine Parts Company)
3150 Boul Des Entreprises, Terrebonne, QC, J6X 4J8

Emp Here 50
SIC 3714 Motor vehicle parts and accessories

Terrebonne, QC J6Y
Terrebonne County

D-U-N-S 25-629-5718   (SL)
9083-7436 QUEBEC INC
DRYTEC TRANS-CANADA
(*Suby of* Coradin Inc)
250 Rue Henry-Bessemer, Terrebonne, QC, J6Y 1T3
(450) 965-0200
Emp Here 26   *Sales* 1,824,018
SIC 3479 Metal coating and allied services

D-U-N-S 24-525-1223   (SL)
9138-7472 QUEBEC INC
CRE TRANSPORT
1060 Rue Armand-Bombardier, Terrebonne, QC, J6Y 1R9
(450) 477-9996
Emp Here 50   *Sales* 2,626,585
SIC 4131 Intercity and rural bus transportation

D-U-N-S 24-827-1202   (SL)
9215-7510 QUEBEC INC
AMPAC
(*Suby of* Proampac LLC)
1041 Boul Des Entreprises O, Terrebonne, QC, J6Y 1V2
(450) 628-4288
Emp Here 75   *Sales* 12,214,139
SIC 3081 Unsupported plastics film and sheet
Pr Gregory R. Tucker
   Eric Bradford

D-U-N-S 24-419-2501   (HQ)
ATIS PORTES ET FENETRES CORP.
FENESTRATION PRO-TECH
(*Suby of* Groupe Atis Inc)
2175 Boul Des Entreprises, Terrebonne, QC, J6Y 1W9
(450) 492-0404
Emp Here 25   *Emp Total* 340
Sales 16,343,197
SIC 2431 Millwork
Pr Robert Doyon
Sec Andre Parent
   Guy Bouille
Dir Mathieu Lalonde

D-U-N-S 24-954-2457   (SL)
AUTOBUS YVES SEGUIN & FILS INC
1730 Rue Effingham, Terrebonne, QC, J6Y 1R7
(450) 433-6958
Emp Here 100   *Sales* 2,845,467
SIC 4151 School buses

D-U-N-S 20-583-3684   (BR)
BELTERRA CORPORATION
1015 Rue Des Forges, Terrebonne, QC, J6Y 0J9
(450) 621-8228
Emp Here 20
SIC 5085 Industrial supplies

D-U-N-S 25-976-1427   (BR)
COMMISSION SCOLAIRE DE LA SEIGNEURIE-DES-MILLE-ILES
COMMISSION SCOLAIRE DE LA SEIGNEURIE-DES-MILLE-ILES
(*Suby of* Commission Scolaire de la Seigneurie-Des-Mille-Iles)
452 Rue De Neuilly, Terrebonne, QC, J6Y 1R2
(450) 621-5642
Emp Here 40
SIC 8211 Elementary and secondary schools

D-U-N-S 25-976-0213   (BR)
COMMISSION SCOLAIRE DE LA SEIGNEURIE-DES-MILLE-ILES
COMMISSION SCOLAIRE DE LA SEIGNEURIE-DES-MILLE-ILES
(*Suby of* Commission Scolaire de la Seigneurie-Des-Mille-Iles)
3415 Place Camus, Terrebonne, QC, J6Y 0C8
(450) 979-9736
Emp Here 50
SIC 8211 Elementary and secondary schools

D-U-N-S 25-706-0293   (SL)
COMPTEC S. G. INC
EQUIPE D'INVENTAIRE F.M.
1115 Rue Armand-Bombardier, Terrebonne, QC, J6Y 1S9
(450) 965-8166
Emp Here 50   *Sales* 2,626,585
SIC 7389 Business services, nec

D-U-N-S 24-893-2209   (SL)
CONSTRUCTION ST LEONAR
1091 Rue Armand-Bombardier, Terrebonne,

QC, J6Y 1S9
(514) 918-1636
Emp Here 50   *Sales* 10,248,960
SIC 1521 Single-family housing construction
Pr Benoit Monette

D-U-N-S 20-997-7156   (SL)
I.M.E. INC
ISOLATION MULTI-ENERGIE
1029 Boul Des Entreprises, Terrebonne, QC, J6Y 1V2
(450) 435-9995
Emp Here 60   *Sales* 6,871,200
SIC 1742 Plastering, drywall, and insulation
Pr Pr Karl Mongrain

D-U-N-S 25-794-8042   (SL)
METAL C.N. INC
1049 Boul Des Entreprises, Terrebonne, QC, J6Y 1V2
(450) 963-4464
Emp Here 40   *Sales* 4,377,642
SIC 3499 Fabricated Metal products, nec

D-U-N-S 20-015-8645   (SL)
PLASTICASE INC
1059 Boul Des Entreprises, Terrebonne, QC, J6Y 1V2
(450) 628-1006
Emp Here 35   *Sales* 3,720,996
SIC 3089 Plastics products, nec

D-U-N-S 24-908-8188   (SL)
PORTES DECKO INC
2375 Rue Edouard-Michelin, Terrebonne, QC, J6Y 4P2
(450) 477-0199
Emp Here 50   *Sales* 4,596,524
SIC 3231 Products of purchased glass

D-U-N-S 24-415-6662   (BR)
RUSSEL METALS INC
ACIER LEROUX
1025 Boul Des Entreprises, Terrebonne, QC, J6Y 1V2
(514) 333-5380
Emp Here 25
SIC 5051 Metals service centers and offices

Terrebonne, QC J7M
Terrebonne County

D-U-N-S 24-192-3312   (BR)
AGNEW, J. E. FOOD SERVICES LTD
TIM HORTONS
5481 Boul Laurier, Terrebonne, QC, J7M 1C3
(450) 477-5736
Emp Here 42
SIC 5812 Eating places

D-U-N-S 20-384-9174   (BR)
CAISSE POPULAIRE DESJARDINS LE MANOIR
4771 Boul Laurier, Terrebonne, QC, J7M 1S9
(450) 474-2474
Emp Here 70
SIC 6062 State credit unions

D-U-N-S 25-233-0055   (BR)
COMMISSION SCOLAIRE DES AFFLU-ENTS
ECOLE DU BOISE
(*Suby of* Commission Scolaire des Affluents)
5800 Rue Rodrigue, Terrebonne, QC, J7M 1Y6
(450) 492-3617
Emp Here 26
SIC 8211 Elementary and secondary schools

D-U-N-S 25-232-9164   (BR)
COMMISSION SCOLAIRE DES AFFLU-ENTS
ECOLE ST-JOACHIM
(*Suby of* Commission Scolaire des Affluents)
10521 Rue Villeneuve, Terrebonne, QC, J7M 0K8

---

(450) 492-3609
Emp Here 35
SIC 8211 Elementary and secondary schools

D-U-N-S 20-026-3908   (BR)
**COMMISSION SCOLAIRE DES AFFLU-
ENTS**
ECOLE PRIMAIRE DU GEAI BLEU
7101 Rue Rodrigue, Terrebonne, QC, J7M
1Y7
(450) 492-3742
Emp Here 65
SIC 8211 Elementary and secondary schools

D-U-N-S 20-712-2420   (BR)
**COMMISSION SCOLAIRE DES AFFLU-
ENTS**
ECOLE PRIMAIRE DE L' AUBIER
1651 Rue Guillemette, Terrebonne, QC, J7M
1Z7
(450) 492-3748
Emp Here 50
SIC 8211 Elementary and secondary schools

D-U-N-S 20-712-2453   (BR)
**COMMISSION SCOLAIRE DES AFFLU-
ENTS**
ECOLES PRIMAIRES DE L' OREE DES BOIS
4960 Rue Rodrigue, Terrebonne, QC, J7M
1Y9
(450) 492-3747
Emp Here 50
SIC 8211 Elementary and secondary schools

D-U-N-S 20-194-6980   (BR)
ECOLAIT LTEE
1591 Ch Sainte-Claire, Terrebonne, QC, J7M
1M2
(450) 478-2055
Emp Here 180
SIC 2011 Meat packing plants

D-U-N-S 25-625-9425   (BR)
PLACEMENTS SELTEC LTEE, LES
MCDONALD'S
5531 Boul Laurier, Terrebonne, QC, J7M 1T7
(450) 968-3322
Emp Here 50
SIC 5812 Eating places

D-U-N-S 20-867-3835   (BR)
SOBEYS QUEBEC INC
5671 Boul Laurier Bureau 117, Terrebonne,
QC, J7M 1T7
(450) 477-4077
Emp Here 70
SIC 5411 Grocery stores

Thetford Mines, QC G6G
Megantic County

D-U-N-S 24-309-4203   (SL)
6410138 CANADA INC
CANATRUSS
1760 Rue Setlakwe, Thetford Mines, QC, G6G
8B2

Emp Here 50   *Sales* 10,365,619
SIC 2493 Reconstituted wood products
Pr Pr Ralph Poulin
Sec Serge Hudon

D-U-N-S 25-093-2642   (BR)
9130-1093 QUEBEC INC
9130-1093 QUEBEC INC.
805 Boul Frontenac E, Thetford Mines, QC,
G6G 6L5
(418) 338-6388
Emp Here 20
SIC 6512 Nonresidential building operators

D-U-N-S 24-016-7978   (BR)
9130-1093 QUEBEC INC
9130-1093 QUEBEC INC.
805 Boul Frontenac E, Thetford Mines, QC,
G6G 6L5

(418) 338-6388
Emp Here 300
SIC 6512 Nonresidential building operators

D-U-N-S 20-332-3035   (BR)
CVTECH INC
CVTECH-AAB
3037 Boul Frontenac E, Thetford Mines, QC,
G6G 6P6
(418) 335-7220
Emp Here 24
SIC 3566 Speed changers, drives, and gears

D-U-N-S 20-580-4565   (BR)
CANADA POST CORPORATION
BUREAU DE POST THETFORD MINES
8 Rue Notre-Dame E, Thetford Mines, QC,
G6G 0C2
(418) 338-2177
Emp Here 41
SIC 4311 U.s. postal service

D-U-N-S 25-232-6780   (BR)
**COMMISSION SCOLAIRE DES AP-
PALACHES**
ECOLE SECONDAIRE JOSEPH FECTEAU
(*Suby of* Commission Scolaire des Ap-
palaches)
561 Rue Saint-Patrick, Thetford Mines, QC,
G6G 5W1
(418) 338-7831
Emp Here 100
SIC 8211 Elementary and secondary schools

D-U-N-S 25-232-8265   (BR)
**COMMISSION SCOLAIRE DES AP-
PALACHES**
ECOLE ST NOEL
(*Suby of* Commission Scolaire des Ap-
palaches)
993 8e Av, Thetford Mines, QC, G6G 2E3
(418) 335-9826
Emp Here 45
SIC 8211 Elementary and secondary schools

D-U-N-S 25-233-6508   (BR)
**COMMISSION SCOLAIRE DES AP-
PALACHES**
ECOLE DU PLEIN SOLEIL
(*Suby of* Commission Scolaire des Ap-
palaches)
507 Rue Saint-Patrick, Thetford Mines, QC,
G6G 4B1
(418) 338-0640
Emp Here 20
SIC 8211 Elementary and secondary schools

D-U-N-S 25-232-8224   (BR)
**COMMISSION SCOLAIRE DES AP-
PALACHES**
ECOLE ST-GABRIEL
(*Suby of* Commission Scolaire des Ap-
palaches)
275 Rue Simoneau, Thetford Mines, QC, G6G
1S8
(418) 335-2110
Emp Here 30
SIC 8211 Elementary and secondary schools

D-U-N-S 25-233-6540   (BR)
**COMMISSION SCOLAIRE DES AP-
PALACHES**
ECOLE DU TOURNESOL
(*Suby of* Commission Scolaire des Ap-
palaches)
285 Rue Houle, Thetford Mines, QC, G6G
5W2
(418) 338-8422
Emp Here 35
SIC 8211 Elementary and secondary schools

D-U-N-S 20-082-5227   (BR)
**COMMISSION SCOLAIRE DES AP-
PALACHES**
*CENTRE DE FORMATION PROFESSIONEL
LE TREMPLIN*
578 Rue Monfette E, Thetford Mines, QC,
G6G 7G9

(418) 335-2921
Emp Here 65
SIC 8331 Job training and related services

D-U-N-S 20-103-2328   (BR)
DOLLARAMA S.E.C.
DOLLARAMA
224 Boul Frontenac O, Thetford Mines, QC,
G6G 6N7
(418) 335-9107
Emp Here 27
SIC 5399 Miscellaneous general merchandise

D-U-N-S 20-367-4226   (SL)
HOCKEY THETFORD INC
555 Rue Saint-Alphonse N, Thetford Mines,
QC, G6G 3X1
(418) 332-4343
Emp Here 20   *Sales* 6,312,800
SIC 7941 Sports clubs, managers, and pro-
moters
Dir Jean Pierre Leffeard

D-U-N-S 24-784-6442   (BR)
HYDRO-QUEBEC
1185 Boul Frontenac E, Thetford Mines, QC,
G6G 8C6
(418) 338-2140
Emp Here 20
SIC 8711 Engineering services

D-U-N-S 25-309-6895   (BR)
**INDUSTRIELLE ALLIANCE, ASSURANCE
ET SERVICES FINANCIERS INC**
1310 Rue Notre-Dame E Bureau 200, Thetford Mines, QC, G6G 2V5
(418) 338-8556
Emp Here 20
SIC 6411 Insurance agents, brokers, and service

D-U-N-S 24-330-1087   (BR)
NAPEC INC
ENTREPRISES NAPEC
3037 Boul Frontenac E, Thetford Mines, QC,
G6G 6P6
(418) 335-7220
Emp Here 50
SIC 3714 Motor vehicle parts and accessories

D-U-N-S 24-358-3171   (BR)
PIONEER HI-BRED LIMITED
ZODIAC QUARTZ SURFACING
(*Suby of* E. I. Du Pont De Nemours and Com-
pany)
1045 Rue Monfette E, Thetford Mines, QC,
G6G 7K7
(418) 338-8567
Emp Here 97
SIC 3299 NonMetallic mineral products,

D-U-N-S 25-299-9099   (BR)
PRISZM LP
PFK
31 Boul Frontenac O, Thetford Mines, QC,
G6G 1M8
(418) 338-4121
Emp Here 20
SIC 5812 Eating places

D-U-N-S 24-125-5137   (BR)
PROVIGO DISTRIBUTION INC
MAXI
805 Boul Frontenac E, Thetford Mines, QC,
G6G 6L5
(418) 338-2136
Emp Here 70
SIC 5411 Grocery stores

D-U-N-S 20-561-4329   (SL)
PULTRALL INC
700 9e Rue N, Thetford Mines, QC, G6G 6Z5
(418) 335-3202
Emp Here 100   *Sales* 11,524,275
SIC 5085 Industrial supplies
Pr Pr Bertrand Aubert
Marc-Andre Drouin
Bernard Drouin

D-U-N-S 25-298-2061   (BR)
**RAYMOND CHABOT GRANT THORNTON
S.E.N.C.R.L.**
257 Rue Notre-Dame O Bureau 2e, Thetford
Mines, QC, G6G 1J7
(418) 335-7511
Emp Here 42
SIC 8721 Accounting, auditing, and book-
keeping

D-U-N-S 20-262-4458   (SL)
ROBERGE, JULES A INC
PHARMACIE JEAN COUTU
926 Rue Labbe Bureau 160, Thetford Mines,
QC, G6G 2A8
(418) 335-2903
Emp Here 80   *Sales* 15,724,750
SIC 5912 Drug stores and proprietary stores
Pr Pr Jules Roberge
Sonia Boutin
Pierre Roberge

D-U-N-S 24-941-1265   (SL)
ROTISSERIES YVES VINCENT INC, LES
ROTISSERIE ST-HUBERT
203 Boul Frontenac O, Thetford Mines, QC,
G6G 6K2
(418) 335-7557
Emp Here 54   *Sales* 1,605,135
SIC 5812 Eating places

D-U-N-S 25-095-5531   (BR)
SABLES OLIMAG INC, LES
(*Suby of* Placements Claude Gosselin Inc)
725 Rue Caouette O, Thetford Mines, QC,
G6G 8C5
(418) 338-4425
Emp Here 37
SIC 5032 Brick, stone, and related material

D-U-N-S 20-804-1710   (BR)
THETFORD MINES, VILLE DE
PISCINE VILLE DE THEDFORD MINES
561 Rue Saint-Patrick, Thetford Mines, QC,
G6G 5W1
(418) 338-8888
Emp Here 25
SIC 7999 Amusement and recreation, nec

D-U-N-S 25-837-5211   (BR)
THETFORD MINES, VILLE DE
CENTRE MARIO GOSSELIN
555 Rue Saint-Alphonse N, Thetford Mines,
QC, G6G 3X1
(418) 338-4477
Emp Here 25
SIC 7999 Amusement and recreation, nec

D-U-N-S 24-207-4222   (BR)
WAL-MART CANADA CORP
WALMART
1025 Boul Frontenac E, Thetford Mines, QC,
G6G 6S7
(418) 338-4894
Emp Here 100
SIC 5311 Department stores

Thetford Mines, QC G6H
Megantic County

D-U-N-S 24-204-0967   (SL)
3358097 CANADA INC
CENTRE DU CAMION (AMIANTE)
4680 Boul Frontenac E, Thetford Mines, QC,
G6H 4G5
(418) 338-8588
Emp Here 120   *Sales* 24,406,321
SIC 6712 Bank holding companies
Pr Clement Poulin
VP VP Jean-Francois Poulin
Chantal Poulin

D-U-N-S 25-231-8415   (HQ)
**CENTRE DE LA PETITE ENFANCE PARC-
EN-CIEL**

(*Suby of* Centre de la Petite Enfance Parc-en-Ciel)
566 Rue Christophe-Colomb, Thetford Mines, QC, G6H 2N6
(418) 423-2004
Emp Here 60   *Emp Total* 65
Sales 1,969,939
SIC 8351 Child day care services

D-U-N-S 25-232-8380   (BR)
COMMISSION SCOLAIRE DES AP-PALACHES
ECOLE ST-LOUIS
(*Suby of* Commission Scolaire des Ap-palaches)
539 Rue Saint-Louis, Thetford Mines, QC, G6H 1J3
(418) 423-2728
Emp Here 30
SIC 8211 Elementary and secondary schools

D-U-N-S 25-232-6665   (BR)
COMMISSION SCOLAIRE DES AP-PALACHES
CENTRE DE FORMATION PROFESSION-NELLE DE BLACK LAKE
(*Suby of* Commission Scolaire des Ap-palaches)
499 Rue Saint-Desire, Thetford Mines, QC, G6H 1L7
(418) 423-4291
Emp Here 75
SIC 8211 Elementary and secondary schools

D-U-N-S 24-863-5505   (SL)
OCEANIA BATHS INC
591 Rue Des Entreprises, Thetford Mines, QC, G6H 4B2
(418) 332-4224
Emp Here 30   *Sales* 6,128,699
SIC 3272 Concrete products, nec
Pr Marc Dussault

Thurso, QC J0X
Papineau County

D-U-N-S 25-174-4678   (BR)
CLEAN HARBORS CANADA, INC
400 Rue Galipeau, Thurso, QC, J0X 3B0

Emp Here 23
SIC 4212 Local trucking, without storage

D-U-N-S 25-240-4447   (BR)
COMMISSION SCOLAIRE AU COEUR DES VALLEES
ECOLE MARIA GORETTI
373 Rue Victoria, Thurso, QC, J0X 3B0
(819) 427-1018
Emp Here 27
SIC 8211 Elementary and secondary schools

D-U-N-S 25-233-5294   (BR)
COMMISSION SCOLAIRE AU COEUR DES VALLEES
ECOLE SECONDAIRE SAINTE FAMILLE AUX TROIS CHEMINS
183 Rue Galipeau, Thurso, QC, J0X 3B0
(819) 427-1017
Emp Here 35
SIC 8211 Elementary and secondary schools

D-U-N-S 24-920-8364   (SL)
LAUZON (THURSO)-RESSOURCES FORESTIERES INC
LAUZON (THURSO)-RESSOURCES FORESTIERES
175 Rue Alexandre, Thurso, QC, J0X 3B0
(819) 985-0600
Emp Here 150   *Sales* 19,593,600
SIC 2421 Sawmills and planing mills, general
Genl Mgr Michel Pitre
Pr David Lauzon

Tingwick, QC J0A
Arthabaska County

D-U-N-S 24-938-8997   (SL)
TINGWICK GARAGE MUNICIPAL
12 Rue De L'Hotel-De-Ville, Tingwick, QC, J0A 1L0
(819) 359-2260
Emp Here 20   *Sales* 20,939,721
SIC 7521 Automobile parking
Dir Benoit Lambert

Trecesson, QC J0Y

D-U-N-S 25-335-9210   (SL)
2645-3530 QUEBEC INC
HARDY CONSTRUCTION
124 Rue Langlois, Trecesson, QC, J0Y 2S0
(819) 732-1493
Emp Here 24   *Sales* 8,842,520
SIC 1541 Industrial buildings and warehouses
Pr Pr Guy Hardy
  Danny Hardy

D-U-N-S 24-254-5833   (BR)
GOUVERNEMENT DE LA PROVINCE DE QUEBEC
MINISTERE RESSOURCES NATURELLES ET FAUNE
164 Ch De La Pepiniere, Trecesson, QC, J0Y 2S0
(819) 444-5447
Emp Here 20
SIC 7389 Business services, nec

Tring-Jonction, QC G0N
Beauce County

D-U-N-S 25-689-0658   (BR)
CAISSE DESJARDINS DE BEAUCE-CENTRE
CENTRE DE SERVICE DE TRING-JONCTION
247 Rue Notre-Dame, Tring-Jonction, QC, G0N 1X0
(418) 397-5238
Emp Here 50
SIC 6062 State credit unions

D-U-N-S 25-232-8349   (BR)
COMMISSION SCOLAIRE DE LA BEAUCE-ETCHEMIN
ECOLE SAINTE-FAMILLE
302 Rue Saint-Cyrille, Tring-Jonction, QC, G0N 1X0
(418) 386-5541
Emp Here 35
SIC 8211 Elementary and secondary schools

D-U-N-S 24-499-3572   (SL)
PLACEMENTS J. L. ROY INC
267 Rue Notre-Dame, Tring-Jonction, QC, G0N 1X0
(418) 426-3005
Emp Here 60   *Sales* 13,492,850
SIC 2435 Hardwood veneer and plywood
Pr Pr Blanche Yvette Giguere Roy

Trois-Pistoles, QC G0L
Riviere-Du-Loup County

D-U-N-S 20-174-2637   (SL)
BAINS OCEANIA INC
(*Suby of* Acrylique Weedon (1995) Inc)
8 Rue Patrice-Cote Bureau 244, Trois-Pistoles, QC, G0L 4K0

(418) 851-1818
Emp Here 20   *Sales* 1,896,978
SIC 3089 Plastics products, nec

D-U-N-S 24-011-7288   (BR)
COMMISSION SCOLAIRE DU FLEUVE ET DES LACS
CENTRE D'EDUCATION DES ADULTES
9 Rue Notre-Dame E, Trois-Pistoles, QC, G0L 4K0
(418) 851-3341
Emp Here 30
SIC 8211 Elementary and secondary schools

D-U-N-S 20-711-9483   (BR)
COMMISSION SCOLAIRE DU FLEUVE ET DES LACS
ECOLE GERARD RAYMOND
84 Rue Raymond, Trois-Pistoles, QC, G0L 4K0

Emp Here 50
SIC 8211 Elementary and secondary schools

D-U-N-S 25-232-7796   (BR)
COMMISSION SCOLAIRE DU FLEUVE ET DES LACS
ECOLE SECONDAIRE L'ARC-EN-CIEL
455 Rue Jenkin, Trois-Pistoles, QC, G0L 4K0

Emp Here 80
SIC 8211 Elementary and secondary schools

D-U-N-S 20-711-9509   (BR)
COMMISSION SCOLAIRE DU FLEUVE ET DES LACS
ECOLE L'ITALIEN
286 Rue Langlais, Trois-Pistoles, QC, G0L 4K0
(418) 851-2346
Emp Here 20
SIC 8211 Elementary and secondary schools

D-U-N-S 25-243-6167   (SL)
TRANSPORT PAUL-EMILE DUBE LTEE
(*Suby of* Groupe Colabor Inc)
489 Rue Notre-Dame E, Trois-Pistoles, QC, G0L 4K0
(418) 724-2400
Emp Here 85   *Sales* 9,333,400
SIC 4212 Local trucking, without storage
Pr Pr Claude Gariepy
  Jean-Francois Neault

D-U-N-S 20-803-1091   (BR)
UNIVERSITY OF WESTERN ONTARIO, THE
ECOLE DE LANGUE FRANCAISE DE TROIS PISTOLES
455 Rue Jenkin Bureau C244, Trois-Pistoles, QC, G0L 4K0
(418) 851-1752
Emp Here 43
SIC 8299 Schools and educational services, nec

Trois-Rives, QC G0X
St-Maurice County

D-U-N-S 25-379-3541   (BR)
SOCIETE DES ETABLISSEMENTS DE PLEIN AIR DU QUEBEC
RESERVE FAUNIQUE DU ST-MAURICE
3773 155 Rte, Trois-Rives, QC, G0X 2C0
(819) 646-5687
Emp Here 22
SIC 7032 Sporting and recreational camps

Trois-Rivieres, QC G8T
St-Maurice County

D-U-N-S 24-346-3101   (BR)
9016-7974 QUA BEC INC
9016-7974 QUEBEC INC

830 Boul Thibeau, Trois-Rivieres, QC, G8T 7A6
(819) 376-6664
Emp Here 45
SIC 5812 Eating places

D-U-N-S 24-518-1248   (SL)
ALERIS ALUMINIUM CANADA S.E.C.
290 Rue Saint-Laurent, Trois-Rivieres, QC, G8T 6G7

Emp Here 500   *Sales* 33,472,560
SIC 3463 Nonferrous forgings
  Scott Mckinley

D-U-N-S 25-004-0045   (BR)
BANQUE NATIONALE DU CANADA
305 Rue Barkoff, Trois-Rivieres, QC, G8T 2A5
(819) 376-3735
Emp Here 22
SIC 6021 National commercial banks

D-U-N-S 20-530-0192   (BR)
CANADA POST CORPORATION
1285 Rue Notre-Dame E, Trois-Rivieres, QC, G8T 4J9
(819) 691-4215
Emp Here 100
SIC 4311 U.s. postal service

D-U-N-S 24-330-1160   (BR)
CASCADES CANADA ULC
CASCADES LUPEL
700 Rue Notre-Dame E Bureau 23, Trois-Rivieres, QC, G8T 4H9
(819) 373-4307
Emp Here 53
SIC 2631 Paperboard mills

D-U-N-S 20-171-8314   (BR)
CENTRE JEUNESSE DE LA MAURICIE ET DU CENTRE-DU-QUEBEC, LE
C J M C Q
(*Suby of* Centre Jeunesse de la Mauricie et du Centre-du-Quebec, Le)
80 Ch Du Passage Bureau 200, Trois-Rivieres, QC, G8T 2M2
(819) 372-0599
Emp Here 50
SIC 8322 Individual and family services

D-U-N-S 20-204-6181   (SL)
CLAUDE CROTEAU ET FILLES INC
500 Rue Barkoff, Trois-Rivieres, QC, G8T 9P5
(819) 379-4566
Emp Here 60   *Sales* 3,648,035
SIC 5651 Family clothing stores

D-U-N-S 20-716-7300   (BR)
COMMISSION SCOLAIRE DU CHEMIN-DU-ROY
ECOLE DE MUSIQUE JACQUES HETU
775 Rue Berlinguet, Trois-Rivieres, QC, G8T 2H1
(819) 691-2501
Emp Here 35
SIC 8211 Elementary and secondary schools

D-U-N-S 25-232-7408   (BR)
COMMISSION SCOLAIRE DU CHEMIN-DU-ROY
ECOLE SACRE COEUR
245 Rue Loranger, Trois-Rivieres, QC, G8T 3V2
(819) 376-3656
Emp Here 30
SIC 8211 Elementary and secondary schools

D-U-N-S 20-716-9132   (BR)
COMMISSION SCOLAIRE DU CHEMIN-DU-ROY
ECOLES PRIMAIRES LOUIS DE FRANCE
881 Rue Louis-De-France, Trois-Rivieres, QC, G8T 1A5
(819) 374-5523
Emp Here 40
SIC 8211 Elementary and secondary schools

D-U-N-S 20-289-7393   (BR)

COMMISSION SCOLAIRE DU CHEMIN-DU-ROY
CENTRE DE FORMATION PROFESSION-NEL QUALITECH
500 Rue Des Erables, Trois-Rivieres, QC, G8T 9S4
(819) 373-1422
Emp Here 120
SIC 8211 Elementary and secondary schools

D-U-N-S 25-232-7325   (BR)
COMMISSION SCOLAIRE DU CHEMIN-DU-ROY
ECOLE DOLLARD
100 Rue Saint-Irenee, Trois-Rivieres, QC, G8T 7C4
(819) 376-3443
Emp Here 35
SIC 8211 Elementary and secondary schools

D-U-N-S 25-232-6574   (BR)
COMMISSION SCOLAIRE DU CHEMIN-DU-ROY
ECOLE STE MADELEINE
445 Boul Sainte-Madeleine, Trois-Rivieres, QC, G8T 3N5
(819) 376-3120
Emp Here 25
SIC 8211 Elementary and secondary schools

D-U-N-S 25-672-1614   (BR)
COMMISSION SCOLAIRE DU CHEMIN-DU-ROY
ACADEMIE LES ESTACADES
501 Rue Des Erables, Trois-Rivieres, QC, G8T 5J2
(819) 375-8331
Emp Here 250
SIC 8211 Elementary and secondary schools

D-U-N-S 25-232-7481   (BR)
COMMISSION SCOLAIRE DU CHEMIN-DU-ROY
ECOLE STE BERNADETTE
730 Rue Guilbert, Trois-Rivieres, QC, G8T 5T6
(819) 378-6562
Emp Here 40
SIC 8211 Elementary and secondary schools

D-U-N-S 20-806-9992   (BR)
COUCHE-TARD INC
365 Rue Saint-Maurice, Trois-Rivieres, QC, G8T 4V1
(819) 379-2999
Emp Here 25
SIC 5411 Grocery stores

D-U-N-S 20-911-3646   (SL)
ECOLE COMMERCIALE DU CAP INC
COLLEGE ELLIS CAMPUS DE TROIS-RIVIERES
90 Rue Dorval, Trois-Rivieres, QC, G8T 5X7
(819) 691-2600
Emp Here 50   *Sales* 3,064,349
SIC 8244 Business and secretarial schools

D-U-N-S 25-233-5005   (SL)
ECOLE VAL MARIE INC
VAL MARIE
88 Ch Du Fassage, Trois-Rivieres, QC, G8T 2M3
(819) 379-8040
Emp Here 70   *Sales* 4,669,485
SIC 8211 Elementary and secondary schools

D-U-N-S 24-224-7914   (SL)
GESTION REJEAN MASSON INC
MARCHE METRO
165 Boul Sainte-Madeleine, Trois-Rivieres, QC, G8T 3L7
(819) 375-4824
Emp Here 70   *Sales* 11,779,113
SIC 5411 Grocery stores
Pr Pr Rejean Masson
Genl Mgr Andre St-Pierre
Pt Jacinthe Masson
Pt Chantale Masson

D-U-N-S 25-896-5003   (SL)
GROUPE SOUCY INC
DIVISION ECOLOBRISS
1060 Boul Thibeau, Trois-Rivieres, QC, G8T 7B2
(819) 376-3111
Emp Here 100   *Sales* 3,137,310
SIC 7381 Detective and armored car services

D-U-N-S 24-329-2328   (BR)
H. MATTEAU ET FILS (1987) INC
15 Rue Philippe-Francoeur, Trois-Rivieres, QC, G8T 9L7
(819) 374-4735
Emp Here 85
SIC 5211 Lumber and other building materials

D-U-N-S 20-545-9741   (BR)
MARCHE VEGETARIEN INC, LE
MARCHE VEGETARIEN
665 Boul Thibeau, Trois-Rivieres, QC, G8T 6Z6

Emp Here 25
SIC 5431 Fruit and vegetable markets

D-U-N-S 20-799-3598   (BR)
MARLU INC
MCDONALD'S
300 Rue Barkoff, Trois-Rivieres, QC, G8T 2A3
(819) 373-7921
Emp Here 75
SIC 5812 Eating places

D-U-N-S 24-207-6347   (BR)
OLYMEL S.E.C.
OLYMEL
531 Rue Des Erables, Trois-Rivieres, QC, G8T 7Z7
(819) 376-3770
Emp Here 170
SIC 5147 Meats and meat products

D-U-N-S 20-002-2379   (BR)
PROVIGO DISTRIBUTION INC
MAXI
320 Rue Barkoff, Trois-Rivieres, QC, G8T 2A3
(819) 378-4932
Emp Here 80
SIC 5411 Grocery stores

D-U-N-S 20-234-8657   (BR)
SOBEYS CAPITAL INCORPORATED
IGA EXTRA
645 Boul Thibeau, Trois-Rivieres, QC, G8T 6Z6
(819) 376-1551
Emp Here 103
SIC 5411 Grocery stores

D-U-N-S 20-013-8837   (BR)
SONOCO CANADA CORPORATION
(*Suby of* Sonoco Products Company)
530 Rue Des Erables, Trois-Rivieres, QC, G8T 8N6
(819) 374-5222
Emp Here 85
SIC 2655 Fiber cans, drums, and similar products

D-U-N-S 20-105-0288   (BR)
STAPLES CANADA INC
BUREAU EN GROS
(*Suby of* Staples, Inc.)
400 Rue Barkoff, Trois-Rivieres, QC, G8T 9P5
(819) 371-4848
Emp Here 35
SIC 5943 Stationery stores

D-U-N-S 25-361-2626   (SL)
TORA CAP-DE-LA-MADELEINE LIMITEE
TIGRE GEANT
(*Suby of* Giant Tiger Stores Limited)
800 Boul Thibeau, Trois-Rivieres, QC, G8T 7A6
(819) 697-3833
Emp Here 50   *Sales* 3,575,074
SIC 5311 Department stores

D-U-N-S 25-991-5965   (BR)
WAL-MART CANADA CORP
300 Rue Barkoff, Trois-Rivieres, QC, G8T 2A3
(819) 379-2992
Emp Here 200
SIC 5311 Department stores

Trois-Rivieres, QC G8V
St-Maurice County

D-U-N-S 24-175-0488   (SL)
SOLIVE AJOUREE 2000 INC
1970 Rue Des Toitures, Trois-Rivieres, QC, G8V 1V9
(819) 374-8784
Emp Here 170   *Sales* 32,354,560
SIC 3441 Fabricated structural Metal
Pr Pr Andre Lemyre

D-U-N-S 20-253-6488   (BR)
STRUCTURES BARRETTE INC
TOITURE MAURICIENNE
(*Suby of* GDTM Inc)
555 Rang Saint-Malo, Trois-Rivieres, QC, G8V 0A8
(819) 374-6061
Emp Here 600
SIC 5031 Lumber, plywood, and millwork

Trois-Rivieres, QC G8Y
St-Maurice County

D-U-N-S 20-053-8978   (BR)
BANK OF MONTREAL
BMO
4125 Boul Des Forges, Trois-Rivieres, QC, G8Y 1W1
(819) 372-4050
Emp Here 20
SIC 6021 National commercial banks

D-U-N-S 20-738-2602   (BR)
CENTRE DE READAPTATION INTERVAL
(*Suby of* Centre de Readaptation Interval)
4100 Rue Jacques-De Labadie, Trois-Rivieres, QC, G8Y 1T6
(819) 378-4083
Emp Here 50
SIC 8361 Residential care

D-U-N-S 20-968-5010   (SL)
CLUB DE VOITURES ANCIENNES DE LA MAURICIE INC
930 Rue Des Saules, Trois-Rivieres, QC, G8Y 2K5
(819) 374-9638
Emp Here 49   *Sales* 7,727,098
SIC 8699 Membership organizations, nec
Pr Justin Brousseau
VP VP Normand Beauchesne

D-U-N-S 25-232-6731   (BR)
COMMISSION SCOLAIRE DU CHEMIN-DU-ROY
ECOLE RICHELIEU
5405 Rue De Courcelette, Trois-Rivieres, QC, G8Y 3V2
(819) 375-8809
Emp Here 20
SIC 8211 Elementary and secondary schools

D-U-N-S 24-338-0107   (BR)
COMMISSION SCOLAIRE DU CHEMIN-DU-ROY
CENTRE DE FORMATION PROFESSION-NELLE BEL-AVENIR
3750 Rue Jean-Bourdon, Trois-Rivieres, QC, G8Y 2A5
(819) 691-3366
Emp Here 110
SIC 8211 Elementary and secondary schools

D-U-N-S 25-232-7051   (BR)
COMMISSION SCOLAIRE DU CHEMIN-DU-ROY
ECOLE ST-THERESE
1405 11e Rue, Trois-Rivieres, QC, G8Y 2Z6
(819) 376-3038
Emp Here 30
SIC 8211 Elementary and secondary schools

D-U-N-S 25-232-7093   (BR)
COMMISSION SCOLAIRE DU CHEMIN-DU-ROY
ECOLE INTEGREE DES FORGES
7625 Rue Lamy, Trois-Rivieres, QC, G8Y 4A8
(819) 373-5155
Emp Here 25
SIC 8211 Elementary and secondary schools

D-U-N-S 25-240-3456   (BR)
COMMISSION SCOLAIRE DU CHEMIN-DU-ROY
ECOLE DU BOIS JOLI
3685 Rue De La Rochelle, Trois-Rivieres, QC, G8Y 5N7
(819) 374-6951
Emp Here 40
SIC 8211 Elementary and secondary schools

D-U-N-S 20-526-6104   (BR)
COMMISSION SCOLAIRE DU CHEMIN-DU-ROY
ECOLE SAINT FRANCOIS XAVIER
3750 Rue Jean-Bourdon, Trois-Rivieres, QC, G8Y 2A5
(819) 379-8714
Emp Here 45
SIC 8211 Elementary and secondary schools

D-U-N-S 25-233-6367   (BR)
COMMISSION SCOLAIRE DU CHEMIN-DU-ROY
ECOLE LES TERRASSES
4675 Cote Rosemont, Trois-Rivieres, QC, G8Y 6R7
(819) 374-1835
Emp Here 34
SIC 8211 Elementary and secondary schools

D-U-N-S 20-284-6812   (BR)
DAVIDSTEA INC
DAVIDSTEA
4225 Boul Des Forges, Trois-Rivieres, QC, G8Y 1W2
(819) 693-9333
Emp Here 20
SIC 5499 Miscellaneous food stores

D-U-N-S 20-886-3092   (SL)
ENTREPRISES DE NETTOYAGE M.P. INC
1621 Rue De Lery, Trois-Rivieres, QC, G8Y 7B3

Emp Here 75   *Sales* 2,188,821
SIC 7349 Building maintenance services, nec

D-U-N-S 20-548-0689   (SL)
GESTION SETR INC
SPORTS EXPERTS
4125 Boul Des Forges Bureau 1, Trois-Rivieres, QC, G8Y 1W1
(819) 376-4343
Emp Here 60   *Sales* 3,429,153
SIC 5699 Miscellaneous apparel and accessory stores

D-U-N-S 20-860-6348   (SL)
GESTIONS GUILTREE INC
PHARMAPRIX
3950 Boul Des Forges Bureau 25, Trois-Rivieres, QC, G8Y 1V7
(819) 375-1730
Emp Here 35   *Sales* 6,832,640
SIC 5912 Drug stores and proprietary stores
Pr Pr Gilles Guillemette
VP VP Celine Trepanier

D-U-N-S 20-742-7951   (BR)
GROUPE SPORTSCENE INC

CAGE AUX SPORTS, LA
4210 Boul Des Forges, Trois-Rivieres, QC, G8Y 1W3
(819) 376-1537
Emp Here 50
SIC 5812 Eating places

D-U-N-S 25-315-7762   (BR)
INVESTORS GROUP FINANCIAL SERVICES INC
GROUPE INVESTORS
4450 Boul Des Forges Bureau 215, Trois-Rivieres, QC, G8Y 1W5
(819) 378-2371
Emp Here 50
SIC 8741 Management services

D-U-N-S 24-016-7820   (BR)
LOBLAWS INC
PROVIGO LE MARCHE
3725 Boul Des Forges, Trois-Rivieres, QC, G8Y 4P2
(819) 374-8980
Emp Here 100
SIC 5411 Grocery stores

D-U-N-S 25-320-4952   (HQ)
M. S. J .N. INC
MCDONALDS
(*Suby of* M. S. J .N. Inc)
3800 Boul Des Forges, Trois-Rivieres, QC, G8Y 4R2
(819) 373-8201
Emp Here 45   *Emp Total* 50
Sales 1,532,175
SIC 5812 Eating places

D-U-N-S 20-657-9976   (BR)
SEARS CANADA INC
4225 Boul Des Forges, Trois-Rivieres, QC, G8Y 1W2
(819) 379-6163
Emp Here 20
SIC 5311 Department stores

D-U-N-S 25-297-8127   (BR)
TOYS 'R' US (CANADA) LTD
TOYS 'R' US
(*Suby of* Toys "r" Us, Inc.)
4125 Boul Des Forges, Trois-Rivieres, QC, G8Y 1W1
(819) 370-8697
Emp Here 24
SIC 5945 Hobby, toy, and game shops

Trois-Rivieres, QC G8Z
St-Maurice County

D-U-N-S 24-168-6351   (SL)
9043-3798 QUEBEC INC
TROIS-RIVIERES TOYOTA
5110 Boul Jean-Xxiii, Trois-Rivieres, QC, G8Z 4A7
(819) 374-5323
Emp Here 30   *Sales* 15,072,000
SIC 5511 New and used car dealers
Pr Luc Lesage

D-U-N-S 25-835-5320   (BR)
AMEUBLEMENTS TANGUAY INC
2200 Boul Des Recollets, Trois-Rivieres, QC, G8Z 3X5
(819) 373-1111
Emp Here 90
SIC 5712 Furniture stores

D-U-N-S 20-855-7439   (HQ)
CRDI TED NCQ IU
UNIVERSITY INSTITUTE
(*Suby of* CRDI TED NCQ IU)
3255 Rue Foucher, Trois-Rivieres, QC, G8Z 1M6
(819) 379-6868
Emp Here 30   *Emp Total* 640
Sales 32,153,600
SIC 8361 Residential care

Mng Dir Sylvie Dupras
Pr Gilles Clutier

D-U-N-S 25-299-0239   (BR)
CRDI TED NCQ IU
CSDI, LE
(*Suby of* CRDI TED NCQ IU)
920 Place Boland, Trois-Rivieres, QC, G8Z 4H2

Emp Here 60
SIC 8399 Social services, nec

D-U-N-S 24-633-1958   (BR)
CANAC-MARQUIS GRENIER LTEE
2350 Boul Des Recollets, Trois-Rivieres, QC, G8Z 3X7
(819) 374-2036
Emp Here 50
SIC 5251 Hardware stores

D-U-N-S 20-270-6545   (BR)
CEGEP DE TROIS-RIVIERES
INNOFIBRE
(*Suby of* Cegep de Trois-Rivieres)
3351 Boul Des Forges, Trois-Rivieres, QC, G8Z 4M3
(819) 376-5075
Emp Here 22
SIC 8732 Commercial nonphysical research

D-U-N-S 24-321-1518   (BR)
CEGEP DE TROIS-RIVIERES
SERVICE DE LA FORMATION CONTINUE DU CEGEP DE TROIS-RIVIERES
(*Suby of* Cegep de Trois-Rivieres)
3500 Rue De Courval, Trois-Rivieres, QC, G8Z 1T2
(819) 378-4911
Emp Here 50
SIC 8221 Colleges and universities

D-U-N-S 24-111-4313   (HQ)
CEGEP DE TROIS-RIVIERES
(*Suby of* Cegep de Trois-Rivieres)
3500 Rue De Courval, Trois-Rivieres, QC, G8Z 1T2
(819) 376-1721
Emp Here 650   *Emp Total* 700
Sales 94,704,065
SIC 8222 Junior colleges
Mark Leblanc
Denise Roy
Renald Cote
Jean Denis Leduc
Genl Mgr Patrick Mangin

D-U-N-S 20-261-8596   (BR)
CENTRE JEUNESSE DE LA MAURICIE ET DU CENTRE-DU-QUEBEC, LE
CENTRE JEUNESSE DE LA MAURICIE ET DU CENTRE-DU-QUEBEC, LE
(*Suby of* Centre Jeunesse de la Mauricie et du Centre-du-Quebec, Le)
2700 Boul Des Forges, Trois-Rivieres, QC, G8Z 1V2
(819) 372-3131
Emp Here 50
SIC 8322 Individual and family services

D-U-N-S 24-405-0795   (HQ)
CENTRE JEUNESSE DE LA MAURICIE ET DU CENTRE-DU-QUEBEC, LE
CJMCQ
(*Suby of* Centre Jeunesse de la Mauricie et du Centre-du-Quebec, Le)
1455 Boul Du Carmel, Trois-Rivieres, QC, G8Z 3R7
(819) 378-5481
Emp Here 65   *Emp Total* 600
Sales 31,705,680
SIC 8322 Individual and family services
Dir Serge Bisaillon

D-U-N-S 24-425-9177   (BR)
CENTRE JEUNESSE DE LA MAURICIE ET DU CENTRE-DU-QUEBEC, LE
PAVILLION BOURGEOIS

(*Suby of* Centre Jeunesse de la Mauricie et du Centre-du-Quebec, Le)
2735 Rue Papineau, Trois-Rivieres, QC, G8Z 1N8
(819) 378-8635
Emp Here 90
SIC 8322 Individual and family services

D-U-N-S 25-959-6997   (BR)
CENTRE JEUNESSE DE LA MAURICIE ET DU CENTRE-DU-QUEBEC, LE
CJMCQ
(*Suby of* Centre Jeunesse de la Mauricie et du Centre-du-Quebec, Le)
1455 Boul Du Carmel, Trois-Rivieres, QC, G8Z 3R7
(819) 378-5590
Emp Here 18,000
SIC 8322 Individual and family services

D-U-N-S 24-773-2782   (BR)
COLLEGE LAFLECHE
CENTRE DE FORMATION CONTINUE COLLEGE LAFLECHE
1687 Boul Du Carmel, Trois-Rivieres, QC, G8Z 3R8
(819) 378-1123
Emp Here 49
SIC 8221 Colleges and universities

D-U-N-S 25-233-4636   (BR)
COMMISSION SCOLAIRE MARGUERITE-BOURGEOYS
ECOLE DU MOULIN
1305 Rue De La Terriere, Trois-Rivieres, QC, G8Z 3J7
(819) 378-4839
Emp Here 30
SIC 8211 Elementary and secondary schools

D-U-N-S 20-716-9041   (BR)
COMMISSION SCOLAIRE DU CHEMIN-DU-ROY
ECOLE SECONDAIRE DES PIONNIERS
1725 Boul Du Carmel, Trois-Rivieres, QC, G8Z 3R8
(819) 379-5822
Emp Here 140
SIC 8211 Elementary and secondary schools

D-U-N-S 25-233-3679   (BR)
COMMISSION SCOLAIRE DU CHEMIN-DU-ROY
ECOLE CURE CHAMBERLAND
3005 Rue Arthur-Guimont, Trois-Rivieres, QC, G8Z 2K2
(819) 378-8780
Emp Here 20
SIC 8211 Elementary and secondary schools

D-U-N-S 25-232-6970   (BR)
COMMISSION SCOLAIRE DU CHEMIN-DU-ROY
ECOLE ST-PIE-X
720 Boul Des Recollets, Trois-Rivieres, QC, G8Z 3W1
(819) 375-0388
Emp Here 40
SIC 8211 Elementary and secondary schools

D-U-N-S 20-703-9855   (BR)
COOP FEDEREE, LA
4225 Rue Saint-Joseph Bureau 379, Trois-Rivieres, QC, G8Z 4G3
(819) 379-8551
Emp Here 250
SIC 5072 Hardware

D-U-N-S 20-806-9950   (BR)
COUCHE-TARD INC
3575 Rue Papineau, Trois-Rivieres, QC, G8Z 1P8
(819) 374-4737
Emp Here 25
SIC 5411 Grocery stores

D-U-N-S 24-714-3829   (BR)
EMCO CORPORATION
WESTLUMD

2400 Rue De La Sidbec S, Trois-Rivieres, QC, G8Z 4H1
(819) 375-4743
Emp Here 24
SIC 5074 Plumbing and heating equipment and supplies (hydronics)

D-U-N-S 25-136-7256   (BR)
EQUIPEMENTS SIGMA INC
(*Suby of* Deere & Company)
2000 Rue De La Sidbec S, Trois-Rivieres, QC, G8Z 4H1
(819) 379-9333
Emp Here 25
SIC 5084 Industrial machinery and equipment

D-U-N-S 24-682-8060   (SL)
GESTION PROKARD INC
TIM HORTONS
5901 Boul Jean-Xxiii, Trois-Rivieres, QC, G8Z 4N8
(819) 373-9799
Emp Here 26   *Sales* 802,568
SIC 5812 Eating places

D-U-N-S 25-815-5142   (HQ)
GESTION R.Y. MENARD INC
TIM HORTONS
(*Suby of* Gestion R.Y. Menard Inc)
2600 Boul Des Recollets Bureau 2205, Trois-Rivieres, QC, G8Z 3X7
(819) 376-3777
Emp Here 20   *Emp Total* 140
Sales 4,231,721
SIC 5812 Eating places

D-U-N-S 24-128-4277   (BR)
GROUPE CRETE DIVISION ST-FAUSTIN INC
MAXI FORET
(*Suby of* Groupe Crete Inc)
6115 Rue Corbeil, Trois-Rivieres, QC, G8Z 4S6
(819) 840-2800
Emp Here 50
SIC 5031 Lumber, plywood, and millwork

D-U-N-S 25-476-1240   (BR)
HEWITT EQUIPEMENT LIMITEE
CATERPILLAR
1850 Rue De La Sidbec S, Trois-Rivieres, QC, G8Z 4H1
(819) 371-1005
Emp Here 35
SIC 7699 Repair services, nec

D-U-N-S 20-926-1531   (BR)
M. S. J .N. INC
MCDONALD'S
5848 Boul Jean-Xxiii, Trois-Rivieres, QC, G8Z 4B5
(819) 378-4114
Emp Here 25
SIC 5812 Eating places

D-U-N-S 20-238-2362   (HQ)
MAGASINS KORVETTE LTEE, LES
2325 Boul Des Recollets, Trois-Rivieres, QC, G8Z 3X6
(819) 374-4625
Emp Here 25   *Emp Total* 632
Sales 64,551,127
SIC 5311 Department stores
Daniel Binette
Dir Andree Binette

D-U-N-S 25-365-0469   (BR)
MOTEURS ELECTRIQUES LAVAL LTEE
SUCCURSALE M ELECTRIC
1330 Rue Cartier, Trois-Rivieres, QC, G8Z 1L8
(819) 374-4687
Emp Here 20
SIC 7694 Armature rewinding shops

D-U-N-S 20-355-6758   (BR)
PNEUS RATTE INC
2420 Boul Des Recollets, Trois-Rivieres, QC, G8Z 3X7

(819) 379-9993
Emp Here 21
SIC 5531 Auto and home supply stores

D-U-N-S 20-170-0601   (BR)
PROVIGO DISTRIBUTION INC
MAXI
5875 Boul Jean-Xxiii, Trois-Rivieres, QC, G8Z 4N8
(819) 378-8759
Emp Here 88
SIC 5411 Grocery stores

D-U-N-S 24-334-6322   (BR)
PUROLATOR INC.
PUROLATOR INC
1885 Rue De La Sidbec S, Trois-Rivieres, QC, G8Z 4M6
(819) 378-8347
Emp Here 25
SIC 4731 Freight transportation arrangement

D-U-N-S 25-517-1555   (BR)
RESTAURANT NORMANDIN INC
1350 Boul Des Recollets, Trois-Rivieres, QC, G8Z 4L5
(819) 691-0507
Emp Here 51
SIC 5812 Eating places

D-U-N-S 20-764-2849   (BR)
SODEXO CANADA LTD
3351 Boul Des Forges, Trois-Rivieres, QC, G8Z 4M3
(819) 376-5215
Emp Here 40
SIC 5812 Eating places

D-U-N-S 20-552-3157   (BR)
SOMAVRAC INC
4600 Rue Saint-Joseph, Trois-Rivieres, QC, G8Z 2Y3
(819) 379-3311
Emp Here 40
SIC 7389 Business services, nec

D-U-N-S 20-531-8640   (BR)
SOMAVRAC INC
TERMINAL 3
2550 Rue De La Sidbec S, Trois-Rivieres, QC, G8Z 4H1
(819) 374-7551
Emp Here 100
SIC 4213 Trucking, except local

D-U-N-S 25-830-6703   (BR)
SUN LIFE ASSURANCE COMPANY OF CANADA
CLARICA
1055 Boul Des Forges Bureau 440, Trois-Rivieres, QC, G8Z 4J8
(819) 375-7737
Emp Here 50
SIC 6311 Life insurance

D-U-N-S 24-378-7376   (BR)
UNIVERSITE DU QUEBEC
UNIVERSITE DU QUEBEC A TROIS-RIVIERES
3351 Boul Des Forges, Trois-Rivieres, QC, G8Z 4M3
(819) 376-5011
Emp Here 1 800
SIC 8221 Colleges and universities

D-U-N-S 24-231-0014   (BR)
WW HOTELS CORP
COMFORT INN
6255 Rue Corbeil, Trois-Rivieres, QC, G8Z 4P9
(819) 371-3566
Emp Here 20
SIC 7011 Hotels and motels

Trois-Rivieres, QC G9A
St-Maurice County

D-U-N-S 20-517-9034   (SL)
2343-7393 QUEBEC INC
DELTA TROIS-RIVIERES
1620 Rue Notre-Dame Centre, Trois-Rivieres, QC, G9A 6E5
(819) 376-1991
Emp Here 100   *Sales* 4,377,642
SIC 7011 Hotels and motels

D-U-N-S 25-978-9196   (SL)
9065-1837 QUEBEC INC
TEMPLE, LE
300 Rue Des Forges, Trois-Rivieres, QC, G9A 2G8
(819) 370-2005
Emp Here 80   *Sales* 2,918,428
SIC 5813 Drinking places

D-U-N-S 24-338-6864   (SL)
9122-6910 QUEBEC INC
RESTAURANT BUFFET DES CONTINENTS
4520 Boul Des Recollets, Trois-Rivieres, QC, G9A 4N2
(819) 370-1099
Emp Here 75   *Sales* 2,685,378
SIC 5812 Eating places

D-U-N-S 20-259-7589   (SL)
9309-6774 QUEBEC INC
9300 Boul Industriel, Trois-Rivieres, QC, G9A 5E1
(819) 539-8058
Emp Here 113   *Sales* 60,309,056
SIC 5142 Packaged frozen goods
Pr Pr Jean-Guy Ladriere

D-U-N-S 25-309-9816   (BR)
AGENCE DE VOYAGES D'AUTOMOBILE ET TOURING CLUB DU QUEBEC INC
AGENCE DE VOYAGES D'AUTOMOBILE ET TOURING CLUB DU
4085 Boul Des Recollets, Trois-Rivieres, QC, G9A 6M1
(819) 376-9394
Emp Here 20
SIC 4724 Travel agencies

D-U-N-S 20-267-0022   (SL)
ANDRE PELISSIER INC
AUBINPELISSIER
3605 Rue Bellefeuille, Trois-Rivieres, QC, G9A 5Z6
(819) 376-3725
Emp Here 50   *Sales* 4,377,642
SIC 1731 Electrical work

D-U-N-S 20-580-5869   (BR)
BANQUE NATIONALE DU CANADA
324 Rue Des Forges Bureau 200, Trois-Rivieres, QC, G9A 2G8
(819) 378-2771
Emp Here 20
SIC 6021 National commercial banks

D-U-N-S 24-707-4045   (SL)
BELLEMARE ENVIRONNEMENT
11450 Boul Industriel, Trois-Rivieres, QC, G9A 5E1
(819) 697-2227
Emp Here 700   *Sales* 51,239,520
SIC 8731 Commercial physical research
Pr Jean-Luc Bellemare
   Daniel Lemire

D-U-N-S 20-520-5383   (BR)
BEST BUY CANADA LTD
FUTURE SHOP 668
(*Suby of* Best Buy Co., Inc.)
4520 Boul Des Recollets Bureau 900a, Trois-Rivieres, QC, G9A 4N2
(819) 379-6161
Emp Here 71
SIC 5731 Radio, television, and electronic stores

D-U-N-S 20-266-1427   (BR)
BIBLIOTHEQUE ET ARCHIVES NATIONALES DU QUEBEC
BANQ

225 Rue Des Forges Unite 208, Trois-Rivieres, QC, G9A 5Z5
(819) 371-6015
Emp Here 30
SIC 8231 Libraries

D-U-N-S 25-525-0540   (HQ)
CAFE MORGANE ROYALE INC
CAFE MORGANE
(*Suby of* Cafe Morgane Royale Inc)
4945 Boul Gene-H.-Kruger, Trois-Rivieres, QC, G9A 4N5
(819) 694-1118
Emp Here 20   *Emp Total* 50
Sales 2,407,703
SIC 5499 Miscellaneous food stores

D-U-N-S 25-860-9288   (HQ)
CAISSE DESJARDINS DES TROIS-RIVIERES
CENTRE DE SERVICE DE LA MONTAGNE
(*Suby of* Caisse Desjardins Des Trois-Rivieres)
1200 Rue Royale, Trois-Rivieres, QC, G9A 4J2
(819) 376-1200
Emp Here 30   *Emp Total* 190
Sales 23,661,244
SIC 6062 State credit unions
Genl Mgr David Belanger
Pr Marili B. Desrochers
VP Louis Brunelle
Sec Andre Gabias
Dir Genevieve Auger
Dir Alexandre Baril
Dir Louis Cloutier
Dir Pierre Gagnon

D-U-N-S 25-517-1381   (SL)
CENTRE DE LA PETITE ENFANCE L'UNIVERS MAMUSE ET MEDUQUE INC
2855 Rue Monseigneur-Saint-Arnaud, Trois-Rivieres, QC, G9A 4L9
(819) 379-6778
Emp Here 50   *Sales* 1,532,175
SIC 8351 Child day care services

D-U-N-S 20-252-3981   (BR)
CHEMINS DE FER QUEBEC-GATINEAU INC
(*Suby of* Genesee & Wyoming Inc.)
900 Rue Bonaventure, Trois-Rivieres, QC, G9A 6G8
(819) 375-4796
Emp Here 50
SIC 4111 Local and suburban transit

D-U-N-S 24-668-6422   (BR)
COCA-COLA LTD
(*Suby of* The Coca-Cola Company)
8500 Boul Industriel, Trois-Rivieres, QC, G9A 5E1
(819) 694-4000
Emp Here 100
SIC 2086 Bottled and canned soft drinks

D-U-N-S 24-762-9611   (BR)
COCA-COLA REFRESHMENTS CANADA COMPANY
COMPAGNIE D'EMBOUTEILLAGE COCA-COLA
(*Suby of* The Coca-Cola Company)
8500 Boul Industriel, Trois-Rivieres, QC, G9A 5E1
(819) 694-4000
Emp Here 60
SIC 2086 Bottled and canned soft drinks

D-U-N-S 24-247-0222   (BR)
COMMISSION SCOLAIRE CENTRAL QUEBEC
THREE RIVERS ACADEMY (TRA)
1875 Rue Nicolas-Perrot, Trois-Rivieres, QC, G9A 1C5
(819) 375-2332
Emp Here 20
SIC 8211 Elementary and secondary schools

D-U-N-S 25-232-0957   (BR)

COMMISSION SCOLAIRE CENTRAL QUEBEC
MAURICIE ENGLISH ELEMENTARY SCHOOL
(*Suby of* Commission Scolaire Central Quebec)
1241 Rue Nicolas-Perrot, Trois-Rivieres, QC, G9A 1C2
(819) 376-7676
Emp Here 50
SIC 8211 Elementary and secondary schools

D-U-N-S 25-232-6939   (BR)
COMMISSION SCOLAIRE DU CHEMIN-DU-ROY
ECOLE ST PHILIPPE MON D'AMI
481 Rue Bureau, Trois-Rivieres, QC, G9A 2M9
(819) 376-3749
Emp Here 50
SIC 8211 Elementary and secondary schools

D-U-N-S 20-716-9082   (BR)
COMMISSION SCOLAIRE DU CHEMIN-DU-ROY
FORMATION GENERALE DES ADULTES
1060 Rue Saint-Francois-Xavier, Trois-Rivieres, QC, G9A 1R8
(819) 379-8714
Emp Here 80
SIC 8211 Elementary and secondary schools

D-U-N-S 25-233-3026   (BR)
COMMISSION SCOLAIRE DU CHEMIN-DU-ROY
ECOLE ST PAUL
946 Rue Saint-Paul Bureau 213, Trois-Rivieres, QC, G9A 1J3
(819) 378-8414
Emp Here 20
SIC 8211 Elementary and secondary schools

D-U-N-S 25-232-7135   (BR)
COMMISSION SCOLAIRE DU CHEMIN-DU-ROY
ST PATRICK ELEMENTARY & SECONDARY SCHOOL
1875 Rue Nicolas-Perrot, Trois-Rivieres, QC, G9A 1C5
(819) 375-2332
Emp Here 20
SIC 8211 Elementary and secondary schools

D-U-N-S 25-026-3803   (BR)
COMMISSION SCOLAIRE DU CHEMIN-DU-ROY
ECOLE SAINT-FRANCOIS DASSISE
636 Rue Sainte-Catherine, Trois-Rivieres, QC, G9A 3L5
(819) 375-1955
Emp Here 35
SIC 8211 Elementary and secondary schools

D-U-N-S 24-179-4015   (SL)
COOPERATIVE DES AMBULANCIERS DE LA MAURICIE
7325 Boul Jean-Xxiii, Trois-Rivieres, QC, G9A 5C9
(819) 376-1414
Emp Here 104   *Sales* 7,405,850
SIC 4119 Local passenger transportation, nec
Pr Pr Pierre Pellerin
   Serge Levesque

D-U-N-S 20-801-2620   (BR)
COSTCO WHOLESALE CANADA LTD
COSTCO
(*Suby of* Costco Wholesale Corporation)
3000 Boul Des Recollets, Trois-Rivieres, QC, G9A 6J2
(819) 693-5758
Emp Here 200
SIC 5399 Miscellaneous general merchandise

D-U-N-S 20-806-9943   (BR)
COUCHE-TARD INC
555 Cote Richelieu, Trois-Rivieres, QC, G9A 5V4

---

(819) 373-9782
Emp Here 25
SIC 5411 Grocery stores

D-U-N-S 20-581-9506   (BR)
DELOITTE & TOUCHE INC
(Suby of Deloitte LLP)
1500 Rue Royale Bureau 250, Trois-Rivieres,
QC, G9A 6E6
(819) 691-1212
Emp Here 80
SIC 8721 Accounting, auditing, and book-keeping

D-U-N-S 20-295-1856   (BR)
DELTA HOTELS LIMITED
WESTMOUNT HOSPITALITY
1620 Rue Notre-Dame Centre, Trois-Rivieres,
QC, G9A 6E5
(819) 376-1991
Emp Here 50
SIC 8741 Management services

D-U-N-S 25-717-2416   (BR)
DESSAU INC
1455 Rue Champlain, Trois-Rivieres, QC, G9A
5X4
(819) 378-6159
Emp Here 50
SIC 8742 Management consulting services

D-U-N-S 24-572-8543   (BR)
DEVELOPPEMENT OLYMBEC INC
125 Rue Des Forges Bureau 200, Trois-Rivieres, QC, G9A 2G7
(819) 374-7526
Emp Here 40
SIC 6512 Nonresidential building operators

D-U-N-S 24-671-2439   (BR)
DOLLARAMA S.E.C.
DOLLARAMA
4445 Boul Gene-H.-Kruger, Trois-Rivieres,
QC, G9A 4N3
(819) 840-8754
Emp Here 22
SIC 5331 Variety stores

D-U-N-S 24-309-7370   (SL)
ELEVATEURS DE TROIS-RIVIERES LTEE,
LES
(Suby of Upper Lakes Group Inc)
2615 Rue Notre-Dame Centre, Trois-Rivieres,
QC, G9A 4Y7
(819) 374-0660
Emp Here 35   Sales 88,574,290
SIC 4221 Farm product warehousing and storage
Sec Guy Bureau
Fin Ex Eric Verville

D-U-N-S 24-126-1838   (BR)
FILTERFAB COMPANY
2305 Rue Jules-Vachon Bureau 2, Trois-Rivieres, QC, G9A 5E1
(819) 691-4104
Emp Here 30
SIC 3569 General industrial machinery, nec

D-U-N-S 25-293-2561   (BR)
FINANCIERE BANQUE NATIONALE INC
7200 Rue Marion, Trois-Rivieres, QC, G9A
0A5
(819) 379-0000
Emp Here 33
SIC 6282 Investment advice

D-U-N-S 24-001-6241   (BR)
FONDATION DU CENTRE DE SANTE ET DE
SERVICES SOCIAUX DE TROIS-RIVIERES
731 Rue Sainte-Julie, Trois-Rivieres, QC, G9A
1Y1
(819) 370-2100
Emp Here 140
SIC 8322 Individual and family services

D-U-N-S 20-284-0484   (SL)
GROUPE ARSENAULT INC.
2875 Rue Saint-Philippe, Trois-Rivieres, QC,

G9A 0A8
(819) 379-5255
Emp Here 50   Sales 5,371,275
SIC 4959 Sanitary services, nec
Pr Michel Arsenault

D-U-N-S 24-054-9345   (BR)
GUAY INC
7100 Boul Jean-Xxiii, Trois-Rivieres, QC, G9A
5C9
(819) 377-4343
Emp Here 35
SIC 7353 Heavy construction equipment
rental

D-U-N-S 20-553-6431   (BR)
HOME DEPOT OF CANADA INC
HOME DEPOT
(Suby of The Home Depot Inc)
4500 Rue Real-Proulx, Trois-Rivieres, QC,
G9A 6P9
(819) 379-3990
Emp Here 100
SIC 5211 Lumber and other building materials

D-U-N-S 24-804-7958   (BR)
INDUSTRIES FOURNIER INC, LES
INDUSTRIES FOURNIER, DIV CONSTRUC-
TION
8605 Boul Parent, Trois-Rivieres, QC, G9A
5E1
(819) 375-2888
Emp Here 40
SIC 1541 Industrial buildings and warehouses

D-U-N-S 24-890-3296   (SL)
INTRAGAZ SOCIETE EN COMMANDITE
6565 Boul Jean-Xxiii Bureau 1, Trois-Rivieres,
QC, G9A 5C9
(819) 377-8080
Emp Here 20   Sales 5,275,400
SIC 4922 Natural gas transmission
Genl Mgr Emil Guilbert

D-U-N-S 20-347-0463   (BR)
JYSK LINEN'N FURNITURE INC
2930 Blvd Des Recollets, Trois-Rivieres, QC,
G9A 6J2
(819) 801-1904
Emp Here 20
SIC 5712 Furniture stores

D-U-N-S 24-370-3738   (SL)
MACO MECANIQUE INC
6595 Boul Jean-Xxiii, Trois-Rivieres, QC, G9A
5C9
(819) 378-7070
Emp Here 50   Sales 5,653,974
SIC 1711 Plumbing, heating, air-conditioning
Pr Pr Mathieu Gagnon
 Martin Gagnon
 Rene Hebert

D-U-N-S 24-351-3889   (BR)
MAGASINS LECOMPTE INC
ESCOMPTES LECOMPTE, LES
(Suby of Magasins Lecompte Inc)
385 Rue Des Forges, Trois-Rivieres, QC, G9A
2H4
(819) 694-1112
Emp Here 20
SIC 5399 Miscellaneous general merchandise

D-U-N-S 24-352-4378   (SL)
MARGARINE THIBAULT INC
GROUPE BERGERON THIBAULT, LE
3000 Rue Jules-Vachon, Trois-Rivieres, QC,
G9A 5E1
(819) 373-3333
Emp Here 55   Sales 29,002,320
SIC 2079 Edible fats and oils
 Danielle Bergeron

D-U-N-S 25-905-3320   (BR)
MARLU INC
MCDONALD'S
4520 Boul Des Recollets, Trois-Rivieres, QC,
G9A 4N2

(819) 373-5408
Emp Here 85
SIC 5812 Eating places

D-U-N-S 25-905-3312   (BR)
MARLU INC
MCDONALDS RESTAURANT
4585 Boul Gene-H.-Kruger, Trois-Rivieres,
QC, G9A 4N4
(819) 375-8202
Emp Here 50
SIC 5812 Eating places

D-U-N-S 20-127-1017   (SL)
MESSAGERIES VALOIS INC
920 Rue Mcdougall, Trois-Rivieres, QC, G9A
2T6
(819) 373-5522
Emp Here 50   Sales 3,939,878
SIC 4212 Local trucking, without storage

D-U-N-S 24-098-0388   (BR)
METALLURGISTES UNIS D'AMERIQUE
METALLURGISTES UNIS D'AMERIQUE
227 Boul Du Saint-Maurice, Trois-Rivieres,
QC, G9A 3N8
(819) 376-6106
Emp Here 100
SIC 8631 Labor organizations

D-U-N-S 20-571-9722   (BR)
METRO RICHELIEU INC
SUPER C
750 Boul Du Saint-Maurice, Trois-Rivieres,
QC, G9A 3P6
(819) 371-1120
Emp Here 100
SIC 5411 Grocery stores

D-U-N-S 25-355-6310   (SL)
ORCHESTRE SYMPHONIQUE TROIS-
RIVIERES INC
1517 Rue Royale, Trois-Rivieres, QC, G9A
4J9
(819) 373-5340
Emp Here 73   Sales 4,669,485
SIC 7929 Entertainers and entertainment
groups

D-U-N-S 20-317-7357   (BR)
PAPIERS DE PUBLICATION KRUGER INC
3735 Boul Gene-H.-Kruger, Trois-Rivieres,
QC, G9A 6B1
(819) 375-1691
Emp Here 340
SIC 2611 Pulp mills

D-U-N-S 20-277-3529   (BR)
PAPILLON & FILS LTEE
MODULES ASSEMBLY PLANT
8420 Boul Industriel, Trois-Rivieres, QC, G9A
5E1
(819) 374-4647
Emp Here 25
SIC 1711 Plumbing, heating, air-conditioning

D-U-N-S 20-263-4135   (HQ)
PAPILLON & FILS LTEE
2300 Rue Jules-Vachon, Trois-Rivieres, QC,
G9A 5E1
(819) 374-4647
Emp Here 50   Emp Total 88
Sales 8,755,284
SIC 1711 Plumbing, heating, air-conditioning
Pr Stephane Champoux
Treas Marilyn Masse

D-U-N-S 20-263-2766   (SL)
PISCINES LAUNIER INC
CLUB PISCINE
5825 Boul Gene-H.-Kruger, Trois-Rivieres,
QC, G9A 4P1
(819) 375-7771
Emp Here 80   Sales 10,550,800
SIC 5999 Miscellaneous retail stores, nec
Pr Pr Serge Turmel
 Serge Massicotte
Treas Martin Rathi

D-U-N-S 25-293-6661   (BR)
RBC DOMINION SECURITIES INC
RBC DOMINION VALEURS MOBILIAIRES
(Suby of Royal Bank Of Canada)
25 Rue Des Forges Bureau 100, Trois-Rivieres, QC, G9A 6A7
(819) 379-3600
Emp Here 30
SIC 6211 Security brokers and dealers

D-U-N-S 24-107-3063   (SL)
RGF ELECTRIQUE INC
2740 Rue Charbonneau Bureau 200, Trois-Rivieres, QC, G9A 5C9
(819) 377-4726
Emp Here 50   Sales 4,377,642
SIC 1731 Electrical work

D-U-N-S 24-363-0667   (BR)
RGIS CANADA ULC
7175 Rue Marion Bureau 240, Trois-Rivieres,
QC, G9A 5Z9
(819) 374-2086
Emp Here 40
SIC 7389 Business services, nec

D-U-N-S 20-700-6425   (BR)
REITMANS (CANADA) LIMITEE
4600 Boul Des Recollets, Trois-Rivieres, QC,
G9A 0A1
(819) 379-6258
Emp Here 25
SIC 5137 Women's and children's clothing

D-U-N-S 25-810-4314   (BR)
ROYAL BANK OF CANADA
ROYAL BANK OF CANADA
(Suby of Royal Bank Of Canada)
3105 Boul Des Recollets, Trois-Rivieres, QC,
G9A 6M1
(819) 691-4150
Emp Here 32
SIC 6021 National commercial banks

D-U-N-S 20-690-8373   (SL)
SERVICE D'IMPARTITION INDUSTRIEL INC
2300 Rue Jules-Vachon, Trois-Rivieres, QC,
G9A 5E1
(819) 374-4647
Emp Here 60   Sales 8,623,250
SIC 1796 Installing building equipment
Pr Pr Stephane Champoux
VP Martin Letendre
Treas Denise St-Pierre
Dir Daniel Caron

D-U-N-S 24-871-8835   (SL)
SERVICES MENAGERS TRIFLUVIENS INC
5224 Boul Gene-H.-Kruger, Trois-Rivieres,
QC, G9A 4N6
(819) 374-7437
Emp Here 60   Sales 1,751,057
SIC 7349 Building maintenance services, nec

D-U-N-S 20-103-2625   (BR)
SOCIETE QUEBECOISE DES INFRAS-
TRUCTURES
100 Rue Laviolette Bureau Rc 01, Trois-Rivieres, QC, G9A 5S9
(819) 371-6035
Emp Here 20
SIC 6512 Nonresidential building operators

D-U-N-S 20-270-6297   (BR)
STANTEC CONSULTING LTD
1455 Rue Champlain, Trois-Rivieres, QC, G9A
5X4
(819) 378-7949
Emp Here 54
SIC 8711 Engineering services

D-U-N-S 25-050-5922   (BR)
STAPLES CANADA INC
BUREAU EN GROS
(Suby of Staples, Inc.)
4000 Boul Des Recollets Bureau 42, Trois-Rivieres, QC, G9A 6K9
(819) 370-8679
Emp Here 30

SIC 5943 Stationery stores

D-U-N-S 24-360-4514   (HQ)
TRANSPORT BELLEMARE INTERNA-TIONAL INC
EXPRESS S.R.S.
(*Suby of* Gestion Bellemare Inc)
8750 Boul Industriel, Trois-Rivieres, QC, G9A 5E1
(819) 379-4546
Emp Here 100   *Emp Total* 1
Sales 19,407,546
SIC 4213 Trucking, except local
  Jean-Luc Bellemare

D-U-N-S 20-703-2074   (BR)
TRANSPORT TFI 1, S.E.C.
TRANSPORT J.C. GERMAIN
1200 Rue Du Parc-Daniel, Trois-Rivieres, QC, G9A 5R6
(819) 370-3422
Emp Here 250
SIC 4213 Trucking, except local

D-U-N-S 24-239-4471   (BR)
TROIS-RIVIERES, VILLE DE
BOREALIS MUSEE
200 Av Des Draveurs, Trois-Rivieres, QC, G9A 0B6
(819) 372-4633
Emp Here 28
SIC 8412 Museums and art galleries

D-U-N-S 24-580-7862   (BR)
UNI-SELECT INC
ACCESSOIRES   D'AUTOMOBILES LEBLANC
3125 Boul Gene-H.-Kruger Bureau 1624, Trois-Rivieres, QC, G9A 4M2
(819) 378-2371
Emp Here 80
SIC 5013 Motor vehicle supplies and new parts

D-U-N-S 24-707-4490   (BR)
VEOLIA ES CANADA SERVICES INDUS-TRIELS INC
VEOLIA ES CANADA INDUSTRIAL SER-VICES INC
2895 Rue Jules-Vachon, Trois-Rivieres, QC, G9A 5E1
(819) 372-0803
Emp Here 35
SIC 8731 Commercial physical research

D-U-N-S 20-520-7124   (BR)
VEOLIA ES CANADA SERVICES INDUS-TRIELS INC
ONYX INDUSTRIES
2895 Rue Jules-Vachon Bureau 2, Trois-Rivieres, QC, G9A 5E1
(819) 372-0803
Emp Here 25
SIC 7699 Repair services, nec

D-U-N-S 20-000-8220   (BR)
WSP CANADA INC
3450 Boul Gene-H.-Kruger Bureau 300, Trois-Rivieres, QC, G9A 4M3
(819) 375-1292
Emp Here 80
SIC 8711 Engineering services

D-U-N-S 20-650-5062   (BR)
WAL-MART CANADA CORP
WALMART MAGASIN
4520 Boul Gene-H.-Kruger, Trois-Rivieres, QC, G9A 4N1
(819) 372-1181
Emp Here 200
SIC 5399 Miscellaneous general merchandise

D-U-N-S 25-293-8550   (BR)
WINNERS MERCHANTS INTERNATIONAL L.P.
WINNERS
(*Suby of* The TJX Companies Inc)
4125 Boul Des Recollets, Trois-Rivieres, QC,

G9A 6M1
(819) 370-2001
Emp Here 80
SIC 5651 Family clothing stores

D-U-N-S 24-226-5572   (BR)
WOLSELEY INDUSTRIAL CANADA INC
(*Suby of* WOLSELEY PLC)
3160 Rue Bellefeuille, Trois-Rivieres, QC, G9A 5R5
(819) 379-0047
Emp Here 30
SIC 5211 Lumber and other building materials

Trois-Rivieres, QC G9B
St-Maurice County

D-U-N-S 25-919-8307   (BR)
4211677 CANADA INC
GROUPE DICOM TRANSPORT CANADA
3700 Boul L.-P.-Normand, Trois-Rivieres, QC, G9B 0G2
(819) 693-0019
Emp Here 28
SIC 4212 Local trucking, without storage

D-U-N-S 20-566-0541   (SL)
CAMIONS FREIGHTLINER M.B. TROIS-RIVIERES LTEE
FREIGHTLINER
300 Rue Quenneville, Trois-Rivieres, QC, G9B 1X6
(819) 377-9997
Emp Here 35   *Sales* 14,295,240
SIC 5511 New and used car dealers
Pr Pr Laurent Deshaies
VP VP Annie Deshaies
  Marc Bellemarre

D-U-N-S 25-233-4552   (BR)
COMMISSION SCOLAIRE DU CHEMIN-DU-ROY
ECOLE SECONDAIRE CHAVIGNY
365 Rue Chavigny, Trois-Rivieres, QC, G9B 1A7
(819) 377-4391
Emp Here 170
SIC 8211 Elementary and secondary schools

D-U-N-S 20-716-7318   (BR)
COMMISSION SCOLAIRE DU CHEMIN-DU-ROY
ECOLES PRIMAIRES NOTRE DAME DU RO-SAIRE
7660 Rue Notre-Dame O, Trois-Rivieres, QC, G9B 1L9
(819) 377-4438
Emp Here 50
SIC 8211 Elementary and secondary schools

D-U-N-S 25-072-0943   (BR)
COMMISSION SCOLAIRE DU CHEMIN-DU-ROY
ECOLE DE POINTE-DU-LAC
101 Rue Elisabeth-Guay, Trois-Rivieres, QC, G9B 7Z4
(819) 377-1312
Emp Here 50
SIC 8211 Elementary and secondary schools

D-U-N-S 25-232-6699   (BR)
COMMISSION SCOLAIRE DU CHEMIN-DU-ROY
ECOLE DE POINTE DU LAC PAVILLON NOTRE DAME
10830 Ch Sainte-Marguerite, Trois-Rivieres, QC, G9B 6N7
(819) 377-1516
Emp Here 25
SIC 8211 Elementary and secondary schools

D-U-N-S 24-509-1533   (HQ)
CONSULTANTS MESAR INC
(*Suby of* Groupe Mesar Inc)
4500 Rue Charles-Malhiot, Trois-Rivieres,

QC, G9B 0V4
(819) 537-5771
Emp Here 80   *Emp Total* 1
Sales 13,862,533
SIC 8711 Engineering services
Pr Pr Yvan Masse
Sec Luc Paulin
Sec Roland Courtemanche
Dir Denis Desaulniers

D-U-N-S 25-027-4495   (BR)
DOMREMY   MAURICIE/CENTRE-DU-QUEBEC
11931 Rue Notre-Dame O, Trois-Rivieres, QC, G9B 6W9
(819) 377-2441
Emp Here 85
SIC 8069 Specialty hospitals, except psychi-atric

D-U-N-S 20-187-3259   (SL)
ENTRETIEN PARAMEX INC
(*Suby of* Groupe Ganotec Inc)
3535 Boul L.-P.-Normand, Trois-Rivieres, QC, G9B 0G8
(819) 377-5533
Emp Here 30   *Sales* 7,821,331
SIC 7699 Repair services, nec
Pr Sebastien Larivee
Sec Michail F. Norton
Dir Richard A. Lanoha

D-U-N-S 24-003-7411   (BR)
GANOTEC INC
3535 Boul L.-P.-Normand, Trois-Rivieres, QC, G9B 0G8
(819) 377-5533
Emp Here 50
SIC 1629 Heavy construction, nec

D-U-N-S 20-577-5526   (BR)
GOUVERNEMENT DE LA PROVINCE DE QUEBEC
SOCIETE DE L'ASSURANCE AUTOMOBILE DU QUEBEC
3235 Boul Saint-Jean, Trois-Rivieres, QC, G9B 1X5
(819) 377-3114
Emp Here 40
SIC 8093 Specialty outpatient clinics, nec

D-U-N-S 25-365-7787   (SL)
GROUPE ROBERT INC
1130 Ch Des Petites-Terres, Trois-Rivieres, QC, G9B 7G9
(819) 377-3003
Emp Here 40
SIC 4213 Trucking, except local

D-U-N-S 20-267-1137   (SL)
MADYSTA TELECOM LTEE
MADYSTA CONSTRUCTIONS
3600 Boul L.-P.-Normand, Trois-Rivieres, QC, G9B 0G2
(819) 377-3336
Emp Here 100   *Sales* 22,615,896
SIC 1623 Water, sewer, and utility lines
  Yvan St-Arnaud

D-U-N-S 24-863-5641   (SL)
RESTAURANT GREC BAIE-JOLIE INC
9151 Rue Notre-Dame O, Trois-Rivieres, QC, G9B 6T2
(819) 377-2511
Emp Here 55   *Sales* 1,678,096
SIC 5812 Eating places

Uashat, QC G4R

D-U-N-S 25-976-4587   (SL)
3232077 CANADA INC
INNU CONSTRUCTION
121 Boul Des Montagnais, Uashat, QC, G4R 5R1
(418) 962-3378
Emp Here 70   *Sales* 3,575,074

SIC 7389 Business services, nec

Umiujaq, QC J0M

D-U-N-S 20-507-4011   (BR)
COMMISSION SCOLAIRE KATIVIK
KILUUTAQ SCHOOL
C.P. 98, Umiujaq, QC, J0M 1Y0
(819) 331-7061
Emp Here 30
SIC 8211 Elementary and secondary schools

Upton, QC J0H
Bagot County

D-U-N-S 20-263-7138   (HQ)
EQUIPEMENTS ADRIEN PHANEUF INC, LES
(*Suby of* 125668 Canada Inc)
292 Rue Principale, Upton, QC, J0H 2E0
(450) 549-5811
Emp Here 35   *Emp Total* 45
Sales 9,776,734
SIC 5083 Farm and garden machinery
Pr Pr Yvon Phaneuf
VP VP Andree Theroux

Val-D'Or, QC J9P
Abitibi County

D-U-N-S 24-391-1463   (SL)
3124673 CANADA INC
1030 Rue Leo-Fournier, Val-D'Or, QC, J9P 6X8
(819) 825-5283
Emp Here 50   *Sales* 6,596,303
SIC 2411 Logging
Pr Pr Jacques Element

D-U-N-S 25-811-4008   (BR)
9017-6165 QUEBEC INC
TIM HORTONS
1690 3e Av, Val-D'Or, QC, J9P 1W2
(819) 825-9118
Emp Here 40
SIC 5812 Eating places

D-U-N-S 25-851-3910   (BR)
9027-3111 QUEBEC INC
MOTEL CONTINENTAL
(*Suby of* 9027-3111 Quebec Inc)
932 3e Av, Val-D'Or, QC, J9P 1T3
(819) 824-9651
Emp Here 35
SIC 7011 Hotels and motels

D-U-N-S 24-820-8126   (SL)
9031-6332 QUEBEC INC
GAREAU TOYOTA
1080 3e Av, Val-D'Or, QC, J9P 1T6
(819) 825-9000
Emp Here 24   *Sales* 12,057,600
SIC 5511 New and used car dealers
Pr Pr Yvon Gareau
Genl Mgr Pascal Gareau
Sls Dir Sebastien Roy

D-U-N-S 24-372-4593   (SL)
9117-6347 QUEBEC INC
S.D.P.F. CONSTRUCTION
2888 Ch Sullivan, Val-D'Or, QC, J9P 0B9
(819) 874-5913
Emp Here 30   *Sales* 7,950,960
SIC 1541 Industrial buildings and warehouses
Pr Patrick Forgues
Treas Serge Duval

D-U-N-S 24-325-9561   (SL)
ACE SERVICES MECANIQUES INC

A.C.E.
1010 Rue Leo-Fournier, Val-D'Or, QC, J9P 6X8
(819) 874-8091
Emp Here 80 *Sales* 4,888,367
SIC 7699 Repair services, nec

D-U-N-S 24-570-5504 (BR)
AGNICO EAGLE MINES LIMITED
AGNICO EAGLE MINES, DIVISION GOLDEX
1953 3rd Av O, Val-D'Or, QC, J9P 4N9
(819) 874-7822
Emp Here 248
SIC 1481 NonMetallic mineral services

D-U-N-S 20-576-1963 (SL)
AUBAINERIE CONCEPT MODE INC, L'
965 Rue Germain, Val-D'Or, QC, J9P 7H7
(819) 824-4377
Emp Here 60 *Sales* 3,648,035
SIC 5651 Family clothing stores

D-U-N-S 24-059-0922 (BR)
AUTOBUS MAHEUX LTEE, LES
855 Boul Barrette, Val-D'Or, QC, J9P 0J8
(819) 825-4767
Emp Here 160
SIC 4151 School buses

D-U-N-S 25-377-3279 (BR)
BELL MEDIA INC
1610 3e Av, Val-D'Or, QC, J9P 1V8
(819) 825-2568
Emp Here 20
SIC 4832 Radio broadcasting stations

D-U-N-S 24-429-7701 (SL)
BETON BARRETTE INC
1000 Boul Barrette, Val-D'Or, QC, J9P 0J8
(819) 825-8112
Emp Here 60 *Sales* 16,785,360
SIC 5032 Brick, stone, and related material
Pr Pr Monique Barrette
  Lynda Barrette
  Guy Barrette
Dir Andree Barrette

D-U-N-S 25-311-3732 (BR)
CANADIAN IMPERIAL BANK OF COMMERCE
CIBC
824 3e Av, Val-D'Or, QC, J9P 1T1
(819) 825-8830
Emp Here 28
SIC 6021 National commercial banks

D-U-N-S 25-379-5082 (BR)
CENTRE DE READAPTATION LA MAISON INC
CENTRE DE READAPTATION LA MAISON INC
(*Suby of* Centre de Readaptation La Maison)
975 Rue Germain, Val-D'Or, QC, J9P 7H7
(819) 825-3337
Emp Here 30
SIC 8093 Specialty outpatient clinics, nec

D-U-N-S 20-963-0821 (HQ)
CENTRE JEUNESSE DE L'ABITIBI TEMIS-CAMINGUE
700 Boul Forest, Val-D'Or, QC, J9P 2L3
(819) 736-7466
Emp Here 235 *Emp Total* 40,000
Sales 23,369,759
SIC 8399 Social services, nec
Pr Rolande Hebert
VP Francis Langlois
VP Anick Robert
Sec Francine Larouche
Dir Martine Humbert
Treas Patrick Perreault
Dir Steve Ethier
Dir Dominic Leclerc
Dir Louise Lemieux

D-U-N-S 20-418-3859 (SL)
CENTRE DE RECYCLAGE UNIVERSEL (1981) LTEE

(*Suby of* 2736-4629 Quebec Inc)
1880 3e Av, Val-D'Or, QC, J9P 7A9
(819) 874-5555
Emp Here 34 *Sales* 5,842,440
SIC 5013 Motor vehicle supplies and new parts
Pr Pr Richard Larochelle
  Benoit Labrie

D-U-N-S 24-389-5690 (BR)
CENTRE DE SANTE ET DE SERVICES SOCIAUX DE LA VALLEE-DE-L'OR
CENTRE D'HEBERGEMENT DE VAL-D'OR
1212 Av Brebeuf, Val-D'Or, QC, J9P 2C9
(819) 825-5858
Emp Here 50
SIC 8062 General medical and surgical hospitals

D-U-N-S 25-443-6264 (BR)
CENTRE DE SANTE ET DE SERVICES SOCIAUX DE LA VALLEE-DE-L'OR
CLSC DE VAL-D'OR
725 6e Rue, Val-D'Or, QC, J9P 3Y1
(819) 825-5858
Emp Here 50
SIC 8062 General medical and surgical hospitals

D-U-N-S 20-998-5084 (BR)
CLAIR FOYER INC
CRDI CLAIR FOYER
1220 7e Rue, Val-D'Or, QC, J9P 5S7
(819) 825-4821
Emp Here 20
SIC 8361 Residential care

D-U-N-S 25-240-3696 (BR)
COMMISSION SCOLAIRE WESTERN QUEBEC
ECOLE GOLDEN VALLEY SCHOOL
(*Suby of* Commission Scolaire Western Quebec)
980 7e Rue, Val-D'Or, QC, J9P 3P8
(819) 825-3211
Emp Here 35
SIC 8211 Elementary and secondary schools

D-U-N-S 25-240-7044 (BR)
COMMISSION SCOLAIRE DE L'OR-ET-DES-BOIS
ECOLE ST SAUVEUR
(*Suby of* Commission Scolaire de l'Or-et-des-Bois)
451 3e Av, Val-D'Or, QC, J9P 1S3
(819) 824-6841
Emp Here 36
SIC 8211 Elementary and secondary schools

D-U-N-S 20-712-6173 (BR)
COMMISSION SCOLAIRE DE L'OR-ET-DES-BOIS
ECOLE POLYVANTE LE CARREFOUR
(*Suby of* Commission Scolaire de l'Or-et-des-Bois)
125 Rue Self, Val-D'Or, QC, J9P 3N2
(819) 825-4670
Emp Here 120
SIC 8211 Elementary and secondary schools

D-U-N-S 20-034-1936 (BR)
COMMISSION SCOLAIRE DE L'OR-ET-DES-BOIS
CENTRE DE L'HORIZON
(*Suby of* Commission Scolaire de l'Or-et-des-Bois)
1241 8e Rue, Val-D'Or, QC, J9P 3P1
(819) 874-3565
Emp Here 40
SIC 8211 Elementary and secondary schools

D-U-N-S 20-712-6256 (BR)
COMMISSION SCOLAIRE DE L'OR-ET-DES-BOIS
CENTRE DE FORMATION PROFESSION-NELLE
(*Suby of* Commission Scolaire de l'Or-et-des-Bois)

125 Rue Self, Val-D'Or, QC, J9P 3N2
(819) 825-6366
Emp Here 75
SIC 8211 Elementary and secondary schools

D-U-N-S 20-712-6165 (BR)
COMMISSION SCOLAIRE DE L'OR-ET-DES-BOIS
ECOLE PRIMAIRE VAL D'OR PAPILLON D'OR
(*Suby of* Commission Scolaire de l'Or-et-des-Bois)
970 Rue Levis, Val-D'Or, QC, J9P 4C1
(819) 825-4356
Emp Here 50
SIC 8211 Elementary and secondary schools

D-U-N-S 25-240-7440 (BR)
COMMISSION SCOLAIRE DE L'OR-ET-DES-BOIS
ECOLE NOTRE DAME DE FATIMA
(*Suby of* Commission Scolaire de l'Or-et-des-Bois)
971 5e Rue, Val-D'Or, QC, J9P 3Y8
(819) 824-2739
Emp Here 30
SIC 8211 Elementary and secondary schools

D-U-N-S 25-240-6962 (BR)
COMMISSION SCOLAIRE DE L'OR-ET-DES-BOIS
ECOLE ST JOSEPH
(*Suby of* Commission Scolaire de l'Or-et-des-Bois)
94 Rue Allard, Val-D'Or, QC, J9P 2Y1
(819) 825-5484
Emp Here 35
SIC 8211 Elementary and secondary schools

D-U-N-S 25-240-0924 (BR)
COMMISSION SCOLAIRE DE L'OR-ET-DES-BOIS
ECOLE SAINTE LUCIE
(*Suby of* Commission Scolaire de l'Or-et-des-Bois)
185 Rue Parent, Val-D'Or, QC, J9P 6E1
(819) 824-6821
Emp Here 35
SIC 8211 Elementary and secondary schools

D-U-N-S 20-294-9470 (BR)
COMMISSION SCOLAIRE DE L'OR-ET-DES-BOIS
ECOLE SECONDAIRE LE TRANSIT
(*Suby of* Commission Scolaire de l'Or-et-des-Bois)
500 6e Av, Val-D'Or, QC, J9P 1B3
(819) 825-3090
Emp Here 45
SIC 8211 Elementary and secondary schools

D-U-N-S 20-804-1835 (BR)
CONSEIL SCOLAIRE DE DISTRICT DES ECOLES CATHOLIQUES DU SUD-OUEST
CONSEIL SCOLAIRE DE DISTRICT DES ECOLES CATHOLIQUES DU SUD-OUEST
370 Rue De L'Eglise, Val-D'Or, QC, J9P 0B8
(819) 874-3355
Emp Here 20
SIC 8211 Elementary and secondary schools

D-U-N-S 24-399-9997 (BR)
CONSTRUCTIONS PEPIN ET FORTIN INC, LES
(*Suby of* Placements Pepin & Fortin Inc)
1925 3e Av, Val-D'Or, QC, J9P 7B8
(819) 824-6300
Emp Here 40
SIC 1521 Single-family housing construction

D-U-N-S 25-337-3104 (BR)
DESSAU INC
1032 3e Av, Val-D'Or, QC, J9P 1T6
(819) 825-1353
Emp Here 20
SIC 8711 Engineering services

D-U-N-S 25-737-9545 (SL)

ENTREPRENEUR MINIER CMAC - THYSSEN INC
GROUPE MINIER CMAC
185 Rue Des Distributeurs Bureau 16, Val-D'Or, QC, J9P 6Y1
(819) 874-8303
Emp Here 295 *Sales* 35,267
SIC 1241 Coal mining services

D-U-N-S 20-179-6427 (BR)
ENTREPRENEUR MINIER PROMEC INC
INDUSTRIAL MECHANICAL SPECIALTY
1400 4e Av, Val-D'Or, QC, J9P 5Z9
(819) 824-2074
Emp Here 30
SIC 7699 Repair services, nec

D-U-N-S 20-914-1311 (BR)
FORAGE SPEKTRA INC
2756 Ch Sullivan, Val-D'Or, QC, J9P 0B9
(819) 824-4435
Emp Here 20
SIC 1799 Special trade contractors, nec

D-U-N-S 24-475-7522 (BR)
GROUPE BELL NORDIQ INC
TELEBEC SEC
555 Av Centrale Bureau 3, Val-D'Or, QC, J9P 1P6
(819) 523-3989
Emp Here 250
SIC 4813 Telephone communication, except radio

D-U-N-S 20-363-3057 (SL)
GROUPE MINIER CMAC-THYSSEN INC
CMAC- THYSSEN MINING GROUP
185 Rue Des Distributeurs, Val-D'Or, QC, J9P 6Y1
(819) 874-8303
Emp Here 250 *Sales* 18,240,175
SIC 1794 Excavation work
Ch Bd Rene Scheepers
Pr Pr Luc Guimond
VP VP Ghislain Blanchet
Sec Pierre Matte
  Jim Haines

D-U-N-S 20-151-7781 (HQ)
GROUPE STAVIBEL INC
1271 7e Rue, Val-D'Or, QC, J9P 3S1
(819) 825-2233
Emp Here 60 *Emp Total* 33,000
Sales 47,527,040
SIC 8711 Engineering services
Pr Pr Gilles Marcotte
VP VP Serge Beaule
Dir Andre Levesque
Dir Steven Campbell

D-U-N-S 25-673-0359 (BR)
HECLA QUEBEC INC
(*Suby of* Hecla Mining Company)
1010 3e Rue, Val-D'Or, QC, J9P 4B1
(819) 874-4511
Emp Here 1,000
SIC 1041 Gold ores

D-U-N-S 20-213-0188 (BR)
HEWITT EQUIPEMENT LIMITEE
CATERPILLAR
1200 3e Av E, Val-D'Or, QC, J9P 0J6
(819) 825-5494
Emp Here 100
SIC 5082 Construction and mining machinery

D-U-N-S 24-820-4844 (SL)
HOTEL FORESTEL VAL-D'OR INC
1001 3e Av, Val-D'Or, QC, J9P 1T4
(819) 825-5660
Emp Here 130 *Sales* 7,837,440
SIC 7011 Hotels and motels
VP Robert F Lariviere
Pr Yvon Gareau

D-U-N-S 20-302-1444 (BR)
HYDRO-QUEBEC
1600 Rue De L'Hydro, Val-D'Or, QC, J9P 6Z1

(819) 825-3320
Emp Here 94
SIC 4911 Electric services

D-U-N-S 20-590-0991   (BR)
HYDRO-QUEBEC
1600 Rue De L'Hydro, Val-D'Or, QC, J9P 6Z1
(819) 825-4880
Emp Here 114
SIC 4911 Electric services

D-U-N-S 24-372-5376   (SL)
IMPRIMERIE LEBONFON INC
(*Suby of* 6505503 Canada Inc)
1051 Rue De L'Echo, Val-D'Or, QC, J9P 4N9
(819) 825-8888
Emp Here 47   *Sales* 3,828,240
SIC 2731 Book publishing

D-U-N-S 25-305-1957   (BR)
INNVEST PROPERTIES CORP
COMFORT INN
(*Suby of* Innvest Properties Corp)
1665 3e Av, Val-D'Or, QC, J9P 1V9
(819) 825-9360
Emp Here 20
SIC 7011 Hotels and motels

D-U-N-S 24-515-7888   (BR)
LOBLAWS INC
MAXI
1500 Ch Sullivan Bureau 24, Val-D'Or, QC, J9P 1M1
(819) 824-3595
Emp Here 60
SIC 5411 Grocery stores

D-U-N-S 25-518-2495   (SL)
MABO WESTERN STAR INC
3100 Boul Jean-Jacques-Cossette, Val-D'Or, QC, J9P 6Y6
(819) 825-8995
Emp Here 50   *Sales* 3,648,035
SIC 7538 General automotive repair shops

D-U-N-S 24-863-0055   (HQ)
MEUBLES MARCHAND INC, LES
1767 3e Av, Val-D'Or, QC, J9P 1W3
(819) 874-8777
Emp Here 50   *Emp Total* 3
Sales 6,566,463
SIC 5712 Furniture stores
Pr Pr Marcel Marchand
 Christian Marchand
 Gisele Marchand
 Dany Marchand

D-U-N-S 25-366-6895   (BR)
MINES RICHMONT INC
776 Ch Perron, Val-D'Or, QC, J9P 0C3
(819) 736-4581
Emp Here 60
SIC 1041 Gold ores

D-U-N-S 25-447-8936   (BR)
PROVIGO INC
LOBLAW
502 Rue Giguere, Val-D'Or, QC, J9P 7G6
(819) 825-5000
Emp Here 120
SIC 5141 Groceries, general line

D-U-N-S 24-334-6330   (BR)
PUROLATOR INC.
PUROLATOR INC
195 Rue Des Distributeurs, Val-D'Or, QC, J9P 6Y1
(819) 825-3238
Emp Here 25
SIC 7389 Business services, nec

D-U-N-S 25-176-0208   (BR)
QMX GOLD CORPORATION
(*Suby of* QMX Gold Corporation)
1900 Ch Brador, Val-D'Or, QC, J9P 0A4
(819) 825-3412
Emp Here 100
SIC 1081 Metal mining services

D-U-N-S 20-697-2247   (BR)
QMX GOLD CORPORATION
1876 3e Av, Val-D'Or, QC, J9P 7A9

Emp Here 39
SIC 1481 NonMetallic mineral services

D-U-N-S 20-034-1928   (BR)
RNC MEDIA INC
COULEUR FM
1729 3e Av, Val-D'Or, QC, J9P 1W3
(819) 825-9994
Emp Here 20
SIC 4832 Radio broadcasting stations

D-U-N-S 24-355-1835   (SL)
ROTISSERIES DU NORD INC, LES
ROTISSERIES ST-HUBERT
1785 3e Av, Val-D'Or, QC, J9P 1W3
(819) 825-8444
Emp Here 70   *Sales* 2,115,860
SIC 5812 Eating places

D-U-N-S 20-536-3315   (BR)
ROYAL BANK OF CANADA
RBC
(*Suby of* Royal Bank Of Canada)
689 3e Av, Val-D'Or, QC, J9P 1S7
(819) 824-5150
Emp Here 20
SIC 6021 National commercial banks

D-U-N-S 20-515-2551   (BR)
SMS EQUIPMENT INC
FEDERAL EQUIPMENT
1085 3e Av E, Val-D'Or, QC, J9P 0J7
(819) 874-3733
Emp Here 22
SIC 5082 Construction and mining machinery

D-U-N-S 25-378-3773   (BR)
SOCIETE DES ETABLISSEMENTS DE PLEIN AIR DU QUEBEC
RESERVE FAUNIQUE LA VERENDRYE
50 Boul Lamaque, Val-D'Or, QC, J9P 2H6
(819) 354-4392
Emp Here 25
SIC 7032 Sporting and recreational camps

D-U-N-S 20-651-9238   (BR)
TELEBEC, SOCIETE EN COMMANDITE
100 Rue Des Distributeurs, Val-D'Or, QC, J9P 6Y1
(819) 824-7451
Emp Here 100
SIC 4813 Telephone communication, except radio

D-U-N-S 25-516-7330   (BR)
TEMABEX INC
375 Av Centrale, Val-D'Or, QC, J9P 1P4
(819) 825-2944
Emp Here 20
SIC 7349 Building maintenance services, nec

D-U-N-S 20-517-5339   (SL)
TIGRE VAL D'OR LIMITEE
TIGRE GEANT
(*Suby of* Giant Tiger Stores Limited)
825 3e Av, Val-D'Or, QC, J9P 1T2
(819) 825-8106
Emp Here 60   *Sales* 4,304,681
SIC 5311 Department stores

D-U-N-S 25-378-0738   (BR)
TRANSCONTINENTAL INC
ECHO ABITIBIEN ET LE CITOYEN DE LA VALLEE DE L'OR, L'
1462 Rue De La Quebecoise, Val-D'Or, QC, J9P 5H4
(819) 825-3755
Emp Here 30
SIC 2721 Periodicals

D-U-N-S 24-308-1218   (BR)
UNIBOARD CANADA INC
UNIRES, DIV DE
2700 Boul Jean-Jacques-Cossette, Val-D'Or,

QC, J9P 6Y5
(819) 825-6550
Emp Here 180
SIC 2493 Reconstituted wood products

D-U-N-S 24-649-7411   (BR)
WSP CANADA INC
1075 3e Av E, Val-D'Or, QC, J9P 0J7
(819) 825-4711
Emp Here 20
SIC 8711 Engineering services

D-U-N-S 20-103-3359   (BR)
WAL-MART CANADA CORP
1855 3e Av Bureau 3139, Val-D'Or, QC, J9P 7A9
(819) 874-8411
Emp Here 225
SIC 5311 Department stores

D-U-N-S 25-670-2643   (SL)
YOUTH PROTECTION
700 Boul Forest, Val-D'Or, QC, J9P 2L3
(819) 825-0002
Emp Here 49   *Sales* 9,193,048
SIC 8399 Social services, nec

Val-David, QC J0T
Terrebonne County

D-U-N-S 20-712-2248   (BR)
COMMISSION SCOLAIRE DES LAURENTIDES
ECOLE ST JEAN BAPTISTE
(*Suby of* Commission Scolaire Des Laurentides)
2580 Rue De L'Eglise, Val-David, QC, J0T 2N0
(819) 324-8670
Emp Here 50
SIC 8211 Elementary and secondary schools

D-U-N-S 25-240-2243   (BR)
COMMISSION SCOLAIRE DES LAURENTIDES
ECOLE PAVILLON SAINTE-MARIE
(*Suby of* Commission Scolaire Des Laurentides)
1350 Rue De L'Academie, Val-David, QC, J0T 2N0
(819) 324-8671
Emp Here 25
SIC 8211 Elementary and secondary schools

D-U-N-S 20-263-8136   (SL)
DUFRESNE, L. & FILS LTEE
METRO DUFRESNE
(*Suby of* Placements Fernand Dufresne Inc)
2500 Rue De L'Eglise, Val-David, QC, J0T 2N0
(819) 322-2030
Emp Here 65   *Sales* 11,698,290
SIC 5411 Grocery stores
Pr Jacques Dufresne

Val-Des-Bois, QC J0X
Papineau County

D-U-N-S 20-284-1248   (BR)
SOCIETE DES ETABLISSEMENTS DE PLEIN AIR DU QUEBEC
SEPAQ RESERVE FAUNIQUE PAPINEAU LABELLE
443 309 Rte, Val-Des-Bois, QC, J0X 3C0
(819) 454-2011
Emp Here 45
SIC 7032 Sporting and recreational camps

Val-Des-Monts, QC J8N
Champlain County

D-U-N-S 25-246-1103   (SL)
3013774 CANADA INC
CONSTRUCTIONS LALONDE & CHARETTE LES
162 Rue De La Cascade, Val-Des-Monts, QC, J8N 1L4
(819) 671-6888
Emp Here 26   *Sales* 5,376,850
SIC 1521 Single-family housing construction
Pr Roger Lalonde

D-U-N-S 20-712-5472   (BR)
COMMISSION SCOLAIRE DES DRAVEURS
ECOLE L'EQUIPAGE
20 Ch De L'Ecole Bureau 215, Val-Des-Monts, QC, J8N 7E7
(819) 503-8022
Emp Here 25
SIC 8211 Elementary and secondary schools

Val-Joli, QC J1S

D-U-N-S 24-020-2085   (HQ)
BESSETTE ET BOUDREAU INC
GESTION SYREBEC
680 Rte 143 S, Val-Joli, QC, J1S 0G6
(819) 845-7722
Emp Here 140   *Emp Total* 1
Sales 14,033,266
SIC 4212 Local trucking, without storage
Pr Jean Rouillard
VP Benoit Rouillard
VP Rene Rouillard
Treas Georgette St-Onge

Val-Morin, QC J0T
Terrebonne County

D-U-N-S 20-264-6535   (SL)
HOTEL FAR HILLS LTEE
HOTEL DU SOMMET
3399 Rue Du Far Hills Inn, Val-Morin, QC, J0T 2R0
(819) 322-2014
Emp Here 70   *Sales* 3,064,349
SIC 7011 Hotels and motels

Valcourt, QC J0E
Shefford County

D-U-N-S 25-093-2279   (BR)
BOMBARDIER INC
MANOIR J. ARMAND BOMBARDIER
794 Rue Saint-Joseph, Valcourt, QC, J0E 2L0
(514) 861-9481
Emp Here 20
SIC 8412 Museums and art galleries

D-U-N-S 24-329-2286   (BR)
BOMBARDIER PRODUITS RECREATIFS INC
BRT
565 Rue De La Montagne, Valcourt, QC, J0E 2L0
(450) 532-2211
Emp Here 70
SIC 5012 Automobiles and other motor vehicles

D-U-N-S 20-956-4488   (BR)
BOMBARDIER PRODUITS RECREATIFS INC
USINE 1
565 Rue De La Montagne Bureau 210, Valcourt, QC, J0E 2L0
(450) 532-2211
Emp Here 100
SIC 3799 Transportation equipment, nec

D-U-N-S 25-233-2556   (BR)
COMMISSION SCOLAIRE DES SOMMETS
ECOLE PRIMAIRE DE LA CHANTERELLE
(*Suby of* Commission Scolaire des Sommets)
1100 Rue Champetre, Valcourt, QC, J0E 2L0
(450) 532-2488
Emp Here 30
SIC 8211 Elementary and secondary schools

D-U-N-S 20-992-6265   (BR)
GOSSELIN EXPRESS LTEE
LOCATION EXPRESS
(*Suby of* Placements Claude Gosselin Inc)
5699 Ch De L'Aeroport, Valcourt, QC, J0E 2L0
(450) 532-3285
Emp Here 25
SIC 4731 Freight transportation arrangement

Vallee-Jonction, QC G0S
Beauce County

D-U-N-S 25-232-7556   (BR)
COMMISSION SCOLAIRE DE LA BEAUCE-ETCHEMIN
ECOLE L'ENFANT JESUS
217 Rue Principale, Vallee-Jonction, QC, G0S 3J0
(418) 253-6018
Emp Here 22
SIC 8211 Elementary and secondary schools

D-U-N-S 25-010-4874   (BR)
OLYMEL S.E.C.
FLAMINGO
568 Ch De L'Ecore S, Vallee-Jonction, QC, G0S 3J0
(418) 253-5437
Emp Here 1,200
SIC 2011 Meat packing plants

D-U-N-S 20-257-8118   (HQ)
TRANSPORT L.F.L. INC
(*Suby of* Turcotte, Dominique Inc)
431 Ch De L'Ecore N, Vallee-Jonction, QC, G0S 3J0
(418) 253-5423
Emp Here 50   *Emp Total* 21
Sales 34,996,540
SIC 4213 Trucking, except local
Pr Pr Dominique Turcotte

Varennes, QC J3X
Vercheres County

D-U-N-S 24-502-6554   (BR)
ABB INC
1600 Boul Lionel-Boulet, Varennes, QC, J3X 1P7
(450) 652-2901
Emp Here 317
SIC 3612 Transformers, except electric

D-U-N-S 20-703-4906   (BR)
ACIER PICARD INC
1951 Ch De L'Energie, Varennes, QC, J3X 1P7
(450) 649-9000
Emp Here 150
SIC 5051 Metals service centers and offices

D-U-N-S 20-650-3265   (BR)
AIR LIQUIDE CANADA INC
3090 Ch De La Baronnie, Varennes, QC, J3X 1P7
(450) 652-9163
Emp Here 20
SIC 4212 Local trucking, without storage

D-U-N-S 20-580-0464   (BR)
AIR LIQUIDE CANADA INC
3575 Boul Marie Victorin, Varennes, QC, J3X 1P9

(450) 652-0611
Emp Here 35
SIC 5169 Chemicals and allied products, nec

D-U-N-S 24-562-8078   (BR)
BAU-VAL INC
PAVAGES VARENNES
3350 Ch De La Butte-Aux-Renards, Varennes, QC, J3X 1P7
(450) 652-9818
Emp Here 40
SIC 2951 Asphalt paving mixtures and blocks

D-U-N-S 24-212-8556   (BR)
BAU-VAL INC
TECH-MIX
3350 Ch De La Butte-Aux-Renards, Varennes, QC, J3X 1P7
(450) 652-0689
Emp Here 30
SIC 2951 Asphalt paving mixtures and blocks

D-U-N-S 25-391-8973   (SL)
CAISSE DESJARDINS DE VARENNES
CENTRE FINANCIER AUX ENTREPRISES DESJARDINS RIVE-SUD
50 Rue La Gabelle Bureau 100, Varennes, QC, J3X 2J4
(450) 652-0607
Emp Here 30   *Sales* 5,992,604
SIC 6062 State credit unions
Genl Mgr Rene Ouellet
Pr Francine Metivier
VP Claire T Bellazzi
Sec Nathalie Jodoin
Dir Marcel Gelineau
Dir Robert Horman
Dir Gino Turcotte
Dir Jean-Francois Morin

D-U-N-S 20-888-6044   (SL)
COMMERCANT DES PEAUX SHEFFREN LTEE
3697 Ch De La Baronnie, Varennes, QC, J3X 1P7
(514) 248-1106
Emp Here 31   *Sales* 9,344,640
SIC 5159 Farm-product raw materials, nec
Pr Pr Harvey Sheffren
VP Eddie Fagen

D-U-N-S 20-712-3204   (BR)
COMMISSION SCOLAIRE DES PATRIOTES
ECOLE PRIMAIRE DU CARROUSEL
230 Rue Suzor-Cote, Varennes, QC, J3X 1L6
(450) 645-2351
Emp Here 50
SIC 8211 Elementary and secondary schools

D-U-N-S 24-636-9222   (BR)
COMMISSION SCOLAIRE DES PATRIOTES
ECOLE SECONDAIRE LE CARREFOUR
123 Ch Du Petit-Bois, Varennes, QC, J3X 1P7
(450) 645-2363
Emp Here 40
SIC 8211 Elementary and secondary schools

D-U-N-S 20-712-3048   (BR)
COMMISSION SCOLAIRE DES PATRIOTES
ECOLE DE LA SOURCE
239 Rue Du Fief, Varennes, QC, J3X 1Z2
(450) 645-2350
Emp Here 40
SIC 8211 Elementary and secondary schools

D-U-N-S 25-233-6037   (BR)
COMMISSION SCOLAIRE DES PATRIOTES
ECOLE J.P.LABARRE
2250 Rte Marie-Victorin, Varennes, QC, J3X 1R4
(450) 645-2354
Emp Here 70
SIC 8211 Elementary and secondary schools

D-U-N-S 25-628-3433   (BR)
ENTREPRISES MARVAIS INC, LES
MCDONALD'S
321 Boul De La Marine, Varennes, QC, J3X 1Z4

(450) 929-0186
Emp Here 48
SIC 5812 Eating places

D-U-N-S 20-984-2504   (BR)
ETHANOL GREENFIELD QUEBEC INC
3300 Rte Marie-Victorin, Varennes, QC, J3X 1P7
(450) 652-1800
Emp Here 30
SIC 2869 Industrial organic chemicals, nec

D-U-N-S 20-203-3242   (SL)
GPCO INC
1471 Boul Lionel-Boulet Bureau 26, Varennes, QC, J3X 1P7

Emp Here 24   *Sales* 2,480,664
SIC 8748 Business consulting, nec

D-U-N-S 24-908-0664   (HQ)
GSI ENVIRONNEMENT INC
BIOSITE
1501 Boul Lionel-Boulet, Varennes, QC, J3X 1P7
(418) 882-2736
Emp Here 40   *Emp Total* 1,318
Sales 21,961,171
SIC 2875 Fertilizers, mixing only
Pr Robert Youden
Sec Linda Beaudin

D-U-N-S 24-167-7525   (BR)
HYDRO-QUEBEC
IREQ
1800 Boul Lionel-Boulet, Varennes, QC, J3X 1P7
(450) 652-8011
Emp Here 750
SIC 8731 Commercial physical research

D-U-N-S 20-264-8424   (BR)
KRONOS CANADA INC
3390 Rte Marie-Victorin, Varennes, QC, J3X 1P7
(450) 929-5000
Emp Here 450
SIC 2816 Inorganic pigments

D-U-N-S 24-698-6012   (HQ)
LABORATOIRES D'ANALYSES S.M. INC
(*Suby of* Le Groupe SMI Inc)
1471 Boul Lionel-Boulet, Varennes, QC, J3X 1P7
(514) 332-6001
Emp Here 100   *Emp Total* 2
Sales 12,907,140
SIC 8731 Commercial physical research
Pr Gerard Laganiere

D-U-N-S 24-667-5177   (SL)
MACONNERIE DEMERS INC
977 Boul Lionel-Boulet Bureau 78, Varennes, QC, J3X 1P7
(450) 652-9596
Emp Here 50   *Sales* 3,648,035
SIC 1741 Masonry and other stonework

D-U-N-S 20-321-5384   (SL)
MAESTRO TECHNOLOGIES INC
1625 Boul Lionel-Boulet Bureau 300, Varennes, QC, J3X 1P7
(450) 652-6200
Emp Here 50   *Sales* 7,000,050
SIC 7372 Prepackaged software
Pr Pr Robert Meunier

D-U-N-S 24-127-6562   (SL)
MARCOTTE SYSTEMES LTEE
1471 Boul Lionel-Boulet Unit9 28, Varennes, QC, J3X 1P7
(450) 652-6000
Emp Here 24   *Sales* 5,472,053
SIC 5084 Industrial machinery and equipment
Pr Pr Fyed Mohamed
Dir Denis-Raymond Marcotte

D-U-N-S 25-523-6176   (BR)
MATERIAUX R.M. BIBEAU LTEE

RONA BIBEAU VARENNES
1527 Ch Du Pays-Brule, Varennes, QC, J3X 1P7
(450) 652-3997
Emp Here 30
SIC 5211 Lumber and other building materials

D-U-N-S 24-419-0224   (BR)
NUVO PHARMACEUTICALS INC
(*Suby of* Nuvo Pharmaceuticals Inc)
3655 Ch De La Cote-Bissonnette, Varennes, QC, J3X 1P7
(450) 929-0050
Emp Here 30
SIC 8731 Commercial physical research

D-U-N-S 24-418-8491   (BR)
NUVO PHARMACEUTICALS INC
(*Suby of* Nuvo Pharmaceuticals Inc)
3655 Ch De La Cote-Bissonnette, Varennes, QC, J3X 1P7
(450) 929-0050
Emp Here 60
SIC 2834 Pharmaceutical preparations

D-U-N-S 25-962-8352   (SL)
PASSION CUISINE ET GOURMET
2020 Boul Rene-Gaultier Bureau 36, Varennes, QC, J3X 1N9
(450) 929-2942
Emp Here 64   *Sales* 4,961,328
SIC 5719 Miscellaneous homefurnishings

D-U-N-S 24-538-8736   (BR)
PROVIGO DISTRIBUTION INC
2020 Boul Rene-Gaultier, Varennes, QC, J3X 1N9
(450) 652-9809
Emp Here 50
SIC 5411 Grocery stores

D-U-N-S 24-323-8144   (SL)
RAIL BONAVENTURE INC
650 Boul Lionel-Boulet, Varennes, QC, J3X 1P7
(450) 652-5400
Emp Here 50   *Sales* 9,536,300
SIC 1629 Heavy construction, nec
Pr Gilles Massicotte
VP VP Rene Massicotte

D-U-N-S 25-627-7302   (SL)
SERVICES DE SANTE JEAN-PHILIPPE PARE INC
UNIPRIX
2020 Boul Rene-Gaultier, Varennes, QC, J3X 1N9
(450) 652-3967
Emp Here 35   *Sales* 6,407,837
SIC 5912 Drug stores and proprietary stores
Pr Pr Jean-Philippe Pare
Dir Marie-Claude Hamelin

D-U-N-S 24-138-0547   (BR)
SOBEYS QUEBEC INC
IGA
1777 132 Rte, Varennes, QC, J3X 1P7
(450) 929-0405
Emp Here 150
SIC 5411 Grocery stores

D-U-N-S 20-984-2850   (BR)
SODEM INC
SELON DE QUILLES CRER
131 Ch Du Petit-Bois, Varennes, QC, J3X 1P7

Emp Here 20
SIC 7999 Amusement and recreation, nec

D-U-N-S 20-264-8895   (HQ)
THOMAS, RENE & FILS INC
HOME HARDWARE
10 Rue Beauregard, Varennes, QC, J3X 1R1
(450) 652-2927
Emp Here 36   *Emp Total* 35
Sales 7,369,031
SIC 5211 Lumber and other building materials
Pr Pr Rene Thomas Jr

Florian Thomas
Hugues Thomas

D-U-N-S 25-392-6869   (BR)
UNIVERSITE DU QUEBEC
*INSTITUT NATIONAL DE LA RECHERCHE
SCIENTIFIQUE ENERGIE & MATERIAUX*
1650 Boul Lionel-Boulet, Varennes, QC, J3X
1P7
(450) 929-8100
Emp Here 80
SIC 8733 Noncommercial research organizations

Vaudreuil-Dorion, QC J7V
Vaudreuil County

D-U-N-S 20-355-7293   (SL)
10052787 CANADA INC
HOUSTON VAUDREUIL
48 Boul De La Cite-Des-Jeunes Bureau 100,
Vaudreuil-Dorion, QC, J7V 9L5
(450) 218-0505
Emp Here 50   *Sales* 1,532,175
SIC 5812 Eating places

D-U-N-S 20-331-7730   (SL)
3367771 CANADA INC
BOULANGERIE PREMIERE MOISSON
189 Boul Harwood, Vaudreuil-Dorion, QC, J7V
1Y3
(450) 455-2827
Emp Here 26   *Sales* 3,720,996
SIC 5149 Groceries and related products, nec

D-U-N-S 24-256-8228   (SL)
3453871 CANADA INC
SUNNY'S RESTAURANT BAR
2400 Rang Saint-Antoine Bureau 3, Vaudreuil-
Dorion, QC, J7V 8P2
(450) 455-1100
Emp Here 60   *Sales* 2,188,821
SIC 5813 Drinking places

D-U-N-S 20-357-3829   (BR)
9631984 CANADA INC
PREMIER MEAT PACKERS
270 Rue Joseph-Carrier, Vaudreuil-Dorion,
QC, J7V 5V5
(800) 361-4045
Emp Here 60
SIC 2011 Meat packing plants

D-U-N-S 20-984-5028   (BR)
**AMENAGEMENT   ET   DESIGN
SPORTSCENE INC**
LA CAGE - BRASSERIE SPORTIVE
47 Boul De La Cite-Des-Jeunes, Vaudreuil-
Dorion, QC, J7V 8C1
(450) 510-3011
Emp Here 30
SIC 1542 Nonresidential construction, nec

D-U-N-S 25-976-3985   (SL)
AMYLIOR INC
AMYSYSTEMS
1650 Rue Chicoine, Vaudreuil-Dorion, QC,
J7V 8P2
(450) 424-0288
Emp Here 55   *Sales* 4,764,381
SIC 2514 Metal household furniture

D-U-N-S 20-564-4615   (BR)
**AVERY DENNISON CANADA CORPORA-
TION**
220 Rue Joseph-Carrier, Vaudreuil-Dorion,
QC, J7V 5V5
(450) 455-7971
Emp Here 20
SIC 2672 Paper; coated and laminated, nec

D-U-N-S 24-249-5625   (BR)
BANK OF NOVA SCOTIA, THE
BANQUE SCOTIA
3070 Boul De La Gare, Vaudreuil-Dorion,

J7V 0H1
(450) 455-2233
Emp Here 20
SIC 6021 National commercial banks

D-U-N-S 24-363-5765   (BR)
BEST BUY CANADA LTD
BEST BUY
(*Suby of* Best Buy Co., Inc.)
3090 Boul De La Gare, Vaudreuil-Dorion, QC,
J7V 0H1
(450) 455-8434
Emp Here 50
SIC 5731 Radio, television, and electronic
stores

D-U-N-S 24-368-9457   (BR)
**CAISSE DESJARDINS DE VAUDREUIL-
SOULANGES**
CENTRE DE SERVICES DORION
170 Boul Harwood, Vaudreuil-Dorion, QC, J7V
1Y2
(450) 455-7901
Emp Here 25
SIC 6062 State credit unions

D-U-N-S 20-530-0481   (BR)
CANADA POST CORPORATION
BUREAU DE POSTE VAUDREUIL DORION
100 Rte De Lotbiniere, Vaudreuil-Dorion, QC,
J7V 2T4
(450) 455-3026
Emp Here 60
SIC 4311 U.s. postal service

D-U-N-S 25-967-5866   (BR)
CASCADES CANADA ULC
NORAMPAC-VAUDREUIL, DIV OF
400 Rue Forbes, Vaudreuil-Dorion, QC, J7V
6N8
(450) 455-5731
Emp Here 170
SIC 2631 Paperboard mills

D-U-N-S 20-532-7955   (BR)
**CENTRE DE LA PETITE ENFANCE DE
L'UNIVERSITE DE MONTREAL**
*CENTRE DE LA PETITE ENFANCE DE
L'UNIVERSITE DE MONTREAL*
418 Av Saint-Charles, Vaudreuil-Dorion, QC,
J7V 2N1
(450) 424-9304
Emp Here 29
SIC 8351 Child day care services

D-U-N-S 20-858-9879   (SL)
CLUB DE GOLF SUMMERLEA INC
1000 Rte De Lotbiniere, Vaudreuil-Dorion, QC,
J7V 0H5
(450) 455-0921
Emp Here 100   *Sales* 4,012,839
SIC 7997 Membership sports and recreation
clubs

D-U-N-S 25-905-4732   (SL)
COJALY INC
ROTISSERIES ST-HUBERT, LES
601 Av Saint-Charles, Vaudreuil-Dorion, QC,
J7V 8G4
(450) 455-0409
Emp Here 80   *Sales* 2,407,703
SIC 5812 Eating places

D-U-N-S 24-346-3150   (BR)
CONSULTANTS LBCD INC, LES
(*Suby of* Consultants LBCD Inc, Les)
1000   Av   Saint-Charles   Bureau   1008,
Vaudreuil-Dorion, QC, J7V 8P5
(450) 455-6119
Emp Here 20
SIC 8711 Engineering services

D-U-N-S 25-527-9655   (HQ)
CONTROLE TOTAL LOGISTIQUE INC
(*Suby of* Controle Total Logistique Inc)
200 Av Loyola-Schmidt, Vaudreuil-Dorion, QC,
J7V 8P2

(514) 426-8521
Emp Here 78   *Emp Total* 100
Sales 7,879,756
SIC 4212 Local trucking, without storage
Ches Nadeau
Ward Goddard

D-U-N-S 20-277-4725   (BR)
**FLS   TRANSPORTATION   SERVICES LIM-
ITED**
454 Rue Aime-Vincent, Vaudreuil-Dorion, QC,
J7V 5V5
(450) 424-9262
Emp Here 30
SIC 4731 Freight transportation arrangement

D-U-N-S 25-362-8283   (BR)
FLYING J CANADA INC
FLYING J TRAVEL PLAZA
2900 Boul De La Gare, Vaudreuil-Dorion, QC,
J7V 9J5

Emp Here 30
SIC 5541 Gasoline service stations

D-U-N-S 25-877-3167   (BR)
**FONDATION DU CENTRE JEUNESSE DE
LA MONTEREGIE**
2555 Rue Dutrisac Bureau 24, Vaudreuil-
Dorion, QC, J7V 7E6
(450) 510-2230
Emp Here 35
SIC 8322 Individual and family services

D-U-N-S 24-330-9197   (BR)
GROUPE EMBALLAGE SPECIALISE S.E.C.
INDUSCORR
22401 Ch Dumberry, Vaudreuil-Dorion, QC,
J7V 8P7
(450) 510-0450
Emp Here 85
SIC 2631 Paperboard mills

D-U-N-S 20-252-3452   (HQ)
GROUPE PREMIERE MOISSON INC
189 Boul Harwood, Vaudreuil-Dorion, QC, J7V
1Y3
(450) 455-2827
Emp Here 50   *Emp Total* 65,000
Sales 13,132,926
SIC 2051 Bread, cake, and related products
Pr Pr Eric R Lafleche
VP VP Bernard Fiset
 Simon Rivet
 Francois Thibault
Dir Serge Boulanger
Dir Christian Bourbonniere

D-U-N-S 25-365-4750   (BR)
HOME DEPOT OF CANADA INC
HOME DEPOT
(*Suby of* The Home Depot Inc)
55 Boul De La Cite-Des-Jeunes, Vaudreuil-
Dorion, QC, J7V 8C1
(450) 510-2600
Emp Here 120
SIC 5251 Hardware stores

D-U-N-S 20-697-6339   (BR)
HYDRO-QUEBEC
3320 Rue F.-X.-Tessier, Vaudreuil-Dorion, QC,
J7V 5V5
(450) 424-3136
Emp Here 25
SIC 4911 Electric services

D-U-N-S 20-543-0150   (SL)
**LABORATOIRES BUCKMAN DU CANADA,
LTEE**
(*Suby of* Bulab Holdings, Inc.)
351 Rue Joseph-Carrier, Vaudreuil-Dorion,
QC, J7V 5V5
(450) 424-4404
Emp Here 138   *Sales* 26,479,445
SIC 2869 Industrial organic chemicals, nec
Pr Pr James Doan
VP VP Davor Mehes
VP VP Ihab Wassef
Treas Rosemary Ghaly

Dir Edson Peredo

D-U-N-S 20-712-3717   (BR)
LESTER B. PEARSON SCHOOL BOARD
*ELEMENTARY   SCHOOLS   PIERRE   ELLIOT
TRUDEAU*
490 Rue Bourget, Vaudreuil-Dorion, QC, J7V
6N2
(514) 798-4454
Emp Here 50
SIC 8211 Elementary and secondary schools

D-U-N-S 20-706-6577   (BR)
METRO RICHELIEU INC
SUPER C
44 Boul De La Cite-Des-Jeunes, Vaudreuil-
Dorion, QC, J7V 9L5
(450) 455-6222
Emp Here 60
SIC 5411 Grocery stores

D-U-N-S 24-411-1014   (BR)
PROVIGO INC
OBLAWS
501 Av Saint-Charles, Vaudreuil-Dorion, QC,
J7V 8V9
(450) 455-6161
Emp Here 20
SIC 5411 Grocery stores

D-U-N-S 20-999-3203   (HQ)
QUADRA CHIMIE LTEE
INGREDIENTS QUADRA
3901 Rue F.-X.-Tessier, Vaudreuil-Dorion, QC,
J7V 5V5
(450) 424-0161
Emp Here 65   *Emp Total* 165
Sales 42,025,363
SIC 5169 Chemicals and allied products, nec
Dir Tony Infilise
Pr Martin Collins
Sec Betty Infilise
 Pierre Thivierge

D-U-N-S 24-590-9387   (SL)
**REGROUPEMENT DES C H S L D DES
TROIS RIVES, LE**
CENTRE D'ACCUEIL VAUDREUIL
408 Av Saint-Charles, Vaudreuil-Dorion, QC,
J7V 7M9
(450) 455-6177
Emp Here 500   *Sales* 31,705,680
SIC 8051 Skilled nursing care facilities
Genl Mgr Lise Belisle

D-U-N-S 24-769-9671   (BR)
RYERSON CANADA, INC
200 Rue Du Cheminot, Vaudreuil-Dorion, QC,
J7V 5V5
(450) 424-0153
Emp Here 55
SIC 5051 Metals service centers and offices

D-U-N-S 20-915-6087   (BR)
**SERVICES   DE   READAPTATION   SUD
OUEST ET DU RENFORT, LES**
401 Boul Harwood Bureau 14, Vaudreuil-
Dorion, QC, J7V 7W1
(450) 455-6104
Emp Here 30
SIC 8051 Skilled nursing care facilities

D-U-N-S 20-852-2552   (BR)
SOBEYS CAPITAL INCORPORATED
*IGA SUPERMARCHE PIERRE PATRY EX-
TRA*
585 Av Saint-Charles, Vaudreuil-Dorion, QC,
J7V 8P9
(450) 424-3549
Emp Here 153
SIC 5411 Grocery stores

D-U-N-S 20-989-4406   (BR)
SOCIETE DE GESTION COGIR S.E.N.C.
SOCIETE DE GESTION COGIR S.E.N.C.
333 Rue Querbes Bureau 210, Vaudreuil-
Dorion, QC, J7V 1J9
(450) 455-6564
Emp Here 25

SIC 8361 Residential care

D-U-N-S 20-363-4642   (SL)
SOLUTIONS BOURASSA BOYER INC
3323 Boul De La Gare, Vaudreuil-Dorion, QC,
J7V 8W5
(450) 424-7000
Emp Here 75   *Sales* 12,243,760
SIC 8748 Business consulting, nec
Pr Claude Boyer

D-U-N-S 24-101-2223   (BR)
STAPLES CANADA INC
BUREAU EN GROS
(*Suby of* Staples, Inc.)
54 Boul De La Cite-Des-Jeunes Bureau 100,
Vaudreuil-Dorion, QC, J7V 9L5
(450) 455-2015
Emp Here 22
SIC 5943 Stationery stores

D-U-N-S 24-228-3497   (SL)
SYSTEMES DE MOBILIER TRIANGLE INC
330 Rue Aime-Vincent, Vaudreuil-Dorion, QC,
J7V 5V5
(450) 424-4040
Emp Here 25   *Sales* 2,042,900
SIC 3843 Dental equipment and supplies

D-U-N-S 24-327-4482   (BR)
WAL-MART CANADA CORP
3050 Boul De La Gare, Vaudreuil-Dorion, QC,
J7V 0H1
(450) 510-3314
Emp Here 150
SIC 5311 Department stores

D-U-N-S 24-357-7827   (BR)
XPO LOGISTICS CANADA INC
KELRON
420 Rue Aime-Vincent, Vaudreuil-Dorion, QC,
J7V 5V5
(450) 424-9365
Emp Here 28
SIC 4731 Freight transportation arrangement

D-U-N-S 20-618-4900   (BR)
YANJACO INC
ST HUBERT ROTISSERIE
(*Suby of* Yanjaco Inc)
435 Boul Harwood, Vaudreuil-Dorion, QC, J7V
7W1
(450) 455-3336
Emp Here 80
SIC 5812 Eating places

D-U-N-S 24-219-4228   (HQ)
YANJACO INC
ST HUBERT ROTISSERIE
(*Suby of* Yanjaco Inc)
640 Rue Chicoine Bureau E, Vaudreuil-
Dorion, QC, J7V 9J4
(450) 455-9615
Emp Here 50   *Emp Total* 130
Sales 3,939,878
SIC 5812 Eating places

Vercheres, QC J0L
Vercheres County

D-U-N-S 24-677-9516   (SL)
TRANSPORT GENERAL LEGAL INC
545 Rue De L'Industrie, Vercheres, QC, J0L
2R0
(450) 583-1177
Emp Here 50   *Sales* 3,939,878
SIC 4212 Local trucking, without storage

Verdun, QC H3E
Hochelaga County

D-U-N-S 24-353-7011   (HQ)
6362222 CANADA INC

CREATECH GROUP, THE
1 Carrefour Alexander-Graham-Bell Bureau A-
7, Verdun, QC, H3E 3B3
(514) 937-1188
Emp Here 120   *Emp Total* 48,090
Sales 17,325,020
SIC 7379 Computer related services, nec
Pr Ivan Mihaljevic
Pr Marinella Ermacora
Sec Michel Lalande
Dir Jenine Krause

D-U-N-S 24-812-1097   (SL)
BCE ELIX INC
14 Place Du Commerce Bureau 510, Verdun,
QC, H3E 1T5
(877) 909-3549
Emp Here 150   *Sales* 26,503,200
SIC 7371 Custom computer programming ser-
vices
Pr Pr Vanda Vicars
    Alain F. Dussault

D-U-N-S 20-174-6786   (BR)
BANK OF CANADA
*AGENCY OPERATIONS CENTRES DEPART-
MENT OF MONTREAL*
1001 Rue Levert, Verdun, QC, H3E 1V4
(514) 888-4310
Emp Here 70
SIC 6011 Federal reserve banks

D-U-N-S 25-334-3545   (BR)
CANADIAN RED CROSS SOCIETY, THE
CANADIAN RED CROSS
6 Place Du Commerce, Verdun, QC, H3E 1P4
(514) 362-2929
Emp Here 75
SIC 8322 Individual and family services

D-U-N-S 24-813-1096   (HQ)
CHARTON-HOBBS INC
VINS VIP, LES
(*Suby of* Herdt & Charton Inc)
3000 Boul Rene-Levesque Bureau 400, Ver-
dun, QC, H3E 1T9
(514) 353-8955
Emp Here 23   *Emp Total* 3
Sales 48,510,056
SIC 5169 Chemicals and allied products, nec
Pr Duncan R. Hobbs
    Gordon M.B. Coburn
Dir Derek Thompson Hobbs
Dir Jonathan Roger Hobbs

D-U-N-S 24-376-8673   (BR)
**COMPAGNIE DE TELEPHONE BELL DU
CANADA OU BELL CANADA, LA**
1 Carref Alexander-Graham-Bell, Verdun, QC,
H3E 3B3

Emp Here 4,000
SIC 4899 Communication services, nec

D-U-N-S 25-524-8411   (BR)
**DATA COMMUNICATIONS MANAGEMENT
CORP**
4 Place Du Commerce Bureau 200, Verdun,
QC, H3E 1J4
(514) 858-6777
Emp Here 50
SIC 2761 Manifold business forms

D-U-N-S 24-659-1358   (HQ)
GROUPE PAGES JAUNES CORP
YELLOW PAGES
16 Place Du Commerce, Verdun, QC, H3E
2A5
(514) 934-2000
Emp Here 800   *Emp Total* 2,800
Sales 306,392,979
SIC 4899 Communication services, nec
Pr Julien Billot
Sec Francois D Ramsay
Dir Ginette Maille

D-U-N-S 24-422-1052   (HQ)
IPEX GESTION INC

3 Place Du Commerce Bureau 101, Verdun,
QC, H3E 1H7
(514) 769-2200
Emp Here 100   *Emp Total* 40
Sales 53,430,054
SIC 8741 Management services
Pr Paul Graddon
Sec Paul Leonard
VP Bruce W Clark
VP Alain Lanthier
VP Franc Yorio
VP Carole Masse
VP Harold Aubie

D-U-N-S 24-612-1219   (BR)
LOBLAWS SUPERMARKETS LIMITED
LOBLAW'S
42 Place Du Commerce, Verdun, QC, H3E
1J5
(514) 761-7207
Emp Here 25
SIC 5411 Grocery stores

D-U-N-S 20-985-8641   (BR)
NAUTILUS PLUS INC
500 Ch Du Golf, Verdun, QC, H3E 1A8

Emp Here 22
SIC 7991 Physical fitness facilities

D-U-N-S 20-297-7455   (BR)
RE/MAX PERFORMANCE INC
RE MAX
1 Place Du Commerce Bureau 160, Verdun,
QC, H3E 1A2
(514) 766-1002
Emp Here 29
SIC 6411 Insurance agents, brokers, and ser-
vice

D-U-N-S 25-307-7432   (BR)
SOCIETE DES ALCOOLS DU QUEBEC
SOCIETE DES ALCOOLS DU QUEBEC
44 Place Du Commerce, Verdun, QC, H3E
1J5
(514) 766-4432
Emp Here 20
SIC 5921 Liquor stores

D-U-N-S 20-332-1682   (SL)
STROM SPA INC
1001 Boul De La Foret, Verdun, QC, H3E 1X9
(514) 761-7900
Emp Here 50   *Sales* 1,678,096
SIC 7991 Physical fitness facilities

D-U-N-S 24-425-1356   (BR)
SYMPHONY SENIOR LIVING INC
325 Ch De La Pointe-Sud, Verdun, QC, H3E
0B1
(514) 767-6792
Emp Here 70
SIC 8741 Management services

Verdun, QC H3G
Hochelaga County

D-U-N-S 25-359-6951   (BR)
**BOMBARDIER PRODUITS RECREATIFS
INC**
1059 Rue De La Montagne Bureau 200, Verdun, QC, H3G 0B9
(514) 732-7003
Emp Here 35
SIC 5012 Automobiles and other motor vehicles

Verdun, QC H4G
Hochelaga County

D-U-N-S 24-308-3545   (BR)
CAISSE DESJARDINS DE L'ILE-DES-

SOEURS-VERDUN
CENTRE D'AFFAIRES WELLINGTON
4162 Rue Wellington, Verdun, QC, H4G 1V7
(514) 766-8591
Emp Here 50
SIC 6062 State credit unions

D-U-N-S 20-290-4074   (BR)
**CENTRE DE SANTE ET DE SERVICES SO-
CIAUX DU SUD-OUEST-VERDUN**
*CENTRE DE SANTE ET DE SERVICES SO-
CIAUX DU SUD-QUES*
4000 Boul Lasalle, Verdun, QC, H4G 2A3
(514) 362-1000
Emp Here 1,600
SIC 8062 General medical and surgical hospi-
tals

D-U-N-S 25-223-7714   (BR)
**CENTRE DE LA PETITE ENFANCE COM-
MUNAUTAIRE LES TROTTINETTES**
*C.P.E. COMMUNAUTAIRE LES TROT-
TINETTES*
(*Suby of* Centre de la Petite Enfance Commu-
nautaire les Trottinettes)
4501 Rue Bannantyne, Verdun, QC, H4G 1E3
(514) 765-7160
Emp Here 22
SIC 8351 Child day care services

D-U-N-S 20-992-8147   (BR)
**CENTRE DE LA PETITE ENFANCE COM-
MUNAUTAIRE LES TROTTINETTES**
202 Rue Galt Bureau 2, Verdun, QC, H4G 2P2
(514) 761-0791
Emp Here 49
SIC 8351 Child day care services

D-U-N-S 25-240-2334   (BR)
**COMMISSION SCOLAIRE MARGUERITE-
BOURGEOYS**
ECOLE LEVIS SAUVE
655 Rue Willibrord, Verdun, QC, H4G 2T8
(514) 765-7585
Emp Here 50
SIC 8351 Child day care services

D-U-N-S 20-518-7060   (BR)
**COMMISSION SCOLAIRE MARGUERITE-
BOURGEOYS**
CARREFOUR MULTI-SERVICES
1100 5e Av, Verdun, QC, H4G 2Z6
(514) 765-7500
Emp Here 25
SIC 8211 Elementary and secondary schools

D-U-N-S 25-240-2250   (BR)
**COMMISSION SCOLAIRE MARGUERITE-
BOURGEOYS**
*ECOLE SECONDAIRE MONSEIGNEUR-
RICHARD*
3000 Boul Gaetan-Laberge, Verdun, QC, H4G
3C1
(514) 765-7666
Emp Here 56
SIC 8211 Elementary and secondary schools

D-U-N-S 25-233-5906   (BR)
**COMMISSION SCOLAIRE MARGUERITE-
BOURGEOYS**
*ECOLE NOTRE DAME DES SEPT
DOULEURS*
320 Rue De L'Eglise, Verdun, QC, H4G 2M4
(514) 765-7575
Emp Here 30
SIC 8211 Elementary and secondary schools

D-U-N-S 20-712-4103   (BR)
**COMMISSION SCOLAIRE MARGUERITE-
BOURGEOYS**
*CENTRE DE FORMATION PROFESSION-
NELLE DE VERDUN*
55 Rue Rheaume, Verdun, QC, H4G 3C1
(514) 765-7683
Emp Here 50
SIC 8211 Elementary and secondary schools

D-U-N-S 25-240-5170   (BR)

COMMISSION SCOLAIRE MARGUERITE-BOURGEOYS
ECOLE NOTRE-DAME-DE-LOURDES
504 5e Av, Verdun, QC, H4G 2Z1
(514) 765-7595
Emp Here 30
SIC 8211 Elementary and secondary schools

D-U-N-S 25-240-2292   (BR)
COMMISSION SCOLAIRE DE LA POINTE-DE-L'ILE
ECOLE PRIMAIRE NOTRE-DAME-DE-LA-PAIX
454 Rue Caisse, Verdun, QC, H4G 2C8
(514) 765-7565
Emp Here 40
SIC 8211 Elementary and secondary schools

D-U-N-S 20-807-1204   (BR)
COUCHE-TARD INC
4460 Rue De Verdun, Verdun, QC, H4G 1M2
(514) 761-1617
Emp Here 25
SIC 5411 Grocery stores

D-U-N-S 25-199-0388   (BR)
GROUPE JEAN COUTU (PJC) INC, LE
PJC JEAN COUTU
(*Suby of* 3958230 Canada Inc)
4061 Rue Wellington, Verdun, QC, H4G 1V6
(514) 761-4591
Emp Here 70
SIC 5912 Drug stores and proprietary stores

D-U-N-S 20-032-6754   (BR)
HOPITAL DOUGLAS
CENTRE WELLINGTON CONTACT
(*Suby of* Hopital Douglas)
4932 Rue Wellington, Verdun, QC, H4G 1X6
(514) 768-2668
Emp Here 20
SIC 8742 Management consulting services

D-U-N-S 25-311-0548   (BR)
MCDONALD'S RESTAURANTS OF CANADA LIMITED
MCDONALD RESTAURANT
(*Suby of* McDonald's Corporation)
4300 Boul Lasalle, Verdun, QC, H4G 2A8
(514) 767-7924
Emp Here 70
SIC 5812 Eating places

D-U-N-S 24-872-0732   (SL)
PLACEMENTS BELCAND MONT-ROYAL INC, LES
211 Rue Gordon, Verdun, QC, H4G 2R2
(514) 766-2311
Emp Here 100   *Sales* 20,899,840
SIC 6712 Bank holding companies
Pr Pierre Beland
VP Pierre Arcand
Renee Lacoursiere
Claude Dufault

D-U-N-S 25-299-9503   (BR)
PRISZM LP
PFK
351 Rue Regina, Verdun, QC, H4G 2G7
(514) 766-9288
Emp Here 20
SIC 5812 Eating places

D-U-N-S 25-258-4180   (BR)
REVERA INC
SAINTE REVERA
Gd Succ Bureau-Chef, Verdun, QC, H4G 3C9

Emp Here 100
SIC 8051 Skilled nursing care facilities

D-U-N-S 25-256-9686   (BR)
VILLE DE MONTREAL
AUDITORIUM DE VERDUN
4110 Boul Lasalle, Verdun, QC, H4G 2A5
(514) 765-7130
Emp Here 100
SIC 7999 Amusement and recreation, nec

D-U-N-S 20-137-2575   (BR)
VILLE DE MONTREAL
VILLE DE MONTREAL
1177 Rue Dupuis, Verdun, QC, H4G 3L4

Emp Here 150
SIC 1611 Highway and street construction

Verdun, QC H4H
Hochelaga County

D-U-N-S 20-573-7591   (BR)
BANQUE LAURENTIENNE DU CANADA
5501 Rue De Verdun, Verdun, QC, H4H 1K9

Emp Here 20
SIC 6021 National commercial banks

D-U-N-S 24-346-5593   (BR)
CENTRE DE SANTE ET DE SERVICES SO-CIAUX DU SUD-QUEST-VERDUN
CENTRE DE SANTE ET DE SERVICES SO-CIAUX DU SUD-QUES
1325 Rue Crawford, Verdun, QC, H4H 2N6
(514) 766-8513
Emp Here 400
SIC 8361 Residential care

D-U-N-S 25-223-7805   (HQ)
CENTRE DE LA PETITE ENFANCE COM-MUNAUTAIRE LES TROTTINETTES
LES TROTTINETTES
(*Suby of* Centre de la Petite Enfance Commu-nautaire les Trottinettes)
1261 Rue Argyle, Verdun, QC, H4H 1V4
(514) 769-1164
Emp Here 50   *Emp Total* 99
Sales 2,991,389
SIC 8351 Child day care services

D-U-N-S 20-712-4087   (BR)
COMMISSION SCOLAIRE MARGUERITE-BOURGEOYS
CENTRE D'EDUCATION DES ADULTES CHAMPLAIN
1201 Rue Argyle, Verdun, QC, H4H 1V4
(514) 765-7686
Emp Here 70
SIC 8211 Elementary and secondary schools

D-U-N-S 25-240-3910   (BR)
COMMISSION SCOLAIRE MARGUERITE-BOURGEOYS
COLLEGE INFORMATIQUE DES ADMINIS-TRATIONS DE VERDUN LA SALLE
1240 Rue Moffat, Verdun, QC, H4H 1Y9
(514) 761-8022
Emp Here 30
SIC 8211 Elementary and secondary schools

D-U-N-S 25-240-2300   (BR)
COMMISSION SCOLAIRE MARGUERITE-BOURGEOYS
ECOLE NOTRE DAME DE LA GARDE
755 Rue Brault, Verdun, QC, H4H 2B3
(514) 765-7611
Emp Here 30
SIC 8211 Elementary and secondary schools

D-U-N-S 20-529-0294   (BR)
HEALTH CANADA
CANADIAN INSTITUTES OF HEALTH RE-SEARCH
6875 Boul Lasalle, Verdun, QC, H4H 1R3
(514) 761-6131
Emp Here 20
SIC 7991 Physical fitness facilities

D-U-N-S 24-636-8117   (SL)
INSTITUT UNIVERSITAIRE EN SANTE MENTALE DOUGLAS
6875 Boul Lasalle, Verdun, QC, H4H 1R3
(514) 761-6131
Emp Here 50   *Sales* 3,502,114
SIC 8062 General medical and surgical hospi-

tals

LESTER B. PEARSON SCHOOL BOARD
RIVERVIEW SCHOOL
971 Rue Riverview, Verdun, QC, H4H 2C3
(514) 762-2717
Emp Here 45
SIC 8211 Elementary and secondary schools

D-U-N-S 20-712-3634   (BR)
LESTER B. PEARSON SCHOOL BOARD
BEURLING ACADEMY
6100 Boul Champlain, Verdun, QC, H4H 1A5
(514) 766-2357
Emp Here 100
SIC 8211 Elementary and secondary schools

D-U-N-S 20-171-0881   (BR)
LESTER B. PEARSON SCHOOL BOARD
VERDUN ELEMENTARY SCHOOL
610 Av Desmarchais, Verdun, QC, H4H 1S6
(514) 767-5344
Emp Here 39
SIC 8211 Elementary and secondary schools

D-U-N-S 25-894-1202   (BR)
ROTISSERIES AU COQ LTEE, LES
5531 Rue De Verdun, Verdun, QC, H4H 1K9
(514) 769-8516
Emp Here 42
SIC 5812 Eating places

Victoriaville, QC G6P
Arthabaska County

D-U-N-S 24-465-2319   (SL)
2166-2440 QUEBEC INC
BAR L'EVASION ENR
19 Boul Des Bois-Francs S, Victoriaville, QC, G6P 4S2
(819) 758-7176
Emp Here 125   *Sales* 4,596,524
SIC 5813 Drinking places

D-U-N-S 24-999-8931   (SL)
2957-3243 QUEBEC INC
CACTUS RESTO BAR
139 Boul Des Bois-Francs S, Victoriaville, QC, G6P 4S4
(819) 758-5311
Emp Here 60   *Sales* 1,824,018
SIC 5812 Eating places

D-U-N-S 25-383-6258   (SL)
3100-2918 QUEBEC INC
D.L. SANITATION ENR
36 Rue Leblanc, Victoriaville, QC, G6P 9B2
(819) 357-5295
Emp Here 50   *Sales* 1,459,214
SIC 7349 Building maintenance services, nec

D-U-N-S 20-514-6025   (SL)
9029-4307 QUEBEC INC
34 Rue De L'Artisan, Victoriaville, QC, G6P 7E3
(819) 752-5743
Emp Here 51   *Sales* 7,915,564
SIC 6712 Bank holding companies
Pr Pr Bertrand Dumond

D-U-N-S 25-002-9105   (BR)
BANQUE NATIONALE DU CANADA
174 Rue Notre-Dame E Bureau 2e, Victoriav-ille, QC, G6P 4A1
(819) 758-5261
Emp Here 30
SIC 6021 National commercial banks

D-U-N-S 25-462-7532   (SL)
BECOTTE INC
483 Rue Notre-Dame O, Victoriaville, QC, G6P 1S7
(819) 758-4436
Emp Here 50   *Sales* 2,845,467
SIC 2321 Men's and boy's furnishings

D-U-N-S 20-028-0597   (BR)
CAISSE DESJARDINS DES BOIS-FRANCS
CAISSE FINANCIER D'ATHABASKA
932 Boul Des Bois-Francs S, Victoriaville, QC, G6P 5V8

Emp Here 30
SIC 6062 State credit unions

D-U-N-S 20-118-9870   (BR)
CANAC-MARQUIS GRENIER LTEE
635 Boul Jutras E, Victoriaville, QC, G6P 7H4
(819) 752-7775
Emp Here 50
SIC 5251 Hardware stores

D-U-N-S 20-537-4965   (BR)
CANADA POST CORPORATION
BUREAU DE POSTE VICTORIAVILLE
133 Rue Saint-Jean-Baptiste, Victoriaville, QC, G6P 0C8
(819) 458-3333
Emp Here 55
SIC 4311 U.s. postal service

D-U-N-S 20-295-5832   (BR)
CENTRE JEUNESSE DE LA MAURICIE ET DU CENTRE-DU-QUEBEC, LE
CENTRE JEUNESSE DE LA MAURICIE ET DU CENTRE-DU-QUEBEC, LE
(*Suby of* Centre Jeunesse de la Mauricie et du Centre-du-Quebec, Le)
38 Rue Monfette, Victoriaville, QC, G6P 1K2
(819) 758-0611
Emp Here 40
SIC 8322 Individual and family services

D-U-N-S 20-984-2116   (BR)
CENTRE POUR HANDICAPES PHYSIQUES DES BOIS-FRANCS INC
C.H.P.B.F.
59 Rue Monfette, Victoriaville, QC, G6P 1J8
(819) 758-9203
Emp Here 60
SIC 8322 Individual and family services

D-U-N-S 20-363-7108   (BR)
CENTRE DE READAPTATION INTERVAL
(*Suby of* Centre de Readaptation Interval)
80 Rue Saint-Paul, Victoriaville, QC, G6P 9C8
(819) 752-4099
Emp Here 25
SIC 8361 Residential care

D-U-N-S 20-292-0757   (SL)
CENTRE DE SANTE ET DE SERVICE SOCI-AUX D'ARTHABASKA-ERABLE
CHSLD ERMITAGE
61 Rue De L'Ermitage, Victoriaville, QC, G6P 6X4
(819) 758-7511
Emp Here 2,300   *Sales* 206,652,750
SIC 8062 General medical and surgical hospi-tals
Genl Mgr Claude Charland

D-U-N-S 20-804-8848   (BR)
COLLEGE D'ENSEIGNEMENT GENERAL ET PROFESSIONNEL DE VICTORIAVILLE
COLLEGE D'ENSEIGNEMENT GENERAL ET PROFESSIONNEL DE VICTORIAVILLE
765 Rue Notre-Dame E, Victoriaville, QC, G6P 4B2
(819) 758-6401
Emp Here 50
SIC 8211 Elementary and secondary schools

D-U-N-S 20-712-0648   (BR)
COMMISSION SCOLAIRE DES BOIS-FRANCS
CENTRE D'EDUCATION DES ADULTES DE VICTORIAVILLE
38 Rue Laurier O, Victoriaville, QC, G6P 6P3
(819) 357-2116
Emp Here 50
SIC 8211 Elementary and secondary schools

D-U-N-S 25-232-9172   (BR)

▲ Public Company   ■ Public Company Family Member   **HQ** Headquarters   **BR** Branch   **SL** Single Location

COMMISSION SCOLAIRE DES BOIS-FRANCS
ECOLE NOTRE DAME DES BOIS FRANCS
(*Suby of* Commission Scolaire des Bois-Francs)
82 Rue Du Cure-Suzor, Victoriaville, QC, G6P 6M8
(819) 357-2451
Emp Here 50
SIC 8211 Elementary and secondary schools

D-U-N-S 25-232-9149   (BR)
COMMISSION SCOLAIRE DES BOIS-FRANCS
ECOLE SAINTE-FAMILLE
(*Suby of* Commission Scolaire des Bois-Francs)
6 Rue Pare, Victoriaville, QC, G6P 2X6
(819) 752-5945
Emp Here 20
SIC 8211 Elementary and secondary schools

D-U-N-S 25-232-8869   (BR)
COMMISSION SCOLAIRE DES BOIS-FRANCS
ECOLE ST-GABRIEL LALLEMAND
(*Suby of* Commission Scolaire des Bois-Francs)
5 Rue Habel, Victoriaville, QC, G6P 4M2
(819) 752-6346
Emp Here 35
SIC 8211 Elementary and secondary schools

D-U-N-S 25-233-8579   (BR)
COMMISSION SCOLAIRE DES BOIS-FRANCS
ECOLE ST DAVID
(*Suby of* Commission Scolaire des Bois-Francs)
155 Rue Olivier, Victoriaville, QC, G6P 5G8
(819) 752-6171
Emp Here 50
SIC 8211 Elementary and secondary schools

D-U-N-S 20-028-5273   (BR)
COMMISSION SCOLAIRE DES BOIS-FRANCS
CENTRE DE FORMATION PROFES-SIONELLE VISION 20 20
595 Rue Notre-Dame E, Victoriaville, QC, G6P 4B2
(819) 751-2020
Emp Here 70
SIC 8331 Job training and related services

D-U-N-S 25-234-0849   (BR)
COMMISSION SCOLAIRE DES BOIS-FRANCS
ECOLE PIE X
(*Suby of* Commission Scolaire des Bois-Francs)
30 Rue Sainte-Victoire, Victoriaville, QC, G6P 2M9
(819) 752-2285
Emp Here 40
SIC 8211 Elementary and secondary schools

D-U-N-S 24-012-1801   (BR)
COMMISSION SCOLAIRE DES BOIS-FRANCS
40 Boul Des Bois-Francs N, Victoriaville, QC, G6P 1E5
(819) 758-6453
Emp Here 100
SIC 8211 Elementary and secondary schools

D-U-N-S 20-712-0754   (BR)
COMMISSION SCOLAIRE DES BOIS-FRANCS
ECOLE MASSICOTTE
57 Rue Monfette, Victoriaville, QC, G6P 1J8
(819) 752-9756
Emp Here 50
SIC 8211 Elementary and secondary schools

D-U-N-S 24-451-3953   (BR)
COMMISSION SCOLAIRE DES BOIS-FRANCS

ECOLE LE TANDEM
20 Rue De L'Ermitage, Victoriaville, QC, G6P 1J5
(819) 752-4591
Emp Here 85
SIC 8211 Elementary and secondary schools

D-U-N-S 25-232-8745   (BR)
COMMISSION SCOLAIRE DES BOIS-FRANCS
ECOLE MONSEIGNEUR GRENIER
(*Suby of* Commission Scolaire des Bois-Francs)
20 Rue Des Plaines, Victoriaville, QC, G6P 2C7
(819) 752-6455
Emp Here 20
SIC 8211 Elementary and secondary schools

D-U-N-S 20-101-4946   (BR)
COMMISSION SCOLAIRE DES BOIS-FRANCS
ECOLE STE-MARGUERITE BOURGEOIS
65 Rue De Versailles, Victoriaville, QC, G6P 1A4
(819) 752-2976
Emp Here 25
SIC 8211 Elementary and secondary schools

D-U-N-S 20-265-2897   (SL)
CUISINES MRS INC
11 Rue De La Nicolet, Victoriaville, QC, G6P 7H2
(819) 758-1594
Emp Here 50   *Sales* 3,793,956
SIC 2752 Commercial printing, lithographic

D-U-N-S 20-722-4528   (HQ)
GARAGE REJEAN ROY INC
TOYOTA VICTORIAVILLE
465 Boul Des Bois-Francs N, Victoriaville, QC, G6P 1H1
(819) 758-8000
Emp Here 23   *Emp Total* 30
Sales 10,944,105
SIC 5511 New and used car dealers
Pr Pr Rejean Roy

D-U-N-S 25-948-7627   (SL)
HOPITAL L'HOTEL DIEU D'ARTHABASKA
5 Rue Des Hospitalieres, Victoriaville, QC, G6P 6N2
(819) 357-1151
Emp Here 800   *Sales* 74,896,080
SIC 8062 General medical and surgical hospitals
Dir Michel Delamarre

D-U-N-S 25-299-0627   (BR)
IMAFLEX INC
CANSLIT DIV OF
355 Boul Labbe N, Victoriaville, QC, G6P 1B1
(819) 758-5542
Emp Here 60
SIC 3081 Unsupported plastics film and sheet

D-U-N-S 20-778-4778   (BR)
LABATT BREWING COMPANY LIMITED
395 Boul Labbe N, Victoriaville, QC, G6P 1B1

Emp Here 50
SIC 5181 Beer and ale

D-U-N-S 20-298-5024   (BR)
LABORATOIRES ABBOTT LIMITEE
LABORATOIRES ABBOTT, LIMITEE
(*Suby of* Abbott Laboratories)
75 Boul Industriel, Victoriaville, QC, G6P 6S9
(819) 751-2440
Emp Here 25
SIC 2834 Pharmaceutical preparations

D-U-N-S 20-543-4348   (HQ)
MAGASINS LECOMPTE INC
(*Suby of* Magasins Lecompte Inc)
119 Rue Notre-Dame E, Victoriaville, QC, G6P 3Z8

(819) 758-2626
Emp Here 40   *Emp Total* 60
Sales 4,888,367
SIC 5399 Miscellaneous general merchandise

D-U-N-S 20-881-3613   (BR)
MEDIAS TRANSCONTINENTAL INC
MEDIAS TRANSCONTINENTAL INC
43 Rue Notre-Dame E, Victoriaville, QC, G6P 3Z4
(819) 758-6211
Emp Here 27
SIC 2711 Newspapers

D-U-N-S 25-540-4782   (BR)
METRO RICHELIEU INC
SUPER C
601 Boul Jutras E, Victoriaville, QC, G6P 7H4
(819) 752-6659
Emp Here 100
SIC 5411 Grocery stores

D-U-N-S 24-464-7566   (SL)
PLACEMENTS F R BOURGEOIS LTEE
6 Rue Du Parc, Victoriaville, QC, G6P 3R5
(819) 752-4512
Emp Here 32   *Sales* 9,231,950
SIC 5039 Construction materials, nec
Pr Pr F Bourgeois

D-U-N-S 24-890-4658   (SL)
POINT PLUS RESTAURANT-BAR INC, AU
192 Boul Des Bois-Francs S, Victoriaville, QC, G6P 4S7
(819) 758-9927
Emp Here 92   *Sales* 2,772,507
SIC 5812 Eating places

D-U-N-S 20-265-3457   (SL)
POUDRIER FRERES LTEE
430 Rue Cantin, Victoriaville, QC, G6P 7E6

Emp Here 90   *Sales* 15,116,050
SIC 3713 Truck and bus bodies
Pr Pr Steve Poudrier
 Stephane Poudrier
VP VP Pierre Poudrier
 Marc Aurele Cliche

D-U-N-S 20-914-6104   (BR)
PROVIGO DISTRIBUTION INC
LOBLAWS VICTORIAVILLE
60 Rue Carignan, Victoriaville, QC, G6P 4Z6

Emp Here 200
SIC 5141 Groceries, general line

D-U-N-S 25-140-0172   (SL)
PUB LE CAMELEON INC
66 Rue Notre-Dame E, Victoriaville, QC, G6P 3Z6
(819) 758-8222
Emp Here 70   *Sales* 2,115,860
SIC 5812 Eating places

D-U-N-S 20-224-6687   (BR)
REDBERRY FRANCHISING CORP
BURGER KING
230 Boul Des Bois-Francs S, Victoriaville, QC, G6P 4T1
(819) 758-4838
Emp Here 25
SIC 5812 Eating places

D-U-N-S 25-531-9485   (BR)
RESIDENCES ALLEGRO, S.E.C., LES
RESIDENCE NOTRE DAME
(*Suby of* Residences Allegro, S.E.C., Les)
222 Rue Notre-Dame O Bureau 315, Victoriaville, QC, G6P 1R9
(819) 758-3131
Emp Here 60
SIC 8361 Residential care

D-U-N-S 24-149-5431   (SL)
RESTAURANT B.C.L. INC
ROTISSERIE ST-HUBERT
609 Boul Des Bois-Francs S, Victoriaville, QC, G6P 5X1

(819) 357-9226
Emp Here 80   *Sales* 2,407,703
SIC 5812 Eating places

D-U-N-S 24-821-4090   (SL)
ROY DESROCHERS LAMBERT S.E.N.C.R.L
450 Boul Des Bois-Francs N, Victoriaville, QC, G6P 1H3
(819) 758-1544
Emp Here 75   *Sales* 3,283,232
SIC 8721 Accounting, auditing, and bookkeeping

D-U-N-S 20-265-4406   (HQ)
VIC MOBILIER DE MAGASINS INC
VIC SOLUTIONS DETAIL
(*Suby of* Vic Mobilier de Magasins Inc)
1440 Rue Notre-Dame O, Victoriaville, QC, G6P 7L7
(819) 758-0626
Emp Here 137   *Emp Total* 140
Sales 10,871,144
SIC 2542 Partitions and fixtures, except wood
 Fabrice Canin
Treas Miguel Lavertu
Dir Jacques Canin

D-U-N-S 20-332-3386   (BR)
VICTORIAVILLE, VILLE DE
COLISEE DESJARDINS, LE
(*Suby of* Victoriaville, Ville de)
400 Rue Jutras E, Victoriaville, QC, G6P 7W7
(819) 758-5211
Emp Here 50
SIC 7999 Amusement and recreation, nec

D-U-N-S 24-791-1787   (SL)
VILLA ST-GEORGES INC
185 Rue Saint-Georges, Victoriaville, QC, G6P 9H6
(819) 758-6760
Emp Here 75   *Sales* 2,772,507
SIC 8361 Residential care

D-U-N-S 24-141-9105   (HQ)
WOOD WYANT CANADA INC
ARISTOCRAT TM
(*Suby of* Groupe Sani-Marc Inc)
42 Rue De L'Artisan, Victoriaville, QC, G6P 7E3
(819) 758-1541
Emp Here 50   *Emp Total* 1
Sales 20,183,648
SIC 2842 Polishes and sanitation goods
 Pierre Goudreault

Victoriaville, QC G6R
Arthabaska County

D-U-N-S 20-791-0050   (HQ)
BLAIS & LANGLOIS INC
345 Rue Cartier, Victoriaville, QC, G6R 1E3
(819) 739-2905
Emp Here 40   *Emp Total* 70
Sales 9,266,009
SIC 1542 Nonresidential construction, nec
Pr Jean Marchand
VP Jean-Francois Marchand
Sec Jacques Marchand
Dir Hugues Marchand
Dir Guillaume Marchand

D-U-N-S 20-871-5334   (HQ)
CONSTRUCTIONS PEPIN ET FORTIN INC, LES
PEPIN FORTIN CONSTRUCTION
(*Suby of* Placements Pepin & Fortin Inc)
371 Av Pie-X, Victoriaville, QC, G6R 0L6
(819) 357-9274
Emp Here 45   *Emp Total* 100
Sales 9,266,009
SIC 1542 Nonresidential construction, nec
 Stephane Mckenzie
 Robert Lamothe

Victoriaville, QC G6S
Arthabaska County

D-U-N-S 20-188-7064   (SL)
CIMENT RO-NO LTEE
1375 Boul Jutras E, Victoriaville, QC, G6S 0M3
(819) 357-8224
Emp Here 35   *Sales* 7,033,600
SIC 3273 Ready-mixed concrete
Pr Pr Jacques Noel
 Nathalie Noel
VP VP Patrick Noel

D-U-N-S 25-293-2520   (BR)
FINANCIERE BANQUE NATIONALE INC
FINANCIERE BANQUE NATIONALE
650 Boul Jutras E Bureau 150, Victoriaville, QC, G6S 1E1
(819) 758-3191
Emp Here 24
SIC 6211 Security brokers and dealers

D-U-N-S 24-000-2134   (BR)
HOME DEPOT OF CANADA INC
HOME DEPOT
(*Suby of* The Home Depot Inc)
160 Boul Arthabaska O, Victoriaville, QC, G6S 0P2
(819) 752-0700
Emp Here 100
SIC 5251 Hardware stores

D-U-N-S 20-652-7645   (BR)
PROVIGO DISTRIBUTION INC
PROVIGO
120 Boul Arthabaska O, Victoriaville, QC, G6S 0P2
(819) 752-7732
Emp Here 40
SIC 5411 Grocery stores

D-U-N-S 25-294-6017   (BR)
SEARS CANADA INC
SEARS DEPARTMENT STORE
1111 Boul Jutras E, Victoriaville, QC, G6S 1C1
(819) 357-4000
Emp Here 20
SIC 5311 Department stores

D-U-N-S 25-498-9882   (BR)
STAPLES CANADA INC
BUREAU EN GROS
(*Suby of* Staples, Inc.)
1111 Boul Jutras E, Victoriaville, QC, G6S 1C1
(819) 357-4484
Emp Here 30
SIC 5943 Stationery stores

D-U-N-S 24-327-4516   (BR)
WAL-MART CANADA CORP
110 Boul Arthabaska O, Victoriaville, QC, G6S 0P2
(819) 758-5136
Emp Here 250
SIC 5311 Department stores

Victoriaville, QC G6T
Arthabaska County

D-U-N-S 24-373-7702   (BR)
9049-3347 QUEBEC INC
IMPART LITHO
383 Boul De La Bonaventure, Victoriaville, QC, G6T 1V5
(819) 758-0667
Emp Here 45
SIC 2752 Commercial printing, lithographic

D-U-N-S 25-618-6144   (BR)
ACKLANDS - GRAINGER INC
AGI
(*Suby of* W.W. Grainger, Inc.)

757 Boul Pierre-Roux E, Victoriaville, QC, G6T 1S7
(819) 758-9991
Emp Here 20
SIC 5085 Industrial supplies

D-U-N-S 20-949-8450   (SL)
ARMATURES BOIS-FRANCS INC
249 Boul De La Bonaventure, Victoriaville, QC, G6T 1V5
(819) 758-7501
Emp Here 500   *Sales* 77,484,263
SIC 3443 Fabricated plate work (boiler shop)
Pr Eric Bernier
VP VP Francois Vallieres

D-U-N-S 25-525-5457   (BR)
CASCADES CANADA ULC
NORAMPAC-VICTORIAVILLE
400 Boul De La Bonaventure, Victoriaville, QC, G6T 1V8
(819) 758-3177
Emp Here 165
SIC 2653 Corrugated and solid fiber boxes

D-U-N-S 20-265-0842   (SL)
CHAREST AUTOMOBILE LTEE
CHAREST INTERNATIONAL
275 Boul Pierre-Roux E Bureau 443, Victoriaville, QC, G6T 1S9
(819) 758-8271
Emp Here 48   *Sales* 25,120,000
SIC 5511 New and used car dealers
Pr Pr Steve Halle
VP VP Alain Bellavance
VP Jean-Francois Poulin
 Claude Larochelle
 Nathalie Halle

D-U-N-S 24-885-0799   (BR)
EXP SERVICES INC
50 Rte De La Grande-Ligne, Victoriaville, QC, G6T 0E6
(819) 758-8265
Emp Here 22
SIC 8711 Engineering services

D-U-N-S 25-275-9274   (SL)
ENTREPRISE G N P INC
750 Boul Pierre-Roux E, Victoriaville, QC, G6T 1S6
(819) 752-7140
Emp Here 50   *Sales* 4,961,328
SIC 8711 Engineering services

D-U-N-S 24-842-4244   (SL)
FOURNITURES FUNERAIRE VICTORIAV-ILLE INC
VIC ROYAL CASKETS
333 Rue De La Jacques-Cartier, Victoriaville, QC, G6T 1Y1
(819) 752-3388
Emp Here 375   *Sales* 16,687,200
SIC 3995 Burial caskets
Pr Pr Alain Dumont
 Claude Dumont
 Louis Parent
 Denis Lacasse
VP Fin Sylvain Hebert

D-U-N-S 24-791-0011   (SL)
METAL GRENIER LTEE
970 Boul Pierre-Roux E, Victoriaville, QC, G6T 2H6
(819) 752-3807
Emp Here 35   *Sales* 5,884,100
SIC 3713 Truck and bus bodies
Pr Pr Gervais Grenier
VP VP Alain Laroche

D-U-N-S 20-695-9681   (SL)
VERTISOFT INC
990 Boul Pierre-Roux E, Victoriaville, QC, G6T 0K9
(819) 751-6660
Emp Here 40   *Sales* 5,277,042
SIC 5734 Computer and software stores
Pr Pr Sylvain Belleau

Dir Martin Dion

D-U-N-S 20-309-5633   (BR)
VICWEST INC
(*Suby of* Vicwest Inc)
707 Boul Pierre-Roux E, Victoriaville, QC, G6T 1S7
(819) 758-0661
Emp Here 150
SIC 3444 Sheet Metalwork

Ville-Marie, QC J9V
Temiscaninque County

D-U-N-S 25-379-9811   (BR)
COMMISSION SCOLAIRE DU LAC-TEMISCAMINGUE
CENTRE FRERE MOFFET
(*Suby of* Commission Scolaire du Lac-Temiscamingue)
9 Rue Notre-Dame-De-Lourdes, Ville-Marie, QC, J9V 1X7
(819) 629-2144
Emp Here 20
SIC 8211 Elementary and secondary schools

D-U-N-S 25-395-0513   (HQ)
COMMISSION SCOLAIRE DU LAC-TEMISCAMINGUE
CSLT
(*Suby of* Commission Scolaire du Lac-Temiscamingue)
2 Rue Maisonneuve, Ville-Marie, QC, J9V 1V4
(819) 629-2472
Emp Here 35   *Emp Total* 325
Sales 28,081,404
SIC 8211 Elementary and secondary schools
Genl Mgr Eric Lariviere
Pr Jean-Claude Bergeron

D-U-N-S 25-377-3873   (BR)
COMMISSION SCOLAIRE DU LAC-TEMISCAMINGUE
ECOLE ST GABRIEL
(*Suby of* Commission Scolaire du Lac-Temiscamingue)
4 Rue Montfort, Ville-Marie, QC, J9V 1W2
(819) 629-2802
Emp Here 35
SIC 8211 Elementary and secondary schools

D-U-N-S 24-126-5193   (BR)
GOUVERNEMENT DE LA PROVINCE DE QUEBEC
MINISTERE DES RESSOURCES NA-TURELLES ET DE LA FAUNE
75a Rue Des Oblats N, Ville-Marie, QC, J9V 1J2
(819) 629-6407
Emp Here 30
SIC 8999 Services, nec

D-U-N-S 25-595-0487   (BR)
GOUVERNEMENT DE LA PROVINCE DE QUEBEC
GOUVERNEMENT DE LA PROVINCE DE QUEBEC
21 Rue Notre-Dame-De-Lourdes Bureau 209, Ville-Marie, QC, J9V 1X8
(819) 629-2676
Emp Here 25
SIC 8322 Individual and family services

Villeroy, QC G0S
Lotbiniere County

D-U-N-S 20-712-0689   (BR)
COMMISSION SCOLAIRE DES BOIS-FRANCS
ECOLE CENTRALE
378 Rue Principale, Villeroy, QC, G0S 3K0

(819) 385-4605
Emp Here 50
SIC 8211 Elementary and secondary schools

Vimont, QC H7M
Ile-Jesus County

D-U-N-S 24-342-7973   (BR)
CARA OPERATIONS LIMITED
HARVEY'S
(*Suby of* Cara Holdings Limited)
2060 Boul Des Laurentides, Vimont, QC, H7M 2R5
(450) 667-1417
Emp Here 20
SIC 5812 Eating places

D-U-N-S 25-542-3154   (SL)
MARCHE DUNN (1990) INC
(*Suby of* Placements C. D. F. G. Inc)
1904 Boul Des Laurentides, Vimont, QC, H7M 2P9
(450) 669-2633
Emp Here 50   *Sales* 8,343,600
SIC 5411 Grocery stores
Pr Gilles Messier
Treas Denis Messier

Wakefield, QC J0X
Gatineau County

D-U-N-S 20-712-5647   (BR)
COMMISSION SCOLAIRE WESTERN QUE-BEC
WAKEFIELD ELEMENTARY
(*Suby of* Commission Scolaire Western Que-bec)
878 Ch Riverside, Wakefield, QC, J0X 3G0
(819) 459-2373
Emp Here 50
SIC 8211 Elementary and secondary schools

Waltham, QC J0X
Pontiac County

D-U-N-S 25-974-6865   (SL)
SOCIETE EN COMMANDITE COULONGE ENERGIE
Gd, Waltham, QC, J0X 3H0
(819) 689-5226
Emp Here 20   *Sales* 12,858,960
SIC 4911 Electric services
Genl Mgr Ronald Lean
Off Mgr Frank Scheer

Warwick, QC J0A
Arthabaska County

D-U-N-S 20-984-2405   (BR)
AKZO NOBEL WOOD COATINGS LTD
274 Rue Saint-Louis Bureau 6, Warwick, QC, J0A 1M0
(819) 358-7500
Emp Here 85
SIC 5198 Paints, varnishes, and supplies

D-U-N-S 24-820-9546   (BR)
ALIMENTS KRISPY KERNELS INC
CROUSTILLES YUM YUM, DIV DE
40 Rue Du Moulin, Warwick, QC, J0A 1M0
(819) 358-3600
Emp Here 200
SIC 2096 Potato chips and similar snacks

D-U-N-S 20-804-8616   (BR)
COMMISSION SCOLAIRE DES BOIS-

FRANCS
ECOLE SAINT-MEDARD
128 Rue Saint-Louis, Warwick, QC, J0A 1M0
(819) 358-2040
Emp Here 24
SIC 8211 Elementary and secondary schools

D-U-N-S 25-232-8984   (BR)
COMMISSION SCOLAIRE DES BOIS-FRANCS
ECOLE SAINT-MEDARD
(*Suby of* Commission Scolaire des Bois-Francs)
128 Rue Saint-Louis Gd, Warwick, QC, J0A 1M0
(819) 358-2260
Emp Here 35
SIC 8211 Elementary and secondary schools

D-U-N-S 24-330-1095   (BR)
JEANS WARWICK INDUSTRIE INC
JEANS DEPOT
3 Rue Menard, Warwick, QC, J0A 1M0
(819) 358-3900
Emp Here 40
SIC 5651 Family clothing stores

D-U-N-S 20-266-3076   (SL)
LES CENTRE FUNERAIRE GREGOIRE & DESROCHERS INC
12 Rue Saint-Joseph, Warwick, QC, J0A 1M0
(819) 358-2314
Emp Here 50   *Sales* 3,648,035
SIC 7261 Funeral service and crematories

D-U-N-S 20-852-2578   (SL)
MARCHE A DESROCHERS INC
IGA MARCHE A DESROCHERS
10 Rue Du Centre-Sportif, Warwick, QC, J0A 1M0
(819) 358-4950
Emp Here 49   *Sales* 8,339,840
SIC 5411 Grocery stores
Pr Andre Desrochers

D-U-N-S 20-266-2987   (SL)
PLASTIQUE D.C.N. INC
250 Rue Saint-Louis, Warwick, QC, J0A 1M0
(819) 358-3700
Emp Here 80   *Sales* 11,162,987
SIC 3089 Plastics products, nec
Pr Pr Charles Letarte
Julie Beliveau

D-U-N-S 24-791-3452   (HQ)
ROLAND BOULANGER & CIE, LTEE
PRODUITS FORESTIERS J.V.
(*Suby of* Gestion Guy Boulanger Inc)
235 Rue Saint-Louis, Warwick, QC, J0A 1M0
(819) 358-4100
Emp Here 330   *Emp Total* 1
Sales 43,659,050
SIC 2431 Millwork
Pr Alexis Boulanger
VP Judith Boulanger
Sec Luce Boulanger
Dir Wilfrid Brunet
Dir Guy Langlois
Dir Richard Boucher
Dir Yves Rheault
Dir Guy Boulanger

Waskaganish, QC J0M
Nouveau-Quebec County

D-U-N-S 24-943-2659   (HQ)
AIR CREEBEC INC
(*Suby of* Cree Regional Economic Enterprises Company (Cree Co) Inc)
18 Rue Waskaganish, Waskaganish, QC, J0M 1R0
(819) 895-8355
Emp Here 96   *Emp Total* 300
Sales 59,827,774
SIC 4512 Air transportation, scheduled

Ch Bd Rusty Cheezo
Pr Matthew Happyjack
VP Randy Bosum
Dir Jack Blacksmith
Emily Whiskeychan
Dir Clarence Jolly
Dir James Bobbish
Dir John Longchap
Dir Neeposh Derrick
Dir Sandy George

D-U-N-S 20-712-6611   (BR)
CREE SCHOOL BOARD
ECOLE WASKAGANISH
(*Suby of* Cree School Board)
Cp 300, Waskaganish, QC, J0M 1R0
(819) 895-8819
Emp Here 50
SIC 8211 Elementary and secondary schools

D-U-N-S 25-377-0234   (BR)
HOSPITAL CHISASIBI
WASKAGANISH COMMUNITY CLINIC
2 Rue Tahktachun Neskanu, Waskaganish, QC, J0M 1R0
(819) 895-8833
Emp Here 40
SIC 8011 Offices and clinics of medical doctors

D-U-N-S 25-270-6205   (BR)
NORTH WEST COMPANY LP, THE
NORTHERN STORES
120 Rue Waskaganish, Waskaganish, QC, J0M 1R0
(819) 895-8865
Emp Here 20
SIC 5411 Grocery stores

Waswanipi, QC J0Y
Abitibi County

D-U-N-S 25-337-1702   (BR)
CREE SCHOOL BOARD
WASWANIPI HIGH SCHOOL
(*Suby of* Cree School Board)
6 Rue Birch, Waswanipi, QC, J0Y 3C0
(819) 753-2583
Emp Here 34
SIC 8211 Elementary and secondary schools

D-U-N-S 24-329-9349   (BR)
CREE SCHOOL BOARD
SABTUAN REGIONAL VOCATIONAL TRAINING CENTRE
(*Suby of* Cree School Board)
1 Rue Elder David Neeposh, Waswanipi, QC, J0Y 3C0
(819) 753-4040
Emp Here 25
SIC 8249 Vocational schools, nec

Waterloo, QC J0E
Shefford County

D-U-N-S 20-005-8381   (BR)
CENTRE DE SANTE ET DE SERVICES SCOIAUX DE LA HAUTE-YAMASKA
(*Suby of* Centre de Sante et de Services Scoiaux de la Haute-Yamaska)
5300 Rue Courville, Waterloo, QC, J0E 2N0
(450) 539-5512
Emp Here 20
SIC 8051 Skilled nursing care facilities

D-U-N-S 25-706-5482   (BR)
CENTRE DE SANTE ET DE SERVICES SCOIAUX DE LA HAUTE-YAMASKA
CLSC DE LA HAUTE YAMASKA
(*Suby of* Centre de Sante et de Services Scoiaux de la Haute-Yamaska)

48 Rue Young, Waterloo, QC, J0E 2N0
(450) 539-3340
Emp Here 20
SIC 8399 Social services, nec

D-U-N-S 25-240-6012   (BR)
COMMISSION SCOLAIRE DU VAL-DES-CERFS
ECOLE ST BERNARDIN
14 Rue Lewis O, Waterloo, QC, J0E 2N0
(450) 539-0522
Emp Here 30
SIC 8211 Elementary and secondary schools

D-U-N-S 25-240-3654   (BR)
COMMISSION SCOLAIRE DU VAL-DES-CERFS
ECOLE SECONDAIRE WILFRID LEGER
185 Rue Lewis O, Waterloo, QC, J0E 2N0
(450) 539-0910
Emp Here 70
SIC 8211 Elementary and secondary schools

D-U-N-S 24-515-3713   (BR)
GROUPE PROMUTUEL FEDERATION DE SOCIETE MUTUELLES D'ASSURANCES GENERALES
PROMUTUEL VALMONT
210 Rue Lewis O, Waterloo, QC, J0E 2N0
(450) 539-0384
Emp Here 32
SIC 6411 Insurance agents, brokers, and service

Waterville, QC J0B
Sherbrooke County

D-U-N-S 24-309-5168   (BR)
PPD HOLDING INC
INDUSTRIES P.P.D. INC
400 Rue Raymond, Waterville, QC, J0B 3H0
(819) 837-2952
Emp Here 200
SIC 2822 Synthetic rubber

D-U-N-S 20-997-3486   (HQ)
WATERVILLE TG INC
10 Rue Du Depot, Waterville, QC, J0B 3H0
(819) 837-2421
Emp Here 728   *Emp Total* 36,679
Sales 106,860,109
SIC 2891 Adhesives and sealants
Ch Bd Maeda Kazuaki
Pr Junichiro Kako
Mario Larose
Treas Hiraku Hiromi
Allan Abdalla
Dir Masayoshi Ichikawa
Dir Mitsuo Mori

Weedon, QC J0B
Wolfe County

D-U-N-S 20-276-6684   (BR)
CENTRE DE SANTE ET DE SERVICE SOCIAUX DU HAUT SAINT-FRANCOIS, LE
CSCL DU HAUT ST FRANCOIS
(*Suby of* Centre de Sante et de Service Sociaux du Haut Saint-Francois, Le)
245 Rue Saint-Janvier, Weedon, QC, J0B 3J0

Emp Here 77
SIC 7041 Membership-basis organization hotels

D-U-N-S 24-975-8061   (HQ)
CENTRE DE SANTE ET DE SERVICE SOCIAUX DU HAUT SAINT-FRANCOIS, LE
CLSC
(*Suby of* Centre de Sante et de Service Sociaux du Haut Saint-Francois, Le)

460 2e Av, Weedon, QC, J0B 3J0
(819) 877-3434
Emp Here 31   *Emp Total* 320
Sales 27,139,075
SIC 8093 Specialty outpatient clinics, nec
Mng Dir Louisette Gosselin

Wemindji, QC J0M
Nouveau-Quebec County

D-U-N-S 25-240-8992   (BR)
CREE SCHOOL BOARD
MAQUATUA EEYOU SCHOOL
(*Suby of* Cree School Board)
Pr, Wemindji, QC, J0M 1L0
(819) 978-0263
Emp Here 45
SIC 8211 Elementary and secondary schools

Wemotaci, QC G0X
Champlain County

D-U-N-S 25-383-7116   (BR)
CONSEIL DES ATIKAMEKW DE WEMOTACI
CONSEIL DES ATIKAMEKW DE WEMOTACI
36 Rue Kenosi, Wemotaci, QC, G0X 3R0
(819) 666-2323
Emp Here 30
SIC 8322 Individual and family services

Wendake, QC G0A
Bellechasse County

D-U-N-S 24-746-9596   (SL)
SIOUI, NORMAND
PREMONTEX
597 Rue Chef-Max-Gros-Louis, Wendake, QC, G0A 4V0
(418) 847-3630
Emp Here 60   *Sales* 4,377,642
SIC 1751 Carpentry work

West Brome, QC J0E
Brome County

D-U-N-S 25-643-6346   (SL)
AUBERGE WEST BROME (CONDOS) INC
AUBERGE & SPA WEST BROME
128 Rte 139, West Brome, QC, J0E 2P0
(450) 266-7552
Emp Here 60   *Sales* 2,626,585
SIC 7011 Hotels and motels

D-U-N-S 24-954-7290   (SL)
SCIERIE WEST BROME INC
15 Ch West Brome, West Brome, QC, J0E 2P0
(450) 266-1480
Emp Here 50   *Sales* 4,742,446
SIC 2421 Sawmills and planing mills, general

Westbury, QC J0B
Compton County

D-U-N-S 25-543-0589   (BR)
CASCADES CANADA ULC
CACADES GROUPE CARTON PLAT EAST ANGUS
2 Rue Angus N, Westbury, QC, J0B 1R0
(819) 832-5300
Emp Here 95
SIC 2631 Paperboard mills

D-U-N-S 20-314-1387   (BR)

ENERKEM INC
551 Av De La Tuilerie, Westbury, QC, J0B 1R0
(819) 832-4411
Emp Here 20
SIC 2869 Industrial organic chemicals, nec

Westmount, QC H3Y
Hochelaga County

D-U-N-S 25-298-5965   (BR)
COMMISSION SCOLAIRE ENGLISH-MONTREAL
ROSLYN SCHOOL
4699 Av Westmount, Westmount, QC, H3Y 1X5
(514) 481-5581
Emp Here 20
SIC 8211 Elementary and secondary schools

D-U-N-S 25-233-8652   (BR)
COMMISSION SCOLAIRE DE MONTREAL
COMMISSION SCOLAIRE DE MONTREAL
11 Ch De La Cote-Saint-Antoine, Westmount, QC, H3Y 2H7
(514) 596-7240
Emp Here 50
SIC 8211 Elementary and secondary schools

D-U-N-S 20-714-2097   (SL)
ECOLE AKIVA, L'
450 Av Kensington, Westmount, QC, H3Y 3A2
(514) 939-2430
Emp Here 60   *Sales* 4,012,839
SIC 8211 Elementary and secondary schools

D-U-N-S 20-860-5931   (SL)
ECOLE MISS EDGAR ET MISS CRAMP
525 Av Mount Pleasant, Westmount, QC, H3Y 3H6
(514) 935-6357
Emp Here 50   *Sales* 3,356,192
SIC 8211 Elementary and secondary schools

D-U-N-S 25-753-1830   (BR)
ECOLE ST-GEORGES DE MONTREAL INC, L'
(*Suby of* Ecole St-Georges de Montreal Inc, L')
3685 The Boulevard, Westmount, QC, H3Y 1S9
(514) 486-5214
Emp Here 40
SIC 8211 Elementary and secondary schools

D-U-N-S 20-928-9057   (SL)
MARIANOPOLIS COLLEGE
4873 Av Westmount, Westmount, QC, H3Y 1X9
(514) 931-8792
Emp Here 185   *Sales* 25,914,240
SIC 8221 Colleges and universities
Ch Bd John Ryan
V Ch Bd Louis Santillo
Sec Elaine O'grady
Sec Diane Quart
Treas Peter Malouf
Francoise Boisvert
Fin Mgr Colleen Feeney
Genl Mgr Len Even

D-U-N-S 20-885-1832   (SL)
STUDY CORPORATION, THE
3233 The Boulevard, Westmount, QC, H3Y 1S4
(514) 935-9352
Emp Here 50   *Sales* 3,356,192
SIC 8211 Elementary and secondary schools

Westmount, QC H3Z
Hochelaga County

D-U-N-S 25-503-3797   (SL)

2809630 CANADA INC
LA CITE, COMPLEXE IMMOBILIER
4150 Rue Sherbrooke O Bureau 400, Westmount, QC, H3Z 1C2
(514) 989-9909
Emp Here 160   *Sales* 36,522,000
SIC 6719 Holding companies, nec
Jean Sylvere

D-U-N-S 24-391-6108   (SL)
7012985 CANADA INC
3500 Boul De Maisonneuve O Bureau 700, Westmount, QC, H3Z 3C1
(514) 380-2700
Emp Here 50   *Sales* 3,648,035
SIC 7379 Computer related services, nec

D-U-N-S 25-672-9211   (SL)
99767 CANADA LTEE
99767 CANADA
4795 Rue Sainte-Catherine O, Westmount, QC, H3Z 1S8
(514) 731-5654
Emp Here 26   *Sales* 8,463,441
SIC 5194 Tobacco and tobacco products
Pr Pr Carrie Garbarino
Garry Garbarino

D-U-N-S 24-388-7929   (BR)
ACCORD FINANCIAL CORP
3500 Boul De Maisonneuve O Bureau 1510, Westmount, QC, H3Z 3C1
(514) 932-8223
Emp Here 70
SIC 6153 Short-term business credit institutions, except agricultural

D-U-N-S 20-580-5729   (BR)
BANQUE LAURENTIENNE DU CANADA
4287 Rue Sherbrooke O, Westmount, QC, H3Z 1C8
(514) 481-0318
Emp Here 20
SIC 6021 National commercial banks

D-U-N-S 24-256-1298   (HQ)
BESSNER GALLAY KREISMAN
BGK CONSULTANTS
(*Suby of* Bessner Gallay Kreisman)
4150 Rue Sainte-Catherine O Bureau 600, Westmount, QC, H3Z 2Y5
(514) 908-3600
Emp Here 52   *Emp Total* 55
Sales 2,407,703
SIC 8721 Accounting, auditing, and bookkeeping

D-U-N-S 20-984-2801   (BR)
CANADIAN UNION OF PUBLIC EMPLOYEES
CUPE LOCAL 3350
6 Rue Weredale Park Bureau 105, Westmount, QC, H3Z 1Y6
(514) 932-7161
Emp Here 300
SIC 8631 Labor organizations

D-U-N-S 20-725-6405   (SL)
CARREFOUR DE L'ESTRIE INC
4141 Rue Sherbrooke O Bureau 400, Westmount, QC, H3Z 1B8
(514) 931-7261
Emp Here 45   *Sales* 5,681,200
SIC 6512 Nonresidential building operators
Pr Pr Sylvan Adams
Sec Diane Pardillo

D-U-N-S 20-691-9487   (SL)
CARSILCO INTERNATIONAL LTD
1 Car Westmount Bureau 1150, Westmount, QC, H3Z 2P9
(514) 384-7440
Emp Here 300   *Sales* 69,355,414
SIC 5131 Piece goods and notions
Pr Robert Carsley

D-U-N-S 20-884-6865   (SL)
CENTRE DES ARTS VISUELS, LE

VISUAL ARTS CENTRE
350 Av Victoria, Westmount, QC, H3Z 2N4
(514) 488-9558
Emp Here 50   *Sales* 2,699,546
SIC 7999 Amusement and recreation, nec

D-U-N-S 20-289-8573   (SL)
CHATEAU WESTMOUNT INC
1860 Boul De Maisonneuve O, Westmount, QC, H3Z 3G2
(514) 369-3000
Emp Here 100
SIC 7041 Membership-basis organization hotels

D-U-N-S 20-858-5067   (SL)
CLUB MED VENTES CANADA INC
3500 Boul De Maisonneuve O Bureau 1500, Westmount, QC, H3Z 3C1
(514) 937-1428
Emp Here 50   *Sales* 11,892,594
SIC 4725 Tour operators
Pr Pr Xavier Mufraggi
Carolyne Doyon
Sec Anne Hong Pham

D-U-N-S 25-240-3118   (BR)
COMMISSION SCOLAIRE DE MONTREAL
ECOLE SAINT-LEON-DE-WESTMOUNT
360 Av Clarke, Westmount, QC, H3Z 2E6
(514) 596-5720
Emp Here 45
SIC 8211 Elementary and secondary schools

D-U-N-S 25-244-4971   (BR)
COMMISSION SCOLAIRE ENGLISH-MONTREAL
WESTMOUNT PARK SCHOOL
15 Place Park, Westmount, QC, H3Z 2K4
(514) 935-7338
Emp Here 40
SIC 8211 Elementary and secondary schools

D-U-N-S 20-712-4897   (BR)
COMMISSION SCOLAIRE ENGLISH-MONTREAL
WESTMOUNT HIGH
4350 Rue Sainte-Catherine O, Westmount, QC, H3Z 1R1
(514) 933-2701
Emp Here 50
SIC 8211 Elementary and secondary schools

D-U-N-S 25-874-1354   (BR)
CONCEPTS ZONE INC, LES
ZONE
5014 Rue Sherbrooke O, Westmount, QC, H3Z 1H4
(514) 489-8901
Emp Here 20
SIC 3999 Manufacturing industries, nec

D-U-N-S 20-575-6500   (SL)
DESIGN & CONSTRUCTION GIFFELS QUEBEC INC
4333 Rue Sainte-Catherine O Bureau 250, Westmount, QC, H3Z 1P9
(514) 931-1001
Emp Here 20   *Sales* 4,677,755
SIC 1541 Industrial buildings and warehouses

D-U-N-S 20-714-2436   (BR)
ECOLE VANGUARD QUEBEC LIMITEE
SECONDAIRE INTER CULTUREL
175 Av Metcalfe, Westmount, QC, H3Z 2H5

Emp Here 50
SIC 8211 Elementary and secondary schools

D-U-N-S 25-368-6497   (SL)
FARO TECHNOLOGIES CANADA INC
BUILDIT SOFTWARE & SOLUTIONS
4999 Rue Sainte-Catherine O Bureau 308, Westmount, QC, H3Z 1T3
(514) 369-4055
Emp Here 20   *Sales* 1,459,214
SIC 7371 Custom computer programming services

D-U-N-S 24-871-5682   (BR)
FINANCIERE ACCORD INC
3500 Boul De Maisonneuve O Bureau 500, Westmount, QC, H3Z 3C1
(514) 932-8223
Emp Here 35
SIC 6153 Short-term business credit institutions, except agricultural

D-U-N-S 25-315-7630   (BR)
INVESTORS GROUP FINANCIAL SERVICES INC
4 Car Westmount Bureau 250, Westmount, QC, H3Z 2S6
(514) 935-3520
Emp Here 40
SIC 6282 Investment advice

D-U-N-S 25-096-1844   (HQ)
IPSOS-ASI, LTD
245 Av Victoria Bureau 100, Westmount, QC, H3Z 2M6
(514) 934-5555
Emp Here 33   *Emp Total* 2
Sales 113,833,343
SIC 8732 Commercial nonphysical research
Pr Jacquie Matthews
Ch Bd Didier Truchot
VP James T. Smith
Sec Sheryl Goodman
Dir James Thompson
Genl Mgr Debra Mason

D-U-N-S 25-857-1272   (BR)
LES CENTRES DE LA JEUNESSE ET DE LA FAMILLE BATSHAW
(*Suby of* Les Centres de la Jeunesse et de la Famille Batshaw)
4515 Rue Sainte-Catherine O, Westmount, QC, H3Z 1R9
(514) 935-6196
Emp Here 60
SIC 8322 Individual and family services

D-U-N-S 20-717-3548   (BR)
LES CENTRES DE LA JEUNESSE ET DE LA FAMILLE BATSHAW
CENTRE DE SERVICES SOCIAUX BASHAW
(*Suby of* Les Centres de la Jeunesse et de la Famille Batshaw)
4039 Rue Tupper Bureau 4, Westmount, QC, H3Z 1T5
(514) 937-9581
Emp Here 100
SIC 8322 Individual and family services

D-U-N-S 24-021-3413   (HQ)
LES CENTRES DE LA JEUNESSE ET DE LA FAMILLE BATSHAW
(*Suby of* Les Centres de la Jeunesse et de la Famille Batshaw)
5 Rue Weredale Park, Westmount, QC, H3Z 1Y5
(514) 989-1885
Emp Here 70   *Emp Total* 1,000
Sales 54,158,720
SIC 8322 Individual and family services
Karen Potter-Bienvenu
Dodo Heppner
Michael Udy
Allan Aitken
Donald Bishop
Michele Dumais
Natasha Mcmullen
Ken Whittingham
Jackie Pinkston
Ronald Jones

D-U-N-S 25-686-1709   (SL)
MADIKAP 2000 INC
4150 Rue Sherbrooke O Bureau 400, Westmount, QC, H3Z 1C2
(514) 989-9909
Emp Here 75   *Sales* 9,840,650
SIC 6531 Real estate agents and managers
Pr Pr Jean Sylvere
Sec Antoine Chawky

D-U-N-S 24-228-9452   (SL)
MANOIR WESTMOUNT INC
4646 Rue Sherbrooke O Bureau 106, Westmount, QC, H3Z 2Z8
(514) 935-3344
Emp Here 65   *Sales* 2,407,703
SIC 8361 Residential care

D-U-N-S 25-746-8470   (BR)
METRO RICHELIEU INC
METRO
4840 Rue Sherbrooke O, Westmount, QC,
H3Z 1G8
(514) 488-4083
Emp Here 150
SIC 5411 Grocery stores

D-U-N-S 25-018-8604   (BR)
ROYAL BANK OF CANADA
RBC
(*Suby of* Royal Bank Of Canada)
1 Car Westmount Bureau 100, Westmount,
QC, H3Z 2P9
(514) 874-5793
Emp Here 20
SIC 6021 National commercial banks

D-U-N-S 20-798-8036   (BR)
STAPLES CANADA INC
BUREAU EN GROS
(*Suby of* Staples, Inc.)
4036 Rue Sainte-Catherine O, Westmount,
QC, H3Z 1P2
(514) 846-0844
Emp Here 20
SIC 5943 Stationery stores

D-U-N-S 24-342-8138   (BR)
VILLE DE WESTMOUNT
HYDRO WESTMOUNT
995 Ch Glen, Westmount, QC, H3Z 2L8
(514) 925-1414
Emp Here 36
SIC 4911 Electric services

D-U-N-S 24-109-7088   (BR)
WESTERN INVENTORY SERVICE LTD
4865 Boul De Maisonneuve O, Westmount,
QC, H3Z 1M7
(514) 483-1337
Emp Here 150
SIC 7389 Business services, nec

Wickham, QC J0C
Drummomd County

D-U-N-S 25-495-1056   (SL)
2161-1298 QUEBEC INC
SIGNATURE
1031 7e Rang, Wickham, QC, J0C 1S0
(819) 398-6303
Emp Here 70   *Sales* 12,072,550
SIC 2491 Wood preserving
Pr Pr Gilles Morin
 Angele Morin
Fin Ex Ian Morin

Windsor, QC J1S

D-U-N-S 20-119-8343   (BR)
ATLANTIC COATED PAPERS LTD
139 Rue Principale N, Windsor, QC, J1S 2E1
(819) 845-7866
Emp Here 45
SIC 2672 Paper; coated and laminated, nec

D-U-N-S 25-161-5647   (SL)
CRDI-TED ESTRIE
CENTRE NOTRE DAME DE L'ENFANT
56 Rue Saint-Georges Bureau 206, Windsor,
QC, J1S 1J5

(819) 845-7200
Emp Here 35   *Sales* 11,402,181
SIC 8322 Individual and family services
 Joanne Demers Blais

D-U-N-S 25-362-7574   (BR)
**CAISSE DESJARDINS DU NORD DE SHER-
BROOKE**
*DESJARDINS ENTREPRISES-ESTRIE - BU-
REAU DU VAL ST-FRANCOIS & ASBESTOS*
89 2e Av, Windsor, QC, J1S 1Z5
(819) 845-2424
Emp Here 22
SIC 6062 State credit unions

D-U-N-S 20-037-3921   (BR)
COMMISSION SCOLAIRE DES SOMMETS
*CENTRE D'EXCELLENCE EN FORMATION
INDUSTRIELLE*
100 Rue Boisjoli, Windsor, QC, J1S 2X8
(819) 845-5402
Emp Here 25
SIC 8249 Vocational schools, nec

D-U-N-S 20-712-1182   (BR)
COMMISSION SCOLAIRE DES SOMMETS
ECOLE DU TOURNESOL
250 Rue Saint-Georges, Windsor, QC, J1S
1K4
(819) 845-2728
Emp Here 75
SIC 8211 Elementary and secondary schools

D-U-N-S 25-233-3638   (BR)
COMMISSION SCOLAIRE DES SOMMETS
ECOLE SAINT PHILIPPE
(*Suby of* Commission Scolaire des Sommets)
101 Rue Ambroise-Dearden, Windsor, QC,
J1S 1H2
(819) 845-3694
Emp Here 51
SIC 8211 Elementary and secondary schools

D-U-N-S 20-270-7683   (BR)
FRUITS & PASSION BOUTIQUES INC
FRUITS ET PASSION - WINDSOR
59 Rue Saint-Georges, Windsor, QC, J1S 1J2
(819) 845-2723
Emp Here 25
SIC 5122 Drugs, proprietaries, and sundries

D-U-N-S 20-252-7545   (BR)
**MASONITE INTERNATIONAL CORPORA-
TION**
PORTES LEMIEUX INC, DIV OF
(*Suby of* Masonite International Corporation)
92 2e Av, Windsor, QC, J1S 1Z4
(819) 845-2739
Emp Here 20
SIC 2431 Millwork

D-U-N-S 25-847-8106   (SL)
TRANSPORT MICHEL MARCOTTE INC
397 Rue Saint-Georges, Windsor, QC, J1S
1K6
(819) 845-2878
Emp Here 50   *Sales* 3,939,878
SIC 4212 Local trucking, without storage

Yamachiche, QC G0X
St-Maurice County

D-U-N-S 24-254-7250   (SL)
GESTION TBL INC.
171 Rue Sainte-Anne Rr 1, Yamachiche, QC,
G0X 3L0

Emp Here 300   *Sales* 53,202,720
SIC 4213 Trucking, except local
Pr Pr Jean-Luc Bellemare

D-U-N-S 24-402-6142   (SL)
PORTE DE LA MAURICIE INC, LA
4 Rue Sainte-Anne, Yamachiche, QC, G0X
3L0

(819) 228-9434
Emp Here 100   *Sales* 2,991,389
SIC 5812 Eating places

Yamaska, QC J0G
Yamaska County

D-U-N-S 20-712-2610   (BR)
**COMMISSION SCOLAIRE DE SOREL-
TRACY**
ECOLE INTEGREE D'YAMASKA
(*Suby of* Commission Scolaire de Sorel-Tracy)
11 Rue Du Pont, Yamaska, QC, J0G 1X0
(450) 746-3513
Emp Here 25
SIC 8211 Elementary and secondary schools

Aberdeen, SK S0K

D-U-N-S 25-288-4564   (BR)
PRAIRIE SPIRIT SCHOOL DIVISION NO. 206
ABERDEEN COMPOSITE SCHOOL
101 Thompson St, Aberdeen, SK, S0K 0A0
(306) 253-4333
Emp Here 52
SIC 8211 Elementary and secondary schools

Air Ronge, SK S0J

D-U-N-S 20-813-8607   (BR)
LAC LA RONGE INDIAN BAND
(*Suby of* Lac La Ronge Indian Band)
54 Far Reserve Rd, Air Ronge, SK, S0J 3G0
(306) 425-2384
Emp Here 80
SIC 8743 Public relations services

Alida, SK S0C

D-U-N-S 20-243-5421   (BR)
AECOM CANADA LTD
Hwy 361, Alida, SK, S0C 0B0
(306) 443-2281
Emp Here 20
SIC 1389 Oil and gas field services, nec

Allan, SK S0K

D-U-N-S 20-251-3867   (BR)
PCS SALES (CANADA) INC
POTASH ALLAN DIV
Gd, Allan, SK, S0K 0C0
(306) 257-3312
Emp Here 500
SIC 1474 Potash, soda, and borate minerals

D-U-N-S 24-233-3326   (BR)
POTASH   CORPORATION   OF SASKATCHEWAN INC
PCS POTASH ALLAN, DIV OF
Gd, Allan, SK, S0K 0C0
(306) 257-3312
Emp Here 290
SIC 1474 Potash, soda, and borate minerals

D-U-N-S 25-096-4913   (BR)
PRAIRIE SPIRIT SCHOOL DIVISION NO. 206
ALLAN SCHOOL
Gd, Allan, SK, S0K 0C0
(306) 257-3311
Emp Here 23
SIC 8211 Elementary and secondary schools

Arcola, SK S0C

D-U-N-S 20-712-8765   (BR)
SOUTH EAST CORNERSTONE SCHOOL DIVISION NO. 209
ARCOLA SCHOOL
(*Suby of* South East Cornerstone School Division No. 209)
302 Souris Ave, Arcola, SK, S0C 0G0
(306) 455-2340
Emp Here 26
SIC 8211 Elementary and secondary schools

Asquith, SK S0K

D-U-N-S 24-618-1601   (BR)
PRAIRIE SPIRIT SCHOOL DIVISION NO. 206
LORD ASQUITH SCHOOL
305 Eagle Ave, Asquith, SK, S0K 0J0
(306) 329-4331
Emp Here 35
SIC 8211 Elementary and secondary schools

Assiniboia, SK S0H

D-U-N-S 20-646-4088   (BR)
CONEXUS CREDIT UNION 2006
ASSINIBOIA BRANCH
400 Centre St, Assiniboia, SK, S0H 0B0
(306) 642-3343
Emp Here 25
SIC 6062 State credit unions

D-U-N-S 25-987-9781   (BR)
FEDERATED CO-OPERATIVES LIMITED
SOUTHLAND COOP 110
(*Suby of* Federated Co-Operatives Limited)
409 Centre St, Assiniboia, SK, S0H 0B0
(306) 642-3347
Emp Here 150
SIC 5411 Grocery stores

D-U-N-S 24-394-9893   (BR)
FIVE HILLS REGIONAL HEALTH AUTHORITY
ASSINIBOIA UNION HOSPITAL
(*Suby of* Five Hills Regional Health Authority)
501 6th Ave E, Assiniboia, SK, S0H 0B0
(306) 642-3351
Emp Here 70
SIC 8062 General medical and surgical hospitals

D-U-N-S 20-697-9234   (BR)
NILSSON BROS. INC
ASSINIBOIA LIVESTOCK AUCTION
200 Railway Ave N, Assiniboia, SK, S0H 0B0
(306) 642-5358
Emp Here 35
SIC 5154 Livestock

D-U-N-S 24-381-1887   (BR)
PATERSON GLOBALFOODS INC
PATERSON GRAIN
717 Highway 2, Assiniboia, SK, S0H 0B0
(306) 642-5900
Emp Here 20
SIC 5153 Grain and field beans

D-U-N-S 24-338-6450   (BR)
PRAIRIE SOUTH SCHOOL DIVISION NO 210
ASSINIBOIA 7TH AVENUE SCHOOL
300 7th Ave E, Assiniboia, SK, S0H 0B0
(306) 642-3566
Emp Here 20
SIC 8211 Elementary and secondary schools

D-U-N-S 24-338-6484   (BR)
PRAIRIE SOUTH SCHOOL DIVISION NO 210
ASSINIBOIA   COMPREHENSIVE   HIGH SCHOOL
200 Bell Rd, Assiniboia, SK, S0H 0B0
(306) 642-3319
Emp Here 25
SIC 8211 Elementary and secondary schools

D-U-N-S 20-264-5859   (BR)
RICHARDSON PIONEER LIMITED
Gd, Assiniboia, SK, S0H 0B0
(306) 642-3612
Emp Here 25
SIC 5153 Grain and field beans

Balcarres, SK S0G

D-U-N-S 24-336-3780   (BR)
PRAIRIE VALLEY SCHOOL DIVISION NO 208
BALCARRES COMMUNITY SCHOOL
420 Lisgar St, Balcarres, SK, S0G 0C0
(306) 334-2520
Emp Here 50
SIC 8211 Elementary and secondary schools

D-U-N-S 24-513-4890   (BR)
PRAIRIE VALLEY SCHOOL DIVISION NO 208
BALCARRES COMMUNITY SCHOOL
420 Listar St, Balcarres, SK, S0G 0C0
(306) 334-2714
Emp Here 50
SIC 8211 Elementary and secondary schools

Balgonie, SK S0G

D-U-N-S 20-716-8274   (BR)
PRAIRIE VALLEY SCHOOL DIVISION NO 208
BALGONIE ELEMENTARY SCHOOL
226 Queen St, Balgonie, SK, S0G 0E0
(306) 771-2345
Emp Here 40
SIC 8211 Elementary and secondary schools

Battleford, SK S0M

D-U-N-S 25-135-8243   (BR)
FINNING INTERNATIONAL INC
(*Suby of* Finning International Inc)
391 Yellowhead Alley, Battleford, SK, S0M 0E0
(306) 445-6151
Emp Here 24
SIC 5082 Construction and mining machinery

D-U-N-S 25-962-3718   (BR)
G.L.M. INDUSTRIES L.P.
14th S And 5th Ave, Battleford, SK, S0M 0E0

Emp Here 65
SIC 3272 Concrete products, nec

D-U-N-S 20-712-7288   (BR)
LIVING SKY SCHOOL DIVISION NO. 202
ST CATHOLIC VITAL SCHOOL
332 23 St, Battleford, SK, S0M 0E0
(306) 937-2233
Emp Here 30
SIC 8211 Elementary and secondary schools

D-U-N-S 25-158-7754   (BR)
LIVING SKY SCHOOL DIVISION NO. 202
BATTLEFORD   CENTRAL   ELEMENTARY SCHOOL
252 23rd St, Battleford, SK, S0M 0E0
(306) 937-2112
Emp Here 60
SIC 8211 Elementary and secondary schools

Beauval, SK S0M

D-U-N-S 20-712-8344   (BR)
NORTHERN LIGHTS SCHOOL DIVISION 113
VALLEY VIEW SCHOOL
Petersen St, Beauval, SK, S0M 0G0
(306) 288-2022
Emp Here 50
SIC 8211 Elementary and secondary schools

Belle Plaine, SK S0G

D-U-N-S 20-833-4532   (BR)
K+S SEL WINDSOR LTEE
Gd, Belle Plaine, SK, S0G 0G0
(306) 345-5200
Emp Here 55
SIC 2899 Chemical preparations, nec

D-U-N-S 24-852-6436   (BR)
YARA BELLE PLAINE INC
2 Kalium Rd, Belle Plaine, SK, S0G 0G0
(306) 345-4200
Emp Here 140
SIC 2874 Phosphatic fertilizers

Bellegarde, SK S0C

D-U-N-S 20-033-3545   (BR)
CONSEIL DES ECOLES FRANSASKOISES
ECOLE DE BELLEGARDE
Gd, Bellegarde, SK, S0C 0J0
(306) 452-6135
Emp Here 20
SIC 8211 Elementary and secondary schools

Bengough, SK S0C

D-U-N-S 25-121-7774   (BR)
SUN COUNTRY HEALTH REGION
BENGOUGH HEALTH CENTRE
(*Suby of* Sun Country Health Region)
400 2nd St W, Bengough, SK, S0C 0K0
(306) 268-2840
Emp Here 50
SIC 8051 Skilled nursing care facilities

D-U-N-S 20-837-0630   (BR)
SUN COUNTRY REGIONAL HEALTH AUTHORITY
BENGOUGH HEALTH CENTRE
400 2nd St W, Bengough, SK, S0C 0K0
(306) 268-2048
Emp Here 60
SIC 8051 Skilled nursing care facilities

Bethune, SK S0G

D-U-N-S 20-342-6010   (BR)
K+S POTASH CANADA GENERAL PARTNERSHIP
Sw 35-19-25-W2, Bethune, SK, S0G 0H0
(306) 638-2800
Emp Here 200
SIC 1474 Potash, soda, and borate minerals

Bienfait, SK S0C

D-U-N-S 20-845-4673   (BR)
PRAIRIE MINES & ROYALTY ULC
(*Suby of* Westmoreland Coal Company)
Gd, Bienfait, SK, S0C 0M0
(306) 388-2272
Emp Here 90
SIC 1221 Bituminous coal and lignite-surface mining

D-U-N-S 20-712-6637   (BR)
SOUTH EAST CORNERSTONE SCHOOL DIVISION NO. 209
BIENFAIT WELDON SCHOOL
(*Suby of* South East Cornerstone School Division No. 209)

802 Weldon Rd, Bienfait, SK, S0C 0M0
(306) 388-2422
Emp Here 30
SIC 8211 Elementary and secondary schools

Big River, SK S0J

D-U-N-S 24-037-6871   (BR)
PRINCE ALBERT PARKLAND REGIONAL HEALTH AUTHORITY
BIG RIVER HEALTH CENTRE
220 1st Avenue North, Big River, SK, S0J 0E0
(306) 469-2220
Emp Here 85
SIC 8051 Skilled nursing care facilities

D-U-N-S 24-121-5891   (BR)
SASKATCHEWAN RIVER SCHOOL DIVISION #119
T D MICHEL COMMUNITY SCHOOL
700 Main St, Big River, SK, S0J 0E0
(306) 469-2128
Emp Here 22
SIC 8211 Elementary and secondary schools

Biggar, SK S0K

D-U-N-S 24-497-1230   (SL)
BULANI AGRO INC
801 Hwy 4, Biggar, SK, S0K 0M0
(306) 948-1800
Emp Here 23   *Sales* 6,219,371
SIC 5191 Farm supplies
Pr Pr Dennis Bulani
   Lynda Bulani

D-U-N-S 20-842-9605   (SL)
DIAMOND LODGE CO LTD
402 2nd Ave W, Biggar, SK, S0K 0M0

Emp Here 100   *Sales* 3,648,035
SIC 8361 Residential care

D-U-N-S 24-324-1093   (BR)
HEARTLAND REGIONAL HEALTH AUTHORITY
BIGGAR HOSPITAL
501 1st Ave W, Biggar, SK, S0K 0M0
(306) 948-3323
Emp Here 70
SIC 8062 General medical and surgical hospitals

D-U-N-S 25-453-9054   (BR)
PARRISH & HEIMBECKER, LIMITED
HANOVER JUNCTION
(*Suby of* Parrish & Heimbecker, Limited)
220 Main St, Biggar, SK, S0K 0M0
(306) 948-1990
Emp Here 20
SIC 5153 Grain and field beans

D-U-N-S 24-334-6876   (BR)
SUN WEST SCHOOL DIVISION NO 207 SASKATCHEWAN
BIGGAR CENTRAL SCHOOL 2000
701 Kings St, Biggar, SK, S0K 0M0
(306) 948-2117
Emp Here 50
SIC 8211 Elementary and secondary schools

Birch Hills, SK S0J

D-U-N-S 20-059-9769   (SL)
BIRCH HILLS CO-OPERATIVE ASSOCIATION LIMITED
1 Wilson St, Birch Hills, SK, S0J 0G0

(306) 749-2255
Emp Here 39   *Sales* 6,496,629
SIC 5171 Petroleum bulk stations and terminals
Genl Mgr Gerry Mccann
Pr Pr Carol Pryznyk
VP VP Stan Bliss
   Darren Sundbo
Dir Mark Rolfes
Dir Joyce Hunter
   Bruce Tilford
Dir Bruce Stevenson

D-U-N-S 20-068-1901   (BR)
PRINCE ALBERT PARKLAND REGIONAL HEALTH AUTHORITY
BIRCH HILLS HEALTH FACILITY
3 Wilson St, Birch Hills, SK, S0J 0G0
(306) 749-3331
Emp Here 65
SIC 8051 Skilled nursing care facilities

D-U-N-S 20-712-7221   (BR)
SASKATCHEWAN RIVER SCHOOL DIVISION #119
BIRCH HILS SCHOOL
110 Mccallum Ave, Birch Hills, SK, S0J 0G0
(306) 749-3301
Emp Here 50
SIC 8211 Elementary and secondary schools

Black Lake, SK S0J

D-U-N-S 20-033-7132   (SL)
FATHER PORTE MEMORIAL DENE SCHOOL
Gd, Black Lake, SK, S0J 0H0
(306) 284-2166
Emp Here 55   *Sales* 3,648,035
SIC 8211 Elementary and secondary schools

Blaine Lake, SK S0J

D-U-N-S 24-612-4825   (BR)
PRAIRIE SPIRIT SCHOOL DIVISION NO. 206
BLAINE LAKE COMPOSITE SCHOOL
627 North Southroad Allowance, Blaine Lake, SK, S0J 0J0
(306) 497-2632
Emp Here 25
SIC 8211 Elementary and secondary schools

Bracken, SK S0N

D-U-N-S 25-977-0154   (SL)
BUTTE COLONY
Gd, Bracken, SK, S0N 0G0
(306) 298-4445
Emp Here 70   *Sales* 3,575,074
SIC 7389 Business services, nec

Bredenbury, SK S0A

D-U-N-S 25-995-2752   (BR)
CANADIAN PACIFIC RAILWAY COMPANY
CPR
101 Railway Ave, Bredenbury, SK, S0A 0H0
(306) 898-2144
Emp Here 50
SIC 4011 Railroads, line-haul operating

Broadview, SK S0G

D-U-N-S 25-705-1870   (BR)
REGINA QU'APPELLE REGIONAL HEALTH AUTHORITY
BROADVIEW CENTENNIAL LODGE
310 Calgary St, Broadview, SK, S0G 0K0
(306) 696-2458
Emp Here 60
SIC 8059 Nursing and personal care, nec

D-U-N-S 25-334-4394   (BR)
REGINA QU'APPELLE REGIONAL HEALTH AUTHORITY
BROADVIEW UNION HOSPITAL
901 Nina St, Broadview, SK, S0G 0K0
(306) 696-5500
Emp Here 50
SIC 8062 General medical and surgical hospitals

Buffalo Narrows, SK S0M

D-U-N-S 24-344-5231   (HQ)
KEEWATIN YATTHE REGIONAL HEALTH AUTHORITY
(*Suby of* Keewatin Yatthe Regional Health Authority)
Gd, Buffalo Narrows, SK, S0M 0J0
(306) 235-2220
Emp Here 20   *Emp Total* 50
Sales 3,502,114
SIC 8062 General medical and surgical hospitals

D-U-N-S 20-034-5986   (BR)
NORTHERN LIGHTS SCHOOL DIVISION 113
TWIN LAKES COMMUNITY SCHOOL
1345 Davies St, Buffalo Narrows, SK, S0M 0J0

Emp Here 40
SIC 8211 Elementary and secondary schools

Bushell Park, SK S0H

D-U-N-S 20-211-0735   (BR)
ATCO STRUCTURES & LOGISTICS LTD
Gd, Bushell Park, SK, S0H 0N0
(306) 694-2780
Emp Here 35
SIC 8741 Management services

Canoe Narrows, SK S0M

D-U-N-S 20-065-9444   (BR)
MEADOW LAKE TRIBAL COUNCIL
CANOE LAKE HEALTH CENTRE
Gd, Canoe Narrows, SK, S0M 0K0
(306) 829-2140
Emp Here 20
SIC 8399 Social services, nec

Canora, SK S0A

D-U-N-S 25-687-4173   (HQ)
CROSSROADS FINANCIAL LIMITED
CROSSROADS CREDIT UNION
(*Suby of* Crossroads Financial Limited)
113 2nd Ave E, Canora, SK, S0A 0L0
(306) 563-5641
Emp Here 34   *Emp Total* 69
Sales 12,627,209
SIC 6062 State credit unions
CEO Perry Wishlow

Pr George Stinka
VP VP Murray Bottcher
VP Gary Herbert
Dir Ardelle Chicilo
Dir Dave W. Harding
Dir Rodney Tetrychyn
Dir Joseph Yacyshyn
Dir Walter Ostofoross

D-U-N-S 24-428-9088   (SL)
GATEWAY LODGE INC
212 Centre Ave E, Canora, SK, S0A 0L0
(306) 563-5685
Emp Here 95   *Sales* 4,304,681
SIC 8051 Skilled nursing care facilities

Canwood, SK S0J

D-U-N-S 25-133-6277   (SL)
AHTAHKAKOOP EDUCATION BOARD
AHTAHKAKOOP SCHOOL
Po Box 280, Canwood, SK, S0J 0K0
(306) 468-2854
Emp Here 60   *Sales* 4,764,381
SIC 8211 Elementary and secondary schools

D-U-N-S 20-713-0241   (BR)
PARKLAND SCHOOL DIVISION NO. 70
CANWOOD PUBLIC SCHOOL
Po Box 370, Canwood, SK, S0J 0K0
(306) 468-2150
Emp Here 50
SIC 8211 Elementary and secondary schools

D-U-N-S 24-626-9182   (BR)
SASKATCHEWAN RIVER SCHOOL DIVISION #119
CANWOOD HIGH SCHOOL
850 1st St E, Canwood, SK, S0J 0K0
(306) 468-2150
Emp Here 20
SIC 8211 Elementary and secondary schools

Carlyle, SK S0C

D-U-N-S 25-020-6844   (BR)
AECOM CANADA LTD
Gd, Carlyle, SK, S0C 0R0

Emp Here 30
SIC 1623 Water, sewer, and utility lines

D-U-N-S 24-365-0731   (BR)
CES ENERGY SOLUTIONS CORP
MOOSE MOUNTAIN MUD
2 Miles S Highway 9, Carlyle, SK, S0C 0R0
(306) 453-4411
Emp Here 60
SIC 1382 Oil and gas exploration services

D-U-N-S 24-876-7308   (BR)
CES ENERGY SOLUTIONS CORP
AES DRILLING FLUIDS
Highway 9 S, Carlyle, SK, S0C 0R0
(306) 453-4470
Emp Here 100
SIC 1382 Oil and gas exploration services

D-U-N-S 25-560-6576   (BR)
REPSOL OIL & GAS CANADA INC
801 Railway Ave W, Carlyle, SK, S0C 0R0
(306) 453-2545
Emp Here 40
SIC 1382 Oil and gas exploration services

D-U-N-S 25-963-5571   (BR)
SASKATCHEWAN INDIAN GAMING AUTHORITY INC
BEAR CLAW CASINO
Gd, Carlyle, SK, S0C 0R0
(306) 577-4577
Emp Here 150

SIC 7999 Amusement and recreation, nec

D-U-N-S 20-712-8773   (BR)
SOUTH EAST CORNERSTONE SCHOOL DIVISION NO. 209
CARLYLE ELEMENTARY SCHOOL
(*Suby of* South East Cornerstone School Division No. 209)
401 Souris Ave E, Carlyle, SK, S0C 0R0
(306) 453-2393
Emp Here 30
SIC 8211 Elementary and secondary schools

D-U-N-S 20-712-8823   (BR)
SOUTH EAST CORNERSTONE SCHOOL DIVISION NO. 209
GORDON F. KELLS HIGH SCHOOL
(*Suby of* South East Cornerstone School Division No. 209)
415 5th St E, Carlyle, SK, S0C 0R0
(306) 453-2500
Emp Here 20
SIC 8211 Elementary and secondary schools

D-U-N-S 20-790-0056   (BR)
SOUTHERN PLAINS CO-OPERATIVE LIMITED
(*Suby of* Southern Plains Co-operative Limited)
214 Main St, Carlyle, SK, S0C 0R0
(306) 453-2222
Emp Here 20
SIC 5411 Grocery stores

D-U-N-S 25-326-1036   (BR)
SUN COUNTRY REGIONAL HEALTH AUTHORITY
MOOSE MOUNTAIN LODGE
6th St W, Carlyle, SK, S0C 0R0
(306) 453-2434
Emp Here 60
SIC 8051 Skilled nursing care facilities

Carnduff, SK S0C

D-U-N-S 24-233-8119   (SL)
BORDER-LINE HOUSING CO (1975) INC
SUNSET HAVEN
415 Spencer St, Carnduff, SK, S0C 0S0
(306) 482-3424
Emp Here 70   *Sales* 3,210,271
SIC 8051 Skilled nursing care facilities

D-U-N-S 24-171-9236   (SL)
COUSINS, GREG CONSTRUCTION LTD
805 Preston Ave, Carnduff, SK, S0C 0S0
(306) 482-5107
Emp Here 95   *Sales* 19,579,850
SIC 1389 Oil and gas field services, nec
Pr Pr Gregory Cousins
 Paulette Cousins

D-U-N-S 20-712-8872   (BR)
SOUTH EAST CORNERSTONE SCHOOL DIVISION NO. 209
CARNDUFF EDUCATION COMPLEX
(*Suby of* South East Cornerstone School Division No. 209)
506 Anderson Ave, Carnduff, SK, S0C 0S0
(306) 482-3491
Emp Here 35
SIC 8211 Elementary and secondary schools

Caronport, SK S0H

D-U-N-S 24-174-0070   (BR)
SODEXO CANADA LTD
528 2nd Ave, Caronport, SK, S0H 0S0
(306) 756-3402
Emp Here 22
SIC 5141 Groceries, general line

Carrot River, SK S0E

D-U-N-S 24-346-7896   (BR)
NORTH EAST SCHOOL DIVISION
CARROT RIVER HIGH SCHOOL
2201 2 St W, Carrot River, SK, S0E 0L0
(306) 768-2433
Emp Here 24
SIC 8211 Elementary and secondary schools

D-U-N-S 20-512-1192   (BR)
PREMIER HORTICULTURE LTEE
Acorder Mile E Circh Rd, Carrot River, SK, S0E 0L0
(306) 768-2794
Emp Here 30
SIC 1499 Miscellaneous nonMetallic minerals, except fuels

Central Butte, SK S0H

D-U-N-S 24-338-5288   (BR)
FIVE HILLS REGIONAL HEALTH AUTHORITY
CENTRAL BUTTE REGENCY HOSPITAL
(*Suby of* Five Hills Regional Health Authority)
601 Canada St, Central Butte, SK, S0H 0T0
(306) 796-2190
Emp Here 49
SIC 8051 Skilled nursing care facilities

D-U-N-S 20-712-9169   (BR)
PRAIRIE SOUTH SCHOOL DIVISION NO 210
CENTRAL BUTTE ELEMENTARY & HIGH SCHOOL
100 4th Ave E, Central Butte, SK, S0H 0T0
(306) 796-2124
Emp Here 20
SIC 8211 Elementary and secondary schools

Chaplin, SK S0H

D-U-N-S 20-068-2144   (SL)
SASKATCHEWAN MINING AND MINERALS INC
1 Railway Ave, Chaplin, SK, S0H 0V0
(306) 395-2561
Emp Here 35   *Sales* 9,517,523
SIC 2819 Industrial inorganic chemicals, nec
Pr Pr Rodney J. Mccann
 Murray J. Mccann

Choiceland, SK S0J

D-U-N-S 24-346-7904   (BR)
NORTH EAST SCHOOL DIVISION
WILLIAM MASON SCHOOL
100 7th St E, Choiceland, SK, S0J 0M0
(306) 428-2157
Emp Here 20
SIC 8211 Elementary and secondary schools

Churchbridge, SK S0A

D-U-N-S 20-060-5954   (SL)
CHURCHBRIDGE CO-OPERATIVE ASSOCIATION LIMITED, THE
Gd, Churchbridge, SK, S0A 0M0
(306) 896-2575
Emp Here 28   *Sales* 10,940,897
SIC 5171 Petroleum bulk stations and terminals

Genl Mgr Bruce Krantz
Pr Pr Brian Swanson
 Al Lutz
VP VP Glen Schaan
Dir Wolodymyr Muzylowski
Dir Gordon Weick

Clavet, SK S0K

D-U-N-S 24-103-9309   (BR)
CARGILL LIMITED
CARGILL CANOLA PROCESSING
Gd, Clavet, SK, S0K 0Y0
(306) 668-5251
Emp Here 70
SIC 3556 Food products machinery

D-U-N-S 25-999-3517   (BR)
CARGILL LIMITED
Gd, Clavet, SK, S0K 0Y0
(306) 668-5105
Emp Here 50
SIC 4221 Farm product warehousing and storage

D-U-N-S 20-712-9680   (BR)
PRAIRIE SPIRIT SCHOOL DIVISION NO. 206
CLAVET COMPOSITE SCHOOL
Gd, Clavet, SK, S0K 0Y0
(306) 933-1022
Emp Here 50
SIC 8211 Elementary and secondary schools

Coleville, SK S0L

D-U-N-S 24-747-8274   (BR)
TRANSGAS LIMITED
Gd, Coleville, SK, S0L 0K0
(306) 965-7370
Emp Here 25
SIC 4923 Gas transmission and distribution

Colonsay, SK S0K

D-U-N-S 20-033-2711   (BR)
PRAIRIE SPIRIT SCHOOL DIVISION NO. 206
COLONSAY SCHOOL
200 Oronsay St, Colonsay, SK, S0K 0Z0
(306) 255-2050
Emp Here 21
SIC 8211 Elementary and secondary schools

Congress, SK S0H

D-U-N-S 20-255-5132   (BR)
CARGILL LIMITED
Railroad Ave, Congress, SK, S0H 0Y0
(306) 642-4956
Emp Here 21
SIC 5153 Grain and field beans

Corman Park, SK S7R

D-U-N-S 25-640-3866   (BR)
ROSENAU TRANSPORT LTD
ACROPOLIS WAREHOUSING
(*Suby of* Mid-Nite Sun Transportation Ltd)
6 Prospect Rd, Corman Park, SK, S7R 0H5
(306) 244-7088
Emp Here 24

SIC 4731 Freight transportation arrangement

Corman Park, SK S7T

D-U-N-S 20-546-6977   (BR)
CANLAN ICE SPORTS CORP
JEMINI ICE SPORTS
2301 Grasswood Rd E, Corman Park, SK, S7T 1C8
(306) 955-3606
Emp Here 55
SIC 7999 Amusement and recreation, nec

Coronach, SK S0H

D-U-N-S 25-686-7649   (BR)
PRAIRIE MINES & ROYALTY ULC
(*Suby of* Westmoreland Coal Company)
Gd, Coronach, SK, S0H 0Z0
(306) 267-4200
Emp Here 160
SIC 1221 Bituminous coal and lignite-surface mining

D-U-N-S 20-747-9119   (BR)
SASKATCHEWAN POWER CORPORATION
SASKPOWER
Gd, Coronach, SK, S0H 0Z0
(306) 267-5200
Emp Here 140
SIC 4911 Electric services

D-U-N-S 20-835-3941   (BR)
SUN COUNTRY REGIONAL HEALTH AUTHORITY
CORONACH HEALTH CENTRE
240 South Ave E, Coronach, SK, S0H 0Z0
(306) 267-2022
Emp Here 30
SIC 8059 Nursing and personal care, nec

Craik, SK S0G

D-U-N-S 24-338-5221   (BR)
FIVE HILLS REGIONAL HEALTH AUTHORITY
CRAIK & DISTRICT HEALTH CENTRE
(*Suby of* Five Hills Regional Health Authority)
620 Mary St, Craik, SK, S0G 0V0
(306) 734-2288
Emp Here 40
SIC 8051 Skilled nursing care facilities

Creighton, SK S0P

D-U-N-S 24-496-7832   (SL)
CREIGHTON SCHOOL DIVISION 111
CREIGHTON COMMUNITY SCHOOL
Gd, Creighton, SK, S0P 0A0
(306) 688-5825
Emp Here 65   *Sales* 4,377,642
SIC 8211 Elementary and secondary schools

D-U-N-S 24-335-8368   (BR)
DYNO NOBEL CANADA INC
115 Roche St, Creighton, SK, S0P 0A0
(306) 688-5209
Emp Here 25
SIC 2892 Explosives

Cudworth, SK S0K

D-U-N-S 20-713-0019   (BR)
HORIZON SCHOOL DIVISION NO 205
CUDWORTH SCHOOL
Gd, Cudworth, SK, S0K 1B0
(306) 256-3411
Emp Here 50
SIC 8211 Elementary and secondary schools

Cumberland House, SK S0E

D-U-N-S 20-034-0805   (BR)
NORTHERN LIGHTS SCHOOL DIVISION 113
CHARLEBOIS COMMUNITY SCHOOL
Gd, Cumberland House, SK, S0E 0S0
(306) 888-2181
Emp Here 38
SIC 8211 Elementary and secondary schools

Cupar, SK S0G

D-U-N-S 20-876-5495   (SL)
CUPAR AND DISTRICT NURSING HOME INC
213 Mills St, Cupar, SK, S0G 0Y0
(306) 723-4666
Emp Here 70   *Sales* 3,210,271
SIC 8051 Skilled nursing care facilities

D-U-N-S 20-656-6155   (BR)
PRAIRIE VALLEY SCHOOL DIVISION NO 208
CUPAR SCHOOL
400 Lansdowne St, Cupar, SK, S0G 0Y0
(306) 723-4660
Emp Here 27
SIC 8211 Elementary and secondary schools

Cut Knife, SK S0M

D-U-N-S 20-843-8887   (SL)
HILLSVALE COLONY HUTTERIAN BRETHEREN LIMITED
Gd, Cut Knife, SK, S0M 0N0
(306) 398-2915
Emp Here 75   *Sales* 6,898,600
SIC 8661 Religious organizations
Pr John Wurz
Treas Mike Wurz

D-U-N-S 20-033-2794   (BR)
LIVING SKY SCHOOL DIVISION NO. 202
CUT KNIFE ELEMENTARY SCHOOL
300 Otter St, Cut Knife, SK, S0M 0N0
(306) 398-4911
Emp Here 23
SIC 8211 Elementary and secondary schools

D-U-N-S 20-033-2802   (BR)
LIVING SKY SCHOOL DIVISION NO. 202
CUT KNIFE HIGH SCHOOL
200 Arthur St, Cut Knife, SK, S0M 0N0
(306) 398-2333
Emp Here 24
SIC 8211 Elementary and secondary schools

Dalmeny, SK S0K

D-U-N-S 24-193-2867   (BR)
PRAIRIE SPIRIT SCHOOL DIVISION NO. 206
DALMENY HIGH SCHOOL
214 3 St Se, Dalmeny, SK, S0K 1E0
(306) 254-2036
Emp Here 27

SIC 8211 Elementary and secondary schools

D-U-N-S 20-033-2984   (BR)
PRAIRIE SPIRIT SCHOOL DIVISION NO. 206
PRAIRIE VIEW ELEMENTARY SCHOOL
205 Ross Crt, Dalmeny, SK, S0K 1E0
(306) 254-2633
Emp Here 30
SIC 8211 Elementary and secondary schools

Davidson, SK S0G

D-U-N-S 25-482-9450   (BR)
HEARTLAND REGIONAL HEALTH AUTHORITY
DAVIDSON HEALTH CENTRE
900 Government Rd, Davidson, SK, S0G 1A0
(306) 567-2801
Emp Here 60
SIC 8062 General medical and surgical hospitals

D-U-N-S 25-705-2837   (BR)
PANTHER INDUSTRIES INC
PRAIRIE PALLET, DIV OF
(*Suby of* J.W. Yuel Holdings Ltd)
108 Internal Rd, Davidson, SK, S0G 1A0
(306) 567-2814
Emp Here 65
SIC 7389 Business services, nec

D-U-N-S 20-150-3765   (BR)
RIVERBEND CO-OPERATIVE LTD
(*Suby of* Riverbend Co-operative Ltd)
912 Railway St, Davidson, SK, S0G 1A0
(306) 567-2013
Emp Here 25
SIC 5411 Grocery stores

D-U-N-S 25-144-9898   (BR)
SUN WEST SCHOOL DIVISION NO 207 SASKATCHEWAN
DAVIDSON SCHOOL
420 Government Rd, Davidson, SK, S0G 1A0
(306) 567-3216
Emp Here 30
SIC 8211 Elementary and secondary schools

Debden, SK S0J

D-U-N-S 20-736-6860   (BR)
BIG RIVER FIRST NATION
MISTAHI SIPIY ELEMENTARY SCHOOL
160 Victorie, Debden, SK, S0J 2X0
(306) 724-2282
Emp Here 36
SIC 8211 Elementary and secondary schools

Deer Valley, SK S2V

D-U-N-S 20-105-6822   (SL)
DEER VALLEY DEVELOPMENT INC
10 Deer Valley Rd, Deer Valley, SK, S2V 1B6

Emp Here 50   *Sales* 2,826,987
SIC 7992 Public golf courses

Delisle, SK S0L

D-U-N-S 20-033-2562   (BR)
PRAIRIE SPIRIT SCHOOL DIVISION NO. 206
DELISLE ELEMENTARY SCHOOL
300 4th Ave E, Delisle, SK, S0L 0P0

(306) 493-2451
Emp Here 22
SIC 8211 Elementary and secondary schools

D-U-N-S 25-289-6956   (BR)
PRAIRIE SPIRIT SCHOOL DIVISION NO. 206
DELISLE COMPOSITE HIGH SCHOOL
400 2nd St E, Delisle, SK, S0L 0P0
(306) 493-2433
Emp Here 40
SIC 8211 Elementary and secondary schools

D-U-N-S 20-714-2642   (SL)
SWANSON CHRISTIAN SCHOOL
Rr 1, Delisle, SK, S0L 0P0
(306) 493-2939
Emp Here 50   *Sales* 3,356,192
SIC 8211 Elementary and secondary schools

Dinsmore, SK S0L

D-U-N-S 20-705-1306   (BR)
HEARTLAND REGIONAL HEALTH AUTHORITY
DISMORE HEALTH CARE CENTER
207 1st St E, Dinsmore, SK, S0L 0T0
(306) 846-2222
Emp Here 47
SIC 8059 Nursing and personal care, nec

Duck Lake, SK S0K

D-U-N-S 24-345-0983   (BR)
PRAIRIE SPIRIT SCHOOL DIVISION NO. 206
STOBART ELEMENTARY COMMUNITY SCHOOL
616 Front St, Duck Lake, SK, S0K 1J0
(306) 467-2128
Emp Here 27
SIC 8211 Elementary and secondary schools

D-U-N-S 25-022-8871   (BR)
PRAIRIE SPIRIT SCHOOL DIVISION NO. 206
STOBART COMMUNITY SCHOOL
556 Front St, Duck Lake, SK, S0K 1J0
(306) 467-2185
Emp Here 48
SIC 8211 Elementary and secondary schools

Dundurn, SK S0K

D-U-N-S 24-134-9666   (SL)
KELSEY PIPELINES LTD
Hwy 11 S, Dundurn, SK, S0K 1K0
(306) 492-2425
Emp Here 70   *Sales* 13,192,606
SIC 4619 Pipelines, nec
Pr Pr Richard Clunie

D-U-N-S 20-033-2547   (BR)
PRAIRIE SPIRIT SCHOOL DIVISION NO. 206
DUNDURN ELEMENTARY SCHOOL
302 3rd Ave, Dundurn, SK, S0K 1K0
(306) 492-2050
Emp Here 20
SIC 8211 Elementary and secondary schools

D-U-N-S 20-712-9706   (BR)
PRAIRIE SPIRIT SCHOOL DIVISION NO. 206
HILCREST COLONY SCHOOL
Gd, Dundurn, SK, S0K 1K0
(306) 492-2345
Emp Here 20
SIC 8211 Elementary and secondary schools

Eastend, SK S0N

D-U-N-S 24-341-9806   (BR)
CYPRESS HEALTH REGION
EASTEND WOLF WILLOW HEALTH CENTER
555 Redcoat Trail, Eastend, SK, S0N 0T0
(306) 295-3534
Emp Here 60
SIC 8011 Offices and clinics of medical doctors

Eatonia, SK S0L

D-U-N-S 20-037-3368   (BR)
SUN WEST SCHOOL DIVISION NO 207 SASKATCHEWAN
EATON SCHOOL
410 1st St E, Eatonia, SK, S0L 0Y0
(306) 967-2536
Emp Here 21
SIC 8211 Elementary and secondary schools

Edam, SK S0M

D-U-N-S 24-343-2783   (BR)
NORTHWEST SCHOOL DIVISION 203
H. HARDCASTLE SCHOOL
123 1st St N, Edam, SK, S0M 0V0
(306) 397-2944
Emp Here 20
SIC 8211 Elementary and secondary schools

Elrose, SK S0L

D-U-N-S 20-746-2529   (BR)
HEARTLAND REGIONAL HEALTH AUTHORITY
ELROSE PHARMACY
203 Main St, Elrose, SK, S0L 0Z0

Emp Here 60
SIC 8051 Skilled nursing care facilities

D-U-N-S 20-787-1299   (BR)
VITERRA INC
AGRICORE UNITED
116 Railway Ave E, Elrose, SK, S0L 0Z0
(306) 378-2242
Emp Here 25
SIC 4221 Farm product warehousing and storage

Emerald Park, SK S4L

D-U-N-S 24-231-7188   (BR)
K-LINE MAINTENANCE & CONSTRUCTION LIMITED
5 Industrial Dr, Emerald Park, SK, S4L 1B7
(306) 781-2711
Emp Here 100
SIC 1623 Water, sewer, and utility lines

Englefeld, SK S0K

D-U-N-S 20-061-2919   (HQ)
SCHULTE INDUSTRIES LTD
(*Suby of* Alamo Group Inc.)
1 Railway Ave, Englefeld, SK, S0K 1N0

---

(306) 287-3715
Emp Here 100   *Emp Total* 3,009
Sales 41,798,207
SIC 3549 Metalworking machinery, nec
Pr Greg Archibald
   Ron Robinson

Esterhazy, SK S0A

D-U-N-S 24-539-5301   (SL)
NOBLE CONSTRUCTION CORP
NOBLE CONSTRUCTION
215 Sumner St, Esterhazy, SK, S0A 0X0
(306) 745-6984
Emp Here 185   *Sales* 36,626,271
SIC 1541 Industrial buildings and warehouses
Pr Chris Miller

D-U-N-S 25-022-9242   (SL)
ST. ANTHONY'S HOSPITAL
Gd, Esterhazy, SK, S0A 0X0
(306) 745-3973
Emp Here 50   *Sales* 3,502,114
SIC 8062 General medical and surgical hospitals

D-U-N-S 24-341-5788   (BR)
SUNRISE REGIONAL HEALTH AUTHORITY
CENTENNIAL SPECIAL CARE HOME
300 James St, Esterhazy, SK, S0A 0X0
(306) 745-6444
Emp Here 100
SIC 8361 Residential care

Estevan, SK S4A

D-U-N-S 20-328-7198   (BR)
ACCEDE ENERGY SERVICES LTD
CAPTIVE OILFIELD RENTALS
Gd Lcd Main, Estevan, SK, S4A 2A1
(306) 634-6868
Emp Here 25
SIC 7353 Heavy construction equipment rental

D-U-N-S 20-810-4856   (BR)
APEX DISTRIBUTION INC
APEX
315a Kensington Ave, Estevan, SK, S4A 2A6
(306) 634-2835
Emp Here 20
SIC 5084 Industrial machinery and equipment

D-U-N-S 25-316-0626   (BR)
BP CANADA ENERGY COMPANY
(*Suby of* BP P.L.C.)
Gd, Estevan, SK, S4A 2A1
(306) 487-2551
Emp Here 34
SIC 1311 Crude petroleum and natural gas

D-U-N-S 24-851-8219   (BR)
BAKER HUGHES CANADA COMPANY
(*Suby of* Baker Hughes, A GE Company)
Devonian Po Box 403 Stn Main, Estevan, SK,
S4A 2A4

Emp Here 45
SIC 1389 Oil and gas field services, nec

D-U-N-S 20-545-6635   (HQ)
BOUNDARY PUBLISHERS LTD
ESTEVAN MERCURY NEWSPAPER
68 Souris Ave, Estevan, SK, S4A 2M3
(306) 634-2654
Emp Here 21   *Emp Total* 1,968
Sales 2,042,900
SIC 2711 Newspapers

D-U-N-S 20-553-8791   (BR)
BOUNDARY PUBLISHERS LTD
ESTEVAN MERCURY NEWSPAPER

134 Perkins St, Estevan, SK, S4A 2K1
(306) 634-9522
Emp Here 40
SIC 2711 Newspapers

D-U-N-S 20-032-8685   (BR)
CEDA INTERNATIONAL CORPORATION
CHEM-EST INDUSTRIES
Gd Lcd Main, Estevan, SK, S4A 2A1
(306) 634-4797
Emp Here 40
SIC 2819 Industrial inorganic chemicals, nec

D-U-N-S 20-069-7550   (BR)
CANADIAN NATURAL RESOURCES LIMITED
206 Souris Ave, Estevan, SK, S4A 1J7
(306) 634-2643
Emp Here 20
SIC 1311 Crude petroleum and natural gas

D-U-N-S 24-850-2838   (BR)
CANYON TECHNICAL SERVICES LTD
548 Bourquin Rd, Estevan, SK, S4A 2A7
(306) 637-3360
Emp Here 85
SIC 1389 Oil and gas field services, nec

D-U-N-S 24-466-7580   (BR)
CORRPRO CANADA, INC
(*Suby of* Aegion Corporation)
318 Superior Ave, Estevan, SK, S4A 2A4

Emp Here 20
SIC 1389 Oil and gas field services, nec

D-U-N-S 24-497-0471   (BR)
DNOW CANADA ULC
ESTEVAN SUPPY
(*Suby of* Now Inc.)
314 Kensington Ave, Estevan, SK, S4A 2A2
(306) 634-4731
Emp Here 49
SIC 5084 Industrial machinery and equipment

D-U-N-S 24-546-3849   (BR)
ENBRIDGE PIPELINES INC
402 Kensington Ave, Estevan, SK, S4A 2K9
(306) 634-2681
Emp Here 130
SIC 4612 Crude petroleum pipelines

D-U-N-S 20-270-3448   (BR)
FINNING INTERNATIONAL INC
(*Suby of* Finning International Inc)
Gd Lcd Main, Estevan, SK, S4A 2A1
(306) 634-3311
Emp Here 30
SIC 7699 Repair services, nec

D-U-N-S 24-353-6633   (BR)
FRONTIER PETERBILT SALES LTD
CERVUS EQUIPMENT PETERBILT
1 Frontier St Suite 1, Estevan, SK, S4A 2K9
(306) 636-6320
Emp Here 30
SIC 5511 New and used car dealers

D-U-N-S 20-068-5431   (BR)
GOLDEN WEST BROADCASTING LTD
CJ 1280
1236 5th St Suite 200, Estevan, SK, S4A 0Z6
(306) 634-1280
Emp Here 20
SIC 4832 Radio broadcasting stations

D-U-N-S 20-656-5116   (BR)
HILL TOP MANOR LTD
HILLVIEW MANOR
(*Suby of* Hill Top Manor Ltd)
1401 1st St Suite 401, Estevan, SK, S4A 2W7
(306) 637-2600
Emp Here 25
SIC 8322 Individual and family services

D-U-N-S 20-071-1575   (BR)
HOLY FAMILY ROMAN CATHOLIC SEPARATE SCHOOL DIVISION 140

ST MARY'S SCHOOL
615 Arthur Ave, Estevan, SK, S4A 1S9
(306) 634-3541
Emp Here 32
SIC 8211 Elementary and secondary schools

D-U-N-S 20-716-8225   (BR)
HOLY FAMILY ROMAN CATHOLIC SEPARATE SCHOOL DIVISION 140
SACRED HEART SCHOOL
1846 Gibbs Rd, Estevan, SK, S4A 1Y2
(306) 634-4249
Emp Here 31
SIC 8211 Elementary and secondary schools

D-U-N-S 24-033-0030   (SL)
INDEPENDENT WELL SERVICING LTD
477 Devonian St, Estevan, SK, S4A 2A5
(306) 634-2336
Emp Here 50   *Sales* 6,566,463
SIC 1389 Oil and gas field services, nec
Pr Pr Paul Chung

D-U-N-S 24-000-4833   (BR)
LML INDUSTRIAL CONTRACTORS LTD
LML
Gd Lcd Main, Estevan, SK, S4A 2A1

Emp Here 40
SIC 7349 Building maintenance services, nec

D-U-N-S 20-061-5284   (SL)
LA FRENTZ & CHRISTENSON TRUCKING LTD
L & C TRUCKING
24 Hwy 39 E, Estevan, SK, S4A 2A2
(306) 634-5519
Emp Here 53   *Sales* 4,937,631
SIC 4212 Local trucking, without storage

D-U-N-S 20-178-5362   (BR)
LOBLAWS INC
REAL CANADIAN WHOLESALE CLUB
137 King St, Estevan, SK, S4A 2T5
(306) 636-1600
Emp Here 40
SIC 5141 Groceries, general line

D-U-N-S 20-355-0731   (BR)
MNP LLP
1219 5th St Unit 100, Estevan, SK, S4A 0Z5
(306) 634-2603
Emp Here 25
SIC 8721 Accounting, auditing, and bookkeeping

D-U-N-S 24-364-7687   (BR)
NATIONAL-OILWELL CANADA LTD
NATIONAL OILWELL VARCO
(*Suby of* National Oilwell Varco, Inc.)
93 Panteluk St, Estevan, SK, S4A 2A6
(306) 634-8828
Emp Here 20
SIC 1389 Oil and gas field services, nec

D-U-N-S 24-572-8290   (BR)
NATIONAL-OILWELL CANADA LTD
TS & M SUPPLIES
(*Suby of* National Oilwell Varco, Inc.)
314 Kensington Ave, Estevan, SK, S4A 2A2
(306) 634-6494
Emp Here 50
SIC 5084 Industrial machinery and equipment

D-U-N-S 24-059-1623   (BR)
PACKERS PLUS ENERGY SERVICES INC
93 Escana St, Estevan, SK, S4A 2A3

Emp Here 20
SIC 1389 Oil and gas field services, nec

D-U-N-S 25-685-1882   (BR)
PRAIRIE MINES & ROYALTY ULC
(*Suby of* Westmoreland Coal Company)
Po Box 3000, Estevan, SK, S4A 2W2
(306) 634-7251
Emp Here 60
SIC 1221 Bituminous coal and lignite-surface

mining

D-U-N-S 20-910-2313   (BR)
PRECISION DRILLING CORPORATION
PRECISION WELL SERVICING
421 Mississipian Dr, Estevan, SK, S4A 2L7
(306) 634-8886
Emp Here 20
SIC 1381 Drilling oil and gas wells

D-U-N-S 20-321-4304   (BR)
REDHEAD EQUIPMENT
Gd Lcd Main, Estevan, SK, S4A 2A1
(306) 634-4788
Emp Here 60
SIC 5084 Industrial machinery and equipment

D-U-N-S 20-913-3755   (BR)
ROCKWELL SERVICING INC
ENSIGN ROCKWELL SERVICING
52 Hwy 39 E, Estevan, SK, S4A 2A5

Emp Here 45
SIC 1389 Oil and gas field services, nec

D-U-N-S 25-952-2068   (BR)
ROYAL BANK OF CANADA
RBC
(*Suby of* Royal Bank Of Canada)
1202 4th St, Estevan, SK, S4A 0W9
(306) 637-4800
Emp Here 22
SIC 6021 National commercial banks

D-U-N-S 20-125-8634   (BR)
SASKATCHEWAN POWER CORPORATION
SASKPOWER
18 Boundary Dam Hwy W, Estevan, SK, S4A
2A6
(306) 634-1300
Emp Here 300
SIC 4911 Electric services

D-U-N-S 20-191-7494   (BR)
SASKATCHEWAN POWER CORPORATION
SASKPOWER SHAND POWER STATION
Gd Lcd Main, Estevan, SK, S4A 2A1
(306) 634-1700
Emp Here 100
SIC 4911 Electric services

D-U-N-S 20-810-4815   (BR)
SASKATCHEWAN   TELECOMMUNICATIONS INTERNATIONAL, INC
SASKTEL
410 Kensington Ave, Estevan, SK, S4A 2A1
(306) 636-5020
Emp Here 30
SIC 4899 Communication services, nec

D-U-N-S 25-685-2856   (BR)
SHAWCOR LTD
GUARDIAN A SHAWCOR COMPANY
341 Imperial Ave, Estevan, SK, S4A 2H8
(306) 634-5959
Emp Here 20
SIC 1389 Oil and gas field services, nec

D-U-N-S 20-553-1176   (BR)
SOBEYS CAPITAL INCORPORATED
SOBEYS ESTEVAN
440 King St, Estevan, SK, S4A 2B4
(306) 637-2550
Emp Here 90
SIC 5411 Grocery stores

D-U-N-S 20-919-9335   (BR)
SOUTH EAST CORNERSTONE SCHOOL DIVISION NO. 209
SPRUCE RIDGE SCHOOL
(*Suby of* South East Cornerstone School Division No. 209)
321 Spruce Dr, Estevan, SK, S4A 2W9
(306) 634-8510
Emp Here 50
SIC 8211 Elementary and secondary schools

D-U-N-S 20-713-0407   (BR)

SOUTH EAST CORNERSTONE SCHOOL DIVISION NO. 209
PLEASANTDALE PUBLIC SCHOOL
(*Suby of* South East Cornerstone School Division No. 209)
1700 Dieppe Cres, Estevan, SK, S4A 1X1
(306) 634-4210
Emp Here 31
SIC 8211 Elementary and secondary schools

D-U-N-S 20-713-0415   (BR)
SOUTH EAST CORNERSTONE SCHOOL DIVISION NO. 209
WESTVIEW PUBLIC SCHOOL
(*Suby of* South East Cornerstone School Division No. 209)
1607 2nd St, Estevan, SK, S4A 0M9
(306) 634-2241
Emp Here 20
SIC 8211 Elementary and secondary schools

D-U-N-S 20-061-4618   (HQ)
SOUTHERN PLAINS CO-OPERATIVE LIMITED
(*Suby of* Southern Plains Co-operative Limited)
826 4th St, Estevan, SK, S4A 0W1
(306) 637-4300
Emp Here 101   *Emp Total* 109
Sales 59,762,752
SIC 5399 Miscellaneous general merchandise
Genl Mgr Bob Declercq
Off Mgr Carol Mckay

D-U-N-S 25-958-8242   (SL)
SYMONS THE BAKER LTD
BEEFEATER MOTOR INN HOTEL
1305 9th St, Estevan, SK, S4A 1J1
(306) 634-6456
Emp Here 85   *Sales* 2,553,625
SIC 5812 Eating places

D-U-N-S 24-853-7461   (BR)
TECHMATION ELECTRIC & CONTROLS LTD
6 Hwy 39 E Unit 3, Estevan, SK, S4A 2H7
(306) 634-5664
Emp Here 21
SIC 5084 Industrial machinery and equipment

D-U-N-S 20-875-4569   (BR)
TRICAN WELL SERVICE LTD
Hwy 39 E, Estevan, SK, S4A 2A7
(306) 637-2060
Emp Here 35
SIC 1389 Oil and gas field services, nec

D-U-N-S 24-572-2939   (SL)
VENTURE WELL SERVICING LTD
36 Hwy 39 E, Estevan, SK, S4A 2L7

Emp Here 35   *Sales* 9,557,852
SIC 1381 Drilling oil and gas wells
Pr Pr Ronald Wanner
Dorothy Wanner

D-U-N-S 25-297-7665   (BR)
WAL-MART CANADA CORP
413 Kensington Ave, Estevan, SK, S4A 2A5
(306) 634-2110
Emp Here 130
SIC 5311 Department stores

Foam Lake, SK S0A

D-U-N-S 20-061-7637   (SL)
FOAM LAKE CO-OPERATIVE ASSOCIATION LIMITED
329 Main St, Foam Lake, SK, S0A 1A0
(306) 272-3301
Emp Here 35   *Sales* 8,481,085
SIC 5411 Grocery stores
Genl Mgr Mario Bouvier
Pr Pr Valerie Block

VP VP Ron Wunder
Lana Helgason
Dir Desa Dukes
Dir Cameron Mckie
Dir Mike Dudley

D-U-N-S 24-628-1880   (BR)
HORIZON SCHOOL DIVISION NO 205
FOAM LAKE COMPOSITE HIGH SCHOOL
200 Alberta Ave E, Foam Lake, SK, S0A 1A0
(306) 272-3307
Emp Here 20
SIC 8211 Elementary and secondary schools

D-U-N-S 25-329-3526   (BR)
SUNRISE REGIONAL HEALTH AUTHORITY
FOAM LAKE HEALTH CENTRE
715 Saskatchewan Ave E, Foam Lake, SK, S0A 1A0
(306) 272-3737
Emp Here 38
SIC 8051 Skilled nursing care facilities

Fort Qu'Appelle, SK S0G

D-U-N-S 25-329-3567   (SL)
FORT QU'APPELLE INDIAN HOSPITAL INC
450 8th St, Fort Qu'Appelle, SK, S0G 1S0
(306) 332-5611
Emp Here 60   *Sales* 4,158,760
SIC 8062 General medical and surgical hospitals

D-U-N-S 24-030-2005   (BR)
PRAIRIE CO-OPERATIVE LIMITED
321 Broadway St W, Fort Qu'Appelle, SK, S0G 1S0
(306) 332-5623
Emp Here 45
SIC 5411 Grocery stores

D-U-N-S 20-716-8357   (BR)
PRAIRIE VALLEY SCHOOL DIVISION NO 208
BERT FOX COMMUNITY HIGH SCHOOL
Po Box 880, Fort Qu'Appelle, SK, S0G 1S0
(306) 332-4343
Emp Here 50
SIC 8211 Elementary and secondary schools

D-U-N-S 20-716-8365   (BR)
PRAIRIE VALLEY SCHOOL DIVISION NO 208
FORT QU'APPELLE ELEMENTARY COMMUNITY SCHOOL
221 4 St E, Fort Qu'Appelle, SK, S0G 1S0
(306) 332-5566
Emp Here 43
SIC 8211 Elementary and secondary schools

D-U-N-S 24-353-8704   (BR)
SERVICE CORPORATION INTERNATIONAL (CANADA) LIMITED
TUBMAN FUNERAL HOME
224 Company Ave S, Fort Qu'Appelle, SK, S0G 1S0
(306) 332-4308
Emp Here 20
SIC 7261 Funeral service and crematories

Frobisher, SK S0C

D-U-N-S 24-520-1876   (SL)
JOHNSTONE TANK TRUCKING LTD
1 Railway Ave, Frobisher, SK, S0C 0Y0
(306) 486-2044
Emp Here 30   *Sales* 3,283,232
SIC 4213 Trucking, except local

Green Lake, SK S0M

D-U-N-S 20-033-2356   (BR)
NORTHERN LIGHTS SCHOOL DIVISION

Furdale, SK S7T

D-U-N-S 25-205-1115   (SL)
WGCC HOLDINGS INC
WILLOWS GOLF & COUNTRY CLUB
382 Cartwright St E, Furdale, SK, S7T 1B1
(306) 956-1100
Emp Here 60   *Sales* 2,553,625
SIC 7992 Public golf courses

Gainsborough, SK S0C

D-U-N-S 20-181-2513   (BR)
SUN COUNTRY REGIONAL HEALTH AUTHORITY
GAINSBOROUGH & AREA HEALTH CENTRE
312 Stephens St, Gainsborough, SK, S0C 0Z0
(306) 685-2277
Emp Here 48
SIC 8051 Skilled nursing care facilities

Goodsoil, SK S0M

D-U-N-S 24-038-0923   (BR)
PRAIRIE NORTH REGIONAL HEALTH AUTHORITY
GOODSOIL HEALTH CENTRE
(*Suby of* Prairie North Regional Health Authority)
100 1st Ave N, Goodsoil, SK, S0M 1A0
(306) 238-2100
Emp Here 20
SIC 8062 General medical and surgical hospitals

Gravelbourg, SK S0H

D-U-N-S 20-656-6148   (BR)
CONSEIL DES ECOLES FRANSASKOISES
ECOLE SECONDARIE COLLEGE MATHIEU
306 1 Ave E, Gravelbourg, SK, S0H 1X0
(306) 648-3105
Emp Here 23
SIC 8211 Elementary and secondary schools

D-U-N-S 24-371-8991   (BR)
CONSEIL DES ECOLES FRANSASKOISES
ECOLE BEAU SOLEIL
306 1 St Ave E, Gravelbourg, SK, S0H 1X0

Emp Here 20
SIC 8211 Elementary and secondary schools

D-U-N-S 24-428-3669   (SL)
CORPORATION DU COLLEGE MATHIEU, LA
308 1st Ave E, Gravelbourg, SK, S0H 1X0
(306) 648-3491
Emp Here 50   *Sales* 3,356,192
SIC 8211 Elementary and secondary schools

D-U-N-S 24-347-5568   (BR)
PRAIRIE SOUTH SCHOOL DIVISION NO 210
GRAVELBOURG ELEMENTARY SCHOOL
7 Arphabasca St, Gravelbourg, SK, S0H 1X0
(306) 648-3277
Emp Here 25
SIC 8211 Elementary and secondary schools

113
ST PASCAL SCHOOL
107 North St, Green Lake, SK, S0M 1B0
(306) 832-2081
Emp Here 25
SIC 8211 Elementary and secondary schools

Grenfell, SK S0G

D-U-N-S 25-013-2966   (BR)
REGINA QU'APPELLE REGIONAL HEALTH AUTHORITY
GRENFELL PIONEER HOME
710 Regina Ave, Grenfell, SK, S0G 2B0
(306) 697-2842
Emp Here 56
SIC 8051 Skilled nursing care facilities

Gull Lake, SK S0N

D-U-N-S 24-546-7964   (SL)
CARMICHAEL HUTTERIAN COLONY INC
Gd, Gull Lake, SK, S0N 1A0
(306) 672-3989
Emp Here 65   *Sales* 3,283,232
SIC 7389 Business services, nec

D-U-N-S 24-340-1234   (BR)
CHINOOK SCHOOL DIVISION NO 211
GULL LAKE SCHOOL
(*Suby of* Chinook School Division No 211)
5175 Kings Ave, Gull Lake, SK, S0N 1A0
(306) 672-3551
Emp Here 30
SIC 8211 Elementary and secondary schools

Hafford, SK S0J

D-U-N-S 25-013-3154   (BR)
LIVING SKY SCHOOL DIVISION NO. 202
HAFFORD CENTRAL SCHOOL
2121 2nd Ave E, Hafford, SK, S0J 1A0
(306) 549-2212
Emp Here 22
SIC 8211 Elementary and secondary schools

D-U-N-S 25-482-4873   (BR)
PRINCE ALBERT PARKLAND REGIONAL HEALTH AUTHORITY
HAFFORD SPECIAL CARE CENTRE
213 South Ave, Hafford, SK, S0J 1A0
(306) 549-2108
Emp Here 50
SIC 8062 General medical and surgical hospitals

D-U-N-S 24-114-5973   (BR)
PRINCE ALBERT PARKLAND REGIONAL HEALTH AUTHORITY
HAFFORD MEDICAL CLINIC
213 South Ave E, Hafford, SK, S0J 1A0
(306) 549-2323
Emp Here 45
SIC 8052 Intermediate care facilities

Hague, SK S0K

D-U-N-S 25-013-3220   (BR)
PRAIRIE SPIRIT SCHOOL DIVISION NO. 206
HAGUE HIGH SCHOOL
320 Saskatchewan Ave, Hague, SK, S0K 1X0
(306) 225-2232
Emp Here 30
SIC 8211 Elementary and secondary schools

D-U-N-S 20-037-7161   (BR)
PRAIRIE SPIRIT SCHOOL DIVISION NO. 206
HAGUE ELEMENTARY SCHOOL
325 Saskatchewan Ave, Hague, SK, S0K 1X0
(306) 225-2104
Emp Here 31
SIC 8211 Elementary and secondary schools

Hanley, SK S0G

D-U-N-S 20-712-9714   (BR)
PRAIRIE SPIRIT SCHOOL DIVISION NO. 206
HANLEY COMPOSITE SCHOOL
316 Bodeman Ave, Hanley, SK, S0G 2E0
(306) 544-2511
Emp Here 50
SIC 8211 Elementary and secondary schools

Hepburn, SK S0K

D-U-N-S 20-713-0035   (BR)
PRAIRIE SPIRIT SCHOOL DIVISION NO. 206
HEPBURN SCHOOL
Po Box 219, Hepburn, SK, S0K 1Z0
(306) 947-2077
Emp Here 50
SIC 8211 Elementary and secondary schools

Herbert, SK S0H

D-U-N-S 20-656-6312   (BR)
CHINOOK SCHOOL DIVISION NO 211
HERBERT SCHOOL
(*Suby of* Chinook School Division No 211)
1 Connaught Ave, Herbert, SK, S0H 2A0
(306) 784-2454
Emp Here 25
SIC 8211 Elementary and secondary schools

D-U-N-S 20-062-3775   (SL)
HERBERT CO-OPERATIVE ASSOCIATION LIMITED
32 Shaw St, Herbert, SK, S0H 2A0

Emp Here 21   *Sales* 8,542,858
SIC 5171 Petroleum bulk stations and terminals
Genl Mgr Jim Paterson
Pr Pr Howard Steinley
VP VP Dale Cannon
 Connie Wiebe
Dir Bob Macfarlane
Dir Les Becker
Dir Dana Schindel
Dir Don Mathies
Dir Richard Forest
Dir Ronda Gerl

Hudson Bay, SK S0E

D-U-N-S 20-889-9364   (BR)
KELSEY TRAIL REGIONAL HEALTH AUTHORITY
HUDSON BAY HEALTH CARE FACILITY
(*Suby of* Kelsey Trail Regional Health Authority)
614 Prince St, Hudson Bay, SK, S0E 0Y0
(306) 865-5600
Emp Here 65
SIC 8093 Specialty outpatient clinics, nec

D-U-N-S 24-347-7226   (BR)
NORTH EAST SCHOOL DIVISION
HUDSON BAY COMPOSITE HIGH SCHOOL
401 Main St, Hudson Bay, SK, S0E 0Y0
(306) 865-2267
Emp Here 25
SIC 8211 Elementary and secondary schools

D-U-N-S 24-347-7259   (BR)
NORTH EAST SCHOOL DIVISION
STEWART HAWKE ELEMENTARY SCHOOL
702 Churchhill St, Hudson Bay, SK, S0E 0Y0
(306) 865-2515
Emp Here 24
SIC 8211 Elementary and secondary schools

D-U-N-S 25-095-2009   (BR)
WEYERHAEUSER COMPANY LIMITED
OSP DIVISION
(*Suby of* Weyerhaeuser Company)
Hiway 9 S, Hudson Bay, SK, S0E 0Y0
(306) 865-1700
Emp Here 200
SIC 2421 Sawmills and planing mills, general

Humboldt, SK S0K

D-U-N-S 24-112-9022   (SL)
BELLA VISTA INN LTD
Hwy 5, Humboldt, SK, S0K 2A1
(306) 682-2686
Emp Here 62   *Sales* 2,699,546
SIC 7011 Hotels and motels

D-U-N-S 20-874-9791   (BR)
FARM WORLD EQUIPMENT LTD
FARM WORLD HUMBOLDT
(*Suby of* Farm World Equipment Ltd)
Hwy 5 E, Humboldt, SK, S0K 2A1
(306) 682-9920
Emp Here 20
SIC 5084 Industrial machinery and equipment

D-U-N-S 20-651-6853   (BR)
HORIZON SCHOOL DIVISION NO 205
HUMBOLDT PUBLIC SCHOOL
509 8th Ave, Humboldt, SK, S0K 2A1
(306) 682-2684
Emp Here 22
SIC 8211 Elementary and secondary schools

D-U-N-S 20-062-5440   (HQ)
HUMBOLDT CO-OPERATIVE ASSOCIATION LIMITED, THE
(*Suby of* Humboldt Co-Operative Association Limited, The)
520 Main St, Humboldt, SK, S0K 2A1
(306) 682-2632
Emp Here 28   *Emp Total* 50
Sales 29,584,006
SIC 5171 Petroleum bulk stations and terminals
Genl Mgr Phil Griffeth
Pr Pr Rick Merkosky
VP VP Chris Weiss
 Shelly Hergott
Dir Mervin Ford
Dir Sharon Cameron
Dir Scott Gehlen
Dir Lloyd Willison
Dir Roger Nordick

D-U-N-S 20-068-2032   (BR)
HUMBOLDT, CITY OF
LEISURE SERVICES
61917 Street, Humboldt, SK, S0K 2A1
(306) 682-2597
Emp Here 40
SIC 7999 Amusement and recreation, nec

D-U-N-S 25-270-1651   (BR)
LOBLAWS INC
EXTRA FOODS
2019 8 Ave, Humboldt, SK, S0K 2A1

(306) 682-8335
Emp Here 50
SIC 5912 Drug stores and proprietary stores

D-U-N-S 24-828-0716   (BR)
PATTISON AGRICULTURE LIMITED
(*Suby of* Pattison Agriculture Limited)
Hwy 5 E, Humboldt, SK, S0K 2A1
(306) 682-2572
Emp Here 30
SIC 5999 Miscellaneous retail stores, nec

D-U-N-S 20-853-5237   (HQ)
PRAIRIE AGRICULTURAL MACHINERY INSTITUTE
PAMI
2215 8 Ave, Humboldt, SK, S0K 2A1
(306) 682-2555
Emp Here 90   *Emp Total* 40,372
Sales 6,428,782
SIC 8734 Testing laboratories
Pr David Gullacher
VP Joanne Forer

D-U-N-S 24-967-4763   (SL)
PRAIRIE PUBLISHING LTD
HUMBOLDT JOURNAL
535 Main St, Humboldt, SK, S0K 2A1
(306) 682-2561
Emp Here 33   *Sales* 2,772,507
SIC 2711 Newspapers

D-U-N-S 20-008-4945   (BR)
RIDLEY INC
FEED RITE
Gd, Humboldt, SK, S0K 2A0
(306) 682-2668
Emp Here 32
SIC 2048 Prepared feeds, nec

D-U-N-S 20-766-7168   (BR)
SASKATOON REGIONAL HEALTH AUTHORITY
SDH-PUBLIC HEALTH SERVICES
515 14th Ave, Humboldt, SK, S0K 2A0
(306) 682-2626
Emp Here 30
SIC 8062 General medical and surgical hospitals

D-U-N-S 24-228-2965   (BR)
SASKATOON REGIONAL HEALTH AUTHORITY
1210 9th St, Humboldt, SK, S0K 2A1
(306) 682-5526
Emp Here 300
SIC 8062 General medical and surgical hospitals

D-U-N-S 24-031-7862   (BR)
SASKATOON REGIONAL HEALTH AUTHORITY
HUMBOLDT DISTRICT HOSPITAL
1210 Ninth St N, Humboldt, SK, S0K 2A1
(306) 682-2603
Emp Here 500
SIC 8062 General medical and surgical hospitals

D-U-N-S 24-126-8825   (BR)
SASKATOON REGIONAL HEALTH AUTHORITY
ST MARYS VILLA
1109 13 St, Humboldt, SK, S0K 2A1
(306) 682-2628
Emp Here 178
SIC 8062 General medical and surgical hospitals

D-U-N-S 25-447-2496   (BR)
SOBEYS CAPITAL INCORPORATED
2304 Quill Ctr, Humboldt, SK, S0K 2A1
(306) 682-2133
Emp Here 100
SIC 5411 Grocery stores

D-U-N-S 20-712-8211   (BR)
ST. PAUL'S ROMAN CATHOLIC SEPARATE SCHOOL DIVISION NO 20

SAINT DOMINIC
706 2nd Ave S, Humboldt, SK, S0K 2A1
(306) 682-1080
Emp Here 28
SIC 8211 Elementary and secondary schools

Ile-A-La-Crosse, SK S0M

D-U-N-S 20-033-3081   (BR)
ILE-A-LA-CROSSE SCHOOL DIVISION NO 112
ROSSIGNOL ELEMENTARY SCHOOL
(*Suby of* Ile-A-La-Crosse School Division No 112)
Gd, Ile-A-La-Crosse, SK, S0M 1C0
(306) 833-2010
Emp Here 35
SIC 8211 Elementary and secondary schools

D-U-N-S 24-343-7089   (BR)
KEEWATIN YATTHE REGIONAL HEALTH AUTHORITY
ST JOSEPH'S HOSPITAL
(*Suby of* Keewatin Yatthe Regional Health Authority)
Gd, Ile-A-La-Crosse, SK, S0M 1C0
(306) 833-2016
Emp Here 75
SIC 8011 Offices and clinics of medical doctors

D-U-N-S 25-271-4530   (BR)
NORTH WEST COMPANY LP, THE
NORTHERN STORES
Gd, Ile-A-La-Crosse, SK, S0M 1C0
(306) 833-2188
Emp Here 21
SIC 5411 Grocery stores

Imperial, SK S0G

D-U-N-S 25-013-3816   (BR)
REGINA QU'APPELLE REGIONAL HEALTH AUTHORITY
LONG LAKE VALLEY INTERGRATED FACILITY
125 Prince St, Imperial, SK, S0G 2J0
(306) 963-2210
Emp Here 40
SIC 8051 Skilled nursing care facilities

D-U-N-S 25-481-5210   (BR)
REGINA QU'APPELLE REGIONAL HEALTH AUTHORITY
LONG LAKE VALLEY INTEGRATED FACILITIES
Gd, Imperial, SK, S0G 2J0
(306) 963-2122
Emp Here 38
SIC 8051 Skilled nursing care facilities

Ituna, SK S0A

D-U-N-S 20-573-8391   (BR)
ROYAL BANK OF CANADA
RBC
(*Suby of* Royal Bank Of Canada)
503 Main St, Ituna, SK, S0A 1N0
(306) 795-2661
Emp Here 20
SIC 6021 National commercial banks

D-U-N-S 24-341-5838   (BR)
SUNRISE REGIONAL HEALTH AUTHORITY
ITUNA PIONEER HEALTH CARE CENTRE
320 5th Ave Ne, Ituna, SK, S0A 1N0
(306) 795-2471
Emp Here 60

SIC 8011 Offices and clinics of medical doctors

Kamsack, SK S0A

D-U-N-S 25-415-2317   (BR)
YORKTON CO-OPERATIVE ASSOCIATION LIMITED, THE
KAMSACK COOP
695 Nykolaishen St, Kamsack, SK, S0A 1S0
(306) 542-2616
Emp Here 20
SIC 5541 Gasoline service stations

Kelliher, SK S0A

D-U-N-S 20-716-8373   (BR)
PRAIRIE VALLEY SCHOOL DIVISION NO 208
KELLIHER SCHOOL
205 2nd Ave, Kelliher, SK, S0A 1V0
(306) 675-2112
Emp Here 30
SIC 8211 Elementary and secondary schools

Kelvington, SK S0A

D-U-N-S 25-013-4103   (BR)
HORIZON SCHOOL DIVISION NO 205
KELVINGTON HIGH SCHOOL
218 1 Ave W, Kelvington, SK, S0A 1W0
(306) 327-4432
Emp Here 22
SIC 8211 Elementary and secondary schools

Kenaston, SK S0G

D-U-N-S 20-033-2489   (BR)
SUN WEST SCHOOL DIVISION NO 207 SASKATCHEWAN
KENASTON HIGH SCHOOL
400 5th Ave, Kenaston, SK, S0G 2N0
(306) 252-2182
Emp Here 45
SIC 8211 Elementary and secondary schools

Kerrobert, SK S0L

D-U-N-S 25-108-7110   (BR)
ENBRIDGE PIPELINES INC
1 Pipeline Rd, Kerrobert, SK, S0L 1R0
(306) 834-2666
Emp Here 24
SIC 4612 Crude petroleum pipelines

D-U-N-S 25-590-1027   (BR)
HEARTLAND REGIONAL HEALTH AUTHORITY
KERROBERT INTEGRATED HEALTH FACILITY
645 Columbia Ave, Kerrobert, SK, S0L 1R0
(306) 834-2463
Emp Here 80
SIC 8361 Residential care

Kindersley, SK S0L

D-U-N-S 25-205-2220   (SL)
600653 SASKATCHEWAN LTD

KINDERSLEY INN
601 11th Ave E, Kindersley, SK, S0L 1S2
(306) 463-6555
Emp Here 65   *Sales* 2,845,467
SIC 7011 Hotels and motels

D-U-N-S 24-345-5545   (BR)
HEARTLAND REGIONAL HEALTH AUTHORITY
KINDERSLEY INTERGRATED HEALTH CARE FACILITY
1003 1st St W Rr 2, Kindersley, SK, S0L 1S2

Emp Here 180
SIC 8051 Skilled nursing care facilities

D-U-N-S 25-486-1396   (BR)
KINDERSLEY AND DISTRICT CO-OPERATIVE LIMITED
KINDERSLEY CO-OP GROCERY STORE
Gd, Kindersley, SK, S0L 1S0
(306) 463-3722
Emp Here 60
SIC 5411 Grocery stores

D-U-N-S 24-915-4790   (SL)
KODIAK ENERGY SERVICES INC
1115 11th Ave W, Kindersley, SK, S0L 1S0
(306) 463-6233
Emp Here 45   *Sales* 8,014,550
SIC 1389 Oil and gas field services, nec
Pr Pr Terry Shea
 Connie Shea
Genl Mgr Brian Reid

D-U-N-S 24-329-4647   (BR)
LOBLAWS INC
EXTRA FOODS
608 12th Ave E Rr 2, Kindersley, SK, S0L 1S2
(306) 463-1651
Emp Here 35
SIC 5411 Grocery stores

D-U-N-S 20-004-4886   (BR)
ROYAL BANK OF CANADA
RBC
(*Suby of* Royal Bank Of Canada)
401 Main St, Kindersley, SK, S0L 1S0
(306) 463-5330
Emp Here 20
SIC 6021 National commercial banks

D-U-N-S 20-033-2513   (BR)
SUN WEST SCHOOL DIVISION NO 207 SASKATCHEWAN
ELIZABETH SCHOOL
200 5th Ave E, Kindersley, SK, S0L 1S0
(306) 463-6547
Emp Here 35
SIC 8211 Elementary and secondary schools

D-U-N-S 20-033-6894   (BR)
SUN WEST SCHOOL DIVISION NO 207 SASKATCHEWAN
KINDERSLEY COMPOSITE HIGH SCHOOL
606 3rd St E, Kindersley, SK, S0L 1S0
(306) 463-3771
Emp Here 40
SIC 8211 Elementary and secondary schools

D-U-N-S 20-063-0572   (SL)
TISDALE SALES & SERVICES LTD
105 11 Ave E, Kindersley, SK, S0L 1S0
(306) 463-2686
Emp Here 32   *Sales* 15,705,600
SIC 5511 New and used car dealers
Pr Pr John Boquist
 Gary Materi
Dir Jeanette Boquist
Genl Mgr Roger Mckenzie

D-U-N-S 24-330-0493   (BR)
WAL-MART CANADA CORP
710 11th Avenue E, Kindersley, SK, S0L 1S2
(306) 463-1330
Emp Here 120
SIC 5311 Department stores

Kinistino, SK S0J

D-U-N-S 24-690-7372   (BR)
PRINCE ALBERT PARKLAND REGIONAL HEALTH AUTHORITY
JUBILEE LODGE
401 Meyers Ave, Kinistino, SK, S0J 1H0
(306) 864-2851
Emp Here 41
SIC 8062 General medical and surgical hospitals

Kinistino, SK S6V

D-U-N-S 20-712-7239   (BR)
SASKATCHEWAN RIVER SCHOOL DIVISION #119
KINISTINO SCHOOL
405 5 St, Kinistino, SK, S6V 1B1
(306) 864-2252
Emp Here 30
SIC 8211 Elementary and secondary schools

Kipling, SK S0G

D-U-N-S 24-227-7122   (BR)
PIC CANADA LTD
(*Suby of* Pic Usa, Inc.)
Gd, Kipling, SK, S0G 2S0
(306) 736-2883
Emp Here 50
SIC 5154 Livestock

D-U-N-S 24-336-3806   (BR)
PRAIRIE VALLEY SCHOOL DIVISION NO 208
KIPLING SCHOOL
401 6th Ave, Kipling, SK, S0G 2S0
(306) 736-2464
Emp Here 40
SIC 8211 Elementary and secondary schools

D-U-N-S 25-326-1119   (BR)
SUN COUNTRY REGIONAL HEALTH AUTHORITY
KIPLING MEMORIAL HEALTH CENTRE
803 1 St, Kipling, SK, S0G 2S0
(306) 736-2553
Emp Here 100
SIC 8062 General medical and surgical hospitals

D-U-N-S 25-326-0954   (BR)
SUN COUNTRY REGIONAL HEALTH AUTHORITY
WILLOWDALE LODGE
200 4th St, Kipling, SK, S0G 2S0
(306) 736-2218
Emp Here 50
SIC 8051 Skilled nursing care facilities

Kyle, SK S0L

D-U-N-S 20-842-6395   (SL)
HUTTERIAN BRETHREN OF KYLE INC
KYLE HUTTERIAN BRETHREN FARM
Gd, Kyle, SK, S0L 1T0
(306) 375-2910
Emp Here 100   *Sales* 6,566,463
SIC 8661 Religious organizations
Pr Micheal J Hofer
Treas Micheal M Hofer

La Loche, SK S0M

D-U-N-S 20-293-8796   (BR)
KEEWATIN YATTHE REGIONAL HEALTH AUTHORITY
LA LOCHE HEALTH CENTRE
(*Suby of* Keewatin Yatthe Regional Health Authority)
Gd, La Loche, SK, S0M 1G0
(306) 822-3201
Emp Here 20
SIC 8062 General medical and surgical hospitals

D-U-N-S 24-851-5249   (BR)
NORTH WEST COMPANY LP, THE
NORTHERN STORES, THE
2 Mission St, La Loche, SK, S0M 1G0
(306) 822-2008
Emp Here 24
SIC 5411 Grocery stores

D-U-N-S 20-033-3016   (BR)
NORTHERN LIGHTS SCHOOL DIVISION 113
LA LOCHE COMMUNITY SCHOOL
Gd, La Loche, SK, S0M 1G0
(306) 822-2024
Emp Here 66
SIC 8211 Elementary and secondary schools

La Ronge, SK S0J

D-U-N-S 20-532-2808   (BR)
CANADIAN BROADCASTING CORPORATION
308 La Ronge, La Ronge, SK, S0J 1L0
(306) 425-3324
Emp Here 20
SIC 4833 Television broadcasting stations

D-U-N-S 20-231-0087   (BR)
CLAUDE RESOURCES INC
(*Suby of* SSR Mining Inc)
Gd, La Ronge, SK, S0J 1L0
(306) 635-2015
Emp Here 250
SIC 1041 Gold ores

D-U-N-S 24-915-1945   (BR)
CLAUDE RESOURCES INC
SEABEE MINE, DIV OF
(*Suby of* SSR Mining Inc)
1112 Finlayson St, La Ronge, SK, S0J 1L0
(306) 635-2015
Emp Here 300
SIC 1041 Gold ores

D-U-N-S 20-740-2967   (SL)
LAC LA RONGE MOTOR HOTEL (1983) LTD
(*Suby of* Lac La Ronge Indian Band)
1120 La Ronge Ave, La Ronge, SK, S0J 1L0
(306) 425-2190
Emp Here 90   *Sales* 5,300,640
SIC 7011 Hotels and motels
 Paul Dicks

D-U-N-S 24-321-9222   (BR)
MAMAWETAN CHURCHILL RIVER REGIONAL HEALTH AUTHORITY
POPULATION HEALTH UNIT, THE
1016 La Ronge Ave, La Ronge, SK, S0J 1L0
(306) 425-8512
Emp Here 24
SIC 8399 Social services, nec

D-U-N-S 20-528-0006   (BR)
NAV CANADA
Gd, La Ronge, SK, S0J 1L0
(306) 425-2369
Emp Here 20
SIC 4899 Communication services, nec

D-U-N-S 20-065-9857   (BR)
NORTHERN LIGHTS SCHOOL DIVISION

113
GORDON DENNY COMMUNITY SCHOOL
108 Finlayson St, La Ronge, SK, S0J 1L0
(306) 425-2997
Emp Here 30
SIC 8211 Elementary and secondary schools

D-U-N-S 20-712-8393   (BR)
NORTHERN LIGHTS SCHOOL DIVISION 113
PRECAM COMMUNITY SCHOOL
600 Boardman St, La Ronge, SK, S0J 1L0
(306) 425-2226
Emp Here 55
SIC 8211 Elementary and secondary schools

D-U-N-S 20-047-1188   (BR)
NORTHERN LIGHTS SCHOOL DIVISION 113
CHURCHILL COMPOSITE HIGH SCHOOL
1201 School Ave, La Ronge, SK, S0J 1L0
(306) 425-2255
Emp Here 63
SIC 8211 Elementary and secondary schools

D-U-N-S 20-656-6569   (BR)
NORTHLANDS COLLEGE
207 Boardman St, La Ronge, SK, S0J 1L0
(306) 425-4353
Emp Here 30
SIC 8221 Colleges and universities

D-U-N-S 24-035-3458   (BR)
PRINCE ALBERT CO-OPERATIVE ASSOCIATION LIMITED, THE
PRINCE ALBERT CO-OPERATIVE ASSOCIATION LIMITED, TH
950 Boardman St, La Ronge, SK, S0J 1L0
(306) 425-2281
Emp Here 70
SIC 5411 Grocery stores

D-U-N-S 20-150-4177   (BR)
PRINCE ALBERT CO-OPERATIVE ASSOCIATION LIMITED, THE
PRINCE ALBERT CO-OPERATIVE ASSOCIATION LIMITED, TH
950 Boardman St, La Ronge, SK, S0J 1L0
(306) 425-2343
Emp Here 76
SIC 5411 Grocery stores

D-U-N-S 20-747-1009   (BR)
TRANSWEST AIR
303 La Ronge Ave, La Ronge, SK, S0J 1L0
(306) 425-2382
Emp Here 25
SIC 4522 Air transportation, nonscheduled

Lafleche, SK S0H

D-U-N-S 25-818-2492   (BR)
FIVE HILLS REGIONAL HEALTH AUTHORITY
LAFLECHE & DISTRICT HEALTH CENTER
(*Suby of* Five Hills Regional Health Authority)
315 Main St, Lafleche, SK, S0H 2K0
(306) 472-5230
Emp Here 30
SIC 8051 Skilled nursing care facilities

Lake Lenore, SK S0K

D-U-N-S 24-345-2757   (BR)
HORIZON SCHOOL DIVISION NO 205
LAKE LENORE SCHOOL
525 Lake Ave Hwy Suite 368, Lake Lenore, SK, S0K 2J0
(306) 368-2333
Emp Here 20
SIC 8211 Elementary and secondary schools

Lampman, SK S0C

D-U-N-S 20-645-9542   (SL)
LAMPMAN COMMUNITY HEALTH CENTRE
309 2nd Ave E, Lampman, SK, S0C 1N0
(306) 487-2561
Emp Here 57   *Sales* 2,699,546
SIC 8059 Nursing and personal care, nec

D-U-N-S 20-712-6645   (BR)
SOUTH EAST CORNERSTONE SCHOOL DIVISION NO. 209
LAMPMAN SCHOOL
(*Suby of* South East Cornerstone School Division No. 209)
910 Coorgan Rd, Lampman, SK, S0C 1N0
(306) 487-2522
Emp Here 28
SIC 8211 Elementary and secondary schools

Langenburg, SK S0A

D-U-N-S 24-717-2323   (SL)
LANGENBURG & DISTRICT ACTIVITY CENTRE INC
ACTIVITY CENTRE
502 Carl Ave, Langenburg, SK, S0A 2A0
(306) 743-5030
Emp Here 36   *Sales* 12,376,900
SIC 8322 Individual and family services
Pr Marj Swejda
VP VP Paulette Koch

D-U-N-S 20-590-0504   (BR)
TORONTO-DOMINION BANK, THE
TD CANADA TRUST
(*Suby of* Toronto-Dominion Bank, The)
139 Kaiser Wilhelm Ave, Langenburg, SK, S0A 2A0
(306) 743-2691
Emp Here 20
SIC 6021 National commercial banks

Langham, SK S0K

D-U-N-S 20-033-2570   (BR)
PRAIRIE SPIRIT SCHOOL DIVISION NO. 206
LANGHAM ELEMENTARY SCHOOLS
102 1 Ave, Langham, SK, S0K 2L0
(306) 283-4455
Emp Here 20
SIC 8211 Elementary and secondary schools

Lanigan, SK S0K

D-U-N-S 20-654-4152   (SL)
CENTRAL PARKLAND LODGE SASKATOON HEALTH REGION
36 Downing Dr E, Lanigan, SK, S0K 2M0
(306) 365-1400
Emp Here 50   *Sales* 2,772,003
SIC 8059 Nursing and personal care, nec

D-U-N-S 20-033-2539   (BR)
HORIZON SCHOOL DIVISION NO 205
LANIGAN CENTRAL HIGH SCHOOL
40 Munster St, Lanigan, SK, S0K 2M0
(306) 365-2830
Emp Here 25
SIC 8211 Elementary and secondary schools

D-U-N-S 25-013-4822   (BR)
HORIZON SCHOOL DIVISION NO 205
LANIGAN ELEMENTARY SCHOOL
24 Wexford St, Lanigan, SK, S0K 2M0

---

(306) 365-2011
Emp Here 26
SIC 8211 Elementary and secondary schools

D-U-N-S 20-447-6006   (BR)
POTASH CORPORATION OF SASKATCHEWAN INC
PCS LANIGAN, DIV
Gd, Lanigan, SK, S0K 2M0
(306) 365-2030
Emp Here 600
SIC 1474 Potash, soda, and borate minerals

Lashburn, SK S0M

D-U-N-S 20-327-8465   (BR)
ALTEX ENERGY LTD
Gd, Lashburn, SK, S0M 1H0
(306) 285-1212
Emp Here 20
SIC 4789 Transportation services, nec

D-U-N-S 24-334-6785   (BR)
NORTHWEST SCHOOL DIVISION 203
LASHBURN HIGH SCHOOL
405 3rd St, Lashburn, SK, S0M 1H0
(306) 285-3505
Emp Here 27
SIC 8211 Elementary and secondary schools

D-U-N-S 24-334-6827   (BR)
NORTHWEST SCHOOL DIVISION 203
J.H. MOORE ELEMENTARY SCHOOL
215 3rd St E, Lashburn, SK, S0M 1H0
(306) 285-3200
Emp Here 27
SIC 8211 Elementary and secondary schools

Leader, SK S0N

D-U-N-S 20-012-5966   (SL)
KONCRETE CONSTRUCTION (SJG) INC
KONCRETE CONSTRUCTION GROUP
609 Miller St, Leader, SK, S0N 1H0
(306) 628-3757
Emp Here 40   *Sales* 8,116,000
SIC 3273 Ready-mixed concrete
Pr Pr Sheldon Guckert

Leask, SK S0J

D-U-N-S 20-034-6919   (BR)
PRAIRIE SPIRIT SCHOOL DIVISION NO. 206
LEASK COMMUNITY SCHOOL
432 3rd Ave, Leask, SK, S0J 1M0
(306) 466-2206
Emp Here 40
SIC 8211 Elementary and secondary schools

D-U-N-S 20-125-7446   (BR)
PRINCE ALBERT PARKLAND REGIONAL HEALTH AUTHORITY
WEATLAND LODGE NURSING HOME
971 2nd St N, Leask, SK, S0J 1M0
(306) 466-4949
Emp Here 53
SIC 8051 Skilled nursing care facilities

Leoville, SK S0J

D-U-N-S 24-227-7841   (BR)
LIVING SKY SCHOOL DIVISION NO. 202
LEOVILLE
Gd, Leoville, SK, S0J 1N0

---

(306) 984-2241
Emp Here 20
SIC 8211 Elementary and secondary schools

D-U-N-S 25-574-7305   (BR)
PRINCE ALBERT PARKLAND REGIONAL HEALTH AUTHORITY
EVERGREEN HEALTH CENTER
Gd, Leoville, SK, S0J 1N0
(306) 984-2136
Emp Here 30
SIC 8051 Skilled nursing care facilities

Lloydminster, SK S9V

D-U-N-S 25-059-6442   (BR)
324007 ALBERTA LTD
HEARTLAND LIVESTOCK SERVICES
(*Suby of* 400369 Alberta Ltd)
Gd Lcd Main, Lloydminster, SK, S9V 0X5
(306) 825-8831
Emp Here 20
SIC 5154 Livestock

D-U-N-S 24-468-8446   (BR)
A S L PAVING LTD
4001 52 St, Lloydminster, SK, S9V 2B5
(306) 825-4984
Emp Here 40
SIC 1611 Highway and street construction

D-U-N-S 20-176-5158   (BR)
B. & R. ECKEL'S TRANSPORT LTD
4609 52 St, Lloydminster, SK, S9V 2B3
(306) 825-4904
Emp Here 60
SIC 1389 Oil and gas field services, nec

D-U-N-S 20-890-4008   (BR)
BAYTEX ENERGY CORP
(*Suby of* Baytex Energy Corp)
Gd Lcd Main, Lloydminster, SK, S9V 0X5
(306) 825-3616
Emp Here 20
SIC 1382 Oil and gas exploration services

D-U-N-S 24-968-0687   (SL)
BERETTA ENTERPRISES (1994) LTD
Gd Stn Main, Lloydminster, SK, S9V 0X5
(780) 875-6522
Emp Here 30   *Sales* 7,067,520
SIC 1623 Water, sewer, and utility lines
Pr Pr Darrell Carter

D-U-N-S 24-098-8241   (SL)
BERETTA PIPELINE CONSTRUCTION LTD
Gd Stn Main, Lloydminster, SK, S9V 0X5

Emp Here 49   *Sales* 11,119,482
SIC 1623 Water, sewer, and utility lines
Pr Darrell Carter

D-U-N-S 24-916-1381   (SL)
BORDER CITY R.V. CENTRE LTD
Gd Lcd Main, Lloydminster, SK, S9V 0X5
(403) 875-0345
Emp Here 28   *Sales* 5,472,053
SIC 5571 Motorcycle dealers
Pr Pr Melvin Joseph (Bud) Kam
Kenneth John Kam, Sr
Prin Ken Kam, Jr

D-U-N-S 25-289-0090   (BR)
CANADA POST CORPORATION
LLOYDMINSTER PO
4616 49 Ave, Lloydminster, SK, S9V 0T2
(306) 825-7510
Emp Here 30
SIC 4311 U.s. postal service

D-U-N-S 25-311-3401   (BR)
CANADIAN IMPERIAL BANK OF COMMERCE
CIBC
4915 50 St, Lloydminster, SK, S9V 0N1

---

(306) 825-4424
Emp Here 30
SIC 6021 National commercial banks

D-U-N-S 24-572-4638   (BR)
FRONTIER PETERBILT SALES LTD
5201 40 Ave, Lloydminster, SK, S9V 2B7
(306) 825-3553
Emp Here 50
SIC 5511 New and used car dealers

D-U-N-S 20-810-1795   (SL)
HURRICANE INDUSTRIES LTD
Gd Lcd Main, Lloydminster, SK, S9V 0X5

Emp Here 60   *Sales* 11,092,080
SIC 1389 Oil and gas field services, nec
Dir Tom Fisher
Dir Blake Fisher
Dir Jason Holtby

D-U-N-S 24-894-6568   (BR)
HUSKY ENERGY INC
HUSKY OIL
4335 44 St, Lloydminster, SK, S9V 0Z8
(306) 825-1196
Emp Here 170
SIC 1311 Crude petroleum and natural gas

D-U-N-S 20-918-5508   (BR)
HUSKY ENERGY INC
Hwy 16 E Upgrader Rd, Lloydminster, SK, S9V 1M6
(306) 825-1700
Emp Here 300
SIC 1311 Crude petroleum and natural gas

D-U-N-S 25-999-1446   (BR)
HUSKY OIL OPERATIONS LIMITED
HUSKY ENERGIE
4335 44 St, Lloydminster, SK, S9V 0Z8
(306) 825-1196
Emp Here 100
SIC 1311 Crude petroleum and natural gas

D-U-N-S 20-713-0456   (BR)
LLOYDMINSTER   ROMAN   CATHOLIC SCHOOL BOARD
FATHER GORMAN COMMUNITY SCHOOL
(*Suby of* LLoydminster Roman Catholic School Board)
3112 47 Ave, Lloydminster, SK, S9V 1G5
(306) 825-4600
Emp Here 45
SIC 8211 Elementary and secondary schools

D-U-N-S 25-486-1412   (BR)
LAKELAND COLLEGE
2602 59th Ave, Lloydminster, SK, S9V 1Z3
(780) 871-5700
Emp Here 100
SIC 8221 Colleges and universities

D-U-N-S 20-655-0050   (BR)
LLOYDMINSTER SCHOOL DIVISION NO 99
JACK KEMP COMMUNITY SCHOOL
(*Suby of* Lloydminster School Division No 99)
3701 47 Ave Suite 3701, Lloydminster, SK, S9V 2C4
(306) 825-9394
Emp Here 55
SIC 8211 Elementary and secondary schools

D-U-N-S 20-531-3765   (BR)
LLOYDMINSTER SCHOOL DIVISION NO 99
E S LAIRD MIDDLE SCHOOL
(*Suby of* Lloydminster School Division No 99)
4808 45 Ave, Lloydminster, SK, S9V 0X4
(306) 825-8826
Emp Here 50
SIC 8211 Elementary and secondary schools

D-U-N-S 20-713-2031   (BR)
LLOYDMINSTER SCHOOL DIVISION NO 99
WINSTON CHURCHILL SCHOOL
(*Suby of* Lloydminster School Division No 99)
4402 27 St, Lloydminster, SK, S9V 1R8
(306) 825-2626
Emp Here 50

SIC 8211 Elementary and secondary schools

D-U-N-S 24-142-9575   (BR)
NORTHWEST SCHOOL DIVISION 203
HILLMOND CENTRAL SCHOOL
1 Hillmond Ave, Lloydminster, SK, S9V 0X7
(306) 825-3393
Emp Here 25
SIC 8211 Elementary and secondary schools

D-U-N-S 20-010-1678   (BR)
PRAIRIE NORTH HEALTH REGION
LLOYDMINSTER HOSPITAL
3820 43 Ave, Lloydminster, SK, S9V 1Y5
(306) 820-6000
Emp Here 300
SIC 8062 General medical and surgical hospitals

D-U-N-S 25-966-7087   (BR)
PRISZM LP
KFC
4411 50 Ave, Lloydminster, SK, S9V 0P3
(306) 820-4532
Emp Here 35
SIC 5812 Eating places

D-U-N-S 24-630-3150   (BR)
REDHEAD EQUIPMENT
4404 37 Ave, Lloydminster, SK, S9V 0X5
(306) 825-3434
Emp Here 50
SIC 5084 Industrial machinery and equipment

D-U-N-S 25-315-1971   (BR)
REMAI INVESTMENT CORPORATION
BEST CANADIAN MOTOR INN
(*Suby of* Remai Investment Corporation)
4320 44 St, Lloydminster, SK, S9V 1Z9
(306) 825-4400
Emp Here 35
SIC 7011 Hotels and motels

D-U-N-S 20-195-0024   (BR)
WASTE MANAGEMENT OF CANADA CORPORATION
(*Suby of* Waste Management, Inc.)
5104 42 Ave, Lloydminster, SK, S9V 2B4
(306) 825-6511
Emp Here 26
SIC 4953 Refuse systems

Loon Lake, SK S0M

D-U-N-S 20-808-4553   (BR)
MAKWA SAHGAIEHCAN BAND FIRST NATION
MAKWA SAHGAIEHCAN FIRST NATION SCHOOL
Gd, Loon Lake, SK, S0M 1L0
(306) 837-2333
Emp Here 50
SIC 8211 Elementary and secondary schools

D-U-N-S 25-325-6226   (BR)
PRAIRIE NORTH REGIONAL HEALTH AUTHORITY
LOON LAKE HOSPITAL & SPECIAL CARE HOME
(*Suby of* Prairie North Regional Health Authority)
510 2nd Ave, Loon Lake, SK, S0M 1L0
(306) 837-2114
Emp Here 40
SIC 8051 Skilled nursing care facilities

Lucky Lake, SK S0L

D-U-N-S 25-483-4252   (BR)
HEARTLAND   REGIONAL   HEALTH   AUTHORITY
LUCKY LAKE HEALTH CENTRE

309 Railway Ave, Lucky Lake, SK, S0L 1Z0
(306) 858-2116
Emp Here 45
SIC 8322 Individual and family services

D-U-N-S 20-038-3607   (BR)
SUN WEST SCHOOL DIVISION NO 207 SASKATCHEWAN
LUCK LAKE SCHOOL
301 2th Ave S, Lucky Lake, SK, S0L 1Z0
(306) 858-2052
Emp Here 23
SIC 8211 Elementary and secondary schools

Lumsden, SK S0G

D-U-N-S 24-690-7778   (SL)
LUMSDEN & DISTRICT HERITAGE HOME INC
10 Aspen Bay, Lumsden, SK, S0G 3C0
(306) 731-2247
Emp Here 70   *Sales* 3,283,232
SIC 8051 Skilled nursing care facilities

D-U-N-S 24-129-7394   (BR)
PRAIRIE VALLEY SCHOOL DIVISION NO 208
LUMSDEN HIGH SCHOOL
300 Broad St, Lumsden, SK, S0G 3C0
(306) 731-2262
Emp Here 30
SIC 8211 Elementary and secondary schools

D-U-N-S 20-621-1042   (BR)
PRAIRIE VALLEY SCHOOL DIVISION NO 208
LUMSDEN ELEMENTARY SCHOOL
200 2nd Ave W, Lumsden, SK, S0G 3C0
(306) 731-3338
Emp Here 46
SIC 8211 Elementary and secondary schools

D-U-N-S 20-890-5161   (BR)
PRAIRIE VALLEY SCHOOL DIVISION NO 208
ARM RIVER SCHOOL
Po Box 570, Lumsden, SK, S0G 3C0
(306) 731-2280
Emp Here 20
SIC 8211 Elementary and secondary schools

Luseland, SK S0L

D-U-N-S 25-000-5949   (BR)
LIVING SKY SCHOOL DIVISION NO. 202
LUSELAND SCHOOL
701 Prospect Ave, Luseland, SK, S0L 2A0
(306) 372-4412
Emp Here 25
SIC 8211 Elementary and secondary schools

Macklin, SK S0L

D-U-N-S 24-345-8507   (BR)
LIVING SKY SCHOOL DIVISION NO. 202
MACKLIN SCHOOL
5001 Herald St, Macklin, SK, S0L 2C0
(306) 753-2375
Emp Here 55
SIC 8211 Elementary and secondary schools

Maidstone, SK S0M

D-U-N-S 24-334-6843   (BR)
NORTHWEST SCHOOL DIVISION 203

MAIDSTONE HIGH SCHOOL
207 2nd St, Maidstone, SK, S0M 1M0
(306) 893-2351
Emp Here 22
SIC 8211 Elementary and secondary schools

D-U-N-S 24-334-6801   (BR)
NORTHWEST SCHOOL DIVISION 203
RATUSHNIAK ELEMENTARY SCHOOL
220 3rd Ave E, Maidstone, SK, S0M 1M0
(306) 893-2634
Emp Here 31
SIC 8211 Elementary and secondary schools

D-U-N-S 20-875-4742   (BR)
PRAIRIE NORTH REGIONAL HEALTH AUTHORITY
MAIDSTONE MEDICAL CLINIC
(*Suby of* Prairie North Regional Health Authority)
214 5 Ave E, Maidstone, SK, S0M 1M0
(306) 893-2689
Emp Here 20
SIC 8011 Offices and clinics of medical doctors

D-U-N-S 24-343-6958   (BR)
PRAIRIE NORTH REGIONAL HEALTH AUTHORITY
MAIDSTONE UNION HOSPITAL
(*Suby of* Prairie North Regional Health Authority)
214 5th Ave E, Maidstone, SK, S0M 1M0
(306) 893-2622
Emp Here 50
SIC 8062 General medical and surgical hospitals

Mankota, SK S0H

D-U-N-S 24-345-2930   (BR)
CYPRESS HEALTH REGION
PRAIRIE VIEW HEALTH CENTRE
241 1st St, Mankota, SK, S0H 2W0
(306) 478-2200
Emp Here 45
SIC 8011 Offices and clinics of medical doctors

Maple Creek, SK S0N

D-U-N-S 20-712-9102   (BR)
CHINOOK SCHOOL DIVISION NO 211
MAPLE CREEK COMPOSITE HIGH SCHOOL
(*Suby of* Chinook School Division No 211)
311 Louis Ave, Maple Creek, SK, S0N 1N0
(306) 662-2655
Emp Here 35
SIC 8211 Elementary and secondary schools

D-U-N-S 24-655-3341   (SL)
HUTTERIAN BRETHERN CHURCH OF DOWNIE LAKE INC
DOWNIE LAKE COLONY
Gd, Maple Creek, SK, S0N 1N0
(306) 662-3462
Emp Here 75   *Sales* 4,961,328
SIC 8661 Religious organizations

D-U-N-S 24-718-1621   (SL)
MAPLE CREEK HOSPITAL
575 Hwy 21 S, Maple Creek, SK, S0N 1N0
(306) 662-2611
Emp Here 66   *Sales* 4,596,524
SIC 8062 General medical and surgical hospitals

D-U-N-S 20-292-8524   (BR)
MIDWEST SURVEYS INC
25 Pacific Ave, Maple Creek, SK, S0N 1N0

(306) 662-3677
Emp Here 25
SIC 8713 Surveying services

D-U-N-S 24-027-9765   (BR)
TRANSGAS LIMITED
728 Pacific Ave, Maple Creek, SK, S0N 1N0
(306) 558-3310
Emp Here 20
SIC 4923 Gas transmission and distribution

Marcelin, SK S0J

D-U-N-S 20-713-0126   (BR)
PRAIRIE SPIRIT SCHOOL DIVISION NO. 206
LAKE VISTA PUBLIC SCHOOL
Gd, Marcelin, SK, S0J 1R0
(306) 683-2800
Emp Here 50
SIC 8211 Elementary and secondary schools

Marengo, SK S0L

D-U-N-S 20-712-9540   (BR)
SUN WEST SCHOOL DIVISION NO 207 SASKATCHEWAN
WEST
2 2nd Ave N, Marengo, SK, S0L 2K0
(306) 968-2933
Emp Here 20
SIC 8211 Elementary and secondary schools

Martensville, SK S0K

D-U-N-S 20-066-0525   (BR)
PRAIRIE SPIRIT SCHOOL DIVISION NO. 206
VENTURE HEIGHTS ELEMENTARY SCHOOL
801 6 St N, Martensville, SK, S0K 2T0
(306) 934-2185
Emp Here 60
SIC 8211 Elementary and secondary schools

D-U-N-S 20-068-2073   (BR)
PRAIRIE SPIRIT SCHOOL DIVISION NO. 206
VALLEY MANOR ELEMENTARY SCHOOL
200 8th Ave S, Martensville, SK, S0K 2T0
(306) 931-2233
Emp Here 50
SIC 8211 Elementary and secondary schools

D-U-N-S 25-013-5225   (BR)
PRAIRIE SPIRIT SCHOOL DIVISION NO. 206
MARTENSVILLE HIGH SCHOOL
115 6th St N Ss 3, Martensville, SK, S0K 2T2
(306) 931-2230
Emp Here 30
SIC 8211 Elementary and secondary schools

D-U-N-S 24-349-7059   (BR)
RANCH EHRLO SOCIETY
CORMAN PARK
Gd, Martensville, SK, S0K 2T0
(306) 659-3100
Emp Here 50
SIC 8361 Residential care

D-U-N-S 25-091-4637   (BR)
SASKATOON CO-OPERATIVE ASSOCIATION LIMITED, THE
MARTENSVILLE CO-OP
7 Centennial Dr Unit 8, Martensville, SK, S0K 2T0
(306) 933-0390
Emp Here 20

SIC 5541 Gasoline service stations

Maymont, SK S0M

D-U-N-S 24-613-9062   (BR)
LIVING SKY SCHOOL DIVISION NO. 202
MAYMONT CENTRAL SCHOOL
200 1st St E, Maymont, SK, S0M 1T0
(306) 389-2045
Emp Here 25
SIC 8211 Elementary and secondary schools

Meadow Lake, SK S9X

D-U-N-S 20-741-6632   (BR)
HUDSON'S BAY COMPANY
FIELDS STORES
719 1st Ave W, Meadow Lake, SK, S9X 1T6
(306) 236-3666
Emp Here 25
SIC 5311 Department stores

D-U-N-S 25-071-9184   (BR)
LOBLAWS INC
EXTRA FOODS 9040, DIV. OF
828 9th St W, Meadow Lake, SK, S9X 1S9
(306) 236-8330
Emp Here 20
SIC 5411 Grocery stores

D-U-N-S 20-588-3403   (SL)
MEADOW LAKE HOME HARDWARE BUILDING CENTRE LTD
HOME HARDWARE BUILDING CTR
802 1st St W, Meadow Lake, SK, S9X 1E2
(306) 236-4467
Emp Here 50   *Sales* 4,815,406
SIC 5251 Hardware stores

D-U-N-S 20-064-3286   (SL)
NORTHLAND CHRYSLER INC
802 1st Ave W, Meadow Lake, SK, S9X 1Z6
(306) 236-4411
Emp Here 20   *Sales* 7,296,070
SIC 5511 New and used car dealers
Pr Pr Jeffery Fechter
 Ginger Fechter

D-U-N-S 20-033-2927   (BR)
NORTHWEST SCHOOL DIVISION 203
JONAS SAMSON JUNIOR HIGH
715 7th Ave W, Meadow Lake, SK, S9X 1A7
(306) 236-5686
Emp Here 46
SIC 8211 Elementary and secondary schools

D-U-N-S 20-033-2935   (BR)
NORTHWEST SCHOOL DIVISION 203
LAKEVIEW ELEMENTARY SCHOOL
304 8th Ave E, Meadow Lake, SK, S9X 1G9
(306) 236-5810
Emp Here 32
SIC 8211 Elementary and secondary schools

D-U-N-S 25-593-5199   (SL)
PINERIDGE FORD SALES LTD
413 4 Hwy S, Meadow Lake, SK, S9X 1Z5
(306) 236-1810
Emp Here 27   *Sales* 13,251,600
SIC 5511 New and used car dealers
Pr Pr Kirt Prete
Pr Pr Larry Moeller

D-U-N-S 24-112-0252   (BR)
PRAIRIE NORTH REGIONAL HEALTH AUTHORITY
MEADOW LAKE UNION HOSPITAL
(*Suby of* Prairie North Regional Health Authority)
711 Centre St Suite 7, Meadow Lake, SK, S9X 1E6

(306) 236-1550
Emp Here 100
SIC 8062 General medical and surgical hospitals

Melfort, SK S0E

D-U-N-S 20-016-8318   (BR)
CERVUS AG EQUIPMENT LTD
2320 Saskatchewan Dr, Melfort, SK, S0E 1A0
(306) 752-9344
Emp Here 45
SIC 5999 Miscellaneous retail stores, nec

D-U-N-S 24-317-9699   (BR)
CUMBERLAND COLLEGE
400 Burns Ave E, Melfort, SK, S0E 1A0
(306) 752-2786
Emp Here 20
SIC 8221 Colleges and universities

D-U-N-S 20-731-8044   (BR)
KELSEY TRAIL REGIONAL HEALTH AUTHORITY
(*Suby of* Kelsey Trail Regional Health Authority)
505 Broadway Ave N, Melfort, SK, S0E 1A0
(306) 752-8700
Emp Here 100
SIC 8062 General medical and surgical hospitals

D-U-N-S 25-174-2482   (BR)
LOBLAWS INC
EXTRA FOODS
620a Sasketchewan Ave, Melfort, SK, S0E 1A0
(306) 752-9725
Emp Here 75
SIC 5411 Grocery stores

D-U-N-S 25-266-6433   (BR)
MNP LLP
601 Main St, Melfort, SK, S0E 1A0
(306) 752-5800
Emp Here 29
SIC 8721 Accounting, auditing, and bookkeeping

D-U-N-S 24-408-9574   (SL)
NORTH EAST OUTREACH AND SUPPORT SERVICES, INC
128 Mckendry Ave W, Melfort, SK, S0E 1A0
(306) 752-9464
Emp Here 40   *Sales* 5,034,288
SIC 8699 Membership organizations, nec
Ch Bd Brenda Ives
Sec Kristin Willerton
Dir Blair Michaliew
Dir Kristin Lee
Dir Katie Adair
Dir Rick Peters
Dir Brandi Moskal
Dir Christine Honeyman
Dir Heather Burns
Dir Peter Waldbillig

D-U-N-S 20-743-3207   (BR)
NORTH EAST SCHOOL DIVISION
MELFORT & UNIT COMPREHENSIVE COLLEGIATE
801 Assiniboia St, Melfort, SK, S0E 1A0
(306) 752-2891
Emp Here 55
SIC 8211 Elementary and secondary schools

D-U-N-S 20-910-2388   (BR)
NORTH EAST SCHOOL DIVISION
BRUNSWICK ELEMENTARY SCHOOL
501 Bemister Ave E, Melfort, SK, S0E 1A0
(306) 752-5771
Emp Here 25
SIC 8211 Elementary and secondary schools

D-U-N-S 20-713-0373   (BR)

NORTH EAST SCHOOL DIVISION
MUDEBURKE COMMUNITY SCHOOL
202 Melfort St, Melfort, SK, S0E 1A0
(306) 752-2391
Emp Here 50
SIC 8211 Elementary and secondary schools

D-U-N-S 24-347-7275   (BR)
NORTH EAST SCHOOL DIVISION
BURKE ELEMENTARY SCHOOL
202 Melfort St E, Melfort, SK, S0E 1A0
(306) 752-2391
Emp Here 25
SIC 8211 Elementary and secondary schools

D-U-N-S 24-346-7870   (BR)
NORTH EAST SCHOOL DIVISION
REYNOLDS CENTRAL SCHOOL
900 Alberta St N, Melfort, SK, S0E 1A0
(306) 752-2525
Emp Here 24
SIC 8211 Elementary and secondary schools

D-U-N-S 24-354-2094   (BR)
PRAIRIE NORTH CO-OPERATIVE LIMITED
Hwy 3 W, Melfort, SK, S0E 1A0
(306) 752-2555
Emp Here 25
SIC 5983 Fuel oil dealers

D-U-N-S 24-917-1075   (BR)
REDHEAD EQUIPMENT
2420 Saskatchewan Dr S, Melfort, SK, S0E 1A0
(306) 752-2273
Emp Here 30
SIC 5084 Industrial machinery and equipment

D-U-N-S 25-315-3050   (BR)
RIDSDALE TRANSPORT LTD
909 Charles St, Melfort, SK, S0E 1A0
(306) 752-5363
Emp Here 20
SIC 4213 Trucking, except local

Melville, SK S0A

D-U-N-S 20-713-0423   (BR)
CHRIST THE TEACHER CATHOLIC SCHOOLS DIVISION 212
ST. HENRY'S SENIOR ELEMENTARY SCHOOL
1255 Prince Edward St, Melville, SK, S0A 2P0
(306) 728-3877
Emp Here 20
SIC 8211 Elementary and secondary schools

D-U-N-S 24-103-9408   (BR)
COMPAGNIE DES CHEMINS DE FER NATIONAUX DU CANADA
C N RAIL
Gd, Melville, SK, S0A 2P0
(306) 728-1751
Emp Here 300
SIC 4111 Local and suburban transit

D-U-N-S 24-357-2893   (BR)
LOBLAWS INC
EXTRA FOODS
100 Halifax St W, Melville, SK, S0A 2P0
(306) 728-6610
Emp Here 50
SIC 5411 Grocery stores

D-U-N-S 25-174-1781   (BR)
LOBLAWS INC
EXTRA FOODS
290 Prince William Dr, Melville, SK, S0A 2P0
(306) 728-6615
Emp Here 75
SIC 5411 Grocery stores

D-U-N-S 20-841-9465   (HQ)
SASKATCHEWAN CROP INSURANCE CORPORATION

---

484 Prince William Dr, Melville, SK, S0A 2P0
(306) 728-7200
Emp Here 121   *Emp Total* 40,372
Sales 370,727,912
SIC 6331 Fire, marine, and casualty insurance
Genl Mgr Cam Swan
 Lorne Warnes
 Alanna Coch
 Nithi Govindasamy
 Glen Clarke
 Doug Gattinger

D-U-N-S 20-656-5249   (BR)
SUNRISE REGIONAL HEALTH AUTHORITY
SUNRISE HEALTH REGION HOME CARE
200 Heritage Dr, Melville, SK, S0A 2P0
(306) 728-7300
Emp Here 25
SIC 8059 Nursing and personal care, nec

Midale, SK S0C

D-U-N-S 24-894-8528   (SL)
PRO CANADA WEST ENERGY INC
Hwy 39 S, Midale, SK, S0C 1S0
(306) 458-2232
Emp Here 100   *Sales* 4,377,642
SIC 8721 Accounting, auditing, and book-keeping

D-U-N-S 24-341-9129   (BR)
SOUTH EAST CORNERSTONE SCHOOL DIVISION NO. 209
MIDALE CENTRAL SCHOOL
(*Suby of* South East Cornerstone School Division No. 209)
610 College Ave, Midale, SK, S0C 1S0
(306) 458-2480
Emp Here 31
SIC 8211 Elementary and secondary schools

D-U-N-S 25-013-5522   (BR)
SUN COUNTRY REGIONAL HEALTH AUTHORITY
MAINPRIZE MANOR AND HEALTH CENTRE
206 South St, Midale, SK, S0C 1S0
(306) 458-2995
Emp Here 35
SIC 8051 Skilled nursing care facilities

Midale, SK S4H

D-U-N-S 24-227-3980   (BR)
APACHE CANADA LTD
(*Suby of* Apache Corporation)
Gd, Midale, SK, S4H 3M8
(306) 458-2884
Emp Here 30
SIC 1389 Oil and gas field services, nec

Middle Lake, SK S0K

D-U-N-S 20-843-1833   (SL)
BETHANY PIONEER VILLAGE INC
Gd, Middle Lake, SK, S0K 2X0
(306) 367-2033
Emp Here 50   *Sales* 2,261,782
SIC 8051 Skilled nursing care facilities

D-U-N-S 20-712-9979   (BR)
HORIZON SCHOOL DIVISION NO 205
THREE LAKES SCHOOL
301 2 Ave S, Middle Lake, SK, S0K 2X0
(306) 367-2122
Emp Here 20
SIC 8211 Elementary and secondary schools

Milestone, SK S0G

D-U-N-S 20-712-6686   (BR)
SOUTH EAST CORNERSTONE SCHOOL DIVISION NO. 209
MILESTONE SCHOOL
(*Suby of* South East Cornerstone School Division No. 209)
415 Prairie Avenue, Milestone, SK, S0G 3L0
(306) 436-2292
Emp Here 20
SIC 8211 Elementary and secondary schools

Montreal Lake, SK S0J

D-U-N-S 25-454-1832   (BR)
PRINCE ALBERT GRAND COUNCIL
MONTREAL LAKE SCHOOL
Gd, Montreal Lake, SK, S0J 1Y0
(306) 663-5602
Emp Here 40
SIC 8351 Child day care services

Moose Jaw, SK S0H

D-U-N-S 20-333-3687   (BR)
SIMPSON SEEDS INC
1170 N Service Rd, Moose Jaw, SK, S0H 0N0
(306) 693-9402
Emp Here 30
SIC 5153 Grain and field beans

Moose Jaw, SK S6H

D-U-N-S 25-803-4263   (BR)
BANK OF NOVA SCOTIA, THE
SCOTIABANK
303 Main St N, Moose Jaw, SK, S6H 0W2
(306) 693-3691
Emp Here 22
SIC 6021 National commercial banks

D-U-N-S 25-168-0393   (BR)
BOMBARDIER INC
BOMBARDIER AERONAUTIQUE
Po Box 5000 Stn Main, Moose Jaw, SK, S6H 7Z8
(306) 694-2222
Emp Here 180
SIC 8299 Schools and educational services, nec

D-U-N-S 20-064-8020   (SL)
CANADAY'S APPAREL LTD
(*Suby of* Four J & M Holdings Ltd)
115 Coronation Dr, Moose Jaw, SK, S6H 4P3
(306) 692-6406
Emp Here 90
SIC 2325 Men's and boys' trousers and slacks

D-U-N-S 25-289-0132   (BR)
CANADA POST CORPORATION
CANADA POST
63 Ross St W, Moose Jaw, SK, S6H 2M2
(306) 691-4770
Emp Here 50
SIC 4311 U.s. postal service

D-U-N-S 20-517-1684   (BR)
CANADA TRUST COMPANY, THE
(*Suby of* Toronto-Dominion Bank, The)
145 Main St N, Moose Jaw, SK, S6H 0V9

Emp Here 29
SIC 6021 National commercial banks

D-U-N-S 25-999-9464   (BR)

CANADIAN PACIFIC RAILWAY COMPANY
CPR
3 Manitoba St W, Moose Jaw, SK, S6H 1P8
(306) 693-5421
Emp Here 125
SIC 4011 Railroads, line-haul operating

D-U-N-S 24-099-0791   (BR)
CANADIAN PACIFIC RAILWAY COMPANY
CPR
3 Manitoba St W, Moose Jaw, SK, S6H 1P8
(306) 693-5422
Emp Here 450
SIC 4011 Railroads, line-haul operating

D-U-N-S 24-466-4702   (SL)
CARDINAL CONSTRUCTION CO. LTD
340 8th Ave Nw, Moose Jaw, SK, S6H 4E7
(306) 692-0677
Emp Here 20   *Sales* 5,006,160
SIC 1542 Nonresidential construction, nec
Pr Pr Brent Waldo
 Grant Robbins

D-U-N-S 20-841-4235   (BR)
CARGILL LIMITED
Gd Lcd Main, Moose Jaw, SK, S6H 4N6
(306) 693-3651
Emp Here 20
SIC 5191 Farm supplies

D-U-N-S 20-755-9477   (SL)
CHARTIER HOTELS LTD
PRAIRIE OASIS COMPLEX
955 Thatcher Dr E, Moose Jaw, SK, S6H 4N9
(306) 692-4894
Emp Here 70   *Sales* 3,064,349
SIC 7011 Hotels and motels

D-U-N-S 25-142-4313   (SL)
CHILLER'S BREW PUB AND EATERY
510 Home St W, Moose Jaw, SK, S6H 7P4
(306) 694-5100
Emp Here 50   *Sales* 1,532,175
SIC 5812 Eating places

D-U-N-S 20-725-5428   (BR)
CONEXUS CREDIT UNION 2006
MOOSE JAW-HIGH BRANCH
80 High St W, Moose Jaw, SK, S6H 1S3
(306) 691-4800
Emp Here 24
SIC 6062 State credit unions

D-U-N-S 20-704-1240   (BR)
CONSEIL DES ECOLES FRANSASKOISES
ECOLE DUCHARME
340 Ominica St W, Moose Jaw, SK, S6H 1X5
(306) 691-0068
Emp Here 20
SIC 8211 Elementary and secondary schools

D-U-N-S 20-268-1941   (BR)
DOEPKER INDUSTRIES LTD
1955 Caribou St, Moose Jaw, SK, S6H 4P2
(306) 693-2525
Emp Here 100
SIC 3715 Truck trailers

D-U-N-S 20-852-7614   (BR)
EXTENDICARE INC
EXTENDICARE MOOSE JAW
1151 Coteau St W, Moose Jaw, SK, S6H 5G5
(306) 693-5191
Emp Here 160
SIC 8051 Skilled nursing care facilities

D-U-N-S 20-654-2453   (BR)
FGL SPORTS LTD
SPORT CHEK
1235 Main St N Unit 13, Moose Jaw, SK, S6H 6M4
(306) 694-7777
Emp Here 25
SIC 5941 Sporting goods and bicycle shops

D-U-N-S 24-338-5338   (BR)
FIVE HILLS REGIONAL HEALTH AUTHORITY

PIONEERS HOUSING
(*Suby of* Five Hills Regional Health Authority)
1000 Albert St, Moose Jaw, SK, S6H 2Y2
(306) 693-4616
Emp Here 105
SIC 8051 Skilled nursing care facilities

D-U-N-S 20-448-7649   (BR)
GATX RAIL CANADA CORPORATION
CORPORATION GATX RAIL CANADA
2200 Caribou St W, Moose Jaw, SK, S6H 4P4
(306) 692-7070
Emp Here 50
SIC 4789 Transportation services, nec

D-U-N-S 25-453-8390   (BR)
GOVERNING COUNCIL OF THE SALVATION ARMY IN CANADA, THE
GOVERNING COUNCIL OF THE SALVATION ARMY IN CANADA, THE
175 1st Ave Ne, Moose Jaw, SK, S6H 0Y9
(306) 692-2844
Emp Here 27
SIC 5932 Used merchandise stores

D-U-N-S 20-712-7726   (BR)
HOLY TRINITY ROMAN CATHOLIC SEPARATE SCHOOL DIVISION #22
ST AGNES SCHOOL
330 Oxford St W, Moose Jaw, SK, S6H 2P2
(306) 694-1767
Emp Here 32
SIC 8211 Elementary and secondary schools

D-U-N-S 25-174-6491   (BR)
HOLY TRINITY ROMAN CATHOLIC SEPARATE SCHOOL DIVISION #22
VANIER COLLEGIATE
324 Macdonald St, Moose Jaw, SK, S6H 2V4
(306) 693-6744
Emp Here 45
SIC 8211 Elementary and secondary schools

D-U-N-S 25-174-8315   (BR)
HOLY TRINITY ROMAN CATHOLIC SEPARATE SCHOOL DIVISION #22
ECOLE ST MARGARET
495 5th Ave Ne, Moose Jaw, SK, S6H 0J9
(306) 694-4044
Emp Here 25
SIC 8211 Elementary and secondary schools

D-U-N-S 20-712-7759   (BR)
HOLY TRINITY ROMAN CATHOLIC SEPARATE SCHOOL DIVISION #22
ST MICHAEL SCHOOL
1111 Brown St, Moose Jaw, SK, S6H 4L2
(306) 693-7693
Emp Here 50
SIC 8211 Elementary and secondary schools

D-U-N-S 20-712-7767   (BR)
HOLY TRINITY ROMAN CATHOLIC SEPARATE SCHOOL DIVISION #22
SACRED HEART COMMUNITY SCHOOL
1020 12th Ave Sw, Moose Jaw, SK, S6H 5X8
(306) 694-1622
Emp Here 36
SIC 8211 Elementary and secondary schools

D-U-N-S 25-360-9218   (BR)
MEDIAS TRANSCONTINENTAL INC
MEDIAS TRANSCONTINENTAL INC
44 Fairford St W, Moose Jaw, SK, S6H 1V1
(306) 692-6441
Emp Here 55
SIC 2711 Newspapers

D-U-N-S 25-177-9880   (BR)
PRAIRIE SOUTH SCHOOL DIVISION NO 210
ECOLE ROSS SCHOOL
350 Oak St, Moose Jaw, SK, S6H 0V6
(306) 692-5796
Emp Here 30
SIC 8211 Elementary and secondary schools

D-U-N-S 25-181-2210   (BR)

PRAIRIE SOUTH SCHOOL DIVISION NO 210
PRINCE ARTHUR SCHOOL
645 Athabasca St E, Moose Jaw, SK, S6H 7Z5
(306) 692-3904
Emp Here 40
SIC 8211 Elementary and secondary schools

D-U-N-S 25-175-7043   (BR)
PRAIRIE SOUTH SCHOOL DIVISION NO 210
PALLISER HEIGHTS SCHOOL
1140 Simpson Ave, Moose Jaw, SK, S6H 4M8
(306) 693-4669
Emp Here 60
SIC 8211 Elementary and secondary schools

D-U-N-S 20-712-7049   (BR)
PRAIRIE SOUTH SCHOOL DIVISION NO 210
KING GEORGE SCHOOL
1150 5th Ave Nw, Moose Jaw, SK, S6H 3Y7
(306) 692-3908
Emp Here 30
SIC 8211 Elementary and secondary schools

D-U-N-S 25-174-6095   (BR)
PRAIRIE SOUTH SCHOOL DIVISION NO 210
CENTRAL COLLEGIATE INSTITUTE
149 Oxford St W, Moose Jaw, SK, S6H 2N4
(306) 693-4691
Emp Here 45
SIC 8211 Elementary and secondary schools

D-U-N-S 25-175-7050   (BR)
PRAIRIE SOUTH SCHOOL DIVISION NO 210
RIVERVIEW COLLEGIATE
650 Coteau St W Suite 210, Moose Jaw, SK, S6H 5E6
(306) 693-1331
Emp Here 36
SIC 8211 Elementary and secondary schools

D-U-N-S 25-174-6079   (BR)
PRAIRIE SOUTH SCHOOL DIVISION NO 210
WESTMOUNT SCHOOL
1100 Currie Cres, Moose Jaw, SK, S6H 5M8
(306) 694-5999
Emp Here 35
SIC 8211 Elementary and secondary schools

D-U-N-S 20-033-2158   (BR)
PRAIRIE SOUTH SCHOOL DIVISION NO 210
EMPIRE COMMUNITY SCHOOL
550 Coteau St W, Moose Jaw, SK, S6H 5E4
(306) 692-3903
Emp Here 35
SIC 8211 Elementary and secondary schools

D-U-N-S 25-091-3381   (BR)
PRAIRIE SOUTH SCHOOL DIVISION NO 210
A E PEACOCK COLLEGIATE
145 Ross St E, Moose Jaw, SK, S6H 0S3
(306) 693-4626
Emp Here 75
SIC 8211 Elementary and secondary schools

D-U-N-S 20-712-7056   (BR)
PRAIRIE SOUTH SCHOOL DIVISION NO 210
WILLIAM GRAYSON SCHOOL
823 Caribou St W, Moose Jaw, SK, S6H 2L2
(306) 692-4659
Emp Here 25
SIC 8211 Elementary and secondary schools

D-U-N-S 25-193-4022   (SL)
PUGLIA, P. M. SALES LTD
CANADIAN TIRE
1350 Main St N, Moose Jaw, SK, S6H 8B9
(306) 693-0888
Emp Here 60   *Sales* 4,888,367
SIC 5399 Miscellaneous general merchandise

D-U-N-S 25-799-5472   (BR)
ROYAL BANK OF CANADA
RBC
(*Suby of* Royal Bank Of Canada)
52 High St W, Moose Jaw, SK, S6H 1S3
(306) 691-4100
Emp Here 45
SIC 6021 National commercial banks

D-U-N-S 24-350-2072   (BR)
SASKATCHEWAN GAMING CORPORATION
CASINO MOOSE JAW
21 Fairford St E, Moose Jaw, SK, S6H 0C8
(306) 694-3888
Emp Here 100
SIC 7011 Hotels and motels

D-U-N-S 20-039-3648   (BR)
SASKATCHEWAN GOVERNMENT INSURANCE
S G I CLAIMS
105 4th Ave Nw, Moose Jaw, SK, S6H 7P1
(306) 691-4500
Emp Here 24
SIC 6331 Fire, marine, and casualty insurance

D-U-N-S 24-733-1291   (BR)
SASKATCHEWAN INSTITUTE OF APPLIED SCIENCE AND TECHNOLOGY
PALLISER CAMPUS
600 Saskatchewan St W, Moose Jaw, SK, S6H 2Z9
(306) 691-8200
Emp Here 330
SIC 8222 Junior colleges

D-U-N-S 24-345-0975   (BR)
SASKATCHEWAN TELECOMMUNICATIONS INTERNATIONAL, INC
SASKTEL WAREHOUSE
55 Ominica St W, Moose Jaw, SK, S6H 1W8
(306) 693-8152
Emp Here 58
SIC 4899 Communication services, nec

D-U-N-S 20-006-0002   (BR)
SEARS CANADA INC
1235 Main St N Suite 28, Moose Jaw, SK, S6H 6M4
(306) 692-7851
Emp Here 80
SIC 5311 Department stores

D-U-N-S 25-272-0040   (BR)
SOBEYS WEST INC
MOOSE JAW SAFEWAY
200 1st Ave Nw, Moose Jaw, SK, S6H 1K9
(306) 693-8033
Emp Here 80
SIC 5411 Grocery stores

D-U-N-S 25-988-7180   (BR)
TEMPLE GARDENS MINERAL SPA INC
HARWOODS
(*Suby of* Temple Gardens Mineral Spa Inc)
24 Fairford St E, Moose Jaw, SK, S6H 0C7
(306) 693-7778
Emp Here 50
SIC 5812 Eating places

D-U-N-S 24-915-8395   (BR)
VITERRA INC
AGPRO GRAIN
2575 24th Ave, Moose Jaw, SK, S6H 4N8
(306) 694-1070
Emp Here 38
SIC 4221 Farm product warehousing and storage

D-U-N-S 24-968-6825   (BR)
WESTCAN BULK TRANSPORT LTD
(*Suby of* The Kenan Advantage Group Inc)
850 Manitoba St E, Moose Jaw, SK, S6H 4P1
(306) 692-6478
Emp Here 80
SIC 4213 Trucking, except local

Moose Jaw, SK S6J

D-U-N-S 24-351-6189   (BR)
BOSTON PIZZA INTERNATIONAL INC
1650 Main St N, Moose Jaw, SK, S6J 1L3
(306) 691-2222
Emp Here 20
SIC 5812 Eating places

D-U-N-S 24-774-6001   (SL)
COR-BON ENTERPRISES LTD
BONANZA RESTAURANT
1707 Main St N, Moose Jaw, SK, S6J 1L6
(306) 692-9891
Emp Here 65   *Sales* 1,969,939
SIC 5812 Eating places

D-U-N-S 20-695-3353   (HQ)
FIVE HILLS REGIONAL HEALTH AUTHORITY
FIVE HILLS HEALTH REGION
(*Suby of* Five Hills Regional Health Authority)
55 Diefenbaker Dr, Moose Jaw, SK, S6J 0C2
(306) 694-0200
Emp Here 100   *Emp Total* 1,700
Sales 3,868,360
SIC 8062 General medical and surgical hospitals

D-U-N-S 25-205-1701   (BR)
GOLDEN WEST BROADCASTING LTD
800 CHAB
1704 Main St N, Moose Jaw, SK, S6J 1L4
(306) 694-0800
Emp Here 35
SIC 4832 Radio broadcasting stations

D-U-N-S 24-234-3028   (SL)
MOOSE JAW EXHIBITION COMPANY, LIMITED, THE
250 Thatcher Dr E, Moose Jaw, SK, S6J 1L7
(306) 692-2723
Emp Here 56   *Sales* 3,064,349
SIC 7999 Amusement and recreation, nec

D-U-N-S 24-113-0095   (SL)
SASCO DEVELOPMENTS LTD
HERITAGE INN
1590 Main St N, Moose Jaw, SK, S6J 1L3
(306) 693-7550
Emp Here 75   *Sales* 3,283,232
SIC 7011 Hotels and motels

D-U-N-S 20-213-7589   (BR)
SASKENERGY INCORPORATED
51 Highland Rd, Moose Jaw, SK, S6J 1M5
(800) 567-8899
Emp Here 25
SIC 4924 Natural gas distribution

D-U-N-S 20-555-0598   (BR)
STAPLES CANADA INC
STAPLES
(*Suby of* Staples, Inc.)
451 Thatcher Dr E, Moose Jaw, SK, S6J 1L8
(306) 694-6800
Emp Here 25
SIC 5943 Stationery stores

D-U-N-S 20-015-8074   (BR)
TAYLOR MOTOR SALES LTD
MOOSE JAW TOYOTA
1743 Main St N, Moose Jaw, SK, S6J 1L6
(306) 694-1355
Emp Here 25
SIC 5511 New and used car dealers

D-U-N-S 25-177-1176   (BR)
WAL-MART CANADA CORP
551 Thatcher Dr E Suite 3173, Moose Jaw, SK, S6J 1L8
(306) 693-3218
Emp Here 200
SIC 5311 Department stores

Moosomin, SK S0G

D-U-N-S 24-116-1801   (BR)
FEDERATED CO-OPERATIVES LIMITED
CO-OP FEEDS
(*Suby of* Federated Co-Operatives Limited)
806 Park Ave, Moosomin, SK, S0G 3N0
(306) 435-3331
Emp Here 24
SIC 5191 Farm supplies

D-U-N-S 25-359-3875   (HQ)
GREENLINE EQUIPMENT LTD
(*Suby of* Cervus Corporation)
Po Box 860, Moosomin, SK, S0G 3N0
(306) 435-3301
Emp Here 30   *Emp Total* 145
Sales 7,234,560
SIC 5999 Miscellaneous retail stores, nec
Pr Pr David Heide

D-U-N-S 25-056-7034   (BR)
MAPLE FARM EQUIPMENT PARTNERSHIP
Hwy 8 N, Moosomin, SK, S0G 3N0
(306) 435-3301
Emp Here 35
SIC 5999 Miscellaneous retail stores, nec

D-U-N-S 25-013-6066   (BR)
REGINA QU'APPELLE REGIONAL HEALTH AUTHORITY
HOME CARE
601 Wright Rd, Moosomin, SK, S0G 3N0
(306) 435-3888
Emp Here 50
SIC 8322 Individual and family services

D-U-N-S 24-347-5527   (BR)
SOUTH EAST CORNERSTONE SCHOOL DIVISION NO. 209
MCNAUGHTON HIGH SCHOOL
(*Suby of* South East Cornerstone School Division No. 209)
908 Gordon St, Moosomin, SK, S0G 3N0
(306) 435-3341
Emp Here 35
SIC 8211 Elementary and secondary schools

D-U-N-S 24-347-5519   (BR)
SOUTH EAST CORNERSTONE SCHOOL DIVISION NO. 209
MACLEOD ELEMENTARY SCHOOL
(*Suby of* South East Cornerstone School Division No. 209)
1016 Gordon St, Moosomin, SK, S0G 3N0
(306) 435-3878
Emp Here 30
SIC 8211 Elementary and secondary schools

Mossbank, SK S0H

D-U-N-S 25-681-0664   (HQ)
SOUTH COUNTRY AG LTD
(*Suby of* South Country AG Ltd)
40 Main St, Mossbank, SK, S0H 3G0

Emp Here 20   *Emp Total* 42
Sales 6,188,450
SIC 6712 Bank holding companies
Pr Pr Robert Linn
 Diana Linn
Dir Duncan Greene
Dir Douglas Sullivan
Dir Chrisopher Clements
Dir Donald Sandbeck
Dir Cari Markewich

D-U-N-S 20-656-5520   (BR)
SOUTH COUNTRY EQUIPMENT LTD
40 Main St N, Mossbank, SK, S0H 3G0
(306) 354-2411
Emp Here 28

SIC 5999 Miscellaneous retail stores, nec

Muenster, SK S0K

D-U-N-S 20-072-1855   (BR)
HORIZON SCHOOL DIVISION NO 205
MUENSTER SCHOOL
301 Scott St, Muenster, SK, S0K 2Y0
(306) 682-4538
Emp Here 25
SIC 8211 Elementary and secondary schools

Naicam, SK S0K

D-U-N-S 24-311-0959   (BR)
CURTIS CONSTRUCTION LTD
(*Suby of* Curtis Construction Ltd)
777 Gird W, Naicam, SK, S0K 2Z0
(306) 874-2299
Emp Here 25
SIC 4953 Refuse systems

D-U-N-S 20-065-2907   (SL)
NAICAM CO-OPERATIVE ASSOCIATION LIMITED, THE
108 Centre St, Naicam, SK, S0K 2Z0
(306) 874-2190
Emp Here 35   *Sales* 10,145,000
SIC 5191 Farm supplies
Genl Mgr Gord Dmytruk
Opers Mgr Denis Sunderland

D-U-N-S 24-346-7862   (BR)
NORTH EAST SCHOOL DIVISION
NAICAM SCHOOL
203 3rd St N, Naicam, SK, S0K 2Z0
(306) 874-2253
Emp Here 25
SIC 8211 Elementary and secondary schools

Neilburg, SK S0M

D-U-N-S 24-334-6819   (BR)
NORTHWEST SCHOOL DIVISION 203
NEILBURG COMPOSITE SCHOOL
410 Gibbons Centre St, Neilburg, SK, S0M 2C0
(306) 823-4313
Emp Here 32
SIC 8211 Elementary and secondary schools

Nipawin, SK S0E

D-U-N-S 20-037-9316   (BR)
BUNGE CANADA
Hwy 35 S, Nipawin, SK, S0E 1E0
(306) 862-4686
Emp Here 72
SIC 2076 Vegetable oil mills, nec

D-U-N-S 25-013-6322   (HQ)
DIAMOND NORTH MANAGEMENT LTD
(*Suby of* Diamond North Management Ltd)
100 First Ave W, Nipawin, SK, S0E 1E0
(306) 862-4651
Emp Here 34   *Emp Total* 50
Sales 9,840,650
SIC 6062 State credit unions
Pr Pr Scott Anderson
VP VP Ray Vandorpe
Genl Mgr John Shenher

D-U-N-S 20-037-8540   (BR)
KELSEY TRAIL REGIONAL HEALTH AUTHORITY
PINEVIEW LODGE

(*Suby of* Kelsey Trail Regional Health Authority)
400 6th Ave E, Nipawin, SK, S0E 1E0
(306) 862-9828
Emp Here 185
SIC 8051 Skilled nursing care facilities

D-U-N-S 24-230-2743   (SL)
KINGFISHER INNS LTD
KINGFISHER INN
1203 8th St W, Nipawin, SK, S0E 1E0
(306) 862-9801
Emp Here 50   *Sales* 2,188,821
SIC 7011 Hotels and motels

D-U-N-S 25-058-2038   (BR)
LOBLAWS INC
EXTRA FOODS 9035
101 Railway Ave W, Nipawin, SK, S0E 1E0
(306) 862-8780
Emp Here 50
SIC 5411 Grocery stores

D-U-N-S 24-346-7938   (BR)
NORTH EAST SCHOOL DIVISION
CENTRAL PARK ELEMENTARY SCHOOL
501 2nd St E, Nipawin, SK, S0E 1E0
(306) 862-5303
Emp Here 35
SIC 8211 Elementary and secondary schools

D-U-N-S 24-346-7912   (BR)
NORTH EAST SCHOOL DIVISION
WAGNER SCHOOL
301 9 Ave W, Nipawin, SK, S0E 1E0
(306) 862-5434
Emp Here 50
SIC 8211 Elementary and secondary schools

D-U-N-S 24-346-7888   (BR)
NORTH EAST SCHOOL DIVISION
WAGNER ELEMEMENTARY SCHOOL
308 9th Ave W, Nipawin, SK, S0E 1E0
(306) 862-5434
Emp Here 20
SIC 8211 Elementary and secondary schools

D-U-N-S 24-347-7218   (BR)
NORTH EAST SCHOOL DIVISION
L P MILLER COMPREHENSIVE SCHOOL
535 6 St E Suite 501, Nipawin, SK, S0E 1E0
(306) 862-4671
Emp Here 64
SIC 8211 Elementary and secondary schools

D-U-N-S 20-191-7650   (BR)
SASKATCHEWAN POWER CORPORATION
SASKPOWER NORTHERN HYDRO
Gd, Nipawin, SK, S0E 1E0
(306) 862-3148
Emp Here 70
SIC 4911 Electric services

Norquay, SK S0A

D-U-N-S 20-065-4879   (SL)
NORQUAY CO-OPERATIVE ASSOCIATION LIMITED, THE
13 Hwy 49, Norquay, SK, S0A 2V0
(306) 594-2215
Emp Here 28   *Sales* 10,039,380
SIC 5211 Lumber and other building materials
Genl Mgr Albert Outhwaite
Pr Pr George Grant
Dir Ken Grywachesky
Dir Ron Perepeluk
Dir Wayne Prokopchuk
Dir Cheryl Holodniuk
Dir Jeremi Korpusik

D-U-N-S 25-013-6439   (SL)
NORQUAY HEALTH CENTRE
Gd, Norquay, SK, S0A 2V0
(306) 594-2133
Emp Here 50   *Sales* 2,261,782

SIC 8051 Skilled nursing care facilities

D-U-N-S 20-532-4747   (BR)
SEARS CANADA INC
11 Main St, Norquay, SK, S0A 2V0
(306) 594-2258
Emp Here 30
SIC 5311 Department stores

North Battleford, SK S9A

D-U-N-S 25-593-7815   (SL)
306632 SASKATCHEWAN LTD
VALLEY FORD SALES
2222 100th St, North Battleford, SK, S9A 0X6
(306) 445-4491
Emp Here 45   *Sales* 32,971,250
SIC 5511 New and used car dealers
Pr Pr Robert Kenny
Treas Todd Heck

D-U-N-S 25-314-4992   (SL)
BATTLEFORD PUBLISHING LTD
NEWS OPTIMIST TELEGRAPH
892 104th St, North Battleford, SK, S9A 1M9
(306) 445-7261
Emp Here 50   *Sales* 4,158,760
SIC 2711 Newspapers

D-U-N-S 20-741-2776   (SL)
BATTLEFORD TRADE & EDUCATION CENTRE INC
702 102nd St, North Battleford, SK, S9A 1E3
(306) 445-6141
Emp Here 20   *Sales* 5,889,600
SIC 8322 Individual and family services
Ex Dir Donald Amos
Pr Julian Stelmaschuk
VP Florence Krilow
Off Mgr Ronda Johnson

D-U-N-S 25-289-0215   (BR)
CANADA POST CORPORATION
1242 100th St, North Battleford, SK, S9A 0V7
(306) 446-4000
Emp Here 20
SIC 4311 U.s. postal service

D-U-N-S 24-455-0724   (BR)
CLIFTON ASSOCIATES LTD
501 104th St, North Battleford, SK, S9A 1M5
(306) 445-1621
Emp Here 40
SIC 8711 Engineering services

D-U-N-S 24-205-8332   (BR)
COMPAGNIE DES CHEMINS DE FER NATIONAUX DU CANADA
75 Railway Ave E, North Battleford, SK, S9A 2P9
(306) 446-5730
Emp Here 40
SIC 4011 Railroads, line-haul operating

D-U-N-S 24-347-1724   (BR)
INNOVATION CREDIT UNION LIMITED
1202 102nd St, North Battleford, SK, S9A 1G3
(306) 446-7000
Emp Here 150
SIC 6062 State credit unions

D-U-N-S 20-361-4180   (BR)
LIGHT OF CHRIST RCSSD
HOLY FAMILY ELEMENTARY
9201 19th Ave, North Battleford, SK, S9A 2W2
(306) 445-2360
Emp Here 28
SIC 8211 Elementary and secondary schools

D-U-N-S 20-835-4055   (BR)
LIGHT OF CHRIST RCSSD
JOHN PAUL II COLLEGIATE SCHOOL
1491 97th St, North Battleford, SK, S9A 0K1
(306) 446-2232
Emp Here 80

SIC 8211 Elementary and secondary schools

D-U-N-S 20-656-6205   (BR)
LIGHT OF CHRIST RCSSD
ECOLE MONSEIGNEUR BLAISE MORAND
1651 96th St, North Battleford, SK, S9A 0H7
(306) 446-2167
Emp Here 32
SIC 8211 Elementary and secondary schools

D-U-N-S 20-033-7041   (BR)
LIGHT OF CHRIST RCSSD
NOTRE DAME SCHOOL
1241 105th St, North Battleford, SK, S9A 1S8
(306) 445-0283
Emp Here 26
SIC 8211 Elementary and secondary schools

D-U-N-S 20-712-7478   (BR)
LIGHT OF CHRIST RCSSD
ST MARY'S COMMUNITY SCHOOL
1352 110th St, North Battleford, SK, S9A 2J1
(306) 445-5152
Emp Here 40
SIC 8211 Elementary and secondary schools

D-U-N-S 20-033-3057   (BR)
LIVING SKY SCHOOL DIVISION NO. 202
BREADY ELEMENTARY SCHOOL
9001 17th Ave, North Battleford, SK, S9A 2V1
(306) 445-4954
Emp Here 25
SIC 8211 Elementary and secondary schools

D-U-N-S 20-033-3073   (BR)
LIVING SKY SCHOOL DIVISION NO. 202
LAWRENCE SCHOOL
1942 102nd St, North Battleford, SK, S9A 1H7
(306) 445-4944
Emp Here 20
SIC 8211 Elementary and secondary schools

D-U-N-S 20-033-2190   (BR)
LIVING SKY SCHOOL DIVISION NO. 202
MCKITRICK SCHOOL
1500 101st St, North Battleford, SK, S9A 1A4
(306) 445-3851
Emp Here 35
SIC 8211 Elementary and secondary schools

D-U-N-S 20-580-6701   (BR)
LIVING SKY SCHOOL DIVISION NO. 202
NORTH BATTLEFORDS COMPREHENSIVE HIGHSCHOOL
1791 110th St, North Battleford, SK, S9A 2Y2
(306) 445-6101
Emp Here 102
SIC 8211 Elementary and secondary schools

D-U-N-S 20-177-9043   (BR)
LOBLAWS INC
REAL CANADIAN WHOLESALE CLUB
11403 Railway Ave E, North Battleford, SK, S9A 2R7
(306) 445-3375
Emp Here 40
SIC 5141 Groceries, general line

D-U-N-S 25-064-8227   (BR)
MAPLE LEAF FOODS INC
MAPLE LEAF CONSUMER FOODS
99 Canola Ave Gd Stn Main Gd Lcd Main, North Battleford, SK, S9A 2X5

Emp Here 27
SIC 2011 Meat packing plants

D-U-N-S 24-818-8195   (HQ)
MIFAB MANUFACTURING INC
(*Suby of* Mifab Manufacturing Inc)
101 Canola Ave, North Battleford, SK, S9A 2Y3

Emp Here 40   *Emp Total* 50
SIC 3431 Metal sanitary ware

D-U-N-S 20-656-4820   (BR)
NORTH BATTLEFORD, CITY OF
AQUATIC CENTRE

1902 106th St, North Battleford, SK, S9A 3G5
(306) 445-1745
Emp Here 24
SIC 7999 Amusement and recreation, nec

D-U-N-S 25-593-7617　　(BR)
PEAVEY INDUSTRIES LIMITED
PEAVEY MART
11442 Railway Ave E, North Battleford, SK, S9A 3P7
(306) 445-6171
Emp Here 20
SIC 5251 Hardware stores

D-U-N-S 20-034-0789　　(BR)
PRAIRIE NORTH HEALTH REGION
COMMUNITY HEALTH
11427 Railway Ave Suite 101, North Battleford, SK, S9A 3G8
(306) 446-6400
Emp Here 30
SIC 8011 Offices and clinics of medical doctors

D-U-N-S 24-343-2858　　(HQ)
PRAIRIE NORTH REGIONAL HEALTH AUTHORITY
PRAIRIE NORTH HEALTH REGION
(*Suby of* Prairie North Regional Health Authority)
1092 107th St, North Battleford, SK, S9A 1Z1
(306) 446-6600
Emp Here 2,000　　*Emp Total* 2,500
Sales 3,766,859
SIC 8062 General medical and surgical hospitals

D-U-N-S 20-034-6208　　(BR)
SASKENERGY INCORPORATED
10010 Fyfe Ave, North Battleford, SK, S9A 3E6

Emp Here 30
SIC 4924 Natural gas distribution

D-U-N-S 20-517-2849　　(BR)
SASKATCHEWAN CROP INSURANCE CORPORATION
1192 102nd St, North Battleford, SK, S9A 1E8
(888) 935-0028
Emp Here 20
SIC 6331 Fire, marine, and casualty insurance

D-U-N-S 25-594-1056　　(BR)
SASKATCHEWAN GOVERNMENT INSURANCE
1002 103rd St, North Battleford, SK, S9A 1K4
(306) 446-1900
Emp Here 20
SIC 6331 Fire, marine, and casualty insurance

D-U-N-S 25-385-8294　　(BR)
SASKATCHEWAN INDIAN GAMING AUTHORITY INC
GOLD EAGLE CASINO
11906 Railway Ave E, North Battleford, SK, S9A 3K7
(306) 446-3833
Emp Here 300
SIC 7999 Amusement and recreation, nec

D-U-N-S 25-451-2023　　(BR)
SASKATCHEWAN TELECOMMUNICATIONS INTERNATIONAL, INC
1201 100th St, North Battleford, SK, S9A 3Z9
(306) 446-5300
Emp Here 35
SIC 4899 Communication services, nec

D-U-N-S 24-101-2264　　(BR)
STAPLES CANADA INC
STAPLES THE BUSINESS DEPOT
(*Suby of* Staples, Inc.)
11429 Railway Ave E, North Battleford, SK, S9A 3G8
(306) 446-5200
Emp Here 20
SIC 5943 Stationery stores

D-U-N-S 20-644-4577　　(SL)
TIM HORTONS
11404 Railway Ave E, North Battleford, SK, S9A 3P7
(306) 445-4474
Emp Here 56　　*Sales* 1,678,096
SIC 5812 Eating places

D-U-N-S 25-593-4895　　(SL)
TROPICAL INN
Gd Lcd Main, North Battleford, SK, S9A 2X5
(306) 446-4700
Emp Here 56　　*Sales* 2,626,585
SIC 7011 Hotels and motels

D-U-N-S 20-447-6212　　(SL)
UNITED ENTERPRISES LTD
HAPPY INN
992 101st St, North Battleford, SK, S9A 0Z3
(306) 445-9425
Emp Here 25　　*Sales* 6,028,800
SIC 7011 Hotels and motels
Pr Pr Pius Pfeifer
　Ida Pfeifer
Genl Mgr Gary Pfeifer
CFO Brian Demonterun

D-U-N-S 25-294-7262　　(BR)
WAL-MART CANADA CORP
601 Carlton Trail Suite 1, North Battleford, SK, S9A 4A9
(306) 445-8105
Emp Here 200
SIC 5311 Department stores

North Portal, SK S0C

D-U-N-S 25-316-1434　　(BR)
COLE INTERNATIONAL INC
528 1st St, North Portal, SK, S0C 1W0
(306) 927-5100
Emp Here 20
SIC 4731 Freight transportation arrangement

Onion Lake, SK S0M

D-U-N-S 20-033-7611　　(BR)
ONION LAKE BOARD OF EDUCATION
EAGLE VIEW COMPREHENSIVE HIGH SCHOOL
(*Suby of* Onion Lake Board of Education)
Gd, Onion Lake, SK, S0M 2E0
(306) 344-2440
Emp Here 40
SIC 8211 Elementary and secondary schools

D-U-N-S 20-038-4167　　(SL)
ONION LAKE HEALTH BOARD INC
ONION LAKE RESERVE
Gd, Onion Lake, SK, S0M 2E0
(306) 344-2330
Emp Here 80　　*Sales* 4,523,563
SIC 8021 Offices and clinics of dentists

Osler, SK S0K

D-U-N-S 20-713-0076　　(BR)
PRAIRIE SPIRIT SCHOOL DIVISION NO. 206
OSLER SCHOOL
205 4th Ave, Osler, SK, S0K 3A0
(306) 239-2077
Emp Here 23
SIC 8211 Elementary and secondary schools

Outlook, SK S0L

D-U-N-S 20-572-2072　　(BR)
BANK OF MONTREAL
BMO
202 Franklin St S, Outlook, SK, S0L 2N0
(306) 867-8689
Emp Here 20
SIC 6021 National commercial banks

D-U-N-S 20-876-5248　　(SL)
OUTLOOK & DISTRICT PIONEER HOME INC
OUTLOOK HEALTH CENTRE
500 Semple St, Outlook, SK, S0L 2N0
(306) 867-8676
Emp Here 80　　*Sales* 3,648,035
SIC 8051 Skilled nursing care facilities

D-U-N-S 20-611-7111　　(HQ)
RIVERBEND CO-OPERATIVE LTD
(*Suby of* Riverbend Co-operative Ltd)
102 Saskatchewan Ave, Outlook, SK, S0L 2N0
(306) 867-8614
Emp Here 70　　*Emp Total* 100
Sales 29,620,122
SIC 5411 Grocery stores
Genl Mgr Jack Nicholson

D-U-N-S 20-716-8399　　(BR)
SUN WEST SCHOOL DIVISION NO 207 SASKATCHEWAN
OUTLOOK ELEMENTARY SCHOOL
515 Franklin St, Outlook, SK, S0L 2N0
(306) 867-8653
Emp Here 31
SIC 8211 Elementary and secondary schools

Oxbow, SK S0C

D-U-N-S 20-712-8898　　(BR)
SOUTH EAST CORNERSTONE SCHOOL DIVISION NO. 209
OXBOW PRAIRIE HEIGHTS SCHOOL
(*Suby of* South East Cornerstone School Division No. 209)
415 Wylie Ave, Oxbow, SK, S0C 2B0
(306) 483-2383
Emp Here 24
SIC 8211 Elementary and secondary schools

D-U-N-S 24-916-9079　　(BR)
SUN COUNTRY REGIONAL HEALTH AUTHORITY
GALLOWAY HEALTH CENTRE
917 Tupper St, Oxbow, SK, S0C 2B0
(306) 483-2956
Emp Here 40
SIC 8099 Health and allied services, nec

Paradise Hill, SK S0M

D-U-N-S 24-343-2809　　(BR)
NORTHWEST SCHOOL DIVISION 203
PARADISE HILL HIGH SCHOOL
Gd, Paradise Hill, SK, S0M 2G0
(306) 344-2055
Emp Here 30
SIC 8211 Elementary and secondary schools

Pelican Narrows, SK S0P

D-U-N-S 24-174-3751　　(BR)
BALLANTYNE, PETER CREE NATION
WAPANACAK ELEMENTARY SCHOOL
(*Suby of* Ballantyne, Peter Cree Nation)
Gd, Pelican Narrows, SK, S0P 0E0

(306) 632-1121
Emp Here 46
SIC 8211 Elementary and secondary schools

Pennant Station, SK S0N

D-U-N-S 20-113-7135　　(SL)
HUTTERIAN BRETHREN OF PENNANT INC
Gd, Pennant Station, SK, S0N 1X0
(306) 626-3369
Emp Here 60　　*Sales* 3,939,878
SIC 8661 Religious organizations

Pierceland, SK S0M

D-U-N-S 20-713-0332　　(BR)
NORTHWEST SCHOOL DIVISION 203
PIERCELAND HIGH SCHOOL
Gd, Pierceland, SK, S0M 2K0
(306) 839-2024
Emp Here 50
SIC 8211 Elementary and secondary schools

Pilot Butte, SK S0G

D-U-N-S 24-951-0418　　(SL)
CROSS BORDERS CONSULTING LTD
CROSS BORDERS DRILLING
Po Box 509, Pilot Butte, SK, S0G 3Z0
(306) 781-4484
Emp Here 80　　*Sales* 28,175,637
SIC 1381 Drilling oil and gas wells
Pr Pr Jared Mills

Pinehouse Lake, SK S0J

D-U-N-S 20-034-6273　　(BR)
NORTHERN LIGHTS SCHOOL DIVISION 113
MINAHIK WASKAHIGAN SCHOOL
Pinehouse Ave, Pinehouse Lake, SK, S0J 2B0
(306) 884-4888
Emp Here 50
SIC 8211 Elementary and secondary schools

Plenty, SK S0L

D-U-N-S 20-712-9805　　(BR)
SUN WEST SCHOOL DIVISION NO 207 SASKATCHEWAN
NORTH WEST CENTRAL SCHOOL
1 Saskatchewan Ave, Plenty, SK, S0L 2R0
(306) 932-2222
Emp Here 24
SIC 8211 Elementary and secondary schools

Ponteix, SK S0N

D-U-N-S 24-496-0951　　(SL)
PONTEIX COLONY OF HUTTERIAN BRETHREN
Gd, Ponteix, SK, S0N 1Z0
(306) 625-3652
Emp Here 83　　*Sales* 4,937,631
SIC 7389 Business services, nec

Porcupine Plain, SK S0E

D-U-N-S 25-824-3989 (BR)
FEDERATED CO-OPERATIVES LIMITED
PARKLAND CO-OP ASSOCIATION
(*Suby of* Federated Co-Operatives Limited)
108 Ash St, Porcupine Plain, SK, S0E 1H0
(306) 278-2022
Emp Here 50
SIC 5251 Hardware stores

D-U-N-S 25-481-3512 (BR)
KELSEY TRAIL REGIONAL HEALTH AU-THORITY
RED DEER NURSING HOME
(*Suby of* Kelsey Trail Regional Health Authority)
330 Oak St, Porcupine Plain, SK, S0E 1H0
(306) 278-6278
Emp Here 70
SIC 8051 Skilled nursing care facilities

D-U-N-S 24-347-7234 (BR)
NORTH EAST SCHOOL DIVISION
PORCUPINE PLAIN COMPOSITE HIGH SCHOOL
319 Pine St, Porcupine Plain, SK, S0E 1H0
(306) 278-2288
Emp Here 20
SIC 8211 Elementary and secondary schools

D-U-N-S 24-949-5180 (BR)
VITERRA INC
CROP PRODUCTION SERVICES
Po Box 760, Porcupine Plain, SK, S0E 1H0
(306) 278-3444
Emp Here 300
SIC 4221 Farm product warehousing and storage

Preeceville, SK S0A

D-U-N-S 25-273-0569 (BR)
MNP LLP
103 Churchill St, Preeceville, SK, S0A 3B0
(306) 547-3357
Emp Here 24
SIC 8721 Accounting, auditing, and book-keeping

D-U-N-S 24-619-4836 (BR)
MAPLE FARM EQUIPMENT PARTNERSHIP
705 Highway Ave E, Preeceville, SK, S0A 3B0
(306) 547-2007
Emp Here 35
SIC 5999 Miscellaneous retail stores, nec

D-U-N-S 24-039-1466 (BR)
SUNRISE REGIONAL HEALTH AUTHORITY
PREECEVILLE LIONS HOUSING
Gd, Preeceville, SK, S0A 3B0
(306) 547-3112
Emp Here 52
SIC 8051 Skilled nursing care facilities

Prince Albert, SK S6V

D-U-N-S 20-981-7696 (BR)
324007 ALBERTA LTD
HEARTLAND LIVESTOCK SERVICES
Gd, Prince Albert, SK, S6V 5R5
(306) 763-8463
Emp Here 20
SIC 5154 Livestock

D-U-N-S 25-684-4887 (BR)
7-ELEVEN CANADA, INC
7-ELEVEN STORE #32250
606 Branion Dr, Prince Albert, SK, S6V 2S1
(306) 764-8355
Emp Here 20
SIC 5411 Grocery stores

D-U-N-S 25-271-3540 (BR)
7-ELEVEN CANADA, INC
7-ELEVEN STORE #26892
215 15th St W, Prince Albert, SK, S6V 3P9
(306) 764-2101
Emp Here 20
SIC 5411 Grocery stores

D-U-N-S 20-066-2195 (SL)
ATHABASKA AIRWAYS LTD
Gd, Prince Albert, SK, S6V 5R4
(306) 764-1404
Emp Here 85 *Sales* 11,159,500
SIC 4522 Air transportation, nonscheduled
Pr Pr Jim Glass
Mamie Glass

D-U-N-S 24-359-6355 (BR)
BANK OF NOVA SCOTIA, THE
SCOTIABANK
800 15th St E Suite 230, Prince Albert, SK, S6V 8E3
(306) 764-3401
Emp Here 20
SIC 6021 National commercial banks

D-U-N-S 20-835-4014 (BR)
BANQUE TORONTO-DOMINION, LA
TORONTO-DOMINION BANK, THE
(*Suby of* Toronto-Dominion Bank, The)
2805 6th Ave E Unit 107, Prince Albert, SK, S6V 6Z6
(306) 953-8230
Emp Here 21
SIC 6021 National commercial banks

D-U-N-S 20-532-2220 (BR)
BANQUE DE DEVELOPPEMENT DU CANADA
BDC
135 21st St E, Prince Albert, SK, S6V 1L9

Emp Here 20
SIC 6141 Personal credit institutions

D-U-N-S 20-304-4321 (BR)
BEST BUY CANADA LTD
FUTURE SHOP
(*Suby of* Best Buy Co., Inc.)
800 15th St E Unit 300, Prince Albert, SK, S6V 8E3
(306) 922-9410
Emp Here 40
SIC 5731 Radio, television, and electronic stores

D-U-N-S 25-537-8721 (BR)
BRICK WAREHOUSE LP, THE
BRICK, THE
1403 Central Ave Unit 1, Prince Albert, SK, S6V 7J4
(306) 763-1775
Emp Here 20
SIC 5712 Furniture stores

D-U-N-S 25-289-0371 (BR)
CANADA POST CORPORATION
9 Marquis Rd W, Prince Albert, SK, S6V 8B9
(306) 953-1900
Emp Here 60
SIC 4311 U.s. postal service

D-U-N-S 20-537-5871 (BR)
CANADA POST CORPORATION
PRINCE ALBERT SHIPPING CENTRE
1403 Central Ave Unit 550, Prince Albert, SK, S6V 7J4
(306) 922-1711
Emp Here 25
SIC 4311 U.s. postal service

D-U-N-S 24-852-8465 (BR)
CANADIAN IMPERIAL BANK OF COM-MERCE
CIBC
1132 Central Ave, Prince Albert, SK, S6V 4V6
(306) 764-6692
Emp Here 49

SIC 6021 National commercial banks

D-U-N-S 20-315-9389 (BR)
CARRIER FOREST PRODUCTS LTD
Gd, Prince Albert, SK, S6V 5S8
(306) 922-6700
Emp Here 30
SIC 2421 Sawmills and planing mills, general

D-U-N-S 24-324-1077 (BR)
CONEXUS CREDIT UNION 2006
PA - SOUTH HILL BRANCH
2800 2nd Ave W, Prince Albert, SK, S6V 5Z4
(306) 953-6100
Emp Here 80
SIC 6062 State credit unions

D-U-N-S 20-065-9162 (BR)
CONSEIL DES ECOLES FRANSASKOISES
ECOLE VALOIS
449 10th St E, Prince Albert, SK, S6V 0Z5
(306) 763-0230
Emp Here 20
SIC 8211 Elementary and secondary schools

D-U-N-S 20-047-2152 (BR)
DELOITTE LLP
77 15th St E Suite 5, Prince Albert, SK, S6V 1E9
(306) 763-7411
Emp Here 20
SIC 8721 Accounting, auditing, and book-keeping

D-U-N-S 24-340-0350 (BR)
FGL SPORTS LTD
SPORT CHEK GATEWAY MALL
1403 Central Ave Unit 500, Prince Albert, SK, S6V 7J4
(306) 922-5791
Emp Here 30
SIC 5941 Sporting goods and bicycle shops

D-U-N-S 20-151-4358 (BR)
GRAINFIELDS PANCAKE & WAFFLE HOUSE INC
600 15th St E, Prince Albert, SK, S6V 8B1
(306) 922-7500
Emp Here 30
SIC 5812 Eating places

D-U-N-S 20-197-2804 (BR)
KJMAL ENTERPRISES LTD
MCDONALD'S
800 15th St E Unit 800, Prince Albert, SK, S6V 8E3
(306) 922-6366
Emp Here 83
SIC 5812 Eating places

D-U-N-S 20-066-5834 (BR)
LOBLAWS INC
REAL CANADIAN SUPERSTORE
591 15th St E Suite 1581, Prince Albert, SK, S6V 1G3
(306) 953-8120
Emp Here 240
SIC 5399 Miscellaneous general merchandise

D-U-N-S 24-264-6966 (SL)
MALENFANT ENTERPRISES LTD
50 North Industrial Dr, Prince Albert, SK, S6V 5R3
(306) 922-0269
Emp Here 50 *Sales* 3,939,878
SIC 4212 Local trucking, without storage

D-U-N-S 20-231-1440 (SL)
MANN MOTOR PRODUCTS LTD
MANN-NORTHWAY AUTO SOURCE OPTI-MUM USED VEHICLES
500 Marquis Rd E, Prince Albert, SK, S6V 8B3
(306) 765-2240
Emp Here 49 *Sales* 13,188,500
SIC 5521 Used car dealers
Pr Roger Mann

D-U-N-S 25-290-8199 (BR)
MARK'S WORK WEARHOUSE LTD

MARK'S WORK WEARHOUSE 42
800 15th St E Suite 540, Prince Albert, SK, S6V 8E3
(306) 922-3414
Emp Here 30
SIC 5651 Family clothing stores

D-U-N-S 20-068-2495 (BR)
MAXIM TRANSPORTATION SERVICES INC
MAXIM TRUCK & TRAILER
Hwy 2 S, Prince Albert, SK, S6V 5S2
(306) 922-1900
Emp Here 27
SIC 5511 New and used car dealers

D-U-N-S 20-185-1602 (BR)
MEDIAS TRANSCONTINENTAL INC
MEDIAS TRANSCONTINENTAL INC
30 10th St E, Prince Albert, SK, S6V 0Y5
(306) 764-4276
Emp Here 50
SIC 2711 Newspapers

D-U-N-S 20-843-8911 (SL)
NORTH SASK. LAUNDRY & SUPPORT SERVICES LTD
NORTH SASK LAUNDRY
1200 24th St W, Prince Albert, SK, S6V 4N9

Emp Here 55 *Sales* 3,137,310
SIC 7218 Industrial launderers

D-U-N-S 24-468-8602 (HQ)
NORTHERN CANADA EVANGELICAL MIS-SION, INC
ARROWHEAD NATIVE BIBLE CENTRE
(*Suby of* Northern Canada Evangelical Mission, Inc)
Lot 6 Block 6 Nw Section 10 Range 17 W Of 2nd, Prince Albert, SK, S6V 7V4
(306) 764-3388
Emp Here 25 *Emp Total* 203
Sales 18,387,840
SIC 8661 Religious organizations
Sec Patricia Elford
Dir Opers Albert Heal
Dir Opers Gary Winger
Roan Elford

D-U-N-S 20-197-9502 (BR)
PRINCE ALBERT CO-OPERATIVE ASSOCI-ATION LIMITED, THE
PRINCE ALBERT CO-OPERATIVE ASSOCI-ATION LIMITED, TH
228 16th St W, Prince Albert, SK, S6V 3V5
(306) 763-3534
Emp Here 21
SIC 7538 General automotive repair shops

D-U-N-S 24-966-5746 (SL)
PRINCE ALBERT DEVELOPMENT CORPO-RATION
PRINCE ALBERT INN
3680 2nd Ave W, Prince Albert, SK, S6V 5G2
(306) 922-5000
Emp Here 115 *Sales* 3,502,114
SIC 5812 Eating places

D-U-N-S 20-518-1873 (BR)
PRINCE ALBERT GRAND COUNCIL
WHITE BUFFALO YOUTH TREATMENT CENTRE
Gd, Prince Albert, SK, S6V 7G3
(306) 764-5250
Emp Here 20
SIC 8093 Specialty outpatient clinics, nec

D-U-N-S 24-114-8670 (BR)
PRINCE ALBERT GRAND COUNCIL
851 23rd St W, Prince Albert, SK, S6V 4M4
(306) 953-7248
Emp Here 40
SIC 8742 Management consulting services

D-U-N-S 20-302-2988 (BR)
PRINCE ALBERT PARKLAND REGIONAL HEALTH AUTHORITY
2345 10th Ave, Prince Albert, SK, S6V 7V6

(306) 765-6055
Emp Here 60
SIC 8093 Specialty outpatient clinics, nec

D-U-N-S 25-484-4236   (HQ)
PRINCE ALBERT PARKLAND REGIONAL HEALTH AUTHORITY
VICTORIA HOSPITAL
1521 6th Ave W, Prince Albert, SK, S6V 5K1
(306) 765-6400
Emp Here 700   Emp Total 40,372
Sales 14,420,549
SIC 8062 General medical and surgical hospitals
Pr Pr Cecile Hunt
VP Fin Cheryl Ellioty
VP Brett Enns
VP Carol Gregoryk
Pers/VP Don Mckay
VP Pat Stuart
Ch Bd Brenda Abrametz
V Ch Bd Bevra Fee
Dir Merv Bender
Dir Don Code

D-U-N-S 20-033-2976   (BR)
PRINCE ALBERT ROMAN CATHOLIC SEPARATE SCHOOL DIVISION NO. 6
ECOLE HOLY CROSS
2051 15th Ave E, Prince Albert, SK, S6V 6T5
(306) 953-7551
Emp Here 30
SIC 8211 Elementary and secondary schools

D-U-N-S 20-033-2257   (BR)
PRINCE ALBERT ROMAN CATHOLIC SEPARATE SCHOOL DIVISION NO. 6
WFA TURGEON SCHOOL
1180 Branion Dr, Prince Albert, SK, S6V 2S8
(306) 953-7558
Emp Here 30
SIC 8211 Elementary and secondary schools

D-U-N-S 20-033-2240   (BR)
PRINCE ALBERT ROMAN CATHOLIC SEPARATE SCHOOL DIVISION NO. 6
ST. JOHN COMMUNITY SCHOOL
1453 7th St E, Prince Albert, SK, S6V 0V3
(306) 953-7536
Emp Here 55
SIC 8211 Elementary and secondary schools

D-U-N-S 20-033-2232   (BR)
PRINCE ALBERT ROMAN CATHOLIC SEPARATE SCHOOL DIVISION NO. 6
ST ANNE CATHOLIC SCHOOL
2245 5th Ave W, Prince Albert, SK, S6V 5J3
(306) 953-7549
Emp Here 25
SIC 8211 Elementary and secondary schools

D-U-N-S 25-389-1972   (SL)
RNF VENTURES LTD
811 Central Ave, Prince Albert, SK, S6V 4V2
(306) 763-3700
Emp Here 45   Sales 8,317,520
SIC 1542 Nonresidential construction, nec
Pr Pr Kelly Miller

D-U-N-S 20-913-3771   (BR)
RANCH EHRLO SOCIETY
Gd, Prince Albert, SK, S6V 6J9
(306) 764-4511
Emp Here 72
SIC 8322 Individual and family services

D-U-N-S 24-390-4674   (SL)
RAVEN ENTERPRISES INC.
HAROLD'S FOODLINER
(Suby of RCS Investments (2003) Inc)
200 28th St E, Prince Albert, SK, S6V 1X2
(306) 922-3663
Emp Here 80   Sales 10,579,302
SIC 5411 Grocery stores
Pr Pr Byron Guy
Heather Guy

D-U-N-S 24-114-5929   (BR)

RIDSDALE TRANSPORT LTD
29 Industrial Dr N, Prince Albert, SK, S6V 6V4
(306) 764-0934
Emp Here 20
SIC 4212 Local trucking, without storage

D-U-N-S 20-226-5307   (SL)
RODEAN ENT LTD
1027 4th St E, Prince Albert, SK, S6V 0L1
(306) 764-1108
Emp Here 30   Sales 7,304,400
SIC 1623 Water, sewer, and utility lines
Dir Dean Brown

D-U-N-S 20-573-8433   (BR)
ROYAL BANK OF CANADA
RBC
(Suby of Royal Bank Of Canada)
801 15th St E, Prince Albert, SK, S6V 0C7
(306) 953-5700
Emp Here 20
SIC 6021 National commercial banks

D-U-N-S 25-315-2268   (BR)
SASKATCHEWAN GOVERNMENT INSURANCE
501 15th St E, Prince Albert, SK, S6V 1G3
(306) 953-8000
Emp Here 36
SIC 6331 Fire, marine, and casualty insurance

D-U-N-S 24-519-6837   (BR)
SASKATCHEWAN HOUSING CORPORATION
800 Central Ave, Prince Albert, SK, S6V 6Z2

Emp Here 30
SIC 6531 Real estate agents and managers

D-U-N-S 25-486-1636   (BR)
SASKATCHEWAN INDIAN GAMING AUTHORITY INC
NORTHERN LIGHTS CASINO
44 Marquis Rd W, Prince Albert, SK, S6V 7Y5
(306) 764-4777
Emp Here 400
SIC 7999 Amusement and recreation, nec

D-U-N-S 24-883-2941   (BR)
SASKATCHEWAN INSTITUTE OF APPLIED SCIENCE AND TECHNOLOGY
SIAST WOODLAND CAMPUS
1100 15th St E, Prince Albert, SK, S6V 7S4
(306) 765-1500
Emp Here 257
SIC 8222 Junior colleges

D-U-N-S 20-033-2166   (BR)
SASKATCHEWAN RIVER SCHOOL DIVISION #119
ARTHUR PECHEY PUBLIC SCHOOL
2675 4th Ave W, Prince Albert, SK, S6V 5H8
(306) 922-9229
Emp Here 26
SIC 8211 Elementary and secondary schools

D-U-N-S 20-231-1747   (BR)
SASKATCHEWAN RIVER SCHOOL DIVISION #119
CARLTON COMPREHENSIVE HIGH SCHOOL
665 28th St E, Prince Albert, SK, S6V 6E9
(306) 922-3115
Emp Here 100
SIC 8211 Elementary and secondary schools

D-U-N-S 20-070-0693   (BR)
SASKATCHEWAN RIVER SCHOOL DIVISION #119
JOHN DIEFENBAKER SCHOOL
1090 Branion Dr, Prince Albert, SK, S6V 2S8
(306) 763-6031
Emp Here 40
SIC 8211 Elementary and secondary schools

D-U-N-S 20-712-7247   (BR)
SASKATCHEWAN RIVER SCHOOL DIVISION #119

WESTVIEW PUBLIC SCHOOL
620 Macarthur Dr, Prince Albert, SK, S6V 8C6
(306) 922-4094
Emp Here 50
SIC 8211 Elementary and secondary schools

D-U-N-S 20-033-2968   (BR)
SASKATCHEWAN RIVER SCHOOL DIVISION #119
W. J. BEREZOWSKY SCHOOL
566 Mcintosh Dr, Prince Albert, SK, S6V 6T2
(306) 763-7404
Emp Here 30
SIC 8211 Elementary and secondary schools

D-U-N-S 20-033-6498   (BR)
SASKATCHEWAN RIVER SCHOOL DIVISION #119
VINCENT MASSEY COMMUNITY SCHOOL
2999 3rd Ave E, Prince Albert, SK, S6V 8G2
(306) 763-7494
Emp Here 25
SIC 8211 Elementary and secondary schools

D-U-N-S 20-033-6621   (BR)
SASKATCHEWAN RIVER SCHOOL DIVISION #119
RIVERSIDE COMMUNITY SCHOOL
511 5th Ave E, Prince Albert, SK, S6V 7Z6
(306) 763-6495
Emp Here 55
SIC 8211 Elementary and secondary schools

D-U-N-S 20-033-2174   (BR)
SASKATCHEWAN RIVER SCHOOL DIVISION #119
KING GEORGE COMMUNITY SCHOOL
421 23rd St E, Prince Albert, SK, S6V 1P9
(306) 763-7571
Emp Here 42
SIC 8211 Elementary and secondary schools

D-U-N-S 20-712-7155   (BR)
SASKATCHEWAN RIVER SCHOOL DIVISION #119
PRINCE ALBERT COLLEGIATE INSTITUTE
45 20th St W, Prince Albert, SK, S6V 4E9
(306) 763-6485
Emp Here 22
SIC 8211 Elementary and secondary schools

D-U-N-S 20-712-7189   (BR)
SASKATCHEWAN RIVER SCHOOL DIVISION #119
RED WING SCHOOL
545 11th St E, Prince Albert, SK, S6V 1B1
(306) 763-5375
Emp Here 22
SIC 8211 Elementary and secondary schools

D-U-N-S 20-033-7801   (BR)
SASKATCHEWAN RIVER SCHOOL DIVISION #119
WESMOR COMMUNITY HIGH SCHOOL
1819 14th Ave W, Prince Albert, SK, S6V 5P1
(306) 764-5233
Emp Here 40
SIC 8211 Elementary and secondary schools

D-U-N-S 20-033-6944   (BR)
SASKATCHEWAN RIVER SCHOOL DIVISION #119
QUEEN MARY COMMUNITY SCHOOL
1010 15th St W, Prince Albert, SK, S6V 3S2
(306) 763-7672
Emp Here 55
SIC 8211 Elementary and secondary schools

D-U-N-S 20-712-7148   (BR)
SASKATCHEWAN RIVER SCHOOL DIVISION #119
PRINCESS MARGARET PUBLIC SCHOOL
333 13th Ave E, Prince Albert, SK, S6V 2N3
(306) 763-5217
Emp Here 50
SIC 8211 Elementary and secondary schools

D-U-N-S 20-034-0474   (BR)

SASKATCHEWAN RIVER SCHOOL DIVISION #119
ECOLE VICKERS SCHOOL
2800 Bradbury Dr, Prince Albert, SK, S6V 7K8
(306) 922-6446
Emp Here 48
SIC 8211 Elementary and secondary schools

D-U-N-S 25-311-2015   (BR)
SEARS CANADA INC
1499 Central Ave, Prince Albert, SK, S6V 4W4
(306) 764-1466
Emp Here 120
SIC 5311 Department stores

D-U-N-S 25-272-0164   (BR)
SOBEYS WEST INC
2995 2nd Ave W, Prince Albert, SK, S6V 5V5
(306) 922-1245
Emp Here 150
SIC 5411 Grocery stores

D-U-N-S 25-145-0243   (BR)
STAPLES CANADA INC
STAPLES BUSINESS DEPOT
(Suby of Staples, Inc.)
800 15th St Suite 240, Prince Albert, SK, S6V 8E3
(306) 922-1711
Emp Here 28
SIC 5943 Stationery stores

D-U-N-S 25-990-9174   (SL)
VC LEMIEUX HOLDINGS INC
1800 6th Ave E, Prince Albert, SK, S6V 2K3
(306) 764-3485
Emp Here 45   Sales 6,674,880
SIC 6719 Holding companies, nec
Pr Curtis Lemieux

D-U-N-S 25-288-5371   (BR)
WAL-MART CANADA CORP
800 15th St E Suite 100, Prince Albert, SK, S6V 8E3
(306) 764-9770
Emp Here 300
SIC 5311 Department stores

D-U-N-S 25-678-2038   (BR)
WAPITI REGIONAL LIBRARY
JOHN M CUELENAERE PUBLIC LIBRARY
145 12th St E, Prince Albert, SK, S6V 1B7
(306) 763-8496
Emp Here 44
SIC 8231 Libraries

D-U-N-S 20-294-8865   (SL)
WESTERN FIRST NATIONS HOSPITALITY LIMITED PARTNERSHIP
914 Central Ave, Prince Albert, SK, S6V 4V3
(306) 922-0088
Emp Here 120   Sales 7,304,400
SIC 7011 Hotels and motels
Pr Pr Ron Michele
Dir Opers Jaime Mcguin

Prince Albert, SK S6W

D-U-N-S 20-273-7672   (SL)
BRODA GROUP HOLDINGS LIMITED PARTNERSHIP
4271 5th Ave E, Prince Albert, SK, S6W 0A5
(306) 764-5337
Emp Here 250   Sales 69,188,900
SIC 1522 Residential construction, nec
Pr Gord Broda

D-U-N-S 20-075-6380   (BR)
INNVEST PROPERTIES CORP
COMFORT INN
(Suby of Innvest Properties Corp)
3863 2nd Ave W, Prince Albert, SK, S6W 1A1
(306) 763-4466
Emp Here 20
SIC 7011 Hotels and motels

D-U-N-S 20-211-3218   (BR)
LOBLAWS INC
REAL CANADIAN WHOLESALE CLUB
4050 2nd Ave W, Prince Albert, SK, S6W 1A2
(306) 922-5506
Emp Here 35
SIC 5141 Groceries, general line

D-U-N-S 20-066-4308   (HQ)
MOKER & THOMPSON IMPLEMENTS LTD
3802 4th Ave E, Prince Albert, SK, S6W 1A4
(306) 763-6454
Emp Here 20   *Emp Total* 482
Sales 8,682,323
SIC 5083 Farm and garden machinery
Pr Pr Gordon Thompson

D-U-N-S 25-056-7104   (BR)
**PRINCE ALBERT CO-OPERATIVE ASSOCI-
ATION LIMITED, THE**
*PRINCE ALBERT CO-OPERATIVE ASSOCI-
ATION LIMITED, TH*
275 38th St E, Prince Albert, SK, S6W 1A5
(306) 764-6491
Emp Here 36
SIC 5211 Lumber and other building materials

D-U-N-S 20-447-4282   (BR)
REDHEAD EQUIPMENT
3802 4th Ave E, Prince Albert, SK, S6W 1A4
(306) 763-6454
Emp Here 64
SIC 5084 Industrial machinery and equipment

D-U-N-S 20-005-4463   (BR)
SASKENERGY INCORPORATED
3855 5th Ave E, Prince Albert, SK, S6W 0A2

Emp Here 30
SIC 4924 Natural gas distribution

Prince Albert, SK S6X

D-U-N-S 25-014-2338   (BR)
**PRINCE ALBERT ROMAN CATHOLIC SEP-
ARATE SCHOOL DIVISION NO. 6**
ST FRANCIS SCHOOL
(*Suby of* Prince Albert Roman Catholic Sepa-
rate School Division No. 6)
1695 Olive Diefenbaker Dr, Prince Albert, SK,
S6X 1B8
(306) 953-7561
Emp Here 26
SIC 8211 Elementary and secondary schools

Punnichy, SK S0A

D-U-N-S 20-712-9417   (BR)
HORIZON SCHOOL DIVISION NO 205
PUNNICHY COMMUNITY HIGH SCHOOL
612 6th Ave, Punnichy, SK, S0A 3C0
(306) 835-2140
Emp Here 20
SIC 8211 Elementary and secondary schools

D-U-N-S 20-712-9409   (BR)
HORIZON SCHOOL DIVISION NO 205
*PUNNICHY ELEMENTARY COMMUNITY
SCHOOL*
200 King St, Punnichy, SK, S0A 3C0
(306) 835-2128
Emp Here 25
SIC 8211 Elementary and secondary schools

D-U-N-S 20-712-9375   (BR)
HORIZON SCHOOL DIVISION NO 205
GEORGE GORDON EDUCATION CENTRE
Gd, Punnichy, SK, S0A 3C0
(306) 835-2222
Emp Here 20
SIC 8211 Elementary and secondary schools

Radville, SK S0C

D-U-N-S 20-572-7097   (BR)
CANADA POST CORPORATION
214 Main St, Radville, SK, S0C 2G0
(306) 869-2433
Emp Here 20
SIC 4311 U.s. postal service

D-U-N-S 24-234-9277   (SL)
MANNATECH INDEPENDENT ASSOCIATE
832 Mann Ave, Radville, SK, S0C 2G0
(306) 869-3237
Emp Here 49   *Sales* 6,784,769
SIC 8748 Business consulting, nec
Owner Oliver Dionne

D-U-N-S 25-325-3348   (SL)
RADVILLE MARIAN HEALTH CENTRE INC
217 Warren St, Radville, SK, S0C 2G0
(306) 869-2224
Emp Here 69   *Sales* 3,137,310
SIC 8051 Skilled nursing care facilities

Raymore, SK S0A

D-U-N-S 24-883-0226   (BR)
LAST MOUNTAIN CO-OPERATIVE LIMITED
(*Suby of* Last Mountain Co-Operative Limited)
Highway 6 Highway 15, Raymore, SK, S0A
3J0
(306) 746-2012
Emp Here 20
SIC 5541 Gasoline service stations

D-U-N-S 24-279-4923   (HQ)
LAST MOUNTAIN CO-OPERATIVE LIMITED
(*Suby of* Last Mountain Co-Operative Limited)
Hwy 6 N, Raymore, SK, S0A 3J0
(306) 746-2019
Emp Here 20   *Emp Total* 55
Sales 16,834,129
SIC 5399 Miscellaneous general merchandise
Genl Mgr Mike Sigouin
Pr Pr Jerry Orthner
VP VP Jim Frohaug
Barry Benson
Dir Stan Larson
Dir Glen Hancock
Dir Ronald Johnston
Dir Mary Anne Grand
Dir Ken Eckel

Redvers, SK S0C

D-U-N-S 20-712-8799   (BR)
**SOUTH EAST CORNERSTONE SCHOOL
DIVISION NO. 209**
REDVERS SCHOOL
(*Suby of* South East Cornerstone School Divi-
sion No. 209)
44 Broadway St, Redvers, SK, S0C 2H0
(306) 452-6161
Emp Here 30
SIC 8211 Elementary and secondary schools

D-U-N-S 25-014-2619   (BR)
**SUN COUNTRY REGIONAL HEALTH AU-
THORITY**
REDVERS HEALTH CENTRE
18 Eichhorst St, Redvers, SK, S0C 2H0
(306) 452-3553
Emp Here 90
SIC 8062 General medical and surgical hospi-
tals

Regina, SK S4M

D-U-N-S 20-300-5269   (BR)
HALTON RECYCLING LTD
ENTERA ENVIRONMENTAL
12214 Rotary Ave, Regina, SK, S4M 0A1
(306) 775-9999
Emp Here 30
SIC 4953 Refuse systems

Regina, SK S4N

D-U-N-S 24-311-9281   (SL)
101087365 SASKATCHEWAN LTD
RESTOREX DISASTER RESTORATION
1465 Mcdonald St Suite A, Regina, SK, S4N
2Y2
(306) 522-3350
Emp Here 70   *Sales* 2,772,507
SIC 8322 Individual and family services

D-U-N-S 20-199-1473   (BR)
668824 ALBERTA LTD
*VISIONS THE BEST NAME IN ELECTRON-
ICS*
2530 E Victoria Ave, Regina, SK, S4N 6M5
(306) 790-7755
Emp Here 20
SIC 5999 Miscellaneous retail stores, nec

D-U-N-S 20-735-3306   (BR)
**AMEC FOSTER WHEELER AMERICAS LIM-
ITED**
EARTH AND ENVIRONMENTAL
608 Mcleod St, Regina, SK, S4N 4Y1

Emp Here 26
SIC 8711 Engineering services

D-U-N-S 25-611-5999   (BR)
ACKLANDS - GRAINGER INC
AGI
(*Suby of* W.W. Grainger, Inc.)
680 Mcleod St, Regina, SK, S4N 4Y1
(306) 721-3200
Emp Here 25
SIC 3569 General industrial machinery, nec

D-U-N-S 25-121-8285   (BR)
ACUREN GROUP INC
(*Suby of* Rockwood Service Corporation)
1135 E Weaver St, Regina, SK, S4N 5Y2
(306) 761-2588
Emp Here 30
SIC 1389 Oil and gas field services, nec

D-U-N-S 20-327-3557   (HQ)
ADOXIO BUSINESS SOLUTIONS LIMITED
(*Suby of* Adoxio Business Solutions Limited)
1445 Park St Suite 200, Regina, SK, S4N 4C5
(306) 569-6501
Emp Here 37   *Emp Total* 50
Sales 5,034,288
SIC 7372 Prepackaged software
Pr Grant Mclarnon

D-U-N-S 20-611-6444   (SL)
ALEX MARION RESTAURANTS LTD
MACDONALDS
940 E Victoria Ave, Regina, SK, S4N 7A9

Emp Here 100   *Sales* 2,991,389
SIC 5812 Eating places

D-U-N-S 25-539-1468   (BR)
ALL-FAB BUILDING COMPONENTS INC
NU-FAB
610 Henderson Dr, Regina, SK, S4N 5X3
(306) 721-8131
Emp Here 75
SIC 5039 Construction materials, nec

D-U-N-S 24-467-3760   (HQ)
ALLIANCE ENERGY LIMITED
504 Henderson Dr, Regina, SK, S4N 5X2

---

(306) 721-6484
Emp Here 100   *Emp Total* 200
Sales 30,643,494
SIC 1731 Electrical work
CEO James Paul Mclellan
Pr Pr Bryan Leverick
Janet Mclellan-Folk

D-U-N-S 20-823-4638   (BR)
ASSOCIATED ENGINEERING (SASK) LTD
(*Suby of* Ashco Shareholders Inc)
199 Leonard St, Regina, SK, S4N 5X5
(306) 721-2466
Emp Here 35
SIC 8711 Engineering services

D-U-N-S 20-651-4155   (BR)
**ASSOCIATED ENGINEERING ALBERTA
LTD**
(*Suby of* Ashco Shareholders Inc)
1922 Park St, Regina, SK, S4N 7M4
(306) 721-2466
Emp Here 45
SIC 8711 Engineering services

D-U-N-S 20-065-0203   (BR)
BAYER CROPSCIENCE INC
295 Henderson Dr, Regina, SK, S4N 6C2
(306) 721-4500
Emp Here 100
SIC 5191 Farm supplies

D-U-N-S 20-801-4196   (BR)
**BEE-CLEAN BUILDING MAINTENANCE IN-
CORPORATED**
1555a Mcdonald St, Regina, SK, S4N 6H7
(306) 757-8020
Emp Here 400
SIC 7349 Building maintenance services, nec

D-U-N-S 20-300-1446   (BR)
BEST BUY CANADA LTD
FUTURE SHOP
(*Suby of* Best Buy Co., Inc.)
1825e Victoria Ave, Regina, SK, S4N 6E6
(306) 791-4000
Emp Here 55
SIC 5731 Radio, television, and electronic
stores

D-U-N-S 20-033-2109   (BR)
**BOARD OF EDUCATION REGINA SCHOOL
DIVISION NO. 4 OF SASKATCHEWAN**
GLEN ELM PUBLIC ELEMENTARY SCHOOL
1225 E 9th Ave, Regina, SK, S4N 0H4
(306) 791-8588
Emp Here 23
SIC 8211 Elementary and secondary schools

D-U-N-S 25-014-2718   (BR)
**BOARD OF EDUCATION REGINA SCHOOL
DIVISION NO. 4 OF SASKATCHEWAN**
COCHRANE HIGH SCHOOL
1069 E 14th Ave, Regina, SK, S4N 0T8
(306) 523-3300
Emp Here 60
SIC 8211 Elementary and secondary schools

D-U-N-S 20-033-7017   (BR)
**BOARD OF EDUCATION REGINA SCHOOL
DIVISION NO. 4 OF SASKATCHEWAN**
F. W. JOHNSON COLLEGIATE
400 Fines Dr, Regina, SK, S4N 5L9
(306) 523-3350
Emp Here 55
SIC 8211 Elementary and secondary schools

D-U-N-S 20-712-6967   (BR)
**BOARD OF EDUCATION REGINA SCHOOL
DIVISION NO. 4 OF SASKATCHEWAN**
JUDGE BRIAN SCHOOL
2828 E Dewdney Ave, Regina, SK, S4N 5G8
(306) 791-8553
Emp Here 42
SIC 8211 Elementary and secondary schools

D-U-N-S 20-037-7104   (BR)
BOARD OF EDUCATION REGINA SCHOOL

DIVISION NO. 4 OF SASKATCHEWAN
ARCOLA COMMUNITY SCHOOL
2315 Abbott Rd, Regina, SK, S4N 2K2
(306) 791-8542
Emp Here 40
SIC 8211 Elementary and secondary schools

D-U-N-S 20-072-4024   (BR)
**BOARD OF EDUCATION REGINA SCHOOL
DIVISION NO. 4 OF SASKATCHEWAN**
STEWART RUSSELL PUBLIC SCHOOL
1920 E 7th Ave, Regina, SK, S4N 6M9
(306) 791-8463
Emp Here 25
SIC 8211 Elementary and secondary schools

D-U-N-S 20-033-2091   (BR)
**BOARD OF EDUCATION REGINA SCHOOL
DIVISION NO. 4 OF SASKATCHEWAN**
*DR GEORGE FERGUSON PUBLIC ELE-
MENTARY*
117 Brotherton Ave, Regina, SK, S4N 0J8
(306) 791-8582
Emp Here 40
SIC 8211 Elementary and secondary schools

D-U-N-S 20-712-6819   (BR)
**BOARD OF EDUCATION REGINA SCHOOL
DIVISION NO. 4 OF SASKATCHEWAN**
DOUGLAS PARK SCHOOL
635 Douglas Ave E, Regina, SK, S4N 1H7
(306) 523-3720
Emp Here 50
SIC 8211 Elementary and secondary schools

D-U-N-S 25-014-3252   (BR)
**BOARD OF EDUCATION REGINA SCHOOL
DIVISION NO. 4 OF SASKATCHEWAN**
HENRY BRAUN ELEMENTARY SCHOOL
710 Graham Rd, Regina, SK, S4N 7A5
(306) 791-8548
Emp Here 36
SIC 8211 Elementary and secondary schools

D-U-N-S 20-712-7361   (BR)
**BOARD OF EDUCATION OF THE REGINA
ROMAN CATHOLIC SEPARATE SCHOOL
DIVISION NO. 81**
ST CATHERINE SCHOOL
150 Brotherton Ave, Regina, SK, S4N 0J7
(306) 791-7325
Emp Here 22
SIC 8211 Elementary and secondary schools

D-U-N-S 20-033-6506   (BR)
**BOARD OF EDUCATION OF THE REGINA
ROMAN CATHOLIC SEPARATE SCHOOL
DIVISION NO. 81**
JEAN VANIER ELEMENTARY SCHOOL
425 15th Ave, Regina, SK, S4N 0V1
(306) 791-7285
Emp Here 20
SIC 8211 Elementary and secondary schools

D-U-N-S 20-712-7353   (BR)
**BOARD OF EDUCATION OF THE REGINA
ROMAN CATHOLIC SEPARATE SCHOOL
DIVISION NO. 81**
ST AUGUSTINE ELEMENTARY SCHOOL
2343 Edgar St, Regina, SK, S4N 3L2
(306) 791-7310
Emp Here 45
SIC 8211 Elementary and secondary schools

D-U-N-S 20-033-7884   (BR)
**BOARD OF EDUCATION OF THE REGINA
ROMAN CATHOLIC SEPARATE SCHOOL
DIVISION NO. 81**
ST THERESA SCHOOL
2707 E 7th Ave, Regina, SK, S4N 5E8
(306) 791-7390
Emp Here 35
SIC 8211 Elementary and secondary schools

D-U-N-S 20-033-2265   (BR)
**BOARD OF EDUCATION OF THE REGINA
ROMAN CATHOLIC SEPARATE SCHOOL**

DIVISION NO. 81
ECOLE ST. ANDREW SCHOOL
621 Douglas Ave E, Regina, SK, S4N 1H7
(306) 791-7300
Emp Here 22
SIC 8211 Elementary and secondary schools

D-U-N-S 20-067-0180   (BR)
BRINK'S CANADA LIMITED
(*Suby of* The Brink's Company)
1761 Wallace St, Regina, SK, S4N 3Z7
(306) 525-8704
Emp Here 35
SIC 7381 Detective and armored car services

D-U-N-S 24-474-2727   (BR)
CALTECH SURVEYS LTD
389 Park St, Regina, SK, S4N 5B2
(306) 775-1814
Emp Here 25
SIC 8713 Surveying services

D-U-N-S 20-580-3294   (BR)
CANADA POST CORPORATION
2223 E Victoria Ave Suite 109, Regina, SK,
S4N 6E4

Emp Here 20
SIC 4311 U.s. postal service

D-U-N-S 24-468-5798   (BR)
**CANADIAN LINEN AND UNIFORM SER-
VICE CO**
QUEBEC LINGE
(*Suby of* Ameripride Services, Inc.)
180 N Leonard St, Regina, SK, S4N 5V7
(306) 721-4848
Emp Here 80
SIC 7213 Linen supply

D-U-N-S 20-001-8955   (BR)
CARA OPERATIONS LIMITED
KELSEY'S
(*Suby of* Cara Holdings Limited)
1875 E Victoria Ave, Regina, SK, S4N 6E6
(306) 949-4955
Emp Here 60
SIC 5812 Eating places

D-U-N-S 24-413-4909   (BR)
CINDERCRETE PRODUCTS LIMITED
1773 Reynolds St, Regina, SK, S4N 7L8
(306) 789-8080
Emp Here 30
SIC 5211 Lumber and other building materials

D-U-N-S 24-008-2060   (BR)
**CLEAN HARBORS ENERGY AND INDUS-
TRIAL SERVICES CORP.**
525 E Dewdney Ave, Regina, SK, S4N 4E9
(306) 546-3322
Emp Here 20
SIC 7349 Building maintenance services, nec

D-U-N-S 24-883-3253   (BR)
**COCA-COLA REFRESHMENTS CANADA
COMPANY**
(*Suby of* The Coca-Cola Company)
355 Henderson Dr, Regina, SK, S4N 6B9
(800) 218-2653
Emp Here 85
SIC 5149 Groceries and related products, nec

D-U-N-S 20-842-5330   (SL)
COMMERCIAL BUILDING SERVICE LTD
819 Arcola Ave, Regina, SK, S4N 0S9
(306) 757-5332
Emp Here 100   *Sales* 2,918,428
SIC 7349 Building maintenance services, nec

D-U-N-S 20-293-2034   (BR)
COMMERCIAL EQUIPMENT CORP
105 N Mcdonald St, Regina, SK, S4N 5W2
(306) 721-9575
Emp Here 20
SIC 5082 Construction and mining machinery

D-U-N-S 20-545-0380   (BR)

CRANE CANADA CO.
CRANE SUPPLY
(*Suby of* Crane Co.)
335 E 6th Ave, Regina, SK, S4N 6A6
(306) 525-1326
Emp Here 20
SIC 5085 Industrial supplies

D-U-N-S 20-546-0587   (BR)
CREATIVE DOOR SERVICES LTD
629 Park St, Regina, SK, S4N 5N1
(306) 721-8515
Emp Here 20
SIC 1751 Carpentry work

D-U-N-S 20-733-5964   (BR)
**CUMMINS WESTERN CANADA LIMITED
PARTNERSHIP**
110 Kress St, Regina, SK, S4N 5Y3
(306) 721-9710
Emp Here 20
SIC 5084 Industrial machinery and equipment

D-U-N-S 20-128-0117   (HQ)
CUSTOM TRUCK SALES INC
520 Park St, Regina, SK, S4N 0T6
(306) 569-9021
Emp Here 40   *Emp Total* 200
Sales 80,982,000
SIC 5511 New and used car dealers
Brent Leach
Dir Ken Leach

D-U-N-S 24-738-8981   (BR)
CUSTOM TRUCK SALES INC
PAC LEASE
520 Park St, Regina, SK, S4N 0T6
(306) 569-9021
Emp Here 50
SIC 5012 Automobiles and other motor vehi-
cles

D-U-N-S 20-152-6451   (BR)
**DATA COMMUNICATIONS MANAGEMENT
CORP**
DATA GROUP OF COMPANY
455 Maxwell Cres, Regina, SK, S4N 5X9
(306) 721-5400
Emp Here 30
SIC 2759 Commercial printing, nec

D-U-N-S 20-800-0930   (BR)
DENCAN RESTAURANTS INC
DENNY'S RESTAURANT
(*Suby of* Northland Properties Corporation)
1800 E Victoria Ave Suite A, Regina, SK, S4N
7K3
(306) 949-2447
Emp Here 40
SIC 5812 Eating places

D-U-N-S 20-447-7558   (HQ)
DIRECT WEST CORPORATION
355 Longman Cres, Regina, SK, S4N 6G3
(306) 777-0333
Emp Here 100   *Emp Total* 40,372
Sales 20,064,193
SIC 7319 Advertising, nec
Pr Gord Farmer

D-U-N-S 25-950-7879   (BR)
DYNAMEX CANADA LIMITED
DYNAMEX
110 N Leonard St, Regina, SK, S4N 5V7
(306) 721-2345
Emp Here 40
SIC 7389 Business services, nec

D-U-N-S 20-576-5030   (BR)
EMCO CORPORATION
615 Vennels St, Regina, SK, S4N 6B1
(306) 525-2311
Emp Here 25
SIC 5074 Plumbing and heating equipment
and supplies (hydronics)

D-U-N-S 20-038-3284   (BR)
ENBRIDGE PIPELINES INC

439 9th Ave N, Regina, SK, S4N 7L5

Emp Here 20
SIC 4612 Crude petroleum pipelines

D-U-N-S 20-859-8313   (BR)
FGL SPORTS LTD
SPORT CHEK
2223 E Victoria Ave, Regina, SK, S4N 6E4
(306) 565-8585
Emp Here 25
SIC 5661 Shoe stores

D-U-N-S 24-264-7782   (BR)
FARM BUSINESS CONSULTANTS INC
F B C
635 Henderson Dr, Regina, SK, S4N 6A8
(306) 721-6688
Emp Here 39
SIC 7291 Tax return preparation services

D-U-N-S 20-699-9448   (BR)
FEDERATED CO-OPERATIVES LIMITED
(*Suby of* Federated Co-Operatives Limited)
2260 Emmett Hall Rd, Regina, SK, S4N 3M3
(306) 782-9000
Emp Here 20
SIC 5984 Liquefied petroleum gas dealers

D-U-N-S 20-067-3259   (BR)
FEDERATED CO-OPERATIVES LIMITED
FCL
(*Suby of* Federated Co-Operatives Limited)
2107 E Turvey Rd, Regina, SK, S4N 3W1
(306) 721-7070
Emp Here 65
SIC 5141 Groceries, general line

D-U-N-S 20-273-8485   (BR)
FIRSTCANADA ULC
FIRST STUDENT CANADA
140 E 4th Ave, Regina, SK, S4N 4Z4
(306) 721-4499
Emp Here 200
SIC 4131 Intercity and rural bus transportation

D-U-N-S 24-916-0003   (BR)
FLYNN CANADA LTD
202 Solomon Dr, Regina, SK, S4N 5A8
(306) 789-1411
Emp Here 50
SIC 1761 Roofing, siding, and sheetMetal
work

D-U-N-S 24-528-4760   (BR)
FRONTIER PETERBILT SALES LTD
CERVUS EQUIPMENT PETERBILT
1507 E Ross Ave, Regina, SK, S4N 7E5
(306) 789-7383
Emp Here 30
SIC 5511 New and used car dealers

D-U-N-S 24-717-9997   (BR)
G4S CASH SOLUTIONS (CANADA) LTD
1810 Mackay St, Regina, SK, S4N 6R4
(306) 522-2671
Emp Here 42
SIC 7381 Detective and armored car services

D-U-N-S 25-514-3117   (BR)
HOME DEPOT OF CANADA INC
HOME DEPOT
(*Suby of* The Home Depot Inc)
1867 E Victoria Ave, Regina, SK, S4N 6E6
(306) 761-1919
Emp Here 200
SIC 5251 Hardware stores

D-U-N-S 24-125-9584   (BR)
HUSSMANN CANADA INC
133 N Mcdonald St, Regina, SK, S4N 5W2
(306) 721-2700
Emp Here 20
SIC 7623 Refrigeration service and repair

D-U-N-S 25-974-7954   (SL)
**INDEPENDENT'S CHOICE DISTRIBUTION
LTD**

I C D
(*Suby of* Pratts Wholesale (Sask.) Ltd)
1450 Park St, Regina, SK, S4N 2G2
(306) 546-5444
Emp Here 50   *Sales* 16,584,990
SIC 5147 Meats and meat products

D-U-N-S 20-611-0009   (HQ)
JAY'S TRANSPORTATION GROUP LTD
555 Park St, Regina, SK, S4N 5B2
(306) 569-9369
Emp Here 40   *Emp Total* 5,515
Sales 62,889,823
SIC 4213 Trucking, except local
Dennis Doehl
Pr Terry Simson

D-U-N-S 20-546-0199   (BR)
JOHN DEERE CANADA ULC
455 Park St, Regina, SK, S4N 5B2
(306) 791-3200
Emp Here 45
SIC 5083 Farm and garden machinery

D-U-N-S 24-914-4924   (BR)
KINDERSLEY TRANSPORT LTD
1601 Elliott St, Regina, SK, S4N 6R5
(306) 721-7733
Emp Here 30
SIC 4213 Trucking, except local

D-U-N-S 20-343-3354   (BR)
KONE INC
KONE ELEVATORS & ESCALATOR
607 Park St, Regina, SK, S4N 5N1
(306) 546-2420
Emp Here 30
SIC 1796 Installing building equipment

D-U-N-S 20-756-5318   (BR)
LORAAS DISPOSAL SERVICES LTD
620 Mcleod St, Regina, SK, S4N 4Y1
(306) 721-1000
Emp Here 40
SIC 4953 Refuse systems

D-U-N-S 25-612-1575   (BR)
LYDALE CONSTRUCTION (1983) CO. LTD
1820 E Ross Ave, Regina, SK, S4N 0R9
(306) 751-4868
Emp Here 20
SIC 8322 Individual and family services

D-U-N-S 20-192-3096   (BR)
MAPLEHURST BAKERIES INC
READY BAKE FOODS INC
1700 Park St, Regina, SK, S4N 6B2
(306) 359-7400
Emp Here 85
SIC 2051 Bread, cake, and related products

D-U-N-S 25-106-8904   (BR)
MASTERFEEDS INC
COWTOWN
745 Park St, Regina, SK, S4N 4Y4
(306) 721-2727
Emp Here 55
SIC 2048 Prepared feeds, nec

D-U-N-S 25-313-1593   (BR)
MAXIM TRANSPORTATION SERVICES INC
MAXIM INTERNATIONAL TRUCKS
475 Henderson Dr, Regina, SK, S4N 5W8
(306) 721-9700
Emp Here 40
SIC 5511 New and used car dealers

D-U-N-S 20-650-8355   (BR)
**MCDONALD'S   RESTAURANTS   OF
CANADA LIMITED**
MCDONALD'S
(*Suby of* McDonald's Corporation)
924 E Victoria Ave, Regina, SK, S4N 7A9
(306) 525-2621
Emp Here 50
SIC 5812 Eating places

D-U-N-S 25-612-2136   (BR)

MIDWEST RESTAURANT INC
MOXIE'S CLASSIC GRILL
2037 Park St, Regina, SK, S4N 6S2
(306) 781-5655
Emp Here 100
SIC 5812 Eating places

D-U-N-S 20-919-3361   (BR)
MIDWEST SURVEYS INC
405 Maxwell Cres, Regina, SK, S4N 5X9
(306) 525-8706
Emp Here 38
SIC 8713 Surveying services

D-U-N-S 24-358-7669   (BR)
**NORTHLAND PROPERTIES CORPORA-
TION**
SANDMAN HOTEL & SUITES REGINA
(*Suby of* Northland Properties Corporation)
1800 E Victoria Ave Suite A, Regina, SK, S4N
7K3
(306) 757-2444
Emp Here 40
SIC 7011 Hotels and motels

D-U-N-S 24-000-4510   (BR)
PLASTIPAK INDUSTRIES INC
235 Henderson Dr, Regina, SK, S4N 6C2
(306) 721-7515
Emp Here 40
SIC 3089 Plastics products, nec

D-U-N-S 24-774-6274   (BR)
POSTMEDIA NETWORK INC
LEADER POST, THE
1964 Park St, Regina, SK, S4N 7M5
(306) 781-5211
Emp Here 275
SIC 2711 Newspapers

D-U-N-S 20-261-1018   (SL)
R & G TRANSPORT LTD
625 Mcdonald St, Regina, SK, S4N 4X1
(306) 721-8677
Emp Here 25   *Sales* 2,338,878
SIC 4212 Local trucking, without storage

D-U-N-S 25-023-4101   (BR)
REIMER EXPRESS LINES LTD
(*Suby of* Yrc Worldwide Inc.)
920 Mackay St, Regina, SK, S4N 4X7
(306) 359-3222
Emp Here 25
SIC 4213 Trucking, except local

D-U-N-S 25-315-3175   (BR)
RIDSDALE TRANSPORT LTD
385 Henderson Dr Suite A, Regina, SK, S4N
5W8
(306) 721-8272
Emp Here 26
SIC 4213 Trucking, except local

D-U-N-S 24-571-7889   (SL)
ROSS MACHINE SHOP LIMITED
40 Kress St, Regina, SK, S4N 5Y3
(306) 721-6680
Emp Here 50   *Sales* 3,648,035
SIC 3599 Industrial machinery, nec

D-U-N-S 24-852-0892   (BR)
RUSSEL METALS INC
RUSSEL STEEL REGINA
475 E 1st Ave, Regina, SK, S4N 4Z3
(306) 721-6411
Emp Here 34
SIC 5051 Metals service centers and offices

D-U-N-S 24-914-1300   (BR)
S.L.H. TRANSPORT INC
745 Park St, Regina, SK, S4N 4Y4

Emp Here 60
SIC 4213 Trucking, except local

D-U-N-S 20-208-1522   (BR)
SASKATCHEWAN ABILITIES COUNCIL INC
SASKATCHEWAN ABILITIES COUNCIL

825 Mcdonald St, Regina, SK, S4N 2X5
(306) 569-9048
Emp Here 25
SIC 8331 Job training and related services

D-U-N-S 24-916-0813   (BR)
**SASKATCHEWAN ASSOCIATION OF RE-
HABILITATION CENTRES**
SARCAN RECYCLING
(*Suby of* Saskatchewan Association of Reha-
bilitation Centres)
1421 Fleury St, Regina, SK, S4N 7N5
(306) 347-3070
Emp Here 25
SIC 4953 Refuse systems

D-U-N-S 20-235-7567   (BR)
**SASKATCHEWAN GOVERNMENT INSUR-
ANCE**
SGI SALVAGE
460 Fleet St, Regina, SK, S4N 7N7
(306) 775-6025
Emp Here 30
SIC 6331 Fire, marine, and casualty insurance

D-U-N-S 25-315-2227   (BR)
**SASKATCHEWAN GOVERNMENT INSUR-
ANCE**
REGINA COMMERCIAL CLAIMS CENTER
440 Fleet St, Regina, SK, S4N 7N7
(306) 775-6000
Emp Here 50
SIC 6331 Fire, marine, and casualty insurance

D-U-N-S 20-770-3385   (BR)
**SASKATCHEWAN GOVERNMENT INSUR-
ANCE**
SGI
440 Fleet St, Regina, SK, S4N 7N7
(306) 775-6000
Emp Here 100
SIC 6331 Fire, marine, and casualty insurance

D-U-N-S 24-104-6478   (BR)
SASKATCHEWAN MOTOR CLUB
105 Kress St, Regina, SK, S4N 5X8
(306) 791-4387
Emp Here 50
SIC 8699 Membership organizations, nec

D-U-N-S 24-000-4858   (BR)
SASKATCHEWAN POWER CORPORATION
SASKPOWER
2901 Powerhouse Dr, Regina, SK, S4N 0A1
(306) 566-3069
Emp Here 25
SIC 4911 Electric services

D-U-N-S 24-340-8478   (BR)
**SASKATCHEWAN   TELECOMMUNICA-
TIONS INTERNATIONAL, INC**
SASKTEL
355 Longman Cres, Regina, SK, S4N 6G3
(306) 777-3584
Emp Here 200
SIC 4899 Communication services, nec

D-U-N-S 24-850-0386   (BR)
SEARS CANADA INC
855 Park St, Regina, SK, S4N 6M1
(306) 566-5104
Emp Here 50
SIC 4225 General warehousing and storage

D-U-N-S 25-271-7467   (BR)
SOBEYS WEST INC
VICTORIA SQUARE SAFEWAY
2223 E Victoria Ave, Regina, SK, S4N 6E4
(306) 789-3191
Emp Here 50
SIC 5411 Grocery stores

D-U-N-S 25-619-3210   (SL)
SOUND STAGE ENTERTAINMENT INC
PUMP ROADHOUSE, THE
641 E Victoria Ave, Regina, SK, S4N 0P1
(306) 359-7440
Emp Here 50   *Sales* 1,824,018

SIC 5813 Drinking places

D-U-N-S 20-068-3514   (SL)
SUN ELECTRIC (1975) LTD
504 Henderson Dr, Regina, SK, S4N 5X2
(306) 721-4777
Emp Here 25   *Sales* 2,826,987
SIC 1731 Electrical work

D-U-N-S 24-344-0232   (BR)
SUPERIOR PLUS LP
WINROC
1048 Fleury St, Regina, SK, S4N 4W8
(306) 721-2010
Emp Here 20
SIC 5039 Construction materials, nec

D-U-N-S 20-840-5076   (HQ)
SUPREME OFFICE PRODUCTS LIMITED
SUPREME BASICS, DIV OF
(*Suby of* Placements Denis Latulippe Inc, Les)
310 Henderson Dr, Regina, SK, S4N 5W7
(306) 566-8800
Emp Here 40   *Emp Total* 300
Sales 14,738,061
SIC 5112 Stationery and office supplies
Pr Pr Doreen Bosche
Diana Bosche
Derek Bosche
Cathy Robinson

D-U-N-S 24-717-2174   (BR)
SYSCO CANADA, INC
SYSCO REGINA
(*Suby of* Sysco Corporation)
266 E Dewdney Ave, Regina, SK, S4N 4G2

Emp Here 130
SIC 5141 Groceries, general line

D-U-N-S 20-514-5837   (BR)
UAP INC
AIR KING REMANUFACTURING
(*Suby of* Genuine Parts Company)
565 Park St, Regina, SK, S4N 5B2

Emp Here 21
SIC 5013 Motor vehicle supplies and new
parts

D-U-N-S 25-153-4988   (HQ)
UPONOR LTD
WIRSBO
662 E 1st Ave Suite 200, Regina, SK, S4N 5T6
(306) 721-2449
Emp Here 45   *Emp Total* 3,869
Sales 45,652,500
SIC 5075 Warm air heating and air condition-
ing
Pr Wade Peterson
Genl Mgr William Gray

D-U-N-S 24-329-3656   (BR)
VIPOND INC
ALSASK FIRE EQUIPMENT
205 E 1st Ave, Regina, SK, S4N 4Z3
(306) 757-0003
Emp Here 25
SIC 5063 Electrical apparatus and equipment

D-U-N-S 20-131-2530   (BR)
WBM OFFICE SYSTEMS INC
414 Mcdonald St, Regina, SK, S4N 6E1
(306) 791-2100
Emp Here 25
SIC 5999 Miscellaneous retail stores, nec

D-U-N-S 20-119-1181   (BR)
WSP CANADA INC
FOCUS SURVEYS
333 Park St, Regina, SK, S4N 5B2
(306) 586-0837
Emp Here 25
SIC 8713 Surveying services

D-U-N-S 20-448-6781   (HQ)
WATERGROUP COMPANIES INC
CULLIGAN

▲ Public Company   ■ Public Company Family Member   **HQ** Headquarters   **BR** Branch   **SL** Single Location

(*Suby of* Clayton, Dubilier & Rice, Inc.)
580 Park St, Regina, SK, S4N 5A9
(306) 761-3210
Emp Here 250   *Emp Total* 33,045
Sales 59,684,694
SIC 3589 Service industry machinery, nec
Dir Maurice Fontaine

Regina, SK S4P

D-U-N-S 25-293-7107   (BR)
6080090 CANADA INC
RBC DOMINION SECURITIES
2010 11th Ave, Regina, SK, S4P 0J3
(306) 777-0500
Emp Here 49
SIC 6211 Security brokers and dealers

D-U-N-S 20-069-9556   (BR)
AON CANADA INC
2103 11th Ave Suite 1000, Regina, SK, S4P
3Z8
(306) 569-6700
Emp Here 30
SIC 6411 Insurance agents, brokers, and service

D-U-N-S 24-519-2984   (BR)
AON REED STENHOUSE INC
2103 11th Ave Suite 1000, Regina, SK, S4P
3Z8
(306) 569-6700
Emp Here 30
SIC 6411 Insurance agents, brokers, and service

D-U-N-S 20-756-0350   (BR)
AECOM CANADA LTD
1621 Albert St Suite 183, Regina, SK, S4P
2S5
(306) 522-3266
Emp Here 52
SIC 8711 Engineering services

D-U-N-S 25-640-3148   (SL)
AFTA RESTAURANT LTD
BOSTON PIZZA
2050 Halifax St, Regina, SK, S4P 1T7
(306) 790-9440
Emp Here 60   *Sales* 1,824,018
SIC 5812 Eating places

D-U-N-S 20-285-1119   (BR)
**ALL SENIORS CARE LIVING CENTRES
LTD**
*COLLEGE PARK RETIREMENT RESI-
DENCE*
(*Suby of* All Seniors Care Holdings Inc)
1535 Anson Rd Suite 140, Regina, SK, S4P
0C2
(306) 565-0515
Emp Here 40
SIC 6513 Apartment building operators

D-U-N-S 24-247-2434   (BR)
ARBOR MEMORIAL SERVICES INC
REGINA MEMORIAL GARDENS
Po Box 4620 Stn Main, Regina, SK, S4P 3Y3
(306) 791-6777
Emp Here 25
SIC 6531 Real estate agents and managers

D-U-N-S 20-298-2208   (BR)
BMO NESBITT BURNS INC
2103 11th Ave Suite 1171, Regina, SK, S4P
3Z8
(306) 780-9700
Emp Here 25
SIC 6211 Security brokers and dealers

D-U-N-S 20-843-2476   (BR)
BANK OF NOVA SCOTIA, THE
SCOTIABANK
1901 Hamilton St, Regina, SK, S4P 2C7
(306) 780-1200
Emp Here 45

SIC 6021 National commercial banks

D-U-N-S 20-572-0100   (BR)
BANK OF MONTREAL
2103 11th Ave Suite 1171, Regina, SK, S4P
3Z8
(306) 569-5602
Emp Here 20
SIC 6021 National commercial banks

D-U-N-S 25-560-4886   (SL)
BANSHEE ENTERPRISES LTD
2330 15th Ave Suite 100, Regina, SK, S4P
1A2

Emp Here 25   *Sales* 6,028,800
SIC 1623 Water, sewer, and utility lines
Pr Pr Randy Bacon
Treas Gary Erickson
Dir Dave Baker
Dir Bryant Conquered
Prin Dwayne Anderson
Prin Glen Eisnor

D-U-N-S 20-712-6900   (BR)
**BOARD OF EDUCATION REGINA SCHOOL
DIVISION NO. 4 OF SASKATCHEWAN**
THOMSON ELEMENTARY SCHOOL
2033 Toronto St, Regina, SK, S4P 1N2
(306) 791-8460
Emp Here 30
SIC 8211 Elementary and secondary schools

D-U-N-S 25-268-1077   (BR)
**BOARD OF EDUCATION REGINA SCHOOL
DIVISION NO. 4 OF SASKATCHEWAN**
BALFOUR COLLEGIATE SCHOOL
1245 College Ave, Regina, SK, S4P 1B1
(306) 523-3200
Emp Here 55
SIC 8211 Elementary and secondary schools

D-U-N-S 20-003-3228   (BR)
**BOARD OF EDUCATION OF THE REGINA
ROMAN CATHOLIC SEPARATE SCHOOL
DIVISION NO. 81**
MILLER COMPREHENSIVE HIGH SCHOOL
1027 College Ave, Regina, SK, S4P 1A7
(306) 791-7230
Emp Here 80
SIC 8211 Elementary and secondary schools

D-U-N-S 25-361-1743   (BR)
BRANDT INDUSTRIES LTD
BRANDT ENGINEERED PRODUCT
302 Mill St, Regina, SK, S4P 3E1
(306) 791-7557
Emp Here 200
SIC 3535 Conveyors and conveying equipment

D-U-N-S 20-174-6943   (SL)
BRANDT PROPERTIES LTD
Hwy 1 E, Regina, SK, S4P 3R8
(306) 525-1314
Emp Here 20   *Sales* 2,355,823
SIC 6512 Nonresidential building operators

D-U-N-S 20-327-5425   (SL)
BRANDT TRACTOR PROPERTIES LTD
Hwy 1 E, Regina, SK, S4P 3R8
(306) 791-7777
Emp Here 20   *Sales* 2,355,823
SIC 8741 Management services

D-U-N-S 25-416-4403   (HQ)
CDSL CANADA LIMITED
CGI
1900 Albert St Unit 700, Regina, SK, S4P 4K8
(306) 761-4000
Emp Here 250   *Emp Total* 485
Sales 164,161,575
SIC 7379 Computer related services, nec
  Serge Godin
Dir Kevin Linder
Dir Francois Boulanger
Dir Benoit Dube

D-U-N-S 25-293-8527   (BR)
CIBC WORLD MARKETS INC
1801 Hamilton St Unit 420, Regina, SK, S4P
4B4
(306) 359-1577
Emp Here 33
SIC 6211 Security brokers and dealers

D-U-N-S 20-514-7809   (BR)
CNH INDUSTRIAL CANADA, LTD
CNH CANADA, LTD
Gd, Regina, SK, S4P 3T6
(306) 721-4250
Emp Here 30
SIC 3523 Farm machinery and equipment

D-U-N-S 24-348-9056   (SL)
CUETS FINANCIAL LTD
(*Suby of* Toronto-Dominion Bank, The)
2055 Albert St, Regina, SK, S4P 2T8
(306) 566-1269
Emp Here 350   *Sales* 21,767,800
SIC 7389 Business services, nec
Dir Stan Kuss
VP VP Ken Kosolofski

D-U-N-S 25-612-2482   (BR)
**CANADA LIFE ASSURANCE COMPANY,
THE**
1901 Scarth St Suite 414, Regina, SK, S4P
4L4
(306) 751-6000
Emp Here 800
SIC 6311 Life insurance

D-U-N-S 25-289-0413   (BR)
CANADA POST CORPORATION
2200 Saskatchewan Dr, Regina, SK, S4P 3V7
(306) 761-6301
Emp Here 350
SIC 4311 U.s. postal service

D-U-N-S 24-426-7209   (BR)
**CANADIAN BROADCASTING CORPORA-
TION**
CBC RADIO CANADA
2440 Broad St, Regina, SK, S4P 0A5
(306) 347-9540
Emp Here 180
SIC 4832 Radio broadcasting stations

D-U-N-S 20-921-0678   (BR)
CANADIAN CANCER SOCIETY
1910 Mcintyre St, Regina, SK, S4P 2R3
(306) 790-5822
Emp Here 28
SIC 8399 Social services, nec

D-U-N-S 25-311-3278   (BR)
**CANADIAN IMPERIAL BANK OF COM-
MERCE**
CIBC
1800 Hamilton St Suite 200, Regina, SK, S4P
4K7
(306) 359-8585
Emp Here 30
SIC 6021 National commercial banks

D-U-N-S 20-104-3242   (BR)
**CANADIAN IMPERIAL BANK OF COM-
MERCE**
CIBC
2412 11th Ave, Regina, SK, S4P 0K3
(306) 337-6000
Emp Here 25
SIC 6021 National commercial banks

D-U-N-S 25-750-6840   (BR)
CANLAN ICE SPORTS CORP
SHERWOOD ICE SPORT CENTRE
Gd Lcd Main, Regina, SK, S4P 2Z4

Emp Here 35
SIC 7997 Membership sports and recreation
clubs

D-U-N-S 24-967-4862   (SL)
CAR RENTALS & SERVICES (2000) LTD

1500 Winnipeg St, Regina, SK, S4P 1E7

Emp Here 53   *Sales* 7,507,300
SIC 7514 Passenger car rental
  Kelvin Leivel
  Daren Sentes
  Wilfred Yauck

D-U-N-S 25-614-6960   (SL)
CATHEDRAL VILLAGE RESTAURANT LTD
CATHEDRAL VILLAGE FREE HOUSE
(*Suby of* Freehouse Asset Management Ltd)
2062 Albert St, Regina, SK, S4P 2T7
(306) 359-1661
Emp Here 60   *Sales* 1,824,018
SIC 5812 Eating places

D-U-N-S 24-684-6674   (BR)
CELERO SOLUTIONS INC
CELERO
(*Suby of* Celero Solutions Inc)
2055 Albert St, Regina, SK, S4P 2T8
(306) 566-1244
Emp Here 65
SIC 8742 Management consulting services

D-U-N-S 20-910-2255   (BR)
CENTRAL CARD SERVICES INC
CUETS
(*Suby of* Toronto-Dominion Bank, The)
2221 Cornwall St, Regina, SK, S4P 2L1
(306) 566-1346
Emp Here 120
SIC 8741 Management services

D-U-N-S 24-468-8461   (BR)
CO-OPERATORS GROUP LIMITED, THE
1920 College Ave, Regina, SK, S4P 1C4
(306) 347-6200
Emp Here 500
SIC 6411 Insurance agents, brokers, and service

D-U-N-S 25-678-6724   (BR)
CONCENTRA BANK
CULEASE FINANCIAL SVC DIV OF
2055 Albert St, Regina, SK, S4P 2T8
(306) 566-7440
Emp Here 22
SIC 6159 Miscellaneous business credit institutions

D-U-N-S 20-514-7601   (BR)
CONEXUS CREDIT UNION 2006
1960 Albert St Suite 205, Regina, SK, S4P
2T1
(306) 244-3702
Emp Here 32
SIC 6162 Mortgage bankers and loan correspondents

D-U-N-S 20-067-1709   (BR)
**CONSUMERS' CO-OPERATIVE REFINER-
IES LIMITED**
(*Suby of* Federated Co-Operatives Limited)
650 E 9th Ave N, Regina, SK, S4P 3A1
(306) 721-5353
Emp Here 500
SIC 2911 Petroleum refining

D-U-N-S 24-231-5190   (BR)
**DELOITTE & TOUCHE MANAGEMENT
CONSULTANTS**
DELOITTE
(*Suby of* Deloitte & Touche Management Consultants)
2103 11th Ave Suite 900, Regina, SK, S4P
3Z8
(306) 525-1600
Emp Here 70
SIC 8721 Accounting, auditing, and bookkeeping

D-U-N-S 20-699-8887   (BR)
DELTA HOTELS LIMITED
1919 Saskatchewan Dr Suite 100, Regina,
SK, S4P 4H2

(306) 525-5255
Emp Here 220
SIC 8741 Management services

D-U-N-S 20-654-1687   (BR)
DYNAINDUSTRIAL INC
277 Sherwood Rd, Regina, SK, S4P 3A2
(306) 359-7088
Emp Here 40
SIC 3599 Industrial machinery, nec

D-U-N-S 20-910-2297   (BR)
ENBRIDGE PIPELINES INC
119 9th Ave N, Regina, SK, S4P 3B2
(306) 791-8181
Emp Here 157
SIC 4612 Crude petroleum pipelines

D-U-N-S 20-067-5734   (HQ)
EVRAZ INC. NA CANADA
EVRAZ REGINA STEEL
(*Suby of* EVRAZ PLC)
100 Armour Rd, Regina, SK, S4P 3C7
(306) 924-7700
Emp Here 1,000   *Emp Total* 98,535
Sales 298,856,595
SIC 3312 Blast furnaces and steel mills
Pr Mike Rewinkel
 Stephen Mcnevitts
Sec Jennifer Murray
 Pavel Tatyanin

D-U-N-S 20-747-1566   (HQ)
FARM CREDIT CANADA
FCC
1800 Hamilton St, Regina, SK, S4P 4L3
(306) 780-8100
Emp Here 700   *Emp Total* 570,000
Sales 855,688,243
SIC 6159 Miscellaneous business credit institutions
Pr Pr Greg Stewart
Sr VP Paul Macdonald
VP Opers Remi Lemoine
 Lyndon Carlson
Ex VP Michael Hoffort
Pers/VP Greg Honey
 Greg Wilmer
CFO Rick Hoffman
 Dale Johnston
Dir Donald Bettle

D-U-N-S 25-950-5121   (BR)
GENERAL ELECTRIC CANADA COMPANY
GE RAILCAR REPAIR SERVICES
(*Suby of* General Electric Company)
Gd, Regina, SK, S4P 3L7
(306) 525-0122
Emp Here 60
SIC 3625 Relays and industrial controls

D-U-N-S 24-718-6463   (BR)
GENERAL SCRAP PARTNERSHIP
WHEAT CITY METALS
2881 Pasqua St N, Regina, SK, S4P 3B1
(306) 775-3611
Emp Here 20
SIC 5093 Scrap and waste materials

D-U-N-S 24-334-7395   (BR)
GOVERNING COUNCIL OF THE SALVATION ARMY IN CANADA, THE
SALVATION ARMY COMMUNITY & FAMILY SERVICES
2240 13th Ave, Regina, SK, S4P 3M7
(306) 757-4600
Emp Here 25
SIC 8322 Individual and family services

D-U-N-S 25-453-1940   (BR)
GOVERNING COUNCIL OF THE SALVATION ARMY IN CANADA, THE
1845 Osler St, Regina, SK, S4P 1W1
(306) 569-6088
Emp Here 20
SIC 8322 Individual and family services

D-U-N-S 20-969-9185   (BR)

GOVERNMENT OF SASKATCHEWAN
MINISTRY OF GOVERNMENT SERVICES PURCHASING BRANCH
1920 Rose St, Regina, SK, S4P 0A9
(306) 787-6871
Emp Here 20
SIC 8741 Management services

D-U-N-S 24-965-7532   (BR)
GOVERNMENT OF SASKATCHEWAN
SASKATCHEWAN VEHICLE STANDARDS AND INSPECTION
2260 11th Ave Suite 18a, Regina, SK, S4P 2N7
(306) 775-6188
Emp Here 22
SIC 8742 Management consulting services

D-U-N-S 25-611-8043   (BR)
GREAT-WEST LIFE ASSURANCE COMPANY, THE
QUADRUS INVESTMENT SERVICES
2010 11th Ave Suite 600, Regina, SK, S4P 0J3
(306) 761-7500
Emp Here 26
SIC 6311 Life insurance

D-U-N-S 20-448-3507   (BR)
HUDSON'S BAY COMPANY
2150 11th Ave, Regina, SK, S4P 0J5
(306) 525-8511
Emp Here 270
SIC 5311 Department stores

D-U-N-S 20-067-5692   (BR)
IBM CANADA LIMITED
(*Suby of* International Business Machines Corporation)
1801 Hamilton St Suite 600, Regina, SK, S4P 4B4
(306) 564-6601
Emp Here 25
SIC 5045 Computers, peripherals, and software

D-U-N-S 25-315-7986   (BR)
IGM FINANCIAL INC
INVESTORS GROUP FINANCIAL
2365 Albert St Suite 100, Regina, SK, S4P 4K1
(306) 757-3511
Emp Here 50
SIC 8748 Business consulting, nec

D-U-N-S 20-179-6591   (BR)
INTRIA ITEMS INC
2220 12th Ave Suite 100, Regina, SK, S4P 0M8
(306) 359-8314
Emp Here 48
SIC 7374 Data processing and preparation

D-U-N-S 20-265-2447   (BR)
JUMP.CA WIRELESS SUPPLY CORP
JUMP.CA
2102 11th Ave, Regina, SK, S4P 3Y6
(306) 569-0062
Emp Here 25
SIC 5999 Miscellaneous retail stores, nec

D-U-N-S 20-798-6816   (BR)
JUMP.CA WIRELESS SUPPLY CORP
JUMP. CA
2221 Cornwall St Suite 500, Regina, SK, S4P 2L1
(306) 790-4525
Emp Here 64
SIC 4899 Communication services, nec

D-U-N-S 24-818-1927   (BR)
KPMG INC
1881 Scarth St Suite 2000, Regina, SK, S4P 4K9
(306) 791-1200
Emp Here 40
SIC 8721 Accounting, auditing, and bookkeeping

D-U-N-S 20-837-0564   (BR)
KPMG LLP
(*Suby of* KPMG LLP)
1881 Scarth St Suite 2000, Regina, SK, S4P 4K9
(306) 791-1200
Emp Here 40
SIC 8721 Accounting, auditing, and bookkeeping

D-U-N-S 20-652-2828   (SL)
LEADON (REGINA) OPERATIONS LP
REGINA INN
1975 Broad St, Regina, SK, S4P 1Y2
(306) 525-6767
Emp Here 100   *Sales* 4,377,642
SIC 7011 Hotels and motels

D-U-N-S 20-558-7467   (SL)
LINNEN, HJ ASSOCIATES LTD
2161 Scarth St Suite 200, Regina, SK, S4P 2H8
(306) 586-9611
Emp Here 42   *Sales* 5,985,550
SIC 8742 Management consulting services
Pr Pr Harvey Linnen

D-U-N-S 20-105-5550   (SL)
LIVEBLOCK AUCTIONS CANADA LTD
2125 11th Ave Suite 200, Regina, SK, S4P 3X3
(306) 523-4004
Emp Here 30   *Sales* 5,681,200
SIC 5045 Computers, peripherals, and software
Dir Walter Dvorak
Dir James P Hallett
Dir Thomas J Caruso

D-U-N-S 20-950-0185   (BR)
LOBLAWS INC
DRUGSTORE PHARMACY
1341 Broadway Ave, Regina, SK, S4P 1E5
(306) 569-7575
Emp Here 20
SIC 5912 Drug stores and proprietary stores

D-U-N-S 24-417-4426   (BR)
LOBLAWS INC
EXTRA FOODS
1341 Broadway Ave, Regina, SK, S4P 1E5
(306) 569-1059
Emp Here 50
SIC 5411 Grocery stores

D-U-N-S 24-337-2013   (BR)
LONDON LIFE INSURANCE COMPANY
FREEDOM 55 FINANCIAL
2010 11th Ave Suite 650, Regina, SK, S4P 0J3
(306) 586-0905
Emp Here 20
SIC 8742 Management consulting services

D-U-N-S 20-841-9051   (BR)
LONDON LIFE INSURANCE COMPANY
2100 Broad St Suite 405, Regina, SK, S4P 1Y5

Emp Here 20
SIC 6411 Insurance agents, brokers, and service

D-U-N-S 20-002-2452   (BR)
MNP LLP
2010 11th Ave Suite 900, Regina, SK, S4P 0J3
(306) 790-7900
Emp Here 42
SIC 8721 Accounting, auditing, and bookkeeping

D-U-N-S 20-273-2546   (BR)
MAGNA ELECTRIC CORPORATION
2361 Industrial Dr, Regina, SK, S4P 3B2
(306) 949-8131
Emp Here 56
SIC 7629 Electrical repair shops

D-U-N-S 25-196-3096   (BR)
MCKERCHER LLP
1801 Hamilton St Suite 800, Regina, SK, S4P 4B4
(306) 565-6500
Emp Here 40
SIC 8111 Legal services

D-U-N-S 24-966-9573   (BR)
MEMORIAL GARDENS CANADA LIMITED
REGINA MEMORIAL GARDENS & CREMATORIUM
Hwy 1 E, Regina, SK, S4P 3Y3
(306) 791-6789
Emp Here 20
SIC 6553 Cemetery subdividers and developers

D-U-N-S 25-682-2078   (BR)
MERIDIAN MANUFACTURING INC
2800 Pasqua St, Regina, SK, S4P 2Z4
(306) 545-4044
Emp Here 150
SIC 3545 Machine tool accessories

D-U-N-S 25-653-0593   (SL)
RANDY KUNTZ CATERING COMPANY LIMITED
Gd Stn Main, Regina, SK, S4P 3C7
(306) 539-0008
Emp Here 50   *Sales* 1,819,127
SIC 5812 Eating places

D-U-N-S 20-733-7804   (BR)
RAWLCO CAPITAL LTD
RAWLCO RADIO
2401 Saskatchewan Dr Suite 210, Regina, SK, S4P 4H8
(306) 525-0000
Emp Here 80
SIC 4832 Radio broadcasting stations

D-U-N-S 24-367-4392   (SL)
RED MOUNTAIN HOLDINGS LTD
SAKUNDIAK EQUIPMENT
2800 Pasqua St N, Regina, SK, S4P 3E1
(306) 545-4044
Emp Here 90   *Sales* 10,871,144
SIC 3523 Farm machinery and equipment
Dir Paul Cunningham
Ch Bd Russ Edwards

D-U-N-S 20-835-7095   (SL)
REGINA EXHIBITION ASSOCIATION LIMITED
REGINA EXHIBITION PARK
1700 Elphinstone St, Regina, SK, S4P 2Z6
(306) 781-9200
Emp Here 1,000   *Sales* 73,129,200
SIC 7999 Amusement and recreation, nec
Pr Mark Allan
Dir Fin Dean Churchill

D-U-N-S 20-545-9217   (SL)
REGINA MOTOR PRODUCTS (1970) LTD
Albert St S Hwy 1-6, Regina, SK, S4P 3A8
(866) 273-5778
Emp Here 74   *Sales* 5,399,092
SIC 7538 General automotive repair shops
 Blaine Ledingham
Pr Pr Jason Ledingham

D-U-N-S 24-655-6583   (SL)
REGINA OPEN DOOR SOCIETY INC
2550 Broad St, Regina, SK, S4P 3Z4
(306) 352-3500
Emp Here 70   *Sales* 2,772,507
SIC 8322 Individual and family services

D-U-N-S 24-335-0068   (BR)
REGINA QU'APPELLE REGIONAL HEALTH AUTHORITY
ADDICTION SERVICES
2110 Hamilton St, Regina, SK, S4P 2E3

Emp Here 50
SIC 8069 Specialty hospitals, except psychiatric

D-U-N-S 20-554-1647　　(BR)
REGINA QU'APPELLE REGIONAL HEALTH AUTHORITY
MENTAL HEALTH CLINIC
2110 Hamilton St Suite 100, Regina, SK, S4P 2E3
(306) 766-7800
Emp Here 60
SIC 8093 Specialty outpatient clinics, nec

D-U-N-S 25-643-6197　　(SL)
REGINA SOCCER ASSOCIATION, THE
1321 Saskatchewan Dr, Regina, SK, S4P 0C9
(306) 352-8040
Emp Here 26　　*Sales* 8,009,797
SIC 8399 Social services, nec

D-U-N-S 20-014-2219　　(BR)
SASKENERGY INCORPORATED
1601 Winnipeg St Suite 9, Regina, SK, S4P 4E7
(306) 777-9200
Emp Here 80
SIC 4924 Natural gas distribution

D-U-N-S 20-153-5056　　(HQ)
SASKATCHEWAN APPRENTICESHIP AND TRADE CERTIFICATION COMMISSION
(*Suby of* Saskatchewan Apprenticeship And Trade Certification Commission)
2140 Hamilton St, Regina, SK, S4P 2E3
(306) 787-2444
Emp Here 50　　*Emp Total* 100
Sales 23,386,295
SIC 8249 Vocational schools, nec
Dir Lily Wong

D-U-N-S 25-417-8072　　(HQ)
SASKATCHEWAN GAMING CORPORATION
CASINO REGINA
1880 Saskatchewan Dr, Regina, SK, S4P 0B2
(306) 565-3000
Emp Here 600　　*Emp Total* 40,372
Sales 137,588,354
SIC 7999 Amusement and recreation, nec
Pr Twyla Meredith
VP Opers Gerry Fischer

D-U-N-S 25-619-3871　　(BR)
SASKATCHEWAN GOVERNMENT INSURANCE
S G I CANADA
2260 11th Ave, Regina, SK, S4P 2N7
(306) 775-6000
Emp Here 24
SIC 6331 Fire, marine, and casualty insurance

D-U-N-S 20-833-4383　　(HQ)
SASKATCHEWAN GOVERNMENT INSURANCE
SGI CANADA
2260 11th Ave Suite 18, Regina, SK, S4P 0J9
(306) 751-1200
Emp Here 1,000　　*Emp Total* 40,372
Sales 1,021,223,304
SIC 6331 Fire, marine, and casualty insurance
　Warren Sproule
　Rick Watson
　Dale Bloom
　William Heidt
　Merin Coutts

D-U-N-S 20-756-4022　　(HQ)
SASKATCHEWAN HOUSING CORPORATION
1920 Broad St Suite 900, Regina, SK, S4P 3V6
(306) 787-4177
Emp Here 100　　*Emp Total* 40,372
Sales 147,133,142
SIC 6531 Real estate agents and managers
Pr Darrell Jones
CFO Don Allen

D-U-N-S 25-611-5718　　(SL)
SASKATCHEWAN LIBERAL ASSOCIATION
2054 Broad St, Regina, SK, S4P 1Y3

Emp Here 52　　*Sales* 4,888,367
SIC 8651 Political organizations

D-U-N-S 24-916-5358　　(HQ)
SASKATCHEWAN TELECOMMUNICATIONS HOLDING CORPORATION
SASKTEL HOLDCO
2121 Saskatchewan Dr, Regina, SK, S4P 3Y2
(306) 777-3737
Emp Here 200　　*Emp Total* 40,372
Sales 1,137,240
SIC 4899 Communication services, nec

D-U-N-S 20-448-3143　　(HQ)
SASKATCHEWAN TELECOMMUNICATIONS INTERNATIONAL, INC
SASKTEL INTERNATIONAL
2121 Saskatchewan Dr, Regina, SK, S4P 3Y2
(306) 777-2201
Emp Here 80　　*Emp Total* 40,372
Sales 11,017,066
SIC 4899 Communication services, nec
Pr Douglas Burnett
S&M/VP Steve Sousa

D-U-N-S 20-068-2177　　(HQ)
SASKATCHEWAN TRANSPORTATION COMPANY
STC
1717 Saskatchewan Dr, Regina, SK, S4P 2E2
(306) 787-3354
Emp Here 75　　*Emp Total* 40,372
Sales 14,518,135
SIC 4131 Intercity and rural bus transportation
Pr Shawn Grice
　Mitch Holash
Dir Jocelyn Hutchinson
Dir John Breakey
Dir Amanda Crashley
Dir Veronique Loewen
Dir Mervin Massier
Dir Mervin Schneider
Dir Delmer Wagner

D-U-N-S 25-002-9378　　(BR)
SEARS CANADA INC
1720 Hamilton St Suite 100, Regina, SK, S4P 4A5
(306) 569-1344
Emp Here 110
SIC 6512 Nonresidential building operators

D-U-N-S 25-219-9260　　(SL)
SIERRA VENTURES CORP
FANTASTIC CLEANING
1810 College Ave, Regina, SK, S4P 1C1
(306) 949-1510
Emp Here 120　　*Sales* 3,502,114
SIC 7349 Building maintenance services, nec

D-U-N-S 20-320-1751　　(BR)
STANTEC ARCHITECTURE LTD
1820 Hamilton St Suite 400, Regina, SK, S4P 2B8
(306) 781-6400
Emp Here 211
SIC 8711 Engineering services

D-U-N-S 24-202-7675　　(BR)
STARTEK CANADA SERVICES LTD
(*Suby of* Startek, Inc.)
2130 11th Ave Suite 301, Regina, SK, S4P 0J5

Emp Here 500
SIC 8741 Management services

D-U-N-S 25-958-8978　　(BR)
STRONGCO LIMITED PARTNERSHIP
WEST CONS EQUIPMENT AND RENTAL
Hwy 1 E, Regina, SK, S4P 3B1
(306) 359-7273
Emp Here 25
SIC 7353 Heavy construction equipment rental

D-U-N-S 24-230-6900　　(BR)

SUN LIFE ASSURANCE COMPANY OF CANADA
2002 Victoria Ave Suite 1200, Regina, SK, S4P 0R7
(306) 757-8631
Emp Here 30
SIC 6311 Life insurance

D-U-N-S 20-548-0820　　(SL)
TOWN & COUNTRY PLUMBING & HEATING (2004) LTD
TOWN & COUNTRY PLUMBING AND HEATING
1450 South Railway St, Regina, SK, S4P 0A2
(306) 352-4328
Emp Here 50　　*Sales* 4,377,642
SIC 1711 Plumbing, heating, air-conditioning

D-U-N-S 24-747-8910　　(HQ)
TRANSGAS LIMITED
1777 Victoria Ave Suite 700, Regina, SK, S4P 4K5
(306) 777-9500
Emp Here 120　　*Emp Total* 40,372
Sales 234,407,521
SIC 4923 Gas transmission and distribution
Pr Doug Kelln
VP VP Daryl Posehn
Pers/VP Robert Haynes
Treas Ken Adams

D-U-N-S 25-368-7040　　(BR)
VARSTEEL LTD
VALUE STEEL & PIPE
2191 Albert St N, Regina, SK, S4P 3E1
(306) 775-3634
Emp Here 20
SIC 5051 Metals service centers and offices

D-U-N-S 20-180-0054　　(BR)
WESTON BAKERIES LIMITED
Gd Lcd Main, Regina, SK, S4P 2Z4
(306) 359-7400
Emp Here 100
SIC 2045 Prepared flour mixes and doughs

D-U-N-S 24-367-3550　　(HQ)
YARA BELLE PLAINE INC
1874 Scarth St Suite 1800, Regina, SK, S4P 4B3
(306) 525-7600
Emp Here 20　　*Emp Total* 545
Sales 23,908,528
SIC 2874 Phosphatic fertilizers
　Edward Cavazuti
　Gordon Dolney
　Peter Valesares

D-U-N-S 24-170-2851　　(SL)
YOUNG WOMEN'S CHRISTIAN ASSOCIATION OF REGINA
Y W C A
1940 Mcintyre St Suite 507, Regina, SK, S4P 2R3
(306) 525-2141
Emp Here 64　　*Sales* 1,896,978
SIC 8351 Child day care services

Regina, SK S4R

D-U-N-S 24-346-3424　　(BR)
511670 ALBERTA LTD
CORAM CONSTRUCTION
845 Broad St Suite 205, Regina, SK, S4R 8G9
(306) 525-1644
Emp Here 180
SIC 1542 Nonresidential construction, nec

D-U-N-S 20-009-2570　　(HQ)
604329 SASKATCHEWAN LTD
HYUNDAI REGINA, DIV OF
(*Suby of* 893353 Alberta Inc)
444 Broad St, Regina, SK, S4R 1X3

(306) 525-8848
Emp Here 40　　*Emp Total* 6
Sales 23,712,228
SIC 5511 New and used car dealers
Pr Pr Ajay Dilawri

D-U-N-S 25-288-0026　　(BR)
A & W FOOD SERVICES OF CANADA INC
JORIDO FOODS
2701 Avonhurst Dr, Regina, SK, S4R 3J3
(306) 545-6441
Emp Here 30
SIC 5812 Eating places

D-U-N-S 24-913-9478　　(BR)
A S L PAVING LTD
2400 1st Ave, Regina, SK, S4R 8G6
(306) 569-2045
Emp Here 70
SIC 1611 Highway and street construction

D-U-N-S 24-375-3266　　(SL)
ABDOULAH ENTERPRISES LTD
LITTLE BAVARIA
433 N Albert St, Regina, SK, S4R 3C3

Emp Here 60　　*Sales* 1,824,018
SIC 5812 Eating places

D-U-N-S 24-717-7264　　(BR)
AUDIO WAREHOUSE LTD
1330 Cornwall St, Regina, SK, S4R 2H5
(306) 352-1838
Emp Here 20
SIC 5731 Radio, television, and electronic stores

D-U-N-S 20-003-3004　　(BR)
BANK OF NOVA SCOTIA, THE
SCOTIABANK
3835 Sherwood Dr, Regina, SK, S4R 4A8
(306) 780-1220
Emp Here 20
SIC 6021 National commercial banks

D-U-N-S 20-712-6959　　(BR)
BOARD OF EDUCATION REGINA SCHOOL DIVISION NO. 4 OF SASKATCHEWAN
GEOGE LEE SCHOOL
180 Wells St, Regina, SK, S4R 5Z7
(306) 791-8510
Emp Here 20
SIC 8211 Elementary and secondary schools

D-U-N-S 20-712-6876　　(BR)
BOARD OF EDUCATION REGINA SCHOOL DIVISION NO. 4 OF SASKATCHEWAN
MCDERMID SCHOOL
139 Toronto St, Regina, SK, S4R 1L8
(306) 791-8502
Emp Here 35
SIC 8211 Elementary and secondary schools

D-U-N-S 20-712-6785　　(BR)
BOARD OF EDUCATION REGINA SCHOOL DIVISION NO. 4 OF SASKATCHEWAN
CORONATION PARK COMMUNITY SCHOOL
3105 4th Ave N, Regina, SK, S4R 0V2
(306) 791-8570
Emp Here 50
SIC 8211 Elementary and secondary schools

D-U-N-S 20-037-7195　　(BR)
BOARD OF EDUCATION REGINA SCHOOL DIVISION NO. 4 OF SASKATCHEWAN
DR L M HANNA ELEMENTARY SCHOOL
55 Davin Cres, Regina, SK, S4R 7E4
(306) 791-8594
Emp Here 40
SIC 8211 Elementary and secondary schools

D-U-N-S 20-712-6777　　(BR)
BOARD OF EDUCATION REGINA SCHOOL DIVISION NO. 4 OF SASKATCHEWAN
MJ COLDWELL ELEMENTARY SCHOOL
103 Fairview Rd, Regina, SK, S4R 0A6
(306) 791-8563
Emp Here 25

▲ Public Company　■ Public Company Family Member　　**HQ** Headquarters　　**BR** Branch　　**SL** Single Location

SIC 8211 Elementary and secondary schools

D-U-N-S 20-966-8339   (BR)
BOARD OF EDUCATION REGINA SCHOOL DIVISION NO. 4 OF SASKATCHEWAN
HENRY JANZEN SCHOOL
222 Rink Ave, Regina, SK, S4R 7T8
(306) 791-8523
Emp Here 37
SIC 8211 Elementary and secondary schools

D-U-N-S 20-033-2141   (BR)
BOARD OF EDUCATION REGINA SCHOOL DIVISION NO. 4 OF SASKATCHEWAN
RUTH PAWSON PUBLIC ELEMENTARY SCHOOL
40 Weekes Cres, Regina, SK, S4R 6X7
(306) 791-8483
Emp Here 25
SIC 8211 Elementary and secondary schools

D-U-N-S 20-033-2117   (BR)
BOARD OF EDUCATION REGINA SCHOOL DIVISION NO. 4 OF SASKATCHEWAN
IMPERIAL COMMUNITY SCHOOL
200 Broad St, Regina, SK, S4R 1W9
(306) 791-8454
Emp Here 32
SIC 8211 Elementary and secondary schools

D-U-N-S 20-712-6884   (BR)
BOARD OF EDUCATION REGINA SCHOOL DIVISION NO. 4 OF SASKATCHEWAN
GLADYS MCDONALD
335 N Garnet St, Regina, SK, S4R 3S8
(306) 791-8500
Emp Here 21
SIC 8211 Elementary and secondary schools

D-U-N-S 20-034-0169   (BR)
BOARD OF EDUCATION REGINA SCHOOL DIVISION NO. 4 OF SASKATCHEWAN
ELSIE MIRONUCK PUBLIC ELEMENTARY SCHOOL
18 Wakefield Cres, Regina, SK, S4R 4T3
(306) 791-8486
Emp Here 40
SIC 8211 Elementary and secondary schools

D-U-N-S 20-712-7379   (BR)
BOARD OF EDUCATION OF THE REGINA ROMAN CATHOLIC SEPARATE SCHOOL DIVISION NO. 81
ST MARY SCHOOL
140 N Mcintosh St, Regina, SK, S4R 4Z9
(306) 791-7365
Emp Here 49
SIC 8211 Elementary and secondary schools

D-U-N-S 25-014-3609   (BR)
BOARD OF EDUCATION OF THE REGINA ROMAN CATHOLIC SEPARATE SCHOOL DIVISION NO. 81
ARCHBISHOP MC O'NEILL HIGH SCHOOL
134 Argyle St, Regina, SK, S4R 4C3
(306) 791-7240
Emp Here 80
SIC 8211 Elementary and secondary schools

D-U-N-S 20-712-7403   (BR)
BOARD OF EDUCATION OF THE REGINA ROMAN CATHOLIC SEPARATE SCHOOL DIVISION NO. 81
ST BERNADETTE ELEMENTARY SCHOOL
727 N Mcintosh St, Regina, SK, S4R 6E4
(306) 791-7320
Emp Here 50
SIC 8211 Elementary and secondary schools

D-U-N-S 20-033-2281   (BR)
BOARD OF EDUCATION OF THE REGINA ROMAN CATHOLIC SEPARATE SCHOOL DIVISION NO. 81
ST PETER ELEMENTARY SCHOOL
150 Argyle St, Regina, SK, S4R 4C3
(306) 791-7380
Emp Here 20

SIC 8211 Elementary and secondary schools

D-U-N-S 20-647-3469   (BR)
BOARD OF EDUCATION OF THE REGINA ROMAN CATHOLIC SEPARATE SCHOOL DIVISION NO. 81
ST GREGORY ELEMENTARY SCHOOL
302 Upland Dr, Regina, SK, S4R 5X3
(306) 791-7340
Emp Here 20
SIC 8211 Elementary and secondary schools

D-U-N-S 25-623-0038   (BR)
BREWSTERS BREW PUB & BRASSERIE INC
BREWSTERS BREWING CO & RESTAU-RANT
480 N Mccarthy Blvd, Regina, SK, S4R 7M2
(306) 522-2739
Emp Here 50
SIC 5812 Eating places

D-U-N-S 25-614-6739   (BR)
BRICK WAREHOUSE LP, THE
BRICK, THE
2425 7th Ave N, Regina, SK, S4R 0K4
(306) 924-2020
Emp Here 20
SIC 5712 Furniture stores

D-U-N-S 20-587-2653   (BR)
CANADIAN PACIFIC RAILWAY COMPANY
CPR
2305 Dewdney Ave, Regina, SK, S4R 8R2
(306) 777-0821
Emp Here 20
SIC 4011 Railroads, line-haul operating

D-U-N-S 20-580-5224   (BR)
CANADIAN PACIFIC RAILWAY COMPANY
2305 Dewdney Ave, Regina, SK, S4R 8R2
(306) 777-0801
Emp Here 20
SIC 7011 Hotels and motels

D-U-N-S 25-614-9477   (BR)
CITY OF REGINA, THE
REGINA TRANSIT
333 Winnipeg St, Regina, SK, S4R 8P2
(306) 777-7780
Emp Here 220
SIC 4131 Intercity and rural bus transportation

D-U-N-S 24-852-9869   (BR)
CITY OF REGINA, THE
TRANSIT DEPARTMENT
333 Winnipeg St, Regina, SK, S4R 8P2
(306) 777-7726
Emp Here 225
SIC 4111 Local and suburban transit

D-U-N-S 24-520-4284   (SL)
CLEAN-BRITE SERVICES OF REGINA LTD
1201 Osler St, Regina, SK, S4R 1W4
(306) 352-9953
Emp Here 75   *Sales* 2,188,821
SIC 7349 Building maintenance services, nec

D-U-N-S 25-167-7696   (SL)
CLOUD-RIDER DESIGNS LTD
1260 8th Ave, Regina, SK, S4R 1C9
(306) 761-2119
Emp Here 50   *Sales* 4,304,681
SIC 3429 Hardware, nec

D-U-N-S 25-170-6800   (SL)
COMMUNITY HEALTH SERVICES ASSOCI-ATION (REGINA) LTD
REGINA COMMUNITY CLINIC
1106 Winnipeg St Suite A, Regina, SK, S4R 1J6
(306) 543-7880
Emp Here 57   *Sales* 3,720,996
SIC 8093 Specialty outpatient clinics, nec

D-U-N-S 20-718-9023   (BR)
CONEXUS CREDIT UNION 2006
NORTH ALBERT BRANCH

265 N Albert St, Regina, SK, S4R 3C2
(306) 780-1845
Emp Here 23
SIC 6062 State credit unions

D-U-N-S 24-117-4812   (BR)
DUCKS UNLIMITED CANADA
1030 Winnipeg St, Regina, SK, S4R 8P8
(306) 569-0424
Emp Here 25
SIC 8999 Services, nec

D-U-N-S 24-348-5195   (BR)
GDI SERVICES (CANADA) LP
1319 Hamilton St, Regina, SK, S4R 2B6

Emp Here 95
SIC 7349 Building maintenance services, nec

D-U-N-S 25-014-3708   (BR)
GOVERNING COUNCIL OF THE SALVA-TION ARMY IN CANADA, THE
GOVERNING COUNCIL OF THE SALVATION ARMY IN CANADA, THE
50 Angus Rd, Regina, SK, S4R 8P6
(306) 543-0655
Emp Here 130
SIC 8361 Residential care

D-U-N-S 20-055-3951   (BR)
H & R BLOCK CANADA, INC
(*Suby of* H&R Block, Inc.)
366 N Albert St, Regina, SK, S4R 3C1
(306) 777-0492
Emp Here 30
SIC 7291 Tax return preparation services

D-U-N-S 24-394-4027   (HQ)
HBI OFFICE PLUS INC
1162 Osler St, Regina, SK, S4R 5G9
(306) 757-5678
Emp Here 40   *Emp Total* 70
Sales 3,793,956
SIC 5112 Stationery and office supplies

D-U-N-S 20-047-2954   (BR)
HARTCO INC
MICROAGE
1060 Winnipeg St, Regina, SK, S4R 8P8
(306) 525-0537
Emp Here 30
SIC 5734 Computer and software stores

D-U-N-S 20-038-2880   (BR)
HYUNDAI CANADA INC
HYUNDAI OF REGINA
444 Broad St, Regina, SK, S4R 1X3
(306) 525-8848
Emp Here 20
SIC 5511 New and used car dealers

D-U-N-S 25-362-4399   (BR)
LENNOX CANADA INC
TOWN & COUNTRY PLUMBING & HEATING
(*Suby of* Lennox Canada Inc)
1901 Dewdney Ave, Regina, SK, S4R 8R2

Emp Here 36
SIC 5075 Warm air heating and air condition-ing

D-U-N-S 24-383-8815   (BR)
LOBLAWS INC
REAL CANADIAN WHOLESALE CLUB
921 Broad St, Regina. SK, S4R 8G9
(306) 525-2125
Emp Here 100
SIC 5411 Grocery stores

D-U-N-S 24-329-4621   (BR)
LOBLAWS INC
DRUGSTORE PHARMACY
336 N Mccarthy Blvd, Regina, SK, S4R 7M2
(306) 924-2620
Emp Here 100
SIC 5912 Drug stores and proprietary stores

D-U-N-S 25-017-0081   (BR)

LONG & MCQUADE LIMITED
LONG & MCQUADE MUSICAL INSTRU-MENTS
1455 Mcintyre St, Regina, SK, S4R 8B5
(306) 569-3914
Emp Here 40
SIC 8299 Schools and educational services, nec

D-U-N-S 20-336-6943   (BR)
LOWE'S COMPANIES CANADA, ULC
LOWE'S 3329
489 N Albert St, Regina, SK, S4R 3C3
(306) 545-1386
Emp Here 135
SIC 5211 Lumber and other building materials

D-U-N-S 25-619-2394   (SL)
MCDONALD'S RESTAURANT
525 N Albert St, Regina, SK, S4R 8E2
(306) 543-0236
Emp Here 80   *Sales* 2,407,703
SIC 5812 Eating places

D-U-N-S 25-987-9773   (BR)
MOORES THE SUIT PEOPLE INC
MOORES CLOTHING FOR MEN
(*Suby of* Tailored Brands, Inc.)
921 Albert St, Regina, SK, S4R 2P6
(306) 525-2762
Emp Here 20
SIC 5611 Men's and boys' clothing stores

D-U-N-S 20-192-3013   (BR)
NORTH WEST COMPANY LP, THE
GIANT TIGER # 405
2735 Avonhurst Dr, Regina, SK, S4R 3J3
(306) 789-3155
Emp Here 90
SIC 5411 Grocery stores

D-U-N-S 24-915-9237   (SL)
NORTHWEST FOOD SERVICES LTD
SMITTY'S
368 N Mccarthy Blvd, Regina, SK, S4R 7M2
(306) 522-7918
Emp Here 50   *Sales* 1,532,175
SIC 5812 Eating places

D-U-N-S 25-388-7814   (BR)
PCL CONSTRUCTION MANAGEMENT INC
1433 1st Ave, Regina, SK, S4R 8H2
(306) 347-4200
Emp Here 25
SIC 1542 Nonresidential construction, nec

D-U-N-S 25-386-9671   (SL)
PRAIRIE MICRO-TECH (1996) INC
2641 Albert St N, Regina, SK, S4R 8R7
(306) 721-6066
Emp Here 25   *Sales* 5,180,210
SIC 5191 Farm supplies
Pr Pr Michelle Tesautelf

D-U-N-S 25-234-4890   (SL)
PRATTS WHOLESALE (SASK.) LTD
1616 4th Ave, Regina, SK, S4R 8C8
(306) 522-0101
Emp Here 80   *Sales* 20,939,721
SIC 5141 Groceries, general line
Pr Pr Leonard Baranyk
Treas Eleane Baranyk
Dir Leonard A .W. Baranyk
 Edward Holowaty

D-U-N-S 20-337-8518   (HQ)
PRINTWEST LTD
MISTER PRINT DIV.
(*Suby of* Printwest Ltd)
1111 8th Ave, Regina, SK, S4R 1E1
(306) 525-2304
Emp Here 48   *Emp Total* 70
Sales 1,479,290
SIC 2759 Commercial printing, nec

D-U-N-S 24-428-6787   (BR)
PUROLATOR INC.
PUROLATOR INC

702 Toronto St, Regina, SK, S4R 8L1
(306) 359-0313
Emp Here 100
SIC 7389 Business services, nec

D-U-N-S 24-400-9366   (BR)
QUOREX CONSTRUCTION SERVICES LTD
(*Suby of* Quorex Construction Services Ltd)
1630a 8th Ave, Regina, SK, S4R 1E5
(306) 761-2222
Emp Here 75
SIC 1542 Nonresidential construction, nec

D-U-N-S 24-363-0949   (BR)
RGIS CANADA ULC
402 Broad St, Regina, SK, S4R 1X3
(306) 757-9180
Emp Here 40
SIC 7389 Business services, nec

D-U-N-S 25-617-4293   (BR)
ROYAL BANK OF CANADA
RBC
(*Suby of* Royal Bank Of Canada)
2441 7th Ave N, Regina, SK, S4R 0K4
(306) 780-2811
Emp Here 35
SIC 6021 National commercial banks

D-U-N-S 25-288-9365   (BR)
RUSSELL FOOD EQUIPMENT LIMITED
1475 Rose St, Regina, SK, S4R 2A1
(306) 525-3333
Emp Here 24
SIC 5046 Commercial equipment, nec

D-U-N-S 25-615-2877   (BR)
SASKATCHEWAN LIQUOR AND GAMING AUTHORITY, THE
416 N Albert St, Regina, SK, S4R 3C1
(306) 787-4261
Emp Here 25
SIC 5921 Liquor stores

D-U-N-S 24-320-2681   (BR)
SASKATCHEWAN TELECOMMUNICA-TIONS HOLDING CORPORATION
SASKTEL
2133 1st Ave, Regina, SK, S4R 8G4
(306) 777-3376
Emp Here 100
SIC 4899 Communication services, nec

D-U-N-S 20-068-2854   (BR)
SEARS CANADA INC
1908 7th Ave, Regina, SK, S4R 5E1
(306) 569-1711
Emp Here 2,000
SIC 5399 Miscellaneous general merchandise

D-U-N-S 24-426-0360   (SL)
SEVEN OAKS MOTOR INN LTD
777 Albert St, Regina, SK, S4R 2P6
(306) 757-0121
Emp Here 105   *Sales* 4,596,524
SIC 7011 Hotels and motels

D-U-N-S 25-364-8950   (BR)
SOBEYS WEST INC
SAFEWAY
353 N Alber: St, Regina, SK, S4R 3C3
(306) 543-8749
Emp Here 50
SIC 5411 Grocery stores

D-U-N-S 25-271-7426   (BR)
SOBEYS WEST INC
3859 Sherwood Dr, Regina, SK, S4R 4A8
(306) 545-6292
Emp Here 105
SIC 5411 Grocery stores

D-U-N-S 25-085-5764   (BR)
STAPLES CANADA INC
STAPLES THE BUSINESS DEPOT
(*Suby of* Staples, Inc.)
660 Albert St, Regina, SK, S4R 2P3

(306) 546-1870
Emp Here 30
SIC 5943 Stationery stores

D-U-N-S 20-645-2695   (BR)
THYSSENKRUPP ELEVATOR (CANADA) LIMITED
1358 Mcintyre St, Regina, SK, S4R 2M8
(306) 352-8608
Emp Here 22
SIC 7699 Repair services, nec

D-U-N-S 25-603-6427   (BR)
VALUE VILLAGE STORES, INC
(*Suby of* Savers, Inc.)
1230 Broad St, Regina, SK, S4R 1Y3
(306) 522-1228
Emp Here 30
SIC 5399 Miscellaneous general merchandise

D-U-N-S 24-748-8059   (BR)
WESTON BAKERIES LIMITED
WESTERN PRE BAKE
1310 Ottawa St, Regina, SK, S4R 1P4
(306) 359-3096
Emp Here 85
SIC 2051 Bread, cake, and related products

D-U-N-S 25-499-6952   (BR)
WESTROCK COMPANY OF CANADA INC
(*Suby of* Westrock Company)
1400 1st Ave, Regina, SK, S4R 8G5
(306) 525-7700
Emp Here 80
SIC 2653 Corrugated and solid fiber boxes

D-U-N-S 20-448-1634   (BR)
WOLSELEY CANADA INC
WOLSELEY MECHANICAL GROUP MID-WEST
(*Suby of* WOLSELEY PLC)
1176 Hamilton St, Regina, SK, S4R 2B2
(306) 525-6581
Emp Here 27
SIC 5074 Plumbing and heating equipment and supplies (hydronics)

Regina, SK S4S

D-U-N-S 25-079-7727   (SL)
101011657 SASKATCHEWAN LTD
TOMAS THE COOK RESTAURANT
3915 Albert St, Regina, SK, S4S 3R4

Emp Here 50   *Sales* 1,532,175
SIC 5812 Eating places

D-U-N-S 25-678-9728   (SL)
617400 SASKATCHEWAN LTD
SOBEYS ALBERT STREET
4250 Albert St, Regina, SK, S4S 3R9
(306) 585-0579
Emp Here 90   *Sales* 15,454,196
SIC 5411 Grocery stores

D-U-N-S 20-515-0381   (BR)
A & W FOOD SERVICES OF CANADA INC
JORIDO FOOD SERVICES
4315 Albert St, Regina, SK, S4S 3R6

Emp Here 30
SIC 5812 Eating places

D-U-N-S 20-034-4187   (BR)
BOARD OF EDUCATION REGINA SCHOOL DIVISION NO. 4 OF SASKATCHEWAN
MASSEY PUBLIC ELEMENTARY SCHOOL
131 Massey Rd, Regina, SK, S4S 4N3
(306) 791-8504
Emp Here 35
SIC 8211 Elementary and secondary schools

D-U-N-S 20-034-0102   (BR)
BOARD OF EDUCATION REGINA SCHOOL DIVISION NO. 4 OF SASKATCHEWAN

ARGYLE PUBLIC ELEMENTARY SCHOOL
2941 Lakeview Ave, Regina, SK, S4S 1G8
(306) 791-8536
Emp Here 30
SIC 8211 Elementary and secondary schools

D-U-N-S 20-712-6983   (BR)
BOARD OF EDUCATION REGINA SCHOOL DIVISION NO. 4 OF SASKATCHEWAN
DR A E PERRY SCHOOL
93 Lincoln Dr, Regina, SK, S4S 6P1
(306) 791-8476
Emp Here 30
SIC 8211 Elementary and secondary schools

D-U-N-S 20-712-6827   (BR)
BOARD OF EDUCATION REGINA SCHOOL DIVISION NO. 4 OF SASKATCHEWAN
GRANT ROAD ELEMENTARY SCHOOL
2501 Grant Rd, Regina, SK, S4S 5E7
(306) 791-8590
Emp Here 30
SIC 8211 Elementary and secondary schools

D-U-N-S 20-712-6850   (BR)
BOARD OF EDUCATION REGINA SCHOOL DIVISION NO. 4 OF SASKATCHEWAN
LAKEVIEW ELEMENTARY SCHOOL
3100 20th Ave, Regina, SK, S4S 0N8
(306) 791-8513
Emp Here 30
SIC 8211 Elementary and secondary schools

D-U-N-S 20-712-6892   (BR)
BOARD OF EDUCATION REGINA SCHOOL DIVISION NO. 4 OF SASKATCHEWAN
MCVEETY MARION SCHOOL
38 Turgeon Cres, Regina, SK, S4S 3Z7
(306) 791-8492
Emp Here 50
SIC 8211 Elementary and secondary schools

D-U-N-S 20-034-0599   (BR)
BOARD OF EDUCATION REGINA SCHOOL DIVISION NO. 4 OF SASKATCHEWAN
SHELDON WILLIAMS HIGH SCHOOL
2601 Coronation St, Regina, SK, S4S 0L4
(306) 523-3550
Emp Here 60
SIC 8211 Elementary and secondary schools

D-U-N-S 20-033-2125   (BR)
BOARD OF EDUCATION REGINA SCHOOL DIVISION NO. 4 OF SASKATCHEWAN
ETHEL MILLIKEN PUBLIC ELEMENTARY SCHOOL
4510 Queen St, Regina, SK, S4S 6K9
(306) 791-8489
Emp Here 30
SIC 8211 Elementary and secondary schools

D-U-N-S 20-522-9870   (BR)
BOARD OF EDUCATION OF THE REGINA ROMAN CATHOLIC SEPARATE SCHOOL DIVISION NO. 81
DR MARTIN LEBOLDUS HIGH SCHOOL
2330 25th Ave, Regina, SK, S4S 4E6
(306) 791-7251
Emp Here 65
SIC 8211 Elementary and secondary schools

D-U-N-S 20-033-2992   (BR)
BOARD OF EDUCATION OF THE REGINA ROMAN CATHOLIC SEPARATE SCHOOL DIVISION NO. 81
DESHAYE CATHOLIC SCHOOL
37 Cameron Cres, Regina, SK, S4S 2X1
(306) 791-7270
Emp Here 29
SIC 8211 Elementary and secondary schools

D-U-N-S 20-572-7600   (BR)
CANADA POST CORPORATION
2625 31st Ave, Regina, SK, S4S 2R3
(306) 761-6373
Emp Here 50
SIC 4311 U.s. postal service

D-U-N-S 25-943-4400   (BR)
CANADIAN TIRE CORPORATION, LIMITED
COCCIMIGLIO RETAIL SALES
2965 Gordon Rd Suite 65, Regina, SK, S4S 6H7
(306) 585-1334
Emp Here 100
SIC 5531 Auto and home supply stores

D-U-N-S 20-303-3212   (BR)
CARA OPERATIONS LIMITED
KELSEY'S
(*Suby of* Cara Holdings Limited)
2655 Gordon Rd, Regina, SK, S4S 6H7
(306) 569-1557
Emp Here 65
SIC 5812 Eating places

D-U-N-S 20-000-7073   (BR)
CONSEIL DES ECOLES FRANSASKOISES
ECOLE MONSEIGNEUR DE LAVAL
1601 Cowan Cres, Regina, SK, S4S 4C4
(306) 584-7558
Emp Here 40
SIC 8211 Elementary and secondary schools

D-U-N-S 20-119-0175   (BR)
DREAM ASSET MANAGEMENT CORPO-RATION
HOMES BY DUNDEE
1230 Blackfoot Dr Suite 105, Regina, SK, S4S 7G4
(306) 347-8100
Emp Here 22
SIC 6553 Cemetery subdividers and developers

D-U-N-S 24-775-4286   (BR)
EARL'S RESTAURANTS LTD
EARL'S RESTAURANTS
(*Suby of* Earl's Restaurants Ltd)
2606 28th Ave, Regina, SK, S4S 6P3
(306) 584-7733
Emp Here 100
SIC 5812 Eating places

D-U-N-S 20-756-6159   (BR)
EXTENDICARE INC
EXTENDICARE SUNSET
260 Sunset Dr, Regina, SK, S4S 2S3
(306) 586-3355
Emp Here 300
SIC 8051 Skilled nursing care facilities

D-U-N-S 20-823-5564   (BR)
EXTENDICARE INC
EXTENDICARE ELMVIEW
4125 Rae St, Regina, SK, S4S 3A5
(306) 586-1787
Emp Here 96
SIC 8051 Skilled nursing care facilities

D-U-N-S 24-352-5123   (BR)
EXTENDICARE INC
EXTENDICARE PARKSIDE
4540 Rae St, Regina, SK, S4S 3B4
(306) 586-0220
Emp Here 308
SIC 8051 Skilled nursing care facilities

D-U-N-S 24-337-3110   (BR)
FGL SPORTS LTD
SPORT CHEK SOUTHLAND MALL
2635 Gordon Rd, Regina, SK, S4S 6H7
(306) 522-2200
Emp Here 40
SIC 5941 Sporting goods and bicycle shops

D-U-N-S 25-619-4325   (HQ)
FUJITSU CANADA
(*Suby of* Fujitsu Canada)
10 Research Dr Suite 350, Regina, SK, S4S 7J7
(306) 545-4344
Emp Here 65   *Emp Total* 67
Sales 4,888,367
SIC 7379 Computer related services, nec

▲ Public Company   ■ Public Company Family Member   **HQ** Headquarters   **BR** Branch   **SL** Single Location

D-U-N-S 24-774-6233   (HQ)
GREYSTONE MANAGED INVESTMENTS INC
1230 Blackfoot Dr Unit 300, Regina, SK, S4S 7G4
(306) 779-6400
Emp Here 100   *Emp Total* 62
Sales 32,657,663
SIC 6282 Investment advice
CFO Robert L Vanderhooft
  Donald W Black
  Frank H Hart
  Louis R Martel
  Ted R Welter
  Donald M Mackay
  Anne E Parker
  William M Wheatley
CFO Tom Mamic

D-U-N-S 24-172-0713   (SL)
HOUSTON PIZZA RESTAURANT LTD
3422 Hill Ave, Regina, SK, S4S 0W9
(306) 584-0888
Emp Here 250   *Sales* 10,449,350
SIC 5812 Eating places
  George Kolitsas
Dir Jim Kolitsas

D-U-N-S 25-055-5018   (BR)
INDIGO BOOKS & MUSIC INC
CHAPTERS
(*Suby* of Indigo Books & Music Inc)
2625 Gordon Rd, Regina, SK, S4S 6H7
(306) 569-6060
Emp Here 55
SIC 5942 Book stores

D-U-N-S 24-266-2559   (BR)
JORIDO FOODS SERVICES LTD
A & W
4315 Albert St, Regina, SK, S4S 3R6
(306) 584-5151
Emp Here 23
SIC 5812 Eating places

D-U-N-S 20-064-3687   (BR)
KJMAL ENTERPRISES LTD
MC DONALD'S
4651 Albert St, Regina, SK, S4S 6B6
(306) 584-5656
Emp Here 90
SIC 5812 Eating places

D-U-N-S 25-623-1143   (BR)
LEIDOS, INC
SAIC CANADA, DIV OF
10 Research Dr Suite 240, Regina, SK, S4S 7J7

Emp Here 60
SIC 7379 Computer related services, nec

D-U-N-S 25-950-5063   (BR)
LOBLAWS INC
DRUGSTORE PHARMACY, THE
3960 Albert St Suite 9037, Regina, SK, S4S 3R1
(306) 584-9444
Emp Here 120
SIC 5411 Grocery stores

D-U-N-S 20-792-0922   (BR)
LOBLAWS INC
3958 Albert St, Regina, SK, S4S 3R1
(306) 790-2550
Emp Here 50
SIC 5541 Gasoline service stations

D-U-N-S 20-197-2788   (BR)
MCDONALD'S RESTAURANTS OF CANADA LIMITED
MCDONALD'S RESTAURANTS
(*Suby* of McDonald's Corporation)
1105 Kramer Blvd, Regina, SK, S4S 5W4
(306) 586-3400
Emp Here 45
SIC 5812 Eating places

D-U-N-S 20-705-5414   (BR)
SASKATCHEWAN OPPORTUNITIES CORPORATION
INNOVATION PLACE
10 Research Dr Suite 140, Regina, SK, S4S 7J7
(306) 798-7275
Emp Here 24
SIC 6519 Real property lessors, nec

D-U-N-S 20-514-2867   (BR)
SASKATCHEWAN RESEARCH COUNCIL, THE
6 Research Dr Suite 129, Regina, SK, S4S 7J7
(306) 787-9400
Emp Here 40
SIC 8733 Noncommercial research organizations

D-U-N-S 25-611-7896   (BR)
SCOTIA CAPITAL INC
SCOTIA MCLEOD
3303 Hillsdale St Suite 305, Regina, SK, S4S 6W9
(306) 352-5005
Emp Here 20
SIC 6211 Security brokers and dealers

D-U-N-S 24-883-6918   (BR)
SHAWCOR LTD
SHAW PIPE PROTECTION
2501 Pasqua St, Regina, SK, S4S 0M3
(306) 543-2552
Emp Here 75
SIC 3479 Metal coating and allied services

D-U-N-S 20-793-0822   (BR)
SOBEYS CAPITAL INCORPORATED
SOBEYS
4250 Albert St, Regina, SK, S4S 3R9
(306) 585-0366
Emp Here 50
SIC 5411 Grocery stores

D-U-N-S 20-722-5967   (BR)
SOBEYS WEST INC
SAFEWAY
2627 Gordon Rd, Regina, SK, S4S 6H7
(306) 586-5140
Emp Here 50
SIC 5411 Grocery stores

D-U-N-S 20-712-7551   (BR)
ST. PAUL'S ROMAN CATHOLIC SEPARATE SCHOOL DIVISION NO 20
ST MATTHEWS SCHOOL
4710 Castle Rd, Regina, SK, S4S 4X1
(306) 791-7370
Emp Here 35
SIC 8211 Elementary and secondary schools

D-U-N-S 20-644-4148   (BR)
TORONTO-DOMINION BANK, THE
TD CANADA TRUST
(*Suby* of Toronto-Dominion Bank, The)
4240 Albert St, Regina, SK, S4S 3R9
(306) 780-0406
Emp Here 20
SIC 6021 National commercial banks

D-U-N-S 25-326-0483   (SL)
TUESDAY RESTAURANT COMPANY LTD, THE
TUESDAY RESTAURANT, THE
3806 Albert St Suite 400, Regina, SK, S4S 3R2
(306) 584-0611
Emp Here 60   *Sales* 2,165,628
SIC 5812 Eating places

D-U-N-S 25-944-6805   (BR)
UNIVERSITY OF REGINA
LUTHER COLLEGE
3737 Wascana Pky Suite 148, Regina, SK, S4S 0A2
(306) 585-5022
Emp Here 100

SIC 8221 Colleges and universities

D-U-N-S 24-330-0501   (BR)
WAL-MART CANADA CORP
2715 Gordon Rd, Regina, SK, S4S 6H7
(306) 584-0061
Emp Here 200
SIC 5311 Department stores

Regina, SK S4T

D-U-N-S 20-712-6769   (BR)
BOARD OF EDUCATION REGINA SCHOOL DIVISION NO. 4 OF SASKATCHEWAN
ELEMENTARY SCHOOLS ALBERT
1340 Robinson St, Regina, SK, S4T 2N4
(306) 791-8539
Emp Here 30
SIC 8211 Elementary and secondary schools

D-U-N-S 20-712-6942   (BR)
BOARD OF EDUCATION REGINA SCHOOL DIVISION NO. 4 OF SASKATCHEWAN
RUTH M F BUCK ELEMENTARY SCHOOL
6330 7th Ave N, Regina, SK, S4T 7J1
(306) 791-8556
Emp Here 50
SIC 8211 Elementary and secondary schools

D-U-N-S 25-268-1069   (BR)
BOARD OF EDUCATION REGINA SCHOOL DIVISION NO. 4 OF SASKATCHEWAN
SCOTT COLLEGIATE
3350 7th Ave, Regina, SK, S4T 0P6
(306) 523-3500
Emp Here 25
SIC 8211 Elementary and secondary schools

D-U-N-S 20-712-6918   (BR)
BOARD OF EDUCATION REGINA SCHOOL DIVISION NO. 4 OF SASKATCHEWAN
WALKER SCHOOL
5637 7th Ave, Regina, SK, S4T 0S9
(306) 791-8526
Emp Here 30
SIC 8211 Elementary and secondary schools

D-U-N-S 20-712-6991   (BR)
BOARD OF EDUCATION REGINA SCHOOL DIVISION NO. 4 OF SASKATCHEWAN
MARTIN COLLEGIATE
1100 Mcintosh St, Regina, SK, S4T 5B7
(306) 523-3450
Emp Here 50
SIC 8211 Elementary and secondary schools

D-U-N-S 20-712-6793   (BR)
BOARD OF EDUCATION REGINA SCHOOL DIVISION NO. 4 OF SASKATCHEWAN
DAVIN SCHOOL
2401 Retallack St, Regina, SK, S4T 2L2
(306) 791-8574
Emp Here 50
SIC 8211 Elementary and secondary schools

D-U-N-S 20-034-0433   (BR)
BOARD OF EDUCATION REGINA SCHOOL DIVISION NO. 4 OF SASKATCHEWAN
ROSEMONT COMMUNITY SCHOOL
841 Horace St, Regina, SK, S4T 5L1
(306) 791-8466
Emp Here 30
SIC 8211 Elementary and secondary schools

D-U-N-S 20-656-0729   (BR)
BOARD OF EDUCATION REGINA SCHOOL DIVISION NO. 4 OF SASKATCHEWAN
KITCHENER COMMUNITY SCHOOL
840 Athol St, Regina, SK, S4T 3B5
(306) 791-8516
Emp Here 38
SIC 8211 Elementary and secondary schools

D-U-N-S 20-712-6926   (BR)
BOARD OF EDUCATION REGINA SCHOOL

DIVISION NO. 4 OF SASKATCHEWAN
WASCANA
4210 4th Ave, Regina, SK, S4T 0H6

Emp Here 50
SIC 8211 Elementary and secondary schools

D-U-N-S 20-712-7338   (BR)
BOARD OF EDUCATION OF THE REGINA ROMAN CATHOLIC SEPARATE SCHOOL DIVISION NO. 81
HOLY ROSARY SCHOOL
3118 14th Ave, Regina, SK, S4T 1R9
(306) 791-7280
Emp Here 25
SIC 8211 Elementary and secondary schools

D-U-N-S 20-712-7460   (BR)
BOARD OF EDUCATION OF THE REGINA ROMAN CATHOLIC SEPARATE SCHOOL DIVISION NO. 81
ST. LUKE SCHOOL
625 Elphinstone St, Regina, SK, S4T 3L1
(306) 791-7248
Emp Here 25
SIC 8211 Elementary and secondary schools

D-U-N-S 25-014-3682   (BR)
BOARD OF EDUCATION OF THE REGINA ROMAN CATHOLIC SEPARATE SCHOOL DIVISION NO. 81
SACRED HEART COMMUNITY SCHOOL
1314 Elphinstone St, Regina, SK, S4T 3M4
(306) 791-7290
Emp Here 40
SIC 8211 Elementary and secondary schools

D-U-N-S 20-033-2273   (BR)
BOARD OF EDUCATION OF THE REGINA ROMAN CATHOLIC SEPARATE SCHOOL DIVISION NO. 81
ST FRANCIS COMMUNITY SCHOOL
45 Mikkelson Dr, Regina, SK, S4T 6B7
(306) 791-7335
Emp Here 40
SIC 8211 Elementary and secondary schools

D-U-N-S 20-033-2307   (BR)
BOARD OF EDUCATION OF THE REGINA ROMAN CATHOLIC SEPARATE SCHOOL DIVISION NO. 81
ST JOAN OF ARC ELEMENTARY SCHOOL
10 Dempsey Ave, Regina, SK, S4T 7H9
(306) 791-7350
Emp Here 25
SIC 8211 Elementary and secondary schools

D-U-N-S 20-656-4721   (BR)
CITY OF REGINA, THE
NEIL BALKWILL CIVIC ART CENTER
2420 Elphinstone St, Regina, SK, S4T 7S7
(306) 777-7529
Emp Here 30
SIC 8641 Civic and social associations

D-U-N-S 20-648-2585   (BR)
MCDONALD'S RESTAURANTS OF CANADA LIMITED
MCDONALD'S
(*Suby* of McDonald's Corporation)
2620 Dewdney Ave, Regina, SK, S4T 0X3
(306) 525-6611
Emp Here 100
SIC 5812 Eating places

D-U-N-S 24-852-2989   (SL)
PIONEER VILLAGE SPECIAL CARE CORPORATION
(*Suby* of Regina Pioneer Village Ltd)
430 Pioneer Dr, Regina, SK, S4T 6L8
(306) 757-5646
Emp Here 600   *Sales* 30,144,000
SIC 8361 Residential care
  Richard (Dick) Chinn
Prs Dir Eugene Kalenchuk
Dir Ferne Creek
  Laura Ross

Bob Thomas
Don Bartel
Fred Clipsham
Jane Kloczko
Debbie Saum
Dir Bea Parker

D-U-N-S 20-105-7648   (BR)
REGINA QU'APPELLE REGIONAL HEALTH AUTHORITY
PASQUA HOSPITAL
4101 Dewdney Ave, Regina, SK, S4T 1A5
(306) 766-2222
Emp Here 1,440
SIC 8062 General medical and surgical hospitals

D-U-N-S 25-359-3560   (BR)
SASKATCHEWAN CANCER AGENCY
ALLAN BLAIR CANCER CENTER
4101 Dewdney Ave Suite 300, Regina, SK, S4T 7T1
(306) 766-2213
Emp Here 150
SIC 8093 Specialty outpatient clinics, nec

D-U-N-S 25-364-9412   (BR)
SOBEYS WEST INC
SAFEWAY
2931 13th Ave, Regina, SK, S4T 1N8
(306) 522-5453
Emp Here 70
SIC 5411 Grocery stores

Regina, SK S4V

D-U-N-S 24-336-2790   (BR)
BEST BUY CANADA LTD
BEST BUY
(*Suby of* Best Buy Co., Inc.)
2125 Prince Of Wales Dr, Regina, SK, S4V 3A4
(306) 546-0100
Emp Here 50
SIC 5731 Radio, television, and electronic stores

D-U-N-S 20-712-7007   (BR)
BOARD OF EDUCATION REGINA SCHOOL DIVISION NO. 4 OF SASKATCHEWAN
WILFRED HUNT PUBLIC ELEMENTARY SCHOOL
101 Mayfield Rd, Regina, SK, S4V 0B5
(306) 791-8451
Emp Here 50
SIC 8211 Elementary and secondary schools

D-U-N-S 20-712-7023   (BR)
BOARD OF EDUCATION REGINA SCHOOL DIVISION NO. 4 OF SASKATCHEWAN
JACK MACKENZIE SCHOO
3838 E Buckingham Dr, Regina, SK, S4V 3A1
(306) 791-8585
Emp Here 160
SIC 8211 Elementary and secondary schools

D-U-N-S 20-712-7015   (BR)
BOARD OF EDUCATION REGINA SCHOOL DIVISION NO. 4 OF SASKATCHEWAN
WF READY SCHOOL
2710 Helmsng St, Regina, SK, S4V 0W9
(306) 791-8471
Emp Here 35
SIC 8211 Elementary and secondary schools

D-U-N-S 20-712-7452   (BR)
BOARD OF EDUCATION OF THE REGINA ROMAN CATHOLIC SEPARATE SCHOOL DIVISION NO. 81
ST GABRIEL SCHOOL
3150 Windsor Park Rd, Regina, SK, S4V 3A1
(306) 791-1717
Emp Here 30
SIC 8211 Elementary and secondary schools

D-U-N-S 20-037-7229   (BR)
BOARD OF EDUCATION OF THE REGINA ROMAN CATHOLIC SEPARATE SCHOOL DIVISION NO. 81
ST. MARGUERITE BOURGEOYS SCHOOL
2910 E Shooter Dr, Regina, SK, S4V 0Y7
(306) 791-7360
SIC 8211 Elementary and secondary schools

D-U-N-S 25-612-2573   (BR)
BOSTON PIZZA INTERNATIONAL INC
BOSTON PIZZA
2660 E Quance St, Regina, SK, S4V 2X5
(306) 779-4500
Emp Here 55
SIC 5812 Eating places

D-U-N-S 25-055-1892   (BR)
CONCORDE FOOD SERVICES (1996) LTD
PIZZA HUT
(*Suby of* Concorde Group Corp)
2525 E Quance St, Regina, SK, S4V 2X8
(306) 791-3020
Emp Here 35
SIC 5812 Eating places

D-U-N-S 25-524-6670   (BR)
COSTCO WHOLESALE CANADA LTD
COSTCO WHOLESALE CANADA
(*Suby of* Costco Wholesale Corporation)
665 University Park Dr Suite 520, Regina, SK, S4V 2V8
(306) 789-8838
Emp Here 150
SIC 5099 Durable goods, nec

D-U-N-S 20-179-9686   (BR)
HUDSON'S BAY COMPANY
HOME OUTFITTERS
2080 Prince Of Wales Dr, Regina, SK, S4V 3A6
(306) 721-1571
Emp Here 30
SIC 5311 Department stores

D-U-N-S 20-799-3879   (BR)
JUMP.CA WIRELESS SUPPLY CORP
3024 E Quance St, Regina, SK, S4V 3B8
(306) 525-5867
Emp Here 36
SIC 4899 Communication services, nec

D-U-N-S 25-170-3229   (BR)
LOBLAWS INC
REAL CANADIAN SUPERSTORES
2055 Prince Of Wales Dr Suite 1584, Regina, SK, S4V 3A3
(306) 546-6518
Emp Here 300
SIC 5411 Grocery stores

D-U-N-S 20-856-5890   (BR)
MICHAELS OF CANADA, ULC
MICHAEL'S ARTS & CRAFTS STORE
(*Suby of* The Michaels Companies Inc)
2088 Prince Of Wales Dr, Regina, SK, S4V 3A6
(306) 585-9892
Emp Here 40
SIC 5945 Hobby, toy, and game shops

D-U-N-S 20-657-9547   (BR)
OLD NAVY (CANADA) INC
(*Suby of* The Gap Inc)
3120 E Quance St, Regina, SK, S4V 3B8
(306) 775-1860
Emp Here 30
SIC 5651 Family clothing stores

D-U-N-S 20-843-3292   (BR)
PEAVEY INDUSTRIES LIMITED
PEAVEY MART
3939 E Quance Gate, Regina, SK, S4V 3A4
(306) 789-9811
Emp Here 30
SIC 5251 Hardware stores

D-U-N-S 24-377-0823   (BR)
PRINCESS AUTO LTD
3701 E Quance Gate, Regina, SK, S4V 3A4
(306) 721-5115
Emp Here 70
SIC 5251 Hardware stores

D-U-N-S 24-915-6522   (BR)
RE/MAX CROWN REAL ESTATE LTD
RE/MAX
234 University Park Dr, Regina, SK, S4V 1A3
(306) 789-7666
Emp Here 35
SIC 6531 Real estate agents and managers

D-U-N-S 20-792-0260   (BR)
SHERWOOD CO-OPERATIVE ASSOCIATION LIMITED
SHERWOOD CO OP
2925 E Quance St, Regina, SK, S4V 3B7
(306) 791-9300
Emp Here 80
SIC 5411 Grocery stores

D-U-N-S 25-498-9361   (BR)
STAPLES CANADA INC
STAPLES THE BUSINESS DEPOT
(*Suby of* Staples, Inc.)
2640 E Quance St Suite 82, Regina, SK, S4V 2X5
(306) 791-7790
Emp Here 40
SIC 5943 Stationery stores

D-U-N-S 20-860-5415   (BR)
TOWN SHOES LIMITED
SHOE COMPANY, THE
2038 Prince Of Wales Dr, Regina, SK, S4V 3A6
(306) 781-0033
Emp Here 25
SIC 5661 Shoe stores

D-U-N-S 24-330-0519   (BR)
WAL-MART CANADA CORP
2150 Prince Of Wales Dr, Regina, SK, S4V 3A6
(306) 780-3700
Emp Here 200
SIC 5311 Department stores

D-U-N-S 20-860-4475   (BR)
WINNERS MERCHANTS INTERNATIONAL L.P.
WINNERS
(*Suby of* The TJX Companies Inc)
2135 Prince Of Wales Dr, Regina, SK, S4V 3A4
(306) 789-9998
Emp Here 25
SIC 5651 Family clothing stores

Regina, SK S4W

D-U-N-S 20-348-5925   (BR)
DREAM UNLIMITED CORP
DREAM UNLIMITED CORP.
4561 Parliament Ave Suite 300, Regina, SK, S4W 0G3
(306) 347-8100
Emp Here 20
SIC 1521 Single-family housing construction

D-U-N-S 25-295-2023   (BR)
FEDERAL EXPRESS CANADA CORPORATION
FEDERAL EXPRESS CANADA LTD
(*Suby of* Fedex Corporation)
2520 Airport Rd Suite 1, Regina, SK, S4W 1A3
(800) 463-3339
Emp Here 50
SIC 7389 Business services, nec

D-U-N-S 20-845-0085   (BR)

KONTZAMANIS   GRAUMANN   SMITH MACMILLAN INC
K G S GROUP
4561 Parliament Ave Suite 200, Regina, SK, S4W 0G3
(306) 757-9681
Emp Here 60
SIC 8711 Engineering services

D-U-N-S 24-773-0034   (BR)
KONTZAMANIS   GRAUMANN   SMITH MACMILLAN INC
KGS GROUP
4561 Parliament Ave Suite 200, Regina, SK, S4W 0G3
(306) 757-9681
Emp Here 60
SIC 8711 Engineering services

D-U-N-S 25-135-5967   (BR)
LOWE'S COMPANIES CANADA, ULC
4555 Gordon Rd, Regina, SK, S4W 0B7
(306) 751-3000
Emp Here 150
SIC 5211 Lumber and other building materials

D-U-N-S 20-528-0402   (BR)
NAV CANADA
5205 Regina Ave, Regina, SK, S4W 1B2
(306) 359-5014
Emp Here 20
SIC 4899 Communication services, nec

D-U-N-S 25-182-8661   (BR)
SHOCK TRAUMA AIR RESCUE SOCIETY
STARS
2640 Airport Rd, Regina, SK, S4W 1A3
(306) 564-7900
Emp Here 50
SIC 4522 Air transportation, nonscheduled

D-U-N-S 25-950-5485   (BR)
WEST WIND AVIATION INC
REGINA AEROCENTRE
3035 Tutor Dr Suite 203, Regina, SK, S4W 1B5
(306) 359-0020
Emp Here 20
SIC 4522 Air transportation, nonscheduled

Regina, SK S4X

D-U-N-S 25-176-7828   (BR)
BOARD OF EDUCATION REGINA SCHOOL DIVISION NO. 4 OF SASKATCHEWAN
MCLURG SCHOOL
125 Paynter Cres, Regina, SK, S4X 2A9
(306) 791-8496
Emp Here 45
SIC 8211 Elementary and secondary schools

D-U-N-S 20-033-3024   (BR)
BOARD OF EDUCATION REGINA SCHOOL DIVISION NO. 4 OF SASKATCHEWAN
MACNEILL PUBLIC ELEMENTARY SCHOOL
6215 Whelan Dr, Regina, SK, S4X 3P6
(306) 791-8507
Emp Here 40
SIC 8211 Elementary and secondary schools

D-U-N-S 20-543-7804   (BR)
BOARD OF EDUCATION REGINA SCHOOL DIVISION NO. 4 OF SASKATCHEWAN
CENTENNIAL COMMUNITY SCHOOL
6903 Dalgliesh Dr, Regina, SK, S4X 3A1
(306) 791-8559
Emp Here 40
SIC 8211 Elementary and secondary schools

D-U-N-S 20-066-0889   (BR)
BOARD OF EDUCATION REGINA SCHOOL DIVISION NO. 4 OF SASKATCHEWAN
WINSTON KNOLL COLLEGIATE
5255 Rochdale Blvd, Regina, SK, S4X 4M8

---

(306) 523-3400
Emp Here 85
SIC 8211 Elementary and secondary schools

D-U-N-S 20-033-7066   (BR)
BOARD OF EDUCATION REGINA SCHOOL DIVISION NO. 4 OF SASKATCHEWAN
W.H. FORD
480 Rink Ave, Regina, SK, S4X 1S7
(306) 791-8623
Emp Here 38
SIC 8211 Elementary and secondary schools

D-U-N-S 20-033-3008   (BR)
BOARD OF EDUCATION OF THE REGINA ROMAN CATHOLIC SEPARATE SCHOOL DIVISION NO. 81
ST JEROME ELEMENTARY SCHOOL
770 Rink Ave, Regina, SK, S4X 1V8
(306) 791-7345
Emp Here 41
SIC 8211 Elementary and secondary schools

D-U-N-S 20-082-5680   (BR)
BOARD OF EDUCATION OF THE REGINA ROMAN CATHOLIC SEPARATE SCHOOL DIVISION NO. 81
ST ANGELA MERICI SCHOOL
6823 Gillmore Dr, Regina, SK, S4X 4J3
(306) 791-7305
Emp Here 50
SIC 8211 Elementary and secondary schools

D-U-N-S 25-014-3666   (BR)
BOARD OF EDUCATION OF THE REGINA ROMAN CATHOLIC SEPARATE SCHOOL DIVISION NO. 81
MICHAEL A RIFFEL HIGH SCHOOL
5757 Rochdale Blvd, Regina, SK, S4X 3P5
(306) 791-7260
Emp Here 70
SIC 8211 Elementary and secondary schools

D-U-N-S 24-345-0280   (BR)
CONEXUS CREDIT UNION 2006
CONEXUS CROSSING BRANCH
1040 N Pasqua St, Regina, SK, S4X 4V3
(306) 780-1892
Emp Here 25
SIC 6062 State credit unions

D-U-N-S 25-959-1147   (BR)
DOMSASK HOLDING LTD
DOMINO'S PIZZA
5875 Rochdale Blvd, Regina, SK, S4X 2P9
(306) 545-4545
Emp Here 20
SIC 5812 Eating places

D-U-N-S 24-309-3155   (BR)
HOME DEPOT OF CANADA INC
(*Suby of* The Home Depot Inc)
1030 N Pasqua St, Regina, SK, S4X 4V3
(306) 564-5700
Emp Here 100
SIC 5251 Hardware stores

D-U-N-S 25-148-1719   (BR)
LOBLAWS INC
REAL CANADIAN SUPERSTORE
4450 Rochdale Blvd Suite 1585, Regina, SK, S4X 4N9
(306) 546-6618
Emp Here 200
SIC 5399 Miscellaneous general merchandise

D-U-N-S 25-366-0575   (BR)
MCDONALD'S RESTAURANTS OF CANADA LIMITED
MCDONALD'S
(*Suby of* McDonald's Corporation)
6210 Rochdale Blvd, Regina, SK, S4X 4K8
(306) 543-6300
Emp Here 80
SIC 5812 Eating places

D-U-N-S 25-633-0192   (BR)
SGI CANADA INSURANCE SERVICES LTD

SGI CANADA REGINA GENERAL CLAIMS
1100 Mcintosh St N, Regina, SK, S4X 4C7
(306) 751-1307
Emp Here 35
SIC 6411 Insurance agents, brokers, and service

D-U-N-S 25-950-7812   (BR)
SHERWOOD CO-OPERATIVE ASSOCIATION LIMITED
CO-OP GAS STATIONS
5805 Rochdale Blvd, Regina, SK, S4X 2P9
(306) 791-9300
Emp Here 22
SIC 5411 Grocery stores

D-U-N-S 20-965-8918   (BR)
SOBEYS CAPITAL INCORPORATED
4101 Rochdale Blvd, Regina, SK, S4X 4P7
(306) 546-5881
Emp Here 100
SIC 5411 Grocery stores

D-U-N-S 25-294-7452   (BR)
WAL-MART CANADA CORP
3939 Rochdale Blvd, Regina, SK, S4X 4P7
(306) 543-3237
Emp Here 290
SIC 5311 Department stores

Regina, SK S4Z

D-U-N-S 20-559-6856   (SL)
628656 SASKATCHEWAN LTD
HOLIDAY INN HOTEL & SUITES
1800 Prince Of Wales Dr, Regina, SK, S4Z 1A4
(306) 789-3883
Emp Here 60   *Sales* 2,626,585
SIC 7011 Hotels and motels

D-U-N-S 25-484-3758   (BR)
CANADIAN UNION OF PUBLIC EMPLOYEES
CUPE SASKATCHEWAN REGIONAL OFFICE
3731 Eastgate Dr, Regina, SK, S4Z 1A5
(306) 525-5874
Emp Here 28
SIC 8631 Labor organizations

D-U-N-S 25-305-3029   (BR)
INNVEST PROPERTIES CORP
W-WESTMONT HOSPITALITY GROUP
(*Suby of* Innvest Properties Corp)
3221 Eastgate Dr, Regina, SK, S4Z 1A4
(306) 789-5522
Emp Here 20
SIC 7011 Hotels and motels

D-U-N-S 20-355-0822   (BR)
MCDONALD'S RESTAURANTS OF CANADA LIMITED
MCDONALD'S
(*Suby of* McDonald's Corporation)
1955 Prince Of Wales Dr, Regina, SK, S4Z 1A5
(306) 781-1340
Emp Here 76
SIC 5812 Eating places

Richmound, SK S0N

D-U-N-S 24-011-4285   (BR)
APACHE CANADA LTD
(*Suby of* Apache Corporation)
Hwy 371 W, Richmound, SK, S0N 2E0

Emp Here 50
SIC 1382 Oil and gas exploration services

Rocanville, SK S0A

D-U-N-S 24-467-7035   (BR)
BORDERLAND CO-OPERATIVE LIMITED
(*Suby of* Borderland Co-operative Limited)
125 Ellis St, Rocanville, SK, S0A 3L0
(306) 645-2160
Emp Here 20
SIC 5411 Grocery stores

D-U-N-S 20-854-9790   (BR)
POTASH CORPORATION OF SASKATCHEWAN INC
PCS POTASH, DIV OF
Gd, Rocanville, SK, S0A 3L0
(306) 645-2870
Emp Here 400
SIC 1474 Potash, soda, and borate minerals

D-U-N-S 24-614-4096   (BR)
SOUTH EAST CORNERSTONE SCHOOL DIVISION NO. 209
ROCANVILLE SCHOOL
(*Suby of* South East Cornerstone School Division No. 209)
1002 Francis Ave, Rocanville, SK, S0A 3L0
(306) 645-2838
Emp Here 35
SIC 8211 Elementary and secondary schools

Rockglen, SK S0H

D-U-N-S 25-014-3955   (BR)
FIVE HILLS REGIONAL HEALTH AUTHORITY
GRASSLANDS HEALTH CENTRE
(*Suby of* Five Hills Regional Health Authority)
1006 Hwy 2, Rockglen, SK, S0H 3R0
(306) 476-2030
Emp Here 35
SIC 8361 Residential care

Rose Valley, SK S0E

D-U-N-S 25-014-3997   (BR)
HORIZON SCHOOL DIVISION NO 205
ROSE VALLEY SCHOOL
517 1st Ave N, Rose Valley, SK, S0E 1M0
(306) 322-2341
Emp Here 24
SIC 8211 Elementary and secondary schools

Rosetown, SK S0L

D-U-N-S 20-068-5290   (BR)
HEARTLAND REGIONAL HEALTH AUTHORITY
HOMECARE
409 Hwy 4 N, Rosetown, SK, S0L 2V0
(306) 882-4175
Emp Here 21
SIC 7363 Help supply services

D-U-N-S 20-842-6080   (SL)
HUTTERIAN BRETHREN OF ROSETOWN
ROSETOWN COLONY
Gd, Rosetown, SK, S0L 2V0
(306) 882-3344
Emp Here 59   *Sales* 4,591,130
SIC 8661 Religious organizations

D-U-N-S 25-269-8816   (BR)
SUN WEST SCHOOL DIVISION NO 207 SASKATCHEWAN
ROSETOWN CENTRAL HIGH SCHOOL
501 Hwy 4 N, Rosetown, SK, S0L 2V0

(306) 882-2677
Emp Here 37
SIC 8211 Elementary and secondary schools

D-U-N-S 20-033-2596   (BR)
SUN WEST SCHOOL DIVISION NO 207 SASKATCHEWAN
WALTER ASELTINE SCHOOL
200 9th Ave E, Rosetown, SK, S0L 2V0
(306) 882-3800
Emp Here 30
SIC 8211 Elementary and secondary schools

D-U-N-S 24-630-6732   (HQ)
WESTERN SALES (1986) LTD
405 Hwy 7 W, Rosetown, SK, S0L 2V0
(306) 882-4291
Emp Here 56   *Emp Total* 2
Sales 28,308,752
SIC 5083 Farm and garden machinery
Pr Pr Grant Mcgrath
  Jason Hintze
  David Kohli
VP VP Carl Persson

Rosthern, SK S0K

D-U-N-S 20-656-6643   (BR)
PRAIRIE SPIRIT SCHOOL DIVISION NO. 206
ROSTHERN HIGH SCHOOL
4000 4 St, Rosthern, SK, S0K 3R0
(306) 232-4868
Emp Here 20
SIC 8211 Elementary and secondary schools

Saltcoats, SK S0A

D-U-N-S 24-394-9901   (BR)
SUNRISE REGIONAL HEALTH AUTHORITY
LAKESIDE MANOR CARE HOME
101 Crescent Lake Rd, Saltcoats, SK, S0A 3R0
(306) 744-2353
Emp Here 54
SIC 8051 Skilled nursing care facilities

Sandy Bay, SK S0P

D-U-N-S 20-712-8385   (BR)
NORTHERN LIGHTS SCHOOL DIVISION 113
THIBOUTOT, HECTOR COMMUNITY SCHOOL
1 Hill St, Sandy Bay, SK, S0P 0G0
(306) 754-2139
Emp Here 60
SIC 8211 Elementary and secondary schools

Saskatoon, SK S7H

D-U-N-S 20-814-3920   (SL)
101055401 SASKATCHEWAN LTD
BEILY'S PUB & GRILL
2404 8th St E, Saskatoon, SK, S7H 0V6
(306) 374-3344
Emp Here 90   *Sales* 2,699,546
SIC 5812 Eating places

D-U-N-S 25-288-0570   (BR)
A & W FOOD SERVICES OF CANADA INC
A & W
2512 8th St E, Saskatoon, SK, S7H 0V6
(306) 374-6464
Emp Here 45
SIC 5812 Eating places

D-U-N-S 25-803-8025   (BR)
BANK OF NOVA SCOTIA, THE
SCOTIABANK
3510 8th St E, Saskatoon, SK, S7H 0W6
(306) 668-1600
Emp Here 25
SIC 6021 National commercial banks

D-U-N-S 25-636-5065   (BR)
BANK OF NOVA SCOTIA, THE
SCOTIABANK
1004 8th St E, Saskatoon, SK, S7H 0R9
(306) 668-1480
Emp Here 20
SIC 6021 National commercial banks

D-U-N-S 20-651-6689   (BR)
**BOARD OF EDUCATION OF SASKA-
TOON SCHOOL DIVISION NO. 13 OF
SASKATCHEWAN, THE**
EVAN HARDY COLLEGIATE
605 Acadia Dr, Saskatoon, SK, S7H 3V8
(306) 683-7700
Emp Here 50
SIC 8211 Elementary and secondary schools

D-U-N-S 20-712-8112   (BR)
**BOARD OF EDUCATION OF SASKA-
TOON SCHOOL DIVISION NO. 13 OF
SASKATCHEWAN, THE**
ROLAND MICHENER SCHOOL
4215 Degeer St, Saskatoon, SK, S7H 4N6
(306) 683-7440
Emp Here 50
SIC 8211 Elementary and secondary schools

D-U-N-S 20-712-7916   (BR)
**BOARD OF EDUCATION OF SASKA-
TOON SCHOOL DIVISION NO. 13 OF
SASKATCHEWAN, THE**
GREYSTONE HEIGHTS SCHOOL
2721 Main St, Saskatoon, SK, S7H 0M2
(306) 242-3555
Emp Here 30
SIC 8211 Elementary and secondary schools

D-U-N-S 20-712-7908   (BR)
**BOARD OF EDUCATION OF SASKA-
TOON SCHOOL DIVISION NO. 13 OF
SASKATCHEWAN, THE**
ECOLE COLLEGE PARK SCHOOL
3440 Harrington St, Saskatoon, SK, S7H 3Y4
(306) 683-7170
Emp Here 50
SIC 8211 Elementary and secondary schools

D-U-N-S 20-712-7874   (BR)
**BOARD OF EDUCATION OF SASKA-
TOON SCHOOL DIVISION NO. 13 OF
SASKATCHEWAN, THE**
BUENA VISTA SCHOOL
1306 Lorne Ave, Saskatoon, SK, S7H 1X8
(306) 683-7140
Emp Here 25
SIC 8211 Elementary and secondary schools

D-U-N-S 20-712-8138   (BR)
**BOARD OF EDUCATION OF SASKA-
TOON SCHOOL DIVISION NO. 13 OF
SASKATCHEWAN, THE**
WILDWOOD SCHOOL
203 Rosedale Rd, Saskatoon, SK, S7H 5H1
(306) 683-7500
Emp Here 50
SIC 8211 Elementary and secondary schools

D-U-N-S 20-071-2938   (BR)
**BOARD OF EDUCATION OF SASKA-
TOON SCHOOL DIVISION NO. 13 OF
SASKATCHEWAN, THE**
HOLLISTON SCHOOL
1511 Louise Ave, Saskatoon, SK, S7H 2R2
(306) 683-7250
Emp Here 30
SIC 8211 Elementary and secondary schools

D-U-N-S 24-418-2908   (BR)
CINEPLEX ODEON CORPORATION

CINEPLEX CINEMAS CENTRE
3510 8th St E, Saskatoon, SK, S7H 0W6
(306) 955-1938
Emp Here 20
SIC 7832 Motion picture theaters, except
drive-in

D-U-N-S 24-914-4148   (SL)
CONCEPT FOODS LTD
GRANARY RESTAURANT, THE
2806 8th St E, Saskatoon, SK, S7H 0V9
(306) 373-6655
Emp Here 60   *Sales* 1,824,018
SIC 5812 Eating places

D-U-N-S 20-119-4722   (BR)
CONCORDE FOOD SERVICES (1996) LTD
PIZZA HUT
3110 8th St E Unit 11, Saskatoon, SK, S7H
0W2
(306) 668-3050
Emp Here 25
SIC 5812 Eating places

D-U-N-S 25-506-0139   (HQ)
CONCORDE GROUP CORP
(*Suby of* Concorde Group Corp)
1171 8th St E, Saskatoon, SK, S7H 0S3
(306) 668-3000
Emp Here 75   *Emp Total* 600
Sales 31,096,857
SIC 6519 Real property lessors, nec
Pr Pr David Dube
VP Fin Sui Ma

D-U-N-S 20-713-0480   (BR)
CONSEIL DES ECOLES FRANSASKOISES
*ECOLE CANADIENNE-FRANCAISE PAVIL-
LON ELEMENTAIRE & INTERMEDIAIRE*
1407 Albert Ave, Saskatoon, SK, S7H 5R8
(306) 653-8498
Emp Here 45
SIC 8211 Elementary and secondary schools

D-U-N-S 20-939-8051   (BR)
**DREAM ASSET MANAGEMENT CORPO-
RATION**
HOMES BY DREAM
2100 8th St E Suite 112, Saskatoon, SK, S7H
0V1
(306) 374-6100
Emp Here 40
SIC 6552 Subdividers and developers, nec

D-U-N-S 24-340-0889   (BR)
FGL SPORTS LTD
*SPORT CHEK CENTRE AT CIRCLE AND
EIGHT*
3310 8th St E Suite 740, Saskatoon, SK, S7H
5M3
(306) 651-3960
Emp Here 60
SIC 5941 Sporting goods and bicycle shops

D-U-N-S 24-230-7437   (BR)
FOOT LOCKER CANADA CO.
FOOT LOCKER
201 1st St E Suite 301, Saskatoon, SK, S7H
1R8
(306) 244-1848
Emp Here 20
SIC 5661 Shoe stores

D-U-N-S 24-581-7577   (BR)
GOLDER ASSOCIATES LTD
1721 8th St E, Saskatoon, SK, S7H 0T4
(306) 665-7989
Emp Here 140
SIC 8711 Engineering services

D-U-N-S 25-652-0099   (BR)
**GRAINFIELDS PANCAKE & WAFFLE
HOUSE INC**
GRAINFIELDS FAMILY RESTAURANT
2105 8th St E Suite 1, Saskatoon, SK, S7H
0T8
(306) 955-1989
Emp Here 35

SIC 5812 Eating places

D-U-N-S 24-776-4350   (HQ)
HARADROS FOOD SERVICES INC
MANO'S FAMILY RESTAURANT
(*Suby of* Haradros Food Services Inc)
1820 8th St E Suite 200, Saskatoon, SK, S7H
0T6
(306) 955-5555
Emp Here 100   *Emp Total* 100
Sales 2,991,389
SIC 5812 Eating places

D-U-N-S 25-652-0040   (BR)
J.H. ENTERPRISES (1969) LIMITED
J & H BUILDERS WAREHOUSE
3331 8th St E, Saskatoon, SK, S7H 4K1
(306) 373-4300
Emp Here 20
SIC 5211 Lumber and other building materials

D-U-N-S 24-654-4753   (SL)
JRK RESTAURANTS LTD
KELSEY'S RESTAURANT
2600 8th St E Unit 340, Saskatoon, SK, S7H
0V7
(306) 955-4616
Emp Here 50   *Sales* 1,532,175
SIC 5812 Eating places

D-U-N-S 25-236-2603   (SL)
JERRY'S FOOD EMPORIUM LTD
1115 Grosvenor Ave Unit 1, Saskatoon, SK,
S7H 4G2
(306) 373-6555
Emp Here 50   *Sales* 1,532,175
SIC 5812 Eating places

D-U-N-S 20-044-5422   (BR)
JUMP.CA WIRELESS SUPPLY CORP
JUMP.CA
3510 8th St E Suite A9, Saskatoon, SK, S7H
0W6
(306) 683-3303
Emp Here 20
SIC 4899 Communication services, nec

D-U-N-S 25-372-0189   (BR)
JYSK LINEN'N FURNITURE INC
JYSK LINEN'N FURNITURE INC
3311 8th St E Suite 12, Saskatoon, SK, S7H
4K1
(306) 651-7360
Emp Here 20
SIC 5712 Furniture stores

D-U-N-S 24-914-5657   (BR)
LOBLAWS INC
REAL CANADIAN WHOLESALE CLUB, THE
2105 8th St E Unit 51, Saskatoon, SK, S7H
0T8
(306) 373-3010
Emp Here 40
SIC 5411 Grocery stores

D-U-N-S 25-270-1172   (BR)
LOBLAWS INC
REAL CANADIAN SUPERSTORE, THE
2901 8th St E Suite 1535, Saskatoon, SK,
S7H 0V4
(306) 978-7040
Emp Here 350
SIC 5411 Grocery stores

D-U-N-S 25-270-1966   (BR)
LOBLAWS INC
EXTRA FOODS
1018 Taylor St E, Saskatoon, SK, S7H 1W5
(306) 343-6690
Emp Here 35
SIC 5411 Grocery stores

D-U-N-S 20-301-3417   (BR)
MNP LLP
701 9th St E, Saskatoon, SK, S7H 0M6
(306) 682-2673
Emp Here 27
SIC 8721 Accounting, auditing, and book-
keeping

D-U-N-S 20-787-8591   (BR)
**MCDONALD'S RESTAURANTS OF
CANADA LIMITED**
MCDONALD'S
(*Suby of* McDonald's Corporation)
1706 Preston Ave, Saskatoon, SK, S7H 2V8
(306) 955-8677
Emp Here 100
SIC 5812 Eating places

D-U-N-S 24-523-9681   (BR)
MCDOUGALL GAULEY LLP
*MCDOUGALL GAULEY BARRISTERS & SO-
LICITOR*
616 Main St Suite 500, Saskatoon, SK, S7H
0J6
(306) 653-1212
Emp Here 90
SIC 8111 Legal services

D-U-N-S 20-354-0575   (SL)
MCDONALDS RESTAURANT
WILDWOOD
3510 8th St E Unit 1, Saskatoon, SK, S7H
0W6
(306) 955-8674
Emp Here 90   *Sales* 2,699,546
SIC 5812 Eating places

D-U-N-S 25-598-6804   (BR)
MORGUARD INVESTMENTS LIMITED
CENTRE AT CIRCLE & EIGHTH, THE
3510 8th St E Suite 10, Saskatoon, SK, S7H
0W6
(306) 955-6611
Emp Here 24
SIC 6512 Nonresidential building operators

D-U-N-S 25-640-8576   (HQ)
POINT2 TECHNOLOGIES INC
(*Suby of* Yardi Systems, Inc.)
3301 8th St E Suite 500, Saskatoon, SK, S7H
5K5
(306) 955-1855
Emp Here 84   *Emp Total* 2,831
Sales 16,489,118
SIC 7371 Custom computer programming ser-
vices
Dir Saul Klein
Ch Bd Jason Golding
Pr Pr Barry Willick
Dir Walt Baczkowski
Dir Scott Macsemchuk

D-U-N-S 20-337-8521   (BR)
PRINTWEST LTD
MISTER PRINT
(*Suby of* Printwest Ltd)
619 8th St E, Saskatoon, SK, S7H 0R1
(306) 934-7575
Emp Here 22
SIC 2759 Commercial printing, nec

D-U-N-S 20-966-6861   (BR)
RAINBOW CINEMAS INC
RAINBOW CINEMAS
3510 8th St E, Saskatoon, SK, S7H 0W6
(306) 955-1937
Emp Here 20
SIC 7832 Motion picture theaters, except
drive-in

D-U-N-S 25-639-9205   (BR)
RED LOBSTER HOSPITALITY LLC
RED LOBSTER RESTAURANTS
(*Suby of* Red Lobster Seafood Co., LLC)
2501 8th St E, Saskatoon, SK, S7H 0V4
(306) 373-8333
Emp Here 90
SIC 5812 Eating places

D-U-N-S 25-300-5201   (BR)
REDBERRY FRANCHISING CORP
BURGER KING
1515 8th St E, Saskatoon, SK, S7H 0T2

Emp Here 35
SIC 5812 Eating places

D-U-N-S 20-535-7572　　(BR)
ROYAL BANK OF CANADA
RBC
(*Suby of* Royal Bank Of Canada)
2802 8th St E, Saskatoon, SK, S7H 0V9
(306) 933-3780
Emp Here 20
SIC 6021 National commercial banks

D-U-N-S 25-636-8093　　(BR)
SASKATCHEWAN LIQUOR AND GAMING AUTHORITY, THE
3120 8th St E Unit 110, Saskatoon, SK, S7H 0W2
(306) 933-5318
Emp Here 25
SIC 5921 Liquor stores

D-U-N-S 24-607-7887　　(SL)
SASKATOON BUTCHER & BAKER INC
FUDDRUCKERS RESTAURANT
2910 8th St E, Saskatoon, SK, S7H 0W1
(306) 955-7777
Emp Here 50　　　*Sales* 1,532,175
SIC 5812 Eating places

D-U-N-S 25-988-9244　　(BR)
SASKATOON CO-OPERATIVE ASSOCIATION LIMITED, THE
SASKATOON COOP GREYSTONE
2511 8th St E, Saskatoon, SK, S7H 0V4
(306) 933-3886
Emp Here 100
SIC 5411 Grocery stores

D-U-N-S 25-066-2814　　(BR)
SASKATOON CO-OPERATIVE ASSOCIATION LIMITED, THE
CO-OP GREYSTONE GAS BAR NO 3
2505 8th St E, Saskatoon, SK, S7H 0V4
(306) 933-3893
Emp Here 25
SIC 5541 Gasoline service stations

D-U-N-S 20-913-7624　　(BR)
SASKATOON CO-OPERATIVE ASSOCIATION LIMITED, THE
2010 8th St E, Saskatoon, SK, S7H 0T9
(306) 933-3817
Emp Here 25
SIC 5211 Lumber and other building materials

D-U-N-S 24-346-3432　　(BR)
SASKATOON PRAIRIELAND PARK CORPORATION
MARQUIS DOWNS RACE TRACK
2615 St Henry Ave, Saskatoon, SK, S7H 0A1
(306) 242-6100
Emp Here 150
SIC 7948 Racing, including track operation

D-U-N-S 20-840-0754　　(SL)
SHERBROOKE COMMUNITY SOCIETY INC
SHERBROOKE COMMUNITY CENTRE
401 Acadia Dr Suite 330, Saskatoon, SK, S7H 2E7
(306) 655-3600
Emp Here 300　　　*Sales* 19,493,120
SIC 8059 Nursing and personal care, nec
　Suellen Beatty
　Lily Krause

D-U-N-S 25-359-9633　　(SL)
SIEMENS TRANSPORT AND SERVICE LTD
815 Patience Lake Rd, Saskatoon, SK, S7H 5P1
(306) 374-6006
Emp Here 20　　　*Sales* 2,858,628
SIC 4213 Trucking, except local

D-U-N-S 20-091-4872　　(BR)
SOBEYS CAPITAL INCORPORATED
SOBEYS
3907 8th St E, Saskatoon, SK, S7H 5M7
(306) 651-1800
Emp Here 200
SIC 5411 Grocery stores

D-U-N-S 20-706-8490　　(BR)

SOBEYS CAPITAL INCORPORATED
1550 8th St E, Saskatoon, SK, S7H 0T3
(306) 477-5800
Emp Here 100
SIC 5411 Grocery stores

D-U-N-S 25-271-7574　　(BR)
SOBEYS WEST INC
3310 8th St E Unit 200, Saskatoon, SK, S7H 5M3
(306) 955-4646
Emp Here 150
SIC 5411 Grocery stores

D-U-N-S 24-363-2077　　(BR)
SOBEYS WEST INC
CUMBERLAND SAFEWAY
1501 8th St E, Saskatoon, SK, S7H 5J6
(306) 373-0030
Emp Here 50
SIC 5411 Grocery stores

D-U-N-S 25-271-7459　　(BR)
SOBEYS WEST INC
1501 8th St E Suite 4, Saskatoon, SK, S7H 5J6

Emp Here 85
SIC 5411 Grocery stores

D-U-N-S 25-174-9482　　(BR)
SOBEYS WEST INC
CO-OP
3310 8th St E, Saskatoon, SK, S7H 5M3
(306) 955-4644
Emp Here 100
SIC 5411 Grocery stores

D-U-N-S 25-106-9563　　(BR)
ST. PAUL'S ROMAN CATHOLIC SEPARATE SCHOOL DIVISION NO 20
SION MIDDLE SCHOOL
2010 7th St E, Saskatoon, SK, S7H 5K6

Emp Here 25
SIC 8211 Elementary and secondary schools

D-U-N-S 20-712-7601　　(BR)
ST. PAUL'S ROMAN CATHOLIC SEPARATE SCHOOL DIVISION NO 20
ST. AUGUSTINE SCHOOL
602 Boychuk Dr, Saskatoon, SK, S7H 4S1
(306) 659-7270
Emp Here 50
SIC 8211 Elementary and secondary schools

D-U-N-S 20-191-7015　　(BR)
STAPLES CANADA INC
STAPLES THE BUSINESS DEPOT
(*Suby of* Staples, Inc.)
2327 8th St E, Saskatoon, SK, S7H 0V4
(306) 955-6536
Emp Here 30
SIC 5943 Stationery stores

D-U-N-S 20-806-3763　　(BR)
STARBUCKS COFFEE CANADA, INC
(*Suby of* Starbucks Corporation)
2311 8th St E Suite A, Saskatoon, SK, S7H 0V4
(306) 955-7434
Emp Here 30
SIC 5812 Eating places

D-U-N-S 25-642-6818　　(BR)
TORONTO-DOMINION BANK, THE
TD CANADA TRUST
(*Suby of* Toronto-Dominion Bank, The)
3020 8th St E, Saskatoon, SK, S7H 0W2
(306) 975-7300
Emp Here 42
SIC 6021 National commercial banks

D-U-N-S 20-184-3203　　(BR)
WINNERS MERCHANTS INTERNATIONAL L.P.
WINNERS
(*Suby of* The TJX Companies Inc)
2319 8th St E, Saskatoon, SK, S7H 0V4

(306) 664-1077
Emp Here 40
SIC 5651 Family clothing stores

Saskatoon, SK S7J

D-U-N-S 20-284-9576　　(BR)
ACTIONWEAR SASKATOON INC
114 Melville St, Saskatoon, SK, S7J 0R1
(306) 933-3088
Emp Here 70
SIC 3842 Surgical appliances and supplies

D-U-N-S 20-712-8013　　(BR)
BOARD OF EDUCATION OF SASKATOON SCHOOL DIVISION NO. 13 OF SASKATCHEWAN, THE
QUEEN ELIZABETH SCHOOL
1905 Eastlake Ave, Saskatoon, SK, S7J 0W9
(306) 683-7420
Emp Here 30
SIC 8211 Elementary and secondary schools

D-U-N-S 25-289-7194　　(BR)
BOARD OF EDUCATION OF SASKATOON SCHOOL DIVISION NO. 13 OF SASKATCHEWAN, THE
LAKERIDGE SCHOOL
305 Waterbury Rd, Saskatoon, SK, S7J 4Z7
(306) 683-7320
Emp Here 45
SIC 8211 Elementary and secondary schools

D-U-N-S 20-656-6692　　(BR)
BOARD OF EDUCATION OF SASKATOON SCHOOL DIVISION NO. 13 OF SASKATCHEWAN, THE
ECOLE ALVIN BUCKWOLD SCHOOL
715 East Drive, Saskatoon, SK, S7J 2X8
(306) 683-7100
Emp Here 25
SIC 8211 Elementary and secondary schools

D-U-N-S 25-289-6758　　(BR)
BOARD OF EDUCATION OF SASKATOON SCHOOL DIVISION NO. 13 OF SASKATCHEWAN, THE
ECOLE LAKEVIEW SCHOOL
527 Kingsmere Blvd, Saskatoon, SK, S7J 3V4
(306) 683-7330
Emp Here 36
SIC 8211 Elementary and secondary schools

D-U-N-S 20-712-8070　　(BR)
BOARD OF EDUCATION OF SASKATOON SCHOOL DIVISION NO. 13 OF SASKATCHEWAN, THE
JOHN DOLAN SCHOOL
3144 Arlington Ave, Saskatoon, SK, S7J 3L5
(306) 683-7290
Emp Here 30
SIC 8211 Elementary and secondary schools

D-U-N-S 25-289-6444　　(BR)
BOARD OF EDUCATION OF SASKATOON SCHOOL DIVISION NO. 13 OF SASKATCHEWAN, THE
WALTER MURRAY COLLEGIATE
1905 Preston Ave, Saskatoon, SK, S7J 2E7
(306) 683-7850
Emp Here 110
SIC 8211 Elementary and secondary schools

D-U-N-S 25-289-7038　　(BR)
BOARD OF EDUCATION OF SASKATOON SCHOOL DIVISION NO. 13 OF SASKATCHEWAN, THE
ADEN BOWMAN COLLEGIATE
1904 Clarence Ave S, Saskatoon, SK, S7J 1L3
(306) 683-7600
Emp Here 72
SIC 8211 Elementary and secondary schools

D-U-N-S 20-712-8005　　(BR)

BOARD OF EDUCATION OF SASKATOON SCHOOL DIVISION NO. 13 OF SASKATCHEWAN, THE
PRINCE PHILIP SCHOOL
1715 Drinkle St, Saskatoon, SK, S7J 0P8
(306) 683-7400
Emp Here 35
SIC 8211 Elementary and secondary schools

D-U-N-S 20-712-7957　　(BR)
BOARD OF EDUCATION OF SASKATOON SCHOOL DIVISION NO. 13 OF SASKATCHEWAN, THE
JOHN LAKE SCHOOL
2606 Broadway Ave, Saskatoon, SK, S7J 0Z6
(306) 683-7300
Emp Here 30
SIC 8211 Elementary and secondary schools

D-U-N-S 20-712-7940　　(BR)
BOARD OF EDUCATION OF SASKATOON SCHOOL DIVISION NO. 13 OF SASKATCHEWAN, THE
HUGH CAIRNS V.C. SCHOOL
2621 Cairns Ave, Saskatoon, SK, S7J 1V8
(306) 683-7270
Emp Here 50
SIC 8211 Elementary and secondary schools

D-U-N-S 25-640-4278　　(BR)
BREWERS' DISTRIBUTOR LTD
B D L
(*Suby of* Brewers' Distributor Ltd)
2630a Jasper Ave, Saskatoon, SK, S7J 2K2
(306) 931-0110
Emp Here 25
SIC 5181 Beer and ale

D-U-N-S 24-170-6985　　(SL)
CHESHIRE HOMES OF SASKATOON
2901 Louise St, Saskatoon, SK, S7J 3L1
(306) 374-6191
Emp Here 60　　　*Sales* 2,188,821
SIC 8361 Residential care

D-U-N-S 24-371-9007　　(BR)
CONSEIL DES ECOLES FRANSASKOISES
ECOLE CANADIENNE-FRANCAISE PAVILLON SECONDAIRE
2320 Louise Ave Suite 200, Saskatoon, SK, S7J 3M7
(306) 653-8490
Emp Here 20
SIC 8211 Elementary and secondary schools

D-U-N-S 24-818-9755　　(BR)
EXTENDICARE (CANADA) INC
EXTENDICARE PRESTON
2225 Preston Ave, Saskatoon, SK, S7J 2E7
(306) 374-2242
Emp Here 110
SIC 8051 Skilled nursing care facilities

D-U-N-S 20-840-9789　　(SL)
MINERS CONSTRUCTION CO. LTD
440 Melville St, Saskatoon, SK, S7J 4M2
(306) 934-4703
Emp Here 30　　　*Sales* 5,545,013
SIC 1542 Nonresidential construction, nec
　Howard Stensrud
　Pr Pr Michael Stensrud
　Aaron Yohnke
　Dave Woodrow

D-U-N-S 20-890-5104　　(BR)
PEPSICO CANADA ULC
FRITO LAY CANADA
(*Suby of* Pepsico, Inc.)
318 Edson St, Saskatoon, SK, S7J 0P9
(306) 242-5918
Emp Here 20
SIC 5145 Confectionery

D-U-N-S 24-654-9695　　(SL)
PLEASURE-WAY INDUSTRIES LTD
302 Portage Ave, Saskatoon, SK, S7J 4C6
(306) 934-6578
Emp Here 150

SIC 3716 Motor homes

D-U-N-S 20-192-3989   (SL)
SASCOPACK INC
106 Melville St, Saskatoon, SK, S7J 0R1

Emp Here 50   *Sales* 2,626,585
SIC 7389 Business services, nec

D-U-N-S 25-289-5560   (BR)
SASKATCHEWAN ASSOCIATION OF RE-HABILITATION CENTRES
SARCAN PECYCLING
(*Suby of* Saskatchewan Association of Rehabilitation Centres)
2605 Broacway Ave Suite 20, Saskatoon, SK, S7J 0Z5
(306) 975-7188
Emp Here 24
SIC 4953 Refuse systems

D-U-N-S 20-080-3232   (BR)
SASKATOON REGIONAL HEALTH AU-THORITY
CALDER CENTRE
2003 Arlington Ave, Saskatoon, SK, S7J 2H6
(306) 655-4500
Emp Here 60
SIC 8069 Specialty hospitals, except psychiatric

D-U-N-S 25-116-7268   (BR)
SASKATOON, CITY OF
SASKATOON LIGHT AND POWER
322 Brand Rd, Saskatoon, SK, S7J 5J3
(306) 975-2414
Emp Here 120
SIC 4911 Electric services

D-U-N-S 25-106-9225   (BR)
ST. PAUL'S ROMAN CATHOLIC SEPARATE SCHOOL DIVISION NO 20
ST PHILIP SCHOOL
1901 Haultain Ave, Saskatoon, SK, S7J 1P4
(306) 659-7450
Emp Here 30
SIC 8211 Elementary and secondary schools

D-U-N-S 20-712-7502   (BR)
ST. PAUL'S ROMAN CATHOLIC SEPARATE SCHOOL DIVISION NO 20
ST FRANCIS
2141 Mcpherson Ave, Saskatoon, SK, S7J 0S8
(306) 659-7310
Emp Here 50
SIC 8211 Elementary and secondary schools

D-U-N-S 25-107-0272   (BR)
ST. PAUL'S ROMAN CATHOLIC SEPARATE SCHOOL DIVISION NO 20
ST. LUKE'S SCHOOL
275 Emmeline Rd, Saskatoon, SK, S7J 5B7
(306) 659-7370
Emp Here 30
SIC 8211 Elementary and secondary schools

D-U-N-S 25-106-9811   (BR)
ST. PAUL'S ROMAN CATHOLIC SEPARATE SCHOOL DIVISION NO 20
ST BERNARD SCHOOL
203 Whiteshore Cres, Saskatoon, SK, S7J 3W4
(306) 659-7280
Emp Here 30
SIC 8211 Elementary and secondary schools

D-U-N-S 20-273-3390   (BR)
THOMAS FRESH INC
THOMAS FRESH SASKATOON
213 Melville St, Saskatoon, SK, S7J 5H7
(306) 933-1900
Emp Here 27
SIC 5148 Fresh fruits and vegetables

D-U-N-S 24-820-0057   (BR)
UPONOR INFRA LTD
348 Edson St, Saskatoon, SK, S7J 0P9

(306) 242-0755
Emp Here 75
SIC 3498 Fabricated pipe and fittings

Saskatoon, SK S7K

D-U-N-S 20-521-5374   (SL)
629112 SASKATCHEWAN LTD
CKBL - FM
366 3rd Ave S, Saskatoon, SK, S7K 1M5
(306) 244-1975
Emp Here 70   *Sales* 4,450,603
SIC 4832 Radio broadcasting stations

D-U-N-S 25-681-4708   (BR)
668824 ALBERTA LTD
VISIONS ELECTRONICS
2731 Faithfull Ave, Saskatoon, SK, S7K 7C3
(306) 664-3666
Emp Here 30
SIC 5731 Radio, television, and electronic stores

D-U-N-S 24-916-6976   (BR)
A & W FOOD SERVICES OF CANADA INC
A & W
822 51st St E, Saskatoon, SK, S7K 0X8
(306) 931-3376
Emp Here 28
SIC 5812 Eating places

D-U-N-S 25-193-5052   (BR)
ADESA AUCTIONS CANADA CORPORA-TION
ADESA SASKATOON
37507 Hwy 12, Saskatoon, SK, S7K 3J7
(306) 242-8771
Emp Here 150
SIC 5012 Automobiles and other motor vehicles

D-U-N-S 25-640-5747   (BR)
AON CONSULTING INC
105 21st St E 8th Fl, Saskatoon, SK, S7K 0B3
(306) 975-8855
Emp Here 25
SIC 8999 Services, nec

D-U-N-S 24-394-2088   (BR)
ATCO POWER CANADA LTD
CORY COGENERATION STATION
8 Hwy 7 W Gd Stn Main Gd Stn Main, Saskatoon, SK, S7K 3J4
(306) 668-8745
Emp Here 29
SIC 4911 Electric services

D-U-N-S 25-639-8975   (BR)
ALLIANCE ENERGY LIMITED
3230 Faithfull Ave, Saskatoon, SK, S7K 8H3
(306) 242-5802
Emp Here 65
SIC 1731 Electrical work

D-U-N-S 24-967-0878   (BR)
ALSCO CANADA CORPORATION
ALSCO UNIFORM & LINEN SERVICE
406 45th St E, Saskatoon, SK, S7K 0W2
(306) 934-0900
Emp Here 50
SIC 7213 Linen supply

D-U-N-S 24-354-8497   (BR)
ANDRITZ HYDRO CANADA INC
ANDRITZ SEPARATION, DIV OF
2600 Wentz Ave, Saskatoon, SK, S7K 2L1
(306) 931-0801
Emp Here 45
SIC 3569 General industrial machinery, nec

D-U-N-S 24-204-8770   (BR)
APPLIED INDUSTRIAL TECHNOLOGIES, LP
HYPOWER SYSTEMS, DIVISION OF
(*Suby of* Applied Industrial Technologies, Inc.)
3077 Faithfull Ave, Saskatoon, SK, S7K 8B3

(306) 934-3366
Emp Here 20
SIC 5084 Industrial machinery and equipment

D-U-N-S 24-344-4200   (HQ)
AQUIFER DISTRIBUTION LTD
(*Suby of* Aquifer Investments Ltd)
227a Venture Cres, Saskatoon, SK, S7K 6N8
(306) 242-1567
Emp Here 35   *Emp Total* 39
Sales 6,931,267
SIC 5074 Plumbing and heating equipment and supplies (hydronics)
Pr Pr Glenn Wig

D-U-N-S 20-645-4873   (BR)
ASSANTE CAPITAL MANAGEMENT LTD
ASSANTE WEALTH MANAGEMENT
500 Spadina Cres E Suite 301, Saskatoon, SK, S7K 4H9
(306) 665-3244
Emp Here 26
SIC 6211 Security brokers and dealers

D-U-N-S 20-211-2723   (BR)
AUDIO WAREHOUSE LTD
AUDIO WAREHOUSE
1601 Quebec Ave, Saskatoon, SK, S7K 1V6
(306) 664-8885
Emp Here 42
SIC 5735 Record and prerecorded tape stores

D-U-N-S 20-843-2534   (BR)
BANK OF NOVA SCOTIA, THE
111 2nd Ave S, Saskatoon, SK, S7K 1K6
(306) 668-1400
Emp Here 35
SIC 6021 National commercial banks

D-U-N-S 25-636-5024   (BR)
BANK OF MONTREAL
BMO
134 Primrose Dr Suite 58, Saskatoon, SK, S7K 5S6
(306) 934-5745
Emp Here 20
SIC 6021 National commercial banks

D-U-N-S 25-115-0140   (BR)
BAYER CROPSCIENCE INC
5 Clumbers Hwy 41, Saskatoon, SK, S7K 7E9
(306) 477-9400
Emp Here 75
SIC 5191 Farm supplies

D-U-N-S 20-188-7390   (BR)
BELL MEDIA INC
CTV SASKATOON
216 1st Ave N, Saskatoon, SK, S7K 3W3
(306) 665-8600
Emp Here 75
SIC 4833 Television broadcasting stations

D-U-N-S 25-652-0313   (BR)
BELOW THE BELT LTD
177 Midtown Plaza Suite 205, Saskatoon, SK, S7K 1J9
(306) 934-8891
Emp Here 20
SIC 5651 Family clothing stores

D-U-N-S 20-644-9394   (BR)
BOARD OF EDUCATION OF SASKA-TOON SCHOOL DIVISION NO. 13 OF SASKATCHEWAN, THE
SASKATOON CHRISTIAN SCHOOL
Rr 5 Lcd Main, Saskatoon, SK, S7K 3J8
(306) 343-1494
Emp Here 40
SIC 8211 Elementary and secondary schools

D-U-N-S 20-712-8146   (BR)
BOARD OF EDUCATION OF SASKA-TOON SCHOOL DIVISION NO. 13 OF SASKATCHEWAN, THE
LAWSON HEIGHTS SCHOOL
430 Redberry Rd, Saskatoon, SK, S7K 5H6
(306) 683-7340
Emp Here 25

SIC 8211 Elementary and secondary schools

D-U-N-S 20-712-8161   (BR)
BOARD OF EDUCATION OF SASKA-TOON SCHOOL DIVISION NO. 13 OF SASKATCHEWAN, THE
BROWNELL SCHOOL
274 Russell Rd, Saskatoon, SK, S7K 7E1
(306) 683-7120
Emp Here 50
SIC 8211 Elementary and secondary schools

D-U-N-S 20-033-7025   (BR)
BOARD OF EDUCATION OF SASKA-TOON SCHOOL DIVISION NO. 13 OF SASKATCHEWAN, THE
MARION M GRAHAM COLLEGIATE
602 Lenore Dr, Saskatoon, SK, S7K 6A6
(306) 683-7750
Emp Here 74
SIC 8211 Elementary and secondary schools

D-U-N-S 20-712-8021   (BR)
BOARD OF EDUCATION OF SASKA-TOON SCHOOL DIVISION NO. 13 OF SASKATCHEWAN, THE
ECOLE RIVER HEIGHTS SCHOOL
60 Ravine Dr, Saskatoon, SK, S7K 1E2
(306) 683-7430
Emp Here 50
SIC 8211 Elementary and secondary schools

D-U-N-S 24-648-7370   (BR)
BOARD OF EDUCATION OF SASKA-TOON SCHOOL DIVISION NO. 13 OF SASKATCHEWAN, THE
SASKATOON PUBLIC SCHOOLS
310 21st St E, Saskatoon, SK, S7K 1M7
(306) 683-8348
Emp Here 150
SIC 8211 Elementary and secondary schools

D-U-N-S 24-916-8352   (BR)
BRANDT TRACTOR LTD
2410 Millar Ave, Saskatoon, SK, S7K 3V2
(306) 664-4141
Emp Here 40
SIC 5084 Industrial machinery and equipment

D-U-N-S 24-368-1850   (HQ)
BRECK SCAFFOLD SOLUTIONS, INC
BRECK CONSTRUCTION
(*Suby of* Breck Scaffold Solutions, Inc)
6 Cory Lane, Saskatoon, SK, S7K 3J7
(306) 242-5532
Emp Here 140   *Emp Total* 150
Sales 13,132,926
SIC 1799 Special trade contractors, nec
Pr Royan Stewart
Dir Bobbylynn Stewart
    Trevor Laughren

D-U-N-S 24-654-4365   (BR)
BRICK WAREHOUSE LP, THE
BRICK, THE
2035 1st Ave N, Saskatoon, SK, S7K 6W1
(306) 244-1400
Emp Here 30
SIC 5712 Furniture stores

D-U-N-S 24-128-6819   (SL)
BUHLER VERSATILE INDUSTRIES
North Corman Industrial Park, Saskatoon, SK, S7K 0A1
(306) 931-3000
Emp Here 22   *Sales* 6,184,080
SIC 5033 Roofing, siding, and insulation

D-U-N-S 25-293-8600   (BR)
CIBC WORLD MARKETS INC
CIBC WORLD MARKETS
119 4th Ave S Suite 500, Saskatoon, SK, S7K 5X2
(306) 975-3800
Emp Here 34
SIC 6211 Security brokers and dealers

D-U-N-S 25-636-7616   (BR)

CP DISTRIBUTORS LTD
CP DISTRIBUTORS LTD.
3719 Kochar Av, Saskatoon, SK, S7K 0B8
(306) 242-3315
Emp Here 50
SIC 5199 Nondurable goods, nec

D-U-N-S 25-995-2166   (BR)
CANADA POST CORPORATION
817 51st St E, Saskatoon, SK, S7K 0G9

Emp Here 135
SIC 4311 U.s. postal service

D-U-N-S 20-510-9551   (BR)
CANADIAN BLOOD SERVICES
BONE MARROW - SASKATCHEWAN
325 20th St E, Saskatoon, SK, S7K 0A9
(306) 651-6600
Emp Here 50
SIC 8099 Health and allied services, nec

D-U-N-S 25-598-6358   (BR)
CANADIAN BROADCASTING CORPORA-TION
CBC
128 4th Avenue S Unit 100, Saskatoon, SK, S7K 1M8
(306) 956-7400
Emp Here 25
SIC 4833 Television broadcasting stations

D-U-N-S 25-636-5826   (BR)
CANADIAN IMPERIAL BANK OF COM-MERCE
CIBC
201 21st St E Unit 21, Saskatoon, SK, S7K 0B8
(306) 668-3488
Emp Here 60
SIC 6021 National commercial banks

D-U-N-S 24-497-0257   (BR)
CANADIAN LINEN AND UNIFORM SER-VICE CO
QUEBEC LINGE
(*Suby of* Ameripride Services, Inc.)
302 1st Ave N, Saskatoon, SK, S7K 1X4
(306) 652-3614
Emp Here 60
SIC 7213 Linen supply

D-U-N-S 20-235-3301   (BR)
CAPITAL INDUSTRIAL SALES & SERVICE LTD
210 48th St E Suite 3, Saskatoon, SK, S7K 6A4
(306) 651-3314
Emp Here 50
SIC 3537 Industrial trucks and tractors

D-U-N-S 24-571-8028   (BR)
CARON TRANSPORTATION SYSTEMS PARTNERSHIP
Rr 4 Lcd Main, Saskatoon, SK, S7K 3J7
(306) 242-5966
Emp Here 40
SIC 4213 Trucking, except local

D-U-N-S 20-069-2333   (HQ)
CAVALIER ENTERPRISES LTD
SHERATON CAVALIER SASKATOON
(*Suby of* Alfour Ventures Inc)
620 Spadina Cres E, Saskatoon, SK, S7K 3T5
(306) 652-6770
Emp Here 250   *Emp Total* 7
Sales 31,096,857
SIC 7011 Hotels and motels
Pr Paul Leier
VP VP Deloris Leier
VP VP Mark Leier
VP VP Scott Leier

D-U-N-S 24-851-3004   (BR)
CERVUS EQUIPMENT CORPORATION
A.R. WILLIAMS MATERIALS HANDLING
210 Faithfull Cres, Saskatoon, SK, S7K 8H8
(306) 933-3383
Emp Here 20

SIC 8731 Commercial physical research

D-U-N-S 24-418-2791   (BR)
CINEPLEX ODEON CORPORATION
SCOTIABANK THEATRE SASKATOON & VIP
347 2nd Ave S, Saskatoon, SK, S7K 1L2
(306) 664-5060
Emp Here 60
SIC 7832 Motion picture theaters, except drive-in

D-U-N-S 24-117-3475   (SL)
CITY MASONRY CONTRACTOR LTD
3042 Faithfull Ave, Saskatoon, SK, S7K 0B1
(306) 934-3599
Emp Here 60   *Sales* 4,377,642
SIC 1741 Masonry and other stonework

D-U-N-S 25-095-0441   (HQ)
CLEARTECH INDUSTRIES INC
(*Suby of* J.W. Yuel Holdings Ltd)
1500 Quebec Ave, Saskatoon, SK, S7K 1V7
(306) 664-2522
Emp Here 30   *Emp Total* 350
Sales 19,923,773
SIC 2819 Industrial inorganic chemicals, nec
James Yuel
Hugh Macgowan
Greg Yuel

D-U-N-S 24-236-7365   (BR)
CLIFTON ASSOCIATES LTD
1925 1st Ave N Suite 4, Saskatoon, SK, S7K 6W1
(306) 975-0401
Emp Here 50
SIC 8711 Engineering services

D-U-N-S 24-883-3212   (BR)
COCA-COLA REFRESHMENTS CANADA COMPANY
(*Suby of* The Coca-Cola Company)
315 Circle Dr E, Saskatoon, SK, S7K 0T7
(306) 244-1577
Emp Here 65
SIC 5141 Groceries, general line

D-U-N-S 20-843-8192   (HQ)
COLLIERS MCCLOCKLIN REAL ESTATE CORP
(*Suby of* Colliers McClocklin Real Estate Corp)
728 Spadina Cres E Suite 101, Saskatoon, SK, S7K 3H2
(306) 653-4410
Emp Here 45   *Emp Total* 50
Sales 4,742,446
SIC 6531 Real estate agents and managers

D-U-N-S 25-359-3354   (BR)
COMPUTER BOULEVARD INC
COMPUTER BOULEVARD SK
1738 Quebec Ave Unit 27, Saskatoon, SK, S7K 1V9
(306) 242-1088
Emp Here 30
SIC 5045 Computers, peripherals, and software

D-U-N-S 25-189-0109   (SL)
CONCEPT GRILLS LTD
2ND AVE GRILL
123 2nd Ave S Unit 10, Saskatoon, SK, S7K 7E6
(306) 244-9899
Emp Here 60   *Sales* 1,824,018
SIC 5812 Eating places

D-U-N-S 24-337-2450   (BR)
CONCORDE FOOD SERVICES (1996) LTD
PIZZA HUT
202 Primrose Dr Suite 8, Saskatoon, SK, S7K 6Y6
(306) 668-3070
Emp Here 20
SIC 5812 Eating places

D-U-N-S 20-071-2953   (SL)
COSMOPOLITAN INDUSTRIES GOLF

CANADA LTD
COSMO GOLF CANADA
(*Suby of* Cosmopolitan Industries Ltd)
1302b Alberta Ave, Saskatoon, SK, S7K 1R5
(306) 477-4653
Emp Here 25   *Sales* 2,845,467
SIC 5091 Sporting and recreation goods

D-U-N-S 24-309-3148   (BR)
CUMMINS WESTERN CANADA LIMITED PARTNERSHIP
3001 Faithfull Ave, Saskatoon, SK, S7K 8B3
(306) 933-4022
Emp Here 24
SIC 5084 Industrial machinery and equipment

D-U-N-S 24-172-0184   (BR)
DELOITTE LLP
122 1st Ave S Suite 400, Saskatoon, SK, S7K 7E5
(306) 343-4400
Emp Here 100
SIC 8721 Accounting, auditing, and book-keeping

D-U-N-S 24-321-9974   (BR)
DIRECT LIMITED PARTNERSHIP
DIRECT TRANSPORT
3030 Cleveland Ave, Saskatoon, SK, S7K 8B5
(306) 956-1760
Emp Here 45
SIC 4212 Local trucking, without storage

D-U-N-S 24-236-6490   (HQ)
DYNAINDUSTRIAL INC
3326 Faithfull Ave, Saskatoon, SK, S7K 8H1
(306) 931-8725
Emp Here 20   *Emp Total* 170
Sales 29,549,084
SIC 3532 Mining machinery
Pr Pr Brian Pickett
Treas Brian Eidem

D-U-N-S 20-810-5077   (BR)
DYNACARE-GAMMA LABORATORY PART-NERSHIP
39 23rd St E Unit 5, Saskatoon, SK, S7K 0H6
(306) 655-4028
Emp Here 65
SIC 8071 Medical laboratories

D-U-N-S 25-643-2246   (BR)
DYNAMEX CANADA LIMITED
DYANAMEX COURIER
3275 Miners Ave, Saskatoon, SK, S7K 7Z1
(306) 975-1010
Emp Here 80
SIC 7389 Business services, nec

D-U-N-S 25-976-4892   (HQ)
EKS HOLDINGS LTD
(*Suby of* EKS Holdings Ltd)
2411 Wentz Ave, Saskatoon, SK, S7K 3V6
(306) 934-1911
Emp Here 20   *Emp Total* 600
Sales 103,090,793
SIC 4213 Trucking, except local
Pr Pr Erwin Siemens

D-U-N-S 24-819-5315   (BR)
EARL'S RESTAURANTS LTD
EARL'S
(*Suby of* Earl's Restaurants Ltd)
610 2nd Ave N, Saskatoon, SK, S7K 2C8
(306) 664-4060
Emp Here 200
SIC 5812 Eating places

D-U-N-S 20-069-4347   (BR)
EMCO CORPORATION
EMCO SUPPLY
3009 Millar Ave, Saskatoon, SK, S7K 6G5
(306) 652-7474
Emp Here 20
SIC 5074 Plumbing and heating equipment and supplies (hydronics)

D-U-N-S 24-818-8542   (BR)

EMCO CORPORATION
WESTERN/WESTLUND
803 58th St E, Saskatoon, SK, S7K 6X5
(306) 652-5545
Emp Here 20
SIC 5085 Industrial supplies

D-U-N-S 20-700-7738   (SL)
FCL ENTERPRISES CO-OPERATIVE
MARKETPLACE AT LORETTE
(*Suby of* Federated Co-Operatives Limited)
401 22nd St E, Saskatoon, SK, S7K 0H2
(306) 244-3311
Emp Here 25   *Sales* 3,378,379
SIC 5411 Grocery stores

D-U-N-S 24-340-0343   (BR)
FGL SPORTS LTD
SPORT-CHEK MIDTOWN PLAZA
201 Midtown Plaza Unit T215c, Saskatoon, SK, S7K 1J9
(306) 955-7733
Emp Here 40
SIC 5941 Sporting goods and bicycle shops

D-U-N-S 25-288-3087   (BR)
FARM CREDIT CANADA
FCC
810 Circle Dr E Suite 109, Saskatoon, SK, S7K 3T8
(306) 975-4248
Emp Here 20
SIC 6159 Miscellaneous business credit insti-tutions

D-U-N-S 20-069-4693   (HQ)
FEDERATED CO-OPERATIVES LIMITED
CO-OPERATIVE
(*Suby of* Federated Co-Operatives Limited)
401 22nd St E, Saskatoon, SK, S7K 0H2
(306) 244-3311
Emp Here 500   *Emp Total* 3,000
Sales 6,825,681,252
SIC 4225 General warehousing and storage
Dusty Macdonald
Valerie Pearson
Judy Clavier
Doug Potentier
Steffen Olsen
Tara Bourke
Russel Wolf
Marc Topola
Brad Schultz
Randy Graham

D-U-N-S 25-742-4445   (BR)
FEDERATED CO-OPERATIVES LIMITED
(*Suby of* Federated Co-Operatives Limited)
604 45th St E, Saskatoon, SK, S7K 3T3
(306) 244-1650
Emp Here 250
SIC 4225 General warehousing and storage

D-U-N-S 24-850-9994   (BR)
FEDERATED CO-OPERATIVES LIMITED
FCL CO-OP WAREHOUSE SASKATOON
(*Suby of* Federated Co-Operatives Limited)
607 46th St E, Saskatoon, SK, S7K 0X1
(306) 244-1690
Emp Here 200
SIC 5141 Groceries, general line

D-U-N-S 24-380-0179   (BR)
FIRSTCANADA ULC
FIRST STUDENT CANADA
110 Faithfull Cres, Saskatoon, SK, S7K 8H8
(306) 343-2125
Emp Here 20
SIC 4151 School buses

D-U-N-S 25-640-0599   (BR)
FLYNN CANADA LTD
134 Faithfull Cres, Saskatoon, SK, S7K 8H8
(306) 242-5909
Emp Here 55
SIC 1761 Roofing, siding, and sheetMetal work

▲ Public Company   ■ Public Company Family Member   **HQ** Headquarters   **BR** Branch   **SL** Single Location

D-U-N-S 24-382-6265   (BR)
FORMER RESTORATION L.P.
103 English Cres, Saskatoon, SK, S7K 8G4
(306) 978-6600
Emp Here 50
SIC 1799 Special trade contractors, nec

D-U-N-S 24-117-3533   (BR)
FORT GARRY INDUSTRIES LTD
FGI
3445 Miners Ave, Saskatoon, SK, S7K 7K9
(306) 242-3465
Emp Here 32
SIC 5013 Motor vehicle supplies and new parts

D-U-N-S 20-012-5461   (BR)
FOUNTAIN TIRE LTD
FOUNTAIN TIRE TRUCK & RETREAD CENTRE
2922 Millar Ave, Saskatoon, SK, S7K 5X7
(306) 242-3233
Emp Here 31
SIC 5531 Auto and home supply stores

D-U-N-S 24-230-0663   (HQ)
FRONTIER PETERBILT SALES LTD
FRONTIER LEASE & RENTAL
303 50th St E, Saskatoon, SK, S7K 6C1
(306) 242-3411
Emp Here 70   *Emp Total* 1,646
Sales 80,256,770
SIC 5511 New and used car dealers
Pr Pr Peter Lacey

D-U-N-S 20-853-1087   (BR)
GVIC COMMUNICATIONS INC
WESTERN PRODUCER PUBLICATIONS
2310 Millar Ave, Saskatoon, SK, S7K 2Y2
(306) 665-3500
Emp Here 75
SIC 2711 Newspapers

D-U-N-S 24-070-3822   (BR)
GAP (CANADA) INC
GAPKIDS
(*Suby of* The Gap Inc)
21st St E, Saskatoon, SK, S7K 0B3
(306) 653-8488
Emp Here 40
SIC 5651 Family clothing stores

D-U-N-S 24-360-1429   (BR)
GAP (CANADA) INC
GAP, THE
(*Suby of* The Gap Inc)
21 St Midtown, Saskatoon, SK, S7K 1J9
(306) 653-8484
Emp Here 40
SIC 5651 Family clothing stores

D-U-N-S 20-651-5715   (BR)
**GOVERNING COUNCIL OF THE SALVA-
TION ARMY IN CANADA, THE**
*GOVERNING COUNCIL OF THE SALVATION
ARMY IN CANADA, THE*
802 Queen St, Saskatoon, SK, S7K 0N1
(306) 244-6758
Emp Here 25
SIC 8361 Residential care

D-U-N-S 24-628-5931   (BR)
**GOVERNING COUNCIL OF THE SALVA-
TION ARMY IN CANADA, THE**
*GOVERNING COUNCIL OF THE SALVATION
ARMY IN CANADA, THE*
410 42nd A St E, Saskatoon, SK, S7K 0V3
(306) 956-4685
Emp Here 20
SIC 8322 Individual and family services

D-U-N-S 25-482-7389   (BR)
GRAHAM GROUP LTD
GRAHAM INDUSTRIAL SERVICES A JV
875 57th St E, Saskatoon, SK, S7K 5Z2
(306) 934-6644
Emp Here 120
SIC 1541 Industrial buildings and warehouses

D-U-N-S 25-636-7178   (BR)
**GRAINFIELDS PANCAKE & WAFFLE
HOUSE INC**
GRANFIELDS
810 Circle Dr E Unit 100, Saskatoon, SK, S7K
3T8
(306) 933-1986
Emp Here 30
SIC 5812 Eating places

D-U-N-S 24-113-5474   (SL)
GRASSWOOD PARK HOLDINGS LTD
GRASSWOOD PARK ESSO
Hwy 11 S, Saskatoon, SK, S7K 4E3
(306) 373-1888
Emp Here 50   *Sales* 1,532,175
SIC 5812 Eating places

D-U-N-S 24-630-6138   (SL)
GREGG'S PLUMBING & HEATING LTD
503 51st St E, Saskatoon, SK, S7K 6V4
(306) 373-4664
Emp Here 50   *Sales* 4,377,642
SIC 1711 Plumbing, heating, air-conditioning

D-U-N-S 24-819-2619   (BR)
HSBC BANK CANADA
321 21st St E Suite 200, Saskatoon, SK, S7K
0C1
(306) 244-2331
Emp Here 26
SIC 6021 National commercial banks

D-U-N-S 24-288-2384   (BR)
HARVARD BROADCASTING INC
105 21st St E Suite 200, Saskatoon, SK, S7K
0B3
(306) 653-9630
Emp Here 30
SIC 4832 Radio broadcasting stations

D-U-N-S 25-685-2070   (BR)
HOME DEPOT OF CANADA INC
HOME DEPOT
(*Suby of* The Home Depot Inc)
707 Circle Dr E, Saskatoon, SK, S7K 0V1
(306) 651-6250
Emp Here 225
SIC 5251 Hardware stores

D-U-N-S 20-069-6599   (BR)
HUDSON'S BAY COMPANY
BAY, THE
201 1st Ave S, Saskatoon, SK, S7K 1J5
(306) 242-7611
Emp Here 200
SIC 5311 Department stores

D-U-N-S 25-619-3103   (BR)
HUSKY OIL OPERATIONS LIMITED
WESTERN ROAD MANAGEMENT
806 50th St E, Saskatoon, SK, S7K 0X6
(306) 934-3033
Emp Here 20
SIC 1311 Crude petroleum and natural gas

D-U-N-S 24-354-8026   (BR)
**IMPRIMERIES TRANSCONTINENTAL 2005
S.E.N.C.**
TRANSCONTINENTAL SASKATOON
838 56th St E, Saskatoon, SK, S7K 5Y8

Emp Here 40
SIC 2752 Commercial printing, lithographic

D-U-N-S 24-967-6016   (HQ)
INDEPENDENT FINANCIAL SERVICES LTD
1001 3rd Ave N, Saskatoon, SK, S7K 2K5
(306) 244-7385
Emp Here 38   *Emp Total* 45
Sales 6,566,463
SIC 6211 Security brokers and dealers
Treas George Clark
Dir Jerome Meckelborg
  Mark Lord

D-U-N-S 24-342-5795   (SL)
INSIGHTRIX RESEARCH INC
3223 Millar Ave Suite 1, Saskatoon, SK, S7K

5Y3
(306) 657-5640
Emp Here 67   *Sales* 2,857,144
SIC 8732 Commercial nonphysical research

D-U-N-S 24-376-7555   (SL)
INTER WEST MECHANICAL LTD
INTER WEST
1839 Saskatchewan Ave, Saskatoon, SK, S7K
1R1
(306) 955-1800
Emp Here 50   *Sales* 4,377,642
SIC 1711 Plumbing, heating, air-conditioning

D-U-N-S 24-915-2380   (BR)
JAY'S TRANSPORTATION GROUP LTD
1730 Alberta Ave, Saskatoon, SK, S7K 1R7
(306) 249-3777
Emp Here 20
SIC 4213 Trucking, except local

D-U-N-S 25-288-0414   (BR)
JORIDO FOODS SERVICES LTD
A & W RESTAURANT
(*Suby of* Jorido Foods Services Ltd)
5 Midtown Plaza, Saskatoon, SK, S7K 1J9
(306) 242-1433
Emp Here 20
SIC 5812 Eating places

D-U-N-S 25-150-4973   (BR)
JUMP.CA WIRELESS SUPPLY CORP
JUMP.CA
134 Primrose Dr Suite 31, Saskatoon, SK,
S7K 5S6
(306) 651-1919
Emp Here 40
SIC 4899 Communication services, nec

D-U-N-S 24-171-1415   (BR)
KPMG LLP
(*Suby of* KPMG LLP)
475 2nd Ave S Suite 500, Saskatoon, SK, S7K
1P4
(306) 934-6200
Emp Here 55
SIC 8721 Accounting, auditing, and book-
keeping

D-U-N-S 25-054-2495   (BR)
KAL TIRE LTD
2907 Faithfull Ave, Saskatoon, SK, S7K 8E8
(306) 931-7133
Emp Here 20
SIC 5531 Auto and home supply stores

D-U-N-S 24-267-6419   (SL)
KEVCOR HOLDINGS LTD
2030 1st Ave N, Saskatoon, SK, S7K 2A1
(306) 242-1251
Emp Here 46   *Sales* 7,255,933
SIC 5013 Motor vehicle supplies and new
parts
Pr Pr Gordon Bell

D-U-N-S 20-069-7449   (HQ)
KINDERSLEY TRANSPORT LTD
2411 Wentz Ave, Saskatoon, SK, S7K 3V6
(306) 934-1911
Emp Here 270   *Emp Total* 600
Sales 129,099,073
SIC 4213 Trucking, except local
Dir Erwen Siemens
Pr Douglas Siemens

D-U-N-S 20-107-8560   (BR)
KINDERSLEY TRANSPORT LTD
KINDERSLEY TRANSPORT TERMINAL
2411 Wentz Ave, Saskatoon, SK, S7K 3V6
(306) 242-3355
Emp Here 150
SIC 4213 Trucking, except local

D-U-N-S 20-099-9238   (BR)
LAFARGE CANADA INC
838 50th St E, Saskatoon, SK, S7K 0X6
(306) 934-7555
Emp Here 25
SIC 3273 Ready-mixed concrete

D-U-N-S 25-645-3937   (BR)
LOBLAWS INC
EXTRA FOODS NO. 9061
2815 Wanuskewin Rd, Saskatoon, SK, S7K
8E6
(306) 249-9200
Emp Here 100
SIC 5411 Grocery stores

D-U-N-S 24-425-4079   (BR)
LOBLAWS INC
EXTRA FOODS
7 Assiniboine Dr, Saskatoon, SK, S7K 1H1
(306) 242-7444
Emp Here 50
SIC 5411 Grocery stores

D-U-N-S 25-303-9291   (BR)
LONDON LIFE INSURANCE COMPANY
606 Spadina Cres E Suite 1400, Saskatoon,
SK, S7K 3H1
(306) 934-7060
Emp Here 40
SIC 6311 Life insurance

D-U-N-S 20-034-7032   (HQ)
MDH ENGINEERED SOLUTIONS CORP
216 1st Ave S, Saskatoon, SK, S7K 1K3
(306) 934-7527
Emp Here 53   *Emp Total* 33,000
Sales 15,217,500
SIC 7373 Computer integrated systems de-
sign
Pr Moir D H Haug

D-U-N-S 20-109-0433   (BR)
MLT AIKINS LLP
MLP
410 22nd St E Suite 1500, Saskatoon, SK,
S7K 5T6
(306) 975-7100
Emp Here 90
SIC 8111 Legal services

D-U-N-S 20-058-8619   (BR)
MNP LLP
119 4th Ave S Suite 800, Saskatoon, SK, S7K
5X2
(306) 665-6766
Emp Here 60
SIC 8721 Accounting, auditing, and book-
keeping

D-U-N-S 20-268-5694   (BR)
MAGNA IV ENGINEERING
3040 Miners Ave Unit 7, Saskatoon, SK, S7K
5V1
(306) 955-8131
Emp Here 33
SIC 5084 Industrial machinery and equipment

D-U-N-S 25-534-7031   (BR)
MARSH CANADA LIMITED
(*Suby of* Marsh & McLennan Companies, Inc.)
122 1st Ave S Suite 301, Saskatoon, SK, S7K
7E5
(306) 683-6960
Emp Here 20
SIC 6411 Insurance agents, brokers, and service

D-U-N-S 20-355-0848   (BR)
**MCDONALD'S   RESTAURANTS   OF
CANADA LIMITED**
MCDONALD'S
(*Suby of* McDonald's Corporation)
102 2nd Ave N, Saskatoon, SK, S7K 2B2

Emp Here 23
SIC 5812 Eating places

D-U-N-S 20-197-2770   (BR)
**MCDONALD'S   RESTAURANTS   OF
CANADA LIMITED**
MCDONALD'S
(*Suby of* McDonald's Corporation)
905 51st St E, Saskatoon, SK, S7K 7E4
(306) 955-8667
Emp Here 40

SIC 5812 Eating places

D-U-N-S 24-389-5369   (HQ)
MERIDIAN SURVEYS LTD
3111 Millar Ave Suite 1, Saskatoon, SK, S7K
6N3
(306) 934-1818
Emp Here 37   *Emp Total* 8
Sales 6,128,699
SIC 8713 Surveying services
Pr Max Putnam
Treas Stuart Hayward
Dir Michael Waschuk
Dir Robert Morrison
Dir Lee Anderson
Dir Murray Redoux
Dir Calvin Fowler

D-U-N-S 25-639-9403   (BR)
MORGUARD INVESTMENTS LIMITED
MALL AT LAWSON HEIGHTS, THE
134 Primrose Dr Suite 20, Saskatoon, SK,
S7K 5S6
(306) 933-2422
Emp Here 22
SIC 8741 Management services

D-U-N-S 24-775-8600   (BR)
NATIONAL ENERGY EQUIPMENT INC
RNG
882 57th St E, Saskatoon, SK, S7K 5Z1
(306) 665-0223
Emp Here 20
SIC 5084 Industrial machinery and equipment

D-U-N-S 24-265-1388   (HQ)
NORTEK AIR SOLUTIONS CANADA, INC
1502d Quebec Ave, Saskatoon, SK, S7K 1V7
(306) 242-3663
Emp Here 105   *Emp Total* 13,114
Sales 51,022,184
SIC 3564 Blowers and fans
Pr Michael Clark
 Ada Lacoursiere

D-U-N-S 24-375-1450   (HQ)
NORTH RIDGE DEVELOPMENT CORPO-RATION
(*Suby of* North Ridge Development Corpora-tion)
3037 Faithfull Ave, Saskatoon, SK, S7K 8B3
(306) 384-5299
Emp Here 95   *Emp Total* 130
Sales 94,232,900
SIC 1522 Residential construction, nec
Pr Pr Walter Mah
 Julius Calyniuk
Dir Colleen Mah
Dir Annette Calyniuk

D-U-N-S 20-833-4425   (HQ)
PCS SALES (CANADA) INC
122 1st Ave S Suite 500, Saskatoon, SK, S7K
7G3
(306) 933-8500
Emp Here 27   *Emp Total* 5,130
Sales 123,822,031
SIC 1474 Potash, soda, and borate minerals
CEO Jochen Tilk
Pr Pr G David Delaney
 Wayne R Brownlee
Fin Ex Denis Sirois

D-U-N-S 24-324-3693   (BR)
PARRISH & HEIMBECKER, LIMITED
P&H MILLING GROUP
(*Suby of* Parrish & Heimbecker, Limited)
75 33rd St E, Saskatoon, SK, S7K 0R8
(306) 667-8000
Emp Here 100
SIC 5153 Grain and field beans

D-U-N-S 25-999-6320   (BR)
PARRISH & HEIMBECKER, LIMITED
P&H MILLING GROUP
(*Suby of* Parrish & Heimbecker, Limited)
817 48th St E, Saskatoon, SK, S7K 0X5

(306) 931-1655
Emp Here 25
SIC 5153 Grain and field beans

D-U-N-S 25-289-7145   (BR)
PEAVEY INDUSTRIES LIMITED
PEAVEY MART
820c 51st St E, Saskatoon, SK, S7K 0X8
(306) 242-0981
Emp Here 25
SIC 5251 Hardware stores

D-U-N-S 24-000-8727   (BR)
POSTMEDIA NETWORK INC
POSTMEDIA NETWORK
204 5th Ave N, Saskatoon, SK, S7K 2P1
(306) 657-6206
Emp Here 98
SIC 2711 Newspapers

D-U-N-S 25-831-8658   (BR)
POTASH   CORPORATION   OF SASKATCHEWAN INC
PCS CORY, DIV
7 Miles West On Hwy 7, Saskatoon, SK, S7K
3N9
(306) 382-0525
Emp Here 300
SIC 1474 Potash, soda, and borate minerals

D-U-N-S 24-129-8442   (BR)
POTASH   CORPORATION   OF SASKATCHEWAN INC
P C S PATIENTS LAKE
1st Ave S, Saskatoon, SK, S7K 3L6
(306) 667-4278
Emp Here 70
SIC 1474 Potash, soda, and borate minerals

D-U-N-S 24-889-9929   (BR)
PRAXAIR CANADA INC
(*Suby of* Praxair, Inc.)
834 51st St E Suite 5, Saskatoon, SK, S7K
5C7
(306) 242-3325
Emp Here 1,700
SIC 2813 Industrial gases

D-U-N-S 20-165-4550   (BR)
PRICEWATERHOUSECOOPERS LLP
PWC MANAGEMENT
123 2nd Ave S Suite 200, Saskatoon, SK,
7E6
(306) 668-5900
Emp Here 52
SIC 8721 Accounting, auditing, and book-keeping

D-U-N-S 25-654-8355   (SL)
Q. C. MAINTENANCE LTD
234 2nd Ave S, Saskatoon, SK, S7K 1K9
(306) 934-6588
Emp Here 50   *Sales* 1,459,214
SIC 7349 Building maintenance services, nec

D-U-N-S 24-851-2105   (BR)
QSI INTERIORS LTD
806 56th St E, Saskatoon, SK, S7K 5Y8
(306) 933-4000
Emp Here 25
SIC 1752 Floor laying and floor work, nec

D-U-N-S 25-293-6943   (BR)
RBC DOMINION SECURITIES INC
RBC INVESTMENTS
(*Suby of* Royal Bank Of Canada)
410 22nd St E Suite 1070, Saskatoon, SK,
S7K 5T6
(306) 956-5200
Emp Here 45
SIC 6211 Security brokers and dealers

D-U-N-S 20-571-5308   (BR)
RAYMOND JAMES (USA) LTD
(*Suby of* Raymond James Financial, Inc.)
105 21st St E Suite 700, Saskatoon, SK, S7K
0B3
(306) 651-4250
Emp Here 20

SIC 6211 Security brokers and dealers

D-U-N-S 25-555-2655   (BR)
REDHEAD EQUIPMENT
MACK TRUCKS DIV OF
Gd Stn Main, Saskatoon, SK, S7K 3J4
(306) 934-3555
Emp Here 30
SIC 5012 Automobiles and other motor vehi-cles

D-U-N-S 24-642-1080   (BR)
REDHEAD EQUIPMENT LTD
9010 North Service Road, Saskatoon, SK,
S7K 7E8
(306) 931-4600
Emp Here 100
SIC 5571 Motorcycle dealers

D-U-N-S 25-057-8887   (SL)
RELY-EX CONTRACTING INC
STEEL MET SUPPLY, DIV OF
516 43rd St E, Saskatoon, SK, S7K 0V6
(306) 664-2155
Emp Here 33   *Sales* 8,521,800
SIC 1542 Nonresidential construction, nec
Pr Pr Richard (Rick) Leier
 Cheryl Leier

D-U-N-S 24-608-2986   (SL)
ROBERTSON STROMBERG LLP
105 21st St E Suite 600, Saskatoon, SK, S7K
0B3
(306) 652-7575
Emp Here 55   *Sales* 4,742,446
SIC 8111 Legal services

D-U-N-S 24-210-5612   (BR)
ROBINSON, B.A. CO. LTD
829 46th St E, Saskatoon, SK, S7K 0X2
(306) 664-2389
Emp Here 30
SIC 5075 Warm air heating and air condition-ing

D-U-N-S 20-841-0050   (BR)
ROYAL BANK OF CANADA
RBC
(*Suby of* Royal Bank Of Canada)
154 1st Ave S, Saskatoon, SK, S7K 1K2
(306) 933-3400
Emp Here 60
SIC 6021 National commercial banks

D-U-N-S 24-852-0819   (BR)
RUSSEL METALS INC
RUSSEL METALS SASKATOON
922 51st St E, Saskatoon, SK, S7K 7K2
(306) 931-3338
Emp Here 35
SIC 5051 Metals service centers and offices

D-U-N-S 20-335-3362   (BR)
RUSSEL METALS INC
RUSSEL METAL PROCESSING
503 50th St E, Saskatoon, SK, S7K 6H3
(306) 244-7511
Emp Here 175
SIC 3599 Industrial machinery, nec

D-U-N-S 20-124-8049   (BR)
SASKENERGY INCORPORATED
1612 Ontario Ave, Saskatoon, SK, S7K 1S8
(306) 777-9200
Emp Here 25
SIC 7389 Business services, nec

D-U-N-S 25-116-6062   (BR)
SASKENERGY INCORPORATED
408 36th St E, Saskatoon, SK, S7K 4J9
(306) 975-8561
Emp Here 120
SIC 4924 Natural gas distribution

D-U-N-S 24-318-5530   (BR)
SASKATCHEWAN ASSOCIATION OF RE-HABILITATION CENTRES
SARCAN RECYCLING
(*Suby of* Saskatchewan Association of Reha-

bilitation Centres)
2327 Faithfull Ave, Saskatoon, SK, S7K 1T9
(306) 975-0650
Emp Here 25
SIC 4953 Refuse systems

D-U-N-S 25-315-2029   (BR)
SASKATCHEWAN GOVERNMENT INSUR-ANCE
623 2nd Ave N, Saskatoon, SK, S7K 0H3
(306) 683-2382
Emp Here 53
SIC 6331 Fire, marine, and casualty insurance

D-U-N-S 24-348-6136   (BR)
SASKATCHEWAN INDIAN GAMING AU-THORITY INC
DAKOTA DUNES CASINO
204 Dakota Dunes Way, Saskatoon, SK, S7K
2L2
(306) 477-7777
Emp Here 50
SIC 7011 Hotels and motels

D-U-N-S 20-080-2861   (BR)
SASKATCHEWAN INDIAN INSTITUTE OF TECHNOLOGIES
229 4th Ave S Suite 201, Saskatoon, SK, S7K
4K3
(306) 373-4777
Emp Here 100
SIC 8299 Schools and educational services,
nec

D-U-N-S 24-748-5394   (BR)
SASKATCHEWAN INSTITUTE OF APPLIED SCIENCE AND TECHNOLOGY
KELSEY CAMPUS OF SIAST
Gd Stn Main, Saskatoon, SK, S7K 3R5
(306) 933-6350
Emp Here 480
SIC 8222 Junior colleges

D-U-N-S 20-338-0217   (BR)
SASKATCHEWAN INSTITUTE OF APPLIED SCIENCE AND TECHNOLOGY
SASKATCHEWAN INSTITUTE OF APPLIED SCIENCE AND TECHNOLOGY
1130 Idylwyld Dr And 33rd St, Saskatoon, SK,
S7K 3R5
(866) 467-4278
Emp Here 1,000
SIC 8222 Junior colleges

D-U-N-S 20-842-0505   (HQ)
SASKATCHEWAN INSTITUTE OF APPLIED SCIENCE AND TECHNOLOGY
SIAST
119 4th Ave S Suite 400, Saskatoon, SK, S7K
5X2
(866) 467-4278
Emp Here 65   *Emp Total* 40,372
Sales 216,521,886
SIC 8222 Junior colleges
Pr Robert Mcculloch
VP Fin Cheryl Mcmillan
 Alan Thomarat
 Jim Plewis
Dir Donna Birkmaier
Dir Ralph Boychuck
Dir Neil Buechler
Dir Brittany Holderness
Dir Bob Loewen
Dir Jean Morrison

D-U-N-S 20-876-4238   (BR)
SASKATCHEWAN   TELECOMMUNICA-TIONS INTERNATIONAL, INC
SASKTEL INTERNATIONAL
410 22nd St E Suite 500, Saskatoon, SK, S7K
5T6
(306) 931-6029
Emp Here 140
SIC 4899 Communication services, nec

D-U-N-S 20-778-5317   (BR)
SASKATCHEWAN   TELECOMMUNICA-TIONS INTERNATIONAL, INC

SASKTEL
446a 2nd Ave N, Saskatoon, SK, S7K 2C3
(306) 683-4922
Emp Here 300
SIC 7372 Prepackaged software

D-U-N-S 20-034-0748   (BR)
SASKATCHEWAN   TRANSPORTATION COMPANY
STC
88 King St, Saskatoon, SK, S7K 6T5
(306) 933-7162
Emp Here 25
SIC 4131 Intercity and rural bus transportation

D-U-N-S 20-841-0639   (BR)
SASKATCHEWAN   TRANSPORTATION COMPANY
50 23rd St E, Saskatoon, SK, S7K 0H8
(306) 933-8000
Emp Here 60
SIC 4131 Intercity and rural bus transportation

D-U-N-S 20-070-2454   (HQ)
SASKATOON BOILER MFG CO LTD
SASKATOON BOILER
(*Suby of* Saskatoon Boiler Mfg Co Ltd)
2011 Quebec Ave, Saskatoon, SK, S7K 1W5
(306) 652-7022
Emp Here 45   *Emp Total* 50
Sales 7,733,834
SIC 3443 Fabricated plate work (boiler shop)
Pr Pr Raymond Graves
  Karl Niedermair
Dir Gerry Svensrud
Dir Ernie Belky

D-U-N-S 24-691-1549   (SL)
SASKATOON FAMILY YOUNG MEN'S CHRISTIAN ASSOCIATION
YMCA SASKATOON
25 22nd St E, Saskatoon, SK, S7K 0C7
(306) 652-7515
Emp Here 90   *Sales* 6,493,502
SIC 8641 Civic and social associations
Dir Dean Dodge

D-U-N-S 20-843-3466   (HQ)
SASKATOON PUBLIC LIBRARY
CARLYLE BRANCH LIBRARY
(*Suby of* Saskatoon Public Library)
311 23rd St E, Saskatoon, SK, S7K 0J6
(306) 975-7558
Emp Here 85   *Emp Total* 150
Sales 6,931,267
SIC 8231 Libraries
  Zenon Zuzak

D-U-N-S 20-040-7323   (BR)
SASKATOON PUBLIC LIBRARY
RUSTY MACDONALD BRANCH LIBRARY
(*Suby of* Saskatoon Public Library)
225 Primrose Dr, Saskatoon, SK, S7K 5E4
(306) 975-7600
Emp Here 20
SIC 8231 Libraries

D-U-N-S 20-840-6363   (HQ)
SASKATOON REGIONAL HEALTH AUTHORITY
PARKRIDGE CENTRE
410 22nd St E, Saskatoon, SK, S7K 5T6
(306) 655-3300
Emp Here 3,500   *Emp Total* 40,372
Sales 1,052,552,335
SIC 8062 General medical and surgical hospitals
Pr Maura Davies
  Deborah Rhodes
VP Shan Landry
VP Sandra Blevins
VP Bonnie Blakley
  Carol Teichrob
  Douglas Finnie
  Jim Rhode
V Ch Bd Colleen Christensen
  Gary Beaudin

D-U-N-S 20-641-4943   (BR)
SASKATOON REGIONAL HEALTH AUTHORITY
122 3rd Ave N Suite 156, Saskatoon, SK, S7K 2H6
(306) 655-4100
Emp Here 26
SIC 8062 General medical and surgical hospitals

D-U-N-S 20-114-5799   (BR)
SASKATOON REGIONAL HEALTH AUTHORITY
SASKATOON CITY HOSPITAL
701 Queen St Suite 1237, Saskatoon, SK, S7K 0M7
(306) 655-8000
Emp Here 700
SIC 8062 General medical and surgical hospitals

D-U-N-S 25-647-3778   (BR)
SASKATOON REGIONAL HEALTH AUTHORITY
CHILD & YOUTH PROGRAM
715 Queen St, Saskatoon, SK, S7K 4X4
(306) 655-7800
Emp Here 25
SIC 8062 General medical and surgical hospitals

D-U-N-S 25-155-9936   (SL)
SASKATOON WHOLESALE TIRE LTD
2705 Wentz Ave, Saskatoon, SK, S7K 4B6
(306) 244-9512
Emp Here 35   *Sales* 5,024,256
SIC 5531 Auto and home supply stores

D-U-N-S 24-033-5864   (BR)
SASKATOON, CITY OF
CIVIC DEPARTMENTS UTILITY SERVICES WASTEWATER TREATMENT & LIFTS
470 Whiteswan Dr, Saskatoon, SK, S7K 6Z7
(306) 975-2541
Emp Here 42
SIC 1629 Heavy construction, nec

D-U-N-S 25-452-1636   (BR)
SCOTIA CAPITAL INC
SCOTIA MCLEOD
410 22nd St E Unit 700, Saskatoon, SK, S7K 5T6
(306) 665-5300
Emp Here 40
SIC 6211 Security brokers and dealers

D-U-N-S 20-546-8853   (BR)
SEARS CANADA INC
1 Midtown Plaza, Saskatoon, SK, S7K 1K1
(306) 653-2060
Emp Here 300
SIC 5311 Department stores

D-U-N-S 24-378-3227   (BR)
SERVICES KAMTECH INC
KAMTECH SERVICES INC
3339 Faithfull Ave, Saskatoon, SK, S7K 8H5
(306) 931-9655
Emp Here 100
SIC 1711 Plumbing, heating, air-conditioning

D-U-N-S 20-070-2009   (BR)
SMUCKER FOODS OF CANADA CORP
(*Suby of* The J M Smucker Company)
95 33rd St E, Saskatoon, SK, S7K 0R8
(306) 665-7110
Emp Here 150
SIC 2041 Flour and other grain mill products

D-U-N-S 25-271-7491   (BR)
SOBEYS WEST INC
134 Primrose Dr, Saskatoon, SK, S7K 5S6
(306) 242-6090
Emp Here 140
SIC 5411 Grocery stores

D-U-N-S 20-860-0416   (BR)
SOURCE (BELL) ELECTRONICS INC, THE
SOURCE, THE

201 1st Ave S Unit 255, Saskatoon, SK, S7K 1J5
(306) 384-7704
Emp Here 25
SIC 5999 Miscellaneous retail stores, nec

D-U-N-S 20-712-7643   (BR)
ST. PAUL'S ROMAN CATHOLIC SEPARATE SCHOOL DIVISION NO 20
ST GEORGE SCHOOL
748 Redberry Rd, Saskatoon, SK, S7K 5H3
(306) 659-7320
Emp Here 20
SIC 8211 Elementary and secondary schools

D-U-N-S 25-021-1950   (BR)
ST. PAUL'S ROMAN CATHOLIC SEPARATE SCHOOL DIVISION NO 20
ST ANGELA SCHOOL
302 Russell Rd, Saskatoon, SK, S7K 6P2
(306) 659-7250
Emp Here 32
SIC 8211 Elementary and secondary schools

D-U-N-S 25-021-2099   (BR)
ST. PAUL'S ROMAN CATHOLIC SEPARATE SCHOOL DIVISION NO 20
ST ANNE SCHOOL
102 Ravine Crt, Saskatoon, SK, S7K 4H6
(306) 659-7260
Emp Here 31
SIC 8211 Elementary and secondary schools

D-U-N-S 25-106-9332   (BR)
ST. PAUL'S ROMAN CATHOLIC SEPARATE SCHOOL DIVISION NO 20
ST MICHAEL COMMUNITY SCHOOL
22 33rd St E, Saskatoon, SK, S7K 0R7
(306) 659-7420
Emp Here 26
SIC 8211 Elementary and secondary schools

D-U-N-S 25-106-9134   (BR)
ST. PAUL'S ROMAN CATHOLIC SEPARATE SCHOOL DIVISION NO 20
ST PAUL SCHOOL
1527 Alexandra Ave, Saskatoon, SK, S7K 3C1
(306) 659-7430
Emp Here 20
SIC 8211 Elementary and secondary schools

D-U-N-S 25-642-9556   (BR)
STAPLES CANADA INC
STAPLES BUSINESS DEPOT
(*Suby of* Staples, Inc.)
810 Circle Dr E Suite 105, Saskatoon, SK, S7K 3T8
(306) 955-6044
Emp Here 50
SIC 5943 Stationery stores

D-U-N-S 20-342-1545   (BR)
STARBUCKS COFFEE CANADA, INC
STARBUCKS COFFEE COMPANY
(*Suby of* Starbucks Corporation)
100 2nd Ave S, Saskatoon, SK, S7K 1K5
(306) 665-5558
Emp Here 26
SIC 5812 Eating places

D-U-N-S 20-855-5623   (HQ)
STEEL-CRAFT DOOR SALES & SERVICE LTD
(*Suby of* Mihalcheon Holdings Ltd)
843 56th St E, Saskatoon, SK, S7K 5Y9
(306) 652-7131
Emp Here 20   *Emp Total* 2
Sales 5,544,006
SIC 5211 Lumber and other building materials
  Arthur Mihalcheon

D-U-N-S 24-344-0059   (BR)
SUPERIOR PLUS LP
ERCO WORLDWIDE
Gd Stn Main, Saskatoon, SK, S7K 3J4
(306) 931-7767
Emp Here 120
SIC 2819 Industrial inorganic chemicals, nec

D-U-N-S 24-819-1348   (BR)
SUPREME OFFICE PRODUCTS LIMITED
SUPREME BASICS
(*Suby of* Placements Denis Latulippe Inc, Les)
2346 Millar Ave, Saskatoon, SK, S7K 2Y2
(306) 667-3210
Emp Here 30
SIC 5943 Stationery stores

D-U-N-S 20-069-9374   (HQ)
T & T TRUCKING LTD
(*Suby of* 601861 Saskatchewan Ltd)
855 60th St E, Saskatoon, SK, S7K 5Z7
(306) 934-3383
Emp Here 45   *Emp Total* 140
Sales 18,094,254
SIC 4213 Trucking, except local
Pr Pr Graham Newton
VP VP Rick Thiessen
Dir Lynn Muyard
  Henry Thiessen

D-U-N-S 24-607-4355   (HQ)
TIGER COURIER INC
705 47th St E, Saskatoon, SK, S7K 5G5
(306) 242-7499
Emp Here 40   *Emp Total* 600
Sales 7,587,913
SIC 7389 Business services, nec
Pr Pr Erwin Siemens

D-U-N-S 25-650-3699   (BR)
TORONTO-DOMINION BANK, THE
TD BANK
(*Suby of* Toronto-Dominion Bank, The)
234 Primrose Dr Suite 242, Saskatoon, SK, S7K 6Y6
(306) 975-7330
Emp Here 20
SIC 6021 National commercial banks

D-U-N-S 25-158-0747   (BR)
TRIMAC TRANSPORTATION SERVICES LIMITED PARTNERSHIP
NATIONAL TANK SERVICES
2945 Millar Ave, Saskatoon, SK, S7K 6P6
(306) 934-2515
Emp Here 35
SIC 4213 Trucking, except local

D-U-N-S 25-642-6065   (SL)
TUCKER CLEANING (1979) INC
901 1st Ave N Suite 9, Saskatoon, SK, S7K 1Y4
(306) 956-3377
Emp Here 60   *Sales* 1,751,057
SIC 7349 Building maintenance services, nec

D-U-N-S 20-191-6827   (BR)
TYCO INTEGRATED FIRE & SECURITY CANADA, INC
SIMPLEXGRINNELL
(*Suby of* Johnson Controls, Inc.)
3006 Cleveland Ave Suite 1, Saskatoon, SK, S7K 8B5
(306) 934-8184
Emp Here 20
SIC 7389 Business services, nec

D-U-N-S 20-069-4933   (BR)
UAP INC
NAPA AUTO PARTS
(*Suby of* Genuine Parts Company)
2815 Faithfull Ave, Saskatoon, SK, S7K 8E8
(306) 244-8187
Emp Here 40
SIC 5015 Motor vehicle parts, used

D-U-N-S 24-099-1518   (BR)
UNITED PARCEL SERVICE CANADA LTD
UPS
2614 Faithfull Ave, Saskatoon, SK, S7K 5W3
(306) 242-3345
Emp Here 28
SIC 7389 Business services, nec

D-U-N-S 20-098-1715   (BR)
VARSTEEL LTD

▲ Public Company   ■ Public Company Family Member   **HQ** Headquarters   **BR** Branch   **SL** Single Location

2607 Wentz Ave, Saskatoon, SK, S7K 5J1
(306) 955-3777
Emp Here 27
SIC 5051 Metals service centers and offices

D-U-N-S 20-152-6857   (BR)
VECTOR CONSTRUCTION LTD
(*Suby of* Vector Management Ltd)
419b 50th St E, Saskatoon, SK, S7K 6K1
(306) 934-3533
Emp Here 20
SIC 1771 Concrete work

D-U-N-S 25-729-7622   (SL)
VEMAX MANAGEMENT INC
Gd Stn Main, Saskatoon, SK, S7K 3J4
(306) 242-8554
Emp Here 60   *Sales* 9,536,300
SIC 8742 Management consulting services
Mgr Shawna Mcmaster
Dir Gordon Sparks
Dir Ray Gerke
Gail Sparks

D-U-N-S 24-389-0873   (SL)
WESTCAP MGT. LTD
410 22nd St E Suite 1300, Saskatoon, SK,
S7K 5T6
(306) 652-5557
Emp Here 22   *Sales* 5,253,170
SIC 6282 Investment advice
Pr Pr Grant Kook
Douglas Banzet
Robert Connoly
VP Wanda Hunchak
VP Jamie Schwitzer
VP Tyler Bradley

D-U-N-S 24-327-5760   (BR)
WESTERN CANADA LOTTERY CORPORA-TION
1935 1st Ave N, Saskatoon, SK, S7K 6W1
(306) 933-6850
Emp Here 81
SIC 7999 Amusement and recreation, nec

D-U-N-S 25-639-9593   (BR)
WESTERN INVENTORY SERVICE LTD
WIS INTERNATIONAL
1736 Quebec Ave Suite 38, Saskatoon, SK,
S7K 1V9
(306) 653-0361
Emp Here 20
SIC 7389 Business services, nec

D-U-N-S 20-446-6866   (SL)
WIG'S PUMPS AND WATERWORKS LTD
227b Venture Cres, Saskatoon, SK, S7K 6N8
(306) 652-4276
Emp Here 25   *Sales* 6,391,350
SIC 5082 Construction and mining machinery
Pr Pr Jodi Wig
Genl Mgr Glenn Wig

D-U-N-S 24-774-4931   (BR)
WILKINSON STEEL AND METALS INC
2325 Mckee Ave, Saskatoon, SK, S7K 2T9
(306) 652-7151
Emp Here 30
SIC 3599 Industrial machinery, nec

D-U-N-S 20-273-1498   (BR)
WOLSELEY CANADA INC
WOLSELEY MECHANICAL
(*Suby of* WOLSELEY PLC)
2744 1st Ave N, Saskatoon, SK, S7K 6M5
(306) 933-1033
Emp Here 30
SIC 5074 Plumbing and heating equipment and supplies (hydronics)

D-U-N-S 25-736-9207   (BR)
WOLSELEY CANADA INC
CENTURY ENVIRONMENTAL SERVICES
(*Suby of* WOLSELEY PLC)
3006 Cleveland Ave Suite 1, Saskatoon, SK,
S7K 8B5

Emp Here 20

SIC 3089 Plastics products, nec

D-U-N-S 20-536-9247   (BR)
WORLD FINANCIAL GROUP INSURANCE AGENCY OF CANADA INC
TRANSAMERICA SECURITIES
20 51 St Suite 200, Saskatoon, SK, S7K 0X8
(306) 651-5260
Emp Here 25
SIC 6311 Life insurance

D-U-N-S 24-608-1103   (SL)
YOUNG WOMEN'S CHRISTIAN ASSOCIA-TION OF SASKATOON
YWCA OF SASKATOON
510 25th St E, Saskatoon, SK, S7K 4A7
(306) 244-0944
Emp Here 110   *Sales* 4,304,681
SIC 8322 Individual and family services

Saskatoon, SK S7L

D-U-N-S 25-085-7711   (BR)
1009833 ALBERTA LTD
PETLAND
300 Confederation Dr Suite 40, Saskatoon,
SK, S7L 4R6
(306) 978-6990
Emp Here 20
SIC 5199 Nondurable goods, nec

D-U-N-S 20-693-7299   (SL)
45TH STREET LIMITED PARTNERSHIP
701 45th St W, Saskatoon, SK, S7L 5W5
(306) 934-0600
Emp Here 130   *Sales* 34,960,406
SIC 5039 Construction materials, nec
Genl Mgr Al Felix

D-U-N-S 20-049-8978   (BR)
ASIG CANADA LTD
(*Suby of* Asig Canada Ltd)
2515 Airport Rd Suite 7, Saskatoon, SK, S7L
1M4
(306) 651-6018
Emp Here 75
SIC 5172 Petroleum products, nec

D-U-N-S 20-066-8978   (HQ)
ASSOCIATED ENGINEERING (SASK) LTD
(*Suby of* Ashco Shareholders Inc)
2225 Northridge Dr Suite 1, Saskatoon, SK,
S7L 6X6
(306) 653-4969
Emp Here 55   *Emp Total* 255
Sales 10,135,137
SIC 8711 Engineering services
Pr Pr Kerry Rudd
Bert Munro

D-U-N-S 20-003-3103   (BR)
BANK OF NOVA SCOTIA, THE
201 Avenue S N, Saskatoon, SK, S7L 2Z7

Emp Here 20
SIC 6021 National commercial banks

D-U-N-S 25-289-6451   (BR)
BOARD OF EDUCATION OF SASKA-TOON SCHOOL DIVISION NO. 13 OF SASKATCHEWAN, THE
BEDFORD ROAD COLLEGIATE
722 Bedford Rd, Saskatoon, SK, S7L 0G2
(306) 683-7650
Emp Here 70
SIC 8211 Elementary and secondary schools

D-U-N-S 20-717-2284   (BR)
BOARD OF EDUCATION OF SASKA-TOON SCHOOL DIVISION NO. 13 OF SASKATCHEWAN, THE
HOWARD COAD SCHOOL
431 Avenue T N, Saskatoon, SK, S7L 3B5
(306) 683-7260
Emp Here 35

SIC 8211 Elementary and secondary schools

D-U-N-S 20-712-7882   (BR)
BOARD OF EDUCATION OF SASKA-TOON SCHOOL DIVISION NO. 13 OF SASKATCHEWAN, THE
CAROLINE ROBINS COMMUNITY SCHOOL
1410 Byers Cres, Saskatoon, SK, S7L 4H3
(306) 683-7150
Emp Here 50
SIC 8211 Elementary and secondary schools

D-U-N-S 20-712-8104   (BR)
BOARD OF EDUCATION OF SASKA-TOON SCHOOL DIVISION NO. 13 OF SASKATCHEWAN, THE
CONFEDERATION PARK COMMUNITY SCHOOL
3555 John A Macdonald Rd, Saskatoon, SK,
S7L 4R9
(306) 683-7180
Emp Here 50
SIC 8211 Elementary and secondary schools

D-U-N-S 20-068-2677   (BR)
BOARD OF EDUCATION OF SASKA-TOON SCHOOL DIVISION NO. 13 OF SASKATCHEWAN, THE
MOUNT ROYAL COLLEGIATE
2220 Rusholme Rd, Saskatoon, SK, S7L 4A4
(306) 683-7800
Emp Here 150
SIC 8211 Elementary and secondary schools

D-U-N-S 20-712-7924   (BR)
BOARD OF EDUCATION OF SASKA-TOON SCHOOL DIVISION NO. 13 OF SASKATCHEWAN, THE
HENRY KELSEY ELEMENTARY
16 Valens Dr, Saskatoon, SK, S7L 3S1
(306) 683-7240
Emp Here 20
SIC 8211 Elementary and secondary schools

D-U-N-S 20-712-8179   (BR)
BOARD OF EDUCATION OF SASKA-TOON SCHOOL DIVISION NO. 13 OF SASKATCHEWAN, THE
DUNDONALD SCHOOL
162 Wedge Rd, Saskatoon, SK, S7L 6Y4
(306) 683-7200
Emp Here 65
SIC 8211 Elementary and secondary schools

D-U-N-S 25-361-0414   (BR)
BOARD OF EDUCATION OF SASKA-TOON SCHOOL DIVISION NO. 13 OF SASKATCHEWAN, THE
WESTMOUNT COMMUNITY SCHOOL
411 Avenue J N, Saskatoon, SK, S7L 2K4
(306) 683-7490
Emp Here 20
SIC 8211 Elementary and secondary schools

D-U-N-S 20-712-8120   (BR)
BOARD OF EDUCATION OF SASKA-TOON SCHOOL DIVISION NO. 13 OF SASKATCHEWAN, THE
LESTER B PEARSON SCHOOL
3620 Centennial Dr, Saskatoon, SK, S7L 5L2
(306) 683-7350
Emp Here 50
SIC 8211 Elementary and secondary schools

D-U-N-S 20-712-7965   (BR)
BOARD OF EDUCATION OF SASKA-TOON SCHOOL DIVISION NO. 13 OF SASKATCHEWAN, THE
MAYFAIR COMMUNITY SCHOOL
510 34th St N, Saskatoon, SK, S7L 0Y2
(306) 683-7360
Emp Here 50
SIC 8211 Elementary and secondary schools

D-U-N-S 20-712-7890   (BR)
BOARD OF EDUCATION OF SASKA-TOON SCHOOL DIVISION NO. 13 OF SASKATCHEWAN, THE

CASWELL COMMUNITY SCHOOL
204 30th St W, Saskatoon, SK, S7L 0N9
(306) 683-7160
Emp Here 40
SIC 8211 Elementary and secondary schools

D-U-N-S 20-712-8054   (BR)
BOARD OF EDUCATION OF SASKA-TOON SCHOOL DIVISION NO. 13 OF SASKATCHEWAN, THE
VINCENT MASSEY COMMUNITY SCHOOL
1001 Northumberland Ave, Saskatoon, SK,
S7L 3W8
(306) 683-7480
Emp Here 45
SIC 8211 Elementary and secondary schools

D-U-N-S 25-075-4442   (BR)
CB PARTNERS CORPORATION
CLARK BUILDERS
2366 Ave C N Suite 273, Saskatoon, SK, S7L
5X5
(306) 979-1106
Emp Here 20
SIC 1542 Nonresidential construction, nec

D-U-N-S 24-358-9587   (SL)
CHIP REIT NO 20 OPERATIONS LIMITED PARTNERSHIP
SASKATOON INN HOTEL AND CONFER-ENCE CENTRE, THE
2002 Airport Dr, Saskatoon, SK, S7L 6M4
(306) 242-1440
Emp Here 221   *Sales* 13,363,840
SIC 7011 Hotels and motels
Pr Ed Pitoniak
Kevin Grayston
Robert Pratt
Dir Stephen Bellringer

D-U-N-S 20-650-3331   (BR)
CANADIAN TIRE CORPORATION, LIMITED
301 Confederation Dr, Saskatoon, SK, S7L
5C3
(306) 384-1212
Emp Here 50
SIC 5531 Auto and home supply stores

D-U-N-S 24-038-8595   (SL)
CENTRAL HAVEN SPECIAL CARE HOME INC
1020 Avenue I N, Saskatoon, SK, S7L 2H7
(306) 665-6180
Emp Here 84   *Sales* 3,793,956
SIC 8051 Skilled nursing care facilities

D-U-N-S 25-650-9266   (BR)
CORUS MEDIA HOLDINGS INC
SHAW MEDIA INC
218 Robin Cres, Saskatoon, SK, S7L 7C3
(306) 665-6969
Emp Here 40
SIC 4833 Television broadcasting stations

D-U-N-S 25-640-5333   (SL)
CUSTOM COURIER CO. LTD
501 Pakwa Pl Suite 2, Saskatoon, SK, S7L
6A3
(306) 653-8500
Emp Here 90   *Sales* 4,523,563
SIC 7389 Business services, nec

D-U-N-S 20-600-5944   (BR)
CUSTOM TRUCK SALES INC
2410 Northridge Dr, Saskatoon, SK, S7L 7L6
(306) 931-1911
Emp Here 45
SIC 5511 New and used car dealers

D-U-N-S 20-740-1431   (HQ)
DEER LODGE HOTELS LTD
SASKATOON TRAVELODGE HOTEL
106 Circle Dr W, Saskatoon, SK, S7L 4L6
(306) 242-8881
Emp Here 240   *Emp Total* 3
Sales 24,077,031
SIC 7011 Hotels and motels
Pr Pr Betty-Anne Latrace-Henderson

VP VP Don Morgan
Brian Henderson
Dave Kelly
Dir Peter Verbeke
Dir Jim Cummings
Dir Bob Webster
Dir Lorrie Surprenant
Dir Mike Stensrud
Dir Thomas Davis

D-U-N-S 25-119-4288   (BR)
DENCAN RESTAURANTS INC
DENNY'S RESTAURANT
(*Suby of* Northland Properties Corporation)
310 Circle Dr W, Saskatoon, SK, S7L 0Y5
(306) 653-7700
Emp Here 50
SIC 5812 Eating places

D-U-N-S 24-330-6292   (BR)
EMERGIS INC
TRI-COMP SYSTEMS
2305 Hanselman Pl, Saskatoon, SK, S7L 6A9

Emp Here 30
SIC 7372 Prepackaged software

D-U-N-S 24-026-8847   (BR)
FGL SPORTS LTD
SPORT CHEK
301 Confederation Drive Unit 120, Saskatoon,
SK, S7L 5C3
(306) 931-8833
Emp Here 55
SIC 5941 Sporting goods and bicycle shops

D-U-N-S 25-360-9333   (BR)
FLOFORM INDUSTRIES LTD
CUSTOM COUNTERTOPS
2209 Speers Ave, Saskatoon, SK, S7L 5X6
(306) 665-7733
Emp Here 80

SIC 2541 Wood partitions and fixtures

D-U-N-S 24-852-9034   (BR)
G4S CASH SOLUTIONS (CANADA) LTD
GARDER CASH LTD
2234a Hanselman Ave, Saskatoon, SK, S7L
6A4
(306) 653-1533
Emp Here 25
SIC 7381 Detective and armored car services

D-U-N-S 20-748-8375   (SL)
GC TELESERVICES CANADA CORP
2600 Koyl Ave, Saskatoon, SK, S7L 5X9

Emp Here 350   *Sales* 24,049,200
SIC 7322 Adjustment and collection services
Genl Mgr Bob Nelson

D-U-N-S 20-040-7174   (BR)
INNVEST PROPERTIES CORP
COMFORT INN
(*Suby of* Innvest Properties Corp)
2155 Northridge Dr, Saskatoon, SK, S7L 6X6
(306) 934-1122
Emp Here 20
SIC 7011 Hotels and motels

D-U-N-S 20-447-3268   (HQ)
J.H. ENTERPRISES (1969) LIMITED
J & H BUILDERS WAREHOUSE
2505 Avenue C N, Saskatoon, SK, S7L 6A6
(306) 652-5322
Emp Here 90   *Emp Total* 110
Sales 20,876,649
SIC 5211 Lumber and other building materials
Pr Pr Donald J Neufeld
Murray Neufeld

D-U-N-S 24-883-2750   (SL)
J.J.-SAKO'S HOLDINGS LTD
TOMAS COOK FAMILY RESTAURANT
305 Idylwyld Dr N Suite 3, Saskatoon, SK, S7L
0Z1
(306) 665-8383
Emp Here 50   *Sales* 1,532,175

SIC 5812 Eating places

D-U-N-S 24-882-9996   (BR)
KONICA MINOLTA BUSINESS SOLUTIONS (CANADA) LTD
KONICA MINOLTA
710 Cynthia St Unit 30, Saskatoon, SK, S7L
6A2
(306) 934-2909
Emp Here 25
SIC 5044 Office equipment

D-U-N-S 20-656-3764   (BR)
LA CAPITALE FINANCIAL SECURITY INSURANCE COMPANY
2345 Avenue C N Suite 5, Saskatoon, SK, S7L
5Z5
(306) 955-3000
Emp Here 20
SIC 6411 Insurance agents, brokers, and service

D-U-N-S 24-350-3385   (BR)
LEON'S FURNITURE LIMITED
126 Cardinal Cres, Saskatoon, SK, S7L 6H6
(306) 664-1062
Emp Here 60
SIC 5712 Furniture stores

D-U-N-S 25-270-1222   (BR)
LOBLAWS INC
REAL CANADIAN SUPERSTORE 1536
411 Confederation Dr, Saskatoon, SK, S7L
5C3
(306) 683-5634
Emp Here 400
SIC 5141 Groceries, general line

D-U-N-S 25-138-8351   (SL)
LOUISVILLE TRUCK CENTRE INC
3750 Idylwyld Dr N, Saskatoon, SK, S7L 6G3
(306) 931-6611
Emp Here 78   *Sales* 39,187,200
SIC 5511 New and used car dealers
Pr Pr Gary Bews

D-U-N-S 20-197-2838   (BR)
MCDONALD'S RESTAURANTS OF CANADA LIMITED
MCDONALD'S RESTAURANTS
(*Suby of* McDonald's Corporation)
1803 Idylwyld Dr N, Saskatoon, SK, S7L 1B6
(306) 955-8665
Emp Here 55
SIC 5812 Eating places

D-U-N-S 20-527-3886   (BR)
NAV CANADA
2555 Airport Dr, Saskatoon, SK, S7L 7M4
(306) 665-4400
Emp Here 20
SIC 4899 Communication services, nec

D-U-N-S 20-106-1913   (BR)
NORTHLAND PROPERTIES CORPORATION
SANDMAN HOTEL SASKATOON
(*Suby of* Northland Properties Corporation)
310 Circle Dr W, Saskatoon, SK, S7L 0Y5
(306) 477-4844
Emp Here 40
SIC 7011 Hotels and motels

D-U-N-S 20-747-8251   (BR)
O.K. TIRE STORES INC
AGLINE INTERNATIONAL
3240 Idylwyld Dr N Suite 103, Saskatoon, SK,
S7L 5Y7
(306) 933-1115
Emp Here 29
SIC 5014 Tires and tubes

D-U-N-S 20-843-3219   (SL)
OLIVER LODGE
1405 Faulkner Cres, Saskatoon, SK, S7L 3R5
(306) 382-4111
Emp Here 126   *Sales* 4,596,524
SIC 8361 Residential care

D-U-N-S 24-038-7662   (BR)
PRINCESS AUTO LTD
2802 Idylwyld Dr N, Saskatoon, SK, S7L 5Y6
(306) 665-8022
Emp Here 40
SIC 5999 Miscellaneous retail stores, nec

D-U-N-S 24-803-2059   (HQ)
QUOREX CONSTRUCTION SERVICES LTD
(*Suby of* Quorex Construction Services Ltd)
142 Cardinal Cres, Saskatoon, SK, S7L 6H6
(306) 244-3717
Emp Here 100   *Emp Total* 175
Sales 32,467,512
SIC 1542 Nonresidential construction, nec
Elphie Bouvier
Brian Crellin
Scott Froese
Bud Green
Micheal Chyzowski
Gary Leontowicz

D-U-N-S 24-054-0310   (HQ)
RSB LOGISTIC INC
219 Cardinal Cres, Saskatoon, SK, S7L 7K8
(306) 242-8300
Emp Here 30   *Emp Total* 10
Sales 15,454,196
SIC 4212 Local trucking, without storage
Pr George Eckel
Dir Ulrich Philippczyk
Dir Johanne Johnson

D-U-N-S 25-300-6266   (BR)
REDBERRY FRANCHISING CORP
BURGER KING
101 Confederation Dr, Saskatoon, SK, S7L
5C3
(306) 382-5310
Emp Here 50
SIC 5812 Eating places

D-U-N-S 25-019-0436   (BR)
ROYAL BANK OF CANADA
RBC
(*Suby of* Royal Bank Of Canada)
15 Worobetz Pl Suite 15, Saskatoon, SK, S7L
6R4
(306) 933-3586
Emp Here 23
SIC 6021 National commercial banks

D-U-N-S 25-452-1339   (BR)
SASK SPORT INC
ADMINISTRATION CENTRE FOR SPORT CULTURE & RECREATION
510 Cynthia St, Saskatoon, SK, S7L 7K7
(306) 975-0873
Emp Here 60
SIC 8699 Membership organizations, nec

D-U-N-S 24-230-6355   (HQ)
SASKATCHEWAN ASSOCIATION OF REHABILITATION CENTRES
SARCAN RECYCLING
(*Suby of* Saskatchewan Association of Rehabilitation Centres)
111 Cardinal Cres, Saskatoon, SK, S7L 6H5
(306) 933-0616
Emp Here 24   *Emp Total* 600
Sales 101,771,532
SIC 4953 Refuse systems
Ex Dir Amy Mcneil
Dir Fin Bob Hnetka
Murray Baird
Dir Dawn Desautel

D-U-N-S 20-518-1386   (BR)
SASKATCHEWAN GOVERNMENT INSURANCE
SGI CANADA
2318 Northridge Dr, Saskatoon, SK, S7L 1B9
(306) 683-2110
Emp Here 35
SIC 6331 Fire, marine, and casualty insurance

D-U-N-S 25-217-8595   (BR)
SASKATCHEWAN HEALTH-CARE ASSOCI-

ATION
SASK ASSOCIATIONS HEALTH ORGAN
2121 Airport Dr Suite 207, Saskatoon, SK,
S7L 6W5

Emp Here 30
SIC 8011 Offices and clinics of medical doctors

D-U-N-S 20-801-2968   (BR)
SASKATCHEWAN LIQUOR AND GAMING AUTHORITY, THE
CONFEDERATION LIQUOR STORES
200 Confederation Dr, Saskatoon, SK, S7L
4R6
(306) 933-5315
Emp Here 20
SIC 5921 Liquor stores

D-U-N-S 25-486-0158   (BR)
SASKATOON CO-OPERATIVE ASSOCIATION LIMITED, THE
SASKATOON CO-OP
1624 33rd St W, Saskatoon, SK, S7L 0X3
(306) 933-3865
Emp Here 110
SIC 5141 Groceries, general line

D-U-N-S 25-788-0971   (BR)
SASKATOON CO-OPERATIVE ASSOCIATION LIMITED, THE
WESTVIEW SERVICE STATION
1628 33rd St W Suite 30080, Saskatoon, SK,
S7L 0X3
(306) 933-3873
Emp Here 26
SIC 5541 Gasoline service stations

D-U-N-S 24-426-8173   (SL)
SASKATOON CONVALESCENT HOME
101 31st St W, Saskatoon, SK, S7L 0P6
(306) 244-7155
Emp Here 80   *Sales* 3,793,956
SIC 8051 Skilled nursing care facilities

D-U-N-S 24-333-5200   (BR)
SASKATOON REGIONAL HEALTH AUTHORITY
SASKATOON DISTRICT HEALTH BOARD
310 Idylwyld Dr N Suite 291, Saskatoon, SK,
S7L 0Z2
(306) 655-4300
Emp Here 120
SIC 8062 General medical and surgical hospitals

D-U-N-S 25-678-3648   (BR)
SASKATOON REGIONAL HEALTH AUTHORITY
SASKATOON HEALTH REGION
310 Idylwyld Dr N, Saskatoon, SK, S7L 0Z2
(306) 655-4620
Emp Here 55
SIC 8062 General medical and surgical hospitals

D-U-N-S 20-332-0700   (BR)
SERVICES D'ENTRETIEN MINIERS INDUSTRIELS R.N. 2000 INC
243 Robin Cres, Saskatoon, SK, S7L 6M8

Emp Here 50
SIC 1241 Coal mining services

D-U-N-S 24-126-4667   (BR)
SHAW COMMUNICATIONS INC
2326 Hanselman Ave, Saskatoon, SK, S7L
5Z3
(306) 664-2121
Emp Here 50
SIC 4841 Cable and other pay television services

D-U-N-S 20-316-1237   (BR)
SHOCK TRAUMA AIR RESCUE SOCIETY
STARS
16 Wayne Hicks Lane, Saskatoon, SK, S7L
6S2

(306) 242-0200
Emp Here 49
SIC 4522 Air transportation, nonscheduled

D-U-N-S 25-271-7616   (BR)
SOBEYS WEST INC
CONFEDERATION SAFEWAY
300 Confederation Dr Suite 100, Saskatoon, SK, S7L 4R6
(306) 384-9599
Emp Here 125
SIC 5411 Grocery stores

D-U-N-S 25-364-9214   (BR)
SOBEYS WEST INC
302 33rd St W, Saskatoon, SK, S7L 0V4
(306) 244-2250
Emp Here 50
SIC 5411 Grocery stores

D-U-N-S 20-600-3543   (SL)
SOUTHCENTER AUTO INC
MAINWAY MAZDA
321 Circle Dr W, Saskatoon, SK, S7L 5S8
(306) 373-3711
Emp Here 27   *Sales* 13,695,750
SIC 5511 New and used car dealers
Pr Pr Wayne Holmes
 Gail Holmes

D-U-N-S 20-853-4362   (SL)
ST. JOSEPH'S HOME
33 Valens Dr, Saskatoon, SK, S7L 3S2
(306) 382-6306
Emp Here 70   *Sales* 2,553,625
SIC 8361 Residential care

D-U-N-S 20-712-7510   (BR)
ST. PAUL'S ROMAN CATHOLIC SEPARATE SCHOOL DIVISION NO 20
ST GERARD SEPERATE SCHOOL
205 Montreal Ave N, Saskatoon, SK, S7L 3N6
(306) 659-7330
Emp Here 50
SIC 8211 Elementary and secondary schools

D-U-N-S 20-712-7585   (BR)
ST. PAUL'S ROMAN CATHOLIC SEPARATE SCHOOL DIVISION NO 20
FATHER VACHON ELEMENTARY SCHOOL
3722 Centennial Dr, Saskatoon, SK, S7L 5K4
(306) 659-7210
Emp Here 40
SIC 8211 Elementary and secondary schools

D-U-N-S 20-712-7676   (BR)
ST. PAUL'S ROMAN CATHOLIC SEPARATE SCHOOL DIVISION NO 20
ST. PETER'S SCHOOL
202 Sumner Cres, Saskatoon, SK, S7L 7A4
(306) 659-7440
Emp Here 50
SIC 8211 Elementary and secondary schools

D-U-N-S 25-106-9837   (BR)
ST. PAUL'S ROMAN CATHOLIC SEPARATE SCHOOL DIVISION NO 20
E.D. FEEHAN HIGH SCHOOL
411 Avenue M N, Saskatoon, SK, S7L 2S7
(306) 659-7550
Emp Here 100
SIC 8211 Elementary and secondary schools

D-U-N-S 25-107-0116   (BR)
ST. PAUL'S ROMAN CATHOLIC SEPARATE SCHOOL DIVISION NO 20
ST GORETTI
301 Avenue Q N, Saskatoon, SK, S7L 2X7
(306) 659-7340
Emp Here 40
SIC 8211 Elementary and secondary schools

D-U-N-S 20-249-1689   (BR)
STERLING TRUCK & TRAILER SALES LTD
2326 Northridge Dr, Saskatoon, SK, S7L 1B9
(306) 242-7988
Emp Here 47
SIC 5511 New and used car dealers

D-U-N-S 24-520-2387   (SL)
VAKHOS RESTAURANT LIMITED
SASKATOON STATION PLACE
221 Idylwyld Dr N, Saskatoon, SK, S7L 6V6
(306) 244-7777
Emp Here 69   *Sales* 2,115,860
SIC 5812 Eating places

D-U-N-S 25-893-5626   (BR)
VECIMA NETWORKS INC
150 Cardinal Pl, Saskatoon, SK, S7L 6H7
(306) 955-7075
Emp Here 700
SIC 8731 Commercial physical research

D-U-N-S 20-861-1918   (BR)
WESTJET AIRLINES LTD
2625 Airport Dr Suite 23, Saskatoon, SK, S7L 7L1
(306) 244-1361
Emp Here 35
SIC 4512 Air transportation, scheduled

Saskatoon, SK S7M

D-U-N-S 20-003-3285   (BR)
BANK OF NOVA SCOTIA, THE
SCOTIABANK
2410 22nd St W Unit 9, Saskatoon, SK, S7M 5S6
(306) 668-1565
Emp Here 24
SIC 6021 National commercial banks

D-U-N-S 25-645-3325   (BR)
BANK OF NOVA SCOTIA, THE
SCOTIABANK
306 20th St W Suite 20, Saskatoon, SK, S7M 0X2
(306) 668-1540
Emp Here 24
SIC 6021 National commercial banks

D-U-N-S 20-656-6338   (BR)
BOARD OF EDUCATION OF SASKATOON SCHOOL DIVISION NO. 13 OF SASKATCHEWAN, THE
KING GEORGE COMMUNITY SCHOOL
721 Avenue K S, Saskatoon, SK, S7M 2E7
(306) 683-7310
Emp Here 35
SIC 8211 Elementary and secondary schools

D-U-N-S 20-712-7999   (BR)
BOARD OF EDUCATION OF SASKATOON SCHOOL DIVISION NO. 13 OF SASKATCHEWAN, THE
PLEASANT HILL COMMUNITY SCHOOL
215 Avenue S S, Saskatoon, SK, S7M 2Z9
(306) 683-7390
Emp Here 45
SIC 8211 Elementary and secondary schools

D-U-N-S 20-705-0662   (BR)
BOARD OF EDUCATION OF SASKATOON SCHOOL DIVISION NO. 13 OF SASKATCHEWAN, THE
W. P. BATE COMMUNICTY SCHOOL
2515 18th St W, Saskatoon, SK, S7M 4A9
(306) 683-7510
Emp Here 40
SIC 8211 Elementary and secondary schools

D-U-N-S 20-712-8153   (BR)
BOARD OF EDUCATION OF SASKATOON SCHOOL DIVISION NO. 13 OF SASKATCHEWAN, THE
JAMES L. ALEXANDER SCHOOL
427 Mccormack Rd, Saskatoon, SK, S7M 5L8
(306) 683-7280
Emp Here 50
SIC 8211 Elementary and secondary schools

D-U-N-S 20-656-0141   (BR)
BOARD OF EDUCATION OF SASKA-

D-U-N-S 20-037-7138   (BR)
TOON SCHOOL DIVISION NO. 13 OF SASKATCHEWAN, THE
PRINCESS ALEXANDRA COMMUNITY SCHOOL
210 Avenue H S, Saskatoon, SK, S7M 1W2
(306) 683-7410
Emp Here 30
SIC 8211 Elementary and secondary schools

D-U-N-S 20-037-7138   (BR)
BOARD OF EDUCATION OF SASKATOON SCHOOL DIVISION NO. 13 OF SASKATCHEWAN, THE
MONTGOMERY SCHOOL
3220 Ortona St, Saskatoon, SK, S7M 3R6
(306) 683-7370
Emp Here 22
SIC 8211 Elementary and secondary schools

D-U-N-S 20-069-1681   (BR)
BRINK'S CANADA LIMITED
BRINK'S CANADA
(*Suby of* The Brink's Company)
538 Avenue L S, Saskatoon, SK, S7M 2H4
(306) 652-9271
Emp Here 34
SIC 7381 Detective and armored car services

D-U-N-S 24-393-6726   (BR)
CANADIAN TIRE CORPORATION, LIMITED
A PARTSOURCE
2305 22nd St W Unit 6, Saskatoon, SK, S7M 0V6
(306) 384-2220
Emp Here 20
SIC 5531 Auto and home supply stores

D-U-N-S 24-344-8672   (BR)
CENTENNIAL FOODSERVICE
2020 St Patrick Ave, Saskatoon, SK, S7M 0L9
(306) 665-2999
Emp Here 20
SIC 5142 Packaged frozen goods

D-U-N-S 20-069-2630   (BR)
CINDERCRETE PRODUCTS LIMITED
605 Avenue P S, Saskatoon, SK, S7M 2W7
(306) 653-3933
Emp Here 25
SIC 3271 Concrete block and brick

D-U-N-S 24-883-0754   (SL)
DUBLINS IRISH PUB LTD
3322 Fairlight Dr, Saskatoon, SK, S7M 3Y4
(306) 382-5467
Emp Here 25   *Sales* 948,489
SIC 5813 Drinking places

D-U-N-S 20-047-8126   (BR)
FINNING INTERNATIONAL INC
(*Suby of* Finning International Inc)
3502 11th St W, Saskatoon, SK, S7M 1K7
(306) 382-3550
Emp Here 100
SIC 5082 Construction and mining machinery

D-U-N-S 25-451-2031   (BR)
GOVERNING COUNCIL OF THE SALVATION ARMY IN CANADA, THE
SALVATION ARMY COMMUNITY CENTRE, THE
339 Avenue C S, Saskatoon, SK, S7M 1N5
(306) 244-6280
Emp Here 38
SIC 8322 Individual and family services

D-U-N-S 20-702-4725   (BR)
HARADROS FOOD SERVICES INC
MANO'S GRILL & BREWHOUSE
(*Suby of* Haradros Food Services Inc)
2202 22nd St W, Saskatoon, SK, S7M 0V4
(306) 683-3333
Emp Here 50
SIC 5812 Eating places

D-U-N-S 25-288-0539   (BR)
JORIDO FOODS SERVICES LTD
A & W

(*Suby of* Jorido Foods Services Ltd)
2222 22nd St W, Saskatoon, SK, S7M 0V4
(306) 382-7123
Emp Here 30
SIC 5812 Eating places

D-U-N-S 20-731-9356   (BR)
LOBLAWS INC
EXTRA FOODS 9068
2410 22nd St W Suite 1, Saskatoon, SK, S7M 5S6
(306) 384-3019
Emp Here 50
SIC 5411 Grocery stores

D-U-N-S 24-329-5289   (BR)
MAPLE LEAF FOODS INC
100 Mcleod Ave, Saskatoon, SK, S7M 5V9
(306) 382-2210
Emp Here 350
SIC 2011 Meat packing plants

D-U-N-S 20-355-0830   (BR)
MCDONALD'S RESTAURANTS OF CANADA LIMITED
MCDONALD'S
(*Suby of* McDonald's Corporation)
2225 22nd St W, Saskatoon, SK, S7M 0V5
(306) 955-8660
Emp Here 100
SIC 5812 Eating places

D-U-N-S 20-740-5288   (BR)
MCDONALD'S RESTAURANTS OF CANADA LIMITED
MCDONALD'S
(*Suby of* McDonald's Corporation)
225 Betts Ave, Saskatoon, SK, S7M 1L2
(306) 955-8676
Emp Here 25
SIC 5812 Eating places

D-U-N-S 24-231-9143   (HQ)
N. YANKE TRANSFER LTD
YANKE GROUP OF COMPANIES
1359 Fletcher Rd, Saskatoon, SK, S7M 5H5
(306) 955-4221
Emp Here 140   *Emp Total* 716
Sales 125,448,480
SIC 4213 Trucking, except local
 Russel Marcoux
VP Fin Scott Fraser
VP Brian Richards
Dir Bonnie Marcoux

D-U-N-S 25-642-8046   (BR)
SGI CANADA INSURANCE SERVICES LTD
SGI
345 Fairmont Dr, Saskatoon, SK, S7M 5N5
(306) 683-4450
Emp Here 20
SIC 6331 Fire, marine, and casualty insurance

D-U-N-S 25-484-0473   (BR)
SASKATCHEWAN ABILITIES COUNCIL INC
1410 Kilburn Ave, Saskatoon, SK, S7M 0J8
(306) 653-1694
Emp Here 70
SIC 8331 Job training and related services

D-U-N-S 25-289-5602   (BR)
SASKATCHEWAN ASSOCIATION OF REHABILITATION CENTRES
SARCAN RECYCLING
(*Suby of* Saskatchewan Association of Rehabilitation Centres)
2305 22nd St W Suite 5, Saskatoon, SK, S7M 0V6
(306) 384-5699
Emp Here 20
SIC 4953 Refuse systems

D-U-N-S 24-346-3374   (BR)
SASKATCHEWAN POWER CORPORATION
SASKPOWER
2211 Spadina Cres W, Saskatoon, SK, S7M 5V5
(306) 934-7995
Emp Here 100

SIC 4911 Electric services

D-U-N-S 20-799-3978   (BR)
SASKATCHEWAN POWER CORPORATION
SASKPOWER
1370 Fletcher Rd, Saskatoon, SK, S7M 5H2
(306) 934-7733
Emp Here 200
SIC 4911 Electric services

D-U-N-S 25-066-2186   (BR)
SASKATOON CO-OPERATIVE ASSOCIA-TION LIMITED, THE
3370 Fairlight Dr, Saskatoon, SK, S7M 5H9
(306) 933-3823
Emp Here 20
SIC 5541 Gasoline service stations

D-U-N-S 20-775-9429   (BR)
SASKATOON REGIONAL HEALTH AU-THORITY
ST. PAUL'S HOSPITAL (GREY NUNS)
1702 20th St W, Saskatoon, SK, S7M 0Z9
(306) 655-5800
Emp Here 49
SIC 8062 General medical and surgical hospitals

D-U-N-S 20-262-8959   (BR)
SASKATOON REGIONAL HEALTH AU-THORITY
PARKRIDGE CENTRE
110 Gropper Cres, Saskatoon, SK, S7M 5N9
(306) 655-3800
Emp Here 500
SIC 8062 General medical and surgical hospitals

D-U-N-S 24-336-8953   (BR)
SASKATOON, CITY OF
WATER TREATMENT PLANT
1030 Avenue H S, Saskatoon, SK, S7M 1X5
(306) 975-2534
Emp Here 500
SIC 4953 Refuse systems

D-U-N-S 20-327-8155   (BR)
SCOULAR CANADA LTD
(*Suby of* The Scoular Company)
1502 17th St W, Saskatoon, SK, S7M 4A4
(306) 249-4151
Emp Here 20
SIC 4221 Farm product warehousing and storage

D-U-N-S 20-712-7544   (BR)
ST. PAUL'S ROMAN CATHOLIC SEPARATE SCHOOL DIVISION NO 20
ST MARY COMMUNITY SCHOOL
337 Avenue O S, Saskatoon, SK, S7M 2R9
(306) 659-7400
Emp Here 50
SIC 8211 Elementary and secondary schools

D-U-N-S 25-021-2495   (BR)
ST. PAUL'S ROMAN CATHOLIC SEPARATE SCHOOL DIVISION NO 20
ST DOMINIC SCHOOL
3301 Dieppe St, Saskatoon, SK, S7M 3S6
(306) 659-7290
Emp Here 28
SIC 8211 Elementary and secondary schools

D-U-N-S 25-107-0363   (BR)
ST. PAUL'S ROMAN CATHOLIC SEPARATE SCHOOL DIVISION NO 20
ST MARK
414 Pendygrasse Rd, Saskatoon, SK, S7M 4M3
(306) 659-7390
Emp Here 30
SIC 8211 Elementary and secondary schools

D-U-N-S 20-712-7536   (BR)
ST. PAUL'S ROMAN CATHOLIC SEPARATE SCHOOL DIVISION NO 20
1205 Avenue N S, Saskatoon, SK, S7M 2R1
(306) 659-7360
Emp Here 35

SIC 8211 Elementary and secondary schools

D-U-N-S 20-712-7668   (BR)
ST. PAUL'S ROMAN CATHOLIC SEPARATE SCHOOL DIVISION NO 20
ST MARGUERITE SCHOOL
1235 Mccormack Rd, Saskatoon, SK, S7M 5L6
(306) 659-7380
Emp Here 50
SIC 8211 Elementary and secondary schools

D-U-N-S 25-297-8366   (BR)
TOYS 'R' US (CANADA) LTD
TOYS 'R' US
(*Suby of* Toys "r" Us, Inc.)
300 Idylwyld Dr S, Saskatoon, SK, S7M 5T4
(306) 653-8697
Emp Here 25
SIC 5945 Hobby, toy, and game shops

D-U-N-S 20-465-3372   (BR)
UNIVERSITY OF SASKATCHEWAN
DEPT OF ACADEMIC FAMILY MEDICINE
(*Suby of* University of Saskatchewan)
3311 Fairlight Dr, Saskatoon, SK, S7M 3Y5
(306) 655-4235
Emp Here 22
SIC 8221 Colleges and universities

D-U-N-S 24-917-3030   (BR)
VITERRA INC
AGRICORE UNITED
3404 11th St W, Saskatoon, SK, S7M 1K5
(306) 384-7900
Emp Here 50
SIC 4221 Farm product warehousing and storage

D-U-N-S 24-826-8737   (BR)
WAL-MART CANADA CORP
WALMART
225 Betts Ave, Saskatoon, SK, S7M 1L2
(306) 382-5454
Emp Here 100
SIC 5311 Department stores

Saskatoon, SK S7N

D-U-N-S 25-679-6996   (BR)
AMEC FOSTER WHEELER AMERICAS LIMITED
AMEC EARTH & ENVIRONMENTAL DIVISION OF
121 Research Dr Unit 301, Saskatoon, SK, S7N 1K2
(306) 477-1155
Emp Here 65
SIC 8711 Engineering services

D-U-N-S 20-348-1783   (SL)
ACADIA PAVING LTD.
(*Suby of* Acadia Construction)
121 105th St E, Saskatoon, SK, S7N 1Z2
(306) 374-4738
Emp Here 50   *Sales* 5,836,856
SIC 1611 Highway and street construction
Wayne Heaslit

D-U-N-S 25-976-3746   (BR)
AGRA FOUNDATIONS LIMITED
121 105th St E, Saskatoon, SK, S7N 1Z2
(306) 373-3762
Emp Here 20
SIC 2491 Wood preserving

D-U-N-S 24-995-9362   (BR)
BEST BUY CANADA LTD
FUTURE SHOP
(*Suby of* Best Buy Co., Inc.)
1723 Preston Ave N Unit 221, Saskatoon, SK, S7N 4V2
(306) 955-6800
Emp Here 50
SIC 5731 Radio, television, and electronic

stores

D-U-N-S 20-712-7841   (BR)
BOARD OF EDUCATION OF SASKA-TOON SCHOOL DIVISION NO. 13 OF SASKATCHEWAN, THE
BRUNSKILL SCHOOL
101 Wiggins Ave S, Saskatoon, SK, S7N 1K3
(306) 683-7130
Emp Here 50
SIC 8211 Elementary and secondary schools

D-U-N-S 20-712-8096   (BR)
BOARD OF EDUCATION OF SASKA-TOON SCHOOL DIVISION NO. 13 OF SASKATCHEWAN, THE
NUTANA COLLEGIATE
411 11th St E, Saskatoon, SK, S7N 0E9
(306) 683-7580
Emp Here 60
SIC 8211 Elementary and secondary schools

D-U-N-S 25-269-0748   (BR)
BOARD OF EDUCATION OF SASKA-TOON SCHOOL DIVISION NO. 13 OF SASKATCHEWAN, THE
DR. JOHN G. EGNATOFF SCHOOL
225 Kenderdine Rd, Saskatoon, SK, S7N 3V2
(306) 683-7190
Emp Here 53
SIC 8211 Elementary and secondary schools

D-U-N-S 20-657-0272   (BR)
BOARD OF EDUCATION OF SASKA-TOON SCHOOL DIVISION NO. 13 OF SASKATCHEWAN, THE
ECOLE FOREST GROVE SCHOOL
501 115th St E, Saskatoon, SK, S7N 2X9
(306) 683-7220
Emp Here 47
SIC 8211 Elementary and secondary schools

D-U-N-S 20-712-8039   (BR)
BOARD OF EDUCATION OF SASKA-TOON SCHOOL DIVISION NO. 13 OF SASKATCHEWAN, THE
SUTHERLAND SCHOOL
1008 Egbert Ave, Saskatoon, SK, S7N 1X6
(306) 683-7460
Emp Here 50
SIC 8211 Elementary and secondary schools

D-U-N-S 20-712-8047   (BR)
BOARD OF EDUCATION OF SASKA-TOON SCHOOL DIVISION NO. 13 OF SASKATCHEWAN, THE
ECOLE VICTORIA SCHOOL
639 Broadway Ave, Saskatoon, SK, S7N 1B2
(306) 683-7470
Emp Here 35
SIC 8211 Elementary and secondary schools

D-U-N-S 25-098-9787   (BR)
CALIAN LTD
SED SYSTEMS
18 Innovation Blvd, Saskatoon, SK, S7N 3R1
(306) 931-3425
Emp Here 230
SIC 4899 Communication services, nec

D-U-N-S 24-174-8842   (BR)
CANADIAN PACIFIC RAILWAY COMPANY
CPR
801 Gray Ave, Saskatoon, SK, S7N 2K6
(306) 931-7426
Emp Here 20
SIC 4111 Local and suburban transit

D-U-N-S 20-814-4522   (SL)
CREEWAY GAS LLP
PETRO CANADA
335 Packham Ave Suite 112, Saskatoon, SK, S7N 4S1
(306) 955-8835
Emp Here 30   *Sales* 5,579,750
SIC 5541 Gasoline service stations
Genl Mgr Troy Larmer

D-U-N-S 24-676-6567   (BR)
CROWN INVESTMENTS CORPORATION OF SASKATCHEWAN
C.I.C.
15 Innovation Blvd Suite 114, Saskatoon, SK, S7N 2X8
(306) 933-6259
Emp Here 25
SIC 6719 Holding companies, nec

D-U-N-S 25-385-0044   (BR)
DOW AGROSCIENCES CANADA INC
DAS
(*Suby of* The Dow Chemical Company)
421 Downey Rd Suite 101, Saskatoon, SK, S7N 4L8
(306) 657-3351
Emp Here 100
SIC 2879 Agricultural chemicals, nec

D-U-N-S 24-426-3786   (SL)
GREEK SPOT FAMILY RESTAURANT INC
ATHENA FAMILY RESTAURANT
900 Central Ave, Saskatoon, SK, S7N 2G8
(306) 249-0900
Emp Here 60   *Sales* 1,824,018
SIC 5812 Eating places

D-U-N-S 24-386-0157   (BR)
HATCH LTD
HATCH ENGINEERING
121 Research Dr Suite 201, Saskatoon, SK, S7N 1K2
(306) 657-7500
Emp Here 60
SIC 8711 Engineering services

D-U-N-S 20-333-8561   (SL)
HERTZ NORTHERN BUS (2006) LTD
330 103rd St E, Saskatoon, SK, S7N 1Z1
(306) 374-5161
Emp Here 110   *Sales* 3,724,879
SIC 4151 School buses

D-U-N-S 20-553-0285   (BR)
HUDSON'S BAY COMPANY
HOME OUTFITTERS
1723 Preston Ave N Unit 211, Saskatoon, SK, S7N 4V2
(306) 955-3790
Emp Here 45
SIC 5311 Department stores

D-U-N-S 25-640-3999   (BR)
LEHIGH HANSON MATERIALS LIMITED
INLAND
136 107th St E, Saskatoon, SK, S7N 3A5
(306) 374-9434
Emp Here 30
SIC 5032 Brick, stone, and related material

D-U-N-S 24-424-3809   (BR)
LOBLAWS INC
EXTRA FOODS
910 Broadway Ave, Saskatoon, SK, S7N 1B7
(306) 242-4764
Emp Here 34
SIC 5411 Grocery stores

D-U-N-S 25-636-6758   (BR)
LOBLAWS INC
EXTRA FOODS
30 Kenderdine Rd, Saskatoon, SK, S7N 4M8
(306) 343-3400
Emp Here 50
SIC 5411 Grocery stores

D-U-N-S 25-290-8116   (BR)
MARK'S WORK WEARHOUSE LTD
MARK'S WORK WEARHOUSE NO. 46
1715 Preston Ave N Suite 101, Saskatoon, SK, S7N 4V2
(306) 477-1444
Emp Here 20
SIC 5651 Family clothing stores

D-U-N-S 20-856-5924   (BR)
MICHAELS OF CANADA, ULC
MICHAELS ARTS & CRAFTS

(*Suby of* The Michaels Companies Inc)
1723 Preston Ave N Unit 201, Saskatoon, SK,
S7N 4V2
(306) 975-1810
Emp Here 65
SIC 5945 Hobby, toy, and game shops

D-U-N-S 24-029-7155 　　(BR)
OLD NAVY (CANADA) INC
OLD NAVY
(*Suby of* The Gap Inc)
1715 Preston Ave N, Saskatoon, SK, S7N 4V2
(306) 653-4420
Emp Here 55
SIC 5651 Family clothing stores

D-U-N-S 24-037-7734 　　(BR)
P. A. FINE FOODS & DISTRIBUTORS LTD
341 105th St E, Saskatoon, SK, S7N 1Z4

Emp Here 20
SIC 5145 Confectionery

D-U-N-S 20-342-1040 　　(BR)
REDBERRY FRANCHISING CORP
BURGER KING
1747 Preston Ave N, Saskatoon, SK, S7N 4V2
(306) 933-9445
Emp Here 20
SIC 5812 Eating places

D-U-N-S 25-289-5644 　　(BR)
SASKATCHEWAN ASSOCIATION OF RE-HABILITATION CENTRES
SARCAN RECYCLING
(*Suby of* Saskatchewan Association of Reha-bilitation Centres)
350b 103rd St E, Saskatoon, SK, S7N 1Z1
(306) 373-3386
Emp Here 20
SIC 4953 Refuse systems

D-U-N-S 25-261-7204 　　(HQ)
SASKATCHEWAN INDIAN GAMING AU-THORITY INC
PAINTED HAND CASINO
103c Packham Ave Suite 250, Saskatoon, SK,
S7N 4K4
(306) 477-7777
Emp Here 90　　　　*Emp Total* 100
Sales 11,253,760
SIC 7999 Amusement and recreation, nec
Pr Zane Hansen
VP Opers Vern Acoose
　Therese McIlymoyl
VP Opers Paul Newton
　Ray Ahenakew

D-U-N-S 25-207-3309 　　(HQ)
SASKATCHEWAN OPPORTUNITIES COR-PORATION
SOCO
15 Innovation Blvd Suite 114, Saskatoon, SK,
S7N 2X8
(306) 933-6295
Emp Here 70　　　*Emp Total* 40,372
Sales 28,671,440
SIC 6519 Real property lessors, nec
Pr Doug Tastad
VP Charlene Callander
Dir Richard Florizone

D-U-N-S 25-640-3965 　　(BR)
SASKATCHEWAN OPPORTUNITIES COR-PORATION
BOFFINS FOOD SERVICES
111 Research Dr Suite 106, Saskatoon, SK,
S7N 3R2
(306) 249-5344
Emp Here 32
SIC 5812 Eating places

D-U-N-S 25-313-8473 　　(HQ)
SASKATCHEWAN RESEARCH COUNCIL, THE
15 Innovation Blvd Suite 125, Saskatoon, SK,
S7N 2X8

(306) 933-5400
Emp Here 180　　　*Emp Total* 40,372
Sales 31,081,258
SIC 8733 Noncommercial research organiza-tions
　Laurier Schramm
　Craig Zawada
　Doug Kelin
Dir Peta Bonham-Smith
Dir Lee Willson
Dir Kathy Palidwar
Dir Shelley Lipon
Dir Patsy Gilchrist

D-U-N-S 25-596-9974 　　(BR)
SASKATCHEWAN RESEARCH COUNCIL, THE
SASKATCHEWAN RESEARCH COUNCIL ANALYTICAL LABORATORY
422 Downey Rd Suite 102, Saskatoon, SK,
S7N 4N1
(306) 933-6932
Emp Here 40
SIC 8733 Noncommercial research organiza-tions

D-U-N-S 24-346-3416 　　(BR)
SASKATOON REGIONAL HEALTH AU-THORITY
KINSMEN CHILDREN'S CENTRE
1319 Colony St, Saskatoon, SK, S7N 2Z1
(306) 655-1070
Emp Here 150
SIC 8062 General medical and surgical hospi-tals

D-U-N-S 20-635-6508 　　(BR)
SOBEYS CAPITAL INCORPORATED
1739 Preston Ave N, Saskatoon, SK, S7N 4V2
(306) 668-9901
Emp Here 140
SIC 5411 Grocery stores

D-U-N-S 25-271-7533 　　(BR)
SOBEYS WEST INC
SAFEWAY
1739 Preston Ave N, Saskatoon, SK, S7N 4V2
(306) 668-9901
Emp Here 104
SIC 5411 Grocery stores

D-U-N-S 25-106-9928 　　(BR)
ST. PAUL'S ROMAN CATHOLIC SEPARATE SCHOOL DIVISION NO 20
DUQUETTE, JOE HIGH SCHOOL
919 Broadway Ave, Saskatoon, SK, S7N 1B8
(306) 659-7730
Emp Here 36
SIC 8211 Elementary and secondary schools

D-U-N-S 20-347-1537 　　(BR)
UNIVERSITY OF SASKATCHEWAN
DEPT OF MEDICAL IMAGING
(*Suby of* University of Saskatchewan)
103 Hospital Dr, Saskatoon, SK, S7N 0W8
(306) 655-2402
Emp Here 22
SIC 8221 Colleges and universities

D-U-N-S 20-646-2624 　　(BR)
UNIVERSITY OF SASKATCHEWAN
DEPT OF ANESTHESIA
(*Suby of* University of Saskatchewan)
103 Hospital Dr, Saskatoon, SK, S7N 0W8
(306) 655-1186
Emp Here 70
SIC 8221 Colleges and universities

D-U-N-S 20-653-9921 　　(BR)
UNIVERSITY OF SASKATCHEWAN
COLLEGE OF DENTISTRY
(*Suby of* University of Saskatchewan)
105 Wiggins Rd, Saskatoon, SK, S7N 5E4
(306) 966-5122
Emp Here 59
SIC 8221 Colleges and universities

D-U-N-S 24-885-4866 　　(BR)

UNIVERSITY OF SASKATCHEWAN
FACILITIES MANAGEMENT
(*Suby of* University of Saskatchewan)
110 Maintenance Rd, Saskatoon, SK, S7N
5C5
(306) 966-4700
Emp Here 34
SIC 8221 Colleges and universities

D-U-N-S 20-787-0689 　　(BR)
UNIVERSITY OF SASKATCHEWAN
CONTINUING AND DISTANCE EDUCATION
(*Suby of* University of Saskatchewan)
221 Cumberland Ave N Suite 232, Saskatoon,
SK, S7N 1M3
(306) 966-5563
Emp Here 50
SIC 8221 Colleges and universities

D-U-N-S 20-347-1180 　　(BR)
UNIVERSITY OF SASKATCHEWAN
DEPARTMENT OF SOIL SCIENCE
(*Suby of* University of Saskatchewan)
51 Campus Dr Rm 5d34, Saskatoon, SK, S7N
5A8
(306) 966-6829
Emp Here 120
SIC 8221 Colleges and universities

D-U-N-S 25-572-5616 　　(BR)
UNIVERSITY OF SASKATCHEWAN
DEPT OF ANIMAL & POULTRY SCIENCE
(*Suby of* University of Saskatchewan)
51 Campus Dr Rm 6d34, Saskatoon, SK, S7N
5A8
(306) 966-4128
Emp Here 60
SIC 8221 Colleges and universities

D-U-N-S 20-653-4497 　　(BR)
UNIVERSITY OF SASKATCHEWAN
DEPT OF CHEMISTRY
(*Suby of* University of Saskatchewan)
110 Science Pl, Saskatoon, SK, S7N 5C9
(306) 966-4655
Emp Here 21
SIC 8221 Colleges and universities

D-U-N-S 20-430-3320 　　(BR)
UNIVERSITY OF SASKATCHEWAN
DEPT OF GEOLOGICAL SCIENCES
(*Suby of* University of Saskatchewan)
114 Science Pl, Saskatoon, SK, S7N 5E2
(306) 966-5683
Emp Here 39
SIC 8221 Colleges and universities

D-U-N-S 20-347-1396 　　(BR)
UNIVERSITY OF SASKATCHEWAN
DEPARTMENT OF CURRICULUM STUDIES
(*Suby of* University of Saskatchewan)
28 Campus Dr Rm 3021, Saskatoon, SK, S7N
0X1
(306) 966-7601
Emp Here 27
SIC 8221 Colleges and universities

D-U-N-S 25-186-5473 　　(BR)
UNIVERSITY OF SASKATCHEWAN
OFFICE OF THE VICE PRESIDENT RE-SEARCH
(*Suby of* University of Saskatchewan)
107 Administration Pl Suite 201, Saskatoon,
SK, S7N 5A2
(306) 966-8514
Emp Here 102
SIC 8221 Colleges and universities

D-U-N-S 20-347-1636 　　(BR)
UNIVERSITY OF SASKATCHEWAN
JOHNSON-SHOYAMA OF GRADUATE SCHOOL OF PUBLIC POLICY
(*Suby of* University of Saskatchewan)
101 Diefenbaker Pl, Saskatoon, SK, S7N 5B8
(306) 966-8525
Emp Here 22
SIC 8221 Colleges and universities

D-U-N-S 20-347-1461 　　(BR)
UNIVERSITY OF SASKATCHEWAN
DEPT OF ELECTRICAL AND COMPUTER ENGINEERING
(*Suby of* University of Saskatchewan)
57 Campus Dr Rm 3b48, Saskatoon, SK, S7N
5A9
(306) 966-5336
Emp Here 35
SIC 8221 Colleges and universities

D-U-N-S 20-347-1669 　　(BR)
UNIVERSITY OF SASKATCHEWAN
DEPARTMENT OF VETERINARY BIOMEDI-CAL SCIENCES
(*Suby of* University of Saskatchewan)
52 Campus Dr Room 1301, Saskatoon, SK,
S7N 5B4
(306) 966-7350
Emp Here 50
SIC 8221 Colleges and universities

D-U-N-S 20-347-1651 　　(BR)
UNIVERSITY OF SASKATCHEWAN
DEPARTMENT OF SMALL ANIMAL CLINI-CAL SCIENCES
(*Suby of* University of Saskatchewan)
52 Campus Dr Rm 2529, Saskatoon, SK, S7N
5B4

Emp Here 42
SIC 8221 Colleges and universities

D-U-N-S 20-347-1610 　　(BR)
UNIVERSITY OF SASKATCHEWAN
SCHOOL OF PHYSICAL THERAPY
(*Suby of* University of Saskatchewan)
104 Clinic Pl 3rd Fl Suite 3400, Saskatoon,
SK, S7N 2Z4
(306) 966-6579
Emp Here 20
SIC 8221 Colleges and universities

D-U-N-S 20-347-1545 　　(BR)
UNIVERSITY OF SASKATCHEWAN
DEPT OF MEDICINE
(*Suby of* University of Saskatchewan)
103 Hospital Dr, Saskatoon, SK, S7N 0W8
(306) 844-1132
Emp Here 122
SIC 8221 Colleges and universities

D-U-N-S 20-347-1594 　　(BR)
UNIVERSITY OF SASKATCHEWAN
COLLEGE OF NURSING
(*Suby of* University of Saskatchewan)
104 Clinic Pl, Saskatoon, SK, S7N 2Z4
(306) 966-6221
Emp Here 75
SIC 8221 Colleges and universities

D-U-N-S 24-245-6197 　　(BR)
UNIVERSITY OF SASKATCHEWAN
LANGUAGE CENTRE
(*Suby of* University of Saskatchewan)
221 Cumberland Ave N Unit 232, Saskatoon,
SK, S7N 1M3
(306) 966-4351
Emp Here 26
SIC 8221 Colleges and universities

D-U-N-S 20-741-3170 　　(HQ)
UNIVERSITY OF SASKATCHEWAN
(*Suby of* University of Saskatchewan)
105 Administration Pl Suite E, Saskatoon, SK,
S7N 5A2
(306) 966-4343
Emp Here 1,100　　　*Emp Total* 8,500
Sales 918,800,689
SIC 8221 Colleges and universities
Pr Peter Stoicheff
VP Michael Atkinson

D-U-N-S 24-951-4071 　　(BR)
UNIVERSITY OF SASKATCHEWAN
DEPARTMENT OF VETERINARY MICROBI-OLOGY
(*Suby of* University of Saskatchewan)

52 Campus Dr Rm 2601, Saskatoon, SK, S7N 5B4
(306) 966-7210
Emp Here 71
SIC 8221 Colleges and universities

D-U-N-S 20-347-1487 (BR)
UNIVERSITY OF SASKATCHEWAN
COLLEGE OF KINESIOLOGY
(Suby of University of Saskatchewan)
87 Campus Dr, Saskatoon, SK, S7N 5B2
(306) 966-1060
Emp Here 35
SIC 8221 Colleges and universities

D-U-N-S 20-997-3283 (BR)
UNIVERSITY OF SASKATCHEWAN
COLLEGE OF LAW
(Suby of University of Saskatchewan)
15 Campus Dr, Saskatoon, SK, S7N 5A6
(306) 966-5869
Emp Here 50
SIC 8221 Colleges and universities

D-U-N-S 20-797-2675 (BR)
UNIVERSITY OF SASKATCHEWAN
COLLEGE OF PHARMACY & NUTRITION
(Suby of University of Saskatchewan)
104 Clinic Pl Rm 3134, Saskatoon, SK, S7N 2Z4
(306) 966-6327
Emp Here 60
SIC 8221 Colleges and universities

D-U-N-S 25-778-8745 (BR)
UNIVERSITY OF SASKATCHEWAN
FACULTY CLUB
(Suby of University of Saskatchewan)
101 Administration Pl, Saskatoon, SK, S7N 5A1
(306) 966-7774
Emp Here 20
SIC 8221 Colleges and universities

D-U-N-S 20-067-5556 (BR)
UNIVERSITY OF SASKATCHEWAN
DEPT OF OBSTETRICS, GYNECOLOGY AND REPRODUCTIVE SCIENCES
(Suby of University of Saskatchewan)
103 Hospital Dr Rm 4544, Saskatoon, SK, S7N 0W8
(306) 844-1059
Emp Here 67
SIC 8221 Colleges and universities

D-U-N-S 24-109-8040 (BR)
UNIVERSITY OF SASKATCHEWAN
COLLEGE OF ENGINEERING
(Suby of University of Saskatchewan)
57 Campus Dr Rm 3b48, Saskatoon, SK, S7N 5A9
(306) 966-5273
Emp Here 150
SIC 8221 Colleges and universities

D-U-N-S 20-976-3205 (BR)
UNIVERSITY OF SASKATCHEWAN
DEPT OF PSYCHOLOGY
(Suby of University of Saskatchewan)
9 Campus Dr Rm 154, Saskatoon, SK, S7N 5A5
(306) 966-6657
Emp Here 36
SIC 8221 Colleges and universities

D-U-N-S 20-327-4238 (BR)
UNIVERSITY OF SASKATCHEWAN
DEPT OF COMPUTER SCIENCE
(Suby of University of Saskatchewan)
110 Science Pl Rm 176, Saskatoon, SK, S7N 5C9
(306) 966-4886
Emp Here 50
SIC 8221 Colleges and universities

D-U-N-S 25-895-6882 (BR)
UNIVERSITY OF SASKATCHEWAN
DEPT OF PATHOLOGY AND LABORATORY MEDICINE

(Suby of University of Saskatchewan)
103 Hospital Drive Rm 2841, Saskatoon, SK, S7N 0W8
(306) 655-2221
Emp Here 65
SIC 8221 Colleges and universities

D-U-N-S 24-666-5202 (BR)
UNIVERSITY OF SASKATCHEWAN
UNIVERSITY OF SASKATCHEWAN
(Suby of University of Saskatchewan)
52 Campus Dr Rm 3101, Saskatoon, SK, S7N 5B4
(306) 966-7477
Emp Here 344
SIC 8221 Colleges and universities

D-U-N-S 20-622-1418 (BR)
UNIVERSITY OF SASKATCHEWAN
UNIVERSITY OF SASKATCHEWAN
(Suby of University of Saskatchewan)
116 Science Pl Rm 163, Saskatoon, SK, S7N 5E2
(306) 966-6393
Emp Here 50
SIC 8221 Colleges and universities

D-U-N-S 20-657-2455 (BR)
UNIVERSITY OF SASKATCHEWAN
DEPT OF ANATOMY AND CELL BIOLOGY
(Suby of University of Saskatchewan)
107 Wiggins Rd Rm 2d01, Saskatoon, SK, S7N 5E5
(306) 966-6362
Emp Here 25
SIC 8221 Colleges and universities

D-U-N-S 24-337-1239 (BR)
UNIVERSITY OF SASKATCHEWAN
DEPT OF PSYCHIATRY
(Suby of University of Saskatchewan)
103 Hospital Dr Rm 119, Saskatoon, SK, S7N 0W8
(306) 844-1310
Emp Here 55
SIC 8221 Colleges and universities

D-U-N-S 20-347-1479 (BR)
UNIVERSITY OF SASKATCHEWAN
SCHOOL OF ENVIRONMENT AND SUSTAINABILITY
(Suby of University of Saskatchewan)
117 Science Pl Rm 323, Saskatoon, SK, S7N 5C8
(306) 966-1985
Emp Here 83
SIC 8221 Colleges and universities

D-U-N-S 20-347-1529 (BR)
UNIVERSITY OF SASKATCHEWAN
DEPT OF EMERGENCY MEDICINE
(Suby of University of Saskatchewan)
107 Hospital Dr, Saskatoon, SK, S7N 0W8
(306) 655-1446
Emp Here 46
SIC 8221 Colleges and universities

D-U-N-S 20-347-1578 (BR)
UNIVERSITY OF SASKATCHEWAN
DEPT OF SURGERY
(Suby of University of Saskatchewan)
107 Wiggins Rd 4th Fl Suite B419, Saskatoon, SK, S7N 5E5
(306) 966-8641
Emp Here 167
SIC 8221 Colleges and universities

D-U-N-S 20-347-1628 (BR)
UNIVERSITY OF SASKATCHEWAN
SCHOOL OF PUBLIC HEALTH
(Suby of University of Saskatchewan)
104 Clinic Pl, Saskatoon, SK, S7N 2Z4
(306) 966-8544
Emp Here 22
SIC 8221 Colleges and universities

D-U-N-S 24-345-0470 (BR)
UNIVERSITY OF SASKATCHEWAN

INFORMATION TECHNOLOGY UNIT, COLLEGE OF MEDICINE
(Suby of University of Saskatchewan)
107 Wiggins Rd Suite B103, Saskatoon, SK, S7N 5E5
(306) 966-1626
Emp Here 1,200
SIC 8221 Colleges and universities

D-U-N-S 25-991-5648 (BR)
UNIVERSITY OF SASKATCHEWAN
DEPT OF MECHANICAL ENGINEERING
(Suby of University of Saskatchewan)
57 Campus Dr Rm 3b48, Saskatoon, SK, S7N 5A9
(306) 966-5440
Emp Here 40
SIC 8221 Colleges and universities

D-U-N-S 20-787-5027 (BR)
UNIVERSITY OF SASKATCHEWAN
DIVISION OF ORTHOPAEDIC SURGERY
(Suby of University of Saskatchewan)
103 Hospital Dr, Saskatoon, SK, S7N 0W8
(306) 244-5561
Emp Here 24
SIC 8221 Colleges and universities

D-U-N-S 24-352-3409 (BR)
UNIVERSITY OF SASKATCHEWAN
PEDIATRICS DEPARTMENT
(Suby of University of Saskatchewan)
103 Hospital Dr, Saskatoon, SK, S7N 0W8
(306) 844-1068
Emp Here 100
SIC 8221 Colleges and universities

D-U-N-S 20-037-4119 (BR)
UNIVERSITY OF SASKATCHEWAN
STUDENT HEALTH CENTER
(Suby of University of Saskatchewan)
91 Campus Dr Suite 145, Saskatoon, SK, S7N 5E8
(306) 966-5768
Emp Here 21
SIC 8221 Colleges and universities

D-U-N-S 20-188-2946 (BR)
UNIVERSITY OF SASKATCHEWAN
UNIVERSITY OF SASKATCHEWAN BOOKSTORE
(Suby of University of Saskatchewan)
97 Campus Dr Suite 227, Saskatoon, SK, S7N 4L3
(306) 966-4638
Emp Here 40
SIC 8221 Colleges and universities

D-U-N-S 20-794-1415 (BR)
UNIVERSITY OF SASKATCHEWAN
COLLEGE OF EDUCATION
(Suby of University of Saskatchewan)
28 Campus Dr Suite 3079, Saskatoon, SK, S7N 0X1
(306) 966-7619
Emp Here 101
SIC 8221 Colleges and universities

D-U-N-S 20-347-1644 (BR)
UNIVERSITY OF SASKATCHEWAN
DEPARTMENT OF LARGE ANIMAL CLINICAL SCIENCES
(Suby of University of Saskatchewan)
52 Campus Dr Rm 2401, Saskatoon, SK, S7N 5B4
(306) 966-7145
Emp Here 34
SIC 8221 Colleges and universities

D-U-N-S 20-347-1446 (BR)
UNIVERSITY OF SASKATCHEWAN
DEPT OF CHEMICAL AND BIOLOGICAL ENGINEERING
(Suby of University of Saskatchewan)
57 Campus Dr Rm 3b48, Saskatoon, SK, S7N 5A9
(306) 966-4762
Emp Here 37

SIC 8221 Colleges and universities

D-U-N-S 20-347-1453 (BR)
UNIVERSITY OF SASKATCHEWAN
DEPT OF CIVIL, GEOLOGICAL AND ENVIRONMENTAL ENGINEERING
(Suby of University of Saskatchewan)
57 Campus Dr Rm 3b48.3, Saskatoon, SK, S7N 5A9
(306) 966-5336
Emp Here 54
SIC 8221 Colleges and universities

D-U-N-S 20-010-7170 (BR)
UNIVERSITY OF SASKATCHEWAN
DEPT OF VETERINARY PATHOLOGY
(Suby of University of Saskatchewan)
52 Campus Dr Suite 1622, Saskatoon, SK, S7N 5B4
(306) 966-7334
Emp Here 64
SIC 8221 Colleges and universities

D-U-N-S 20-657-8403 (SL)
USASK SMALL ANIMAL CLINICAL STUD
52 Campus Dr, Saskatoon, SK, S7N 5B4
(306) 966-7068
Emp Here 49   Sales 7,727,098
SIC 8699 Membership organizations, nec
Dir Jenn Molley

D-U-N-S 25-294-8187 (BR)
WAL-MART CANADA CORP
1706 Preston Ave N Suite 3084, Saskatoon, SK, S7N 4Y1
(306) 373-2300
Emp Here 150
SIC 5311 Department stores

Saskatoon, SK S7P

D-U-N-S 25-681-7776 (BR)
ACKLANDS - GRAINGER INC
INDUSTRIAL DIVISION
(Suby of W.W. Grainger, Inc.)
3602 Millar Ave, Saskatoon, SK, S7P 0B1
(306) 664-5500
Emp Here 100
SIC 5085 Industrial supplies

D-U-N-S 24-718-6190 (BR)
AKZO NOBEL CHEMICALS LTD
3910 Wanuskewin Rd, Saskatoon, SK, S7P 0B7
(306) 242-3855
Emp Here 30
SIC 2869 Industrial organic chemicals, nec

D-U-N-S 25-101-7240 (HQ)
APPLIED INDUSTRIAL TECHNOLOGIES, LP
A I T
(Suby of Applied Industrial Technologies, Inc.)
143 Wheeler St, Saskatoon, SK, S7P 0A4
(306) 931-0888
Emp Here 25   Emp Total 5,569
Sales 138,167,035
SIC 5085 Industrial supplies
Dir Peter Wallace
Pr Ron Sowinski
VP Fin Mark Eisele
 Thomas Armold
Dir Benjamin Mondics
 Neil Schrimsher

D-U-N-S 25-238-4818 (BR)
CWS LOGISTICS LTD
(Suby of CWS Logistics Ltd)
115 Marquis Crt, Saskatoon, SK, S7P 0C4
(306) 384-9696
Emp Here 24
SIC 4225 General warehousing and storage

D-U-N-S 24-233-1510 (BR)
ECCO HEATING PRODUCTS LTD

ECCO SUPPLY
311 70th St E, Saskatoon, SK, S7P 0E1
(306) 242-5525
Emp Here 38
SIC 5075 Warm air heating and air conditioning

D-U-N-S 20-012-4100 (BR)
HARRIS STEEL ULC
(*Suby of* Nucor Corporation)
3810 Wanuskewin Rd, Saskatoon, SK, S7P 0B7
(306) 242-8455
Emp Here 30
SIC 3449 Miscellaneous Metalwork

D-U-N-S 24-916-0094 (HQ)
HYFLEX ASSEMBLIES LTD
3711 Mitchelmore Ave, Saskatoon, SK, S7P 0C5
(306) 934-8886
Emp Here 38   *Emp Total* 200
Sales 3,939,878
SIC 5251 Hardware stores

D-U-N-S 24-040-6798 (BR)
MOTION INDUSTRIES (CANADA), INC
COMMERCIAL SOLUTIONS
(*Suby of* Genuine Parts Company)
40 3903 Arthur Rose Ave, Saskatoon, SK, S7P 0C8
(306) 931-7771
Emp Here 20
SIC 5085 Industrial supplies

D-U-N-S 20-841-0241 (SL)
NORAC SYSTEMS INTERNATIONAL INC
3702 Kinnear Pl, Saskatoon, SK, S7P 0A6
(306) 664-6711
Emp Here 50   *Sales* 3,866,917
SIC 3625 Relays and industrial controls

D-U-N-S 24-678-5781 (BR)
NORSEMAN INC
NORSEMAN STRUCTURES DIV.
3815 Wanuskewin Rd, Saskatoon, SK, S7P 1A4
(306) 385-2888
Emp Here 114
SIC 3448 Prefabricated Metal buildings and components

D-U-N-S 24-916-0854 (BR)
SASKATCHEWAN ASSOCIATION OF REHABILITATION CENTRES
SARCAN RECYCLING
(*Suby of* Saskatchewan Association of Rehabilitation Centres)
3720 Kochar Ave, Saskatoon, SK, S7P 0C2
(306) 934-8879
Emp Here 40
SIC 4953 Refuse systems

D-U-N-S 20-303-3964 (BR)
VICWEST INC
(*Suby of* Vicwest Inc)
3542 Millar Ave, Saskatoon, SK, S7P 0B6
(306) 664-8420
Emp Here 30
SIC 5039 Construction materials, nec

Saskatoon, SK S7R

D-U-N-S 24-692-2541 (BR)
AG GROWTH INTERNATIONAL INC
AGI
201 Industrial Drive, Saskatoon, SK, S7R 0H4
(306) 934-0611
Emp Here 30
SIC 3496 Miscellaneous fabricated wire products

D-U-N-S 24-717-4196 (SL)
BECKER UNDERWOOD CANADA LTD
BECKER UNDERWOOD

3835 Thatcher Ave, Saskatoon, SK, S7R 1A3
(306) 373-3060
Emp Here 31   *Sales* 4,815,406
SIC 2874 Phosphatic fertilizers

D-U-N-S 20-794-9475 (BR)
COSTCO WHOLESALE CANADA LTD
COSTCO
(*Suby of* Costco Wholesale Corporation)
115 Marquis Dr W, Saskatoon, SK, S7R 1C7
(306) 933-4262
Emp Here 275
SIC 5099 Durable goods, nec

D-U-N-S 24-519-5326 (SL)
DAIRYLAND AGRO SUPPLY LTD
4030 Thatcher Ave, Saskatoon, SK, S7R 1A2
(306) 242-5850
Emp Here 45   *Sales* 9,776,734
SIC 5083 Farm and garden machinery
Pr Pr Ronald Elder
 Gwen Elder

D-U-N-S 20-108-3222 (BR)
RIDSDALE TRANSPORT LTD
210 Apex St, Saskatoon, SK, S7R 0A2
(306) 931-1138
Emp Here 30
SIC 4231 Trucking terminal facilities

D-U-N-S 20-105-5618 (BR)
SAPUTO INC
122 Wakooma St, Saskatoon, SK, S7R 1A8
(306) 668-6833
Emp Here 250
SIC 2023 Dry, condensed and evaporated dairy products

D-U-N-S 20-112-8670 (BR)
WESTCAN BULK TRANSPORT LTD
(*Suby of* The Kenan Advantage Group Inc)
110 71st St W, Saskatoon, SK, S7R 1A1
(306) 242-5899
Emp Here 100
SIC 4213 Trucking, except local

D-U-N-S 24-915-2216 (BR)
WESTERN FOOD SERVICES LTD
WESTERN CONCESSIONS, DIV OF
(*Suby of* Western Food Services Ltd)
3515 Thatcher Ave Suite 301, Saskatoon, SK, S7R 1C4
(306) 242-2912
Emp Here 60
SIC 5812 Eating places

Saskatoon, SK S7S

D-U-N-S 24-132-1061 (BR)
BOARD OF EDUCATION OF SASKATOON SCHOOL DIVISION NO. 13 OF SASKATCHEWAN, THE
CENTENNIAL COLLEGIATE
160 Nelson Rd, Saskatoon, SK, S7S 1P5
(306) 683-7950
Emp Here 70
SIC 8211 Elementary and secondary schools

D-U-N-S 25-636-5941 (BR)
CO-OPERATORS GROUP LIMITED, THE
407 Ludlow St Suite 101, Saskatoon, SK, S7S 1P3
(306) 934-7317
Emp Here 20
SIC 6331 Fire, marine, and casualty insurance

D-U-N-S 24-821-6041 (BR)
DOLLARAMA S.E.C.
DOLLARAMA
513 Nelson Rd, Saskatoon, SK, S7S 1P4
(306) 651-1265
Emp Here 25
SIC 5331 Variety stores

D-U-N-S 24-683-5008 (BR)

INVESTORS GROUP FINANCIAL SERVICES INC
1848 Mcormond Dr Suite 102, Saskatoon, SK, S7S 0A5
(306) 653-3920
Emp Here 30
SIC 8741 Management services

D-U-N-S 20-712-7718 (BR)
ST. PAUL'S ROMAN CATHOLIC SEPARATE SCHOOL DIVISION NO 20
MOTHER THERESA SCHOOL
738 Konihowski Rd, Saskatoon, SK, S7S 1M4
(306) 659-7240
Emp Here 50
SIC 8211 Elementary and secondary schools

D-U-N-S 20-712-7700 (BR)
ST. PAUL'S ROMAN CATHOLIC SEPARATE SCHOOL DIVISION NO 20
ST JOSEPH HIGH SCHOOL
115 Nelson Rd, Saskatoon, SK, S7S 1H1
(306) 659-7650
Emp Here 90
SIC 8211 Elementary and secondary schools

Saskatoon, SK S7T

D-U-N-S 24-883-3824 (SL)
CIRCLE DRIVE SPECIAL CARE HOME INC
3055 Preston Ave, Saskatoon, SK, S7T 1C3
(306) 955-4800
Emp Here 80   *Sales* 3,793,956
SIC 8051 Skilled nursing care facilities

D-U-N-S 20-407-7788 (BR)
CO-OP SASKATOON STONEBRID
106 Stonebridge Blvd, Saskatoon, SK, S7T 0J1
(306) 933-0306
Emp Here 40   *Sales* 5,630,632
SIC 5411 Grocery stores

D-U-N-S 24-390-5895 (BR)
GOLF TOWN LIMITED
GOLF TOWN
3015 Clarence Ave S Unit 110, Saskatoon, SK, S7T 0B4
(306) 652-4571
Emp Here 20
SIC 5941 Sporting goods and bicycle shops

D-U-N-S 24-350-3450 (BR)
HOME DEPOT OF CANADA INC
(*Suby of* The Home Depot Inc)
3043 Clarence Ave S Suite 1, Saskatoon, SK, S7T 0B5
(306) 657-4100
Emp Here 100
SIC 5251 Hardware stores

D-U-N-S 25-315-8083 (BR)
INVESTORS GROUP FINANCIAL SERVICES INC
203 Stonebridge Blvd Suite 300, Saskatoon, SK, S7T 0G3
(306) 955-9190
Emp Here 50
SIC 6799 Investors, nec

D-U-N-S 25-499-2217 (BR)
MICROSEMI STORAGE SOLUTIONS LTD
510 Cope Way Unit 230, Saskatoon, SK, S7T 0G3
(306) 651-4700
Emp Here 33
SIC 3674 Semiconductors and related devices

D-U-N-S 20-165-4543 (BR)
WSP CANADA INC
WSP
203 Wellman Cres, Saskatoon, SK, S7T 0J1
(306) 665-6223
Emp Here 35
SIC 8711 Engineering services

D-U-N-S 24-330-0543 (BR)
WAL-MART CANADA CORP
3035 Clarence Ave S, Saskatoon, SK, S7T 0B6
(306) 653-8200
Emp Here 200
SIC 5311 Department stores

Saskatoon, SK S7V

D-U-N-S 25-363-0198 (BR)
LOBLAWS INC
EXTRA FOODS
315 Herold Rd, Saskatoon, SK, S7V 1J7
(306) 664-5033
Emp Here 100
SIC 5411 Grocery stores

D-U-N-S 20-311-9953 (SL)
TC GREEN TRADING INC
739 Bayview Close, Saskatoon, SK, S7V 1B7
(306) 612-3339
Emp Here 22   *Sales* 6,184,080
SIC 5033 Roofing, siding, and insulation
Pr Ken Foord

Saskatoon, SK S7W

D-U-N-S 20-285-0178 (BR)
MICHELS CANADA CO
(*Suby of* Michels Corporation)
100 Mcormond Dr, Saskatoon, SK, S7W 0H4
(306)
Emp Here 40
SIC 1381 Drilling oil and gas wells

Shaunavon, SK S0N

D-U-N-S 24-971-6291 (BR)
CHINOOK SCHOOL DIVISION NO 211
SHAUNAVON HIGH SCHOOL
(*Suby of* Chinook School Division No 211)
301 7th Ave W, Shaunavon, SK, S0N 2M0
(306) 297-2733
Emp Here 20
SIC 8211 Elementary and secondary schools

D-U-N-S 20-712-8641 (BR)
CHINOOK SCHOOL DIVISION NO 211
SHAUNAVON PUBLIC SCHOOL
(*Suby of* Chinook School Division No 211)
Gd, Shaunavon, SK, S0N 2M0
(306) 297-2751
Emp Here 50
SIC 8211 Elementary and secondary schools

D-U-N-S 20-793-3180 (BR)
SHAUNAVON CO-OPERATIVE ASSOCIATION LIMITED
HOME & AGRO
591 3rd St W, Shaunavon, SK, S0N 2M0
(306) 297-2663
Emp Here 40
SIC 5411 Grocery stores

Shellbrook, SK S0J

D-U-N-S 24-389-3380 (BR)
AFFINITY CREDIT UNION
31 Main St, Shellbrook, SK, S0J 2E0
(306) 934-4000
Emp Here 25
SIC 6062 State credit unions

D-U-N-S 24-371-2531 (SL)
HANNIGAN'S HONEY INC

Gd, Shellbrook, SK, S0J 2E0
(306) 747-7782
Emp Here 35   *Sales* 5,034,288
SIC 5149 Groceries and related products, nec
Pr Murray Hannigan
VP VP Ruby Hannigan

D-U-N-S 20-065-9345   (BR)
PARKLAND SCHOOL DIVISION NO. 70
W P SANDIN
110 4 St E, Shellbrook, SK, S0J 2E0
(306) 747-2191
Emp Here 30
SIC 8211 Elementary and secondary schools

Simmie, SK S0N

D-U-N-S 20-712-8625   (BR)
CHINOOK SCHOOL DIVISION NO 211
SIMMIE HUTTERIAN SCHOOL
(*Suby* of Chinook School Division No 211)
Gd, Simmie, SK, S0N 2N0
(306) 297-3387
Emp Here 50
SIC 8211 Elementary and secondary schools

Sintaluta, SK S0G

D-U-N-S 20-287-1468   (SL)
CARRY THE KETTLE HEALTH ADMINIS-TRATION
Carry The Kettle Indian Rsv, Sintaluta, SK, S0G 4N0
(306) 727-2101
Emp Here 27   *Sales* 9,029,050
SIC 8399 Social services, nec
Dir Jeff Eashappie

Spiritwood, SK S0J

D-U-N-S 20-535-6715   (BR)
LIVING SKY SCHOOL DIVISION NO. 202
SPIRITWOOD HIGH SCHOOL
216 4th St W, Spiritwood, SK, S0J 2M0
(306) 883-2282
Emp Here 26
SIC 8211 Elementary and secondary schools

D-U-N-S 20-731-8036   (BR)
PRINCE ALBERT PARKLAND REGIONAL HEALTH AUTHORITY
SPIRITWOOD AND DISTRICT HOUSE COM-PLEX
400 1st St E, Spiritwood, SK, S0J 2M0
(306) 883-2133
Emp Here 100
SIC 8051 Skilled nursing care facilities

St Brieux, SK S0K

D-U-N-S 20-647-1133   (BR)
BOURGAULT INDUSTRIES LTD
PRECISION PROFILES PLUS
501 Barbier Dr, St Brieux, SK, S0K 3V0
(306) 275-4800
Emp Here 100
SIC 1761 Roofing, siding, and sheetMetal work

D-U-N-S 25-678-2996   (BR)
WAPITI REGIONAL LIBRARY
ST. BRIEUX PUBLIC LIBRARY
503 3rd Ave, St Brieux, SK, S0K 3V0
(306) 275-2133
Emp Here 25

SIC 8231 Libraries

St Isidore De Bellevue, SK S0K

D-U-N-S 24-371-9015   (BR)
CONSEIL DES ECOLES FRANSASKOISES
ECOLE ST-ISIDORE
Gd, St Isidore De Bellevue, SK, S0K 3Y0
(306) 423-5354
Emp Here 20
SIC 8211 Elementary and secondary schools

St Louis, SK S0J

D-U-N-S 20-713-0027   (BR)
HORIZON SCHOOL DIVISION NO 205
ST LOUIS PUBLIC HIGH SCHOOL
205 2nd St, St Louis, SK, S0J 2C0
(306) 422-8511
Emp Here 25
SIC 8211 Elementary and secondary schools

D-U-N-S 20-656-6783   (BR)
SASKATCHEWAN RIVER SCHOOL DIVI-SION #119
ST LOUIS PUBLIC SCHOOL
167 2nd St, St Louis, SK, S0J 2C0
(306) 422-8511
Emp Here 21
SIC 8211 Elementary and secondary schools

St Walburg, SK S0M

D-U-N-S 24-343-2791   (BR)
NORTHWEST SCHOOL DIVISION 203
ST. WALBURG SCHOOL
Gd, St Walburg, SK, S0M 2T0
(306) 248-3602
Emp Here 50
SIC 8211 Elementary and secondary schools

D-U-N-S 20-735-1805   (BR)
PRAIRIE NORTH REGIONAL HEALTH AU-THORITY
ST WALBURG HEALTH COMPLEX
(*Suby* of Prairie North Regional Health Authority)
410 3 Ave W, St Walburg, SK, S0M 2T0
(306) 248-3355
Emp Here 65
SIC 8099 Health and allied services, nec

Stoughton, SK S0G

D-U-N-S 20-712-8807   (BR)
SOUTH EAST CORNERSTONE SCHOOL DIVISION NO. 209
STOUGHTON SCHOOL
(*Suby* of South East Cornerstone School Division No. 209)
101 Government Rd, Stoughton, SK, S0G 4T0
(306) 457-2533
Emp Here 20
SIC 8211 Elementary and secondary schools

Strasbourg, SK S0G

D-U-N-S 20-642-5725   (BR)
HORIZON SCHOOL DIVISION NO 205
WILLIAM DERBY SCHOOL
321 Mountain St, Strasbourg, SK, S0G 4V0

---

(306) 725-3441
Emp Here 35
SIC 8211 Elementary and secondary schools

Swift Current, SK S9H

D-U-N-S 24-312-3275   (SL)
101084058 SASKATCHEWAN LTD
2180 Oman Dr, Swift Current, SK, S9H 3X4
(306) 773-0644
Emp Here 200   *Sales* 32,490,960
SIC 3523 Farm machinery and equipment
Pr Pr Frank Rempel
Dir Helen Rempel

D-U-N-S 20-840-2268   (BR)
BIG COUNTRY ENERGY SERVICES LIM-ITED PARTNERSHIP
2105 North Service Rd W, Swift Current, SK, S9H 5K9
(306) 778-1500
Emp Here 20
SIC 1623 Water, sewer, and utility lines

D-U-N-S 25-119-6077   (SL)
BOSTON PIZZA #209
1601 North Service Rd E, Swift Current, SK, S9H 3X6
(306) 778-7666
Emp Here 60   *Sales* 1,824,018
SIC 5812 Eating places

D-U-N-S 25-191-6078   (SL)
CAN-AM GEOMATICS SASK CORP
15 Dufferin St W, Swift Current, SK, S9H 5A1
(306) 773-3333
Emp Here 20   *Sales* 1,751,057
SIC 8713 Surveying services

D-U-N-S 24-340-6605   (HQ)
CHINOOK SCHOOL DIVISION NO 211
(*Suby* of Chinook School Division No 211)
2100 Gladstone St E, Swift Current, SK, S9H 3W7
(306) 778-9200
Emp Here 20   *Emp Total* 1,000
Sales 86,317,336
SIC 8211 Elementary and secondary schools
Ch Bd Gary Shaddock

D-U-N-S 20-712-6728   (BR)
CHINOOK SCHOOL DIVISION NO 211
(*Suby* of Chinook School Division No 211)
520 6th Ave Se, Swift Current, SK, S9H 3P6

Emp Here 50
SIC 8211 Elementary and secondary schools

D-U-N-S 20-325-1400   (BR)
CRESCENT POINT ENERGY CORP
330 Central Ave N Suite 220, Swift Current, SK, S9H 0L4
(306) 294-7002
Emp Here 60
SIC 1311 Crude petroleum and natural gas

D-U-N-S 24-346-3382   (BR)
CYPRESS HEALTH REGION
PALLISER REGIONAL CARE CENTRE
440 Central Ave S, Swift Current, SK, S9H 3G6

Emp Here 200
SIC 8361 Residential care

D-U-N-S 24-804-6117   (BR)
CYPRESS HEALTH REGION
CYPRESS REGIONAL HOSPITAL
2004 Saskatchewan Dr, Swift Current, SK, S9H 5M8
(306) 778-9400
Emp Here 100
SIC 8062 General medical and surgical hospitals

D-U-N-S 25-483-1779   (BR)

DUBE MANAGEMENT LTD
PIZZA HUT
(*Suby* of Concorde Group Corp)
1121 6th Ave Ne, Swift Current, SK, S9H 4S1
(306) 778-4840
Emp Here 21
SIC 5812 Eating places

D-U-N-S 25-386-2957   (SL)
DURA PRODUCTS INC
(*Suby* of Now Inc.)
506 Fenton'S Cres, Swift Current, SK, S9H 4G6
(306) 773-0627
Emp Here 25   *Sales* 547,205
SIC 3561 Pumps and pumping equipment

D-U-N-S 24-947-5323   (SL)
DYNAMIC HEAVY HAUL LTD
301514 W 3, Swift Current, SK, S9H 3W8
(306) 773-8611
Emp Here 30   *Sales* 22,617,817
SIC 1382 Oil and gas exploration services
Dir Eric Eckert

D-U-N-S 25-963-2396   (SL)
ELMWOOD GOLF CLUB INC
2015 Hillcrest Dr, Swift Current, SK, S9H 3V8
(306) 773-9500
Emp Here 55   *Sales* 2,334,742
SIC 7992 Public golf courses

D-U-N-S 24-428-7769   (BR)
GOLDEN WEST BROADCASTING LTD
94.1 FM
134 Central Ave N, Swift Current, SK, S9H 0L1
(306) 773-4605
Emp Here 30
SIC 4832 Radio broadcasting stations

D-U-N-S 24-916-6521   (BR)
GOLDEN WEST BROADCASTING LTD
CIMG THE EAGLE 94.1 FM
134 Central Ave N, Swift Current, SK, S9H 0L1

Emp Here 25
SIC 4832 Radio broadcasting stations

D-U-N-S 20-712-7775   (BR)
HOLY TRINITY ROMAN CATHOLIC SEPA-RATE SCHOOL DIVISION #22
ST PATRICK SCHOOL
751 Lorne St W, Swift Current, SK, S9H 0J7

Emp Here 30
SIC 8211 Elementary and secondary schools

D-U-N-S 25-315-2391   (BR)
KINDERSLEY TRANSPORT LTD
KINDERSLEY TRANSPORT A M DELIVER-IES
(*Suby* of EKS Holdings Ltd)
910 North Railway St W, Swift Current, SK, S9H 0A3
(306) 778-3683
Emp Here 20
SIC 4213 Trucking, except local

D-U-N-S 25-000-7671   (BR)
LOBLAWS INC
REAL CANADIAN WHOLESALE CLUB, THE
1501 North Service Rd E, Swift Current, SK, S9H 3X6
(306) 778-5640
Emp Here 62
SIC 5141 Groceries, general line

D-U-N-S 25-273-0627   (BR)
MNP LLP
50 1st Ave Ne, Swift Current, SK, S9H 4W4
(306) 773-8375
Emp Here 50
SIC 8721 Accounting, auditing, and book-keeping

D-U-N-S 20-651-9154   (BR)
MEDIAS TRANSCONTINENTAL INC
MEDIAS TRANSCONTINENTAL INC
30 4th Ave Nw, Swift Current, SK, S9H 0T5

---

(306) 773-9321
Emp Here 25
SIC 2711 Newspapers

D-U-N-S 20-913-8986   (BR)
PEAVEY INDUSTRIES LIMITED
PEAVEY MART
1150 Central Ave N Suite 1005, Swift Current,
SK, S9H 4C8
(306) 773-9558
Emp Here 20
SIC 5251 Hardware stores

D-U-N-S 25-384-5473   (SL)
PEL INDUSTRIES LTD
2180 Oman Dr, Swift Current, SK, S9H 3X4
(306) 773-0644
Emp Here 69   *Sales* 11,190,240
SIC 3523 Farm machinery and equipment
Pr Pr Frank Rempel

D-U-N-S 20-192-2692   (BR)
**PIONEER CO-OPERATIVE ASSOCIATION
LIMITED, THE**
PIONEER CO-OP AGRO CENTER
1150 Central Ave N Suite 2000, Swift Current,
SK, S9H 0G1
(306) 778-8876
Emp Here 20
SIC 5999 Miscellaneous retail stores, nec

D-U-N-S 24-886-6928   (BR)
PLAINS MIDSTREAM CANADA ULC
Gd Lcd Main, Swift Current, SK, S9H 3V4
(306) 773-9381
Emp Here 500
SIC 4612 Crude petroleum pipelines

D-U-N-S 24-040-1794   (BR)
REDHEAD EQUIPMENT
2604 South Service Rd W, Swift Current, SK,
S9H 5J9
(306) 773-2951
Emp Here 42
SIC 5084 Industrial machinery and equipment

D-U-N-S 25-451-2114   (BR)
ROYAL BANK OF CANADA
RBC
(*Suby of* Royal Bank Of Canada)
261 1st Ave Nw, Swift Current, SK, S9H 0N1
(306) 778-4100
Emp Here 30
SIC 6021 National commercial banks

D-U-N-S 24-231-7758   (BR)
SAM'S GENERAL TRUCKING LTD
1433 North Railway St W, Swift Current, SK,
S9H 4K5

Emp Here 20
SIC 1389 Oil and gas field services, nec

D-U-N-S 24-114-8720   (BR)
SASKENERGY INCORPORATED
Gd Lcd Main, Swift Current, SK, S9H 3V4
(306) 778-4166
Emp Here 25
SIC 4924 Natural gas distribution

D-U-N-S 25-481-3223   (BR)
SASKATCHEWAN ABILITIES COUNCIL INC
1551 North Railway St W, Swift Current, SK,
S9H 5G3
(306) 773-2076
Emp Here 93
SIC 8331 Job training and related services

D-U-N-S 20-519-0940   (BR)
**SASKATCHEWAN CROP INSURANCE
CORPORATION**
350 Cheadle St W, Swift Current, SK, S9H
4G3
(888) 935-0007
Emp Here 20
SIC 6331 Fire, marine, and casualty insurance

D-U-N-S 25-315-2417   (BR)
**SASKATCHEWAN GOVERNMENT INSUR-
ANCE**

SGI
110 3rd Ave Nw, Swift Current, SK, S9H 0R8
(306) 778-4900
Emp Here 20
SIC 6331 Fire, marine, and casualty insurance

D-U-N-S 24-344-8466   (BR)
SASKATCHEWAN POWER CORPORATION
SASKPOWER
1800 Aberdeen St, Swift Current, SK, S9H
3W4
(306) 778-7510
Emp Here 50
SIC 4911 Electric services

D-U-N-S 25-060-6472   (BR)
SMITTY'S CANADA LIMITED
CYPRESS INVESTMENT
105 North Service Rd E, Swift Current, SK,
S9H 3T4
(306) 773-5353
Emp Here 30
SIC 5812 Eating places

D-U-N-S 25-271-7475   (BR)
SOBEYS WEST INC
SWIFT CURRENT SAFEWAY
1 Springs Dr, Swift Current, SK, S9H 3X6
(306) 773-6325
Emp Here 60
SIC 5411 Grocery stores

D-U-N-S 20-656-5405   (SL)
SWIFT CURRENT CARE CENTRE
700 Aberdeen St Suite 22, Swift Current, SK,
S9H 3E3

Emp Here 80   *Sales* 3,648,035
SIC 8051 Skilled nursing care facilities

D-U-N-S 25-144-8288   (BR)
SWIFT CURRENT, CITY OF
CHINOOK GOLF COURSE
663 6th Ave Se, Swift Current, SK, S9H 3P5
(306) 778-2776
Emp Here 20
SIC 7992 Public golf courses

D-U-N-S 20-315-9827   (BR)
TARPON ENERGY SERVICES LTD
2071 Sidney St W, Swift Current, SK, S9H 5K3
(306) 773-8237
Emp Here 30
SIC 1389 Oil and gas field services, nec

D-U-N-S 25-270-7997   (BR)
VITERRA INC
AGRICORE UNITED
2200 North Railway St W, Swift Current, SK,
S9H 5H9
(306) 773-6425
Emp Here 25
SIC 4221 Farm product warehousing and stor-
age

D-U-N-S 25-294-8708   (BR)
WAL-MART CANADA CORP
1800 22nd Ave Ne, Swift Current, SK, S9H
0E5
(306) 778-3489
Emp Here 140
SIC 5311 Department stores

Tisdale, SK S0E

D-U-N-S 20-071-5399   (HQ)
**BEELAND CO-OPERATIVE ASSOCIATION
LIMITED**
(*Suby of* Beeland Co-operative Association
Limited)
1101 99 St, Tisdale, SK, S0E 1T0
(306) 873-2688
Emp Here 81   *Emp Total* 85
Sales 29,748,983
SIC 5171 Petroleum bulk stations and termi-

nals
Genl Mgr Todd Svenson
Fin Ex Linda Alvis
Dir Robert Haller
Dir Gary Rice
Dir Bj Madsen
Dir Evelyn Keays
Dir Dianne Wallington
Dir Lorne Luck
Dir Christina Friske
Dir Barry Thesen

D-U-N-S 24-346-3390   (BR)
**KELSEY TRAIL REGIONAL HEALTH AU-
THORITY**
TISDALE HOSPITAL
(*Suby of* Kelsey Trail Regional Health Author-
ity)
Gd, Tisdale, SK, S0E 1T0

Emp Here 200
SIC 8062 General medical and surgical hospitals

D-U-N-S 20-068-2099   (HQ)
**KELSEY TRAIL REGIONAL HEALTH AU-
THORITY**
(*Suby of* Kelsey Trail Regional Health Author-
ity)
Gd, Tisdale, SK, S0E 1T0
(306) 873-6600
Emp Here 50   *Emp Total* 200
Sales 17,998,484
SIC 8062 General medical and surgical hospi-
tals
Ch Bd Jim Taylor

D-U-N-S 24-347-7309   (BR)
NORTH EAST SCHOOL DIVISION
TISDALE MIDDLE & SECONDARY SCHOOL
800 101st St, Tisdale, SK, S0E 1T0
(306) 873-2352
Emp Here 67
SIC 8211 Elementary and secondary schools

D-U-N-S 24-347-7291   (BR)
NORTH EAST SCHOOL DIVISION
TISDALE ELEMENTARY SCHOOL
513 105th Ave, Tisdale, SK, S0E 1T0
(306) 873-4533
Emp Here 42
SIC 8211 Elementary and secondary schools

D-U-N-S 20-152-7053   (SL)
PASQUIA PUBLISHING LTD
1004 102 Ave, Tisdale, SK, S0E 1T0
(306) 873-4515
Emp Here 20   *Sales* 1,678,096
SIC 2711 Newspapers

Turtleford, SK S0M

D-U-N-S 24-343-2916   (BR)
NORTHWEST SCHOOL DIVISION 203
FACILITIES & TRANPORTATION, DIV OF
Gd, Turtleford, SK, S0M 2Y0
(306) 845-2150
Emp Here 20
SIC 4173 Bus terminal and service facilities

D-U-N-S 24-628-7713   (BR)
NORTHWEST SCHOOL DIVISION 203
TURTLEFORD SCHOOL
336 Birk St, Turtleford, SK, S0M 2Y0
(306) 845-2079
Emp Here 40
SIC 8211 Elementary and secondary schools

D-U-N-S 24-773-0083   (BR)
**PRAIRIE NORTH REGIONAL HEALTH AU-
THORITY**
RIVERSIDE HEALTH COMPLEX
(*Suby of* Prairie North Regional Health Au-
thority)
1st Street South Highway 303, Turtleford, SK,

S0M 2Y0
(306) 845-2195
Emp Here 60
SIC 8062 General medical and surgical hospitals

Unity, SK S0K

D-U-N-S 25-593-4986   (BR)
COMPASS MINERALS CANADA CORP
(*Suby of* Compass Minerals International,
Inc.)
Hwy 14th E, Unity, SK, S0K 4L0
(306) 228-2641
Emp Here 55
SIC 1479 Chemical and fertilizer mining

D-U-N-S 25-268-8940   (BR)
LIVING SKY SCHOOL DIVISION NO. 202
UNITY COMPOSITE HIGH SCHOOL
300 3rd Ave E, Unity, SK, S0K 4L0
(306) 228-2657
Emp Here 38
SIC 8211 Elementary and secondary schools

D-U-N-S 24-949-3631   (BR)
PATTISON AGRICULTURE LIMITED
(*Suby of* Pattison Agriculture Limited)
Highway 14 W, Unity, SK, S0K 4L0
(306) 228-2696
Emp Here 24
SIC 5999 Miscellaneous retail stores, nec

D-U-N-S 25-453-1973   (BR)
TRANSGAS LIMITED
Gd, Unity, SK, S0K 4L0
(306) 228-7200
Emp Here 22
SIC 4923 Gas transmission and distribution

Val Marie, SK S0N

D-U-N-S 20-032-4171   (BR)
**ENVIRONMENT AND CLIMATE CHANGE
CANADA**
*GRASSLANDS NATIONAL PARK OF
CANADA*
101 Center St, Val Marie, SK, S0N 2T0
(306) 298-2257
Emp Here 45
SIC 7996 Amusement parks

D-U-N-S 20-757-2223   (SL)
SAND LAKE HUTTERIAN BRETHREN
Gd, Val Marie, SK, S0N 2T0
(306) 298-2068
Emp Here 80   *Sales* 4,012,839
SIC 7389 Business services, nec

Vanscoy, SK S0L

D-U-N-S 20-446-9050   (BR)
AGRIUM INC
(*Suby of* Agrium Canada Partnership)
16 Agrium Rd, Vanscoy, SK, S0L 3J0
(306) 668-4343
Emp Here 600
SIC 1474 Potash, soda, and borate minerals

D-U-N-S 20-039-2137   (BR)
AGRIUM INC
AGRIUM VANSCOY POTASH OPERATIONS
(*Suby of* Agrium Canada Partnership)
Gd, Vanscoy, SK, S0L 3J0
(306) 683-1280
Emp Here 400
SIC 1011 Iron ores

D-U-N-S 20-034-4195   (BR)

▲ Public Company   ■ Public Company Family Member   **HQ** Headquarters   **BR** Branch   **SL** Single Location

PRAIRIE SPIRIT SCHOOL DIVISION
VANSCOY SCHOOL
309 Main St, Vanscoy, SK, S0L 3J0
(306) 668-2056
Emp Here 22
SIC 8211 Elementary and secondary schools

Vonda, SK S0K

D-U-N-S 20-033-2554   (BR)
CONSEIL DES ECOLES FRANSASKOISES
ECOLE PROVIDENCE
316 Main St, Vonda, SK, S0K 4N0
(306) 258-2181
Emp Here 20
SIC 8211 Elementary and secondary schools

Wadena, SK S0A

D-U-N-S 20-033-2646   (BR)
HORIZON SCHOOL DIVISION NO 205
WADENA ELEMENTARY SCHOOL
318 Main St N, Wadena, SK, S0A 4J0
(306) 338-2455
Emp Here 22
SIC 8211 Elementary and secondary schools

D-U-N-S 24-188-7558   (BR)
HORIZON SCHOOL DIVISION NO 205
WADENA SCHOOL
621 6th St Ne, Wadena, SK, S0A 4J0
(306) 338-2235
Emp Here 20
SIC 8211 Elementary and secondary schools

Wakaw, SK S0K

D-U-N-S 20-567-6534   (BR)
ENVIRONMENT AND CLIMATE CHANGE CANADA
PARKS CANADA AGENCY
Gd, Wakaw, SK, S0K 4P0
(306) 423-6227
Emp Here 20
SIC 7999 Amusement and recreation, nec

D-U-N-S 20-656-6817   (BR)
HORIZON SCHOOL DIVISION NO 205
WAKAW SCHOOL
Gd, Wakaw, SK, S0K 4P0
(306) 233-4683
Emp Here 25
SIC 8211 Elementary and secondary schools

D-U-N-S 24-748-5535   (SL)
LAKEVIEW PIONEER LODGE INC
400 1st St N, Wakaw, SK, S0K 4P0
(306) 233-4621
Emp Here 63   *Sales* 2,845,467
SIC 8051 Skilled nursing care facilities

D-U-N-S 24-233-0397   (BR)
SASKATOON REGIONAL HEALTH AUTHORITY
WAKAW HOSPITAL
300 1st St N, Wakaw, SK, S0K 4P0
(306) 233-4611
Emp Here 60
SIC 8062 General medical and surgical hospitals

Waldeck, SK S0H

D-U-N-S 24-347-5477   (BR)
CHINOOK SCHOOL DIVISION NO 211

WALDECK ELEMENTARY
(*Suby of* Chinook School Division No 211)
1 Warrior Way, Waldeck, SK, S0H 4J0

Emp Here 25
SIC 8211 Elementary and secondary schools

Waldheim, SK S0K

D-U-N-S 20-713-0092   (BR)
PRAIRIE SPIRIT SCHOOL DIVISION NO. 206
WALDHEIM SCHOOL
4008 2nd Ave E, Waldheim, SK, S0K 4R0
(306) 945-2211
Emp Here 26
SIC 8211 Elementary and secondary schools

Warman, SK S0K

D-U-N-S 20-044-5414   (SL)
LEGENDS GOLF CLUB INC, THE
WARMAN GOLF CLUB
415 Clubhouse Blvd W, Warman, SK, S0K 4S2
(306) 931-8814
Emp Here 50   *Sales* 2,042,900
SIC 7997 Membership sports and recreation clubs

D-U-N-S 20-713-0043   (BR)
PRAIRIE SPIRIT SCHOOL DIVISION NO. 206
WARMAN ELEMENTARY SCHOOL
403 4th St W, Warman, SK, S0K 4S0
(306) 933-2066
Emp Here 45
SIC 8211 Elementary and secondary schools

D-U-N-S 20-713-0100   (BR)
PRAIRIE SPIRIT SCHOOL DIVISION NO. 206
WARMAN HIGH SCHOOL
201 Central St E, Warman, SK, S0K 4S0
(306) 933-2377
Emp Here 45
SIC 8211 Elementary and secondary schools

D-U-N-S 20-098-1657   (SL)
WARMAN MENNONITE SPECIAL CARE HOME INC
201 Centennial Blvd, Warman, SK, S0K 0A1
(306) 933-2011
Emp Here 55   *Sales* 2,042,900
SIC 8361 Residential care

Watrous, SK S0K

D-U-N-S 25-366-2407   (BR)
AFFINITY CREDIT UNION
210 Main St, Watrous, SK, S0K 4T0
(306) 946-3312
Emp Here 23
SIC 6062 State credit unions

D-U-N-S 24-668-9785   (BR)
CERVUS AG EQUIPMENT LTD
FARM GARDEN CENTRE
406 1 St Ave W, Watrous, SK, S0K 4T0
(306) 946-3362
Emp Here 35
SIC 5999 Miscellaneous retail stores, nec

D-U-N-S 20-712-9359   (BR)
HORIZON SCHOOL DIVISION NO 205
WINSTON HIGH SCHOOL
202 6th Ave E, Watrous, SK, S0K 4T0
(306) 946-3309
Emp Here 22

SIC 8211 Elementary and secondary schools

D-U-N-S 20-037-3343   (BR)
HORIZON SCHOOL DIVISION NO 205
WATROUS ELEMENTARY SCHOOL
602 Main St, Watrous, SK, S0K 4T0
(306) 946-3366
Emp Here 21
SIC 8211 Elementary and secondary schools

D-U-N-S 20-734-9239   (BR)
SASKATOON REGIONAL HEALTH AUTHORITY
NOKOMIS HEALTH CENTER
103 2nd Ave E, Watrous, SK, S0K 4T0
(306) 528-4355
Emp Here 30
SIC 8059 Nursing and personal care, nec

D-U-N-S 24-337-1544   (BR)
SASKATOON REGIONAL HEALTH AUTHORITY
WATROUS HOSPITAL
702 4th St E, Watrous, SK, S0K 4T0
(306) 946-1200
Emp Here 50
SIC 8062 General medical and surgical hospitals

Watson, SK S0K

D-U-N-S 24-655-2566   (SL)
QUILL PLAINS CENTENNIAL LODGE
400 3rd Ave N, Watson, SK, S0K 4V0
(306) 287-3232
Emp Here 80   *Sales* 3,769,316
SIC 8361 Residential care

D-U-N-S 25-329-3419   (BR)
SASKATOON REGIONAL HEALTH AUTHORITY
WATSON COMMUNITY HEALTH CENTRE
402 2nd St Ne, Watson, SK, S0K 4V0
(306) 287-3791
Emp Here 50
SIC 8062 General medical and surgical hospitals

Wawota, SK S0G

D-U-N-S 25-326-0996   (BR)
SUN COUNTRY REGIONAL HEALTH AUTHORITY
DEERVIEW LODGE
201 Wilfred St, Wawota, SK, S0G 5A0
(306) 739-2400
Emp Here 70
SIC 8051 Skilled nursing care facilities

Weyburn, SK S4H

D-U-N-S 25-128-3842   (BR)
GOLDEN WEST BROADCASTING LTD
AM 1190 RADIO STATION
305 Souris Ave, Weyburn, SK, S4H 0C6
(306) 848-1190
Emp Here 20
SIC 7922 Theatrical producers and services

D-U-N-S 20-647-9128   (BR)
MNP LLP
8 4th St Ne, Weyburn, SK, S4H 0X7
(306) 842-8915
Emp Here 25
SIC 8721 Accounting, auditing, and bookkeeping

D-U-N-S 25-999-7372   (SL)
MINARD'S LEISURE WORLD LTD

921 Government Rd S, Weyburn, SK, S4H 3R3
(306) 842-3288
Emp Here 40   *Sales* 9,182,261
SIC 5561 Recreational vehicle dealers

D-U-N-S 20-259-8793   (BR)
PARRISH & HEIMBECKER, LIMITED
WEBURN SIDING GRAIN ELEVATOR
(*Suby of* Parrish & Heimbecker, Limited)
Hwy 39, Weyburn, SK, S4H 2K8
(306) 842-7436
Emp Here 50
SIC 5153 Grain and field beans

D-U-N-S 24-000-0351   (BR)
SASKENERGY INCORPORATED
1835 1st Ave Ne, Weyburn, SK, S4H 0A1
(306) 848-4417
Emp Here 20
SIC 4923 Gas transmission and distribution

D-U-N-S 24-341-9137   (BR)
SOUTH EAST CORNERSTONE SCHOOL DIVISION NO. 209
WEYBURN JR HIGH SCHOOL
(*Suby of* South East Cornerstone School Division No. 209)
600 5th St, Weyburn, SK, S4H 1A1
(306) 842-7474
Emp Here 40
SIC 8211 Elementary and secondary schools

D-U-N-S 20-712-6660   (BR)
SOUTH EAST CORNERSTONE SCHOOL DIVISION NO. 209
WEYBURN COMPREHENSIVE SCHOOL
(*Suby of* South East Cornerstone School Division No. 209)
107 2nd Ave Nw, Weyburn, SK, S4H 1P7
(306) 842-7494
Emp Here 65
SIC 8211 Elementary and secondary schools

D-U-N-S 20-712-6652   (BR)
SOUTH EAST CORNERSTONE SCHOOL DIVISION NO. 209
HAIG SCHOOL
(*Suby of* South East Cornerstone School Division No. 209)
1113 Coteau Ave, Weyburn, SK, S4H 0H5
(306) 842-2812
Emp Here 50
SIC 8211 Elementary and secondary schools

D-U-N-S 25-962-3726   (HQ)
SUN COUNTRY HEALTH REGION
(*Suby of* Sun Country Health Region)
808 Souris Valley Rd, Weyburn, SK, S4H 2Z9
(306) 842-8399
Emp Here 100   *Emp Total* 2,000
Sales 444,733,263
SIC 8099 Health and allied services, nec

D-U-N-S 25-329-3534   (BR)
SUN COUNTRY REGIONAL HEALTH AUTHORITY
WEYBURN GENERAL HOSPITAL IN SCHR
201 1st Ave Ne, Weyburn, SK, S4H 0N1
(306) 842-8400
Emp Here 150
SIC 8062 General medical and surgical hospitals

D-U-N-S 24-317-1811   (BR)
WAL-MART CANADA CORP
WALMART
1000 Sims Ave, Weyburn, SK, S4H 3N9
(306) 842-6030
Emp Here 130
SIC 5311 Department stores

D-U-N-S 24-852-0827   (HQ)
WEYBURN CREDIT UNION LIMITED
(*Suby of* Weyburn Credit Union Limited)
205 Coteau Ave, Weyburn, SK, S4H 0G5

---

(306) 842-6641
Emp Here 67   *Emp Total* 100
Sales 19,493,120
SIC 6062 State credit unions
CEO Don Shumlich

D-U-N-S 20-656-4838   (BR)
WEYBURN, CITY OF
WEYBURN LEISURE CENTER
532 5th St, Weyburn, SK, S4H 1A1
(306) 848-3280
Emp Here 20
SIC 7999 Amusement and recreation, nec

D-U-N-S 24-273-5848   (BR)
YOUNG'S EQUIPMENT INC
350 South Service Rd, Weyburn, SK, S4H 2L2
(306) 842-2629
Emp Here 28
SIC 5083 Farm and garden machinery

White City, SK S4L

D-U-N-S 24-679-8714   (BR)
AECOM CANADA LTD
CARSON WELDING
Highway 1 East 3 North Service Rd, White City, SK, S4L 5B1
(306) 779-2200
Emp Here 100
SIC 1389 Oil and gas field services, nec

D-U-N-S 20-716-8332   (BR)
PRAIRIE VALLEY SCHOOL DIVISION NO 208
WHITE CITY SCHOOL
30 Kingsmere Ave, White City, SK, S4L 5B1
(306) 781-2115
Emp Here 43
SIC 8211 Elementary and secondary schools

Whitewood, SK S0G

D-U-N-S 24-116-3281   (SL)
WHITEWOOD COMMUNITY HEALTH CENTRE
921 Gambetta St, Whitewood, SK, S0G 5C0
(306) 735-2010
Emp Here 60   *Sales* 3,378,379
SIC 8051 Skilled nursing care facilities

Wilkie, SK S0K

D-U-N-S 24-115-5134   (BR)
HEARTLAND REGIONAL HEALTH AUTHORITY
WILKIE & DISTRICT HEALTH CENTRE
304 7th St E, Wilkie, SK, S0K 4W0
(306) 843-2644
Emp Here 90
SIC 8062 General medical and surgical hospitals

D-U-N-S 20-910-2479   (BR)
HEARTLAND REGIONAL HEALTH AUTHORITY
Gd, Wilkie, SK, S0K 4W0
(306) 843-2531
Emp Here 85
SIC 8011 Offices and clinics of medical doctors

D-U-N-S 20-712-9912   (BR)
LIVING SKY SCHOOL DIVISION NO. 202
MCLURG HIGH SCHOOL
202 5th Ave E, Wilkie, SK, S0K 4W0
(306) 843-2288
Emp Here 25
SIC 8211 Elementary and secondary schools

Wolseley, SK S0G

D-U-N-S 25-735-2070   (BR)
REGINA QU'APPELLE REGIONAL HEALTH AUTHORITY
WOLSELEY MEMORIAL UNION HOSPITAL
801 Ouimet St, Wolseley, SK, S0G 5H0
(306) 698-2213
Emp Here 30
SIC 8062 General medical and surgical hospitals

D-U-N-S 20-295-0767   (BR)
REGINA QU'APPELLE REGIONAL HEALTH AUTHORITY
LAKESIDE NURSING HOME
701 Ouimet St, Wolseley, SK, S0G 5H0
(306) 698-4400
Emp Here 120
SIC 8059 Nursing and personal care, nec

Wynyard, SK S0A

D-U-N-S 25-678-8274   (BR)
LILYDALE INC
LILYDALE FOODS
502 Bosworth St, Wynyard, SK, S0A 4T0
(306) 554-2555
Emp Here 400
SIC 2015 Poultry slaughtering and processing

Yorkton, SK S3N

D-U-N-S 25-410-8012   (BR)
324007 ALBERTA LTD
HEARTLAND LIVESTOCK SERVICES
(*Suby of* 400369 Alberta Ltd)
107 York Rd E, Yorkton, SK, S3N 2W4
(306) 783-9437
Emp Here 23
SIC 5154 Livestock

D-U-N-S 25-289-0256   (BR)
CANADA POST CORPORATION
70 Bull Cres, Yorkton, SK, S3N 3W7
(306) 783-4647
Emp Here 30
SIC 4311 U.s. postal service

D-U-N-S 20-712-7791   (BR)
CHRIST THE TEACHER CATHOLIC SCHOOLS DIVISION 212
ST MARY SCHOOL
212 Independent St, Yorkton, SK, S3N 0S8
(306) 782-2889
Emp Here 45
SIC 8211 Elementary and secondary schools

D-U-N-S 25-156-0124   (BR)
CHRIST THE TEACHER CATHOLIC SCHOOLS DIVISION 212
SACRED HEART HIGH SCHOOL
280 Gladstone Ave N, Yorkton, SK, S3N 2A8
(306) 783-3128
Emp Here 40
SIC 8211 Elementary and secondary schools

D-U-N-S 25-156-0082   (BR)
CHRIST THE TEACHER CATHOLIC SCHOOLS DIVISION 212
ST ALPHONSUS SCHOOL
81 Henderson St E, Yorkton, SK, S3N 0A8
(306) 783-4121
Emp Here 30
SIC 8211 Elementary and secondary schools

D-U-N-S 20-712-7809   (BR)
CHRIST THE TEACHER CATHOLIC SCHOOLS DIVISION 212

ST PAUL'S ELEMENTARY SCHOOL
487 Parkview Rd, Yorkton, SK, S3N 2L6
(306) 783-9212
Emp Here 30
SIC 8211 Elementary and secondary schools

D-U-N-S 20-712-7817   (BR)
CHRIST THE TEACHER CATHOLIC SCHOOLS DIVISION 212
ST MICHAELS
407 Darlington St E, Yorkton, SK, S3N 3Y9
(306) 782-4407
Emp Here 37
SIC 8211 Elementary and secondary schools

D-U-N-S 24-497-9977   (SL)
DEDMAN, DAVID PONTIAC BUICK GMC LTD
115 Palliser Way, Yorkton, SK, S3N 4C6
(306) 783-8080
Emp Here 22   *Sales* 11,052,800
SIC 5511 New and used car dealers
Pr Pr David Dedman
 Ronald Dedman

D-U-N-S 25-329-3450   (SL)
EAST CENTRAL DISTRICT HEALTH BOARD
YORKTON REGIONAL HEALTH CENTRE
Po Box 5027 Stn Main, Yorkton, SK, S3N 3Z4
(306) 786-0113
Emp Here 1,400   *Sales* 134,140,800
SIC 8062 General medical and surgical hospitals
Pr James Miller
 Mary Anderson
VP Christina Denysek
Dir David Myall
 Sheriff Rahaman
 Jae K Choi
 Heather Torrie
 Ron Merriman
 Sherryl D Mydonick
Dir Sherrell Fox

D-U-N-S 20-601-3435   (SL)
KEY CHEVROLET CADILLAC LTD
441 Broadway St E, Yorkton, SK, S3N 3G3
(306) 782-2268
Emp Here 37   *Sales* 18,768,250
SIC 5511 New and used car dealers
Pr Pr Evan Ortynsky
Genl Mgr Joel Martinuk

D-U-N-S 25-018-6988   (BR)
MORRIS INDUSTRIES LTD
85 York Rd W, Yorkton, SK, S3N 3P2
(306) 783-8585
Emp Here 150
SIC 3523 Farm machinery and equipment

D-U-N-S 24-327-1272   (BR)
PARKLAND REGIONAL COLLEGE
200 Prystai Way, Yorkton, SK, S3N 4G4
(306) 783-6566
Emp Here 30
SIC 8221 Colleges and universities

D-U-N-S 20-853-2051   (HQ)
PARKLAND REGIONAL LIBRARY
(*Suby of* Parkland Regional Library)
Hwy 52 W, Yorkton, SK, S3N 3Z4
(306) 783-7022
Emp Here 20   *Emp Total* 120
Sales 7,381,120
SIC 8231 Libraries
Ex Dir Deirdre Crischton

D-U-N-S 20-703-8303   (BR)
PREMIUM BRANDS OPERATING LIMITED PARTNERSHIP
HARVEST MEATS
501 York Rd W, Yorkton, SK, S3N 2V6
(306) 783-9446
Emp Here 200
SIC 2011 Meat packing plants

D-U-N-S 24-037-0452   (BR)

REMAI INVESTMENT CORPORATION
TRAVELLODGE YORKTON
(*Suby of* Remai Investment Corporation)
345 Broadway St W, Yorkton, SK, S3N 0N8

Emp Here 50
SIC 7011 Hotels and motels

D-U-N-S 20-232-2900   (BR)
REVERA INC
BENTLEY RETIREMENT COMMUNITY
94 Russell Dr, Yorkton, SK, S3N 3W2
(306) 782-5552
Emp Here 24
SIC 6513 Apartment building operators

D-U-N-S 24-418-0431   (BR)
RICHARDSON OILSEED LIMITED
Hwy 16 3 Miles W, Yorkton, SK, S3N 2W1
(306) 828-2200
Emp Here 70
SIC 2079 Edible fats and oils

D-U-N-S 25-729-2029   (BR)
SASKATCHEWAN ABILITIES COUNCIL INC
162 Ball Rd, Yorkton, SK, S3N 3Z4
(306) 782-2463
Emp Here 65
SIC 8331 Job training and related services

D-U-N-S 25-156-0207   (BR)
SASKATCHEWAN ASSOCIATION OF REHABILITATION CENTRES
SARCAN RECYCLING
(*Suby of* Saskatchewan Association of Rehabilitation Centres)
144 Ball Rd, Yorkton, SK, S3N 3Z4
(306) 782-4213
Emp Here 20
SIC 4953 Refuse systems

D-U-N-S 20-568-1146   (BR)
SASKATCHEWAN CROP INSURANCE CORPORATION
YORKTON CUSTOMER SERVICE
38 Fifth Ave N, Yorkton, SK, S3N 0Y8
(306) 786-1375
Emp Here 150
SIC 6331 Fire, marine, and casualty insurance

D-U-N-S 25-315-2292   (BR)
SASKATCHEWAN GOVERNMENT INSURANCE
276 Myrtle Ave, Yorkton, SK, S3N 1R4
(306) 786-2430
Emp Here 27
SIC 6331 Fire, marine, and casualty insurance

D-U-N-S 25-966-0538   (BR)
SASKATCHEWAN INDIAN GAMING AUTHORITY INC
PAINTED HAND CASINO
30 Third Ave N, Yorkton, SK, S3N 1B9
(306) 786-6777
Emp Here 160
SIC 7993 Coin-operated amusement devices

D-U-N-S 20-174-8543   (SL)
SECURTEK MONITORING SOLUTIONS INC
70 First Ave N, Yorkton, SK, S3N 1J6
(306) 786-4331
Emp Here 90   *Sales* 3,137,310
SIC 7382 Security services services

D-U-N-S 25-053-7172   (BR)
SOBEYS CAPITAL INCORPORATED
PARKLAND SOBEYS, READY TO SERVE
277 Broadway St E, Yorkton, SK, S3N 3G7

Emp Here 70
SIC 5411 Grocery stores

D-U-N-S 25-187-7619   (BR)
STAPLES CANADA INC
STAPLES THE BUSINESS DEPOT
(*Suby of* Staples, Inc.)
210 Hamilton Rd Suite 167, Yorkton, SK, S3N 4E5

▲ Public Company   ■ Public Company Family Member   **HQ** Headquarters   **BR** Branch   **SL** Single Location

(306) 782-9300
Emp Here 35
SIC 5943 Stationery stores

D-U-N-S 24-330-0584   (BR)
WAL-MART CANADA CORP
240 Hamilton Rd, Yorkton, SK, S3N 4C6
(306) 782-9820
Emp Here 200
SIC 5311 Department stores

D-U-N-S 25-359-7298   (BR)
WATERGROUP COMPANIES INC
CULLIGAN
(*Suby of* Clayton, Dubilier & Rice, Inc.)
76 Seventh Ave S Suite 1, Yorkton, SK, S3N
3V2
(306) 782-0718
Emp Here 100
SIC 5999 Miscellaneous retail stores, nec

D-U-N-S 20-072-8913   (HQ)
WEBER CONSTRUCTION LTD
WEBER BUILDING CENTRE
(*Suby of* Weber Construction Ltd)
175 York Rd W, Yorkton, SK, S3N 3P3
(306) 783-8516
Emp Here 53   *Emp Total* 60
Sales 12,275,450
SIC 5211 Lumber and other building materials
Pr Pr Brent Weber
 Brian Weber

D-U-N-S 24-914-4213   (SL)
YORKTON PUBLISHING LTD
YORKTON THIS WEEK
20 Third Ave N, Yorkton, SK, S3N 1B9
(306) 782-2465
Emp Here 40   *Sales* 3,283,232
SIC 2711 Newspapers

D-U-N-S 20-087-0561   (BR)
YORKTON, CITY OF
AQUATIC OFFICE
455 Broadway St W, Yorkton, SK, S3N 2W3
(306) 786-1740
Emp Here 30
SIC 7389 Business services, nec

D-U-N-S 24-375-0036   (BR)
YORKTON, CITY OF
GALLAGHER CENTRE
455 Broadway St W, Yorkton, SK, S3N 2X1
(306) 786-1740
Emp Here 56
SIC 7999 Amusement and recreation, nec

Young, SK S0K

D-U-N-S 20-179-7102   (BR)
CONEXUS CREDIT UNION 2006
109 Main St, Young, SK, S0K 4Y0
(306) 259-2122
Emp Here 50
SIC 6062 State credit unions

Beaver Creek, YT Y0B

D-U-N-S 25-898-1729   (BR)
WESTMARK HOTELS OF CANADA LTD
202 Alaska Hwy, Beaver Creek, YT, Y0B 1A0
(867) 862-7501
Emp Here 45
SIC 7011 Hotels and motels

Dawson, YT Y0B

D-U-N-S 25-892-9140   (BR)
WESTMARK HOTELS OF CANADA LTD
WESTMARK INN DAWSON
Gd, Dawson, YT, Y0B 1G0
(867) 393-9717
Emp Here 60
SIC 7011 Hotels and motels

Whitehorse, YT Y1A

D-U-N-S 20-065-9139   (BR)
A & W FOOD SERVICES OF CANADA INC
WHITE FERN ENTERPRISES
2222 2nd Ave, Whitehorse, YT, Y1A 1C8
(867) 633-3772
Emp Here 30
SIC 5812 Eating places

D-U-N-S 25-316-7555   (BR)
ATCO ELECTRIC LTD
ATCO ELCTRIC YUKON
1100 Front St Suite 100, Whitehorse, YT, Y1A 3T4
(867) 633-7000
Emp Here 48
SIC 4911 Electric services

D-U-N-S 25-523-8792   (BR)
BANK OF NOVA SCOTIA, THE
SCOTIABANK
212 Main St, Whitehorse, YT, Y1A 2B1
(867) 667-6231
Emp Here 23
SIC 6021 National commercial banks

D-U-N-S 25-288-8995   (BR)
CANADA POST CORPORATION
300 Range Rd, Whitehorse, YT, Y1A 0H8
(867) 668-2195
Emp Here 50
SIC 4311 U.s. postal service

D-U-N-S 24-042-7138   (BR)
CANADIAN BROADCASTING CORPORATION
CBC YUKON RADIO
3103 3rd Ave, Whitehorse, YT, Y1A 1E5
(867) 668-8400
Emp Here 26
SIC 4832 Radio broadcasting stations

D-U-N-S 24-227-8880   (BR)
CANADIAN IMPERIAL BANK OF COMMERCE
CIBC
110 Main St, Whitehorse, YT, Y1A 2A8
(867) 667-2534
Emp Here 20
SIC 6021 National commercial banks

D-U-N-S 20-622-9213   (SL)
DUNCAN'S LIMITED
106 Copper Rd, Whitehorse, YT, Y1A 2Z6
(867) 668-3805
Emp Here 35   *Sales* 5,796,872
SIC 1761 Roofing, siding, and sheetMetal work
Pr Pr Stephen Duncan

James Duncan
Laurie Warner
Gordon Duncan

D-U-N-S 24-350-8020   (BR)
FRASERWAY RV LIMITED PARTNERSHIP
9039 Quartz Rd, Whitehorse, YT, Y1A 4Z5
(867) 668-3438
Emp Here 27
SIC 7519 Utility trailer rental

D-U-N-S 24-886-9406   (BR)
GOVERNING COUNCIL OF THE SALVATION ARMY IN CANADA, THE
GOVERNING COUNCIL OF THE SALVATION ARMY IN CANADA, THE
311 Black St, Whitehorse, YT, Y1A 2N1
(867) 668-2327
Emp Here 35
SIC 8322 Individual and family services

D-U-N-S 24-074-1132   (BR)
KEITH PLUMBING & HEATING CO LTD
KEITH PLUMBING
(*Suby of* Keith Plumbing & Heating Co. Ltd)
14 Burns Rd, Whitehorse, YT, Y1A 4Y9
(867) 668-6611
Emp Here 20
SIC 1711 Plumbing, heating, air-conditioning

D-U-N-S 25-367-5052   (BR)
LOBLAWS INC
REAL CANADIAN SUPERSTORE
2270 2nd Ave Suite 1530, Whitehorse, YT, Y1A 1C8
(867) 456-6618
Emp Here 50
SIC 5141 Groceries, general line

D-U-N-S 25-315-0460   (BR)
MARK'S WORK WEARHOUSE LTD
WORK WORLD
2 Chilkoot Way, Whitehorse, YT, Y1A 6T5
(867) 633-8457
Emp Here 20
SIC 5699 Miscellaneous apparel and accessory stores

D-U-N-S 20-299-5168   (BR)
NAV CANADA
50 Fairchild Pl Unit 215, Whitehorse, YT, Y1A 0M7
(867) 667-8425
Emp Here 26
SIC 4899 Communication services, nec

D-U-N-S 25-195-7759   (HQ)
NORTH 60 PETRO LTD
146 Industrial Rd, Whitehorse, YT, Y1A 2V1
(867) 633-8820
Emp Here 36   *Emp Total* 130
Sales 3,137,310
SIC 4226 Special warehousing and storage, nec

D-U-N-S 24-152-9189   (HQ)
NORTHWESTEL INC
301 Lambert St Suite 2727, Whitehorse, YT, Y1A 1Z5
(867) 668-5300
Emp Here 275   *Emp Total* 48,090
Sales 139,935,857
SIC 4899 Communication services, nec
  Terry Mosey
Pr Pr Paul Flaherty
VP Don Pumphrey
VP Curtis Shaw
Div VP Mark Walker
Manager Barb Szabo
Sec Leslie Mcrae
  Jason Bilsky
Dir Rob Hunt
Dir Andrew Smith

D-U-N-S 24-777-3005   (BR)
NORTHWESTEL INC
301 Lambert St Suite 2727, Whitehorse, YT, Y1A 1Z5

(867) 668-5300
Emp Here 300
SIC 4899 Communication services, nec

D-U-N-S 20-303-6731   (BR)
NORTHWESTEL INC
183 Range Rd, Whitehorse, YT, Y1A 3E5
(867) 668-5475
Emp Here 250
SIC 4899 Communication services, nec

D-U-N-S 20-355-0376   (BR)
PASLOSKI, DARRELL PHARMACY LTD
SHOPPERS DRUG MART
211 Main St Suite 100, Whitehorse, YT, Y1A 2B2
(867) 667-2485
Emp Here 45
SIC 5912 Drug stores and proprietary stores

D-U-N-S 25-087-4310   (BR)
ROYAL BANK OF CANADA
RBC
(*Suby of* Royal Bank Of Canada)
4110 4th Ave, Whitehorse, YT, Y1A 4N7
(867) 667-6416
Emp Here 26
SIC 6021 National commercial banks

D-U-N-S 25-158-6046   (SL)
SILVER GREEN HOLDINGS LIMITED
BOSTON PIZZA
2241 2nd Ave, Whitehorse, YT, Y1A 5W1
(867) 667-4992
Emp Here 50   *Sales* 1,532,175
SIC 5812 Eating places

D-U-N-S 25-453-5651   (SL)
SKOOKUM ASPHALT LTD
1 Ear Lake Rd, Whitehorse, YT, Y1A 6L4
(867) 668-6326
Emp Here 50   *Sales* 3,648,035
SIC 1794 Excavation work

D-U-N-S 24-330-0576   (BR)
WAL-MART CANADA CORP
9021 Quartz Rd, Whitehorse, YT, Y1A 4P9
(867) 667-2652
Emp Here 200
SIC 5311 Department stores

D-U-N-S 24-855-4024   (HQ)
WESTMARK HOTELS OF CANADA LTD
WESTMARK KLONDIKE INN
2288 2nd Ave, Whitehorse, YT, Y1A 1C8
(867) 668-4747
Emp Here 100   *Emp Total* 82,200
Sales 10,395,012
SIC 7011 Hotels and motels
Pr Pr Steve Leonard

D-U-N-S 20-558-0397   (BR)
WESTMARK HOTELS OF CANADA LTD
201 Wood St, Whitehorse, YT, Y1A 2E4
(867) 393-9700
Emp Here 100
SIC 7011 Hotels and motels

D-U-N-S 20-786-1167   (BR)
WHITEHORSE, CITY OF
FIRE DEPARTMENT
305 Range Rd, Whitehorse, YT, Y1A 3E5
(867) 668-2462
Emp Here 35
SIC 7389 Business services, nec

D-U-N-S 24-898-6820   (HQ)
YUKON ENERGY CORPORATION
2 Miles Canyon Rd, Whitehorse, YT, Y1A 6S7
(867) 393-5300
Emp Here 70   *Emp Total* 5,000
Sales 35,688,736
SIC 4911 Electric services
Pr Pr Andrew Hall
VP Michael Brandt
  Kells Bowland
  Sue Craig
  Blair Hogan
  John Jensen

Cam Malloch
Clint Mccuaig
Wendy Shanks
Curtis Shaw

This Page left intentionally blank